Who's Who in Religion

Biographical Titles Currently Published by Marquis Who's Who

Who's Who in America
  Who's Who in America supplements:
    Who's Who in America Birthdate Index
    Who's Who in America Classroom Project Book
    Who's Who in America College Alumni Directory
    Who's Who in America Index:
      Geographic Index, Professional Area Index
Who Was Who in America
  Historical Volume (1607-1896)
  Volume I (1897-1942)
  Volume II (1943-1950)
  Volume III (1951-1960)
  Volume IV (1961-1968)
  Volume V (1969-1973)
  Volume VI (1974-1976)
  Volume VII (1977-1981)
  Index Volume (1607-1981)
Who Was Who in American History—Arts and Letters
Who Was Who in American History—The Military
Who Was Who in American History—Science and Technology
Who's Who in the World
Who's Who in the East
Who's Who in the Midwest
Who's Who in the South and Southwest
Who's Who in the West
Who's Who in American Law
Who's Who of American Women
Who's Who in Finance and Industry
Who's Who in Frontiers of Science and Technology
Who's Who in Religion
World Who's Who in Science
Directory of Women in Marquis Who's Who Publications
Index to Who's Who Books
Directory of Medical Specialists
Marquis Who's Who Directory of Online Professionals
Marquis Who's Who Directory of Computer Graphics
Marquis Who's Who in Cancer: Professionals and Facilities
Marquis Who's Who in Rehabilitation: Professionals and Facilities
Marquis International Who's Who in Optical Science and Engineering

Who's Who
in Religion

3rd edition

MARQUIS
Who'sWho

Marquis Who's Who, Inc.
200 East Ohio Street
Chicago, Illinois 60611 U.S.A.

Library of Congress Catalog Card Number 76-25357
International Standard Book Number 0-8379-1603-8
Product Code Number 030228

Distributed in Europe by
Thompson, Henry Limited
London Road
Sunningdale, Berks
SL5 OEP, England

Distributed in Asia by
United Publishers Services Ltd.
Kenkyu-Sha Bldg.
9, Kanda Surugadai 2-Chome
Chiyoda-Ku, Tokyo, Japan

Manufactured in the United States of America

Table of Contents

Preface

The third edition of *Who's Who in Religion* provides biographical information on more than 7,000 religious leaders and religion professionals in North America. These individuals, approximately 4,000 of whom are new to this edition, represent the following general categories:

Church officials — national and regional, both lay and clergy of all denominations, and heads of orders;
Clergy — priests, rabbis, ministers, and other clergy, selected for their contributions to the various activities of their faith;
Religious educators — professors of religion, theology, or divinity at theological seminaries, denominational colleges, and other colleges and universities with schools of religion or theology;
Lay leaders — founders or directors of religious charities, lay organizations, lay writers and editors of religious publications, and many other professionals working on every aspect of religious endeavor.

The names recorded in *Who's Who in Religion* reflect the culmination of a two-year process of research, writing, and editing by the Marquis Who's Who editorial staff. In addition to careful examination of literature, communications media, and other available data sources, the editors worked with a distinguished Board of Advisors, whose members nominated outstanding individuals in their own denominations for inclusion in this volume.

As with all Marquis Who's Who biographical directories, final selection of names rests on one principle: reference value. Therefore, in the editorial evaluation that resulted in the collection of sketches published herein, an individual's desire to be listed was not a determining factor. Rather, it was demonstrated merit in an area of religious activity that prevailed.

In the majority of cases, the men and women listed in *Who's Who in Religion* supplied their own data. They reviewed proofs of their sketches to assure accurate, current information. In some instances where individuals failed to furnish data, the Marquis editorial staff engaged in careful independent research to compile factual biographical information. Each sketch prepared in this manner is denoted by an asterisk. Brief key information is provided in sketches of selected individuals, new to this edition, who did not submit data. Cross-references to current information in *Who's Who in America* appear for others.

Each biographical sketch includes name, religious and/or secular occupation, denomination, vital statistics, parents, marriage and children (where applicable), education, professional certification, religious activities, creative works, civic and political activities, awards and other special achievements, professional memberships, political party, clubs, lodges, and address.

Marquis Who's Who exercises the greatest care in preparing each sketch for publication. Occasionally, however, errors do occur despite all precautions taken. Users of this directory are invited to report such errors to the publisher so that corrections can be made in a later edition.

Board of Advisors

Marquis Who's Who gratefully acknowledges the following distinguished individuals who have made themselves available for review, evaluation, and general comment with regard to the publication of the third edition of *Who's Who in Religion*.
The advisors have enhanced the reference value of this edition by the nomination of outstanding individuals for inclusion. However, the Board of Advisors—either collectively or individually—is in no way responsible for the final selection of names appearing in this volume, nor does the Board of Advisors bear reponsibility for the accuracy or comprehensiveness of the biographical information or other material contained herein.

CONSULTANT

Constant H. Jacquet, Jr.
Editor
Yearbook of American and Canadian Churches

ADVISORS

Rev. James E. Andrews
Stated Clerk
Presbyterian Church (U.S.A.)

Fr. Alexander Doumouras
Convenor
Study and Planning Commission
  of the Standing Conference
  of Canonical Orthodox Bishops
  in the Americas

Rev. Cedric Earl Gibb
Executive Director
National Conference of
  Black Churchmen

Dr. Archibald Goldie
Associate Secretary
Baptist World Alliance

Dr. Joe Hale
General Secretary
World Methodist Council

Nihad Hamed
Secretary General
Federation of Islamic
  Associations in the
  United States and Canada

Milton Himmelfarb
Editor
American Jewish Yearbook

Dr. Robert E. A. Lee
Executive Director
Lutheran Council in the U.S.A.

Bishop James W. Malone
President
National Conference of
  Catholic Bishops

Prof. Martin E. Marty
Divinity School
University of Chicago

Prof. Charles Winquist
Department of Religious Studies
California State University, Chico

Standards of Admission

The foremost consideration in selecting biographees for *Who's Who in Religion* is the extent of an individual's reference interest. Such reference interest is based on either of two factors: (1) the position of responsibility held, or (2) the level of significant achievement attained.

Admission based on the factor of position includes:

Presiding clergy of organized religious groups in North America

U.S. and Canadian bishops of all churches

Executive directors or heads of major religious agencies or organizations

Leaders of religious orders

Presidents and deans of major theological seminaries and schools

Leading publishers of religious books and periodicals

Religion editors of major daily newspapers

Admission based on individual achievement is based on objective qualitative criteria. To be selected, a person must have attained conspicuous achievement.

Key to Information

❶ JAMIESON, Burton Carter, ❷ minister, ❸ Churches of Christ; ❹ b. Chgo., Jan. 20, 1930; ❺ s. William and Elizabeth Mary (Donne) J.; ❻ m. Janice Deanne Clark, May 11, 1954; ❼ children: Elizabeth, Carter, Monica. ❽ A.B. in Theology, Southeastern Bible Coll., 1952; M.Div., Harvard U., 1955. ❾ Ordained to ministry Churches of Christ, 1952. ❿ Chaplain U.S. Naval Res., 1955-57; pastor chs., Minn. and Wis., 1957-62; pastor First Ch. of Christ, Mundelein, Ill., 1962-68, Main St. Christian Ch., Danville, Ill., 1968-70; exec. sec. Midwestern region Chs. of Christ, Chgo., 1970-73; sr. pastor First Christian Ch., Elmhurst, Ill., 1973 –; ⓫ bd. dirs. Christian Home for the Aged, Monroeville, Wis., 1981 –. ⓬ Contbr. articles to religious jours. ⓭ Area capt. Crusade of Mercy, Elmhurst, 1980-84. ⓮ Served with USNR, 1955-59. ⓯ Recipient award of honor Danville Ministerial Assn., 1970. ⓰ Mem. Assn. Pastoral Counselors, Am. Bible Research Assn. ⓱ Republican. ⓲ Home: 1345 Ave Elmhurst IL 60126 ⓳ Office: 1352 Forest Ave Elmhurst IL 60126

KEY

❶ Name
❷ Religious occupational title
❸ Denomination
❹ Vital statistics
❺ Parents
❻ Marriage
❼ Children
❽ Education
❾ Ordination and certifications
❿ Career (Clergy)
      Religious activities (Lay people)
⓫ Career-related religious activities (Clergy)
      Current secular employment (Lay people)
⓬ Religious writings and creative works
⓭ Civic or political activities
⓮ Military record
⓯ Awards
⓰ Professional and
      association memberships
⓱ Political affiliation
⓲ Home address
⓳ Office address

Table of Abbreviations

The following abbreviations and symbols are frequently used in this book.

*An asterisk following a sketch indicates that it was researched by the Marquis Who's Who editorial staff and has not been verified by the biographee.

A.A. Associate in Arts
AAAL American Academy of Arts and Letters
AAAS American Association for the Advancement of Science
AAHPER Alliance for Health, Physical Education and Recreation
AAU Amateur Athletic Union
AAUP American Association of University Professors
AAUW American Association of University Women
A.B. Arts, Bachelor of
AB Alberta
ABA American Bar Association
ABC American Broadcasting Company
AC Air Corps
acad. academy, academic
acct. accountant
accg. accounting
ACDA Arms Control and Disarmament Agency
ACLU American Civil Liberties Union
ACP American College of Physicians
ACS American College of Surgeons
ADA American Dental Association
a.d.c. aide-de-camp
adj. adjunct, adjutant
adj. gen. adjutant general
adm. admiral
adminstr. administrator
adminstrn. administration
adminstrv. administrative
ADP Automatic Data Processing
adv. advocate, advisory
advt. advertising
A.E. Agricultural Engineer (for degrees only)
A.E. and P. Ambassador Extraordinary and Plenipotentiary
AEC Atomic Energy Commission
aero. aeronautical, aeronautic
aerodyn. aerodynamic
AFB Air Force Base
AFL-CIO American Federation of Labor and Congress of Industrial Organizations
AFTRA American Federation TV and Radio Artists
agr. agriculture
agrl. agricultural
agt. agent
AGVA American Guild of Variety Artists
agy. agency
A&I Agricultural and Industrial
AIA American Institute of Architects
AIAA American Institute of Aeronautics and Astronautics
AID Agency for International Development
AIEE American Institute of Electrical Engineers

AIM American Institute of Management
AIME American Institute of Mining, Metallurgy, and Petroleum Engineers
AK Alaska
AL Alabama
ALA American Library Association
Ala. Alabama
alt. alternate
Alta. Alberta
A&M Agricultural and Mechanical
A.M. Arts, Master of
Am. American, America
AMA American Medical Association
A.M.E. African Methodist Episcopal
Amtrak National Railroad Passenger Corporation
AMVETS American Veterans of World War II, Korea, Vietnam
anat. anatomical
ann. annual
ANTA American National Theatre and Academy
anthrop. anthropological
AP Associated Press
APO Army Post Office
Apr. April
apptd. appointed
apt. apartment
AR Arkansas
ARC American Red Cross
archeol. archeological
archtl. architectural
Ariz. Arizona
Ark. Arkansas
ArtsD. Arts, Doctor of
arty. artillery
ASCAP American Society of Composers, Authors and Publishers
ASCE American Society of Civil Engineers
ASHRAE American Society of Heating, Refrigeration, and Air Conditioning Engineers
ASME American Society of Mechanical Engineers
assn. association
assoc. associate
asst. assistant
ASTM American Society for Testing and Materials
astron. astronomical
astrophys. astrophysical
ATSC Air Technical Service Command
AT&T American Telephone & Telegraph Company
atty. attorney
AUS Army of the United States
Aug. August
aux. auxiliary
Ave. Avenue
AVMA American Veterinary Medical Association
AZ Arizona

B. Bachelor
b. born
B.A. Bachelor of Arts
B.Agr. Bachelor of Agriculture

Balt. Baltimore
Bapt. Baptist
B. Arch. Bachelor of Architecture
B.A.S. Bachelor of Agricultural Science
B.B.A. Bachelor of Business Administration
BBC British Broadcasting Corporation
B.C., BC British Columbia
B.C.E. Bachelor of Civil Engineering
B. Chir. Bachelor of Surgery
B.C.L. Bachelor of Civil Law
B.C.S. Bachelor of Commercial Science
B.D. Bachelor of Divinity
bd. board
B.E. Bachelor of Education
B.E.E. Bachelor of Electrical Engineering
B.F.A. Bachelor of Fine Arts
bibl. biblical
bibliog. bibliographical
biog. biographical
biol. biological
B.J. Bachelor of Journalism
Bklyn. Brooklyn
B.L. Bachelor of Letters
bldg. building
B.L.S. Bachelor of Library Science
Blvd. Boulevard
bn. battalion
B.&O.R.R. Baltimore & Ohio Railroad
bot. botanical
B.P.E. Bachelor of Physical Education
br. branch
B.R.E. Bachelor of Religious Education
brig. gen. brigadier general
Brit. British. Britannica
Bros. Brothers
B.S. Bachelor of Science
B.S.A. Bachelor of Agricultural Science
B.S.D. Bachelor of Didactic Science
B.S.T. Bachelor of Sacred Theology
B.Th. Bachelor of Theology
bull. bulletin
bur. bureau
bus. business
B.W.I. British West Indies

CA California
CAA Civil Aeronautics Administration
CAB Civil Aeronautics Board
Calif. California
C.Am. Central America
Can. Canada, Canadian
CAP Civil Air Patrol
capt. captain
CARE Cooperative American Relief Everywhere
Cath. Catholic
cav. cavalry
CBC Canadian Broadcasting Company
CBI China, Burma, India Theatre of Operations
CBS Columbia Broadcasting System
CCC Commodity Credit Corporation
CCNY City College of New York
CCU Cardiac Care Unit
CD Civil Defense

C.E. Corps of Engineers, Civil Engineers (in firm's name only or for degree)
cen. central (To be used for court system only)
CENTO Central Treaty Organization
CERN European Organization of Nuclear Research
cert. certificate, certification, certified
CETA Comprehensive Employment Training Act
CFL Canadian Football League
ch. church
Ch.D. Doctor of Chemistry
chem. chemical
Chem.E. Chemical Engineer
Chgo. Chicago
chirurg. chirurgical
chmn. chairman
chpt. chapter
CIA Central Intelligence Agency
CIC Counter Intelligence Corps
Cin. Cincinnati
cir. circuit
Cleve. Cleveland
climatol. climatological
clin. clinical
clk. clerk
C.L.U. Chartered Life Underwriter
C.M. Master in Surgery
C.&N.W.Ry. Chicago & Northwestern Railway
CO Colorado
Co. Company
COF Catholic Order of Foresters
C. of C. Chamber of Commerce
col. colonel
coll. college
Colo. Colorado
com. committee
comd. commanded
comdg. commanding
comdr. commander
comdt. commandant
commd. commissioned
comml. commercial
commn. commission
commr. commissioner
condr. conductor
Conf. Conference
Congl. Congregational, Congressional
Conglist. Congregationalist
Conn. Connecticut
cons. consultant, consulting
consol. consolidated
constl. constitutional
constn. constitution
constrn. construction
contbd. contributed
contbg. contributing
contbn. contribution
contbr. contributor
Conv. Convention
coop. cooperative
CORDS Civil Operations and Revolutionary Development Support
CORE Congress of Racial Equality
corp. corporation, corporate
corr. correspondent, corresponding, correspondence

C.&O.Ry. Chesapeake & Ohio Railway
C.P.A. Certified Public Accountant
C.P.C.U. Chartered Property and Casualty Underwriter
C.P.H. Certificate of Public Health
cpl. corporal
CPR Cardio-Pulmonary Resuscitation
C.P.Ry. Canadian Pacific Railway
C.S. Christian Science
C.S.B. Bachelor of Christian Science
CSC Civil Service Commission
C.S.D. Doctor of Christian Science
CT Connecticut
ct. court
crt. center
CWS Chemical Warfare Service
C.Z. Canal Zone

d. daughter
D. Doctor
D.Agr. Doctor of Agriculture
DAR Daughters of the American Revolution
dau. daughter
DAV Disabled American Veterans
D.C., DC District of Columbia
D.C.L. Doctor of Civil Law
D.C.S. Doctor of Commercial Science
D.D. Doctor of Divinity
D.D.S. Doctor of Dental Surgery
DE Delaware
dec. deceased
Dec. December
def. defense
Del. Delaware
del. delegate, delegation
Dem. Democrat, Democratic
D.Eng. Doctor of Engineering
denom. denomination, denominational
dep. deputy
dept. department
dermatol. dermatological
desc. descendant
devel. development, developmental
D.F.A. Doctor of Fine Arts
D.F.C. Distinguished Flying Cross
D.H.L. Doctor of Hebrew Literature
dir. director
dist. district
distbg. distributing
distbn. distribution
distbr. distributor
disting. distinguished
div. division, divinity, divorce
D.Litt. Doctor of Literature
D.M.D. Doctor of Medical Dentistry
D.M.S. Doctor of Medical Science
D.O. Doctor of Osteopathy
D.P.H. Diploma in Public Health
D.R. Daughters of the Revolution
Dr. Drive, Doctor
D.R.E. Doctor of Religious Education
Dr.P.H. Doctor of Public Health, Doctor of Public Hygiene
D.S.C. Distinguished Service Cross
D.Sc. Doctor of Science
D.S.M. Distinguished Service Medal
D.S.T. Doctor of Sacred Theology

D.T.M. Doctor of Tropical Medicine
D.V.M. Doctor of Veterinary Medicine
D.V.S. Doctor of Veterinary Surgery

E. East
ea. eastern (use for court system only)
E. and P. Extraordinary and Plenipotentiary
Eccles. Ecclesiastical
ecol. ecological
econ. economic
ECOSOC Economic and Social Council (of the UN)
E.D. Doctor of Engineering
ed. educated
Ed.B. Bachelor of Education
Ed.D. Doctor of Education
edit. edition
Ed.M. Master of Education
edn. education
ednl. educational
EDP electronic data processing
Ed.S. Specialist in Education
E.E. Electrical Engineer (degree only)
E.E. and M.P. Envoy Extraordinary and Minister Plenipotentiary
EEC European Economic Community
EEG Electroencephalogram
EEO Equal Employment Opportunity
EEOC Equal Employment Opportunity Commission
EKG Electrocardiogram
E.Ger. German Democratic Republic
elec. electrical
electrochem. electrochemical
electrophys. electrophysical
elem. elementary
E.M. Engineer of Mines
ency. encyclopedia
Eng. England
engr. engineer
engring. engineering
entomol. entomological
environ. environmental
EPA Environmental Protection Agency
epidemiol. epidemiological
Episc. Episcopalian
ERA Equal Rights Amendment
ERDA Energy Research and Development Administration
ESEA Elementary and Secondary Education Act
ESL English as Second Language
ESSA Environmental Science Services Administration
ethnol. ethnological
ETO European Theatre of Operations
Evang. Evangelical
exam. examination, examining
exec. executive
exhbn. exhibition
expdn. expedition
expn. exposition
expt. experiment
exptl. experimental

F.A. Field Artillery
FAA Federal Aviation Administration

FAO Food and Agriculture Organization (of the UN)
FBI Federal Bureau of Investigation
FCA Farm Credit Administration
FCC Federal Communication Commission
FCDA Federal Civil Defense Administration
FDA Food and Drug Administration
FDIA Federal Deposit Insurance Administration
FDIC Federal Deposit Insurance Corporation
F.E. Forest Engineer
FEA Federal Energy Administration
Feb. February
fed. federal
fedn. federation
FERC Federal Energy Regulatory Commission
fgn. foreign
FHA Federal Housing Administration
fin. financial, finance
FL Florida
Fla. Florida
FMC Federal Maritime Commission
FOA Foreign Operations Administration
found. foundation
FPC Federal Power Commission
FPO Fleet Post Office
frat. fraternity
FRS Federal Reserve System
FSA Federal Security Agency
Ft. Fort
FTC Federal Trade Commission

G-1 (or other number) Division of General Staff
Ga., GA Georgia
GAO General Accounting Office
gastroent. gastroenterological
GATT General Agreement of Tariff and Trades
gen. general
geneal. genealogical
geod. geodetic
geog. geographic, geographical
geol. geological
geophys. geophysical
gerontol. gerontological
G.H.Q. General Headquarters
G.N. Ry. Great Northern Railway
gov. governor
govt. government
govtl. governmental
GPO Governmental Printing Office
grad. graduate, graduated
GSA General Services Administration
Gt. Great
GU Guam
gynecol. gynecological

hdqrs. headquarters
HEW Department of Health, Education and Welfare
H.H.D. Doctor of Humanities
HHFA Housing and Home Finance Agency
HHS Department of Health and Human Services
HI Hawaii
hist. historical, historic

H.M. Master of Humanics
homeo. homeopathic
hon. honorary, honorable
Ho. of Dels. House of Delegates
Ho. of Reps. House of Representatives
hort. horticultural
hosp. hospital
HUD Department of Housing and Urban Development
Hwy. Highway
hydrog. hydrographic

IA Iowa
IAEA International Atomic Energy Agency
IBM International Business Machines Corporation
IBRD International Bank for Reconstruction and Development
ICA International Cooperation Administration
ICC Interstate Commerce Commission
ICU Intensive Care Unit
ID Idaho
IEEE Institute of Electrical and Electronics Engineers
IFC International Finance Corporation
IGY International Geophysical Year
IL Illinois
Ill. Illinois
illus. illustrated
ILO International Labor Organization
IMF International Monetary Fund
IN Indiana
Inc. Incorporated
ind. independent
Ind. Indiana
Indpls. Indianapolis
indsl. industrial
inf. infantry
info. information
ins. insurance
insp. inspector
insp.gen. inspector general
inst. institute
instl. institutional
instn. institution
instr. instructor
instrn. instruction
intern. international
intro. introduction
IRE Institute of Radio Engineers
IRS Internal Revenue Service
ITT International Telephone & Telegraph Corporation

JAG Judge Advocate General
JAGC Judge Advocate General Corps
Jan. January
Jaycees Junior Chamber of Commerce
J.B. Jurum Baccolaureus
J.C.B. Juris Canoni Baccalaureus
J.C.D. Juris Canonici Doctor, Juris Civilis Doctor
J.C.L. Juris Canonici Licentiatus
J.D. Juris Doctor
j.g. junior grade
jour. journal
jr. junior
J.S.D. Juris Scientiae Doctor

J.U.D. Juris Utriusque Doctor
jud. judicial
Kans. Kansas
K.C. Knights of Columbus
K.P. Knights of Pythias
KS Kansas
K.T. Knight Templar
Ky., KY Kentucky

La., LA Louisiana
lab. laboratory
lang. language
laryngol. laryngological
LB Labrador
lectr. lecturer
legis. legislation, legislative
L.H.D. Doctor of Humane Letters
L.I. Long Island
lic. licensed, license
L.I.R.R. Long Island Railroad
lit. literary, literature
Litt.B. Bachelor of Letters
Litt.D. Doctor of Letters
LL.B. Bachelor of Laws
LL.D. Doctor of Laws
LL.M. Master of Laws
Ln. Lane
L.& N.R.R. Louisville & Nashville Railroad
L.S. Library Science (in degree)
lt. lieutenant
Ltd. Limited
Luth. Lutheran
LWV League of Women Voters

m. married
M. Master
M.A. Master of Arts
MA Massachusetts
mag. magazine
M.Agr. Master of Agriculture
maj. major
Man. Manitoba
Mar. March
M.Arch. Master in Architecture
Mass. Massachusetts
math. mathematics, mathematical
MATS Military Air Transport Service
M.B. Bachelor of Medicine
MB Manitoba
M.B.A. Master of Business Administration
MBS Mutual Broadcasting System
M.C. Medical Corps
M.C.E. Master of Civil Engineering
mcht. merchant
mcpl. municipal
M.C.S. Master of Commercial Science
M.D. Doctor of Medicine
Md, MD Maryland
M.Dip. Master in Diplomacy
mdse. merchandise
M.D.V. Doctor of Veterinary Medicine
M.E. Mechanical Engineer (degree only)
ME Maine
M.E.Ch. Methodist Episcopal Church
mech. mechanical
M.Ed. Master of Education
med. medical
M.E.E. Master of Electrical Engineering
mem. member

meml. memorial
merc. mercantile
met. metropolitan
metall. metallurgical
Met.E. Metallurgical Engineer
meteorol. meteorological
Meth. Methodist
Mex. Mexico
M.F. Master of Forestry
M.F.A. Master of Fine Arts
mfg. manufacturing
mfr. manufacturer
mgmt. management
mgr. manager
M.H.A. Master of Hospital Administration
M.I. Military Intelligence
MI Michigan
Mich. Michigan
micros. microscopic, microscopical
mid. middle (use for Court System only)
mil. military
Milw. Milwaukee
mineral. mineralogical
Minn. Minnesota
Miss. Mississippi
MIT Massachusetts Institute of Technology
mktg. marketing
M.L. Master of Laws
MLA Modern Language Association
M.L.D. Magister Legnum Diplomatic
M.Litt. Master of Literature
M.L.S. Master of Library Science
M.M.E. Master of Mechanical Engineering
MN Minnesota
mng. managing
Mo., MO Missouri
moblzn. mobilization
Mont. Montana
M.P. Member of Parliament
M.P.E. Master of Physical Education
M.P.H. Master of Public Health
M.P.L. Master of Patent Law
Mpls. Minneapolis
M.R.E. Master of Religious Education
M.S. Master of Science
MS, Ms. Mississippi
M.Sc. Master of Science
M.S.F. Master of Science of Forestry
M.S.T. Master of Sacred Theology
M.S.W. Master of Social Work
MT Montana
Mt. Mount
MTO Mediterranean Theatre of Operations
mus. museum, musical
Mus.B. Bachelor of Music
Mus.D. Doctor of Music
Mus.M. Master of Music
mut. mutual
mycol. mycological

N. North
NAACP National Association for the Advancement of Colored People
NACA National Advisory Committee for Aeronautics
NAD National Academy of Design
N.Am. North America
NAM National Association of Manufacturers

NAPA National Association of Performing Artists
NAREB National Association of Real Estate Boards
NARS National Archives and Record Service
NASA National Aeronautics and Space Administration
nat. national
NATO North Atlantic Treaty Organization
NATOUSA North African Theatre of Operations
nav. navigation
N.B., NB New Brunswick
NBC National Broadcasting Company
N.C., NC North Carolina
NCCJ National Conference of Christians and Jews
N.D., ND North Dakota
NDEA National Defense Education Act
NE Nebraska
NE Northeast
NEA National Education Association
Nebr. Nebraska
NEH National Endowment for Humanities
neurol. neurological
Nev. Nevada
NF Newfoundland
NFL National Football League
Nfld. Newfoundland
N.G. National Guard
N.H., NH New Hampshire
NHL National Hockey League
NIH National Institutes of Health
NIMH National Institute of Mental Health
N.J., NJ New Jersey
NLRB National Labor Relations Board
NM New Mexico
N.Mex. New Mexico
No. Northern
NOAA National Oceanographic and Atmospheric Administration
NORAD North America Air Defense
NOW National Organization for Women
Nov. November
N.P.Ry. Northern Pacific Railway
nr. near
NRC National Research Council
N.S., NS Nova Scotia
NSC National Security Council
NSF National Science Foundation
N.T. New Testament
NT Northwest Territories
numis. numismatic
NV Nevada
NW Northwest
N.W.T. Northwest Territories
N.Y., NY New York
N.Y.C. New York City
NYU New York University
N.Z. New Zealand

OAS Organization of American States
ob-gyn obstetrics-gynecology
obs. observatory
obstet. obstetrical
O.D. Doctor of Optometry
OECD Organization of European Cooperation and Development

OEEC Organization of European Economic Cooperation
OEO Office of Economic Opportunity
ofcl. official
OH Ohio
OK Oklahoma
Okla. Oklahoma
ON Ontario
Ont. Ontario
ophthal. ophthalmological
ops. operations
OR Oregon
orch. orchestra
Oreg. Oregon
orgn. organization
ornithol. ornithological
OSHA Occupational Safety and Health Administration
OSRD Office of Scientific Research and Development
OSS Office of Strategic Services
osteo. osteopathic
otol. otological
otolaryn. otolaryngological

Pa., PA Pennsylvania
P.A. Professional Association
paleontol. paleontological
path. pathological
P.C. Professional Corporation
PE Prince Edward Island
P.E.I. Prince Edward Island (text only)
PEN Poets, Playwrights, Editors, Essayists and Novelists (international association)
penol. penological
P.E.O. women's organization (full name not disclosed)
pfc. private first class
PHA Public Housing Administration
pharm. pharmaceutical
Pharm.D. Doctor of Pharmacy
Pharm. M. Master of Pharmacy
Ph.B. Bachelor of Philosophy
Ph.D. Doctor of Philosophy
Phila. Philadelphia
philharm. philharmonic
philol. philological
philos. philosophical
photog. photographic
phys. physical
physiol. physiological
Pitts. Pittsburgh
Pkwy. Parkway
Pl. Place
P.&L.E.R.R. Pittsburgh & Lake Erie Railroad
P. O. Post Office
PO Box Post Office Box
polit. political
poly. polytechnic, polytechnical
PQ Province of Quebec
P.R., PR Puerto Rico
prep. preparatory
pres. president
Presbyn. Presbyterian
presdl. presidential
prin. principal
proc. proceedings
prod. produced (play production)

prodn. production
prof. professor
profl. professional
prog. progressive
propr. proprietor
pros. atty. prosecuting attorney
pro tem pro tempore
PSRO Professional Services Review Organization
psychiat. psychiatric
psychol. psychological
PTA Parent-Teachers Association
ptnr. partner
PTO Pacific Theatre of Operations, Parent Teacher Organization
pub. publisher, publishing, published
pub. public
publ. publication
pvt. private

quar. quarterly
q.m. quartermaster
Q.M.C. Quartermaster Corps.
Que. Quebec

radiol. radiological
RAF Royal Air Force
RCA Radio Corporation of America
RCAF Royal Canadian Air Force
RD Rural Delivery
Rd. Road
REA Rural Electrification Administration
rec. recording
ref. reformed
regt. regiment
regtl. regimental
rehab. rehabilitation
rep. representative
Rep. Republican
Res. Reserve
ret. retired
rev. review, revised
RFC Reconstruction Finance Corporation
RFD Rural Free Delivery
rhinol. rhinological
R.I., RI Rhode Island
R.N. Registered Nurse
roentgenol. roentgenological
ROTC Reserve Officers Training Corps
R.R. Railroad
Ry. Railway

s. son
S. South
SAC Strategic Air Command
SALT Strategic Arms Limitation Talks
S.Am. South America
san. sanitary
SAR Sons of the American Revolution
Sask. Saskatchewan
savs. savings
S.B. Bachelor of Science
SBA Small Business Administration
S.C., SC South Carolina
SCAP Supreme Command Allies Pacific
Sc.B. Bachelor of Science
S.C.D. Doctor of Commercial Science
Sc.D. Doctor of Science
sch. school

sci. science, scientific
SCLC Southern Christian Leadership Conference
SCV Sons of Confederate Veterans
S.D., SD South Dakota
SE Southeast
SEATO Southeast Asia Treaty Organization
sec. secretary
SEC Securities and Exchange Commission
sect. section
seismol. seismological
sem. seminary
s.g. senior grade
sgt. sergeant
SHAEF Supreme Headquarters Allied Expeditionary Forces
SHAPE Supreme Headquarters Allied Powers in Europe
S.I. Staten Island
S.J. Society of Jesus (Jesuit)
S.J.D. Scientiae Juridicae Doctor
SK Saskatchewan
S.M. Master of Science
So. Southern
soc. society
sociol. sociological
S.P. Co. Southern Pacific Company
spl. special
splty. specialty
Sq. Square
sr. senior
S.R. Sons of the Revolution
SS Steamship
SSS Selective Service System
St. Saint, Street
sta. station
stats. statistics
statis. statistical
S.T.B. Bachelor of Sacred Theology
stblzn. stabilization
S.T.D. Doctor of Sacred Theology
subs. subsidiary
SUNY State University of New York
supr. supervisor
supt. superintendent
surg. surgical
SW Southwest

TAPPI Technical Association of Pulp and Paper Industry
Tb Tuberculosis
tchr. teacher
tech. technical, technology
technol. technological
Tel.&Tel. Telephone & Telegraph
temp. temporary
Tenn. Tennessee
Ter. Territory
Terr. Terrace
Tex. Texas
Th.D. Doctor of Theology
theol. theological
Th.M. Master of Theology
TN Tennessee
tng. training
topog. topographical
trans. transaction, transferred
transl. translation, translated

transp. transportation
treas. treasurer
TV television
TVA Tennessee Valley Authority
twp. township
TX Texas
typog. typographical

U. University
UAW United Auto Workers
UCLA University of California at Los Angeles
UDC United Daughters of the Confederacy
U.K. United Kingdom
UN United Nations
UNESCO United Nations Educational, Scientific and Cultural Organization
UNICEF United Nations International Children's Emergency Fund
univ. university
UNRRA United Nations Relief and Rehabilitation Administration
UPI United Press International
U.P.R.R. United Pacific Railroad
urol. urological
U.S. United States
U.S.A. United States of America
USAAF United States Army Air Force
USAF United States Air Force
USAFR United States Air Force Reserve
USAR United States Army Reserve
USCG United States Coast Guard
USCGR United States Coast Guard Reserve
USES United States Employment Service
USIA United States Information Agency
USMC United States Marine Corps
USMCR United States Marine Corps Reserve
USN United States Navy
USNG United States National Guard
USNR United States Naval Reserve
USO United Service Organizations
USPHS United States Public Health Service
USS United States Ship
USSR Union of the Soviet Socialist Republics
USV United States Volunteers
UT Utah

VA Veterans' Administration
Va., VA Virginia
vet. veteran, veterinary
VFW Veterans of Foreign Wars
V.I., VI Virgin Islands
vice pres. vice president
vis. visiting
VISTA Volunteers in Service to America
VITA Volunteers in Technical Service
vocat. vocational
vol. volunteer, volume
v.p. vice president
vs. versus
Vt., VT Vermont

W. West
WA Washington (state)
WAC Women's Army Corps

Wash. Washington (state)
WAVES Women's Reserve. U.S. Naval
    Reserve
WCTU Women's Christian Temperance
    Union
we. western (use for court system only)
W. Ger. Germany, Federal Republic of
WHO World Health Organization
WI, Wis. Wisconsin
W.I. West Indies
WSB Wage Stabilization Board
WV West Virginia
W.Va. West Virginia
WY Wyoming
Wyo. Wyoming

YK Yukon Territory (for address)
YMCA Young Men's Christian Association
YMHA Young Men's Hebrew Association
YM & YWHA Young Men's and Young
    Women's Hebrew Association
Y.T. Yukon Territory
YWCA Young Women's Christian
    Association
yr. year

zool. zoological

Alphabetical Practices

Names are arranged alphabetically according to the surnames, and under identical surnames according to the first given name. If both surname and first given name are identical, names are arranged alphabetically according to the second given name. Where full names are identical, they are arranged in order of age—with the elder listed first.

Surnames beginning with De, Des, Du, however capitalized or spaced, are recorded with the prefix preceding the surname and arranged alphabetically, under the letter D.

Surnames beginning with Mac and Mc are arranged alphabetically under M.

Surnames beginning with Saint or St. appear after names that would begin Sains, and are arranged according to the second part of the name, e.g., St. Clair before Saint Dennis.

Surnames beginning with prefix Van are arranged alphabetically under letter V. Surnames containing the prefix Von or von are usually arranged alphabetically under letter V, any exceptions are noted by cross references.

Compound hyphenated surnames are arranged according to the first member of the compound. Compound unhyphenated surnames are treated as hyphenated names.

Parentheses used in connection with a name indicate which part of the full name is usually deleted in common usage. Hence Abbott, W(illiam) Lewis indicates that the usual form of the given name is W. Lewis. In such a case, the parentheses are ignored in alphabetizing. However if the name is recorded Abbott, (William) Lewis, signifying that the entire name William is not commonly used, the alphabetizing would be arranged as though the name were Abbott, Lewis.

Who's Who in Religion

AADLAND, MARLIN BENNIE, pastor, Evangelical Lutheran Church of Canada; b. Strongfield, Sask., Can., June 12, 1936; s. Bennie George and Mavis Evelyn (Jackson) A.; m. Jeanette Lorraine Quenzer, July 18, 1964; children: Jeffrey Scott, Jill Michele. B.A. magna cum laude, Augsburg Coll., 1962; M.Div., Luth. Theol. Sem., Saskatoon, Sask., 1966; Th.D., Boston U., 1981. Ordained to ministry Evangelical Lutheran Church of Canada, 1966. Pastor, Wetaskiwin Parish, Alta., Can., 1966-70, Grace Luth. Ch., Burnaby, B.C., Can., 1973—; asst. minister Centre Meth. Ch., Malden, Mass., 1971-73; protestant chaplain Malden Hosp., 1971-73; mem. bd. govs. Luth. Theol. Sem., Saskatoon, 1974-80; mem. Bd. Congregational Life, Saskatoon, 1976-78. Contbr. articles to religious publs. Tchr., Parent Effectiveness Tng., Calif., 1978—; mem. Sask. Bd. Edn., 1980—. Recipient sem. grad. award Luth. Life (formerly Luth. Brotherhood), Waterloo, Ont., Can., 1967. Home: 7325 Nelson Ave Burnaby BC V5J 4C5 Canada Office: Grace Luth Ch 7283 Nelson Ave Burnaby BC V5J 4C2 Canada

AARON, WILLIAM JOSEPH, priest, Roman Catholic Ch.; b. Wichita, Falls, Tex., Nov. 2, 1947; s. Joseph Elmer and Dorothea Leona (Koehler) A.; B.A., U. Dallas, 1969; S.T.B., Pontifical Gregorian U. (Italy), 1972. Ordained priest, Roman Catholic Ch., 1973; asso. pastor St. John the Apostle, Ft. Worth, Tex., 1973-76, Our Lady Queen of Peace, Wichita Falls, Tex., 1976—. Mem. youth ministries team Diocese of Fort Worth, 1973-77; sec.-treas. priests senate, 1975-76; mem. Liturgical Conf. U.S.A., 1973-77. Mem. Common Cause, Composers Forum. Address: 2510 Lansing Blvd Wichita Falls TX 76309

AARONSON, DAVID RICHARD, minister Presbyn. Ch. in U.S.; b. Trenton, Sept. 15, 1927; s. Edward Shreve and Margaret Jeanne (Lewis) A.; B.A., Wheaton Coll., 1948; M.Div., Princeton Theol. Sem., 1951; postgrad. Evang. Bible Coll. and Sem., 1951-53; D.D., Pacific Western U., 1966; m. Sue Grover, Sept. 16, 1950; children—Karen, Kevin, Kathy. Ordained to ministry, 1951; pastor Harmony Presbyn. Ch., Phillipsburg, N.J., 1950-58, Calvary Presbyn. Ch., Newburgh, N.Y., 1958-69; sr. pastor 1st Presbyn. Ch., Sparta, N.J., 1969—. Moderator Newton Presbytery, 1956-57, 73-75, Sparta Ecumenical Council Chs., 1971, 76; pres. Warren County Council Chs., 1952-56; religious civil def. coordinator Warren County, 1950-58; commr. to Gen. Assembly, 1964, 74; bd. mgrs., chaplain St. Lukes Hosp., Newburgh, 1963-69; pres. Newburgh Ministerium, 1962, 67; instl. chaplain N.J. Glen Gardner State Hosp., 1954-58, Masons, 1959; instl. ministries chmn. Sussex County Council Chs., 1972-75. Bd. dirs. Warren County Mental Health Assn., Orange County Mental Health Assn., 1960-69; pres. bd. dirs. Family Counseling Assn. Orange County, 1962-68; Chmn. Family Counseling Sussex County, 1969-73; vice chm., dir. Mental Health bd. mgrs. Sussex County, 1969—. Mem. Acad. Parish Clergy Sussex County. Home: 29 Main St Sparta NJ 07871 Office: 32 Main St Sparta NJ 07871

ABATA, RUSSELL JAMES, priest, author, Roman Catholic Church; b. North East, Pa., May 30, 1930; s. Joseph and Josephine (Cuccia) A.; D. in Moral Guidance, Angelicum, Rome, 1962; Licentiae, Academia Alfonsiana, Rome, 1959. Joined Order Redemptorist Fathers; ordained priest Roman Cath. Ch., 1957; preacher missions, Eastern seacoast, 1962; tchr. Mt. St. Alphonsus Sem., Esopus, N.Y., 1963-85; counselor mental health Our Lady of Perpetual Help, 1966—; prof. comparative religions Fordham U., N.Y.C., 1969. Author: Love Is a Rainbow, 1971; Double Dare To Be You, 1972; Sex Sanity in the Modern World, 1975; Helps for the Scrupulous, 1976; You and the Ten Commandments, 1976; How to Develop a Better Self-Image, 1980; Unlocking the Doors of Your Heart, 1984; Is Love In and Sin Out, 1985; (with W. Weir) Dealing with Depression, 1982; A Book of Poetry, 1984; contbg. author: All Things to All Men, 1967. Home: 323 E 61st St New York City NY 10021

ABATIE, RODGER PAUL, minister, Lutheran Church-Missouri Synod; radio executive; b. LaJolla, Calif., May 16, 1951; s. John Robert and Margaret Jane (Moore) A.; m. Robin Ruth York, Aug. 4, 1973; children: Kristen Michelle, Justin Paul. A.A., Concordia Coll., Ann Arbor, Mich., 1971; B.A., Concordia Coll., Ft. Wayne, Ind., 1973, M.Div., 1977; M.A. in Communications, Sangamon State U., 1975. Pastor St. Mark Luth. Ch., Muskegon, Mich., 1977-82; gen. mgr. Sta. KFUO, St. Louis, Mo., 1982—; zone leader Mo. Fedn. Aid Assn. for Lutherans, St. Louis, 1983—; chmn. Word of Life Sch. Bd., St. Louis, 1983—; exec. sec. bd. Sta. KFUO, 1983—; bd. edn. mem. Concordia Luth. Ch., 1983-84. Recipient Cert. of Merit, Boy Scouts Am., Pottawatomie Council, 1971. Mem. Nat. Assn. Broadcasters, Mo. Broadcasters Assn., St. Louis Radio Assn.

ABBOTT, ALVIN RICHARD, minister, Presbyterian Church in the U.S.A.; b. Chgo., May 12, 1929; s. Richard Thomas and Lauretta Marie (Lieser) A.; m. Donna Jean Bailey, Dec. 16, 1956; children: Alvin Richard, Bradley Roy, Chrystal Jean. B.A., Park Coll., 1952; diploma McCormick Theol. Sem., 1957, M.Div., 1974, D. Ministry, 1980. Ordained to ministry, Presbyn. Ch. in U.S.A., 1957. Student intern First Presbyn. Ch., Watford City, N.D., 1953-54, Williston, N.D., 1954; student, then pastor 1st Presbyn. Ch., Green Valley, Ill., 1954-62; pastor Presbyn. Ch., Clinton, Ill., 1963-68, Westminster Presbyn. Ch., Joliet, Ill., 1969—; moderator Blackhawk Presbytery, Oregon, Ill., 1976, chmn. council, 1978-83; pres. Joliet Ecumenical Clergy Assn., 1983—. Chmn. Joliet Renewal Task Force. Mem. Alpha Phi Omega, Mu Sigma. Home: 417 Tana Ln Joliet IL 60435 Office: Westminster Presbyn Ch Clara and Larkin Aves Joliet IL 60435

ABBOTT, DAVID LLOYD, minister, United Pentecostal Church International; b. Carlsbad, N.Mex., Jan. 11, 1949; s. Chester Lewis and Leveta (Johnson) A.; m. Darcy Renee Cleveland, Nov. 27, 1971; children: Dustin, David, Devi, Daniel. Th.B., Christian Life Coll., 1971. Ordained to ministry United Pentecostal Ch. Internat., 1976. Evangelist, United Pentecostal Ch., U.S. and Can., 1971-81; campus evangelist Pentecostal Students Fellowship, Northwest U.S., 1972-75; pastor Landmark Pentecostal Ch., Scottsdale, Ariz., 1981—; sec. Ariz. Youth United Pentecostal Ch., Phoenix, 1983—. Songwriter, singer gospel albums, tapes, 1976—. Home: 2343 N 80th Pl Scottsdale AZ 85257

ABBOTT, GARY LOUIS, minister, So. Bapt. Conv.; b. Millen, Ga., Sept. 26, 1947; s. Albert Louis and Viola Rose (Kingston) A.; A.B., Mercer U., 1969; M.Div., Southwestern Bapt. Theol. Sem., 1972; postgrad. Columbia Theol. Sem., 1974-76, New Orleans Bapt. Theol. Sem., 1977—; m. Billie Avalie Uselton, July 26, 1969; 1 son, Gary Louis. Ordained to ministry, 1968; pastor Antioch Bapt. Ch., Godfrey, Ga., 1967-69, Pleasant Grove Bapt. Ch., Sandersville, Ga., 1969; interim pastor 1st Bapt. Ch., Waynesboro, Ga., summer 1970; pastor Fairview (Tex.) Bapt. Ch., 1970-72; asso. pastor 1st Bapt. Ch., Washington, Ga., 1972-73; pastor 1st Bapt. Ch., Hogansville, Ga., 1973—. Chmn. exec. com. Western Bapt. Assn., 1974-76; pres. Hogansville Ministerial Assn., 1974-75. Chmn. edn. funds crusade Am. Cancer Soc., Wilkes County, Ga., 1973; chmn. gift of life Hogansville Kidney Found., 1976—; bd. dirs. Kidney Found. Ga. Home: PO Box 402 Boyd Rd Hogansville GA 30230 Office: PO Box 402 E Main St Hogansville GA 30230

ABBOTT, JOHN DAVID See *Who's Who in America*, 43rd edition.

ABDELSAYED, GABRIEL H.A. See *Who's Who in America*, 43rd edition.

ABEL, PAUL FREDERICK, minister, United Methodist Church; b. Tokyo, Oct. 22, 1921; s. Frederick and Dora Florella (Schenk) A.; came to U.S., 1924; A.B., Asbury Coll., 1945; M.Div., Asbury Theol. Sem., 1948; M.A., Columbia U., 1951; m. Alma Wilmetta Turkington, Aug. 24, 1945; children: Paul Frederick Jr., Emily Carol. Ordained to ministry, 1950; pastor Knickerbocker Ave. Meth. Ch., Bklyn., 1949-51; assoc. pastor Hanson Place Central Meth. Ch., Bklyn., 1951-54; pastor, Rye, N.Y., 1954-60, Flushing, N.Y., 1960-63, Lynbrook, N.Y., 1963-65; exec. sec. N.Y. Conf. Bd. Missions, 1965-68, assoc. program dir., 1968-72, conf. program dir., 1972-73; pastor Golden Hill United Meth. Ch. Bridgeport, Conn., 1973-78; pres. Greater Bridgeport Council of Chs., 1977-78; mem. Gen. Bd. Discipleship United Meth. Ch., 1972-80; supt. Met. Dist., N.Y. conf. United Meth. Ch., 1978-80; pastor United Meth. Ch. Port Washington, N.Y., 1980—. Home: 12 Hampton Rd Port Washington NY 11050

ABELSON, KASSEL ELIJAH, rabbi, Conservative Jewish Congregations; b. Bklyn., June 26, 1924; s. George and Elizabeth (Kasnowitz) A.; m. Shirley Raskin, Dec. 23, 1947 (dec.); children; David, Elissa, Samuel, B.A., NYU, 1943; Masters in Hebrew Lit., Jewish Theol. Sem., 1948, Doctor Hebrew Letters (hon.), 19—. Ordained rabbi, 1948. Rabbi Beth El Synagogue, Mpls., 1948-51, 57—; rabbi Shearith Israel, Columbus, Ga., 1953-57. Author numerous responsa on applications of Jewish faith. Served as lt. (chaplain) USAF, 1951-53. Mem. Rabbinical Assembly (exec. com. 1981-84, v.p. 1984—). Office: Beth El Synagogue 5224 W 26th St Minneapolis MN 55416

ABERNATHY, DAVID MYLES, clergyman, United Methodist Church; b. Connelly Springs, N.C., June 27, 1933; s. James William and Lorena Mae (Alexander) A.; m. Evelyn Diane Davis, Nov. 24, 1962 (div. Apr. 1970); m. Kathryn Lynn Fordham, Oct. 16, 1971; children: Marc Alexander, Chadwick Myles. B.A., High Point Coll., 1955; M.Div., Emory U., 1962; S.T.M., Union Theol. Sem., N.Y.C., 1964; diploma RCA Insts., N.Y.C., 1964; Litt.D. (hon.), Rust Coll., Holly Springs, Miss., 1974; L.H.D. (hon.), Tex. Wesleyan U., 1980. Ordained deacon United Meth. Ch., 1960, ordained elder, 1963. Instr. Interdenominational Theol. Ctr., Atlanta, 1961-63; tutor asst. Union Theol. Sem., N.Y.C., 1963-64, tutor, 1964-65; adj. prof. Emory U., 1965-72; exec. dir. Joint Communications Com., Atlanta, 1974—; mem. adv. bd. Protestant Radio & TV Ctr., Atlanta., 1972—; mem. Religious Pub. Relations Council, N.Y.C., 1972—; mem. Southeast Jurisdictional Conf. Council on Ministries, Lake Junaluska, N.C., 1974—; mem. Western N.C. Ann. Conf., 1960—; mem. charge conf. Northside United Methodist Ch., Atlanta, 1978—. Author: Hello, Japan!, 1957; A Child's Guidebook to Rome, 1964; Ideas, Inventions and Patents, 1973; Understanding the Teaching of Jesus, 1983. Served to capt. USAF, 1956-59; PTO, Japan. Recipient Gold Mike award Far East Network, Japan, 1959; Gold medal Internat. Film and TV Festival, 1983; Ralph W. Sockman grad. fellow, 1964-65; churchman in residence Candler Sch. Theology, 1985. Mem. Pub. Relations Soc. Am.,-Internat. Assn. Bus. Communications, Nat. Acad. TV Arts and Scis. (Emmy award 1972), United Methodist Assn. Communicators, Am. Film Inst., Am. Acad. Polit. and Social Sci., Soc. Bibl. Lit., Nat. Acad. Rec. Arts and Scis. (gov. 1984—), ASCAP, Authors League Am. Democrat. Home: 935 Bream Ct NE Marietta GA 30067 Office: Joint Communications Com 159 Ralph McGill Blvd NE Atlanta GA 30365

ABERNETHY, JOHN GREGORY, minister, Ind. Christian Chs. and Chs. of Christ; b. San Diego, May 16, 1946; s. John Wayne and Elsie Lorraine Ethridge (Aldridge) A.; student Pacific Christian Coll., Fullerton, Calif., 1966-68; m. Claire Ellen Kennedy, Feb. 16, 1974; children—Robin, Rebekah, John. Ordained to ministry, 1969; pastor chs. in Maricopa and Norwalk, Calif., 1966-67; pastor First Christian Ch., Elsinore, Calif., 1968-70, Wasco (Calif.) Christian Ch., 1974—; mus. dir., producer Wasco Bicentennial Choir Pageant, 1976, also rec. I Love Am., 1976; condr. revivals, singer gospel mus. groups, also soloist. Lions Club scholar, 1967. Mem. Wasco Ministerial Fellowship, Shafter Christian Businessmen's Com. (asso.). Address: 7815 Downing Ave Bakersfield CA 93308

ABEYWICKREMA, LIONEL AUGUSTINE, priest, Roman Catholic Ch.; b. Sri Lanka, July 26, 1926; s. Francis Xavier and Alice Beatrice (Siriwardena) A.; came to U.S., 1963, naturalized, 1969; Th.M., Pontifical U. of the Propagation of the Faith, Rome, 1952. Ordained to priesthood, 1951; asso. pastor, Negombo, Sri Lanka, 1952-53; prof. St. Joseph's Coll., Colombo, Sri Lanka, 1953-56; asso. pastor St. Lucy Cathedral, Colombo, 1956-59; asso. pastor St. Joseph's Ch., Pamunugama, Sri Lanka, 1959-61; asso. pastor St. Sebastian's Ch., Moratwwa, Sri Lanka, 1961-62; asso. pastor St. Bernadette Ch., Albuquerque, 1963-71; co-pastor Our Lady of Fatima, Albuquerque, 1971-77; pastor Sacred Heart Ch., Albuquerque, 1977—. Chaplain Bernalillo County Med. Center, Albuquerque, 1963-64; aide-de-camp to gov. of N. Mex., 1968—. Mem. K.C. Home: 412 Stover SW Albuquerque NM 87108

ABNEY, JAMES WARREN, minister, So. Bapt. Conv.; b. Greenfield, Tenn., Feb. 2, 1932; s. Willis and Odelle (Coats) A.; student Union U. (Tenn.), 1949-53, U. Tenn., 1957, Tex. Wesleyan U., 1959; B.R.E., Southwestern Bapt. Theol. Sem., 1964; m. June Eloise Dowdy, May 30, 1954; children—Michael Wayne, Terry Ray. Ordained to ministry, 1951; pastor Mt. Moriah Bapt. Ch., Whiteville, Tenn., 1951-53, Liberty Bapt. Ch., Somerville, Tenn., 1953-55, South Fork Bapt. Ch., Halls, Tenn., 1955-57, First Bapt. Ch., Troy, Tenn.,

1957-58, Vashti Bapt. Ch., Bowie, Tex., 1958-60, Mayfield Bapt. Ch., Hillsboro, Tex., 1962-64, Mt. Pelia Bapt. Ch., Martin, Tenn., 1964-68, West Bapt. Ch., Hickman, Ky., 1968-72, First Bapt. Ch., Sharon, Tenn., 1972—. Moderator Fulton County (Ky.) Bapt. Assn., 1970-71; com. on bds. Tenn. Bapt. Conv., 1974-77; moderator Weakley County (Tenn.) Bapt. Assn., 1974-76, chmn. constitution study revision com., 1974-76; chmn. Bapt. Student Union steering com., U. Tenn., Martin 1972—; bd. trustees Jonathan Creek Assembly, Ky. Bapt. Conv., 1970-72; v.p. West Tenn. Pastors Conf., 1975. Pres. Civic Club of Sharon, Tenn., 1975. Mem. Hickman C. of C. (dir. 1969-72). Home: 220 N Highway Ave POB 96 Sharon TN 38255 Office: POB 96 Sharon TN 38255

ABRAHAM, DEZSO, bishop, Hungarian Reformed Church in Am. Address: 18700 Midway Ave Allen Park MI 48101

ABRAHAM, MICHAEL LEWIS, rabbi, Reform Jewish Congregations; b. N.Y.C., Aug. 7, 1938; s. Arthur and Mina (Simon) A.; m. Sandra Faust, Dec. 26, 1962; children: Joel, Daniel. B.A., Johns Hopkins U., 1959; B.A. in Hebrew Lit., Hebrew Union Coll., 1962, M.A. in Hebrew Lit., 1965. Ordained rabbi Reform Jewish Congregations, 1965. Chaplain U.S. Army, Verdun, France, 1965-67, Munich, W. Ger., 1967-68; rabbi Temple Beth-El, Somerville, N.J., 1968—; dir. Jewish Family Service, Somerville, 1980—; mem. faculty Sch. Edn., Hebrew Union Coll., N.J., 1970-71. Contbr. articles to profl. jours. Pres. Somerset Community Action Program, N.J., 1968-72, Somerville Area Ministerial Assn.; bd. dirs. Family Counseling Services, Somerset, 1968-73. Served to capt. U.S. Army, 1965-68. Recipient Hannah Solomon award Nat. Council Jewish Women, 1971. Mem. Central Conf. Am. Rabbis, N.J. Assn. Reform Rabbis (pres. 1981-83), Nat. Fedn. Temple Youth (life). Home: 2006 Holland Brook Rd Somerville NJ 08876 Office: Temple Beth El 67 Route 206 S Somerville NJ 08876

ABRAMOWICZ, ALFRED L. See *Who's Who in America*, 43rd edition.

ACERRA, ANGELO THOMAS, bishop, Roman Catholic Church. Titular bishop of Lete, aux. bishop Mil. Vicariate, N.Y.C., 1983—. Office: Mil Vicariate 1011 First Ave New York NY 10022*

ACHE, HARVEY ELLSWORTH, JR., minister, Christian and Missionary Alliance; b. Allentown, Pa., Nov. 29, 1927; s. Harvey Ellsworth and Ruth Beatrice (Parton) A.; B.A. in Bible, Ft. Wayne (Ind.) Bible Coll., 1952; B.S. in Edn., Kent (Ohio) State U., 1970, M.Ed., 1972; m. Jane Leona Ford, May 25, 1951; children—Jewel (dec.), Joy, Andy. Ordained to ministry, 1954; missionary to W.Africa, 1954-58; evangelist, 1958-59; pastor chs. in Ohio, Ill., Mich. and Pa., 1959—; pastor People's Ch., Geneva, Ohio, 1975—; elementary guidance counselor Geneva Pub. Schs., 1976—. Mem. S. Amherst (Ohio) Tchrs. Assn. (pres.) 1971-73, Ohio Guidance Counselors Assn. Home: 270 S Ridge St Geneva OH 44041 Office: 300 S Ridge St Geneva OH 44041

ACKERSON, CHARLES STANLEY, minister, American Baptist Churches of the U.S.A., social worker; b. St. Louis June 19, 1935; s. Charles Albert Ackerson and Glenda Mae (Brown) Ackerson Cooper; m. Carol Jean Stehlick, Aug. 18, 1957; children: Debra Lynn, Charles Mark, Heather Sue. A.B., William Jewell Coll., 1957; M.Div., Colgate Rochester Div. Sch., 1961. Ordained to ministry American Baptist Churches in the U.S.A., 1961. Pastor, Soc. of Friends Ch., Glens Falls, N.Y., 1961-65; assoc. pastor Delmar Bapt. Ch., St. Louis, 1965-68; ecumenical ministry Block Partnership, Inc., Am. Bapt. Ch., St. Louis, 1968-71; assoc. supply pastor St. Jordan's United Ch. Christ, Jeffriesburg, Mo., 1970—, St. John's United Ch. Christ, Casco, Mo., 1970—; adj. instr. Mo. Bapt. Coll., St. Louis County, 1981—; developer, mem. com. for interracial communication, Glen's Falls, 1964-65; mem. planning com. med. communication, St. Louis Met. Ch. Fedn., 1965-68; chmn. conf. com. violence and the ch., St. Louis, 1982; mem. ordination com. Area V Great Rivers Region, Am. Bapt. Ch. U.S.A., 1982-84. Group home supr. Juvenile Ct. St. Louis, 1973-74; dir. Youth Opportunities Unltd., St. Louis County, 1974-76; case work supr. Juvenile Ct. St. Louis County, 1976-81; youth specialist Office County Youth Programs, Dept. Human Resources, St. Louis County, 1985—. Cartoonist Wilbur, 1959-61, Willers, 1984—. Mem. adult edn. adv. bd., Glens Falls, 1961-65; mem. urban renewal bd., Glens Falls, 1961-65; mem. citizen adv. bd. Parkway Sch. Dist., Manchester, Mo., 1967-68; mem. New Democratic Coalition, St. Louis, 1967-68; chmn. group home com. Mo. Council on Criminal Justice, 1973-76; chmn. cts. and instns. sub-com. Juvenile Delinquency Task Force for Gov. Bonds' Mo. Action Plan for Pub. Safety, 1976; dir. residential treatment program N. Side YMCA Group Home, St. Louis, 1971-73. Mem. Mo. Juvenile Justice Assn. (treas. 1980-82, v.p. 1983-84), Mo. Assn. Child Care Agys. (assoc.), Nat. Council Juvenile and Family Ct. Judges (assoc.), Lambda Chi Alpha (pledge trainer 1955-57). Clubs: 3 Rivers Kennel of Mo. (pres. 1984-85). Cairn Terrier Am., Trappers of Starved Rock (St. Charles, Mo.). Home: 1221 Havenhurst Manchester MO 63011

ACTON, ALFRED, minister, administrator General Church of the New Jerusalem; b. Bryn Athyn, Pa., Aug. 21, 1934; s. Kesniel Carswell and Renee (Odhner) A.; m. Henrietta Palmer Gourdin, July 23, 1960; 1 child, Kesniel Carswell. B.A., Haverford Coll., 1958; B.Th., Acad. New Ch., 1964. Ordained to ministry, 1964. Pastor, Sharon Ch., Chgo., 1964-68; asst. pastor/headmaster Immanuel Ch., Glenview, Ill., 1968-73; pastor/pres. Immanuel Ch.-Midwestern Acad., Glenview, 1973-76; pres. Acad. of the New Ch., Bryn Athyn, Pa., 1976-83; Bishop's rep. Gen. Ch. of New Jerusalem, Bryn Athyn, 1983—; prin. Midwestern Acad. of New Ch., Glenview, 1968-73. Bd. dirs. Bryn Athyn Civic and Social Club, 1962, 84. Served with U.S. Army, 1959-61. Mem. Assn. for Curriculum Devel., Am. Philological Assn., Swedenborg Soc., Swedenborg Scientific Assn. Republican. Home: 2880 Quarry Rd Bryn Athyn PA 19009 Office: Gen Ch of New Jerusalem Cairncrest Bryn Athyn PA 19009

ACTON, THOMAS R., minister, Lutheran Church-Missouri Synod; b. Elmhurst, Ill., Sept. 5, 1953; s. Raymond and Margaret (Bell) A.; m. Carol Jevne, Aug. 17, 1974; children: John, Mark, Kimberly. B.A., No. Ill. U., 1975; M.Div., Concordia Theol. Sem., 1979. Ordained to ministry, 1979. Missionary, Luth. Ch. in Philippines, 1979-82; campus pastor Concordia Coll., River Forest, Ill., 1982—; synodical rep. Nat. Luth. Campus Ministries World Task Force, Chgo., 1984—. Contbr. articles to profl. jours. Mem. Luth. Hist. Conf. Home. 1115 Bonnie Brae River Forest IL 60305 Office: Concordia Coll 7400 Augusta River Forest IL 60305

ADAIR, TOBY WARREN, JR., retired minister, Southern Baptist Convention; b. Beaumont, Tex., Sept. 8, 1922; s. Toby Warren and Mildred Lee (Muldrow) A.; B.S., Centenary Coll., 1947; M.Div., Golden Gate Bapt. Theol. Sem., 1973; M.R.E., 1974; Doctor of Ministry, San Francisco Theol. Sem.; m. Ann Ivareese Redden, May 8, 1943; 1 child, Robin Lee Adair Fleming. Ordained to ministry Baptist Ch., 1973; pastor South Reno (Nev.) Bapt. Ch., 1973-77, Bancroft Bapt. Ch., Spring Valley, Calif., 1977-81, Mt. Zion Bapt. Ch., Prairieville, La., 1982-85; ret., 1985; pres. pastors conf. San Diego So. Bapt. Assn., 1981, Ascension Bapt. Assn., 1984; rotating prayer-time host Sta. KNIS, Reno-Carson City, Nev., 1974-76. Served to maj. USAFR, 1943-67, ret. Decorated DFC, air medal with 2 oak leaf clusters; named Boss of Yr., Sierra chpt. Am. Bus. Women's Assn., 1975. Home: 803 W 12th St Pine Bluff AR 71601

ADAM, JOHN, Synodical bishop Lutheran Church in America. Office: Luth Ch in Am 13 Kingswood Rd Danbury CT 06810*

ADAMCIO, JOHN STEPHENS, priest, Orthodox Church in America; b. Herkimer, N.Y., Dec. 26, 1951; s. Stephen and Barbara (Sweda) A.; m. Marlene Melania Rinish, June 3, 1973; children: Anysia, Matthew. Diplomate, St. Tikhon's Sem., 1974. Ordained deacon Orthodox Church in America, 1973, priest, 1974. Rector St. John's Ch., Philipsburg, Pa., 1974-76, St. Nicholas Ch., Fort Lauderdale, Fla., 1976-77, St. Nicholas Ch., McKees Rocks, Pa., 1977-79, St. Michael's Ch., Old Forge, Pa., 1979—; night chaplain Wilkes Barre Gen. Hosp., Pa., 1982-84; sec. Wilkes-Barre Deanery, 1983-84; mem. exec. bd., mem. ethics com. Community Med. Ctr. Chaplains (Night), Scranton, Pa., 1983-84. Home and Office: 512 Summer St Old Forge PA 18518

ADAMO, SALVATORE JOSEPH, priest, Roman Catholic Church; b. N.Y.C., Feb. 2, 1919; s. Vito and Orsola (LaDolce) A.; B.A., N.Y. U., 1941; postgrad. St. Joseph's Coll. and Sem., 1939-44, St. Mary's Sem., Balt., 1944-45. Ordained priest, 1945; editor Cath. Star Herald, 1962—; rector Immaculate Conception Cathedral, Camden, N.J., 1967-84; pastor St. Vincent Pallotti Ch., Hadden Twp., N.J., 1984—; pro-synodal judge Matrimonial Tribunal, 1963-66; pres. Priests Council, Diocese of Camden, 1971, 76. Active, N.J. Com. of Capital Punishment, 1964, N.J. Crime Commn., 1966, Camden Econ. Devel. Adv. Com., 1967-72. Recipient Human Relations award Phila. chpt. Am. Jewish Com., 1963. Author: While the Winds Blew, 1968. Press columnist Am. Mag., 1965-74; author weekly column Phila. Daily News, 1973—. Office: St Vincent Pallotti Ch Hopkins Rd Haddon Township NJ 08033

ADAMS, CONNIE WILSON, minister, Ch. of Christ; b. Hopewell, Va., Sept. 22, 1930; s. Joyner Wilson and Nollie Matilda (Stotesberry) A.; B.A., Fla. Coll., 1953; postgrad. U. Bergen (Norway), 1957-59; m. Barbara Rose Colley, Aug. 14, 1950; children—Doron Wilson, Martin Weldon. Minister chs., Atlanta, 1954-57, Newbern, Tenn., 1960-62, Orlando, Fla., 1962-65, Akron, Ohio, 1965-70, Louisville, 1970—; missionary to Norway, 1957-59; asso. editor Truth Mag., Marion, Ind., 1965-73; editor/pub. Searching the Scriptures, Brooks, Ky., 1973—. Evangelist, various states and countries, 1950—. Mem. nat. adv. council Fla. Coll., 1972—; chmn. Hilbrook Farms Assn. Property Owners, Bullitt County, Ky., 1975—. Named Hon. Ky. Col., 1971; recipient Ann. Friendship award Ky. Alumni Assn., 1973. Author: Premillennialism, True or False?, 1966; Miraculous Divine Healing: Faith or Fake?, 1967; also tracts and booklets. Home: 52 Yearling Dr Brooks KY 40109 Office: PO Box 68 Brooks KY 40109

ADAMS, DOUGLAS GLENN, educator, minister, United Church of Christ; b. DeKalb, Ill., Apr. 12, 1945; s. Glenn Hammer and Harriet (Engstrom) A.; m. Margo Alice Miller, June 7, 1968. B.A., Duke U., 1967; M.A., Pacific Sch. Religion, 1970, M.Div., 1970; Th.D., Grad. Theol. Union, 1974. Ordained to ministry, 1970. Pastor, Coll. Hts. Ch., San Mateo, Calif., 1970-72; asst. prof. U. Mont., Missoula, 1975-76, Pacific Sch. Religion, Berkeley, Calif., 1976-79, assoc. prof., 1979-84, prof. Christianity and art, 1984—; bd. dirs. United Ch. Christ Fellowship in the Arts, N.Y.C., 1979—. Author: Meeting House to Camp Meeting, 1981; Humor in the American Pulpit, 1975; Congregational Dancing in Christian Worship, 1971. Editor: Dancing Christmas Carols, 1978. Editorial bd. Modern Liturgy, 1977—. Bd. dirs. Body and Soul Dance Co., Berkeley, Calif., 1978—. Smithsonian Instn. fellow in art history, 1974-75; Third Internat. Congress on Religion, Art and Arch. overseas fellow, Jerusalem, 1973; Library prize, Duke U., 1967. Fellow Arts Religion and Contemporary Culture, N. Am. Acad. Liturgy; mem. Nat. Sacred Dance Guild (dir. and pres. 1977-79), The Polayi Soc. (dir.), Am. Acad. Religion, College Art Assn. Home: 6226 Bernhard St Richmond CA 94805 Office: Pacific Sch Religion 1798 Scenic Ave Berkeley CA 94709

ADAMS, ELLSWORTH ROBERT, minister, Church of God (Cleveland, Tenn.); b. Thompsonville, Mich., Nov. 30, 1910; s. Lester Duane and Elizabeth Emily (Whiteside) A.; m. Ethel Adeline Dial, May 18, 1937 (dec. Dec. 1983); children: Joyce Ann, Ellsworth Robert. A.S., Frontier Community Coll., 1984. Ordained to ministry Bethel Full Gospel Assemblies, 1931, Internat. Pentecostal Assemblies, 1946, Church of God, 1951. Asst. pastor, pastor Bethel Full Gospel Assembly, McDaniel Crossroads, Gallia, Ohio, 1931-36; gen. treas. Internat. Pentecostal Assembly, Newcastle, Wyo., 1946-48; instr. Black Hills Bible Inst., Newcastle, 1946-49; pastor Full Gospel Assembly, Sturgis, S.D., 1948-49; pastor Church of God, Sheboygan, Wis., 1950-52, McClellan, Mt. Vernon, Ill., 1952-55, Fairfield, Ill., 1955—; co-founder, then interim pastor Beacon Gospel Assembly, Detroit, 1946; mem. Ill. State Council Church of God, Decatur, 1972-74, 1974-76. Co-founder, editor: Bridegroom's Messenger, official mag. Internat. Pentecostal Assemblies, Detroit, 1941-46, Newcastle, 1946-48. Producer, host radio program: A Voice for Holiness, 1971—. Composer gospel songs. Pres. Wayne County Anti-Poverty Group, Fairfield, Ill.; bd. dirs., founder Wabash Area Devel. Inc. Rural Resource Ctr. Mem. Fairfield Ministerial Alliance (sec. 1956-58). Home: 115 Young Dr PO Box 22 Fairfield IL 62837 Office: Church of God 815 W Main St PO Box 232 Fairfield IL 62837

ADAMS, F(REDERICK) JOHN, minister, United Church of Canada; b. Burin, Nfld., Can., May 13, 1939; s. Frank K. and Maggie K. (Downer) A.; m. Dallas Judith George, Feb. 14, 1969; children: Lynette, John, Corey. B.A., Mount Allison Coll., 1963; M.Div., Pine Hill Div. Hall, 1965. Ordained to ministry, United Ch. of Can., 1965. Sr. minister First United Ch., Corner Brook, Nfld. Sec. Nfld. Conf. United Ch. of Can., St. John's, 1970-73, pres., 1973-74; gen. council exec., sub-exec. United Ch. of Can., Toronto, 1974-77. Scoutmaster Exploits council Boy Scouts of Can., 1970-75; chaplain Royal Can. Legion, Botwood, Corner Branch, 1977-84; St. John Ambulance Brigade Botwood, 1977-80; mem. Bay of Islands Sch. Bd., Corner Brook, 1981-85. Mem. Humber Presbytery (chmn. ministry, personnel and edn.). Lodges: Masons, Rotary. Home: 25 Park St Corner Brook NF A2H 2W8 Canada Office: United Ch of Can 19 Park St Corner Brook NF A2H 2W8 Canada

ADAMS, FRED LEVIE, minister, American Baptist Churches in the U.S.A.; b. Atlanta, Nov. 12, 1937; s. Levie Newton and Annie Bertie (Harrelson) A.; m. Frances Elizabeth Williams, Aug. 9, 1959; children: Catherine Belinda Adams Wallace, Alan Craig. B.A., Baylor U., 1959; M.Div., So. Sem., 1962; D.Ministry, McCormick Sem., 1984. Ordained to ministry Am. Bapt. Chs., 1962. Pastor First Bapt. Ch., Salem, Ind., 1962-67; campus minister Univ. Bapt. Ch., Normal, Ill., 1967-76; pastor First Bapt. Ch., Jacksonville, Ill., 1976-79; area minister Gt. Rivers Region, St. Louis, 1979—; bd. dirs. Hudleston Children's Home, Centralia, Ill., 1979—; mem. Mo. Christian Leadership Forum, Jefferson City, 1982—; bd. dirs. Am. Bapt. Campus, Columbia, Mo., 1983—, Shuntleff Found., 1972—; mem. Ministers Council. Lodge: Kiwanis (Jacksonville). Home: 811 Weatherhwood Dr Saint Louis MO 63011 Office: Am Bapt Chs of Gt Rivers Region 225 E Cook St Springfield IL 62708

ADAMS, JACK HOWARD, minister, Ch. of God (Cleveland, Tenn.); b. Birmingham, Ala., Aug. 9, 1929; s. Kyle Kaiser and Murzie Etrula (Kelley) A.; B.A., Lee Coll., 1956; postgrad. Tenn. Temple Coll., 1956; m. Elma Reba Crane, Apr. 6, 1951; children—Cheri, Janice, Pamela. Ordained to ministry, 1960; pastor N.Y. Ave. Ch. of God, Chattanooga, 1955-56, Kenosha

(Wis.) Ch. of God, 1956-62, Salisbury (Md.) Ch. of God, 1962-65, Central Pkwy. Ch. of God, Cin., 1966-69, Harlan Park Ch. of God, Middletown, Ohio, 1969-74; state overseer Chs. of God (Cleveland, Tenn.) Wis., Milw., 1974—. Pres., Greater Cin. Ch. of God Ministerial Assn., 1967-69, Evang. Ministerial Assn., Middletown, 1971-73; mem. pres.'s council N.W. Bible Coll., Minot, N.D., 1975—. Home and Office: 4536 N 110th St Milwaukee WI 53225

ADAMS, JAMES BENJAMIN, minister, Baptist Missionary Association America; b. Bachconton, Ga., Mar. 10, 1907; s. Douglas Appolas and Hattie Irene (Frazier) A.; m. Willie Mae Christie, Oct. 23, 1976; children by previous marriage: Willie, Joyce. Student, Fla. A&M U., 1926-28; D.D., Fla. Sem., 1954. Ordained to ministry, 1938. Pastor, First Bapt. Ch., Dundee, Fla., 1938-40, Bethel Bapt. Ch., Lake Alford, Fla., 1942-45; missionary First S. Fla. Assn., Fla. Dist., 1940-45; pastor Mt. Gilboa Ch., Bartow, Fla., 1945-50, St. John Ch., Belle Glade, Fla., 1950—; chmn. edn. bd. M & E Progressive Conf., Fla., 1950—; moderator Greater S. Fla. Assn., 1951—; chmn. edn. bd. Nat. Bapt. Conv. Am., 1974—, pres., Lakeland, Fla., 1980—. Pres., Interdenomination Alliance, Belle Glade, Fla., 1955, Wee Care, Inc. for Migrant Workers, 1976, Glade Area Assn. Retarded, 1976. Mem. Ministerial Interdenomination Assn. (pres. 1970). Democrat. Address: 609 SW 9th St Belle Glade FL 33430

ADAMS, JERE VARNELL, minister, Southern Baptist Convention; b. Douglasville, Ga., Mar. 3, 1937; s. Willard Varnell and Mildred Louise (Yeager) A.; B.A., Georgia State U., 1964; B.Christian Music, Southwestern Bapt. Theol. Sem., 1972, M.R.E., 1972, M.Christian Music, 1973; m. Polly Pattillo, July 23, 1960; children: Kimberly, Patrick Dean, Lorianne. Ordained to ministry, 1968; music tchr. Tenn. Bapt. Youth Music Camp, Newport, 1974, 75, Ala. Youth Music Camp, Talladega, 1976; minister of music chs., Tex., 1969-73, Camden (Ala.) Bapt. Ch., 1973-74, Loudon County Bapt. Ch., Lenoir City, Tenn., 1974—, Hamilton County Bapt. Ch.-Hixson First Bapt. Ch., Tenn., 1982-83; program assoc. ch. music dept. Tenn. Bapt. Conv., mem. arrangements com., 1980-82; music dir. Loudon County Bapt. Assn. Guest musician Lenoir City Pub. Schs., 1976. Mem. Am. Choral Dirs. Assn., So. Bapt. Ch. Music Conf. Club: Optimists. Lodges: Masons, Scottish Rite. Home: 470 S Fawn Ct Murfreesboro TN 37130 Office: 205 Franklin Rd Box 347 Brentwood TN 37027

ADAMS, JOHN A., minister, So. Bapt. Conv.; b. Morgan City, La., June 21, 1944; s. John J. and Winnifred Maude (Underwood) A.; B.S. in Bus. Adminstrn., U. Southwestern La., 1974; m. Susan A. Stierheim, May 18, 1966; children—John Scott, Shane Mark, Walter Matthew, Jennifer Ruth. Ordained to ministry, 1974; evangelist, 1972-77; asso. pastor Trinity Bapt. Ch., Blytheville, Ark., 1974-75; founder, tchr. E. New Orleans Vietnamese Bapt. Mission, 1975—. Home: 411 Crawford St Lafayette LA 70506 Office: 411 Crawford St Lafayette LA 70506

ADAMS, JOHN HURST, bishop, African Methodist Episcopal Church; b. Columbia, S.C., Nov. 27, 1929; s. Eugene Avery and Charity A. (Nash) A.; A.B., Johnson C. Smith Coll., 1948; S.T.B., Boston U., 1951, S.T.M., 1953; D.D., Wilberforce U., 1956, Paul Quinn Coll., 1972; m. Dolly Desselle, Aug. 25, 1956; children—Gaye Desselle, Jann Hurst, Madelyn Rose. Ordained to ministry African Methodist Episcopal Ch. as deacon, 1948, elder, 1952, bishop, 1972; pastor Bethel A.M.E. Ch., Lynn, Mass., 1950-52; prof. Wilberforce U., 1952-56; pres. Paul Quinn Coll., Waco, Tex., 1956-62, chmn. bd., 1972—; pastor 1st A.M.E. Ch., Seattle, 1962-68, Grant A.M.E. Ch., Los Angeles, 1968-72; 87th A.M.E. bishop 10th dist., Tex., from 1972, now bishop 2d dist. Bd. dirs. Nat., Tex. councils chs., Nat. Conf. Black Churchmen, Nat. Bd. Black United Funds, Nat. Council Chs., PUSH (People United to Save Humanity). Named Man of Year B'nai B'rith, 1964, Urban League, Seattle, 1965. Mem. Boulé, Alpha Phi Alpha. Author: Ethnic Education in Black Church, 1970. Office: 615 G St SW Washington DC 20024*

ADAMS, LESLIE, church musician, American Baptist Assn.; b. Cleve., Dec. 30, 1932; d. Harrison Leslie and Jessie (Beatrice) A. Bachelor in Music Edn., Oberlin Conservatory, 1955; M.A., Calif. State U.-Long Beach, 1965; Ph.D., Ohio State U., 1973. Organist West Side United Church of Christ, Cleve., 1980—. Composer-in-residence Cleve. Music Sch. Settlement, 1980—. Composer: Blake (opera), 1984; Symphony No. 1, 1983; Ode to Life (orchestral work), 1980; A Kiss in Xanadu (orchestral work), 1953, 74. Recipient Nat. Composition award Christian Arts Choral Composition Competition, 1973. Nat. Endowment Arts fellow, 1979; Yaddo Artist fellow, 1980, 84. Mem. Am. Choral Dirs. Assn. (life), Phi Kappa Phi, Phi Kappa Lambda, Phi Mu Alpha Sinfonia, Phi Delta Kappa. Home: 9409 Kempton Ave Cleveland OH 44108 Office: Cleve Music Sch Settlement 11125 Magnolia Dr Cleveland OH 44106

ADAMS, MENDLE EUGENE, minister, United Church of Christ; b. Bath County, Va., July 1, 1938; s. Earl and Margaret M. (Godsey) A.; m. N. Ruth Williams, Feb. 2, 1957; children: David Mendle, Brian Richard, Josef Wayne, Vicki Ruth. A.B., Marion Coll., 1967; M.A.R., Christian Theol. Sem., 1969; postgrad. in mgmt. Aquinas Coll., 1977; postgrad. in health adminstrn. Harvard U., 1978. Ordained to ministry Meth. Ch., 1968, United Ch. of Christ, 1981. Pastor Windfall Pilgrim Ch., Ind., 1960-63, Mt. Olive Meth. Ch., Marion, Ind., 1963-67, Mt. Comfort United Meth. Ch., Indpls., 1967-69, Hope Congl. United Ch. Christ, Granville, N.D., 1980-82, First Congl. United Ch. Christ, McPherson, Kans., 1982—; mem. Kans.-Okla. Conf. Camp Com., 1983—. Mem. Ind. Ho. of Reps., 1975-76; chmn. McPherson Community Nursing Home Com., 1984; bd. dirs. McPherson Family Life Ctr., 1983-84. Recipient Honored Legislator citation Ind. Council Chs. 1976. Mem. McPherson Ministerial Alliance (sec. 1983-84). Democrat. Home and Office: 208 S Maple McPherson KS 67460

ADAMS, TERRY MARTIN, music and youth minister, Southern Baptist Convention; b. Cunningham, Ky., Dec. 22, 1951; s. Robert Martin and Rachel Lee (Terry) A.; m. Beverly Rae Kinard, Oct. 19, 1972 (div. Aug. 1981); children: Kindra Rae, Shanna Leigh. Student So. Bapt. Coll., 1969-71; B.A. in Music, Union U., 1971-74; M.A. in Ch. Music, Southwestern Bapt. Theol. Sem., 1974-76. Ordained to ministry So. Bapt. Conv., 1980. Minister of music and youth various chs., Ark., Tenn., Tex., Colo., 1971-81; minister of music and youth First Bapt. Ch., Fulton, Ky., 1981—; choral dir. Bapt. Student Union Choir So. Bapt. Coll., 1971-73. Composer: Go Forth and Let Me Reach Out, 1984; You Are My Everything, 1983; Bless His Holy Name, 1983. Mem. Ky. Bapt. Chorale, Fulton Bapt. Assn. (youth dir. 1982—). Democrat. Lodge: Lions (dir. men's chorus 1982—). Avocations: snow and water skiing, racquetball, songwriting, photography. Home: PO Box Hickory Ln Rd Fulton KY 42041 Office: 1st Bapt Ch 2d and Eddings Sts Fulton KY 42041

ADAMS, THURMAN LEON, JR., minister, Southern Baptist Convention; b. Jackson, Miss., Dec. 21, 1945; s. Thurman Leon and Erma Frances (Evans) A.; m. Mary Eloise Hardwick, Nov. 24, 1965; children: Stephanie Rene, Lori Marie. B.A., Miss. Coll., 1969; postgrad. New Orleans Bapt. Theol. Sem., 1977-79, 81-82. Ordained to ministry, 1968. Pastor, Salem Bapt. Ch., Preston, Miss., 1970-72, Mashulaville, Bapt. Ch., Macon, Miss., 1972-73, Macedonia Bapt. Ch., Louisville, Miss., 1973-76, Arkadelphia Bapt. Ch., Bailey, Miss., 1976-80, Oak Grove Bapt. Ch., Meridian, Miss., 1980—; bd. dirs. Am. Christian TV Network, Meridian, 1983—; chaplain Meridian Police Dept., 1981—. Mem. Internat. Conf. Police Chaplains. Home: 1000 Oak Grove Dr Meridian MS 39301 Office: Oak Grove Bapt Ch 1002 Oak Grove Dr Meridian MS 39301

ADAMSON, STANLEY ERROL, minister, Presbyterian Church (U.S.A.); b. Van Nuys, Calif., June 19, 1948; s. Raymond Ferris and Barbara Lela (Dunham) A.; m. Linda-Marie Mayer, June 13, 1970; children: Daniel Elias, Nathan John, Michael Andrew, Joel James. A.A., L.A. Pierce Coll., 1968; B.A., UCLA, 1970; M.Div., Fuller Theol. Sem., 1973; D.Min., McCormick Theol. Sem., 1985. Ordained to ministry United Presbyn. Ch. in U.S.A., 1973. Youth dir. Union Ch. of Los Angeles, 1970-71; lay asst. First Presbyn. Ch., Sherman Oaks, Calif., 1972; pastor United Presbyn. Ch., Jetmore, Kans., 1973-80, First Presbyn. Ch., Halstead, Kans., 1980—; chmn. adv. council on ch. and society Synod of Mid-Am., Overland Park, Kans., 1975-77; mem. ministerial relations com. Presbytery So. Kans., Wichita, 1979-84; commr. 192d Gen. Assembly, Detroit, 1980. Cubmaster Quivira council Boy Scouts Am., Halstead, Kans., 1983—. Club: Optimists (pres. 1983-84). Avocations: backpacking, cycling, writing, photography, vocal music. Home: 120 E 4th St Halstead KS 67056 Office: First Presbyterian Ch PO Box 309 Halstead KS 67056

ADCOCK, MARTHA J., lay minister, Free Methodist Church; automotive consultant executive; b. Lenzsiding, Oreg., Aug. 17, 1938; d. Johnnie B. and Ruth V. (Parton) Bivens; m. Jack H. Adcock, Sept. 8, 1956; children: R. Denice, Rodney D., Ryan D. Christian edn. dir. Free Methodist, Chico, Calif., 1962-65, lay minister, 1955-65, asst. pastor, Hayward, Calif., 1970-74, assoc. pastor, Macon, Ga., 1978-80; dir. musical group Nazarene Ch., Jackson, Ga., 1982—. Vice pres. ADCO Automotive Cons., Jackson, 1983—. Author: What the Bible Says About the Return of Christ, bible study, 1982; musical dramas, 1984, 85; co-author Living Faith for Families, family life seminar, 1977. Home: Route 2 Box 539 Jackson GA 30233 Office: ADCO Automotive Cons Inc Route 2 Box 539 Jackson GA 30233

ADDISON, CARL VERNON, JR., minister, Church of God, Anderson, Indiana; b. Welch, W. Va., Mar. 19, 1957; s. Carl Vernon and Jo Anne (Gammon) A.; m. Valerie Ann Hartshorn, July 28, 1979; children: Matthew Paul, Steven Andrew. B.A., Anderson Coll., 1978; M.Div., Anderson Sch. Theology, 1981. Ordained to ministry, 1982. Assoc. pastor Evanswood Ch. of God, Troy, Mich., 1980-82; pastor First Ch. of God, West Chester, Ohio, 1983—; chmn. Bd. Christian Edn., S.W. Ohio Assembly, Hamilton, 1983—; treas. Ohio State Bd. Christian Edn., Columbus, 1984—; mem. exec. com. S.W. Ohio Assembly, 1984—; instr. Towne Bible Inst., Middletown, Ohio, 1985—. Mem. Lakota Ministerial Assn. Republican. Home: 7904 3d St West Chester OH 45069 Office: First Church of God 7904 3d St West Chester OH 45069

ADDISON, LESLIE WAYNE, minister, Southern Baptist Convention; b. Balt., Sept. 6, 1954; s. Raleigh Evans and Margaret Evelyn (Whitt) A.; B.A., Graham Bible Coll., 1976; m. Lora Kay Carr, May 18, 1974; children: Hannah Kay, Rachel Lynne, Deborah Leigh. Ordained to ministry, 1974; pastor Pleasant Home Bapt. Ch., Laurel Bloomery, Tenn., 1974-83; assoc. pastor 1st Bapt. Ch., Mountain City, Tenn., 1983-84; pastor Beulah Bapt. Ch., Kingsport, Tenn., 1984—; pres. Graham Bible Coll. student body, 1975-76; tchr. Southwest Va. Christian Acad., 1978-79. Recipient Dan Graham Service award, 1976. Mem. Holston Bapt. Assn. Home: Route 11 Box 162 Kingsport TN 37663 Office: Route 11 Kingsport TN 37663

ADENEY, BERNARD TEMPLE, religion educator; b. Shanghai, China, Sept. 28, 1948; s. David H. and Ruth Adeney; m. Frances Screnock, Dec. 16, 1967; children: Jennifer, Rina, Peter. B.A. with honors, U. Wis., 1970; diploma theology Discipleship Tng. Ctr., Singapore, 1973; B.D., U. London, 1974; Ph.D. with distinction, Grad. Theol. Union, Berkeley, Calif., 1982. Asst. prof. social ethics, dir. cross cultural ministry program New Coll. of Berkeley, Calif., 1982—; bd. dirs. Berkeley Christian Coalition, 1974—. Contbr. articles, revs. to various publs. Grad. Theol. Union tuition grantee. Mem. Am. Acad. Religion, Soc. Christian Ethics, Evangs. for Social Action, Bread for the World, Amnesty Internat. Home: 1545 Dwight Way Berkeley CA 94703 Office: Dept Ethics New Coll of Berkeley 2600 Dwight Way Berkeley CA 94704

ADKERSON, WILLIAM HALLIBURTON, minister religious edn., So. Bapt. Conv.; b. Lauderdale County, Tenn., Sept. 18, 1936; s. James H. and Maude Elizabeth (Jennings) A.; B.A., Union U., 1960; M.R.E., Southwestern Bapt. Theol. Sem., 1963; m. Mary Janet Southall, Dec. 28, 1958; children—Lori Katherine, Norma Suzanne, Mary Amanda. Minister music edn. First Bapt. Ch., Joana, S.C., 1963-64; minister of edn. First Bapt. Ch., Clinton, N.C., 1964-66, First Bapt. Ch., Mobile, Ala., 1967-76, First Bapt. Ch., Winston-Salem, N.C., 1976—, also ch. adminstr., 1976—. Conf. leader Ala. Bapt. Conv., 1968-76; mem. missions com. Mobile (Ala.) Bapt. Assn., 1970-73. Mem. Mobile com. for President's Com. on Aging, 1972; bd. dirs. Mobile Presch. for the Deaf, 1975-76. Mem. So. Bapt., Southeastern Bapt., Ala. Bapt., Mobile Bapt. religious edn. assns. Home: 8815 Merry Hill Court Clemmons NC 27012 Office: First Baptist Church Fifth and Spruce Streets Winston-Salem NC 27101

ADKINS, FRED KLINE, JR., minister, Southern Baptist Convention; b. Columbia, S.C., June 11, 1952; s. Fred Kline and Mary (Smith) A.; m. Dorothy Sue Carroll, July 6, 1974; 1 child, Fred Kline. B.A., Gardner-Webb Coll., Boiling Springs, N.C., 1974; M.R.E., Southwestern Bapt. Theol. Sem., Fort Worth, 1976. Ordained to ministry So. Bapt. Conv., 1980. Minister of music East Side Bapt. Ch., Kings Mountain, N.C., 1970-72, Campfield Meml. Bapt. Ch., Mooresboro, N.C., 1972-73, Westview Bapt. Ch., Shelby, N.C., 1973-74; minister of music and youth 1st Bapt. Ch., Alvarado, Tex., 1974-76, 2d Bapt. Ch., Kershaw, S.C., 1976-79, Mt. Pleasant Bapt. Ch., Colonial Heights, Va., 1979—; chaplain Petersburg Hosp, Va., Colonial Heights Police Dept. Mem. Colonial Heights Clergy (pres. 1981-83), Associated Pastoral Counselors Colonial Heights (bd. dirs. 1985—), Va. Bapt. Religious Edn. Assn., Am. Guild Organists, Inst. Indsl. and Comml. Ministries. Home: 906 Dogwood Dr Colonial Heights VA 23834 Office: Mt Pleasant Bapt Ch 3110 Greenwood Ave Colonial Heights VA 23834

AEBI, CHARLES JERRY, minister, educator, Church of Christ; b. Webster, Pa., Feb. 15, 1931; s. Jerry and Nadeline (Stipes) A.; m. Imogene D. McDonough, Aug. 5, 1955; children: Ruth, Joy, Mark, Mary. B.S., Pa. State U., 1952; M.A., Abilene Christian U., 1959; Ph.D., Ohio U., 1972. Part-time minister Ch. of Christ, Vanceville, Pa., 1954-55; minister Ch. of Christ, Corapolis, Pa., 1956-61, Sistersville, W.Va., 1962-64, Vienna, W.Va., 1971-82, Parkersburg, W.Va., 1964-70, 82—; v.p., acad. dean Ohio Valley Coll., Parkersburg, 1970—. Author: Old Testament Survey, 1964; Herzberg's Job Satisfaction Theory, 1972; Lamp to My Feet, A Thorough Study of the Bible, 1978; New Testament Survey, 1984. Editor: The New Birth and Its Implications, 1980; Educating to Service, OVC Self Study, 1977, 2d edit. 1982. Mem. Am. Assn. Higher Edn., W.Va. Council Acad. Deans, Phi Delta Kappa. Lodge: Kiwanis. Home: Route 1 Vincent OH 45784 Office: Ohio Valley Coll College Parkway Parkersburg WV 26101

AESCHLIMANN, HILDEGARDE JOSEPHINE (MRS. ORVEL A. AESCHLIMANN), lay church worker, American Lutheran Church; b. Bethune, Colo., Dec. 1, 1922; d. Walter H. and Pauline (Kramer) Kloeckner; grad. Blair Bus. Coll., Colorado Springs, 1942; m. Orvel A. Aeschlimann, Sept. 20, 1944;

children: William A., Rodney L. Sunday Sch. tchr., supt. First St. Pauls Luth. Ch., Burlington, Colo., 1944-73; mem. evangelism com., parish edn. com. Central Dist., Am. Luth. Ch., 1964-70, first woman lay rep. Central Dist. and Am. Luth. Ch. Council, 1971-80, also mem. exec. com. Central Dist. and Dist. Council; sec., treas., pres. Am. Luth. Ch. Women, also sec. Tri-State Conf. Chmn., Colo. Farm Bur. Women's Com., 1966—. Mem. Community Concert Assn., Burlington, 1974—. Recipient Master Farm Homemaker award, 1974. Home: 21543 Route 58 Burlington CO 80807

AGEE, JAMES WILLARD, minister, Church of Brethren; b. Spray, N.C., Dec. 20, 1923; s. Charles Willard and Catherin Amanda (Smith) A.; A.B., McPherson Coll., 1948; B.D., Bethany Theol. Sem., 1951; postgrad. Mich. State U., 1956—, Phillips U., 1964-74; m. Geneva Lorayne Bowman, Mar. 4, 1945; children: JoEtta, Krista Leigh, James Willard, Mary Beth. Ordained to ministry, 1943; diplomate Am. Assn. Pastoral Counselors. Pastor ch., Parsons, Kans., 1951-52; chaplain Eastern N.C. Tb Sanatorium, Wilson, 1953-56; teaching chaplain Polk (Pa.) State Sch. and Hosp., 1956-64; chaplain supr. Enid (Okla.) State Sch., from 1964; now chaplain Western State Hosp., Staunton, Va.; adj. prof. Phillips U., Enid, 1964-74; founder, Northwest Okla. Pastoral Care Assn., 1968, Contact, Northwest Okla., 1970; trustee Okla. Pastoral Inst. Fellow Am. Hosp. Chaplain's Assn., Assn. Clin. Pastoral Edn. Contbr. articles to profl. jours. Home: PO Box 2485 Staunton VA 24401 Office: Western State Hosp Staunton VA 24401

AGUILERA, FRANCISCO MARIA, bishop, Roman Catholic Church; b. Guanajuato, Mex., Apr. 27, 1918; s. Gregorio A. and Maria de la Luz (Gonzalez) A. M.Philosophy, Gregorian U., Rome, 1940, D.D., 1946, M.History, 1947. Ordained priest Roman Cath. Ch., 1943, consecrated bishop, 1979. Prof. philosophy, theology Seminario Concilar, Mexico City, Mex., 1947-66; dir. Nat. Catechetical Office, 1958-72; dean studies Colegio Mexicano, Rome, 1973-75; prof. catechetics Ateneo Salesiano, Rome, 1974—; aux. bishop Archdiocese of Mex., Mexico City, 1979—; Holy See observer UN, UNICEF; trustee Christian Children Fund, Mexico City, 1983—. Author: Theology of Francisco Suarez, 1946. Contbr. articles to religious jours. Pres., Found. Buena Nueva, Mexico City, 1981—; bd. dirs. nat. pastoral care programs. Mem. Sociedad Teologica Mexicana, Consejo Episcopal Latinoamericano. Office: Episcopal Vicariate Archidiocese Mexico Plaza San Jacinto 18 bis Mexico City Distrito Federal Mexico 01000

AH CHICK, MARY DAVILYN, nun, religion educator, Roman Catholic Church; b. Honolulu, Feb. 27, 1941; d. John Sonee Sr. and Dorothy Amy (Chun-Leong) Ah C. Student Maria Regina Coll., 1960, LeMoyne Coll., 1970; B.A., Cath. U., 1972, M. Ch. Adminstrn., 1973. Joined Third Franciscan Order, Minor Conventuals, 1959. Prof. theology Maria Regina Coll., Syracuse, N.Y., 1974-80; novice directress Sisters of St. Francis, Washington, 1972-74, postulant/novice dir., Syracuse, N.Y., 1974-80, del. community's gen. chpt., 1970-80; mem. constn. com., 1972-80; prin. Our Lady of Angels Sch., Albany, N.Y., 1982—; chmn. parish council liturgy/spiritual com., Albany, 1982; exec. dir. Albany Sch. Bd., 1982. Sec. Peace and Justice Com., Syracuse, 1982. Mem. Nat. Cath. Edn. Assn., Cath. Adminstrs. Assn. of N.Y. Democrat. Home: 145 Sherman St Albany NY 12206 Office: Our Lady of Angels Sch 400 Sheridan Ave Albany NY 12206

AHLSTROEM, GOESTA WERNER, religious educator; b. Sandviken, Sweden, Aug. 27, 1918; came to U.S., 1962; s. Tage K.J. and Ester V. (Carlsson) Ahlström; m. E. Maria A. Brorson Fich, Dec. 20, 1952; children: B. Pernille, Hans G. Teol.Kand., U. Uppsala, Sweden, 1950, Teol.lic., 1954, Teol.Dr., 1959, Fil.Kand., 1961. Mem. faculty U. Chgo., 1963—, prof. O.T. and ancient Palestinian studies, 1976—. Author: Psalm 89, 1959; Aspects of Syncretism in Israelite Religion, 1963; Joel and the Temple Cult, 1971; Royal Administration and National Religion in Ancient Palestine, 1982; Who Were the Israelites, 1985. Mem. N. Soederblom Soc. (sec. 1960-62), Am. Oriental Soc., Am. Schs. Oriental Research (steering com. Jerusalem Inst. 1970-74), Am. Inst. Archeology, Soc. Bibl. Lit. (pres. Midwest sect. 1976-78). Office: Swift Hall U Chicago Chicago IL 60637

AHN, PETER PYUNGCHOO, minister, United Methodist Ch.; b. Chorwon, Korea, May 21, 1917; s. Kyung Sam and Oak Bong (Lee) A.; came to U.S., 1948, naturalized, 1961; student Methodist Theol. Sem., Seoul, 1938-40, St. Paul's U., Tokyo, 1940-43, Nippon Union Theol. Sem., Tokyo, 1943-44; B.D., Garrett Theol. Sem., Evanston, Ill., 1949; M.A., Northwestern U., 1951; Ph.D., Boston U., 1962; m. Grace Whayoung Chung, June 10, 1950; children—David Avery and John Avery (twins). Ordained deacon United Methodist Ch., 1954, elder, 1954; pastor S.F. Korean Meth. Ch., 1953-60; asst. prof. philosophy and religion Los Angeles Pacific Coll., 1963-65; Bible translator Lockman Found., La Habra, Calif., 1965-67; asso. minister Woodland (Calif). United Meth. Ch., 1967-69; pastor Knights Landing (Calif.) United Meth. Ch., 1969-73, Marina-Seaside (Calif.) United Meth. Ch., 1973—; research dir. New Am. Standard Bible Concordance, 1970-75. Mem. bd. edn. Calif.-Nev. ann. conf. United Meth. Ch., 1971-73, mem. commn. religion and race, 1970-73, chairperson div. higher edn., 1973-76; trustee conf., 1970-73; mem. exec. com. United Ministries in Higher Edn. No. Calif. and Nev., 1973-75. Vol. fireman, Knight's Landing, 1969-73. Mem. Soc. Bibl. Lit., Asian-Am. Caucus (Western jurisdiction coordinating com.). Republican. Compiler English-Korean, Korean-English dictionaries. Home: 3282 Michael Dr Marina CA 93933 Office: 1340 Hilby Ave Seaside CA 93955

AHRONI-FISCH, DOV, rabbi, Jewish Orthodox Church; b. Bklyn., Oct. 26, 1953; s. Aaron and Shirley (Shapiro) F.; m. Linda Yellin Fisch, Jan. 19, 1975; children: Yael Reviva, Kineret Yardena, Ayalet Geula. B.A., Columbia U., 1975; M.A., Yeshiva U., 1981. Ordained rabbi, 1981. Dir. community outreach Lincoln Sq. Synagogue, N.Y.C., 1980; rabbinical faculty Robosin Yeshiva High Sch., Jersey City, N.J., 1981-82, Shephardic Yeshiva High Sch., Bklyn., 1982-83; sr. rabbi Cottage St. Synagogue, Jersey City, 1980-82, Freedom Synagogue, Jersey City, 1982—; nat. exec. dir. Herut Zionists of Am., N.Y.C., 1983—; bd. dirs. United Jewish Appeal, Jersey City, 1980—; exec. com. Am. Zionist Fedn., 1978—; del. Conf. of Pres. of Major Am. Jewish Orgns., N.Y.C., 1980—. Author: Jews for Nothing, 1984. Contbg. editor: Hamevaser, 1981-83. Contbr. articles to profl. jours. Recipient Community Leadership award Cottage St. Synagogue, 1982; Breath of Life award Am. Red Magen David for Israel, 1982. Mem. Rabbinical Council Am., Am. Jewish Hist. Soc., Assn. Jewish Studies. Office: Herut Zionists of Am 41 E 42d St Rm 617 New York NY 10017

AILSHIE, GLENN EDGAR, minister, So. Bapt. Conv.; b. Green County, Tenn., Feb. 19, 1939; s. James Willis and Dora Dussie (Rader) A.; student U. Tenn., Tusculum Coll., So. Bapt. Conv. Sem. Extension; m. Betty Jean Hartman, Oct. 25, 1957; children—Lyle, Lee, Lynne, Lana Lori. Deacon Sunday Sch. supt., tng. dir., Sunday Sch. tchr. Concord Bapt. Ch., Mohawk, Tenn., 1960-70; ordained to ministry, 1971; pastor Woodlawn Park Bapt. Ch., Mullins, S.C., 1971—. Pres. Pastors' Conf.; Sunday Sch. dir. Marion Bapt. Assn., Mullins. Home: 618 S Main St Mullins SC 29574 Office: Cypress St Mullins SC 29574

AIZENBERG, ISIDORO, rabbi, Conservative Jewish Congregations; b. Buenos Aires, Argentina, Nov. 25, 1939; s. Moises and Rebeca (Rajchenberg) A.; came to U.S., 1960; m. Edna Sitchin, June 16, 1963; children: Gabriel, Salo. B.S., Columbia Univ., 1964; M.A., NYU, 1967; M. Hebrew Letters, Jewish Theol. Sem., 1965. Ordained rabbi, 1967. Rabbi, B'nai B'rith, Caracas, Venezuela, 1967-74, Conservative Synagogue, Jamaica, N.Y., 1974—; del. Synagogue Council, N.Y.C., 1980—; mem. Law Com. Rabbinical Assembly, N.Y.C., 1983—. Author; The Jews of Coro, 1983. Office: Conservative Synagogue of Jamaica 182-69 Wexford Terr Jamaica Estates NY 11432

AKAMINE, TOKI NAKASONE, lay church worker, United Methodist Church; b. Hana, Maui, Hawaii, June 9, 1913; d. Kokyu and Ushi (Teruya) Nakasone; m. Ernest Kisei Akamine, June 11, 1938; children: Carol Linden Matsushita, Faye Ruth McCoy, Harry Ernest. B.E., U. Hawaii, 1935, 5th yr. cert., 1936, postgrad. edn., summers 1965, 68, 69, 71. Choir dir. Wesley United Meth. Ch., Honolulu, 1952-66, chpt. pres. United Meth. Women, 1981-82, tchr., mem. various bds., 1930—; pres. local chpt. Woman's Soc. Christian Service, 1947, 50-52, 60-62, 69-71, v.p. ter. of Hawaii, 1954-56, pres. 1956-59. Bd. dirs. Susannah Wesley Community Ctr., Honolulu, 1963-68; officer, mem. PTA, various schs., Hawaii, 1936-78; mem. Kalihi-Palama Congress Model Cities Program, Honolulu, 1966-70; vol. tutor Fern Elem. Sch., Palolo Community Ctr., 1981—. Recipient award of merit City and County of Honolulu, 1970, Change Agent award Pacific Southwest Annual Conf. United Meth. Women, 1984. Mem. Oahu Ret. Tchrs. Assn., Hawaii State Ret. Tchrs. Assn., Nat. Ret. Tchrs. Assn., U. Hawaii Alumni Assn., Pi Gamma Mu, Phi Kappa Phi. Avocations: reading; family history; music. Home: 2255 Hulali Pl Honolulu HI 96819

AKIN, JAMES DELBERT, minister, Nat. Assn. Free Will Bapts.; b. Maud, Okla., Nov. 22, 1927; s. Daniel Robert and Anna Earsy (Black) A.; B.A., Okla. Bapt. U., 1952; postgrad. E. Central U., Ada, Okla., 1960, Okla. U., Norman, 1966-67; m. Dorothy Mae Christian, June 11, 1948; children—Judith Elaine, Jan Irene, James Philip. Ordained to ministry, 1950; pastor chs., Tecumseh, Okla., 1951-56, Ada, 1956-63, Norman, Okla., 1963-67, Spencer, Okla., 1967-68; pastor 1st Free Will Bapt. Ch., Ada, 1968-77, 1st Free Will Bapt. Ch., Ardmore, Okla., 1977—. Mem. nat. home mission bd. Nat. Assn. Free Will Bapts., 1974—, mem. Okla. mission bd., 1955-75; pres. Ada Ministerial Alliance, 1976. Sec., United Comml. Travelers Am., Ada., 1970—, grand counselor Okla., 1976—; trustee Hillsdale Coll., Moore, Okla., 1975—. Mem. Okla. State Ministers Conf. Free Will Bapts. Contbr. articles to religious jours. Home: 706 D St NW Ardmore OK 73401 Office: 805 Grand Ave Ardmore OK 73401

AKINS, GLENN LEE, minister, administrator, Southern Baptist Convention; b. Bartlesville, Okla., Sept. 4, 1952; s. Herbert Glenn and Dorothy Lee (Harris) A.; m. Elizabeth Anne Cantrell, Oct. 25, 1980; 1 son, Andrew Lee. A.A., Missouri Bible Coll., 1972, B.A., 1974; M. Divinity in Relgion, Southern Bapt. Theol. Seminary, 1980; Ordained to ministry So. Bapt. Conv., 1980. Minister of youth Third Bapt. Ch., St. Louis, 1974-77, Rosemont Bapt. Ch., Lexington, Ky., 1978-79; ch. planter Home Mission Bd., So. Bapt. Conv., Charlotte, N.C., 1981-83; adminstrv. assoc. Mecklenberg Bapt. Assn., Charlotte, 1983—. Pres. ACTS of Charlotte, Inc., 1984—. Office: Mecklenburg Bapt Assn 209 S Kings Dr Charlotte NC 28204

AKOGNON, EMMANUEL OLUFEMI, minister, seminary instructor, American Baptist Churches in the U.S.A.; b. Lagos, Nigeria, Nov. 23, 1953; s. Bernard Sisa and Toivi Lucy (Adidemeh) A.; m. Alfreda Marie Small, Mar. 14, 1981; 1 child: Shola Nokwegnon. B.Th., Northwest Bapt. Sem., Vancouver, B.C., Can., 1977; M.R.E., Golden Gate Sem., 1979, M.Div., 1980, Th.M., 1983. Ordained to ministry American Baptist Churches in the U.S.A., 1979. Pastor Frazier Canyon Bapt. Ch., Boston Bar, B.C., Can., 1976-78, Village Bapt. Ch., Marin City Calif., 1978—; instr. Golden Gate Sem., Mill Valley, Calif., 1983—; dir. Village Oduduwa Corp., Marin City, 1981—; pres. So. Marin Interdenominational Ministerial Alliance, 1983—. Pres. Marin City Community Credit Union, 1984—. Home: 895 Drake Ave Marin City CA 94965 Office: Village Bapt Ch 825 Drake Ave Marin City CA 94965

ALBERS, EDWIN OMER, priest, Roman Cath. Ch.; b. St. Louis, Feb. 21, 1934; s. Anton Bernard and Margaret (Wienstroer) A.; Ph.B., Quincy Coll., 1957; B.Th., St. Joseph Sem., Teutopolis, Ill., 1962. Joined Franciscan Order of Sacred Heart, 1954; ordained priest, 1961; asso. pastor Guardian Angels Ch., Chaska, Minn., 1962, St. Christopher Ch., Midlothian, Ill., 1963-67; asso. pastor St. Francis Ch., Humphrey, Nebr., 1967-70, pastor, 1970—; supt. St. Francis Grade and High Schs., Humphrey, 1970—. Chaplain, Midlothian K.C., 1963-67, Humphrey K.C., 1967—, Holy Name and Christian Mothers, 1970—, Humphrey Fire and Rescue Squad. Recipient Chaplain award Midlothian Boy Scouts Am., 1967; citation Nebr. K.C., 1970. Mem. Humphrey Community Club. Home and Office: Box 116 Humphrey NE 68642

ALBERT, DONALD LEROY, minister, Lutheran Church in America; b. Youngstown, Ohio, Dec. 17, 1925; s. Lawrence Le Roy and Alice Edna (Kirkwood) A.; m. Joan Audrey Ranges, Sept. 7, 1956; children: Mark David, Ruth Louise. B.A., Midland Luth. Coll., 1952; B.Div., Central Luth. Sem., Fremont, Nebr., 1955; M.Div., Chgo. Luth. Sem., 1972. Ordained to ministry Lutheran Ch., 1955. Pastor St. Paul Luth Ch., Newcomerstown, Ohio, 1963-69, First English Luth. Ch., Crestline, Ohio, 1969-72; assoc. pastor First Luth. Ch., Shelby, Ohio, 1972-82; pastor Calvary Luth. Ch., Lancaster, Ohio, 1982—; mem. various coms. Ohio Synod, Luth. Ch. in Am., 1960—, sec. camping unit Ohio Synod, 1967-73, dean Mansfield dist., 1975-81. Served with A.C., U.S. Army, 1944-46; ETO. Recipient awards from various local groups. Mem. Lancaster/Fairfield Luth. Pastors (chmn. 1982—), Crestline C. of C. (dir. 1972). Republican. Lodge: Kiwanis. Office: Calvary Luth Ch 508 N Broad St Lancaster OH 43130

ALBRACHT, JUANITA ANNA, nun, religious organization administrator, Roman Catholic Church; b. Castro County, Tex., Feb. 13, 1933; d. Cyril Joseph and Mary (Schaefer) A. B.S. in Nursing, Incarnate Word Coll., 1971; M.A. in Health Adminstrn., St. Louis U., 1980. Joined Sisters of Charity of Incarnate Word, Roman Cath. Ch., 1951; registered nurse, Mo., Tex. Infirmarian Incarnate Word Convent, St. Louis, 1956-67; assoc. dir. nursing service, dir. nursing service, head nurse med.-surg. unit Incarnate Word Hosp., St. Louis, 1971-75; cons. health services St. Louis Province, 1972-78, provincial superior, 1981-84; health systems services dir. Incarnate Word Generalate, San Antonio, 1980, gen. counselor, 1984—; trustee Incarnate Word Health Services Corp., San Antonio, 1981—, St. Anthony's Hosp., Amarillo, Tex., 1981—, Yoakum Cath. Hosp., Tex., 1984—; chmn. bd. Incarnate Word Hosp., St. Louis, 1982-84; mem. Cath. initiative adv. com. St. Louis U., 1982—; lectr. in field. Mem. Midtown Med. Ctr. Redevel. Corp., St. Louis, 1983-84, chmn. pub. relations com., 1984; active CASE, St. Louis; bd. dirs. Cath. Charities, 1972-78. Recipient Flanagan award St. Louis U., 1980. Mem. Leadership Conf. Women Religious (family life com. 1983), Am. Coll. Hosp. Adminstrs., Kappa Gamma Pi. Home and Office: Incarnate Word Generalate 4503 Broadway San Antonio TX 78209

ALBRECHT, ARDON DU WAYNE, minister, Lutheran Church-Missouri Synod; television producer; b. Burlington, Wis., Sept. 2, 1936; s. Franklin William Albrecht and Esther Maria (Braatz) Albrecht Silbernagel; m. Edith Elizabeth Spillner, Aug. 2, 1960; children: Kim, Rebekah, Suzanne, Matthew, Marc. A.A., Concordia Coll., Milw., 1956; M.Div., Concordia Sem., St. Louis, Mo., 1962; M.S., Syracuse U., 1969. Ordained to ministry Luth. Ch.-Mo. Synod, 1962.

Missionary to Taiwan Luth. Ch. Mo. Synod, Taipei, 1962-71; TV producer Luth. TV, St. Louis, Mo., 1971—; bd. dirs. Joint Luth. TV, Taipei, 1968-70, asst. exec. sec., 1970-71; v.p. Taiwan Christian Audio Visual Assn., Taipei, 1970-71; trustee Luth. Film Assocs., N.Y.C., 1980—. Translator: Taiwanese Customs and Superstitions, 1965; author: Essential Christian Doctrines, 1965. Recipient Gold award Internat. Film and TV Festival, N.Y.C., 1973, 84, Silver award, 1976, 78, 79, 80, Bronze, 1982, 83; Angel award Religion in Media, Los Angeles, 1977, 85. Mem. Acad. TV Arts and Scis., Writers Guild Am. Republican. Home: 2016 Alscot Ave Simi Valley CA 93063 Office: Luth TV 14622 Lanark St Panorama City Ca 91402

ALBRIGHT, JIMMY LEE, minister, educator, Southern Baptist Convention; b. Lubbock, Tx., Nov. 25, 1942; s. Jimmie W. and Margie M. (Tew) A.; m. Janice Jeanne Lain, Aug. 24, 1962; children: Jana Lynn, Jennifer Lee. A.B., Stephen Austin U., 1965; B.D., N. Am. Theol. Sem., 1968; M.Div., Southwestern Sem., 1976, Ph.D., 1980. Ordained to ministry Bapt. Ch., 1964. Pastor, First Bapt. Ch., Mount Selman, Tex., 1963-65, Davis St. Bapt. Ch., Sulphur Springs, Tex., 1968-75, Wyatt Park Bapt. Ch., St. Joseph, Mo., 1980—; interim pastor First Bapt. Ch., Lipan, Tex., 1976-77; youth minister First Bapt. Ch., Burleson, Tex., 1978-79; 1st v.p. Mo. Bapt. Conv., Jefferson City, Mo., 1983—, mem. nominating and Christian Life coms., 1982-84, exec. bd., 1983—; prof. Mo. Western State Coll., St. Joseph, 1981—; adj. prof. Southwestern Theol. Sem., Ft. Worth, 1978-80, Midwestern Theol. Sem., Kansas City, Mo., 1983-84. Contbr. articles and photographs to profl. publs. Div. dir. United Fund, Sulphur Springs, 1972-73; bd. dirs. Am. Cancer Soc., St. Joseph, 1982—; city chmn. tax levy campaign St. Joseph Sch. Systems, 1984; supr. Tel Batash Archaeol. Expedition, 1978-79, Tel 'Uza Archaeol. Expdn., 1981-84. Recipient David Meier Internat. Study League award Southwestern Sem., 1979. Mem. Am. Schs. Oriental Research, Soc. Bibl. Lit., Alpha Chi. Lodges: Lions, Kiwanis. Home: 2209 Elephant Trail Saint Joseph MO Office: Wyatt Park Bapt Ch 2739 Mitchell Saint Joseph MO 64507

ALBRIGHT, WILLIAM EDWARD, minister, educator United Meth. Ch.; b. Bluefield, W. Va., Mar. 18, 1920; s. William Edward and Bertha Lucile (Thompson) A.; A.B., Emory and Henry Coll., 1941; M.Div., Duke, 1944; M.A., Marshall U., 1969; m. Catherine Cobb, Sept. 6, 1945; children—Lynne, William Edward, Mary Elizabeth, David Wesley. Ordained to ministry, 1944; pastor Kinnakeet Chs., Avon, N.C., 1944-45, Fort Ashby (W.Va.) Meth. Ch., 1945-48, Amherstdale (W.Va.) Community Ch., 1948-51, Highlawn Meth. Ch., Huntington, W.Va., 1951-57, 1st Meth. Ch., Welch, W.Va., 1957-59, Thompson United Meth. Ch., Wheeling, W.Va., 1959-63, Humphreys Meml. United Meth. Ch., Charleston, W.Va., 1963-65; chaplain Morris Harvey Coll., Charleston, W. Va., 1965—, prof. sociology, 1965—. Mem. gen. assembly Nat. Council Chs., 1963, 66, 69. Contbr. articles to religious jours. Home: 817 Springdale Dr Charleston WV 25302 Office: Morris Harvey Coll Charleston WV 25304

ALCANTARA, MIGUEL BACCAY, priest, Roman Catholic Church; b. Atimonan, Quezon, Philippines, Sept. 26, 1940; came to U.S., 1970, naturalized, 1984. B.S. in Philosophy, Ateneo de Manila U., Quezon City, 1960; B.S.T. magna cum laude, Lateran U., Rome, 1965; M.A. in Philosophy Edn., Loyola U., Chgo., 1971; M.A. in Sociology, DePaul U., 1973; Litt.D. (hon.), Colegio Estadual de Jandaia do Sul, Brazil, 1980. Ordained priest Roman Cath. Ch., 1965. Curate St. Isidore Ch., Cuenca, Batangas, Philippines, 1966-67, Cathedral of St. Sebastian, Lipa City, Philippines, 1967-68; dean of studies Major Sem. Bauan, Philippines, 1968-70, also curate of city parish; resident St. John Berchmans Ch., Chgo., 1970-74; assoc. pastor St. Rocco's Ch., Pittston, Pa., 1974-78; missionary, Brazil, 1978-81; assoc. pastor St. Sebastian Parish, Middletown, Conn., 1981, St. Andrew's Parish, Calumet City, Ill., 1982—. Named Cidadao Benemerito, City Council of Jandaia do Sul, Brazil, 1981, Outstanding New Citizen of 1984, Chgo. Met. Council for Citizenship, 1984. Address: 768 Lincoln Ave Calumet City IL 60409

ALCARÁZ FIGUEROA, ESTANISLAO, archbishop, Roman Catholic Church; b. Patzcuaro, Michoacán, Méx., Oct. 23, 1918; s. Estanislao Alcaráz and Rafaela (Figueroa) A.; Humanidades, Morelia Sem., 1937; Filosofiá y Teologiá, Montezuma Sem., 1943. Ordained priest Roman Catholic Ch., 1942, consecrated bishop, 1959; bishop of Matamoros, Tamaulipas, 1959-68, San Luis Potosí, 1968-72; archbishop of Morelia, Michoacán, 1972—. Office: Apartado 17 Morelia Michoacán México

ALCORN, WALLACE ARTHUR, minister, General Association Regular Baptist Church; b. Milw., Aug. 29, 1930; s. William Keith and Dora Mildred (Brazee) A.; student Marquette U., 1950; A.B., Wheaton Coll., 1952; B.D., Grand Rapids Bapt. Theol. Sem., 1959; A.M., Wheaton Grad. Sch. Theology, 1959; postgrad. Mich. State U., 1959-60, U. Mich., 1960-61; Th.M., Princeton Theol. Sem., 1965; Ph.D., NY U, 1974; m. Ann Margaret Carmichael, June 5, 1958; children: John Mark, Allison Ann, Stephen Paul. Ordained to ministry, Gen. Assn. Regular Bapt. Chs., 1957. Pastor Caddy Vista Bapt. Ch., Caldonia, Wis., 1955-57; nation editor Christian Life, Wheaton, Ill., 1956-59; pastor Bloomfield Hills (Mich.) Bapt. Ch., 1960-61, Community Bapt. Ch. Shark River Hills, Neptune, N.J., 1961-67; bible prof. Moody Bible Inst., Chgo., 1967-73; radio tchr. Moody Radio Network, 1968-74; assoc. prof. N.T., N.W. Bapt. Sem., Tacoma, 1974-76; affiliate chaplain Madigan Army Med. Center, Tacoma, 1974-76; N.T. editor The Living Bible Commentary, 1975-76; pastor 1st Bapt. Ch., Austin, Minn., 1976-83; prin. Wallace Alcorn Assocs., Austin, 1983—; U.S. Army Res. chaplain, 1957—; mem. profl. adv. council Pub. Edn. Religion Studies Center, Wright State U., Ohio, 1972—; dir. The Good News Hour, Austin, 1976—. Mem. citizens' adv. council Neptune (N.J.) Bd. Edn., 1965-67. Mem. Evang. Theol. Soc., Soc. Evang. Press Assn., Nat. Assn. Religious Broadcasters, Mil. Chaplains Assn. (pres. Chgo. chpt. 1970-74). Author: The Bible as Literature, 1965; Knowing and Using the Bible, 1974; Press On—Don't Fall Back, 1984. Contbr. to Wycliffe Bible Ency., 1974, Tyndale Family Bible Ency., 1976. Home: 1010 7th Ave NW Austin MN 55912 Office: Wallace Alcorn Assocs PO Box 733 Austin MN 55912

ALDERINK, LARRY JON, religion educator, United Presbyterian Church in the U.S.A.; b. Holland, Mich., Aug. 2, 1940; s. John and Hazel Kathryn (Knoll) A.; m. Lynda Ann Nyhoff, Aug. 26, 1961; children: MariaLyn, Anna Marie. B.A., Calvin Coll., 1962; B.D., Calvin Sem., 1965; M.A., U. Chgo., Divinity Sch. 1967, Ph.D., 1974. Ordained to ministry United Presbyterian Ch. U.S.A., 1975. Instr. religion Elmhurst Coll., (Ill.), 1968-69; instr. Greek, Luth. Sch. Theology at Chgo., 1968; assoc. prof. religion Concordia Coll., Moorhead, Minn., 1969—. Author: Creation and Salvation in Ancient Orphism, 1981; contbr. articles to profl. jours. Bush fellow, 1984. Mem. Am. Acad. Religion, Soc. Bibl. Lit. Democrat. Home: 819 5th Ave S Moorhead MN 56560 Office: Dept Religion Concordia Coll Moorhead MN 56560

ALDERSON, CAROLYN WALLOP, lay church worker; b. Sheridan, Wyo., July 7, 1939; d. Oliver Malcolm and Jean (Moore) W.; m. Donald A. Guthrie, Dec. 29, 1984; children by previous marriage: Natalie Moore, Jean Catherine, Mary Roberts. B.A., Sarah Lawrence Coll., 1961. Mem. Nat. Episcopal Task Force on Energy and Environment, N.Y.C., 1977-78; mem. ch. and society commn. Diocese of Mont., 1978-82, co-chmn., 1982—; mem. standing com. Diocese of Mont., 1983—; trustee St. George's Sch., Newport, R.I., 1982—. Contbr. articles to profl. jours. A founder, No. Plains Resource Council, Billings, Mont., bd. dirs. 1971-80; bd. dirs. Environ. Policy Inst., Washington, 1976—, pres., 1978-81; co-chmn. Coalition Against Stripmining, 1975-77. Democrat. Office: 409 Edith St Missoula MT 59801

ALDERSON, LEONA RUTH, educator, Seventh-day Adventist Church; b. Bosanquet, Ont., Can., June 4, 1930; d. Roy Ernest and Vivian Geneva (Collingwood) A. B.A., Atlantic Union Coll., 1964; M.A., Andrews U., 1969. Tchr. Ont. Conf., Seventh-day Adventist Ch., 1951-62; faculty Kingsway Coll., Oshawa, Ont., 1962—. Active various charitable orgns. Mem. Can. Home Econs. Assn., Ont. Family Studies of Home Econs. Educators Assn. Home: 1156 King St E PO Box 605 Oshawa ON L1H 7M6 Canada Office: Kingsway Coll 1156 King St E Oshawa ON Canada L1H 7M6 Canada

ALDRICH, JOSEPH COFFIN, evangelist, religious school administrator; b. Portland, Oreg., Nov. 16, 1940; s. Willard Maxwell and Doris Virginia (Coffin) A.; m. Ruthe Miles Aldrich, Aug. 18, 1962; children: Stephen, Kristin. Diploma, Multnomah Sch. Bible, 1961; B.A., So. Oreg. State Coll., 1963; Th.M., Dallas Theol. Sem., 1968, Th.D., 1971. Staff mem. Campus Crusade for Christ, 1963-64; teaching fellow Dallas Theol. Sem., 1969-70, instr., 1970-71; part-time faculty Talbot Theol. Sem., La Mirada, Calif., 1973-77; pastor Mariners Ch., Newport Beach, Calif., 1971-78; pres., mem. faculty Multnomah Sch. of the Bible, Portland, 1978—. Author: Life-Style Evangelism, 1981; Secrets to Inner Beauty, 1977. Producer/star video/film series: Life-Style Evangelism, 1984. Contbr. articles to profl. jours. Recipient Lewis Sperry Chafer award, Dallas Theol. Sem. Address: Multonmah Sch of Bible 8435 NE Glisan Portland OR 97220

ALEXANDER, EDWIN REECE, minister, So. Bapt. Conv.; b. Savannah, Tenn., Jan. 14, 1922; s. Edwin Nelson and Nymtha Adeline (Duckworth) A.; A.A., So. Bapt. Coll., Walnut Ridge, Ark., 1948; A.B., Union U., Jackson, Tenn., 1951; m. Juanita Gaston Basey, Nov. 16, 1946; 1 son, Edwin Reece. Ordained to ministry, 1946; supt. missions William Carey Bapt. Assn., Fayetteville, Tenn., 1951-53, 55-61; pastor ch., Memphis, Tenn., 1961-67, Rutherford, Tenn., 1967-76; pastor Grace Bapt. Ch., Springfield, Tenn., 1976—. Sec., Tenn. Bapt. Pastors Conf., 1973; chmn. Gibson County (Tenn.) House Conf. Com., 1970. Contbr. articles to denominational publs. Home: 1802 Meadowbrook St Springfield TN 37172

ALEXANDER, JAMES EDWIN, minister, United Meth. Ch.; b. Indianola, Iowa, Feb. 16, 1930; s. James Eugene and Lillian Esther (Gamble) A.; B.A., U. Pacific, 1959; S.T.B., Boston U., 1962; M.A., Claremont Grad. Sch., 1967; Ph.D., Vanderbilt U., 1972; m. Joan Frances Harris, June 28, 1952; children—James Michael, Michele Alene, Marsha Ann. Ordained to ministry, 1960; chief engr. sta. KJOY, Stockton, Calif., 1955-56; instr. broadcasting U. Pacific, 1956-59; lectr. Bible, 1963-65; owner/operator Stockton-Teletronics, Stockton, 1956-59; studio engr. sta. WHDH, Boston, 1960; pastor Gleasondale (Mass.) Methodist Ch., 1960-62; teaching fellow Boston U. Coll. Bus. Adminstrn., 1960-62; asso. pastor Central Methodist Ch., Stockton, 1962-65; asso. pastor Claremont (Cal.) Methodist Ch., 1966-67; dir. printed resources Methodist Bd. Edn., 1967-70, asst. gen. sec. Bd. Discipleship, 1970—. Mem. exec. bd. Christian Youth Publs., 1967—. Mem. Soc. Bibl. Lit., Am. Mgmt. Assn., Am. Acad. Religion, Assn. Ednl. Communication and Tech., Nat. Assn. Ednl. Broadcasters, Pub. Service Satellite Consortium, Religious Pub. Relations Council. Author: Abstracts from Federal Communication Law, 1958; Audiovisual Facilities and Equipment for Churchmen, 1970; Ethical Factors in Management Decision, 1972; Mass Media Models of Education, 1974; Emerging Developments in Educational Television, 1976; Religious Applications of Satellite Communications, 1977—. Editor, Basic Edn. series, 1970, Resource System for Council of Ministries, 1970-74. Home: 712 Adkisson Ln Nashville TN 37205 Office: POB 840 Nashville TN 37202

ALEXANDER, JOSEPH JOHN MURPHY, priest, educator, Roman Catholic Church; b. Lafayette, La., Aug. 20, 1933; s. Frederick O. and Elizabeth (Rubin) A.; B.L.Mus., St. John U., Collegeville, Minn., 1957; B.A., Western Ky. U., 1968; M.Div., St. Meinrad (Ind.) Sem., 1974; M.A., Ind. U., 1977, Ph.D. in Speech Communication, 1980; postgrad. Cath. U. Am., 1983-84. Joined Order of St. Benedict, 1955, ordained priest, 1973. Choir master, organist St. Mark's Monastery, South Union Ky., 1955—, infirmarian, 1955—, trustee, 1958—: mem. faculty St. Maur Sem. and High Sch., 1955-66; asst. chaplain St. Thomas Aquinas Newman Center, Western Ky. U., 1966-70, Bowling Green, Ky., 1974; prof. homiletics, liturgy and lituriguical law and music St. Mark's Sch. Theology, South Union, 1974-83, also dean students and student affairs, vice rector, 1975-77, rector, 1977-83; sub-prior St. Mark's Priory, 1975-77, prior, 1977-83; faculty dept. speech communication Western Ky. U., Bowling Green, 1984; adminstr. Wisdom Cath. Studies Ctr., U. Southwestern La., 1984—. mem. area ministry Barren River Area Cath. Enterprise, Diocese Owensboro, 1974—; tchr. Confrat. Christian Doctrine secondary and elementary schs., Russellville, Ky.-Bowling Green area; active Shaker Pageant Festival, 1966-72, dir., 1967; trustee Order St. Benedict; mem. Ky. Humanities Council, 1982-84. Mem. St. Meinrad Sch. Theology, Western Ky. U. alumni assns., Speech Communication Assn., Ind. U. Alumni Assn., So. Speech Communication Assn., Lituriigical Conf., Black Cath. Clergy Caucus Nat. Cath. Music Assn., Ky. Music Educators Assn., Ky. Bluegrass Music Assn. Address: Wisdom Cath Student Ctr USL Box 42371 U Southwestern La Lafayette LA 70504

ALGER, DAVID TOWNLEY, religious association executive, Presbyterian Church, U.S.A.; b. Warsaw, N.Y., June 4, 1945; s. Clifton and Dorothy (Townley) A.; m. Sarah I. Cheaney, Aug. 17, 1928; 1 dau., Hannah I. B.A., Coll. Wooster, 1967; M. Div., McCormick Theol. Sem., 1971; M.S.W., U. Ill.-Chgo., 1971. Ordained to ministry Presbyn. Ch., U.S.A., 1971. Assoc. pastor First Presbyn. Ch., Grand Forks, N.D., 1971-75; pastor Riverside Presbyn. Ch., Clinton, Iowa, 1975-80; exec. dir. Associated Ministries of Tacoma/Pierce County, Wash., 1980—; mem. adv. council on ch. and soc. Presbyn. Ch., U.S.A., 1978-84, liaison council on ch. and race, 1984; chmn. dept. mission strategy Olympia Presbytery, Wash., 1983—. Mem. Clinton City Council, 1978-79. Recipient Key to City, Clinton City Council, 1979. Mem. Nat. Assn. Ecumenical Staff, Presbyn. Health, Edn. and Welfare Assn. Democrat. Office: Associated Ministries of Tacoma/Pierce County 2520 6th Ave Tacoma WA 98406

ALIX, JACQUELYN JANET, Roman Catholic nun, administrator of home for aged; b. Webster, Mass., Oct. 30, 1940; d. Leonard Phillip and Janet Evelyn (Fournier) A. A.S., Becker Jr. Coll., 1960; B.S., Annhurst Coll., 1970; L.H.D., (hon.), Assumption Coll., 1984. Lic. nursing home adminstr., Mass. Asst. adminstr. St. Francis Home, Worcester, Mass., 1970-75, adminstr., 1975—. Trustee Becker Jr. Coll., Worcester, 1983—; bd. dirs. Occupational Tng. Ctr., Auburn, Mass., 1982—, Assn. Mass. Homes for Aging, 1985—. Mem. Am. Coll. Health Care Adminstrs., Assn. Mass. Homes for Aging (membership chmn. 1976-82), New Eng. Conf. Cath. Health Assn. (program com. 1979-82). Office: Saint Francis Home 101 Plantation St Worcester MA 01604

ALLAN, HUGH JAMES PEARSON See *Who's Who in America*, 43rd edition.

ALLEN, GAIL JANET GARDNER, lay church worker, Southern Baptist Convention; b. Suffolk, Va., Oct. 24, 1941; d. Moody Harrison and Mae (Rexrode)

G.; B.S., Old Dominion U., 1965; m. Neil Gordon Allen, Dec. 30, 1967; 1 son, Wesley Gardner. Ch. organist Beaverdam Bapt. Ch., Franklin, Va., 1957-60, soloist, 1960-65; mem. music com. Epworth United Meth. Ch., Norfolk, Va., 1966-67, choir mem., dir. spl. singing group, 1966-67; mem. nominating com. Beaver Dam Bapt. Ch., 1972-73, minister of music, 1971—, mission study chmn. Women Missionary Union, 1975—. Music tchr. Nansemond-Suffolk Acad., Suffolk, Va., 1971-75. Mem. Sigma Alpha Iota (Rose of Honor award 1967). Home: 7921 Harvest Dr Suffolk VA 23437

ALLEN, GREGORY JOHN, minister, Seventh-day Adventist Church; b. Bklyn., July 16, 1950; s. William Anthony and Mary Elizabeth (Bell) A.; m. Carol Maureen Easley, June 1, 1980. B.S., Atlantic Union Coll., 1976; M.Div., Seventh-day Adventist Theol. Sem., 1981. Ordained to ministry, 1985. Pastor Sun Village Seventh-day Adventist Ch., Little Rock, Calif., 1981, Mid-City Seventh-day Adventist Ch., Los Angeles, 1982-83; pastor Ivy Ave. Seventh-day Adventist Ch., Monrovia, Calif., 1983—; mem. phase II structure com. Pacific Union Conf., Seventh-day Adventists, Westlake Village, 1982—; sec., regional adv. com. So. Calif. Conf., Glendale, 1983-84. Editor Viewpoint, a Jour. of Ministry and Mission, 1983—. Mem. Black Ministerial Fellowship, Young Pastors Assn. Home: 1017 E Dolores Dr Altadena CA Office: Ivy Ave Seventh-Day Adventist Church 1003 S Ivy Ave Monrovia CA 91016

ALLEN, HARRY EVANS, JR., priest, Episcopal Church; b. Nashville, Aug. 29, 1930; s. Harry Evans and Myrtle Mae (Hill) A.; student So. Bapt. Theol. Sem., 1951-53; B.A., George Peabody Coll., 1952, M.A., 1955; G.S.T., U. of South, 1958; postgrad. St. Lukes Sem., Canterbury, summer 1974; m. Vivien Azilee Gore, Aug. 14, 1962; children: Harry Evans, III, Warren Andrw Lawton, Stephen Henry. Ordained priest, 1959; So. Baptist pastor, 1947-56; pastor St. Agnes Episcopal Ch., Cowan, Tenn., 1956-58; deacon St. Johns Ch., Knoxville, 1958-59; vicar St. Marks Ch., Copperhill, Tenn., 1959-61; chaplain La. State U., 1961-63; rector St. Andrews Ch., Clinton, La., 1963-83; rector St. Patricks Ch., Zachary, La., 1963—; headmaster St. Patricks Epis. Day Sch.; lt. col., chaplain Tenn. Wing, CAP, 1951-56, E. La. State Hosp., 1963-76. Pres. Baton Rouge Area Ministerial Assn.; pres., bd. dirs. Family Counselling Service; social worker Greater Baton Rouge Kidney Center. Bd. dirs. Isrouma Area council Boy Scouts Am., ARC. Mem. La. Hosp. Chaplains Assn., La. Episcopal Sch. Assn., Council Nephrology Social Workers. Home: 3816 N Main St Zachary LA 70791 Office: PO Box 208 Zachary LA 70791

ALLEN, HORACE THADDEUS, JR., educator, minister, United Presbyterian Church in the U.S.A.; b. Phila., Jan. 14, 1933; s. Horace Thaddeus and Dorothy (Miller) A. A.B. magne cum laude, Princeton U., 1954; M.Div., Harvard U., 1957; postgrad. Princeton Theol. Sem., 1954-56; M.Ph., Union Theol. Sem., 1976, Ph.D., 1980. Ordained to ministry Presbyn. Ch. U.S., 1957. Rural pastor Presbytery of Greenbrier, Renick, W.Va., 1957-62; asst. minister Towson Presbyn. Ch. (Md.), 1962-65; warden Iona Abbey, Iona Community (Scotland), 1966-68; dir. worship and music Presbyn. Ch. U.S. and U.S.A., Phila. and N.Y., 1970-76; asst. prof. worship Boston U. Sch. Theol., 1979—; mem. worship com. Consultation on Ch. Union, Princeton, N.J., 1970—; mem. Consultation on Common Texts, Washington, 1970—, chmn., 1982—; chmn. Iona Cornerston Found., Boston, 1980—; convenor English Lang. Liturgical Consultation, Boston, 1985. Author: A Handbook for the Lectionary, 1980. Contbr. to encyclopedias and dictionary. Fellow N. Am. Acad. Liturgy, Societas Liturgica (councilor); mem. Presbyn. Assn. Musicians, Boston Ministers' Club. Democrat. Clubs: St. Andrews Soc. (N.Y.); Princeton Terrace Club (N.J.). Home: 82 Ivy St Apt 9 Brookline MA 02146 Office: Boston U Sch Theol 745 Commonwealth Ave Boston MA 02215

ALLEN, JIMMY RAYMOND, minister, So. Baptist Conv.; b. Hope, Ark., Oct. 26, 1927; s. Earl Lester and Edna May (Ray) A.; B.A., Howard Payne U., 1948; B.D., Southwestern Bapt. Theol. Sem., 1951, Th.D., 1958; m. Wanda Ruth Massey, Aug. 20, 1949; children—Michael Wayne, Stephen Ray, Kenneth Scott. Ordained to ministry, 1945; youth evangelist, Dallas, 1944-47; exec. sec. Royal Ambassadors, Bapt. Gen. Conv. of Tex., 1948-51; pastor First Bapt. Ch., Van Alstyne, Tex., 1951-53, Wills Point, Tex., 1953-56, Cockrell Hill Bapt. Ch., Dallas, 1956-60; dir. Christian Life Commn., Bapt. Gen. Conv. Tex., Dallas, 1960-67; pastor First Bapt. Ch., San Antonio, 1968—. Pres. Bapt. Gen. Conv. Tex., San Antonio, 1969-70, mem. adminstrn. com., 1971; mem. exec. com. So. Bapt. 0onv., 1975—; nat. pres. Ams. United for Separation of Church and State, 1972—. Trustee Howard Payne U., 1969—. Recipient Distinguished Service award Christian Life Commn. of So. Bapt. Conv., 1972; Legion of Honor award Tex. Bapt. Men, 1971. Columnist San Antonio Express-News, 1969—. Home: 7618 Vinewood St San Antonio TX 78209 Office: 515 McCullough San Antonio TX 78215

ALLEN, JOHN GORDON, priest, Roman Cath. Ch.; b. Richmond, Va., Jan. 1, 1944; s. Robert Lawrence and Dorothy Julia (Plath) A.; B.A. in Philosophy, St. Francis Coll., Loretto, Pa., 1966. Ordained priest, 1970; coordinator Cathedral Sch., Harrisburg, Pa., 1971-76; exec. sec. Liturgical Commn., Diocese of Harrisburg, 1973—, mem. com. on evangelization, dir. Office of Youth and Vocations, asst. dir. Permanent Deaconate, 1976—. Recipient award for Distinguished and Meritorious Community Service, Harrisburg, 1976. Home and Office: 4800 Union Deposit Rd Box 3557 Harrisburg PA 17105

ALLEN, JOHN HOUSTON, Presbyterian minister; b. Hartford, Conn., July 9, 1932; s. William Phelps and Martha (Houston) A.; m. Elizabeth Speissegger, June 7, 1955 (div. 1975); children: William S., Elizabeth H., Robert A., John O.; m. O'Lynn Armstrong, May 27, 1977; step-children: Melinda Ann Armstrong, Timothy Edward Armstrong. B.S., Va. Poly. Inst., 1955; Th.M., Columbia Sem., Decatur, Ga., 1975. Ordained to ministry, Presbyterian Ch., 1965; asst. minister Rock Spring Presbyn. Ch., Atlanta, 1965-66; dir. Atlanta Presbyn. Mass Media Ministry, 1966-69; exec. dir. Atlanta Interfaith Broadcasting, Inc., 1969-84, pres., 1984—. Editor: John's Guide, 1968—; Nat. Religious Cable Connection, 1984—. Mem. Assn. Regional Religious Communications, Internat. TV Assn., Tau Beta Pi, Alpha Pi Mu. Office: Atlanta Interfaith Broadcasters 1580 Peachtree St Atlanta GA 30309

ALLEN, JON HUGHES, minister, Southern Baptist Convention; b. Fredrick, Okla., May 13, 1944; s. Milton Hughes Allen; m. Diane Saucier, Sept. 30, 1978; children: Collin, Rachel. B.A., Calif. Bapt. Coll., 1967; M.Div., Golden Gate Sem., 1970, M.Th., 1973; D.Min., Southwestern Sem., 1976. Ordained to ministry, So. Bapt. Conv., 1967. Pastor Crockett Bapt. Ch., Calif., 1970-72; intern minister Broadway Bapt. Ch., Fort Worth, 1973-76; resort missionary Grand Canyon Nat. Park, Ariz., 1976-81; sr. pastor Whispering Lakes Community Ch., Ontario, Calif., 1981—. Contbr. articles to profl. jours. Fellow Am. Assn. Marriage and Family Counselors. Lodge: Rotary (Chino, Calif.), (pres. 1980-81). Office: Whispering Lakes Community Ch 1401 E Riverside Dr Ontario CA 91761

ALLEN, JOSEPH LAND, educator, minister, United Methodist Church: b. Burlington, N.C., Nov. 17, 1928; s. Louis Carr and Bess (Land) A.; m. Mary David Ritter, Aug. 5, 1953; children: Robert Bruce, Joyce Leigh. B.A., Duke U., 1950; B.Div., Yale Div. Sch., 1953; Ph.D., Yale U., 1958. Ordained to ministry, 1952. Instr., Perkins Sch. Theology, So. Meth. U., Dallas, 1957-58, asst. prof., 1958-63, assoc. prof., 1963-70, prof. Christian ethics, 1970—. Author: Love and Conflict: A Covenantal Model of Christian Ethics, 1984. Contbr. articles to profl. jours. Kent fellow, 1956; Assn. Theol. Schs. faculty research fellow, 1970-71. Mem. Soc. Christian Ethics (exec. sec. 1980-84), AAUP. Office: Perkins Sch Theology So Meth Univ Dallas TX 75275

ALLEN, MARGARET SUE, music evangelist, Southern Baptist Convention; b. Purcell, Okla., Sept. 2, 1946; d. R.V. and Alice Elizabeth (Alcorn) Langley; student U. Okla., 1964-65, Inst. Basic Youth Conflicts, 1973; Billy Graham Sch. Evangelism, 1975; m. Loyd Vernon Allen, Feb. 13, 1965; children: Lavena Dawn, Tammy Sue, Natalie Deanne. Soloist, Pleasant Valley Bapt. Ch., Norman, Okla., 1962-66; mem. choir, soloist Met. Bapt. Ch., Cambridge, Mass., 1966-67; soloist Chinle (Ariz.) Bapt. Mission, 1967-68; mem. choir, soloist Bethel Bapt. Ch., Norman, Okla., 1968-69; choral dir. Internat. Friendship Club of Bapt. Chs., Austin, Tex., 1969-70, Norman, 1975-76; acteen dir., teenage sponsor Girlstown U.S.A., Pecan Springs Bapt. Ch., 1969-71, mem. choir, soloist, 1969-71; youth advisor for girls, jr. choir dir. Bethel Bapt. Ch., Norman, 1973-74, music evangelist, 1974—. Mem. Okla. Bapt. Evangelists (sec. 1976-80, music dir. 1981-82, v.p. 1983-84), Conf. So. Bapt. Evangelists, Margaret Allen Music Evangelism, Inc. Composer: Perfect Love, 1973; Life, 1975. Home and Office: 11331 Burning Oak Rd Midwest City OK 73110

ALLEN, O. TOM, literature evangelist, Seventh-day Adventist Ch.; b. Worthville, Ky., Apr. 24, 1950; s. Glen Oris and Margia Mae (Merritt) A.; m. Martha Ann Evans, Jan. 3, 1970; children: Timothy Steven, Thomas Charles, Lauri Michelle. Ordained elder Seventh-Day Adventists, 1977; cert. drug prevention educator. Personal ministries dir. Seventh-day Adventists, Jonesboro, Ga. 1975-79, lit. evangelist, Atlanta, 1978-80, assoc. pub. dir., Nashville, 1980-82, drug prevention educator, Portland, Tenn., 1984—; owner The Bible Story, Portland, 1984—. Author: High Rider, 1983; editor Adventist Health Network newsletter, 1984—; contbr. articles to religious publs. Recipient cert. of achievement Rev. and Herald Pub. Assn., 1983. Office: Home Health Edn Service PO Box 293 Portland TN 37148

ALLEN, PAUL HEFLIN, minister, Cumberland Presbyterian Church; b. Elizabeth City County, Va., May 23, 1928; s. Mathews Franklin and Eunice Tinsley (Pyron) A.; student Midwestern U., Wichita Falls, Tex., 1949-52; B.A. in Biology, Bethel Coll., McKenzie, Tenn., 1955; B.D., Memphis Theol. Sem., 1958; Th.D., Four-States U., 1968; postgrad. East Tex. State U., Commerce, 1970-71; m. Ann Middleton, Apr. 9, 1955; 1 child, Paul Michael. Ordained to ministry, 1955; pastor in Milan and Ramer, Tenn., Joinerville and Longview, Tex., 1956-67; pastor Centre Presbyn. Ch., Longview, 1967-68, Canton-Van Presbyn. Ch., Tex., 1968-70, Troup-Overton (Tex.) Parish, 1970-83. Officer, Presbyn. bds. missions, Christian edn. and finance, 1956—; dir. camps for children and youth, 1957-68; moderator Presbytery, 1957, 59, Synod, 1965-66; commr. Gen. Assembly, 1957, 60. Mem. Tex. Employment Commn., Longview, 1970—; chmn. steering com. to secure Mental Health Clinic for Gregg County, Tex., 1965-67; team capt. United Fund, 1966. Recipient Counselors certificate in Mental Health, Rusk State Hosp., Tex., 1961. Mem. Tex. Pub. Employees Assn., Internat. Assn. Personnel in Employment Security, Missionary Orgn. Cumberland Presbyn. Ch. (life). Contbr. articles to ch. mags. Home: 1814 Swan St Longview TX 75604 Office: 412 S High St Longview TX 75604

ALLEN, R. EARL, minister, Southern Baptist Convention; b. Fort Worth, May 26, 1922; s. James Roy and Mary Ellen (Coker) A.; B.A., Howard Payne Coll., 1946; B.S., Midwestern U., 1947; postgrad. Southwestern Bapt. Theol. Sem., 1946, 53, 57; D.D., Howard Payne U., 1953; D.Laws, Atlanta Law Sch., 1968; D.Litt., John Brown U., 1971; D.Humanities, Linda Vista Bapt. Coll., 1968, Th.B., 1975, M.A., 1977; D.Sacred Theology, Southwest Bapt. U., 1984; m. Norma Joyce Lovelace, Dec. 25, 1941; children—Norma, James Todd, Joy Earline. Ordained to ministry So. Baptist Conv., 1940; pastor First Bapt. Ch., Archer City, Tex., 1945-47, First Bapt. Ch., Seagraves, Tex., 1947-50, First Bapt. Ch., Floydada, Tex., 1950-56, Rosen Heights Bapt. Ch., Fort Worth, 1956—; adj. prof. SW Bapt. Theol. Sem., Fort Worth; mem. exec. com. So. Baptist Conv., 1973-81, mem. Home Mission Bd., 1964-73, mem. Sunday Sch. Bd., 1957-64; trustee Howard Payne Coll., 1984—. Author: Bible Paradoxes, 1963; Memorial Messages, 1964; Trails, Tragedies and Triumphs, 1965; Christian Comfort, 1965; Strength from Shadows, 1967; Sign of the Star, 1968; Silent Saturday, 1968; Personal Jesus, 1972; Person of the Passion, 1972; Bible Comparatives, 1973; Speaking in Parables, 1973; Divine Dividends, 1974; Days to Remember, 1974; Good Morning, Lord: Devotions for Hospital Patients, 1975; Prayers That Changed History, 1978; The Hereafter, What Jesus Said About It, 1978; For Those Who Grieve, 1978; Jesus Loves Me, 1979; Seven Words of Christ, 1981; Good Morning, Lord: Devotions for Times of Sorrow, 1983; A Man Like No Other, 1984; Let it Begin in Me, 1985. Recipient George Washington Honor medal awards, Freedoms Found. at Valley Forge, 1964, 68, 79; disting. alumnus award, Howard Payne Coll., 1967. Address: 2524 Roosevelt St Fort Worth TX 76106

ALLEN, RAYMOND CLYDE, minister, So. Bapt. Conv.; b. St. Petersburg, Fla., Sept. 20, 1945; s. Harold Bennett and Marjorie Gertrude (Glidden) A.; B.S., Toccoa Falls Bible Coll., 1969; M.R.E., Gordon-Conwell Theol. Sem., 1972; m. Myrtie Carolyn Shifflett, Jan. 20, 1968; children—Michelle Rene, Stephen Brent. Ordained to ministry, 1969; interim pastor New Colony Bapt. Ch., Billerica, Mass., 1970-72; founder, pastor Judson Meml. Bapt. Ch., North Andover, Mass., 1972—; founding pastor New Life Bapt. Chapel, Dracut, Mass., 1976—. Dir., Sunday sch. Mass. Bapt. Assn., 1973-76, dir. ch. tng., 1976—; mem. exec. bd. Bapt. Gen. Assn. New Eng., 1975—; treas. Merrimack Valley Evang. Ministers Assn., 1975—; mem. Ministerial Bicentennial Com. North Andover (Mass.) Chs., 1975-76. Home: 60 Andover St Andover MA 01810 Office: Box 306 33 Johnson St North Andover MA 01845

ALLEN, RUSSELL THOMAS, minister, Ind. Fundamental Chs. Am.; b. Phillipsburg, N.J., July 6, 1929; s. Edward Van Dyke and Elise Erma (Berisch) A.; B.A., Muhlenberg Coll., Allentown, Pa., 1953; student Nyack Coll., 1950, Bibl. Sem. N.Y.C., 1955-56, Reformed Episcopal Sem., Phila., 1957-58, Temple U., 1958-59; D.D., Ridgedale Theol. Sem., Chattanooga, 1975; B.Th., Colo. Coll. and Sem., 1961; m. Dorith E. Stoneback, June 17, 1950; children—Cheryl, David, Daniel, Cherene. Ordained to ministry, 1958; pastor Non-Sectarian Fellowship Ch., Phillipsburg, N.J., 1968—; youth conf. speaker, Pa., Mass., Tenn., N.J.; adviser to Billy Graham Crusades, N.Y.C., Phila.; dean Lancaster Sch. of Bible-Phillipsburg Extension. Mem. Lopat Twp. Bd. Edn., 1972-75, bd. edn. Phillipsburg Christian Acad., 1974—; mem. Gospel Mission to S.Am., 1969, Bible Club Movement Bd., 1970; chaplain Warren Hosp., 1950, Police Dept., 1973; host radio programs. Active Bicentennial Com. of Lopat Twp., 1975—. Mem. Nat. Religious Broadcasters. Author: Over the River to Challie, 1967. Contbr. articles to religious publs. Home: 222 4th St Phillipsburg NJ 08865 Office: 3d and Cromwell Sts Phillipsburg NJ 08865

ALLEY, EDDIE RAY, minister to youth, So. Bapt. Conv.; b. San Angelo, Tex., Jan. 3, 1946; s. Otis and Ruth (Mattson) A.; B.A., Baylor U., 1968; postgrad. Southwestern Bapt. Theol. Sem., 1968-70; m. Betty Allan, Dec. 17, 1966; children—Kimberly Ann, Jana Michele. Ordained to ministry, 1967; summer missionary Home Mission Bd., So. Bapt. Conv., 1966; minister to youth, asso. pastor Alice Ave. Bapt. Ch., Waco, Tex., 1966-68; minister to youth Cockrell Hill Bapt. Ch., Dallas, 1968-70; journeyman missionary Fgn. Mission Bd. Baptist Ch., Salzburg, Austria, 1970-71; minister to youth Calvary Bapt. Ch., Garland, Tex., 1971-76, First Bapt. Ch., Houston, 1976—; tchr. ch. tng. week Glorieta (N.Mex.) Bapt. Assembly, 1972. Chmn. youth com. Waco Bapt. Assn., 1967-68, Dallas Bapt. Assn., 1973-74; v.p. Religious Edn. Music Conf., Dallas Bapt. Assn., 1974-75, mem. Mt. Lebanon com., 1973-75; dir. of recreation Mt. Lebanon Bapt. Encampment, 1971. Contbr. articles to religious publs. Home: 5731 Knobby Knoll Houston TX 77092 Office: 7401 Katy Freeway Houston TX 77024

ALLIN, JOHN MAURY, bishop, Episcopal Church; b. Helena, Ark., Apr. 22, 1921; s. Richard and Dora (Harper) A.; B.A., U. South, 1943, M.Div., 1945, D.D. (hon.), 1962; M. Ed., Miss. Coll., 1960; m. Frances Ann Kelly, Oct. 18, 1949; children—Martha May, Kelly Ann, John Maury (twins), Frances Elizabeth. Ordained priest Episcopal Ch., 1945; vicar St. Peter's Ch., Conway, Ark., 1945-49; curate St. Andrew's Ch., New Orleans, 1950-51; chaplain to Episcopal students and instns., New Orleans, 1950-51; rector Grace Ch., Monroe, La., 1952-58; pres., rector All Saints Jr. Coll., Vicksburg, Miss., 1958-61; bishop coadjutor Diocese of Miss., 1961-66; bishop of Miss., 1966-74; presiding bishop Protestant Episcopal Ch. in U.S., 1974—. Mem. exec. council Episcopal Ch., 1970—, steering com. exec. council, 1971—, chmn. program adv. com. on communications, 1970-74; chmn. Miss. Religious Leadership Conf., 1972-73; mem. Joint Commn. on Ecumenical Relations, 1964—, chmn., 1973. Mem. exec. bd. County Health Improvement Project Miss., 1968—. Trustee All Saints Sch., Vicksburg, 1961—; trustee U. South, 1961—, chancellor, 1973—, bd. regents, 1965-71. Home: 338 Round Hill Rd Greenwich CT 06830 Office: 815 2d Ave New York City NY 10017

ALLISON, GRADY NED, church official, Presbyterian Church U.S.A.; b. Eastland, Tex., May 2, 1928; s. Joseph Carroll and Lillie Mae (Shelburne) A.; B.A., Hardin-Simmons U., 1949; B.D., Southwestern Bapt. Theol. Sem., 1954; m. Glorietta Travis, June 2, 1950; children—Carroll Edwin, Melissa Louise. Ordained to ministry Bapt. Ch., 1945, transferred to United Presbyn. Ch. in U.S.A., 1966. Minister Bapt. chs. in Tex., 1945-59, Wooster Bapt. Ch., Baytown, Tex., 1959-66; organizer, minister St. Thomas United Presbyn. Ch., Houston, 1966-73; program dir. for evangelism Program Agy., United Presbyn. Ch. in U.S.A., N.Y.C., 1973-85, Presbyn. Ch. (U.S.A.), 1985—; pres. West Meml. Drive Christian Community, Houston, 1970, 73; chmn. evangelism working group Nat. Council Chs. of Christ, 1975-76, 84—, mem. program planning and evaluating com., div. of ch. and society, 1975-76, 84—; mem. planning com., workshop leader Washington Roundtable on Evangelism, 1982—; mem. staff Spl. Com. on Evangelism and Ch. Growth, 1983-84. Mem. service unit Salvation Army, 1958; sec. Munday Little League, Tex., 1958; pub. relations officer Baytown Civil Def. Orgn., 1961-66; chmn. crime prevention com. Exchange Club, Houston, 1970-71. Precinct capt. Rep. Party, Houston, 1970-71. Home: 30 Wiltshire Pl Bronxville NY 10708 Office: 475 Riverside Dr New York NY 10115

ALLISON, WILLIAM LANDON, minister, Ch. of God, Anderson, Ind.; b. Johnson City, Tenn., Sept. 15, 1921; s. Walter Rupert and Flora Bell (Carriger) A.; B.Sc., East Tenn. State U., 1943; M.Ed., U. Miami, 1949; M.R.E., U. So. Calif., 1955; Ed.D., Luther Rice Sem., 1974; m. Virginia Lee Murray, July 27, 1957. Ordained to ministry Ch. of God, Anderson, Ind., 1954; founding pastor Arcadia (Calif.) Community Ch. of God, 1954; founding registrar Arlington Coll., Riverside, Calif., 1955; asso. pastor Tacoma Ch. of God, Johnson City, Tenn., 1963-72; sr. minister First Ch. of God, Bristol, Tenn., 1972—. Mem. state bd. Christian Edn. Ch. of God, Anderson, Ind., 1965-70, bd. publs., 1972—; area religious edn. cons., 1963-75. Mem. adv. bd. Warner So. Coll., Lake Wales, Fla., 1969-72, Am. Security Council, 1973—. Recipient Distinguished Achievement award Warner So. Coll., 1969, Apple award, 1968; certificate ednl. achievement U. Tenn., 1970, Fla. State U., 1968, U.S. Air Force, 1959. Mem. NEA, Am. Legion (chaplain 1963-65), Mil. Chaplains Assn., PTA, Air Force Assn., Tenn. Assn. Pub. Sch. Adult Edn. (sec. 1968-71), Tenn., Kingsport (chmn. human relations com. 1973-74) edn. assns., Internat. Platform Assn. Home: 301 Georgia Ave Bristol TN 37620 also: 1430 Watauga St Kingsport TN 37664

ALLRED, JANICE MARILYN, evangelist, minister, Church of God of Prophecy; b. Muskogee, Okla., Feb. 28, 1942; d. Theodore Alonzo and Frances Elizabeth (Fuller) A.; student Tulsa Tech. Inst., 1961; certificates Bible Tng. Inst., Ch. of God of Prophecy, Cleveland, Tenn., 1969-75; Ordained to ministry, 1971; pastor Ch. of God of Prophecy, Lovington, N.Mex., 1971-72; sec. Okla., 1972-73; pastor Worstell Ch., Ada, Okla., 1973-74; evangelist, lay worker, Tahlequah, Okla., 1974-75; pastor Ch. of God of Prophecy, Raton, N.Mex., 1975-84; evangelist, Muskogee, Okla., 1984—. Mem. Raton Ministerial Alliance, Ch. Women United (pres.). Address: 900 Erie St Muskogee OK 74403

ALLSHOUSE, JOHN, minister, Independent Fundamental Churches of America, educator; b. Struthers, Ohio, Jan. 13, 1951; s. John and Marilyn (Maggianetti) A. B.A. in Edn., Youngstown State U., 1978; M.S. in Edn., Westminster Coll., 1978; M. Religion, Cin. Christian Sem., 1980, D. Religious Edn., 1983; Th.D., Christian Bible Coll., 1984. Ordained to ministry Baptist Bible Fellowship Ch., 1980. Intern Higginsport Bapt. Ch., Ohio, 1978-79, Moscow Bapt. Ch., Ohio, 1979-80; interim pastor Butler Bapt. Ch., Ind., 1980-81, Boonsboro Bapt. Ch., 1981-82; tchr. Ohio, Ind., Md. schs., 1978-85; instr. Christian Study Ctr., Campbell, Ohio, 1983-85; substitute tchr. Youngstown area sch., 1978-85. Contbr. articles to religious jours. Republican. Address: 491 W Wilson St Struthers OH 44471 (216) 755-9285

ALMEIDA MERINO, ADALBERTO, clergyman, Roman Catholic Church. Archbishop of Chihuahua, Mex., Office: Archdiocese of Chihuahua City of Chihuahua Aparato Postal N7 Mexico*

ALMEN, LOWELL GORDON, minister, editor, American Lutheran Church; b. Grafton, N.D., Sept. 25, 1941; s. Paul O. and Helen E. (Johnson) A.; m. Sally Arlyn Clark, Aug. 14, 1965; children: Paul Simon, Cassandra Gabrielle. B.A., Concordia Coll., 1963; M.Div., Luther Theol. Sem., 1967; Litt.D. (hon.), Capital U., 1981. Ordained to ministry Lutheran Ch., 1967. Pastor, St. Peter's Ch., Dresser, Wis., 1967-69; assoc. campus pastor and dir. communications Concordia Coll., Moorhead, Minn., 1969-74; mng. editor The Luth. Standard, Mpls., 1974-78, editor, 1979—. Editor: (curricula) World Religions and Christian Mission, 1967, Our Neighbor's Faith, 1968. Bush Found. grantee, 1972; recipient Disting. Alumnus award Concordia Coll., 1982. Mem. Associated Ch. Press (bd. dirs. 1981-84), Evang. Press Assn., Minn. Press Club. Home: 1453 Lincoln Terr NE Minneapolis MN 55421 Office: The Lutheran Standard PO Box 1209 Minneapolis MN 55440

ALSPAUGH, CHARLES EDWARD, minister, Lutheran Church-Missouri Synod; b. Hickory, N.C., Oct. 13, 1941; s. Kermit Edison and Ida Bell (Timberlake) S.; s. Donna Kay Robenstein, May 29, 1966; children: Robert Charles, Deanna Lynn. A.A., St. John Coll., Kans., 1963; B.A., U. Tex.-El Paso, 1965; B.D., Concordia Sem., Springfield, Ill., 1968. Ordained to ministry, Luth. Ch., 1968. Minister of youth and edn. Trinity Luth. Ch., San Bernardino, Calif., 1968-69; pastor St. John Luth. Ch., Yuma, Colo., 1969-73, Bethany Luth. Ch., Osburn, Idaho and Emmanuel Luth. Ch., Mullan, Idaho, 1973-77, St. John Luth. Ch., Palmer, Alaska, 1977—; mem. State Youth Bd., Luth. Ch.-Mo. Synod, Washington, 1976, Alaska, 1977-83, cir. counselor, 1980-81. Bd. dirs. Little League Baseball, Palmer, 1979-80; mem. symposium Cooperative Extension Service, Anchorage, 1983; chaplain coordinator Valley Hosp., Palmer, 1980—; cross-country coach Palmer Community Schs., 1982. Mem. Ministerial Assn. (chmn. 1983—). Luth. Women's Missionary League (pastoral advisor 1970-71), Luth. Layman's League (pastoral advisor 1983—). Home: PO Box 774 Palmer AK 99645 Office: St John Luth Ch PO Box 774 Palmer AK 99645

ALTMAN, GARDNER HOWARD, minister, Assemblies of God; b. Sampson County, N.C., Dec. 21, 1924; s. Polie Gardner and Mildred (Smith) A.; A.B., Atlantic Christian Coll., 1957; m. Velma Lee Beasley, Aug. 5, 1944; children—Gardner Howard, Constance Lee. Founding pastor Calvary Assembly, Angier, N.C., 1958-60, Calvary Assembly, Fayetteville, N.C., 1960—. Youth dir. Assemblies of God, N.C., 1956-57; contact chaplain Ft. Bragg, N.C. and Pope AFB, 1962—; pres., chaplain Sta. WQTI, 1976—; chaplain Radio Sta. WFLB, 1962-77. Home: 2502 Lochwood Rd Fayetteville NC 28303 Office: 2512 Fort Bragg Rd Fayetteville NC 28303

ALTMAN, TIMOTHY ALAN, Christian video publisher; b. Lancaster, Ohio, June 8, 1952; s. Charles Richard and RoseMary (Murphy) A.; m. Janice Ellen Vanderhorst, Dec. 8, 1973; children: Jennifer, Tamara. B. Bibl. Sci., Western Bible Coll., 1983. News dir., announcer Sta. KWBI, Morrison, Colo., 1978-83; video publisher Nat. Cable TV Inst., Denver, 1983—. Recipient Western Bible Coll. Trustees award, 1981. Mem. Delta Epsilon Chi. Republican. Office: Nat Cable TV Inst 330 1 W Hampton Denver CO

AMALFITANO, JOSEPH ANTHONY, priest, Roman Catholic Church; b. Ridley Park, Pa., Mar. 23, 1935; s. James Francis and Grace Rose (Ponci) A. B.A., St. Charles Sem., Phila., 1959. Ordained priest Roman Catholic Ch., 1963. Asst. pastor Annunciation Ch., Phila., 1963-69, Our Lady of Mt. Carmel, Bridgeport, Pa., 1969-73, St. Paul's Ch., Phila., 1973-78, St. Stanislaus Ch., Lansdale, Pa., 1978-82; pastor Our Lady of Pompeii, Phila., 1982—; spiritual dir. Cause of Padre Pio, Norristown, Pa., 1968—, Risen Christ Young Adult Prayer Group, Warminster, Pa., 1978—. Democrat. Home and Office: Our Lady of Pompeii Ch 632 W Erie Ave Philadelphia PA 19140

AMAN, NORMAN, minister, Lutheran Church-Missouri Synod. B. Lehr, N.D., Oct. 30, 1933; s. Jacob K. and Martha (Miller) A.; m. Dolores Anne Roberts, Apr. 24, 1965: children: Timothy, Faith, James, Hope. Diploma, Concordia Theol. Sem., Springfield, Ill., 1961, B.Th., 1972. Ordained to ministry Luth. Ch., 1961. Pastor, Trinity Luth. Ch., Moosomin, Sask., Can., 1961-64, St. Paul's Luth. Ch., Beach, N.D., 1964-67, Christ Luth. Ch., Goodrich, Mich., 1967-77, St. Matthew's Luth. Ch., Esko, Minn., 1977—; circuit counselor Mich. dist. Luth. Ch.-Mo. Synod, 1975-77, mem. campus ministry sub-com. Minn. N. Dist., 1980—, pastoral counselor Luth. Women's Missionary League, 1980—, Luth. Laymen's League, Lake Superior Circuit, 1982—. Vice chmn. Carlton County Edn. for Marriage (Minn.), 1978-84, chmn., 1984—. Served to cpl. U.S. Army, 1953-55. Home: 10 Elizabeth Ave Esko MN 55733 Office: St Matthews Luth Ch 1 Elizabeth Ave Esko MN 55733

AMBROSIEWICZ, MARY FIDELISE, nun, Roman Cath. Ch.; b. Phila., Apr. 1, 1915; d. Mathew and Honora (Ester) A.; R.N., St. Francis Sch. Nursing, 1945; B.S., St. Louis U., 1947; postgrad. Cornell U., 1960. Joined Felician Sisters, 1933; hosp. adminstr. Blackwell Gen. Hosp. (Okla.), 1947-53, St. Joseph's Hosp., Phila., 1954-61; adminstr. St. Mary's Hosp., Orange, N.J., 1962—, sec., treas. bd. trustees, 1962—. Fellow Am. Coll. Hosp. Adminstrs.; mem. Am. Acad. Med. Adminstrs., Am. Nurses Assn. Home and Office: 135 S Center St Orange NJ 07050

AMBUHL, FRANK JERROLD, priest, religious organization executive, Episcopal Church; psychotherapist. B. Toronto, Ont., Can., Apr. 27, 1925 (parents Am. citizens); s. Frank Frederick and Martha Lillian (Sasser) A.; m. Susan Tandy Durrett, Sept. 5, 1960; children: Elizabeth, Daniel, Robert, Susanne, Tandy, Frank, Donald, Martha, Paul. B.A.Sc., U. Toronto, 1952; M.B.A., Harvard U., 1954; M.Div. with honors, Church Div. Sch. of Pacific, 1968; D.Min., Austin Presbyterian Theol. Sem., 1980. Ordained to ministry Episcopal Ch., 1968. Assoc. rector St. Pauls-on-the-Plains, Lubbock, Tex., 1968-70; priest in charge St. Stephen's Ch., Sweetwater, Tex., 1970-72, Holy Cross Ch., San Antonio, 1972-83; dir. counseling ministries St. Mark's Ch., San Antonio, 1982—. Psychotherapist in pvt. practice, San Antonio, 1980—. Fellow Am. Assn. Pastoral Counselors; mem. Am. Assn. Marriage and Family Therapists, Internat. Transactional Analysis Assn., Am. Assn. Sex Educators, Counselors, and Therapists, U.S. Transactional Analysis Assn. Republican. Lodge: Masons. Home: 342 Maplewood San Antonio TX 78216 Office: 3030 Nacogdoches Rd Suite 208 San Antonio TX 78217

AMES, DAVID ATWATER, priest, Episcopal Church; b. Glendale, Ohio, Sept. 12, 1938; s. Malcolm McEwan and Jane Elizabeth (Whitcher) A.; m. Carol Landau, Jan. 30, 1982; 1 child by previous marriage, John Winthrop. A.B., Miami U., Oxford, Ohio, 1960; M.Div., Episc. Theol. Sch., 1966; D.Min., Episc. Div. Sch., Cambridge, 1984. Ordained priest Episcopal Ch., 1967. Asst. pastor Ch. of St. Edward, Columbus, Ohio, 1966-69, Grace Ch., Providence, 1969-71; chaplain R.I. Coll., Providence, 1971-74, R.I. Sch. Design, Providence, 1974—, Brown U., Providence, 1974—; supr. field edn. Episc. Div. Sch., Cambridge, 1974—, pres. alumni/alumni edn. assn., 1985—; v.p. bd. dirs. Interfaith Health Care Ministries, 1984—; mem. steering com. Ministers in Med. Edn., Soc. Health and Human Values, 1984—; parish cons. Diocese of R.I., 1982—. Co-author: Good Genes?: Emerging Values for Science, Religion and Society, 1984. Mem. research com. Women and Infants' Hosp., Providence, 1975—; parish cons. Diocese of R.I., 1982—. Fellow Coll. Preachers; mem. Episc. Soc. Ministry in Higher Edn., Inst. Soc., Ethics and Life Scis., ACLU. Home: 130 Slater Ave Providence RI 02906 Office: 114 George St Providence RI 02906

AMMONS, EDSEL A., Bishop, The United Methodist Church, West Ohio Conf., Columbus. Office: The United Meth Ch 471 Broad St Suite 1106 Columbus OH 43215*

AMUNDSEN, DALE JONATHAN, minister, Evangelical Free Church; b. Seattle, Aug. 14, 1952; s. John Alexander and Lillian Astrid (Larson) A.; m. Charlene Marie Nickle, Feb. 18, 1956; children: Jonathan Edward, Stephanie Marie. B. Religious Edn., Grace Bible Coll., 1974; B.A., Seattle Pacific Coll., 1975, M. Christian Ministry, 1976; M. Div., Fuller Theol. Sem., 1979. Licensed to ministry Evangelical Free Ch., 1976. Minister of youth Grace Bible Ch., Port Orchard, Wash., 1975-77, Emmanuel Evangelical Free Ch., Burbank, Calif., 1978-80; sr. pastor Elim Evangelical Free Ch., Puyallup, Wash., 1980—; chaplain Tacoma Police Dept., Wash., 1983—, Pierce County Sheriff's Office, Tacoma, 1985—. Republican. Avocations: travel; gourmet seafood cooking. Office: Elim Evangelical Free Ch PO Box 73639 Puyallup WA 98373

ANDERL, HENRY BERNARD, priest, Roman Cath. Ch.; b. Chippewa Falls, Wis., Oct. 7, 1918; s. Henry and Katherine (Schneider) A.; B.A. in Philosophy, St. John's U., Collegeville, Minn., 1941; postgrad. in Bds. Adminstrn. and Econs., U. Minn., 1945-48. Ordained priest, 1945; joined Order of St. Benedict of St. John's Abbey; pastor St. John's Parish, Grand Marais, Minn., 1967—. Pres., Cook County unit Am. Cancer Soc., Grand Marais, 1971—; bd. dirs. Cook County Hist. Soc., 1969. Address: PO Box 548 Grand Marais MN 55604

ANDERSEN, FRANCES ELIZABETH, religious leadership educator; b. Hot Springs, Ark., Feb. 11, 1916; d. Benjamin Knox and Pearl Scott (Smith) Gold; B.A., UCLA, 1936, secondary teaching credential, 1937; student various grad. courses in edn.; m. Robert Thomas Andersen, June 27, 1942; children: Nancy Ruth (Mrs. Bernd Neumann), Robert Thomas. Mem. nat. bd. missions United Methodist Ch., 1940-44; mem. nat. bd. Bible sch. and youth Baptist Gen. Conf., 1966-71; coordinator leadership tng. insts. Greater Los Angeles Sunday Sch. Assn., 1956—; exec. dir. San Bernardino—Riverside Sunday Sch. Assn., 1959—; dir. Christian edn. 1st Presbyn. Ch., Phoenix, 1944-46, Trinity Meth. Ch., Los Angeles, 1953-55, 1st Bapt. Ch., Lakewood, Calif., 1955-57, Grace Bapt. Ch., Riverside, 1958-83, chmn. nursery sch. bd., 1969-83; mem. Christian edn. bd. S.W. Bapt. Conf., 1956-59, 63-66, 72-75, 80-83; bd. dirs. Women's Guild, Calif. Bapt. Coll., Riverside, 1983—. Pres. Univ. Jr. High Sch. P.T.A., Riverside, 1963-64, Poly High Sch. P.T.A., Riverside, 1965-67. Life mem. P.T.A.; mem. Sons of Norway, Alpha Delta Chi (nat. pres. 1950-51, exec. sec. 1952-54), Pi Mu Epsilon, Author: How to Organize Area Leadership Training Institutes, 1964. Address: 1787 Prince Albert Dr Riverside CA 92507

ANDERSEN, RICHARD, minister Am. Luth. Ch.; b. Kansas City, Kans., Aug. 23, 1931; s. Marius Teador and Ellen Kjstine (Christensen) A.; B.A., Dana Coll., 1953; B.D., Trinity Theol. Sem., 1960; Ph.D., Calif. Grad. Sch. Theology, 1972; m. Lois Jeanette Petersen, June 9, 1957; children—Kristyn, Deryk, Jennifer. Ordained to ministry, 1960; intern pastor, Whittier, Calif., 1958-59; asso. pastor, North Hollywood, Calif., 1960-62; founding pastor Ch. of the Holy Cross, Ojai, Calif., 1962-64; pastor Grace Am. Luth. Ch., Rancho Cordova, Calif., 1964-68; sr. pastor Luth. Ch. of the Master, La Habra, Calif., 1968-73; founding pastor Community Ch. of Joy, Glendale, Ariz., 1974—. Chmn. pub. relations com. S. Pacific Dist.; dist. rep., standing com. for office communication and missions support Am. Luth. Ch.; chaplain Glendale Samaritan Hosp., 1974—. Mem. Deer Valley Ministerial Assn. Author: Devotions Along the Way, 1972; Loving in Forgiveness, 1973; Your Keys to the Executive Suite, 1973; Flights of Devotion, 1973; For Those Who Mourn, 1974; Highways to Health, 1974, 75; Now the Good Wine, 1974; The Love Formula, 1974; Living Lenten Portraits, 1975; For Grieving Friends, 1975; The Bread of Christmas, 1975; The Joy of Easter, 1975; Devotions for Church School Teachers, 1976; Grace and Rest of Life, 1976. Contbr. articles to profl. publs. Home: 5510 West Beck Ln Glendale AZ 85306 Office: 16635 N 51st Ave Glendale AZ 85306

ANDERSON, A(NDREW) WALLACE, minister, American Lutheran Church; b. Rockville, Md., May 17, 1953; s. Arnold Windsor and Arcadia Maria (Ramos) A.; m. Susan Jean Schnell, July 21, 1979; children: Andrew Woodruff, Sarah Kay. B.A. in Religion, Gettysburg Coll., 1976; M.Div., Trinity Luth. Sem., Columbus, Ohio, 1981. Ordained to ministry American Lutheran Church, 1981. Minister, Cogswell Luth Parish, N.D., 1981—; missionary intern Central African Republic, 1978-80. Organizer rural stress workshops, 1984. Named Eagle scout, Nat. Capital Area council Boy Scouts Am., 1971. Mem. Sargent County Ministerium (pres. 1982-85). Democrat. Home and Office: Cogswell Luth Parish PO Box 9 Cogswell ND 58017

ANDERSON, ALAN BRAUER, religion educator, administrator, United Methodist Church; b. Oklahoma City, Dec. 4, 1934; s. Homer Spaulding and Margaret Frances (Brauer) A.; m. Deborah H. Nelson, Aug. 11, 1956 (div. 1976); children: Amy Elizabeth, Margaret Hunt; m. Gwyneth B. Davis, Apr. 22, 1978. B.A., Knox Coll., 1956; B.D., U. Chgo., 1959, M.A., 1966, Ph.D., 1975. Ordained to ministry United Meth. Ch., 1961. Instr., asst. prof. Div. Sch., U. Chgo., 1966-75; prof. interdisciplinary studies Wilberforce U., Ohio, 1976-78; head dept. religious studies U. N.C., Greensboro, 1978-83; head dept. philosophy and religion Western Ky. U., Bowling Green, 1985—. Author: Civil Rights and Civil Religions, 1986. Editor: Desegregation and Chicago Public Schools, 1976; Rockefeller Bros. Theol. fellow, 1956-57, Danforth Grad. fellow, 1957-59, 62-66. Mem. Am. Acad. Religion (chmn. ethics sect. 1983—, bd. dirs. 1983—), Southeastern Am. Acad. Religion (sec.-treas. 1983—), Soc. Christian Ethics (bd. dirs. 1984—, editor Ann. of Soc. Christian Ethics, 1985—), Phi Beta Kappa. Office: Western Ky U Bowling Green KY 42101

ANDERSON, ALBERT ESTEN See *Who's Who in America*, 43rd edition.

ANDERSON, ANNE RESPOL, lay church worker, Roman Catholic Church; computer company executive; b. N.Y.C., Aug. 15, 1943; d. John J. and Lillian (Mannello) Respol; m. Bruno Andersson, July 23, 1966; children: Christopher, Michael. B.A., Hunter Coll., 1965, M.S., 1969. Cert. tchr., N.Y.; lic. IRS enrolled agt. Founder, dir. Christian Women: Quo Vadis?, Weston, Conn., 1983—; co-planner, panel moderator for conf. on women Diocese of Bridgeport Roman Cath. Ch., 1984-85. Pres. Micromatic Programming Co., Weston, 1979—. Author poetry, 1958, 59, 75. Co-author Computer Income Tax Software, 1980, 81. Creator, editor, publisher Christian Women: Quo Vadis? monthly newsletter, 1983. Designer adult edn. course, 1976-77. Bd. dirs. NOW Huntington chpt., N.Y., 1974-77, chmn. edn. com., 1974-77; co-convener edn. conf. NOW Long Island chpts., 1975; adv. regents external degree program U. State of N.Y., Albany, 1975-77. Mem. Nat. Soc. Pub. Accts., Nat. Assn. Enrolled Agts., NETWORK. Home: 24 Old Farm Rd Weston CT 06883

ANDERSON, BRUCE TIMOTHY, minister, Lutheran Church in America; b. Chgo., Sept. 16, 1941; s. Oscar V. and Lilly Viola (Flodden) A.; m. Karen Adelade Thomas, Dec. 21, 1963; 1 child, Constance A. B.A. in History, Augustana Coll., 1963; M.Div., Northwestern Luth. Theol. Sem., St. Paul. 1974; D.Min., Luther Northwestern Theol. Sem., St. Paul, 1984. Ordained to ministry Lutheran Church in America, 1974. Pastor, Luth Ch. of the Resurrection, Niles, Ill., 1974—. Participant, N. Shore Peace Initiative, Niles Nuclear Freeze Com.; mem. YMCA, Northbrook, Ill. Mem. Niles Clergy Assn. (organizer), N. Suburban dist. Ill. Synod, Luth. Ch. in Am. Home: 7147 W Keeney St Niles IL 60648 Office: Luth Ch of Resurrection 8450 N Shermer Rd Niles IL 60648

ANDERSON, C. L. Bishop, mem. gen. bd. The Church of God in Christ, Detroit. Office: The Ch of God in Christ 20485 Mendota Detroit MI 48221*

ANDERSON, DENNIS A., minister, Lutheran Church; b. Glenwood, Minn., July 8, 1937; s. Albin G. and Florence E. Anderson; m. Barbara Ann Forse, Dec. 30, 1960; children: Kristin E., Charles. A.B., Gustavus Adolphus Coll., 1959; B.D., Luth. Sch. Theology, Chgo., 1963; D.Div., Gustavus Adolphus, 1978; L.H.D., Midland Luth. Coll., 1980. Ordained to ministry Luth. Ch. Am. Mission developer, pastor Holy Cross Ch., Austin, Tex., 1963-66; pastor Ch. of Good Shepherd, Prospect Heights, Ill., 1966-71; regional sec. Bd. Am. Missions, N.Y.C., 1971-72; pastor St. Paul Ch., Grand Island, Nebr., 1973-78; bishop Nebr. Synod Luth Ch. Am., Omaha, 1978—. Author: Searching for Faith, 1976; Jesus, My Brother in Suffering, 1977. Home: 15141 Arbor St Omaha NE 68144

ANDERSON, DONALD WHIMBEY, priest, council executive, Anglican Church of Canada; b. Ottawa, Ont., Can., Oct. 14, 1931; s. Roland Kumpf and Florence Catharine (Whimbey) A.; m. Veronica Agnes Ryan, Sept. 11, 1954; children: Hilary Mary, Mark Ryan. B.A., U. Toronto, 1954, M.A., 1958; S.T.B., U. Trinity Coll., Toronto, 1957; Th.D., Toronto Sch. Theology, 1971; postgrad. Harvard U., 1959-60. Ordained priest, Anglican Ch. of Can., 1957. Priest asst. St. James Cathedral, Toronto, 1957-59; lectr. Central Theol. Coll., Tokyo, 1960-61; rector Ch. of the Holy Wisdom, Japan, 1961-64; prof. Central Theol. Coll., St. Paul's U., Tokyo, 1964-73; prof. St. Andrew's Sem., Manila, Philippines, 1974-75; gen. sec. Can. Council Chs., Toronto, 1975—. Sidney Childs fellow, 1969-71. Office: Can Council Churches 40 St Clair Ave E Toronto ON M4T 1M9 Canada

ANDERSON, EDWARD WALFRID, JR., minister, Assemblies of God; b. Seattle, Nov. 4, 1923; s. Edward Walfrid and Signe Naomi (Persson) A.; m. Mary La Verne Stading, Feb. 11, 1955; children: Harriet, Mary, Hazel, Dorothey. B.A. in Religious Edn., Northwest Coll. Assemblies of God, Kirkland, Wash., 1949. Ordained to ministry Assemblies of God, 1953. Pastor Lake Terrace Assembly, Seattle, 1949-57, Cottage Brook Assembly, Woodinville, Wash., 1961-75; Christian edn. dir. Faith Center Assembly, Monroe, Wash., 1975—; chaplain Evergreen Hosp., Kirkland, 1974-75. Mem. Seattle Full-Gospel Ministerial Fellowship, Northshore Ministerial Assn. Author articles. Address: 18044 167th Ave NE Woodinville WA 98072

ANDERSON, EDWARD WILLIAM, minister, Assemblies of God; b. San Francisco, Mar. 16, 1910; s. Eric William and Esther (Hasselroth) A.; student Bethany Bible Coll., 1929; m. Goldia Irene Stone, Nov. 22, 1933; children: Delores Ruth Anderson Boyd, Marlene Alyce Anderson Hamilton. Ordained to ministry, 1934; traveling evang. ministry, U.S. and Can., 1931-40; pastor, Temple Ch., Oakland, Calif., 1940-46; field rep. Ch. Extension Plan, Salem, Oreg., 1957-67 West Coast rep. Dept. Benevolences, Assemblies of God, Springfield, Mo., 1967-69; field rep. Ch. Builders Plan, Springfield, 1972-73; dir. Calif. Plan of Ch. Fin., Fresno, 1976-79, Broadway Plan, Houston, 1974-75; assoc. pastor First Assembly of God Life Ctr., Tacoma, 1979—. Mem. Assemblies of God Ministers Benevolent Fund Assn. Home: 1145 N Fir Tacoma WA 98406

ANDERSON, GERALD HARRY, minister, educator, United Methodist Church; New Castle, Pa., June 9, 1930; s. Elmer Arthur and Dorothy Emma (Miller) A.; B.S. in Commerce, Grove City Coll., 1952; M.Div., Boston U., 1955, Ph.D., 1960; postgrad. (Fulbright scholar) U. Marburg (Germany), 1955-56, U. Geneva (Switzerland) Grad. Sch. Ecumenical Studies, 1956-57, U. Edinburgh (Scotland), 1957; m. Joanne Marie Pemberton, July 9, 1960; children: Brooks Arthur, Allison Hope. Ordained to ministry, 1955; Protestant chaplain Philmont Nat. Boy Scout Ranch, Cimarron, N.Mex., summer 1954; interim pastor Kenai Circuit, Alaska, summer 1955, Iona, Scotland, summer 1957; asso. minister Trinity United Meth. Ch., Providence, 1957-60; missionary to Philippines, 1960-70; vis. lectr. Harris Meml. Coll., Manila, Philippines, 1961-62; prof. ch. history and ecumenics Union Theol. Sem., Manila, 1961-70, acad. dean, 1963-66, dir. grad. studies, 1968-70; pres., prof. world Christianity, Scarritt Coll., Nashville, 1970-73; vis. sr. research asso. S.E. Asia Program, Cornell U., 1973-74; asso. dir. Overseas Ministries Study Center, Ventnor, N.J., 1974-76, dir., 1976—; lectr. in field, participant internat. confs. Trustee Found. Theol. Edn. SE Asia, 1971—, United Bd. Christian Higher Edn. in Asia, 1973-79, Am. Leprosy Missions, 1978—, Mission Soc. for United Methodists, 1984—. Mem. Am. Am. Soc. Ch. History, Am. Soc. Missiology (pres. 1972-75, sec.-treas. 1976-79), Assn. Asian Studies, Assn. Profs. Missions N. Am., Deutsche Gesellschaft für Missionswissenschaft, Internat. Assn. Mission Studies (exec. com. 1971-76, pres. 1982-85), Fellowship of Reconciliation, Philippine Bible Soc. (life), U.S. Cath. Mission Assn., Omicron Delta Kappa. Author: Bibliography of the Theology of Missions in the 20th Century, 1958, 3d edit., 1966. Editor, co-author The Theology of the Christian Mission, 1961; Christ and Crisis in Southeast Asia, 1968; Studies in Philippine Church History, 1969; Concise Dictionary of the Christian World Mission, 1971; editor Sermons to Men of Other Faiths and Traditions, 1966; editor, compiler Christianity in Southeast Asia: A Bibliographical Guide, 1966; Asian Voices in Christian Theology, 1976; Witnessing to the Kingdom, 1982; Internat. Bull. Missionary Research, 1977—; (with others) Mission Trends, 5 vols., 1974-81. Editorial bd. South East Asia Jour. Theology, 1968-70, Missiology: An International Review, 1972-79. Contbr. articles to jours. Home: 12 S Sacramento Ave Ventnor NJ 08406 Office: PO Box 2057 Ventnor NJ 08406

ANDERSON, HERMAN LEROY, bishop, African Methodist Episcopal Zion Church; b. Wilmington, N.C.; s. Felix Sylvester and Bessie Bernice (Bizzell) A.; m. Ruth Rosetta Rogers, July 6, 1946; children: Deborah Anderson Kareem, Herman L., Derrick R. B.S., Tuskegee Inst., 1943; B.Div., Hood Theol. Sem., Salisbury, N.C., 1959; D.Div. (hon.), Livingstone Coll., Salisbury, 1980. Pastor, St. James A.M.E. Zion Ch., Ithaca, N.Y., 1959-62, Soldiers Meml. A.M.E. Zion Ch., Salisbury, N.C., 1962-72, Broadway Temple A.M.E. Zion, Louisville, Ky., 1972-76; gen. sec. A.M.E. Zion Ch., Charlotte, N.C., 1976-80, bishop, 1980—. Co-author: Churches and Church Membership, 1980. Bd. dirs. World Meth. Council; trustee Livingstone Coll. Served with USNR, 1944-46. Mem. Congress Nat. Black Churchmen (dir. 1984—).

ANDERSON, JOHN KERBY, religious organization executive, Northwest Bible Ch.; writer; b. Berkeley, Calif., Dec. 7, 1951; s. John A. and M. Lorraine (Allen) A.; m. Susanne Elise Pardey, Aug. 3, 1974; children: Amy, Jonathan, Catherine. B.S., Oreg. State U., 1974; M.S., Yale U., 1976; M.A., Georgetown U., 1980. Vice pres. Probe Ministries, Dallas, 1976—; nat. syndicated columnist. Author: Fossils In Focus, 1977; Life, Death and Beyond, 1980; Genetic Engineering, 1982. Contbr. articles to Moody and Eternity mags. Mem. Am. Sci. Affiliation. Republican. Avocations: writing; basketball, tennis. Home: 4121 Longleaf Garland TX 75042 Office: Probe 1900 Forman Dr #100 Richardson TX 75081

ANDERSON, JUSTICE CONRAD, religious educator, Southern Baptist Convention; b. Bay City, Tex., Feb. 13, 1929; s. Conrad Roy and Eunice Mae (Justice) A.; m. Mary onn Elmore, June 1, 1949; children: Sandra Jean, Timothy Justice, Bradley Pryse, Suzanne Renee. B.A., Baylor U., 1950, M.A., 1951; M.Div., Southwestern Sem., 1955, Th.D., 1965; Spanish Degree, Escuela de Idiomas, San Jose, Costa Rica, 1958. Ordained to ministry, 1955. Fgn. missionary Fgn. Mission Bd., So. Bapt. Conv., Argentina, 1957-74; pastor various chs., Stranger, Osage, Franklin, Tex., 1949-57; guest prof. various sems., 1981, 74, 70-71; v.p. Argentine Bapt. Conv., 1962, 65; prof. missions Southwestern Sem., Ft. Worth, 1974—; dir. World Mission and Evangelism Ctr., Ft. Worth, 1981—; pres. Argentine Bapt. Mission, 1965, 72; interim pres. Internat. Bapt. Sem., 1968-69; vol. missionary Residence Canary Islands, Spain, 1980. Assoc. editor Southwestern Jour. Theology. Author: A Manual of Homiletics in Spanish; A History of the Baptists, vol. I; A Study of Baptist Ecclesiology. Named Baylor U. Man of Merit, 1979. Mem. Argentine Bible Soc., Bapt. Hist. Soc., Am. Soc. Missiology, Assn. Profs. Missions,

Asociacion de Institutos y Seminarios Teologicos del Rio de la Plata. Home: 4628 Brandingshire Fort Worth TX 76133 Office: Southwestern Bapt Theol Sem PO Box 22206 Fort Worth TX 76122

ANDERSON, LAURENCE ERNEST, retired minister, United Church of Canada; psychologist; b. Fir Mountain, Sask., Can., Feb. 4, 1914; s. Leonard Elvin and Mary Aquina (Price) A.; m. Edna Fern Gladys Haverfield, June 15, 1937; children: Karlene, Lornel, Starla, Dalton, Cheryl, Vickie. B.A., U. Sask., 1934; B.D., St. Andrew's, Saskatoon, Sask., 1940; M.Ed., U. Mont., 1959; Ph.D., U. W.I., Kingston, Jamaica, 1973. Ordained to ministry United Ch. Can., 1937, United Ch. Christ, 1947. Minister United Ch. Christ, Glendive, Mont., 1947-54, Minto United Ch., Moose Jaw, Sask., 1954-60; tutor Ch. Tchrs. Coll., Kingston, 1968-72; supply pastor United Ch., Empress, Alta., Can., 1974-84; senator St. Andrew's Coll., 1955; chmn. Presbytery, Moose Jaw, 1957-58; chmn. Christian edn. So. Alta. Presbytery, 1973-74. Psychologist in pvt. practice, Medicine Hat, Alta., 1973—. Teaching fellow U. Mont., 1960; Bursary grantee Govt. Sask., 1961. Mem. Alta. Psychol. Assn., Can. Psychol. Assn., Am. Psychol. Assn. Club: Kiwanis (lt. gov. So. Alta. 1982-83). Lodge: Masons (past grand chaplain Mont., past master). Address: 1390 24th St SE Medicine Hat AB T1A 2E6 Canada

ANDERSON, LEROY R. Bishop, mem. gen. bd. The Church of God in Christ, Amherst, N.Y. Office: The Ch of God in Christ 265 Ranch Trail W Amherst NY 14221*

ANDERSON, MARK MAGNUS, ch. ofcl., Am. Lutheran Ch.; b. Neenah, Wis., Dec. 13, 1933; s. Fridtjof B. and Lavinia M. (Larsen) A.; B.A., St. Olaf Coll., 1955; B.D., Luther Theol. Sem., 1959, Th.M., 1965; m. Donna Mae Aga, Aug. 26, 1956; children—Scott, Nathan, Karn. Ordained to ministry, Am. Lutheran Ch., 1959; pastor Grace Lutheran Ch., Ukiah, Calif., 1959-63; chaplain resident Fairview Hosp., Mpls., 1963-66; dir. chaplaincy services, supr. clin. pastoral edn. Met. Med. Center, Mpls., 1966—. Fellow Am. Assn. Pastoral Counselors; mem. Assn. Mental Health Chaplains. Home: 5341 Clinton Ave S Minneapolis MN 55419 Office: 900 S 8th St Minneapolis MN 55404

ANDERSON, MOSES B., bishop, Roman Catholic Church. Titular bishop of Vatarba, aux. bishop, Detroit, 1983—. Office: 14155 Abington Rd Detroit MI 48227*

ANDERSON, OTIS LEE, JR., minister, Progressive Nat. Bapt. Conv.; b. Crossett, Ark., Apr. 16, 1933; s. Otis L. and Geneva (Harris) A.; student U. Ill., 1949-50, Wilson Jr. Coll., Chgo., 1960; A.A., Chgo. Bapt. Inst., 1961; D.D. (hon.), Universal Bible Inst., 1973; m. Lois Jean Samuels, Jan. 12, 1954; children—Dawna B., Brian Scott, Geoffrey C. Ordained to ministry, 1960; asso. minister Greater New Morning Star Ch., Los Angeles, 1960-61; asst. pastor Greater Mt. Olive Ch., Chgo., 1961-63; adminstrv. asst. Monumental Bapt. Ch., Chgo., 1963-69; pastor Broadview (Ill.) Bapt. Ch., 1969-72; pastor Old Ship of Zion Missionary Bapt. Ch., Chgo., 1972-75; pastor Cathedral Bapt. Ch., Chgo., 1975—. Pres. of preachers Parents Police Orgn., Chgo., 1968. Recipient Service award Manteno Mental Hosp., 1973. Mem. Ministers Alliance (sec. 1970), So. Christian Leadership Conf., NAACP. Home: 35 Timberlane Rd Matteson IL 60443 Office: 4821 S Wabash Chicago IL 60615

ANDERSON, PAUL FRANCIS, bishop, Roman Catholic Church; b. Boston, Apr. 20, 1917; s. Philip Leo and Mary Elizabeth (Doyle) A.; B.A., St. John's Sem., Mass., 1943. Ordained priest Roman Catholic Ch., 1943; pastor Sioux Falls (S.D.) Diocese, 1946-68; consecrated bishop; coadjutor bishop of Duluth (Minn.) 1968-69, bishop, 1969-82, aux. bishop of Sioux Falls, 1982—. Office: 516 N Lake Dr Watertown SD 57201*

ANDERSON, PAUL HILTON, pastor, Evangelical Free Church; b. Chgo., Aug. 4, 1920; s. Hans Christian and Gunda Elida (Abrahamson) A.; m. June Cecelia Aldeen, July 20, 1946; children: Barton Paul, Bradley Steven, Timothy Janes. Student Moody Bible Inst., 1940-43; B.A., Wheaton Coll., 1946; M.A., Boston U., 1948. Asst. pastor Cornerstone Bapt. Ch., Cambridge, Mass., 1946-48; pastor Calvary Evangelical Free Ch., Bridgeport and Trumbull, Conn., 1948—; sec.-chmn. eastern dist. assn. Evangelical Free Ch., 1968-69, 70-71, camp sec., chmn., 1948-50, 51-52; founder, chmn. Greater Bridgeport Fellowship of Evangelicals, 1950-53; founder Christian Heritage Sch., Trumbull, 1976. Pres. Wheaton Alumni, 1946-48; trustee Kings Coll. Briarcliff Manor, N.Y., 1973—; pres. Heritage Found., Inc., Trumbull, 1967—; chaplain Trumbull Vol. Fire Dept., 1962-72; mem. com. Housing for Elderly, 1983-84. Avocations: golfing, skiing. Home: 601 White Plains Rd Trumbull CT 06611 Office: Calvary Evangelical Free Ch 498 White Plains Rd Trumbull CT 06611

ANDERSON, ROBERT ROUSE, priest, Episcopal Church; b. Ten Sleep, Wyo., May 20, 1926; s. Rouse W. and Zula (Arnold) A.; m. Ruby Elizabeth Anderson, May 21, 1955; children: Katherine Jean Bedient, Elizabeth Marie Osborn. B.A., U. Wyo., 1960. Ordained priest Episcopal Ch., 1982. Vicar, Ch. of Good Shepherd, Sundance, Wyo., 1982—, Christ Ch., Newcastle, Wyo., 1984—; mem. Ecclesiastical ct., Diocese of Wyo., 1983-84. Pres. Wyo. Dept. Classroom tchrs., 1967-68, Wyo Edn. Assn., 1969-70. Served with U.S. Army, 1944-46, PTO. Lodge: Masons. Home: 608 Main Sundance WY 82729 Office: Box 246 Sundance WY 82729

ANDERSON, VINTON R. Bishop for spl. assignment African Methodist Episcopal Church. Office: 7748 Peachtree Ln University City MO 63130*

ANDRE, PAUL REVERE, minister, Free Methodist Church North America; b. Nesbit, Nebr., Oct. 25, 1935; s. George Martin and Iva Elsie (Cassens) A.; A.A., Central Coll., McPherson, Kans., 1957; B.A., Greenville (Ill.) Coll., 1959; M. Div., Asbury Seminary, Wilmore, Ky., 1962; m. Anna Katherine Jones, June 7, 1953; children: Paul, Georgia, Iva, Katherine. Ordained to ministry, 1962; pastor Free Meth. Ch., Amelia, Nebr., 1962-64, Kearney, Nebr., 1964-66, Colville, Wash., 1966-70, Bellevue, Nebr., 1970-85, MacArthur Free Meth. Ch., Oklahoma City, 1985—; asst. supt. Nebr. Conf. Free Meth. Ch. N. Am., 1977-79, supt., 1979-83, gen. conf. del., 1979, 85. Mem. mayor's commn. on preservation of historic sites City of Bellevue, 1984—. Recipient Outstanding Citizen of Omaha award, 1976. Mem. Nebr. Assn. Evang. (v.p. 1976), Met. Assn. Evangs. Omaha (pres. 1973-76), Greater Omaha Christian Edn. Assn. (pres. 1976-77), Bellevue Ministerial Assn. (v.p. 1971-73, pres. 1973-75, 84—, sec. 1982-83). Lodge: Rotary (pres. Bellevue 1978-79, Paul Harris fellow 1981). Home: 6001 NW 62 St Oklahoma City OK 73122 Office: 6000 N MacArthur Blvd Oklahoma City OK 73122

ANDREW, JOHN GERALD BARTON, priest, Episcopal Church; b. Scarborough, Yorkshire, Eng., Jan. 10, 1931; s. Thomas Barton and Eva Maud (Friend) A.; came to U.S., 1959; B.A., Keble Coll., Oxford (Eng.) U., 1955, M.A., 1957; sem. tng. Cuddesdon Coll., 1954-56; D.D. (hon.), Cuttington Coll., Liberia, 1976, Epis. Theol. Sem., Lexington, Ky., 1976. Ordained deacon, 1956, priest, 1957; curate Redcar Parish Ch., York, Eng., 1956-59; asst. to rector St. George's-River Ch., Rumson, N.J., 1959-60; chaplain to Archbishop of Canterbury, 1960-69; Six preacher Canterbury (Eng.) Cathedral, 1966-71; vicar, rural dean, Preston, Lancashire, Eng., 1969-72; rector St. Thomas Ch., N.Y.C., 1972—. Chaplain, Most Venerable Order Hosp. St. John Jerusalem; priest asso. Order St. Margaret, London, Boston; trustee, hon. alumnus Nashotah (Wis.) Theol. Sem.; trustee House of Redeemer, N.Y.C. Contbr. articles to ch. periodicals. Office: Saint Thomas Ch 1 W 53d St New York NY 10019

ANDREWS, JAMES EDGAR, church official, minister, Presbyterian Church U.S.; b. Whittenburg, Tex., Dec. 29, 1928; s. Bryan McEvrie and Rose Ellen (Simpson) A.; B.A., Austin Coll., 1952, M.A., 1953, D.D., 1974; B.D., Austin Presbyn. Theol. Sem., 1956; m. Sarah Elizabeth Crouch, Sept. 16, 1962; children—Charis Megan, Bryan Hugh. Ordained to ministry, 1956; asst. minister St. Andrews Presbyn. Ch., Houston, 1956-58; sec. for info. World Alliance of Ref. Chs., Geneva, Switzerland, 1958-60; dir. info. Princeton (N.J.) Theol. Sem., 1960-68, asst. to pres., 1963-71; asst. to stated clk. Presbyn. Ch. U.S., 1971-73, stated clk., 1973—. Mem. Common Council of Borough of Princeton, 1968-70. Office: 341 Ponce de Leon Ave NE Atlanta GA 30308

ANDREWS, ROBERT FREDERICK, bishop, Free Meth. Ch. N.Am.; b. Sedalia, Mo., Nov. 26, 1927; s. Milton Paul and Lydia (Newberry) A.; A.A., Central Coll., 1946; B.A., Greenville Coll., 1949; B.D., Asbury Theol. Sem., 1952; m. Genevieve Arlene Hendricks, June 25, 1949; children: Robert Frederick, Mary Louise, Melva Arlene, Vondria Beth. Ordained to ministry, 1953; pastor Free Meth. Ch., Caldwell, Kans., 1952-55; No. regional dir. Free Meth. Youth, 1955-60; pres. Wessington Springs Coll., 1960-65; speaker, dir. Light and Life Hour internat. broadcast Free Meth. Ch., Winona Lake, Ind., 1965-79; exec. dir. Light and Life Men Internat., Winona Lake, 1968-71; gen. dir. Evangelistic Outreach, Winona Lake, 1971-79; bishop Free Meth. Ch. N. Am., 1979—. Mem. Nat. Religious Broadcasters (dir.), Christian Holiness Assn., Nat. Assn. Evangs. Republican. Editor-in-chief Transmitter, 1966—. Contbg. editor several denominational mags. Office: 901 College Ave Winona Lake IN 46590

ANGELL, KENNETH ANTHONY, bishop, Roman Catholic Church; b. Providence, Aug. 3, 1930; s. Henry L. and Mae T. (Cooney) A.; student Our Lady of Providence Sem., 1945-50, St. Mary's Sem., 1950-56. Ordained priest, 1956; asst. St. Mark's Ch., Jamestown, R.I., 1956, Sacred Heart Ch., Pawtucket, R.I., 1956-60; asst. pastor St. Mary's Ch., Newport, R.I., 1960-68; asst. chancellor and bishop's sec., Diocese of Providence, 1968-72, chancellor, 1972-74; consecrated bishop, 1974; Titular Bishop of Settimunicia, aux. bishop of Providence, 1974. Invested as prelate of honor to His Holiness, Pope Paul VI, 1972. Home: 57 Sutton St Providence RI 02903 Office: Chancery Office Cathedral Square Providence RI 02903

ANGLIN, JOHN FRANCIS, priest, Roman Cath. Ch.; b. Boston, Dec. 9, 1944; s. John Francis and Mary Genevieve (Brown) A.; A.B., Immaculate Conception Sem., Troy, N.Y., 1967; B.D., St. John Sem., Boston, 1970; M.A., Cath. U. Am., 1974; postgrad. Iona Coll., 1974—. Ordained priest, 1971; dir. dept. religion Christopher Columbus High Sch., Boston, 1971-73; staff St. Francis Ch., N.Y.C., 1974—, dir. adult religious edn., 1974—; team priest Worldwide Marriage Encounter, Bergen County, N.J., 1975—. Mem. Religious Edn. Assn. Am. Home and Office: 135 W 31st St New York City NY 10001

ANKROM, ROBERT LYNN, religious music manager, Assemblies of God; b. Youngstown, Ohio, Sept. 2, 1959; s. Alonzo Everett and Edity Ann (Moore) A. Sound engr. Omega Sonship Music, Austintown, Ohio, 1978-83, pub. relations dir., 1983, also dir.; exec. dir. Anchor Artist Mgmt., Austintown, 1984—; founder, dir. Youngstown chpt. Fellowship of Contemporary Christian Ministries, 1985—; head shiping and receiving Namco Industries, Inc., Youngstown, 1980—. Republican. Home and Office: 2509 Bainbridge St Austintown OH 44511

ANTHONY (ANTHONY GERGIANNAKIS). Bishop of San Francisco, Greek Orthodox Archdiocese of N. and S. Am. Office: 826 Junipero Serra Blvd San Francisco CA 94127*

ANTHONY (ANTHONY MEDVEDEV, archbishop, The Russian Orthodox Ch. Archbishop of Western Am. and San Francisco. Office: 372 Santa Clara Ave San Francisco CA 94127

ANTREASSIAN, ELISE J., religious education administrator, Armenian Orthodox Church. b. N.Y.C., Mar. 20, 1951; d. Jack Antreassian and Alice (Eksouzian) A.; m. Papken Bayizian, Nov. 25, 1983. Student, Vassar Coll., 1969-70; B.A., Hunter Coll., N.Y.C., 1974; student St. Vladimir's Sem., Crestwood, N.Y., 1977-78; M.Div., Union Theol. Sem., N.Y.C., 1979-80; postgrad. Columbia U., 1981—. Dir. religious edn. Diocese of the Armenian Ch., N.Y.C., 1981—. Author: Mesrob Mashdotz: A Fifth Century Life, 1984. Editor: (mag.) DRE Bull., 1981—. Compiler: The Life of Jesus, 1984. Translator: Men Without Childhood, 1985. Avocations: Painting, writing. Office: Diocese of the Armenian Ch 630 Second Ave New York NY 10016

APONTE MARTINEZ, LUIS CARDINAL, archbishop, Roman Catholic Church; b. Lajas, P.R., Aug. 4, 1922; s. Santiago E. Aponte and Rosa Martinez. Student San Ildefonso Sem., 1944, St. John's Sem., Boston, 1950; LL.D. (hon.), Fordham U., 1965. Ordained priest Roman Catholic Ch., 1950. Asst. in Patillas, P.R.; pastor chs., Maricao, P.R., Station Isabel, P.R., 1953-55; sec. to bishop of Ponce, P.R., 1955-57; pastor ch., Aibonito, P.R., 1957-60; aux bishop of Ponce, 1960-63, consecrated bishop, 1963, bishop of Ponce, 1963-64; archbishop of San Juan, 1964—, elevated to cardinal, 1973; chancellor Cath. U. P.R., Ponce, 1963—; pres. Puerto Rican Episc. Conf. Served as chaplain USNG, 1957-60. Lodge: Lions. Address: 50 Cristo St PO Box S-1967 San Juan PR 00903

APPELQUIST, A RAY. Exec. sec. Nat. Assn. Congregational Christian Churches. Office: Nat Assn Congregational Christian Churches PO Box 1620 Oak Creek WI 53154*

APPLETON, JON GILBERT, minister, So. Bapt. Conv.; b. Louisville, Aug. 9, 1934; s. Zack Yeargan and Kate (Chappell) A.; A.B., Samford U., 1955; M.Div. (Eli Lily scholar), So. Baptist Theol. Sem., 1959; M.A., Auburn U., 1968; D.D., Judson Coll., 1976; m. Virginia Jo Bell, Aug. 19, 1956; 1 dau., Catherine Anne. Ordained to ministry, 1953; youth dir. Deer Park Baptist Ch., Louisville, 1957-59; asso. pastor First Baptist Ch., Gadsden, Ala., 1959-61; pastor First Baptist Ch., Opelika, Ala., 1961-68; dir. dept. campus ministry Ala. Bapt. Conv., Montgomery, 1968-75; pastor First Bapt. Ch., Athens, Ga., 1976—. Trustee Am. Baptist Theol. Sem., Nashville, 1967-75, Bapt. Village, Home for Aged, Waycross, Ga.; mem. youth com. Bapt. World Alliance, 1975—. Recipient History award Colonial Dames Am., 1955. Mem. Am., So. hist. assns., Ala. Baptist Hist. Soc., Am. Assn. for Higher Edn., State Student Dirs. Assn. (pres. 1975-76), Phi Alpha Theta, Omicron Delta Kappa. Office: 355 Pulaski St Athens GA 30601

ARANDA DIAZ MUÑOZ, PEDRO, bishop Roman Catholic Church; b. Leon, Mex., Apr. 29, 1933. Ordained priest Roman Catholic Ch., 1956. Named bishop of Tulancingo, Mex., 1975. Address: Obispado Apartado 14 Tulancingo Mexico

ARAUJO, DENIS ARASARKADAVIL, priest, Roman Cath. Ch.; b. Alleppey, India, Feb. 6, 1917; s. John-Chrysostom Thomas Arasarkadavil and Christina Denis Therath; came to U.S., 1956, naturalized, 1976;

B.A. with honors, U. Madras, 1950, M.A., 1951, B.Ed., 1952; M.A., U. San Francisco, 1958; Ph.D., U. Calif., Berkeley, 1961. Ordained priest, 1944; tchr. St. Francis Assisi High Sch., Alleppey, 1950-56, head master, 1961-67; vice prin., dean dept. econs. St. Michael's Coll., Alleppey, 1967-69; supt. schs. Roman Cath. Diocese Alleppey, 1950-56, dir. social service, 1961-69, insp. schs., 1961-69; pastor St. Francis Assissi Ch., Thykal, Alleppey, 1964; assoc. pastor St. Agnes Ch., Concord, Calif., 1970-74, St. Michael's Ch., Livermore, Calif., 1974-77; pastor St. John the Bapt. Ch., El Cerrito, Calif., 1977-82, Our Lady of Mercy Ch., Point Richmond, Calif., 1982—; dean West Contra Costa County of Diocese of Oakland, Calif., 1981-84; senator Diocese of Oakland, 1981-84; consultor to bishop of Oakland, 1984— chaplain Cath. Daus. Am., Ct. De La Salle, Italian Cath. Fedn. of Contra Costa County. Founder, Fish Indsl. Coop. Soc. #2201, Shertallay, India, 1953, St. Sebastians Hosp., Arathinkal, Alleppey, 1965. Mem. Phi Delta Kappa. Author: Secondary School Leaving Examination in India, 1963. Address: 301 W Richmond Ave Point Richmond CA 94801

ARBOGAST, JAMES BERT, minister, United Meth. Ch.; b. Thornwood, W.Va., Aug. 11, 1927; s. Parker Henry and Rella Katherin (Waybright) A.; B.A., W. Va. Wesleyan U., 1957; B.D., Wesley Sem., 1962; postgrad. Salem Coll., 1963-64; m. Rheba Violet Hoffman, June 10, 1946; children—Sue Ellen, Sherry Lynn. Ordained to ministry, 1962; pastor Volga, W.Va., 1957-59, Stonewood, W. Va., 1959-62, Bethany Meth. Ch., Parkersburg, W.Va., 1962-71, St. Paul's Meth. Ch., Nitro, W. Va., 1971—. Chaplain Union Protestant Hosp., Clarksburg, W.Va., 1959-62, Fire Dept., Nitro, 1971—; mem. health welfare com., United Meth. Conf., 1962-71, sec. bd. dirs., 1963-71. Bd. dirs. housing for low income families, Nitro, 1974—. Named Minister of Yr., Charleston (W.Va.) Dist. Conf., 1976. Home: 1813 18th St Nitro WV 25143 Office: PO Box 278 20th St Nitro WV 25143

AREGOOD, ROBERT GEORGE, minister, United Church of Christ; b. Greensburg, Pa., Oct. 7, 1941; s. John Mosgrove and Alma Suzanna (Trout) Aregood; B.S., Albright Coll., 1965; B.D., Lancaster Theol. Sem., 1968; m. Barbara Marie Crnkovich, Sept. 12, 1970; children: Robert George, Katherine Elizabeth. Ordained to ministry, 1968; interim pastor Circular Congregation Ch., Charleston, S.C., 1968; pastor Zion United Ch. Christ, Reading, Pa., 1968—, 2d Reformed Ch., Reading, 1972-79; chmn. Taskforce Chs. in Transition Pa. SE Conf. United Ch. Christ, 1972, bd. dirs. conf., 1984—, chmn. audio-visual com. Reading Assn., 1984-85, mem. planning com. Reading Assn., 1984-85; bd. dirs. Council United Ch. Ministry, Reading, pres., 1975; bd. dirs. SW Christian Ministry; bd. dirs. Fellowship House of Reading, pres., 1975-77. Pres. Mayor's Policy Adv. Bd., Reading, 1975, v.p., 1976; mem. alumni council Lancaster Theol. Sem., 1972-74, sec., 1972-73. Mem. Greater Reading Council Chs., Berks County United Ch. Christ Ministerium (pres. 1974). Home: 107 A Windsor St Reading PA 19601 Office: 45 S 6th St Reading PA 19602

ARENAS, ERASTO LEGASPI, minister, United Church of Christ; b. Mindoro, Philippines, Dec. 14, 1939; came to U.S., 1976; s. Pantaleon Arenas and Julia (Legaspi) A.; m. Jesusa Naidas, May 14, 1964; children: May Laurette, Erastus Murray, Marion Grace, Michael Jason. B.A. cum laude, Luna Colls., 1960; Div.B. cum laude, Union Theol. Sem., 1964; postgrad. Taipei Lang. Inst., 1967-69. Ordained to ministry United Ch. of Christ, 1965. Pastor, United Ch. of Christ, Paranguqe, Rizal, Philippines, 1961-65; dir. Div. Chinese Mission-United Ch. of Christ, Manila, 1965-70, Div. of Mission-United Ch. of Christ, 1965-70; sec. dept. distbn.-Philippine Bible Soc., 1971-76; pastor 1st Fil-Am. United Ch. of Christ, Hawaii, 1976-79, San Bruno, Calif., 1979—, founder, adminstrv. pastor; mem. (del.) Pacific-Asian Ministries, Nationwide, United Ch. of Christ, 1979—, No. Calif. Conf., 1979—. Recipient Achievement award Ministers of New Chs. of United Ch. of Christ, 1983. Republican. Home: 2736 Wilbur Ave San Jose CA 95127 Office: 1st Filipino-Am United Ch of Christ 461 Linden Ave San Bruno CA 94066

ARENDALL, EDGAR MULLINS, retired minister, Southern Baptist Convention; b. Richmond, Va., June 26, 1920; s. Charles Baker and Kate (Peacock) A.; B.A., U. Richmond, 1941, D.D. (hon.), 1983; Th.M., So. Bapt. Theol. Sem., 1944; D.D. (hon.), Samford U., 1956; m. Sara Trimble Goode, Aug. 3, 1942; children—Douglas Tyson, Sara Lynn (Mrs. Curt Newell), David Randall. Ordained to ministry, 1944; pastor ch., Atmore, Ala., 1944-48, Dawson Meml. Bapt. Ch., Birmingham, Ala., 1948-84. Pres. Ala. Bapt. Pastor's Conf., 1949-50; chmn. social service commn. Ala. Bapt. Conv., 1949-54, mem. exec. bd. and adminstrn. com., 1955-65, pres. home mission bd., 1965-66, mem. stewardship commn., 1970—; mem. radio and TV commn. So. Bapt. Conf., 1954-61, chmn. radio and TV commn., 1959-61; trustee Birmingham Sunday Sch. Council, 1949-54, Birmingham Bapt. Hosp., 1950-65. Home: 144 Lucerne Blvd Birmingham AL 35209

ARENT, RICHARD FREDERICK, minister, United Ch. Christ; b. Benton Harbor, Mich., Jan. 22, 1930; s. Vernon Lloyd and Norene Roberta (Klett) A.; A.A., Benton Harbor Jr. Coll., 1951; B.A., Elmhurst Coll., 1953; B.D., Eden Theol., Sem., 1956, M.Div., 1971. Ordained to ministry, 1956; pastor Port Hope-Forestville (Mich.) United Chs. Christ, 1956-61, Salien-Three Oaks (Mich.) charge, 1962—. tchr. pub. schs. Port Hope, 1958-59; Chmn. commn. on town and country ch., Mich. Conf., United Ch. Christ; pres. Three Oaks Ministerial Assn., 1962-63. Home and Office: 10 W Ash St Three Oaks MI 49128

ARIAS, DAVID, bishop, Roman Catholic Church; b. Metaluengas, Leon, Spain, July 22, 1929; came to U.S., 1958; s. Atanasio and Magdalena (Perez) A. Ph.B., St. Rita's Coll., San Sebastian, Spain, 1948; M.Th., Good Counsel Theologate, Granada, Spain, 1952; postgrad. Teresianum, Rome, Italy, 1964. Ordained priest, Order Augustinian Recollect Fathers, Roman Catholic Ch., 1952; ordained aux. bishop of Newark, N.J., 1983; Tchr., St. Rita's Coll., San Sebastian, Spain, 1953; prefect St. Augustine Sem., Kansas City, Kans., 1964-66, tchr., 1964-66; assoc. pastor Lourdes Parish, Mexico City also Tex., 1958-63; dir. Cursillo Movement, N.Y.C., 1966-78; dir. Spanish Apostolate, Archidiocese of N.Y., 1978-83, vicar provincial Augustinian Recollects, W. Orange, N.J., 1981-83, aux. bishop Archdiocese of Newark, N.J., 1983—. Author: Luz Y Vida, 1979. Mem. Nat. Conf. Cath. Bishops, U.S. Cath. Conf.

ARLIN, CHARLES NOSS, priest, Episcopal Ch.; b. Cuba, N.Y., May 1, 1938; s. William Aubrey and Edith Elizabeth (Noss) A.; B.A., Hobart Coll., 1961; M.Div., Gen. Theol. Sem., 1964; postgrad. N.Y. U., 1968-69; m. Jane Carolyn McDonough, Oct. 10, 1964; children—Patricia Grace, Jennifer Brewster, Amy Elizabeth, John Charles. Ordained to ministry, 1964; missionary Ch. of St. Ambrose, Groton, N.Y., 1964-66; asst. St. John's in the Village, N.Y.C., 1966-68; tchr. Grace Ch. Sch., N.Y.C., 1968-70, asst. headmaster, 1970-72, acting headmaster, 1972-73, headmaster, 1973—; asst. St. Luke's Ch., Roselle, N.J., 1968-76; priest-in-charge, Holy Cross Ch., Perth Amboy, N.J., 1976—. Chaplain USAR, 1970. Trustee Hillsdale (N.J.) Bd. Edn., 1971—, v.p., 1975—. Mem. Nat. Assn. Episcopal Schs., N.Y. Guild Ind. Schs., N.J. Sch. Bds. Assn., Res. Officers Assn., Non-Pub. Sch. Ofcls. N.Y. Home: 94 Baylor Ave Hillsdale NJ 07642 Office: 86 4th Ave New York City NY 10003

ARMENTROUT, DONALD SMITH, educator, minister, Lutheran Ch. Am.; b. Harrisonburg, Va., Apr. 22, 1939; s. Louis Smith and Edith Irene (Moomaw) A.; B.A., Roanoke Coll., 1961; B.D., Luth. Theol. Sem., 1964; Ph.D., Vanderbilt U., 1970; m. Sue Ellen Gray, Mar. 26, 1967; children—Emily Gray, Ellen Scherer, Philip Donald. Ordained to ministry Lutheran Ch. Am., 1972; mem. examining com. Southeastern Synod, Luth. Ch. Am., 1972—; mem. Commn. on Publs., Luth. Hist. Conf., 1973-74; chmn. subcom. on continuing edn. Southeastern Synod, 1973—; tchr. ch. history Sch. Theology, Sewanee, Tenn., 1967—; bd. dirs. Vanderbilt/Sewanee Joint D. Min. Program, 1975—. Treas., Sewanee Nursery and Kindergarten, 1974-75; trustee U. of South, 1974—; asst. treas. Sewanee PTA, 1976-77; mem. Sewanee Vol. Fire Dept., 1977—. Mem. Am. Ch. History Soc., Luth. Hist. Conf., Concordia Hist. Inst., Luth. Peace Fellowship, Episcopal Peace Fellowship, AAUP, ACLU, Common Cause. Democrat. Home: Alabama Ave Sewanee TN 37375 Office: Sch Theology Sewanee TN 37375

ARMSTRONG, ARTHUR JAMES, former bishop; b. Marion, Ind., Sept. 17, 1924; s. Arthur J. and Frances (Green) A.; m. Phyllis Jeanne Shaeffer, Feb. 26, 1942; children: James, Teresa, John, Rebecca (Mrs. Ed Putens), Leslye (Mrs. David Hope). A.B. Fla. So. Coll., 1948; B.D., Candler Sch. Theology, Emory U., 1952; D.D., Fla. So. U., 1960, DePauw U., 1965; L.H.D., Ill. Wesleyan U., 1970, Dakota Wesleyan U., 1970, Westmar Coll., 1971, Ind. Central U., 1982, Emory U. Ordained to ministry Meth. Ch., 1948; minister in Fla., 1945-58; sr. minister Broadway Meth. Ch., Indpls., 1958-68; bishop United Meth. Ch., Dakotas area, 1968-80, Ind. area, Indpls., from 1980; vis. prof. Iliff Sch. Theology, Denver, 1985-86; instr. Christian Theol. Sem., Indpls., 1961-68; del. 4th Gen. Assembly World Council Chs., 1968, 6th Gen. Assembly World Council Chs., 1983, Nat. Council Chs., 1970, pres., 1982-84; pres. bd. ch. and society United Meth. Ch., 1972-76, chmn. com. for peace and self-devel. of peoples, 1972-76, pres. commn. on religion and race, 1976—. Author: The Journey That Men Make, 1969, The Urgent Now, 1970, Mission: Middle America, 1971, The Pastor and the Public Servant, 1972, United Methodist Primer, 1973, 77, Wilderness Voices, 1974, The Nation Yet To Be, 1975, Telling Truth: The Foolishness of Preaching in a Real World, 1977, The Miracle of Easter, 1980, From the Underside, 1981, Preaching on Peace, 1982; contbg. author: The Pulpit Speaks on Race, 1966, War Crimes and the American Conscience, 1970, Rethinking Evangelism, 1971, What's a Nice Church Like You Doing in a Place Like This?, 1972. Vice-chmn. Hoosiers for Peace, 1968; mem. Ind. State Platform Com. Democratic Party, 1968, Nat. Coalition for a Responsible Congress, 1970; trustee, exec. com. Christian Century Found.; trustee Ewha U., Seoul, Korea, DePauw U., U. Evansville, Ind. Central U., United Theol. Sem., Dayton, Ohio. Served with USNR, 1942. Recipient distinguished service award Indpls. Jr. C. of C., 1959. Office: care Iliff Sch Theology 2201 S University Blvd Denver CO 80210

ARMSTRONG, GREGORY TIMON, educator, minister Presbyterian Church U.S.A.; b. Evanston, Ill., Dec. 23, 1933; s. John Robert and Clara Joanna (Carlson) A.; m. Edna Louise Stagg, May 11, 1957; children: Edna Louisa Armstrong Montague, Elizabeth Stagg. B.A., Wesleyan U., Middletown, Conn., 1955; B.D., McCormick Theol. Sem., Chgo., 1958; D.Theol., U. Heidelberg, 1961. Ordained to ministry Presbyterian Ch., U.S.A., 1961. Instr. ch. history McCormick Theol. Sem., Chgo., 1961-62; asst. prof. ch. history Vanderbilt U. Div. Sch., Nashville, 1962-68; assoc. prof. religion Sweet Briar Coll., Va., 1968-75, prof., 1975-81, Charles A. Dana prof., 1981—; vis. prof. hist. studies Union Theol. Sem., Richmond, Va., 1983; moderator Presbytery of So. Va., 1980. Author: Die Genesis in der Alten Kirche, 1962; contbr. articles to profl. jours. Mem. Nashville United Givers Fund, 1966-68; pres. Amherst PTA, Va., 1971-72; v.p. Amherst County Council of PTAs, 1972-73; mem. Wesleyan U. Alumni Fund, 1971-74. Fellow Rotary Internat., 1958-59, Rockefeller Found., 1959-61, Am. Council of Learned Societies Study, 1965-66, NEH, 1971, Fulbright-Hays Sr. Research, 1974-75, Am. Philos. Soc., 1981; Sweet Briar faculty fellow, 1981-82. Mem. Am. Hist. Assn., Am. Soc. Ch. History, Am. Cath. Hist. Assn., AAUP (chpt. pres. 1976-77, exec. com. Va. Conf. 1984-86), Am. Acad. Religion, Archaeol. Inst. Am., Phi Beta Kappa (chpt. pres. 1976-78). Democrat. Office: Dept Religion Sweet Briar Coll PO Box AY Sweet Briar VA 24595

ARMSTRONG, HART REID, editor, publisher; b. St. Louis, May 11, 1912; s. Hart Champlin and Zora Lillian (Reid) A.; m. Iona Rhoda Mehl, Feb. 21, 1932; 1 child, Hart Reed. A.B., Christian Temple U., 1938; Litt.D., Geneva Theol. Coll., 1967; Th.M., Evang. Bible Sem., 1968; Th.D., 1970; D.D. (hon.), Central Sch. Religion of Surrey, Eng., 1972; Ph.D. (hon.), Berean Ch. Coll., 1980. Ordained to ministry Assemblies of God, 1932. Dean Bible Standard Coll., Eugene, Oreg., 1935-40; editor Gospel Pub. House, Springfield, Mo., 1946-53; crusade adminstr. editor Oral Roberts Assn., Tulsa, 1955-62; pres.-editor Defenders of Christian Faith, Wichita, Kans., 1967-81, Christian Communications, Wichita, 1981—; curriculum com. Nat. Sunday Sch. Assn., Chgo., 1948-54. Author: To Those Who Are Left, 1950; How Do I Pray?, 1968; The Story of Lebanon, 1983; Comment on Gospel of John, 1985. Mem. Evang. Press Soc. (pres. 1951-52), Pope County Hist.

ARMSTRONG, HERBERT W., minister, Worldwide Church of God; b. Des Moines, July 31, 1892; married; 4 children including Richard David (dec.), Garner Ted. Ordained to ministry, 1931. Founder Worldwide Ch. of God, 1933, now pastor gen. and chmn. Founder, chancellor Ambassador Coll.; founder, chmn. Ambassador Found. Author: The Missing Dimension in Sex, 1964; The Autobiography of Herbert W. Armstrong, 1967; The United States and Britain in Prophecy, 1967; The Incredible Human Potential, 1978; The Wonderful World Tomorrow, 1979; Mystery of the Ages, 1984. Editor-in-chief, founder The Plain Truth, 1934—; The Good News, 1951—; Youth '85, 1981—. Broadcaster "The World Tomorrow" TV and radio program, 1934—. Address: Worldwide Ch of God PO Box 111 Pasadena CA 91123

ARMSTRONG, RICHARD STOLL, minister, Presbyterian Church USA; b. Balt., Mar. 29, 1924; s. Herbert Eustace and Elsie Davis (Stoll) A.; m. Margaret Childs, Jan. 31, 1948; children: Ellen, Richard, Andrew, William, Elsie. B.A., Princeton U., 1947; M.Div., Princeton Theol. Sem., 1958; D.Min., Christian Theol. Sem.-Indpls., 1978; postgrad. Temple U., 1962-68. Ordained to ministry, 1958. Pastor, Oak Lane Presbyn. Ch., Phila., 1958-68; dir. devel. Princeton Theol. Sem., 1968-71, v.p. for devel., 1971-74; pastor 2nd Presbyn. Ch., Indpls., 1974-80; prof. ministry and evangelism Princeton Theol. Sem., 1980—; life trustee Fellowship of Christian Athletes, Inc., Kansas City, Mo., 1979—; trustee Princeton Theol. Sem., 1979-80; ch. ministers adv. bd. Christian Theol. Sem., 1975-80; bd. dirs. Nat. Conf. Christians and Jews, Indpls., 1975-80, Indiana Inter-Religious Commn. on Human Equality, 1975-80. Author: The Oak Lane Story, 1971; Service Evangelism, 1979; The Pastor as Evangelist, 1984. Contbg. author Westminster Dictionary of Christian Theology, 1983. Bd. dirs. Indpls. Symphony Orch., 1978-80; trustee Am. Boychoir Sch., 1980—, McDonogh Sch., Md., 1980—; mem. adv. bd. Surveyors Ministry, 1972—; mem. alumni council Princeton U., 1964-71. Served to lt. (j.g.), USN, 1942-46. Recipient

Disting. Service award Fellowship of Christian Athletes, 1965, Branch Rickey Meml. award, 1974; Outstanding Service award Nat. Conf. Christians and Jews, 1980; Alumni Service award Princeton Theol. Sem., 1974; Man of the Week, Princeton Town Topics, 1957, 68. Mem. Presbytery of New Brunswick, Acad. for Evangelism. Home: 3620 Lawrenceville Rd Princeton NJ 08540 Office: Princeton Theol Sem CN821 Princeton NJ 08542

ARNETT, LOREN E., clergyman. Exec. minister Wash. Assn. Chs. Office: Wash Assn Chs 4759 15th Ave NE Seattle WA 98105*

ARNOLD, HUGH DELLIS, minister; b. Hoboken, Ga., Aug. 4, 1940; s. Hugh Dorsey and Edna Lucile (Carter) A.; diploma in pastoral tng. Bapt. Bible Inst., 1968; B.A., William Carey Coll. 1970; M.R.E., New Orleans Bapt. Theol. Sem., 1972; m. Bonnie Fay Berryhill, June 14, 1964; children: Della Veronica, Angel Bona. Ordained to ministry; pastor Bapt. Ch., Lyons, Ga., 1961-62; assoc. pastor, minister of music and edn. Limestone Bapt. Ch., Cochran, Ga., 1962-65; pastor First Bapt. Ch., Southport, Fla., 1965-68, Sandhill (Miss.) Bapt. Ch., 1968-72, First Bapt. Ch., Nahunta, Ga., 1972—; pastor, founder Ivory Pl. Ch. and Internat. Ministries, Nahunta; tchr. Bible study Ivory Pl. Ch. World Mission Tng. Ctr.; preacher Brantley County High Sch., 1972—; active evangelistic youth work, 1967-68; active worker youth camps, retreats; leader various Bible study groups; chaplain Pulaski Prison br., Hawkinsville, Ga., 1964-65. Author prose and poetry including Your Need No Greater than a Mustard Seed; also composer songs. County wide chmn., Community Action Com., Office Econ. Opportunity, Brantley County, Ga., 1973-76; chmn. Brantley County Heart Fund, 1976; mem. governing bd. Slash Pine Community Action Agy., S.E. Ga., 1974-76. Mem. Nashville Gospel Music Assn., Okefenokee-Piedmont Bapt. Assn. Address: PO Box 587 Nahunta GA 31553

ARNOLD, WILLIAM MEREDITH, III, minister, Southern Baptist Convention; b. Memphis Mar. 7, 1947; s. William and Eunice Leigh A.; B.S., Miss. Coll., 1969; M.R.E., Southwestern Theol. Sem., 1971; postgrad. Am. Mgmt. Assn., 1984; m. Margaret Grantham Hale, May 17, 1969; children: Meredith Leigh, Jonathan William. Ordained to ministry, 1968; minister of youth Willow Meadows Bapt. Ch., Houston, 1971-73; dir. lay ministries div. Dallas Bapt. Assn., 1973-79; cons. Sunday Sch. div. Bapt. Gen. Conv. of Tex., 1979-84, centennial offering coordinator, 1984—. Vice pres. Tex. Bapt. Men, 1972-76, dir.-at-large, 1976—; mem. Tex. Bapt. Disaster Relief Team, 1973—; mem. Dallas Ind. Sch. Dist. Religious Task Force, 1976—; v.p. Aviation Ministries, 1970-72. Pres. Tex. Voluntary Orgns. Active in Disaster, 1983-84. Recipient Legion of Honor award Tex. Royal Ambassadors, 1976; cert. of recognition So. Bapt. Fgn. Mission Bd., 1976; Key Service award Tex. Bapt. Men, 1972, Key Young Man award, 1975; diploma of gratitude Govt. Honduras, 1975. Mem. Southwestern Religious Edn. Assn., Fellowship Christian Athletes, Tex. Bapt. Wireless Assn. (trustee 1975—). Contbr. articles to religious jours. Home: 11021 Ridgemeadow St Dallas TX 75218 Office: 511 N Akard St Dallas TX 75201

ARONCHICK, SAMUEL JAMES, church official; Jewish Traditional Orthodox Congregations; b. Lechowitz, Russia, Feb. 11, 1903; s. Abraham and Bessie (Kroshin) A.; came to U.S., 1906, naturalized, 1919; grad. Pace Inst. Accounting, 1925; m. Betty Sherman, Apr. 17, 1921 (dec. Aug. 1947); m. Ida Cooper, Sept. 18, 1949 (dec. Dec. 7, 1979); 1 son, Edward (dec.); m. Helen Brown, Feb. 3, 1985. Pres. Temple Knesseth Israel of Hollywood, Los Angeles, 1963-84, now hon. life pres., treas., 1961, v.p., 1962; rep. mem. Jewish Fedn. Council, 1965-84. Mem. B'nai B'rith, Telephone Pioneers. Home: 11936 Weddington #8 Hollywood CA 91607 Office: 1260 N Vermont Ave Los Angeles CA 90029

ARONSON, DAVID See Who's Who in America, 43rd edition.

ARPINO, BIAGIO MICHAEL, principal, Roman Catholic Church; b. Jamaica, N.Y., Oct. 28, 1951; s. Alphonse D. and Mildred (Strocchia) A.; m. Leona R. Ancona, Oct. 23, 1982; 1 dau., Alyse Nicole. A.A., St. John's U., 1971, B.S., 1973; M.S., C.W. Post Coll., 1975, Profl. Diploma, 1980. Tchr., St. Mary Sch., East Islip, N.Y., 1973-79, vice prin., 1979-80, prin., 1980—; religious edn. coordinator Our Lady of Perpetual Help, Lindenhurst, N.Y., 1976—; mem. Diocesan Prins. Council, Rockville Centre, N.Y., 1982-84; lectr. dept. child study St. Joseph's Coll., Patchogue, N.Y., 1985—. Editor: School Handbook and Calendar, 1983, 84. Democrat. Office: Saint Mary Sch 16 Harrison Ave East Islip NY 11730

ARRINGTON, JUANITA ROBY, elder, Apostolic Overcoming Holy Church of God; b. Birmingham, Ala.,

Dec. 15, 1936; d. Jasper and Malinda (Sanders) Roby; B.S., Ala. State Coll., 1957; M.S. in Edn., Samford U., 1972, postgrad. m. Joe Arrington, Aug. 21, 1955; children: Joe Ronaldo, Jovita Richelle, Jasper Randale. Ordained elder Apostolic Overcoming Holy Church of God. Ch. clk. Apostolic Overcoming Holy Ch. of God, Birmingham, 1968-83, nat. sec., 1972—; regional sec. North Ala. Ministerial Council, 1965-79, editor People's Mouthpiece, 1974—; pres. Apostolic Overcoming Holy Ch. Theol. Sem., 1982—. High Sch. tchr., 1961-71; counselor, Banks High Sch., Birmingham, 1972-79, Phillips High Sch., Birmingham, 1980-81. Mem. Ala. Soc. Crippled Children and Adults. Mem. Ala. Assn. Counseling and Devel. (dist. IV), Assn. Religious and Value Issues in Counseling, Kappa Delta Pi. Home: 909 Jasper Rd W Birmingham AL 35204 Office: 1120 N 24th St Birmingham AL 35234

ARZUBE, JUAN ALFREDO See Who's Who in America, 43rd edition.

ASHE, BOOKER TALIAFERRO, monk, Roman Catholic Church; b. Columbia S.C., Jan. 30, 1932; s. Booker T. and Evelyn C. (Livingston) A.L.L.D. (hon.), Marquette U.; H.H.D. (hon.), Marian Coll. Joined Capuchin Order, 1951. Dir. House of Peace Community Ctr., Milw., 1967—. Bd. dirs. Nat. Office of Black Caths., 1970—, Nat. Black Clergy Assn., 1968—, Cath. Social Services, 1969—. Home and Office: 1702 W Walnut St Milwaukee WI 53205

ASHJIAN, MESROB See Who's Who in America, 43rd edition.

ASHLEY, GEORGE NORMAN, minister, Southern Baptist Convention; b. Edenton, N.C., May 7, 1903; s. George Valentine and Clara Virginia (Satterfield) A.; B.A., Wake Forest U., 1928; M.A., Duke, 1931, B.D., 1932; postgrad. Am. Sch. Oriental Research, Jerusalem, 1934; m. Alice Freeman Jones, Dec. 12, 1931; children: Sara Roberts, Norma Satterfield, George Norman. Ordained to ministry, 1926; pastor Rawls Bapt. Ch. and Collins Grove Bapt. Ch., 1926-33, Salemburg (N.C.) Bapt. Ch., 1935-58, Roseboro (N.C.) Bapt. Ch., 1935-75, Elizabeth Bapt. Ch., Roseboro, 1936-73, Long Br. Bapt. Ch., Autryville, N.C., 1944—; dean Bible dept. Pineland Coll., Salemburg, 1934-39, v.p., trustee, 1934-42, pres., 1945-49; lectr. So. Bapt. Assembly, Ridgecrest, N.C., 1935-36; prof. N.T., Southeastern Theol. Sem. Extension, Fayetteville, N.C., 1941-46. Trustee, Sampson Tech. Inst., 1964-68. Recipient Conservation award Woodmen of World, 1973; named Conservation Farmer of Year, Sampson Conservation Dist., 1972. Mem. N.C. Forestry Assn. (treas. 1970-72), Sampson County Assn. for Retarded Children. Home: PO Box 267 Salemburg NC 28385 Office: Route 1 Autryville NC 28318

ASHLEY, THOMAS HAZEL, minister, Ch. of God Cleveland, Tenn.; b. Rock Hill, S.C., May 11, 1928; s. Thomas Clay and Dessie Mae (Benton) A.; diploma Lee Coll., 1951; m. Dorothy Rosella Weaver, Nov. 16, 1946; children—Thomas Hazel, Rebecca Doris, Byron Eugene. Ordained minister, 1958; pastor, S.C., 1952-70, Saluda St. Ch., Chester, 1960-67, West Ashley Ch., Charleston, 1967-70, also dist. overseer, 1967-70; state supt. Churches of God N.Mex., Albuquerque, 1970-74; pastor Park Pl. Ch. of God, Greenville, S.C., 1975-76; pastor Crichton Ch. of God, Mobile, Ala., 1976—, also dist. overseer Crichton dist. also dist. overseer North Greenville dist. Mem. S.C. Youth Bd., 1960-66. Bd. dirs. Home for Children Ch. of God S.C. Mauldin, S.C., 1966-70, West Coast Bible Coll. Fresno, Calif., 1970-74. Address: 18 Berkley Ave Greenville SC 29609

ASHLOCK, JAMES ALLEN, minister, Church of Christ; b. Flint, Mich., Aug. 10, 1955; s. James Andrew and Lowanda June (Proctor) A.; m. Mary Beth Wood, Aug. 20, 1977; children: Sarah Elizabeth, Jason Allen. B.S., Freed-Hardeman Coll., Henderson, Tenn., 1977; postgrad. Harding Coll., 1978-79, Tenn. Bible Coll., 1979-80; M.A., Ala. Sch. Religion, 1987. Ordained to ministry Ch. of Christ, 1977. Minister, Ch. of Christ, Toone, Tenn., 1977, Bay, Ark., 1977—; promoter Crowley's Ridge Acad. of Christian Edn., Jonesboro, Ark., 1983-84, bd. dirs., 1983—. Author: (booklet) Christian Evidences, 1978. Contbr. articles to religious jours. Recipient Outstanding Service award Freed-Hardeman Coll., 1977, Appreciation award Soc. Disting. High Sch. Students, 1984-85. Mem. Freed-Hardeman Coll. Alumni Assn. Republican. Lodges: Optimist (bd. dirs. 1983-84), Toastmasters. Avocations: stamp collecting, fishing, reading, gardening. Home: PO Box 159 222 Central St Bay AR 72411

ASHMAN, JOYCE ELAINE, lay church worker, National Fellowship Brethren Churches; bookkeeper; b. Peru, Ind., June 17, 1939; d. Robert Allen and Bernice (Miller) Ashman; student Internat. Bus. Sch., Ft. Wayne, Ind., 1957-58. Mem. ch. choir Nat. Fellowship

Brethren Chs., 1959—, mem. Sunday sch. secretarial staff, 1965—, nat. pres. Sisterhood of Mary and Martha, 1960-64, fin. sec.-treas., 1964-68, fin. sec.-treas. Women's Missionary Council, 1971—; name tag, prayer favor chmn. Christian Bus. and Profl. Women, 1968-69, 76-77, treas., 1970-71, 80-81, telephone chmn., 1972-73, 78-79, decorations chmn., 1974-75, ticket chmn., 1982, music chmn., 1983, contact adviser, 1984. Bookkeeper, Grace Schs., Winona Lake, Ind., 1961—. Home: 602 Chestnut Ave Winona Lake IN 46590 Office: 200 Seminary Dr Winona Lake IN 46590

ASHTON, MARVIN J., church official. Mem. Quorum of the Twelve, The Church of Jesus Christ of Latter-day Saints. Office: The Church of Jesus Christ of Latter-Day Saints 50 E North Temple St Salt Lake City UT 84150*

ASKEW, WILLIAM FRANCIS, minister, Baptist Bible Fellowship; b. Elberta, Mich., Jan. 20, 1922; s. Francis Ivan and Violet May (Ives) A.; A.S., Jones Coll., Jacksonville, Fla., 1967; m. Doris Irene Dillman, June 15, 1946; children: Charles, Judith, Margaret, David, Carol, Stephen, Martha, Alice, William. Ordained to ministry, 1953; pastor Arlington Heights Bapt. Ch., Jacksonville, Fla., 1953-68, Noble Hill Bapt. Ch., Springfield, Mo., 1969—; mgr. Sta. KWFC, Springfield, 1968—; prof. speech Bapt. Bible Coll., Springfield, 1969—. Pres. North Springfield Betterment Assn., 1975-76; bd. dirs. Mo. Moral Majority, Midwest Soc. for Protection of Environment. Home: 3516 E Fruitwood Ln Springfield MO 65804 Office: PO Box 5027 Springfield MO 65801

ASSAD, DAVUD AHMAD, religious organization executive, Muslims; b. Jerusalem, Dec. 23, 1931; s. Ahmad A. Radwan and Nazha (Ismael) Atiyyah; m. Amena Radwan, July 4, 1953; children: Fareed, Rashid, Maryam. B.S. in Mech. Engring., Northeastern U., 1959; M.S., Polytech, Inst. Bklyn., 1975. Pres. Islamic Service Organ., Old Bridge, N.J., 1968—; funding mem. Supreme Council of Mosques, Makkah, Saudi Arabia, 1975—; sec. Gen. Council of Masajid, U.S.A., Inc., N.J., 1978—; chmn. bd. dirs. Islamic Soc. Central Jersey, South Brunswick, 1978—; assoc. dir. Muslin World League, N.Y.C., 1976—; pres. Fed. Islamic Assn. U.S.A. and Can., N.Y.C., 1976-78. Traveling lectr. on Islam. Mem. World Congress of Mosques (founding mem.), ASME.

ATEN, WILBUR ROY, minister, Christian Churches (Churches of Christ); b. Iola, Kans., Dec. 1, 1931; s. William Roy and Rebecca May (Rhodes) A.; A.B., Midwest Christian Coll., 1954; student Phillips U., 1954-55; m. Lois Earle Hamilton, Apr. 8, 1955; children—Mark, Scott, Lane, Todd. Ordained to ministry, 1954; pastor 1st Christian Ch., Peabody, Kans., 1955-57, Pierre (S.D.) Ch. of Christ (Christian), 1957-63, Univ. Heights Ch., Borger, Tex., 1963-67, Central Christian Ch., Brownsville, Tex., 1967-77; exec. chaplain Internat. Seamen's Ctr., Brownsville, Tex., 1977—. Sec., Nat. Key 73 Com., Christian Chs.-Chs. of Christ, 1970-73; mem. Nat. Bicentennial Com. for Christian Chs.-Chs. of Christ, 1975—; pres. Brownsville Ministerial Assn., 1972-73, 76-77; sec. Nat. Ch. Growth Research Center, Washington, 1973—; participant Internat. Congress on World Evangelization, Lausanne, Switzerland, 1974. Co-founder, pres. Port of Brownsville Internat. Seamen's Center, 1974—; mem. Brownsville Bicentennial Commn., 1975—; mem. Nat. Evangelization Forum. Author: The Great Commission Festival, 1975. Contbr. articles to The Christian Standard, The Lookout and Devotion. Address: PO Box 4033 Brownsville TX 78523

ATHANASSOULAS, SOTIRIOS, bishop, Greek Orthodox Archdiocese of North and South America; b. Lepiana, Epirus, Greece, Feb. 19, 1936; came to Can., 1962; s. George and Anastasia A. Athanassoulas. B.D., U. Athens, 1961; M.A., U. Montreal, 1971. Ordained priest Greek Orthodox Archdiocese of North and South Am., 1962. Parish priest St. George Ch., Edmonton, Alta., Can., 1962-65; dean St. George Cathedral, Montreal, Que., Can., 1965-73; bishop Greek Orthodox Diocese, Toronto, Ont., Can., 1973—; head Greek Orthodox Ch. of Can., 1973—; mem. exec. com. Can. Council of Chs., Toronto, 1974—; mem. Archdiocesan Council Greek Orthodox, 1968—; mem. del. to China, Can. Council of Chs., Toronto, 1981; v.p. Christian Pavillion, Expo 67, Montreal, 1967. Mem. governing council U. Toronto, 1975-78; hon. pres. Thalassemia Fund, 1975. Home and Office: Greek Orthodox Diocese of Toronto 27 Teddington Park Ave Toronto ON M4N 2C4 Canada

ATHIMOS (ANTHIMOS DRAKONAKIS). Bishop of Denver, Greek Orthodox Archidiocese of N. and S. Am. Office: 10225 E Gill Pl Denver CO 80231*

ATKINSON, FREDERICK OREN, minister, United Methodist Church; b. Mankato, Minn., May 31, 1942; s. Archie Lawrence and Olga Ann (Haenze) A.; B.A. cum laude, Mankato State U., 1964; M.Div. with highest honors, Garrett-Evang. Sem., 1969; M.A., U. Iowa, 1969; postgrad. Oxford (Eng.) U., U. St. Andrews (Scotland); m. Vonda Rae Quesenberry, Aug. 14, 1964; children: Christopher John, Lisa Beth. Ordained to ministry, 1970; college chaplain Bemidji (Minn.) State U., 1969-71; pastor Blaine-Bethlehem Ch., Mpls., 1971-74; assoc. pastor Homstead Ch., Rochester, Minn., 1974-76; pastor Preston-Lanesboro Ch., Preston, Minn., 1976-83, Ortonville Ch., Minn., 1983—. Mem. commn. on worship, Minn. Conf., United Meth. Ch., 1974-80, Conf. Bd. of Diaconal Ministry, 1973-78, commn. on sessions, 1975-80. Nat. Humanities fellow in history U. Iowa, 1964-66 Mem. Acad. Parish Clergy. Office: 803 Roy St Orthonville MN 56278

ATKINSON, JOE MORRIS, evangelist, Southern Baptist Convention; b. Bryan, Tex., Aug. 4, 1943; s. Joseph Morris and Elizabeth (Pittman) A.; B.A., Baylor U., 1967; M.R.E., Southwestern Bapt. Theol. Sem., 1970; m. Judith Covey, June 21, 1963; children: Jason Drew, Jennifer Paige. Ordained to ministry, 1965; gospel singer, rec. artist Imperial Sound label, Arlington, Tex., 1961—; pres. Imperial Enterprises Unltd., Inc., Arlington, 1975—. Mem. Nat. Assn. Religious Broadcasters, Fellowship Christian Athletes, So. Bapt. Conf. Evangelists, Am. Radio Relay League, Nat. Assn. Broadcasters, Gospel Music Assn., Dan Vestal Evang. Assn. Home: 1821 Lakeside Dr Arlington TX 76013 Office: PO Box 13535 Arlington TX 76013

ATTER, GORDON FRANCIS, minister, Pentecostal Assemblies of Canada; b. Abingdon, Ont., Can., Nov. 13, 1905; s. Arthur Manley and Jessie Mernelva (Snyder) A.; student Canadian Pentecostal Bible Coll., Winnipeg, 1928; D. Sacred Lit., Trinity So. Bible Coll. and Sem., 1963; m. Margaret Hope McKinney, Apr. 2, 1940; 1 son, Arthur James. Ordained to ministry, 1929; pastor chs. in Ont., 1925-26, 1933-56, Sask., 1928-29, Alta., 1930-32; asst. dist. supt. Western Ont. conf. Pentecostal Assemblies of Can. 1942-54, mem. gen. exec., 1946-54; prof. Eastern Pentecostal Bible Coll., Peterborough, Ont., 1956-72. Mem. Canadian Wild Life Fedn., Nat. Geog. Soc. Author: Messages for the Last Days, 1954; Rivers of Blessing, 1960; The Students' Handbook on Divine Healing, 1960; The Third Force, 1962; Friendship, Courtship and Marriage, 1961; God's Financial Plan, 1962; Cults and Heresies, 1963; Rethinking Bible Prophecy, 1967; Interpreting the Scriptures, 1964; Down Memory's Lane, 1974. Editor Full Gospel Advocate, 1943-54, Glad Tidings Messenger, 1955-57. Home: 6042 Murray St Suite 210 Niagara Falls ON L2G 2K3 Canada Office: 10 Overlea Blvd Toronto ON M4H 1A5 Canada

ATTISON, KATHLEEN THERESA, special education administrator, Roman Catholic; learning consultant; b. Manhattan, N.Y., July 9, 1949; d. William and Sophie (Lucas) A. B.A., Coll. St. Elizabeth, 1972; Ed.M., William Paterson Coll., 1979, Learning Disabilities Tchr. Cons., 1981. Nurse's aide several hosps. in Wis., 1967-68; domestic supr. high sch. girls Madonna High Sch., Milw., 1968; Kindergarten tchr. St. Mary's Elem. Sch., Denville, N.J., 1972-76, elem. music tchr., Confrat. Christian Doctrine, 1972-76; asst. supr. candystripers St. Clare's Hosp., Denville, 1974; English tutor to Vietnamese refugees Our Lady Sorrows Convent, Denville, 1976-77; mental health aide Dover Social Club MHA, Dover, Morristown, N.J., 1973-76; music, art tchr. Family Corner, Paterson, N.J., 1972-74, Mt. St. Joseph Psychiat. Ctr. for Children, Totowa, N.J., 1975-76; co-founder, co-house supr. Sisters of the Sorrowful Mothers, Transitional Residence Emotionally Handicapped Women, Boonton, N.J., 1976-78; head tchr. spl. edn. Mt. St. Joseph Psychiat. Ctr., 1976-85; Confrat. Christian Doctrine tchr., cons., artist St. Alphonse Ch., Sweetwater, Tex., 1982; sec. to provincial chpt. Missionary Sisters of Immaculate Conception of Mother of God, West Paterson, N.J., 1982; pres. Sisters Council Paterson Diocese, 1975-76. Cons. learning disabilities Hillside Bd. Edn., N.J., 1985—. Artist and illustrator, Bd. dirs. Mental Health Assn. Passaic County, Clifton, N.J., 1983—. Mem. Council for Exceptional Children, Nat. Mental Health Assn., N.J. Assn. Learning Cons., Pi Lambda Theta. Democrat. Avocations: art and music appreciation; archeology; geology; drawing; illustration.

AU, LAWRENCE, minister, Southern Baptist Convention; b. Nanking, China, Jan. 14, 1938; s. Ka-Ying and Wai-Chun (Lee) A.; student Hong Kong Christian and Missionary Alliance Bible Sem., 1958, Hong Kong Bapt. Coll., 1960; B.Th., Hong Kong Bapt. Theol. Sem., 1963; M.R.E., Golden Gate Bapt. Theol. Sem., 1969, M.Div., 1972, D.Min., 1975; D.D., Conroe Coll., 1974; postgrad. Coll. Jewish Studies, 1971, Logos West Family Therapist Tng. Center, 1976, Oxford U., 1978, San Francisco Police Acad., 1982; B.S., U. San Francisco, 1979; m. Panie Chitavet, Dec. 8, 1963; 1 son, Lorenzo. Came to U.S., 1967, naturalized, 1973. Ordained minister, 1967; asst. minister Hong Kong English Bapt. Ch., 1961-62; minister Macao Bapt. Ch., 1963-65; dir. religious edn. Macao Bapt. High Sch., 1963-65; minister Ipoh (Malaysia) Bapt. Ch., 1965-67, 1st Chinese So. Bapt. Ch., San Francisco, 1967—; instr. Bay Area Theol. Sch. Conroe Coll., Tex., 1968—; chaplain San Francisco Police Dept., 1983—; pres. Christian Witness Theol. Sem., Berkeley, Calif., 1984—. Instr. Berlitz Sch. Langs., San Francisco, 1968—. Mem. nat. adv. bd. Am. Security Council, 1973—. Mem. San Francisco Peninsula So. Bapt. Assn., San Francisco Council Chs. (v.p.), San Francisco Zool. Soc., Calif. Acad. Scis., Nat. Trust for Hist. Preservation, Smithsonian Instn. Home: 639 38th Ave San Francisco CA 94121 Office: 1525 Solano Ave Berkeley CA 94707

AUDET, LIONEL See *Who's Who in America,* 43rd edition.

AUDET, MAURICE, priest, Roman Catholic Church. b. Montreal, Que., Can., Nov. 26, 1930; s. Louis-Napoleon and Marie-Louise (Blais) A. B.A., College Brebeuf, Montreal, 1951; M.A. in Pastoral Theology, U. Montreal, 1966; cert. in teaching Ministere de l'Education du Que., 1970. Ordained priest Roman Catholic Ch., 1955. Curate St. Michael Parish, Rouyn, Que., 1955-57; asst. procurer Timmins Diocese, Haileybury, Ont., 1957-59; chaplain Assumption Acad., Kirkland Lake, Ont., 1959-64; curate Assumption Parish, Kirkland Lake, 1960-64; asst. dir. Centre de Catechese, Montreal, 1966-67; pastoral coordinator Commn. des Ecoles catholiques de Montreal, 1968-71; dir. Office Christian Edn., Montreal, 1971—; chmn. Institut Catholique de Montreal, 1978; adminstr. Coll. Stanislas, Montreal, 1979, Coll. Ville-Marie, Montreal, 1981; counselor Assn. des Commns. Scolaires de la region de Montreal, 1971. Author: Jalons vers Dieu, 1959; Bazar a Bagamak, 1983. Coordinator Table des mouvements laics interesses a l'education chretienne, Montreal, 1980—. Mem. Assn. des directeurs diocesains d'education chretienne du Que. Club: Chevaliers de Colomb-Conseil Lafontaine, Montreal. Office: Diocesan Edn Office 2000 Sherbrooke St W Montreal PQ H3H 1G4 Canada

AUDET, RENE, bishop, Roman Catholic Church; b. Montreal, Que., Can., Jan. 18, 1920. Ordained priest, 1948; titular bishop of Chonochora and aux. bishop of Ottawa (Ont., Can.), 1963-68; bishop of Joliette (Que.), 1968—. Address: 2 Rue Saint Charles Borromee Nord CP 470 Cité de Joliette PQ J6E 6H6 Canada*

AUERBACH, SELIG SIEGMUND, rabbi, Jewish Congregations; b. Hamburg, Germany, Oct. 20, 1906; came to U.S., 1941; s. Joseph and Rosa (Cahn) A.; m. Hilda Fromm, Dec. 9, 1934; children: Hannah Helene Auerbach Isaaco, Ruth Wilma Auerbach Lebowitz, Nancy Joy Auerbach Rosenblum. B.A., City of London Coll., 1939; Ph.D., Maximilian U., Bavaria, 1934; rabbi, Hildesheimer Rabbinical Sem., 1933; D.D. (hon.), Jewish Theol. Sem., 1981; Golden Doctorate Maximilian U., 1982. Ordained rabbi, 1933. Rabbi, Congregation Beth El, Torrington, Conn., 1958-61, Congregation Agudas Achim, Alexandria, Va., 1955-58, Congregation Beth El, Superior, Wis., 1951-55, Lake Placid Synogogue, N.Y., 1961—; chaplain N.Y. Dept. Corrections, Ray Brook, 1961—, N.Y. Mental Health, Tupper Lake, N.Y., 1961—, Fed. Bur. Prisons, Ray Brook, 1981—. Author: The Rabbinical Assemblies of the Rhine Communities in the 12th Century, 1934. Contbr. articles to profl. jours. Active, bd. dirs. Boy Scouts Am., 1979—, Essex County Mental Health Assn., Elizabethtown, N.Y., 1968—, No. Elba Hist. Soc., Lake Placid, 1962—. Mem. Rabbinical Assembly of Am. (exec. council and commn. on Jewish law), N.Y. Bd. Rabbis, Assn. Mental Health Chaplains, Am. Assn. Correction Chaplains. Republican. Lodges: Lions (pres. 1966-67), Rotary. Home: 30 Saranac Ave Lake Placid NY 12946 Office: Lake Placid Synogogue 30 Saranac Ave Lake Placid NY 12946

AUFDERHAR, GLENN ALVIN, minister, Seventh-day Adventists; b. Pierce, Colo., Aug. 13, 1933; s. Lloyd Herman and Leva Violet (Enke) A.; B.A. cum laude, Walla Walla Coll., 1961; M.A. cum laude, Andrews U., 1962; m. Barbara M. Salter, Dec. 21, 1953; children: Nancy Marie, Kenneth Glenn, Michael James. Ordained to ministry Seventh-day Adventist Ch., 1966. Pastor, Port Townsend, Wash., 1962-63; evangelist, Western Wash., 1963-64; North Pacific Union Conf., 1964-65, Idaho Conf., 1965-68; pastor, evangelist, Milw., 1968-69; dir. trust services, stewardship sec., communications sec., exec. sec. Wis. Conf. Assn. Seventh-day Adventists, 1969-75; pres. Mid Am. Health Services, Marshfield, Wis., 1972-77, Mid-Am. Supply & Equipment, 1976-77, Fireside Apts., Inc., 1976-77, Norris Manor, Inc., 1976-77, Chula Vista Manor, Inc., 1976-77; ministerial dir. Wash. Conf. Seventh-day Adventists, 1977-78, pres., 1978-85; pres. Mich. Conf. Seventh-day Adventists, Lansing, 1985—. Corr., Lake Union Herald, religious jour., 1970-75. Bd. dirs. Wis. Acad., Columbus, 1974—. Mem. Am. Nursing Home Assn., Wis. Assn. Nursing Homes, AMA. Office: 320 W St Joseph St PO Box 19009 Lansing MI 48901

AUKEE, HENRY TARMO, minister, Lutheran Church in America; b. Ironwood, Mich., Mar. 15,1927; s. Frank Josef and Hulda Kirstina (Ilman) A., m. Gladys Eleanor Mayry, Sept. 22, 1951; children: Dwight Henry, Timothy Elias, Marys Ilona Michelle, Dale Martin. A.A., Suomi Coll., 1947; B.Div., Suomi Theol. Sem., 1950. Ordained to ministry Lutheran Ch., 1950. Assoc. pastor Bethlehem Luth. Ch., Detroit, 1950-51; pastor Central Wis. Pasrotal Parish, Owen and Brantwood, Almena, Wia., 1951-54, St. James Luth. Ch., Rudyard, Mich., 1954-60; mission developer Zion Luth. Ch., Port Arthur, Ont., Ca., 1960-62; sr. pastor Messiah Luth. Ch., Duluth, Minn., 1962-; pres. Suomi conf. Minn. Dist., 1963-84; chmn. Lakeshore Luth. Bd., Duluth, 1980-82; turstee Bd. Social Ministry, Mpls., 1980-84. Pres. East Hillside Community Club, Duluth, 1970-75. Home: 922 E 11th St Duluth MN 55805 Office: Messiah Luth Ch 302 E 4th St Duluth MN 55805

AULT, JAMES MASE, bishop, United Methodist Church; b. Sayre, Pa., Aug. 24, 1918; s. Tracey Everett and Bessie (Mase) A.; m. Dorothy Mae Barnhart, Dec. 22, 1943; children: James Mase, Kathryn Louise, Elizabeth Ann, Christopher John (dec.). A.B. magna cum laude, Colgate U., 1949; B.D. magna cum laude, Union Theol. Sem., N.Y.C., 1952, S.T.M., 1964; postgrad. St. Andrews U., Scotland, 1966; D.D., Am. U., Washington, 1968; LL.D., Albright Coll., 1973, Ohio Wesleyan U., 1973. Ordained to ministry United Meth. Ch., 1951. Tool engr., Ingersoll-Rand Co., 1936-42; pastor Meth. Ch., Preston, N.Y., 1946-49, Carlton Hill Meth. Ch., East Rutherford, N.J., 1951-53, Meth. Ch., Leonia, N.J., 1953-58, First Meth. Ch., Pittsfield, Mass., 1958-61; dean students, assoc. prof. practical theology Union Theol. Sem., N.Y.C., 1961-64, prof. practical theology, dir. field edn., 1964-68; dean, prof. pastoral theology, Theol. Sch., Drew U., Madison, N.J., 1968-72; bishop Phila. area United Meth. Ch., 1972-80, Pitts. area, 1980—, sec. council of bishops, 1980-84. Mem. governing bd. Nat. Council Chs. of Christ in U.S.A.; mem. central com. World Council of Chs., exec. com. World Meth. Council, 1981—. Author: Responsible Adults for Tomorrow's World, 1962. Served to 1st lt. AUS, 1942-46. Faculty fellow Am. Assn. Theol. Schs., 1965-66. Mem. AAUP, Acad. Polit. and Social Sci., Phi Beta Kappa. Office: 223 4th Ave Pittsburgh PA 15222

AULTMAN, PAUL DAVID, minister, Southern Baptist Convention; b. Sumrall, Miss., June 19, 1930; s. Clifford Condee and Nanie Mae (Watts) A.; student Clarke Meml. Jr. Coll., 1949, U. So. Miss., fall 1950, Miss. Coll., 1955-56; B.Th., New Orleans Bapt. Theol. Sem., 1960; Th.M., Luther Rice Sem., 1973, D.Min., 1975, Th.D., 1977; m. Kathleen Bell, Aug. 9, 1953; children—James David, Jonathan Paul, Mark Andrew. Ordained to ministry, 1950; pastor Franklin Bapt. Ch., Flora, Miss., 1955-57, Cenerville Bapt. Ch., Tylertown, Miss., 1957-59, Hays Creek Bapt. Ch., Franklinton, La., 1959-62, Improve Bapt. Ch., Columbia, Miss., 1962-65, 1st Bapt. Ch., Ocean Springs, Miss., 1965—. Chalk artist. Served with USMC, 1951-54; Korea. Home: 610 Bellande St Ocean Springs MS 39564 Office: 1st Baptist Ch Washington St at Porter St Ocean Springs MS 39564

AUSTIN, JAMES HAROLD, minister, Lutheran Church in America, psychotherapist; b. Bryn Mawr, Pa., Aug. 18, 1927; s. James Harold and Thelma Frances (Wood) A.; m. Sonia H. Seeber, Oct. 21, 1950 (div.); children: Bruce Bancroft, Andrew Christian, B.A., U. Pa., 1950; M.Div., Luth. Theol. Sem., 1956; M.A., U. Colo. Springs, 1979. Ordained to ministry Lutheran Ch. in Am., 1956. Asst. pastor St. John's Luth. Ch., Phila., 1956-59; pastor St. Andrew's Luth. Ch., Audubon, Pa., 1959-64, Hope Luth. Ch., Pueblo, Colo., 1964-69, Shepherd of the Hills, Colorado Springs, Colo., 1969-77; psychotherapist Pikes Peak Mental Health Center, Colorado Springs, 1979—; pastoral counselor Bethany Lutheran Ch., Colorado Springs, 1982—; dean S. Colo. Dist. Rocky Mountain Synod, Luth. Ch. Am., 1972-77. Counselor Domestic Violence Prevention Ctr., Colorado Springs, 1983—; instr. Am. Red Cross, Colorado Springs, 1982—; naturalist Bear Creek Nature Ctr., 1983—. Mem. Am. Assn for Marriage and Family Therapy, Am. Assn of Pastoral Counselors. Republican. Clubs: Vail (Colo.) Athletic; Pikes Peak Y (Colorado Springs). Home: 1538 Gatehouse Circle S E-2 Colorado Springs CO 80904 Office: Pikes Peak Mental Health Ctr 25 N Spruce St Colorado Springs CO 80905

AUSTIN, MILES JONATHAN, minister, Am. Baptist Chs., U.S.A.; b. Sanford, Fla., July 10, 1933; s. Simeon Louis and Charity (Delancy) A.; B.S., Fla. A. and M. U., 1959; B.D., Howard U., 1964; D.Min., Drew U., Madison, N.J., 1976; m. Jeanne Mary Sistrunk, June 28, 1959; children—Miles Jonathan, II, Maria Jeannae. Vice prin. Fla. Sch. Boys, Okeechobee, 1959-60; youth counselor D.C. Welfare Dept., 1960-62; social worker Jr. Police Citizens Corp., Washington, 1962-64; ordained to ministry, 1970; with research devel. dept., then youth dir. YM-YWCA, Newark, N.J., 1964-67; dir. Essex County Neighborhood Youth Corps, Orange, N.J., 1967-68; dir. disaster relief for Essex County, ARC, 1968-74; pastor Calvary Bapt. Ch., Vauxhall, N.J., 1970-74, Bethel Bapt. Ch., Westfield, N.J., 1974—; condr. symposiums, lectr. Adj. faculty Immaculate Conception Sem., Darlington, N.J., Essex County Coll., Newark. Pres. Urban Housing Corp., Newark, 1972—; bd. dirs. Westfield United Fund, 1974—. Recipient appreciation and achievement awards. Mem. Middlesex Assn. Chs., YMCA, Kappa Alpha Psi. Address: 537 Trinity Pl Westfield NJ 07090

AUSTIN, WILLIAM EDGAR, JR., minister, Christian Church (Disciples of Christ); b. Balt., Mar. 7, 1941; s. William E. and Annie Laurie (Wagster) A.; m. Karen Sue Lawson, Dec. 23, 1967; children: William Todd, Richard Brian. B.A., Culver-Stockton Coll., 1963; M.Div., Lexington Theol. Sem., 1967, D.Min., 1982. Ordained to ministry, 1967. Pastor-dir. Applachia Unity, Hazel Green, Ky., 1967-69; 1st pastor Virginia Beach Christian Ch. (Va.), 1969—; chmn. Direct Ministries of Va. Council of Chs., Richmond, 1981—; bd. mem. Tidewater Pastoral Counseling, Norfolk, 1981. Pres. Mental Health Assn., Norfolk, 1983; bd. dirs. Serenity Lodge, Chesapeake, Va., 1980. Recipient Jacob's Trophy, Culver-Stockton Coll., 1963. Office: Virginia Beach Christian Ch 2225 Rose Hall Dr Virginia Beach VA 23454

AUTREY, C. ELIJAH, minister, educator, So. Baptist Conv.; b. Columbia, Miss., Sept. 17, 1904; s. Adam Elijah and Lee Rose (Yates) A.; B.A., La. Coll., 1929; Th.M., New Orleans Bapt. Theol. Sem., 1932; Th.D., New Orleans Bapt. Theol. Sem., 1934; D.D., La. Coll., 1961; m. Aline Hilton, Oct. 16, 1964; children—Carroll, Jerry. Ordained to ministry, 1924; pastor Temple Bapt. Ch., Ruston, La., 1934-38, First Bapt. Ch., Union City, Tenn., 1938-41, First Bapt. Ch., W. Monroe, La., 1941-49; asso. dir. evangelism Home Mission Bd., Alexandria, La., 1949-52, Dallas, 1952-55; prof. evangelism Southwestern Bapt. Theol. Sem., Ft. Worth, 1955-60; dir. evangelism So. Bapt. Conv., Atlanta, 1960-69; prof. evangelism New Orleans Bapt. Theol. Sem., 1969-71; evangelist, missionary, Utah, Idaho, 1973-76; prof. evangelism Mid-Am. Bapt. Theol. Sem., Memphis, 1976—; interim pastor Oak Haven Bapt. Ch., Memphis, 1976—. Mem. Shelby County So. Bapt. Assn. Author: Basic Evangelism, 1959; Revivals of the Old Testament, 1960; You Can Win Souls, 1961; Evangelistic Sermons, 1962; Evangelism in the Acts, 1964; Theology of Evangelism, 1966; others. Home: 1461 Mink St Memphis TN 38111 Office: 70 Bellevue St Memphis TN 38103

AYALA, ARMAND MARIE, nun, Roman Catholic Church; b. San Juan, P.R., Jan. 16, 1947; d. Armando and Carmen (Torres) A. B.A., Coll. Notre Dame, 1970; M.A., U. P.R., 1980. Community leader Sch. Sisters Notre Dame, San Juan, 1984-85; prin. Academia Perpetuo Socorro, Miramar, P.R., 1982—. Mem. adv. com. Middle States Assn., San Juan, 1984—. Mem. Nat. Cath. Edn. Assn., Middle States Assn. Secondary Schs. (adv. commn.), Nat. Assn. Secondary Sch. Prins., Assn. for Curriculum Devel. Avocations: jogging; music; reading. Home and Office: Academia Perpetuo Socorro Marti esq Central Miramar PR 00907

AYCOCK, BOBBY HUGH, minister, educator, Free Will Baptists; b. Lucama, N.C., Apr. 1, 1935; s. Hugh Gordon and Debbie Ellen (Cuddington) A.; m. Edith Sue White, June 14, 1957; children: Debra Dianne, Rebecca Hellen, David Gordon. B.A., Free Will Bapt. Bible Coll., 1957; postgrad. Trinity Evang. Div. Sch., 1983—. Ordained to ministry Free Will Bapt. Ch., 1953. Pastor Fellowship Free Will Bapt. Ch., Washington, N.C., 1957-58, Plymouth Free Will Bapt. Ch., N.C., 1959-60; missionary Free Will Bapt. Fgn. Mission Bd., Brazil, 1960-82; missionary, founder Igrega Batista Livre Araras, Sao Paulo, Brazil, 1962-65, Igrega Batista Livre Pirassununga, 1962-65, Igrega Batista Livre Barbacena, Minas Gerais, Brazil, 1972-82; prof. missions Free Will Bapt. Bible Coll., Nashville, 1982—; dir. Inst. Biblico, Jaboticabal, Sao Paulo, 1967-69; radio narrator Palavra da Esperanca, Araras, 1964-65, Jabotical, 1969-70, Barbacena, Minas Gerais, 1972-81; mem. Presbytery of Cumberland, Assn. Free Will Bapts. Contbr. articles to mags. Republican. Home: 531 Achievement Dr Nashville TN 37209 Office: Free Will Bapt Bible Coll 3606 West End Ave Nashville TN 37209

AYCOCK, DALE, minister, So. Baptist Conv.; b. Moffatt, Tex., Feb. 3, 1930; s. Bobby Hugh and Elsie Ora (Norman) A.; student Hardin Simmons U., 1949-50, Baylor U., 1950-52, Long Beach State U., 1959, San Jose State U., 1962-63; B.A., Calif. Bapt. Coll., 1965; postgrad. U. Calif. at Riverside, 1965-66, Golden Gate Sem., Los Angeles, 1975-76; m. Patricia Ann Brandes, Mar. 2, 1951; children—Norman Scott, Patricia Yvonne (Mrs. Steven Lynn Shumaker), Timothy Dale, Benjamin Glen. Ordained minister, 1950; pastor Tex., 1950-52, Calif., 1952—, Olive St. Bapt. Ch., Colton, Calif., 1963-67, 1st So. Bapt. Ch., Long Beach, 1967—. Mem com. on coms. So. Bapt. Conv., 1973-74; mem. exec. bd. So. Bapt. Gen. Conv. Calif., 1974—. Mem. human relations council Jordon High Sch., Long Beach, 1974-75, booster club, 1971-74. Mem. Long Beach Harbor So. Bapt. Assn. (moderator 1972-73), Pastor's Conf. (pres. 1968-69). Kiwanian (local pres. 1973-74). Home: 1330 E 57th St Long Beach CA 90805 Office: 5640 Orange Ave Long Beach CA 90805

AYERS, GEORGE WASHINGTON, minister, Apostolic Overcoming Holy Church of God, Inc.; B. Maben, Ala., Nov. 24, 1927; s. Lester and Rosa (Tibbs) A.; m. Verley Mildred Smith, Feb. 3, 1946; 1 child, LaTanja Verley. B.A., Booker T. Washington Bus. Coll., 1953; B.Th., Bethel Sch. Theology, 1967; Th.M., Maranatha Bible Coll., 1979; Th.D., Internat. Bible Inst., 1981; D.D. (hon.), Internat. Bible Inst., 1980, LL.D. (hon), 1980. Ordained to ministry Apostolic Overcoming Holy Ch. of God, 1951, elected to bishopric, 1963. Pastor, Apostolic Overcoming Holy Ch. of God, Tuskeegee, Ala., 1951-55, Pratt City, Ala., 1952-56, Marin City, Calif., 1956-58, Richmond, Calif., 1958—; gen. trustee Aposolic Overcoming Holy Ch. of God, Inc., Birmingham, Ala., 1972—, chmn. trustees bd. edn. dept., 1981—, 2d co-chmn. exec. bd., 1980—; pres Western Regional Bible Coll., Richmond, Calif., 1975—, police chaplain Richmond Police Dept., 1984. City councilman, Marin City, Calif., 1981; v.p. Bay Cities and Richmond Interdenom. Ministers Alliance, 1984. Served with U.S. Army, 1946-49. Recipient Alumni Merit award Booker T. Washington Coll. Bus., 1981, Merit award, 1984; Service award, Western States Sunday Sch. Conv., 1983. Mem. NAACP. Democrat. Home: 1717 Arlington El Cerrito CA 94530 Office: Apostolic Overcoming Holy Ch of God Inc 309 36th St Richmond CA 94805

AYERS, JAMES RAY, minister, educator non-denominational Bible College; b. Hanover, Pa., Jan. 6, 1953; s. Nathaniel Ray and Helen Louise (Wentz) A.; m. Rae Ann Sterner, Aug. 25, 1972; children: Jared, Joel. B.S. in Bible, Lancaster Bible Coll., 1980; M.A. in Counseling Services, Rider Coll., 1985. Ordained to ministry Calvary Bible Ch., 1980; cert. Evangelism Explosion tchr./trainer, 1982. Youth dir. Calvary Bible Ch., Hanover, Pa., 1975-80, asst. pastor, 1976-80; camp adminstr. Rocky Spring Bible Camp, Dillsburg, Pa., 1979-80; dean of men Phila. Coll. Bible, Langhorne, Pa., 1981-82, dir. Christian service, 1982—; chaplain Met. Hosp., Phila., 1983—; speaker in field. Recipient Homiletics award and Student Council award Lancaster Bible Coll., 1980; named Faculty Mem. of Yr., Phila. Coll. Bible, 1984. Mem. Assn. Christian Service Personnel. Republican. Home: 731 Newportville Rd Croydon PA 19020 Office: Phila Coll of Bible Langhorne Manor Langhorne PA 19047

AYERS, JOHN JOSEPH, priest, Roman Catholic Church; b. Waterbury, Conn., Feb. 1, 1926; s. John Joseph and Gertrude Rose (Flaherty) A.; B.Th., Grand Sem., Montreal, Que., Can., 1951. Ordained priest Roman Cath. Ch., 1951. Assoc. pastor Our Lady of the Valley Ch., Sheffield, Mass., 1951, St. Agnes Parish, Dalton, Mass., 1951-68, Annunciation Parish, Florence, Mass, 1968-70, St. Brigids Parish, Amherst, Mass., 1970-72; pastor Immaculate Conception Ch., West Springfield, Mass., 1972-78, St. Francis of Assisi Ch., Belchertown, Mass., 1978—; bd. dirs. Diocesan Bd. for Vocations, Springfield, 1984—. Mem. Exec. Bd. for Elderly, Belchertown, 1980—.

AYERS, ROBERT CURTIS, priest, Episcopal Church, educator; b. Roanoke, Va., Nov. 20, 1927; s. Walter Curtis and Lena Mae (Anderson) A.; m. Vivian Eleanor Harper, Sept. 4, 1950. A.B., Roanoke Coll., 1947; M.Div., Luth. Sem., 1950; Ph.D., Syracuse U., 1981. Ordained priest, 1953. Mission developer United Luth., Massapequa, Park, N.Y., 1950-52; rector Episcopal Ch., Adams, N.Y., 1952-58, chaplain Episcopal Diocese, Syracuse U., 1958-80; rector Episcopal Ch., Camden, N.Y., 1983—; adj. prof. SUNY Coll. Tech., Utica, 1982—; chaplain Utica Coll., 1958-65, USNR, 1956-67. Editor, Messenger, 1970-73. Contbr. articles to profl. jours. Author: F.X. Kraus and Americanists, 1981. Regional rep. Staff, U.S. Senator A. D'Amato, Syracuse, 1981; mgr. election Jack Plumley, Utica, N.Y., 1983. Served to lt. (j.g.) USNR, 1956-67. Danforth Found. fellow, 1965-66. Fellow Coll. Preachers; mem. Am. Cath. Hist. Soc., Sigma Chi. Republican. Address: 818 Ostrom Ave Syracuse NY 13210

AYLOR, GARY LEON, minister, So. Bapt. Conv.; b. Oklahoma City, Mar. 8, 1947; s. Leon Pershing and Ruth Maxine (DeGraffenreid) A.; B.A., Okla. Bapt. U., 1969; m. Juanita Joyce Hardgraves, May 26, 1968; children—Gary Bradley, Steven Andrew. Ordained to ministry, 1969; asso. pastor Meadowood Bapt. Ch., Midwest City, Okla., 1969-76; asso. pastor, ch. adminstr. 1st So. Bapt. Ch., Phoenix, 1976—. Youth tchr. Falls Creek Bapt. Assembly, 1969-76; past chmn. Capitol Bapt. Youth Com.; mem. exec. bd. So. Bapt. Conv., Oklahoma City, Phoenix. Meme. program bd. YMCA, Midwest City, 1970-76. Home: 5825 N 39th Ave Phoenix AZ 85019 Office: 3100 W Camelback Phoenix AZ 85019

AZIZ, GEORGE KALIB, priest, Roman Catholic Ch.; b. Brownsville, Tex., Aug. 2, 1927; s. George Kalib and Lillian (Essey) A.; M.A., Gonzaga U., 1951; S.T.M., Santa Clara U., 1958; postgrad. Cath. U., 1970-71; Ordained priest, 1957; instr. English, Bellarmine Coll. Prep. Sch., San Jose, Calif., 1951-53; instr. logic Loyola U., Los Angeles, 1953-54, instr. metaphysics, 1959-63; tchr. Ryan Prep. Sem., Fresno, Calif., 1963-69; instr. San Joaquin Meml. High Sch., Fresno, also Spiritual dir. priest trainees, 1969-70; asso. pastor St. Bernard's Ch., Eureka, Calif., 1971-76, St. Helena (Calif.) Cath. Ch., 1976—. Sec. Eureka Ministerial Assn., 1973-74; lectr., producer Challenge: Issues and Answers for Christians Today, Sta. KIEM-TV, Eureka, 1975. Mem. Cath. Theol. Soc. Am. Address: 1340 Tainter St St Helena CA 94574

BABB, W. SHERRILL, college president, minister, Independent Baptist; b. Greenville, S.C., Aug. 20, 1940; s. J. Wylie and Sally P. Babb; m. Linda Witmer, June 30, 1963; children: Corinne, Michelle, David. B.A., C.W. Post Coll., 1963; Th.M., Dallas Sem., 1967; Ph.D., U. Pitts., 1978. Ordained to ministry Bapt. Ch., 1967. Pastor, Scottsdale Bible Ch., Ariz., 1967-71; acad. dean Lancaster Bible Coll., Pa., 1971-76; dean faculty Moody Bible Inst., Chgo., 1976-79; pres. Phila. Coll. of Bible, Langhorne, Pa., 1979—; corp. mem. Keswick, Whiting, N.J., 1982-84. Trustee Citizens' Crime Commn., Phila., 1984—. Mem. Am. Council on Edn., Lower Bucks County C. of C., Phi Delta Kappa. Club: Union League (Phila.). Home: 161 Andrew Dr Newtown PA 18940 Office: Phila Coll of Bible Langhorne PA 19047

BABCOCK, WENDELL KEITH, minister, religion educator, Independent Fundamental Churches of America; b. Mt. Morris, Mich., Nov. 21, 1925; s. George Dewey and Nettie (Miller) B.; m. Esther Marie Winger, Aug. 23, 1951; children: Timothy Keith, Stephen Craig. B.A., Bob Jones U., 1967; M.A., Ph.D., Columbia Pacific U., 1984. Ordained to ministry Free Will Baptist Ch., 1952. Pastor, Free Will Bapt. Ch., Timmonsville, S.C., 1951-53; instr. Free Will Bapt. Coll., Nashville, 1953-55; instr. Grand Rapids Sch. of Bible and Music, Grand Rapids, Mich., 1955—, editor, 1960-84; interim pastor Ch of Open Door, Wyoming, Mich., 1964-67; organist Gideons Internat., Nashville, 1977-83. Author: Favorite Hymn Duets, 1964; Hymn Stylings, I and II, 1968. Contbr. articles to profl. publs. Recipient plaque for composition and music prodn. Grand Rapids Sch. of Bible and Music, 1970; named Alumnus of Yr. Bob Jones U. Alumni Assn., 1975. Republican. Home: 3455 Williamson NE Grand Rapids MI 49505 Office: Grand Rapids Sch of Bible and Music 1331 Franklin SE Grand Rapids MI 49506

BABINSKY, JOSEPH ANTHONY, minister, religion educator, United Pentecostal Church International, mechanical engineer; b. South River, N.J., May 20, 1935; s. Andrew and Julie (Kayati) B.; m. Maryruth Prose, June 21, 1963 (dec. 1973); children: Elizabeth Julia, Catherine Vera; m. Donna Carter, Sept. 18, 1982. Student U. Buffalo, 1953-58; B.A. in Philosophy, Monmouth Coll., 1961; M.Div., Union Theol. Sem., 1966. Ordained to ministry United Presbyterian Ch., 1964, United Pentecostal Ch. Internat., 1975. Pastor, United Presbyn. Ch., Vineland, N.J., 1964-67, Sharon, Pa., 1967-71; evangelist United Pentecostal Internat., 1976-78; educator United Pentecostal, Tucson, Ariz., 1978—; del. Ecumenical Council, Sharon, Pa., 1970-71; coordinator, del. United Presbyn. Ch./Voter Registration, Selma, Ala., 1965. Mech. engr. designer Anderson DeBartolo and Pan, Architects and Engrs., Tucson, 1978-83, 1984—. Author: One Day in the Desert, 1978. Served with U.S. Army, 1955-57. Home: 5941 E Sun County Blvd Tucson AZ 85712

BACALIS, NICHOLAS GEORGE, priest, Greek Orthodox Archdiocese of North and South America. B. Norfolk, Va., Aug. 19, 1942; s. George Nicholas and Katherine (Gretakis) B.; m. Vivian Couchell, May 24, 1970; children: Katrina Nicole, Anastasia Dawn. B.A. in Religion, U. Va., 1964; B.D. in Theology, St. Vladimir's Sem., 1968; cert. The Ecumenical Inst., Geneva, 1968-69. Ordained as deacon Greek Orthodox Ch., 1971, as priest, 1972. Dir. Youth Ministry, Greek Orthodox Cathedral, Charlotte, N.C., 1969-71; parish priest St. Nicholas Ch., Jamestown, N.Y., 1972-76, Holy Trinity Ch., Roanoke, Va., 1976—; assoc. chaplain VA Med. Ctr., Salem, Va., 1976—; del. Va. Council Chs., Richmond, 1980—; state youth dir. Diocese of N.J., Va., 1984—. Rep. PTA Central Council, Roanoke, 1982, Multiple Sclerosis Soc., Roanoke, 1980. Mem. NCCJ (mem. steering com. 1980—; Brotherhood citation 1981), Nat. Presbyters Conf., Roanoke Valley Ministerial Assn. (pres. 1978-79), Va. Council Greek Orthodox Chs. (pres. 1981-83), Philo Soc. Office: Holy Trinity Greek Orthodox Ch 30 Huntington Blvd Roanoke VA 24012

BACHELDER, HORACE LYMAN, minister, New Haven Congl. Assn.; b. Cambridge, Mass., June 18, 1915; s. Everett Edward and Margaret (Toole) B.; B.A., Washington and Lee U., 1937; postgrad. Heidelberg U., Germany, 1937-38; M.A., Duke, 1942; M.Th., Yale, 1946; m. Evangeline Grammer Morris, Dec. 16, 1942; children—Ann Lyman (Mrs. James E. Goulka), Margaret Claire, Stephen Morris, Edward Lee. Ordained to ministry, 1946; minister ch., Ansonia, Conn., 1944-46, First Congl. Soc. Oreg., Oregon City, 1946-71, First Parish Ch., Plymouth, Mass., 1971—. Chmn., Oreg. Constl. Rights Com., 1958-60; pres. Willamette Falls (Oreg.) YMCA, 1954, dir., 1954-61; mem. Oregon City Centennial Commn., 1948. Bd. dirs. Plymouth County Devel. Commn., 1972—, treas., 1974-75. Recipient Jr. 1st Citizen Oregon City award, 1948. Mem. Fellowship Religious Humanists, Soc. Descs. Colonial Clergy, Ballou-Channing Unitarian Universalist Ministers Assn. (pres. 1974-75). Author: The Liberal Church at the End of the Oregon Trail, 1969; Another Jesus Book, 1971. Home: 17 Evergreen St Kingston MA 02364 Office: First Parish Town Sq Plymouth MA 02360

BACHELDER, ROBERT STEPHEN, minister, United Church of Christ; b. Middletown, N.Y., Nov. 2, 1951; s. Stephen and Dorothy Esther (Gunderson) B.; m. Beverly June Brandt, Sept. 17, 1977. A.B., Dartmouth Coll., 1973; M.Div., Yale U., 1978. Ordained to ministry, United Ch. Christ, 1978. Pastor United Reformed Ch., Pangbourne, Eng., 1978-79; minister First Congl. Ch., Shrewsbury, Mass., 1980-84; minister for mission and service Worcester City Missionary Soc., Mass., 1984—; dir. central assn. Mass. Conf. United Ch. Christ, 1983—, chmn. social responsibility in investments, 1983—; del. Commn. on Mission and Ministry, Worcester County Ecumenical Council, 1981—; jr. secretariat World Conf. Religion and Peace, Princeton, N.J., 1979; invited speaker Bentley Coll., Waltham, Mass., 1983, DePaul U., Chgo., 1984. Author: Mystery and Miracle, 1983; Between Dying and Birth, 1983; Contbr. articles to profl. jours. Bd. dirs. Central Mass. Human Services Coalition, Worcester, 1981-82, Mass. Conv. Congl. Ministers, 1985—, Worcester Com. on Homeless, 1984—, Boston City Missionary Soc., 1984—; pres. Habitat Worcester, Inc., 1984—. Mem. Nat. Acad. Polit. Social Sci., Soc. Descendants of Colonial Clergy, Kappa Kappa Kappa. Republican. Lodge: Masons. Home: 71 Ennis Rd North Oxford MA 01537 Office: Worcester City Missionary Soc 911 Main St Worcester MA 01610

BACHERT, ALAN HAROLD, minister, Lutheran Church-Missouri Synod; b. Aurora, Ill., Apr. 24, 1942; s. Harold C.L. and Esther E. (Holtz) B.; m. Judith Ann Sweatman, Aug. 21, 1965; children: Kristianna, Jennifer, Jason. B.A., Aurora Coll., 1965; B.D., Concordia Sem., Springfield, Ill., 1969, M.Div., 1971. Ordained to ministry Luth. Ch., 1969. Pastor, St. Paul Luth. Ch., Steelville, Ill., 1969-72, Good Shepherd Chapel, Cape Girardeau, Mo., 1972-74; mission developer, campus pastor, Murfreesboro, Tenn., 1974-77; minister discipleship St. Peter Luth. Ch., Arlington Heights, Ill., 1978-81; sr. pastor Trinity Luth. Ch., Tinley Park, Ill., 1981—; chaplain Howe Devel. Ctr., Tinley Park, 1981—. Pres. Carl Sandburg High Sch. Music Parents, Orland Park, Ill., 1984, Bellwood PTA, Murfreesboro, 1979. Named Outstanding PTA Pres., Tenn. PTA, 1979. Mem. Luth. Ch. Mo. Synod Edn. Assn. (bd. evangelism 1982—), Tinley Park Ministerial Assn. Lodge: Rotary (sec. 1970-72). Home: 14015 Chelsea Dr Orland Park IL 60462 Office: Trinity Luth Ch 6850 W 159th St Tinley Park IL 60477

BACHMAN, JAMES VERNON, minister, Lutheran Church-Missouri Synod; b. Council Bluffs, Iowa, June 14, 1946; s. Merle Edward and Louise Clara (Meyermann) B.; m. Susan Happel Ortmeyer, June 14, 1969; children: Henry Nathaniel, Katherine Jeanne, Joshua Karl. B.S. in Math. and Philosophy, Valparaiso U., 1968; B.A. with honors, Cambridge U., Eng., 1970; M.Div., Concordia Sem., St. Louis, 1972; M.A. in Theology, Cambridge U., 1974; M.A. in Philosophy, Fla. State U., 1984. Ordained to ministry Luth. Ch., 1972. Pastor, Our Redeemer Luth. Ch., Lake City, Fla., 1972-81; pastor, dir. Univ. Luth. Chapel, Tallahassee, Fla., 1981—; instr. philosophy and world religions Lake Community Coll., 1971-81; chmn. com. to restructure Fla.-Ga. dist. Luth Ch.-Mo. Synod, Orlando, Fla., 1974-78, sec. council on ministry in higher edn., 1974-80, chmn., 1981—, campus Ministry dist. coordinator, St. Louis, 1981—; treas. campus ministries Fla. State U., Tallahassee, 1981—. Contbr. articles to religious publs. Mem. Lake City Community Choir (Fla.), 1975-80; mem. Tallahassee Bach Parley, 1981—. Fulbright grantee, 1968-70; fellow Fla. State U., 1982-83—. Mem. Am. Philos. Assn. Republican. Home: 4108 Zermatt Dr Tallahassee FL 32303 Office: Univ Luth Chapel 925 W Jefferson St Tallahassee FL 32304

BACHMEIER, ADAM BERNARD, priest, Roman Catholic Church; b. nr. Balfour, N.D., Aug. 21, 1938; s. Ignatius and Ethel (Lauinger) B. B.A., in Journalism, U. N.D., 1961; B.Div., St. John's Sem., 1968. Ordained priest, Roman Cath. Ch., 1968. Assoc. pastor St. Mary's Cathedral, Fargo, N.D., 1968-73, St. Alphonsus Ch., Langdon, N.D., 1973-74; pastor St. Francis Ch., Marion, N.D., 1974-79, Assumption Ch., Dickey, N.D., 1974-79, Holy Family Ch., Grand Forks, N.D., 1979—; mem. Ecumenical Commn. Diocese of Fargo, 1979—, Liturgy Commn., 1970-75. Active Community Bd., Grand Forks, 1981—, Community Task Force on Chem. Use and Awareness, Grand Forks, 1983—. Democrat. Home and Office: Holy Family Ch 1122 18th Ave S Grand Forks ND 58201

BACKS, HERMAN HENRY, minister, Lutheran Church, Missouri Synod; b. Nashville, Ill., Apr. 1, 1905; s. Charles Herman Henry and Emma (Maschoff) B.; m. Edna Mary Fetter, June 29, 1930; children: Marcile Elizabeth, Vincent John. B.S., Concordia Theol. Sem., 1929; postgrad. European Sch. Music, 1925-26. Ordained to ministry, 1929. Pastor Mt. Calvary Luth. Ch., Ft. Wayne, Ind., 1929-79, asst. pastor, 1979—; chmn. Ft. Wayne Instn. Missions, 1960-75; sec., v.p. Luth. Deaconess Assn., 1942-60; chmn. Allen County Crippled Children's Soc., 1945-47; founder, tchr. Mt. Calvary Luth. Sch., Ft. Wayne, 1929-44; chmn. Ft. Wayne Pastoral Conf., 1950-65; chmn. pub. relations Central dist. Mo. Synod, 1950-60, circuit counselor, 1938-48; civilian chaplain U.S. Air Base, Bar Field, Ft. Wayne, 1940-45; adv. mem. U.S. Selective Service of Allen County, 1936-47. Contbr. articles to profl. jours. Bd. dirs. Ind. Soc. Crippled Children, 1947-50. Recipient Award of Achievement, Concordia Sem., 1979; Servus Ecclesiae Christi award, Concordia Sem., 1979; Service award, Armed Forces Commn., Luth. Ch., Mo. Synod, 1946; commendations, Pres. Franklin D. Roosevelt, Jimmie Carter, Gerald Ford for loyal civilian service; citation, Gov. Otis R. Bonen, Gov. Ind., 1979. Address: 6310 Maywood Cir Fort Wayne IN 46819

BACKUS, JOHN LEROY, II, minister, American Lutheran Church; b. Aurora, Ill., Sept. 7, 1953; s. John LeRoy and Josephine Mary (Bartucci) B.; m. Elizabeth Louise Danko, May 8, 1976; 1 child, Emily Mi Ie. B.A. in Philosophy, U. Nebr., 1975; M.Div., Wartburg Sem., 1979. Ordained to ministry, 1979. Youth pastor Cross of Glory Luth. Ch., Mpls., 1979-82; co-pastor Bethlehem and Union Prairie Luth. Parish, Lanesboro, Minn., 1982—; nat. convention del. Am. Luth. Ch., Lanesboro, 1984. Local organizer Ground Zero, Washington, D.C., 1983—. Home: 702 Fillmore St Lanesboro MN 55949 Office: Bethlehem and Union Prairie Luth Parish 200 Kenilworth St Lanesboro MN 55949

BACON, BOB JOE, minister, So. Bapt. Conv.; b. Redding, Calif., Dec. 19, 1939; s. Clyde Lowry and Mabel (Coleman) B.; B.A., Ouachita Bapt. U., 1962; M.Div., Southwestern Bapt. Theol. Sem., 1966; m. Martha L. Scrimshire, June 14, 1962; children—Debra Dawn, Gay Lynn. Ordained to ministry, 1961; pastor Gilead Bapt. Ch., Malvern, Ark., 1960-62, Stockard Bapt. Ch., Athens, Tex., 1963-64, 1st Bapt. Ch., Detroit, Tex., 1964-66, Calvary Bapt. Ch., Greenfield, Ind., 1966-68; asso. pastor, minister edn. 1st Bapt. Ch., Hobbs, N. Mex., 1969-72; pastor Del Norte Bapt. Ch., Albuquerque, 1973—. Pres. Hobbs Recreation League, 1969-72. Mem. Bapt. Ministers Assn. Home: 6624 Lafving St NE Albuquerque NM 87109 Office: 6124 Montgomery St NE Albuquerque NM 87109

BACON, JOHN THOMAS RICHARD, deacon, Orthodox Church in America, security guard; b. Barnstable, Mass., July 26, 1948; s. Paul Daniel and Vera Irene (Hawes) B.; m. Elizabeth Pamela Hill Gates, June 26, 1971; children: Daniel, Juliana. B.A., Bridgewater State Coll., 1970; M.Theol. Studies, Holy Cross Greek Orthodox Sch. Theology, Brookline, Mass., 1985. Ordained deacon Orthodox Church in America, 1983. Assoc. pastor Trinity Episcopal Ch., Bridgewater, Mass., 1970-79; Mass. dist. dir. United Evangelical Chs., Morovia, Calif., 1973-77; nat. adminstrv. asst., 1975-77; deacon Holy Trinity Orthodox Ch., Boston, 1983—; pres. parish council Holy Trinity Orthodox Cathedral, 1980-82; assembly del. New Eng. diocese Orthodox Church in Am., 1981, 82, 83, del. 7th all-Am. council, Phila., 1983. Adv., Bridgewater Bicentennial Commn., 1975-76; asst. co-ordinator Bridgewater Civil Defense, 1978. Gargas Meml. scholar Holy Cross Greek Orthodox Sch. Theology, 1983, 84. Mem. Am. Inst. Patristic and Byzantine Studies, Brockton Evangelical Ministers Assn. (v.p. 1974-75), Nat. Eagle Scout Assn. Home: 47 Church St PO Box 302 Bridgewater MA 92324 Office: Holy Trinity Orthodox Cathedral 165 Park Dr Boston MA 02215

BACON, PAUL E., minister, Lutheran Church-Missouri Synod; b. Oak Park, Ill., Mar. 5, 1942; s. Herman Erwin Greifendorf and Lydia Marie (Geiseman) B.; m. Annette Louis Voth, June 5, 1965; children: Paul M., Dean M., Elizabeth. B.A., Concordia Coll., Ft. Wayne, Ind., 1963; M.Div., Concordia Sem., St. Louis, 1967; M.S.T., Luth. Sch. Theology, Chgo., 1976. Ordained to ministry Luth. Ch., 1967. Pastor, St. John Luth. Ch., 1967-70, St. Paul Luth. Ch., Glenwood City., Wis., 1967-70, Good Shepherd Luth. Ch., Maywood, Ill., 1970-76, Trinity Luth. Ch., New Lenox, Ill., 1976—; sec. English dist. Luth. Ch.-Mo. Synod, Detroit, 1976—; bd. dirs. Luth. Child and Family Services, River Forest, Ill., 1974—. Pres. Maywood Rotary Club, 1973-74. Home: 515 N Cedar Rd New Lenox IL 60451 Office: Trinity Luth Ch N Cedar and Elm Sts New Lenox IL 60451

BACON, TOM LEE, minister, Southern Baptist Convention; b. Winnsboro, Tex., Sept. 14, 1936; s. Tom Wilson and Myrtle Lee (Inman) B.; m. Thelma Clamp, June 11, 1955; children: Charles Alan, Tom Wayne, Michael Bruce, Gladys Amilee. B.A., Calif. Bapt. Coll., 1965; M. Div., Golden Gate Bapt. Theol. Sem., 1970. Ordained Southern Baptist Convention, 1960. Pastor chs., Riverside, Chino, and Belmont, Calif., 1960-73; pastor 1st So. Bapt. Ch., Hawthorne, Nev., 1974—; vice moderator Nev. Bapt. Assn. of No. Nev., 1974-75; moderator Nev. Bapt. Assn., 1975—, chmn. missions com., 1974; v.p. Nev. Bapt. Fellowship, 1975; pres. Mineral County Ministers Assn., Nev., 1974-76; mem. study com. for formation Nev. Bapt. Conv., 1977-78; v.p., mem. exec. bd. Nev. Bapt. Conv., 1979; dir. missions Lahontan and N.E. Bapt. Assn., 1980—. Bd. dirs., pres. Consol. Agencies for Human Services of Mineral County, 1977—; bd. dirs. Assn. Retarded Citizens of Mineral County, Mineral County Council Alcohol Drug Abuse, 1974—. Named Clergyman of Yr., Hawthorne (Nev.) Kiwanis Club, 1976. Home and Office: PO Box 1364 Hawthorne NV 89415

BADER, CARL DAVIS, minister, United Church of Christ; b. Phila., Nov. 15, 1924; s. Carl and Anna Mildred (Davis) B.; m. Anna Marie Scott, June 7, 1948; 1 child, Carl Scott. B.S. in Edn., Temple U., 1946, M.Div., 1949, S.T.M., 1950; M.S., U. Pa., 1952. D.D. (hon.), Onyang Acad., On Yang On Chun, Chung Nam, Korea, 1977. Ordained to ministry Congregational Christian Chs., 1949. Pastor, 1st Congl. Ch., Germantown, Pa., 1949-51, 1st Christian Ch., Phila., 1951-58, Newportville United Ch. Christ, (Pa., 1959-82; lectr., preacher, Phila., 1983—; moderator, Delaware Valley Assn. Congl. Christian Chs., 1957; vis. chaplain Friends Hosp., Phila., 1952-77. Sr. counselor Abraham Lincoln High Sch., Phila., 1981—. Contbr. articles to religious publs.; composer hymns. Mem. Phila. Assn. United Ch. Christ, Internat. Soc. Preachers (pres. 1979—), Pa. Prison Soc., Kappa Phi Kappa. Republican. Lodge: Masons.

BADGER, W. BRUCE, chairman Bethel Ministerial Association, Inc. Address: 511 W Cedar St Leroy IL 61752

BADURINA, GABRIEL DINKO, priest, Roman Cath. Ch.; b. Lun, Croatia, Yugoslavia, Jan. 19, 1935; s. Romulo and Kleofina B.; came to U.S., 1966, naturalized, 1971; B. Degree in Philosophy, Theol. U., Zagreb, Yugoslavia, 1958, M. Degree in Theology, 1963; M. Counseling Guidance, Duquesne U., Pitts., 1970. Joined Provincial Commisary Croatian Fathers, 1972, ordained priest, 1962; pastor asst., Preko, Yugoslavia, 1963-66; asst. pastor Croatian Parish St. Nicholas, Milvale, Pa., 1966-70; pastor Croatian Parish Sacred Heart, McKeesport, Pa., 1970—. Mem. civil service bd. City of McKeesport, 1970—; mem. McKeesport Central Cath. Sch. Bd., 1970—. Mem. Croatian Fraternal Union, Croatian Cath. Union. Home and office: 705 Shaw Ave McKeesport PA 15132

BAER, JAMES FREDERICK, minister, American Baptist Churches in the U.S.A.; b. Bklyn., Aug. 13, 1952; s. Berthold Bartley and Stella (Tabershaw) B.; m. Allison Jane Levin, Oct. 15, 1977; children: Melissa Kay, Benjamin Charles. B.A. cum laude, Loyola U., Chgo., 1976; M.Div., Northern Bapt. Theol. Sem., 1981. Ordained to ministry Am. Bapt. Chs. U.S.A., 1982. Pastor, Ch. on the Hill, Oak Creek, Wis., 1981—. Presidential scholar No. Bapt. Theol. Sem., 1978-79, recipient Teaching Asst. Bibl. Studies award, 1980-81. Lodge: Kiwanis (bd. dirs., 1983—, v.p., 1984—). Home: 242 E Groveland Dr Oak Creek WI 53154

BAERG, HENRY RALPH, educational administrator, minister, Mennonite Brethren Church; b. Ukraine, Russia, Aug. 12, 1918; s. John Jacob and Margaret (Wiebe) B.; came to Can., 1925, naturalized, 1930; student Coaldale Bible Inst., 1935-38, Prairie Bible Inst., 1938-40, Mennonite Brethren Bible Coll., 1945-46; B.A., Tabor Coll., 1949, B.D., 1951; M.A., Wichita U., 1953; Ph.D. candidate U. N.D., 1975; m. Justina Anne Wiebe, Feb. 23, 1941; children: Donald, Eleanor, Sam, Charity-Anne, Paul, David. Ordained to ministry Baptist Ch., 1951; pastor First Bapt. Ch., 1948-53; pastor Mennonite Brethren Ch., Henderson, Nebr., 1953-56; prof. Mennonite Brethren Bible Coll., Winnipeg, Man., Can., 1956-62; pastor Portage Ave. Mennonite Brethren Ch., Winnipeg, 1962-69, Kingwood Bible Ch., Salem, Oreg., 1969-82, Valleyview Bible Ch., 1982-83, Grace Mennonite Ch., Winkler, Man., 1983-84, Mennonite Brethren Ch., Elm Creek, Man., 1984—; pres. Winkler (Man.) Bible Inst., 1968-69. Chmn. bd. Christian Edn. Canadian Mennonite Brethren Conf., 1960-63. Camp dir. Camp Arnes, Man., 1957-59. Contbr. numerous articles to Voice of Mennonite Brethren Bible Coll. mag. Home: Box 104 Elm Creek MB R0G 0N0 Canada

BAERWALD, KATHRYN. Gen. sec. Am. Lutheran Ch., Mpls. Office: Am Lutheran Ch 422 5th St Minneapolis MN 55415*

BAGBY, DANIEL GORDON, minister, So. Baptist Conv.; b. Porto Alegre, Brazil, May 30, 1941; s. Albert Ian and Thelma (Frith) B.; B.A., Baylor U., 1962, M.S., 1964; B.D., So. Bapt. Theol. Sem., Louisville, 1967, Ph.D., 1973; m. Janet Glee Pitman, June 12, 1965; 1 son, Douglas Ian. Ordained to ministry, 1968; chaplain Louisville Detention Center, 1964-68; asso. pastor Ravensworth Bapt. Ch., Annandale, Va., 1968-71; chaplain Ky. Correctional Instn. for Women, Pewee Valley, 1971-74; marriage and family counselor Jeffersonville Personal Counseling Center, Clarksville, Ind., 1971-74; instr. psychology of religion So. Bapt. Theol. Sem., Louisville, 1973-74, state alumni pres., 1975-76; pastor Calvary Bapt. Ch., West Lafayette, Ind., 1973—. Pres., Tippecanoe County Ministerial Assn.; trustee Midwestern Baptist Theol. Sem., Kansas City, Mo., sem. extension dir., W. Lafayette, Ind. Active, Ind. InterReligious Commn. on Human Equality. Mem. Am. Assn. Marriage and Family Counselors (clin.), Omicron Delta Kappa. Contbr. articles to religious publs. Home: 307 Sharon Rd West Lafayette IN 47906 Office: 2552 Soldiers Home Rd West Lafayette IN 47906

BAGGER, RALPH WILLIAM, minister, Lutheran Church in America; b. Butler, Pa., June 12, 1923; s. Henry Horneman and Margaret (Finck) B.; A.B.,

Muhlenberg Coll., 1948; B.D., Luth. Theol. Sem., Phila., 1951; A.M., U. Pa., 1951; m. Elizabeth Louise Hodges, Aug. 26, 1950; Ordained to ministry, 1951; pastor St. Mark's Luth. Ch., Allentown, Pa., 1951-55, Immanuel Luth. Ch., East Lansdowne, Pa., 1955-59, Friedens Luth. Ch., Hegins, Pa., 1959-68; periodicals editor bd. publ. Luth. Ch. Am., Phila., 1968—, editor Light for Today, 1968—; dir. Luth. Theol. Sem., Phila., 1981—. Author: (with Elizabeth Bagger) Ofcl. Summary of Biennial Convs. of United Luth. Ch. in Am., 1954-60, Ofcl. Summary of Biennial Convs. of Luth. Ch. in Am., 1964—. Charter mem. East Lansdowne Civic Assn., Pa., 1956-59. Served as sgt. AUS, 1943-46, ETO, PTO. Mem. Hymn Soc. Am., Omicron Delta Kappa. Home: 9 Terrace Rd Norristown PA 19401 Office: Bd Publ Luth Ch in Am 2900 Queen Ln Philadelphia PA 19129

BAHL, JANICE MIRIAM, nun, religious education director, Roman Catholic Church; b. Allentown, Pa., Apr. 13, 1937; d. Franklin Clayton and Emma (Kosharek). B.A. in Social Sci. and History, Our Lady of Angels (now Newmann Coll.), 1976; M.A. in Sacred Scripture and Religious Studies, St. Charles Sem., Overbrook, Pa., 1984. Joined Sisters of St. Francis of Phila., Roman Cath. Ch., 1965. Tchr. St. Mary of Assumption, Phila., 1965-71, St. Mary Sch., Delphi, Pa., 1971-73, St. Benedict Sch., Phila., 1973-76, Resurrection Sch., Chester, Pa., 1976-79, St. Coleman-Neumann, 1979-80; tchr. St. Stanislaus Sch., Lansdale, Pa., 1980-82; dir. learning ctr., 1982-84, dir. religious edn., 1984—; mem. religious curriculum com. Archdiocese of Phila., 1974-84. Leader Lehigh council Girl Scouts U.S., 1956-62. Mem. Nat. Cath. Ednl. Assn., Educators for Social Responsibility, Network. Democrat. Avocations: woodcutting; photography; painting; camping; music. Home: Franciscan Convent 485 F Main St Lansdale PA 19446 Office: St Stanislaus Parish Religious Edn Office 493 E Main St Lansdale PA 19446

BAHR, GORDON JOHN, religious studies educator; b. Berlin, Wis., Oct. 4, 1926; s. John Ernest and Anna Bertha (Braun) B. B.A., Wartburg Coll., 1951; B.D., Wartburg Sem., 1954; postgrad. U. Gottingen, W. Ger., 1954-56; Ph.D., Hebrew Union Coll., 1962. Instr., Wartburg Coll., Waverly, Iowa, 1956-57; asst. prof. Wayne State U., Detroit, 1963-65; asst. prof. Marquette U., Milw., 1965-69; prof. religion Claflin Coll., Orangeburg, S.C., 1969—. Served with U.S. Army, 1945-47. Mem. Soc. Bibl. Lit. Republican. Home: 1120 Gloria St NE Orangeburg SC 29115 Office: Claflin Coll Orangeburg SC 29115

BAIER, PAUL MATHIAS, priest, Roman Catholic Ch.; b. Bastress, Pa., Jan. 25, 1918; s. Robert Charles and Rebecca Cecelia (Stopper) B.; B.A., Pontifical Coll. Josephinum, 1940. Ordained priest, 1944; asst. pastor St. Mary's Ch., Scranton, Pa., 1944-51; chaplain Divine Providence Hosp., Williamsport, Pa., 1951-53; asst. pastor St. Boniface Ch., Wilkes-Barre, Pa., 1953-66, Our Lady of the Snows Ch., Clarks Summit, Pa., 1966-67; pastor St. John's Ch., Troy, Pa. and St. Michael's Ch., Canton, Pa., 1967—. Moderator Council of Cath. Women, Diocese of Scranton. Mem. Religious Edn. Assn., Liturgical Conf., Josephinum Alumni Assn. Author: Supernatural Life, 1953, 55; Go, Teach All Nations, 1964, 66; These Are My Roots, 1969; Prayer of the Believer, 1972; Love Is What Christianity Is All About, 1974; contbr. articles to religious jours. Home and Office: 140 Canton St Troy PA 16947

BAILEY, AMOS PURNELL, minister, columnist, United Methodist Church; b. Grotons, Va., May 2, 1918; s. Louis William and Evelyn Kate (Charnock) B.; m. Ruth Martin Hill, Aug. 22, 1942; children: Carol (Mrs. Thomas T. Harriman), Anne (Mrs. Peter S. Page), Beth (Mrs. David L. Richardson II), Jeanne (Mrs. Paul H. Dodge). B.A., Randolph-Macon Coll., 1942, D.D., 1956; B.D., Duke, 1948; Th.M., Union Theol. Sem., 1957. Ordained to ministry United Methodist Church, 1942; Pastor, Va., 1938-61; dist. supt. Richmond, Va., 1961-67; sr. pastor Reveille Ch., Richmond, 1967-70; assoc. gen. sec., div. chaplains, bd. higher edn. and ministry United Meth. Ch., Washington, 1970-79; v.p. Nat. Meth. Found., 1979-82; pres. Nat. Temple Ministries, Inc., 1982—; chmn. communications com. S.E. jurisdiction United Meth. Ch., 1968-76; del. Gen. Conf., 1964, 66, 68, 70, World Meth. Conf. London, 1966, Denver, 1970, Dublin, 1976; vice chmn. div. overseas ministries Nat. Council Chs., 1973-79; chmn. adv. com. VA Chaplaincy, 1973-79; author syndicated column Daily Bread, Los Angeles Times syndicate, 1945—, syndicated radio program Daily Bread, 1945-69; trustee So. Sem., 1961-76; bd. vistors Duke Div. Sch., Durham, N.C., 1962-68. Dir. Reeves Parvin Co., 1978—. Trustee Randolph Macon Coll., Ashland, Va., 1960-82. Group chmn. industry div. United Givers Fund Richmond, 1961. Home: 7815 Falstaff Rd McLean VA 22101 Office: 1835 N Nash St Arlington VA 22209

BAILEY, ELMER F., minister, So. Bapt. Conv.; b. Detroit, Dec. 24, 1916; s. George W. and Caroline Frederica (Bofinger) B.; A.B., Okla. Bapt. U., 1939; m. Virginia Louise Shipman, July 11, 1941; children—James Carroll, Roger Bradley, Richard Ramsey. Ordained to ministry, 1943; dir. music and

edn. Avondale Bapt. Ch., Chattanooga, 1940-42, 1st Bapt. Ch., Port Arthur, Tex., 1944-45, 1st Bapt. Ch., Jacksonville, Fla., 1945-47; asst. pastor Broadway Bapt. Ch., Knoxville, Tenn., 1948-60; asso. pastor Bellevue Bapt. Ch., Memphis, 1960—; asst. prof. Mid-Am. Bapt. Theol. Sem., Memphis, 1976. Pres. Southwestern Religious Edn. Assn., 1967; dir. music So. Bapt. Conv., 1960, bd. trustees Bapt. Sunday Sch., 1967-74; vice pres. So. Bapt. Religious Edn. Assn., 1968, pres.-elect, 1976. Mem. Met. Religious Edn. Assn., Nat. Conf. Ch. Bus. Adminstrs. Home: 379 N Highland St Memphis TN 38122 Office: 70 N Bellevue St Memphis TN 38104

BAILEY, GEORGE ELDENE, minister, United Methodist Church; b. Adrian, Mich., Feb. 8, 1926; s. Charles Finney and Ethel (Shreve) B.; m. Betty Jean Weber, Sept. 21, 1948; children: Charles Alan, Carol Ann, Christine Alise (dec.). A.B., Asbury Coll., 1949; M.Div., Pitts. Theol. Sem., 1953. Ordained to ministry Meth. Ch., as deacon, 1951, as elder, 1954. Pres. Bellaire Council Chs., Ohio, 1964-66; del. World Meth. Conf., London, 1966; pres. Interfaith Campus Kent, Canton, Ohio, 1976-79; sec. East Ohio Conf., Bd. Global Ministries, 1980-81; supt. Mansfield dist. East Ohio Conf., 1981—, cabinet rep. bd. discipleship, 1984—; cabinet rep. bd. diaconal ministry, 1984—, camps and confs., 1984—, conf. program, 1984—. Served with USAF, 1944-46, ETO. Mem. Ohio Council Chs. (life). Republican. Home: 1155 Burkwood Rd Mansfield OH 44907 Office: Mansfield Dist Office 446 Park Ave W Mansfield OH 44906

BAILEY, J(AMES) MARTIN, minister, United Ch. Christ; b. Emmetsburg, Iowa, July 28, 1929; s. Allen Ransom and Kathryn Gunver (Ausland) B.; B.A., State U. Iowa, 1951; B.D., Eden Theol. Sem., 1954; M.S., Northwestern U., 1956; D.D., Eden Theol. Sem., 1965, Lakeland Coll., 1967; m. Betty Jane Bailey, June 5, 1954; children—Kristine Elizabeth, Susan Ruth. Ordained to ministry, 1954; editorial asst. The Messenger, Evang. and Ref. Ch., 1951-54; bus. mgr. Internat. Jour. Religious Edn., 1954-60; dir. circulation, advt. and promotion United Ch. Herald, 1960-63, editor, 1963-72; editor A.D. Publs., Inc., N.Y.C., 1972-83; editor "Connections", Ch. World Service, 1983-85; assoc. gen. sec. Nat. Council of Chs. of Christ in the U.S.A., 1985—; former pres. Associated Ch. Press. Former chmn. Interchurch Features. Mem. Democratic Com. Montclair County; former mem. Nat. Council Chs. Communications Com. Recipient Merit awards Associated Ch. Press. Mem. Sigma Delta Chi. Author: Windbreaks, 1958; Youth and the Town and Country Church, 1958; (with Betty Jane Bailey), Worship with Youth, 1963; Steps of Bonhoeffer, 1969. Home: 45 Watchung Ave Upper Montclair NJ 07043 Office: 475 Riverside Dr Room 804 New York City NY 10115

BAILEY, J. S., bishop The Church of God in Christ, Detroit. Office: 17370 Pontchartrain Detroit MI 48203*

BAILEY, MARK LEROY, minister, religion educator, Conservative Baptist Association of America; b. Monte Vista, Colo., Sept. 28, 1950; s. Arthur Charles and Martha Virginia (Jones) B.; m. Barbara Kay Green, June 23, 1972. A.A., Maricopa Tech. Coll., 1970; B.A., Southwestern Coll., 1972; M.Div., Western Sem., 1975, Th.M., 1977; Th.D. candidate Dallas Sem. Ordained to ministry Conservative Baptist Association of America, 1972. Gospel magician Southwestern Coll., Phoenix, 1970-72; conf. speaker Western Sem., Portland, Oreg., 1972-75, teaching fellow, 1975-76; bible tchr. Southwestern Coll., 1976-85; assoc. pastor Palmcroft Bapt. Ch., Phoenix, 1980-85; asst. prof. Bible exposition Dallas Theol. Sem., 1985—; bd. dirs. Valley Bible Inst., Phoenix, 1982—; nominating com. Conservative Bapt. Fgn. Mission Soc., Wheaton, Ill., 1983—. Mem. Am. Registry Radiol. Technicians, Creation Research Soc., Bibl. Archeol. Soc., Evang. Theol. Soc., Delta Epsilon Chi. Republican. Home: 13601 N 41st St Phoenix AZ 85032 Office: Southwestern Coll 2625 E Cactus Rd Phoenix AZ 85032

BAILEY, PRESTON TIMOTHY, SR., minister, So. Baptist Conv.; b. Newport News, Va., Nov. 4, 1928; s. Otis Cecil and Georgie Christine (Mathews) B.; diploma Moody Bible Inst., 1954; B.S., Samford U., 1959; M.Ed., William and Mary Coll., 1967; Th.M., Luther Rice Sem., 1975, D.Ministry, 1976; m. Dolores Joan Burwell, Mar. 2, 1952; children—Rebecca Ann, Preston Timothy, Catherine Ruth, Judith Lynn, Lynda Joan, Christine Delores, Babette Darlene. Ordained to ministry, 1950; pastor in Ill. and Ala., 1952-58, N.C., 1960-64, Va., 1967-72; pastor Highland View Bapt. Ch., St. Charles, Mo., 1973—; host weekly radio program, 1971—. Chaplain, St. Charles County Sheriff's Dept., 1973—. Mem. adv. com. St. Charles Bd. Edn., 1975—; bd. dirs. Caribbean Centre for the Deaf, Mandeville, Jamaica. Named hon. citizen Jung Ju City, Korea, 1974. Mem. St. Louis Bapt. Assn., St. Louis Bapt. Pastors' Conf., Mo. Bapt. Conv., St. Charles Geneal. Soc., Kappa Delta Pi. Author: After Death - What Then?, 1972; After Marriage - What Then?, 1974; also daily newspaper column. Home: 2613 Cypress St Saint Charles MO 63301 Office: 3750 Droste Rd Saint Charles MO 63301

BAILEY, ROBERTA, nun, day care administrator, Roman Catholic Ch.; b. Wilmington, Del., Oct. 24, 1938; d. William Thomas and Elizabeth (Donahue) B. B.S., Bellamarine Ursuline U., Louisville 1969; M.A., U. S. Fla., 1973, cert. Mid West Montessori Tchr. Tng. Center, Chgo., 1969. Perpetual profession Benedictine Order; cert. tchr., Fla. Tchr. Catholic schs., Jacksonville and Miami, Fla., 1959-67; prin. St. Martha's Sch., Sarasota, Fla., 1969-70; admintr. Montessori Sch., St. Leo, Fla., 1970-76, 79—, Ocala, Fla., 1976-79. Del. Sister's Council, Diocese of St. Petersburg, 1970—; mem. commn. Diocesan Liturgy Council, 1982—. Mem. child adv. bd. Community Coll. Ocala, 1976-79; tchr. Pasco County Adult Edn., Dade County 1979—. Mem. Fla. Assn. Children Under Six (editor 1983—), Am. Montessori Soc. Democrat. Home: PO Drawer H Saint Leo FL 33574 Office: Priory Early Childhood Center Route 3 Box 683 Dade City FL 33525

BAILEY, SCOTT FIELD See *Who's Who in America*, 43rd edition.

BAILEY, THOMAS IRVIN, ednl. adminstr., minister, Christian and Missionary Alliance; b. Elma, Wash., July 13, 1942; s. Harry Arnton and Violet Rose (Robinson) B.; B.S. in Missions, Nyack Missionary Coll., 1964; M.Div., Wheaton Grad. Sch. Theology, 1974. m. Janice Gail Walton, July 27, 1963; children—Jennifer Lynn, Kimberly Erin, Natalie Rae. Ordained to ministry, 1970; pastor Wayside Chapel Community Ch., Rosamond, Calif., 1968—. Chaplain Antelope Valley Hosp. Med. Center, Lancaster, Calif., 1970—; Christian Edn. dir., mem. dist. exec. com. South Pacific Dist., Christian and Missionary Alliance, Fullerton, Calif., 1972—. Mem. steering com. chaplaincy program Antelope Valley Hosp. Med Center, Lancaster, 1972—; chmn. steering com., 1976—; chief adminstr. Rosamond Christian Sch., 1976—; chmn. bd. Antelope Valley Youth for Christ, Lancaster, 1969-75. Chmn. secondary curriculum com. So. Kern Unified Sch. Dist., Rosamond, 1971—. Mem. Rosamond Ministerial Assn. (sec. 1972-74, pres. 1974—), Evang. Theol. Soc. Home: 2134 Alexander POB F Rosamond CA 93560 Office: 3275 Glendower Rosamond CA 93560

BAIN, DOUGLAS COGBURN, JR., minister, religion educator, Southern Baptist Convention; b. Poplarville, Miss., Nov. 30, 1940; s. Douglas Cogburn and Audrey (Smith) B. B.A., Miss. Coll., 1962; M.Div., Southwestern Sem., Fort Worth, 1967, Th.D., 1973. Ordained to ministry So. Bapt. Conv., 1962. Assoc. prof. religion and psychology Blue Mountain Coll., Miss., 1976—. Pres. Bd. Ministerial Edn., Miss. Bapt. Conv., 1982—. Mem. Nat. Assn. Bapt. Profs. Religion. Address: Blue Mountain Coll Box 337 Blue Mountain MS 38610

BAIRD, JOHN STOCKTON, minister, Presbyterian Church, educator; b. Princeton, N.J., Oct. 8, 1928; s. Richard Hamilton and Golden (Stockton) B.; m. Mary Elizabeth Hamelman, Apr. 19, 1951; children: Richard Hamelman, Cynthia Louise, Bonnie Lynn, John Mark. Ordained to ministry Presbyterian Ch., 1954. B.A., Maryville Coll. (Tenn.), 1951; B.D., San Francisco Theol. Sem., 1954; S.T.M., Temple U., S.T.D., 1960. Asst. pastor 1st Presby. Ch., Ambler, Pa., 1954-56; pastor Deerfield Presbyn. Ch. (N.J.), 1956-67, S. Hollywood Presbyn. Ch. (Calif.), 1967-76; instr. religion Rutgers U., Camden, N.J., 1966-67; Denise prof. homiletics U. Dubuque Theol. Sem. (Iowa), 1976—; bd. dirs. Native Am. Theol. Edn. Consortium, 1982—. Contbr. to Bakers Dictionary of Evang. Theology, 1984. Bd. dirs. YMCA, Dubuque, 1984. Mem. Assn. for Practical Theology (bd. dirs. 1982—), Acad. Homiletics, N.Am. Acad. Liturgy, Am. Theol. Soc., Soc. Bibl. Lit., Am. Acad. Religion. Republican. Home: 56 Hill St Dubuque IA 52001 Office: Univ of Dubuque Theol Sem 2050 University Ave Dubuque IA 52001

BAIRD, LARRY DON, minister, United Pentecostal Church International, nurse; b. Abilene, Tex., Sept. 23, 1949; s. Delmar Lee Baird and Frances Elizabeth (Robertson) Weathers; m. Mary Margaret Ledbetter, Dec. 22, 1970; 1 child, Shannon Kirk; 1 foster child: Rober Dale Stembridge, Jr. Student San Diego State U., 1971-72, Cisco Jr. Coll., Clyde, Tex., 1977-78; diploma in nursing Hendrick Meml. Hosp., Abilene, 1972-73. Ordained to ministry United Pentecostal Ch. Internat., 1973. Evangelist United Pentecostal Ch., 1973-78, pastor, Hamlin, Tex., 1979-82; campus dean Tupelo Children's Mansion, Miss., 1983-84, residential dir., 1982-84; co-pastor First Pentecostal Ch., Abilene, 1984—; asst. choir dir., musician, dir. and interpreter for deaf United Pentecostal Ch., Abilene, 1984—; dir. Spirit of Freedom Alcoholic Ministeries, United Pentecostal Ch., Abilene, 1984—. Pvt. nurse coordinator Health Care Services, Abilene, 1984—. Active various health support groups, Abilene, 1984—; chmn., mem. exec. bd. Abilene Coordinating Council, 1984—. Served with USNR, 1970-76. Fellow Ministerial Alliance (pres. 1980-82). Republican. Home: 757 Westview Abilene TX 79603 Office: First Pentecostal Ch 741 S 11th St Abilene TX

BAIRD, ROBERT DAHLEN, religion educator, United Presbyterian in U.S.A.; b. Phila., June 29, 1933; s. Jesse Dahlen and Clara (Sonntag) B.; m. Patty Lo

Lutz, Dec. 18, 1950; children: Linda Sue, Stephen Robert, David Bryan, Janna Ann. B.A., Houghton Coll., 1954; B.D., Fuller Theol. Sem., Pasadena, Calif., 1954-57; S.T.M., So. Meth. U., 1959; Ph.D., U. Iowa-Iowa City, 1964. Ordained to ministry, United Presby. Ch. U.S.A., 1971. Asst. prof. religion U. Omaha, 1962-65; asst. prof. religion U. Iowa, Iowa City, 1966-69, assoc. prof., 1969-74, prof., 1974—. Author: Category Formation and the History of Peligions, 1971; (with W. R. Comstock, et. al) Religion and Man: An Introduction, 1971; (with A. Bloom) Indian and Far Eastern Religious Traditions, 1972. Editor, contbr.: Methodological Issues in Religious Studies, 1975; Religion in Modern India, 1981. Contbr. articles to profl. jours. Ford Found. fellow, 1965, 66, Soc. Religion in Higher Edn. fellow, 1965-66, Am. Inst. Indian Studies fellow, 1972. Mem. Am. Acad. Religion (co-chmn. sect. of South Asian Religion 1983-84), Assn. Asian Studies. Democrat. Office: Sch Religion Univ Iowa Iowa City IA 52242

BAKELY, DONALD CARLISLE, minister, United Methodist Church; b. Elwood, N.J., Aug. 23, 1929; s. Edwin Paul and Margaret Catherine (Decker) B.; m. Jeanne Flagg; children: Paul, Stephen, Claudia, Peter, Matthew, Lois, Bethany. B.S. in Edn., Temple U., 1952; M.Div., Temple Sch. Theology, 1955. Ordained to ministry, 1955. Assoc. pastor Centenary Tabernacle Meth. Ch., Camden, N.J., 1949-50; pastor Fairview Meth. Ch., Camden, 1950-53, Brooklawn Meth. Ch., N.J., 1953-58, Centenary Tabernacle Meth. Ch., Camden, 1958-65; exec. dir. Cross-Lines Coop. Council, Kansas City, Kans., 1965—; chmn. Commn. on Vol. Service & Action, N.Y.C., 1983—; chmn. Cross Lines Towers, 1980—. Author: If—A Big Word With the Poor, 1976; Bethy and the Mouse, 1984. Served with U.S. Army, 1946-48. Recipient Bicentennial award, Pres. Gerald Ford, 1976; Service to Mankind award Sertoma, 1978; Liberty Bell award, 1969; Appreciation award Nat. Community Action, 1981. Mem. Nat. Assn. Ecumenical Staff, Kans. E. Conf. United Meth. Ch. Home: 1708 Southwest Blvd Kansas City KS 66103 Office: Cross Lines Cooperative Council 1620 S 37th St Kansas City KS 66106

BAKER, A(RTHUR) NAPIER, minister, chaplain, American Baptist Churches in the U.S.A.; b. Balt., Oct. 17, 1939; s. Guilford LeRoy and Ella (Napier) B.; m. Louise Royston, June 16, 1961; 1 child, Linda Elisabeth. B.A. cum laude, Wake Forest Coll., 1961; B.D., Colgate Rochester Div. Sch., 1964; M.Th., 1972. Ordained to ministry Am. Bapt. Chs. the U.S.A., 1964. Pastor, Ogden Bapt. Ch., Spencerport, N.Y., 1965-72; chaplain, supr. St. Vincent Health Ctr., Erie, Pa., 1972-76; dir. pastoral care N.C. Meml. Hosp., Chapel Hill, 1976—. Contbg. author; Pastoral Care, 1983. Vice pres. Spencerport Vol. Ambulance, N.Y., 1971, Erie County Council Chs., Erie, 1975; bd. dirs. Janus Tree House, Chapel Hill, 1981—. Fellow Coll. Chaplains, Am. Protestant Hosp. Assn.; mem. N.C. Chaplains Assn., Interchurch Ministeries NW Pa. (pres. 1976), Assn. Clin. Pastoral Edn. (accreditation commn. chmn., nominating com. 1981—, cert. supr.). Democrat. Home: 206 Lexington Rd Chapel Hill NC 27514 Office: Dept Pastoral Care 6002 Patient Support Tower NC Meml Hosp Chapel Hill NC 27514

BAKER, CHARLES ESTELL, minister, Gospel Fellowship Association; b. Shelby County, Mo., Mar. 17, 1939; s. Estell S. and Lena Fay (Bowman) B.; m. Guyanne Drew, Dec. 27, 1966; children: Wesley Drew, Mayme Estelle, Samuel Woodford, Grace Anna, Charles Robert Ian. B.A., Bob Jones U., 1969, D.D., 1976. Lic. minister Southern Methodist Church, 1967; ordained to ministry Gospel Fellowship Association, 1970. Pastor So. Meth. chs. S.C. and Ala., 1968-70; pastor Ind. Meth. Ch., Tarrant, Ala., 1970-72; founder, pastor Center Point Ind. Ch., Birmingham, Ala., 1972—. Contbr. articles to mags. and newspapers. Mem. Gospel Fellowship Assn., Bob Jones U. Alumni Assn., SAR (pres. Birmingham chpt., chaplain Ala. soc.), Soc. War of 1812, United Daus. Confederacy (hon.), Soc. Cincinnati, Sons Confederate Vets (chaplain-in-chief, comdr. Ala. div.). Home: 652 16th Ave NW Birmingham AL 35215 Office: 1269 Center Point Rd Birmingham AL 35215

BAKER, HOWARD EUGENE, minister, Ch. of God (Anderson, Ind.); b. Oilton, Okla., Mar. 2, 1926; s. Oran Clint and Edith Elsie (Holeman) B.; B.Th., Warner Pacific Coll., 1952; m. Elizabeth Mae Rowden, Aug. 1, 1947; children—John, Joanne, Janet. Ordained to ministry, 1953; pastor Floyd Dist. Ch. God, Fresno, Calif., 1952-54, 1st Ch. of God, Roseburg, Oreg., 1955-59, 1st Ch. of God, Coalinga, Calif., 1959-62, San Bernardino, Calif., 1962-69, 1st Ch. of God, Walla Walla, Wash., 1969—. Chmn., Walla Walla Ministerial Fellowship, 1975-76; mem. bd. Christian edn. Ch. of God (Anderson, Ind.), 1974—, chmn., 1976—; trustee Warner Pacific Coll., 1953-69, chmn. bd., 1965-69. Mem. Walla Walla C. of C. Contbr. articles to religious jours. Home: 714 Liberty Pl Walla Walla WA 99362 Office: 928 Sturm Ave Walla Walla WA 99362

BAKER, HOWARD GLENN, minister, Lutheran Church in America; b. Concord, N.C., Feb. 14, 1955; s. Martin Flowe and Rosa Jane (Gregory) B.; m. Susan Carol Brown, July 12, 1980; 1 child, Michael Jacob. B.A. in History, Lenoire-Rhyne Coll., 1977; M.Div., Luth. Theol. Sem., 1981. Ordained to ministry Lutheran Church in America, 1981. Pastor, Holy Cross Luth. Ch., Mocksville, N.C., 1981-83, Mt. Moriah Luth. Ch., China Grove, N.C., 1983—. Recipient Eagle Scout award Boy Scouts Am., 1971, Pro deo et Patria award 1971, Vigil Order of the Arrow award, 1973; Arian Music award Rotary Club, 1976. Home: Route 3 Box 349 China Grove NC 28023

BAKER, JAMES ALLEN, minister, Lutheran Church-Missouri Synod; b. Defiance, Ohio, Feb. 7, 1952; s. Lester Elmer Baker and Marilyn Jean (Vogel-Dirr) Keeferle; m. Sandra Lee King, June 24, 1977; children: Paul David, Jonathan Adam. A.A., Concordia Luth. Jr. Coll., Ann Arbor, Mich., 1975; B.A., Concordia Sr. Coll., Ft. Wayne, Ind., 1977; M.Div., Concordia Theol. Sem., Ft. Wayne, 1982. Ordained to ministry Luth. Ch., 1982. Vicar, Zion Luth. Ch., Bancroft, Nebr., 1980-81; pastor Immanuel Luth. Congregation, Athens, Ill., 1982-84, King of Glory Luth. Ch., Sylvania, Ohio, 1984—. Office: King of Glory Luth Ch 6517 Brint Rd Sylvania OH 43560

BAKER, JAMES FREDERICK, minister, Southern Baptist Convention; b. Paris, Tenn., Apr. 4, 1952; s. Donald Trovillion and Mary Catherine (Miller) B.; m. Lisa Helen Bourgoyne, Apr. 8, 1978. B.A., Rhodes Coll., 1974; M.R.E., Southwestern Baptist Theol. Sem., 1976. Ordained to ministry Baptist Ch. 1982. Asst. minister of activities First Bapt. Ch., Memphis, 1970-74; minister of activities Immanuel Bapt. Ch., Alexandria, La., 1976-78, Park Cities Bapt. Ch., Dallas, 1978-81, First Baptist Ch., Jackson, Miss., 1981—; bd. dirs. Mikel Williams Evangelistic Ministry, Houston, 1983—, Light of the World Ministries, Jackson, 1983—, Ch. Recreation Specialities, Ft. Worth, 1984. Author: Church Recreator's Survival Guide to Publicity and Promotion, 1984; co-editor: The Best of Church Recreation Magazine, 1984. Contbr. articles to mags. Mem. La. Bapt. Recreation Assn. (pres. 1978), Miss. Bapt. Recreation Assn. (pres. 1985), Tex. Bapt. Recreation Assn. (pres. 1981). Home: 3426 Galloway Ave Jackson MS 39216 Office: First Bapt Ch 430 N President St Jackson MS 39205

BAKER, JAMES WESLEY, religious organization adminstrator, communication arts educator, General Association of Regular Baptists; b. North Hornell, N.Y., Aug. 27, 1950; s. Zane Wesley and Marilyn June (Woolever) B.; m. Rebecca Glenn McGuire, Aug. 17, 1973; children: Vanessa Grace, Nathaniel Lason. B.A., Bob Jones U., 1972; M.A., U. S.C., 1980. Asst. prof. Cedarville Coll., Ohio, 1977—; asst. dir. pub. relations Gen. Assn. Regular Bapt. Chs. Nat. Conf., Rochester, N.Y., 1968, Internat. Council Christian Chs, Cape May, N.J., 1968; pres. bd. Proclaimers, Cedarville, 1978—; cons. Radio Luce, Perugia, Italy, 1982. Contbr. articles to profl. jours. Mem. Broadcast Edn. Assn., Nat. Religious Broadcasters. Republican. Home: 46 Center St Cedarville OH 45314 Office: Cedarville Coll PO Box 601 Cedarville OH 45314

BAKER, LYLE LEE, minister, Lutheran Church; b. Robinson, Ill., Feb. 20, 1932; s. Fred and Elsie Mable (Shipman) B; children: Rodney, Jeffrey, Brian. B.A., No. Ill. U., 1960; B.D., Concordia Sem., 1970. Ordained to ministry, 1970. Pastor Zion Luth. Ch., Ocheyedan, Iowa, 1970-73, Christ Our Saviour Luth. Ch., 1973-77; pastor Celebration Luth. Fellowship, Ballwin, Mo., 1977—. Address: 658 Amberjack Ballwin MO 63111

BAKER, MARVIN WILLIAM, minister, Church of God, Anderson, Indiana; b. French Lick, Ind., July 1, 1922; s. Earl Forrest and Daisy Isabelle (Scruggs) B.; m. Faye Lucille Davidson, Sept. 5, 1943; children: Judith, Janet, Jeanne. B.Th., Anderson Coll., 1945; M.Min., Anderson Sem., 1975. Ordained to ministry, 1945. Pastor, Chs. of God, Wis., Ind. Kans., Ohio, 1945-76; assoc. state minister Ind. Ministries of the Ch. of God, Indpls., 1977-80; pastor Ch. of God, Anderson, Ind., 1980—; trustee Anderson Coll. and Sch. Theology, 1958—, chmn. coll. bd., 1976-78, 79-81; mem. exec. bd. Ind. Assn. Ch. God., 1983—. Contbr. articles to profl. jours. Recipient Disting. Alumnus award Alumni Assn. Anderson Sem., 1976. Mem. Madison County Ministerial Assn. Republican. Home: 4224 Alhambra Dr Anderson IN 46013 Office: Maple Grove Ch of God 2729 E 38th St Anderson IN 46013

BAKER, NATHAN LARRY, seminary dean, Southern Baptist Convention; b. Frierson, La., Oct. 31, 1937; s. Nathan Forrest and Anner Lara (Looper) B.; m. Wanda Marie Campbell, June 16, 1959; children: Anne Elisabeth, Angela Eileen, Andrew Nathan. B.S., East Tex. Bapt. Coll., 1959; B.D., Southwestern Bapt. Theol. Sem., 1963, Th.M., 1966, Th.D., 1974. Ordained to ministry Southern Baptist Convention, 1958. Pastor, Doddridge Bapt. Ch., Ark., 1957-59, Dial Bapt. Ch., Honey Grove, Tex., 1960-63, First Bapt. Ch., Hamilton, Tex., 1967-70, Parkview Bapt. Ch., Monroe, La., 1970-73, First Bapt. Ch., Fayetteville, Ark., 1975-78; interim pastor Leesville Bapt. Ch., Manchester, Tex., 1960, Ctr. Point Bapt. Ch., Denton, Tex., 1965, Parkview Bapt. Ch., 1973-74, Broadway Bapt. Ch., Oak Grove, Mo., 1979, First Bapt. Ch., Tarkio, Mo., 1980, Northgate Bapt. Ch., Kansas City, Mo., 1983-83, First Bapt. Ch., Sedalia, Mo., 1984-85; assoc. pastor Grace Temple Bapt. Ch., Denton, 1965-67; dir. Bapt. student union, instr. Bible Tex. Woman's U., Denton, 1963-65; mem. Tri-Rivers Bapt. Area Com., 1968-70; mem. order bus. com. La. Bapt. Conv., 1972-73; asst. prof. Christian ethics and pastoral ministry Southwestern Bapt. Theol. Sem., Fort Forth, 1973-75; chmn. resolutions com. So. Bapt. Conv., 1978; adj. prof. Christian ethics Midwestern Bapt. Theol. Sem., 1976; prof. Boyce Bible Sch., Little Rock Ctr., 1977, 78, 80, prof. Bible Ouachita Bapt. U. Extension Ctr., Fayetteville, Ark., 1976; mem. Christian Life commn. Mo. Bapt. Conv., 1980—; mem. exec. bd. Ark. Bapt. Conv.; officer Ouachita Parish Bapt. Pastor's Conf.; pres. exec. bd. Northeast La. Bapt. Student Union Corp.; mem. steering com. third century campaign Ark. Bapt. State Conv.; frequent preacher, lectr. and Bible tchr. for youth and student groups, conf. and workshop leader, leader; speaker religious emphasis weeks and family life confs. Author: Mission Action Guide: Combating Moral Problems, 1968. Contbr. articles, chpts., curriculum materials and book revs. to religious publs. Bd. dirs. Tex. Alcohol Narcotics Edn., Inc., 1967-70, Ozark Literacy Council; dir. Hamilton county unit Am. Cancer Soc., 1968-70; mem. adv. com. NEH, Northeast La. U.; participant emerging needs survey City of Monroe, 1972; mem. United Community Services Northwest Ark., Northwest Regional Alcoholism Council; mem. bicentennial com. Fayetteville, 1976. Teaching fellow Southwestern Bapt. Theol. Sem., 1967-68. Mem. Assn. Am. Marriage and Family Therapists (adv. council Kansas City chpt. 1982—), Assn. Profl. Edn. for Ministry, Soc. Christian Ethics. Lodge: Rotary. Office: Midwestern Bapt Theol Sem 5001 N Oak St Kansas City MO 64118

BAKER, RALEIGH OTTO, JR., ch. ofcl., Baptist Ch.; b. Charlotte, N.C., Sept. 1, 1922; s. Raleigh Otto and Ruth Lillian (Bickett) B.; A.A., Mars Hill Coll., 1948; B.A. cum laude, Wake Forest U., 1950; B.D., Southwestern Bapt. Theol. Sem., 1953; D. Ministry, Luther Rice Sem., 1974; m. Phyllis Ann McKinnon, Dec. 19, 1948; children—Jeannie Lynn, William Raleigh. Ordained to ministry So. Baptist Conv., 1950; minister Stanfield (Tex.) Bapt. Ch., 1951-53, Commonwealth Bapt. Ch., Charlotte, N.C., 1953-58, First Bapt. Ch., Cramerton, N.C., 1958-63, Norview Bapt. Ch., Norfolk, Va., 1963-73; asso. exec. dir. Va. Bapt. Homes, Inc., Culpeper, Va., 1973—. Mem. City Sch. Bd., Cramerton, N.C., 1962-63; mem. Rappahannock-Rapidan Planning Dist. Commn., 1974—. Trustee Gardner Webb Coll., 1961-63; bd. dirs., v.p., pres.-elect Va. Assn. of Homes for Aging, 1973-77. Recipient Citizens award Mars Hill Coll., 1948. Mem. Bapt. Pub. Relations Assn., Va. Assn. of Homes for Aging. Rotarian. Contbr. articles to profl. jours. Book reviewer So. Bapt. Sunday Sch. Bd., 1971-73. Office: Box 191 Culpeper VA 22701

BAKER, WILLIAM JOHN, lay church worker, Assemblies of God; b. Galsgow, Mont., Apr. 11, 1947; s. John Alfred and Sue (Penner) B.; m. Marvel Ann Daywitt, Jan. 21, 1978; children: Lori Lynn, Chad Allen. B.S. in Computer Sci., Nat. Coll.-Rapid City, S.D., 1974. Christ ambassador's pres. Assembly of God, Lead, S.D., 1977-79; youth tchr. Sunday Sch. Assemblies of God, Lead, 1975-80; comdr. Royal Rangers, Lead, 1976-81, 83—. Data processing control scheduler Homestake Mining Co., Lead, 1974—. Served with USMC, 1969-73. Club: Mixed Bowling League (pres.). Lodge: Kiwanis (pres. 1985-86). Avocations: painting; coin and stamp collecting; 10K races. Office: Homestake Mining Co 215 W Main St Lead SD 57754

BAKER, WILLIAM THOMAS, minister, So. Baptist Conv.; b. Springfield, Ill., Sept. 4, 1943; s. Harold Thomas and Leta Elizabeth (Hamilton) B.; B.A., Ouachita Bapt. U., 1966; M.R.E., Southwestern Bapt. Theol. Sem., 1970; m. Mari Kay Kirkpatrick, Aug. 20, 1964; children—William Harold, Kristi Kay. Ordained to ministry, 1974; minister of youth Watson Chapel Bapt. Ch., Pine Bluff, Ark., 1963-66; minister of edn. 1st Bapt. Ch., Grapevine, Tex., 1968-70; minister of edn. and youth Spring (Tex.) Bapt. Ch., 1970-72, LaBelle Haven Bapt. Ch., Memphis, 1972-74; minister of youth and recreation Green Acres Bapt. Ch., Tyler, Tex., 1974—; guest lectr. East Tex. Bapt. Coll., Glorieta Bapt. Conf. Center. Organizer ch. softball and basketball leagues Tyler, 1974-76; instl. rep. Boy Scouts Am., Tyler, 1975—. Mem. Smith County Bapt. Assn., S.W. Football Ofcls. Assn., S.W. Basketball Ofcls. Assn. Contbr. articles to religious jours. Home: 3823 Belle Mere St Tyler TX 75701 Office: 1612 Leo Lynn St Tyler TX 75701

BAKEWELL, ANDERSON EDWARD, priest, Roman Cath. Ch.; b. St. Louis, Sept. 18, 1913; s. Edward Lilburn and Mildred Cecilia (Anderson) B.; B.A., St. Louis U., 1937, postgrad., 1937-39; postgrad. Woodstock Coll., 1944-47, St. Mary's Coll., India, 1948-52. Joined S.J., 1942; ordained priest Roman Catholic Ch., 1951; asst. pastor Raj Anandpur, Bihar, India, 1952-54; adminstr. De Britto House, Gomoh, Bihar, 1954-55; asst. pastor Holy Trinity Ch., Georgetown, Washington, 1955-67; pastor Our Lady of Sorrows Ch., Delta, Alaska, 1967—. Fellow Royal, Am. geog. socs.; mem. Arctic inst. North Am., Am. Polar Soc., Am. Alpine Club, Himalayan Club. Home and office: Our Lady of Sorrows Box 446 Delta AK 99737

BAKKER, JAMES ORSEN See *Who's Who in America*, 43rd edition.

BALAS, JOHN PAUL, III, minister; Lutheran Church in America; b. Charleroi Pa., June 5, 1940; s. John P. Jr. and Mary (Mihovich) B.; m. Karen Ann Schall, Nov. 24, 1962; children: John Paul IV, James Andrew, Michael Thomas. B.A., Thiel Coll., 1962; B.D., Luth. Sem., Gettysburg, Pa., 1966; M.Ed., U. Pitts., 1971, Ph.D., 1980. Ordained to ministry Lutheran Ch Am., 1966. Pastor Ascension Luth. Ch., McKees Rocks, Pa., 1966-69; campus pastor Luth. Student Found., Pitts., 1969-74; pastor Prince of Peace Luth. Ch., Pleasant Hills Pa., 1974-78; coll. pastor Thiel Coll., Greenville, Pa., 1978—; trustee The Luth. Theol. Sem., Gettysburg, Pa., 1982—. Mem. Luth. Campus Ministry Assn., Luth. Acad. for Scholarship, Am. Assn. for Counseling and Devel. Republican. Home: 16 Holiday Ln Greenville PA 16125 Office: Thiel Coll Greenville PA 16125

BALCH, GLENN MCCLAIN, JR., minister, United Methodist Church; b. Shattuck, Okla., Nov. 1, 1937; s. Glenn McClain and Marjorie (Daily) B.; m. Diana Gale Seeley, Oct. 15, 1970; children: Bryan, Gayle, Wesley, John Rodden. B.A., Southwestern State U., Okla., 1962; B.D., Phillips U., 1965; LL.D. (hon.), Los Angeles Coll. Law, 1968, J.D., 1969, LL.M., 1971; M.A., Chapman Coll., 1973, 75; Ph.D., U.S. Internat. U., 1978. Ordained to ministry United Meth. Ch. as deacon, 1962, as elder, 1964. Asst. dean. Chapman Coll., Orange, Calif., 1970-75; assoc. to v.p. Pepperdine U., Los Angeles, 1975-76; minister Goodrich Meml. United Meth. Ch., Norman, Okla., 1965-66, First United Meth. Ch., Barstow, Calif., 1966-70, Brea United Meth. Ch., Calif., 1977—; mem. conf. bd. evangelism, 1968-70, conf. camp bd., 1969-70, conf. bd. global ministries, 1979-81. Co-author: Investigating Child Abuse, 1985. Contbr. articles to profl. jours. Mem. Orange County Human Services Adv. Bd., Calif., 1984—, Orange County Child Abuse Council, 1984—, Brea Econ. Devel. Council, 1985—, Served with USMC, 1956-58. Named Man of Yr., Barstow Jaycees, 1969, Humanitarian of Yr., Los Angeles Chiropractic Assn., 1977. Mem. Calif-Pacific Conf. United Meth. Ch., Calif. Marriage and Family Therapists Assn., Am. Soc. Clin. Hypnosis, Brea Ministerial Assn. (past pres.), Brea C. of C. (bd. dirs.). Lodges: Masons, Shriners, Elks, Rotary. Avocation: piloting. Home: 1016 Steele Dr Brea CA 92621 Office: Brea United Meth Ch 480 N State College Blvd Brea CA 92621

BALCOMB, RAYMOND EVERETT, church official, United Methodist Church; b. Bernardino, Calif., Feb. 8, 1923; s. Jean Bart and Rose (Gibbs) B.; m. Hazel F. Schlasser, June 18, 1944; children: Bernice, Rosemary, Joanne, Gene, Scott. A.B., San Jose State Coll., 1944; S.T.B., Boston U., 1947, Ph.D., 1951. Ordained deacon United Meth. Ch., 1946, elder, 1948. Pastor, Holbrook, Mass., 1945-49, Federated Ch., Ashland, Mass., 1949-51, Sellwood Meth. Ch., Portland, Oreg., 1951-54, Medford 1st Meth. Ch. (Oreg.), 1954-57, Corvallis 1st Meth. Ch. (Oreg.), 1957-63, 1st United Meth. Ch., Portland, 1963-82; dist. supt. United Meth. Ch., Portland, 1982—. Author: Stir What You've Got!, 1967; Try Reading the Bible, 1970, also articles. Republican. Home: 868 SW Troy Portland OR 97219 Office: United Meth Ch Center 1505 SW 18 Portland OR 97201

BALDWIN, LEWIS V., minister, religion educator, National Baptist Convention U.S.A.; b. Camden, Ala., Sept. 17, 1949; s. L.V. and Flora Bell (Holt) B.; m. Jacqueline Loretta Laws, Sept. 29, 1979. B.A., Talladega Coll., 1971; M.A., Colgate-Rochester Div. Sch., 1973, M.Div., 1975; Ph.D., Northwestern U., 1980. Ordained to ministry Nat. Bapt. Conv., 1978. Asst. pastor Englewood United Meth. Ch., Chgo., 1976, Sherman United Meth. Ch., Evanston, Ill., 1977-79; asst prof. Coll. of Wooster, Ohio, 1981-82, Colgate U., Hamilton, N.Y., 1982-84, Vanderbilt U., Nashville, 1984—. Author: Invisible Strands in African Methodism, 1983. Contbr. articles to profl. jours. Recipient Key to the City award Wilmington, Del., 1981; named Outstanding Young Man of Am., U.S. Jaycees, 1975, 1980. Mem. Am. Soc. Ch. History, Am. Acad. Religion, Soc. for Study of Black Religion, NAACP. Home: 2006 26th Ave S Nashville TN 37212

BALKE, VICTOR, bishop, Roman Catholic Church; b. Meppen, Ill., Sept. 29, 1931; ed. St. Mary of the Lake Sem. Ordained priest, 1958; bishop of Crookston (Minn.), 1976—. Address: 1200 Memorial Dr PO Box 610 Crookston MN 56716*

BALL, ALICE E., religious organization executive. Gen. sec. Am. Bible Soc., N.Y.C. Office: Am Bible Soc 1865 Broadway New York NY 10023*

BALL, HAROLD GENE, minister, Southern Baptist Convention; b. Newport, Tenn., June 29, 1944; s. Wiliam Robert and Nancy Belle (Holbert) B.; m. Geraldine Vess, June 16, 1963; children: Terry Lynn, Ronny Darin. B.A., Carson-Newman Coll., 1977; M.Div. with Langs., Southeastern Bapt. Theol. Sem., 1981. Ordained to ministry Bapt. Ch., 1968. Pastor, Calvary Bapt. Ch., Newport Ch. (Tenn.), 1968-73, Flat Gap Bapt. Ch., New Market, Tenn., 1973-77, Grassy Creek Bapt. Ch., Bullock, N.C., 1977-81, Eastlawn Bapt. Ch., Burlington, N.C., 1981—; moderator East Tenn. Bapt. Assn., Newport, 1972-73, Jefferson County Bapt. Assn., Jefferson City, 1976-77; pres. Mount Zion Bapt. Assn. Pastor's Conf., Burlington, 1982-83. Mem. Pi Tau Chi. Democrat. Home: 2258 Wilkins St Burlington NC 27215 Office: Eastlawn Bapt Ch 432 N Sellars Mill Rd Burlington NC 27215

BALL, IRVING R., minister, Free Meth. Ch.; b. Glens Falls, N.Y., Sept. 5, 1920; s. Owen Levi and Mable Lillian (Varney) B.; grad. Chesbro Sem., North Chili, N.Y., 1942; m. Luona Agnes Harvey, July 26, 1941; children—Irving, Marvin, Kevin. Ordained to ministry, 1945; pastor chs., Balt., Washington, Tulsa, Oklahoma City; pastor Largo (Fla.) Free Meth. Ch., 1976—. Mem. Fla. Conf. Free Meth. Ch. Home: 3093 Meadowview Ave Largo FL 33540 Office: 380 Fulton Dr S Largo FL 33540

BALL, LARRY K., minister, educator, Presbyterian Church; b. Decatur, Ill., Nov. 4, 1939; s. Bill O. and Dorothy (DeVore) B.; m. Kristin Ann Wiedbush, June 8, 1960; 1 child, Mindy Kay. B. Music Edn., Millikin U., 1962, Mus.M., 1964; D.Mus. Arts., U. So. Calif., 1981. Cert. ch. musician Presbyterian Ch., 1979. Minister of music Trinity Lutheran Ch., Decatur, Ill., 1960-62, Central Christian Ch., Decatur, 1962-66, First Presbyn. Ch., Orange, Calif., 1966—. Bd. dirs. Choristers Guild, Dallas, 1976—. Dir. choral studies Rancho Santiago Coll., Santa Ana, Calif., 1975—. Author music edn. materials. Mem. Choristers Guild, Am. Choral Dirs. Assn., Hymn Soc. Am., Am. Guild English Handbell Ringers, Calif. Choral Condrs. Guild. Avocations: golf, gardening, reading. Home: 2320 N Lowell Ln Santa Ana CA 92706 Office: First Presbyn Ch 191 N Orange St Orange CA 92666

BALL, ROBERT JAMES, minister, Churches of Christ; b. Mammoth Spring, Ark., July 2, 1949; s. George Gray and Ruth Lyle (Charlton) B.; m. Kathy Sharlene Haney, June 1, 1967; children: Kathy Michelle, Carolyn Jean. A.A. Internat. Bible Coll., Florence, Ala., 1983, B.A., 1984; M.A., Ala. Christian Sch. Religion, 1985, postgrad., 1985—. Ordained to ministry Churches of Christ. Evangelism dir. Coll. Ch. of Christ, Florence, 1980-81; evangelist Priceville Ch. of Christ, Decatur, Ala., 1981—; chapel Bible instr. Tri-County Bible Sch., Decatur, 1984—. Contbr. articles to Fulton County Gospel News, 1981, Hoffman Heights Herald, 1984. Named one of Outstanding Young Men of Am., U.S. Jaycees, 1982. Republican. Avocations: golf; fishing. Home and Office: Route 4 Box 186 Decatur AL 35603

BALL, VARL LEROY, minister, So. Bapt. Conv.; b. Eagle Rock, Mo., Oct. 31, 1931; s. Ethel Omen and Edith Pansy (Carter) B.; A.A., SW Bapt. Coll., 1958; B.A., Baylor U., 1960; B.D., Golden Gate Bapt. Theol. Sem., 1964; m. Ilene Faye Comstock, June 27, 1954; children—Tony, Carol, Artie, Kyle. Ordained to ministry, 1958; pastor Rock Creek Bapt. Ch., Auburn, Calif., 1964-67, 1st Bapt. Ch., Carrizozo, N.Mex., 1967-70, 1st Bapt. Ch., Hermitage, Mo., 1970-76, Roaring River Bapt. Ch., Eagle Rock, 1976—. Steward chmn. Sierra Foothills Assn., 1965-66; ch. tng. dir. Mountain Valley Assn., 1967-70; chmn. inner bd. Osage Pomme de Terre and Benton County Assn., 1971-76, moderator, 1975-76; active Resort Lake Ministry. Mem. Hermitage Sch. Bd., 1974-75; mem. Election Bd., 1970-75. Home and Office: PO Box 77 Eagle Rock MO 65641

BALL, WILLIAM LOCKHART, JR., retired minister, Southern Baptist Convention; b. Richmond, Va., June 24, 1914; s. William L. and Marion S. (Terrell) B.; B.S. cum laude, Furman U., 1935; D.D. (hon.), 1955; Th.M., So. Bapt. Theol. Sem., 1939; m. Bessie Bagby Rice, May 2, 1947; children: William Lockhart III, Blair Terrell, David Alderman, Joel Drake, Betsy. Ordained to ministry So. Bapt. Conv., 1942. Bapt. campus minister U. Ala., 1939-40; assoc. pastor First Bapt. Ch., Clinton, Miss., 1940-42; pastor First Bapt. Ch., Belton, S.C., 1946-51, Oakland Bapt. Ch., Rock Hill, S.C., 1951-60, Fernwood Bapt. Ch., Spartanburg, S.C., 1960-76; assoc. pastor, pastoral ministries First Bapt. Ch., Spartanburg, 1976—; pastor emeritus Oakland Bapt. Ch., Rock Hill, S.C., 1984—; trustee So. Bapt. Theol. Sem., Louisville, 1950-64; treas. Spartan Bapt. Assn., 1960—; pres. Gen. Bd. S.C. Bapt. Conv., 1968-70; mem. exec. com. Greater Spartanburg Ministries, 1975—. Mem. mayor's com. Crime Prevention, 1964-65, Gov.'s Council on Mental Retardation, 1965; pres. Council Spartansburg (S.C.) County, 1968-70; bd. dirs. S.C. Bd. Mental Health, 1961-65; United Way, Spartanburg, 1974; trustee Anderson (S.C.) Coll., 1948-52, Furman U., Greenville, S.C., 1969-74, S.C.-Piedmont chpt. Nat. Multiple Sclerosis Soc., 1975—, Connie Maxwell Children's Home, 1980—; mem. Spartanburg FACT Bd., 1977-80; mem. adv. com. Community Long-Term Care, 1980-85. Served as chaplain USN, 1943-46. Recipient Katherine Hamilton Vol. of Year award Ind. Mental Health Meml. Found. 1964. Mem. Spartanburg County Ministerial Assn. (pres. 1965), Spartanburg County Mental Health Assn. (dir. 1960-62). Lodge: Kiwanis (pres. 1970-71, Citizen of Yr. 1980). Home: 201 Emory Rd Spartanburg SC 29302 Office: 250 E Main St Spartansburg SC 29302

BALLARD, RONALD DOYLE, minister, educator, United Methodist Church; b. Houston, June 25, 1934; s. Brents Larimore and Irene Mae (Hodges) B.; B.S., N. Tex. State U., 1956; M.Div., Candler Sch. Theology, 1960; Ph.D., U. Glasgow (Scotland), 1971; m. Wanda Marie Tatum, Nov. 15, 1960; children: Rhonda Leigh, Ronald Kyle, Christa Lynn. Ordained to ministry, 1960; pastor Allgood Rd. United Meth. Ch., Stone Mountain, Ga., 1960-66, 1st United Meth. Ch., Forsyth, Ga., 1968-70, Allen Meml. United Meth. Ch., Oxford, Ga., 1970-71; prof. religion, dean Sch. Sci. and Humanities, Tex. Wesleyan Coll., Fort Worth, 1979—. Pres. Diakoneo, Inc., Fort Worth, 1973—, Ronald D. Ballard Enterprises, Inc., 1984—. Named Educator of Year, Student Assn., 1974. Mem. Am. Acad. Religion, Coll. Theology Soc., Hastings Ctr., Am. Assn. Higher Edn., Am. Council Edn. Office: PO Box 50010 Fort Worth TX 76105

BALLENTINE, WYMAN WAYNE, minister, United Meth. Ch.; b. Blythewood, S.C., Mar. 25, 1925; s. Walter James and Eula Mae (Ethredge) B.; B.S., Clemson U., 1950; M.Div., Duke U., 1953; M.A., Ball State U., 1973; M.A., L.I. U., 1974; m. Martha Ann Burnette, Mar. 1, 1958; children—Barry Wendell, Cary Layne, Ann Marie, Dennis Brent. Ordained deacon, 1952, full connection and elder, 1954; pastor chs., S.C., 1952-66; chaplain U.S. Army, 1966—, Fort Leonard Wood, Mo., 1974—. Asst. sec. Conf. Bd. Christian Social Concerns, 1954-60; mem. Conf. Bd. Pensions, 1960-65; pres. Union County Ministerial Assn., 1965; chaplain S.C. Assn. Rescue Squards, 1958-60, Union Civil Air Patrol, 1962-64. Bd. dirs. U.S.C. Wesley Found., 1964-65; mem. Mayor's Com. on Alcohol, Hartsville, S.C., 1958-61; rep. S.C. Gov.'s Council on Alcoholism, 1959. Mem. Assn. U.S. Army, Mil. Chaplains Assn., Am. Assn. Sex Educators, Counselors and Therapists. Home: 22 Kirby St Fort Leonard Wood MO 65473 Office: Office of the Post Chapel Center Pastor Fort Leonard Wood MO 65473

BALSER, GLENNON, clergyman. Pres. Advent Christian Church, Wilmington, N.C. Office: Advent Christian Ch 5540 S College Rd Wilmington NC 28403*

BALTAKIS, PAUL ANTANAS, Roman Catholic bishop; b. Troskunai, Panevezys, Lithuania, Jan. 1, 1925; came to U.S., 1954; s. Juozas and Apolonia (Lauzikaite) B. B.Ph., Franciscan U., Rekem, Belgium, 1948; B.Th., Franciscan U., St. Truiden, Belgium, 1953. Ordained priest, Roman Catholic Ch. Asst. pastor Resurrection Parish, Toronto, Ont., Can., 1953-69; adminstr. Lithuanian Cultural Ctr., Bklyn., 1969-79; counselor Franciscan Fathers, Kennebunkport, Maine, 1964-79, superior, Toronto, Ont., Can., 1964-67, Superior, Bklyn., 1973-79, provincial superior, Kennebunkport, Maine, 1979-84; bishop Lithuanian Roman Catholics, Bklyn., 1984—; nat. spiritual dir. Lithuanian Scouts., Bklyn., 1964—.

BALTZELL, ANNE POMEROY, hospital chaplain, American Baptist Churches in the U.S.A.; b. Richmond, Va., July 8, 1945; d. Clinton Jesse and Nancy Burwell (Williams) P.; m. James Ellsworth Baltzell III, Aug. 30, 1969. B.A, Westhampton Coll., 1967; M.Div., Colgate Rochester Divinity Sch., 1971. Ordained to ministry Am. Bapt. Chs. U.S.A., 1971. Campus minister, Miami U., Oxford, Ohio, 1974-75; staff chaplain Bethesda, Hosp., Cin., 1974-75, chaplain resident, 1975-76; dir. chaplains dept. Mpls. Childrens Med. Center, 1976—. Mem. statements of concern com. Am. Bapt. Chs. U.S.A., Valley Forge, Pa., 1981—; del. Am. Bapt. Conv., Cleve., 1983. Mem. adv. bd. Childhood Cancer, Mpls., 1980-81. Recipient Leadership cert. Mpls. YWCA, 1978. Fellow Coll. Chaplains Am. Protestant Hosp. Assn.; mem. Assn. Clin. Pastoral Edn. (gen. assemby 1983—), AAUW. Office: Mpls Children's Med Center 2525 Chicago Ave S Minneapolis MN 55404

BANCROFT, STEPHEN HALTOM, priest, Episcopal Church; b. Kansas City, Mo., Aug. 7, 1946; s. John Sidney and Myrah Allen (Haltom) B.; m. Margaret Jane Kubin, Dec. 28, 1971; children: Nathan Paul, Aaron Stephen, Jessica Margaret. B.A., Tex. A&M U., 1969; M.Div., Va. Theol. Sem., 1972. Ordained priest, 1972. Chaplain, Stephen F. Austin State U., Nacogdoches, Tex., 1972-75; asst. rector St. John the Divine Ch., Houston, 1975-78; rector St. Cyprian's Ch. and Sch., Lufkin, Tex., 1978—; mem., chmn. camping com. Camps and Conf. Ctr., Diocese of Tex., 1982—, chmn. youth dept., 1976-81, mem. steering com. div. coll. ministry, 1983—. Trustee Palmer Drug Abuse program, Dallas, 1982—, Lufkin Family Practice Residency Clinic, Lufkin, 1984—; pres. Christian Info. and Service Ctr., Lufkin, 1983. Mem. Angelina County Ministerial Alliance (pres. 1981). Republican. Lodge: Rotary. Home: 116 W Menefee Lufkin TX 75901 Office: Saint Cyprians Episcopal Church and Sch 919 S John Redditt Dr Lufkin TX 75901

BANDY, BETTE LINDE, ch. music dir.; b. Galveston, Tex., Apr. 16, 1926; d. Knud Wolmer and Alice (Lasserre) Linde; grad. St. Cecelia Sch. Music, Fernandina, Fla., 1943; student John R. Neal Coll. Law, Knoxville, Tenn., 1945-47. Soloist, asst. choir dir., Sunday sch. pianist St. Peter's Episcopal Ch., Fernandina, 1940-43; pipe organist, choir dir. Okolona

Presbyn. Ch., Louisville, 1958-67; organist, choir dir. Beechmont Presbyn. Ch., Louisville, 1968-74; dir. music Kenwood Bapt. Ch., Louisville, 1974—. Legal sec. and bookkeeper law firm, Louisville, 1968—. Composer ch. music. Home: 4501 Walton Ct Louisville KY 40213 Office: 26th Floor Citizens Plaza Louisville KY 40202

BANDY, JOHN JAMES, JR., minister, Southern Baptist Convention; b. Atlanta, Aug. 14, 1918; s. John James and Ruth (Brannon) B.; B.C.S., U. Ga., 1948; M.Div., So. Bapt. Theol. Sem., 1951, Th.M., 1952; postgrad. Ind. U., 1953-55; m. Ala Jones, Jan. 12, 1952; children—Darla Alane, John James. Ordained to ministry, 1949; pastor Avoca (Ind.) Bapt. Ch., 1949-55, Judson Bapt. Ch., Greenville, S.C., 1955-77; trustee S.C. Bapt. Hosp., 1969-72, Bethea Home, Darlington, S.C., 1975-79; organizer 14 world mission seminar tours; chmn. study com. on housing for aged Greenville Bapt. Assn., 1974-76; founder, chmn. bd. trustees Greenville Bapt. Retirement Community, 1976—, minister of devel., 1977-81; cons. Countryside Manor Retirement Community, Easley, S.C., 1984—. Mem. Greenville County Council for Aging, 1968-84. Address: 16 Hampton Ct Greenville SC 29609

BANKS, MICHAEL PAT, lay religious worker, So. Bapt. Conv.; b. Pittsburg, Tex., Aug. 17, 1955; s. Harrom Marshall and Mary Louise (Parrish) B.; student E. Tex. State U., 1973—. Dir. music and youth 1st Bapt. Ch., Omaha, Tex., 1973-75, music dir. jr. high choir 1st Bapt. Ch., Mount Pleasant, Tex., summer, 1975; interim music dir. 1st Bapt. Ch., Naples, Tex., 1975; music dir. Pine St. Bapt. Ch., Winnsboro, Tex., 1976—. Pvt. tchr. voice, Mount Pleasant, 1974—. Mem. Tex. Music Educators Assn., Phi Mu Alpha Sinfonia. Home: 808 W 5th St Mount Pleasant TX 75455 Office: 611 W Pine St Winnsboro TX 75494

BANNAN, MARGARET M., Roman Catholic provincial minister; b. Tacoma, Wash., Sept. 9, 1925; d. James Dennis and Margaret Ann (Creedican) B. B.A., Rosary Hill Coll., 1961; M.A. in Psychology, Cath. U., 1963. Entered Order Sisters of St. Francis of Penance and Christian Charity; prin. Annunciation Sch., Arcadia, Calif., 1955-60; dir. novices Sisters of St. Francis, Redwood City, Calif., 1964-68; counselor Alverno High Sch., Sierra Madre, Calif., 1970-78; provincial minister Sisters of St. Francis, Redwood City, Calif., 1978—; trustee Marian Med. Ctr., Santa Maria, Calif., 1976-83, St. Francis Med. Ctr., Lynwood, Calif., 1976-81, Sisters of St. Francis, Redwood City, 1978—, St. Mary Ctr., Toledo, 1982—. Mem. Leadership Conf. of Women Religious (v.p. 1981-84). Democrat. Office: Sisters of St Francis of Penance and Christian Charity 3910 Bret Harte Dr PO Box 1028 Redwood City CA 94064

BARBER, CYRIL JOHN, author, counselor, educator; b. Baxley, Eng., May 18, 1934; came to U.S., 1962, naturalized, 1976; s. Charles Stanley and Muriel (Cook) B.; Th.M., Dallas Theol. Sem., 1968; D.Lit., U. London, 1968; M.A. in L.S., Rosary Coll., 1971; D.Ministry, Talbot Theol. Sem., 1979; m. Aldyth Ayleen, Apr. 13, 1957; children—Allan, Stephen. Ordained to ministry Ind. Fundamental Chs. of Am., 1963. Chmn. dept. Bible expn. Winnipeg Bible Coll., Man., Can., 1967-69; instr. N.T., head librarian Trinity Evang. Div. Sch., Deerfield, Ill., 1969-72; asso. prof., dir. library Rosemead Grad. Sch. Psychology, Calif., 1972-82; prof. Internat. Christian Grad. U., Calif., 1979-83; counseling assoc. Insight for Living, 1982—. Author: The Minister's Library, 1974, rev., 1985; God Has The Answer, 1974; Searching for Identity, 1975; Nehemiah and The Dynamics of Effective Leadership, 1976; Leadership: The Dynamics of Success, 1982; Introduction to Theological Research, 1982; Ruth: A Story of God's Grace, 1983; (with A. Barber) Your Marriage Has Real Possibilities, 1984; (with A. Barber) You Can Have a Happy Marriage, 1984; Habakkuk and Zephaniah, 1985; numerous others; contbg. author: Zondervan's Pictorial Ency. of The Bible, 1975; contbg. editor: Jour. of Psychology and Theology, 1972—. Mem. ALA, Am. Theol. Library Assn., Royal Soc. Lit., Beta Phi Mu. Home: 2729 Fragancia Ave Hacienda Heights CA 91745 Office: 211 E Imperial Hwy Suite 100 Fullerton CA 92635

BARBOUR, JOHN DICKINSON, religious studies educator, United Church of Christ; b. Kalamazoo, Aug. 8, 1951; s. Ian G. and Deanne (Kern) B.; m. Margaret Ann Ojala, Aug. 26, 1978. B.A., Oberlin Coll., 1973; M.A., U. Chgo., 1975, Ph.D., 1981. Asst. prof. St. Olaf Coll., Northfield, Minn., 1982—. Author: Tragedy as a Critique of Virtue, 1984; contbr. articles to religious jours. U. Chgo. fellow, 1980, Susan Rosenberger prize, 1983. Mem. Am. Acad. Religion. Home: PO Box 83 Dundas MN 55019 Office: Dept Religion St Olaf Coll Northfield MN 55057

BARCUS, DANIEL DEAN, minister, Christian Ch.; b. Champaign, Ill., Mar. 20, 1943; s. Ernest A. and Frances G. (Jones) B.; student Lincoln Christian Coll.; B.Christian Edn., Platte Valley Bible Coll., 1967; m. Joyce Elaine Halladey, Mar. 3, 1967; children—Mark Daniel, Amber Joyce, Shelli Jean, Danette Elaine. Ordained to ministry, 1967; pastor Morrill, Nebr., 1966-68; caretaker Colo. Christian Service Camp, Como, summer 1968; minister Christian Ch., Elbert, Colo., 1969; asso. minister N.E. Christian Ch., Grand Junction, Colo., 1971-72; maint. man, dorm dad Intermountain Bible Coll., Grand Junction, 1971; pastor 1st Christian Ch., Wheatland, Wyo., 1972—. Pres. Wyo. Evangelistic Assn., 1975-76; sch. bus driver Platte County Sch., Dist. No. 1, part-time 1974-76; salesman Cactus Jack's Western Wear, Wheatland, Wyo., part-time 1972-76; instr. Wheatland Jr. Riding Club, 1972—; mem. Wyo. Emergency Med. Technicians, 1973—. Home: 1255 Walnut St Wheatland WY 82201 Office: 13th St Walnut St Wheatland WY 82201

BARDES, GEORGE FRANCIS, priest, Roman Catholic Church. b. N.Y.C., Nov. 3, 1918; s. George F. and Mary E. (Gowlan) B. B.A., St. Joseph's Coll., 1940; S.T.B., Cath. U., 1944, S.T.L., 1945, S.T.D., 1952. Ordained priest Roman Catholic Ch., 1944. Assoc. pastor St. John the Evangelist Ch., White Plains, N.Y., 1949-70; pastor Ch. Sts. John and Paul, Larchmont, N.Y., 1970-81, St. Thomas More Ch., N.Y.C., 1981—; prof. theology Good Counsel Coll., White Plains, 1952-53; prof. social scis. St. Joseph's Sem., Yonkers, N.Y., 1960-70; campus minister Westchester Community Coll., White Plains, 1950-70; exec. sec. Commn. for Inter-Parish Financing, Archdiocese N.Y., 1969—. Author: Distribution of Rights in a Modern Corporation, 1952. Mem. Pub. Employment Relations Br., White Plains, 1967. Mem. Cath. Theol. Soc. Am., Cath. Sch. Assn. (bd. dirs.). Home and Office: 65 E 89th St New York NY 10128

BARDSLEY, JOHN WALLACE, minister, United Methodist Church; b. Appalachia, Va., Mar. 1, 1921; s. John Wallace and Mamie Josephine (Hartsock) B.; m. Sara Jo Greever, Sept. 5, 1953; children: Donna Jane, John Joseph. B.A., Emory and Henry Coll., 1951; M.Div., Drew Theol. Sem., 1954; postgrad. Drew Theol. Sch., 1959-60; D.Religion, Geneva-St. Albans Theol. Coll., 1976. Ordained to ministry, 1953. Pastor, Grace United Meth. Ch., St. Albans, N.Y., 1954-60, Smithtown United Meth. Ch., N.Y., 1960-83, Huntington/Cold Spring Harbor United Meth. Ch., Huntington, N.Y., 1983—; trustee Geneva-St. Albans Theol. Coll., Knoxville, 1976-80; pres. Huntington Clergy Assn., 1983—. Pres. bd. visitors Kings Park Psychiat. Ctr., 1974—; mem. Fire Dept., Smithtown, N.Y., 1960-70, chief of chaplains, 1962-70; founding mem. Smithtown Narcotics Council, 1964; trustee Harbor Country Day Sch., 1962-72; chmn. com. of clergy/adminstrs. Smithtown Central Sch. Dist., 1976; arbitrator Better Bus. Bur., 1981—. Mem. Christian Assn. for Psychol. Studies, Am. Assn. Christian Counsellors, Order of St. Luke the Physician. Lodges: Rotary, Masons. Address: 75 Tanyard Ln Huntington NY 11743

BARELA, RICHARD LEO, priest, Roman Cath. Ch.; b. Santa Fe, Apr. 12, 1948; s. Leo and Stella (Martinez) B.; B.S., Coll. of Santa Fe, 1970; M.Div., St. Meinrad Sem., 1974. Ordained priest, 1974; asso. pastor Our Lady of Guadalupe Ch., Albuquerque, 1974-76, St. Bernadette Ch., Albuquerque, 1976—. Mem. Priests' Senate, Archdiocese of Santa Fe; chaplain Boy Scouts Am.; participant religious TV programs, Santa Fe. Bd. dirs. Camp Fire Girls, Job Corps of Albuquerque. Home and Office: 1311 Avenida Aliso Santa Fe NM 87501

BARFIELD, KENNY DALE, minister, religion educator, Church of Christ; b. Florence, Ala., Nov. 17, 1947; s. Henry Perry and Bernice Elizabeth (Olive) B.; m. Nancy Ann Cordray, Aug. 7, 1970; children: Amber Elizabeth, Lora Allyn. B.A., David Lipscomb Coll., 1969; M.A., U. Ala., 1972. Minister, Highland Park Ch. of Christ, Muscle Shoals, Ala., 1969-74, Jackson Heights Ch. of Christ, Florence, Ala., 1974-78, Sherrod Ave. Ch. of Christ, Florence, 1978—; educator Mars Hill Bible Sch., Florence, 1969—. Dir. T.B. Larimore Forensic Soc., Florence, 1969—. Editor: 50 Golden Years: NFL Nationals, 1980. Recipient Coach of Yr. award Commercial Appeal, 1976; Tchr. of Yr. award Ala. Speech and Theatre Assn., 1977; Outstanding Young Religious Leader award Ala. Jaycees, 1977; Disting Service award Nat. Forensic League, 1981. Mem. Ala. Forensic Educator's Assn. (pres. 1976, 81, 85), Deep South Forensic League (chmn. 1976-79, 82-85), Am. Forensic Assn. (ednl. practices com. 1984—), Speech Communication Assn., So. Speech Assn. Home: 2030 Saxton Dr Florence AL 25630 Office: Mars Hill Bible Sch 698 Cox Creek Pkwy Florence AL 35630

BARGE, JEAN MARIE, minister, Lutheran Church in America; b. Milw., Nov. 23, 1927; d. Charles B. and Genevieve (Schul) Wright; divorced; children: Lynn, Marc, Karl. B.A., U. Rochester, 1949; M.A., SUNY-Albany, 1953; M.Div., Luth. Sch. Theology at Phila., 1981. Ordained to ministry Lutheran Ch., 1981. Pastor, Holy Cross Luth. Ch., Farnham, N.Y., 1981—; bd. dirs. Luth. Theol. Sem. at Phila., 1983—. Bd. dirs. Community Concern, Derby, N.Y., 1981—; 1st v.p. LWV, Princeton, N.J., 1958-62. Home: 556 Commercial St Farnham NY 14061

BARGER, LOUISE B., minister of education, Southern Baptist Convention, American Baptist Churches in the U.S.A.; b. Mexia, Tex., Nov. 7, 1938; d. Curtis Arthur and Vada Irene (Barker) Baldwin; m. Billy Joe Barger, June 15, 1957; children: Kenneth Gene, Keith Dean, Kimberly Ann. B.S., Tex. Woman's U., 1961; M.S.N., St. Louis U., 1974, Ph.D. in Higher Edn., 1981; M.R.E., So. Bapt. Theol. Sem., 1982. Minister Christian edn. Third Bapt. Ch., St. Louis, 1980—; instr. St. Louis U., 1974-80, Mo. Bapt. Hosp. Sch. Nursing, 1973; rep. Christian Edn., Area V Gt. Rivers Region Am. Bapt. Chs. Mo. and Ill., 1981—. Contbr. curriculum materials to So. Bapt. Sunday Sch. Bd., 1982. Grantee, Fund of Renewal Am. Bapt. Chs. U.S.A., 1980, Hazle Fund, 1984; Handicapped Ministry, Home Mission Bd. So. Bapt. Conv., 1983. Mem. Downtown Religious Edn. Assn. (sec., 1979), So. Bapt. Religious Edn. Assn., Eastern Bapt. Religious Edn. Assn., Mo. Bapt. Religious Edn. Assn., Am. Bapt. Chs. U.S.A. Ministers Council. Home: 12402 Dawn Hill Dr Maryland Heights MO 63043 Office: Third Bapt Ch 620 N Grand Blvd Saint Louis MO 63103

BARKER, VERLYN LLOYD, minister, United Church of Christ; b. Auburn, Nebr., July 25, 1931; s. Jack Lloyd and Olive Clara (Bollman) B.; A.B., Doane Coll., 1952; B.D., Yale, 1956, S.T.M., 1960; postgrad. U. Chgo., 1960-61; Ph.D., St. Louis U., 1970. Ordained to ministry United Ch. of Christ, 1956; instr. history, chaplain Doane Coll., 1954-55; pastor U. Nebr., 1956-59; sec. ministry higher edn. United Ch. Bd. Homeland Ministries, N.Y.C., 1961—; pres. United Ministries in Higher Edn., N.Y.C., from 1971. Mem. Am. Assn. Higher Edn., Am. Hist. Assn., Am. Studies Assn., Acad. Polit. Sci., Am. Acad. Polit. and Social Sci., ACLU, Soc. Health and Human Values, Yale Club N.Y., Doane Coll. Alumni Assn. (pres. 1957-58). Contbg. author: Campus Ministry, 1964; editorial adv. com. Jour. Current Social Issues; contbr. articles to Jour. Current Social Issues, 1972—. Office: care United Ch of Christ 475 Riverside Dr S New York NY 10115*

BARKER, WILLIAM FRAZIER, minister, Southern Baptist Convention, insurance broker; b. Charlston, W.Va., Sept. 16, 1951; s. William Frazier and Elfa Mae (McDerment) B.; m. Elizabeth Arlene Hawkins, Dec. 7, 1974; children: Wiliam Bradford. A.A., Dalton Jr. Coll., 1984; student Tenn. Temple U., 1969-72, Trevecca Nazarene Coll., Nashville, 1975-77; B.A., Covington Bible Sch., 1984; M.Div., Covington Sem., 1985. Ordained to ministry So. Bapt. Conv., 1979. Pastor, Ch. Nazarene, Dalton, Ga., 1974-75, Louisville, Ga., 1976, Nashville, 1977; Mt. Pisgah Bapt. Ch., Chatsworth, Ga., 1979-84, Cohutta 1st Bapt. Ch. (Ga.), 1984—. Ins. broker North Ga. Agy., Dalton, 1980—. Mem. Murray County Bapt. Assn. (moderator 1983-84, Sunday Sch. dir. 1980-83), Murray Chaplains Assn. (pres. 1981-84). Democrat. Lodge: Optimist (v.p. 1981-83). Home: 148 Wolfe St PO Box 300 Cohutta GA 30710 Office: PO Box 537 Dalton GA 30722

BARKLEY, WILLIAM INGERSOLL, JR., minister, Southern Baptist Convention; b. Louisville, Oct. 21, 1928; s. William Ingersoll and Rachel (Gibson) B.; B.A., Mercer U., 1950; B.D., Southwestern Bapt. Theol. Sem., 1954; D.Ministry, So. Bapt. Theol. Sem., 1980; m. Barbara Jane Minter, July 6, 1954; children: Beverly Gayle, William Burtis. Ordained to ministry, 1949. Student pastor chs., Ellerslie, Raleigh, Columbus, Ga., 1949-52; pastor 1st Bapt. Ch., Gene Autry, Okla., 1954-57, East Baltimore Bapt. Ch., Md., 1957-62, Catonsville Bapt. Ch., Balt., 1962-67; dir. associational missions Potomac Bapt. Assn., Waldorf, Md., 1967—. Mem. Radio and TV Commn. So. Bapt. Conv., 1967-74. Mem. Balt. County Decency Com., 1963-67, Religious Heritage Com., Charles County (Md.) Bicentennial Com. Named Outstanding Missionary Leader in a Rural-Urban Assn. for eastern U.S., So. Bapt. Home Mission Bd., 1982. Mem. Potomac Bapt. Pastors Conf., Charles County Ministerial Assn., So. Bapt. Conv. Associational Dirs. Conf. Contbr. articles to Outreach Mag. Home: 807 Roxbury Ct Waldorf MD 20601 Office: PO Box 736 Waldorf MD 20601

BARKLIND, JOHN DEAN, minister, Presbyterian Ch. in the U.S.; b. St. Paul, Jan. 21, 1943; s. Albert Leonard and Bonnie Marjorie (Baker) B.; m. Rosemary Jean Zuroff, June 4, 1966; children: Sharla, Stacy, Tracy. Student U. Minn., 1962; B.A., Rocky Mountain Coll., 1966; M.Div., Louisville Presbyn. Sem., 1969; D. Ministry, San Francisco Sem., 1984. Ordained to ministry United Presbyterian Ch. in the U.S., 1969. Minister 1st Presbyn. Ch., Fullerton, Nebr., 1969-74, Fairbury, Nebr., 1974-79, Holdrege, Nebr., 1979—; pres. Holdrege Ministerial Assn., 1982-83; chairperson vocation dept. Presbytery of Central Nebr., 1982—; chairperson leadership devel. Synod of Lakes and Prairies, 1983—. Chairperson Community Improvement, Fullerton/Fairbury, 1970-74. Recipient Alumni award Rocky Mountain Coll., 1966. Lodges: Lions, Kiwanis (bd. dirs. Fairbury chpt. 1976-78), Rotary (pres. Holdrege chpt. 1984—). Home: 1125 Sheridan St Holdrege NE 68949 Office: 1st Presbyn Ch 1103 Sheridan St Holdrege NE 68949

BARLOW, AUGUST RALPH, JR., minister, United Churches of Christ; b. Sewickley, Pa., Oct. 9, 1934; s. August Ralph and Kathryn (Adams) B.; B.A., Haverford Coll., 1956; m. Elizabeth Evone Anderson, Aug. 27, 1960; children: Paul Martin, Andrew Ralph, Ann Kathryn. B.D., Yale, 1959, S.T.M., 1964. Ordained to ministry United Churches of Christ, 1959. Pastor chs.

n Pa. and Ohio, 1959-63; teaching minister Beneficent Congl. Ch., Providence, 1964-70, minister, 1970—; v.p. Pastoral Counseling Center Greater Providence, Providence Intown Chs. Assn., Interfaith Urban Ministry; chmn. social action com. R.I. Conf., United Chs. Christ, 1985—; pres. Steere House, 1983—. Author articles. Bd. dirs. Providence Leisure and Learning for Ret. Persons; mem. adv. com. Providence Pub. Library, 1968-71; bd. dirs. Citizens United Renewal Enterprises, 1970-75; bd. govs. Beneficent House Apts., Providence, 1970—; pres. Mouthpiece Coffee House, 1974-75. Mem. R.I. Assn. United Chs. Christ Ministers, Dodeka Soc., Phi Beta Kappa. Home: 95 Cole Ave Providence RI 02906 Office: 300 Weybosset St Providence RI 02903

BARNES, BILL LLOYD, seminary administrator, Christian Church; b. Kansas City, Mo., July 16, 1926; s. William Lloyd and Augusta B. (Moore) B.; student Kansas City Jr. Coll., 1943-44; B.A., Drake U., 1948; M.Div., Christian Theol. Sem., 1952; M.S., Butler U., 1957; postgrad. U. Mich., 1973; m. Shirley Nadine Malone, Oct. 9, 1945; children: Judith Diane (Mrs. Robert S. Stall), Janis Caryl (Mrs. Kent A. Barnard). Ordained to ministry Christian Ch., 1947; pastor Iowa and Ind. chs., 1946-52, Affton Christian Ch., St. Louis, 1952-60; dir. devel. Christian Theol. Sem., Indpls., 1960-67, v.p. devel., 1967—; mem. home and state missions planning council Disciples of Christ, 1956-60; sec. Mo. Disciples State Conv., 1954; pres. St. Louis Ministers, 1957, Disciple Ministers, St. Louis, 1959; mem. bd. higher edn. Disciples of Christ, 1961-78, mem. theol. edn. commn., 1979—. Chmn. St. Louis Counseling Center, 1959; bd. dirs. Repertory Theater, 1969—. Recipient award of merit Hoosier Power Squadron; service award Christian Theol. Sem., 1970, Distinguished Alumnus award, 1975. Mem. Sem. Mgmt. Assn. (pres. 1972-74), Hoosier Power Squadron (chaplain 1971—), Theta Phi. Contbr. articles to religious publs. Home: 411 Braeside S Dr Indianapolis IN 46260 Office: 1000 W 42d St Indianapolis IN 46208

BARNES, DALE RICHARD, minister, independent Christian Church; b. Ft. Fairfield, Maine, Aug. 2, 1949; s. Otis Richard and Anna Louise (Cumming) B.; m. Janice Todd Littlefield, June 7, 1978; children: Robert, Christine. B.A., Gordon Coll., 1977; M.R.E., Gordon-Conwell Theol. Sem., 1979. Ordained to ministry, 1980. Gospel team coordinator Gordon Coll., Wenham, Mass., 1973-76; lic. minister E. Gloucester Community Ch., Mass., 1978-79; minister Irasburg United Ch., Vt., 1979—; dir. pastoral services Orleans & No. Essex Home Health, Newport, Vt., 1984—; mem. bd. dirs. Christian Ministries, Inc., Gloucester, 1984—. Vol. hospice Orleans and Northern Essix Hospice, Newport, 1980—; tng. coordinator Reach Out Bereavement Program, 1982—; bd. dirs. Vt. State Hospice Council, Randolf, 1983—; capt. Irasburg Vol. Fire Dept., 1984—. Served as cpl. USMC, 1967-69, Vietnam. Mem. Bibl. Archaeology Soc., Evang. Theol. Soc., VFW, Am. Legion (asst. chaplain 1984—). Avocations: landscape photography; reading; fishing; travel. Home: PO Box 167 Irasburg VT 05845 Office: Irasburg United Ch Irasburg Common Irasburg VT 05854

BARNES, EUGENE WILLIAM, minister, General Association Regular Baptist Churches; b. Dayton, Ohio, Mar. 28, 1928; s. William McKinley and Lucy (Hawk) B.; B.A., Los Angeles Bapt. Coll., 1952; Ph.D., Calif. Grad. Sch. Theology; m. Virginia Dora Cullers, Aug. 7, 1947; children—Marcia Graves, Timothy, Stephen. Ordained to ministry, 1953; pastor Calif. Heights Bapt. Ch., Long Beach, 1953-58, Pleasant Valley Bapt. Ch., Chico, Calif., 1958-62, Temple Bapt. Ch., Tacoma, 1962-67, 1st Bapt. Ch., Ceres, Calif., 1967-73, El Monte, Calif., 1973—; chmn. Northwest Regular Bapt. Fellowship, 1963-67; chmn. Council of Seven, Calif. Assn. Regular Bapt. Chs., chmn. Council of Nine; trustee Western Bapt. Bible Coll., Salem, Oreg., 1968-73, Los Angeles Bapt. Coll., Newhall, Calif., 1973—; chmn. Glendawn Bapt. Ch. Camp, Auburn, Wash., 1964-67; mem. NW Bapt. Home Missions Bd., 1963-67, Western Bapt. Home Missions Bd., 1967-73, SW Bapt. Home Missions, 1973-75; chaplain CAP, 1975—. Home: 3803 Daleview Ave El Monte CA 91731 Office: PO Box 5711 El Monte CA 91734

BARNES, JOSEPHINE AUNER, minister, United Church of Christ; b. Algona, Iowa, Feb. 28, 1925; d. Joseph Sturgis and Frances (Kate) Auner; m. Walter Clement Barnes, June 18, 1947; children: Thomas, Annie, Susan. B.A., U. Colo., 1946; M.Div., Drake U., 1967; D.Min., United Theol. Sem., New Brighton, Minn., 1982. Ordained to ministry United Ch. of Christ, 1967; cert. vol. adminstr. Dir. Christian edn. St. Paul's Episcopal Ch., Des Moines, 1968-80; interim minister various South Iowa chs., 1970-81; exec. dir. Bidwell Riverside Ctr., Des Moines, 1981-84; pres. Des Moines Area Religious Council, 1984. Dir. vols. Des Moines Pub. Schs., 1970-81. Mem. Altrusa, Profl. Women's League (pres. 1984-85), Colonial Dames, DAR (regent 1980), P.E.O. Club: Jr. League (Des Moines). Home Route 10 West Des Moines IA 50265

BARNES, LOU RAY, minister, Baptist Missionary Association of America; b. Bethel, N.C., Dec. 27, 1911; d. Jobie and Daisy (Brown) Banks; m. William Rufus Barnes, Dec. 21, 1960; children: Anett, Lou Ray. Diploma, Sondenling High Sch., 1966; D.D., Mt. Zion Bible Sch., 1980. Ordained to ministry Baptist Ch., 1982. Pres. Progressive State Conv. Ushers, Brentwood, N.Y., 1969-74; pres. Progressive Assn. Ushers, Brentwood, 1973—, pres. emeritus, advisor; pres. Womens aux. Ushers, Sunday sch. tch. Broadcaster, producer of program WNYS and WIAM. Recipient Usher Yr. award Bible Coll., Balt.; Praise of Age award, Islip, N.Y. Lodge: Eastern Star. Home: 183 Merrill Brentwood NY 11717

BARNES, RANDOLPH, JR., minister, Am. Bapt. Ch.; b. Phila., Mar. 1, 1927; s. Randolph and Margaret Elizabeth (Williams) B.; B.A., Va. Theol. Sem. and Coll., 1957; B.Theol., Sch. Religion, Balt., 1960; m. Kitty Imre, Dec. 5, 1972; children—Randolph, John Patrick. Ordained to ministry, 1958; founder, pastor Mt. Gilead Bapt. Ch., Bronx, N.Y., 1962—. Mem. Bapt. Ministers Conf., 1962-74; founder Bapt. Evening Conf., 1959-63. Dir., Central Complaint Bur., City N.Y., 1965-67, dir. Community Affairs, 1967-72; asst. commr. housing N.Y.C., 1970-74; pres. South Bronx Civic Improvement Assn., 1966; coordinator election of John V. Lindsay, 1965, 1969, 1972; chmn. bd. Mt. Gilead Fed. Credit Union, 1974—. Sec., Meml. Library and Art Collection, N.Y.C., 1963-65. Mem. Empire State Bapt. Assn. Home: 20-29 W Mosholu Pkwy S Bronx NY 10468 Office: 1682 Morris Ave Bronx NY 10457

BARNHILL, FREDRICK ATKINSON, priest, Episcopal Church; b. Los Angeles, Nov. 20, 1907; s. James Fred and Roberta (Atkinson) B.; A.B., Occidental Coll., 1934; M.Th., Andover Newton Theol. Sch., 1936; D.D., Pacific Sch. Religion, 1955; D.Ministry, San Francisco Theol. Sem., 1985; m. Jean Marie Pickford, Sept. 22, 1972; 1 child, Richard Alan. Ordained priest, 1958. Pastor Community Ch., Melvin Village, N.H., 1934-39; pastor in Hemet and Brea, Calif., 1939-42; chaplain AUS, 1942-46; pastor First Congl. Ch., Phoenix, 1946-56, Oneonta Congl. Ch., South Pasadena, Calif., 1956-58, St. Pauls in the Desert Episcopal Ch., Palm Springs, Calif., 1959-66, Emmanuel Episcopal Ch., Kailua, Hawaii, 1966-72; chaplain Beatitudes Retirement Home, Phoenix, 1972-76; asso. rector All Saints Episcopal Ch., 1976—. Pres., Ariz. Council Chs., Windward Oahu Coalition Chs. Pres., Camp Fire Girls Council, Phoenix, 1953-56, Phoenix United Fund, 1954-56, Palm Springs United Fund, 1964-66, Windward Oahu C. of C., Kailua, 1971-72. Decorated Silver Star, Bronze Star, Purple Heart; recipient Freedoms Found. award, 1955. Contbr. articles to ch. publs. Home: 805 W State Ave Phoenix AZ 85021 Office: 6300 N Central Ave Phoenix AZ 85012

BARR, CHARLES BEECHER, minister Christian Ch. (Disciples of Christ); b. Mt. Vernon, Ill., Aug. 28, 1921; s. Manning Granville and Wretha (Talbott) B.; m. Martha Bernhart, Apr. 2, 1944; children: Allan, Carol Barr Rippe, Vivian Barr Pinegar, Wayne, Patricia. B.S., U. Ill., 1942; postgrad. U. Chgo., 1942-45; B.D., Christian Theol. Sem., Indpls., 1959; M.S., Butler U., 1962. Ordained to ministry Christian Ch. (Disciples of Christ), 1945. Pastor, congregations Ill., Mo., Kans., Ind., 1945-66; dist. minister Christian Ch. Dist. 10, Fredericktown, Mo., 1966-83; area minister S.E. Gateway Area Christian Ch., St. Louis/Fredericktown, 1984—. Bd. dirs. Chritian Ch. (Disciples of Christ) Mid Am., Jefferson City, 1963-66, Lenoir Meml. Home, Columbia, Mo., 1978-84. Me. Christian Ch. Area Ministers (sec. treas. 1975-77), Nat. Evangelistic Assn. (bd. dirs. 1977-81). Home: PO Box 351 Fredericktown MO 63645 Office: Southeast Gateway Area PO Box 351 Fredericktown MO 63645

BARRERA, GUSTAVO CLEMENTE, priest, Roman Catholic Church; b. Falfurrias, Tex., Dec. 11, 1951; s. Octavio Clemente and Adelaida (Benavides) B. Student Del Mar Coll., Corpus Christi, Tex., 1971-73; B.Mus., Our Lady of the Lake U., San Antonio, 1975; M.Div., St. Meinrad Sem., Ind., 1979. Ordained priest Roman Cath. Ch., 1979; Pastor, 1979; master of ceremonies Diocese of Brownsville, Tex., 1979—, asst. chancellor, 1980-81, mem. tribunal, defender of the bond, 1980—, dir. seminarians, 1980—, chancellor, 1981—, trustee Priests' and Lay Pension Plans, 1981—, pro-synodal judge of matrimonial tribunal, 1982—, mem. Presbyteral Council, 1984—; sec. Coll. of Consultors, 1980—; pres. Sta. KEVD-TV, Brownsville, 1980-84. Sec., bd. dirs. San Juan Nursing Home, 1980—. Office: PO Box 2279 1910 E Elizabeth St Brownsville TX 78520

BARRETT, JOHN FRANCIS, priest, Roman Catholic Church; b. Chgo., Apr. 24, 1933; s. Francis Joseph and Hildegarde Cecilia (Parr) B.; B.A., St. Mary of the Lake Sem., Mundelein, Ill., 1955, S.T.B., 1957, M.A., 1958, D.Min., 1983. Ordained priest, 1959; assoc. pastor Saints Peter and Paul Ch., Naperville, Ill., 1959-64; assoc. pastor Notre Dame Ch., Clarendon Hills, Ill., 1964-69, pastor, 1972-84; assoc. pastor St. Alexander Ch., Villa Park, Ill., 1969-72, pastor, 1984—; chaplain Naperville Dominic Club, 1962—; nat. chaplain Dominic Club; diocesan consultor to bishop Diocese of Joliet, Roman Cath. Ch., 1972-74, mem. Priests' Senate, 1972-74, treas., 1972-74, chmn. liturgical commn., 1976—, diocesan tribunal, 1984—. Address: 300 S Cornell Villa Park IL 60181

BARROW, GILBERT ERWIN, minister, So. Baptist Conv.; b. Pensacola, Fla., Oct. 14, 1932; s. George Lemont and Alma Louise (Miller) B.; A.A., Pensacola Jr. Coll., 1956; B.S., Miss. Coll., 1958; B.D., New Orleans Bapt. Theol. Sem., 1962; m. Barbara Jane Edwards, Aug. 30, 1959; children—Donna Elise, Gilbert Erwin, Jane Allison. Ordained to ministry, 1959; pastor Concord Bapt. Ch., Franklin County, Miss., 1959-62; asso. pastor First Bapt. Ch., Panama City, Fla., summer 1962; pastor Westview Bapt. Ch., Panama City, Fla., 1962-65, First Bapt. Ch., Prichard, Ala., 1965-68, First Bapt. Ch., Leesburg, Fla., 1968-76, Capitol Heights Bapt. Ch., Montgomery, Ala., 1976—. Chaplain Christian Athlete Fellowship, Panama City, Fla., 1964. Pres. Boys Club, Panama City, 1964; bd. dirs. Sunrise Workshop for Handicapped, Leesburg, Fla., 1974; trustee Bapt. Med. Center, Montgomery, 1976—. Recipient Jr. C. of C. award for Outstanding Young Man of Am., 1967. Mem. New Orleans Bapt. Theol. Sem. Alumni Assn. (nat. alumni pres. 1974-75). Home: 540 Chatsworth Dr Montgomery AL 36109 Office: PO Box 7428 Montgomery AL 36107

BARROWS, DOUGLAS (STEPHEN), retired minister, educator, United Church of Christ; b. Tampa, Tenn., Feb. 13, 1908; s. Irvin and Jennie V. (Pulling) B.; student Moody Bible Inst., 1926-27; B.S., Wheaton (Ill.) Coll., 1928; m. Katherine Ruth Sisson, May 19, 1934; children: William Irvin, Kenneth Douglas, Clara Lavanchie, Charles Gordon. Ordained to ministry, 1952; supply pastor Meth., Congl. and Presbyn. Chs., 1931-39; pastor Lebanon (S.D.) Congl. Ch., 1939-42, Sunbeam Congl. Ch., St. Lawrence, S.D., 1942-66, Wheaton Congl. Ch., Zell, S.D., 1942-66, Selby-Java Parish United Ch. Christ, 1966-76, ret., 1976; specialized tchr. and counselor various Dakota Indian groups, 1939-76. Clk., LaFoon Twp., Faulk County, S.D., 1940-67; treas. LaFoon Sch. Dist., 1942-57. Named hon. mem. Ptaye Owohdake Dakota. Mem. Oahe Assn. S.D. Conf. United Ch. Christ. Author: History of Congregational Indian Churches of South Dakota For The Past Century, 1976. Home and Office: SheepFold Mitchell St Java SD 57452

BARRY, JAMES FRANCIS, priest, Roman Cath. Ch.; b. Phila., Feb. 6, 1941; s. James Francis and Mary Jane (Fisher) B.; diploma in philosophy Resurrection Coll., Kitchener, Ont., Can., 1963; diploma in theology St. Vincent Sem., Latrobe, Pa., 1967; M.A. in Econs., Notre Dame U., 1975. Ordained priest, 1967; asso. pastor Our Lady of Angels Ch., Cape May Court House, N.J., summer 1967, St. Joan of Arc Ch., Camden, N.J., 1967-70, St. Francis de Sales, Barrington, N.J., 1970-72; tchr. theology Camden Cath. High Sch., Cherry Hill, N.J., 1972—. Dir. Camden County Cath. Youth Orgn., 1969-72. Mem. Haddonfield Juvenile Conf. Com., 1970—. Mem. Religious Edn. Assn., Assn. Profs. and Researchers in Religious Edn., Nat. Cath. Edn. Assn. Producer, coordinator slide and sound presentations ch. history, edn., death and dying. Home: 199 Willmont Ave Barrington NJ 08007 Office: Camden Catholic High Sch Route 38 and Cuthbert Blvd Cherry Hill NJ 08002

BARRY, RICHARD LIVINGSTON, minister, Episcopal Ch.; b. Miami, Nov. 14, 1940; s. Albert James and Olive Pauline (Rahmning) B.; B.A., St. Augustine's Coll., Raleigh, N.C., 1962; M.Div., Va. Episcopal Theol. Sem., 1968; postgrad. Emory U., 1975; m. Virla C. Rolle, Aug. 18, 1962; 1 dau., Diana Lacha. Ordained to ministry, 1968; priest-in-charge St. Monica's Ch., Stuart, Fla., 1968-74; chaplain Ft. Pierce (Fla.) Meml. Hosp., 1968—, Indian River Community Coll., Ft. Pierce, 1968—. Mem. planning com. Episcopal Diocese Central Fla., 1970-73, exam. chaplain, 1971-74, bd. dirs., 1974—. Treas., Lincoln Park Child Care Center, 1970-73; 1st v.p. NAACP, Ft. Pierce, 1971-75. Named Humanitarian of Year, Sigma Gamma Rho, 1971, Man of Year, Fla., Phi Beta Sigma, 1973. Mem. Order St. Luke, Union Black Episcopalians. Home: 2504 Ave P Fort Pierce FL 33450 Office: 1147 Fort Pierce FL 33450

BARTEL, BRUCE ALLAN, minister, United Meth. Ch.; b. Madison, Wis., Nov. 10, 1943; s. Bernard Benjamin and Edith Amelia (Dauner) B.; B.S., U. Wis., Stevens Point, 1966; M.Div., Garrett Evang. Sem., 1970; postgrad. Iliff Sch. Theology, Denver, 1974—; m. Kathleen Ann Jepsen, June 1, 1969; children—Tami, Brian, Trina. Ordained elder, 1970; pastor Milladore (Wis.) Meth. Ch., 1965-67; asst. minister Wisconsin Rapids (Wis.) United Meth. Ch., 1965-70; asso. minister Anchorage First United Meth. Ch., 1970-71; minister Kenai (Alaska) Ch. of New Covenant, 1971-76; sr. minister 1st United Meth. Ch., Anchorage, 1976. Mem. council on ministries Alaska Missionary Conf., 1971—, chmn. Christian Outreach com., 1976—. Mem. Bd. Edn., Kenai Peninsula Borough Sch. Dist., 1974-76; chmn. bd. Kenai Peninsula Community Care Center, 1973-76; active Kenai Peninsula Conservation Soc., 1971-76, Kenai chpt. Am. Cancer Soc., 1971—. Named Outstanding Young Man Am., 1974, Citizen of Month, Kenai C. of C., 1976. Mem. Assn. Couples for Marriage Enrichment. Author: (with Herbert A. Otto) The Family and the Church: A Survey of Needs, 1976.

Home: 2112 Esquire Dr Anchorage AK 99503 Office: 725 9th Ave Anchorage AK 99501

BARTHOLOMEW, ALFRED CLINTON, clergyman, United Church of Christ; b. Catasauqua, Pa., Nov. 18, 1918; s. Edwin Jonas and Meda Mae (Wenner) B.; m. Joyce Tillman Studenmund, June 27, 1942; children: Jocelyn, Alan, Philip. A.B., Ursinus Coll., 1939, D.D. (hon.), 1960; B.D., Lancaster Theol. Sem., 1942; Ph.D., Drew U., 1950. Ordained to ministry United Ch. of Christ. Pastor Pleasantville Ch., Chalfont, Pa., 1942-49; prof. ch. and community Lancaster Theol. Sem., Pa., 1949-71; gen. sec. div. world service United Ch. Bd. for World Ministries, N.Y.C., 1971-83, ret., 1983; cons. Ch. World Service, N.Y.C., 1984—, CODEL, N.Y.C., 1984—; bd. dirs. CARE, N.Y.C., 1971—, Technoserve, Norwalk, CT, 1971—. Recipient citation for ecumenism Lutheran Ch. Am., 1956. Fellow Am. Social. Assn., Rural Sociol. Soc., Religious Research Assn. Club: Cliosophic Soc. (pres. 1967), Fortnightly (pres. 1960) (Lancaster).

BARTLE, JOHN CURTIS, minister, Christian Church; b. Indpls., Jan. 4, 1942; s. Melvin Curtis and Grace Virginia (Fike) B.; B.A., Cin. Bible Sem., 1963; m. Donna Kay Schmeuszer, May 26, 1962; children—Julie Ann, David Curtis. Ordained to ministry, 1964; minister Liberty Christian Ch., Madison, Ind., 1962-63; youth minister First Christian Ch., Inglewood, Calif., 1963-65; minister Quartz Hill Christian Ch., Lancaster, Calif., 1965-66; asso. minister Gardenside Christian Ch., Lexington, Ky., 1966-67; minister Stanton Christian Ch., Stanton, Ky., 1967-70; minister 1st Christian Ch., Pleasant Hill, Calif., 1970-72; minister 1st Christian Ch., Castro Valley, Calif., 1972-80, Christian evangelist, 1980—. Mem. Presdl. adv. bd. San Jose Bible Coll. Home and Office: 48775 Flagstaff Ct Fremont CA 94539

BARTLETT, ALLEN LYMAN, JR., priest, Episcopal Church; b. Birmingham, Ala., Sept. 22, 1929, s. Allen Lyman and Edith Buell (West) B.; m. Jerriette Luehring Kohlmeier, Dec. 28, 1957; children: Christopher, Stephen, Catherine. B.A., U. of the South, Sewanee, Tenn., 1951; M.Div., Va. Theol. Sem., 1958, D.Ministry, 1980; D.D. (hon.), Episc. Theol. Sem. of Ky., 1984. Ordained to ministry Episcopal Ch. as deacon, 1958, as priest, 1959. Vicar St. James Ch., Alexander City, Ala., 1958-61; rector Zion Ch., Charles Town, W.Va., 1961-70; dean Christ Ch. Cathedral, Louisville, 1970—; trustee U. of the South, 1960-63, 78-80, Va. Theol. Sem., Alexandria, 1964-69; deputy Gen. Conv. Episc. Chs., 1964—; bd. dirs. exec. council Episc. Chs., N.Y.C., 1979-85. Vice chair Human Relations Commn., Louisville, 1979-81. Served to lt. (j.g.) USN, 1952-55. Mem. Louisville Council on Peacemaking and Religion (chair 1979-82), Phi Beta Kappa. Democrat. Home: 5905 Brittany Valley Rd Louisville KY 40222 Office: Christ Ch Cathedral 421 S 2d St Louisville KY 40202

BARTLETT, ROSS ALLEN, minister, educator, American Baptist Association; b. Everett, Wash., Mar. 8, 1915; s. William and Adelia Vera (Pede) B.; m. Dorothy Ellen, Aug. 21, 1938; children: Ross Eugene, James Oliver. B.A., Linda Vista Coll. Sem., 1964, B.Th., 1964, D.D., 1970, B.D., 1971; M.A., Evang. Sem.; S.T.D., Galilean U., San Antonio, 1973. Ordained to ministry American Baptist Association, 1951. Pastor Oak Park Bapt. Ch., San Diego, 1951—; instr. bibl. archaeology So. Calif. Bible Coll., San Diego, 1970—; prof. theology and bibl. archaeology Linda Vista Sem. Author 7 religious books, 1 hist. novel. Editor monthly publ. The Trumpet. Composer several hymns. Recipient Merit award Dictionary of Internat. Biography, 1970. Mem. Ams. Preserving Religious Liberty (founder, nat. pres.). Home: 23477 Japatul Valley Rd Alpine CA 92001 Office: 3200 Star Acres Dr Spring Valley CA 92078

BARTLETT, WILLIAM DONALD, JR., minister, educator, Independent Baptist Chs.; b. Clarksburg, W.Va., Oct. 12, 1950; s. William Donald and Mary Louvina (Shawhan) B.; m. Gloria Ann Cole, June 4, 1972; children: Angela Marie, William Derek, William Brandon. Diploma, Appalachian Bible Coll., 1971; B.A., Cedarville Coll., 1973; M.A., W.Va. Coll. Grad. Studies, 1984; postgrad. Grand Rapids Bapt. Sem., Mich., 1985—. Ordained to ministry Independent Baptist Chs., 1973. Sr. Pastor, 1st Bapt. Ch., Mantua, N.J., 1973-77, Bethany Bapt. Ch., St. Albans, W.Va., 1977-78; interim pastor 2d Bapt. Ch., Ravenswood, W.Va., 1978; adintr., instr. Appalachian Bible Coll., Bradley, W.Va., 1978—, registrar, dir. Christian Service, 1983—. Copywriter, editor newsletter Introspect, 1978-83. Mem. Assn. Christian Service Personnel, Assn. N. Am. Missions, Beckley Fundamental Pastors Fellowship, Appalachian Bible Coll. Alumni Assn. (pres. 1977-79), Delta Epsilon Chi. Office: Appalachian Bible Coll Bradley WV 25818

BARTON, CHARLES ANDREWS, retired church official, United Methodist Church; b. Memphis, Apr. 25, 1916; s. Charles Andrews and Martha Lee (Stewart) B.; B.S., Rhodes Coll., 1937, D.D., 1968; Sc.M., N.Y.U., 1939; M.Div., Union Theol. Sem., 1952; m. Jane Irby Teague, Aug. 19, 1950; children: Martha Jane, Carol Anne, Stewart Teague, Susan Lee. Ordained to ministry, 1952; pastor Trinity United Meth. Ch., City Island, N.Y., 1952-54, Crawford Meml. United Meth. Ch., Bronx, N.Y., 1954-56, First United Meth. Ch., Jamaica, N.Y., 1956-67, Mt. Kisco United Meth. Ch. (N.Y.), 1967-73; assoc. exec. dir. United Meth. City Soc., N.Y.C., 1973-84, ret., 1984; del. United Meth. Jurisdictional Conf., 1964, 68, 72, United Meth. Gen. Conf., 1972. Chmn. Narcotics Guidance Council, Mt. Kisco, N.Y., 1970-72; sec. ethics com., Mt. Kisco, 1968-73; mem. Park Commn., Mt. Kisco, 1968-72. Bd. dirs. Five Points Mission, N.Y.C., Chinese Meth. Community Center, N.Y.C., Anchor House, N.Y.C. Parish hall at Wakefield-Grace United Meth. Ch., Bronx, named in his honor, 1980; edn. bldg. at 1st United Meth. Ch., Jamaica, N.Y., named in his honor, 1982; swimming pool at Camp Olmsted, Five Points Mission, named in his honor, 1984. Mem. Pi Kappa Alpha, Omicron Delta Kappa, Tau Kappa Alpha. Home: 3945 Back Trails Clarkston GA 30021

BARTON, GEORGE EDWARD, religion educator, pastor, Fellowship of Evangelical Baptist Churches in Canada; b. Toronto, Ont., Can., Dec. 26, 1933; s. Clarence Aikman and Ruth Milner (Watkins) B.; m. Margaret Ellen Ware, Sept. 4, 1954; children: Stephen, Andrew, Colleen. M.Div., Central Bapt. Sem., Toronto, 1960, M.Th., 1962; M.A., U. Toronto, 1965; D.Min. Studies, Trinity Theol. Sem., Deerfield, Ill., 1984; postgrad. Brandeis U. and U. Toronto, 1967-70. Ordained, 1961. Registrar, Central Bapt. Sem., Toronto, 1965-80, dean, 1980-85; sr. pastor Port Perry Bapt. Ch., Ont., 1985—; pastor various chs. Fellowship of Evang. Bapt. Chs. Can., Toronto area, 1960-78; mem. ch. ministries bd. fellowship, Fellowship of Evang. Bapt. Chs. Can., 1982-84. Author study guides: Acts to Revelation, 1983. Can. Council grantee, 1968-69. Home: Rural Route 3 Port Perry ON L0B 1N0 Canada Office: Port Perry Bapt Ch PO Box 25 Port Perry ON L0B 1N0 Canada

BARWIG, REGIS NORBERT JAMES, priest, Roman Catholic Church; b. Chgo., Jan. 16, 1932; s. Ladislas-Joseph and Josepha Agnes (Neugebauer) B. A.B., St. Procopius Coll., 1954; postgrad. Georgetown U., 1957, Pontifical Lateran U., Rome, 1959-61. Ordained priest, 1959. Sec. to abbot of Lisle, 1955-61; sec. gen. Christian unity apostolate, 1961-64; founding prior Claremont Priory, Cedarburg, Wis., 1964-67; prior Community of Our Lady, Oshkosh, Wis., 1968—; co-chmn. 1st Festival of Faith, Milw., 1966; chmn. Ecumenical Conf. Spiritual and Liturgical Renewal Religious Life, 1969—; mem. Green Bay Diocese Ecumenical Commn., 1970-73; theol. cons. Consortium Perfectae Caritatis, 1974—; preacher, U.S. and Europe; U.S. liaison for beatification of Pope Pius IX, 1975—; assoc. Wanda Landowska Music Ctr., Lakeville, Conn., 1969; bd. dirs. Inter-Cath. Press Agy., N.Y., 1967-72. Author: Changing Habits, 1971; Waiting for Rain, 1975; Reflections on Spiritual Life for Order of Malta, 1982. Translator: His Will Alone, 1971; Wanda Landowska Diaries, 1971; Pius XI-A Close-up, 1975; Pius IX—More Than a Prophet, 1977; Writings of Blessed Maximilian Maria Kolbe, 1977; Evaluations of the Possibility of Constructing a Christian Ethics on the Assumptions of the Philosophy of Max Scheler, 1982. Editor: Conferences of Mother Mary of Jesus, 1968. Contbr. articles to religious publs. Decorated bruderschaft Collegio Teutonico, Vatican City, 1959; knight comdr. Order Isabel la Catolica, Spain, 1959; cross of merit Sovereign Mil. Order of Malta, also magistral chaplain, conventual chaplain of honor. Mem. Selden Soc., Queen Mary Coll., Polish-Am. Assn. Wis. (chaplain 79—). Club: Polish Arts. Home and office: 2804 Oakwood Ln Oshkosh WI 54901

BASELER, JAMES EDWARD, minister, Luth. Ch. Am.; b. Bloomington, Ill., Oct. 21, 1946; s. George Edward and Ruth Marie (Mardorf) B.; B.A., Wartburg Coll., Waverly, Iowa, 1969; M.Div., Pacific Luth. Theol. Sem., 1973; m. Elizabeth E. Brooks, Aug. 29, 1970; 1 dau., Elizabeth Ruth. Ordained to ministry, 1973; youth worker Centro Latino, San Francisco, 1971, Luth. Ch. of the Cross, Berkeley, Calif., 1972; chaplain-intern Lenoir Rhyne Coll., Hickory, N.C., 1973; intern-pastor St. Andrews Luth. Ch., Hickory, 1973; asso. pastor Bethel Luth. Ch., Manassas, Va., 1973-76; pastor Toms Brook (Va.) Luth. Parish, 1976—. Youth counselor The Bridge, Hickory, 1973; sec.-treas. Western Prince William Ministerial Assn., Manassas, 1974; chairperson Task Force on Amnesty and Vietnam Vets., Va. Synod, Luth. Ch. Am., 1976—, mem. home missions mng. group Va. Synod, 1976—. Mem. Serve, Inc., Manassas; bd. dirs. Manassas Choral Soc., 1975, Bread for the World. Named Best Supporting Actor, Wartburg Coll., 1969. Home and Office: PO Box 104 Toms Brook VA 22660

BASHORE, GEORGE W., Bishop The United Methodist Church, Maine Conf. and So. New Eng. Conf. Office: The United Meth Ch PO Box 277 Winthrop ME 04364 also RFD 3 Box 36 Concord NH 03301*

BASINGER, EARL. Bishop Reformed Mennonite Church, Ephrata, Pa. Office: Reformed Mennonite Ch 1036 Lincoln Heights Ave Ephrata PA 17522*

BASS, JOSEPH OSCAR, minister, American Baptist Churches; b. Vicksburg, Miss., Jan. 23, 1933; s. Sylvester and Jeanette (Sims) B.; B.R.E., Western Baptist Coll., Kansas City, Mo., 1956; B.A., Nat. Coll., Kansas City, 1958; M.R.E., Central Bapt. Sem., Kansas City, Kan., 1959; M.A., U. Mo., 1969, postgrad. 1975-76; M.Div., Mo. Sch. Religion, Columbia, 1971; L.H.D. (hon.), Va. Coll., Lynchburg, 1974; Ph.D., Walden U., Naples, Fla., 1976; m. Charline Delores Sanders, June 5, 1955; children: Karen Sue, Julie Yvette. Ordained minister Am. Bapt. Chs., 1954; pastor chs. in Kans. and Mo., 1955-62; indsl. missionary to Thailand, Am. Bapt. Conv., 1962-69, asso. exec. dir. world mission support, 1969-72; nat. dir. fund of renewal Progressive Nat. Bapt. Conv. and Am. Bapt. Conv., Valley Forge, Pa., 1972-74; exec. dir. home mission bd. Progressive Bapts.; Pastor, founder Alpha Bapt. Ch., also Alpha Acad. Christian Growth, Willingboro, N.J., 1977—; mem. adv. council internat. affairs Nat. Council Chs., Washington, 1974-81; mem. men's. com. Japan Internat. Christian U., 1972. Sec. Burlington County (N.J.) Community Action Program, 1972-73, pres., 1973—. Mem. Am. Sociol. Assn., Nat. Doctoral Assn. Educators, World Wide Acad. of Scholars. Author: These Are They, 1970; The History of the Progressive National Baptist Convention, 1976; co-author: The Black American Experience, 1974. Co-author: One in Nine Americans is Black, 1973. Home: 2 Normont Ln Willingboro NJ 08046 Office: 175 Somerset Dr Willingboro NJ 08046

BASS, LAWRENCE ARVIL, JR., minister, Christian Church (Disciples of Christ); b. Maryville, Mo., Jan. 26, 1948; s. Lawrence Arvil and Elva Pauline (Duff) B.; m. Jennifer Sue Sanford, Nov. 28, 1971; children: Sayard Ellen, Jacob Isaiah. B.A. cum laude, Eureka Coll., 1970; M.Div., Yale U., 1974. Ordained to ministry Christian Ch. (Disciples of Christ), 1974. Student asst. United Ch. of Christ, Devon, Conn., 1970-71; asst. First Christian Ch., Centralia, Ill., 1971-72; student asst. United Meth. Ch., New London, Conn., 1972-74; minister Central Christian Ch., Havana, Ill., 1974—; chmn. camp facilities devel. commn., mem. regional bd., mem. div. adminstrn. Christian Ch. (Disciples of Christ), 1975-81, mem. camp program mgmt. team, mem. steering com. Dist. Men's fellowship, mem. Disciples Peace Fellowship in Ill. and Wis., dir. regional family camp, 1982—, mem. youth dept., 1983—; bd. dirs. Lewistown Area Devel. Corp, Christian Ch. Nat. Benevolent Assn., St. Louis, 1983—. Bd. dirs. Sr. Citizens Havana Twp., 1974-78, v.p. bd., 1979-80, pres. bd., 1981-83, mem. adv. bd., 1983—; sec. Havana Ch. Softball League, Basketball League, 1979—, Volleyball League, 1983—; pres. Thursday Night Ch. Bowling League, 1979—; bd. dirs. Community Emergency Food Pantry, 1983—; mem. Mason County Welfare Com., 1984—; commr. Mason County Housing Authority, 1984—. Recipient Vigil Honor award Boy Scouts Am., 1965; Eureka Coll. scholar, 1968, 69; named An Outstanding Young Man of Am., U.S. Jr. C. of C., 1977, 81, 83. Mem. Havana Ministerial Assn. (sec. 1975-76, pres. 1976-77), Coll. Profl. Ministers (dean New Hope cluster 1979), Havana C. of C., Havana Jr. C. of C. (Jaycee of Month 1980, 81, Merit cert. 1981, Community Action Project of Yr. award 1981-82, Presdl. Honor award 1981-82).

BASTIAN, DONALD NOEL, bishop, Free Methodist Church; b. Estevan, Sask., Can., Dec. 25, 1925; s. Josiah and Esther Jane (Millington) B.; B.A., Greenville (Ill.) Coll., 1953; B.D., Asbury Theol. Sem., 1956; D.D. (hon.), Seattle Pacific U., 1965; S.T.D. (hon.), Greenville Coll., 1974; m. Kathleen Grace Swallow, Dec. 20, 1947; children: Carolyn Dawn, Donald Gregory, Robert Wilfrid, John David. Ordained to ministry, 1956, bishop, 1974; pastor, Lexington, Ky., New Westminster, B.C. and Greenville, 1953-74; bishop Free Meth. Ch. N.Am., Winona Lake, Ind., 1974—. Chmn. bd. Light & Life Pub. House, chmn. editorial com. Light and Life mag., 1974-76; mem. bd. adminstrn. Free Meth. Ch., 1974-76, mem. hymnal commn., 1970-76. Recipient Alumnus of Year award Asbury Theol. Sem., 1974, citation for community service Police Dept., Greenville, 1974. Mem. Nat. Assn. Evangelicals U.S.A., Canadian Holiness Fedn., Evang. Fellowship Can. Contbr. weekly guest editorial to Brit. Columbian, New Westminster, 1959, also articles to religious publs. Home: 3 Harrowby Ct Islington ON M9B 3H3 Canada Office: 833-D Upper James St Hamilton ON L9C 3A3 Canada

BASTILLE, EDWARD CHARLES, JR., pastor, United Church of Christ; b. Gardner, Mass., Apr. 21, 1943; s. Edward Charles and Evelyn Emma Nicholas) B. B.S. Springfield Coll., 1966; M.Div., Andover Newton Theol. Sch., 1975, D.Min., 1980; cert., Jung Inst., Zurich, Switzerland, 1982, 84. Ordained to ministry United Ch. Christ, 1975. Pastor, Park/St. Marks Parish, Meadville, Pa., 1977, Trinity United Ch. Christ, Delmont, Pa., 1980—; chaplain USAF, 1977-79; pres. Delmont Salvation Army Service Unit, Pa., 1980—, named Vol. of Yr. 1983. Editor Greensburg Ostomy Assn. Newletter, 1980—. Coordinator Delmont council Boy Scouts Am., 1982—; bd. dirs. Westmoreland County Commn's Vets. Adv. Bd., Greensburg, Pa., 1982—. Served to capt. USAF, 1967-78. Hayden Found. grantee Boys Clubs Am., 1965; named Vol. of Yr. Mohegan Council Boy Scouts Am., 1978; Hon. Fireman, Delmont Fire Dept., 1984.

Mem. Assn. Clin. Pastoral Edn. (clin. mem.), Delmont Ministerium (treas. 1984), Westmoreland Assn. Ministerial Assn., Mil. Chaplains Assn., Am. Legion benefits counselor 1980—). Club: Westmoreland County Choral Soc.; Allwine Civic Centre Supper. Lodge: Lions (bd. dirs., program chmn. 1982—). Home: 110 W Pittsburgh St Delmont PA 15626

BASTUSCHECK, BURTON CHARLES, minister, United Meth. Ch.; b. Drums, Pa., Aug. 15, 1910; s. Raymond Ernst and Gertrude Mae (Eroh) B.; B.A., Pa. State U., 1936; B.D., Drew U., 1938; S.T.M., Wesley Theol. Sem., 1952; Th.D., Iliff Sch. Theology, 1958; m. Ruth Mae Peters, Aug. 9, 1935 (dec. Jan. 1963); children—Herbert Carl, Donald Earl; m. 2d, Gladys Laura Shank Kelty, July 18, 1965. Ordained to ministry, 1936; pastor in Central Pa., 1931-49; dir. Fulton County Group Ministry, 1946-49; pastor in Keosauqua, Iowa, dir. Van Buren County Group Ministry, 1949-54; prof. Willamette U., 1954-66; counselor Town and Country Ch., Oreg., 1954-64; pastor in Oreg., 1961—, Marquam, 1966—. Chaplain, Order Eastern Star; grand chaplain Masonic Lodge in Oreg. Bd. dirs. Molalla Telephone Co. Mem. United Meth. Rural Fellowship, Am. Sociol. Assn., Pi Gamma Mu. Contbr. articles to religious jours. Home and Office: Box 207 Marquam OR 97362

BATE, CHARLES THOMAS, lay church worker, Church of God-Anderson, Ind.; lawyer; b. Muncie, Ind., Nov. 14, 1932; s. Thomas E. and Vina F. (Jackson) B.; A.B., Butler U., 1955; postgrad. Christian Theol. Sem., 1956-57; J.D., Ind. U., 1962; m. Barbara K. Dailey, June 16, 1955; children: Charles Thomas, Gregory A., Jeffrey S. Mem. Nat. Gen. Assembly, Ch. of God-Anderson, Ind., 1969-76; trustee Glendale Ch. of God, Indpls., 1958-77, dir., 1976—; family life lay speaker, Ohio, Ind., Ky., Mich., Ill.; mem. nat. pension bd. Ch. of God, 1969-73, sec. nat. by-laws com., 1969-76; trustee Anderson Coll., Ind. Admitted to Ind. bar, 1962; practiced in Indpls., 1962-67, Shelbyville, 1967—; partner firm Soshnick, Bate & Harrold, Shelbyville, 1967—; city atty. City of Shelbyville, 1981—. Mem. Am., Ind. bar assns., Ind. Bar Found., Am., Ind. trial lawyers assns., Am. Judicature Soc., Indpls., Shelby County bar assns., Am. Bd. Trial Advs., Mcpl. Lawyers of Ind. Assn., Tex. Trial Lawyers Assn., Am. Arbitration Assn. Clubs: Columbia (Indpls.); Elks Blue River Country (Shelbyville). Home: POB 26 Shelbyville IN 46176 Office: POB 477 Shelbyville IN 46176

BATSON, JOSEPH RAY, minister, So. Baptist Conv.; b. Sumter, S.C., July 3, 1926; s. Paul Otis and Rose Eva (Lyons) B.; B.A., Carson-Newman Coll., 1947; B.D., So. Bapt. Theol. Sem., 1950, M.Div., 1969; m. Nancy Sloan, June 8, 1951; children—Nancy Elizabeth, Jennie Ruth, Rosanne, Donna Rae. Ordained to ministry, 1947; pastor chs., S.C., 1950-68; dir. associational missions Spartanburg County So. Bapt. Conv., 1968—. Mem. gen. bd. S.C. Bapt. Conv.; preaching missions to Jamaica, Panama, Alaska, Tanzania, Zimbabwe Home: 907 Brentwood Spartanburg SC

BATTLE, WALTER LEROY, clergyman, Church of God in Christ; b. Battle, Miss., July 1, 1921; s. Nathaniel and Bessie (Waynewright) B.; m. Willa Grant, July 4, 1941; 1 child, Glarushia. Grad. North Central Bible Coll., Mpls., 1950; postgrad. U. Minn., 1953; D.D. (hon.), Trinity Theol. Inst., Newark, N.J., 1971, Payne Acad. Jackson, Miss., 1984. Pastor, Gospel Temple, St. Paul, 1949—; preacher radio and TV. Served with U.S. Army, 1942-45. Home: 220 E 42d St Minneapolis MN 55409

BATTS, TERRY MILBURN, minister, Primitive Baptists; b. Memphis, Nov. 2, 1914; s. William Douglas and Annie Dee (Maclin) B.; M.Th., Midwestern Grad. Bible Sch., Indpls., 1960; D.D., Am. Div. Sch., Chgo., 1964; m. Mamye Sue Crutcher, Dec. 19, 1943; children—Terry M., Harold E., Carl D. Ordained to ministry, 1933; pastor Zion Mount Church, Hudsonville, Miss., 1934-42, Springhill Ch., Holly Springs, Miss., 1936-42, St. Stephens Ch., Decatur, Ala., 1937-45, St. Mary Ch., Pratt City, Ala., 1942-45, El Beth El Primitive Bapt. Ch., Mobile, Ala., 1945-68, New Sardis Primitive Bapt. Ch., Cleve., 1968—. Moderator W. Ala. Primitive Bapt. Assn., 1951-68; pres. Ala. State Conv. Primitive Bapts., 1947-63; founder, pres. Midwestern States Conv., 1972—; dean Chicago River Dist. Sch. of Methods; pres. Cleve. Bapt. Ministers Credit Union. Active Mt. Pleasant Community Council, 1970, 21st Dist. Caucus, Cleve., 1973, Clergyman's Polit. Com., 1976—. Recipient citation Ala. Coordinating Com., 1954. Mem. Nat. Primitive Bapt. Conv. Am., Bapt. Ministers Conf. Cleve. and Vicinity, Bapt. Pastors Council, Interdenominational Ministers Alliance Cleve., Mt. Pleasant Ministerial Assn. Cleve. (pres.), Chicago River Primitive Bapt. Assn. (clk.). Chmn. Nat. Primitive Bapt. Pub. Bd.; editor Nat. Primitive Bapt. Clarion. Home: 4076 E 147th St Cleveland OH 44128 Office: 3474 E 147th St Cleveland OH 44120

BAUGH, HORACE GRENVILLE, priest, Anglican Church of Canada; b. Arundel, Que., Can., Mar. 14, 1916; s. C. Wesley Palmer and Ellen Rose (Judd) B.; student McGill U., 1938-42; B.A., Diocesan Theol. Coll., Montreal, Que., 1943; m. Dorothy Eleanor McCubbin, Apr. 10, 1942; 1 dau., Marlena Dorothy. Ordained to ministry Anglican Ch. Can., as deacon, 1943, priest, 1944; priest parish of Ludlow (N.B.), 1944-48, Blissfield, N.B., 1948-50; rector St. Paul's Ch., Grand Manan, N.B., 1948-50, parish of Mille Isles, Morin Heights and St. Sauveur, Que., 1950-83; aviation chaplain Diocese of Montreal, 1975—; dir.-at-large Que. Assn. Protestant Sch. Bds., 1984—; pres. Laurentian Planning and Counselling Services Inc., 1984—; chaplain Res. Army Corps., Can., 1952-70. Justice of Peace, Dist. Terrebonne, Que., 1951—; vice chmn. Laurentian Sch. Bd., 1970-74; regional dean of the Laurentians, 1974—; hon. canon Christ Ch. Cathedral, Montreal, 1975—. Home: POB 114 Morin Heights PQ J0R 1H0 Canada Office: The Rectory Morin Heights PQ Canada

BAUGH, ODIN ALBERTUS, minister, Presbyterian Church (U.S.A.); b. Nevada, Mo., Dec. 24, 1918; s. Fred Edward and Luella Lydia (Thurston) B.; B.A., Whitworth Coll., 1947, D.D., 1967; M.Div., Princeton Theol. Sem., 1950; m. Nearine Marcus, Aug. 21, 1948; children—Michelle Nearine, Gregory Odin. Ordained minister, 1950; pastor 1st Presbyn. Ch., Quincy, Wash., 1950-53; sr. pastor Opportunity Presbyn. Ch., Spokane, 1953-68; pastor 1st Presbyn. Ch., Kalispell, Mont., 1968—; moderator, Presbytery of Glacier, 1971-72, chmn. gen. council, 1972-73. Chmn. Selection Com., Am. Field Service, 1971-76. Bd. dirs. Youth Guidance Home, Kalispell, 1975—. Mem. Mont. Assn. Chs. (chmn. Christian unity com. 1978-81, bd. dirs. 1981-84), Kalispell Ministerial Assn. (pres. 1970-72), Flathead Valley Genealogy Soc. (pres. 1974-79), Kalispell C. of C. Home: 900 West Reserve Dr Apt 100 Kalispell MT 59901

BAUGHER, JAMES WILLARD, minister, United Methodist Church; b. Eldorado, Ill., Dec. 16, 1926; s. Edward Leander and Effie Mae Baugher; B.A., So. Ill. U., Carbondale, 1950; B.D., Emory U., Atlanta, 1957, M.Div., 1972; m. Judith Helen Holmes, Aug. 21, 1971; children: Renee, Kent, Karen Baugher. Ordained to ministry, 1959; pastor So. Ill. Conf., 1960-64, Fla. Conf., 1960-71; sr. pastor College Park United Meth. Ch., Orlando, Fla., 1971—; mem. Fla. Conf. Bd. Evangelism, 1967-72; mem. sch. com. Sch. Christian Mission Fla. Conf. United Meth. Ch., 1968-75; Pres., North Port Ministerial Assn., 1974-75; trustee Asbury Towers, Bradenton, Fla., 1976. Tenor soloist Englewood (Fla.) Community Chorus, 1971—; mem. sch. adv. com., 1974-75; sec. South County Comprehensive Health Planning Council, 1975—; mem. advisory bd. Fla. Home Health Services, Inc., 1976-77; mem. Citizens Adv. Com., North Port, 1975—; bd. dirs. North Port Civic Assn., 1971-72, Hardee County Spanish Ministry, 1977—; mem. bd. health and welfare Fla. Conf., United Meth. Ch., 1979-84, mem. adult ministries, 1984—. Lodge: Orlando Rotary. Home: 1300 Radclyffe Rd Orlando FL 33804 Office: 644 W Princeton St PO Box 7777 Orlando FL 33854

BAUM, RITA ANN, Roman Catholic social agency administrator; b. Prosser, Wash., Mar. 4, 1941; d. Joseph Nicholas and Agnes Regina (Conway) B. B.A. in English, Incarnate Word Coll., 1970, M.A., 1971. Registered Interpreter for the Deaf. Entered Order Sisters of St. Joseph, 1960. Tchr. elem. sch. St. Theresa Sch., Coral Gables, Fla., 1962-68; tchr. English and religion Cardinal Mooney High Sch., Sarasota, Fla., 1968-72, St. Joseph Acad., St. Augustine, Fla., 1972-75; dir. religious edn. Fla. Sch. for Deaf and Blind, St. Augustine, 1972-80; dir. ministery with handicapped persons Diocese of St. Augustine, Fla., 1980-82; exec. dir. Nat. Cath. Office for Persons with Disabilities, Washington, 1982—; dir. Nat. Cath. Office for Deaf, Silver Springs, Md., 1982—, Nat. Apostolate with Mentally Retarded Persons, Bklyn., 1982—, Cath. Assn. Visually Impaired Persons, Pitts., 1982—. Contbr. articles to religious, profl. jours. Liaison, Internat. Yr. of Disabled Persons, 1981-82, Nat. Office on Disability, 1984—. Recipient Service award KC, 1981. Mem. Am. Assn. Mental Deficiency, Am. Assn. Deaf-Blind, Nat. Conf. Cath. Charities. Democrat.

BAUMAN, WALTER LYNN, lay worker, United Methodist Church; b. Kansas City, Mo., Apr. 29, 1951; s. Andrew Lamar and Roxie Joyce (Goodwin) B.; m. Mary Martha Roberts, Aug. 8, 1971; children: Ceciley Lynn, Whitney Albert, Andrew France. B.Mus., Henderson State U., 1973. Organist First United Meth. Ch., DeWitt, Ark., 1967-69, First Presbyn. Ch., Camden, Ark., 1970-71; organist, choir youth dir. First United Meth. Ch., Hope, Ark., 1972-75; organist, choir dir. Grand Ave. United Meth. Ch., Stuttgart, Ark., 1975-77, First United Meth. Ch., Hot Springs, Ark., 1977-82, Little Rock, 1982—. Mem. Am. Guild Organists (Central Ark. Chpt.), Am. Guild English Handbell Ringers (Ark. state chmn. 1978—), Fellowship of United Methodists in Worship, Music and Other Arts, Royal Acad. Ch. Music. Democrat. Avocations: restoring Victorian homes, cross stitch, fishing. Office: First United Meth Ch 723 Center St Little Rock AR 72201

BAUMANN, EDWARD JOSEPH, priest, Roman Catholic Ch.; b. Newport, Ky., July 30, 1927; s. Edward Isidore and Susan Josepha (Enzweiler) B.; B.A., St. Paul Sem., 1947, M.A., 1950. Ordained priest, 1950; asso. pastor Cathedral Basilica of the Assumption, Covington, Ky., 1950-60, St. Bernard Ch., Dayton, Ky., 1960-63; resident chaplain St. Charles Nursing Home, Covington, 1964-76; tchr. history Thomas More Coll., Fort Mitchell, Ky., 1953-64, dean continuing edn., 1964-76; planner for continuing edn. St. Ambrose Coll., Davenport, Iowa, 1976—. Bd. dirs. Nat. Fedn. Christian Life Communities, 1961-69, nat. dir., 1967-69; moderator Covington Diocesan Fedn. of Christian Life Communities, 1957—. Mem. Ky. State Adv. Council on Title I, 1966-71; nat. councillor Alpha Sigma Lambda, 1968—. Mem. Assn. Continuing Higher Edn., Nat. Cath. Edn. Assn., Adult Edn. Assn. U.S.A. Contbg. author New Cath. Ency., 1967. Home: 1906 Scott St Davenport IA 52803 Office: 518 W Locust St Davenport IA 52803

BAUMHART, RAYMOND CHARLES, priest, Roman Catholic Ch., univ. pres.; b. Chgo., Dec. 22, 1923; s. Emil and Florence (Weidner) B.; B.S., Northwestern U., 1945; B.A., Loyola U., 1950, Licentiate in Philosophy, 1952, Licentiate in Theology, 1958; M.B.A., Harvard, 1953, D.B.A. 1963. Joined S.J., 1946, ordained priest Roman Catholic Ch., 1957; faculty St. Xavier High Sch., Cin., 1953-54; vis. lectr. bus. ethics Boston Coll., 1961-62; asst. prof. Loyola U. Sch. Bus. Adminstrn., 1962-64, dean, 1964-66, acting v.p. for Med. Center, 1968-69, exec. v.p., 1968-70; research asso. Cambridge Center for Social Studies, 1966-68; pres. Loyola U. Chgo., 1970—. Cons. Fabricast div. Gen. Motors, Bedford, Ind., 1957; dir. Jewel Co. Inc., Continental Ill. Corp. Mem. Ill. Bd. Higher Edn.'s Commn. on Financing of Higher Edn., 1971; bd. dirs. Council Better Bus. Burs., others. Mem. Ind. Ill. Colls. and Univs. Fedn. (exec. com. 1973-80), Am. Mgmt. Assn. (mem. theologians' adv. council 1964-69), Nat. Conf. Christian Employers and Mgrs. (cons. 1963-67), Assn. Jesuit Colls. and Univs. Author: An Honest Profit: What Businessmen Say About Ethics in Business, 1968; (with Garrett, Purcell, Roets): Cases in Business Ethics, 1968. Office: Loyola U Chgo 820 N Michigan Ave Chicago IL 60611

BAUR, FRANCIS GODFREY, priest, educator, Roman Catholic Church; b. Los Angeles, Sept. 12, 1930; s. Anton and Antonia (Krist) B.; A.B., San Luis Rey Coll., 1952; S.T.B., Old Mission Theol. Sem., 1956; M.A. in Theology, U. San Francisco, 1968; Ph.D., Grad. Theol. Union, 1976. Joined Order of St. Francis, 1948, ordained priest, 1955; tchr., adminstr. high schs., Ariz., Calif., Oreg., 1956-64; dir. Holy Cross Retreat House, Las Cruces, N.M., 1964-66; instr. theology U. San Francisco, 1969-74; prof. philos. theology Grad. Theol. Union, Berkeley, Calif., 1971—; asst. pastor St. Thomas Ch., San Francisco, 1971-78. Mem. Am. Acad. Religion, Soc. Sci. Study Religion, Cath. Theol. Soc. Author: Life in Abundance: A Contemporary Spirituality, 1983. Contbr. articles to religious jours. Office: 1712 Euclid Ave Berkeley CA 94709

BAXLEY, JOHN COY, minister, Bapt. Ch.; b. St. Pauls, N.C., Aug. 21, 1926; s. Coy Stephen and Susan (Edge) B.; diploma in theology Southwestern Bapt. Sem., 1958, Asso. Religious Edn., 1960; m. Mary Earlene Lewis, Feb. 26, 1949; children—Imogene, Annette, Marilyn. Ordained to ministry Bapt. Ch., 1950; pastor Bethlehem Bapt. Ch., Conway, S.C., 1952-54, Rock Creek Ch., Weatherford, Tex., 1958-60, Northside Ch., Mineral Wells, Tex., 1960-63, Patillo (Tex.) Ch., 1963-65, K Street Ch., Ardmore, Okla., 1965—. Mem. Ardmore Grievance Com. City Govt., 1975—; chmn. bd. trustees Ardmore Pub. Library; trustee Chickasaw-Multi County Library System. Mem. Conservative Preachers Fellowship, Ministeral Alliance. Home: 522 NW Ave Ardmore OK 73401 Office: 708 K St Ardmore OK 73401

BAXTER, CHARLES CLAYTON, minister, Am. Baptist Conv.; b. Birmingham, Ala., Mar. 26, 1927; s. Charles Clayton and Una Glenn (Breedlove) B.; student U. Ala., 1946-47, John B. Stetson U., 1947-49, B.A., Evang. Bible Coll. 1959; B.Th., Evang. Sem., 1958; D.Div., Judson Coll., Elgin, Ill., 1976; m. Dottie Alice Gower, Aug. 15, 1949; children—Charles Clayton IV, Robert Stephen. Ordained to ministry Am. Bapt. Conv., 1956; pastor Sandcreek Bapt. Ch., Greensburg, Ind., 1955-57, Franklin Rd. Bapt. Ch., Indpls., 1957-70, Greensburg First Bapt. Ch., 1970—. Dir., founder Haiti and Africa Task Force Indpls., 1966—. Mem. Indpls. Bapt. Assn. (moderator 1970—), Decatur County Bapt. Assn. (moderator 1974—). Mason, Lion. Home: Rural Route 7 Greensburg IN 47240 Office: 209 W Washington Greensburg IN 47240

BAYANG, MARTIN EUGENIO, minister, Episcopal Church; b. Sagada, Philippines, Mar. 10, 1935; came to U.S., 1964, naturalized, 1979; s. Eugenio and Agustina (Alipit) B.; m. Veronica A. Guitelen, June 10, 1965; children: Martin Knox, Beverly Jean, Charles Kim, Rebecca Lynne, Josephine Faith. A.B. in History, U. Philippines, Quezon, 1960; B.Th. cum laude, St. Andrew's Sem., Manila, 1961; student Episcopal Theol. Sch., Cambridge, Mass., 1964-65; S.T.M., Boston U., 1966, Ph.D., 1974; student in Sociology, U. Philippines, 1967-69. Ordained to ministry as deacon, 1961, as priest, 1962. Minister, Upi Missions, Cotabato, Philippines, 1961-64; vice-prin. St. Francis High Sch., Upi, 1961-64; asst. minister St. Peter's Ch., Beverly, Mass., 1964-66; Trinity Ch., Topsfield, Mass., 1964-66;

instr. sociology and history Trinity Coll. Quezon City, Philippines, 1966-67, head discipline of sociology, acting chaplain, 1967-69; research assoc. Inst. Ethnic Studies in S.E. Asia, Manila, Philippines, 1967-69; staff mem. Dakota Tng. Program, Fort Yates, N.D., 1969-70; supply clergy Episcopal Diocese of Mass., Boston, 1971-74; prof. sociology U. N.Mex., Gallup, 1974-75; vicar All Saints' Ch., Grants, N.Mex., 1974—. Recipient faculty award Trinity Coll., Philippines, 1968-69; scholar St. Andrew's Sem., Manila, 1954-61, U. Philippines, 1968-69; Topsfield-Beverly scholar, 1964-66. Home: 1406 S Cliff Dr Gallup NM 87301 Office: All Saints Episcopal Ch PO Box 157 Grants NM 87020

BAYENS, PATRICK JAMES, minister, Lutheran Church-Missouri Synod; b. Sheboygan, Wis., Sept. 19, 1951; s. James and Fay Jane (Puls) B.; m. Denise Runge, June 10, 1978; children: Seth, Daniel, David. A.A., Concordia Coll., Milw., 1971; B.S. in Edn., Concordia Tchrs. Coll., Seward, Nebr., 1973; M.Div., Concordia Theol. Sem., Fort Wayne, Ind., 1977. Ordained to ministry Luth. Ch., 1977. Asst. pastor St. John's Luth. Ch., Mayville, Wis., 1977-78; second pastor Trinity Luth. Ch., Racine, Wis., 1978—; mem. religious life evaluating com. Racine Luth. High Sch., 1983, dean chapel, 1984—. Composer religious song: Blow the Trumpet Loud in Zion, 1982. Home: 2804 Green St Racine WI 53402 Office: Trinity Luth Ch 2035 Geneva St Racine WI 53402

BAZAR, KENNETH LAVERNE, minister, editor, American Baptist Association; Pittsburg, Tex., Mar. 6, 1930; s. Albert Curtis and Thelma Eva (Culpepper) B.; grad. Missionary Bapt. Sem., 1951; D.D., Okla. Missionary Bapt. Sem., 1968; m. Mary Elizabeth York, Oct. 2, 1952; children: Steven Paul, Rebekah Gaye. Ordained to ministry, 1947; pastor, Ark., Tex., 1948-65, Liberty Bapt. Ch., Hope, Ark., 1965-73, Unity Bapt. Ch., Little Rock, 1973-78. Asst. editor publs. Am. Bapt. Assn. 1965-72, sec.-treas. missions, 1978-80, editor-in-chief publs., 1980—; dir. S.W. Ark. Youth Camps, 1968-71; dir. publicity Ark. State Assn. Missionary Chs., 1962-67; vis. lectr. Missionary Bapt. Sem., Little Rock. Pres., Texarkana (Ark.) High Sch. PTA, 1971-72; active Boy Scouts Am.; mem. adv. council City Hope, 1972. Mem. Alumni Assn. of Missionary Bapt. Sem. Little Rock (pres.). Author: The Missionary Baptist Pulpit, vol. 1, 1966, vol. 2, 1968; Your Spiritual Diet, 1976; Biblical Sex Standards, 1976; Curtis Has a New Address, 1977. Contbr. articles to religious publs. Home: 4803 Sanderson Ln Texarkana AR 75502 Office: 4605 N State Line Ave Texarkana AR 75503

BEACH, RICHARD ALLEN, minister, Christian Ch. (Disciples of Christ); b. Cleve., Sept. 1, 1947; s. James Edward and Annabelle (Bates) B.; B.A., Tex. Christian U., 1969; M.Div., Lexington Theol. Sem., 1972; m. Diane Davis, Aug. 15, 1969; 1 son, Martin Davis. Ordained to ministry, 1972; pastor Crittenden (Ky.) Christian Ch., 1970-72, Waverly (Ill.) Christian Ch., 1972-76, Franklin (Ill.) Christian Ch., 1972-76, 1st Christian Ch., Brunswick, Ohio, 1976—; part-time prof. Lincoln Land Community Coll., Springfield, Ill., 1973-74. Chaplain, Ill. Nat. Guard, Springfield, 1975-76; dir. Ill. Disciples Camp, Effingham, Ill., 1973-74; chaplain Waverly Lions Club, 1975-76; chpt. dean Ill. Coll. Ministers, 1973-76; mem. Ill. Christian Youth Commn., 1972. Mem. Delta Sigma Pi. Book reviewer Christian Mag., 1972—, Disciple Mag., 1972—. Home: 4130 Center Rd Brunswick OH 44212 Office: 3611 Center Rd Brunswick OH 44212

BEACH, WILLIAM WALDO, educator, United Methodist Church; b. Middletown, Conn., Aug. 2, 1916; s. William Deverne and Edith (Waldo) B.; m. Mary Joyce Heckman, Jan. 2, 1943; children: Richard Waldo, Margot Sullivan, Betsy Beach. B.A., Wesleyan U., 1937; B.D., Yale Div. Sch., 1940; Ph.D., Yale U., 1944. Ordained to ministry, 1940. Coll. pastor and assoc. prof. religion Antioch Coll., Yellow Springs, Ohio, 1942-46; prof. Duke Div. Sch., Durham, N.C., 1946—, dir. grad. studies in religion, 1959-69; trustee Wesleyan U., 1960-70. Author: Conscience on Campus, 1955; The Christian Life, 1966; Christian Community and American Society, 1969; The Wheel and the Cross, 1979. Co-editor: Christian Ethics, 1955, 2d edit. 1973. Mem. Acad. Ind. Scholars (fellow), Soc. Christian Ethics (pres. 1978), Am. Theol. Soc. (treas. 1972-75), Phi Beta Kappa. Democrat. Home: 130 Pinecrest Rd Durham NC 27705 Office: Div Sch Duke Univ Durham NC 27706

BEACHAM, A. D. Clergyman, gen. supt. Pentacostal Holiness Church Internat. Office: Heritage Bible Coll PO Box 1628 Dunn NC 28334*

BEACHAM, JAMES LEON, minister, Southern Baptist Convention; b. Shreveport, La., Sept. 3, 1928; s. Clyde Columbus and Ruth Naomi (Simpson) B.; B.A., Hardin-Simmons U., 1949; B.D., Southwestern Bapt. Theol. Sem., 1953; postgrad. Luth. Sem., 1975-76; m. Bennie Marie Reneau, June 30, 1952; children: Ruth Ann, James Leon. Ordained to ministry, 1949; pastor chs., Abilene, Tex., 1947-49, Shreveport, 1950-52, Anna, Tex., 1952-53, Bristol, Va., 1953-55, Enoree, S.C., 1955-59, Spartanburg, S.C., 1959-64; Royal Ambassador leader, camp dir. S.C. Bapt. Conv., 1964-75; 1st dir. White Oak Conf. Center, S.C. Bapt. Conv., Columbia, 1975—. Mem. Am. Camping Assn. (chmn. liaison com. to S.C. Health Dept. 1971-72), Internat. Assn. Conf. Ctr. Adminstrs., So. Bapt. Conv. Assembly and Camp Mgrs. Conf. (pres. 1977-78), Christian Camping Internat. Home: 1 Brookview Rd White Oak SC 29176 Office: White Oak Conf Ctr White Oak SC 29176

BEAHEN, JOHN, bishop, Roman Catholic Church. Titular bishop of Phoaghe, aux. bishop, Ottawa, Ont., Can., 1977—. Office: 256 Kings Edward Ave Ottawa ON K1N 7M1 Canada*

BEAL, CHARLES HUGH, minister, Southern Baptist Convention; b. Atlanta, Jan. 31, 1927; s. John Franklin and Ida Kate (Bannister) B.; B.A., Columbia Bible Coll., 1948; B.D., So. Bapt. Theol. Sem., 1953, Th.M., 1954, D.Min., 1975; m. Mary Winona Roark, Aug. 6, 1949; children: Jeremy Lawrence, Eric David. Ordained to ministry, 1948; pastor Field of Rural Chs., Washington, Ga., 1948-50, Freedom Bapt. Ch., N. Vernon, Ind. and Butlerville (Ind.) Bapt. Ch., 1951-54, Bay Haven Bapt. Ch., Sarasota, Fla., 1954-68; assoc. pastor, minister edn. Columbia Dr. Bapt. Ch., Decatur, Ga., 1968-71; pastor Bay Haven Bapt. Ch., Sarasota, Fla., 1971—; dir. ch. tng. S.W. Fla. Bapt. Assn., 1955-57, moderator, 1962-63, chmn. missions com., 1976—, chmn. budget com., 1974-76; mem. state bd. missions Fla. Bapt. Conv., 1966-68, 80—. Tchr. Sem. extension center, Stetson U. extension center, Sarasota, 1955-65. Chmn. study and planning com. Bay Haven Elementary Sch., 1967-68. Home: 638 Beverly Dr Sarasota FL 33580 Office: 3200 Bradenton Rd Sarasota FL 33580

BEALL, DICKSON HUGH, minister, United Church of Christ; b. Winston Salem, N.C., June 22, 1940; s. Edward Leyburn and Mildred Lee (Warfield) B.; m. Darlyn Dawn Hartmann, Feb. 3, 1968; 1 child, Brook Darrett. B.A. magna cum laude, U. Mo., 1975; M.Div., Eden Theol. Sem., 1978. Ordained to ministry United Ch. Christ, 1978. Asst. minister St. Paul United Ch. of Christ, Belleville, Ill., 1978-80; dir. United Christian Found., So. Ill. U., Edwardsville, 1980—; v.p. ch. council St. Paul Ch., Edwardsville, 1984—; bd. dirs. Ecumedia, St. Louis, 1982—; bd. dirs. video communications Ill. South Conf. United Ch. Christ, Highland, Ill., 1983—. Producer TV series Life Patterns, 1982-83 (Cert. Merit 1984), (with Walter Brueggemann) Covenants to Keep, 1985. Bd. dirs. Rape and Sexual Abuse Ctr., So. Ill. U., 1980—, Friends of Theatre and Dance, 1982—. Mem. Nat. Campus Ministry Assn. Home: 7490 Bruno St Saint Louis MO 63117 Office: United Christian Found Religious Ctr Box 59 So Ill U Edwardsville IL 62026

BEAM, WILLIAM HAROLD, minister, So. Bapt. Conv.; b. Shelby, N.C., May 11, 1942; s. Reviere Rufus and Alice Eugenia (Mode) B.; student Gardner Webb Coll., 1961-62, Fruitland Bapt. Bible Inst., 1971-74; m. Alice Frances Grady, Mar. 31, 1962; 1 son, William Scott. Ordained to ministry, 1974; resort ministry Chimney Rock, Lake Luce, N.C., 1973-74; pastor Red Bud Bapt. Ch., Castalia, N.C., 1974-76, Tabernacle Bapt. Ch., Troy, N.C., 1976—. Mem. evangelism com. Montgomery County, 1976—, chmn. preaching com., 1976—. Mem. com. for removal pornographic materials Christian Action League Franklin County, 1975. Home: 412 Bell St Troy NC 27371

BEAMAN, LESTER HENRY, minister, Disciples of Christ Church; b. Enid, Okla., Dec. 8, 1936; s. Henry Virgil Beaman and Evelyn Arvila (Setchell) Parrish; b. Lois Evan Barnard, Feb. 6, 1959 (div. 1977); children: Bonnie Beaman Rucker, Cheri Lynn; m. 2d Martha Alice Gadberry, Dec. 16, 1978; 1 dau., Beth Gibbons. B.Th., N.W. Christian Coll., 1966; M.Div., Lexington Theol. Sem., 1969; postgrad. Boston U., 1983—. Ordained, 1966. Minister 1st Christian Ch., Forrest City, Ark., 1969-71, 1st Christian Ch., Searcy, Ark., 1971-74, 1st Christian Ch., Pine Bluff, Ark., 1974-77, 1st Christian Ch., Russellville, Ark., 1977-79, Havelock Christian Ch., Lincoln, Nebr., 1979—; mem. adv. bd. Phillips U. Grad. Sem., Enid, 1974-78; bd. dirs. Lincoln Fellowship Chs., 1982-84; chmn. dept. ministry Christian Ch. Nebr., 1982-84, bd. dirs., 1982-84, cons., 1982—; chaplain Lincoln Police and Fire Chaplaincy Corps, 1979—, sr. chaplain, 1981-83. Served with U.S. Army, 1954-56. Estral scholar Eastern Star, Oreg., 1966; recipient commendation Forrest City Human Relations Council, 1970; Doulos award Lincoln Fellowship of Chs., 1983. Mem. Congress of Disciple Clergy. Democrat. Home: 6511 Ballard Lincoln NE 68507 Office: Havelock Christian Ch 6520 Colfax Lincoln NE 68507

BEAN, MARVIN DAY, minister, administrator, United Methodist Church; b. Tampa, Fla., Sept. 8, 1921; s. Marvin Day and Lillian (Howell) B.; children: Bethany Louise, Thomas Holmes, Carole Sue. A.B., Fla. So. Coll., 1946; M.S. in Social Work, Vanderbilt U., 1948; M.Div., Garrett Theol. Sem., 1950; postgrad. Northwestern U., 1950-51, Ohio State U., 1951-52. Ordained to ministry United Methodist Church, 1950. Assoc. minister San Marcos Methodist Ch., Tampa, 1947; minister Lena Vista United Meth. Ch., Fla., 1946, Cedar Lake Meth. Ch., Ind., 1948-50, Shepard United Meth. Ch., Columbus, Ohio, 1951-68, Stonybroo United Meth. Ch., Gahanna, Ohio, 1960-65, Obet United Meth. Ch., Ohio, 1968-73, Neil Ave. Unite Meth. Ch., Columbus, 1973-79, St. Andrew Unite Meth. Ch., Gahanna, 1979—; dir. intake United Meth Children's Home, Worthington, Ohio, 1974—, truste 1973-74; trustee Meth. Retirement Ctr., Wesley Glen Columbus, 1964—; sec. United Meth. Hist. Soc. c Ohio, Columbus, 1983—; chmn. commn. on Archive and history, Ohio Wesleyan U., Delaware, 1983— Author: A Guide to United Methodist Building, 1973 You Are On The District Board, 1974; Unto The Leas of These, 1981. Pres. bd. trustees Neil Ave. Found Columbus, 1973-79. Served to sgt. U.S. Army, 1943-46 Recipient Recognition award Wolfley Fund, 1961 Outstanding Service award Shepard Community Assn. 1968; named Outstanding Citizen, City of Obetz, 1973 Mem. Columbus Meth. Ministerial Assn. (pres 1960-61), Acad. of Cert. Social Workers, Nat. Assn. o Social Workers, Central Ohio Coalition on Services t Children and Youth. Home: 122 W Henderson R Columbus OH 43214 Office: United Methodist Hom for Children 1033 High St Worthington OH 43085

BEASLEY, ANNE WILLIAMS, minister of music Southern Baptist Convention; b. Swansea, S.C., Apr. 16 1930; d. Burton Eugene and Marie (Shull) Williams A.B. in Music Edn., U. S.C., 1951; M.Ch. Music Golden Gate Bapt. Sem., Mill Valley, Calif., 1956; m Clyde E. Beasley, June 26, 1952; children: Deborah Lawrence, Kent, Kurt. Organist chs. in Calif. and Tenn. 1952-71; minister of music Cherokee Creek Bapt. Ch. Gaffney, S.C., 1971-75, First Bapt. Ch., Matthews, S.C. 1975—; choir dir., organist Swansea Bapt. Ch., N.C. 1976—. Pvt. piano tchr., Swansea, 1976—. Music chmn. San Rafael (Calif.) Sch. PTA, 1963-64. Mem Delta Omicron. Address: Box 486 Swansea SC 2916

BEASLEY, DEWEY ELDRIDGE, minister, So Baptist Conv.; b. Dale County, Ala., Oct. 18, 1930; s. Dewey Roscoe and Emma Clara (Nolin) B.; B.A., Mercer U., 1957; B.D., New Orleans Bapt. Theol. Sem., 1960; M.Ed., Valdosta (Ga.) State Coll., 1976; m. Cleo Maybelle Burdette, Aug. 12, 1950; children—Joseph Keith, Eldridge Eugene. Ordained to ministry, 1953; pastor chs. in Ga., Ala., Miss., Fla., 1953-76; pastor Lenox (Ga.) Bapt. Ch., 1971—. Moderator, Dale Bapt. Assn., 1963; moderator Coffee Bapt. Assn., 1969-70, also chmn. evangelism; tng. union dir. Dale County Bapt. Assn., Mem. Mell Bapt. Ministerial Assn. Address: POB 376 Lenox GA 31637

BEATTIE, ROBERT ALLEN, minister, So. Baptist Conv.; b. Lincoln, Nebr., Oct. 26, 1926; s. James Allen and Luella Maude (Barker) B.; student Grand Canyon Coll., Phoenix, 1959-62; m. Margaret Nell Robinson, June 29, 1945; children—Katherine Maudine, Patricia Marie, Arnella Kay. Licensed to ministry, 1958; dir. Tng. Union, North Park Bapt. Ch., Evansville, Ind., 1957-58; dir. tng., dir. Sunday sch., edn. dir. Elsinore Bapt. Ch., Phoenix, 1958-70; edn. dir. W. Dunlap Bapt. Ch., Phoenix, 1970-72; minister edn. First So. Bapt. Ch., Peoria, Ariz., 1973—. Mem. So. Ind., Central Phoenix Bapt. assns., Estrella Bapt. Assn. Ariz., Greater Phoenix Bowling Assn. (v.p. 1968—). Home: 2132 W Laurel Ln Phoenix AZ 85029 Office: PO Box 610 Peoria AZ 85345

BEATTY, ROBERT CLINTON, theology educator, administrator, non-denominational; b. Needham, Mass., May 19, 1935; s. Henry Russell and Alice Cornelia (van Schagen) B.; m. Carolyn Phyllis Caton, Oct. 5, 1957; children: Robert Russell, Daniel Clinton, Melissa Lynn, Alicia Felicity. A.B. in Econs., Northeastern U., 1957; M.B.A. in Mgmt. summa cum laude, Fairleigh Dickinson U., 1973; M.Div., Columbia Grad. Sch. Bible and Missions, 1983, M.A. in Bible, 1985. Ordained to ministry Harmony Ch., 1984. Commd. 2d lt. U.S. Army, 1957, advanced through grades to lt. col., 1980; stationed in France, Germany and Vietnam; part-time chaplain S.C. Dept. Corrections, Columbia, 1981—; dir. U.S. Extension Ctrs., Columbia Bible Coll., S.C., 1983—; vice chmn. bd. Victory Ctr., Inc., Columbia, 1981—; bible study tchr. U.S. Army, Ft. Jackson, S.C., 1981-83, Prison Fellowship, Columbia, 1981—, vol. tng. coordinator, 1983—. Author: Extension Coordinators Handbook, 1984. Editor: Adjunct-Extension Faculty Handbook, 1984. Decorated Legion of Merit, Bronze Star medal with oak leaf cluster, Air medal, Joint Services Commendation medal, Army Commendation medal with oak leaf cluster; recipient Vol. of Yr. award Goodman Correctional Instn., 1985. Mem. Am. Protestant Correctional Chaplains Assn., Assn. Evang. Instl. Chaplains, Near East Archeol. Soc., Evang. Theol. Soc., Nat. Assn. Evangs., DAV, Ret. Officers Assn., Signal Corps Assn. Republican. Avocations: Music; traveling. Home: 213 Bosworth Field Rd Columbia SC 29210 Office: Columbia Sch Biblical Edn 7435 Monticello Rd Columbia SC 29230-3122

BEAUBIEN, IRÈNEE, priest, administrator, Roman Catholic Church; b. Shawinigan, Que., Can., Jan. 26, 1916. D.D. (hon.), McGill U., 1970. Joined Soc. Jesus, Roman Cath. Ch., 1936, ordained priest, 1949. Faculty, St. Boniface Coll., Man., 1943-46; founder Cath. Inquiry Forum, Montreal, 1952-62; pres. Diocesan Ecumenical Commn. of Montreal, 1962-73; founder, dir. Centre for Ecumenism, 1963-84; dir. Office National d'Oecumenisme, 1966-74; chmn. bd. dirs. Christian Pavilion, Montreal, 1967; consultor, Secretariat for Christian Unity, Rome, 1968-73; mem. World Assembly of World Council Chs., Uppsala, Sweden, 1968-69; tutor Ecumenical Inst., Bossey, Switzerland, 1968-69; pres. Joint Working Group of Canadian Chs., 1968-80; chmn. Joint Research Com. on Relations Between Freemasons and Roman Catholics in Que., 1973-75; mem. Nat. Dialogue Commn. between Anglican Ch. of Can. and Roman Catholic Ch., 1971-81; mem. Nat. Dialogue Com., United Ch. of Can. and Roman Cath. Ch., 1975-83; founder, mem. steering com. Montreal Inter-Ch. Coordination Com., 1980-84; founder, dir. Pathways of Faith, Montreal, 1984—. Mem. Military and Hospitaller Order of St. Lazarus of Jerusalem. Home: 25 Jarry St W Montreal PQ H2P 1S6 Canada Office: 1200 Bleury St Montreal PQ H3B 3J3 Canada

BEAUMONT, JERROLD FOSTER, priest, Episcopal Church, management consultant; b. Highland Park, Mich., Jan. 23, 1926; s. Francis Wellington and Clara Winifred (Pett) B.; m. Marjorie Doris Hesman, June 2, 1951; children: Gordon Foster, Susan Elizabeth, Douglas Allen. B.A.M.E., Lawrence Coll., 1961; B.Theology, Sacred Heart Sem., 1975. Ordained to ministry Epis. Ch., 1973. Lay reader St. Barnabas Ch., Chelsea, Mich., 1962-73, priest-vicar, 1974—; asst. deacon St. Stephen Ch., Hamburg, Mich., 1973-74, vicar of Order of St. Paul, Diocese of Mich., 1975-76; dean Huron Valley Convocation, Diocese of Mich., 1976-78; pres. Faith In Action, Chelsea, 1981—; sr. counselor Pastoral Counseling Ctr., Chelsea, 1983—; vis. lectr. Madonna Coll., Livonia, Mich., 1981—, St. John's Sem., Plymouth, Mich., 1982—; commd. lt. RCAF, 1941 advanced through grades to maj., 1954. Pres. Beaumont Mgmt. Assocs., Ltd., Ann Arbor, Mich., 1975—. Author: Success Begins With Me, 1984. Editor: Totel—Law, 1964. Republican election worker County Clerk's Office, Washtenow County, Mich., 1983. Recipient Service Recognition award Civitan, 1982; Exceptional Services award Mich. Dept. Corrections, 1982. Mem. Engring. Soc. Detroit, Rho Delta Phi. Lodge: Kiwanis (bd. dirs.) Home: 335 Washington St Chelsea MI 48118 Office: Beaumont Mgmt Assocs Ltd 610 Church St Ann Arbor MI 48104

BEAVER, ROBERT PIERCE, minister, United Church of Christ; b. Hamilton, Ohio, May 26, 1906; s. Joseph Earl and Caroline (Nuesch) B.; A.B., M.A., Oberlin Coll., 1928; Ph.D. in History, Cornell U., 1933; postgrad. U. Munich, 1931-32, Yale, 1938, Coll. Chinese Studies, Peking, 1938-39, Union Theol. Sem., N.Y.C., 1943-44, Columbia, 1943-45; D.D., Concordia Sem., St. Louis, 1972; m. Wilma Manessier, Aug. 22, 1927; children—Ellen Barbara (dec.), David Pierce, Stephen Robert. Ordained to ministry United Ch. Christ, 1932; pastor chs., Ohio, Md., 1932-36; mem. China Mission of Evang. and Ref. Ch., 1938-46; prof. Central China Union Theol. Sem., Lingling, Hunan, 1939-42, Lancaster (Pa.) Theol. Sem., 1944-48; dir. Missionary Research Library, N.Y.C., research sec. Fgn. Missions Confs. N.Am. and div. fgn. missions Nat. Council Chs., 1948-55; prof. missions U. Chgo. Div. Sch., 1955-71, emeritus, 1971—; dir. Overseas Ministries Study Center, Ventnor, N.J., 1973-76. Trustee Found. Theol. Edn. in S.E. Asia; hon. trustee Missionary Research Library. Mem. Am. Soc. Ch. History, Am. Soc. Missiology (exec., editorial bd.), Assn. Profs. of Missions, Internat. Assn. Mission Studies, Deutsche Gesellschaft für Missions-wissenscaft. Democrat. Author: American Protestant Women in World Mission; Church, State and the American Indians; Ecumenical Beginnings in Protestant World Mission-A History of Comity; Envoys of Peace; From Missions to Mission; The Gospel and Frontier Peoples; The Missionary Between the Times; Pioneers in Mission; To Advance the Gospel-Selections from the Writings of Rufus Anderson; Christianity and African Education; American Missions in Bicentennial Perspective; Contbr. numerous articles to profl. jours. Editor: Eerdmans' Christian World Mission Books. Home: 766 La Huerta Green Valley AZ 85614

BEAVER, W. LEE, JR., lay church administrator, Southern Baptist Convention, financial executive; b. Kuttawa, Ky., June 16, 1917; s. William Lee and Ida Malinda (Perryman) B.; m. Mary Eva Rodgers, June 18, 1940; children: Douglas Alden, Betsy Lee. Cert. in acctg., commerce and fin. St. Louis U., 1939. Vice chmn. bd. trustees Mo. Bapt. Hosp., St. Louis, 1955—; chmn. bd. trustees Southeastern Bapt. Theol. Sem., Wake Forest, N.C., 1979—; gen. chmn. 75th Anniversary Commn. Mo. Bapt. Hosp., St. Louis, 1959, co-chmn. 100th Anniversary Commn., 1984. Vice-chmn. Sachs Holdings, Inc., St. Louis, 1962—. Bd. dirs. Centerre Bank of Chesterfield, St. Louis; treas., trustee Children's Home Soc. Mo., St. Louis. Served to capt. USAF, 1942-45. Recipient Outstanding Community Leadership award Religious Heritage Am., 1978. Mem. Fin. Execs. Inst., Mo. Soc. C.P.A.s, Nat. Assn. Accts., Am. Inst. C.P.A.s Republican. Clubs: Mo. Athletic, Norwood Hills Country, Noonday, Media (St. Louis). Home: 1587 Milbridge Dr Chesterfield MO 63107 Office: Sachs Holdings Inc PO Box 96 St Louis MO 63166

BEAVON, JOSEPH C., minister, United Methodist Church; b. Wheeling, W.Va., Nov. 18, 1943; s. Joseph Charles and Anna Martha (Marx) B.; m. Jennie Elizabeth Gross; children: J. Clark, Kevin Martin, Jason Cash. B.S., Union Coll., 1966; M.Div., Meth. Theol. Sch., 1969. Ordained elder, 1969. Student pastor Alton Meth. Ch., Columbus, Ohio, 1966-68, Morristown-Lloydsville-Bannock United Meth. Chs., Belmont County, Ohio, 1968-69; pastor Lockwook United Meth. Ch., Youngstown, Ohio, 1969-73, Hyatts United Meth. Ch., Delaware County, Ohio, 1977-78, Hyatts-Powell United Meth. Chs., Delaware County, 1978-79; assoc. pastor Normandy United Meth. Ch., Dayton, Ohio, 1979-84; dir. communications and community relations Luth. Social Services of the Miami Valley, Dayton, 1984—; instr. speech U. Dayton, 1983—; lectr., cons. in field of rational behavior therapy. Mem. curriculum adv. com. Centerville Pub. Schs., 1982—; bd. dirs. United Health Services, 1983—. Mem. Assoc. Photographers Internat., Internat. Assn. Bus. Communicators, United Meth. Assn. Communicators. Office: 6445 Far Hills Ave Dayton OH 45459

BECK, JAMES PIERCE, minister, So. Baptist Conv.; b. Shawnee, Okla., Feb. 18, 1937; s. Marvin Edward and Reba (Greene) B.; B.A., Okla. Bapt. U., 1970; m. Bobbie H. Cottrell, May 25, 1956; children—James, Michael, David A., Alicia May. Ordained to ministry, 1967; pastor Trinity Bapt. Ch., Seminole, Okla., 1968-70, East Side Bapt. Ch., Paragould, Ark., 1970-72, 1st Bapt. Ch., Leedey, Okla., 1972-74, N.W. Bapt. Ch., Norman, Okla., 1974-76, 1st Bapt. Ch., Thornton, Colo., 1976—. Home: 8620 Ogden St Denver CO 80229 Office: 8900 Hoffman Way Thornton CO 80229

BECKELHYMER, BETTY JANE, minister, Christian Church (Disciples of Christ); b. Chauncey, Ohio, Apr. 23, 1921; d. Gilbert Birge and Helen Marguerite (Bradfield) Courtney; B.S. in Edn., Ohio U., 1943; B.D., Yale, 1950; m. Paul Hunter Beckelhymer, Aug. 19, 1951; children: Helen Corinne, Anna Christine, Carolyn Jean. Ordained to ministry, 1975; student dir. Disciples Found, Ohio U., 1942-43; asst. pastor Lakewood Christian Ch., Cleve., 1943-47; assoc. sec. Ohio Soc. Christian Chs., Cleve., 1950-51; assoc. minister University Christian Ch., Fort Worth, 1972-78; pres. Ft. Worth Assn. Disciples Ministers, 1980-81; mem. central study com. World Conv. Chs. of Christ, 1963-65, 68-70; mem. youth ministry council Christian Ch. in Tex., 1969-72, chmn. 1972-73; pres. Fort Worth Area Council Chs., 1975-76. Bd. dirs. Tarrant County (Tex.) Assn. for Mental Health, Fort Worth, 1968-73, 75-78, Ft. Worth Southside Area Ministries, 1979—; chmn. adv. com. Parents Anonymous Tarrant County, 1982—. Mem. Nat. Christian Ch. Educators. Author: (with Hunter Beckelhymer): Reconciliation in a Broken World, 1969. Contbr. articles to profl. jours. Home: 5725 Whitman Ave Fort Worth TX 76133

BECKER, JACOB JOSEPH, lay worker, Conservative Jewish Congregations; b. Yakovlev, Poland, Dec. 18, 1905; s. Mathis and Chaye Leah (Richman) B.; came to U.S., 1921, naturalized, 1927; student Jewish Theol. Sem., Columbia, 1945-46; m. Sue F. Balter, Aug. 3, 1933; 1 son, Mayer Gil. Pres., Zionist Orgn., Jacksonville, Fla., 1946-49; trustee Hebrew Home for Aged—River Garden, Jacksonville, 1949-59; chmn. United Synagogue campaign, Jacksonville, 1955-60; founder Solomon Schechter Day Sch., Jacksonville, 1962; pres. Jacksonville Jewish Center Synagogue, 1966-67; founder, pres. Men's ORT, Jacksonville, 1971-74; gen. chmn. United Jewish Appeal, Jacksonville, 1973-74; pres. Jacksonville Jewish Community Council, 1974-75; del. Jewish Agency Assembly, Jerusalem, Israel, 1976; active Jewish Nat. Fund; pres. Jewish Family and Children's Services, Jacksonville, 1977; organizer, tchr. Talmud and Bible study groups. Recipient citation of honor Jewish Nat. Fund, 1962; Israel Bond Prime Minister's award, 1967. Mem. Zionist Orgn. Am. (nat. exec. com.), NCCJ, B'nai B'rith. Home: 859 S Waterman Rd Jacksonville FL 32207

BECKER, RUSSELL JAMES, minister, United Church of Christ; b. Rochester, N.Y., July 1, 1923; s. William Henry and Alcey Mae (Cole) B.; B.A., Kalamazoo Coll., 1944; B.D., Colgate-Rochester Div. Sch., 1946; Ph.D., U. Chgo., 1950; m. Dorothy Jane Kiefth, July 1, 1945; children—Jonathan Cole, Carl Richard, Kurt Merrill. Ordained to ministry, 1945; instr. Federated Theol. Faculty, U. Chgo., 1951-52; dean of men Kalamazoo (Mich.) Coll., 1952-53; asst. prof. psychology Coll. Wooster, Ohio, 1953-56, assoc. prof., 1956-57; minister of pastoral care Glenview (Ill.) Community Ch., 1957-60; assoc. prof. pastoral theology Yale, New Haven, Conn., 1960-69, coordinator field edn., 1964-69; pastor Glencoe (Ill.) Union Ch., 1969—. Author: Family Pastoral Care, 1965, When Marriage Ends, 1971; contbr. articles in field to religious jours. Home: 229 Park Ave Glencoe IL 60022 Office: 263 Park Ave Glencoe IL 60022

BECKERDITE, DAVID VERN, minister, United Church of Christ; b. Springfield, Mo., May 28, 1953; s. David Vern Beckerdite and Carol Sue (Douglas) Beckerdite Morrison; m. Linda Ann Griffin, June 19, 1972; children: Bethany Dawn, Sara Elizabeth. B.S. in Sociology, Southwest Mo. State U., 1975; M.Div., St. Paul Sch. Theology, 1979. Ordained to ministry United Meth. Ch., 1977. Assoc. minister Platte Woods United Meth. Ch., Kansas City, Mo., 1979-80; asst. pastor Grandview United Meth. Ch., Mo., 1980-81; pastor Sloan United Ch. Christ, Iowa, 1981—; liaison for peace 6th congl. dist. United Ch. Christ, Northwest Iowa Conf., 1982—, chmn. ministry with adults com. 1982—; chaplain for the day Iowa Legis., Feb. 1982. Regional vice chmn. Platte County ARC, 1979-80; mem. campaign com. D. Rauch election assn., Napoleon, Mo., 1978; judge, 1976, 1978 elections; chmn. Dem. Caucus, Salix, Iowa, 1984; treas. Sloan Library Bd., 1983—. Mem. Westwood Ministerium, Monona County Crop Assn. (chmn. 1983—), Iowa State U. Clergy Extension, Pleasant View Nursing Home (care rev. bd.). Home: PO Box 50 Sloan IA 51055

BECKWITH, PETER HESS, priest, Episcopal Church; (chaplain); b. Battle Creek, Mich., Sept. 8, 1939; s. Robert Edgar and Florence Catheryn (Hess) B.; m. Melinda Jo Foulke, July 10, 1965; children: Peter Hess II, Michael Joseph. A.B., Hillsdale Coll., Mich., 1961; M.Div., Sch. Theology, U. South, 1964; S.T.M., Nashotah House, Wis., 1974. Ordained deacon Episcopal Ch., 1964, priest, 1965. Asst. rector St. John's Ch., Plymouth, Mich., 1964-66, St. Paul's Ch., Jackson, Mich., 1966-70; rector St. Matthew's Ch., Saginaw, Mich., 1970-78, St. John's Ch., Worthington, Ohio, 1978—; chaplain inmates So. Mich. State Prison, Jackson, 1966-70, Jackson Fire Dept., 1967-70; chmn. congregational devel. com. Central Ohio Regional Episcopalian Council, 1984—; asst. 4th Marine Aircraft Wing Chaplain, New Orleans, 1984—. Served to comdr., chaplian USNR, 1972—. Recipient Alumni Achievement award Hillsdale Coll., 1982; Navy Achievement medal Sec. Navy, 1983. Mem. Worthington Pastors Assn., Mil. Chaplains Assn., Naval Res. Assn., Navy League, Res. Officers Assn., Marine Corps Res. Officers Assn., SAR, Delta Tau Delta. Club: Sawmill Athletic (Columbus). Avocations: jogging, golf, auto mechanics, flying. Home: 6472 Tonbridge St Worthington OH 43085 Office: St John's Episcopal Ch 700 High St Worthington OH 43085

BEDNARIK, JOHN FRANCIS, priest, Roman Catholic Church; b. Pitts., Oct. 27, 1942; s. John Joseph and Antoinette Clare (Pernatozzi) B.; B.A., St. Fidelis Coll., 1965; M.A., Cath. U. Am., 1968. Ordained priest, 1968; asst. Santa Teresita Ch., Ponce, P.R., 1969-72; advisor Juventud Acciòn Católica, Ponce, 1969-72; dir., founder youth retreats Centro Capuchino, Río Piedras, P.R., 1972-84, dir. formation, 1984—; chaplain, CAP, Ponce, 1970—; spiritual dir. Colegio Santa Cruz, Trujillo Alto, P.R., 1975—; chaplain NG, Ponce, 1971-72, Marist High Sch., 1982—. Address: PO Box 21235 Río Piedras PR 00928

BEEKMANN, DAROLD HENRY, minister, parish services coordinator, Am. Luth. Ch.; b. Ft. Dodge, Iowa, Jan. 12, 1935; s. Jake and Tena (DeWall) B.; B.A., Wartburg Coll., 1957; B.D., Wartburg Theol. Sem., 1963; M.S.T., in Old Testament, Union Theol. Sem., N.Y.C., 1970; m. Marlene June Thews, Aug. 11, 1963; children—Heidi Lajune, Timothy David. Ordained to ministry, 1964; instr. missions seminar, Neuendettelsau, Germany, 1959-60; class asst., Old Testament dept. Union Theol. Sem., N.Y.C., 1963-64; asst. pastor Our Saviors Luth. Ch., Greeley, Colo., 1964-67; instr. Ecumenical Religious Seminar Program, Colo. State U., Ft. Collins, U. No. Colo., Greeley, 1965-67; pastor St. John-Trinity Luth. Parish, Hector, Minn., 1967-72; asst. pastor Our Redeemers Luth. Ch., Benson, Minn., 1972-75; coordinator parish services Southwestern Minn. Dist. Am. Luth. Ch., 1975—. Instr., Parents Effectiveness Tng., 1974—. Mem. bd. Renville County (Minn.) Assn. Mentally Retarded, 1971-72, mem. bd. Right To Read Program, 1973-75. Translator editor: Our Controversial Bible, 1969; author: (with Terrance Frethein) Our Old Testament Heritage, Vols. I and II, 1970-71; Instructors Guide for Our Old Testament Heritage I & II, 1970-71. Office: 619 SW 11th St Wilmar MN 56201*

BEHR, MARLENE ANN, educator, Seventh-day Adventist Church; b. Oswego, Kans., Nov. 21, 1931; d. Fred C. and Eunice (Cannard) Stevens; m. Robert D. Behr, June 16, 1954; 1 dau., Cynthia Kay. B.S., Union Coll., 1954; M.A., San Jose State U., 1966; postgrad. U. Hawaii, 1967. Tchr. home econs., dean Oak Park Acad., Nevada, Iowa, 1954-55; tchr., home econs. registrar Campion Acad., Loveland, Colo., 1955-60; tchr. hom econs. Golden Gate Acad., Oakland, Calif., 1960-66, Hawaiian Mission Acad., Honolulu, 1966-69, Orangewood Acad., Garden Grove, Calif., 1969-83; tchr. comsumer related sci. Hawaiian Mission Acad., 1984—; home econs. rep. N. Am. div. curriculum com. Gen. Conf., Washington, 1970-75, chmn. home econs. curriculum com., S.E. Calif., 1970-78; tchr. child devel. and devel. psychology Loma Linda U. Extension, 1969-83. Coordinator work experience child devel. classes Orangewood Acad., 1969-83. Named Tchr. of Year, Orangewood Acad., 1979, 82. Mem. Seventh-day Adventist Home Econs. Assn. Republican.

BEHREND, WILBUR. Bishop, Moravian Church of America, pres. Provincial Elder's Conf., 1982. Office:

Moravian Ch Am 69 W Church St Bethlehem PA 18018*

BEHRENS, CRAIG ALAN, minister, Lutheran Church - Missouri Synod; b. Worthington, Minn., Feb. 4, 1956; s. Dale Cobus and Marianne (Brinkman) B.; m. Tamara Marie Backus, Apr. 22, 1978; children: Katrina Elizabeth, Natascha Marie. B.A., Concordia Coll., St. Paul, 1978; M.Div., Concordia Sem., St. Louis, 1982. Ordained to ministry Luth. Ch. - Mo. Synod, 1982. Pastor Grace Evangelical Luth. Ch., West Lorne, Ont., Can., 1982—. Republican. Home: 110 Graham St West Lorne ON N0L 2P0 Canada

BEIL, MARY EUGENE, nun, educator, Roman Catholic Ch.; b. Youngstown, Ohio, Nov. 2, 1913; d. Eugene Jacob and Nellie Theresa (Knox) Beil; B.S. in Edn., Sisters Coll., Cleve., 1940; M.S. in Edn., Akron U., 1964; postgrad. John Carrol U., 1963-64, St. Louis U., 1967-68. Joined Sisters of St. Dominic, 1929; tchr. St. Bernard Sch., Akron, Ohio, 1930-40, St. Paul's Sch., Akron, 1941-42, St. Augustine Sch., Barberton, Ohio, 1942-46, Our Lady of Elms Sch., 1947-49, 63-64, Immaculate Conception Sch., Ravenna, Ohio, 1954-55; prin. St. Bernard Sch., Akron, 1949-55, 57-63, St. Felicitas Sch., Euclid, Ohio, 1953-57; adminstr. St. Edward Nursing Home, Akron, 1964—. Active Confraternity Christian Doctrine, 1930-64, Summit County United Way. Mem. Nat. Conf. Catholic Charities, Nat. Catholic Edn. Assn., Gerontology Soc., Missionary Assn. of Mary Immaculata, Bath Hist. Soc., Nursing Home Adminstrs. Assn., Am. Assn. Homes for Aging, Ohio Health Care Assn., Assn. Ohio Philanthropic Homes for Aging (legis. com. 1972). Home and office: 3131 Smith Rd Akron OH 44313

BELCHER, JOE CORNELIUS, minister, So. Bapt. Conv.; b. Spartanburg, S.C., Nov. 6, 1917; s. Enock Kenneth and Agnes Martha (Bryant) B.; student Campbell Coll., 1945-46; A.A., Gardner Webb Coll., 1947; B.A., Limestone Coll., 1949; m. Ellen Grubb, May 23, 1936; children—Joe William, Kenneth, Daniel. Ordained to ministry, 1945; pastor Pleasant Memory Bapt. Ch., Coats, N.C., 1945-46; asst. pastor Cherokee Ave. Bapt. Ch., Gaffney, S.C., 1946, Temple Bapt. Ch., Gaffney, 1946-59; pastor South Point Bapt. Ch., Belmont, N.C., 1960, Central Bapt. Ch., Gaffney, 1961-63, Flint Hill Bapt. Ch., Shelby, N.C., 1963-66, Rose Hill Bapt. Ch., Gaffney, 1966—. Mem. Broad River Bapt. Assn. Author: Gospel Call Booklet, 1950; Gospel Call Sermons, 1951; The Life and Ministry of Joe C. Belcher, 1975. Address: Route 8 PO Box 580 Gaffney SC 29340

BELISLE, GILLES See *Who's Who in America*, 43rd edition.

BELL, J.S., minister, Southern Baptist Convention; educator; b. Henderson County, Tenn., May 10, 1911; s. Charles D. and Ida Jane; B.A., Union U., 1933; Th.M., So. Bapt. Seminary, 1936; D.D., Georgetown Coll., 1949; M.S., U. Louisville, 1971; D.Min., Lexington Theol. Sem., 1980; m. Beulah Garland Threlkeld, June 12, 1936; children: Dorothy Ellis, Mary Garland, Ida Charlene, James Ernest. Ordained to ministry, 1929; pastor rural chs. Tenn., Ky., 1929-36, First Baptist Ch., Whiteville, Tenn., 1936-37, Fleming (Ky.) Baptist Ch., 1937-40, Hindman First Baptist Ch., 1940-58, 59-76, Temple Baptist Ch., Champaign, Ill., 1958; prof. Bible, Alice Lloyd Coll., Pippa Passes, Ky., 1959-69, asst. pastor First Bapt. Ch., Hindmon, Ky., 1984—; moderator Three Forks Bapt. Assn., 1955-57, 60-61, dir. missions, 1980-82; evangelist crusades in Alaska, 1966, 70, Kaduna and Minna, Nigeria, 1973; trustee Oneida Baptist Inst., 1973-76; prof. Clear Creek Bapt. Sch., Pineville, Ky., 1976-79; exec. bd. Ky. Baptists, 1952-54, 61-63; mem. Home Mission Bd., So. Baptist Conv., 1951-57. Chmn. Minimum Found. Com. for Knott County, 1974; trustee Alice Lloyd Coll., 1953-74, Georgetown Coll., 1961-67. Recipient Mountain Minister award Clear Creek Baptist Sch., 1956, citation Alice Lloyd Coll., 1966, 68, commemoration by Ky. Gov., 1976, Disting. Service award Union U., 1978. Gave ann. sermon Ky. Bapt. Conv., 1948; weekly sermon for Knott County News, Hindman, Ky., 1972-76; radio program Sta. WTCW, 1953-76. Home and Office: PO Box 306 Hindman KY 41822

BELL, JERRY LEE, minister, General Association of Regular Baptist Churches; b. Wabash, Ind., May 9, 1944; s. Paul Marion and Lenora Estella (Rogers) B.; m. Janie Irene Reed, Dec. 27, 1966; children: Andrew Wayne, Jonathan Michael, Matthew Alan. B.A., Bob Jones U., 1966; M.Div., Grace Theol. Sem., 1972. Ordained to ministry Bapt. Ch., 1973. Expediter Union Gospel Press, Cleve., 1967; bookstore mgr. Mid-South Bible Coll., Memphis, 1967-69; pastor Struthers Bapt. Tabernacle, Ohio, 1972—; sec. Bethany Assn. of Regular Bapt. Chs., Northeastern Ohio, 1975, 76, 83, 85, treas., 1984. Amateur Radio Club (v.p. 1983, ambassador 1984, vol. examiner 1984, 85). Contbr. articles to religious mags. Home: 2066 Lyon Blvd Poland OH 44514 Office: Struthers Bapt Tabernacle 305 Elm St Struthers OH 44471

BELL, KEITH ANDREW, minister, counselor United Methodist Church; b. Keldron, S.D., Apr. 16, 1913; s. John Andrew and Clara Katherine (Herrmann) B.; m. Genevieve Bertha Sill, Sept. 7, 1940. B.A., Whitworth Coll., 1941; B.D., Western Conservative Bapt. Sem., 1947; M.Ed., U. Oreg., 1951; Ed.D., Oreg. State U., 1959. Ordained to ministry United Meth. Ch., 1941. Pastor, United Meth. Ch., Seattle, 1938-39, Spokane, Wash., 1940-41, Portland, Oreg., 1941-48; asst. prof. Cascade Coll., Portland, 1948-58; asst. dean of students Portland State U., 1958-63; dean of students Malone Coll., Canton, Ohio, 1963-66; dean of students Seattle Pacific U., 1966-70, profl counseling psychology, 1970-81; dir. counseling CRISTA Ministries, Seattle, 1981—. Mem. adv. council for adult rehab. ctr. Salvation Army, Seattle, 1980—, chmn., 1984—, mem. adv. bd., 1984—; bd. dirs. Christian Conciliation Services, Seattle, 1981—. Contbr. to books: Adult Education in Church, 1970; Ventures in Family Living, 1971. Fellow, Seattle Pacific U., 1969. Mem. Oreg. Psychol. Assn., Christians Associated for Psychol. Studies. Republican. Avocations: photography, gardening, fishing, travel. Home: 22906 72d Pl W Mountlake Terrace WA 98043 Office: CRISTA Ministries 19303 Fremont Ave N Seattle WA 98133

BELL, L. M., bishop, Apostolic Overcoming Holy Church of God. Office: 200 Pio Nono Ave Macon GA 31206

BELL, LEON, minister, Nat. Bapt. Conv. U.S.A., Inc.; b. Liberty, Miss., July 14, 1930; s. Julius and Verline (Williams) B.; Th.B., Miss. Bapt. Sem., 1957; B.S., Jackson State U., 1959; M.S. U. So. Miss., 1969, M.A., 1974; D.D., (hon.), Miss. Bapt. Sem., 1975; postgrad. Wheaton Coll., summers 1963, 65, 66. Ordained minister, 1958; state dir. vacation bible schs. Miss. Bapt. Sem., 1958-59, also dir. Bapt. Student Union, Jackson State U.; dean Central Center Miss. Bapt. Sem., Jackson, 1959-67; pastor Hyde Park Bapt. Ch., Jackson, Miss., 1967—, New Mt. Zion Bapt. Ch., Jackson, 1969—. Part time pastor Priestley Chapel Bapt. Ch., Canton, Miss., 1961-64, Fairview Bapt. Ch., 1963-65, Pilgrim br. Bapt. Ch., Fannin, Miss., 1964-69, 1st Bapt. Ch., Monticello, Miss., 1965-66; chaplain Jackson State U., 1965-69, chmn. steering com. for religious activities, 1969-75; asst. sec. Progressive Bapt. State Conv. Miss., 1969—. Instr. English, Jackson State U., 1969-75. Active Boy Scouts Am., Community Service Assn., N.A.A.C.P. Bd. dirs. Com. of Concern, 1960-64, YMCA, Fairsh St., 1971—, Operation Shoestring, 1974—; trustee Miss. Bapt. Sem., 1971—; bd. dirs. Progressive Bapt. State Conv., 1967—, Gen. Bapt. State Conv., 1969—. Recipient certificate profl. excellency Miss. Tchrs. Assn., 1962. Mem. Miss. Bapt. Sem. Nat. Alumni Assn. (treas. 1970—), Internat. Platform Assn., V.F.W., Met. Bapt. Ministrial Fellowship Jackson, Phi Delta Kappa. Democrat. Mason. Home: 4322 Beacon Pl Jackson MS 39213 Office: 140 W Maple St Jackson MS 39213

BELL, WAYNE H., seminary adminstrator. Pres. Lexington Theol. Sem. (Disciples of Christ). Office: Lexington Theol Sem 631 Limestone St Lexington KY 40508*

BELL, WILLIAM WAKEFORD, minister, educator, Church of the Nazarene; b. Toronto, Ont., Can., Dec. 27, 1932; came to U.S., 1970; s. William Alfred Bell and Hilda Aloha (Dobney) Bellamy; m. Deborah Jean Franklin, June 19, 1971; children: Jennifer, Suzanne. B.A. with honors, Wheaton Coll., 1961; postgrad. Jaffray Sch. Missions, 1962-63, Toronto Inst. Linguistics, 1964; M.A. with honors, Wheaton Coll. Grad. Sch., 1967; Ph.D. with honors, Northwestern U., 1974. Ordained to ministry Christian and Missionary Alliance, 1964, Ch. of Nazarene, 1981. Asst. pastor, Christian and Missionary Alliance, Flint, Mich., 1963-64, missionary, India, 1964-66; prof., chmn. dept. psychology Olivet Nazarene Coll., Kankakee, Ill., 1970—; speaker confs. Bd. dirs., pres. Kankakee County Mental Health Ctr., 1971—; founding pres. Kankakee County Mental Health Council, 1975—. Graduate fellow Northwestern U., 1968, Garret Theol. Sem., 1968-70; named Tchr. of Yr., Olivet Nazarene Coll., 1973; recipient Disting. Service award Kankakee County Mental Health Ctr., 1978, Disting. Service award Kankakee County Mental Health Council, 1984. Mem. Christian Assn. Psychol. Studies. Home: 442 Francis St Bourbonnais IL 60914 Office: Olivet Nazarene Coll Kankakee IL 60901

BELLO, PATRICIA HARMON, religious educator, Roman Catholic Church; b. Chgo., Nov. 27, 1926; d. Patrick Thomas and Mary Josephine (Reilly) H.; m. Anthony Bello, July 11, 1959; 1 child: Sean Harmon. B.A. in Speech Edn., Mich. State U., 1949; M.A., U. Mich., 1951; B.S., Chgo. Tchrs. Coll., 1955. Cert. tchr., Pa. Coordinator preschool CCD, Pitts., 1969-71, tchr., 1969-79; nat. coordinator Wm. H. Sadlier Inc., N.Y.C., 1977-80; writer-dir. Telecreed Prodns., Pitts., 1982—; mgr. Anthony Bello Assocs., Pitts., 1982—; dir. Religious TV Telecreed Prodns., Pitts., 1982—. Author: Prayer Celebrations, New Life Liturgies I, 1977, II, 1978; writer Children's TV religious shows, Rainbow Country, 1984—. Home: 7321 Perrysville Ave Ben Avon Pittsburgh PA 15202

BELOTE, THOMAS ROBERT, SR., minister, Southern Baptist Convention; b. Townsend, Va., Apr. 30, 1922; s. Grover Cleveland and Edna Mae (Barker) B.; student Ventura Jr. Coll., 1969-70, U. Santa Barbara, 1968—, Golden Gate Theol. Sem., 1974; m. Helen Louise Speight, Sept. 18, 1946; children: Barbara Louise, Thomas R. Ordained to ministry, 1974; asst. youth minister 1st So. Baptist Ch., Oxnard, Calif., 1970-72; missionary assoc. So. Baptist Home Mission Bd., dir. Fillmore Community Center, San Francisco, 1972-77; chaplain Portsmouth City Jail, Va., 1977-82; dir. Downtown Ministry Ctr., Bpat. Home Mission project, 1982-84. Chmn. Western Addition Council of Youth Serving Agencies, San Francisco, 1975-76; mem. Westside Mental Health Advisory Bd., San Francisco. Named Outstanding Missionary of Yr., Christian Social Ministries Dept. Calif., 1976. Mem. San Francisco Peninsula Assn. of Calif. So. Baptist Conv. Home: 320 Florida Ave Portsmouth VA 23707

BELTER, EDGAR WILLIAM, clergyman, hospital administrator, Lutheran Church in America; b. Guttenberg, Iowa, Jan. 6, 1929; s. Robert Rudolf and Erna Dora (Teegan) B.; m. Deloris Ann Koenig, July 10, 1954; children: Timothy William, Christine Ann. B.A., Carthage Coll., 1948; D.D., 1969; M.Div., N.W. Luth. Theol. Sem., 1951. Ordained to ministry, 1951. Pastor Peace Luth. Ch., Steelville, Ill., 1951-57; asst. to pres. Wartburg Synod, United Luth. Ch. in Am., 1958, 59; sr. pastor Emmanuel Luth. Ch., Racine, Wis., 1959-69; pres., exec. dir. A-Center, Racine, 1969—; dir. Carthage Addiction Inst., 1969-80; chmn. legis. com. Alcohol/Drug Problems Assn. N. Am. 1972—, bd. dirs., chmn. bd. mgrs., council of agys., 1977-80; chmn. Gov.'s Task Force Alcohol-Drug Ins., 1970-76; chmn. Nat. Invitational Policy Forum on Alcohol/Drugs, 1982—; cons. Nat. Inst. Drug Abuse, Wis. Bur. Alcohol and Other Drug Abuse; mem. program rev. com. S.E. Wis. Health Systems Agy.; mem. alcohol/drug adv. com. Mission in N. Am. div. Luth. Ch. Am., 1977—; dir. Wis. Upper Mich. Synod, Luth. Ch. Am., Strength for Mission Campaign, 1977-78. Pres. Racine County Mental Health Assn., 1969-72; v.p. Wis. Mental Health Assn., 1972-74; mem. Alcohol/drug problems assn. N. Am. (treas. 1980-82). Mem. Wis. Alcohol Drug Treatment Providers Assn. (pres. 1982-83), Racine Mfg. and Employers Assn. (dir.). Home: 30 E Four Mile Rd Racine WI 53402

BELTER, SIEGFRIED RUDOLF, minister, educator, Church of God (Anderson, Ind.); b. Petrikan, Germany, Mar. 16, 1944; s. Martha Belter; came to Can., 1948, naturalized, 1963; Th.B., Alta. Bible Inst., 1966; B.A., U. Alta., 1970; D.D. (hon.), Gardner Bible Coll., 1984; m. Elaine Francis Frederick, Apr. 11, 1966 (dec. 1978); children: Desiree, Michelle; m. Donnalyn Kay Switzer, Dec. 22, 1979. Alumni chmn. Alta. Bible Inst., Camrose, 1968-70, alumni dir., 1970-73, mem., vice chmn. study commn., 1970-71, instr. Bible and Contemporary Theology, 1971-84, dean of men, 1971, acad. chmn., 1973-84, acad. dean, 1979-84; vice chmn. conv. program com. Ch. of God, Western Can., 1972-75. Mem. Alta. Theol. Soc., Assoc. Photographers Internat. Contbr. articles in field to religious jours. Home: 6701 45 Ave Camrose AB T4V 2P7 Canada Office: 4704 55 St Camrose AB T4V 2B6 Canada Died Jan. 19, 1984.

BELTRAN, EUSEBIUS JOSEPH See *Who's Who in America*, 43rd edition.

BENAVIDES, ALBERT J., priest, Roman Catholic Ch.; b. San Antonio, Tex., Dec. 25, 1943; s. Raul J. and Carmen (Chacon) B.; B.A., St. Mary's U., 1966, M.A., 1970. Ordained priest, 1970; asso. pastor St. John's Parish, San Antonio, 1970-73; pastor St. Timothy's Parish, San Antonio, 1973—. Regional dir. Padres Asociados Para Derechos Religiosos, Educativos, Sociales, 1975—. Mem. utilities action com. Communities Organized for Pub. Service, 1974—; treas. Mexican Am. Unity Council, 1975—; bd. dirs. Barrio Betterment and Devel. Corp., San Antonio, 1973—. Named Chicano of Yr., Raza Unida, 1975. Home: 1515 Saltillo St San Antonio TX 78207

BENDER, CORTLANDT SCHUYLER, religious music and arts educator, Presbyterian Church; b. Denver, Apr. 3, 1943; s. William Benton Bender and Eleanor (Schuyler) Bender Woodhull; m. Annette Savage, Aug. 14, 1964; children: Emily Juliette, Rebecca Kathleen. B.A., Tarkio Coll., 1964; M.F.A., Calif. Inst. Arts, 1973. Minister of music Luth. Ch., Westboro, Mo., 1963-64, First Meth. Ch., Los Angeles, 1966-69, Pacific Palisades Presbyn. Ch., Calif., 1969-75; minister music and arts Trinity Presbyn. Ch., San Carlos, Calif., 1981-83; sr. arts cons. Schuyler Creative Arts Inst., San Carlos, 1984—; dir. Body and Soul Dance Co., Berkeley, Calif., 1985. Actor, singer, dancer, producer, dir. various theaters throughout U.S., 1971—. Composer choral and instrumental works. Contbr. articles to profl. jours. Religious emphasis chmn. Santa Monica Jaycees, 1972. Rockefeller Found. fellow, 1970-71; Calif. Inst. Arts scholar, 1971-73. Mem. SAG, Actor's Equity Assn., Choral Condrs. Guild Los Angeles (pres. 1975-76), v.p. state bd. govs. 1983-85), Presbyn. Assn. Musicians. Office: Schuyler Creative Arts Inst 2757 Melendy Dr Suite 15 San Carlos CA 94070

BENDERLY, SHLOMO, educator, religious organization executive; b. Safed, Israel, Sept. 19, 1938; s. Joshua and Henia (Schneider) B.; came to U.S., 1972; diploma Ministry of Edn. Israel, 1961; M.S., Drake U., 1975; m. Victoria Moryoseph, Mar. 22, 1961; children—Joseph, Rakefet. Dir. Jewish Community Program, Cleve., 1967-69; a founder Hebrew House, Oberlin Coll., instr. Hebrew, 1968-69; cons., asst. Hebrew High Sch., Calgary, Alta., Can., 1969; dir. culture, youth and sport dept. Ministry of Edn., Safed, Israel, 1970-72; tchr., dir. Hebrew Sch., Des Moines, 1972—; exec. dir. Bur. Jewish Edn. and Jewish Community Center, Des Moines, 1973—; instr. Hebrew, Drake U., 1973-77. Home: 223 Aikapa Kailua HI 96734

BENDHEIM, CHARLES H., rabbi, Orthodox Jewish, chemical company executive; b. Bklyn., 1917; m. Els Salomon; 7 children. B.S. in Metall. Engring., Lafayette Coll., 1939. Bd. trustees Yeshiva U., 1961—, chmn. bd. trustees Rabbi Isaac Elchanan Theol. Sem., 1977—; past chmn. bd. dirs. Yeshiva U. High Schs.; pres. Am. Com. for Shaare Zedek Hosp., Jerusalem, 1979—; pres. Manhattan Day Sch.; bd. dirs. Jewish Edn., Inc., Beth Medrash Govoha, Lakewood, N.J., Ponevez Yeshiva, Israel, Congregation Shearith Israel, Manhattan, N.Y., Congregation Bachurei Chemed, Long Beach; active United Jewish Appeal-Fedn. Jewish Philanthropies; chief exec. officer, pres. Philipp Bros. Chem., Inc. Office: Philipp Bros Chemicals Inc New York NY

BENINCASA, PIUS A. See *Who's Who in America,* 43rd edition.

BENNETT, BILLY RAY, minister, Disciples of Christ Church; b. Goldsboro, N.C., Dec. 18, 1925; s. Losker Brian and Sarah S. (Herring) B.; m. Evie Cox, Jan. 11, 1946; children: Billy Ray, Tonya Kay Bennett Green. Student Draughon's Bus. Coll., Atlanta, 1947; A.B., Atlantic Christian Coll., 1955; postgrad. Lexington Theol. Sem., 1964-67. Ordained, 1955. Minister, Central Christian Ch., Merritt Island, Fla., 1967-69, Guyton Christian Ch. (Ga.), 1969-75, Crestwood Christian Ch., Birmingham, Ala., 1975-77, 1st Christian Ch., Macon, Ga., 1977—; treas. Greater Macon Area Christian Chs., 1983-85; bd. dirs., program dir. Inst. of Religion, Macon, 1979—; sec., bd. dirs. Christian Chs. in Ga., 1981-83; pres. All Faiths Com. Med. Ctr., Macon, 1983. Pres. Western Auto Supply Co., Greensboro, N.C., 1948-55; host radio show: Point of View, 1963, radio spot: Bright Spot, 1982-83. Author booklet: Twelve Most Asked Questions About the Christian Church, 1980. Bd. dirs., treas. March of Dimes, Macon, 1980-84; pres. Speech and Hearing Ctr. Central Ga., 1985. Served with U.S. Army, 1945-46. Recipient Outstanding Vol. Service award March of Dimes, 1982, Soc. Disting. High Sch. Students, 1982-85. Mem. Macon Ministerial Assn. (pres. 1979-80). Democrat. Club: Civitan (pres. Versailles, Ky. 1967). Office: 1st Christian Ch 2306 Vineville Ave Macon GA 31204

BENNETT, HAROLD CLARK, minister, religious organization administrator, Southern Baptist Convention; b. Asheville, N.C., July 30, 1924; s. Charles C. and Emily H. (Clark) B.; m. Phyllis Jean Metz, Aug. 17, 1947; children: Jeffrey Clark, John Scott, Cynthia Ann Bennett Howard. Student, Asheville Biltmore Jr. Coll., 1946, Mars Hill Coll., 1946-47; B.A., Wake Forest U., 1949; postgrad. Duke U. Div. Sch., 1949-51; M.Div., So. Bapt. Theol. Sem., 1953; LL.D. (hon.), Stetson U., 1968; D.D., Campbell U., 1982. Ordained to ministry Bapt. Ch., 1948. Pastor, Glen Royal Bapt. Ch., Wake Forest, N.C., 1948-51, Beech St. Bapt. Ch., Texarkana, Ark., 1955-60; chaplain Ky. State Reformatory, LaGrange, 1951-53, Ky. Woman's Prison, 1951-53; pastor Westpoint Bapt. Ch., Ky., 1952; asst. pastor First Bapt. Ch., Shreveport, La., 1953-55; supt. new work Sunday Sch. Dept. Sunday Sch. bd. So. Bapt. Conv., Nashville, 1960-62; interim pastor Little West Fork Bapt. Ch., Hopkinsville, Ky., 1960, Tow Rivers Bapt. Ch., Nashville, 1962; sec. met. missions home mission bd. So. Bapt. Conv., Atlanta, 1962-65; dir. missions div. Bapt. Gen. Conv. Tex., Dallas., 1965-67; exec. sec., treas. Fla. Bapt. Conv., Nashville, 1979—; bd. dirs. Religion in Am. Life, 1980—. Dir. Bapt. Life Ins. Co., 1982—; Author: Glimpses of Faith, 1983. Compiler: God's Awesome Challenge, 1980. Contbr. articles to religious publs. Mem. adv. council Fla. State Alcoholism, 1973-78; trustee Fla. Meml. Coll., Miami, 1967-74. Served with USN Air Corps, 1942-45. Named Ky. Col. Mem. Assn. Bapt. State Exec. Secs. (pres. 1978-79), Assn. Bapt. State Conv. Ch. Bond Plans (pres. 1978-79), Fla. Bapt. State Bd. Missions (sec. 1967-79), Am. Bible Soc., (bd. govs. 1979—). Lodge: Rotary. Home: 202 Long Valley Rd Brentwood TN 37027 Office: 460 James Robertson Pkwy Nashville TN 37219

BENNETT, WILLIAM EVERETT, lay church worker, deacon, Southern Baptist Convention; b. Forsyth County, Ga., Apr. 16, 1933; s. Luther L. and Mary Edith (Mamgum) B.; B.B.A., Ga. State U., 1967; m. Nancy Teresa Fowler, May 8, 1954; children—David William, Debra Teresa. Chmn. bd. deacons Bapt. Ch., 1970, 72, 74, 76; mem. exec. com. Atlanta Bapt. Conv., also internat. studies com., nominating com.; dir. Sunday sch. Briarlake Bapt. Ch., 1974-77. Pres., Bennett Bros. Printing Co., 1968—. Trustee, Peachtree Inn, Inc., Atlanta; Decatur Hosp. Home: 2156 Saren Ct Tucker GA 30084 Office: 2930 Flowers Rd South Atlanta GA 30341

BENSON, DAVID VANDERMEER, religious broadcaster, minister, Conservative Congl. Christian Conf.; b. Los Angeles, Sept. 18, 1929; s. Amos Searle and Bertha (VanDermeer) B.; student U. So. Calif., 1947-48, Wheaton Coll., 1948-49, Occidental Coll., 1950-51; B.D., U. Calif. at Los Angeles, 1953; postgrad. Harvard U., 1953-55; B.D., Fuller Theol. Sem., 1958; postgrad L'Alliance Française and U. Lausanne, 1960-61; m. Mary Carolyn Ware, July 4, 1964; children—Duke VanDermeer, David Ware. Ordained to ministry, 1967; founder Russia for Christ, Inc., Santa Barbara, Calif., 1958—; preacher, author, tchr., missionary; founder, pres. Miracle Publs., Inc.; with U.S. Dept. State in Russia, 1959; composer classical music; lectr. in various countries. Mem. bd. reference GLINT, 1965-77. Author: Henrietta Mears and How She Did It, 1965; Christianity, Communism and Survival, 1967; A New Look at Colossians, 1973; Miracle in Moscow, 1973. Home: 910 Crestwood Dr Santa Barbara CA 93105 Office: 3009 A De La Vina St Santa Barbara CA 93105

BENSON, EZRA TAFT, church official. Mem. Quorum of the Twelve, The Church of Jesus Christ of Latter-Day Saints. Office: The Church of Jesus Christ of Latter-Day Saints 50 E North Temple St Salt Lake City UT 84150*

BENSON, JAMES LOUIS, minister, So. Baptist Conv.; b. Oct. 5, 1932; s. William Carroll and Mayme Magdalene (O'Leary) B.; B.A., U. Corpus Christi, Tex., 1959; B.D., So. Bapt. Theol. Sem., Louisville, 1962, M.Div., 1970; m. Margie Mae Johnson, May 22, 1953; children—James Ray, Donald Wayne, John Mark, Stephen Earl, Cheryl LaMae. Ordained to ministry, 1956; pastor Papalote (Tex.) Bapt. Ch., 1956-59, Hay Crossing Bapt. Ch., Morehead, Ky., 1959-60, Bramlette Bapt. Ch., Sanders, Ky., 1960-62, Bellepoint Bapt. Ch., Frankfort, Ky., 1962-65; Spanish missionary to Mexican Americans, Tex., 1965-74; lang. missions dir. Home Mission Bd., So. Bapt. Conv. and Bapt. Conv. N.Y. State, N.Y.C., 1974—. Owner, operator Med. Clinic, San Antonio, 1966-72. Active, Protestants and Others United for Separation of Ch. and State. Mem. Christian Med. Soc. Home: 345 Maolis Ave Glen Ridge NJ 07028 Office: Box 383 Ansonia Sta New York City NY 10023

BENSON, JEFFREY RHODES, theology educator; b. Eau Claire, Wis., July 8, 1955; s. Charles William and Marlys Estella (Rhodes) Adams; m. Denise Susan Julian, Aug. 7, 1976. B.A., Pillsbury Coll., 1976; M.Div., Central Bapt. Sem., 1979, Th.M., 1981; Th.D. candidate Dallas Theol. Sem., 1984. Teaching fellow Central Sem., Mpls., 1978-81, prof. N.T., 1981—, registrar, 1981—; dean 4th Bapt. Bible Inst., Mpls., 1981-83. Editor, Central Testimony, 1981-83. Mem. Evang. Theol. Soc., Soc. Bible Lit. Office: Central Bapt Theol Sem 2105 Freemont Ave N Minneapolis MN 55411

BENSON, LEONARD AXEL, minister, American Lutheran Church; b. Egan, S.D., Dec. 8, 1919; s. Iver and Lena Sophia (Lorentson) B.; B.A., Augustana Coll., 1943; diploma Luther Theol. Sem., St. Paul, 1948; postgrad. U. Wis., 1948-51; m. Noreen Jessie Obrecht, Aug. 12, 1950; children: Rolf, Martha, Lisa, Sonia, Arne, Solveig. Ordained to ministry, 1948; pastor Bethel Luth. Ch., Madison, Wis., 1948-51, English Luth. Ch., Ellsworth, Wis., 1951-58, Bethlehem Luth. Ch., Ellsworth, 1951-54, Bethany Luth. Ch., Mauston, Wis., 1958—. Chmn. fgn. missions com. S. Wis. Dist., Am. Luth. Ch., 1968-70, v.p. dist., 1973—, v.p. dist. council, 1972-74, mem. exec. com., 1973—. Sec. Juneau County Blood Assn., 1964-76; pres. chpt. Am. Field Service, 1972-73; pres. Mauston PTA, 1965-66; bd. dirs. Hess Meml. Hosp. Assn., 1966—. Recipient Distinguished Citizen award Mauston Jr. C. of C., 1972; Twenty-five year service award Am. Luth. Ch., 1976; named Citizen of Yr., Mauston C. of C., 1984. Mem. Juneau County Mental Health Soc. Home: 702 Grove St Mauston WI 53948 Office: 701 Grove St Mauston WI 53948

BENSON, WILLIE, JR., clergyman. Chief pastor Free Christian Zion Church of Christ, Nashville, Ark. Office: Free Christian Zion Ch of Christ 1315 Hutchinson St Nashville AR 71852*

BENZ, NORMAN DAVID, minister, Ch. of God (Cleveland, Tenn.); b. New Sharon, Iowa, June 8, 1947; s. Ray Charles and Violet V. (Matherly) B.; B.S., Lee Coll., 1969; postgrad. U. Louisville, 1973, Purdue U., 1972-73; grad. Ch. of God Bible Inst. program, 1976; m. Judy Carol Denham, Aug. 26, 1967; children—Jonathan David, Kristopher Erik. Ordained to ministry, 1976; clk. records Ch. of God radio ministry, Forward in Faith, Cleveland, 1969; pastor Ch. of God, Cohutta, Ga., 1969-70, Franklin, Ind., 1974—; dir. Christian edn. Farmdale Ch. of God, Louisville, 1970-74. Sec., Central Ind. Ch. of God Ministerial Assn.; tchr. Bible Inst. classes, Franklin. Chmn. Johnson County (Ind.) Salvation Army social services unit; chmn. bd. dirs. Kandy Kane Child Care Center, Franklin. Mem. Johnson County Ministerial Assn. Named Dist. Youth and Christian Edn. Dir. of Year, Ky. Ch. of God, 1971-72. Home: 860 N Main St Franklin IN 46131 Office: 856 N Main St Franklin IN 46131

BEREN, SHELDON, Jewish organization executive. Chmn. Nat. Bd. Torah Umesorah-Nat. Soc. for Hebrew Day Schs. Office: Torah Umesorah-Nat Soc for Hebrew Day Schs 160 Broadway New York NY 10038*

BERG, RICHARD DAVID, religious official Orthodox Judaism; engineer, b. Bklyn., Feb. 24, 1943; s. Max and Mildred (Amrom) B.; m. Janet Barbara Marks, Feb. 24, 1968; children: Brian, Cheri, Abby. Student Bklyn. Coll., 1960-62; cert. elec. engring. RCA Inst., 1969. Bd. dirs. Congregation Bet Tefilah, Matawan, N.J.; pres., Aberdeen, N.J., chmn. bd., 1983—. Supervising engr. Westinghouse Electric Corp., Hillside, N.J., 1969—. Membership chmn. U.S. Submarine Vets., Elmont, N.Y., 1967. Served with USN, 1962-68. Republican. Lodge: Erste Baranower K.U. Verien (pres. 1979—).

BERGENDOFF, CONRAD LUTHER, minister, Lutheran Church in America; b. Chgo., Feb. 14, 1924; s. Conrad John Immanuel Gertrude (Carlson) B.; m. Marlom E. Thompson, June 26, 1948 (div. 1976); children: Bruce, Rondi; m. Jean Rulf, Feb. 9, 1980. B.A., Augustana Coll., 1944; M.A., U. Chgo., 1948; M.Div., Luth. Sem., Phila., 1948. Ordained to ministry Luth. Ch. of Am., 1948. Pastor St. Luke's Luth. Ch., Bay Shore, N.Y., 1957-66, Reformation Luth. Ch., New Britain, Conn., 1967-72; mgr. communications Profl. Leadership div. Luth. Ch. in Am., Phila., 1974-77; chaplain Riverside Retreat, Rock Island, Ill., 1977-80; pastor Faith Luth. Ch., Brookfield, Ill., 1981-84; vis. scholar U. Chgo., 1985—; mem. task force on alcoholism and drug dependence Ill. Synod, Chgo., 1981—. Author: (pamphlet) Pastoral Care for Alcoholism, 1981. Editor Profl. Leadership Exchange jour, 1974. Democratic committeeman, Conn., 1972. Served with USN, 1943-45. Fulbright fellow London Sch. Econs., 1949. Mem. Brookfield Ministerial Alliance. Lodge: Kiwanas. Home: 9523 Jefferson Ave Brookfield IL 60513

BERGER, ALAN LEWIS, educator; b. New Brunswick, N.J., Nov. 16, 1939; s. Michael and Ruth (Baum) B.; A.B., Upsala Coll., 1962; A.M., U. Chgo. Div. Sch., 1970; Ph.D., Syracuse U., 1976; m. Naomi Berger, Aug., 1971; 3 sons. Faculty dept. religion Syracuse (N.Y.) U., 1973—, chmn. Jewish studies program, 1980—. Bd. dirs. Inst. for Study of Genocide, 1985—. Mem. Am. Acad. Religion, Nat. Assn. Holocaust Educators, Assn. for Sociology of Religion. Author: Crisis and Covenant: The Holocaust in American Jewish Fiction. Contbr. articles to profl. and religious jours., to Ency. Brit. 1985—. Office: 505 H L Religion Dept Syracuse Syracuse NY 13210

BERGER, GEORGE DONALD, minister, Southern Baptist Convention; b. Baton Rouge, Apr. 2, 1942; s. Beverly Benjamin and Florence Omelia (Dunn) B.; m. Jo Ann Patton, Aug. 17, 1963; children: Pamela Donise, Kimberly Dawn. Student, La. State U., 1960-62; B.S., William Carey Coll., 1964; Th.M. New Orleans Bapt. Theol. Sem., 1969; Th.D., Clinton Theol. Sem., 1977; postdoctoral Southwestern Bapt. Theol. Sem., Nicholls State U., 1980-81. Ordained to ministry So. Bapt. Ch., 1963. Pastor Indian Hill Bapt. Ch., Greene County, Miss., 1963-64, 1st Bapt. Ch., Springfield, La., 1965-69, Sumrall, Miss., 1969-73, Plaquemine, La., 1973-83, Calvary Bapt. Ch., Pascagoula, Miss., 1982—; mem. Miss. Bapt. Conv. Bd., Jackson, 1970-73; moderator Lamar Bapt. Assn., Miss., 1972-73; pres. Judson Pastor's Conf., Baton Rouge, 1974-75; family life dir. Jackson County Bapt. Assn., Miss., 1982—. Chmn. Tri-Parish Substance Abuse Council, Plaquemine, 1975-77; active mem. Mental Health Bd., Donaldsonville, La., 1980-82; mem. allocation com. United Way, Pascagoula, 1984—. Served to capt. U.S. Army. Named to Gov's. staff Gov. Bill Waller, Miss., 1972, Gov. Dave Treen, La., 1980; recipient Legion of Honor Internat. Supreme Order of Demolay, Kansas, 1981. Mem. Jackson County Ministerial Assn., Baton Rouge Area Ministerial Assn. (v.p. 1981-82), Jackson County C. of C. (membership com. 1984—), Jaycees (pres. local chpt. 1972-73). Lodges: Masons, Rotary. Home: 3607 Catalina St Pascagoula MS 39567 Office: Calvary Bapt Ch PO Box 2278 Pascagoula MS 39567

BERGER, PHILMORE, rabbi, Reform Jewish Congregations; b. Cleve., Apr. 10, 1927; s. Harry W. and Rose (Reich) B.; B.A., U. Cin., 1950; M. Hebrew Lit., Hebrew Union Coll., 1953; diploma in pastoral counseling Post Grad. Center for Mental Health, N.Y.C., 1967; m. Anita Silberstein, Nov. 21, 1951; children—Debra, Daniel, David, Diane. Ordained rabbi, 1953; rabbi Temple Avodah, Oceanside, N.Y., 1963—, now life tenure. Pres. N.Y. Assn. Reform Rabbis, 1976-78; rabbinic dir., counsellor N.Y. Fedn. Reform Synagogues, 1970—; chmn. family life com. Central Conf. Am. Rabbis, 1973-75; chaplain South Nassau Communities Hosp., L.I., 1972—. Mem. B'nai B'rith. Home: 333 Niles St Oceanside NY 11572 Office: 3050 Oceanside Rd Oceanside NY 11572

BERGERON, LILLY ROSE, religious music administrator, Roman Catholic Church; b. Berlin, N.H., Oct. 25, 1933; d. Honore Damas and Sophie Aurore (LeFrancois) B. B.Mus. in Applied Music, Rivier Coll., 1969; M.Mus. Edn., Duquesne U., 1977. Tchr. elem. schs. Presentation of Mary, Woonsocket, R.I., 1955-56, Concord, N.H., 1957-58, Phenix, R.I., 1958-61, Cascade, N.H., 1961-66; choir dir., N.H., 1958-79, organist, Manchester, N.H., 1961-79; elem. tchr. music Hudson Acad., N.H., 1967-71; instr., chmn. dept. music Rivier Coll., Nashua, N.H., 1974-79; dir. ministry of music St. John the Evangelist Ch., Davison, Mich., 1979—. Music tchr., organist Keene Cultural Ctr., N.H., 1972-73; mem. Manchester Music Com., N.H., 1972-74, N.H. Commn. on Arts, 1973-74. Arranger church music, liturgies. Author exptl. study on aesthetic experience as approach in teaching music listening skills. Mem. Am. Choral Dirs. Assn., Nat. Pastoral Musicians. Avocations: tennis; golf; mountain climbing. Home: 215 W South St Davison MI 48423 Office: Saint John the Evangelist Church 404 N Dayton St Davison MI 48423

BERGESON, ERNEST AXEL EUGENE, minister, Lutheran Church in America; b. Deep River, Conn., Nov. 3, 1920; s. Ernest Hjalmer Andrew and Elsie (Bjorkman) B.; m. Martha Magdeline Julius, June 27, 1943; children: Marvin E., Rachel Bergeson Margolis, Mark. Ordained to ministry Lutheran Church in America, 1945. A.B., Bethany Coll., 1942; B.D., Augustana Theol. Sem., 1945; M.Div., Luth. Sch. Theology, 1972. Pastor Emmanuel Luth. Ch., Mason City, Iowa, 1945-49, Peace Luth. Ch., Seattle, 1949-61, Bethel Luth. Ch., Auburn, Mass., 1961-69, First Luth. Ch., Waltham, Mass., 1970—; dean Western Mass. Dist. New Eng. Synod, 1966-69; mem. Mass. Comn. Christian Unity, 1969—; v.p. Lord's Day League of New England, Boston, 1972—; trustee Waltham Hosp., 1978-81; pres., dir. Mass. Council Chs., Boston, 1983—; mem. bd. mgrs. Lord's Day Alliance of U.S., Atlanta, 1981—. Chmn. trustees City of Waltham's Leland Charity Fund, 1974—; exec. bd. Minuteman council Boy Scouts Am., Stoneham, Mass., 1970—; commr. Mayor's Cable TV Commn., Waltham, 1982—. Recipient Silver Beaver award Boy Scouts Am., 1970, Lamb award Luth. Council, U.S.A., 1972. Mem., organizer Ecumenical Theol. Study Group, Worcester, Mass., 1963—. Lodge: Kiwanis (pres. 1974). Home: 1714 Trapelo Rd Waltham MA 02154 Office: First Luth Ch 8 Eddy St Waltham MA 02154

BERGGREN, PAUL WALTER, minister, Evangelical Free Church; b. Runnels, Iowa, Aug. 22, 1922; s. Walter Carl and Fern (Temple) B.; m. Dorothea F. Bierma, July 14, 1943; children: Nancy Ann, Susan Elaine, Jane Marie. B.A., Kletzing Coll., 1944; student Trinity Evang. Div. Sch., Deerfield, Ill., 1967-69. Ordained to ministry Evang. Free Ch., 1942. Pastor chs., Madric, Iowa, 1944-46, Keene, Nebr., 1947-49, Mpls., 1950-55, Wayzata, Minn., 1955-63, Kenosha, Wis., 1963-66, 1st Evang. Free Ch., Moline, Ill., 1966-76; traveling evangelist, 1947—; ch. extension dir., evangelist North Central dist. Evang. Free Ch. Am., Mpls., 1976-79, evangelist, Bible tchr., nationally, 1979—; treas. Free Ch. Internat. Ministerial Assn., 1958-60; pres. Miss. Valley Nat. Assn. Evangelicals, 1968-69; sec. overseas mission bd. Evang. Free Ch., 1971-76, chmn. Great Lakes dist., 1975-76; bd. dirs. Ozark Bible Inst., 1964-76. Home: 585 Old Crystal Bay Rd Long Lake MN 55356 Office: 1515 E 66th St Minneapolis MN 55423

BERGH, HENRY THEODORE, minister, Seventh-day Adventist Ch.; b. Spokane, May 24, 1918; s. Paul Bennie and Anna Marie (Meyer) B.; B.A. in Bus., Walla Walla Coll., 1940; m. Miriam Lorraine Jackson, Aug. 24, 1939; children—Karen, Judi, Della, Cyndi. Ordained to ministry Seventh-day Adventist Ch., 1948; served Seventh-day Adventist chs., Milwaukie, Oreg., 1940-43, St. Johns, Oreg., 1943-46; asst. mgr. book dept., advt. mgr. Pacific Press Pub. Assn., Mountain View, Calif., 1946-48; dir. youth activities, dir. Wawona summer camp Central Calif. Conf. Seventh-day Adventists, 1948-54; dir. youth activities, dir. Cedar Falls summer camp So. Calif. Conf. Seventh-day Adventists, 1954-57; sec.-treas. Ariz. Conf. Seventh-day Adventists, 1957-63; adminstr. Hanford Community Hosp., 1963-69; asso. adminstr. St. Helena Hosp. and Health Center, 1969-71; sec.-treas. No. Calif. Conf. Assn. Seventh-day Adventists, 1971—, also dir. trust services, sec. Leoni Meadows Devel. Com. Retreat Camp. Author: Upward Trails, 1963; author, composer Pathfinders, 1952. Home: 371 Ridgeview Dr Pleasant Hill CA 94523 Office: Box 23165 Pleasant Hill CA 94523

BERGSMA, DERKE PETER, educator, minister, Christian Reformed Church in America; b. Racine, Wis., Aug. 29, 1927; s. John Sietze and Johanna Jacoba (Vlaardingerbroek) B.; m. Doris Elaine Bielema, Oct. 28, 1950; children: Deborah, Derk, Diann, Danette. A.B., Calvin Coll., 1951; B.D., Calvin Sem., 1954; M.A., Northwestern U., 1962; Th.D., Free U.-Amsterdam, 1964; Rel.D., Chgo. Theol. Sem., 1968. Ordained to ministry, 1954. Instr., Calvin Coll., Grand Rapids, Mich., 1950-52; pastor Christian Reformed Ch., Grand Rapids, 1954-62; prof. Trinity Christian Coll., Palos Hts., Ill., 1968-81, Westminster Theol. Sem., Escondido, Calif., 1981—; co-founder Christian Counseling Ctr., Palos Hts., 1974-76; trustee Bd. Publs., Christian Ref. Ch., Grand Rapids, 1970-76. Author: Voices, 1976, Predestination: Islam and Calvinism, 1984. Contbr. articles to profl. jours. Chaplain USNR, Chgo., 1968-75, USMCR, Glenview, Ill., 1975-77. Served with USN, 1945-47. Chgo. Ch. Fedn. grantee, 1977. Mem. Evang. Theol. Soc., DAV. Lodge: Lions. Home: 2751 Crownpoint Pl Escondido CA 92027 Office: Westminster Theol Sem PO Box 2215 Escondido CA 92025

BERGSTROM, CHARLES VERNE, minister, religious organization official, Lutheran Church in America; b. Orion, Ill., July 9, 1922; s. J. Edward and Emily Marie (Swanson) B.; m. Lois Janet Johnson, Aug. 5, 1945; children: Cheryl Ann (dec.), Paul Scott, Gail Janet. B.A., Augustana Coll., Rock Island, 1945; M.S., Augustana Theol. Sem., Rock Island, 1948; postgrad. Andover-Newton Theol. Sch., 1959-61; D.D., (hon.), Upsala Coll., 1973. Ordained to ministry Lutheran Ch., 1948. Pastor St. Mark's Ch., Bridgeport, Conn., 1948-53, Bethesda Ch., Springfield, Mass., 1954-63, Trinity Ch., Worcester, Mass., 1963-77; advocate Office for Govtl. Affairs, Luth. Council in the U.S.A., Washington, 1977—; mem. bd. of social ministry Luch. Ch. in Am., 1962-72, pres. bd. of social ministry, 1972-77, mem. exec. council; chmn. commission on ecumenical relations, N.E. Synod, Worcester, Mass., 1969-74; chmn. Mass. Com. on Christian Unity, Worcester, 1969-77; pres. Luth. Resource Mobilization, Worcester, 1970-74; chmn. Washington Interreligious Staff Council, 1980-81. Author: The Gospel We Preach, 1958. Chmn. Citizens Com. on Police Practices, Springfield, Mass., 1955-60; mem. Personnel Police Bd., Springfield, 1960-63, Planning Council, Worcester, Mass., 1966-70, Citizens Action Com., Worcester, 1964-70; chmn. IMPACT, 1982-84. Recipient Alumni citation Augustana Coll., 1962, Outstanding Service award, 1974. Democrat. Home: 5424 Bromyard Ct Burke VA 22105 Office: Office for Governmental Affairs Lutheran Council in the USA 122 C St NW Suite 300 Washington DC 20001

BERISFORD, MARTIN ANDREW, JR., minister, United Meth. Ch.; b. Clarksburg, W.Va., Mar. 28, 1937; s. Martin Andrew and Florence Mae (Alley) B.; A.B., W.Va. U., 1959; M.Div., United Theol. Sem., 1963; m. Sandra Lou Turner, Aug. 13, 1960; children—Martin Andrew, Sarah Emily, Susan Margaret. Ordained to ministry, 1963; asso. pastor in Dayton, Ohio, 1959-63, Evang. United Brethren Ch., New Haven, 1963-67; with extension staff W.Va. U., 1967-68; pastor 4th Ave United Meth. Ch., Huntington, W.Va., 1968-69; conf. program council staff, dir. camps and conf., family life and mgmt. EvUnBreth Acres, Ednl. Center, Buckhannon, W.Va., 1969-71; pastor Evang. United Meth. Ch., Buckhannon, 1971-73, Christ Ch., Sutton, W.Va., 1973-76, Trinity United Meth. Ch., Glenville, W.Va., 1976—. Home: PO Box 128 Glenville WV 26351 Office: 122 Main St Glenville WV 26351

BERKEDAL, DAVID JAMES, minister, American Lutheran Church. B. Manitowoc, Wis., May 21, 1948; s. Robert Marvin and Marilyn Deane (Hansen) B.; m. Sally Ann Welch, Oct. 14, 1983. B.A., St. Olaf Coll., 1973; cert. in Clin. Pastoral Edn., Luth. Gen. Hosp., Park Ridge, Ill., 1975; M.Div. with honors, Pacific Luth. Theol. Sem., 1977, D.Min. candidate, 1981—. Ordained to ministry American Lutheran Church, 1977. Pastor, Christ Luth. Ch., Compton, Calif., 1977—; mem. Luth. Soc. Service of So. Calif. Bd., Los Angeles, 1977-81, Ecumedia, Los Angeles, 1978-81, Bishop's Commn. on Hispanic Ministry, Fresno, Calif., 1980—; facilitator/dir. Gospel Worship Service, 1982; treas. Religious Access Cable TV Bd., Compton, 1982—. Author (weekly newspaper col.) The Amen Corner, 1980—. Founder, pres. Hub City Cert. Farmer's Market, Compton, 1981—; mem. standing com. on crime City of Compton, 1982—; mem. pres.'s adv. com. Compton Coll., 1983-84. Served to cpl. USMC, 1969-71. Recipient cert. of participation Drake Relays Marathon, Des Moines, 1976, Order Blistered Toe award Livermore Marathon, Calif., 1976, First Pl. trophy City of Compton 5K Race, 1982. Mem. Compton Ministerial Assn. (community outreach chairperson 1980—). Democrat. Office: Christ Luth Ch 530 W Alondra Blvd Compton CA 90220

BERKOWITZ, WILLIAM, rabbi, Conservative Jewish Congregations; b. Phila., June 28, 1924; s. Albert Lewis and Pauline (Obod) B.; B.S., Temple U., 1948; M.H.L., Jewish Theol. Sem., 1952; D.H.L., Spertus Coll. of Judaica, 1972; m. Florence Elster, Dec. 22, 1946; children—Perry Ethan, Adena Karen, Leah Daphne. Ordained rabbi, 1952; asso. rabbi Congregation B'nai Jeshurun, N.Y.C., 1951-60, rabbi, 1960—. Pres. N.Y. Bd. Rabbis, 1972-74, also chmn. exec. com.; nat. pres. B'nai Zion, nat. orgn. hdqrs. N.Y.C., from 1974; founder, dir. Inst. Adult Jewish Studies. Editor: I Believe, 1961; Ten Vital Jewish Issues, 1964; Heritage and Hope, 1965; Let Us Reason Together, 1970; Conversation With . . ., 1975. Office: 270 W 89th St New York NY 10024

BERLAT, NORMAN, rabbi, Orthodox Jewish Congregations; b. N.Y.C., Oct. 20, 1940; s. Joseph Solomon and May (Goodman) B.; B.A., Yeshiva U., 1962, M. Hebrew Lit., 1965, rabbi, 1965, M.S., 1973; doctorate Hebrew Theol. Coll., 1980; m. Roslyn H. Metzger, Mar. 22, 1964; 1 son, Hillel. Rabbi, 1965; rabbi congregations in Pa., Ga., Ohio, Minn., 1965-73; chaplain Rochester (Minn.) Meth. Hosp., 1970-73, St. Mary's Hosp., Rochester, 1970-73; Luth. Gen. Hosp., Park Ridge, Ill., 1973—. Fellow Coll. Chaplains, Rabbinical Council Am., Assn. for Clin. Pastoral Edn., Chgo. Bd. Rabbis, Chgo. Rabbinical Council, Am. Chem. Soc., Assn. Orthodox Jewish Scientists. Contbr. articles to profl. publs. Home: 7135 N Carpenter Rd Skokie IL 60077 Office: Lutheran Gen Hosp 1775 W Dempster St Park Ridge IL 60068

BERLIN, DONALD ROBERT, rabbi, Jewish religion; b. Montreal, Que., Can., June 30, 1936; s. Saul Schnair and Isabel (Riven) B.; B.A., U. Toronto and U. Cin., 1961; B.H.L., Hebrew Union Coll., 1963, M.A. in Hebrew Lit., 1969; m. Norma Brass, Nov. 26, 1959; children: Seth Daniel, Sharon Leah. Rabbi, 1965; rabbi Temple Emanuel, Roanoke, Va., 1965-71, Congregation Keneseth Israel, Allentown, Pa., 1971-76; sr. rabbi Temple Oheb Shalom, Balt., 1976—; chaplain VA Hosp., Salem, Va., 1965-71; instr. Va. Western Community Coll., Roanoke, Va., 1968-71, Northampton Sem., Pa., 1972-73, Ecumenical Inst., St. Mary's Sem. and U., 1978—, Goucher Coll., 1977—; cons., Commn. Ecumenical Affairs Roman Catholic Diocese Richmond, 1966-71; exec. com. Camp Harlam, Kresgeville, Pa., 1975—; Pres., Ronaoke Valley Assn. Mental Health, 1968-70; rep. Roanoke Valley Mental Health, Mental Retardation Services Bd., 1968-71; 2d v.p. Family Service Travelers Aid, Roanoke Valley, 1969-71; chmn. Drug Abuse Coordinating Com. Roanoke Valley, 1969-71; mem. exec. com. Va. adv. bd. Anti Defamation League, 1967-71, exec. com. United Jewish Appeal, 1966-71; mem. religious relations com. Minsi Trails council Boy Scouts Am., 1972-76, exec. council Balt. Area council, 1981-83; vice-chmn. Allentown Youth Commn., 1975-76; adviser Allentown Council Youth, 1974—; bd. dirs. Lehigh County Council on Alchol and Drug Abuse, 1971-74, United Fund Lehigh County, 1972-76, Lehigh County Mental Health-Mental Retardation Services Program, 1972-76, Jewish Fedn. Allentown, 1971-76, Jewish Community Relations Council, 1971-76, Allentown Jewish Day Sch., 1971-76, Greater Balt. Assn. Mental Health, 1977-81; bd. dirs., 1st v.p. Valley Youth House, 1974-76; chmn. Pastoral Care com. Allentown-Sacred Heart Hosp., 1975-76; mem. nat. rabbinic cabinets United Jewish Appeal, State of Israel Bonds, World Union for Progressive Judaism; mem. Jewish culture and identity com. Assoc. Jewish Charities and Welfare Funds; mem. nat. Jewish edn. com. Am. Jewish Com.; pres. Balt. Blacks and Jews in Dialogue, 1984; chmn. council of clergy Md. Dept. Health and Mental Hygiene, 1983—. Mem. Central Conf. Am. Rabbis (exec. com., pres. Mid-Atlantic region 1984-86), Am. Jewish Hist. Soc., Assn. Reform Zionists in Am. (nat. bd. dirs., exec. com. 1982—), Zionist Orgn. Am. (bd. dirs. Balt. region), Jewish Book Council Am., Balt. Jewish Council (1st v.p. 1983—), Balt Bd. Rabbis (pres. 1983-85). Lodge: B'nai B'rith. Home: 28 Millstone Rd Randallstown MD 21133 Office: 7310 Park Heights Ave Baltimore MD 21208

BERLING, JUDITH A., religion educator; b. Jacksonville, Fla., Sept. 8, 1945; d. Sigmund Arthur Berling and Frances Marie (Schilling) Youtzy; B.A., Carleton Coll., 1967; M.Phil., Columbia U., 1975, Ph.D., 1976. Assoc. prof. religious studies Ind. U., Bloomington, 1975—. Author: The Syncretic Religion of Lin-Chao-en, 1980. Fellow Woodrow Wilson Found., 1967, Nat. Def. Fund, 1968-71, Danforth Found., 1971-74, Am. Council Learned Socs., 1981-82; NEH grantee, summer 1984. Mem. Am. Acad. Religion (co-chmn. comparative studies of religion sect. 1982—), Assn. Asian Studies (bd. dirs. China and Inner Asia Council 1985—), Am. Soc. Study Religion, Am. Council Learned Socs. (com. on history of religion 1985—). Office: Dept Religious Studies Ind U Bloomington IN 47405

BERMAN, JULIUS, religious organization executive. Pres. Union of Orthodox Jewish Congregations in Am., N.Y.C. Office: Union of Orthodox Jewish Congregations in Am 116 E 27th St New York NY 10016*

BERMUDES, ROBERT WILLIAM, minister, United Church of Christ; b. Springfield, Mass., Jan. 15, 1930; s. Ralph Angel Bermudes and Charlotte (Meserve) Bermudes Cox; m. Sally Ruth Brown, Mar. 18, 1956; children: Robert William, Mark Richard, Peter Andrew. B.A., Hiram Coll., 1952; M.Div., Hartford Sem., 1955; D.Min., Colgate/Rochester Div. Sch., 1980. Ordained to ministry Congregational Christian Chs., 1955. Asst. minister 1st Congl. Ch., Lorain, Ohio, 1955-57; assoc. minister 1st Congl. Ch., New Britain, Conn., 1957-62; minister 1st Ch. of Christ, Groton, Conn., 1962-72; sr. minister Irondequoit United Ch. of Christ, Rochester, N.Y., 1972—; mem. bd., pres. Commn. Human Rights, New Britain, 1973-76; mem. com. structure N.Y. conf. United Ch. of Christ, 1975-78; pres. West Irondequoit Ministers Assn., 1978-79; bd. dirs. Metro-planning Task Force, Rochester, 1978-81, Mutuality in Mission, Rochester, 1980-84, St. John's Home for Aging, Rochester, 1981—. Author: Conquering Cancer, 1983;

also articles in religious publs. Frequent speaker tng. and support groups Am. Cancer Soc., 1984—; mem. adv. bd. Hi-Sch. Guidance Dept., West Irondequoit, 1984—. Recipient Outstanding Leader award Rochester Gen. Hosp. Chaplaincy Com., 1982. Home: 126 Bellehurst Dr Rochester NY 14617

BERNABE, POLIENATO FERRER, priest, Roman Cath. Ch.; b. Labrador, Pangasinan, Philippines, Feb. 13, 1941; s. Julio and Leoncia (Ferrer) B.; came to U.S., 1973; B.A., Vigan Maj. Sem., Philippines, 1963. Ordained priest, 1966; asso. pastor, then pastor chs. in Philippines and Fla., 1966-74; asst. dir. Royal Carpenter Acad., Philippines, 1969-72; pastor Infanta Ch., Pangasinan, 1973-75; asso. pastor Holy Name Ch., Gulfport, Fla., 1975—; chaplain Sons of Italy, 1975—. Recipient Thanks award Philippine Boy Scouts, 1971. Mem. Legion of Mary (dir. praesidium and curia of St. Petersburg). Address: 5806 15th Ave S Gulfport FL 33707

BERNARD, DAVID KANE, religion educator, college dean and official, United Pentecostal Church International; b. Baton Rouge, Nov. 20, 1956; s. Elton David and Loretta (Artigue) B.; m. Connie Jo Sharpe, June 6, 1981. B.A. magna cum laude, Rice U., 1978; J.D. with honors, U. Tex., 1981. Ordained to ministry United Pentecostal Ch., 1984; bar: Tex. 1981. Youth minister United Pentecostal Ch., Austin, Tex., 1978-81; dean of students Jackson Coll. Ministries, Miss., 1981-82, dean of missions, 1981—, asst. v.p., 1982—; mem. publicity com. Miss. dist. United Pentecostal Ch., Jackson, 1984—. Author: In Search of Holiness, 1981; The Oneness of God, 1983; The New Birth, 1984; Essentials of Oneness Theology, 1984; Practical Holiness: A Second Look, 1985. Contbr. articles to religious publs. Mem. Order of Coif, Phi Beta Kappa. Home: 236 Pine Knoll Dr Jackson MS 39211 Office: Jackson Coll Ministries 1555 Beasley Rd Jackson MS 39206

BERNARDIN, JOSEPH LOUIS CARDINAL, archbishop, Roman Catholic Church; b. Columbia, S.C., Apr. 2, 1928; s. Joseph and Maria M. (Simion) B.; A.B. in Philosophy, St. Mary's Sem., Balt., 1948; M.A. in Edn., Cath. U. Am., 1952. Ordained priest Roman Cath. Ch., 1952: consecrated bishop, 1966; asst. pastor Diocese Charleston (S.C.), 1952-54, vice chancellor, 1954-56, chancellor, 1956-66, vicar gen., 1962-66, diocesan consultor, 1962-66, administr., 1964-65; aux. bishop Atlanta, 1966-68; pastor Christ the King Cathedral, 1966-68; sec., mem. exec. com. Nat. Conf. Cath. Bishops-U.S. Cath. Conf., gen. sec., 1968-72; archbishop of Cin., 1972-82, of Chgo., 1982—; elevated to Sacred Coll. of Cardinals, 1983. Mem. Sacred Congregation Bishops, 1973-78, Permanent Council Synod Bishops, 1974—; del. World Synod of Bishops, 1974; pres. Nat. Conf. Cath. Bishops-U.S. Cath. Conf., 1974—; mem. Pontifical Commn. Social Communications, 1970-72. Mem. Am. Revolution Bicentennial Adv. Com., 1975, Pres.'s Adv. Com. on Refugees, 1975. Address: 1555 N State Pkwy Chicago IL 60610*

BERNEY, JAMES EDWARD, campus chaplin; b. Medford, Oreg., Dec. 31, 1937; came to Can., 1981; s. Edward Alfred and Lou Ella (Ponath) B.; m. Margery Ann Black, Sept. 3, 1960; children: Christine, Sarah. B.S., Oreg. State U., 1959, M.S., 1961; M.A., Young Life Inst., Pasadena, Calif., 1967. Ordained to ministry, Plymouth Brethren Assemblies, 1961. Campus staff mem. Inter-Varsity Christian Fellowship, Madison, Wis., 1961-65, area dir., 1965-68, regional dir., 1968-81, gen. dir., Toronto, Ont., Can., 1981—; adj. instr. Fuller Theol. Sem., Pasadena, Calif., 1976-81. Editor: You Can Tell the World, 1979. Mem. Am. Sci. Affiliation. Office: Inter-Varsity Christian Fellowship 745 Mount Pleasant Rd Toronto ON M4S 2N5 Canada

BERNSTEIN, IRVING See *Who's Who in America,* 43rd edition.

BERNTSON, TERRANCE WILFRED, priest, Roman Catholic Ch.; b. St. Paul, Aug. 3, 1934; s. Wilfred Clarence and Catherine Bernadine (Sullivan) B.; B.A., St. Paul Sem., 1956; J.C.B., Lateran U., Rome, Italy, 1963, J.C.L., 1964, J.C.D., 1965. Ordained priest, 1960; chancellor Archdiocese of St. Paul and Mpls., Roman Catholic Ch., 1965-73; chaplain Coll. St. Catherine, St. Paul, 1966-71; named monsignor, 1973; pastor Basilica of St. Mary, Mpls., 1973—. Mem. bd. consultors Archdiocese of St. Paul and Mpls., Roman Catholic Ch., 1967—, mem. ecumenical commn., 1973—; chaplain Minn. Senate, 1976. Mem. Canon Law Soc. Am., Knight of Equestrian Order of Holy Sepulchre. Contbr. articles to religious jours. Home and office: 88 N 17th St Minneapolis MN 55403

BERRY, JAMES TERRANCE, religious organization, administrator, Roman Catholic Church; b. St. Paul, Sept. 19, 1946; s. James Graham and Molana Jane (Duxbury) B.; m. Paula Jeanne Justice, Apr. 18, 1969; children: Paul Justice, Pamela Justice. B.F.A., U. Minn., 1972; M.A., Coll. St. Thomas, St. Paul, 1980; D.Min., Luther Northwestern Theol. Sem., St. Paul. Dir. adult edn. St. Richard's Cath. Community, Richfield, Minn., 1978-80; dir. family ministry St. Mary of Lake Ch., Plymouth, Minn., 1980-85; dir. King's House of Retreats, Buffalo, Minn., 1985—; cons. Sycamore Cons., Mpls., 1980-83; research asst. Faith Devel. in Adult Life Cycle Project, St. Paul, 1980-81; continuing edn. specialist Coll. St. Thomas, 1980-82. Contbr. articles to religious jours. Served with USN, 1964-68. Mem. Assn. Coordinators Religious Edn., Assn. Pastoral Ministers. Avocations: photography; writing; sports. Home: 4504 Rutledge Ave Edina MN 55436 Office: King's House of Retreats 621 S 1st Ave Buffalo MN 55313

BERRY, ROBERT COURTLAND, minister, Baptist Federation Canada; b. Moncton, N.B., Can., Apr. 3, 1931; s. Harry Allison and Bernice Catherine (Steeves) B.; B.A. in Theology, Gordon Coll., 1954; B. Div., Gordon Div. Sch., 1958; m. Grace Ethel Lambert, May 23, 1953; children—Richard, Donald, Paul, Glen. Ordained to ministry, 19—; pastor chs., Grand Falls, N.B., Can., 1958-62, Calvary Baptist Ch., North Sydney, N.S., 1962-67, Forest Hills Baptist Ch., St. John, N.B., 1967-70; asso. sec. Canadian Baptist Overseas Mission Bd., Toronto, Ont., 1970—. Mem. Baptist Ministers Fellowship Ont. and Que., Toronto Inst. Linguistics (mem. exec. com.). Asso. editor The Enterprise, 1973—; contbr. articles to religious jours. Office: care Can Bapt Fedn 217 Saint George St Toronto ON M5R 2M2 Canada

BERRY, ROBERT EDWARD FRASER, bishop, Anglican Church Canada; b. Ottawa, Ont, Jan. 21, 1926; s. Samuel and Clara (Hartley) B.; m. Margaret Joan Trevorrow, May 12, 1951; children: Christopher Fraser, Elisabeth Joan. B.A., Sir George Williams Coll., 1950; Th.L., Montreal Diocesan Theol. Coll., 1953, D.D. (hon.), 1972; B.D., McGill U., 1953. Ordained deacon Anglican Ch. Can., 1953, priest, 1954, consecrated bishop, 1971. Rector, St. Margaret's Ch., Hamilton, Ont., 1955-61, St. Mark's Ch., Orangeville, Ont., 1961-63, St. Luke's Ch., Winnipeg, Man., Can., 1963-67; rector St. Michael and All Angels Ch., Kelowna, B.C. and supervisory pastor Central Okanagan region, 1967-71; bishop of Kootenay, B.C., 1971—. Served with RCAF, 1943-45. Home: 1857 Maple St Kelowna BC V1Y 1H4 Canada Office: PO Box 549 Kelowna BC V1Y 7P2 Canada

BERRY, RONALD THOMAS, minister, United Meth. Ch.; b. Covington, Ky., May 11, 1946; s. Ollie Thomas and Virgie Lee (Adkins) B.; A.B., Asbury Coll., 1968; M.Div., Candler Sch. Theology, Emory U., Atlanta, 1972. Ordained to ministry, 1969; pastor Wesley United Meth. Ch., Ludlow, Ky., 1972—. Mem. dist. bd. ministry United Meth. Ch., 1972; bd. mgrs. Lake Junatucka Assembly, United Meth. Ch., 1976—. Named Rotarian of the Year, Ludlow (Ky.) Rotary Club, 1976. Address: 449 Victoria St Ludlow KY 41016

BERTHOLD, FRED, JR., minister, United Church of Christ, educator; b. St. Louis, Dec. 9, 1922; s. Fred and Myrtle Bernice (Williams) B.; A.B., Dartmouth Coll., 1944; B.D., Chgo. Theol. Sem., 1947; Ph.D., U. Chgo., 1954; D.D., Middlebury Coll., 1959, Concord Coll., 1960, U. Vt., 1964; m. Laura Bell McKusick, Dec. 27, 1945; children: Marjorie Chase, Daniel Stephen, Timothy Marshall, Sarah Megan. Ordained to ministry United Ch. of Christ, 1949; prof. religion, Dartmouth Coll., 1954—, dean William Tucker Found., 1957-62, dean of humanities, 1976-81. Recipient Harbison award for disting. teaching, 1962. Mem. Am. Theol. Soc., Am. Acad. Religion, Nat. Soc. Values in Higher Edn. Author: The Fear of God, 1959; Basic Sources of the Judeo-Christian Tradition, 1962. Contbr. articles to religious periodicals. Office: Dartmouth College Hanover NH 03755

BERTMAN, JOHN CHARLES, priest, Roman Catholic Ch.; b. Jerseyville, Ill., June 17, 1914; s. John Charles and Mary Theresa (Schmieder) B.; A.B., Pontifical Coll., Josephinum, 1940. Ordained priest Roman Cath. Ch., 1940, became monsignor, 1974; asst. pastor St. Aloysius Ch., Springfield, Ill., 1940-49; chaplain St. Francis Hosp., Litchfield, Ill., 1949-50; pastor St. Valentine Ch., Oblong, Ill., 1950-52, St. Michael Ch., Michael, Ill., 1952-59, St. Aloysius Ch., Litchfield, 1959-67, St. Michael Ch., Sigel and St. Mary Ch., Neoga, Ill., 1967-69, St. Boniface Ch., Quincy, Ill., 1969—. Dean Quincy Deanery, 1969; mem. Diocesan Bd. Consultors, Springfield, 1975—; sec. Springfield Diocesan Rural Life Conf., 1945—. Diocesan dir. Legion of Mary, 1970—. Bd. dirs. Western Cath. Newspapers, 1970—, Cath. Boys High Sch. (now Quincy Notre Dame), 1970—, Parochial Secondary Edn. Found., 1970—, United Community Services of Adams County, Ill., 1969—. Decorated Papal Chamberlain, 1974. Mem. Farm Bur., Western Cath. Union, Roman Cath. Cemetery Assn. (pres.), Internat. Medicale du Lourdes (hon.), C. of C. K.C. (4 deg., chaplain). Home and office: 117 N 7th St Quincy IL 62301

BEST, JAMES RICHARD, minister, Southern Baptist Convention. B. Woodville, Tex., Aug. 22, 1933; s. James Fletcher and Annie Floy (Maclin) B.; m. Bobbie Jean Benton, May 30, 1952; children: Theresa Floy, Daveta Elaine, James Timothy Milton. B.S., East Tex. Bapt. U., 1955; B.D., Southwestern Bapt. Theol. Sem., 1965; D.Min., Luther Rice Sem., 1981. Lic., 1950; ordained, 1954. Pastor various Tex. chs., 1955-66, Clawson Bapt. Ch., Lufkin, Tex., 1966-67, 1st Bapt. Ch., Alpine, Tex., 1967-69, Parkview Bapt. Ch., Decatur, Ala., 1969-75, Vestavia Hills Bapt. Ch., Decatur, 1975-78, 1st Bapt. Ch., Colmesneil, Tex., 1978-85, Lincoln St. Bapt. Ch., Portland, Oreg., 1985—; exec. bd. Bapt. Gen. Conv. Tex., 1981-85; area com. Sabine Neches Bapt. Area, Kirbyville, Tex., 1982-85; vice moderator New Bethel Bapt. Assn., Woodville, Tex., 1982-85; trustee Paisano Bapt. Assembly, Alpine, 1967-70; assn. clk. Assn. Annual, Big Bend Bapt. Assn., 1968, 69 (awards), chaplain Masons, Rising Sun, 1977-78, Yellow Pine, 1983—; tchr. Bible jr. colls. Author: A View from Bethel, 1983; A Continuing Witness, 1984. Bd. dirs. Morgan County Concerned Citizens Against Alcohol and Drug Problems, Decatur, 1973; mem. Tex. Sesquicentennial Com., Tyler County, 1984. Lodge: Rotary (pres. Woodville 1981-82, editor Alpine 1967-69). Home: 3240 SE Lincoln St Portland OR 97214 Office: Lincoln St Bapt Ch Portland OR 97214

BETHEA, JOSEPH BENJAMIN, minister, United Meth. Ch.; b. Dillon, S.C., Sept. 9, 1932; s. Rufus Emery and Ella Blumer (Johnson) B.; A.B., Claflin Coll., 1953; M.Div., Gammon Theol. Sem., 1956, D.D., 1974; postgrad. Union Theol. Sem., Richmond, 1966-68; m. Shirley Ann Cundiff, June 7, 1958; 1 dau., Josefa Elizabeth. Ordained to ministry, 1954; pastor in S.C., 1953-56, N.C., 1956-65; dist. supt., Richmond, Va., 1965-68; pastor in Greensboro, N.C., 1968-72; dir. The Black Ch. Studies Center, Duke Div. Sch., Durham, N.C., 1972—. Del., United Meth. Gen. and Jurisdictional Confs., 1967-72, ann. conf. Ch. in Caribbean and the Americas, 1976; chmn. Black Methodists for Ch. Renewal; Mem. Western N.C. conf. bd. discipleship, bd. ordained ministry; chmn. N.C. Regional Commn. on Higher Edn. and Campus Ministry. Pres., Bragtown Elementary Sch. PTA, 1976-77; bd. dirs. Edgemont Community Center, Durham; trustee High Point (N.C.) Coll., 1972—. Mem. NAACP, Alpha Phi Alpha. Home: 5600 Old Well St Durham NC 27704 Office: Duke Div Sch Durham NC 27706

BETTENDORF, JAMES BERNARD, priest, Roman Catholic Church; b. Jackson, Mich., Oct. 22, 1933; s. Bernard Anthony and Kathryn Marie (Vaughan) B.; B.A., Sacred Heart Sem., Detroit, 1955; S.T.B., St. John Sem., Plymouth, Mich., 1959; M.A., Western Mich. U., 1970; postgrad. U. Detroit, summer 1956, U. Notre Dame, summer 1957, Cath. U. Am., summer 1958, St. Mary's U., Balt., 1981—. Ordained priest Roman Catholic Ch., 1959; assoc. pastor Holy Trinity Ch., Fowler, Mich., 1959-60; assoc. pastor St. Phillip Ch., Battle Creek, Mich., 1960-63, Sacred Heart Ch., Flint, Mich., 1963-66; dir. Flint Newman Center, Flint Cath. Info. Center, 1966—; pastor Good Shepherd Parish, Montrose, Mich., 1983—; pres. Interfaith Action Council Flint, 1970-71; diocesan dir. Campus Ministry, Diocese of Lansing, Mich., 1971—; chmn. Interfaith Met. Agy. Planning, Flint, 1971-74. Mem. exec. bd. Genesee-Lapeer-Shiawasee Health Planning Commn., 1971—, Tall Pine Council Boy Scouts Am.; mem. exec. bd. Urban Coalition, Flint, 1973-74, 76—, pres., 1976—; treas. Regional Ecumenical Broadcasting Commn., 1971—. Mem. Am. Cath. Hist. Assn., Catholic Campus Ministers Assn., Flint Ministerial Assn., Medieval Acad. Rotarian. Home: 1802 E Court St Flint MI 48503 Office: 609 E 5th Ave Flint MI 48503

BETTIS, CRESTON ALAN, religious educator, American Baptist Churches in the U.S.A.; recreational vehicle center executive; b. Merced, Calif., May 27, 1959; s. Creston Amberson and Betty Jean (Lynn) B.; B.A. in Social Service, Fresno Pacific Coll., 1981; M.A. in Counseling, Valley Christian U., 1985. Dir. theatre arts First Bapt. Ch., Merced, Calif., 1982—, sr. high sch. staff mem., 1982—; resident counselor Fresno Pacific Coll., Calif., 1979-81, dir. religious drama, 1980-81; dir. child devel. Readyland Day Care, Fresno, 1981-82. Ptnr. Recreational Vehicle Bettis Ctr., Merced, Calif., 1981—. Author: textbook, Christian Counseling - A Primer, 1985. Mem. Nat. Assn. Christians in Social Work. Home: 3056 N Trindade Rd Merced CA 95348

BETTIS, JOSEPH DABNEY, religious studies educator, United Methodist Church; b. Graham, Tex., Sept. 19, 1936; s. Jack and Jo (Dabney) B.; m. Lynne S. Masland; 5 children. B.A., So. Meth. U., 1958; B.D. cum laude, Drew U., 1961; M.A., Princeton U., 1963, Ph.D., 1964. Ordained to ministry United Meth. Ch., 1960. Instr. religion Douglass Coll., Rutgers U., 1962-64; asst. prof. religion U. Ala., 1964-66, assoc. prof., chmn. dept. religious studies, 1966-72, Thompson lectr., 1967; disting. prof. humanities, scholar in residence Sch. Pub. Affairs and Community Services, U. Nebr.-Omaha, 1972-73, assoc. dean, prof. in residence, 1973-75, grad. faculty fellow, 1974; dean, prof. Fairhaven Coll., Western Wash. U., Bellingham, 1975-78, prof. religious studies, 1978—; sr. fellow William O. Douglas Inst. for Study Contemporary Social Problems, 1975—; bd. dirs., sr. cons. Youth Seminar on World Religions, 1982-84; mem. bd. advisors Internat. Coalition against Religious and Racial Intolerance, 1981-84; exec. dir. N.W. Council on Religious Liberty, 1984. Editor: Phenomenology of Religion, 1969; (with Stanley Johannesen) The Return of the Millenium, 1984. Contbr. articles and revs. to religious jours. Cons. tech. assistance panel So. region

OEO/Community Action Program, 1966-72; mem. regional selection com. Danforth Assoc. Program, 1968-70; mem. acad. council Nat. Inst. on Holocaust, 1977; mem. panel experiential edn. resources Council for Advancement Experiential Edn., 1978-79; mem. Wash. Com. on Religious Liberty, 1981; mem. acad. adv. bd. Inst. on Comparative Polit. and Econ. Systems, 1981-83; bd. dirs. New Sch., Omaha, 1973, Inst. for Social Encounters, 1974, NW Concert Assn., 1981-83. Tipple scholar Drew U., 1958-60; fellow in religious studies Princeton U., 1961-63; research grantee U. Ala., 1965, 66, 68-71; Danforth assoc., 1966-75; internat. studies grantee U. Ala., 1970; fellow Inst. for Ecumenical and Cultural Research, St. Johns U., 1970, NEH, 1970; Met. Life ednl. grantee, 1977; cons. program grantee NEH, 1978. Mem. Am. Religious Liberty Assn. (planning coordinator 1983—), Am. Acad. Religion (chmn. N.W. region sect. on modern religious movements 1983—). Home: 1327 Scenic Ave Bellingham WA 98226 Office: Fairhaven College Western Wash Univ Bellingham WA 98225

BETTON, FARRISH EARL, minister, United Pentecostal Church International; b. Little Rock, July 29, 1946; s. TeRoy and Thelma (Odom) B.; m. Carolyn McCoy, Dec. 28, 1968; children: Samuel F., Benjamin E. B.S.E.E., U. Ark., 1969. Ordained to ministry United Pentecostal Ch. 1983; cert. fin. planner; registered investment advisor. Sr. elder United Pentecostal Ch., Houston, 1978—; sec., trustee Life Temple, United Pentecostal Ch., Houston, 1977—. Pres., chief exec. officer Betton and Co. Group, Bellaire, Tex., 1978—. Treas. Child Care Council of Houston, 1978—. Mem. Internat. Assn. Fin. Planners, Inst. Cert. Fin. Planners. (713) 667-0094

BETZ, HANS DIETER, minister, Presbyn. Ch., educator; b. Lemgo, Germany, May 21, 1931; s. Ludwig and Gertrude (Vietor) B.; student Sch. Theology, Bethel, Germany, 1951-52; postgrad. (World Council Chs. fellow) U. Cambridge (Eng.), 1954-55; Dr. Theology, U. Mainz, 1957, Habilitation, 1966; m. Christel H. Wagner, Nov. 10, 1958; children—Martin, Ludwig, Arnold. Came to U.S., 1963, naturalized, 1973. Ordained to ministry Presbyn. Ch., 1961; pastor Evangelische Landeskirche, Germany, 1958-63; prof. N.T., Sch. Theology, Claremont (Calif.), 1964-78, also prof. religion Claremont Grad. Sch., 1963-78, project dir. Inst. Antiquity and Christianity, Claremont, 1965-78; prof. N.T., U. Chgo. Divinity Sch., 1978—, chmn. dept. N.T. and early Christian lit. Humanities Div., 1985—; vis. prof. U. Mainz, 1967, U. Uppsala, 1973-74, U. Zürich, 1977, Oxford U., 1981, Cambridge U., 1984. Recipient Gutenberg Stipendium, 1953, several research fellowships Nat. Endowment for Humanities. Mem. Studiorum Novi Testamenti Societas, Soc. Bibl. Lit., Chgo. Soc. Bibl. Research. Author: Lukian von Samosata und das Neue Testament, 1961; Nachfolge und Nachahmung Jesu Christi im Neuen Testament, 1967; Der Apostel Paulus und die sokratische Tradition, 1972; Galatians, 1979; Essays on the Sermon on the Mount, 1985; 2 Corinthians 8 and 9, 1985. Contbr. articles and book reviews to periodicals. Office: 1025 E 58th St Chicago IL 60637

BEUSSE, ROBERT BERNARD, religious communication consultant, Roman Catholic Church; b. Utica, N.Y., Aug. 10, 1930; s. Harry A. and Christina (Collins) B.; m. Patricia M. Welsh, Apr. 6, 1953; children: Claire, Robert G., Patricia, Brian, Donna, Barbara, Thomas. A.B., Fordham U., 1952, M.F.A., 1960. Sec. for communication Nat. Conf. Roman Catholic Bishops and U.S. Catholic Conf., N.Y.C., 1970-79; pres. Robert B. Beusse, Inc., N.Y.C., 1979—; organizer, creator Campaign for Human Devel., 1970, Cath. Communication Campaign, 1978; bd. mgrs. Internat. Cath. Assn. for Radio-TV, 1972; cons. Pontifical Commn. for Social Communication, 1973-84. trustee N. Am. Vatican Radio Found. Vice pres. N.Y. Bd. Trade, 1970, bd. dirs., 1967-70; bd. dirs. Greater N.Y. chpt. ARC, 1968-71. Recipient UNDA award for Best Religious Film Program, 1968; Gabriel award for Best TV spot series, 1971, for personal achievement, 1979. Mem. Knights of Malta, Nat. Acad. TV Arts and Scis. (chmn. edn. com. 1968), NCCJ (nat. TV campaign chmn. 1968). Lodge: K.C. Home: 41 Overlook Rd Caldwell NJ 07006 Office: 404 Park Ave S New York NY 10016

BEUTEL, EUGENE WILLIAM, mission administrator, American Lutheran Church; b. Sanborn, N.Y., July 27, 1927; s. Edwin William and Alice Ruth B. (Williams) B.; m. Dolores Mae Hanson, June 24, 1950; children: David Lee, Paul Christian, Jonathan Andrew. B.A., Capital U., 1949; B.D., Evangelical Luth. Theol. Sem., Columbus, Ohio, 1952; Th.M., Princeton Sem., 1970, D.Min., 1975. Ordained to ministry American Lutheran Church, 1952. Pastor, Holy Trinity Luth. Ch., Balt., 1955-61, Redeemer Luth. Ch., Nepture, N.J., 1961-74; area service mission dir. Am. Luth. Ch., Farmingdale, N.J., 1974—; chaplain Hamilton Fire Co., Neptune, N.J., 1962-74; chmn. ch. and soc. com. Eastern dist. Am. Luth. Ch., Washington, D.C., 1971-73; advisor soc. service agys., Springfield, Va., 1974-84; mem. task force on D.Min. standards Am. Assn. Theol. Schs., Vandalia, Ohio, 1975-77; mem. nat. task force on internationalization of Mission Am. Luth. Ch., Mpls., 1978—; lectr. on China reflections J. J.

Murphy Lectures, 1983. Reviewer various publs. Bd. dirs. Shore Area YMCA, Asbury Park, N.J., 1962-69; advisor, mem. Juvenile Conf. Com., Neptune, N.J., 1965-74; con. Hope Community Counseling Ctr., Freehold, N.J., 1976—. Served with U.S. Army, 1952-55; Korea, Col. Res. (ret.). Decorated Bronze Star, Legion of Merit, Meritorious Service medal; recipient Man Yr. award Shore Area YMCA, Asbury Park, 1968. Mem. Mil. Chaplains Assn. Republican. Home: 21 Schaeffer Ln Freehold NJ 07728 Office: Am Luth Ch Area Office 8 W Main St Farmingdale NJ 07727

BEVILACQUA, ANTHONY JOSEPH, bishop, Roman Catholic Church; b. Bklyn., June 17, 1923; s. Louis and Maria Giuseppa (Codella) B.; J.C.D., Gregorian U., Rome, 1956; M.A., Columbia, 1962; J.D., St. John's U., 1975. Ordained priest, 1949; asst. pastor chs., N.Y., 1949-50; prof. history Cathedral Coll. Sem., Bklyn., 1950-53; asst. chancellor in Tribunal, 1957-65; prof. canonllaw Sem. of Immaculate Conception, Huntington, N.Y., 1968-80; vice-chancellor Diocese of Bklyn., 1965-76; dir. Cath. Migration Office, Diocese of Bklyn., 1971—; aux. bishop of Bklyn., 1980-83; bishop of Pitts., 1983—; Chaplain, Sisters of Mercy Motherhouse, 1972—; v.p. Bklyn. Diocesan Priests Senate, 1971-72; chancellor Diocese of Bklyn., 1976-80. Adj. prof. law St. John's U., 1976—. Mem. Canon Law Soc. Am., Am. Cath. Philos. Assn., Cath. Theol. Soc. Am., Am. Bar Assn., Assn. Immigration and Nationality Lawyers, N.Y. State, Bklyn. bar assns. Contbr. articles to profl. and religious jours. Office: 111 Blvd of Allies Pittsburgh PA 15222*

BEVINS, CHARLES REX, clergyman, United Methodist Church; b. Cedar Rapids, Nebr., May 5, 1932; s. Charles Franklin and Maggie Lavina (Cox) B.; m. Ardis Dee Dappen, June 21, 1953; children: Michael, Mark, Deborah. B.A., Nebr. Wesleyan U., 1955, D.D. (hon.), 1979; M. Div., Pacific Sch. Religion, 1959. Ordained deacon, United Meth. Ch., 1956, elder, 1959. Pastor chs., Calif., Nebr., 1956-74; exec. dir. ministry Nebr. Conf. United Meth. Ch., Lincoln, 1974-80; sr. minister St. Paul Ch., Lincoln, 1980—; mem. Gen. Bd. Global Ministries, United Meth. Ch., N.Y.C., 1976-84, chmn. research and devel. com., 1980-84; chmn. legis. com. Gen. Conf. Global Ministries, United Meth. Ch., 1980, 84; chmn. legis com. Gen. Bd. Discipleship, United Meth. Ch., Nashville, 1984-88. Chmn. treatment and rehab. com. Commn. on Drugs, Lincoln, 1974-80. Democrat. Lodge: Kiwanis (local club Kiwanis Man of Yr. 1973). Office: St Paul United Meth Ch 1144 M St Lincoln NE 68508

BEYER, DOUGLAS DEAN, minister, American Baptist Church in the U.S.A.; b. Hutchinson, Kans., Apr. 17, 1935; s. Harold A. and Julia J. (Kealiher) B.; m. Martha A. Edwards, May 20, 1957; children: Catherine, Deborah, Elizabeth. B.A., Baylor U., 1957; M.Div., Fuller Theol. Sem., 1969; Th.M., Southwestern Bapt. Theol. Sem., 1961; D.Min., San Francisco Theol. Sem., 1974. Ordained to ministry Baptist Ch., 1961. Pastor First Bapt. Ch., Ness City, Kans., 1961-65, First Bapt. Ch., Atchison, Kans., 1965-69, West Side Bapt. Ch., Topeka, Kans., 1969-82, First Bapt. Ch., Temple City, Calif., 1982—; chaplain Topeka Police Dept., 1969-82. Author: Basic Beliefs of Christians, 1981; Commandments for Christian Living, 1983; Parables for Christian Living, 1985. Home: 9906 Bogue St Temple City CA 91780 Office: First Bapt Ch 6019 Baldwin St Temple City CA 91780

BEYER, FREDERICK WILLIAM A., pastor, United Church of Christ; b. Billings, Mo., Jan. 19, 1914; s. John Martin and Emma (Krug) B.; m. Rayetta Cantrell, Mar. 25, 1939; children: Judith Ann (Mrs. Reiner Arnott), John Raymond. B.A., Drury Coll., Springfield, Mo., 1941; B.Div., Eden Theol. Sem., Webster Groves, Mo., 1944, M.Div., 1970. Ordained minister United Ch. of Christ, 1944. Pastor, St. Martin United Ch. of Christ, Dittmer, Mo., 1944-50, St. Peter United Ch. of Christ, Centralia, Ill., 1950-60, Zion United Ch. of Christ, Central City, Ill., 1950-60; pastor St. John United Ch. of Christ, Chicago Heights, Ill., 1960-80, now pastor emeritus. Named Disting. Past Pres., Kiwanis Internat., 1980; Citation for Pastoral service United Ch. of Christ, 1980. Lodge: Downtown Kiwanis (bd. dirs. 1984—, sec. 1985—) (Springfield,Mo.). Republican. Home: Rural Route 1 Box 113 Billings MO 65610

BIALKIN, KENNETH J., organization executive, Jewish. Nat. chairperson Anti-Defamation League of B'nai B'rith, N.Y.C. Office: 823 United Nations Plaza New York NY 10017*

BIBZA, JAMES, minister, religion educator, Presbyterian Ch. U.S.A.; b. Tarentum, Pa., Feb. 18, 1950; s. John and Ingrid (Binner) B.; m. Karen Jane Lawrence, June 12, 1971; children: Jason Andrew, Matthew Thomas, Ryan Michael. B.A., C.W. Post Coll., 1972; M.Div., Gordon Conwell Sem., 1975; postgrad., Princeton Sem., 1975-84. Ordained to ministry Presbyterian Ch., 1981. Asst. to pastor Am. Bapt. Ch., Peabody, Mass., 1974-75; instr. in religion Grove City Coll., Pa., 1977—; supply pastor Amity-Irwin Presbyn. Chs. U.S.A., Grove City, 1980; stated supply pastor Hadley Presbyn. Ch., Pa., 1981—; mem. higher edn. com. Shenango Presbyn. Ch., New Castle, Pa., 1983—;

speaker Lay Academy Covenant Presbyn. Ch., Sharon, Pa., 1978. Mem. bd. edn. Lawrence County Christian Sch., Grove City, 1983—. Mem. Soc. Bibl. Literature, Evangelical Theol. Soc., Am. Scientific Assn. (assoc.), Phi Alpha Chi. Republican. Home: 140 Garden Ave Grove City PA 16127 Office: Grove City College Memorial Ave Grove City PA 16127

BICKES, PAUL FRANK, minister, Ch. of the Nazarene; b. Clinton, Ill., May 20, 1926; s. George L. and Mildred Leone (Andrews) B.; A.B., Asbury Coll. 1954; m. Mary Anna Barrett, July 6, 1947; 1 dau., Cindi. Ordained to ministry, 1955; pastor First Ch. of the Nazarene, Columbia, Ky., 1954-56, Lake City, Fla., 1956-59, Ocala, Fla., 1959-60, Sanford, Fla., 1960-66, Winter Haven, Fla., 1966-69, Lakeland, Fla., 1969-75, Central Ch. of the Nazarene, Orlando, Fla., 1975—. Home: 790 Apt D South Conway Rd Orlando FL 32807 Office: 300 E Jackson St Orlando FL 32801

BIEDERMAN, HAROLD ROBERT, minister, United Methodist Church; b. Whittier, Calif., Dec. 4, 1937; s. Marvin H. and Ardath (Berry) B.; m. Karen Ruth Mosimann, Aug. 22, 1958; children: Linda Ruth, Mark Harold. A.B., Westmar Coll., 1959; M.Div., United Theol. Sem., 1963; D.Min., NAB Sem., 1983. Ordained to ministry, 1969. Minister, EUB-UCC Chs., Grey Eagle, Minn., 1963-66, EUB-Meth. Chs., Hendricks, Minn., 1966-68; minsiter of edn. United Meth. Ch., Fairmont, Minn., 1968-70; minister Renville-Echo United Meth. Ch., Minn., 1970-77, Tracy United Meth. Ch., Minn., 1977-84; sr. minister First United Meth. Ch., Worthington, Minn., 1984—; pres. bd. mgrs. Decision Hills Camp, Spicer, Minn., 1980—; men. DHC Bd. Mgmt., Spicer, 1969—; mem. bd. camps Minn. United Meth. Ch., 1969-75, 80-84. Author: Preparation for Discipleship, 1983; contbr. articles to profl. jours. Vice chmn. County Park Bd., Ivanhoe, Minn., 1967-68; clk. Sch. Bd., Renville, 1972-75; treas. Ednl. Service Unit, Marshall, Minn., 1974-75. Mem. Christian Educators Fellowship. Lodges: Lions, Kiwanis (dir. 1967-68). Office: First United Meth Church 408 11th St Worthington MN 56187

BIELICKE, NORMAND LAWRENCE, priest, Roman Cath. Ch.; b. St. Louis, June 22, 1917; s. Louis Aloysius and Rose Cecilia (Baer) B.; student St. Joseph Sem. Jr. Coll., 1935-37, St. Francis Novitiate, Teutopolis, Ill., 1937-38, Our Lady of Angels, Cleve., 1938-41, St. Joseph Sem., Teutopolis, 1941-45. Ordained priest, 1944; asso. pastor Our Lady Help of Christians Ch., Bastrop, La., 1945-51, St. Mary Ch., Waterloo, Iowa, 1951-54, St. Francis of Assisi Ch., Oakville, Mo., 1954-60, St. Charles Ch., W. Monroe, La., 1960-68, St. Paschals Ch., W. Monroe, 1968-70, 76—, Corpus Christi Ch., Chgo., 1970-71, St. Anthony of Padua, St. Louis, 1973-76; police clergy liaison St. Louis Police Dept., 1973-76. Active CYC sports program, St. Louis, 1954-60, 72-76, OEO program Monroe Ouachita Parish, La., 1964-70, Boy Scouts Am., St. Louis, 1972-76. Recipient Leadership award Boy Scouts Am., 1975. Home and Office: 711 N 7th St PO Box 1227 West Monroe LA 71291

BIER, LOUIS HENRY GUSTAV, minister, Lutheran Church-Missouri Synod; b. Chgo., Jan. 12, 1933; s. Louis Wilfred Maximillian and Ethel Lea (Laue) B.; m. Helene Anne Mueller, July 29, 1962; children: Richard A., Karen E., Lisa A. B.Ed., Chgo. Tchr's. Coll., 1954; B.Th., Concordia Sem., 1959, M.Div., 1975; M.Ed., Boston State Coll., 1962; resident Boston State Hosp., 1970-72. Ordained to ministry Lutheran Ch., 1959. Vicar Redeemer Luth. Ch., Phila., 1957, First Luth. Ch., Holyoke, Mass., 1957-58; pastor St. Paul's Luth. Ch., West Frankford, Ill., 1959-61, Trinity Luth. Ch., Boston, 1961—; staff chaplain Boston VA Med. Ctr., 1968—, West Roxbury VA Med. Ctr., Mass., 1978—, Arbour Psychiat. Hosp., 1969—; clk., trustee, chaplain German Home for Elderly, Boston, 1961—; incorporator, mem. bd. mgrs. Roxbury Home for Aged Women, Boston, 1974—; pastoral adv. Boston Zone, 1974-76, New England dist. Luth. Women's Missionary League, 1978-80; dir. Interfaith Bible Readings Inc., Boston, 1975—; cir. counselor Luth. Ch.-Mo. Synod, 1976—, commn. on services to mentally retarded Luth. Ch. - Mo. Synod, 1977-79; trustee German Aid Soc., Boston, 1978-84; incorporator Faulkner Hosp., Boston, 1981—; part-time instr. psych. Boston State Coll., 1968-81. Editor New England Lutheran Witness, 1976. Chaplain Boy Scout Troop 400, Boston council Boy Scouts Am., 1975—, Boy Scout Internat. Jamboree, Morraine State Park, Pa., 1976, Headquarters Staff Mass. State Guard, 1981—; pres. Branch 1982, Aid Assn. for Luths., 1980—; Colonial Br. Luth. Brotherhood Ins. Co., 1976-80; rep. Wheat Ridge Found., New England, 1975—; bd. dirs. Health Planning Council Greater Boston, 1972-75, Arboretum Dist. Boston Council Boy Scouts Am., 1976-79, Fed. Credit Union, Boston, 1982—, USO New Eng., Boston, 1982—, New Eng. Fraternal Congress, 1976-80. Recipient Honored Citizens award Kennedy VFW Post, 1973; Lamb award Luth. Council U.S.A., 1975; Community Service award Greater Boston Assn. Retarded Citizens, 1974; Medal of St. Herman of Alaska, Russian Orthodox Diocese of Sitka, 1982; George Meaney Youth Award AFL-CIO, 1983; (with wife) Humanitarian award Region X, Am. Assn. Mental

Deficiency, 1984. Mem. Assn. Mental Health Chaplains (cert.), Mil. Chaplain Assn. U.S.A. (life) (various offices), Civil Air Patrol (chaplain, lt. col., 1974—), Luth. Edn. Assn. (life), Concordia Hist. Inst. (life), Concordia Sem. Alumni Assn. (Servus Eccelsia Christ; award, 1976). Home: 169 Nahatan St Westwood MA 02090 Office: Trinity Lutheran Ch 1195 Centre St Box C Roslindale MA 02131

BIERMANN, LAWRENCE JOHN, minister, Southern Baptist Convention; b. Chgo., Nov. 8, 1936; s. Frank Lawrence and Dorothy Alice (Thompson) B.; student Jacksonville U., 1958-59; m. Mary Ann Basford, Oct. 9, 1954; children: Lori Ann, Susan Renee, Jennifer Lynn. B.A., Miss. Coll., 1961; B.D., New Orleans Bapt. Theol. Sem., 1964, M.Div., 1975; student clin. pastoral edn. Bapt. Hosp., Miami, 1969-70; Ordained to ministry Southern Baptist Convention, 1963. Pastor, Kentwood, La., 1963-64, South Daytona, Fla., 1964-68, Coral Villa Bapt. Ch., Miami, 1968-73; chaplain VA Med. Ctr., Hampton, Va., 1973—, now chief Chaplain Service; moderator, Halifax Bapt. Assn., Daytona Beach, Fla., 1967-68; mem. bd. missions Fla. Bapt. Conv., 1972-73. Mem. Mil. Chaplains Assn. Home: 3324 W Lewis Rd Hampton VA 23666 Office: VA Center Hampton VA 23667

BIERY, PAUL LELAND, minister, United Methodist Church; b. Ravenna, Ohio, Aug. 2, 1937; s. Willis C. and Virginia A. (Fox) B.; A.A., Ventura Coll., 1957; A.B., Mount Union Coll., 1960; B.D., Oberlin Coll., 1967; M.Div., Vanderbilt U., 1974; certificate Pastoral Psychology Service Inst., Case Western Res. U., 1976; m. Joan Irene Alworth, July 31, 1960; children: Raymond, Michelle Lynn, Anne Marie. Ordained to ministry, 1967; pastor Lanham, Emory and Lay Hill Meth. chs., Washington, 1960-62, Moreland (Ohio) Meth. Ch., 1962-67; asso. pastor Westlake (Ohio) Meth. Ch., 1967; pastor Aldersgate United Meth. Ch., Warrensville Heights, Ohio, 1970-77; program dir. Cleve. dist. United Meth. Ch., 1977—; chaplain Apple Creek (Ohio) State Hosp., 1963-67, Brentwood Hosp., Cleve., 1971—; dir. ecumenical edn. Cleve. Council of Chs., 1969; chmn. bd. of ch. and soc. E. Ohio Conf., United Meth. Ch.; lectr. psychology Cuyahoga Community Coll., 1976; cons. transitional communities Gen. Bd. Religion and Race; bd. advisers Pastoral Psychology Service Inst., Case Western Res. U., Cleve. Mem. staff Congressman Louis Stokes, 21st dist. Ohio, 1974—. Certified fellow Clergy Internship in Urban Ministry, Case Western Res. U., 1970. Mem. Urban League, NAACP (mem. Cleve. exec. com. 1976—), Black Methodists for Ch. Renewal, Warrensville Heights Community Caucus. Home: 3711 Rawnsdale Rd Shaker Heights OH 44122 Office: 3000 Euclid Ave Cleveland OH 44115

BIEVER, BRUCE FRANCIS, priest, Roman Catholic Ch.; b. Milw., July 24, 1933; s. Franklyn Peter and Helene Mary (Ahern) B.; student Marquette U., 1951-54; A.B., St. Louis U., 1958, Ph.L., 1959, M.A., 1960; M.A., U. Pa., 1962, Ph.D., 1965; S.T.L., St. Louis U., 1967. Joined Soc. of Jesus, 1953, ordained priest Roman Catholic Ch., 1966; asst. prof. sociology Marquette U., Milw., 1967-72, v.p., 1979-83; asst. provincial Wis. Province, Soc. Jesus, Milw., 1967-72, provincial, 1972—; dir. nat. self-study Soc. Jesus N.Am., 1967-69; exec. v.p. Cath. League for Religious and Civil Rights, Milw., 1984—. Bd. dirs. U. Detroit, 1979—, Sacred Heart Sch. Theology, 1980—. Author: Guardian of the Faith: The Social Role of the Catholic Church in Ireland, 1965. Home: 1404 W Wisconsin Ave Milwaukee WI 53233 Office: 1100 W Wells St Milwaukee WI 53233

BIGLIARDI, MATTHEW PAUL, bishop, Episcopal Church; b. Charleroi, Pa., Sept. 14, 1920; s. Achille and Regina (Bonaccinni) B.; B.S., U. Calif. at Berkeley, 1950; M.Div., Ch. Div. Sch. of the Pacific, 1953, D.D., 1974; m. Jeanne C. Gross, Feb. 19, 1949; 1 child, Aidan. Ordained priest Protestant Episcopal Ch., 1954; curate Trinity Ch., Seattle, 1953-55; vicar Emmanuel Ch., Mercer Island, Wash., 1955-60; rector, 1960-74; bishop Diocese of Oreg., Lake Oswego, 1974—. Bd. trustees Good Semaritan Hosp., chmn., 1974—; mem. bd. trustees Oreg. Episcopal Schs., chmn. 1974—. Mem. Assn. for Creative Change, Sigma Xi, Phi Beta Kappa. Office: PO Box 647 Lake Oswego OR 97034

BILANIUK, PETRO BORYS, educator; b. Zalishchyky, Ukraine, Aug. 4, 1932; s. Terentyj and Paraskevia (Romanko) B.; came to Can., 1949, naturalized, 1955; B. Th., U. Montreal (Que., Can.), 1955; postgrad. Pontifical Urbanian U., 1955-56; Th.D. magna cum laude, U. Munich (Germany), 1961; Dr. Phil. summa cum laude (Can. Council fellow), Ukrainian Free U., Munich, 1971-72; m. Franziska Maria Theresa von Limbach, Jan. 9, 1960; children: Stefan, Nykolai, Mykhail, Josyf. Lectr. theology and religious knowledge St. Michael's Coll. U. Toronto (Ont., Can.), 1962-65, asst. prof., 1965-69, asso. prof., 1969-74, prof. theology and religious studies, 1974—, acad. sec. Inst. Christian Thought, 1969-72, also bd. admissions, chmn. Can. Council Bd., 1972—. Mem. Ukrainian Catholic Brotherhood Can., 1967—; mem. central com. def. rite, tradition and lang. Ukrainian Cath. Ch. U.S. and Can., 1966—. Recipient Gold medal Pope Paul VI, 1966. Mem. N. Am. Acad. Ecumenists, Coll. Theology Soc., Canadian, Ukrainian theol. socs., Cath. Theol. Soc. Am., Soc. Sci. Study Religion, Shevchenko Sci. Soc., Am. Teilhard de Chardin Assn., Nat. Assn. Pastoral Renewal, Ukrainian Geneal. and Heraldic Soc., Karl Barth Soc. N. Am. Author several religious works in Ukrainian, English and Latin. Editor-in-chief Bull. Za Ridnu Cerkwu, 1966—. Home: 41 Parkway Ave Toronto ON M6R 1T6 Canada

BILDSTEIN, WALTER JOHN, educator, Roman Cath. Ch.; b. Edmonton, Alta., Can., Sept. 17, 1929; s. Alphonse Isidore and Rosetta Agnes (Schell) B.; B.A. with honours in Philosophy, U. Western Ont., 1953; S.T.B., Pontifical Gregorian U., Rome, 1955, S.T.L., 1956; S.T.L., Angelicum, U., 1957; diploma secondary edn. Ont. Coll. Edn., 1961; M.A. in Religious Studies, U. Windsor, 1970; S.T.D., Pontifical U. Thomas Aquinas, Rome, 1971. Joined Congregation of Resurrection 1949, ordained priest, 1956; laicized, 1974; pastor St. Michael's Parish, Bermuda, 1957-61, also sec. to bishop of Bermuda; pub. Cath. News, Hamilton, Bermuda, 1957-61; tchr. high sch., Kitchener, Ont., Can., 1961-63; pastor Blessed Sacrament Ch., Burford, Ont., 1963-67; chancellor Diocese Bermuda, 1967-69; rector St. Theresa's Cathedral, Hamilton, 1967-69; chmn. religious studies St. Jerome's Coll., Waterloo, Ont., 1973—. Author: Secularization, 1972; Radical Response, 1974. Address: St Jerome's Coll Waterloo ON N2L 3G3 Canada

BILLINGS, DAVID J., III, clergyman. Sec. gen., treas. The Church of God in Christ Internat., Bklyn. Office: The Ch of God in Christ Internat 315 Clinton Ave Brooklyn NY 11205*

BILLINGS, GEORGE CRESSWELL, minister, So. Bapt. Conv.; b. Toronto, Ont., Can., June 3, 1931; s. Cresswell S. and Lillie V. (Porter) B.; student Dominion Bus. Coll., 1948-49; B.A., Bob Jones U., 1954; B.D., Southwestern Bapt. Theol. Sem., 1958; Th.D., Luther Rice Sem., 1972; m. Margaret Catherine Klemm, May 14, 1955; children—Barbara Cay, John Cresswell. Ordained minister, 1954; missionary, British West Indies, 1954-55; pastor 1st Bapt. Ch., Strathroy, Ont., 1958-60, 1st Av. Bapt. Ch., Toronto, 1960-66, 1st Bapt. Ch., Woodstock, Ont., 1966-68, Idlewild Bapt. Ch., Tampa, Fla., 1968—. Prof. Ont. Bible Coll., Toronto, 1965-66. Bd. devel. St. Joseph's Hosp., Tampa, 1973—. Kiwanian, Mason (32 deg., Shriner, chaplain). Author: Poems of Great Blessing, 3 vols., 1970, 71, 72, Words of Life, 1974. Contbr. articles to theol. publs. Home: 12005 Hope Ln Tampa FL 33618 Office: 6018 Highland Ave Tampa FL 33604

BILOCK, JOHN M. See *Who's Who in America*, 43rd edition.

BINGHAM, ARLES LEE, minister, So. Baptist Conv.; b. Spurger, Tex., June 27, 1934; s. William Ramsey and Bulah Mae (Ratcliff) B.; B.A., Tenn. Temple Coll., 1962; M.Div., Southwestern Bapt. Theol. Sem., 1965, M.R.E., 1965; m. Ann Marie Hicks, Dec. 21, 1956; children—Michael, Bethwyn, Torrey, Kim, Chip. Ordained to ministry, 1965; pastor Strongsville (Ohio) Bapt. Ch., 1965—. Asst. rec. sec. Ohio State Bapt. Conv., 1975—; moderator Greater Cleve. Bapt. Assn., 1971-73; mem. exec. bd. Ohio State Bapt. Conv., 1970-74. Home: 14710 Fetterman Dr Strongsville OH 44136 Office: 19543 Lunn Rd Strongsville OH 44136

BINGHAM, WALTER DOTTIE, minister, Third Christian Church; b. Memphis, June 3, 1921; s. Willie and Lena (Allen) B.; m. Rebecca T. Bingham, Oct. 27, 1957; 1 child, Gail Elaine Simmons Bingham. A.B., Talladega Coll., 1945; M.Div., Harvard U., 1948; D.D. (hon.), Christian Theol. Sem., 1969; L.H.D. (hon.), Drury Coll., 1972, Transylvania U., 1973. Ordained to ministry, 1946. Prof. religion Jarvis Christian Coll., Hawkins, Tex., 1949-57; pastor Pine St. Christian Ch., Tulsa, 1957-61, Third Christian Ch., Louisville, 1961—; moderator Christian Ch. (Disciples of Christ) U.S.A. and Can., 1971-73; chmn. Council on Christian Unity, Indpls., 1982—; del. assembly World Council of Chs., 1975, 83. Bd. dirs. Vols. of Am., Louisville, 1962-67; overview com. Norton's Hosp., Louisville, 1984—. Named Pastor of the Year, WLOU Radio, 1979. Lodge: Masons (32 deg.). Home: 3608 Dumnesnil St Louisville KY 40211 Office: Third Christian Ch 3900 W Broadway Louisville KY 40211

BINGMAN, TIMOTHY WAGNER, minister, Lutheran Church in America; b. Harrisburg, Pa., Sept. 10, 1950; s. Glen Nevin and Dorothy Virginia (Wagner) B.; B.A., Susquehanna U., 1972; M.A., Bucknell U., 1974; M.Div., Luth. Theol. Sem., 1979. Ordained to ministry Lutheran Church in America 1979. Assoc. pastor Moxham Luth. Ch., Johnstown, Pa., 1979—; pres. Moxham Ministerium, Johnstown, 1981—; sec., treas. Johnstown Dist. Luth. Ch. Am., 1980-84. Home: 538 Park Ave Johnstown PA 15902 Office: Moxham Luth Ch 538 Park Ave Johnstown PA 15902

BINKLEY, WALTER VIRGIL, minister, Church of the Brethren; b. Allen County, Ohio, July 12, 1904; s. William and Anna Marie (Desenberg) B.; B.S., Ohio No. U., 1932; m. Cora May Ballinger, Aug. 14, 1928; children: Norma Jean, Donald Eugene. Ordained to ministry, 1947; pastor, Sand Ridge, Ohio, 1947-57, Ross Ch. of the Brethren, Mendon, Ohio, 1957-80, pastor emeritus, 1980-85, moderator, 1985. Pastoral advisor, No. Ohio, 1971-74. Chmn. community affairs Ret. Tchrs. Assn., Allen County, Ohio, 1970-82. Mem. Nat. Tchrs. Assn. (life), Ohio Tchrs. Assn., Ohio Ret. Tchrs. Assn. (life), Allen County Tchrs. Assn. Home: 980 W High St Lima OH 45805

BIONDA, BONAVENTURE BRUNO, priest, Roman Catholic Church. b. N.Y.C., Oct. 2, 1927; s. Domenic and Mary (Castignoli) B. B.A. in Philosophy, Mt. Alvernia Coll., 1955, B.A. in Religion, 1959. Ordained priest Roman Catholic Ch., 1959. Tchr. sci. St. Francis Sem., Lowell, Mass., 1962-64; tchr. math. Columbus High Sch., Boston, 1960-62, 64-83, dean studies, 1967-70; co-dir. postulants Scotus Friary, Brighton, Mass., 1983—; pastoral asst. St. Ann's, Marlboro, Mass., 1984—. Served with U.S. Army, 1946-48. Home: Scotus Friary 284 Foster St Brighton MA 02135

BIRCH, DAVID LADONNE, minister, General Association of Regular Baptist Churches. B. Effingham, Ill., July 28, 1944; s. Ardeth Arlie and Marjorie Sue (Pursell) B.; m. Frances Marie McCann, June 26, 1963; children: Donna Sue Birch Beight, Timothy, Laurie. B.A. in Bible, Graham Bible Coll., 1968; M.R.E., Grand Rapids Bapt. Sem., 1982; grad. student Ohio State U., 1980-81. Ordained to ministry Waukegan Bible Ch., Ill., 1968. Dir., Tri-State Independent Ch., Princeton, Ind., 1969-72, Child Evangelism Extension Fellowship, Indpls., 1972-77, state dir. Westerville, Ohio, 1977-80; asst. pastor Grace Bapt. Ch., Westerville, 1980-81; pastor First Bapt. Ch., Wellington, Ohio, 1982—. Mem. Hebron Assn. Regular Bapt. Chs. (clerk NE Ohio sect. 1984—). Home: 19121 St R 58 N Wellington OH 44090 Office: First Bapt Ch 125 Grand Ave Wellington OH 44090

BIRD, PETER ROBERT, lay church worker, Episcopal Church, insurance agent; b. Kansas City, Mo., June 20, 1943; s. Robert Adam and Nellie Flora (Worthing) B.; B.A. in Polit. Sci., Ripon Coll., 1966; J.D., So. Meth. U., 1972, M.A. in Divine Theology, 1977. Bar: Tex. 1973. Lay dir. Vocare In Wis. Fond du Lac, 1982; dir. Diocese of Fond du Lac Youth Ministry Workshop, Wis., 1982. Prin. Bird Ins., Brownsville, Wis., 1980—. Pres. Dallas-Forth Worth Refugee Interagency, Tex., 1979-80, bd. atty., 1978-79; mem. Gov.'s Task Force on Refugees, Tex., 1979-80. Served with U.S. Army, 1968-70, Viet Nam. Mem. State Bar Tex., Happening Nat. Com. (treas. 1983), Nat. Vocare Assn. (convenor 1984). Republican. Avocations: golf; travel. Home and Office: Route 1 Box 207 Brownsville WI 53006

BIRD, THOMAS EDWARD, church official, Roman Catholic Church, educator; b. Rome, N.Y., Mar. 28, 1935; s. Harry J. and Paula W. (Boyce) B.; A.B. magna cum laude, Syracuse U., 1956; postgrad. Harvard U., 1958-59; M.A., Middlebury Coll., 1960; A.M., Princeton U., 1965; m. Mary Lynne Miller, Aug. 23, 1958; children: Matthew David, Lisa Bronwen. Mem. Boston Archdiocesan Ecumenical Commn., 1963-66, Bklyn. Diocesan Ecumenical Commn., 1975—, Bklyn. Diocesan Justice and Peace Commn., 1979—; spl. cons. Nat. Conf. Cath. Bishops, 1970—; dir. Pax Romana Grad. and Profl. Commn., 1974-78, pres., 1978-81; mem. Roman Cath.-Eastern Orthodox Bilateral Dialogue Commn., 1965—, gen. sec., 1978—; U.S. Roman Cath.-Russian Patriarchal Theol. Dialogue Com., 1969—; del. Holy See to 1st World Conf. on Religion and Peace, Kyoto, Japan, 1970; U.S. rep. Centre for Study Religion and Communism, 1971-75; mem. adv. bd. Cath. Interracial Council N.Y., 1976-80; mem. U.S. Cath. Bishops Com. for Dialogue with Oriental Orthodox Chs., exec. sec., 1976-80; dir. Council for Study of Ethics and Pub. Policy, 1977—. Faculty, Queens Coll., CUNY, 1965—, asst. chmn. dept. Slavic langs. and lits., 1973-75. Fellow Soc. for Values in Higher Edn.; mem. St. Davids Soc. of State N.Y. (pres. 1985—), Am. Cath. Hist. Assn., Am. Assn. Advancement Slavic Studies, Modern Lang. Assn., AAUP, N.Am. Acad. Ecumenists, Nat. Interreligious Task Force on Soviet Jewry, SAR, Columbia U. Faculty Seminars, Dobro Slovo, Phi Beta Kappa, Phi Kappa Alpha. Club: Princeton (N.Y.C.). Author: Patriarch Maximos IV, 1964; Orthodoxy in Byelorussia: 1917-80, 1985. Editor: Modern Theologians: Christians and Jews, 1967; Aspects of Religion in the Soviet Union: 1917-1967, 1971; Archiepiscopal and Patriarchal Autonomy, 1972; The Ecumenical World of Orthodox Civilization, 1974; In the Image and Likeness of God, 1974; The Third Hour, 1976; editor religion sect. Am. Bibliography Russian and East European Studies, 1962-65; founding editor Diakonia, 1966-75. Home: Little Neck NY Office: Queens Coll CUNY 65-30 Kissena Blvd Flushing NY 11367

BIRKENFELD, ROSE MARIA, parish minister, nun Roman Catholic Church; b. Amarillo, Tex., Sept. 13, 1931; d. John Simon and Dora Elizabeth (Moore) B. B.S. in Elem. Edn., U. Mo., 1974; B.A. in Religious Studies, Coll. of St. Scholastica, Duluth, 1976; M.A. in Theology, St. Mary's U., San Antonio, 1986. Joined Benedictine Sisters, 1949, Found. of Our Lady of Peace, 1968. Part time tchr. Holy Rosary Sch., Stuttgart, Ark., 1959-63; with personnel dept. St. Joseph's Orphanage, North Little Rock, Ark., 1956-59, 63-68; religious edn.

coordinator St. Jude's Ch., Jacksonville, Ark., 1966-68, St. Joseph's Ch., Pilot Grove, Mo., 1970-73; parish minister St. Mary's Ch., Shelbina, Mo., 1976—. Home: 208 E Chestnut St Shelbina MO 63468

BIRNEY, DAVID B., IV, bishop Episcopal Ch., Idaho Area. Office: PO Box 936 Boise ID 83701*

BISCOE, B. ROBERT. Clergyman, Bible Protestant Church; exec. sec. Am. Council Christian Churches. Office: PO Box 816 Valley Forge PA 19482*

BISHOP, BERNARD TAYLOR, minister, Nat. Bapt. Conv., U.S.A., Inc.; b. Bloomfield, Ky., May 26, 1933; s. Allen Richard and Selena (Edwards) B.; B.Th., Simmons Bible Coll., 1966, D.D. (hon.), 1977; m. Gloria Samuels, Dec. 21, 1957; children—Anthony Jerome, Bernard Taylor. Ordained to ministry, 1960; minister Beargrass Bapt. Ch., Louisville, 1960-66, First Bapt. Ch., Elizabethtown, Ky., 1966—. Vice-chmn. pub. bd. Gen. Assn. Ky. Baptist, 1975-79; mem. Sunday Sch. pub. bd. Nat. Bapt. Conv. U.S.A., Inc., 1975-79. Mem. Elizabethtown Housing Authority. Mem. NAACP, Elizabethtown Ministerial Assn. Home and Office: PO Box 813 New Glendale Rd Elizabethtown KY 42701

BISHOP, CECIL, bishop, African Methodist Episcopal Zion Church, Tenth Episc. Area. Office: 5401 Broadwater St Temple Hill MD 20748*

BIXLER, R(OY) RUSSELL, minister, Christian broadcasting company executive, Church of the Brethren; b. Boston, Apr. 24, 1927; s. Roy Russell and Bertha Lurah (Stiles) B.; m. Norma Kathryn Bowman, Jan. 25, 1948; children: Kathryn, Paul, Harold, John. B.A., Bridgewater Coll., 1947; M.A., George Washington U., 1949; M.Div., Bethany Theol. Sem., 1959. Ordained to ministry Ch. of the Brethren, 1958. Pastor Pitts. Ch. of the Brethren, 1959-72; pres., chmn. Sta. WPCB, Channel 40, Wall. Pa., 1970—; regent Melodyland Sch. of Theology, Anaheim, Calif., 1975—; chmn. Interfaith Ministers Fellowship, Pitts., 1968—; bd. dirs., chmn. TV com. Nat. Religious Broadcasters, Morristown, N.J., 1983-84; pres., chmn. Sta. WKBS-TV, Channel 47, Altoona, Pa., 1984—. Author: It Can Happen to Anybody, 1970, When Nothing Happens, 1981, Learning to Know God as Provider, 1982. Author: (with others) Eyes to Behold Him, 1972, Sunrise at Evening, 1974, Chosen to Live, 1983. Editor: The Spirit Is A'Movin', 1974. Contbr. articles to profl. jours. Served with USNR, 1945-46. Mem. Nat. Religious Broadcasters. Home: 4722 Baptist Rd Pittsburgh PA 15227 Office: Western Pennsylvania Christian Broadcasting Co Channel 40 Wall PA 15148

BJERKOE, GEORGE OLAF BOE, coll. pres. emeritus, chancellor minister, Luth. Ch. in Am.; b. Bklyn., July 2, 1895; s. Johan Arnt and Alvilde O. (Boe) Bjerkoe; A.B., Muhlenberg Coll., 1922, Litt.D., 1946; M.Div., Luth. Theol. Sem., 1925; A.M., N.Y. U., 1935; postgrad. Boston U., 1935-36, Harvard, summer 1936, Columbia, 1938-39; Litt.D., U. Cin., 1971; m. Eleanor Tupper, June 21, 1933; children—Priscilla Tupper, Barbara Tupper. Ordained to ministry Lutheran Ch. in Am., 1925; pastor, organizer, founder Luth. Ch. of the Good Shepherd, Bellaire, L.I., 1924-35; instr. Boston YMCA, 1936-38; co-founder, 1st pres., Chaplain Endicott Coll., Beverly, Mass., 1939-71, emeritus 1971—, chancellor, 1976—, also trustee. Asst. to dir. Luth. Inner Mission Soc., 1923-24; asst. to supt. Home Missions bd. Luth. Synod of N.Y. and New Eng., 1924-25; co-founder Prince of Peace Luth. Ch., Beverly, Mass., 1962. Beverly Ministers Assn., Beverly C. of C. (edn. com.). Rotarian (chaplain 1943—) . Organized, founded two ch. bldgs. and a parsonage at Ch. of Good Shepherd, 1924-35. Home: 868 NW Fourth Court Boca Raton FL 33432

BJORNLIE, C(LARENCE) LLOYD, minister, religious school official, Church of the Lutheran Brethren; b. Cooperstown, N.D., July 25, 1925; s. Lars and Bertha (Agre) B.; m. Eleanor Alvina Eastvold, Oct. 29, 1949; children: Cheryl, David, Ethan, Lori, Teresa. B.A., Concordia Coll., Moorhead, Minn., 1950; postgrad. Luth. Brethren Sem., 1954, U. Minn., 1970, Concordia Sem., St. Louis, 1984-85; M.A., U. Minn., 1970. Ordained to ministry Lutheran Ch., 1971; cert. tchr., Minn., sch. adminstr. Instr. Hillcrest Luth. Acad., Fergus Falls, Minn., 1950-54, prin., 1954-65; asst. to v.p. U. Minn., Mpls., 1964-70; exec. sec. U. Minn. Senate-Accreditation, 1965-70; pastor Immanuel Luth. Ch., Eugene, Oreg., 1970-72, Berea Luth. Brethren Ch., Alexandria, Minn., 1984—; pres. Luth. Brethren Schs., Fergus Falls, 1972-84; sec. Synod com. for restructuring of orgn. of ch. body Ch. of the Luth. Brethren, Fergus Falls, 1984—; sec. Central Dist. Ch. of the Luth. Brethren of U.S.A., 1960-62; mem. Synodical Bd. Edn., 1970-72, mem. bd. publs., 1958-60; treas., sec., exec. ex officio World Mission Soc. of Luth. Brethren Schs., Ch. of Am., 1951-84. Editor accreditation evaluations of Minn. schs., 1965-70. Served with U.S. Army, 1944-46, ETO. Mem. Minn. Non-Pub. Accrediting Assn. (pres. 1978-83). Republican. Home: 713 Nissen Ave Alexandria MN 56308 Office: Berea Luth Ch 1405 E Lincoln Alexandria MN 56308

BLACKBURN, ROBERT MCGRADY, bishop, United Methodist Church; b. Bartow, Fla., Sept. 12, 1919; s. Charles Fred and Effie Frances (Forsythe) B.; B.A., Fla. So. Coll., 1941; M.Div., Emory U., 1943, LL.D., 1973; D.D. (hon.), LaGrange Coll., 1961; m. Mary Jeanne Everett, Nov. 16, 1943 (dec. 1977); children—Jeanne Marie (Mrs. Ramon Cox), Robert M., Frances Lucille; m. Jewell Haddock, Sept. 9, 1978. Ordained to ministry United Methodist Ch., 1943; pastor United Meth. Ch., Boca Grande, Fla., 1943-44; chaplain U.S. Army, 1944-46; asso. pastor First Meth. Ch., Orlando, Fla., 1946-48, Mt. Dora, Fla., 1948-53, DeLand, Fla., 1953-60, Jacksonville, Fla., 1960-68; pastor First Meth. Ch., Orlando, 1968-72; bishop United Meth. Ch., Raleigh, N.C., 1972-80, Va. Conf., 1980—. Mem. program council United Meth. Ch., 1963-72; del. to Meth. Gen. Confs., 1968-70, 72. Trustee Fla. So. Coll., Meth. Coll., Fayetteville, N.C., N.C. Wesleyan Coll., Rocky Mountain, Louisberg (N.C.) Coll., Meth. Home for Children, Raleigh. Office: PO Box 11367 Richmond VA 23230*

BLACKETOR, PAUL GARBER, minister, Southern Baptist Convention; b. Birmingham, Ala., Feb. 10, 1927; s. Everly B. and Marie (Scokel) B.; B.S., Samford U., Birmingham, 1953; M.A., Auburn (Ala.) U., 1954, M.A., 1955, Ed.D., 1956; m. Jean Barbara Fitch, Aug. 1, 1971; children: Arnold Wade, Paula Dawn. Ordained minister So. Baptist Conv., 1951; pastor chs. in Ala. and Tenn., 1950-57; dean Judson Coll., Marion, Ala., 1957-61; dean students Union Coll., Barbourville, Ky., 1961-63; pastor chs. in Ky. and Pa., 1961-66; pastor Wilmington (Vt.) Bapt. Ch., 1968—. Prof. research, law and statistics Keene (N.H.) State Coll., 1966—; dean Keystone Jr. Coll., La Plume, Pa.; mem. N.H. Ho. of Reps., 1984-85. Bd. dirs. New Hope Center, Keene, 1967-69, 71-72. Named Ky. col., 1961. Mem. Kappa Delta Kappa, Kappa Delta Pi, Phi Delta Kappa. Mason (32 deg., Shriner). Co-author: Basic Statistics, 1974. Editor: Career Opportunities in Greater Keene, 1968. Address: 383 Main St Keene NH 03431

BLACKMAN, HERMAN ELLIOTT CONSTANTINE, priest, Episcopal Ch.; b. Barbados, West Indies, Dec. 25, 1912; s. Joseph Constantine and Amanda Rosaline (Barrow) B.; came to U.S., 1946, naturalized, 1951; B.A., Oxford U., 1940; M.A., N.Y. U., 1953; M.Div., Va. Theol. Sem., 1949; D.D., Allen U., 1955, Ph.D., 1954; m. Henrietta Henry, June 12, 1950. Ordained priest, 1949; curate St. Augustine's Ch., Bklyn., 1949-50; missionary, Bklyn., 1951-53; vicar St. Martin's, Bklyn., 1953-54; rector St. Stephen's and St. Martin's Ch., Bklyn., 1954—. Vice-pres. Long Island Clericus; mem. Diocesan Council exec. com. Anglican Soc. Pres. Bklyn. Borough Community Planning Bd., 1965-70. Mem. Va. Theol. Sem. Alumni Soc. Home: 541 Franklin Ave Brooklyn NY 11238 Office: 809 Jefferson Ave Brooklyn NY 11221

BLACKMAN, MURRAY, rabbi, Reform Jewish Congregations; b. N.Y.C., Nov. 18, 1920; s. Maxwell and Sarah (Levy) B.; B.S., Coll. City N.Y., 1940; B.Hebrew Lit., Hebrew Union Coll., 1943, M.Hebrew Lit., 1949, D.D. (hon.), 1974; Ph.D., Walden U., 1975; m. Martha Dora Mecklenburger, Aug. 31, 1947; children: Michael Simon, Margaret Jo, Barbara Sarah. Rabbi, Reform Jewish Congregation, 1949; asst. rabbi Temple B'nai Jeshurun, Newark, 1949-50; rabbi, Binghamton, N.Y., 1950-51, Paterson, N.J., 1953-56, Rockdale Temple, Cin., 1956-67, St. Thomas (V.I.) Synagogue, 1967-70, Temple Sinai, New Orleans, 1970—; nat. chmn. Commn. on Jewish Edn., Union Am. Hebrew Congregations, Central Conf. Am. Rabbis, 1983—. Instr., La. State U., Baton Rouge, 1971-75, U. New Orleans, 1974—. Chmn. community relations com. Jewish Welfare Fedn., New Orleans, 1972—; pres. Rabbinical Council New Orleans, 1973-76; vice-chmn. Nat. Jewish Community Relations Adv. Council, N.Y.C., 1976—. Home: 1408 Frankfort St New Orleans LA 70122 Office: 6227 St Charles Ave New Orleans LA 70118

BLAES, CHARLES EMMET, lay church official, Roman Catholic Church; b. Wichita, Kans., Nov. 24, 1936; s. Emmet Andrew and Anna Rose (Kranda) B.; m. Mary Susan Campbell, June 26, 1965; children: Charles, Michael, Lisa, Peter. A.A., Cardinal Glennon Coll., 1956; Ph.B., Gregorian U., Rome, 1958; M.S.W., St. Louis U., 1967; Social worker Cath. Social Services, Wichita, Kans., 1967-69; diocesan dir. Cath. Social Services, Mobile, Ala., 1969—; mem. planning com. diocesan pastoral council, Mobile, 1972-74, pres. diocesan pastoral council, 1979-82; pres. St. Joan of Arc Parish Council, Mobile, 1978-82; mem. nat. standing com. dirs. Nat. Conf. Cath. Charities, Washington, 1973-75, bd. dirs., 1981-82. Bd. dirs. FISH of Mobile, Inc., 1970-78, Christian Home Service Bd., 1972—, Villa Mercy Nursing Home, 1973—, Legal Aid Soc. of Mobile, Inc., 1974-80. Mem. Nat. Assn. Social Workers, Acad. Cert. Social Workers. Home: 206 Volanta Ave Fairhope AL 36532 Office: PO Box 759 Mobile AL 36601

BLAINE, ALLAN, rabbi, Jewish religion; b. N.Y.C., Mar. 4, 1931; s. Arthur and Frances (Perlmutter) B.; degree Herzliah Hebrew Tchrs. Inst., 1952; B.A., Univ. Coll., N.Y. U., 1952; M.H.L., Jewish Theol. Sem., 1957, D.D., 1982; m. Suzanne Iteld, Jan. 28, 1962; children: Deena Seelenfreund, Ari. Rabbi, 1957; U.S. chaplain, Munich and Berlin, 1957-59; rabbi Temple Israel, Somerville, N.J., 1960; assoc. rabbi East Midwood Jewish Ctr., Bklyn., 1960-68; rabbi Temple Beth-El of Rockaway Park, N.Y., 1968—, prin. Beth-El Day Sch., 1968—; lectr. Jewish Welfare Bd. Lecture Bur., 1968-75; weekly host The Jewish Scene, NBC-TV, 1964-82; chmn. commn. on adult edn. Met. Region, United Synagogue of Am., N.Y.C., 1974, now nat. chmn. day sch. edn. com.; chmn. nat. curriculum com. Solomon Schechter Day Sch. Movement. Recipient Massada award State of Israel, 1974. Author brochures. Editor: Alcoholism in the Jewish Community; Definitive Volume, Alcoholism in the Jewish Community. Home: 466 Beach 136th St Belle Harbor NY 11694 Office: 445 Beach 135th St Rockaway Park NY 11694

BLAIR, LEROY ROBERT, minister, A.M.E. Zion Ch.; b. Pitts., Apr. 3, 1929; s. Eutaw and Daisy (Thomas) B.; B.S., U. Pitts., 1951; M.Ed., Chgo. Tchrs. Coll., 1964; M.A. in Evangelism, Scarritt Coll., Nashville, 1974; D.D., Teamer Sch. Religion, Charlotte, N.C., 1975; Ordained to ministry, 1965; pastor St. John A.M.E. Zion Ch., Hammond, Ind., 1965-67, St. Paul A.M.E. Zion Ch., Carnegie, Pa., 1967-68, Wright Meml. Ch., Washington, Pa., 1968-70, Mount Pleasant A.M.E. Zion Ch., Danbury, Conn., 1970-73, Warner Temple, Wilmington, N.C., 1973—; tchr. sci. Dunbar Vocat. High Sch., Chgo., 1955-64; counselor Loop Jr. Coll., Chgo., 1964-67. Dir. teaching staff dept. evangelism A.M.E. Zion Ch., 1968—, sec. Allegheny Conf., 1969-70, sec. Cape Fear Conf., 1975—, dean Ministers' Inst., 1976—; bd. dirs. Assn. Religious Communities Danbury, 1971-73. Alcoholism counselor, Wilmington, 1973-74; mem. Wilmington Bicentennial Com., 1975-76. Mem. Wilmington Interdenominational Alliance (sec. 1975), NAACP (v.p. Danbury br. 1971-73). Contbr. articles to religious jours. Home: 620 S Kerr Ave Wilmington NC 28401 Office: 620 Nixon St Wilmington NC 28401

BLAISDELL, RUSSELL CARTER, minister, Presbyterian Church U.S.A.; b. Chgo., Oct. 19, 1936; s. Russell Lloyd and Viola Evelyn (Hagen) B.; m. Anita Fay Cone, Jan. 4, 1964; children: David Scott, Valerie Ruth, Sarah Jane, John Milton. B.A., U. Calif.-Berkeley, 1959; M.Div., McCormick Theol. Sem., 1965. Ordained to ministry, 1965. Pastor, Community Presbyn. Ch., Lawton, Iowa, 1965-73, First United Presbyn. Ch., Portage, Wis., 1973-79; assoc. gen. sec. Presbyn. and Reformed Renewal Ministries, Internat., Oklahoma City, 1979—, editor Renewal News, 1983—; chmn. Christian Edn., N.W. Iowa Presbytery, Storm Lake, 1969-73; commr. 191st Gen. Assembly, United Presbyn. Ch. U.S.A., 1979. Actor/singer Portage Players, Wis., 1974; organizer, singer, bd. dirs. Portage Ecumenical Chorus, 1974-79; Served as 1st lt. USAF, 1959-62. Calif. Alumni scholar, 1954-55; Rotary scholar, 1954-57. Mem. Presbytery of Indian Nations (new ch. devel. com.). Republican. Lodge: Kiwanis (bd. dirs. 1976-79). Office: Presbyn and Reformed Renewal Ministries 2245 NW 39th St Oklahoma City OK 73112

BLAKE, J. A. Mem. gen. bd., 2d asst. presiding bishop The Church of God in Christ, San Diego. Office: The Ch of God in Christ 2192 Harrison Ave San Diego CA 92113*

BLANCHET, BERTRAND, bishop, Roman Catholic Church; b. Montmagny, Que., Can., Sept. 19, 1932; s. Louis and Alberta (Nicole) B.; B.A., Coll. Ste-Anne-de-la-Pocatière, 1952; L.Th., U. Laval, 1956, D.Sc., 1975. Ordained priest, 1956; consecrated bishop, 1973; tchr. biology Coll. and Cegep, La Pocatiere, Que., 1963-73; bishop of Gaspe (Que.), 1973—. Mem. Com. Catholique (Ministere de Edn.), Chevaliers de Colomb, Fonds de Recherches Forestières. Home and office: Rue Jacques Cartier Gaspe PQ GOC 1RO Canada

BLANCO, JACK JOHN, religion educator, Seventh-day Adventist Church; B. Chgo., June 17, 1929; s. Frederick and Katherine (Kiesling) Ross; stepson Lee Joseph Blanco; m. Marion June Blasius, Sept. 26, 1952; children: Cheryl Ann, Stephen Jon. B.A., Union Coll., 1955; M.A., Andrews U., 1957, B.D., Seventh-day Adventist Theol. Sem., 1958; M.Th., Princeton Sem., 1965; D.D., U. South Africa, Pretoria, 1970. Ordained, 1961. Prof. religion Solusi Coll., Bulawayo, Rhodesia, 1965-70; chmn. grad. sch. religion Philippine Union Coll., Manila, 1970-72; acad. dean, prof. Columbia Union Coll., Takoma Park, Md., 1972-77; assoc. editor Adventist Rev., Rev. and Herald Pub. Assn., Washington, 1977-79; prof. religion and ethics So. Coll., Collegedale, Tenn., 1983—. Mem. Com. of One Hundred, Collegedale, 1984—. Mem. Soc. Bibl. Lit., Andrews Soc. Religious Studies. Office: Southern Coll Collegedale TN 37315

BLANEY, ROBERT WILLIAM, minister, religious studies educator, United Methodist Church; b. Los Angeles, Apr. 18, 1931; m. Laurel H. Blaney; children: Martha, Joy. A.B., UCLA, 1953, M.Pub. Adminstrn., 1958; S.T.B., Boston U., 1959, Th.D., 1966; cert. Grad. Inst., Bossey, Switzerland, 1960. Ordained to ministry United Meth. Ch., 1957. Assoc. dir. UCLA Wesley Found, 1962-64; pastor Brentwood United Meth. Ch., Los Angeles, 1962-64, Los Feliz United Meth. Ch., Los

Angeles, 1964-66; dir., assoc. prof. Pacific Ctr. for Study of Social Issues, U. Pacific, Stockton, Calif., 1966-76, chmn., prof. religious studies, 1975—; minister in residence Holy Cross United Meth. Ch., Stockton, 1974—; del. Christian Peace Conf., Prague, Czechoslovakia, 1979; mem. div. ordained ministry Calif.-Nev. Conf., bd. dirs. pastors sch., United Meth. Ch., San Francisco, 1980—; pres., bd. dirs. Stockton Metro Ministry, 1974—; vis. scholar Chs. Ctr. for Study Theology and Pub. Policy, Washington, 1979, Cambridge U., Eng., 1984. Pres. San Joaquin County Mental Health Assn., Calif., 1974-75; mem. cancer com. and instnl. rev. bd. Dameron Hosp., Stockton, 1978—; chmn. Crime Awareness and Prevention Commn., San Joaquin County, 1980-81. Fellow Rockefeller Found., 1956, NEH, 1980; recipient Outstanding Educator award Am. Ednl. Assn., 1975. Mem. Soc. Christian Ethics (pres. Pacific sect. 1981-82), Am. Acad. Religion, Christians Associated for Relationships with Eastern Europe (chmn. task force 1968-80), Nat. Orgn. for Changing Men, AAUP, Phi Kappa Phi, Sigma Pi. Democrat. Home: 2221 Dwight Way Stockton CA 95204 Office: U Pacific Stockton CA 95211

BLAYLOCK, DONALD LYNN, minister, Southern Baptist Convention; b. Bristol, Va., July 31, 1938; s. Orville Roscoe and Mary Belle (Hutton) B.; B.A., Carson-Newman Coll., 1960; M. Div., So. Bapt. Theol. Sem., 1969; m. Phyllis Joyce Moyers, Mar. 26, 1960; 1 child, Mary Donice Jackson. Ordained to ministry, 1962. Minister of music Unaka Ave. Bapt. Ch., Johnson City, Tenn., 1960-61; assoc. pastor Beaumont Ave. Bapt. Ch., Knoxville, Tenn., 1961-63; tchr. Fulton High Sch., Knoxville, 1963-64; asso. pastor Island Home Bapt. Ch., Knoxville, 1964-65; minister of music Buechel Park Bapt. Ch., Louisville, 1965-68; campus minister Morehead State U., Ky., 1968-70; assoc. pastor 1st Bapt. Ch., Cullman, Ala., 1970-71; asso. student dept. Ky. Bapt. Conv., Middletown, 1971-73, state dir. student dept., 1976—. Mem. So. Bapt. State Student Dirs. Assn., Religious Edn. Assn. U.S. and Can., Am. Mgmt. Assn. Author and composer of religious works. Home: 2503 Browns Lane Louisville KY 40220 Office: Box 43433 Ky Baptist Conv Middletown KY 40243

BLAYLOCK, JAMES CARL, minister, Baptist Missionary Association of America; b. Guntown, Miss., Jan. 27, 1938; s. Carl Houston and Katie Lee (Pugh) B.; m. Jo Ann Enlow, May 3, 1962; children: Jacquelyn Ann, John Thomas. A.A., Southeastern Baptist Coll., Laurel, Miss., 1962; B.Th., Bapt. Missionary Assn. Theol. Sem., Jacksonville, Tex., 1964; B.A., Tex. Eastern U., Tyler, 1976; M.R.E., Bapt. Missionary Assn. Theol. Sem., 1977; M.S.L.S., East Tex. State U., 1980. Ordained minister Baptist Missionary Association of America, 1962. Pastor Mt. Pleasant Ch., Bedias, Tex., 1962-64, Buena Vista Ch., Timpson, Tex., 1964-70, 1st Bapt. Ch., Maydelle, Tex., 1970—; asst. dir. Bapt. News Service, 1969—; asst. editor Directory and Handbook of the Baptist Missionary Assn. Am., 1969—; librarian Bapt. Missionary Assn. Theol. Sem., 1972—. Democrat. Editor: Mt. Olive Evangel, 1965-70. Home: 625 Kickapoo St Jacksonville TX 75766 Office: PO Box 1797 Jacksonville TX 75766

BLECKER, MICHAEL J., school administrator. Pres. Grad. Theol. Union (Interdenom.). Office: 2465 LeConte Ave Berkeley CA 94709*

BLEDSOE, CHARLES ADAIR, ednl. adminstr., Episcopal Ch.; b. Perry, Ga., July 23, 1933; s. Daniel Webster and Lillian Elaine (Adair) B.; A.B., Vanderbilt U., 1955, M.A., 1956; M. Div., U. of the South, 1960; divorced; children—Mary Capers, Charles Adair, Thorne Sparkman. Ordained priest, 1961; founder, headmaster Episc. Day Sch., Bristol, Va., 1966—. Pres., Abingdon Convocation, 1963-64, dean, 1976-77; mem. dept. coll. work Episc. Ch., 1964-65, mem. exec. bd., 1964-65, del. Provincial Synod, 1964. Bd. govs. Bristol Meml. Hosp.; founder Bristol Theatre and Ballet Co.; active Bristol Arts Council. Mem. Bristol C. of C. (dir.). Editorial asst. The Sewanee Rev., 1959-61; author: (with R. R. Purdy) The Fugitives' Reunion, 1956. Home: 926 Sycamore St Bristol VA 24201 Office: PO Box 897 Bristol VA 24201

BLEDSOE, JOHN L., minister, So. Baptist Conv.; b. Franklin, Ga., Feb. 17, 1933; s. John L. and Bernice Estelle (Camp) B.; B.A., Mercer U., 1954; B.D., So. Bapt. Theol. Sem., 1959, M.Div., 1970; postgrad. San Francisco Theol. Sem., 1973-75; m. Joann Coulter, June 23, 1957; children—Sherri Ann, Christie Lynnette, Jonna Carole. Ordained to ministry, 1954; pastor Pineview Bapt. Ch., LaGrange, Ga., 1954-55, Greenup Fork Bapt. Ch., Owenton, Ky., 1956-58, Long Ridge Bapt. Ch., Owenton, Ky., 1958-60, First Bapt. Ch., Clay, Ky., 1960-63, First Bapt. Ch., Calhoun, Ga., 1963-71, Trinity Bapt. Ch., Moultrie, Ga., 1971—. Vice pres. N.W. Ga. Bapt. Pastor's Conf., 1966-67, pres., 1967-68; mem. adminstrn. com. Ga. Bapt. Conv., 1968-71, exec. com., 1966-71; vice moderator Colquitt County Bapt. Assn., Moultrie, Ga., 1971, 76; chmn. chaplaincy program, Colquitt County Meml. Hosp., Moultrie, 1975-76; chapel speaker Bethel Coll., Hopkinsville, Ky., 1961, Truett McConnel Coll., Cleveland, Ga., 1968; mem. city bi-racial com., Calhoun, Ga., 1970-71; vice chmn. spl. com. to study drug and juvenile delinquency problem in Colquitt County, Ga., 1974; speaker various civic clubs and events; bd. dirs. Colquitt chpt. Am. Cancer Soc., 1973-75; chmn. Mental Health Assn. of Colquitt County (Ga.), 1976-77; chmn. bd. dirs. Green Oaks Center for Developmental Disabilities, Moultrie, 1976-77; bd. dirs. Moultrie YMCA, 1976-77. Mem. Assn. Christian Counselors and Psychotherapists. Contbr. articles in field to religious jours. Office: PO Box 1235 Moultrie GA 31768

BLEDSOE, THOMAS LEE, minister, So. Baptist Conv.; b. Hot Springs, Ark., Jan. 3, 1939; s. Thomas Filmore and Ruby Lee (Young) B.; B.A., Baylor U., 1967; m. Teresa Nell Phelps, Mar. 28, 1969. Ordained to ministry, 1972; asso. choral dir. Seventh and James Bapt. Ch., 1957—; minister music Western Heights Bapt. Ch., Waco, Tex., 1957-58, Oaklawn Bapt. Ch., Bellmead, Tex., 1959-60, Queen St. Bapt. Ch., Tyler, Tex., 1967-68, Northwest Bapt. Ch., Oklahoma City, 1968-70; music coordinator Billy Graham Asso. Crusade Program, 1970—; minister music Forest Meadow Bapt. Ch., Dallas, 1972—. Named Outstanding Cadet, USAF, 1965. Recorded albums Oh, How I Love Jesus, 1972; Tom and Terry, 1977; compiler Associate Crusades Choir Book, 1972. Home: 9339 Locarno St Dallas TX 75243 Office: 9150 Church Rd Dallas TX 75231

BLEDSOE, TOMMY DALTON, minister, Southern Baptist Convention; b. Carrollton, Ga., July 23, 1942; s. Johnson Dalton and Mary Doris (Cooley) B.; A.B., Ga. State Coll., 1964; Th.M., New Orleans Bapt. Theol. Sem., 1967; M.Ed., Ga. State U., 1972, Ph.D., 1980; m. Donna Lee Shores, June 25, 1966; children: Tommy Dalton, Jonathan Lee, Jennifer Leigh. Ordained to ministry, 1966; asso. pastor Temple Bapt. Ch., New Orleans, 1968; pastor Mt. Ararat Bapt. Ch., Gaffney, S.C., 1969-70, Arbor Heights Bapt. Ch., Douglasville, Ga., 1973-77; minister counseling Douglasville Fedn. Bapt. Chs., 1977-80; interim pastor Adairsville Bapt. Ch., 1983-84; pastor Unity Bapt. Ch., Newnan, Ga., 1984—; dir. Pastoral Counseling Assocs., Douglasville, 1982—. Tchr. Atlanta Pub. Schs., 1970-74, counselor, 1974-84. Mem. Am. Assn. Marriage and Family Therapy, Ga. Assn. Marriage and Family Therapy (editor newsletter 1984—). Home: 4881 Old Briar Trail Douglasville GA 30135

BLEVINS, LEON WILFORD, educator, minister, Southern Baptist Convention; b. Brownfield, Tex., Oct. 2, 1937; s. Bernice Wilford and Virgie Opal (Bevers) B.; B.A., Wayland Bapt. Coll., Plainview, Tex., 1961; postgrad. Southwestern Bapt. Theol. Sem., Ft. Worth, 1961-63; M.A., U. Tex., El Paso, 1967; m. Shannah Pharr, Aug. 28, 1960; children: Tab, Keith, Shaleah. Ordained to ministry So. Baptist Conv., 1957. Dir., counselor Phila. Girls Home, Fort Worth, 1961; pastor chs., Tex., N.Mex., Calif., 1962-65; various interim pastorates, 1967-70; chaplain Interfaith Chapel, Tex. State Tech. Inst., Amarillo, 1971-72; lectr. Tchr. polit. sci. U. Tex., El Paso, 1965-67, Tex. Tech. U., 1967-70, West Tex. State U., 1970-72; instr. polit. sci. El Paso Community Coll., 1972—. Author: The Young Voters Manual: A Topical Dictionary of American Government and Politics, 1973; Texas Government in Comparative Perspective, 1985. Contbr. articles to profl. jours. Mem. El Paso Citizens Adv. Com. on Constl. Revision, 1973-74, El Paso Bicentennial Commn., 1975-76. Del., Tex. Dem. convs., 1972, 74, 76. Mem. Alpha Chi, Alpha Psi Omega, Alpha Mu Gamma, Phi Alpha Theta, Pi Sigma Alpha, Pi Gamma Mu. Home: 10305 Ashwood Dr El Paso TX 79925

BLEVINS, THOMAS L. bishop, Lutheran Church of Am. Office: 5519 Phinney Ave N Seattle WA 98103*

BLICK, WARREN SCOTT, priest, Episcopal Church; b. Joplin, Mo., Dec. 5, 1952; s. Sherman Herald and Elizabeth Margaret (Leard) B.; m. Esther Deann Gade, May 22, 1979; 1 child, Scott Matthew; stepchildren: Vicki Lynn Moore, Lowell Jeffery Ahl. B.A., Phillips U., 1974; M.Div., U. South, 1977; postgrad. Coll. Preachers, 1982, Grad. Theol. Found., 1984—. Ordained priest, 1978. Canon St. Paul's Cathedral, Oklahoma City, 1977-79; vicar Polk Meml. Episcopal Ch., Leesville, La., 1979-82; rector Trinity Episcopal Ch., DeRidder, La., 1979-82; chaplain St. Mark's Episcopal Day Sch., Shreveport, La., 1982-84; asst. rector St. Mark's Episcopal Ch., Shreveport, 1982—; mentor Edn. for Ministry, U. South, 1975—; alt. del. Provincial Synod, Province VII, El Paso, Tex., 1984; mem. cursillo secretariat Episcopal Ch., Diocese of Western La., 1984—; priest advisor task force on ministry of the aging Episcopal Ch., 1983—. Mem. Child Abuse and Neglect Task Force, DeRidder, La., 1982; bd. dirs. Help Line Telephone Crisis Intervention, DeRidder, 1979-82, Creative Life Ctr., Oklahoma City, 1977-79; troop com. Boy Scouts Am., Shreveport, La., 1982—. Republican. Lodge: Lions. Home: 2765 Fairfield Shreveport LA 71104 Office: Saint Marks Episcopal Ch 908 Rutherford Shreveport LA 71104

BLOCK, LARRY LEROY, minister, Assemblies of God; b. Des Moines, July 29, 1942; s. Gust Fredrick and Vernita Irene (Ackerman) B.; m. Carol Esther Newby, Aug. 19, 1961 (dec. 1969); children: David LeRoy, Rodney Ray; m. Nancy Joe Girdner, Aug. 29, 1971; children: Brandon Elliott, Jonathan Andrew. D.D., Jameson Bible Inst., Phila., 1978, Th.D. (hon.), 1978; D.Ministries (hon.), Mid-States Bible Coll., Des Moines, 1978. Ordained to ministry, Assemblies of God Ch., 1983. Pastor Open Bible Ch., Fremont, Calif., 1971-75, Assembly of God, Creston, Iowa, 1983—; nat. evangelist Evangelistic Ministries, Inc., Stockton, Calif., 1975-81; exec. dir., prin. Kingsway Christian Sch., Des Moines, 1982-83; exec. dir. Kingsway Christian Coll. and Theol. Sem., Des Moines, 1981-83. Recipient Outstanding Accomplishment in Area of Ch. Growth and Co operation award Open Bible Standard Churches, Inc., Des Moines, 1973. Avocations: flying, golf, skiing. (515) 782-4236

BLOOMER, DONALD LEE, minister, Ch. of God (Anderson, Ind.); b. Lansing, Mich., Aug. 6, 1944; s. Edward A. and Beulah B. (Reed) B.; A.A., John Wesley Coll., 1976; m. Barrara Ann Lee, Aug. 10, 1968; children—Lee Edward, Kimberly Dawn. Ordained to ministry, 1974; pastor Jackson (Ky.) First Ch. of God, 1973-74, Sanford (Mich.) Ch. of God, 1974—. Treas., Jackson (Ky.) Clergy Assn., 1973-74; usher coordinator St. Louis Camp meeting Ch. of God, 1975, prayer chmn., 1976. Mem. Sanford Ministerial Assn. (pres. 1976-77). Home and Office: 1938 Seven Mile Rd Sanford MI 48657

BLOOMFIELD, EDWARD HENRY, minister, United Church of Christ; philosophy educator; b. Orange, Calif., May 24, 1938; s. Henry Martin and Mabel Edna (Hicks) B.; m. Veronica Little, Apr. 22, 1967; 1 child, Veronica Elizabeth. B.A., Whittier Coll., 1960; M.Div., Harvard Div. Sch., 1963; M.A., Claremont Grad. Sch., 1969, Ph.D., 1975. Ordained to ministry United Ch. of Christ, 1966. Asst. minister Plymouth Congregational Ch., Whittier, Calif., 1965-67, Hillcrest Congl. Ch., La Habra Heights, Calif., 1972—; pres. bd. St. Mark's Sch., Downey, Calif., 1980—; pres. bd. dirs. Interchurch Samaritan Counseling Ctr., Whittier, 1983—. Prof. philosophy Cerritos Coll., Norwalk, Calif., 1969—, staff devel. coordinator, 1983—. Author: Understanding Our Religious Heritage, 1983; The Opposition to the English Separatists, 1982. Editor Music Odyssey newsletter, 1981. Vice pres. bd. dirs. So. Calif. Consortium for Community Coll. Television, 1979-82; registered reader Huntington Library, San Marino, Calif., 1970—. Woodrow Wilson fellow, 1960; NEH grantee, 1983, ALA grantee, 1983. Mem. Am. Acad. Religion, Am. Philos. Assn., Western Assn. for Theol. Discussion, Calif. Tchrs. Assn., AAUP, Cerritos Coll. Faculty Assn., Alpha Gamma Sigma (faculty advisor 1973-83). Democrat. Home: 18703 S Clarkdale Ave Artesia CA 90701 Office: Cerritos College 11110 E Alondra Blvd Norwalk CA 90650

BLOOMFIELD, OREE, SR. Bishop, Christian Methodist Episcopal Church (Seventh Dist.), chair Gen. Bd. of Missions. Office: 6524 16th St NW Washington DC 20012*

BLOSKAS, JOHN D., religious organization executive, Southern Baptist Convention; b. Waco, Tex., July 13, 1928; s. George and Alvina (Schrader) B.; B.A., Baylor U., 1953; m. Ann Louise Nelson, Feb. 7, 1955; children: Suzzanne (Mrs. Robert L. Webb) (dec.), John D., Kenneth Douglas. Supr. press relations Annuity Bd., So. Baptist Conv., Dallas, 1958-63, dir. publs. and communications, 1963-70, v.p. and dir. pub. relations, 1970—, v.p. endowment, 1984—; regional corr. Bapt. Press, 1958—; ordained deacon First Bapt. Ch., Dallas, 1968; del. Pres.'s Conf. on Aging, 1961, 71. Trustee Dallas Christian Acad., 1967-73. Mem. So. (pres. 1967), Tex. (pres. 1961, 73) Bapt. pub. relations assns., Pub. Relations Soc. Am., Religious Pub. Relations Council, Waco Jr. C. of C., Sigma Delta Chi. Author: Staying in the Black Financially, 1973; (tape) Living Within Your Means, 1979. Editor: The Years Ahead, 1958—. Home: 5816 Clendenin St Dallas TX 75228 Office: 511 N Akard Bldg Dallas TX 75201

BLOUNT, OUIDA POOL, lay worker; b. Tennille, Ga., Apr. 6, 1916; d. Ernest Vanderver and Jimmye (Futrill) Pool; m. Willie Brown Blount, July 15, 1932 (dec. Mar. 1958); children: Linda, David Brown, Evelyn, Louise, Richard William. Pres. Woman's Missionary Union First Bapt. Ch., Winder, Ga., 1940-42, 46-48, 60-64, 69, dir., 1970-74, 78-80, 82—; dir. Bapt. Women, Winder, Ga., 1976-77, 80, 81; divisional v.p. Bapt. Woman's Missionary Union, Ga., 1970-75, mem. exec. bd., 1970-75; mem. exec. com. Appalachee Assn. of Bapt. Woman's Missionary Union, Ga., 1971—, chmn. missions com., 1977-79, 82-84, conf. leader, Ridgecrest, N.C., 1978, conf. leader, Toccoa, Ga., 1984, Norman Park, Ga., 1984; bd. dirs. So. Bapt. Home Mission Bd., Atlanta, 1975-83, sec., 1981-83, interfaith witness assoc., 1984—, tchrs., 1978—, speaker world missions confs., 1977—; tchr. Sunday Sch., First Bapt. Ch., Winder, Ga., 1931—, choir mem., 1933—, dir. children's choir, 1966-68, dir. cherub choir, 1969-79. Pres. Am. Legion Aux., 1946-48; pres. Parent Tchr. Assn., Winder, Ga., 1949-50, 53-56; v.p. Winder Woman's Club, 1959-61; pres. Winder Garden Club, 1962-64, 70-72, 74-75; vol. Mental Health Clinic, Winder, 1971-82. Home: 207 Partridge Trail Winder GA 30680

BLUMBERG, HERSCHEL W., religious organization executive Jewish. Pres. United Jewish Appeal, Inc., N.Y.C. Office: United Jewish Appeal Inc 1290 Ave of Americas New York NY 10019*

BOADT, LAWRENCE EDWARD, priest, educator, Roman Catholic Church; b. Los Angeles, Oct. 26, 1942; s. A. Loren and Eleanor (Power) B. M.A. in Religion, St. Paul's Coll., 1968; S.T.L., Cath. U. Am., 1971, M.A. in Semitic Langs., 1972; Lic. in Scripture, Pontifical Bibl. Inst., Rome, 1973, S.S.D., 1976. Ordained priest Roman Catholic Ch., 1969. Parish priest Cath. Ch., Clemson, S.C., 1969-70, Rome Bibl. Inst., 1971-74; tchr. theology dept. Fordham U., N.Y.C., 1974-76; prof. Bibl. studies Washington Theol. Union, Silver Spring, Md., 1976—; editor Paulist Press, Ramsey, N.J., 1975—. Author: Ezekiel's Oracles Against Egypt, 1980; Jeremiah 1-25: A Commentary, 1982; Jeremiah 26-52, Zephaniah, Habakkuk, Nahum, 1983; Ezekiel's Oracles Against Egypt, 1980; Reading the Old Testament: An Introduction, 1984; Introduction to Wisdom Literature and Proverbs, 1985. Mem. Soc. Bibl. Lit. (regional pres. Chesapeake Bay 1980-81), Cath. Bibl. Assn., Cath. Theol. Soc. Am., Am. Schs. Oriental Research. Office: Washington Theol Union 9001 New Hampshire Ave Silver Spring MD 20910 also Paulist Press 545 Island Rd Ramsey NJ 07446

BOATRIGHT, RICHARD ROLAND, minister, Bapt. Missionary Assn. Am.; b. Kansas City, Kans., Mar. 9, 1933; s. Walter Salem and Pearl Lee (Roland) B.; B.S., Kans. State Coll., 1956, M.S., 1962; student Bapt. Missionary Assn. Theol. Sem., 1956-58, Central Mo. State U., 1971-74; m. Glayds Gertrude Dillion, Mar. 9, 1956; children—Michael, Patricia, Sheryl, Lauraleen. Ordained to ministry Baptist Missionary Assn. Am., 1956; pastor Kans. and Tex. chs., 1956-62, Mt. Zion Bapt. Ch., Garland, Kans., 1962-67, S.W. Chgo. Bapt. Ch., 1967-69, Mt. Zion Bapt. Ch., Garland, 1969-70, Broadview Bapt. Ch., Kansas City, Mo., 1970-74, Mt. Zion Bapt. Ch., Kansas City, Mo., 1974—. Tchr. Kansas City Pub. Schs., 1960—. Pres. Kansas City Assn. Community Councils, 1973—, N.E. Area Community Council, 1963-65, 69-71, 73—; life mem. Nat. Congress Parents and Tchrs. Mem. NEA (life), Kansas City Edn. Assn., Mo. Tchrs. Assn., Phi Belta Kappa. Home: 3530 Gladstone Blvd Kansas City MO 64123 Office: 4447 Sunrise Dr Kansas City MO 64123

BOBB, DOUGLAS CAMPBELL JOSIAH, minister, United Meth. Ch.; b. Ann's Grove, Demerara, Guyana, Feb. 8, 1907; s. Jehoshaphat Ahijah and Elsie Mary Ann (Dey) B.; came to U.S., 1963, naturalized, 1970; M.S. in Edn., U. Pa., 1965; m. Myrtle Agnes Rholehr Pollard, Aug. 21, 1941; children— Hyacinth, Lucille, Daphne Elsie, Avril Patricia, Hilary Penelope, Douglas John, Myrtle Asala, Joy Ann Eleanor. Ordained to ministry, 1941; jr. minister Tobago Circuit Trinidad (W.I.) and Tobago Island (W.I.) Dist. of Brit. Conf., 1941-43, supt. Chateaubelair circuit, St. Vincent, 1941-43, supt. British Guiana dist., Mahaica, 1943-53, Georgetown, 1953-63; asso. pastor Midtown Parish, Phila., 1963-69; pastor Trinity United Meth. Ch., Phila., 1969—. Mem. legislature Brit. Guiana, 1950, 53-57. Recipient New Testament Greek prize Meth. Ch. Great Brit., 1938. Home: 6337 Baynton St Philadelphia PA 19144

BODE, RICHARD PAUL, minister, Lutheran Church - Missouri Synod; b. Detroit Lakes, Minn., Apr. 6, 1934; s. Reinhold Ludwig Martin and Adeline Minnie Mary (Tietgens) B.; m. Kathleen Frances Peradotto, July 13, 1957; 1 child, Theresa Kay. M.Div., Concordia Sem., 1959, S.T.M., 1969; postgrad. U. Edinburgh (Scotland), 1970-71; Th.D., Concordia Sem., 1977. Ordained to ministry Luth. Ch., 1959. Missionary to Philippines, Luth. Ch. - Mo. Synod Bd. for Missions, 1959-70; pastor St. John's Luth. Ch., Hooker, Okla., 1972-84, Grace Luth. Ch., Liberal, Kans., 1984—; pres. Mindanao Dist. Luth. Ch. in Philippines, 1967-70; v.p. Luth. Ch. in Philippines, 1967-70; dir. Okla. Dist. Luth. C. - Mo. Synod, 1972-83. Republican. Home: 1241 S Pershing Liberal KS 67901

BOEHLKE, CRAIG ALAN, minister, Am. Lutheran Ch.; b. Cleve., Aug. 25, 1947; s. Frank Carl and Polly (Connelly) B.; B.A., Capital U., 1969; postgrad. Ohio State U., 1970; M.Div., Luth. Theol. Sem., 1973; m. Georgia Clemens Stokes, Sept. 9, 1972. Ordained to ministry, 1973; intern St. Pauls Lutheran Ch., Charleston, W. Va., 1971-72; pastor edn., youth Grace Luth. Ch., St. Paul, Minn., 1973—. Del. nat. conv. Am. Luth. Ch., 1976; supr. interns Luth. Sem., Concordia Coll., 1973—. Instr. extension div. dept. social work U. Minn., 1975—. Mem. St. Paul Task Force on Youth, 1974—. Mem. St. Paul Clergy Assn. Home: 7564 Carillon Plaza W St Paul MN 55119 Office: 1730 Old Hudson Rd St Paul MN 55106

BOEHNKE, JOHN HENRY, minister, Christian Church (Disciples of Christ); b. Hooper, Nebr., Dec. 17, 1932; s. John F. and Emma Mae (Schwanamann) B.; m. Joyce Jeannine Boehnke, Apr. 11, 1954; children: Terri Lynn, Tommy Lee. B.A., Phillips U., 1960, M.Ed., 1967; M.Div., Grad. Sem., Enid, Okla., 1977. Ordained to ministry Christian Ch., 1960. Tchr. social studies Hazel Green Acad., Ky., 1962-67; dir. counseling Cowley County Community Coll., Arkansas City, Kans., 1967-75; assoc. pastor First Christian Ch., Blackwell, Okla., 1975-80; sr. pastor First Christian Ch., Lake Jackson, Tex., 1980—; vice-moderator dist. IV, Christian Chs. Okla., 1978-80; sec. coastal plains area chs., Tex., 1982-84; del. Internat. Conv. Christian Chs., Kans., Okla., Tex., 1969-84. Vice-chmn. Women's Shelter of Brazoria County, Angleton, Tex., 1982; mem. Com. to Reelect Pres., Washington, 1983-84. Served with USAF, 1952-56. Recipient Master Tchr. award Cowley County Community Coll., Arkansas City, Kans., 1974-75. Mem. NEA (life), Profl. Counselors Assn., Tex. Dow Employees Credit Union, Brazosport Ministerial Alliance (pres. 1981-82), Nat. Rifle Assn. Democrat. (Washington). Lodge: Masons. Office: First Christian Ch 503 Oyster Creek Dr Lake Jackson TX 77566

BOGER, RICHARD EDWIN, JR., minister, Lutheran Church in America; b. Atlanta, May 13, 1952; s. Richard Edwin and Marie Yoder (Leonard) B.; m. Jill Roberta Howard, Apr. 26, 1980. A.B., Lenoir-Rhyne, 1973, Hamma Sch Theol., 1975; M.Div., Pacific Luth. Theol. Sem., 1978. Ordained to ministry Luth. Ch. in Am., 1980. Vesper intern Vesper Soc., San Leandro, Calif., 1975-76; coordinator volunteers Care Network, San Francisco, 1978; intern Christ Our Shepherd, Peachtree City, Ga., 1979-80; pastor Luth. Ch. of Our Savior, Jacksonville, N.C., 1980—; counselor Neighborhood Ch. Clinic, Springfield, Ohio, 1974; pastoral counselor Eden Hayward Pastoral Counsel Service, Hayward, Calif., 1975-76; mem. worship com., music com. N.C. Synod, Luth. Ch. in Am., 1982, 1984—. Bd. dirs. ARC, Jacksonville N.C., 1981—. Mem. Jacksonville Ministerial Assoc., 1980-81, Onslow County Ministerial Fellowship, 1984; assoc. mem. N.C. Chaplains Assoc, 1984. Office: Luth Ch of our Savior PO Box 687 Jacksonville NC 28541-0687

BOGGS, JAKE WOODYARD, JR., evangelist, American Baptist Convention; b. Gassaway, W.Va., May 9, 1924; s. Jake W. and Ruby O. (Paisley) B.; student Prairie Bible Inst., 1942-46, Nat. Bible Inst., 1946-47, Bob Jones U., 1948-51; m. Betty R. White, Nov. 23, 1950; children: Deborah, Jonathan. Ordained to ministry Am. Bapt. Chs. in U.S.A., 1952; evangelist W.Va. Conv. chs., 1951-56, also radio broadcaster, 1951-56; evangelist Am. Bapt. Conv. chs., 1957—; pres. Evangelistic Ministries, Inc. Home: 2716 Rummelbrown Dr Charleston WV 25302

BOHLMANN, RALPH ARTHUR, seminary president, minister, Luth. Ch.-Mo. Synod; b. Palisade, Nebr., Feb. 20, 1932; s. Arthur Erwin and Anne Fredericka (Weeke) B.; student St. John's Coll., Winfield, Kans.; B.A., Concordia Sem., 1953, M.Div., 1956, S.T.M., 1966; Fulbright scholar U. Heidelberg, 1956-57; Ph.D., Yale, 1968; m. Patricia Anne McCleary, Apr. 19, 1959; children—Paul, Lynn. Ordained to ministry, 1958; instr. history and religion Concordia Coll., 1957-58; pastor Mt. Olive Luth. Ch., Des Moines, 1958-60; prof. systematic theology Concordia Sem., St. Louis, 1960-71, acting pres., 1974-75, pres., 1975-81; now pres. Luth. Ch.-Mo. Synod; exec. sec. Commn. Theology and Ch. Relations, Luth. Ch.-Mo. Synod. St. Louis, 1971-74; mem. Faith and Order Commn., Nat. Council Chs., 1973-76. Author: Principles of Biblical Interpretation in the Lutheran Confessions, 1968. Office: 1333 S Kirkwood Rd Saint Louis MO 63122*

BOHMFALK, JOHNITA SCHUESSLER, lay ch. worker, United Methodist Ch.; b. Austin, Tex., Mar. 4, 1916; d. John and Ida Wilhelmina (Jordan) Schuessler; student Southwestern U., 1933-35; B.A., So. Meth. U., 1938; m. Milton F. Bohmfalk, July 28, 1937; children—Joan (Mrs. James Ullrich), Robert. Ch. sch. tchr. Methodist Chs., Tex., 1935-65; dist. dir. children's work United Meth. Ch., 1939-42, mem. conf. bd. Christian Vocations, 1964-68; coordinator Wesleyan Service Guild, 1949-71; mem. conf. bd. Christian edn. Southwest Tex. Ann. Conf., 1969-72; conf. sec. campus ministry Women's Soc. Christian Service, 1964-68, conf. chmn. com. nominations, 1971-72, zone pres., 1940-42; conf. chmn. membership United Meth. Women, 1972-76; v.p. Southwest Tex. Meth. Conf. Ministers Wives, 1951; del. Regional Sch. Missions, 1964-68, 71-76, Nat. Assembly United Meth. Women, 1966, 70, 73; chmn. Conf. Shepherdess Task Force, 1975-76; co-dean Conf. Youth Assemblies; speaker in field, lay witness missions. Tchr. pub. schs., 1935-37. Active United Fund. Recipient dedication service certificate Women's Soc. Christian Service, others. Mem. governing bd. Kirby Hall of U. Tex., 1964-68. Mem. Ch. Women United, AAUW, Internat. Platform Assn. Home: 437 Delaine Dr Corpus Christi TX 78411

BOHN, JAY M., minister, Lutheran Church in America; b. Hagerstown, Md., Dec. 7, 1935; s. C. Elmo and Madeline (Jacobs) B.; m. Christel M. Hinsch, May 21, 1960 (div. 1979); children: Heide M., Erik D.; m. Mary Jane Weller, Jan. 3, 1981; 1 child, Mark J. A.A., Hagerstown Jr. Coll., 1975; A.B., Gettysburg Coll., 1957; M.Div., Luth. Theol. Sem., 1960, S.T.M., 1974. Ordained to ministry, 1960. Pastor, St. Christopher Luth. Ch., Lykens, Pa., 1980—; pastor Rockingham Luth. Parish, Harrisonburg, Va., 1960-62, Christ Luth. Ch., Spring Grove, Pa., 1962-67, Holy Trinity Luth. Ch., York Springs, Pa., 1967-74, St. John Evang. Luth. Ch., Meyersburg, Pa., 1974-79; bd. dirs. Mercersburg/Tuscarora Bicentennial Commn., 1975-77; chmn. Festival of Faith com., Chambersburg dist. Luth. Ch. Am., 1977, mission group dir., 1977; pres. Lykens Ministerium, 1981—, active various coms. in the past. Sec-treas. Mercersburg Area Youth Orgn., 1977; chmn. supervisory com. Luth. Credit Union, York, Pa., 1977-78, others. Mem. Am. Philatelic Soc., Am. Auto. Assn., Luth. Family Campers Assn., Lincoln Fellowship of Pa., Pa. German Soc. Democrat. Club: Avon Literary. Home: 637 N 2d St Lykens PA 17048 Office: Saint Christopher Evang Luth Ch 635 N 2d St Lykens PA 17048

BOL, DOUGLAS JOHN, minister, General Association Regular Baptist Churches, educator; b. Grand Haven, Mich., July 31, 1935; s. J. Edward and Jean B. (Putnam) B.; LL.B., LaSalle Extension U., 1960; B.B.A., Western Mich. U., 1963; B.D. cum laude, Grand Rapids Bapt. Theol. Sem., 1966, M.Div., 1970; M.Ed., U. Ariz., 1972, Ed.D., 1973; m. Marylin Seman, July 31, 1954; children: Gary Douglas, Julie Ann. Ordained to ministry Gen. Assn. Regular Baptist Chs., 1966; chaplain AUS, 1966-70; pastor Eastview Bapt. Ch., Tucson, 1970-73; chaplain Ariz. Army N.G., 1970—. Psychologist, pastoral counselor, Tucson 1970—; speaker, dir. radio broadcast Psychology in the Bible, Tucson, from 1973, Let's Talk. bd. dirs., pres. Inst. Family Living, 1970—. Mem. Am. Personnel and Guidance Assn., Western Assn. Christians for Psychol. Studies (dir.), Am. Psychol. Assn. Home: 9249 E 39th St Tucson AZ 85730

BOLAND, EDWARD GEORGE, priest, Roman Catholic Church; B. Phila., Aug. 20, 1926; s. William Aloysius and Alice (Patton) B. B.A., St. Charles Borromeo Sem., 1951; postgrad. Temple U. Sch. Journalism, 1970-72. Ordained priest Roman Cath. Ch., 1951. Asst. pastor St. Joseph Ch., Summit Hill, Pa., 1951-53, St. Michael Archangel, Levittown, Pa., 1953-60, St. George Ch., Glenolden, Pa., 1960-65, Presentation Blessed Virgin Mary Ch., Cheltenham, Pa., 1965-70, St. Joachim Ch., Phila., 1970-72, St. James Ch., Elkins Park, Pa., 1972-83; pastor St. Mary of the Assumption Ch., Phoenixville, Pa., 1983—; mem. com. Jewish-Catholic Com. Archdiocese Phila., 1969—. Author: Isaac My Son, 1980. Contbr. Articles to profl. jours, mags., newspapers. Mem. Cardinal's Commn. on Human Relations, 1969—. Home and Office: St Marys Ch 212 Dayton St Phoenixville PA 19460

BOLANOS, ROBERT JOSEPH, priest, Roman Cath. Ch.; b. N.Y.C., Feb. 24, 1937; s. Raymond Perfecto and Consuelo de los Angeles (Ortega) B.; M.A., Fordham U., 1962; Ph.L., Woodstock Coll., 1961, S.T.L., 1968. Joined S.J., 1954; ordained priest, 1967; dir. vocations N.Y. Soc. of Jesus, 1968-74, mem. bd. admissions, 1969-76; dir., superior Gonzaga Jesuit Center for Renewal, Monroe, N.Y., 1972—. Mem. Intercommunity Task Force on Spiritual Direction. Translator, Concilium series, vols. 8, 10. Home and office: Jesuit Center for Renewal Monroe NY 10950

BOLING, CHARLES WALKER, minister, So. Bapt. Conv.; b. Greenville, S.C., Aug 16, 1931; s. John Harold and Mae Inez (Wooten) B.; B.A., Furman U., 1953; B.D., Southwestern Baptist Theol. Sem., Ft. Worth, 1957, M.Div., 1973; m. Betty Jean Harbin, Aug. 31, 1952; children—Anne Elizabeth, Debra Jean, Charla Kay. Ordained minister, 1953; music dir. Lima Bapt. Ch., Greenville, 1949-51; youth and music dir. Siloam Bapt. Ch., Easley, S.C., 1951-53; summer missionary home mission bd. So. Bapt. Conv., 1954; music and edn. minister, Springtown, Tex., 1955; minister, Azle, Tex., 1955-57, Easley, 1958-68, 1st Bapt. Ch., Pinckneyville, Ill., 1968—. Dir. sem. extension Easley area, 1959-62; mem. hist. commn. So. Bapt. Conv., 1970-74; chmn. trustees Piedmont Bapt. Assn., S.C., 1963-67, moderator, 1961-62, chmn. exec. com., 1961-62; pres. Piedmont Bapt. Pastors Conf., 1960, Easley Ministerial Alliance, 1966; mem. stewardship com. S.C. Bapt. Conv., 1966, mem. nominating com., 1967; parliamentarian Ill. Bapt. Assn., 1969-72 mem. com. on coms., 1970-72, chmn. spl. ministries com., 1972—; preacher S. Pacific Crusade, summer 1970; moderator Nine Mile Bapt. Assn, Ill., 1971; pres. Pinckneyville Ministerial Alliance, 1972. Chmn. Christmas Parade, Easley, 1964, W. Perry County (Ill.) chpt. A.R.C., 1974; chmn living endowment for N. Greenville Coll., Greenville, 1959-62. Trustee S.C. Bapt. Hosps., 1965-68, Judson Bapt. Coll., Elgin, Ill., 1973—, New Orleans Bapt. Theol. Sem., 1975—. Mem. N. Greenville Coll. Alumni Assn. (pres. S.C. 1959-62), Ill. State Bapt. Assn. (dir. 1976—). Home: 310 W St Louis St Pinckneyville IL 62274 Office: PO Box 157 Pinckneyville IL 62274

BOLLMER, JACOB ANDREW, priest, Roman Catholic Church, religious social services administrator; b. Reading, Ohio, Mar. 27, 1942; s. Jacob Andrew and Irma (Topmiller) B. B.A. in Philosophy, St. Bernard, Rochester, N.Y., 1964; M.S.W. in Social Work, Atlanta U., 1972. Ordained priest, Roman Catholic Ch., 1968; asst. pastor Christ the King Cathedral, Atlanta, 1968-69; asst. dir. Cath. Social Services, Atlanta, 1969-70, exec. dir., 1971—, archdiocesan dir. Campaign for Human Devel., Atlanta, 1972—, regional coordinator Diocesan Dirs. Assn. Campaign for Human Devel., 1973-77, resettlement dir. Indochinese

Program, U.S. Cath. Conf., 1976—. Mem. Nat. Alliance for Family Life, Nat. Conf. Cath. Charities, Nat. Assn. Social Workers, Acad. Cert. Social Workers, Ga. Social Welfare Conf., Nat. Orthropsychiatry Soc. Office: Catholic Social Services Inc 680 W Peachtree St NW Atlanta GA 30308

BOLTON, DENNIS RUDOLPH, minister; Lutheran Church in America; b. Highpoint N.C., Mar. 24, 1953; s. Rudolph Alexander and Gerda Sophia (Gemar) B.; m. Angela Polk, May 25, 1974; 1 child, Jessica Kristen. B.A. in Religious Studies, U. S.C., 1975; M.Div., Luth. Theol. Southern Sem., 1979; D.Min., Union Theol. Sem., 1984. Ordained to ministry Lutheran Ch. in Am., 1979. Chaplain S.C. Bapt. Hosp., Columbia, S.C., 1976, S.C. State Mental Hosp., Columbia, 1977; intern pastor Indian/Black Ministry, Greensboro, N.C., 1977-78; pastor Shepherd of The Sea Ch., Atlantic Beach, N.C., 1979-81, Christus Victor Ch., Durham, N.C., 1981—; dir. Indian Ministry, N.C. Synod, 1980—, Inclusive Ministry Commn., N.C. Synod, 1980—, Luth. Family Service, Durham, N.C., 1982—; sec. Luth. Campus Ministry, Durham, N.C., 1981—. Author and editor articles. Adviser Nat. Indian Luth. Bd., Chgo., 1978—, Indian Treaty Rights and Concerns, State of N.C., 1979—; bd. dirs. World Hunger, Morehead City, 1981—. Mem. Acad. Parish Clergy. Home: 14 Vanguard Ct Durham NC 27713 Office: Christus Victor Luth PO Box 12343 Research Triangle Pk NC 27709

BONAR, CLAYTON LLOYD, minister, Church of the Nazarene; b. Washington County, Kans., Nov. 5, 1934; s. Earl Albert and Violet May (Doane) B.; m. Helen Ann Harmaning, Sept. 12, 1958; children: Renee, Scott. B.A., Northwest Nazarene Coll., 1960; postgrad., Fuller Theol. Sem., 1974-75; M.A., Point Loma Coll., 1975; postgrad., Rosemead Grad. Sch., 1975. Ordained to ministry Church of the Nazarene, 1963. Pastor, Ch. of Nazarene, Caldwell, Idaho, 1961-63, Pocatello, Idaho, 1963-68, Inglewood, Calif., 1968-73, Alhambra, Calif., 1973-78, Richland, Wash., 1978—; del. Gen. Nazarene World Missionary Soc., Conv. Nazarene Ch., Kansas City, 1968; regent Northwest Nazarene Coll., Nampa, Idaho, 1967-68; dist. sec. Ch. Nazarene, Los Angeles, 1976-78, adv. bd., Northwest Dist., 1984—; committeeman Nazarene Fed. Credit Union, Whittier, Calif., 1974-78; mem. curriculum com. The Enduring Word Series. Author: From Behind Closed Doors, 1981; The Spoken Law, 1985; (with others) Tough Questions: Christian Answers, 1982. Contbr. articles to mags. Served with USAF, 1953-56. Mem. Wesleyan Theol. Soc., Speakers and Writers Ink. Republican. Lodge: Kiwanis. Avocation: photography. Home: 2207 Humphreys Richland WA 99352 Office: First Ch of the Nazarene 603 Wright Ave Richland WA 99352

BONDARIN, AV, religious organization executive, Jewish. Exec. dir. Jewish Chautaugua Soc., Inc., N.Y.C. Office: Jewish Chautaugua Soc Inc 838 Fifth Ave New York NY 10021*

BONENBERGER, OMER EDMOND, religious educator, General Association of Regular Baptists. b. Jeffersonville, Ind., May 29, 1938; s. Omer Albright and Bertha Geraldine (Baker) B.; m. Rbecca Sharon Hughes, Dec. 22, 1961; children: Joyce, Todd. B.A. in Bible, Bob Jones U., 1960; M.A. in Edn., Ariz. State U., 1968; Dr. Edn., U. Maine, 1981. Asst. pastor Calvary Bapt. Ch., Tempe, Ariz., 1961-62, interim pastor, 1962; deacon Bible Bapt. Ch., Saco, Maine, 1973-81; tchr., dept. supt. Grace Bapt. Ch., Cedarville, Ohio, 1981-84; mem. faculty Cedarville, Ohio, 1981—, assoc. prof. edn., 1981—. Mem. Internat. Reading Assn., Nat. Council Tchrs. English, Reading Excellence Through Arts, Phi Delta Kappa, Phi Kappa Phi. Home: PO Box 601 Cedarville OH 45314 Office: Cedarville Coll Cedarville OH 45314

BONHAM, TAL D., minister, Southern Baptist Conv.; b. Cordell, Okla., July 20, 1934; s. Woodrow and Esther Pairlee (Gray) B.; B.A., Okla. Bapt. U., Shawnee, 1957; B.D., Southwestern Bapt. Theol. Sem., Ft. Worth, 1958, Th.D., 1963; D.D., Campbellsville Bapt. Coll. Ky., 1982; m. Clara Faye Wright, July 25, 1958; children: Marilyn, Randy, Daniel, Tal David. Ordained to ministry, 1954; pastor First Bapt. Ch., Marlow, Okla., 1960-63, South Side Bapt. Ch., Pine Bluff, Ark., 1964-73; dir. evangelism Bapt. Gen. Conv. Okla., 1973-80; exec. dir., treas. State Conv. Baptists in Ohio, 1980—; moderator, Millins Bapt. Assn., 1962, Harmony Bapt. Assn., 1965; pres. exec. bd. Ark. Bapt. Conv., 1969, pres. conv., 1970-71; pres. Pine Bluff Ministerial Assn., 1970, Marlow Ministerial Assn., 1961; chaplain Babe Ruth World Series, Ark., 1972; vice chmn. chapel com. Cummins Prison, Ark., 1972. Named Disting. Citizen, Pine Bluff, 1970, Outstanding Young Man Ark. Jaycees, 1970. Author: The Demands of Discipleship, 1967; Back to the Mountain, 1971; God Doesn't Want Your Money, 1975; Lift for Life, 1976; Victory in Jesus Crusade Manual, 1976; Victory in Jesus, 1981; The Treasury of Clean Jokes, 1981; Another Treasury of Clean Jokes, 1983; other joke collections. Home: Route 2 Box 196 Yukon OK 73099 Office: 2232 Stratingham Dr Dublin OH 43017

BONIGIOVANNI, GUY. Clergyman, gen. overseer Christian Church of North America. Office: 3740 Longview Rd West Middlesex PA 16159*

BONNER, CHARLES GARY, pastor, Southern Baptist Convention; b. Shreveport, La., Mar. 5, 1937; s. Curtis G. and Flossie (Tapscott) B.; m. Ann Harper, June 27, 1959; children: Christopher Graham, Andrea Lynn. B.A., Baylor U., 1959; M.A., S.W. Tex. U., 1972; M.Div., S.W. Bapt. Theol. Sem., Fort Worth, 1963, D.Ministry, 1979. Ordained to ministry, 1963. Pastor, First Bapt. Ch., Schulenburg, Tex., 1963-65, Baytown, Tex., 1969-76, Huntsville, Tex., 1976—; assoc. pastor Highland Park Ch., Austin, Tex., 1965-67, First Bapt. Ch., Abilene, Tex., 1967-69; leader youth revival, Springhill, La., 1953, 54, Selfs Bapt. Ch., Honeygrove, Tex., 1962, Layman's Crusade, Los Angeles, 1962, First Baptist Ch., Eden, Tex., 1969, Los Angeles, 1970; youth pastor Broadway Bapt. Ch., Fort Worth, 1963; clk. Gonzales Bapt. Assn., Schulenburg, Tex., 1964-65; tchr. sr. high sch. students Sunday Sch. Week, Glorieta Bapt. Assembly, N.Mex., 1967; tchr. adult leadership of sr. high sch. students, 1969; tchr. high sch. students Ridgecrest Bapt. Assembly, N.C., 1968; mem. missions com. Abilene Bapt. Assn., 1969-70; tchr. Lueders Bapt. Encampment, Abilene, 1969; Paisano Bapt. Encampment, Alpine, Tex., 1972, Brownwood Bapt. Camp, Tex., 1972; sec. Baytown Ministerial Alliance, Tex., 1970-71, pres., 1972-73; pres. Bapt. Pastors' Conf., Baytown, 1970, Huntsville Ministerial Alliance, Tex.; mem. com. to nominate exec. bd. mems. Bapt. Gen. Conv. Tex., 1971-74, 77-79; leader pastoral ministry seminar N.Mex. Bapt. Conv., 1974; mem. com. to nominate trustees Bapt. Hosps. S.E. Tex., Bapt. Gen. Conv. Tex., Beaumont, 1974; moderator San Jacinto Bapt. Assn., Baytown, 1975-76, chmn. Christian life com., chmn. long range planning com.; speaker Community Thanksgiving Worship, Huntsville; chmn. community ministries com. Tryon-Evergreen Bapt. Assn., 1984, mem. missions com., 1981-83; bd. dirs. Lueders Bapt. Encampment, Abilene, 1968-69; chmn. bd. dirs. Good Shepherd Mission, Huntsville, 1983—. Author: Good News for Modern Man, 1969, Parenthood Enrichment Activities, 1970; Marks of Maturity, 1972. Contbr. articles to religious publs. Vice. pres. Baytown Welfare League Bd., 1974, pres., 1976; mem. Bayshore Mental Health Mental Retardation Bd., 1973-74; speaker Lee High Sch. Baccalaureate, Baytown, 1974; bd. dirs. Baytown YMCA; chmn. Gov.'s Com. on Aging, Fayette County, Tex.; asst. dist. commr. Live Oak dist. Boy Scouts Am.; mem. Citizens Com. on Child Care, Schulenburg, Tex.; vol. counselor Suicide Prevention Service, Abilene; establisher mission action groups to meet needs of multi-cultural transition community, Baytown; mem. com. United Fund, Huntsville; co-founder Child Devel. Ctr., Huntsville. Mem. Huntsville C. of C. (banquet program participant). Lodge: Rotary. Home: 209 Magnolia Way Huntsville TX 77340 Office: First Bapt Ch 1229 Ave J Huntsville TX 77340

BONNER, DISMAS WILLIAM, priest, educator, Roman Catholic Ch.; b. Fort Wayne, Ind., Sept. 15, 1929; s. William Lewis and Rose (Orr) B.; A.B. in Philosophy, Quincy Coll., 1955; J.C.B., Pontificio Athenaeo Antoniano (Rome, Italy), 1961; J.C.L., Cath. U. Am., 1962, J.C.D., 1963. Ordained priest, 1958; canonical asst. Poor Clare Nun's Fedn., Western U.S. and Can., 1965—; prof. canon law Cath. Theol. Union, Chgo., 1968-78. Del. to Gen. Chpts., Medellin, Colombia, 1971, Madrid, Spain, 1973, Assisi, Italy, 1976, 85; mem. Internat. Commn. for Chpt. Preparation, Rome, 1972; expert Gen. Chpt. of Franciscan Order, Assisi, 1967; visitor general Byzantine-Slavonic Custody of Franciscan Order, 1974-75, Calif. Province of Franciscan Order, 1976; mem. provincial council Sacred Heart Province, Franciscan Order, 1975-78, minister provincial Sacred Heart Province, 1978—; mem. Priests Senate, Archdiocese Chgo., 1971-72; trustee Quincy (Ill.) Coll. Mem. Canon Law Soc. Am. Author: The Pastoral Companion, 1966, supplements annually, 1967—; The Church Under Tension, 1972. Contbr. articles to The New Catholic Ency. Office: 3140 Meramec St Saint Louis MO 63118

BONNER, JOHN WILLIAM, minister, Am. Baptist Conv.; b. Wetzel County, W.Va., Sept. 23, 1905; s. John W. and O'Ella Mae (Boggs) B.; A.B. in Elementary Edn., Salem Coll., 1936, B.A. in Secondary Edn., 1942; D.D., Alderson-Broaddus Coll., 1964; m. Ovah Byrl Wallace, June 9, 1926; children—Ernestine O'Ella, June L., John Wallace. Ordained to ministry, 1930; pastor Bethany Bapt. Ch., 1929-38, Wallace First Bapt. Ch., 1932-38, Smith Bapt. Ch., 1929-38, Coon's Run Bapt. Ch., 1929-38, Simpson Creek Bapt. Ch., 1938-44, Bapt. Temple, Fairmont, W.Va., 1944-70, Clarksburg (W.Va.) Bapt. Ch., 1975—. Dir. Week Day Religious Edn., Marion County, W.Va.; pres. W.Va. Bapt. Conv. Recipient Silver Beaver and Silver Antelope awards Boy Scouts Am., 1964; named Man of Year, Woodmen of the World, 1953. Mem. Am. Bapt., W.Va. Bapt., Union Bapt. assns., Clarksburg Ministerial Assn. Author: History of Simpson Creek Baptist Church, 1943; History of the Baptist Temple, Fairmont, W.Va., 1975; History of Clarksburg Baptist Church, 1976. Contbr. articles to religious mags. Home: 709 Maryland Ave Fairmont WV 26554 Office: 6th and Pike St Clarksburg WV 26301

BONNER, W. L., bishop; sr. apostle Church of Our Lord Jesus Christ of The Apostolic Faith, Inc. Office: 2081 Adam Clayton Powell Jr Blvd New York NY 10027*

BONNEY, ROLLIN BRIAN, ch. ofcl., Free Methodist Ch.; b. Mitchell, S.D., Oct. 8, 1929; s. Clarence Roy and Edith Irene (Ward) B.; A.A., Wessington Springs Coll., 1949; B.A., Greenville Coll., 1958; B.D., Asbury Sem., 1962; m. Mary-Ellan Schantz, June 1, 1950; children—Roger, Carol, Mary, Joy, Julie. Pastor, Free Meth. Ch., S.D., 1954-56, Ky., 1957-63, Atlanta, 1963-66; supt. Free Meth. Ch. Ky., 1966—. Mem. gen. bd. adminstrn. Free Meth. Ch. Trustee Greenville Coll. Mem. Allen County Ministerial Assn. Contbr. articles to religious jours. Home: Route 8 Box 2 Scottsville KY 42164

BOOK, JOHN BUTLER, minister, Churches of Christ; b. Orlando, Fla., June 14, 1937; s. Morris Butler and Connie Elizabeth (Brannon) B.; student Cin. Bible Sem., 1956-57; m. Sue Hodges, Oct. 6, 1962; children—John, James, Joni Sue. Ordained to ministry, 1970; founder, dir. syndicated TV show Christian Viewpoint; pastor Ch. of Christ at Southside Ch., Richmond, Va., 1966-71, Northside Ch. of Christ, Maitland, Fla., 1971—; founder, dir. Northside Christian Sch., Maitland, 1971—. Nominated for Gov. Va., Am. Ind. Party, 1969. Home: 230 Ventris Ave Maitland FL 32751

BOOMHOWER, CHARLES EZRA, minister, Lutheran Church in America; b. Troy, N.Y., Jan. 15, 1947; s. Everett Peckham and Cecelia Mary (Prespare) B.; m. Rosemary Katherine Fellers, Aug. 21, 1971; children: Matthew, Daniel, John. B.A., Midland Luth. Coll., 1969; M.Div., Hamma Sch. Theology, 1973. Ordained to ministry Lutheran Ch., 1973. Minister Emmanuel Luth. Ch., Stuyvesant Falls, N.Y., 1973-77, St. Luke's Luth. Ch., Valatie, N.Y., 1973-77, St. Peter's Luth. Ch., Holgate, Ohio, 1977—; mem. Ohio Synod Task Force on Aging, 1978—, chmn., 1980-84; dean N.W. dist. Ohio Synod, Luth. Ch. Am., 1983—; mem. Ohio Synod Parish Services Unit, 1983—. Author: Aging Ministry Workshop, 1980. bd. dirs. Henry County Food Bank, Napoleon, Ohio, 1984; coordinator vols. Holgate Community Festival Com., 1984; cubmaster Pack 169, Cub Scouts, Holgate, 1984; mem. troop com. Boy Scouts Am., Holgate, 1984. Mem. Henry County Ministers Assn. (pres. 1982, 83). Home: 310 Kaufman St Holgate OH 43527 Office: St Peter's Luth Ch 300 Kaufman St PO Box 307 Holgate OH 43527

BOONE, WILLIAM JAMES, priest, vicar general, Roman Catholic Church. B. St. John's, Nfld., Can., Apr. 18, 1924; s. William Frederick and Margaret Francis (O'Reilly) B. Cert. in Philosophy, Boston Coll., 1957; Baccalaureate in Theology, Regina Cleri Sem., Sask., Can., 1957-61; lic. in Canon Law, St. Paul's U., Ottawa, Ont., Can., 1980; M. in Canon Law, Ottawa U., 1982. Ordained priest Roman Catholic Church, 1961. Sec. to bishop St. George's Diocese, Corner Brook, Nfld., 1969-70, chancellor, 1970—, vicar gen., 1984, also sec., mem. bd. consuctors, sec. mem. bd. adminstrn. Diocese, 1970—; asst. judicial vicar Halifax Regional Tribunal, Halifax, N.S., Can., 1978—; judicial vicar Diocesan Curia, Corner Brook, 1978—. Editor: The Diocesan Rev., 1964—. Named Prelate of Honor, Holy See, Vatican City, 1984. Mem. Can. Canon Law Soc., Canon Law Soc. Am., Canon Law Soc. Gt. Britain and Ireland. Club: Blomidon Country. Lodge: K.C. Home and Office: Chancery Office 16 Hammond Dr Corner Brook NF A2H 2W2 Canada

BOOTH, LAVAUGHN VENCHAEL, minister, Progressive National Baptist Convention; b. Miss., Jan. 7, 1919; s. Fredrick Douglas and Mamie (Powell) B.; A.B., Alcorn A. and M. Coll., 1940; B.D., Howard U., 1943; M.A., U. Chgo., 1945; L.H.D., Wilberforce U., 1964; D.D. (hon.), Morehouse Coll., 1967; L.H.D., Central State U., 1969; m. Georgia Anna Morris, June 3, 1943; children: Lavaughn Venchael, William Douglas, Anna Marie, Georgia Annita, Paul Michael. Ordained to ministry Progressive Nat. Bapt. Conv., Inc., 1941; pastor First Bapt. Chs., Warrenton, Va., 1943-44, Gary, Ind., 1944-52, Zion Bapt. Ch., Cin., 1952-84, Olivet Bapt. Ch., Silverton, Ohio, 1984—; founder Progressive Nat. Conv., Inc., 1961. Founder, chmn. bd. Hamilton County State Bank. Chmn. bd. Progress Assn. for Econ. Devel., Cin., 1969—; campaign chmn. Municipal Ct. Judge, Cin., 1965. Bd. dirs. Blue Cross of S.W. Ohio; trustee U. Cin. Recipient Push award for excellence, 1974. Author: (radio sermons) Shower of Blessings, 1950; Who's Who in Baptist America, 1960. Composer: Brothers Joined in Heart, 1960. Home: 6753 Siebern Ave Cincinnati OH 45236

BOOTH, PAUL WAYNE, minister, president council of Twelve, Reorganized Ch. of Jesus Christ of Latter Day Saints; b. Caraway, Ark., July 30, 1929; s. Arthur Irvin and Martha Belle (Wood) B.; B.S. with honors in Sociology, Bus., Ark. State U., 1963; M.A. in Sociology U. Louisville, 1968; postgrad. religious theory and practice Sch. of Restoration, Independence, Mo., 1974; M.Div., St. Paul Sch. Theology, 1975; m. Lavanda Joan Colbert, Dec. 29, 1949; children—Dennis Paul, Donald

Wayne, Karen Sue. Ordained to ministry, 1953; pastor in Caraway, 1953-60; dist. pres. Reorganized Ch. of Jesus Christ of Latter Day Saints, Louisville, 1963-66, adminstr. Colo., Wyo., Kans. and Nebr. region, 1966-68, Mo., Ill., Ind., Ky. region, 1969-70, dir. div. program planning, Gen. Ch., 1970-76, coordinator ch. relationship to Institutions of Higher Edn., Independence, Mo., 1976—. Chmn. Gen. Ch. Commn. on Theology, Evangelism and Zionic Community, 1970-76; pres. Outreach Internat. Found. for 3d World Comprehensive Community Devel. Chmn., Indsl. Devel. Com., Caraway, 1958-60. Mem. World Future Soc. (bd. dirs. human values sect. 1976). Author: The Church and Its Mission, 1971. Contbr. articles in field to profl. jours. Home: 401 W Walnut St Independence MO 64051 Office: The Auditorium Independence MO 64050

BOOTH, WALTER LANGLEY, officer, The Salvation Army; b. Staten Island, N.Y., Aug. 4, 1934; s. Walter and Marie (Bawor) B.; grad. The Salvation Army Sch. for Officers Tng., 1971; m. Jean Harvey, May 28, 1966; children—Paul, Mark, Brian. Corps officer The Salvation Army, Erie, Pa., 1971, Beaver Falls, Pa., 1972; chaplain on call Holiday Inn, Beaver Falls, 1973—. Mem. Beaver County Civil Def. Council, 1976. Mem. Beaver County Fire Chief Assn. Home: 515 Main St PO Box 1146 Middletown CT 06457

BOOTH, WILLIAM DOUGLAS, minister; b. Gary, Ind., Sept. 16, 1944; s. Lavaughn Venchael and Georgia Anna (Morris) B.; B.A., Howard U., 1966; M.Div. (Rockefeller fellow), Crozer Theol. Sem., 1969; m. Ruth Ann Barnes, Sept. 27, 1969; children—William Douglas, David Michael. Ordained to ministry Shiloh Baptist Ch., 1965; asst. to pastor, Washington, 1967-68; minister to youth First Bapt. Ch., Phila., 1968-69; asst. to pastor Zion Bapt. Ch., Cin., 1969-73; pastor Mt. Zion Bapt. Ch., Knoxville, Tenn., 1973—. Mem. Knoxville Bapt. Dist. Assn., Bapt. Missionary and Edn. Conv. Tenn., 1973—, Progressive Nat. Bapt. Conv., 1973; host TV Ten Report, Sta. WBIR, 1976; instr. Black theology Xavier U., Cin., 1973; instr. N.T., Temple Bible Coll., Cin., 1972, 73. Mem. Knoxville Roundtable NCCJ Bd., Black Community Devel. Policy Com.; treas. Knoxville Area Urban League; mem. Ambulatory Patient Care Bd., Cin., 1972-73. Recipient Jr. C. of C. Outstanding Young Men of Am. award, 1974. Mem. Knoxville Interdenoml. Christian Ministers Alliance, Alpha Kappa Delta. Contbr. to The Worker. Home: 1621 Kenro Dr SE Knoxville TN 37915 Office: 2714 Brooks Rd SE Knoxville TN 37915

BOOTY, JOHN EVERITT See *Who's Who in America*, 43rd edition.

BORCHARDT, BORUCH B., religious organization executive, Jewish. Exec. dir. Agudath Israel of America, N.Y.C. Office: Agudath Israel of Am 5 Beckman New York NY 10038*

BORCHERT, GERALD LEO, minister, educator, Baptist Union of West Canada; b. Edmonton, Alta., Can., Mar. 20, 1932; came to U.S., 1963. s. Leo Ferdinand and Lillian Violet (Bucholz) B.; student U. Calgary, 1951-52; B.A., U. Alta., 1955, LL.B., 1956; M.Div. summa cum laude, Eastern Bapt. Theol. Sem., 1959; Th.M., Princeton Theol. Sem., 1961, Ph.D. cum laude (Research fellow in N.T.), 1967; postgrad. Princeton U., 1961-63, Am. Inst. Holy Land Studies and Albright Inst. Archeol. Research, 1974, Duke U. and Southeastern Bapt. Sem., 1981, Southwestern Bapt. Sem., 1985; m. Doris Ann Cox, May 23, 1959; children—Mark, Timothy. Ordained to ministry Baptist Union of West Can., 1959. Asst. minister Christ West Hope Presbyn. Ch., Phila., 1958-60; teaching fellow and lectr. in Greek, Princeton Theol. Sem., 1961-63; asso. prof. N.T., North Am. Bapt. Sem., Sioux Falls, S.D., 1963-68, prof. N.T., 1968-77, academic v.p. and dean, 1970-77; dean, prof. N.T., No. Bapt. Sem., Lombard, Ill., 1977-80; prof. N.T. So. Bapt. Sem., Louisville, 1980. Sec. commn. on cooperative Christianity Bapt. World Alliance, 1968-76, mem. commn. doctrine, 1976-80, 85—; rep. Bapt. Joint Com. on Pub. Affairs for U.S.A. and Can., 1971-76, sec., 1973-75, vice chmn., 1975-76. Bd. dirs. Sioux Empire Drug Edn. Com., 1970-77, treas. and chmn. speaker's bur., 1970-72; trustee Tabor Coll., Hillsboro, Kan., 1972-78, North Am. Bapt. Coll., Edmonton, 1973-77, Sioux Falls Community Coll., 1975-77; bd. dirs. Am. Inst. Holy Land Studies, Jerusalem, 1971,74,84—, exec. bd., 1972-74; resource scholar Christianity Today Inst., 1985—. Mem. Soc. Bibl. Lit. and Exegesis, Am. Schs. Oriental Research, Chgo. Soc. Bibl. Research, Novi Testamenti Societas. Kiwanian (pres. 1974-75). Author: Great Themes From John, 1966; The Dynamics of Pauline Evangelism, 1969; Today's Model Church, 1971; Dynamics of Evangelism, 1976; Paul and His Interpreters, 1985. Co-editor: Spiritual Dimensions of Pastoral Care, 1985. Co-tchr.: (TV) Hidden Treasures of the Bible; Studies in the Gospel of John, 1977-78. Columnist The Baptist Herald, 1969-76. Contbr. articles to various publs. and jours. Office: 2825 Lexington Rd Louisville KY 40280

BORDEN, ARTHUR CLIFFORD, religious organization administrator, minister, Evangelical Free Church; b. Mt. Holly, N.J., June 26, 1929; s. Arthur and Anna (Cordery) B.; m. Alice Marie Holsopple, July 11, 1959; children by previous marriage: David, Janet; children by present marriage: Steven, Bruce, Susan. B.A., King's Coll., 1953; Th.M., Dallas Theol. Sem., 1957; postgrad. Spanish Lang. Inst., Costa Rica, 1961. Ordained to ministry Evang. Free Ch., 1957. Missionary, Orinoco River Mission, Venezuela, 1959-63; exec. sec. United Bible Soc., Venezuela and Central Am., 1963-70; sec. ch. relations Am. Bible Soc., N.Y.C., 1973-80; dir. mktg. Genesis Project, Falls Church, Va., 1980-81; exec. dir. Evang. Council for Fin. Accountability, Oakton, Va., 1981—. Mem. Christian Ministries Mgmt. Assn. (bd. dirs. 1983—, Christian Mgmt. award 1983), Nat. Assn. Evangs. (bd. dirs. 1984—, ind. sector devel. com., evang. joint acctg. com., Merit award 1984). Home: 14723 Saint Germain Dr Centreville VA 22020 Office: Evang Council Fin Accountability 2915 Hunter Mill Rd Suite 17 Oakton VA 22124

BORDENARO, DONALD RAY, minister Christian Ch. (Disciples of Christ); b. New Castle, Pa., July 11, 1938; s. Joseph F. and Mildred I. (Fry) B.; B.S.L., Cin. Bible Sem., 1963; postgrad Youngstown State U., 1975—; m. Martha D. Kenemuth, Sept. 16, 1966; children—Andria Lynn, Michelle Ann, Dianna Rae. Ordained to ministry, 1962; youth minister Bridgetown Ch. of Christ, Cin., 1960-62; minister Hartsville (Ind.) Ch. of Christ, 1962-63, Shadeland Ave Christian Ch., Pitts., 1963-64; minister Wickliffe Christian Ch., Youngstown, Ohio, 1973—. Exec. Mahoning Valley-Youngstown dist. Boy Scouts Am., 1966-69; exec. dir. Am. Cancer Soc., 1969-73. Mem. Austintown Clergy Assn. Home: 2225 Oran Dr Youngstown OH 44511 Office: 3939 Potomac Ave Youngstown OH 44515

BORDERS, WILLIAM D., archbishop, Roman Cath. Ch.; b. Washington, Ind., Oct. 9, 1913; ed. St. Meinrad Sem., Notre Dame Sem., U. Notre Dame. Ordained priest, 1940; rector St. Joseph Cathedral, Baton Rouge; consecrated bishop, 1968; bishop of Orlando (Fla.), 1968-74; archbishop Balt., 1974—. Address: 320 Cathedral St Baltimore MD 21201

BORECKY, ISIDORE, bishop, Ukrainian Greek Catholic Church in Canada; b. Ostrovec, Ukraine, Russia, Oct. 1, 1911. Ordained priest, 1938; titular bishop of Amathus in Cypro and exarch of Toronto (Ont., Can.), 1948-56; bishop of Toronto (Ukrainian), 1956—. Address: Ukrainian Cath Eparchy of Toronto 61 Glen Edyth Dr Toronto ON M5B 1G1 Canada*

BOREN, JAMES EARL, minister, educator, United Presbyterian Church in U.S.A.; b. Fort Branch, Ind., July 28, 1910; s. James Sherman and Versa Alice (Smith) B.; B.A., Coll. Wooster, 1935; M.Div., McCormick Theol. Sem., 1938; M.A., U. Minn., 1965; m. Marcelle Virginia Alexander, Aug. 27, 1938; children: James Edward, Virginia Lucille. Ordained to ministry, 1938; pastor Olivet Inst. Ch., Chgo., 1937-39; instr. Presbyn. Coll. Christian Edn., Chgo., 1938-39; missionary United Presbyn. Ch., Thailand, 1939-44; univ. pastor, dir. Westminster Found., U. Minn., Mpls., 1944-65; assoc. pastor Flossmoor (Ill.) Community Ch., 1965-75; tchr. adult edn. 1st Presbyn. Ch., Dallas, 1980—; del. World Ch. Conf., Oxford, Eng., 1937; founder student hostel, Bangkok, Thailand, 1939; mem. exec. com. Assn. Presbyn. Univ. Pastors, 1945-54, pres., 1954-57; chmn. Minn. Council Religions, U. Minn., 1946-48; mem. com. on edn. Presbytery of Mpls., 1946-60, moderator, 1959, stated clk., 1962-65; treas. Mpls. Clergy Council, 1949-50; mem. com. on standardized exams. for ministry Gen. Assembly, United Presbyn. Ch., 1964-68, co-convenor Chgo. reading group of com., 1970-74; mem. com. on candidates Presbytery of Chgo., 1967-73; sec., treas. Homewood-Flossmoor Ministerial Assn., 1968-70. Chmn. PTA Council, Mpls., 1964-65; mem. 15 Year Evaluation Com. of Homewood-Flossmoor High Sch., 1964-65; mem. Com. on Open Housing, Flossmoor, 1966-67. Recipient Good Neighbor award Sta. WCCO, Mpls., 1964. Mem. Am., Ill. personnel and guidance assns., Insts. of Religion and Health, Order of Geneva. Lodge: Masons. Contbr. articles to profl. jours. and books; editor jour. Minn. Council of Religions 1964. Home: 3440 Binkley St Dallas TX 75205

BORER, ANTON JOSEPH, priest, Roman Catholic Church; b. Buesserach, Switzerland, Aug. 16, 1916; s. Arnold and Mathilda (Jeker) B.; B.A., Bruder Klausen Sem., 1939, B.A. in Theology, 1943. Ordained priest Roman Catholic Ch., 1943; missionary to China, 1946-48; asst. pastor ch., Denver, 1949-66; dist. superior Bethlehem Fathers U.S.A., 1959-70; founder Bethlehem Center, Broomfield, Colo., 1966, dir., 1966-78, spiritual dir., 1978—; dir. Papal Vols. in Denver, 1968-74; Newman chaplain Denver colls., 1969—; personal rep. of archbishop to Charismatic Community in Archdiocese of Denver, 1974-81. Bd. dirs. Spirit's Runway, Denver, 1970-76. Mem. Liturg. Com. Am., Cath. Campus Ministry Assn. Co-author: New Life: Preparation of Religious for Retirement, 1973; editor: Bethlehem Call, 1974—; contbr. articles to religious jours. Home: 5630 E 17th Ave Denver CO 80220 Office: W 128th St at Zuni Broomfield CO 80020

BORIS (BORIS GEEZO). Bishop of Chgo., Orthodox Ch. in America. Office: 8200 S Country Line Rd Hinsdale IL 60521*

BORLAND, JAMES ALLEN, religion educator, Baptist Bible Fellowship. b. Santa Monica, Calif., July 11, 1944; s. Howard James and Marguerite Agnes (Weaver) B.; m. Cheryl Lee Lindner, Aug. 25, 1967; children: Sarah, Ruth, Hannah, Jonathan, Daniel, Andrew. B.A., Los Angeles Bapt. Coll., 1966, M.Div., 1969; Th.M., Talbot Theol. Sem., 1971; Th.D., Grace Theol. Sem., 1976. Prof. N.T., Central Bapt. Theol. Sem., Mpls., 1973-74; prof. Bible, Maranatha Bapt. Bible Coll., Watertown, Wis., 1974-77; assoc. prof. religion Liberty Bapt. Coll., Lynchburg, Va., 1977-79, prof. theology and Bible, 1979—. Author: Christ in the Old Testament, 1978; Liberty Bible Commentary, 1978-81. Treas., Campbell County Republican Com., Va., 1984—. Mem. Evang. Theol. Soc. (chmn. Eastern region (1981-83). Home: 112 Russell Woods Dr Lynchburg VA 24502 Office: Liberty Bapt Theol Sem Lynchburg VA 24506

BORUM, HERMAN EDWARD, minister, So. Bapt. Conv.; b. Deepwater, Mo., June 25, 1918; s. Leland Kelly and Sarah Maye (Henne) B.; A.B., Central Mo. State U., 1955; M.R.E., Central Bapt. Theol. Sem., 1956; B.D., Midwestern Baptist Theol. Sem., 1961, M.Div., 1971; m. Edna Dorothy Robison, July 18, 1945; children—Kenneth Austin, Ellen Louise. Ordained to ministry, 1952; pastor First Baptist Ch., Vista, Mo., 1952-54, New Harmony Bapt. Ch., Martinsville, Mo. and Winston (Mo.) Bapt. Ch., 1954-56, First Bapt. Ch., Maysville, Mo., 1956-58, First Bapt. Ch., Union Star, Mo., 1958-64, First Bapt. Ch., Winterset, Iowa, 1964-74, First Bapt. Ch., Dexter, N.Mex., 1974—. Field rep. Christian Civic Found. Mo., 1962-63. Sec. Iowa Council on Alcohol Problems, 1969-74; mem. bd. dirs. varsity athletics program high sch., Winterset, 1968-72; bd. dirs. Central Bapt. Theol. Sem. Fed. Credit Union, 1955-56. Recipient recognition for work with youth, pub. sch. system Union Star, Mo., 1963; cited for services and devotion rendered to Bapt. Youth Assn., St. Joseph, Mo., 1964; cited for initiating orgn. and funding of full time chaplaincy program for nursing homes and hosps., Madison County, Iowa, 1974; authorized tchr. coll. level courses So. Bapt. Sem. Extension Dept., 1976. Home: 111 W 3d St Dexter NM 88230 Office: 101 W 3d St Dexter NM 88230

BOSCO, ANTHONY G., bishop, Roman Catholic Church. Titular bishop of Labicum, aus. bishop, Pitts. Office: 5246 Clarion Ave Pittsburgh PA 15229*

BOSSENBROEK, ALBERTUS GEORGE, minister, Reformed Church in America; b. Brandon, Wis., Oct. 16, 1910; s. Henry and Matilda (Bysbers) B.; m. Hilda Laating, June 10, 1936; children: Nina Kay, Margaret, Donna Louise. B.A., Hope Coll., 1932; M.Div., Western Theol. Sem., Holland, Mich., 1936; D.D. (hon.), Hope Coll., 1977. Ordained to ministry Reformed Ch., 1936. Pastor Helderberg Reformed Ch., Guilderland Center, N.Y., 1936-41, First Reformed Ch., Chatham, N.Y., 1941-47, First Reformed Ch., Hastings-on-Hudson, N.Y., 1947-65; exec. sec. Synod of N.Y., Reformed Ch. Am., 1964-79; acting prof. practical thenology Theol. Sem., New Brunswick, N.J., 1979-81; pres. Warwick Conf. Ctr., N.Y., 1983-87; pres. Synod of Albany, Reformed Ch. Am., N.Y., 1946-47, pres. N. Am. missions, 1961-63; trustee Hope Coll., Holland, Mich., 1964-78; pres. Reformed Ch. in Am., N.Y.C., 1977-88; chaplain Fire Dept., Hastings-on-Hudson, N.Y., 1947. Welfare chmn. CD, Hastings-on-Hudson, 1947. Republican. Club: Exchange (pres. 1943-44) (Chatham, N.Y.). Home: 18 Olinda Ave Hastings-on-Hudson NY 10706

BOST, RAYMOND MORRIS, theology educator, Lutheran Ch. Am.; b. Maiden, N.C., Aug. 18, 1925; s. Loy Robert and Virginia Marie (Anderson) B.; m. Margaret Martha Vedder, Aug. 16, 1947; children: Timothy Lee, Penelope Ruth Judd, Peter Raymond, Jonathan Otto. B.A., Lenoir-Rhyne, Coll., 1947-49; B.D., Lutheran Sem., 1952; M.A., Yale U., 1959, Ph.D., 1963; D.D. (hon.), Lenoir-Rhyne Coll., 1976. Ordained minister United Lutheran Ch. in Am., 1952. Pastor Nativity Luth. Ch., Spartanburg, S.C., 1952-53, Holy Trinity Luth. Ch., Raleigh, N.C., 1953-57; pres. Lenoir-Rhyne Coll., Hickory, N.C., 1968-76, Luth. Sem., Phila., 1976-85. Contbr. hist. texts, 1971, 1981. Pres. Ind. Coll. Fund of N.C., Winston-Salem, 1975, Piedmont U. Ctr. N.C., Winston-Salem, 1976; v.p. Bd. of Pub. Luth. Ch. Am. Served as chaplain USAR. 1956-58. Nat. Luth. Edn. Conf. Martin Luther fellow, 1959; Am. Assn. Theol. Schs. faculty fellow, 1960. Mem. Am. Soc. Ch. Hist., Luth. Hist. Conf., Orgn. Am. Historians. Republican. Club: Yale (N.Y.C.). Home: 7333 Germantown Ave Philadelphia PA 19119 Office: Lutheran Seminary 7301 Germantown Ave Philadelphia PA 19119

BOST, RAYMOND MORRIS See *Who's Who in America*, 43rd edition.

BOSWELL, GEORGE MARION, JR., lay church worker, United Methodist Church; b. Grand Prairie, Tex., May 12, 1920; s. George Marion and Viola (Scarborough) B.; B.S., Tex. Tech. Coll., 1940; M.A., U.

Tex., 1941; M.D., Southwestern Med. Sch., Dallas, 1950; m. Veta F. Fuller, Oct. 30, 1958; children: Brianna, Kama, Maia. Chmn. ofcl. bd. 1st United Meth. Ch., Dallas, 1963-65, charge lay leader, 1965—; chmn. council Central dist., 1972—; del. Gen. Jurisdictional Conf., 1972, 76, chmn. legis. com. fin. adminstrn., 1976; mem. Gen. Council on Ministries, United Meth. Ch., 1976—; del. Meth. Conf. of U.K., 1985. Practice medicine, Dallas, 1955—. Bd. dirs. pension found. N.W. conf. United Meth. Ch.; mem. lay adv. council Perkins Sch. Theology. Diplomate Am. Bd. Orthopedic Surgeons. Fellow A.C.S.; mem. Am., So., Tex. med. assns., Dallas County Med. Soc., Am. Acad. Orthopedic Surgeons, Western Orthopedic Assn., Am. Coll. Traumatic Surgeons, Am. Acad. Sports Medicine, Tex. Flying Physicians Assn. (pres. 1964-65), Alumni Assn. Southwestern Med. Sch. (pres. 1971-72). Republican. Author papers. Home: 7249 Wabash Ave Dallas TX 75214 Office: 4849 Lawther Dr Dallas TX 75214

BOTHWELL, JOHN CHARLES, bishop, anglican Church of Canada; b. Toronto, Ont., Can., June 29, 1926; s. William Alexander and Anne (Campbell) B.; m. Joan Cowan, Dec. 29, 1951; children: Michael, Timothy, Nancy, Douglas, Ann. B.A., Trinity Coll., U. Toronto, 1948, B.D., 1951, D.D. (hon.), 1972. Ordained deacon Anglican Ch. Can., 1951, ordained priest, 1952. Asst. priest St. James' Cathedral, Toronto, 1951-53; sr. asst. Christ Ch. Cathedral, Vancouver, B.C., Can., 1953-56; rector St. Aidan's Ch., Oakville, Ont., 1956-60, St. James' Ch., Dundas, Ont., 1960-65; canon Christ's Ch. Cathedral, Hamilton, Ont., 1963; program dir. Niagara Diocese, Hamilton, 1965-69, elected coadjutor bishop, 1971, installed eighth bishop of Niagara, Hamilton, 1973—; exec. dir. of program Nat. Hdqrs. Anglican Ch., Toronto, 1969-71; consecrated bishop Ch. of God, 1971; succeeded to See of Niagaga, 1973; mem. gen. synod and Ont. provincial synod Anglican Ch. Can.; ofcl. visitor Ridley Coll., St. Catharines, Ont., 1973—, St. John's Boys Sch., Elora, Ont., 1973—, St. Margaret's Sch., Elora, 1973—, Community of the Sisters of the Ch., Oakville, 1973—. Author: Taking Risks and Keeping Faith, 1985. Exec. mem. Hamilton Social Planning Council, 1972-76, pres., 1976-78; bd. mem. Hamilton United Way and Ont. Council for Social Devel.; pres. Hamilton United Way, 1984-85; dir., pres. Hamilton Found., 1984-85. Club: Dundas Valley Golf and Country. Office: Synod of Diocese of Niagara 67 Victoria Ave S Hamilton ON L8N 2S8 Canada

BOTSFORD, DONALD GEORGE, minister, Evangelical Free Church America; b. Toronto, Ont., Can., Aug. 3, 1931; s. Harold Nelson and Beatrice (Frogley) B.; came to U.S., 1950, naturalized, 1955; B.A., Bob Jones U., 1954; m. Liela Jean Rose, Apr. 28, 1959; children—Robert Nelson, Betsy Lynn. Ordained to ministry, 1954. Pastor Evang. Free Ch. of the Canyons, Calif., 1973—. Founding dir. Athletes in Action, Campus Crusade for Christ, 1956—; program dir. Forest Home Christian Conf. Center, Forest Falls, Calif., 1957-60, asst. conf. dir., 1961-73. Bd. dirs. Forest Home, Inc., 1966—; resource and founding cons. No. Pines of Minn., Inc., Family Conf. Center, 1973. Mem. Christian (regional pres.), Am. camping assns. Home: 15250 Lotusgarden Dr Canyon Country CA 91351 Office: PO Box 1162 Canyon Country CA 91351

BOTTOMS, JESSE VOYDE, minister, Progressive Nat. Bapt. Conv., Inc.; b. Versailles, Ky., July 11, 1905; s. Charlie Tipton and Harriette (Butler) B.; B.D., Simmons U., 1942; D.D., 1950; B.D., So. Bapt. Theol. Sem., 1952; m. Florence Carter, Dec. 27, 1924; children—Doris (Mrs. Winstead), Jesse Voyde, Barbara (Mrs. Millhouse). Ordained minister, 1934; supr. Louisville Detention Home for Juveniles, 1934-41; pastor Green St Bapt. Ch., Louisville, 1950—. Acting pres. Simmons U., Louisville, 1953-55: chmn. Gen. Assn. Com. Ky., 1964; chmn. Orthodox Com., 1965; chmn. publ. bd. Am. Bapt. Jour., 1972; counselor Louisville City Jail, 1964-66. Recipient Outstanding Citizen award Pan-Hellenic Council Louisville, 1961, Inst. award Nat. Progressive Bapt. Bible Inst., 1974. Editorial writer Bapt. State Jour., 1960. Home: 1200 Cecil Ave Louisville KY 40211 Office: 519 E Gray St Louisville KY 40202

BOTTOMS, LAWRENCE WENDELL, minister, Presbyterian Church in the U.S.: b. Selma, Ala., Apr. 9, 1908; m. Elizabeth Stallworth; 4 children. A.B., Geneva Coll., Beaver Falls, Pa.; postgrad., Reformed Presbyn. Sem., Atlanta U.; D.D. (hon.), Davis and Elkins Coll., 1966. Ordained to ministry Presbyn. Ch. Pastor, Reformed Presbyn. Ch., Selma, Ala., Grace Presbyn. Ch., Louisville, Oakhurst Presbyn. Ch., Decatur, Ga.; interim pastor in exptl. ministry New Covenant Presbyn. Ch., Miami, Fla. Sec. Dept. Negro Work Presbyn. Ch. in U.S., Atlanta, 1953-64; Presbyn. Ch. in U.S. rep. to Commn. on Missionary Edn., Nat. Council Chs., 1963-73, Conf. on Third World, World Council Ch., 1972; moderator Louisville Presbytery, 1963, Synod Ky., 1963; asst. sec. div. home missions Bd. Ch. Extension, Atlanta, 1964-66, assoc. sec., 1964-66; assoc. sec. div. interpretation and research Bd. Nat. Ministries, 1966-69, coordinator support services, 1969-71, coordinator social concerns, 1971-73; Bible leader Women of the Chapel, U.S. Air Force, Fed. Republic Germany, 1972, Great Britain, 1973; mem. coordinating council Synod of the Southeast. 1973—. Recipient Disting. Service award Geneva Coll., 1960. Home: 381 Peyton Rd SW Atlanta GA 30311 Office: Oakhurst Presbyn Ch 118 Second Ave Decatur GA 30030

BOUCHARD, SISTER JEANNE, nun, Roman Catholic Church provincial leader; b. St. Agathe, Maine, Apr. 1, 1924; d. Alphonse and Agnes (Tardif) B. B.S., St. Joseph Coll., North Windham, Maine, 1962; M.S., Cath. U. Entered Order Daughters of Wisdom, Roman Cath. Ch., 1941. Superior, Lille, Maine, 1960-62, Chesapeake, Va., 1962-65; superior, provincial councillor, Port Jefferson, N.Y., 1965-70; vicar provincial Daughters of Wisdom, Islip, N.Y., 1977-80, provincial, 1980—; adminstr. Maryhaven Ctr. of Hope Facility for Handicapped, Port Jefferson, N.Y., 1965-77. Bd. dirs. Religious Consultation Services, Rockville Centre Diocese, 1970—, St. Charles Hosp., Port Jefferson, 1965—; trustee Maryhaven Ctr. of Hope, Port Jefferson, 1984—. Mem. Leadership Conf. Women Religious (treas. diocese 1982—). Republican. Office: Daughters of Wisdom 385 S Ocean St Box 430 Islip NY 11751

BOUCHER, CHARLES VICTOR, minister, American Baptist Churches of the U.S.A.; b. North Adams Maine, Mar. 20, 1955; s. Victor Henry and Ruth Arlene (Wheeler) B.; m. Madelyn Cherryl Klose, Jan. 11, 1975; 1 child: Elissa Joy. B.A. cum laude, N. Adams State Coll., 1976; M.Div., Gordon-Conwell Theol. Sem., 1980. Ordained to ministry American Baptist Churches in the U.S.A., 1981. Dir. Camp Advenchur, Alton Bay, N.H., 1977-79; minister of youth First Baptist Ch., Belmont, Mass., 1977-80; program assoc. Camp Grotonwood, Groton, Mass., 1980-81, assoc. dir., 1981-82, dir., 1985—; dir. Camp Oceanwood, Ocean Park, Maine, 1982-85; trustee Camp Ashmere, Hinsdale, Mass., 1975-77; pres. Am. Bapt. Students Gordon-Conwell Sem., S. Hamilton, Mass., 1978-80; deacon United Bapt. Ch., Saco, Maine, 1984—. Mem. Christian Camping Internat., Conf. Bapt. Ministers, Evang. Tchr. Tng. Assn. Home: Prescott St Groton MA 01450 Office: Camp Grotonwood Prescott Groton MA 01450

BOUDREAUX, WARREN LOUIS, bishop, Roman Catholic Church; b. Berwick, La., Jan. 25, 1918; s. Alphonse Louis and Loretta Marie (Senac) B.; student St. Joseph's Sem., Benedict, La., 1931-36; student Notre Dame Sem., New Orleans, 1937, 42, LL.D., 1963; student Grand Sem. de St. Sulpice, Paris, France, 1938-39; J.C.D., Cath. U. Am., 1946; D.D. (hon.), Pope John XXIII, 1962. Ordained priest Roman Catholic Ch., 1942; asst. pastor, Crowley, La., 1942-43; vice chancellor Diocese of Lafayette (La.), 1946-54, officialis, 1949-54, vicar gen., 1957-61, consecrated bishop, 1962, aux. bishop, 1962-71; pastor St. Peter's Ch., New Iberia, La., also dean New Iberia Deanery, 1954-71; bishop Diocese of Beaumont (Tex.), 1971-77; bishop of Houma-Thibodaux, La., 1977—. Vice pres. Southwest La. Registry Newspaper, 1957—; mem. U.S. Bishops Liturgical Commn., 1966-70, adv. council U.S. Cath. Conf., 1969—; chmn. liaison com. Nat. Conf. Cath. Bishops, 1972-75, mem. liturgy commn., from 1975, mem. com. canon law, 1975—; nat. bishop moderator of marriage encounter, 1974; pres. bd. La. Cath. Conf., 1984; Tex. chaplain K.C., 1975—. Mem. New Iberia Community Relations Council, 1963-71. Bd. dirs. Southwest Ednl. Devel. Lab., Iberia Paris Youth Home, Consolata Home for Aged, New Iberia.; bd. dirs. New Orleans Archdiocesan Conf. Chancery Ofcls., 1952-55, pres., 1950-51. Address: Diocese of Houma-Thibodaux 1220 Aycock St Houma LA 70361

BOURNE, SAMUEL WALKER, minister, Christian Church (Disciples of Christ); b. Mt. Sterling, Ky., Apr. 8, 1944; s. Henry Walker and Elizabeth Graves (Ledford) B.; m. Elizabeth Ann Eatman, June 12, 1971; children: Jennifer Lane, Robert Walker. B.A., Transylvania Coll., 1966; D.Min., Lexington Theol. Sem., 1975. Ordained to ministry Christian Ch. (Disciples of Christ), 1974. Minister Mt. Zion Christian Ch., Frankfort, Ky., 1971-72; minister of youth Harrodsburg Christian Ch., Ky., 1972-74; minister First Christian Ch., Millersburg, Ky., 1974-75; chaplain, resident supr. U. Ky. Med. Ctr., Lexington, 1974-77; dir. pastoral services Hamot Med Ctr., Erie, Pa., 1977—; trustee Chautauqua Assn. of Christian Ch. (Disciples of Christ), N.Y., 1981—; bd. dirs. Inter-Ch. Ministries of Northwestern Pa., Erie, 1978-84; pres., 1983; chaplain Erie They Help Each Other Spiritually, Pa. 1977—; bd. dirs. Erie Compassionate Friends, 1982—, Erie County Crippled Children's Soc., 1984—. Served with USAF, 1962. Recipient Ecumenical Service award Inter-Ch. Ministries Northwestern Pa., Erie, 1984. Fellow Coll. Chaplains (state rep. 1984—); mem. Assn. Clin. Pastoral Edn. (clin. mem.), Pa. Soc. Chaplains (pres. 1984-85), Disciples Chaplains Assn., Disciples of Christ Hist. Soc. (life), Disciples Peace Fellowship, Hosp. Assn. of Pa. (chmn. conf. affiliated soc. presidents 1985—). Democrat. Office Hamot Med Ctr 201 State St Erie PA 16550

BOWEN, ERNEST THOMAS HARRISON, III, priest, Roman Cath. Ch.; b. Gainesville, Fla., Nov. 10, 1945; s. Ernest Thomas Harrison and Alma Theresa (Stefanilo) B.; B.A. in Philosophy, St. Mary's Coll., St. Mary, Ky., 1967. Ordained deacon, 1970, priest, 1971; deacon Our Lady of Peace Parish, North Augusta, S.C., 1971; priest Our Lady of Peace Ch., North Augusta, 1971; asso. pastor chs., S.C., 1971-75; pastor Sacred Heart Ch., Abbeville, S.C. and Ch. of the Good Shepherd, McCormick, S.C., 1976—. Vice-pres., McCormick County Ministerial Assn., 1976—. Counselor, Abbeville County Commn. on Alcohol and Drug Abuse, 1976—; bd. dirs. Abbeville County Mental Health Assn., 1976—, area 6 br. S.C. Lung Assn., 1977—. Mem. Nat. Hist. Soc., Navigator Corp. Columbia (charter), Spirit of '76 Soc. (charter). Named Outstanding Program Dir., S.C. Jaycees, 1975-76; recipient Outstanding Accomplishment certificate U.S. Jaycees, 1976; Distinguished Service award Abbeville Jaycees, 1976. Author: The Heartbeat of the Holy Spirit, 1973. Address: PO Box 812 Abbeville SC 29620

BOWEN, GILBERT WILLARD, minister, Presbyterian Church in the U.S.; b. Muskegon, Mich., Dec. 30; s. Bruce Oliver and Beatrice Lillian (Sibley) B.; m. Marlene Mary Michell, July 31, 1954; children: Kathryn Leigh, Mark Kevin, Stephen James. B.A., Wheaton Coll. (Ill.), 1955; M.Div., McCormick Theol. Sem., 1957, D.Min., 1976; cert. Ctr. for Religion and Psychotherapy, Chgo., 1976. Ordained to ministry Presbyn. Ch. in U.S., 1956. Minister, 1st United Presbyn. Ch., Blue Earth, Minn., 1956-63; exchange minister Johanneskirche, Neuwied, W. Ger., 1961-62; minister, Faith United Presbyn. Ch., Tinley Park, Ill., 1963-65, Community Presbyn. Ch., Mt. Prospect, Ill., 1965-70, Kenilworth Union Ch. (Ill.), 1970—; pres. bd. dirs. Ctr. for Religion and Psychotherapy, Chgo., 1980—; dir. Anatolia Coll., Thessaloniki, Greece, 1974—, Presbyn. Home, Evanston, Ill., 1974—, Am. Waldensian Aid Soc., N.Y.C., 1982—. Author sermon collection: Mit Anderen Zungen Geredet, 1963; On Being a Real Person, 1976; translator: Man and His Hope in the Old Testament, 1968. Chmn., Instnl. Rev. Bd., Evanston Hosp., 1980—. Mem. Am. Assn. Pastoral Counselors, Acad. Parish Clergy. Home: 417 Warwick Rd Kenilworth IL 60043 Office: Kenilworth Union Ch 211 Kenilworth Ave Kenilworth IL 60043

BOWENS, JOSEPH T. Bishop, gen. pres. United Holy Church of America, Inc., Chillum, Md. Office: United Holy Ch of Am Inc 825 Fairoak Ave Chillum MD 20783*

BOWER, RICHARD JAMES, minister, Congl. Christian Chs., Nat. Assn.; b. Somerville, N.J., June 9, 1939; s. Oneil Anthony and Mildred Rhoda (Goss) B.; student Sorbonne, Paris, 1959-60; B.A., Wesleyan U., Middletown, Conn., 1961; B.D., Drew U., 1965; m. Helen Ann Cheek, Dec. 29, 1962; 1 son, Christopher Scott. Ordained to ministry, 1965; minister, Kewaunee, Wis., 1965-67; sr. minister Congl. Ch., Bound Brook, N.J., 1967—. Mem. commn. on Christian edn. Nat. Assn. Congl. Christian Chs., 1965-68, chmn., 1967-68, mem. nominating com., 1970-72, chmn., 1971-72, mem. exec. com., 1973—, chmn., 1976-77; mem. Bound Brook Ministerium. Organizer, 1st pres. Kewaunee chpt. Am. Field Service, 1966-67; bd. dirs. Bound Brook Coop. Nursery Sch., pres., 1975—. Contbr. poetry, articles to various publs. Home: 762 Watchung Rd Bound Brook NJ 08805 Office: Congl Ch Church and High Sts Bound Brook NJ 08805

BOWER, ROY DONALD, minister, counselor, Christian Call Fellowship; b. Pitts., June 20, 1939; s. Roy Clare and Evelyn June (Moorhead) B.; m. Sandra Marie Daugherty, Mar. 16, 1963 (dec. 1976); children: Christine, Roy, Donald, Kathleen; m. Robin Jeanette Cook, Aug. 20, 1976; children: Daniel, Robin, William. Student Ind. U. of Pa., 1958, Geneva Coll., 1959-61; B.S. in Edn., Slippery Rock U., 1972; postgrad. Am. Bible Coll., 1980. Ordained to ministry Christian Call Fellowship, 1970; cert. counselor United Assn. Christian Counselors Internat. Instr. Colorado Springs Free U., Colo., 1976-80; counselor La Casa Contenta, Colorado Springs, 1976-78, Cheyenne Village, Manitou Springs, Colo., 1979-80; therapist Giles Edn. Ctr., Colorado Springs, 1978-79; Christian counselor, instr. Tutoring and Counseling Service, Confluence, Pa., 1980—; chaplain Spencer Nursing Home, Slippery Rock, Pa., 1971-73; comdr., acting chaplain CAP, Confluence, 1982; mem. West Pa. Conservancy, Pitts., 1980; founder Yough Valley Symposium, Confluence, 1982; resource network counselor Family Research Council Am., 1985—. Recipient citation El Paso Dept. Social Service, 1975; Menninger Found. fellow, 1984. Mem. Am. Ministerial Assn., Nat. Council for Social Studies, Am. Council of Christian Chs., Kappa Delta Pi. Democrat. Lodge: Order of De Molay. Avocations: philately, tennis, nature study. Home: 709 Oden St Confluence PA 15424 Office: Tutoring and Counseling Service 709 Oden St Confluence PA 15424

BOWERS, FRANCES WEMPLE, practitioner, Church of Christ, Scientist; b. Fergus Falls, Minn., Feb. 11, 1904; d. Daniel Schuyler and Nancy Alice (Close) Wemple; m. Edward Arden Bowers, May 14, 1925; children: Demorest Bowers Morrow, Cyrus Arden, Schuyler Wemple. Student pub. schs. Practitioner Ch. of Christ, Scientist, 1937—; clk. Fargo (N.D.) First Ch. of Christ, Scientist, 1937, chmn. bd., 3 terms, vice-chmn.,

1st reader, 1946-49. Address: 37 N 7th St Fargo ND 58102

BOWLES, JOSEPH ARTHUR, minister, Southern Baptist Convention; b. Lebanon, Ind., July 15, 1952; s. Joseph Fay and Loueva Mae (Evans) B.; m. Susan Elaine Wall, June 25, 1976; 1 dau., Brittany Jo. B.A., U. S. Fla., 1976; postgrad. New Orleans Bapt. Theol. Sem. Ordained to ministry Bapt. Ch., 1978. Assoc. pastor Shiloh Bapt. Ch., Plant City, Fla., 1976-78, pastor, 1978—; ch. growth cons. Fla. Bapt. Conv., Jacksonville, 1980—. Author weekly newspaper column Successful Living, 1979—. Trustee S. Fla. Bapt. Hosp., 1984—. Democrat. Home: 408 Alice St Plant City FL 33566 Office: Shiloh Bapt Ch PO Box 1226 905 W Terrace Dr Plant City FL 33566

BOWMAN, ELMER JESSE, JR., minister, United Church of Christ; b. St. Louis, Mar. 29, 1942; s. Elmer Jesse and Velma Leona (Schutte) B.; m. Linda Rae Hartman, Aug. 15, 1969; children: Steven Kyle, Melissa Eileen. B.S. in Edn., So. Ill. U., 1966; M.Div., Eden Theol. Sem., 1971. Ordained to ministry United Ch. Christ, 1971. Student minister Friedens/St. Hecker/Freeburg Ill., 1968-71; minister Zion United Ch. Christ, New Baden Ill., 1971-78, St. John's Ch., Summerfield, Ill., 1971-78; minister Immanuel United Ch. of Christ, Carlyle, Ill., 1979—; mem. com. on pastoral care Human Sources Ministries Consortium, Ill. Conf. Chs., Springfield, 1984. Mem. East St. Louis Met. Ministries (treas. 1973—), Carlyle Ministerial Assn. (chmn. 1981). Lodge: Lions (pres. New Baden 1973-74). Home: Rural Route 1 WP 64 Carlyle IL 62231 Office: Immanuel United Ch Christ 1970 Clinton Carlyle IL 62231

BOWMAN, JESSE EMMERT, minister, educator, Southern Baptist Convention; b. Callaway, Va., Apr. 4, 1911; s. Levi Abraham and Cora Ann (Bowman) B.; m. Elizabeth Laurel Wray, Sept. 23, 1930; children: Jesse, Jr., Douglas, Paige. D.Sacred Music, Mt. Vernon U., 1945; M.Ed., Luther Rich Sem., 1975; Th.D., Brown Theol. Sem., 1983. Ordained to ministry Bapt. Ch., 1938. Pastor, Olivet Bapt. Ch., Shanghi, Va., 1938-41, Liberty Bapt., Lanexa, Va., 1941-47, James River Bapt. Ch., Williamsburg, Va., 1947-56, Smith Meml. Bapt. Ch., 1956—; prof. So. Bapt. Sem. Extension, Fredricksburg, Va., 1971-73, Peninsula Bible Inst., Newport News, Va., 1973-79, Boyce Bible Sch., Newport News, 1979-83, Fredricksburg Bible Inst., 1983—. Author: History of James City Baptist Church, 1953; Notes on Exodus, 1972; Personal Evangelism, 1975. Home: PO Box 9 Lightfoot VA 23090 Office: Smith Meml Bapt Ch PO Box 9 Lightfoot VA 23090

BOWMAN, MARLIN LEONARD, priest, Episcopal Church; b. Santa Barbara, Calif., May 30, 1930; s. Leonard Leon and Christina Ruth (Glasco) B.; B.A., San Francisco State U., 1953; M.Div., Ch. Div. Sch. of Pacific, 1958. Ordained to ministry, 1959; chaplain Protestant Chapel, John F. Kennedy Internat. Airport, N.Y.C., 1970—; vicar St. James of Jerusalem Ch., Long Beach, N.Y., 1969—. Founder Bishop Wright Air Industry Awards luncheon, Senator William Reynolds of Long Beach Civic Awards. Recipient Good Scout award N.Y. council Boy Scouts Am. Home: 220 West Penn St Long Beach NY 11561 Office: Protestant Chapel John F Kennedy Airport Jamaica NY 11430

BOWMAN, WILLIAM MCKINLEY, minister, Progressive National Baptist Convention, Inc.; b. near St. George, S.C., Feb. 7, 1914; s. Joseph and Earline B.; A.B., Morris Coll., 1938, B.Th., 1939, D.D., 1963; m. Annie Mae Jones, July 14, 1942; children—William McKinley, Beverly (Mrs. Wesley Dennis), Joseph A., Audrey (Mrs. Bruce Brown). Ordained to ministry, 1938. Pastor, Granger Bapt. Ch., Elloree, S.C., 1938-46, Creston, S.C., 1940-42, Mt. Carmel Bapt. Ch., Cameron, S.C., 1942-48, St. Paul Bapt. Ch., Orangeburg, S.C., 1944-48, 2d Nazareth Bapt. Ch., Columbia, S.C., 1949—, Friendship Bapt. Ch., Hopkins, S.C., 1960-85; dir. pub. relations Bapt. Ednl. and Missionary Conv. S.C., 1942-85; pres. Gethsemane Bapt. Sunday Sch. Conv., Columbia, 1960—; sec.-treas. Interracial Bapt. Ministers Union Greater Columbia, 1970—; pres. Bapt. Fellowship of S.C., Council Black and White Bapts. of S.C.; v.p. Mt. Hebron Sunday Sch. Conv.; sales mgr. Radio WQXL, Christian radio for S.C. Mem. adv. bd. Midland Planning Council, 1969-74; chmn. emergency assistance program Sch. Dist. 1, 1970—; treas. Palmetto Action League, 1970—; pres., Dem. Com. Ward 9, Richland County, 1966-74; chmn. OEO, Richland-Lexington, Newberry counties, 1970-72; pres. NAACP, Columbia, 1960-72; trustee Morris Coll. Sumter, S.C., 1950-84; bd. dirs. Victory Service Ctr., 1970—; chmn. adv. bd. Children's Bur. S.C.; mem. Dist. 1 Sch. Bd., 1978—, Richland County. Mem. Columbia Ministers Assn. (pres. 1970-72, 84-86), Columbia Evang. Fellowship (sec. 1970-75), Mt. Hebron Progressive Assn. (exec. bd. 1967-85). Lodges: Masons, Elks. Address: 2012 Hydrick St Columbia SC 29203

BOX, LLOYD CLIFTON, III, minister, Baptist Missionary Association of America; b. Dallas, Jan. 12, 1951; s. Lloyd Clifton Jr. and Katherine Louise (Woelfley) B.; m. Vicki Lynn Folks, Dec. 23, 1972; children: Amy Leigh, Joshua David, Zachary Paul. Student Dallas Bapt. Coll., 1976-77; B.A., Criswell Ctr. Bibl. Studies, 1980; postgrad., 1980, Bethany Theol. Sem., 1983-85. Ordained to ministry Baptist Missionary Association of America, 1972. Pastor various chs., Tex., 1972-84; counselor Mission Ministries, Balch Springs, Tex., 1984—; vice-chmn. Desoto Community Outreach Council, Tex., 1983-84; mem. Dallas Bapt. Assn., 1980-84, Desoto Ministerial Alliance, Tex., 1979-84, Dallas Bapt. Assn. Pastors Conf., 1980-84; Desoto Mens Prayer Breakfast, 1981-82, Desoto Mens Inst., 1980-84, instr., 1982-84. dir. Onesimus Ministries, Balch Springs, 1985—. Coordinator Meals on Wheels, Desoto, 1983-84; advisor Glenn Heights Police Dept., Tex., 1982-84, Desoto Police Dept., 1982—; mgr. Ruby Young Elem. PTA, Desoto, 1980-84, Belt Line Elem. PTA, Desoto, 1982-84, Desoto Preschool PTA, 1979-82. Served to E-3 USAF, 1970-71. Ford Found. grantee 1969. U. Tex. scholar 1969. Avocations: collecting books; coaching football; reading; computers. Home: 2327 Peachtree Rd Balch Springs TX 75180 Office: Mission Ministries 2327 Peachtree Rd Balch Springs TX 75180

BOX, RAYMOND MARSHALL, minister, Ch. of the Nazarene; b. St. Arnaud, Victoria, Australia, Aug. 20, 1928; s. Albert and Rosina Catherine (Reyne) B.; came to U.S., 1965; diploma Bible with distinction, Nazarene Bible Coll., N.S.W., Australia, 1955; A.B., Northwest Nazarene Coll., Nampa, Idaho, 1965-68; M.R.E., Nazarene Theol. Sem., Kansas City, Mo., 1972; m. Maureen Helen Hodgens, Jan. 28, 1956; children—Stephen Marshall, Sharon Joy. Ordained to ministry, 1959; pastor chs. in Australia, Idaho and Mo., 1956-70; asso. pastor Rainbow Ch. of Nazarene, Kansas City, Kans., 1970-72; pastor Covina (Calif.) Ch. of Nazarene, 1973—. Mem. Covina Area Ministerial Assn. (pres.), Covina C. of C. Contbr. articles to religious jours. Home: 1150 W Grovecenter St Covina CA 91722 Office: 260 E College St Covina CA 91723

BOYD, HELEN, lay church worker, United Church of Christ; b. Sewickly, Pa., Nov. 28, 1906; d. John Logan Jr. and Nellie Eurydice (Taylor) B. B.A., U. Wash., 1928; student Chgo. Theol. Sem., 1932-33; M.A., Columbia U., 1940. Dir. religious edn. Mich. Congl. Christian Conf., Lansing, 1933-39; dir. religious activities, instr. New Testament Women's Coll., U. N.C., Greensboro, 1940-42; dean women, instr. Bible and Christian edn. Elon Coll., N.C., 1942-43; dir. religious edn. St. Anthony Park Congl. Ch., St. Paul, 1943-44; dir. Christian edn. Plymouth Congl. Ch., Fort Wayne, Ind., 1944-48; chmn. bd. Christian edn. Plymouth Congl. Ch.-United Ch. of Christ, Seattle, 1950-52, mem. adminstrv. council, 1962-64, trustee, 1966-70, mem., chmn., bd. deacons, 1971-73, chmn. bd. parish care, 1973-77, ch. council, 1976-83, chmn. pastoral relations com., 1977-79, mem., 1981-84, mem., chmn. nominating com., 1980-84; corp. mem. Nat. Bd. for Homeland Ministries-United Ch. of Christ, N.Y.C., 1975—, bd. dirs., exec. com., mem., chmn. personnel and salaries com., mem. nominating com., 1981-85, mem. search com. for exec. v.p., 1984; mem. personnel com. Wash.-N. Idaho Conf.-United Ch. of Christ, Seattle, 1975-77. Exec. dir. Seattle-King County council Camp Fire Cirls, 1948-72 (citation Merit 1972, life membership 1983); mem. Mcpl. League Seattle, 1950—; mem. health and welfare council United Way, Seattle, 1955-60; mem. YMCA Girl Reserve Soc., Seattle, Muskegon, Mich., 1929-32. Recipient citation merit, Camp Fire Girls, Inc., N.Y.C., 1971, Leadership award Plymouth Congl. Ch., 1975; named one of Matrix Table Women of Achievement, Women in Communication, 1972. Mem. PEO (Washington state treas. 1974-75), Mortar Bd., Kappa Delta Pi, Phi Lamda Theta, Kappa Delta (pres. 1927-28). Lodge: Soroptimist (pres. Seattle sect. 1966-67). Home: 900 University St #2A Seattle WA 98101

BOYD, JOHN ERIC, minister, United Baptist Convention; b. Windsor, N.S., Can., Jan. 11, 1950; s. Eric Burton and Sarah Margaret (Smith) B.; m. Deborah Joan Cuthbertson, July 1, 1978; children: Anthony Blair, John Adam. B.A., Acadia U., 1971, M.Div., 1974. Ordained to ministry, 1974. Student minister Bapt. Ch., Advocate, N.S., 1969-71, Kentville, N.S., 1971-74; minister Bapt. Ch., Mahone Bay, N.S., 1974-82; sr. minister First Bapt. Ch., Amherst, N.S., 1982—; v.p. Atlantic Ecumenical Council, Can., 1984—; chmn. Atlantic Seminar in Theol. Edn., Truro, N.S., 1982—; mem. senate Acadia Div. Coll., Wolfville, N.S., 1980-82; dir. N.S. Dist. Canadian Bible Soc., Halifax, N.S., 1983—; pres. Atlantic Bapt. Fellowship, Can., 1981-82. Mem. N.S. Social Services Council, Halifax, 1980-82; bd. dirs. United Way, Amherst, N.S., 1982—. Home: 2 N Adelaide St Amherst NS B4H 3M4 Canada Office: First Bapt Ch 90 Victoria St PO Box 637 Amherst NS B4H 4B8 Canada

BOYD, JULIA MARGARET (MRS. SHELTON B. BOYD), lay church worker, United Methodist Church; b. Newton Grove, N.C., Mar. 7, 1921; d. Isaiah and Mary Lela (Blackman) Tart; B.S., East Carolina U., 1942; m. Shelton Bickett Boyd, Feb. 21, 1944; children: Mary (Mrs. James M. Berdine, Jr.), Deborah (Mrs. John Wayne Pearson). Pres., United Meth. Women, 1st United Meth. Ch., Mt. Olive, N.C., 1951-55, 57-59, mem. and sec. adminstrv. bd. and council ministries, 1955—, mem. local work area on edn., 1960—, chmn., 1971-75, chmn. spiritual growth, 1968-72; counselor United Meth. Youth Fellowship, 1960-67; adult del. Nat. Convocation Meth. Youth, 1964; pres. Godsboro dist. United Meth. Women, 1955-59; mem. N.C. Conf. Bd. Edn., 1964-72; mem. N.C. Conf. Council on Youth Ministries, 1964-82, chmn., 1972-76, mem. adult staff youth, sr. high ministries, 1962-81; mem. N.C. Conf., 1970-76, Goldsboro Dist. Council on Ministries, 1971— also coordinator youth ministries Goldsboro Dist., 1964-82; Goldsboro dist. lay rep. Conf. Council on Ministries, 1982—. Pres., Mt. Olive P.T.A., 1955-56, Mt. Olive High Sch. and So. Wayne High Sch. Band Patron's Club, 1964-66; leader Girl Scouts, 1956-57; active Community Chest. Named Lay Person of Yr., N.C. Conf. United Meth. Ch., 1979. Mem. Women's Aux. of N.C. Pharm. Assn. (pres. 1980-81). Club: Southern Wayne Country. Home: 400 W Main St Mount Olive NC 28365

BOYD, MALCOLM, priest, author, priest Episcopal Ch.; b. Buffalo, June 8, 1923; s. Melville and Beatrice (Lowrie) B.; B.A., U. Ariz., 1944; B.D., Ch. Div. Sch. of the Pacific, 1954; postgrad. Oxford (Eng.) U., 1955; S.T.M., Union Theol. Sem., 1956. Ordained priest Episcopal Ch., 1955; rector ch., Indpls., 1957-59; chaplain Colo. State U, 1959-61, Wayne State U, 1961-65; nat. field rep. Episcopal Soc. for Cultural and Racial Unity, 1965-70; canonical res. Episcopal Diocese of N.Y., 1971—; asso. fellow Yale U., 1968—; writer-priest-in-residence, St. Augustine by-the-Sea, Santa Monica, 1980—. Pres., TV Producers Assn., 1950. Active voter registerations in Miss. and Ala., 1963, 64; mem. Los Angeles City and County AIDS task force, 1984—. Mem. film awards com. Nat. Council Chs., 1965—; mem. nat. bd. Clergy and Laity Concerned; co-chmn. Jerusalem Conf. Christians and Israelis, 1977. Recipient award for Christian-Jewish Understanding, Union Am. Hebrew Congregations, 1980. Mem. NAACP, Integrity, Authors Guild, PEN (pres. Los Angeles Ctr. 1984—). Author: Crisis in Communication, 1957; Are You Running with Me, Jesus?, 1965; Free to Live, Free to Die, 1967; As I Live and Breathe, 1970; Christian, 1975; Am I Running with You, God?, 1977; Take Off the Masks, 1978; Look Back in Joy, 1981. Contbr. articles to Christian Century, Nat. Cath. Reporter, The Advocate, N.Y. Times, Los Angeles Times, Washington Post, MS. Malcolm Boyd Collection, permanent archive of letters and papers established at Boston U. Address: 1227 4th St Santa Monica CA 90401

BOYER, BARRY CHARLES, minister, Presbyterian Church U.S.A.; b. LaJolla, Calif., Jan. 25, 1947; s. Hilbert L. and Loetta Irene (Jacobsen) B.; m. Delores JoAnne Leafblad, Sept. 11, 1973; 1 child, Laurel Ann. B.A., Macalester Coll., 1968; M.Div., San Francisco Theol. Sem., 1971; D.Min., McCormick Theol. Sem., 1984. Ordained to ministry Presbyterian Ch. U.S.A., 1971. Minister, Bayfield Presbyn. Ch., Wis., 1971-79; assoc. minister Glen Avon Presbyn. Ch., Duluth, Minn., 1979—; pres. Arrowhead Council Chs., Duluth, 1982—. Columnist Bayfield Sun, Washburn, Wis., 1975-77. Bds. dirs. Lake Superior council Boy Scouts Am., Duluth, 1985, Nat. Polinsky Rehab. Ctr., Duluth, 1985. KT scholar, 1970. Office: Glen Avon Presbyn Ch 2105 Woodland Duluth MN 55803

BOYES, GLENN MERVIN, minister, religion educator, The Missionary Church; b. Owen Sound, Ont., Can., Jan. 24, 1955; s. Mervin Edwin and Dorothy Margaret (Filsinger) B.; m. Beverly Jean Francey, Sept. 3, 1977; 2 children: Ehren, Kristen. B.A. in Philosophy, U. Regina, 1977, M.Div., Can. Theol. Sem., 1980. Ordained to ministry, 1982, Missionary Church. Clergy Missionary Ch., Listowel, Ont., 1980-82; part-time prof. Emmanuel Bible Coll, Kitchener, Ont., 1981-83, full-time prof., 1983—. Mem. Evang. Theol. Soc., Evang. Fellowship of Can. Home: 49 Betzner Ave N Kitchener ON N2H 3B8 Canada Office: Emmanuel Bible Coll 100 Fergus Ave Kitchener ON N2A 2H2 Canada

BOYLE, LAWRENCE PETER, Episcopal vicar, Roman Cath. Ch.; b. Millville, N.J., June 29, 1928; s. William Augustine and Margaret Mary (Connolly) B.; A.B., St. Mary's Ch., Balt., 1958. Ordained priest, 1962; asso. pastor Star of the Sea, Atlantic City, 1962-66, St. Joseph's Ch., Somers Point, N.J., 1966-70, St. John's Ch., Collingswood, N.J., 1970-74; pastor St. Monica's Ch., Atlantic City, 1974—; Episc. vicar of Atlantic City, 1975—. Mem. personnel bd. Diocese of Camden (N.J.), Roman Cath. Ch., 1974—, diocesan consultor, 1975—; chaplain Serra Internat., Atlantic City, 1975—; chmn. Cath. Com. Atlantic City, 1975—; mem. exec. bd. St. Nicholas Regional Sch., Atlantic City, 1974—. Trustee Atlantic Human Resources, 1975-76. Address: 108 N Pennsylvania Ave Atlantic City NJ 08401

BRADFIELD, CECIL DAVID, educator, minister, Am. Lutheran Ch.; b. Rio, W.Va., Nov. 6, 1939; s. Jasper Hall and Beulah B.; B.A., Capital U., 1961; M.Div., Lutheran Theol. Sem., 1965; M.A., Madison Coll., 1968; Ph.D., Am. Univ., 1975; m. Barbara Jeanne Hanne, Mar. 26, 1961; 1 dau., Anne Cecilia. Ordained to ministry Am. Lutheran Ch., 1965; pastor The Franklin W. Va. Lutheran Parish, 1965-71; asst. prof. sociology Madison Coll., Harrisonburg, Va., 1971—. Mem. Assn. Sociology of Religion, Religious Research

Assn., Am. Sociol. Assn. Office: Madison Coll Harrisonburg VA 22801

BRADLEY, DAVID IRA, editor, United Methodist Church; b. Reedpoint, Mont., June 8, 1938; s. James Ira and Ruth Daisy (Nutting) B.; m. Velma Grace Krebs, Aug. 12, 1960; children: Susan Annette, Sandra Kay, David Jonathan. B.A., Westmar Coll., 1960; M.Div., United Theol. Sem., 1964; postgrad. Vanderbilt Div. Sch., 1980-82. Cert. lab. tchr. Clergy/group ministry Residence Park Ch., Dayton, Ohio, 1963-66; editor Otterbein Press, Dayton, 1963-68; children's editor United Meth. Ch., Nashville, 1968-77, adult editor/family, 1977-81; editor/dir. The Upper Room, Nashville, 1981—; chmn. editor's sect. Nat. Council Chs. of Christ, Dayton, 1965-68, chmn. children's sect., Nashville, 1973-76; bd. dirs. Sch. of Hope, Franklin, Tenn., 1970—; mem. exec. com. Commn. on Family, United Meth. Ch., 1978-81. Author/editor: Celebrating Marriage, 1982. Pres., Grassland Sch. PTO, Franklin, 1976-78; organizer Franklin High Sch. PTO, 1982; v.p. Williamson County Parent Assn., 1982—. Served with U.S. Army, 1956-60. Mem. Nat. Assn. Marriage Enrichment, Council Affiliated Marriage Enrichment Orgns. Home: 108 Williamsburg Pl Franklin TN 37064 Office: The Upper Room 1908 Grand Ave Box 189 Nashville TN 37202

BRADLEY, LAWRENCE VERBLE, JR., minister, So. Bapt. Conv.; b. Marion, N.C., Dec. 2, 1920; s. Lawrence V. and Tennie Mae (Brooks) B.; grad. Mars Hill Jr. Coll., 1939; B.A., Georgetown Coll., 1940; postgrad. So. Sem., Ky., 1944-45; LL.D. (hon.), Augusta Law Sch., 1971; m. Evelyne G. Davis, June 13, 1938; children—Robert Lawrence, Carlyn Delaine. Ordained to ministry, 1939; pastor Orchard Knob Bapt. Ch., Atlanta, 1946-52, Stanton Meml. Bapt. Ch., Miami, Fla., 1952-54, Grove Ave. Bapt. Ch., Richmond, Va., 1954-60, Curtis Bapt. Ch., Augusta, Ga., 1960—; chaplain U.S. Army, 1945-47. Vice pres. Ga. Bapt. Conv., 1972-74; mem. Africa, Europe and Near-East Com. Fgn. Mission Bd. So. Bapt. Conv., 1957-60. Trustee Hill Crest Meml. Park, Augusta, Ga., 1970—; founder largest Bapt. Ch. in Japan, 1945; founder Curtis Bapt. Sch., 1963; founder Curtis Bapt. Found.; ch. was named in his honor in Bijnor, India. Contbr. numerous articles to religious publs. Home: 2205 Dartmouth Dr Augusta GA 30904 Office: 1316 Broad St Augusta GA 30901

BRADLEY, WILLIAM LEE, found. exec., minister, United Ch. Christ; b. Oakland, Calif., Sept. 6, 1918; s. Dwight Jaques and Kathryn Lee (Culver) B.; A.B., Oberlin Coll., 1941; Ph.D., Edinburgh U., 1949; B.D., Andover Newton Theol. Sch., 1950; m. Paula Anne Elliott, Aug. 7, 1947; children—James Richard, Dwight Culver, Paul William. Ordained to ministry, 1950; instr. to prof. philosophy of religion Hartford (Conn.) Sem. Found., 1950-66; vis. prof. Thammasat U., Bangkok, 1964-66; asst. to asso. dir. humanities and social sci., arts and humanities Rockefeller Found., N.Y.C., 1966-70; pres. Hazen Found., New Haven, 1970—. Mem. AAAS, Council Fgn. Relations, Am. Acad. Religion, Am. Theol. Soc., Am. Anthrop. Soc. Author: P.T. Forsyth, The Man and His Work, 1952; The Meaning of Christian Values Today, 1965; Introduction to Comparative Religion, 1965. Home: 245 E Rock Rd New Haven CT 06511 Office: 400 Prospect St New Haven CT 06511

BRAITHWAITE, GILBERT GEORGE, educator, minister, General Association of Regular Baptist Churches; b. Bellingham, Wash., Nov. 7, 1947; s. John Alfred and Joyce Elinor (Gunderson) B.; m. Pamela Ann Worley, Sept. 24, 1977; children: Joyanne Michelle, Annette Kathleen. B.S., Wash. State U., 1968; Th.M., Dallas Theol. Sem., 1972, Th.D., 1976. Ordained to ministry, 1983. Mem. faculty, Faith Bapt. Bible Coll., Ankeny, Iowa, 1976—, prof., 1983—, chmn. div. gen. studies, 1984—; bd. dirs. Dallas Bible Memory Assn. Council, 1970-72; deacon Urbandale Bapt. Ch., Iowa, 1977-78; chmn. Bapt. Friends of Israel, Des Moines, 1981-83. Bd. dirs. Greentree Condominium Corp. #1 Ankeny, 1984—. Mem. Creation Research Soc., Bible Sci. Assn., Commodore Computer Users Group of Iowa. Republican. Office: Faith Bapt Bible Coll 1900 NW 4th St Ankeny IA 50021

BRAMLETT, THOMAS KEITH, minister, Assemblies of God. b. Paragould, Ark., June 12, 1953; s. Tom and Margie (Johnson) B.; m. Cheryl Lynn Center, Aug. 24, 1973; children: Jennifer, Adrienne, Cassie; 1 fosterchild, Lisa. B.A. in Religious Edn., Central Bible Coll., 1975. Ordained to ministry Assemblies of God, 1981. Pastor First Assembly of God, Marlin, Tex., 1979-84; assoc. Pastor Trinity Temple Ch., Fayetteville, Ark., 1977-79; asst. pastor N.W. Assembly of God, Wichita Falls, Tex., 1975-77; Christian lay worker Parkcrest Village A/G Springfield, Mo., 1973-75; sectional youth rep. Assemblies of God, Marlin region, 1980-81; officer Ministerial Alliance, Marlin, 1982-84; pastor First Assembly of God Ch., Sulphur, Okla., 1984—. Writer, columnist Possibilities Unlimited, 1983-84. Home: 900 E Oklahoma Sulphur OK 73806 Office: First Assembly of God HW 7E Sulphur OK 73086

BRAMMER, DON HARLO, minister, Chs. of Christ; b. Henry County, Ind., Jan. 28, 1924; s. Harlo M. and Sara L. (Bouslog) B.; B.A., Christian Restoration Assn., Cin., 1971; m. Louise E. Livingston, Dec. 7, 1961. Ordained to ministry Chs. of Christ, 1971; minister Domestic Ch. of Christ, Geneva, Ind., 1972-74, Greenville (Ohio) Ch. of Christ, 1974-80, New Testament Ch. of Christ, Hagerstown, Ind., 1980—. Writer weekly article for Bible page Eastern Ind. Farmer, 1970-72. Home: Route 1 Box 375 Greens Fork IN 47345

BRANDEL, BERNICE PETERSON STEGE (MRS. PAUL W. BRANDEL), church official, Covenant Church of America; b. Chgo., May 10, 1914; d. Emil R. and Mildred M. (Anderson) Peterson; m. Henry F. Stege, June 5, 1943 (dec.); m. Paul W. Brandel, Jan. 3, 1976. Student North Park Coll., 1933-35, Northwestern U., 1936. Dir. and sec. Bd. of Benevolence, Evang. Covenant Ch. of Am., Chgo., 1964—; chmn. bldg. com., fin. com. and bd. trustees Northbrook (Ill.) Covenant Ch., 1964—, also Sunday Sch. tchr., 1960—; dir. Covenant Retirement Communities mem. pres.'s adv. bd. North Park Coll. and Theol. Sem. Vice pres. Paul W. Brandel Enterprises, Inc., Chgo., 1969—. Area chmn. United Fund Drive, Northbrook, 1968-70; bd. dirs., sec. Swedish Retirement Assn., 1960-70, Swedish Covenant Hosp., 1950—; trustee, sec. Mary Thompson Hosp., 1950-60, Michigan Av. Hosp., 1963-67, bd. dirs., past sec. The Lambs, Inc. Mem. Assn. of Chgo. Bank Women. Clubs: Chicago Women's, Everglades. Home: 2513 Mayapple Court Northbrook IL 60062 Office: 641 Landwehr Northbrook IL 60062

BRANDENBURG, ARTHUR LEWIS, minister, United Meth. Ch.; b. Haralson, Ga., Jan. 7, 1931; s. Henry Lewis and Inez (Todd) B.; B.A., Emory U., 1952; B.D., Union Theol. Sem., 1955; M.Th., Chgo. Theol. Sem., 1967; m. Rebecca Brown, July 17, 1956; 1 son, Mark. Ordained to ministry, 1957; chaplain Duke U., Durham, N.C., 1955-61; dir. Wesley Found., Greater New Haven, Conn., 1961-68; Meth chaplain Yale, New Haven, 1961-68; fellow Pierson Coll., Yale, 1965-70; assoc. chaplain, assoc. pastor Ch. of Christ in Yale, New Haven, 1968-70; instr. sociology and anthropology So. Conn. State Coll., New Haven, 1968-70; assoc. pastor 1st United Meth. Ch. of Germantown, Phila., 1970-73; pastor, dir. Calvary United Meth. Ch., Phila., 1973—; instr. Trinity Coll. Singapore, summer 1968. Pres. Nat. Assn. Coll. and Univ. Ministers, 1966-69; chmn. Nat. Conf. Univ. Christian Movement, 1967; chmn. commn. on urban ministries Eastern Pa. Annual Conf., United Meth. Ch., 1975-76; vice chmn. regional personnel com. Bd. of Global Ministries, United Meth. Ch., 1974-76; v.p. Met. Christian Council Phila., 1982—; bd. dirs. Pub. Interest Law Ctr., 1981—; exec. com. West Phila. Partnership, 1980—. Contbr. articles to religious jours. Home: 4702 Springfield Ave Philadelphia PA 19143 Office: 48th St and Baltimore Ave Philadelphia PA 19143

BRANDON, JAMES OSCAR, minister, So. Bapt. Conv.; b. Wellman, Tex., Oct. 26, 1935; s. Oscar Elbert and Edith Lolee (Record) B.; B.A., Hardin-Simmons U., 1958; M.Div., Southwestern Bapt. Theol. Sem., 1967; Th.D., Luther Rice Sem., 1972; m. Barbara Nell Williams, Aug. 6, 1956; children—Elesha, Janna, Nessa, Sarita. Ordained to ministry, 1956; pastor chs., Stanford, Tex., 1956-57, Cottonwood, Tex., 1957-60, Tarzan, Tex., 1960-63, Amarillo, Tex., 1963-68; pastor missionary fgn. mission bd. So. Bapt. Conv., Richmond, Va., 1968-73; exec. sec. Bapt. Gen. Conv. Fed. Dist. Brazil, Brazilia, 1968-72; pastor 1st Bapt. Ch., Clarendon, Tex., 1973—; prof. phil. of religion Clarendon Coll., 1975—. Sec.-treas. Donley County Ministerial Alliance, 1974—; pres. bd. dirs. Panfork Bapt. Camp, Top of Tex. Bapt. Area, 1974—, mem. exec. bd., 1974—. Mem. Panfork Bapt. Assn. Columnist Clarendon Press, 1973—; contbr. articles to religious jours. Home: Box 944 402 E 4th St Clarendon TX 79226 Office: Box 944 1st Bapt Ch Clarendon TX 79226

BRANDT, KENNETH EDWARD, minister, Churches of God General Conference; b. Lancaster, Pa., June 14, 1959; s. Kenneth Ebersole and Jean Marie (Brandt) B.; m. Kelley Ann Rice, Aug. 18, 1979; children: Jennifer Dorlane, Kristopher Edward, Zachary Elwood. A.A., Findlay Coll., 1979, B.A., 1981; student Winebrenner Sem., 1981-82; M.Div., Princeton Theol. Sem., 1985. Ordained to ministry Churches of God General Conference, 1985. Pastor Zion Ch. of God, Hamler, Ohio, 1979-82, Newport Ch. of God, Pa., 1984—; asst. pastor Simpson United Meth. Ch., Old Bridge, NJ., 1982-84; del. E. Pa. Conf., Mechanicsburg, 1977, Middletown, 1979, Youth Ministries, Bear Lake, Ind., 1980; mem. Perry County Ministerium, 1984—, W. Shore Ministerium, 1984—. Contbr. articles to profl. jours. Bd. dirs. Sr. Citizens Bd., Newport, Pa., 1984, Perry County Human Services, New Bloomfield, 1985, Local Adv. Council, New Bloomfield, 1985. Club: Owls. Avocations: kite flying; magic; coins. Home: 515 S 4th St Newport PA 17074 Office: Newport First Ch of God 390 S 5th St Newport PA 17074

BRANDT, STEVEN RUSSELL, librarian; b. Garden City, Kans., Aug. 22, 1949; s. Jacob Herbert and Henrietta Rachel (Siemens) B.; m. Emily Stewart Battles, May 29, 1976; children: Hannah, Peter. B.A., Pacific Coll., 1971; M.Div., Princeton Theol. Sem., 1980; M.L.S., U. Calif.-Berkeley, 1982. Assoc. librarian Fresno Pacific Coll., Calif., 1980-82; dir. library Mennonite Brethren Bibl. Sem.-Fresno Pacific Coll., 1982—; bd. dirs. Immanuel High Sch., Reedley, Calif., 1983—; sec. West Coast Mennonite Brethren Hist. Soc., Fresno, 1984—. Mem. ALA, Assn. for Coll. and Research Libraries, Am. Theol. Library Assn., Beta Phi Mu. Home: 4847 E Heaton Fresno CA 93727 Office: Fresno Pacific Coll-Mennonite Brethren Bibl Sem 1717 S Chestnut Ave Fresno CA 93702

BRANHAM, DANIEL C., minister, educator, Assemblies of God; b. Granby, Mo., Mar. 14, 1927; s. John Moss and Jennie Ellen (Bowman) B.; B.A., Manhattan (Kans.) Bible Coll., 1948; m. Irene Lucille Brent, Dec. 30, 1949; children—David M., Debra E., Dea Anna. Ordained to ministry, 1944; evangelist, Midwest Area, 1948-51; pastor ch., Ulysses, Kans., 1951-59, Neosho, Mo., 1959—; founder, pres. Ozark Bible Inst., Neosho, Mo., 1969—, Ozark Christian Acad., Neosho, 1973—. Bd. dirs. Neosho Housing Authority. Editor, writer Standard Bearer, 1969—. Home: 6021 N High St Neosho MO 64850 Office: 614 N High St Neosho MO 64850

BRANHAM, MACK CARISON, JR., minister, Lutheran Church America; b. Columbia, S.C., Apr. 20, 1931; s. Mack Carison andLaura Pauline (Sexton) B.; B.S., Clemson U., 1953; B.D., Luth. Theol. So. Sem., 1958, S.T.M., 1963; M.Div., 1972; M.S., George Washington U., 1968; Ph.D., Ariz. State U., 1974; distinguished grad. Command and Staff Coll., Air Force Inst. Tech., 1974; m. Jennie Louise Jones, Dec. 17, 1953; children—Kenneth Gary, Charles Michael, Keith Robert, Laurie Lynn. Ordained to ministry, 1958; pastor Providence Nazareth Luth. Parish, Lexington, S.C., 1958-59; chaplain U.S. Air Force, 1959, Lackland AFB, Tex., 1959, Sheppard AFB, Tex., 1959-62, Chateauroux Air Sta., France, 1962-65, Wright Patterson AFB, Ohio, 1965-67, Maxwell AFB, Ala., 1967-68, Cam Ranh Bay, Viet Nam, 1968-69, chief Profl. Services Hdqrs., Air Tng. Command, Randolph AFB, Tex., 1969-73, mem. Air Force Chaplain Resource Bd., Maxwell AFB, Ala., 1974-77; pres. Luth. Theol. So. Sem., 1982—. Instr. Far East div. U. Md., College Park, 1968. Exec. com. Greater Dayton Planned Parenthood, 1966-67; bd. dirs. Cam Ranh City Christian Orphanage, Cam Ranh City, Viet Nam, 1968-69. Decorated Bronze Star medal, Air Force Commendation medal with Oak leaf cluster, Meritorious Service medal; recipient Outstanding Achievement award, Cam Ranh City Christian Orphanage, 1969. Mem. Assn. for Creative Change. Editor Air Force Chaplain Newsletter, 1974-77, Chaplain Interchange, 1974-77. Office: Luth Theol So Sem 4201 N Main St Columbia SC 29203*

BRANNON, RONALD R., clergyman, gen. sec. The Wesleyan Church. Office: PO Box 200 Marion IN 46953*

BRANNON, THOMAS JAY, religious denomination official, Southern Baptist Convention; b. Greer, S.C., Dec. 26, 1937; s. J.A. and Lettie Mae (Emory) B.; m. Sandra Raines, July 27, 1965. A.A., North Greenville Coll., 1958; B.A., Furman U., 1960; student Southeastern Bapt. Theol. Sem., 1960-61, 63-64. Dir. pub. relations Bapt. Gen. Conv. of Tex., 1980—; pres. So. Bapt. Pub. Relations Assn., 1972-73, Religious Pub. Relations Council, Inc., 1980-82; dir. pub. relations S.C. Bapt. Conv., 1965-80, chmn. prodn. and budget com. So. Bapt. Conv. Videotape Service, 1981—. Mem. Religious Pub. Relations Council, (bd. govs. 1976-79, 80—), Pub. Relations Soc. Am., Bapt. Pub. Relations Assn., Tex. Bapt. Pub. Relations Assn., S.C. Bapt. Hist. Soc., Alston-Wilkes Soc., Southeastern Bapt. Theol. Sem. Alumni Assn. (past sec.).

BRASSARD, RONALD ERNEST, priest, Roman Catholic Church; b. Attleboro, Mass., Feb. 12, 1947; s. Ernest Joseph and Cecile Gertrude (Gousie) B. B.A., Our Lady of Providence Sem. Coll., Warwick, R.I., 1968; S.T.B., Cath. U., 1972. Ordained priest Roman Catholic Ch., 1974. Chaplain to deaf Diocese of Providence, 1973-75, dir. of liturgy, 1975-83, asst. chancellor, 1980-83; dir. of liturgy Nat. Shrine of Our Lady of the Snows, Belleville, Ill., 1983—; bd. dirs. Fedn. Diocesan Liturgical Commns., 1979-83; chmn. Nat. Pastoral Musicians Regional Conf., 1980, 82; chmn. spl. events Nat. Pastoral Musician Nat. Conf., 1981, 83; instr., bd. dirs., music ministry certification program Fontbonne Coll., St. Louis, 1983—. Mem. Nat. Pastoral Musicians, Liturgical Conf. Democrat. Avocations: swimming; walking; music; reading; films. Home: 7506 W Main St Belleville IL 62223 Office: Nat Shrine of Our Lady of Snows 9500 W Illinois Route 15 Belleville IL 62223

BRASWELL, CHARLES VERNON, minister, So. Bapt. Conv.; b. Johnston County, N.C., Apr. 10, 1936; s. John Gardner and Euzelia Tabitha (Denning) B.; A.A., Gardner-Webb Coll., 1959; B.A., Atlantic Christian Coll., 1962; M.Div., Southeastern Theol. Sem., 1965; postgrad. Dorothea Dix Hosp., Raleigh, N.C., 1968; m. Janice Marie Woodard, Sept. 11, 1956;

children—Vickie LaVerne, Lloyd Vernon. Ordained to ministry, 1962; pastor Micro (N.C.) Bapt. Ch., 1962-65, Stephens Chapel Bapt. Ch., Smithfield, N.C., 1962-65, Cove City (N.C.) Bapt. Ch., 1965-67, Trenton (N.C.) Bapt. Ch., 1965-67; Immanuel Bapt. Ch., Clinton, N.C., 1967-82, Wilson Grove Bapt. Ch., Charlotte, N.C., 1982—; Pres. Clinton Ministerial Assn., 1970-72; moderator Eastern N.C. Bapt. Assn., 1972-74; chaplain Clinton CAP, 1973-82; mem. exec. com. N.C. Christian Action League, 1972—; mem. com. of ministers Campbell Bapt. Coll., Bule's Creek, N.C., 1970—; chmn. Sampson County Christian Action League, 1974-82. Mem. Assn. for Handicapped Sampson County. Home: 9418 Central Dr Charlotte NC 28212 Office: 6624 Wilgrove Mint Hill Rd Charlotte NC 28212

BRAUER, JERALD CARL, educator, minister, Lutheran Church America; b. Fond du Lac, Wis., Sept. 14, 1921; s. Carl Lewis and Anna (Linde) B.; A.B., Carthage Coll., 1943, LL.D., 1957; B.D., Northwestern Luth. Theol. Sem., Mpls., 1945; Ph.D., U. Chgo. 1948; D.D. (hon.), Miami U., Oxford, Ohio, 1956; S.T.D. (hon.), Ripon (Wis.) Coll., 1961; L.H.D., Gettysburg Coll., 1963; m. Muriel Nelson, Mar. 18, 1945; children: Christopher Nelson, Marian Ruth, Thomas Carl. Instr. ch. history and history Christian thought Union Theol. Sem., N.Y.C., 1948-50; ordained to ministry, 1951; mem. faculty U. Chgo., 1950—, prof. history Christianity, 1959—, dean Federated Theol. Faculty, 1955-60; dean Div. Sch., 1960-70, Naomi Shenstone Donnelley prof., 1969—; vis. prof. U. Frankfurt (Germany), spring 1971; vis. lectr. U. Tokyo and U. Kokugakuin (Japan), 1966. Mem. bd. social missions United Luth. Ch. Am., 1954-60; del. founding Luth. Ch. Am., 1961, Luth. World Fedn., Helsinki, Finland, 1963, Vatican Council II, Rome, 1964, 65; exec. com. theol. fellowship program Rockefeller Bros., 1956-68; bd. dirs. Ch. Fedn. Greater Chgo., 1955-58; mem. bd. theol. edn. Luth. Ch. Am., 1961-71, pres., 1961-69. Cons. N.Y. State Dept. Edn., 1969—; mem. Center Policy Studies, U. Chgo., 1968—. Vis. fellow Center Study Democratic Instns., Santa Barbara, Calif., 1972, 74. Trustee Augustana Coll., 1964-66, Carthage Coll., 1958-62; trustee Council Religion and Internat. Affairs, 1966-83, chmn., 1979-83; bd. dirs. Inst. Advanced Pastoral Care, 1956-62; bd. govs. Internat. House of U. Chgo., 1958—, chmn., 1973—. Mem. Am. Assn. Theol. Schs. (exec. com. 1956-61), Am. Soc. Ch. History (pres. 1961), Midwestern Brit. Hist. Assn., Am. Hist. Assn. Author: Protestantism in America, 2d edit., 1965; Basic Questions for the Christian Scholar, rev. edit., 1963; Luther and the Reformation, 1953; Images of Religion in America, 1967; also articles, monographs, chpts. in books. Editor: The Impact of the Church Upon Its Culture, Vol. II, 1966, The Reinterpretation of American Church History, Vol. V, 1968; (Paul Tillich) The Future of Religions, 1966; (Paul Tillich) My Travel Diary, 1970; Westminster Dictionary of Church History, 1971; gen. editor Essay in Divinity, 7 vols., 1967-69; Religion and the American Revolution, 1976.

BRAUN, BARBARA ANN, lay church worker, Episcopal Church; b. Whitewater Twp., Mich., Nov. 13, 1933; d. Ben Adrian and Mabelle Juliette (Corey) Watson; m. Gilbert L. Braun, Sept. 1, 1947; children: Virginia, Phyllis, Gilbert, David, Dennis. Grad. in stenography, Ferris Inst., Big Rapids, Mich., 1941. Sunday sch. tchr. Christ Ch. Cathedral, Eau Claire, Wis., 1965—, pres. Episcopal Ch. Women, Diocese of Eau Claire, 1971-73, 76-78, chmn. united thank offering, 1978—; del. to Episc. Ch. Women Triennial (nat.), 1973, 76, 79, 82, 85; pres. Chippewa Valley Deanery, 1974-76, Ch. Women United, Eau Claire, 1978-80; rectora first women's cursillo Diocese of Eau Claire, 1977, mem. evangelism commn., ch. periodical club chmn., 1982—; dir. Teen's Encounter Christ, 1978-82; sec. Province V Town and Country, 1978—, chmn. ch. periodical club Diocese of Eau Claire, 1982—, chmn. nat. books fund, bd. dirs. 1984—; mem. Pewsaction Bd., 1983—; area chmn. State Bd. for Ch. Women United, 1979—. Editor Cursillo Newsletter, 1978—. Discussion chmn. LWV State Conv., 1963, state conv. chmn., 1977; leader Eau Claire Council Camp Fire, 1954-79, pres., 1978-81, bd. dirs., 1978—, del. nat. conf., 1981; co-chmn. handicapped swim program State of Wis., 1965-72. Home: 5724 Iona Beach Rd Eau Claire WI 54703

BRAY, EDDIE ATLAS, JR., minister, United Church of Christ; b. Bluefield, W.Va., July 25, 1950; s. Eddie Atlas and Joyce Lorraine (White) B.; m. Karen Lee Jackson, Aug. 1, 1970; children: Tami Leigh, Adam Robert. A.A., Lakeland Community Coll., 1970; B.A. in Psychology, Lake Erie Coll., 1972; M.Div., Ashland Sem., 1975; postgrad., 1978—. Ordained to ministry United Church of Christ, 1975. Pastor Ripley Congregational Ch., Greenwich, Ohio, 1973-75, Mt. Zwingli United Ch. Christ, Wadsworth, Ohio, 1976-81, Emanuel United Ch. Christ, Doylestown, Ohio, 1976-81; organizing pastor East Gate United Ch. Christ, Batavia, Ohio, 1981—; dir. Ohio Conf. Camps, 1977-80; trustee Ohio Conf., United Ch. Christ, Columbus, 1977-80; chmn. Southwest Ohio United Ch. Christ Dept. Stewardship and Mission, 1984—, council mem., 1984—. Treas. Operation H.O.P.E., Clermont County, Ohio, 1984—. Mem. Cin. United Ch. Christ Ministerium, Nat. Honor Soc. in Psychology, Southwest Ohio Assn. of United Ch. Christ, Clermont County C. of C. Home: 4638 Locust Grove Ct Batavia OH 45103 Office: East Gate United Ch Christ 4638 Locust Grove Ct Batavia OH 45103

BRAY, JACQUELYN MONELL, church musician, Southern Baptist Convention, accountant; b. Washington, Dec. 31, 1946; d. Arnold Scott and Elizabeth (Archibald) Monell; divorced; children: Mark Allen, Robelyn Andrea, Stephen Scott. Assoc. Music Edn., Daytona Beach Jr. Coll., 1965. Ch. organist, pianist First Congl. Ch., Lake Helen, Fla., 1960-65; chapel music dir. U.S. Army, Aschaffenburg, W. Ger., 1965-68; music dir. First United Meth. Ch., McGregor, Tex., 1970-73, Primrose Dr. Bapt. Ch., Waco, Tex., 1979-81; ch. pianist First Bapt. Ch., Laguna Park, Tex., 1981-83; ch. musician First Bapt. Ch., Crawford, Tex., 1974-79, 1983—; ch. sec. Primrose Dr. Bapt. Ch., Waco, 1981-82; del. Bapt. Gen. Conv., Waco., 1982—; tchr. spl. adults class First Bapt. Ch., Crawford, 1983—; acct., v.p. Graham Embroidery Co., Waco, 1981—. Composer of music. Christian life chmn. PTO, McLennan County, Tex., 1981-82; bicentennial com. McLennan County, 1976; Centennial com., Mc Gregor, 1980; active in Women for Reagan, 1984. Republican. Avocations: reading; sewing, camping. Home: PO Box 221 Crawford TX 76638 Office: Graham Embroidery Co Waco TX 76702

BRAY, JAMES FRANKLIN, minister, So. Baptist Conv.; b. Macon, Ga., Mar. 19, 1930; s. John Alfonza and Mattie Lillian (Cardell) B.; A.B., Mercer U., Macon, 1951; M.Div., So. Bapt. Theol. Sem., Louisville, 1955; m. Ruby Edna Pou, Feb. 15, 1964; children—Jennifer, Jessica, Jonathan T. Ordained to ministry, 1956; pastor Isle of Hope Bapt. Ch., Savannah, Ga., 1956-60; commd. 1st lt. Chaplains Corps, U.S. Army, 1960, advanced through grades to lt. col., 1971; assigned U.S., Ger. and Vietnam, 1960-75; staff chaplain, Ft. Buchanan, P.R., 1975—. Mem. council USO, Waynesville, Mo., 1972-75, San Juan, P.R., 1975—. Mem. Mil. Chaplains Assn., Assn. U.S. Army. Address: PO Box 34125 Fort Buchanan PR 00934

BRAY, JOHN LESTER, minister, Christian Ch. (Disciples of Christ); b. Columbus, Ohio, Dec. 10, 1925; s. Lester J. and Alice Edith (Jones) B.; B.A., Transylvania U., 1952; B.D., Lexington (Ky.) Theol. Sem., 1955; m. Helen Vice Felty, Jan. 1, 1954; children—Helen Edward, Susan Darlene, Margaret Louise. Ordained to ministry, 1954; student pastor in Ky., 1948-54; minister 1st Christian Ch., Tiffin, Ohio, 1955-57, Community Christian Ch., Las Cruces, N.Mex., 1957-58; minister edn. Monte Vista Christian Ch., Albuquerque, 1959-61; minister 1st Christian Ch., Marceline, Mo., 1961-65, Watson Terrace Christian Ch., St. Louis, 1965-70, Cynthiana (Ky.) Christian Ch., 1971-76, Prairie Ave. Christian Ch., Decatur, Ill., 1976—. Dist. pres. Mo. and Ky. Assembly of Christian Ch.; chmn. credentials com. Gen. Assembly Christian Ch., 1969, 71. Councilman at large Marceline, Mo., 1962-64; pres. Harrison County (Ky.) Commn. on Aging, 1972-76. Home: 236 Bristol Dr Decatur IL 62521 Office: 2201 E Prairie Ave Decatur IL 62521

BRAZAUSKAS, PIUS, priest, Roman Catholic Ch.; b. Pilviskiai, Lithuania, Nov. 28, 1905; s. Pius and Catherine (Dicpinigaityte) B.; came to U.S., 1949, naturalized, 1958; ed. Gizai Sem., Vilkaviskis, Lithuania, 1924-30; student Fine Arts Sch., Kaunas, Lithuania, 1932-36. Ordained priest, 1930; chaplain at Displaced Persons Camp in Salzburg, Austria, 1945-49; chaplain Sacred Heart Hosp., Eugene, Oreg., 1952-71, St. Catherine's Nursing Center, North Bend, Oreg., 1971—; chaplain, North Bend, Oreg., 1971—. Recipient 1st and 2d prizes Premium Art Oreg., 1962-63. Mem. Ateitininkai. Address: 3959 Sheridan North Bend OR 97459

BRAZIL, RUDOLPH EDWARD, religious organization administrator, Roman Catholic Ch.; b. Gustine, Calif., Nov. 2, 1923; s. Manuel Silveira and Maria Merces Brazil. B.B.A., San Jose State U., 1959. Catechist, Holy Spirit Ch., Fremont, Calif., 1969-80, prin. Sch. of Religion, 1980-84, dir. religious edn., 1984—. Served to lt. cdr. USN, 1944-58, PTO, Korea. Recipient South Korea. Pres. Unit citation, 1950. Mem. Oakland Diocese (catechist 1983-85, master catechist 1985—). Lodges: KC (grand knight 1967-68, chapt. pres. 1970-71), Luso Am. (pres. 1970-74), St. Anthony Soc. (pres. 1973-76). Avocations: reading; swimming; gardening. Home: 37434 Jason Way Fremont CA 94536 Office: Holy Spirit Sch Religion 37588 Fremont Blvd Fremont CA 94536

BREDESON, JAMES CLEMENS, minister, Lutheran Church - Missouri Synod; b. Forest City, Iowa, June 3, 1956; s. Clemens and Marilyn (Winkelmann) B.; m. Susan M. Waldschmidt, Aug. 29, 1981. B.A., Concordia Coll., Ann Arbor, Mich., 1978; M.Div., Concordia Sem., St. Louis, 1982. Ordained to ministry Lutheran Ch.-Mo. Synod, 1982. Intern, Golden Valley Luth. Ch., Minn., 1980-81; pastor St. Johns Luth. Ch., Chillicothe, Mo., 1982-85, Luth. Ch. Good Shepherd, York, Pa., 1985—; tchr. spl. edn. religion Trinity Luth. Ch., Ann Arbor, 1977-78; tchr. spl. religious edn., St. Johns Cath. Ch., Ypsilanti, Mich., 1977-78. Vol., St. Louis Assn. Retarded Children, 1980; bd. dirs. Operation Help, Chillicothe, 1983. Mem. Chillicothe Ministerial Alliance, Evangelicals for Social Action, Prolifers for Survival, Evang. Ministers Fellowship, Christians for Peace and Justice. Democrat. Lodge: Optimists (Chillicothe) (bd. dirs. 1984—). Home: 135 S Hartley St York PA 17404

BREIGHNER, JOSEPH FRANCIS, priest, Roman Cath. Ch.; b. Balt., Mar. 1, 1945; s. William James and Mary Elizabeth (Stansbury) B.; B.A., St. Mary's - Paca St., 1967; M.Div., Mary's Sem. and U., 1971; certificate in pastoral psychotherapy Pastoral Counseling and Consultation Centers Greater Washington, 1975. Ordained deacon, 1970, priest, 1971; deacon intern St. Joseph's Parish, Fullerton, Md., 1970-71; asso. pastor Shrine of the Little Flower, Balt., 1971-73, St. Charles Ch., Pikesville, Md., 1973—. Pastor weekly radio show Country Road. Author: Reflections from the Country Road, 1977. Home and Office: 101 Church Ln Baltimore MD 21208

BREITENBECK, JOSEPH M., bishop, Roman Catholic Church; b. Detroit, Aug. 3, 1914; s. Matthew J. and Mary A. (Quinlin) B.; student U. Detroit, 1932-35; B.A., Sacred Heart Sem., Detroit, 1938; postgrad. Gregorian U., Rome, Italy, 1938-40; S.T.L., Cath. U. Am.; J.C.L., Lateran U., Rome, 1949. Ordained priest Roman Catholic Ch., 1942; asst. St. Margaret Mary Parish, Detroit, 1942-44; sec. to Cardinal Mooney, 1944-58; sec. to Cardinal Dearden, 1959; pastor Assumption Grotto, 1959-67; consecrated bishop, 1965; bishop of Grand Rapids (Mich.), 1969—. Mem. Nat. Conf. Cath. Bishops. Office: 265 Sheldon Ave SE Grand Rapids MI 49502

BRELAND, FRED AZOR, minister, Baptist Missionary Association of America; b. Perry County, Miss., Sept. 29, 1912; s. Henry Levi and Serena (Breland) B.; m. Gertrude Sarah Rester, Aug. 25, 1934; children: Peggy Jolene, Keith Alvan. Student Southwestern Bapt. Coll., 1972—. Ordained to ministry Baptist Missionary Association of America, 1971. Pastor Cyrpess Creek Bapt. Ch., Brooklyn, Miss., 1971-72, Fairview Bapt. Ch., Laurel, Miss., 1972-82, Palestine Bapt. Ch., Lovin, Miss., 1982—; com. sec. for youth, Harvest Revival, 1973-76; moderator Ten Mile Bapt. Assn., Miss., 1963, 64. Mem. Perry County Bd. Suprs., 1948-52; game warden Miss. State Game and Fish Commn., 1958-68. Mem. Bapt. Missionary Assn. Miss., Big Creek Missionary Bapt. Assn. Home: Route 1 Box 74 Brooklyn MS 39425 Office: Route 6 Laurel MS 39440

BRELAND, JAMES ANDREW, minister, Southern Baptist Convention; b. McDonald, Miss., Feb. 10, 1927; s. Luther Clifton and Onie May (Rice) B.; B.S., Delta State Coll., 1950, M.Ed., 1970; postgrad. New Orleans Bapt. Theol. Sem., 1953; m. Billie A. Wasson, June 8, 1954; 1 child, Brenda Carol. Ordained to ministry, 1950; pastor chs., 1950-51; dir. Bapt. campus ministry Delta State U., Cleveland, Miss., 1951—. Mem. Bolivar Bapt. Pastors' Conf., Omicron Delta Kappa. Home: 200 Sostes Dr Cleveland MS 38732 Office: 903 S Court St Cleveland MS 38732

BRESLIN, LAWRENCE KENNY, priest, Roman Catholic Church; b. Cincinnati, Oct. 25, 1932; s. Leo Joseph and Margaret Mary (McDevitt) B. A.B., Athenaum of Ohio, 1954; S.T.L., Gregorian U.-Rome, 1958; Ph.D., Xavier U., 1981. Ordained priest Roman Catholic Ch., 1957. Tchr., Purcell High Sch., Cin., 1958-62; tchr., adminstr. Alter High Sch., Kettering, Ohio, 1962-68; vice rector N. Am. Coll., Rome, 1968-74; pastor St. Bartholomew Ch., Cin., 1974-78; pres., rector Atheneum of Ohio, Cin., 1978-84; pastor St. Vivian's Ch., Cin., 1984—; mem. Papal Vis. Team for Sem.; dir. Fountain Sq. Pools, Cin. Contbr. articles to profl. jours. Named Prelate of Honor, Holy See, Vatican City, 1972. Home: 7600 Winton Rd Cincinnati OH 45224 Office: Saint Vivians Parish 7600 Winton Rd Cincinnati OH 45224

BRETHAUER, HERBERT ALLAN, minister, United Church of Christ; b. Buffalo, N.Y., Aug. 22, 1927; s. Herbert Andrew and Clara Marie Louise (Weiman) B.; m. Shirley Olga Ullmann, Sept. 16, 1950; children: Douglas, Steven, Marilyn, Gloria. B.A., Heidelberg Coll., 1949; B.Div., Eden Sem., 1952; D.Min., San Francisco Theol. Sem., 1983. Ordained to ministry United Ch. Christ, 1952. Minister Zion Meml. United Ch. Christ, Dayton, Ohio, 1952-56; commd. 1st lt. U.S. Air Force, 1953, advanced through grades to lt. col. 1979, served as chaplain; minister Carondelet United Ch. Christ, St. Louis, 1979—. Decorated Legion of Merit, 1979. Republican. Lodge: Masons. Home: 3844 Loughborough Saint Louis MO 63116 Office: Carondelet United Ch Christ 7423 Michigan St Saint Louis MO 63111

BREWER, DENNIS LEE, minister, Southern Baptist Convention; b. Booneville, Ky., Jan. 9, 1948; s. Robert and Emma (Bowman) B.; m. Lucille Sebastian, Oct. 7, 1967; children: Scottie Joe, John Bowman. B.S., Eastern Ky. U., 1969; Th.M., Luther Rice Sem., Jacksonville, Fla., 1975; D.Ministry, So. Bapt. Ctr. for Bibl. Studies, Folkston, Ga., 1982. Ordained to ministry So. Bapt. Conv., 1968. Pastor Beattyville Bapt. Ch. (Ky.), 1972—; bd. advisers Cumberland Coll., Williamsburg, Ky.,

1980—; trustee Temperance League Ky., Louisville, 1983—. Author: Tales from Skurgeon Creek, 1979; The Land of Lee, 1983. Bd. dirs. Lee-Owsley Health Exchange, Beattyville, 1976, Lee County Indsl. Devel. Bd., 1977-80, Southside Water Assn., Beattyville 1978—; bd. dirs. Ky. Oil Mus., 1984—, Lee County Little League, 1984—; chmn. Lee County Concerned Citizens League, 1978. Recipient Leadership award U.S. Jaycees, 1969; Ky. Col. award, 1970; Mem. Red River Assn. So. Bapts. (exec. bd. 1972—, moderator 1976, 80-82, clk. 1974, 75, dir. of mission, 1976-84), Lee County Ministerial Assn. (pres. 1975-78, 82-83), Lee County Softball League (chmn. 1979—), Assn. So. Bapts. Club: Kiwanis (pres. 1981-82, sec. 1983—; Disting. Pres. award 1982). Lodge: Masons. Home: PO Box 488 Beattyville KY 41311 Office: Beattyville Bapt Ch PO Box 439 Beattyville KY 41311

BREWSTER, DANIEL FERGERSON, minister, religious organization executive, United Methodist Church; b. Newnan, Ga., Dec. 23, 1916; s. Daniel Fergerson and Sara Josephine (Stevens) B.; m. Helen Howe Glawson, June 7, 1943. A.B. Emory U., 1945; M.Div., Candler Sch. Theology, 1948; D.D. (hon.) LaGrange Coll., 1966. Ordained to ministry, United Meth. Ch., 1948. Pastor 5 chs. in Ga., 1943-64; exec. dir. Ga. Meth. Commn. on Higher Edn., Atlanta, 1964-84, retired 1984; trustee LaGrange Coll., Ga., 1965—; mem. exec. com., sec. Southeastern Jurisdiction Commn. on Higher Edn., Atlanta, 1980-84; dean Ga. Meth. Pastors Sch., 1960-64; sec. Conf. Bd. of Edn., 1956-60. Editor: Higher Education in Southeastern Jurisdiction 1787-1984 (United Methodist Church), 1984; North Ga. Conf. Handbook, 1963-70. Chmn. history-writing com. Newnan-Coweta County Hist. Soc., 1983; dist. commr. Flint River council Boy Scouts Am., 1985—. Recipient Special Achievement award 9 Meth. Colls., 1983, Brewster Endowment in Liberal Arts, Ga. Meth. Commn. on Higher Edn.; fellow La Grange Coll., Ga., 1981. Mem. Soc. Advancement Continuing Edn., Nat. Eagle Scout Assn. Democrat. Home: 20 W Broad St Newnan GA 30263

BRIAN, ALEXIS MORGAN, JR., lay preacher, deacon, So. Baptist Conv.; b. New Orleans, Oct. 4, 1928; s. Alexis Morgan and Loyola Evelyn (Thibaut) B.; B.A., La. State U., 1949, J.D., 1956; M.S., Trinity U., 1954; m. Elizabeth Louise Graham, Mar. 17, 1951; children—Robert Morgan, Ellen Graham. Ordained deacon So. Bapt. Conv., 1957; mem. Port Sulphur Bapt. Ch., 1951, First Bapt. Ch., Baton Rouge, 1951, 55-56, First Bapt. Ch., San Antonio, 1951-55; mem. First Bapt. Ch., New Orleans, 1956—, deacon, 1957—, first vice chmn., 1958, 61, chmn., 1963, 72, trustee, 1971—, bible tchr., 1956—, doctrines class tchr., 1958—, chmn. deacon nomination com., 1970, chmn. activities and recreation com., 1957-58, 65-69, chmn. music com., 1964, also mem. various coms.; lay preacher throughout So. Bapt. Conv., 1957—, mem. com. bds., 1969; mem. exec. bd. New Orleans Bapt. Assn., 1957-63, trustee, 1967-70, sec., 1968-70, chmn. radio-TV com., 1958-59; mem. exec. bd. New Orleans Fedn. Chs., 1965-68; also mem. various coms.; statewide Christian Witness leader La. Bapt. Conv., 1962-64. Asso. law firm Deutsch, Kerrigan & Stiles, New Orleans, 1956-60, partner, 1961-79; sr. ptnr. Brian, Simon, Peragine, Smith & Redfearn, New Orleans, 1979-80, counsel, 1981-82; sr. ptnr. Fawer, Brian, Hardy & Zatskis, New Orleans, 1982—. Asst. scoutmaster Boy Scouts Am., 1963-70; mem. steering com. United Fund, New Orleans, 1964; mem. Sponsor Club, WYES-TV Channel 12, 1974—. Bd. dirs. New Orleans Bapt. Theol. Sem. Found., 1972—, Inter-Varsity Christian Fellowship, 1974—; bd. dirs. Goodwill Industries, Inc., New Orleans, 1968—, 2d v.p., mem. exec. com., 1975—; trustee New Orleans Bapt. Theol. Sem., 1961-74, pres., chmn. exec. com., 1968-74, mem. bd. devel., 1961-63; mem. La. State U. Found.; mem. legal advisory council Ams. United for Separation Ch. and State; v.p. Upper Carrollton Neighborhood Assn., 1976—. Recipient Boss of Year award New Orleans Legal Secs. Assn., 1966. Mem. Internat. Assn. Ins. Counsel, Am., La., New Orleans bar assns., La. Assn. Def. Counsel, Def. Research Inst., Am. Arbitration Assn., La. State U. Alumni Fedn. (Century Club), La. Civil Service League, Trinity U., La. State U. Law Sch. alumni assns., Internat. House, Christian Legal Soc., Christian Businessmen's Com., Gideons Internat., Phi Delta Phi, Theta Xi. Contbr. articles to profl. jours. Home: 1738 S Carrollton Ave New Orleans LA 70118 Office: 2355 Pan-Am Life Ctr 601 Poydras St New Orleans LA 70130

BRIDGES, BOBBY LAWRENCE, minister, Southern Baptist Convention; b. Knoxville, Tenn., Aug. 23, 1949; s. Lawrence and Mary Elizabeth (Swaggerty) B.; m. Judith Ann Freeman, June 24, 1978; 1 child, Jonathan Christian. B.A., Belmont Coll., 1974; M.Div., Southwestern Bapt. Theol. Sem., 1977. Ordained to ministry Baptist Ch., 1973. Minister of youth Belmont Heights Bapt. Ch., Nashville, 1974-76; asst. pastor Travis Ave. Bapt. Ch., Ft. Worth, 1977-79; minister youth and edn. First Bapt. Ch., Grapevine, Tex., 1979-80; sr. pastor Woods Chapel Bapt. Ch., Arlington, Tex., 1980—; a founder Arlington Park Bapt. Ch.; dir. Arlington Children's Camp, Glen Rose, Tex., 1982, 83, 85; pres. Arlington So. Bapt. Fellowship, 1983-84. Co-founder, bd. dirs. Children in Med. Crisis Intervention, Arlington, 1984-85. Mem. Arlington Ministerial Assn., Tarrant Bapt. Assn. (exec. bd.). Avocations: skiing; golf; book collecting. Home: 2812 Monties Ln Arlington TX 76015 Office: Woods Chapel Bapt Ch 2424 California Ln Arlington TX 76015

BRIDGES, CLARENCE REGINALD, chaplain, So. Bapt. Conv.; b. Corsicana, Tex., Aug. 3, 1925; s. Clarence Odell and Minnie Velma (Willis) B.; B.A., Corpus Christi U., 1950; B.D., Southwestern Bapt. Theol. Sem., 1964; m. Addie Verlyne Dillard, June 14, 1949; children—Thelma Renee, Reginald Lowell, Merry Christine, Cheryl Ann. Ordained to ministry, 1950; pastor New Hope Bapt. Ch., Parker County, Tex., 1950-51, Oletha Bapt. Ch., Limestone County, Tex., 1951-55, Alta Mesa Bapt. Ch., Dallas, 1955-59, Calvary Bapt. Ch., Stephenville, Tex., 1959-63, Eureka Bapt. Ch., Weatherford, Tex., 1963-64, Highland Bapt. Ch., Pampa, Tex., 1964-69; chaplain Lubbock (Tex.) State Sch., 1969—. Mem. vol. council Lubbock State Sch., 1973—; organizer vol. chaplains program Highland County Hosp., Pampa, 1965. Home: Box 133 Idalou TX 79329 Office: Box 5396 Lubbock TX 79417

BRIDGES, ZEBADEE, minister, National Baptist Convention U.S.A.; b. Summit, Miss., Mar. 1, 1926; s. Jim and Cassie (Haynes) B.; m. Lorraine Johnson, Aug. 21, 1948; children: Zebadee, Jr., Juliette Bridges Perez, Andra. B.Th., Union Bapt. Theol. Sem., 1958, M.Th., 1963, D.D. (hon.), 1976. Ordained to ministry Bapt. Ch., 1954. Pastor, Community Bapt. Ch., New Orleans, 1956-61, Asia Bapt. Ch., New Orleans, 1961—, organizer, dir. Asia Day Care Ctr., 1974—. Treas. bd. trustees Union Bapt. Theol. Sem., New Orleans, 1979; gen. coordinator Nat. Assembly Black Chs., Nat. Bapt. Conv. U.S.A., 1984; gen. Black history dir. Black History Documentary Presentation, 1975—. Compiler: Parliamentary Procedure, 1984. Statewide chmn. Push/Excel, La., 1978-79; gen. chmn. 7th Ward Civil and Polit. Group, New Orleans, 1980—; chmn. Concerned Clergy, New Orleans, 1981—; polit. adviser, activist various polit. orgns. and candidates, New Orleans, 1981—; ch. campaign mgr. Mayoral Election, New Orleans, 1981—; mem. Am. Fedn. Chs., 1985—. Recipient Community Ednl. Involvement Christian Ministers award Edward H. Phillips Elem. Sch., 1981, Human Relations award Met. Area Com., 1981. Mem. First Dist. Missionary Bapt. Assn. (statistician, mem. exec. bd. 1984—), Interdenominational Ministerial Alliance (treas., chmn. polit. affairs 1980—), La. State Bapt. Conv. (instr., bd, dirs. 1980), Nat. Bapt. Conv. (bd. dirs., past chmn. Bapt. Tng. Union), New Orleans Fedn. Chs. Democrat. Avocations: hunting; little league baseball, ranching. Home: 4241 Jumonville St New Orleans LA 70122 Office: Asia Bapt Ch 1400 Sere St New Orleans LA 70122

BRIGGS, GLENN ALLISON, minister, Conservative Bapt. Assn. Am.; b. Shelby, Ohio, Mar. 19, 1930; s. Earl H. and Rilla M. (Roberts) B.; B.A., Trinity Coll., 1957; M.Ed., Westfield State Tchrs. Coll., 1967; m. Ruth May Davis, Jan. 17, 1953; children—Linda, Timothy, Sandra, Charles, William, Cheri, Laurie, Peter. Ordained to ministry, 1952; minister youth, asso. pastor First Bapt. Ch., Shelby, 1952-53; pastor United Ch., Chesterfield, Ill., 1953-57; Christian edn. dir. Bowmanville Bapt. Ch., Chgo., 1961-63; pastor East Chatham (N.Y.) United Meth. Ch., 1965-75; youth program dir. New Eng. Keswick Youth Camp, Adult Conf. and Retreat Center, Monterey, Mass., 1953-65, gen. dir., 1965—. Tchr. pub. schs., 1957—. Mem. Christian Camping Internat., NEA, Mass. Tchrs. Assn. Ednl. curriculum writer, local sch. dist. Home: Chestnut Hill Rd Monterey MA 01245 Office: PO Box 156 Monterey MA 02145

BRIGGS, MARK LELAND, minister, United Pentecostal Church; b. Alexandria, La., Dec. 11, 1959; s. Leland Paul and Bernell Lavela (Roberts) B.; m. Laquita Ann Lott, June 15, 1979; 1 child, Mark Leland. Student, Tex. Bible Coll., 1979; B.Theology, Internat. Bible Inst., 1985. Ordained to ministry, United Pentecostal Ch. Internat., 1979. Mem. youth com. United Pentecostal Ch., Tioga, La., 1980-82; evangelist, United Pentecostal Ch., Tioga, 1979—; pastor United Pentecostal Ch., Mansfield, La., 1984—; del. Internat. Youth Core, Athens, Greece, 1983; "Rally Time" evangelist Crusaders Youth Camp, Tioga, 1984. Named Staff Mem. of Yr., Jr. Crusaders Youth Camp, 1984. Democrat. Home: PO Box 1593 Mansfield LA 71052 Office: First United Pentecostal Ch 1202 Jenkins St Mansfield LA 71052

BRIGHT, JOHN CALVIN, minister, Church of Brethren; b. Liao Chow, Shansi, People's Republic China, Sept. 19, 1915; s. Jacob Homer and Minnie Minerva (Flory) B. (parents Am. citizens); B.S., Berea Coll., 1943; M.A., Bethany Theol. Sem., 1947; m. Harriett Louise Howard, May 26, 1945. Ordained to ministry, 1943. Pastor, Peoria, Ill., 1945-47; missionary to China, West China Union U., Chengtu, Szechwan, 1947-51; exec. sec. West China Border Research Soc., 1948-51; dist. exec. sec. So. Ind., and pastor in Richmond, Ind., 1952-62; pastor, Decatur, Ill., 1962-66, East Dayton Ch. of Brethren, Ohio, 1966—. Mem. Gen. Brotherhood Bd., 1957-61; mem. standing com., 1954, 56, 63-64; denom. rep. Nat. Council Chs., 1959-61; tchr. West China Union Theol. Sem., also dir. West China Union U. Mus. Art, Archaeology, Ethnology and Anthropology, 1948-50. Mem. bd. Boy Scouts Am., Peoria, 1945-47, Family Service, Richmond, 1954-59; bd. dirs., life mem. Eastern Area Council, 1967-73; mem. Parole Bd., Decatur, 1963-64; bd. dirs. Sun Rise Center, 1974—; mem. Human Service Bd. Montgomery County, 1978—; mem. sch. com., Dayton, 1981-83. Mem. Brethren Ministers Assn., Dayton Ministers Assn. Author: Missionary Letters of Minnie Flory Bright, 1973; contbr. articles to religious jours. Home: 528 Gondert Ave Dayton OH 45403 Office: 3520 E 3d St Dayton OH 45403

BRINKLEY, THOMAS ELSTON, church musician, Southern Baptist Convention; b. Memphis, June 17, 1933; s. Albert Madison and Rosalie (Dean) B.; Mus.B., Union U., Jackson, Tenn., 1957; M.Ch. Music, Southwestern Bapt. Theol. Sem., 1960. Ordained to ministry, 1974; organist Bapt. chs. in Memphis, 1951-57, Dallas, 1958, Ft. Worth, 1958-60; organist, music assoc. First Bapt. Ch., Midland, Tex., 1960-67, First Bapt. Ch., Wichita Falls, Tex., 1967-70, 76—, First Bapt. Ch., Dallas, 1970-76; trustee So. Bapt. Radio and TV Commn. Recipient Service award Union U., 1971. Mem. Am. Guild Organists, Am. Guild English Handbell Ringers, Alpha Tau Omega. Composer. Home: 2009 Heather Ln Wichita Falls TX 76308 Office: 1200 9th St Wichita Falls TX 76301

BRINSON, ROBERT RANDOLPH, lay church worker, Southern Methodist Church; physician. B. Miami, Fla., July 11, 1957; s. Robert Jefferson and Corinne (Butler) B.; m. Pamela Rayette Bennett, Apr. 4, 1981; 1 child, Christopher Bennett. B.S., Valdosta State Coll., 1978; M.D., Med. Coll. Ga., 1981. Ordained to ministry, Methodist Ch., 1979; diplomate Nat. Bd. Med. Examiners. Supply pastor Tifton So. Meth. Ch., Ga., 1974-75, Live Oak So. Meth. Ch., Fla., 1978; youth pastor Augusta First So. Meth. Ch., Ga., 1978-81. Resident physician U. Fla. Affiliated Hosps., Jacksonville, 1982-84; practice medicine specializing in internal medicine, Jacksonville, 1984—. Served to 1st lt. USAF. Mem. ACP, Christian Med. Soc. Republican. Home: 11756 Tyndel Creek Dr Jacksonville FL 32217

BRISBIN, LAWRENCE E. Presiding bishop, Pentacostal Assemblies of the World Inc. Office: 3841 Wedgewood Dr SW Grand Rapids MI 49509*

BRISBY, OCIE LEE, minister, Southern Baptist Convention; hospital administrator; b. Dallas, Nov. 25, 1944; s. Fred and Ruby (Sanders) B.; m. Linda Dolores Jordan, Dec. 21, 1968; 1 child, Kevin Darrell. B.S. in Journalism, North Tex. State U., 1973. Ordained to ministry Bapt. Ch., 1983. Instr. St. John Bapt. Ch., Dallas, 1972-81, minister, 1975-83; minister, tchr. Cornerstone Bapt. Ch., Dallas, 1981-83; pastor Found. Bapt. Ch., Dallas, 1984—; del. Bapt. Gen. Conv., Dallas, 1982—. Med. adminstr. VA Hosp., Dallas, 1984—. Editor Ch. newspaper Revelations of St. John, 1980. Campaign mgr. Charles Rose for state rep., Dallas, 1978-82. Served with USAF, 1970. Recipient Community Service award Black Knights Youth Found. 1974, Youth Sports Cert. Bishop Coll., 1980, Vol. Service award Tex. Dept. Human Resources, 1983. Mem. Dallas Pastors Assn. (bd. dirs. 1982—), Dallas Bapt. Assn. (del. 1982—). Democrat. Avocations: recording and sound systems. Home: 3411 Frosty Trail Dallas TX 75241

BRISCO, OSCAR HIAWATHA, minister, Baptist Missionary Association of America; educator; b. Bryans Mill, Tex., Dec. 20, 1938; s. Vannie and Alma (Warren) B.; m. Vera Mae Hall, July 4, 1982; children by previous marriage: Mitchell W., Michael L., Gabriel L., Timothy R., Deborah D.; stepchildren: Kimberly Walker, Jessie J. Hall. B.A., Bishop Coll., 1957; M.A., Prairie View Coll., 1976. Ordained to ministry, Bapt. Ch., 1964. Pastor Paradise Bapt. Ch., Dallas, 1971—; vice moderator Dist. Assn. Dallas, 1972—; rep. Nat. Bapt. Youth of Am., 1981—; coordinator Gen. Bapt. Youth, State of Tex., 1980—; advisor Dallas Citywide Jr. Miss, 1981—; founder, dir. Dallas Citywide Youth, 1973—; vice moderator Trufellowship Dist., Dallas, 1972—; dep. head Gen. Bapt. Youth, State Tex., 1980—. Tchr. Dallas Ind. Sch. Dist., 1971. Author: (pamphlets) What the Church Is, 1975; Scriptures for Hospitals, 1976. Coordinator voter registration, Dallas, 1971-81, Community Crime Watch, Dallas, 1983. Mem. Fed. Employee Assn. Dallas, Internat. Airline Assn. Dallas. Democrat. Office: Paradise Bapt Ch PO Box 24338 Dallas TX 75224

BRIX, JAMES ALAN, minister, American Baptist Churches in the U.S.A.; b. Summit, N.J., Aug. 15, 1948; s. George Christian and Hazel May (Bowers) B.; m. Carol Lynn Tmpleton, June 26, 1971; children: Michael James, Elizabeth Lynn, Patricia Anne. B.A., Barrington Coll., 1970; M.Div., Trinity Evangelical Div. Sch., 1974; D.Ministry, Eastern Bapt. Theol. Sem., Phila., 1983. Ordained to ministry Bapt. Ch., 1974. Minister of youth First Bapt. Ch., Oak Park, Ill., 1971-74; pastor First Bapt. Ch., Greenfield, Ill., 1974-78, First Bapt. Ch. Grantwood, Cliffside Park, N.J., 1978-84, First Bapt. Ch., Freehold, N.J., 1984—; gen. chmn. Greenfield Area Crusade Exec. Com., 1976-77; counselor Clergy Cons., Flanders, N.J., 1981-84. Contbr. articles to profl. jours. Active March for Life, Washington, 1983, 85. Eljabar Found. scholar, 1966-70. Mem. Am. Bapt. Chs.

N.J. (mem. adminstrv. council 1980-83), Bergen County Right to Life, Policemen's Benevolent Assn. (chaplain 1979-84), Am. Assn. Marital and Family Therapy (assoc.), Ministers Council Am. Bapt. Chs., Profl. Soc. Drs. of Ministry, Avocations; racquetball; theater, science fiction fantasy literature reading. Home: 79 W Main St Freehold NJ 07728 Office: 1st Bapt Ch 81 W Main St Freehold NJ 07728

BROCK, RAYMOND THEODORE, counselor; b. Skiatook, Okla., Feb. 20, 1927; s. Clarence Columbus and Hazel Mae (Boyer) B.; diploma Central Bible Coll., 1946; B.A., Phillips U., 1949, B.S., 1950; M.A., U. Tulsa, 1953, Ed.D., 1972; m. Lynita Corinne Kennemer, Sept. 2, 1949; children: Cynthia Lynne, Andrea Joan, Robert Clarence. Ordained to ministry Assemblies of God, 1950; asst. prof. Great Lakes Bible Inst., Zion, Ill., 1949-51; assoc. pastor West Tulsa Assembly of God, 1951-52; prin. Nigeria Central Bible Inst., Nigeria, West Africa, 1953-55; asst. prof. Southwestern Assemblies of God Coll., Waxahachie, Tex., 1956-59, Central Bible Coll., Springfield, Mo., 1960-63; assoc. pastor First Assembly, Glendora, Calif., 1964-65, Oak Cliff Assembly of God, Dallas, 1965-66; assoc. prof. Evangel Coll., Springfield, 1966-75, prof., 1975—; counselor Christian Counseling and Guidance Services, Denver, 1976-77, also minister counseling First Assembly of God, Aurora, Colo., 1976-77; dir. Christian Family Counseling Services, 1980—. Bd. dirs. Royale Convalescent Hosp., Santa Ana, Calif., 1965-74, Park Central Hosp., Springfield, 1973-76, PEACE Counseling Services, 1975-76. Mem. Am. Assn. Counseling and Devel., Christian Assn. Psychol. Studies, Nat. Vocat. Guidance Assn., Am., Mo. psychol. assns., Am. Assn. Marriage and Family Therapy. Author: Into the Highways and Hedges, 1961; Let's Go!, 1962; Billy Wasn't There, 1976; Dating and Waiting for Marriage, 1982; The Emotions of a Man, 1983. Editor Fgn. Missions Pubs. Assemblies of God, 1959-63. Columnist Christ's Ambassador's Herald, 1961-70. Home: 1128 W Arlington Dr Springfield MO 65803 Office: 1111 N Glenstone Springfield MO 65802

BROM, ROBERT H., bishop, Roman Catholic Church. Bishop of Duluth, Minn., 1983—. Office: 215 W 4th St Duluth MN 55806*

BRONFMAN, EDGAR MILES See *Who's Who in America*, 43rd edition.

BRONKEMA, FREDERICK HOLLANDER, minister, church official, Presbyterian Church (U.S.A.) and Christian Church (Disciples of Christ); b. Albany, N.Y., Feb. 1, 1934; s. Frederick and Sadie (Hollander) B.; m. Marguerite Cobble, June 5, 1959; children; Frederick David, Timothy Dunning, John Hollander, Robert Kelton. B.A. magna cum laude, Whitworth Coll., 1956; M.Div., Princeton Theol. Sem., 1959, Th.M., 1965; postgrad. New Coll., U. Edinburgh, Scotland, 1959-60, Union Theol. Sem., 1971-72, Ctr. for Intercultural Documentation, Cuernavaca, Mexico, 1972. Ordained to ministry United Presbyn. Ch., 1960. Asst. minister Craigsbank Ch. of Scotland, Edinburgh, 1959-60; minister Atlantic Highlands Presbyn. Ch., N.J., 1960-63; assoc. minister Red Clay Creek Presbyn. Ch., Wilmington, Del., 1963-65; fraternal worker United Presbyn. Ch., Lisbon and Figueira de Foz, Portugal, 1965-72; prof. Evangelical Theol. Sem., Carcavelos, Portugal, 1967-70; dir. Reconciliation Ecumenical Ctr., Figueira da Foz, 1966-71; missionary Christian Ch. (Disciples of Christ) and Commn., assoc./fraternal worker United Presbyn. Ch., Rome, 1972-77; dir., mng. editor The Future of the Missionary Enterprise, documentation/publs. project Internat. Documentation and Communication Ctr., Rome, 1972-76, assoc. gen. sec., 1974-76; U.S.A. rep. Ecumenical Devel. Coop. Soc., N.Y.C., 1977—; pres. Ecumenical Group of Portugal, 1967-69; cons. Commn. on World Mission and Evangelism, World Council of Chs., 1973-75, advisor central com. meeting, Geneva, 1984; advisor 7th Assembly of Luth. World Fedn., Budapest, Hungary, 1984. Contbr. articles on ecumenism, theology, mission, corp. responsibility, investment, and Latin Am. to ch. jours. Mem. Ecumenical Assn. of Acads./Laity Ctrs. in Europe, 1969—. Democrat. Home: 22 N Portland Ave Ventnor NJ 08406 Office: Ecumenical Devel Coop Soc 475 Riverside Dr Room 1003 New York NY 10115

BRONSTEIN, HERBERT, rabbi, educator, Jewish Congregation; b. Cin., Mar. 1, 1930; s. Morris and Lillian (Weisberg) B.; B.A. with high honors, History, U. Cin., 1952, M.A. with honors in History, 1953; B. Hebrew Letters with honors, Hebrew Union Coll., 1954, M. Hebrew Letters with high honors, 1956; m. Tamar Blumenfield, June 12, 1954; children—Deborah Ruth, Miriam, Daniel Mosheh. Ordained rabbi, 1957; rabbi B'rith Kodesh, Rochester, N.Y., 1957-72; sr. rabbi North Shore Congregation Israel, Glencoe, Ill., 1972—; lectr. on religion and lit.; prof. history and philosophy of religion U. Rochester, 1962-72; now teaching U. Ill. Circle Campus, Chgo., 1975—. Mem. liturgy com. Central Conf. Am. Rabbis, 1962—; editor Haggadah, 1972, nat. chmn. Joint Commn. on Worship, 1973—. Mem. Rochester Police Adv. Bd., 1965-70; mem. Joint Met. Housing Com. of Rochester, 1966-71; bd. dirs. Rochester Jobs, Inc., founder, 1968; founder, chmn. Rochester Inst. Pastoral Counseling, 1960-70; mem. exec. com. Nat. Jewish Community Relations Adv. Council. Recipient Faculty award Hebrew Union Coll., 1951. Contbr. articles to religious publs. Home: 595 Sheridan Rd Glencoe IL 60022 Office: North Shore Congregation Israel 1185 Sheridan Rd Glencoe IL 60022

BROOKINS, HAMEL HARTFORD See *Who's Who in America*, 43rd edition.

BROOKS, ALEXANDER DOBBIN, minister, administrator, Bethany Fellowship, Inc.; b. Dumbarton, Scotland, June 10, 1940; came to U.S., 1960; s. Thomas Gillespie and Mary (Bovil) B.; m. Joanie Carol Hegre, Oct. 11, 1963; children: David Scott, Diane Carol. Diploma, Bethany Fellowship Missionary Tng. Ctr., Mpls., 1963. Ordained to ministry Bethany Missionary Ch., 1974. Tchr. Bethany Fellowship Missionary Tng. Ctr., Mpls., 1970, dean of men, 1972-80; pastor Bethany Missionary Ch., Mpls., 1974—; prin. Bethany Acad., Mpls., 1975-81; editor-in-chief Bethany House Pubs., Mpls., 1966-80; pres. Bethany Fellowship, Inc., Mpls., 1980—, Bethany Corp., Mpls., 1980—; internat. dir. Bethany Fellowship Missions, Mpls., 1983—; bd. dirs. Greater Mpls. Assn. Evangs., 1983-85, Faith Ventures, Clarkesville, Ga., 1983—. Contbg. author Message of the Cross mag., 1975—, editor, 1982—. Home and Office: Bethany Fellowship 6820 Auto Club Rd Minneapolis MN 55438

BROOKS, CLARENCE MARTIN, minister, religious educator, marriage and family therapist, Southern Baptist Convention; b. Gastonia, N.C., Aug. 8, 1935; s. Clarence Edward and Mary Odessa (Merrill) B.; m. Anna Beth Reeves, Dec. 27, 1964; children: Bethani Anne, Darissa Lynn. B.A., Carson-Newman Coll., 1960; M.Div., Southwestern Bapt. Theol. Sem., 1965, M.R.E., 1975, Ed.D., 1978. Ordained to ministry, So. Baptist Conv., 1962. Pastor Shiloh Bapt. Ch., Bartonville, Tex., 1962-63, Lois Bapt. Ch., Tex., 1965, Kirkwood Bapt. Ch., Bozeman, Mont., 1965-67; commd. 2d lt. U.S. Army, 1967, advanced through grades to maj. 1974, served as chaplain; mem. faculty Cumberland Coll., Williamsburg, Ky., 1978—; deacon First Bapt. Ch., Williamsburg, 1982—; pastoral counselor Ky. Bapt. Conv., Middletown, Ky., 1984—; dir. family ministries Gambrell St. Baptist Ch., Ft. Worth, 1975-77. Author 6 video programs on marriage and family, 1983. Pres., life mem. Williamsburg PTA, 1979; coordinator pres. War On Drugs, Williamsburg, 1983. Decorated Nat. Def. Service medal, Air medal, Vietnam Cross of Gallantry, Meritorious Service medal, Vietnam Commendation medal. Mem. Am. Assn. Marriage and Family Therapists, So. Bapt. Assn. of Family Ministers, Res. Officers Assn., Men of the Century. Democrat. Lodge: Rotary (v.p. Williamsburg chpt. 1980-81, sec. 1981-82). Home: Box 990 CC Station Williamsburg KY 40769 Office: Cumberland Coll Box 990 CC Station Williamsburg KY 40769

BROOKS, CLAUDE OTIS, minister, Southern Baptist Convention; b. Grayson, Ga., Mar. 2, 1923; s. Clinton D. and Mayfus (Wood) B.; m. Olive Hansen, Aug. 30, 1947; children: Leigh Brooks Collier, Mark, Clint. B.A., Emory U., 1947; B.D., So. Bapt. Theol. Sem., 1950, Th.M., 1951. Ordained to ministry So. Bapt. Conv., 1948. Minister, Belleview Bapt. Ch., Grant, Ky., 1949-51, First Bapt. Ch., Eatonton, Ga., 1951-56, Swainsboro, Ga., 1956-61, Florence, Ala., 1961-68, Parkview Bapt. Ch., Monroe, La., 1968-69, Vestavia Hills Bapt. Ch., Birmingham, Ala., 1969—; mem. state exec. com., state adminstrv. com., state calendar com., chmn. budget com. Ga. Bapt. Conv.; mem. exec. bd., past chmn. bd. aid Ala. Bapt. Conv., also mem. adminstrv. com.; sec. bd. trustees Bapt. Med. Ctrs. Contbr. articles to profl. jours. Served with U.S. Army, 1943-46. Avocations: gardening, furniture refinishing. Home: 2110 Montreat Pkwy Birmingham AL 35216 Office: Vestavia Hills Bapt Ch 2600 Vestavia Dr Birmingham AL 35216

BROOKS, DAVID EARL, minister, television broadcaster, Assemblies of God; b. Olton, Tex., Mar. 21, 1950; s. Thomas Earl and Imaleta (Williamson) B.; m. Linda Jean Lewis, July 19, 1969; children: Quint Allen, Chadwick Aaron. Student Central Bible Coll., 1968-69, E. Central U., 1969-70; B.Th., Internat. Bible Inst. and Sem., 1982; grad. Fifth U.S. Army Grad. Sch., 1971. Ordained to ministry Assemblies of God Ch., 1981. Youth minister Putnam City Assembly of God, Bethany, Okla., 1976-77; youth, assoc. minister Cloverdale Assembly of God Ch., Little Rock, 1977-78; sr. pastor First Assembly of God Ch., DeQueen, Ark., 1978—; chmn. bd., broadcaster Communication Dynamics, Sta. KOBKF-TV, DeQueen, 1983—; pres. DeQueen Ministerial Alliance, 1980-81; mem. bd. Community Broadcasters Assn., Washington, 1984—. Served with USNG, 1969-75. Avocations: vocalist; fishing; woodworking. Home: 116 W Northgate DeQueen AR 71832 Office: Hwy 70-W PO Box 146 DeQueen AR 71832

BROOKS, DORIS AGNES, educator, Seventh-day Adventist Ch.; b. Bklyn., Mar. 6, 1920; d. Kenneth Paul and Minnie Sunbeam (Barton) Stearns; student Walla Walla Coll., 1938-39, 46-49, 57, 69, Portland (Ore.) State U., 1965-69, Clackamas Community Coll., 1968; B.S., Lewis and Clark Coll., 1970, M.A.T., 1973; m. Chester Willard Brooks, May 18, 1940; children—William Chester, Robert Allen. Tchr. Seventh-day Adventist Schs., 1956—; teaching prin. Rivergate Elementary Sch., Gladstone, Oreg., 1956-69; tchr. Portland Elementary Adventist Sch., 1970—; dir. Vacation Bible Sch., 1956-57, leader Jr. Sabbath Sch. Div., 1958-59, craft leader, 1963-64; leader primary Sabbath Sch. Lents Seventh-day Adventist Ch., Gladstone Seventh-day Adventist Ch., 1960-61, Cradle Roll, 1954, Kindergarten Sabbath Sch., 1955, tchr. Youth Adult Sabbath Sch., class, 1961-62, deaconness, 1968-69, supt. Sabbath Sch., 1964-65; mem. curriculum com. Seventh-day Adventist Schs. Ore., 1969, reading com. N. Pacific Union, 1974; mem. greater Portland Adv. Bd., Seventh-day Adventists Schs. Oreg., 1969-71; mem. lay adv. com. Oreg. Conf. Seventh-day Adventists, 1982—. Mem. Assn. Seventh-day Adventist Educators (charter), Quesitor. Home: 12505 SE Crest Dr Portland OR 97236 Office: 3990 NW 1st St Gresham OR 97030

BROOKS, GEORGE ANDREW, lay church worker, Roman Catholic Church; b. N.Y.C., May 11, 1900; s. George H. and Mary Winifred Agnes (O'Hara) B.; A.B., Fordham U., 1924, J.D. cum laude, 1927, LL.D., 1952; LL.M., NY U, 1951; LL.D., Scranton U., 1953. Tchr. Roman Catholic schs., 1924-34; lector Our Lady of Fatima Ch., Scarsdale, N.Y. Admitted to N.Y. State bar., 1928; practiced in N.Y.C. and Tuckahoe, 1928-34; with Gen. Motors Corp., 1934-65, in charge legal staff, 1941-65, corp. sec., 1947-65; lectr., adj. asst. prof. law Fordham U., 1965-70, adj. assoc. prof., 1970-72, adj. prof., 1972—. Trustee, Lavelle Sch. for Blind, N.Y. Archdiocese, 1956—, v.p., 1971-78, pres., 1978-80; bd. dirs. Legal Aid Soc. Westchester County 1964-75, sec., 1965-72, pres., 1972-74; bd. dirs. Westchester Legal Services, Inc., 1967-85; trustee emeritus Fordham U., mem. nat. adv. bd. Fordham Alumni Fedn.; trustee St. Agnes Hosp., White Plains, N.Y.; bd. dirs. Rosehill Housing Devel. Fund Corp. Recipient Alumni Achievement award Fordham U., 1959, Encaenia award Fordham Coll., 1959; Bene Merenti medal Fordham U., 1979, award Fordham Law Sch., 1984; decorated Knight of Malta. Fellow N.Y. Bar Found.; mem. Am., Fed. bar. assns., Assn. Bar City N.Y., N.Y. County Lawyers Assn. (dir. 1965-71), N.Y. State Bar Assn. (ho. of dels. 1972-77), Westchester County Bar Assn., Guild Cath. Lawyers (past dir.), U.S. Cath. Hist. Assn. (bd. dirs. 1958-84, pres. 1966-68), Newman Assn. (Eng.), Religious Edn. Assn., Am. Soc. Ch. History, Fordham Law Alumni Assn. (medal of achievement 1968). Home: Eton Hall 127 Garth Rd Scarsdale NY 10583 Office: 140 W 62d St New York NY 10023

BROOKS, LEO CALVIN, minister, Nat. Baptist Conv., U.S.A., Inc.; b. New Orleans, May 26, 1915; s. Frank Henry and Dorothy Elenora (Harden) B.; B.Th., Union Bapt. Sem., 1955, Th.M., 1957, D.D. (hon.), 1972; m. Thelma Corinne Parker, Dec. 17, 1938; 1 dau., Alma Elenora Brooks Lyle. Ordained to ministry, 1949; pastor Amozion Bapt. Ch., New Orleans, 1949—. Treas. First Dist. Bapt. Assn., New Orleans, 1960—, chmn. fin. com., 1960—; treas. Bapt. Faith Nursing Home, New Orleans; mem. faculty Christian edn. dept. Union Bapt. Sem. Mem. Nat., La. Bapt. convs. Home: 4017 Pauger St New Orleans LA 70122 Office: 907 Deslonde St New Orleans LA 70117

BROOKS, PORTER HARRISON, priest, Episcopal Ch.; b. Chgo., July 5, 1926; s. Hugh Moore and Lucy Elizabeth (Brooks) Woods; B.A., McMurry Coll., 1948; M.Div., Va. Theol. Sem., 1951; m. Norma Margaret Singer, Aug. 21, 1954; children—Beverly Agnes, Roland Ignatius, Gloria Lucy. Ordained priest, 1951; chaplain U.S. Army, 1951-53; rector St. Matthew's Episc. Ch., Pampa, Tex., 1953-55; chaplain U.S. Army, Tex., Japan, Kans., Germany, Va., N.Y., Vietnam, 1955-70; post chaplain, Fort Myer, Va., 1971-74; community chaplain Hdqrs. U.S. Army Europe, 1974-75, Heidelberg, Germany, 1976—. Chmn. Gray County, Tex. Cancer Soc., 1953-54. Home: 16 San Jacinto Dr Patrick Henry Village Heidelberg Germany Office: Office of Chaplain Hdqrs US Army Military Community Heidelberg APO NY 09102

BROOKS, ROBERT JOHNSON, priest, Episcopal Church; b. Austin, Tex., Mar. 25, 1947; s. Robert Max and Marietta (Moody) B.; B.A. in History cum laude, St. Edwards U., 1970; M.Div., Ch. Div. Sch. of Pacific, 1973; M.A., U. Notre Dame, 1980; postgrad. Cath. U. Am., 1984—. Ordained to ministry Episcopal Ch., 1973; vicar All Saints Ch., Baytown, Tex., 1973—; mem. Council of Associated Parishes for Liturgy and Mission, 1982—; mem. Societas Liturgica, 1983—; assoc. mem. N. Am. Acad. Liturgy, 1981—; mem. Internat. Consultation Anglican Liturgists, 1984—; cons. Standing Liturgical Commn. of Episc. Ch., 1978-80; lectr. liturgics U. St. Thomas, 1981-82; mem. Diocese of Tex. Liturgical Commn., 1977-83; guest lectr. Episc. and Roman Cath. seminaries; conf. leader U.S. and abroad; Commissary of Bishop of Namibia to the Am. Ch., 1974—. Author numerous articles and book revs. Commr., State of Tex. Health Coordinating Council, 1985—; bd. dirs. People for Am. Way, 1985—; mem. Democratic Bus. Council, 1984—; del. Dem. Nat. Conv., 1980; bd. dirs. Houston Grand Opera, 1980-84.

BROOKS, SHADRACH RICHARD, minister, Southern Baptist Convention; b. Jena, La., July 26, 1922; s. Leonidas Hill and Lilly Eloise (Randall) B.; m. Bessie Marie Little, Sept. 9, 1943; children: Ann, Eloise, Richard, Pamela, Patricia. B.A., La. Coll., 1943; Th.M., So. Western Bapt. Theol. Sem., 1946. Ordained to ministry, 1939. Pastor, Searcy Bapt. Ch., La., 1939-43, Ouachita Bapt. Ch., Enterprise, La., 1943-45, Pisgah Bapt. Ch., Manifest, La., 1943-45, First Bapt. Ch., Carrollton, Tex., 1945-46, Merryville, La., 1948-56; pastor Parkerson Ave. Bapt. Ch., Crowley, La., 1956—; moderator Acadia Bapt. Assn., La.; pres. Ministerial Assn. Crowley, La.; mem. com. on com. La. Bapt. Conv., 1980-83. Active Salvation Army, Right to Life, Bi-Racial Com. and Hospital Ministry, Crowley, La. Mem. Ministerial Assn. Crowley. Home: 1106 N Parkerson Ave Crowley LA 70526 Office: Parkerson Ave Bapt Ch 1116 N Parkerson Ave Crowley LA 70526

BROOKSHIER, DUANE ANDREW, minister, United Pentecostal Church International; project engineer. b. Clovis, N.Mex., July 30, 1946; s. David Andrew and Doris Anna (Durham) B.; m. Carol Elaine Bloom, Jan. 1, 1965; children: John Duane, David Charles, Jim Paul. Student Internat. Corr. Schs., 1969; grad. in electronics Utah State U., 1974; student Ind. Bible Coll., 1984—. Ordained to ministry Pentecostal Ch., 1982. Asst. pastor United Pentecostal Ch., Elmo, Utah, 1965-68, assoc. pastor, Logan, Utah, 1969-74; asst. pastor Apostolic Bible Ch., Mesa, Ariz., 1974-82; pastor Truth Tabernacle, Hemet, Calif., 1982—, trustee, 1982-84; sec.-treas. sect. 2 western dist. United Pentecostal Ch. Internat., So. Calif., 1983—. Project engr., sales adminstr. Rama Corp., San Jacinto, Calif., 1982—. Home: 26158 Hemet St Hemet CA 92344 Office: Truth Tabernacle United Pentecostal Ch 25637 1st St Hemet CA 92344

BROOME, RONALD ALLEN, religious educator, elder, Seventh-day Adventist; b. Chicago Heights, Ill., Nov. 12, 1942; s. Earl Robert and Lila Elizabeth (Martin) B.; m. Linda Patricia Karr, June 14, 1968; children: Robert Allen, Julie Lynn Elizabeth. B.S., Andrews U., 1965, postgrad., 1969, Rollins U., 1976, U. Central Fla., 1984. Cert. elem. tchr., Fla. Elder, Altamonte Springs Seventh-day Ch. (Fla.), 1977—, jr. early teen Sabbath Sch. dir., 1981—, state workshop dir., 1984—; chmn. sch. bd. South Suburban Seventh-day Adventist Sch., Chicago Heights, 1970-76. Tchr. fifth grade Forest Lake Elem. Edn. Ctr., Longwood, Fla., 1977—, computer program developer, 1984; tchr. sci. and math. Ft. Myers, Fla., 1977; dir. Natural Cheese Co., Altamonte Springs, 1982—. Contbg. author pamphlets. Active Young Republicans, Orlando, Fla., 1982. Recipient Scholarship award Kiwanis, 1965; Service award Fla. Conf. Seventh-day Adventists, 1982. Club: Pathfinder (master guide 1982-84) (Orlando). Home: 104 Dogwood St Altamonte Springs FL 32714

BROUWER, ARIE RAYMOND, minister, Reformed Church in America; b. Inwood, Iowa, July 14, 1935; s. Arie and Gertie (Brands) B.; A.A., Northwestern Coll., Orange City, Iowa, 1954; B.A., Hope Coll., 1956; B.D., Western Theol. Sem., Holland, Mich., 1959; m. Harriet Korver, Aug. 16, 1955; children—Milton, Charla, Steven, Patricia. Ordained to ministry, 1959; pastor chs., Mich., 1959-63, N.J., 1963-68; sec. for program Ref. Ch. in Am., N.Y.C. 1968-70, exec. sec., 1970—; gen. sec. Nat. Council Chs., 1984—. First chmn. Bd. Theol. Edn., Reformed Ch., 1967-68; v.p. Bd. World Missions, 1967-68; mem. Theol. Commn., 1967-68; mem. gen. bd. Nat. Council Chs., 1969-72, gov. bd., 1973-83; bd. dirs. Bread for the World, 1975-82. Contbg. editor The Church Herald, 1967-68. Office: 475 Riverside Dr New York NY 10027

BROWN, BRUCE RITCHIE, minister, Conservative Congregational Christian Conference; b. Yonkers, N.Y., Apr. 27, 1936; s. Hugh Ritchie and Helen Louise (Bullock) B.; m. Shirley Ann Storie, June 9, 1962; children: Mark, Rebekah, Elisabeth, Kent. A.B., Temple U., 1958; postgrad. Westminster Theol. Sem., 1957-61; B.D., Gordon Div. Sch., 1962, M.Div., 1974. Ordained to ministry Congl. Ch., 1963. Asst. pastor First Confg. Ch., N. Collins, N.Y., 1962-63, pastor, 1963-76; pastor San Dieguito Bible Ch., Encinitas, Calif., 1976-81, Marion Community Ch., Mich., 1981-84, First Congl. Ch., Middleboro, Mass., 1984—. Dir. Peniel High Sch. Camp, Luzerne, N.Y., 1963-76, 79; chmn. Inter-Varsity Local Com., Buffalo, 1973-76; 2d v.p. Conservative Congl. Christian Conf., 1975-78, 1st v.p., 1978-81, pres., 1981-84; mem. teaching mission to Micronesia, Marshalls, Ponape, Kosrae, Truk, 1984, 85. Mem. So. Erie County Community Migrant Com., N. Collins, 1960's; mem. Village Planning Commn., N. Collins, 1964-74; pres. Eden-N. Collins Rotary, 1972-80. Mem. Buffalo Evang. Ministers Fellowship (pres. 1969-70), San Dieguito Ministers Assn. (pres. 1977-78). Republican. Club: Community Men's (Marion, Mich) (v.p. 1984). Home: 4 Plymptom St Middleboro MA 02346 Office: First Congl Ch 6 Plympton St Middleboro MA 02346

BROWN, DAVID CLIFFORD, minister, United Ch. of Christ; b. Plainwell, Mich., Jan. 12, 1938; s. Maynard Fred and Geraldine Louise (Fish) B.; B.A., Kalamazoo Coll., 1960; B.D., Colgate Rochester Div. Sch., 1964; D.Rel., Chgo. Theol. Sem., 1970; m. Gertrude Wilhelmina DeHoog, Aug. 19, 1961; children—Gordon Clifford, Mason Alan, Stuart Evan. Ordained to ministry United Meth. Ch., 1964; pastor chs. in N.Y., 1961-67; part-time instr. English, Niagara County Community Coll., Niagara Falls, N.Y., 1966; pastor Geneseo United Meth. Ch., dir. Wesley Found., State U. N.Y. at Geneseo, 1967-1969; doctoral student, sr. resident fellow, acting clin. dir. Chgo. Inst. Pastoral Care, 1969-70; asso. minister First United Meth. Ch., Jackson, Mich., 1971; sr. minister Community Ch., East Williston, N.Y., 1971—. Mem. nat. bd. Religion in Am. Life, 1971—; bd. govs. L.I. Council Chs., 1971—; trustee, mem. commn. ecumenical relations Nat. Council Community Chs., 1971—; exec. com. Commn. on Inter-Religious Affairs, Am. Zionist Fedn. Hon. Woodrow Wilson fellow, 1960. Fellow Am. Assn. Pastoral Counselors, Pi Kappa Delta; mem. Acad. Parish Clergy. Contbr. articles, book revs. to profl. publs. Home: 202 Ward St East Williston NY 11596 Office: Community Ch E Williston Ave East Williston NY 11596

BROWN, DOUGLAS LEO, priest Roman Catholic Church; b. Bklyn., Mar. 29, 1937; s. Leo Francis and Sophie Margaret (Wyshnevska) B. A.B., Cathedral Coll., 1959; S.T.B., Cath. U., 1963; S.T.M., N.Y. Theol. Sem., 1968. Ordained priest Roman Cath. Ch., 1963. Assoc. pastor Epiphany Ch, Bklyn., 1963-68; assoc. dir. St. Paul's Ctr., Bklyn., 1968-76; sec. for clergy personnel Roman Cath. Diocese Bklyn., 1976—; dir. Diocesan Lang. Inst., Bklyn., 1976-81; chmn. Personnel Bd. Roman Cath. Ch., Bklyn., 1976—; mem. Priest's Retirement Bd., 1976—, Sem. Admissions Bd., 1977—; cons. Priest Spirituality Adv. Bd., 1978—. Mem. Nat. Assn. Ch. Personnel Adminstrs., Canon Law Soc. Am., Nat. Clergy Council on Alcoholism. Office: Personnel Office Roman Catholic Diocese 75 Greene Ave PO Box C Brooklyn NY 11202

BROWN, EARL KENT, minister, United Methodist Church; b. Kent, Ohio, July 26, 1925; s. Earl Royal and Bernice Blanche (Howard) B.; B.A., Columbia, 1948; S.T.B., Boston U., 1953, Ph.D., 1956. Ordained to ministry, 1957. Teaching fellow, Boston U. Sch. Theology, 1953-56; asst. prof. history Baldwin Wallace Coll., Berea, Ohio, 1956-63; asso. prof. ch. history Boston U., 1963-70, prof. ch. history, 1970—; vis. prof. Western Res. U., Cleve., 1961, Union Theol. Sem., Manila, Philippines, 1970, United Theol. Coll., Bangalore, India, 1978, U. Manchester, Eng., 1979. Howard fellow, 1953-54; Dempster fellow, Meth. Ch., 1954-55; Fulbright fellow, 1962. Mem. Am. Soc. Ch. History, Am. Acad. Religion Am. Hist. Assn., Am. Cath. Hist. Soc., United Meth. Commn. on Archives and History, Phi Beta Kappa. Author: Women of Mr. Wesley's Methodism, 1983. Contbr. articles in field to religious jours. Home: 580 Commonwealth Ave Boston MA 02215 Office: 745 Commonwealth Ave Boston MA 02215

BROWN, ELLIS MOSS, lay ch. worker, United Methodist Ch.; b. Dallas, Jan. 13, 1906; s. Ernest and Nancy Annette (Cochran) B.; B.S. in Mech. Engring., Ga. Sch. Tech., 1930; m. Rose Marie Loupot, June 27, 1936; children—Marie Annette, Louise Kathleen (Mrs. Steven L. Smith). Mem. Cochran Chapel United Methodist Ch., Dallas, 1912—, supt. ch. sch., 1965-68, chmn. council ministries, supt. study, vice chmn. adminstrv. bd., also bd. dirs. child care center, 1968-71, lay leader, chmn. ednl. material study, bd. dirs. child care center, mem. adminstrv. bd., also ex-officio mem. all ch. commns. and coms., 1971-73, trustee, 1973-76, pres., 1975-76, chmn. greeting com. in membership drive, chmn. sound equipment com. for new Fellowship Hall, also mem. numerous coms. and bds. including pastor parish relations com., finance com., council ministries, 1974-76, chmn. adminstrv. bd., 1977—. Instr. Dale Carnegie Leadership courses, 1955-74. Mem. Am. Mgmt. Assn., ASME Sigma Xi.

BROWN, FRANK KARL, minister, Christian Church; b. Boise, Idaho, Dec. 20, 1948; s. Claude Earl and Margaret Elenor (Barnes) B.; m. Laura Marie Kramer, Aug. 8, 1970. B.S. in Pastoral Theology, Western Bapt. Coll., 1975. Youth pastor Valley Bapt. Ch., San Rafael, Calif., 1970-71, Halbert Bapt. Ch., Salem, Oreg., 1971-72; assoc. pastor Valley Bapt. Ch., Dallas, Oreg., 1973-81; pastor Grace Community Ch., Salem, Oreg., 1981—. Home: 2505 E Ellendale St Dallas OR 97338 Office: Grace Community Ch 4515 Salem Dallas Hwy Salem OR 97304

BROWN, HERMAN, fund raising executive, consultant; b. Bklyn., May 16, 1928; s. Sam and Anna (Grushkin) B.; m. Anita Lepzelter, Sept. 29, 1956; children: Lori, Kenneth, Terri. B.A., Bklyn. Coll., 1953; postgrad. CCNY, 1954-55. Regional dir. Am. Jewish Congress, Queens and L.I., N.Y., 1963-68, dir. N.Y. met. council, 1968-72; exec. dir. Jewish Community Council of Met. Boston, 1972-75; dir. New Eng. area Jewish Nat. Fund, 1976—; fund raising cons.; New Eng. dir. Am. Assocs., Ben-Gurion U of Neyov, 1976—; U.S. coordinator Israel Coll. Optometry, 1984—; pres. Cardinal sales trustee Temple Israel, Boston, 1976—. Mem. Comprehensive Health Planning Agy., N.Y.C., 1971; pres. Friends of Needham Pub. Library, Mass., 1975-79. Mem. N.Y. Civil Liberties Union (dir. 1968-71), Bklyn. Coll. Alumni Assn. (co-chmn. New Eng. chpt. 1976—), Phi Beta Kappa, Alpha Kappa Delta. Lodge: B'nai B'rith (chmn. Israel com. Greater Boston Council 1979—). Home and Office: 33 Cynthia Rd Needham MA 02194

BROWN, JAMES ALAN, minister, Churches of Christ; educator; b. Knoxville, Tenn., Dec. 2, 1956; s. Clarence Hubert Jr. and Mary Agnes (Geer) B.; m. Cynthia Dianne Thompson, Jan. 30, 1982; 1 child, Rachel Melissa. A.A. in Bible, Bellview Preacher Tng. Sch., 1982; A.A., Pensacola Jr. Coll., 1982; B.A., U. West Fla., 1984. Ordained to ministry Churches of Christ, 1976. Evangelist Chs. of Christ, 1977-81; evangelist Pace Ch. of Christ, Fla., 1981-84, Briggs Ch. of Christ, Tex., 1984—; cons. editor Landmark Books, 1985—. Tchr. pub. schs., Burnett County, Tex., 1984—. Contbr. articles to Defender & Beacon mag., 1982—. Fire chief Briggs Vol. Fire Dept., 1985—. Served to sgt. USAF, 1975-79. Republican. Avocations: computers, cars, reading, gardening. Home: Loop 308 Briggs TX 78608 Office: Briggs Ch of Christ PO Box 21 Briggs TX 78608

BROWN, JAMES DONNELL, religious educator, minister, Assemblies of God. b. Frisco City, Ala., Oct. 30, 1930; s. Eunice and Omie Dee (Pipkin) B.; m. D'Ann Pellow, Sept. 12, 1953. B.A. in Bibl. studies Central Bible Coll., 1955; M.A. in Speech Communication, U. Minn., 1968, Ph.D., 1977; postgrad. Northwestern U., 1962-63, Garrett Theol. Sem., 1963-64. Ordained to ministry, 1953. Evangelist Assemblies of God, 1955-64; pres. Southeastern Coll. of Assemblies of God, Lakeland, Fla., 1968-70; pastor Westside Assembly of God, West Columbia, S.C., 1973-75, First Assembly of God, Leesburg, Fla., 1975-76, Southside Assembly of God, Jacksonville, Fla., 1976-78, First Assembly of God, Terre Haute, Ind., 1978-79; v.p. acad. affairs Valley Forge Christian Coll., Phoenixville, Pa., 1979-80; exec. v.p. Assemblies of God Theol. Sem., Springfield, Mo., 1983—; mem. Bd. Edn., Assemblies of God, Springfield, Mo., 1968-70, chmn. adv. bd. evangelism, 1960-61, mem. commn. on doctrinal purity, 1978—. Cons. editor: Paraclete, 1965-68. Author: Pentecostal Evangel, 1959, 65, 82. Contbr. articles to profl. jours. Garrett Theol. Sem. scholar, 1964. Mem. Fellowship of Evang. Sem. Pres., Acad. for Evangelism in Theol. Edn. Republican. Lodge: Rotary. Home: 2476 E Meadow Springfield MO 65804 Office: Assemblies of God Theol Sem 1445 Boonville Ave Springfield MO 65802

BROWN, JAMES ROBERT, minister, United Church of Christ; b. Little Rock, Aug. 20, 1947; s. John Hardy and Dorothy (Conn) B.; m. Karen Jean Snyder, June 3, 1972; children: James Eric, Mark Edward. B.A., Northwestern U., 1969; postgrad. U. Mo., 1969-70, U. Ark., 1970-71; Th.M., Perkins Sch. Theology, So. Meth. U., 1974. Ordained to ministry United Meth. Ch., 1976. Assoc. pastor Oak Forest United Meth. Ch., Little Rock, 1974-75, First United Meth. Ch., Camden, Ark., 1975-78; interim pastor Marysville-Silver Hill United Meth. Ch., Marysville, Ark., 1978; pastor St. Peter United Ch. of Christ, Granite City, Ill., 1980-84, assoc. pastor Shiloh Ch., Dayton, Ohio, 1984—; chmn. continuing edn. and leadership devel. Ill. So. Conf., United Ch. of Christ, 1981-84, chmn. music and worship, 1984, mem. peace task force, 1982-84; Ill. So. Conf. rep. to Ill. Conf. of Chs. Consortium on Govtl. Concerns, Springfield, 1981-83; Ill. So. Conf. rep. to United Ch. of Christ Peace Seminar, Fed. Republic Germany, 1982. Advancement chairperson Ouchita Council Boy Scouts Am., 1977-78. Recipient Flinn Sr. Award, Perkins Sch. of Theology, 1974, James Bible award Perkins Sch. of Theology, 1974. Mem. Quad-City Ministerial Alliance (program chmn. 1982-83). Democrat. Lodge: Lions. Home and Office: 4135 Colemere Circle Dayton OH 45415

BROWN, KATHLEEN JANE, teacher educator, Independent Bible Church. b. Chgo., July 3, 1947; d. William Philip Sr. and Dorothy Jane (Kouba) Brown. B.A., Southeastern Bible Coll., 1970; M.Ed., Univ. Montevallo, 1974; postgrad., U. Ala., 1981—. Cert. elem., secondary tchr. Tchr. Alliance Christian Schs., Birmingham, Ala., 1970-76, Plymouth Christian Acad., Plymouth, Mich., 1976-79; assoc. prof. Southeastern Bible Coll., Birmingham, Ala., 1979—. Named to Outstanding Young Women Am., 1983. Mem. Internat. Reading Assn., Ala. Reading Assn., Assn. Tchr. Educators, Phi Delta Kappa, Kappa Delta Pi. Republican. Home: 3924 Fifth Ave S Apt E Birmingham AL 35222 Office: Southeastern Bible Coll 2901 Pawnee Ave Birmingham AL 35256

BROWN, KENNETH IRA, minister, college administrator, General Association of Regular Baptist Churches; b. Sayre, Pa., Sept. 23, 1928; s. Laurence Eugene and Irene Naomi (Carmen) B.; B.S., Mansfield State Coll., 1951; m. Zelda Joyce Luce, June 30, 1951; children: Judy, Alan, Laurence, Mark, Kurt. Th.B., Bapt. Bible Sem., 1956; Th.M., Westminster Theol. Sem., 1959; Th.D., Grace Theol. Sem., 1965. Ordained to ministry General Association of Regular Baptist Churches, 1956. Assoc. faculty Bapt. Bible Sem., Johnson City, N.Y., 1952-58; pastor Stanfordville Bapt. Ch., Hallstead, Pa., 1954-58, Calvary Bapt. Ch., Cadasia, N.Y., 1958-61; prof. Bibl. langs., chmn. N.T.

dept. Bapt. Bible Sem., Johnson City, N.Y., 1962-70; pastor Park Ave. Bapt. Ch., Binghamton, N.Y., 1970-72; dean faculty, chmn. N.T. dept. San Francisco Bapt. Theol. Sem., 1972-76, Detroit Bapt. Div. Sch., Allen Park, Mich., 1976-83. Bible Conf. speaker, 1962—. Home: 255 Owego St Montour Falls NY 14865 Office: Glen Bapt Ch N Glen Ave Box 82A Watkins Glen NY 14865

BROWN, LEE ROY, minister, National Baptist Convention U.S.A.; b. Memphis, June 4, 1949; s. Mitchell Anderson and Emma Lee (Ross) B.; m. Charles Etta Jackson, Feb. 25, 1979; children: Felicha, LeCarl. Student Memphis State U., 1967-69, Mid-South Bible Coll., Memphis, 1969-70; B.A. in Bible Study, Moody Bible Coll., Chgo., 1973-74; postgrad., Trinity Theol. Sem., Newburgh, Ind., 1983—. Ordained to ministry Nat. Bapt. Conv. U.S.A., 1971. Intern minister East Trigg Bapt. Ch., Memphis, 1970-71; assoc. minister Keel Ave. Bapt. Ch., Memphis, 1971-74; asst. to pastor Oak Grove Bapt. Ch., Memphis, 1974-79; sr. pastor Springdale Bapt. Ch., Memphis, 1979—; instr. Greater Memphis Sunday Sch., Bapt. Tng. Union, 1982—; minister's council Operation PUSH, Memphis, 1983—; trustee Memphis Gen. Sch. of Religion, 1984—. Editor: Christian Discipleship Guidebook, 1984. Trustee Sky Lake Land Devel., Memphis, 1984. Mayors' Aide de Camp Memphis Mayor Patterson, 1982, Memphis Mayor Hackett, 1983; recipient Outstanding Religious Leader Memphis Comml. Appeal Newspaper, 1983; scholar L.K. Williams Ministers' Inst., 1973-76, Ruby C. Howe Ministers' Lectures, 1981—. Mem. Nat. Bapt. Congress (committeeman, local gen. sec. 1983), Memphis Bapt. Ministers' Assn. (sec.-treas. 1982-84), Memphis Dist. Assn. (edn. chmn. 1980—). Lodges: Elks, Masons. Home: 2740 Lakecrest Circle South Memphis TN 38127-8438 Office: Springdale Bapt Ch 1193 Springdale St Memphis TN 38108-2232

BROWN, MARIE ELIZABETH, lay ch. worker, Ch. of God; b. Alexander City, Ala., Nov. 3, 1900; d. James Menger and Dessie Ann (Slaughter) Edwards; student Barber Meml. Sem., 1919; m. Sept. 9, 1947; stepchildren—Samuel, Evelyn, Jay, Margurett, Fredrick, Franklin, Moses, Lucy. Asst. to husband in traveling ministry, U.S., Can., Mex., 1952-71; officer local missionary soc., tchr. Contbr. articles to religious publs. Home: 105 N Grimes St San Antonio TX 78202

BROWN, OSCAR PATRICK JOHNSON, minister, Ch. of God in Christ; b. Mobile, Ala., Mar. 9, 1923; s. James and Essie (Felton) J.; m. Anna Pearl Whittaker, June 12, 1953; children—Jeanette, Essie Belinda, Anna Frances, Oscar, Cynthia Jean, Connie Lee. Ordained to ministry, 1964; youth leader, pastor Williams Temple; treas., financer Southeastern and Western Ill. Dist. No. 5. Mem. exec. bd. local P.T.A. Home: 4184 W Belle Pl St Louis MO 63108

BROWN, PAUL EARNEST, minister, So. Baptist Conv.; b. Paragould, Ark., Oct. 19, 1931; s. Henry Silas and Lora Mae (Shettles) B.; B.A., Miss. Coll., 1953; Th.M., New Orleans Bapt. Theol. Sem., 1972; M.A., U. Miss., 1972, Ph.D., 1974; m. Cornelia Smith, June 6, 1956; children—Lynn, Mark, Dan, Beth. Ordained to ministry, 1952; pastor Kilmichael (Miss.) Bapt. Ch., 1956-59, Oakhaven Bapt. Ch., Memphis, 1959-68; admissions counselor Union U., Jackson, Tenn., 1968-70; div. chmn. instr. Clarke Coll., Newton, Miss., 1970-76; v.p., dean acad. affairs Hannibal-LaGrange Coll., Hannibal, Mo., 1976—. Mem. edn. com., exec. bd. Tenn. Bapt. Conv., 1965-68; pres. Memphis Bapt. Pastors Conf., 1963; mem., pres. bd. ministerial edn. Miss. Bapt. Conv., 1970-76; mem. Edn. Commn., So. Bapt. Conv., 1982—. Author: Sermons on Tithing, 1968. Home: 4513 W Ely Rd Hannibal MO 63401

BROWN, RAYMOND EDWARD, educator, priest, Roman Catholic Church; b. N.Y.C., May 22, 1928; s. Robert H. and Loretta Brown. Student St. Charles Coll., 1945-46; B.A., Cath. U. Am., 1948, M.A., 1949; S.T.B., St. Mary's Sem., Balt., 1951, S.T.L., 1953, S.T.D., 1955; Ph.D., Johns Hopkins, 1958; S.S.B., Pontifical Bibl. Commn., Rome 1959, S.S.L., 1963; D.D. (hon.), U. Edinburgh (Scotland), 1972, Glasgow U., 1978; Th.D. (hon.), U. Uppsala (Sweden), 1974, U. Louvain (Belgium), 1976, St. Anselm's Coll., 1977; Litt.D., Villanova U., 1975, Boston Coll., 1977; L.H.D., DePaul U., 1974, Hofstra U., 1985, others. Joined Soc. St. Sulpice, 1951, ordained priest Roman Cath. Ch., 1953; prof. sacred scripture St. Mary's Sem., Balt., 1959-71; Auburn prof. Bibl. studies Union Theol. Sem., 1971—; Am. mem. Roman Pontifical Bibl. Commn., 1972—, Joint Theol. Commn. of World Council Chs. and Roman Cath. Ch., 1967-68; named Consultor of Vatican Secretariat for Christian Unity, 1968-73; mem. faith and order commn. World Council Chs., 1968—; adviser to Archbishop Hurley of St. Augustine at Vatican II Council, 1963; lectr. Aquinas Inst. Theology, 1963, Duke U. Div. Sch., 1967, U. Sydney (Australia), 1969, Lancaster Theol. Sem., 1971, So. Bapt. Theol. Sem., 1971; Thomas More lectr. Yale U., 1966, Shaffer lectr., 1978; lectr. U. Coll., Dublin, 1971, Vanderbilt Divinity Sch., 1980, others. Mem. Soc. N.T. Studies (pres. elect 1986), Am. Schs. Oriental Research, Cath. Bibl. Assn. (pres. 1971-72), Soc. Bibl. Lit. (pres. 1976-77), Bibl. Theologians, Am. Theol. Soc., Phi Beta Kappa. Author: New Testament Essays, 1965; The Gospel According to John, 1966, 70 (Nat. Cath. Book award, Christopher award); Jesus, God and Man, 1967; The Jerome Biblical Commentary (Nat. Cath. Book award), 1968; Priest and Bishop: Biblical Reflections, 1970; The Parables of the Gospels, 1963; (with P.J. Cahill) Biblical Tendencies Today: An Introduction to the Post-Bultmanians, 1969; Peter in the New Testament, 1973; Virginal Conception and Bodily Resurrection of Jesus (Nat. Cath. Book award), 1973; Biblical Reflections on Crises Facing the Church, 1975; The Birth of the Messiah (Nat. Religious Book award), 1977; The Critical Meaning of the Bible, 1981; The Epistles of John (Anchor Bible), 1982; Biblical Exegesis and Church Doctrine, 1985; many others. Contbr. articles to religious jours.; editorial bd. Cath. Bibl. Quarterly, Jour. Bibl. Lit., Theol. Studies, New Testament Studies. Address: 3041 Broadway at Reinhold Niebuhr Pl New York NY 10027

BROWN, ROBERT MCAFEE, educator, minister, Presbyn. Ch. in U.S.; b. Carthage, Ill., May 28, 1920; s. George William and Ruth Myrtle (McAfee) B.; B.A., Amherst Coll., 1943, D.D., 1958; B.D., Union Theol. Sem., N.Y.C., 1945; Ph.D., Columbia, 1951; Fulbright grantee Mansfield Coll., Oxford (Eng.) U., 1949-50; Am. Assn. Theol. Schs. grantee, St. Mary's Coll, St. Andrews (Scotland) U., 1959-60; Litt.D., U. San Francisco, 1964; L.H.D., Lewis and Clark Coll., 1964, St. Louis U., 1966, Kenyon Coll., 1981, Hebrew Union Coll., 1982; LL.D., Loyola U., Chgo., 1965, U. Notre Dame, 1965, Boston U., 1965, St. Mary's Coll., 1968; D.D., Pacific Sch. Religion, 1967, Hamilton Coll., 1969, Kalamazoo Coll., 1980, Macalester Coll., 1985; m. Sydney Elise Thomson, June 21, 1944; children—Peter, Mark, Alison, Thomas. Ordained to ministry, 1944; chaplain USNR, 1945-46; asst. pastor, Amherst, Mass., also asst. chaplain Amherst Coll., 1946-48; prof. religion Macalester Coll., 1951-53; prof. systemtic theology Union Theol. Sem., N.Y.C., 1953-62, prof. ecumenics and world Christianity, 1976-76; prof. religious studies Stanford U., 1962-76; prof. theology and ethics Pacific Sch. Religion, 1979-85. Recipient Harbison award Danforth Found., 1966; Peacemaker award Presbyn. Peace Fellowship, 1971; Triennial award excellence ecumenical lit. Sacred Heart U., 1968. Author: P.T. Forsyth: Prophet for Today, 1952; The Bible Speaks to You, 1955; The Significance of the Church, 1956; (with Father Gustav Weigel) An American Dialogue, 1960; The Spirit of Protestanism, 1961; Observer in Rome: A Protestant Report on the Vatican Council, 1964; The Collected Writings of St. Hereticus, 1964; (with others) Vietnam: Crisis of Conscience, 1967; The Ecumenical Revolution, 2d edit., 1969; The Pseudonyms of God, 1972; Religion and Violence, 1973; Frontiers for the Church Today, 1973; Is Faith Obsolete?, 1974; Theology in a New Key, 1978; The Hereticus Papers, 1979; Creative Dislocation: The Movement of Grace, 1980; Gustavo Gutierrez, 1981; Making Peace in the Global Village, 1981; Elie Wiesel: Messenger to All Humanity, 1983; Unexpected News: Reading the Bible with Third World Eyes, 1984. Editorial bd. Theology Today, Christianity and Crisis, Christian Century. Home: 2090 Columbia St Palo Alto CA 94306

BROWN, TOD DAVID, priest, Roman Catholic Church; b. San Francisco, Nov. 15, 1936; s. George Wilson and Edna Anne (Dunn) B. B.A., St. John's Coll., 1958; S.T.B., Gregorian U., Rome, 1960; M.A., U. San Francisco, 1970, M.A.T., 1974. Ordained priest Roman Catholic Ch., 1963. Dir. edn. Diocese of Monterey, Calif., 1970-80, vicar gen./clergyman, 1980-82, chancellor, 1982—, vicar gen./chancellor, 1983—, moderator of Curia, 1984—; pastor St. Francis Xavier, Seaside, Calif., 1977-82; sec. Edn. and Welfare Corp., Monterey, 1982, Catholic Charities Corp. Bd., Monterey, 1984. Mem. Community Coll. Adv. Bd., Bakersfield, Calif., 1964-67; mem. adv. council City of Seaside, 1971-75. Named Papal Chaplain, Pope Paul VI, 1975. Mem. Cath. Theol. Soc. Am., Cath. Bibl. Assn., Canon Law Soc. Am. Home: PO Box 247 Seaside CA 93955 Office: PO Box 2048 Monterey CA 93942

BROWN, VICTOR LEE, bishop, Church of Jesus Christ of Latter-day Saints; b. Cardston, Alta., Can., July 31, 1914; s. Gerald S. and Maggie C. (Lee) B.; came to U.S., 1931, naturalized, 1942; student U. Utah, 1934, Latter-day Saints Bus. Coll., 1937; m. Lois Kjar, Nov. 13, 1936; children—Victor L., Gerald E., Joanne (Mrs. Steven Soderberg), Patricia (Mrs. Larry Glade), Stephen M. Ordained bishop Ch. of Jesus Christ of Latter-day Saints, 1953; bishop 4th Ward, Denver, 1953-54; counselor Denver Stake Presidency, 1954-60; 2d counselor Presiding Bishopric, Salt Lake City, 1961-72; presiding bishop, Salt Lake City, 1972—. Pres. Hotel Utah Corp., Salt Lake City, 1972—, also dir., chmn. exec. com.; v.p., dir. Murdock Travel, Salt Lake City, 1963-74; dir. Western Air Lines, 1974—, also mem. exec. com.; dir. O.C. Tanner Jewelry Co., Salt Lake City, Deseret News Pub. Co.; pres., chmn. bd. Desert Mut. Benefits Assn.; vice chmn. bd. Deseret Trust Co. Mem. Utah Am. Revolution Bicentennial Commn., 1973—, chmn. festival com., 1973-77; chmn. bd. Welfare Services Corp., Salt Lake City, 1972—; mem. nat. exec. bd. Boy Scouts Am.; bd. dirs. Utah Symphony; trustee Brigham Young U. Mem. Beta Gamma Sigma. Office: 50 E North Temple Salt Lake City UT 84150

BROWN, WILLIAM, minister, Christ Temple Church, Inc.; b. Birmingham, Ala., June 4, 1945; s. Eddie and Ann (Brown) B. B.A., Cornell U., 1969, M.A., 1972, Ph.D., 1978; Ph.D. (hon.), Northeastern U., 1979. Ordained to ministry, 1970. Gen. overseer and bishop Salvation and Deliverance Ch., Inc., N.Y.C., 1975—; v.p. Lift Up Jesus Movement, N.Y.C., 1981—; pres. Com. for a Better Human Relationship, N.Y.C., 1982—. Author: Cast Them Out, 1982; The Glorified Church, 1985; The Just Shall Live by Faith, 1985. Editor Deliverance mag., 1982. Named Man of Yr., Citizen of Harlem, 1974; Pastor of Yr., Radio Sta. WTHE, Mineola, N.Y., 1984; recipient Cert. of Appreciation, Girl Scouts U.S.A., 1984, Ministers Prayer Group, N.Y.C., 1984. Mem. NAACP, Urban League. Avocations: tennis; golf. Address: Salvation and Deliverance Church Inc 37 W 116th St New York NY 10026

BROWNBACK, PAUL TIMOTHY, college president, minister; b. Royersford, Pa., Aug. 13, 1940; s. Lloyd F. and Helen (Reed) B.; m. Constance M. Didden, May 20, 1964; children: Stephanie, Stephen. B.S., U.S. Mil. Acad., 1963; M.Div. magna cum laude, Talbot Theol. Sem., Calif., 1970; Ph.D., NY U, 1982. Ordained to ministry, 1972. Dir. Christian edn. Grace Brethren Ch., Westminster, Calif., 1967-68; pastor Downey Baptist Ch., Calif., 1969-70; dean Word of Life Bible Inst., Pottersville, N.Y., 1970-74; pres. Citadel Bible Coll., Ozark, Ark., 1974—. Author: Danger of Self-Love, 1982. Served to capt. U.S. Army, 1963-67; Ger., Vietnam. Republican. Office: Citadel Bible College Ozark AR 72949

BROWNE, BENJAMIN PATTERSON, minister, Baptist Church, college administrator; b. Wicasset, Maine, Jan. 25, 1893; s. Benjamin Randall and Lena Evelyn (Patterson) B.; student Harvard, 1924, Boston U., 1926-27, Sch. Theology, 1928-30, Andover-Newton Sem., 1930-32; D.D., Eastern Bapt. Theol. Sem., 1947, William Jewell Coll., 1962; L.H.D., Hillsdale Coll., No. Bapt. Theol. Sem., 1963; Litt.D., Ottawa U., 1961; Ed.D., Judson Coll., 1967; m. Rachel Eunice Sprague, Apr. 3, 1915; children—Rachel Sprague (Mrs. Lloyd Diggs), Priscilla Alden (Mrs. Nicholos Wagner), Benjamin Judson, Marcia Carol Hoff. Ordained to ministry Baptist Ch., 1912; pastor Bapt. chs., Me. and Mass., 1912-41; dir. promotion Mass. Bapt. Conv. hdqrs. Tremont Temple, Boston, 1941-44; exec. sec. Pa. Bapt. Conv., Phila., 1944-47; editorial exec. Christian publs. Bd. Edn. and Publs., Am. Bapt. Conv., Phila., 1947-62, pres. conv., 1962-63, also pres. Asso. Ch. Press; pres. No. Bapt. Theol. Sem., 1959-64; pres. Judson Coll., Elgin, Ill., 1962-66, chancellor, 1967-76. Pres., founder Christian Writers' Conf., 1948; exec. dir. Nat. Christian Authors' Guild; chmn. edn. Bapt. World Alliance, 1955. Trustee David C. Cook Found., 1967-74, Lincoln Acad. Republican. Club: Holyoke Literary. Author: Let There Be Light, 1956; The Writers Conference Comes to You, 1956; Techniques of Christian Writing, 1959; Signal Flares, 1960; Gateway to Morning, 1961; Tales of Baptist Daring, 1962; Story of the Browne Family, 1973; History of Judson College in Illinois, 1974; Christian Journalism for Today; Illustrations for Preachers, 1976; also booklets, poems, hymns, story sermons. Staff editor Mass. Bapt. Bull., 1941-44; editor Penn Baptist, 1944-47, The Baptist Leader, 1947-63; compiler-editor Christian Journalism for Today, 1952. Died Aug. 3, 1976. Home: 622 Washington St Alhambra CA 91801

BROWNING, ASA G., JR., minister, Bapt. Missionary Assn. Am.; b. Social Circle, Ga., June 6, 1934; s. Asa G. and Carrie Elizibath (Pace) B.; B.A., Cedarville Coll., 1973; M.Div., United Theol. Sem., 1976; children—Artrenia, Asa, Stranton, Thelma. Ordained to ministry, 1972; chaplain Miami Valley Hosp., Dayton, Ohio, 1975—. Sr. data clk. Inland Mfg. Co. div. Gen. Motors Corp., Dayton, 1960—. Counselor, Prisoners Helpers Inc., Dayton. Home: 522 Shoop Ave Dayton OH 45407

BROWNING, EDMOND LEE, bishop, Episcopal Church; b. Corpus Christi, Tex., Mar. 11; s. Edmond Lucian and Cora Mae (Lee) B.; B.A., U. of South, Sewanee, Tenn., 1952, B.D., 1954, D.D., 1970; m. Patricia Sparks, Sept. 10, 1953; children—Robert Mark, Patricia Paige, Philip Myles, Peter Sparks, John Charles. Ordained priest Episcopal Ch., 1954, bishop, 1968; curate Ch. of the Good Shepherd, Corpus Christi, 1954-56; rector Redeemer Ch., Eagle Pass, Tex., 1956-59, All Souls Ch., Okinawa, 1959-63, St. Matthews Ch., Okinawa, 1965-67; archdeacon Okinawa Episcopal Ch., 1965-67; first missionary bishop of Okinawa, 1968-71; bishop of Convocation, Episcopal Chs. in Europe, 1971-74; exec. Nat. and World Mission Exec. Council, N.Y.C., 1974-76, 82—. Bd. dirs. Anglican Center, Rome, St. Stephens Sch., Rome; mem. Anglican Consultative Council, 1983—. Hon. canon St. Michaels Cathedral, Kobe, Japan. Office: Queen Emma Sq Honolulu HI 96813

BROWNSON, WILLIAM CLARENCE, minister, Christian broadcasting company executive, Reformed Church in America; b. Charlotte, N.C., June 27, 1928; s. William C. and Juanita V. (Clements) B.; m. Helen Christine Stewart, Aug. 25, 1951; children: William C. (dec.), David A., James V., Jonathan C. A.B., Davidson

Coll., 1949; M.Div., Columbia Sem., 1952; Th.D., Princeton Sem., 1963; D.D. (hon.), Central U., 1984. Ordained to ministry Reformed Ch. in Am., 1953. Pastor 2d Reformed Ch., Lod, N.J., 1953-59, 1st Reformed Ch., Chgo., 1959-64; prof. preaching Western Theol. Sem., Holland, Mich., 1964-74; pres. broadcast minister Words of Hope, Grand Rapids, Mich., 1974—; mem. gen. synod exec. com. Reformed Ch. in Am. Hdqrs., N.Y.C., 1983—, pres., 1984-85. Author: Tried by Fire, 1975; Distinctive Lessons from Luke, 1976; Do You Believe?, 1976, and others. Pres. Heritage Homes, Holland, Mich., 1972-74; del. World Alliance of Reformed Chs. Mem. Nat. Religious Broadcasters, Phi Beta Kappa. Home: 1347 Heather Dr Holland MI 49423 Office: Words of Hope 700 Ball Ave Grand Rapids MI 49503

BRUBAKER, RAY METZLER, news commentator (religious); b. Mt. Joy, Pa., Apr. 5, 1923; s. Harry L. and Theda Jane (Metzler) B.; m. Darlene Beatrice Robertson, June 1, 1946; children: Jay Marlin, Danny Ray, Kaye Marlene. Editor news Sta. WMBI-WDLM, Chgo., 1945-47; commentator God's News Behind the News, St. Petersburg, Fla., 1956—; pres., dir. Cathedral Caravan, Inc., St. Petersburg, 1947—; pastor, Tierra Verde Christian Ctr., St. Petersburg, 1984—. Author 80 small books on prophecy. Editor news pub. Radar, 1954—. Recipient Angel award Religion in Media, 1982-83, 83-84, 84-85. Home: 6639 Date Palm St S St Petersburg FL 33707 Office: 6550 Mango Ave S Box 10475 Zone 33733 St Petersburg FL 33707

BRUMMETT, BILLY RAY, minister, Assemblies of God; b. Jenks, Okla., Sept. 17, 1936; s. James Oscar and Elsie May (Crowl) B.; student Ouchita Bapt. U., 1970-71, Concordia Luth. Coll., 1973-75; student Okla. U., 1968-69; m. Shirley Cooleen Sixkiller, Nov. 23, 1955; children—Sharon Renee, Billy Ray, Gary Dewayne, Doyle Gene. Ordained to ministry, 1959; youth dir. Tulsa dist., Assemblies of God, 1963-67; ednl. dir. Camden (Ark.) Dist., 1969-70; youth dir. Austin (Tex.) Dist., 1971-72; pastor, Austin, Tex., 1970-75, First Assembly of God, Levelland West, Tex., 1975—. Dist. sectional committeeman, Assemblies of God, 1972-74, sec.-treas., 1973-74, dist. presbyter, 1974-75. Coach Little League Baseball, Levelland, 1976—. Recipient Spl. Recognition, Nat. Headquarters of Assemblies of God, 1969. Mem. Levelland Ministerial Alliance. Home: 220 Detroit Dr Levelland TX 79336 Office: PO Box 1054 Levelland TX 79336

BRUN, CAROL JOYCE, clergywoman, sec. United Church of Christ, N.Y.C. Office: 105 Madison Ave New York NY 10016*

BRUNER, BENJAMIN ROGERS, minister, Southern Baptist Convention; lawyer; b. Richmond, Va., July 29, 1911; s. Weston and Maria (Gwathmey) B.; m. Virginia Wilford, Oct. 23, 1936; 1 son, Roger Ellis. B.A., Coll. William and Mary, 1932, B.L., 1933, J.D., 1958; Th.M., So. Bapt. Theol. Sem., Louisville, 1945; postgrad. U. Tenn., 1932. Ordained to ministry So. Bapt. Conv., 1942; pastor chs., Ky., Fla., Va., 1943-55; pastor Edgemont Bapt. Ch., Durham, N.C., 1955-58, Temple Bapt. Ch., Norfolk, Va., 1958-64, 1st Bapt. Ch., Cumberland, Md., 1964-76; interim pastor chs., Richmond, Va., 1977—. Trustee, Fork Union Mil. Acad. (Va.), 1952-78, So. Bapt. Theol. Sem., Louisville, 1968-77; v.p. Bapt. Conv. Md., 1970-71, 73-74; sec., pastoral care dept. Meml. Hosp., Cumberland, Md., 1971-76. Author: (with others) Which Bible Can You Trust, 1972; contbr. to Bapt. publs.; producer religious radio and TV programs, 1946—. Mem. Va. Bapt. Hist. Soc., So. Bapt. Hist. Soc., Assn. Preservation Va. Antiquities, Phi Kappa Phi. Home: 604 Maple Ave Richmond VA 23226

BRUNETT, ALEX JOSEPH, priest, Roman Catholic Church; b. Detroit, Jan. 17, 1934; s. Raymond Henry and Cecilia Una (Gill) B.; B.A., Sacred Heart Sem., 1955; S.T.B., Gregorian U., Rome, 1957, S.T.L., 1959; M.A., U. Detroit; postgrad. Marquette U., 1964-68. Ordained priest, 1958; pastor chs., Mich., 1958-62; chaplain U. Mich., 1962-64; prof. Marquette U., 1964-68; dean St. John's Provincial Sem., 1968-72; pastor St. Aidan's Parish, Livonia, Mich., 1973—; Dir. ecumenical and interreligious affairs, Detroit, 1973—; chmn. Archdiocese of Detroit Theol. Commn., 1973—; bd. dirs. Midwest Assn. Theol. Schs., 1970-72; v.p. research and devel. com. Nat. Assn. Diocesan Ecumenical Officers, 1975—; nat. chmn. Christian-Jewish Dialogue, 1976—; exec. dir. St. Aidan's Cultural Soc. Mem. Nat. Cath. Edn. Assn., Cath. Theol. Soc., Acad. Ecumenists. Home: 17500 Farmington Rd Livonia MI 48152 Office: 305 Michigan Ave Detroit MI 48226

BRUNGARDT, MARTHA ANN, director of religious education, Roman Catholic Church; b. Hays, Kans., Dec. 14, 1951; d. Marcellus Francis and Mary Ann (Jacobs) Schmeidler; m. Edward Joseph Brungardt, May 11, 1984; 1 child, Ann Marie. B.A., Marian Coll., Wis., 1974; M.S., Fort Hays State U., Kans., 1981. Tchr., Immaculate Conception High Sch., Elmhurst, Ill., 1974-78, Marian High Sch., Hays, Kans., 1978-79; youth minister Immaculate Heart of Mary, Hays, 1979-80; youth minister St. Patrick Parish, Pasco, Wis., 1981-82; dir. religious edn. St. Joseph Parish, Hays, 1982—. Contbr. article to communication jour. Cert. master catechist Diocese of Salina, Kans., 1985. Mem. Nat. Assn. Female Execs., Phi Kappa Phi. HomeP PO Box 447 Victoria KS 67671 Office: St Joseph Parish 215 W 13th Hays KS 67601

BRUSO, ROBERT ARTHUR, minister, Wesleyan Ch.; b. Plattsburgh, N.Y., June 26, 1939; s. Truman Archie and Marion Isabell (Thompson) B.; student Plattsburgh State U., 1957-61; m. Diane Frances Chellis, July 25, 1959; children—Nancy Mae, Robert Alan, Mark Thomas. Ordained to ministry, 1972; pastor chs., Ticonderoga, N.Y., 1969-70; pastor Wesleyan Ch., Long Lake, N.Y., 1970—. Mem. dist. bd. adminstrn. Wesleyan Ch. Chmn., Planning Bd. Long Lake. Mem. Nat. Assn. Evangelicals, Christian Holiness Assn., Nat. Assn. Christian Marriage Counselors. Editor Challenger newspaper, Champlain dist., 1976—. Home and Office: Box 322 Deerland Rd Long Lake NY 12847

BRUST, LEO T., bishop, Roman Catholic Church. Titular bishop of Svelli, aux. bishop, Milw., 1969—. Office: 3501 S Lake Dr Milwaukee WI 53207*

BRYANT, GARY, clergyman. Chmn. exec. council United Church of Christ, N.Y.C. Office: United Ch of Christ 105 Madison Ave New York NY 10016*

BRYANT, MARCUS DAVID, pastoral care educator, minister, Christian Church (Disciples of Christ); b. Gilbert, Ark., July 18, 1924; s. Morton Dillard and Anna May (Boyd) B.; m. Virginia Rae Stevenson, Aug. 9, 1953; children: Barbara Lynn Bryant Martin, Steven Mark. B.A., Lynchburg Coll., 1949; M.A., Columbia U., 1950; M.Div., Lexington Theol. Sem., 1953; Ph.D., U. Nebr., 1958. Ordained to ministry Christian Church (Disciples of Christ), 1949. Minister Newtown Christian Ch., Georgetown, Ky., 1950-54; assoc. minister 1st Christian Ch., Lincoln, Nebr., 1954-58, pastor, Waukegan, Ill., 1958-61; assoc. prof. Div. Sch., Drake U., Des Moines, 1961-67; prof. pastoral care Brite Div. Sch., Tex. Christian U., Fort Worth, 1967—; elder South Hills Christian Ch., Fort Worth, 1984—. Author: (curriculum books) Come Alive, 1971; (with others) The Church and Community Resources, 1977; The Art of Christian Caring, 1979. Contbr. articles to religious publs. Served with U.S. Army, 1943-46, ETO. Research grantee Tex. Christian U., 1978, 81. Mem. Am. Assn. Pastoral Counselors (diplomate, chmn. profl. relationships 1977-80), Tex. Council on Family Relations. Democrat. Home: 3956 Wosley Dr Fort Worth TX 76133 Office: Brite Div Sch Tex Christian U Fort Worth TX 76129

BRYANT, ROY, bishop, Bible Church of Christ; b. Armour, N.C., July 18, 1923; s. Augusta and Susan (Granger) B.; m. Sissieretta Burney, Oct. 11, 1942; children: Eurnetha, Roy, Larry, Ruth, Seth. D.Div., Fla. State Christian Coll., 1966. Ordained to ministry, The Bible Church of Christ. Elder Phila. Bible Ch., N.Y.C., 1959-61; bishop The Bible Ch. of Christ, Inc., Bronx, N.Y., 1961—; pres. The Bible Ch. of Christ Theol. Inst., Bronx, 1976—; dir. The Bible Ch. of Christ Christian Bookstore, 1978—, The Bible Ch. of Christ Resort Community and Summer Camp, Monticello, N.Y., 1971—. Exec. editor: The Voice; producer, host Radio and Television Ministry. Office: The Bible Church of Christ Inc 1358 Morris Ave Bronx NY 10456

BRYANT, THERMAN VIRGIL, cons., So. Bapt. Conv., U.S.A.; b. Pontotoc, Miss., Feb. 5, 1913; s. Bailey Bruce and Mattie (Russell) B.; B.A., U. Miss., 1951, M.Ed., 1953; m. Annie Grace McCord, Sept. 21, 1934; children—Therman Harold, William Bruce, Doris Carolyn (dec.) Tchr. Longview Consol. High Sch., Pontotoc, 1933-36; prin. Bankhead High Sch., 1936-40; supr. Pontotoc Pub. Schs., 1940-52, supr. instrn., 1952-55; instr. adult edn. Miss. State U., Starkville, 1952-56; tchr. math. Batesville (Miss.) High Sch., 1955-56; dean, asst. to pres. Clarke Coll., Newton, Miss., 1956-65; cons. coop. missions dept. Miss. Bapt. Conv. Bd., Jackson, 1956—. Chmn. March of Dimes, Pontotoc County, 1950-51, Pontotoc County unit ARC, 1952-53. Mem. Miss. Registrars Assn., Miss., Nat. edn. assns., Phi Delta Kappa. Home: 1302 Arlington St Clinton MS 39056 Office: 515 Missippi St Jackson MS 39205

BRYANT, THURMON EARL, educator, So. Bapt. Conv.; b. Claud, Okla., May 25, 1930; s. Allen Walter and Nannie Pairlee (McClellan) B.; A.B., Baylor U., 1951; B.D., Southwestern Baptist Theol. Sem., Ft. Worth, 1954, Th.D., 1959; m. Doris Marie Morris, Aug. 8, 1948; children—Larry Joe, Danny Earl, David Wayne, John Randall. Ordained minister, 1950; pastor chs. in Tex., 1950-58; teaching fellow Southwestern Bapt. Theol. Sem., 1957-58; vis. prof. missions So. Sem., Louisville, 1963-64; missionary, educator, pastor, translator, administr., Brazil, 1958-72; prof. religion, dir. in-service tng. William Jewell Coll., Liberty, Mo., 1972—. Founder, pres. Bapt. Theol. Sem., San Paulo, 1963-72. Vice pres. trustees Pan Am. Christian Acad., Sao Paulo, 1970-72. Contbr. articles to profl. jours. Editor Teologica, 1967-72. Home: Caixo Postal 30259 01000 Sao Paulo Brazil

BRYER, IRVINE ALAFIA, JR., minister, United Church of Christ; b. Beacon, N.Y., May 22, 1946; s. Irvine and Carolyn Marie (Givens) B.; 1 child, Stacy. B.A., City U. N.Y., 1975; M.Div., Union Theol. Sem., 1980. Ordained to ministry 1974. Asst. pastor Nazarene Congl. Ch., Bklyn., 1974-75; pastor Resurrection Ch., N.Y.C., 1975-78, Hollis Ave. Congl. Ch., Queens Village, N.Y., 1978—; chaplain N.Y. Guard, N.Y.C., 1982—; campus minister York Coll., Jamaica, N.Y., 1982—; chmn. affirmative action commn. N.Y. Conf. United Ch. Christ, 1982—; sec. Inter Ch. Ministers, Jamaica, 1981—; chmn. Metro Black Clergy United Ch. Christ, N.Y., 1982-84; chaplain 33d Regular Democratic Club, Queens, N.Y., 1983. Active Community Bd. 13, Queens, 1982, Wayanada Civic Assn., Queens, Village, 1982; exec. dir. Guy R. Brewer Learning Ctr. Queens, 1980. Served with U.S. Army, 1966-69. Recipient Community Service award St. Albans Congl. Ch., 1982; named Man of Yr. Hunt-E Entertainment, 1982; Benjamin Mays fellow, 1978. Home: 213-02 110th Ave Queens Village NY 11429

BRZANA, STANISLAUS JOSEPH, bishop, Roman Catholic Church; b. Buffalo, July 1, 1917; s. Frank and Catherine (Mikosz) B.; B.A., St. Bonaventure Coll., 1938; S.T.L., Gregorian U., 1951, S.T.D., 1953. Ordained priest Roman Catholic Ch., 1941; with Buffalo Missionary Apostolate, 1941; asst. St. Josephs Ch., Gowanda, N.Y., 1942, Saints Peter and Paul Ch., Jamestown, N.Y., 1943, 46-49; chaplain AUS, 1944-46; dir. Cath. Info. Center, Buffalo, 1949; weekend asst. Transfiguration Ch., Buffalo, 1949, asst., 1953-54; weekend asst. St. John Kanty Ch., Buffalo, 1950; Diocesan examiner of clergy, 1953, censor of books, 1954-64; vice-officialis Tribunal of Diocese of Buffalo, 1954-56, officialis, 1958-64; weekend asst. Our Lady of Grace Parish, Woodlawn, N.Y., 1956-57, adminstr., 1957; weekend asst. St. Barbara's Parish, Lackawanna, N.Y., 1957, St. Adalberts Parish, Buffalo, 1957-58; adminstr. Resurrection Parish, Cheektowaga, N.Y., 1959, Queen of Peace Parish, Buffalo, 1959; apptd. domestic prelate, 1959; pastor Queen of Peace Parish, Buffalo, 1961-64; titular bishop of Cufruta, aus. bishop of Buffalo, 1964; consecrated bishop, 1964; chmn. Diocesan Commn. on Sacred Liturgy, Music and Art, 1964-66; vicar gen., Diocesan consultor, 1966-68; bishop Diocese of Ogdensburg, N.Y., 1968—. Address: 622 Washington St Ogdensburg NY 13669

BUBY, BERTRAND ANDREW, priest, theology educator, Roman Catholic Church; b. Braddock, Pa., June 18, 1934; s. Andrew C. and Helen J. (Gyurik) B. B.A., U. Dayton, 1955; Licentiate Theol., U. Fribourg, Switzerland, 1964; Licentiate Scripture, Biblicum, Rome, 1966; S.T.D., U. Dayton, 1980. Ordained priest Roman Cath. Ch., 1964. Chaplain, Marianist Coll., Dayton, Ohio, 1967-69; asst. for religious life Marianists of Cincinnati Province, 1970-77, provincial, 1981—; tchr. N.T., U. Dayton, 1981—, trustee, 1982—; pres. Jewish-Christian Dialogue Group, Dayton, 1977-79. Author: Exegesis — Patristics, 1979. Mem. Cath. Bibl. Assn., Mariol. Soc. Am., Democrat. Office: Marianists 4435 E Patterson Rd Dayton OH 45430

BUCHANAN, KING LANDISS, minister, Church of Christ; b. Orange, Tex., Dec. 21, 1929; s. King Robert and Sharlet Vanona (Lee) B.; m. Winnie Ruth Bates, July 31, 1953; children: King Landiss, Landra Cay, Celia Lynn. B.A., Harding Coll., 1957; M.A., Harding Grad. Sch. Bible and Religion, 1959. Ordained to ministry Ch. of Christ, 1948. Dir. Ch. of Christ Bible Chair, Arlington State Coll., Tex., 1960-64; minister Elmwood Ch. of Christ, Dallas, 1965-70; tchr. Preston Rd. Sch. of Preaching, Dallas, 1970-76; minister Del City Ch. of Christ, Okla., 1980—; lectr. in field. Served with U.S. Army, 1953-55. Lodge: Kiwanis (pres. 1982). Home: 4753 Koelsch Dr Del City OK 73117 Office: Del City Church of Christ 1901 Vickie Dr Del City OK 73115

BUCHANAN, PAUL MARCUS (MARK), minister, United Methodist Ch.; b. Knoxville, Tenn., Oct. 6, 1955; s. William Woodrow and Clara Elizabeth (Marshall) B. B.A., U. Evansville, 1978; M.Th., So. Meth. U., 1983. Ordained deacon, N. Ind. Ann. Conf., United Meth. Ch., 1979, elder, Southwest Tex. Ann. Conf., 1985. Youth dir. Aldersgate United Meth. Ch., 1976-78; assoc. minister and Wesley Found. dir. 1st United Meth. Ch., Southeastern Okla. State U., Durant, Okla., 1980-81; minister Tipton Meth. Ch., England, 1981-82; minister to youth Alamo Heights United Meth. Ch., San Antonio, 1983—; youth del. N. Ind. Ann. Conf., 1972-74; co-convenor Perkins Student Assn., So. Meth. U., 1982-83. Contbr. to Meth. Reporter. Vol. solicitor San Antonio Mus. Assn., 1985; partipant Target-90 Phys. Resources Council, San Antonio, 1985. A.J. Bigney scholar U. Evansville, 1975-77. Mem. Christian Educators Fellowship, Religious Edn. Assn. Amnesty Internat. Democart. Avocations: bicycling; travel; skiing. Office: Alamo Heights United Meth Ch 5101 Broadway San Antonio TX 78209

BUCHIN, RICHARD JAMES, lay church worker, Presbyterian Church in the U.S.A., tax collector; b. Allentown, Pa., Dec. 15, 1952; s. Harry and Rachel Irene (Gehman) B.; B.A., Messiah Coll., 1976; M.A. in Religion, Eastern Bapt. Sem., 1980; postgrad.,

Kutztown U., 1985—. Editor Cedar Crest Bible Ch., Allentown, Pa., 1971-72; com. mem. First Presby. Ch., Bethlehem, Pa., 1980—. Tax collector Borough of Macungie, Pa., 1978—. Reviewer for periodical, 1981. Mem. Acad. Political Sci., Am. Library Assn. Republican. Home: 19-21 E Main St Macungie PA 18062 Office: Buchin Electric and Hardware 19-21 E Main St Macungie PA 18062

BUECHLEIN, DANIEL MARK, monk, priest, seminary administrator Roman Catholic Church; b. Jasper, Ind., Apr. 20, 1938; s. Carl Bernard and Rose (Blessinger) B.; B.A., St. Meinrad Coll., 1960; student St. Meinrad Sch. Theology, 1960-64; S.T.L., Internat. Benedictine U. of St. Anselmo, Rome, 1966. Ordained priest, Order of St. Benedict, Roman Cath. Ch., 1964; asst. dean students St. Meinrad Coll. Liberal Arts, 1966-68, chmn. div. religion, 1967-71, spiritual dir., 1968-71, pres., rector, 1982—, pres., rector St. Meinrad Sch. Theology, 1971—; mem. formation com. Conf. Major Superiors of Men of the U.S.A., 1971—; cons. Nat. Conf. Cath. Bishops Com. on Priestly Formation, 1971—; mem. exec. bd. Sem. div. Nat. Cath. Edn. Assn., 1972-75; mem. continuing edn. of priests Commn. Archdiocese of Indpls., ad hoc prep. com. 1977 Congress Benedictine Abbots; dir. First Nat. Conf. Sem. Spiritual Dirs., 1971. Mem. Nat. Assn. Sem. Spiritual Dirs. (coordinator founding 1972), Midwest Assn. Theol. Schs. (pres. exec. bd. 1974-75), Theol. Edn. Assn. Mid-Am. (pres. exec. bd. 1976-78). Address: St Meinrad Sch Theology St Meinrad IN 47577

BUGDEN, LOUIS JAMES, minister, Seventh-day Adventist Ch. in Can.; b. Halifax, N.S., Can., June 7, 1930; s. Arthur James and Mabel Louise (Muise) B.; B.Sc., Andrews U., Berrien Springs, Mich., 1973; m. Stella Marie Corkum, July 19, 1949; children—Shauna Marie, Cynthia Louise, Louis Paul. Ordained to ministry; tchr. Toronto Jr. Acad., Willowdale, Ont., 1958-65, prin., 1966-71; youth dir. Man.-Sask. Conf. Seventh-day Adventists, Saskatoon, 1974-75; deacon, elder, choir dir., pastor Warren (Mich.) Seventh-day Adventist Ch., 1966-69. Temperance lectr. in pub. schs.; Boy Scout leader, 1947-49; dir. Pathfinders. Home: Box 296 Beiseker AB T0M 0G0 Canada

BUGTONG, LEONARDO ROBLES, minister, Luth. Ch.—Mo. Synod; b. Atok, Benquet, Philippines, Dec. 30, 1933; s. James Barry and Dolores Peralejo (Robles) B.; A.A., Baguio Colls., Philippines, 1955, A.B., 1970; B.Th., Luth. Theol. Sem., Manila, 1961; m. Estela Ganibi, Dec. 30, 1961; children—Reuben, Ruth, Barry, Rachel. Ordained to ministry, 1961; pastor chs., Philippines, 1961-69; dist. missionary Benquett Tribe, Philippines, 1969-71; pastor St. Peter Ch., New Hamburg, Ont., Can., St. Paul Ch., Tavistock, Ont., 1973—. Dist. pres., mem. bd. dirs., Luth. Ch. Philippines, 1964-66, 68-71; mem. dist. mission bd., 1974-76; counselor Ont. dist. Luth. Women's Missionary League, 1975—; treas. Wilmot Ministerial Assn. Home: 144 Huron St New Hamburg ON N0B 2G0 Canada Office: Box 609 New Hamburg ON N0B 2G0 Canada

BUHL, GEORGE SAMUEL, JR., minister, Conservative Congl. Christian Conf.; b. Phila., Oct. 14, 1916; s. George Samuel and Lottie Wentz (Herr) B.; student Temple U., 1943-44, Drexel Inst. Tech., 1936-38; grad. Phila. Coll. Bible, 1946; m. Grace Forrest Bowers, Oct. 21, 1939; children: David Robert, Richard John. Ordained to ministry, 1949; pastor First Congl. Ch., Port Leyden, N.Y., 1947-56, Mayflower Congl. Ch., Kingston, Mass., 1958-84. Moderator New Eng. Assn. Congl. Christian Chs., 1970-73; bd. dirs. Conservative Congl. Christian Conf., 1971-73, first v.p., 1975-78, pres., 1978-81. Chmn. youth commn. Town of Kingston (Mass.), 1974. Address: 5 Sunset Rd Kingston MA 02364

BUHLER, ALLEN, minister, So. Bapt. Conv.; b. Lebanon, Tenn., Apr. 26, 1916; s. John William and Minnie Mai (Bingham) B.; B.A., Carson-Newman Coll., 1949; m. Amy Lee Graves, Apr. 26, 1939; children—Franchot, Beverly Buhler Bains, Lynn, Victor, Lera Buhler Jones, Richard. Ordained to ministry, 1944; interim pastor First Chilhowee Bapt. Ch., Seymour, Tenn., 1944-45; pastor Montview Bapt. Ch., Morristown, Tenn., 1945-47, Fairview Bapt. Ch., Lebanon, 1947-71, Shelby Ave. Bapt. Ch., Nashville, 1971—. Moderator Wilson County (Tenn.) Bapt. Assn., 1953-54. Home: 918 Mitchell Rd Nashville TN 37206 Office: 1008-1014 Shelby Ave Nashville TN 37206

BULKA, REUVEN P., rabbi; b. London, 1944; m. Naomi Jakobvits; children: Yocheved Ruth, Shmuel Refael, Rena Dvorah, Eliezer Menachem, Binyomin Dovid. Ph.D., U. Ottawa, 1971. Ordained: Rabbi, Rabbinical Sem., N.Y., 1965. Rabbi, Congregation Machzikei Hadas, Ottawa, Ont., Can., 1967—; chmn. Rabbinical Council of Am. Family & Marriage Com., editor Family & Marriage Newsletter, 1976—; founder, editor Jour. of Psychology & Judaism, Ottawa, 1976—. Author: The Wit and Wisdom of the Talmud, 1974, 83; Mystics and Medics: A Comparison of Mystical and Psychotherapeutic Encounters, 1979; Sex and the Talmud: Reflections on Human Relations, 1979; The Quest for Ultimate Meaning: Principles and Applications of Logotherapy, 1979; As a Tree by the Waters-Pirkey Avoth: Psychological and Philosophical Insights, 1980; Holocaust Aftermath: Continuing Impact on the Generations, 1981; Dimensions of Orthodox Judaism, 1983; Torah Therapy: Reflections on the Weekly Sedra and Special Occasions, 1983. Editor: Dimensions of Orthodox Judaism, 1983. Author: Loneliness, 1984; The Haggadah For Pesah, with Translation and Thematic Commentary, 1985. Co-editor: Logotherapy in Action, 1979; A Psychology-Judaism Reader, 1982. Mem. editorial bd. Tradition, Jour. of Religion & Health, The Internat. Forum for Logotherapy and Pastoral Psychology, Dictionary of Pastoral Care and Counseling. Sect. editor: Rabbianical Council of America Sermon Manual, 1977-82. Contbr. articles to profl. jours. Host TV series: About Ourselves. Chmn. Rabbinic Cabinet, State of Israel Bonds of Canada; co-chmn. Ottawa Soviet Jewry Com.; mem. pastoral care adv. com. Children's Hosp. of Eastern Ont. Address: Jour of Psychology & Judaism 1747 Featherston Dr Ottawa ON K1H 6P4 Canada

BULL, HOWARD ELWOOD, minister, Conglist. Ch.; b. Oakland, Calif., Jan. 24, 1916; s. Homer Elwood and Florence Edith (Felton) B.; student, U. Mich., 1944; Garrett Theol. Sem., 1955; m. Doris Muriel Revheim, June 30, 1939 (dec. 1973); children—Harvey, Donald, Marjorie (Mrs. Eric O. Witt), Marilyn. Ordained to ministry Conglist. Ch., 1961; minister chs., Mich., 1954-68, Birmingham, Mich., 1961-68, Pioneer Congl. Ch., Santa Rosa, Calif., 1968-70, Community Ch. of the Monterey Peninsula, Carmel, Calif., 1970—; chmn. exec. com. Nat. Assn. Congl. Christian Chs., 1969-70; pres. No. Calif. Assn. Community and Congl. Chs., 1972-73. Mem. Ret. Officers Assn. (founder, pres. Monterey chpt. 1971-72). Author: Pulpit Prayers for Protestant Pulpits. Home: POB 1219 Carmel CA 93921 Office: POB 3627 Carmel CA 93921

BULLARD, JOHN MOORE, religion educator, minister, United Methodist Church; b. Winston-Salem, N.C., May 6, 1932; s. Hoke Vogler and May Evangeline (Moore) B. A.B., U. N.C.-Chapel Hill, 1953, A.M., 1955; M.Div., Yale U., 1957, Ph.D., 1962. Ordained elder, 1963. Asst. prof. religion Wofford Coll., Spartanburg, S.C., 1961-65, assoc. prof., 1965-70, chmn. dept. religon, 1962—, Albert C. Outler-prof. religion, 1970—; vis. prof. bibl. lit. U. N.C.-Chapel Hill, summers 1966-67, U. N.C.-Charlotte, summer 1974; vis. prof. comparative religion Converse Coll., Spartanburg, S.C., 1984; minister music Bethel United Meth. Ch., Spartanburg, 1972—. Adv. editorial bd. LIGHT, Contbr. articles, book revs. to profl. jours. Fund for Study of Great Religious grantee, 1970-71; U. London, 1975, Nat. Endowment Humanities grantee, Harvard U., 1982; Nat. Endowment Humanities travel grantee, Pakistan, 1973. Mem. Am. Acad. Religion, Soc. Bibl. Lit. (so. sect. pres. 1968-69), Fellowship of Meth. Musicians (state pres. 1980-81), Am. Guild Organists (chpt. dean 1965-67), Neu BachGesellschaft. Democrat. Home: 1514 Fernwood-Glendale Rd Spartanburg SC 29302 Office: 227 Main Bldg Wofford Coll Spartanburg SC 29301

BULLEN, VOY M., bishop, Church of God. Gen. overseer, bishop Ch. of God. Address: 2504 Arrow Wood Dr SE Huntsville AL 35803

BULLINGER, EMMANUAL, pastor, Church of the Brethren; b. Belleville, Ill., Sept. 3, 1930; s. Hienrich and Anna Marie (Knapp) B.; m. Mary Lou Ecookson, Apr. 15, 1946. B.D., Zion Faith Coll., Ind., 1952; M.Div., Georg Sch. of Theology, Germany, 1955; D.Th., Brethren Sem., England, 1962, D.D. (hon.), Brooks Divinity Sch., Denver, 1980. Ordained: Minister. Pastor, Brethren Ch., St. Louis, 1962-66, The English Ch., Stuttgart, Germany, 1967-77, Reformed Chapel, Zurich, 1978-82, Brethren Ch., Cleveland, Tenn., 1983—; trustee Georg Sch. Theology, Baden Baden, Germany, 1981—. Author: Ephrata: A Beginning, 1975; Church Management Cases, 1980; Personal Computer's in Church Management, 1983. Decorated Order of St. John's, St. John's Abbey, England, 1973. Mem. Ch. Computer Users Assn. Office: Brethren Ch PO Box 2424 Cleveland TN 37320

BULLOCK, CLIFTON VERNICE, minister, United Methodist Church; b. Lincoln County, Miss., Feb. 12, 1928; s. Obie and Gertrude (Hughes) B.; m. Voncile C. Bowman, Sept. 28, 1951; children: Vidette K., Kim V. Bullock Joseph, Ivan A. B.S., Nebr. Wesleyan U., 1967; M.Th., So. Meth. U., 1971. Ordained to ministry United Methodist Ch., 1971. Minister, Newman United Meth. Ch., Lincoln, Nebr., 1962-67; pastor/dir. Eastwood Ministry, Ft. Worth, 1968-71, Washington Heights United Meth. Ch., Battle Creek, Mich., 1976—; chaplain Nebr. Wesleyan U., Lincoln, 1971-76; mem. Council of Ministries, North Central Jurisdiction, United Meth. Ch., 1976—; chmn. Commn. on Religion and Race, West Mich. Ann. Conf., United Meth. Ch., 1978-84, New Black Ch. Task Force, Black Meths. for Ch. Renewal, 1978-82; founder, pres. United Community Ministerial Alliance, Battle Creek, 1979—; del. to gen. and jurisdictional confs. United Meth. Ch., 1980, 84, World Meth. Council, 1981. Mem. Battle Creek City Commn., 1982—, Police-Community Relations Com.; bd. dirs. Community Alternatives Program. Recipient George award Battle Creek Enquirer & News, 1980; named Religious Leader Mich. Religious Heritage Am., Inc., 1982. Mem. Forward in Faith Clergy Fellowship, Urban League, NAACP. Home: 26 W Roosevelt Battle Creek MI 49017 Office: Washington Heights United Meth Ch 153 N Wood St Battle Creek MI 49017

BULLOCK, DONALD MELVIN, minister, Churches of Christ; b. Reading, Ohio, Feb. 15, 1933; s. Coy and Leta Pearl (Herrin) B.; m. Jewel Willene Beal, May 10, 1952; children: Pamela Kay, Denise Diane, Lynnette Lynn, Rebecca Joy, Timothy Coy. A.B., Ky. Christian Coll., 1955; B.A., St. Francis Coll., 1969; M. Ministry, Ky. Christian Coll., 1984; Ordained to ministry Churches of Christ, 1953. Minister Stinson, Ky., 1952, Higginsport, Ohio, 1952-53, Waco, Ky., 1953-55, Tollesboro, Ky., 1955-56, Butler, Ind., 1956-57, Edgerton, Ohio, 1957-67, St. Joe, Ind., 1967-69, Parkview Ch. of Christ, Findlay, Ohio, 1969-74, Kenwood Ch. of Christ, Livonia, Mich., 1974-75, W. Village Christian Ch., Oak Ridge, 1975—. Contbr. articles to religious jours. Home: 639 Robertsville Rd Oak Ridge TN 37830 Office: 637 Robertsville Rd Oak Ridge TN 37830

BULLOCK, HENRY MORTON, minister, editor, United Methodist Church; b. Chgo., Dec. 6, 1902; s. Hugh Morton and Alma Pauline (Smith) B.; m. Julia Sargent, Aug. 16, 1937; 1 child, David Morton. Ph.D., Emory U., 1924, B.D., 1925; B.S.T., Yale U., 1927, Ph.D., 1932. Ordained elder, 1929. Pastor, Union City Meth. Cir., Ga., 1924-25, Concord Park Ch., Orlando, Fla., 1925-26, Jefferson St. Meth. Ch., Natchez, Miss., 1942-45, First Meth. Ch., Gulfport, Miss., 1945-49, Capitol St. Meth. Ch., Jackson, Miss., 1949-53; prof. English Bible, Blackburn Coll., Carlinville, Ill., 1929-34; head dept. religion Millsaps Coll., Jackson, Miss., 1934-42; vis. prof. Scarritt Coll., Nashville, 1939; minister edn. United Meth. Ch., Brentwood, Tenn., 1972-81; editor ch. sch. publs. Meth. Ch., Nashville, 1953-72; gen. bd. mem. Nat. Council Chs. in Am., N.Y., 1954-68; mem. World Conf. on Ch. Sch. Curriculum, World Council Chs., Lucerne, Switzerland, 1964. Author: A History of Emory University, 1936; The Divine Fatherhood, 1945. Editor: Young Readers Bible, 1964. Trustee Scarritt Coll., 1955-84. Mem. Phi Beta Kappa (hon.), Omicron Delta Kappa (hon.). Democrat. Lodge: Kiwanis. Home: 2145 Chickering Ln Nashville TN 37215 Died Oct. 24, 1984

BULLOCK, WILLIAM H. See *Who's Who in America*, 43rd edition.

BUMBA, RUTH BECKLER, practitioner, Ch. of Christ, Scientist; b. Crawford, Neb., Oct. 6, 1905; d. Joseph Albert and Ida Jane (Moulton) Beckler; A.B., Chadron (Nebr.) State Tchrs. Coll., 1931; M.A., Northwestern U., 1948; m. Joseph Bumba, June 15, 1933; 1 son, Lincoln Joseph. Practitioner chs., U.S. and Can.; Reading Room librarian 1st Ch. of Christ, Scientist, Park Forest, Ill., 1973—; bd. dirs. 17th Ch. of Christ, Scientist, Chgo., 1949-52, clk. of bd., supt. Sunday Sch., 1955-56. Mem. Christian Sci. Assn. of Students of Mary Sands Lee. Home and Office: 3023 Commercial Ave South Chicago Heights IL 60411

BUNCH, ALBERT WILLIAM, minister, Southern Baptist Convention; b. Eldon, Mo., Feb. 3, 1933; s. Tade W. and Leta Beatrice (Hees) B.; A.B., William Jewell Coll., 1954; B.D., Central Bapt. Theol. Sem., Kansas City, 1958, M.Div., 1972; postgrad. U. Mo., 1971, Mo. Valley Coll., 1970-75. Ordained to ministry Southern Baptist Convention, 1954. Pastor Bethlehem Bapt. Ch., Carrollton, Mo., 1957-61, New Salem Bapt. Ch., Marshall, Mo., 1961—; clk. Saline Bapt. Assn., 1965-67, 75-84; mem. joint mission bd. Carroll-Saline Bapt. Assns., 1966-69, 71-73, 73—; bd. dirs. Grand Oaks Assembly, So. Bapt. Conv., 1971—. Chmn. student work com. Mo. Valley Coll., Marshall, Mo., 1975—. Author: History of the Saline Baptist Assn., 1976. Recipient cert. Saline County Bapt. Assn., 1976; Alumnus of Yr. award Central Bapt. Theol. Sem., Kansas City, 1983. Mem. ACLU, Saline County Assn. for Mental Health, Nat. Cathedral Assn., State Hist. Soc. Mo., Ky. Hist. Soc. Home: Route 1 Marshall MO 65340 Office: Interstate Hwy 70 at US Hwy 65 Marshall MO 65340

BUNGE, JOHN ERIC, minister, American Lutheran Church; b. Dubuque, Iowa, Dec. 1, 1951; s. Richard John and Myrene (Larson) B.; m. Connie Rae Walters, Aug. 22, 1982. B.A. in Psychology, Wartburg Coll., 1974; M.Div., Wartburg Sem., 1978. Intern Hope Luth. Ch., Annandale, Va., 1976-77; assoc. minister Morningside Luth. Ch., Sioux City, Iowa, 1978-79, Atonement Luth. Ch., Overland Park, Kans., 1979—; youth coordinator Sioux City Council Chs., 1978-79; chmn. program com. Central Dist. Youth Conv., 1983—; chmn. Central Dist. Task Force, Ch. and Soc., 1983—; clergy dean Kansas City Conf., Am. Luth. Ch., 1984—. Author: Liturgy for Holy Communion, 1980; Stories for Easter, 1984. Democrat. Office: Atonement Luth Ch 9948 Metcalf Overland Park KS 66212

BUNTING, JOSIAH, college president; b. Phila., Nov. 8, 1939; s. Josiah II and Mary (Duncan) B.; m. Diana Cunningham, Aug. 21, 1965; children: Elizabeth, Josiah IV. B.A., Va. Mil. Inst., 1963; M.A., Oxford U., Eng.,

1966, doctoral candidate Columbia U., 1970. Formerly asst. prof. history U.S. Mil. Acad.; mem. faculty dept. strategy Naval War Coll., Newport, R.I., 1972; formerly resource fellow Aspen Inst.; pres. Briarcliff Coll., 1973-77; pres. Hampden-Sydney Coll., Va., 1977—. Served with USMCR; served U.S. to maj. Army, 1966-72; Vietnam. Author: The Lionheads, 1972: The Advent of Frederick Giles. Contbg. editor Harper's mag. Mem. Council on Fgn. Relations. Office: Office of Pres Hampden-Sydney Coll Hampden-Sydney VA 23943

BUNTYN, JOHN RAY, JR., minister, Progressive National Baptist Church; b. Memphis, Jan. 3, 1942; s. John Ray and Johnetta (Staples) B.; m. Loretta Louise Batts, July 6, 1963; children: John Ray III, Cynthia D., Angela M., Anthony E. B.A., Park Coll., 1972; A.A., Southwestern Coll., 1976, B.A., 1976; M.Bible Theology, Internat. Bible Inst. and Sem., Orlando, Fla., 1979; M.A., Webster Coll., 1978. Ordained to ministry Baptist Ch., 1961. Pastor Mt. Moriah Ch., Knob Noster, Mo., 1970-74, Gospel Tabernacle, Minot, N.D., 1974-77, Sandy Plains, Whiteville, N.C., 1977-79, Prince's Chapel, Blytheville, Ark., 1982-83, New Bethel Bapt. Ch., Memphis, 1983-84, Blessed Trinity Bapt. Ch., Memphis, 1984—; chief social actions USAF, 1962-84, chaplain corps augmentee, 1962-84; mem. clergy adv. com. Memphis Regional Med. Ctr., 1984. Mem. Memphis Bapt. Pastor's Alliance, Saber and Quill, Alpha Phi Omega. Lodges: St. Luke (worshipful master), Acacia (worshipful master), O'Misawa (worshipful master), Order Eastern Star (worthy patron). Home: 5330 Wnitworth St Memphis TN 38116

BURAKOWSKI, HENRY FRANCIS, elementary school administrator, Roman Catholic Church; b. Detroit, Nov. 12, 1940; s. Henry F. and Rose (Bialy) B.; m. Gloria J. Cherry, Feb. 12, 1960; children: Michael, Jeffrey, Suzanne, Jonah, Matthew. B.A. in Elem. Edn., U. Detroit, 1965; M.A. in Ednl. Leadership, Wayne State U., 1974. Prin. St. Augustine Sch., Richmond, Mich., 1981—; worship commr. St. Malachy Ch., Sterling Heights, Mich., 1974-78. Author: Imagination Unlimited, 1980; (with others) Expeditions, Flights and Passages, 1980; Flamboyance, 1980; also filmstrips. Foster parent Cath. Social Services, Wayne County, Mich., 1970—; scoutmaster Detroit Area Council Boy Scouts Am., 1970-80. Recipient Ed Crowe award Cath. Youth Orgn., 1970; Spl. Recognition for Community Service award City of Warren, 1976; named Tchr. of Yr., Lakeview Schs., St. Clair Shores, Mich., 1974. Mem. Assn. Supervision and Curriculum Devel., Mich. Assn. Educators for Gifted, Talented, Creative, Mich. Assn. Non-Pub. Schs. Home: 3074 Foxhill Sterling Heights MI 48077 Office: St Augustine Sch 67901 Howard Richmond MI 48062

BURBURY, WILLIAM CLARENCE, minister, Wesleyan Ch.; b. Presque Isle, Maine, Feb. 19, 1928; s. Alexander John and Alice Sarah (Neddeau) B.; diploma Bethan Bible Coll., 1957; postgrad. U. Maine, 1962; B.Theology, God's Bible Sch. and Coll., 1965, B.A., 1966; M.Ed., U. Cin., 1969, postgrad., 1975—; m. Wilma June Jordan, June 19, 1952; children—Wanda (Mrs. George Anthony Oliver), Carolyn, Elaine, Warren. Ordained to ministry, 1957; pastor Wesleyan Ch., Sandy Point, N.S., Can., 1957-61, Wesleyan Ch., Old Town, Me., 1961-64; dean men, instr. God's Bible Sch. and Coll., Cin., 1966-68; dean men, instr. Bethany Bible Coll., Sussex, N.B., Can., 1968-69, pres., 1969-74, academic dean, prof., 1974—. Mem. pres.'s council Wesleyan Edn. Com., Marion, Ind., 1972-74. Vice pres. P.T.A., Cutter (Cin.) Jr. High Sch., 1967-68, Sussex, N.B., Can., 1969-72; rep. to St. John (N.B.) Regional Library System, 1972-73. Trustee Maine Tb and Mental Health Assn., 1962-64, Sussex Pub. Library, 1972-73; sec. bd. Bethany Bible Coll., Sussex, N.B., 1958-64, trustee, 1969-75. Mem. Atlantic Dist. Ministerial Assn. (sec. ministerial standing com. 1970-74). Home: 66 Summit Ave Sussex NB Canada Office: Bethany Bible Coll Summit Ave Sussex NB E0E 1P0 Canada

BURCH, BOBBY DEE minister, Southern Baptist Convention; b. Lawton, Okla., Apr. 29, 1926; s. George W. and Moseller (Ledford) B.; m. Roberta L. Faries, Oct. 20, 1950; children: Dorthy, Kathy, Penny. Th.B., Okla. Missionary Bible Inst., 1972; D.D., Universal Bible Inst., Alama, Tenn., 1975; Th.D., So. Bible Sem., 1976. Ordained to ministry Southern Baptist Convention 1966. Pastor, Richard Spur Ch., Lawton, Okla., 1966-68, Gatlin Bapt. Ch, Duncan, Okla., 1968-72, Second Bapt. Ch., Okmulgee, Okla., 1972—. Served with USMC 1944-46. Democrat. Home: 1000 N Griffin St Okmulgee OK 74447 Office: Second Bapt Ch 1003 N Alabama St Okmulgee OK 74447

BURCH, CHARLES HENRY, pastor, Independent Baptist Ch.; college administrator. b. Port Huron, Mich., May 31, 1940; s. Archie W. and Thelma (Draper) B.; m. Nancy Coleen Hodgin, May 16, 1964; children: Kimberly, Mark, Keri, Kristie. B.S. in Secondary Edn., Bethel Coll., 1968; B.R.E., Bapt. Bible Coll., 1971. Ordained to ministry Independent Baptist Ch., 1973. Asst. pastor First Bapt. Ch., Elkhart, Ind., 1971-73; assoc. pastor Evangel Bapt. Ch., Taylor, Mich., 1973-83; faculty adminstr. Bapt. Bible Coll., Clarks Summit, Pa., 1983—, Christian service dir., 1983—; pastor First Bapt. Ch., Hollisterville-Moscow, Pa., 1983—. Mem. Clarks Summit Alumni Assn. (v.p. 1978—). Home: Rural Route 1 Box 279 Moscow PA 18444 Office: Baptist Bible Coll 538 Venard Rd Clarks Summit PA 18411

BURCHFIELD, LEE DEAN, minister, Assemblies of God; b. Charleston, Ark., Feb. 26, 1934; s. Eulas Andrew and Ruby Mae (Graham) B.; B.S., Coll. Ozarks, Clarksville, Ark., 1967; M.Ed., Northeastern State Coll., Tahlequah, Okla., 1972; m. Esther Joyce Wesson, Dec. 26, 1954; 1 son, Gregory Dean. Ordained to ministry, 1976; pastor chs. in Ark., 1955-69; home missionary, 1970—; missionary to Navajo Indians, N.Mex., 1970-74; pastor Indian Assembly of God Ch., Manuelito, N.Mex., 1974—. Sec., treas. Indian Fellowship, N.Mex. Assemblies of God, 1974—; organizer Royal Rangers group, 1967. Recipient Leaders award Cub Scouts Am., 1972. Address: PO Box 209 Gallup NM 87301

BURDICK, GARY LEE, minister, United Church of Christ; b. Pasadena, Calif., Apr. 19, 1952; s. James Alfred and Roberta (Jones) B.; m. Jacqueline Ruth Massaro, Oct. 8, 1978; children: James Vincent, Caralyn Ruth. B.A., Point Loma Coll., 1974; M.Div., Princeton Sem., 1977. Ordained to ministry United Ch. Christ, 1977. Chaplain, Meth. Hosp., Bklyn., 1977-78; assoc. minister Mary E. Wilson Ch., Watchung, N.J., 1978-82, East Congregational Ch., Grand Rapids, 1982—; chmn. Div. Christian Nurture, Grand Rapids, 1982-84; chmn. Clergy Adv. Com. Community Counseling, Grand Rapids, 1984—; trustee Branch Ministries, Plainfield, N.J., 1980-82; bd. dirs. Plainfield Assn. Religious Orgns., Plainfield, 1980-81; chmn. Youth Ministry Task Force Central Atlantic Conf. United Ch. Christ, 1980-82. Mem. adv. bd. West Mich. Dental Soc., Grand Rapids, 1984—; chaplain Watchung Police and Fire Dept., N.J., 1978-82; counselor Safe Home Project for Battered Women, Bklyn., 1977-78. Mem. Grand Rapids Clergy Assn. Republican. Lodge: Lions (asst. sec. 1981-82, chaplain 1983—, significant achievement award 1979, 81). Home: 1333 Philadelphia SE Grand Rapids MI 49506 Office: East Congl Ch 1005 Giddings SE Grand Rapids MI 49506

BURDICK, OSCAR CHARLES, theological librarian, Seventh Day Baptist; b. Milton, Wis., Jan. 2, 1929; s. Charles Crandall and Fereida (Fowler) B.; m. Dora Caroline McConnell, July 8, 1979; children from previous marriage: John, Ruth, Richard. B.A. and Cert. in Pipe Organ, Milton Coll., 1950; B.D., Alfred U., 1953; postgrad. Pacific Sch. Religion, 1952-54; M.L.S., U. Calif.-Berkeley, 1958. Ordained to ministry, 1955. Pastor, Seventh Day Bapt. Ch., Daytona Beach, Fla., 1954-56; co-pastor Bay Area Seventh Day Bapt. Ch., Berkeley, Calif, 1963-73; assoc. librarian for collection devel. Grad. Theol. Union Library, Berkeley, Calif., 1966—; del. Nat. Council Chs. of Christ in U.S.A. Gen. Assembly, 1960, 63, mem. Nat. Council Gen. Bd., 1960-65. Author Seventh Day Baptist history articles. Mem. Am. Theol. Library Assn. (pres. 1974-75), Am. Guild Organists, Seventh Day Bapt. Hist. Soc., Guild of Carillonneurs N. Am. Office: Grad Theol Union Library 2400 Ridge Rd Berkeley CA 94709

BURGE, GARY MITCHELL, educator, minister, Presbyterian Church U.S.A.; b. Covina, Calif., Apr. 28, 1952; s. John T. and Shirlee E. (Horn) B.; m. Carol Elizabeth Wright, June 19, 1976; 1 child, Ashley Elizabeth. B.A. with honors, U. Calif.-Riverside, 1974; M.Div., Fuller Theol. Sem., 1978; Ph.D., King's Coll., Aberdeen U., Scotland, 1983. Ordained to ministry, 1982. Asst. prof., chmn. dept. religion King Coll., Bristol, Tenn., 1981—. Contbr. articles to profl. jours. Author: The Anointed Community: Christ, Christians and the Spirit According to the Fourth Gospel, 1985. Recipient Everett Harrison award in N.T. studies Fuller Theol. Sem., 1978. Mem. Soc. Bibl. Lit., Evang. Theol. Soc. (chmn. S.E. region 1982-83), Tyndale Fellowship for Bibl. Research (Eng.). Address: Dept Religion King Coll Bristol TN 37620

BURGHARDT, WALTER JOHN, priest, theologian, author, Roman Catholic Church; b. N.Y.C., July 10, 1914; s. John Albert and Mary (Krupp) B.; M.A., Woodstock Coll., 1937, Ph.L., 1938; S.T.D., Cath. U. Am., 1957. Joined S.J., 1931, ordained priest, 1941; prof. hist. theology Woodstock (Md.) Coll., 1946-74; prof. patristic theology Cath. U. Am., Washington, 1974-78; author: The Image of God in Man According to Cyril of Alexandria, 1957; The Testimony of the Patristic Age Concerning Mary's Death, 1957; (with William F. Lynch) The Idea of Catholicism, 1960; All Lost in Wonder: Sermons on Theology and Life, 1960; Saints and Sanctity, 1965; Towards Reconciliation, 1974; Seven Hungers of the Human Family, 1976; Tell the Next Generation, 1980; Sir, We Would Like to See Jesus, 1982; Still Proclaiming Your Wonders, 1984; mng. editor Theol. Studies, 1946-67, editor-in-chief, 1967—. Mem. U.S. dialogue group Luth.-Roman Cath. Theol. Conversations, 1965-76; mem. faith order commn. World Council Chs., 1968-75, Nat. Council Chs., 1971-75; mem. Internat. Papal Theol. Commn., 1969-80. Recipient Mariological award, 1958; Cardinal Spellman award Outstanding Contbns. Sacred Theology, 1962; Andrew White medal Loyola Coll., 1968; Cath. Press award, 1979; Pres.'s medal Cath. U. Am., 1982; recipient 12 hon. degrees. Address: Jesuit Community Georgetown Univ Washington DC 20057

BURGIE, RICHARD RAY, minister, Lutheran Church in America. b. Toledo, Dec. 8, 1936; s. Frederick William and Alethea Anne (Reichert) B.; m. Arline K. Arnold, Aug. 22, 1966; children: Robert F., Leslie A., Marcy R. B.S. in Metallurgy, MIT, 1958; M.B.A., U. Mich., 1960; M.Div., Hamma Sch. Theology, 1969; D.Ministry, United Sem., 1980. Ordained to ministry Luth. Ch. in Am., 1969. Pastor, Sugarcreek Parish, Ohio, 1969-81, Christ Evang. Luth. Ch., Heath, Ohio, 1981—; sec. Hamma Sch. Theology, Springfield, Ohio, 1972-78; del. conv. Luth. Ch. in Am., 1976, 80. Bd. dirs., pres. Family Services, Dover, Ohio, 1978-79; bd. dirs. Home Health Agy., Dover, 1983—. Mem. Ministerial Assn. Newark (treas. 1982—). Home: 860 Village Pkwy Newark OH 43055 Office: Christ Lutheran 732 Hebron Rd Heath OH 43056

BURGREEN, CHARLES LEE, bishop, Episcopal Church; b. Davis, W.Va., Mar. 6, 1924; s. Alsace Lorraine and Zella (Poling) B.; m. Helen Florence Lord, Mar. 31, 1948; children: Amy Lord, Beth Poling. B.A., Maryville Coll., 1944; B.D., U. South, 1946, D.D. (hon.), 1979. Ordained priest, 1948, bishop, 1978. Curate, Holy Trinity Ch., W. Palm Beach, Fla., 1946-48; pastor St. Marks Ch., Haines City, Fla., 1948-51; chaplain U.S. Army, 1951-73; asst. to bishop Episcopal Ch. Ctr., N.Y.C., 1973-78, bishop Armed Forces, 1978—. Served with U.S. Army, 1951-73. Office: Episcopal Church Center 815 2nd Ave New York NY 10017

BURGWIN, GEORGE C., III, lay church worker, Episcopal Church; lawyer; b. Pitts., Aug. 24, 1921; s. George C. and Rebecca (White) B.; m. Lela Hill, Nov. 29, 1949; children: Rebecca White, George C., Kathryn Cochran, Maury Hill, Lela Hill. B.A., Yale U., 1943; LL.B., U. Pitts., 1949. Former vestryman Calvary Episcopal Ch., Pitts.; former trustee, pres. Episcopal Ch. Home, Pitts., former chmn. com. on canons, former mem. com. on structure Episcopal Diocese of Pitts. Ptnr. Berkman Ruslander Pohl Lieber & Engel, Pitts., 1968—. Served to lt. USN, 1943-46. Mem. St. Barnabas Inc. (chmn.). Democrat. Clubs: Rolling Rock, Harvard-Yale-Princeton, Pitts. Golf (past gov.). Home: 5700 Fair Oaks St Pittsburgh PA 15217 Office: One Oxford Centre Pittsburgh PA 15219

BURKE, AUSTIN EMILE, bishop, Roman Catholic Church; b. Sluice Point, N.S., Can., Jan. 22, 1922. Ordained priest, 1950; bishop of Yarmouth (N.S.), 1968—. Address: 53 Rue Park Yarmouth NS B5A 4B2 Canada*

BURKE, JOHN, priest, Roman Catholic Church; b. Washington, Sept. 15, 1928; s. William Francis and Grace Allison (Logan) B.; A.B., Cath. U. Am., 1950, M.A., 1965, S.T.D., 1969; S.T.L., Immaculate Conception Faculty, 1961. Joined Order Preachers, ordained priest, 1960; prof. homiletics St. Stephen's Coll., Dover, Mass., 1961-64, Immaculate Conception Faculty, 1964-67; lectr. sacred theology Cath. U. Am., 1964-68, asst. prof., summers, 1964-69, asst. prof. drama, 1968-72, dir. Preaching Workshop, 1965-67, dir. Preachers Inst., 1967-72; mem. faculty Washington Theol. Coalition, 1968-69; coordinator Nat. Congress Word of God, 1972; founder, 1972, since exec. dir. Word of God Inst., Washington. Mem. Christian Preaching Conf. (past dir.), Speech Assn. Am., Liturgical Conf., Nat. Assn. Ednl. Broadcasters, Nat. Acad. TV Arts and Scis., Radio-TV Dirs. Guild, AFTRA, Nat. Cath. Theatre Conf., AAUP, Phi Beta Kappa. Author: The Sunday Homily, 1966; also articles. Producer TV film Chimbote, 1964. Address: 487 Michigan Ave NE Washington DC 20017

BURKE, KENYON CLINTON, religious organization executive, Episcopal Church; counseling psychologist; b. Cin., Sept. 25, 1930; s. Kenyon Tucker and Pathenia (Clinton) B.; m. Dorothy McIntyre, Oct. 10, 1953; children: Gregory Paul, Steven Allan. B.A., Bowling Green State U., 1956; M.A., Columbia U., 1961; Ed.D., Rutgers U., 1983. Assoc. exec. dir. Urban League Essex, Newark, 1964-67; nat. urban affairs dir. Anti-Defamation League, N.Y.C., 1968-73; community affairs dir. Planned Parenthood/World Population, N.Y.C., 1977-79; assoc. program dir. NAACP, N.Y.C., 1977-79; assoc. gen. sec. Nat. Council Chs. of Christ, N.Y.C., 1980—; cons. Meharry Med. Coll., 1976—, Rutgers U. Sch. Social Work, 1969—, Tex. So. U., 1971-76. Syndicated columnist Community Affairs, 1974-79. Bd. dirs. South Mountain YMCA, Maplewood, N.J., 1971-83, Pastoral Counseling Service, Maplewood, 1971—, Nat. Coalition for Black Voter Participation, 1983, Nat. Com. against Discrimination in Leadership Conf. on Civil Rights; mem. equal opportunity adv. com. U.S. Dept. Agr., 1977. Mem. Sigma Pi Phi, One Hundred Black Mem. Office: Nat Council Chs of Christ 475 Riverside Dr New York NY 10115

BURKE, MAURICE GLYNN, JR., minister, Christian Church (Disciples of Christ); b. Junction City, Ky., Nov. 21, 1929; m. Maurice Glynn and Nancy E. (Fox) B.; m. Betty Jean Clarkson, June 27, 1948; children: Rebecca Ann, Maurice Glynn III, Rosemary Burke Dawson.

B.A., Transylvania U., 1953, D.D. (hon.), 1976; B.D., Lexington Theol. Sem., 1957. Ordained to ministry Christian Ch., 1955. Minister 1st Christian Ch., Maysville, Ky., 1955-63, Columbia, Mo., 1963-70, Central Christian Ch., Lexington, Ky., 1970—; pres. Christian Chs. in Ky., 1961-62; pres. Peace Fellowship, Indpls., 1966-68; trustee Mo. Sch. Religion, Columbia, 1963-70. Sect. chmn. United Way of Blue Grass, Lexington; chmn. Youth Adv. Com., Maysville, Ky., 1955-63; bd. dirs. Fellowship of Reconciliation, Nyack, N.Y., 1965-68; trustee Christian Coll., Columbia, Mo., 1963-70; trustee, vice-chmn. Lexington Theol. Sem., Ky., 1971—. Mem. Nat. Acad. Parish Clergy, Lexington Alliance of Religious Leaders (pres. 1982). Theta Phi. Lodges: B'nai Brith, Rotary (pres. 1976-77). Home: 212 S Ashland Ave Lexington KY 40502 Office: Short and Walnut Sts PO Box 1459 Lexington KY 40591

BURKEY, FREDERICK THEODORE, educator, Brethren Ch. (Ashland, Ohio); b. La Grange, Ind., Sept. 29, 1940; s. Lendel E. and Nila I. (Ringler) B.; B.A., Ashland Coll. and Theol. Sem., 1963, B.D., 1966; M.R.E., So. Bapt. Theol. Sem., 1967; M.A., Ohio State U., 1971, Ph.D., 1975; m. Marilyn Jean Thomas, Aug. 24, 1963; children—Lynne Marie, Brian Thomas. Ordained to ministry, 1964; pastor Ch. of the Master, Steuben, Ohio, 1963-66; dir. Christian edn. Brethren Ch., Ashland, 1967—. Mem. Nat. Assn. Evangs., Religious Edn. Assn. U.S. and Can., Assn. Ch. Tchrs., Adult Edn. Assn. U.S.A., Christian Resource Assos., Nat. Council on Family Relations, Ashland County Family Life Com., Nat. Brethren Ministerial Assn. Contbr. articles to profl. publs. Home: 1385 Meadow Ln Ashland OH 44805 Office: 524 College Ave Ashland OH 44805

BURKHART, JOHN ERNEST, educator, minister, Presbyterian Ch. (U.S.A.); b. Riverside, Calif., Oct. 25, 1927; s. Joseph Ernest and Lockie Louisa (Dryden) B.; B.A., Occidental Coll., 1949; D.D., 1964; B.D., Union Theol. Sem., 1952; Ph.D., U. So. Calif., 1959; postgrad. U. Coll. (London), 1972; m. Virginia Bell French, Sept. 16, 1951; children—David Aaron, Audrey Elizabeth, Deborah Ann. Ordained to ministry United Presbyn. Ch. U.S.A., 1952; Presybn. univ. pastor U. So. Calif., 1953-59, lectr. religion, 1955-59; instr. McCormick Theol. Sem., Chgo., 1959-62, asst. prof., 1962-65, asso. prof., 1965-68, prof. systematic theology, 1968-81, prof. theology, 1981—; mem. adv. council theology program U. Notre Dame, 1971-79. Mem. pres.'s council St. Scholastica High Sch., Chgo. 1970-76; mem. N.Am. area council World Alliance Ref. Chs., 1974-78; exec. com. Council Theol. Sems. of United Presbyn. Ch. in U.S.A., 1975-79; chmn. theol. cons. com. United Presbyn. Ch. in U.S.A., 1975-83. Fellow Soc. Values in Higher Edn., Royal Anthropol. Inst., Am. Anthropol. Assn.; mem. Am. Acad. Religion, Cath. Theol. Soc. Am., N. Am. Acad. Liturgy, Am. Theol. Soc. (pres. 1969-70), Blue Key, Phi Beta Kappa. Author: Understanding the Word of God, 1964; Worship, 1982. Editor: McCormick Quarterly, 1968-70. Home: 1700 E 56th St Chicago IL 60637 Office: 5555 S Woodlawn Ave Chicago IL 60637

BURKHOLDER, ALVIN CHRISTIAN, minister, Brethren in Christ Church; b. Upland, Calif., Mar. 19, 1907; s. Christian Charles and Fannie Elizabeth (Zook) B.; B.R.E., Los Angeles Bapt. Theol. Sem., 1945; m. Vera Mae Fike, Apr. 7, 1927; children—Phyllis Jo, Charles C. Ordained to ministry, 1927; pastor Upland Brethren in Christ Ch., 1931-40, 52-57; bishop Pacific and Midwest confs. Brethren in Christ Ch., 1957-67; chmn. stewardship commn. Nat. Assn. Evangelicals, 1964-76; dir. stewardship Brethren in Christ Ch., 1967—. Capitol fund raiser, 1970-80; bd. adminstrn. Nat. Holiness Assn.; mem. bd. adminstrn. Nat. Assn. Evangelicals; bd. dirs. Mennonite Aid Plan, 1978—. Mem. Upland Bicentennial Commn. Mem. Mennonite World Presidium. Home: 548 N 2d Ave Upland CA 91786

BURKS, ERNEST SEDESSIE, practitioner, Ch. of Christ Scientist; b. Logansport, Ind., Feb. 18, 1906; s. Charles Franklin and Dora Ann (Anderson) B.; student U. Toledo, 1926-27; m. Roma Story, Dec. 25, 1952. First reader 6th Ch. of Christ, Scientist, St. Louis, 1974—, bd. trustees, 1952-73, treas., 1954—. Mem. Assn. Pupils Elizabeth McArthur Thomson. Contbr. articles to religious jours. Home and Office: 1811 Veronica Ave Saint Louis MO 63136

BURKS, JAMES TITUS, minister, Church of God in Christ; b. Samson, Ala., Mar. 22, 1916; s. Alto Lee and Ethel (Thomas) B.; student Columbia U., 1947-52; B.A., Shelton Coll., 1953; B.Th., N.Y. Theol. Sem., 1953, Th.M., 1956, S.T.D., 1973; m. Viola Brown, July 2, 1966; children—John, Aaron; stepchildren—Lorraine, Charles. Ordained to ministry, 1942; pastor Evergreen Ch. of God in Christ, Bklyn., 1972—; dean O.M. Kelly Religious Tng. Inst., Bklyn., 1967—. Mem. planning com. Council of Chs. in City of N.Y., 1976—. Home: 25-14 97th St East Elmhurst NY 11369 Office: 489 Washington Ave Brooklyn NY 11238

BURKS, ROBERT EDWARD, educator, Southern Baptist Convention; b. Washington, Aug. 20, 1930; s. Jesse Audie and Elizabeth (Morton) B.; m. Norma Jean Banner, Sept. 5, 1953; children: Jennifer Burks Dawson, Kari Beth Burks Parchment, Robert Tucker. B.A., Mercer U., 1951; B.D., So. Bapt. Theol. Sem., 1954, Th.M., 1955, Ph.D., 1961. Ordained to ministry Bapt. Ch., 1953. Pastor, Bethel Bapt. Ch., Scottsburg, Ind., 1955-60; assoc. pastor First Bapt. Ch., Anderson, S.C., 1961-65; prof., chmn. dept. Anderson Coll., 1965—. Chmn. bd. dirs. ARC, Anderson, 1962-77; pres. bd. dirs. Anderson Scholastic Loan Fund, 1963—. Recipient Service to Community award Kiwanis, 1965. Mem. Soc. Bibl. Lit., Nat. Assn. Bapt. Profs. of Religion (mem. editorial bd. 1980—, sec. S.E. region 1984—). Democrat. Home: 1117 Springdale Rd Anderson SC 29621 Office: Anderson Coll Anderson SC 29621

BURLEW, CLAUDE LESLIE, JR., minister, American Baptist Churches of the U.S.A.; educator; b. Chester, Pa., July 2, 1933; s. Claude Leslie and Katherine (Lindenburg) B.; m. Hazel Grace Dishner, June 3, 1961; children: C. Edwin, Jonathan W., Christopher M. B.A., Eastern Coll., 1962; M.Div., 1965; D.Min., Eden Theol. Sem. Ordained to ministry Am. Bapt. Chs. in the U.S.A., 1965. Minister Hornerstown Bapt. Ch., Cream Ridge, N.J., 1961-65, First Bapt. Ch., Salamanca, N.Y., 1965-68, First Bapt Ch., Newfane, N.Y., 1968-74, Morningside Bapt. Ch., Pittsfield, Mass., 1974-80, First Bapt. Ch., Gem, Kans., 1980—; instr. Colby Community Coll., Kans., 1982—; rep. Gen. Bd. Am. Bapt. Chs., Valley Forge, Pa., 1983—, bd. dirs. Am. Bapt. Chs., Topeka, 1983—; cons. World Mission Support, Topeka, 1984—; chmn. evangelism com. Great Plains Assn. Topeka, 1984—. Served with USN, 1951-53. Democrat. Lodge: Lions (2d v.p. 1984—). Home: PO Box 177 Gem KS 67734 Office: First Bapt Ch Gem KS 67734

BURNETT, FREDRICK WAYNE, religious studies educator; b. Birmingham, Ala., Dec. 18, 1944; s. Arthur Fredrick and Pauline Nellie (Gunn) B.; m. Carol Jean Struthers, June 23, 1967; children: Brian, Kelli. B.A., Anderson Coll., 1967; M.Div., Anderson Theol. Sem., 1970; D. Ministry, Vanderbilt Div. Sch., 1973; M.A., Vanderbilt U., 1976, Ph.D., 1979. Minister Post Oak Presbyn. Ch., Cookeville, Tenn., 1971-74; teaching asst. religion Vanderbilt U., Nashville, 1975-76; instr. Greek, Am. Bapt. Sem., Nashville, 1975-76; assoc. prof. religion Anderson Coll., Ind., 1976—; asst. youth dir. YMCA, Anderson, 1967-70. Author: The Testament of Jesus-Sophia, 1981; contbr. articles and revs. to religious jours. NEH grantee, 1980, 83; Andrew Mellon Found. grantee, 1981. Mem. Soc. Bibl. Lit., Am. Acad. Religion, Cath. Bibl. Assn. Office: Anderson Coll Anderson IN 46012

BURNETTE, ROBERT MITCHELL, minister, Baptist Missionary Assn. Am.; b. Oine, N.C., Nov. 25, 1917; s. George Fenall and Mary Ann (Edwards) B.; diploma in theology Ittrell Coll., 1959; certificate in religion Shaw U., 1964; postgrad. Mars Hill Coll., 1970-74; m. Louise Richardson, July 8, 1944; children—Annie, Louise, Barbara. Ordained to ministry, 1948; pastor chs., N.C., 1948—, Spring St. Bapt. Ch., Henderson, N.C., 1961—. Co-chmn. Howard Lee's Fin. Com. for Warren County, N.C., 1976. Recipient Vance County Community award, 1973. Mem. Shiloh Bapt. Union, Middle Bapt. Union, Reedy Creek Bapt. Union, NAACP. Home: Route 3 PO Box 25 Warrenton NC 27589 Office: Spring St Henderson NC 27536

BURNS, ALBERT REESE, minister, Progressive National Baptist Convention, Inc.; b. Enterprise, Miss., Feb. 9, 1911; s. John and Annie Letetita (Chapman) B.; m. Mary Edna Hunter, Oct. 10, 1936; children: Annie Laura, Albert Reese, Mary Louise, Franklin Douglas, Margaret Lee, Charles, Theresa May, Gwendolyn, Christal, Victor, Reecenda, Vincent, Eunice. Student Moody Bible Inst., 1945-47, Chgo. Bapt. Inst., 1947-49; D.D., Universal Bible Inst., 1975. Ordained to ministry Progressive National Baptist Convention, Inc., 1945. Pastor Mt. Zion Bapt. Ch., Hammond, Ind., 1945—; moderator New Era Dist. Bapt. Assn., 1968-72; pres. Martin Luther King, Jr., Meml. Bapt. State Conv. Ind., 1972-76; trustee Morehouse Sch. Religion, Atlanta, 1975—. Pres. Mt. Zion Housing Authority, Hammond, 1976—; trustee City Redevel., Hammond, 1977—; pres. Mental Health Clinic of Lake County, 1967-69. Recipient Keys to City of Indpls., 1975. Mem. Am. Orthopsychiat. Assn. Street named in his honor, Hammond, 1976. Home: 1104 Highland St Hammond IN 46320 Office: PO Box 347 1047 Kenwood St Hammond IN 46325

BURNS, CLAY LEE, minister, So. Baptist Conv.; b. Temple, Tex., Dec. 31, 1927; s. Raymond and Rettie Lee (Gribble) B.; B.A., Baylor U., 1951; B.D., Southwestern Bapt. Theol. Sem., Ft. Worth, 1956; clin. pastoral edn. Parkland Hosp., Dallas, 1969, Bapt. Meml. Hosp., San Antonio, 1971; m. Margaret Ann Dillard, Aug. 25, 1951; children—Brenda Burns Groves, Bridget. Ordained to ministry, 1947; pastor Heights Bapt. Ch., Temple, 1948-53, First Bapt. Ch., Florence, Tex., 1956-59, Walnut Creek Bapt. Ch., Austin, Tex., 1959-63, First Bapt. Ch., Clifton, Tex., 1963-70; chaplain intern Bapt. Meml. Hosp., San Antonio, 1970-71; chaplain S.E. Bapt. Hosp., San Antonio, 1971—. Moderator, Williamson County Bapt. Assn., 1957-59; pres. Austin Bapt. Pastors Fellowship, 1961; moderator Meridian Bapt. Assn., 1963-65; chmn. Trinity Brazos Area, 1968. Pres., Walnut Creek Elementary PTA, 1960. Fellow Coll. Chaplains, Am. Protestant Hosp. Assn. Home: 123 Verdant St San Antonio TX 78209 Office: 4214 E Southcross St San Antonio TX 78286

BURNS, J(AMES) PATOUT, priest, educator, Roman Catholic Church; b. New Orleans, Oct. 14, 1939; s. James Patout and Theodosia (Weber) B. B.A., Springhill Coll., 1963, M.A., 1964; M.Div., Regis Coll., 1970; M.Th., St. Michael's Coll., 1971; Ph.D., Yale U., 1974. Ordained priest, 1970. Asst. prof. Jesuit Sch. Theology, Chgo., 1974-79, assoc. prof., 1979-80; chaplain Misericordia Home, Chgo., 1984—; assoc. prof. theology, chmn. dept., Loyola U., Chgo., 1980-85. Author: The Development of Augustine's Doctrine of Operative Grace, 1980; Theological Anthropology, 1981; The Holy Spirit, 1984. Editor: Grace and Freedom: Operative Grace in the Thought of St. Thomas Aquinas, 1971. Trustee, Loyola U. South, New Orleans, 1982-85. Mem. Am. Acad. Religion, Cath. Theol. Soc. Am., Coll. Theology Soc., N. Am. Patristic Soc. Office: Loyola Univ Chgo 6525 N Sheridan Rd Chicago IL 60626

BURNS, JOHN LANIER, religion educator, minister, Bible Church; b. Knoxville, Tenn., Nov. 8, 1943; s. David Brantley and Lollie Ellis (Newton) B.; m. Katherine Gaines Oates, July 8, 1966; children: John, Laura, Katherine, Mary. B.A., Davidson Coll., 1965; Th.M., Dallas Theol. Sem., 1972, Th.D., 1979; postgrad. in humanities U. Tex.-Dallas, 1981—. Ordained to ministry Plano Bible Ch., 1973. Minister, Plano Bible Ch., Tex., 1972-82; co-founder Asian Christian Acad., India, 1973, pres. Am. council, 1973-82; asst. prof. systematic theology Dallas Theol. Sem., 1979-82, assoc. prof., 1982-84, prof., chmn. dept., 1982—. Contbr. articles to religious jours. Served to capt. M.P., U.S. Army, 1965-68. W.H. Griffith Thomas scholar. Mem. Soc. Bibl. Lit., Am. Philol. Soc., Evang. Theol. Soc. Home: 3505 Wentwood Dallas TX 75225 Office: Dallas Theol Sem 3909 Swiss Dallas TX 75204

BURNS, ROBERT EDWARD, retired religious publishing company executive, Roman Cath. Ch.; b. Chgo., May 14, 1919; s. William Joseph and Sara (Foy) B.; student DePaul U., 1937-39; Ph.B., Loyola U., Chgo., 1941; m. Brenda Coleman, May 15, 1948; children: Maddy F., Martin J. Pub. relations dir. Cath. Youth Orgn., Chgo., 1943-45, 47-49; exec. dir. NCCJ, No. Ind., 1946; exec. editor U.S. Cath., gen. mgr. Claretian Publs., Chgo., 1949-84. Author: The Examined Life, 1980; Catholics on the Cutting Edge, 1983. Trustee Rosary Coll., River Forest, Ill., 1970-84; bd. dirs. Thomas More Assn., Chgo., 1960—. Recipient St. Francis de Sales award Cath. Press Assn., 1973. Home: 616 High Rd Glen Ellyn IL 60137

BURNS, VINCENT L., Roman Catholic priest, seminary president; b. Phila., Aug. 30, 1926; s. Earl Michael and Anne Estelle (Crowe) B. B.A., St. Charles Sem., Phila., 1952; M.A., Villanova U., 1964; Ph.D., Cath. U., 1966. Ordained priest, Roman Catholic Ch., 1956. Tchr., Bishop Kenrick High Sch., Norristown, Pa., 1958-64, prin., 1966; vice-rector St. Charles Sem., Phila., 1966-74, rector, pres., 1974—. Mem. Pa. Gov.'s Adv. Council on Pub. Libraries, Harrisburg, 1979—. Sec., trustee Free Library of Phila. Served with USNR, 1945-46. Named Domestic Chaplain, Pope Paul VI, 1969, Domestic Prelate, 1976. Mem. East Coast Conf. Major Sem. Rectors (chmn. 1979—).

BURRELL, ADONIRAM JUDSON, church official, minister, Southern Baptist Convention; b. Princeton, S.C., Aug. 12, 1912; s. Thaddeus A. and Sarah R. (Fleming) B.; A.B., Mercer U., 1934, D.D. (hon.), 1951; M.A., Winona Lake Sch. Theology, 1953; m. Martha Howard Edwards, May 24, 1931; children—Theodore Hamilton, Olivia Burrell Williams, Jr., Ann Judson Burrell Pinson. Ordained to ministry, 1930. Pastor Bapt. chs. in Conyers, Ga., 1934-36, Warrenton, Ga., 1936-39, Millen, Ga., 1939-42, Bradenton, Fla., 1942-45, Rose Hill Bapt. Ch., Columbus, Ga., 1945-69, pastor emeritus, 1969—. Vice pres. Ga. Bapt. Conv., 1948-53, sec. stewardship and annuity dept., 1969-79; interim pastor, Lyons, Ga., 1983, Tifton, Ga., 1984, Winder, Ga., 1985; exec. com. So. Bapt. Conv., 1955-61; bd. dirs. Christian Index, 1969; trustee Ga. Bapt. Children's Home, 1960-65. Contbr. articles to religious publs. Mem. Mercer Alumni Assn., Ga. Bapt. Hist. Soc. Home: 1495 Ontario Ct Tucker GA 30084 Office: Baptist Center Flowers Rd Atlanta GA

BURRELL, DAVID BAKEWELL, priest, educator, Roman Catholic Ch.; b. Akron, Ohio, Mar. 1, 1933; s. Roger Allen and Nancy (Bakewell) B.; B.A., U. Notre Dame, 1954; S.T.L., Gregorian U., Rome, 1960; Ph.D., Yale, 1965. Joined Congregation Holy Cross, 1955, ordained priest, 1959; tchr. philosophy U. Notre Dame, 1964—, chmn. dept. theology, 1971-80, assoc. prof., 1969-77, prof., 1977—. Fulbright fellow, 1954-55, Woodrow Wilson fellow, 1954-55, Kent fellow, 1963. Mem. Soc. Values in Higher Edn., Am. Philos. Assn. Author: Analogy and Phiosophical Language, 1973;

Exercises in Religious Understanding, 1974; Aquinas: God and Action, 1979. Home: Box 402 Notre Dame IN 46556

BURRILL, RUSSELL CLAYTON, clergyman, Seventh-day Adventists. B. Haverhill, Mass., June 19, 1941; s. Arnold Franklin and Norma Ruth (Ward) B.; m. Cynthia Lynn Hartman, Aug. 25, 1963; children: James David, Ruth Anne. B.A., Atlantic Union Coll., 1963; M.A., Andrews U., 1964, M.Div. Equivalency, 1983. Ordained to ministry Seventh-day Adventists, 1968. Pastor, So. New Eng. Conf. Seventh-day Adventists, Willimantic, Conn., 1964-68; pastor Mountain View Conf. Seventh-day Adventists, Cumberland, Md., 1968-70, evangelist, Parkersburg, W.Va., 1970-72; evangelist Chesapeake Conf. Seventh-day Adventists, Columbia, Md., 1972-75; evangelist Upper Columbia Conf. Seventh-day Adventists, Spokane, Wash., 1975-77, pastor, 1977-83; pastor Kans./Nebr. Conf. Seventh-day Adventists, Wichita, 1983—; mem. com. Mountain View Conf. Seventh-day Adventists, 1968-72, Kans./Nebr. Conf. Seventh-day Adventists, Topeka, 1983—. Home: 924 W 25th St S Wichita KS 67217 Office: Seventh-day Adventist Ch S 820 W 27th St S Wichita KS 67217

BURSON, OSCAR BURRELL J., minister, Nat. Bapt. Conv., U.S.A., Inc.; b. Patterson, N.C., Oct. 9, 1924; s. John H. and Ada (Johnson) B.; B.A., Shaw U., 1948, B.D., 1950, M.Div., 1974; D.D., Friendship Coll., 1963; LL.D., Va. Sem., 1966; m. Katie B. Leake, Aug. 24, 1952; children—Anita, Marissa, Oscella L., Jonada R., Jayson Eric. Ordained to ministry, 1942; pastor Mt. Pleasant Ch., Belmont, N.C., 1948-49, Shiloh Ch., Henderson, N.C., 1949-63, Coley Springs Ch., Warrenton, N.C., 1953-65, 1st Bapt. Lambert's Point-Norfolk (Va.), 1963-69, Holy Trinity Bapt. Ch., Bklyn., 1969—. Exec. council Bapt. World Alliance, 1970; spl. asst. to pres. Nat. Bapt. Conv. U.S.A., Inc., 1971. Mem. NAACP (v.p. Norfolk br. 1966-69), Omega Psi Phi. Home: 1349 President St Brooklyn NY 11213 Office: 10-14 Ralph Ave Brooklyn NY 11221

BURT, JOHN HARRIS, bishop, Episcopal Church; b. Marquette, Mich., Apr. 11, 1918; s. Bates G. and Emily May (Bailey) B.; m. Martha May Miller, Feb. 16, 1946; children: Susan, Emily, Sarah, Mary. B.A. cum laude, Amherst Coll., 1940, D.D., 1960; postgrad. Columbia, 1941, New Sch. for Social Research, 1941; M.Div. cum laude, Va. Theol. Sem., 1943, D.D., 1967; D.D., Youngstown U., 1954, Kenyon Coll., 1967. Ordained deacon Episcopal Church, 1943, priest, 1944, consecrated bishop, 1967. Canon, rector chs., St. Louis, 1943-44; chaplain U. Mich., 1946-50; rector St. John's Ch., Youngstown, Ohio, 1950-57, All Saints Ch., Pasadena, Calif., 1957-67; bishop coadjutor, Ohio, 1967-68; Episc. bishop of Ohio, Cleve., 1968-84; chmn. joint commn. deployment Episc. Ch., 1967-73, chmn. joint commn. on ecumenical relations, 1974-80, chmn. theol. com. House of Bishops, 1972-82; pres. So. Calif. Council Chs., 1962-65; trustee Va. Theol. Sem., 1967-72, Colgate Rochester Div. Sch., 1968-84; chaplain USNR, 1943-46. Bd. dirs. Cleve. Urban Coalition, 1968-70; trustee Pomona Coll., 1963-66, Kenyon Coll., 1967-84. Recipient Arvona Lynch Human Relations award City of Youngstown, 1956, Rissica Human Relations award Jewish War Vets., 1966, Pasadena Community Relations award, 1967, Simon Bolivar award, 1973. Mem. Ams. for Energy Independence (dir.), Inst. Am. Democracy (dir.), Nat. Council Chs. (gen. bd. 1968-78), Phi Gamma Delta. Author: (with Homer Jack) World Religions and World Peace, 1969. Home: Middle Island Point 450 Marquette MI 49855 Office: 2230 Euclid Ave Cleveland OH 44115

BURTCH, THOMAS WARREN, minister, American Lutheran Church. B. Waupaca, Wis., July 19, 1946; s. Anthel Dee and Hildegarde Iola (Knutson) B. B.A. cum laude, St. Olaf Coll., 1968; M.Div., Luther Theol. Sem., St. Paul, 1971. Ordained to ministry, Am. Luth. Ch., 1973. Asst. pastor Luther Meml. Ch., South St. Paul, 1973-81, sr. pastor, 1981—. Mem. Democratic Farmer Labor Party Office: Luther Meml Ch 315 15th Ave N South Saint Paul MN 55075

BURTON, NORMA JEAN, minister, United Church of Christ; b. Mpls., Feb. 21, 1925; d. Norman Scott and Lillian Eva (Plaisance) Schroder; m. Robert Van Burton, Jan. 3, 1947; children: David Scott, Marc Niles. Student, U. Minn., 1943-44; cert. Met. State U., 1974; M.Div., United Theol. Sem., New Brighton, Minn., 1978. Ordained to ministry United Ch. of Christ, 1980. Para-profl., Christian educator Bd. Edn., United Meth. Ch., Nashville, 1954-72; student pastor Hobart United Meth. Ch., Mpls., 1974-78; pastor Olivet United Meth. Ch., St. Paul, 1978-79; pastor Faith United Ch. of Christ, Mpls., 1980—; chmn. religious affairs com. Planned Parenthood Minn., Mpls., 1982-84; alt. del. gen. synod Minn. Conf. United Ch. Christ, 1982—; Sunday Sch. tchr. United Meth. Chs.; resource leader Mpls. Council Chs.; lay rep. Roman Catholic Community. Creator and developer Christian edn. materials for mentally retarded, 1960-72. Editor: Mathematical Guide Book, 1973. Active vol. for area hosps. Mem. LWV. Address: 4301 1st Ave S Minneapolis MN 55409

BURTON, ROBERT LEON, minister, Christian Ch.; b. Bloomington, Ind., Dec. 22, 1927; s. Leon and Augusta Marie (Foltz) B.; B.A., Butler U., 1953, postgrad., fall 1966; postgrad. in criminology, Ind. State U., spring 1966, in religion, Midwest Christian Coll., Oklahoma City, 1976; m. Rosetta Kathryn Adams, Oct. 6, 1957. Ordained to ministry, 1950; pastor chs., Ind., 1950—, Liberty Christian Ch., Madison, 1972-74, Spearsville Ch. of Christ, Trafalgar, 1974—. Aux. chaplain 972d Battalion C.E. USAR, 1968-72, 76; chmn. Que. Christian Mission, Indpls. Speaker on Am. history. Recipient Citizen of Day award Sta. WIFN-FM, Franklin, Ind., 1976. Contbr. articles to religious jours., including Christian Standard; developed reading assignment and study approach to ch. services. Home and office: 4653 Young Ave Indianapolis IN 46201

BURY, DAVID ALFRED, minister; b. Mpls., June 19, 1933; s. Alfred Frank and Annie Viola (Howard) B.; B.Th., N. Central Bible Coll., 1956; postgrad. in Sociology and Psychology, Seattle Pacific U., 1968-70; m. Joyce Annette Steen, Aug. 6, 1955; children—Michael David, Diane Joyce, Steven George, Cheryl Jean. Ordained to ministry, 1959; youth pastor Peoples Ch., Mpls., 1955-57; instr. music N. Central Bible Coll., Mpls., 1955-56; youth pastor, music dir. Fremont Tabernacle, Seattle, 1958-60; club dir. Seattle Youth for Christ, 1960-63, exec. dir., 1963-71; Pacific N.W. area v.p. Youth for Christ Internat., 1964-68, dir., 1964-70; exec. dir. Portland (Oreg.) Youth for Christ, 1975-84; exec. dir. San Gabriel-Pomona Valley Youth for Christ, 1984—. Mem. adv. bd. Campus Life Mag., 1966-69; producer religious radio and multi media presentations. Office: 461 N Grand Ave Covina CA 91723

BUSCH, JOSEPH NEWTON, II, minister, American Baptist Churches in the U.S.A.; b. Parkersburg, W.Va., Jan. 4, 1953; s. Joseph Newton and Ruth Beryl (VanWay) B.; m. Gloria Dawn Flowers, May 17, 1975; 1 child; Jennifer Dawn. B.A., Alderson-Broaddus Coll., 1975; M.Div., No. Bapt. Theol. Sem., 1978. Ordained to ministry Am. Bapt. Chs. in the U.S.A., 1978. Pastor Worthington Bapt. Ch., W.Va., 1973-75; youth dir. Grace Bapt. Ch., Downers Grove, Ill., 1975-77; pastor Broad Run Bapt. Ch., Jane Lew, W.Va., 1978—; exec. bd. W.Va. Bapt. Conv., Parkersburg, 1982—; pres. Broad Run Assn. Pastors, Pa., 1983—. Bd. dirs. Potomic House Nursing Home, Jane Lew, 1982—. Home: Rural Route 2 Box 34B Jane Lew WV 26378

BUSDIECKER, ALBERT DANIEL, minister, Christian Church (Disciples of Christ); b. Kansas City, Mo., May 5, 1944; s. Roy Frederick and Adelaide Lillian (Linder) B.; m. Linda Bell, Aug. 24, 1968; children: Sara Lynn, Debra Joy. B.A., Kalamazoo Coll., 1966; M.Div., Colgate Rochester Div. Sch., 1969; D.Ministry, Drew U., 1978. Ordained to ministry Baptist Ch., 1969. Student asst. minister Bapt. Temple, Rochester, N.Y., 1966-69; pastor Grace Bapt. Ch., Meriden, Conn., 1969-75, Ramapo Valley Bapt. Ch., Oakland, N.J., 1975-76; adminstr. Temple Ahavath Sholom, Bklyn., 1977-79; assoc. minister Northway Christian Ch., Dallas, 1979—; Disciples campus minister So. Meth. U., Dallas, 1982—; bd. dirs. Christian Youth Found., Athens, Tex., 1983—; edn. chair Dallas Assn. Christian Chs., Dallas, 1984-85. Bd. dirs. Meriden Community Action Agy., Conn., 1972-75; mem. Oakland Student Aid Com., N.J., 1976; bd. dirs. Tex. Drug and Alcohol Program, Dallas, 1983—. Mem. Assn. Christian Ch. Educators, S.W. Assn. Christian Ch. Educators. Democrat. Office: Northway Christian Ch 8400 Airline Rd Dallas TX 75225

BUSH, JOHN CHARLES, minister, United Presbyterian Church in U.S.A.; b. Century, Fla., Mar. 8, 1938; s. William Ernest and Anna Lee (Vaughn) B.; B.A., Samford U., 1960; M.Div., Midwestern Bapt. Theol. Sem., 1963; postgrad. U. Mo., 1968, San Francisco Theol. Sem., 1972—; m. Sara Lucile Fulton, Dec. 18, 1959; children—Michael David, Janet Lucile. Ordained to ministry, So. Bapt. Conv., 1956; received to ministry United Presbyn. Ch. in U.S.A., 1963; student pastor chs., Ala., 1956-58, Mo., 1960-63; student asst., Birmingham, 1958-60; pastor chs., Kans., 1963-68, Mo., 1968-70; exec. dir. Interch. Coordinating Council W.Central Mo., Clinton, 1970-73; exec. dir. Ky. Council Chs., Lexington, 1974—. Mem. nat. com. self-devel. people United Presbyn. Ch., 1973-76; mem. Ky. Hunger Task Force, Ky. Rural Devel. Com., Commn. Religion in Appalachia, Gov.'s Spl. Adv. Commn. Ky. Penal Instns., 1975-76, Gov.'s Adv. Com. on Bicentennial Festival of Faith, 1976, Ky. Adv. Com. Youth for Understanding, 1976. Bd. dirs. Ky. Assn. Older Persons, 1975-77. Recipient Distinguished Citizen award Americus (Kans.) C. of C., 1967, Conservation award Mo. Conservation Fedn., 1970. Mem. Nat. Assn. Ecumenical Staff, N.Am. Acad. Ecumenists, Fellowship of Reconciliation, NAACP. Contbr. articles to religious publs. Office: Ky Council of Chs 1410 B Versailles Rd Lexington KY 40504*

BUSH, L. RUSS, religious educator, minister, Southern Baptist Convention; b. Alexandria, La., Dec. 25, 1944; s. Luther Russell and Sara Frances (Warnock) B.; m. Cynthia Ellen McGraw, June 2, 1968; children: Joshua, Bethany. B.A., Miss. Coll., 1967; M.Div., Southwestern Bapt. Theol. Sem., 1970, Ph.D., 1975. Ordained to ministry, 1968. Assoc. to minister for adults First Bapt. Ch., Dallas, 1974-75; prof. philosophy of religion Southwestern Bapt. Theol. Sem., Ft. Worth, 1973—, chmn. philosophy of religion dept., 1984—. Author: Baptists and the Bible, 1980; editor: Classical Readings in Christian Apologetics, 1983. Mem. Evang. Philos. Soc. (regional pres. 1983—), Evang. Theol. Soc. (regional pres. 1982-83). Address: Southwestern Sem Box 22000 Fort Worth TX 76122

BUSHFIELD, DONALD CARL, pastoral counselor, minister, Am. Baptist Chs. U.S.A.; b. Pontiac, Mich., Apr. 26, 1929; s. Carl William and Pearl Lillian (Ferguson) B.; A.B., Calif. Baptist Theol. Sem., 1959; M.Div., Am. Bapt. Sem. of the West, 1962; Ph.D., Calif. Grad. Sch. Theology, 1973; m. Celia Carolyn Frick, Aug. 10, 1957; children—Mark Andrew, Lisa Ann. Ordained to ministry Am. Bapt. Chs. in the U.S.A., 1962; pastor chs., Joshua-Tree, Calif., 1962-64, Los Angeles, 1964-65; chaplain Help Line Telephone Clinic, Los Angeles, 1965-72; dir. Am. Bapt. Chs. Counseling Service, Gardena, Calif., 1972—. Mem. Am. Assn. Pastoral Counselors, Calif. Assn. Marriage and Family Counselors, Am. Bapt. Sem. of the West Alumni Assn. (pres.). Contbr. to Community Mental Health: The Role of Church and Temple, 1970. Home: 1203 Teri Ave Torrance CA 90503 Office: 16010 S Crenshaw Blvd Gardena CA 90249

BUSHY, TIMOTHY FRANCIS, priest, Roman Catholic Church; b. Crookston, Minn., May 11, 1953; s. Ronald and Dolorose (Demarais) B.; B.A. in Journalism, U. N.D., 1975; M.Div., St. Thomas Sem., 1983. Ordained priest Roman Catholic Ch., 1983. Deacon St. Mark's Ch., Bottineau, N.D., 1982-83; assoc. pastor Ch. of the Nativity, Fargo, N.D., 1983—; clergy counselor Crossroads at St. John's Hosp., 1983—; bd. dirs. Clin. Pastoral Edn. Adv. Bd. St. Luke's Hosp., Fargo, 1983—; mem. religious edn. bd. Diocese of Fargo, 1984—. State Bd. mem. N.D., Mental Health Assn., Bismarck, 1983—; bd. dirs. Ctr. for Parents and Children, Moorhead, Minn., 1984—, Red River Valley Mental Health Assn., Fargo, 1983—; mem. Dakota Hosp. Community Relations Com., Fargo, 1985—. Club: Moorhead Country. Lodge: K.C. (Fargo); Elks. Office: Ch of Nativity 1825 S 11th St Fargo ND 58103

BUSICHIO, SALVATORE ANTHONY, priest, Roman Cath. Ch.; b. Elizabeth, N.J., June 12, 1934; s. Salvatore and Julia (Skarzynski) B.; B.A., Seton Hall U., 1956; postgrad. classical langs. Immaculate Conception Sem., Darlington, N.J., 1960. Ordained priest, 1960; asso. pastor Our Lady of Peace Parish, New Providence, N.J., 1961—. Chaplain, New Providence Police Dept. Fire Dept.; mem. priests senate Roman Cath. Archdiocese Newark, since 1972. Mem. New Providence Juvenile Conf. Com. Certified hypnotist. Mem. Cath. Priests Eucharistic League, Cath. Clergy Conf., Tri-Community Interfaith Clergy Assn., Confraternity Cath. Clergy. Advisory bd. The Advocate. Address: 111 South St New Providence NJ 07974

BUSSINO, FLORA FRANCES (SISTER MARY DOMINIC), nun, Roman Catholic Church; b. Los Angeles, Mar. 23, 1934; d. Giuseppe and Rita (Bava) B. B.A., Immaculate Heart Coll., 1956. Joined Cloistered Dominican Nuns of the Order of Preachers, Roman Catholic Ch., 1962. Subprioress Monastery of the Angels, Los Angeles, 1980-83, prioress, 1983—. Address: Monastery of the Angels 1977 Carmen Ave Los Angeles CA 90068

BUTLER, ALBERT BOARDMAN, III, minister, administrator, Seventh-day Adventist Ch.; b. Waterbury, Conn., Sept. 27, 1908; s. Albert B. and Alice Adelaide (Koch) B. II; B.A., Columbia Union Coll.; m. Lois Edith Howeth, June 12, 1938; children—Albert B., Gayle Howeth (Mrs. Gayle Butler Rowe), Carol Mae (Mrs. Carol Butler Peterson), Harold Engle. Ordained to ministry; pastor, chs. Tex., Del., 1941-46; treas., sec. Chesapeake Conf., Seventh day Adventist Ch., Balt., 1946-59, pres., 1959-63; pres. N.J. Conf., Trenton, 1963-67; treas., sec. Columbia Union Conf., Takoma Park, Md., 1967-69, exec. treas., 1969-75; pres. Eastern States Adventist Health Services, Inc., Takoma Park, 1975-79; pres. Hackettstown (N.J.) Community Hosp., 1975-79, Washington Adventist Hosp., 1975-79, Hadley Meml. Hosp., Washington, 1975-79; chmn. bd. dirs. Kettering Med. Ctr., 1975-79. Instr., ARC, 1941-63; pres. Nat. Capital Hosp. Council, 1973-79. Mem. Md. Hosp. Assn. (bd. presidents), Conn. Nat. Guard Assn. Contbr. articles to denominational publs. Home: 10213 MacGill Ave Columbia MD 21044 Office: 7710 Carroll Ave Takoma Park MD 20012

BUTLER, CHARLES DEAN, minister, Southern Baptist Convention; b. Newport, Ark., July 18, 1923; s. Charles Henry and Edna Novella (McGinnis) B.; m. Anna Elizabeth Angier, May 7, 1949; children: Philip Henry, Stephen Don. B.A., Southeast Mo. State U., 1948, B.D., 1952; Th.M. Southwestern Bapt. Theol. Sem., Ft. Worth, 1961; postgrad. Concordia Luth. Sem., St. Louis, 1968-71. Ordained to ministry So. Bapt. Conv. 1947. Pastor 1st Bapt. Ch., Commerce, Mo., 1946-48, 1st Bapt. Ch., Leon, Okla., 1948-51, Senath,

Mo., 1951-57, 1st Bapt. Ch., Marietta, Okla., 1957-59, Murray Lane Bapt. Ch., Sikeston, Mo., 1959-67, Hanley Hills Bapt. Ch., St. Louis, 1967-73, 1st Bapt. Ch., Senath, Mo., 1973-80; cons. ch. minister relations Mo. Bapt. Conv., Jefferson City, Mo., 1980—; trustee Bapt. Sunday Sch. Bd., Nashville, 1977-85. Served with U.S. Army, 1942-46. Lodge: Lions (pres. Senath chpt. 1978). Home: 1423 Boss Terr Jefferson City MO 65101 Office: Mo Bapt Conv 400 E High St Jefferson City MO 65101

BUTLER, JOHN ALLEN, minister, Southern Baptist Convention; b. Laurel, Miss., Apr. 23, 1932; s. Berlin Earl and Neva Merle (Temple) B.; A.A., Jones County Jr. Coll., Ellisville, Miss., 1958; B.S., U. So. Miss., Hattiesburg, 1961; M.R.E., New Orleans Bapt. Theol. Sem., 1965; postgrad. Ga. State U., Atlanta, 1973-76; m. Kathryne Jordan, Nov. 13, 1954; children—John Randall, Pattie Annelle. Ordained to ministry, 1972; minister edn. University Bapt. Ch., Huntsville, Ala., 1965-68; minister edn. and adminstrn. Briarlake Bapt. Ch., Decatur, Ga., 1968—. Mem. Sunday sch. and fin. coms. Atlanta Bapt. Assn.; conf. leader Ga. Bapt. Chs.; pres. Atlanta Bapt. Religious Edn. Assn., 1975—; mem. exec. com. Ga. Bapt. Conv., 1983—, mem. adminstrn. com., 1985—; chmn. Met. Religious Edn. Assn., 1983; v.p. Ga. Religious Edn. Assn., 1976. Recipient Outstanding Civitan award Laurel, 1961. Mem. So. Bapt., Metro religious edn. assns., Rho Epsilon. Contbr. articles to religious mags. Home: 2182 Skytop Dr Stone Mountain GA 30087 Office: 3715 LaVista Rd Decatur GA 30033

BUTLER, PAUL THURMAN, minister, educator, educational administrator, Christian Church; b. Springfield, Mo., Nov. 17, 1928; s. Willard Drew and Verna Lois (Thurman) B.; m. Gale Jynne Kinnard, Nov. 20, 1948; children: Sherry Lynne Butler Lankford, Mark Stephen. B.Th., Ozark Bible Coll., 1961, M.Bibl. Lit., 1973. Minister, Washington Christian Ch., Lebanon, Mo., 1958-60, Westside Christian Ch., Carthage, Mo., 1960-63; prof., dean of admissions, Ozark Bible Coll., Joplin, Mo., 1961—. Author textbook-commentary: Gospel of John, 1961; Minor Prophets, 1968; Daniel, 1970; Isaiah, 3 vols., 1975; Esther, 1978; Gospel of Luke, 1981; Revelation, 1982; I Corinthians, 1985. Served with USN, 1946-56. Mem. Am. Legion, SAR (pres. chpt. 1985). Republican. Home: 2502 Utica Joplin MO 64801 Office: Dean of Admissions Ozark Bible Coll 1111 N Main St Joplin MO 64801

BUTLER, RICHARD EDMUND, priest, Roman Catholic Church; b. Salem, Mass., Dec. 14, 1918; s. Joseph Ignatius and Clara Agatha (Sylvester) B. B.A., Catholic U., 1942; Lector Sacred Theology, Dominican House Studies, 1949; Ph.D. Angelicum U. (Italy), 1952. Ordained priest Roman Catholic Ch., 1949. Tchr. philosophy Loras Coll., Dubuque, Iowa, 1952-53, U. Albuquerque, 1953-56; chaplain U. N.Mex., Albuquerque, 1953-62; nat. chaplain Newman Orgn. Catholic Ch. U.S.A., 1962-64; chaplain U. Ariz., Tucson, 1968-76; tchr. theology and journalism Fenwick High Sch., Oak Park, Ill., 1977—; nat. dir. Campus Ministry Ch. in the U.S.; Dominican dir. Newman Apostolate; consultor Vatican's Secretariat for Unbelivers, 1965. Author: The Mind of Santayana; The Life and World of George Santayana; Religious Vocation, An Unnecessary Mystery; God on the Secular Campus; Themes of Concern; Witness to Change, A Cultural Memoir, 1976; God Calls You, 1984: Responding to God, 1982; Jesus is the Way, 1985. Home: Priory Sts Dominic & Thomas 7200 W Division St River Forest IL 60305

BUTMAN, SHMUEL M., rabbi, youth organization director; b. Frunze, Russia; s. Schneur Zalman and Yehudis (Schneerson) B.; m. Rochel Geisinsky; children: Velvel, Yoseph Yitzchock, Yehudis, Chana, Basya D'Vorah. Ed., Lubavitcher Yeshivas, France, Israel, Can., U.S. Ordained rabbi, Lubavitcher Yeshivas, 1965. With Lubavitch Youth Orgn., Bklyn., 1966—, nat. dir.; chmn. Internat. Conv., Lubavitch World Hdqrs.; cons. and lectr. Jewish affairs; organizer world's largest Chanukah Menorah, N.Y.C., Internat. Succah. Author: (weekly column) Challenge, Jewish Press. Lectr., prin. Beth Rivka Acad., Montreal. Chmn., Assn. of Descs. of Rabbi Schneur Zalman, Founder of Chabad-Lubavitch Movement; mem. Community Planning Bd., Bklyn. Address: Community Planning Bd Crown Heights Sect Brooklyn NY 11200

BUTOSI, JOHN, bishop, United Ch. of Christ; b. Nyirgyulaj, Hungary, Dec. 18, 1919; s. Mihaly and Erzsebet (Becsei) B.; came to U.S., 1947, naturalized, 1951; B.A., Kossuth Gimnazium, Cegled, Hungary, 1939; B.D., U. Debrecen (Hungary), 1946; Th.M., Princeton Theol. Sem., 1949; Ph.D., U. Pitts., 1961; m. Lorraine F. Nickel, Aug. 16, 1953; children—Ann Elizabeth, Jarah Joan. Ordained to ministry, 1946; field sec. Christian Endeavor Soc., Hungary, 1945-47; pastor Hungarian Ref. Ch., Hammond, Ind., 1950-55, McKeesport, Pa., 1955-59, South Norwalk, Conn., 1960-76, Bridgeport, Conn., 1976—; bishop Calvin Synod Conf., United Ch. of Christ, 1975—. Sec. Magyar Synod, United Ch. of Christ, 1959-63; pres. Calvin Synod, 1967-71; rep. nat. council, United Ch. of Christ, 1963-67, world council chs., 1967-71, World Alliance of Ref. Chs., Nairobi, 1970; mem. exec. council United Ch. of Christ, 1971-75, del. to six gen. synod meetings, 1957-75; supervising pastor Yale Div. Sch., New Haven, 1963—. Mem. community devel. citizens action council, Norwalk, Conn., 1974—; chmn. Springwood Neighborhood Assn., Norwalk, 1974—; chmn. ethnic council, Norwalk, 1973—; chmn. Hungarian Assn. of Norwalk and Vicinity, 1963—; bd. dirs. Internat. Inst. Conn., 1972—, Hungarian Studies Found., 1967—. Mem. Am. Hungarian Fedn. (dir. 1967—), Doctoral Assn. Educators, Norwalk Ministerial Assn. Author: Theological Principles in the Great Awakening, 1949; Church Performance of Three Generations, 1961; A Half Century in the Balances, 1958; columnist The Calvin Synod Herald, 1952—. Address: 963 Laurel Ave Bridgeport CT 06604

BUTT, GEORGE BOYD, minister, United Ch. of Can.; b. Blackhead, Nfld., Can., Aug. 8, 1928; s. Henry George and Elizabeth Ann (Thistle) B.; student Mount Allison U., 1957-59; B.Th., Pine Hill Div. Hall, 1961; m. Hilda Charity Cassell, Feb. 1, 1951; children—Glenda Luann, Sharon Emily, Jacquelyn Hilda. Ordained to ministry, 1961; pastor chs., Bell Island, Nfld., 1961-63, Cape Breton, N.S., 1963-71; pastor St. Andrew's-Wesley United Ch., Spring Hill, N.S., 1971-74; commr. to Gen. Council, United Ch., Niagara Falls, Ont., Can., 1971; dist. sec. Canadian Bible Soc., 1974—; chmn. Inverness-Guysborough Presbytery United Ch. Can., 1969; mem. United Ch. of Can. Conf. Exec., 1969-70. Home: 60 Creighton Ave St John NB E2J 3G7 Canada Office: 117 Germain St St John NB E2L 2E9 Canada

BUURSMA, BRUCE MARTIN, religion editor; b. Holland, Mich., Aug. 18, 1951; s. William Douwe and Althea Faye (Kass) B.; m. Judith Lynn Wobbema, May 26, 1973; children by previous marriage: Benjamin Paul, David Andrew. Student Calvin Coll., Mich., 1969-73. Religion editor Chgo. Tribune, 1980—. Panelist TV show Everyman, 1982—. Mem. Religion Newswriters Assn. (sec. 1983, 2d vp. 1984). Mem. Christian Reformed Ch. Office: Chgo Tribune 435 N Michigan Ave Chicago IL 60611

BYERS, EDITH J., evangelist, Pentacostal Church of God; b. Long Branch, N.J., Jan. 18, 1932; d. Thomas and Martenia (Lee) Riley; m. Parker Byers, Jr., Sept. 21, 1947; children: Martenia E. Cupe, Theresa M. Mosley (dec.), Joan Byers. A.A.S., Gloucester County Coll., Sewell, N.J., 1971; B.A., Jameson Ministry Coll., Phila., 1982; D.D., Jameson Christian Coll., Phila., 1985. Ordained to ministry Pentacostal Ch.; registered nurse. Asst. pastor St. John Pentacostal Ch., Cedarville, N.J., 1979-84; trustee, tchr. Sunday sch., asst. supt. Tabernacle of Deliverance Ch., Quinton, N.J., 1984—. Home: PO Box 304 Bridgeton NJ 08302 Office: Vineland Devel Ctr Main Rd & Landis Ave Vineland NJ 08360

BYLAMA, OTTO JOHN, minister, American Baptist Churches in U.S.A.: b. Lynden, Wash., Jan. 7, 1921; s. Charles and Nancy (Meenderinck) B.; m. Phyllis Priscilla Land, Feb. 27, 1946; children: Beverly Ann, Robert Charles. B.A. with honors, UCLA, 1951; B.D. magna cum laude, Calif. Bapt. Theol. Sem., 1953. Ordained to ministry, 1952. Pastor First Bapt. Ch., Coalinga, Calif., 1956-62, First Bapt. Ch., Red Bluff, Calif., 1962-68, First Bapt. Ch., Willows, Calif., 1968-76, First Bapt. Ch. of North Sacramento, Calif., 1976—. Bd. dirs. Calif. Council on Alcohol Problems, 1964—. Served with U.S. Army, 1944-46. Mem. Ministers Council Am. Bapt. Chs. Republican. Home: 4649 Freeway Circle Sacramento CA 95841 Office: First Bapt Ch of North Sacramento 2601 Del Paso Blvd Sacramento CA 95815

BYRD, GLENN NELSON, minister, So. Baptist Conv.; b. Hartford, Ala., May 21, 1922; s. William Arthur and Jimmie Gertrude (Stewart) B.; certificate Christian tng., Samford U., Birmingham, Ala., 1954; A.B., Mercer U., Macon, Ga., 1959; m. Melba Kyser, June 27, 1948; children—Joel Glenn, Jeanene Karen. Ordained to ministry, 1951; pastor chs. in Ga., 1952-70; pastor Richmond Hill (Ga.) Bapt. Ch., 1969-70; dir. missions Grady County Bapt. Assn., Cairo, Ga., 1970—. Pres. Ga. Bapt. Tng. Union Conv., 1964-65. Recipient Wilburn S. Smith award Grady County Bapt. Youth Assn.; Scouter's Key, Boy Scouts Am., 1970—. Mem. Grady County Ministerial Assn. (past pres., sec.), So. Bapt. Conv. Dirs. Missions Assn. Home: 1405 Platt Ave SE Cairo GA 31728 Office: PO Box 609 Cairo GA 31728

BYRD, JAMES FRANKLIN, minister, Ch. of God; b. McMinnville, Tenn., Oct. 6, 1939; s. Woodrow Curtis and Tannis Geneva (Ellis) B.; A.A., Lee Coll., 1959; B.A., Tenn. Wesleyan Coll., 1961; postgrad. Christian Theol. Sem., 1966-68; m. Genie Ard, June 8, 1963; children—Kimberly Rene, Kevin Anthony, Kelley Velinda. Ordained to ministry, 1968; asso. minister Lake Wire Ch. of God, Lakeland, Fla., 1963-64; youth and Christian Edn. dir. Md., Del. and D.C., 1964-66, Ind., Indpls., 1966-68, Fla., Tampa, 1969-74; pastor Tallahassee Ch. of God, 1974—. Supt., Big Bend dist. Ch. of God, 1974—; mem. State Fla. Sch. Bd. for Ch. of God, 1974-76; mem. State Evang. and Home Missions Bd., 1974-76; mem. gen. bd. youth and Christian edn. Ch. of God Internat., 1968—, chmn., 1974—; mem. Fla. State Council Ch. of God, 1976—. preacher, various univs. Named Fla. Lee Coll. Alumnus of Year, 1974; named Outstanding Young Man of Year, Fla., 1970. Mem. Pentecostal Fellowship N. Am. (pres. 1976—), Big Bend Ministerial Assn. Contbr. articles in field to religious jours. Home: 1703 Monticello Dr Tallahassee FL 32303 Office: 9th and Branch Sts Tallahassee FL 32303

BYRDWELL, FRANK MEARN, JR., minister, Am. Baptist Conv.; b. Fresno, Calif., June 30, 1937; s. Frank Mearn and Lula Ethelyn (Morris) B.; B.A., Fresno State Coll., 1960; M.Div., Berkeley Bapt. Divinity Sch., 1963; m. Phyllis Maria McDonald, Nov. 17, 1963; children—Frank Mearn III, Frederick Morris. Ordained minister Am. Baptist Conv., 1963; minister edn. and music Grace Bapt. Ch., San Jose, Calif., 1963-65; asst. minister music and edn. Mt. Zion Bapt. Ch., Seattle, 1966—. Spl. asst. for student counseling U. Wash., Seattle, 1968-74, regional adminstr. Office Admissions, 1974-75, asst. registrar, 1975—. Mem. Calif. Scholarship Fedn. (life), Western Area Dirs. Christian Edn. (pres., 1971-73), Am. Guild Organists, Seattle Urban League. Kiwanian. Democrat. Office: 1634 19th Ave Seattle WA 98122

BYRNE, HARRY J., priest, Roman Catholic Ch.; b. N.Y.C., Feb. 7, 1921; s. Harry T. and Mary E. (Whelen). B.A., Cathedral Coll., 1942; J.C.D., Catholic U., 1948. Ordained priest Roman Cath. Ch., 1945. Sec. to marriage tribunal Archdiocese of N.Y., 1950-63, asst. chancellor, 1963-68, chancellor, 1968-71; pastor St. Joseph's Ch., N.Y.C., 1971-82, Epiphany Ch., N.Y.C., 1982—. Pub. mem. Rent Guidelines Bd., N.Y.C., 1978-81; bd. dirs. Doctor's Hosp., N.Y.C., 1978—, Boys Brotherhood Republic, N.Y.C., 1960—, Burden Ctr. for Aging, N.Y.C., 1972—. Democrat. Address: Ch of the Epiphany 239 E 21st St New York NY 10010

BYRNE, PATRICK JAMES, priest, editor, Roman Catholic Church; b. Toronto, Ont., July 15, 1931; s. James Patrick and Catherine (Wigglesworth) B. J.C.L., St. Thomas U., Rome, 1960; M.A. in Liturgical Studies, U. Notre Dame, 1977; M.Div., Immaculate Conception Sem., 1981. Ordained priest Roman Cath. Ch., 1956. Pastoral minister, Diocese of Peterborough Ont., 1956-71; asst. dir. and editor Nat. Liturgical Office, Ottawa, Ont., 1971—. Editor Nat. Bull. on Liturgy, 1972—; Canadian Liturgical Books, 1972—; ann. issues Worship, 1982, 83. Served to capt. Chaplains Corps, Can. Army, 1961-66. Recipient Medal of Merit, Boy Scouts of Can., 1969, Silver Acorn, 1975. Fellow N.Am. Acad. Liturgy (del. 1982-83, editorial com. 1982—); mem. Societas Liturgica, Can. Liturgical Soc. (dir. 1975—, pres. 1981-83). Lodge: K.C. Home: 90 Parent Ave Ottawa ON K1N 7B1 Canada Office: National Liturgical Office 90 Parent Ave Ottawa ON K1N 7B1 Canada

BYRNE, ROBERT HENRY, priest, Roman Catholic Church; b. Saginaw, Mich., Sept. 1,1947; s. Edward and Louise (Keeler) B. Student, St.Paul Sem., 1961-65; B.A., Catholic U. Am., 1969, M.A., 1970; S.T.B., N. AM. Coll.-Rome, 1973, S.T.L., 1978. Ordained to ministry, 1975. Deacon internship St. Matthew Parish, Zilwaukee, Mich., 1974-75; assoc. pastor St. Stanislaus Parish, Bay City, Mich., 1975-77; asst. prof. moral theology St. John's Provincial Sem., Plymouth, Mich., 1978-80, rector, pres., 1980——; inst. lay ministries program Diocese Saginaw, 1975—; instr. Permanent Diaconate program, Archdiocese of Detroit, 1978-80, popular inst./lectr., 1978—; mem. Bioethics Group Detroit, 1979-82. Author: Sacraments and Morality in Juan Luis Segundo, 1978; Equality in the Thought of Alexis deTocqueville, 1970. Contbr. articles to profl. jours. Basselin scholar, Cath. U., 1967-70. Mem. Midwest Assn. Theol. Schs. (treas.), Nat. Cath. Edn. Assn., Assn. Theol. Schs. Address: Saint Johns Provincial Sem 44011 Five Mile Rd Plymouth MI 48170

BYRNES, ROBERT R., priest, Roman Catholic Ch.; b. McKeesport, Pa., Aug. 1, 1941; s. Andrew Albert and C. Aileen (Wolf) B.; B.A. in Philosophy, St. Vincent Coll., 1964, M. Div., 1966. Ordained priest, 1967; asso. pastor Our Lady of Grace Ch., Greensburg, Pa., 1967-70, Holy Family Ch., Latrobe, Pa., 1970-71, Immaculate Conception Ch., Connellsville, Pa., 1971-74; pastor St. Hubert Ch., Point Marion, Pa., 1974—. Chaplain State Regional Correctional Facility, Greensburg, 1967-71, Cath. Bus. and Profl. Women, Connellsville, 1973-74; instr. St. Joseph Hall Minor Sem., Greensburg, 1968-70; dir., chaplain Boy Scouts Am., Diocese of Greensburg, 1969-71; chaplain, vol. Mut. Aid Ambulance Service, Greensburg, 1969-74. Bd. dirs. Connellsville Community Ambulance Service, pres., 1974-76; vice chmn. Fayette County (Pa.) Emergency Med. Services Council; v.p. Southwestern Pa. chpt. Am. Heart Assn., 1974-80; mem. Westmorland County (Pa.) Citizens Advisory Council to Dist. Atty.'s Office, 1968-71; mem. exec. com., bd. dirs. Pa. State affiliate Am. Heart Assn., 1973—, chmn. bd., 1983-84. Recipient numerous awards from Am. Heart Assn. and emergency service groups. Home and Office: 9 Sadler St Point Marion PA

BYRON, WILLIAM JAMES See *Who's Who in America*, 43rd edition.

CADDEN, THOMAS JAMES, priest, educator, Roman Catholic Church; b. Chillicothe, Ohio, Apr. 24, 1930; s. Daniel Anthony and Leone Margaret (Streitenberger) C. B.A., St. Charles Coll., 1952; M.Ph., Atheneum Ohio, 1956; postgrad. Notre Dame U., 1961—. Ordained priest, 1955. Asst. chancellor Diocese of Columbus, Ohio, 1959-60; prof. philosophy St. Charles Coll., Columbus, 1964-67; vice chancellor, asst. vicar for adminstrn. Archdiocese of San Juan, P.R., 1968-71; Episcopal vicar Cath. Charities, Columbus, 1979—; instr. philosophy Pontifical Coll. Josephinum, Columbus, 1982—; pro-synodal judge Matrimonial Ct., Columbus, 1983—; diocesan rep. Columbus, 1979—; cath. rep. PEA Planning, United Way, Columbus, 1983. Mem. Nat. Conf. Cath. Charities, Ohio Cath. Conf. Social Concerns Dept. Lodge: K.C. (4 degree). Home: 212 E Broad St Columbus OH 43215 Office: Cath Charities Social Concerns 197 E Gay St Columbus OH 43215

CAFFERTY, MARGARET, nun, Roman Catholic Church; b. San Francisco, Dec. 8, 1935; s. John A. and Mildred (Sinks) Cafferty. B.A., U. San Francisco, 1964; M.S.W., U. Calif.-Berkeley, 1971. Entered Sisters of the Presentation, Roman Catholic Ch., 1953. Tchr., Sisters of the Presentation, San Francisco, Los Angeles, 1956-68; parish minister Sacred Heart Parish, San Francisco, 1968-71; community organizer Catholic Social Services, San Francisco, 1971-75; program dir. bicentennial Nat. Conf. Catholic Bishops, Washington, 1975-77; exec. dir. Catholic Commn. Urban Ministry, Notre Dame, Ind., 1977-78; parish outreach dir. Catholic Charities, San Francisco, 1978-81; congl. superior Sisters of the Presentation, San Francisco, 1981—; pres. Network, Washington, 1970-71; bd. dirs. Nat. Conf. Catholic Charities, 1980-81; v.p. Leadership Conf. Women Religious, 1983-84, pres., 1984—. Office: Sisters of the Presentation 2340 Turk Blvd San Francisco CA 94118

CAHILL, JOSEPH THOMAS, university president, priest, Roman Catholic Church; b. Phila., June 1, 1919; s. Joseph T. and Mary (Hayes) C.; student St. Joseph's Coll., Mary Immaculate Sem., M.A., St. John's U., 1950; LL.D., Niagara U., 1967, China Acad., 1969, Nat. Chengchi U., Taipei, Taiwan, 1971, St. Mary's U., 1973; L.H.D., Mercy Coll., 1974. Ordained priest Roman Catholic Ch., 1946; dir. students, prof. history St. Joseph's Coll., 1946-53; prof. history, dir. dramatics Niagara U., 1953, moderator athletics, 1956-58, dean Grad. Sch. and Sch. Edn., 1958-59, acad. v.p., dean Coll. Arts and Scis., 1959-62; pres., superior St. Joseph's Coll., 1962-64; pres., superior Niagara U., 1964-65; pres. St. John's U., 1965—. Hon. adv. mem. Queensboro Council for Social Welfare; mem. Regents Regional Coordinating Council for Postsecondary Edn. N.Y.C., Trustee Commn. on Ind. Colls. and Univs. State N.Y. Mem. Nat. Catholic Ednl. Assn., Am. Council on Edn., Assn. Am. Colls., Middle States Assn. Colls. and Secondary Schs., Assn. Colls. and Univs. State N.Y., Am. Assn. Ind. Coll. and Univ. Presidents, N.Y. Acad. Pub. Edn., Italian Hist. Soc. (bd. govs.). Office: St John's U Jamaica NY 11439

CAHILL, LISA SOWLE, theology educator, Roman Catholic Church. b. Phila., Mar. 27, 1948; d. Donald Edgar and Gretchen Elizabeth (MacRae) Sowle; m. Lawrence Robert Cahill, Mar. 25, 1972; children: Charlotte Mary, James Donald. B.A., U. Santa Clara, 1970; M.A. in Theology, U. Chgo., 1973, Ph.D. in Theology, 1976. Instr. religion Concordia Coll., Moorhead, Minn., 1976; asst. prof. theology Boston Coll., Chestnut Hill, Mass., 1976-82, assoc. prof., 1982—; adv. bd. Logos: Philosophic Issues in Christian Perspective, 1983—. Assoc. editor: Religious Studies Rev., 1981—, Jour. of Religious Ethics, 1981—, editorial bd., 1978-81; contbr. articles to publs. including Jour. Medicine and Philosophy, Linacre Quar., Jour. Religious Ethics, Theol. Studies, Interpretation, Religions Studies Rev., Chgo. Studies, Thought. Mem. instl. rev. bd. Harvard Community Health Plan, Boston, 1979—. Summer research grantee, Boston Coll., 1977. Mem. Am. Acad. Religion, Soc. Christian Ethics (bd. dirs. 1983—), Cath. Theol. Soc. Am. (moral theology steering com. 1983—), Coll. Theology Soc. (assoc. editor Horizons 1983—), Hastings Inst. Democrat. Office: Boston Coll Theology Dept Chestnut Hill MA 02167

CAILLOUET, ADRIAN JOSEPH, priest, Roman Catholic Church; b. Houma, La., July 24, 1923; s. Adrian Joseph and Effie Amelia (Briggs) C.; A.A., St. Joseph Sem., St. Benedict, La., 1943; B.A., Little Rock Coll., 1952; student Notre Dame Sem., 1946-47, St. John's Sem., Little Rock, 1946-52. Ordained priest Roman Catholic Ch., 1952; assoc. dir. Propagation of Faith, New Orleans, 1952-54; pastor St. Andrew Ch., Amelia, La., 1965-72; pastor Holy Family Ch., Grand Caillou, La., chaplain Amelia (La.) Fire Dept., 1965-72, Grand Caillou Fire Dept., 1973-85, Terrebonne (La.) CB Club, 1976, Amelia Fire Dept. Rescue Squad, from 1965. Dioscesan dir. Holy Name Socs. Mem. John Sem., Notre Dame Sem., St. Joseph Sem. Coll. alumni assns. Address: 5101 Grand Caillou Rd Houma LA 70363

CAIN, JOHN FRANCIS, priest, Roman Cath. Ch.; b. Owens, Iowa, Feb. 3, 1923; s. James Patrick and Maria Ellen C.; B.A., Loras Coll., 1971; postgrad. Drake U. Ordained priest, 1956; asst. pastor Corpus Christi Ch., Ft. Dodge, Iowa, 1956-63; pastor St. John's Ch., Gilmore City, Iowa, 1963-69, St. Malachy's Ch., Madrid, Iowa, 1969—; chaplain Woodward State Hosp.-Sch., 1969—. Bd. dirs. Cath. Charities, Ft. Dodge, 1958-63; chaplain Girl Scouts U.S.A., Camp Fire Girls, Sioux City, 1963—. Bd. dirs. N. Central Iowa Mental Health Center, Ft. Dodge, 1963-70, Sudden Infant Death Syndrome, Des Moines, 1976—. Mem. Am. Assn. Mental Deficiencies, Nat. Assn. Cath. Chaplains, Nat. Apostolate to Mentally Retarded, Iowa Chaplains Assn. (pres. 1977—). Home: 207 Gerald St Madrid IA 50156 Office: Woodward State Hosp Woodward IA 50276

CAIN, RICHARD WILSON, minister, United Methodist Church; b. Marlow, Okla., Feb. 26, 1926; s. Lloyd D. and Zelma (Leddy) C. A.B., U. So. Calif., 1949; S.T.B., Boston U., 1952, S.T.M., 1954; D.D., U. Pacific, 1964. Ordained to ministry, 1952. Minister, Silverado United Meth. Ch., Long Beach, Calif., 1954-58, Mont Park United Meth. Ch., Calif., 1958-62; dist. supt. Los Angeles Dist., 1962-68; minister Phoenix United Meth. Ch., 1968-77; pres. Sch. Theology Claremont, Calif., 1977—. Address: Claremont Sch Theology 1325 N College Ave Claremont CA 91711

CALBERT, WILLIAM EDWARD, minister, American Baptist Churches in the U.S.A.; b. Lemoore, Calif., June 11, 1918; s. William Riley and Sadie Emma (Hackett) C.; m. Katie Rose Baker, Sept. 4, 1942 (div. 1961); children: William E. (dec.), Rose M. Calbert Findley, Muriel L., Katherine E. Calbert Jackson; m. Madlyn Gwendolyn Williams, June 15, 1963; 1 child, William Eugene. A.B., San Francisco State U., 1949; M.Div., Berkeley Bapt. Div. Sch., 1942; M.A., Columbia U., 1963; postgrad. Am. U., 1969-70. Ordained to ministry Am. Bapt. Chs. U.S.A., 1952. Orgn. chaplain U.S. Army, Korea, and Germany, 1952-62; dir. religious edn. Concord Bapt. Ch., Bklyn., 1964-67; instr. U.S. Army Chaplain Sch., Bklyn., 1963-67; asst. chaplain ops. tng. U.S. Army, Ft. Meade, Md., 1968-69; chaplain St. Elizabeth Hosp., Washington, 1973-81; minister edn. Shiloh Bapt. Ch., D.C., 1981—; del. Council Chs., Washington, 1981—. Contbr. articles to profl. jours. Asst. dir., exec. dir. Far East Community Services, Washington, 1970-73; bd. dirs. Housing Devel. Corp., Washington, 1972-76; mem. Com. Mayor's Health Planning, Washington, 1972-77. Recipient Cert. Appreciation D.C. Govt., 1973, U.S. Army Chief of Chaplains, Ft. Meade, 1969; Spl. Fraternal Leadership award Sigma Gamma Rho Soroity, 1983. Mem. Fairfield Travis Ministerial Assn. (v.p. 1960-61), Far East Ministerial Assn. (pres. 1973-74), Nat. Mil. Chaplains Assn. (trustee 1984—), Assn. Mental Health Chaplains, Bapt. Ministers Conf. D.C., NAACP, Urban League, Alpha Phi Alpha (chaplain 1980-81, pres. 1982-83). Democrat. Home: 1261 Kearny St NW Washington DC 20017 Office: Shiloh Bapt Ch 1500 9th St Washington DC 20001

CALCOTE, ALAN DEAN, priest, headmaster, Episcopal Church; b. Shreveport, La., July 25, 1933; s. Aucei Daniel and Patty Lewis (Redditt) C.; m. Maree Elizabeth Minturn, Aug. 12, 1961; children: Alan, Sarah. B.A., Tulane U., 1955; M.Div., Gen. Theol. Sem., 1958, S.T.M., 1963. Ordained priest, 1959. Curate, St. Paul's Episcpal Ch., New Orleans, 1958-61; lectr. Gen. Theol. Sem., N.Y.C., 1962-63; chaplain, asst. headmaster All Saints Episcopal Sch., Vicksburg, Miss., 1963-69; asst. headmaster Episcopal High Sch., Baton Rouge, La., 1969-74; headmaster All Saints Episcopal Sch., Beaumont, Tex., 1974—; assoc. rector St. Mark's Episcopal Ch., Beaumont, 1974—; chmn. Bishop's Commn. on Schs., Diocese of Tex., 1978—. Mem. S.W. Assn. Episcopal Schs. (pres.), Nat. Assn. Episcopal Schs. (governing bd.). Club: Rotary. Home: 5615 Duff Beaumont TX 77706 Office: All Saints Episcopal Sch PO Box 7188 Beaumont TX 77706

CALDER, ALEXANDER JAMES, minister, Presbyterian Church in Canada; b. Twp. of Thorah, Ont., Can., July 21, 1915; s. Donald James and Eva Lauretta (Laird) C.; m. Helen Isabella Keenan McKay, Nov. 3, 1946; children: Donald, Judith (Mrs. Wm. Fawcett), William, Grace. B.A., U. Toronto, 1941; M.Div., Knox Coll., Toronto, 1944, D.D. (hon.), 1983. Ordained to ministry Presbyterian Church in Canada, 1944. Minister Knox Presbyn. Ch., Norwich, Ont., 1945-48, Georgetown, Ont., 1948-61, St. Paul's Presbyn. Ch., Peterborough, Ont., 1961—; moderator Presbyn. Ch. in Can., Peterborough, 1984—. Home: 1314 Barlesan Rd Peterborough ON K9H 6W3 Canada Office: St Paul Presbyn Ch 120 Murray St Peterborough ON K9H 2S5 Canada

CALDWELL, CHARLES FRANCIS, clergyman, Episcopal Church; b. DeLand, Fla., May 5, 1935; s. Charles Barret and Adelaide (Lettia Carusi) C.; m. Eleanor Marguerite Trump, May 26, 1956; children: Catherine, Margaret, Stephen, Mark. B.A. in History, U. Fla., 1957; B.D., Seabury-Western Sem., 1961; S.T.M., U. South, 1972; Ph.D., U. Notre Dame, 1978. Ordained priest, 1962. Asst., St. Andrew's Ch., Tampa, Fla., 1962-63; rector St. Mary of the Angels Ch., Orlando, Fla., 1963-65; asst. rector St. Barnabas and chaplain Stetson U., Deland, Fla., 1965-68; vicar Gloria Dei Ch., Cocoa, Fla., 1968-73; vis. prof. theology U. Notre Dame, Ind., 1978-79; assoc. prof. pastoral theology St. Meinrad Sch. Theology, Ind., 1979-82; vicar St. Thomas Ch., Salem, Ill. and St. John's Ch., Centralia, Ill., 1982—; mem. Commn. on Ministry, Diocese of Springfield, Ill. Danforth fellow, 1959-60. Address: 111 S Sycamore Apt 209 Centralia IL 62801

CALDWELL, WILLIAM GERALD, educator, minister, Southern Baptist Convention; b. Atlanta, Jan. 21, 1934; s. George Wesley and Evelyn (Albright) C.; B.A., Howard Coll. (now Samford U.), 1954; M.R.E., Southwestern Bapt. Theol. Sem., 1956, D.R.E., 1963, Ed.D., 1972; m. Emily Dianne Clemm, May 29, 1954; children—William Gerald, Janis Marie. Ordained to ministry, 1971; minister of edn. First Bapt. Ch., Ferguson, Mo., 1959-63; minister edn. Hunter St. Bapt. Ch., Birmingham, Ala., 1963-66; minister edn. Cliff Temple Bapt. Ch., Dallas, 1966-69; prof. religions edn. Bapt. Bible Inst., 1969-73; cons. adult work Bapt. Sunday Sch. Bd., Nashville, 1973-76; prof. adminstrn. Southwestern Bapt. Theol. Sem., Ft. Worth, 1976—. Mem. So., Southwestern, Eastern (pres. 1974-75) Bapt. religious edn. assns. Contbr. articles, curriculum materials to So. Bapt. periodicals. Home: 3905 Wosley Dr Fort Worth TX 76133 Office: Box 22000 Fort Worth TX 76122

CALER, STEVEN EDWIN, minister, Lutheran Church in America; b. Hanover Pa., Aug. 30, 1950; s. Sterling Edwin and Mary Louise (Resh) C.; m. Gretchen Cranz, Aug. 25, 1973; children: Sterling Edward, Julie Marion. B.A., SUNY-Binghamton, 1972; M.Div., Gettysburg Sem., 1976. Ordained to ministry Lutheran Ch. in Am., 1976. Pastor Turbotville Parish, Turbotville, Pa., 1976-84, St. Luke Ch. Williamsport, Pa., 1984—; del. Luth. Ch. in Am. Conv., Seattle, 1980, Louisville, 1982; dir. Luth. Social Services, Camp Hill, Pa., 1982—. Vol. fireman Turbotville, 1978-84. Democrat. Office: St Luke Luth Ch 1400 Market St Williamsport PA 17701

CALHOUN, WILLIAM CARL, minister, American Baptist Churches U.S.A., Progressive National Baptist Convention, TV producer; b. Frankfort, Ky., Oct. 28, 1949; s. William Taylor and Myrtle Lorraine (Scott) Johnson; m. Philathia Yvonne Reese, Oct. 5, 1974; 1 child, William Carl, Jr. B.A., Judson Coll., 1971; M.Div., Va. Union U., 1974; D.D. (hon.), Va. Sem., 1980. Ordained to ministry, 1974. Pres., Area III Great Rivers Region Am. Bapt. Youth, 1967-68; chaplain Judson Coll., Elgin, Ill., 1970-71; asst. minister Moore St. Bapt. Ch., Richmond, Va., 1971-74, minister to youth, 1971-74; pres. Progressive Bapt. Conv. Md. Inc., Balt., 1979-81; exec. producer Lift Every Voice Sta. WMAR-TV 2, Balt., 1980—; trustee Md. Bapt. Aged Home, Balt., 1980-81; mem. adv. com. for Religious Studies Community Coll. Balt.; commentator Bapt. Minister's Conf. Balt., 1980-84. Bd. dirs. YMCA, Balt., Opportunities Industrialization Ctr., Balt.; mem. Minority Adv. for Interstate Hwy., Balt. Recipient Student Senate Service award Judson Coll., 1971, Alumnus of the Yr. award Judson Coll, 1978, Disting. Service award Conner Alumni chpt. Va. Union U., 1979. Yokefellow, Frontiers Internat. Mem. Interdenominational Minister's Alliance, Md. Chs. United, NAACP (bd. dirs.). Home: 932 N Central Ave Baltimore MD 21202 Office Trinity Bapt Ch 1601 Druid Hill Ave Baltimore MD 21217

CALIAN, CARNEGIE SAMUEL, educator, United Presbyterian Church in U.S.A.; b. N.Y.C., July 1, 1933; s. Frank and Zekieh (Halijian) C.; B.A., Occidental Coll., 1955; M.Div., Princeton Theol. Sem., 1958; Th.D. magna cum laude, U. Basel (Switzerland), 1962; m. Doris Zobian, Sept. 12, 1959; children—Lois, Philip, Sara. Ordained to ministry, 1958; student asst. First Presbyn. Ch., Haddonfield, N.J., 1956-58; asst. pastor Calvary Presbyn. Ch., Hawthorne, Cal., 1958-60; vis. prof. U. Dubuque Theol. Sem., 1963-67, asso. prof., 1967-72, prof., 1972—; J.Omar Good vis. prof. evang. Christianity, Junction Coll., Huntingdon, Pa., 1975-77; bd. dirs. U.P. Commn. on Ecumenical Mission and Relations, 1971-73. Mem. Am. Theol. Soc., Am. Acad. Religion, Am. Assn. U. Profs., Catholic Theol. Soc., Soc. Sci. Study of Religion. Author: The Significance of Eschatology in the Thoughts of Nicolas Berdyaev, 1965; Icon and Pulpit, The Protestant-Orthodox Encounter, 1968; Berdyaev's Philosophy of Hope, 1968; Grace, Guts and Goods, 1971; The Gospel According to the Wall St. Journal, 1975; Today's Pastor for Tomorrow's World, 1977. Contbr. to Ency. Brit. 1974. Office: 2570 Asbury Rd Dubuque IA 52001

CALIVAS, ALKIVIADIS, clergyman, educational administrator. Pres. Holy Cross Greek Orthodox Sch. of Theology, Brookline, Mass. Office: Holy Cross Greek Orthodox Sch of Theology 50 Goddart Ave Brookline MA 02146*

CALLAHAN, NELSON JAMES, priest, theology educator, Roman Catholic Church; b. Cleve., Aug. 20, 1927; s. Nelson James and Mary Katherine (Mulholland) C. Student St. Mary Sem., 1947-53; Lumen Vitae Ctr., Belgium, 1962. Ordained priest, Roman Cath. Ch., 1953. Asst. pastor 2 parishes, Cleve.,

1953-65; dir. guidance St. Peter High Sch., Cleve., 1965-67; resident chaplain, asst. prof. theology St. John Coll., Cleve., 1967-74; pastor St. Raphael Ch., Bay Village, Ohio, 1974—; historian and archivist Diocese of Cleve., 1967-68; moderator First Friday Club of Cleve., 1968—; prof synodal judge Cleve. Diocese Matrimonial Tribunal, 1969—; bd. dirs. Nat. Ethnic Studies Assembly, Cleve. State U., 1974—; co-dir. Area Bus. Clergy Dialog, Cleve., 1978—. Author: A Case For Due Process In the Church, 1971; (with others:) Irish Communities of Cleveland, 1978. Editor: Diary of Richard Burtsell (1865-68), 1978; Catholic Journey Through Ohio, 1976; The History of St. Ignatius High School: 100 years, 1986. Mem. Canon Law Soc. Am., Cath. Hist. Soc., Coll. Theol. Soc., Great Lakes Hist. Soc. Home and Office: St Raphael Ch 525 Dover Rd Bay Village OH 44140

CALLENDER, JEFFREY THOMAS, minister, Presbyterian Church in the U.S.; b. Peoria, Ill., Sept. 3, 1950; s. Clarence Robert and Joanne (Prosser) C.; m. Jana Ialeen Barros, June 18, 1976; children: Molly Joleen, Andrew Jeffrey. B.A. in Sociology, Whittier Coll., 1972; M.Div., Pacific Sch. Religion, 1979. Ordained to ministry Presbyn. Ch., 1978. Asst. pastor Calvary Presbyn. Ch., Enumclaw, Wash., 1979-82; pastor 1st Presbyn. Ch., Davenport, Wash., 1982—. Coordinator Food Bank, Enumclaw, Wash., 1981; vol. Suicide Prevention, Berkeley, Calif., 1976-77, Tacoma Crisis Clinic, 1975. Mem. Presbytery of Inland Empire, Kappa Delta Lambda.

CALLIGIURI, NADINE JULIANA, lay ch. worker, Roman Cath. Ch.; b. Hibbing, Minn., Oct. 5, 1938; d. Charles Carmen and Mary Ann (Alimenti) Calligiuri; student parochial schs., San Francisco. Foundress Calif. Handicapables, Inc. Decorated Cross Pro Ecclesia et Pontifice; recipient Phoebe Apperson Hearst award, 1967; Nat. Volunteer award, 1972; K.C. award, 1975, 76, 77; Pope John XXIII award, 1975; also awards from state of Calif., and cities of Los Angeles and San Francisco. Home: 2326 Jones St San Francisco CA 94133

CALLIS, KENNETH RIVERS, minister, United Methodist Church; b. Louisville, Aug. 26, 1925; s. George Washington and Fannie Lou (Hutcherson) C.; m. Anne Ruth Smith, Sept. 1, 1949; children: Kenneth Rivers, Annette VanderPloeg, Cheryl Callis deGier. B.S.E., U. Mich., 1947; M.Div., Asbury Theol. Sem., 1950; D.D. (hon.), Albion Coll., 1975. Ordained elder Meth. Ch., 1950. Sr. minister First United Meth. Ch., Saginaw, Mich., 1959-63, Franklin Community Ch., Mich., 1963-65, First United Meth. Ch., Ypsilanti, Mich., 1965-72, Court St. United Meth. Ch., Flint, Mich., 1972-77, Utica United Meth. Ch., Sterling Heights, Mich., 1977—; pres. bd. trustees United Meth. Retirement Homes, Detroit and Chelsea, Mich., 1980—; dean Mich. Pastor's Sch., United Meth. Ch., 1971-75; bd. dirs., exec. com. Asbury Theol. Sem., Wilmore, Ky., 1979—. Contbr. articles to profl. jours. Mem., sec. Sterling Heights Housing Commn., Mich., 1977—; mem. Housing Commn., Ypsilanti, Mich., 1968-72. Served with USN, 1943-46, PTO. Margaret Kraus Ransdell fellow U. Mich., 1947-48. Home: 8506 Clinton River Rd Sterling Heights MI 48078 Office: Utica United Meth Ch 8650 Canal Rd Sterling Heights MI 48078

CALLOS, STEPHEN, priest, Greek Orthodox Archdiocese of North and South America; b. Lewisburg, Pa., July 19, 1953; s. John George and Priscilla Ann (Swanger) C.; m. Christina Tomaras, May 14, 1977; children: George, Priscilla, Yiannis. B.A., Hellenic Coll., Brookline, Mass., 1975; M.Div., Holy Cross Orthodox Sch. Theology, 1978. Ordained as deacon Greek Orthodox Ch., 1978, as priest, 1978. Assoc. pastor, Sts. Constantine and Helen Greek Orthodox Cathedral, Merrillville, Ind., 1978-79; pastor All Saints Greek Orthodox Ch., Weirton, W.Va., 1979-82; dean Sts. Constantine and Helen Greek Orthodox Cathedral, Cleveland Heights, Ohio, 1982—; pres. Greater Cleve. Council of Orthodox Clergy, 1984—. Recipient Oikonomos award Greek Orthodox Diocese Pitts., 1984. Mem. Clergy of Cleveland Heights North, St. John Chrysostom Clergy Assn. (treas. 1983—). Office: Sts Constantine and Helen Cathedral 3352 Mayfield Rd Cleveland Heights OH 44118

CAMACHO FLORES, FELIXBERTO See *Who's Who in America*, 43rd edition.

CAMANDARI, MANUEL TALAMAS, bishop, Roman Catholic Church; b. Chihuahua, Mex., June 16, 1917; s. Felix and Isabel (Camandari) Talamas. Philosophy Degree of Licenciate, Gregorian U., Rome, 1939. Ordained priest Roman Cath. Ch., 1943. Prof. philosophy Sem. Chihuahua, Mex., 1944-52, rector, 1945-57; bishop of Cuidad Juarez, Mex., 1957—; pres. Episcopal Commn. for Mas Media, Cath. Conf. Mexican Bishops, 1976—. Author: Cuál es su Excusa?, 1975; Buen humor de un obisgo, 1978, others. Contbr. articles to profl. jours. Home: Zavagoza 1119 Ciudad Juarez Chihuahua Mexico 32000 Office: Diocesis de Cuidad Juarez Mejia y Peru Ciudad Juarez Mexico 32000

CAMERON, KARON LEE, musical and fine arts director, United Methodist Church; music educator; b. Birmingham, Ala., Mar. 16, 1948; d. Lucien Lee and Alice Virginia (Caradine) C. B. Mus. Edn., Birmingham So. Coll., 1970; M. Mus. Edn., La. State U., 1972; postgrad. Eastman Sch. Music, 1983, Westminster Choir Coll., 1984. Organist, dir. music North Birmingham Presbyn. Ch., Ala., 1967-70; gen. music Ensley Highlands Presbyn. Ch., Birmingham, 1975-76; dir. music Lake Highlands United Meth. Ch., Birmingham, 1976-80; organist, dir. music St. Teresa's Cath. Ch., Midfield, Ala., 1980-81; dir. music, fine arts First United Meth. Ch., Gadsden, Ala., 1981—; mem. com. role and status of women No. Ala. Conf. United Meth. Ch., 1981—; music tchr., Gadsden, 1981—. Campaigner Democratic Nat. and State Candidates, 1970—. Mem. Am. Fedn. Music Clubs, Am. Choral Dirs. Assn., Music Educators Nat. Conf., Christian Educators Fellowship, Phi Kappa Lambda. Avocations: gourmet cooking; dancing; art history. Home: 110 Argyle Circle Apt 10 Gadsden AL 35901 Office: First United Meth 115 S 5th St Gadsden AL 35901

CAMIN, BALDWIN ALBERT, minister, Lutheran Church-Missouri Synod; b. Helmstedt, Germany, Nov. 8, 1940; came to U.S., 1953; naturalized, 1963; s. Albert and Emmi Loni (Meyer) C.; m. Janet Mina Nahodyl, June 12, 1965; children: Timothy, Jonathan, Marc. B.A., Montclair State U., 1963; B.D., Concordia Theol. Sem., 1967, M.Div., 1972. Ordained to ministry Lutheran Ch.-Missouri Synod, 1967. Pastor Duncan-Trinity (B.C.) Luth. Ch., 1967-69, Youbou (B.C.) Luth. Ch., 1967-69, chs. in Alta.; founder mission Grande Cache, Alta., 1969-72; pastor Zion Luth. Ch., Decatur, Ind., 1972-76, Messiah Luth. Ch., Marysville, Wash., 1976—; sec. Edson Ministerial Assn. and Pastoral Group, 1970-71; chmn., 1971-72; vice chmn. Ind. Dist. Youth Commn., 1974-76; instr. Bible Stony Plain and Decatur Circuits Luth. Ch.—Mo. Synod, 1967. Home: 8710 46th Dr NE Marysville WA 98270 Office: 9209 Smokey Point Blvd Marysville WA 98270

CAMP, THOMAS EDWARD, theological librarian, Episcopal Church; b. Haynesville, La., July 12, 1929; s. Charles Walter and Annie Laura (Brazzel) C.; m. Elizabeth Anne Sowar, Sept. 4, 1952; children: Anne Winifred, Thomas David. B.A., Centenary Coll. of La., 1950; postgrad. Div. Sch. Vanderbilt U., 1950-51; M.L.S., La. State U., 1953. Circulation librarian Perkins Sch. Theology So. Meth. U., Dallas, 1955-57; librarian Sch. Theology U. of South, Sewanee, Tenn., 1957—, assoc. univ. librarian, 1976—; mem. vestry, organist, sr. warden Otey Meml. Parish Ch., 1959—. Co-author: Using Theological Books and Libraries, 1963; contbr. articles to profl. jours. Active Sewanee Civic Assn., 1958—, Franklin County Assn. for Retarded, Winchester, Tenn., 1960-73. Mem. Am. Theol. Library Assn. (exec. sec. 1965-67), ALA, AAUP (v.p. local chpt. 1983—), Tenn. Theol. Library Assn. (pres. 1980-81), Tenn. Library Assn. Democrat. Home: Carruthers Rd Sewanee TN 37375 Office: Univ of the South Library of Sch of Theology Sewanee TN 37375

CAMPBELL, ALAN RICHARD WILLIAM, minister, United Church of Christ; b. Ft. Wayne, Ind., Feb. 7, 1937; s. Joe Richard and Neva Alice (Lintz) C.; m. Janet Lee Updike, Sept. 28, 1957; children: Bruce Alexander, Brian Alan. A.B., Baldwin-Wallace Coll., 1958; S.T.B., M.Div., Boston U. Sch. Theology, 1961; M.S.T., Oberlin Grad. Sch. Theology, Vanderbilt Div. Sch., 1967, D.Min., 1974. Ordained to ministry Congregational Christian Ch. (now. United Church of Christ), 1961. Student pastor Union Congregational Ch., Medford, Mass., 1958-61; pastor East Oberlin Community Ch., United Ch. of Christ, Ohio, 1961-65; assoc. minister Mariemont Community Ch., Cin., 1965-68, Bushnell Congl. Ch., Detroit, 1968-71; sr. minister Washington Park United Ch. of Christ, Denver, 1971-77, First Congl. Ch., United Ch. of Christ, Fremont, Nebr., 1977-81, St. Lucas United Ch. of Christ, St. Louis, 1981—; field supr. Eden Theol. Sem., Webster Groves, Mo., 1981—; chmn. Chgo.-United-Eden com. Mo. Conf. United Ch. of Christ, St. Louis, 1982—; participant large ch. growth com. Evangelism Div., United Ch. of Christ, N.Y.C., 1983—. Author: (booklet) A Festival of Banners, 1975. Bertha Walker fellow Boston U. Sch. Theology, 1958, Frank D. Howard fellow Boston U. Sch. Theology, 1961. Mem. St. Louis Ministerium (pres. 1983—), Crestwood Ministerium, Jeffco Pastors Ministerium, Assn. United Ch. Educators. Democrat. Office: St Lucas United Ch of Christ 11735 Denny Rd Saint Louis MO 63126

CAMPBELL, ALLAN NEAL, minister, Am. Baptist Chs., U.S.A.; b. Pitts., May 10, 1947; s. Ralph R. and Grace Philips (Lorig) C.; B.S., Indiana U. of Pa., 1970, M.Ed., 1977; postgrad. Kent (Ohio) State U., 1971-72, No. Bapt. Theol. Sem., Oak Brook, Ill., 1972-75; m. Dorothy Muirhead, Mar. 9, 1974. Ordained to ministry, 1971; asso. pastor, interim pastor First Bapt. Ch. of Indiana, Indiana (Pa.) U., 1970-74; pastor First Bapt. Ch., Glen Campbell, Pa. and Pine Flats Bapt. Ch., 1974—. Moderator, Indiana Bapt. Assn., 1974-77; chmn. statement of concerns com. Am. Bapt. Chs., U.S.A. of Pa. and Del., 1976; bd. dirs. Greater Indiana Council Chs.; mem. Ministers Council of Am. Bapt. Chs., U.S.A. Dir. devel. and mktg. Lee Hosp.; exec. dir.

Lee Health Services Found., 1984—. Vice pres. Indiana County Human Relations Commn., Inc., 1972-74; chmn. Indiana County Campaign to elect John Heinz to U.S. Senate, 1976, 82; mem. exec. com. Indiana County Republican Com., 1976—; pres. bd. dirs. Indiana County Clothing Exchange, Inc.; exec. dir. Pa. Highlands chpt. Am. Heart Assn., 1977-84. Named Tchr. of Month, United Comml. Travelers of Am., 1975. Home: 231 N 6th St Indiana PA 15701 Office: Richard F Seifert Med Arts Ctr Suite 4-H Johnstown PA 15901

CAMPBELL, BYFORD LEE, minister, United Free Will Baptist Ch.; b. Spring Garden, Ill., June 3, 1927; s. Trellie D. and Lillian (Allen) C.; student pub. schs., Mt. Vernon; grad. pub. relations course Dale Carnegie, 1967; m. Wastina Faye McCann, Apr. 21, 1947; 1 dau., Sherry Leah. Ordained to ministry, 1954; pastor Hoits Addition Ch., Mt. Vernon, Ill., 1962-64, Salem Ch., Bluford, Ill., 1966, Oak Valley Ch., Geff, Ill., 1966-80, Salem Free Will Bapt. Ch., Wayne City, Ill., 1983—; chaplain Ina Ruritan Club, 1966-75; sec., Ill. Assn. Free Will Baptists, 1971-72, 82—; ministerial exam. bd. East Central Dist. Assn. Free Will Baptists of Ill., 1965-76. Home: PO Box 36 Ina IL 62846

CAMPBELL, CAROL LOUISE, religious educator; Seventh-day Adventists; b. Grandview, Tex., Oct. 6, 1955; s. Aaron and Dorothy Lee (Heffington) C. B.S., Walla Walla Coll., 1978; M.Ed., Tex. Christian U., 1982. Cert. profl. tchr. Seventh-day Adventists, Tex. Tchr., Seventh-day Adventists, Lewiston, Idaho, 1978-80, Arlington, Tex., 1980—. Mem. Internat. Reading Assn., Phi Delta Kappa. Home: 3525 Willow Wood St #1001 Arlington TX 76015 Office: Burton Adventist Acad 4611 Kelly Elliott Arlington TX 76010

CAMPBELL, DAVID GEORGE, minister, Christian Ch.; b. Saginaw, Mich., Sept. 29, 1938; s. Paul Francis and Clara Rosemond (Allee) C.; B.A., Cin. Bible Sem., 1962; M.R.E., Zion Theol. Sem., 1973; postgrad. U. S. Africa, 1968-71, S.W. Minn. State Coll., 1972-73; Th.D., Berean Christian Sem., 1977; m. Hela Marie Storey, Oct. 3, 1958; children:—Enya Marlene, Kyle Jane, Deanne Noel. Ordained to ministry, 1959; minister Christian Ch., Elizabethtown, Ind., 1957-61, College Park, Ga., 1962-65; sr. minister, Griffith, Ind., 1965-68; missionary Central Africa Mission, Rhodesia, 1968-71; minister Ch. of Christ, Redwood Falls, Minn., 1971-74; chaplain resident Rochester (Minn.) Meth. Hosp., 1974-75; sr. minister Mt. View Ch. of Christ, Phoenix, 1975—; dir. dept. religion and pastoral care Desert Samaritan Hosp., Mesa, Ariz. Hosp. chaplain cons.; bd. dirs. Chgo. Dist. Evangelistic Assn., 1965-68, Ariz. Evangelizing Assn., 1975—; mem. steering com. S.W. Christian Edn. Conv., 1975—. Bd. dirs. Ariz. Kidney Found., 1976—. Mem. Assn. for Clin. Pastoral Edn., Minn. Evangelizing Assn. (pres. 1972-74), Am. Protestant Hosp. Assn., Coll. of Chaplains, Am. Assn. Christian Edn. Home: 4429 N 29th St Phoenix AZ 85016 Office: 2927 E Campbell Ave Phoenix AZ 85016

CAMPBELL, DENNIS MARION, educator, United Methodist Church; b. Dalhart, Tex., Aug. 23, 1945; s. Francis Marion and Margaret (Osterberg) C.; m. Leesa Heydenreich, June 13, 1970; children: Margaret Heyden, Robert Trevor. A.B., Duke U., 1967; B.D., Yale U., 1970; Ph.D., Duke U., 1973. Ordained to ministry, 1974. Assoc. pastor Trinity Meth. Ch., Durham, N.C., 1970-74; prof. religion and chmn. dept., Converse Coll., Spartanburg, S.C., 1974-79; dir. continuing edn. Duke U. Div. Sch., Durham, 1979-82; dean and prof. theology Duke U. Div. Sch., 1982—; pres. Meth. Student Movement, 1968-70; bd. dirs. Bd. Higher Edn. & Ministry, United Meth. Ch., 1968-72, del. gen. conf., 1984; mem. Oxford Inst. Meth. Technology, 1973, 82. Author: Authority and Renewal of American Theology, 1976; Doctors, Lawyers, Ministers: Christian Ethics in Professional Practice, 1982. Danforth fellow, 1985—; Gurney Harriss Kearns fellow, 1970-73. Mem. Am. Acad. Religion, Am. Soc. Christian Ethics, Phi Beta Kappa, Omicron Delta Kappa. Home: 2802 Friendship Cir Durham NC 27705 Office: The Divinity Sch Duke Univ Durham NC 27706

CAMPBELL, ELIZABETH JOSEPHINE, missionary, So. Baptist Conv.; b. Chesterville, Ill., Jan. 22, 1915; d. Robert Franklin and Jessie Margaret (Bentley) Campbell; diploma Mars Hill Jr. Coll., 1934; B.R.E., Southwestern Bapt. Theol. Sem., 1944. Associational missionary N.C. Caldwell Missionary Bapt. Assn., So. Bapt. Conv., 1944—; mem. staff numerous vacation Bible sch. and clinics; chaplain home life dept. Lenoir (N.C.) Women's Club, Gen. Woman's Club, Lenoir, 1972-74; v.p. N.C. Conf. Associational Missionaries, 1956, officer, 1965, pres., 1969-70; mem. exec. bd. N.C. Woman's Missionary Union, 1946-48, 56-58, 64-67, 74—; now dir. missions Caldwell Missionary Bapt. Assn.; mem. gen. bd. N.C. Bapt. Conv., 1969-70, mem. program com. So. Bapt. Conv., 1965, 71, 73, mem. com. on coms. 1963, 70. Writer gospel hymns. Home: 516 Main St SW Lenoir NC 28645 Office: 208 Nu-Way Circle NE Lenoir NC 28645

CAMPBELL, GORDON PAUL, minister, United Pentecostal Church International; b. Belfast, No. Ireland, May 10, 1951; came to U.S., 1969; naturalized, 19—; s. David and Jane Nelson (Beattie) C.; m. Lillian

Grace White, June 5, 1971; children: David Leon, Gordon Scott, Robert James. B.A.T.H., Christian Life Coll., 1973. Ordained to ministry, United Pentecostal Ch. Internat., 1977. Nat. evangelist United Pentecostal Ch. Internat., Eng., 1973-76, nat. youth pres., Eng., 1973-76, evangelist, U.S., 1976-79, pastor, Binghamton, N.Y., 1979—. Home and Office: 1256 Vestal Ave Binghamton NY 13903

CAMPBELL, JOHN DOUGLAS, minister, Church of God (Anderson, Indiana); b. Blyth, Ont., Can., Jan. 8, 1943; s. Albert Douglas and Gladys Laura (Good) C.; m. Betty Lou Campbell, Aug. 17, 1963; children: Laura Lee, Douglas Bruce. Ministerial Diploma, Gardner Bible Coll., 1967. Ordained to ministry Ch. of God (Anderson, Ind.), 1969. Pastor, Ch. of God, Schuler, Alta., Can., 1967-72, Swift Current, Sask., Can., 1972-75, Grand Bend, Ont., 1975—; chmn. Ch. of God Ministerial Assembly of Ont., 1976-84; vice chmn. Ch. of God Gen. Assembly, Ont., 1984—, mem. missionary bd., 1980—, bd. dirs., 1982—. Census enumerator Fed. Govt. Can., 1970. Address: 8 Gill Rd PO Box 225 Grand Bend ON N0M 1T0 Canada

CAMPBELL, KENNETH LIVINGSTONE, clergyman, Fellowship of Evangelical Baptist Churches in Canada; b. Hartford, Ont., Can., Jan., 1934; s. Robert Duncan and Mary Jean (Scott) C.; m. Alice Joyce McLeod, Jan. 15, 1958 (dec. 1960); children: Annette, Jennie; m. Norma Sylvie Nandrea, Nov. 27, 1960; children: David, Kathy, Shelly. B.A. in History, Bryan Coll., 1956; D.D. (hon.), Richmond Coll., 1973. Ordained to ministry Bapt. Ch., 1958. Pastor, Emmanuel Bapt. Ch., Milton, Ont., 1958-60, 82—; pres. Ken Campbell Evangelistic Assn., Inc., Milton and South Bend, Ind., 1960—; pres. Richmond Coll., Milliken, Ont., 1979-81, chancellor, 1981-83; pres., bd. dirs. Golden Horseshoe Christian Youth Ctr., Milton, Ont., 1964—, Renaissance Can., Inc., Milton, 1974—; founder, pres. Renaissance Internat., Milton, 1974—; founder, chancellor Coronation Coll., Milton, 1983—. Author: A Live Coal from the Altar, 1964, 68, 73; Tempest in a Teapot, 1975; No Small Stir, 1980. Pub. religious quar. Liberation, 1971—. Home: Rural Route 6 Milton ON L9T 2Y1 Canada Office: Ken Campbell Evangelistic Assn Inc 245 Commercial St Milton ON L9T 2J3 Canada

CAMPBELL, MAYNARD L., JR., minister, So. Baptist Conv.; b. Beaver, Okla., Apr. 9, 1943; s. Maynard L. and Anna Lois (Armstrong) C.; B.A., Hardin-Simmons U., Abilene, Tex., 1967; M.Div., Southwestern Bapt. Theol. Sem., Ft. Worth, 1970, Th.D., 1977; m. Janice Lynne Robertson, Dec. 26, 1970; 1 dau., Melynda Ruth. Ordained to ministry, 1960; pastor Fairview Bapt. Ch., Duncan, Okla., 1960-63, Patterson Ave. Bapt. Ch., Comanche, Okla., 1964-67, Irving Bapt. Ch., Ryan, Okla., 1971-73, Springdale Bapt. Ch., Tulsa, 1974-76. Solicitor, Am. Cancer Soc., Ft. Worth, 1974. Recipient Baker Bookhouse award Hardin-Simmons U., 1967. Home and office: Box 715 Ava MO 65608

CAMPBELL, ROBERT CHARLES, church executive, American Baptist Chs., U.S.A.; b. Chandler, Ariz., Mar. 9, 1924; s. Alexander Joshua and Florence (Betzner) C.; A.B., Westmont Coll., 1944; B.D., Eastern Bapt. Theol. Sem., 1947, Th.M., 1949, Th.D., 1951, D.D. (hon.), 1974; M.A., U. So. Calif., 1959; postgrad. Dropsie U., 1949-51, U. Pa., 1951-52, N.Y. U., 1960-62, U. Cambridge (Eng.), 1969; D.Litt. (hon.), Calif. Bapt. Theol. Sem., 1972; Hum.D. (hon.), Alderson-Broaddus Coll., 1979; L.H.D., Linfield Coll., 1982; m. Lotus Idamae Graham, July 12, 1945; children—Robin Carl, Cherry Colleen. Ordained to ministry, 1947; pastor 34th St. Bapt. Ch., Phila., 1945-49; instr. Eastern Bapt. Theol. Sem., Phila., 1949-51; asst. prof. Eastern Bapt. Coll., St. Davids, Pa., 1951-53; asso. prof. N.T., Am. Bapt. Sem. of West, Covina, Calif., 1953-54, dean, prof., 1954-72; gen. sec. Am. Bapt. Chs., U.S.A., Valley Forge, Pa., 1972—. Pres., N.Am. Bapt. Fellowship, 1974-76; mem. exec. com. Bapt. World Alliance, 1972—, v.p., 1975-80; mem. exec. com., governing bd. Nat. Council Chs., 1972—; mem. central com., del. World Council Chs.; del. World Council of Chs., 1975, 83; Author: Great Words of the Faith, 1965; The Gospel of Paul, 1973; Teachings of Jesus, 1985. Home: 1000 Valley Forge Circle King of Prussia PA 19406 Office: Am Bapt Chs Valley Forge PA 19481

CAMPBELL, ROBERT WILLIAM, minister, Southern Baptist Convention; b. Charlotte, N.C., Apr. 20, 1949; s. Robert Lee and Irene Elizabeth Campbell; m. Dawne Mary Batchleor, Apr. 16, 1983. B.R.E., Gardner-Webb Coll., 1971; M.R.E., Southeastern Sem., 1974; D.Min., Luther-Rice Sem., 1980. Ordained to ministry Southern Baptist Convention, 1968. Minister of youth and edn. Oakhurst Bapt. Ch., Charlotte, 1980-82; pastor Calypso Bapt. Ch., N.C., 1973-76, Mount Lebanon Bapt. Ch., Bostic, N.C., 1976-80, Liberty Hill Bapt. Ch., Pageland, S.C., 1982—; pres. Mid-Atlantic Sem., Rockhill, S.C., 1985—; dir. music Chesterfield Bapt. Assn., Ruby, S.C., 1983—; mem. bd. of assocs. Gardner-Webb Coll., Boiling Springs, S.C., 1973. Author: Facing and Conquering Death in the Life of A Christian, 1980. Chmn. ARC, Calypso, 1975, Cystic Fibrosis Assn., Calypso, 1974. Recipient Christian Devel. award So. Bapt. Conv., 1985; Kesie Found. scholar, 1971-73. Mem. Ministers Growth Conf., 300 Club of S.C. Democrat. Lodge: Masons. Avocations: music; volleyball; softball. Home and Office: Liberty Hill Bapt Ch PO Box 84 Pageland SC 29728

CAMPION, OWEN FRANCIS, editor, priest, Roman Catholic Ch.; b. Nashville, Apr. 24, 1940; s. Owen Finnegan and Joanna Frances (Bass) C.; B.A., St. Bernard Coll., 1962; postgrad. theology St. Mary's Sem., 1964-66; postgrad. Cath. U. Am., 1967-68. Ordained priest Roman Cath. Ch., 1966; asso. pastor St. Jude Ch., Chattanooga, 1966-69; tchr. Notre Dame High Sch., Chattanooga, 1966-69; asso. editor The Tenn. Register, Nashville, 1968-71, editor, 1971—; asso. pastor Holy Ghost Ch., Knoxville, Tenn., 1969-71; asso. diocesan dir. of religious edn. Confrat. Christian Doctrine, Nashville, 1967-71; chmn. ecumenical commn. Diocese of Nashville, 1972-77. Mem. Am., Tenn. hist. assns., S.A.R., Cath. Press Assn., (treas. 1981-84, pres. 1984—), Nat. Press Club, Sigma Delta Chi. Author: A History of the Diocese of Nashville, 1962. Home: 3909 Cambridge Ave Nashville TN 37205 Office: 2400 21st Ave South Nashville TN 37212

CANCRO, FRANCIS THOMAS, priest, Roman Catholic Church; b. Phila., June 12, 1950; s. Frank T. and Mary Elizabeth (Tallett) C. B.A. in Theology, St. Mary Sem. and U., 1977, M.A., 1980, S.T.B., 1981; M.A., Trinity Coll., 1978. Ordained to priesthood Roman Cath. Ch., 1981. Pastor, Bishop McGuinness High Sch., Winston-Salem, 1981-85; dir. Office Communications, Diocese of Charlotte, N.C., 1983—; dir., founder Cath. Telecommunications N.C., Charlotte, 1984—; bd. dirs. N.C. Cath. Newspaper, Raleigh, 1983—; faculty Deacon Prep Program, Sacred Heart Coll., Belmont, N.C., 1984—. Co-author: Focus on Preaching, 1985. Mem. Human Relations Council, Winston-Salem, 1982; youth advisor ARC, 1983. U.S. Cath. Conf. grantee, 1984; FADICA grantee, 1985. Mem. N.C. Assn. Broadcasters, Am. Fedn. TV and Radio Artists, Allied Cath. Communicators, Cath. Telecommunications Network of Am. Home: PO Box 1274 Clemmons NC 27012 Office: Catholic Ctr 1524 E Morehead St Charlotte NC 28206

CANFIELD, FRANCIS X., priest, Roman Catholic Church; b. Detroit, Dec. 3, 1920; s. Edward and Adelle Mary (Berg) C. B.A., Sacred Heart Sem., 1941; M.A., Cath. U., 1945; M.A.L.S., U. Mich., 1949; Ph.D., U. Ottawa, Ont., 1950. Ordained priest, 1945. Instr., Sacred Heart Sem., Detroit, 1946-49, prof., librarian, 1949-63, rector, pres., 1963-70; pastor St. Paul Parish, Grosse Pointe, Mich., 1971—. Author: History: Archdiocese of Detroit, 1983; Co-author: With Eyes of Faith, 1984. Recipient Community Service award Grosse Point Inter-Faith Ctr., 1979; award, Pregnancy Aid Ctr., Gross Point, 1984. Mem. Grosse Pointe Inter-Faith Ctr., Grosse Point Ministerial Assn. (pres. 1973-74), Cath. Library Assn., Am. Friends of Vatican Library (pres.). Address: 157 Lake Shore Grosse Point MI 48236

CANFIELD, MARTHA RUSSELL, lay ch. worker, Christian Sci. Ch.; b. Sedalia, Mo., July 18, 1923; d. Wallace William and Mary Susan (Milburn) Russell; student Kan. City Jr. Coll., 1940-41; m. Lloyd Hugh Canfield, Aug. 25, 1951 (dec.); children—Pamela Canfield Peck, Sandra Canfield Leffingwell. Reader Christian Sci. Ch., 1969-73, pres., chmn. bd. dirs., Kansas City, Mo., 1973, 74, chmn. Christian Sci. Monitor Com.; librarian Christian Sci. Reading Room; practitioner Crown Center, Kansas City; bd. dirs. Cedars Camp for Christian Sci. Children, Lebanon, Mo. Mem. Longyear Found. and Hist. Soc. Home: 2004 Condolea Dr Leawood KS 66209 Office: 2420 Pershing Rd Suite 130 Crown Center Kansas City MO 64108

CANFIELD, RICHARD MAURICE, minister, Conservative Baptist Assn. Am.; b. Munden, Kans., Aug. 25, 1921; s. Roy Alfred and Lois Mary (Williams) C.; B.S., Wheaton Coll., 1944; B.D., No. Sem. (Chgo.), 1945; m. Juanita Fern Lortz, Dec. 21, 1944; children—Ron, Cheryl, David, Patti, Judy, Jan, Rich, Bob, Joyce. Ordained to ministry, 1950; pastor DuPage Presbyn. Ch., Plainfield, Ill., 1945-47; asst. pastor First Presbyn. Ch., Aurora, Ill., 1948-49; pastor First Bapt. Ch., Maxwell, Nebr., 1950-52; asst. to dir. Back to the Bible Broadcast, Lincoln, Nebr., 1952-64; pres. Keys to Better Living, Inc., Mt. Joy, Pa., 1964—. Chaplain Nebr. State Penitentiary, 1955-56; counselor Philhaven Psychiatric Hosp., Lebanon, Pa., 1967-75; dir. Keys Counseling Center, Manheim, Pa., 1975—; exec. bd. Nat. Religious Broadcasters, 1965-75. Author: Keys to Better Mental Health, 1976; Keys for Unlocking Depression, 1975; Keys to Better Behavior for your Child, 1974; Happy Marriages Make Happy Homes, 1973; Keys to Happiness, 1972, many others. Home: Route 1 Manheim PA 17545 Office: Route 2 Mount Joy PA 17552

CANN, ROGER CARL, council of churches administrator, Baptist Federation of Canada; b. Yarmouth, N.S., Can., Mar. 2, 1932; s. Lawrence Wyman and Myra Genevieve (McGray) C.; m. Sadie Katryn Campbell, Sept. 7, 1955; children: Paul, Carl, Scott. B.A., Acadia U., N.S., 1954, B.D., 1956. Ordained to ministry Baptist Fedn. Can. 1956. Dir. Suvartha Vani Studio, India, 1962-68; Missionary Orientation Can. Sch. Missions, 1970-72; exec. sec. communications Bapt. Conv., Ont., Que., 1971-78; project officer Relief and Devel., India, 1978-79; assoc. sec. Can. Council Chs., Toronto, 1979—. Editor Council Communicator, 1979—. Organizer Inter-faith Celebrations, Toronto, 1984. Served to 2d lt. Can. Army, 1954. Mem. Internat. Communication Assn. Mem. New Democratic Party. Home: 215 Gainsborough Rd Toronto ON M4L 3C7 Canada Office: Can Council Chs 40 St Clair Ave E Toronto ON M4T 1M9 Canada

CANNON, ALBERRY CHARLES, JR., priest, Episcopal Ch.; b. Greenville, S.C., May 12, 1936; s. Alberry Charles and Mary (Cogswell) C.; student U. Ga., 1953-55; B.A., The Citadel, 1957; M.Div., U. South, Sewanee, Tenn., 1960-63; postgrad. The Citadel, 1970, Coll. Preachers, Mt. St. Alban, Washington, 1965, 68, 73, Sch. Pastoral Care, Monteagle, Tenn., 1975; m. Nancy Estelle Sterling, June 15, 1957; children—Alberry Charles III, John Maxwell Sterling, Jane Caroline Alexander, Michael David Winslow. Ordained to ministry, as deacon, 1963, as priest, 1964; rector Ch. of the Nativity, Union, S.C., 1963-67; asst. rector Grace Ch., Charleston, S.C., 1967-70; Episcopal chaplain The Citadel, Charleston, S.C., 1967-73; Episcopal campus minister, Charleston, S.C., Episcopal Diocese S.C., 1970-73; rector St. Mark's Ch., pres. St. Mark's Parish Day Sch., Cocoa, Fla., 1973-76; rector St. Thomas Ch., Miami, Fla., 1976—. Trustee, St. Mary's Coll., Raleigh, N.C., 1966-67; bishop and council Diocese S.C., 1969-70; chmn. Div. Coll. Work, 1967-72, mem. Commn. on Ministry, 1972-73, mem. Liturgical Commn., 1969-73; dir. Episcopal Soc. for Ministry in Higher Edn., 1969-72, treas., 1969-70, v.p., 1970-72; chmn. Liturgical Commn., Diocese Central Fla., 1975-76, mem. Melbourne Deanery Council, 1973-74, examining chaplain Commn. on Ministry, 1976, dep. gen. conv., 1976; lectr. liturgics Inst. Christian Studies, 1975-76; pres. Brevard Deanery Clericus, 1976. Bd. dirs. Union (S.C.) Mental Health Assn., 1963-67, v.p., 1966-67; dir., sec. Spartanburg (S.C.) Mental Health Center, 1965-67; bd. dirs. Union (S.C.) Teen Club, 1964-67, ARC, Cocoa, Fla., 1976—. Mem. Huguenot Soc. S.C., Preservation Soc. Charleston (S.C.), Soc. of Cin. of State S.C., Assn. Citadel Men, Pi Kappa Phi. Address: St Thomas Ch 5690 N Kendall Dr Miami FL 33156

CANNON, WILLIAM RAGSDALE, bishop, United Meth. Ch.; b. Dalton, Ga., Apr. 5, 1916; s. William R. and Emma (McAfee) C.; A.B., U. Ga., 1937; B.D., Yale, 1940, Ph.D., 1942; LL.D., Temple U., 1955; D.D., Asbury Coll., 1959; L.H.D., Emory U., 1969. Ordained to ministry, 1940; pastor Allen Meml. Meth. Ch., Oxford, Ga., 1942-43, Stewart Ave. Meth. Ch., Atlanta, 1944; prof. ch. history Emory U. Candler Sch. Theology, 1944-68, dean, 1953-68; elected bishop, 1968; bishop Raleigh (N.C.) Area, 1968-72, Richmond (Va.) Area, 1970-72, Atlanta Area, 1972—. Del. jurisdictional, gen. confs. United Meth. Ch., 1948, 52, 56, 60, 64, 68; ecumenical conf. United Meth. Ch., Oxford U. (Eng.), 1952; del. World Meth. Council to World Council on Faith and Order, Lund, Sweden, 1953; accredited visitor World Council Chs., Evanston, Ill., 1953; del. World Council Chs., New Delhi, India, 1961, Upsalla, Sweden, 1968, Nairobi, Kenya, 1975; observer II Vatican Council, 1964, 65, 66, World Meth. Council rep. Conversations with Roman Caths. on Christian Unity, 1966—; mem. Commn. on Ritual and Worship, 1948-60; chmn. dept. ministry Gen. Bd. Edn., 1971; chmn. Commn. on Doctrine and Doctrinal Standards, Commn. to Study Ministry, 1972-76; vis. prof. ch. history Garrett Bibl. Inst., summer 1949; Richmond Coll. U. London (Eng.), 1950; vis. lectr. Wesley Works project. Chmn. bd. trustees Protestant Radio and TV Center; vice-chmn. bd. trustees Emory U.; trustee Andrew, LaGrange, Paine, Reinhardt, Young Harris, Ga. Wesleyan colls. Mem. Am. Hist. Soc., Am. Soc. Ch. History, Oxford Inst., Phi Beta Kappa, Phi Kappa Phi, Theta Phi. Author: A Faith for These Times, 1944; The Christian Church, 1945; The Theology of John Wesley, 1946; Our Protestant Faith, 1949; Our Faith in Love, 1949; The Redeemer, 1950; The History of Christianity in the Middle Ages, 1960; The Journeys After Saint Paul, 1963; Evangelism in a Contemporary Context, Tidings, 1974; A Disciple's Profile of Jesus: Gospel of Luke, 1975; Jesus the Servant: Gospel of Mark, 1978; The Gospel of Matthew, 1982; The Gospel of John, 1985. Home: 2575 Peachtree Rd NE Atlanta GA 30305

CANNY, JAMES WALDO, minister, United Methodist Church; b. Buffalo, Oct. 15, 1924; s. Thomas Vincent and Ceora Belle (Boardman) C.; m. Sarah Caroline Porter, Aug. 8, 1953; children: Debra, Dennis, Kristin. B.A., Millikin U., 1951; M. Div., Christian Theol. Sem., 1955. Ordained to ministry United Meth. Ch., 1955. Pastor chs., 1955—; pastor 1st United Meth. Ch., Windsor, Ill.; dir. edn. Springfield Dist. United Meth. Ch., 1963-65; team leader Mattoon Dist. United Meth. Ch., Ill., 1980-82; Mattoon dist. rep. Conf. Deaf Ministry, Jacksonville, Ill., 1983—. Lodges: Rotary, Kiwanis. Office: 1st United Meth Ch 1200 Ohio St Windsor IL 61957

CANTRELL, ALMOS CALVIN, minister, Southern Baptist Convention; b. Haynesville, La., June 27, 1932; s. David DeVan and Clara Bell (Bruer) C.; m. Dorothy Mae Adcock, Dec. 28, 1952; children: Beth Cantrell Lord, Calvin, Paul E. D.Div., 1980. Ordained to ministry So. Baptist Conv., 1952. Pastor Gilliam Bapt. Ch., La., 1952-58, Bethany Bapt. Ch., La., 1958-65, Chapel Hill Bapt. Ch., West Monroe, La., 1965-73; assoc. dir. evangelism La. Bapt. Conv., Alexandria, 1973—. Named Outstanding Pastor of Yr., La. Bapt. Conv., 1973. Home: PO Box 7552 Alexandria LA 71306 Office: PO Box 311 Alexandria LA 71309

CANTRELLE, EARL PAUL, minister, United Methodist Church; b. New Orleans, May 12, 1934; s. Clay J. and Josophine (Trosclair) C.; B.S., Centenary Coll., 1960; Th.M., Perkins Sch. Theology, 1964; m. Hilda Sue Myers, Aug. 29, 1958; 1 son, Steven Clay. Ordained to ministry, 1961; minister Summit United Meth. Ch., Marshall, Tex., 1955-56; pastor, Scottsville, Tex., 1956-57, Elysian Fields, Tex., 1957-59, Winfield, Tex., 1960-63, Colfax, Tex., 1963-64, Bullard-Flint, Tex., 1964-65, Kemah (Tex.) United Meth. Ch., 1965-69, Wesley United Meth. Ch., Nederland, Tex., 1969-73, Van (Tex.) United Meth. Ch., 1973-76, Crocket (Tex.) First United Meth. Ch., 1976—, Bethany United Meth. Ch., Houston. Vice chmn. bd. high edn. div. Tyler Jr. Coll., 1976, prof. Biblical Studies, 1975-76; bd. discipleship, and auditor, Tyler Dist. Meth. Ch., 1975-76; chmn. bd. dirs. Wesley Found., 1974-76; auditor Palestine dist. United Meth. Ch. Recipient citation, Tex. Meth. Coll. Assn., 1976. Mem. Van C. of C., Tex. Assn. Mental Health. Address: First United Meth Ch Crockett TX

CAPOZZELLI, ANTHONY MICHAEL, priest, Roman Catholic Ch.; b. Olean, N.Y., Mar. 21, 1943; s. Samuel and Laura C.; B.A., St. Bonaventure U., 1969; M. Div., Christ the King Sem., 1975. Ordained priest, 1973; deacon St. Luke's Ch., Erie, Pa., 1972-73; deacon St. Jude the Apostle Ch., Erie, 1973, asst. rector, 1973-74; asst. rector St. Catherine's Ch., DuBois, Pa., 1974—. Chaplain K.C., Legion of Mary, DuBois, DuBois Hosp., Maple Ave. Hosp. dir. Religious edn. program, DuBois. Home: 116 S State St DuBois PA 15801

CAPPS, ROBERT VANBUREN, minister, Southern Baptist Convention; b. Atlanta, Aug. 19, 1938; s. Homer Buren and Grace Ione (Ward) C.; B.A., Furman U., 1960; B.Div., Southwestern Bapt. Theol. Sem., 1963, M.Div., 1973; m. Nancy Patricia Radford, Feb. 14, 1964; 1 child, Joy Lynn. Ordained to ministry, 1961; pastor Poynor (Tex.) Bapt. Ch., 1961-62; assoc. pastor First Bapt. Ch., Enterprise, Ala., 1963-65; pastor Pine Crest Bapt. Ch., Tampa, Fla., 1965-67; evangelist, founder Van Capps Evangelistic Assn., Lake Hamilton, Fla., 1967—. Mem. Conf. So. Bapt. Evangelists, Alpha Phi Gamma. Home: 3 E Lake Dr Paradise Island Haines City FL 33844 Office: PO Box 337 Lake Hamilton FL 33851

CARAWAY, JAMES JULIUS, minister, religious organization executive, United Methodist Church; b. Winnfield, La., Jan. 8, 1926; s. Porter Myers and Minnie Merle (Youngblood) C.; m. Mary Linn Miller, July 14, 1947 (dec. 1981); children: Linn Caraway Richardson, James Jay, Jan Caraway Humphries, Ann Caraway Wideman, Ray Miller; m. Carol Louise Zimmerman, May 8, 1982. B.A., East Tex. State U., 1948; M.Th., So. Meth. U., 1951; D.D. (hon.), Centenary Coll., 1978. Ordained to ministry, United Meth. Ch., 1951. Dist. supt. La. Conf. Hammond, La., 1969-72; sr. minister Asbury United Meth. Ch., Lafayette, La., 1972-77; dist. supt. La. Conf. United Meth. Ch., Monroe, La., 1977-79, dir. fin. affairs, Baton Rouge, 1979—; mem. gen. council fin. and administrn., United Meth. Ch., 1984—, chmn. ofcl. forms and records com., 1984—, sec. fin. services com., 1984—, mem. investment com., 1984—; del. Jurisdictional Conf., 1972, 80, 84; chmn. Jurisdictional Council on Fin. and Adminstrn, South Central Jurisdiction, 1980—; trustee United Meth. Ch., 1984—, Mt. Sequoyah Assembly, 1980—, Ind. Coll. Fund of La., 1982—, St. Paul Sch. Theology, 1980—, Lydia Patterson Inst., 1980-84. Pres. Homer (La.) PTA, 1966. Served with USN, 1944-46, PTO. Named Vol. of Yr. Perkins Sch. Theology, So. Meth. U., 1984. Lodge: Lions (pres. Homer 1967). Home: 15422 N Firewood Baton Rouge LA 70816 Office: 527 North Blvd Baton Rouge LA 70802

CARDEN, DANA HARMON, minister, Church of God (Anderson, Indiana); b. Elizabethton, Tenn., Mar. 17, 1915; s. Richard Presley and Mathilde E. (Carden) C.; m. Dorothy L. Leonard, Aug. 24, 1935. Diploma in Higher Acctg., Internat. Corr. Sch., 1954; Diploma in Fin. and Banking, Am. Savs. and Loan Inst., 1970. Ordained to ministry Ch. of God (Anderson, Ind.), 1980. Sec., treas. East Tenn. Gen. Assembly, Ch. of God, Greensville, Tenn., 1958-79, chmn., treas., 1966-73; sec., treas. East Tenn. Ministerial Assembly, Elizabethton, 1970-72; assoc. pastor First Ch. of God, Johnson City, Tenn., 1983—; exec. com. mem. East Tenn. Ministerial Com., Greensville, 1970-72; chmn. bd. trustees First Ch. of God, Elizabethton, 1959-63, chmn. ch. council, 1959-71, interim pastor, 1968, 71, 74. Contbr. articles to profl. jours. Active United Fund, Johnson City, 1969-72; treas. East Tenn. Kingdom Builders, 1975-77. Served with USN, 1944-46. Recipient award in Am. history DAR, 1933. Mem. C. of C. Address: Route 1 Box 3175 Elizabethton TN 37643

CARDONE, NICHOLAS, univ. adminstr., Assemblies of God; b. Pittston, Pa., Feb. 22, 1919; s. Joseph and Congetta (Squiccimarra) C.; student pub. schs., Pittston; m. Lydia Martella, Oct. 13, 1947; children—Shirley, Nicholas, Donna. Deacon, Calvary Temple, Pittston, 1950—, Sunday sch. youth supt., 1970—; founding regent Oral Roberts U., Phila., 1965—. Pres., chief exec. officer Cardo Automotive Products, Inc., Phila., 1968—. Named Automotive Rebuilder of Yr., Automotive Service Industry Assn., 1968. Mem. Automotive Service Industry Assn. (dir. 1970-76), Automotive Parts Rebuilders Assn. (dir. 1960-66), Automotive Warehouse Distbrs. Assn., Full Gospel Bus. Fellowship, Internat. (internat. dir. 1970—), Gideon. Home: 247 Barclay Circle Cheltenham PA 19012 Office: 11500 Norcom Rd Philadelphia PA 19154

CARFREY, DAVID EUGENE, minister, Wesleyan Ch.; b. Athens, Ohio, Oct. 14, 1945; s. Charles Rex and Mary (Witter) C.; student Ariz. Bible Coll., 1964-65, Liberty Bapt. Coll., Lynchburg, Va., 1974; m. Georgia Anna Haews, Oct. 14, 1966; children—David Eugene, Rose Marie, Anna Marie. Ordained to ministry, 1964; music dir. Acacia Ave. Bapt. Ch., Hawthorne, Calif., 1967-70; music evangelist, pub. relations work Open Door Children's Home, Hazard, Ky., 1970-72; asso. pastor, minister music Old Forest Rd. Bapt. Ch., Lynchburg, 1973-74, Lynchburg Wesleyan Ch., 1975-76; pastor Calvary Meml. Ch., Roanoke, Va., 1976—. Music evangelist ann. Wesleyan Crusades, Roanoke; dir. Teens 'n Talent, Va. Wesleyan Ch.; guest singer Jr. Miss Pageant, Lynchburg, 1975. Home: 822 Queen Ave NW Roanoke VA 24012 Office: 2226 Colonial Ave SW Roanoke VA 24015

CARIGNAN, RONALD, clergyman, Roman Catholic. Pres. Conf. Major Superiors of Men, Silver Spring, Md. Office: Conf Major Superiors of Men 8808 Cameron St Silver Spring MD 20910*

CARLEN, CLAUDIA, religious, Roman Catholic Church; b. Detroit, July 24, 1906; d. Albert Bernard and Theresa Mary (Ternes) Carlen; A.B. in L.S., U. Mich., 1928, M.A. in L.S., 1938; postgrad. U. Chgo., 1953; L.H.D., Marygrove Coll., 1981, Loyola U., Chgo., 1983; Litt.D., Cath. U. Am., 1983. Joined Servants of Immaculate Heart of Mary Sisters, Roman Catholic Ch., 1930. Asst. librarian Marygrove Coll., Detroit, 1929-44, librarian, 1944-69; library cons. grad. div. North Am. Coll., Rome, 1971-72; librarian St. John's Sem. Library, Plymouth, Mich., 1972—. Trustee Marygrove Coll., Detroit, 1976—; scholar-in-residence St. John's Sem., 1981—; library cons., Cuernavaca, Mex., 1983-84. Recipient Marygrove Library Guild award, 1958; U. Mich. Sch. Library Sci. Disting. Alumnus award, 1974. Mem. ALA (mem. council 1958-61, 68-71), Cath. Library Assn. (pres. 1965-67), Am. Friends Vatican Library (founder, v.p.), Phi Beta Kappa, Phi Kappa Phi, Beta Phi Mu. Author: Guide to the Encyclicals, 1939; Guide to the Documents of Pius XII, 1951; Dictionary of Papal Pronouncements, 1958; The Papal Encyclicals, 5 vols., 1982. Editor (index): New Catholic Encyclopedia, 1963-67; editor Corpus Pubs. Inc., 1968-70, v.p., 1969-70. Adv. bd. mem. The Pope speaks, 1963—. Contbr. articles to religious jours. Office: St John's Sem 44011 Five Mile Rd Plymouth MI 48170

CARLETON, ALSIE HENRY, bishop, United Methodist Church; b. Oglesby, Tex., June 22, 1910; s. Thomas Jefferson and Ethel (Hudson) C.; B.A., McMurry Coll., 1933, LL.D., 1969; B.D., So. Meth. U., 1935, D.D., 1971; postgrad. U. Chgo., 1935-36, Boston U., 1947; D.D., Tex. Wesleyan Coll., 1952; m. Artha Blair Crutchfield, Oct. 13, 1936; children: Thomas B., Jonathan C., Carolyn A. Ordained to ministry United Meth. Ch., 1938; pastor 1st Ch., Trent, Tex., 1936-38, Clyde, Tex., 1938-40, Baird, Tex., 1940-42, St. John's Ch., Lubbock, Tex., 1942-48, 1st Ch., Big Spring, Tex., 1948-53; pastor University Park Ch., Dallas, 1953-61; supt. Dallas N.E. dist. United Meth. Ch., 1961-64; prof. Perkins Sch. Theology So. Meth. U., 1964-68; elected bishop N.W. Tex.-N.Mex. area, 1968—, sec. Coll. Bishops, 1969-73, pres, 1973-74; pres. Gen. Bd. Pensions, United Meth. Ch., 1972-80; mem. exec. council, 1974-80; mem. Gen. Bd. Discipleship, United Meth. Ch., 1972-76. Trustee McMurry Coll., Tex. Wesleyan Coll., So. Meth. U.; pres. bd. trustees Lydia Patterson Inst. 1973. Recipient Disting. Alumnus award So. Meth. U., 1973. Lodges: Masons, Kiwanis. Home: 810 Morningside Pl SE Albuquerque NM 87108

CARLIN, ADAM BURL, minister, Southern Baptist Convention; b. Plaquemine, La., June 23, 1922; s. George and Lydia (Myon) C.; grad. La. Bapt. Coll., 1950; postgrad. Luther Rice Sem., 1970—; m. Virginia Fowler, June 27, 1943; children—George Kenneth, Clifford Ray, Rebecca Ann. Ordained to ministry, 1944; pastor Cannan Bapt. Ch., Leesville, La., 1944-45, Hollow Way Bapt. Ch., Deville, La., 1945-46, Wardville Bapt. Ch., Pineville, La., 1946-50, First Bapt. Ch., Voth, Tex., 1951-52, Calvary Bapt. Ch., Port Arthur, Tex., 1953-63, Emanuel Bapt. Ch., Beaumont, Tex., 1963-66, First Bapt. Ch., Buna, Tex., 1966—. Moderator, Emmanuel Bapt. Assn., 1970-72; preacher, Alaska, 1958, India, 1972; mem. exec. bd. Tex. Bapt. Conv. Chmn. Mental Health Assn., Buna 1975; trustee Bapt. Hosp., Beaumont, 1967—; active Boy Scouts Am. Mem. So. Bapt. Pastor's Fellowship, Buna Ministerial Brotherhood, C. of C. Home and Office: PO Box 280 Buna TX 77612

CARLISLE, JAMES PATTON, religious organization administrator, United Methodist Church; b. Miami Beach, Fla., May 7, 1946; s. William Olin and Evelyn Obie (Ogden) C.; m. Sally-Anne Hart, July 7, 1982. B.A., Auburn U., 1969; M.Div., Emory U., 1976. Ordained to ministry as elder, 1979; cert. ch. bus. adminstr., United Meth. Ch.; clin. chaplain Emory U. Hosp., Atlanta. Assoc. pastor First United Meth. Ch., Alexander City, Ala., 1973-75, 10th St. United Meth. Ch., Atlanta, 1975-78; dir. continuing edn. Northern Ga. Conf., United Meth. Ch., Atlanta, 1976-78; program dir. Ctr. for Profl. Devel. in Ministry of Lancaster Theol. Sem., Pa., 1978-80, dir., 1980—; ednl. cons. United Meth. Consultation on Continuing Edn., 1979; cons. on continuing edn. Mid Atlantic region United Ch. of Christ, 1980-81; cons., mem. task force Minority Recruitment in Theol. Edn., Nat. Council Chs., 1983-84. Author, editor, research research reports on continuing edn. of clergy. Campaign organizer Tom Radney for Lt. Gov., Alexander City, Ala., 1969, Elliot Levitas for Congress, Atlanta, 1975; campaign worker United Way, Lancaster, 1979. Mem. Soc. Advancement Continuing Edn. in Ministry (bd. dirs. 1984—). Democrat. Home: 112 Willow Valley Dr Lancaster PA 17602 Office: Ctr for Profl Devel in Ministry 555 W James St Lancaster PA 17603

CARLOCK, HERBERT WILLIAM, JR., minister, Cumberland Presbyterian Church; b. Pine Bluff, Ark., July 14, 1933; s. Herbert William and Edna Tempi (Elgin) C.; m. Betty Jane Thompson, Sept. 1, 1957; children: Herbert William, Jon Thompson. B.A., Bethel Coll., 1955; M.Div., Cumberland Presbyn. Theol. Sem., 1972. Ordained to ministry, 1954. Pastor, First Cumberland Presbyn. Ch., Humboldt, Tenn., 1957-60, Fairview Cumberland Presbyn. Ch., Marshall, Tex., 1960-63, E. Lake Cumberland Presbyn. Ch., Birmingham, Ala., 1963-68, Oak Ridge Cumberland Presbyn. Ch., Oak Ridge, 1968—; mem. judiciary com. Cumberland Presbyn. Ch., Memphis, 1984—. Contbr. articles to profl. jours. Mem. E. Tenn. Assn. Chs. (pres.), Tenn. Assn. Chs. (v.p.). Democrat. Lodges: Optimist, Masons. Home: 122 Netherland Rd Oak Ridge TN 37830 Office: Cumberland Presbyn Ch 127 Lafayette Oak Ridge TN 37830

CARLSON, ALAN NILS, minister, Luth. Ch. Am.; b. Aberdeen, Wash., Dec. 11, 1933; s. Carl Gustav Edwin and Anna Amelia (Anderson) C.; student U. Wash., 1951-52; B.A., Pacific Luth. U., 1955; B.D., Augustana Sem., Rock Island, Ill., 1959; m. Lois Lorraine Weber, Aug. 18, 1957; children—Lucinda Lois, Steven Alan, Luther Nils. Mission developer Resurrection Luth. Ch., Tacoma, Wash., 1959-65; pastor Good Shepherd Luth. Ch., Veradale, Wash., 1965-70; sr. pastor St. Andrew's Ch., Beaverton, Oreg., 1970—. Mem. exec. bd., v.p. Luth. Outdoor Ministries; mem. witness and life com. Ecumenical Ministries Oreg.; exec. bd. Pacific N.W. Synod Luth. Ch. Am. Recipient Outstanding Alumnus award Aberdeen High Sch., 1974. Home: 3550 NW 179th Pl Portland OR 97229 Office: 12405 SW Butner Rd Beaverton OR 97005

CARLSON, DENNIS NOBEL, religious organization executive, Seventh-day Adventists; b. Lincoln, Nebr., Mar. 26, 1946; s. Nobel August and Hildur Eulila (Bengtson), C.; m. Annalee Whieldon, Aug. 10, 1968; children: Jonathan Dennis, Julie Ann. Ordained to ministry Seventh-day Adventists, 1974. Pastor, Seventh-day Adventist Ch., East Dayton, Ohio, 1970-72, Willoughby and Brooklyn, Ohio, 1972-74, Mansfield, Ohio, 1974-80, Puyallup, Wash., 1980-84; dir. stewardship edn. and communication Wash. Conf. Seventh-day Adventists, Bothell, Wash., 1984—; mem. exec. com. Ohio Conf. Seventh-day Adventists, Mount Vernon, Ohio, 1978-80, mem. K-16 Bd. Edn., 1978-80; mem. exec. com. Wash. Conf. Seventh-day Adventists, 1981-83. Contbr. articles to profl. jours. Alt. del. Pierce County Republican Conv., 1984. Club: Exchange. (bd. dirs. 1977). Office: Wash Conf Seventh-day Adventists 20015 Bothell Way SE Bothell WA 98012

CARLSON, DONALD DEAN, journalist, educator; b. Kewanee, Ill.; s. Alfred Cecil and Alfaretta Louise (Frick) C.; m. Sharon Louise Carlson, Jan. 21, 1966; children: Jessica Marie, Tipton Braun. A.A., Fullerton Community Coll., Calif., 1968; B.A. in Edn., Ariz. State U., 1970. Cert. tchr., Ariz. Pres. Campus Ministries of Am., Redlands, Calif., 1978—. Exec. editor: (newspaper) The Campus Times, 1980. Republican. Home: 1345 Pacific St Redlands CA 92373 Office: Campus Ministries of Am PO Box 1345 Redlands CA 92373

CARLSON, JAMES LESLIE, minister, Lutheran Church in America; b. Canton, Ill., May 26, 1932; s. Leslie A.F. and Helen Marie (Teed) C.; m. Greta Adair Nelson, June 24, 1954; children: Kristen, Gretchen,

Marcus, Steffen. B.A., Bethany Coll., 1954; B.D., Augustana Sem., Rock Island, Ill., 1958; M.Div., Luth. Sch. Theology, Chgo., 1964, D.Min., 1983. Ordained to ministry Lutheran Ch., 1958. Pastor Luth. Ch. of the Good Shepherd, Largo, Fla., 1958-61, Gloria Dei Luth. Ch., Durant, Iowa, 1961-63; chaplain resident Austin State Hosp., Tex., 1963-64; sr. pastor Trinity Luth. Ch., Victoria, Tex., 1964—; mem. planning council Tex.-La. Synod, Luth. Ch. Am., 1973-75, synodical dean, 1975—, mem. synod council, 1975—. Bd. dirs., mem. founders group Gulf Bend Ctr., Victoria, 1964; pres. Victoria County Sr. Citizens Assn., 1979; pres. City PTA, Victoria, 1975; pres. DeLeon Villa-HUD 302 Housing, Victoria, 1983. Fellow Assn. Large Luth. Chs.; mem. Ministerial Alliance Victoria. Home: 2403 Terrace St Victoria TX 77901 Office: Trinity Evangelical Lutheran Ch 106 N DeLeon St Victoria TX 77901

CARLSON, RICHARD PAUL, minister, Evangelical Free Church America; b. Hazard, Ky., Apr. 7, 1945; s. Harold Nathaniel and Verma Elnora (Granlund) C.; m. Virginia Ann Piatt, June 16, 1967; children: Amy Marie, Heather Adele, Gretchen Ann, Audrey Joy, Aaron Richard, Nathaniel August. B.A. cum laude, Trinity Coll., Ill., 1967; M.Div. magna cum laude, Trinity Evang. Div. Sch., 1970. Ordained to ministry Evang. Free Ch. Am., 1973. Pastor Evang. Free Ch. of Bloomington-Normal, Ill., 1970-76, Evang. Free Ch., Rock Springs, Wyo., 1976—; v.p. McLean County Ministerial Assn., 1970-73; chmn, co-chmn. Evang. Ministerial Fellowship, 1974-76; Christian edn. coordinator So. Ill. Area 7, Great Lakes Dist. Evang. Free Ch. Am., 1970-76; pres. Sweetwater County Ministerial Alliance, 1979-81. Author: Hope for the Home, in press; contbr. articles to Evang. Beacon. Mem. Youth Services Agy., Bloomington, 1973-74, assoc. mem., 1975-76; v.p., sec., treas. Right to Read, Inc., 1977-83; v.p., bd. dirs. Travelers Assistance of Sweetwater County, 1982— (chmn., bd. dirs. 1977—); chmn. intermountain dist. satellite Evang. Free Ch. of Am., vice-sec., bd. dirs. Rocky Mt. dist.; v.p., sec. Right to Read, Inc., 1977-82. Mem. Key '73, Evang. Free Ch. Am. Ministerial Assn. (chmn. Rock Springs/Green River 1979-81), Sweetwater County Right to Life (bd. dirs. 1983—). Home and Office: 523 D St Rock Springs WY 82901

CARLSON, ROBERT J., bishop, Roman Catholic Church. Titular bishop of Avioccala, aux. bishop, St. Paul and Mpls., 1984—. Office: 226 Summit Ave St Paul MN 55102*

CARLSON, ROBERT WARREN, religion educator, priest, Episcopal Church; b. Bklyn., July 5, 1928; s. Arthur Muritz and Ruth Alva (Johnson) C.; m. Faith Elisabeth Cabarga, June 3, 1951; children: Arthur, Paul, Edward. B.A., Drew U., 1950, M.Div., 1953; D.Min., Wesley Sem., 1974. Ordained to ministry, 1956. Asst. minister St. Matthew's Episcopal Ch., Hyattsville, Md., 1955-59; rector Nativity Episcopal Ch., Camp Springs, Md., 1959-76; prof. ministries and dir. field edn. Seabury-Western Sem., Evanston, Ill., 1976—; dir. Episcopal Soc. for Ministry on Aging, Milford, N.J., 1983—, Ecumenical Ctr. for Stewardship Studies, Evanston, 1980—. Pres. Md. Assn. for Mental Health, Balt., 1970-72; mem. Gov.'s Adv. Com. on Mental Health, Annapolis, 1970-72; mem. Evanston Commn. on Aging, 1984—. Angus Dunn fellow, Diocese of Washington, 1971-72; Dieffendorf fellow in Religion and Health, 1953. Mem. Assn. for Theol. Field Edn. Home: 2145 Orrington Ave Evanston IL 60201 Office: Seabury-Western Theol Sem 2122 Sheridan Rd Evanston IL 60201

CARLTON, JOHN WAYNE, minister, So. Baptist Conv.; b. Tuscalooda, Ala., Sept. 7, 1946; s. Myers Cecil and Dorothy (Morgan) C.; student U. S.Fla., 1963-66, Mercer U., 1973-74; m. Mary Jean Johnson, July 6, 1968; children—Joel Wayne, Joy Alicia. Ordained to ministry, 1977. Minister music and youth Shurlington Bapt. Ch., Macon, Ga., 1971-73, Glover Bapt. Ch., Norcross, Ga., 1973-74, Calvary Bapt. Ch., Jesup, Ga., 1974—. Sec. Altamaha Bapt. Pastor's Conf., 1975-78; music dir. Altamaha Bapt. Assn., 1974-84; area rep. Ga. Bapt. Ch. Music Conf., 1976-78. Mem. Wayne County Ministerial Assn. Home: 1109 S Palm St Jesup GA 31545 Office: 411 E Cherry St Jesup GA 31545

CARMICHAEL, JOHN CURTIS, minister, United Methodist Church; b. Glenwood, Ala., May 14, 1922; s. Edward Alonza and Laura Eva (Curtis) C.; m. Reba LaMerle Johnson, June 5, 1946; children: Keitha Elaine Duncan, Daniel Asher Carmichael. B.S., Troy State U., 1945; postgrad. Candler Sch. Theology, 1949, 56. Ordained deacon United Meth. Ch., 1946, elder, 1949. Pastor Columbia Meth. Charge, Ala., 1944, 47-48, Shady Grove Meth. Charge, Troy, Ala., 1945-46, Warrington Meth. Ch., Pensacola, Fla., 1948-60, 68-75, Port St. Joe Meth. Ch., Fla., 1960-62, Lafayette St. Meth. Ch., Dothan, Ala., 1962-66, Mary Esther Meth. Ch., Fla., 1975-76, First Meth. Ch., Opp, Ala., 1976-80, Elba, Ala., 1980—; supt. Meth. Assembly, Andalusia, Ala., 1966-68; conf. statistician Ala.-West Fla. Meth. Conf., 1952-73, trustee, chmn. 1977—; mem. conf. bd. ministry ch. scholarships, 1964-76; credit chmn. bd. dirs. Conf. Credit Union, 1972—; chaplain Civitan Club, Port St. Joe, Fla., 1961-62. Club: Rotary (pres. Elba, Ala. 1983-84). Home: 1438 Highland Dr XPO Drawer L Elba AL 36323 Office: First United Meth Ch Davis at Claxton Sts Elba AL 36323

CARMICHAEL, MARGARET SUSAN, theology educator, United Methodist Church; b. Laurel, Miss., Dec. 25, 1923; d. William Merritt and Mary Annie (Williams) C. A.A., Jones County Jr. Coll., 1943; B.A., Scarritt Coll., 1948, M.A., 1959. Ordained deaconess United Meth. Ch., 1960, diaconal minister, 1977. Dir. Christian edn. St. Luke's United Meth. Ch., Jackson, Miss., 1948-61; assoc. prof. Christian edn. Pfeiffer Coll., Misenheimer, N.C., 1961—; mem. bd. diaconal ministries N.C. Conf. United Meth. Ch., 1983—; dist. dir. childrens ministries Albermarle dist., Western N.C. Conf., 1978—. Sec., Stanly County Council Status of Women, 1984-85. Mem. Nat. Christian Educators Fellowship, Western N.C. Christian Educators Fellowship, Southeastern Jurisdiction Deaconess and Home Missionary Assn., United Meth. Assn. Profs. Christian Edn., Albermarle Bus. and Profl. Womens Club (scholarship chmn.). Home: Box 561 Misenheimer NC 28109 Office: Pfeiffer Coll Misenheimer NC 28109

CARNEY, JAMES F., archbishop, Roman Catholic Church; b. Vancouver, B.C., Can., June 28, 1915; s. John and Ethel (Crook) C.; ed. Vancouver Coll. and Jr. Sem. of Christ the King, 1930-38, St. Joseph's Sem., Alta., Can., 1938-42. Ordained priest 1942; pastor Corpus Christi Ch., Vancouver, later vicar gen., domestic prelate; consecrated bishop, 1966; aux. bishop of Vancouver, 1966-69; installed as archbishop for Vancouver, 1969. Office: Archdiocese of Vancouver 150 Robson St Vancouver BC V6B 2A7 Canada

CARNEY, RANDALL GALE, minister, writer, editor, religious institute administrator; b. Christopher, Ill., July 28, 1949; s. Roy Hansel and Coeva Mae (Johnson) C.; A.A., Rend Lake Coll., 1969; B.S., So. Ill. U., 1971; M.Div., Memphis Theol. Sem., 1974; D.Min., Luther Rice Sem., 1979; m. Rhonda Lynn Miller, June 10, 1972; children: Rachelle Dorene, Ralanna Gale, Rita Beth, Roy Rustin. Ordained to ministry, 1974; pastor Pine Level Free Will Bapt. Ch., Chester, Ga., 1974-76; prin., supr. Berean Christian Sch., Eatonton, Ga., 1976-83; asst. pastor Berean Bapt. Ch., Eatonton, 1977-83; ednl. cons. Accelerated Christian Edn., Ga. and Ill., 1980-84; prin., supr. Calvary Bapt. Ch., Marion, Ill., 1983-84; asst. pastor, 1983-84; adminstrv. asst. Accelerated Christian Edn., Lewisville, Tex., 1984, writer, editor, 1984-85; supr. Internat. Inst., Grace Fundamental Ch., 1985—; chaplain, Chester Lions Club, 1975-76; sec.-treas. Bd. Christian Edn., Ga. Union Assn. Free Will Baptists, 1974-76. Home: 1818 El Paso Lewisville TX 75067 Office: 2600 Ace Ln Lewisville TX 75067

CARON, WILFRED RENE, lawyer, Roman Catholic Church; b. N.Y.C., July 23, 1931; s. Joseph W. and Eva (Berube) C.; m. Anne T. Flanagan, Aug. 2, 1958. J.D., St. John's U., 1956. Bar: D.C. 1977, N.Y. 1956, U.S. Dist. Ct. (no., so. and ea. dists.) N.Y., U.S. Ct. Appeals (2d, 3d, 5th, 6th, 8th, 9th and D.C. Cirs.), U.S. Supreme Ct. 1961. Gen. counsel U.S. Cath. Conf., Washington, 1980—, Nat. Conf. Cath. Bishops, 1980—, Cath. Telecommunications Network Am., N.Y.C., 1981—. Author legal articles. Served to 1st lt. U.S. Army, 1952-54; Korea. Mem. ABA, D.C. Bar Assn., Fed. Bar Council, Canon Law Soc. Am., Supreme Ct. Hist. Soc. Club: University (Washington). Office: US Catholic Conf 1312 Massachusetts Ave NW Washington DC 20024

CARR, CHARLES LOUIS, missionary adminstr., minister, Gen. Baptists; b. Rockport, Ind., Sept. 9, 1930; s. Louis E. and Loris B. (Lindsey) C.; student Ind. State U., 1949-50, Oakland City Coll., 1958-59, So. Baptist Theol. Sem., 1965-67; m. Shirley R. Cron, Nov. 15, 1950; children—Kathleen (Mrs. Paul J. Wright), Charles Stephen, Jeffrey Louis, David Wayne. Ordained to ministry, 1957; pastor East Oolitic Gen. Bapt. Ch., Bedford, Ind., 1959-63, Mt. Zion Gen. Bapt. Ch., Indpls., 1963-65, Hunsinger Lane Gen. Bapt. Ch., Louisville, 1965-67; missionary to Saipan, Marianas Islands, 1967-73; exec. dir. Gen. Bapt. Fgn. Mission Soc., Poplar Bluff, Mo., 1973—. Mem. Am. Soc. Missiology, Evang. Fgn. Missions Assn. Editor: Capsule. Contbr. articles to various publs. Home: 706 South 9th Poplar Bluff MO 63901 Office: 100 Stinson Dr Poplar Bluff MO 63901

CARR, JAMES RUSSELL, religious organization executive, American Lutheran Church; b. Fort Dodge, Iowa, Dec. 28, 1934; s. Russell M. and Anna (Anderson) C.; m. Karen Olson, Feb. 12, 1955; children: Daniel, Andrew, Kathryn. B.A., U. Iowa, 1956; M.Div., Wartburg Theol. Sem., 1960; M.A. with distinction, U. Calif., Fresno, 1970; D.Div. Wartburg Theol. Sem., 1984. Assoc. pastor St. Peter Luth. Ch., Santa Ana, Calif., 1960-62; pastor Atonement Luth. Ch., Sacramento, 1962-65; campus pastor Calif. State U., Fresno, 1965-76; regional dir. Nat. Luth. Campus Ministry, Aurora, Colo., 1975-81; dir. Nat. Luth. Campus Ministry, Chgo., 1981—; official observer, Pre-Assembly Youth Gathering, Luth. World Fedn., Budapest, Hungary, 1984; dir. Ctr. for Study of Campus Ministry, Valparaiso, Ind., 1981—. Contbg. editor Campus Ministry Communications, ENTREE, Campus Ministry Communications. Bd. dirs. King of Kings Community Ctr., Fresno, 1967-71. Mem. Luth. Student Movement-USA, Phi Kappa Phi. Office: Luth Council USA Nat Luth Campus Ministry 35 E Wacker Dr 1847 Chicago IL 60601

CARR, MARILYN MARIE, minister, Church of God (Anderson, Indiana); b. Chgo., Dec. 4, 1947; d. Eddie B. and Dorothy (Price) Davidson; m. James A. Carr, Nov. 13, 1971 (dec. 1976). B.S., Chgo. State U., 1969; M.A., Concordia Coll., 1983; postgrad. U. Ill.-Chgo. Youth counsellor Emerald Ave. Ch. of God, Chgo., 1974-82; Bible study tchr., 1977—; from missionary student to evangelist Ch. of God, St. Kitts, W.I., 1977—; assoc. minister Emerald Ave. Ch. of God, Chgo., 1980—. nat. conv. speaker Nat. Assn. Ch. of God, San Diego, 1981, nat. campmeeting speaker, West Middlesex, Pa., 1976; evangelistic speaker, 1972—. Tchr. Chgo. Pub. Schs., 1970—. Mem. Nat. Montford Point Marine Assn., Chgo., 1971-76; prin. Chgo. Operation Push Alternative Sch. Program, 1979-80. Mem. Nat. Assn. Exec. Females. Democrat. Home: 2034 W 79th Pl Chicago IL 60620 Office: Beale Elem Sch 6006 S Peoria St Chicago IL 60621

CARR, OWEN CLAUD, minister, Assemblies of God; b. Okmulgee, Okla., May 19, 1923; s. Claud Clarence and Alvina Louise (Thorman) C.; student pub. schs. Arkansas City, Kans.; m. Priscilla Faye Seidner, Jan. 1, 1942; children—Stanley David, Marilyn Faye. Ordained to ministry, 1945; pastor Assembly of God Chs. in Gerlane, Kans., 1942-43, Corwin, Kans., 1943-44, Pomona, Kans., 1944-46; Iola, Kans., 1946-51, Lyons, Kans., 1951-53; dir. state youth and edn. Assemblies of God Kans., Wichita, 1953-58; pastor in Topeka, 1958-61; nat. dir. youth Assemblies of God Internat. Hdqts., Springfield, Mo., 1961-65; pastor in Beaumont, Tex., 1965-66, Edwards St. Assembly of God, Alton, Ill., 1966-70, Stone Ch. Chgoland, Chgo., 1970-76; pres. Christian Communications Chgoland, Inc., Christian Television sta. WCFC-TV, 1976—. Missionary ministry in 25 countries; religious speaker; asst. supt. Ill. Assemblies of God; bd. regents N. Central Bible Coll., Mpls., Served Mayor's Commn., Alton, Ill.; established Alton Youth Center, 1968. Named Dist. Youth Leader of Yr., Assemblies of God, 1955, Pastor of Yr., Greater Chgo. Sunday Sch. Assn., 1975, 1976. Mem. Nat. Assn. Evangelicals, Nat. Religious Broadcasters Assn., Assemblies of God Gen. Presbytery. Editor: The Harvester, History of the Assemblies of God in Kans., 1955. Home: 15420 Arroyo Dr Oak Forest IL 60452 Office: 20 N Wacker Dr Suite 1345 Chicago IL 60606

CARR, RONALD ALTON, minister, Church of God (Anderson, Ind.). b. Roanoke, Va., Aug. 30, 1946; s. Samuel Donald and Joan (Cook) C.; m. Andrea Manning, Sept. 1, 1973. B.A., Anderson Coll., 1970; M.Div., Anderson Sch. Theology, 1978; cert. reality therapy Inst. Mental Devel., Houston, 1980; cert. in clin. pastoral edn. Richmond Meml. Hosp., Va., 1985. Ordained to ministry Ch. of God, 1973. Missionary tchr. Ch. of God, Grand Caymon, B.W.I., 1970-71, assoc. pastor, Canton, Ohio, 1972-75, pastor, Cross Lanes, W.Va., 1978-80; dir. sports and recreation St. Luke's United Meth. Ch., Houston, 1981-84; counseling staff Richmond Meml. Hosp., Va., 1985—. Pres. council Scottish Clan Assn., 1982—; vol. ARC, 1962—. Mem. Scottish Heritage Club U.S.A., Royal Scottish Country Dance Soc. (trustee 1981-82, tchr. 1982—), Houston Highland Games Assn. (v.p.). Home: 3948 Bridgeton Rd Richmond VA 23234 Office: Richmond Meml Hosp Richmond VA 23234

CARRINGER, JERRY WAYNE, minister, Southern Baptist Convention; b. Robbinsville, N.C., Aug. 24, 1947; s. Wayne and Willa Mae (Orr) C.; m. Donna Jean McGuire, Dec. 28, 1974; children: Sara Elizabeth, Leah Rachel. B.A., Western Carolina U., 1969; postgrad. Southwestern Bapt. Sem., 1973; M. Div., So. Bapt. Theol. Sem., 1975. Ordained to ministry So. Bapt. Conv., 1978. Youth dir. Carter Park Meth. Ch., Ft. Worth, 1973, Meadows Bapt. Ch., College Park, Ga., 1974; pastoral intern Highland Bapt. Ch., Louisville, 1974, Trinity Bapt. Ch., 1975; pastor N. Linden Bapt. Ch., Columbus, Ohio, 1978—; exec. bd. State Conv. Bapt. Ohio, Columbus, 1983—; ch. tng. dir. Greater Columbus Bapt. Assn., 1983—, student com. chmn., 1981—, vice-moderator, 1982-83. Editor The Uplifter, 1981—. Active Moral Majority, Columbus, 1980—, Nat. Fedn. Decency, 1983—. Served with U.S. Army, 1969-72, Vietnam. Decorated Bronze Star with oak leaf cluster. Recipient Gov.'s Personal Service award State of N.C., 1976. Republican. Home: 2151 Colfax Ave Columbus OH 43224 Office: North Linden Bapt Ch 1783 Melrose Ave Columbus OH 43224

CARRINGTON, ROBERT, minister, Assemblies of God; b. Birkenhead, Eng., Sept. 9, 1915; s. William and Florence (Sillet) C.; came to U.S., 1922, naturalized, 1940; grad. So. Calif. Bible Coll., 1939; D.D., Bethany Bible Coll., 1976; m. Josephine Annie Seal, Aug. 27, 1939; children—Fred, Dennis, Ann. Ordained to ministry, 1941; pastor, Nevada City, Calif., 1939-43, St. Helena, Calif., 1944, Assembly of God Bethel Temple, Turlock, Calif., 1947-75, Ch. of the Highlands, San Bruno, Calif., 1976—. Chmn. bd. Bethany Coll., Santa Cruz, Calif., 1970-75; pres. Turlock Council Chs., 1952,

56, Turlock Ministerial Union, 1947-75; pres. Christ Ambassadors, Assemblies of God, 1945-47, organizer, mem. nat. bd. fgn. missions, 1955-59, gen. presbyter, 1974-75, exec. presbyter No. Calif. and Nev. Dist., 1935-45, mem. world evangelism bd., 1965—; co-founder Speed of Light. Mem. Turlock Safety Council, 1952-53. Recipient citation Bethany Bible Coll., 1976. Home: 380 Vallejo #204 Millbrae CA 94030 Office: 1900 Monterey Dr San Bruno CA 94066

CARROLL, CARMAL EDWARD, priest, Episcopal Church; b. Grahn, Ky., Oct. 8, 1923; s. Noah Washington and Jessie (Scott) U.; m. Greta Seustrom, June 11, 1960; 1 child, Mehran Sabouhi. Ph.B., U. Toledo, 1947, M.A., 1950, B.Ed., 1951; M.L.S., UCLA, 1961; Ph.D., U. Calif.-Berkeley, 1969; postgrad. Duke U., 1947-50; Episcopal Div. Sch., 1980. Ordained priest Episcopal Ch., 1982. Asst. priest Calvary Episcopal Ch., Columbia, Mo., 1982-84; vicar Trinity Episcopal Ch., Marshall, Mo., 1984—; mem. bishop's council Diocese of Mo., St. Louis, 1981—. Author: The Professionalization of Education for Librarianship, 1970. Contbr. articles to profl. jours. Prof. library sci. U. Mo., Columbia, 1970—. Named hon. Ky. Col. Mem. ALA, Nat. Assn. Self-Supporting Clergy, Assn. Info. and Image Mgmt., AAUP (state pres. Mo. 1981-83), N.Y. Acad. Scis., Phi Delta Kappa, Beta Phi Mu. Democrat. Lodge: Rotary. Home: 2001 Country Club Dr Columbia MO 65201 Office: U Mo 105 Stewart Hall Columbia MO 65211

CARROLL, JAMES ARCHIE, minister, So. Bapt. Conv.; b. Carter County, Ky., Jan. 23, 1937; s. Kenneth Edward and Laura Lottie (Smith) C.; student pub. schs., Garyson, Ky.; m. Lois Naomi Burton, Jan. 19, 1957; children—Daniel Thomas, John Anthony, Charles Robert, James Matthew. Ordained deacon, 1970, pastor, 1974; asso. pastor First Bapt. Ch., Mt. Vernon, Ind., 1973-74; pastor First Bapt. Ch., New Harmony, Ind., 1974—. Dir. Associational Sunday sch. Southwestern Ind. Bapt. Assn., Evansville, 1974-75, chmn. nominating com., 1975-77, trustee, 1975-77. Claims rep. Cin. Ins. Co., Mt. Vernon, Ind., 1975-76. Pres., Mt. Vernon (Ind.) Pony League, 1976—. Home and office: 327 E 3d St Mt Vernon IN 47620

CARROLL, MARY JUDE, nun, Roman Catholic Church; b. Stamford, Conn., Jan. 3, 1942; d. John Anthony and Ruth Ione (Adams) C. B.A., U. Conn., 1964; M.A., Fairfield U., 1979. Joined Congregation Holy Family of Nazareth, Roman Catholic Ch., 1976. Dir. religious edn. St. Hyacinth Roman Cath. Ch., Glen Head, N.Y., 1980-83; pastoral assoc. Our Lady of the Lakes Roman Cath. Ch., Oakdale, Conn., 1983—; dir. retreat. Contbr. articles to Insights newspaper. Named to Outstanding Young Women Am., U.S. Jaycees, 1976. Avocations: writing; photography. Home: 120 Cliff St Norwich CT 06360 Office: Our Lady of the Lakes Roman Cath Ch Box 85 Route 82 Oakdale CT 06370

CARROLL, STEVEN EDWARD MICHAEL, priest, Episcopal Church; b. Detroit, Sept. 23, 1949; s. Edward James and Helen Ruth (Harrison) C.; m. Rosemary Calabro, May 26, 1979. B.A. in History, Wayne State U., 1976; M.Div., Trinity Coll., U. Toronto, 1979. Ordained priest Episcopal Ch., 1980. Curate Grace Episcopal Ch., Port Huron, Mich., 1979-80; rector St. John's Episcopal Ch., Howell, Mich., 1980—. Chmn. adv. com. Hospice/Home Care, Howell, 1984—; mem. Comprehensive Health Planning Council of Southeastern Mich., Livingston County, 1984—. Mem. Howell Jaycees. Democrat. Home: 420 W Caldonia St Howell MI 48843 Office: Saint Johns Episcopal Ch 504 Prospect St Howell MI 48843

CARRUTH, THEODORE RAYMOND, religious educator, Churches of Christ; b. Pampa, Tex., May 20, 1941; s. Glenn Raymond and Lela Silverene (Grant) C.; m. Georgia Carolyn Ridgeway, Oct. 7, 1966; children: Amy, Ellen, Karen. B.A., Harding U., 1964, Th.M., 1966; Ph.D., Baylor U., 1973. Ordained to ministry Chs. of Christ, 1963. Instr. Lubbock Christian Coll., Tex., 1971-73, asst. prof., 1973-76; asst. prof. David Lipscomb Coll., Nashville, 1976—, assoc. prof. religion, 1976—. Mem. editorial bd. Restoration Quar., 1977—. Contbr. articles to profl. jours. Bd. dirs. Coronado Children's Home, Lubbock, 1971-76. David Lipscomb Coll. grantee, 1982. Named Outstanding Tchr., David Lipscomb Coll., 1983. Home: 755 Elysian Fields Rd Nashville TX 37204 Office: David Lipscomb Coll 3901 Granny White Pike Nashville TN 37203

CARTER, ALEXANDER, bishop, Roman Catholic Church; b. Montreal, Que., Can., Apr. 16, 1909; s. Thomas and Mary (Kerr) C.; M.Th., M.C.L., LL.D., Montreal Coll. 1930; ed. Sem. Philosophy and Grand Sem. Montreal, 1936; M.Th., M.C.L., Canadian Coll., Rome, 1939; LL.D., (hon.) Laurentian U., Sudbury, Ont., 1962. Ordained priest, 1936; bishop of Sault Ste. Marie, 1957—. Chancellor U. Sudbury, 1962—. Pres. Canadian Cath. Conf., 1967-69; pres. Ont. Conf. Cath. Bishops, 1977-81. Mem. Vanier Inst., Pontifical Mission Aid Socs. Can. (nat. dir. 1971-77). Address: PO Box 510 480 McIntyre St W North Bay ON P1B 2Z4 Canada*

CARTER, GERALD EMMETT CARDINAL, archbishop, Roman Catholic Church; b. Montreal, Que., Can., Mar. 1, 1912; s. Thomas Joseph and Mary (Kelty) C. B.Th., Grand Sem. Montreal, 1936; B.A., U. Montreal, 1933, M.A. 1940, Ph.D., 1947, L.Th., 1950, D.H.L., Duquesne U., 1962; LL.D., U. Western Ont., 1966, Concordia Univ., 1976, U. Windsor, 1977, McGill U., 1980, U. Notre Dame (Ind.), 1981; Litt.D., St. Mary's U., Halifax, N.S., 1980. Ordained priest, 1937, consecrated bishop, 1962, elevated to cardinal, 1979; prin., prof. St. Joseph Tchrs. Coll., Que., 1939-61; chaplain Newman Club, McGill U., 1941-56; charter mem., 1st pres. Thomas More Inst. Adult Edn., Montreal, 1945-61; mem. Montreal Cath. Sch. Commn., 1948-61; hon. canon Cathedral Basilica Montreal, 1952-61; aux. bishop London and titular bishop Altiburo, 1961-62; bishop of London, Ont., 1964-78; archbishop of Toronto, 1978—, cardinal, 1979—. Chmn. Episcopal Commn. Liturgy Can., 1966; mem. Consilium of Liturgy, Rome, 1965; mem. Council on Econ. Affairs, Vatican, 1981; mem. Sacred Congregation for Divine Worship, 1970; chmn. Internat. Com. for English in the Liturgy, 1971. Vice pres. Can. Cath. Conf., 1973, pres., 1975; mem, Synod of Bishops, 1977. Decorated companion Order of Can. Author: The Catholic Public Schools of Quebec, 1957; Psychology and the Cross, 1959; The Modern Challenge to Religious Education, 1961. Office: 355 Church St Toronto ON M5B 1Z8 Canada

CARTER, GLENN THOMAS, minister, Seventh-day Adventists; lawyer; b. Beaumont, Tex., July 20, 1934; s. Glenmore Rust and Sarah Elizabeth (Woods) C.; m. Janette Lucile Mullikin, Aug. 1, 1954; children: Penny Lucile Carter Loucks, Sylvia Lee Carter DeVries. Student Andrews U., 1952-53; B.A. in Religion, Union Coll., 1956; J.D., Emory U., 1967. Bar: Ga. 1968, Tex. 1969, D.C. 1976, Md. 1976, Calif. 1984; ordained to ministry Seventh-day Adventists, 1960. Pastor, Tex. Conf. Seventh-day Adventists, Pharr, Nacadoches and Beaumont, 1956-63, dir. trust services and pub. affairs, Ft. Worth, 1969-76; pastor Wyo. Conf. Seventh-day Adventists, Casper, 1963-65; pastor, spl. legal counsel GA.-Combination Conf. Seventh-day Adventists, Decatur, 1965-69; assoc. dir. trust services Gen. Conf. Seventh-day Adventists, Washington, 1976-81; dir. pub. affairs Southwestern Union Conf. Seventh-day Adventists, Burleson, Tex., 1981-83; dir. trust services Pacific Union Conf. Seventh-day Adventists, Westlake Village, Calif., 1983—; sec., mgr. Pacific Union Conf. Assn. Seventh-day Adventists, 1983—; mem. standing com. Gen. Conf. Seventh-day Adventists, N.Am. div. Mem. ABA. Home: 3015 Shirley Dr Newbury Park CA 91320 Office: Pacific Union Conf Seventh-day Adventists 2686 Townsgate Rd Westlake Village CA 91359

CARTER, JAMES CLARENCE, priest, university president, Roman Catholic Church; b. N.Y.C., Aug. 1, 1927; s. Clarence S. and Elizabeth (Dillon) C. B.S., Spring Hill Coll., 1952; M.S., Fordham U., 1953; Ph.D., Cath. U. Am., 1956; S.T.L., Woodstock Coll., 1959. Joined S.J., Roman Catholic Ch., ordained priest, 1958. Asst. prof. physics Loyola U., New Orleans, 1960-67, assoc. prof., 1967—, acad. v.p., 1970-74, pres., 1974—; dir. edn. New Orleans Province, S.J., 1968-70; mem. La. Higher Edn. Facilities Com., 1971-73; chmn. New Orleans Mayor's Com. on Ednl. Uses of CATV, 1972; mem. Am. Council's Commn. on Leadership Devel. in Higher Edn., 1975-78; mem. adv. com. to New Orleans Pub. Library for NEH Grant, 1975; mem. La. Ednl. TV Authority, 1977-83; trustee Xavier U., Cin., 1979—, Regis Coll., Denver, 1980—, Loyola U., Chgo., 1981—. Contbr. articles to sci. jours. Bd. dirs. Met. Area Com. New Orleans, 1975—, chmn. bus. of govt. task force, 1981—; bd. dirs. United Way for Greater New Orleans Area, 1976—, chmn. govt. group, United Way Fund Dr., 1981, chmn. program effectiveness criteria com.; hon. mem. bd. dirs. Internat. Trade Mart, 1975—. Named to St. Stanislaus High Sch. Hall of Fame, 1974; recipient Palmes Academiques, 1974, Torch of Liberty award Anti Defamation League of B'nai B'rith, 1983. Mem. Am. Phys. Soc., Am. Assn. Physics Tchrs., Nat. Assn. Ind. Colls. and Univs. (bd. dirs. 1979-80, 81-83), Assn. Jesuit Colls. and Univs. (bd. dirs., mem. exec. com., chmn. fed. relations com.), So. Assn. Colls. and Schs. (exec. council of commn. on colls. 1983—), Sigma Xi. Office: Loyola U 6363 Saint Charles Ave New Orleans LA 70118

CARTER, JAMES EDWARD, minister, So. Bapt. Conv.; b. New Edinburg, Ark., Jan. 19, 1935; s. Edward Floyd and Carrie Sue (Reaves) C.; B.A., La. Coll., 1957; B.D., M.Div., Southwestern Bapt. Theol. Sem., 1960, Ph.D., 1964; m. Carole Ann Hunter, Sept. 4, 1955; children—James Craig, Edward Keith, Chyrisse Ann. Ordained to ministry, 1955; pastor Wise Meml. Bapt. Ch., Lena, La., 1955-57, John T. White Bapt. Ch., Fort Worth, 1958-61, Temple Bapt. Ch., Gainesville, Tex., 1961-64, First Bapt. Ch., Natchitoches, La., 1964—. Pres. La. Bapt. Conv., 1973. Trustee Southwestern Baptist Theol. Sem., Ft. Worth; mem. exec. bd., v.p. La. Bapt. Conv., 1971. Mem. Am. Soc. Ch. History, So. Bapt. Hist. Soc., Natchitoches Parish C. of C. Author: A Sourcebook for Stewardship Sermons; People Parables; The Mission of the Church, 1974; What Is to Come?, 1975. Contbr. articles to religious publs. Home: 220 Williams Ave Natchitoches LA 71457 Office: 508 2d St Natchitoches LA 71457

CARTER, JERRY ARTHUR, minister, American Baptist Association; b. Hamburg, Ark., Mar. 1, 1936; s. Arthur Ervin and Allie Myrtle (Carpenter) C.; student U. Ark., 1954-55; Th.B., La. Missionary Bapt. Inst. and Sem., Minden, 1974, Th.M., 1975; m. Annie Clara Jeffers, June 15, 1956; children—Debra, Karen, Barry. Ordained to ministry, 1958; pastor Egypt Missionary Bapt. Ch., Hamburg, 1958-60, Maplevale Missionary Bapt. Ch., Hamburg, 1961-63; missionary to Tallulah, La., 1964-67; pastor Central Missionary Bapt. Ch., Warren, Ark., 1968—. Moderator, Judson Bapt. Assn., 1971—; instr. La. Missionary Bapt. Inst. and Sem., 1972-75, chmn. fin. com., 1974—; trustee Missionary Bapt. Student Fellowship, U. Ark., Monticello, 1972—. Author: Repentance, 1974; Effective Homiletics, 1975. Home: 609 Bond St Warren AR 71671 Office: 406 Seminary St Warren AR 71671

CARTER, JOAN LENEA, layworker, Presbyterian Church in the U.S.A.; liturgical designer; b. Seattle, Feb. 20, 1936; d. James Alexander and Sigrid Linnea (Forsberg) Brix; children: Joseph Mentor Jr., James Mentor, Judith Mentor, Jennifer Mentor; m. Jack Limerick Carter, June 13, 1982. B.A., U. Wash., 1970; M.A., San Francisco Theol. Sem., 1981; postgrad. Grad. Theol. Union, 1982—. Tchr. Lifetime Learning Ctr., Seattle, 1976-81, Religious Learning Inst., Seattle, 1982; liturgical artist Sausalito Presbyn. Ch., Calif., 1982—, co-chmn. worship, 1983—, elder, 1985—. Owner, mgr. Pacific Design Co., Seattle, 1970—. Exhibited in group shows at San Francisco Arts Commn. Invitational, Olympic Artists Annual, U. Wash. Alumni Invitational, U. Puget Sound Invitational, North Kitsap County Regional, others; numerous one-woman shows; represented in numerous pub. and pvt. collections. Mem. Interfaith Forum on Religion, Art and Architecture, The Visual Word, United C. of C. Fellowship in Arts, Ecumenical Council for Drama and Other Arts, Inc., San Francisco Mus. of Modern Art, The Visual Word, Pacific Sch. Religion Christianity and the Arts Com. Home: 100 South St #208 Sausalito CA 94965 Office: Pacific Design 3710 E High Ln Seattle WA 98112

CARTER, KENNEDY JAMES, minister, Southern Baptist Convention; b. Newport News, Va., Feb. 12, 1947; s. Melvin Brozier and Eunice Rose (Shanko) C.; B.Mus., Va. Commonwealth U., 1969; M.Ch. Music, So. Bapt. Theol. Sem., 1971; m. Mary Helen Gupton, Aug. 2, 1969; 1 child, Kimberly Ann. Ordained to ministry, 1972. Minister of music and youth chs., Richmond, Va., 1965-66, Williamsburg, Va., 1966, 67, Chester, Va., 1967-69, Richmond, 1966-67, 69, Verona, Ky., 1969-70, Hampton, Va., 1970, Louisville, 1970-71, Vienna, Va., 1972—; youth ministry cons. Mem. Va. Bapt. Male Chorale. Composer ch. music; pianist at confs.; songleader at revivals and youth camps; summer missionary Jamaica, 1968. Mem. So. Bapt. Conv. Ch. Music Conf., Va. Bapt. Ch. Music Conf. (pres., 1st v.p., 1978-79), Royal Ambassadors (pres. 1964-66), Phi Mu Alpha. Home: 1854 Patton Terr McLean VA 22101 Office: 8120 Leesburg Pike Vienna VA 22180

CARTER, RANDOLPH COLEMAN, minister, Southern Baptist Convention; b. Dublin, Ga., May 25, 1932; s. Joseph Kelly and Jennie Lucile (Renfroe) C.; m. Mary M. Gray, Feb. 20, 1955; children: Randy, Danny, Rhonda. A.B., Mercer U., 1965; M.Div., Midwestern Theol. Sem., Kansas City, Mo., 1968; postgrad. Luther Rice Sem., 1978-80; Th.D., Trinity Theol. Sem., 1985. Ordained to ministry So. Bapt. Conv., 1956. Pastor various chs., Ga. and Mo., 1957-68, First Bapt. Ch., St. Clair, Mo., 1968-82, Immanuel Bapt. Ch., Hannibal, Mo., 1982—; mem. exec. bd. Ga. Bapt. Conv., 1961-63; bd. mgrs. Mo. Bapt. Children's Home; mem. exec. bd., mem. time-place com., mem. order of bus. com., mem. com. on coms. Mo. Bapt. Conv.; v.p. Mo. Bapt. Pastor's Conf.; mem. adv. bd. Mo. Bapt. Coll.; rep. Franklin County Head Start Program; pres. St. Clair Ministerial Alliance, 1975-78; vis. prof. Hannibal-LaGrange Sch., 1984-85; condr. revivals, Mo., Ga. Kans., Ill., Fla. Served to 1st Sgt. U.S. Army, 1952-54. Named Outstanding Minister, Mercer U., 1963. Home: 3322 Pleasant St Hannibal MO 63401 Office: Immanuel Bapt Ch 3600 McMasters Ave Hannibal MO 63401

CARTER, ROY LLEWELLYN, minister, Presbyterian Church USA; b. El Salvador, Central Am., Apr. 9, 1921 (parents Am. citizens); s. Harry L. and Lucila (Rodriguez) C.; m. Jeanette Sanchez, Feb. 12, 1981; children by previous marriage: Marguerite, Myrna, Roy Llewellyn, Naphtali. Diploma Los Angeles Spanish Sem., 1949; B.A., San Francisco Bible Coll., 1955; M.Div., Berkely Bapt. Div. Sch., 1958; M.A., Jersey City State Coll., 1970; D.Min., McCormick Theol. Sem., 1975; Ed.D., NY U, U., 1979. Ordained to ministry Am. Bapt. Ch., 1948; lic. phys. therapist, Calif., 1954. Student pastor Bapt. Chs., San Francisco, Richmond and Oakland, Calif., 1948-58; pastor First Presbyn. Ch., Hoboken, N.J., from 1959; pastor Bilingual Presbyn. Ch., Superior, Ariz., 1980—; chmn. com. for Hispanic Spiritual Concern, Presbytery de Cristo; pub. safety chaplain, Hoboken, 1967—; coordinating council mem. Palisade Presbytery, 1976—, vice moderator, 1977, moderator, 1978; mem. vocation agy. Synod of N.E., 1974-75, mem. racial and ethnic concerned team, 1974-75; condr. seminars for Spanish ministers, 1974-77. Mem. Anti-Poverty Bd.,

Hoboken, 1965-76, sec., 1973-76; chmn. juvenile conf. for juvenile ct., Hoboken, 1967—; mem. Hoboken Welfare Bd., 1969-77; mem. foster care rev. bd. Superior Ct. Ariz.; bd. dirs. Intermountain Behavioral Health Assn., Inc., Ariz. Recipient citation Joint Meml. Com. of War Vets, 1974. Mem. Hudson County Ministerial Assn. Lodges: Masons (32 deg.), Rotary (pres. Superior club 1983-84). Author: Behavior Patterns of the Puerto Rican Poor; The Religious Question in Mexico, 1910 to 1928; Self Renewing Mechanism for a Bilingual Congregation in an Urban Setting; The Bible, The Key for Awakening the Spiritual Dimension of Children. Address: Box 772 Superior AZ 85273

CARTER, STEPHEN JAMES, minister, theology educator, Lutheran Church-Missouri Synod; b. Indpls., Mar. 23, 1941; s. Homer James and Irene Laura (Olsen) C.; m. Gail Roane Dobberstein, June 27, 1964; children: Mark Stanton, Amy Elizabeth, Rebecca Dawn. B.A. with high distinction, Concordia Sr. Coll., Ft. Wayne, Ind., 1962; M.Div., Concordia Sem., St. Louis, 1966, S.T.M., 1967; D. Ministry, United Theol. Sem., 1984. Ordained to ministry Luth. Ch., 1967. Asst. pastor St. Paul Luth. Ch., Decatur, Ill., 1967-71; assoc. pastor Trinity Luth. Ch., Utica, Mich., 1971-74; sr. pastor St. John's Luth. Ch., Peru, Ind., 1974-82; asst. prof. Concordia Theol. Sem., Ft. Wayne, 1982—; dist. archivist Central Ill. dist. Luth. Ch.-Mo. Synod, 1967-71, founder, leader marriage emrichment retreats Ind. dist., Ft. Wayne, 1975-82, chmn. adult edn. com. Ind. dist., 1980—, mem. denominational edn. com., St. Louis, 1984—; dir. continuing edn. Concordia Theol. Sem., 1983—; pres. Decatur Christian Found., 1970-71. Author: (with others) Keeping a Good Thing Going, 1979, More of A Good Thing, 1982; (workshop materials) Learning Plan Worshop, 1984. Mem. exec. com. C. of C., Peru, Ind., 1979-80; mem. exec. bd. Decatur Mental Health Assn., 1968-70. Luth. Brotherhood Grad. scholar Concordia Sem., 1966-67, scholar Aid Assn. for Luths., United Theol. Sem., 1982-84. Mem. Soc. Advancement Continuing Edn. for Ministry, Concordia Hist. Inst. Republican. Home: 3212 Stepping Stone Ln Fort Wayne IN 46815 Office: Concordia Theol Sem 6600 N Clinton Fort Wayne IN 46825

CARTER, THOMAS EDWARDS, minister, American Baptist Churches U.S.A.; b. Balt., June 8, 1950; s. John Merriken and Helen (Day) C.; m. Mary Christine Sampietro, July 31, 1982; 1 child, Andrea Christine. B.A., U. Idaho, 1972; M.Div., Fuller Theol. Sem., 1975; D.Min. with highest honors, Internat. Sem., 1979. Ordained to ministry Baptist Ch., 1976. Assoc. pastor First Bapt. Ch., Menlo Park, Calif., 1976-77, Visalia, Calif., 1977-82; pastor First Bapt. Ch., Dinuba, Calif., 1982—; teaching fellow Fuller Sem., Pasadena, Calif., 1972-75, extension prof., San Jose, Calif., 1976-77; sec. Visalia Ministerial Assn., Calif., 1982, Dinuba Ministerial Assn., 1984. Author: Cover to Cover, 1984. Named Best Preacher in Graduating Class, Fuller Sem., 1975. Republican. Home: 1497 Newton Ave Dinuba CA 93618 Office: First Baptist Ch 288 N J St Dinuba CA 93618

CARTER, TROY HAROLD, minister music, So. Baptist Conv.; b. Hattiesburg, Miss., Aug. 13, 1941; s. Leroy and Verma Idella (Stringer) C.; B.M., U. So. Miss., 1964; M. Ch. Music, New Orleans Baptist Theol. Sem., 1972; m. Earline Ellison, Aug. 17, 1963; children—Catherine Suzanne, Wesley Troy. Minister music chs., Miss., Fla., Tex., La., 1962-72; minister of music 1st Baptist Ch., Kerrville, Tex., 1972—. Mem. So. Baptist Ch. Music Conf., Am. Guild English Handbell Ringers, Ministerial Alliance of Kerrville, Tex. Home: 1103 4th St Kerrville TX 78028 Office: 625 Washington St Kerrville TX 78028

CARTER, WILLIAM CURTIS, minister, Christian Ch. (Disciples of Christ); b. Indpls., May 22, 1946; s. Ola Martin and Mary Elsie Juanita (Mauck) C.; B.A., Culver Stockton Coll., 1969; M.Ministry, Christian Theol. Sem., 1974; m. Janet Lee Miller, Aug. 4, 1968; children—Paul William, Lisa Marie. Ordained to ministry, 1974; student pastor Peaksville (Mo.) Christian Ch. and Warren (Mo.) Christian Ch., 1966-69; worship asst. Garden City Christian Ch., Indpls., 1969-72; pastor Hobbs (Ind.) Christian Ch., 1972-75; adminstrv. asst. Kennedy Meml. Christian Home, Martinsville, Ind., 1975—. Mem. ecumenical laity conf. com. Disciples of Christ Regional Commn. on Aging, 1975—, mem. men's retreat com., 1972-76; chmn. Ecumenical Laity Commn., 1976-77; bd. dirs. Morgan County Rehab. Services, 1977. Mem. Nat. Geriatrics Assn., Martinsville Ministerial Assn. Home: 315 W Pike St Martinsville IN 46151 Office: 210 W Pike St Martinsville IN 46151

CARTER, WILLIAM HOUSTON, minister, Southern Baptist Convention; b. Birmingham, Ala., Oct. 22, 1935; s. Robert Julian and Martha Louise (Wilkerson) C.; m. Catherine Ann Upshaw, Aug. 15, 1958; children: William Russell, Robert Scott, Catherine Leigh, Richard Houston. A.B., Samford U., 1956; B.D., So. Bapt. Theol. Sem., Louisville, 1960, M.Div., 1959. Ordained to ministry So. Bapt. Conv., 1956. Asst. pastor for youth Shades Mountain Bapt. Ch., Birmingham, 1956-57; pastor Cash Creek Bapt. Ch., Henderson, Ky., 1958-60, Summerville Bapt. Ch., Phenix City, Ala., 1960-72, Terry Parker Bapt. Ch., Jacksonville, Fla., 1972-79, Hunter St. Bapt. Ch., Birmingham, 1979—; mem. various associational offices and coms., Phenix City, Jacksonville, Birmingham, 1960-72; exec. com. Ala. Bapt. Assn., 1970—; mem. various coms. Fla. Bapt. Mission Bd., Jacksonville, 1972-79; trustee Bapt. Towers Retirement Home, Jacksonville, 1977-79. Active Phenix City Com. of 100, 1963-72, Phenix City Bd. Edn., 1964-68, Phenix City Girls Club, 1964-68, United Givers. Named Young Man of Yr., Phenix City Jr. C. of C., 1967. Office: Hunter St Bapt Ch PO Box 3970 Birmingham AL 35208

CARVER, LOYCE C., general overseer, Apostolic Faith; b. Decaturville, Tenn., Dec. 13, 1918; s. Oscar Price and Mae (Chumney) C.; student pub. schs.; m. Mary Rebecca Frymire, Dec. 14, 1940. Ordained to ministry Apostolic Faith Mission of Portland, Oreg., 1947; pastor chs. Dallas, Oreg., 1948-49, San Francisco, 1950-52, Los Angeles, 1953-56; pastor Apostolic Faith Mission, Medford, Ore., 1956-65; gen. overseer Apostolic Faith mission of Portland, 1965—. Office: 6615 SE 52d St Portland OR 97209*

CARYL, EARL OTIS, minister, American Baptist Churches in U.S.A.; b. Davison Mich., Mar. 5, 1928; s. Frank Silas and Ida Grace (Hollingshed) C.; m. Martha Eva Riggs, June 13, 1948; children: Marcia, Frank, Myrna, Marilynn. Student Ottawa U., 1946-48; B.S., Kans. State U., 1952; B.D., Central Bapt. Sem., 1956, M.Div., 1976; postgrad. U. Western Mich., 1961-63. Ordained to ministry Am. Bapt. Chs. in U.S.A., 1955. Pastor, tchr. Ceresco Bapt. Ch., Mich., 1956-64, Desert Ministries, Beatty, Nev., 1964-66; pastor Zenobia Bapt., Pawnee, Ill., 1966-68; pastor, tchr. Maple Hill Bapt. Ch., Kansas City, Kans., 1968-73; supt. of bldgs. Central Sem., Kansas City, 1973-81; dir. Ch. Relations, 1981—; county chmn. Christian Rural Overseas Program, Marshall, Mich., 1957-60; adult chmn. Mo. River Assn., Kansas City, 1968-72; mem. Minister's Council, 1968—; deacon, pres. Grandview Bapt. Ch., 1982. Bd. dirs. Bethel Neighborhood Ctr., Kansas City, 1972-80. Mem. Intercity Cluster (pres. 1984). Republican. Club: Toastmaster's Internat. (Kansas City). Lodge: Kiwanis (dir. 1978-80). Home: 4352 Garfield Kansas City KS 66102 (913) 287-9054 Office: Central Bapt Theol Sem Seminary Heights Kansas City KS 66102

CASATI, LAWRENCE WILLIAM, III, priest, Orthodox Church in America; b. Bklyn., Sept. 3, 1953; s. Lawrence William II and Gloria Anna (Donato) C. B.A. in Theol. Studies, U. Dayton, 1974; M.A. in Bibl. Studies, Athenaeum of Ohio, 1983, M.A. in Sacred Theology, 1983. Ordained priest Orthodox Church in America, 1983; cert. catechist Roman Catholic Church. Tchr. Chaminade-Julienne High Sch., Dayton, Ohio, 1979-80; deacon Holy Spirit Ch., Parma, Ohio, 1981, St. Mary's Byzantine Ch., Cleve., 1981-82, St. Michael Orthodox Ch., Wright-Patterson AFB, Dayton, 1982-83; rector Sts. Cyril and Methodius Orthodox Ch., Lorain, Ohio, 1983—; sec. Greater Cleve. Council of Orthodox Clergy, 1984—. Notary public, State of Ohio, 1978—. Author: The Anaphora of St. John Chrysostom, 1982; Pentecostal Narratives in the Acts of the Apostles, 1983. Editor Italian Genealogist. Newspaper columnist What's On Your Mind?, 1981-82. Fellow Octavian Soc.; mem. Montgomery County Hist. Soc., Augustan Soc. (chmn. Italian com.), Fellowship of St. Alban and St. Sergius, Heraldry Soc. (USA), Am. Numismatic Assn., St. Charles Alumni Assn., U. Dayton Alumni Assn. Lodge: Sons of Italy in Am. (chaplain Dayton 1983—).

CASE, M. ROSE CECILIA, nun, Roman Catholic Church; b. Pottstown, Pa., Apr. 9, 1917; d. Earl John and Mary Rachel (Pyle) Case. B.Mus., Cath. U., 1950; M.A. in Theology, St. Bonaventure U., 1955. Entered Convent of Our Lady of Angels, 1940. Tchr., Archdiocese of Phila., 1942-47, 57-74; faculty Our Lady of Angels Coll., Aston, Pa., 1950-56, 68; vicar gen. Sisters of St. Francis, Aston, Pa., 1974-78, gen. minister, 1978—; corp. mem. Franciscan Health System, Chadds Ford, Pa., 1981—; chmn. bd. trustees Neumann Coll., Aston, 1978—. Author: The Fatherhood of God and St. Francis, 1972. Mem. Franciscan Fedn. (del. 1981-82, pres. 1983—), Leadership Conf. Women Religious, Nat. Cath. Edn. Assn. Address: Convent of Our Lady of Angels Aston PA 19014

CASE, STEVEN CHARLES, minister, American Baptist Churches in the U.S.A.; b. Mariemont, Ohio, Sept. 4, 1951; s. Charles Robert and Estelle Margaret (Bryan) C.; m. Gayle Louise Milay, June 23, 1973. B.A., Judson Coll., 1973; M.Div., Eastern Bapt. Sem., 1978. Ordained to ministry Am. Bapt. Chs. in the U.S.A., 1978. Minister Norwayne Bapt. Ch., Westland, Mich., 1970-73, First Bapt. Ch., Somerdale, N.J., 1974-79, Bergen Point Community Ch., Bayonne, N.J., 1979-80, Grace Bapt. Ch., Westmont, N.J., 1981—; mem., chmn. com. pub. mission Am. Bapt. Chs. in N.J., 1982—, chmn. ann. session, 1979; trustee, v.p. bd. trustees Bapt. Home of S. Jersey, Riverton, 1982—, chmn. personnel com., 1982—; organizer community food pantry Grace Bapt. Ch., Haddon Twp., N.J., 1983—. Mem. Bapt. Peace Fellowship. Democrat. Home: 23 Reeve Ave Westmont NJ 08108 Office: Grace Baptist Ch 25-27 Reeve Ave Westmont NJ 08108

CASEY, DANIEL JOSEPH, priest, Roman Catholic Church; b. County Kerry, Ireland, Jan. 25, 1935; s. Daniel D. and Julia Ann (Collins) C.; student All Hallows Coll., Dublin, Ireland, 1952-58; M.S.W., Sacramento State U., 1972. Came to U.S., 1958, naturalized, 1964. Ordained priest Roman Cath. Ch., 1958; assoc. pastor Holy Rosary Ch., Woodland, Calif., 1958-65, St. Isidore's Ch., Yuba City, Calif., 1965-66, Cathedral of Blessed Sacrament, Sacramento, 1966-69; founding dir. Dept. Mexican Am. Affairs, Diocese of Sacramento, 1969-71; coordinator for Spanish-speaking Apostolate, Diocese of Sacramento, 1971-76; mem. Commn. for Spanish-speaking West Coast Bishops, 1973-76; producer Mexican Am. Cath. Forum and Chicano Press Conf. TV shows, 1973-76; pastor St. Mary's Ch., Vacaville, Calif., 1977—; dir. community devel. Diocese of Sacramento, 1976-77. Mem. Sacramento Redevel. Commn., 1973-75; mem. Calif. State Office Econ. Opportunity Bd., 1973-76. Mem. Calif. State Marriage Counselors Assn., Nat. Assn. Social Workers, Sacramento Bd. of Realtors, Acad. Cert. Social Workers, Nat. Conf. Cath. Charities. Home and Office: 350 Stinson Ave Vacaville CA 95688

CASEY, JAMES VINCENT, archbishop, Roman Catholic Church; b. Osage, Iowa, Sept. 22, 1914; s. James G. and Nina (Nims) C.; A.B., Loras Coll., 1936, LL.D., 1959; postgrad. Gregorian U., Rome, Italy, 1936-40; J.C.D., Cath. U. Am., 1949. Ordained priest Roman Catholic Ch., 1939; asst. pastor St. John's Parish, Independence, Iowa, 1940-44; sec. Archbishop Leo Binz, Dubuque, Iowa, 1946-49; consecrated bishop, 1957; bishop of Lincoln (Nebr.), 1957-67; archbishop of Denver, 1967—. Chaplain USN, 1944-46. Office: Archdiocese of Denver 200 Josephine St Denver CO 80206*

CASIANO VARGAS, ULISES See *Who's Who in America*, 43rd edition.

CASLOW, DANIEL ERNEST, minister, Seventh-day Adventist Church; b. Rochester, Ind., Aug. 14, 1916; s. Ernest Thomas and Orah (Alspach) C.; m. Olive Wilson, Jan. 16, 1939. R.N., Fla. Hosp. Sch. Nursing, Orlando, 1941; B.A. cum laude, Andrews U., 1944. Ordained, 1948. Pastor-evangelist, Ind. Conf. Seventh-day Adventists, 1944-52, dept. dir. personal ministries, 1952-58; dept. dir. personal ministries N.Y. Conf., 1958-60, Atlantic Union Conf., 1960-63, N.Pacific Union Conf., 1963-81; researcher, developer 1st discipling ministry Seventh-day Adventist Ch., 1980—; discipling cons., condr. seminars, ministerial and lay leadership groups N. Am., 1981—. Author: Winning-Lay Bible Ministry, 1981; Discipling-New Member Ministry, 1982; Profile Nurture Series 1, 2, 3, 4, 1982; Accenting Your Life, 1985. Recipient Dean of Dirs. award Gen. Conf. Seventh-day Adventists, 1981. Home: 14343 NE Siskiyou Ct Portland OR 97230

CASSEL, EARL OWEN, minister, American Baptist Churches U.S.A.: b. Phila., Aug. 29, 1947; s. Earl Ruth and Mary Millicent (Williard) C.; m. Linda Sue Baker, June 1, 1974; children: Earl Owen, Melissa Joy. B.A., Wash. Bible Coll., 1973; M.Div., Reformed Presbyterian Theol. Sem., 1978. Ordained to ministry Baptist Ch., 1978. Minister Mars Hill Bapt. Ch., Rillton, Pa., 1975-78, Emmanuel Bapt. Ch., Pitts., 1978-81, East End Bapt. Ch., Williamsport, Pa., 1981—. Home: 815 Washington Blvd Williamsport PA 17701 Office: 801 Washington Blvd Williamsport PA 17701

CASSELS, ROSALIE VERNON, lay church worker, Presbyterian Church in the U.S.; b. Columbia, S.C., Jan. 1, 1909; d. Frank Littleton and Vernon Rosamond (Tyler) Outlaw; m. William Tobin Cassels, July 31, 1928; 1 child William Tobin. Student Chicora Coll. for Women, Columbia, 1924-25, U. S.C., 1930, 35; Bible tchr., adult adviser to youth groups Presbytery and Synod levels Presbyn. Ch. in U.S., 1932-44; pres. Women of Ch., Congaree Presbytery, 1943-45; dir. Interdenomn. Christian Leadership Tng. Sch. for Women, Benedict Coll., Columbia, 1946-64; pres. Women of Ch., Synod of S.C., 1967-68; dean Synodical Tng. Sch., Presbyn. Coll., Clinton, S.C., 1967-68; mem. com. women's concerns, gen. assembly Presbyn. Ch. in U.S., 1973-74; trustee Mission Haven, Decatur, Ga., 1967-69; bd. visitors Presbyn. Coll., Clinton, S.C., 1968-70, 73-75, 78-82. Active S.C. Mental Health Assn., Crippled Children's Soc. Richland County; trustee Queens Coll., Charlotte, N.C., 1980-84. Mem. Women's Symphony Assn., U. S.C. Soc., Columbia Mus. Art, Columbia Hist. Soc. Address: 835 Kilbourne Rd Columbia SC 29205

CASTELLANO-HOYT, DONALD WAYNE, educator, Church of the Nazarene; b. Nampa, Idaho, Aug. 21, 1945; s. Robert Lyman and Lulu Mae (Wagoner) H.; B.A., Pasadena Nazarene Coll., 1967, M.A., 1968; postgrad. in Hebrew Studies, U. Tex. at Austin, 1968—; M.S.W., Our Lady of the Lake U., 1984; m. Julia Castellano, Mar. 22, 1974. Asst. minister S. Austin (Tex.) Ch. of the Nazarene, 1968-70; Hebrew tchr. Austin Ind. Sch. Dist., 1968-70, U. Tex. at Austin, 1969-70; asst. prof. Bibl. lit. Olivet Nazarene Coll., Kankakee, Ill., 1971-75; instr. St. Philips Coll., 1975—; pvt. practice group psychotherapy, 1975—; condr. workshops. Counselor Travis and Bexar counties alcohol treatment programs, 1972—. Mem. Am.

Orthopsychiat. Assn., Nat. Assn. Social Workers. Office: 227 Old Guilbeau San Antonio TX 78205

CASTLEBERRY, JAMES MICHAEL, minister, So. Baptist Conv.; b. Montgomery, Ala., Oct. 26, 1943; s. Richard Steven and Frances Inez (Mason) C.; B.A., Samford U., Birmingham, Ala., 1966; Th.M., New Orleans Baptist Theol. Sem., 1969; m. Marsha Joette Bush, Aug. 23, 1970; children—James Brian, Jon Bart. Ordained to ministry, 1961; minister Brewer Meml. Baptist Ch., Cecil, Ala., 1961-69, Pike Road (Ala.) Baptist Ch., 1969-72, 1st Baptist Ch., Wetumpka, Ala., 1972—. Vice pres. Ala. Baptist Pastors Conf., 1973-74; moderator Elmore County Baptist Assn., 1975—; sec. Montgomery Baptist Ministers Conf.; area rep. Ala. Bible Soc. Mem. Montgomery Ministerial Assn., Elmore Baptist Ministers Conf. Home: 304 Marshall St Wetumpka AL 36092 Office: 205 W Bridge St Wetumpka AL 36092

CASTRO, EMILIO, clergyman; gen. sec. World Council of Churches, 1984—. Office: World Council of Chs 475 Riverside Dr Room 1062 New York NY 10115*

CASTRO RUIZ, MANUEL, archbishop, Roman Catholic Church; b. Morelia, Michoacan, Mex., Nov. 9, 1918; s. Castro Tinoco and Mercedes (Ruiz de) C. Student, Morelia Sem., 1930-37; Pontifical Pius, Latin Am. Coll., 1940; Gregorian U., Rome, 1940, Puebla Sem., 1943. Ordained priest Roman Cath Ch., 1943. Pvt. sec. to archbishop of Morelia, 1943; prefect of Valladolid Inst.; spiritual dir. Minor Sem., 1947-50; spiritual dir. major Sem. of Morelia, prof. math. and philosophy, 1950-65; aux. bishop of Yucatan, 1965-69, archbishop of Yucatan, 1969—; asst. to Episcopal Synod, 1974. Office: 501 58th Merida Yucatan Mexico

CATANZARO, FRANK JAY, JR., minister, ednl. adminstr., So. Bapt. Conv.; b. Pitts., Feb. 18, 1931; s. Frank J. and Lois Margaret (Walcroft) C.; student Kings' Coll., Briarcliff Manor, N.Y., 1948-50; B.A., Baldwin Conservatory, 1951; postgrad. Western Res. U., 1955-56, Central (S.C.) Wesleyan Coll., 1969, Rice Sem., 1969-71, Moody Bible Inst., 1972; Th.D., Brainerd Theol. Sem., Anderson, S.C., 1972; H.H.D. (hon.), Kans. Coll. Human Relations, 1969; m. Lois Ann Harris, Jan. 8, 1954; children—Frank Jay III, Barbara Ann. Concert pianist and organist, 1954-58; minister of music, asso. pastor Oakland Bapt. Ch., Roanoke, Va., 1958-60; ordained to ministry, 1961; pres. Anderson Sch. Music, 1961-70; dir. Confidential Counseling Service, Anderson, 1963-73; pres. Brainerd Theol. Sem., Spartanburg, S.C., 1973—. Dir., producer religious news broadcast Anderson Coll., 1965-68; speaker numerous commencements, ch. events. Contbr. articles to religious jours.; introduced extension edn. for pastors and religious workers at Brainerd Theol. Sem. Home: PO Box 555 Anderson SC 29622 Office: Brainerd Theol Sem PO Box M Anderson SC 29622

CATE, WILLIAM BURKE, church official, minister, United Methodist Church; b. Itasca, Tex., Mar. 25, 1924; s. Emmet and Irene (Kincaid) C.; B.A., Willamette U., 1945; S.T.B., Boston U., 1948, Ph.D., 1953; D.D., Lewis and Clark Coll., 1965; m. Janice Mcleod Patterson, Aug. 20, 1946; children—Lucy Cate (Mrs. Keith Warren), Nancy (Mrs. James Lawler), Michael, Sara, Rebecca, Mary. Ordained to ministry, 1952; exec. dir. Interch. Council of Greater New Bedford (Mass.), 1953-58, Greater Portland (Oreg.) Council Chs., 1958-70; pres., dir. Ch. Council of Greater Seattle, 1970—. Recipient Anti-Defamation League Torch of Liberty award, 1972. Mem. Nat. Assn. Ecumenical Staff. Author: The Ecumenical Scandal on Main Street, 1965. Office: 4759 15th NE Seattle WA 98105

CATHELL, RICHARD BRUCE, chaplain, Seventh-day Adventists. B. Lynwood, Calif., July 11, 1946; s. Raymond Hannah Cathell and Elma Chrystelle (McCulloch) Cathell Spoden; m. Donna May Yeoman, Aug. 20, 1967; children: Kirsten, Ebbe. B.A. in Theology, Loma Linda U., 1969; M.Div., Andrews U., 1972; Ph.D. candidate in Marriage and Family Counselling, Columbia Pacific U., 1985—. Ordained to ministry Seventh-day Adventists, 1977; cert. chaplain, 1982. Chaplain, Adventist Med. Ctr., Okinawa, Japan, 1971-72, Porter Meml. Hosp., Denver, 1981—; pastor Morristown Seventh-day Adventist Ch., N.J., 1972-75; clin. pastoral edn. resident intern Kettering Med. Ctr., Ohio, 1975-76; minister youth and family Takoma Park Seventh-day Adventist Ch., Md., 1976-79; sr. pastor Leesburg Seventh-day Adventist Ch., Va., 1979-81. Founder-speaker (weekly radio program) Crisis: On Call, 1976-79; Happiness Homemade, 1979-81; editorial counsel Insight Mag., 1977-81. Mem. Met. Washington Family Life Com., Washington, 1977-79; mem. youth resources com. Gen. Conf., Washington, D.C., 1977-81; founder-chmn. Lincoln Norris Meml. Symposium on Grief, 1981—; founder-facilitator Single Again, Denver, 1982—, Values for Creative Lifestyle, Denver, 1983—. Fellow Coll. Chaplains Am. Protestant Hosp. Assn. (cert. 1982); mem. Loudoun County Ministerial Assn. (sec.-treas. 1979-81). Republican. Home: 9728 S Turkey Creek Rd Morrison CO 80465 Office: Porter Meml Hosp 2525 S Downing St Denver CO 80210

CATLIN, MARTHA CORINNE, lay ch. worker, Evansville Meeting of Friends; b. Bartholomew County, Ind., July 31, 1906; s. Alfred and Zella Newby (Cox) C.; A.B., Earlham Coll., 1930; postgrad. Ind. U., 1936-39, Evansville Coll., 1951-52. Organizer, Evansville (Ind.) Meeting of Friends, 1957, rec. clk., 1963-65, presiding clk., 1966—; rep. on del. council Evansville Council Chs., 1964—, sec. exec. com., 1967-69, 71-74; presiding clk. So. Area Meeting of Friends, 1971-74; rep. on exec. com., sec. Western Yearly Meeting of Friends, 1970-74. Bd. dirs. Tri-State Epilepsy Assn., 1960—, sec., 1970—; bd. dirs. Mental Health Assn. Vanderburgh County, 1957—, pres., 1973—. Named Dietitian of Yr., Ind. Dietetic Assn., 1971. Mem. AAUW, Am., Ind., S.W. Ind. dietetic assns., Bus. and Profl. Women's Club. Home: 127 Locust St Apt 315 Evansville IN 47708

CAUBLE, HERMAN W., Synodical bishop Lutheran Church in America, Columbia, S.C. Office: Lutheran Ch in Am 1003 Richland St Columbia SC 29202*

CAUGHMAN, WOFFORD BOSWELL, JR., minister of education and youth, Southern Baptist Convention; b. Camden, S.C., Mar. 1, 1953; s. Wofford Boswell Sr. and Betty Jean (Baker) C.; m. Catherine Leila Bailey, May 23, 1976; children: Wofford Boswell III, Rachel Catherine. A.A., Anderson Jr. Coll., 1973; B.A., Gardner-Webb Coll., 1975; M.Div., So. Bapt. Theol. Sem., 1978. Ordained to ministry So. Bapt. Conv., 1977. Minister of youth New Hope Bapt. Ch., Raleigh, N.C., 1976-78, assoc. pastor, 1978-81; minister of edn. and youth Bethel Bapt. Ch., Greenville, S.C., 1981—. Contbr. articles to profl. jours. Mem. Berea Area Bus. Community Assn., S.C. Bapt. Religious Edn. Assn., Eastern Bapt. Religious Edn. Assn., So. Bapt. Conv. Religious Edn. Assn., Berea Area Ministers Assn. Republican. Avocations: softball, painting. Home: 1 Wheatridge Dr Greenville SC 29609 Office: Bethel Bapt Ch 403 Sulphur Springs Rd Greenville SC 29611

CAUSEY, GERALD DAVID, lay church worker, Southern Baptist Convention; b. Hendersonville, N.C., July 9, 1934; s. Herman Columbus and Tempie Faye (Bagwell) C.; B.A., Wayland Coll., 1962; M.A., Appalachian State U., 1963; m. Beverly Jean Hicks, Nov. 2, 1956; children—Mark David, Steven Craig, Tara Renee, Amber Jean. Minister music First Bapt. Ch., Alamogordo, N.Mex., 1957-59, First Bapt. Ch., Edmundson, Tex., 1959-62, First Bapt. Ch., Hendersonville, N.C., 1963-70, First Bapt. Ch., Tucker, Ga., 1970-76; pres. Master Media, Tucker, Ga., 1976—; mem. nat. evangelism support team So. Bapt. Conv. Recipient Certificate of Appreciation, DeKalb County Juvenile Ct., 1976, Certificate of Merit, Southeastern U.S. Fair, 1975; Exceptional Achievement award for media prodn. Nat. Council Advancement and Support of Edn., 1983. Mem. Am. Guild English Handbell Ringers, Am. Choral Dirs. Assn., Nat. Assn. Tchrs. Singing, Nat. Audio Visual Assn., Phi Mu Alpha Sinfonia. Photographer, multi-media producer. Home: 1441 Camelot Lane Tucker GA 30084

CAUSEY, RICHARD WAYNE, minister Southern Baptist Convention; b. Meridian, Miss., May 26, 1935; s. Harry and Genevieve (Davis) C.; m. Mary Elizabeth May, July 18, 1959; children: Kimberly Ann, Richard Wayne. B.S., Miss. Coll., 1957; B.D., So. Bapt. Theol. Sem., Louisville, 1960, M.Div., 1967, D.Ministry, 1983. Ordained to ministry Bapt. Ch., 1959. Youth dir. 1st Bapt. Ch., Meridian, Miss., 1957-58; assoc. pastor 1st Bapt. Ch., Greensboro, N.C., 1960-66; pastor 1st Bapt. Ch., Gaffney, S.C., 1966-74, Pendleton St. Bapt. Ch., Greenville, S.C., 1974—; chaplain Wesley Long Community Hosp., Greensboro, 1964-66; trustee Bapt. Courier, Greenville, 1971-75, N. Greenville Coll., Tigerville, S.C., 1977-81; pastor adviser Bapt. Student Union Furman U., Greenville, 1976-81; pub. relations council Southeastern Bapt. Theol. Sem., Wake Forest, N.C., 1978-84. Contbr. curriculum materials, articles to Youth Alive mag., 1970—. Mem. Greenville Ministerial Alliance. Club: Greenville Kiwanis (dir. 1979-81). Home: 228 Compton Dr Greenville SC 29615 Office: Pendleton St Bapt Ch 422 Pendleton St Greenville SC 29601

CAVANAGH, KAREN MARIE, nun, religious educator, administrator, Roman Catholic Church. b. Bklyn., Apr. 10, 1941; d. Joseph James and Agnes Rita (Fasan) C. B.S. in Edn., Brentwood Coll., 1966; M.S. in Edn., CUNY, 1972; M.A. in Religion and Family Ministry, Fordham U., 1982. Joined Congregation of Sisters of St. Joseph Roman Catholic Ch. Tchr. religion grade schs., Bklyn.-Queens, 1962-77; sacrament coordinator Immaculate Conception Sch., Jamaica, N.Y., 1971-77; religion tchr. Immaculate conception and St. Rita, Queens, N.Y., 1965-77; sch. adminstr. Blessed Sacrament Sch., Bklyn., 1977—; Eucharistic minister to homebound Immaculate Conception Parish, 1973-77, Blessed Sacrament Parish, 1977—; retreat coordinator Cong. of St. Joseph, Brentwood, N.Y., 1975—; clown minister, Bklyn., 1979—; coordinator workshops. Poverty rep. Qualicap Civic Orgn., L.I., 1967-69. Home: 189 Chestnut St Cypress Hills NY 11208 Office: Blessed Sacrament Sch 187 Euclid Ave Cypress Hills NY 11208

CAVERLY, PATRICK JOSEPH, priest, Roman Cath. Ch.; b. Cork, Ireland, June 22, 1933; s. James and Agnes Catherine (Hegarty) C.; came to U.S., 1961; naturalized, 1967; B.A., Mt. Melleray Coll., 1957; M.A. Carlow Coll., 1961, 67. Ordained priest, 1961; prof. English and Latin, St. Petersburg (Fla.) Cath. High Sch., 1961-65; pres. Santa Fe High Sch., Lakeland, Fla., 1967-72; pastor St. Mary Magdalen Ch., Maitland, Fla., 1972—. Recipient Philosophy award Mt. Melleray Coll., 1957. Home and Office: 700 Spring Lake Rd Altamonte Springs FL 32750

CAVETT, LOIS JEAN, religious organization librarian, Christian Church (Independent); b. Ada, Okla., Oct. 20, 1946; d. Leon Joseph and Lenna Mae (McClure) Myers; m. Danny Lee Cavett, July 12, 1968; children: Mark Allen, Tonya Lynn. B.S. in Elem. Edn., Southwestern State U., Okla., 1968; M.L.S., U. Okla., 1981. Asst. librarian Midwest Christian Coll., Oklahoma City, 1976-78, library dir., 1978—. Mem. Assn. Christian Librarians, Assn. Library and Learning Ctrs. Dirs. (sec. 1979-80), Okla. Library Assn., Friends of Libraries in Okla., Okla. Assn. Coll. Research Libraries. Office: Midwest Christian Coll 6600 N Kelley Oklahoma City OK 73111

CAYCE, W. H., elder Primitive Baptists. Address: S 2d St Thornton AR 71766

CECIL, EARL IVAN, minister, Evangelical Mennonite Church; b. Fort Wayne, Ind., Mar. 31, 1946; s. Kenneth Everett and Amy Ilene (Leonard) C.; m. Cheryl Ann Roth, July 8, 1967; children: Angela Beth, Aric Nathan, Andrew Jon, April Joy. B.A. in Pastoral Ministries, Ft. Wayne Bible Coll., 1968; postgrad. Trinity Evang. Div., 1972-74, Grace Theol. Sem., 1976-79; M. Christian Ministries, Huntington Grad. Sch. Christian Ministries, 1983. Ordained to Mennonite Ch. as minister, 1971. Minister, pastor First Evang. Mennonite Ch., Lafayette, Ind., 1968-72; houseparent, counselor Salem Children's Home, Flanagan, Ill., 1972-73, asst. pastor, chaplain, 1973-76; pastor Thorncreek Ch. of God, Columbia City, Ind., 1976-77, Woodburn Evang. Mennonite Ch., Ind., 1977—; chmn. Evang. Mennonite Conf. Commn. on Christian Edn., Ft. Wayne, 1980-84; program chmn. Miracle Camp, Lawton, Mich., 1980-85; bd. dirs. Gen. Bd. Evang. Mennonite Ch., Ft. Wayne, 1980-84. Vice-pres. PTA, Woodburn, 1983. Home: 4114 Becker Rd Woodburn IN 46797 Office: Woodburn Evang Mennonite Ch 4100 Becker Rd Woodburn IN 46797

CECIRE, ROBERT CLYDE, minister, American Baptist Association; educator; b. Norwalk, Conn., Nov. 3, 1940; s. Bernard Francis and Elva Louise (Buchannon) C.; m. Sarah Marie Hull, June 19, 1971. A.B., Wheaton Coll., 1962; B.D., Gordon Div. Sch., 1965; M.A., U. Kans., 1976, postgrad., 1976. Ordained to ministry Am. Bapt. Churches, U.S.A., 1967. Pastor, Biddeford United Bapt. Ch., Maine, 1967-70, Southwest Bapt. Ch., Topeka, 1970-80; interim pastor Gage Park Bapt. Ch., Topeka, 1980, Terra Heights Bapt. Ch., Topeka, 1980-81, First Bapt. Ch., Silver Lake, Kans., 1981—. Teaching asst. U. Kans., Lawrence, 1981—; acad. leader Gordon Coll. European seminar, 1984. Mem. Soc. Bibl. Lit., Phi Alpha Theta. Home: 2900 Evensingside Dr Topeka KS 66614

CEGIELKA, FRANCIS ANTHONY, priest, educator, Roman Catholic Church; b. Grabow, Poland, Mar. 16, 1908; s. Martin and Maryann (Nieszczesna) C.; student Collegium Marianum, Wadowice (Krakow), Poland, 1924-27; Th.D., Pontifical Gregorian U., Rome, 1931. Came to U.S., 1948, naturalized, 1954. Joined Soc. Cath. Apostolate, 1926; ordained priest Roman Cath. Ch., 1931; chaplain Polish Cath. Mission, Caen, Calvados, France, 1931-32; tchr. minor sem. Soc. Cath. Apostolate, Chelmno, Poland, 1932-34; instr. maj. sem. Soc. Cath. Apostolate, Wadowice, Poland, 1934-36; rector Polish Cath. Mission, Paris, France, 1937-47; lectr., retreat master U.S., Europe, Africa, 1948-67; prof., chmn. dept theology Felician Coll., Lodi, N.J., 1967-71; prof., chmn. religious studies Holy Family Coll., Phila., 1971-76. Named Outstanding Educator Am., Holy Family Coll., 1972, 74-75. Mem. AAUP, Polish Inst. Arts and Scis. in Am. Author 10 books in Polish, 12 books in English, including The Pierced Heart, 1955, Spiritual Theology for Novices, 1961, Three Hearts, vol. 1, 1963, vol. 2, 1964, All Things New, 1969, Handbook of Ecclesiology and Christology, 1971; Toward a New Spring of Humankind. 1985. Home: 3452 Niagara Falls Blvd North Tonawanda NY 14120

CERLING, CHARLES EDWARD, JR., minister, American Baptist Chs. U.S.A.; b. Elmhurst, Ill., Oct. 7, 1943; s. Charles Edward and Agnes Macintosh (Muir) C.; m. Geraldine Lee Bock, June 11, 1966; children: David Bruce, Jonathan Mark, Peter James. A.B., Taylor U., 1965; M.A., Trinity Evangelical Div. Sch., 1968, M.Div., 1969; D.Min., Talbot Theol. Sem., 1983. Ordained to ministry Baptist Church, 1978. Minister United Methodist Ch., North Liberty, Iowa, 1970-72, Scales Mound, Ill., 1972-74; minister edn. Hopevale Bapt. Ch. Saginaw, Mich., 1976-78; minister First Bapt. Ch. Tawas City, Mich., 1978—; pres. Saginaw Ministers Assn., 1978. Author: Holy Boldness, 1979, Assertiveness and the Christian, 1983, The Divorced Christian, 1984; Freedom from Bad Habits, 1985. Profl.

advisor Parents Without Partners, Tawas City, 1983—. Mem. Pastor/Church Relations Com. Mich. Ministers Council, 1984—, Assn. for Couples for Marriage Enrichment. Home: PO Box 457 405 Second St Tawas City MI 48763 Office: First Bapt Ch 401 Second St Tawas City MI 48763

CERVENY, FRANK STANLEY, bishop, Episcopal Ch.; b. Springfield, Mass., June 4, 1933; s. Frank Charles and Julia Victoria (Kulig) C.; B.A., Trinity Coll., Hartford, Conn., 1955, D.D. (hon.), 1977; M.Div., Gen. Theol. Sem., N.Y.C., 1958, D.D. (hon.), 1975; D.D. (hon.), U. of South, 1975; m. Emmy Thomas Pettway, Nov. 1, 1961; children—Frank Stanley, Emmy Thomas Pettway, William DeMoville Pettway. Ordained priest, 1958, bishop, 1974; asst. rector Ch. of Resurrection, Miami, Fla., 1958-60; asso., dir. Christian edn. Trinity Ch., N.Y.C., 1960-63; rector St. Lukes Ch., Jackson, Tenn., 1963-68, St. Johns Ch., Knoxville, Tenn., 1969-72; dean St. John's Cathedral, Jacksonville, Fla., 1972-74; bishop Diocese of Fla., Jacksonville, 1975—. Chmn. evangelism House of Bishops, Nat. Ch.; Episc. adviser Center for Christian Spirituality; nat. bd. mem., adviser Brotherhood of St. Andrew; trustee U. of South, Gen. Theol. Sem. Mem. Jacksonville Mayor's Com. on Human Relations, 1975-76; mem. Jacksonville Bicentennial Commn., 1975-76; bd. dirs. Urban Crisis Com., Christian Social Relations, Heart Fund, Mental Health Assn., YMCA, Cerebral Palsy, Jacksonville Area Council on Alcoholism, Jacksonville and Knoxville travelers aid socs., Community Planning Council Jacksonville. Home: 4949 Vandiveer Rd Jacksonville FL 32210 Office: 325 Market St Jacksonville FL 32202

CEVETELLO, JOSEPH F. X., priest, Roman Cath. Ch.; b. Jersey City, Oct. 21, 1919; s. John and Lucy (Bonifer) C.; A.B., Seton Hall U., 1943. Ordained priest, 1947; asso. pastor and pastor chs., N.J., 1947-72; instr. scripture and theology Seton Hall U., Newark, 1952-63; chaplain, instr. scripture theology Villa Walsh Coll., Morristown, N.J., 1964-68; instr. scripture and pastoral theology Consolata Theol. Coll., Somerset, N.J., 1969-74; pastor Our Lady Mt. Virgin Parish, Garfield-Lodi, N.J., 1972—. Nat. chaplain Cath. War Vets. Am. Aux., 1975—; chaplain N.J. Cath. War Vets., 1970—, N.J. Cath. War Vets. Aux., 1971—. Chmn. Garfield (N.J.) Bicentennial Com., 1975. Mem. Cath. Theol. Assn. Am., Mariological Soc. Am., Canon Law Soc. Am., Cath. Bibl. Assn. Am., Internat. Narcotics Enforcement Officers Assn. Author: From Peasant to Pope, 1953; Getting to Know the Bible, 1957; contbg. author, editor: All Things to All Men, 1965-67; contbr. articles to religious jours. Home and Office: 188 MacArthur Ave Garfield NJ 07026

CHABLE, EDWARD ROBERT, minister, senior pastor emeritus, United Church of Christ; b. Cleve., June 7, 1920; s. Eugene Ray and Marion Margaret (Skym) Chable Hohman; m. Marion Hayes Boynton, Oct. 26, 1946. B.B.A., Cleve. State U., 1944; M.Div., Colgate-Rochester Div. Sch., 1946; M.A., U. Rochester, 1948; Ph.D., Columbia U., 1955; D.D. (hon.), Piedmont Coll., 1975. Ordained to ministry Am. Bapt. Ch., 1946. Student assoc. Brighton Presbyn. Ch., Rochester, N.Y., 1944-45; minister First Bapt. Ch., Palmyra, N.Y., 1945-51; interim minister Wyckoff Reformed Ch., N.J., 1951-53; assoc. pastor Park Ave. Meth. Ch., N.Y.C., 1953-54; founding minister, sr. pastor emeritus Venice United Ch. Christ, Fla., 1962—; dir. student personnel Hillsdale Coll., Mich., 1954-57, assoc. prof. history, 1954-57; dean student personnel, acting registrar, prof. philosophy and religion Rio Grande Coll., Ohio, 1957-59; past pres. United Chs. Palmyra-Macedon Area N.Y., Palmyra Clergymen's Council. Incorporator, mem. exec. founding com. New Coll., Inc., Sarasota, Fla.; trustee, 1968-74; past lectr. SBA; mem. sponsoring com. Manatee Jr. Coll., Venice. Vice pres., bus. rep. Venice-Nokomis Bank, Fla., 1959-63, cons., 1963-66. Contbr. articles, poems to Masonic publs. Past pres. bd. dirs. Palmyra Community Ctr.; v.p. Palmyra Betterment (Civic) Club; past mem. bd. dirs. Wayne County Tb and Pub. Health Assn.; bd. dirs. Sarasota County Community Health and Welfare Council, 1968-70, 1st v.p., 1969-70; pres. bd. dirs. Manatee-Sarasota Guidance Ctr., 1961-62; bd. dirs. South Sarasota County Retarded Children's Assn., 1961-63, South Sarasota County Meml. Hosp. Assn., Venice-Nokomis Art Assn., 1961-62, life mem. Venice Art League; past dir. Venice Council Navy League U.S.; bd. dirs. Venice Little Theatre, Venice Area Vol. Talent Pool; bd. govs. NCCJ, Sarasota-Manatee chpt., 1965-70. Named Col. Confederate Air Corps. Ala., Col. Gov. Ky. staff; many other honors. Mem. Soc. Bibl. Lit. Am. Council Learned Socs., Fla. Conf. United Ch. Christ (dir. 1971-72), Council on Epilepsy, Sarasota Mental Health Assn., Delta Sigma Phi (Delta Omega chpt. Alumni Disting. Achievement award 1972). Republican. Clubs: Chalet (Lake Lure, N.C.); Venice Yacht (Fla.). Lodge: Mason (33 deg.). Home: 104 Alba St W Venice FL 33595

CHABOT, GILBERT, priest, Roman Catholic Church. B. Montreal, Que., Can., June 8, 1930; s. J. Norbert and Marie-Rosalie (Thibodeau) C.; B.A., Montreal U., 1962. B.Th., 1966. Ordained priest, 1966. Curate, St. Georges Parish, Montreal, 1966-70, St. Bonaventure Parish, Montreal, 1970-81; nat. dir. Eucharistic Movement of Can., Montreal, 1980—. Office: Mouvement Eucharistique du Canada 2335 rue Sherbrooke ouest Montreal PQ H3H 1G6 Canada

CHACKO, PHILIP CHACKUPURACKAL, minister, Christian Church (Disciples of Christ); b. Piraventhoor, India, Apr. 27, 1944; came to U.S., 1970; s. Chackupurackal Varghese Philip and Aleyamma (Mathai) P.; m. Elizabeth Malayil, Mar. 20, 1969; children: Vincent, Stephen, Sarah Beth. Grad. theology So. Asia Bible Coll., Bangalore, India, 1970; B.A., Oral Roberts U., 1972; M.Div., Tex. Christian U., 1975, Dr. Ministries, 1976. Ordained to ministry Christian Ch. (Disciples of Christ), 1976. Student pastor Assemblies of God, Bangalore, 1967-70; youth minister United Meth. Ch., Fort Worth/Gainsville, 1973-75; student minister Christian Ch. (Disciples of Christ), Grapeland and Crockett, Tex., 1975-76; minister First Christian Ch., Crockett, 1976-80; sr. minister Hillside-Meml. Christian Ch., Fort Worth, 1980—; pres. India Theol. Student Assn., Bangalore, 1968-69, Houston County Ministerial Assn., Crockett, 1977-80; bd. dirs. Women's Aglow Fellowship, Fort Worth. Author project: Evangelism Calling, 1976; author devotional programs: Love on the Cross, 1977, Meditations for Thanksgiving, 1978. Bd. dirs. Community Concert Assn., Crockett, 1978-80; adv. bd. dirs. Mental Health and Mental Retardation, Crockett, 1978-80; founder Youth Encounter and Solutions, Crockett, 1978-80. Recipient Book award Brite Divinity Sch., 1973, Henson scholar, 1974; named Man of Yr. Crockett C. of C., 1980. Mem. Internat. Soc. Theta Phi, Disciple Minister's Fellowship (treas. 1982), Southwest Ministerial Assn., Nat. Evangelism Assn. (nat. recognition for ch. growth 1979, 81, 83; internat. recognition 1980, 82, 84). Lodge: Lions (program chmn.). Home: 236 Hallmark Dr W Fort Worth TX 76134 Office: Hillside-Meml Christian Ch 6410 S Freeway Fort Worth TX 76134

CHADDICK, LIONEL GERALD, minister, So. Baptist Conv.; b. Beaumont, Tex., Nov. 1, 1929; s. Richard Kelley and Jimmie Dell (Summeral) C.; B.A., La. Coll., Pineville, 1951; B.D., M.Div., Southwestern Bapt. Theol. Sem., Ft. Worth, 1956; postgrad. Golden Gate Sem.; m. Anna Laura Seymour, May 30, 1952; children—Gerald Wayne, Deborah Kay, Bryan Keith. Ordained to ministry, 1950; pastor chs. in La., Tex., Calif., 1950-71; dir. Child Care and Family Services, Pico Rivera, Calif., 1971-72; dir. home missionary family services Los Angeles area, Pico Rivera, 1972—. Pres. child care bd. So. Bapt. Gen. Conv. Calif., 1970-71; assoc. dir. Christian Social Ministries, Calif. So. Bapt. Conv., 1972; bd. dirs. So. Calif. Voluntary Agys. Active in Disaster, 1980. Mem. Nat. Assn. Social Workers, So. Bapt. Social Services Assn. Home: 7337 Finevale Dr Downey CA 90240 Office: 9617 Lakewood Blvd Downey CA 90240

CHALMERS, DOUGLAS, lay church worker, United Ch. of Christ; b. Manchester, N.H., Feb. 13, 1913; s. Thomas and Maude V. (Smith) C.; student Rollins Coll., Fla., 1931-32; B.S., Mass. Inst. Tech., 1936; postgrad. U. Denver, U. Colo., 1945-49; m. Betty Beetley, Feb. 11, 1939; 1 dau., Martha Jo Breunig. Mem., chmn., moderator local chs., deacon, trustee Hyde Park Congl. Ch., Los Angeles and Corona del Mar United Ch. of Christ, Newport Beach, Calif., 1951—; pres. Ch. Mens Fellowship, So. Calif. and S.W. Conf., United Ch. of Christ, 1963-65, gen. chmn. Black Coll. Fund, 1973-74; mem. exec. com. United Ch. Men, Los Angeles Council Chs., 1964; moderator So. Calif. Conf., 1966-67; vice chmn. Nat. Council for Lay Life and Work, 1965-71; mem. Nat. Budget Com., 1967-71, Nat. Task Force on World Hunger, 1974; mem. strategy and structures com. United Ministries for Higher Edn., 1969-71; chmn. com. for econ. justice for agrl. com. Calif. Council Chs., 1966-71; 1st lay pres. So. Calif. Council Chs.; vice chmn. Calif. Ch. Council, 1968-69; del. Nat. Council Chs. St. Louis Conf. on Internat. Relations, 1968, Detroit Conf. on Ch. and Soc., 1969; adminstrv. organizer First Calif. World Hunger Conf., 1969; treas., financial sec. So. Calif. Council Chs., 1969-71; So. Calif. Council radio commentator KABC, 1968-69. Chief chemist, asst. research dir. Gates Rubber Co., Denver, 1939-50; founder, pres., gen. mgr. Golden State Rubber & Latex Corp., Gardena, Calif., 1950—. Recipient Lay Service award So. Calif. Council Chs., 1973; Outstanding Community Leadership award Religious Heritage Am., 1978. Fellow Am. Inst. Chemists; mem. ASTM, Acad. Polit. Sci., Los Angeles Rubber Group, U.S. Power Squadron. Contbr. articles to profl. jours. Home: 3411 Finley Ave Newport Beach CA 92660

CHALMERS, ROBERT LAWTON, minister, Presbyn. Ch. U.S.A.; b. Madison, Minn., Apr. 28, 1916; s. George Hugh and Florence (Westby) C.; B.A., Augsburg Coll., 1939; B.D., M.Div., U. Dubuque, 1950; m. Shirley Mae Pladsen, Mar. 31, 1940; children—Philip, George, Mary Ann. Ordained to ministry, 1950; minister Claremont (Minn.) Presbyn. Ch., 1950-56, Kasson, Minn., 1950-56, Shenandoah, Iowa, 1957-59, St. James, Minn., 1959-61, John Knox larger parish, Redwood County, Minn., 1961-66; field rep. Ch. World Service, Nat. Council Chs., 1966-68; minister Presbyn. Ch., Shakopee, Minn., 1968-74; chaplain, minister Minn. Masonic Home, Mpls., 1975—. Stated clk., Mpls. Presbytery, 1968-74; mem. Presbyn. Nat. Rural Fellowship; leader Ecumenical Council, Shakopee, 1969-74. Fund chmn. ARC, 1954-55. Asst. editor Scottish Rite Monthly Sun. Home and Office: 11400 Normandale Blvd Minneapolis MN 55437

CHAMBERLAIN, DAVID MORROW, priest, Episcopal Church; b. Chattanooga, Oct. 10, 1946; s. Augustus Wright and Myrle Delano (Hancock) C.; m. Patricia Ann Magill, Jan. 8, 1972; children: Michael, Carolyn. B.A., U. Chattanooga, 1968; M.Div., Va. Theol. Sem., 1971. Ordained to ministry, 1972. Asst. rector Calvary Episc. Ch., Memphis, 1972-73; asst. to rector St. Andrews Episc. Ch., Arlington, Va., 1973-76; rector St. John's Episc. Ch., Arlington, 1976-80; dean Region III, Episc. Diocese of Va., 1978-80; canon educator, sr. canon Cathedral of St. Philip, Atlanta, 1980—; field edn. supr. Va. Theol. Sem., Alexandria, 1973-80; exec. com. Region III, Diocese of Va., 1978-80, com. of ann. council, Diocese of Atlanta, 1980—, com. overseeing bishop election, 1983. Film critic in The Tennessee Churchman, 1972-73. Served to 1st lt., U.S. Army, 1968-73. Lodge: Kiwanis. Home: 2952 Vinings Forest Way Atlanta GA 30339 Office: Episcopal Cathedral of Saint Philip 2744 Peachtree Rd NW Atlanta GA 30363

CHAMBERS, BILLY JOE, minister, Southern Baptist Convention; b. Ft. Worth, Dec. 13, 1932; s. Joseph Yancy and Bertha Clara (McMillen) C.; m. Ima Louise Tyson, Aug. 22, 1954; children: Joseph Thurman, Marc William, Carol Lynn. B.A., Baylor U., 1955; postgrad. Golden Gate Sem., 1955-58; B.D., Southwestern Bapt. Sem., 1960. Ordained to ministry So. Bapt. Conv., 1956. Missionary, Sunday sch. dir. Bapt. Conv. Mich., Detroit, 1973-77; pastor Eastgate Bapt. Ch., Burton, Mich., 1977-81; ch. services dir. Minn.-Wis. So. Bapt. Conv., Rochester, Minn., 1981-84; pastor First Bapt. Ch., Ranger, Tex., 1984—; trustee Golden Gate Bapt. Sem., 1970-73, Midwestern Bapt. Sem., 1977-81. Contbr. articles to profl. jours. Address: 907 Cherry St Ranger TX 76470

CHAMBERS, WILL EARL, minister, Christian Methodist Episcopal Church; educator; b. South Fulton, Tenn., Nov. 23, 1938; s. Hall and Sallie Louise (Hunter) C.; m. Judith Tilghman, Dec. 26, 1964; 1 dau., Carissa Jean. B.A., Paine Coll., 1961; B.D., Phillips Sch. Theology, 1965; M.S.T., Boston U., 1971. Ordained to ministry, 1966. Assoc. editor bd. edn. Christian Meth. Episc. Ch., Memphis, 1965-67; pastor, St. John Christian Meth. Episcopal Ch., Washington, 1967-68, Parkwood Christian Meth. Episcopal Ch., Charlotte, N.C., 1968-70; instr. Miles Coll., Birmingham, Ala., 1971-72; asst. prof. religion and philosophy Livingstone Coll., Salisbury, N.C., 1972—. Artist, logo, Centennial Marker, 1970 (citation 1974); author booklets: Primer for Youth Leaders, 1979, CME Membership, 1971, 72; author articles. Bd. dirs. Dial Help, Salisbury, 1980-84. Mem. AAUP, United Ministerial Alliance, N.C. Religious Studies Assn., N.C. Philos. Soc., Caroline Conf. Bd. Christian Edn. (citation 1982). Democrat. Home: 124 Lloyd St Salisbury NC 28144

CHAMPION, MARY EMMA, lay worker, Southern Baptist Convention, educator; b. Bayou, Ky., Nov. 11, 1923; d. Quincey Allard and Laura Lottie (Sharp) Thompson; m. Jesse Otis Champion, May 2, 1942; children: Donna Kaye, Patricia Gayle. B.S., Ind. State U.-Evansville, 1971; M.S., U. Evansville, 1975. Dept. dir. Tng. Union of Grace Bapt. Ch., Evansville, 1954-64, chmn. com. on coms., 1969-82, asst. ch. clk., 1979-84, tchr. adult Bible class Sunday Sch., 1948—; trustee Sunday Sch. bd. Southern Baptist Convention, Nashville, 1975-83. Tchr. South Gibson Sch. Corp., Ft. Branch, Ind., 1971—. Vol. worker Laubach Literacy Internat. Author poetry (1st and 3rd place prizes, 2d place hon. mention award), short story (3rd prize non-fiction). Democrat. Home: 724 Cardinal Dr Evansville IN 47711

CHAN, DAVID TAK-YAN, minister, Presbyterian Church in Canada; b. Hong Kong, June 15, 1925; s. Kwan Cheung and Chiu Ying (Yau) C.; came to Can., 1964, naturalized, 1969; m. Roseanna Woon-Tsang Yuen, Apr. 2, 1963; children: Eugene, Victoria, John. B.D., Chgo. Luth. Sem., 1955, S.T.M., 1956; Ph.D., U. Edinburgh, 1959. Ordained to ministry Presbyn. Ch. in Can., 1965; prin. Tsung Tsin Coll., 1960-64; lectr. theology Chung Chi Coll., 1961-62, bd. govs., 1961-63; external examiner for post-secondary colls. in Hong Kong, 1962; mem. exec. com. Hong Kong Christian Council, 1961-63, Chinese Christian Lit. Soc., 1961-63; minister Presbyn. Ch. in Can., Windsor, Ont., 1964—; chaplain, Royal Canadian Legion, 1967-71; chmn. bd. dirs. Tsung Tsin Ch., Hong Kong, 1960-64; chmn. Conf. for All Chinese Presbyn. Chs. in Can., Toronto, 1969. Chmn. bd. dirs. Chinese Hosp. in Victoria, B.C., 1965-66; commr. for taking affidavits in Ont., 1981-84; patron Chinese-Can. Intercultural Assn., 1984—. Home: 1827 Pelletier St Windsor ON N9B 1S7 Canada

CHANCE, JAMES BRADLEY, religion educator, Southern Baptist Convention; b. Topeka, May 17, 1954; s. James Melvin and Myrtle Annette (Huke) C.; m. Mary Venters Jenkins, Aug. 16, 1975; 1 child, Marianne. B.A., U. N.C., 1975; M.Div., Southeastern Sem., 1978; Ph.D., Duke U., 1984. Ordained to ministry Baptist Ch., 1977. Minister youth, edn., Woodland Baptist Ch., Wake Forest, N.C., 1977-78; vis. instr.

N.T., Southeastern Sem., 1978-82; interim pastor Second Bapt. Ch., Henderson, N.C., 1981-82, First Bapt. Ch., Lexington, Mo., 1984-85; asst. prof. religion William Jewell Coll., Liberty, Mo., 1982—. Contbr. book reviews to Faith and Mission, Perspectives. Mem. Assn. Bapt. Profs. Religion, Soc. Bibl. Lit. Democrat. Office: William Jewell Coll Liberty MO 64068

CHANDLER, CHARLES HOWARD, minister, Southern Baptist Convention. B. Cedartown, Ga., July 26, 1935; s. Gordon Russell and Kathleen Maude (Green) C.; m. Betty Lou Horton, Mar. 22, 1957; children; Charles Howard, Sheri Lynn, Clayton Anthony, Cynthia Dawn. A.B., Samford U., 1957; M.Div., So. Bapt. Theol. Sem., 1961, M.R.E., 1964, D.Min., 1974. Ordained, 1957. Pastor Fellowship Bapt. Ch., Harrodsburg, Ky., 1960-62; assoc. pastor Deer Park Bapt. Ch., Louisville, 1962-65; pastor Bapt. Tabernacle Ch., Paducah, Ky., 1965-71, 1st Bapt. Ch., Metropolis, Ill., 1971-76, Pennsylvania Ave. Bapt. Ch., Urbana, Ill., 1976—; bd. dirs. Bapt. Bd. Child Care, Ky., 1968-71; pres. Ill. Bapt. State Assn., 1984—, bd. dirs., 1973-78, 79-82, chmn. spl. ministries com., 1976-78, mem. exec. stewardship adv. council, 1973—, host pastor, speaker convs., retreats, confs.; condr. revivals, numerous states; pres. Paducah Area Ministerial Assn., 1967, Massac County Ministerial Alliance, Metropolis, 1975-76, Champaign-Urbana Ministerial Assn., 1981-83; participant devotional Sta. WCIA-TV, Champaign; mem. com. on coms., So. Bapt. Conv., 1981; field supr. D.Min. program, So. Bapt. Theol. Sem., Louisville, 1975—, tchr. Ctr. of Boyce Bible Sch., Springfield, Ill., 1979—. Author: The Deacon Family Ministry Plan Really Works, 1982; contbr. chpt. to book, articles to denominational publs. Bd. dirs. Devel. Services Ctr., Champaign, 1982—, C. of C., Metropolia, 1975-76; chmn. Metropolis Little League Football Program, 1972-75; mem. Mayor's Adv. Com. for City Improvement through HUD, Metropolis, 1975-76. Recipient Duke of Paducah award, 1967; Superman of Metropolis award, 1972; Ky. Col. award, 1976. Mem. So. Bapt. Theol. Sem. Alumni Assn. (pres. Ill. chpt. 1980-81). Lodge: Rotary. Home: 507 Park Ln Champaign IL 61820 Office: Pennsylvania Ave Bapt Ch 600 E Pennsylvania Ave Urbana IL 61801

CHANDLER, DANIEL DAVID, minister, Ch. of God in Christ; b. Bells, Tenn., Oct. 9, 1927; s. John Reubin and Eliza Ellen (Cobb) C.; student Ware Bible Sch., 1958-60, Moody Bible Inst., 1972-74; B.Th., Universal Bible Inst., Birmingham, Ala.; m. Hazel Ernestine McKinney, Mar. 9, 1948; children—Daniel David, Ann (Mrs. Charles Barrett), Carolyn, Sylvia, Ellen, Jonathan. Ordained minister, 1955; pastor, 1955-60; pastor, founder New Prospect Ch. of God in Christ, Memphis, 1965—; dist. supt. Sunday sch., Memphis, 1960-68; mem. Tenn. Sunday sch. staff Tenn. 1st Jurisdiction, 1970—, chmn. state conv., 1973-74; 2d v.p. Dickerson Bros. Christian Alliance of Am., 1974—. Recipient Man of Year award Religious Workers Guild, 1972. Home: 532 George St Memphis TN 38109 Office: 2524 Carne S Ave Memphis TN 38114

CHANDLER, DAVID THOMAS, minister, Christian Ch.; b. Lexington, Ky., July 29, 1924; s. Houston and Nellie Belle (Wright) C.; B.R.E., Dallas Christian Coll., 1957; postgrad. Phillips U., 1958-59; m. Betty Lee Kimble, June 12, 1946; children—Ruth Marie, Sharon Lee, Dorothy Sue. Ordained to ministry, 1949; pastor various chs. Ill., Tex., Okla., Oreg., Idaho, Ky., Wash., 1949-74, Hartford (Ky.) Christian Ch., 1974—. Prof. N.T., Dallas Christian Coll., 1955-58, Coll. Scriptures, Louisville, 1965-66; dir. pub. relations Midwest Christian Coll., Oklahoma City, 1958-59; pres. Boise (Ida.) Bible Coll., 1971-72; police chaplain Tacoma (Wash.) Police Dept. 1974. Pres. PTA, Newberg, Oreg., 1964; chmn. Beautification project, Klamath Falls, Oreg., 1969; ARC chmn. fund dr., Sallisaw, Okla., 1961, Hartford, Ky., 1976; vice chmn. RSVP of Ohio County, Hartford, Ky., 1975-76. Recipient Kiwanian of the Year award, Kiwanis Club Klamath Falls, 1970. Mem. Ohio County Ministerial Assn. (chmn. 1975-76). Address: PO Box 122 Hartford KY 42347

CHANDLER, JOHN RICHARD, minister, Lutheran Church in America. B. Boulder, Colo., July 28, 1933; s. John Theodore and Thelma M. (Young) C.; m. Dana Sue O'Dell-Daniell, March 14, 1955; children: Timothy John, Mary Sue. Ph.B. U. Colo., Boulder, 1958; M.Div., Central Luth. Theol. Sem., Fremont, 1962. Ordained to ministry Lutheran Church in America, 1962. Asst. pastor St. Pauls Luth. Ch., Albuquerque, 1962-63; mission developer Atonement Luth. Ch., Oklahoma City, 1964-67; pastor St. John's Luth. Ch., Westboro, Mo., 1967-77; assoc. pastor Trinity Luth. Ch., Boulder, 1977-78; pastor Olsburg-Walsburg Parish, Leonardville Kans., 1978-83, St. Paul's Luth. Ch., Darrouzett, Tex., 1983—; chaplain Randolph VFW, Kans., 1980-83, Am. Legion, Darrouzett, 1983—; workshop leader Luth. Youth Encounter, 1978-80; letrs. in field. Author: (booklet) I'm Still a Lutheran, 1981. Contbr. articles to mags. Inst. rep., asst. scoutmaster Last Frontier and Pony Express councils Boy Scouts Am., 1965-75; leader 4-H Club, Westboro, 1967-72; precinct chmn. Republican Party, Atchison County, Mo. 1972-76; mem. Lipscomb County Child Welfare Bd., 1983—. Home: PO Box 327 Darrouzett TX 79024 Office: St Paul Lutheran Church Darrouzett TX 79024

CHANEY, EDGAR LEE, JR., minister, So. Baptist Conv.; b. Muskogee, Okla., June 1, 1937; s. Edgar Lee and Dora Steele (Colbert) C.; B.A., Okla. Bapt. U., Shawnee, 1960; M.Div., Southwestern Bapt. Theol. Sem., Ft. Worth, 1964; m. Vivian Imadell Burks, Sept. 26, 1964; children—Julie, Janet, Joanna, Jamie. Dir. Bapt. Student Union, Eastern Okla. State Coll., Wilburton, 1958; evangelist, 1958-64; ordained to ministry, 1957; pastor chs. in Tex. and Okla., 1965-71; pastor First Bapt. Ch., Marietta, Okla., 1971-72; minister evangelism Putnam City Bapt. Ch., Oklahoma City, 1972-77, 1st Bapt. Ch., Muskogee, Okla., 1977—. Bd. dirs. Bapt. Gen. Conv. Okla., 1971-75; mem. evangelism com. Capital Bapt. Assn., 1974-76. Office: 111 S 7th St Muskogee OK 74401

CHANEY, JERRY EUGENE, minister, Independent Baptist Chs.; b. Chillicothe, Ohio, May 20, 1943; s. Clark and Ardith (King) C.; m. Loretta Sue Burns, Sept. 11, 1964; children: James, Todd. B.A., Heritage Bapt. U., 1983, M.A., 1985, postgrad., 1983—, D.D. (hon.), 1983. Ordained to ministry Baptist Ch., 1978. Pastor Ch. Christ Christian Union, Ohio, Mich., N.Y., W.Va., 1964-74; founder, pastor Open Door Bapt. Ch., Marietta, Ohio, 1977—; founder, adminstr. Open Door Bapt. Christian Acad., Marietta, 1980—; founder, dean Marietta-Parkersburg Br. Heritage Bapt. U., Marietta, 1984—; founder, pres. Jerry Chaney Ministries Assn., Marietta, 1984—; owner ch. bookstore Browse and Buy Bookstore, Marietta; mgr. Open Door Bapt. Printshop, Marietta; bd. dirs. Heritage Bapt. U., North Jackson, Ohio, Mt. Salem Revival Grounds, Salem, W.Va.; Rudy Pennington Evangelistic Assn., Lima, Ohio; mem. Sword Evangelism Council, Tenn. Author of numerous booklets. Recipient Plaque Heritage Bapt. U. 1984, Cert. Mt. Salem Revival Ground 1982, Cert. Bapt. Evangelistic Missionary Assn. 1983. Home: 103 Gates Ave Marietta OH 45750 Office: Open Door Bapt Ch 301 Franklin St Marietta OH 45750

CHANG, KEITH SUNG, lay church worker, Seventh-day Adventist; printing plate maker. B. Nammyon, Jungson, Korea, June 20, 1929; came to U.S., 1974, naturalized, 1979; s. Cnul Ee and Joon Hee (Kim) C.; married, Mar. 22, 1959; children: Kent Jin Hoon, James Jin Woong. Minister, Sam Yook Coll., Seoul, Korea, 1959; B.A. in English, 1974; postgrad. U. Alta., Edmonton, 1983—. Bible tchr. Seventh-day Adventist Acad., Seoul, 1958-60; Bible worker Seventh-day Adventist Ch., Hwachun, Korea, 1960-63, Alta. Conf., Edmonton, 1977-80; translator Sam Yook Children's Rehab. Ctr., Seoul, 1963-70; elder Seventh-day Adventist Ch., Lacombe, Alta., 1983—. Fourcolor stripper and plate maker, Parkland Color Press, College Height, Alta., 1981—. Served as sgt. Korean Army, 1955-58. Home: Box 527 College Heights AB T0C 0Z0 Canada Office: Parkland Color Press Box 490 College Heights AB T0C 0Z0 Canada

CHAO, CALVIN, minister; b. China, Mar. 15, 1906; s. Chao Kun-Yuen and Lee-Sze C.; ed. Hangchow Coll.; m. Faith Chang, Apr. 20, 1934; children—Calvin, Sophie, Andrew, John, Jean, Joyce, James, Ruth. Ordained to ministry, 1949; evangelist, China, 1935-37, U.S., 1956-59; head extension dept. Hunan (China) Bible Inst., 1939-40; pastor ch., Yunnan, China, 1940-42, Kweiyang, China, 1941-44; prin. Southwestern Bible Inst., Yunnan, 1940-41; supt. Chinese Native Evangelistic Crusade, China, 1943-46; gen. sec. All China Christian Univ. Students Assn., 1945-51; supt. spiritual activities Singapore Inter-ch. Union, 1951-56; acting pres. Singapore Bible Coll., 1952-56; gen. sec. Youth Gospel Center, Manila, 1952-56; regional sec. for Orient, Internat. Fellowship Evang. Students, 1947-50; mem. exec. com. World Evang. Fellowship, 1953-56; exec. dir. Chinese for Christ, Inc., Los Angeles, 1959—. Contbr. articles to religious jours.; columnist Chinese newspapers. Address: 922 N Edgemont St Los Angeles CA 90029

CHAPMAN, IRVIN CLARKE, lay church worker, Christian Churches; b. Fullerton, Calif., Feb. 14, 1911; s. Charles Clarke and Clara Jassamine (Irvin) C.; A.B., Chapman Coll., 1933; m. Zelda McNamee, June 21, 1936 (div.); children: Cherie Chapman Hull, Claire Chapman Nichols; m. Edythe Boland, Feb. 14, 1976. Chmn. bd. First Christian Ch., Fullerton, 1940-42, 52-54; mem. nat. bd. YMCA, 1960—, mem. exec. com., 1967-77; chmn. bd. Christian Chs. So. Calif. and So. Nev., 1964; bd. dirs. Unified Promotion, Inc.; mem. governing bd. Nat. Council Chs., 1969-75; chmn. internat. div. YMCAs of U.S., 1971-77; mem. exec. com. World Alliance YMCAs, 1973-85. Sec., gen. mgr. Placentia Orchard Co., 1934—. Mem. Orange County Fair Bd., 1949-77; mem. City Council, Fullerton, 1946-50, 52-54, mayor, 1948-50; sec. bd. trustees Chapman Coll., 1942—; trustee Hoag Meml.-Presbyn. Hosp., Newport Beach, Calif., 1947-54; mem. Calif. Juvenile Justice and Delinquency Commn., 1984—. Mem. Calif. Farm Bur. Editor: History of California-Nevada-Hawaii Dist. of Kiwanis, 1917-74; History of Valencia Orange - for 1930 History of Orange County, 1973. Home: 2782 Bayshore Dr Newport Beach CA 92663 Office: 2962 Airway Ave Costa Mesa CA 92626

CHAPMAN, MICHAEL RAY, minister, Church of God; b. Laurens, S.C., Aug. 22, 1951; s. Ray Calhoun and Sara (Davis) C.; m. Trudy Elaine Leverette, Dec. 19, 1970. B.A. summa cum laude, Lee Coll., 1973; Th.M., Luther Rice Sem., 1977; postgrad. Faith Evang. Luth. Sem. Ordained to ministry Ch. of God, 1968. Asst. pastor ch., Cleveland, Tenn., 1972-73; pastor chs., Fremont, Calif., 1973-74, Chattanooga, 1976—; state youth and Christian edn. dir. Chs. of God in Hawaii, 1974-76; mem. pres.'s council West Coast Bible Coll., Fresno, Calif., 1974-76; mem. clergy bd. Moccasin Bend Mental Health Inst., 1980—; mem. Ch. of God State Edn. Bd. for Tenn., 1982-84, Ch. of God Evangelism Bd. for Tenn., 1984—. Mem. exec. bd. dirs. Chattanooga Teen Challenge, 1978-82; advisor Women's Aglow Fellowship of Chattanooga, 1980—. Mem. Chattanooga Ministerial Assn., United Assn. Christian Counselors. Recipient Bibl.-Hist. award Lee Coll., 1973; Youth World Evangelism award Ch. of God Dept. Christian Edn., 1975, 76; named Outstanding Young Man Am., 1975; contbr. articles to religious jours. Home: 6708 Larkwood Ln Chattanooga TN 37421 Office: 7120 Lee Hwy Chattanooga TN 37421

CHAPMAN, PATRICIA ANN, religion educator, Christian and Missionary Alliance; b. Chgo., Jan. 17, 1932; d. Edgar Slayton Hussey and Verna (Spence) Hussey Baldwin; m. Earl Wilson Chapman, Dec. 11, 1954 (dec. 1960); children: Cynthia Ann, Katherine Jean. B.A., Biola U., 1954; M.A., Talbot Theol. Sem., 1977; postgrad. in edn. U. San Francisco, 1986—. Children's dir. Bethany Baptist Ch., Long Beach, Calif., 1973-76; children's dir. 1st Nazarene Ch., Long Beach, 1976-77, dir. Christian edn., 1977-78; prin. Crescent Avenue Christian Sch., Buena Park, Calif., 1979-81; prof. Christian edn. Simpson Coll., San Francisco, 1981—; Christian edn. cons. David C. Cook Pubs., Elgin, Ill., 1980, various chs. in San Francisco Bay Area, 1983; lectr. in field, 1974—; curriculum writer Success with Youth, Pioneer Girls, Nazarene Pub. House, Bapt. publ. Gospel Light, also others, 1970—. Editor jr. curriculum Gospel Light Pubs., 1978-79. Contbr. articles to religious jours. Mem. Nat. Assn. Profs. Christian Edn. (editor newsletter 1983—), Kappa Tau Epsilon. Republican. Home: 109 Serrano Dr San Francisco CA 94132 Office: Simpson Coll 801 Silver Ave San Francisco CA 94134

CHAPMAN, SARAH FRANCIS, religious organization executive, nurse, Southern Bapt. Convention; b. Clarksville, Tenn., Aug. 23, 1944; d. John Elmer and Bonnie Lee (Nelson) Francis; m. Morris Hines Chapman, Aug. 31, 1963; children: Christopher Morris, Stephanie Suzanne. Student Miss. Coll., 1962-63; A.A.S., McClennan Community Coll., 1973; Assoc. Nursing, 1973. Sec., treas. Conf. Ministers' Wives So. Bapt. Conv., 1973; dir. Women's Missionary Union, Albuquerque, 1974, Bapt. Young Women's Orgn., Albuquerque, 1975-78; charter mem., organizer Ministers' Wives Fellowship of N.Mex., Albuquerque, 1978; dir. Sunday Sch. First Bapt. Ch., Wichita Falls, Tex., 1979; trustee So. Bapt. Sunday Sch. Bd., Nashville, 1982—; mem. personnel com. Wichita-Archer-Clay Assn., Wichita Falls, 1983-84. Mem. Women's Forum, Wichita Falls, 1981—, Wichita Falls Hist. Soc., 1981.

CHAPPELL, BONNIE DELL, religious educator; b. Silverton, Tex., Feb. 1, 1927; d. Andrew Houston and Glen Josephine (Graham) C. A.A., Wayland Coll., 1946; B.S., Howard Payne Coll., 1948; M.R.E., Southwestern Bapt. Theol. Sem., 1950. Edn. sec. First Bapt. Ch., Brownfield, Tex., 1950-51, Greenville, Tex., 1951-54, Beech St. Bapt. Ch., Texarkana, Ark., 1954-55, First So. Bapt. Ch., Costa Mesa, Calif., 1955-60; assoc. chmn. tng. dept., field worker So. Bapt. Conv., Fresno, Calif., 1960-64; asst. to bus. mgr. Calif. Bapt. Coll., Riverside, Calif., 1964-70; instr. Golden Gate Bapt. Sem., Mill Valley, Calif., 1970—. Mem. So. Bapt. Religious Edn. Assn., Western Bapt. Religious Edn. Assn. Home: 203 Gill Hall Mill Valley CA 94941 Office: Golden Gate Bapt Sem Strawberry Point Mill Valley CA 94941

CHAPPELL, LARRY ALLEN, minister, Ind. and Fundamental Baptist Ch.; b. Cortez, Colo., Apr. 3, 1942; s. Paul Bryan and Edith Louise (Ince) C.; B.S., Maranatha Bapt. Bible Coll., 1973; Ph.D., Bapt. Christian U., 1976; m. Maxine Estelle Brennan, Sept. 8, 1961; children—Paul, Mark, Elisabeth, Stephen. Ordained to ministry, 1964; asst. pastor Calvary Bapt. Ch., San Francisco, 1964-65; pastor Calvary Bapt. Ch., Avenal, Calif., 1965-66, United Bapt. Ch., San Jose, Calif., 1966-75, Bethany Bapt., Whittier, Calif., 1975-77; missionary to Korea, 1977—; lectr. in field. Office: PO Box 85 Pomona CA 91769

CHAPPELL, PAUL GALE, minister, educator, Assemblies of God; b. Norfolk, Va., July 2, 1947; s. Carlton William and Anne Bell (Hollowell) C.; m. Marilyn Joyce Fisk, Sept. 10, 1971; 1 child, Bradley Paul. B.A. summa cum laude, Oral Roberts U., 1968; M.Div. with honors, Asbury Theol. Sem., 1971; Th.M., Princeton Theol. Sem., 1972; M.Phil., Drew U., 1979, Ph.D., 1982. Ordained to ministry, 1979. Assoc. pastor Capital Assemblies of God, Trenton, N.J., 1971-75; prof. theol. studies dept. theology Oral Roberts U., Tulsa, 1975-78, asst. to vice provost of theology,

1978-79, assoc. dean acad. affairs, prof. Am. ch. history Grad. Sch. Theology, 1979—. Author: Great Things He Hath Done, 1984. Contbr.: Religious Periodicals of the United States, Evang. Theol. Dictionary. Contbr. articles to profl. jours. Mem. Tulsa County Republican Party; reviewer NEH, 1981—. Named Outstanding Faculty of Yr., Oral Roberts U. Sch. Theology, 1984. Mem. Am. Acad. Religion, Soc. Am. Ch. History, Wesleyan Theol. Soc., Soc. Pentecostal Studies, Soc. Am. Historians, Alpha Kappa Delta, Soc. Theta Phi. Home: 7408 S Granite Tulsa OK 74136 Office: Sch Theology Oral Roberts Univ 7777 S Lewis St Tulsa OK 74171

CHAPPELL, ROY MACK, minister, Pentecostal Church of God of America, Inc.; b. Pollard, Ark., May 1, 1932; s. Frank and Velma (Garrett) C.; B.A., Pentecostal Bible Coll., 1973, D.D., 1976; m. Willie Mae Haggard, Nov. 6, 1954; children: Steven Roy, Janiece Marie. Ordained to ministry, 1956; pastor chs., Calif. and Mo., 1954-66; missions rep. western div. Pentecostal Ch. of God, 1963-66, missions exec., 1969-74, dist. supt., 1974-75, conf. speaker, 1954-76, conv. chmn., 1969-76, pres., gen. supt., 1974—; supr. office mgmt., 1974-76, seminar and workshop coordinator, 1969-76. Camp speaker, 1963-76. Mem. Joplin C. of C., Pentecostal Bible Coll. Alumni Assn. Contbr. monthly articles to Pentecostal Messenger mag. Home: 1313 W 17th St Joplin MO 64801 Office: PO Box 850 Joplin MO 64801

CHAPPELLE, RICHARD ALLEN, SR., Gen. sec. African Methodist Episcopal Church, St. Louis. Office: African Meth Episcopal Ch PO Box 183 Saint Louis MO 63166*

CHARLES, OTIS, bishop, Episcopal Ch.; b. Norristown, Pa., Apr. 24, 1926; s. Jacob Otis and Elizabeth (Abraham) C.; B.A., Trinity Coll., 1948; S.T.B., Gen. Theol. Sem., 1959, D.D., 1983. m. Elvira Latta, May 26, 1951; children—Christopher, Nicholas, Emilie, Timothy, Elvira. Ordained priest, Episcopal Ch., 1951; curate St. John's Ch., Elizabeth, N.J., 1951-53; priest-in-charge St. Andrews Ch., Beacon, N.Y., 1953-59; rector St. John's Ch., Washington, Conn., 1959-68; asso. dir. Montford House Ecumenical Center, Litchfield, Conn., 1968-69; exec. sec. Asso. Parishes, Inc., Mt. St. Alban, Washington, 1968-71; consecrated bishop, 1971; bishop of Utah, Salt Lake City, 1971—; dean Episcopal Div. Sch., Cambridge, Mass., 1985—; mem. Standing Liturgical Commn. Episcopal Ch.; bishop-in-charge Navajo Episcopal Council. Trustee Rowland Hall-St. Mark's Sch., Salt Lake City, Episcopal Radio and TV Found.; pres. bd. trustees St. Mark's Hosp.; bd. dirs. Asso. Parishes; mem. Utah Health Systems Agy., 1981—, State Health Coordinating Council, 1981. Mem. Delta Psi, Alta Club, St. Anthony Club (N.Y.C.). Office: 231 E 1st S Salt Lake City Ut 84111

CHARLESWORTH, JAMES HAMILTON, educator, minister, United Methodist Church; b. St. Petersburg, Fla., May 30, 1940; s. Arthur Riggs and Martha Jean (Hamilton) C.; m. Jerrie Lynn Pittard, Apr. 10, 1965; children: Rachel Michelle, Eve Marie, James Hamilton. A.B., Ohio Wesleyan U., 1962; B.D., Duke Div. Sch., 1965; Ph.D., Duke U., 1967; E.T., Ecole Biblique de Jerusalem (Israel), 1969. Ordained to ministry, 1963. Fulbright fellow U. Edinburgh, Scotland, 1967-68; Thayer fellow in Am. Sch. Oriental Research, Jerusalem, 1968-69; prof. dept. religion Duke U., Durham, N.C., 1969-84; dir. Internat. Ctr. on Christian Origins, Duke U., 1975-82; George L. Collord prof. N.T. lang. and lit. Princeton Theol. Sem., 1984—. Editor/translator: The Odes of Solomon, 1973. Author: The Pseudepigrapha and Modern Research, 1976, 2d edit., 1981, The Pseudepigrapha and the New Testament, 1985. Editor, translator: The History of the Rechabites, 1982. Editor: The Old Testament Pseudepigrapha, 1983. Eleve Titulaire de l'Ecole Biblique avec la mention, Tres Honorable, Jerusalem, 1968; Am. Council Learned Socs. fellow, 1973-74; Alexander von Humboldt fellow, 1983-84. Mem. Soc. Bibl. Lit. (sec. Pseudepigrapha Group 1969—), Soc. N.T. Studies (editorial bd. 1979-83), Am. Acad. Religion, Found. Christian Origins (pres.), Bibl. Archaeology Soc. (editorial bd.). Democrat. Home: 60 Wittmer Ct Princeton NJ 08540 Office: Princeton Theol Sem CN 821 Princeton NJ 08542

CHARLOP, ZEVULUN, rabbi, seminary administrator, Jewish; b. N.Y.C., Dec. 14, 1929; s. Jechiel Michael and Ida (Schocher) C.; m. Judith Rosner, Dec. 27, 1954; children: Betty, Rochelle, Anna Riva, Shishana, Zev, Alexander Z., Fay Gila, Miriam. B.A., Yeshiva Coll., 1951; M.A., Columbia U., 1959; student The Rabbi Isaac Elchanan Theol. Sem.; postgrad. Columbia U. Ordained: Rabbi, 1954. Rabbi, Young Israel of Mosholu Pkwy., Bronx, 1954—; instr. Talmud Yeshiva U., 1967-71, lectr. Am. history, 1967; dir. Rabbi Isaac Elchanan Theol. Sem., 1971—. Editor: Chavrusa, 1967. Mem. exec. com. Bronx chpt. Am. Cancer Soc. Named Grand Chaplain Free deg.ons of Israel, 1956-58. Mem. Nat. Council Young Israel (pres. council rabbis 1968-71), Rabbinical Council Am. (co-chmn. coll. campus com. 1966-68). Home: 3037 Bainbridge Ave New York NY 10458 Office: Rabbi Isaac Elchanan Theol Sem 2540 Amsterdam Ave New York NY 10033

CHARLTON, JOHN F., III, minister, American Baptist Churches in the U.S.A.; b. Elgin, Ill., July 24, 1944; s. John F. and Ivagene E. (Householder) C.; children: Tamah Lynn, John F. IV, Candice Louise. Student U. Tenn.—Knoxville, Tenn., 1962-63; B.A., Judson Coll., 1963-66; M.Div., Eastern Bapt. Theol. Sem., 1970; D. Ministry, McCormick Theol. Sem., 1978; teaching cert. Central Mich. U., 1985. Ordained to ministry American Baptist Churches in the U.S.A., 1970. Youth dir. First Bapt Ch., Pedricktown, N.J., 1966-67; pastor First Bapt. Ch., Browns Mills, N.J., 1967-69; missionary Phila. Bapt. Assn., 1969-70; pastor First Bapt. Ch., Harbor Beach, Mich., 1970-73, First Bapt. Ch., Alma, Mich., 1973—; pres. Harbor Beach Ministerial Assn., 1971-73, Alma Minsterial Assn., 1975-81, Gratiot County Minsterial Assn., 1976-81. Chmn. Personal Growth and Devel. Adv. Com., 1980-83. Lodge: Rotary (chaplain 1970-73, 1973-76). Home: 507 Woodworth Ave Alma MI 48801 Office: First Bapt Ch 534 N State St Alma MI 48801

CHARNOV, BRUCE HIRSCHL, rabbi, Conservative Jewish Congregations; b. Grand Rapids, Mich., Nov. 16, 1946; s. Abraham and Winona (Fuller) C.; B.A., U. Mich., 1968; M.A., Jewish Theol. Sem. Am., 1971; Ph.D., U.S. Internat. U., 1975; m. Naomi Ostroff, Sept. 5, 1971; children—Miryam Esther. Rabbi, 1972. Tchr. Congregation Beth Israel, Ann Arbor, Mich., 1966-67, Cliffside Park, N.J., 1968-69, Congregation Temple Shalom, Greenwich, Conn., 1969-71, asst. prin., 1970-71; asst. prin. Hebrew High Sch. of the Five Towns, Lawrence, L.I., 1971-72; vis. asst. prof. Coll. Judaic Studies, San Diego, 1972-75; chaplain USN, San Diego, 1972-75, Seattle, 1975-77, Camp Lejeune, N.C., 1977—. Guest lectr. Grossmont Sch. Vocat. Nursing, San Diego, 1972-75, CPE Inst., Navy Regional Med. Center, San Diego, 1973-74; cons. Jewish Family Service of San Diego, 1974-75; advisor Navy Relief Soc. San Diego, 1972-75. Recipient Bessie and Morris Greenberg prize in modern Hebrew Lit., 1971; Alexander Lamport Prize in Talmud, 1971; Mich. State Regents scholar, 1964-68. Mem. Rabbinical Assembly, Assn. Mil. Chaplains, Naval Acad. Assn., Am. Personnel and Guidance Assn., Am. Psychol. Assn. Contbr. articles in field to religious jours. Home: Care Ostroff 13 Audubon St Rochester NY 14610 Office: Office of Chaplain HQ Bn 2d Mardiv FMF Camp Lejeune NC 28540

CHASE, J. RICHARD, seminary administrator. Pres. Talbot Theol. Sem. (Interdenom.), La Mirada, Calif. Office: Talbot Theol Sem 13800 Boila Ave La Mirada CA 90639*

CHAVANZ, JOSÉ LUCIO, community services administrator, Seventh-day Adventists; b. Panamá, Republic of Panama, June 13, 1933; came to U.S., 1965, naturalized, 1972. S. José Lucio and Francisca (Quezada) F.; m. Apr. 23, 1961 (div. June 1971); 1 child, Tania; m. Blanca Ramírez, Dec. 29, 1974. B.S. in Bus. Adminstrn., Columbia Union Coll., 1968; M. Urban Affairs, Howard U., 1974. Ordained to ministry Seventh-day Adventists, 1969. Treas. Seventh-day Adventist Mission fo Honduras Central Am. Union, 1955-56; treas. Seventh-day Adventist Conf. Panama Central Am. Union, 1957-61, pres., 1968-70; bus. mgr. Central Am. Union Coll., Costa Rica, 1962-66; acct. Columbian Union Coll., Takoma Park, Md., 1970-73; bus. mgr. Antillan Union Coll., Mayaguéz, P.R., 1973-75; dir. inner city dept. So. Calif. Conf. Seventh-day Adventists, Glendale, 1975-80; dir. community services/inner city dept. Pacific Union Conf. Seventh-day Adventists, Westlake Village, Calif., 1980—; mem. Hispanic coordinating com. Seventh-day Adventist Ch., Westlake Village, 1975—, mem. exec. com., 1980—, chmn. community-services/inner city com., mem. minority com., 1981—; mem. Adventist Health Systems W. Exec. Com., Westlake Village, 1981—. Author/editor Inner City Manual, 1978, 83. Mem. vol. orgns. active in disaster, So. Calif., 1980—. Democrat. Home: 4288 Tecolote Ct Moorpark CA 93021 Office: Pacific Union Conf Seventh-day Adventists 2686 Townsgate Rd Westlake Village CA 91361

CHAVERS, ELMA LOUISE, interdenominational lay church worker; librarian; b. Kingston, Ark., Jan. 16, 1941; d. Bert Allen and Fannie Malissie (Thomas) Burney; m. Ben Chavers, Nov. 21, 1964; children: Timothy Ben, Michael Bert. Student in bus. Twin Falls Bus. Coll., 1958-59. Sunday sch. tchr. First United Brethren Ch., Twin Falls, Idaho, 1962-63, youth co-dir., 1973-74; social dir. West Oakey Bapt. Ch., Las Vegas, 1975; Sunday sch. tchr. First So. Bapt. Ch., Pocatello, Idaho, 1976-77; dir. women's ministries Inkom Community Bible Ch., Idaho, 1983—. Administrv. asst., circulation services coordinator Pocatello Pub. Library, 1976—. Named Employee of Yr., Pocatello Pub. Library, 1978, Employee of Month, Pocatello Pub. Library, 1983. Mem. Exec. Christian Women, Ins. Women of Idaho (chairperson membership Twin Falls chpt. 1973-74). Republican. Avocations: needlecraft, reading, camping, fishing. Home: 2023 N Inkom Rd Inkom ID 83245 Office: Pocatello Pub Library 812 E Clark St Pocatello ID 83201

CHAVES, SERAFIN GERMINO, minister, United Church of Christ; b. Iloilo, Philippines, Oct. 22, 1928; came to U.S., 1974, naturalized, 1981. B.A. in Sci., Central Philippine U., 1957, B.S. in Chemistry, 1959; B.D., magna cum laude, Union Theol. Sem., Manila, Philippines, 1964. Ordained to ministry United Ch. of Christ, 1965; cert. chemist, Philippines, 1960. Minister United Ch. of Christ, Pasig, Philippines, 1966-74, Honolulu, 1974-79, San Jose, Calif., 1979—, Salinas, Calif., 1984—; coordinator Santa Clara Outreach-Counseling Project, 1979—; chaplain on call San Jose Hosp., 1984—. Mem. LINK (Downtown Ministerial Assn. San Jose), Filipino Santa Clara Valley Assn. Republican. Home: 743 Kevenaire Dr Milpitas CA 95035 Office: Cosmopolitan Evang United Ch of Christ 97 S Jackson Ave San Jose CA 95116

CHAVEZ, GILBERT ESPIHOZA, bishop, Roman Catholic Church. Titular bishop of Magarmel, aux. bishop, San Diego. Office: 2020 Alaquinas Dr San Ysidro CA 92073*

CHAVEZ, JUAN, minister, Seventh-day Adventists; b. Sorochuco, Peru, Dec. 7, 1939; s. Gonzalo and Maria Teodocia (Medina) C.; B.A., Inca Union Coll., 1964; postgrad. Andres U., 1975-76; m. Magda Odicio, July 11, 1965; children—John, Esther. Ordained to ministry, 1970; pastor chs., Lima, Peru, 1965, N.J., 1966—, Newark and Passaic, 1977—. Home: 48 Fairhaven Ave Midland Park NJ 07432 Office: 2160 Brunswick Ave Trenton NJ 08638

CHAYA, PAUL EDWARD, minister, American Baptist Churches in the U.S.A.; b. Hazleton, Pa., Dec. 7, 1951; s. Thaddeus Thomas and Jean Wanda (Talkowski) Ch.; m. Jean Ann Rathfon, Oct. 26, 1974; children: Jennifer, Sarah Louise; B.S. in Health and Phys. Edn., E. Stroudsburg State U., 1969-73; student Dallas Theol. Sem., 1980; M.Div., Eastern Bapt. Sem., 1981. Ordained to ministry American Baptist Churches in the U.S.A., 1981. Pastoral intern Roxborough Bapt. Ch., Phila., 1978-81; pastor Olney Bapt. Ch., Phila., 1981—. Author (research project on evangelism) Growth Study of an Urban Church, 1981). Mem. Olney Community Council, Pa., 1984—. Recipient Herbert Stillwell Prize in Evangelism, Eastern Bapt. Sem., 1981, service award Chapel of Four Chaplains 1983. Mem. Am. Bapt. Ministers Council, Am. Bapt. Men, Olney Clergy Assn., Phila. Bapt. Assn. (adv. bd., 1981—, evangelism com., 1984, exec. ministers com., 1984—, pastor, counselor Am. Bapt. Men, 1984—). Democrat. Home: 241 W Chew Ave Philadelphia PA 19120 Office: Olney Baptist Church American & Chew Ave Philadelphia PA 19120

CHEEK, RANDY MICHAEL, minister, broadcaster, Southern Baptist Convention; b. Atlanta, Aug. 14, 1952; s. James Lee and Frances Odene (Richards) C.; m. Connie Lois Brantley, Nov. 17, 1972; 1 son, Michael James. B.A. cum laude, Mercer U., 1974; M.Div., So. Bapt. Sem., 1978. Ordained to ministry So. Bapt. Conv., 1975. Sunday worship leader Autumn Breeze Nursing Home, Marietta, Ga., 1970-74; assoc. pastor music and youth First Bapt. Ch., Shepherdsville, Ky., 1975-78; pastor First Bapt. Ch., Grantville, Ga., 1978-79; minister to youth Mount Zion Bapt. Ch., Snellville, Ga., 1979-82, First Bapt. Ch., Smyrna, Ga., 1982—; music programmer, disc jockey Sta. WYNX-Christian Radio, Smyrna, 1983—. Author church drama The Shepherd and His Gift, 1984. Avocations: Christian broadcasting; gardening; yard work; woodworking. Home: 2434 Josh Ct Marietta GA 30064 Office: First Bapt Ch 1275 Church St Smyrna GA 30080

CHEEKS, JOHN RAYMOND, minister, Church of God (Anderson, Indiana); b. Ellisville, Miss., July 27, 1939; s. Walter Lee and Lillie Mae (Johnson) C.; m. Garlyn Faye Mitchell, July 13, 1963; children: John Marty, Patricia Hope. A.A., Jones Jr. Coll., 1959; B.S., U. So. Miss., 1963; postgrad. Anderson Sch. Theology, 1975—. Ordained to ministry Ch. of God (Anderson, Ind.), 1966. Pastor, First Ch. of God, Pascagoula, Miss., 1965-68, Goodwill Ch. of God, Oak Grove, La., 1968-74, First Ch. of God, Lena, La., 1974-81, Capital City Ch. of God, Jackson, Miss., 1981—; exec. council Gulf Coast Bible Coll., Houston, 1975-76; chmn. dept. evangelism La. Assembly, Lena, 1976-80; chmn. Miss. Gen. Assembly, Jackson, 1983—, John Wesley Fellowship, 1983-84. Mem. Right to Life Orgn., Jackson, 1984—. Served with USN, 1959-61. Recipient appreciation for youth work award Ch. of God Youth,

La., 1974-75, 78. Home: 1737 Camellia Dr Jackson MS 39204 Office: Capital City Ch of God PO Box 20145 Jackson MS 39209

CHELETTE, BAYNARD BRIAN, minister, United Pentecostal Church International; b. Montgomery, La., July 24, 1932; s. Peter Lee and Pearl Vivian (Shelton) C.; m. Regina Annette Lanier, Jan. 18, 1957; children: Brian Keith, Denise Darcelle. Th.B., Tex. Bible Coll., 1968; Th.B., Apostolic Bible Inst., 1966. Ordained to ministry, United Pentecostal Ch., 1968. Tchr., instr. Tex. Bible Coll., Houston, 1967-68; pastor United Pentecostal Ch., Port Lavaca, Tex., 1968-69, First Pentecostal Ch., Dallas, 1969-70; supt. Tupelo-Childrens Mansion, Miss., 1970-76; pastor United pentecostal Ch., Tioga, La., 1976-78; exec. asst. La. dist. United Pentecostal Ch., Tioga, 1976-78; missionary United Pentecostal Ch., Ghana, West Africa, 1979-80, pastor, Eunice, La., 1980-82, missionary, Zimbabwe, Africa, 1982-83, evangelist, Montgomery, La., 1984-85; pastor Rosepine Pentecostal Ch., La., 1985—. Editor Miss. Dist. News Mag., 1973-75. Contbr. articles to profl. jours. Served with USAF, 1951-60. Democrat. Lodge: Civitan. Home and Office: Route 1 Box 271-J Montgomery LA 71454

CHEN, CROMWELL CHIAN CHEUN, minister, religious organization executive, The Lutheran Church-Missouri Synod; b. Tinghai, Chekiang, China, Aug. 1, 1929; came to U.S., 1958; naturalized, 1971; m. Paula Chee; children: Connie, Cammie, Chris, Candie. Th.B., Bethel Sem., 1952; M.A., Concordia Sem., 1966; Th.M., Golden Gate Sem., 1970; S.T.D., San Francisco Theol. Sem., 1980. Ordained to ministry Lutheran Church, 1960. Pastor, Trinity Luth. Resurrection Luth., Hong Kong, 1952-58, 63-64, Zion Luth., San Francisco, 1968-82; prof. Concordia Sem. Hong Kong, 1966-68; dir. and prof. Asian Luth. Theol. Tng. Ctr., Daly City, Calif., 1983—. Author: Christian Doctrine, 1985. Translator: Luther's Commentary on Galatians, 1966. Office: Asian Luth Theol Training Ctr 55 San Fernando Way Daly City CA 94015

CHENDO, JOHN CHARLES, minister, United Ch. of Christ and United Presbyn. Ch. U.S.A.; b. Washington, Dec. 7, 1944; s. John Charles and Anne Marie (Bollenbacher) C.; B.A., Columbia, 1966; M.Div., Union Theol. Sem., 1971; m. Judith Gray Fink, May 18, 1969; 1 son, John Michael Gray. Ordained to ministry, 1971; chaplain Roosevelt Hosp., N.Y.C., 1968-69; youth minister St. Albans United Ch. of Christ, St. Albans, N.Y., 1970-71; summer pastor Vt. Ecumenical Council, Albany, Vt., 1970; research asst. United Meth. Office for UN, N.Y.C., 1971 pastor San Juan Larger Parish, Bayfield, Colo., 1971-75; asso. pastor Rye (N.Y.) Presbyn. Ch., 1975—. Student chaplain San Quentin Penitentiary, Calif., 1967, Colo. State Reformatory, Arboles, Colo., 1972-75. Chmn. Council on Alcoholism and Drug Abuse Program, Ignacio, Colo., 1973-75; Dem. committeeman, Precinct 9, La Plata County, Colo., 1974-75. Columbia U. internat. fellow, 1970-71. Mem. Assn. for Clin. Pastoral Edn., Common Cause, ACLU, Covenant Players, Faith at Work, Amnesty Internat. Editor-in-chief Union Sem. Quarterly Review, 1968-69. Home: 430 64th St West New York NJ 07093 Office: Boston Post Rd Rye NY 10580

CHERNOFF, ROBERT, rabbi, Conservative Jewish Congregations; b. Bklyn., Sept. 4, 1922; s. Louis and Sarah Dorothy (Grotsky) C.; B.A., Elysion Coll., 1978, Ph.D., 1979; m. Lea Rosen, Nov. 23, 1943; children—Howard, Shira, Frances. Rabbi, Rabbinical Acad. Am., 1972; rabbi Congregation Beth Knesset Bamidbar, Lancaster, Calif., 1950-56, Har Brook Hebrew Congregation, Balt., 1956-68, Congregation Shaare Tikvah, Temple Hills, Md., 1968-69, Congregation Sons of Israel, Chambersburg, Pa., 1974—; Jewish chaplain South Mountain Restoration Center, 1974—; lectr. Shippensburg U., Wilson Coll., various chs., civic groups. Recipient Meritorious Service award Dept. Air Force, 1956, Commendation award Dept. Def., 1972, Merit award Mayor of Chambersburg, 1980. Mem. Chambersburg Ministerium (pres. 1979-80), Jewish Chaplains Orgn. Pa., Am. Assn. Rabbis (nat. sec. 1981—), Assn. Mental Health Clergy. Author: Shechitah, The Jewish Method of Slaughtering; and Attendant Dietary Laws, 1973; Aspects of Judaism, 1975; Biblically Inspired Dietary Laws Recast in Contemporary Society, 1979. Club: Cumberland Valley Torch. Lodges: B'nai B'rith, Kiwanis (pres. 1979-80). Office: King and 2d Sts Chambersburg PA 17201

CHERNUS, IRA, religion educator; b. Newark, Oct. 29, 1946; s. Solomon and Miriam (Katchen) C. B.A., Rutgers Coll., 1968; M.A., Temple U., 1973, Ph.D., 1975. Asst. prof. philosophy U. Nev., Las Vegas, 1974-76; asst. prof. religious studies U. Colo., Boulder, 1976-82, assoc. prof. religious studies, 1982—. Author: Mysticism in Rabbinic Judaism, 1982. Columnist Colo. Daily newspaper, 1981—. Contbr. articles to profl. jours. Mem. Am. Friends Service Com., Denver, 1977-83. Danforth Grad. fellow, 1968. Mem. Am. Acad. Religion (co-chmn. religion, peace and war group 1984-85). Office: Dept Religious Studies U Colo Boulder CO 80309

CHERRY, C. CONRAD, publishing company executive; b. Mar. 31, 1937; s. Charles Curry and Laura (Owens) C.; m. Mary Ella Bigony, Aug. 21, 1959; children: Charles Kevin, Cythia Diane. B.A., McMurry Coll., 1958; M.Div., Drew U., 1961, Ph.D., 1965. Dir. Scholars Press, Atlanta, 1980—. Author: Theology of Jonathan Edwards, 1966, God's New Israel, 1971. Contbr. articles to profl. jours. Dempster fellow, 1962-63; Am. Quar. award, 1969; Soc. Religion in Higher Edn. fellow, 1970-71; Inst. for Ecumenical and Cultural Research fellow, 1973; Inst. Arts and Humanistic Studies fellow, 1977. Mem. Am. Studies Assn., Am. Acad. Religion, Am. Soc. Ch. History, Soc. for Values in Higher Edn. Address: Scholars Press 1552 Clifton Rd NE Atlanta GA 30322

CHESNEY, WILLIAM DEAN, minister, counselor, So. Baptist Conv.; b. Spartanburg, S.C., Feb. 28, 1926; s. James Horace and Lottie May (Harmon) C.; student North Greenville Coll., 1952, New Orleans Bapt. Theol. Sem., 1957; D.D., Pioneer Acad. and Theol. Sem., 1960; M.A., Trinity Christian U., 1972, Ph.D., 1974; m. Dorothy Allen, Jan. 19, 1948; children—Adeana Sue, William Rodger, Nancy Kay, Judy Ann. Ordained to ministry, 19—; pastor, counselor Ala. Ave. Bapt. Ch., 1952-55, New Hope Bapt. Ch., Franklinton, La., 1955-56, Isabel (La.) Bapt. Ch., 1956-58, Motlow Creek Bapt. Ch., Campobello, S.C., 1958-62, Mt. Pisgah Bapt. Ch., Jefferson, S.C., 1962-65, Hill Crest Bapt. Ch., York, S.C., 1966-70, Westerly Hills Bapt. Ch., Ft. Mill, S.C., 1970—; pvt. practice family therapy Family Counseling Services, 1970—; faculty LeLand Coll., Baker, La., 1957; chaplain USAF, 1960-62. Mem. Internat. Assn. for Spiritual Psychology, Am. Assn. Sex Educators and Counselors, Nat. Assn. Christian Marriage Counselors, Christian Assn. Psychol. Studies, Am. Assn. Higher Edn., Nat. Council Family Relations. Home and Office: Route 3 Box 259 Sutton Rd Fort Mill SC 29715

CHESNUT, FRANKLIN GILMORE, minister, Cumberland Presbyterian Church; b. Bowling Green, Ky., Mar. 2, 1919; s. Walter Franklin and Fannie (Meador) C.; m. Laurelyn Travillian, Aug. 19, 1950; children: Franklin Gilmore, Kathryn Lynne. B.A., Bethel Coll., 1941; B.D., Cumberland Presbyn. Theol. Sem., 1943. Ordained to ministry Cumberland Presbyn. Ch., 1940. Pastor, Brunswick, Tenn., 1943-44; denom. youth dir., 1944-53; mgr. Cumberland Presbyn. Book Store, 1953-54; pastor Calico Rock, Ark., 1954-58, Russellville, Ark., 1958-75, Booneville, Ark., 1975—; moderator Logan Presbytery, Ky. Synod, 1941, White River and Ewing Presbyteries, Ark. Synod, 1956, 59, 61, 64; moderator West Tenn. Synod, 1945, Cumberland Presbyn. Gen. Assembly, 1963, Porter Presbytery, Caulksville, Ark., 1975; stated clk. Ark. Synod, 1956—, Porter Presbytery, 1977—; trustee Cumberland Presbyn. Children's Home, 1962-71; mem. denom. com. on unification, 1963-68, denominational commn. on The Ministry, 1975-84; synodic editorial com. on synodic history, 1977-84. Home: 908 N Erie St Russellville AR 72801 Office: PO Box 163 Booneville AR 92927

CHESNUT, SAMUEL JOSEPH, minister, Ch. of God-Anderson, Ind.; b. Oklahoma City, May 1, 1948; s. Lawrence James and Jesse Mae (Hill) C.; student Bethany Peniel Coll., 1966-67, Oklahoma City U., 1967-68; D.D., Universal Bible Inst., 1974; m. Norma Jean Frolich, May 6, 1966; children—Darla Sue, Angela Renee. Ordained to ministry Ch. of God-Anderson, Ind., 1970; asso. pastor Capitol Hill Ch. of God, Oklahoma City, 1963—; minister of music, 1966—; youth dir., 1963—; musical dir. Ministerial Convs., Ch. of God., 1971—; musical evangelist Camp Meetings Ch. of God, 1972—. Owner Chesnut Constrn. Co., Oklahoma City, 1966—; owner, stock prodr. C-Ranch, Oklahoma City, 1968—. Mem. S. Okla. City C. of C., Okla. Cattlemen's Assn., Nat. Rifle Assn. Address: 3206 S Harvey Ave Oklahoma City OK 73109

CHI, RICHARD SEE YEE, educator, Buddhist religion; b. Peking, China, Aug. 3, 1918; s. Mi Kang and Teng (Pao) C.; B.Sc., Nankai U., 1937; M.A., Oxford U., 1962, D.Phil., 1964; Ph.D., Cambridge (Eng.) U., 1964. Came to U.S., 1965. Lectr., Buddhist thought and texts Oxford U., 1962-65; faculty Ind. U., Bloomington, 1965—, prof. Chinese lang., lit., 1971—, acting chmn., summer 1972. Cons. Inst. for Advanced Studies World Religions, 1972—; adviser film Buddhism in China, 1972; mem. sub-com. on Buddhist philos. materials Nat. Endowment for Humanities, 1974; mem. com. on constrn. Lama Temple at Ind., 1976—; architect Buddhist Monastery at N.Y. State, 1976—; Chinese rep. Internat. Seminar on History of Buddhism, U. Wis., 1976. Fellow China Acad., Royal Asiatic Soc. (Eng.); mem. Mind Assn., Aristotelian Soc., Buddhist Soc., King's Coll. Assn. (Eng.), Assn. for Symbolic Logic, Assn. for Asian Studies, Soc. Asian and Comparative Philosophy, Linguistic Soc. Am. Author: On Fallacies, 1947; Buddhist Formal Logic, 1969. Contbr. articles to profl. jours. Home: PO Box 2717 Bloomington IN 47402

CHIASSON, DONAT, archbishop, Roman Catholic Church; b. Paquetville, N.B., Can., Jan. 2, 1930. Ordained priest, 1956; archbishop of Moncton (N.B.), 1972—. Address: PO Box 248 Moncton NB E1C 8K9 Canada*

CHICHESTER, DONALD WALLACE, minister, United Presbyn. Ch. U.S.A.; b. Amityville, N.Y., Aug. 23, 1933; s. Jesse Ketcham and Ingar Elizabeth (Shaller) C.; B.S. in Applied Physics, Hofstra U., 1955; M.Div., Pitts. Theol. Sem., 1964; m. Jane A. Reid, Apr. 26, 1958; children—Deborah Louise, Elizabeth Mae, Stephen Wallace. Ordained to ministry, 1964; asst. and interim pastor 6th Presbyn. Ch., Pitts., 1964-67; asso. pastor 1st Presbyn. Ch., Monongahela, Pa., 1967-68, Southampton, N.Y., 1968-72; pastor Eastminster United Presbyn. Ch., Erie, Pa., 1972—. Commr. to Synod of Trinity, United Presbyn. Ch. U.S.A., 1976, resource staff synod sch., Wilson Coll., 1976. Pres. bd. dirs. Erie Family and Child Service, 1976—; active radio talking library, Erie Center for the Blind, 1974—. Mem. L.I. Council of Chs. (award for religious broadcasting 1972), Lake Erie Presbytery. Contbg. author Contemporary Worship Services, (James L. Christensen), 1971. Home: 1953 E 2d St Erie PA 16511 Office: 232 E Lake Rd Erie PA 16511

CHILD, CHARLES JUDSON, JR., bishop of Atlanta, Episcopal Church; b. North Bergen, N.J., Apr. 25, 1923; s. Charles Judson and Alice Sylvia (Sparling) C. B.A., U. of the South, 1944, M.Div., 1947, D.D. (hon.), 1978; Lic. in Theology, St. Augustine Coll. (Eng.), 1961. Ordained priest Episcopal Ch., 1948, bishop, 1978. Asst. St. Paul's Episc. Ch., Paterson, N.J., 1947-51; rector St. Bartholomew's Episc. Ch., Ho-Ho-Kus, N.J., 1951-67; canon pastor Cathedral of St. Philip, Atlanta, 1967-78; bishop suffragan Diocese of Atlanta, 1978-83, bishop, 1983—. Home: 3138 Peachtree Dr NE Atlanta GA 30305 Office: Episcopal Diocese of Atlanta 2744 Peachtree Rd NE Atlanta GA 30363

CHILDS, JOSEPH MICHAEL, evangelist, Assemblies of God; b. Middletown, Ohio, June 3, 1951; s. John S. Childs and Peggy (Williams) Childs Buzek; m. Marjorie Gail Tasker, Sept. 14, 1974. B.S., So. Bible Coll., Houston, 1977; D.D. (hon.), Midwestern Sch. Theology, Hamilton, Ohio, 1984. Ordained to ministry Assemblies of God, 1985. Ind. evangelist, Hamilton, Ohio, 1968-78; assoc. minister Hamilton Christian Ctr., 1978-83; evangelist Mike Childs Ministries, Hamilton, 1983—; dir. MCM Mission Ministries, Hamilton, 1983—; adviser Midwestern Sch. Theology, Hamilton, 1984. Editor Millennium, 1983. Recipient cert. of service City of Hamilton, 1970. Mem. Tri-State Ministers Fellowship. Avocations: gardening; sports. Republican. Home: 1320 Glenbrook Dr Hamilton OH 45013 Office: Mike Child Ministries 1320 Glenbrook Dr Hamilton OH 45013

CHILES, JERRY EDWARD, minister, Southern Baptist Convention; b. Falmouth, Ky., Feb. 20, 1946; s. James Allen and Ruth Faye (Bentle) C.; m. Patsy Irene Copeland, Apr. 8, 1972. B.A., Georgetown Coll., 1968; M.R.E., So. Sem., 1970, G.S.R.E., 1971. Ordained to ministry So. Bapt. Conv., 1971; minister youth and music Woodland Ave Bapt. Ch., Lexington, Ky., 1967-68, chs. in Lawrence, Ky., 1968-71, Decatur, Ga., 1972-74; minister of youth 1st Bapt. Ch., Dalton, Ga., 1974-80, minister edn., 1980—; pastor adviser Bapt. Student Union Dalton Jr. Coll. Mem. Ga. Religious Edn. Assn. (2d v.p. 1978, pres. 1983), So. Bapt. Religious Edn. Assn., So. Bapt. Assn. Ministries with the Aging, Nat. Assn. Bapt. Sr. Adults, Dalton-Whitfield Ministerial Assn. (pres. 1980), Eastern Bapt. Religious Edn. Assn. (v.p. 1983, pres. 1984), Phi Mu Alpha. Home: 614 Valley Dr Dalton GA 30720 Office: 311 N Thornton Ave Dalton GA 30720

CHILSON, MICHAEL WAYNE, minister, Independent Baptist Churches; b. McPherson, Kans., Nov. 13, 1956; s. Billy Gene and Linda Marie (Shawly) C.; m. Christina Jo King, Sept. 24, 1983; 1 child, Jonathan Michael. Th.G., Bapt. Bible Coll., 1977, B.S., 1978; M.R.E., Temple Bapt. Theol. Sem., Chattanooga, 1981. Ordained to ministry Ind. Bapt. Chs., 1985. Youth pastor Broadway Bapt. Ch., Indpls., 1981-83; assoc. pastor Grace Bible Ch., McPherson, Kans., 1983-85, also youth pastor, minister visitation. Republican. Home: 910 S Ash St PO Box 1062 McPherson KS 67460 Office: Grace Bible Ch 1215 N Grimes St PO Box 1234 McPherson KS 67460

CHILSTROM, HERBERT W., Bishop, Lutheran Ch. in America. Office: 122 W Franklin Ave Rm 600 Minneapolis MN 55404*

CHILTON, CLAUDE LYSIAS, minister, Church of the Nazarene; b. N.Y.C., Feb. 19, 1917; s. Claude Lysias and Clara Caroline (Weidman) C.; m. Juanita Christine Eastis, Aug. 17, 1939; children: Robert H., Claudia Jeanne, Chilton Britt, Linda Christine. B.Th., Bethany Nazarene Coll., 1939, B.A., 1940; M.A., Calif. Grad. Sch. Theology, Glendale, 1974, Ph.D., 1975. Ordained to ministry Ch. of the Nazarene, 1939. Pastor, Ch. of the Nazarene, Ala., Okla., Ohio, 1936-43, Calif. and Ala., 1946-51, Phoenix, 1971-79, ret., 1979; chaplain U.S. Army, 1943-46, U.S. Air Force, 1951-71, ret. lt. col., 1971. Trustee, Trevecca Nazarene Coll., Nashville,

1949-53; pres. Mobile Ministerial Assn., Ala., 1950-51. Author: The Nazarene Serviceman, 1953; co-author: Chaplains See World Missions, 1946; contbr. articles to profl. jours. Active Ministerial Assns., Phoenix, 1976—. Recipient various mil. awards and decorations. Mem. USAF Assn., Ret. Officers Assn., Christian Holiness Assn., Nat. Assn. Evangelicals, Ariz. Christian Writers Assn., Wesleyan Theol. Soc. Republican. Avocation: collector religious periodicals. Home: 13215 N 56th Ave Glendale AZ 85304

CHIMY, JEROME ISIDORE, bishop, Ukrainian Cath. Ch.; b. Radway, Alta., Can., Mar. 12, 1919; s. Stanley and Anna (Yahnij) C.; J.C.D., Lateran U., Rome, 1966. Ordained priest, 1944; consecrated bishop, 1974; consultor to Provincial Superior, 1958-61; sec. to Superior Gen. of Basilian Order, Rome, 1961-63, consultor, 1963-74; rector St. Josaphat Ukrainian Pontifical Coll., Rome, 1966-74; consultor Sacred Congregation for Eastern Congregation, 1973—; former commissario for matrimonial cases at Sacred Congregation for Doctrine of Faith; bishop, New Westminster, B.C., 1974, Vancouver, B.C., 1974—. Author: De Figura Iuridica Archiepiscopi Maioris in Iure Canonico Orientali Vigenti, 1968. Home and Office: 502 5th Ave New Westminster BC V3L 1S2 Canada

CHIN, SYBIL MARION LUM, lay ch. worker, Roman Cath. Ch.; b. San Francisco; d. Yun-Yow and Margaret (Chew) Lum; m. John Yehall Chin, May 1, 1943; children—Thomas Louis, Terence Paul. Vol., St. Mary's Chinese Mission, San Francisco, 1931-40; pres. St. Mary's Chinese Sch. Parent-Tchr. Groups, 1962-64; exec. sec. San Francisco Archdiocesan Council Cath. Women, 1970-72, 74—, rec. sec., 1972-74; mem. informational bd. The Monitor, 1966—; mem. San Francisco Archdiocesan Bd. Edn., 1970-73; pres. San Francisco Archdiocesan Parent-Tchr. Groups, 1968-69; lector Old St. Mary's Ch., San Francisco, 1973—. Sec., San Francisco County Parent-Tchr. Groups, 1964-66, pres., 1966-68; pres. Chinese Hosp. Aux., 1969-70; mem. budget panel United Bay Area Crusade, United Way, 1974—. Bd. dirs. Cath. Social Service of San Francisco, 1971—, San Francisco Archdiocesan Cath. Com. for Aging, 1969—, Nat. Found. March of Dimes, 1966-76, San Francisco unit Am. Cancer Soc., 1974-76, Archdiocesan Bicentennial Com., 1975-76, San Francisco Interfaith Bicentennial Com., 1975-76, Services for Seniors, Inc., 1976—. Home: 3146 Lyon St San Francisco CA 94123 Office: 913 Stockton St San Francisco CA 94108

CHING, RONALD FAH KUI, minister, United Church of Christ; psychology educator; b. Honolulu, Nov. 28, 1937; s. En Chong and Alma Lok Tsin (Chong) C.; m. Betty Anne Sing, Sept. 2, 1961; children: Darlene Oi Sim, David En Chong. B.B.A., U. Hawaii, 1959; M.Div., Fuller Sem., 1966. Ordained to ministry United Ch. Christ, 1966. Asst. pastor United Ch. Christ, Honolulu, 1966-67; pastor Kaimuki Evang. Ch., Honolulu, 1967—; founder, dir. Nat. Clergy Conf. in Transactional Analysis, Honolulu, 1978—. Lectr. Continuing Edn., U. Hawaii, 1969—. Contbg. author: I Am a Winner, 1984. Mem. adv. com. Big Sisters of Hawaii, 1973, Multiple Sclerosis Soc., Honolulu, 1978. Mem. Hawaii Conf. United Ch. Christ, Kaimuki Bus. Profl. Assn. Democrat. Home: 5290 Kalanianaole Hwy Honolulu HI 96821

CHING, WINSTON WYMAN, priest, Episcopal Ch.; b. Honolulu, June 23, 1943; s. Carl Lin Kau and Ellen Kam Chin (Wong) C.; B.A., U. Hawaii, 1965; M.Div., Ch. Div. Sch. Pacific, Berkeley, Calif., 1968; postgrad. Pacific Sch. Religion. Ordained deacon and priest Episcopal Ch., 1968; asso. chaplain Herrick Meml. Hosp., Berkeley, 1968-70, Alameda County Juvenile Hall, San Leandro, Calif., 1968-69; dir. youth div. Episcopal Diocese Calif., 1971-74; pastoral counselor psychiat. emergency service Herrick Meml. Hosp., 1970; vicar St. John the Evangelist Ch., San Francisco, 1970-74; exec. officer Episcopal Asiamerica Ministry, Exec. Council Episcopal Ch., N.Y.C., 1974—. Mem. bishop's prayer commn. Diocese Calif., 1969-70, bishop's rep. Am. Indian work, 1971-73; alt. dep. to gen. conv., 1973; mem. nat. policy and planning com. United Ministries in Pub. Edn., Washington, 1971-73; mem. met. planning br. Diocese Calif., 1970-74, futures planning council, 1974—; bd. dirs. San Francisco Council Chs., 1972-74; mem. gov. bd. Nat. Council Chs., 1973—, mem. adminstrv. com. China program, 1975—; mem. nat. bd. A Christian Ministry in Nat. Parks, 1975—; bd. govs. Asia Center for Theology and Strategies, 1976—. Mem. city wide com. alcoholism City and County of San Francisco, 1972-74. Bd. dirs. St. John's Ednl. Thresholds Center, San Francisco, 1972—. Mem. Guild Psychol. Studies, Assembly Episcopal Hosps. and Chaplains, Assn. Clin. Pastoral Edn. Address: 815 2d Ave New York City NY 10017

CHITTY, ARTHUR BENJAMIN, JR., educational consultant; b. Jacksonville, Fla., June 15, 1914; s. Arthur Benjamin and Hazel Talitha (Brown) C.; student U. Fla., summer 1933; B.A., U. South, 1935; M.A., Tulane U., 1953; L.H.D., Canaan Coll., 1970; LL.D., Cuttington Coll., 1974; D.H.L., St. Paul's Coll., 1984; m. Elizabeth Nickinson, June 16, 1946; children—Arthur Benjamin, John A.M., Miss Em Turner, Nathan H.B. Dir. pub. relations U. South, Sewanee, Tenn., 1946-65, 70-73, historiographer, 1954—. Sr. warden Otey Parish, Episcopal Ch., Sewanee, 1954-60; mem. Bishop's Council Diocese of Tenn., 1953-60, Presiding Bishop's Com. on Prayer and Devotional Life, 1968-73; mem. program com. Nat. Council Chs., 1975-79. Pres., Sewanee Civic Assn., 1948-50; former trustee St. Augustine's Coll., St. Paul's Coll., St. Andrew's Sch., Living Ch. Found. Mem. Ch. Hist. Soc., Assn. Episcopalian Colls. (pres. 1965-70, 73-79), English Speaking Union (nat. bd. 1973-81), Brotherhood St. Andrew (nat. v.p. 1968—) , Phi Beta Kappa (pres. Sewanee chpt. 1960-61), Sigma Epsilon, Pi Gamma Mu, Phi Alpha Theta, Sigma Nu (pres. Ednl. Fedn. 1972—). Author: Reconstruction at Sewanee, 1954; Men Who Made Sewanee, 1981; monographs: Archdeacon of Yukon, 1958, First Bishop of Texas, 1959; bicentennial series: History of Episcopal Church in Education, 1976; editor: Sewanee News, 1946-65; Ely-Too Black Too White, 1969; mem. editorial bd. Ch. Hist. Mag., St. Luke's Jour. Theology. Home: 100 South Carolina Ave Sewanee TN 37375 Office: 815 2d Ave New York City NY 10017

CHITWOOD, BILLY JAMES, minister, Southern Baptist Convention; b. Estill Springs, Tenn., Sept. 5, 1931; s. Charles Wilbur and Bertha Angeline (Fagg) C.; m. Elizabeth Jane Knight, Apr. 3, 1954; B.A. summa cum laude, Belmont Coll., 1957; M.A. with highest honors, Middle Tenn. State U., 1962; B.D., Luther Rice Sem., 1967, Th.D., 1971. Ordained to ministry Bapt. Ch., 1954. Pastor, First Bapt. Ch., Flintville, Tenn., 1968-70, Tusculum Hills Bapt. Ch., Nashville, 1970-74, Mount Zion Bapt. Ch., Huntsville, Ala., 1974-83, First Bapt. Ch., Madison, Tenn., 1983—; part time chaplain Tinley Park Mental Hosp., Ill., 1964; mem. exec. bd. Ill. Bapt. Conv., Springfield, 1968; pres. Bapt. Ministers' Conf., Huntsville, Ala., 1975-76; instr. Adult Edn. Program, Samford U., Birmingham, Ala., 1976-83. Author: A Faith That Works, 1969; Meet the Real Jesus, 1976; What the Church Needs Now, 1973; (Bible commentary) Romans, 1983. Contbr. articles, study materials to religious publs. Served as staff sgt. USAF, 1950-54. Named Minister of Yr., Duck River Bapt. Assn., 1956; Tchr. of Yr., Franklin County Jaycees, 1962. Mem. Nashville Bapt. Assn., Tenn. Bapt. Conv., So. Bapt. Conv. (del. 1964—). Home: 222 Cumberland Hills Dr Madison TN 37115

CHOO, SAMUEL KAM-CHEE, minister, United Ch. of Can.; b. Malaysia, Mar. 16, 1916; s. Seng and Foon (Wong) C.; B.Sc., Lingnan U., Canton, China, 1941; M.R.E., Golden Gate Bapt. Theol. Sem., Berkeley, Calif., 1955-58; postgrad. U. Calif. at Berkeley, 1958-59; m. King Cheung Man, Feb. 4, 1950. Came to Can., 1960, naturalized, 1968. Tchr. Lingnan Middle Sch., Hong Kong, 1945-55; ordained to ministry United Ch. of Canada, 1962; minister Ottawa (Ont.) Chinese United Ch., 1960-68, Chinese United Ch., Winnipeg, Man., 1968-77. Pres., Chinese United Ch. Conf. Can., 1963-67. Bd. dirs. Chinatown Redevel. Non-Profit Housing Corp., Winnipeg, 1982—, sec., 1984; sec. Sr. Citizen's Home Bldg. Com., Winnipeg, 1975-82. Recipient Community Service award City of Winnipeg, 1984. Home: 415 Beverley St Winnipeg MB R3G 1T9 Canada Office: 281 Pacific Ave Winnipeg MB R3B 0M7 Canada

CHOY, WILBUR WONG YAN, bishop, United Meth. Ch.; b. Stockton, Calif., May 28, 1918; s. Lie Yen and Ida (Lee) C.; A.A., Stockton Jr. Coll., 1944; B.A., Coll. Pacific, 1946; M.Div., Pacific Sch. Religion, 1949, D.D., 1969; L.H.D., U. Puget Sound, 1973; m. Grace Ying Hom, Sept. 26, 1940 (dec. 1977); children—Randolph W., Jonathan W., Phyllis W., Donnell W. Ordained to ministry United Methodist Ch. as deacon, 1947, elder, 1949, consecrated bishop, 1972; asso. pastor Chinese Meth. Ch., Stockton, 1943-49, pastor, 1949-54; pastor St. Mark's Meth. Ch., Stockton, 1954-59; asso. pastor Woodland (Calif.) Meth. Ch., 1959-60; pastor Oak Park Meth. Ch., Sacramento, 1960-69, Chinese Meth. Ch., Sacramento, 1968-69; dist. supt. Bay View Dist. Calif.-Nev. Conf. United Meth. Ch., 1969-72; resident bishop Seattle area, 1972-80, San Francisco area, 1980—; chaplain Calif. State Senate, 1967; mem. exec. com. Nat. Conf. Chinese Chs., 1971-74; exec. com. World Meth. Council, from 1972; v.p., gen. bd. ch. and soc. United Meth. Ch., 1972—, chmn. div. gen. welfare, from 1972; mem. Meth. Gen. Bd. Temperance, 1952-56. Del. Western Jurisdictional Conf., 1952, 56, 60, 64, 72, alternate rep., 1968; del. Gen. Conf., 1972. Rep. Chinese Assn. of Stockton to Nat. Conf. Chinese Communities in U.S.A., 1954; mem. exec. com. Oak Park Neighborhood Council, Sacramento, 1964-67. Trustee Pacific Sch. Religion, U. Puget Sound. Mem. Asian Am. Ministries (mem. adv. com. 1968-72). Office: 800 Olympic Nat Bldg 920 2d Ave Seattle WA 98104

CHRISTELL, ROY ERNEST, minister, Lutheran Church in America; b. Oak Park, Ill., Sept. 21, 1952; s. Jack Vally and Shirley Eleanor (Quenzer) C.; m. Theresa Lynn Jensen, Aug. 18, 1973; 1 child, Kelly Jean. B.A., Augustana Coll., 1974; M.Div., Luth. Theol. Sem., 1978. Ordained to ministry Luth. Ch. in Am., 1978. Asst. pastor Bethany Luth. Ch., Crystal Lake, Ill., 1978-80; pastor, developer Living Lord Luth. Ch., Lake St. Louis, Mo., 1980-81, pastor, 1981—; dist. resource person, witness St. Louis Dist., Ill. Synod, 1982-83, mem., witness com., 1983—; chaplain Lake St. Louis Police Dept., 1981—; Ill. synod rep. Mo. Christian Leadership Forum, Jefferson City, Mo., 1983—. Editor: The Wood Works, 1978-81. Blood drive chmn. Crystal Lake Jaycees, 1979-80; bd. dirs. ARC, St. Louis, 1983—; mem. St. Charles County adv. bd. council ARC, 1982—; com. mem., chaplain Mo. state program Am. Jr. Miss, 1983-84. Ill. State scholar, 1970. Mem. Lake St. Louis Ambassadors (bd. dirs. 1981-82, sec. 1983-84). Home and Office: Living Lord Luth Ch 51 Normandy Dr Lake Saint Louis MO 63367

CHRISTENSON, ALFRED MANDT, minister, American Lutheran Church; b. Hartford, Wis., Mar. 16, 1943; s. Robert Irving and Esther Synneva (Lunde) C.; m. Sylvia Febus, July 26, 1980; children: Selene, Sylvia Esther, Mark. Student Capital U., 1961-64; B.A., U. Wis.-Milw., 1970; M.Div. cum laude, Luth. Theol. Sem., Columbus, Ohio, 1974. Ordained to ministry American Lutheran Church, 1975. Pastor, Kingsbridge Luth. Ch., Bronx, N.Y., 1975-81, Community Luth. Ch., Butler, Pa., 1981, Bethlehem Luth. Ch., Baldwin, N.Y., 1982—; campus pastor Lehman Coll., Bronx, 1975-81; mem. Riverdale Clergy Conf., Bronx, 1975—, chmn., 1980; bd. dirs. Luth. Charities Fund, N.Y.C., 1977-81, 82—, chmn., 1980, sec., 1984—; mem. com. for life and mission in congregation Am. Luth. Ch., eastern dist., 1977-81, 82—, chmn. 1978-81, 83—; chaplain Aux. Police Benevolent Assn., N.Y.C., 1976-81; coordinator Planning Assn. Bronx Luth. Chs., 1980-81. Staff, Citizens League Twin Cities, Mpls., 1974-75. Served to sgt. USAF, 1964-68. Recipient cert. Action Tng. Coalition, Luther Sem., St. Paul, 1975. Mem. Baldwin Clergy Fellowship (chmn. 1984—). Republican. Home: 743 Sprague St Baldwin NY 11510 Office: Bethlehem Luth Ch 1375 Grand Ave Baldwin NY 11510

CHRISTENSON, CARLTON GEORGG, minister, American Baptist Churches in the U.S.A.; b. St. Paul, July 14, 1925; s. Gustaf Adolph and Georgina Cecilia (Berg) C.; m. Marian Edith Peterson, June 18, 1947; children: Jeanne, John, JoAnn, James, Judith. B.S. in Edn., Valley State Coll., 1951. Ordained to ministry American Baptist Churches in the U.S.A., 1952. Pastor, First Baptist Ch., Valley City, N.D., 1948-52, Williston, N.D., 1952-56, Crawfordsville, Ind., 1956-64, Jerseyville, Ill., 1964-72, Galesburg, Ill., 1972-82, Newton, Iowa, 1982—; pres. Bd. Nat. Ministries, Valley Forge, Pa., 1980, 81; chmn. Ministry Care & Support Mid-Am. Bapt. Chs., 1982-84. Recipient Guardsman's award Ind. Nat. Guard, 1964. Mem. Am. Bapt. Chs. U.S.A. (sec. Ministers Council exec. com. 1971-73, mem. gen. bd., 1975-81). Lodge: Rotary (pres. 1962-63) (Crawfordsville). Home: 833 E Main St Havana IL 62644 Office: First Baptist Church Main and Charlotte Havana IL 62644

CHRISTI, FRANCIS, educational administrator Roman Catholic Church, nun; b. Phila., Aug. 9, 1940; d. Francis J. and Mary (Creitz) B. B.S., Chesnut Hill Coll., 1969; M.A., William Patterson Coll., 1976. Joined Order Sisters of St. Joseph, Roman Catholic Church, 1958. Tchr., elem. schs., Phila., 1959-74; tchr. spl. edn. mentally retarded students, Phila., 1974-80; adminstr. Queen of the Universe Day Ctr., Levittown, Pa., 1980—; chmn. liturgy Sisters Council, Phila., 1976—; tchr. Archdiocesan religious edn. tchr. tng. programs, Phila., 1976—; bd. dirs. Ednl. Spl. Religious Adv. Council, Archdiocese of Phila., 1976—. Mem. ednl. adv. bd. Bucks Community Coll., 1982—. Recipient Elizabeth Seton award Nat. Cath. Edn. Assn., 1984. Mem. Nat. Apotolate Mentally Retarded Persons. Office: Queen of the Universe Day Center Trenton Rd Levittown PA 19056

CHRISTIAN, EDWIN ERNEST, minister, Seventh-day Adventists. b. Port of Spain, Trindad, Dec. 14, 1928; s. Rolland J. and Marion Elvina (Darrell) C.; came to U.S., 1929; naturalized, 1951; m. Gloria Ola deBruen, June 16, 1952; children: Edwin, Connie, Mark, Marlene. B.A., Columbia Union Coll., 1952; postgrad. Andrews Univ., 1959-61. Ordained to ministry Seventh-day Adventists, 1955. Pastor chs. Blacktone, Va., Alexandria, Va.; dir. chaplaincy service St. Helena Hosp. and Health Ctr., Calif., 1962-67; Porter Meml. Hosp., Denver, 1967-85; dir. patient relations dept., 1975—; lectr. Union Coll. of Lincoln, Nebr. Denver campus, 1967-77; adj. prof. pastoral care St. Thomas Sem., Denver, 1973-80; Iliff Sem., Denver, 1976-85; pres. chaplains' sect. Western Hosp. Assn., 1976-77; pres. Seventh-day Adventists Hosp. Chaplains' Assn., 1976-78; pres. Met. Denver Chaplains Assn., 1975-76. Editor The Chaplain, 1973-75. Contbr. articles to religious publs. Pres. Inter-Agy Council Smoking and Health, State of Colo. and Wyo., 1970-73; Colo. Soc. Patients Reps., 1975-77; bd. dirs. Arapahoe County Cancer Soc., 1975—, Investigational Rev. Bd. Colo. Regional Cancer Ctr., 1978-81; Instl. Rev. and Research Bd. for Human Experimentations, 1977—. Fed. Bur. Prisons grantee, 1973. Fellow Coll. Chaplains Protestant Hosp. Assn., Seventh-day Adventists Hosp. Assn. (div. of chaplains); mem. Acad. Religion and Health, Royal Soc. Health (England), Am. Hosp. Assn., Nat. Soc. Patient Reps. Lodge: Rotary. Republican. Office: 2525 S Downing St Denver CO 80210

CHRISTIANSEN, FREDERICK WILLIAM, minister, Presbyterian Church U.S.A.; b. Orange, N.J., Oct. 30, 1913; s. William Frederick and Marie Theresa (Erdmann) C.; B.A. cum laude, Tusculum Coll., 1934; M.A., N.Y. U., 1937; M.Div., Union Theol. Sem., 1948. Ordained to ministry, 1948. Youth minister Community Ref. Ch., Bloomfield, N.J., 1946-47; minister Park Presbyn. Ch., Newark, 1947-52; chaplain Combat Command B, 50 Armored Div., N.J. N.G., 1949-52; minister Holland and Milford (N.J.) Presbyn. Chs., 1952-80, minister emeritus, 1980—. History instr. Secondary schs. N.J., 1934-42. Trustee, bd. sec. Presbyn. Homes, Synod of N.J., 1969-72; commr. Gen. Assembly, United Presbyn. Ch. U.S.A., 1951, 63; trustee, sec., v.p. The Sunday League, Inc., 1950-74, pres., 1974—; vice moderator Presbytery of New Brunswick, 1957, moderator, 1963; chaplain VFW Post, Milford-Frenchtown, 1954—. Mem. Milford Bd. Health, 1965-68; adv. com. Reigel Community Found., 1969-72; trustee N.J. Council on Alcohol Problems, 1960-74, hon. trustee, 1974—. Served to sgt. U.S. Army, 1942-45, ETO, NATOUSA. Mem. VFW (nat. chaplain 1984-85, chaplain Eastern States Conf. 1983—, state chaplain N.J. 1981—). Address: RD 3 Box 264 Milford NJ 08848

CHRISTIANSON, CONRAD JOHAN, JR., minister, church official, Lutheran Church in America; b. Stoughton, Wis., Oct. 13, 1935; s. Conrad Johan and Edith Lysle (Thomas) C.; m. Eva Elisabeth Strasser, June 24, 1965; 1 child, Katrin M. B.A., U. Ill., 1957; B.Div., Luth. Theol. Sem., Gettysburg, Pa., 1966, S.T.M., 1973, D.Min., 1984. Ordained, 1966. Minister, Bethel Luth. Ch., Winchester, Va., 1966—; pres. Social Services Council, Winchester, 1975, 76; pres. Ministerial Assn., Winchester/Frederick County, Va., 1982-83; dean No. Valley Area, Va. Synod Luth. Ch. Am., 1983—; bd. dirs. Catholic Charities, Winchester, 1978-81; chaplain West Va. State Soc. SAR, 1983. Contbr. articles to ch. periodicals. Bd. mem. Big Bros., Winchester, 1982—. Served with U.S. Army, 1958-59. Lodge: Lions. Home: Rural Route 5 Box 894 Winchester VA 22601 Office: Bethel Luth Ch Bloomery Route Box 117A Winchester VA 22601

CHRISTMAS, JIMMY, minister, ch. exec., Jesus People Revolution Movement; b. Bakersfield, Calif., Mar. 9, 1939; s. Donald Earl and Ruth Caroline Blanchard Adams; B.Th., Covenant Coll., 1964; postgrad. Luth. Theol. Sem., 1964-66; Ph.D. in Humanities, Ohio Coll., 1971; U.S. Office Edn. diploma, U. Calif., Berkeley, 1973; certificate Oxford U., Eng., 1973, Harvard Law Sch., 1974; J.D., Blackstone Law Sch., 1975. Ordained to ministry, 1964; adminstrv. asst. Ch. of Jesus Christ, Nat. Hdqrs. in Calif., 1963-64; youth minister, sch. tchr. Luth. Ch., Costa Mesa, Calif., 1964-66; founder, street minister Jesus People Revolution Movement, Balboa Beach, Calif. and Haight-Ashbury, San Francisco, 1965-68; youth minister Am. Luth. Ch., Tustin, Calif., 1968-69; exec. dir. Laguna Beach (Calif.) Free Counseling Clinic, 1970-74; founder, pres., sr. minister Celebrate Life Ch. and exec. dir. Sunshine House Counseling Center, Laguna and Newport Beach, Calif., 1974—. Missionary to orphanages in Mexico and to Am. Indian children; area dir. Young Life; dir. Youth for Christ, Campus Life Clubs; high sch. dir. Bal Week, Campus Crusade for Christ; co-sponsor Dr. Paul Carlson's Med. Found. of Africa; chaplain Orange County Empire council Boy Scouts Am., Hoag and South Coast Hosp.; del. Am. Luth. Ch. Nat. Conv.; lectr. on drug abuse USMC officers; producer, moderator television talk show Insight; bd. dirs. Athletes in Action; developer first Christian nite clubs Snoopy's Place and High Life. Event coordinator March of Dimes, Toys for Tots, Children's Hosp., United Way, Sunshine Kids, City of Children, Am. Indian Thunderbird Children's Found., Tustin Rap Center for Youth; cons. Orange County Mental Health Dept.; adminstr. Fed. OEO Program, Long Beach Sr. Citizens Nutrition Project; atty. mgmt. Sunshine House Calif. Legal Plan. Recipient awards YMCA, 1969, Kiwanis, 1970, Lions, 1970, Rotary, 1971, TWA, 1972, Alpha Psi Omega, Nat. Journalism award Pasadena Coll., 1957. Mem. Ralph Nader Pub. Citizen Raiders, Ministerial Assn., Gestalt Inst., Transactional Analysis Assn., Nat. Council Family Relations, Am. Humanistic Psychology Assn., Am. Assn. Sex Educators and Counselors, Esalen Inst., Am. Assn. Pastoral Counselors. Author: Both Sides Now, 1976. Home: Box 444 Laguna Beach CA 92652 Office: 1201 Dove St Suite 600 Newport Beach CA 92660 also care James Adams ABC Entertainment Center 2040 Ave of the Stars Atty Suite 400 Los Angeles Century City CA 90067

CHRISTOPHER, (VELIMIR KOVACEOVICH), Bishop of Eastern Am., Serbian Eastern Orthodox Ch. in the U.S.A. Office: Way Hollow Rd Edgeworth Sewickley PA 15143*

CHRISTOPHER, JAMES ALEXANDER, minister, United Church of Christ; b. Pulaski, Tenn., June 28, 1938; s. James Hayden and Helen (Moore) C.; m. Nancy Ada Trites, Apr. 2, 1960 (div. 1982); m. Carole Ann Snyder, May 7, 1983; children: Cynthia, Karen, Jonathan. B.A., Colgate U., 1961; B.D., Iliff Sch. Theol., 1963; D.Min., Andover Newton Sch. Theol., 1973. Ordained to ministry United Ch. of Christ, 1964. Pastor, Ashburnham Community Ch., Mass., 1965-69, Ridgeview Ch., White Plains, N.Y., 1969-76; sr. pastor Faith United Protestant Ch., Park Forest, Ill., 1976-82, First Congl. Ch., Elgin, Ill., 1982—; dir. Ill. Conf. United Ch. Christ, Westchester, 1984—. Bd. dirs. C.G. Jung Ctr., Evanston, Ill., 1983; adv. bd. C.G. Junt Inst., 1984; v.p. Econ. Devel. Commn., Park Forest, 1981-82. Mem. Clergy Assn. Greater Elgin, Profl. Assn. Clergy, Assn. Clin. Pastoral Edn. Democrat. Club: Current History. Office: 1st Congregational Ch 256 E Chicago St Elgin IL 60120

CHRISTOPHERSON, KENNETH EUGENE, religious educator; b. Viborg, S.D., July 7, 1926; s. Harry Adiel and Clara Olea (Bedin) C.; m. Phyliss Genevieve Larson, Sept. 13, 1947; children: David, Dan, Jené, Bruce. B.A., Augustana Coll., 1946; B.Th., Luther Theol. Sem., 1950; Ph.D., U. Minn., 1972. Ordained to ministry, American Luth. Ch., 1950. Assoc. pastor Grace Luth. Ch., Watertown, S.D., 1950-51; pastor Hudson Luth. Ch., S.D., 1951-55; assoc. pastor Univ. Luth. Ch. of Hope, Mpls., 1956-58; asst. prof. religion Pacific Luth. U., Tacoma, Wash., 1958-72, assoc. prof., 1972-76, prof., 1976—. Author: Norwegian Historiography of Norway's Reformation, 1972. Fulbright scholar, 1955-56. Mem. Am. Acad. Religion (chpt. pres. 1984-85), Am. Soc. Ch. History, Am. Soc. for Reformation Research, Norwegian Am. Hist. Assn. Democrat. Home: 809 Tule Lake Rd S Tacoma WA 98444 Office: Pacific Lutheran U Dept Religion Tacoma WA 98447

CHRISTOPHERSON, SIDNEY JULIUS, minister, Evangelical Lutheran Church of Canada; b. Sutton, N.D., Feb. 27, 1912; went to Can., 1964; s. Olaf and Thora (Mørck) C.; m. Nina Christine Dybwad, Mar. 27, 1937; children: Duane Phillip, Lynn Leroy, Mark Olav. Diploma Luther Sem., St. Paul, 1964. Ordained to ministry American Lutheran Church, 1964, Evangelical Lutheran Church of Canada, 1964. Pastor Am. Luth. Ch., Froid, Mont., 1957-60, Wolf Point, Mont., 1960-61, Culbertson, Mont., 1961-63; pastor Evang. Luth. Ch. of Can., Sedgewick, Alta., 1964-68, Red Deer, Alta., 1968-77; pres. Central Alta. Conf., Evang. Luth. Ch. of Can., 1969-75, chmn. bd. edn., 1976-79. Editor Eternity for Today, 1978—. Pres. Sedgewick Bd. of Trade, 1966-67; state sec., office mgr. Minn. Farmers Union, Willmar, 1947-49. Home: PO Box 207 Blind Bay BC V0E 1H0 Canada

CHRYSTAL, WILLIAM GEORGE, minister, United Church of Christ; b. Seattle, May 22, 1947; s. Francis Homer and Marjorie Isabell (Daubert) C.; m. Mary Frances King, Aug. 24, 1970; children: Shelley Diane, Sarah Frances, John Canfield, Philip George. B.A., U. Wash, 1969, M.Ed., 1970; M.Div., Eden Theol. Sem., 1977; M.A., Johns Hopkins U., 1984. Ordained to ministry United Ch. Christ, 1977. Minister, St. Peter United Ch. Christ, Granite City, Ill., 1978-79; sr. minister First Congl. Ch., Stockton, Calif., 1979-83; minister, Trinity United Ch. Christ, Adamstown, Md., 1983—; mem. hist. council United Ch. Christ, N.Y.C., 1983—; coordinator oral history project United Ch. Christ, 1983—. Author: Young Reinhold Niebuhr: His Early Writings, 1911-1931, 1977; A Father's Mantle: The Legacy of Gustav Niebuhr, 1982. Contbr. articles to religious and hist. jours. Mem. Am. Soc. Ch. History, Congl. Hist. Soc., Evang. and Reformed Hist. Soc. Home: 5605 Mountville Rd Adamstown MD 21710 Office: Trinity United Ch Christ 5603 Mountville Rd Adamstown MD 21710

CHUN, RICHARD CHEW PUNG, minister, United Ch. of Christ; b. Honolulu, Apr. 28, 1924; s. Kan Yen and Ruth (Tseu) C.; student Temple U., 1942-44; B.A., Parsons Coll., 1946; M.Div., Hartford Sem. Found., 1949; postgrad. LaSalle Coll., 1944, U. Hawaii, 1954, Lancaster Sem., 1969-70; m. Thelma H. T. Lau, Aug. 19, 1950; children—Dennis James, Malcolm Joh, Jonathan Joel, Deborah Ruth. Ordained to ministry, 1950; asst. pastor First Chinese Ch., Honolulu, 1949; pastor Lanai Union Ch., Lanai City, Hawaii, 1950-53, Federated Ch., Granville, Mass., 1953-54, United Community Ch., Hilo, Hawaii, 1955-60, Lihue (Hawaii) Christian Ch., 1960-72, Kapoa (Hawaii) First Hawaiian Ch., 1973—. Pres., Kauai Evangel. Assn., 1964, Kauai Ministerial Union, 1967, Hawaii Conf. United Ch. Christ, 1973-74, chmn. long range planning, 1974-75, del. Gen. Synod, 1958, 1965, 1973, 1975. Bd. dirs. Lanai Community Assn., 1952-53, Kauai Economic Opportunity, Inc., 1965-69, 1971—, chmn. bd., 1968-69, Kauai Immigrant Service Com., 1970—, Kauai Community Chest, 1970, Vol. Orgn. Concern for Elderly, 1972—, chmn. bd., 1972-73; chmn. task force home health care and health screening Comprehensive Health Planning, Kapaa, 1975-76; advisory council Kauai Med. Group, 1975—; sec. State Hawaii Library Commn., 1976—; chmn. Title XX Advisory Council, Kapaa, 1976—; project coordinator Office Elderly Affairs County Kauai, 1972—. Recipient Recognition for Meritorious Service award, Gov. of Hawaii, 1969. Mem. Hawaii Govt. Employees Assn. Home: 2831 Mokoi St Lihue HI 96766 Office: Box 111 Lihue HI 96766

CICHANSKI, TIMOTHY JOHN, church official, Roman Catholic Church, educational administrator, director; b. Chgo., Jan. 24, 1952; s. John Anthony and Mary Esther (Janczak) C. B.S., Loyola U., Chgo. and Rome, 1974; M. Edn., Loyola U., 1975; Ph.D., U. Chgo., 1978. Cert. in adminstrn., Ill. Dir. religious edn. St. Benedict Parish, Chgo., 1975-77, St. Mary Parish, Buffalo Grove, Ill., 1977-79, St. Scholastica Parish, Woodridge, Ill., 1979—, Christ the King Parish, Lombard, Ill., 1984—; prin. Christ the King Sch., Lombard, 1984—; speaker Diocese of Joliet, Ill., 1980—; faculty mem. Nat. Coll. of Edn., Evanston, Ill., 1977—. Dir. med. ethics Cook County Hosp., Chgo., 1979—. Speaker, Am. Arthritis Found., Chgo., 1979—, Am. Cancer Soc., Chgo., 1979—, Am. Heart Assn., Chgo., 1979—. Mem. AAUP, Am. Coll. Hosp. Adminstrs., The Hastings Ctr., Phi Delta Kappa. Home: 917 S Lancaster Mount Prospect IL 60056 Office: Christ the King 115 E 15th Lombard IL 60148

CILKE, ROBERT HENRY, clergyman, educator, Assemblies of God Church; b. Petoskey, Mich., June 27, 1941; s. Robert Emil and Eleanor (Baines) C.; m. Barbara Eleene Hatch, Dec. 28, 1963; children: Debra, Brenda, Robert F. Diploma in music North Central Bible Coll., 1962; B.Music Edn., MacPhail Coll. Music, 1963; M.A., Central Mich. U., Mt. Pleasant, 1969. Ordained minister Assemblies of God Ch., 1966. Minister music and youth Bethel Assembly of God, Rapid City, S.D., 1963-64; pastor chs. in Mich., 1964-72, First Assembly of God, Cheboygan, Mich., 1964-65, Faith Assembly of God, Rogers City, Mich., 1965-72; assoc. pastor, minister music Brookdale Assembly of God, 1972-74, assoc. pastor, 1976—; chmn. music dept. North Central Bible Coll., 1972-76; music dir. State of Minn. Assemblies of God, 1972-76; assoc. Pastor Brookdale Christian Ctr. Assembly of God, Bklyn. Ctr., Minn., 1976—; Christ ambassador rep. Northeast sect. Mich. for Assemblies of God Ch., 1966-68. Bd. dirs. King's Acad., 1976—; mem. Bklyn. Ctr. Housing Commn., 1977-83; bd. dirs. Ohio Teen Tempo, 1975-76; dir. Northwest Suburbs Cable TV Commn., 1982—. Mem. Bklyn. Ctr. C. of C. (chmn. legis. affairs com. 1979-81), North Twin Cities Ministers Assn. (sec./treas. 1982). Lodge: Rotary (v.p. 1981-82, pres. 1982-83). Home: 3307 Mumford Rd Brooklyn Center MN 55429 Office: 6030 Xerxes Ave North Brooklyn Center MN 55430

CIUBA, EDWARD JOSEPH, priest, Roman Catholic Church; b. Elizabeth, N.J., Mar. 20, 1935; s. Joseph and Anna Ciuba. B.A., Seton Hall U., 1955; S.T.L., Pontifical Gregorian U.-Rome, 1959, S.S.L., 1962; Cert., Ecole Biblique et Archeologique, 1963. Ordained priest, 1959. Assoc. pastor St. Ann's Ch., Jersey City, N.J., 1960; prof. Sacred Scripture, Immaculate Conception Sem., Darlington and Sch. Theology and Pastoral Ministry, Seton Hall U., 1963—; rector, pres. Immaculate Conception Sem., Mahwah, N.J., 1974, rector/dean, 1984—; prof. sacred scripture Immaculate Conception Sem., 1963—; vis. prof. Fordham U., 1974, Fairfield U., 1971-73, Felician Coll., 1970, Notre Dame U., 1969, St. Louis U., 1968; mem. nat. consultation for discussion between United Meth. Ch. and Roman Cath. Ch., 1971-76; mem. senate of priests Archdiocese of Newark, 1966-73, sec. for ministerial formation, 1979-82, dir. office ministerial formation, 1982—, mem. council of priests, 1984—. Author: Who Do You Say That I Am?, 1974. Contbr. articles to profl. jours. Mem. licensure and adv. bd. State N.J. Ind. Colls. and Univs., 1978-81; participant Warren H. Deem Inst. for Theol. Edn. Mgmt., 1981. Mem. Inst. for Theol. Edn. Mgmt., Assn. Theol. Schs. (exec. com. 1982), Cath. Theol. Soc., Soc. Bible Lit., Cath. Bibl. Assn. Address: Immaculate Conception Sem Seton Hall University South Orange NJ 07079

CLAAR, RICHARD LEE, minister, Ind. Fundamental Chs. Am.; b. Columbus, Ohio, Nov. 19, 1926; s. Lawrence McKinley and Millie (Hayes) C.; grad. Dallas Bible Coll., 1954; postgrad. Moody Bible Inst., 1973; m. Kathleen C. Foley, Oct. 20, 1943; children—Terry Lee, Richard Lee. Ordained to ministry, 1957; pastor Decatur Chapel Ch., Little Hocking, Ohio, 1956-58, Dalton (Wis.) Bible Ch., 1958-59, Branson (Mo.) Bible Ch., 1959—. Vice pres. Wis. region Ind. Fundamental Chs. Am., 1958-59, pres. Ozark region, 1961-62; chmn. bd. Mid-Am. Mission, 1969-74; treas. Wilderness Ch. Fund, 1962—. Mem. Mo. State Welfare Commn., 1976—, Mo. Study Rehab. Council, 1968; program chmn. Branson PTA, 1969. Named Alumnus of Year Dallas Bible Coll., 1961. Mem. Dallas Bible Coll. Alumni Assn. (pres. 1962-63). Home: Hillcrest Addition Branson MO 65616 Office: N Hwy 65 Box 123 Branson MO 65616

CLAAS, GERHARD, general secretary Baptist World Alliance; b. Wetter, Germany, Aug. 31, 1928; s. Ernest and Anna (Schroeder) C.; m. Irmgard Lydia Saffran, July 29, 1954; children: Regina, Gabriele, Martin. Diploma Bapt. Theol. Sem., Rueschlikon, Switzerland, 1951, Hamburg, Germany, 1950; D.D. (hon.), Ouachita Bapt. U., 1974. Ordained, Union Evang. Free Chs. in Germany, 1956. Pastor, First Bapt. Ch., Duesseldorf, Germany, 1953-58; youth sec. German Bapt. Union, Hamburg, 1958-64; pastor J.G. Oncken Bapt. Ch., Hamburg, 1964-67; gen. sec. German Bapt. Union, Bad Homburg, 1967-76; assoc. sec. for Europe, Bapt. World Alliance, Bad Homburg, 1976-80, gen. sec., Bapt. World Alliance, Washington, 1980—; tchr. of religion Jacobi Gymnasium, Duesseldorf, 1953-58; dir. Youth Leaders

Sem., Bad Homburg, 1958-64; chmn. exec. bd. Bapt. Theol. Sem., Rueschlikon, 1975-80. Author: Missionary Church Work, 1960; editor: Working Material for Youth Workers, 1958-64. Exec. bd. Bread for the World, Bad Homburg, 1967-76; bd. dirs. Albertinen Hosp., Hamburg, 1964-80; chmn. exec. bd. Evang. Free Ch. Social Work, Hannover, Germany, 1967-80. Office: Bapt World Alliance 1628 16th St NW Washington DC 20009

CLAPP, STEVEN EVERENT, minister, United Meth. Ch.; b. Urbana, Ill., Sept. 7, 1947; s. Everett E. and Mary Jo (Baker) C.; B.S., U. Ill., Urbana, 1968; M.Div., Garrett Theol. Sem., 1971; m. Elizabeth Jane Yother, May 17, 1968; children—Debbie, Sandy. Ordained to ministry; pastor Henning-Jamesburg United Meth. Chs., Henning, Ill., 1967-68, Seymour-Centerville United Meth. Chs., Seymour, Ill., 1968-70; asso. pastor Kewanee (Ill.) First United Meth. Ch., 1970-74, Univ. United Meth. Ch., Peoria, Ill., 1974-76; dir. camping, coordinator youth ministries Central Ill. Conf., United Meth. Ch., Bloomington, 1976—. Mem. leadership devel. commn. Ill. Conf., United Meth. Ch., 1973-76; bd. dirs. Kewanee Salvation Army, 1970-74. Mem. tng. com. Girl Scouts U.S.A., Peoria, 1974-76; mem. advisory bd. Boy Scouts Am., 1974-76. Recipient Distinguished Service award Ill. Dept. Children and Family Services, 1974. Mem. Christian Edn. Fellowship, Fellowship of Adult Workers in Youth Ministry, Am. Camping Assn. Contbr. articles to religious jours. Home: 5104 W Greenridge St Charter Oak Village Peoria IL 61614 Office: Council on Ministries 1211 N Park St Bloomington IL 61701

CLARK, BETH, minister, United Church of Christ; b. Bradford, N.H., Apr. 15, 1914; d. John Scott and Bessie Gordon (Murdock) Pendleton; m. John Guill Clark, June 20, 1940 (dec. 1955); children: John Guill, Jr., Beverly Estelle Daggett. B.A., Colby Coll., 1935; B.D., Andover Newton Theol., 1938; M.Div., Eastern Bapt. Theol., 1968; D.Min., Lancaster Theol. Sem., 1981. Ordained to ministry United Ch. of Christ, 1967. Interim minister Penn Central Conf., United Ch. Christ, Harrisburg, Pa., 1968—; interim pastor St. Lukes United Church of Christ, Lock Haven, Pa., 1984; bd. mgrs. Bethany Childrens Home, Womelsdorf, Pa., 1982—; mem. adv. bd. Sun Home Nursing Services, Northumberland, Pa., 1982—; corp. mem. United Ch. Bd. World Ministries, N.Y.C., 1983—. Editor: Meditations on the Lord's Supper (John G. Clark), 1958; Author: Grief in the Loss of a Pastor, 1981. Recipient Albion Woodbury Small Prize Colby Coll., 1935. Mem. Interim Network, Washington Assn. Ret. State Employees, Alban Inst. Democratic. Clubs: Interagency (pres. 1966-68), Triangle (pres. 1960-64). Home: 709 N 9th St Selinsgrove PA 17870

CLARK, EARL, pastor, religion educator, Southern Baptist Convention; b. Burning Springs, Ky., Nov. 14, 1926; s. Vernon C. and Ada Pearl (Hacker) C.; m. Vada Robinson, Feb. 2, 1946; children: Carol Sue Clark Everman, Patricia Ann Clark Collier, Sherman Earl. B.A., Eastern Ky. U., 1960; M.Div., So. Bapt. Theol. Sem., Louisville, 1971; D.Ministry, Lexington Theol. Sem., 1980. Ordained to ministry, 1953. Pastor, New Prospect Bapt. Ch., Manchester, Ky., 1954-57, Corinth Bapt. Ch., London, Ky., 1962-72, East Bernstadt 1st Bapt. Ch., Ky., 1981—; prof. N.T., Clear Creek Sch., Pineville, Ky., 1972—; syndicated newspaper writer internat. Sunday Sch. lessons, 1975-78. Served with U.S. Army, 1945-48. Named Ky. Col., 1972. Mem. Laurel River Bapt. Assn. (moderator 1964-65). Republican. Home: Route 12 Box 490 London KY 40741 Office: Clear Creek Bapt Sch Pineville KY 40977

CLARK, EUGENE VINCENT, priest, Roman Catholic Church; b. N.Y.C., Dec. 1, 1925; s. Eugene Vincent and Kathryn (Vandervoort) C.; B.A., St. Joseph's Sem., 1947, M.A., 1951; M.A., Fordham U., 1956; Ph.D., Notre Dame U., 1966. Ordained priest Roman Cath. Ch., 1951; curate St. Francis Ch., Mt. Kisco, N.Y., 1951-53; tchr. Dubois High Sch., N.Y.C., 1953-56; Lingard fellow U. Notre Dame, South Bend, Ind., 1956-57; prof. Notre Dame Coll., N.Y., 1957-61; tchr. Cardinal Spellman Sch., N.Y.C., 1961-66; editor U.S. Cath. Hist. Soc., 1962-66; sec. to Cardinal Spellman, N.Y.C., 1967, Cardinal Cooke, 1968-71; dir. Office of Communications Archdiocese of N.Y., N.Y.C., 1971—. Trustee St. John's U., N.Y.C. Mem. Am. Hist. Assn., Am. Cath. Hist. Assn., U.S. Cath. Hist. Soc., Com. Religion and Art in Am., Patrons of Arts Vatican Museums (pres.). Home: 470 Westchester Ave Crestwood NY 10707 Office: 1011 1st Ave New York NY 10018

CLARK, GEORGE TRUETT, minister, So. Baptist Conv.; b. Marlin, Tex., Nov. 8, 1932; s. George Washington and Lela Mae (Mauldin) C.; B.S., Hardin-Simmons U., 1955; B.Div., Southwestern Baptist Theol. Sem., 1961; m. Barbara Jean Smith, Jan. 30, 1954; children—Jeana Georgette, Jennifer Leigh, George Taylor. Ordained to ministry, 1953; pastor 1st Baptist Ch., Guthrie, Tex., 1953-55, 1st Baptist Ch., Dumont, Tex., 1953-55, Carey, Tex., 1955-61, Nacogdoches, Tex., 1961-64, Timpson, Tex., 1964-66, Nederland, Tex., 1966-73; editor Church Adminstrn. Baptist Sunday Sch. Bd., Nashville, 1973—; v.p. pub. relations com. So. Baptist Conv. Mem. Baptist Pub. Relations Assn. Contbr. articles to religious periodicals. Home: 808 Irma Dr Antioch TN 37013 Office: 127 9th Ave N Nashville TN 37234

CLARK, JAMES RATCLIFFE, educator, Ch. of Jesus Christ of Latter-day Saints; b. Grantsville, Utah, Feb. 2, 1910; s. Edwin Marcellus and Matilda Curtis (Ratcliffe) C.; A.B., Brigham Young U., 1936, M.A., 1944; postgrad. U. Denver, 1940, Harvard, 1945; Ed.D. in Ednl. Adminstrn., Utah State U., 1958; m. Helen Virginia Jorgensen, Oct. 6, 1937; children—Virginia (Mrs. Donald Grant Bragg), Stephen Marcellus, James Bruce. Ordained high priest Ch. of Jesus Christ of Latter-day Saints, 1948; dist. clk. Brit. Mission, 1929-31; prin. Latter-day Saints Sem., 1936-38; Sunday sch. tchr. gospel doctrine, 1939-42; stake missionary, Provo, Utah, 1942-45; pres. 282 Quorum of 70, 1946-48; counselor in bishopric, 1948-52; pres. East Sharon Stake Mission, 1952-54; prof. religious instrn. Brigham Young U., 1963-75, prof. emeritus, 1975—, also dir. research Centennial History of Brigham Young U., Provo, 1973-76. Mem. Utah Acad. Arts, Scis. and Letters, Soc. Early Hist. Archaeology (gen. officer 1959-64), NEA, Phi Delta Kappa. Republican. Author: Messages of the First Presidency of the Church of Jesus Christ of Latter-day Saints, 6 vols., 1965-75. Home: 1213 E Ash Ave Provo UT 84604

CLARK, JOHN DANIEL, JR., minister, Full Gospel Southern Baptist Convention; b. Detroit, May 19, 1944; s. John Daniel and Phyllis Bea (Ellingsworth) C.; m. Joyce Mary Edwards, May 9, 1969; children: Violet, Sherry, Bernard, Velvet, Milton, Margaret, Cricket, Steven. Student, Calif. Bapt. Coll., 1965-67. Ordained to ministry, 1977. Pastor, Miracle Church of Our Lord, Valinda, Calif., 1975-76; evangelist Crusades, Kingman, Ariz., Victorville, Calif., 1976-77; pastor Westmont Bapt. Ch./First Gospel Ch., Alhambra, Calif., 1977—; mem. evangelism com. First Gospel So. Bapt. Ch., 1983—, mem. evangelism devel. com., evangelism media devel. com. Producer cable TV program, First Gospel Hour, 1984. Chaplain, Alhambra Police Dept., 1983—. Served with USAF, 1962-65. Mem. Los Angeles So. Bapt. Assn. Evangelists Com., Moral Majority, Underground Evangelism. Republican. Home: 16512 Arvid St Valinda CA 91744 Office: First Gospel Church 3228 W Main St Alhambra CA 91801

CLARK, MALCOLM GRAY, minister, Presbyterian Church in the U.S.; b. Lumberton, N.C., Oct. 1, 1947; s. George Ellis and Martha (Cromartie) (Campbell) C.; m. Sandra Lynn Crank, Oct. 31, 1976; children: Joshua Gray, William Daniel, Kelly Elizabeth. B.A., St. Andrews Coll., Laurinburg, N.C., 1969; postgrad Union Theol. Sem., 1969-70; M. Div., Eden Theol. Sem., 1973; D. Min., McCormick Theol. Sem., 1979. Ordained to ministry Presbyn. Ch., 1974. Pastor Little River Presbyn. Ch., Hundle Mills, N.C., 1974-76; assoc. pastor First Presbyn. Ch., Asheboro, N.C., 1977-79; pastor Fellowship Presbyn. Ch., Greensboro, N.C., 1979—; chmn. budget preparations Orange Presbytery, Durham, N.C., 1979-83. Contbr. articles to religious publs. Del. Mo. State Democratic Conv., Jefferson City, 1972, N.C. State Dem. Conv., Raleigh, 1976. Home: 2705 Asbury Terr Greensboro NC 27408 Office: Fellowship Presbyterian Ch 3713 Richfield Rd Greensboro NC 27410

CLARK, MARGARET OWEN (PEGGY), minister, church administrator, theology educator Christian Church (Disciples of Christ). b. Miami, Fla.; d. George Earle and Margaret (Richards) Owen; m. Gerald Daniel Clark, Sept. 1, 1973. B.A. in Comparative Lit., Ind. U., 1970; M.A. in Comparative Religion, Columbia U., 1973; D. Ministry, N.Y. Theol. Sem., 1981. Ordained to ministry Christian Ch. (Disciples of Christ), 1976. Asst. minister Park Ave Christian Ch., N.Y.C., 1971-73; minister Union Meml. Ch., Stamford, Conn., 1977-79; assoc. regional minister Christian Ch. Northeastern region, N.Y.C., 1980-84, regional minister, 1984—; assoc. prof. New Brunswick Theol. Sem., N.J., N.Y., 1984—; chmn. Com. Denominational Execs., N.Y.C.; chmn. Tri-State Media Ministry; v.p. World Conv. Chs. of Christ. Author, contbr: Go Quickly and Tell, 1969; Voices, 1981. Mem. Nat. Assn. Female Execs. Home: 527 E 84th St New York NY 10028 Office: 132 W 31st St #1541 New York NY 10028

CLARK, MATTHEW HARVEY See *Who's Who in America*, 43rd edition.

CLARK, ROBERT EUGENE, minister, Independent Baptist Churches; b. Pontiac, Mich., May 30, 1935; s. Vera M. Clark; m. Nelda I. Parrish, Oct. 29, 1969; children: David, Robert, Shane. B.A., Trinity Bapt. Coll., D.D., 1984, D.D. (hon.), 1985. Ordained to ministry Ind. Bapt. Chs. Gospel musician, 1955—; mem. gospel quartets, 1955-69; pastor, founder First Bapt. Ch., Winter Springs, Fla., 1974—. Tenor Orlando Opera. Author: Story of The Cross, 1982; Woman Preachers, 1983; Message of the Blood, 1985. Republican. Home: 640 Silvercreek Rd Winter Springs FL 32708 Office: First Bapt Ch Winter Springs 290 E Bahama Rd Winter Springs FL 32708

CLARK, ROY CLYDE See *Who's Who in America*, 43rd edition.

CLARK, VIRGIL LEE, missionary, So. Bapt. Conv.; b. West Frankfort, Ill., Apr. 11, 1916; s. Harmon and Mary Adeline (Gunter) C.; B.A., Georgetown (Ky.) Coll., 1949; M.Div., Southwestern Baptist Theol. Sem., Ft. Worth, 1955; m. LaVora Rose Ing, May 18, 1942; 1 son, Paul David. Ordained to ministry So. Bapt. Conv., 1947; minister chs. in Ky., Tex., Ill. and Ind., 1947-70; missionary, 1967—; pres. State Conv. Bapts. in Ind., 1965-66, chmn. camp planning com., 1964-71; dir. associational ministries, 1967—; mem. fgn. mission bd. So. Bapt. Conv., 1965-71, also mem. coms. missionary personnel, missionary edn. and promotion and com. on Europe and Middle East. Mem. Christian Business Men's Com. U.S. Address: 1129 Wood Ln Terre Haute IN 47802

CLARK, WILLIAM HAWLEY, bishop, Episcopal Ch.; b. Escanaba, Mich., May 10, 1919; s. William James and Katherine Elsie (Hawley) C.; B.A., U. Mich., 1942; postgrad. Chgo. Theol. Sem., 1942-44; B.D., Episc. Theol. Sem., 1945; S.T.M., Yale U., 1952; postgrad. St. Augustine Coll., Eng., 1960-61; m. Rosemary Ellen Lehman, June 12, 1943; 3 children. Ordained deacon, 1945, priest, 1946; asst. rector St. Paul's Ch., Flint, Mich. and vicar Trinity Ch., Flushing, Mich., 1945-49; priest-in-charge St. Peter's Ch., Monroe, Conn., 1949-51; rector Trinity Ch., Concord, Mass., 1951-62; asso. sec. World Council Chs., Geneva, 1962-65; rector St. Andrew's Ch., Wellesley, Mass., 1965; now bishop Diocese of Del., Wilmington. Tutor, Episc. Theol. Sem., 1953-54; pres. Mass. Clerical Assn., 1953-54; chmn. refugee resettlement com. Episc. Ch., 1954-56, com. on ecumenical relations, 1956-60, 67—, mem. exec. council, 1958-60; exchange preacher Brit. Council Chs., 1969. Office: 2020 Tatnall St Wilmington DE 19802*

CLARKE, ALBERT EMANUEL, minister, United Meth. Ch.; b. Alston, Ga., Feb. 15, 1936; s. Andrew Thomas and Katie (McLain) C.; A.B., Emory U., 1957; B.D., 1960; m. Elizabeth Anne Stuckey, June 21, 1960; 1 son, Alan Stuckey. Ordained to ministry, 1958; pastor Vidette Circuit, S. Ga. Conf., 1958-60; conf. dir. youth work S. Ga. Conf., 1960-64; minister Bass Meth. Ch., Macon, Ga., 1964-66; asso. minister St. Mark Meth. Ch., Atlanta, 1966-67, Peachtree Rd. United Meth. Ch., Atlanta, 1967—. Mem. Christian Council Met. Atlanta, 1976; chaplain troop Boy Scouts Am., 1970-76, dist. chaplain N. Atlanta Dist., 1976; chaplain Lenox Square Civitan Club, 1968-76, pres., 1975-76, chaplain Ga. dist. North, 1976-77. Pres., Heritage Ga. Corp., 1975-77. Recipient Operation Search award Civitan Club, 1975, Bicentennial award Boy Scouts Am., 1976. Life mem. Ga. Dist. N. Civitan Found. Home: 95 Pine Lake Dr NW Atlanta GA 30327 Office: 3180 Peachtree Rd NE Atlanta GA 30305

CLARKE, CAROLYN CARPENTER, minister, American Baptist Churches in the U.S.A.; b. Attleboro, Mass., Apr. 9, 1937; d. Lloyd Wesley and Elsie Marvis (Hager) Carpenter; m. James Davis Clarke, July 13, 1963; children: Sabra, Benjamin, Heather. B.S., Ursinus Coll., 1959; cert. in occupational therapy U. Pa., 1961; M.Div., Andover Newton Theol. Sch., 1985. Ordained to ministry American Baptist Churches in the U.S.A., 1985. Asst. pastor Am. Baptist Chs. of Strafford, N.H., 1981-83; pastor 2d Bapt. Ch., Strafford, 1983—; sec. Am. Bapt. Charismatic Fellowship N.H., 1984—; sec. bd. dirs. United Campus Ministry, U. N.H., 1984—. Mem. Ministers Council Am. Bapt. Chs. U.S.A., Dover Women's Aglow Fellowship. Home: Route 126 H C 71 Box 29 Center Strafford NH 03815-9705

CLARKE, E. KENT, bishop, Anglican Church of Canada; b. Ranking, Ont., Can., Jan. 21, 1932; s. J. Roy and Margaret G. (Brown) C.; m. Norma L. Griffith, July 25, 1964; children: John, Susan, Myles. B.A., Bishop's U., Lennoxville, Que., Can., 1954, L.S.T., 1956; M.R.E., Union Theol. Sem., 1960; D.D. (hon.), Huron Coll., London, Ont., 1977. Ordained to ministry Anglican Church of Canada. Curate All Saint's Westboro, Ottawa, Ont., 1956-59; dir. Christian edn. Diocese of Ottawa, 1960-66; rector St. Barnabas Parish, St. Lambert, Que., Can., 1966-73; archdeacon of Niagara, Hamilton, Ont., 1973-76, suffragan bishop of Niagara, 1976-79; bishop of Edmonton, Alta., Can., 1979—. Office: Diocese of Edmonton 10033 84th Ave Edmonton AB T6E 2G6 Canada

CLARKE, J. RICHARD, Presiding bishop The Church of Jesus Christ of Latter-day Saints, Salt Lake City. Office: The Ch of Jesus Christ of Latter-day Saints 50 E N Temple St Salt Lake City UT 84150*

CLARKE, WILLIAM DARRELL, minister, So. Bapt. Conv.; b. Henderson County, Tenn., Oct. 11, 1947; s. William Andrew and Mattie Elizabeth (Smith) C.; B.A., Union U., 1969; M.Div., Midwestern Bapt. Theol. Sem., 1974; m. Susan Diane Long, Aug. 18, 1968. Ordained to ministry, 1968; pastor Northern's Chapel Bapt. Ch., Rutherford, Tenn., 1968, Three Way Bapt. Ch., Bells, Tenn., 1969-72, Eureka Valley Bapt. Ch., St. Joseph, Mo., 1972-74, Mt. Tirzah Bapt. Ch., Newbern, Tenn., 1972—. Vol. dir. Bapt. Student Union, Dyersburg State Community Coll., 1972. Home and Office: Rt 1 Newbern TN 38059

CLARKE, WILLIAM FRANCIS, minister, United Church of Canada; b. Hall's Bridge, Ont., Can., May 24, 1918; s. Francis John and Susan (Weir) C.; m. Ruth Lee Ballard, Sept. 1, 1944; children: Ruth Lynne (Mrs. Larry Alfred Bredesen), Donald Ballard. Tchr.'s cert. Sask. Tchr's. Coll., 1937; B.A., U. Sask., 1942; diploma in theology St. Andrews Theol. Coll., 1943, B.D., 1945, D.D., 1967; M.A., Columbia U. and Union Theol. Sem., N.Y.C., 1948, Ed.D., 1949. Ordained to ministry United Ch. of Can., 1943. Minister Climax (Sask., Can.) United Ch., 1943-44; field sec. Christian edn. Sask., 1944-47; supr. field work Union Theol. Sem., N.Y.C., 1947-48, field staff asst., 1948-49; survey asst. N.Y.C. Mission Soc., N.Y.C., 1948; ministerial cons. N.Y. State League Planned Parenthood, N.Y.C., 1948-49; minister Trinity United Ch., Portage la Prairie, Man., Can., 1949-52; prin., founder Prairie Christian Tng. Centre for Lay Leadership, United Ch. of Can., Ft. Qu'Appelle, Sask., 1952-59; minister Zion United Ch., Moose Jaw, Sask., 1959-64; field sec. Christian edn. Alta. Conf. United Ch. Can., Edmonton, 1964-69; missionary, asso. prof. Christian edn., head dept. pastoralia and Christian edn. United Theol. Coll., Bangalore, India, 1969-72; minister St. Giles United Ch., Vancouver, B.C., Can., 1972-76; Grace-Westminster United Ch., Saskatoon, Sask., 1976—. Pres., Sask. Conf. United Ch. of Can., 1961-62; presbyter Ch. S. India at St. Marks' Cathedral, Bangalore, 1969-72; lectr. Indian Social Inst., Bangalore, 1969-72, Roman Cath. Nat. Centre for Continuing Edn., India, 1969-72; prof. India Nat. YMCA Tng. Coll., Bangalore, 1970-72; staff trainer Deena Seva Sangh Hindu Secondary Sch., Bangalore, 1971-72. Bd. dirs. Sask. Centre for Community Studies, 1958-60. Mem. Sask. Assn. Adult Edn. (chmn. study com. Continuing Edn. Centre 1962-64), World Council Christian Edn. (sec. leadership devel. sem., Nishinomiya, Japan 1958, conf. group coordinator study groups Nairobi, Kenya 1967). Author: The Clue To The Mystery, 1965. Home: 2504 Underwood Ave Saskatoon S7J 0W3 Canada Office: 505 10th St E Saskatoon SK S7N 0E3 Canada

CLARY, GEORGE ESMOND, JR., minister, United Methodist Ch.; b. Chatham County, Ga., Sept. 25, 1917; s. George Esmond and Ruby (Mottweiler) C.; A.B., Emory U., 1940; S.T.B., Boston U., 1942; M.Ed., U. Ga., 1962, Ed.D., 1965; m. Sarah Miller, June 18, 1943; children—George Esmond III, Lucy Dian, William Edwin. Ordained to ministry, 1942; student missionary, Cuba, 1941; pastor United Meth. Chs., Ga., 1942-62; faculty Paine Coll., Augusta, Ga., 1962-83; supply pastor East Macon Circuit, United Meth. Ch., Franklin, N.C., 1983—. Mem. Am. Hist. Assn., So. Hist. Assn. Author: Our Methodist Heritage in South Georgia, 1960; The Founding of Paine College, 1965; The Beginnings of the South Georgia Methodist Conference, 1967. Home and Office: 80 Clark's Chapel Rd Franklin NC 28734

CLARY, WILLIAM VICTOR, minister, United Church of Christ; b. Baraboo, Wis., May 27, 1946; s. Harry Theone and Ruth Margaret (Harris) C.; m. F. Marie Bush, Aug. 12, 1966; children: Donna, Vicki, William. A.A., Mich. Christian Coll., 1966; B.S., Okla. Christian Coll., 1968; postgrad. Abilene Christian U., 1972, No. Ill. U., 1973. Ordained to ministry United Church of Christ, 1966. Minister, Church of Christ, Clinton, Ill., 1974-78, Church of Christ, Lincoln, Ill., 1978-84, Church of Christ, Anchorage, Alaska, 1984—; v.p. Ill. Christian Camp, Decatur, 1978-84, camp dir., 1976-84; dir. Ill. Ch. of Christ Exhibit, Springfield, 1977-84; chaplain Abraham Lincoln Hosp., Lincoln, 1978-84, Logan County Jail, Lincoln, 1983-84. Contbr. articles to profl. publs. Recipient award Coe Found., 1972. Republican. Avocations: reading; athletics; fishing; photography; traveling. Home: 1031 W 73d Ave Anchorage AK 99502 Office: Church of Christ 7800 Stanley St Box 4-1735 Anchorage AK 99509

CLAY, HENRY CARROL, JR., church district administrator, clergyman; b. Yazoo City, Miss., June 8, 1928; s. Henry Carrol and Clara (Washington) C.; m. Effie Jean Husbands, Dec. 24, 1955; 1 child, Henry Carroll. B.A., Rust Coll., Holly Springs, Miss., 1952; M.Div., Gammon Theol. Sem., Atlanta, 1956; D.Div. (hon.), Rust Coll., 1969. Ordained deacon United Methodist Ch., 1954, elder, 1956. Pastor, St. Mark United Meth. Ch., Gulfport, Miss., 1956-61, St. Paul's United Meth. Ch., Laurel, Miss., 1961-67; dist. supt. Jackson Dist. United Methodist Ch., Jackson, Miss., 1967-73, dist. supt. East Jackson Dist., 1980—; assoc. dir. Miss. Conf. Council on Ministries, Jackson, 1973-78; pastor Central United Methodist Ch., Jackson, 1978-80; del. World Meth. Conf., Denver and Dublin, Ireland, 1971-76; del. Gen. Conf. United Methodist Ch., 1976-84; dir. Gen. Bd. Ch. & Soc., 1980—; mem. Clin. Pastoral Edn. Adv. Com., Jackson. Contbr. articles to profl. jour. Mem. Mississippians for Ednl. TV., Jackson; bd. dirs. Goodwill Industries, Jackson, 1980; trustee Rust Coll., 1964-79, chmn. 1971-77. Mem. Miss. Religious Leadership Conf. (chmn. 1975-76, Outstanding Churchman award 1975), NAACP, Omega Psi (Citizen of Yr. 1960). Democrat. Office: East Jackson Dist United Methodist Ch PO Box 303 Jackson MS 39205

CLAY, JOEL ROY, minister, United Methodist Church; b. Miami, Okla., Mar. 30, 1952; s. J.T. and Ruth Janice (Hulsman) C.; m. Peggy Lee Brown, May 31, 1974; 1 child, Shawn Christopher. B.A. in Religion, U. Tulsa, 1975; Th.M., Perkins Sch. Theology, 1978. Ordained United Meth. Ch. as deacon, 1976, elder, 1979. Asst. to pastor Trinity United Meth. Ch., Tulsa, 1971-75; youth dir. Ridgewood Park United Meth. Ch., Dallas, 1975-76, dir. family ctr., 1976-77; intern pastor Linwood United Meth. Ch., Oklahoma City, 1977-78; youth minister Boston Ave. United Meth. Ch., Tulsa, 1978-80; minister Grace United Meth. Ch., Lawton, Okla., 1980-84, First United Meth. Ch., Choctaw, Okla., 1984—. Cert. facilitator Human Sexuality Program, United Meth. Ch. Okla., 1981—; adult co-chmn. Conf. Council on Youth Ministries, Okla. Ann. Conf., 1979-81; adult mem. project rev. com. Nat. Youth Ministry Orgn., Gen. Conf. United Meth. Ch., 1981-83; adult sponsor youth service fund CCYM Okla. Ann. Conf., 1983—, dist. youth coordinator Tulsa Dist., 1978-80, Lawton Dist., 1981-83. Chmn. Rape Crises Coalition, Comanche County, Okla., 1982-84; chmn. Rape Crises Vols. Comanche County, 1982-84; chaplain Choctaw Police Dept., 1984—; del. county, state Democratic Party, 1983. Mem. Christian Educators Fellowship, Nat. Christian Educators Fellowship. Democrat. Lodges: Kiwanis (Lawton, Okla. and Choctaw). Avocations: model building; flying; racquetball; computers. Office: First United Meth Ch PO Box 100 Choctaw OK 73020

CLEGG, ALBERT LAWRENCE, minister, Southern Baptist Convention; b. Crystal Springs, Miss., Feb. 16, 1931; s. Cecil Grey and Winnie (Gardner) C.; A.A., Jones County Jr. Coll., 1951; B.A., Miss. Coll., 1953; B.D., New Orleans Bapt. Theol. Sem., 1956, Th.D., 1958; m. Dorothy Ann Beckman, Feb. 11, 1956; children—Lauranne, Lawrence, Ronald, David. Ordained to ministry, 1953; pastor Coyt Bapt. Ch., Waynesboro, Miss., 1955-57, Silver Creek Bapt. Ch., McComb, Miss., 1957-59, First Bapt. Ch., Greensburg, La., 1959-61, First Bapt. Ch., Ponchatoula, La., 1961-80; dir. Associational Missions for S.E. La., La. Bapt. Conv., 1980—. Vice pres. La. Bapt. Conv., 1974-75, chmn. missions com., 1968-72, mem. exec. bd., 1966-72; pres. Dist. 11 Bapt. Conv., 1963-65; pres. Dist. Bapt. Pastor's Conf., 1961-63, 66-68. Bd. dirs. Tangipahoa Home Health Agy., 1969—. Mm. Ponchatoula C. of C. Home: 221 S 2d St Ponchatoula LA 70454 Office: 501 W Dakota Hammond LA 70401

CLEMENS, DAVID ALLEN, minister, Independent Baptist Church; b. Camden, N.J., Aug. 8, 1941; s. Arleigh Allen and Mae Elizabeth (Browne) C.; m. Janice Ruth Bonino, Feb. 13, 1965; children: Stephen David, Daniel Lee. B.A. magna cum laude, Houghton Coll., 1963; M.A., Nat. Christian U., 1972; Th.D., Clarksville Sch. Theology, 1980. Ordained to ministry Ind. Bapt. Ch., 1963. Missionary Pocket Testament League in Argentina, Paraguay, Brazil, S. Am., 1963-66; minister Richfield (Pa.) Mennonite Ch., 1966-67; itinerant Bible tch. Bible Club Movement Inc., Upper Darby, Pa., 1968-71, nat. rep., 1971-77, dir. family adult ministries dept., 1977-80; minister-at-large, 1980—; preaching/teaching tours Eng., Holland, Belgium, Sweden, Spain, Can., Middle East. Mem. Nat. Home Missions Fellowship. Author: Steps to Maturity, Vols. I-III, 1973-79. Home: 72 Knox Blvd Marlton NJ 08053 Office: 237 Fairfield Ave Upper Darby PA 19082

CLEMENT, (JERMAN KAPALIN), vicar bishop Russian Orthodox Church in the U.S.A.; bishop of Serpukhov, 1982. Office: St Nicholas Patriarchal Cathedral 15 E 97th St New York NY 10029*

CLEMENTS, L(EWIS) FREDERICK, lay worker, Southern Baptist Convention; b. Petersburg, Va., Oct. 29, 1938; s. Leroy Franklin and Nellie Rachael (Wrenn) C.; B. Mus. Edn., Richmond Profl. Inst., 1960; Mus.M., Va. Commonwealth U., 1970; m. Shirley Ann Beasley, Aug. 23, 1960; children—Freddy, David. Choir dir., organist Broad St. Meth. Ch., Richmond, Va., 1960-61; minister of music Chamberlayne Bapt. Ch., Richmond, 1962-65, Colonial Heights (Va.) Bapt. Ch., 1966-69, 1st Bapt. Ch., Petersburg, Va., 1970-74; youth choir dir., organist Washington St. United Meth. Ch., Petersburg, 1974-84; dir. music, organist Washington Street United Meth. Ch., 1984—. Tchr. music Colonial Heights Pub. Schs., 1974—; mem., accompanist Va. Bapt. Male Chorale, 1963-73. Mem. Nat., Colonial Heights (treas. 1976—) edn. assns., Asso. Friends Marcel Dupre's Artistry, Music Educators Nat. Conf., Nat. String Orch. Assn., Va. Band and Orch. Dirs. Assn., Am. Guild Organists. Composer ch. anthems. Home: 1846 Fairfax Petersburg VA 23805

CLENDANIEL, DONALD OTIS, minister, United Meth. Ch.; b. Milton, Del., Apr. 21, 1924; s. Henry David and Eliza (Webb) C.; B.A., U. Del., 1950; B.S.T., Temple U., 1953, M.Div., 1973; D.Min., Drew U., 1975; m. Helen Dickerson, Sept. 26, 1946; children—Donald Otis, Karin Sue. Ordained to ministry, 1951; pastor United Meth. Ch., Church Hill, Md., 1951-55, Federalsburg, Md., 1956-63, Calvary Ch., Milford, Del., 1964-71, Atonement Ch., Claymont, Del., 1972; grand chaplain Del. Grand Lodge Masons, Wilmington, 1975—; mem. Peninsula Conf. Worship Commn., 1960-64, dist. program council, 1966-71; chaplain Del. Senate, 1965-71, Md. Senate, 1962-63, Boy Scout Troop 116, Milford, 1965-71; assisting chaplain Sussex County Correctional Instn.; contbg. chaplain City Council of Milford, 1965-71; chaplain Claymont Lions Club, 1972-74; sec. Peninsula Conf. Bd. Pensions, United Meth. Ch., 1972—. Pres., Milford Area Ministerium Assn., 1970-71; chmn. ch. and community dept., mem. exec. bd. Del. Council Chs., 1965-71; pres. N.E. Ecumenical Parish of Greater Wilmington, 1973-74; mem. Wilmington Dist. Ch. Location Bd., 1972—. Adviser-counsellor Sussex County Mental Hygiene Clinic, Del. Dept. Mental Health, 1964-71; mem. exec. com. Claymont Community Council, 1972—; mem. Ofcl. Del. Am. Revolution Bicentennial Planning Commn., 1975—. Mem. Del.-Md. Sch. Theology Alumni Temple U. (chmn.). Author: God's Greatest Gamble, 19S9. Home: 44 Seminole Ave Claymont DE 19703 Office: 3519 Philadelphia Pike Claymont DE 19703

CLINTON, STEPHEN MICHAEL, educator, minister, Evang. Free Ch. Am.; b. Wichita, Kans., Aug. 21, 1944; s. Thomas Francis and Bettie Lee (Harrison) C.; B.A. in Social Sci., Trinity Coll., 1967; M.A. cum laude, Trinity Evang. Div. Sch., 1969, M.Div. cum laude, 1970; Ph.D. in Systematic Theology, Calif. Grad. Sch. Theology, 1979; m. Virginia Ann Schoonover, Aug. 30, 1964; children—Matthew Walter, Michael Alan, Shanna Michele. Ordained to ministry Evang. Free Ch. Am., 1973; asst. to dean Trinity Evang. Div. Sch., Deerfield, Ill., 1967-69; instr. Bible, philosophy Tabor Coll., Hillsboro, Kans., 1969-71; instr. theology Friends U., 1973-74; campus dir. Campus Crusade for Christ, Wichita, Kans., 1971-74; acad. dir. Inst. Bibl. Studies, Arrowhead Springs, San Bernardino, Calif., 1974-80; dir. bibl. tng. Campus Crusade for Christ, 1974-80; assoc. prof. theology Internat. Sch. Theology, 1978—; asst. pastor Highlander Evang. Free Ch. Mem. Evang. Theol. Soc., Soc. Christian Philosophy, Calif. Assn. for the Gifted. Address: Arrowhead Springs San Bernardino CA 92414

CLOSTERHOUSE, WILBUR RAYNOR, minister, United Presbyn. Ch. U.S.A.; b. Jenison, Mich., June 28, 1914; s. John and Bessie Maud (Cheyne) C.; A.B., Calvin Coll., 1938; Th.B., Princeton Theol. Sem., 1941; Th.M., Butler U., 1958; D.D., Hanover Coll., 1960; postgrad. U. Mich., 1972—; m. Fannie Mae Reid, June 17, 1941; children—Carole Ann, Joyce Ellen, Marcia Lynn. Ordained to ministry, 1941; pastor Union Presbyn. Ch., North Kingsville, Ohio, 1941-43, Blvd. Presbyn. Ch., Cleve., 1943-49, Northminster Presbyn. Ch., Indpls., 1949-62, Calvin W. Presbyn. Ch., Detroit, 1962-64; organizing pastor new ch. devel. Presbytery Chgo., 1964-66; asso. pastor Worthington (Ohio) Presbyn. Ch., 1966-67; pastor First Presbyn. Ch., Spring Lake, Mich., 1967—. Pres., Tri-Cities Counseling Services, 1974—; lectr. philosophy Muskegon Community Coll., 1971-73. Lyndon Baines Johnson Found. study grantee, 1976. Mem. Am. Soc. Ch. History, Phi Kappa Phi, Theta Phi. Home: 16045 Harbor Point Dr Spring Lake MI 49456 Office: 760 E Savidge St Spring Lake MI 49456

CLOTHEY, FREDERICK WILSON, educator, Advent Christian Ch.; b. Madras, South India, Feb. 29, 1936; s. Frederick Bateman and Vesta Averill (Wilson) C. (parents Am. citizens); B.A., B.Th., Aurora Coll., 1957; B.D., Evang. Theol. Sem., Naperville, Ill., 1959; M.A., U. Chgo., 1965, Ph.D., 1968; m. Ann Irene Forbes, June 30, 1962; children: Phillip Warren, Rebecca Anneli, Frederick Michael, Sharmali Jean, Fathima. Ordained to ministry Advent Christian Ch., 1959; dir. youth work Advent Christian Gen. Conf., 1959-62; asst. prof. history of religions Boston U., 1967-74; asst. prof. religious studies U. Pitts., 1975-78, assoc. prof., 1978-84, prof., 1984—, chmn. dept., 1978—; chmn. Conf. South Indian Religion, 1970-71; resident coordinator GLCA Year in India Program, 1971-72. Nat. Def. Edn. Act fellow, 1963-66; Am. Inst. Indian Studies fellow, 1966-67, 71-72, 81; Fulbright-Hays fellow, 1978, 82; Mem. Am. Acad. Religion, Assn. Asian Studies, Soc. South Indian Studies, Conf. Religion in South India. Author: The Many Faces of Murukan: the History and Meaning of a South Indian God, 1978; Rhythm and Intent: Ritual Studies from South India; Quiescence and Passim: The Vision of Arunakiri, 1985. Co-editor: Experiencing Síva: Encounters With a Hindu Deity, 1983; dir., producer film series on festival experience in South India. Office: Dept Religious Studies U Pitts Pittsburgh PA 15260

CLOWER, JERRY ANDREW, minister, So. Baptist Conv.; b. Lamesa, Tex., Aug. 9, 1941; s. George Everett and Mary Rachel (Geddie) C.; A.B., Howard Payne U., 1963; M.Th., New Orleans Baptist Theol. Sem., 1969; m. Barbara Frances Hooker, Aug. 28, 1965; children—Jeri Ann, Todd Everett. Ordained to ministry, 1965; pastor Richard Spur Baptist Ch., Elgin, Okla., 196S-66, First Baptist Ch., Gilchrist, Tex., 1967-68, Mt. Hermon (La.) Baptist Ch., 1969-72, First Baptist Ch., Forks, Wash., 1972-73, First Baptist Ch., Wayne, Okla., 1973—. State cons. on ch. renewal Baptist Gen. Conv. Okla. Chaplain Mt. Hermon Ruritan Club, 1970-73. Home and office: Box 117 Wayne OK 73095

CLUTTS, CURTISS RAY, lay ch. worker, So. Bapt. Conv.; b. Murphysboro, Ill., Sept. 24, 1947; s. Raymond Cluster and Geneva (Qualls) C.; certificate bookkeeping Office Tng. Sch., Cape Girardeau, Mo., 1967. Minister youth, librarian, dir. ch. tng. dir., dir. Bible Sch., dir. dept. youth, trustee 1st Bapt. Ch., Grand Tower, Ill., 1970—. Asst. grade sch. basketball coach and baseball coach, Grand Tower, 1976—; tour guide Historic Huthmacher House, Grand Tower, 1972—; custodian Meredith Funeral Parlor, Grand Tower, 1975—. Mem. Nat. Hist. Soc., Jackson County Hist. Soc., Huthmacher House Assn. Home: PO Box 203 Main St Grand Tower IL 62942

COATES, FREDERICK ALVIN HERBERT, minister, Presbyterian Church in the U.S.A.; b. Kingston, Ont., Can., Oct. 1, 1950; came to U.S., 1956, naturalized, 1965; s. Herbert Wright Coates and Kathleen Freda (Wheeler) Coates Bates; m. Jean Barton Caldwell, Apr. 15, 1973; children: Andrew Ian, Ashley Elaine. B.S. in Bus. Adminstrn. U. N.C., 1972; D.Min., Union Theol. Sem., 1979. Ordained to ministry Presbyn. Ch. in the U.S.A., 1979. Assoc. pastor First Presbyn. Ch., Mooresville, N.C., 1979—, media intern, 1977-79; dir. Alzheimer's Support Services, Charlotte, N.C., 1984—. Mem. adv. bd. Community Schs., Mooresville, 1984; bd. dirs. Mooresville Spl. Olympics, 1982-83. Mem. Mooresville Area Ministers Assn. Lodges: Civitan, Masons. Home: 363 W McLelland Ave Mooresville NC 28115 Office: First Presbyn Ch 249 W McLelland Ave Mooresville NC 28115

COATIE, CHARLES EVERETT, minister, Ch. of God in Christ; b. Mound City, Ill., Apr. 14, 1929; s. Dixon C. and Hazel Vivian (Henry) C.; student Ind. Bus. Coll., 1954-56; m. Ann Barbara Dennis, Aug. 25, 1953; children—Shenetia Gail, Sheila Ann, Charlotte, Beth Ann. Ordained to ministry, 1964; pastor Mt. Calvary Ch. of God in Christ, Muncie, Ind., 1973—, Faith Ch. of God in Christ, Richmond, Ind., 1961—; dist. supt. No. Ind.; dist. pres. Young People's Willing Workers. Vice pres. Charisma Ch. of God Cosmetic Plant. Active, Longfellow Sch. PTA. Recipient awards Salvation Army, 1975, Heart Fund, 1976. Hon. All Am. Airborn. Mem. Delaware County Evangelistic Assn., Fraternal Order Police, Vis. Nurse Assn. Home: 1800 Carver Dr Muncie IN 47303 Office: 1525 E Butler St Muncie IN 47303

COBB, JOHN BOSWELL, JR., theology educator, minister, United Methodist Church. b. Kobe, Japan, Feb. 9, 1925; s. John Boswell and Theodora Cook (Atkinson) C.; m. Jean Olmstead Loftin, June 18, 1947; children: Theodore, Clifford, Andrew, Richard. Student Emory U.-Oxford, 1941-43, U. Mich., 1943; M.A., U. Chgo., 1949, Ph.D., 1952; Th.D. (hon.), U. Mainz, 1968; D.Litt. (hon.), Emory U., 1971; D.D. (hon.), Linfield Coll., 1983. Ordained to ministry United Meth. Ch., 1950. Pastor, Towns County Circuit, Ga., 1950-51; instr. Young Harris Coll., Ga., 1950-53; asst. prof. Emory U., Atlanta, 1953-58; prof. theology Sch. Theology, Claremont, Calif., 1958—; mem. Commn. on Doctrine and Doctrinal Standards, United Meth. Ch., also mem. Commn. on Mission; pub. Process Studies jour., 1970—. Author: Living Options in Protestant Theology, 1962; A Christian Natural Theology, 1965; The Structure of Christian Existence, 1968; Christ in a Puralistic Age, 1975; Beyond Diologue, 1982. Contbr. numerous articles to profl. jours. Served to capt. U.S. Army, 1943-46. Recipient Disting. Alumnus award U. Chgo., 1976; Woodrow Wilson Ctr. fellow, 1976. Mem. Ctr. for Process Studies (dir. 1973—). Democrat. (714) 626-2686

COBURN, CHARLES GRAHAM, III, minister, Southern Baptist Convention; b. Mobile, Ala., Feb. 26, 1951; s. Charles Graham and Lydia (McAuley) C.; m. Angie Elizabeth Canady, July 23, 1977; 1 child, Shelby Canady. B.S. in Music Edn., Mobile Coll., 1984. Ordained to ministry Baptist Ch., 1972. Asst. bus. minister Dauphin Way Bapt. Ch., Mobile, 1970-72; minister music and youth Berean Bapt. Ch, Mobile, 1972-75, First Bapt. Ch., Grand Bay, Ala., 1975-77, Airport Blvd. Bapt. Ch., Mobile, 1977, Daphne Bapt. Ch., Ala., 1977-84, First Bapt. Ch., Houma, La., 1984—; assoc. music dir. Baldwin Bapt. Assn., Baldwin County, Ala., 1981-83. Chaplain, Fellowship of Christian Athletes, Fairhope, Ala., 1982-84; active Community Patriotic Festival, Daphne, 1983. Recipient Golden Flop award for best leader Centrifuge Camp, Mobile, 1984. Office: First Bapt Ch 901 W Main St Houma LA 70360

COBURN, HAROLD MONROE, minister, So. Bapt. Conv.; b. Shreveport, La., July 17, 1946; s. Harold M. and Ruby Helen (Burkhalter) C.; B.A. in Sociology, NE La. State U., 1969; M.R.E., New Orleans Bapt. Theol. Sem., 1975; m. Mary Ann Timon, July 23, 1966; children—Scott Erik, Marci Mikel. Ordained to ministry, 1967; pastor chs., La., 1966-70; tchr. Bossier Parish (La.) Schs., 1969-70; social worker La. Welfare Dept., Bossier Parish, 1969-70; juvenile probation officer, La. Dept. Welfare, Shreveport and Monroe, 1971-73; pastor New Henley Field Bapt. Ch., Carriere, Miss., 1973-75; asso. pastor, youth and edn., 1st Bapt. Ch., Belle Chasse, La., 1975-76; asso. pastor edn. adminstrn. Ridge Ave Bapt. Ch., W. Monroe, La., 1976—. Bd. dirs. New Bethany Home for Girls, Arcadia, La.; mem. human relations council Ouachita Parish,(La.), 1971-73, Pub. Housing Coalition Shreveport (La.). Home: 65 Pine Grove Circle West Monroe LA 71291 Office: 1009 Ridge Ave West Monroe LA 71291

COBURN, JOHN BOWEN, priest, ch. ofcl., Episcopal Ch.; b. Danbury, Conn., Sept. 27, 1914; s. Aaron Cutler and Eugenia Bowen (Woolfolk) C.; A.B., Princeton, 1936, D.D., 1960; B.D., Union Theol. Sem., 1942; D.D., Amherst Coll., 1955, Huron Coll., 1964, Harvard, 1964, Middlebury Coll., 1970, Bucknell U., 1971; S.T.D., Berkeley Div. Sch., 1958, Hobart and William Smith Coll., 1967, Gen. Theol. Sem., 1968; D.C.L., Kenyon Coll., 1968, Episcopal Theol. Sch., Trinity Coll., Williams Coll.; m. Ruth Alvord Barnum, May 26, 1941; children—Thomas Bowen, Judy C. (Mrs. James H. Klein), Michael Cutler, Sarah E. (Mrs. Steven E. Borgeson). Ordained priest Episcopal Ch., 1943; instr., Robert Coll., Istanbul, Turkey, 1936-39; asst. Grace Ch., N.Y.C., 1942-44; chaplain USNR, 1944-45; rector Grace Ch., Amherst, Mass., 1946-53; chaplain Amherst Coll., 1946-53; dean Trinity Cathedral, Newark, 1953-57; dean Episcopal Theol. Sem., Cambridge Mass., 1957-69; tchr. Urban League Street Acad., N.Y.C., 1968-69; rector St. James Ch., N.Y.C., 1969-75; bishop Diocese of Mass., Boston, 1976—; dir. Corning Glass Works. Pres. House of Deps., Gen. Convs. of Episcopal Ch., 1967-70, 70-73, 73-76. Trustee Princeton, Wooster Sch., Union Theol. Sem. Mem. Century Assn. Author: Prayer and Personal Religion, 1957; Minister: Man in the Middle, 1963; Anne and the Sand Dobbies, 1964; Twentieth Century Spiritual Letters, 1967; (with Norman Pittinger) Viewpoints, 1959; A Life to Live-A Way to Pray, 1973; A Diary of Prayers, 1975; The Hope of Glory, 1976; Feeding Fire, 1980; Christ's Life: Our Life, 1978. Office: 1 Joy St Boston MA 02108

COCCO, ANTOINETTE MARIE, religion educator, administrator, nun, Roman Catholic Church. B. Phila., Apr. 5, 1929; d. Pasquale and Mary (Farrell) C. B.Mus., Manhattanville Coll., 1961; B.A., Villanova U., 1963; M.Mus., Cath. U. Am., 1971; M.A., St. Charles Sem., 1978. Joined Sisters of Mercy, Roman Catholic Ch., 1946. Assoc. prof. religious studies Gwynedd-Mercy Coll., Gwynedd Valley, Pa., 1975—, profl. lectr., 1975—; adminstr. Phila. Inst. of Ministerial Music, 1981—; liturgist, musician St. Charles Sem., Overbrook, Pa., summer 1982; cantor Phila. Cathedral; profl. singer. Author article in field. Recipient service citation, plaque, Eucharistic Congress, Phila., 1976; named hon. mem. Chapel of Four Chaplains, 1981. Home: Gwynedd-Mercy Coll Gwynedd Valley PA 19437

COCKERILL, GARETH LEE, religion educator, Wesleyan Church; b. Arlington, Va., July 13, 1944; s. Welby Lee and Daisy Virginia (Mateer) C.; m. Rosa Bishop, Aug. 15, 1969; children: Allene Rose, Ginny Dora, Kathy Lee. B.A., summa cum laude, Central Wesleyan Coll., 1966; M.Div., Asbury Theol. Sem., 1969; Th.M., Union Theol. Sem., Va., 1973, Ph.D., 1976. Ordained to ministry Wesleyan Ch., 1969. Missionary, Wesleyan Ch., Sierra Leone, West Africa, 1969-72, 76-79; asst. prof. Wesley Bibl. Sem., Jackson, Miss., 1979-81, mission coordinator, Sierra Leone, 1981-84; prof. Wesley Bibl. Sem., Jackson, 1984—; hon. del. Gen. Conf. Wesleyan Ch., Columbus, Ohio, 1984. Mem. Soc. Bibl. Lit., Evang. Theol. Soc., Inst. Bibl. Research, Theta Phi. Office: Wesley Biblical Sem PO Box 9938 Jackson MS 39206

COCORIS, GEORGE MICHAEL, minister; b. Pensacola, Fla., Sept. 22, 1939; s. George Theodore and Laura Belle (Rutherford) C.; m. Judith Iola Eaves, June 2, 1962; children: James Michael, Careth Ruth, Christine Hope. B.A., Tenn. Temple U., 1962; Th.M., Dallas Theol. Sem., 1966; D.D. (hon.), Biola U., 1984. Ordained to ministry, Southern Baptist Convention, 1963. Pastor 1st Bapt. Ch., Pattonville, Tex., 1963-66; evangelist, Chattanooga, 1966-74; staff evangelist, v.p. EvanTell, Dallas, 1974-79, also dir. to present; sr. pastor Ch. of the Open Door, Glendora, Calif., 1979—; adj. prof. Dallas Sem., 1974-79; bd. dirs. S.O.S., Irvine, Calif., 1979—; speaker The Open Door radio, Los Angeles, 1979—; founder, tchr. Torrey Bible Inst., Los Angeles, 1982—. Author: Evangelism: A Biblical Approach, 1984; (booklet) Lordship Salvation, Is it Biblical?, 1983. Contbr. articles to profl. jours. Arbitrator Better Bus. Bur., 1984. Home: 1162 Paloma Dr Arcadia CA 91006 Office: Church of the Open Door 701 W Sierra Madre Ave Glendora CA 91740

COFFEY, DAVID LEE, minister, So. Bapt. Conv.; b. Birmingham, Ala., Aug. 7, 1945; s. Marion Truett and Mary Frances (Walker) C.; B.S., Jacksonville State U., 1969; M.R.E., Southwestern Bapt. Theol. Sem., 1971; m. Nalda Jean Ragsdale, Aug. 18, 1965; children—David Lee, Daniel Scott. Ordained to ministry, 1976; minister Oakwood Bapt. Ch., Chattanooga, 1971-73, Lakewood Bapt. Ch., Birmingham, 1973-75, Woodlawn Bapt. Ch., Vicksburg, Miss., 1975-77; minister of evangelism 1st Bapt. Ch., Camden, S.C., 1977—. Dir. Sunday schs. Warren County Bapt. Assn., 1975-77; dir. children's camps Birmingham Bapt. Assn., 1973-75. Mem. Miss., Ala. Bapt. religious edn. assns. Home: 1710 Woodside Dr Camden SC 29020 Office: 1201 Broad St Camden SC 29020

COFFEY, JACK FRANKLIN, minister, Southern Baptist Convention; b. Granite Falls, N.C., Nov. 18, 1928; s. Frank Byrum Coffey and Lottie (Lefevers) Coffey Hill; m. Sarah Buie, May 9, 1959; children: Jack F. Jr., Sarah Catherine. Student Mars Hill Coll., 1949-50; B.A., Wake Forest Coll., 1954; postgrad. Duke Div. Sch., 1955; B.D., Southeastern Bapt. Sem., 1958. Ordained to ministry, Southern Baptist Convention, 1954. Pastor, Island Creek Bapt. Ch., Henderson, N.C., 1954-58; assoc. pastor Montgomery Hills Bapt. Ch., Silver Spring, Md., 1958-62; pastor Downtown Bapt. Ch., Alexandria, Va., 1962-67, New Hope Bapt. Ch., Raleigh, N.C., 1967—; bd. ministers Campbell U., Buies Creek, N.C., 1976—, trustee, 1983—; moderator Raleigh Bapt. Assn., 1982—; bd. dirs. Life Enrichment Ctr., Raleigh, 1975—. Democrat. Lodges: Masons, Kiwanis. Home: 3801 Valley Stream Dr Raleigh NC 27604 Office: New Hope Bapt Ch 4301 Louisburg Rd Raleigh NC 27604

COFFIN, ROY RIDDELL, JR., priest, Episcopal Church; b. Bryn Mawr, Pa., Mar. 9, 1932; s. Roy Riddell and Catharine Marie (Pfingst) C.; m. Caroline Compton Clarkson, Mar. 9, 1963; children: Cynthia Parker, Deborah Osborne, John Tristram. B.A., Dartmouth Coll., 1954; M.B.A., U. Mich., 1959; M.Div., Va. Theol. Sem., 1977. Ordained priest Episcopal Ch., 1978. Interim rector Diocese of Washington, 1978—; asst. St. Columbo's Ch., Washington, 1977-78; chaplain St. Patrick's Elem. Day Sch., Washington, 1977-79; mem. steering com. Interim Network, Washington, 1981—. Address: 124 Hesketh St Chevy Chase MD 20815

COFFMAN, EDWARD F(ELAND), JR., minister, Christian Church (Disciples of Christ); b. Russellville, Ky., Jan. 25, 1922; s. Edward F. and Emma M. (Hill) C.; m. Carol Jean Alexander, June 5, 1949; children: Catherine Ann Coffman McCandless, Carol Lee, Constance Sue Coffman Burke. A.B., Vanderbilt U., 1942, B.D., 1944, D.Min., 1972; M.A., N.E. Mo. State Coll., 1968. Ordained, 1944. Pastor 1st Christian Ch., Leitchfield, Ky., 1945-46; dir. religious edn. 1st Christian Ch., Mayfield, Ky., summer 1946; campus minister 1st Christian Ch., Columbia, Mo., 1946-58; pastor, 1st Christian Ch., Kirksville, Mo., 1958-67; sr. minister 1st Christian Ch., Madisonville, Ky., 1967—; bd. dirs. Mo. Sch. of Religion, Columbia, 1958-67; bd. dirs., pres. Christian Ch. in Ky., 1976-82; bd. dirs. Christian Ch. (Disciples of Christ), Indpls., 1980-84, Christian Ch. Homes of Ky., Louisville, 1977—. Pres. Pennyrile Performing Arts Assn., Madisonville, 1976; with Community Band, Madisonville, 1980—; pres. St. Louis Regional Blood Program ARC, 1963-66; dist. chmn. Boy Scouts Am., Kirksville, 1964-66. Mem. Phi Kappa Psi. Republican. Club: Kiwanis (pres. Madisonville 1979-80). Home: 560 Park Ave Madisonville KY 42431 Office: 1st Christian Ch PO Box 672 College Dr at N Main Madisonville KY 42431

COHEN, ARMOND E., rabbi, Conservative Jewish; b. Canton, Ohio, June 5, 1909; m. Samuel and Rebecca (Lipowitz) C.; m. Anne Lederman; children: Rebecca Long, Deborah Long (dec.), Samuel. B.A., NY U, 1931; rabbi, Jewish Theol. Sem. Am., 1934; M. Hebrew Lit., 1945, D.D., 1966; LL.D., Cleve. State U., 1969. Ordained rabbi, 1934. Rabbi, Park Synagogue, Cleve., 1934—; vis. prof. psychiatry Jewish Theol. Sem. Am., N.Y.C., 1970-75; dir. Inst. Religion and Health, N.Y.C. Author: All God's Children, Selected Readings on Zionism, Outline of Jewish History, Readings in Medieval Jewish Literature. Editorial bd. dirs. Jour. Religion and Health, 1943-67. Contbr. articles to profl. jours. Bd. govs. Hebrew U. Jerusalem; trustee Am. Friends of Hebrew U.; bd. dirs. Consumers League Ohio, Cleve., Jewish Community Fed., Cleve., Council World Affairs, Cleve.; hon. v.p. Zionist Organ. Am. Recipient Nat. Humanitarian award NCCJ, 1983. Mem. Rabbinical Assembly Am., Cleve. Bd. Rabbis (founder). Club: Lotos (N.Y.C.). Home: 3273 Euclid Heights Blvd Cleveland Heights OH 44118 Office: The Park Synagogue 3300 Mayfield Rd Cleveland Heights OH 44118

COHEN, GERSON D., rabbi, theologian, seminary administrator, Conservative Jewish Congregation; b. N.Y.C., Aug. 26, 1924; s. Meyer and Nahama (Goldin) C.; B.A., City Coll. N.Y., 1944; B.H.L., The Jewish Theol. Sem. Am., 1944, M.H.L., 1948; Ph.D., Columbia U., 1958; D.D. (hon.), Princeton, 1976; m. Naomi Wiener, May 26, 1948; children—Jeremy, Judith. Rabbi, Conservative Jewish Congregation, 1948; mem. faculty Columbia, 1963-70, prof. history, dir. Center of Israel and Jewish Studies, 1963-70; librarian The Jewish Theol. Sem. Am., 1950-57, Jacob H. Schiff prof. history, 1970—, chancellor, 1972—. Bd. visitors Harvard Div. Sch., 1975-83; bd. dirs. Alliance Israelite Universelle, 1975—. Recipient Townsend Harris medal City Coll. N.Y., 1975. Fellow Am. Acad. Jewish Research (editor 1969-72), Jewish Publ. Soc. (dir. 1970, chmn. publ. com. 1970-72), Leo Baeck Inst. (dir. 1968), Conf. Jewish Social Studies (dir.). Author: Story of the Four Captives, 1961; Sefer Ha Qabbalah, 1967; Gaonim in Modern Jewish Historiography, 1972; Aliyah, 1968; contbg. author The Talmudic Age in Great Ages and Ideas of the Jewish People, 1956; Rabbinic Judaism in Ency.

Brit. Recipient Townsend Harris medal CCNY, 1961. Mem. Alliance Israelite Universelle (bd. dirs.), Conf. Jewish Social Studies (bd. dirs.), Leo Baeck Inst. (bd. dirs.), Jewish Pub. Soc. (bd. dirs., chmn. publ. com. 1970-72). Home: 416 W 255th St Bronx NY 10471 Office: Jewish Theol Sem of Am 3080 Broadway New York City NY 10027

COHEN, JACOB, Bishop, mem. gen. bd. The Church of God in Christ, Miami, Fla. Office: The Ch of God in Christ 3120 NW 48th Terrace Miami FL 33142*

COHEN, MYRA H., broadcasting company executive; b. Toronto, Ont., Can., Aug. 14, 1943; came to U.S., 1946; d. Oscar and Eva (Margolis) Cohen. B.A., Hunter Coll., 1966. Dir., Israel Broadcasting Service, N.Y.C., 1981—. Writer/producer radio features "Footnotes from the Holy Land", 1982—; writer/producer musical plays: Imagine Me, 1973, Animal Lib, 1974; writer TV show, That's Cat, 1976; (play) Next Stop Magic, 1978. Contbg. author: Accent on Reading Skills, 1979. Vol., Ronald McDonald House, N.Y.C., 1984, Rancho Los Amigos Hosp., Downey, Calif., 1978-80. Address: Israel Broadcasting Service 800 Second Ave New York NY 10017

COHN, ROBERT ALLEN, lay religious worker, newspaper editor; b. St. Louis, Sept. 4, 1939; s. Harold and Lilian (DeWoskin) C.; A.B. in English, Washington U., St. Louis, 1961, J.D., 1964, B.S. in Polit. Sci., 1965, B.S. in Philosophy, 1967; m. Barbara Florence Berg, Dec. 19, 1965; children—Scott Harold, Julie Francine, Emily Mara. Editor in chief St. Louis Jewish Light, St. Louis, 1969—; dir. pub. relations Jewish Fedn. St. Louis, 1970-77; v.p., dir. Congregation Shaare Emeth, University City, Mo., 1972-76. Atty., St. Louis., 1964—. Adminstrv. asst. St. Louis County Supr., 1964-69; chmn. St. Louis County Human Relations Commn., 1970—; chmn. Regional Forum, Met. St. Louis, 1972-76; treas. East-West Gateway Coordinating Council, 1984—. Recipient Fred A. Goldstein Meml. Service award Jewish Fedn. St. Louis, 1974, Boris Smolar award Council Jewish Fedns. and Welfare Funds, 1974, 75. Mem. Am., Mo., St. Louis County Bar assns., Bar Assn. St. Louis, Am. Jewish Press Assn. (pres. 1972-77, 84—), Omicron Delta Kappa, Alpha Sigma Lambda, Phi Delta Phi, Pi Lambda Phi. Author: History and Growth of St. Louis County, 1969. Editor: The Record, 1965. Home: 629 S Central St Clayton MO 63105 Office: 12 Millstone Campus Dr Saint Louis MO 63146

COKLEY, JAMES BENJAMIN, minister, A.M.E. Zion Ch.; b. McCleny, Fla., July 17, 1931; s. John M. and Rena Mae; B.M., N.Y. Coll. of Music, 1957; M.S.W., Adelphi U., 1972; D.Div., Universal Bible Inst., 1973, Ph.D., 1978; postgrad. in pastoral counseling, N.Y. Theol. Sem.; m. Thelma Lee, Aug. 17, 1952; children—James B., Rodney, Melinda. Ordained to ministry, 1964; pastor Abraham Thompson Meml. A.M.E. Zion Ch., Jamaica, N.Y., 1962—; instr. CUNY, 1980-82, Bronx Community Coll., 1980-83. Supreme grand chaplain Mason, Southern, Western U.S.A., 1972—, state grand chaplain, 1972—; field supr. Adelphi undergrad. students in S.W.; bd. dirs. Tic Toc Day Sch., 1969—, Al. Care Inc., 1967—. Pres. 33rd Zone Civic Assn., 1963-67; exec. dir. Assn. for Coney Island Devel. Inc., 1975—; chmn. gen. social services adv. bd. Dist 9-12; bd. dirs. South Jamaica Ctr. for Children and Parents, Inc. Mem. A.M.E. Zion Ministers Alliance, NAACP, Jamaica C. of C., Black Social Works Assn. of N.Y.C. Club: Kiwanis. Home: 167 01 110th Rd Jamaica NY 11433 Office: 169 03 107th Ave Jamaica NY 11433

COLAW, EMERSON S., Bishop The United Methodist Church, Minn. Conf., Mpls. Office: The United Meth Ch 122 W Franklin Ave Room 400 Minneapolis MN 55404*

COLE, BRUCE KASNER, rabbi, Reform Jewish Congregations; b. Cleve., Feb. 28, 1939; s. Morris and Pauline (Kasner) C.; B.A., U. Mich., 1961; B.H.L., Hebrew Union Coll., 1964, M.A., 1966; m. Marianne Presner, June 20, 1965; children—Michael Edward, Jennifer Karen. Ordained rabbi, 1966; community cons. Columbus (Ohio) regional office Anti-Defamation League B'nai B'rith, 1966-68, N.Y. dir. interreligious affairs, 1968—; rabbi East End Temple, N.Y.C., 1974—. Exec. co-sec. Cath.-Jewish Relations Com., Diocese Bklyn. and Anti-Defamation League, 1970—; mem. exec. com., commn. on inter-religious affairs Am. Zionist Fedn., 1976-80; co-chmn. adv. com. on Jewish relations Episc. Diocese N.Y., 1975—; mem. religious adv. com. N.Y. State Div. Human Rights, 1975-81. Bd. dirs. Ralph W. Alvis Halfway House for Prisoner Rehab., Columbus, 1967-68; mem. exec. com. Civil Rights Council, Columbus, 1966-68; mem. exec. com. Civil Rights Legis., Columbus, 1966-68; vice-chmn. Raoul Wallenberg Com. of U.S., 1980—; mem. Cath.-Jewish relations com. Archdiocese of N.Y., 1982—. Mem. Central Conf. Am. Rabbis, N.Y. Assn. Reform Rabbis. Co-editor: The Future of Jewish-Christian Relations, 1982. Contbr. articles to religious jours. Home: 166 E 63d St New York City NY 10021 Office: 823 United Nations Plaza New York NY 10017

COLE, JAMES KENNETH, minister, So. Baptist Conv.; b. Coolidge, Tex., Mar. 28, 1939; s. Albert James and Ruby Mae (Wootonn) C.; B.A., Wayland Bapt. Coll., 1969; M.R.E., Southwestern Bapt. Theol. Sem., 1976; m. Roberta Nell Breeding, Dec. 22, 1962; children—Sherrie Lynn, Robert James, Michael Dale. Ordained to ministry, 1973; pastor Central Bapt. Ch., Thornton, Tex., 1973—. Mem. exec. bd. Bi-Stone Bapt. Assn. Home: PO Box 56 Thornton TX 76687

COLE, JOHN DEAN, minister, Pillar of Fire Church; b. Jewell County, Kans., Apr. 18, 1921; s. Luke Chapen and Minerva Iola (Thatcher) C.; B.A., Alma White Coll., 1945; grad. Belleview Bible Sem., 1956; M.A., U. Colo., 1973, Ph.D., 1978; m. Mary Marie Haffner, Sept. 1, 1940; 1 son, John Paul. Ordained to ministry, 1942; pastor chs., Newark, 1945, Cin., 1945-48, Phila., 1948-52, New Haven, 1952-53, Boulder, Colo., 1953-56, 70-77, 84—; dir. pub. info. Alma White Coll., Zarephath, N.J., 1977, dean, 1977-80, dean Zarephath Bible Sem., 1981-84; ch. recorder Pillar of Fire Chs. Trustee N.J. Council Alcohol Problems; radio broadcaster Pillar of Fire stas. Mem. Am. Ednl. Studies Assn., Internat. Platform Speakers Assn., Phi Delta Kappa. Contbr. articles to newspapers, religious publs. Home: 2951 Sugarloaf Rd Boulder CO 80302 Office: 2245 16th St Boulder CO 80302

COLE, LESLIE EUGENE, minister, Christian Church (Disciples of Christ); b. Marion, Ind., Feb. 8, 1951; s. Leslie E. Stone and Omega M. (Weesner) Morgan; m. Bonnie Rankin, Dec. 5, 1970; children: Les Matthew, Melynn Renee. B.S., Tex. Tech U., 1977; M.Div., Phillips U., 1980. Ordained to ministry, Christian Ch., 1980. Youth minister First Christian Ch., Lubbock, Tex., 1975-77; sr. minister First Christian Ch., Crescent, Okla., 1977-80, First Christian Ch., Marion, Ind., 1980-82, So. Hills Christian Ch., Edmond, Okla., 1982—; resource person Task Force on Image and Media, Oklahoma City, 1983—; dir. new church devel. Christian Ch. in Okla., Edmond, 1982-84. Author: Chaplain: Puppet or Prophet?, 1977. Served with USAF, 1971-74. Mem. Am. Assn. Pastoral Counselors, Edmond Ministerial Alliance. Democrat. Lodge: Kiwanis (Kiwanian of Yr. 1980). Home: 2308 Cypress Ct Edmond OK 73034 Office: So Hills Christian Ch 3207 S Blvd Edmond OK 73034

COLE, WILLIAM JOSEPH, priest, educator, Roman Catholic Ch.; b. Camden, N.J., June 12, 1923; s. James Vincent and Clara Chrysostoma (Dalton) C.; B.S., U. Dayton, 1947; S.T.B., U. Fribourg (Switzerland), 1952, S.T.L., 1954, S.T.D., 1955. Joined Soc. of Mary, 1942; ordained priest, 1953; mem. faculty U. Dayton, 1956-62, 64—, prof. theol. studies, 1966—, dir. religion in life, 1957-61, 72—. Retreatmaster, 1956—; speaker in ecumenical movement in Cath. and Protestant circles; asst. to Provincial Cin. Province Soc. Mary, 1962-64; chaplain various interracial councils; co-chmn. Interfaith Com., Dayton, 1962-68; co-chmn. Interfaith Com. to Aid Farmworkers, 1973—; mem. social action commn. Archdiocese of Cin., 1976—; mem. Pax Christri. Mem. SCLC, Coll. Theology Soc. (past pres., officer Louisville region 1959), Mariological Soc., Cath. Interracial Conf., Urban League, UN Assn., Internat. Peace Acad., Univs. and Quest for Peace, Common Cause, AAUP. Editor Mariam Library Studies, 1956-62; asso. editor Marianist, 1958-62; contbr. to religious publs. Address: U Dayton Box 466 Dayton OH 45469

COLEMAN, C. COOPER, minister, American Baptist Churches in the U.S.A.; b. Mark, Miss., June 1, 1934; s. Ben and Lula C.; m. Virgie Lee Espress, Feb. 17, 1955 (div. 1965); children: Ben, Toni, Cynthia, Debbie, Anglia; m. JoAnn F. Darensburg, Dec. 20, 1975; 1 child, Kristal. B.S., Wayne U., 1953; B.Th., Linda Vista Bapt. Coll., 1963; M., Fuller Theol. Sem., 1973. Asst. to pastor New Providence Bapt. Ch., Los Angeles, 1957-58, 68; dir. Christian edn., dir. youth dept. Imperial Bapt. Ch., San Diego, 1958-63, pastor, 1960-63; pastor Ajalon Temple of Truth Bapt. Ch., Los Angeles, 1969-75, New Life Bapt. Ch. of Lynwood, Calif., 1977—; instr. New Testament theology Reed Christian Coll., Compton, Calif., 1970-73; laymen counsel Providence Missionary Bapt. Assn., 1963-67, Bible instr., 1964-72, congress pres., 1964-74; pres. Providence Congress of Christian Edn., 1970-74; pres. Providence Congress of Christian, 1984. First v.p. Lynwood Community Coordinating Council, 1981. Mem. Sr. Ministers Council Am. Bapt. Chs. of Pacific S.C., Los Angeles Bapt. Ministers Conf., Lynwood Ministerial Assn. (pres. 1981). Home: 3356 Josephine St Lynwood CA 90262 Office: New Life Baptist Ch 11516 State St Lynwood CA 90262

COLEMAN, C. D. Bishop, chmn. dept. legal affairs Christian Methodist Episcopal Church, 8th dist., Dallas. Office: Christian Methodist Episcopal Ch 2330 Sutter St Dallas TX 75216*

COLEMAN, CLARENCE LOUIS, JR., ednl. orgn. exec.; b. Chgo., Aug. 31, 1903; s. Clarence L. and Bella F. (Freund) C.; B.A., Princeton, 1924; m. Lillian Suffrin, Feb. 21, 1927; children—Thomas D., Nancy (Mrs. James J. White), Patricia J. Pres., Am. Council for Judaism, Manhattan, N.Y., 1955-67, 1969—; chmn. founders' com., first pres. Lakeside Congregation for Reform Judaism, Highland Park, Ill., 1955-59, chmn. building com., 1969-73. Sec., Coleman Floor Co., Rolling Meadows, Ill., from 1964. Clubs: Standard (Chgo.); Lake Shore Country (Glencoe, Ill.); LaQuinta Country (La Quinta, Calif.). Office: care of Am Council for Judaism 307 Fifth Ave Suite 1006 New York NY 10016

COLEMAN, CLINTON R., bishop, African Methodist Episcopal Zion Church, 5th Episc. Area. Office: 3513 Ellamont Rd Baltimore MD 21215*

COLEMAN, DONALD CARL, minister, Church of God (Anderson, Ind.); b. Punxsutawney, Pa., July 31, 1946; s. Vernon Albert and Ruth Louise (McMullen) C.; m. Darlene Louise Manners, Apr. 19, 1969; children: Sheila, D. Bradley, Salinda. B.A., Warner So. Coll., 1977; postgrad. La. Tech. U., 1979. Ordained to ministry Ch. of God (Anderson, Ind.), 1979. Pastor Highway Chapel Ch. of God, Quitman, La., 1977-79, Berwick Ch. of God, Columbus, Ohio, 1979-82, Paradise Valley Ch. of God, Alta., Can., 1982—; chmn. La. Bus. Com., 1978-79; sec. Canadian Bd. Missions, Camrose, Alta., 1984—. Served with AUS, 1965-68, Vietnam. Decorated Silver Star; Army Commendation medal. Mem. Alta. Ministers (chmn. 1983—), Canadian Gen. Assembly. Home: PO Box 28 Paradise Valley AB T0B 3R0 Canada Office: Paradise Valley Ch of God PO Box 30 Paradise Valley AB T0B 3R0 Canada

COLEMAN, EMMETT WAYNE, minister, So. Baptist Conv.; b. Louisville, Miss., Feb. 15, 1924; s. Emmett Clifton and Minnie Lee (Reynolds) C.; B.A., Miss. Coll., 1949; M.Div., So. Bapt. Theol. Sem., Louisville, 1958; m. Margaret Hood, May 16, 1953; children—Ann Cameron, Mary Leigh. Ordained to ministry, 1948; pastor chs. in Miss., 1956—, including First Bapt. Ch., Natchez, 1953-56, First Bapt. Ch., Oxford, 1962-73; asst. pastor Woodland Hills Bapt. Ch., Jackson, Miss., 1973-76; pastor First Bapt. Ch., Terry, 1976—. Trustee Miss. Bapt. Hosp., Jackson, 1966-70. Mem. spl. planning com. Miss. Council Aging, 1974. Home: PO Box 527 Terry MS 39170 Office: PO Box 159 Terry MS 39170

COLEMAN, NEIL CONWAY, minister, Christian Ch.; b. Hutchison, Kans., June 29, 1925; s. Reuben Wesley and Viloe Ione (Hutchins) C.; B.A., Wittenberg U., 1954; M.S., Ohio State U., 1955; D.Religion, Sch. Theology Claremont, Calif., 1971; m. Evelyn Aikins Fearnley, July 28, 1967; children—Neil Conway, Linda Joy. Ordained to ministry Christian Ch., 1969; minister chs., Frederick, Ohio, 1950-53, South Vienna, Ohio, 1953-55, La Verne, Calif., 1967-71, Sunnyvale, Calif., 1971-74; chaplain Nat. Benevolent Assn. Health Services Corp., Los Gatos, Calif., 1974-76; pastor 1st Christian Ch., San Mateo, Calif., 1976—. Community sec. YMCA, Dayton, Ohio, 1955. Field exec. Boy Scouts Am., 1956-57; pres. San Dimas (Calif.) Area Coordinating Council, 1969-70. Bd. dirs. Pomona (Calif.) Am. Nat. Red Cross, 1969-71. Mem. Internat. Transactional Analysis Assn., Asso. Smithsonian Instn. Author: Event and Response, A Study in the Problem of Hermaneutics, 1971. Home: 2714 All View Way Belmont CA 94002 Office: 2701 Flores San Mateo CA

COLEMAN, ROGER LEON, minister, Christian Church (Disciples of Christ); b. Raleigh, N.C., Apr. 7, 1943; s. Leon Blease and Louise (Bradshaw) C.; m. Elizabeth Alice Cockrell, July 8, 1972; children: Lauren Grace, Amy Louise, Annalise Bradshaw. B.A., Bethany Coll., 1965; M.Div., Tex. Christian U., 1968; M.Th., Mo. Sch. Religion, 1972; M.Edn., U. Mo., 1973; D.Min., St. Paul Sch. Theology, Kansas City, Mo., 1985; D.D. (hon.), Mo. Sch. Religion, 1981. Ordained to ministry Christian Ch., 1968. Minister Olivet Christian Ch., Columbia, Mo., 1968-70; dir., founder Everyday People, Inc., Columbia, 1970-73; exec. dir. Westport Coop. Services, Kansas City, 1973-83; assoc. minister Swope Pkwy. United Christian Ch., Kansas City, 1978—; exec. dir. Westport Allen Ctr., Kansas City, 1983—; pres. Clergy Referral Service of Greater Kansas City, 1982—. Chmn. Mayor's Task Force on Food and Hunger, Kansas City, 1984, Kansas City Vision Com., 1984. Lodge: Rotary. Home: 4938 Holly St Kansas City MO 64112 Office: Westport Allen Ctr 706 W 42d St Kansas City MO 64111

COLEMAN, THEODORE CHARLES (TED), minister, Disciples of Christ Church and United Methodist Church; b. Crystal City, Mo., Sept. 4, 1939; s. Harry Myers and Ethelda Viola (Hamilton) C.; m. Judith Ann Chrum, Aug. 8, 1958 (div. 1970); children: Timothy Robert, Cynthia Ann, Thomas Charles; m. 2d Edna Frieda Heller, Aug. 13, 1971; children: Terri Lynn, Linda Sue; stepchildren: Donna Midkiff, Frank Midkiff, Jr., Edward Midkiff, Michael Midkiff. B.A. in Religion and Philosophy, Culver-Stockton Coll., 1978; M.Div., Lexington Theol. Sem., 1982. Ordained, 1981. Lay worker 1st Christian Ch., Festus, Mo., 1972-74; lic. student minister Meyer/Lima Unity Ch., Meyer and Lima, Ill., 1974-78, Mt. Sinai Christian Ch., Durham, Mo., 1975-78, 1st Christian Ch., Taylorsville, Ky., 1978-81; minister Lancaster Christian Ch. (Ky.), 1981-84; minister United Parish, First Christian Meth. Ch., Coggon, Iowa, 1984—; mem. Stewardship Com. Christian Ch. in Ky., 1982-84. Contbr. weekly column Spencer Magnet, 1978-81; contbg. author jour. articles.

Chmn. Garrard County Inter-Agy. Council, Lancaster, Ky., 1981-84; mem. Spouse Abuse Ctr. Adv. Council, Lexington, 1982-84; county exec. Blue Grass council Boy Scouts Am., Lancaster, 1981-84. Named Disting. Disciple, Culver-Stockton Coll., 1974-78, recipient Robert Jacobs award in religion, 1977-78; entrance scholar, Lexington Theol. Sem., 1978; commd. Ky. Col., 1979. Mem. Nat. Evangelistic Assn., Garrard County Ministerial Assn. (pres. 1982-84), Spencer County Ministerial Assn. (v.p. 1980-81), Garrard County C. of C. (dir. 1983-84). Republican. Clubs: Rotary (pres. Lancaster 1984-85), Ruritan (sec. Taylorsville 1980-81). Home: S 3d St PO Box 585 Coggon IA 52218 Office: United Parish Christian and Meth Ch 3d and Main St Coggon IA 52218

COLEMAN, WILLIAM VINCENT, writer, publisher; b. Waterbury, Conn., Jan. 27, 1932; s. William Vincent and Ethel Marguerite (Brennan) C.; m. Patricia Marie Register, Nov. 27, 1974; children: Lisa, James, Angel. A.B., St. Bernard Coll., Rochester, N.Y., 1953, M.Div., 1973; M.A., Fairfield U., 1962; Ph.D., Fla. State U., 1975. Ordained priest Roman Catholic Ch., 1957, resigned, 1973. Sem. rector, supt. edn., pastor Diocese of Savannah, Ga., 1957-73; free lance writer, editor, Mystic, Conn., 1974-79; publisher, writer Growth Assocs., Weston, Vt., 1979—. Author numerous books including: Mine is the Morning, 20 vols., 1973-85; Daybreak, 10 vols., 1974-78; Only Love Can Make It Easy, 1975; God's Own Child; 1976, Prayer Talk, 1983, Special Days, 1985, Lent '82 (and ann. edits.), Advent '84. Editor: Synthesis, 1979—. Democrat. Home and Office: PO Box 215 Weston VT 05161

COLEMON, JOHNNIE, minister; b. Centerville, Ala., Feb. 18, 1920; d. John Haley and Lula M. (Parker) C.; B.A., Wiley Coll., 1943, D.D. (hon.), 1977; D.D. (hon.) L.H.D. (hon.), both Monrovia Coll. Ordained to ministry Christ Unity Temple; pastor Christ Universal Temple, Chgo., 1956—. Founder, pres. Universal Found. for Better Living Inst., 1974—; pres. Assn. Unity Chs., Unity Village, Mo., 1969-70; speaker weekly TV program Better Living with Johnnie Colemon; founder Johnnie Colemon Inst., 1975. Recipient numerous awards Assn. Unity Chs., 1969-70, Civic Liberty League, 1974, Alpha Kappa Alpha, 1972, Hillside Chapel, Atlanta, 1974, Boy Scouts Am., 1975, Internat. New Thought Alliance, 1975, Push Found., 1975, others. Home: 5008 S Greenwood Ave Chicago IL 60615 Office: 8601 S State St Chicago IL 60619

COLES, JOSEPH C., JR., Bishop Christian Methodist Episcopal Church, 6th dist., Atlanta. Office: Christian Methodist Episcopal Ch 2780 Collier Dr Atlanta GA 30018*

COLLER, EDWARD WILLIAM, minister, United Presbyterian Church U.S.A.; b. Indpls., Feb. 2, 1918; s. Charles Edward and Rosa Clara (Owen) C.; A.B., Hanover Coll., 1942; M.Div., McCormick Theol. Sem., 1945; m. Joyce Caldwell, May 30, 1942; children—Morris C., Harry E. (dec.), Stephen C., Stanley A. Ordained to ministry, 1945; pastor ch., La Grange, Ind., 1945-47; asst. pastor, Fort Wayne, Ind., 1947-50; pastor, Evansville, Ind., 1950-55, Granby, Colo., 1955-57, Manor Presbyn. Ch., Jennings, Mo., 1957-70, Gasconade County Presbyn. Chs., Bethel and Owensville, Mo., 1970—; pres., Owensville Ministeriels Alliance; chmn. radio and TV dept. Evansville Council Churches; chmn. Westward Ho Cluster of Presbytery. Bd. dirs. Central Mo. Area Agy. on Aging, 1973-82; chmn. bd. dirs. Gasconade Manor Nursing Home Dist., 1974—; pres., bd. dirs. Owensville Sr. Citizens Housing Corp., 1978-85. Home: 205 W Madison St PO Box 119 Owensville MO 65066 Office: 201 W Madison St Owensville MO 65066

COLLIER, HERMAN EDWARD, JR. See *Who's Who in America,* 43rd edition.

COLLINS, J.C., minister, So. Baptist Conv.; b. Greer, S.C., July 28, 1943; s. Leo Hampton and Lucille Edna (Patterson) C.; A.A., North Greenville Coll., 1964; B.A., Furman U., 1966; M.Div., Southwestern Bapt. Theol. Sem., 1969, Th.D., 1974; m. Mary Ruth Mitchell, June 15, 1969; children—Jason Chadwick, J. Clifton. Ordained to ministry, 1967; interim pastor Fairview (S.C.) Bapt. Ch., 1964-65; asso. pastor Victor Bapt. Ch., Greer, S.C., 1967, pastor Olin (Tex.) Bapt. Ch., 1969-71; tchr. sem. extension, Fort Worth, 1970-71; pastor Eastview Bapt. Ch., Rock Hill, S.C., 1973-77, Connie Maxwell Bapt. Ch., Greenwood, S.C., 1977—. Counselor, Pastoral Counseling Center, 1971-72. Co-therapist Mental Health Center, Rock Hill, S.C., 1973—. Mem. Rock Hill Ministerial Assn., York County Mental Health Assn. Home and Office: POB 1178 Greenwood SC 29646

COLLINS, JACK, minister, So. Bapt. Conv.; b. Cullman County, Ala., Apr. 26, 1931; s. Otto Otis and Gertrude Marie (Watson) C.; A.B., Howard Coll., 1964; m. Peggy L. Smith, Sept. 3, 1949; children—Sheila Kay, Gregory Stephen. Ordained to ministry, 1958; pastor West Side Ch., Demopolis, Ala., 1960-70, Northside Ch., Cullman, Ala., 1970—. Vice-moderator Bethel Bapt. Assn., 1967; chmn. missions com. Cullman-West Assn., 1969-74, dir. Vacation Bible Schs., 1972-74; dir. Christian Action Com., Cullman County, 1971—; chmn. bd. dirs. Cullman West Assn. Group Home, 1973-76; moderator Cullman West Bapt. Assn., 1974-76; pres. Cullman County Ministerial Assn., 1974-76; chmn. Cullman Here's Life America, 1976; chaplain Demopolis Fire Dept., 1964-70; state exec. bd. mem. Ala. Bapt. Assn., 1975-77; chmn. exec. bd. Cullman-West Bapt. Assn., 1974-76. Mem. adv. council Sheriff's Council on Alcohol and Drug Problems, 1976—. Mem. Am. Council on Alcohol Problems. Home and office: 1223 Katherine St Cullman AL 35055

COLLINS, MICHAEL EDWARD, editor; b. Columbus, Ohio, Nov. 17, 1938; s. Martin Patrick and Monica Louise (Metzger) C.; student Mass. Inst. Tech., 1956-57, Ohio State U., 1957-61. Staff writer Catholic Times, 1962-66, news editor, 1966-70, editor, 1970—; pres. Cath. Men's Luncheon Club, 1972-73; pres. Holy Name parish council, 1972-73; chmn. communcations Diocesan Council Catholic Men, 1964-67; chmn. communications sect. Cath. Conf. Ohio, 1978-80; instr. Gabriel Richard Inst., 1963-69. Mem. Cath. Press Assn. (various coms.), Press Club of Ohio, Mensa, Sigma Delta Chi (pres. Central Ohio chpt. 1980-82). Contbr. articles to religious jours. Home: 82 Georgetown Dr Columbus OH 43214 Office: POB 636 Columbus OH 43216

COLYN, JAMES ANTHONY, minister, educator, Independent Baptist; b. Pueblo, Colo., Aug. 29, 1947; s. Anthony Colyn, Jr. and Lenora Mae (Corsentino) Lee; m. Linda Susan Hillman, Aug. 31, 1968; children: David Allen, Deborah Lynn. Student Ariz. State U., 1965-66, Southwestern Bapt. Coll., 1966-70; D.D. (hon.), San Francisco Bapt. Theol. Sem., 1983. Ordained to ministry Independent Baptist Ch., 1971. Asst. pastor Del Norte Bapt Ch., Tucson, Ariz., 1970-73; asst. pastor Temple Bapt. Ch., Albuquerque, 1973-76; pastor Glendale Bible Ch., Ariz., 1976—; pres. Glendale Bapt. Schs., Ariz., 1981—; v.p. Christian Schs. Ariz., 1984—; trustee San Francisco Bapt. Theol. Sem., 1981—, Internat. Bapt. Coll., Tempe, Ariz., 1982—, Internat. Bapt. Missions, Tempe, 1982—; v.p. Bapt. Arabic Missions, Greenville, S.C., 1983—. Author: Why?, 1980; Every Pilgrim Should Make Progress, 1982; Steering Through Moral and Spiritual Anarchy, 1984. Republican. Lodge: Rotary. Avocations: fishing; golf. Home: 6535 W Purdue Glendale AZ 85302 Office: Glendale Bible Bapt Ch 7101 N 55th Dr Glendale AZ 85301

COMER, JACK DERWIN, minister, missionary, Southern Baptist Convention; b. Beaumont, Tex., June 24, 1926; s. Willie Ray and Bertha Beryl (Lindsey) C.; B.A., E. Tex. Bapt. Coll., 1954; B.D., New Orleans Bapt. Sem., 1962; m. Betty Rae Newsome, Aug. 24, 1947; children—Derwin Ray, Lloyd Bernard, Lindsey Lee. Ordained to ministry, 1954; pastor Bon Wier (Tex.) Bapt. Ch., 1955-58, First Bapt. Ch., Fisher, La., 1958-61; mem. Home Mission Bd., So. Bapt. Conv., 1961—; pastor Spring River Indian Bapt. Ch., Quapaw, Okla., 1961-64, First Indian Bapt. Ch., Gallup, N.Mex., 1964-67; regional missionary to Navajo Indians in Northwest N.Mex., 1967-75; gen. missionary to Choctaw-Chickasaw Indians, S.E. Okla., 1976-83. Home and office: PO Box 461 Atoka OK 74525

COMSTOCK, ALLEN MITCHELL, minister, United Ch. Christ; b. Cleve., July 13, 1942; s. Allen and Gladys June (Mitchell) C.; B.A., Coll. of Wooster, 1965; M.Div., Hartford Sem. Found., 1968, M.A., 1975; m. Linda Elaine Piper, Aug. 23, 1964. Ordained to ministry, 1970; pastor Heath (Mass.) Union Ch. and Rowe (Mass.) Community Ch., 1970-74, Stockbridge (Mass.) United Ch. Christ, 1974—; mem. task force on hunger Mass. Conf., United Ch. Christ, 1975—, mem. worship commn., 1975-76; chaplain Franklin County Pub. Hosp., Greenfield, Mass., 1972-73. Chmn. bd. dirs. Franklin County Sr. Services, Greenfield, 1973-74, Harvest of Hope, Stockbridge; chmn. personnel com., bd. dirs. Berkshire Homecare Corp., Pittsfield, Mass., 1975—. Recipient Bennet Tyler prize in systematic theology, 1968, Richard Ernest Weingart prize for original research in theol. studies Hartford Sem. Found., 1972. Mem. Inst. for Study Religion in an Age of Sci. Home and office: Box 246 Stockbridge MA 01262

CONFORTI, SISTER PASCAL, nun, provincial superior Roman Catholic Church; b. Bklyn., July 29, 1934; d. Pasquale E. and Lena (Petrone) C. B.A., Coll. New Rochelle, 1956; M.A., Cath. U. Am., 1961. Entered Order Ursuline Sisters, Roman Cath. Ch., 1956; local prioress Ursuline Community, Coll. New Rochelle, N.Y., 1969-74, Malone, N.Y., 1975-79, provincial prioress Ea. Province, Ursuline Sisters, Bronx, N.Y., 1979—. Mem. Leadership Conf. Women Religious. Office: Ursuline Provincialate 323 E 198th St Bronx NY 10458

CONGDON, ROGER DOUGLASS, minister, educator, Conservative Baptist Assn. Am.; b. Ft. Collins, Colo., Apr. 6, 1918; s. John Solon and Ellen Avery (Kellogg) C.; B.A., Wheaton Coll., 1940; student Nyack Missionary Coll., 1940, Eastern Bapt. Theol. Sem., 1940-41; Th.M., Dallas Theol. Sem., 1945, Th.D., 1949; m. Rhoda Gwendolyn Britt, Jan. 2, 1948; children—Rachel Anita (Mrs. Scott Lidbeck), James Roland, Rodney Steven, Jonathan Blanchard, Philip Fred, Robert Neilson, Bradford Britt, Ruth Alethia, Rebecca York (Mrs. Paul Skones), Rhoda Jane, Marianne Custis, Douglas Mark (dec.), Mark Alexander. Ordained to ministry Conservative Baptist Assn. Am., 1945; pastor Wash. and Oreg. chs., 1950-55; Far Western dir. N.Am. Assn. Bible Insts. and Bible Colls., 1956-59; pastor Oreg. chs., 1959-70, Glendoveer Community Chapel, Portland, Oreg., 1970—. Chmn. library dept. Multnomah Sch. of the Bible Coll., 1953-80, mem. faculty, 1950—, v.p., dean edn., 1956-62, chmn. Bible and theology dept., 1970-80; founder, pres. Preaching Print, Inc., 1954—. Chmn. Citizens Com. Spl. Action, 1960-80. Mem. Am. Assn. Bible Colls. Contbr. reviews to religious publs. Home: 16539 N E Halsey St Portland OR 97230 Office: 8435 N E Glisan St Portland OR 97220

CONLIN, J. F. S., bishop, Anglican Church of Canada. Office: 341-13th St Brandon MB R7A 4P8 Canada*

CONNALLY, DAN A., minister, Southern Baptist Convention; b. Breckenridge, Tex., Dec. 4, 1937; s. Houston D. and Jessie (Reid) C.; B.A., Howard Payne U., 1960; M.R.E., Southwestern Bapt. Theol. Sem., 1963; m. Oma Dale Shelton, Dec. 28, 1956; children—Michael Dan, Kelli Elaine. Ordained to ministry, 1958; pastor, chs. Tex., N.Y., 1958—, including First Bapt. Ch., Orchard Park, N.Y., 1966-71, First Bapt. Ch., Goldthwaite, Tex., 1971-78; dir. missions Heart of Tex. Bapt. Area, Brownwood, 1978—. Mem. state exec. bd. Tex. Bapt. Gen. Conv., 1973-78; mem. cabinet Heart of Tex. Bapt. Area, 1971-78; missions chmn. Mills County Assn., 1973—; pres. Mills County Ministerual Assn., 1971—; trustee Heart of Tex. Bapt. Encampment, 1971-78. Mem. Tex. Council Alcoholism, 1972-78, County Com. Aging, 1971-78. Home: PO Box 512 Goldwaite TX 76844 Office: PO Box 1646 Brownwood TX 76804

CONNALLY, GENEVA VADA, lay church worker, United Methodist Church; retired government official; b. Mart, Tex., Mar. 3, 1922; d. Daniel Thomas and Lyde May (Crafton) Stodghill; student Robert B. Green Sch. Nursing, San Antonio, 1939-41; B.A., U. Md.; m. Willis Glenn Connally, Aug. 2, 1941; 1 child, Donna Jean Connally Harrington. Leader adult Bible class Cokesbury United Meth. Ch., San Antonio, 1955—, treas., 1967-68; certified lay speaker, 1967; del. Southwest conf. United Meth. Ch., 1968-78, now vol. nurse free clinics; tchr., counselor to Mexicans. Med. sec. Wilford Hall Med. Center, 1958-81, ret., 1981. Home: 238 Sussex Ave San Antonio TX 78221

CONNARE, WILLIAM GRAHAM, bishop, Roman Cath. Ch.; b. Pitts., Dec. 11, 1911; s. James J. and Nellie T. (O'Connor) C.; B.A., Duquesne U., 1932, Litt.D., 1961; M.A., St. Vincent Coll., Latrobe, Pa., 1934, L.H.D., 1962; LL.D., Seton Hill Coll., 1960. Ordained priest Roman Catholic Ch., 1936; asst. pastor St. Canice, Pitts., 1936-37, St. Paul's Cathedral, 1937-49; adminstr. St. Richard's Ch., Pitts., 1949-55, pastor, 1955-60; domestic prelate, 1955; chaplain Univ. Cath. Club, Pitts., 1947-60, Cath. Interracial Council Pitts., 1953-60; dir. Soc. Propogation of the Faith, 1950-59; vicar for religious as rep. to Bishop of Pitts., 1959-60; consecrated bishop, 1960; bishop Diocese of Greensburg (Pa.), 1960—. Mem. Pitts. Commn. Human Relations, 1953-60, Allegheny County Council Civil Rights, 1953-60; episcopal chmn. Nat. Cath. Com. on Scouting, Boy Scouts Am., 1962-70; episcopal moderator div. youth activities U.S. Cath. Conf., 1968-70; mem. Bishop's Commn. for Liturgical Apostolate; chmn. commn. on missions Nat. Conf. Cath. Bishops, 1967-71. Bd. dirs., chmn. community sers. com. Urban League Pitts., 1950-60; bd. dirs. Pitts. br. NAACP, 1959-60. Address: Diocese of Greensburg 723 E Pittsburgh St Greensburg PA 15601

CONNELL, JOHN STEPHEN, minister, Southern Baptist Convention; b. Atlanta, July 22, 1953; s. Fredric Rivers and Bobbie Lee (Sikes) C.; m. Donna Kay Cooper, Nov. 23, 1977; children: Trey Askew, John Jacob, Brittany Suzanne. B.S., U. North Ala. 1975; M.Div., New Orleans Bapt. Theol. Sem., 1982, postgrad., 1982—. Ordained to ministry Southern Baptist Conv., 1977; minister music, youth and activities Highland Park Bapt. Ch., Muscle Shoals, Ala., 1976-79; pastor Jerusalem Bapt. Ch., Hammond, La., 1980—. Mem. Colbert Lauderdale Bapt. Assn. (youth dir. 1976-78), Latangi Bapt. Assn. (chmn. stewardship com. 1983—, chmn. credentials com. 1982, 84). Republican. Home: 571 Jerusalem Church Rd Hammond LA 70401

CONNER, JACK WASHINGTON, minister, So. Baptist Conv.; b. El Reno, Okla., Jan. 14, 1932; s. George W. and Minnie M. (Harriage) C.; B.A., Howard Payne Coll., 1957; B.D., Golden Gate Bapt. Theol. Sem., 1962; m. Bonna Faye Murray, Oct. 14, 1950; children—Sharon Ann, Diana Louise, Janet Kay, Gary Lee. Ordained to ministry, 1954; pastor Monroe Ave. Bapt. Ch., Wichita, Kans., 1954-55, Cross Cut (Tex.) Bapt. Ch., also Rockwood (Tex.) Bapt. Ch., 1956-57, Alder Ave. Bapt. Ch., Fremont, Calif., 1959-66, First So. Bapt. Ch., Santa Paula, Calif., 1966-70, Westside Bapt. Ch., Santa Paula, 1969-72, Scarborough Bapt. Ch., Prince Albert, Sask., Can., 1972—; dir. Assn. Sunday Sch., 1966—; mem. exec. bd. Bapt. Gen. Conv. Calif., 1965-69; moderator Harmony Bapt. Assn., Santa Paula,

1970-71; pres. Canadian So. Bapt. Conf., 1974-76; prof. New Testament, Greek, evangelism, co-founder Christian Tng. Center, 1972—. Named Alumnus of Year, Golden Gate Bapt. Theol. Sem., 1972. Home: 161 23d St W Prince Albert SK S6V 4L5 Canada Office: PO Box 1174 Prince Albert SK S6V 5S7 Canada

CONNER, RONALD PARKS, priest, Episcopal Church; b. Washington, June 15, 1945; s. Francis Willard and Vivian (Parks) C.; B.A. magna cum laude, U. of South, 1967; S.T.B. cum laude, Gen. Theol. Sem., 1970, S.T.M., 1971; Th.M., Princeton Theol. Sem., 1980; D.Min., Drew U., 1982. Ordained priest, 1970; curate Holy Trinity Ch., Hicksville, N.Y., 1970-71; teaching fellow Gen. Theol. Sem., 1971-72, Princeton Theol. Sem., 1972-74; assoc. All Saints Ch., Princeton, N.J., 1974-75, curate, 1975-78; staff Trinity Ch., Princeton, 1976-78, St. Columba's Ch., Washington, 1978; vicar St. Martin's Ch., Martinsville, N.J., 1978-81, dean Providence Deanery, 1982—; chmn. Diocesan Continuing Edn. Com., 1982—, Diocesan Commn. on Higher Edn., Phi Beta Kappa. Editor: Prayers For Eastertide, 1970. Office: St Stephen's Church in Providence 114 George St Providence RI 02906

CONNOLLY, THOMAS JOSEPH, bishop, Roman Cath. Ch.; b. Tonopah, Nev., July 18, 1922; s. John and Katherine (Hammel) C.; student St. Joseph's Prep. Sem., 1936-42, St. Patrick Sem., Menlo Park, Calif., 1942-47; J.C.L., Cath. U. Am., 1951; J.C.D., Pontifical Lateran U., Rome, 1952. Ordained priest, 1947, consecrated bishop, 1971; asst. Nev. chs., 1947-48, 52-53; sec. to bishop, 1948-49; asst., rector St. Thomas Aquinas Cathedral, Reno, 1953-55; pastor St. Joseph Ch., Elko, Nev., 1955-60, St. Albert Great Ch., Reno, 1960-68, St. Theresa Ch., Carson City, Nev., 1968-71; bishop Diocese of Baker (Oreg.), 1971—. Officialis Diocese of Reno, 1953-54, chmn. bldg. commn., 1960-71, dir. Cursillo Movement, 1961-71, dean, mem. personnel bd. Priest's Senate, 1969-70; mem. Nat. Bishops' Com. Liturgy, 1973-76; moderator Reno Deanery Council Cath. Women, 1960-65, Italian Cath. Fedn., 1960-62. Mem. Nat. Council Cath. Bishops (com. on liturgy 1973-75, adv. com. 1974-76; joint rep. U.S. Conf. Cath. Bishops Region XII 1973-76). Home: 3805 N Cedar Baker OR 97814 Office: Diocese of Baker 2215 1st St PO Box 826 Baker OR 97814

CONNORS, EDWARD M., clergyman, seminary administrator, Roman Catholic. Pres. St. Joseph's Sem., Yonkers, N.Y. Office: St Joseph's Sem 201 Seminary Ave (Dunwoodie) Yonkers NY 10704*

CONRAD, FLAVIUS LESLIE, JR., minister, Lutheran Church Am.; b. Hickory, N.C., May 5, 1920; s. Flavius Leslie and Mary Wilhelmina (Huffman) C.; A.B., Lenoir Rhyne Coll., 1941; M.Div., Luth. Theol. So. Sem., 1944; S.T.M., Temple U., 1955, S.T.D., 1959; m. Mary Elizabeth Isenhour, Nov. 4, 1944; children—Ann (Mrs. Bruce E. Meisner), Susan (Mrs. James A. Amis). Ordained to ministry, 1944; pastor St. Timothy Luth. Ch., Hickory, 1944-49, Holy Comforter Luth. Ch., Belmont, N.C., 1949-50; youth dir. United Luth. Ch. Am., Phila., 1950-60; pastor St. Lukes Luth. Ch., Richardson, Tex., 1960—. Dean, Dallas and E. Tex. dist. Luth. Ch. Am., 1973-77, mem. bd. publ., 1974-82; del. convs. Luth. Ch. Am., 1968, 74, 76; exec. sec. Luther League Am., 1950-60; mem. exec. bd. and gen. assembly Nat. Council Chs. of Christ in U.S.A., 1954-60. Vice pres. Piedmont council Boy Scouts Am., N.C., 1948-49. Winner, Nat. Poetry Contest, 1960. Author: A Study of Four Non-Denominational Youth Movements, 1955; Poetic Potshots at People and Preachers, 1977. Corr. The Lutheran from S.W., 1962—; contbg. editor Ch. Mgmt. mag., 1966-74. Contbr. sermons, articles and poems to various mags. Home: 1108 Pueblo Dr Richardson TX 75080 Office: 1200 Belt Line Rd Richardson TX 75080

CONSTANTELOS, DEMETRIOS JOHN, priest, educator, Greek Orthodox Archdiocese of North and South America; b. Spilia, Greece, July 27, 1927; came to U.S., 1955, naturalized, 1958; s. John and Christine (Psilopoulos) C.; m. Stella Croussouloudis, Aug. 15, 1954; children: Christine, John, Eleni, Maria. B.Th., Holy Cross Sch. Theology, 1958; Th.M., Princeton Theol. Sem., 1959; M.A., Rutgers U., 1963, Ph.D., 1965. Ordained priest Greek Orthodox Ch., 1955. Pastor, St. Demetrios, Perth Amboy, N.J., 1964-65, St. Nicholas Ch., Lexington, Mass., 1965-67; interim pastor St. Barbara Ch., Toms River, N.J., 1972-74, St. Anthony Ch., Vineland, N.J., 1975-82, Holy Trinity Ch., Northfield, N.J., 1982-85; prof. Holy Cross Sem., Brookline, Mass., 1965-71; prof. history Stockton Coll., Pomona, N.J., 1971—; mem. Orthodox-Cath. Theol. Consultation, 1965-84. Author: Byzantine Philanthropy, 1968; Understanding the Greek Orthodox Church, 1982; Byzantine Society and Church Philanthropy, 1985. Editor Encyclicals, 1976; Orthodox Theology, 1981; assoc. editor Greek Theol. Rev., Holy Cross Theol. Sem., 1971—, Jour. Ecumenical Studies, Temple U., Phila., 1976—. Lane Cooper fellow Rutgers U., 1962; Jr. fellow Dumbarton Oaks, 1964. Mem. Orthodox Theol. Soc. (pres. 1968-71), Soc. for Ch. History, Am. Hist. Assn., Medieval Acad. Am., Modern Greek Studies Assn. Home: 304 Forest Dr Linwood NJ 08221 Office: Stockton State Coll Pomona NJ 08240

CONTE, JOHN PHILIP, priest, Roman Cath. Ch.; b. New Haven, Aug. 5, 1936; s. Frank and Erminia Theresa (Grande) C.; B.A., St. Mary's Sem. and U., Balt., 1960. Ordained priest, 1964; asst. pastor chs. in Conn., 1964—; co-pastor St. Rose Ch., E. Hartford, 1971—. Mem. priests senate Roman Cath. Archdiocese of Hartford, 1972-75, mem. personnel bd., 1975-76; pres. E. Hartford Ecumenical Clergy Assn., 1971-74. Address: 33 Church St East Hartford CT 06108

COOK, HAROLD GENE, minister, So. Baptist Conv.; b. Denton, Tex., Nov. 18, 1937; s. Dennis Wiley and Daisy Murrell (Calk) C.; B.S., Tex. Christian U., 1966; M.Div., Southwestern Bapt. Theol. Sem., 1973; m. Patricia Ann Walls, June 27, 1959; children—Camille D'Ann, Craig Alan, Christopher Scott. Ordained to ministry, 1967; pastor Valdasta Bapt. Ch., Blue Ridge, Tex., 1967-70, 1st Bapt. Ch., Godley, Tex., 1970—. Clk., Johnson County Bapt. Assn., chmn. budget com., mem. mission study com.; bd. dirs. Latham Springs Bapt. Camp, Aquilla, Tex., 1973—. Pres., Concerned Citizens Godley, Tex., 1976. Bd. dirs. Tex. Alcohol Narcotic Edn. Assn., 1976, Am. Council on Alcohol Problems. Editor (with Bill Malone): Coordinated Vocational Academic Education, 1967. Home and office: Box 630 Taylor TX 76574

COOK, JAMES IVAN, minister, Reformed Church in America; b. Grand Rapids, Mich., Mar. 8, 1925; s. Cornelius Peter and Cornelia (Doornbos) C.; m. Jean Rivenburgh, July 8, 1950; children: Mark James, Carol Jean, Timothy Scott, Paul Brian (dec.). A.B., Hope Coll., 1948; M.A., Mich. State U., 1949; B.D., Western Theol. Sem., 1952; Th.D., Princeton Theol. Sem., 1964. Ordained to ministry Reformed Ch. Am. 1953. Pastor, Blawenburg Reformed Ch., N.J., 1953-63; instr. Biblical langs. Western Theol. Sem., Holland, 1963-65, asst. prof., 1965-67, prof., 1967-77, Anton Biemolt prof. New Testament, 1977—; chmn. ch. extension com. Particular Synod of N.J., 1961-63; chmn. theol. commn. Reformed Ch. Am., N.Y.C., 1980-85, pres. Gen. Synod, 1982-83. Author: Edgar Johnson Goodspeed, 1981. Editor, contrb.: Grace Upon Grace, 1975, Saved By Hope, 1978; editor: The Church Speaks, 1985. Served with U.S. Army, 1943-45; ETO. Mem. Soc. Bibl. Lit. Office: Western Theol Sem 86 E 12th St Holland MI 49423

COOK, MILTON GERARD, minister, International Ch. of Foursquare Gospel; b. Lewistown, Mont., July 10, 1938; s. Milton Burdett and LaVerne (Rozell) C.; B.A., Seattle Pacific Coll., 1961; B.D., Fuller Theol. Sem., 1965; m. Barbara Lou Paulson, July 1, 1961; children—Carmen Beth, Christi Linn, Timothy James, Sundar John. Ordained to ministry, 1965; minister East Hill Ch., Portland, Oreg., 1965-84. Founder Ministries Unlimited, 1974, pres., 1974-75. Recipient Golden Mike award for best youth program Am. Legion, 1970. Mem. Life Bible Coll. (hon.), Seattle Pacific Coll., Fuller Theol. Sem. alumni assns., Nat. Assn. Evangelicals, Gresham Ministerial Assn., Nat. Assn. Religious Broadcasters, Greater Portland Pentacostal Fellowship, Greater Portland Assn. Evangelicals, Oreg. Assn. Evangelicals, Gresham C. of C. Author: Where the Rubber Meets the Road, 1969; Love, Acceptance and Forgiveness, 1978; Choosing to Love, 1981. Contbr. articles to mags. Home: 1420 NW Division St Gresham OR 97030 Office: 1525 NW Division St Gresham OR 97030

COOK, WILLIAM HARLESTON, minister, Southern Baptist Convention; b. Little Rock, Jan. 1, 1931; s. Thomas Lee and Jamie (Reynolds) C.; B.A., Hardin Simmons U., 1952; B.D., Southwestern Bapt. Sem., 1955, Th.D., 1960; m. Rachel Lee Quattlebaum, Aug. 29, 1954; children—Camille, William Craig, Pamela Kay. Ordained to ministry, 1950; pastor 1st Bapt. Ch., Harrison, Ark., 1957-60, Levelland, Tex., 1960-69, Bartlesville, Okla., 1969—. Speaker at revivals, motivational confs.; 1st v.p. Bapt. Gen. Conv. of Okla., 1973, pres., 1982-84. Author: Success, Motivation, and the Scriptures, 1974; contbr. articles to religious jours. Home: 214 E 15th St Bartlesville OK 74003 Office: First Bapt Ch POB 1080 4th and Cherokee Sts Bartlesville OK 74003

COOKE, MARK GRISHAM, minister of music, American Baptist Churches, U.S.A.; b. Abilene, Tex., May 24, 1954; s. Paul Raymond and Bette (Grisham) C.; m. Roseann Beha, Aug. 11, 1979; 1 child, Matthew Shawn. Student, Baylor U., 1975-77; B.A. in music, U. Louisville, 1979; M.A. in music, So. Bapt. Theol. Sem., 1981. Ordained to ministry Pioneer Baptist Ch. Minister Music & Youth, First Bapt. Ch., Kenova, W.Va., 1982—; sec. C-K Ministerial Assn., Kenova, 1983—. Served in U.S. Army, 1972-75. Mem. Fellowship of Am. Bapt. Musicians, C-K Ministerial Assn., Phi Eta Sigma, Gamma Beta Phi Soc. Office: First Baptist Ch PO Box 475 12th and Poplar Kenova WV 25530

COOKE, WILLIAM THOMAS, JR., minister, United Meth. Ch.; b. Surry County, N.C., Oct. 5, 1925; s. William Thomas and Annie (Arrington) C.; student Furman U.; B.A., Central Wesleyan U., 1970; Th.B., Holmes Theol. Sem., 1946, D.D. (hon.), 1973; postgrad. Chandler Sch. Theology, Emory U.; m. Marian Juanita Bradley, June 10, 1950; children—William Thomas, III, Cynthia Bralley, Anne Clarice, Celeste Marian. Ordained to ministry, 1963; pastor Bethel United Meth. Ch., Simpsonville, S.C., 1959, Bethel and Ebernezer United Meth. Ch., 1960-63, Salem United Meth. Ch., Greenville, S.C., 1963-76; vol. chaplain Greenville Hosp. System; chaplain Gantt Dist. Vol. Fire Dept., White Horse Rd. Sertoma Club. Pres., Greer Ministerial Alliance. Pres. Greenville dist. PTA, 1973-74, also past pres. other elementary, middle sch. and high sch. PTA's; treas. S.C. PTA, 1975-76, character and spiritual life chmn., 1972-73, also life mem.; active Bd. Drug and Alcohol of Greenville County, Citizens Adv. Com. Greenville County; bd. dirs. Young Life. Mem. Greenville Ministerial Alliance, Nat. PTA (life). Home: Route 8 Davis Dr Greenville SC 29611 Office: POB 8213 Greenville SC 29604

COOLEY, ROBERT E., educational administrator. Pres. Gordon-Conwell Theol. Sem. (Interdenom.), South Hamilton, Mass. Office: Gordon-Conwell Theol Sem South Hamilton MA 01982*

COOLIDGE, ROBERT TYTUS, educator, Episcopal Ch.; b. Boston, Mar. 30, 1933; s. Lawrence and Victoria Stuart (Tytus) C.; grad. Groton (Mass.) Sch., 1951; A.B., Harvard, 1955; M.A., U. Calif. at Berkeley, 1957; B.Litt., Oxford (Eng.) U., 1966; m. Ellen Osborne, Sept. 10, 1960; children—Christopher, Miles, Matthew. Ordained deacon Episcopal Ch., 1967; non-stipendiary ministry Christ Ch. Cathedral, Montreal, Que., Can., 1967-69, 71—, St. Marylebone Ch. and London (Eng.) Clinic, 1969-71; faculty, Loyola Coll. (now Concordia U.), Montreal, 1963—, asso. prof. history, 1968—. Fellow Royal Hist. Soc.; mem. Am. Soc. Ch. History, Ecclesiastical History Soc., Medieval Acad. Am., Am. Hist. Assn., Soc. d'Histoire de L'Eglise de France. Club: Oxford and Cambridge (London). Contbr. to hist. vol. Home: POB 4070 Westmount PQ H3Z 2X3 Canada

COONEY, PATRICK RONALD, bishop, Roman Catholic Church; b. Detroit, Mar 10, 1934; s. Michael and Elizabeth (Dowdall). B.A., Sacred Heart Sem., 1956; S.T.B., Gregorian U., Rome, Italy, 1958, S.T.L., 1960; M.A., Notre Dame U., 1973. Ordained priest, Roman Cath. Ch., 1959; consecrated bishop, 1983. Asst. pastor St. Catherine Parish, Detroit, 1960-62; asst. chancellor Archdiocese of Detroit, 1962-69; chaplain Mercy Coll., Detroit, 1967-72; dir. worship Archdiocese of Detroit, 1969-83, aux. bishop, Detroit Archdiocese, 1983—.

COONS, DOUGLAS ARTHUR, lay ch. worker, United Methodist Ch.; b. Troy, N.Y., Jan. 31, 1947; s. Robert Milton and Elizabeth Jane (Landmesser) C.; certificate in culinary Arts, So. Me. Vocational Tech. Inst., 1967. Christian edn. instr. First United Meth. Ch., Rochester, N.H., 1967-68; dir. Christian edn. dir., 1968-71, lay leader, 1971—; certified United Meth. lay speaker, 1971—; mem. United Meth. Conf. Council on Ministries, 1973—; mem. United Meth. Conf. Work Area-Lay Life and Work, 1973—. Vocational instr. Dover (N.H.) High Sch., 1970—. Mem. Friends of the Rochester Music Theatre, 1968-73. Bd. dirs. So. Main Vocat. Tech. Inst. Alumni Assn. Mem. Dover Tchrs. Assn. (1st v.p. 1976—), N.H. Edn. Assn., Nat. Edn. Assn. Research for State Dept. of Edn. on Task Analysis for Culinary Arts, 1974-75. Home: 21 Calef Hwy Rochester NH 03867

COOPER, EDGAR MAUNEY, minister, Lutheran Ch. Am.; b. Kings Mountain, N.C., Oct. 17, 1922; s. Edgar Claudius and Vera (Mauney) C.; A.B., Lenoir Rhyne Coll., 1943; B.D., Mt. Airy Luth. Sem., 1945; S.T.M., 1950; m. Jacqueline Wyrick, Apr. 16, 1977. Ordained to ministry, 1945; pastor New Hanover (Pa.) Luth. Ch., 1945—. Luther League advisor Norristown (Pa.) Conf., 1953; sec. Trappe Dist., 1969; bd. mgrs. Artman Home for Aging, Ambler, Pa., 1962-69; chaplain Pottstown Auto Club, 1947-68. Mem. adv. bd. Nat. Bank of Boyertown, 1961—; mem. Pottstown Selective Service Bd., 1966-73. Mem. Eastern Pa. Luth. Hist. Soc. (pres. 1974-80), Boyertown Ministerium (pres. 1961). Author: Mark Her Bulwarks, 1950; History of the New Hanover Lutheran Ch. Organized 1700, 1974. Home: 2971 Lutheran Rd Gilbertsville PA 19525 Office: PO Box 272 Pottstown PA 19464

COOPER, FRED HANDEL, lay ch. worker, univ. ofcl., Baptist Ch.; b. Pontotoc, Miss., June 2, 1930; s. Fred Handel and Martha Augusta (Bigham) C.; student Tulane, 1947-49; A.B., Am. U., 1952; m. Shirley Jo Miller, Oct. 22, 1950; children—Fred Handel III, Joe Richard, Mem. Fla. Bapt. Conv., State Bd. Missions, 1968-69, 70-73, vice chmn., 1972-73, v.p. conv., 1973-74; minister edn. Powers Dr. Bapt. Ch., Orlando, Fla., 1969-70; mem. com. on bds. So. Bapt. Conv., 1970-71. Dir. information Stetson U., DeLand, Fla., 1970—. Pres., Sarasota Citizens League, 1959-61. Recipient award Freedoms Found, 1961, Orlando Press Club, 1972, 74. Mem. Pub. Relations Soc. Am. (dir.), Fla. (pres. 1973-74), Bapt. pub. relations assns. Mason. Club: Sertoma (internat. dir. 1960-64). Contbr. articles to denominational publs. Home: 6139 Pickering Ct Orlando FL 32808 Office: Stetson U DeLand FL 32720

COOPER, JAMES VERNON, minister, Assemblies of God; b. Harrison, Ark., Feb. 23, 1936; s. Guss Sewell and Ava Francis (Norton) C.; B.A., Ark. Poly. Coll., 1962; M.S.W., U. Tenn., 1966; m. Hazel Dean Smith, Aug. 1, 1958; children—Dan, Verna, Marie, Jason, Dawn. Ordained to ministry, 1966; pastor N.W. Assembly of God Ch., N. Little Rock, 1967-68; asso. minister 1st Assembly of God Ch., Russellville, Ark., 1968-69; adminstr. Highland Child Placement Service, Kansas City, Mo., 1969—. Mem. Ark. Gov.'s Com. on Early Childhood Devel., 1966-67; Ark. rep. to White House Conf. on Rural Am., 1967. Mem. Nat. Assn. Social Workers, Acad. Certified Social Workers, Am. Assn. Marriage and Family Counselors (clin.), Nat. Assn. Christians in Social Work. Contbr. articles to religious jours.

COOPER, JOSEPH, minister, Assemblies of God; b. Raywick, Ky., Nov. 3, 1926; s. Joseph B. and Anna Mary (Brannon) C.; Ph.B., Golden Gate Bapt. Theol. Sem., 1969, Th.M., 1973; m. Mattie Deen Jennings, July 21, 1943; children—Robert Joseph, Sherry, Joann, James, Verna, Susan. Ordained to ministry, 1971; asso. minister Bethel Bapt. Ch., Oakland, Calif., 1961-71; pastor Mt. Eden Assembly of God, Hayward, Calif., 1972—. Dir. Black Ministers Outreach for No. Calif. and Nev. Dist., Assemblies of God, 1976-78; bd. supervision to planning commn., 1975—. Home: 320 Stoneford Ave Oakland CA 94603 Office: 24540 Mohr Dr Hayward CA 94541

COOPER, RICHARD RANDOLPH, priest, Episcopal Ch.; b. Ashland, Ky., June 24, 1940; s. Francis Marion and Marian Elizabeth (Coleman) C.; student U.S. Air Force Acad., 1959-62; B.A., U. of South, 1964, M.Div., 1966; m. Susan Elizabeth Tuthill, July 10, 1965; children—Frances Elizabeth, Anne Elizabeth. Ordained priest, 1967; asst. rector Grace Episcopal Ch., Ocala, Fla., 1966-68; vicar St. Christopher's Ch., Tampa, Fla., 1968-70, rector, 1970-72, Trinity Episcopal Ch., Baytown, Tex., 1972-76, St. George's Episcopal Ch., San Antonio, 1976—. Mem. exec. bd. Tampa Ministerial Assn., 1968-69; diocesan chaplain Daus. of the King, 1969-72; regional coordinator Faith Alive, 1971-72; bd. dirs. St. James House, 1973-76; mem. corp. Sch. of Pastoral Care, 1973—; chaplain Order of St. Luke the Physician, 1970—, asso. warden, 1975—. Home: 105 S Gardenview San Antonio TX 78213 Office: 6904 West Ave San Antonio TX 78213

COOPER, VIRGIL DAVID, minister, chaplain, Christian Church (Disciples of Christ); b. Kennett, Mo., Sept. 18, 1949; s. Millage Franklin and Helen (Glessnor) C.; m. Sherry Malyn Martin, May 15, 1971; children: Amy Beth, Jarred David, Ryan Martin. B.A., Sch. of Ozarks, 19—; M.Div., Lexington Theol. Sem., 1978, D.Min., 1985. Ordained to ministry Disciples of Christ Ch., 1978. Assoc. minister Victory Christian Ch., Lexington, Ky., 1975-76; minister Newtown Christian Ch., Georgetown, Ky., 1976-78, Central Christian Ch., Beaufort, S.C., 1978-83, First Christian Ch., Covington, Ky., 1984—; mem. S.C. Regional Evangelism Com., Charleston, 1979-80, N.C.-S.C. Alignment Com., Charleston, 1979-81; del. S.C. Regional Bd., Charleston, 1979-83; chmn. S.C. Regional Com. on Ministry, Charleston, 1980-83, Beaufort Ministerial Assn., S.C., 1980; chaplain U.S. Air Force Res., 1981—. Adviser HELP Orgn., Beaufort, 1980; chmn. Wheels for Life, St. Jude Hosp., Beaufort, 1982-83, mem. Cin. Symphony-Chorus, 1984—. Recipient Key to City mayor of Hollister, Mo., 1974, George V. Moore award Lexington Theol. Sem., 1977; Lexington Theol. Sem. scholar, 1976. Mem. Mil. Chaplain's Assn., Disciples's Chaplains Assn., Res. Officers Assn. Lodge: Kiwanis Internat. (funding chmn. 1983). Avocations: camping, canoeing, tennis, golf, music. Office: First Christian Ch 14 W 5th St Covington KY 41011

COPACIA, LEONTE SIMION, JR., deacon, Romanian Orthodox Episcopate of America; automobile company administrator; b. Salem, Ohio, Apr. 4, 1932; s. Leonte Simion Sr. and Elena (Buta) C.; m. Mary Bogdan, Aug. 21, 1954; children: Terry Lee, Timothy George, Tod Leo, Trevor John. Student Ohio State U., 1951-53, Akron U., 1955-56; B.S. in Indsl. Mgmt. and Supervision, Central Mich. U., 1984. Ordained to ministry Romanian Orthodox Episcopate of America as deacon, 1979. Choir condr. Sts. Peter and Paul Romanian Orthodox Ch., Dearborn Heights, Mich., 1966-73, cantor, 1973-79; deacon, 1979-83; deacon St. George Romanian Orthodox Cathedral, Southfield, Mich., 1982—; nat. auditor Am. Romanian Orthodox Youth, Grass Lake, Mich., 1957-58, nat. v.p., 1958-59, nat. pres., 1959-60; bus. mgr. Solia News, 1963-65. Specialist advance program planning mfg. engring. staff Chrysler Corp., Detroit, 1957—. Bicentennial festival commr. Shelby Twp., Utica, Mich., 1976, chmn. chartered commn., 1980, mem. econ. devel. corp., 1982, mem. planning commn., 1983. Served to Sgt. USMC, 1953-55, Korea. Recipient scholarship N.Y. Mil. Acad., 1947-50. Fellow Engring Soc. Detroit, Chrysler Corp. Mgmt. Club. Democrat. Lodge: Rotary (sec. 1980-81). Home: 5993 Wilmington Dr Utica MI 48087

COPELAND, ROGER, minister, So. Bapt. Conv.; b. Maud, Okla., Mar. 16, 1942; s. Finis Earl and Alpha Lee (Sammons) C.; B.A., Okla. Bapt. U., 1964; M.R.E., Southwestern Bapt. Theol. Sem., 1973; m. Karen Sue Merritt, Mar. 9, 1968; children—Kami Sheree, Jeremy Scott. Liscensed to ministry, 1961; minister of music and youth 1st Bapt. Ch., McLoud, Okla., 1961, Okemah, Okla., 1962, Holdenville, Okla., 1963-64, Tabernacle Bapt. Ch., Ennis, Tex., 1964-68, Bellevue Bapt. Ch., Hurst, Tex., 1970-75, 2d Bapt. Ch., Little Rock, 1975—. Composer sacred music. Home: 11423 Southridge St Little Rock AR 72212 Office: 222 E 8th St Little Rock AR 72202

CORBETT, GORDON LEROY, minister, Presbyterian Church in the U.S.A.; b. Melrose, Mass., Dec. 11, 1920; s. Winfield Leroy and Lalia (Fiske) C.; m. Winifred Pickett, Sept. 7, 1946; children: Christine, Douglas, Patricia, Carolyn. B.A., Bates Coll., 1943; M.Div., Yale U., 1948. Ordained to ministry, 1948. Pastor, Montowese Bapt. Ch., North Haven, Conn., 1948-52; assoc. pastor Presbyn. Ch., Glens Falls, N.Y., 1952-59; synod exec. United Presbyn. Synod of Ky., Lexington, 1959-71; assoc. synod exec. Synod of Alaska N.W., Anchorage, 1971-84; pastoral services, Anchorage, 1984—; chmn. Alaska Pipeline Chaplaincy Task Force, 1974-78; trustee Sheldon Jackson Coll., Sitka, Alaska, 1971-84; bd. dirs. Presbyn. Hospitality House, Fairbanks, Alaska, 1971-84; mem. exec. bd. Alaska Christian Conf., 1971-84. Dist. chmn. Republican party, Anchorage, 1974-78; trustee Appalachian Regional Hosps., 1968-72; bd. dirs. Buckhorn Children's Ctr., Ky., 1959-71. Served to 1st lt. USAAF, 1943-45. Recipient Christian Citizenship award Sheldon Jackson Coll., 1984. Mem. Yukon Presbytery (moderator of presbytery 1980, chmn. bd. trustees 1985—). Home: 2324 Sonstrom Dr Anchorage AK 99503

CORBETT, W. LYNN, clergyman, pres. Southern Methodist Church. Office: PO Box 132 Orangeburg SC 29116*

CORCORAN, JOHN JOSEPH, priest, Roman Catholic Church; b. Newport, R.I., May 2, 1931; s. Edward John and Mary Stella (Walsh) C. A.B., Brown U., 1953; M.R.E., Maryknoll Sem., 1963; M. Div., Maryknoll Sch. Theology, 1963, M.A., 1983. Joined Maryknoll Fathers and Bros., Roman Catholic Ch., 1957, ordained priest, 1963. Missionary Maryknoll Mission, Republic of Korea, 1963-79, regional superior Maryknoll in Korea, 1972-78; rector Maryknoll Sem., Ossining, N.Y., 1980-84; vicar gen. Maryknoll, Ossining, 1984—. Served to lt. (j.g.) USN, 1953-57. Democrat. Office: Maryknoll Ossining NY 10545

CORDELL, RALPH LUCIAN, minister, So. Bapt. Conv.; b. LaFollette, Tenn., Mar. 13, 1921; s. John Edward and Leona (Nelson) C.; certificate Carson-Newman Coll., Jefferson City, Tenn., 1962; postgrad. course missions Southwestern Bapt. Theol. Sem., Ft. Worth, 1964; m. Mary Helen Grant, Nov. 17, 1945; children—Linda Faye, Margaret Sue, Doris Jean, Debra Kay, Paul Edward, Stephen Earl. Ordained to ministry, 1944; pastor chs. in Tenn., 1944-60; missionary Campbell County Bapt. Assn., LaFollette, 1960—. Adv. com. Cumberland Coll., Williamsburg, Ky. Mem. S. Campbell County Ministerial Assn. Club: Shriner. Home: 810 W Central Ave LaFollette TN 37766 Office: 721 W Central Ave LaFollette TN 37766

CORDUAN, WINFRIED, religious educator, minister, Independent Protestant. b. Hamburg, West Germany, Aug. 17, 1949; s. Bruno Max Paul and Ursula (Woehlbrand) C.; came to U.S., 1963; m. June Ellen Anderson, Aug. 28, 1971; children: Nicholas, Seth. B.S., Univ. Md., 1970; M.A., Trinity Evang. Div. Sch., 1973; Ph.D., Rice U., 1977. Ordained to ministry, 1981. Asst. prof. religion and philosophy Taylor Univ., Upland, Ind., 1977-81, assoc. prof., 1981—; pastor Union Chapel Community Ch., Summitville, Ind., 1981-84; del. to Summit conf. Internat. Council on Bibl. Inerrancy, Chgo., 1979, 83. Author: Handmaid to Theology, 1981; also articles, book revs. Com. chmn. Cub Scout Pack 183 Boy Scouts Am., Alexandria, Ind., 1983-84. Mem. Evang. Theol. Soc. (chmn. Midwest region 1982-83), Evang. Philos. Soc. (pres. 1984—), Soc. Christian Philosophers, Am. Philos. Assn. Home: 214 N West St Alexandria IN 46001 Office: Taylor Univ Upland IN 46989

CORIATY, GEORGE MICHAEL, priest, religious organization executive, Roman-Byzantine Catholic Church; b. Avare Sao Paulo, Brazil, Jan. 1, 1933; came to Can., 1960. Student U. Boston, 1957-58, U. Montreal, Que., Can., 1961-63; Ph.D. in Social Psychology and Polit. Sch., Columbia Pacific U., 1983; lic. in Canon Law, Strasbourg U., France, 1985. Ordained priest Roman-Byzantine Cath. Ch., 1956. Asst. pastor Our Lady Annunciation Ch., Boston, 1957-60; pastor St. Savior's Ch., Montreal, 1960; vicar gen., chancellor Melkite Eparchy of Can., 1981—; superior Basilian Salvatorian Order in Can.; founder Our Lady Assumption Parish, Toronto, Ont., Can., St. Ann's Parish, Quebec City, Que., Can., St. George's Ch., Vancouver, B.C., Can.; pres. Melkite Community Ctr.; active Ecumenical Movement, Can.; chaplain Golden and Silver Age Assn. for Elderly People; founder, chaplain Young Women Club of St. Sanveur Community; mem. Conf. Religieuse Can. Founder, pub., editor Trait d' Union, 1963—. Founder Middle-East Immigrant Aid Soc. of Can., 1963, Byzantine Mus., 1975; mem. Can. Consultative Council on Multiculturalism, 1973-79; founder pres. Ctr. Multicultural Bois de Boulogne, 1973—; active Mus. Arts of Montreal, House of Trade, Montreal, Cedars Cancer Fund, Royal Victoria Hosp., Montreal; adminstrv. mem. Soc. Québécoise pour Les Refugies, 1980. Decorated Order of Can.; officer mil. and hospitaller Order of St. Lazarus of Jerusalem; recipient Citizen of Honour award Civic Council Montreal, 1973. Mem. Ecumenical Assn. Can., Assn. Can. Wildlife Assn., UN Assn. Club: Internat. Tennis. Office: PO Box 578 Sta C Montreal PQ H2L 4K4 Canada

CORIGLIANO, ANTHONY MARY, priest, Roman Catholic Church; b. Bklyn., May 29, 1929; s. Joseph Gregory and Mary Grace (Blasi) C. Student Elm Bank Sem., 1950-52; student in theology St. Thomas U., Rome, 1952-55; M.S.Ed., Iona Coll., 1966. Ordained priest, Roman Cath. Ch., 1955. Parish asst. Sacred Heart Ch., Milford, Mass., 1955-58, St. Ann's Ch., West Springfield, Mass., 1958-61, Mt. Carmel Ch., White Plains, N.Y., 1961-64; dir. House of Studies, Washington, 1964-67; provincial N.Am. Province, Stigmatine Fathers and Bros., Newton, Mass., 1980—; team mem. Marriage Encounter, White Plains, N.Y., 1972-75. Office: Stigmatine Fathers and Bros 36 Fairmont Ave Newton MA 02158

CORRELL, WALTER HERBERT GRIFFITH, priest, Episcopal Ch.; b. Chgo., Aug. 2, 1907; s. Herbert Eugene and Caroline Clair (Griffith) C.; student Skagit Coll., 1960-62; student Ch. Divinity Sch. of the Pacific, 1962-63, U. Wash., 1965-66; m. Margaret Mary Julia Shore, Sept. 15, 1934; 1 dau., Colleen Evelyn. Ordained priest, 1963; curate St. Pauls Ch., Bremerton, Wash., 1963-64; vicar St. Catherin's Ch., Enumclaw, Wash., 1964-66; asso. Trinity Episcopal Ch., Everett, Wash., 1966-70; vicar St. Aidans Ch., Camano Island and Stanwood, Wash., also Ch. Transfiguration, Darrington, Wash., 1970—. Moderator Uncle Walter's Children's Hour, Vancouver, Wash., 1940-42. chaplain, Providence and Gen. hosps., 1966-74; asso. priest Order Holy Cross Monastery. Mem. Assn. Clergy Diocese Olympia. Contbr. poetry to mags. Home and office: PO Box 145 Stanwood WA 98292

CORRIPIO AHUMADA, ERNESTO, archbishop, Roman Catholic Church; b. Tampico, Méx., June 29, 1919; Ordained priest Roman Catholic Ch., 1942; aux. bishop, Zapara, Méx., 1953, named bishop of Tampico, 1956, bishop of Artequera, 1967, bishop of Puebla de los Angeles, 1976, now archbishop of Mexico City, primate of Mex.; prof. sem., Tampico, 1945-50. Address: Apartado Postal 24-433 México 7 DF México

CORTES, EDELMIRO, Synodical bishop Lutheran Church in America, San Juan, P.R. Office: Lutheran Ch in Am 415 Bellavista St PO Box 14426 Barrio Obrero Sta San Juan PR 00915*

CORTESI, DAVID JOHN, priest, Roman Cath. Ch.; b. Highland Park, Ill., Mar. 11, 1937; s. John Joseph and Jean Helen (Hendrickson) C.; A.B., St. Mary of the Lake Sem., Mundelein, Ill., 1959, M.A., 1963; M.Ed., Loyola U., 1972, M.A., 1977. Ordained priest, 1963; asso. pastor St. Joan of Arc Ch., Skokie, Ill., 1963-68, Santa Maria del Popolo, Mundelein, Ill., 1968-70, Divine Infant Ch., Westchester, Ill., 1970—. Exec. dir. Cath. Family Consultation Service, 1976; moderator Archdiocesan Council of Cath. Women, 1976; coordinator Office of Edn. and Leadership tng. Office of Laity, 1974; chaplain Combined Counties Police Assn., 1974; mem. adj. faculty St. Mary of Lake Sem. Bd. dirs. Mental Health Assn. Greater Chgo., 1976. Mem. Ill. Personnel and Guidance Assn., Nat. Council Family Relations, Psychologists Interested in Religious Issues, Nat. Conf. Cath. Charities. Home: 10120 Kent St Westchester IL 60153 Office: 155 E Superior St Chicago IL 60605

COSTELLO, THOMAS JOSEPH See *Who's Who in America*, 43rd edition.

COSTEN, JAMES H., minister, educator. Pres., Interdenom. Theol. Ctr., Atlanta. Office: Interdenom Theol Ctr 671 Beckwith St SW Atlanta GA 30314*

COTTINGHAM, WATSON OCTAVUS, minister; b. Centreville, Ala., Dec. 13, 1919; s. Walter Watson and Ellorea (Pratt) C.; A.B., Samford U., 1956; M.Div., New Orleans Baptist Sem., 1961; m. Alpha Hollifield, June 8, 1920; children—Katherine Sue, Mary Jessie, Watson Allen, William Barnes. Ordained to ministry So. Baptist Conv., 1953; pastor Eastmont Bapt. Ch., Birmingham, Ala., 1953-54, First Bapt. Ch., St. Rose, La., 1959—. Home missionary, 1963—; chaplain CAP, New Orleans, 1978—, St. Charles Parish Sheriff's Dept., Hahnville, La., 1979—, New Orleans Bapt. Assn., So. Bapt. Hosp., 1979—. Bd. dirs. River Parish Drug and Alcohol Abuse Council, Destrehan, La., 1979—. Mem. New Orleans Bapt. Assn. (pres. pastors conf. 1974-75). Home: PO Box 218 Destrehan LA 70047 Office: 406 St Rose Ave St Rose LA 70087

COUCHELL, DIMITRIOS GEORGE, priest, religious organization executive, Greek Orthodox Archdiocese of North and South America; b.

Greenville, S.C., Feb. 17, 1938; s. George James Pleicones and Iphigenia (Trakas) Couchell. B.Th., Holy Cross Theology Sch., Brookline, Mass., 1963. Ordained priest Greek Orthodox, Archdiocese of N. and S. Am., 1983, elevated to archimandrite, 1985. Exec. sec. Campus Commn., Standing Conf. of Canonical Orthodox Bishops, N.Y.C., 1964-71; English editor Orthodox Observer, N.Y.C., 1971-81; ecumenical officer Greek Orthodox Archdiocese, N.Y.C., 1979-81; exec. dir. St. Photios Found., Inc., St. Augustine, Fla., 1981—; mem. exec. com. Nat. Council of Chs., N.Y.C., 1976-78; pres. Syndesmos, World Orgn. Orthodox Youth, Helsinki, Finland, 1977-80; mem. adv. bd. Assoc. Ch. Press, Media, Pa., 1980-81. Editor: Concern mag., 1965-71, Contemporary Issues, 1976. Mem. Orthodox Theol. Soc. in Am. (sec. 1977-79). Office: St Photios Found Drawer AF Saint Augustine FL 32085

COUEY, DUANE EMERSON, ch. ofcl., Reorganized Ch. of Jesus Christ of Latter-day Saints; b. Milw., Sept. 13, 1924; s. Ralph Emerson and Hazel Viola (Lindsey) C.; student U. Wis., 1946-47, Park Coll., Kansas City, Mo., 1976-77; m. Edith Rosalyn Griswold, Sept. 6, 1947; children: Patricia L., Ralph F. Ordained to ministry Reorganized Ch. of Jesus Christ of Latter-day Saints, 1948; pastor chs. in Appleton, Wis., 1948-52, Milw., 1952-54; pres. Memphis dist., 1954-58; asst. 1st presidency, 1958; pres. Los Angeles County (Calif.) Stake, 1958-60; mem. Council of 12 Apostles, Southwestern U.S. and Hawaii, 1960-66; mem. first presidency Reorganized Ch. of Jesus Christ of Latter-day Saints, Independence, Mo., 1966—, presiding patriarch, 1982. Editor-in-chief Herald House, Independence, 1966—. Mem. corporate bd. Independence Sanitarium and Hosp.; trustee Sch. of Restoration. Mem. John Whitmer Hist. Soc. Contbr. articles to ch. mags., ednl. materials. Office: Central Profl Bldg PO Box 1059 Independence MO 64051

COULTER, WILLIAM ROBERT, clergyman, ch. ofcl., Ch. of God (Seventh Day); b. Parkersburg, W.Va., July 21, 1930; s. Jesse Henderson and Mary Jamison (Hensworth) C.; student Salem Coll., 1950-51, U. Colo., 1953-54; m. Flora Emogene Fletcher, June 9, 1951; children—William Robert, James Eric, Jill Marie, Alan Lee. Ordained to ministry Ch. of God (Seventh Day), 1957; pastor, New Auburn, Wis., 1956-61; dist. overseer Great Lakes dist. Ch. of God (Seventh Day), Detroit, 1961-63, chmn. Gen. Conf., Denver, 1963—. Mem. Nat. Assn. Parlimentarians. Office: 330 W 152d Ave PO Box 33677 Denver CO 80233

COURTER, WALTER MERLE, II, minister, Lutheran Church in America; b. Evansville, Ind., May 18, 1949; s. Walter Merle and Mary Marie (Matthews) C.; m. Karen Sue Gourley, June 21, 1975; children: Marie Elizabeth, Michelle Christine. B.A., U. Evansville, 1971; M.Div., Luth. Theol. Sem., 1975. Ordained to ministry Lutheran Ch. in Am., 1975. Pastor, Christ Luth. Ch., Evansville, 1975-77; chaplain Beale AFB, Calif., 1977-80, U.S. Air Force Acad., Colo., 1980-83, Andersen AFB, Guam, 1983-85; chmn. Ecumenism Task Force Ind.-Ky. Synod, 1975-76, Youth Ministry Task Force, 1976-77; del. Ind. Council of Chs., 1976. Contbr. articles to theol. jours. Mem. Internat. Assn. Police Chaplains. Home: 37 Poinciana Circle FPO San Francisco CA 96630 Office: 43d CSG APO San Francisco CA 96334

COUSIN, PHILIP R., bishop, African Methodist Episcopal Church; pres. Nat. Council of Church of Christ In the U.S. Office: Nat Council Chs of Christ 475 Riverside Dr New York NY 10115*

COUTURE, JEAN-GUY, bishop, Roman Catholic Church; b. St. Jean-Baptiste de Quebec, Que., Can., May 6, 1929. Ordained priest, 1953; bishop of Hauterive, Que., 1975-79, of Chicoutimi, Que., 1979—. Address: 602 Rue Racine est CP 278 Chicoutimi PQ G7H 5C3 Canada*

COUTURIER, GUY, priest, educator, Roman Catholic Church; b. St. Joseph, N.B., Can., Apr. 22, 1929; s. Treffle and Leona (Cyr) C. Licentiate in theology, Angelicum, Rome, 1956; M.A., Johns Hopkins U., 1957; Licentiate in Bible, Vatican, 1959; Ph.D., Ecole Biblique, Jerusalem, 1961. Ordained priest Roman Cath. Ch., 1955. Mem. faculty U. Montreal, Que., Can., 1963—, prof. theology, 1962—. Trustee Stonehill Coll., North Easton, Mass., 1976—. Mem. Am. Schs. Oriental Research, Archaeol. Inst. Am. (pres. 1979—), Soc. Bibl. Lit., Brit. Sch. Archeology, Israel Exploration Soc. Office: U Montreal Montreal PQ H3C 3J7 Canada 343-7026A

COVENEY, MAURICE JOHN, minister, Pentecostal Assemblies of Can.; b. London, July 2, 1933; s. John Herbert and Mary Ann (Roden) C.; came to Can., 1957, naturalized, 1977; grad. Western Pentecostal Bible Coll., Vancouver, B.C., 1963; m. Eileen Lois Ryba, Aug. 16, 1958; children—Graham Brent, Caren Lynn. Ordained to ministry, 1968; pastor Salmo Pentecostal Ch., Salmo, B.C., Can., 1965-67, Cache Creek (B.C.) Pentecostal Ch., 1967-70; asst. pastor Williams Lake Pentecostal Tabernacle, 1970-74; teaching ministry How to Deal with Jehovah's Witnesses, 1974—. Author tape: How to Witness to the Jehovah's Witnesses, 1976. Home: 685 Fraser Rd Kelowna BC V1X 4K6 Canada Office: PO Box 2212 Station R Kelowna BC V1X 4K6 Canada

COVERDALE, GERALD DEAN, priest, Roman Cath. Ch.; b. Minot, N.D., May 25, 1923; s. Earl Sylvester and Bernice Irene (Bucklin) C.; B.A., Aquinas Inst., 1951, Licentiate of Philosophy, 1955, M.A. in Systematic Philosophy, 1955. Ordained priest, 1954; parish asst. priest St. Dominic's Ch., Denver, 1955-57; assigned S.W. Okla. missions, work with migratory workers, 1957-62; commd. capt. U.S. Air Force, 1962; advanced through grades to maj., 1973; chaplain Vandenberg AFB, Calif., Anderson AFB, Guam, McClellan AFB, Sacramento, Itazuke AFB, Japan, Tainan AFB, Taiwan, ret., 1973; participant team pastorate Ch. of Risen Savior, Kansas City, Mo.; pastoral counsellor Dial-A-Priest, Kansas City, Mo., 1973—; participant Marriage Encounter program, 1973—. Named Outstanding Chaplain Logistic Command USAF, 1968. Mem. K.C. Columnist Key to the News, Kansas City Diocese, Roman Cath. Ch., 1973—. Author: Snowflakes in the Desert, 1977. Home: 2127 Benton Blvd Kansas City MO 64127 Office: 18 E 11th St Kansas City MO 64106

COVINO, PAUL FRANCIS XAVIER, religious executive, Roman Catholic; b. Methuen, Mass., Aug. 3, 1958; s. Benjamin Gene and Lorraine Mary (Gallagher) C.; m. Anne Elizabeth Hallisey, Apr. 23, 1983. B.A., Georgetown U., 1980; M.A., U. Notre Dame, 1981. Mem. staff Diocesan Office for Worship, Worcester, Mass., 1980; assoc. dir. The Georgetown Ctr. for Liturgy, Spirituality and the Arts, Washington, 1981—; Dormitory minister-in-residence Georgetown U., Washington, 1981-83. Mem. N. Am. Acad. Liturgy (assoc.), Nat. Assn. for Lay Ministry. Office: The Georgetown Center for Liturgy Spirituality and the Arts 3514 O St NW Washington DC 20007

COWGILL, FRANCIS ANTHONY, priest, Roman Catholic Church. b. Spokane, June 27, 1927; s. James Daniel and Kathryn (Salchert) C. B.A., St. Thomas Sem., 1948. Ordained priest Roman Catholic Ch., 1952. Prin. PXM High Sch., Skagway, Alaska, 1952-59; pastor St. Mary's Ch., Kodiak, Alaska, 1964-66; chancellor Archdiocese of Anchorage, 1966-70; pastor St. Andrew's Ch., Eagle River, Alaska, 1967-68, St. Anthony's Ch., Anchorage, 1968—; sec. edn. Archdiocese of Anchorage, 1966-70, prelate, monsignor, 1966—. Treas. Anchorage Mental Health Assn., 1964. Decorated Knight of Holy Sepulchre, 1971, vicar gen., 1983. Address: St Anthony's Ch 825 S Klevin St Anchorage AK 99508

COX, DAVID ELMER, minister, American Lutheran Church; b. Bellingham, Wash., Apr. 15, 1955; s. Chester William Cox and Eleanor Mae (Layton) Cox-Knutzen; m. Brenda Susan Bailes, July 16, 1977; children: Kyle Patrick, Brian Christopher. B.A. in Religion, Pacific Luth. U., 1977; M.Div., Wartburg Theol. Sem., 1979, S.T.M., 1986. Ordained to ministry Luth. Ch., 1980. Interim pastor Ch. of Indian Fellowship, Tacoma, 1974-77, St. Paul's Luth. Ch., Sherill, Iowa, 1978-79; pastor Grade Luth. Ch., Des Moines, Wash., 1980-83, Burlington Luth. Ch., Wash., 1983—. Mem. devel. asst. program N. Pacific Dist. Am. Luth. Ch., 1981—, mem. evangelism com., 1984—; bd. dirs. Luth. Camp Assocs., Bellingham, Wash., 1984—; pres. Burlington Ministerial Assn., 1983—. Co-author, editor stage play: People of Passion, 1981; People of Faith, 1982. Co-author stage play: The Problem of Temptation, The Seven Deadly Sins, 1983. Mem. Soc. Biblical Lit. Lodge: Rotary. Avocations: gardening, acting, music, opera. Home: 831 Rio Vista Burlington WA 98233 Office: Burlington Luth Ch 134 Victoria Ave Burlington WA 98233

COX, HARVEY GALLAGHER, theologian; b. Phoenixville, Pa., May 19, 1929; s. Harvey Gallagher and Dorothea (Dunwoody) C.; A.B. with honors in history, U. Pa., 1951; B.D. cum laude, Yale, 1955; Ph.D., Harvard 1963; m. Nancy Nieburger, May 10, 1957; children—Rachel Llanelly, Martin Stephen, Sarah Irene. Dir. religious activities Oberlin Coll., 1955-58; program asso. Am. Baptist Home Mission Soc., 1958-62; fraternal worker Gossner Mission, East Berlin, 1962-63; asst. prof. Andover Newton Theol. Sch., 1963-65; asso. prof. church and soc. Harvard, 1965-70, Victor Thomas prof. divinity, 1970—; cons. Third Assembly World Council Chs., New Delhi, India, 1961. Chmn. bd. Blue Hill Christian Center, 1963-66; chmn. Boston Indsl. Mission. Author: The Secular City, 1965; God's Revolution and Man's Responsibility, 1965; The Feast of Fools, 1969; The Seduction of the Spirit: The Use and Misuse of People's Religion, 1973; Turning East: The Promise and Peril of the New Orientalism, 1977. Editorial bd. Christianity and Crisis. Office: Harvard U Div Sch Cambridge MA 02140

COX, HENRIETTA TAYLOR, lay church worker, United Methodist Church; retired educator, poet; b. Spartanburg, S.C., Nov. 2, 1922; d. L.B. and Alma Jane (Coggins) Taylor; m. William Edgar Cox, Jan. 12, 1947; children: Linda Dawn Cox Walker, William David. B.S. cum laude, Asheville Coll., 1943; postgrad. U. S.C., 1949-51. Tchr. Sunday Sch. Meth. Ch., Greer, S.C., 1947—; zone leader Greer Area Meth. Chs., 1958-60, leader adult studies, 1958—; leader Meth. Youth Fellowship, Sharon United Meth. Ch., Greer, 1961-65, chmn. missions, 1980—, organizer and chairperson tape ministry, 1981—, chmn. council on ministries, 1984; pres. Woman's Missionary Soc., Victor Meth. Ch., Greer, 1958-60; lay witness, leader, speaker missions Meth. Ch., S.C., N.J., Va., N.C., Tenn., Ga., 1971-77; lay speaker Greenville dist. Meth. Ch., S.C., 1978—. Chairperson Heart Vols., Am. Heart Assn., Reidville, S.C., 1979-85. Named Tchr. of Yr., Dist. V Schs., Spartanburg County, S.C., 1969; recipient citation Am. Heart Assn., 1982, 83, 84, citation Statue of Liberty Ellis Island Centennial Commn., 1984; Presbyn. Bd. Nat. Missions scholar Asheville Coll., 1939-43. Mem. Nat. Ret. Tchrs. Assn., Woman's Missionary Soc. (life), DAV Comdrs. Club (charter). Avocations: writing, reading, hiking. Home: Route One Box 141 Woodruff SC 29388

COX, J. ARTHUR, minister, Lutheran Church-Missouri Synod. B. Utica, N.Y., Aug. 5, 1940; s. James F. and Margaret (Craig) C.; m. Mahailie Tillson, Dec. 29, 1962; children: Deborah Jean, James Andrew. A.Applied Sci., Mohawk Valley Community Coll., 1961; B.Th., Concordia Sem., 1975. Ordained to ministry Lutheran Ch., 1975. Pastor, Grace Luth. Ch., Bradford, Pa., 1975—; counselor Cattaraugus Cir., Bradford, 1978-82; del. Synodical Conv., Dallas, 1977; chmn. Dist. Open House, Bradford, 1982, Dist. Extension Fund, Buffalo, 1982—; dist. chmn. Alive in Christ, Eastern Dist.; bd. dirs. Mission Services, Eastern Dist. Bd. dirs. Evergreen Hylands, 1979, Am. Cancer Soc., 1980, Vis. Nurse Assn., 1980—. Republican. Lodge: Rotary (bd. dirs. 1978-82, pres. 1982-83). Home: 465 Interstate Pkwy Bradford PA 16701 Office: Grace Luth Ch 79 Mechanic St Bradford PA 16701

COX, JOHN B., minister, Southern Baptist Convention; b. Rochester, Tex., July 20, 1932; s. Arthur Boyd and Leora (Bradley) C.; diploma in theology Southwestern Baptist Sem., 1965; postgrad. Nebr. Sch. Religion, 1970-71; D.Arts in Ministry, Ebert Profls. Inst., 1980; m. Mozelle Davis, May 20, 1949; children: Roy L., Timothy B., Robin J., Michelle D. Ordained to ministry So. Bapt. Conv., 1968; pastor Yankton (S.D.) Bapt. Ch., 1965-68, Bethel Bapt. Ch., Lincoln, Nebr., 1968-73, First Bapt. Ch., Papillion, Nebr., 1973-83, Millard Bapt. Ch., Omaha, 1983—; mem. Com. on Bds. So. Bapt. Conv., 1973—; mem. exec. com., exec. bd. Kan.-Nebr. Bapt. Conv., 1972-79, parliamentarian, 1979-83; bd. dirs. Home Mission Bd., So. Bapt. Conv., 1979-84. Pres. adv. council Papillion Sch. Dist., 1973—, United Cerebral Palsy Assn. of Nebr., 1972—. Bd. dirs. Nebr. Bapt. Fellowship, Nat. United Cerebral Palsy Assn., Nebr. Council on Alcohol Narcotic Edn. Mem. Eastern Nebr. Bapt. Assn. (moderator 1969-70), Southwestern Sem. Alumni Assn. (pres. 1973-74), Christian Counseling Assos. (pres. bd. dirs. 1976—), Assn. Christian Marriage Counselors, Assn. Christian Therapists, Papillion C. of C. Home: 4203 Walnut St Omaha NE 68105 Office: 2100 S 51st St Omaha NE 68106

COX, JOSEPH CLARENCE, JR., minister, So. Baptist Conv.; b. Marceline, Mo., June 25, 1905; s. Joseph Clarence and Zona V. (Bowman) C.; student U. Richmond (Va.), 1926; grad. New Orleans Bapt. Theol. Sem., 1959; D.D.; m. Billie Louise Neal, June 16, 1937; 1 dau., Suzan. Ordained to ministry, 1959; mission pastor 1st Bapt. Ch., Shreveport, La., 1959-64; preaching mission, Jamaica, 1961; sr. chaplain La. State Penitentiary, 1964-69; evangelist, 1969-72; ret., 1973; 1st chaplain Shreveport Police Dept., 1960-64. Bd. dirs. CODAC, Shreveport, Birth Defects, Shreveport. Home: 16 Wasson Rd Blanchard LA 71009

COX, W. F., official, United Free Will Baptist Church. Chmn. exec. bd. United Free Will Baptist Ch. Address: 1106 Holt St Durham NC 27701

COX, WILLIAM ALBERT, JR., educator, minister, Southern Baptist Convention, ch. musician; b. Jefferson, Tex., May 2, 1927; s. William Albert and Dollye (Spradley) C.; B.S., E. Tex. Bapt. Coll., 1949; M.R.E., Southwestern Bapt. Theol. Sem., 1954; m. Catherine Ann Ward, Dec. 5, 1948; children—Catherine Rose (Mrs. Kenneth W. Jones), Carole Nan (Mrs. Bobby Hammock). Ordained to ministry So. Baptist Conv., 1952; minister of music and edn. Barksdale Bapt. Ch., Bossier City, La., 1948-49, Parkview Bapt. Ch., Shreveport, La., 1949-50, First Bapt. Ch., Sulphur Springs, Tex., 1950-52, Tabernacle Bapt. Ch., Ennis, Tex., 1952-54, First Bapt. Ch., Palestine, Tex., 1954-55; supt. intermediate work Bapt. Sun. Sch. Bd., Nashville, 1955-60; minister of edn. First Bapt. Ch., Dallas, 1960-63; minister of music and edn. First Bapt. Ch., West Palm Beach, Fla., 1963-65, Miami Springs Bapt. Ch., Miami, 1965-67; supr. field sales Broadman div. Bapt. Sunday Sch. Bd., Nashville, 1967-74, Broadman Music Cons., 1974-75; trade sales supr. Broadman Press, 1975-80; promotion and program supr. So. Bapt. Conf. Ctrs., 1980—. Soloist for many meetings and confs. Long play record God Gave Me Love, 1973, From Glory to Heaven, 1983. Compiler: (music book) The Time of Salvation, 1973. Home: 104 Blue Hills Ct

Nashville TN 37214 Office: 127 Ninth Ave N Nashville TN 37234

COX, WILLIAM EDWARD, priest, Roman Cath. Ch.; b. Janesville, Wis., Aug. 21, 1916; s. Charles Edward and Catherine Elizabeth (Crowley) C.; B.A., B.D., St. Francis Sem., Milw., 1938. Ordained priest, 1942; asst. pastor, then pastor chs. in Wis., 1942—; founder, 1963, since pastor St. Paul the Apostle Parish, Racine, Mem. Clergy Assn. Racine, Wis. Hist. Soc., Alumni Assn. St. Francis Sem. (exec. bd.). Address: 5700 Washington Ave Racine WI 53406

COYLE, LARRY WALTER, minister, Christian Churches and Churches of Christ; b. Savannah, Mo., Dec. 11, 1933; s. Joseph Walter and Thelma Grace (Gibson) C.; m. Shirley Carol Twigg, Nov. 27, 1954; children: Larry Wayne, Sherri Lynne, Joseph Scott, James Charles. B.A., Roanoke Bible Coll., 1963; M.A., Pacific Christian Coll., 1985. Ordained to ministry Christian Chs. and Chs. of Christ, 1961. Pastor, Ch. of Christ, Jarvisburg, N.C., 1960-62, Ch. of Christ, Portsmouth, Va., 1962-64; sr. pastor First Christian Ch., Compton, Calif., 1964-68; evangelist Ch. of Christ, West Covina, Calif., 1968-81; sr. pastor First Christian Ch., Escondido, Calif., 1981—; news dir. Ch. Broadcasting Network, Portsmouth, 1962-64; exec. v.p. Webb Advt., Hollywood, Calif., 1968-71; pres. Coyle Advt., West Covina, Calif., 1971-78; TV media dir. No. Am. ChristianConv., 1984-85. Exec. producer video spl.: The Passover (Merit award 1970), 1969; writer, producer video spl.: Pass It On (Merit award 1974), 1973; editor, speaker weekly radio program: Your Reason For Living (Merit award 1985), 1980. Pres. various Republican clubs, 1960—. Served with USAF, 1953-57. Recipient Merit award Life Underwriter Tng. Council, 1958; named Salesman of Yr., Prudential Ins. Co., 1958, Minister of Yr., Christian Crusade, 1966. Mem. So. Calif. Ministerial Assn., Escondido Ministerial Assn. Lodge: Masons (chaplain local club 1966-68). Avocations: collecting baseball cards and other memorabilia; rare religious books; film and video techniques and development. Office: First Christian Ch 1300 S Juniper St Escondido CA 92025

CRABB, FREDERICK HUGH WRIGHT, archbishop, Anglican Church of Canada; b. Eng., Apr. 30, 1915; came to Can., 1957, naturalized, 1977; s. William Samuel and Florence Mary (Wright) C.; m. Margery Coombs, Sept. 26, 1946; children: John, Alison, Elizabeth, Peter. B.D. with 1st class honors, U. London, 1939; D.D. (hon.), Wycliffe Coll., Toronto, Ont., Can., 1958, St. Andrew U., Saskatoon, Sask, Can., 1963, Coll. Emmanuel and St. Chad, Saskatoon, 1979. Ordained to ministry Ch. of England, 1939. Engaged in farming, 1935; asst. priest, Teignmouth and Plymouth, Eng., 1939-42; dist. missionary, Akot, So. Sudan, 1942-45; prin. Bishop Gwynne Coll., Mundri, So.Sudan, 1945-51; vice prin. London Coll. Div., 1951-57; prin. Coll. Emmanuel and St. Chad, 1957-67; asst. Christ Ch., Calgary, Alta., Can., 1967-69; rector St. Stephen's Ch., Calgary, 1969-75; bishop of Athabasca, Alta., 1975-77, archbishop of Athabasca, met. of Ruperts Land, 1977-83; assoc. rector St. Cyprian's Ch., Calgary, 1983—; mem. gen. synod and coms. Anglican Ch. Can.; dir. Anglican Sch. Lay Ministry; chaplain Calgary Dist. Royal Can. Mounted Police Vets. Contbr. articles to profl. publs. Lodge: Rotary.

CRABTREE, ERNEST RICHARD, minister, non-denominational church; b. Wheelersburg, Ohio, Feb. 11, 1928; s. Ernest E. and Ethel Alice (Burke) C.; m. June Elizabeth Lord, June 24, 1949; 1 child, Steven Richard. A.B., Cin. Bible Sem., 1948; B.S. in Edn., U. Cin., 1957; D.D. (hon.), Pacific Christian Coll., 1973. Sr. minister White Oak Christian Ch., Cin., 1950-69, First Christian Ch., Canton, Ohio, 1969-83, Acad. Christian Ch., Colorado Springs, Colo., 1983—; instr. Cin. Bible Sem., Cin., 1950-52. Pub. com. mem. Standard Pub. Co., Cin., 1969—; pres. N. Am. Christian Conv., Cin., 1972; v.p. World Conv. of Christian Chs., Mexico City and Dallas, 1974-79. Author column for Christian Standard. Contbr. articles to religious publs. Boys work chmn. Central YMCA, Cin., 1958-69; chmn. Citizens for Better Pub. Schs. NW Dist., Cin., 1963-66, Tom Skinner Evangelistic Crusade, Canton, Ohio, 1974. Mem. So. Pacific Christian Fellowship (pres. 1970—), Christian Benevolent Assn. (pres. 1958-69), Disciples of Christ Hist. Soc. (bd. dirs. 1980—, life mem.), Open Forum on the Future of Christian Chs./Chs. of Christ (treas.-registrar 1983—), N. Am. Christian Conv. (pres. 1972, treas. 1967-70). Republican. Club: Glen Eagle Country (Colorado Springs). Lodge: Kiwanis. Avocations: fishing; golfing. Home: 14405 River Oaks Dr Glen Eagle Colorado Springs CO 80908 Office: Acad Christian Ch 1635 Old Ranch Rd Colorado Springs CO 80908

CRABTREE, WALTER GAYLE, lay church worker, Southern Baptist Convention; educator; b. Lawton, Okla., Aug. 14, 1939; s. Maurice Edwin and Sarah-Margaret (Foster) C.; B.A., Calif. Bapt. Coll., 1962; M.R.E., Golden Gate Bapt. Theol. Sem., 1965; cert. in elem. teaching Pacific Coll., 1976; m. Marilyn Jean Greenlee, June 10, 1961; children: Cameron Eugene, Melodee Ruth, Todd Alan. Minister of music, music dir. chs., Whittier, Riverside, and Antioch, Calif., 1959-67; minister of edn. 1st Bapt. Ch., Westminster, Calif., 1967-68, Greenleaf Ave. Bapt. Ch., Whittier, 1968-69; assoc. dir. Sunday sch. dept. So. Bapt. Conv. Calif., 1969-74; music dir. Trinity So. Bapt. Ch., Fresno, Calif., 1972-74, 76—; trustee Calif. Bapt. Coll., 1967-69; producer weekly TV program for the deaf Signs of Life. Tchr., Clovis (Calif.) Unified Sch. Dist., also asst. varsity football coach and head varsity track coach. Mem. Fresno Community Council, San Joaquin Valley Health Consortium, Fresno Health Round Table. Named Alumnus of Yr., Calif. Bapt. Coll., 1968. Mem. Western Religious Edn. Assn., Fresno Mental Health Assn. Contbr. articles to So. Bapt. publs. Home: 976 W Holland St Clovis CA 93612

CRADDOCK, FRANCES SMITH, church official, Christian Church (Disciples of Christ). b. Alleghany, Va., Sept. 30, 1922; d. Charles Calvin and Lelia Belle (Fridley) S.; m. James Richard Craddock, Aug. 20, 1943; 1 child, Lynn. B.S., James Madison U. and Va. Poly. Inst., 1943. Program dir. Met. Ch. Fedn., St. Louis, 1959-61; exec. Christian Ch. (Disciples of Christ) Dept. Ch. Women, Indpls., 1974—; v.p. div. homeland ministries, 1975—; pres. Christian Women's Fellowship, Ill.-Wis., 1964-70; bd. dirs. Christian Ch. (Disciples of Christ), Ill.-Wis., 1964-72, pres., 1970-72; v.p. Interant. Christian Women's Fellowship, 1970-74; mem. gen. bd., adminstrv. com., bus. com. Christian Ch. (Disciples of Christ), 1969-75, mem. adv. com., office of communication, 1971—, chmn., 1971-73; trustee United Christian Missionary Soc., 1966-73, vice chmn. bd. dirs. div. homeland ministries, 1973-74; del. Consultation on Ch. Union, Princeton, N.J., 1970; mem. Women's Task Force, 1974-85; del. World Council of Chs. Assembly, Nairobi, Kenya, 1975, accredited visitor, Vancouver, B.C., Can., 1983; bd. dirs. Christian Ch. Services, 1977—, mem. ch. fin. council, 1975—; bd. mgrs. Ch. Women United, N.Y.C., 1975-84, mem. exec. com., 1980-83; mem. women's com. Internat. Christian U., Tokyo, 1972—. Contbr. articles to profl. jours. Leader neighborhood bd. Girl Scouts U.S.A., Richmond, Mo., 1957; bd. dirs. PTA, Richmond, 1954-57. Christian Ch. (Disciples of Christ) scholar, Indpls., 1975—. Mem. Denominational Coordinators for Women (pres. 1980-83), NOW, Internat. Christian Women's Fellowship (sec. 1975—), World Christian Women's Fellowship (sec.-treas. 1975—), PEO (pres. 1969-70), Phi Kappa Phi. Democrat. Club: Zanafra (Indpls.). Home: 3445 W 71st St Indianapolis IN 46268 Office: Div Homeland Ministries 222 S Downey Ave Indianapolis IN 46219

CRAIG, DAVID BRIAN, minister, Moody Memorial Church; b. Salamanca, N.Y., Nov. 15, 1959; s. George W. and Darlene Mae (Kroohn) C.; m. Alice R. Guth, Aug. 8, 1981. Diploma, Moody Bible Inst., Chgo., 1982; student Northeastern U., 1983—. Ordained to ministry Moody Meml. Ch., 1984. Pastoral intern Lakeside Bapt. Ch., Muskegon, Mich., 1979; with pub. relations Moody Bible Inst., Chgo., 1980-82; minister of youth Moody Meml., Chgo., 1982—; assoc. mem. Youth for Christ, Chgo., 1983—; cons. Sonlife Ministries, Chgo., 1984—. Mem. Evang. Tchr. Training Assn., Soc. Disting. High Sch. Students. Office: Moody Meml Ch 1609 N LaSalle Dr Chicago IL 60614

CRAIG, GORDON NEVILLE, JR., minister, United Methodist Ch. B. Abington, Pa., Aug. 9, 1925; s. Gordon Neville and Elizabeth (Anderson) C.; m. Lois Mae Meyer, Aug. 8, 1948; children: Carol Craig Vincent, Gordon Paul. B.B.A., U. Miami, 1948; B.D., Crozer Theol. Sem., 1957; postgrad. Mansville Coll., Oxford, Eng., 1965; M.A., Scarritt Coll., 1972; D. Ministry, Drew U., 1978. Ordained deacon United Methodist Ch., 1957, elder, 1958. Pastor Main St. United Meth. Ch., Jacksonville, Fla., 1969-73; Organizing pastor Isle of Palms United Meth. Ch., Jacksonville Beach, Fla., 1973-78; assoc. council dir. Fla. Conf. United Meth. Ch., Lakeland, Fla., 1978-82; sr. pastor First United Meth., Ormond Beach, Fla., 1982—; dir. Internat. Child Care, Port au Prince, Haiti, 1982—; chaplain Bd. Counselors Bethune-Cookman Coll., Daytona Beach, Fla., 1982—; mem. council fin. and Adminstrn. Fla. Conf. United Meth. Ch., 1982—. Contbr. World Meth. Ency., 1969. Served with USCG, 1943-45, PTO. Recipient Religion & Human Relations award Bethune Cookman Coll., 1968. Fellow Acad. of the Parish Clergy; mem. Pa. Soc. of the Cin., Halifax Area Ministerial Assn., St. Augustine Hist. Soc., Fla. Hist. Soc. Lodge: Rotary. Office: First United Meth Ch 336 S Halifax Dr Ormond Beach FL 32074

CRAIG, HELEN CECIL, religion educator, Seventh-day Adventists; b. Albion, Pa., Aug. 25, 1926; d. Carl Arden and Edith Zilda (Walton) Craig. B.S., Andrews U., 1967, M.A., 1972. Tchr. day sch. Pa. conf. Seventh-day Adventists, 1944-57, acad. dean girls Ind. conf., Cicero, 1957-59, tchr., prin. N.J. conf., 1959-76, ednl. supr., dir. Sunday sch. Chesapeake conf., Md., 1975-83, assoc. dir. Sabbath Sch. dept. Gen. Conf., Takoma Park, Washington, 1983—. Contbr. articles to ch. ednl. and religious jours. Editor children's religious material. Office: Gen Conf of Seventh-day Adventists 6840 Eastern Ave NW Takoma Park Washington DC 20012

CRAIG, JUDITH, Bishop The United Methodist Church, Detroit Conf. and W. Mich. Conf. Office: PO Box 6247 Grand Rapids MI 49506 also 155 W Congress St Suite 200 Detroit MI 48226*

CRAIG, MANFORD RODRICK, chaplain, Assemblies of God; b. Lincoln, Maine, Feb. 14, 1941; s. Vincent Albert and Thelma (Thomas) C.; B.A., Central Bible Coll. and Sem., 1964, M.A. in Theology, 1969; m. Jeanette Eldine Herman, Aug. 11, 1962; children—Todd, Jerald, Constance, Tamara, Wendy. Ordained to ministry, 1968; pastor North Barre Chapel, Barre, Vt., 1965-71; chaplain U.S. Bur. Prisons, Lewisburg (Pa.) Penitentiary, 1971-73, Leavenworth (Kans.) Penitentiary, 1973—; asso. pastor Tiffany Fellowship, Kansas City, Mo., 1973—. Dir. men's ministries Maine, N.H., Vt., Assemblies of God, 1969-71; bd. dirs. Salvation Army, Leavenworth, 1974—; bd. dirs. Coll. of Fellows, Am. Protestant Correctional Chaplains Assn., 1976-77. Named Chaplain of Year, Am. Congress of Corrections, 1975-76. Mem. Yolkfellow Internat. Masterkey. Editor: Am. Protestant Correctional Chaplains Assn. Jour., 1976—. Home: 1700 Miami St Leavenworth KS 60048 Office: US Penitentiary Leavenworth KS 66048

CRANE, CHARLES ARTHUR, minister, Chs. of Christ; b. Sweet Home, Oreg., July 4, 1938; s. Claude Carl and Jessie LaVelle (Waters) C.; B.A., NW Sch. Religion, 1962; M.A., Lincoln Christian Sem., 1975, M.Div., 1977, D. Min., 1978; m. Margaret Lucile Ross, Nov. 28, 1957; children: Carol Elizabeth, Douglas Gorden, Steven Alan. Ordained to ministry, 1962; pastor Sutherlin, Oreg., 1962-66, Salt Lake City, 1966-73, Moweaqua, Ill., 1973-76, First Caldwell, Idaho, 1976-83, Ch. of Christ, Eugene, Oreg., 1983—; assoc. prof. Lincoln Christian Sem., 1975-76; prof. Boise Bible Coll., 1977-83; trustee Intermountain Bible Coll., 1967-73, Puget Sound Christian Coll., 1984—. Author: Do You Know What the Mormon Church Teaches, 1974; The Bible and Mormon Scriptures Compared, 1976; Mormon Missionaries in Flight, 1978; Bold Ones for Christ, 1985; (movie) The God Makers, 1983. Office: 2600 Belmont St Eugene OR 97404

CRANER, MAX WELLS, educator, Church of Jesus Christ of Latter-day Saints; b. Burley, Idaho, July 29, 1928; s. John Thomas and Lauretta (Wells) C.; m. Evelyn Parke, Sept. 17, 1948; children: Diane, Brenda, Maxine, Teresa, Susan, Veanne. B.S., Ricks Coll., 1954; M.S. in Ednl. Adminstrn., Brigham Young U., 1958, D.R.E., 1965; postdoctoral Mich. State U., 1966. Missionary, Ch. of Jesus Christ of Latter-day Saints, N.C., 1949-51, bishop, Ephraim, Utah, 1961-63, stake pres., Pocatello, Idaho, 1984—, area dir. Ch. Ednl. System, Pocatello, 1968—, Holy Land tour dir., Israel, Middle East, Egypt and Europe, 1979—. Author: (with Ron R. Munns) Hey, Wait for Me, I'm Your Leader, 1982. Mem. Pocatello City Task Com., 1979-80; chmn. fund raising ARC, Burley, Idaho, 1956; chmn. fin. com. Tendoy Area council Boy Scouts Am., 1971-72. Recipient Supervision award Ch. of Jesus Christ of Latter-day Saints, Salt Lake City, 1984. Club: Lions. Home: 1478 Los Altos Way Pocatello ID 83201 Office: CES Area Offices PO Box 8132 Pocatello ID 83209

CRANNY, TITUS FRANCIS, priest, Roman Cath. Ch.; b. Sioux City, Iowa, Apr. 15, 1921; s. Daniel Joseph and Theresa P. (Clarke) C.; B.A., Cath. U. Am., 1944, M.A., 1949, Th.D., 1953. Ordained priest, 1948; rector Atonement Sem., 1951-54; dir. Unity Apostolate, Graymoor, 1954-68; staff mem. R.I. Council Chs., 1968-70; tchr. various colls., 1951-72; dir. League of Prayer for Unity, Garrison, N.Y., 1956—. Recipient Marian Library medal, 1963. Mem. Cath. Theol. Soc., Internat. Marian Acad., Internat. Scotistic Acad. Author: Mary and Reunion, 1962; Father Paul and Christian Unity, 1963; Is Mary Relevant?, 1970. Home and Office: League of Prayer for Unity Graymoor Garrison NY 10524

CRAWFORD, DAN REAVIS, educator, So. Baptist Conv.; b. Temple, Tex., Dec. 30, 1941; s. William Edwin and Mary Inez (Gilliam) C.; B.A., Howard Payne U., 1964; B.D., Southwestern Baptist Theol. Sem., 1967, M.Div., 1976; student U. Tex., summer 1973, East Tex. State U., summer 1976; m. Joanne Cunningham, Aug. 8, 1964; children—Danna Ruth, James Edwin. Ordained to ministry So. Baptist Conv., 1963; pastor Robinson Springs Baptist Ch., DeLeon, Tex., 1963-64; pastor Pisgah Bapt. Ch., Frankston, Tex., 1966-67; dir. Bapt. Student Union, Bible instr. Pan Am. U., Edinburg, Tex., 1967-73; dir. Bapt. Student Union, instr. Bible East Tex. State U., 1973-76; dir. Bapt. Student Union, U. Tex., 1976—. Program supr. City of Irving (Tex.) Parks and Recreation Dept., 1965-66. Mem. Tex. Assn. Coll. Teachers, Fellowship of Christian Athletes. Home: 2505 Ashdale Austin TX 78758 Office: 2204 San Antonio Austin TX 78705

CRAWFORD, LARRY PAUL, priest, Roman Catholic Ch. B. Owensboro, Ky., July 26, 1940; s. Charles Leonard and Elizabeth Lucille (Coomes) C. B.S., St. Meinrad Coll., Ind., 1962. Ordained Priest Roman Catholic Ch., 1966. Asst. pastor Holy Spirit Ch., Indpls. and instr. Scecina High School., Indpls., 1966-68; asst. pastor Holy Family Ch., Richmond, Ind., 1968-71; assoc. pastor St. Gabriel Ch., Indpls., 1971-76; pastor Holy Trinity Ch., Indpls., 1976—; dir. Archdiocese of Indpls. Office Pro-Life Activities, 1982—; chaplain

Richmond State Hosp., 1968-71; deanery dir. Cath. Youth Orgn., 1969-71; v.p., then pres. Speedway Ministerial Assn., Indpls., 1972-76; pres. West Deanery Bd. Edn., Indpls., 1976-78; v.p. Indpls. Deaneries Coordinating Com., 1977-82; mem. edn. planning commn. Archdiocesan Bd. of Edn., 1977-79; chmn. fin. com. Urban Ministry Study, 1982-84; bd. dirs. Christamore House, Indpls., 1982—. Pres. WESCO (local neighborhood orgn.), Indpls., 1978-80. Mem. Ind. Pro-Life Activities Dirs. (chmn.), Archdiocese of Indpls. Bd. Edn. Democrat. Club: Indpls. Athletic. Home: 2618 W Saint Clair St Indianapolis IN 46222 Office: Office of Pro-Life Activities 1400 N Meridian St PO Box 1410 Indianapolis IN 24106

CRAWFORD, VELMA VELORE, school administrator; b. La Verne, Calif., July 4, 1905; d. Leslie Walter and Pearl Elzada (Akers) Raley; student Normal Sch., McComb, Ill., 1924-26, Whittier Coll., 1951, Los Angeles Pacific Coll., 1957, Riverside City Coll., 1960; m. Vance Wesley Mason, Feb. 14, 1931 (dec.); m. William McKinley Crawford, June 17, 1962 (dec.). Prin., Light and Life Christian Sch., Corona, Calif., 1951-59, Corona Christian Day Sch., Norco, Calif., 1959—. Home: 1649 Elm Dr Norco CA 91760 Office: 2518 Hamner Ave PO Box 336 Norco CA 91760

CRAWFORD, WILLIAM GEORGE, minister, So. Baptist Conv.; b. Newport, Ky., Aug. 8, 1910; s. Ray and Luella (Schell) C.; B.S. cum laude, Tex. Wesleyan U., Ft. Worth, 1951; M.R.E. magna cum laude (John M. Price award), Southwestern Bapt. Theol. Sem., Ft. Worth, 1953; m. Ruth Warwood, Oct. 17, 1935; 1 dau., Bonnie Mary Crawford Hammons. Ordained to ministry, 1959; assoc. pastor First Bapt. Ch., Newport, Ky., 1946-48; minister edn. chs. in Tex. and Ky., 1953-63; minister edn. Grace Bapt. Ch., Lexington, Ky., 1963-66, First Bapt. Ch., Franklin, Ky., 1966-76; dir. missions Simpson Bapt. Assn., Franklin, 1977-82; dir. Simpson County World Missions Conf., 1977, 81; cons. religious edn., 1982—. Mem. exec. bd. Simpson County Right to Life Com., Franklin, 1974-76. Mem. Ky. Bapt. Religious Edn. Assn. (pres. 1976), Franklin County Simpson Ministerial Assn. (pres. 1973-75), Southwestern Bapt. Theol. Sem. Alumni Assn. (pres. Ky. 1973). Author articles. Home and Office: 6050 Luwista Ln Cincinnati OH 45230

CREECH, PRESTON ALLEN, JR., minister, Southern Baptist Convention; b. Augusta, Ga., Sept. 4, 1940; s. Preston Allen and Marybelle E. (Boyd) C.; m. Nancy Elaine Clegg, Aug. 20, 1966; children: Preston A., Nathan B. B.A., Augusta Coll., 1967; M.Div., Southeastern Sem., 1979. Ordained to ministry, 1977. Pastor, Enon Bapt. Ch., Oxford, N.C., 1977—; USAF Res. chaplain, Denver, 1981—; interim pastor Pollocksville Bapt. Ch., N.C., 1977; supr. ministry program Southeastern Bapt. Theol. Sem., 1980— pres. minister's conf. Flat River Bapt. Assn., 1979-80, exec. com. mem., 1977—, associational stewardship chmn., 1978—. Chaplain, Oxford Wildlife Club, 1979-85; adv. bd. Granville County Bd. Edn., Oxford, 1979-81, Granville County Nursing Home, 1980-82. Served with USAF, 1959-62. Mem. Flat. River Bapt. Assn., Air Force Assn. (life). Democrat. Lodges: Rotary (pres.), Masons (chaplain 1980-81). Address: Route 1 Box 369F Oxford NC 27565

CREEL, THURMAN ORESTER, lay ch. worker, Bapt. Ch.; b. College Park, Ga., June 5, 1920; s. Thomas Orester and Susie Ozella (Cook) C.; student Draughon Jr. Coll., 1938-39; m. Catherine Juanita Middlebrooks, Oct. 18, 1923; children: Gary M., Phyllis Theresa. Dir. music College Park (Ga.) 2d Bapt. Ch., 1936—. Inventory analyst Internat. Harvester Co., Atlanta, 1939—. Mem. Broadcast Music Inc. Composer: A Morning Prayer, 1967; I Stood One Day, 1971; Our Father in Heaven, 1971; Blest Be the Tie, 1951; Just the Lord and I, 1971. Home: 2305 Sandgate Rd College Park GA 30349 Office: 1500 Norman Dr College Park GA 30349

CREMEANS, JAMES L., minister, non-denominational; b. Rayland, Ohio, Dec. 22, 1939; s. Leroy and Waneda (Montgomery) C.; m. Mary McCormick, Oct. 4, 1956; children: James, David, Jeffery, Diane, Janet. D.D. (hon.), Internat. Bible. Sem., 1985. Ordained to ministry First Tabernacle Ch., Ironton, Ohio, 1967. Pastor, City Mission Ch., Ironton, 1967—; exec. dir. City Welfare Mission, Ironton, 1967—; corr. sch. dir. Evangelistic Outreach, Pedro, Ohio, 1982—, v.p., 1975—, also dir. Mem. Lawrence County Welfare Adv. Bd., Ohio, 1980-82, Home Health Care Bd., Ironton, 1980-85. Named Citizen of Yr. Community Betterment Club, Lawrence County, 1979. Mem. Lawrence County Ministerial Assn. (chmn. radio and TV 1975-80). Home: Route 1 Box 18 Pedro OH 45659 Office: City Mission Ch 710 N 5th St Ironton OH 45638

CRENSHAW, JAMES L(EE), theology educator, Southern Baptist Convention; b. Sunset, S.C., Dec. 19, 1934; s. B. D. and Bessie (Aiken) C.; m. Juanita Rhodes, June 10, 1956; children: James Timothy, David Lee. A.A., North Greenville Coll., 1954; B.A., Furman U., 1956; B.D., So. Bapt. Theol. Sem., 1960; Ph.D., Vanderbilt U., 1964. Asst. prof. religion Atlantic Christian Coll., Wilson, N.C., 1964-65; assoc. prof. Mercer U., Macon, Ga., 1965-69; prof. O.T., Vanderbilt Div. Sch., Nashville, 1970—. Author 8 books, editor, contbg. author 4 books. Contbr. articles to profl. jours. Grantee NEH, 1974, Am. Council Learned Socs., 1981; fellow Soc. Values in Higher Edn., 1972-73, Assn. Theol. Schs., 1978-79, Guggenheim Found., 1984-85. Mem. Soc. Bibl. Lit. (editor 1978—), Cath. Bibl. Assn., Soc. Values in Higher Edn., Colloquium Bibl. Research, Internat. Orgn. Study of O.T. Democrat. Club: Freolac (Nashville). Home: 3807 Brighton Rd Nashville TN 37205 Office: Vanderbilt Div Sch Nashville TN 37240

CRESS, JAMES REID, minister United Church of Christ, religious organization executive; b. Rowan County, N.C., July 7, 1931; s. Joseph Franklin and Mary Ophelia (Patterson) C.; m. Anna Mardelle Bayler, Sept. 22, 1956; children: Karen Elaine, Jennifer Ann, Janet Marie, Philip Reid, Richard Bryan, Theresa Lynn. B.A., Catawba Coll., 1953; B.Div., Lancaster Theol. Sch., 1956, M.Div., 1976. Ordained to ministry United Church of Christ, 1956. Pastor Brick United Ch. Christ, Whitsett, N.C., 1956-62, Ursinus United Ch. Christ, Rockwell, N.C., 1962-69; exec. dir. Rowan Coop. Christian Ministry, Salisbury, N.C., 1969—; chmn. Health and Welfare So. Conf. United Ch. Christ, 1983—; bd. dirs., cons. Sr./Jr. Friends, Salisbury, N.C., 1983—, Dial Help, Salisbury, 1971—; bd. dirs., cons. Yokefellow Prison Ministry, Salisbury, 1970—. Sec. Rowan Council Human Services, Salisbury, 1980-83; bd. dirs. Greater Salisbury Track Club, Salisbury, 1977—, Rowan Council on Aging, Salisbury, 1962-83; cons. Mental Health Assn., Salisbury, 1982-83; mem. The Concert Choir, Salisbury, 1978-83; performer Piedmont Players Theatre, 1961-83. Recipient Brotherhood award NCCJ, 1972, Good Samaritan award Salisbury Civitan Club, Rowan County, 1974, 25 Years Outstanding Service award United Ch. Christ, 1981; winner age group trophies and medals for various road races in N.C. and S.C., 1977—; participant 100 Mile Run for Hunger CROP/Church World Service, 1982. Mem. Salisbury/Rowan Ministers Assn., Rowan Dist. Ministers United Ch. Christ, Internatl. Christian Youth Exchange (bd. dirs. N.C. and S.C. 1977-83), Nat. Com. Persons with Disabilities (corresponding mem. 1984), N.C. Dept. Corrections (community volunteer 1971—). Home: Route 9 Box 93 Salisbury NC 28144 Office: Rowan Coop Christian Ministry 117 W Fisher St Salisbury NC 28144

CRIBBIN, AUSTIN JOSEPH, priest, Roman Cath. Ch.; b. Ballyhaunis, Mayo, Ireland, Feb. 19, 1929; s. Thomas Martin and Margaret Mary (Lyons) C.; came to U.S., 1956, naturalized, 1962; M.A., St. Kieran's Coll., Kilkenny, Ireland, 1956. Ordained priest, 1956; pastor chs. in Oreg., 1956—, St. Elizabeth's Ch., John Day, Oreg., 1968-73, St. Augustine's Ch., Merrill, Oreg., 1973—. Mem. health and retirement bd. Roman Cath. Diocese Baker. Address: Box 340 Merrill OR 97633

CRIST, BURTON WAYNE, minister, Ch. of the Brethren; b. Quinter, Kans., Sept. 14, 1921; s. Daniel Floyd and Nellie Mae (Jamison) C.; A.B., McPherson Coll., 1943; B.D., Bethany Theol. Sem., 1946; student Chgo. Div. Sch., 1954-56; D.Ministry, San Francisco Theol. Sem., 1982; m. Dorothy Elizabeth Jones, Dec. 25, 1951; children: Danese Ann, Robert Floyd, David Wayne, Thomas Owen. Ordained to ministry, 1943; pastor Polo (Ill.) Ch. of the Brethren, 1946-52, Wenatchee (Wash.) Ch. of the Brethren, 1956-61, Imperial Heights Ch. of the Brethren, Los Angeles, 1961-69, Pomona (Calif.) Ch. of the Brethren, 1961-72, McPherson (Kans.) Ch. of the Brethren, 1972—; vis. prof. Bethany Theol. Sem., 1955-56. Moderator No. Ill. Dist., 1949-50, Wash. State Dist., 1958-59; mem. gen. bd. Ch. of the Brethren, 1959-64; mem. standing com. Ann. Conf., 1949, 50, 59, 67, 68, curriculum study com. for denom., 1968-69; mem. central com. Ann. Conf., 1973—, worship coordinator, 1973—; chmn. S.W. Los Angeles Ministerial Assn., 1965-66, Ministerial Assn. Pomona, 1971-72, Chs. United In Ministry of McPherson, 1973-75, Ministerial Assn. of McPherson, 1973-75. Mem. Brethren Pastors' Assn. Contbr. articles to religious jours.; contbg. author: Brethren Preaching Today, 1947. Home: 1322 E Euclid Ave McPherson KS 67460 Office: 1500 E Euclid Ave McPherson KS 67460

CRISTO, GEORGE LUIS, minister, Assemblies of God Church; b. Cruces, Santa Clara, Cuba, Mar. 29, 1958; came to U.S., Jan. 1961, naturalized, 1976; s. Ellodoro Cristo and Marie Cristo Pallas. B.A. in Bibl. Studies, Bus. Adminstrn. and Fgn. Lang., Azusa Pacific U., 1983, B.A. in Edn., 1984. Ordained to ministry Assemblies of God, 1980. Treas. Royal Ranger Templo De La Fe, Assemblies of God, San Francisco, 1968-70, sec., 1970-73, religion educator, 1974-79, asst. ch. sec., 1984—, treas. Sunday Sch., 1985—; choir, drama dir. Latin Am. Bible Coll., La Puente, Calif., 1979-82; bilingual interpretor Azusa Pacific Mexicali Outreach Ministry, Calif., 1982-83; lang. interpretor Youth Ministries, Assemblies of God, San Francisco, 1979—. Adminstr. IBM, Oakland, Calif., 1985—. Contbr. articles to newspaper. Pub. educator Glendora High Sch., Calif., 1984; bilingual host Los Angeles Olympic Organizing Com., 1984; mem. Democratic organizing com., San Francisco, 1980-84. Mem. Nat. Assn. Campers Orgn. West, Alpha Chi. Avocations: tennis, running, stamp and coin collecting, aerobics, bowling. Home: 2522 Folsom St San Francisco CA 94110 Office: IBM 475 14th St 10th Floor Oakland CA 94612

CROCKER, LARRY J., minister, Christian Church (Disciples of Christ); b. Dallas, July 11, 1948; s. Wilson N. and Doris J. (Montgomery) C.; m. Gloria Ann Scott, Aug. 11, 1978; 1 child, Patrick Wayne. B.S. in Criminal Justice, Am. Tech. U., Killeen, Tex., 1978; M.Div., Tex. Christian U., 1984; diploma Tex. Coll. Mortuary Sci., 1969. Ordained to ministry Christian Ch. (Disciples of Christ), 1984. Youth dir. Cove Christian Ch., Copperas Cove, Tex., 1976-78; youth minister Rockwood Christian Ch., Ft. Worth, 1978-80; minister Central Christian Ch., Hillsboro, Tex., 1980-84, First Christian Ch., Rockdale, Tex., 1984—; vice chmn. Outdoor Christian Edn. Com., Ft. Worth, 1981—. Vice chmn. Kickapoo Indian Land Acquisition Com., Eagle Pass, Tex., 1982—. Lodges: Masons, Shriners, K.T. Home: 1708 Murray Rockdale TX 76567 Office: First Christian Ch 231 N Burleson St Rockdale TX 76567

CROFT, HERMAN COLBERT, evangelist, So. Baptist Conv.; b. Berlin, Ga., May 4, 1941; s. Arley William and Josephine (Griffin) C.; A.A., Norman Coll., 1969; B.Th., Luther Rice Sem., 1971; m. Joyce Smith, June 26, 1964; Ordained to ministry, 1965; pastor 1st Bapt. Ch., Lake Park, Ga., 1969-71, Northside Bapt. Ch., Quitman, Ga., 1971-73, 1st Bapt. Ch., New Brockton, Ala., 1973-75; evangelist, Jasper, Fla., 1975—. Radio broadcasts. Named Gospel Disc Jockey of Am., 1972. Mem. Gospel Music Assn. Composer gospel songs including I Believe He Died for Me, 1973. Home and Office: PO Box 125 Jasper FL 32052

CROMIE, RICHARD MARLIN, minister, religious organization executive, Presbyterian Church in the U.S.; b. Pitts., Apr. 9, 1936; s. Harry Marlin and Margaret (Good) C.; children: Catherine Alice, Anne Campbell, Courtney Beth. B.A., U. Pitts., 1957; M. Div. magna cum laude, Pitts. Theol. Sem., 1961; Ph.D., U. St. Andrews (Scotland), 1974; D.D. (hon.), Grove City Coll., 1981. Pastor Carnegie Mellon U., Pitts., 1960-62; assoc. pastor Shadyside Presbyn. Ch., Pitts., 1961-66; pastor Parkwood Ch., Pitts., 1968-72; sr. pastor Southminster Ch., Mt. Lebanon, Pa., 1972-83, First Presbyn. Ch., Fort Lauderdale, Fla., 1983—; pres. Desert Ministries Inc., Pitts., 1982—; trustee Pitts. Theol. Sem., 1980—, Eckerd Coll., St. Petersburg, Fla., 1984—; chmn. supporting mission com. Nat. Assembly Ch., 1976. Author: Sometime Before The Dawn, 1982; The Future is Now, 1984; Christ Will See You Through, 1985. Contbr. articles to profl. jours. Bd. dirs. Freshair Camp, Pitts., 1970—; chmn. devel. com. Sta. WQED, Pitts., 1979-83. Recipient George Washington award Freedoms Found, 1970; Rotary Internat. fellow 1958-59. Mem. Acad. Parish Clergy, After Many Days Club (U. St. Andrews, Scotland). Republican. Lodges: Rotary, Masons (33d deg.). Avocations: golf; tennis; reading. Office: First Presbyn Ch 401 SE 15 Ave Fort Lauderdale FL 33301

CRONIN, DANIEL ANTHONY, bishop, Roman Catholic Church; b. Newton, Mass., Nov. 14, 1927; s. Daniel George and Emily Frances (Joyce) C.; S.T.L., Gregorian U., 1953, S.T.D. summa cum laude, 1956; LL.D., Suffolk U., 1969. Ordained priest Roman Catholic Ch., 1952; attache Apostolic Internunciature, Addis Ababa, Ethiopia, 1957-61; attache Secretariat of State, Vatican City, 1961-68; became monsignor, 1962; consecrated bishop, 1968; titular bishop of Egnatia, aux. bishop of Boston, 1968; pastor St. Raphael Ch., Medford, Mass., 1968-70; bishop of Fall River (Mass.), 1970—. Address: 47 Underwood St PO Box 2577 Fall River MA 02722

CRONIN, WILLIAM FRANCIS, priest, Roman Catholic Church; b. Bklyn., Dec. 21, 1948; s. Francis John and Cecilia Lucille (De Nike) C. B.A., Marquette U., 1971; M. Div., Sacred Heart Sem., 1974; cert. in geriatrics U. So. Calif., 1976. Joined Order of St. Camillus, 1968; ordained priest Roman Catholic Ch., 1976; lic. nursing home adminstr., Ariz., Wis. Chaplain, St. Luke's Hosp., Milw., 1970-72, St. Joseph's Hosp., Milw., 1976-78, St. Joseph's Hosp., Phoenix, 1982-84; dir. pastoral care St. Camillus Hosp., Milw., 1978-79; asst. dir. pastoral care St. Joseph's Hosp., Phoenix, also nursing home adminstr., 1984—; adminstrv. asst. St. Camillus Hosp., Milw., 1975-77; nursing home adminstr. Catholic Diocese Phoenix, 1979-82; provincial counselor, sec. ministry Order of St. Camillus, Milw., 1979—, supr., Phoenix, 1979—; trustee St. Camillus Hosp., Whitinsville, Mass., 1982—. Mem. White House Conf. on Aging, Phoenix, 1980; chaplain Phoenix Police Vol. Res., 1981; mem. Ariz. Com. on Long-Term Care, Phoenix, 1982. Mem. Nat. Assn. Cath. Chaplains (cert.), Am. Coll. Health Care Adminstrs., Gerontol. Soc. Am., Nat. Council on Aging, Nat. Interfaith Coalition on Aging, Cath. Hosp. Assn., Acad. for Cath. Health Care Leadership (bd. dirs.), Alpha Kappa Delta, Pi Gamma Mu, Sigma Phi Omega, Cath. Youth Orgn., YMCA. Ind. Democrat. Lodge: KC. Home: 3124 N 53d St Phoenix AZ 85018 Office: St Joseph's Hosp 350 W Thomas Rd Phoenix AZ 85013

CRONLEY, MARGARET MARY, provincial superior, Roman Cath. Ch.; b. N.Y.C., Oct. 26, 1926; d. Thomas and Elizabeth (Melsopp) Cronley; B.S. in Edn., Fordham U., M.S. in Edn. Joined Marianites of Holy Cross, 1945; tchr. New Orleans, Algiers, La., N.Y.C., Ridgefield, Conn.; prin. Our Lady of Perpetual Help, Ardsley, N.Y., 1959-63, St. Colman's Sch., Brockton, Mass., 1963-69; provincial Marianites of Holy Cross, Princeton, N.J., 1969—, gen. councillor, LeMans, France, 1974—; provincial superior Our Lady of Princeton, 1969—. Address: Our Lady of Princeton Princeton NJ 08540

CROSE, LESTER ALTON, minister, Ch. of God (Anderson, Ind.); b. Santa Cruz, Calif., July 28, 1912; s. John Davis and Pearl Parthenia (Conrad) C.; B.A., Anderson Coll., 1945, D.D., 1959; m. Ruthe Marie Hamon, Sept. 26, 1934; children: Alta Ruthe (Mrs. Ronald Jack), John Lester. Ordained to ministry Ch. of God (Anderson, Ind.), 1937; overseas missionary, 1933-54; sec.-treas., Barbados, Trinidad, 1941-44, Lebanon, 1945-50, Egypt, 1950-52; exec. sec.-treas. missionary bd. of Ch. of God, 1954-75, mem. exec. council, div. world service, div. gen. service, 1954-75, sec. for research and devel., 1975-76, prof. missions Sch. Theology, 1976-78, mem. missionary bd. and gen. assembly Ch. of God; mem. Commn. on Christian Unity; cons. Mediterranean Bible Coll., Beirut, Lebanon. Author: Passport for a Reformation, 1981. Mem. Am. Soc. Missiology, Middle East Inst. Home: 303 Central Ave Anderson IN 46012 Office: Ch of God Exec Offices Anderson IN 46012

CROSS, JAMES ADAM, minister, Chs. of God; b. Crawfordville, Fla., Dec. 12, 1911; s. William Henry and Agnes Elizabeth (Walker) C.; B.A., Lee Coll., D.D., 1967; m. Nell B. McClure, Oct. 26, 1934; children: Marvin Holbert, Allen Henry, Norman James. Ordained to ministry Ch. of God, 1933; pastor chs. in S.D., Fla., Tenn., 1934-50; pres. Lee Coll., Cleveland, Tenn., 1966-70; evangelist, Bible lectr. Ch. of God, Cleveland, 1974—; chmn. bd. dirs. Home for Children, 1945-50; bd. dirs. Lee Coll., 1950-54, chmn. 1952-54; chmn. World Missions Bd., 1970—; chmn. bd. dirs. Pentecostal Fellowship N.Am., 1960-62; mem. adv. bd. World Pentecostal Fellowship, 1959-62; asst. gen. overseer Chs. of God, 1954-58, gen. overseer, 1958-62; state overseer Chs. of God in Nebr., 1936-38, Pa., 1950-52, S.C., 1952-54, Fla., 1962-66, Ala., 1970-74; mem. Chs. of God 1986 Centennial Commn. Mem. Phi Delta Kappa, Phi Delta Omicron. Author: Glorious Gospel, 1956; Healing in the Church, 1960; A Study of the Holy Ghost, 1973; Answers From the Word, 1974. Contbr. articles to religious publs. Address: PO Box 185 Valrico FL 33594

CROUCH, EMMA MAY, educator, minister, Pentacostal Holiness Church; b. Paoia, Kans., Dec. 17, 1925; d. Fred Samuel and Alice (Neff) Everett; student N.W. Coll., 1943-45; diploma Foothills Bible Inst., 1967; B.A. in Religious Edn., Southwestern Coll,. 1974; B.Th., Christianview Bible Coll., 1979. Ordained to ministry Pentecostal Holiness Ch., 1958; active in children's work Pentecostal Holiness Ch., and other denominations, 1940—, approved tchr. Evang. Tchr. Tng. Assn., 1959—; christian edn. dir., tchr. Foothills Bible Inst., Winfield, Alta., Can., 1964-75, pres., 1972-75 Christian edn. dir., adminstr., tchr. Christianview Bible Coll., Ailsa Craig, Ont., 1975—. Cons. Scripture Press Found. of Can., Whitby, Ont. 1972—. Active Sunday sch. and Christian edn. confs. and convs. Pentecostal Holiness Ch., 1952—; pres. N.W. Conf. Sunday Sch. Assn., 1958-64, sec.-treas. N.W. Conf., 1960-64, pres Western Can. Conf. Sunday Sch. Assn., 1970-75; mem. gen. bd. adminstrn. Pentecostal Holiness Ch. of Can., 1972—, mem. gen. bd. edn., 1974—, dir. Can. Gen. Christian Edn. Dept., 1982—. Pub. dispensations chart God's Plan of the Ages, 1954. Address: Box 25 Ailsa Craig ON N0M 1A0 Canada

CROUCH, PAUL FRANKLIN, minister, church official, Assemblies of God; b. St. Joseph, Mo., Mar. 30, 1934; s. Andrew Franklin and Sarah Matilda (Swingle) C.; B.Th., Central Bible Coll. and Sem., Springfield, Mo., 1955; m. Janice Wendell Bethany, Aug. 25, 1957; children: Paul F., Matthew W. Ordained to ministry, 1955; dir. fgn. missions film and audio-visual dept. Assemblies of God, 1955-58; asso. pastor 1st Assembly of God, Rapid City, S.D., 1958-60, Central Assembly of God, Muskegon, Mich., 1960-62; gen. mgr. TV and film prodn. center Assemblies of God, Burbank, Calif., 1962-65; gen. mgr. Sta. KREL, Corona, Calif., 1965-71, Sta. KHOF, KHOF-TV, Glendale, Calif., 1971-73; founder, pres. Sta. KLXA-TV, Trinity Broadcasting Network, Los Angeles, 1973—. Recipient Best Religious Film award Winona Lake Film Festival, 1956. Mem. Nat. Assn. Religious Broadcasters, Western Religious Broadcasters Assn., Assn. Christian TV Stas. (founder). Home: 1973 Port Clelsea Pl Newport Beach CA 92660 Office: Box A Santa Ana CA 92711

CROUNSE, REXFORD KNIFFIN, minister, United Meth. Ch.; b. Meadowdale, N.Y., May 6, 1912; s. Freeman Carlisle and Edna (Kniffin) C.; A.A., Keystone Coll., 1951; A.A., Wyo. Sem., 1934; postgrad. Emory U., 1954-55; m. Ruth LaCoe Thompson, Jan. 1, 1936; children—Ina May, Judith Ann, John Rexford. Ordained to ministry, 1948; pastor Plymouth (N.Y.) United Meth. Ch., 1937-39, Sidney Center (N.Y.) United Meth. Ch., 1940-42, New Milford (Pa.) United Meth. Ch., 1943-47, Derr Meml. United Meth. Ch., Wilkes-Barre, Pa., 1948-51, Bennett Meml. United Meth. Ch., 1948-51, Sherburne (N.Y.) United Meth. Ch., 1951-56, Simpson Ch., Scranton, Pa., 1957-64, Central United Meth. Ch., Honesdale, Pa., 1965—. Pres. Oneonta Dist. Ministers Assn., 1954-55, Scranton Dist. Ministers Assn., 1971-72; treas. entertainment fund. Wyo. Conf., United Meth. Ch., 1950-58, sec. missionary, 1965-72, dir. homes for aging, 1966-76. Religious broadcaster Windows of Hope, Sta. WGBI, Scranton, 1957—. Home: 207 11th St Honesdale PA 18431 Office: 205 11th St Honesdale PA 18431

CROUSE, KEITH ALBERT, minister, Lutheran Church in America; b. Lunenburg, N.S., Can., Dec. 13, 1938; s. Kinsman Eleazor and Doris Emma Victor (Spindler) C.; m. Grethe Edna Kristiansen, Sept. 10, 1962; children: Kelly, Daniel, Joel, Ted. B.A., Wilfrid Laurier U., Waterloo, Ont., 1960, B.Div., 1969. Ordained to ministry Lutheran Ch., 1963. Pastor Mahone Bay Luth. Parish, N.S., 1963-69, Good Shepherd Luth. Ch., Brockville, Ont., 1969-82, St. Matthews Luth. Ch., Welland, Ont., 1982—. Creator-dir. maritime power lifting championships, Mahone Bay, 1964-68; chmn. Living In A Free Environment, 1983. Named Mr. Ont. Physique, Ont. Body Builders Assn., 1961; Mr. Eastern Can., Power Lifting and Physique, Halifax, N.S., 1965-67; Mr. Atlantic Provinces, 1st Power Lifting and Physique, St. John, N.B., 1968. Mem. Clergy Fellowship (treas. Welland 1984—). Home and Office: 59 Griffith St Welland ON L3B 4G6 Canada

CROUTER, RICHARD EARL, educator; b. Washington, Nov. 2, 1937; s. Earl C. and Neva J. (Crain) C.; A.B., Occidental Coll., 1960; B.D., Union Theol. Sem., 1963, Th.D., 1968; postgrad. U. Heidelberg, 1965-66, U. Toronto, Can., 1972-73, U. Marburg, 1976-77; m. Barbara Williams, Jan. 30, 1960; children: Edward Clinton, Frances Elizabeth. Prof. religion Carleton Coll., Northfield, Minn., 1967—. Resident dir. Northfield ABC Program, 1968-70. Post-doctoral Cross-disciplinary fellow, 1972-73; Am. Council Learned Socs., Fulbright scholar, 1976-77. Mem. Soc. for Values in Higher Edn., Am. Acad. Religion, Hegel Soc. Am., Am. Soc. for Ch. History. Office: Carleton College Northfield MN 55057

CROW, CHARLES DELMAR, minister, Ch. of Nazarene; b. Sutherland, Nebr., Oct. 16, 1945; s. Elmer Joseph and Ruth Vivian; A.B., Bethany Nazarene Coll., 1968; M.Div., Nazarene Theol. Sem., 1971, postgrad., 1972; m. Imalee Ruth Smith, July 1, 1967; 1 dau., Annette Lynn. Ordained to ministry, 1965; adminstrv. asst. Nazarene Gen. Headquarters, Kansas City, Mo., 1973-76; church growth cons. Fuller Evangelistic Assn., Pasadena, Calif., 1976—. Mem. forum steering com. Internat. Cong. on World Evangelization. Mem. Nat. Assn. of Ch. Bus. Adminstrs. Author: Biblical Basis for Church Growth, 1976; contbr. articles to religious mags. Home: 1508 Stagecoach Dr Olathe KS 66061

CROW, PAUL ABERNATHY, JR., minister, religious orgn. exec., educator, Christian Ch. (Disciples of Christ); b. Birmingham, Ala., Nov. 17, 1931; s. Paul A. and Beulah Elizabeth (Parker) C.; B.S., U. Ala., 1954; B.D., Lexington Theol. Sem., 1957; S.T.M., Hartford Sem. Found., 1958, Ph.D., 1962; m. Mary Evelyn Matthews, Sept. 11, 1955; children: Carol Ann, Stephen Paul, Susan Margaret. Ordained to ministry, 1957; campus minister U. Ala., Tuscaloosa, 1953-54; minister chs., Ala., Ky., Mass., 1953-61; assoc. prof. ch. history Lexington (Ky.) Theol. Sem., 1961-66, prof. ch. history, 1966-68; gen. sec. Consultation Ch. Union, Princeton, 1968-74; pres. Council Christian Unity, Christian Ch. (Disciples Christ), Indpls., 1974—; vis. prof. ch. history Princeton Theol. Sem., 1970—, Christian Theol. Sem., Indpls., 1974—. Moderator bd. World Council Chs. Ecumenical Inst., Bossey, Switzerland; del. to 4th Assembly World Council Chs., Uppsala, Sweden, 1968, 5th Assembly, Nairobi, Kenya, 1975, 6th Assembly, Vancouver, B.C., 1983; mem. central com. and commn. faith and order World Council Chs.; mem. exec. com. and governing bd. Nat. Council Chs. U.S.A.; exec. com. Consultation on Ch. Union; co-moderator Disciples of Christ-Roman Cath. Internat. Dialogue, 1977—; gen. sec. Disciples Ecumenical Consultive Council, 1979—. Author: Church Union at Midpoint, 1972; No Greater Love: Gospel and Its Imperatives, 1967; Ecumenical Movement in Bibliographical Outline, 1965; Where We Are in Church Union, 1965; Christian Unity: Matrix for Mission, 1982; contbr. over 150 articles to religious jours. Editor: Mid-Stream, an ecumenical jour., Indpls., 1974—. Home: 7215 Vauxhall Rd Indianapolis IN 46250 Office: PO Box 1986 Indianapolis IN 46206

CROWDER, CHARLES LINFIELD, minister, Assemblies of God; b. American Falls, Idaho, Nov. 13, 1929; s. Charles David and Elizabeth Elle (Dille) C.; B.A., N.W. Coll., Kirkland, Wash.; m. Nellie Luella Fuller, June 7, 1952; children—Linelle, Alice, Leilani, Sarah. Ordained to ministry, 1956; missionary evangelist Singapore, Greece, Guam and Marshall Islands, 1956-64, Micronesia, Kwajalien, others, 1964-67, Korea, 1967-75, Weisbaden, W.Ger., 1976; cons. Assemblies of God, American Falls, 1969—. Judge, Boise Valley, Idaho, 1953-57. Named Alumnus of Year, N.W. Coll., 1973. Mem. Ch. of God in Christ (hon.), Stanley Found. Coll. Lectrs. Contbr. articles to religious jours. Address: 448 Garfield St American Falls ID 83211

CROWE, DONA JON, minister, So. Bapt. Conv.; b. Louisville, Ky., July 13, 1938; d. Cad Wallace and Dona Dolores (Albrecht) Crowe; B.A., Ky. So. Coll., 1969; M.R.E., So. Bapt. Theol. Sem., 1974. Minister of edn. 18th St. Bapt. Ch., Louisville, 1974—. Vol. entertainer Masonic Home for Widows, 1968-76; mem. program com. Long Run Religious Educators Assn., 1975-76; vol. tutor Bapt. Tabernacle, Louisville, 1972. Bd. dirs. Portland Area Council of Louisville Community Action Commn., 1971-73, sec. bd., 1972-73; sec. Louisville Neighborhood Health Bd., 1973; bd. dirs. Neighborhood House, Louisville, 1973-76, sec. bd., 1975-76; mem. Louisville Mayor's Task Force for Neighborhood Improvement, 1972. Named Disting. Citizen, City of Louisville, 1972; recipient Cert. of Service Louisville Pub. Sch. System, 1972. Mem. Nat. Religious Educators Assn. Home: 202 N 28th St Louisville KY 40212 Office: 2001 Dixie Hwy Louisville KY 40210

CROWE, OLEN C(LYDE), minister, Church of God of Prophecy; nuclear quality assurance engineer; b. Oliver Springs, Tenn., Oct. 14, 1952; s. Chester E. and Ruth Lucille (King) C.; m. Glenna K. Buck, Aug. 5, 1972; children: Christi R., Rebecca L. A.A., Hinds Jr. Coll., 1981; student U. New Orleans, 1982-84. Ordained bishop Church of God of Prophecy, 1983. Pastor Ch. of God of Prophecy, Newellton, La., 1979-81; pastor, dist. overseer Ch. of God of Prophecy, Pearl River, La., 1981—; state fin. com. man Ch. of God of Prophecy, La., 1982—, sr. camp dir., La., 1983-84, camp coordinator, 1984—; police chaplain Pearl River Police Dept., 1984—; chaplain 1984 World's Fair, New Orleans, 1984. Served as specialist 5, U.S. Army, 1971-74. Avocations: flying; pilot. Home and Office: Ch of God of Prophecy 309 Saint Paul Dr Pearl River LA 70454

CROWLEY, JOSEPH R., bishop, Roman Catholic Church. Titular bishop of Maraguis, aux. bishop, Fort Wayne, 1971—. Office: 1701 Miami St South Bend IN 46613*

CRUMBLY, JOHN QUANTOCK, priest, Episcopal Church; b. Union Point, Ga., Nov. 2, 1916; s. Frank Walden and Anna Rebecca (Walden) C.; m. Meda Lamb Crouch, May 31, 1936. B.Div., U. of the South, 1952, M.Div., 1971; M.Ed., The Citadel, 1984. Ordained priest Episcopal Ch., 1949. Vicar, rector Diocese of S.C., Charleston, 1947-51; rector Diocese of S. Fla., Orlando, 1951-58, Diocese of Washington, 1958-63, Diocese of Upper S.C., Columbia, 1963-79; chaplain VA Med. Ctr., Charleston, S.C., 1979—; mem. prison ministry com. Diocese S.C., Charleston, 1983—. Mem. Assn. Episcopal Hosps. and Chaplains, Assn. Mental Health Clergy. Home: Ashley House Charleston SC 29401 Office: VA Med Ctr 109 Bee St Charleston SC 29403

CRUMLEY, JAMES ROBERT, JR. See *Who's Who in America*, 43rd edition.

CRUPI, FRANCIS JOSEPH, priest, Roman Catholic Church. B. Mileto, Catanzaro, Calabria, Italy, Jan. 2, 1926; came to U.S. 1938; s. Dominick Anthony and Isabella Mazzeo C. Student Charles Coll., Catonsville, Md., 1943-47; St. Mary's Sem., 1947-52; B.A., S.T.B., U. Balt., 1950, S.T.L., 1952. Ordained priest Roman Cath. Ch. 1952. Assoc. pastor St. Edward's Ch., Milford, N.J., Mission Ch. of Our Lady of Victories, Baptistown, N.J., 1952-54; assoc. pastor, dir. athletics St. Philip and St. James Ch., Phillipsburg, N.J., tchr. Religion Phillipsburg Cath. High Sch., 1954-62; asst. pastor St. Mary of Mount Virgin Ch., New Brunswick, N.J., 1962-70; pastor St. Mary of Mount Virgin Ch., Mission Ch. of St. Theresa, Edison, N.J., 1970—; chaplain Middlesex County Park Police, N.J. Dept. Weights and Measures, Middlesex County Correctional Inst., Golden Age Club; Mem. St. Peter's Med. Ctr. Found. cons. to Bishop, mem. Priests Senate, Diocese of Metuchen, N.J.; former dir. Middlesex County Cath. Youth Orgn. Bd. dirs. First Jersey Bank, North Brunswick N.J., Middlesex County Heart Assn.; trustee Pub. Employees Retirement System of N.J., 1976-84; adv. council N.J. Bell Telephone Co., Raritan Valley area; founding mem. New Brunswick Human Relations Commn., past mem. Rutgers Mental Health Bd.; mem. Fee Arbitration com. Middlesex County of Supreme Ct. N.J.; fundraiser Italian Earthquake Relief Fund; sponsoring agt. Sr. Citizens Housing program; mem. exec. com. Tercentennial City of New Brunswick; liturgy chmn. Italian Festival Garden State Arts Ctr., Holmdel, N.J., 1982; others. Recipient Outstanding Citizen award, North Brunswick; Brotherhood award NCCJ, 1983; named Citizen of Week, Middlesex County Tercentennial Celebration, 1983; Grand Marshall 1st ann. Columbus Day Parade, North Brunswick, 1982; L'Onorificenzodi Commendatore, Republic of Italy, 1983. Lodge: KC (chaplain). Home and Office: St Mary of Mt Virgin Ch 190 Sandford St New Brunswick NJ 08901

CRUTCHER, GABRIEL, bishop, Apostolic Overcoming Holy Church of God. Office: 529 E Bethune St Detroit MI 48202*

CRYDERMAN, WILLIAM DALE, bishop, Free Meth. Ch. N.Am.; b. Detroit, July 4, 1916; s. William and Mary Belle (McPhee) C.; ed. Spring Arbor Coll., LL.D., 1975; m. Dorothy C. Gates, Oct. 19, 1935; children: William Leon, Dale Leroy, Lyn Dean, Richard Burton. Ordained to ministry, 1943; pastor chs, Albion, Mich., 1940-42, Winona Lake, Ind., 1949-52; regional dir. Young People's Missionary Soc., Free Meth. Ch. N. Am., 1943-46; field dir. Spring Arbor Coll., 1947-48; dir. Youth for Christ Internat., Japan, Korea, 1953-55; supt. So. Mich. Conf., 1956-68, bishop, 1969-85. Chmn. commn. on evangelistic outreach Free Meth. Ch. N.Am.; chmn. bd. bishops and gen. council for ch. in mission, 1975-76; chmn., organizer Commn. Evangelism and Spiritual Life, Nat. Assn. Evangs.; mem. adv. council Am. Bible Soc., 1969—. Mem. Gov's Com. on Food for the Hungry, 1958-60. Trustee Spring Arbor Coll., sec. exec. com., 1960-75. Mem. Nat. Assn. Evangs., Christian Holiness Assn., World Relief Commn. Office: 901 College Free Methodist Mdqrs Winona Lake IN 46590

CRYNES, JOSEPH PETER, priest, Roman Catholic Church; b. Jamaica, N.Y., Oct. 31, 1941; s. Joseph P. and Anne Marie (Lawlor) C. B.A., St. Mary's Sem. and U., Balt., 1963, S.T.B., 1965. Ordained priest Roman Cath. Ch., 1967. Program dir. Camp St. Andrew, Tunkhannock, Pa., 1967; asst. pastor St. Patrick's Ch., White Haven, Pa., 1967-68, Holy Rosary Ch., Scranton, Pa., 1968-72; dir. religious forma Bishop Hannan High Sch., Scranton, 1972-73; chaplain St. Joseph's Ctr., Scranton, 1972-75; dir. Our Lady of Fatima Ctr., Elmhurst, Pa., 1975—, Office of Youth Ministry, Diocese of Scranton, 1978-85; trustee Scranton Prep. Sch., 1982—; del. Scranton Diocesan Synod II, 1984—; dir. Internat. Student Leadership Inst., Cleve., 1980—, Scranton Cath. Youth Ctr., 1982—. Bd. dirs. ARC of Northeast Pa., 1982—, Planning Council of Northeast Pa. Mem. Pa. Province Youth Dirs. Club: Foxhill Country (Pittston, Pa.). Home: PO Box 163 Elmhurst PA 18416 Office: Our Lady of Fatima Ctr Griffin Rd Elmhurst PA 18416

CULLINAN, ALICE RAE, educator, So. Baptist Conv.; b. Richmond, Va., May 21, 1939; d. James Michaux and Sarah Elizabeth (Burger) C.; B.A., Carson-Newman Coll., 1963; M.R.E., Southwestern Bapt. Theol. Sem., 1965, Ed.D., 1974. Minister music and edn. Triangle (Va.) Bapt. Ch., 1966-70; counselor Southwestern Sem. Counseling Clinic, 1971-73; instr. psychology Tarrant County Jr. Coll., 1972; cons., tchr. tng. dept. Va. Bapt. Gen. Assn., 1973-74; prof. religion and religious edn. Gardner-Webb Coll., Boiling Springs, N.C., 1974—; interim music dir. Stanley (N.C.) Bapt. Ch., 1974-75, Upper Fair Forest Bapt. Ch., Union, S.C., 1975-76; minister of music and edn. Mt. Sinai Bapt. Ch., Shelby, N.C., 1979-83; minister edn. Zoar Bapt. Ch., Shelby, 1983—. Mem. So. Bapt. Religious Edn. Assn., Religious Edn. Assn. Am., N.C. Bapt. Profs. Religion, AAUP. Home and Office: PO Box 833 Boiling Springs NC 28017

CULLUM, ROBERT FRANCIS, hospital chaplain, Southern Baptist Convention; b. St. Louis, Aug. 9, 1932; s. Ralph Francis and Mildred (Hanson) C.; B.A., So. Ill. U., 1960; B.D., Southwestern Bapt. Theol. Sem., Fort Worth, 1965; Th.D., Luther Rice Sem., 1973; D.D., Internat. Free Protestant Episc. U., Switzerland, 1972; m. Shirley Rose Harvengt, Dec. 22, 1957; children: Pamela Kay, Barbara Lynn, Christi Coleen. Ordained to ministry, 1963. Chaplain, counselor Masonic Home and Sch., Fort Worth, 1962-65; chaplain Bapt. Meml. Hosp., San Antonio, 1966, San Antonio State Hosp., 1966—; lectr., Tex. Alcoholic and Narcotics Edn. Found., 1967—; pres. Half-Way House of San Antonio, 1967—; pastor, restored mental patients Harmony House, San Antonio, 1967—; coordinator chaplains Tex. Dept. Mental Health and Retardation. Pres., Mental Health Assn. Bexar County, 1975. Recipient spl. vol. award SASH Vol. Council, 1984. Fellow Coll. Chaplains; mem. Acad. Religion (pres. San Antonio 1973-74), Tex. Pub. Employees Assn. (pres. San Antonio 1973-74, Outstanding Service award 1974), So. Bapt. Chaplains Assn., Am. Assn. Pastoral Counselors (assoc.), So. Assn. Marriage Counselors, Assn. Clin. Pastoral Edn., Am. Assn. Mental Health Clergy. Lodge: Lions (pres. 1984-85). Home: 446 Saipan St San Antonio TX 78221 Office: PO Box 14353 Harlandale Station San Antonio TX 78214

CULLY, KENDIG BRUBAKER, seminary president, educator, Episcopal Church; b. Millersville, Pa., Nov. 30, 1913; s. William B. and Emma L. (Kendig) C.; m. Iris Virginia Arnold; children: Melissa Iris Cully Mueller, Patience Allegra Cully Ecklund. A.B. cum laude, Am. Internat. Coll., Springfield, Mass., 1934; B.D., Hartford Sem. Found., Conn., 1937, M.R.E., 1938, Ph.D., 1939; S.T.M., Seabury-Western Theol. Sem., 1953; S.T.D., Episcopal Theol. Sem., 1984. Ordained to ministry, Congregational Ch., 1937, Episcopal Ch., 1955. Parish minister, Mass., 1937-51; minister edn. First Meth. Ch., Evanston, Ill., 1951-54; prof. religious edn. Seabury-Western Theol. Sem., Evanston, Ill., 1954-64; prof., dean N.Y. Theol. Sem., N.Y.C., 1964-71; pres., dean Episc. Theol. Sem., Lexington, Ky., 1980—; founding editor Rev. of Books and Religion, 1971-84. Author: The Search for a Christian Education, 1965. Editor: The Westminster Dictionary of Christian Education, 1963; (with Iris V. Cully) From Aaron to Zerubbabel, 1976; numerous others. Assn. Theol. Schs. fellow, 1970-71; Danforth vis. lectr. Mem. Religious Edn. Assn., Assn. Profs. and Researchers in Religious Edn., Nat. Council Chs. (chmn. sect. 1968-69), Tau Kappa Epsilon. Democrat. Home: 1027 Gainesway Dr Lexington KY 40508

CULP, WAYMON ALTON, minister, Southern Baptist Convention; b. Petersburg, Tex., Nov. 3, 1931; s. Walter Albert and Laura Rosa (Wyatt) C.; m. Dortha Dee Tally, Aug. 30, 1952; children: Debra, Kirby Randall, Wayne Alan, Kevin Ray. B.A., Wayland Bapt. U., 1963; student Golden Gate Bapt. Theol. Sem., 1966-67, Calif. State U.-Fresno, 1968-71. Ordained to ministry Southern Baptist Convention, 1952. Pastor 1st So. Bapt. Ch., Reedley, Calif., 1952-54, Parksdale So. Bapt. Ch., Madera, Calif., 1956-60, Martin Bapt. Ch., Clarendon, Tex., 1961-63, Tanglewood Bapt. Ch., Santa Maria, Calif., 1963-66, Pacifica Bapt. Ch., Calif., 1966-69, Beacon Light Bapt. Ch., Madera, 1969-71, Happy Union Bapt. Ch., Plainview, Tex., 1971-72, First Bapt. Ch., Chillicothe, Tex., 1972-76, First Bapt. Ch., Buckhorn, Mo., 1976-80, First Bapt. Ch., Eula, Tex., 1980—. Recipient spl. diplomas Sunday Sch. Bd. of So. Bapt. Conv., 1983. Home: Rte 1 Box 227 Clyde TX 79510 Office: Rte 1 Box 227 Clyde TX 79510

CULVER, CHESTER PAUL, minister, So. Baptist Conv.; b. Louisville, Apr. 14, 1929; s. Sidney Vail and Mary Sybyl (Collins) C.; student U. Louisville, 1948-49, Georgetown Coll., 1953, 58, Cumberland Coll., 1960-62, Eastern Ky. U., 1973; m. Freda Marie Wells, June 2, 1959; 1 dau., Paula Marie. Ordained to ministry, 1951; pastor, Bedford, Ky., 1950-52; chaplains asst. AUS, 1954-56; pastor Elm Grove, Ind., 1956-58, First Bapt. Ch., Wooten, Ky., 1958-63, 76—, Belfry, Ky., 1963-67, Flatwoods, Ky., 1967-70, Kirksville, Ky., 1970-74, Hamilton, Ohio, 1974-76. Pres. local sch. PTA, Hamilton, Ohio, 1974-76, Wooten, 1976—. Mem. Three Forks Bapt. Assn., So. Bapt. Conv. Home and office: Box 169 Wooton KY 41776

CULVER, JOHN BLAINE, minister, United Church of Christ; history educator; b. Urbana, Ill., Nov. 3, 1938; s. Lawson Blaine and Sunray Lillian (Cooper) C.; m. Rosa Bertha Diaz-Mori, Feb. 28, 1970; children: Janice Lillian, John Manuel, Edward Blaine. B.A., U. Ill., 1962, M.A., 1962-64; M.Div. cum laude, Chgo. Theol. Sem., 1972; postgrad. Escuela de Idiomas, Sociedad de Santiago Apostol, Lima, Peru, 1969-70. Ordained to ministry United Ch. of Christ, 1973. Pastor, adminstr. Winnebago Indian Mission, United Ch. of Christ, Black River Falls, Wis., 1972-75; pastor Bethany United Ch. of Christ, San Antonio, Tex., 1975-78, Bethany Congregational Ch., San Antonio, 1978—; interim pastor Pilgrim Congl. Ch., San Antonio, 1978, Iglesia Unida de Cristo Betania, San Antonio, 1982-83; part-time instr. San Antonio Coll., 1978, 81—; pres. Jackson County Ministerial Assn., Black River Falls, 1974-75; bd. dirs. Greater San Antonio Community of Chs., 1976-80, San Antonio Urban Council, 1984—; sec.-registrar South Tex. Assn. United Ch. of Christ, San Antonio, 1982—, bd. dirs. South Central Conf., Austin, Tex., 1982, 84—. Program chmn. Illini Young Republicans, Urbana, 1963; sec. Tobin Hill Neighborhood Assn., San Antonio, 1978-79. Lodge: Masons (chaplain 1981-82, tiler 1980-81, 84—). Home: 102 Shadywood Ln San Antonio TX 78216 Office: Bethan Congl Ch 500 Pilgrim Dr San Antonio TX 78213

CUMMINGS, CLINTON SAXTON, educator, Missionary Seventh-day Adventist Church; b. Glendive, Mont., Nov. 19, 1939; s. Saxton Delancy and Enid Valentine (Sorenson) C.; children: Craig Thomas, Susan Diane. B.A., Walla Walla Coll., 1964; M.A.T., Andrews U., 1970. Tchr., missionary/Seventh-day Adventist Ch., Lebanon, Oreg., 1970—; tchr., prin. Songa Mission Sch., Kamira, Zaire, 1974-77. Developer, Kilubi Devel. Project, 1984. Mem. Oreg. Math Tchrs. Assn. Home: 40011 McDowell Circle Dr Lebanon OR 97355 Office: 10th and W Sherman Lebanon OR 97355

CUMMINGS, FRANK C., bishop, African Meth. Episcopal Ch., ch. ofcl.; b. Minter, Ala., Apr. 4, 1929; s. Edmond and Annie (Moultrie) C.; B.A., Daniel Payne Coll., 1949; B.D., Seattle Pacific Coll., 1952; D.D., Shorter Coll., 1970; m. Martha Coleen Colly, Mar. 5, 1954; 1 dau., Paschell Coleen. Ordained to ministry African Methodist Episcopal Ch., 1949; pastor, Alridge, Ala., 1948-49, Bremerton, Wash., 1952-53, Santa Barbara, Calif., 1954-60, St. Louis, 1960-68; sec.-treas. ch. extension dept. .AM.E. Ch., St. Louis, 1968-76, bishop ch., 1976—, presiding bishop 8th Epis. Dist. in LA an Miss. 1976— 1984, bishop, 1st district, Bala Cynwyd, PA 1984—. Formerly pres. A.M.E. Mgmt. Agy. Pres., Allen Travel Service, Inc. Vice-chmn. St. Louis Civil Service Commn. Bd. dirs. West End Hosp. Assn. Mem. Alpha Phi Alpha. Address: #1 Bala Ave Suite 3-C Bala Cynwyd PA 19004

CUMMINS, JOHN STEPHEN, bishop, Roman Cath. Ch.; b. Oakland, Calif., Mar. 3, 1928; s. Michael and Mary (Connolly) C.; A.B., St. Patrick's Coll., 1949; M.Div., St. Patrick's Sem., 1973. Ordained priest, 1953; asst. pastor Mission Dolores Ch., San Francisco, 1953-57; mem. faculty Bishop O'Dowd High Sch., Oakland, 1957-62; chancellor Diocese of Oakland, 1962-71; exec. dir. Calif. Cath. Conf., Sacramento, 1971—; consecrated bishop, 1974; aux. bishop of Sacramento, 1974-77; bishop of Oakland, 1977—. Campus minister San Francisco State Coll., 1953-57, Mills Coll., Oakland, Calif., 1957-71. Trustee St. Mary's Coll., 1968-79. Named Domestic Prelate, 1967. Office: Diocese of Oakland 2900 Lakeshore Ave Oakland CA 94610

CUNNINGHAM, JAMES HAMPSHIRE, minister, United Church Christ; b. Lancaster, Ohio, Apr. 23, 1945; s. Gail Biddison and Mary Georgina (Jones) C.; m. Julie Marie Myers, Nov. 21, 1981; 1 child, Jessica Erin; m. Marilyn Mae Bell, June 10, 1967 (div. 1981); children: Teresa Emma, Mark Allen. B.A., Heidelberg Coll., 1968; M.Div., Lancaster Theol. Sem., 1971; Ordained to ministry United Ch. of Christ, 1971. Pastor, Farmersville United Ch. Christ, Ohio, 1972-79; resident chaplain Luth. Gen Hosp., Park Ridge, Ill., 1976-77; pastor Washington Congl. United Ch. Christ, Toledo, 1979-81; chaplain Toledo Hosp., 1981—; pres. Maumee Bay United Ch. Christ Ch. Profls., 1979—; mem. Toledo United Ch. Christ Clergy Support Group, 1981—; bd. dirs. NW Ohio Sudden Infant Death Syndrome Found., Toledo, 1983—; chaplain C.A.R.E. bereaved parent support group, Toledo, 1981—, Narcoleptic Support Group, 1985—. Author: (with M. and J. Johnson) Newborn Death, 1982, Death of an Infant Twin, 1984, A Most Important Picture (A Very Tender Manual for Taking Pictures of Stillborn Babies and Infants Who Die), 1985. R.C. and J.D. Spring scholar, 1968. Fellow Coll. Chaplains, (Am. Protestant Health Care Assn.); mem. Assn. Care Childrens Health, Ohio Perinatal Assn., Ohio Health Care Chaplains Assn., Ohio Hosp. Assn., Parents of Premature and High Risk Infants Internat., Inc., Stepfamily Assn. Am. Home: 2010 Wellesley Dr Toledo OH 43606 Office: Toledo Hosp 2142 N Cove Blvd Toledo OH 43606

CUNNINGHAM, LAWRENCE DAVID, minister of edn., Bapt. Ch.; b. Little Rock, Nov. 5, 1936; s. L.E. and Eunice (Woods) C.; B.A. in Ch. Music Edn., Ouachita Bapt. U., 1959; M.R.E., Southwestern Bapt. Theol. Sem., 1965; m. Sarah Frances Watson, Mar. 31, 1961; children—David Edward, Shannah Delise. Minister of music and youth Towson Ave Bapt. Ch., Fort Smith, Ark., 1955-57, First Bapt. Ch., Cullendale, Ark., 1957-59, Field City Bapt. Ch., Dallas, 1961-62, First Bapt. Ch., Durant, Okla., 1963-65; minister of music Ridgecrest Bapt. Ch., Ozark, Ala., 1959-61; minister of music and edn. First Bapt. Ch., Seagoville, Tex., 1962-63, Pleasant Valley Bapt. Ch., Amarillo, Tex., 1965-68; minister edn. Plymouth Park Bapt. Ch., Irving, Tex., 1968-73, First Bapt. Ch., Orlando, Fla., 1973—. Tng. union dir. Amarillo Bapt. Assn. 1965-68; conf. leader and speaker So. Bapt. Idaho-Utah State Tng. Union Conv., 1969; mem. Mt. Lebanon Encampment Com., Dallas Bapt. Assn., 1969-71, vacation Bible sch. dir., 1971-73; mem. spl. emphasis com. Fla. Bapt. Conv., 1975-76; chmn. Arrangements Fla. Bapt. Vocat. Guidance Conf., 1973. Mem. Metro, Fla. Bapt., So. Bapt. religious edn. assns. Contbg. author: Ideas for Vacation Bible School Promotion, 1973; contbr. articles to religious publs. Home: 3201 Lake Anderson Ave Orlando FL 32806 Office: 100 E Pine St Orlando FL 32801

CUNNINGHAM, MILTON EMERY, JR., minister, So. Bapt. Conv.; b. Victoria, Tex., Sept. 13, 1928; s. Milton Emery and Bertha (Smith) C.; B.A., Baylor U., 1950; B.D., Southwestern Bapt. Theol. Sem., 1953; D.D., Corpus Christi U., 1962; m. Barbara Jean Schultz, Mar. 2, 1956; children—Milton Emery, Miller Vaughn. Ordained to ministry, 1948; dean students, asst. to pres. U. Corpus Christi (Tex.), 1954-57; missionary, Rhodesia, Africa, 1957-62, Zambia, Africa, 1962-67; cons. mass media S. Africa, 1967-72; pastor Westbury Bapt. Ch., Houston, 1973—. Trustee Southwestern Bapt. Theol. Sem., Ft. Worth; trustee, mem. exec. com. Houston Bapt. Univ.; exec. bd. Union Bapt. Assn. Tex.; exec. bd. Bapt. Gen. Conv. Tex., 1t v.p., 1976, also nominating com.; founder, chmn. bd. trustees Lusaka (Zambia) Internat. Sch., 1964-67; rep. planning translation com. United Bible Socs. Eng., Scotland, 1965-66. Author: People Who Walked With Jesus, 1965; My Walk With Christ, 1966; Parables of Jesus, 1966; New Drums Over Africa, 1970. Home: 5835 Dumfries St Houston TX 77096 Office: 10425 Hillcroft St Houston TX 77096

CUNNINGHAM, WILLIAM PATRICK, editor, Roman Catholic Church; insurance executive; b. San Antonio, Jan. 22, 1947; s. William Gregory and Jewel (Hamilton) C.; m. Carolyn Louise Caldwell, Aug. 7, 1971; children: Amy, Lisa, Julie. B.A., St. Mary's U., San Antonio, 1969, M.A. in Theology, 1977; M.A. in Edn., Stanford U., 1970. Choral dir. St. Mary Magdalen Ch., San Antonio, 1972-75, Blessed Sacrament Ch., 1975-77; chmn. San Antonio Diocesan Music Commn., 1975-77; music dir. Fort Sam Houston, Tex., 1977-80, St. Anthony Parish, San Antonio 1980-84. Sales mgr.

Conn. Mut., San Antonio, 1982—. Editor, composer: Cast into the Deep, 1976; editor, adapter: Chants for the Church Year, 1982. Editor The Music Locator Resource Publ., 1975—, Pastorale Music, 1973—. Contbr. articles to profl. jours. Mem. Organ Hist. Soc., San Antonio Pipe Organ Soc. (sec. 1977—). Republican. Lodges: Lions, K.C. Avocations: building historic keyboard instruments; swimming; gardening. Home: 235 Sharon Dr San Antonio TX 78216 Office: Conn Mut Cos 85 NE Loop 410 #603 San Antonio TX 78216

CURLEE, ROBERT C., JR., minister, So. Bapt. Conv.; b. Ellaville, Ga., Apr. 2, 1935; s. Robert C. and Grace (Willis) C.; B.A., Samford U., 1957; B.D., So. Sem., 1962; m. Sue Lenox, July 11, 1959; children—Robert, Lisa, Cathy, Jamey. Ordained to ministry, 1956; pastor Ashland (Ala.) Bapt. Ch., 1963-67, Ensley Bapt. Ch., Birmingham, Ala., 1967-72, Centercrest Bapt. Ch., Birmingham, 1972—. Exec. dir. Jonah Missions, 1969—. Trustee Birmingham Bapt. Camp. Recipient Brother Bryan award, Birmingham, 1973. Mem. Ministers' Assn. Greater Birmingham (pres. 1976). Author: Jonah and the Whale, 1969; From Haystacks to Skylabs, 1974. Home: 2533 5th St NE Birmingham AL 35215 Office: 3025 Wood Dr NE Birmingham AL 35215

CURRIE, CHARLES LEONARD See *Who's Who in America*, 43rd edition.

CURRY, EVERETT WILLIAM, JR., minister, American Baptist Churches U.S.A.; b. Glendale, Calif., Mar. 7, 1942; s. Everett William and Sylvia Pauline (Burkholder) C.; m. Barbara Kay Orman, June 13, 1964; children: Kimberly Suzanne, Kevin Everett. B.A., Calif. State U.-Northridge, 1964; M.Div., Am. Bapt. Sem. of West, 1967; D.Min., San Francisco Theol. Sem., 1977. Ordained to ministry, 1967. Asst. pastor Valley Park Bapt. Ch., Sepulveda, Calif., 1962-66; assoc. pastor First Bapt. Ch., Thermal, Calif., 1966-67; pastor Lake View Terrace Bapt. Ch., Calif., 1968-71; dir. media ministries Los Angeles Bapt. City Soc., 1971-74; pastor Community Bapt. Ch., Honolulu, 1974-78, First Bapt. Ch., Coos Bay, Oreg., 1978—; dir. pub. affairs KYTT-F M, Coos Bay, 1978—; chief chaplain's corps Coos Bay Police Dept., 1979—; dir. Am. Bapt. Chs. Oreg., 1983—; senator Nat. Am. Bapt. Ministers Council, 1984—; council mem. Am. Bapt. Ministers Council Oreg., 1982—; chmn. Centennial Celebration, Am. Bapt. Ch. Oreg., 1984—. Assoc. producer film: Faith in Action, 1973; producer: Potpourri, 1984—; producer/host: Got a Minute, 1979-83. Bd. dirs. Sch. Dist. 9, Coos Bay, 1985—, Temporary Help in Emergency House, 1979-84; pres. Bay Area Ministerial Assn., 1982-84. Named Citizen of Yr., Lake View Terrace Assn., 1971; nat. scholarship awardee Am. Bapt. Chs., 1960; recipient Founder's award Hawaii TV for Youth, 1977. Mem. Am. Bapt. Ministers Council, Bay Area Ministerial Assn. Lodge: Kiwanis. Republican. Avocations: backpacking; computing; reading. Home: 1056 Central Ave Coos Bay OR 97420 Office: First Bapt Ch of Coos Bay 1140 S 10th PO Box 38 Coos Bay OR 97420

CURRY, MELVIN DOTSON, JR., educator; b. Orlando, Fla., May 22, 1931; s. Melvin Dotson and Bessie Leora (Belue) C.; B.S., Fla. Coll., 1953; postgrad. Nazarene Theol. Sem., 1954-56; A.B., Harding Coll., 1957; M.A., Wheaton Coll., 1963; postgrad. U. Ill., 1963; Ph.D. Fla. State U., 1980; m. Shirley Marie Castleberry, May 30, 1952; children—Thomas Mark, Rebecca Lynn, Barbara Jean, David Lee, Erin Kathleen. Prof. div. of Bible, chmn. div. humanities Fla. Coll., Temple Terrace, 1963—. Sponsor, Pi Gamma chpt. Nat. Phi Theta Kappa. Mem. Evang. Theol. Soc., Soc. Sci. Study Religion, Soc. Bibl. Lit. Contbr. articles to profl. publs. Home: 209 Willowick Ave Temple Terrace FL 33617

CURRY, MICHAEL DENNIS, minister, Church of God (Anderson, Ind.); b. Ft. Lauderdale, Fla., May 27, 1950; s. Manuel and Catherine (Strachon) C.; m. Carol Blackwell, Aug. 1, 1981; children: Shanna, Michael. B.A. in Religious Studies, Anderson Coll., 1978, M.A. in Pastoral Ministry, 1982. Ordained to ministry Church of God (Anderson, Ind.), 1983. Youth counselor Arlington Ch. of God, Akron, Ohio, 1975; assoc. pastor Sherman St. Ch. of God, Anderson, Ind., 1981-82, interim pastor, 1982-83; pastor First Ch. of God, Evanston, Ill., 1983—; elected mem. Ministerial Program Com., Gen. Assembly Ch. of God, Mt. Zion, Ill.; mem. Gen. Assembly, 1981—. Author: A Historical Study of the Growth of Black Congregations of the Church of God, 1983. Vice pres. Operation PUSH, Anderson, Ind., 1979-83. Recipient Outstanding Male Leadership award Minority Student Council, Anderson Coll., 1978. Mem. Evanston Ministerial Alliance, Evanston Ecumenical Action Council (rep.). Democrat. Club: Adelphos Social (pres. 1976-78). Home: 1721 Leland Ave Evanston IL 60201 Office: First Church of God 1524 Simpson St Evanston IL 60202

CURRY, MITCHELL LEE, minister, African Methodist Episcopal Church; psychotherapist. b. Augusta, Ga., Feb. 5, 1935; s. Walter Lee and Ernestine (Battle) C.; m. Carolyn Davenport, Sept. 11, 1974; children: Rachael, Michele; children by previous marriage: Sonja, Reuben. B.A., Morris Brown Coll., 1960; M.Div., Andover Newton Theol. Sem., 1964; M.S.W. in Social Work, U. Louisville, 1972; Ph.D., D.Min., Sch. Theology at Claremont, 1979; L.H.D. (hon.), Reed Christian Coll., 1976. Ordained elder African Meth. Episcopal Ch., 1951. Exec. dir. Harlem div. Protestant Council N.Y.C., 1963-65; pastor Richard Allen African Meth. Episcopal Ch., St. George's, Bermuda, 1965-69; interim pastor Florence Ave. Presbyn. Ch., Los Angeles, 1976-79, Imperial Heights Ch., Los Angeles, 1980-84; assoc. pastor Allen African Meth. Episcopal Ch., San Bernardino, Calif., 1985—; psychotherapist Los Angeles County Mental Health Dept.; bd. dirs. Crenshaw Counseling Services, Los Angeles, 1976—; bd. govs. Nat. Council Chs., N.Y.C., 1981—; mem. So. Calif. Council Chs., Los Angeles, 1982—; mem. Los Angeles Council Chs., 1973—. Scholarship grantee Am. Missionary Assn., N.Y.C., 1960-64, NIMH, Md., 1970-72. Fellow Am. Assn. Pastoral Counselors; mem. Acad. Cert. Social Workers, NAACP, Alpha Phi Alpha. Club: Watt Businessmen's (Los Angeles). Home: 1809 Virginia Rd Los Angeles CA 90019 Office: Crenshaw Counseling Service 4306 Crenshaw Blvd Los Angeles CA 90008

CURRY, STANLEY THURSTON, minister, So. Bapt. Conv.; b. Green County, Ky., Aug. 12, 1928; s. Roy Alton and Louvie Christine (Chaudoin) C.; student Cleark Creek Bapt. Sch., 1973, Lindsey Wilson Coll., 1974, Boyce Bible Sch. Sem., 1975; m. Betty Francis Tucker, June 19, 1948; children—Beverly, Patty, Becky, Shelia, Sherry, Stan. Ordained to ministry, 1973; pastor Dunbar Hill Bapt. Ch., Greensburg, Ky. Chaplain, Civil Def. Mem. Russell Creek Assn. Home: 104 Texas St Greensburg KY 42743 Office: PO Box 372 Greensburg TX 42743

CURTIS, JOHN ARTHUR, minister, American Baptist Churches in the U.S.A.; b. Chatsworth, Ill., May 12, 1941; s. Harley Lynwood and Eva (Basara) C.; m. Kathy Ellen Waggoner, June 8, 1968; children: Arinne, Braden. B.S., U. Wis., 1964; M.Div., No. Bapt. Sem., 1968; D.Min., So. Bapt. Sem., 1979. Ordained to ministry American Baptist Churches in the U.S.A., 1968. Assoc. pastor Meadow Lane Bapt. Ch., Hammond, Ind., 1968-70; pastor Cambridge Bapt. Ch., Ill., 1970-76, Community Bapt. Ch., Aurora, Ill., 1974-76, First Bapt. Ch., Newton, Ill., 1976-82, Muncie Bapt. Ch., Ill., 1982—; chaplain Cambridge Fire Dept., Ill., 1971-74; trustee Bapt. Student Foudn., Champaign, Ill., 1982—; del. Congress '84, No. Bapt. Sem., Lombard, Ill., 1984; pres. Eastern Rural Ill. Chs., Muncie, 1984. Mem. Ministers Council Great Rivers Region of Am. Assn. (pres. 1979-82). Bapt. Chs. (treas. 1977-78, editor 1982—), Newton Ministerial. Home: Box 298 Muncie IL 60857 Office: Muncie Bapt Ch Box 407 Muncie IL 61857

CURTIS, LYLE EDGAR, minister, Assemblies of God. b. Poynette, Wis., Feb. 17, 1909; s. Edgar F. and Jennie Estella (Teeter) C.; m. Grace Iva Curtis, June 29, 1934 (dec. Dec. 1971); children: Ruth, Dorothy, Faith; m. Ruth Blenda Anderson Abbalt, Nov. 3, 1972. Student N. Central Bible Coll., Mpls., 1933-35. Ordained to ministry Assemblies of God, 1938. Minister Assemblies of God chs., Randolph, Lodi, Adams, Wis., 1936-40, Watertown, Monroe, Wisconsin Rapids, Wis., 1940-66, Marshfield, Wis., 1974-82; mem. Gen. Presbytery Bd., Assemblies of God, 1947-74, Fgn. Missions Bd., 1959-62, dist. Sunday Sch. dir., Wis. and No. Mich., 1945-47, dist. sec., 1948-60, asst. dist. supt., 1960-66, dist. supt., 1966-74. Author: When Dreams Come True, 1977. Editor Full Gospel Tidings, 1948-57, 66-74. Hon. life mem. Presbyter of Assemblies of God, Dist. Presbyter. Home: 1404 Berlin St Waupaca WI 54981

CURTIS, RAY CHARLES, minister, American Baptist Association; b. Little Rock, Aug. 1, 1942; s. Raymond Thomas and Carol Lee (Lusby) C.; m. Glenda Gale Woodworth, Aug. 27, 1963; children: John Richard, Robert Mark. B.Bible Langs., Missionary Bapt. Sem., 1970, M. Bible Langs., 1971; D.Th., Gulf Coast Bapt. Sem., 1973. Ordained to ministry Am. Bapt. Assn., 1963. Pastor Bethlehem Bapt. Ch., Star City, Ark., 1967-69, Park Ave. Bapt. Ch., Stuttgart, Ark., 1970-72, Overlook Bapt. Ch., Mobile, Ala., 1973—. Dean, Gulf Coast Bapt. Sem., 1973—; moderator Magnolia Bapt. Assn., 1973-74; dir. Miss. Bama Bapt. Youth Encampment, 1976. Author: Portraits in the Smoke and Other Sermons, 1976; The Burning Bush, 1976. Editor, publ. The Shepherd's Voice, monthly, 1974—. Home: 6809 Norfolk Ct Mobile AL 36608 Office: 6455 Overlook Rd Mobile AL 36608

CURTIS, WALTER W., bishop, Roman Catholic Church; b. Jersey City, May 3, 1913; student Fordham U., Seton Hall U., Immaculate Conception Sem., N.Am. Coll. and Gregorian U. (Rome), Cath. U. Am. Ordained priest, 1937; titular bishop of Bisica and aux. Bishop of Newark, 1957-71; bishop of Bridgeport (Conn.), 1961—. Address: 238 Jewett Ave Bridgeport CT 06606*

CURTISS, ELDEN F., bishop, Roman Catholic Church; b. Baker, Oreg., June 16, 1932; s. Elden F. and Mary (Neiger) C.; B.A., St. Edward Sem., Seattle, M.Div., 1958; M.A. in Ednl. Adminstrn., U. Portland, 1965; postgrad. Fordham U., U. Notre Dame. Ordained priest, 1958; campus chaplain, 1959-64, 65-68; supt. schs. Diocese of Baker (Oreg.), 1962-70; pastor, 1968-70; pres./rector Mt. Angel Sem., Benedict, Oreg., 1972-76; bishop of Helena (Mont.), 1976—. Mem. priests senate Diocese of Portland; mem. ecumenical ministries State of Oreg., 1972; mem. pastoral services com. Oreg. State Hosp., Salem, 1975—. Mem. Nat. Cath. Ednl. Assn. (Outstanding Educator 1973). Address: PO Box 1729 612 Harrison Ave Helena MT 59601*

CUSACK, GREGORY DANIEL, religious organization executive, Roman Catholic Ch. B. Davenport, Iowa, May 6, 1943; s. Daniel I. and Jeannette M. (Heaney) C. B.A., St. Ambrose Coll., 1965; M.A., U. Iowa, 1967. Exec. dir. Nat. Cath. Rural Life Conf., Des Moines, 1981—; bd. dirs. Edwin Vincent O'Hara Inst. for Rural Ministry Edn., Washington, 1981—, Rural Coalition, Washington, 1983—; observed U.S. Cath. Conf. Com. on World Peace and Social Devel., Washington, 1981—. Mem. City Council, Davenport, 1970-73; mem. Iowa Ho. of Reps., Des Moines, 1973-81; bd. dirs. Iowa Commn. on Aging, 1973-81. Mem. Am. Hist. Soc. Democrat. Office: Nat Cath Rural Life Conf 4625 N W Beaver Des Moines IA 50310

CUSACK, JAMES C., priest, vicar, Roman Catholic Church. b. Hubbardston, Mich., Oct. 13, 1929; s. Philip Edward and Margaret Minerva (Kane) C. Student St. Joseph Sem., 1946-50, Sem. of Philosophy (Can.), 1950-52; M.Div., St. John's Provincial Sem., 1956. Ordained priest Roman Catholic Ch., 1956. Tchr. Muskegon Cath. Central High Sch., Mich., 1956-57; asst. diocesan dir. religious edn., Grand Rapids, Mich., 1957-64; coll. chaplain Ferris State Coll., Big Rapids, Mich., 1964-67; vicar Women Religious, Grand Rapids, 1976—; pastor St. Thomas Ch., Grand Rapids, 1978—; trustee Aquinas Coll., Grand Rapids, 1978-83; co-dir. Diocesan Cemeteries, Grand Rapids, 1979—; chaplain Western Mich. Law Enforcement, 1972-79; dir. Nat. Vicar for Religious Assn., 1976. Recipient award Grand Rapids Area Ctr. for Ecumenism, 1985. Club: Penninsular. Address: St Thomas the Apostle Ch 1449 Wilcox Pk SE Grand Rapids MI 49506

CUSHING, BRUCE LEON, minister, evangelist, Christian Ch.; b. Kanosh, Utah, Mar. 17, 1916; s. William H. and Nellie Mae (Barney) C.; student Pacific Bible Coll., 1954-58; m. Edna M. Braden Beardsley, Mar. 22, 1943; children—Linda, Ronald, Kevin. Ordained to ministry, 1954; founding Palmdale Ch., 1954, 6 other chs. in Calif.; evangelist in revivals in various western states of U.S., 1958-74; dir. Christian camps, Calif., 1958-59, 64-68, 65-68; founder, pastor Central Christian Ch., Vallejo, Calif., 1976—. Bd. dirs. San Jose Bible Coll., 1962-68. Recipient Outstanding Achievement awards Tustin (Calif.) C. of C., 1972, City of Tustin. Author: Mormonism vs. the Bible, 1968; also newspaper articles. Home: 386 Oak St Orange CA 92667 Office: PO Box 1192 Vallejo CA 94590

CUSHING, VINCENT DEPAUL, priest, theology educator, college president, Roman Catholic Church; b. N.Y.C., Apr. 6, 1934; s. Joseph Patrick and Anna Veronica (O'Connell) C. B.A., St. Bonaventure U., 1960; S.T.L., Cath. U., 1964, S.T.D., 1972; D.Litt. (hon.), Villanova U., 1984. Joined Order of St. Francis; ordained priest Roman Catholic Ch. Instr. theology Christ the King Sem., Olean, N.Y., 1964-66, Holy Name Coll., Washington, 1966-69; asst. prof. theology Washington Theol. Union, Silver Spring, Md., 1970—, pres., 1975—; trustee St. Bonaventure U., Olean, 1969-78, Siena Coll., Loudanville, N.Y., 1969-75, Christ the King Sem., 1972-74. Mem. Cath. Theol. Soc. Am., Assn. Theol. Schs. in U.S. and Can. (pres. 1982-84). Office: Washington Theol Union 9001 New Hampshire Ave Silver Spring MD 20903

CUTRELL, BENJAMIN ELWOOD, lay ch. worker; b. Scottdale, Pa., Mar. 28, 1923; s. George W. and Frances (Nissley) C.; B.S., Carnegie-Mellon U., 1945; m. Dorothy L. Stutzman, Dec. 2, 1944; children—Kathleen (Mrs. Wayne Royer), David B. Bus. mgr. Mennonite Pub. House, Scottdale, 1955-61, pres., pub., 1961—. Mem. coordinating council Mennonite Gen. Bd., 1971—. Mem. Protestant Ch.-Owned Pubs. Assn. (pres. 1974-76), Phi Kappa Phi. Mennonite. Home: Rt 1 Box 244A Scottdale PA 15683 Office: 616 Walnut Ave Scottdale PA 15683

CYR, CLAUDETTE FERNANDE, consecrated secular, religious association administrator, Roman Catholic Church; b. St. Leonard, N.B., Can., Dec. 30, 1940; came to U.S., 1941, naturalized, 1958; d. Alphonse Remi and Blanche Marie (Durepos) C. B.A. in Home Econs. Edn., Inst. Familial, St. Jerome, P.Q., Can., 1962; B.A. in Human Services Adminstrn., Merrimack Coll., 1979. Lic. cert. social worker, Mass.; immigration law accredited rep. Team animator Oblate Missionaries of Mary Immaculate, Lowell, Mass., 1962-68, area coordinator, Lawrence, Mass., 1972-79; sec. exec. council U.S. Conf. Secular Insts., Lawrence, 1973-81, pres., Watertown, Conn., 1981—; del. gen. assembly Oblate Missionaries of Mary Immaculate, Can., 1976, 85, dir. formation, Watertown, 1982—. Supr. Internat. Inst. Conn., Inc., Bridgeport, 1981—. Mem. Conn. Citizen Action Group. Democrat.

Avocations: quilting; Sewing and needlework; oil painting; cooking. Home: 121 Greenwood St Watertown CT 06795 Office: 670 Clinton Ave Bridgeport CT 06605 also 247 Pearl St Hartford CT 06103

DABNER, JACK DUANE, minister, film and television director, writer, Evangelical Church of North America; b. Billings, Mont., Jan. 29, 1930; s. Charles Duane and Violet Virginia (Prout) D.; m. Mary Lousie Nelson, Sept. 10, 1950; children: Donald Duane, Timothy Carl, Richard Dana, Jayne Marie. Student Westmar Coll., 1948-49, Eastern Mont. Coll., 1949-50, U. Oreg., 1951-52, Mont. State U., 1952-53, 64-67. Ordained to ministry Evangelical United Brethren Ch., 1964. Dir. prodn. Good New Prodns., Chester Springs, Pa., 1953-56; asst. to pres. Yellowstone Boys Ranch, Billings, 1958-60; pastor Evang. Ch., Bozeman and Billings, Mont., 1960-70; asst. dir. Campus Radio-TV Crusade, San Bernardino, Calif., 1970-75; pres. Seven Star Prodns., Long Beach, Calif., 1975—; exec. dir. Nat. Assn. for Media Evangelism, Hollywood, Calif., 1978—; bd. dirs. Fellowship of Christians In The Arts, Media, and Entertainment, 1977—, World Gospel Crusade, Upland, Calif., 1982—. Writer, dir. films: The Genesis Flood and Noah's Ark, 1977; A Sure Foundation (Pres.'s award 1983), 1982; producer, dir. film: The Silent Scream (So. Calif. Motion Picture Council award 1985), 1984. Instr. Haggai Inst., Singapore. Republican. Avocations: designing and building motion picture equipment. (213) 633-1777

DABNEY, DELMAR MORRISON, pastor, Assemblies of God; b. Mattoon, Ill., May 3, 1925; s. James Franklin and Olive Mahettable (Morrison) D.; m. Cleo Gazolee Lile, Dec. 30, 1947; children: Delmar Lyle, Michael Lynn, James Blake. Bible degree, Great Lakes Bible Inst., 1946-50; postgrad., South Central Bible Coll., 1950-51. Ordained to ministry Assemblies of God, 1952. Pastor various chs. Ill, Mo., 1948-70, Cathedral In The Pines Assemblies of God, Beaumont, Tex., 1970—. Served to cpl. USMC, 1942-46, PTO. Republican. Lodge: Kiwanis. Avocations: golf; writing. Office: Cathedral In The Pines Christian Ctr 2350 Eastex Freeway Beaumont TX 77706

DADE, TOMMIE JAMES, JR., evangelist, outreach ministry, Christian Ch. (Disciples of Christ); b. Macon, Miss., Nov. 19, 1927; s. Tommie James and Inez (Williams) D.; student Chgo. Bapt. Inst., 1959, No. Theol. Coll., 1962; B.Ministry, M.Ministry, Internat. Bible Inst. and Sem., 1982; m. Ursula Izetta White, July 2, 19S0; children: Tommie James III, Katrice, Karen, Christopher. Ordained to ministry, 1961; asst. pastor Faith Tabernacle Bapt. Ch., Chgo., 1969-71; pastor Beacon Hill Missionary Bapt. Ch., Chicago Heights, Ill., 1971-84; overseer Disciples for Christ, Park Forest, Ill., 1984—. chaplain Nat. Interdenominational Conv., Phila., 1959. Communications cons. Ill. Bell Telephone Co. Vol., East Chicago Heights Day Care Center, 1976. Mem. Internat. Bible Inst. and Sem. Alumni Assn., Internat. Platform Assn. Home: 362 Niagara St Park Forest IL 60466

DAFFERN, JANICE EISEMAN, clergyman, Seventh-day Adventist Church; b. St. Helena, Calif., Oct. 25, 1953; d. Paul Frederick and Joanne Alice (Peterson) Eiseman; m. Gene Marion Daffern, Aug. 29, 1976. B.A. in Theology, Loma Linda U., 1978; M.Div., Andrews U., 1985. Commd. minister's license. Assoc. pastor Sligo Seventh-day Adventist Ch., Takoma Park, Md., 1980—; dir. Assn. of Adventist Women, Takoma Park. Author numerous articles in profl. jours. Mem. Am. Acad. Religion, Assn. of Adventist Forums. Democrat. Office: Sligo Seventh-day Adventist Ch 7700 Carroll Ave Takoma Park MD 20903

DAGINO, JAMES WILLIAM, minister, American Baptist Churches in the U.S.A.; b. Milo, Maine, Jan. 20, 1924; s. William McCloud and Edna Mae (Scott) D.; m. Ruth Noma Libby, Aug. 7, 1977; children: Charles, Libby. Diploma in Bible, Barrington Coll., 1944; A.B. in Theology, Berkshire Christian Coll., 1952; B.D., Eastern Bapt. Theol. Sem., 1959. Ordained to ministry American Baptist Churches in the U.S.A. 1952. Pastor Hancock Bapt. Ch., also Winter Harbor Bapt. Ch., Maine, 1944-47, Cape Heddick Bapt. Ch., Maine, also High Pine Bapt. Ch., Maine, 1947-53, Littlefield Meml. Ch., also Owls Head Bapt. Ch., Rockland, Maine, 1953-54, Malvern Bapt. Ch., Pa., 1955-60, Greenwood Bapt. Ch., Bklyn., 1965-71, 79—; sec. alumni affairs Eastern Bapt. Theol. Sem. and Coll., Phila., 1961-65. Office: Greenwood Baptist Church 461 6th St Brooklyn NY 11215

D'AGOSTINO, ANGELO, priest, Roman Cath. Ch.; b. Providence, Jan. 26, 1926; s. Luigi and Julia (Lonardo) D'A.; B.S., St. Michael's Coll., 1945; M.D., Tufts U., 1949. Joined S.J., 1955; ordained priest, 1966; dir. Center for Religion and Psychiatry, Washington, 1971—; clin. assoc. prof. George Washington U. Med. Sch., 1969—; dir. med. services Cath. Relief Service, Phanatnikhom Refugee Ctr., Thailand, 1980-81; Africa coordinator Jesuit Refugee Service, 1982-84. Mem. nat. adv. council, chief chaplains VA, Washington; adj. prof. Washington Theol. Coalition; bd. dirs Washington Archdiocesan Consultation Center; vice chmn. task force on religion and psychiatry Am. Psychiat. Assn.; chmn. com. on religion and medicine D.C. Med. Soc. Pvt. practice psychiatry, Washington, 1959—. Mem. AMA, Italian Execs. Am. (pres. 1974-76), Am. Psychiat. Assn., Eastern Psychoanalytic Assn., Am. Coll. Psychoanalysts, Washington Acad. Medicine, Soc. Sci. Study Religion, N.Y. Acad Sci., R.I. Med. Assn., Nat. Com. for Mental Health Edn., Nat. Assn. Cath. Chaplains, D.C. Mental Health Assn., Assn. Clin. Pastoral Edn. Editor: Family, Church and Community, 1965. Home: Jesuit Community Georgetown Univ Washington DC 20057 Office: 2201 L St NW Washington DC 20037

DAHLBERG, GILBERT EDWARD, priest, Episcopal Church; b. Chgo., Oct. 11, 1933; s. Gilbert Edward and Helen Miriam (Watkiss) D.; m. Mary Garrett Price, Feb. 2, 1985; children: Martha Jean Aitken, Anne Katherine. A.B., U. Chgo., 1954; M.Div., Seabury Western Theol. Sem., 1962; Ordained priest Episcopal Ch., 1962. Curate, St. Gregory's Episcopal Ch., Deerfield, Ill., 1962-65; asst. to rector St. Barnabas Parish, Denver, 1965-69, rector, 1969-83; pres. Extensive Care, Inc., Denver, 1984—; mem. diocesan council Diocese of Colo., Denver, 1968-71, chmn. dept. Christian social relations, 1970-71; treas. ch. community service Colo. Council Chs., 1978-79, mem. cabinet, 1983-84; ecumenical officer Diocese of Colo., 1983-84. Chmn., Deerfield Youth Council, Ill., 1963-65; treas., bd. dirs. Capitol Hill Community Ctr., Denver, 1977-80; precinct leader Colo. Republican Orgn., 1982-83; bd. dirs. Rocky Mountain Kidney Found., Denver, 1966-68. Served with U.S. Army, 1957-58. Recipient Leadership award Village of Deerfield, 1966. Fellow Coll. Preachers; mem. Colo. Clericus. Lodge: Sertoma (chmn. 1969-73). Home and Office: 1530 Adams St Apt 2 Denver CO 80206

DAKE, CHARLES SAFELY, JR., minister, Evangelical Free Church of America; b. St. Paul, Nov. 11, 1952; s. Charles Safely and Margaret Lorraine (Zakariasen) D.; m. Sharon Gail Houston, June 24, 1978. B.A. in History and Philosophy summa cum laude, Trinity Coll., Deerfield, Ill., 1975; M.Div. summa cum laude, Trinity Evang. Div. Sch., 1979. Ordained to ministry Evang. Free Ch. Am., 1984. Intern pastor Elim Mission Ch., Cokato, Minn., 1976; pastor Saguaro Evang. Free Ch., Tucson, 1979—, sr. pastor, 1983—; bd. dirs. S.W. Border Dist., Evang. Free Ch. Am., Phoenix, 1980-83, vice chmn., 1981-82. Recipient Lincoln Medallion State of Ill., 1975; Z. Albin E. Anderson award Trinity Evang. Div. Sch., 1979. Mem. Evang. Free Ch. Ministerial Assn., Trinity Evang. Div. Sch. Alumni Assn. (bd. dirs., sec. 1981-85). Democrat. Home: 2626 S Camino Seco Tucson AZ 85730 Office: Saguaro Evang Free Ch 10111 E Old Spanish Trail Tucson AZ 85748

D'ALBRO, THOMAS GREGORY, priest, Roman Catholic Ch.; b. N.Y.C., Apr. 22, 1945; s. Vincent James and Rose Anna (Riccobono) D'A.; B.A., Bklyn. Coll., 1966; M.Div., Niagara U., 1970, M.A., 1971; S.T.L., Pontifical U. St. Thomas (Rome, Italy), 1975, S.T.D. candidate, 1975. Asso. pastor, liturgical coordinator, dir. communications St. Andrew Avellino Roman Catholic Ch., Flushing, N.Y., 1976—; founder, dir. Sch. Adult Religious Edn., St. Joan Arc Roman Cath. Ch., Jackson Heights, N.Y., 1972—. Coordinator Ecumenical activities Cath. parishes N.W. Queens, 1974—. Mem. community health planning agy. Elmhurst Gen. Hosp., 1973—, community affairs bd. 110th Precinct, Queens, N.Y.C., 1971-74. Home and office: 35-60 158th St Flushing NY 11358

DALE, JOHN FRANKLIN, minister, United Methodist Church; b. Peoria, Ill., July 26, 1932; s. Franklin and Gladys May (Clark) D.; m. Jean Esther Kendall, May 28, 1955; children: Esther E., Barbara R., Arthur K., Julia J. B.A., Ill. Wesleyan U., 1954; S.T.B., Boston U., 1957; S.T.M., Iliff Sch. Theology, 1965; D.Min., Bethany Theol. Sem., 1978. Ordained to ministry, 1957. Pastor, United Meth. Chs., Ill., Vt., Colo., 1953-68, United Meth. Ch., Fowler, Colo., 1968-74, Wymore, Nebr., 1974-78, Faith United Meth. Ch., Kearney, Nebr., 1978-81; dist. supt. S.W. Dist., Nebr. Conf., United Meth. Ch., McCook, 1981—; trustee Hester Meml. Home, Benkelman, Nebr., 1981—. Bd. chmn. Community United Fund, Fowler, 1970-74, City Housing Authority, Wymore, 1981; bd. dirs. Pioneers' Meml. Hosp., Rocky Ford, Colo., 1969-74; trustee Meth. Meml. Homes, Holdrege, Nebr., 1981-83. Decorated Legion of Honor, Order of DeMolay, 1963. Mem. Sigma Chi. Lodges: Rotary, Masons, K.T. Home: 508 ELizabeth Ln McCook NE 69001 Office: SW Dist United Meth Ch PO Box 406 McCook NE 69001

DALEY, BRIAN EDWARD, priest, theology educator, Roman Catholic Ch.; b. Orange, N.J., Jan. 1, 1940; s. John Joseph and Florence Catherine (McKenna) D. B.A., Fordham U., 1967; M.A., Oxford U., 1964; Lic. Theol., Hochschule Skt. Georgen, Frankfurt, Germany, 1972; D. Philosophy, Oxford U., 1978. Ordained priest Roman Cath. Ch., 1970. Asst. prof. Weston Sch. Theology, Cambridge, Mass., 1978—; trustee Le Moyne Coll., Syracuse, N.Y., 1979—, Georgetown U., D.C., 1984—; cons. N.Y. Province Soc. of Jesus, N.Y.C., 1979—. Editor jour. Tradition, 1979—. Rhodes Trust scholar, 1961; Danforth Found. fellow, 1961, Dumbarton Oaks fellow Harvard U., 1981. Fellow Soc. Religion in Higher Edn.; mem. Assn. Am. Rhodes Scholars. Home: 39 Kirkland St Cambridge MA 02138 Office: Weston Sch Theology 3 Phillips Pl Cambridge MA 02138

DALEY, JOSEPH T., bishop, Roman Cath. Ch. Ordained priest Roman Catholic Ch., June 4, 1941, consecrated bishop, 1963; titular bishop Barca, aux. Harrisburg, Pa., 1963-67; coadjutor bishop with right of succession, Harrisburg, 1967-71; bishop of Harrisburg, 1971—. Address: 4800 Union Deposit Rd Harrisburg PA 17105

DALTON, RONNIE THOMAS, minister, Church of the Nazarene; b. Dayton, Ohio, Apr. 25, 1953; s. Merl Thomas and Luttie (Scrimager) D.; m. Martha Gomer, Oct. 15, 1977; children: John Thomas, James Douglas. A.A., Mt. Vernon Nazarene Coll., 1973; B.A., Trevecca Nazarene Coll., 1975; M.Div., Nazarene Theol. Sem., 1979; D.Min., Vanderbilt U., 1984. Ordained to ministry Ch. of Nazarene, 1983. Pastor, Ch. of Brethren, St. Joseph, Mo., 1977-78; assoc. pastor Grace Nazarene Ch., Chattanooga, Tenn., 1979-80; v.p. Nazarene Youth Internat., Dist. of East, Tenn., 1982-84; teaching asst. Vanderbilt Div. Sch., Nashville, 1983-84; pastor West View Nazarene Ch., Lebanon, Tenn., 1980-85, Montana Ave Nazarene Ch., Cin., 1985—. Mem. Soc. Bibl. Lit., Religious Research Assn., Wesleyan Theol. Soc. Avocations: computer programming and design; golf; antique auto rebuilding. Home and Office: 2559 Montana Ave Cincinnati OH 45211

DALY, ALEXANDER JOSEPH, minister, Lutheran Church in America; b. Jersey City, May 23, 1930; s. Alexander Joseph and Viola (Fell) D.; m. Mary Kay Baughman, Aug. 20, 1960. B.A., Lenoir-Rhyne Coll., 1958; M.D., Luth. Sch. Theol., 1962. Ordained to ministry Lutheran Ch. in Am., 1962. Pastor St. James Luth. Ch., Folsom, N.J., 1962-64; assoc. pastor Trinity Luth. Ch., Lemoyne Pa., 1964-71, Redeemer Luth. Ch., Atlanta, 1971-80; campus pastor Georgia Tech. Atlanta, 1980—; chaplain Luth. Towers, Atlanta, 1980—. Coordinator Community Head Start Program, Lemoyne, Pa., 1977-78; chmn. County-Wide Meals on Wheels, Lemoyne, 1978-79; cons. Downtown Atlanta Sr. Services, 1983-84. Office: Luth Towers 727 Juniper St NE Atlanta GA 30308

DALY, JAMES JOSEPH See *Who's Who in America*, 43rd edition.

DALY, JAMES ROBERT, bishop, Roman Catholic Church. Titular bishop of Castra Nova, aux. bishop, Rockville Centre, N.Y., 1977—. Office: St Joseph's Villa 984 N Village Ave Rockville Centre NY 11570*

DAMKOEHLER, CHARLES ROBERT, minister, American Baptist Churches in the U.S.A.; b. Milw., Dec. 23, 1937; s. Enno Frank and Doris Edna (Schrump) D.; m. Paulette Belle Korzeniewski, July 20, 1963; children: Cynthia, Daniel, Laura. B.S., Western Bapt. Coll., 1965; M.Div., Trinity Evang. Div. Sch., 1969; Min.D., Am. Bapt. Sem. of West, 1984. Ordained to ministry American Baptist Churches in the U.S.A., 1970. Pastor Buena First Bapt. Ch., Wash., 1969-71, Shoreline First Bapt. Ch., Seattle, 1971-74, Community Bapt. Ch., Waterford, Calif., 1974—; area rep., bd. mgrs. Am. Bapt. Chs. West, 1984—, chmn. area bd. Central San Joaquin Area, 1984—; chergy rep., ethics rev. com. Modesto City Hosp., Calif., 1984—. Mem. gifted edn. planning com. Oakdale Union High Sch., Calif., 1984—. MacMillan fellow, 1980. Mem. Ministers Council Am. Bapt. Chs., Western Continuing Edn. Assocs., Waterford Ministerial Assn. (sec. 1983-84). Home: 425 N Western Ave PO Box 155 Waterford CA 95386 Office: Community Baptist Church 328 D St PO Box 155 Waterford CA 95386

DAMM, JOHN SILBER, minister, Lutheran Church in America; b. Union City, N.J., June 21, 1926; s. John William and Lillian (Meisse) D. B.A., M.Div., B.D., Concordia Sem., St. Louis, 1945-51; M.A., Columbia U., 1952; Ed.D., Tchrs. Coll. N.Y., 1959; D.D. (hon.), Susquehanna U., 1982. Ordained to ministry Luth. Ch. in Am., 1951. Prof., Concordia Sem. in Exile, St. Louis, 1974-81, acting pres., 1974-75, acad. dean, 1974-81; sr. pastor St. Peter's Ch., N.Y.C., 1981—; vice chmn. bd. trustees Hosp. Chaplaincy, Inc., N.Y.C., 1983—; mem. nat. adv. com. Forum for Corp. Responsibility, N.Y.C., 1982; synod rep. Luth. Ch. Dialogue with Archdiocese of N.Y., 1984. Editorial staff Concordia Theol. Monthly, 1966-74; mng. editor Am. Luth., 1962-66. Contbr. articles to profl. jours. Asst. chmn. Community Scholarship Fund, Teaneck, N.Y., 1964; chmn. Cerebral Palsy Lily campaign, 1965. Fulbright scholar, 1959; Amerika-Kreis-Meunster Auslands scholar, 1960; Case Study Inst. fellow, 1972; Luth. Brotherhood ann. faculty scholar, 1981. Home: 30 Waterside Plaza 34D New York NY 10010 Office: Saint Peter's Ch 619 Lexington Ave New York NY 10022

DAMON, ROBERT ARTHUR, associate minister, teacher, Christian Churches and Churches of Christ; b. Orville, Ohio, July 26, 1958; s, William Eugene and Joanne Elaine (Poll) D.; m. Michelle Ruth Robinson, May 9, 1981. Student Mankato State U., 1977-78,

Rochester Community Coll., Minn., 1976, 83, 84; B.A., Minn. Bible Coll., 1985. Coordinator, mgr. Lighthouse Coffeehouse, Rochester, 1977-79; minister of music Plainview Ch. Christ, Minn., 1978; co-founder, dir. Assn. Interdenominational Ministries, Inc., Mpls., 1978-81; coffeehouse dir. Greater Mpls. Assn. Evangelicals, 1980-81; intern minister Alexandria Christian Ch., Minn., 1983; assoc. minister, tchr. Bloomington Ch. Christ, Minn., 1984—; tchr., counselor Pine Haven Christian Assembly, Park Rapids, Minn., 1975—; chmn. spiritual com. Minn. Bible Coll., 1983-85; music leader Campus Crusade for Christ, Minn., 1977-79, U. Minn. Christian Student Fellowship, 1979-81, Formosa Christian Radio Program, 1978-83. Author-compiler: History of the Minnesota Churches of Christ, 1985. Program worker Gra-Y Rochester YMCA, 1982-83. Avocations: collecting antique books; camping. Home: 10225 S Lyndale Ave Bloomington-Minneapolis MN 55420 Office: Bloomington Ch Christ 9000 Bloomington Freeway East Bloomington MN 55431

DAMROW, WILLIAM JOSEPH, minister, Lutheran Church in America; b. Barton, N.Y., Sept. 9, 1952; s. Joseph William and Emily Dorothy (Jenchen) D.; m. Patricia Mary Stevens, Aug. 18, 1973; children: Jessica Lee, Matthew Joseph William. B.A., SUNY-Fredonia, 1975; M.Div., Luth. Theol. Sem., 1979; cert. Cambridge U., 1973; Th.M., Yale Divinity Sch., 1982. Ordained to ministry Lutheran Church in America, 1979. Student Chaplain Phila. State Hosp., 1976; pastor St. Mark's Luth. Ch., Elmsford, N.Y., 1979—; pres. Clergy Assn., Elmsford, 1981—; mem. Personnel Commn., Metro Synod, N.Y., 1980-83, Commn. Alcoholism, 1983—. Contbr. articles to profl. jours. Pres. Elmsford Ecumenical Refugee Assn., 1980-82; bd. dirs. Search for Change, White Plains, N.Y., 1980-81, Community Cable Television Assn., Greenburgh, N.Y., 1983—; mem. N.Y. Coalition for the Children of Alcoholic Families, Hempstead, N.Y., 1984—. Mem. Yale Alumni Assn. Democrat. Club: Adirondack Mountain (Glens Falls, N.Y.). Lodge: Rotary. Home and Office: 2170 Saw Mill River Rd Elmsford NY 10523

DANCY, PAUL BARTLETT, minister, Lutheran Church-Missouri Synod; b. Detroit, June 23, 1954; s. Robert Bartlett and Joan Arda (LeMond) D.; m. Heidi Lynn Scherfling, Aug. 28, 1976; children: Rachel, Adam, Rebecca. B.A. in Edn., Concordia Coll., 1976; M.Div., Concordia Theol. Sem., Ft. Wayne, Ind., 1980. Ordained to ministry, 1980. Pastor, Trinity Luth. Ch., Pontiac, Ill., 1980—; clergy counselor mentally retarded Martin Luther Homes, Pontiac, 1983—; v.p. Pontiac Area Ministerial Assn., 1984—; vacancy pastor Emmanuel Luth. Ch., Dwight, Ill., 1984. Bd. dirs. Christian Action Council of Pontiac, 1984—. Republican. Home: 301 Center Dr Pontiac IL 61764 Office: Trinity Evang Luth Ch 520 N Oak St Pontiac IL 61764

DANFORTH, JOHN CLAGGETT, priest, Episcopal Church, senator; b. St. Louis, Sept. 5, 1936; s. Donald and Dorothy (Claggett) D.; m. Sally Dobson, Sept. 7, 1957; children: Eleanor, Mary, D.D., Jody, Tom. A.B., Princeton U., 1958; LL.B., B.D., Yale U., 1963, M.A. (hon.); D.D. (hon.), Lewis and Clark Coll.; L.H.D. (hon.), Lindenwood Coll., Ind. Central U.; H.H.D. (hon.), William Jewell Coll.; D.S.T. (hon.), S.W. Bapt. U.; LL.D. (hon.), Drury Coll., Maryville Coll., Rockhurst Coll., Westminster Coll., Culver-Stockton Coll. Ordained priest Episcopal Ch. Asst. rector Ch. of Epiphany, N.Y.C., 1963-66; assoc. rector St. Michael and St. George Ch., Clayton, Mo., 1966-68, Grace Ch., Jefferson City, Mo., 1969-76; hon. assoc. St. Alban's Ch., Washington, 1977—. U.S. senator from Mo., 1976—. Atty. gen. State of Mo., Jefferson City, 1968-76; chmn. Mo. Law Enforcement Assistance Council, 1973-74. Recipient Disting. Service award St. Louis Jaycees; Disting. Missourian award, Brotherhood award, NCCJ; Truman Disting. Lectr. award Avila Coll. Mem. Mo. Acad. Squires, Alpha Sigma Nu (hon.). Republican. Home: 5101 Van Ness NW Washington DC 20016 Office: US Senate 497 Russell Office Bldg Washington DC 20510

DANGLMAYR, AUGUSTINE, priest, Roman Catholic Church; b. Muenster, Tex., Dec. 11, 1898; s. Joseph Dangelmayr and Theresia (Muck) D. B.A., M.A., Subiaco Coll.-Ark.; LL.D., St. Edwards Coll., 1943. Ordained priest, 1922. Priest various chs., Dallas, 1922-72; bishop Diocese of Dallas, 1942—. Address: Route 2 Box 67 Muenster TX 76252

DANIEL, ELEANOR ANN, educator; b. Milton, Ill., Feb. 28, 1940; d. Donal Wayne and Eva Bernice (Hillig) D. A.B., Lincoln Christian Coll., 1962, M.A., 1965; Ed.M., U. Ill., 1969, Ph.D., 1975. Youth minister First Christian Ch., Tuscola, Ill., 1961-65; dir. Christian Edn., Ch. of Christ, Buchanan, Mich., 1965-67; instr. Christian edn., Lincoln Christian Coll., Ill., 1964-65, 72, 74-78; prof. Christian edn. Midwest Christian Coll., Oklahoma City, 1967-71, 78-81; minister Christian edn. Christian Ch., Lincoln, Ill., 1971-73, 73-78; prof. Christian edn. Cin. Bible Sem., 1978—; cons. Standard Pub. Co., Cin., 1982—; bd. dirs. Pioneer Bible Translators, Dallas, 1981—; mem. adv. bd. Chinese Christian Sem., Hong Kong, 1979—. Author: Teaching, 1975; VBS Ideas: How To's for a Successful Summer Ministry, 1977; Teach with Success, 1979; What the Bible Says About Sexual Identity, 1982; The ABC's of VBS, 1983; (with Charles Gresham and John Wade) Introduction to Christian Education, 1980. Recipient Restoration award Alumni Assn. of Lincoln Christian Coll., 1979. Mem. Am. Ednl. Research Assn., Nat. Assn. Profs. Christian Edn., AAUW, Delta Kappa Gamma, Gamma Alpha Chi, Delta Epsilon Chi. Home: 459 Dartmouth Cir Cincinnati OH 45244 Office: Cincinnati Bible Sem 2701 Glenway Ave Cincinnati OH 45204

DANIEL, JOSEPH EUGENE, minister of music, So. Baptist Conv.; b. Okmulgee, Okla., Nov. 28, 1912; s. Decatur and Latha (Vance) D.; B.M., Hardin Simmons U., 1948; B.C.Th., New Orleans Baptist Theol. Sem., 1942; m. Flota Grace Smith, Dec. 24, 1940; children: Flota Delatha, Lella Faith, Joseph Emmett. Minister of music chs., La., N.Mex., Okla., Tex., Calif., 1940-57; asst. supt. Los Angeles City Missions, 1957-62; minister of music 1st Bapt. Ch., Mar Vista, Calif., 1966-68, Green Hills Bapt. Ch., La Habra, Calif., 1968-78, 1st Bapt. Ch., Norwalk, Calif., 1978-84; dir. music for numerous Bapt. and community activities. Recipient 1st Joseph Daniel award for outstanding contbn. to church music, 1983. Mem. Western Religious Edn. Assn., Western Music Dirs. Assn. Composer music for song I Know a Name, 1946. Home: 18917 Belshire Cerritos CA 90701

DANIEL, KENNETH VICTOR, minister, United Church of Christ. B. Allentown, Pa., Apr. 22, 1955; s. Victor Asher and LaRue Elizabeth (Laubach) D. B.A. magna cum laude, Kutztown State Coll., 1977; M.Div., United Theol. Sem., St. Paul, Minn., 1981. Ordained to ministry United Church of Christ, 1981. Pastor, St. Andrew's United Ch. of Christ, Reading, Pa., 1981—; v.p. Council for United Ch. Ministry in Reading, 1981—; del. Pa. Southeast Conf., Collegeville, 1981—; chmn. Pub. Advocacy Commn., Reading, 1982—; bd. dirs., mem. exec. com. Berks Women In Crisis, Reading, 1984—. Presdl. scholar United Theol. Sem., 1978, 81. Mem. Assn. Clin. Pastoral Edn., Berks United Ch. of Christ Ministerium. Democrat. Home: 117 N 8th St Reading PA 19601 Office: St Andrew's United Ch of Christ 1320 Spruce St Reading PA 19602

DANIELS, BENJAMIN FRANKLIN, minister, Progressive National Baptist Convention Inc.; b. Weldon, N.C., Mar. 19, 1935; s. Walter Pete and Corinthian (Richards) D.; m. Bronnie Marian Harris, Apr. 11, 1970. B.A., Norfolk State Coll., 1960; B.D., Shaw Div. Sch., 1965, M.Div., 1974; D.Ministry, St. Mary's Sem. and U., 1980. Ordained to ministry Bapt. Ch., 1965. Dormitory counselor Shaw U., Raleigh, N.C., 1962-65, dean of men, 1965-66; missionary Bapt. State Conv., Raleigh, 1966-74; pastor First Bapt. Ch., Lexington, N.C., 1969-81, Union Bapt. Ch., Winston-Salem, N.C., 1981—; tchr. Seminary Extension, 1974—. Pres. Forsyth County Tng. Union, Winston-Salem, 1983—; bd. of friends Shaw Div. Sch., Raleigh, 1984—. Treas. Emancipation Proclamation, Winston-Salem, 1981—; mem. Christmas Toy Shop, United Way, Winston-Salem, 1981-85; mem. exec. bd. Crisis Control Ministries, Winston-Salem, 1981-83. Recipient Plaque, Lexington Ministerial Assn., 1972, Elks of N.C., 1981, Cert. Appreciation, Shaw Div. Sch., 1985. Mem. Bapt. Ministers Conf. and Assocs. (program com.), Rowan Bapt. Assn. (chmn. benefit com.), Gen. Bapt. State Conv. (co-chmn. transp. and housing), Progressive Nat. Bapt. Conv., Lott Carey Fgn. Missionary Conv., Pilot Mountain Bapt. Assn. (strategy com.), NAACP (exec. bd. 1981—), Forsuth Chaplain Assn., Eta Beta Beta, Omega Psi Phi. Lodges: Masons, Shriners. Avocations: reading, golf, meditation. Home: 3911 Tony Dr NE Winston-Salem NC 27105 Office: Union Bapt Ch 406 Northwest Blvd Winston-Salem NC 27105

DANIELS, GEORGE MORRIS, religious publications editor, United Methodist Church; b. St. Louis, July 9, 1927; s. Stafford Cecil and Hattie W. (Nichols) D.; B.A. in Journalism, Drake U., 1951; M.A. in Journalism, Columbia U., 1970; m. Cecilia Adams, 1959 (div. 1960); 1 child, Margaret Ann; m. June Aline Smith, July 20, 1961 (div. 1973); 1 child, Lisa Marguerite. Assoc. news dir. United Meth. Bd. Missions, 1961-67; dir. interpretive services United Meth. Bd. Global Ministries, 1967-81, exec. editor New World Outlook, 1981—; editor Renewal Mag., N.Y.C., 1974—. Free lance writer, 1951—; specialist in African/Caribbean affairs. Recipient Page One award Chgo. Newspaper Guild, 1955. Ralph Stoody fellow, 1969. Columbia U. mag. grantee, S.Am., 1970. Mem. NAACP, Columbia U. Grad. Sch. Journalism Nat. Alumni Assn. (pres. 1983-85), Alpha Phi Alpha, Sigma Delta Chi. Author: The Church in New Nations, 1964. Editor: Southern Africa: A Time for Change, 1969; Drums of War: the continuing crisis in Rhodesia, 1974. Home: 392 Central Park West New York NY 10025 Office: 475 Riverside Dr New York NY 10115

DANIELS, IVERY, minister, aging administrator, White Rock Baptist Church; b. Timmonsville, S.C., June 11, 1938; s. Henry and Alberta (Green) D.; m. Audrey Rosina Winley, July 26, 1958; children: Cynthia, Jerome, Linda, Ivery Jr., Karla, Iris. B.A., SUNY-Buffalo, 1973, M.S., 1976, Ph.D., 1982; D.D. (hon.), U. Bible Inst., 1975. Ordained to ministry, White Rock Baptist. Ch., 1969. Pastor White Rock Bapt. Ch., Buffalo; 1984. moderator Brotherhood Assn., Buffalo, 1976-80 organizer weekly radio ministry Sta. WUFO, Buffalo, 1978-85. Producer rec. sermons, 1984. Bd. dirs. HEAR Erie County, Buffalo, 1978-84; active NAACP, So. Christian Leadership Conf., Operation Push. Recipient Service award White Rock Bapt. Ch., 1984, Community Service award Masten Dist. Republican Orgn., 1984. Republican. Lodge: St. Matthews (sec. 1976-80). Home: 136 Stanton St Buffalo NY 14206 Office: White Rock Bapt 480 E Utica Buffalo NY 14208

DANIELS, THOMAS WILLIAM, evangelist, So. Bapt. Conv.; b. St. Johnsbury, Vt., Sept. 28, 1949; s. Roland Oscar and Betty Patricia (Labounty) D.; grad. Grand Rapids Sch. Bible and Music, 1971; m. Kay Michele Fish, June 27, 1975. Ordained to ministry, 1971; audio arts dir. New Eng. Fellowship of Evangelicals, Rumney, N.H., 1967-69; news dir., announcer Sta. WMPC, Lapeer, Mich., 1971-73; minister of music and youth Riverside Bapt. Ch., Newport News, Va., 1973—. Music dir. Hampton Rds. Crusade, 1976; v.p. Peninsula Citizens for Decency through Law, Hampton, Va., 1976; sponsor Greater Peninsula Crusade for Christ Com., 1976; mem. campus ministries com. Peninsula Bapt. Assn., 1976—. Pres., Peninsula Citizens for Decency through Law, 1977—. Res. officer Lapeer County Sheriffs Dept., 1972-73; squadron commander CAP, 1973. Home: 187 Turrill Rd Lapeer MI 48446 Office: 187 Turrill Rd Lapeer MI 48446

D'ANJOU, HENRY GENET, priest, Roman Catholic Ch.; b. Gemzin, Poland, Nov. 18, 1922; s. Ignace and Anne (Folque) d'A.; came to U.S., 1960, naturalized, 1966; D.S.T., U. Warsaw, Poland, 1950; Licentiate Biblical Scis., Pontifical Biblical Inst., Rome, 1959; Ph.D., U. Vienna, 1960. Ordained priest, 1948; chancellor Wloclawek Diocese, Poland, 1951-53; prof. Biblical Scis. Diocesan Sem., Wloclawek, Poland, 1951-57; lectr. Columbia U., N.Y.C. and St. Thomas Aquinas Coll., Sparkill, N.Y., 1965; asso. pastor Immaculate Heart of Mary Ch., Scarsdale, N.Y., 1972, St. Thomas More Ch., N.Y.C., 1974; pastor Sacred Heart Ch., Port Chester, N.Y., 1975—. Founder Cath.-Jewish Councils, Port Chester, N.Y., 1975. Mem. British Bibl. Assn. Home and office: 229 Willett Ave Port Chester NY 10573

DARBY, SAMUEL EDWARD, religious educator, administrator, Seventh-day Adventists. B. Cuba, N.Y., June 15, 1952; s. Samuel E. and Jayne (Doswell) D.; m. Diane Miller, July 21, 1974; children: Kelly, Krystal. B.A., Columbia Union Coll., 1974; student Temple U., 1978; M.Ed., Trenton State Coll., 1981. Ordained lay elder Seventh-day Adventists; cert. profl. denominational educator, Pa., Del., N.J. Instr., Columbia Union Coll., Takoma Park, Md., 1974-75; tchr., prin. Allegheny East Conf. Seventh-day Adventists, Pine Forge, Pa., 1975-84; vice prin. Pine Force Acad., 1984—. Named Outstanding Young Man Am., 1984. Mem. Assn. Supervision and Curriculum Devel. Office: Pine Forge Acad Pine Forge PA 19548

DARBY, WESLEY ANDREW, minister, Conservative Bapt. Assn. Am.; b. Glendale, Ariz., Sept. 19, 1928; s. Albert Leslie and Beulah Elvirah (Lamb) D.; student Bible Inst. Los Angeles, 1947, No. Ariz. State U., 1947-48; B.A., Rockmont Coll., 1950; postgrad. Ariz. State U., 1968, St. Anne's Coll., Oxford, Eng., 1978; m. Donna Maye Bice, May 29, 1947; children: Carol Darby Eyman, Lorna, Elizabeth, Andrea. Ordained to ministry, 1950; pastor Sunnyside Bapt. Ch., Flagstaff, Ariz., 1947-48, 1st Bapt. Ch., Clifton, Ariz., 1950-55, West High Bapt. Ch., Phoenix, 1955—; pres. Phoenix Gospel Mission, 1975-77; v.p. Ariz. Bapt. Conv., 1975-84; pres. Conservative Bapt. Found., 1974-84; chaplain CAP, 1952-55, Ariz. Breakfast Club, 1970—. Instr. English and homiletics Southwestern Coll., Phoenix, 1961—. Pres., Ariz. Alcohol-Narcotic Edn. Assn., 1968—; precinct committeeman, capt. Republican party, Phoenix, 1962-69. Chmn. bd. Ariz. Bapt. Found., Phoenix, 1974—, Gospel Wings Inc., 1960—. Mem. Greater Phoenix Evang. Ministers Assn. (pres. 1960-63). Office: 3301 N 19th Ave Phoenix AZ 85015

DARCY, HAROLD PATRICK, sem. pres., Roman Cath. Ch.; b. Newark, July 10, 1929; s. Michael and Annie (Keaney) D.; A.B., Seton Hall U., 1951; S.T.L., Gregorian U., Rome, 1955, J.C.D., 1960. Ordained priest, Roman Catholic Ch., 1954; asso. pastor St. Joseph's of the Palisades Ch., West New York, N.J., 1955-56; asst. chancellor-actuary of Tribunal, Archdiocese of Newark, 1956-57; sec. to apostolic del., Washington, 1961-71; pastor St. Vincent DePaul Ch., Bayonne, N.J., 1971-72; rector-pres. Immaculate Conception Sem., Darlington, N.J., 1972-74; rector N. Am. Coll., Rome, 1974—. Trustee Seton Hall U. Papal chamberlain, 1962; hon. prelate of His Holiness, 1971; mem. Pastor Council Peregrinatio Ad Petri Sedem, 1976—. Editorial bd. The Advocate, ofcl. newspaper of Archdiocese of Newark, 1973-74. Home: N Am Coll Via del Gianiculo 14 00120 Vatican City

D'ARCY, JOHN M., bishop, Roman Catholic Church. Titular bishop of Mediana, aux. bishop, Boston, 1975—. Office: 70 Lawrence St Lowell MA 01852*

DARK, PHILLIP RAY, minister, Southern Baptist Convention; b. Tulsa, May 25, 1945; s. Clarence Harold and Bertie Mae (Woolley) D.; m. Betty Irene Williams, Aug. 10, 1968; children: Terry Wade, Stephen Ryan. B.A., Okla. State U., 1970; M.Div., Midwestern Bapt. Sem., 1973. Ordained to ministry Bapt. Ch., 1968. Interim pastor Morrison Bapt. Ch., Okla., 1968; pastor Pleasant View Bapt. Ch., Ponca City, Okla., 1968-70, Little Platte Bapt. Ch., Edgerton, Mo., 1970-73, First Bapt. Ch., Lindsay, Okla., 1973-78, Trinity Bapt. Ch., Tulsa, 1978-84, First Bapt. Ch., Hugo, Okla., 1984—. Bd. dirs. Westside YMCA, 1983-84. Mem. Tulsa Bapt. Assn., S.W. Tulsa Ministers Fellowship, Midwestern Bapt. Sem. Alumni Assn. Democrat. Lodges: Rotary (pres. 1984—). Home: 611 E Duke Hugo OK 74743 Office: First Baptist Ch 3rd and Jackson Hugo OK 74743

DARLING, EDNA PEARLENE, chaplain, American Baptist Churches in the U.S.A.; b. Wartrace, Tenn., July 19, 1934; d. Willie Lee and Rosie Lee (Scott) Phillips; m. George C. Darling, May 1, 1960 (div. 1973); children: Charles Adams, Curtis William. M.Div., Meth. Theol. Sch. in Ohio, 1975; B.S., Franklin U., 1977. Ordained to ministry American Baptist Churches in the U.S.A., 1975. Asst. pastor Zion Meth. Ch., Delaware, Ohio, 1972-76; pastoral counselor Cin-Thy-Care Community Ctr., Columbus, Ohio, 1976-79, Pastoral Counseling Services, Middletown, Ohio, 1980-81; chaplain resident Hospice and Miami Valley Hosp., Dayton, Ohio, 1979-80; chaplain St. Elizabeth Med. Ctr., Dayton, Ohio, 1981—; mem. Ch. Women United, Delaware, Ohio, 1966-70; workshop instr. Tehol. Sch. Reynoldsburg, Ohio, 1973; retreat leader First Bapt. Ch., Delaware, Ohio, 1983. Mem. Delaware Community Service, 1965-68, Hospice Dayton, Inc., 1980; vol. activities therapist Harding Mental Hosp., Worthington, Ohio, 1974-76; co-facilitator Make Today Count, Dayton, 1980, Perinatal Grief Support Group, Dayton, 1983—. Fellow Coll. Chaplains (cert.; condr. workshop nat. conv. 1984, 85); mem. Interdenominational Ministerial Alliance, Dayton Area Bapt. Assn., Assn. Clin. Pastoral Edn. (clin. mem.), Dayton Area Chaplains Assn. Democrat. Home: Dayton OH Office: St Elizabeth Med Ctr 601 Edwin Moses Blvd W Dayton OH 45426

DARMODY, STEVEN GRADY, minister, Seventh-day Adventist Church; b. Huntsville, Tex., Nov. 13, 1956; s. Gordon Richard and Virginia Carol (Brown) D.; m. Joni Louise Whitacre, Aug. 14, 1977; children: Alan Whitacre, Jaclyn Nicole. B.A. in Theology, So. Missionary Coll., 1978; M.Div., Andrews Theol. Sem., 1982. Ordained to ministry Seventh-day Adventists, 1985. Pastor Ga.-Cumberland Conf. Seventh-day Adventists, Brunswick Ch., Ga., 1978-80; assoc. pastor Belevedere Seventh-day Adventist Ch., Decatur, Ga., 1982-83; pastor Smyrna Seventh-day Adventist Ch., Ga., 1983—; pres. Morning Song Concerts, Smyrna, 1982—. Recs. include Shall We Learn to be Friends, 1982; producer: Morning Song Prodns., 1984—. Mem. Smyrna Ministerial Assn. (sec.-treas.). Home: 3390 Navaho Trail Smyrna GA 30080 Office: Smyrna Seventh Day Adventist Ch PO Box 1821 Smyrna GA 30081

DARRAH, WILLIAM STANLEY, minister, Churches of God General Conference; b. Cresap, W.Va., Sept. 11, 1933; s. Clarence Eugene and Alma Bernice (Estep) D.; m. JoAnn Faler, Oct. 5, 1957; children: Daniel, William, Chriss, David, Amy. B.S., Findlay Coll., 1955; M. Div., Winebrenner Sem., 1972. Ordained to ministry Chs. of God Gen. Conf., 1957. Pastor Grove City Ch., Pa., 1957-60, Centennial Ch., Aleppo, Pa., 1960-65, Kingwood Ch., Markleton, Pa., 1965-70, Fort Wayne Ch., Ind, 1970-79, Shippensburg Ch., Pa., 1984—; trustee Winebrenner Sem., Findlay, Ohio, 1973—; chmn. World Missions Commn., Findlay, 1977—; mem. exec. com., mem. adminstrv. council Chs. of God, Findlay, 1977—. Republican. Lodge: Rotary. Office: Chs of God Gen Conf 123 E King St Shippensburg PA 17257

DARST, HARRY WALTER, minister, Bapt. Missionary Assn. Am.; b. Steelville, Mo., May 18, 1909; s. William Patrick and Emma Caroline (Forester) D.; student Springfield (Mo.) State Coll., 1930, Rolla (Mo.) State Coll., 1940, Pittsburg (Kans.) State Coll., 1946-47; m. Marie Roena Britton, May 21, 1938; 1 dau., Marilyn Ruth Darst Orr. Pastor chs., Kans., 1953-57, Ala., 1957-62, Mo., 1940-48, Okla., 1962-65, Miss., 1965-70, Parkview Ch., Arnold, Mo., 1970—; tchr. schs., Mo., 1937-45, Galena, Kans., 1947-48. State missionary Bapt. Missionary Assn. Mo., Arnold; Writer jr. high Sunday Sch. Quarterly, Bapt. Missionary Assn. Am., 1953-62; mem. bldg. corp., 1955—, sec.-treas. missions, 1977—; pres. Bapt. Bldg. Bonds, Inc., 1972-76. Editor Ala. Bapt. Banner, 1959-62; asst. editor Mo. Missionary Bapt., 1972-77, editor, 1977-84. Home and Office: 1169 Whispering Wind Dr Arnold MO 63010

DASAL, ROBERT LARIDO, minister, So. Baptist Conv.; b. Charleston, SC., Sept. 5, 1946; s. Domingo Larido and Annie Eloise (Pruett) D.; B.A., Southwest Bapt. Coll., 1968; student Southwestern Bapt. Theol. Sem., 1973; m. Barbara Jean Perry, Dec. 24, 1946; children—Scott Allen, Stephanie Ann. Ordained to ministry, 1965; pastor Elk Creek Bapt. Ch., Cabool, Mo., 1965, Mt. Nebo Bapt. Ch., Lockwood, Mo., 1966-68, Grace Temple Bapt. Chapel, Muscatine, Iowa, 1968-70; youth minister Blvd. Bapt. Ch., Springfield, Mo., 1970-72, pastor, 1973—; minister youth edn. Handley Bapt. Ch., Fort Worth, 1972-73. Police chaplain Springfield (Mo.) Police Dept., 1971-72; prayer chmn. Mo. Bapt. Conventions Bible Conf., 1975. Mem. Greene County Bapt. Assn. (mem. exec. bd. 1974-77, associational Sunday Sch. dir. 1975-76). Preacher revival crusades. Home: 2856 E Bergman St Springfield MO 65803 Office: 1722 N National St Springfield MO 65803

D'ASTOUS, RITA, nun, Roman Catholic Church; b. St. Fabien, Que., Apr. 21, 1916; d. Desire and Eugenie (Belzile) D'A. Diploma Sup. Enseignement menager U. Montreal, 1952; Licence Pedagogie, U. Laval, 1958. Joined Sisters of Our Lady of Holy Rosary, Roman Cath. Ch. Prof., Normal Schs., Que., 1942-52, directress, 1952-63; regional superior Sisters of Our Lady of the Holy Rosary, Portland, Maine, 1967-72; superior gen. Congregation of Sisters of Our Lady of the Holy Rosary, Rimouski, Que., 1979—; mem. corp. adminstrv. council Sisters of Our Lady of the Holy Rosary Conf. of Can. Religious of Que., 1980—. Contbr. articles to profl. jours. Recipient Merite Scolaire, 2d degree, Ministire de l'education, Que., 1955. Home: 300 Ave du Rosaire Rimouski PQ G5L 3E3 Canada Office: Sisters of Our Lady of Holy Rosary 375 Lasalle Rimouski PQ G5L 3V6 Canada

DATTLER, LESTER LIONEL, minister, Presbyterian Ch. in U.S.; b. Waterloo, Iowa, Aug. 25, 1933; s. Carl Richard (stepfather) and Elda Marie (Leege) Kline; A.A., Young Harris Coll., 1955; B.A., U. Ga., 1957; M. Div., Erskine Theol. Sem., 1960; m. Betty Helen Gunter, June 3, 1956; children—Frederick Dorrington, Eric Dana. Ordained to ministry, 1960; pastor chs., Tucker, Ga. and Charlotte, N.C., 1960-69; pastor Edgemont Associated Ref. Presbyn. Ch., Covington, Va., 1970-76, First Presbyn. Ch., Carthage, N.C., 1976—. Vis. prof. Lynchburg (Va.) Sem.; moderator N.C. Presbytery, 1964, Va. Presbytery, 1970, 76; chmn. Pan-Presbyn. Com., Charlotte, 1967-68; pres. released time religious edn. program, Covington, 1972-73. Active Boy Scouts Aml; bd. dirs. Westgate Civic Club, Charlotte, 1968; mem. Charlotte Police Community Council, 1969; pres. Edgemont PTA, Covington, 1970-71. Recipient Alleghany County (Va.) Sesquicentenial award, 1972. Mem. Covington-Alleghany Ministerial Assn. Contbr. articles to religious jours. Home: 3068 S Wildwood Dr Covington VA 24426 Office: 2306 S Church Ave Covington VA 24426

DAUSEY, GARY RALPH, religious association executive; b. Chgo., Jan. 8, 1940; s. Ralph S. and Theresa (Campbell) D.; student Moody Bible Inst., 1958-59; A.B., Taylor U., 1962; M.A., Wheaton Grad. Sch. Theology, 1965; m. Barbara Elaine Carman, June 29, 1963; children: Julie, Greg. Ordained to ministry, 1963; pastor Noble (Ind.) Congl. Christian Ch., 1959-62; asst. dir. audiovisual dept. Moody Bible Inst., Chgo., 1962-63; v.p. Youth for Christ Internat., Wheaton, 1964-81; exec. v.p. Youth for Christ/USA, 1982—. Author: Youth Leaders Sourcebook; contbg. author: Parents and Teenagers. Contbr. articles to religious mags. and jours. Bd. dirs. Am. Evangelism Assn., 1963-66; chmn. bd. Wheaton Bible Ch. Recipient Editorial award Evang. Press Assn., 1967; Gold Medallion Book award Evang. Christian Pubs. Assn., 1984. Mem. Fellowship of Congl. Christian Chs., Assn. for Ednl. Communication and Tech. Home: 309 Brookside Circle Wheaton IL 60187 Office: Box PO 419 Wheaton IL 60189

DAVES, OTIS MAXION, minister, So. Baptist Conv.; b. Jesup, Ga., Sept. 21, 1940; s. Otis Wells and Jewel Bertie (Dotson) D.; B.E., Ga. So. Coll., 1969; M.Div., Southwestern Bapt. Theol. Sem., 1974; D.Min., Luther Rice Sem., 1976; m. Dorothy Lorene Windham, June 20, 1964; 1 son, Otis Maxion. Ordained to ministry, 1960; pastor Elza Bapt. Ch., Reidsville, Ga., 1959-61, El Bethel Bapt. Ch., Twin City, Ga., 1962-65, New Bethel Bapt. Ch., Sandersville, Ga., 1966-71, First Bapt. Ch., Jean, Tex., 1972-74, Northside Bapt. Ch., Elberton, Ga., 1974—; chaplain Elbert County (Ga.) Fire Dept., 1974—. Full time radio ministry, Sta. WSGC, Elberton; mem. exec. com. Ga. Bapt. Convention, 1969-71; evangelism dir. Hebron Bapt. Assn., 1975—; v.p. Elbert County Ministerial Assn., 1974—. Home: 507 Ridgecrest Dr Elberton GA 30635 Office: N Oliver St Elberton GA 30635

DAVID, GEORGE EMMANUEL, minister, United Methodist Church; b. Aligarh, Uttar Pradesh, India, Sept. 3, 1944; came to U.S., 1970; s. Lawrence Vincent and Champawati (Pershadi Lall) D.; m. Rajkumari Myra Lyall, June 22, 1972; children: Sonia Marion, Merrill Vincent, Shannon Myra. B.A., Agra U., India., 1965; M.A., Meerut U., India, 1969; M.A., Wheaton Grad. Sch. Theology, 1973; M.Div., U. Dubuque Theol. Sem., 1980, now postgrad. Ordained elder The Wesleyan Church, 1975. Asst. pastor Wheaton Wesleyan Ch., Ill., 1973-74; pastor Hoopeston Wesleyan Ch., Ill., 1974-76, Free Meth. Ch., Chgo., 1976-77, United Meth. Ch., Tampico, Ill., 1977-81, Hope United Meth. Ch., Ill., 1981-85; assoc. prof. First United Meth. Ch., Palatine, Ill., 1985—; mem. dist. bd. Ordained Ministry, Rockford, Ill., 1984—, Commn. of Race and Religion. Home: 240 E Colfax St Palatine IL 60067 (312) 358-5121 Office: 123 N Plum Rd Palatine IL 60067

DAVIDS, PETER HUGH, minister, religious educator, Plymouth Brethren Church; b. Syracuse, N.Y., Nov. 22, 1947; s. Hugh Harold and Doris Marie (Dunning) D.; m. Judith Lee Bouchillon, Aug. 19, 1967; children: Elaine Marie, Gwenda Lee, Ian Hugh. A.B., Wheaton Coll., 1968; M.Div., Trinity Evang. Div. Sch., 1971; Ph.D., U. Manchester, 1974. Commended Plymouth Brethren Church, 1974; ordained to ministry Episcopal Ch., 1979. Theologischer lehrer Bibelschule Wiedenest, Bergneustadt, Fed. Republic Germany, 1974-76; assoc. prof. bibl. studies Trinity Episcopal Sch. Ministry, Ambridge, Pa., 1976-83; adj. prof. N.T., Regent Coll., Vancouver, B.C., Can., 1983—; vis. prof. N.T., Trinity Evang. Div. Sch., Deerfield, Ill., 1978, New Coll., Berkeley, Calif., 1982-83; elder Austin Ave. Chapel, Coquitlam, B.C., Can., 1983—. Author: Epistle of James, 1982, James, 1983. Contbg. editor Sojourners, 1981—. Contbr. articles to various publs. Fellow Inst. Bibl. Research (editor microcomputer newsletter 1983—); mem. Studiorum Novi Testamenti Societas, Tyndale Fellowship for Bibl. Research, Soc. Bibl. Lit., Evang. Theol. Soc., Evang. for Social Action. Democrat. Home: 120 Brookside Dr Port Moody BC V3H 3H4 Canada Office: Regent Coll 2130 Westbrook Mall Vancouver BC V6T 1W6 Canada

DAVIDSON, GLENN OSCAR, minister, pastoral counselor, Am. Luth. Ch.; b. Floyd, Iowa, Apr. 1, 1931; s. Alfred O. and Nora A. (Skogen) D.; A.A., Waldorf Coll., 1956; B.A., Augsburg Coll., M.Div., Luther Theol. Sem., 1962; m. Ruth M. Zacher, Dec. 28, 1958; children—Nathan Erik, Amy Sarah. Ordained to ministry, 1962; pastor N. Kickapoo and S. Kickapoo Luth Chs., Soldiers Grove, Wis., 1962-64, Kickapoo United Luth. Ch., Soldiers Grove, Wis., 1964-68, Peace Luth. Ch., Readstown, Wis., 1965-68, St. Stephen's Luth. Ch., Rogersville, Wis., also Peace Luth. Ch., Rosendale, Wis., 1968-72; pastoral counselor Unified Bd., Fond du Lac County, Wis., 1972—. Bd. dirs. Fon du Lac Luth. Home, 1967-71; cons. to bd. dirs. Blandine Halfway House for Alcoholics, 1976—. Mem. Alcoholism Services Com., Fond du Lac County, 1969—. Mem. Assn. Mental Health Clergy, Wis. Assn. on Alcoholism and Other Drug Abuse. Contbr. articles to religious jours. Home: 310 E 19th St Fond du Lac WI 54935 Office: 459 E 1st St Fond du Lac WI 54935

DAVIDSON, NEAL RUSSELL, minister, chaplain, Lutheran Church in America; b. Milw., Nov. 25, 1934; s. Russell Norman Davidson and Eleanor Clara (Geller) Davidson Biegler; children: Craig, Roger; m. Jean Colette Okstel, Feb. 14, 1982; stepchildren: William, Jean, Robert. B.S., Iowa State U., 1956; M.Div., Luth. Sch. Theology at Chgo., 1963; Th.M., Princeton U., 1974; Ed.M., Columbia U., 1981, Ed.D., 1983. Ordained to ministry Lutheran Ch., 1963. Mission developer Luth. Ch., Portland, Tex., 1963-64; pastor St. Stephen Luth. Ch., Portland, 1964-70; commd. lt. U.S. Army, 1966, advanced through grades to maj., 1981; chaplain U.S. Army, 1985—; dir. U.S. Army Drug and Alcohol Rehab. Ctr., Fort Monmouth, N.J., 1972-74; instr. U.S. Army Chaplain Sch., Fort Monmouth, 1979-82; instr. communications U. Md. European Div., Rheinberg, Fed. Republic Germany, 1982—. Contbr. articles to profl. jours. Bd. dirs. Portland Little League, 1966-70. Mem. Internat. Communication Assn. Lodge: Rotary (pres. 1969). Republican. Home: Selfridge ANGB MI 48045 Office: US Army Tank Automotive Command Warren MI 48090

DAVIDSON, WILLIAM, bishop, Episcopal Church; b. Miles City, Mont., July 20, 1919; s. Thomas and Catherine Annie (Gold) D.; B.S., Mont. State U., 1940; S.T.B., Berkeley Divinity Sch., 1946, D.D., 1966; m. Mary Ernestine Shoemaker, June 3, 1942; children: Carol (Mrs. Ronald Carpenter), Thomas, George, Robert. Ordained deacon Episcopal Ch., 1946, priest, 1947, consecrated bishop, 1966; priest-in-charge St. John's Ch., Townsend, Mont., Grace Ch., White Sulphur Springs, Mont., Trinity Ch., Martinsdale, Mont., 1946-51, 52-56, St. James Ch., Lewistown, Mont., 1952-56; assoc. sec. nat. council, div. town and country Home Dept. Episcopal Ch., N.Y.C., 1956-62; rector Grace Ch., Jamestown, N.D., 1962-66; bishop Diocese Western Kans., Salina, 1966-80; asst. bishop Diocese of Ohio, 1980—. Ex-officio chmn. bd. trustees St. John's Mil. Sch., Salina; ex-officio chmn. bd. dirs. St. Francis Boys' Homes, Salina. Named Lewistown Jr. C. of C. Young Man Year, 1954. Mem. Salina C. of C., Episcopal Soc. Rural Workers Fellowship (pres. 1949-50), Episcopal Peace Fellowship, Alpha Gamma Rho. Office: 2230 Euclid Ave Cleveland OH 44115

DAVIES, ARCHIBALD DONALD, bishop, Episcopal Ch.; b. Pitts., Apr. 15, 1920; s. Archibald Decimus and Velma Mercedes (Harris) D.; B.A., U. Tulsa, 1944; S.T.B., S.T.M., 1947; m. Mabel Myrtle Roberts, Dec. 25, 1939. Ordained priest Episcopal Ch., 1951; deacon in charge, El Dorado, Kans., 1950-51; rector St. Paul Ch., Manhattan, Kans., 1952-54, chapel Kan. State U., Manhattan, 1952-54; sec. standing com. Episcopal Ch., 1953-54; asso. sec. adult div. dept. Christian edn., 1954-56; rector Grace Ch., Monroe, La., 1958-61; dean Trinity Cathedral, Omaha, 1968-70; consecrated bishop, 1970; bishop Episcopal Diocese of Dallas, 1970-83; bishop of Ft. Worth, Tex., 1983—. Trustee Episcopal Found., E.D. Farmer Found., St. Mark's Sch., Gaston Episcopal Hosp., Dallas, So. Meth. U., Dallas. Author: Adventure in Renewal, also booklets. Contbr. articles to religious mags. Office: 3572 Southwest Loop 820 Fort Worth TX 76133

DAVIES, JAMES ALAN, religious educator, Christian and Missionary Alliance; b. Akron, Ohio, Nov. 5, 1948; s. Thomas and Mable Jane (Piefer) D.; m. Cheryl Suzanne Gregg, May 17, 1970; children: James Alan II, Jeffrey Trevor, Jennifer Elizabeth. Student, Akron State U., 1966-67; B.S., Calvary Bible Coll., 1971; M.A. cum laude, Trinity Evang. Div. Sch., 1982; Ed.D. candidate, U. Ga. Minister of edn. Wealthy St. Bapt. Ch., Grand Rapids, Mich., 1971-73, Immanuel Bapt. Ch., Fort Wayne, Ind., 1973-76; ednl. pastor No. Valley Evang. Free Ch., Cresskill, N.J., 1978-82; assoc. prof. Christian edn. Toccoa Falls Coll., Ga., 1982—; Christian edn. com. 1st Alliance Ch., Toccoa, 1984—; bd. Christian edn. Evang. Free Ch. Am., Eastern Dist., 1979-82; bd. dirs. ednl. com. Creation Research Inst., Chgo., 1976-77. Author: Evangelistic Home Bible Studies, 1975; Small Groups In The Church-A Ministry Manual, 1984. Contbr. articles to profl. jours. Active on Mayors Council Civic Affairs, Cresskill, 1980-82; umpire Am. Softball Assn., 1980—. Recipient Mayor's Service award Cresskill, 1981, 82. Mem. Nat. Assn. Profs. Christian Edn., Am. Assn. Adult and Continuing Edn., Evang. Tchr. Tng. Assn., Nat. Assn. Dirs. Christian Edn., Tugaloo Bapt. Assn. (tng. dir. 1984—). Republican. Home: Rural Route 6 Box 395 Toccoa GA 30577 Office: Toccoa Falls Coll PO Box 800248 Toccoa Falls GA 30598

DAVIGNON, CHARLES PHILIAS, priest, Roman Catholic Church; b. Albany, Vt., Nov. 5, 1930; s. Leo and Nellie Mae (Pudvah) D. S.T.L., U. Montreal, 1956; M.A., Cath. U. Am., 1960, Ph.D., 1973. Ordained priest Roman Cath. Ch., 1956. Prin., St. Michael's High Sch., Montpelier, Vt., 1960-66; dir. Communication Ctr., Puno, Peru, 1969-72, Ctr. Mission Studies, Maryknoll, N.Y., 1977-79; pastor St. Mary's Ch., Newport, Vt., 1980—; dean Orleans-Essex Deanery, Diocese of Burlington, Vt., 1980-84; mem. peace com. Vt. Ecumenical Council. Contbr. articles to profl. jours. Mem. Orleans County Hist. Soc. (bd. dirs. 1981-84). Lodge: K.C. Address: 5 Clermont Terr Newport VT 05855

DAVIS, BENJAMIN FRANKLIN, minister United Methodist Ch.; b. Cleveland County, N.C., Aug. 14, 1933; s. Forrest Andrew and Nettie Erma (Morrison) D.; A.A., Charlotte Coll., 1961; B.A., U. N.C., Charlotte, 1966; M.Div., Duke U., 1969; m. Patsy Jean Bridges, Sept. 8, 1960. Ordained elder W.N.C. Conf. United Meth. Ch., 1970; pastoral counselor Piedmont Clinic, Lawndale, N.C., 1969-72; clin. chaplain, dir. Alcohol and drug div. Cleveland County Mental Health Center, Shelby, N.C., 1972—. Pres., Cleveland County Ministerial Assn., 1976; dir. Camp for Mentally Retarded, 1970—; counselor Shelby unit Dept. Corrections, 1969-73; vice pres. N.C. Chaplains Assn., 1975-76. Mem. com., eagle rev. bd. Piedmont council Boy Scouts Am., 1970—; organizing com. Upper Cleveland Area Needs, Inc.; pres. Cleveland County Mental Health Assn., 1974-75; bd. dirs. Assn. Retarded Citizens, 1974-75; bd. dirs. Cleveland County Mental Health Assn. Bd., 1974-76. Mem. Upper Cleveland Group Ministry, Cleveland County Pub. Adminstrs. Assn. (v.p. 1976), Alcohol Profls. N.C. Home: PO Box 167 Lawndale NC 28090 Office: Cleveland County Mental Health Center Shelby NC 28150

DAVIS, CHARLES DEBRELLE, minister, Am. Bapt. Chs. in U.S.A.; b. Cochran, Ga., Nov. 14, 1927; s. Charles Debrelle and Mary Claire (Wade) D.; B.A., Mercer U., 1950; M.Div., Yale, 1954; postgrad. Boston U., 1971—; m. Betty Jean Morgan, Sept. 4, 1952; children—Charles, Bill. Ordained to ministry Am. Baptist Chs. in U.S.A., 1952; minister chs., Center Brook, Conn., 1952-54, Pulaski, Va., 1954-59, Mars Hill (N.C.) Bapt. Ch., 1959-66, Myers Park Bapt. Ch., Charlotte, N.C., 1966-71; minister edn. First Bapt. Ch., Needham, Mass. since 1971—. Jr. staff psychologist Kennedy Meml. Hosp., Brighton, Mass., 1974-75; staff psychologist Framingham (Mass.) Youth Guidance Center, 1976—; intern Danielsen Pastoral Counseling Center, Boston U.; mem. Christian life com. N.C. Bapt. Conv., 1963-66; staff adult library conf. Am. Bapt. Chs. in U.S.A., Greenlake, Wis., 1968-71. Mem. Citizens Com. for Better Govt., Mars Hill, 1961-66; bd. advisers Mars Hill Coll., 1970—. Mem. Religion and Fgn. Policy Assn., Blue Key, Kappa Phi Kappa. Home: 151 Warren St Needham MA 02192 Office: 895 Great Plain Ave Needham MA 02192

DAVIS, CLAUDIA MAE HARPER, lay church worker, Christian Methodist Episcopal Church; educator; b. Marshall, Tex., Apr. 2, 1922; d. Joe and Clara (Adkins) Harper; m. Percy Singleton, 1940 (div.

1945); children: Harold L., Percy Jr., Orchid DeLois Singleton Mitchell; m. Lester A. Davis, Apr. 6, 1974. B.S., Bishop Coll., 1950; M.Ed., U. Tex., 1960; postgrad., Tex. A&M U., 1966. Cert. tchr.; lic. cosmetology instr. Dir. Mission Outreach, 1979—; dir. Christian edn. Abilene dist. Christian Meth. Episc. Ch., 1979-82, dir. youth Northwest Tex. Conf., 1980—; music dir. St. Paul Ch., Midland, Tex., 1960—, supt. Ch. Sch., 1967, 70, 80—, chmn. steward bd., 1969-72, sec. trustee bd., 1976—. Tchr. Midland Sch. Dist., 1958—. Youth dir. ARC, Midland, 1967; mem. Parks and Recreation Commn., Midland, 1968-71; voter registrar Community Devel. Bd., Midland, 1975-76; bd. dirs. Community Day Nursery, Midland, 1975-77. Named Tchr. of Yr., Midland Kiwanis Club, 1964, Outstanding Tchr., Midland Ind. Schs., 1965, Laity of Yr., Northwest Tex. Conf., 1979. Mem. Tex. State Tchrs. Assn., NEA, Nat. Hairdressers and Cosmetologists, Am. Vocat. Assn., Tex. Classroom Tchrs., Vocat. Club (nat. sponsor 1968—), Instrs. Club (state treas. 1976-80), Delta Sigma Theta (treas. 1967-69). Avocations: sewing, cake decorating. Home: 118 E Nobles St Midland TX 79701 Office: Midland High Sch 906 W Illinois St Midland TX 79701

DAVIS, DAVID, rabbi, Reform Jewish Congregations; b. Balt., Aug. 18, 1936; s. Alexander Alvin and Anne Lillian (Frank) D.; B.A., Am. U., 1958; B. Hebrew Literature, Hebrew Union Coll., 1962, M.A. in Hebrew Lit., 1965, D.D., 1965; m. Ulla Zimmermann, Dec. 8, 1974; children—Amy, Allyson. Ordained rabbi, 1965; rabbi, coll. instr., San Rafael, Calif., 1970—. Dir. Nat. Fedn. Temple Youth, 1967-70; chaplain San Quentin Prison, 1972—; mem. ecumenical housing com. Lloyd Edn. Center, 1972-73. Mem. Central Conf. Am. Rabbis, Pacific Assn. Reform Rabbis (mem. exec. bd. 1973-75), No. Bd. Rabbis, Contbr. articles to religious jours. Home: 170 Wilson Way Larkspur CA 94939 Office: 4340 Redwood Hwy San Rafael CA 94903

DAVIS, DAWSON ALAN, minister, Lutheran Church in America; b. Bellevue, Ky., Feb. 16, 1938; s. William Jennings and Gwendolyn A. (Dawson) D.; m. Ann Beck Arnold, June 24, 1961; children: Timothy Alan, Mark Edward. A.B., Wittenberg Coll., 1960; B.D., Hamma Div. Sch., 1963; postgrad., Eberhardt-Karls U., Tuebingen, Fed. Republic Germany, 1963-64. Ordained to ministry Luth. Ch. in Am., 1965. Asst. pastor 1st English Luth. Ch., Platteville, Wis., 1964-67, Redeemer Luth. Ch., Milw., 1967-70; campus pastor Marquette U., Milw., 1970-82; dir. Christcross, Milw., 1983—; bd. dirs. Broadcasting Commn., Wis. Conf. Chs., Milw., 1968—; host TV program; Look-In, Milw., 1975—; creator, founder Christcross, 1983. Bd. dirs. Bulimic Edn. and Support Tng., Milw., 1984. Home: 1805 N 69th St Wauwatosa WI 53213 Office: Christcross 3200 W Highland Blvd Milwaukee WI 53208

DAVIS, D'EARCY PAUL, JR., lay worker, Presbyn. Ch. in U.S.; b. Isle of Wight, Va., Sept. 12, 1917; s. D'Earcy Paul and Laura Mae (Joyner) D.; B.S., Va. Poly. Inst., 1940, postgrad. U. Va., 1940, 42; m. Frances Brooks, Apr. 11, 1942; children: D'Earcy Paul III, Wayne Howard. Deacon, First Presbyn. Ch. of Harrisburg, 1960, elder, 1966; pres. Presbyn. Bible Conf. Center, Massanetta Springs, Va., 1964-70, trustee, 1956—; moderator Shenandoah Presbytery, Presbyn. Ch. in U.S., 1984. Home: 539 S Dogwood Dr Harrisonburg VA 22801 Harrisonburg VA 22801 Office: 110 Newman Ave Harrisonburg VA 22801

DAVIS, DONALD JAMES, bishop, Episcopal Church; b. New Castle, Pa., Mar. 12, 1929; s. LeRoy Francis and Rya Anne (Stewart) D.; B.A., Westminster Coll., 1949; B.D., Princeton U., 1952; M.A., Bowling Green State U., 1971; m. Mary-Gray Schofield, Sept. 6, 1952; 3 children. Ordained priest, 1955; asst. minister Epiphany Ch., Washington, 1954-56; asso. rector Christ Ch. and chaplain House of Mercy, Washington, 1956-57; rector St. Christopher's Ch., Carmel, Ind., 1957-63, Trinity Ch., Toledo, 1963-71; rector Trinity Ch. and chaplain Ind. U., Bloomington, 1971-74; bishop Diocese of Erie (Pa.), 1974—. Chmn. youth div. Md., Episc. Ch., 1957; chmn. Province 5 and mem. Nat. Adv. Commn., 1960-63; dean central deanery and mem. exec. council, 1960-63; dept. missions, 1960-63, 66-69, dept. lay ministries, 1968-71, ministries of higher edn., 1971. Office: 145 W 6th St Erie PA 16501*

DAVIS, EARL CLINTON, minister, Southern Baptist Convention; b. Madison, Fla., Aug. 26, 1938; s. Edward Clinton and Jessie Evelyn (Seago) D.; m. Pegeen Smith, June 10, 1960; children: Deryl, Dawn. B.A., Stetson U., 1960; B.D., Southeastern Bapt. Theol. Sem., 1963; Ph.D., So. Bapt. Theol. Sem., 1967. Ordained to ministry So. Bapt. Conv., 1959. Pastor 1st Bapt. Ch., Marianna, Fla., 1967-70, 1st Bapt. Ch., Dalton, Ga., 1970-76, 1st Bapt. Ch., Memphis, 1976—; trustee Bapt. Sunday Sch. Bd., 1981—; mem. study commn. on pastoral leadership Bapt. World Alliance, 1981—; chmn. hunger com. Tenn. Bapt. Conv., 1978—. Author: Forever, Amen, 1982; Somebody Cares, 1983; Christ at the Door, 1985; contbr. sermon to publ. Active Leadership Memphis, 1980—. Home: 85 W Chickasaw Pkwy Memphis TN 38111 Office: First Bapt Ch PO Box 12105 200 E Parkway N Memphis TN 38112

DAVIS, FRANCE ALBERT, minister, National Baptist Convention, U.S.A., Inc.; educator; b. Gough, Ga., Dec. 5, 1946; s. John Hildery and Julia (Cooper) D.; m. Willene Witt, Sept. 1, 1973; children: Carolyn Marie, Grace Elaine, France Albert II. A.A., Laney Coll., 1971, Merritt Coll., 1972; B.A., U. Calif.-Berkeley, 1972; B.S., Westminster Coll., 1977; M.A., U. Utah, 1978. Ordained to ministry Nat. Bapt. Conv. U.S.A., 1972. Assoc. minister Center St. Bapt. Ch., Oakland, Calif., 1970-72; vice moderator Utah-Idaho Assn., Salt Lake City, 1974-76, moderator 1977-80; sec.-treas. Salt Lake Ministerial Assn., 1979-81; pastor Calvary Bapt. Ch., Salt Lake City, 1973—; instr. Bapt. Sem. Extension, Salt Lake City, 1978-79. Instr. U. Utah, Salt Lake City, 1972—. Chmn., Utah Opportunity Industrialization Ctr., 1973—, Utah Bd. Correction, 1974—; bd. dirs. Albert Henry Edn. Found., Utah, 1980—, Opportunities Industrialization Ct. Am., Phila., 1982—. Served with USAF, 1966-70. Recipient citation U. Utah, 1974, Pres.' award NAACP, Salt Lake City, 1975, Service award Beehive Elks, 1975, Torch Bearer award Opportunities Industrialization Ctrs., Phila., 1979, Civil rights worker award NAACP, Salt Lake City, 1984. Mem. Utah-Idaho Bapt. Assn. (moderator 1977-80). Home: 1912 Meadow Dr Salt Lake City UT 84121 Office: Calvary Bapt Ch 532 East 700 South Salt Lake City UT 84102

DAVIS, FRANCIS RAYMOND, priest, Roman Catholic Church; b. Washington, Feb. 10, 1920; s. Frank Raymond and Ruth Madeline (Donovan) D. B.A., St. Bernard's Sem., 1941; M.S. in Library Sci., Cath. U. Am., 1953. Ordained priest Roman Cath. Ch., 1945. Asst. pastor St. Ambrose Ch., Rochester, N.Y., 1945-50; librarian St. Bernard's Sem., Rochester, 1950-69; pastor Our Lady of Lourdes Ch., Elmira, N.Y., 1969-78, St. Mary's Ch., Dansville, N.Y., 1978-80, St. Patrick's Ch., Corning, N.Y., 1980—; chaplain Cath. Daus. Am., Corning, 1980—; mem. sch. bd. Cath. Sch. South, Corning, 1980—; spiritual advisor, bd. dirs. Legion of Mary Praesidium, Corning, 1981—. Mem. Cath. Library Assn., ALA, Eastern Communication Assn., Speech Communication Assn., Ch. and Synagogue Library Assn. Address: 274 Denison Pkwy E Corning NY 14830

DAVIS, GARY WAYNE, religious writer, Roman Catholic Church; educational administrator; b. Bismarck, N.D., June 15, 1944; s. Gale Wayland and Mary Lorraine (McGillic) D.; m. Amy C. Johnson, Aug. 7, 1965 (div. 1983); 1 child, Alexandra Ellen. B.A., Morningside Coll., 1965; Ph.D., U. Iowa, 1972. Asst. v.p. for acad. affairs Ill. State U., Normal, 1981-84; asst. to pres., sec. to bd. control Saginaw Valley State Coll., University Center, Mich., 1984—. Contbr. articles on religious topics to jours. U. Iowa teaching fellow, 1984. Mem. Midland C. of C., Saginaw C. of C., Am. Acad. Religion, AAUP, Assn. for Higher Edn. Lodge: Kiwanis. Office: Office of Pres Saginaw Valley State Coll University Center MI 48710

DAVIS, GEORGE WASHINGTON, minister, A.M.E. Ch.; b. Brundidge, Ala., Sept. 10, 1932; s. Samuel Moses and Minnie (Flowers) D.; A.B., Morris Brown Coll., 1957; S.T.B., Boston U., 1960; A.M., Univ. City N.Y., 1970; m. Alice Faye Clarke, Aug. 26, 1972; 1 dau., Germaine Alisha. Ordained to ministry, A.M.E. Ch., 1956; coll. chaplain Alcorn Coll., Lorman, Miss., 1960-63; asso. pastor St. Marks United Meth. Ch., N.Y.C., 1963-65, Bethel A.M.E. Ch., Copaigue, L.I., 1965-69; pastor St. Paul Community Ch., N.Y.C., 1969—. Chaplain N.Y. State Prison, Ossining, N.Y., 1975—; mem. Nat. Council Community Chs., 1970—. Mem. Am. Correction Chaplains Assn., NAACP, Poverty for Law Center, Manhattan Council Chs. Contbr. to The Minister's Manual, 1978. Commentator radio series WCHN, Norwich, N.Y., 1968-69. Home: 1150 E 221st St Bronx NY 10469 Office: 256 W 145th St New York City NY 10039

DAVIS, GORDON BELL, priest, Episcopal Ch.; b. Beaufort, N.C., Jan. 3, 1926; s. Clarence Leslie and Claudia (Morris) D.; B.S., East Carolina U., 1948; diploma Va. Theol. Sem., 1954, St. Augustine's Central Coll. of Anglican Communion, 1965; m. Virginia Mary Ritchie, Feb. 16, 1963; children: Katharine Isabella, Nicholas Stuart Ritchie. Ordained priest, 1955; priest-in-charge, rector St. John's, Chester, Va., 1954-57; rector Grace Colonial Ch., Yorktown, Va., 1957-64, St. Augustine's Ch., Canterbury, England, 1964-65; assoc. rector All Saint's Ch., Richmond, Va., 1965-71, Christ Ch., Gordonsville, Va., 1971—. Mem. exec. bd. Diocese of Va., 1975—; mem. Diocesan Stewardship Commn., 1982—. Bd. dirs. Tide Water Guidance Clinic, Williamsburg, Va.; trustee Orange County Library, 1979—, pres., 1982—. Mem. Richmond Antiquarian Soc. Home and Office: PO Box 217 Gordonsville VA 22942

DAVIS, HAROLD, organization executive. Pres. YMCA of U.S.A., Chgo. Office: 101 Wacker Dr Chicago IL 60606*

DAVIS, HARRELL DUANE, minister, Presbyterian Church USA; b. Carson City, Nev., Mar. 5, 1950; s. Neil Sexton and Ethel Pearl (Ocobo) D.; m. Carol Louise West, Mar. 21, 1970; children: Allison Kay, Sarah Jane. B.S., Central State U., 1976; M.Div., Louisville Presbyn.

Theol. Sem., 1981. Ordained to ministry, 1981. Prof., dir. native Am. Studies United Theol. Sem. of Twin Cities, New Brighton, Minn., 1981-83; exec. dir. Native Am. Theol. Assn., Mpls., 1983—; instl. rep., bd. dirs. Nat. Am. Theol. Assn., 1981-83. Gen. editor Jour. Native Am. Theology. Vol., Stilwater State Prison, Minn., 1982-83. Mem. Nat. Fellowship Indian Workers, Nat. Council Chs. (ethnic minority ministries). Address: Native Am Theol Assn 122 W Franklin #303 Minneapolis MN 55404

DAVIS, HARRY CLIFTON (H. CLIFF), minister, association director of missions, Southern Baptist Convention; b. Ludlow, Miss., Sept. 4, 1930; s. Joe Stanley and Willie (Vick) D.; m. Mary Doyle Ferguson, Apr. 25, 1958; children: Gary, Larry, Angela, Keith. A.A., Clarke Coll., 1952; B.A., Miss. Coll., 1965; M.Div., So. Bapt. Theol. Sem., 1967. Ordained to ministry So. Bapt. Conv., 1951. Pastor several chs. Central Miss., 1951-60; instr. and dir. Bapt. Student Union, Murray State Jr. Coll., Tishomingo, Okla., 1962-63; pastor churches Okla., Md., Ind., W.Va., 1963-82; dir. missions Mountain State Bapt. Assn., Bluefield, W.Va., 1982—; chmn. constn. com. W.Va. Conv. So. Baptists, St. Albans, 1983—; bd. dirs. Friendly W.Va. Conv. So. Baptists, Ridgecrest, N.C., 1984—; supr. ministers Southeastern Bapt. Theol. Sem., Wake Forest, N.C., 1984; active founding new chs. W.Va. Conv. So. Baptists, 1982; prof. So. Bapt. Theol. Sem. Extension Ctr.; dir. edn. ctr. for Mountain State Bapt. Assn.; mem. So. Bapt. Conf. of Dirs. of Missions. Contbr. chpt. to book on founding new chs. Served with USN, 1948-49. Republican. Club: Lions (Tishomingo). Home and Office: 109 Willowbrook Rd Princeton WV 24740

DAVIS, HOWARD DELANO, SR., minister, Lumber River Baptist Missionary Association; educational administrator; b. Southport, N.C.; m. Mildred Elizabeth Thompson, May 30, 1959; children: Howard Delano Jr., Sherwood Tyrone, Millicent Alisia, Kevin Craig, Ivan Terrence, Leatine. A.B., Livingstone Coll., 1958; M.A., N.C. Central U., 1966; D.Div. (hon.), Urban Bible Coll., 1984. Ordained to ministry Lumber River Bapt. Missionary Assn., 1979. Trustee, First Bapt. Ch., Lumberton, N.C., 1959-71, deacon, 1971-79, pastor, 1978—; pastor Jones Chapel Bapt. Ch., Laurinburg, N.C., 1984—; Prin. R. B. Dean Sch., Maxton, N.C., 1983—. Mem. Robeson County Bd. Social Services, N.C., 1982—; mem. Lumberton Mayor's Com. For Program, 1983-85; chmn. Lumberton Democratic Precinct 6 Com., 1982-84. Served with U.S. Army, 1954-55, Korea. Recipient cert. of award and appreciation Dem. Party, Washington, 1981, Rural Pastor's award Gen. Bapt. State Conv. N.C., 1983. Mem. Lumberton Ministerial Alliance (pres. 1982-84), Lumber River Bapt. Assn. (moderator 1982—), Phi Delta Kappa (pres. chpt. 1983-84), Omega Psi Phi (baselus 1979-81). Lodge: Masons. Avocations: woodwork; gardening; reading; music. Home: 226 Side St Lumberton NC 28358 Office: R B Dean Sch 216 W Fourth St Maxton NC 28364

DAVIS, JAMES ALBERT, minister, educator, Presbyterian Church in the U.S.; b. Paducah, Ky., Mar. 29, 1953; s. Clifford Glenwood and Helen Jeanette (Matson) D.; m. Ruth Anne Holzer, June 28, 1975; 1 child, Sarah Jeanne. B.A., Coll. of Wooster, 1975; M.Div., Trinity Evang. Div. Sch., 1979; Ph.D., U. Nottingham, Eng., 1982. Ordained to ministry Presbyn. Ch. in the U.S., 1983. Vis. asst. prof. Western Ky. U., Bowling Green, 1982-83; asst. prof. Trinity Episcopal Sch. for Ministry, Ambridge, Pa., 1983—. Author: Wisdom and Spirit, 1984. Recipient A.T. Olson prize Trinity Evang. Div. Sch., 1979; fellow Rotary Found., 1980, Tyndale Bibl. Research Found., 1981. Mem. Soc. Bibl. Lit., Inst. Bibl. Research, Tyndale Fellowship. Office: Trinity Episcopal Sch for Ministry 311 11th St Ambridge PA 15003

DAVIS, JOE WALTER, organization official, United Methodist Ch.; b. Hobart, Okla., Aug. 11, 1913; s. Lee and Willie (Stewart) D.; B.S., Southwestern U., 1935, postgrad., 1935-36; B.C.S., Benjamin Franklin U., 1942; m. Ethel Lois Wiemers, Apr. 24, 1937; children: Edith Marie (Mrs. Alan W. Loveland), Eugene Stewart, George Edward, Mary Ellen (Mrs. Phillip H. Arnold), Elizabeth Ann (Mrs. Michael Hime). Fingerprint expert FBI, 1937-43, spl. agt., 1943-45; auditor, Southwestern U., 1945-54; financial sec. First Meth. Ch., Georgetown, Tex., 1945-54; treas., bus. mgr., Meth. Radio and Film Commn. (name now United Methodist Communications), 1954-73; asst. gen. treas. Meth. Council on Finance and Adminstrn., 1973; staff treas. Joint Com. on Communications, United Methodist Ch., Nashville, 1974—. Active Boy Scouts Am., 1952-62. Sec. Georgetown (Tex.) Ind. Sch. Dist., 1951-54. Home: 210 Emery Dr Nashville TN 37214

DAVIS, JOHN JAMES, theology educator, Fellowship of Grace Brethren Churches; b. Phila., Oct. 13, 1936; s. John James and Cathrine Ann (Nichols) D.; m. Carolyn Ann Clark, June 28, 1958; 1 child, Debbie Ann. B.A., Trinity Coll., 1959, D.D. (hon.), 1968; M.Div., Grace Theol. Sem., 1962, Th.M., 1963, Th.D., 1965; postgrad., Near East Sch. Archaeology, Jerusalem, 1963, Ind. U., 1972. Ordained to ministry Grace Brethren Chs., 1960. Pastor Faith Bible Ch., Tampa, Fla., 1956-59, Centerview Community Ch., South Whitley, Ind., 1973-77; instr. Grace Coll., Winona Lake, Ind., 1963-65; prof. O.T. Grace Theol. Sem., Winona Lake, 1965—, dir. admissions, 1972-76; exec. v.p. Grace Coll. and Sem., 1976-82; exec. dean Near East Inst. of Archaeology, Jerusalem, 1970-71; dir. Brethren Men and Boys, Winona Lake, 1984—; corr. Warsaw Times-Union, 1972-79, writer, 1979—; corr. Columbia City Post, 1972-76; sports broadcaster Sta. WRSW, WRSW-FM, Warsaw, Ind., 1976-80, WOWO, Ft. Wayne, Ind., 1974-79, Cable Sports TV, Ind., 1978-80. Bd. dirs. Riverwood Ranch, Warsaw, 1972-74; bd. dirs. Koscivsko County Lakes Assn., 1982—. Recipient Book of Yr. B.M.H. Book Pubs., 1975, 79. Author: Biblical Numerology, 1968; The Birth of a Kingdom: Studies in the Books of Samuel and I Kings, 1970; Mummies, Men and Madness, 1972; Paradise to Prison: Studies in Genesis, 1975; Demons, Exorcism and the Evangelical, 1977; A History of Israel: From Conquest to Exile, 1980; A Lake Guide to Fishing and Boating in Kosciusko County, Indiana (with Arthur W. Davis), 1981. Contbr. articles to profl. jours. Translator: New International Version Bible (study edit.). Mem. Soc. Bibl. Lit., Near East Archeol. Soc. (bd. dirs. 1973—, editor 1973-75), Am. Schs. Oriental Research, Hoosier Outdoor Writers Assn. (pres. 1984-85). Republican. Club: Chapman Lake Conservation (Warsaw). Lodge: Kiwanis. Home: PO Box 635 Winona Lake IN 46590 Office: Grace Theol Sem 200 Seminary Dr Winona Lake IN 46590

DAVIS, KEITH, minister, Lutheran Church in America; lawyer; b. Scotts Bluff, Nebr., July 23, 1941; s. Keith and Dorothy (Garritt) D. B.A., U. Nebr., 1963; M.Div., Luth. Sch. Theology, 1967; J.D., DePaul U., 1976. Ordained to ministry Luth. Ch. in Am., 1967. Assoc. pastor St. Matthew's Ch., Phila., 1967-68; pastor 1st Luth. Ch., East St. Louis, Ill., 1968-70, Holy Spirit Ch., Chgo., 1970-72; assoc. pastor Christ the King Ch., Chgo., 1984—. Mng. ptnr. Murphy, Peters, Davis & O'Brien, Chgo., 1976—; teaching atty. IIT Kent Coll. Law, 1983—; mem. faculty Nat. Inst. Trial Advocacy, 1984—. Guest columnist USA Today, 1984. Mem. ABA, Ill. Bar Assn., Chgo. Bar Assn., Chgo. Council Lawyers (bd. govs. 1981—, chmn. criminal justice com. 1981—). Democrat. Office: 205 W Randolph Suite 1310 Chicago IL 60606

DAVIS, MALCOLM FLETCHER, priest, Episcopal Ch.; b. Cleve., Sept. 20, 1935; s. Kenneth Culp and Carol Margaret (Seeds) D.; A.B., Harvard, 1958; M.Div., Ch. Div. Sch. of the Pacific, 1961; m. Jane Elizabeth Nilan, Aug. 15, 1959; children—Heather Ann, Peter Andrew. Ordained priest Episcopal Ch., 1961; asst. rector St. Paul's Ch., Visalia, Calif., 1960; vicar Christ Ch., Lemoore, Calif., 1961-63; rector St. John's Ch., Porterville, Calif., 1963-68; missionary to Mmadinare, Botswana, S.Africa, 1968; rector St. Columba's Ch., Fresno, Calif., 1969—; sec.-registrar Diocese of San Joaquin (Calif.) 1968—; dep. to gen. conv. Episcopal Ch., 1969, 70, 73, 76. Trustee St. Paul's Sch., 1967-70, Camp San Joaquin, 1966-70. Fellow Coll. Preachers. Contbr. to religious and psychol. jours. Home: 4235 N Maroa Ave Fresno CA 93704 Office: 5073 N Palm Ave Fresno CA 93704

DAVIS, MILTON HOLDER, minister, United Churches of Christ; b. St. Thomas, V.I., Feb. 15, 1926; s. Reginald Gormanston and Adelita Christina (Simmonds) D.; m. Alyce Virginia Ligon, Sept. 13, 1950; 1 son, Milton Holder. A.B. magna cum laude, St. John's U., N.Y., 1948; M.A. in Religion, Harvard, 1949; B.D., Union Sem., N.Y., 1951; Ph.D., Oxford U., 1952; J.D., U. So. Calif., 1971. Ordained to ministry United Chs. Christ, 1948. Pastor Wesley Meth. Ch., Hempstead, N.Y., 1952-55; instr. Harvard, Cambridge, Mass., 1956-58; pastor Meth. Chs., Calif., 1958-65; prof. Redlands and Whittier Colls., Calif., 1965-69; sr. minister Ch. of the Master (United Chs. Christ), Los Angeles, 1966—; legal counsel to chs. and non-profit orgns.; lectr. contemporary legal studies; asst. dir. research and survey dept. Nat. Council Chs., 1952-53; bd. dirs. Los Angeles Council Chs. Author: O For a Trumpet Voice, 1951. Recipient Outstanding Achievement Award, Profl. League Virgin Islanders in N.Y., 1952, Outstanding Citizen Award, Bd. Suprs. Los Angeles County, 1969, 72. Mem. Ministers for Racial and Social Justice, ACLU, NAACP. Home: 3503 Westmount Ave Los Angeles CA 90043 Office: 2811 W 54th St Los Angeles CA 90043

DAVIS, MOSHE See *Who's Who in America,* 43rd edition.

DAVIS, RICHARD LEE, minister, Southern Baptist Conv.; b. Toccoa, Ga., Apr. 30, 1950; s. Tyrus L. and Naomi (Brookshire) D.; m. Nan Lucia Davis, May 26, 1973; children: Lee, Joy. B.S. in Sociology, William Carey Coll., 1972; postgrad. New Orleans Bapt. Theol. Sem., 1978. Licensed to ministry Bapt. Ch., 1968. Minister music and youth Rich Fork Bapt. Ch., Thomasville, N.C., 1972-75; minister youth First Bapt. Ch., Poplarville, Miss., 1975-78; minister of youth and coll. Temple Bapt. Ch., Hattiesburg, Miss., 1978—; sponsor Fellowship of Christian Athletes. Contbr. articles to profl. jours. Fellow Miss. Bapt. Religious Edn. Assn., Metro Coll. Minister Assn., So. Bapt. Religious Edn. Assn. Avocations: family; travel; gardening; sports. Home: 19 Sharmont Dr Hattiesburg MS 39401 Office: Temple Bapt Ch 1508 Hardy St Hattiesburg MS 39401

DAVIS, ROBERT RICHARD, minister, Presbyterian Church in America; b. Cleve., Dec. 1, 1933; s. George Milton and Edith Manila (Randall) D.; m. Betty E. Godsey, Sept. 7, 1958; children: Deborah Annette, Rebekah Louise. Student Toccoa Falls Coll., 1953-56; A.B., Taylor U., 1958; M.Div., United Theol. Sem., Dayton, Ohio, 1961, B.D., 1961; postgrad. Scarrett Sch. Religion, 1961; D.Div., Toccoa Falls Coll., 1981. Ordained to ministry Methodist Ch., 1961, Presbyn. Ch., 1964. Minister Williamsburg Meth. Ch., Ind., 1959-61, Alto Meth. Ch., Kokomo, Ind., 1961-64; assoc. minister 1st Presbyn. Ch., Miami, Fla., 1964-66; minister Hazelwood Presbyn. Ch., N.C., 1966-72; adminstrv. v.p. Westminster Christian Sch., Miami, Fla., 1971-72; sr. minister Old Cutler Presbyn. Ch., Miami, 1972—. Author: Portraits from the Pages, 1978. Contbr. articles to religious jours. Recipient medal Freedom Found., 1969, 75, cert., 1974, 77, George Washington Honor medal, 1981. Republican. Home: 17824 SW 83d Ct Miami FL 33157 Office: Old Cutler Presbyn Ch 14401 Old Cutler Rd Miami FL 33158

DAVIS, RONNIE DALE, minister, United Pentecostal Church; b. Vivian, La., Nov. 18, 1948; s. Clarance Danny and Thelma Lucille (Wiggins) D.; m. Myrna Gayle Latham, July 12, 1968; children: Shayla Gayle, Ronald Dale. Student pub. schs., 1956-67. Ordained to ministry, 1976. Evangelist, United Pentecostal Ch., Mich., 1971-73, pastor, Laramie, Wyo., 1973-75, evangelist, La., Tex., 1975-76, pastor, Longview, Tex., 1976-81, evangelist, La., Tex., 1981-82; founder, pastor Christians Hope Tabernacle Ch., Waco, Tex., 1982—; staff mgr. Prudential Ins. Co., Waco, 1983-84; youth coordinator United Pentecostal Ch., Longview, 1979-80, Sunday sch. dir., 1980-81. Served with U.S. Army N.G., 1968-70. Named Waco Rookie of Year, Prudential Ins. Co., 1982. Democrat. Home: Route 1 Box 141 Lorena TX 76655

DAVIS, ROY WILLIAM, minister, So. Bapt. Conv.; b. Canton, Ohio, Mar. 30, 1950; s. Roy Beasley and Elizabeth Mathilda (Marquart) D.; A.A., Pensacola Jr. Coll., 1970; B.A., U. W.Fla., 1972; M.R.E., New Orleans Bapt. Theol. Sem., 1974; m. Cynthia Ann Huggins, Apr. 22, 1972. Ordained to ministry, 1975; minister edn. Smithwood Bapt. Ch., Knoxville, Tenn., 1974-76, First Bapt. Ch., Burlington, N.C., 1976—. Mem. Eastern Bapt. Religious Edn. Assn., Vols. for People. Home: 2638 Hyde St Burlington NC 27215 Office: Box 2686 Burlington NC 27215

DAVIS, RUBY ICIS JONES, minister, Church of Christ (Disciples of Christ); b. Wayne County, Iowa, Mar. 12, 1919; d. Newton Jasper and Clara Icis (Adams) Jones; student pub. schs. Plano, Iowa; m. Lewis Davis, July 16, 1950. Licensed to ministry, 1939, Iowa State Soc., 1943-50. Pastor Antioch Christian Ch., Seymour, Iowa, 1939, Promise City Ch. of Christ, Iowa, 1940, Hilltown Ch. of Christ, Dean, Iowa, 1940-44, Walnut City Christian Ch., Mystic, Iowa, 1940-42, Clio Ch. of Christ, Iowa, 1944-47, Van Wert Ch. of Christ, Iowa, 1945-46, Sharon Chapel Community Ch., Centerville, Iowa, 1980—; broadcaster radio programs Sta. KCOG-AM and Sta. KDMI-FM. Author: And Call a Young Woman to Preach; What God Told Me. Address: PO Box 16 Plano IA 52581

DAVIS, WALTER BOND, minister, United Church of Christ; b. Balt., Jan. 16, 1930; s. Everett Fogg and Fanny Fern (Smith) D.; m. Barbara Buschmeyer; children: Martha Ellen, Thomas Merrill, Ward, Peter, Eric, Craig, Jean, Neil. B.A., Cornell U., 1951; M. Div., Yale U., 1954; postgrad. Harvard Div. Sch., 1958-60. Ordained to ministry United Ch. Christ 1954. Assoc. pastor Oberlin Coll., Ohio, 1954-57, instr. dept. religion, 1954-57; assoc. pastor Central Congl. Ch., Newtonville, Mass., 1957-60; pastor First Congl. Ch., United Ch. Christ, Verona, N.J., 1960-65, sr. pastor, Santa Barbara, Calif., 1965-71, Winchester, Mass., 1971—; sec. United Ch. Christ Bd. World Ministries, 1980-84, Congl. Christian Hist. Soc., 1981—; exec. com., bd. dirs. Mass. Conf. United Ch. Christ, 1980, gen. Synod del., 1970's; founder Family to Family Fellowship, Santa Barbara, Calif., 1967; founding chmn. Winchester Interagency Council, 1970's; pres. Winchester Ecumenical Assn., 1983-84. Author religious poetry and hymns. Contbr. articles to profl. jours. Chmn. Community Relations Commn., Santa Barbara, 1966-70; bd. govs. Mass. Dept. Mental Health, 1970-74; parole assistance bd. Dept. Corrections, Calif., 1965-68. Recipient Outstanding Service award News Pub. Co. 1970-71, Cert. Service award City Santa Barbara, 1970, Exchange Club speakers award 1969-70. Mem. Winthrop Club (pres. 1982-84), Congl. Christian Hist. Soc. (sec. 1981—), Winchester Interagency Council (coordinator 1978—). Lodge: Rotary. Avocations: music; photography; sailing; writing; woodworking. Office: First Congl Ch United Ch Christ On The Common Winchester MA 01890

DAWIDIUK, WASYL, minister, Ukrainian Pentecostal Ch.; b. Boryatyn, USSR, Apr. 6, 1928; s. Ephrem and Helena (Waszchuk) D.; came to Can., 1953, naturalized, 1961; m. Shirley Ann Kalinsky, May

22, 1976. Ordained to ministry, 1961; missionary, S.Am., 1957-60; minister Ukrainian Pentecostal Temple, Bonnyville, Alta., Can., 1960-63, Ukrainian Pentecostal Ch., Liege, Belgium, 1964-67, 1st. Ukrainian Pentecostal Ch., Toronto, Ont., Can., 1967-72; missionary to Soviet Ukraine. Radio broadcaster to Ukrainian Evang. Lighthouse, Portugal. Editor Ukrainian Evang. Voice, 1968-72; author Ukrainian and evang. song books and poems.

DAWSON, CONRAD HUGHES, JR., minister, Christian Church (Disciples of Christ); b. Monticello, Ind., Aug. 18, 1935; s. Conrad Hughes and Gail (Allen) D. A.A., Broward Community Coll., 1972; B.Div., Faith Bible Coll., 1962, D.D., 1965, D.D. (hon.), 1963; postgrad. Fla. Atlantic U., 1972-75. Ordained to ministry Christian Ch., 1963. Chaplain Boy Scouts Am., Pompano Beach, Fla., 1962-64; minister Hope Christian Ch., Pompano Beach, 1967—, ch. counselor, 1969-72; chaplain Fire Dept., Parkland, Fla., 1982—. Composer children's music. Editor Hope News, 1969. Counselor Big Bros., Fort Lauderdale, Fla., 1975. Recipient Community Service award Broward Action Ctr., Fort Lauderdale, 1978. Mem. Broward Community Coll. Alumni Assn. (membership com. 1978). Home: 266 NE 42d Pompano Beach FL 33060

DAWSON, GENE, minister, Full Gospel; b. West Palm Beach, Fla., Feb. 9, 1941; s. Joseph W. and Josephine (Stephens) D.; M.A., Lone Mountain Coll., 1976; m. Irene Ramirez Sanchez, Oct. 18, 1975; children—Joseph Eugene, Antonio Eugene, Michael Gordon. Ordained to ministry, 1966; youth dir., music dir. Faith Tabernacle, Aberdeen, Wash., 1964-67; founder, adminstr. Drug Abuse Preventive Soc. Calif., Santa Cruz, 1967—; founder, pres. World Alliance Rehab. and Edn., 1973—. Bd. dirs. A.R.C., 1973; bd. dirs. Joychild, Inc., Project Back.; chaplain Capitola Police Dept., 1968-76. Mem. Full Gospel Fellowship. Home: PO Box 132 Soquel CA 95073 Office: PO Box 2727 Santa Cruz CA 95063

DAWSON, LEWIS EDWARD, chaplain, air force officer, So. Bapt. Conv.; b. Louisville, Oct. 26, 1933; s. Lewis Harper and Zelma Ruth (Hocutt) D.; B.A., Baylor U., 1954; M.Div., So. Bapt. Sem., 1960; postgrad. Presbyn. Sch. Christian Edn., 1977—; m. Margaret Ellen Poor, July 29, 1956; children—Edward Rhodes, David Harper, Deborah Louise, Virginia Ruth. Ordained to ministry, 1960; pastor Fincastle (Va.) Bapt. Ch., 1960-63, Zion Hill Bapt. Ch., Fincastle, 1960-63, 1st So. Bapt. Ch., Great Falls, Mont., 1963-67; commd. capt. U.S. Air Force, 1967; advanced through grades to maj., 1977; chaplain McCoy AFB, 1967-69, Vietnam, 1969-70, Sheppard AFB, 1971-73, RAF, Chicksands, Eng., 1973-76. Clk., Triangle Bapt. Assn., 1965-66; chmn. Mont. Indian mission com. Mont. So. Bapt. Fellowship, 1965-66, treas., 1965-66. Mem. exec. council Save the Children Fund, Shefford, Eng., 1973-76. Decorated Bronze Star, Air Force Commendation medal. Home: 3210 Noble Ave Richmond VA 23222 Office: 1205 Palmyra Ave Richmond VA 23227

DAY, ARTHUR RUSSELL, JR., minister, United Presbyn. Ch. U.S.A.; b. Washington, Pa., Apr. 3, 1922; s. Arthur Russell and Bertha Edna (Dunn) D.; B.A., Washington and Jefferson Coll., 1948; Th.M., Western Theol. Sem., 1952; m. Jean Marie Swingle, July 2, 1949 (dec. Aug. 1980); children: Lydia, Rebekah, Mary Edna. Ordained to ministry, 1952; pastor Upper Ten Mile Presbyn. Ch., Prosperity, Pa., 1952-54, Claysville (Pa.) Presbyn. Ch., 1954-62, West Newton (Pa.) United Presbyn. Ch., 1962—. Chmn. youth com. Washington Presbytery, 1952-62, moderator, 1954-55; mem. camp and conf. com. Redstone Presbytery, 1963-69, mem. mission and strategy com., 1975-76, jud. commn., 1975, spl. camp task force, 1975, ecclesiastical responsibilities com., 1965-68; dir. Jr. High Camps, 1962-72; faculty Sr. High Confs., 1959-60. Mem. youth commn., West Newton, 1974—; dir. McGuffey Sch. Dist., 1962-63; chaplain West Newton Fire Co., 1967; sec. bd. dirs. West Newton Community Fund. Mem. West Newton Ministerial Assn. Chs. (pres. 1962), West Newton Hist. Soc. (bd. dirs. 1983), Phi Beta Kappa, Alpha Kappa Alpha, Eta Sigma Phi, Phi Alpha Theta. Contbr. poems to anthologies. Home: 115 S 3d St West Newton PA 15089 Office: Corner Main and 3d Sts West Newton PA 15089

DAY, HOWARD MALCOLM, minister, So. Bapt. Conv.; b. Mulberry, Fla., Dec. 14, 1914; s. James Samuel and Olive Beatrice (Wilhelm) D.; B.A., Stetson U., 1936; M.Div., So. Bapt. Theol. Sem., 1940, M.Ed., 1962; m. Elizabeth Marie Ransom, June 5, 1939; 1 son, James Frederick. Ordained to ministry, 1936; chaplain U.S. Navy, 1940-61; instr. history, sociology and philosophy St. John River Jr. Coll., Palatka, Fla., 1962-63, dir. student activities, 1963-64, spl. asst. to pres., 1965-66, dir. student services, 1966-70, counselor, instr., 1971-76, vets. counselor, 1976—; pastor Paran Bapt. Ch., Grandin, Fla., 1964—. Pres., Putnam County Community Concert Assn., 1963-65; pres. Palatka Rotary Club, 1971-72. Mem. Palatka Civic Round Table (pres. 1973-74), Fla. Assn. Community Colls. (pres. St. Johns River Jr. Coll. chpt. 1973-74), Pi Kappa Phi, Theta Alpha Phi. Home: 120 Crestwood Ave Palatka FL 32077

DAYRINGER, RICHARD, minister, educator, Southern Baptist Convention; b. Carthage, Mo., Feb. 3, 1934; s. Joseph Allen and Sarah Marlin (Rupert) D.; A.A., S.W. Bapt. Coll., Boliver, Mo., 1953; A.B., William Jewell Coll., Liberty, Mo., 1955; M.Div., Midwestern Bapt. Theol. Sem., 1961; Th.D. (ESTARL scholar, Family Life Edn. fellow), New Orleans Bapt. Theol. Sem., 1968; m. E. Janet Dayringer; children—Stephen, David, Deborah, Daniel, James. Ordained to ministry, 1952; pastor Mentor Bapt. Ch., Rogersville, Mo., 1951-53, Enon Bapt. Ch., Pittsville, Mo., 1954-55, First So. Bapt. Ch., Eudora, Kans., 1955-61, First Bapt. Ch., Madisonville, La., 1961-63, Norwood (La.) Bapt. Ch., 1963-65; interim pastor Golden Gate Bapt. Ch., Clinton, Mo., 1968-69, Santa Fe Hills Bapt. Ch., Kansas City, Mo., 1972-73; instr. pastoral care Immaculate Conception (Mo.) Sem., 1967-72; clin. pastoral edn. So. Bapt. Hosp., New Orleans, 1961-63; resident in psychiatry Tulane U. at E.La. State Hosp., Jackson, 1963-64; dir. dept. pastoral care and counseling Bapt. Meml. Hosp., Kansas City, 1965-74; vis. prof. Midwestern Bapt. Theol. Sem., Kansas City, 1967-69, clin. instr. pastoral care, 1968-72, adj. prof., 1972-74; instr. religion and pastoral counseling U. Mo. at Kansas City Sch. Medicine, 1971-74; asso. prof. med. humanities So. Ill. U. Sch. Medicine, Springfield, 1974—, dir. clin. edn. in psychosocial care, asso. prof. dept. family practice, sec. instructional delivery team for med. edn., soc. and the humanities; med. staff affiliate, clin. counselor St. John's Hosp., Springfield; mem. allied med. services sect. of med. staff Meml. Med. Center, Springfield; cons. and lectr. in fields medicine and religion. Chmn. student work com. Kansas City Bapt. Assn., 1968-74; moderator Kaw Valley Bapt. Assn., 1960. Bd. dirs. Council on Alcoholism, Kansas City Area, 1966-74, Kansas City chpt. Nat. Found. for Sudden Infant Death, 1973-74. Diplomate Am. Assn. Pastoral Counselors. Fellow Coll. Chaplains, Am. Protestant Hosp. Assn. (chmn. research com. 1968, editorial com. 1973-74); mem. Am. Assn. Marriage and Family Counselors, Assn. Clin. Pastoral Edn. (chaplain supr., chmn. certification and accreditation com. S.Central region 1969, chmn. research com. 1973-74), Assn. Mo. Chaplains (pres. 1967-68), Jackson County (Mo.) Med. Soc., Soc. Health and Human Values, Soc. Tchrs. Family Medicine. Author books and monographs, including Pastor and Patient, 1982; God Cares for You, 1983; also essays, articles and poems. Home: 3221 Dorchester St Springfield IL 62704 Office: 913 N Rutledge St PO Box 3926 Springfield IL 62708

DAYTON, DONALD WILBER, theology educator, writer, Wesleyan Church of America; b. Chgo., July 25, 1942; s. Wilber Thomas and Donna Irene (Fisher) D.; m. Lucille Faythe Sider, June 9, 1969 (div. 1985); 1 child, Charles Soren. B.A. in Philosophy and Math. magna cum laude, Houghton Coll., 1963; postgrad. Columbia U., 1963-64, Union Theol. Sem., 1963-64, Am. Inst. Holy Land Studies, 1967, Asbury Theol. Sem., U. Tubingen; B.D., Yale Div. Sch., 1969; M.S. in Library Sci., U. Ky., 1969; Ph.D. in Christian Theology, U. Chgo., 1983. Asst. prof. bibliography and acquisitions library Asbury Theol. Sem., Wilmore, Ky., 1969-72; assoc. prof. theology North Park Theol. Sem., Chgo., 1972-79; faculty mem. Sem. Consortium Urban Pastoral Edn., Chgo., 1976-82; prof. theology and ethics No. Bapt. Theol. Sem., Lombard, Ill., 1979—, librarian, 1979-82; adj. faculty mem. Wesleyan Urban Coalition, Olive Branch Missions, Chgo., 1980—; bd. dirs. John Wesley Theol. Inst., 1981—, New Ecumenical Research Assn., 1980—; speaker numerous profl. and ednl. groups. Author: Discovering an Evangelical Heritage, 1976; Theological Roots of Pentecostalism, 1985. Editor: Sojourner, 1975-78, The Post-American, 1974—, The Higher Christian Life: Sources for The Study of Holiness, Pentecostal and Keswick Movements, 1984, Five Sermons and A Tract by Luther Lee, 1974, Contemporary Perspectives on Pietism, 1975, Reflections on Revivals, 1979, The Coming Kingdom: Essays in American Millenialism and Eschatology, 1983; editor The Covenant Quar., The Other Side, The Epworth Pulpit, TSF Bull., Studies in Evangelism, Sources in American Spirituality. Contbr. articles to profl. jours. and chpts. to scholarly books. Bd. dirs. Urban Life Ctr., Chgo., 1972-79, Olive Branch Mission, Chgo., 1980-84. Woodrow Wilson Found. fellow, 1964-65; grantee Assn. Theol. Schs. 1980, 84. Mem. Karl Barth Soc. N. Am. (sec. 1972—), Wesleyan Theol. Soc. (mem. exec. com. 1974—, liaison rep. to Nat. Council Chs. 1983—), Am. Acad. Religion (chmn. evang. theology sect. 1984—), Oxford Inst. Meth. Theol. Studies (mem. core planning com. 1982, 87), Theta Phi. Office: No Bapt Theol Sem 660 Butterfield Rd Lombard IL 60148

DAYTON, DONNA FISHER, religion educator, librarian, Wesleyan Church; b. Flushing, Ohio, Sept. 26, 1914; d. Joseph A. and Bertha Newcomer (Kraybill) Fisher; F.; m. Wilber Thomas Dayton, Dec. 24, 1938; children: Donald Wilber, Carol Jo (Mrs. Walter D. Mayer), Deane Kraybill, Janet Elizabeth (Mrs. Michael Manley). Student Asbury Coll., 1932-35, Ohio U., 1935; B.R.E., No. Bapt. Theol. Sem., 1945; M.A., U. Ky., 1963. Cert. pub. sch. tchr., library adminstr., Ohio, S.D., Ind., Ky., N.Y. Supr. student tchrs. Wessington Springs Coll., S.D., 1939-41; tchr. of Bible, pub. schs., Marion, Ind., 1946-47; instr. Edn. Marion Coll., Ind., 1954-56; librarian, asst. prof. edn. Asbury Coll., Wilmore, Ky., 1965-70; Marion Coll., 1971-72; asst. to head librarian, Houghton Coll., N.Y., 1973-76; librarian, asst. prof. Christian edn. Wesley Bibl. Sem. Jackson, Miss., 1976-83, prof. emeritus, 1983—; active lay worker in local ch. mem. ch. bds. and coms.; lectr. in field; cons. ch. and sch. libraries in U.S. and S. Am. Author Sunday Sch. curriculum for children, 1958-62. Contbr. articles and book reviews to religious and profl. jours. Leader 4H Club; Cub scout den mother; charity fundraiser; active Nat. Trust for Hist. Preservation, 1977—, Richwood Estates Homeowner's Assn., 1981—. Scholarship for sem. students named in her honor Wesleyan Sem. Found. at Asbury Theol. Sem., 1970. Mem. Ky. Retired Tchrs. Assn., Ky. Edn. Assn., NEA, Internat. Students' Fellowship (organizer, sponsor 1981-83), Jackson Arts Alliance, Delta Kappa Gamma. Home: 1912 Hamilton Blvd Jackson MS 39213 Office: Wesley Bibl Sem PO Box 9938 Jackson MS 39206

DEAN, BENNETT WAYNE, lay church worker, United Methodist Church; community relations manager; b. Mobile, Ala., Dec. 11, 1942; s. Bennett and Dorothy Lucile (Seymour) D.; m. Doris Jean Allinson, Apr. 13, 1968; children: Lillian Doris, Timpy Anna, Bennett Wayne, Jr. B.S. in Biology, U. Ala.-Tuscaloosa, 1965; B.S. in Psychology, 1966; postgrad. U. Ark., 1966-67, Miss. State U., 1971. Mem. parish devel. com. Govt. St. United Meth. Ch., Mobile, 1979-80, chmn. ecumenical concerns and race relations com., 1980-81, mem. council on ministries, 1980—, mem. adminstrv. bd., 1981—, chmn. adminstrv. bd., 1984—, trustee, 1983-85, usher, 1982—; official dist. circuit rider Mobile dist. United Meth. Ch., 1984—; mem. Meth. Bicentennial, Mobile dist., 1984. Community relations mgr. Hampton Assocs., Inc., Mobile, 1984—. Author: A Mobile Mardi Gras Handbook, 1967; Mardi Gras: Mobile's Illogical Whoop-de-doo, 1971; The Swarming Bee Hive-A History of Mobile's Mother Church of Methodism, 1984. Dir. film Mardi Gras: Mobile's Big Blast! (U.S. Navy citation 1981). Editor ch. newsletter Bee Hive, 1982—. Contbr. articles to profl. jours and mags. Treas. Mobile Community Action Com., 1972-73; pres. Gulf Coast Area Childbirth Edn. Assn., 1973-74; officer Shrine Bowl Classic, 1976-78; v.p. Soc. Restoration and Beautification of Church St. Graveyard, Inc., 1977—; bd. dirs. Toy Bowl Classic, 1975-76; mem. Downtown Mobile Unltd. Christmas Parade Com., City of Mobile's Mardi Gras Spl. Events Com., 4th of July Com. Served with U.S. Army, 1967-69. Recipient Patriot award City of Mobile, 1981, M.O. Beale Scroll of Merit, Mobile Press Register, 1975, Award of Excellence, Ala. Bus. Jour., 1985. Mem. Mobile Jaycees (v.p. 1973-74, bd. dirs. 1974-76, Outstanding Jaycee Officer 1973-74), Internat. Assn. Personnel in Employment Security (pres. 1974-75, dist. VIII rep. 1978-79, chmn. internat. pub. relations 1982-83, editor conv. newspaper 1983, Internat. Award of Merit 1973, Internat. Group Award of Merit 1980, 81, Ala. Hall of Fame 1984, Spl. Life-Saving award 1984). Clubs: Ala.-Gulf RR (pres. 1975), Mardi Gras Doubloon Collectors (pres. 1977-78), Sons of Confederate Vets. Lodges: Masons, Shriners. Avocations: genealogical research and writing; Mardi Gras history; model railroading. Home: 1064 Palmetto St Oakleigh Garden Dist Mobile AL 36604 Office: Hampton Assocs Inc 601 Bel Air Blvd Mobile AL 36606

DEAN, BETTE JO, lay ch. worker, So. Bapt. Conv.; b. Hattiesburg, Miss., Sept. 14, 1933; d. Joseph Colen and Eudora Inez (Hamm) Runnels; B.S., Miss. U. for Women, 1955; M.R.E., New Orleans Bapt. Theol. Sem., 1957; m. David F. Dean, Sept. 13, 1959; children—Jodi, Dahn, David. Dir. youth 1st Bapt. Ch., Pascagoula, Miss., 1956; interim minister of edn., 1973; minister of edn. So. Bapt. Ch., Spartanburg, S.C., 1957-59; asso. minister of edn., dir. youth Citadel Square Bapt. Ch., Charleston, S.C., 1960-62; youth minister 1st Bapt. Ch., Bellevue, Nebr., 1966; minister of edn. 1st Bapt. Ch., Ocean Springs, Miss., 1974-75; dir. sr. youth dept. Cottage Hill Bapt. Ch., Mobile, Ala., 1975—. Mem. Med. Assn. Aux., Univ. Women's Club. Author: (with David Jenkins) God's People, United for Conquest, 1973; Getting Ready for Youth Sunday School Work, 1976; Teaching Youth in Sunday School, 1976. Home: 612 Montclaire Way W Mobile AL 36609

DEAN, DAVID EDWARD, minister, evangelist, Assemblies of God; b. Landour, Mussoorie, India, Oct. 2, 1921; s. Bartholemew and Edith (Petterson) D.; came to U.S., 1924, naturalized, 1954; grad. Bible Coll. Central, Springfield, Mo., 1939-42; m. Mary Elizabeth Rice, Aug. 30, 1942; children—Rachel, Samuel, David, John, Paul. Ordained to ministry, 1954; founder, pastor Calvary Assembly of God, Union City, Ind., 1951-64; evangelist Christ Life Revivals Inc., Dallas, 1965—, pres., 1972-76. Author: The Way Of The Christ Life, 1967; Meat For The Household, 1974; numerous sermons rec. on cassette tapes; evang. tours include 3 around-the-world trips, covering 40 countries. Home and Office: 6929 Sperry St Dallas TX 75214

DEAN, EDWIN GAYLE, minister, So. Baptist Conv.; b. New Orleans, May 6, 1936; s. Edwin Gayle and Emma Elizabeth (Carraway) D.; student La. Coll., 1954-56; B.A., Hamilton State U., 1973; M.Theology,

Internat. Bible Inst. and Sem., 1982, D.Div., 1983; m. Susie Francis Wilson, Mar. 7, 1953; children: Elizabeth Sue, Stephen Gayle, Rachel Alison. Ordained to ministry, 1956; pastor Alexandria, La., 1955-56, Ferriday, La., 1956-58, Jonesville, La., 1958-60, Rhinehart, La., 1960-63, Alexandria, 1964, Simmesport, La., 1964-68, Archibald, La., 1968-70, Shiloh Bapt. Ch., Bernice, La., 1970-71, Newlight Bapt. Ch., Mangham, La., 1971-74, First Bapt. Ch., Gilbert, La., 1974—. Mem. Deer Creek Bapt. Assn., La. Bapt. Conv., So. Bapt. Conv. Home: PO Box 697 Dawn Ave Gilbert LA 71336 Office: Govt and McCain Sts Gilbert LA 71336

DEAN, J. LARRY, Christian edn. minister, Independent Baptist Ch.; b. Springfield, La., Nov. 19, 1946; s. Richard A. and Lela (Wilson) P.; m. Diane Ciardi Dean, July 26, 1968; children: Lisa, David, Jonathan. B.A., Tenn. Temple U., 1968, M.R.E., 1970; Ed.D., Luther Rice Sem., 1976. Ordained to ministry Bapt. Ch., 1970. Tchr. Christian High Sch., San Diego, 1970-71; asst. prof. Christian Heritage Coll., El Cajon, Calif., 1971-82; instr. Walk Thru the Bible, Atlanta, 1981—; minister Christian edn. Scott Meml. Bapt. Ch., San Diego, 1971—; v.p. San Diego Sunday Sch. Conv., 1971—. Author: (booklet) Why Can't I Be Baptized?, 1972; How to Have a Family Emphasis Month, 1978. Named Boardman of Yr. WDYN-FM Radio, 1970. Mem. Nat. Assn. Dirs. Christian Edn. (dir. pub. relations 1978-80), Nat. Assn. Profs. Christian Edn.

DEAN, JACK OSBON, minister, Church of God; b. Bath, S.C., Feb. 25, 1934; s. James M. and Viola (Hall) D.; m. Jean Carolyn Trammell, Dec. 20, 1958; children: Jack Osbon, Janice, Jennifer. M.S., Ch. of God Grad. Sch. Theology, 1981. Ordained to ministry Ch. of God, 1962. Pastor Ch. of God, 1959-82; state overseer Ch. of God, Iowa, Nebr., 1982—, dir. evangelism, dir. youth and Christian edn., dir. finances, 1982—. Contbr. articles to profl. jours. Bd. dirs. Freedom Council, Iowa, 1984. Recipient awards Ch. of God, 1970-82. Home: 14011 Pierce St Omaha NE 68144 Office: Ch of God State Office 14011 Pierce St Omaha NE 68144

DEAN, JOHN CRAMER, minister, So. Bapt. Conv.; b. Oxford, N.C., Apr. 21, 1933; s. Alfred Beecham and Hallie Ruth (Daniel) D.; B.A., Wake Forest U., 1955; M.Div., Southeastern Bapt. Theol. Sem., 1960; m. Mary Elizabeth Jordan, Apr. 7, 1956; children—Beth, Amy, Alan, Susan. Ordained to ministry, 1956; pastor Whitakers (N.C.) Bapt. Ch., 1958-60, Hickory Bapt. Ch., Whitakers, 1958-60, Severn (N.C.) Bapt. Ch., 1960-67; chaplain U.S. Navy, 1967-70; pastor Southport (N.C.) Bapt. Ch., 1970-72; asso. pastor Highland Bapt. Ch., Hickory (N.C.), 1972-76; pastor Victoria (Va.) Bapt. Ch., 1976—. Home and Office: PO Box 911 Victoria VA 23974

DEAN, ROBERT CHOLLAR, priest, Episcopal Church; b. Cleve., Feb. 24, 1921; s. Robert Charles and Ella Mary (Chollar) D.; m. Nancy Jane Weaver, Nov. 25, 1944; children: Robert Paul, Timothy Andrew, Mary Patricia, Anne Christopher. B.S., Case Inst. Tech., 1942; B.D., Kenyon Coll., 1953; M.Div., Bexley Hall, 1973. Ordained priest Episc. Ch., 1953. Rector, Ch. of Good Shepherd, Lyndhurst, Ohio, 1959-76; family and marriage therapist in pvt. practice, Cleve., 1977-80; chaplain and group therapist Horizon Ctr. Hosp., Warrenville Twp., Ohio, 1980-81; rector St. John's Ch., Farmington, N.Mex., 1981—; chmn. task force on alcohol and drug awareness Episc. Diocese of Rio Grande, Albuquerque, 1982—. Mem. San Juan Council Community Agys., 1981—. Served to lt. USNR, 1942-45. Watson fellow, 1961; Wates Seabury Exchange fellow, Kent, Eng., 1964-65; Rossiter scholar, 1983. Fellow Coll. of Preachers; mem. ch. Mems. United, Assoc. Parishes. Democrat. Home: 1221 E 18th St Farmington NM 87401 Office: St John's Church 312 N Orchard Ave Farmington NM 87401

DEANE, GUY MOORMAN, JR., minister, Southern Baptist Convention; b. Owensboro, Ky., July 13, 1924; s. Guy Moorman and Ruby Belle (Harreld) D.; m. Eulah May (Judy) Wells, Sept. 17, 1954; children: Donald Clark, Elizabeth Lynn Deane Floyd. Diploma in theology New Orleans Bapt. Theol. Sem., 1953, B.R.E., 1953; M.Div., Luther Rice Internat. Sem., Fla., 1979; Th.D., Internat. Bible Inst. and Sem., Orlando, Fla., 1981. Ordained to ministry Bapt. Ch. Pastor Maceo Bapt. Ch., Ky., 1980—; moderator Red River Ministerial Assn., Campton, Ky., 1963; mem. exec. bd. Ky. Bapt. Conv., 1963-65, 76, 79, 82, mem. nominating com., 1983; mem. ch. relations adv. bd. Cumberland Coll., Williamsburg, Ky., 1983—. Contbr. articles to theol. jours. Trustee Bethel Coll., Ky., 1966. Served with USN, 1943-46. Mem. New Orleans Bapt. Theol. Sem. Alumni Assn. (pres. 1978), Daviess-McLean Bapt. Assn. (trustee 1984), others. Club: TPA (chaplain 1955) (Owensboro, Ky.). Home: PO Box 57 Maceo KY 42355

DEANS, WILLIAM ANDERSON, III, minister, American Baptist Churches in the U.S.A.; b. Lumberton, N.C., Feb. 3, 1941; s. George Thomas Jr. and Emma Marjalene (Tolar) D.; m. Mary Elizabeth Morgan, June 23, 1962; children: Donna Elizabeth, Sarah Louise, Rachel Marie, Michael William. B.A. in History, Mars Hill Coll., 1965; M.R.E., So. Bapt. Theol. Sem., Louisville, 1974, M.Div., 1978, D.Min., 1979, M.A. in Christian Edn., 1984. Ordained to ministry So. Bapt. Conv., 1966, transferred credentials to Am. Bapt. Chs. in U.S.A., 1979. Community minister West Side Bapt. Ch., Louisville, 1974-78; pastor Lake Dreamland Bapt. Ch., Louisville, 1978-79, Meml. Bapt. Ch., Ft. Wayne, Ind., 1979—; asst. to dir. ministry studies So. Bapt. Theol. Sem., Louisville, 1977-79; pres. Fedn. Ch. Soc. Agys., Louisville, 1977-78; bd. dirs. Assoc. Chs., Ft. Wayne, 1980-83, Samaritan Pastoral Counseling Ctr., Ft. Wayne, 1980-83, Ind. Office for Campus Ministry, Indpls., 1982—; state rep. Met. Ministry Conf., Phila., 1982. Author: An Evaluation and Redesign of the Supervised Ministry Studies Staff Development Program for Campus Ministries at Southern Baptist Theological Seminary, 1979; senator Ministries Council Am. Bapt. Chs. in the U.S.A., 1983—. Bd. dirs. Coalition on Housing, Louisville, 1978; panelist, bd. dirs. LaLeche League Internat. Conv., Atlanta, 1979; v.p. Brentwood Elem. Sch. PTA, Ft. Wayne, 1983. Mem. Am. Bapt. Peace Fellowship, Pastors Roundtable Club, So. Bapt. Theol. Sem. Alumni Assn. (pres. Ind. chpt. 1982, pres. nat. chpt. 1983—). Home: 2410 Santa Rosa Dr Fort Wayne IN 46805 Office: Meml Bapt Ch 2900 N Anthony Blvd Fort Wayne IN 46805

DEATS, RICHARD BAGGETT, religious agency executive, United Methodist Church; b. Big Spring, Tex., Feb. 28, 1932; s. Charles Wesley Deats Sr. and Helen Marie (Mueller) Horton; m. Janice Baggett, June 2, 1956; children: Mark, Stephen, Elizabeth, Katherine. B.A. magna cum laude, McMurry Coll., 1953; B.D. with honors, So. Meth. U., 1956; Ph.D., Boston U., 1964. Ordained to ministry United Meth. Ch., 1954. Assoc. pastor First Meth. Ch., Big Spring, 1956-57; prof. social ethics Union Theol. Sem., Manila, Philippines, 1959-72; dir. inter-faith activities Fellowship of Reconcilation, Nyack, N.Y., 1972-79, 84—, exec. sec., 1979-84; chmn. bd. dirs. Meth. Social Ctr., Manila, 1969-71; sec., treas. Philippine Theol. Soc., Manila, 1964-66; exec. com. Internat. Fellowship Reconcilation, Alkmoor, Holland, 1976-84. Author: The Story of Methodism in the Philippines, 1964; Nationalism and Christianity in the Philippines 1967; (with others) Studies in Philippine Church History, 1968; Responsible Parenthood in the Philippines, 1970. Co-editor: The Filipino in the Seventies, 1973. Trustee, Philippine Wesleyan Coll., Cabanatuan, 1964-70; chmn. Fred Johnson Congl. Campaign, Spring Valley, N.Y., 1978; steering com. 20th Anniversary King March on Washington, 1983; treas. Nyack Coop. Market, 1981-82; vice-chmn. June 12th Com., N.Y.C., 1982; active in Martin Luther King Singers, Spring Valley, 1982—. Mem. Am. Soc. Christian Ethics. Democrat. Home: 117 N Broadway Nyack NY 10960 Office: Fellowship of Reconciliation Box 271 Nyack NY 10960

DEBOER, JOHN CHARLES, church official, United Church of Christ; b. Kodaikanal, India, May 23, 1923; s. John and Erma Elizabeth (Eardley) DeB. (parents U.S. citizens); B.S., U. Mich., 1944; B.D., N.B. Theol. Sem., 1950; S.T.M., Drew U., 1954; m. Clara L. Merritt, Apr. 29, 1944; children: John L., Katharine L., David C. Ordained to ministry Congl. Christian Chs., 1950; minister 1st Congl. Ch., Union, N.J., 1949-53, Maple Shade (N.J.) Congl. Ch., 1953-59; assoc. minister Vt. Congl. Conf., 1959-65; nat. sec. to ch. extension United Ch. of Christ, 1965-77; exec. dir. Joint Strategy and Action Com., Inc., N.Y.C., 1977—; founder and sec. Cornucopia Network of N.J. Inc., 1983-85. Mem. Sigma Xi, Phi Kappa Phi, Tau Beta Pi. Author: Let's Plan—a Guide to the Planning Process for Voluntary Organizations, 1970; How to Succeed in the Organization Jungle Without Losing Your Religion, 1972; Energy Conservation Manual for Congregations, 1980; Primer on Food Fellowship, 1982. Editor: (with others) Are New Towns for Lower Income Americans Too?, 1974. Office: 475 Riverside Dr New York NY 10027

DEBORD, PAUL CHILTON, minister, American Baptist Churches-Southern Baptist Convention; b. Charleston, W.Va., Aug. 20, 1931; s. Charles Arthur and Valaria Marie (Griffith) D.; m. Christina Lee Akers, July 11, 1958; children: Steven Paul, Mark Gregory. Ordained to ministry Am. Bapt. Chs. in U.S.A., 1958. Pastor, Pine Grove Bapt. Ch., McCorkle, W.Va., 1957-58, Olive Br. Ch., Turtle Creek, W.Va., 1958-61, Sycamore Grove Ch., Alkol, W.Va., 1958-61, Naomi Bapt. Ch., Quincy, W.Va., 1961-65, Evans Meml. Bapt. Ch., Charleston, W.Va., 1965-67, Union Bapt. Ch., Milton, W.Va., 1967—; mem. W.Va. Bapt. Ordination Bd., 1975; also radio broadcaster. Mem. Guyandotte Bapt. Assn. (moderator 1972-73, chmn. nominating com. 1983-84), Milton Ministerial Assn. (pres. 1974), Greater Huntington Bapt. Assn. of So. Bapt. Conv. (exec. bd. 1985—). Home and Office: Union Bapt Ch Route 1 Box 60-A Milton WV 25541

DEBRUYN, HARRY EDWARD, church administrator, Reformed Church in America; b. Chgo., Sept. 25, 1931; s. Neal and Henrietta (Brink) DeB.; m. Joan Buis Reininga, Dec. 27, 1952; children: Deborah L., James E., Steven G. J.D., John Marshall Law Sch., 1954. Pres., Gen. Synod Reformed Ch. in Am., N.Y.C., 1972-73, pres. bd. direction, 1979—; sr. ptnr. DeBruyn, Lockie, Voorn & Taylor, Ltd., Palos Hts., Ill., 1956—; pres. Temple Time, Grand Rapids, Mich., 1968-72, Bethesda Hosp., Denver, 1968-72, 83—. Address: 672 Wyandot Dr Palos Heights IL 60463

DEBUES, VERA, Christian organization executive Pres. Young Women's Christian Assn. in Can. Office 80 Gerrard St E Toronto ON M5B 1G6 Canada*

DECELLES, CHARLES EDOUARD, theolog educator, Roman Catholic Church; b. Holyoke, Mass May 17, 1942; s. Fernand Pierre and Stella Mari (Shooner) D.; m. Mildred Manzano Valdez, July 17 1978; children: Christopher Emanuel, Mark Joshua Salvador Isaiah. B.A. in Philosophy, U. Windsor, 1964 M.A. in Theology, Marquette U., 1966; M.A. i Religion, Temple U., 1979; Ph.D., Fordham U., 197(Instr. theology Dunbarton Coll. Holy Cross Washington, 1969-70; instr. theology Marywood Coll Scranton, Pa., 1970-72, asst. prof. religious studies Scanton, 1972-75, assoc. prof., 1975-80, prof., 1980— group leader, advisor Marywood Charismatic Praye group, Scranton, 1970-76; columnist Nat. Cath Register, Los Angeles, 1983—; mem. Pro-Lif Preparatory Commn. Scranton Diocesan Synod 1984—. Author: Paths of Belief study guide, 1977; (with others) Psyche and Spirit, 1976. Contbr. articles to religious jours. Bd. dirs. Pennsylvanians For Human Life, Scanton, 1983—; moderator Students Organized to Uphold Life, Marywood, 1982—. Recipient Disting Service award UN Assn. U.S., 1974; Cert. o Appreciation, U.S. Cath. Conf., 1976; Best Mag. Article award Cath. Press Assn. Am., 1976. Mem. UN Assn U.S. (chmn. UN Day 1974), Coll. Theology Soc. Am. Theta Alpha Kappa (moderator Marywood 1982—) Home: 923 E Drinker St Dunmore PA 18512 Office Marywood Coll 2300 Adams Ave Scranton PA 1850

DECHANT, VIRGIL C., fraternal executive, Roman Catholic Church; b. Antonino, Kans., Sept. 24, 1930; s Cornelius J. and Ursula Legleiter D.; m. Amm L Schafer, Aug. 20, 1951; children: Thomas, Daniel Karen, Robert. Ed. Josephinum Pontifical Coll. Worthington, Ohio, D.Litt. (hon.), 1978; ed. St Joseph's Mil. Acad., Hays, Kans., Salt City Bus. Coll. Hutchinson, Kans.; LL.D. (hon.), St. Anselm's Coll. Manchester, N.H., Providence Coll., 1980; D.Litt., St Leo's Coll., Fla., 1978, Mt. St. Mary's Coll. Emmitsburg, Md., 1979, St. John's U., S.I., 1979. Chmn bd. Dechant Motor Co. Inc., La Crosse, Kans., 1956-74 Former pres. Dodge City Diocesan Devel., Kans.; bd dirs. High Plains Mental Health Assn., 1964-66, Nat Cath. Ednl. Assn., 1978—; trustee Albertus Magnus Coll., New Haven, 1977—. Decorated Order Knighthood of St. Gregory the Great, 1967, Comdr. with silver star, 1978. Mem. La Crosse C. of C. (dir.), New Haven C. of C. Roman Catholic. Lodge: KC (Supreme sec. 1967-77, Supreme knight 1977—). Office: 1 Columbus Plaza New Haven CT 06507

DECHENT, HERMAN ARTHUR, minister, Southern Baptist Convention; b. Buie'S Creek, N.C., July 14, 1921; s. Herman Arthur and Nolie (Burt) D.; m. Anne Jones, July 14, 1946; children: Patricia Anne, Sidney Arthur, Lorene Alysia. A.A., Campbell Coll., 1940; B.A., Wake Forest Coll., 1950; B.D., Crozer Theol Sem., 1953, M.Div., 1972. Ordained to ministry Bapt. Ch., 1953. Pastor, Drummondtown Bapt. Ch., Accomac, Va., 1953-57, Falling Creek Bapt. Ch., Goldsboro, N.C., 1957-64, Clover Bapt. Ch., Va., 1964-69, Hermitage Bapt. Ch., Church View, Va., 1969-76, Ruckersville Bapt. Ch., Va., 1976—. Tng. officer Central Middlesex Vol. Rescue Squad, Urbanna, Va., 1974-77. Served with U.S. Army, 1943-45, ETO. Mem. Albemarle Bapt. Pastor's Conf. (pres. 1984), Greene County Ministerial Assn. (pres. 1982, 84). Republican. Lodges: Masons, K.T. Home: PO Box 86 Ruckersville VA 22968

DE CORNEILLE, ROLAND BARTO, priest, Anglican Church of Canada; member Canadian Parliament; b. Lausanne, Switzerland, May 19, 1927; s. Jacques Andre and Muriel Hilda (Schlager) de C.; came to Can., 1951, naturalized, 1956; B.A. cum laude, Amherst Coll., Mass., 1946; Licentiate in Theology, Trinity Coll., Toronto, Ont., Can., 1953, S.T.B., 1954, Th.M., 1961; postgrad. McGill U., 1954-55, Yale, 1959, U. Toronto, 1958; m. Margaret Elizabeth Cleland, June 5, 1954; children: Christopher Charles Martin, Pamela Michelle Denys. Statistician, Time, Inc., N.Y.C., 1946-47; with advt. dept. Proctor & Gamble, Inc., Eastern region U.Sa, 1948-51; ordained deacon, 1952, priest, 1953; curate St. Johns Ch., West Toronto, Ont., 1952, St. John the Evangelist Ch., Montreal, Que., 1953; rector St. Andrew-by-the-Lake Ch., Toronto, 1954-55, St. Laurence Ch., Toronto, 1956-62; dir. Christian-Jewish Dialogue, Anglican Ch., Toronto, 1962-70; nat. dir. League for Human Rights, B'nai B'rith, Toronto, 1971-79; chaplain Canterbury Club of McGill U., 1953, Sir George Williams Coll., 1953, Northwestern Hosp., Toronto, Bell Clinic, Toronto, 1956-62; hon. asst. St. Hilda's Anglican Ch., Toronto, 1979—; lectr. Ecumenical Inst. Can., 1965-66. Chmn. Martin Luther King Fund, Toronto, 1965-68; dir. Internat. Conf. Christians and Jews, 1968; mem. religious adv. com. Ont. Ednl. Communication Authority, Toronto, 1973-79; mem. com. religious edn. in schs. Anglican Diocese Toronto, 1952-53, religious edn. com. on youth, 1952-53, com. on hosp. chaplaincy, 1955-61, council social service, 1959-65, exec. com.,

1960-61, com. on doctrine and worship, 1973-74; mem. com. on ch. and Jewish people World Council Chs., 1962-72; mem. Nat. Council Chs. of Christ, 1962-72; mem. commn. on research and tng. Canadian Council Chs., 1968-73; M.P. for Eglinton. Lawrence, 1979—, parliamentary sec. to Minister of Vets Affairs, 1981-83;ofel. opposition critic for Sec. of State, 1984—; chmn. Toronto and Region Liberal Caucus, 1984—; mem. Primates Adv. Group on Jewish/Christian Relations, 1975-82; chmn. sub-com. on racist propaganda Metro-Toronto Interfaith Task Force on Racism, 1976-78. Recipient Mass Media and Brotherhood award NCCJ, 1966. Author: Christians and Jews: The Tragic Past and the Hopeful Future, 1966; contbr. articles to religious jours. Home: 9 Bernick Rd Willowdale ON M2H 1E3 Canada Office: House of Commons Ottawa ON K1A 0A6 Canada

DE COSTA, GEORGE DONALD, priest, Roman Cath. Ch.; b. Hilo, Hawaii, Oct. 7, 1937; s. George Donald and Katherine Agnes (DeMello) DeC.; B.A., St. Patrick's Sem., Menlo Park, Calif., 1960, H.M., 1964. Ordained priest, 1964; asst. pastor St. Theresa's Ch., Honolulu, 1964-68; dir. religious edn. Diocese of Honolulu, 1968-72; pastor Malia Puka O Kalani Ch., Hilo, Hawaii, 1972—. Chmn., Am. Lung Assn., Hilo. Office: 326 Desha Ave Hilo HI 96720

DEDMON, LEROY, clergyman; b. Ringgold, Ga., June 27, 1939; s. Gordon Lee and Ruby (Dickson) D.; m. Jane Glasscock, Apr. 5, 1959; children: Gary, Swen Dedmon Rawls. B.A., Ala. Christian Sch. Religion, Montgomery, 1976, M.A. Ordained to ministry Ch. of Christ. Minister, Ch. of Christ, Gurley, Ala., 1960-64, Manchester, Tenn., 1964-68, Morrison, Tenn., 1968-72, Springfield, Tenn., 1972—; speaker daily radio program Sta. WDBL, Springfield, Tenn., 1972—; dir. Summber Bible Camp, Woodbury, Tenn., 1972—; vol. chaplain Jesse Holman Jones Hosp., 1972—; dir. Home Health Care Inc., Springfield, 1983—; speaker in field. Mem. Robertson County Job Opportunity Com., 1974, Robertson County Food Bank, 1976—. Lodges: Kiwanis. Office: Ch of Christ PO Box 310 318 N Main St Springfield TN 37172

DEE, RICHARD STOCKING, minister, United Meth. Ch.; b. Sioux Falls, S.D., Oct. 18, 1938; s. Harry Paul and Helen Anita (Beamer) D.; B.A., Sioux Falls Coll., 1961; M.Div., Iliff Sch. Theology, 1974; m. Teresa Ann Greiner, June 1, 1963; children: Catharine Marie, Anna Maria, Charity Grace, Susanna Abigail. Ordained to ministry, 1972; treas. Ministerial Assn. Council Bluffs (Iowa), 1976—; pastor Sheldon United Meth. Ch., Iowa; vice chmn. Iowa United Meth. Conf. Bd. Evangelism, 1978-79; founder Fellowship Wesleyan Renewal, 1982; organizer, coordinator Police Chaplaincy Council Bluffs, 1974; moderator religious radio talk program Shorty Dee, Denver, 1971-73; dist. rep. to Iowa Conf. Bd. Worship Evangelism, 1975-76; mem. task force Conf. Holy Spirit, 1976. Mem. Sch. Bd. Task Force Council Bluffs, 1976. Mem. Sheldon Ministerial Assn. (chmn.). Home: 1616 5th Ave Council Bluffs IA 51501 Office: 505 8th St Sheldon IA 51201

DEEDS, MOSES EARNSHAW, missionary Free Will Baptist Church; b. Oilton, Okla., Oct. 31, 1932; s. Franklin Pierce and Gracie Fanny (Johnson) D.; m. Willie Jean Barker, June 18, 1957; children: Lyndon, LaDonna, Jeffrey, James, Daniel. B.A., Free Will Bapt. Bible Coll., 1958. Ordained to ministry Free Will Bapt. Ch., 1958. Pastor, First Free Will Bapt. Ch., Warren, Ark., 1958-60, First Free Will Bapt. Ch., Conway, Ark., 1960-62; missionary Brazil Free Will Bapts., Nashville, 1962—; prof. Free Will Bapt. Bible Inst., Jaboticabal, Sao Paulo, 1968-70; radio broadcaster Free Will Bapt. Mission/Brazil, 1969-72, 74—, field chmn., 1975—. Contbr. articles to profl. jours. Served with U.S. Army, 1951-54. Home: Caixa Postal 35 Conselheiro Lafaiete Minas Gerais Brazil 36400 Office: Free Will Bapt Fgn Missions PO Box 1088 Nashville TN 37202

DEEGAN, JOHN EDWARD, priest, Roman Catholic Church, college president; b. Newburgh, N.Y., Mar. 31, 1935; s. John Francis and Kathleen Marguerite (McGrath) D. B.A., Villanova U., 1957, M.A. in History, 1960, M.A. in Secondary Sch. Adminstrn., 1965, Ph.D. in Student Personnel Adminstrn. in Higher Edn., Am. U., 1971. Ordained priest Roman Cath. Ch., 1961. Dir. studies Msgr. Bonner High Sch., Drexel Hill, Pa., 1961-69; assoc. dean student activities Villanova U., 1972-73, asst. prof. edn., 1972-81, chmn. dept. edn., 1975-76, v.p. student life, 1976-81; pres. Merrimack Coll., North Andover, Mass., 1981—. Mem. Am. Personnel and Guidance Assn., Nat. Assn. Student Personnel Adminstrs., Phi Delta Kappa, Kappa Delta Pi. Club: K.C. Office: Merrimack Coll Office of the Pres North Andover MA 01845

DEERING, RONALD FRANKLIN, seminary librarian, minister, Southern Baptist Convention; b. Ford County, Ill., Oct. 6, 1929; s. Mor Franklin and Grace Gilmore (Perkins) D.; m. Edith Ann Proctor, June 12, 1966; children: Mark David, Daniel Timothy. B.A. summa cum laude, Georgetown (Ky.) Coll., 1951; M.Div., So. Bapt. Theol. Sem., Louisville, 1955, Ph.D., 1962; M.S. in L.S. (Lilly Endowment scholar), Columbia U., 1967. Ordained to ministry So. Baptist Conv., 1950. Instr. Bible, Georgetown Coll., 1950-51; pastor chs., Ohio, Ind., 1951-59; instr. Greek, So. Bapt. Theol. Sem., 1958-61, mem. library staff, 1962—, head librarian, 1973—. Mem. ALA, Am. Theol. Library Assn., Am. Acad. Religion, Soc. Bibl. Lit., Sigma Tau Delta, Phi Alpha Theta, Beta Phi Mu. Home: 3111 Dunlieth Ct Louisville KY 40222

DEES, JAMES PARKER, bishop, Anglican Orthodox Church; b. Greenville, N.C., Dec. 30, 1915; s. James Earl and Margaret Burgwin (Parker) D.; A.B., U. N.C., 1938, postgrad., 1938-39; B.D., Va. Theol. Sem., 1949; D.D. honoris causa, Bob Jones U., 1965; m. Margaret Lucinda Brown, Aug. 10, 1940; children—Margaret Lucinda, Eugenia Johnston. Ordained priest Episcopal Ch., 1949; priest, Aurora, N.C., 1949-52, Beaufort, N.C., 1952-55, Statesville, N.C., 1955-63; resigned, 1963; founder Anglican Orthodox Ch., Statesville, 1963; consecrated bishop, 1964, bishop met. Anglican Orthodox Communion, 1969, presiding bishop, 1964—. Pres. P.T.A., 1964-66; founder, pres. N.C. Defenders States' Rights, Inc., 1956; mem. editorial bd. Citizens' Councils Publ., Jackson, Miss., 1959; mem. policy bd. Liberty Lobby, Washington. Bd. dirs. Fedn. Constl. Govt., New Orleans, 1957-60, Independence Found., Portland, Ind., Nat. Conservative Council, Richmond, Va. Recipient Liberty award Congress of Freedom, 1969, 70. Mem. Mayflower Soc. Home: 618 Walnut St Statesville NC 28677 Office: 323 Walnut St Statesville NC 28677

DEFOOR, TERRY WALTON, minister, So. Bapt. Conv.; b. nr. Haleyville, Ala., Jan. 14, 1928; s. Amos Elvin and Willie Adelia (Barber) DeF.; B.A., Samford U., 1948; M.Div., So. Bapt. Theol. Sem., 1959; m. Vira June Swinney, Oct. 30, 1951; children—Jerry, Greg. Ordained to ministry So. Baptist Conv., 1946; pastor, tchr., missionary, 1946-59; pastor 1st Bapt. Ch., Phil Campbell, Ala., 1959-65, Cahaba Heights Bapt. Ch., Birmingham, Ala., 1965-68, Crestway Bapt. Ch., 1968—; preaching mission, Jamaica, Haiti, 1974; evangelist numerous revivals, including Philippines, 1978. Trustee Bapt. Med. Ctr., Birmingham. Mem. Franklin County Bapt. Assn. (moderator 1960-61), Birmingham Bapt. Assn. (chmn. finance com. 1969-70, moderator 1984—). Home: 1020 50th Pl S Birmingham AL 35222 Office: 6400 Crestwood Blvd Birmingham AL 35212

DEFOOR, W. ROBERT, minister, Southern Baptist Convention; b. Atlanta, Dec. 2, 1941; s. Joseph T. and Mary Louise (Sheriff) DeF.; m. Sandra Bailey, June 22, 1962; children: Jennifer Louise, W. Robert, Stephanie Ruth. B.A., Baylor U., 1964; M.Div., So. Bapt. Theol. Sem., Louisville, 1968, D.Min., 1975. Ordained to ministry So. Bapt. Conv., 1965; pastor. Mt. Moriah Bapt. Ch., Boston, Ky., 1965-68, Gilead Bapt. Ch., Glendale, Ky., 1969-73, Harrodsburg Bapt. Ch., Ky., 1979—; assoc. pastor Druid Hills Bapt. Ch., Atlanta, 1973-75, pastor, 1976-79; evangelist So. Bapt. Home Mission Bd., Atlanta, 1977-83; pres. Ga. Bapt. Pastor's Conf., 1978-79; dir. Western Recorder, Middletown, Ky., 1983—. Author Sunday sch. lessons for religious publs. Coach Harrodsburg Little League, 1980-83; bd. dirs. Harrodsburg YMCA, 1983—; mem. Harrodsburg Bd. Edn., 1982—. Mem. Mercer Ministerial Assn. (pres. 1981-83). Democrat. Lodge: Rotary (bd. dirs. 1984; Rotarian of Yr. 1983). Home: 486 Beaumont Ave Harrodsburg KY 40330 Office: Harrodsburg Bapt Ch Main at Office St Harrodsburg KY 40330

DEGAN, JEAN LAFRAMBOISE, musician, administrator, Roman Catholic Church; b. Putnam, Conn., Oct. 10, 1956; d. Francis Bernard and Pauline Elizabeth (LaVigne) LaFramboise; m. William Lawerence Degan, Dec. 31, 1983. B.S. in Music Edn., U. Conn., 1978; B.Mus. in Organ Performance, Hartt Sch. Music, 1983, M.Mus. in Liturgical Music, 1985. Organist U.S. Naval Submarine Base, Groton, Conn., 1979-82; minister of music Sts. Peter and Paul Roman Cath. Ch., Waterbury, Conn., 1982—. Self employed piano tchr., 1976—. Contbr. articles to profl. jours. Mem. Commn. Sacred Liturgy and Sacred Music, Am. Guild Organists (sec. 1983—), Nat. Pastoral Musician. Home: 159 Prospect St Plantsville CT 06479 Office: Sts Peter and Paul Ch 67 Southmayd Rd Waterbury CT 06705

DEGROFT, STEVEN CRAIG, minister, Independent Baptist Church; b. Ft. Ord, Calif., Aug. 9, 1954; s. Lester Robert and Lois Maxine (Shank) DeG.; m. Linda Marie Smith, June 27, 1976. Diploma, Word of Life Bible Inst., 1973; B.S., Liberty Bapt. Coll., 1976. Ordained to ministry Ind. Bapt. Ch., 1983. Youth staff Thomas Road Bapt. Ch., Lynchburg, Va., 1973-76; area rep. Word of Life Fellowship, Schroon Lake, N.Y., 1976-79; youth pastor Liberty Bapt. Ch., Irvine, Calif., 1979-81, First Bapt. Ch., Long Beach, Calif., 1981—; assoc. rep. Word of Life, Schroon Lake, 1979—, pres., youth league basketball coach, Long Beach, 1981—. Named Outstanding Young Man of Am., U.S. Jaycees, 1980. Republican. Office: First Baptist Ch 1000 Pine Long Beach CA 90813

DEHAVEN, E(RNEST) THOMAS, minister, Christian Church (Disciples of Christ); association executive; b. Hiram Twp., Ohio, Aug. 7, 1928; s. Ernest Roy and Bertha Catherine (Thomas) DeH.; m. Barbara Ann Hoskin, Aug. 21, 1955; children: Matthew, Stephen, Catherine. A.B., Hiram Coll., 1949; M.H.A., Va. Commonwealth U., 1957; postgrad. Lexington Theol. Sem., Ky., 1957-58. Ordained to ministry Christian Ch. (Disciples of Christ), 1958. United Christian Missionary Soc. hosp. adminstr. Albert Schweitzer Meml. Hosp., St. Mark, Haiti, 1958-59, Jackman Meml. Hosp., Bilaspur, India, 1959-64; asst. adminstr. Lake County Meml. Hosp., Painesville, Ohio, 1964-67; adminstr. Carroll County Meml. Hosp., Carrollton, Ky., 1967-77; exec. dir. Wesley Manor, Frankfort, Ind., 1977-82; adminstr. Ramsey Meml. Home (Nat. Benevolent Assn.), Des Moines, 1982—; regional ops. dir. Nat. Benevolent Assn., 1985—; chmn. evangelism com. 1st Christian Ch., Des Moines, 1984-85; bd. dirs. Christian Ch. in Upper Midwest, Des Moines, 1982—. Served with AUS, 1952-54, Korea. Bd. dirs. Des Moines Choral Soc., 1984—. Mem. Am. Coll. Hosp. Adminstrs., Am. Coll. Health Care Adminstrs. Lodges: Des Moines Rotary, Masons (32 degree), Shriners. Home: 7008 Townsend St Des Moines IA 50322 Office: Ramsey Memorial Home 1611 27th St Des Moines IA 50310

DEHEYMAN, WILLIAM MARQUAD, minister, Lutheran Church in America; b. Sept. 3, 1933; s. Frank Grover and Luella (Marquand) deH.; m. Martha Ann Diana, June 4, 1960; children: Elizabeth, Deborah. B.A., Wagner Coll., 1955; M.Div., Luth. Theol. Sem., 1960. Ordained to ministry Luth. Ch. in Am., 1960. Pastor, mission developer King of Kings Luth. Ch., New Windsor, N.Y., 1960-63; assoc. pastor St. Paul's Luth. Ch., Allentown, Pa., 1963-69; pastor St. John's Luth. Ch., Phoenixville, Pa., 1969-70, Good Shepherd Luth. Ch., King Of Prussia, Pa., 1971-82, Christ's Luth. Ch., Oreland, Pa., 1984—; trustee Luth. Home at Germantown, Phila., 1981—. Recipient Youth award KYW-TV, 1966. Republican. Home: 117 Rech Ave Oreland PA 19075 Office: Christ Luth Ch Pennsylvania and Rech Aves Oreland PA 19075

DEIFELL, JOHN JEY, JR., minister, Presbyterian Ch. in U.S.A.; b. Florence, S.C., Dec. 31, 1939; s. John Jey and Louise (Holliday) D.; B.S., U. N.C., Chapel Hill, 1962; M.Div. cum laude, Columbia Theol. Sem., 1966; Ph.D. in Theology, U. Edinburgh, 1969; m. Joan Thomson Chapman, June 5, 1964; children—Anthony, David, Heather. Ordained to ministry, 1966; student pastor St. Cuthberts Parish Ch., Edinburgh, Scotland, 1966-69; pastor Gaithersburg (Md.) Presbyn. Ch., 1969—. Pres., Gaithersburg Area Clergy Assn.; trustee Presbyn. Home of Washington. Pres., Gaithersburg Help; bd. advisers Washington Kidney Found., Met. Washington Parents Without Partners, Upper Montgomery County YMCA. Recipient Paul T. Fuhrmann Ch. History award, 1966, Columbia Sem. Alumni fellow, 1966. Mem. Gaithersburg Pastoral Counseling Center, Community Ministry of Montgomery County, Nat. Capital Union Presbytery, Synod of the Virginias. Home: 7332 Muncaster Mill Rd Derwood MD 20855 Office: 16700 Frederick Rd Gaithersburg MD 20760

DEJONG, JAMES A., seminary administrator. Pres. Calvin Theol. Sem., (Christian Reformed). Office: 3233 Burton St SE Grand Rapids MI 49506*

DEJULIO, ROBERT JAMES, priest, Roman Cath. Ch.; b. New Rochelle, N.Y., June 25, 1946; s. James Thomas and Carmela (Serena) DeJ.; A.B. in Sociology, St. Anselm's Coll., Manchester, N.H., 1968; M.Div., St. Joseph's Sem., Yonkers, N.Y., 1971; postgrad. N.Y. Theol. Sem. Ordained priest, 1972; asso. pastor St. Catharine's Ch., Blauvelt, N.Y., 1972—. Cath. chaplain Rockland Children's Center, Orangeburg, N.Y., 1973—; vicariate vocation coordinator, 1974-76; mem. N.Y. Senate Priests, 1972-74; regional dir. Cath. Charities, 1973-77; advocate Met. Tribunal, 1977. Mem. Assn. Cath. Clergy Rockland County. Address: 148 Western Hwy Blauvelt NY 10913

DEKAR, PAUL RICHARD, minister, religion educator, Baptist Convention of Ontario and Quebec; b. San Francisco, Feb. 8, 1944; s. Paul George and Ariadne Spiradoneva (Dovjenko) D.; m. Nancy Rose, Dec. 31, 1967; children: Nathaniel Paul, Matthew Paul. A.B., U. Calif.-Berkeley, 1965; M.Div., Colgate Div. Sch., 1971; A.M., U. Chgo., 1973, Ph.D., 1978. Ordained to ministry Am. Bapt. Chs., 1971. Pastor English lang. congregation, Yaounde, Cameroon, 1968-70; asst. chaplain U. Rochester, N.Y., 1970-71; asst. to editors Ch. History, U. Chgo., 1973-75; instr. religion Central Mich. U., Mt. Pleasant, 1975-76; assoc. prof. Christian history McMaster Div. Coll., Hamilton, Ont., Can., 1976—, also chmn. com. on study of peace; bd. dirs. Bapt. Peace Fellowship of N. Am. Editor: In the Great Tradition, 1982. Contbr. numerous articles, booklets, revs., denom. pieces. Mem. Amnesty Internat. (chair 1977-79), Can. Bapt. Peace Group (chair 1981), Am. Soc. Ch. History, Can. Soc. Ch. History (bd. dirs. 1980-82), Hamilton Disarmament Coalition (chair 1981), McMaster Campus Ministries Council (chair 1979-81).

DEKICH, MILAN BROWN, minister, Church of God (Anderson, Ind.); b. Chattanooga, Oct. 23, 1954; s. Milan Hall and Lois Edith (Hicklen) D.; m. Barbara Jo Blevins, July 16, 1983. B.E. magna cum laude, U. Ga., 1977; M.Div., Anderson Sch. Theology, 1980.

Ordained to ministry Church of God (Anderson, Ind.), 1982. Pastor Fairview Ch. of God, Falkville, Ala., 1980—; active North Anderson Prison Ministry, Ind., 1978-80. Coach, basketball dir. Falkville Recreation Bd., 1980-82. Mem. Falkville Ministerial Assn. (pres. 1980-81), North Ala. Ministerial Assn. (pres. 1984-85, sec. 1982). Lodge: Lions. Home and Office: Fairview Ch of God Route 2 Box 177 Falkville AL 35622

DEKKER, LOIS ANN, lay church worker, Lutheran Church in America; b. Sheboygan, Wis., Apr. 1, 1929; d. Theodore R. Stuedeman and Gladys R. (Eichenberger) Stuedeman Kaufmann; m. Russell E. Rydberg, June 4, 1949; (dec. 1973); children: Marcia A. Rydberg Soerens, Sandra R. Rydberg Miller, Virginia L.; m. John Dekker, June 29, 1977; step-children: Ruth Evan Dekker, Gary J., Debra L. Dekker Leftwich. Student U. Wis.-Sheboygan, 1974-75; C.Ed.D. (hon.), Carthage Coll., 1984. Cert. lay profl. leader, Luth. Ch. in Am., 1982. Christian edn. coordinator First United Luth. Ch., Sheboygan, 1963-83; assoc. dir. dept. leadership support div. for profl. leadership Luth. Ch. in Am., Phila., 1983—; synod rep. Wis. Broadcast Ministry, Wis. Council Chs., Madison, 1970-74; del. convs. Luth. Ch. in Am., Boston, 1976, Chgo., 1978, mem., v.p. bd. publs., Phila., 1976-83; communicator Luth. Brotherhood, Mpls., 1983. Editor Life Without newsletter, 1975-76. Contbr. articles to publs., 1966-83. Trainer Sheboygan County council Girl Scouts U.S.A., 1957-62; trustee Mead Pub. Library, Sheybogan, 1975-83, Sheboygan County Federated Library, 1978-83; mem. Women for Greater Phila., 1983-84; mem. budget com. United Way, Sheboygan, 1978-79; dist. chairperson Heart Fund, Sheboygan, Community Fund, Sheboygan, Mothers' March, Sheboygan. Recipient Citation award Sheboygan Jaycettes, 1963. Office: Div Profl Leadership Luth Ch in Am 2900 Queen Ln Philadelphia PA 19129

DELANEY, JOSEPH PATRICK, bishop, Roman Catholic Church; b. Fall River, Mass., Aug. 29, 1934; s. Joseph R. and Jane (Burke) D. A.B., Cath. U. Am., 1956, M.A., 1957; S.T.B., S.T.L., Gregorian U., Rome, 1961; M.Ed., R.I. Coll., 1964. Ordained priest, Roman Cath. Ch., 1960; consecrated bishop, 1981. Bishop, Diocese of Ft. Worth, Tex., 1981—.

DELAQUIS, NOEL JACQUES, bishop, Roman Catholic Church; b. Notre-Dame de Lourdes, Man., Can., Dec. 25, 1934; s. Louis and Therese (Hebert) D.; B.A., U. Man., 1954; Th.L., U. Laval, Que., 1958; J.C.L., U. Latran, Rome, 1962. Ordained priest, 1958; consecrated bishop, 1974; bishop of Gravelbourg, (Sask., Can.), 1974—. Address: CP 690 Gravelbourg SK S0H 1X0 Canada

DELEERY, SETH MABRY, priest, Episcopal Church; b. Glaveston, Tex., Oct. 11, 1946; s. Joseph Sutherland and Mildred (Mabry) D.; m. Cynthia Lou Scott, Apr. 21, 1967. B.A., U. Houston, 1969, M.S., 1981; M.Div., Episc. Sem. of Southwest, 1974. Ordained priest Episc. Ch., 1974. Asst. rector St. Martin's Episc. Ch., Houston, 1974-76; chaplain to Bishop of Iran, Diocese of Iran, Isfahan, 1976; assoc. rector Trinity Episc. Ch., Houston, 1977-78; rector St. Michael's Ch., LaMarque, Tex., 1978-83; chaplain U. Tex.-Austin, 1984—; dir. youth ministry Diocese of Tex., Houston, 1983—; trustee St. James' House, Baytown, Tex., 1978-82, Camp Allen, Houston, 1979—. Author: The Christian Socialist Movement, 1981. Served with USAF, 1969-71. Address: 1102 Huntridge Austin TX 78758

DELONG, MICHAEL BEN, minister, college president, Independent Baptist Churches; b. Bellefonte, Pa., Sept. 24, 1956; s. Bernard Lincoln and Priscilla (Hobson) DeL.; m. Terry Arlene Stone, Dec. 3, 1978; children: Benjamin Joel, Jonathan Michael, Matthew Jesse. Grad., Centreville Bible Coll., 1978; B.A., Temple Bapt. Coll., 1981. Ordained to gospel ministry Ind. Bapt. Chs., 1979. Assoc. evangelist Harvest Time Ministries Eng., Hatherleigh, Devon, 1976; music dir. First Bapt. Ch. Centerville, Ohio, 1976—; registrar, bus. adminstr. Centreville Bible. Coll., Centerville, 1978-85, pres., 1985—; assoc. minister First Bapt. Ch. Centerville, 1978—. Editor The Light newsmag., 1976-83. Mem., Dayton Right to Life Orgn., Ohio Right to Life Orgn. Republican. Home: 148 Washington Mill Rd Bellbrook OH 45305 Office: Centreville Bible Coll 38 N Main St Centerville OH 45459

DE LUCA, MICHAEL GRAY, minister, American Baptist Churches in U.S.A.; b. Long Beach, Calif., Jan. 12, 1943; m. Karen. B.A., Biola U., 1967; M.Div., Talbot Theol. Sem., 1973. Ordained to ministry Am. Bapt. Chs. in U.S.A., 1974. Youth pastor First Bapt. Ch., Buena Park, Calif., 1961-66, First Bapt. Ch., Paramount, Calif., 1966-69; Christian edn. dir. Garfield Bapt. Ch., Long Beach, Calif., 1969-72; asst. pastor First Bapt. Ch., Whittier, Calif., 1972-77; sr. pastor First Bapt. Ch., Darrington, Wash., 1977—. Office: First Baptist Ch 1205 N Emens St Darrington WA 98241

DELVAUX, AUGUSTE JOSEPH, priest, Roman Cath. Ch.; b. Woonsocket, R.I., Mar. 19, 1933; s. Auguste Joseph and Emilia Marie (Casse) D.; Ph.B., Louvain U.. Belgium, 1955, B.A., 1958; M.A., Assumption Coll., 1963. Ordained priest, 1958; parish asst. St. Rita Ch., 1958-59, Notre Dame Ch., Phenix, R.I., 1959-63; prof. Our Lady of Providence Sem., Warwick, 1959-69; founding dir. Diocesan Media Center, Providence, 1971-76; pastor St. Joan's Parish, Cumberland, R.I., 1976—. Police and fire chaplain, Warwick and Providence, 1964-76; diocesan media cons. Mem. AAUP, R.I. Police Chaplains Assn. Home: 3357 Mendon Rd Cumberland RI 02864

DEMAREST, GARY WILLIAM, minister, United Presbyn. Ch. U.S.A.; b. Santa Monica, Calif., Jan. 16, 1926; s. Garrett Wilson and Viola Victoria (Rusthoi) D.; B.S. in C.E., U. Calif., Berkeley, 1947; B.D., Fuller Theol. Sem., 1950, Th.M., Princeton Theol. Sem., 1957; m. Marily Evans, Aug. 28, 1959; children: Anne Marie, Patti Lynn, Kathleen. Ordained to ministry, 1950; minister to youth, Seattle, 1950-55, Jacksonville, Fla., 1956-58; program dir. Fellowship Christian Athletes, Kansas City, Mo., 1959-61; pastor Hamburg (N.Y.) Presbyn. Ch., 1961-65, La Canada (Calif.) Presbyn. Ch., 1965—. Moderator, Synod So. Calif., Presbytery of San Fernando; dir. United Presbyn. Center for Mission Studies, 1970- ; trustee Whitworth Coll., 1973- , Fuller Theol. Sem., 1973—. Author: Christian Alternatives Within Marriage; Colossians: The Mystery of Christ Within Us; Commentary on Thessalonians and Timothy. Mem. Los Angeles County Commn. on Human Relations, 1965-75, pres., 1972-74; mem. La Canada Sch. Bd., 1972-81, pres., 1973-75; chmn. bd. dirs. African Enterprise. Named Nat. Presbyn. Preacher of Yr., 1976; recipient La Canadan of Yr. community award, 1976, Distinguished Citizens award La Canada PTA, 1970. Home: 820 Chehalem Rd LaCanada CA 91011 Office: PO Box 188 La Canada CA 91011

DEMARINIS, JOHN HENRY, priest, Roman Catholic Church; b. Youngstown, Ohio, Oct. 2, 1937; s. John and Lucille Elizabeth (Pavone) DeM. B.A., Athenaeum Ohio, Cin., 1959, M.Div., 1963; M.A., Xavier U., Cin., 1962; Ordained priest Roman Cath. Ch., 1962. Assoc. Pastor St. Paul's Ch., Canton, Ohio, 1963-66; theology instr. Ursuline High Sch., Youngstown, 1966-73; pastor St. Anthony Ch., Youngstown, 1973—; pro-synodal judge Diocesan Priests Senate, Youngstown, 1976-83; treas. Diocese of Youngstown, 1981—, dir. adult edn., 1963, 65, mem. ins. bd., 1981—, priorities study steering com., 1983—, chmn. fin. adv. bd., 1981—; mem. adv. bd. Oblate Sisters, 1966—; mem. com. Synod 76, Youngstown, 1976; tchr. rep. Diocesan Tchr. Confedn., Youngstown, 1968-70; chaplain Mahoning Valley council Boy Scouts Am., 1963-66; moderator Home and Sch. Assn. Ursuline High Sch., 1969-73. Democrat. Home: 1125 Turin Ave Youngstown OH 44510 Office: Diocesan Treas 144 W Wood St Youngstown OH 44503

DEMONG, LAWRENCE LAVERNE, priest, educator, Roman Catholic Church; b. Cudworth, Sask., Can., Aug. 29, 1937; s. Henry William and Anna Marie (Wedewer) DeM. B.A., St. John's U., 1959; B.A. in Catechetics, Laval U., Que., Can., 1966, M.A. in French, 1968, Licentiate in Catechetics, 1969. Joined Benedictine Order, Roman Cath. Ch., 1957, ordained priest, 1963. Tchr. high sch. religion St. Peter's Coll., Muenster, Sask., 1964-65, 69-70; dir. religious edn. St. Peter's Abbacy, Muenster, 1969-74, 77-82; pastor Marysburg Parish, Sask., 1976-82; dir. nat. office religious edn., Can. Conf. Cath. Bishops, Ottawa, Ont., Can., 1982—. Contbr. articles to religious publs. Home: St Elizabeth Rd Cantely PQ J0X 1L0 Canada Office: Nat Office Religious Edn 90 Parent Ave Ottawa ON K1N 7B1 Canada

DEMPSEY, JOSEPH PAGE, minister, Bapt. Missionary Assn. Am.; b. Nash County, N.C., Mar. 8, 1930; s. Sidney Hilliard and Irene Alice (Vick) D.; B.S., Fayetteville State U., 1958; B.D., Shaw Div. Sch., 1964, M.Div., 1972; M.A., N.C. Central U., 1972; postgrad. behavioral scis. Nova U.; m. Evelyntyne Humphrey, May 31, 1958; children—Denise Paige, Joseph Todd, Eric Humphrey, Kathy Denyne. Ordained to ministry, 1954; pastor First Bapt. Ch., Lillington, N.C., 1961-64; asst. pastor White Rock Bapt. Ch., Durham, N.C., 1962-63, Oberlin Bapt. Ch., Raleigh, N.C., 1964—. Tchr. ministers Wake Bapt. Assn., 1964-70, mem. ministerial bd., 1964-74. Mem. precinct exec. com. Wake Democratic party, 1974—. Named Father of Yr., Oberlin Bapt. Ch., 1965, Christmas Christian Family of Yr., Raleigh, 1972. Mem. NAACP. Home: 1409 E Martin St Raleigh NC 27610 Office: 1707 Fayetteville St Durham NC 27707

DEMPSEY, RAYMOND LEO, JR., evangelist, writer, non-denominational Christian; b. Providence, June 18, 1949; s. Raymond Leo and Louise (Gambuto) D.; m. Patricia Ann Batchelder, Dec. 15, 1978; children: Joab, Jahdeam, Deezsha, Nathaniel, Talitha. B.A., R.I. Coll., 1973. Elder, Church of the Redeemer, Providence, 1979—, auditor, 1985; freelance writer specializing in Christianity, Providence, 1980—; Author of interviews, reviews, articles. Producer cable TV presentations, 1982—; guest speaker on radio and TV. Bd. dirs. R.I. State Right to Life Com., Edgewood, 1978—; pres. A Pro-Life Gathering, Inc., Providence, 1980—; legis. witness R.I. Gen. Assembly. Recipient 5 Yr. Vol. award A.R.C., 1982. Home: 75 Marion Ave Providence RI 02905

DEMPSEY, ROBERT BRINKERHOFF, minister Nat. Assn. Congl. Christian Chs.; b. East Paterson, N.J. Sept. 26, 1926; s. Joseph Gordon and Eleanor (Brinkerhoff) D.; grad. Moody Bible Inst., 1946; B.A. Gordon Coll., 1948; Th.M., Gordon Div. Sch., 1952 Th.D., Boston U., 1963; m. Priscilla Jean Mills, May 6, 1972; children—Gordon Arthur, Sunday Arlene, Wendi Joy. Ordained to ministry, 1948; pastor Union Evangelical Ch., Stow, Mass., 1948-54, Carlisle Congl. Ch. (Mass.), 1954-64; supply minister, Rockland, Maine, 1967—. Exec. sec. Conservative Congl Christian Conf., 1956-64; gen. dir. Camp Fireside, 1960-64. Mem. Evangel. Theol. Soc., Near East Archaeol. Soc., Phi Alpha Chi. Contbr. articles to religious jours. and encys. Home: 130 Union St Rockland ME 04841 Office: PO Box 223 Florence MA 01060

DEMSHUK, VLADIMIR VLADIMUOVITCH, priest, Orthodox Catholic Church; Russian educator; b. Sharon, Pa., Jan. 12, 1944; s. Walter and Anna (Patrick) D.; m. Katherine Marie Parimuha, Sept. 10, 1972; children: Larisa, Jonathan. Student Ohio State U., 1962-63, Iona Coll., St. Vladimir's Orthodox Theol. Sem., 1963-65; B.A. in Russian Lang. and Lit., The Youngstown U., 1967; B.A. in Religion, Mich. State U., 1968; M.A. in Humanities, U. Detroit, 1981. Ordained priest Russian Orthodix Church in the U.S. and Can., 1973. Parish priest various parishes, 1973—; adj. faculty Oakland Community Coll., Farmington Hills, Mich., 1974, Grand Island Tech Community Coll., Kearney, Nebr., 1978, Mohawk Valley Community Coll., Utica, N.Y., 1984, Herkimer County Community Coll., 1984. Author: Russian Sainthood and Canonization, 1978. Contbr. articles to profl. mags. Newspaper columnist Kearney Daily Hub, 1978, The Evening Telegram, 1984. Commentator The Ethnic Hour, Kearney State Coll., 1977-78, Orthodox View, TV 13, 1978-79, Chicagoland Ch. Hour, WGN-TV, 1980.

DEMSKE, JAMES MICHAEL See *Who's Who in America,* 43rd edition.

DENDE, CORNELIAN EDMUND, priest, radio program director, Roman Catholic Church; b. Scranton, Pa., Aug. 8, 1915; s. John and Mary (Borowski) D. Student Seminaire de Philosophie, Montreal, U. Lwow, Poland, Gregorian U., Rome, St. Hyacinth Sem./Coll., Granby, Mass. Ordained priest Roman Cath. Ch., 1941. Dir., Cath. Press Agy., N.Y.C., 1943; master novices Order Friars Minor Conventual, 1948-58; rector St. Hyacinth Coll., Sem., Granby, Mass., 1959; dir. Father Justin Rosary Hour, Athol Springs, N.Y., 1959—. Author radio speeches in Polish, 25 ann. vols., 1959-85. Recipient Medal of Merit, Cath. U. Lublin, Poland, 1984. Office: Father Justin Rosary Hour Station F Box 217 Buffalo NY 14212

DENEF, LAWRENCE WALTER, church official, American Lutheran Church. b. Erie County, N.Y., Feb. 5, 1931; s. Walter J.H. and Gertrude I. (Belling) D.; m. Ruth C. Bargmann, June 23, 1959. B.S., Capital U., 1952; B.D., Trinity Sem., 1956; postgrad., U. Hamburg, 1956-58. Ordained to ministry Lutheran Church, 1958. Assoc. prof. systematic theol. Trinty Sem., Columbus, Ohio, 1958-59; pastor St. John and Christ Luth. Ch., Wapella and Kipling, Sask., Can., 1960-61, Mt. Olivet Luth. Ch., North Vancouver, B.C., Can., 1961-65; editor Augsburg Pub. House, Mpls., 1965-70; dir. for theol. and adult ministries Am. Luth. Ch., Mpls., 1970—; chmn. Consultation on the Whole Person, Mpls., 1978; moderator Consultation on the Poor and Economic Justice, Mpls., 1979; official visitor Luth. World Fedn. Mem. World Council Chs., Vancouver, B.C. Assembly, 1983. Author: The Kingdoms of Israel and Judah, 1965. Translator: Beyond Mere Obedience, 1966; Evangelical Catechism, 1982; Paul: Rabbi and Apostle, 1984; Luther: The Man and His Work, 1985. State adv. com. White House Conf. on Family, Minn., 1980. Recipient Samuel Scheiner Human Relations award Jewish Community Relations Council-Anti-Defamation League, 1980; named One of 10 Most Influential Lutherans, Luth. Perspective, 1982. Mem. Minn. Adult Edn. Assn., Am. Acad. Religion. Home: 1105 2222 Bellevue West Vancouver BC V7V 1C7 Canada Office: Am Luth Ch 422 S 5th St Minneapolis MN 55415

DENHAM, MICHAEL THOMAS, lay church worker, minister, Presbyterian Ch. N. Am.; opera singer; b. Tulsa, June 29, 1955; s. Leonard Patrick and Jeanne (Dowdy) D.; m. Elizabeth Jarrell Callender, June 6, 1981. B.A. in Music, Wheaton Coll., 1978; postgrad. North Tex. State U., 1983; M.A. in Music, U. Ill., 1984; Th.M. (candidate) Dallas Theol Sem., 1986. Assoc. music staff Twin City Bible Ch., Urbana, Ill., 1978-80; with music staff Northwest Bible Ch., Dallas, 1981—, intern, 1983-84. Soloist, U. Ill. Chamber Orchestra, Urbana, 1979, 80. Named finalist young artist auditions Okla. Symphony Orch., 1985; recipient Wheaton Coll. Performance award Wheaton Conservatory of Music, Ill., 1978. Mem. World Evang. Fellowship (life), Theol. Students Fellowship, Evang. Theol. Soc. (student assoc.). Republican. Home: 609 Goodwin Dr Richardson TX 75081 Office: Dallas Theol Sem 3909 Swiss Ave Dallas TX 75204

DENNIS, GARY OWEN, minister, Presbyterian Church; b. Waynesville, N.C., Feb. 17, 1946; s. Daniel Shaefer and Shirley Carlene (Owen) D.; m. Sara Bright, June 14, 1969; children: Cory, Jennifer. B.A., Taylor U., 1968; M.Div., Princeton Theol. Sem., 1972. Ordained to ministry Presbyn. Ch., 1972. Assoc. pastor Second Presbyn. Ch., Memphis, 1972-73; asst. pastor Hollywood Presbyn. Ch., Los Angeles, 1973-76; adj. prof. religion Fuller Theol. Sem., Pasadena, Calif., 1973-76; sr. pastor Westlake Hills Presbyn. Ch., Austin, Tex., 1976—; founder, dir. Youth Leadership Devel. Am., Los Angeles, 1974-76; mem. edn. com. Mission Presbytery, San Antonio, 1976-80, mem. stewardship com., 1980-83. Cons. Lilly Endowment, Indpls., 1974-76; bd. dirs. Central City Counseling Ctr., Austin, 1982-84; mem. com. Ronald McDonald House, Austin, 1984—. Contbr. articles to profl. jours. Named One of Outstanding Young Men in Am., 1974. Democrat. Lodge: Rotary. Home: 1300 Circle Ridge Austin TX 78746 Office: Westlake Hills Presbyn Ch 101 Westlake Dr Austin TX 78746

DENNIS, GEORGE THOMAS, priest, Roman Catholic Ch.; b. Somerville, Mass., Nov. 17, 1923; s. George Thomas and Helen Gertrude (Caldwell) D. B.A., U. Santa Clara, 1947; Ph.D., Oriental Inst., Rome, 1960. Ordained priest Roman Cath. Ch., 1954. Faculty Cath. U. Am., Washington, 1967—, now prof. history. Author: Letters of Manuel II, 1977; Palaeologus Byzantium and The Franks, 1982. Contbr. articles to profl. jours. Bd. dirs., chmn. Neighborhood Planning Council 3, 1970—. Mem. Medieval Acad. Am., Byzantine Studies Conf., Cath. Hist. Assn. Democrat. Office: Cath U Am Washington DC 20064

DENNIS, JOHN DAVISON, minister, United presbyterian Ch. in U.S.A.; b. Pitts., Sept. 18, 1937; s. John Wellington and Helen Isabella (Davison) D.; A.B., Wesleyan U., 1959; B.D., Princeton Theol. Sem., 1962, Th.M., 1965; m. Nancy Schumacher, Jan. 7, 1967; children: Michael, Andrew. Ordained to ministry, 1962; asst. pastor First Presbyn. Ch. in Germantown, Phila., 1962-69; sr. pastor First Presbyn. Ch., Corvallis, Oreg., 1969—; exchange minister St. Columba's Presbyn. Ch., Johannesburg, South Africa, 1978. Mem. United Presbyn. Ch. consulting com. on continuing edn., 1974—; Chaplain Germantown Hosp., 1965-69; W. Coast dean Presbyn. Young Pastors Seminars, 1983-85. Mem. Westminster Found. of Oreg., 1969-76, vice chmn., 1974-76; vice chmn. Madison Ave. Task Force; pres. Corvallis Community Improvement, Inc.; founder Corvallis Summer Music Festival, 1979, v.p., 1979-83; trustee, charter mem. Good Samaritan Hosp. Found.; mem. Benton County Mental Health Bd., 1972-76, chmn., 1975-76; founder, exec. com. Corvallis Fish Emergency Aid Service, 1969-76. Lodge: Rotary (charter, dir.). Author: Study Guide on Religion and Race, 1964. Home: 2760 NW Skyline Dr Corvallis OR 97330 Office: 114 SW Eighth St Corvallis OR 97330

DENNIS, ROBERT EARL, minister, Prog. Nat. Baptist Conv., Inc.; b. Greenville, S.C., May 27, 1942; s. James Walter and Rosie Anna (Bowling) D.; B.Th., Morris Coll., 1977; m. Mary Elizabeth Croft, Feb. 22, 1963; 1 dau., Caroline. Ordained to ministry, 1969; pastor Cedar Grove Baptist Ch., Simpsonville, S.C., 1969—. Moderator Reedy River Union of Chs., Greenville County, S.C.; dir. Cedar Grove Day Care Center. Bd. dirs. Community Action, Mental Health of Simpsonville; mem. Greenville Housing Bd. Adjustment and Appeal. Mem. S.C. Congress Christian Edn., NAACP, Greenville County Ministerial Union. Home: Route 3 Box 188A Simpsonville SC 29681 Office: Moore St Simpsonville SC 29681

DENNIS, ROGER DEE, minister, Lutheran Church in America; educator; b. Robinson, Ill., July 24, 1947; s. Charles Demorris and Virginia Maxine (Cantwell) McQuin; m. Barbara Jean Rutter, Mar. 15, 1979; children: Lucas Michael, Aaron Kyle. B.S. in Mass Communication, Kans. State U., 1970; M.P.A., La. State U., 1977; M.Div., Luth Sch. Theology, Chgo., 1981. Ordained to ministry Luth. Ch. in Am., 1981. Pastor, Faith Luth. Ch., Wichita Falls, Tex., 1981—; com. mem. Tex.-La. Synod, Austin, Tex., 1976-77; bd. dirs. Interfaith Ministries Inc., Wichita Falls, 1981—, Hospice, Wichita Falls, 1984—. Author: (poetry) Peace Be With You Brother, 1970. Contbr. articles to profl. jours. Cons. (film) Jerusalem City of Peace, 1984. Bd. dirs. Clergy for Nuclear Awareness, 1984—. Served to lt. U.S. Army, 1971-74. Mem. Wichita Falls Ministerial Fellowship (v.p. 1982, pres. 1982—). Home: 7 Briandale Ct Wichita Falls TX 76310 Office: Faith Luth Ch 1437 Southwest Pkwy Wichita Falls TX 76302

DENNIS, WALTER DECOSER, suffragan bishop, Episcopal Church; b. Washington, Aug. 23, 1932. B.A., Va. State Coll., 1952; M.A., NY U, 1953; M.Div., Gen. Sem., 1958, D.D. (hon.), 1983; D.D. (hon.), Absalom Jones Sem., 1977; L.H.D. (hon.) Va. State and Sem. of Southwest, 1983. Ordained priest Episcopal Ch, 1958, bishop, 1979. Curate St. Philip's Ch., Bklyn., 1956; residentiary canon Episcopal Ch., N.Y.C., 1956-60, suffragan bishop, 1979—; vicar St. Cyprian Ch., Hampton, Va., 1960-65. Contbr. articles to profl. jours. Bd. dirs. SEICUS, N.Y.C., 1979-82; bd. dirs. Planned Parenthood, N.Y.C., 1980-83. Home and Office: Episcopal Ch 1047 Amsterdam Ave New York NY 10025

DENNIS, WILLIAM EARL, minister, Luth. Ch. Am.; b. Stroudsburg, Pa., Feb. 13, 1927; s. Earl Dewitt and Sadie Young (Houck) D.; A.B., Muhlenberg Coll., 1948; M.Div., Phila. Luth. Theol. Sem., 1950, S.T.M., 1959; m. Sarah Evelyn Moll, June 3, 1950; children: John Earl, Sarah Louise, Catharine Elizabeth. Ordained to ministry, 1950; pastor Trinity Luth. Ch., Clarks Summit, Pa., 1949-55, Trinity Luth. Ch., Bangor, Pa., 1955-68, St. Michael's Ch., Sellersville, Pa., 1968—. Mem. Synod Publicity Com., 1951-71; statistician Wilkes-Barre Conf., 1952-55; mem. Synod Pension Com., 1953-54; chmn. Synod Nominating Com., 1957; del. conv. Luth. Ch. Am., 1964, 68; sec., Easton Dist., 1958-68; chmn. Synod Registration and Excuse, 1973-75; evangelism com. SE Pa. Synod, 1971—; writer; weekly religious columnist Bangor Daily News, 1959-67. Chmn. Bucks br. SE Pa. chpt. ARC, 1972-74, mem. bd., 1972-74, recipient commendation, 1975. Mem. Lambda Chi Alpha. Home: 328 E Church St Sellersville PA 18960 Office: 111 E Church St Sellersville PA 18960

DENNISON, JACK LEE, minister, American Baptist Churches in the U.S.A.; b. Ft. Wayne, Ind., July 7, 1951; s. Lawrence Caldwell and Barbara Jean (Stilwell) D.; m. Janice Louise Hoffman, Apr. 17, 1971; children: Stephen Michael, David Allan. A.A., Mt. San Antonio Coll., 1974; B.A., Biola U., 1976; M.Div., Talbot Theol. Sem., 1980; postgrad. Fuller Theol. Sem., 1983—. Ordained to ministry Am. Bapt. Chs. in U.S.A., 1981. Assoc. pastor Whittier Hills Bapt. Ch., Whittier, Calif., 1978-80, First Bapt. Ch., Yakima, Wash., 1981-82, Northlake Bapt. Ch., Longview, Wash., 1982—; cons. David C. Cook Pub. Co., Elgin, Ill., 1981—, Farwest area Am. Bapt. Ch., Longview, 1984. Served as sgt. U.S. Army, 1968-72, Vietnam, chaplain Res. Recipient Charles Lee Feinberg award Talbot Theol. Sem., 1979. Mem. Alpha Gamma Sigma. Home: 1144 22d Ave Longview WA 98632 Office: Northlake Bapt Ch 2614 Ocean Beach Hwy Longview WA 98632

DENNISON, MARY ELIZABETH, nun, religious educator, Roman Catholic Church; b. Alton, Ill., Apr. 24, 1928; d. John Thomas and Emelie Ann (Grschwend) D.; B.S., St. Louis U., 1949; M.R.E., Loyola U., 1969; Ed.D., U. Houston, 1984. Joined Religious of the Cenacle, Roman Cath. Ch. Staff Cenacle Retreat House, Ill., Mo., Calif. and Tex., 1951-59; staff office Religious Edn., Sacramento Diocese, Calif., 1957-63, Houston Diocese, 1964-69; dir. religious edn. St. John Vianney, Houston, 1968-80; assoc. prof. U. St. Thomas, Houston, 1968—, acting dir. M.R.E. Program, 1983—. Co-author: (high sch. text) Church, 1982; Guides 1 and 2, God With Us, 1983. Contbr. articles to religious jours. Recipient Constantin award for faculty devel. U. St. Thomas, 1982. Mem. Assn. Profs. and Researchers in Religious Edn., Religious Edn. Assn., Assn. Dir. Grad. Religious Edn. Programs (treas. 1972-74), World Future Soc., Nat. Cath. Edn. Assn. Home: Cenacle Retreat House 420 N Kirkwood St Houston TX 77079 Office: U St Thomas 3812 Montrose St Houston TX 77006

DENNY, JOHN LAWRENCE, priest, Episcopal Church; b. Cambridge, Ohio, May 4, 1920; s. Silas Webster and Artlissa (Erven) D.; m. Jane Irene Stewart, Feb. 15, 1958. Student, Univ. of South, 1947-49, NYU, 1950-51; Cert. Theology, Gen. Theol. Sem., 1958. Ordained priest, 1958. Lay asst. chaplain Rockland State Hosp., Orangeburg, N.Y., 1946-47; vicar Ch. of Good Shepherd, Ringwood, N.J., 1957-60, Ch. of Transfiguration, Towaco, N.J., 1958-61; rector Christ Episcopal Ch., Teaneck, N.J., 1961-85, rector emeritus, 1985—; lay analyst, counselor, 1961—; exec. dir. Inst. Christian Dynamics, Hackensack, N.J., 1978—; trustee Teaneck Scholarship Fund, 1984—; commn. mem. Communications com. Episcopal Diocese of Newark, 1981—; founder, priest Anglican/Roman Catholic Covenanted Parishes, 1978. Author: The Demon Makers, 1984. Contbr. articles to profl. jours. Bd. dirs. Teaneck Community Chest, 1963-66; trustee Bergenstage Prof. Theatre, 1978-83; chaplain Nat. Air Service Post 501, Am. Legion, 1971-82; pres. Teaneck Clergy Assn., 1966-67. Served to 2d lt. USAAF, 1942-46. Mem. Delta Tau Delta. Clubs: Shattemuc Yacht, White Beeches Country. Home: 321 Prospect Ave Hackensack NJ 07601

DENNY, ROBERT STANLEY, religious orgn. exec., Baptist World Alliance; b. Somerset, Ky., July 23, 1914; s. Arny Sherman and Ada (Thurston) D.; B.S. in Commerce, U. Ky., 1937, LL.B., 1939, J.D., 1970; H.H.D., Georgetown Coll., 1961; m. Mary Gunn Webb, 1939 (dec. Jan. 1959); children—Robert S., Allie Webb, Julia Gunn; m. 2d, Jane Ray Bean, Dec. 19, 1959. Dir., Baptist Student Union, La. State U., 1939-41; dir. religious activities Baylor U., 1941-45; staff mem. Nat. Studen Ministries, So. Baptist Conv., Nashville, 1945-55; asso. sec. Baptist World Alliance, Washington, 1956-69, gen. sec., 1969—. Office: 1628 16th St NW Washington DC 20009

DENSMAN, JAMES L., minister, Southern Baptist Convention; b. Marlin, Tex., Dec. 4, 1948; s. Lloyd W. Densman and Avalyn J. (Saxon) Densman Williams; m. Elaine R Burt, Apr. 30, 1972; children: Sarah, Joshua, Mary. B.A., Baylor U., 1973; M.A., Southwestern Bapt. Theol. Sem., Ft. Worth, 1976; postgrad. Luther Rice Sem., Jacksonville, Fla. Ordained to ministry So. Bapt. Conv., 1970; pastor Navarro Mills Bapt. Ch., Purdon, Tex., 1972-76. Eastwood Bapt. Ch., Gatesville, Tex., 1976-77, 1st Bapt. Ch., Smithville, Tex., 1977-79, 1st Bapt. Ch., Groesbeck, Tex., 1979—. Chmn. Smithville Salvation Army, 1977, Groesbeck Salvation Army, 1977-83. Republican. Lodges: Odd Fellows, Lions. Office: 1st Bapt Ch PO Box 388 406 N Ellis St Groesbeck TX 76642

DENTON, DONALD D., minister, Presbyterian Church in the U.S.; b. Rockford, Ill., Mar. 19, 1948; s. Donald D. and Marjorie Lois (Bell) D.; m. Elisabeth Ann Beckon, Jan. 23, 1971; children: Matthew James, Andrew William, Luke Allen. B.A. magna cum laude, Trinity Coll., Deerfield, Ill., 1973; M.Div., McCormick Theol. Sem., Chgo., 1978. Ordained to ministry Presbyn. Ch. in the U.S., 1979. Intern LaSalle St. Ch., Chgo., 1973-76; sec. Sem. Consortium for Urban Pastoral Edn., Chgo., 1976-77; sem. asst. Lincoln Park Presbyn. Ch., Chgo., 1977-78; minister Cutler Presbyn Ch., Ind., 1978-84; pastoral counselor Buchanan Counseling Ctr., Indpls., 1984—; chmn. hunger com. Synod of Lincoln Trails, Indpls., 1981—; chmn. hunger task force Wabash Valley Presbytery, West Lafayette, Ind., 1981-84; chmn. dept. peace and justice Ind. Council Churches, Indpls., 1985-87. Contbr. articles to religious publs. Author simulation game Charlottesville 1980, 1983. Parish assoc. Wabash Valley Hosp-Mental Health Ctr., West Lafayette, 1979-84; founder Carroll County Food Pantry, Flora, Ind., 1981. Served with USMC, 1966-69, Vietnam. Mem. Assn. Religious Values in Counseling, Am. Assn. Counseling and Devel., Presbyn. Hist. Soc., Presbyn. Health Edn. and Welfare Assn., Am. Assn. Pastoral Counselors, Assn. Clin. Pastoral Edn. Home: 3038 W Hiland Dr Indianapolis IN 46268

DENTON, PRESTON MARVIN, minister, So. Baptist Conv.; b. Big Spring, Tex., July 21, 1923; s. Madison Mitchell and Mabel May (Hill) D.; B.A., Hardin-Simmons Coll., Abilene, Tex., 1949; B.D., Southwestern Bapt. Theol. Sem., Ft. Worth, 1952; m. Mildred Louise Sullivan, Mar. 28, 1948; children—David Preston, Mary Mildred, Philip Charles, Sharon Kay, James Ray. Ordained to ministry, 1944; pastor chs. in Tex. and Ill., 1943-45, 49-56; chaplain AUS, 1945-46; missionary Westfield Bapt. Assn., 1956-58; area missionary, Rockford, Ill., 1958-63; met. missionary Chgo. Met. Bapt. Assn., 1963-73; dir. Billy Graham Crusade, 1970-71; dir. missions Lakeland Bapt. Assn., Milw., 1973-76; exec. sec. St. Louis Bapt. Assn., 1976—. Trustee Milw. Inst. Theology, 1974-76. Treas. Greater Milw. Bi-Racial Exec. Com., 1974-76; bd. dirs. Chgo. Council Appalachia, 1965-73, Ill. Temperance League, 1958-62. Home: 828 Clayton Rd Ballwin Saint Louis MO 63011 Office: 3526 Washington Blvd Saint Louis MO 63103

DEPAUW, GOMMAR ALBERT, priest, educator, Roman Catholic Church; b. Stekene, Belgium, Oct. 11, 1918; s. Désiré Marie and Anna Philomena (Van Overloop) DeP.; J.C.B., Louvain U., 1943, J.C.L., 1945; J.C.D., Cath. U. Am., 1953. Ordained priest Roman Catholic Ch., 1942. Parish priest, Ghent, Belgium, 1945-49, N.Y.C., 1949-52; prof. theology, canon law, acad. dean Mt. St. Mary's Sem., Emmitsburg, Md., 1953-66; founder, pres. Cath. Traditionalist Movement, N.Y.C., 1964—. Theol. adviser, procurator 2d Vatican Ecumenical Council, Rome, 1962-65; producer Latin Radio Mass, 1970—. Mem. Internat. Platform Assn., Cath. Theol. Soc., Canon Law Soc., Univ. Profs. for Acad. Order, Am. Cath. Philos. Assn. Author: The Educational Rights of the Church, 1953; The Traditional Roman Catholic Mass, 1977; Weighed and Found Wanting, 1983. Editor: Sounds of Truth and Tradition, 1953—; Quote . . . Unquote, 1980—. Home: 210 Maple Ave Westbury NY 11590 Office: Pan Am Bldg 200 Park Ave New York NY 10017

DEPPA, DENNIS ERNEST, minister, Ch. of Christ; b. Foley, Minn., June 10, 1940; s. Bernard Frank and Kathryn Pauline (Katchmarzenski) D.; B.S., Pacific Christian Coll., 1969; m. Delores Anne Dray, May 21, 1960. Ordained to ministry, 1969; pastor Ronneby (Minn.) Ch. of Christ, 1966, Victory Center Ch. of Christ, North Hollywood, Calif., 1969-71, Faith Christian Ch., Van Nuys, Calif., 1971-74, Valley Christian Ch., Arleta, Calif., 1974-75, Knollwood Ch. of Christ, St. Louis Park, Minn., 1975—; mem. St. Louis Park Police Chaplincy. Mem. St. Paul Ministerial Assn. (pres. 1976—). Home: 2744 Idaho Ave S Saint Louis Park MN 55426 Office: 3639 Quebec Ave S Saint Louis Park MN 55426

DERBY, ROGER SHERMAN, minister, Episcopal Church; b. Bklyn., Mar. 15, 1935; s. Irving Marsh and Helen Georgia (Bennett) D.; m. Nancy Elizabeth Tyner, Jan. 7, 1961; children: Sarah Bennett, Martha Elizabeth. B.A., Hamilton Coll., 1957; B.D., Episcopal Div. Sch., 1960. Ordained priest Episcopal Ch., 1961. Curate Church Ch., Pittsford, N.Y., 1960-62; vicar St. Paul's Ch., Angelica, N.Y. and St. Andrew's Ch., Friendship, N.Y., 1962-63; rector Ch. of Epiphany, Gates, N.Y., 1963-69; rector Calvary Ch., Utica, N.Y.,

1969-74, All Saints Ch., Pontiac, Mich., 1974—; dir. Camp Davenport Phelps, Diocese of Rochester, 1963-68; dean Oakland Convocation, Diocese of Mich., 1980-82, pres. standing com., 1980, mem. Commn. on Ministry, 1983—; treas. Pontiac Ecumenical Ministry, 1976. Founder, advisor Cornhill People United, Utica, 1971; mem. United Way Planning Commn., Pontiac, 1981; trustee Women's Survival Ctr., Pontiac, 1984. Va. Theol. Sem. fellow, 1984. Lodge: Rotary. Home: 34 Niagara Pontiac MI 48053 Office: All Saints Episcopal Church PO Box 357 Pontiac MI 48056

DEREA, PHILIP, priest, Roman Catholic Church; b. Roseto, Pa., Mar. 26, 1942; s. Philip and Irene Elizabeth (Bajan) DeR. B.S. in Philosophy, Sacred Heart Sem., Shelby, Ohio, 1965, M.Div., 1969. Ordained priest Roman Cath. Ch., 1968. Devel. dir. Missionaries of Sacred Heart, Aurora, Ill., 1969-76, vocation and communications dir., Center Valley, Pa., 1976-79; assoc. pastor Our Lady of Guadalupe, Cali, Colombia, 1979-80; chaplain Sacred Heart Hosp., Allentown, Pa., 1980-81; nat. dir. Missionary Vehicle Assn., Washington, 1981—; canon Cathedral of La Paz, Bolivia, 1985—; mem. Nat. Cath. Devel. Conf., Hempstead, N.Y., 1969—. Mem. Nat. Assn. Cath. Chaplains, Wings of Hope. Democrat. Lodge: K.C. (3d and 4th deg.). Address: 1326 Perry St NE Washington DC 20017

DE ROO, REMI JOSEPH, bishop, Roman Catholic Church; b. Swan Lake, Man., Can., Feb. 24, 1924; s. Raymond Peter and Josephine Elodie (De Pape) DeR.; S.T.D., Angelicum U., Rome. With Holy Cross Parish, St. Boniface, 1952-53, 60-62; diocesan dir. Cath. Action, 1953-54; sec. to Archbishop Baudoux, 1954-56; diocesan dir. Confraternity of Christian Doctrine, 1956; v.p. English sect. Catechetical Commn., 1957; sec. Man. Cath. Conf., 1957-58; diocesan consultor, 1958-60; bishop of Victoria, B.C., 1962—. Canadian Episcopal rep. Internat. Secretariat, Apostleship of the Sea; mem. pastoral team and adminstrv. bd. Canadian Cath. Conf. of Bishops. Chairperson, Human Rights Commn. of B.C. Author: (with Douglas Roche) Man-to-Man, 1969. Office: 740 View St Victoria BC V8W 1J8 Canada

DERR, THOMAS SIEGER, educator, minister, United Ch. of Christ; b. Boston, June 18, 1931; s. Thomas Sieger and Mary Ferguson (Sebring) D.; A.B., Harvard, 1953; B.D., Union Theol. Sem., 1956; Ph.D., Columbia, 1972; m. Virginia Anne Bush, June 9, 1956; children—Peter Bulkeley, Laura Seely, Mary Williams. Ordained to ministry United Ch. of Christ, 1956; asst. chaplain Stanford, 1956-59; research asso. World Council Chs., Geneva, 1961-62; asst. chaplain Smith Coll., 1963-65, prof. religion, 1965—, chmn. dept. religion, 1971-75; cons. dept. on ch. and soc. World Council Chs., 1966—, cons. commn. faith and order, 1974-75. Dir. No. Ednl. Service, Springfield, Mass., 1963-70. Danforth Found. fellow, 1961-62. Mem. Am. Soc. Christian Ethics, AAUP. Author: Ecology and Human Liberation, 1973; Ecology and Human Need, 1975; The Political Thought of the Ecumenical Movement, 1900-1939, 1972; also articles. Home: 72 Dryads Green Northampton MA 01060 Office: Smith Coll Northampton MA 01060

DERRICKSON, DONALD LEE, minister, Ch. of God in Christ; b. Nashville, Jan. 25, 1929; s. Curry and Hattie Mae (Graves) D.; D.D. (hon.), Marantha Bible Sem., 1972; m. Velma Ree Ferrell, Aug. 30, 1954 (dec.); children: Donald Lee, Debra M., Kenneth R., Stacy E.; m. Ruth M. Davis, May 18, 1984. Ordained elder, 1957; minister Faith Temple Ch., Livingston, Tenn., 1961-62, Faith Temple, Nashville, 1962-66, Algood (Tenn.) Ch., 1965-66, Rock Temple Ch. God in Christ, Knoxville, 1966—. Jurisdictional sec. State Exec. Bd. Ch. of God in Christ, Nashville, 1958-74, fin. sec., 1969-79, sec. Tenn. Ordination Bd., 1967—; 2d adminstrv. asst. to jurisdictional bishop, Knoxville, 1974-81, 1st adminstrv. asst., 1981-83. Home: 5108 Skyline Dr Knoxville TN 37914 Office: 814 Maria Ave Knoxville TN 37912

DE SALVO, RAPHAEL, abbot, Roman Catholic Ch.; b. Center Ridge, Ark., Oct. 7, 1919; s. Anthony Luke and Josephine (Rossi) DeS.; A.B., Subiaco Coll. and Sem., 1942; S.T.L., Cath. U. Am., 1946, S.T.D., 1948. Joined Order St. Benedict; ordained priest, 1945; novice master, New Subiaco Abbey, Subiaco, Ark., 1960-63, prior, 1968-74, abbot, 1974—; rector Subiaco Sem., 1948-63; missionary, Nigeria, 1963-67; pastor, Paris, Ark., 1968. Home and Office: New Subiaco Abbey Subiaco AR 72865

DES GROSEILLERS, LIONEL MARIE, priest, Roman Catholic Church; b. Montreal, Que., Can., Oct. 16, 1931; s. Georges and Germaine (Fournier) DesG. B.A., Laval U., Que., Can., 1954; B. in Pegagogy, Montreal U., 1958; B. in Theology, Inst. de Pastorale, Montreal, Can., 1974. Ordained priest Roman Catholic Ch., 1957. Tchr. of tongues Montfort Sem., Papineauville, Que., 1958-60, Coll. Notre Dame de Lourdes, Port-de-Paix, Haiti, 1960-66, Ecole Louis-Joseph Papineau, Que., 1967-73; animator Montfort Shrine, Montreal, 1974-78; rector Vincent de Paul Parish, NorthBay, Ont., 1984—; missionary Montfort Fathers, Port-de-Paix, 1960-66; prof. Polyvalente Papineau, Que., 1967-73; shrine animator Queen of all Hearts, Montreal, 1974-78; vice rector Our Lady of Lourdes, Vanier, Ont., 1978—. Mem. Mouvement Couple et Famille (animateur diocesain). Home: 1265 Wyld St North Bay ON P1B 2A9 Canada Office: Paroisse Saint Vincent de Paul North Bay ON P1B 2A9 Canada

DESHAY, SAMUEL LEE, missionary physician, minister, Seventh-day Adventists; b. Columbus, Ohio, Jan. 1, 1933; s. William Henry and Aleatha Delilah (Brantley) D.; m. Bernice Anita Moore, Feb. 28, 1960; children: Joy Lynette, Teymi Elise. B.A. in Chemistry, Union Coll., 1954; M.D., Loma Linda U., 1959, M.P.H., 1974; M.A., Andrews U., 1957; D.Min., Howard U., 1982. Ordained to ministry Seventh-day Adventists, 1966. Health dir. West African Seventh-day Adventists, Accra, Ghana, 1966-73, Seventh-day Adventists World Ch., Washington, 1976-80, assoc. dir. health and temperance, 1980-84, Pan African health services dir., Nairobi, Kenya, 1984—; bd. dirs. Loma Linda U., Calif., 1977-80, Christian Med. Coll., Vellore, India, 1978-84, Montemorelos U., Mexico, 1980-84. Pres. Pan African Devel. Corp., Washington, 1982—. Author/editor: Adventist and Genetic Engineering; editor Health and Happiness, 1968. Contbr. articles to religious and secular jours. Mem. Am. Temperance Soc., Washington, 1976—, Nat. Council Internat. Health, Washington, 1981—. Named Alumnus of Yr., Loma Linda U., 1972. Mem. Internat. Health and Temperance Assn. (bd. dirs. 1982—). Home: 6360 Guilford Rd Clarksville MD 21029 Office: Pan African Devel Corp 4801 Massachusetts Ave NW Suite 400 Washington DC 20016

DESHAY, WILLIAM LESLIE, minister, Seventh-day Adventists; b. Columbus, Ohio, Sept. 23, 1930; s. William Henry Dewey and Aleatha Delilah (Brantley) DeS.; m. Corinne Fauntleroy, Oct. 25, 1959; children: William Leslie, Mark Antoine. B.A. in Theology, Oakwood Coll., 1952; M.S. in Counseling Psychology, A&M U., Normal, Ala., 1971; Ph.D. in Counseling, Ohio State U., 1975. Ordained to ministry Seventh-day Adventists, 1959. Pastor Allegheny Conf. Seventh-day Adventists, 1954-64, Dupont Park Ch., Washington, 1965-69; chaplain, counselor adminstr. Oakwood Coll., Huntsville, Ala., 1969-72; adminstr. So. Calif. Conf. Seventh-day Adventists, Glendale, 1976—, dir. black affairs, 1976—, exec. com., 1976—; trustee So. Calif. Conf. Assn., Glendale, 1976—, minority groups com. Pacific Union Conf., 1976—; del. youth congress Columbia Union Conf., Paris, 1951. Named hon. citizen State of Tenn., 1977; recipient Century Soul award South Central Conf., Huntsville, 1972. Democrat. Home: 18951 Milmore Ave Carson CA 90746 Office: Southern Calif Conf Seventh-Day Adventists 1535 E Chevy Chase Dr Glendale CA 91206

DESIMONE, LOUIS A. See *Who's Who in America*, 43rd edition.

DESJARDINS, GEORGE ALBERT, priest, Roman Catholic Church; b. Dover, N.H., Nov. 12, 1932; s. Albert George and Albertine G. (Morin) D. B.A., St. Bonaventure U., 1955; postgrad. Christ the King Sem., 1955-59. Ordained priest, Roman Cath. Ch., 1959. Assoc. pastor St. Anthony Ch., Manchester, N.H., 1959-66, Sacred Heart Ch., Lebanon, N.H., 1966-68, St. John the Baptist, Manchester, 1968-73; pastor Holy Redeemer Ch., West Lebanon, 1973-74, Sacred Heart Ch., Manchester, 1974—; exec. sec. Diocesan Liturgical Com., Manchester, 1962-75; defender of the marriage bond Diocesan Tribunal, Manchester, 1973-80. Home and Office: Sacred Heart Ch 223 S Main St Manchester NH 03102

DESMARAIS, MARCEL MARIE, priest; b. Montreal, Que., Can., Apr. 6, 1908; s. Charles and Rose Anna (Mayer) D. B.A., U. Montreal, 1927, Cert. in Physics, Chemistry and Natural Scis., 1927; Th.D., Angelicum, Rome, 1934; Ph.D., Institut Catholique, Paris, 1935; Certificate in French Lit., English Lit. and Psychology, Sorbonne, Paris, 1938. Ordained priest Roman Cath. Ch., 1932. Prof. psychology Dominicans, Ottawa, Ont., Can., 1939-40; preacher on radio and TV Canadian networks, 1940—. Author: L'Amour a l'age Atomique, 1950, La Vie En Rose, 1951, Capsules D'Optimisme, 1954, La Clinique du Coeur, numerous others. Home: 5375 Ave Notre Dame De Grace Montreal PQ H4A 1L2 Canada

DESPATIE, ROGER, bishop, Roman Catholic Church; b. Sudbury, Ont., Can., Apr. 12, 1927. Ordained priest, 1952; titular bishop of Usinaza and aux. bishop of Sault Ste. Marie (Can.), 1968-73; bishop of Hearst (Ont.), 1973—. Address: CP 1330 Hearst ON P0L 1N0 Canada*

DETERDING, PAUL E., minister, Lutheran Church-Missouri Synod; b. Jacksonville, Ill., Feb. 19, 1953; s. George H. and Velda J. (Fricke) D. B.A., Concordia Sr. Coll., Ft. Wayne, Ind., 1975; M.Div., Concordia Sem., St. Louis, 1978, S.T.M., 1979, Th.D., 1981. Ordained to ministry Luth. Ch.-Mo. Synod, 1981. Pastor, Our Savior Luth. Ch., Sattelite Beach, Fla., 1981—. Author: Echoes of Pauline Concepts in the Speech at Antioch, 1980.

DETJE, DAVID, educational administrator, Roman Catholic Church; b. N.Y.C., Aug. 6, 1936; s. Henry John and Cecilia Caroline (Gutberlet) D. B.A., Cath. U. Am., 1959; M.A., Rensselaer Poly. Inst., 1968; Cert. in Not for Profit Mgmt., Columbia U., 1978. Ordained Brother, Roman Cath. Ch., 1954. Vice-prin. Mater Christi High Sch., Astoria, N.Y., 1967-70, prin., 1970-72; exec. dir. Martin De Porres Community Service Ctr., L.I., 1972-78; provincial L.I.-New Eng. Province, Bros. of the Christian Schs., Narragansett, R.I., 1978-84; pres., headmaster LaSalle Mil. Acad., Oakdale, N.Y., 1984—; del. for superior gen. to Ethiopia, Bros. of the Christian Schs., Rome, Italy, 1979—, mem. provincial council Bros. of the Christian Schs., Narragansett, R.I., 1976—. Contbr. articles to profl. jours. Bd. dirs. Steinway Child and Family Devel. Ctr., Astoria, N.Y. Am. Assn. Supervision and Curriculum Devel., Nat. Assn. Secondary Sch. Prins., Ind. Sch. Mgmt.

DETTERLINE, MILTON ELMER, JR., minister, United Church Christ; b. Bethlehem, Pa., Nov. 16, 1929; s. Milton E. and Mary Elizabeth (Ault) D.; m. Elaine Hughes; children: James Lee, Jon Scott, Peter Kirk. B.A., Moravian Coll., 1951; M.Div., Drew U., 1954; postgrad. (pastoral fellow) Yale, 1968. Ordained to ministry United Ch. Christ, 1954; pastor, Pottsville, Pa., 1954-57, Allentown, Pa., 1957-61, Tamaqua, Pa., 1961-68, St. Peters, Pa., 1974—. Chaplain, adminstr. Ursinus Coll., Collegeville, Pa., 1969-74; chaplain Holland-Am. Line Cruises, 1973—; exec. dir. Walden III Communications, 1973—; moderator Schuylkill Assn. Pa., 1965-67; bd. dirs. Pa. S.E. Conf., 1968-72; sec. Collegeville Summer Assembly, 1969-74; del. Gen. Synod del. Pa. Faith and Order Confs., 1967, 69. Bd. dirs. Schuylkill County Welfare, 1963-68, Appalachian Trail council Boy Scouts Am., 1964-68, Tamaqua Indsl. Devel. Enterprise, 1967-69, Tamaque C. of C., 1963-69, Pottstown Area Bicentennial Commn., 1976. Named Man of Year, Tamaqua Area C. of C., 1968. Mem. St. Peters Village Mchts. Assn., Ursinus Assn. Editor: Decisions in Philosophy of Religion, 1975; editor Religious and Theol. Abstracts, 1967-71; contbr. articles to religious jours. Home: Box 156 Saint Peters PA 19470

DEUSCHLE, EDWIN JOHN, minister, Southern Baptist Convention; b. Pitts., Sept. 24, 1946; s. Edwin Bryant and Dorothy Cecilia (Richardson) D.; m. Rita Lynn Fraiser, Aug. 28, 1967; children: Edwin Bryant II, Jennifer Ann, Holly Maria. B.S. in Phys. Edn., U. Miss., 1969; M.Div., S.W. Bapt. Theol. Sem., 1974; D.Ministry, New Orleans Bapt. Theol. Sem., 1983. Ordained to ministry Calvary Bapt. Ch., 1974. Pastor Eastside Bapt. Ch., Marietta, Okla., 1974-75, Morgan Chapel Bapt. Ch., Sturgis, Miss., 1975-79, Trinity Bapt. Ch., Fulton, Miss., 1979—; state bd. mem. Miss. Bapt. Conv. Bd., Jackson, 1982—. Served to 1st lt. U.S. Army, 1969-71. Decorated Air medal. Mem. Itawamba County Bapt. Assn. (moderator), Am. Legion. Home: PO Box 638 Fulton MS 38843 Office: Trinity Bapt Ch Hwy 25S and Wiygul St PO Box 638 Fulton MS 38843

DEVIK, RUDOLF, priest, Episcopal Church; b. Tacoma, Wash., Nov. 12, 1923; s. Toralf and Ann (Stormanns) D.; m. Claire Van Sant, Aug. 12, 1945; children: Susan, Jeffry, Karin, Timothy, Mary Claire. B.S., Northwestern U., 1945; M.Div., Seabury-Western U., 1953. Ordained priest Episc. Ch., 1953. Rector, St. Mark's Parish, Des Moines, Iowa, 1953-56; canon missioner Diocese of Olympia, Seattle, 1956-64, archdeacon, v.p., 1964-72; rector Grace Ch., Lawrence, Mass., 1974—. Pres., chief exec. office Consultation/Search Inc., Cambridge, Mass., 1972-74. Editor Olympia Churchman, 1959. Contbr. articles to profl. jours. Pres. bd. Friends of Youth, Seattle, 1968-72; pres., bd. dirs. Internat. Inst., Lawrence, Mass., 1976-82; exec. com., bd. dirs. Lawrence Strategy Inc., 1980—; trustee Cheswick Ctr., Boston, 1971-73. Served to lt. col. USAR, 1943-83, PTO. Named Canon of Honor, Diocese of Olympia, 1972. Mem. Clericus of Boston. Democrat. Clubs: Hamblet. Home: 46 Olive St Metuan MA 01844 Office: Grace Ch PO Box 467 Lawrence MA 01842

DEVINE, MARIETTA, nun, center adminstr., retreat dir., Roman Cath. Ch.; b. N.Y.C., Oct. 6, 1926; d. John Henry and Catherine Virginia (McNamara) D.; B.A., Coll. New Rochelle (N.Y.), 1948; certificate journalism Marquette U., Milw., 1961; M.S. in Math. Edn., Dominican Coll., San Rafael, Calif., 1970. Joined Ursuline Order, 1949; prin. St. Rose Sch., Santa Rosa, Calif., 1966-69; prin. superior St. Malachys Sch., Los Angeles, 1969-72; superior, adminstr., retreat directress, hon. pres. bd. Ursuline Centre, Great Falls, Mont., 1972—. Sec. ecumenical commn. Great Falls Diocese; treas. 3-sister team Diocesan Sisters Senate; mem. city-wide pastoral commn., Great Falls, 1975—. Mem. core group Aglow Womens' Fellowship. Recipient certificate of Merit in Journalism Marquette, Wall St. Jour., 1961. Cons. and writer ednl. program and handbook. Home and Office: Ursuline Centre 2300 Central Ave Great Falls MT 59401

DEVITT, THOMAS KIRKLAND, minister, Christian Church (Disciples of Christ); b. Birmingham, Mich., June 25, 1939; s. Charles Samuel and Florence Gertrude (Ellis) Kiltz D.; m. Jean Mary Teggerdine, Dec. 22, 1956; children: Victoria Lynn, Douglas T.K., Lisa Rose.

.S., Mich. State U., 1966; M.Div., Sch. of Theology, Claremont, Calif., 1977, D.Ministry, 1978. Ordained to ministry Christian Ch., 1977. Student minister Ingelside Christian Ch., Phoenix, 1975-76; student assoc. First Christian Ch., Pomona, Calif., 1976-78; minister First Christian Ch., Woodbine, Iowa, 1978-80, First Christian Ch., Helena, Mont., 1980—; chmn. Ch. in Soc. Com., Mont. regional Christian Ch., 1983—; mem. regional bd. Christian Ch. in Mont., 1980—; mem. gen. bd. Christian Ch. in U.S. and Can., 1982—, mem. gen. adminstrv. com., 1983—; vice moderator Christian Ch. in Mont., 1985—. Served to lt. col. Mont. N.G., 1957—. Mem. Helena C. of C. (mil. affairs com. 1982—), Helena Ministerial Assn. (pres. 1984). Democrat. Lodge: Kiwanis (v.p. 1978-80). Home: 311 Power St Helena MT 59601 Office: First Christian Ch 311 Power St Helena MT 59601

DEVRIES, KIM THOMAS, minister, Lutheran Church-Missouri Synod; b. Cherokee, Iowa, Apr. 25, 1950; s. Richard Philip and Jessie Elizabeth (Elder) DeV.; m. Cathy Lyn Domann, July 25, 1976; children: Thomas, Timothy. A.A., Concordia Jr. Coll., Austin, Tex., 1970; B.A. with honors, Concordia Sr. Coll., Ft. Wayne, Ind., 1972; M.Div. with honors, Concordia Sem., St. Louis, 1976. Ordained to ministry Luth. Ch., 1976. Pastor, Faith Luth. Ch., Greenville, Miss., 1976-80, Good Shepherd Luth. Ch., Cleveland, Miss., 1976-80, St. Michael Luth. Ch., Houston, 1980-84, Mt. Calvary Luth. Ch., San Antonio, 1984—; v.p. Houston area council Luth. Ch.-Mo. Synod, 1982-84; pastoral adviser Bayou zone Women's Missionary League, Houston, 1983-84. Editor newsletter Dunbarton Oaks Civic Club, Houston, 1983-84. Contbr. articles to religious publs. Home: 552 Crosswinds St San Antonio TX 78239 Office: Mt Calvary Luth Ch 308 Mt Calvary St San Antonio TX 78209

DEWEESE, CHARLES WILLIAM, minister, editorial adminstr., educator, So. Bapt. Conv.; b. Asheville, N.C., Oct. 7, 1944; s. James Philip and Faye (Warren) D.; B.A., Mars Hill (N.C.) Coll., 1967; M.Div., So. Bapt. Theol. Sem., 1970, Ph.D., 1973; m. Mary Jane Eisenhauer, July 29, 1967; 1 dau., Dana Marie. Ordained to ministry, 1968; pastor Mt. Pleasant Bapt. Ch., Madison, Ind., 1968-69, Friendship Bapt. Ch., Oakland, Ky., 1971-73; asst. dir. editorial and research services Hist. Commn. So. Bapt. Conv., Nashville, 1973-76, dir. editorial services, 1976—; instr. sem. extension dept. So. Bapt. Conv., 1974—. Recipient Davis C. Woolley Meml. award Hist. Commn. So. Bapt. Conv., 1972. Author: (with A. Ronald Tonks) Faith, Stars, and Stripes, 1976; contbr. articles and book revs. to denominational publs. Home: 309 Ash Grove Ct Nashville TN 37211

DEWIRE, NORMAN (NED) EDWARD, minister, United Meth. Ch.; b. Cin., Mar. 5, 1936; s. Ormsby and Lucille (Binder) D.; B.S. in Edn. with honors, Ohio U., 1958; M.Div. with honors, Boston U., 1962; D.Div., Adrian Coll., 1976; D.Min., McCormick Theol. Sem., 1979; m. Shirley Jean Woodman, June 16, 1957; children: Cathy Lynn, Deborah Kay. Ordained to ministry United Methodist Ch., 1962; exec. dir. Joint Strategy and Action Com., 1969-75; exec. sec. bd. missions and ch. extension Detroit conf. United Methodist Ch., 1967-69; pastoral staff Central Methodist Ch., Detroit, 1962-67; pastor chs., Charlton City, Mass., 1958-62, Jacksonville Circuit, Athens County, Ohio, 1957-58; chair Montclair (N.J.) Inter-ch. Com., 1972-73; chair social and internat. affairs com., exec. com. World Meth. Council; gen. sec. Gen. Council on Ministries United Meth. Ch., 1975—; mem., officer United Meth. and Pan Meth. Bicentennial; Chairperson organizing bd. Offenders Aid Restoration-U.S.A., 1973-74, Religious Leaders of N.J. for McGovern-Shriver, 1972. Bd. dirs. United Theol. Sem., Otterbein Home; governing bd. Nat. Council Chs. of Christ; v.p., chair fin. com. Ch. World Service Bd., Inc. Mem. Am. Mgmt. Assn., Kappa Delta Pi. Contbr. chpts. to books; interpreter Editorial Adv. Group. Home: 34 W Dixon Ave Dayton OH 45419 Office: 601 W Riverview Av Dayton OH 45406

DE WITT, JESSE R., bishop, United Methodist Ch.; b. Detroit, Dec. 5, 1918; s. Jesse A. and Bessie G. (Mainzinger) DeW.; B.A., Wayne State U.; B.D., Garrett Theol. Sem.; D.D. (hon.), Adrian Coll., Lakeland Coll.; m. Annamary Horner, Apr. 19, 1941; children—Donna Lee (Mrs. William Wegryn), Darla Jean (Mrs. William Inman). Ordained deacon United Methodist Ch., 1945, elder, 1948; minister chs., Detroit, 1946-52, Oak Park, Mich., 1952-58; exec. sec. Bd. Missions, Detroit Conf., 1958-67; dist. supt. Detroit West Dist., 1967-70; asst. gen. sec., sect. ch. extension, nat. div. Bd. Missions, 1970-72, del. Gen. Conf., 1964, 66, 68, 70, 72, 76, head ministerial dels. of Detroit Conf. delegation, 1968, 70, 72; chmn., dean Mid-West Conf. Christian World Mission; mem. Task Force on Ch. Devel., chmn. new towns work group; past mem. Bd. Ch. and Soc., Emerging Social Issues, Role and Status of Women; resident bishop Wis. area, 1972-80; bishop Chgo. area, 1980—. Mem. Task Force Urban Network, North Central Jurisdiction; pres. North Central Jurisdiction Coll. Bishops; pres. nat. div. Gen. Bd. Global Ministries; chmn. pastoral concerns com., overseas visitation com. Council Bishops; head Meth. delegation Consultation Ch. Union, also mem. exec. com.; mem. steering com. Nat. Consultation Equitable Salaries. Bd. dirs. North Central Coll., Naperville, Ill., Evergreen Manor, Oshkosh, Wis., Meth. Manor West Allis, Wis., Meth. Hosp., Madison, Wis., Wis. United Meth. Found., Project Equality. Address: 77 W Washington St Suite 1806 Chicago IL 60602

DEWITT, LEONARD WALTER, minister, Missionary Church, Inc.; b. Galahad, Alta., Can., Nov. 17, 1937; came to U.S., 1957; s. Paul W. and Clara (Reniger) DeW.; m. Joyce Marie DeWitt, Sept. 5, 1964; children by previous marriage: Pamela J., Sheldon B. B.S.L., Mt. View Bible Coll., 1960; D.D. (hon.), Azusa Pacific U., 1981; D.Humanities Bethel Coll., 1982. Ordained to ministry, 1963. Pastor, Missionary Ch., Yakima, Wash., 1960-64, Wapato, Wash., 1964-71, Ventura, Calif., 1971-81; pres. Missionary Ch., Inc., Ft. Wayne, Ind., 1981—; trustee Ft. Wayne Bible Ch., 1981—; bd. adminstrn. Nat. Assn. Evangelicals, Wheaton, Ill., 1981—; trustee Asbury Theol. Sem., 1983—, Bethel Coll., 1981—. Author (periodical): Emphasis, 1981—. Home: 5411 Tomahawk Trail Fort Wayne IN 46804 Office: Missionary Church Inc 3901 S Wayne Ave Fort Wayne IN 46807

DEWOLFE, WILLIAM ARTHUR, minister, church official, Unitarian Universalist Association; b. Boston, Aug. 21, 1927; s. John Campbell and Miriam Elbridge (Ford) DeW.; m. Barbara Louise Mosher, Sept. 10, 1949; children: Mark Edward, Richard Scott, Paul Howard. B.A., Tufts Coll., 1950; B.Th., Harvard U., 1953; M.Ed., Springfield Coll., 1964. Ordained to ministry Unitarian Universalist Association, 1952. Minister, 1st Universalist Ch., Wakefield, Mass., 1953-55, Stoughton, Mass., 1956-60, Unitarian Universalist Ch., Springfield, Mass., 1960-64, 1st Unitarian Ch., San Antonio, 1964-70, 1st Unitarian Ch., St. Louis, 1970-73; interdist. rep. Unitarian Universalist Assn., Berea, Ohio, 1973—; pres. Mass. Universalist Conv., 1958-61. Bd. dirs. ACLU, N.Y.C., 1968-70; pres. Tex. Civil Liberties Union, Austin, 1967-70; pres. San Antonio Civil Liberties Union, 1965-67; v.p. Project Equality of South Tex., 1966-70; pres. Universalist Hist. Soc., Medford, Mass., 1958-63. Served with U.S. Army, 1945-47. Mem. Unitarian Universalist Ministers Assn. (trustee 1981-83), Liberal Religious Edn. Dirs. Assn. Democrat. Home: 200 Meadow Circle Berea OH 44017 Office: Unitarian Universalist Assn 16 Beacon St Boston MA 02108

DEYNEKA, PETER, JR., religious association executive; b. Chgo., Sept. 13, 1931; s. Peter and Vera (Demidovich) D.; m. Anita Marson, June 14, 1968. B.A. in Bibl. Lit., Wheaton Coll., 1953; M.Div., No. Bapt. Sem., 1957. Missionary, Slavic Gospel Assn., Ecuador, Argentina, 1961, 62-63; dir. Russian Bible Inst., Buenos Aires, Brazil, 1962-63; missionary/chaplain SGA/U.S. Army, Seoul, Republic of Korea, 1963-65; asst. dir. Slavic Gospel Assn., Chgo., 1966-74, gen. dir., Wheaton, Ill., 1975—; bd. elders Coll. Ch., Wheaton, 1983-85; guest lectr. Fuller Theol. Sem., summer 1984, Wheaton Coll. Grad. Sch., 1984; guest speaker TV and radio programs. Co-author: A Song in Siberia, 1977; Peter Dynamite, 1975; Christians in the Shadow of the Kremlin, 1974. Cons. on religion in USSR & EE, Billy Graham Assn., Trans World Radio, others; cons. in field. Mem. Interdenominational Fgn. Mission Assn. (dir.), S. Am. Crusades (dir.), Soc. for Study of Religion and Communism (dir. 1979-81), Romanian Missionary Soc. (dir.), Soc. for Central Asian Nationalities (council advisors). Home: 1263 Casa Solana Wheaton IL 60187 Office: Slavic Gospel Assn 139 N Washington Box 1122 Wheaton IL 60189

D'HEEDENE, WALTER OCTAAF, priest, Roman Catholic Church; b. Lichtervelde, Belgium, Apr. 2, 1941; came to U.S., 1968; s. Albert Gerard and Gilberthe (Vandekerckhove) D'h. M.A., Cath. U., Washington, 1971. Ordained priest Roman Cath. Ch., 1967. Asst. master, master of novices Missionhurst-Congregation of Immaculate Heart of Mary, Arlington, Va., 1969-73, provincial superior, 1981—; assoc. pastor Dolores Mission, Los Angeles, 1973-76, pastor, 1976-80; pastor St. Jude's Cath. Ch., San Antonio, 1980-81. Mem. Conf. Major Superiors of Men (chmn. mission com. Silver Spring, Md. 1983—). Home and Office: Congregation of Immaculate Heart of Mary Missionhurst-CICM 4651 N 25th St Arlington VA 22207

DICK, HENRY H., ch. ofcl., minister, Gen. Conf. Mennonite Brethren Chs.; b. Russia, June 1, 1922; s. Henry H. and Marie (Unger) D.; Th.B., Mennonite Brethren Bible Coll., 1950; m. Erica Penner, May 25, 1946; children—Janet (Mrs. Arthur Enns), Judith (Mrs. Ron Brown, James Henry. Ordained to ministry Gen. Conf. Mennonite Brethren Chs., 1950; pastor chs. Coldwater, Ont., Can., 1950-54; dir. pub. relations Tabor Coll., 1954-55; pastor ch., Lodi, Calif., 1955-57; pastor, Shafter, Calif., 1958-69; gen. sec. U.S. Conf. Mennonite Brethren Chs., 1969-72; pres. Mennonite Brethren Bibl. Sem., 1972-76; pastor Reedley Mennonite Brethren Ch., 1976—; mem. bd. reference and counsel Gen. Conf. Mennonite Brethren Chs., now vice moderator, also chmn. bd. missions and services, 1984—; mem. exec. com. Mennonite Central Com.; staff rep. Gen. Conf. Mennonite Brethren; pres. Council Mennonite Sems.; moderator Pacific dist. Conf. Mennonite Brethren Chs.; chmn. Pacific dist. Home Missions Bd.; columnist Pulsebeats in Christian Leader. Recipient Shafter C. of C. Humanitarian award, 1970, citation of merit, bd. dirs. Bibl. Sem., 1976. Mem. Nat. Assn. Evangs. (bd. adminstrn.), Calif. Tchrs. Assn. Home: 783 W Carpenter St Reedley CA 93654 Office: 4824 E Butler St Fresno CA 93727

DICKENS, TYRONE TERRY, minister, So. Baptist Conv.; b. Madison, Wis., Sept. 28, 1939; s. Raymond William and Velva Leola (Riddle) D.; B.S., Howard Payne U., 1969; M.Div., Southwestern Bapt. Theol. Sem., 1979; m. Betty Lue Stephens, Nov. 23, 1957; children: Tammie, Stephanie, Candace. Ordained to ministry, 1965; pastor So. Copperas Bapt. Ch., Comanche, Tex., 1965-66, Pecan Grove Bapt. Ch., San Saba, Tex., 1966-69, Ravenhill Bapt. Ch., San Antonio, 1969-71, Mt. Zion Bapt. Ch., Lufkin, Tex., 1969-76, Westwood Bapt. Ch., Palestine, Texas, 1977—. Pres., Ministerial Alliance Howard Payne U., 1966; chmn. missions com. Unity Assn. Lufkin, 1974, 75; pastor Camp Tomahawk, Livingston, Tex., 1974, Pineywoods Bapt. Encampment, 1975; past moderator Saline Bapt. Assn., rep. Archway to the '80's Conf.; past trustee, now pres. Pineywoods Bapt. Encampment. Chmn. citizens com. Westwood Ind. Sch. Dist., 1977. Mem. Angelina County Ministerial Alliance, PTA, Kappa Delta Pi, Gamma Beta Phi. Home: 107 Chestnut Dr Palestine TX 75801 Office: Bassett Rd Palestine TX 75801

DICKERSON, EUGENE ELLIS, minister, Ch. of God in Christ; b. nr. Bells, Tenn., May 26, 1920; s. John and Ida Mae (Chandler) D.; student Lane Coll., Jackson, Tenn., 1946-47, Lemoyne Coll., Memphis, 1947-49; B.Th., R.R. Wright Jr. Sch. Religion, Memphis, 1952; D.D., Universal Bible Inst., Alamo, Tenn., 1973; m. Martha Louise Flagg, Dec. 15, 1946; 1 dau., Gloria Jean (Mrs. Charles Rodgers). Ordained to ministry Ch. of God in Christ, 1951; asst. pastor in Bells, Jackson and Bell Eagle, Tenn., 1946-50; asst. pastor New Chicago Ch. of God in Christ, Memphis, 1959-62, pastor, 1962—; co-founder Emanuel Ch. of God, Chgo., 1956, asst. pastor, 1956; state sec. So. Ill. Ministers Alliance, 1954-56; founder, pres. Dickerson Bros. Christian Alliance Am., Inc., 1933—; founder Brotherly Love Club, 1962. Mem. Memphis and Shelby County Ministers Alliance. Address: 4852 Hornlake Rd Memphis TN 38109

DICKEY, JAMES ROSS, minister, Presbyterian Church in Canada; b. Prescott, Ont., Can., Jan. 11, 1943; s. Mervyn Eldon and Nell (Ross) D.; m. Carol Anne Edgley, May 13, 1967; children: Alice Elizabeth, Stephen Ross, Rachel Anne. B.A., Sir George Williams U., 1963; B.D., Presbyn Coll., 1967. Ordained to ministry Presbyn. Ch. in Can., 19—. Minister, Presbyn. Ch. in Can., Creston B.C., 1967-69, Wabush, Labrador, 1969-72, Thompson, Man., 1972-77; editor The Presbyn. Record, Don Mills, Ont., 1977—. Editor articles, editorials, 1972-77. Writer, performer radio programs, 1970-77. Speechwriter New Labrador Party, Wabush, 1970-72; chmn. Labrador West Integrated Sch. Bd., Wabash, 1970-72; bd. dirs. Alcohol and Drug Found., Thompson, Man., 1972-77. Mem. Can. Ch. Press (pres. 1980-81), Assoc. Ch. Press (bd. execs. 1983). Home: 3481 Ellesmere Rd Scarborough ON M1C 1H4 Canada Office: Presbyn Record 50 Wynford Dr Don Mills ON M3C 1J7 Canada

DICKEY, ROBERT CLEMENT, JR., minister, religious organization executive, Presbyterian Church in (U.S.A.); b. San Antonio, Dec. 4, 1934; s. Robert Clement and Mary Mack (Vineyard) D.; m. Patricia Gayle Bitterman, Jan. 31, 1964; children: Lori Brooks, David Clement. A.A., Schreiner Coll., 1954; B.A., Southwestern (now Rhodes) Coll., 1956; M.Div., Austin Presbyn. Theol. Sem., 1959; D.Min., McCormick Theol. Sem., 1976. Ordained to ministry, Presbyn. Ch. (U.S.A.), 1959. Pastor First Presbyn. Ch., Aransas Pass, Tex., 1960-64; assoc. gen. Presbyter South Tex. Presbytery, Corpus Christi, Tex., 1964-70, gen. presbyter, 1970-72; assoc. gen. presbyter Presbytery del Salvador, Corpus Christi, 1972-74; Presbytery exec. Norfolk Presbytery, Va., 1976—; trustee Westminster-Canterbury, Virginia Beach, Va., 1977—. Vice pres. Virginians Organized for Informed Community Expression, Norfolk, 1976—. Mem. Assn. of Exec. Presbyters. Lodge: Theophilus. Home: 106 Carlisle Way Norfolk VA 23505 Office: Norfolk Presbytery 405 Brackenridge Ave Norfolk VA 23505

DICKINSON, BUFORD ALLEN, minister, United Methodist Church; b. Hattiesburg, Miss., Nov. 7, 1933; s. Homer Eugene and Ella Ruth (Ward) D.; m. Mary Eugenia Clegg, June 4, 1957; children: Timothy Allen, Kathryn Clegg. B.S., U. So. Miss., 1954; B.D., Emory U., 1957; Rel.D., Sch. Theology at Claremont, 1967, Ph.D., 1976. Ordained to ministry, 1957. Asst. to pres. Sch. Theology Claremont, Calif., 1966-72, dir. continuing edn., asst. to pres., 1972-75, personnel dir., 1978-81, v.p. adminstrn., 1975-81; pres. Meth. Theol. Sch. Ohio, Delaware, 1981—; bd. trustees Riverside Meth. Hosp., Columbus, 1981—; ministerial mem. Calif.-Pacific Conf. United Meth. Ch. Home: 901 Clubview Blvd N Worthington OH 43085 Office: Meth Theol Sch Ohio 3081 Columbus Pike Delaware OH 43015

DICKS, PHILIP DUANE, minister, United Methodist Ch.; b. Albia, Iowa, Nov. 5, 1951; s. Cecil Duane and Norma Darlene (DeVos) D.; m. Constance Leigh Derby, June 21, 1974; children: Carla Marie Darlene, Joshua Philip Arie, Elijah Philip Paul. B.S., Drake U., 1974; B.A., Asbury Coll., 1976; M.Div., Asbury Theol. Sem., 1979; postgrad. Illiff Sch. Theology, Aspen, Colo., 1982, Candler Sch. Theology, 1983, St. Paul Sch. Theology, Kansas City, Mo., 1984—. Ordained to ministry United Methodist Ch., 1980. Youth pastor, Bartlesville United Meth. Ch., Okla., 1974; chaplain Eastern State Mental Hosp., Lexington, Ky., 1976; music dir. United Meth. Ch., Wilmore, Ky., 1978-79; pastor Trimble United Meth. Ch., Sioux City, Iowa, 1979-85, Grace United Meth. Ch., Davenport, Iowa, 1985—; chaplain clin. pastoral edn. Iowa Meth. Med. Ctr., Des Moines, 1978; del. Inst. for World Evangelism, Atlanta, 1982; vice chairperson Iowa Ann. Conf. Bd. of Evangelism & Spiritual Formation, 1982, chairperson, 1984—; escort, del. United Meth. Bicentennial Study/Tour, London, Paris, Brussels, Amsterdam, 1984. Contbg. author: Self-Pity, 1982; The Ministers Manual, 1983. Contbg. editor: Emphasis Mag., 1984. Bd. dirs. Council on Domestic Violence-Sexual Assault, Sioux City, 1981-84, Goodwill Industries, Sioux City, 1984. Westinghouse Sci. scholar, 1968; Gen. Motors Sci. scholar, 1969; Craig E. Brandenburg scholar United Meth. Bd. Higher Edn., 1983-84. Fellow Am. Assn. Religious Therapists; mem. Siouxland Ministerial Assn., Inter-Faith Resource. Democrat. Avocations: writing, traveling, hunting. Home: 105 McManus St Davenport IA 52804 Office: Grace United Meth Ch 2651 Telegraph Rd Davenport IA 52804

DIEFENDERFER, PAUL TILTON, lay church worker, United Church of Christ; b. Fullerton, Pa., Sept. 8, 1903; s. Eugene Edgar and Omie Alice (Tilton) D.; m. Anna Estella Ulrich, Jan. 1, 1930 (dec. 1967); m. Minnie Ella Ulrich, June 9, 1968. B.S., Bradley U., 1923; postgrad. U. Chgo., 1925-27. Research anthropologist Bernice P. Bishop Mus., Honolulu, 1927-31; with Met. Life Ins. Co., Reading, Pa., 1931-68, dist. mgr., 1935-60; numerous offices and positions in church and ch. schs., 1932—; mission interpreter United Ch. of Christ, Worldwide, 1973—. Chmn., War Bond and ARC drives Berks County; bd. dirs. United Ch. Bd. for World Ministries, N.Y.C., 1981—. Republican. Lodges: Masons, Lions. Home: 3600 Kent Ave Laureldale-Reading PA 19605

DIEHM, FLOYD LEE, minister, Christian Ch. (Disciples Christ); b. Red Rock, Okla., May 1, 1925; s. John William and Hortence (Russell) D.; B.Th., NW Christian Coll., 1951; M.Div., Phillips Sem., 1954; Rel.D., Sch. Theology, Claremont, Calif., 1970; m. Emily Louise, Helseth, Dec. 21, 1951; children—Kenneth John, Janet Kay. Nat. evangelist, 1955-58; pastor chs., Va., Calif., 1958-66; pastor Midwest Blvd. Christian Ch., Midwest City, Okla., 1970-76, 1st Christian Ch., Alhambra, Calif., 1976—. Trustee Phillips U., pres. alumni assn.; chaplain local C. of C. Author: How to be Fully Alive, 1976; How to Evangelize Effectively, 1977; also religious booklets. Office: 220 S 5th St Alhambra CA 91801

DIEMER, CARL JOHN, JR., minister, seminary dean Independent Baptist Churches; b. Mobile, Ala., July 2, 1938; s. Carl John and Nellie Mary (Robine) D.; m. Gayle Carolyn Sparks, July 6, 1963; children: Curtis, Christy. B.S. in Mech. Engring., Va. Inst. Tech., 1960; M.Div., Southwestern Bapt. Theol. Sem., 1965, Th.D., 1972. Ordained to ministry, Ind. Bapt. Chs., 1966. Pastor, Forestburg Bapt. Ch., Tex., 1966-69, Villebrook Bapt. Ch., Hazelwood, Mo., 1969-73; prof. Liberty Bapt. Theol. Sem., Lynchburg, Va., 1973-83, asst. dean, 1984—. Contbr. articles to profl. jours. Mem. Evang. Theol. Soc., Am. Hist. Soc., Va. Bapt. Hist. Soc., Profl. Tennis Registry. Home: 105 Pacos St Lynchburg VA 24502 Office: Liberty Bapt Theol Sem 3765 Candlers Mountain Rd Lynchburg VA 24506

DIERINGER, DENNIS DEAN, minister, General Association of Regular Baptist Churches; b. Celina, Ohio, Nov. 14, 1948; s. Robert E. and Gladys (Hundly) D.; m. Joyce L. Mobler, Aug. 19, 1972; children: Andrea Joy, Aaron Joel, Daniel Dean. B.A., Cedarville Coll., 1971; M.Div., Grace Theol. Sem., 1974; postgrad. Luther Rice Sem., 1984—. Ordained to ministry, 1967. Youth pastor Community Bapt. Ch., Winamac, Ind., 1972-73; asst. pastor Shoaff Park Bapt. Ch., Ft. Wayne, Ind., 1973-74; pastor Fresno Bible Ch., Ohio, 1974-79; pastor Anchor Bapt. Ch., Seville, Fla., 1980—; chmn. Orlando area Gen. Assn. Regular Bapt. Chs. Pastor's Fellowship, 1983-84. Forest fire worker Ohio Dept. Natural Resources, 1976-79. Republican. Address: PO Box 274 Seville FL 32090

DIERSING, LEO THEODORE, priest, Roman Catholic Ch.; b. Hobson, Tex., Nov. 4, 1905; s. August Herman and Mary (Henke) D.; B.A., Subiaco (Ark.) Coll., 1936; religious edn. New Subiaco Abbey, 1940. Ordained priest, 1939; tchr. Subiaco Coll.-Acad., 1940-41; pastor St. Scholastica Ch., New Blaine, Ark., 1941-47, St. Joseph Ch., Rhineland, Tex., 1947-55; tchr. Corpus Christi (Tex.) Acad., 1955-56; chaplain St. Mary of the Plains Hosp., Lubbock, Tex., 1956-57; pastor St. Joseph's Ch., Stanton, Tex., 1957-59, St. Joseph's Ch., Rotan, Tex., 1959-62; pastor St. Boniface Ch., Olfen, Tex., 1962-65, St. Margaret's Ch., Big Lake, Tex., 1965-67, San Angelo, Tex., 1967-69, Sacred Heart Ch., Coleman, Tex., 1970—. Vice pres., youth dir. Cath. Central League Am., St. Louis, 1945-47. Contbr. articles to religious jours. Home and Office: 303 E College Ave Coleman TX 76834

DIETRICH, EDWARD JOSEPH, priest, Roman Catholic Church; b. Cleve., Jan. 2, 1943; s. Edward A. and Mildred (Maloney) D. B.Ph., St. Charles Morromeo U., Cleve., 1967; M.Div., St. Mary U., Cleve., 1971; Ph.D. candidate Inst. Advanced Study of Human Sexuality, San Francisco, 1979. Ordained priest, Roman Cath. Ch., 1971; assoc. pastor St. Rita Ch., Solon, Ohio, 1971-76; campus ministry Cleve. State U., 1976-77; hosp. ministry St. Joseph Hosp., Albuquerque, 1978-79, 79-84; exec. dir. Nat. Assn. Cath. Chaplains, Milw., 1984—. Editor: Camillian, 1984—. Fellow Am. Coll. Sexologists; mem. Nat. Assn. Cath. Chaplains, Acad. Health Care Leadership. Office: Nat Assn Cath Chaplains 3257 S Lake Dr Milwaukee WI 53207

DIETZ, PAUL THEODORE, minister, Lutheran Ch.-Missouri Synod; b. Milw., Sept. 7, 1922; s. Paul and Elsie (Imse) D.; m. Corinne B. Braeger, Dec. 27, 1950; children: Christine Dietz Kush, Mary, David. B.A., Concordia Theol. Sem., 1944, M.Div., 1949; M.A. in History, Marquette U., 1951; M.A., U. Wis.-Madison, 1957. Ordained to ministry Luth. Ch.-Mo. Synod, 1950. Pastor St. Paul and St. Luke's Luth. Parishes, Green Grove, Wis., 1950-52; prof. Concordia Coll., Milw., 1952-78; adminstrv. pastor Grace Evang. Luth. Ch., Menomonee Falls, Wis., 1978—; archivist So. Wis. dist. Luth. Ch.-Mo. Synod, Milw., 1957-78; bd. dirs. Luth. High Sch. Assn., Greater Milw., 1979—; mem. bd. regents Concordia Coll.-Wis., Mequon, 1982—. Mem. Council on Library Devel., State of Wis., Madison, 1968-73; pres. Wis. Library Assn., Madison, 1972. Mem. Menomonee Falls Ministerial Assn., Concordia Coll. Pastor Conf. Home: W158 N6301 Cherry Hill Dr Menomonee Falls WI 53051 Office: Grace Evang Luth Ch N87 W16171 Kenwood Blvd Menomonee Falls WI 53051

DIETZE, CHARLES EDGAR, minister, Disciples of Christ Church; b. Savannah, Ga., Jan. 21, 1919; s. Ernest and Mary Edith (Fetzer) D.; m. Mary Nettie Peavyhouse, Dec. 28, 1940 (dec. 1980); children: Mary Katherine Dietze Ballance, Charles William; m. 2d Irma Spencer, Nov. 30, 1980. B.A., Transylvania U., 1940; B.D., Lexington Theol. Sem., 1944; D.D. (hon.), Atlantic Christian Coll., 1965. Ordained minister Disciples of Christ Ch., 1941. Minister, First Christian Ch., Morehead, Ky., 1943-47; minister First Christian Ch., Henderson, Ky., 1948-52, minister emeritus, 1983—; minister Christian Ch., North Middletown, Ky., 1952-55; v.p. Lexington Theol. Sem., Ky., 1966-76; regional minister Christian Ch. N.C., Wilson, 1965-81; nat. pres. Disciples Peace Fellowship, 1956-57; nat. v.p. Bd. Higher Edn., 1968-69; pres. N.C. Council Chs., Durham, 1970-71; nat. pres. Conf. Regional Ministers, 1974-76. Author: God's Trustees, 1976; The Henderson Crusade, 1983. Pres., St. Anthony's Hospice, Henderson, 1983. Recipient Spl. Centennial Citation, Lexington Theol. Sem., 1965. Democrat. Club: Lions (chmn. sight conservation com. Henderson 1983-84). Home: 322 Hancock St Henderson KY 42420

DIETZSCHOLD, BEVERLY JANE, minister, religion educator, Southern Baptist Convention; b. Cameron, Mo., Feb. 14, 1939; d. John Herman and Helen Ruby (Doak) D. B.A., William Jewell Coll., 1961; M.R.E., So. Bapt. Theol. Sem., 1966. Minister to children Central Bapt. Ch., Chattanooga, 1966-73; presch. and children's minister First Bapt. Ch., Montgomery, Ala., 1973-76, First Bapt. Ch., Hendersonville, N.C., 1976—; summer missionary Home Mission Bd. of So. Bapt. Conv., Ga., Calif., 1959-60; cons. tchr. for various vacation Bible schs. and Sunday sch. preschs. and children leadership, 1966—; v.p. Ala. Religious Edn. Assn., 1975-76; equipper and cert. witness for continuing witnessing tng. Home Mission Bd., So. Bapt. Conv., 1983-85. Author curriculum Preschool Bible Teacher, 1985. Writer for music leader. Vol. Hendersonville City Schs., N.C., 1980-84, Henderson County Schs., N.C., 1984; mem. scholarship com. Hendersonville Women's CLub, 1981. Named one of Outstanding Young Women Am., 1970. Mem. N.C. Religious Edn. Assn., Southeastern Religious Edn. Assn. Republican. Avocations: rock hounding; hiking; travel. Home: 1736 Lower Ridgewood Blvd Hendersonville NC 28739 Office: First Bapt Ch 312 5th Ave W Hendersonville NC 28739

DIFFEE, ROBERT BRUCE, minister, Baptist Independent Church; b. Hammon, Okla., May 22, 1936; s. Wadie D. and Dorene W. (Cunningham) D.; m. Barbara Gayle Bishop, Oct. 26, 1938; children: Donna Sue, Robert Carl. Th.B., Bapt. Bible Coll., Springfield, Mo., 1965; B.A., South Tex. Bapt. Coll., 1973, M.A., 1975; Ph.D., Bapt. Christian U., 1976, LL.D. (hon.), 1976; D. Min. (hon.), Tri-State Bapt. Coll., 1979. Ordained to ministry Bapt. Ch., 1965; lic. marriage and family counselor. Sr. pastor Eagle Crest Bapt. Ch., Indpls., 1965-69, Halstead Bapt. Ch., Kans, 1970-73, Maranatha Bapt. Ch., Oxon Hill, Md., 1974-77, Tri-State Bapt. Ch., Charlestown, W.Va., 1977—; mem. council Sword of Evandelism, Murfreeboro, Tenn., 1982—. Contbr. articles to newspapers. Sustaining mem. Republican Nat. Com., 1984. Recipient Nat. Leadership award ACTV, 1984. Mem. Nat. Assn. Marriage and Family (cert. 1983), Am. Assn. Christian Schs., Smithsonian Assocs., Mo. Bapt. Bible Fellowship (pres. 1975-76). Republican. Home: Rural Route 2 Box 692 Harpers Ferry WV 25425 Office: Tri-State Bapt Ch 211 E 2d Ave Charlestown WV 25414

DIIANNI, ALBERT RALPH, priest, Roman Catholic Church; b. Woburn, Mass., May 12, 1933; s. Modesto and Marcia (Grossi) DiI. Ph.D., U. Louvain, Belgium, 1963; Ph.L., Angelicum, Rome. Ordained priest Roman Catholic Ch., 1960. Asst. prof. philosophy Marist Coll., Framingham, Mass., 1963-66; from asst. prof. to assoc. prof. philosophy Coll. of Holy Cross, Worcester, Mass., 1966-79, chmn. dept. philosophy, 1973-79; provincial superior Marist Fathers of Boston, Chestnut Hill, Mass., 1979—; sec. social issues com. Boston Area Sem. Faculties, 1961-68; radio, TV speaker on morality. Contbr. articles on moral philosophy to profl. jours. Mem. Am. Assn. Philosophy, Am. Cath. Philosophy Assn. Office: 72 Beacon St Chestnut Hill MA 02167

DILDAY, RUSSELL HOOPER, JR., seminary administrator, Southern Baptist Convention; b. Amarillo Tex., Sept. 30, 1930; s. Russell Hooper and Opal (Spillers) D.; m. Betty Doyen, Aug. 15, 1952; children: Robert, Nancy, Ellen. B.A., Baylor U., 1952, LL.D. (hon.), 1978; B.D., Southwestern Bapt. Sem., 1955, Ph.D., 1976; D.D. (hon.), Mercer U., 1975; L.H.D. (hon.), William Jewell Coll., 1979; postgrad. in advanced mgmt. Emory U., 1978. Ordained to ministry Southern Baptist Convention, 1952. Pastor First Bapt. Ch., Antelope, Tex., 1952-56, Clifton, Tex., 1956-59, Tallowood Bapt. Ch., Houston, 1959-69, Second-Ponde de Leon Bapt. Ch., Atlanta, 1969-77; pres. Southwestern Bapt. Theol. Sem., Ft. Worth, 1978—; instr. religion Baylor U., 1957-58; 1st v.p. Bapt. Gen. Conv. Tex., 1965-66; chmn. com. on resolutions So. Bapt. Conv., 1969, 2d v.p., 1970-71, pres. home mission bd., 1974-76, mem., chmn. coms.; moderator Atlanta Bapt. Assn., 1973-74, pres. pastors conf., 1974-75; exec. com. Ga. Bapt. Conv., 1970-75, adminstrn. com. of exec. com., 1973-75; field supr. dir. of ministries program So. Bapt. Theol. Sem., Louisville, 1973-77; mem. rev. com. for research project Mercer Sch. Pharmacy, 1975-77. Author: You Can Overcome Discouragement, 1977; Prayer Meeting Resources, vol. I, 1977; contbr. writings to teachers' commentaries, sermon collections, Sunday Sch. materials; worldwide speaker. Trustee Pace Acad., Atlanta, 1973-75; mem. clin. pastoral edn. adminstrv. and adv. com. Ga. Bapt. Hosp., Atlanta, 1974-77; bd. dirs. Sch. Religion Morehouse Coll., Atlanta, 1976-77; Recipient Valley Forge award for sermon, 1976, Outstanding Alumni award Omicron Delta Kappa, Baylor U., 1977, Disting. Alumni award Southwestern Sem., 1979. Mem. Am. Acad. Religion, AAUP, Soc. for Sci. Study of Religion. Republican. Clubs: Ft. Worth Rotary, Ft. Worth C. of C., Atlanta Kiwanis. Office: Southwestern Bapt Theol Sem PO Box 22000 Fort Worth TX 76122

DI LELLA, ALEXANDER ANTHONY, priest, Biblical studies educator, Roman Catholic Church; b. Paterson, N.J., Aug. 14, 1929; s. Alessandro and Adelaide (Grimaldi) D.; B.A., St. Bonaventure U., 1952; S.T.L., Cath. U., 1959, Ph.D., 1962; S.S.L., Pontifical Bibl. Inst., Rome, 1964. Ordained priest, 1955. Franciscan friar Order of Friars Minor, N.Y.C., 1949—; asst. pastor St. Francis Parish, Long Beach Island, N.J., summers 1956, 70; sem. instr. Holy Name Coll., Washington, 1964-69; mem. faculty Cath. U., Washington, 1966—, prof. Bibl. studies, 1977—; adj. prof. O.T., Washington Theol. union, Silver Spring, Md., 1969-72; mem. Revised Standard Version Bible com. Nat. Council Chs., N.Y.C., 1982—. Author: The Hebrew Text of Sirach, 1966; Proverbs, Old Testament in Syriac, 1979; (with others) The Book of Daniel, 1978. Contbr. articles to religious and scholarly publs. Mem. instl. rev. bd. Dubroff Eye Ctr., Silver Spring, 1982—; mem. oncology unit adv. com. George Washington U. Hosp., Washington, 1983—. Fellow Am. Schs. Oriental Research, Jerusalem,

DILLON, CLARENCE EDWARD, minister, Church of God (Anderson, Indiana); b. South Charleston, W.Va., Jan. 30, 1933; s. James Wesley and Hurtle Gladys (King) D.; m. Shirley Ann Hill, Apr. 3, 1953; children: Karen Lynn, Sharon Kay, Angela Carol, Judith Ann. Student Morris Harvey Coll., 1963-64; B.S. in Chemistry, W.Va. State U., 1964. Ordained to ministry Ch. of God (Anderson), 1965. Pastor 1st Ch. of God, Point Pleasant, W.Va., 1964-67, Rock Creek Ch. of God, Bessemer, Ala., 1967-72, Parkview Ch. of God, Meridian, Miss., 1972-75, 1st Ch. of God, Princeton, W.Va., 1975—; trustee Warner So. Coll., 1973-82; chmn. W.Va. Gen. Assembly, 1981; chmn. W.Va. Credentials Commn., 1983—. Served with U.S. Army, 1953-55. Home: 1815 Honaker Ave Princeton WV 24740 Office: First Church of God 301 Mahood Ave Princeton WV 24740

DIMINO, JOSEPH T., bishop, Roman Catholic Church. Titular bishop of Carini, aux. bishop Mil.

Vicariate, N.Y.C. Office: 1011 First Ave New York NY 10022*

DIMMERLING, HAROLD J., bishop, Roman Cath. Ch.; b. Braddock, Pa., Sept. 23, 1914. Ed. St. Fidelis Preparatory Sem., Herman, Pa., St. Charles Sem., Columbus, Ohio, St. Francis Sem., Loretto, Pa. Ordained priest Roman Catholic Ch., 1940; consecrated bishop, 1969; bishop Diocese of Rapid City, S.D., 1969—. Address: Diocese of Rapid City 606 Cathedral Dr POB 678 Rapid City SD 57701

DIMMICK, WILLIAM ARTHUR, bishop, Episcopal Ch.; b. Paducah, Ky., Oct., 1919; s. James Oscar and Annis (Crouch) D.; B.A., Berea Coll., 1946; B.D., Yale U., 1949; M.A., George Peabody Tchrs. Coll., 1955. Ordained priest, 1955; priest-in-charge St. Philip's Ch., Nashville, 1955-60; canon St. Mary's Cathedral, Memphis, 1960-62, dean, 1962; now bishop Diocese of No. Mich., Menominee. Exam. chaplain, 1962. Address: 922 Tenth Ave Menominee MI 49858*

DINGMAN, MAURICE J., bishop, Roman Cath. Ch. Ordained priest Roman Catholic Ch., 1939; consecrated bishop, 1968; bishop Diocese of Des Moines, 1968—. Address: 818 5th Ave POB 1816 Des Moines IA 50306

DI NOIA, JOSEPH AUGUSTINE, educator, priest, Roman Catholic Church; b. N.Y.C., July 10, 1943; s. Giacomo and Matilda (Carucci) Di N.; student Providence Coll., 1961-63; B.A., St. Stephen's Coll., 1966, M.A., 1970; S.T.B., Pontifical Faculty Immaculate Conception Sem., 1969, S.T.L., 1971; Ph.D., Yale U., 1980. Ordained Dominican priest Roman Catholic Ch., 1970; instr. dept. religious studies Providence Coll., 1971—, asst. chaplain, 1971-74; assoc. prof. Systematic Theology Dominican House of Studies, 1980—; subprior Dominican Community. Editor-in-chief The Thomist. Mem. Cath. Theol. Soc. Am., Am. Acad. Religion. Home and office: 5 Hillhouse Ave New Haven CT 06505

DIONNE, GERARD JOSEPH, bishop, Roman Catholic Church; b. St. Basile, N.B., Can., June 19, 1919; s. Aurele and Octavie (Pelletier) D. B.A., Laval U., 1944; Th.B., Holy Heart Sem., 1948; Ph.D. in Canon Law, Angelicum, Rome, 1963. Ordained priest Roman Cath. Ch., 1948. Asst. pastor Edmundston Ch., N.B., Can., 1948-56, pastor, 1971-75; chaplain Orphanage, Edmundston, 1956-60; dir. office of missions Conf. of Bishops, Ottawa, Ont., Can., 1967-71; bishop (aux.) Diocese of Sault-Ste. Marie, Sudbury, Ont., Can., 1975-84; bishop Diocese of Edmundston, 1984—. Home and Office: Centre Diocesain Edmundston NB E3V 3K1 Canada

DIPPOLD, DAVID OTTO, minister, Assemblies of God; b. Phila., Mar. 3, 1935; s. Otto Earnest and Mabel Alma (Zimmerman) D.; diploma Eastern Bible Inst., Green Lane, Pa., 1956, Northeast Bible Inst., Green Lane, 1964; M.A., Villanova (Pa.) U., 1968; D.Min., Drew U., 1982; m. Ruth Ann Dobromilski, June 16, 1956; children: Judith Ruth, David Michael. Ordained to ministry, 1959; pastor ch. in N.J., 1956-59; pastor N.E. Assembly of God, Phila., 1959-68, Gospel Tabernacle, New Kensington, Pa., 1968-73, Green Ridge Pentecostal Assembly of God, Scranton, Pa., 1973-85, 1st Assembly of God, Lancaster, Pa., 1985—. Sec. bd. dirs. Messiah Mission, Phila.; vice chmn. Teen Challenge Western Pa.; chmn. resolution com. Eastern dist. council Assemblies of God; pres. G.R. Ministerium, pastoral counseling, Scranton. Mem. Am. Assn. Counseling and Devel. Author: The Bible and Astronomy, 1957; Lest We Forget, 1964; The Plus Factor in Pastoral Counseling, 1969; Who Ministers to the Minister?, 1976. Address: 130 Roosevelt Blvd Lancaster PA 17601

DIRKS, DENNIS HAROLD, minister, Evangelical Free Church of America, seminary educator; b. South Gate, Calif., Mar. 14, 1944; s. Harold Kenneth and Ruth (Dyck) D.; m. Karen Marie Sommer, Mar. 29, 1969; children: Matthew Dirks, Jennifer Dirks. B.A., Calif. State U.-Fresno, 1966; M.A., Talbot Theol. Sem., 1970; postgrad. Calif. State U.-Fullerton, 1978; Ph.D., Claremont Grad. Sch., 1982. Ordained to ministry, Evang. Free Ch. Am., 1982. Minister Christian edn. First Covenant Ch., Mpls., 1974-76; assoc. prof. Talbot Theol. Sem. and Sch. Theology, Biola U., La Mirada, Calif., 1976— assoc. dean, 1983—; seminar leader Internat. Ctr. for Learning, Ventura, Calif., 1975-84; pres. Twin Cities Dirs. Christian Edn., Mpls., 1975-76, San Diego Dirs. Christian Edn., 1973-74; Christian sch. tchr. First Evang. Free Ch., Fullerton, 1977-83. Contbg. editor Ch. Sch. Curriculum, 1980-83. Author: The Renewed Mind, 1983; Bible Teacher Training Series, 1983. Mem. Nat. Assn. Profs. Christian Edn., Religious Edn. Assn., Assn. Profs. and Researchers in Religious Edn. Republican. Office: Talbot Theol Sem and Sch Theology 13800 Biola La Mirada CA 90639

DISCHER, GERALD ROGER, minister, Lutheran Church-Missouri Synod; b. Wausau, Wis., July 20, 1929; s. William Frederick and Lillie (Bloedel) D.; m. Betty Jane Halgardier, Jan. 17, 1951; children: Claryllie, Cynthia, Stephen. B.Th., Concordia Sem., Springfield, Ill., 1961; M.Div., Concordia Sem., Ft. Wayne, Ind., 1980; postgrad. Tex. A&M U., 1965-75. Ordained to ministry Luth-Ch.-Mo. Synod. Pastor Ascension Luth. Ch., Apple Valley, Calif., 1961-65, Trinity Luth. Ch., Navasota, Tex., 1965-82; chaplain Tex. Dept. Corrections, Navasota, 1982—; circuit counsellor Tex. dist. Luth. Ch.-Mo. Synod, also mem. town and country com., 1965-71. Chmn. Crimes Substance Abuse Council, Navasota, 1965-82; scout master Sam Houston council Boy Scouts Am.; chaplain Tex. Wing, CAP, 1981-82. Served with USAF, 1947-55. Recipient Honor cert. Freedoms Found., 1977, Outstanding Service award Brazos Valley Devel. Council, 1980-82. Mem. Am. Assn. Protestant Correctional Chaplains, Air Force Assn., Mil. Chaplains Assn. Alpha Kappa Delta. Lodge: Kiwanis (named Kiwanian of Yr. 1970). Home: Rural Route 3 Box 300 Navasota TX 77868

DISTLER, CHARLES, minister, Conf. Fundamental Churches of America; b. N.Y.C., June 21, 1915; s. William and Anna Elizabeth (Weisskoff) D.; m. Daisy Smith, Mar. 21, 1936; children: Charles Alfred, Daisy (Mrs. Paul H. Powell), Ruth Gabel. Grad. Nat. Bible Inst. (now Shelton Coll., Cape Canaveral, Fla.), 1947; student Eastern Bapt. Theol. Sem., Pa., summers 1949-51. Ordained to ministry Conf. Fundamental Chs. of Am., 1945. Pastor Woodside (N.Y.) Bapt. Ch., 1947-56, Faith Bapt. Ch., 1956-62, Goodyear Heights Community Ch., Akron, Ohio, 1962-70, Sutter Salem Bible Ch., Warsaw, Ill., 1970-77, Fenton (Mich.) Bible Ch., 1977—; broadcaster, Bible tchr. radio sta. WCAZ, Carthage, Ill., 1971—; chaplain N.Y.C. Civilian Def., 1950-56, Carthage (Ill.) Meml. Hosp., 1974—; pres. Ohio Regional Sect. Ind. Fundamental Chs. Am., 1st v.p. Central Ill. Regional Sect.; bd. dirs. Ill. Bible Ch. Mission. Instl. rep. Boy Scouts Am., Woodside, 1948-56. Mem. Am. Numis. Assn. (life), Keokuk (Ill.), Hannibal (Mo.) coin clubs, Franklin Mint Soc., Smithsonian Instn. Address: 303 S Holly Rd Fenton MI 48430

DITTY, WILLIAM ALFRED, minister, Gen. Assn. Regular Bapt. Chs.; b. DuBois, Pa., May 16, 1924; s. Alfred William and Mary (Laing) D.; B.Th., Shelton Coll., 1951; B.A., 1951; Th.D., Trinity So. Bible Coll. and Sem., 1960; m. Katherine Phyllis Duncan, June 6, 1948; children: Karen Ditty Herron, Marilyn Ditty Malcolm, Cheryl. Ordained to ministry, 1960; pastor 1st Bapt. Ch., Damascus, Pa., 1952-61, Cornwall (N.Y.) Bapt. Ch., 1961-76, 1st Bapt. Ch., Butler, Pa., 1976—. Chaplain, lt. col. CAP and U.S. Air Force, 1964-76; sec. Council of Ten, Empire State Fellowship Regular Bapt. Chs.; mem. council of ten Pa. Assn. Regular Bapt. Chs.; mem. dist. com. Fellowship of Baptists for Home Missions, Elyria, Ohio. Vol., Cornwall Ambulance Corps, 1969-70; organizer, mgr. Little League, Damascus, Pa., 1958-61. Author: Current Developments in New Evangelicalism, 1973. Home: N Duffy Rd Butler PA 16001 Office: 221 New Castle St Butler PA 16001

DIXON, ERNEST T., bishop, United Methodist Church; b. San Antonio, Oct. 13, 1922; m. Lois F. Brown, July 20, 1943 (dec.); children: Freddie Brown, Ernest Reese, Muriel Jean, Leona Louise; m. 2d, Ernestine Gray Clark, May 18, 1979; 1 step-dau., Sherryl D. Clark. B.A. magna cum laude, Samuel Huston Coll., 1943; B.D., Drew Theol. Sem., 1945; D.D. (hon.) Huston-Tillotson Coll., 1962; L.H.D. (hon.), Southwestern Coll., 1973; LL.D. (hon.), Baker U., 1973; Litt.D. (hon.), Westmar Coll., 1978; H.H.D. (hon.), Kans. Wesleyan Coll., 1980. Ordained to ministry, United Methodist Ch.; pastor Brackettville (Tex.) Meth. Ch., 1943; asst. pastor East Calvary Meth. Ch., Harlem, N.Y., 1943-44; asst. pastor Wallace Chapel A.M.E. Zion Ch., Summit, N.J., 1944-45; dir. religious ext. service Tuskegee Inst., 1945-51, coorganizer Bosen Meth. Ch., Tuskegee, 1945-51; exec. sec. West Tex. Conf. Bd. Edn., 1951-52; mem. staff div. local ch. Bd. Edn. Meth. Ch., 1952-64; pres. Philander Smith Coll., Little Rock, 1965-69; asst. gen. sec. div. coordination, research and planning Program Council, United Meth. Ch., 1969-72; elected bishop, 1972; bishop Kans. Area United Meth. Ch., 1972-80, San Antonio Area, Rio Grande and Southwest Tex. Confs., 1980—, bd. mgrs. United Meth. Communications, 1976—. Mem. Citizens Adv. Com. to Gov. Ark., 1967-69; mem. exec. com. Civic Com. on Pub. Edn., Nashville and Davidson County, Tenn., 1962-64. Trustee, Gammon Theol. Sem., Gulfside Assembly, Waveland, Miss., pres. bd., 1978—, Huston-Tillotson Coll., Holding Inst., Laredo, Tex., Lydia Patterson Inst., El Paso, Meth. Mission Home, San Antonio, Mission Home of Tex., Waco, Morningside Manor Inc., San Antonio, Mt. Sequoyah Assembly, Fayetteville, Ark., So. Meth. U., S.W. Tex. Meth. Hosp., San Antonio, Southwestern U., Georgetown, Tex. Office: 535 Bandera Rd PO Box 28509 San Antonio TX 78228

DIXON, FREDDIE BROWN, SR., minister, United Meth. Ch.; b. San Antonio, June 6, 1944; s. Ernest T. and Lois Freddie (Brown) D.; B.A., Philander Smith Coll., 1967; M.Div., Gammon Sem., 1970; m. Barbara Watson, June 1, 1968; children: Freddie Brown, Douglass L. Ordained to ministry, 1970; assoc. pastor First United Meth. Ch., Beeville, Tex., 1970-73; pastor Wesley United Meth. Ch., Austin, 1973—. Mem. Alpha Phi Alpha. Home: 1602 Astor Pl Austin TX 78721 Office: 1164 San Bernard St Austin TX 78702

DIXON, JONATHAN LEE, minister, Free Methodist Church of North America; b. Miltonvale, Kans., Sept. 11, 1947; s. George Benjamin and Frances Clara (Murphy) D.; m. Ellen Lois Trice, Aug. 8, 1970; children: Jonathan Lee II, Rebekah Sue, Rachel Ann. A.A., Central Coll., 1967; B.A. with honors, N.Mex. State U., 1970; M. Div., Western Evangelical Sem., 1976; postgrad., St. Louis U., 1984—. Pastor Free Meth. Ch., Las Cruces, N.Mex., 1970-72; asst. pastor, Beaverton, Oreg., 1974-76, pastor, Ione, Calif., 1976-81, Hillsboro, Ill., 1981—; chmn. bd. Durley Camp, Greenville, Ill., 1982—; pres. Conf. Ministers Fellowship, Calif. and Nev., 1976-78; speaker Youth Camps and Retreats, Calif. and Ill., 1980-84, Sr. Adult Retreat, Central Ill., 1983; tchr. adult Bible class Durley and Cowden Family Camps, 1982, 83, 84; zone leader, sec., treas. Central Ill. Conf., 1982, 1983—. Bd. dirs. Citizens for Drug Free Youth, Montgomery County, Ill., 1983—; campaign vol. Dominici for Gov., Las Cruces, 1969-70; co-founder Ione Youth Council, Calif., 1978-79; rally participant Right to Life Orgns., Montgomery County and Springfield, Ill., 1984; active Moral Majority Voter Registration Drive, Sacramento, Calif., 1980, Springfield, 1984. Western Evang. Sem. scholar and loan grantee, 1972-76, St. Louis U. grad. fellow, 1984. Mem. County Ministerial Assn. (pres. Amador County, Calif. 1977-81), Weslyan Theol. Soc., Evang. Theol. Soc. (assoc. mem.), Christian Holiness Assn. (nat. conv. del. 1983), Nat. Assn. Evangs., Hillsboro Ministerial Assn., Pi Gamma Mu. Republican. Clubs: Philosophy (pres. 1969-70). Home: 202 Walnut Dr Hillsboro IL 62049 Office: Hillsboro Free Meth Ch 202 Walnut St Hillsboro IL 62049

DIXON, LYNNE KATIE, minister, Church of God (Anderson, Indiana); b. Ithaca, N.Y., Sept. 14, 1951; d. John Fitzgerald and Ruth Elizabeth (Hoerber) Dixon; B.A., Wittenberg U., 1973; B.Th., Gulf Coast Bible Coll., 1978. Ordained to ministry Ch. of God (Anderson), 1981. Pastor, Ch. of God, Saratoga, Ind., 1978—; del. Ch. of God Gen. Assembly, Anderson, 1978—; forwarding agt. Friends of Turkey, 1984—; alumni recruiter Gulf Coast Bible Coll., 1982—; bd. dirs. Haven Ministries, 1984—. Pres. R.E.A.C.H. Services, Inc., Winchester, Ind., 1981-82; chmn. St. Jude's Children's Hosp. Bike-a-thon, Saratoga, 1983-84; chmn. Cystic Fibrosis Bike-athon, Saratoga, 1981, 82. Mem. Winchester Area Ministerial Assn. (pres. 1981-82, sec.-treas. 1983-85), Randolph County Hosp. Chaplains Assn. (pres. 1982-83), Youth Explosion. Republican. Home: Washington St PO Box 11 Saratoga IN 47382 Office: Saratoga Church of God PO Box 11 Saratoga IN 47382

DIXON, ROBERT LEROY, minister, Ch. of the Nazarene; b. Ashland, Ky., Aug. 9, 1936; s. Delbert William and Mary (Hall) D.; A.B. in Religion, Trevecca Nazarene Coll., Nashville, 1962; m. Ella Marie Preston, Apr. 30, 1955; children—Kenneth Neil, David Michael. Ordained to ministry, 1962; pastor chs. in Tenn., Ky. and Ind., 1960-70; pastor Ch. of Nazarene, Pennsville, N.J., 1970-76, Ch. of Nazarene, Huntington, W.Va., 1976—; vol. chaplain Salem (N.J.) County Hosp., 1973-76. Pres. Pennsville Ministerial Assn., 1974-76; sec. Phila. dist. Ch. of Nazarene Sunday Sch. Bd., 1974-76, also mem. bd. orders and relations. Pres. Maysville (Ky.) Jr. High Sch. PTA, 1969. Named Ky. col., 1965. Mem. Huntington East End Ministers Assn. Home: 2978 4th Ave Huntington WV 25702 Office: 321 30th St Huntington WV 25702

DIXON, RONALD WAYNE, minister, So. Baptist Conv.; b. Montrose, Colo., June 13, 1939; s. Donald David and Atta Faye (Andrews) D.; B.Music Edn., U. Colo., 1962; M.Mus., Southwestern Theol. Sem., Ft. Worth, 1966; m. Carrie Lee Brown, Aug. 29, 1959; children—Donnie, Kimberly. Ordained to ministry, 1967; minister music N.Cleburne (Tex.) Bapt. Ch., 1964; minister music, edn. and youth Northside Bapt. Ch., Duncanville, Tex., 1965-66; minister music First Bapt. Ch., Texas City, Tex., 1967—. Pianist, program chmn. Kiwanis Internat., 1968-70; soloist Honors Chapel, 1965. Sem. Quartet scholar, 1964-65. Mem. Ministerial Alliance, Singing Churchmen Tex., So. Bapt. Ch. Music Conf., Galveston Bapt. Assn. Composer: Homes, 1972. Home: 2214 19th Ave N Texas City TX 77590 Office: Box 2788 Texas City TX 77590

DMITRI, (ROBERT ROYSTER), Bishop of Dallas, Orthodox Church in America. Office: 4112 Throckmorton Dallas TX 75219*

DOAN, GILBERT EVERETT, JR., minister, Lutheran Church in America; b. Phila., Sept. 14, 1930; s. Gilbert Everett and Alice Curtis (Olney) D.; m. Janice Yelland (div. 1976); children: Gilbert Everett III, Robert Bruce, Stephen Olney, James Sibbald; m. Roberta McKaig, A.B., Harvard U., 1952; M.Div., Luth. Theol. Sem., Phila., 1955; M.A., U. Pa., 1962; D.D. (hon.), Wagner Coll., 1984. Ordained to ministry Luth. Ch. in Am., 1955. Campus pastor Luth. Found., Phila., 1955-61; regional dir. Luth. Council U.S.A., Phila., 1961-84; pastor Luth. Ch. of Holy Communion, Phila., 1984—; chmn. com. on hymn texts Inter-Luth. Commn. on Worship, 1972-78, sec., 1972-78; mem. council Acad. of Preachers, Phila., 1982—. Editor: Preaching of F.W. Robertson, 1964; (with others) Oremus, 1962.

Recipient Campus Ministry award Danforth Found., 1964. Republican. Home: 142 Drexel Rd Ardmore PA 19003 Office: Ch of Holy Communion 2111 Sansom St Philadelphia PA 19103

DOANE, GILBERT HARRY, priest, Episcopal Ch.; b. Fairfield, Vt., Jan. 28, 1897; s. Harry Harvey and Charlotte Maude (Gilbert) D.; A.B., Colgate U., 1918; LL.D. (hon.), Nashotah Sem., 1955; m. Susan Howland Sherman, June 23, 1923; children—Cynthia Gilbert Doane Nickerson, John Philip. Ordained deacon, 1943, priest, 1956; asst. to rector St. Andrew's Ch., Madison, Wis., 1943-51, Shrivenhan, Berkshire, Eng., 1944, Grace Ch., Madison, 1951-68; historiographer Diocese of Milw., 1955-68. Lectr. genealogy Nat. Archives, Washington, 1973, 74, 76, Harvard, summer 1976. Fellow Am. Soc. Genealogists, Soc. Genealogists (London); mem. Newport Hist. Soc. (v.p. 1974—), Harleian Soc. (council 1968—). Author: Searching for Your Ancestors, 1937, 4th edit., 1974; History of Grace Church, Madison, Wis., 1958. Editor New Eng. Hist. Geneal. Register, 1960-70. Contbr. articles in field to profl. jours. Home: 1 Cottage St Newport RI 02840

DOBBS, DAVID LEE, minister, Tri-City Christian Center; b. Seminole, Okla., May 14, 1943; s. Claude Oliver Dobbs and Catherine (Trimble) Dobbs Maddox; m. Pamela Joyce Wilks, May 13, 1972; children: Tosha, Sonya, Dina, Amanda. Student Okla. State U., 1961-64; B.Th., Life Bible Coll., 1970; postgrad. Rio Hondo Coll., 1974, Long Beach City Coll., 1974-76. Ordained to ministry Deliverance Temple, 1961. Evangelist, tchr. Ch. of Deliverance, San Diego, 1961-73; assoc. pastor Calif. Evangelistic Assn., Long Beach, Calif., 1973-76; radio minister Sta. KYMS, Santa Ana, Calif., 1976-77; prof. Columbia Basin Coll., Pasco, Wash., 1977-80; pastor, missionary Barrow Christian Ctr., Alaska, 1980-84; pres. Sion Internat. Inc., Richland, Wash., 1984—; TV minister Columbia Cable, Kennewick, 1984-85; radio minister Sta. KBRW, Barrow, 1980-84; elder, tchr. Tri-City Christian Ctr., Pasco, 1984-85; mem. Kingsmen Quartet, 1979—, mgr., 1984-85. Author: Prayer in the Christian Life, 1976; Spiritual Life, 1985. Counselor, Boys Club Am., Okmulgee, Okla., 1962-63. Recipient Model Preparation award Calvary Christian Ctr., Kennewick, 1985. Mem. Tri-City Exec. Assn., Alaska Peach Officers Assn., Nat. Rifle Assn. Republican. Avocations: chess; boating; flying. Home: 5610 W Melville Rd Pasco WA 99301 Office: Sion Internat Inc 1776 Fowler Suite 11 Richland WA 99352

DOBRINSKY, HERBERT COLMAN, rabbi, educational administrator, Orthodox Jewish; b. Montreal, Que., Can., Apr. 6, 1933; came to U.S., 1962; s. Victor and Lillian (Honigman) D.; m. Dina Loebenberg, Dec. 26, 1954; children: Deborah Dobrinsky Kramer, Tova Dobrinsky Cohen, Aaron David. B.A., Yeshiva Coll., 1954; M.S. in Edn., Ferkauf Grad. Sch., Yeshiva U., 1959, Ed.D., 1980. Ordained rabbi, 1957. Rabbi Beth Israel Synagogue, Halifax, N.S., Can., 1958-62; assoc. dir. Max Stern Div. Communal Services, Rabbi Isaac Elchanan Theol. Sem., N.Y.C., 1962-73, dir. rabbinic placement, dir. Sephardic community activities, 1964-73; exec. asst. to pres. Yeshiva U., N.Y.C., 1973-81, v.p. for univ. affairs, 1981—; cons. Sephardic programs Rabbi Isaac Elchanan Theol. Sem. and Yeshiva U.; bd. dirs. Camp Morasha, Edn. Council Am. Author: A Treasury of Sephardic Laws and Customs, 1985. Mng. editor The Am. Sephardi, 1964—. Founder Interdisciplinary Conf. on Bereavement and Grief, Yeshiva U., 1974. Recipient Disting. Humanitarian award Yeshiva U. and Interdisciplinary Conf. on Bereavement and Grief, 1981. Mem. Rabbinical Council Am., Jewish Communal Works Am., Am. Soc. Sephardic Studies (co-founder). Office: Yeshiva U 500 W 185th St New York NY 10033

DOCHERTY, ROBERT KELLIEHAN, II, minister, United Presbyterian Church USA; b. Newton, Mass., May 27, 1935; s. Alexander Harper and Mollie (Campbell) D.; m. Eileen Joyce Rockefeller, June 14, 1958; children: Robert Kelliehan III, Scott Rockefeller, Stacy Jean. Student Gordon Coll., 1953-54, Boston U., 1954-55; diploma Moody Bible Inst., 1958, B.A., 1970; B.A., Sterling Coll., 1961; M.S., Kans. State Coll., 1972; Ph.D., Kans. State U., 1981. Ordained to ministry Bapt. Ch. 1963; minister First Bapt. Ch., Frederick, Kans., 1959-63, First Bapt. Ch., Russell, Kans., 1963-67; campus minister Kans. State Coll., Pittsburg, 1967-77. Mem. campus Ministry state staff Kans. Bapt. Conv., Topeka, 1972-77; sr. pastor United Presbyn. Ch., 1977—. Mem. Bi-Centennial Com. of Pittsburg, 1974—; gen. dr. chmn. United Way Campaign, Pittsburg, 1974; mem. exec. com. Kans. Spl. Olympics for Retarded Citizens, 1973-77; bd. dirs. Elm Acres Youth Home, Girard, Kans., 1973-75; mem. adv. bd. Help Now, 1972-73. Mem. Ministerial Assn. Pitts., Pvt. Pilots Assn., Alpha Kappa Delta, Kappa Delta Pi, Phi Delta Kappa. Kiwanian (gov. Kans. dist.). Office: 401 N Walnut St Pittsburg KS 66762

DOCKER, JOHN THORNLEY, JR., priest, Episcopal Church; b. Reading, Pa., June 2, 1937; s. John Thornley and Evelyn Clara (Deam) D.; m. Georgie Elizabeth Dawson, Dec. 31, 1968; children: Sean Thornley, Robert Kenneth. B.A., Lehigh U., 1960; M.Div., Gen. Theol. Sem., 1963; postgrad. Rochester Ctr. for Theol. Studies, 1972-74, St. George's Coll., Jerusalem, 1982. Ordained priest Epis. Ch., 1964. Rector, St. Mary-St. Joseph's Ch., Wind Gap, Pa., 1963-68, Nativity Ch., Newport, Pa., 1968-74; canon Christ Ch. Cathedral, Rochester, N.Y., 1974-76; program dir. Diocese of Bethlehem, Pa., 1976-82; coordinator ministry devel. Episcopal Ch. Ctr., N.Y.C., 1982—; program asst. Diocese of Central Pa., Harrisburg, 1968-74. Trainer Mid-Atlantic Assn. for Tng. and Cons., Washington, 1970—; cons. Alban Inst., Washington, 1980-81. Designer: Guide for Congregational Self-Evaluation, 1982; How to Organize for Evangelism, 1979. Contbr. articles to profl. jours. Mem. Assn. for Creative Change. Democrat. Home: 27 Linden Ave Ossining NY 10562 Office: Episcopal Church Ctr 815 2d Ave New York NY 10017

DODD, LOUIS EDMUND, minister, Advent Christian Church, b. Elkview, W.Va., Feb. 24, 1936; s. Giles R. and Carrie Alspie (Cummings) D.; m. Mary Anna Butler, Oct. 29, 1954; children: Cindy, Steven, Pamela, Gregory, Andrew. B.S. in Bus. Adminstrn., U. Charleston, 1959; grad. cert. Bank Adminstrn. Inst., U. Wis.-Madison, 1973; postgrad. in clin. pastoral edn. St. Francis Hosp., Charleston, W.Va., 1981-83. Ordained to ministry, Advent Christian Ch., 1969. Pastor Banner Advent Christian Ch., Spencer, W.Va., 1967-69, First Advent Ch., Dunbar, W.Va., 1969-74, Elmore Meml. Ch., Charleston, W.Va., 1974—; pres. Clergy Assn. for Pastoral Services, St. Francis Hosp., 1982—, Gen. Appalachian Advent Christian Fellowship, Blowing Rock, N.C., 1969-71; mem. Nat. Advent Christian Youth Bd., 1967-71; camp dir. Camp Whitney, Clendenin, W.Va., 1977-84; chmn. bd. Christian edn. Appalachian Advent Ch. Assn., Blowing Rock, N.C., 1982-83, W.Va. Advent Christian Conf., Clendenin, 1972-82; pres. 2d Dist. Advent Christian Ch. Conf., Charleston, 1984—. Mem. pastoral adv. bd. for Charleston Area Med. Ctr., 1981—; cubmaster, scoutmaster Buckskin council Boy Scouts Am., 1960-69; pres. Kenton Sch. PTA, Blue Creek, W.Va., 1950-59. Mem. Greater Charleston Ministerial Assn. (past pres., v.p.). Republican. Lodge: Masons. Home: 5176 Elk River Rd N Elkview WV 25071 Office: Elmore Meml Advent Christian Ch 1001 Crescent Rd PO Box 6807 Charleston WV 25362-0807

DODD, WILLIAM PORTER, priest, Episcopal Ch.; b. San Diego, Dec. 25, 1933; s. William Porter and Lois (Rockhold) D.; m. Margaret Rose Miller, June 11, 1954; children: Kathleen Elizabeth, William Alexander. A.A., Long Beach City Coll., 1958; B.A., U. Calif.-Long Beach, 1960; M.Div., Seabury-Western Theol. Sem., 1964. Ordained to ministry Episcopal Ch. as deacon, 1964, as priest, 1964. Curate Trinity Episc. Ch., Marshall, Mich., 1964-67; rector St. Paul and St. John's Episc. Ch., Montour Falls and Catherine, N.Y., 1967-71, St. John's Episc. Ch., Wellsville, N.Y., 1971-79; exec. dir. Greater Bethlehem Area Council Chs., Pa., 1979—; chairperson, mem. adv. bd. Dept. Pastoral Care St. Luke's Hosp., Bethlehem, 1979-83; bd. dirs. Christmas City Com., Bethlehem, 1979, Cities-in-Schs., Bethlehem, 1982; mem. Select Com. on Moral Teachings in Schs., Bethlehem, 1980; mem. bd. mgrs. Bethlehem Found., 1983—. Vice-chmn. Sayre Child Care Ctr., Bethlehem, 1980. Served as sgt. U.S. Army, 1954-56. Mem. Pa. Bible Soc. (bd. mgrs. 1981—). Republican. Home: 1955 Windson Rd Bethlehem PA 18017 Office: Greater Bethlehem Area Council Chs 520 E Broad St Bethlehem PA 18018

DODGE, LAWRENCE JOHN, youth worker. b. Skagway, Alaska, Aug. 27, 1947; s. John Knott and Elsie Linea (Erickson) D.; m. Patricia Ann Fritz, Feb. 16, 1974; children: Joshua Eric, Sarah Elizabeth. B.S. in Edn., Ill. State U., 1969. Exec. dir. South East Youth for Christ, Burlington, Iowa, 1977—. Mem. Youth Evangelism Assn. (conv. dir. 1982, bd. dirs. 1981—). Home: 600 N Central St Burlington IA 52601 Office: South East Iowa Youth Christ 2700 Division St Box 382 Burlington IA 52601

DOGGETT, MAURINE, pastoral psychotherapist, United Church of Christ; b. Eustis, Fla., Dec. 20, 1943; d. Robert Caxton and Julia Rebecca (Ashton) D.; m. James Thacker, Apr. 5, 1975; 1 child, Jorge. M.Div., Union Sem., 1972. Ordained to ministry United Ch. of Christ, 1972. Chaplain trainee Osawatomie State Hosp., Kans., 1972-73; co-dir. Christian Assn., U. Pa., Phila., 1973-79; pastoral psychotherapist Pa. Found. Pastoral Counselors, Warrington, 1981—; pres. Pa. Religious Coalition for Abortion Rights, 1977-79; bd. dirs. Well-Woman, Phila., 1977-79; mem. corp. bd. dirs. Bd. for Homeland Ministries, 1983—; mem. steering com. 1st ann. nat. meeting United Ch. Christ Women. Contbr. chpt. to Sistercelebrations, 1974. Mem. Am. Assn. Marriage and Family Therapy. Democrat. Office: Pa Found Pastoral Counselors Inc 968 Easton Rd Warrington PA 18976

DOHERTY, DENIS JOSEPH, priest, Roman Cath. Ch.; b. Enniskillen, N. Ireland, Mar. 19, 1922; s. Michael and Ellen (Reynolds) D.; came to U.S., 1946, naturalized, 1952; A.B., Nat. U. Ireland, 1942; S.T.B., J.C.L., Maynooth, Ireland, 1945. Ordained priest, 1946; vicar gen. Diocese of Fresno, Calif., 1972; dir. Soc. Propogation of the Faith, 1960—; consultor Diocese of Fresno, 1960—, mem. adminstrn. bd., 1967—, bd. edn., 1964—, dir. bldg. com., 1969—, dir. cemeteries, 1972—, chancellor, 1967-72, vocation dir., 1954-67; apostolate of Christian Action; dir. Confraternity of Christian Doctrine, 1954-67; officialis Diocesan Tribunal, 1960-67; named papel chamberlain, 1963, domestic prelate, 1968. Office: PO Box 1668 Fresno CA 93717

DOLAN, JOSEPH MICHAEL, priest, Roman Catholic Church; b. N.Y.C., Nov. 7, 1924; s. John Joseph and Bertha (Lyoos) D. B.A., Mt. Carmel Coll., 1948; M. Div., Immaculate Conception, 1981. Ordained priest Roman Cath. Ch., 19—. Dir. pastoral care of sick, Cath. Charities, Bklyn., 1972—, dir. Prison Ministries, Bklyn., 1976—. Author: Give Comfort to My People, 1979. Mem. Nat. Assn. Cath. Chaplains (diplomate 1980), U.S. Cath. Conf., Acad. Pastoral Counselors, Am. Correctional Chaplains. Democrat. Home: 88-25 153 St Jamaica NY Office: Cath Charities Pastoral Care Sick 191 Joralemon St Brooklyn NY 11201

DOLINAY, THOMAS V. See *Who's Who in America*, 43rd edition.

DOLLAHITE, DEWITT GENE, priest, Episcopal Ch.; b. Yukon, Okla., Nov. 2, 1939; s. LouisC. and Mabel Lucille (Jackson) D.; A.A., Coll. Marin, 1971; B.A., Antioch Coll., 1976; m. Loni Jeanne Dill, June 19, 1976. Ordained deacon, 1973; youth dir. Holy Innocents Ch., Corte Madera, Calif., 1961—, lay reader, sub deacon, 1962-73, vestryman, 1970-73; acolyte dir., 1974—. Founder, Bread for Life Ministries in Marin, 1974, pres., chmn. bd., 1974—. Meterman, Pacific Gas and Electric Co., San Rafael, Calif., 1962—. Clergy asso., Order of Holy Cross, West Park, N.Y. Home: 135 Redwood Ave #8 PO Box 521 Corte Madera CA 94925 Office: 2 Redwood Ave Corte Madera CA 94925

DOLOROSA, SISTER MARIA, nun, hospital administrator, Roman Catholic Church; b. Bronx, Aug. 25, 1917; s. Patrick and Helena Mary (Hassett) Grealis. Normal Cert., Fordham U., 1948; B.S. in Nursing, NY U, 1958, postgrad. 1958. Joined Order of St. Francis, Roman Cath. Ch., 1934. Tchr. parochial schs., Astoria, L.I., S.I. and Westchester, N.Y., 1936-48; clin. instr. Sch. Nursing, St. Mary's Hosp., Orange, N.J., 1956-59; coordinator Health service Mission of Immaculate Virgin, S.I., 1954-56, 66-77; obstet. supr. St. Agnes Hosp., White Plains, N.Y., 1951-54, adminstr., 1959-65, pres., 1977—, sec. bd. trustees, 1977—, mem. corp., 1977—, mem. found., 1984—. Bd. dirs. Hospice Planning and Edn. Found. of Westchester, Inc., White Plains, 1978-84. Recipient Seguere Deum award Stepinac High Sch., 1982, Medallion award Westchester Community Coll. Found., 1982. Mem. Am. Coll. Hosp. Adminstrs., Cath. Health Assn. U.S., No. Met. Hosp. Assn., Westchester Hosp. Consortium, Hosp. Assn. N.Y. Address: Saint Agnes Hosp 305 North St White Plains NY 10605

DOLSINA, JOHN, priest, Roman Catholic Church; b. Podsmreka, Yugoslavia, Aug. 21, 1909; came to U.S., 1948, naturalized, 1954; s. Frank and Frances (Mihelcic) D. M.Theol., U. Ljubljana (Yugoslavia), 1934. Ordained priest Roman Cath. Ch., 1934. Various assignments Diocese of Ljubljana; pastor Deerwood-St. Joseph Ch., also Our Lady of Fatima Ch., Garrison, Minn., 1952-56, St. Emily Ch., Emily, Minn., 1956-60, Crosslake, Minn., 1957-60, St. Cecilia's Ch., Nashwauk, Minn., 1960-67, St. Anthony Ch., Ely, Minn., 1967-72, Holy Rosary Ch., Aurora, Minn., 1972—; Episcopal Vicar Virginia Area, Minn., 1978-84; mem. Priests' Senate, Duluth, Minn., 1978-84; bishop's cons. Diocese of Duluth, 1978-84. Home and Office: Holy Rosary Ch 16 W 5th Ave N Aurora MN 55705

DOMOTOR, TIBOR GYULA, bishop, Free Hungarian Reformed Church; b. Budapest, Hungary, May 29, 1929; came to U.S., 1957; s. Gyula and Azuzsanna (Bakoss) D.; m. Elizabeth Guba, June 22, 1957; children: Elizabeth, Tibor. Ordained to ministry, Free Hungarian Reformed Ch., 1954; minister Free Hungarian Reformed Ch., Akron, 1966—, dean, 1971-82, dep. bishop, 1978-82, bishop, 1982—; pres. Lorantffy Care Ctr., Akron, 1971—; pres. Gaspar Karoly Theol. Sem., Akron, 1976—. Editor: Magyar Egyhaz, 1971-82; Szabad Egyhaz, 1982—; author: Ketelu Kard, 1971; Istentol Krisztusig, 1974. Chmn., Am. Hungarian Fedn., 1978—; vice-chmn. Hungarian Found., Akron, 1975—; bd. dirs. Polish-Hungarian World Fedn., Chgo., 1976—; v.p. Transylvanian World Fedn., 1977—; pres. Hungarian Freedomfighters Assn., 1957—; chmn. Synod Free Hungarian Reformed Ch., 1982—. Mem. Hungarian Reformed Fedn. Am. (dir. 1976—), Hungarian Ministerial Assn. (v.p. 1981-82). Clubs: Kiwanis, Hungarian Home (dir. 1970-72). Office: Free Hungarian Reformed Ch 2631 Copley Rd Copley OH 44321

DOMSCH, JOHN FRANCIS, minister, Lutheran Church-Missouri Synod; b. Council Bluffs, Iowa, Dec. 13, 1941; s. John Traugott and Constance Concordia (Mencke) D.; m. Linda Ellen Patzer, June 8, 1968; children: Lara Lyn, Jeremy John, Jeffrey James. B.A., Concordia Sr. Coll., 1964; M.Div., Concordia Theol. Sem., St. Louis, 1968. Ordained to ministry Luth.

Ch.-Mo. Synod, 1968. Pastor 1st Luth. Ch., Sabetha, Kans., 1968-76, Redeemer Luth. Ch., Marshalltown, Iowa, 1976—; del. Luth. Ch.-Mo. Synod Nat. Conv., Milw., 1971, del., mem. floor com., Dallas, 1977, St. Louis, 1983; circuit counselor Iowa Dist. East, 1981—. Bd. dirs. Service to Mil. Families; bd. dirs. Nemaha County chpt. ARC, Sabetha, 1973, county chmn., 1975. Republican. Home: 1603 S 2nd Ave Marshalltown IA 50158 Office: Redeemer Luth Ch 1600 S Center St Marshalltown IA 50158

DONADIO, PATRICK JAMES, minister, Assemblies of God; b. Schenectady, Apr. 17, 1940; s. James Vincent and Florence (Madelone) D.; B.S., N.E. Bible Coll., 1963; B.A., Central Bible Coll., 1965; student Pine Crest Bible Inst., 1960-61, Phila. Coll. of Bible, 1962-63; m. Ruth Spuler, Apr. 7, 1962; children—Dale Patrick, Doreen Patricia. Ordained to ministry, 1964; missionary Assemblies of God, 1966—; pastor chs., Alaska, 1966—; v.p. Alaska Youth Crusade, 1975—. Pres. Alaska dist. Christ Ambassadors, Assemblies of God, 1971-76; pres. Italian dist., 1974-76; bd. chaplains Central Peninsula Hosp., Soldotna, Alaska, 1974-76. Camp dir. Little Beaven Camp, Wasilla, Alaska, 1972-75. Author: By God's Grace or I Should Have Raised Pigs, 1976. Home and office: 102 Dayton Ave Collingswood NJ 08108

DONAGHEY, JOHN JAMES, priest, Roman Catholic Ch.; b. Boston, June 2, 1928; s. Hugh and Fanny Ann (Canney) D.; B.A., St. Mary's Mission Sem., 1951; M.A., Gregorian U., Rome, 1957, Ph.D., 1959. Ordained priest Roman Catholic Ch., 1954; instr. philosophy and liturgy St. Mary's, Techny, Ill., 1959-61; instr. philosophy, acad. dean, dean students St. Michael's Conesus, N.Y., 1961-65; instr. philosophy, dean students Divine Word Coll., Epworth, Iowa, 1965-70; provincial superior Divine Word Missionaries, Techny, 1970—. Chmn. formation com. Conf. of Maj. Superiors of Men, Washington, 1970—. Chmn. bd. trustees Divine Word Coll., Epworth, 1970-75; trustee Cath. Theol. Union, Chgo., 1970-74. Mem. Am. Cath. Philos. Assn. Democrat. Home: Society of the Divine Word Techny IL 60082

DONALDSON, CLIFFORD MERLE, minister, Church of God (Anderson, Indiana); b. Corpus Christi, Tex., Aug. 20, 1952; s. Earl Frank and Lois Matilda (Janes) D.; m. Kirsti Jo Hillstrom, Aug. 20, 1974; children: Kristopher, Amy, Corey. B.A., Gulf Coast Bible Coll., 1976. Ordained to ministry, Ch. of God (Anderson). Assoc. pastor 1st Ch. of God, Dewey, Okla., 1975-76, Big Spring, Tex., 1976-78; sr. pastor Woodmere Ch. of God, Muskegon, Mich., 1978—— chmn. Dist. Ministerial Assn., Cedar Springs, Mich., 1980-81; chmn. Div. Christian Edn., Lansing, Mich., 1980—; dir. youth camps Youth Camping in Mich., Grand Junction, 1983-84; chmn. Holiness Assn., Muskegon, 1984—; mem. steering com. North Central Pastors Fellowship, Lincoln Park, Mich., 1983—; chmn. Warner Camping Assn., Mich., 1984—; musician/vocalist Christian Evangelistic Music Ministry-Theophilus, 1972-75. Mem. adv. bd. Right to Life, Muskegon, 1983. Republican. Home: 1635 Kregel St Muskegon MI 49442 Office: Woodmere Ch of God 1630 Southland Muskegon MI 49442

DONALDSON, MARCIA JEAN, lay church worker, Conservative Baptist Church; b. Wilmington, Del., June 20, 1925; d. Aubrey Smith and Marcia Allen (Hall) Whitman; m. Robert Donald Donaldson, Jan. 8, 1944; children: Robert Gary, Pamela Lynn, David Keith. Student pub. schs., Wilmington. Sunday sch. tchr., Del. and N.J., 1943-70; tchr. Child Evangelism Fellowship, Wilmington, 1943-55, tchr., bd. dirs., N.J., 1955-64, dir., Ocean County, N.J., 1964-73; pres. Christian Children's Assocs., Toms River, N.J., 1973—. Mem. Nat. Religious Broadcasters Assn. (bd. dirs.), Gideons Aux. Writer radio and television syndicated programs for children; producer, hostess radio and TV program Adventure Club. office: 322 Dover Rd Toms River NJ 08754

DONFRIED, KARL PAUL, minister, Luth. Ch. Am., educator; b. N.Y.C., Apr. 6, 1940; s. Paul and Else (Schmuck) D.; A.B., Columbia, 1960; B.D., Harvard, 1963; S.T.M., Union Theol. Sem., 1965; Th.D., U. Heidelberg, 1968; m. Katharine E. Krayer, Sept. 10, 1960; children—Paul Andrew, Karen Erika. Ordained to ministry, 1963; named ecumenical canon Christ Ch. Cathedral, 1977; asso. pastor ch., N.Y.C., 1963-64; acting Luth. chaplain Columbia U., 1963-64; asso. prof. N.T. and early Christianity, Smith Coll., 1968—; mem. N.T. panel Nat. Luth.-Roman Cath. Dialogue, 1971-73, 75—; chmn. Columbia Seminar for Study of N.T., 1976—; vis. prof. Assumption Coll., Worcester, Mass., 1975, Amherst (Mass.) Coll., 1976, St. Hyacinth Coll. and Sem., Granby, Mass., 1976. Mem. Am. Acad. Religion (dir. 1972-73, pres. New Eng. region 1971-73), Studiorum Novi Testamenti Societas (chmn. Paul seminar 1975—), Soc. Bibl. Lit., Cath. Bibl. Assn. (pres. New Eng. region 1975—). Author: (with R.E. Brown J. Reumann) Peter in the New Testament, 1973; The Setting of Second Clement in Early Christianity, 1974. Editorial bd. Jour. Bibl. Lit., 1975—. Address: 157 Aubinwood Rd Amherst MA 01002

DONNELL, JAMES KNOX, minister, Presbyterian Church (USA); b. Waterloo, Iowa, Dec. 27, 1931; s. Allan Douglas and Anita Louise (Rath) D.; B.A., Princeton, 1953; B.D., Yale, 1958; m. Barbara Doan Pendleton, June 18, 1955; children: Bridget Stevens, Jane Knox, Calvin Rath. Ordained to ministry, 1958; pastor First Presbyn. Ch., West Carrollton, Ohio, 1958-72, College Hill Presbyn. Ch., Beaver Falls, Pa., 1972-85; assoc. exec. presbyter for ministry and candidates Pitts. Presbytery, 1985—; dir. summer youth camps, 1963-68; commr. to Gen. Assembly, 1965, 78; commr. to Synod, Ohio, 1961, 66, Trinity, 1973, 80; del. Ohio Council Chs., 1960-64, 70-72; chmn. Presbytery's Com. on Ministerial Relations, Miami Presbytery, 1969-72, Beaver-Butler Presbytery, 1972-79, 80-85; pres. West Carrollton Council Religious Edn., 1958-66. Pres., West Carrollton Bd. Edn., 1966-72; chmn. steering com. Meals on Wheels, Beaver Falls, 1972-85; bd. dirs. FISH, 1972-75, Big Bros. Assn. Greater Dayton, 1965-72; mem. adv. group profl. personnel Home Health Agy., Med. Center Beaver County, Pa., 1973-81. Mem. College Hill Ministerial Assn., Beaver Falls Ministerium. Home: 141 Dillon St Beaver Falls PA 15010 Office: 801 Union Ave Pittsburgh PA 15212

DONNELLAN, THOMAS ANDREW, archbishop, Roman Cath. Ch.; b. Bronx, N.Y., Jan. 24, 1914; s. Andrew and Margaret (Egan) D.; A.B., Cathedral Coll., N.Y.C.; postgrad. St. Joseph's Sem., Yonkers, N.Y.; J.C.D., Catholic U., Washington. Ordained priest Roman Catholic Ch., 1939; consecrated bishop, 1964; asst. pastor St. Patricks Cathedral, N.Y.C., 1942-44; asst. chancellor Archdiocese of N.Y., 1944-50, synodal judge, 1950-54, sec. to Cardinal Spellman, 1954, vice chancellor, 1954-57, archdiocesan vocation dir., 1957-58, chancellor, 1958-62; rector St. Josephs Sem., Yonkers, 1962-64; bishop of Ogdensburg, N.Y., 1964-68; archbishop of Atlanta, 1968—. Chaplain del.-vicar gen. Mil. Ordinariate for states of Ga., Fla., N.C., S.C., 1972—; treas. Nat. Conf. Cath. Bishops/U.S. Cath. Conf., 1972—; mem. Atlanta Community Relations Commn.; v.p. bd. trustees, chmn. devel. com. Cath. U.; trustee St. Vincent de Paul Sem., Boynton Beach, Fla., Christian Council Metro Atlanta; adv. bd. Atlanta's Neighborhood Justice Ctr., Inst. on Religious Life; bd. govs. Cath. Ch. Extension Soc.; mem. Ga. Christian Council Com. on Nominations and Personnel, Ga. Lord's Day Alliance; bd. dirs. Cath. Near East Relief. Decorated knight grand cross Knights of Holy Sepulchre; papal chamberlain, 1958, domestic prelate, 1958, prothonotary apostolic, 1962; named Clergyman of Yr., Ga. Region NCCJ, 1970. Office: 680 W Peachtree St NW Atlanta GA 30308

DONNELLY, GEORGE RICHARD, minister, United Methodist Church, counselor. b. Pitts., July 14, 1954; s. George Henderson Jr. and Jeannette Ruth (Polk) D.; m. Deborah Ann Johnson, June 5, 1976; 1 child, George. B.A., Ashland Coll., 1972-76; M. Div., Pitts. Theol. Sem., 1976-80; postgrad. Duquesne U., 1981—. Ordained to ministry United Methodist Ch. 1980. Assoc. pastor Greenstone United Meth. Ch., Bellevue, Pa., 1977-78; pastor Brush Run United Meth. Ch., Beaver Falls, Pa., 1978-79, Wampum United Meth. Ch., Pa., 1979—. Counselor, St. Francis Hosp. Hospice, New Castle, Pa., 1981—. Republican. Lodge: Lions. Home: Rural Route 2 Box 2509 Newport Rd Wampum PA 16157 Office: Wampum United Meth Ch Main St Wampum PA 16157

DONNELLY, ROBERT WILLIAM, bishop, Roman Catholic Church. Titular bishop of Garba, aux. bishop, Toledo, 1984—. Office: 2544 Parkwood Ave Toledo OH 43610*

D'ONOFRIO, ALICE MARIE, nun, Roman Catholic Church; b. N.Y.C., Dec. 20; d. Saverio and Mildred Louise (Johnson) D'Onofrio. A.A.S., Queen of the Apostles Coll., 1965; B.S., Fordham U., 1970; M.A., Seton Hall U., 1974, Ed.S., 1980. Entered Sisters of Catholic Apostolate, 1962. Tchr., Mt. Carmel-St. Benedicta Sch., S.I., N.Y., 1965-68, St. Bartholomew Sch., Providence, 1968-69, Sacred Heart Sch. Boys, Kearny, N.J., 1969-73, Holy Rosary Acad. High Sch., Union City, N.J., 1973-78; prin. Immaculate Conception Sch., Bronx, N.Y., 1978—; trustee Astor Home Guidance, Bronx, 1979-81; formation team mem. Pallottine Sisters, Harriman, N.Y., 1977—. Editor: Yearning of a Soul, 1978. Mem. Cath. Sch. Adminstrs. Assn. N.Y., Nat. Assn. Secondary Sch. Prins., Assn. Sch. Curriculum Devel., Middle States Assn. Schs. and Colls., Nat. Assn. Elem. Sch. Prins. Home: Immaculate Conception Convent 3305 Wallace Ave Bronx NY 10467 Office: Immaculate Conception Sch 760 E Gun Hill Rd Bronx NY 10467

DONOGHUE, JOHN F., bishop, Roman Catholic Church. Bishop, Charlotte, N.C., 1984—. Office: PO Box 3776 Charlotte NC 28203

DONOHUE, ROBERT AUSTIN, minister, Southern Baptist Convention; b. Las Cruces, N.Mex., Feb. 24, 1938; s. Robert E. and Mabel E. (Rhoads) D.p m. A. June Meek, Aug. 23, 1960; children: Dana June, David Sean, Dawn Erin. B.A., U. Tex.-El Paso, 1968, M.A. in Psychology, 1973; D.Adminstrn., Calif. Grad. Sch. Theology, 1978. Ordained deacon Baptist Ch., 1966, minister, 1970. Pastor, First Bapt. Ch., Dell City, Tex., 1970-71; assoc. pastor First So. Bapt. Ch., Casper, Wyo., 1971-73; pastor/organizer Evansville Bapt. Mission, Wyo., 1972-73; pastor Eastside Bapt.-TLC, Riverside, Calif., 1974—. Div. mgr. A.L. Williams Co., Riverside, 1981—; rep. First Am. Nat. Securities, Inc., Riverside, 1984—. Instr., Calif. Bapt. Coll., 1980-82. Mayor, City of Evansville, Wyo., 1973-74. Served with USAR, 1955-62. Mem. Nat. Assn. Ch. Bus. Adminstrs. (com. 1981). Republican. Home: 5798 Wisteria Dr Riverside CA 92504

DONOVAN, BARBARA JEAN, nun, hospital administrator, Roman Catholic Church. b. Pitts., Apr. 4, 1942; d. James Donald and Eleanor Louise (Whitman) Donovan. B.S., Duquesne U., 1967, M.Ed. in L.S., 1970; M.A. in Health Care Adminstrn., George Washington Univ., 1977. Joined Sisters of St. Francis of the Providence of God, Roman Cath. Ch., 1960. Tchr., Diocese of Pitts., 1962-67, 68-73, diocese Greensburg, Pa., 1967-68, diocese Milw., 1973-74; hosp. adminstr. St. Joseph's Hosp., Alton, Ill., 1977—, pres. bd. dirs., 1981—; mem. formation work Srs. St. Francis, 1971-73; dir. Good Samaritan Hosp., Mt. Vernon, Ill., 1982—; mem. profl. affairs com. St. Mary's Hosp., East St. Louis, Ill., 1983—. Mem. George Washington Alumni Assn., Greater Alton C. of C. (accreditation com. 1982). Home and Office: 915 E 5th St Alton IL 62002

DOOLEY, MARY A., nun, Roman Catholic Ch.; b. Somerville, Mass., Mar. 5, 1923; d. Richard A. and Mary A. (O'Neill) Dooley; A.B., Coll. of Our Lady of Elms, Chicopee, Mass., 1944; M.A., Assumption Coll., Worcester, Mass., 1960; postgrad. Laval U., Que., Can.; Ph.D., Sorbonne, U. Paris, 1968. Joined Sisters of St. Joseph, 1944; faculty St. Joseph's High Sch., North Adams, Mass.; chmn. dept. langs. Coll. of Our Lady of Elms, Chicopee, Mass., 1968-71, trustee, 1971—; maj. superior Sisters of St. Joseph, Springfield, Mass., 1971—. Chmn. New Eng., Region I., Leadership Conf. of Women Religious, 1974—, mem. nat. bd., 1974—, mem. exec. com., 1975—. Address: Mont Marie Holyoke MA 01040

DOOLIN, SYLVA ALPHA, minister, Assemblies of God; b. Selvin, Ind., Nov. 3, 1913; d. James Oliver and Emma Cordillia (Thiry) Bolin; grad. Glad Tidings Bible Inst., 1937; certificate Bethany Bible Coll., 1937; master diploma worker's tng. Assemblies of God, Springfield, 1958; diploma Christian Writers Inst., 1963; m. Marvin Lawson Doolin, July 15, 1939 (dec. 1972); children: Marvin, Roy Edward, Daniel Lee. Ordained to ministry, 1947. Pastor Assemblies of God chs., Carrollton, Ill., 1939-40, Jerseyville, Ill., 1940-45, Renault, Ill., 1945-53, Olney, Ill., 1953-63, Browning, Ill., 1963-70; Bible tchr., music tchr., evangelist, christian writer, Browning, 1970—. Mem. advisory council for ch. sch. lit. Assemblies of God, 1958; treas. Salvation Army; WCTU worker, Olney; mem. Schuyler County Sr. Citizens Council; active Ret. Sr. Vols. Program. Recipient Manuscript award Harvest Publs., 1966. Contbr. short stories and articles to numerous religious mags. and jours. Home and Office: Route 1 Browning IL 62624

DOOLING, J(OHN) STUART, priest, Roman Catholic Church; b. Phila., June 27, 1913; s. John Aloysius and Sarah Dermitt (Love) D. A.B., Catholic U., 1936, Ph.D., 1951; LL.D. (hon.), Lehigh U., 1978, Muhlenberg U., 1974. Ordained priest, Roman Catholic Ch., 1940. Mem. faculty Catholic U. Am., 1949-64; pres. Allentown Coll., Center Valley, Pa., 1964-78; superior Deshairs Hall, Washington, 1962-64, Wills Hall, Center Valley, Pa., 1965-70; provincial Oblates of St. Francis de Sales, Wilmington, Del., 1978—. Contbr. articles in field quantum mechanics to tech. jours. Club: Saucon Valley.

DORFF, MARCELLA ADABELLE, missionary, Assemblies of God; b. Moorhead, Minn., Mar. 14, 1923; d. Walter Fritz and Emma (Nokelby) D.; B.A. in Missions, N. Central Bible Coll., Mpls., 1963; postgrad. Grad. Sch. Assemblies God, Springfield, Mo., 1974. Ordained to ministry, 1950; founding pastor ch., Owatonna, Minn., 1947-52; sec. Youth for Christ, Owatonna-Faribault area, 1950-52; youth leader S.E. Minn., Assemblies of God Ch., 1950-52; missionary to Indonesia, 1953—; tchr. Bible schs., Indonesia, 1953—, founder, dir. Salatiga (Java) Bible Sch., 1976—. Home: 1445 Boonville Ave Springfield MO 65802 Office: Kotak Pos 25 Salatiga Java Indonesia

DORN, LOUIS OTTO, minister, Lutheran Church-Missouri Synod, editor; b. Detroit, July 1, 1928; s. Theodore Herman and Thekla Maria (Frederkig) D.; m. Erna Ruth Koessel, June 14, 1953; children: Margaret Ligaya Dorn White, Peter Bayani, Martin Louis, Judith Anne. B.A., Concordia Theol. Sem., St. Louis, 1951, B.Div., 1962; M.A. in Linguistics, Ateneo de Manila U., Quezon City, Philippines, 1974; Th.D., Luth. Sch. Theology, Chgo., 1980. Ordained to ministry, 1953. Missionary, Luth. Ch. in Philippines, Manila, 1953-74; candidate Ohio dist. Luth. Ch.-Mo. Synod, 1975-80, N.J. dist. Luth. Ch.-Mo. Synod, 1980—; translations research assoc. Am. Bible Soc., N.Y.C., 1979—; chmn. Luth. Philippine Mission, Manila, 1962-63, 71-72; sec. Luth. Ch. in Philippines, Manila, 1962-63, sec. commn. for ecumenical affairs, 1964-74, dir. translations dept., 1966-74; hon.

translations advisor Philippine Bible Soc., Manila, 1968-74; bd. dirs. Interchurch Lang. Sch., Quezon City, 1964-74, chmn. bd., 1967-74. Contbr. articles and revs. to religious publs. Grantee Central dist. Luth. Ch.-Mo. Synod, 1944-53; scholarship grantee Luth. Sch. Theology, Chgo., 1974-78. Mem. Soc. Bibl. Lit. Democrat. Office: Am Bible Soc 1865 Broadway New York NY 10023

DORNETTE, RALPH MEREDITH, evangelist, Christian Ch.; b. Cin., Aug. 31, 1927; s. Paul August and Lillian (Bauer) D.; A.B., Cin. Bible Coll., 1948; postgrad. Cin. Bible Sem., 1948-51, Talbot Theol. Sem., 1966-67; m. Betty Jean Pierce, May 11, 1948; 1 dau., Cynthia Anne. Ordained to ministry, 1947; minister Indian Creek Christian Ch., Cynthiana, Ky., 1946-51, First Christian Ch., Muskogee, Okla., 1951-57; organizing minister Bellaire Christian Ch., Tulsa, 1957-59; faculty Cin. Bible Coll., 1948-51, Midwest Christian Coll., Oklahoma City, 1955-56; guest lectr. Cin. Christian Sem., 1972, 76-79, Pacific Christian Coll., 1982, 83, 85; exec. dir. So. Calif. Evangelistic Assn., 1959-62; founding minister Eastside Christian Ch., Fullerton, Calif., 1962-68; exec. dir. So. Calif. Evangelistic Assn. and Ch. Devel. Fund, Inc., Torrance, 1968-77; mem. faculty Cin. Bible Coll., 1977-79; devel. officer Cin. Bible Sem., 1977-79; exec. dir. Ch. Devel. Fund Inc., 1979—; sr. minister LaHabra Christian Ch., Calif., 1983—. Vice pres. N.Am. Christian Conv., 1972; trustee Cin. Bible Sem. Named Churchman of Year, Pacific Christian Coll., 1973. Author: Bible Answers to Popular Questions-Book I, 1954, Book II, 1961; Walking With Our Wonderful Lord, 1955. Contbr. articles to religious jours. Address: Church Devel Fund Inc 18436 Hawthorne Blvd Suite 207 Torrance CA

DORPH, SHELDON ARTHUR, religious educator, rabbi, Conservative, Judaism. b. Phila., Mar. 30, 1941; s. Philip and Hannah (Cantor) D.; m. Gail Zaiman, Dec. 27, 1964; children: Michele, Rena, Yonina. A.B., Temple U., 1963; M. Hebrew Lit., Jewish Theol Sem., 1965; Ed.D., Columbia U., 1976. Ordained rabbi, 1968. Dir., Camp Ramah, N.Y.C., 1968-71; prin. Los Angeles Hebrew High Sch., 1971-84; headmaster Golda Meir Sch., Los Angeles, 1979—. Editor: Jewish Education Issues at Irvine, 1979; Shalav Aleph, Bet, Gimmel, 1980-83. Jewish Community Found. grantee, 1973-75. Mem. Jewish Educators Assembly. Home: 245 S LaPeer Dr Beverly Hills CA 90211 Office: Golda Meir Sch 15339 Saticoy Ave Van Nuys CA 91406

DORSEY, LAWRENCE JOSEPH, priest, Roman Cath. Ch.; b. Cedar Rapids, Iowa, Sept. 18, 1933; s. Robert Michael and Marie Margurite (Burvenich) D.; B.A., Immaculate Conception Sem., Mo., 1959; M.S., Creighton U., 1968; D.Min., San Francisco Theol. Sem., 1977. Ordained priest, 1959; urban asso. pastor, Omaha, 1959-64, 66-68; rural asso. pastor, Creighton, Nebr., 1964-66; senator Omaha Senate of Priests, 1970-71; dir. guidance Dominican High Sch., Omaha, 1968-72; dir. Grad. Program in Pastoral Ministry, Creighton U., 1972—; dir. continuing edn. Omaha Archdiocese; mem. exec. bd. Nat. Fedn. Priest Council. Active, Citizens Concerned for Orderly Implimentation Ct. Ordered Busing to Achieve Integrated Pub. Schs. Named Counselor of Year, Omaha Notre Dame Acad., 1973. Adm., Nebr. Navy. Mem. AAUP (chmn. acad. freedom com. Creighton chpt.), Nat. Assn. for Continuing Edn. Roman Cath. Clergy, Am., Nebr. personnel and guidance assns. Contbr. articles to religious publs. Home: 2617 S 31st St Omaha NE 68105 Office: Creighton U Omaha NE 68178

DORST, RICHARD RALPH, minister, Presbyterian Church of the U.S.A.; b. Pitts., Mar. 15, 1945; s. Ralph August and Mary Margaret (Bitzer) D.; m. Connie Lynette Smith, June 15, 1968; children: Stephen, Keri, Brian. B.A., Houghton Coll., 1967; M.Div., McCormick Theol. Sem., 1970; D.Min., Fuller Theol. Sem., 1982. Ordained to ministry Presbyn. Ch., 1971. Asst. and assoc. minister Meml. Park Community United Presbyn. Ch., Pitts., 1970-75; assoc. minister Second Presbyn. Ch., Memphis, 1976-80; sr. minister Kirk of the Hills Presbyn. Ch., Tulsa, 1981—; adv. trustee Literacy and Evangelism Internat., Tulsa, 1981—. Author doctoral dissertation Renewal through Ministry to New Members. Bd. dirs. Prison Fellowship, Memphis, 1977-80. Republican. Avocations: sports; travel. Home: 6204 S Pittsburgh Ave Tulsa OK 74136 Office: 4102 E 61st St Kirk of the Hills Presbyn Ch Tulsa OK 74136

DORTCH, RICHARD WILLIAM, minister, educator Assemblies of God; b. Granite City, Ill., Oct. 15, 1931; s. Harry and Mary C. (Brown) D.; m. Mildred V. Nickles, July 11, 1952; children: Deanna R., Richard William. Student N. Central Bible Coll., Minn., 1949-52, U. Liège (Belgium), 1960-62. Ordained to ministry Assemblies of God, 1954. Pastor, Watertown, S.D., 1952-55, Garden City, Kan., 1955-57, Alton, Ill., 1963-67; pres. Emmanuel Bible Inst., Andrimont, Belgium, 1957-62; field fellowship sec. Assemblies of God of Europe, 1959-62; exec. sec. Assemblies of God of Ill., 1967-70, state supt., 1970-84; exec. presbyter Assemblies of God, 1971—; exec. dir. P.T.L. Television Ministries; dir. P.T.L. Television Network. Bd. dirs. Ch. Growth Internat., Grad Sch. Theology of Assemblies of God, Evangel Coll. Contbr. articles to religious jours. Home: Lake Wylie Charlotte NC 28220 Office: PO Box 11245 Charlotte NC 28220

DOSTER, JUNE MARKEN, minister, Christian Church (Disciples of Christ); b. Des Moines, June 10, 1930; d. DeLoss Irving and Helen (Roberts) Marken; m. Harold Charles Doster, June 19, 1955; children: Deborah, Diana, Donald, Denise. B.A., magna cum laude, State U. Iowa, 1952; M.R.E., Yale U., 1957. Ordained to ministry, Christian Ch. (Disciples of Christ), 1982. Dir. religious edn. Meml. Christian Ch., Ann Arbor, Mich., 1966-68; instr. society Bethany Coll., W.Va., 1961-62; minister Ch. edn. First Christian Ch., Wilson, N.C.; assoc. regional minister Christian Ch. Ga., Macon, 1984—; mem. Church Women Fellowship regional cabinet Canton, Mo., 1975-77, Wilson, N.C., 1979-83, mem. exec. com. Indpls., 1985—. Author retreat, jr. camp curriculum, Christian Ch. in N.C. Leader, Girl Scouts U.S.A., Ky., W.Va., 1968-73, treas. neighborhood council Wilson, N.C., 1978-83; bd. dirs. Wilson Concerts, 1981-83; mem. adv. bd. Villa Internat., Atlanta, 1985—; bd. dirs. Parents Anonymous, Wilson, N.C., 1982-83; mem. adv. bd. Christmount Christian Assembly, 1985—. Recipient Adelaide L. Burge award Iowa State U., 1951, Sr. Woman Scholar, 1952, Mortar Bd., 1951. Mem. PEO, Phi Beta Kappa, Alpha Xi Delta. Republican. Clubs: Gen. Fedn. Women (Keyser, W.Va. and Canton, Mo.); Wilson Women's. Avocations: music (cello, piano, organ); swimming; water skiing; golf. Home: 2452 Stonington Rd Dunwoody GA 30338 Office: Christian Church in Georgia 2370 Vineville Ave Macon GA 31204

DOTSON, JAMES BENJAMIN, minister, So. Bapt. Conv.; b. Belltown, Tenn., Jan. 14, 1924; s. Only Robert and Mary Jane (Farr) D.; B.S., San Francisco Bapt. Coll., 1953; B.D.. Golden Gate Bapt. Sem., 1954; B.A., Carson Newman Coll., 1965; m. Gladys Longley, Dec. 1950; children—Raymond, James Benjamin, Mary, Rebecca, Ruth, Sarah. Ordained to ministry, 1940; pastor numerous chs., Tenn., 1940-50, Cooper Ridge Bapt. Ch., Rockford, Tenn., 1973—; dir. Tellico River Camp and Home, Knoxville, 1970—. Pres. Alaska Bapt. Conv., 1961-63; missionary Europe, Asia, Alaska, 1954-63; tchr. Knoxville City schs., 1963—. Editor The Outreach Pub., 1970—. Home: Route 2 Rockford TN 37853 Office: Route 4 Madisonville TN 37354

DOUD, JOHN FOSTER, minister, National Association of Congregational Christian Churches; b. Milw., Feb. 7, 1953; s. Donald Budlong and Jane Ellen (Foster) D.; m. Catherine Ellen Roberts, Aug. 21, 1976. B.A., Albion Coll., 1975; M.Div., Duke U., 1978. Ordained to ministry Nat. Assn. Congl. Christian Chs., 1978. Chaplain, U. N.C. Hosp., Chapel Hill, 1978; minister First Congl., Lake Odessa, Mich., 1978-80; sr. minister Arbor Grove Congl. Ch., Jackson, Mich., 1981—; chmn. Commn. Christian Edn., Nat. Ass. Congl. Christian Chs., 1983-85; moderator Central Mich. Assn. Congl. Christian Chs., 1983-84; chmn. ch. and pastoral counselling Mich. Conf., Congl. Christian Chs., 1983-84; pres. Jackson Area Ministerial Assn. (Mich.), 1983-84. Author pamphlets for church devotions. Vice pres. Big Bros./Big Sisters, Jackson County, 1983-84; mem. Voice of Reason, Jackson, 1982-84. Fellow Internat. Congl. Fellowship; mem. Ecumenical Inst. Jewish/Christian Studies, Fellowship of Religious Humanists, Soc. Congl. Christian Educators, Found. for Econ. Edn. Inc. Republican. Club: High Twelve 16 (Jackson). Lodges: Lions (Lake Odessa), Masons (Jackson). Home: 2510 Spring Arbor Rd Jackson MI 49203 Office: Arbor Grove Congl Church 2621 McCain Rd Jackson MI 49203

DOUGHERTY, JOHN JOSEPH See *Who's Who in America,* 43rd edition.

DOUGLAS, ALBAN HECTOR, minister, religious educator, Evangelical Free Church. B. Swift Current, Sask., Can., Nov. 21, 1920; s. Alex A. Douglas and Bessie J. Douglas Foged; m. Anna Schmidt, Nov. 4, 1949; children: Heather, Trevor. M.A. In Missions, Grace Theol. Sem., India, 1982. B.R.E., Briercrest Bible Coll., Sask., 1983. Missionary, China Inland Mission-Overseas Missionary Fellowship, China, 1947-51, Philippines, 1954-64; pastoral work Presbyterian Ch. of Can., Sask., 1952-54; tchr. Prairie Bible-Inst., Three Hills, Alta., 1965—. Author: Bible Doctrine, 1969; transl. 100 bible lessons into Chinese, Indonesian, Korean, Indian langs. Home and Office: Prairie Bible Inst Three Hills AB T0M 2A0 Canada

DOUGLAS, JESSIE MAE, religious educator, Baptist Missionary Association of America; medical consultant; b. Ethel, La., Jan. 25, 1929; s. John and Edna Irene (Payne) H.; m. Silas Douglas; children by previous marriage: Carl Russel, Ronald Vernon, Ira Adrian. Diploma Coinson Nursing Sch., 1949; B.A. in Religious Edn., U. Bibl. Studies, 1983; student Leland Coll. Extension, 1952-53, La. State U., 1976-77. Cert. health coordinator 1983. Pres. Woman's Missionary Soc., Baton Rouge, 1956-66; mem. edn. bd. New Sunlight Baptist Ch., Baton Rouge, 1968—, chmn., 1966-84; bd. dirs. Eden Park Referral Ctr., Baton Rouge, 1973-77; instr. Fourth Dist. Religious Inst., Baton Rouge, 1983—; del. Nat. Baptist Sunday Sch. Conv., Memphis, 1983. Health cons. Head Start programs Tex. Tech. U., Lubbock, 1984—. Editor health coordinating manual, 1982; author: Job-A Perspective on Suffering, 1985. (pamphlet) Medicaid and Headstart, 1976. Founder Baton Rouge Sickle Cell Found., 1974; del. Nat. Sickle Cell Conf., Detroit, 1984; counselor sickle cell patients, Baton Rouge, 1974—; trainer S. Baton Rouge Adv. Com., 1967—; liaison Earl K. Long and Community Agys., Baton Rouge, 1983—. Named Hon. Col. State La., 1984, Hon. Lt., 1984; recipient Outstanding Service award Mayor's office, 1977; Nurse of Yr. award Baton Rouge Assn. Community Action, 1975. Mem. NAACP. Democrat. Lodge: Order Eastern Star, Stars of Jupiter. Avocations: crocheting, quilting. Home: 8968 Hyacinth St Baton Rouge LA 70810 Office: Baton Rouge Sickle Cell Found 2301 North Blvd Baton Rouge LA 70802

DOUGLASS, ALBERT IRVIN, minister, Lutheran Church in America; b. Phila., Feb. 24, 1945; s. Albert and Dorothy Katherine (Moths) D.; m. Carol Louise McClay, July 8, 1967; children: Sharon Louise, Katherine Marie. A.B., Muhlenberg Coll., 1967; M.Div., Luth. Theol. Sem., Phila., 1971. Ordained to ministry Lutheran Ch., 19—. Pastor St. Luke's Ch., Obelisk, Pa., 1971-77, Little Zion Ch., Telford, Pa., 1977—; chmn. examining com. South East Pa. Synod, Luth. Ch. Am., 1980—. Mem. Task Force for Continuing Care, Penn Found. for Mental Health, 1980—; chmn. Montgomery County Com. Office of Children and Youth, Norristown, Pa., 1983—. Democrat. Home and Office: 267 Morwood Rd Telford PA 18969

DOUGLASS, HERBERT EDGAR, JR., minister, jour. editor, Seventh-day Adventists; b. Springfield, Mass., May 16, 1927; s. Herbert Edgar and Mildred Jennie (Munson) D.; A.B., Atlantic Union Coll., 1947; M.A., Andrews U., 1956; B.D., Seventh-day Adventist Theol. Sem., 1957; Th.D., Pacific Sch. Religion, 1964; m. Norma F. Campbell, Nov. 16, 1974; children by previous marriage—Janelle, Herbert, Reatha, Vivienne Sue. Ordained to ministry, 1951; pastor chs., Ill., 1947-53; mem. theol. faculty Pacific Union Coll., Angwin, Calif., 1953-60; head, theol. faculty, Atlantic Union Coll., S. Lancaster, Mass., 1960-64, dean, 1964-67, pres., 1967-70; asso. editor Rev. and Herald, Washington, 1970-76. Vice pres. Pacific Leadership Seminar; chmn. bd. Trans World Found. Named Distinguished Alumnus Andrews U., 1976. Author If I Had One Sermon to Preach; Why I Joined; We Found This Faith; Why Jesus Waits; Perfection: The Impossible Possibility; Jesus-The Benchmark of Humanity; What Ellen White Means to Me; contbr. articles to religious jours. Home: 419 Browning Ave Bismarck ND 58501

DOUGLASS, SAMUEL KARL, minister, So. Baptist Conv.; b. Corpus Christi, Tex., Apr. 3, 1950; s. Ransom Samuel and Martha Jean (Balzer) D.; B.S., Tex. A. and M. U., 1972; postgrad. Southwestern Bapt. Theol. Sem., 1976—; m. Nancy Kay Nelson, July 22, 1972; 1 son, Mark Nelson. Ordained to ministry, 1973; youth dir. Calvary Bapt. Ch., Bryan, Tex., 1969-71; pastor Oakland Bapt. Ch., Roans Prairie, Tex., 1971-72, Rock Prairie Bapt. Ch., Bryan, 1972-73; summer minister of youth 1st Bapt. Ch., Bryan, 1973, asst. pastor, minister of youth and recreation, 1974-76; minister of youth 1st Bapt. Ch., Corsicana, Tex., 1973-74; dir. Bapt. Student Union, Kilgore (Tex.) Coll., Bapt. Gen. Conv. Tex., Kilgore, 1976—, Panola Jr. Coll., Carthage, Tex., 1976—. Mem. Am. Council Alcohol Problems, Kilgore Ministerial Alliance, Religious Workers Assn. Kilgore Coll., Fellowship of Christian Athletes, Farm Bur., Tex., Nat. recreation and park socs., Gregg County, Rusk-Panola Bapt. assns. Home: 532 Camp St Kilgore TX 75662 Office: 809 Nolen St Kilgore TX 75662

DOUHAN, JOHN, minister, American Baptist Churches in the U.S.A.; b. Boston, May 9, 1933; s. John and Svea Evelyn (Karlson) D.; m. Beverly Ann Pearson, Aug. 20, 1955 (div. Dec. 1975); children: John III, Paul, Karl; m. Mary Zelinda Makepeace, June 26, 1982. B.A., Harvard U., 1956; B.Div., Bethel Sem., 1958; M.S.T., Andover Newton Theol. Sch., 1962; D.Min., 1981. Ordained to ministry Baptist Ch., 1960. Pastor, South Bapt. Ch., Worcester, Mass., 1959-63; area minister Am. Bapt. Chs. of Mass., Boston, 1963-77, assoc. exec. minister, 1977—; lectr. O.T., Barrington Coll., R.I., 1962-63; lectr. Andover-Newton Theol. Sch., 1969-81, Gordon-Conwell Theol. Sch., 1972-79; vis. lectr. Bapt. Seminaries, Scandanavia, 1983. Bd. dirs. Found for Campus Ministry, Boston, 1966—, Bapt. Home of Mass., 1978—; chmn. bd. Center for the Ministry, Newton, Mass., 1982—; mem. Human Rights Commn., Bapt. World Alliance, Washington, 1980—; mem. Democratic Town Com., Arlington, Mass., 1972, Dartmouth, Mass., 1983. Mem. Religious Research Assn., Conf. Bapt. Ministers. Clubs: Beverly Yacht (Marion, Mass.); New Bedford Yacht; Harvard (bd. dirs). Office: Am Bapt Chs of Mass 88 Tremont St Boston MA 02108

DOUKAS, JAMES ANDREAS, priest, Greek Orthodox Archdiocese of North and South America; b. Cleve., Nov. 13, 1950; s. Andreas Demetrios and Matilda (Miconitis) D.; m. Goldie Chrysanthe Pirovolos, July 6, 1974; children: Demetria, Dianna. B.A., Hellenic Coll., 1973; M.Div., Holy Cross Greek Orthodox Theol. Sch., 1976. Ordained priest Greek

Orthodox Archdiocese of N. and S. Am., 1976. Priest St. Demetrios Greek Orthodox Ch., Astoria, L.I., N.Y., 1976-78, Holy Trinity Greek Orthodox Ch., Fort Wayne, Ind., 1978-82, Nativity of the Virgin Mary Greek Orthodox Ch., Plymouth, Mich., 1982—; spiritual advisor Orthodox Christian Fellowship, Detroit, 1984—; mem. Archdiocesan Spiritual Renewal Com., 1980-82; mem. youth commn. Diocese of Detroit, 1985—. Fellow Eastern Orthodox Council of Chs. Home: 14595 Shadywood Dr Plymouth MI 48170 Office: Nativity of the Virgin Mary Greek Orthodox Ch 39851 W Five Mile Rd Plymouth MI 48170

DOUMA, HARRY HEIN, minister, independent nondenominational church; b. Richmond, N.Y., Mar. 12, 1933; s. Hein and Ida D.; B.A., Shelton Coll., 1960; M.Div., Faith Theol. Sem., 1965; m. Carole Marie Evelyn Piening, June, 1958; children: Daniel, Deborah Joy, Crystal. Ordained to ministry, 1965; chaplain Edward R. Johnstone Tng. and Research Center, Bordentown, N.J., 1960-65; pastor Times Beach (Mo.) Bible Ch., 1965-67, 1st Bapt. Ch., Pilot Knob, Mo., 1967-76. Pres., Penuel Inc., Lake Killarney, Ironton (Mo.) Children's Camp and Retreat Center, 1973—; pastor Penuel Fellowship, 1976—; guide Holy Land tours; radio and TV speaker. Author: The Book of Revelation for the Layman, 1971. Home: 326 Michael St Ironton MO 63650 Office: Lake Killarney Ironton MO 63663

DOUMOURAS, ALEXANDER, priest, Greek Orthodox Church; b. Sheboygan, Wis., Dec. 8, 1936; s. Demetrios and Ioanna (Benos) D. B.A., U. Wis., 1960; M.Div., St. Vladimir Sem., Crestwood, N.Y., 1964; M.A., Fordham U., 1971. Ordained priest Greek Orthodox Ch. With Study and Planning Commn., Standing Conf. Orthodox Bishops in Am., N.Y.C.; bd. dirs. Council of Chs., N.Y.C., 1982—, Religion in Am. Life, N.Y.C.; mem. exec. com. Faith and Order Commn., ecumenical officer Greek Orthodox Archdiocese of North and S. Am. Office: Study and Planning Commn Standing Conf Orthodox Bishops in America 8-10 E 79th St New York NY 10021

DOW, THOMAS EDWARD, college dean, Missionary Church. B. Royal Oak, Mich., Feb. 5, 1940; s. Harold Walter D. and Herbena May (Buckner) LeNeve; m. Carolyn Ruth Spice, Sept. 23, 1961; children: Stephen Thomas, Beverly Susan, Marianne Elizabeth. Th.B., Emmanuel Bible Coll., 1961; B.A., Wilfrid Laurier U., 1963, M.A., 1972; B.D., Waterloo Luth. Sem., Ont., Can., 1966; Ph.D., U. Waterloo, 1981. Ordained to ministry Missionary Church, 1963. Pastor, Missionary Ch., Stratford, Ont., Can., 1962-66, Lincoln Heights Missionary Ch., 1967-72, Beechwood Missionary Ch., 1980—; prof. Emmanuel Bible Coll., Kitchener, Ont., 1966-72, 74-79, acad. dean, 1979—; missionary Missionary Ch., Nigeria, 1972-74; sec./treas., bd. dirs. Missionary Ch. Can., 1979—. Recipient scholarship U. Waterloo, 1979-80. Mem. Can. Assn. Bible Colls. (exec. com. 1980—). Home: 30 Simpson Ave Kitchener ON N2A 1L3 Canada Office: Emmanuel Bible Coll 100 Fergus Ave Kitchener ON N2A 2H2 Canada

DOWD, KARL EDMUND, priest, camp dir., Roman Cath. Ch.; b. Nashua, N.H., May 3, 1934; s. Karl Edmund and Edna Louise (Burque) D.; B.S., Coll. of Holy Cross, 1956; B.Th., U. Ottawa, 1958, S.T.L., 1960; M.Ed., Rivier Coll., 1964. Ordained priest Roman Catholic Ch., 1960; tchr. Bishop Bradley High Sch., Manchester, N.H., 1960-62; asst. camp dir. Camp Fatima, Gilmanton, N.H., 1960-62; tchr., athletic dir. St. Thomas Aquinas High Sch., Dover, N.H., 1962-68; adminstr. St. Marys, Rollinsford, N.H., 1967; asso. pastor St. Bernards Parish, Keene, N.H., 1968-69, St. Josephs Parish, Nashua, N.H., 1969-71; diocesan dir. Cath. Camps Fatima and Bernadette, Manchester, N.H., 1971—; assoc. Immaculate Heart of Mary, Concord, N.H., 1971-75; pastor St. Joseph's Ch., Salem, N.H., 1975—; mem. New Eng. Liturgical Com., 1961—, dir., 1976-77; dean Salem Deanery Diocese of Manchester, 1980—; chaplain K.C., 1970-75. Bd. dirs., mem. exec. com. Concord Mental Health Clinic; chmn. Interfaith Service Council N.H. Hosp., Concord, 1974-75; past pres., bd. dirs. Salemhaven Inc. Recipient Noyes medal in speaking, 1952. Mem. Am. Camping Assn. (chmn. New Eng. Ch. Camp com. 1973, program chmn. 1975-77, mem. nat. execs. group 1982—, v.p. New Eng. sect. 1984—), N.H. Camp Dirs. Assn. (sec. 1971-74, pres. 1974—) , U.S. Cath. Conf. on Cath. Camping (nat. adv. bd. 1972—) . Home: 33 Main St Salem NH 03079 Office: 153 Ash St Manchester NH 03105

DOWDELL, JOSEPH MICHAEL, priest, Roman Catholic Church. b. Buffalo, Aug. 14, 1935; s. Michael Joseph and Rose Mary (Burkhardt) D. B.B.A., Canisius Coll., 1957; M.A. in Theology, Christ The King Sem., 1976. Ordained priest Roman Catholic Ch., 1963. Tchr., Cardinal Mindszenty Sch., Dunkirk, N.Y., 1964-75; asst. pastor St. Peter's Ch., Lewiston, N.Y., 1976-78; hosp. chaplain Roswell Park Hosp., Buffalo, 1978-80; pastor Blessed Sacrament Ch., Andover, NY, 1980-83, St. Mary's Ch., Lockport, N.Y., 1983—. Served to 2d lt. U.S. Army, 1958. Dept. Def. scholar for Spanish, 1968. Mem. Lockport Clergy Assn. Address: 5 Saxton St Lockport NY 14094

DOWDY, JOHN WESLEY, JR., minister, Baptist Ch.; b. Muskogee, Okla., Nov. 15, 1935; s. John Wesley and Floy Weaver (Thurston) D.; A.A., Southwest Bapt. Coll., 1954; B.A., Southwest Mo. State U., 1956; M.Div., Midwestern Bapt. Theol. Sem., 1962, D.Ministry, 1974; m. Joycelyn Adele Pinnell, June 9, 1956; children—Barbara Annette, Gina Marie. Ordained to ministry Baptist Ch., 1956; pastor chs. Cedar City, Mo., 1956-59, Maysville, Mo., 1959-64, Tabernacle Bapt. Ch., Kansas City, Mo., 1964-75; dir. Christian Social Ministries, Met. So. Bapt. Mission Bd., Kansas City, Mo., 1975—; supr. pastoral ministries seminar Midwest Bapt. Theol. Sem., 1975—. Vice moderator Kansas City (Mo.) Bapt. Assn., 1969-71, mem. exec. com., 1966-75, chmn. missions com., 1972-75; mem. adv. com. for nat. Bapt. work Mo. Bapt. Conv., 1972-74. Vol. probation officer Kansas City, Mo., 1970-75; mem. adv. com. clin. pastoral edn. Bapt. Meml. Hosp., Kansas City, Mo., 1976—. Mem. Midwestern Bapt. Theol. Sem. Alumni Assn. (nat. pres. 1972-74, sec. Mo. chpt. 1970-72). Mason; mem. Order Eastern Star. Home: 11 NE Englewood Rd Kansas City MO 64118 Office: Suite 310 910 Pennsylvania Ave Kansas City MO 64105

DOWHOWER, RICHARD LEE, minister, Lutheran Church in America, b. Saginaw, Mich., Nov. 13, 1936; s. Howard Young and Anne M. (Myers) D.; m. Kay E. Scanlon, Aug. 20, 1960; children: Deidre Ann, Andrea Lyn. B.A., Thiel Coll., 1958; B.D., Northwestern Luth. Sem., Mpls., 1961. Ordained to ministry Lutheran Ch. in Am., 1961. Pastor Zion's First Ch., Ambridge, Pa., 1961-65; assoc. pastor Luth. Ch. of the Holy Comforter, Balt., 1966-69; sr. pastor Berkeley Hills Luth. Ch., Pitts., 1969-76, Trinity Luth. Ch., Camp Hill, Pa., 1976—; pastor, evangelist Luth. Ch. in Am., 1979-80; exec. bd. Central Pa. Synod, 1982—; del. Luth. Ch. in Am. Conv., 1984. Citizens adv. com. Juvenile Ct., Beaver County, Pa., 1962-65; active Northeast Balt. Community Orgn., 1966-68; adv. com. mem. North Hills Schs., Pitts., 1972-76. Mem. Am. Family Found., World Future Soc., Luth. Ch. in Am. Found. (bd. dirs.), Republican. Club: YMCA (Harrisburg, Pa.). Home: 2106 Ridge Rd Camp Hill PA 17011 Office: Trinity Luth Ch 2000 Chestnut St Camp Hill PA 17011

DOWNIE, SANDRA CARROLL, lay church worker, Roman Catholic Church; b. St. Joseph, Mo., Feb. 10, 1939; d. William Harry and Beverly (Carroll) Minger; m. R. Hayden Downie, June 1, 1963 (div. 1979); children: Whitney Anne, Timothy, Allyson Diane. B.S. in Recreation Therapy, Tex. Women's U., 1960. Mem. parish council Christ the King Ch., Tulsa, 1971-74, chmn. social action com., 1971-74; bd. dirs. Neighbor for Neighbor, Tulsa, 1972-74; bd. dirs. Cath. Ctr., Cath. Diocese Tulsa, 1972-75, mem. permanent diaconate, 1975-78; chmn. Tulsa Met. Ministry, 1980—. Asst. mgr. Met. Tulsa C. of C., 1983—; exec. dir. Tulsa Bus. Health Group, Inc., 1983—. Exec. com. bd. dirs. ARC, Tulsa, 1970-73, Family and Children's Services, Tulsa, 1972-75, YWCA, Tulsa, 1974-75; chmn. suburban div. Tulsa United Way, 1970-72, Social Action, Christ the King Ch., Tulsa, 1970-74, Hillcrest Med. Ctr. safety com., 1980-82; mem. Tulsa Human Services Commn., 1980-82, others.

DOWNING, CHRISTINE ROSENBLATT, religious educator, Society of Friends; b. Leipzig, Ger., Mar. 21, 1931; came to U.S., 1935; d. Edgar F. and Herta (Fischer) Rosenblatt; m. River Malcolm, Sept. 2, 1984; children by previous marriage; Peter, Eric, Scott, Christopher, Sandra. B.A., Swarthmore Coll., 1952; Ph.D., Drew U., 1966; M. A., U.S. Internat. U., 1982. Chmn., prof. religion San Diego State U., 1974—; faculty Calif. Sch. Profl. Psychology, 1974—. Author: Face to Face to Face, 1976; The Goddess, 1981. Editor: Quaker Religious Thought, 1969-74. Kent fellow, 1961-63; Cross Disciplinary fellow, 1967-68; NEH fellow, 1983. Mem. Am. Acad. Religion (pres. 1973-74), Soc. for Values in Higher Edn. (dir. 1966-81), Pendle Hill Grad. Study Ctr. (chmn. bd. 1971-74). Home: 625 Serpentine Dr Del Mar CA 92014 Office: Religious Studies San Diego State Univ San Diego CA 92014

DOWNING, FREDERICK LEE, minister, educator, Southern Baptist Church; b. Brewton, Ala., Aug. 24, 1948; s. Fred and Clara Lee (Norsworthy) D.; m. Linda Pugh, Dec. 19, 1970; children: Amy Leigh, Jonathan Wiley. A.B., Samford U., 1970; Th.M., New Orleans Bapt. Sem., 1973, Th.D., 1976; M.A., Princeton Theol. Sem., 1984; postgrad. Emory U., 1984-85. Ordained to ministry, 1967. Minister, Sepulga Bapt. Ch., Evergreen, Ala., 1967-70, Grace Bapt. Ch., New Orleans, 1974-76; faculty Union Bapt. Sem., New Orleans, 1970-74; asst. prof. Cumberland Coll., Williamsburg, Ky., 1976-77; chaplain USAR, 1971—; assoc. prof. religon La. Coll., Pineville, 1977—. Contbr. articles to profl. jours. Mem. Assn. Bapt. Profs. of Religion, Soc. Bibl. Lit. Home: 3222 Cloverland Dr Pineville LA 71360 Office: Religion Dept Louisiana Coll 1140 College Dr Pineville LA 71359

DOWNS, DAVID WILLIAM, minister, Southern Baptist Convention; b. Birmingham, Ala., Jan. 31, 1954; s. Orville Clinton and Eula Elizabeth (Reno) D.; m. Dorothy Susan Sanford, Dec. 18, 1976; children: Deidre Michelle, Drew Sanford. B.A., Samford U., 1976; M.Div., So. Bapt. Sem., 1979, Th.M., 1980, Ph.D.; 1984; postgrad. Oxford U., Eng., 1981. Ordained to ministry Baptist Ch., 19—. Staff minister First Bapt. Ch., Marietta, Ga., 1977, St. Matthews Meth. Ch., Louisville, 1978; teaching fellow So. Bapt. Sem., Louisville, 1979-82; pastor Macedonia Bapt. Ch., Madison, Ind., 1978-85; adj. prof. theology Bellarmine Coll., Louisville, 1985; pastor Edison Bapt. Ch., Ga., 1985—. Mem. Am. Soc. Ch. History, So. Bapt. Hist. Soc. Democrat. Club: Grad. (So. Bapt. Sem.) (pres. 1983-84). Home: Box 296 Edison GA 31746

DOYLE, DAVID PAUL, minister, United Meth. Ch.; b. Bath Springs, Tenn., Mar. 13, 1915; s. Arthur Ewell and Minnie Valentine (Bethune) D.; B.A., U. Ala., 1938; M.Div., Emory U., 1940; D.D., Athens (Ala.) Coll., 1975; m. Lonya Mae Shirley, Dec. 25, 1935; 1 dau., Mary Janice. Ordained to ministry, 1941; pastor Kellyton United Meth. Ch., 1940-42, 62-66, Woodlawn Ch., 1966-72, Bluff Park Ch., 1972-76; sec. Conf. Bd. Missions, 1956-66; dist. dir. evangelism, missions and health and welfare, 1966; chaplain Choccolocca council Boy Scouts Am. Mem. N.Ala. Conf. Council on Ministries; mem. bd. superannuate homes N.Ala. Conf.; del. Southeastern Conf., 1972; supt. Sylacauga Dist., 1976—; trustee Athens Coll. Contbr. articles to religious publs. Home and office: 709 S Norton Ave Sylacauga AL 35150

DOYLE, JAMES LEONARD, bishop, Roman Catholic Church; b. Chatham, Ont., Can., June 20, 1929; s. Herbert Lawrence and Mary Josephine (Ennett) D.; B.A., U. Western Ont., 1950; D.D., St. Peters Sem., London, 1954. Ordained priest, then consecrated bishop; assoc. rector St. Peters Cathedral, London, Ont., 1954-60, rector, 1974-76; pastor Sacred Heart Ch., Windsor, Ont., 1960-66; prin. Brennan High Sch., Windsor, 1966-68; pastor Holy Name Ch., Windsor, 1968-74; bishop of Peterborough (Ont.), 1976—. Home and Office: 350 Hunter St W Peterborough ON K9T 6Y8 Canada

DOYLE, JAMES MARSHALL, pastor, Southern Baptist Church; b. Jeffersonville, Ind., Apr. 9, 1947; s. Marvin Bransford and Elizabeth Mae (Lamstus) D.; m. Peggy Fay Hargrove, Aug. 18, 1971; children: James Marshall, II, Charisa Fay, Cara Leigh. B.A., Belmont Coll., 1970-74; M. Div., Southern Bapt. Seminary, Louisville, 1978. Ordained to ministry Inglewood Bapt. Ch., 1971. Mission pastor Cross Keys Bapt. Chapel, College Grove, Tenn., 1971-73; pastor Brookside Bapt. Nashville, 1973-75, Parkwood Bapt., Clarksville, Ind., 1975-79, Robinson Street, Jackson, Miss., 1979-83, Midlane Park Bapt., Louisville, 1983—; pres. Belmont Ministerial Assn., Nashville, 1973-74; mem. assn. council Hinds-Madison Assn., Jackson, Miss., 1980-83, stewardship dir., 1980-83; mem. program com. Southeast Bapt. Assn., Memphis, Ind., 1978-79, assn. clk., 1977-79; field edn. supr. So. Bapt. Theol. Sem., 1977-79, 83-85. Served with U.S. Navy, 1966-70. Mem. Longrun Exec. Bd., Long Run Ministerial Assn., South East Area Assoc. Ministeries. Republican. Home: 4119 Wimpole Rd Louisville KY 40218 Office: Midlane Park Bapt Ch 6500 Six Mile Ln Louisville KY 40218

DOYLE, WILFRED EMMETT, bishop, Roman Cath. Ch.; b. Calgary, Alta., Can., Feb. 18, 1913; s. John Joseph and Mary Anne (O'Neill) D.; B.A.; U Alta.,, 1935; J.C.D., Ottawa U., 1949. Ordained priest, 1938; chancellor Archdiocese Edmonton (Alta.), 1940-58; bishop of Nelson, B.C., 1958—; chancellor Notre Dame U. Nelson, 1963-69, chmn. bd. govs., 1968-73; pres. Bishop's Commn. Religious Edn., 1961-74. Address: 813 Ward St Nelson BC V1L 1T4 Canada

DOZIER, CARROLL T., bishop, Roman Cath. Ch.; b. Richmond, Va., Aug. 18, 1911; s. Curtis M. and Rose A. (Conatry) D. A.B., Holy Cross Coll., 1932, LL.D. (hon) 1973; postgrad. North Am. Coll., Gregorian U., Rome. Ordained priest Roman Catholic Ch., 1937. Curate St. Vincent's Ch., Newport News, Va., 1937-41, St. Joseph's Ch., Petersburg, 1941-45; dir. Soc. Propagandation of Faith, 1945-54; pastor Christ the King Ch., Norfolk, Va., 1954-71; consecrated bishop, 1971; bishop Diocese of Memphis, 1971—. Author pastoral letters. Named papal chamberlain, 1954, domestic prelate, 1962, proto. apost., 1967; recipient Bill of Rights award ACLU, 1972, Cath. Human Relations award, Memphis, 1973. Address: 1325 Jefferson Ave Memphis TN 38104

DRACE, JERRY LEE, minister, Southern Baptist Convention; b. South Fulton, Ky., Jan. 1, 1947; s. J.T. and Virginia (Tucker) D.; m. Rebecca Carol Hight, Aug. 10, 1969. B.S., Union U., Jackson, Tenn., 1968; M.Div., So. Bapt. Theol. Sem., 1971; Ordained to ministry So. Baptist Conv., 1969. Pastor chs. in Tenn., Ind. and Ga., 1968-70; minister to youth Southside Bapt. Ch., Jacksonville Fla., 1972-75; evangelist, pres. Jerry Drace Evangelistic Assn., Jacksonville, 1975—; overseas crusades in South Korea and Philippines, 1977, 78, Korea and Hong Kong, 1981, 84; producer, emcee TV program Why?, 1974-75, radio program Reflections, 1975; producer Video Series Revival with Effect, 1984; participant, keynote speaker evang. confs. U.S. and abroad. Mem. Evangelistic Assn. of So. Bapt. Conv., Am. Clin. Chaplains Assn. Author: The Devil, Witchcraft and Hell, 1976; The Family, 1977; also articles; contbg. editor Courage Mag. Home: 3452 San Jose Blvd Jacksonville FL 32207 Office: PO Box 10513 1833 Atlantic Blvd Jacksonville FL 32207

DRAINVILLE, GERARD See *Who's Who in America*, 43rd edition.

DRAKE, FLOYD DONALD, religion educator, General Association of Regular Baptist Churches; b. Rochester, N.Y., Nov. 20, 1918; s. William Louis and Georgia Helen (Sherman) D.; m. Dorothea Louise Flint, Nov. 19, 1942; children: Floyd Donald, David Alan, Reginald Thomas. Grad. Bapt. Bible Sem., Johnson City N.Y., 1947; Th.B., Pikes Peak Coll. and Sem., Colorado Springs, Colo., 1955; postgrad. Coll. of DuPage, Glen Ellyn, Ill., 1972, 74. Ordained to ind. ministry 1941, now affiliated with Gen. Assn. Regular Bapt. Chs. Pastor Trinity Temple, Rochester, N.Y., 1941-42, First Bapt. Chs., Marathon, N.Y., 1949-57, Dunkirk, N.Y., 1957-63, Grace Bapt. Ch., Springfield, Mass., 1963-67; book editor Regular Bapt. Press, Des Plaines, Ill., 1967-76; developmental officer Bapt. Bible Coll. and Sch. Theology of Pa., Clarks Summit, 1976-82, faculty sem. div., 1982—; mem. adminstrv. staff Gen. Assn. Regular Bapt. Chs. Home Office, Des Plaines, 1969-76; mem. Council of Ten, N.Y. State, 1956-63, Council of Seven in New Eng., 1964-67; mem. Exec. Council Fellowship of Bapt. for Home Missions, 1958-72; mem. Nat. Council Fellowship of Bapts. for Home Missions, 1954—. Mem. Citizens Com. for Community Improvement, Marathon, 1950-57; bd. dirs. Camp Northfield Youth Camp, 1964-67. Editor: My Devotion, 1967-75; Doctrine and Administration of the Church, 1968; Missionary Administration in the Local Church, 1970.

DRAMSTAD, HARRY OSCAR, lay minister, Luth. Ch.—Mo. Synod; b. Binford, N.D., Nov. 7, 1918; s. Hans and Bergine (Hagen) D.; A.A., Concordia Coll., 1973; m. Lorraine Wanetha Arneson, Oct. 12, 1941; children—Russel Leroy, Roger Kent, Duane Lyle. Congregational chmn., Luth. Ch., Kensal, N.D., 1969-70; Sunday sch. tchr., Mabel Luth. Ch., Sutton, N.D., Zion Luth. Ch., Binford, N.D., 1935-66; zone chmn. Luth. Laymen's League, 1961-63, dist. dir., 1961-63; lay minister Luth. Ch., Jamison, Nebr., 1973—. Mem. Assn. of Christian Marriage Counselors. Home and office: Jamison NE 68744

DRAPER, ALBERT LEE, minister, Southern Baptist Convention; b. Beaumont, Tex., July 20, 1938; s. Chester Oren and Mary Elizabeth (Cash) D.; m. Linda Lou Burgess, Jan. 30, 1960; children: Lori Rae, Derek Jackson. B.S., U. Houston, 1964; M.R.E., Southwestern Bapt. Theol. Sem., 1968. Ordained to ministry So. Baptist Conv., 1959. Pastor Joy Bapt. Ch., Gladewater, Tex., 1959-62, Lakeview Park Bapt. Ch., Houston, 1962-65, Justin Bapt. Ch., Tex., 1966-69, First Bapt. Ch., Wylie, Tex., 1969—; Mem. exec. bd. Bapt. Gen. Conv. Tex., 1975-78, mem. mission funding com., 1981—; bd. dirs. Lake Lavon Bapt. Encampment, Tex., 1975-77; cons. for bldg. Today's Challenge, Bapt. Gen. Conv. Tex., 1973—, cons. life style evangelism, 1975—; pres. Wylie Ministerial Alliance, 1973-75; chaplain Wylie Vol. Fire Dept., 1969-79; moderator exec. bd. Collin Bapt. Assn., McKinney, Tex., 1975—, chmn. missions com., 1983-84, mem. steering com., 1984. Field rep. Salvation Army, Wylie, 1970—; v.p. Wylie Community Edn. Adv. Council, 1976—; bd. dirs. Tex. Alcohol Narcotics Edn., Dallas; mem. citizens adv. com. Wylie Pub. Sch., 1973-74. Named Wylie Area Citizen of Yr., 1980. Home: 100 Tanglewood Ct Wylie TX 75098 Office: 100 N 1st St Wylie TX 75098

DRAVES, ROGER EDWARD, minister, Conservative Baptist Assn. Am.; b. Webster City, Iowa, Feb. 4, 1943; s. Emil William and Jean Blanche (Shafer) D.; B.A., Biola Coll., La Mirada, Calif., 1969; M.Div., Western Conservative Bapt. Sem., Portland, Oreg., 1973; m. Linda Misao Sase, Aug. 30, 1963; children—Christine Lynette, Karen Jeanette. Ordained to ministry, 1975; deacon First Bapt. Ch., Milwaukie, Oreg., 1972-73; pastor Calvary Bapt. Ch., Cove, Oreg., 1973-77, Treasure Valley Bapt. Ch., Ontario, Oreg., 1977—. Sec., Blue Mountain Assn. Conservative Bapt. Chs., 1974-75, Pastors Prayer Fellowship, 1974—; trustee Conservative Bapt. Assn. Oreg., 1976—. Recipient Jr. Class Scholastic Achievement award Western Conservative Bapt. Sem., 1970. Home: 1366 NW 4th Ave Ontario OR 97914 Office: 386 N Verde Dr Ontario OR 97914

DREIBELBIS, JOHN LAVERNE, priest, Episcopal Church; b. Miles City, Mont., Dec. 1, 1934; s. John Calvin and Regina Theresa (Pestka) D.; m. Patricia Ann Wagner, June 11, 1960; children: Anne, Catherine, David, Rachel. Student, U. Chgo., 1952-56; M.Div., Seabury-Western Sem., 1959; Ph.D., U. Chgo., 1985. Ordained priest, 1959. Curate, St. Matthew's Episcopal Ch., Evanston, Ill., 1959-60; pastor Good Samaritan Ch., Oak Park, Ill., 1960-63, Christ Episcopal Ch., Chgo., 1964-71; rector Grace Episcopal Ch., Huron, S.D., 1971-75; asst. St. Christopher's Ch., Oak Park, Ill., 1981—; dir., profl. programs, continuing edn. U. Chgo., 1983—; mem. Diocese of Chgo. council, 1963-66, chmn. Commn. on Met. Affairs, 1968-71; mem. bishop and council Diocese of S.D., 1971-74. Dir. White Farm Equip. Co., Oak Brook, Ill., 1983—; cons., educator Borg Warner Fin. Services, Chgo., 1977—; del., mem. Woodlawn Orgn., Chgo., 1964-68. Mem. Episcopal Clergy Assn. Chgo. (nat. del. 1970, pres. 1970-71). Club: Quadrangle. Office: U Chgo 5835 S Kimbark Ave Chicago IL 60637

DREISBACH, ALBERT RUSSEL, JR., priest, Episcopal Church; b. Watertown, N.Y., Apr. 27, 1934; s. Albert Russel and Florence (Agnew) D.; m. Jane Corey, June 1, 1957; children: Diane Corey, Daniel Agnew. A.B., Wesleyan U., Middletown, Conn., 1956; M. Div., Union Theol. Sem., 1962. Ordained to ministry as deacon Episcopal Ch., 1962. Asst. to dean Cathedral of St. John, Wilmington, Del., 1962-64; assoc. dir. Episc. Soc. Cultural and Racial Unity, Atlanta, 1965-67, exec. dir., editor newsletter, 1967-70; rector Ch. of Incarnation, Atlanta, 1973-85; founder, pres. Atlanta Internat. Ctr. Continuing Study and Exhibit of Shroud of Turin, 1977—, exec. dir., 1985—; dean Southwest convocation Diocese of Atlanta, 1973-75; reader gen. bd. examing chaplains Nat. Episcopal Ch., 1978-82; dean Lay Readers Acad., Diocese of Atlanta, 1981. Served to capt. USMC, 1956-59. Mem. Shroud of Turin Research Project (liaison to bd. dirs. 1984—), Assn. Scientists and Scholars of Shroud of Turin (liaison to bd. dirs. 1984—), Brit. Soc. Turin Shroud (liaison to bd. dirs. 1984—), Holy Shroud Guild. Avocations: travel, photography, collection of Shroud related materials. Home: 2657 Vance Dr East Point GA 30344 Office: Atlanta Internat Ctr for Continuing Study and Exhibit of Shroud of Turin Inc 323 Omni Internat Atlanta GA 30335

DREVLOW, ARTHUR HERMAN, minister, Lutheran Church, Missouri Synod. B. Long Prairie, Minn., Jan. 12, 1918; s. Otto Herman and Clara Anna (Schutt) D.; m. Virginia Ruth Uttech, June 19, 1943; children: David, Ronald, Daniel. B.Th., Concordia Sem., Springfield, Ill., 1941; B.A., Gustavus Adolphus Coll., 1966; M.A., Mankato State U., 1972; M.Div., Concordia Sem., Ft. Wayne, 1977, D.Min., 1982. Ordained, 1941. Minister, St. Peter's Luth. Ch., Randall, Minn., 1941-43, St. Peter's Luth. Ch., Goodhue, Minn., 1943-51, St. John's Luth. Ch., St. James, Minn., 1951—, St. John's Luth. Ch., Truman, Minn. (2d charge), 1958; mem. Minn. bd. dirs. Luth. Ch., Mo. Synod, St. Paul, 1956-58, 82—; counselor Luth. Women's Missionary League, Truman, 1968-78, Truman Cir., 1978-82; chmn. Pastoral Conf., Gruman and Fairmont, 1960; pres. Luth. Edn. Assn. Truman, 1966—; mem. bd. Minn. So. bd. dirs., Burnsville, 1982; del. synodical conv, 1960-79. Lectr., contbr. articles, essays to religious jours. Mem. Concordia Hist. Inst. Home: Rural Route 1 Box 90 Saint James MN 56081 Office: Rural St James Route 1 Box 90 Saint James MN 56081

DRICKAMER, JOHN MARTIN, minister, Lutheran Ch. - Missouri Synod; theology educator; b. Cleve., Dec. 5, 1949; s. George Henry and Ruth Alma (Schuette) D.; m. Jean Anne Laing, Aug. 11, 1973; 1 child, Faith Anne. B.A., Capital U., 1971; M.Div., Concordia Theol. Sem., 1975, Th.D., 1978. Ordained to ministry Luth. Ch., 1977. Vicar Zion Luth. Ch., Chamberlain, S.D., 1973-74; instr. in religion Concordia Coll., Ann Arbor, Mich., 1977-80; pastor Immanuel Luth. Ch., Georgetown, Ont., 1980—; adjunct instr. Concordia Sem., St. Catherines, Ont., 1980—. Editor: Lutheranism in America, 1979. Translator: Walther and the Church, 1981. Editor, author: Kept in the Faith, 1983. Author: (poems) Bible Verse, 1983. Mem. Concordia Historical Inst. (com. on hist. studies & resources, 1978—). Home: 111 Delrex Blvd Georgetown ON L7G 4C5 Canada Office: Immanuel Lutheran Church Box 6 Georgetown ON L7G 4T1 Canada

DRIGGERS, BENJAMIN CARLISLE, minister, So. Bapt. Conv.; b. Hartsville, S.C., Aug. 27, 1937; s. Benjamin Carl and Zula Mae (Hilton) D.; A.A., Mars Hill Coll., 1957; B.A., Carson-Newman Coll., 1959; M.Div., So. Bapt. Theol. Sem., 1964, M.R.E., 1967; D.Ministry, Pitts. Theol. Sem., 1976; m. Carole Jeanette Roberts, Aug. 16, 1959; children: Jana Carole, Benjamin Dave. Ordained to ministry, 1962; pastor 23d and Broadway Bapt. Ch., Louisville, 1963-69; asso. minister First Bapt. Ch., Birmingham, Ala., 1969-70, Bapt. Ch. of the Covenant, Birmingham, 1970-71; pastor Calvary Bapt. Ch., Morgantown, W.Va., 1971-75; assoc. dir. dept. coop. ministeries with Nat. Baptists, So. Bapt. Home Mission Bd., Atlanta, 1975-78, regional coordinator Bd., 1978—. Student dir. W.Va. Conv. So. Bapts., 1972-75; dir. chaplaincy services W.Va. U. Med. Center, 1973-74; pres. W.Va. Conv. So. Bapts., 1973-75. Author: Churches in Changing Communities: Crisis or Opportunities?, 1977. Contbr. articles to religious jours. Home: 5180 Whispering Pines Ln Conyers GA 30207 Office: 1350 Spring St NW Atlanta GA 30309

DRIGGERS, HARRY JEFFERSON, minister Southern Baptist Convention; b. Elba, Ala., Mar. 12, 1946; s. Johnny and Exa (Wambles) D.; m. Penny Ree Stricklin, Mar. 8, 1968; children: Jeff, Rena Lee. Diploma in Christian Tng., Samford U., 1982. Ordained to ministry So. Bapt. Conv., 1979. Minister, Calvary Bapt. Ch., Brantley, Ala., 1979-81, Bethel Bapt. Ch., Goshen, Ala., 1981—; dir. youth Ala.-Crenshaw Bapt., Luverne, 1982-84, dir. evangelism, 1983-84. Fire chief Bullock Fire Dept., Ala., 1984—. Coach Pee Wee Football, Brantley, 1984—. Recipient Sustained Superior Performance award U.S. Govt., Fort Rucker, Ala., 1975, 78, 82. Address: Route 2 Box 18 Brantley AL 36009

DRIGGERS, RAYMOND ROLAND, minister, Assemblies of God; b. Coleman, Fla., May 2, 1923; s. John Jonas and Mable L D.; B.A., Southeastern Bible Coll., 1966; postgrad. in edn. U. Miss., 1969-76; m. Mary Pearl Golden, Jan. 25, 1946; children: Sharon Mary Driggers Blanton, Larry Raymond. Ordained to ministry, 1955; pastor 1st Assembly, Coleman, Fla., 1952, Polk City, Fla., 1953-55; asst. pastor Auburndale 1st Assembly, 1955-62; pastor 1st Assembly, Arcadia, Fla., 1964-65; asst. pastor 1st Assembly, Winter Haven, Fla., 1973—. Chaplain, dist. chartering officer Royal Rangers, Winter Haven. Home: 110 Rose St Auburndale FL 33823

DRISCOLL, CECIL LILLIAN, religion educator; b. Apr. 23, 1915; d. Andrew Melville and Linnie (DeWeese) D. A.B., Cascade Coll., 1948. Ordained to ministry Ky. Mt. Holiness Assn., 1941, transferred to Faith Missionary Assn., 1953. Co-pastor, Ky. Mount Holiness Assn., Vancleve, 1940-41; missionary World Gospel Mission, Honduras, 1943-48, Caribbean Missions, Camaguey, Cuba, 1950-52; missionary Faith Missionary Assn., Oriente, Cuba, 1953-60, refugee Worker, Miami, Fla., 1961-63; faculty mem. Hobe Sound Bible Coll. (Fla.), 1963-72, 73—; with Pilgrim Pub. House, Indpls., 1960, 61. Author: Cloud By Day: Fire By Night, 1983; (play) The Message of Christmas, 1947. Asst. editor religious periodical The Torch, 1970—. Contbr. articles, lessons to religious publs. Republican. Home: PO Box 1065 Hobe Sound FL 33455 Office: Hobe Sound Bible Coll 11305 SE Gomez Rd Hobe Sound FL 33455

DRISCOLL, JUSTIN ALBERT, bishop, Roman Cath. Ch.; b. Bernard, Ia., Sept. 30, 1920; s. William J. and Agnes (Healey) D.; B.A., Loras Coll., 1942; Ph.D., Cath. U. Am., 1952. Ordained priest Roman Catholic Ch., 1945; consecrated bishop, 1970; faculty Loras Acad., 1945-48; sec. to Archbishop Henry P. Rohlman, Dubuque, Ia., 1948-49; sec. to Archbishop Leo Binz, Dubuque, 1952-53; supt. schs. Archdiocese Dubuque, 1953-67, dir. confrat. Christian doctrine, 1953-67; moderator Archdiocesan Council Cath. Women, Dubuque, 1953-67; dir. Confrat. Blessed Sacrament, Archdiocese Dubuque, 1954-67; chaplain Mt. St. Francis Convent Motherhouse, Dubuque, 1954-67; pres. Loras Coll., 1967-70; bishop diocese of Fargo, N.D., 1970—. Named papal chamberlain Pope Pius XII, 1954, reappointed by Pope John XXIII, 1958; apptd. domestic prelate Pope John XXIII, 1960. Author: We Pray for our Priests, 1965; The Pastor and The School, 1966; With Faith and Vision, Schools of the Archdiocese of Dubuque, 1836-1966. Home: 608 Broadway St Fargo ND 58102 Office: Queen of Peace Cath Center Diocese of Fargo 1310 Broadway Box 1750 Fargo ND 58102

DRISKELL, RONALD CLIFTON, minister Southern Baptist Convention; gas company executive; b. Houston, Dec. 5, 1943; s. Alto William and Annie (Bagwell) D.; m. Judy Carleen Stacy, Jan. 24, 1970; children: Ryan M., Monica R. Student Sam Houston State U., 1962-70. Ordained to ministry Southern Baptist Convention, 1980; pres. Bapt. Student Union Sam Houston State U., Huntsville, Tex., 1967-68; chmn. deacons 1st Bapt. Ch., Marshall, Tex., 1976-77, tchr. Sunday Sch., 1975-77; chmn. deacons Central Bapt. Ch., Carthage, Tex., 1978-79; pastor Oletha Bapt. Ch. (Tex.), 1980-82; tchr., deacon Central Bapt. Ch., Thornton, Tex., 1982—. Safety rep. Lone Star Gas Co., Dallas, 1982—. Trustee, Sch. Bd. Groesbeck, Tex., 1982—. Mem. Soc. Safety Engrs. Am., Carthage C. of C. (bd. dirs. 1978). Lodge: Lions. Republican. Home: Route 3 Box 36B Thornton TX 76687 Office: Lone Star Gas Co Box 30 Mexia TX 76667

DRISKILL, JOSEPH DENVER, minister, Christian Ch. (Disciples of Christ); b. Peoria, Ill., Jan. 7, 1946; s. Joseph Abraham and Evelyn Jane (Skinner) D.; B.A., Culver-Stockton Coll., 1968; M.Div., Vanderbilt Div. Sch., 1971; M.A., U. Regina, 1976—; m. Anne Louise Cummings, June 2, 1971. Ordained to ministry, 1971; minister Mt. Zion Christian Ch., Hannibal, Mo., 1965-68, Union Chapel Christian Ch., Center, Mo., 1965-68, Marion (Ky.) Christian Ch., 1969-71, Regina Ave. Christian Ch., Regina, Sask., Can., 1971-75; chaplain U. Western Ont., London, 1976—. Exec., Regina Gen. Ministerial Assn., 1974-76; mem. com. on union and joint mission Anglican United and Disciples Chs. Can., 1972-75; mem. consultation com. Sask. Council for Internat. Coop. Govt. and Agy., 1974-76. Exec., Regina Housing Assn., 1973-75. Recipient Oreon E. Scott Found. award Culver-Stockton Coll., 1968. Mem. Can. Council Supervised Pastoral Edn., Congress Disciples Clergy, Am. Acad. Religion. Home: 146 Arbour Glen Cr London ON N5Y 2A4 Canada Office: Room 4 UCC Univ Western Ontario London ON N6A 5B8 Canada

DRIVER, GEORGE JAMES, JR., lay ch. worker, Seventh-day Adventist Ch.; b. St. Louis, Jan. 14, 1912; s. George James and Stella May (Cooper) D.; B.A., Jefferson Coll., St. Louis, 1937; postgrad. Washington

U., St. Louis, 1945-47, U. So. Cal., 1950-51, Fullerton Jr. Coll., 1957-66, U. Calif. at Los Angeles, 1972-75; m. Betty Lou Polly, Apr. 19, 1947; children—Polly Ann (Mrs. Jeffery Smith), Thomas Alan, Richard Edward, George James IV. Deacon, Anaheim (Calif.) Seventh-day Adventist Ch., 1960-67, Arlington Seventh-day Adventist Ch., Riverside, Calif., 1971-74; elder White Meml. Seventh-day Adventist Ch., Los Angeles, 1974—. Dir. budgets White Meml. Med. Center, Los Angeles, 1971-75, mgmt. engr., 1975—. Recipient Merit awards Rockwell Internat., 1960-71. Mem. Am. Inst. Indsl. Engrs., Nat. Assn. Accountants. Patentee high speed bearings. Home: 607 N Bailey St Los Angeles CA 90033 Office: 1720 Brooklyn Ave Los Angeles CA 90033

DRIVER, TOM FAW, theology educator, writer; b. Johnson City, Tenn., May 31, 1925; s. Leslie Rowles and Sarah (Broyles) D.; m. Anne L. Barstow, June 7, 1952; children: Katharine Anne, Paul Barstow, Susannah Ambrose, A.B., Duke U., 1950; M.Div., Union Theol. Sem., 1953; Ph.D., Columbia U., 1957; D.Litt., Denison U., 1970. Ordained to ministry United Methodist Ch., 1951. Dir. youth work Riverside Ch., N.Y.C., 1955-56; faculty Union Theol. Sem., N.Y.C., 1956—, Paul J. Tillich prof. theology and culture, 1973—; drama critic Christian Century, 1956-62, Sta. WBAI-FM, 1960-61, The Reporter, 1963-64; vis. assoc. prof. English, Columbia U., 1964-65; vis. assoc. prof. religion Barnard Coll., 1965-66, Fordham U., 1967; cons. humanities and arts Coll. Old Westbury, N.Y., 1970; William Evans vis. prof. religion U. Otago, N.Z., 1976; vis. prof. religion Vassar Coll., 1978, Montclair State Coll., 1981; vis. prof. English lit. Doshisha U., Kyoto, Japan, 1983; bd. dirs. dept. worship and arts Nat. Council Chs., 1958-63, Found. for Arts, Religion and Culture, 1963-67. Author: liberetto for oratorio The Invisible Fire, 1957; The Sense of History in Greek and Shakespearean Drama, 1960, Jean Genet, 1966, Romantic Quest and Modern Query: A History of The Modern Theater, 1970, Patterns of Grace: Human Experience as Word of God, 1977, Christ in a Changing World; Toward an Ethical Christology, 1981; Editor: (with Robert Pack) Poems of Doubt and Belief, 1964. Contbr. articles to profl. jours. Served with AUS, 1943-46. Kent fellow, 1953; Guggenheim fellow, 1962-63. Mem. Am. Acad. Religion, New Haven Theol. Group, Soc. Values in Higher Edn., AAUP, ACLU, Clergy and Laity Concerned, Phi Beta Kappa, Omicron Delta Kappa. Office: Union Theol Sem Broadway at 120th St New York NY 10027

DROBENA, THOMAS JOHN, minister, Lutheran Church in America; researcher Slavic cultures; b. Chgo., Aug. 23, 1934; s. Thomas and Suzanne (Durec) D.; m. Wilma S. Kucharek, Dec. 27, 1980. B.Th., Concordia Sem., Springfield, Ill., 1961, M.Div., 1974; B.A., Valparaiso U., 1965; M.A., Hebrew U., Jerusalem, 1968; Ph.D., Calif. Grad. Sch., 1975; D.Sc. (hon.), London Inst., 1973. Ordained to ministry Luth. Ch.-Mo. Synod, 1962. Pastor Emmanuel Luth. Ch., Britton, Mich., 1962-67, Luth. Ch. of Redeemer, Jerusalem, 1967-68, St. Mark Luth. Ch., Bklyn., 1968-69, Ascension Luth. Ch., Binghamton, N.Y., 1969-78, Holy Emmanuel Luth. Ch., Mahanoy, Pa., 1981—; chaplain U.S. Air Force Aux., Hazelton, Pa., 1965—. Researcher Slavic Heritage Inst., Mahoney, 1981—. Co-author: Heritage of the Slavs, 1979. Contbr. articles to profl. jours. Grantee Russian and East European Ctr., U. Ill., 1980-84, Dept. State, Israel, 1967-68. Fellow Istituto Slovacco; mem. Am. Assn. for the Advancement of Slavic Studies, Am. Assn. Slavic and East European Langs., Czechoslovak Soc. for Arts and Scis.

DROWN, DOUGLAS WARREN, minister, National Association Congregational Christian Churches; b. Gardner, Mass., Aug. 31, 1951; s. Charles Abner and Marian Louise (Kopper) D.; Student Gordon Coll., 1969-71, Skidmore Coll., 1984—, Bangor Theol. Sem., 1977—. Ordained to ministry Congregational Christian Chs., 1979. Pastor First Congl. Ch., Royalston Ctr., Mass., 1974-76, 2d Congl. Ch., South Royalston, Mass., 1975-76, First Congl. Ch., Bingham, Maine, 1977—, Congl. Ch., West Forks, Maine, 1980—; exec. sec. Congl. Christian Council of Maine, 1981—; dir. Christian Civic League Maine, 1982—; mem. exec. com. Maine Council of Chs., 1985—; host Good News Radio Program WQMR-AM, Skowhegan-Waterville, Maine, 1982—; v.chmn. Am. Com. for the Internat. Congl. Fellowship, 1983—; mem. program com. Nat. Assn. Congl. Christian Chs., 1984—. Instr. in Art Longfellow Sch., Pleasant Ridge, Maine, 1978—; substitute tchr. Maine Sch. Adminstrv. Dist., Bingham, 1978-79, 1983—. Contbr. articles to The Congregationalist, 1979, 1984. Pres., Bingham Area Health Council, 1978-80; trustee Bingham Union Library, 1978-80; bd. dirs. Athol Salvation Army, Mass., 1974-76, Mt. Grace Regional Transp. Commn., Athol, 1975-76. Republican. Lodges: Lions, Grange (chaplain 1977-84), Masons (jr. deacon 1982-84). Home: Box 253 Meadow St Bingham ME 04920

DRUMMOND, LEWIS ADDISON, educator, Southern Baptist Church; b. Dixon, Ill., July 11, 1926; s. Wendall Addison and Elsie Lottie (Newbury) D.; m. Betty Rae Love. B.A., Samford U., 1950; B.D., Southwestern Sem.-Ft. Worth, 1955, Th.M., 1958; Ph.D., U. London-Eng., 1963. Ordained to ministry, 1948. Pastor, New Bethel Bapt. Ch., Ft. Worth, Tex., 1951-53, First Bapt. Ch., Granbury, Tex., 1953-56, Geln Iris Bapt. Ch., Birmingham, Ala., 1956-61, Ninth and O Bapt. Ch., Louisville, 1964-68; faculty Spurgeon's Theol. Coll., London, 1968-73; Billy Graham prof. evangelism So. Bapt. Theol. Sem., Louisville, 1973—, div. chmn. sem. and head evangelism dept.; lectr. in field; mem. com. on evangelism and edn. Bapt. World Alliance, 1975—; mem. commn. on lay ministry Bapt. World Alliance, mem. gen. council on lay ministry; assoc. evangelist Billy Graham Evangelistic Team, Poland, Australia; condr. evangelistic crusades worldwide; pres. Louisville Bapt. Pastor's Conf. Author: Evangelism: The Counter-Revolution, 1972; Leading Your Church in Evangelism, 1976; Life Can be Real, 1974; The Awakening That Must Come, 1979; Witnessing for God to Men, 1980; The Revived Life, 1982; Chrles G. Finney: The Birth of Modern Evangelism, 1982. Editor: Here They Stand: Sermons from Eastern Europe, 1976; What the Bible Says, 1974. Contbr. articles to profl. jours. Mem. Royal Inst. Philosophy (Eng.), Evang. Philos. Soc., Acad. of Profs. of Evangelism (pres. 1978-80). Address: So Bapt Theol Sem 2825 Lexington Rd Louisville KY 40206

DRUMMOND, RICHARD HENRY, religious educator, Presbyterian Church U.S.A.: b. San Francisco, Dec. 14, 1916; s. John Albert and Clara (Jacobson) D.; m. Pearl Estella Oppegaard, June 5, 1943; children: Donald Craig, Angela Claire, Lowell Henry. B.A., UCLA, 1939, M.A., 1939; Ph.D., U. Wis., 1941; B.D., Gettysburg Theol. Sem., 1944. Ordained to ministry, 1947. Fraternal worker United Presbyn. Ch. U.S.A., Japan, 1949-62; prof. Christian studies and classical langs. Meiji Gakuin U., Tokyo, 1958-62; Florence Livergood Warren prof. comparative religions U. Dubuque Theol. Sem., 1962—. Author: A History of Christianity in Japan, 1971; Gautama the Buddha, 1974; Unto the Churches, 1978; Toward a New Age in Christian Theology, 1985. Served with U.S. Army, 1945-46. U. Wis. fellow, 1940-41; Sealntic Fund fellow, 1968-69. Mem. Fellowship Christian Missionaries in Japan (pres. 1960-61), Midwest Fellowship of Profs. Mission (pres. 1966-67), Am. Soc. Missiology, Am. Acad. Religion, N. Am. Acad. Ecumenists, Internat. Assn. Mission Studies. Democrat. Lodge: Rotary. Home: 135 Croydon Crest Dubuque IA 52001 Office: Univ Dubuque Theol Sem 2000 University Ave Dubuque IA 52001

DUBNEAC, FELIX, archmandrite, artist, Romanian Missionary Orthodox Ch. Am.; b. Voloavele, Romania, July 29, 1912; s. David and Stefania; came to U.S., 1967, naturalized, 1973; B.A. in Theology and Philosophy, U. Bucharest, 1949; diploma Acad. of Arts, Bucharest, 1949, Superior Sch. of Ch. Painting of the Romanian Orthodox Patriarchate, 1951. Ordained priest Romanian Orthodox Ch., 1955; monk, 1938; deacon, 1939; archmandrite, 1973—. Organizer choirs of Byzantine church music, Romania, N. Am.; authorized restourator and painter of Christian hist. monuments and icons. Licensed church and icon artist; recipient Romanian Patriarchal Cross, 1965. Mem. Romanian Assn. "Gheorghe Lazar". Author: The Problem of Senses in Christian Spirituality-Sources of Christian Edn., 1972; The Beauty of Christianity and its Distinguished Personalities, 1977; American Romanians Defend Romania's Integrity and Its Independence, 1977. Editor: Thinking and Art, 1979—. Painter altar screens Romanian Orthodox Chs., Lansing, Ill., Cleve., Hollywood, Fla., Windsor, Ont., Can., Edmonton, Alta., Can., fresco on Romanian history Wayne State U., Detroit. Home: 19959 Riopelle St Detroit MI 48203

DU BOSE, FRANCIS MARQUIS, educator, minister, Southern Baptist Convention; b. Elba, Ala., Feb. 27, 1922; s. Hansford Arthur and Mayde Frances (Owen) Du B.; B.A. cum laude, Baylor U., 1947; M.A., U. Houston, 1958; B.D., Southwestern Baptist Theol. Sem., 1957, Th.D., 1961; postgrad. U. Okla., 1954, Oxford U., 1972; m. Dorothy Ann Sessums, Aug. 28, 1940; children—Elizabeth (Mrs. Herbert Parnell), Frances (Mrs. Daniel Stevens), Jonathan Michael, Celia Danielle Carmichael. Ordained to ministry So. Baptist Conv., 1939; pastor chs., Tex., Ark., 1939-61; supt. missions, Detroit, 1961-66; prof. missions, dir. urban ch. studies Golden Gate Baptist Theol. Sem., 1966—; mem. exec. bd. San Francisco Peninsula So. Baptist Assn., 1967—, San Francisco Conf. Religion and Race, 1967—. Mem. Am. Acad. Religion, Assn. Mission Profs., Am. Soc. Missiology, Alpha Chi. Author: How Churches Grow in an Urban World, 1978; Classics of Christian Missions, 1979; God Who Sends, 1983. Home: 21 Platt Ct Mill Valley CA 94941 Office: Strawberry Point Mill Valley CA 94941

DUCHOW, GILBERT JULIUS, minister, Lutheran Church-Missouri Synod; b. Albany, N.Y., July 8, 1942; s. Martin Christian and Julia Elmira (Anderson) D.; m. Linda Louise Mengerink, May 29, 1966; children: Julie, Cheryl, Sara, Rachel. B.A., Concordia Sr. Coll., 1964; M.Div., Concordia Sem., 1968. Ordained to ministry Luth. Ch.-Mo. Synod, 1968. Minister, Faith Luth. Ch., Rome, N.Y., 1968-72, Good Shepherd Luth. Ch., Sylvan Beach, N.Y., 1968-72, St. Paul Luth. Ch., Parkersburg, W.Va., 1972-80, Immanuel Luth. Ch., Hamilton, Ohio, 1980—; vice chmn. Ohio Dist. Bd. of Parish Services, Luth. Ch.-Mo. Synod, Cleve., 1978—; commr. Commn. on Religion in Appalachia, Knoxville, 1975-81. Treas., trustee Transitional Living Corp., Hamilton, Ohio, 1980—; mem. region V Mental Health Council, W.Va., 1974-76; chmn. Community Service Council, Parkersburg, 1977-78; mem. Foster Care Citizens Rev. Council, 1979-80; mem. ethics com. Mercy Hosp., Hamilton, Ohio, 1985—. Mem. Hamilton/Fairfield Ministerial Assn. (pres. 1984-85). Home: 41 Dover Pl Hamilton OH 45013 Office: Immanuel Lutheran Church 1285 Main St Hamilton OH 45013

DUCKETT, PHILLIP ANSEL, SR., minister, Southern Baptist Convention; b. Union, S.C., July 18, 1929; s. Homer E. and Lucia M. (Gaddis) D.; m. Jeanette Holseunback, Aug. 9, 1947; children: Patricia, Phillip, Phyllis. Ordained to ministry Baptist Ch., 1953. B.S., Newberry Coll., S.C., 1958; postgrad. Southeastern Bapt. Theol. Sem., N.C., 1959-61; M.Min., Luther Rice Sem., Fla., 1979, D.Min., 1980. Sr. minister Sharon Bapt. Ch., S.C., 1958-60, Mount Home Bapt. Ch., Morganton, N.C., 1960-63, McCabe Meml. Bapt. Ch., Martinsville, Va., 1965-73, 80—, Enon Bapt. Ch., Chester, Va., 1973-80; v.p. Pastors Conf. Va., 1983-84, pres., 1984-85; mem. gen. bd. Va. Bapt. Conv., 1983—; youth Bible leader Eagle Eyrie State Assembly, Lynchburg, Va., 1976-79. Trustee Va. Bapt. Children's Home, Petersburg, 1977-80; bd. dirs. family Council on Mental Health, Martinsville, 1969-72; pres. bd. dirs. Home for Alcoholics, Martinsville, 1968-72; devotional leader Va. State Senate, 1977-78; chaplain Martinsville Police Dept., 1981-82. Democrat. Lodge: Masons. Home: 920 Ainsley St Martinsville VA 24112 Office: McCabe Meml Ch 107 Clearview Dr Martinsville VA 24112

DUCKETT, ZELMA ELEWESE, minister, A.M.E. Ch.; b. Chattanooga, Dec. 25, 1906; d. William Hayden and Callie Donna (Baker) Ferguson; B.S., State U. N.Y. at Brockport, 1954; B.S., N.Y. U., 1954; grad. Buffalo Bible Inst., 1968; m. Gilbert Chilwalder Duckett, Nov. 25, 1945. Ordained to ministry, 1963; pastor A.M.E. chs., 1956—; home mission dir. and pastor A.M.E. Zion Mission, Albion, N.Y., 1956—. Mem. NAACP. Contbr. lit. essays to jours. Home: 129 Clarendon St PO Box 92 Albion NY 14411 Office: PO Box 92 Albion NY

DUCKWORTH, JOHN HOWARD, minister, American Baptist Churches of the U.S.A., b. b. Parkersburg, W. Va., Mar. 27, 1949; s. James Wellington and Fern Mildred (Larsen) D.; m. Patricia Gaye Nichols, Aug. 14, 1976; 1 child, Jonathan Douglas. B.A., Sioux Falls Coll., 1977; M.Div., Central Bapt. Sem., 1980. Ordained to ministry American Baptist Churches of the U.S.A., 1980. Interim, student pastor Burke/Lucas Parish, Burke, S.D., 1976-77; student pastor Wyandotte Bapt. Ch., Kansas City, 1979-80; pastor First Bapt. Ch., Greybull, Wy., 1980-84; pastor First Bapt Ch., Ridgecrest, Calif., 1984—; bd. dirs. New Ch. Devel., Denver, 1980-84. Contbr. article to profl. jour. Served to E4 U.S. Navy, 1967-71. Recipient Scripture Reading award Am. Bible Soc., 1979. Mem. Acad. Parish Clergy, Minister's Council Am. Bapt. Chs. (sec., tres. 1983-84), South Big Horn County Ministerial Assn. (pres. 1981-83), Indian Wells Valley Ministerial Assn. (pres. 1985—). Lodge: Rotary (sec., treas. 1981-83). Office: First Bapt Ch 1350 South Downs Ridgecrest CA 93555

DUDICK, MICHAEL JOSEPH, bishop, Roman Cath. Ch.; b. St. Clair, Pa., Feb. 23, 1916; s. John and Mary (Jurick) D.; B.A., Ill. Benedictine Coll., 1942; B.A., St. Procopius Sem., 1942-45. Ordained priest Roman Catholic Ch., 1945; consecrated bishop, 1968; vice-chancellor Byzantine Catholic Diocese of Pitts., 1946-55; chancellor Byzantine Catholic Diocese of Passaic (N.J.), 1963-68, bishop, 1968—; pastor St. Nicholas Ch., Old Forge, Pa., 1955-61; pastor St. Mary's Ch., Freeland, Pa., 1961-63, St. George Ch. Newark, 1963-68. Mem. Roman Curia-Sacred Congregation for Eastern Cath. Chs.; mem. exec. bd. Nat. Cath. Conf. on Ethnics and Neighborhood. Trustee Seton Hall U., 1968—. Project Equality of N.J. Home: 56 Highland Ave Montclair NJ 07042 Office: 101 Market St Passaic NJ 07055

DUDLEY, CARL SAFFORD, educator, Presbyterian Church U.S.A.; b. Balt., Oct. 27, 1932; s. Harold Jenkins and Margaret (Safford) D.; m. Shirley Sanford, June 18, 1955; children: Nathan, Rebecca, Andrew, Debora, Steven. B.A., Cornell U., 1954; postgrad. N.Y. Sch. Social Work, 1954-56; M.Div., Union Theol. Sem., 1959; D.Min., McCormick Theol. Sem., 1974. Social worker Manhattanville Community Ctr., N.Y.C., 1954-56; asst. pastor First Presbyn. Ch., Buffalo, 1959-62; pastor Berea Presbyn. Ch., St. Louis, 1962-73; prof. McCormick Theol. Sem., Chgo., 1973—; exec. dir. Ctr. for Congl. Ministries, Chgo., 1982—, Religious Research Assn. N.Y.C., 1979-82; assoc. editor Religious Research Rev., 1980-82. Author: Making the Small Church Effective, 1978; Where Have All Our People Gone, 1979; Orientations to Faith, 1982. Editor: Building Effective Ministry, 1983. Commr., St. Louis Housing Authority, 1970-73; bd. dirs. Sch. Bd. #200, Oak Park, Ill., 1981—. Mem. Religious Research Assn., Soc. Sci. Study Religion, Assn. Sociology of Religion.

Home: 210 S Elmwood Ave Oak Park IL 60302 Office: McCormick Theol Sem 5555 S Woodlawn Ave Chicago IL 60637

DUDLEY, CHARLES EDWARD, elder, Seventh-day Adventists; b. South Bend, Ind., Feb. 1, 1927; s. Joseph and Julia (Talley) D.; B.A., Oakwood Coll., Huntsville, Ala., 1947; LL.D., Bapt. Theol. Sem., 1969; m. Etta Mae Maycock, Dec. 28, 1947; children—Bonita Andrea, Charles Edward, Albert LeRoy. Ordained elder, 1951; pastor in Tenn., Ala., La., Tex., 1947-62; pres. S.Central Conf. Seventh-day Adventists, Nashville, 1962—; rep. to African mems. World Seventh-day Adventist Ch., 1975; pres. S. Central Conf. Seventh-day Adventist Ch. Office: 715 Youngs Ln Nashville TN 37207

DUDLEY, MERLE BLAND, minister, Presbyterian Church in U.S.; b. Norfolk, Va., Feb. 19, 1929; s. Harry Roy and Merle (Garrett) D.; B.A., Lynchburg Coll., 1950; M.Div., Union Theol. Sem., 1954; M.A., Presbyn. Sch. Christian Edn., Richmond, Va., 1969; Ph.D., U. Glasgow (Scotland), 1973; m. Lillie Pennington, Oct. 12, 1950; children: Carter Bland, Jane Merle. Ordained to ministry, 1954; pastor McQuay Meml. Presbyn. Ch., Charlotte, N.C., 1954-56, Holmes Presbyn. Ch., Bayview, Va., 1956-59; asst. pastor 1st Presbyn. Ch., Roanoke, Va., 1959-60; pastor Christ Presbyn. Ch., Virginia Beach, Va., 1960-67; assoc. pastor 1st Presbyn. Ch., Winston-Salem, N.C., 1967-70; pastor Westminster Presbyn. Ch., Waynesboro, Va., 1971—. Bd. dirs. Massanetta Springs, Inc., Harrisonburg, Va., 1972—; trustee Sunnyside Presbyn. Home, Harrisonburg, 1972—. mem. adv. bd. Salvation Army, Waynesboro, 1972-75; bd. dirs. YMCA, Waynesboro, 1973-75. Mem. Am. Acad. Religion, Soc. Bibl. Lit., Am. Sch. for Oriental Research, Church Service Soc., Va. Hist. Soc., Jamestowne Soc., SAR (state chmn. 1985—). Author: New Testament Preaching and Twentieth Century Communications, 1973. Lodge: Rotary. Home: 1900 Mt Vernon St Waynesboro VA 22980 Office: 1904 Mount Vernon St Waynesboro VA 22980

DUDLEY, PAUL V. See *Who's Who* in America, 43rd edition.

DUDLEY, THOMAS ALLEN, minister, Lutheran Church in America; b. Granville, Ohio, Mar. 4, 1944; s. Melvin John and Mabel Mary (Greiner) D.; m. Elizabeth C. Stroh, Dec. 24, 1972. A.B., Wittenberg U., 1966; M.Div., Hamma Sch. Theology, 1969. Ordained to ministry Lutheran Ch., 1969. Assoc. pastor Grace Luth. Ch., Toledo, Ohio, 1969-72; pastor North Riverdale Luth. Ch., Dayton, Ohio, 1972-76; pastor, developer Christ The King Ch., Birmingham, Ala., 1976-81, Christ The King Ch., Gt. Falls, Va., 1981—; chmn. stewardship mng. group Va. Synod, Luth. Ch. Am., 1983—. Mem. adv. bd. Center for Community Mental Health, Fairfax County, Va. Lodge: Optimist. Home: 930 Cup Leaf Holly Ct Great Falls VA 22066 Office: Christ the King Lutheran Ch PO Box 251 Great Falls VA 22066

DUDNEY, BENNETT, minister Church of the Nazarene; b. Nashville, Ark., Dec. 23, 1921; s. Ira and Evadna (Landers) D.; m. Cathryn Baker, Jan. 4, 1942; children: Sherry, Glenda, Kaye. B.A. in Religion, Bethany Nazarene Coll., 1950; student Garrett Bibl. Inst., Evanston, Ill., 1954-55; D.D. (hon.) Trevecra Nazarene Coll., Nashville, 1976. Ordained to ministry, Church of the Nazarene, 1950; minister of ch. edn. Bethany Ch. of Nazarene, Bethany, Okla., 1950-53, First Ch. of Nazarene, Chgo., 1953-56; pastor First Ch. of Nazarene, Kankakee, Ill., 1956-59; dir. lay tng. Denomination Hdqrs., Gen. Bd., Ch. Nazarene, Kansas City, Mo., 1959-71; pastor First Ch. of Nazarene, Atlanta, 1971-76; pres. European Nazarene Bible Coll., Busingen, W. Ger., 1976-82; dir. publs. Ch. of Nazarene Internat. Hdqrs., Kansas City, Mo., 1982—. Author: Planning Church Growth, 1969; The Sunday School, 1965; Superintendent Records That Build the Sunday School, 1963. Served with USAAF, 1942-45. Office: Ch of Nazarene Internat Hdqrs 6401 The Paseo Kansas City MO 66212

DUER, RONALD EUGENE, minister, Lutheran Church-Missouri Synod; b. Chgo., Sept. 1, 1938; s. Harry K. and Wilhelmine (Nehring) D.; m. Phyllis E. Schumm, Aug. 11, 1962; children: Mark, Paul, Kristen. B.A., Concordia Sr. Coll., Ft. Wayne, 1960; M.Div., Concordia Sem., St. Louis, 1964; S.T.M., Christ Sem., 1978. Ordained to ministry, 1964. Pastor, Holy Cross Ch., Anita, Iowa, 1964-68, St. Louis, 1968-75, Gloria Dei Ch., Hudson, Ohio, 1975—; mem. youth and stewardship bd. Iowa Dist. West, Ft. Dodge, 1966-68; chaplain St. Louis Jaycees, 1972-75; counselor Ohio Dist., Akron, Canton, Youngstown circuits, 1982—; pres. Hudson Ministerial Assn., 1976-77. Mem. Cleve. Ministerial Assn., Akron Ministerial Assn. Democrat. Office: Gloria Dei Luth Ch 2113 Ravenna Rd Hudson OH 44236

DUERBECK, JULIAN JOSEPH FRANCIS, priest, Roman Catholic Church, educator. b. Chgo., May 3, 1949; s. Joseph and Frances (Dankowski) D. B.A. in Eng. Lit., St. Procopius Coll., 1971; M.A. Theology in Liturgy, St. John's U., Collegeville, Minn., 1975; postgrad. U. Toronto, summers 1981, 82, 84. Professed Benedictine monk, 1970; ordained priest Roman Cath. Ch., 1976. Instr. religious studies Ill. Benedictine Coll., Lisle, 1975-78; instr. monastic novices St. Procopius Abbey, Lisle, 1976-83, liturgist, 1976-84; Sunday asst. Joliet Diocese Parishes, DuPage County, Ill., 1976-84; campus minister Benet Acad., Lisle, 1978—; lectr. in field, Du Page County, 1975—; cons. liturgy for parishes and religious houses, 1975—. Editor 3 vol. Liturgy of the Hours, 1979; author short story. Mem. Liturgical Conf., Field Mus. Chgo. Home: St Procopius Abbey 5601 College Rd Lisle IL 60532 Office: Benet Academy Lisle IL 60532

DUERKSEN, EDWARD HARRY, minister, educator, Conservative Baptist Assn. Am.; b. Reedley, Calif., Apr. 10, 1922; s. Jacob Toews and Catherine Pearl (Neufeld) D.; grad. Multonomah Sch. Bible, 1950; Th.B., Multnomah Sch. Bible, 1975; m. Edna Rosalie Goertzen, Feb. 8, 1942; children—Roger Lee, Rosalie Sharon, Catherine Ann, Michael Ray. Ordained to ministry, 1950; pastor various chs., Oreg., 1950-63; pastor First Bapt. Ch., Pollock Pines, Calif., 1964-68, Valley Bapt. Ch., San Jose, Calif., 1969-72, Westside Bapt. Ch., Alameda, Calif., 1972—; evangelist, Germany, summer 1949; profl exposition E. Bay Sch. Bible, San Leandro, Calif., 1975—. Dir. Wolf Mountain Conf. Assn., Grass Valley, Calif., 1963-64; treas. No. Calif. Nat. Assn. Evangelicals, 1970—. Dir. Enemy Aircraft Alert Skywatch, Palouse, Wash., 1950-51. Mem. Fellowship Christian Magicians. Author: Outline Studies in Daniel, 1976. Home: 1338 St Charles St Alameda CA 94501 Office: POB 534 Alameda CA 94501

DUFF, FLOYD PAUL, minister, Lutheran Church, Missouri Synod; b. Detroit, Sept. 26, 1929; s. Floyd and Evelyn (Malokey) D.; m. Bobbie Ann Wessinger, June 12, 1955; children: Timothy, Paul, Jonathan, Evelyn, Marion, Katherine, Lois. B.A., Concordia sem., St. Louis, 1952. Ordained to ministry Luth. Ch., 1955. Pastor, Redeemer Luth. Ch., Auburn, N.Y., 1955-59, Bethel Luth. Ch., Glenshaw, Pa., 1959-67, Emmanuel Luth. Ch., Preston, Md., 1967-71, Trinity Luth. Ch., New Orleans, 1981—; adminstr., exec. dir. Augsburg Luth. Home, Balt., 1971-80; exec. dir. St. John's Luth. Home, Mars, Pa., 1980; sec.-treas. fin. com. Luth. Welfare, Pitts., 1960-67. Mem. adv. bd. Adminstrv. div. Md. State Bd. Health, 1978; bd. dirs. Nursing Home Liaison Com., Balt., 1978, Central Md. Profl. Service Rev. Orgn. Adv. Bd., Balt., 1979. Mem. Am. Assn. Homes for Aged (service award 1976-79, 79, ho. dels, membership com., fin. com. 1972-80), Md. Assn. Non-profit Homes for Aged (pres. 1972-78). Republican. Home: 3521 Mimosa Ct New Orleans LA 70114 Office: Trinity Luth Ch 624 Eliza St New Orleans LA 70114

DUFFEY, PAUL ANDREWS, bishop, United Methodist Church; b. Brownsville, Tenn., Dec. 13, 1920; s. George Henderson and Julia Griffin (McKissach) D.; m. Anna Louise Calhoun, June 20, 1944; children: Melanie Claire, Paul A., Jr. A.B., Birmingham So. U., 1942, D.D. (hon.), 1966; M.Div., Vanderbilt U., 1945; D.H.L.(hon.), Union Coll., Barbourville, Ky., 1981; LL.D. (hon.), Ky. Wesleyan U., 1984. Ordained to ministry United Meth. Church. Pastor various chs. in Tenn., Ala., Fla., 1944-79; bishop Louisville Area United Meth. Ch., 1980—. Recipient Trustees award Sue-Bennett Coll., 1982, Disting. Service award Lindsy-Wilson Coll., 1983. Democrat. Office: 4010 Dupont Circle Louisville KY 40207

DUFFY, GLENN ALAN, priest, Episcopalian Church, telecommunications aeronatuics company executive; b. Jamaica, N.Y., Oct. 30, 1940; s. Philip Frederick and Ernestine (Braun) D.; m. Marie A. Dietrich, July 2, 1960; children: Glenn John, Kathleen Marie. Grad. George Mercer Sch. Theology, 1975. Ordained to ministry Episcopal Church as deacon, 1974, as priest, 1975. Assoc., St. James Episcopal Ch., Long Beach, N.Y., 1974-81; rector, Christ Episcopal Ch., Lynbrook, N.Y., 1981—; mem. Christian Jewish relations commn. Diocese of L.I., 1975—. Mgr. communications planning Societe Internationale de Telecommunications Aeronautiques, Bohemia, N.Y., 1984—. Assoc. editor, author Fragments lit. jour., 1970—; patetee specialized data communications equipment, 1975. Served to E5 USN, 1958-62. Mem. Am. Legion. Clubs: Freeport Tuna, Jones Beach Power Squadron. Lodge: Masons. Home: 51 Blake Ave Lynbrook NY 11563 Office: Soc Internat de Telecommunications Aeronautiques 45 Orville Dr Bohemia NY 11716

DUGAN, HERSCHEL CEDRIC, minister Christian Church (Disciples of Christ); b. Mankato, Minn., Apr. 13, 1931 s. Charles E. and Harriet (Van Buren) D.; m. Shirley Joan Tietsort, July 28, 1960; children: Denise, Mark. B.A., Phillips U., 1953; M.Div., Drake U., 1956; D.Min., Phillips U., 1981. Ordained to ministry Christian Church (Disciples of Christ), Assoc. minister 1st Christian Ch., Omaha, 1956-60; minister No. Heights Christian Ch., Tulsa, 1960-63, 1st Christian Ch., Aurora, Nebr., 1963-68, Olathe, Kans., 1968—. Moderator, Christian Ch. Greater Kansas City, 1984-85; chn. com. on ministry Christian Ch. in Kans., 1979-81; bd. dirs. Christian in Kans, 1981—. Mem. Nebr. adv. com., U.S. Civil Rights Commn., 1965-68. Mem. Disciple Ministers Assn. Greater Kansas City (pres. 1972-73), Ministers and Wives Assn. Christian Ch. Kans. (pres. 1978). Republican. Lodges: Lions, Masons (master 1978). Office: PO Box 544 Olathe KS 66061

DUGAS, KENNETH, minister, So. Baptist Conv.; b. Campbellton, N.B., Can., Aug. 8, 1947; s. Joseph Julien and Annie Wagstaff (Young) D.; B.Music Edn., Capital U., Columbus, Ohio, 1969; m. Patricia Ann Walker, Dec. 6, 1969; children—Jason Bradley, Heather Michelle. Ordained to ministry, 1970; minister music and youth Hillcrest Bapt. Ch., Carlisle, Ohio, 1969-73, First Bapt. Ch., Heath, Ohio, 1973—; dir. Morningstar Singers, 1973—. Recipient Good Deeds award Exchange Club Cleve., 1969. Mem. Phi Mu Alpha. Home: 508 Hudson Ave Newark OH 43055 Office: 525 S 30th St Heath OH 43055

DUGGAN, JOHN PHILIP, priest, Roman Catholic Ch.; b. Niagara Falls, N.Y., Dec. 3, 1907; s. James and Bridget (Mitchell) D.; came to U.S., 1930, naturalized, 1936; student St. John's Coll., Ireland, 1927-30; B.Th., Niagara U., 1934, LL.D., 1963. Ordained priest, 1934; asst. pastor Nativity Ch., Buffalo, 1934-37, St. Mary's Ch., Niagara Falls, N.Y., 1937-42; served with U.S. Army, 1942-61; chaplain K.C., Niagara Falls, 1965—; pastor St. Mary's Ch., Niagara Falls, N.Y., 1961—. Bd. dirs. Mt. St. Mary's Hosp. Recipient K.C. award, 1963-65. Mem. VFW, Cath. War Vets., Mil. Chaplains Assn. U.S., Niagara U. Alumni Assn., USCG Aux., Amvets, Air Force Aid Soc., Air Force Assn. (charter), USAF Acad. Assn. Clubs: Rotarians, Fin, Feather and Fur Sportsmen's. Address: 259 4th St Niagara Falls NY 14303

DUKE, JAMES O., theology educator, Christian Church (Disciples of Christ); b. Balt.; s. James Roy and Florence (Hanes) D.; m. Jean Ortgies, Jan. 29, 1969 (div. Feb. 1984); children: Cassandra L., C. Nicole. B.A., U Md., 1968; M.Div., Vanderbilt Divinity Sch., 1971; Ph.D., Vanderbilt U., 1975. Ordained to ministry Christian Church (Disciples of Christ). Vis. asst. prof. U Mont., Missoula, 1975-76; assoc. prof. Brite Divinity Sch., Tex. Christian U., Fort Worth, 1976—. Mem. Theology Commn. Consulation on Ch. Union, 1977—, Theology Commn. Council on Chritian Unit, 1976—. Author: Horace Bushnell, 1984. Grantee: Fulbright-Daad, 1973, Assn. Theol. Schs., 1984. Mem. Am. Acad. Religion (co editor 1981—), Am. Soc. Ch. History. Office: Brite Divinity Sch Tex Christian U Fort Worth TX 76129

DUKES, DOROTHY (MRS. LEONARD DUKES), lay ch. worker, Ch. of God in Christ; b. Birmingham, Ala., Jan. 24, 1926; d. Charlie and Elizabeth (Smiler) Dixon; grad. Detroit Bible Coll., 1976; D.H. (hon.), Trinity Hall Coll. and Sem., 1981; m. Leonard Dukes, Mar. 11, 1957; children: Charlie Mae (Mrs. Robert Johnson), Lauretta. Evangelist, Ch. of God in Christ, 1965; state dean Sunday sch. dept. Ch. of God in Christ, 1969-71, chmn. lay del., internat. Sunday sch. conv., 1971, internat. coordinator Sunday sch. conv. pageant, 1974—, chmn. edn. com. S.W. Mich. Dist. 9, 1982—; pub. relations dir. Baileys Temple Ch. of God in Christ, 1976—. Owner Dorothy Dukes House de Coiffure, Detroit, 1957—. Mem. Women's Conf. of Concern, 1974, Nat. Council Negro Women, 1974. Bd. dirs. Charles Harrison Mason Systems of Bible Coll., Detroit, 1972. Recipient Religious Workers Guild Honorium award Ch. of God in Christ, 1982. Mem. Bus. and Profl. Womans Fedn. S.W. Mich. (state dir. 1968), Internat. Platform Soc. Democrat. Assoc. editor Cogic womens mag., 1973. Home: 4181 Burns Dr Detroit MI 48214 Office: 7414 E Canfield Detroit MI 48214

DUKES, JAMES EDWARD, JR., minister, Lutheran Church in America; b. Columbia, S.C., Feb. 28, 1938; s. James Edward and Ruby Avis (Bolen) D.; m. Gladys Irene Canada, Dec. 21, 1968; children: Diane, Christina. B.A. in Edn., U. Fla., 1961; B.D., Candler Sch. Theology, 1965; M.A. in Philosoph, U. S.C., 1974; cert. Luth. Theol. So. Sem., 1975. Ordained to ministry Lutheran Ch., 1975. Instr. Bible and philosophy U. S.C., Lancaster, 1971-75; minister New Bethel Luth. Ch., Richfield, N.C., 1975-78, St. Mark Luth. Ch., Lumberton, N.C., 1978-83, Christus Victor Luth. Ch., Bonita Springs, Fla., 1983—; mem. world hunger and justice coms. N.C. Synod, Luth. Ch. in Am., 1975-77; Fla. Synod rep. The Lutheran, Phila., 1984—. Chmn. Bointa Springs Coordinating Council, 1984; precinct committeeman Republican Party, Naples, Fla., 1984. Mem. S. Lee County Clergy Assn. (pres. 1984-85). Home: 537 104th Ave N Naples FL 33963 Office: Christus Victor Luth Ch US 41 PO Box 867 Bonita Springs FL 33923

DULLES, AVERY, educator, priest, Roman Catholic Ch.; b. Auburn, N.Y., Aug. 24, 1918; s. John Foster and Janet Pomeroy (Avery) D.; A.B., Harvard, 1940; Ph.L., Woodstock Coll., 1951, S.T.L., 1957; S.T.D., Gregorian U., 1960; LL.D., St. Joseph's Coll., Phila., 1969; L.H.D., Georgetown U., 1977, Creighton U., 1983; Th.D., U. Detroit, 1978; D.D., St. Anselm Coll., 1981. Joined Soc. of Jesus, 1946, ordained priest Roman Catholic Ch., 1956; instr. philosophy Fordham U., 1951-53; prof. theology Woodstock (N.Y.) Coll., 1960-74, asst. prof., 1960-62, asso. prof., 1962-69, prof., 1969-74; prof. systematic theology Cath. U., Washington, 1974—. Bd.

dirs. Georgetown U., 1966-68; trustee Fordham U., 1969-72. Woodrow Wilson Internat. Center for Scholars fellow, 1977. Mem. Cath. Theol. Soc. Am. (dir. 1970-72, 74-77, pres. 1975-76), Am. Theol. Soc., Cath. Commn. Intellectual and Cultural Affairs, Gustave Weigel Soc. (bd. dirs. 1966—), Phi Beta Kappa. Consultor to Papal Secretariat for dialogue with non-believers, 1966-73. Author: A History of Apologetics, 1971; The Survival of Dogma, 1971; Revelation Theology: A History, 1969; Revelation and the Quest for Unity, 1968; The Dimensions of the Church, 1967; Models of the Church, 1974; The Resilient Ch., 1977; A Church to Believe In, 1982; Models of Revalation, 1983. many others; also articles. Asso. editor for ecumenism Concilium, 1963—. Address: Cath U Am Caldwell Hall Washington DC 20064

DULOHERY, M. CORNILE, retired hospital administrator, nun, Roman Catholic Church; b. Longford, Kans., Nov. 10, 1909; d. Cornelius Jerome and Margaret Mary (Berry) Dulohery; B.S., Cath. U. Am., 1940, M.S., 1941. Entered Order Sisters of Mercy, 1933, became nun, 1936. Supt. med. nursing Mercy Hosp., Balt., 1936, pediatric nursing 1936-39; dir. sch. nursing St. Joseph Hosp., Savannah, Ga., 1941-42, 1959-60, hosp. adminstr., 1960—; dir. hosp. St. Joseph Infirmary, Atlanta, 1943-52; supr. Leprosarium, Convent of Mercy, Chachacare, Trinidad, B.W.I., 1952-55. Mem. Community Planning Council of Atlanta, 1943-52; vice chmn. Supts. Council of Atlanta, 1948-50; mem., pres. State Bd. Examining Nurses Ga., 1947-52, chmn. bd., 1950-51. Named Woman of Yr., Bus. and Profl. Women's Club, 1973; recipient Brotherhood award NCCJ, 1975. Mem. Ga. (pres. 1943-45, treas. 1945-47, trustee 1945-57) Cath. hosp. assns., Am. Coll. Hosp. Adminstrs., Alumnae Assn. St. Joseph Hosp. Sch. Nursing, Pi Gamma Mu. Home: 11806 McAuley Dr Savannah GA 31406 Office: 11705 Mercy Blvd Savannah GA 31406

DUMAINE, MAURICE PHILIPPE, priest, Roman Catholic Church. B. St. Guillaume d'Upton, Que., Can., July 21, 1916; s. Omer and Emma (Melancon) D. Grad. Theology Scolasticat St. Jean, Cite de Vanier, Ont., Can., 1943; Lic. Canon Law, Sem. St. Paul, Ottawa, 1961; Bachillerate Library Sci., Ottawa U., 1965. Ordained priest Roman Cath. Ch., 1943. Missionary, Haiti, 1943-49, Colombia, 1950-56; prof. canon law and moral theology Scolasticat St. Jean, Cite de Vanier, Ottawa, 61; hosp. chaplain Grace Dart Hosp., Montreal, Que., 1963-85; lawyer, defender bond Ch. Tribunal, Montreal, 1965—. Mem. Assn. Des Bibliothecaires de Langue Francaise, Assn. des Bibliothecaires Profls. du Que., Cath. Library Assn., Canon Law Soc. Home and Office: 4000 rue Bossuet Montreal PQ H1M 2M2 Canada

DUMAINE, PIERRE, Bishop of San Jose, Roman Catholic Church, 1981—. Office: St Joseph Ctr 7600-Y St Joseph Ave San Jose CA*

DUMOND, FRANKLIN R., minister, General Association of General Baptists; b. Tahlequah, Okla., June 11, 1952; s. Franklin Theodore and Norma Rose (Jamison) D.; m. Winda Thompson, May 21, 1976; children: Joseph Franklin, Jeffrey Steven. B.A., Northeastern State U., 1974; M. Div., So. Bapt. Theol. Sem., 1979. Ordained to ministry Gen. Assn. Gen. Baptists, 1971. Pastor Caney Gen. Bapt. Ch., Tahlequah, Okla., 1971-74, Blue Springs Gen. Bapt. Ch., Hulbert, Okla., 1974-76, First Gen. Bapt. Ch., McLeansboro, Ill., 1977-80, Lane Ave. Bapt. Ch., Kansas City, Mo., 1980—; pres. Mission Point Assn. Home Missions, Springfield, Mo., 1984—; v.p. Home Missions Ozarks Inc., Branson, Mo., 1984—; moderator Mission Point Assn. Gen. Baptists, 1980-81; program dir. Mission Point Youth Camp, Rogersville, Mo., 1982-84; mem. planning com. gen. bd. Gen. Bapts., chmn. 1984—. Author Sunday Sch. materials. Contbr. articles to profl. jours. Mem. Gen. Bapt. Hist. Soc. (chmn. 1979-80). Avocations: gardening, historical and genealogical research, writing. Office: Lane Ave Bapt Ch 9003 E 87th Kansas City MO 64138

DUMOUCHEL, PAUL, archbishop, Roman Cath. Ch.; b. Winnipeg, Man., Can., Sept. 19, 1911; s. Joseph and Josephine D.; grad. St. Boniface (Man.) Coll., 1930; student U. Man., 1929-30; Sem. Lebret, Sask., Can., 1931-36. Ordained priest, 1936; missionary to Indians of Man., 1936-50; retreat master, 1940-50; sch. prin., 1950-55; bishop of Keewatin, Can., 1955-67; 1st archbishop Keewatin-Le Pas, 1967—. Author: Saulteux Grammar, 1942. Address: 108 1st St W The Pas MB R9A 0A4 Canada

DUNAHOO, CHARLES, minister, religious educator, Presbyterian Church USA; b. Winder, Ga., Feb. 24, 1940; s. Charles Wynn and Myrtle (Everette) D.; m. Colleen Roberts, Dec. 27, 1963; children: John Charles, Melanie Colleen, Mark Wynn. A.B., U. Ga., 1962; M.Div., Columbia Theol. Sem., 1965; postgrad. Westminster Theol. Sem., 1985—. Ordained to ministry, 1965. Student asst., camp dir. Westminster Presbyn. Ch., Atlanta, 1962-67, asst. pastor, 1954-67; pastor Oak Park Presbyn. Ch., Montgomery, Ala., 1967-71, Smyrna Presbyn. Ch., Ga., 1971-76; coordinator, Presbyn. Ch. Am. Christian Edn. and Pubs., Decatur, Ga., 1977—; adv. mem. bd. dirs. Covenant Theol. Sem., St. Louis, 1982—. Covenant Coll., Chattanooga, 1982—, Ridge Haven, Rosman, N.C., 1982—; ex officio bd. dirs. Great Commn. Pubs., Phila., 1977—; bd. trustees Westminster Theol. Sem., Phila., 1981—; cons. in field. Editor Effective Ch. Leadership, 1983. Chaplain, capt. Civil Air Patrol, Atlanta, 1979. Served with USAR, 1958-60. Mem. Am. Mgmt. Assn., Performax Systems Internat., Time Mgmt. Ctr. Club: Lions. Home: 1207 Berkley Rd Avondale Estates GA 30002 Office: Presbyn Ch Am Christian Edn and Pubs 4319 Memorial Dr Suite F Decatur GA 30031

DUNAWAY, JOHN THOMAS, minister, Southern Baptist Convention; b. Stanford, Ky., Nov. 25, 1932; s. John Thomas and Rachel M. (Bailey) D.; m. Mary Jayne Cutter, Aug. 22, 1954; children: Susan Elaine, John Mark. B.A., Georgetown Coll., Ky., 1954; B.D., So. Sem., 1958, M.Div., 1973; D.Min., Lexington Theol. Sem., 1983; D.D. (hon.), Cumberland Coll., 1980. Ordained to ministry So. Bapt. Conv., 1952. Pastor, Harris Creek Bapt. Ch., Stanford, 1952-55, Antioch Bapt. Ch., Bedford, Ky., 1956-58, Little Flock Bapt. Ch., Shepherdsville, Ky., 1958-62, Eaton Meml. Bapt. Ch., Owensboro, Ky., 1962-69, 1st Bapt. Ch., Corbin, Ky., 1969—; trustee Bethel Coll., Hopkinsville, Ky., 1965, Clear Creek Bapt. Sch., Pineville, Ky., 1970-76; pres. Ky. Bapt. Conv., Middletown, Ky., 1980-81; chmn. exec. com. So. Bapt. Conv., Nashville, 1981-83. Contbr. editorials to religious publs. Chmn. spl. com. to study city utilities, Corbin, 1976; chmn. Owensboro Human Rights Commn., 1967-69. Recipient spl. recognition for fund raising Cumberland Coll., 1979. Mem. Corbin Ministerial Assn. Democrat. Lodge: Rotary. Home: 326 N Hamlin Corbin KY 40701 Office: 1st Bapt Ch 401 N Laurel Ave Corbin KY 40701

DUNCAN, HENRY CLARK, minister, United Meth. Ch.; b. Thayer, Mo., Feb. 4, 1922; s. Byrd and Vida (Clark) D.; A.B., Drury Coll., 1946; B.D., Duke, 1949, M.Div., 1971; postgrad. Union Theol. Sch., N.Y.C., 1957-58; m. Esta Lee Keele, June 30, 1946; children: Ann Rosella, Henry Clark. Ordained deacon, 1947, elder, 1949, to ministry, 1949; pastor St. John's Meth. Ch., Charlotte, N.C., 1949-51; commd. lt. j.g. U.S. Navy, 1950, advanced through grades to capt., 1968; sr. chaplain U.S. Naval Acad., Annapolis, Md., 1970-72; base chaplain Camp Lejeune, N.C., 1972-73, Guantanamo Bay, Cuba, 1965-67, Newport, R.I., 1967-69; ret., 1973; pastor Village Chapel, Pinehurst, N.C., 1973—. Mem. Ret. Officers Assn., Nat. Assn. Uniformed Services. Recipient Disting. Alumni Service award Drury Coll., 1971. Columnist weekly sermon Pinehurst Outlook, 1975-79. Lodges: Rotary, K.T. Home: PO Box 1895 Pinehurst NC 28374 Office: PO Box 1060 Pinehurst NC 28374

DUNCAN, JILES HERBERT, minister, Church of God (Cleveland, Tenn.); b. Kings Mountain, N.C., Aug. 17, 1923; s. Jiles Herbert and Olive Annie (Allen) D.; m. Mildred Elizabeth Bynum, Mar. 11, 1951; children: Carol, Brenda, Sandra, Amy. Student Holme Bible Coll., 1950's, Moody Bible Inst., 1970's. Ordained to ministry Church of God, 1983. Evangelist Ch. of God, Greenville, S.C., 1976-78, pastor, Lewiston, Idaho, 1978, Nampa, Idaho, 1978-80, Honolulu, 1980—; mem. state council, state ministerial examining bd. Ch. of God., Ajea, Hawaii. Served with U.S. Army, 1948-50, Japan. Republican. Avocation: deep sea fishing. Home and Office: 822 Coolidge St Honolulu HI 96826

DUNCAN, JOHN EBLEN, church official, So. Bapt. Conv.; b. Chattanooga, Aug. 1, 1925; s. Ronald Clarence and Nellie Mae (Gray) D.; student Wis. State U., 1943-44, Tenn. Temple Coll., 1951-53; A.B., Samford U., 1955, M.S., 1968; postgrad. Carver Sch. Missions and Social Work, 1962, So. Bapt. Theol. Sem., 1963; m. Eleanor Kathleen Gardenhire, June 29, 1946; 1 son, John Charles. Asst. pastor Roebuck Plaza Bapt. Ch., Birmingham, Ala., 1954-55; pastor, Mt. Pleasant Bapt. Ch., Pell City, Ala., 1956-59; dir. missions St. Clair Bapt. Assn., Ashville, Ala., 1959-62; dir. missions Shelby Bapt. Assn., Columbiana, Ala., 1962—. Mem. Am. Assn. Counseling and Devel., Ala. Assn. Counseling and Devel., Assn. Specialists in Group Work, Mental Health Assn. Club: Civitan (pres. 1963-64) (Columbiana). Contbr. articles to publs. Home: 125 Myrtle St Columbiana AL 35051 Office: PO Box 888 Columbiana AL 35051

DUNCAN, POPE ALEXANDER, religious college president, Southern Baptist Convention; b. Glasgow, Ky., Sept. 8, 1920; s. Pope Alexander and Mable (Roberts) D.; m. Margaret Flexer; children: Mary Margaret Duncan Jones, Annie Laurie Duncan Kelly, Katherine Duncan Maxwell. B.S. in Physics and Math, U. Ga., 1940, M.S. in Physics, 1941; Th.M., So. Bapt. Theol. Sem., 1944, Ph.D. in Ch. History, 1947; postgrad. Union Theol. Sem., N.Y.C., 1954, U. Zurich, Switzerland, 1960-61, Oxford U., England, 1952. Ordained to ministry, 1941. Pastor, River View Bapt. Ch., Ky.; dir. religious activities Mercer U., Macon, Ga., 1945-46, Roberts Prof. Ch. History, 1948-49; prof. religion Stetson U., DeLand, Fla., 1946-48, 49-53, pres., 1977—; prof. ch. history Southeastern Bapt. Theol. Sem., Louisville, 1953-63, acting dir. student recruitment, 1962-63; prof. Bapt. Theol. Sem., Ruschlikon, Switzerland, 1960-61; dean Brunswick Coll., Ga., 1964; S. Ga. Coll., Douglas, 1964-68; v.p. Ga. So. Coll., Statesboro, 1968-71, pres., 1971-77; interim pastor First Bapt. Ch., DeLand, Fla., Lynchburg, Va., Gastonia, N.C., Wieuca Rd. Bapt. Ch., Atlanta; mem. com. on history Ga. Bapt. Conv., 1964-66. Past curator, sec. Fla. Bapt. Hist. Commn.; sec. Council Deans and Vice Pres., Univ. System Ga., 1969-70, chmn., 1970-71; vice chmn. Council Presidents, So. Consortium for Internat. Edn., Inc., 1973-74, chmn., 1974-75; pres. Coastal Empire council Boy Scouts Am., 1973-74; mem. Ga. Com. for Humanities, 1972-77, Ga. Statewide Adv. Com. for Am. Issues Forum, 1975; cons. NEH, 1975; bd. dirs. Fla. Endowment for Humanities, 1978-79, United Fund, Volusia County, Fla., 1978-81; mem. Fla. Council of 100; chmn. Fla. Independent Coll. Fund, 1980-81; dir. DeLand-West Volusia Com. of 100, 1982-85; mem. 7th Judicial Circuit Nominating Commn., Fla., 1978-82. Recipient Charbonnier prize U. Ga., 1941; Carnegie grantee 1951, 52; faculty fellow Southeastern Bapt. Theol. Sem., 1960-61. Mem. Am. Hist. Soc., Am. Soc. Ch. History (Brewer prize com. 1957, com. on program and local arrangements for spring meeting 1959), So. Bapt. Hist. Soc., Newcomen Soc., Ga. Assn. Colls. (v.p. 1967-68, pres. 1968-69), Am. Assn. State Colls. and Univs. (com. on workshops and confs. 1975-77), So. Assn. Colls. and Schs. (commn. on colls. 1978-82), Fla. Assn. Colls. and Univs. (bd. dirs. 1978-84, pres. 1982-83), Nat. Assn. So. Bapt. Colls. and Schs. (pres. 1980-81), Nat. Assn. Ind. Colls. and Univs. (bd. dirs. 1979-83), Ind. Colls. and Univs. in Fla. (chmn. 1981-82), Nat. Collegiate Athletic Assn. (pres.'s commn. 1984—), DeLand Area C. of C. (bd. dirs. 1978-81, v.p. 1980-81), Phi Beta Kappa (pres. Wake County alumni chpt. 1956-60, pres. Coastal Ga.-S.C. chpt. 1974-76), Phi Kappa Phi (pres. Ga. So. chpt. 1971-72), Phi Mu Epsilon, Phi Eta Sigma, Omicron Delta Kappa, Phi Delta Kappa, Kappa Delta Pi, Pi Omega Pi. Democrat. Lodge: Rotary. Office: Stetson Univ 421 N Blvd DeLand FL 32720

DUNCAN, RICHARD LEO, religious media executive, United Church of Christ; TV host, producer; b. Plymouth, Ill., Dec. 7, 1936; s. Gilbert Leo and Vera Viola (Payne) D.; m. Mary Rose Hackett, Dec. 16, 1962 (div. Nov., 1981). B.A. in Chemistry, Knox Coll., 1958; M.Div., Pacific Sch. Religion, 1969; postgrad. San Diego Community Coll., 1977-81. Ordained to ministry United Ch. of Christ, 1970. Youth minister 1st Congregational Ch., San Mateo, Calif., 1967-68; minister youth and education Kensington Community Ch., San Diego, 1969-74; campus minister Calif. State U.-Long Beach, 1975-77; exec. dir. Religious Media Ministry, San Diego, 1978—; bd. dirs., v.p., treas. Ecumedia, Los Angeles, 1980—, interim exec. dir., 1982; host, producer KFMB-TV, San Diego, 1977—; producer Focus Sive, KGTV, San Diego, 1977—; co-producer Wordways, KNXT-TV, Los Angeles, 1980; moderator United Ch. Christ San Diego Assn., 1982-83. Bd. dirs. Centro de Asuntos Migratorios, San Diego, 1981-84; bd. dirs., v.p. The Great Day, San Diego, 1975—; Adv. bd. Congressman Jim Bates, San Diego, 1980—, Calif. Assemblywoman Lucy Killea, San Diego, 1984. Served to capt. U.S. Army, 1960-64. Recipient Emmy award Nat. Acad. TV Arts and Scis., 1980, 84, Award of Merit Religious Pub. Relations Council, 1983, Gabriel Cert. of Merit, Nat. Cath. Assn. Broadcasters and Allied Communicators, 1978, video award of merit Internat. TV Assn., 1984. Mem. World Assn. Christian Communication, Nat. Assn. Better Broadcasting (bd. dirs. 1981—, editorial com. You Own More than Your Set 1983), Assn. Regional Religious Communicators, Telecommunications Consumer Coalition. Home: PO Box 151135 San Diego CA 92115 Office: Religious Media Ministry 4778 Soria Dr San Diego CA 92115

DUNCAN, WILLIAM ADAM, JR., church official, minister, Southern Baptist Convention; b. Newton Centre, Mass., Apr. 27, 1918; s. William A. and Milner F. (Sammons) D.; A.A., Gordon Mil. Coll., 1936; A.B., Mercer U., 1947; B.D., Southwestern Bapt. Theol. Sem., 1951; m. Edna Shaw, Apr. 11, 1946; children—Adam Chandler, Malcomb, Sammons, Robert Bruce. Ordained to ministry, 1946; pastor First Bapt. Ch., Hahira, Ga., 1951-52, First Bapt. Ch., Screven, Ga., 1952-54, Gordon Rd. Bapt. Ch., Mableton, Ga., 1976—. Supt. associational missions, Daniell Bapt. Assn., Vidalia, Ga., 1954-57; supt. missions O'Geechee River Bapt. Assn., Statesboro, Ga., 1957-58; dir. associational programs Piedmont Bapt. Assn., 1958-76; v.p., dir. missions N.C. Conf., 1969; chaplain USAF, 1968—; ministers trustee adviser Gardner Webb Coll. N.C. Mem. Greensboro Community Council, 1965-67. Recipient Sculpture Purchase prize Ga. Artists League, 1947. Mem. Nat. Geog. Soc. (life), Nat. Rifle Assn., Southwestern Theol. Alumni (past pres.), Ga. Sport Shooters Assn., Ga. State Chaplains Assn. Pi Kappa Alpha. Republican. Home: 2239 Headland Dr East Point GA 30344

DUNCAN, ZERDEN BILLIE, minister, Advent Christian Ch.; b. Hickory, N.C., May 29, 1921; s. Ernest Lee and Daisy Emma (Page) D.; grad. high sch.; m. Verlie Estelle Brown, Dec. 24, 1941; children—Patricia Ann (Mrs. Jerry A. Clontz), Paul David, Wanda Elaine (Mrs. Jimmy D. Keller), Timothy Wayne. Ordained to ministry, 1952, in Ch. of God, 1973; tchr. men's Bible class Advent Christian Ch., Hickory, 1948-51; pastor

Calvary Advent Christian Ch., Lenoir, N.C., 1951-61, Ch. of God of Resurrection Hope, Lenoir, 1961—. Radio broadcaster, 1952—; condr. revival meetings in U.S., Can., 1962—. Contbr. tracts, poems, articles to ch. publs. Address: 232 Walt Arney Rd Lenoir NC 28645

DUNETS, JOSEPH, evangelist, retired minister, Assemblies of God Church; b. Bethlehem, Pa., Jan. 2, 1916; s. William and Mary (Zmaya) D.; grad. Central Bible Coll., Springfield, Mo., 1937; m. Helen Aline Edwards, Sept. 10, 1937; children: Judith Ann Dunets Cole, Joseph Richard. Ordained to ministry, 1941; evangelistic work, 1939-41, 85—; pastor Goshen (Ind.) Gospel Tabernacle, 1941-46; dir. of Youth for Christ, Goshen, 1943-46; pastor First Assembly of God, Cheyenne, Wyo., 1946-53; wing chaplain of Wyo. CAP, 1952-53; pastor Evangel Temple, Portland, Oreg., 1953-85, ret., 1985; evangelist campaigns in Europe, Asia, Africa, S.Am., 1966—. Asst. dist. supt. of Assemblies of God, State of Wyo., 1953; mem. bd. of elders of World Evangelism, San Diego, 1966—; chmn. Greater Portland Full Gospel Fellowship, 1956-74; bd. dirs. Youth for Christ, 1953-65. Home: 1645 SE 72d Ave Portland OR 97215 Office: 5001 W Powell Blvd Gresham OR 97030

DUNHAM, DUANE ARTHUR, minister, educator, Conservative Baptist Association of America; b. Norwood, Colo., Dec. 2, 1933; s. Lois Ann and Clifton Davis Dunham; m. Gail Ellen Hein, Oct. 24, 1953; children: Rebecca Ann, Ethan Allen, Daniel Alfred, Lois Catherine. B.A. in Bible, Biola U., 1959; B.D. in Theology, Talbot Theol. Sem., 1962; Th.M., Western Conservative Bapt. Sem., 1964; Th.D., Grace Theol. Sem., 1974. Ordained to ministry Conservative Bapt. Assn. Am., 1970. Pastor, 1st Bapt. Ch., Grass Valley, Oreg., 1962-64; prof. N.T., Western Christian Bapt. Sem., Portland, Oreg., 1964—; pastor Burlingame Bapt. Ch., Portland, 1971-74. Contbr. articles to profl. jours. Served with USAF, 1951-55. Mem. Evang. Theol. Soc., Internat. Council on Bibl. Inerrancy (del. 1978). Republican. Home: Route 1 Box 412 Beaverton OR 97007 Office: Western Conservative Bapt Theol Sem 5511 SE Hawthorne Blvd Portland OR 97215

DUNKERLEY, DONALD AUSTIN, minister, Presbyterian Church in America; b. Passaic, N.J., Oct. 8, 1936; s. John Raymond and Beatrice Ethel (Chamberlain) D.; m. Eileen Joy Tomlinson, June 24, 1961; children: David, Joy Anne (dec.), Kathleen. B.A., Rutgers U., 1958; M.Div., N.Y. Theol. Sem., 1961. Ordained to ministry Presbyn. Ch., 1961. Asst. pastor Second Presbyn. Ch., Rahway, N.J., 1961-62; pastor Hope Presbyn. Ch., Tarrytown, N.Y., 1963-67, McIlwain Meml. Presbyn. Ch., Pensacola, Fla., 1971-80; assoc. pastor First Presbyn. Ch., Babylon, N.Y., 1967-71; evangelist Presbyn. Evangelistic Fellowship, Decatur, Ga., 1980-84, bd. dirs., 1972-80; dir. Proclamation Internat., Inc., Pensacola, Fla., 1984—; ministerial adv. bd. mem. Reformed Theol. Sem., Jackson, Miss., 1970-80; mem. exec. com. European Missionary Fellowship, Eng., 1970-84; bd. dirs. Pensacola Theol. Inst., Fla., 1971-80, adv. bd. Affirmative Evang., Pine Bush, N.Y., 1983—. Mem. editorial bd. Presbyn. Layman, N.Y.C., 1968-71. Contbr. columns to religious publs. Founding bd. dirs. Alpha Ctr., Pensacola, 1972-76. Mem. Evang. Theol. Soc. Home: 3941 McClellan Rd Pensacola FL 32503 Office: Proclamation Internat Inc 3941 McClellan Rd Pensacola FL 32503

DUNN, ARVIN GAIL, minister, Churches of God, General Conference; b. Columbia City, Ind., Jan. 11, 1930; s. Thomas Henry Arvin and Mary Ruth (Pritchard) D.; A.B., Findlay (O.) Coll., 1952; B.D., Winebrenner Theol. Sem., 1955; D.D. (hon.), Findlay Coll., 1983; m. Marilyn Joan Reames, Jan. 1, 1950; children: Stephen Leslie, Gaye Lynn, Karen Lou, Mark Lee. Ordained to ministry Chs. of God, Gen. Conf., 1952; student pastor Sugar Ridge Ch. of God, Convoy, Ohio, 1952-53, Anthony Wayne First Ch. of God, Ft. Wayne, Ind., 1953-55; pastor Anderson Bethel Ch. of God, Mendon, Ohio, 1955-60, First Ch. of God, Mendon, 1955-67, First Ch. of God, Harrisburg, Pa., 1967-83; supt. E. Pa. Conf. Chs. of God Gen. Conf., 1984—; pres. pres. Ohio Conf., 1965-67; mem. bd. adminstrn. Ohio Council Chs., 1965-67; mem. Commn. on Edn., Gen. Conf., 1971-76, Commn. on Ch. Vocations, 1980—; mem. Commn. on Ministerial Tng. and Ordination, E.Pa. Conf., 1974-75. Adviser, Neighborhood Action Center, 1968-70; mem. scholarship com. Urban Black Cultural Com., 1973-76; bd. dirs. Harrisburg Council Chs., 1972-76, pres., 1975-76. Trustee Winebrenner Theol. Sem., Findlay, Ohio, 1971—, pres. bd., 1974-83; trustee Chs. of God Home, Carlisle, Pa., 1968-75, pres. bd., 1972-75; bd. dirs. Pa. Council Chs., 1984—. Contbr. to The Church Advocate, 1960—. Office: 900 S Arlington Ave Room 200 Harrisburg PA 17109

DUNN, DAVID L., rabbi; pres. Am. Assn. Rabbis. Office: Am Assn Rabbis 350 Fifth Ave Suite 3308 New York NY 10001*

DUNN, DAVID LAMONT, minister, American Baptist Churches; b. Gardiner, Maine, Feb. 2, 1940; s. John Leo and Grace Roberta (Linton) D.; m. Carolyn Althea Pitts, June 22, 1963; children: Paula Elisabeth, Bethany Joy, Krista Leigh. B.A., Barrington Coll., 1964; M.R.E., Gordon-Conwell Theol. Sem., 1968. Ordained to ministry, 1968. Asst. pastor Court St. Bapt. Ch., Auburn, Maine, 1961-65; pastor No. Livermore Bapt. Ch., No. Livermore, Maine, 1965-68; minister of Christian edn. Penney Meml. Bapt. Ch., Augusta, Maine, 1968-73; pastor Littlefield Meml. Bapt. Ch., Rockland, Maine, 1973-76; pastor First Bapt. Ch., Gettysburg, Pa., 1976—; rep. gen. bd. Am. Bapt. Chs. U.S.A., Valley Forge, Pa., 1984—, Am. Bapt. Ch. Pa. and Del., 1982—; bd. dirs. Adams Rescue Mission, Gettysburg, 1983—. Author: A Year of Discipleship, 1977. Pres. Band Boosters, Gettysburg, 1984-85. Mem. Am. Bapt. Ministers, Gettysburg Ministerium (pres. 1978-82). Republican. Home: 490 Marsh Creek Rd Gettysburg PA 17325 Office: First Bapt Church 1015 Chambersburg Rd Gettysburg PA 17325

DUNN, FRANCIS JOHN See *Who's Who in America*, 43rd edition.

DUNN, GERALD EDWARD, priest, Roman Catholic Church. b. Rochester, N.Y., May 6, 1923; s. Edward Raymond and Harriet Jane (Sanders) D. B.A., St. Bernard's Coll., 1945, M. Div., 1980. Ordained priest Roman Catholic Ch., 1948. Asst. pastor Immaculate Conception Ch., Rochester, 1948-55, St. Patrick's Ch., Corning, N.Y., 1955-58, St. Monica Ch., Rochester, 1958-68; family life dir. Diocese of Rochester, 1959-69; pastor St. Theodore Ch., Rochester, 1968—; treas. Clergy Relief Soc., Rochester, 1976-83; co-chmn. Priests Retirement Residence, Rochester, 1984—; chaplain Police and Ambulance, Gates, N.Y., 1973—. Cons. Gates-Chili Sch. Dist., 1982; pres. Dunn Tower Apts. and Dunn Tower II, 1975—. Recipient Citizen of Yr. award, 1980. Clubs: Lions (dir. 1975-81); Eagles. Address: 168 Spencerport Rd Rochester NY 14606

DUNN, JARIUS WILSON, minister, Baptist Chs.; b. Wilkes, Ga., Mar. 7, 1916; s. Pope and Kizzie (Freeman) D.; m. Pauline Gloria Gibson, July 14, 1941; 1 child, Richard Paul. B.S., Fla. Meml. U., 1964. Ordained to ministry Baptist Ch., 1964. Minister, Drake Meml. Baptist Ch., 1966—; adminstr. Drake Meml. Day Care Ctr., Miami, Fla., 19—; pres. Fifth Sunday Mission, Miami, 1982—. Mem. Self-Help Community Ctr., Miami, Acorn Community Orgn., Miami, People United to Lead the Struggle for Equality, Miami. Mem. Ministers and Deacons Union (chrm. program comm., 1967-74), Fla. East Coast Bapt. Assn. Conv., Omega Psi Phi. Democrat. Lodge: Masons. Home: 1895 NW 57 St Miami FL 33142 Office: Drake Memorial Bapt Church 5800 NW 2d Ave Miami FL 33127

DUNN, JOHN LEO, JR., minister, American Baptist Churches in U.S.A.; b. Gardiner, Maine, Nov. 4, 1937; s. John Leo and Grace Roberta (Linden) D.; m. Shirley Elaine Alexander, Feb. 23, 1957; children: Pamela, Susan, Steven, Kay, Rebekah. Asso. Theology, Christian Internat. Coll., 1977. Ordained to ministry Am. Bapt. Churches in U.S.A., 1977. Minister, North Windsor Bapt. Ch., Windsor, Maine, 1966-73, First Bapt. Ch., Dexter, Maine, 1973-81, Morse's Corner Bapt. Ch., Corinna, Maine, 1973-81, United Bapt. Ch., Ellsworth, Maine, 1981—; chmn. adequate ministries dept. Am. Bapt. Chs./Maine, 1981-82, sec. dept. pastoral support and small ch. ministries, 1983—. Served with USAF, 1956-60. Mem. Ellsworth Area Ministerial Assn. (chmn. 1983—). Republican. Home: 38 Pine St Ellsworth ME 04605 Office: United Baptist Church Hancock and Pine Sts Ellsworth ME 04605

DUNN, NORWOOD CARROLL, minister, Christian Church (Disciples of Christ); educator; b. Bentonville Twp., N.C., Oct. 30, 1929; s. Paul and Edna Lucille (Wade) D.; m. Mary Ada Watts, Aug. 29, 1953. B.A., Atlantic Christian Coll., Wilson, N.C., 1951; M.B.A., U. Chgo., 1961; M.A., Ashland Theol. Sem., 1978, M.Div., 1980. Ordained to ministry Christian Ch. (Disciples of Christ), 1980. Pastor, Shenandoah Christian Ch., Shiloh, Ohio, 1978—; dist. del. State Youth Commn. Christian Ch. Ohio, Elyria, 1978-84; subs. tchr. Shelby Sch. Dist., Ohio. Mem., baritone Fun Ctr. Chordsmen, Mansfield, Ohio, 1983—. Served to lt. col. USAF, 1952-75. Decorated Korean Service medal, UN Service medal, Air Force Commendation with 2 oak leaf clusters. Democrat. Clubs: Bicycling USA, League Am. Wheelman. Lodge: Masons. Avocations: bicycling, knitting, music theory. Home: 171 W Smiley Ave Shelby OH 44875 Office: Shenandoah Christian Ch Route 2 State Route 13 Shiloh OH 44878

DUNN, OWEN GALE, minister, Southern Baptist Convention; b. Clinton, Okla., Oct. 19, 1913; s. Albert Jackson and Mabel Clair (Owens) D.; B.F.A., Okla. Bapt. U., 1936; M.R.E., Southwestern Bapt. Theol. Sem., 1939, M.Sacred Music, 1939; m. Florence Adele Long, Aug. 24, 1937; children—Richard Albert, Dorothy Gale. Ordained to ministry, 1942; minister music and edn. Temple Bapt. Ch., Memphis, 1939-42, First Bapt. Ch., Pine Bluff, Ark., 1943-45, Second Bapt. Ch., Little Rock, 1945, Bapt. Temple, Houston, 1946-47, Gaston Ave. Bapt. Ch., Dallas, 1948-57, Highland Bapt. Ch., Shreveport, La., 1958-66, Richardson Heights (Tex.) Bapt. Ch., 1967-80; minister of music TimberRidge Bapt. Ch., Dallas, 1980; Mem. exec. bd. Dallas Pastor's Conf., 1966—; chmn. sr. adult coordinating com. Dallas Bapt. Assn. Mem. Religious Edn. Music Conf., So. Southwestern (Service award) Bapt. religious edn. assns., Dallas Bapt. Assn. Composer, compiler: Songs for Today, 1948; composer, pub.: My Picture Book of Scripture Songs, 1951; composer: Hail to the King, Christmas cantata, 1948. Home: 2214 Ridgecrest St Richardson TX 75080 Office: 701 W Beltline St Richardson TX 75080

DUNN, PAUL HAROLD, church official, Church of Jesus Christ of Latter-day Saints; b. Provo, Utah, Apr. 24, 1924; s. Joshua Harold and Geneve (Roberts) D.; m. Jeanne Alice Cheverton; children: Janet Dunn Gough, Marsha Jeanne Dunn Winget, Kellie Colleen Dunn McIntosh. A.B., Chapman Coll., 1953; M.S., U. So. Calif., 1954, Ph.D., 1959. Religious edn. adminstr. high schs. and colls. Ch. of Jesus Christ of Latter-day Saints, Calif., 1951-64, mem. gen. authority, Salt Lake City, 1964—. Author 20 books including: You and Your World, 1977; Horizons, 1981; Success Is, 1983; The Human Touch, 1983. Named Utah's Father of Yr., 1981. Served with U.S. Army, 1943-46. Decorated Bronze Star. Address: 47 E South Temple Salt Lake City UT 84150

DUNN, RICHARD ALBERT, minister, So. Bapt. Conv.; b. Pine Bluff, Ark., June 15, 1944; s. Owen Gale and Florence Adele (Long) D.; B.A. in Music Edn., La. Coll., 1968; M.R.E., Southwestern Bapt. Theol. Sem., 1970; m. DeRema Darlene LeFevre, July 15, 1967; children—Dawn Denel, Dannah Delaiah, Derek Richard. Ordained to ministry, 1976; youth and recreation asst. Highland Bapt. Ch., Shreveport, La., summer 1965; minister of music and youth 1st Bapt. Ch., Oakdale, La., 1965-66; minister to youth Richardson Heights Bapt. Ch., Richardson, Tex., 1966—. Vice pres. La. Bapt. Tng. Union Conf., 1966; pres. youth com. Dallas Bapt. Assn., 1970; v.p. religious edn. and music dirs. conf., 1972; tchr., conf. leader Glorieta (N.Mex.) Bapt. Conf. Center, 1974—. Mem. Dallas Inter-Racial Inst. Com., 1968-69. Mem. S.W. Football Ofcls. Assn., S.W. Basketball Ofcls. Assn., S.W. Baseball Ofcls. Assn. Home: 1318 Cheyenne Dr Richardson TX 75080 Office: 701 W Belt Line Rd Richardson TX 75080

DUNN, RONALD LOUIS, minister, Southern Baptist Convention; b. Poteau, Okla., Oct. 24, 1936; s. Cecil and Eunice (Bridges) D.; B.A., Okla. Bapt. U., 1958; B.D., Southwestern Bapt. Theol. Sem., 1962, M.Div.; m. Rita Kaye Mitchell, Dec. 21, 1956; children—Ronald (dec.), Stephen, Kimberly. Ordained minister So. Baptist Conv. 1954; evangelist, 1963-65; pastor Valley View Bapt. Ch., Dallas, 1961-63, Munger Pl. Bapt. Ch., 1965-66; pastor MacArthur Blvd. Bapt. Ch., Irving, Tex., after 1966, now minister-at-large; pres. Life Style Ministries, Inc. Author: Any Christian Can, 1976; The Faith Crisis, 1984; Victory, 1984. Home: 2705 Vancouver St Irving TX 75062 Office: 2616 MacArthur Blvd Irving TX 75062

DUNNAM, SPURGEON M., III, minister, United Meth. Ch.; b. Panama City, Fla., Jan. 10, 1943; s. Spurgeon M. and Thelma Naomi (Byers) D.; B.A., Tex. Wesleyan Coll., 1965; M.Div., So. Methodist U., 1968; m. Dottie Cox, Aug. 5, 1966; children: Delilah Denise, Delayna Dawn, Daniel Spurgeon. Ordained to ministry United Methodist Ch. as deacon, 1967, elder, 1969; asst. editor Tex. Meth. News, 1965-69; editor-gen. mgr. Tex. Meth./United Meth. Reporter News, Dallas, 1969—. Winner numerous awards of merit for reporting Associated Ch. Press. Office: United Meth Reporter PO Box 221076 Dallas TX 75222

DUNPHY, JOHN JOSEPH, priest, Roman Catholic Church. b. Morell, P.E.I., Can., Oct. 15, 1928; s. Wilfred William and Mary Josephine (Kelly) D. B.A., St. Dunstan's U.; B.Th., Holy Heart Sem., Halifax, N.S., Can.; postgrad. in scripture and family life St. Paul's U., 1979-80. Ordained priest Roman Cath. Ch., 1958. Asst. pastor St. Mary's Parish, Souris, P.E.I., 1958-66, Ch. Immaculate Conception, St. Louis, P.E.I., 1966-71; pastor St. Columba Ch., Fairfield, P.E.I., 1971-79, St. Pius X Ch., Parkdale, P.E.I., 1980—; team leader Marriage Encounter, Ottawa, Ont., Can. and Charlottetown, P.E.I., 1976-81, Engaged Encounter, Ottawa and Charlottetown, 1979—; mem. Council of Priests, Charlottetown, 1983-85; cons. Charlottetown Diocese, 1983-88. Chmn. Cancer Soc., Souris, 1961-66; bd. dirs. Rural Devel. Council, Charlottetown, P.E.I., 1972-76. Home: 106 St Peter's Rd Parkdale PE C1A 5P2 Canada

DUNSTON, ALFRED GILBERT, JR., bishop, African Meth. Episcopal Ch.; b. Coinjock, N.C., June 25, 1915; s. Alfred Gilbert and Cora Lee (Charity) D.; A.B., Livingstone Coll., 1938; student Drew U., 1938-39, 41-42; m. Permilla Rollins Flack, June 18, 1940 (div. 1947); children—Carol (Mrs. Clifton L. Goodrich), Aingred (Mrs. Vincent James), Armayne (Mrs. Christopher Pratt). Ordained elder African Methodist Episcopal Zion Ch., 1938, then minister; consecrated bishop; minister chs., Advance, N.C., 1936, Thomasville, N.C., 1937-38, Atlantic City, N.J., 1941-43, Summit, N.J., 1946-48, Knoxville, Tenn., 1948-52; Chaplain AUS, World War II; minister Wesley A.M.E. Zion Ch., Phila., 1952-63; minister Mother A.M.E. Zion Ch., N.Y.C., 1963-64; prof. Black Ch. History Inst. for Black Ministries, Phila., 1971—.

Featured in TV documentary The Run from Race, 1963. Mem. Alpha Phi Alpha. Author: Black Man in Old Testament and Its World; narrator film The Rising New Africa, 1958. Office: A521 City Line and Presidential Blvd Philadelphia PA 19131

DUONG, SAU, minister, Seventh-day Adventist Ch. B. Quangnam, Vietnam, May 4, 1938; came to U.S., 1975; s. Cong and Nguyen D.; m. Tam Do Thai, July 28, 1957; children: Tung, Ky, Viet, An, Thuy Trang. Grad., Bible Tng. Sch., Saigon, Vietnam, 1960. Ordained to ministry Seventh-Day Adventist Ch., 1970. Intern, Seventh-Day Adventist Ch., Vietnam Mission, Cantho, 1960-61, pastor, 1970-74; pastor, Tam Ky, 1961-63; dist. pastor, Danang, 1964-66, Dalah, 1967-75; minister pastor Oreg. Conf. 7th Day Adventists, Portland, 1975—; pres. Viet Young People, Inc., Portland, 1976—; bd. dirs. Sponsoring Orgn. Asian Refugees, Portland, 1977-83. Mem. Vietnamese Refugee Christian Assn. (v.p. 1975-77). Home: 2016 S E 89th Ave Portland OR 97215 Office: 1001 S E 60th Ave Portland OR 97216

DUPIN, CLYDE CLEMENT, minister, Wesleyan Church; b. East View, Ky., Feb. 22, 1933; s. Kendrick W. and Polly (McGuffin) D.; m. Grace E. Spencer, June 15, 1951; children: Wesley, Kenneth, Joy Beth. Student United Wesleyan Coll., 1953, Evansville U., 1968; D.D. (hon.) Central Wesleyan Coll., 1983. Ordained elder Wesleyan Ch., 1953. Evangelist, Clyde Dupin Evangelistic Assn., Indpls., 1954-59; pastor Trinity Wesleyan Ch., Evansville, Ind., 1959-69; pres. Clyde Dupin Ministries, Kernersville, N.C., 1974—. Del. Internat. Wesleyan Conf., Anderson, Ind., 1964-68; speaker, del. Jerusalem Conf., 1978, Amsterdam Conf., Netherlands, 1983. Author: Wake Up America, 1976; New Life in Christ, 1979. Cons. editor Evangelical Review, 1984—. Named Outstanding Minister, United Wesleyan Coll., 1964, Alumni of Yr., United Wesleyan Coll., 1980. Mem. Delta Epsilon Chi. Avocations: golf, reading, travel. Office: PO Box 565 402 E Mountain St Kernersville NC 27284

DUPRIEST, TRAVIS TALMADGE, priest, Episcopal Church; b. Richmond, Va., Aug. 15, 1944; s. Travis Talmadge and Mildred Elizabeth (Abbitt) DuP.; m. Mabel Ann Benson, Sept. 1, 1972; children: Travis Edgerton, Benson Hunter. B.A., U. Richmond, 1966; Ph.D., U. Ky., 1972; M.T.S., Harvard U., 1974; postgrad. U. Durham-Eng., 1972-73. Ordained priest, 1974. Deacon, priest St. Matthew's Ch., Kenosha, Wis., 1974-76; asst. to rector St. Luke's Ch., Racine, Wis., 1976—; chaplain DeKoven Found., Racine, 1980—; assoc. prof. English, Carthage Coll., Kenosha, 1974—; editorial asst. The Living Church mag., 1983—. Editorial asst. The Episcopal Ch. Ann., 1966. Author: Soapstone Wall, 1980. Editor: Jeremy Taylor's Discurse on Friendship, Intro., 1985. Contbr. articles to profl. jours., poems to lit. jours. Danforth fellow, 1977; Clark Library fellow, 1981-82; Cambridge U. vis. fellow, 1982-83; Carthage Coll. Disting. Tchr., 1980. Mem. Episcopal Peace Fellowship, Wis. Hugunot Soc., Nat. Collegiate Honors, Conf. on Christianity and Lit. Home: 508 DeKoven Ave Racine WI 53403 Office: Carthage Coll Kenosha WI

DURAN, FRASCUELO ELI, minister, educator, Assemblies of God; b. Greeley, Colo., June 2, 1938; s. Frank L. and Salome (Torrez) D.; diploma Latin Am. Bible Inst., El Paso, Tex., 1962; B.A. in Liberal Arts, So. Colo. U., Pueblo, 1974; B.A. in Christian Ministry, Southwestern Assemblies of God Coll., Waxahachie, Tex., 1969; M.A., Assembly of God Theol. Sem., Springfield, Mo., m. Elaine Maes, June 23, 1962; children—Annette, Duane, Danelle, Damon. Ordained to ministry, 1967; instr. theology Latin Am. Bible Inst., El Paso, 1962-73, prin., 1968-73; pastor Templo Cristiano, Pueblo, Colo., 1973-76; pres. So. Ariz. Bible Coll., Hereford, 1976—. Chmn., Evang. Ministers' Prayer Fellowship, Pueblo, 1975-76. Mem. Delta Epsilon Chi. Home and Office: So Ariz Bible Coll Hereford AZ 85615

DURAND, EUGENE FRANK, minister, editor, Seventh-day Adventist Church. B. Takoma Park, Md., Sept. 23, 1928; s. Clarence and Elizabeth Elsa (Hansch) D.; m. Evelyn Louise Cunningham, Aug. 27, 1950; children: Martha Faye, Rebecca Maye. B.A. in Theology, Columbia Union Coll., 1951; M.A. in Religion, George Washington U., 1971, Ph.D. in Am. Religious Ottistorl, 1978. Ordained to ministry Seventh-Day Adventist Ch., 1956. Pastor, Phillipsburg, As, N.J., 1951-56; pastor-evangelist, missionary Venezuela, Colombia, 1957-65; instr. Spanish, Columbia Union Coll., Takoma Park, Md., 1965-68; Inst. to editor Adventists Rev., Washington, 1975-83, asst. editor, 1983. Author: Yours in the Blessed Hope, 1980, also articles. Mem. Assn. Seventh-day Adventist Historians. Home: 5006 Bald Hill Rd Adamstown MD 21710 Office: Gen Conf Seventh-day Adventists 6840 Eastern Ave Washington DC 20012

DURAND, GUY, theology educator; b. Dunham, Que., Can., May 30, 1933; s. Leopold and Marie (Lemieux) D.; m. Jocelyne Masse, June 10, 1961; children: Stephane, Guy-Laine, Isabelle. M.A., U. Montreal, 1960, Licence en Droit, 1961; Th.D., Faculte Cath., Lyon, France, 1967. Prof. theology U. Montreal, 1968—. Author: Sexualite et Foi, 1977; Quelle Vie?, 1981, Quel Avenir?, 1981, Ethique de la Rencontre Sexuelle, 1971. Mem. Societe Canadienne de Theologie. Office: Faculte de Theologie Universite de Montreal CP 6128 Montreal PQ H3C 3J7 Canada

DURMAN, KENNETH THOMAS, religious organization executive, Evangelical Free Church; b. London, Sept. 22, 1920; came to U.S., 1965, naturalized, 1970; s. Thomas Joseph and Edith (Buttell) D.; m. Jessie J. Dare, Sept. 1, 1945; children: Barry K., Jeanette K., Daryl J., Frank R. Internat. dir. The Pocket Testament League, Lincoln Park, N.J., 1978—. Home: 960 Bloomfield Ave Glen Ridge NJ 07028 Office: Pocket Testament League 117 Main St Lincoln Park NJ 07035

DURNBAUGH, DONALD FLOYD, minister, Church of the Brethren; b. Detroit, Nov. 16, 1927; s. Floyd Devon and Ruth Elsie (Tombaugh) D.; m. Hedwig Therese Raschka, July 10, 1952; children: Paul D., Christopher S., Renate E. B.A., Manchester Coll., 1949; M.A., U. Mich., 1953; Ph.D., U. Pa., 1960; L.H.D. (hon.), Manchester Coll., 1980. Ordained to ministry Ch. of Brethren, 1962. Dir. program Brethren Service Commn., Austria, 1953-56; asst. prof. Juniata Coll., 1958-62; assoc. prof. Bethany Theol. Sem., Oak Brook, Ill., 1962-69, prof., 1970—, moderator Ch. of the Brethren, 1985-86. Author: European Origins of the Brethren, 1958; The Brethren in Colonial America, 1967; Guide to Research in Brethren History, 1968; The Believers' Church: The History and Character of Radical Protestantism, 1968; Every Need Supplied: Mutual Aid and Christian Community in the Free Churches (1525-1675), 1974; editor: Die Kirche der Brueder: Vergangenheit and Gegenwart, 1971; The Church of the Brethren: Past and Present, 1971; To Serve the Present Age: The Brethren Service Story, 1975; On Earth Peace: Discussions on War/Peace Issues Between Friends, Mennonites, Brethren and European Churches, 1935-1975, 1978; editor-in-chief: The Brethren Encyclopedia, 1983-84; contbr. numerous articles to scholarly jours., denominational periodicals. Recipient U. Pa. Fellowship award, 1957-58. Mem. Am. Soc. Ch. History, Orgn. Am. Historians, Brethren Jour. Assn., Am. Soc. Reformation Research, Inst. Mennonite Studies. Office: Bethany Theol Sem Meyers and Butterfield Rds Oak Brook IL 60521

DURRETT, MADISON WINFREY, minister, Southern Baptist Convention; b. Knifley, Ky., Apr. 8, 1915; s. James Madieon and Myrtle Susan (Watson) D.; m. Carmen Elsie Gibbs, May 25, 1946; children: Dale Dwight, Glen Winfrey. B.A., East Tex. Bapt. Coll., 1949; M.Div., So. Bapt. Theol. Sem., 1973. Ordained to ministry So. Bapt. Conv., 1948. Pastor, Oak Park Bapt. Mission, Jeffersonville, Ind., 1954-55, East Toledo Bapt. Mission, 1956-57, Greenfield Bapt. Ch., Meadowview, Va., 1951-54, Mountain View Bapt. Ch., Meadowview, 1951-54, 57-62, 81—; dir. associational missions New Lebanon Bapt. Assn., Lebanon, Va., 1962-81, ch. tng. dir., Abingdon, Va., 1959-60, clk., treas., 1960-62; sec. Russell County Ministers' Fellowship, Lebanon, 1964-66. Clubs: Meadowview Civic, Ruritan (sec., 1984) (Meadowview). Mem. Maumee Valley Bapt. Assn. (clk. 1956-57). Home and office: Route 2 Box 37-B Meadowview VA 24361

DURST, MOSE, president Unification Church of America; b. N.Y.C., Sept. 5, 1939; s. Samuel and Lillian (Farb) D.; m. Onni Lim, Dec. 20, 1974; children: Isaac, Chaim, Yeondo. B.A., Queens Coll., 1961; M.A., U. Ore.-Eugene, 1963, Ph.D., 1967. Dir., Unification Ch. of Calif., San Francisco, 1974-80; pres. Unification Ch. of Am., N.Y.C., 1980—; chmn. Unification Theol. Sem., Barrytown, N.Y., 1979—; chmn. Internat. Relief Friendship Found., N.Y., 1978—. Author: To Bigotry, No Sanction, 1984; contbr. articles to religious jours. Pres., chmn. Project Volunteer, Inc., San Francisco, 1976—; mem. Oakland (Calif.) Mayor's Sm. Bus. Task Force, 1977. NDEA Fellowship awardee, 1961-64. Clubs: Metropolitan, Commonwealth. Office: Unification Church of Am 4 W 43d St New York NY 10036

DUSEK, GARY ALLAN, minister, American Baptist Churches in the U.S.A.; b. Chgo. May 11, 1940; s. Clifford Frank and Laura Alma (Frees) D.; m. Nancy Lou Neher, July 31, 1965; children: Michelle, Nicole. Diploma Moody Bible Inst., 1960; B.A. in Philosophy, N. Central Coll., 1963; M.Div., Wheaton Coll., 1967; M.A., Brandeis U., 1970. Ordained to ministry American Baptist Churches in the U.S.A., 19—. Pastor First Bapt. Ch., Chelmsford, Mass., 1970-77; sr. pastor First Bapt. Ch., Sunnyvale, Calif., 1977—; bd. dirs. Am. Bapt. Chs. Mass., 1973-76; pres. Am. Bapt. Fellowship Mass., 1973-77; bd. dirs. Mass. Bapt. Charitable Soc., 1975-77; western v.p. Am. Bapt. Fellowship U.S.A., 1977-82. Author numerous devotional articles. Recipient Spl. Recognition award House of Rep. Mass., 1977. Office: First Bapt Ch Sunnyvale 445 South Mary Ave Sunnyvale CA 94086

DUSING, MICHAEL LEE, religious educator, Assemblies of God; m. Hagerstown, Md., Nov. 26, 1954; s. Linwood Charles and Wanda Lee (Dixon) D.; m. Ruth Elaine Spruill, June 6, 1981. B.A., Southeastern Coll., 1976; postgrad. Tex. Christian U., 1976-77; M. Divinity, Emory U., 1979; M. Theology, Columbia Theol. Seminary, 1984. Ordained to ministry Assemblies of God, 1981. Asst. pastor Fleming Heights Assembly of God, Orlando, Fla., 1975-76, Calvary Assembly of God, Atlanta, 1977-78; hosp. chaplain Emory U. Hosp., Atlanta, 1979; asst. prof. theology Southeastern Coll., Lakeland, Fla., 1979—, chmn. dept. theology, dept. philosophy, 1984-85, mem. student ministry life com., 1979—, sponsor married students fellowship, 1981—, mem. acad. affairs, 1984-85. Contbg. author book series The Complete Bible Library, 1984. Mem. Evangel. Theol. Soc., So. Pentecostal Studies. Democrat. Office: Southeastern Coll 1000 Longfellow Blvd Lakeland FL 33801

DUSMAN, PRESTON HENRY, minister, Lutheran Church in America; b. Hanover, Pa., Mar. 15, 1927; s. George Henry and Gertie (Hahn) D.; m. Virginia Florence Wentz, June 15, 1952; 1 child, Karl Wayne. B.A., Gettysburg Coll., 1951; M.Div., Gettysburg Luth. Theol. Sem., 1954. Ordained to ministry Luth. Ch. in Am., 1954. Pastor, Easton-Cordova Parish, Md., 1954-60, Christ Luth. Ch., Fredericksburg, Va., 1960-66, Williamsburg Parish, Pa., 1966-75, Redeemer Luth. Ch., Williamsport, 1975—; dir. Personal Counseling Service, Fredericksburg, 1965-66. Lodge: Lions. Address: 804 Sherman St Williamsport PA 17701

DUVALL, JOHN ALLEN, minister, United Meth. Ch.; b. West Jefferson, N.C., Jan. 27, 1939; s. Raymond Spencer and Osie (Graybeal) D.; A.A., Brevard Coll., 1959; B.S. in Edn., Appalachian State U., 1961; M.M.S., Duke, 1968; m. Newassa Taylor, Dec. 26, 1964; 1 dau., Osie Ellen. High sch. tchr., 1962-65; ordained to ministry, 1968; pastor Bridle Creek (Va.) Circuit, 1966-68, First Ch., Hillsville, Va., 1969-72, Trinity Ch., Wise, Va., 1973-75, First Ch., Pennington Gap, Va., 1976—. Mem. Va. Council on Social Welfare, 1970-74. Author: Light to March By, 1969. Home and office: POB 248 Pennington Gap VA 24277

DYCUS, WILLIAM FRED, minister, Southern Baptist Convention; b. Dallas, Dec. 11, 1952; s. Ray and Ola Fay (McGibboney) D.; m. Marinell Dunlop, June 15, 1974. Student Dallas Bapt. Coll., 1973-75, Midwestern Bapt. Theol. Sem., 1985—. Ordained to ministry So. Bapt. Conv., 1974. Youth evangelist, 1972-74, pastor-evangelist, 1974—; pastor, Westwood Park Bapt. Ch., Irving, Tex., 1974-75, Grace Bapt. Ch., Iola, Kans., 1975-79, 1st Bapt. Ch. of Udall, Kans., 1979—. Served with USAF, 1972. Mem. Southcentral Bapt. Assn. Kans. (chmn. evangelism 1979-84, moderator 1984—). Democrat. Home: 208 Larry St Udall KS 67146

DYE, DWIGHT LATIMER, minister, Ch. of God (Anderson, Ind.); b. Parkersburg, W.Va., Jan. 29, 1931; s. Clyde E. and Mona Pearl (Marshall) D.; A.B., Anderson Coll., 1953; M.A., U. Tulsa, 1963; postgrad. U. Okla., 1966-67; m. Carolyn Sue Priest, Oct. 13, 1951; children: Linda Lee, Mark Evan. Ordained to ministry, 1954; pastor First Ch. of God, Pryor, Okla., 1956-59, Westridge Hills Ch. of God, Oklahoma City, 1959-69, East Side Ch. of God, Anderson, 1969—; vice chmn. Nat. Bd. Christian Edn., 1970-71; state chmn. Okla. Ministers of Ch. of God; exec. sec.-treas. mass communication bd. Ch. of God (Anderson, Ind.); pres. Oklahoma City chpt. Nat. Assn. Evangelicals, 1967; speaker All-India Assembly of Ch. of God, 1971, Jamaican Assembly, Kingston, 1973. Author: A Kingdom of Servants, 1979. Home: 409 Sylvan Rd Anderson IN 46012 Office: 2620 E 5th St Anderson IN 46012

DYER, HENRY RAY, minister, teacher, evangelist, American Baptist Churches in the U.S.A.; b. Terre Haute, Ind., Dec. 31, 1925; s. Cecil Ray and Josephine Irene (Brown) D.; m. Doris Janet Clark, Aug. 7, 1955; children: Steven Ray, Dan Bradley, Karen Irene. LL.B., LaSalle U., Chgo., 1963; Th.M., Internat. Bible Inst. and Sem., Orlando, Fla., 1978; Th.D., 1979. Ordained to ministry Gospel of Jesus Christ, 1977. Mem. bd. Montrose Methodist Ch., Terre Haute, 1957-64; bible tchr. Maryland Ch., Terre Haute, 1964-76; minister Zion Ch., Cory, Ind., 1976-77, First Bapt. Ch., Prairie Creek, Ind., 1977—; dir. Youth for Christ, Terre Haute, 1970-75; chaplain Am. Legion, Prairie Creek, 1979, 1983, 84; with U.S. Postal Service, Terre Haute, 1959—. Contbr. articles to profl. jours. Served to sgt. USMC, 1944-46; PTO. Recipient award Am. Legion, 1980. Home: 1019 Elizabeth Ln Terre Haute IN 47802 Office: First Prairie Creek Bapt Ch Prairie Creek IN 47869

DYKES, WEEMS SYLVERTER, clergyman, educator; b. Quitman, Tex., June 18, 1918; s. Richard Wilson and Mary Jane (Weems) D.; m. Verne Ella Allison, Dec. 25, 1962; 1 child, Susan Jane Harrison. B.A., Tex. Christian Coll., Ft. Worth, 1942; B.D., 1946, M.Div., 1972. Pres. Ministerial Alliance, Colorado City, Tex., 1968-69; poet laureate of Tex., 1980-81. Author: (poetry) A Cup of Thoughtfulness, 1976, My Cup of Tea, 1978, The Listening Cup, 1981. Bd. dirs. March of Dimes, McCamey, Tex, 1957; chmn. Salvation Army, McCamey, 1978, Mendoza Trail Mus., McCamey, 1978; del. State of Tex. Democratic Conv., McCamey, 1957. Recipient Certificate of Appreciation for work with elderly State of Tex., 1977.

DYRNESS, WILLIAM ARTHUR, college president; b. Geneva, Ill., Jan. 23, 1943; s. Enock and Grace D.; m. Grace Strachan Roberts, Mar. 16, 1968; children: Michelle, Andrea, Jonathan. B.A., Wheaton Coll., 1965; B.D., Fuller Theol. Sem., 1968; D.Theol., U. Strasbourg-France, 1970; Doctorandus, Free U. Amsterdam, 1976. Minister to students Hinson Bapt. Ch., Portland, Oreg., 1971-73; prof. theology Asian Theol. Sem., Manila, Philippines, 1974-82; prof. theology and missions Gordon Conwell Sem., S. Hamilton, Mass., 1978-82; program dir. Inst. for Studies in Asian Ch. and Culture, 1979-82; pres. prof. theology New Coll. Berkeley, Calif., 1982—. Author: Roualt: A Vision of Suffering and Salvation, 1971; Themes in Old Testament Theology, 1979; Christian Apologetics in a World Community, 1983; Let the Earth Rejoice, 1983. Mem. Am. Acad. Religion. Home: 1335 ML King Jr Way Berkeley CA 94709 Office: New Coll Berkeley for Advanced Christian Studies 2600 Dwight Way Berkeley CA 94704

DYRUD, AMOS OLIVER, minister, educator, Association of Free Lutheran Congregations; b. Newfolden, Minn., June 6, 1915; s. Petter Andrew and Marie (Hanson) D.; m. Ovidie Marie Evenson, June 15, 1948; children: Peter, Naomi, Rebecca, Samuel. B.A., Augsburg Coll., 1949, Candidatus Theologiae, 1949; cert. L'Alliance Francaise, Paris, 1950. Ordained to ministry Luth. Ch., 1949. Pastor, missionary Luth. Free Ch., and Am. Luth. Ch., Madagascar, 1949-69; instr. Assn. Free Luth. Congregation, Mpls., 1969—, dean theol. sem., 1971-81; chmn. World Missions Com. of Assn. Free Luth. Congregation, Mpls., 1982—. Served with USN, 1943. Home: 4509 Jersey Ave N Minneapolis MN 55428 Office: Assn Free Luth Congregations 3110 E Medicine Lake Blvd Minneapolis MN 55441

DYTTMER, JOYCE ARLINE, lay church worker, Roman Catholic Church; b. Buffalo, June 14, 1926; d. Millard Vincent and Esther Carolyn (Mingen) Jeffery; m. Leonard Chester Dyttmer, July 1, 1948 (dec. June 1984); children: Dorn, Dyan. B.E., U. Buffalo, 1948, B.F.A., Albright Art Sch., 1948. Staff mem. Lay Ministry and Permanent Diaconate, Toledo, 1980-82, dir. parish ministry program, 1982—; pres. altar rosary soc. St. Aloysius Ch., Bowling Green, Ohio, 1975-76, 79-80, trainer eucharistic ministers and lectors, 1982—, liturgy chmn., 1982—. Illustrator: (workbook) Parish Ministry, 1983. Mem. AAUW (chmn. fine arts 1979-81). Democrat. Avocations: drawing; sewing; needlecrafts. Home: 10106 Devil's Hole Rd Bowling Green OH 43402 Office: Lay Ministry and Permanent Diaconate 1933 Spielbusch Ave Toledo OH 43624

EADS, ORA WILBERT, church official The Christian Congregation, Inc. Gen. supt. The Christian Congregation, Inc. Address: 804 W Hemlock St LaFollette TN 37766

EAKER, GLORIA JEAN, religious organization executive, Seventh-day Adventists; b. Bradford, Pa., Aug. 16, 1929; d. George Edward and Myrtle Jeanette (Scriven) Eaker. Student pub. schs. Bradford, Pa. Ins. underwriter asst. Gen. Conf. Seventh-day Adventists, Washington, 1952—. Registered vol. Gen. Conf. Seventh-day Adventists; asst. Sabbath Sch. Sec. Sligo Seventh-day Adventist Ch. Republican Office: Gen Conf Seventh-day Adventists 6840 Eastern Ave NW Washington DC 20012

EANES, KENNETH RAY, religious organization executive, Southern Baptist Convention; financial executive; b. South Boston, Va., June 8, 1943; s. Joseph R. and Thelma (Osborne) E.; m. Faye L. Laughan, May 12, 1962 (div. 1969); children: Sabra Lee, Anglea Denise; m. Ila Sue Davis, Mar. 7, 1982. Degree in pastoral ministries So. Bapt. Sems., Nashville, 1979; M.A., Columbia Pacific U., 1980, Ph.D. in Theology, 1980, Ph.D. in Bus. Adminstrn., 1983. Ordained to ministry Southern Baptist Convention, 1979. Pastor, Villa Heights Bapt. Ch., Martinsville, Va., 1978-84; pres. Ctr. for Bibl. Understanding, Martinsville, 1984—; v.p. fin. Vrain Corp., Martinsville, 1984—. Co-organizer Divorce Recovery, Martinsville, 1983. Home: PO Box 3496 Martinsville VA 24115

EARGLE, ANDREW DAVID, minister, Lutheran Church in America. b. Newberry, S.C., Aug. 27, 1942; s. Willie Andrew and Lurleen (Halfacre) E.; m. Janie Mayer, May 26, 1966; children: David, Dee Ann. A.B., Newberry Coll., 1964; B.D., Southern Sem., 1968. Ordained to ministry Lutheran Church in America, 1968. Pastor, Grace Luth. Ch., Gilbert, S.C., 1968-79, St. Jacob's Luth. Ch., Chapin, S.C., 1979—. Home and Office: Route 2 Box 536 Chapin SC 29036

EARLEY, NEAL CHRISTOPHER, minister, Presbyterian Church (USA); b. Cin., Dec. 14, 1946; s. Neal Norman and Margery May (Qualheim) E.; B.A., Columbia U., 1969; M.Div., Union Theol. Sem., 1972; m. Judith Ann Warner, June 16, 1973; children: Neal Howard, Joyce Ann. Ordained to ministry, 1972; pastor 1st United Presbyn. Parish, White Haven, Pa., 1972-76, Chester (N.Y.) Presbyn. Ch., 1976-80, Georgetown (Ohio) Presbyn. Ch., 1980—. Pres., Meals on Wheels, Weatherly, Pa., 1974-76. Home: 206 W North St Georgetown OH 45121

EARNST, LOU ANN, minister, United Church of Christ; b. Spring Grove, Pa., Sept. 30, 1953; d. Preston Robert and Edna Mae (Warrenfeltz) Earnst; B.A. in Music, York Coll., 1975; M. Div., Lancaster Sem., 1982. Ordained to ministry United Church of Christ, 1982. Organist St. Paul's United Ch. Christ, York, Pa., 1977-80; student asst. Willow Street United Ch. Christ, Willow Street, Pa., 1980-82; minister St. John's United Ch. of Christ and Christ Congl. United Ch. of Christ, Ashland, Pa., 1982—; mem. chaplain tng. com. Leisure Ministry for Pa. Council Chs., Harrisburgh, Pa., 1982—; v.p. Ashland Area Ministerium, Ashland, 1983—; sec. Schuylkill United Ch. of Christ Ministerium Pa., 1983-84. Pres. bd. Schuylkill County Task Force on Abused Women, Pottsville, Pa., 1983; bd. dirs. Ashland Area Community Hosp., Ashland, 1984. Republican. Home and Office: 134 Broad St Ashland PA 17921

EASON, RONALD LEE, minister, Southern Baptist Convention; b. Norfolk, Va., Mar. 3, 1949; s. Kelly Lee and Mabel E. (Harrell) E.; m. Deborah Moore, Aug. 22, 1970; children: Amy Leigh, Scott Brandon. B.A. in Religion, U. Richmond, 1971; M.Div., Southeastern Bapt. Theol. Sem., 1974. Ordained to ministry Southern Baptist Convention, 1971. Pastor Mt. Hope Bapt. Ch., Mannboro, Va., 1970-71, Aenon Bapt. Ch., Elm City, N.C., 1971-74, Meherrin Bapt. Ch., Murfreesboro, N.C., 1974-77; assoc. pastor Tabernacle Bapt. Ch., Salem, Va., 1977-80; pastor Dan River Bapt. Ch., Halifax, Va., 1980—; moderator Dan River Bapt. Assn., 1984—, chmn. evangelism com., 1980—; mem. meml. com. Va. Bapt. Gen. Assn., 1984—. Bd. dirs. South Boston YMCA, 1983—, Halifax Welfare Com., 1983. Mem. Halifax Ministerial Assn. (pres. 1982), Dan River Bapt. Ministers Assn. Republican. Clubs: Ruritan (chaplain 1983), Concord (chaplain 1974-76). Home: Rt 2 Box 615 Halifax VA 24558 Office: Dan River Baptist Ch Rt 2 Box 615 Halifax VA 24558

EAST, DAVID HAROLD, minister, Church of God (Anderson, Indiana); b. Martinsville, Ind., Sept. 10, 1941; s. Edgar Harold and Esther Irene (Schafer) E.; m. Jacqueline Jo Sellers, July 6, 1968; (div. 1983); 1 child, Brian David. B.S., Ball State U., 1964, M.A., 1969; M.Div., Sch. Theology, Anderson, 1979. Ordained to ministry Ch. of God (Anderson), 1979. Assoc. pastor Fifth Street United Meth. Ch., Anderson, 1977-78, Glendale Ch. of God, Indpls., 1978-79; pastor Dorr Street Ch. of God, Toledo, 1979—; mem. exec. council Ohio Ch. of God, Columbus, 1981—; chmn. N.W. Ohio Ch. of God, 1983—. Home: 5454 Glenridge Toledo OH 43614 Office: Dorr Street Church of God 5509 Dorr St Toledo OH 43615

EAST, WADE BUTLER, minister, So. Baptist Conv.; b. Everman, Tex., Jan. 17, 1917; s. Joel Odes and Essie Myrtle (Bowling) E.; B.A., Okla. Bapt. U., Shawnee, 1940, H.H.D., 1975; B.Th., Southwestern Bapt. Theol. Sem., Ft. Worth, 1944; m. Lora Lucile Cochran, Nov. 23, 1938; children—Wade David, Janette East Arterburn. Ordained to ministry, 1939; pastor chs. in Okla., 1942-46; field sec. Bapt. Children's Home, Oklahoma City, 1946-51; supt., treas. Bapt. Children's Home. Carmi, Ill., 1951-58; 1st exec. dir. Lee and Beulah Moor Children's Home, El Paso, Tex., 1958-62; supt., treas. La. Bapt. Children's Home, Monroe, La., 1962—. Charter mem. Child Care Execs. of So. Bapt. Conv.; mem. Nat., Southwestern assns. homes for children. Club: Monroe Rotary. Author articles, newspaper column. Home: 7103 De Siard Rd Monroe LA 71203 Office: PO Box 4196 Monroe LA 71203

EAST, WILLIAM EUGENE, minister, ch. adminstr., So. Baptist Conv.; b. Carter, Okla., May 25, 1929; s. Henry Melton and Mamie Virginia (Forrester) E.; A.B., Okla. Baptist U., Shawnee, 1951; B.D., Golden Gate Baptist Theol. Sem., Mill Valley, Calif., 1957, Th.M., 1960, D. Ministry, 1973; m. Shirley Jean Eddy, Aug. 26, 1950; children—Carol, David, Virginia, Donna, Melton. Ordained to ministry, 1951; pastor 1st Baptist Ch., Newark, Calif., 1951-54, Calvary Baptist Ch., Auburn, Calif., 1954-55, 1st Baptist Ch., El Sobrante, Calif., 1956-58, 1st Baptist Ch., Folsom, Calif., 1959-62; dir. missions Kern County (Calif.) So. Baptist Assn., Bakersfield, 1962—. Pres., Greater Bakersfield Ministerial Assn.; v.p. Calif. Ministers Orgn.; mem. Bakersfield Rescue Mission Bd.; bd. dirs. Ch. of Sequoia, a ministry to the nat. parks. Pres., Bakersfield Suicide Prevention Bd. Home: 230 17th St Bakersfield CA 93301 Office: 427 18th St Bakersfield CA 93301

EASTERLY, ORVILLE EDWARD, minister, Assemblies of God; b. Pitcher, Okla., Sept. 15, 1942; s. Orville Ray and Margaret (Metz) E.; B.A., Bethany Bible Coll., 1965; M.Div., Golden Gate Bapt. Theol. Sem., 1976; m. Sylvid Juliene Rogers, June 10, 1967; children—Rodney, Ronald. Ordained to ministry, 1965; pastor chs., Santa Clara, Calif., 1962-65, Reedly, Calif., 1965-66, Hayward, Calif., 1966-67, San Francisco, 1967-69, San Bruno, Calif., 1969-72; pastor 1st Assembly of God, Roseville, Calif., 1972—. Exec. dir., founder Sunrise Christian Schs., Roseville; pres. Ministerial Assn. Roseville, 1973; v.p. youth ministries dept. No. Calif. and Nev. Dist. Assemblies of God, 1972-76. Home: 1041 Audrey Way Roseville CA 95678 Office: 202 Bonita Ave Roseville CA 95678

EASTLACK, ROBERT DAVID, minister, Lutheran Church in America; b. Trinidad, Colo., Jan. 3, 1948; s. John William and Margaret Ella (Bond) E.; m. Vickie Colleen Wirt, Sept. 21, 1974; children: Heather Elizabeth, Benjamin Sean-Thomas. B.A., Gettysburg Coll., 1970; M.Div., Luth. Theol. Sem., Gettysburg, Pa., 1974. Ordained to ministry Lutheran Ch., 1974. Pastor Klingerstown Parish, Pa., 1974-79, Grace Luth. Ch., Berwick, Pa., 1979—; treas. Berwick Area Ministerium, 1984. Democrat.

EASTMAN, JANIS ELIZABETH, educator, Seventh-day Adventists; b. Berkeley, Calif., July 7, 1953; d. Bennie Franklinaand Maureen Mae (Healzer) Roth; m. David O. Eastman, Jan. 1, 1976. B.S. in Elem. Edn., Walla Walla Coll., 1976; M.S. in Learning Disabilities, Portland State U., 1984. Tchr. Portland Adventist Elem. Sch., 1976—. Republican. Home: 3966 SE 174th Ave Portland OR 97236 Office: Portland Adventist Elem Sch 3990 NW 1st St Portland OR 97236

EATON, GLENN ALAN, minister, Episcopal Church; b. North Bend, Oreg., July 15, 1917; s. Clyde Lester and Blanche Elizabeth (Howell) E.; m. Jeannette Alice Christensen, Feb. 21, 1942; children: Lillian Alice, Glenn Alan. B.S., B.A., U. Oreg., 1940; grad. Command and Gen. Staff Coll., 1953. Ordained deacon Episcopal Ch., 1954. Deacon, Episc. Diocese of Oreg., Salem, 1954—; fin. officer Episc. Diocese of Oreg., Portland, 1960-77; planned giving dir. Episc. Bishop of Oreg. Found., Portland, 1977-83, William Temple House, Portland, 1983—; exec. dir. Willamette View Manor Found., 1978—; pres. Episcopal Bishop of Oreg. Found. 1984-85; bd. dirs., trustee Good Samritan Hosp., 1980—; bd. dirs. Good Samaritan Hosp. Found., 1982-85, Eumenical Ministries of Oreg., 1981-85. Author planned giving pamphlets: Estate Planning, 1979. Sr. v.p. Boy Scouts Am., Portland, 1967-69; pres. Parkrose Lions, 1964-65, Sons./Daus. Oreg. Pioneers, 1966; v.p., regional v.p. Bro. St. Andrew, 1972-84. Served to col. U.S. Army, 1940-60. Recipient Clint Duncgan award Jaycees, 1953; Silver Beaver award Boy Scouts Am., 1956; decorated Legion of Merit, Bronze Star. Mem. Mil. Order World Wars (pres. 1973-74), Am. Legion, Res. Officers Assn. Republican. Lodge: Masons. Office: William Temple House 615 NW 20th Ave Portland OR 97220

EBACHER, ROGER See*Who's Who in America*,43rd edition.

EBERHARD, DAVID, minister, Lutheran Church; city councilman; b. Louisville, Jan. 1, 1934; s. Carl Alfred and Clara (Schowlert) E.; m. Beverly Ott Jacobs, July 11, 1959; children: Michael, Mark, Timothy, Paul, David. B.A., Concordia Sem., St. Louis, 1959, B.Div., 1959, Th.M., 1959. Ordained to ministry Luth. Ch., 1959. Pastor Riverside Luth. Ch., Detroit, 1959-76, Holy Trinity Polish Ch., Detroit, 1970-80, Historic Trinity Ch., Detroit, 1981—; mem. Luth. High Sch. Assn., Luth. Nat. Med. Missions Bd.; bd. dirs. Mich. dist. Social and Urban Ministry. Mem. Detroit City Council, 1969—; bd. dirs. Riverside Civic Fund, Inc., 1966-76, Sobriety House; mem. Berry Subdiv. Assn., United Negro Coll. Fund, Detroit Urban Studies Commn., Northeast Child Guidance Ctr., mem. legal aid com. Detroit Bar Assn. Named Detroit's Young Man of Yr., 1968; recipient Liberty Bell for Leadership award, 1968. Mem. Friends of Greenfield Village, German-Am. Cultural Ctr., Detroit Hist. Soc., NAACP, Detroit Urban League, Mich. Mcpl. League, Nat. Urban Planning Inst., Nat. League Cities. Home: 357 Lodge Dr Detroit MI 48214 Office: 1340 City County Bldg Detroit MI 48226

EBERLY, WILLIAM ROBERT, biology educator, Church of the Brethren; b. North Manchester, Ind., Oct. 4, 1926; s. John H. and Ollie M. (Heaston) E.; m. Eloise Lenore Whitehead, June 30, 1946; children: Diana Sue Eberly Bucher, Brenda Eberly Bibbee, Sandra Eberly Person. A.B., Manchester Coll., 1948; A.M., Ind. U., 1955, Ph.D., 1958. Ordained to ministry Church of the Brethren, 1943. Pastor, Ch. of Brethren, Portland, Ind., 1945, South Whitley, Ind., 1946-47, Roann, Ind., 1949-52, Clay City, Ind., 1953-54, Buffalo, Ind., 1956-58; prof. biology Manchester Coll., North Manchester, Ind., 1955—; dist. moderator Ch. of the Brethren, Ind., 1962, 79; chmn. hist. com. Ch. of Brethren, sec. ann. conf., 1967-77, moderator ann. conf., 1979-80. Author: History of the Church of the Brethren in N.W. Ohio, 1982. Editor numerous sci. and ch. volumes. Contbr. articles to sci. and religious publs. Cons. Ind. Dept. of Natural Resources, Indpls., 1976-80. Recipient Sagamore of Wabash award Gov. of Ind., 1983. Fellow Ind. Acad. Sci. (pres. 1982). Republican. Home: 304 Sunset Ct North Manchester IN 46962 Office: Manchester Coll North Manchester IN 46962

EBLING, WILLIAM LUNDER, minister, American Baptist Churches in the U.S.A. B. Barnesville, Minn., Sept. 25, 1930; s. Paul Ebling and Irine (Lunder) Ebling Crowe; m. JoAnne Mildred Erickson, Apr. 25, 1952; children: Jennifer Jo Ebling Trevithick, Milissa Milrine Ebling Ware. B.A., U. Minn., 1952; M.Div., Fuller Sem., 1959. Ordained to ministry, Am. Bapt. Chs. U.S.A. 1959. Pastor Roger Williams Bapt. Ch., Los

Angeles, 1959-65, Creek Valley Bapt. Ch., Edina, Minn., 1965-67, Redeemer Bapt. Ch., Los Angeles, 1967-74; sr. pastor First Baptist Ch., Burlingame, Calif., 1974-79, Bellflower, Calif, 1979—; dir. Am. Bapt. Chs., Phila.; v.p. Am. Bapt. Fgn. Mission Soc., Phila., 1984—; bd. mgrs. Am. Bapt. Ch. Pacific Southwest, Covina, Calif., 1980—. Mem. Am. Bapt. Ministers COuncil, Los Angeles Bapt. Ministers Council (pres. 1964). Lodge: Rotary. Home: 12829 Alconbury Cerritos CA 90701 Office: First Bapt Ch 9603 Belmont Bellflower CA 90706

ECKARDT, ALICE LYONS, religion studies educator, United Church of Christ; b. Bklyn., Apr. 27, 1923; d. Henry Egmont and Almira Blake (Palmer) Lyons; m. A. Roy Eckardt, Sept. 2, 1944; children: Paula Jean Eckardt Strock, Stephen Robert. B.A., Oberlin Coll., 1944; M.A., Lehigh U., 1966. Adj. asst. prof. religion studies dept. Lehigh U., Bethlehem, Pa., 1972—; mem. Christian Study Group on Judaism and the Jewish People, sponsored NCCJ, 1973—, chmn. 1977-79; exec. bd. Zachor: Holocaust Resource Ctr., 1978—; bd. dirs. Nat. Inst. on the Holocaust, 1981—; vis. scholar Oxford Ctr. for Postgrad. Hebrew Studies, Eng., 1982. Editorial bd. Holocaust Publs., Inc., 1984—; Holocaust and Genocide Studies: An Internat. Jour.; editor, contbr.: Jerusalem: City of the Ages, 1985; co-author: Long Night's Journey into Day: Life and Faith After the Holocaust, 1982, Encounter with Israel, 1970; contbr. articles to jours. Spl. advisor U.S. Holocaust Meml. Council, Washington, 1981—; spl. cons. Pres.'s Commn. on the Holocaust, 1979; adv. com. Holocaust Resource Ctr., Allentown, Pa., 1984—; founding officer Citizens Adv. Com. for So. Lehigh Schs., 1958-60. Recipient Human Relations award Am. Jewish Com., 1971; Myrtle Wreath Achievement award Hadassah, Allentown, 1971, Eastern Pa. Region, 1975, So. N.J. Region, 1979. Mem. Am. Acad. Religion, Am. Profs. for Peace in the Middle East, Assn. Jewish Studies. Democrat. Club: Lehigh U. Women's (pres. 1960-61). Home: Beverly Hill Rd Box 619A Coopersburg PA 18036 Office: Maginnes Hall #9 Lehigh Univ Bethlehem PA 18015

ECKELKAMP, DAVID ROBERT, priest, Roman Catholic Church; b. Washington, Mo., June 4, 1927; s. William Anton and Mary Ann (Straatmann) E. B.A. in Philosophy, Quincy Coll., Cleve. Extension, 1950; M.A. in Theology, Cath. U. Am., St. Joseph Sem. Extension, Teutopolis, Ill., 1954. Joined Franciscan Order, Roman Cath. Ch., 1946, ordained priest, 1953. Chaplain St. Louis Chronic Hosp. and St. Anthony Hosp., St. Louis, 1956-60; sec./U.S.A. liaison to curia gen. Order Friars Minor, Rome, 1960-61; sec. Sacred Heart OFM Province, St. Louis, 1961-64; exec. sec. Internat Order Friars Minor English-Speaking Conf., Rome/St. Louis, 1964—; vicar provincial Sacred Heart Province, Order Friars Minor, St. Louis, 1969-75; nat. spiritual asst. Secular Franciscan Order, St. Louis/Rome, 1979—; cons. Franciscan Sisters, Wheaton, Ill., 1963—, apostolic visitor, Paterson, N.J., Europe, Brazil, 1970-75; retreat dir. Sacred Heart Province, Order Friars Minor; spiritual asst. secular Franciscans, Sacred Heart Secular Province Community, Oak Brook, Ill., 1979—. Contbr. articles to Franciscan Herald Press. Mem. Nat. Assn. Cath. Chaplains (cert.). Office: 3140 Meramec St Saint Louis MO 63118

ECKERMANN, CHARLES HENRY, priest, Roman Cath. ch.; b. Syracuse, N.Y., May 10, 1931; s. Charles Henry and Grace B. (Bruna) E.; A.A., St. Andrews Sem., Rochester, N.Y., 1951; B.A., St. Bernards Sem., 1953; Licentiate in Sacred Theology, Gregorian U., 1957; M.A., Syracuse U., 1963. Ordained priest, 1956; asst. pastor St. Brigid Ch., Syracuse, 1956-63; dean students, chmn. religion and lang. depts., guidance counselor, athletic dir. Bishop Ludden High Sch., 1963-70, prin., 1970-76; pastor St. John the Baptist Ch., Syracuse, 1976—; chmn. bd. adminstrv. rev. which oversees due process procedure Diocese of Syracuse, 1973-76, treas. Priests Senate, 1973-74, bd. dirs. Clerical Fund, 1975—. Co-founder, exec. chmn. Cath. Sch. Adminstrs. Assn. N.Y. State, 1972-74; regional dir. Northeastern region Nat. Cath. Edn. Assn. of Secondary Schs., 1972-74, mem. exec. bd., 1974—. Vice pres. Central N.Y. Cities League, 1969-70. Home and Office: St John the Baptist Ch 406 Court St Syracuse NY 13208

ECKLEBARGER, KERMIT ALLEN, religion educator, minister, Conservative Baptist Association of America. B. Chgo., Dec. 10, 1935; s. Kermit Arthur and M. Marie (Wilson) E.; m. Shirley Jean Hawkins, June 9, 1956; children: Kae Anne, Kermit Andrew. Pastor's diploma, Moody Bible Inst., 1956; B.A., Wheaton Coll., 1958, M.A., 1961; postgrad. U. Chgo., 1963—. Ordained, 1960. Assoc. prof. N.T. and dean of students, London Coll. Bible and Missions, London, Ont., Can., 1960-68; prof. N.T., dean of students, Ont. Bible Coll., Toronto, Ont., 1968-71, asst. to pres., 1970-72; assoc. prof. N.T., Denver Conservative Bapt. Sem., 1972—. Co-editor Bible Dictionary: Lockyer's Bible Dictionary, 1985; contbr. articles to publs. in field. Assn. Theol. Schs. grantee, 1977-78. Mem. Soc. Bibl. Lit., Evang. Theol. Soc. Home: 1704 E Euclid Ave Littleton CO 80121 Office: Denver Seminary Box 10000 Denver CO 80210

ECKLEY, DAVID OLMSTEAD, priest, Greek Orthodox Archdiocese of North and South America; b. Blue Island, Ill., Apr. 5, 1932; s. Gerald Olmstead and Marguerite (Kasten) E.; m. Vasiliki Costas, Apr. 5, 1960; children: David Mark, Marika. B.A., Knox Coll., 1954; M.Div., Holy Cross U., 1975; Teaching credential, Northwestern U., 1959. Ordained priest Greek Orthodox Archdiocese of N. and South Am., 1975. Priest, Greek Orthodox Ch., Denver, 1975-78, Pueblo, Colo., 1978; priest Assumption Greek Orthodox Ch., Galveston, Tex., 1979—; del. Tex. Conf. Chs., Austin, Tex., 1980—; mem. U. Tex. Chaplaincy, Galveston, 1981—; pastoral care co-ordinator Galveston Hospice Group, Tex., 1983—. Author: Who Am I, 1975. Contbr. articles to profl. publs. Sculptor figurative sculpture, I Care, 1970 (first place award). Mem. Galveston Arts Bd., 1980-81, Nuclear Freeze, Galveston, 1982-83, Anti-Gambling Com., Galveston, 1984. Served to 1st lt. inf. U.S. Army, 1954-56, Korea. ESEA Title IV fellow U. Calif.-Berkeley, 1965, U. San Francisco, 1966, Notre Dame Coll., 1967. Mem. Denver Diocese Clergy Assn. (v.p. 1984-86), Greater Galveston Ministerial Alliance, Nat. Released Time Assn., Galveston Hist. Found., Eastern Orthodox Clergy. Democrat. Home: 1819 Sealy St Galveston TX 77550 Office: Assumption Greek Orthodox Ch PO Box 655 Galveston TX 77550

EDDINS, JAMES THOMAS, religion educator, Churches of Christ; b. Henderson, Ky., Nov. 7, 1946; s. James Thomas and Ann (Kennedy) E.; m. Ginger Melody Brackeen, June 26, 1970; children: Amanda Ginger, Olivia Jill. B.A., Freed-Hardeman Coll., 1966; B.A., David Lipscomb Coll., 1968; M.A., Harding U., 1970, M.Th., 1972. Pulpit minister Washington Ave Ch. of Christ, Evansville, Ind., 1972-74; asst. prof. Bible, Harding U., Searcy, Ark., 1975—; campaign dir. Harding U. Internat. Campaign to Australia, 1982—. Home: 24 Jenny Lind Searcy AR 72143 Office: Harding U Box 800 Station A Searcy AR 72143

EDELHEIT, JOSEPH ALLEN, rabbi, Jewish Reform Congregation; b. San Francisco, Nov. 11, 1946; s. Bernard and Shirley Jean (Fortgang) E.; children: Esther Rachel, Shanan Angel. B.A., U. Calif.-Berkeley, 1968; B.H.L., Hebrew Union Coll.-Jewish Inst. Religion, 1970, M.H.L., 1973. Ordained rabbi, 1973. Asst. rabbi Emanuel Congregation, Chgo., 1973-76, assoc. rabbi, 1985—; rabbi Sinai Temple, Michigan City, 1976-85; adj. assoc. prof. theology Valparaiso U., Ind., 1977-84; exec. bd. Central Conf. Am. Rabbis, N.Y.C., 1982—. Author: Introduction to Judaism, 1978; Divre Gerut, 1984. Contbr. articles to profl. jours. Fuerstenberg fellow U. Chgo., 1984. Mem. Chgo. Assn. Reform Rabbis (pres.), Am. Acad. Religion, Michigan City Ministerial Assn. (pres.). Lodge: B'nai B'rith. Home: 532 Boyd Cir Michigan City IN 46360 Office: Sinai Temple 2800 Franklin St Michigan City IN 46360

EDGE, THOMAS LESLIE, minister, Luth. Ch.-Mo. Synod; b. Detroit, Dec. 20, 1935; s. Leslie Joseph and Flora Marie (Dirksen) E.; B.A., Concordia Sem., St. Louis, 1957, M.Div., 1960; m. Betty Ruth Maxwell, Aug. 22, 1959; children—Elizabeth Anne, Christopher Thomas Gregory, Angela Michelle Marie. Ordained to ministry, 1960; founding pastor Luth. Ch. of St. Ambrose, Pennsville, N.J., 1960-67; pastor All Saints Luth. Ch., Charlotte, N.C., 1967-70, Christ the King Luth. Ch., Ringwood, N.J., 1970—; chmn. commn. on worship N.J. Dist. Luth. Ch.-Mo. Synod, 1972-74, mem. bd. adjudication, 1974—; mem. Luth. Hour Research Com., 1973—; chaplain Fire Dept., Ringwood, 1970—. Co-founder Charlotte Citizens for Peace in Viet-Nam, 1967; dir. Ambulance Corps, Ringwood, 1970—. Contbr. articles to religious mags. Home: 222 Skylands Rd Ringwood NJ 07456 Office: 50 Erskine Rd Ringwood NJ 07456

EDIE, WAYNE PAUL, minister, Church of God (Anderson, Indiana); b. Canton, Ohio, Feb. 3, 1942; s. Wayne Arthur and Dora Mae (Hinchliff) E.; m. Norma Jean Craddock, Aug. 21, 1965; children: Gregory Paul, Jill Renee. B.A., Anderson Coll., 1968. Ordained to ministry Ch. of God (Anderson), 1969. Pastor 1st Ch. of God, Lincoln, Nebr., 1968-70, Danville, Ky., 1970-77, Vero Beach, Fla., 1977-81, Cape Coral, Fla., 1981-82, Bloomington, Ind., 1982—; bd. dirs. City Mission, Lincoln, 1968-70, Nebr. Council on Alcoholic Edn., 1968-70; com. mem. Youth for Christ, Lincoln, 1968-70; bd. dirs. Ind. Evangelistic Bd., Bloomington, 1982—. Republican. Home: 1203 Matlock Rd Bloomington IN 47401 Office: First Church of God 1203 Matlock Rd Bloomington IN 47401

EDMAN, DAVID ARTHUR, priest, Episcopal Church; b. Worcester, Mass., Jan. 9, 1930; s. Victor Raymond and Edith Marie (Olson) E.; children: Sarah, Peter, Brita. B.A., Wheaton Coll., 1955; M.A., Columbia U., 1959; M.Div., Union Theol. Sem., 1959. Ordained priest Episcopal Ch., 1959. Assoc. rector Christ Ch., Bronxville, N.Y., 1959-62; priest-in-charge Christ the King Ch., Stone Ridge, N.Y., 1962-65; chaplain Rochester Inst. Tech., N.Y., 1965-69; rector Grace Ch., Scottsville, N.Y., 1969-84, St. Thomas Ch., Camden, Maine, 1984—. Author: Of Wise Man and Fools, 1972; A Bit of Christmas Whimsy, 1975; One Upon an Eternity, 1984; (with Wendell Castle) Book of Laminations, 1979. Served to lt. U.S. Army, 1951-53. Address: PO Box 631 Camden ME 04843

EDWARDS, BLAKE EDISON, minister, American Baptist Churches in the U.S.A.; b. Dublin, Va., May 11, 1938; s. Garland Anderson and Ruby Jane (Melton) E.; m. Ann Arlayne Steinbright, May 13, 1967. B.A., Eastern Coll., St. Davids, Pa., 1973; M.Div., Eastern Bapt. Theol. Sem., Phila., 1976. Ordained to ministry Baptist Ch., 1976. Pastor Andorra Bapt. Ch., Phila., 1973-75, Taylor Meml. Bapt. Ch., Paulsboro, N.J., 1975-78, Brandywine Bapt. Ch., Chadds Ford, Pa., 1978—; mem. commn. on the ministry Am. Bapt. Chs. Pa. and Del., 1979—; coordinator Tri-County Fellowship of Christian Chs., 1979—; moderator Riverside Bapt. Assn., 1981-84. Served with USAF, 1956-69. Mem. Am. Bapt. Chs. of Pa. and Del. Ministers Council, Eastern Bapt. Theol. Sem. Alumni (treas. 1981-84). Office: Brandywine Baptist Church PO Box 162 Chadds Ford PA 19317

EDWARDS, BRUCE LEE, JR., minister, Churches of Christ; English educator; b. Akron, Ohio, Sept. 5, 1952; s. Bruce Lee and Betty Lou (Klever) E.; m. Joan Christine Lungstrum, Sept. 28, 1973; children: Matthew, Mary, Justin, Michael. B.A., U. Mo., 1977; M.A., Kans. State U., 1979; Ph.D., U. Tex., 1981. Ordained to ministry Churches of Christ 1973. Minister Ch. Christ, St. James, Mo., 1973-77, Manhattan, Kans., 1977-79, Bowling Green, Ohio, 1981—; asst. prof. English, Bowling Green State U., Ohio, 1981—. Author: Roughdrafts, 1985. Contbr. articles to profl. jours. Ednl. dir. Right to Life, Bowling Green, 1982. U. Tex. fellow, 1980-81. Named Outstanding Young Man, Jaycees, 1984. Mem. Conf. Christianity and Lit., Nat. Council Tchrs. of English, Ohio Right to Life Orgn., N.Y. C.S. Lewis Soc. Republican. Office: Bowling Green State U Dept English Bowling Green OH 43403

EDWARDS, DON RABY, priest, Episcopal Ch.; b. Tarboro, N.C., June 13, 1931; s. Charles Kenneth and Mable Hester (Craft) E.; A.B., East Carolina U., 1955; M.Div., Va. Theol. Sem., 1958, D.D., 1978; m. Jane Mann Credle, June 3, 1957; children: Charles Blount, Nathaniel Carter. Ordained priest, 1959; vicar St. Christopher's Ch., Havelock, N.C., 1958-61; rector St. Paul's Ch., Wilmington, N.C., 1961-63, St. Stephen's Ch., Goldsboro, N.C., 1963-68, Emmanuel Ch., Athens, Ga., 1968-73, St. Stephen's Ch., Richmond, Va., 1973—; fellow Sch. Continuing Edn., Va. Theol. Sem., Alexandria, 1971—; chmn. com. on vacancy consultation and parish devel. Diocese of Va., 1973-75, chmn. commn. on ministry, 1976—, mem. standing com., 1976—; dep. Gen. Conv. Episcopal Ch., 1961-68, 79, 82, 85; trustee St. Paul's Coll., Lawrenceville, Va., 1980—, Ch. Schs. in Va., 1980—, St. Margaret's Sch., Tappahannock, Va., 1981-84, St. Christopher's Sch., Richmond, Va., 1974-80. Trustee, Emma G. Scott Found., Richmond, 1978—. Mem. Va. Sem. Alumni Assn. (exec. com. 1976—). Home: 311 Cloverly Rd Richmond VA 23221

EDWARDS, ELWYN GERALD, minister, So. Baptist Conv.; b. Tampa, Fla., June 10, 1928; s. Seeber Iverson and Beulah (Franklin) E.; A.B., Stetson U., DeLand, Fla., 1952; B.D., Southwestern Bapt. Theol. Sem., Ft. Worth, 1958, M.Div., 1973; m. Joyce Lavonne Trawick, Aug. 24, 1950; children—Lawyn Clayton, Dawana Jo. Ordained to ministry, 1951; commd. 1st lt. Chaplain Corps, U.S. Army, 1953, advanced through grades to col., 1972; sr. pastor Benjamin Franklin Village Chapel, Mannheim, W. Ger., 1972-73; dist. chaplain U.S. Army Support Dist., Baden-Wurtemberg, Stuttgart, Ger., 1973-74; post chaplain, Ft. Huachuca, Ariz., 1974—; regtl. chaplain 4th Cav. Regt. (Meml.), Ft. Huachuca, 1974-76; troop comdr. B Troop, 4th Cav. Regt. (Meml.), 1977—. Active local Boy Scouts Am. Certified tchr., Fla. Mem. Mil. Chaplains Assn., Assn. U.S. Army, Sierra Vista (Ariz.) Ministerial Assn. (pres. 1976-77), Scabbard and Blade, Pi Kappa Phi, Theta Alpha Phi. Home: PO Box 104 Homosassa Springs FL 32647 Office: Post Chaplain Fort Huachuca AZ 85613

EDWARDS, GERALD (JERRY) WILLIAM, minister, So. Baptist Conv.; b. St. Louis, Apr. 15, 1943; s. Carl Burnette and Doris Edith (Edwards) E.; B.A., William Jewell Coll., 1966; M.R.E., So. Bapt. Theol. Sem., 1968; M.S. in Social Work, Kent Sch. Social Work, U. Louisville, 1977; m. Bonnye Beth Hackworth, Apr. 10, 1967; children—Bryan Anthony, Kymberlee Beth. Ordained to ministry, 1967; dir. So. Bapt. Refugee Resettlement, Fort Chaffee, Ark., 1975-76; dir. Christian social ministries N.C. Bapt. Conv., 1968-70, Greater Boston Bapt. Ministries, 1970-75. Organist/choir master Met. Bapt. Ch., Cambridge, Mass., 1972-75. State rep. Office for Children, Boston, 1974-75. Recipient Dir.'s citation HEW, Dallas, 1976. Mem. So. Bapt. Social Service Assn., Nat. Assn. Social Workers. Address: 3132 Radiance Rd Louisville KY 40220

EDWARDS, JAMES ROBERT, minister, educator, Presbyterian Church USA; b. Colorado Springs, Colo., Oct. 28, 1945; s. Robert Emery and Mary Eleanor (Callison) E.; m. Mary Jane Pryor, June 22, 1968; children: Corrie Jane, Mark James. B.A., Whitworth Coll., Spokane, Wash., 1963-67; M.Div., Princeton Theol. Sem., 1970; postgrad. U. Zurich, Switzerland,

1970-71; Ph.D., Fuller Theol. Sem., 1978. Ordained to ministry Presbyterian Church USA, 1971. Minister students First Presbyn. Ch., Colorado Springs, 1971-78; prof. religion Jamestown Coll., N.D., 1978—. Contbr. articles to profl. jours. Author: Commentary of Epistle to Romans, 1984. Mem. steering com. CROP Hunger Walk, Jamestown, 1983, 84; lectr. in field. Named Prof. of Yr., Jamestown Coll., 1984. Mem. Soc. Bibl. Lit., N.Y. C.S. Lewis Soc. Address: 524 5th St NE Jamestown ND 58401

EDWARDS, JEFFERSON DAVID, JR., pastor, non-denominational; b. Chgo., July 7, 1951; s. Jefferson David Edwards and Mary Etta (Ohio) Jones; m. Debra Venice Stegall, Dec. 19, 1981; 1 dau., Honesty Joy. Student Northwest Mo. State U. Ordained as pastor Evangelistic Ctr. Ch., 1977. Pastor, Inner-City Christian Ctr., Kansas City, Mo., 1977—; pres. Inner-City Christian Bible Coll., Kansas City, 1980—, Inner-City Christian Ministries, 1977—; prin. Inner-City Christian Acad., Kansas City, 1981-83. Author: Perfect Will, Perfect Heart, Perfect Love, 1981; The Call of God, 1985. Contbr. articles to newspaper. Pres. New Breed Club of 1969, Kansas City, 1969, 74; 1st pres., founder Operation Push/Kansas City, 1974. Avocations: organ playing; song writing; singing. Office: Inner City Christian Ctr 3600 Indiana Kansas City MO 64128

EDWARDS, LELAND BRETON, clergyman, administrator, International Church of the Foursquare Gospel; b. San Jose, Calif., Aug. 15, 1919; s. Arthur Farmer and Edith Lillian (Breton) E.; m. Barbara Nell Noyes, Aug. 31, 1941; children: Arthur Noyes, Loren Jonathan. D.D. (hon.), Life Bible Coll., 1968. Ordained to ministry, 1941. Missionary, Internat. Ch. of Foursquare Gospel, Republic of Panama, 1937-47, missionary supr., 1947-59, Republic of Panama and Chile, 1959; asst. dir. Foursquare Missions, Los Angeles, 1960-65, dir., 1965—; sec. Internat. Ch. of the Foursquare Gospel, 1973—; pres. Istmian Religious Fedn., Panama and Panama Canal Zone, 1957; chmn. Billy Graham Crusade, Panama, 1958; instr. missions Life Bible Coll., Los Angeles, 1964-72. Mem. Evang. Fgn. Missions Assn. Republican. Office: Internat Church of the Foursquare Gospel 1100 Glendale Blvd Los Angeles CA 90026

EDWARDS, OTIS CARL, JR., educator, priest, Episcopal Ch.; b. Bienville, La., June 15, 1928; s. Otis Carl and Margaret Lee (Hutchinson) E.; B.A., Centenary Coll., 1949; S.T.B., Gen. Theol. Sem., 1952; S.T.M., So. Methodist U., 1962; M.A., U. Chgo., 1963, Ph.D., 1971; D.D., Nashotah House, 1976; m. Jane Hanna Trufant, Feb. 19, 1957; children—Carl, Sam. Louise. Ordained to priesthood Episcopal Ch., 1954; curate ch., Baton Rouge, 1953-54; vicar ch., Abbeville, La., 1954-57, Waxahachie, Tex., 1960-61; rector ch., Morgan City, La., 1957-60; priest-in-charge ch., Chgo., 1961-63; instr. Wabash Coll., 1963-64; asst. prof. Nashotah (Wis.) House, 1964-69, asso. prof., 1969-72, prof. N.T., 1972-74, sub-dean, 1973-74, acting dean, 1973-74; pres., dean Seabury-Western Theol. Sem., Evanston, Ill., 1974-83, prof. preaching, 1983—; vis. prof. Immanuel Coll. and Trinity Coll., Nigeria, 1983, Vancouver Sch. Theology, summer 1984; Bd. dirs. Council Episcopal Sem. Deans, Inc., U. Chgo. Div. Sch. Inst. Advanced Study of Religion (panel of cons.), Native Am. Theol. Assn. Trustee Kendall Coll. Recipient Spl. award Mystery Writers of Am., 1965. Mem. Soc. Bibl. Lit., Am. Acad. Religion, Cath. Bibl. Assn., Acad. of Homiletics. Book rev. editor: Anglican Theol. Review, 1971—. Contbr. articles to religious jours. Address: Seabury Western Theological Seminary 2122 Sheridan Rd Evanston IL 60201

EDWARDS, REX DANIEL, minister, Seventh-day Adventist Ch.; b. Christchurch, New Zealand, Nov. 14, 1934; came to U.S., 1970; s. Leslie Ernest and Daphne (James) E.; m. Zelma Beryl Harris, Nov. 20, 1956; children: Davina Janelle, LeRoy Paul, Antony Shane. L.Th., Avondale Coll., 1955, B.A., 1956; M.A., Andrews U., 1971, M.Div., 1973; D.Div., Vanderbilt U., 1974. Ordained to ministry Seventh-Day Adventist Ch., 1963. Pastor, evangelist Seventh-Day Adventist Chs., Australia, Eng., U.S., 1956-75; prof. Columbia Union Coll., Takoma Park, Md., 1975-81; editorial assoc. and field dir. Ministry Mag., Washington, 1981—. Author: Every Believer A Minister, 1979. Contbr. articles to religious publs. Vanderbilt U. grantee, 1973. Mem. Coll. Preachers, Soc. Bibl. Lit., Am. Acad. Religion, Bibl. Research Inst. Home: 7401 Aspen Ave Takoma Park MD 20912 Office: Ministry Mag 6840 Eastern Ave NW Washington DC 20012

EDWARDS, RICHARD ALAN, theology educator, Lutheran Church in America. b. West Mahanoy, Pa., Dec. 31, 1934; s. Francis Reed and Helen Irene (Mates) E.; m. June Caroline Kirkhuff, Sept. 3, 1958; children: Jennifer Lynne, Emily Katharine, Jonathan Alan. B.A., Princeton U., 1956; postgrad. Phila. Luth. Sem., 1956-57; M.A., U. Chgo., 1962, Ph.D., 1968. Instr. Bethany Coll., Lindsborg, Kans., 1962-63; asst. prof. Susquehanna U., Selinsgrove, Pa., 1963-66; from asst. prof. to assoc. prof. Thiel Coll., Greenville, Pa., 1968-72; assoc. prof. Va. Tech. U., Blacksburg, 1972-78; assoc. prof. Marquette U., Milw., 1978—, asst. chmn. theology dept., 1982—. Author: Sign of Jonah, 1970; Theology of Q, 1975; Matthew's Story of Jesus, 1985; editor, translator: Sentences of Sextus, 1982; contbr. articles to religious jours. Mem. Soc. Biblical Lit., Studiorum Novi Testament Socs., Cath. Biblical Assn. Home: 2623 N 66th St Wauwatosa WI 53213 Office: Marquette U Theology Dept Milwaukee WI 53233

EDWARDS, ROBERT J., minister, counselor, Southern Baptist Convention; b. Valley Park, Mo., Mar. 3, 1923; s. Albert H. Edwards and Myrtle I. Holloway; m. Blanche Lestean Sparks, May 9, 1942 (dec. 1974); m. Ruth Belle Hewitt, June 1, 1975; children: Robert Eugene, Preston Keith. B.A., Ouachita Bapt. U., 1954; B.D., M.Div. Southwestern Bapt. Theol. Sem., 1956; D. Ministry, Luther Rice Sem., 1982. Ordained to ministry Bapt. Ch., 1947. Pastor, South Haven Bapt. Ch., Springfield, Mo., 1956-60; commd. lt. (j.g.) U.S. Navy, 1957, advanced through grades to lt. comdr., 1966, retired, 1982; chaplain U.S. Navy, 1960-82; pastor, adminstr. Mo. Bapt. chs., St. Louis, Perryville and Bismark, 1966-82; educator, counselor Christian Civic Found., St. Louis, 1968—; asst. dir. devel. Southwestern Bapt. Coll., Bolivar, Mo., 1974-76; adminstr. Bapt. Towers Retirement Home, Kansas City, Mo., 1977-79, 83; speaker to profl. and service orgns. Author series on grief and drug awareness for local newspapers. Pres. Ministers Alliance, Bismarck, Mo., 1967, Vol. Chaplains, Bonne Terre, Mo., 1969, Southeastern Mo. Ministers Fellowship, Cape Girardeau, Mo., 1980. Mem. Res. Officers Assn., VFW. Clin. Pastoral Edn. Assn. Home: 4520 Prague Ave St Louis MO 63109 Office: Dir Missions Box 547 Salem MO 65560

EDWARDS, THOMAS CLARKE, priest, Orthodox Church in America, psychiatric social worker; b. Washington, D.C., Jan. 30, 1937; s. Raymond Joseph and Jane Christine (Willett) E.; m. Evelyn Ruzila, Aug. 13, 1967; children: Laura, Mary-Clarke, Daniel. B.A. in Philosophy, Duquesne U., 1965; student, S.S. Cyril and Methodious Sem. of Byzantine Rite, 1959-65; M.Div. in Theology, St. Vladimir's Orthodox Theol. Sem., 1968. Ordained priest Orthodox Church in America, 1968. Pastor, Holy Annunciation Ch., Maynard, Mass., 1968-71, Holy Transfiguration Ch., Pearl River, N.Y., 1972-75, Holy Apostles Orthodox Ch., Saddle Brook, N.J., 1974—. Psychiat. social worker N.Y. Office Mental Retardation and Devel. Disabilities, Thiells, 1973—. Author: The Waggamans and their Allied Families, 1983. Recipient Kamalavka, Holy Synod of Bishops, Orthodox Ch. in Am., 1981, Gold Cross, Holy Synod of Bishops of Orthodox Ch. in Am., 1984. Republican. Home: 147 Midwood Rd Paramus NJ 07652 Office: Holy Apostles Orthodox Ch 17 Platt Ave Saddle Brook NJ 07662

EDWARDS, WALTER ROSS, minister, So. Baptist Conv.; b. Star City, Ark., Aug. 20, 1910; s. Samuel John and Linnie Jane (Waters) E.; B.A., Ouachita U., Arkadelphia, Ark., 1935; Th.D., So. Bapt. Theol. Sem., Louisville, 1938; Th.M., Central Bapt. Theol. Sem., Kansas City, Kans., 1945; m. Lorraine Maurice Sinks, Feb. 10, 1937; children—Wanda Ross Edwards Buehre, James Douglas. Ordained to ministry, 1931; pastor chs. in Ark. and Mo., 1938-67; editor Word and Way, 1967-75; pastor Noland Rd. Bapt. Ch., Independence, Mo., 1975—; tchr. pastoral adminstrn. Central Bapt. Theol. Sem., 1953-55; evangelistic tours in Eng., Australia, Japan, Indonesia, Brazil. Bd. dirs. Mo. Bapt. Hosp., 1950-65, Bapt. Meml. Hosp., 1965-67, Midwestern Bapt. Theol. Sem., 1956-67; mem. bd. social service commn. So. Bapt. Conv., 1950-56; mem. So. Bapt. Found., 1961-63; pres. Mo. Bapt. Conv., 1956-59; v.p. So. Bapt. Pastors Conf., 1963-64. Bd. govs. Citizens Assn. Kansas City, Mo., 1948-67; chmn. Citizens Adv. Com. for Community Improvement in Workable Program, 1965-67. Mem. Pi Kappa Delta. Home: 8629 Rhinehart Rd Kansas City MO 64139 Office: 4505 S Noland Rd Independence MO 64055

EFIRD, JAMES MICHAEL, theology educator, Presbyterian Church USA; b. Kannapolis, N.C., May 30, 1932; s. James Rufus and I.Z. (Christy) E.; m. Vivian Lee Poythress, Mar. 7, 1975; 1 dau., Whitney Michelle; 1 stepson Anthony Kevin Crumpler; m. Joan Shelf, June 30, 1951 (div. Nov. 1971). Ordained to ministry Presbyterian Ch. U.S.A., 1958. Asst. prof. Duke Divinity Sch., Durham, N.C., 1962-68, assoc. prof., 1968—, dir. acad. affairs, 1971-75; interim minister Presbyn. Ch., Roxboro, N.C, 1983-84, Bethesda Presbyn. Ch., Aberdeen, N.C, 1982-83, others. Author: How to Interpret the Bible, 1984; Biblical Books of Wisdom, 1983; Old Testament Writings, 1982; others. Duke U. scholar, 1958-62. Mem. Soc. Bibl. Lit., Phi Beta Kappa. Home: 2609 Heather Glen Rd Durham NC 27712 Office: Duke Divinity Sch Durham NC 27706

EGAN, HARVEY DANIEL, priest, Roman Catholic Church, theology educator. B. Putnam, Conn., Nov. 6, 1937; s. Harvey Joseph and Alice Blanche (LaCroix) E. B.S. E.E., Worcester Poly. Inst., 1959; M.A. in Philosophy, Boston Coll., 1965; M.A. in Theology, Woodstock Coll., 1969; Th.D., U. Muenster, 1973. Joined S.J., 1960; ordained priest Roman Catholic Ch., 1969. Priest, Roman Cath. Ch., Boston, 1969—; Roman Cath. chaplain NATO Base, Drierwalde, Germany, 1969-72; Research elec. engr. Boeing Airplane Co., Seattle, 1959-60, Kaman Helicopter, Moosup, Conn., 1960; lectr. Holy Cross Coll., Worcester, Mass., 1965-66; asst. prof. Santa Clara U. (Calif.), 1973-75; assoc. prof. theology Boston Coll., 1975—. Author: The Spiritual Exercises, 1976; What Are They Saying about Mysticism, 1982; Christian Mysticism, 1984. Mem. Cath. Theology Soc., Cath. Theol. Soc. Am., Boston Theology Soc., Am. Acad. Religion. Home: St Mary's Hall Boston College Chestnut Hill MA 02167

EGELSTON, CHESTER GERALD, minister, church official, Church of God (Anderson, Indiana); b. Middletown, Ohio, Oct. 2, 1931; s. Carl Chester and Minnie Marie (Day) E.; m. Kathleen Ann Snider, May 22, 1954; children: David Lynn, Douglas Brian, Dale Kevin. B.A., Anderson Coll., 1953; M.A., Morehead State U., 1977. Ordained to ministry Ch. of God (Anderson); 1953. Pastor, Ch. of God, Melvern, Kans., 1956-60, Vincennes, Ind., 1960-63, Liberal, Kans., 1963-69, Morehead, Ky., 1969-73, Tulsa, 1973-79; exec. sec. Okla. Assembly of Ch. of God, Tulsa, 1979—; cons. Cornerstone Mgmt. Cons., Inc., Oklahoma City, 1984—; trustee Gulf Coast Bible Coll., Houston, 1970-80; chmn. Kans. Conv., Ch. of God, 1964-69; vice chmn. bus. com. Gen. Assembly of Ch. of God, Anderson, 1966-69; chmn. Nat. Assn. State Coordinators, Ch. of God, 1982. Named Paster of Yr., State of Kans., 1958. Mem. Phi Alpha Theta. Republican. Home: 6849 W 35th Pl Tulsa OK 74107 Office: Okla Assembly of Church of God 3319 W 41st St Tulsa OK 74107

EGGENSCHILLER, ROBERT EMIL, priest, Episcopal Church; b. Paterson, N.J., Jan. 2, 1940; s. Marcel Francis and Jean Rose (Incremona) E.; B.A., Am. U., 1961; M.Div., Episcopal Theol. Sch., Cambridge, Mass., 1964; m. Patricia Nancy Scola, Sept. 12, 1964; children—Michele Lynn, Denise Noel. Ordained deacon, 1964, priest, 1964; asst. Ch. of Saviour, Denville, N.J., 1964-66; rector Christ Ch., Lockport, N.Y., 1966-77, Ch. of the Advent, Kenmore, N.Y., 1977—; chmn. Diocesan dept. Christian Social Relations, 1967-70; mem. Diocesan Council, 1968-71, 73-76; chmn. Diocesan Task Force on Leadership Devel., 1974-76; chmn. Commn. on Clergy Devel., 1976—; mem. Diocesan Standing Com., 1975-79, Diocesan Planning Commn., 1982-83; chmn. Stewardship Devel. Com., Diocese of Western N.Y., 1981-84; head 8-mem. del. to Nat. Ch. Conv., 1979. Pres. Lockport Area Council of Chs., 1973-74; chaplain Niagara County Infirmary, 1970—; clin. asst. Western N.Y. Psychiat. Group, Niagara Falls. Councilman, Town of Lockport, 1971-77. Mem. Niagara County Planned Parenthood, Inc. (past mem. exec. bd.). Home: 381 Louviane Dr Kenmore NY 14223 Office: 54 Delaware Rd Kenmore NY 14217

EHLERT, ARNOLD DOUGLAS, librarian, minister, Evang. Free Ch. Am.; b. Mondovi, Wis., Apr. 22, 1909; s. Richard J. and Cora E. (Hakes) E.; A.B., John Fletcher Coll., 1932; Th.M., Dallas Theol. Sem., 1942, Th.D., 1945; M.S.L.S., U. So. Calif., 1953; m. Thelma A. Adolphs, Dec. 25, 1933; children—A. Benjamin, Susan Elizabeth (Mrs. Ronald Weiss), Eunice Yvonne (Mrs. Bruce Castle). Ordained to ministry Evang. Free Ch. Am., 1943; librarian Dallas Theol. Sem., 1942-48, Fuller Theol. Sem., Pasadena, Calif., 1948-55, Biola Coll., La Mirada, Calif., 1955-69, Talbot Theol. Sem., La Mirada, 1969-74; dir. libraries Christian Heritage Coll., 1974-80, Inst. for Creation Research, El Cajon, Calif., 1980—. Mem. Internat. Soc. Bible Collectors (founder 1964, pres. 1964—), Beta Phi Mu. Author: The Biblical Novel, a Checklist, 1961; Bibliographic History of Dispensationalism, 1965; Brethren Writers, a Checklist, 1969; editor The Bible Collector, 1965-84. Home: 1262 Camillo Way El Cajon CA 92021 Office: 2100 Greenfield Dr El Cajon CA 92021

EHMAN, JACOB, minister, North American Baptist Conference; b. Lehr, N.D., Sept. 14, 1923; s. Fred and Emila (Kranzler) E.; m. Helen Fischer, June 2, 1946; children: David, Dorothy, Deborah, Donna. B. Th., N. Am. Bapt. Sem., Sioux Falls, 1951; Ordained to ministry North American Baptist Conference, 1951. Minister, First Bapt. Ch., Bessie, Okla., 1951-56, Sidney, Mont., 1956-61, Goodrich, N.D., 1961-67, Steamboat Rock, Iowa, 1967-74, Ripley Blvd Bapt. Ch., Alpena, Mich., 1974—. Dir., Ch. Extension Investors Corp., Oakbrook Terrace, Ill., 1970—. Mem. Alpena Ministerial Assn. (chmn. 1979), Gt. Lakes Bapt. Assn. (chmn. 1982, chmn. extension com. 1983, 84). Republican. Home: 1104 Greenhaven Ln Alpena MI 49707 Office: Ripley Blvd Bapt Ch 318 Ripley Blvd Alpena MI 49707

EICHMAN, CHARLES W., minister, Moravian Church; b. Easton, Pa., Oct. 11, 1923; s. Charles and Pearl Mae (Smith) E.; m. Geraldine Miller Paules, June 5, 1948; children: David P., Beth R., Kurt S., Irgrid R. B.A., Moravian Coll., 1948; B.D., Moravian Theol Sem., 1951. Ordained to ministry Moravian Ch., 1951. Pastor Palmyra Moravian Ch., N.J., 1951-57, Canadensis Moravian Ch., Pa., 1957-61, Bethel Moravian Ch., Alaska, 1961-64, Hope Moravian Ch., Ind., 1964-67, Nazareth Moravian Ch., Pa., 1967-77, Castleton Hill Moravian Ch., S.I., N.Y., 1977—; trustee Moravian Theol. Sem., Bethlehem, Pa., 1981—; mem. bd. Christian Edn., Bethlehem, 1968-80; pres. S.I. Council Chs., 1983-85. Pres., bd. dirs. Nazareth YMCA, 1976-77; active S.I. Health Systems Agy.,

1977-80, S.I. Selective Service Bd. 160, 1982—. Served with USN, 1943-46, PTO. Democrat. Lodge: Lions (v.p. S.I., chpt.) Home: 1646 Victory Blvd Staten Island NY 10314 Office: Castleton Hill Moravian Ch 1657 Victory Blvd Staten Island NY 10314

EICKWORT, KATHLEEN RUTH, priest, Episcopal Church; biologist; b. Balt., Jan. 3, 1945; d. George Robert and June Meredith (Quinan) Hoddinott; m. George Campbell Eickwort, Mar. 20, 1965; children: Mary Kathleen, Robert Campbell, Jeffrey Matthew. B.S. in Zoology, Mich. State U., 1962; M.A. in Entomology, Kans. U., 1968; Ph.D. in Ecology, Cornell U., 1971; postdoctoral Bexley Hall, 1981-83. Ordained deacon Episcopal Ch., 1983, priest, 1984; cert. pastoral care. Coordinator ministries Episc. Ch. at Cornell U., Ithaca, N.Y., 1979-82; seminarian intern St. John's Ch., Ithaca, 1982; priest assoc. Episc. parishes of Schuyler County, Watkins Glen, N.Y., 1984—; coordinator Loaves and Fishes Hospitality and Advocacy Ministry, Ithaca, 1983—; mem. Jubilee Ministries Task Force, Diocese of Central N.Y., 1983—; mem. Coll. Work Commn., 1979-84. Contbr. articles to Ecology Mag., Evolution Mag., and other biology jours. Danforth fellow, 1965, Woodrow Wilson fellow, 1965; NSF fellow, 1965-68. Mem. Soc. St. Francis (novice 3d order). Home: 105 Birchwood Dr Ithaca NY 14850 Office: Loaves and Fishes 210 N Cayuga St Ithaca NY 14850

EIKERENKOETTER, FREDERICK J., II (REVEREND IKE), minister, Sci. of Living Ch.; b. Ridgeland, S.C., June 1, 1935; s. Frederick Joseph and Rema Estelle (Matthews) E.; B.Th., Am. Bible Coll., 1956; D.Sci. of Living, Sci. of Living Inst., 1971; m. Eula Mae Dent, Feb. 7, 1964; 1 son, Xavier Frederick III. Founder, pres. United Christian Evangelist Assn., 1962—, United Ch. Sci. of Living, 1969—, Rev. Ike Found., 1973—. Vis. lectr. dept. psychiatry Harvard Med. Sch., May 1973, U. Ala., Jan. 1975, Atlanta U. Center, Nov., 1975, Rice U., Houston, 1977. Served with chaplain sect. USAF, 1956-58. Recipient World Service award for outstanding contribns. to mankind Prince Hall Masons, 1975. Mem. NAACP (life). Founder of the Science of Living philosophy, church, and inst. Office: GPD Box 50 New York NY 10116

EIKLOR, FRANK FRED, minister, Evangelical Ch., broadcaster; b. Chgo., June 16, 1936; s. David Fred and Laura (Lipps) E.; m. Norma Dean Dysart, June 10, 1960; 1 dau.: Dawn Melody. B.A., Baptist Christian Coll. Ordained to ministry Evangelical Ch., 1961. Dean, Christians in Action, Long Beach, Calif., 1961-70, v.p., 1970-79; pres. Shalom Fellowship, Keene, N.H., 1979—. Rep. Nat. Christian Leadership Council for Israel, N.Y.C., 1962; del. Internat. Conv. on Soviet Jewry (Jerusalem), Boston, 1983; pres. Cheshire County Ministerial, Keene, N.H., 1982, 83; daily broadcaster Shalom Radio, 1979—. Editor: The Shalom Letter; contbr. articles to profl. jours.; instr. TV, radio, cassettes. Nat. organizer Christian Holocaust Dialogues, Keene, 1982—. Served to corp. USMC, 1956-58. Mem. Evang. Counsel for Fin. Accountability, Nat. Religious Broadcasters. Home: Rural Route 9 E Keene NH 03431

EISENBERG, FREDERICK AARON, rabbi, Reform Jewish Congregations; b. Boston, Jan. 26, 1931; s. Moses Joel and Violet (Hirshon) E.; B.A., Clark U., 1952; B.H.L., Hebrew Union Coll., 1955, M.A., 1958; m. Helen Louise Finer, Sept. 1, 1957; children—Matthew, Elizabeth, Rachel. Rabbi, 1958; student rabbi congregations in Petoskey and Saginaw, Mich., Marion, Ind., 1952-56; ednl. dir., tchr., Muncie, Ind., 1956-58; dir. audio-visual dept. Wise Temple Religious Sch., Cin., 1956-58; chaplain USAF, 1960-62; asst. rabbi Temple Sholom, Chgo., 1962-64; rabbi Temple Emanuel, Grand Rapids, Mich., 1964-72; rabbi Young Peoples Congregation, rabbi B'rith Emeth Temple, Cleve., 1972—; mem. Jewish Fedn. Hunger Task Force, Task Force for Soviet Jewery; dean N.E. Lakes Fedn. Temple Youth, 1976. Mem. broadcasting commn. Chgo. Bd. Rabbis; bd. dirs. Inst. Pastoral Care, Chgo., Acad. Religion and Mental Health; mem. steering and clergy coordinating com. Lakeview Council Chs.; rabbinic liaison Chgo. office Jewish Welfare Bd.; mem. radio and TV commn. Grand Rapids Area Council Chs.; commr. cemeteries Mich., 1971; rabbinic adviser to Cleve. and Lake Erie Fedn. Temple Youth; mem. com. for continuing edn. Central Conf. Am. Rabbis; lectr. for Jewish Chautauqua Soc. at Purdue U., Hope Coll., Aquinas Coll., Mich. State U., Calvin Coll.; Jewish chaplain Aquinas Coll., 1970. Bd. dirs. USO, Mental Health Soc. Greater Chgo., Jewish Community Fund of Grand Rapids, Spectrum; mem. ministerial adv. com. Kent County Planned Parenthood Assn.; clergy chmn. United Way, 1984. Recipient Nelson and Helen Glueck prize in Bibl. Archaeology, 1956. Mem. Cleve. Bd. Rabbis. Author articles, sermons, film strips. Recorded: What Is A Jew? What Is Judaism? Home: 2879 Coleridge St Cleveland Heights OH 44118 Office: 27575 Shaker Blvd Cleveland OH 44124

EISENMAN, VICTORIA, educational administrator, nun Roman Catholic Church; b. Covington, Ky., Apr. 25, 1928; d. Francis Alfonse and Margaret Camille (Fusinger) E. B.A., Thomas More Coll., 1953; M.A., Catholic U., 1958; Ph.D., St. Louis U., 1962. Joined Order St. Benedict, Roman Catholic Church, 1946. Tchr. elem. schs. Diocese of Covington, Ky., 1948-58, 68-71, diocesan supr. elem. edn., 1971-76; tchr. Thomas More Coll., Edgewood, Ky., 1962-68; prin. St. Paul Sch., Florence, Ky., 1976—. Bd. dirs. Villa Madonna Acad., Covington, 1982-85. Mem. Nat. Cath. Edn. Assn.

EISNER, JANET MARGARET See *Who's Who in America,* 43rd edition.

EITRHEIM, NORMAN D., bishop, American Lutheran Church; b. Baltic, S.D., Jan. 14, 1929; s. Daniel T. and Selma (Thompson) E.; m. Clarice Yvonne Pederson, Aug. 23, 1952; children: Daniel, David, John, Marie. B.A., Augustana Coll., Sioux Falls, S.D., 1951; B.Th., Luther Theol. Sem., St. Paul, 1956. Ordained to ministry Am. Lutheran Ch., consecrated bishop, 1980. Pastor 1st English Luth. Ch., Tyler, Minn., 1956-63, St. Philips Luth. Ch., Fridley, Minn., 1963-76; asst. to pres. Luther Theol. Sem., St. Paul, 1976-80; bishop S.D. dist. Am. Luth. Ch., Sioux Falls, 1980—. Home: 1605 Cedar Ln Sioux Falls SD 57103 Office: Augustana College Sioux Falls SD 57197

EITTREIM, KINLEY OWEN, minister, American Lutheran Church; b. Decorah, Iowa, Sept. 29, 1932; s. Oliver Maurice and Mable Clarissa (Rohm) E.; m. Tucky Ann Neiswanger, Aug. 6, 1960; children: Susan Ann, Mark Owen. B.A., Luther Coll., 1959; B.D., Luther Theol. Sem., 1963, M.Div., 1972. Ordained to ministry Am. Lutheran Ch., 1963. Pastor Sarles/Hannah Luth. Parish, N.D., 1963-65, McVille (N.D.) Luth. Parish, 1965-69, Trinity Luth. Ch., Newman Grove, Nebr., 1969-72, Messiah Luth. Ch., Vestavia Hills, Ala., 1974—; exec. dir. Vestavia Counseling Ctr., Vestavia Hills; chaplain Naval Tng. Ctr., Orlando, Fla., summer, 1972; hosp. chaplain intern Winter Haven (Fla). Hosp., 1972-73; instr. Parish Edn. Inst., Epping, N.D., 1964. Bd. dirs. Mid-Nebr. Luth. Home for the Aged, Newman Grove, 1972—; mem. Dist. Com. on World Mission and Inter-Ch. Cooperation, 1975—, Elections Com. Am. Luth. Ch. Conv., Ohio dist., 1975; bd. dirs. Multiple Sclerosis Br. of Norfolk, Nebr., 1971-72; bd. dirs. Parents Anonymous, Birmingham, Ala., pres., 1976—. Mem. Clergy on Call for U. Hosp., Naval Res. Assn. Home: 1205 Lincoya Dr Vestavia Hills AL 35216 Office: 1360 Montgomery Hwy S Vestavia Hills AL

ELBAZ, MARCEL, religious organization executive, Jewish. Exec. dir. Can. Sephardi Fedn. Office: Can Sephardi Fedn 4755 Cote Ste Catherine St Montreal PQ H3W 1M1 Canada*

ELCOCK, JOHN BASIL, lay church worker, Independent Fundamental Churches of America; systems programmer; b. Georgetown, Guyana, Jan. 20, 1957; came to U.S., 1979, naturalized, 1986; s. Leon Basil and Doreen (Dookhoo) E. Diploma in systems Herzing Inst., Montreal, 1975; B.S., Concordia U., Montreal, Que., Can., 1979; diploma in Biblical studies, Word of Life Inst., N.Y.C., 1980. Cert. dir. Christian Edn., Assoc. Gospel Chs. Children's choir dir. People's Ch., Montreal, 1978-79, dir. Christian edn., 1979-80; tchr. Grace Chapel, Havertown, Pa., 1981—, camp dir., 1981—, elder, 1984—, interim youth pastor, 1983-84. Systems programmer Gen. Accident Ins., Phila., 1984—. Sr. patrol leader St. George's Council Boy Scouts Guyana, 1974. Mem. Aircraft Owners and Pilots Assn. Avocations: flying; sports; traveling; applied theology; music. Home: 557 S Orange St Media PA 19063 Office: Gen Accident Ins Co 414 Walnut St Philadelphia PA 19105

ELDER, GERALD CAUSEY, minister, Southern Baptist Convention; b. Atlanta, Sept. 21, 1956; s. James Charles and Jaqueline (Causey) E.; m. Phyllis Westbury, Mar. 10, 1979; 1 child, Philip Causey. A.A., Brewton Parker Coll., Mount Vernon, Ga., 1976; B.Music Edn., Samford U., Birmingham, Ala., 1979; M. Church Music, So. Bapt. Theol. Sem., Louisville, 1981. Ordained to ministry So. Bapt. Conv., 1982. Minister of music and youth Warsaw Bapt. Ch., Ky., 1980-82, 1st Bapt. Ch., Jesup, Ga., 1982—; dir. youth Altamaha Bapt. Assn., Jessup, 1983-84, dir. music, 1984—; asst. dir. Sons of Jubal Brass, Ga., 1983—; instrumental specialist Ga. Bapt. Music Dept., 1984—. Cons. Wayne County Theatrical Groups, Jesup, 1984—. Mem. So. Bapt. Ch. Music Conf., Ga. Bapt. Ch. Music Conf. Democrat. Lodge: Kiwanis. Avocations: photography; printing; electronics. Home: 138 Greenwood St Jesup GA 31545 Office: 1st Bapt Ch Brunswick at Cherry St Jesup GA 31545

ELFVIN, ROBERT ROGER, minister, Episcopal Church; b. Charleston, S.C., Jan. 25, 1945; s. Charles Donald and Gloria Audrey (Bell) E.; m. Karon Jean Kerber, Mar. 5, 1966; children: Stephen, David, Jared, John. B.A., Ohio U., 1966; M.Div., Berkeley-Yale Div. Sch., 1969. Ordained priest, 1970. Asst. to rector Christ Ch., Lima, Ohio, 1969-71; rector Trinity Ch., Findlay, Ohio, 1971-78, St. Luke's Ch., Des Moines, Iowa, 1978—; mem. Commn. on Ministry, Des Moines, 1981-84, Mission Bd., Diocese of Iowa, 1979-82. Religious rep. Child Abuse & Neglect Council, Des Moines, 1984—; care rev. bd. Convalescent Home for Children, Des Moines, 1984—, Covenant St. Michaels Roman Cath. and Trinity Episcopal, Findlay, Ohio, 1976; chmn. Ohio Council of Chs. task force on nat. farm worker ministry, 1978. Diocese of Iowa tuition grantee, 1984—. Home: 2816 Eula Des Moines IA 50322 Office: Saint Lukes Episcopal Ch 3424 Forest Des Moines IA 50311

ELI, JUDE RONALD, priest, education; Dominican Order, Roman Catholic Church; b. San Mateo, Calif., July 12, 1946; s. Albert Raymond and Mary Marie (Piedemonte) E. B.A. in Anthropology, San Francisco State Coll., 1970; B.A. in Philosophy, St. Albert's Coll., 1975; M.Div., St. Alberts Coll., 1977; M.A. in Theology, Grad. Theol. Union, 1981. Joined Dominican Order; ordained priest Roman Cath. Ch., 1976. Instr. Moreau High Sch., Hayward, 1970-72; instr. Daniel Murphy High Sch., N. Hollywood, Calif., 1972-73, Holy Rosary Coll., Mission San Jose, Calif., 1977-79; prof. Dominican Coll., San Rafael, Calif., 1979—; campus minister Dominican Coll., 1978—. Illustrator: Braille for A Storm of Loss by William Ruddy, 1978 (book of poetry). San Francisco grant sabbatical to Israel, 1983-84; Buck Found. grantee, 1983-84. Democrat. Lodge: KC (minister). Home: 2401 Ridge Rd Berkeley CA 94709 Office: Dominican Coll 1520 Grand Ave San Rafael CA 94901

ELIADE, MIRCEA, historian, author; b. Bucharest, Romania, Mar. 9, 1907; s. Gheorghe and Ioana (Stonenescu) E.; M.A., U. Bucharest, 1928, Ph.D., 1932; student U. Calcutta, 1928-31; m. Georgette C. Cottescu, Jan. 9, 1950. Assoc. prof. faculty letters Bucharest U., 1933-39; vis. prof. Ecole des Hautes Etudes, Sorbonne, Paris, 1946-48; Haskell lectr. U. Chgo., 1956, vis. prof. history religion, 1956-57, prof., 1958—, Sewell L. Avery distinguished service prof., 1963—; lectr. univs. Rome, Lund, Marburg, Munich, Frankfurt, Strasbourg, Padua; cultural attache Romanian legation, London, Eng., 1940-41; cultural conseiller Romanian legation, Lisbon, Portugal, 1941-44; dir. Zalmoxis, Revue des études religieuses, Paris, Bucharest, 1938-42; pres. Centre Roumain de Recherches, Paris, 1950-55. Mem. Am. Soc. for Study Religion (pres. 1963-67), Romanian Writers Soc. (Sec. 1937), Société Asiatique, Frobenius Institut. Author: Yoga, 1936; Techniques du Yoga, 1948; Traité d'Histoire des Religions, 1949; Le Chamanisme, 1951; Images et Symboles, 1952; The Myth of the Eternal Return, 1954; Forêt Interdite, 1954; Forgerons et Alchimistes, 1956; Patterns in Comparative Religions, 1958; Birth and Rebirth, 1958; Myths, Dreams and Mysteries, 1959; Images and Symbols, 1960; The Forge and the Crucible, 1962; Myth and Reality, 1963; Shamanism, 1964; The One and the Two, 1965, From Primitives to Zen, 1967; The Quest, 1969; Zalmoxis, the Vanishing God, 1972; Australian Religions, 1973; Occultizm, Witchcraft and Cultural Fashions, 1976; No Souvenirs, 1977; The Forbidden Forest, 1978; A History of Religious Ideas, Vol. 1, 1979. Address: Swift Hall U Chgo Div Sch Chicago IL 60637

ELKO, NICHOLAS THOMAS See *Who's Who in America,* 43rd edition.

ELLEDGE, CARL RAY, minister, Southern Baptist Convention; b. Ronda, N.C., Feb. 14, 1947; s. Travis J. and Minnie Louise (Dancy) E.; B.A., Wake Forest U., 1969; M.Div., Southeastern Baptist Theol. Sem., 1972; m. Sandra Joyce Gambill, June 17, 1967; children—Ronald Scott, Kimberly Rae. Ordained to ministry, 1973. Youth minister Boulevard Bapt. Ch., Raleigh, N.C., 1969-73; pastor Welcome Home Bapt. Ch., North Wilkesboro, N.C., 1973-79, Pleasant Grove Bapt. Ch., Ronda, N.C., 1979—; ch. tng. dir. Brushy Mountain Bapt. Assn.; pres. bd. dirs. Wilkes County Coop. Christian Ministry, 1976-77; vice moderator Elkin Bapt. Assn., 1983-84; mem. hist. com. N.C. Bapt. State Conv., 1979-81, chmn., 1981. Bd. dirs. Wilkes Day Center, 1976—, Clingman Med. Ctr., 1981-83, Clingman Community Ctr., 1983—; bd. dirs. Hospice of Wilkes, 1983—, pres., 1984-85. Home and Office: Route 2 Box 81 Ronda NC 28670

ELLENBOGEN, RAPHAEL, ch. ofcl.; b. N.Y.C., Dec. 9, 1924; s. Saul and Hilda Irene (Goldberg) E.; B.A., Yeshivah U., 1945; M.B.A., N.Y.U., 1947; m. Florence Lischinsky, Aug. 24, 1947; children—Marvin, Sanford. Exec. dir. Shaare Torah Community Center, Bklyn., 1947-48; exec. dir. br. YM and YWHA, Williamsburg, N.Y., 1948-54; exec. dir. Young Israel of Eastern Pkwy., Bklyn., 1954-55, Rego Park Jewish Center, Queens, N.Y., 1957-70, Temple Beth El, Cedarhurst, N.Y., 1970—. Active United Jewish Appeal, Israel Bonds. Mem. Assn. Synagogue Adminstrs. (pres. 1962), Nat. Assn. Synagogue Adminstrs., Am. Israel Numis. Assn., Am. Numis. Assn., Soc. Am. Magicians, Internat. Brotherhood Magicians, Jewish Communal Assn. Home: 105-55 Flatlands 2d St Brooklyn NY 11236 Office: Broadway and Locust Ave Cedarhurst NY 11516

ELLER, JOHN LESTER, minister, Assemblies of God; b. Tucapau, S.C., Mar. 20, 1939; s. Lester Nevels and Annie Mae (Williams) E.; diploma Berean Sch. Bible, Springfield, Mo., 1963; journalism student S W Mo. State U., Springfield, 1970; m. Bonnie Marie Ruble, July 6, 1963; children—Johna Marie, Bonnie Jean, John

David. Ordained to ministry, 1963; asso. evangelist, 1953-55; asso. pastor, then evangelist, 1956-63; pastor chs. in Ark. and Mo., 1963-70; dir. youth and edn. So. Mo. for Assemblies of God, 1970-73; pastor 1st Assemblies of God Ch., Milan, Tenn., 1973-77, Hannibal, Mo., 1977—. Presbyter, Milan sect. Assemblies of God, 1976-77; pres. Christian Sch., Milan Ministerial Assn., 1975-76. Instr., A R C; bd. dirs. Milan Community Camp; mem. Mayor Milan Com. Aging. Mem. Evang. Press Assn., Christian Camping Internat., Royal Rangers Frontiersmen (past pres.). Author, editor in field. Home: 1921 Missouri Ave Hannibal MO 63401 Office: PO Box 1106 Hannibal MO 63401

ELLER, JOHN THEODORE, minister, United Church of Christ; development and consulting company executive; b. Cleve., Nov. 14, 1942; s. Ralph T. and Ruth (Fortune) E.; m. Sandra Hamm, Sept. 12, 1964; children: Jonna Lynn, Laurel Elizabeth. B.A., Hiram Coll., 1964; postgrad. Ford Found. program U. Mass., 1968-69; M.Div., Andover Newton Theol. Sch., 1968. Ordained to ministry United Ch. of Christ, 1969. Asst. pastor Ch. of Christ, Millis, Mass., 1965-67, 1st Ch., Newton, Mass., 1967-70; council mem. Met. Boston Assn. United Ch. of Christ, 1969-73; trustee 1st Ch. Legacy Fund, 1981—; lectr. pub. adminstrn. Newton Theol. Sch., 1966-77. Exec. officer devel. and cons. firm, Boston, 1981—. Contbr. articles to profl. jours. Mem. state bd. Ams. for Democratic Action, 1970—, pres., 1977; editor Mass. Democrat, 1976-77; bd. dirs. Nat. Council State Housing Agys., Washington, 1980; bd. dirs. Newton Community Service Ctrs., 1975—, pres., 1979-82; bd. dirs. Newton Community Devel. Found., 1983—, pres.-elect, 1985. Recipient commendation Mass. Mental Health Assn., 1970, Mass. Dept. Youth Services, 1970; B. Fliegel Pub. Service award Nat. Assn. Social Workers, 1976; named One of 10 Outstanding Young Leaders, Boston Jaycees, 1978; award Mass. Housing Fin. Agy., 1980, HUD, 1980; Excellence award Nat. Morgan Mus., 1983. Home: 18 Albion St Newton Centre MA 02159 Office: Suite 3160 One Post Office Sq Boston MA 02109

ELLER, RAYMON ERNEST, minister, Ch. of the Brethren; b. Roanoke County, Va., Mar. 31, 1910; s. Christian Emory and Rebecca Martha (Henry) E.; A.B., Bridgewater Coll., 1937; B.D., Bethany Theol. Sem., 1938; postgrad. Gettysburg Theol. Sem., 1949; m. Anna Belle Whitmer, June 13, 1937; children—Rebecca Ann Eller Replogle, Stanley, Jerry, Rufus. Ordained to ministry, 1933, as elder, 1944; pastor chs. Danville, Va., 1938-40, Bassett, Va., 1940-44, Dundalk, Md., 1944-55, Richmond, Va., 1955-59, Madison Ave. Ch., York, Pa., 1959-63, Oakland Ch., Gettysburg, Ohio, 1963-69, First Ch., Wichita, Kans., 1969-71, First Ch., Akron, Ohio, 1971—. Mem. Akron Met. Interch. Ministries Bd., 1971—; vice chmn. Campus Ministry Commn., Akron, 1975—; mem. Eastern Md. dist. bd. Ch. of Brethren, 1948-54, chmn., 1953-54, mem. SE regional bd., 1949-56, chmn., 1953-56, mem. standing com. ann. conf., 1943-44; denominational rep. Balt. City Ch. Planning Commn., 1953-55, Wichita State U. Campus Ministry, 1967-69. Bd. dirs. No. dist. Ohio West View Manor Homes for Aging, 1972—, vice chmn., 1975—. Mem. Akron Ministerial Assn. (sec. 1974—), Denominational Arts and Crafts Assn., Bridgewater Coll. Alumni Assn. (founder, 1st pres. Richmond and Dayton). Host for tours Mid-East and Europe; author hymns: God of the People, Lord of Glory, God of Grace, Table Grace. Home: 358 Selden Ave Akron OH 44301 Office: 1812 Marigold Ave Akron OH 44301

ELLIOTT, JOHN FRANKLIN, minister, Independent Presbyterian Church; b. Neosho, Mo., June 11, 1915; s. William Marion and Charlotte Jeanette (Crump) E.; m. Winifred Margaret Key, July 6, 1939; children: Paul Timothy, Stephen Marion, Andrew Daniel. Student Maryville Coll., 1933-35; A.B., Austin Coll., 1937; postgrad., Louisville Presbyn. Sem., 1937-38, U. Tenn., 1938, Dallas Theol. Sem., 1939-40; B.D., Columbia Theol. Sem., 1942, M.Div., 1971; D.Litt (hon.), Internat. Acad., 1964. Ordained to ministry Independent Presbyterian Ch., 1942. Founder Emory Presbyn. Ch., Atlanta, 1941. Wildwood Presbyn. Ch., Salem, Va., 1950; pastor Wylam Presbyn. Ch., Birmingham, Ala., 1942-47, Salem Presbyn. Ch., 1947-51, Calvary Presbyn. Ch. Ind., Ft. Worth, 1952—; founder, pastor Grace Presbyn. Ch. Ind., Roanoke, Va., 1951-52; headmaster Colony Christian Sch., Ft. Worth, 1968-84, chancellor, 1984—. Bd. dirs., pres. Salem Nursing Assn., 1949; charter mem. Fellowship Ind. Evang. Chs., 1950—, pres. 1967, nat. sec., 1971; founder, dir. Ft. Worth Home Bible Classes, 1954—; dir. Scofield Bible Publs., Inc., bd. dirs. Ind. Presbyn. Home Missions, 1956-74; dist. committeeman Longhorn council Boy Scouts Am., Ft. Worth, 1960-66; bd. dirs. Union Gospel Mission, Ft. Worth, 1965-70, pres., 1968; mem. U.S. Coast Guard Aux., Ft. Worth, 1967—; pilot, chaplain, col. CAP, Ft. Worth, 1970—, chmn. nat. chaplain, com., 1979-80, chief of chaplains, 1980-82; ministerial adviser bd. dirs. Reformed Theol. Sem., Jackson, Miss., 1973-83; chaplain Tex. Constl. Conv., 1974; bd. dirs. Scripture Memory Fellowship Internat., 1979-83, Graham Bible Coll., 1966-74. Recipient Disting. Service award CAP, 1982, Order of the Arrow,

Boy Scouts Am., 1976. Fellow Philos. Soc. Gt. Britain (Victoria Inst.), Royal Geog. Soc., Huguenot Soc. of London. Clubs: Ft. Worth, Ridglea Country, Ft. Worth Boat. Lodge: Rotary. Home: 3980 Edgehill Rd Ft Worth TX 76116 Office: 4800 El Campo Ave Fort Worth TX 76107

ELLIOTT, RALPH HARRISON, minister, religion educator, American Baptist Church; b. Swansonville, Va., Mar. 2, 1925; s. Earl A. and Consuela (Arnn) E.; m. Virginia Case, Aug. 21, 1945; children: Virginia Lee, Beverly Ann Rose. B.A., Carson Newman Coll., 1949; B.D., So. Bapt. Theol. Sem., 1952, Th.S., 1956. Ordained to ministry Southern Baptist Convention, 1947, American Baptist Churches, 1962. Asst. prof. O.T., So. Bapt. Theol. Sem., Louisville, 1955-58; prof. O.T., Midwestern Bapt. Theol. Sem., Kansas City, 1958-62; sr. pastor Emmanuel Bapt. Ch., Albany, N.Y., 1964-72; prof. O.T., Crozer Theol. Sem., Chester, Pa., 1963-64, sr. pastor First Bapt. Ch., White Plains, N.Y., 1972-77, North Shore Bapt. Ch., Chgo., 1977—; lectr. in ecumenism Our Lady of Angels Sem., Glenmont, N.Y., 1965-72, Siena Coll., Albany, N.Y., 1965-72; pres. Council of Chs., Albany, White Plains, N.Y.; v.p. Ch. Fedn. Chgo.; vice chmn. commn. profl. leadership Bapt. World Alliance, 1981—. Author: The Message of Genesis, 1962; God's Doing - Man's Undoing, 1967; Reconciliation and the New Age, 1973; Church Growth That Counts, 1982. Contbr. articles to profl. jours. Served with U.S. Army, 1943-45, ETO. Mem. Soc. Profl. Ch. Leaders (pres. 1984). Home: 5415 N Francisco Chicago IL 60625 Office: North Shore Bapt Ch 5244 N Lakewood Chicago IL 60640

ELLIOTT, RICHARD HAROLD, minister, Lutheran Church in America; pharmaceutical assistant; b. Pitts., June 1, 1953; s. John Edward Elliott and Shirley Jean (Pfiester) Elliott Morgan; m. Jane Ruth Miley, June 11, 1977; 1 child, Jennifer. B.S. summa cum laude, Thiel Coll., 1975; M.Div., Luth. Sem., Gettysburg, Pa., 1979; S.T.M., Luth. Sem., Phila., 1984. Ordained to ministry Lutheran Ch., 1979. Student pastor Trinity Luth. Ch., Lansdale, Pa., 1977-79, assoc. pastor, 1979-81; pastor Luther Meml. Luth. Ch., Blacksburg, Va., 1981—; mem. 1st profl. degree com. Council for Luth. Theol. Edn. in the N.E., 1976-78; adv. mem. Luth. Campus Ministry Council, Va. Tech. U., 1981—; mem. youth com. Southeastern Pa. Synod, Luth. Ch. in Am., 1980-81; mem. lay leadership taskforce Va. Synod 1981-83, dean New River area Va. Synod, 1983—; mem. New River Area Mission Strategy Study Team, 1983—, New River Area Luth. Council, 1981—. Pharm. asst. Standlanders Pharmacy, Pitts., 1975-76. Mem. Alcoholism Task Force, Southeastern Pa., 1979-81; bd. dirs. Am. Cancer Soc., Phila., 1980. Bradley scholar Thiel Coll., 1973; Luth. Brotherhood scholar, 1975; Luth. Brotherhood grantee, 1980. Mem. Blacksburg Ministerial Assn. (pres. 1983-84); Montgomery County Hosp.'s Vol. Chaplains Orgn. Democrat. Home: 2800 Wellesley Ct Blacksburg VA 24060 Office: Luther Memorial Lutheran Ch 600 Prices Fork Rd Blacksburg VA 24060

ELLIOTT, WESLEY GARLAND, minister, Pentecostal Holiness Church; b. Danville, Va., Nov. 15, 1921; s. Claude Hutcherson and Gracie Mae (Whisnant) E.; m. Susan Foster, Dec. 20, 1942; children: David Wesley, Ronald Garland, Mark Timothy. Grad. Holmes Theol. Sem., 1943. Ordained to ministry Pentecostal Holiness Ch., 1943. Pastor various chs., N.C., Va., 1943-64, Maiden PEntecostal Holiness Ch., 1964—; regional teen talent dir. Youth Dept., Pentecostal Holiness Ch., 1974-75, mem. gen. youth bd., 1976; chmn. home and family life Western N.C. Conf., 1979-82, youth div., 1971-77, sec.-treas. youth dept., 1975; del. Worlds Conf., Jerusalem, 1961; pres. Ministerial Assn., Maiden, 1975; leader tour of Europe, Asia, Egypt, 1975; chaplain Sr. Citizens, Maiden, 1977—; aux. chaplain Catawba Meml. Hosp., Hickory, N.C., 1984. Chmn. Heart Fund, Maiden, 1973; pres. PTA, Hamptonville, N.C., 1956. Avocations: swimming; reading; travel; horseback riding. Home: 502 E Main St Maiden NC 28650 Office: Maiden Pentecostal Holiness Ch PO Box 647 Maiden NC 28650

ELLIS, F. PATRICK, religious educator, priest, Roman Catholic Church; b. Balt., Nov. 17, 1928; s. Harry James and Elizabeth Alida (Evert) E. A.B., Cath. U. Am., 1951; M.A., U. Pa., 1954, Ph.D., 1960; L.H.D. (hon.), Assumption Coll., 1982. Tchr., chmn. West Cath. High Sch., Phila., 1951-60; mem. dept. English, LaSalle Coll., Phila. 1960-62, dir. honors, 1964-69, dir. devel., 1969-76, pres., 1977—; prin. LaSalle High Sch., Miami, Fla., 1962-64; bd. dirs. Greater Phila. First Corp., 1984—; bd. dirs. Manhattan Coll., 1979—, St. Mary's Coll., Winona, Minn., 1977—, St. John's Coll. High Sch., 1982—. Trustee, Afro-Am. Hist. & Cultural Mus., Phila., 1981-84; chmn. Camp William Penn, Phila., 1981-82, Campus Blvd. Corp., Phila., 1977—; bd. dirs. Roman Cath. Diocesan Council Mgrs., Phila., 1980—; former trustee Community Leadership Seminars, Better Bus. Bur.; pres. James A. Finegan Fellowship Found.; bd. dirs. Urban Affairs Partnership, 1980—; mem. Commn. on 21st Century and Econ. Roundtable, Phila. Mem. Pa. Assn. Colls. and Univs.

(sec., treas.), Am. Council on Edn. (dir.), Assn. Cath. Colls. and U. (chmn.), Phi Beta Kappa. Democrat. Club: Friends of Independence Hall, Union League. Address: LaSalle Univ 20th St and Olney Ave Philadelphia PA 19141

ELLIS, HERMAN JEFFERSON, minister, Southern Baptist Convention; b. Smithville, Tenn., May 27, 1919; s. Claude Jefferson and Nealie Jane (Malone) E.; A.B., Carson-Newman Coll., 1949; M.Div., So. Bapt. Theol. Sem., 1959; m. Louise Johnson, Aug. 8, 1947; children—John Leslie, David Neal, Sidney Martin (dec.). Ordained to ministry, 1949; pastor First Bapt. Ch., Norris, Tenn., 1949-52, North Springfield (Tenn.) Bapt. Ch., 1952-55, Forks of Elkhorn Bapt. Ch., Midway, Ky., 1956-59, Joelton (Tenn.) Bapt. Ch., 1959-61, Trace Creek Bapt. Ch., New Johnsonville, Tenn., 1962-67, First Bapt. Ch., Lafayette, Tenn., 1967-70, Rutledge (Tenn.) Bapt. Ch., 1970-81; ednl. dir. Bell Ave Bapt. Ch., Knoxville, Tenn., 1981-83, McCalla Ave Bapt. Ch., Knoxville, 1983-84; pastor Thorn Grove Bapt. Ch., Strawberry Plains, Tenn., 1984—. Chmn. Macon County chpt. ARC, 1968-69; Grainger County rep. E. Tenn. Council on Aging, 1975. Bd. dirs. Grainger County Housing Devel. Mem. So. Bapt., E. Tenn. hist. assns., Robertson, Truett, Grainger assns., Nashville Bapt. Assn. Home and Office: 9705 Thorn Grove Pike Strawberry Plains TN 37871

ELLIS, JAMES WELBORN, minister, Southern Baptist Convention; b. Covington County, Ala., July 22, 1926; s. Edward Welborn and Alma (Langford) E.; m. Betty Gentry Ellis, Oct. 28, 1958; children: James Welborn, Jr., Elizabeth Sue. B.S., Auburn U., 1948; B.D., Southern Bapt. Theol. Seminary, 1954, M. Theology, 1956; D. Ministry, Union Theol. Seminary Virginia, 1978. Ordained to ministry Bapt. Ch., 1949. Assoc. pastor Univ. Heights Bapt. Ch., Springfield, Mo., 1957-59; pastor First Bapt. Ch., Livingston, Ala., 1959-69, First Bapt. Ch., Ashland, Va., 1969—. Asst. prof. religion Livingston U., Ala., 1964-69; state advisor Bapt. Youth Fellowship Mo., Springfield, 1958-59; pres. Sumter County Ministerial Alliance, Livingston, 1961-62, 1964-65; moderator Bigbee Bapt. Assn., Livingston, 1962-63, 1967-68; mem. Ala. Bapt. State Exec. Bd., 1965; pres. Dover Bapt. Pastor's Conf., 1973-74, Richmond Area Bapt. Pastor's Conf., 1975-76; mem. Virginia Bapt. Gen. Bd., 1974-78; mem. exec. com. Va. Bapt. Gen. Bd., 1978; chmn. study com. Adult Mental Retardation Va. for Va. Bapt. Gen. Bd., 1977-78; moderator Dover Bapt. Assn., 1980-82; mem. Ministers Adv. Com., Averett Coll., Danville, Va., 1981-85. Pres. Internat. Relations Club, Springfield, Mo., 1958-59; bd. dirs. West Ala. Mental Health Assn., 1967-69, Hanover County Mental Health Assn., 1972-73; bd. trustees Alcohol-Narcotics Edn. Council Va., 1973-75, The Religious Herald, Richmond, 1985—. Mem. Ashland Clergy Assn., Richmond Area Bapt. Pastors Conf., Dover Bapt. Pastor's Conf., Pi Tau Chi. Home: 110 Stebbins St Ashland VA 23005 Office: First Bapt Ch 800 Thompson St Ashland VA 23005

ELLIS, JOHN LUCIAN, minister, American Baptist Churches in U.S.A.; flight instr.; b. Memphis, Sept. 22, 1935; s. Ernest Leander and Marie LaBelle (Cannon) E.; m. Phyllis Elaine Chaney, Aug. 10, 1957; children: Ann Stone, John B., Nancy L. B.A., U. Redlands, 1957; M.Div., Am. Bapt. Sem. 1961. Ordained to ministry American Baptist Churches in the U.S.A., 1961. Dir. youth First Bapt. Ch., Livermore, Calif., 1958-60; pastor First Bapt. Ch., Huron, Calif., 1961-64, First Bapt. Ch., Exeter, Calif., 1964-70, Mayhew Bapt. Ch., Sacramento, Calif., 1970-81, Thornton Avenue Bapt. Ch., Fremont, Calif., 1981—; bd. mgr. Am. Bapt. Chs./West, 1983—, v.p. ministers council, 1983—, chmn. placement rev. com., 1981-84; pres. Interfaith Service Bur., Sacramento, 1977. Flight instr. Calif. Airways, Hayward, Calif. 1982—. Capt., chaplain CAP, Sunnyvale, Calif., 1975-84. Recipient Outstanding Leadership award Ch. Service Bur., Sacramento, 1978; named Outstanding Sr. Mem., GAP Squadron, Mather AFB, Calif., 1976. Mem. Am. Bapt. Ministers Council. Republican. Home: 34566 Colville Pl Fremont CA 94536 Office: Thornton Ave Baptist Ch 4500 Thornton Ave Fremont CA 94536

ELLIS, JOHN TRACY See Who's Who in America, 43rd edition.

ELLWANGER, JOHN PAUL, minister, Lutheran Church-Missouri Synod; b. St. Louis, Nov. 7, 1931; s. Walter Henry and Jessie Lorraine (Hanger) E.; m. Jane Alice Taylor, Jan. 15, 1967; children: Jennifer, Jeremy. B.A., Concordia Sem., St. Louis, 1953, M.Div., 1956. Ordained to ministry Luth. Ch., 1956. Pastor, Luth. Ch. of Redeemer, Melbourne, Fla., 1956-62, Columbus, Ga., 1962-70; pastor Hope Luth. Ch., Austin, Tex., 1970—; sec. Fla.-Ga. Dist., Luth. Ch.-Mo. Synod, Orlando, Fla., 1965-70, counselor Austin cir., 1971-73; bd. regents Concordia Coll., Austin, 1973-77; mem. Social Ministry Com., Tex. Dist. Luth. Ch.-Mo. Synod, 1978—. Author: (children's devotions) My Devotions, 1964. Editor mag. Fla.-Ga. edit. Luth. Witness,

1960-65. Pres. Muscogee County Am. Cancer Soc., Columbus, Ga., 1965; vice chmn. Mayor's Com. on Fluoridation, Columbus, 1966-67; mem. Human Relations Bd., Columbus, 1968-70. Democrat. Lodge: Kiwanis (chpt. pres. 1985-86). Home: 7406 Barcelona Dr Austin TX 78752 Office: Hope Luth Ch 6414 N Hampton Dr Austin TX 78723

ELLWOOD, ROBERT SCOTT, JR., educator; b. Normal, Ill. July 17, 1933; s. Robert Scott and Knola Lorraine (Shanks) E.; B.A., U. Colo., 1954; M.Div., Berkeley Div. Sch., 1957; M.A., U. Chgo., 1965, Ph.D., 1967; m. Gracia Fay Bouwman, Aug. 28, 1965; 1 son, Richard. Pastor Episcopal ch., Central City, Nebr., 1957-60; chaplain USNR, 1961-62; asst. prof. religion U. So. Calif., 1967-71, assoc. prof., 1971-75, prof., 1975—. Mem. Am. Acad. Religion, Assn. Asian Studies, Religious Soc. of Friends. Author: Religious and Spiritual Groups in Modern America, 1973; One Way: The Jesus Movement and Its Meaning, 1973; The Feast of Kingship, 1973; The Eagle and the Rising Sun, 1974; Many Peoples, Many Faiths, 1976; Words of the World's Religions, 1977; Alternative Altars, 1979; Introducing Religion, 1983; An Introduction to Japanese Civilization, 1980; Tenrikyo: A Pilgrimage Faith, 1982.

ELMORE, MICHAEL HIRAM, minister, Christian Church (Disciples of Christ); b. Cliffside, N.C., June 21, 1943; s. Henry Hiram and Lois Virginia (Jackson) E.; m. Phyllis Annette Hughes, May 31, 1964; children: Michele Annette, Jonathan Scott. A.A., Gardner-Webb Coll., 1963; B.A., Limestone Coll., 1965; M.Div., So. Bapt. Sem., Louisville, 1969; postgrad. Lexington Sem., 1982—. Ordained to ministry So. Bapt. Conv., 1969, Christian Ch., 1982. Student minister Bewleyville Bapt. Ch., Ky., 1967-69; minister Healing Springs Bapt. Ch., Va., 1969-72; clin. pastoral edn. Va. Bapt. and N.C. Bapt. Hosp., 1972-74; minister First Bapt. Ch., Dobson, N.C., 1974-81, First Christian Ch., Fayetteville, N.C., 1982—; instr. religion Surry Community Coll., Dobson, N.C., 1974-81; chmn. Christian Life Com., Mt. Airy, N.C., 1976-81; tng. class dir. Contact Tele-Ministry, Fayetteville, N.C., 1984—; chmn. Shalom Congregation Program, N.C. Disciple Chs., 1984—. Mem. Dobson Community Coll., N.C., 1975-81; mem. Surry County Arts Council, Mt. Airy, N.C. 1980-81; mem., local pres. Assn. Couples for Marriage Enrichment, Surry County, 1976-81; v.p. Dobson Elem. Sch. P.T.A., Dobson, N.C., 1977-78. Mem. The Alban Inst. Democrat. Lodge: Lions. Home: 2629 Elmhurst Dr Fayetteville NC 28304

ELSON, EDWARD LEE ROY, minister, United Presbyn. Ch. in U.S.A.; b. Monongahela, Pa., Dec. 23, 1906; s. Leroy and Pearl (Edie) E.; A.B., Asbury Coll., 1928; Th.M., U. So. Calif., 1931; m. Helen Chittick, Feb. 8, 1937; children—Eleanor Elson Heginbotham, Beverly Elson Gray, Mary Faith Elson MacRae, David Edward. Ordained to ministry, 1930; asst. minister First Presbyn. Ch., Santa Monica, Calif., 1929-31; minister First Presbyn. Ch., LaJolla, Calif., 1931-41; chaplain U.S. Army, ETO, 1941-46; minister Nat. Presbyn. Ch., Washington, 1946-73, minister emeritus, 1973—; chaplain U.S. Senate, 1969—; moderator Presbytery of Los Angeles, 1938, Presbytery of Washington, 1966; Western regional dir. Presbyn. Post War Fund, 1946; nat. chaplain DAV, 1950-51; chaplain Mil. Order World Wars, Inc., 1952—; Presbyn. rep. World Alliance Presbyn. and Reformed Chs.; commr. Gen. Assembly, United Presbyn. Ch. in U.S.A., six times. Mem. Presbyn. Council for Chaplains and Mil. Personnel, 1947-57; pres. Washington Fedn. Chs., 1952-54, Mil. Chaplains Assn., 1957-59; bd. dirs. Maryville Coll. (Tenn.), 1948-71; bd. dirs. Wilson Coll. (Pa.), 1953-73, pres. bd., 1961-72; bd. dirs. Greenbrier Coll. (W.Va.). Chmn. nat. council, v.p. Am. Friends of Middle East, 1950-73; chmn. clergy adv. council NAM, 1954-66; mem. adv. com. on arts John F. Kennedy Center for Performing Arts, 1959—; mem. nat. adv. council Welfare of Blind, 1961; mem. U.S. Mission to observe Vietnamese elections, 1967; mem. adv. council Center for Study of Presidency, 1975—; bd. dirs. Am. Colony Charities Assn., Jerusalem, 1950-74, pres., 1970; bd. dirs. Religious Heritage of Am., 1950—, v.p., 1965—; bd. dirs. Freedoms Found. at Valley Forge, 1950—, Am. Near East Relief Assn., Damavand Coll., Tehran, Iran, Gustave Weigel Soc. Decorated Legion of Merit, Bronze Star, Army Commendation medal, Croix de Guerre avec palme, medal of Freedom, Arms of City of Colmar (France), comdr. Order medal of merit (Lebanese), Silver Star (Kingdom of Jordan); recipient Clergy Churchman of Year award Religious Heritage of Am., 1954, Freedoms Found. awards, 1951-73, Distinguished Citizen of Year award City of Los Angeles, 1975; named hon. citizen Dallas, Charlotte (N.C.), Alliance (Ohio), Knoxville (Tenn.); designated Edward L.R. Elson Monumental Wall at Nat. Presbyn. Ch., 1971. Mem. English-Speaking Union, Assn. U.S. Army, Newcomen Soc. N.Am., Internat. Platform Assn., Scottish Am. Heritage, U.S. Capitol Hist. Soc., Pa. State Soc., Am. Soc. Ch. History, Ch. Service Soc., Acad. Religion and Mental Health, Theta Sigma, Phi Chi Phi. Author: One Moment with God, 1951; America's Spiritaul Recovery, 1954; And Still He Speaks, 1960; The Inevitable Encounter, 1962; 4 vols. prayers offered in 91st-94th Congresses. Home: 4000 Cathedral Ave NW Washington DC 20016 Office: 220 Russell Senate Office Bldg Washington DC 20510

EMERY, OREN DALE, minister, ch. ofcl., Wesleyan Ch.; b. Indpls., May 30, 1927; s. Oren and Jean Roberta (Dodd) E.; B.Religion, Marion Coll./Ind. U., 1950; postgrad. No. Baptist Theol. Sem., 1954-56; D.D., Pa. Wesleyan Coll., 1969; m. Ruthanne Adams, Aug. 5, 1946; children—Steven, Paul, Deborah (Mrs. L. Andrew Weaver), David, Timothy, Elizabeth. Ordained to ministry, 1949; pastor, Marion, Ind., 1947-49, Michigantown, Ind., 1949-50, Terre Haute, Ind., 1950-52, Hillsboro, Wis., 1952-54, Milw., 1954-57, Pontiac, Mich., 1957-58; dist. supt. Wis. Dist., 1951-59, Ariz. Dist., 1959-62; gen. sec. Sunday schs. and youth Wesleyan Ch., Marion, 1962-68, gen. sec. youth, 1968-70, gen. sec. ch. edn., 1972—; exec. dir. Christian Holiness Assn., 1970-72. Author: Concepts to Grow By, 1976; Effective Ministry through Multiple Staff, 1976; also ednl. articles. Home: 1202 Lincolnshire Blvd Marion IN 46952 Office: Box 2000 Marion IN 46952

EMLER, DONALD GILBERT, minister, Christian education educator, United Methodist Church; b. Kansas City, Mo., June 1, 1939; s. Earl Cecil and Esther Margaret (Brier) E.; m. Lenore Suzanne Plummer, Aug. 9, 1968; children: Matthew Kirk, David Earl. B.A. in History and Govt., U. Mo.-Kansas City, 1960; M.Div., Garrett-Evang. Theol. Sem., 1963; M.S.Ed., Ind. U., 1972, Ed.D. in Adult Edn., 1973. Ordained to ministry United Meth. Ch., 1963. Minister edn. Broadway United Meth. Ch., Kansas City, 1963-66, Platte Woods United Meth. Ch., Kansas City, 1968-70, St. John's United Meth. Ch., Kansas City, 1973-76; instr. Christian edn., chaplain Central Meth. Coll., Fayette, Mo., 1966-68; minister Gosport/Quincy United Meth. Ch., Ind., 1970-73; assoc. prof. Christian edn., chmn. dept. religion Centenary Coll., Shreveport, La., 1976—; mem. adv. bd. Centenary Sch. Ch. Careers, 1976; chmn. La. Bd. Diaconal Ministry, 1978—, Shreveport Dist. Council on Ministries, 1981—, Ecumenical Lecture Series, Shreveport, 1984—; dir. Inter-Faith Com., Shreveport, 1981, NCCJ, Shreveport, 1984; dir., loan officer La. Meth. Conf. Credit Union, Shreveport, 1980. Author: Program Planning with Adults, 1976; Understanding and Using the Bible in Teaching, 1979; author, TV presenter Church School Series. Contbr. articles to religious publs. Mem. Christian Educators Fellowship, Religious Edn. Assn., United Meth. Assn. Profs. Christian Edn. (sec.-treas. 1983-84), Assn. Profs. and Researchers in Religious Edn., Nat. Council on Religion and Pub. Edn., Omicron Delta Kappa. Home: 136 Adger St Shreveport LA 71105 Office: Centenary Coll La PO Box 41188 Shreveport LA 71134

ENDERLE, MARVIN FRANK, priest, Roman Catholic Ch.; b. Beaumont, Tex., Nov. 8, 1925; s. Martin F. and Pauline Monica (Matzke) E.; B.A. in Philosophy, St. Mary's U., Tex., 1957; M.A. in Counseling Psychology, U. Notre Dame, 1968. Ordained priest Roman Catholic Ch., 1961, named domestic prelate, 1976; asst. pastor Holy Name Ch., Houston, Tex., 1961, St. Mary's Ch., Galveston, Tex., 1961; asst. pastor St. Anthony's Cathedral, Beaumont, Tex., 1964, 1969-72, pastor, 1972—; asst. pastor St. Mary's Ch., Texas City, 1961; head religious edn. dept. Kelly High Sch., Beaumont, Tex., 1963; diocesan dir. of vocations, Beaumont, 1966-71; supt. St. Anthony's Sch., Beaumont, 1972—; chaplain John Sealy Hosp., Galveston, 1961, Cath. Daus. Am. Recipient Padre of Youth award, 1965, Pontifical award for Ecclesiastical Vocations, 1974. Mem. Nat. Council of Vocation Dirs., Serra Internat., Beaumont Mental Health Assn., Nat. Cath. Guidance Assn., Southwest Liturgical Conf., Am. Personnel and Guidance Assn., Nat. Guidance and Counseling Assn., Am. Legion, Diocesan Pastoral Council. Home: 753 Archie St Beaumont TX 77701 Office: POB 3309 Beaumont TX 77704

ENDRUSCHAT, ROBERT WILLIAM, religious publisher, minister, Lutheran Church in America; b. Buffalo, Apr. 15, 1930; s. William and Helen (Unverzagt) E.; m. M. Louise Dellwig, May 17, 1952; children: Robert Louis, John Stephen. B.A., Wittenberg U., 1950; postgrad. U. Pa., 1950-51; M.Div., Luth. Sem., Phila., 1953. Ordained to ministry Luth. Ch. in Am., 1953. Pastor Trinity Luth. Ch., New Haven, 1953-68; editor Fortress Press Bd. Publs., Luth. Ch. Am., Phila., 1968-70, asst. gen. mgr. Bd. Publs., 1970-79, pres., gen. mgr., 1980—; mem. cabinet of execs. Luth. Ch. in Am., N.Y.C., 1980—. Mem. Protestant Ch. Pubs. Assn. (bd. dirs. 1972—), Coop. Pubs. Assn. (bd. dirs. 1972—). Republican. Club: Union League (Phila.). Lodge: Rotary (pres.)(New Haven). Home: 1439 Stephen Rd Meadowbrook PA 19046 Office: Bd Publs Luth Ch in Am 2900 Queen Ln Philadelphia PA 19129

ENGEBRETSON, MILTON BENJAMIN, minister, ch. exec., Evang. Covenant Ch. Am.; b. Grand Forks, N.D., Dec. 29, 1920; s. Hans Emil and Anna Sophie (Huss) E.; B.A., U. Wash., 1950; grad. North Park Theol. Sem., Chgo., 1954; D.D., Seattle Pacific Coll., 1967, North Park Coll., 1975; m. Esther Rhoda Hollenbeck, Dec. 12, 1945; children—Jon Philip, Donn Norman. Ordained to ministry, 1956; pastor Stotler Mission Covenant Ch., Osage City, Kans., 1951-52, Mission Covenant Ch. Mankato, Minn., 1954-57, Elim Covenant Ch., Mpls., 1957-62; exec. sec. Evang. Covenant Ch. Am., 1962-67, pres., 1967—. Conf. chmn. meeting U.S. Churchmen, 1972, U.S. Ch. Leaders, 1972-79; pres. Internat. Fedn. Free Evang. Chs., 1979. Decorated comdr. Royal Order Polar Star (Sweden). Office: 5101 N Francisco Ave Chicago IL 60625

ENGEL, RONALD PAUL, minister, Luth. Ch.-Mo. Synod; b. Indpls., Aug. 30, 1944; s. Henry Frank and Mildred Geraldine (Kasting) E.; A.A., Concordia Jr. Coll., 1964; B.A., Concordia Sr. Coll., 1966; M.Div., Concordia Sem., 1970; m. Jan Arlene Scheel, Aug. 17, 1968; children—Paul, Rebecca. Ordained to ministry, 1972; asso. pastor Emmaus Luth. Ch., Denver, 1972—. Chmn. youth ministry com. Colo. dist. Luth. Ch.-Mo. Synod, 1974—. Home: 3125 Stuart St Denver CO 80212 Office: 3268 West 32d St Denver CO 80211

ENGLAND, JOHN MELVIN, minister, Presbyterian Church U.S.; lawyer; b. Atlanta, June 29, 1932; s. John and Frances (Brown) E.; LL.B., U. Ga., 1956, J.D., 1969; B.D., Columbia Theol. Sem., 1964; m. Jane Cantrell, Aug. 2, 1953; children: Kathryn, Janette, John, Kenneth, James, Samuel. Ordained to ministry U.P. Ch. U.S.A., 1964; pastor Mullins (S.C.) Presbyn. Ch., 1964-67; evangelist Presbyn. Ch. U.S., 1967—; evangelist Christian Businessmen's Coms. U.S.A., Atlanta, 1967—, chmn., 1971-73, 77—. Admitted to Ga. bar, 1959; asst. dist. atty. Fulton County, Atlanta, 1967-75; sole practice law, Atlanta, 1975; sr. ptnr. firm England & Weller, Atlanta, 1976—. Bd. dirs. Met. Atlanta Council on Alcohol and Drugs, 1971-73. Mem. ABA, Atlanta Bar Assn., State Bar Ga. Home: 217 Skyland Dr Roswell GA 30075 Office: 1220 Atlanta Center Ltd 250 Piedmont Ave NE Atlanta GA 30308

ENGLE, CHARLES E., minister, Brethren in Christ Ch.; b. Junction City, Kans., Apr. 1, 1896; s. Benjamin Franklin and Susan (Shelley) E.; A.B., Upland Coll.; children—Ardys Engle Thuma, Mary Lou Engle Bert, Phyllis Jeanne Engle Saltzman. Ordained to ministry, 1926; pastor Mooretown Ch., Sandusky, Mich., 1926-28; medical worker India, 1929-33; evangelist Bays Sch. and Hostel, 1933-35, acting mission supt., 1935-37; village evangelist and missionary, India, 1939-62; chaplains asst. State Sch. for Boys, Chino, Calif., 1965-70. Working to establish new church congregations, 1976—. Mem. Christian Bus. Mens Com., Pomona Valley Nat. Assn. of Evangelism. Home: 355 W Arrow Hwy Upland CA 91786

ENGLISH, BARNEY WILLIAM, minister, Pentecostal Free Will Baptist Church; b. Wallace, N.C., Aug. 22, 1918; s. Thomas Smith and Laura (Bland) E.; m. June 3, 1938; children: Elizabeth, William James. A.B., So. Methodist U., 1940; M.S., Union Theol. Sem., Richmond, Va., 1953, Th.B., 1954, Th.M., 1955; Ph.D., Temple U., Phila., 1956, Th.D., Evang. Sem., Goldsboro, N.C., 1959; D.D. (hon.), Carter Coll., Goldsboro, 1960; Mus.D. (hon.), Evang. Sem., 1964. Ordained to ministry Pentecostal Free Will Bapt. Ch., 1942. Gen. sec. Free Will Bapt. Ch., Wilmington, N.C., 1937-55; pastor Free Will Bapt. Ch., Wilmington, 1940-59, Pentecostal Free Will Bapt. Ch., Dunn, N.C., 1959—; v.p. Carter Coll., Goldsboro, 1952—; lectr. on music and psychology; v.p. Evang. Sem., Goldsboro, 1954—, vice chmn. regents, 1954—. Author: Play Piano 10 Lessons, 1948; Music Appreciation, 1976. Contbr. articles on religion, psychology, psychology and econs. to profl. publs. Composer over 100 songs. Mem. pres. council Lee Coll., Cleve., 1976—. Mem. Internat. Speakers Platform. Republican. Lodge: Masons. Home: 207 W Carroll St Magnolia NC 28453 Office: 202 W Carroll St Magnolia NC 28453

ENGLISH, JAMES MILES, priest, Roman Catholic Ch.; b. Phila., Oct. 11, 1935; s. Thomas Joseph and Helen Rose (Gilmore) E.; A.B., Fordham U., 1959, M.A. in Theology, 1962, Ph.L., 1960; M.Div., Woodstock Coll., 1967. Ordained priest, 1966; faculty Loyola High Sch., Jamshedpur, India, 1960-63; asst. pastor Holy Trinity Ch., Georgetown, 1968-75; pastor Holy Trinity Ch., Washington, 1975—; prin. Gonzaga Coll. High Sch., 1971-73. Home and office: 3514 O St NW Washington DC 20007

ENGSTRAND, FLORENCE SIGRID, minister, Assemblies of God; b. Wilton, N.D., Nov. 6, 1916; d. Thure A. and Anges Marie (Asplund) Johnson; m. Arnold N. Engstrand, May 29, 1942; children—Gloria Carolee, Donna Jean, Agnes Marie (dec.), Arnold N. Ordained to ministry, 1944; evangelist, 1934-36; pastor chs., N.D., 1942-54; pastor Holy Spirit Fellowship, Steele, N.D., 1977—. Women's missionary pres. N.D. Assemblies of God, 1971-76; tchr. Bible study, Bismarck, N.D., 1971—. Program chmn. Richholt Sch.

PTA, Bismarck, 1955. Contbr. articles to denominational publs. Home and office: 812 19th St N Bismarck ND 58501

ENGSTROM, THEODORE WILHELM, lay church worker; b. Cleve., Mar. 1, 1916; s. David W. and Ellen L. (Olson) E.; A.B., Taylor U., 1938, L.H.D., 1955; LL.H., John Brown U., 1984; Litt.D., Seattle Pacific U., 1985; m. Dorothy E. Weaver, Nov. 3, 1939; children: Gordon, Donald, Jo Ann. Pres. Youth for Christ, Internat., Wheaton, Ill., 1957-63; chmn. Lake Av. Congl. Ch., Pasadena, Calif., 1972—. Pres. v.p. World Vision, Internat., Monrovia, Calif., 1963—. Trustee Taylor U., Upland, Ind., African Enterprise, Pasadena, Azusa Pacific U., Calif. Mem. Nat. Assn. Evangelicals, Am. Mgmt. Assn. Author: Managing Your Time, 1970; The Making of a Christian Leader, 1976; Strategy for Living, 1976; The Pursuit of Excellence, 1980; Your Gift of Administration, 1983; The Fine Art of Friendship, 1985. Office: 919 W Huntington Dr Monrovia CA 91016

ENSLEY, MILTON, JR., minister, United Presbyn. Ch. in U.S.A.; b. Colfax, Wash., July 6, 1925; s. Milton and Merle (Arresmith) E.; B.A., Whitworth Coll., 1957; postgrad. Asbury Theol. Sem., 1957-58, Pacific Sch. Religion, 1958-59; B.D., Golden Gate Bapt. Theol. Sem., 1961; m. Shirley J. Metcalf, Dec. 9, 1948; children—Myra Gwen Ensley Taylor, Bruce Milton, Paul Keith, Timothy John, David Earl. Ordained to ministry, 1962; founding pastor First So. Bapt. Ch., Camarillo, Calif., 1961-63; asst. pastor First Presbyn. Ch., Fillmore, Calif., 1964-66; pastor Queen Anne United Presbyn. Ch., Seattle, 1966-71, Mt. View Presbyn. Ch., Seattle, 1971-76, West Vale Presbyn. Ch., Salt Lake City, 1976—; chaplain coordinator Burien Gen. Hosp., mem. bd. govs., 1974-76; chapel speaker Kenney Home, Exeter House, Kingston Village. Mem. Queen Anne adv. bd. Seattle Park Dept., 1969-71; bd. dirs. White Center C. of C., 1972-76. Mem. White Center, South Suburban ministerial assns., Seattle Assn. Evangelicals, Queen Anne Ecumenical Parish. Mem. Whitworth Coll. study tour to Europe, 1966; sponsor, host Holy Land Tour, 1973. Home: 3610 S 4400 West Salt Lake City UT 84120 Office: West Vale Presbyn Ch Salt Lake City UT

ENSTROM, WALTER GORDON ANDREW, minister, Evangelical Ch.; b. Chgo., Oct. 15, 1931; s. Walter August and Edla Viola Linnea (Carlson) E.; B.S., U. Ill., 1952; M.S. in Agronomy, U. Minn., 1953; M.Div. magna cum laude, North Park Theol. Sem., 1961; m. Helen Marie Fahning, June 29, 1957; children: Karen, Mark, Jon Erick. Ordained to ministry, 1962; pastor Evang. Covenant Ch., Savonburg, Kans., 1957-59, Evang. United Brethren Ch., Kimball, Kans., 1959, Evang. Covenant Chs., New Richland, Minn., 1961-66, Lanyon, Iowa, 1966-67, United Presbyn. Ch., Livermore, Iowa, 1968, United Meth. Ch., Danbury, Iowa, 1968-78, United Ch. of Christ, Oto, Iowa, 1969-78, St. John Evang. Ch., 1978—; Conf. officer, Bible Camp work, evangelism clinics; mem. Dist. Youth Bd., Assn. nominating com. Recipient Scholarship Key, U. Ill., 1952. Mem. Alpha Zeta, Gamma Sigma Delta. Contbr. articles to religious publs. Home: Hornick IA 51026

ENYART, JOSEPH ALLEN, minister, Soc. of Friends; b. LaPaz, Bolivia, Apr. 15, 1939; s. Paul Cleophas and Mary Huldah (Barnard) E.; diploma Union Bible Sem., 1961; m. DeLoris Ann Thomas, June 17, 1961; 1 son, Mark Allen. Ordained to ministry Soc. of Friends, 1961; pastor, Kempton, Ind., 1961-62, Fishers, Ind., 1962, Niles, Mich., 1963-65, Terre Haute, Ind., 1965-75, Westfield, Ind., 1975—; bd. dirs. Union Bible Sem., Westfield, Ind., 1977—. Supt. fgn. missions Central Yearly Meeting of Friends, 1970—, mem. exec. com., 1969—; pres. Vigo County Youth for Holiness, 1967-75; treas. Vigo County Union Holiness Assn., 1965-75. Parts mgr. Sears Roebuck & Co., 1965-75. Home: POB 542 Westfield IN 46074 Office: 535 S Union St Westfield IN 46074

EPP, ELDON JAY, educator; b. Mountain Lake, Minn., Nov. 1, 1930; s. Jacob Jay and Louise (Kintzi) E.; A.B. magna cum laude, Wheaton Coll., 1952; B.D. magna cum laude, Fuller Theol. Sem., 1955; S.T.M., Harvard, 1956, Ph.D., 1961; m. ElDoris Balzer, June 13, 1951; children—Gregory Thomas, Jennifer Elizabeth. Spl. research asst. Princeton Theol. Sem., 1961-62; asst. prof. religion U. So. Calif., 1962-65, asso. prof., 1965-67, asso. prof. classics, 1966-68; asso. prof. religion Case Western Res. U., 1968-71, prof. religion, Harkness prof. bibl. lit., 1971—, dean humanities and social scis., 1977—. Bd. mgrs. St. Paul's Cathedral (Episcopal), Los Angeles, 1964-68, clk., 1967-68. Mem. Am. exec. com. Internat. Greek New Testament Project, 1968—. Recipient Christian Research Found. award, 1960-61; Rockefeller doctoral fellow, 1959-60; Guggenheim fellow, 1974-75. Mem. Inst. Antiquity and Christianity (corr.), Am. Acad. Religion (pres. Pacific Coast sect. 1965-66), Soc. Bibl. Lit. (chmn. textual criticism seminar 1966, 71—) , Studiorum Novi Testamenti Societas, Cath. Bibl. Assn., New Testament Colloquium, Soc. Mithraic Studies, AAUP. Author: The Theological Tendency of Codex Bezae Cantabrigiensis in Acts, 1966. Asso. editor: Jour. Bibl. Lit., 1971—; mem. editorial bd. Studies and Documents, 1971—, Hermeneia: A Critical and Historical Commentary on the Bible, 1966—, monograph series Soc. Bibl. Lit., 1969-72, Soc. Bibl. Lit. Centennial Publs., 1975—. Contbr. articles and revs. to profl. jours. Office: Dept Religion Case Western Res Univ Cleveland OH 44106

EPP, THEODORE HERMAN, minister, Mennonite Church; b. Oraibi, Ariz., Jan. 27, 1907; s. Jacob and Nettie (Harmes) E.; m. Matilda S. Schmidt, Aug. 10, 1930; children: Gerald (dec.), Eleanor, Herbert, Berniece, Mari Lyn, Virginia. Th.M., Southwestern Bapt. Theol. Sem., 1932; D.D. (hon.), Bob Jones U., 1955, Wheaton Coll., 1959; D.Hm. (hon.), John Brown U., 1982. Ordained to ministry, 1938. Pastor, Mennonite Ch., Coltry, Okla., 1932-36; independent evangelist, Enid, Okla., 1936-39; founder, dir. Back to the Bible Broadcast, Lincoln, Nebr., 1939-84, founding dir., 1984—; radio minister, 1939—. Author of numerous books on religion (65). Named Nebraskan of the Yr., Nebr. Broadcasters Assn., 1966; Disting. Service award Nat. Religious Broadcasters, 1983; Disting. Christian Service award Am. Indians, 1981. Republican. Office: 12th at M St Lincoln NE 68501

EPSTEIN, HARRY HYMAN, rabbi; b. Lithuania, Apr. 1, 1903; s. Ephraim and Hannah (Israelowitz) E.; came to U.S., 1911, naturalized, 1917; B.A., Emory U., 1931, M.A., 1932; D.D., Jewish Theol. Sem., N.Y.C., 1966; m. Rebecca Chashesman, Jan. 13, 1929; children—Renana (Mrs. Bennet B. Lavin), Davida (Mrs. James H. Weiss). Rabbi, 1925; rabbi Ahavath Achim Synogogue, Atlanta, 1928—; mem. Rabbinical Assembly, 1952—; mem. Rabbinic Cabinet, Jewish Theol. Sem., 1960-73; pres. Rabbinical Assembly S.E. Region, 1966-67, mem. law com., 1955-62; chmn. Atlanta Jewish Welfare Fund, 1949-50; del. Am. Jewish Conf., 1943-45; vice chmn. Nat. Rabbinic Ort Com. Mem. City of Atlanta Community Relations Com. Bd. dirs. Jewish Home; trustee Atlanta Jewish Welfare Fedn. Recipient Distinguished Service award Jewish War Vets., 1968, Human Relations award B'nai B'rith, 1970; named Ort Man of Yr., 1971. Author: Judaism and Progress, 1935. Home: 2545 Arden Rd NW Atlanta GA 30327 Office: 600 Peachtree Battle Ave NW Atlanta GA 30327

ERENRICH, DAVID EUGENE, minister, United Methodist Ch.; b. Morgantown, W.Va., Sept. 16, 1948; s. Melvin Donald and Carolyn Joy (Pierce) E.; B.A. with honors, W.Va. U., 1970; M.Div. with honors, Meth. Theol. Sch., 1973, M.A., 1974; m. Janice Elaine Backus, Sept. 1, 1973; children—Tonya Marie, John David. Ordained minister, 1971; minister Hope United Meth. Ch., Morgantown, 1969-70; minister Middleburg (Ohio) United Meth. Ch., 1970-73; marriage and family therapist Open Door Clinic Columbus (Ohio) Area Community Mental Health, 1973-74; minister Lakeview United Meth. Ch., St. Albans, W.Va., 1974-77, Follansbee (W.Va.) United Meth. Ch., 1977—; Instr., guest speaker W.Va. State Coll., Meth. Theol. Sch., 1974—; part-time pvt. practice marriage-family therapist, 1974—; mem. W.Va. United Meth. Bd. Higher Edn. and Ministry, 1976—. Chmn. W.Va. United Meth. Task Force on Hunger, 1977—. Bd. dirs. Kanawha Pastoral Counseling Center, Charleston, W.Va., 1975—. Mem. St. Albans Ministerial Assn. (v.p. 1975-77), Am. Assn. Marriage and Family Counselors. Home: 179 Tartan Dr Follansbee WV 26037

ERICKSON, GEORGE VERNER, minister, United Presbyn. Ch. in U.S.A.; b. Phillipsburg, Pa., Sept. 19, 1931; s. Clifford Henning and Caroline Anna (Musselman) E.; A.B., U. Redlands, 1952, M.A., 1954; M.Div., Fuller Theol. Sem., 1961; J.D., Valley U., 1976; m. Margaret A. Heacock, Sept. 5, 1952; children—Catherine Anne, Sandra Sue. Ordained to ministry, 1955; pastor Trinity Presbyn. Ch., Camarillo, Calif., 1966—, Calvary Presbyn. Ch., S. Pasadena, Calif., 1961-66. Moderator, Synod of So. Calif., 1974-75; pastor, Christian and Missionary Alliance, Modesto and Petaluma, Calif., 1953-61. Bd. dirs., v.p. Pleasant Valley Hosp., 1974—. Named Young Man of Year, S. Pasadena, 1961. Home: 1740 Loma Dr Camarillo CA 93010 Office: PO Box 586 Camarillo CA 93010

ERICKSON, JOHN DAVID, minister, religious society official, Lutheran Church America; b. Wesleyville, Pa., Apr. 28, 1933; s. Arvid and Julia (Anderson) E.; m. Nancy Ann Olson, June 2, 1956; children: Alana, Julia Ann, John David, Ronald. B.A., Augustana Coll., Rock Island, Ill., 1955; B.Div., 1959; postgrad. U. Minn., 1959-60; D.Div. (hon.), Va. Sem., 1973. Ordained to ministry Luth. Ch. Am., 1959. Missionary to Japan, 1960-62; asst. pastor Elim Luth. Ch., Robbinsdale, Minn., 1962-65; exec. sec. ways and means dept. Am. Bible Soc., N.Y.C., 1969-76, dep. gen. sec., 1976-78, world service officer, 1976—, gen. sec., 1978—; world service officer United Bible Socs., N.Y.C., 1976—. Bd. dirs. Leonia Pub. Sch. Dist., 1974-77; pres. Leonia Civic Conf., 1969; officer Leonia Citizens for Pub. Schs., 1967-69. Mem. Nat. Soc. Fund Raisers. Office: Am Bible Soc 1865 Broadway New York NY 10023

ERICKSON, PAUL E., Synodical bishop Lutheran Church in America, Chgo. Office: Luth Ch in Am 18 S Michigan Ave Room 800 Chicago IL 60603*

ERICSON, CARL ERLAND, minister, United Presbyn. Ch. in U.S.A.; b. Jacksonville, Ill., Mar. 20, 1913; s. Carl August and Ethel Jane (Plummer) E.; B.A., Ill. Coll., 1934, D.D., 1963; M.Div., Princeton Theol. Sem., 1959; m. Mary Katherine Shaw, Jan. 19, 1936; children—Mary Karin, Carl Eric Jon, Helen Jane. Ordained to ministry, 1959; city editor Jacksonville Daily Jour., 1940-43; picture editor AP, Chgo., 1943-45, Washington, 1945-56; pastor Knox Presbyn. Ch., Falls Church, Va., 1959-67, 6th Presbyn. Ch., Pitts., 1967-69, Beulah Presbyn. Ch., Orion, Ill., 1969—; moderator, Great Rivers Presbytery, 1974, del. to Nigerian independence, 1960. Columnist, The Daily Dispatch, Moline, Ill. Chmn. jail rehab. program, Fairfax County, Va., 1960-67; mem. Fed. Community Action Unit, 1962-65. Named Man of Year, Squirrel Hill Kiwanis, Pitts., 1968. Home: 8212 162d Ave Orion IL 61273

ERKKINEN, ERIC JOHANNES, minister, Lutheran Ch. - Missouri Synod; b. Concord, Mass., Sept. 19, 1951; s. Paavo Johannes and Vieno Elizabeth (Maki) E.; m. Linda Nancy Jones, Aug. 4, 1973; children: Aaron, Joel, Leah. A.A., Concordia Coll., 1969-71, B.A., 1973; M.Div., Concordia Sem., 1977. Ordained to ministry Lutheran Ch., 1977. Pastor Gloria Dei Luth. Ch., Virginia, Minn., 1977-81, Hope Luth. Ch., Hudson, Fla., 1981—; dist. pastoral youth adviser Minn. No. Dist., Brainerd, 1978-81. Contbr. My Devotions, devotional for children. Bd. dirs. Right to Life of West Pasco, Hudson, 1984—. Serving as chaplain Army NG, 1978—. Club: Sertoma. Republican. Home: 9118 Scot St Hudson FL 33562 Office: Hope Lutheran Church 12321 Canton Ave Hudson FL 33562

ERMAKOV, DIMITRI H., priest, Russian Orthodox Church; b. Homestead, Pa., Oct. 4, 1926; s. Herasim Vladimirovich and Ksenia (Zaitsov) E.; m. Martha Sweda, July 26, 1950; children: Larissa, Kyra, Juliane, Martha, Dimitri D. Diploma, St. Tikhon Theol. Sem.-Pa., 1950. Ordained priest, 1957. Parish tchr., choir master Holy Resurrection Cath. Ch., Wilkes Barre, Pa., 1950-53, Holy Ascension Ch., Frackville, Pa., 1953-56, Sts. Peter/Paul Ch., Jersey City, 1956-57; priest Holy Virgin Protection, Carnegie, Pa., 1957-61, St. John's Ch., Canonsburg, 1961-68, Sts. Peter and Paul Ch., Buffalo, 1968-70, Holy Virgin Dormition, McKeesport, Pa., 1970—; dir. Pitts. Russian Orthodox Male Chorus, 1958-68, 75-81; editor diocesan news monthly, Light of Orthodoxy, 1963-68; dir., narrator radio talk Light of Orthodoxy, 1980—. Editor translation/music transposition: Orthodox Feasts, 1979; Marriage, 1981; 3 Prayer Services, 1982; Christmas Epiphany, 1983, Orthodox Feasts, 1984. Mem. City Charter Rev. Com., McKeesport, 1975. Served with U.S. Army, 1945-46. Club: Federated Russian Orthodox Clubs (spiritual dir. 1972-75). Address: 330 Shaw Ave McKeesport PA 15132

ERNO, KIMBER DANA, minister, Lutheran Church in America, b. St. Albans, Vt., Dec. 5, 1952; s. Hayden Louis and Virginia Phyllis (Fadden) E.; m. Kelly Ann Corrigan, July 27, 1974; 1 child, Kathryn Kelly. B.S. in Biology, Bates Coll., 1975; M.Div., Luth. Theol. Sem., Gettysburg, Pa., 1980. Ordained to ministry Lutheran Church in America, 1980. Asst. pastor Faith Luth. Ch., Oxon Hill, Md., 1980-84; mission developer Trinity Luth. Ch., St. Albans, Vt., summer 1984; pastor St. Stephen Luth. Ch., Silver Spring, Md.; exec. dir. Luths. Affirming Ministry in a Pluralistic Soc., Oxon Hill, 1980-81; advocate Luth. Coalition on South Africa, Md. Synod, Luth. Ch. in Am., 1980—; mem. Community Ministry of Prince George's County, 1980—; rep. Am. Luth. Ch. Commn. on Racism, N.Y.C., 1980—, Minority Ministry Task Force, Balt., 1983—; coordinator Building Rainbows Youth Retreat, Washington, D.C., 1981-82, Black Worship Workshop, Balt., 1982. Organizer local neighborhood forums, Prince George's County, Md., 1983. Mem. IMPACT, Luth. Human Relations Assn. Am. Office: St Stephen Luth Ch 11612 New Hampshire Ave Silver Spring MD 20904

ERVIN, GARY MITCHELL, minister, Southern Baptist Convention; b. Metcalfe County, Ky., June 16, 1950; s. Mitchell and Norma Lee E.; B.S., Campbellsville Coll., 1973; M.A., Western Ky. U., 1977; Th.D., Internat. Bible Inst., 1981; m. Marcella Hubbard, June 20, 1970. Ordained to ministry, 1969. Minister Harrodsfork Bapt. Ch., Columbia, Ky., 1970-71, Antioch Bapt. Ch., Knob Lick, Ky., 1970-72, Bethlehem Bapt. Ch., Greensburg, Ky., 1972—. Asst. moderator Russell Creek Bapt. Assn., 1975-76. Mem. Ky. Tchrs. Assn. Contbr. weekly articles to Greensburg Record Herald, 1975—; weekly Gospel Song and Evangelism Hour, radio sta. WGRK; Bethlehem Baptist Hour WGRB-tv sta. Address: Rt 5 Greensburg KY 42743

ESCHBACH, VICTOR JOSEPH, priest, Roman Catholic Church. b. Phila., Apr. 6, 1944; s. Victor J. and Margaret M. (McGivney) E. B.A., St. Charles Sem., 1968, M.Div., 1972. Ordained priest Roman Catholic Ch., 1972. Asst. pastor various chs., Pa., 1972-79; asst.

pastor Most Precious Blood Ch., Phila., 1979-82, adminstr., 1982-83, pastor, 1983—; exec. dir. Finley Place, Inc., Phila., 1980—; mem. Priests' Council, Phila., 1973-75; dir. Phila. Council Community Advancement, 1981—. Recipient Mayor's award City of Phila., 1971; Signum Fidei award LaSalle Coll. Alumni, 1982. Democrat. Home: Most Precious Blood Ch 2814 W Diamond St Philadelphia PA 19121

ESCHLIMAN, ROGER WAYNE, minister, United Meth. Ch.; b. Columbus, Nebr., Jan. 14, 1945; s. Jasper Wayne and Frances Louise (Klaus) E.; B.A., Kearney (Nebr.) State Coll., 1968; M.Div., St. Paul Sch. Theology, Kansas City, Mo., 1971; m. Carolyn Toomey, Aug. 4, 1968; children—Diane, Sonya. Ordained to ministry, 1972; pastor Winchester (Kans.) United Meth. Ch., 1969-71; coordinating pastor KBR Coop. Parish, Bassett, Nebr., 1971-75; sr. pastor Stephens Creek Coop. Parish, Lincoln, Nebr., 1975—. Mem. parish devel. commn. Lincoln dist. Nebr. Conf. Bd. Ministry, mem. bd. ch. and soc. Bd. dirs. Lincoln Family Services Assn., Lincoln. Mem. Kappa Sigma Beta. Home: 5810 Dogwood Dr Lincoln NE 68516 Office: 8320 South St Lincoln NE 68520

ESPOSITO, LUIGI, priest, educator, Roman Cath. Ch.; b. Casoria, Italy, Aug. 23, 1940; s. Pasquale and Colomba (Memoli) E.; came to U.S., 1960, naturalized, 1970; B.A., Collegio Bianchi, Naples, Italy, 1960; M.Div., Mary Immaculate Coll., 1964; M.L.A., Johns Hopkins, 1975. Ordained priest, 1964; tchr. religion, counselor Our Lady of Pompei High Sch., Balt., 1964—; marriage counselor, asso. pastor Our Lady of Pompei Ch., Balt., 1975—. Chaplain K.C., 1971—, retreat group Balt. Police Dept., 1976, Cath. War Vets., 1972—. Instl. rep., committeeman Boy Scouts Am., Balt., 1965—; guidance counselor Girl Scouts U.S.A., 1965—; clergy mem. Md. Council of Blind, 1975—. Contbr. articles to religious jours. Home: 3600 Claremont St Baltimore MD 21224 Office: 201 S Conkling St Baltimore MD 21224

ESTILL, ROBERT WHITRIDGE, bishop, Episcopal Ch.; b. Lexington, Ky., Sept. 7, 1927; s. Robert Julian and Elizabeth Pierpont (Whitridge) E.; A.B., U. Ky., 1949; M.Div., Episc. Theol. Sch., Cambridge, Mass., 1952; S.T.M., U. of the South, 1960; D.Min., Vanderbilt Sem., 1977; m. Joyce Haynes, June 19, 1950; children—Helen Haynes, Robert Whitridge, Elizabeth Rodes. Ordained priest, 1953; rector ch., Middlesboro, Ky., 1952-55, Lexington, Ky., 1955-63, Washington, 1969-73; dean Christ Ch. Cathedral, Louisville, 1963-69; dir. center for continuing edn. Va. Theol. Sem., 1973-76; rector St. Michael and All Angels Ch., Dallas, 1976-80; bishop Diocese of N.C., 1980—. Mem. Nat. Episc. Ch. Standing Liturgical Commn.; bd. dirs. Ky. Council Chs.; chmn. Com. on Human Rights, 1962-69; mem. Nat. Bd. Exam. Chaplains. Bd. dirs. Planned Parenthood, Actor's Theatre, Louisville. Mem. Phi Delta Theta. Editor prayer books. Address: 201 St Alban's PO Box 17025 Raleigh NC 27609

ETHERTON, RAYFORD LEE, minister, United Meth. Ch.; b. DeKalb County, Ala., Apr. 27, 1936; s. Acie Oscar and Grace Leona (Strange) E.; B.A. with high honors, U. Ala., 1968; M.Div., Duke U., 1972; m. Swannelle Cassidy, Mar. 20, 1954; children—Rayford Lee, Claudia Beth. Ordained to minister, 1969; pastor Henryville Ch., Guntersville, Ala., 1964-68, Louisburg (N.C.) charge, 1968-72, Southside Ch., Gadsden, Ala., 1972-76, Vernon (Ala.) First Ch., 1976—. Mem. equitable salaries commn. N. Ala. Ann. Conf., United Meth. Ch., 1976—, dist. dir. evangelism, 1974-76, dist. dir. health and social welfare ministries, 1977-78; chaplain Ala. Dist. N. Civitan Internat., 1967. Recipient Town and Country award N. Ala. Ann. Conf., 1967. Mem. Phi Theta Kappa. Home: PO Box 608 102 1st St Vernon AL 35592 Office: PO Box 608 104 1st St Vernon AL 35592

EUBANK, GEOFFREY LYNN, minister, Missionary Church; b. Lima, Ohio, June 14, 1954; s. Richard Charles and Dorothy Jane (Williams) E.; m. Pamela Nell Padgett, June 24, 1978; children: Nathan Paul, Sarah Elizabeth. B.A., Fort Wayne Bible Coll., 1976; M.Div., Trinity Evang. Div. Sch., 1981. Lic. minister Missionary Ch., Pastor, Pandora Missionary Ch., Ohio, 1981—. Mem. Pandora Ministerial Assn. (pres. 1984). Republican. Home: 207 E Monroe Pandora OH 45877 Office: Pandora Missionary Ch 210 E Main Box 173 Pandora OH 45877

EUBANKS, HAZEL BENTLEY, lay church worker, Southern Baptist Convention; b. Leathersville, Ga., Dec. 3, 1919; d. Benjamin Franklin and Gladys (Bennett) Bentley; m. Joseph Robert Eubanks, Oct. 4, 1942; children: Gary Franklin, Thomas Marshall. Cert. bus. Garretts Comml. Coll., 1937; student Ga. State Coll. for Women, 1939-40. Supt. Intermediate I Sunday Sch. Roswell St. Bapt. Ch., Marietta, Ga., 1948-50; pres. Women's Missionary Union, 1949; mem. Second-Ponce de Leon Bapt. Ch., Atlanta, 1950—; mem. exec. com. Atlanta Assn. Bapt. Women's Missionary Union, 1958-61; mem. budget com. Atlanta Assn. Bapt. Women's Missionary Union, 1958-60, mem. nominating com., 1964; supt. Intermediate I Sunday Sch. Soncond-Ponce de Leon Bapt. Ch., 1950-59; pres. Women's Missionary Union, 1959-61, hostess, 1966-76, chmn. sr. citizen's orgn., 1966-70, mem. mission com., 1957-67, 78-81, chmn. reception com. 125th ann., 1979, mem. social com., 1980-82; mem. exec. com. So. Bapt. Conv., 1982—; restored with husband Greenwood Bapt. Ch., Lincoln County, Ga., 1978-84; mem. Heritage Com., 1978—; tchr. Sunday Sch. King's Men Bible Class, 1981—; restored with husband Chapel Bldg. at Shorter Bapt. Coll., Rome, Ga., 1984—. Various positions with Girls' Clubs of Am., Inc. including: pres., 1968-70, dir., 1956-78, nat. adv. com., 1966-77, hon. mem., 1978—, chmn. region I, 1957-64, founder Hazel B. Eubanks Expansion Trophy, 1957—; historian, 1964-65, historian, 1971-73; organizing com. of Atlanta Girls' Club, 1952, charter dir., 1952-64, 68-77, pres., 1955-58; mem. Freedoms Found. at Valley Forge, Atlanta chpt., 1975—, Ga. Bapt. Hist. Soc., 1978—; past v.p. Jr. Atlanta Woman's Club; mem. Atlanta Hist. Soc., 1963-74, Parliamentary Study Club, 1952-65. Recipient numerous awards including: Girls' Clubs of Am. Twenty-Five Year award, 1977; W.S. Beaver award, 1961, 68, 69, 73; Boys' Clubs of Am. cert., 1968; Lucile M. Wright Citizenship award, 1970; named Gracious Lady of Ga., 1982. Mem. Hughenot Soc. of Founders of Namakin in the Colony of Va. (state pres. Ga. 1961-63, state parliamentarian, 1967-81), Nat. Soc. Magna Charta Dames (sec. Ga. div. 1963-65), Nat. Soc. Daughters of Am. Colonists (past regent James Edward Oglethorpe chpt. 1979-81; hon. regent 1981—).

EUBANKS, ODUS KAY, educator, minister, Ch. of God (Anderson, Ind.); b. Russellville, Ark., July 14, 1933; s. O.K. and Clarsa (Simmons) E.; B.E., S.E. Mo. State U., 1959; M.R.E., Southwestern Bapt. Sem., 1961; M.Div., Anderson Coll., 1975; m. Patsy Ann Musgrave, Oct. 2, 1953; children—Gary, Pamella Kay, Timothy LeBaron. Ordained to ministry, 1959; missionary, Colombia, S.Am., 1961-63; pastor in Fort Worth, 1964-67; academic dean Calif. Christian Coll., Fresno, 1967-69; minister edn. Glenview Bapt. Ch., Ft. Worth, 1969-71; pastor Saratoga (Ind.) Ch. of God, 1972-75; asst. prof. Christian edn. Gulf-Coast Bible Coll., Houston, 1975—, also campus minister, 1976—, dir. Christian services, 1975—. Exec. sec. Tex. Assn. Free Will Baptists, 1965-67; adviser Coll. Missions Club, 1975—, job placement, 1975—. Recipient Ellis Preaching award Anderson Coll., 1975. Mem. Tex. Jr. Coll. Assn., Assn. Christian Edn. Profs. Contbr. articles to religious mags. Home: 6022 Golden Forest St Houston TX 77092 Office: 911 W 11th St Houston TX 77008

EUBANKS, WALTER SHELTON, JR., minister, United Methodist Ch.; b. Augusta, Ga., Oct. 12, 1931; s. Walter Shelton and Sarah Ann (Baird) E.; sci. diploma Jr. Coll. Augusta, 1952; A.B., U. Ga., 1954; M.Div., Emory U., 1957; m. Joyce Christine Kesler, Aug. 4, 1956; children—Shelton, Krystyna. Ordained elder, 1957; pastor chs., West Putnam Charge, Eatonton, Ga., 1954-55, Trinity Ch., Austell, Ga., 1955-56, McEachern Meml. Ch., Powder Springs, Ga., 1956-60, Clayton (Ga.) 1st Ch., 1960-67, Maple Ave Ch., Marietta, Ga., 1967-71, Monroe (Ga.) 1st Ch., 1971-76, St. Paul Ch., Gainesville, Ga., 1976—. Dist. sec. missions, 1971-76; mem. dist. bd. ministry, 1972-76; pres. Monroe-Walton Ministerial Assn., 1973-76; 76, Rabun County (Ga.) Ministerial Assn., 1961-63. Recipient awards for service Ga. Youth Temperance Council. Home: 1104 Lanier Ave Gainesville GA 30501 Office: POB 804 Gainesville GA 30501

EULER, FRANK OTTO, JR., minister, Independent Baptist Churches; b. Freeport, Ill., May 10, 1926; s. Frank Otto Sr. and Florence Edna (Juluis) E.; m. Marjorie Mae Bennett, Dec. 1, 1946; children: Michael Dennis, Daniel Frank, Timothy Lee, Andrew Joel. Student, Bob Jones U., 1943-45, Ind. Central U., 1945-46; B.A., Rockmont Coll., 1951; postgrad. Purdue U., 1963; D.D. (hon.), Ill. Bapt. Coll., 1971; H.H.D., Ind. Bapt. Coll., 1976. Ordained to ministry, 1950. Pastor, First Bapt. Ch., Louisville, Colo., 1945-51, Grace Bapt. Ch., Moweadua, Ill., 1963-66, Indpls., 1966-70, Pinehill Bapt. Ch., Columbus, Ohio, 1970-76, Riverview Bapt. Ch., Casper, N.Y., 1976-82, Valley Bapt. Ch., Palm Desert, 1982—; missionary in Japan, 1951-62; trustee Ind. Bapt. Coll., Indpls., 1970-84, Ill. Bapt. Coll., Pekin, 1970-84.

EUSDEN, JOHN DYKSTRA, educator, college chaplain, United Ch. of Christ; b. Holland, Mich., July 20, 1922; s. Ray A. and Marie (Dykstra) E.; A.B., Harvard, 1943; B.D., Yale, 1949, Ph.D., 1954; m. Joanne Reiman, June 14, 1950; children—Andrea B., Alan T., John Dykstra, Sarah J. Ordained to ministry, 1949; interim minister chs. in Conn., 1953-54, 60; asso. of chaplain Yale, part-time, 1947-49, asst. to dean Div. Sch., 1949-52, instr., then asst. prof. religion, 1953-60; asso. prof. religion, chaplain Williams Coll., 1960-65, prof. religion, 1965-70, chaplain, 1960-68, Nathan Jackson prof. Christian theology, 1970—; research fellow, lectr. faculty of letters Kyoto (Japan) U., 1963-64; theologian-in-residence Am. Ch., Paris, 1972; research fellow Center Study of Japanese Religions, Kyoto, 1976. Mem. adv. council Danforth Found. Campus Ministry program, 1966-70. Trustee Lingnan U., Hong Kong. Kent. fellow Soc. Values in Higher Edn., 1949. Mem. Am. Acad. Religion, AAUP, Am. Soc. Ch. History, Nat. Assn. Coll. and Univ. Chaplains. Author: Puritans, Lawyers and Politics in Early 17th-Century England, 1958; Zen and Christian: The Journey Between, 1981; The Spiritual Life: Learning East and West, 1982; also articles. Editor, translator: The Marrows of Theology (William Ames). Clubs: Berzelius (hon.), Elizabethan (Yale). Address: Stetson Hall Dept Religion Williams Coll Williamstown MA 02167

EUTSLER, R(ALPH) KERN, bishop, United Methodist Church; b. Bridgewater, Va., Aug. 2, 1919; s. Robert Lee and Nora Lillian (Zepp) E.; m. Eva Rebecca Vines, Oct. 10, 1945; children: Rebecca Ann Eutsler Coulter, Mary Margaret Eutsler Abramson. B.A., Berea Coll., 1940; M.Div., Union Theol. Sem., N.Y.C., 1943; D.Div. (hon.), Randolph-Macon U., 1963. Ordained deacon, United Methodist Ch., 1942, elder, 1944; pastor Greenville-Mint Spring, Va., 1943-45, Elkton, Va., 1945-49, Luray, Va., 1949-53, South Roanoke, Va., 1953-60, Ginter Park, Richmond, Va., 1960-65, Washington Street Ch., Alexandria, Va., 1965-66, Reveille, Richmond, 1978-82; exec. dir. Va. Meth. Homes, Inc., 1966-73; supt. Alexandria Dist., United Meth. Ch., 1973-78; dir. Va. Conf. Council on Ministries, 1982-84; elected bishop, 1984; resident bishop Holston Area United Meth. Ch., 1984—, mem. bd. discipleship, 1980—, bd. global ministries, 1972-76, mem. Southeastern Jurisdictional Council on Ministries, 1980—. Office: Holston Area United Meth Ch 3606 Western Ave Knoxville TN 37921

EVANS, CALVIN CURTIS, minister, National Association Free Will Baptist Church; b. Pedro, Ohio, Mar. 30, 1930; s. Ersel and Ruby Mae (Roth) E.; m. Doris Irene Henry; children—Sharon, Keith, Jimmy, Patricia, Pamela, Calvin, Angela. B.Min., Luther Rice Sem., 1981; Th.M., Emmaus Bible Sem., 1982; D.Min., Internat. Bible Sem., 1984; D.D., Bethel Bible Coll., 1977. Ordained to ministry, 1957; pastor chs. in Ky. and Ohio, 1961-78; pres., dir. Evangelistic Outreach, Inc. Bd. dirs. Ohio Assn. Free Will Baptists; weekly speaker radio and TV programs. Mem. Nat. Religious Broadcasters Assn. Editor: Evangelistic Outreach Mag., 1974—. Office: PO Box 56 Pedro OH 45659

EVANS, GEORGE R., bishop Roman Catholic Church; titular bishop of Tubyza and aux. bishop of Denver, 1969—. Office: St Rose of Lima Ch 1320 W Nevada Pl Denver CO 80223*

EVANS, JAMES LEE, minister, Southern Baptist Convention; construction company executive; b. Boger, Tex., Jan. 31, 1930; s. Dwight Taft and Gracie Mae (Morris) E.; m. Wanda Fay Stephens, Feb. 23, 1948; children: Rita Fay, James Dale, Stephen Dwight. B.S., Addison State U., 1959, M.S., 1969; B.Th., Southwestern Sem., 1965; D.Religion (hon.), Northwestern Coll., 1979; D.Div. (hon.) Addison State U., 1983. Ordained to ministry So. Bapt. Conv., 1956. Sunday sch. tchr. Morris Meml. Ch., Ada, Okla., 1955-57; pastor Bapt. Ch., Ada, 1957-62, Maud, Okla., 1962-67, Konawa, Okla., 1977—; bd. dirs. Okla. Bapt. Gen. Conv.; dir. evangelism, chmn. annuities, chmn. coop. program, mem. planning and promotion com., 1985—; pres. Ministerial Alliance, Konawa, Okla., 1980, 84, Jenks, Okla., 1976; pres. Associational Pastors' Conf., 1985—. Author: Within the Shadow, 1965; also poems, booklets. Chmn. United Dry Organization, Pontotoc, Okla., 1959. Recipient Appreciation award Okla. Bapt. U., 1981, 82, Teaching awards Falls Creek Bapt. Assembly, 1965-80. Mem. Southwestern Sem. Alumni Assn. Republican. Lodge: Lions. Home: Ada OK Office: First Bapt Ch 129 S Broadway Konawa OK 74849

EVANS, JOSEPH ROBERT, minister, United Presbyterian Ch. in U.S.A.; b. Sierra Madre, Calif., July 25, 1924; s. Joseph Ratcliff and Mary Frances (Wilson) E.; B.S., U. Calif., Berkeley, 1949; M.Div., San Francisco Theol. Sem., San Anselmo, Calif., 1956; m. Edith Dorothy Luke, Nov. 20, 1953; children—Lorilee Anne, James Ratcliff, Elizabeth Anne. Ordained to ministry, 1956; pastor South Park Presbyn. Ch., Seattle, 1956-58; organizing minister Berean Presbyn. Ch., Tacoma, Wash., 1958-59, pastor, 1959-69; pastor Westminster United Presbyn. Ch., Anacortes, Wash., 1969—. Developer, Ednl./Counseling Center, 1974-76; speaker civic affairs at high sch. baccalaureate services. Mem. Internat. Platform Assn. Club: Rotary. Office: 1300 9th St Anacortes WA 98221

EVANS, MARLENE JUNE, editor, Independent Baptist Ch.; educator. B. Beatrice, Nebr., Nov. 11, 1933; d. Alvin Dale and Mary Helen (Fauver) Zugmier; m. Wendell Lee Evans, Dec. 22, 1955; children: Joy Lynn Evans Ryder, David Lee. B.S., Bob Jones U., 1955, M.A., 1956; M.Ed., U. Tenn., 1962; L.H.D. (hon.), Hyles-Anderson Coll., 1978. Editor, founder Christian Womanhood mag., Crown Point, Ind., 1975—, dir. ann. Christian Womanhood Spectacular, 1975—; pres. Bus. Women's Sunday sch. class, Chattanooga, Tenn., 1962-64; dir. tng. Union Highland Park Ch., Chattanooga, 1962-63, Sunday sch. promotion coordinator, 1965, mem. ch. bus ministry, 1969-72. Dean of women, coll. activities coordinator Hyles-Anderson Coll., Crown Point, 1972—; hostess radio program Woman to Woman, 1969-70; speaker in field. Author: Through a Woman's Eyes, vol. 1, 2, 1975-76. Founder, bd. dirs. Blue Beret Girls service group, Hammond, Ind., 1975-76. Republican. Home: 38 Risch Schererville IN 46375 Office: Christian Womanhood 8400 Burr St Crown Point IN 46307

EVANS, ROBERT FRANKLIN, minister, Southern Baptist Convention; b. Clyde, Ohio, May 12, 1924; s. Frank Lincoln and Laura Nannearl (Forgerson) E.; B.A., Okla. Bapt. U., Shawnee, 1950; M.R.E., Southwestern Bapt. Theol. Sem., 1952; m. Norma Sue Francis, June 1, 1946: children: Robin Sue, Donna Gay, David Lee. Ordained to ministry, 1965. Minister edn. chs. in Okla., Ill., N.Mex., Ky., Tex., La., 1952-74, First Bapt. Ch., Springfield, Mo., 1974-85, Roswell St. Bapt. Ch., Marietta, Ga., 1985—; mem. faculty Mid-Am. Sunday Sch. Leadership Conf., Kansas City, Kans., 1981, Denver Metro Clinic, 1984, Houston Metro Clinic, 1985, Glorieta Sunday Sch. Leadership Conf., 1985. Pres. Ill. Religious Edn. Assn., 1956, Okla. Religious Edn. Assn., 1964, Mo. Bapt. Religious Edn. Assn., 1979-80. v.p. Southwestern Bapt. Religious Edn. Assn., 1969-70; pres. Waco Ministerial Fellowship, Tex., 1972. Mem. action team Springfield C. of C. Home: 1251 Morgan Chase Dr Marietta GA 30066 Office: 774 Roswell St Marietta GA 30060

EVANS, THOMAS, minister, Bapt. Ch.; b. Ramer, Ala., Aug. 11, 1925; s. Allen and Mattie (Day) E.; B.S., Ala. U., 1953; M.Ed., Wayne State U., 1971; m. Irene Parks, Aug. 13, 1946; children—Tommie Mae, Deborah Ann. Ordained to ministry, 1947; dir. christian edn. Ch. of Our Father Bapt., Detroit, 1957-74, pastor, 1974—. Mem. NAACP. Home: 13950 Robson St Detroit MI 48227 Office: 5333 E 7 Mile Rd Detroit MI 48234

EVANS, WENDELL LEE, minister, religious educator, Independent Baptist Chs.; college president; b. Linn Grove, Iowa, Jan. 26, 1935; s. Clarence and Wilma (Long) E.; m. Marlene June Zugmier, Dec. 22, 1955; children: Joy Lynn, David Lee. B.A., Bob Jones U., Greenville, S.C., 1956, M.A., 1957, Ph.D., 1962; postgrad. U. Tenn.-Knoxville, 1964-71. Ordained to ministry Ind. Bapt. Chs., 1959. Pastor, Faith Bible Ch., Hendersonville, N.C., 1959-60; chmn. dept. religious edn. Temple Bapt. Theol. Sem., Chattanooga, 1961-72; acad. dean Tenn. Temple Bible Coll., Chattanooga, 1967-72; exec. v.p. Hyles-Anderson Coll., Crown Point, Ind., 1972-76, pres., 1976—. Author: Analysis of 7th Day Adventism and its Relation to Present Day Evangelicalism, 1962. Del. Ind. Republican. Conv., 1976. Mem. So. Hist. Assn., Orgn. Am. Historians, Conf. Faith and History. Office: Hyles-Anderson Coll 8400 Burr St Crown Point IN 46307

EVANSON, CHARLES JOHN, minister, Luth. Ch.-Mo. Synod; b. Elmhurst, Ill., Feb. 26, 1936; s. Charles Olaf and Louise Marietta (Case) E.; B.A., Valparaiso U., 1959; B.D., Luth. Sch. Theology, Chgo., 1964; postgrad. Concordia Sem., St. Louis, 1964-66; m. Lenore Mary Clark, Mar. 16, 1964; children—James, Anne Marie, Charles. Ordained minister, 1964; asst. pastor, then pastor chs. in N.Y., Ont., Can. and Mich., 1961-70; pastor Christ English Luth. Ch., Chgo., 1970-74, Redeemer Luth. Ch., Ft. Wayne, Ind., 1975—; asst. sec. Ont. dist. Luth. Ch.-Mo. Synod, 1964-67, circuit counselor English dist., 1972—; treas. Joint Luth. Pastoral Conf., Detroit, 1968-70; mem. exec. com. Luth. Council Greater Chgo., 1974—; mem. exec. bd. Luth. Assn. Elementary Edn., 1975—; guest instr. St. Francis Coll., 1976; sec. com. on liturgical texts and music Commn. on Worship, Luth. Ch. Mo. Synod, 1979-81, sec. standing com. on worship Bd. Parish Services, 1981-83, sec. Commn. on Worship, 1983—. Sec. Stratford (Ont.) and Dist. Social Work Conf., 1966-67. Mem. Alpha Tau Omega (historian 1955-56). Author, translator articles. Home: 4510 Lafayette Esplanade Fort Wayne IN 46806

EVELER, GERALDINE LEE, nun, ednl. adminstr., Roman Cath. Ch.; b. Jefferson City, Mo., Apr. 10, 1930; d. John Paul and Leona Elizabeth (Schulte) Eveler; B.A., Marillac Coll., 1966; M.A. in Ednl. Adminstrn., U. Mo., 1973. Joined Sisters of Charity of Incarnate Word, 1945; tchr. Roman Cath. elementary schs., Mo., Tex., Ill., 1948—, high sch., St. Francis Xavier Parish, Taos, Mo., 1970-73; instr. coll. bus. English, Instituto Miguel Angel, Mexico City, 1967-68; vocation dir. Mary Immaculate Sch., Kirksville, Mo., 1961-64; prin., local superior Our Lady of Valley Sch. and Convent, El Paso, Tex., 1964-67; prin. St. Mary's Sch., Amarillo, Tex., 1974—, superior, 1974-76. Vice pres. Diocesan Assembly of Women Religious, Jefferson City (Mo.), 1970-71, pres., 1971-72; v.p., Diocesan Assembly of Women Religious, Amarillo, 1975-76, pres., 1976—; active Cursillo Movement, Charismatic Renewal; mem. renewal resource team Sisters Charity Incarnate Word; minister of communion, lectr., reader, song leader St. Francis Xavier, Taos, also St. Mary's, Amarillo. Mem. Nat. Cath. Edn. Assn., Nat. Assembly Women Religious, Am. Assn. Supervision and Curriculum Devel. Home: 1407 W 11th St Amarillo TX 79102 Office: 1200 S Washington St Amarillo TX 79102

EVEREST, QUINTON JAMES, minister, Missionary Church; b. Goshen, Ind., Sept. 11, 1907; s. Walter C. and Annetta (Boyer) E.; grad. Ft. Wayne Bible Coll., 1928; student Winona Lake Sch. Theology, 1937-38; D.D., Bethel Coll., 1974; m. Malinda Mae Yoder, Feb. 16, 1929; children: Charlene (Mrs. Dale Sherry), Quinton James, Sharon Everest Fry, Cynthia (Mrs. Michael McKee). Ordained to ministry, 1932; pastor Missionary Chs., Union, Mich., 1928-31, Elkhart, Ind., 1931-38, Goshen, 1938-43, South Bend, Ind., 1943-65; Your Worship Hour Broadcast, 1933—. Pres., Fgn. Missionary Dept. Missionary Ch., 1950-73; Bible Conf. speaker and evangelist; mem. Gen. Ch. Bd., 1935-73; mem. exec. bd. Nat. Religious Broadcasters. Chmn. bd. Bethel Coll., 1947-54, mem. bd., 1954-73; mem. bd. Ft. Wayne Bible Coll., 1937-42. Mem. Delta Epsilon Chi (hon.). Author numerous devotional, sermon books. Home: 52845 Swanson Dr South Bend IN 46635 Office: POB 6366 South Bend IN 46660

EVERETT, GARY GENE, minister, Assemblies of God; b. Ft. Worth, Tex., July 30, 1951; s. Thomas Belle and Erma Lee (Holderby) E.; B.S., Southwestern Assemblies of God Coll., 1975. Ordained to ministry, 1977; pastor youth 1st. Assembly of God Ch., Mineral Wells, Tex., 1974; youth music dir. N. Side Assembly of God, Ft. Worth, Tex., 1974-75; minister youth, ch. sec., asst. pastor U. Assembly of God, Waxahachie, Tex., 1975—; sec., treas. S. Dallas Sect. Christ Ambassadors, 1975—; mem. gen. council Assemblies of God. Active Seminard, Youth Camps, Assemblies of God Chs. Mem. Waxahachie Ministerial Assn. (treas. 1976-77), Tex. Sunday Sch. Assn. (registration com., 1973-76, bd. dirs. 1973-76), Southwestern Assemblies of God Coll. Ex Students Assn. Home: 607 John Arden Dr Waxahachie TX 75165 Office: 908 Syamore St Waxahachie TX 75165

EVERETT, ROBERT ANDREW, minister, United Church of Christ; b. Middleboro, Ky., Oct. 30, 1948; s. Robert Lester and Jurl Ann (Patton) E.; m. Marie Anna Iselborn, Jan. 10, 1982. A.B., U. Ga., 1970; M.Div., Yale U., 1973, S.T.M., 1975; M.Ph., Columbia U., 1979, Ph.D., 1983. Ordained to ministry United Ch. of Christ, 1974. Asst. pastor Union Meml. Ch., Glenbrook, Conn., 1973-75; pastor Emanuel United Ch. of Christ, Irvingston, N.J., 1975—; adj. prof. religion Albright Coll., 1982-83; adj. prof. religion studies Lehigh U. mem. exec. com. Nat. Christian Leadership Conf. for Israel, N.Y.C., 1980-83; v.p. Am. Friends of Nes Ammim, Teaneck, N.J., 1983—. Contbr. articles and book revs. to profl. publs. Advisor Youth Inst. for Peace in Middle East, Pitts., 1982—; speaker, advisor Ams. Concerned for Peace in Middle East, Paramus, N.J., 1983—. Travel grantee Am. Friends Tel Aviv U., 1974; fellow Columbia U. Grad. Sch., 1976-77, 77-78; recipient Outstanding Teaching award Albright Coll. Students, 1983. Democrat. Home: 23 Lincoln Pl Irvington NJ 07111 Office: Emanuel United Ch of Christ Lincoln Pl and Nye Ave Irvington NJ 07111

EWALD, ELWYN ELDEN, lay church worker, Association of Evangelical Lutheran Churches; b. Shobnoier, Ill., Nov. 8, 1941; s. Urban R. and Helen A. (Matthews) E.; m. Phyllis Marie Meseke, June 8, 1963; children: Craig A., Pamela M., Kurt T., Brett E. B.A.Ed., Concordia Tchrs. Coll., River Forest, Ill., 1963; M.S.W., Washington U., St. Louis, 1970; D.D. (hon.), Christ Sem./Seminex, St. Louis, 1980. Tchr., New Guinea Luth. Mission, Wobag, Papua New Guinea, 1963-68, pres., 1970-73, adv. to pres., 1972-73; exec. dir. Evang. Luths. in Mission, St. Louis, 1973-77; exec. sec. Assn. Evang. Luth. Chs., St. Louis, 1977—, mem. Commn. for a New Luth. Ch., 1982—, staff adv. council on theol. edn., 1980—; mem. Luth. Domestic Disaster Relief Bd., 1977—. Mem. Bread for the World, 1970—. Democrat. Home: 747 Sherwick Terr Manchester MO 63011 Office: Assn Evang Luth Chs 12015 Manchester St Saint Louis MO 63131

EXNER, ADAM, archbishop, Roman Catholic Church; b. Killaly, Sask., Can., Dec. 24, 1928. Ordained priest, 1957; bishop of Kamloops, B.C., Can., 1974-82; archbishop of Winnipeg, Man., Can., 1984—. Office: 50 Stafford St Winnipeg MB R3M 2V7 Canada*

EXUM, J. MADISON, Bishop, Christian Methodist Episcopal Church (Tenth Dist.). Office: 650 McKellar Memphis TN 38106*

EZELL, WILLIAM BRUCE, JR., seminary administrator. Pres. Erskine Theol. Sem. (Reformed Presbyterian). Office: Erskine Theol Sem PO Box 171 Due West SC 29639*

FAATUI, TUSAPA LAOLAGI, minister, Congregational Christian Church of American Samoa; b. Olosega, Am. Samoa, Jan. 19, 1931; s. Tusapa Fonoti and Faapupula (Tuiolosega) L.; m. Elisapeta Saelua, Aug. 28, 1965; children: Faatui, Zenora, Dorothea, Alofagia, Upumoni. B.A., So. Calif. Coll., 1957; M.A. in Edn. and Adminstrn., San Francisco State U., 1961; M.Div., Am. Bapt. Sem. of West, 1971. Ordained to ministry United Ch. of Christ, 1971. Mem. fin. com. Congregational Christian Ch., Am. and Western Samoa, 1973-79, dir. Christian edn., 1980-82, mem. edn. com., 1980-82, pastor, 1973—; tchr. Gov. of Am. Samoa High Sch., 1961-63, counselor, 1963-64, vice prin., 1964-67; dir. tng. programs Govt. of Am. Samoa, 1971-73. Mem. Arts Council, Govt. Am. Samoa, 1981—; active ARC, Am. Samoa, 1981-83, Vocat. Rehab. Am. Samoa, 1982-84; mem., chmn. Criminal Justice Planning Agy., Am. Samoa, 1982—. Home: PO Box PPC Pago Pago AM 96799

FABER, JELLE, minister, religious educator, theological college principal, Canadian Reformed Churches; b. Drogeham, Netherlands, May 12, 1924; immigrated to Can., 1969; s. Anne and Geeske (Pruiksma) F.; m. Wietske Holwerda, Jan. 12, 1952; children: Trijntje, Harmen, Geeske, Riemer, Benne. Matriculation, Gereformeerd Gymnasium, Amsterdam, 1943; Candidaat, Theologische Hogeschool, Kampen, Netherlands, 1951, Doctorandus, 1958, Doctor Theologiae, 1969. Ordained to ministry Can. Ref. Chs. 1969. Minister Gereformeerde Kerk, Deventer, Netherlands, 1952-58, Rotterdam, Netherlands, 1958-69, Can. Ref. Ch., Hamilton, Ont., 1969—; prin., prof. dogmatology Theol. Coll. Can. Ref. Ch., Hamilton, 1969—; vis. prof. Westminster Theol. Sem., Phila., 1981; del. Internat. Conf. Christian Higher Edn., 1978. Author: Vestigium Ecclesiae (Cypriánns, Optatus, Augustinus), 1969; (with others) The Bride's Treasure, 1979. Editor Jour. Lucerna, 1958-69, Clarion, 1979-83. Mem. Calvin Soc. N. Am. Home: 226 Columbia Dr Hamilton ON L9C 3Y9 Canada Office: 110 W 27th St Hamilton ON L6C 5A1 Canada

FABIAN, JOHN LEONARD, priest, Roman Cath. Ch.; b. Mocanaqua, Pa., July 30, 1922; s. John Andrew and Anna Mary (Polasko) F.; student U. Scranton (Pa.), 1940-42, St. Peter's Sem., London, Ont., Can., 1948. Ordained to priesthood, 1948; pres. Slovaks of Luzerne County, Wilkes-Barre, Pa., 1958-64; asst. pastor Holy Rosary Ch., Ashley, Pa., 1964-66, Holy Trinity Ch., Hazelton, Pa., 1966-67; pastor Ascension Ch., Mocanaqua, 1967-71, St. John's Ch., Taylor, Pa., 1971-76, Holy Trinity Ch., Simpson, Pa., 1976—; chaplain Am. Slovak Soc., Scranton, Pa., 1971—; treas. Father Murgas Meml. Fund, Taylor, Pa., 1975; supreme chaplain Pa. Slovak Cath. Union, Wilkes-Barre, 1976; chaplain Cath. War Vets., Ashley, Pa., 1976; chaplain, Boy Scouts Am., Ashley, 1976. Recipient Certificate of Merit, Scranton U., 1973. Mem. K.C., Slovak Fedn. Am., 1st Cath. Slovak Union. Office: 37 Prospect St Simpson PA 18407

FACKENHEIM, EMIL LUDWIG See *Who's Who in America,* 43rd edition.

FAGAN, A. RUDOLPH, minister, church official, Southern Baptist Convention; b. Richton, Miss., Jan. 1, 1930; s. Lemuel Thad and Grace (Smith) F.; m. Florrie Linda Bateman, Feb. 12, 1954; children: Vicki, Max, Myra, Amanda. A.B., Howard Coll., 1951; B.D., M.Div., Southwestern Bapt. Theol. Sem., 1955. Ordained to ministry So. Bapt. Conv., 1948. Pastor 1st Bapt. Ch., Kirbyville, Tex., 1951-55, Sebring, Fla., 1955-63, Delaney Street Bapt. Ch., Orlando, Fla., 1963-72, 1st Bapt. Ch., Bradenton, Fla., 1972-74; pres. Stewardship Commn., Nashville, 1974—; pres. Fla. Bapt. Conv., 1973. Author: What the Bible Says About Stewardship, 1975. Office: Stewardship Commn 901 Commerce St Nashville TN 37203

FAGER, EVERETT DEAN, minister, United Methodist Church; b. Redkey, Ind., Apr. 6, 1947; s. Luther Von and Nola Marceil (Elliott) F.; m. Kathy Jo McKean, Mar. 17, 1973; children: Holly Renee, Ryan Christopher. B.A., U. Evansville, 1969; Th.M., Boston U., 1972; D.Min., Drew U., 1981. Ordained to ministry Methodist Ch., 1973. Minister of youth and edn. First United Meth. Ch., also St. Mark's United Meth. Ch., Decatur, Ind., 1972-76; minister Albany United Meth. Ch., Ind., 1976-82, Osceola United Meth. Ch., Ind., 1982—; ptnr. GROW Ministries, South Bend, Ind., 1983—; assoc. faculty Bethel Coll.; youth coordinator N. Ind. Conf., United Meth. Ch., 1976-80, chmn. communications services, 1980—, mem. exec. com. conf. council on ministries, 1980—, mem. program com., 1984—; mem. area communications com. Ind. Area, United Meth. Conf., 1980—; chaplain Jaycees, Decatur, Ind., 1975-76. Chmn. of Walkathon, March of Dimes, Adams County, Ind., 1973-75; mem. publicity com. Osceola Days, 1984—; vice-chmn. Osceola Bd. Zoning Appeals, 1985—. Mem. Osceola Ministerial Assn. (v.p. 1984-85). Democrat. Avocations: church sports; photography. Home: PO Box 300 423 N Beech Rd Osceola IN 46561 Office: Osceola United Meth Ch 431 N Beech Rd Osceola IN 46561

FAGGART, BRADY YOUNG, minister Lutheran Church in America; b. Concord, N.C., Apr. 17, 1930; s. Brady and Annie Lee (Aycock) F.; m. Lois Barrier McEachern, Aug. 1, 1952; children: Laura, Lois A., Luther. A.B., Lenoir Rhyne Coll., 1952; M.Div., Luth. Sch. Theology, 1956; D.D., Lenoir Rhyne Coll., 1975. Ordained to ministry Luth. Ch. in Am., 1956. Minister Good Shepherd Luth. Ch., Hickory, N.C., 1956-60, St. Mark Luth. Ch., China Grove, N.C., 1960-63; sec. Christian edn. N.C. Luth. Synod, Salisbury, N.C., 1963-67; exec. dir. Lutheridge, Arden, N.C., 1967-69; asst. to pres. Luth. Ch. Am., N.Y.C., 1969-75, exec. council, 1978—, mem. mgmt. com. Profl. Service div., Phila., 1976-78; minister 1st Luth. Ch., Greensboro, N.C., 1975—; chaplain, Wesley Long Hosp., Greensboro, 1977—. Trustee, Lenoir Rhyne Coll. Hickory, N.C., 1979-82, 83—; Recipient History Alumnus award Lenoir Rhyne Coll., 1982. Home: 3206 Robin Hood Dr Greensboro NC 27808 Office: 1st Luth Ch 3600 W Friendly Ave Greensboro NC 27410

FAIR, HAROLD LLOYD, minister, editor, United Methodist Church; b. Tyronza, Ark., Aug. 2, 1924; s. James A. and Clara (Williamson) F.; m. Agnes Hunt, Apr. 2, 1976; children: Kathryn Robert. B.A., U. Miss., 1952; B.D., Vanderbilt U., 1954, M.A., 1968, Ph.D., 1971. Editor, Bd. Edn., United Meth. Ch., Nashville, 1958-72, mng. editor Bd. Discipleship, 1972-81, gen. mgr. Abingdon Press, 1981-84, assoc. book editor, 1984—. Author: Class Devotions, ann. 1975—; also religious articles. Democrat. Office: United Methodist Pub House 201 8th Ave S PO Box 801 Nashville TN 37202

FAIR, JAMES WOODSON, minister, Church of God (Anderson, Ind.); b. Oak Grove, La., Mar. 18, 1927; s. Iverson J. and Effie C. (Skinner) F.; m. Esther Lillian Ikast, June 19, 1949; children: Pamela Diane Fair Sower, James Douglas. B.A., Anderson Coll., 1951; postgrad. Candler Sch. Theology, Emory U., 1964. Ordained to ministry Ch. of God (Anderson, Ind.), 1952. Pastor chs. Cadiz, Ohio, 1951-54, Reading, Pa., 1954-57; missionary to Denmark, 1957-62; pastor Ch. of God chs. Atlanta, 1962-65, Baton Rouge, 1965-68, Milw., 1968-74, Norfolk, Va., 1974-78, Bethany Ch. of God., Sterling Heights, Mich., 1978—; cons. to exec. council, mem. div. gen. service Ch. of God, 1973-78, chmn. ordination and ratification State of Va., 1976-77, pres. Va. Assembly, 1977-78; vice chmn. div. ministerial credentials Ch. of God in Mich., 1981—; rep. to World Conf. Ch. of God, 1959, 70, 80; pres. Norfolk Clergy Assn., 1976-78; chmn. program com. Norfolk Interfaith Bicentennial Commn., 1976; ann. lectr. Fritzlar Bibelschule, Germany, 1957-62. Contbg. editor Vital Christianity, 1963-69, Pulpit Digest, 1983-85; former curriculum writer Warner Press, Inc. Mem. Crime Resistance Edn. Com., Norfolk, 1976-78, Norfolk Action Com. for Foster Children, 1976-78, Ad hoc Crime Com., 1976-78, Mayor's Youth Commn., 1976-78. Home: 17832 Costello Mount Clemens MI 48044 Office: Bethany Ch of God 11600 Clinton River Rd Sterling Heights MI 48078

FAIRFAX, ROGER DAVID, minister, American Baptist Churches in the U.S.A.; educator; b. Clarksburg, W.Va., Aug. 30, 1944; s. Lawrence Buckner and Sarah Jane (Gaines) F.; m. Constance Barrett Umberger, Dec. 5, 1962; children: Crystal Dawn, Laura Beth. B.A., Glenville State Coll., W.Va., 1984. Ordained to ministry, Am. Bapt. Ch. in U.S.A., 1980. Minister Marshville Bapt. Ch., W.Va., 1977-79, Good Hope Bapt. Ch., Shultz, W.Va., 1979-81, Elizabeth Bapt. Ch., W.Va., 1981—; founder Project Good Samaritan, Elizabeth, 1982, exec. dir. to present; chaplain Camden Clark Meml. Hosp., Parkersburg, W.Va., 1983—. Tchr. homebound students, Wirt County Bd. Edn., Elizabeth, 1984-85. Mem. adv. bd. Consumer Homemakers, Elizabeth, 1981—; bd. dirs. Wirt County Community Action Assn., 1985; coordinator local council Boy Scouts Am. Served with USN, 1962-65. Mem. Wirt County Ministerial Assn., W.Va. Ministerial Assn., Am. Bapt. Ministerial Assn. Democrat. Avocations: golf; fishing.

FALCINI, RODOLFO ALESSANDRO, priest, Roman Catholic Ch.; b. Usella, Italy, June 11, 1913; s. Dante and Ersilia (Barbieri) F.; came to U.S., 1965, naturalized, 1972; Th.D. with specialization in History, Pontificio Athenaeo Antoniano, Rome, 1940. Joined Franciscan Order, 1929, ordained priest, 1936; instr. theology Franciscan Sems., Arezzo, Italy, 1939-44, Alverna, Italy, 1944-45, Fiesole, Italy, 1945-61, Interdiocesan Sem. Florence (Italy), 1961-65; superior of monasteries San Francesco, Fiesole, 1958-61, Monte alle Croci, Florence, 1961-64, St. Lucia, Lastra Signa, 1964-65; asst. pastor Our Lady Pity Ch., Bronx, N.Y., 1966-70. Radio speaker, religion and related topics, Stas. WEVD and WHBI, N.Y.C., 1970—. Organizer Italian partisans, World War II. Author religious books in Italian. Home and Office: 151 Thompson St New York City NY

FALCONE, SEBASTIAN ANTHONY, educator, priest, Roman Catholic Ch.; b. Rochester, N.Y., Oct. 15, 1927; s. Augustine Michael and Rose Elizabeth (Lanteri) F.; S.T.L., Catholic U. Am., 1959, postgrad., 1958-61. Ordained priest Roman Catholic Ch., 1951; prof. English, St. Lawrence Sem., Beacon, N.Y., 1951-54, prof. theology, 1954-58; prof. scripture Immaculate Heart Sem., Geneva, N.Y., 1961-67; prof. N.T., St. Bernard's Sem., Rochester, 1967—, acad. dean, 1972—. Mem. bd. Rochester Center for Theol. Studies, from 1973. Pres. Capuchin Ednl. Conf., 1958-60; asso. Sisters Formation Bd., 1969-72; mem. Priests Council, Diocese of Rochester, 1972-74; mem. Acad. Deans Eastern Conf. Theologates, 1972—; dir. Diocesan Pastoral Assts. Task Force, 1973-74, mem. pastoral assts. com., 1974—; coordinator Diocesan Permanent Diaconate Task Force, from 1976. Editor: Perspectives on Parish-based Ministries: Survey Report, 1975. Contbr. to encys. Address: St Bernard's Inst 1100 S Goodman St Rochester NY 14620

FALK, HARVEY, rabbi, Orthodox Jewish Congregations; b. N.Y.C., Apr. 30, 1932; s. Isadore and Sadie (Eisen) F.; student City Coll. N.Y., 1954; Rabbi, Mesivta Torah Sodaath, 1955; postgrad. Acad. for High Learning and Research, Monsey, N.Y., 1956; m. Hedy Rhoda Braun, June 9, 1958; children—Sharon, Barbara, Civia. Ordained rabbi, 1955; rabbi, instr. Young Israel of Claremont Pkwy., Bronx, N.Y., 1956-59; Yeshiva rabbi, religious instr. various synagogues N.Y., 1960-73; rabbi Flushing Jewish Center, Queens, N.Y., 1973-75, Congregation Ahavath Israel, Liberty, N.Y., 1975-76. Lectr. Nat. Jewish Welfare Bd., Bnai Brith. Mem. Rabbinical Council Am., N.Y. Bd. Rabbis. Author: Days of Judgement, 1972. Home and Office: 1888 48th St Brooklyn NY 11204

FALLON, EDWARD J., brother, Roman Catholic Ch.; b. Chgo., Apr. 7, 1934; s. Edward Francis and Mary Alice (O'Hagan) F.; B.A., St. Mary Coll., Minn., 1956, M.Ed., 1964. Joined Christian Brothers Order, 1949; tchr. De La Salle High Sch., Mpls., 1956-59, Christian Brothers High Sch., Quincy, Ill., 1959-60; missionary, tchr. Nicaragua, Honduras and Guatemala, 1960-62; tchr. Christian Brothers Coll., Memphis, 1963; prin. Price Coll., Amarillo, Tex., 1964-66, Driscoll High Sch., Addison, Ill., 1966-71; prin. Internat. LaSallian Center, Rome, Italy, 1972; supt. schs. Christian Brothers Central States Province, Lockport, Ill., 1973-75; supt. St. Patrick High Sch., Chgo., 1975—. Mem. Sch. Bd. Archdiocese Chgo.; mem. Ill. Cath. Conf. exec. bd.; mem. nat. ednl. council Christian Bros.; trustee Lewis U., Lockport, 1968—. Mem. Nat. Assn. Secondary Sch. Prins., Nat. Assn. Sch. Adminstrs., Assn. Supervision and Curriculum, Devel., Nat. Cath. Edn. Assn., Ill. Assn. Sch. Prins., Ill. Assn. Cath. Sch. Prins., Phi Delta Kappa. Home and office: 5900 W Belmont Ave Chicago IL 60634

FALWELL, JERRY LAYMAN, clergyman, Independent Baptist, association executive; b. Lynchburg, Va., Aug. 11, 1933; s. Cary H. and Helen V. (Beasley) F.; m. Macel Pate, Apr. 12, 1958; children: Jerry L., Jeannie, Jonathan. B.A., Bapt. Bible Coll., Springfield, Mo., 1956; D.D. (hon.), Tenn. Temple U., LL.D., Calif. Grad. Sch. Theology, Central U., Seoul, Korea. Ordained to ministry Bapt. Ch. Founder, 1956; since sr. pastor Thomas Rd. Bapt. Ch., Lynchburg; founder Moral Majority Inc., 1979, since pres. Author: Listen, America!, 1980, The Fundamentalist Phenomenon, 1981, Finding Inner Peace and Strength, 1982, When It Hurts Too Much to Cry, 1984, Wisdom for Living, 1984, Stepping Out on Faith, 1984; co-author: Church Aflame, 1971, Capturing a Town for Christ, 1973, Recipient Clergyman of Yr. award Religious Heritage Am., 1979, Jabotinsky Centennial medal, 1980; named Christian Humanitarian of Yr., Food for the Hungry Internat., 1981, One of 20 Most Influential People in Am. U.S. News & World Report, 1982, Man of Yr., Nat. Religious Broadcasters, 1984. Mem. Nat. Assn. Religious Broadcasters (dir.). Conservative. Address: Thomas Rd Bapt Ch Lynchburg VA 24514

FANDREY, JAMES EDWARD, minister, Lutheran Church-Missouri Synod; b. St. Paul, Apr. 15, 1951; s. Paul and Katherine Augusta (Mueller) F.; m. Ruth Ann Akkerman, May 29, 1971; children: Sara, Rachel, Anne. B.S. in Edn., Concordia Coll., Seward, Nebr., 1974; M.Div., Concordia Sem., Ft. Wayne, Ind., 1980. Ordained to ministry Luth. Ch., 1980. Parochial sch. tchr. Concordia Acad., St. Paul, 1975-76; pastor Zion Luth. Ch., Tobias, Nebr., 1980-82, Our Redeemer Luth. Ch., Jackson, Miss., 1982—; circuit counselor Minn. So. dist. Luth. Ch.-Mo. Synod, Jackson, 1983—; Del. Jackson County Republican Conv., Lakefield, Minn., 1984, Legis. Dist. 28B Republican Endorsing Conv., 1984. Mem. Luth. Pastors' Assn. Jackson (chmn. 1983—). Home: 400 Morrison St Jackson MN 56143 Office: Our Redeemer Luth Ch South and Kimball Sts Jackson MN 56143

FANNING, KATHERINE WOODRUFF See *Who's Who in America,* 43rd edition.

FANNING, ROBERT ALLEN, lay church worker, Southern Baptist Convention; b. Dallas, Nov. 3, 1931; s. Charles Allen and Beryl Julia (Buckner) F.; m. Carolyn Parker Hedges, Aug. 6, 1960; children: Barry H., Marc H. B.B.A., Baylor U., 1953; J.D., So. Meth. U., 1960. Trustee annuity bd. So. Bapt. Conv., 1972—; chmn. bd. trustees San Marcos Bapt. Acad., 1973—; mem. nat. bd. dirs. Fellowship Christian Athletes, 1972—; mem. adv. council Southwestern Bapt. Theol. Sem., 1966-72; mem. bd. advs. Dallas Bapt. Coll., 1984-85, found. dir., 1985; pres. bd. trustees San Marcos Bapt. Acad., 1985. Ptnr. law firm Fanning & Harper, Dallas, 1960—. Mem. devel. council Baylor U., 1965—. Mem. Am., Tex., Dallas bar assns., S.W. Legal Found., Am. Judicature Soc., Delta Theta Phi. Home: 3605 Crescent St Dallas TX 75205 Office: 4040 1st Nat Bank Bldg Dallas TX 75202

FARES, LAWRENCE TANNOUSE, priest, Roman Cath. Ch.; b. Kobayath, Lebanon, May 2, 1925; s. Tannouse J. and Nejme Abraham (Antoun) F.; M.A., St. Joseph Coll., Becharry, Lebanon, 1946; B.D., Internat. U. Theology, Rome, 1948, LL.D., 1950. Ordained priest, 1950; prin. elementary and high schs. of Becharre, 1951-56; apostolic missionary in Middle and Far East, 1951-65; tchr. theology, moral and canon law Carmelite Sacred Heart Sem., 1956-60; tchr. English lit. St. Elias Coll., Tripoli, 1956-60; chaplain U.S. bases in Turkey, 1965-66; ofcl. translator, co-sec. gen. World Lebanese Union, 1966-68, mem. council, 1966-68; faculty U. Sydney (Australia), 1968-69; coordinator Internat. Yoga Conv., 1968-69; asso. pastor Our Lady of Good Counsel Ch., Detroit, 1970—. Translator: The Works of St. Theresa of Avila, 1959; The Works of St. John of the Cross, 1964; Beloved Prophet, 3 vols., 1974; The Prophet in Miniature, 1973. Translator, Arabic works of Gibran; Mary in the Koran. Home: 17142 Rowe St Detroit MI 48205

FARGASON, EDDIE WAYNE, orchestra director, arranger; b. Lubbock, Tex., Feb. 19, 1948; s. Claude Patrick and Winnie Bertinia (Howell) F.; m. Terri Lee Rousser, Aug. 30, 1968; children: Jason Kyle, Kevin Wray. Mus.B., U. Tex., 1971, Mus.M., 1973. Arranger, orchestrator First Bapt. Ch., Dallas, 1978-83, orch. condr., 1983—. Free-lance arranger Songline Prodns., Richardson, Tex., 1975—. Composer numerous musical works. Mem. Internat. Trombone Soc., Tex. Composer's Guild, Broadcast Music Inc., Christian Instrumental Dir.'s Assn., Gospel Music Assn., Pi Kappa Lambda. Avocations: water skiing; fishing. Home: 1909 Clemson Dr Richardson TX 75081 Office: First Bapt Ch 1707 San Jacinto St Dallas TX 75201

FARIAS, JOSEPH GUS, priest, Roman Cath. Ch.; b. Passaic, N.J., June 3, 1949; s. Joseph James and Anita Marie (Lembo) F.; B.A., St. Mary's Sem., Balt., 1971, S.T.M. in Liturgy, 1975. Ordained priest, 1975; deacon St. Philip Apostle Ch., Clifton, N.J., 1974-75; asso. pastor Our Lady of Mountain Ch., Schooleys Mountain, N.J., 1975-76; dir. youth ministry Roman Cath. Diocese Paterson, N.J., 1976—. Dir. Students Participating in Aging Needs, Passaic County; bd. advisers bilingual program William Paterson Coll.; adv. council Youth Haven. Mem. Nat. Cath. Youth Orgn. (bd. advisers), Nat. Liturg. Conf. Contbg. editor Catholic Liturgy Book, 1975. Home: 41 Nosenzo Pond Rd West Milford NJ 07480 Office: 374 Grand St Paterson NJ 07505

FARMER, DAVID ALBERT, minister, Southern Baptist Convention; publisher. B. Knoxville, Tenn., Feb. 13, 1954; s. Albert Junior and Martha Dorissa (Foust) F.; m. Lindon Elizabeth Fowler, July 28, 1980; children: Jarrett Logan, Carson Gregory. B.A., Carson-Newman Coll., 1976; M.Div., So. Bapt. Theol. Sem., 1981, Ph.D., 1984. Ordained to ministry So. Bapt. Conv., 1975. Dir. youth activities Broadway Bapt. Ch., Maryville, Tenn., 1974-76; youth dir. Grace Bapt. Ch., Knoxville, 1976-77, asst. pastor, minister of youth, 1977-78; pastor Hebron Bapt. Ch., Madison, Ind., 1978-80, Harrison Hills Bapt. Ch., Lanesville, Ind., 1981-84; adj. prof. Christian preaching So. Bapt. Theol. Sem., Louisville, spring 1985; vis. prof. homiletics European Bapt. Theol. Sem., Ruschlikon, Switzerland, fall 1985. Author: Minister's Manual, 1984, 85. Assoc. editor Pulpit Digest, Louisville, 1982-84, pub., editorial dir., 1984—. Contbr. articles to publs. in field. Mem. Pi Tau Chi. Office: Pulpit Digest Inc PO Box 6405 Louisville KY 40206

FARMER, RALPH SAMUEL, minister, Ch. of God Can.; b. South Bend, Ind., Feb. 9, 1932; s. William Maxwell and Helen Janette (Grody) F.; came to Can., 1957; B.Th., Warner Pacific Coll., 1968; m. Gertrude Reimchen, Aug. 6, 1954; children—Sheryl Marie, Grant Timothy. Ordained to ministry, 1950; evangelist, Eastern and Midwestern U.S., 1949-51; pastor Asheville, N.C., 1951-52, Kelso, Oreg., 1953-56; evangelist Western Can., 1956-57; pastor Vernon, B.C., Can., 1958; co-founder World Missionary Fellowship of Ch. of God Can., Medicine Hat, Alta., Can., 1958, exec. sec., 1972—; co-founding missionary, Tanzania, E. Africa, 1959-72; pastor Ash Ave Ch. God, Medicine Hat, 1976—. Devel. dir. Alta. Bible Inst., 1974-75; mem. Medicine Hat Ministerial Assn., Evang. Fellowship Can. Home: 141 Hull Crescent St Medicine Hat AB T1C 1C9 Canada Office: Box 983 Medicine Hat AB T1A 7G8 Canada

FARMER, RICHARD ALLEN, minister, American Baptist Churches in the U.S.A.; b. N.Y.C., Nov. 16, 1951; s. Russell Vanis and Catherine (English) Robinson; m. Rosemary Simmons, June 13, 1981. Mus.B., Nyack Coll., 1975; M.Div., Princeton Theol. Sem., 1980. Ordained to ministry Am. Bapt. Chs. in U.S.A., 1980. Minister of music Trinity Bapt. Ch., Bronx, N.Y., 1974-77; evangelist, concert artist, 1977-80; sr. minister Bethany Bapt. Ch., Pitts., 1980—; instr. Bible Distbn. Ctr., Pitts., 1982—; bd. dirs. Coalition for Christian Outreach, Pitts., 1983—, Youth Guidance, Inc., Pitts., 1984—, United World Mission, St. Petersburg, Fla., 1985—; pres. RAF Ministries, Inc., Pitts., 1985—. Mem. Nat. Black Evang. Assn. Home: 174 Briarwood Dr Pittsburgh PA 15236

FARMILIAN, HIS GRACE, see Ocokoljich, Farmilian

FARR, CHARLES ELBERT, priest, ch. ofcl., Episcopal Ch.; b. Dearborn, Mich., May 15, 1934; s. Charles Albert and Ethel Mary (Jack) F.; B.A., Central Mich. U., 1958; M.Div., U. Toronto, 1961; M.A. Biblical Edn., Columbia U., 1966; Th.D., NY U, 1979; m. Jean Corrine Hudson, June 24, 1961; children—David Charles Mark, Gwyneth Mary Corrine. Ordained priest, 1961; rector Trinity Episcopal Ch., Irvington, N.J., 1970-76, Ch. of the Epiphany, Denver, 1976—; trustee Anglican Fellowship of Prayer,

1976—; mem. Presiding Bishops Com. Prayer Network for Gen. Conv., 1976; mem. Evangelism Commn., Diocese of Newark, 1969-76; vice warden Internat. Order of St. Luke the Physician, 1973—. Mem. Hudson County Clergy Assn. (pres. 1966-69). Author: Children Who Really Count, 1968; What Love is This?, 1973; The Shared Prayer Book, 1974; The Children's Book of Prayers (Big Hearts and Little Hands), 1976. Home: 101 Albion Denver CO 80220 Office: 100 Colorado Blvd Denver CO 80206

FARR, DAVID DONALD, organist, choirmaster, Episcopal Church; b. Coquille, Oreg., Feb. 28, 1942; s. Donald Haines and Emma Frances (Mulkey) F.; m. Kathleen Ann McIntosh, June 19, 1968 (div. June 1976). B.A., U. Oreg., 1965, Mus.M., 1966; postgrad. Grad. Theol. Union, Berkeley, Calif., 1979—. Organist, choirmaster St. Stephen's Episc. Ch., McLean, Va., 1967-68, St. Mark's Episc. Ch., Berkeley, 1968-72, All Sts. Episc. Ch., Pasadena, Calif., 1972-78, St. Mary Magdalen Ch., Berkeley, 1979—; cons. liturgy, dir. of chapel music St. Mary's Coll., Moraga, Calif., 1981-83; chairperson diocesan com. liturgy and music Episcopal Diocese of Los Angeles, 1975-78; adv. mem. standing com. ch. music Episcopal Ch., 1976-79; mem. com. liturgical renewal Diocese of Calif., 1983—. Clk., Law Office Ray W. Sherman, Jr., P.C., Oakland, Calif., 1980—. Composer cycle of alleluia verses. Fellow Coll. Ch. Musicians; mem. Assn. Anglican Musicians (pres. 1976-77, adv. com. 1984—), Am. Guild of Organists (bd. dirs. San Francisco chpt. 1984—). Democrat. Home: 1506 Chestnut St Berkeley CA 94702 Office: Grad Theol Union 2465 Le Conte Ave Berkeley CA 94709

FARRALL, ROBERT TRACEY, minister, Southern Baptist Convention; b. Washington, May 24, 1927; s. Victor Guy and Corinne Henrietta (Tracey) F.; B.A., Baylor U., Waco, Tex., 1948; B.D., So. Bapt. Theol. Sem., Louisville, 1951, Th.M., 1974; postgrad. Fla. State U., 1955-56, 59, Peabody Conservatory, 1966, Ga. State U., 1976; m. Betty Jane Hammett, July 23, 1954. Ordained to ministry, 1953. Asst. pastor, minister music and youth chs. in Ala. and Ga., 1954-64; minister music, pastoral asst. First Bapt. Ch., Silver Spring, Md., 1964-69; minister music and youth First Bapt. Ch., Athens, Ga., 1970—; faculty mem. Ga. Bapt. Youth Music Camps, 1955-64, 70—; condr. concerts, guest soloist; music dir. Thomas County (Ga.) Bapt. Assn., 1955-57, Valdosta (Ga.) Bapt. Assn., 1961-63; pres. Ga. Bapt. Ch. Music Conf., 1956-58. Mem. Am. Choral Dirs. Assn. (charter), So. Ch. Music Conf., Ga. Bapt. Ch. Music Conf., Phi Mu Alpha Sinfonia. Home: 385 Forest Heights Dr Athens GA 30606 Office: 355 Pulaski St Athens GA 30606

FARRELL, DOUGLAS GEORGE, minister, American Baptist Churches in the U.S.A.; b. Waverly, Iowa, May 17, 1946; s. Arthur Leslie and Erda Mae (Erxleben) F.; B.A., Judson Coll., 1968; M.Div., Am. Bapt. Sem. of West, Covina, Calif., 1972. Ordained to ministry Am. Bapt. Chs. in U.S.A., 1973. Assoc. pastor First Bapt. Ch., South Gate, Calif., 1971-72; chaplain Los Angeles County-U. So. Calif. Med. Ctr., Los Angeles, 1972-73; supr. Help Line Contact Teleministry, Los Angeles, 1973-77; minister higher edn. Orange County Campus Ministry, Orange, Calif., 1979—; seminar leader Hosp. Learning Ctrs., North Hollywood, Calif., 1981-82; bd. dirs. Interfaith Peace Ministry Orange County, 1984—, v.p., 1985—; exec. com. higher edn. and compus ministry Pacific and Southwest Conf., United Meth. Ch., 1984—; mem. com. on edn. Los Ranchos Presbytery of Presbyn. Ch. U.S.A., 1980—; mem. com. on theol. studies Orange Ctr., 1984—. Treas. Wellness Promotion Network, Orange County, 1984—; mem. Draft Counseling and Registration Info. Service, U. Calif.-Irvine, 1984—, mem. human subjects rev. com., 1983—, also bd. dirs. Interfaith Found. Mem. Christians for Latim Am. Study and Solidarity, Am. Bapt. Peace Fellowship. Democrat. Office: Orange County Campus Ministry 161 S Orange St Orange CA 92666

FARRELL, LEIGHTON KIRK, minister, United Methodist Church; b. Hillsboro, Tex., Oct. 13, 1930; s. Aubrey Lee and Lorene (Kirk) F.; m. Charlotte Ann Underwood, May 31, 1952; children: Becky Ann, Scott Gregory. B.A., So. Meth. U., 1951, Th.M., 1953; Th.D., U. Denver, 1956; L.H.D. (hon.), Alaska Pacific U., 1983. Ordained to ministry United Meth. Ch. as elder, 1954. Pastor Edge Park United Meth. Ch., Ft. Worth, 1956-65; adminstrv. asst. to bishop of Dallas-Ft. Worth area United Meth. Ch., 1965-67; sr. minister 1st United Meth. Ch., Richardson, Tex., 1967-72, Highland Park United Meth. Ch., Dallas, 1972—; trustee Meth. Mission Home, San Antonio, 1972-80, So. Meth. U., Dallas, 1972—; bd. dirs. Meth. Hosps. of Dallas, 1972-77, chmn. bd., 1977-83; del. Gen. Conf. United Meth. Ch., 1976, 80, 84. Trustee C.C. Young Home for Aged, Dallas, 1968-83; bd. dirs. Hope Cottage, Dallas, 1975-82. Recipient Valley Forge medal Freedoms Found., 1977-79, Disting. Alumnus award So. Meth. U., 1979, George Washington Medal of Honor, Freedoms Found., 1980-82. Home: 6301 Westchester St Dallas TX 75205 Office: Highland Park United Meth Ch 3300 Mockingbird Ln Dallas TX 75205

FARRELL, PATRICK JOSEPH, priest, Roman Catholic Church; b. Galway, Ireland, Feb. 26, 1937; came to U.S., 1960; s. Patrick Joseph and Mary (Kelly) F. M.A., Cath. U. Am., 1962. Ordained priest Roman Cath. Ch., 1960. Asst. pastor Nativity Ch., Biloxi, Miss., 1960-62, St. Peter's Ch., Jackson, Miss., 1962-63, Our Lady of Victory Ch., Pascagoula, Miss., 1963-65; rector Diocesan Sem., Jackson, 1965-68; dir. pastoral services Diocese of Jackson, 1968-75; pastor St. Richard Ch., Jackson, 1975—; v.p. Priest's Council, Jackson, 1976-79, pres. personnel bd., 1974-78. Bd. dirs. Jackson Council on Alcoholism, 1976-84. Mem. Jackson Ministerial Alliance (v.p. 1976-77), Nat. Council on ALcoholism (outstanding service award 1984). Home: 1213 Lynnwood Dr Jackson MS 39206

FARRIS, DONN MICHAEL, librarian; b. Welch, W.Va., Nov. 4, 1921; s. Robert Coleman and Aileen Virginia (Hutson) F.; A.B., Berea Coll., 1943; M.Div., Garrett Theol. Sem., 1947; M.L.S., Columbia, 1950; student Northwestern U., 1944-47; student Yale, 1947-48; m. Joyce Gwendolyn Lockhart, Nov. 20, 1956; children—Evan Michael, Amy Virginia. Librarian, Duke U. Div. Sch., 1950—, asst. prof. theol. bibliography, 1959-63, asso. prof., 1964-70, prof., 1971—. Mem. Am. Theol. Library Assn. (mem. exec. com. 1953-56, v.p. 1961-62, pres. 1962-63), N.C. Library Assn. Editor: Am. Theol. Library Assn.'s Newsletter, 1953—; book rev. editor Duke Div. Sch. Review, 1959—; editor: Aids to a Theological School Library, 1958, Aids to a Theological Library, Selected Basic Reference Books and Periodicals, 1969. Home: 921 N Buchanan Blvd Durham NC 27701

FARWELL, LYNDON JAMES, priest, education administrator, Roman Catholic Church; b. Los Gatos, Calif., Oct. 29, 1940; s. Lyndon James and Louise Catherine (Bacigalupi) F. B.A. in Philosophy, Gonzaga U., 1964; M.A. in History, UCLA, 1968, S.T.M., Jesuit Sch. Theology, 1972; Ph.D. in Religion, Claremont Grad. Sch., 1976. Ordained priest Roman Catholic Ch., 1971, entered Society of Jesus, 1958. Instr., Loyola High Sch., Los Angeles, 1965-68; parish asst. Our Lady of the Assumption Ch., Claremont, Calif., 1971-73; asst. prof. theology and religious studies U. San Francisco, 1976-78; exec. asst. Calif. province Soc. Jesus, Los Gatos, Calif., 1978-81; pres. Jesuit Sch. Theology, Berkeley, Calif., 1981—. Trustee U. San Francisco, 1981—, Grad. Theol. Union, Berkeley, 1981—, U. Santa Clara, Calif., 1977-84; bd. dirs. Cath. Charities Archdiocese San Francisco, 1979-81; editorial bd. Company, Nat. Jesuit mag., 1981—. Mem. Am. Acad. Religion, Internat. Assn. for Hist. Religions, North Am. Acad. Liturgy, Am. Hist. Assn., Soc. Calif. Pioneers. Democrat. Home: 2535 Le Conte Ave Berkeley CA 94709 Office: Jesuit Sch Theology 1735 Le Roy Ave Berkeley CA 94709

FATORA, JOACHIM ROBERT, priest, Roman Cath. Ch.; b. Blairsville, Pa., June 7, 1928; s. John A. and Susan Elizabeth (Ritz) F.; B.A., St. Vincent Coll., 1950; M.Div., St. Vincent Sem., 1976. Joined Order St. Benedict, 1948; ordained priest, 1954; asso. pastor St. Joseph Ch., Johnstown, Pa., 1954-57, Queen of the World Parish, St. Marys, Pa., 1957-59, St. Benedict Ch., Canton, Ohio, 1959-66, St. Boniface Ch., Pitts., 1966-70, St. Marys, Pitts., 1970-72; adminstrv. prin. St. Marys Sch., Pitts., 1972-73; pastor Immaculate Conception, New Germany, Pa., 1974-76; St. Vincent Basilica, Latrobe, Pa., 1976—. Chaplain, K.C., 1962-76. Home: St Vincent Archabbey Latrobe PA 15650 Office: St Vincent Basilica Latrobe PA 15650

FAULKENBURY, LONNIE ALVIN, minister, evangelist, Bapt. Ch.; b. Monroe, N.C., Sept. 13, 1928; s. Henry M. and Lillie Florence (Plyler) F.; student Wingate Coll., 1948-49; diploma Fruitland Bible Inst., 1952; A.B., Bapt. Bible Inst., 1956; B.Th., Clarksville Sch. Theology, 1960, D.D., 1963; B.A., Burton Coll., 1961; m. Naomi H. Huneycutt, Aug. 16, 1952; children—Phyllis Ann, Patricia Elaine. Ordained to ministry, 1949; supply pastor West Concord (N.C.) Bapt. Ch., 1949; interim pastor Bapt. Ch., Locust, N.C., 1950; pastor chs., N.C., 1950-54, 56—, Ala., 1955-56, Roberdel Bapt. Ch., Rockingham, N.C., 1974—; tchr. Bible, schs. and chs., 1970-76; evangelistic tract Ministry various states, 1965-76, C.Am., 1974, S.Am., 1974, Europe, 1974, Near East, 1974-76. Gen. bd. Bapt. State Conv. of N.C., 1972-74; worker Home Mission Bd., So. Bapt. Conv., 1975—. Pres. Norwood (N.C.) PTA, 1969-70. Home: 786 Richmond Rd Rockingham NC 28379 Office: 789 Richmond Rd Rockingham NC 28379

FAUST, CHARLES ELMER, minister, Churches of Christ; b. Pitts., Dec. 12, 1929; s. Philip Vincent and Mable Josephine (Snyder) F.; A.B., Ky. Christian Coll., 1951; m. Norma Jean McCallie, May 18, 1951; children—Cynthia Lee, Cathryn Louise, Candice Lynn, Carol Layne. Ordained to ministry, 1950; pastor chs., Salineville, Ohio, 1951-53, Hicksville, N.Y., 1953-63; dir. publicity, promotion and evangelism Eastern Christian Coll., Bell Air, Md., 1963-65; minister Ch. of Christ, West Islip, N.Y., 1965-68; dir. Go Ye Chapel Mission, East Islip, N.Y., 1968—. Trustee New York Christian Inst., Clarence, N.Y., Love Mission, N.Y.C.; mem. Continuation Com. N.Am. Christian Conv., Cin., 1971-74, 76-79, 81-84; pres. Eastern Christian Conv.,

1972; trustee Lifeline Mission to Haiti, 1979—; sec. Nat. Missionary Conv., Copeland, Kans., 1975-76, continental v.p., 1977, pres. 1978. Home: 886 Udall Rd West Islip NY 11795 Office: 886 Udall Rd West Islip NY 11795

FAUST, JAMES E., church official. Mem. Quorum of the Twelve, The Church of Jesus Christ of Latter-day Saints. Office: The Church of Jesus Christ of Latter Day Saints 50 E North Temple Salt Lake City UT 84150*

FAVRET, J(AMES) RAYMOND, priest Roman Catholic Church; b. Cin., Sept. 18, 1923; s. James Raymond and Helen (Gilligan) F. B.A., Athenaeum Ohio, 1945, B.S. in Edn., 1952; S.T.L., Angelicum, Rome, 1949, S.T.D., 1950. Ordained priest Roman Cath. Ch., 1948. Mem. adminstrv. staff Cath. U. Am., Washington, 1956-71, sec. of Univ., 1967-69, head chaplain, 1969-71; rector, pres. Mt. St. Mary Sem., Cin., 1971-78; dir. priestly formation Archdiocese of Cin., 1978-79, judge Matrimonial Tribunal, 1983-84 pastor Guardian Angels Ch., Cin., 1979—; dean, St. Francis de Sales Deanery, Cin., 1983-84; del. Southeastern Ecumenical Ministry, Cin., 1979-84. Assoc. Ctr. for Human Devel., Washington, 1979—; appeals judge Matrimonial Appeals Ct. of Ohio and D.C., 1983-84; trustee, Phi Kappa Theta Found., Worcester, Mass., 1971—. Recipient Disting. Service award Phi Kappa Theta Found., 1981. Address: 6531 Beechmont Ave Cincinnati OH 45230

FEARON, MARY, religious educator, nun, Roman Catholic Church; b. Chgo., Feb. 25, 1924; d. Thomas and Margaret (McNamara) F. B.A., St. Xavier Coll., Chgo., 1958; M.R.E., Loyola U., Chgo., 1971, postgrad., 1972. Joined Sisters of Mercy, 1944. Tchr. Mercy Schs., Ill., Iowa, 1946-67; religious educator Archdiocesan Confraternity of Christian Doctrine, Chgo., adult religious educator, 1979-81, coordinator religious edn., Ch./Sch., Chgo., 1974-76, Wilmette, Ill., 1976-79; tchr., writer St. Bernardine Sch., Forest Park, Ill., 1981—; with William C. Brown Pub. Co., part-time, 1980—. Co-author Catechetical manuals, 1980, 83, 84, 85, manuals and texts, 1981, 83, vacation sch. series: We Catholics, 1982—. Address: 816 Marengo Forest Park IL 60130 Office: St Bernardine Sch 815 Elgin Forest Park IL 60130

FEASTER, ROBERT KEITH, religious organization executive, United Methodist Church; b. Petersburg, W.Va., Feb. 28, 1930; s. Edwin G. and Louella V. (Rinehart) F.; m. Barbara Ann Lowman, June 20, 1953; children: Alicia Lynn, Victoria Glenn, Robert Keith, II, Richard Lowman. A.B., Lebanon Valley Coll., 1951; M.Div., United Theol. Sem., 1954; M.Ed., Shippensburg U., 1967. Pres., pub. The United Meth. Pub. House, Nashville, Tenn., 1983—. Vice pres. Ginn & Co., Lexington, Mass., 1968-83. Office: The United Meth Pub House 201 Eighth Ave S Nashville TN 37202

FEDJE, RAYMOND NORMAN, minister, United Meth. Ch.; b. Bklyn., Nov. 7, 1924; s. Roy Anderson and Norma (Iverson) F.; A.B., Williamette U., 1949, D.D. (hon.), 1968; S.T.B., Boston U., 1952, Ph.D., 1964; m. Betty Thompson, Aug. 31, 1949; 1 dau., Bettyrae. Ordained to ministry United Methodist Ch., 1950; youth dir. First Meth. Ch., Salem, Oreg., 1947-49; asst. ministry First Congregation Ch., Hyde Park, Mass., 1949-52; pastor Meth. Ch., East Pepperell, Mass., 1952-54, Wesley Meth. Ch., Amherst, Mass., 1954-61; sr. pastor Carter Meml. United Meth. Ch., Needham Heights, Mass., 1961-69, Asbury First United Meth. Ch., Rochester, N.Y., 1969—. Pres., Vols. in Partnership, 1974—; bd. dirs. Ashram Internat. Stowell scholar, 1967. Clubs: Masons, Shrine, Rotary. Home: 24 Oak Manor Ln Pittsford NY 14534 Office: 1050 East Ave Rochester NY 14607

FEINBERG, JEFFREY ENOCH, lay church worker, Messianic Jewish Congregation; b. Chgo., Mar. 10, 1951; s. Sidney Theodore and Sher Lee (Pelinski) F.; m. Patricia King, June 15, 1979; 1 child, Avraham David. B.A., U. Calif.-Berkeley, 1972; M.B.A., U. Chgo., 1974, M.A., 1976; M.Div., Trinity Sem., 1985; postgrad. in edn., 1985—. Deacon, Adat haTikvah, Chgo., 1977-79, elder, 1981—, also fin. adviser; fin. adviser Tyndale Theol. Sem., Netherlands; fin. mgr. Wycliffe Bible Transls., Peru, 1980-81, youth adviser, 1980-81; del. Union Messianic Jewish Congregations, Washington, 1983—; co-laborer Internat. Christian Embassy of Jerusalem, Montreat, N.C., 1982—; instr. Trinity Coll., Deerfield, Ill., 1982-83, chmn. dept. econs. and mgmt., 1984—. Author: Plans for Feast, 1983. Trinity chpt. adviser Am. Soc. Personnel Adminstrn., 1982-84. Recipient award Am. Soc. Personnel Adminstrn., 1984-85. Stanford U. scholar, 1979-80. Home: 2065 Half Day Rd D532 Deerfield IL 60015 Office: Trinity Coll 2077 Half Day Rd Deerfield IL 60015

FEINSTEIN, MOSHE, rabbi. Pres. Union of Orthodox Rabbis of the US and Can. Office: Union of Orthodox Rabbis of the US and Can 235 E Broadway New York NY 10002

FELDHEIM, PHILIPP, Jewish religious books publisher; b. Vienna, Austria, Dec. 1, 1901; came to U.S., 1939; s. Hermann and Josephine (Weissman) F.; m. Gisela Kalisch, Apr. 6, 1930; children: Eva, Felix,

Miriam R., Yitzchak. Student Rabbinical Acad., 1921. Pres., Philipp Feldheim, Inc., N.Y.C., 1941—; treas. K'hall Adas Yereim, Bklyn., 1941-51, Adas Jeshurun, N.Y.C., 1954-63. Office: Philipp Feldheim Inc 96 E Broadway New York NY 10002

FELDMAN, RUTH S., organization executive, Jewish. Exec. dir. B'nai B'rith Women, Washington. Office: B'nai B'rith Women 1640 Rhode Island Ave NW Washington DC 20036*

FELDMANN, ROBERT M., minister, Association of Evangelical Lutheran Churches; b. Ramsey, N.J., May 27, 1929; s. William Peter and Ellen Margaret (Leach) F.; m. Ethel Dorothy Winter, June 9, 1951; children: Douglas R., John M., Martha S. B.S. in Chem. Engring., Newark Coll. Engring., 1951; S.T.M., Concordia Theol. Sem., Springfield, Ill., 1960. Ordained to ministry Assn. Evang. Luth. Chs., 1960. Pastor Shepherd of the Hills Luth. Ch., Simsbury, Conn., 1960—; trustee Assn. of Evang. Luth. Chs. in New Eng., Falls Village, Conn., 1979—; mem. Peace Ctr. Communications Ministry of Christian Conf. of Conn., 1980—; bd. dirs., chmn. social concerns dept. Capitol Region Conf. of Chs., Hartford, Conn., 1982—. Contbg. editor The New Eng. Luth., 1978—. Treas. Hartford br. NAACP, 1970—; bd. dirs. Valley Net, Simsbury, 1980—, Simsbury Handicapped Advocacy Group, 1980—, Simsbury-Granby Disarmament Groups, 1980—. Mem. Hymn Soc. Am. Republican. Home: 68 Canal Rd Granby CT 06035 Office: Shepherd of the Hills Luth Ch 7 Wescott Rd Simsburg CT 06070

FELDSTEIN, DONALD, organization executive, Jewish. Exec. v.p. Am. Jewish Com., N.Y.C. Office: Am Jewish Com 165 E 56th St New York NY 10022*

FELLMAN, ERIC JOHN, editor, publisher, Baptist General Conference; b. Harvey, Ill., Apr. 18, 1954; s. John Arthur and JoAnn (Trittipoe) F.; m. Joy Annette Fickett, Sept. 6, 1975; children: Jason Eric, Nathan Eric, Jonathan Eric. Diploma, Moody Bible Inst., 1975; B.S., U. Wis.-Oshkosh, 1976; M.A. in Communications, Wheaton Coll.-Ill., 1981. Lic. minister, Minn. Media coordinator, pub. relations Moody Bible Inst., Chgo., 1977-78, asst. dir. pub. relations, 1978-79, pub. relations dir., 1979-81; dir., editor Moody Monthly Mag., Chgo., 1981—; owner JNJ Communications, Glen Ellyn, Ill., 1982—; deacon Evangel Bapt. Ch., Wheaton, 1982—; exec. com. Christian Coll. Coordinating Council, Spring Arbor, Mich., 1979-81. Publisher/editor Total Mag., 1983. Mem. Evang. Press Assn., Christian Ministries Mgmt. Assn. Office: Moody Monthly Mag Moody Bible Inst 820 N LaSalle Dr Chicago IL 60610

FELLOWS, ROBERT EDWARD, minister, Luth. Ch. in Am.; b. Milw., Sept. 14, 1926; s. Irving C. and Marie (Kovasch) F.; B.A., Carthage Coll., 1950; M.Div., Northwestern Lutheran Theol. Sem., 1953; m. Edith Alice Butterfield, May 22, 1953; children—Mark, John, Mary. Ordained to ministry Lutheran Ch. in Am., 1953; pastor United Luth. Ch., Butte, Mont., 1953-57, Redeemer Evang. Luth. Ch., Livingston, Mont., 1957-60, Lord God of Saboath Luth. Ch., Christiansted, St. Crox, V.I., 1960-64, Trinity Luth. Home, Round Rock, Tex., 1964-71, Luth. Home, Puyallup, Wash., 1971-73, Va. Synod Luth. Home, Roanoke, 1973—; sec. Carribbean Synod, Luth. Ch. in Am., 1962. Sec. Welfare Territorial Bd. I., 1962-64, child welfare adviser, 1962-64; pres. Tex. Assn. Homes for Aging, 1966, bd. dirs., 1964-71; treas. Va. Assn. Homes for Aging, 1976-77. Mem. Am., Va. (dir. 1974—) assns. homes for aging, Luth. Welfare Council. Home: 5119 Sugar Loaf Dr SW Roanoke VA 24018 Office: 3804 Branden Ave SW Roanoke VA 24018

FELTON, CATHERINE, nun, Roman Cath. Ch.; b. Providence, Aug. 4, 1916; d. James Joseph and Julia Adelaide (Prior) Felton; M.Ed., Cath. Tchrs. Coll., 1948. Entered religious soc. of Sisters of Mercy, 1934; tchr. Tyler Sch., Providence, 1937-45, St. Patrick's Sch., Providence, 1945-49, St. Catherine's Sch., Belize City, Brit. Honduras, 1954-56; prin. Our Lady of Mercy Sch., East Greenwich, R.I., 1956-60; provincial sec. Sisters of Mercy, Province of Providence, 1960-69, asst. provincial, 1982—; exec. sec. Instituto S. Pius XII, Rome, 1969-72; adminstr. Eastgate Renewal Center, Portsmouth, R.I., 1972-74; adminstr. Mt. St. Rita Health Centre, Cumberland, R.I., 1974—. Co-chmn. diocesan health consortium, Providence, 1975—; trustee St. Joseph Hosp., Providence, 1977—. Home: 255 Mercycrest Convent Wrentham Rd Cumberland RI 02864 Office: Sisters of Mercy Provincialate RD3 Cumberland RI 02864

FENERTY, LAURIE DONALD, minister, United Baptist Conv. of Atlantic Provinces; b. Wolfville, N.S., Can., Nov. 14, 1936; s. Freeman Chambers and Ethel Maude Fenerty; B.A., Meml. U. of Nfld., St. Johns, 1959; B.D., Acadia U., Wolfville, 1962; m. Marion Mabel King, May 19, 1959; children—Marion Celeste, Laurie Shawn King, Marilee Dawn, Myria Cairine. Ordained to ministry, 1962; pastor First Bapt. Ch., Thompson, Man., 1962-67, Brentwood United Bapt. Ch., Moncton, N.B., 1967-70, Berwick (N.S.) Bapt. Ch., 1970-76, Marysville United Bapt. Ch., Fredericton, N.B., 1976—; pres. United Bapt. Conv. of Atlantic Provinces, 1975-76; bd. dirs. Atlantic Bapt. Coll., 1970-76, Kingswood Camp Mens Retreats. Pioneer new ch. devel. work for Bapt. Union of Western Can. in No. Man., 1962-67. Home: 50 Hollybrook St Fredericton NB E3A 4N7 Canada

FENHAGEN, JAMES CORNER, seminary dean and president, priest, Episcopal Church; b. Nov. 4, 1929; s. Frank Donald and Mary (McLanahan) F.; m. Eulalie McFall, July 14, 1950; children: Leila, James, John. B.A., U. of South, 1951; M. Div., Va. Theol. Sem., 1954, D.D. (hon.), 1978. Ordained priest Episcopal Ch., 1955. Rector St. Mark's Ch., Brunswick, Md., 1955-58, St. Michael's Ch., Columbia, S.C., 1958-63; dir. Christian edn. Diocese D.C., Washington, 1963-67; dir. ch. and ministries Hartford Sem., Conn., 1973-78; dean, pres. Gen. Theol. Sem., N.Y.C., 1978—; dep. Gen. Conv. Episcopal Ch., 1967, 70, 77; mem. Bd. for Theol. Edn., N.Y.C., 1983—. Co-author: Prescription for Parishes, 1972; author: Mutual Ministry, 1977; More Than Wanderers, 1978; Ministry and Solitude, 1981. Mem. Assn. Theol. Schs. (council 1984—). Democrat. Office: Gen Theol Sem 175 9th Ave New York NY 10011

FERGUSON, LARRY NEIL, lay ch. worker, Conservative Baptist Assn. Am.; clinical psychologist; b. Hillsdale, Mich., June 24, 1944; s. Neil Webster and Laura Bertha (Schultz) F.; B.A., San Fernando Valley State Coll., 1967; M.Div., Conservative Bapt. Theol. Sem., 1970; Ph.D., Fuller Theol. Sem., 1975; lic. clin. psychologist, Calif.; m. Rosalinda Ison, June 7, 1969; children: Gregory-Paul Ison, Tiffany-Lin Ison. Clin. dir. Link Care Ctr., Fresno, Calif., 1980—; crisis supr. Valley Med. Ctr., Fresno, 1981—; lectr. psychology Calif. State U., Fresno, 1980—; guest lectr. Central Philippines U., 1984; trainer cross-cultural workers and missionaries. Contbr. Christian mags. and jours. Unit commr. Boy Scouts Am., 1975—. Mem. Am. Psychol. Assn., Gerontol. Assn., Christian Assn. Psychol. Studies (bd. dirs. 1980-86, pres. 1983-85), Calif. State Psychol. Assn., Evang. Theol. Soc. Home: 8104 Shirley Ave Reseda CA 91335 Office: 1734 W Shaw Ave Fresno CA 93711

FERGUSON, MILTON, seminary administrator. Pres. Midwestern Baptist Theol. Sem. (Southern Baptist), Kansas City, Mo. Office: 5001 N Oak St Trafficway Kansas City MO 64118*

FERGUSON, ROBERT URIEL, minister, ch. adminstr., So. Bapt. Conv.; b. Webster Groves, Mo., Dec. 31, 1925; s. Lloyd Ernest and Elsie Virginia (Neidringhaus) F.; A.B., Samford U., 1949; Th.M., New Orleans Baptist Sem., 1953; D.D., Ark. Bapt. Coll., 1972; m. Mary Edna Creighton, Aug. 25, 1946; children—Susan, Robert, Kathryn, Nancy, Lloyd. Ordained to ministry, 1948; pastor chs., Randolph County, Ala., 1948, Harrisonburg, La., 1949-52, Summerdale, Ala., 1953-54, Bogalusa, La., 1954-57; dir. race relations La. Bapt. Conv., 1958-60; pastor Oakdale Bapt. Ch., Mobile, Ala., 1960-70; dir. coop. ministries Ark. Bapt. Conv., 1970—. Pres. Mobile Pastors Assn., 1964-65; bd. dirs. Home Missions So. Bapt. Conv., 1966-68. Bd. trustees Mobile Coll., 1960-64. Home: Route 1 Box 524 Mabelvale AR 72103 Office: Box 552 Little Rock AR 72202

FERGUSON, ROGER NEAL, pastor, Southern Baptist Convention; b. Enid, Okla., May 13, 1955; s. John L. and Beatrice D. (Hart) F.; m. Marla Sue Moore, Dec. 29, 1979; child: Christopher Loren. B.A., Okla. Bapt. U., 1977; M.Div., Southwestern Bapt. Theol. Sem., 1980; cert. clin. edn. Bapt. Med. Ctr., 1980. Ordained to ministry Baptist Ch., 1980. Speaker, Tex. Alcohol-Narcotics Edn., Inc., Dallas, 1978-80; chaplain Bapt. Med. Ctr., Oklahoma City, 1980-81; pastor Trinity Bapt. Ch., Enid, 1981—; pres. Pastor/Staff Conf., Enid, 1984—; Okla. moderator Perry Bapt. Assn., Enid, 1982; sr. worker CONTACT, U.S.A., Enid, 1981—. Author numerous studyguides. Pres. N.W. Okla. Pastoral Care and CONTACT, 1982. Mem. Okla. Bapt. U. Alumni Assn. (pres. 1984—). Republican. Home: 926 Wild Oak Enid OK 73701 Office: Trinity Bapt Ch 1818 E Chestnut Enid OK 73701

FERRARA, LOUIS FRANCIS, priest, Episcopal Ch.; b. Bklyn., Jan. 27, 1933; s. Frank Ralph and Martha Anna (Hoeber) F.; B.A., Wagner Coll., S.I., N.Y., 1954; M.Div., Yale, 1957. Ordained priest, 1957; dir. Glenridge Sr. Citizens Multiservice and Adv. Center, Bklyn., 1974—; instr. George Mercer Sch. Theology, Garden City, N.Y., 1958—. Mem. commn. ministry and commn. on life and human health Episcopal Diocese L.I.; treas. Queens Interagy. Council Aging. Past mem. N.Y.C. Sch. Bd. 29. Mem. N.Y.C. Council Against Poverty. Home: 126 Pierrepont St Brooklyn NY 11201 Office: 67-16 Myrtle Ave Glendale NY 11227

FERRARIO, JOSEPH ANTHONY See *Who's Who in America,* 43rd edition.

FERRAZZI, THOMAS AUGUSTUS, priest, Roman Catholic Church; b. Tivoli, Italy, Mar. 14, 1912; came to U.S. 1934, naturalized, 1940; s. Joackim Ferrazzi and Bernadine Ferrazzi Moreschini. Ph.D., Propaganda Fide, Rome, 1930, D.D., 1934. Ordained priest Roman Cath. Ch., 1934. Pastor Assumption Ch., Chgo., 1938—; provincial St. Joseph Province, 1951-58; builder St. Joseph Minor Sem., St. Charles, Ill., Major Sem., Riverside, Calif., New Rectory, Perth, Australia, New Covent, Mapallapuram, India, Ch. Batticaloa, Sri Lanka, New Rectory, Chgo. Author: 26 books and 10 manuscripts on various subjects. Contbr. numerous articles to Inter Servos Mag. Home and Office: Assumption Ch 323 W Illinois St Chicago IL 60610

FERREIRA, JOE AUGUSTO, priest, Roman Cath. Ch.; b. Ribeira Grande, Sao Miguel, Azores, Dec. 31, 1935; s. Benjamin and Alice (Silva) F.; came to U.S., 1955, naturalized, 1958; student Angra's Sem., Azores Islands, 1946-55, St. Patrick's Sem., Menlo Park, Calif., 1955-58. Tchr. Bishop O'Dowd High Sch., Oakland, Calif., 1958; ordained priest, 1959; asst. pastor various chs. in Calif., 1959-72; pastor Our Lady of Good Counsel Cath. Ch., San Leandro, Calif., 1972—. Free lance writer, 1952—. Chaplain San Leandro K.C., San Leandro Young Men's Inst., Luso Am. Fraternal Fedn., Portuguese Soc. Queen St. Isabel, Portuguese Protective Union Calif., Protective Assn. Madeirense Union Calif., Brotherhood of Divine Holy Spirit, Brotherhood of St. Anthony, Brotherhood of St. Mary Magdalene, San Leandro Serra Club, Brotherhood Santo Cristo, Portuguese Am. Civic Club, Cabrillo Civic Club; organizer Parish Men's Club, Parish Youth Choir, Parish Thanksgiving Pageant; builder parish house, 1974. Named San Leandro Young Man of Year, 1963, Outstanding Portuguese Immigrant to U.S., Internat. Inst. East Bay, 1975; recipient Community Service award Observer Newspapers, 1973, Cardinal Spellman award San Leandro Eagles, 1974. Home: 14112 Azores Pl San Leandro CA 94577

FERRER, LUIS ELIEZER, minister, Christian Church (Disciples of Christ); m. Humacao, P.R., June 26, 1944; s. José and Carmen Rosa (Calzada) F.; m. Elsie Bonés, July 31, 1965; children: David Rubén, Michelle Elise. B.Th., N.W. Christian Coll., 1970; postgrad. McCormick Theol. Inst., 1979-81, Christian Theol. Inst., 1983—. Ordained to ministry Christian Ch. (Disciples of Christ), 1975. Sr. pastor 1st Spanish Christain Ch., Gary, Ind., 1970-82; dir. Christian Ch. (Disciples of Christ)-Div. Homeland Ministries, Indpls., 1982—, dir. Hispanic and Bilingual Congregations, 1984—; pres. Midwest Hispanic Fellowship, 1978-81, Nat. Hispanic Fellowship, 1981-83. Exec. dir. Asociacion Latina de Servicios Educaionales, East Chicago, Ind., 1978-82; pres. Concerned Latins Orgn., Lake County, Ind., 1975-77. Democrat. Office: Christian Ch-Div Homeland Ministries PO Box 1986 Indianapolis IN 46206

FERRIS, ROGER HOCKEY, minister, religious educator, Seventh-day Adventists; b. Port Chester, N.Y., May 7, 1933; s. Irving Edward and Louise (Hockey) F.; m. Ida Marie Kleinsmith, May 16, 1954; children: Jeffrey Paul, Jeri Beth, Jay Timothy. A.B., Atlantic Union Coll., 1955; M.A., Andrews U., 1957, Ed.D., 1985. Ordained to ministry, 1960. Intern, Seventh-day Adventist Ch., Buffalo, 1955-56, pastor, dist. leader, Oswego County, N.Y., 1957-62, Chicago Heights, Ill., 1962-68, Winnipeg, Man., Can., 1968-71; exec. dir. Health Edn. Centre, Victoria, B.C., Can., 1971-73; pastor vol. Park Seventh-day Advenist Ch., Seattle, 1973-84; tchr. Cypress Adventist Sch., Lynnwood, Wash., 1984—; mem. exec. com. Man.-Sask. Conf., 1968-71, Seventh-day Adventist Ch. in Can., 1969-71; trustee Can. Union Coll., 1969-71, Resthaven Hosp., Sidney, B.C., 1971-73; western v.p. Assn. Couples for Marriage Enrichment, Winston-Salem, 1980-83, Am. Counseling Assn., 1978—; trustee Wash. Conf. Bd. Edn., Bothell, Wash., 1983—. Contbr./co-editor: Family, Family, Family, 1973; contbr. to Pastoral Care of the Handicapped, 1983; co-author: Couple Workbook: Communication Skills in Marriage, 1976; Contbg. editor Ministry mag., 1966-70. Fellow Am. Coll. Counselors; mem. Nat. Council on Family Relations, Groves Conf. on Marriage and Family, Nat. Model R.R. Assn. (supt. 4th div. Pacific N.W. region). Home: 19929 2d Ave NW Seattle WA 98177 Office: Cypress Adventist Sch 21500 Cypress Way Lynnwood WA 98036

FERRIS, RONALD CURRY, bishop, Anglican Church; b. Toronto, Ont., Can., July 2, 1945; s. Herald Bland and Marjorie May (Curry) F.; m. Janet A. Waller, Aug. 14, 1965; children: Elisa, Jill, Matthew, Jenny, Rani, Jonathan. Diploma, Toronto Tchrs. Coll., 1965; B.A., U. Western Ont., 1972; M.Div., 1972, D.Div., 1982. Ordained deacon Anglican Ch., 1970, priest, 1971, bishop, 1981. Incumbent St. Luke's Ch., Old Crow, Can., 1970-72; rector St. Stephens Meml. Ch., London, Ont., 1973-81; bishop of Yukon, Whitehorse, Yukon, Can., 1981—. Home: 41 Firth Rd Whitehorse YT YIA 4R5 Canada Office: 4th and Elliott Sts Whitehorse YT Canada YIA 3T3

FESSENDEN, LUKE EBEN, minister, Bible teacher Seventh-day Adventist Ch.; b. Fulford, Que., Can., Oct. 25, 1943; B.A., Atlantic Union Coll., 1966; m. Geraldine Renee Dyke, Aug. 30, 1964; children: Trevor Scott, Tammie Sue. Ordained to ministry, 1974. Assoc. dean of boys Monterey Bay Acad., Watsonville, Calif., 1966-68; Bible tchr. San Pasqual Acad., Escondido, Calif., 1969-75; Bible tchr., assoc. pastor Upper

Columbia Acad., Spangle, Wash., 1975-76; pastor Ephrata and Grand Coulee (Wash.) Seventh-day Adventist Chs., 1976-78; Bible tchr. Spring Valley Acad., Centerville, Ohio, 1978-80; pastor Willoughby and Chardom Seventh-day Adventist Chs., Ohio, 1980; pastor, youth dir. Maritime Conf. in Can., 1981-83; Bible tchr. Columbia Adventist Acad., Battle Ground, Wash., 1983—; worked with youth groups on various community projects; established 2 churches with youth help. Mem. Ministerial Assn. of Seventh-day Adventists, Bible Tchrs. Assn. of North Pacific Union Conf. Home and Office: 308 NE 189th St Battle Ground WA 98604

FETTERHOFF, HOWARD J., religious organization executive, Roman Catholic Church; b. Scranton, Pa., Jan. 22, 1924; s. Howard Talmedge and Sadie A. (Neville) F.; m. Gloria Elizabeth Cahill, May 8, 1948; children: Mary, William, Robert, Margaret, Therese. H.H.D. (hon.), Thiel Coll., 1979. Dir. Pa. Cath. Conf., Harrisburg, 1969—. Home: 3415 Logan St Camp Hill PA 17011 Office: Pa Cath Conf 222 North St Harrisburg PA 17105

FICZERI, PAUL DANIEL, minister, Christian Church (Disciples of Christ); b. Cleve., Feb. 16, 1946; s. Paul and Bertha Helen (Toth) F.; m. Linda Kay Auble, July 12, 1967 (div. Oct. 1970); m. Mary Elizabeth Markley, June 12, 1981; children: Susan Elizabeth. B.A., Tex. Christian U., 1968; M.R.E., Brite Div. Sch., 1972. Ordained to ministry Christian Ch., 1972. Assoc. minister, interim minister 1st Christian Ch., Mineral Wells, Tex., 1972-73; organizing minister 1st Christian Ch., Coppell, Tex., 1974-75; minister 1st Christian Ch., Monahans, Tex., 1975-78, Mesquite, Tex., 1978-82; minister Community Christian Ch., San Antonio, 1982—; bd. dirs. Randolph Area Christian Assistance Program, Schertz, Tex., 1983—, treas., 1985—; assembly planner Bluebonnet Area Christian Ch., San Antonio, 1983-84. Contbr. articles to religious jours. Organizing dir. Footlight Players, Monahans, Tex., 1977. Recipient award Am. Bible Soc., 1970. Mem. Northeast San Antonio Commodore Owner's Group (organizer, 1st pres. 1984-85). Republican. Club: Optimists (Monahans, Tex.) (chaplain 1976-78). Lodges: Ancon, Panama Canal Bodies. Home: 5339 Maple Vista San Antonio TX Office: Community Christian Ch 16402 Front Royal St San Antonio TX 78247

FIELDS, JAMES BERYL, minister, Evangelical Methodist Church; b. Kingsport, Tenn., Mar. 20, 1938; s. James Hubert and Flora Elizabeth (Bates) F.; m. Mary Elizabeth Rogers, July 31, 1960; children: Kimberla, Katina. B.A., Bob Jones U., 1969; M.A., Manahath Sch. Theology, 1979. Ordained to ministry Evang. Meth. Ch. Am. Treas. Bible Meth. Missions, Kingsport, 1974-80, vice-chmn., 1980-82, chmn., 1982—; pastor Cedar View Meth. Ch., Kingsport, 1970—; gen. supt. Evang. Meth. Ch. Am., 1982—; mem. exec. com. Am. Council Christian Chs., Valley Forge, Pa., 1981—; chief adminstr. Cedar View Christian Schs., Kingsport, 1979—; bd. dirs. Manahath Sch. Theology, Hollidaysburg, Pa., 1978—; del. Tenn. Assn. Christian Schs., Chattanooga, 1981—. Served with USN, 1956-59; Atlantic.

FIELDS, WILMER CLEMONT, minister, So. Bapt. Conv., ch. ofcl.; b. Saline, La., Mar. 16, 1922; s. F.B. and Eva Mae (Corbitt) F.; B.A., La. Coll., 1943; Th.M., So. Bapt. Theol. Sem., 1946, Th.D., 1950; m. Rebecca Elizabeth Hagan, June 22, 1946; children—Randall Hagan, Christy Alderson, Rebecca Elizabeth. Ordained to ministry So. Baptist Conv., 1941; student pastor, Woodworth, Belcher and Gilliam, La., 1941-43; music and edn. dir. Carlisle Av. Bapt. Ch., Louisville, 1943-48; pastor Bethany Bapt. Ch., Louisville, 1948-51; pastor First Bapt. Ch., Yazoo City, Miss., 1951-56; editor Bapt. Record jour. Miss. Bapt. Conv., 1956-59; asst. to exec. sec. also dir. pub. relations So. Bapt. Conv. Exec. Com., Nashville, Tenn., 1959—. Nat. pres. Asso. Ch. Press, 1967-69. Trustee Council on Religion and Internat. Affairs; bd. dirs. Religion in Am. Life, Nat. Conf. Christians and Jews. Mem. Religious Pub. Relations Council (nat. pres. 1966-67), Pub. Relations Soc. Am., Bapt. Pub. Relations Assn. (pres. 1970-71), So. Bapt. Press Assn. Author: The Chains Are Strong, 1963; Trumpets in Dixie, 1968; (with James Daniel and others) The 70's Opportunities for Your Church, 1969; (with H. Franklin Paschall and others) The Teacher's Bible Commentary, 1972. Editor Pub. Relations Handbook, 1976. Home: 2223 Woodmont Blvd Nashville TN 37215 Office: 460 James Robertson Pkwy Nashville TN 37219

FILEVICH, BASIL, bishop, Ukrainian Catholic Church; b. Mundare, Alta., Can., Jan. 13, 1918; s. Euvenaly and Anna (Pelech) F. B.Th., St. Joseph's Sem., Edmonton, 1942. Ordained priest, Ukrainian Cath. Ch., 1942. Pastor, Dauphin, Man., Can., 1942-43, Kitchener, Ont., 1943-48, St. Catharine's Ch., On., 1948-51; rector St. Josaphat's Cathedral, Toronto, Ont., Can., 1951-78; pastor Holy Cross Parish, Thunder Bay, Ont., 1978-83; named Chancellor Eparchy of Toronto, 1951; named Monsignor, domestic prelate, 1959; named Vicar-Gen. Eparchy of Toronto, 1962; named Mitred Archpriest, 1972; consecrated Bishop of Saskatoon, 1983. Address: Ukrainian Cath Eparchy of Saskatoon 866 Saskatchewan Crescent E Saskatoon SK S7N 0L4 Canada

FINEOUT, ARTHUR JOHN, minister, Southern Baptist Convention; b. Mountaindale, Pa., Nov. 16, 1923; s. Lloyd Edwin and Esther Louise (Gates) F.; m. Virginia Ellen Sims, Aug. 20, 1953; children: Arthur John II, James Mark, Lynne Ellen, Myron Paul. B.S., E. Tenn. State U., 1951; M.Div., Southwestern Bapt. Theol. Sem., Fort Worth, 1955. Ordained to ministry So. Bapt. Conv., 1941. Minister, Doe River Bapt. Ch., Elizabethton, Tenn., 1941-51, First Bapt. Chs., Princeton, Tex., 1952-55, Plano, Tex., 1955-61, Terrell, Tex., 1961—; trustee Lavon Bapt. Encampment, McKinney, Tex., 1953—; trustee E. Tex. Bapt. U., Marshall, 1965—, vice pres. bd., 1982-84; mem. exec. bd. Bapt. Gen. Conv. of Tex., Dallas, 1979—. Mem. Terrell Ministerial Alliance (pres. 1984), Assn. Photographers Internat. Lodges: Terrell Rotary (bd. dirs.). Home: 1000 Griffith Ave Terrell TX 75160 Office: First Bapt Ch 403 N Catherine St Terrell TX 75160

FINGER, WOODROW W., minister, Conservative Bapt. Assn. Am.; b. Saugerties, N.Y., July 29, 1918; s. Floyd Elting and Lilly Ann (Darringer) F.; B.A., Bob Jones Coll., 1943; B.D., Eastern Bapt. Theol. Sem., 1945; Ph.D., Bob Jones U., 1957; m. Lydia Fedynich, Aug. 30, 1944; children—Betty Finger Camp, Robert David. Pastor Third St. Bapt. Ch., Cordele, Ga., 1945-52, Blvd. Bapt. Ch., Greenville, S.C., 1952-55, Immanuel Bapt. Ch., Utica, N.Y., 1955-63, Norwood Park Bapt. Ch., Chgo., 1963-66, First Bapt. Ch., Sheridan, Wyo., 1966-78, Ponderosa Bapt. Ch., Payson, Ariz., 1981—. Pres. Conservative Bapt. Assn. N.Y. State, 1958-59; bd. dirs. Conservative Bapt. Home Mission Soc., 1966-72, Conservative Bapt. Assn. Am., 1960-63; trustee Conservative Bapt. Theol. Sem., Denver, 1965-83; mem. adminstrv. bd. Rocky Mountain Conservative Bapt. Assn., 1972-78; NW regional v.p. Conservative Bapt. Assn. Am., 1974, 75. Bd. dirs. Sheridan County YMCA, 1969-75. Address: 1402 N Matterhorn Payson AZ 85541

FINK, ARNOLD GOODFRIEND, rabbi, Reform Jewish; b. Buffalo, June 2, 1935; s. Joseph Lionel and Janice Florence (Gutfreund) F; m. Karen Faith Hoffman, June 14, 1958; children: Daniel Bruce, Jonathan Alan, Julie Lynn. B.A., Princeton U., 1957; B.H.L., M.A., Hebrew Union Coll., 1957-62; postgrad. Temple U., 1963-64, Va. Theol. Sem., 1980-84. Rabbi, 1962. Assoc. rabbi Congregation Keneseth Israel, Phila., 1962-69; rabbi Beth El Hebrew Congregation, Alexandria, Va., 1969—; chmn. No. Va. Synagogue Council, 1972-73; del. Nat. Com. on Synagogue Rabbinical Relations, 1981—. Preceptor, Inter/Met, Washington, 1972-77. Mem. Wash. Bd. Rabbis, Alexandria Clergy Assn. (pres. 1978-79). Lodge: Rotary (chaplain Alexandria 1974-75). Home: 6558 Wolftree Ln Annandale VA 22003 Office: Beth El Hebrew Congregation 3830 Seminary Rd Alexandria VA 22304

FINK, JOHN FRANCIS, religious newspaper executive, Roman Catholic Ch.; b. Ft. Wayne, Ind., Dec. 17, 1931; s. Francis Anthony and Helen Elizabeth (Hartman) F.; B.A., U. Notre Dame, 1953; m. Marie Therese Waldron, May 31, 1955; children—Regina Marie, Barbara Ann, Robert Paul, Stephen Lawrence, Therese Rose, David Lawrence, John Noll. Dir., Catholic Press Assn. of U.S. and Can., 1965-75, pres., 1973-75; exec. v.p. Our Sunday Visitor, Inc., Huntington, Ind., 1971-76, pres., 1976-82, pub. 1982-84; editor-in-chief The Criterion, Indpls., 1984—; pres. Internat. Fedn. Ch. Press Assns., 1981—; dir. and exec. com. council Internat. Cath. Union Press. Chmn. United Fund Dr., 1963; pres. United Way Huntington County, 1973-74, dir., 1971-74. Bd. dirs. Catholic Journalism Scholarship Fund, 1968—. Recipient Distinguished Service award Jr. C. of C., 1960. Home: 7043 N Delaware St Indianapolis IN 46220 Office: 1400 N Meridian St Indianapolis IN 46206

FINKBEINER, ROBERT GLYNN, minister, Luth. Ch. Am.; b. Laurens, S.C., Dec. 26, 1941; s. Robert Adam and Madera Crystal (Glynn) F.; B.A., Newberry Coll., 1964; M.Div. Luth. Theol. So. Sem., 1968; m. Phyllis Kay Wade, Apr. 11, 1964; children—Paul Glynn, Christine Lynn, Amy Lee. Ordained to ministry, 1968; pastor Holy Cross Luth. Ch., Lincolnton, N.C., 1968-71, St. John's Luth. Ch., Beaufort, S.C., 1971-72; Immanuel Luth. Ch., Jamestown, N.Y., 1972—. Mem. youth com., minority recruitment task force Synod; bd. dirs. Luth. Social Services of Jamestown; mem. exec. bd. Upper N.Y. Synod, Luth. Ch. Am. Mem. narcotics guidance council county bd.; bd. dirs. Am. Field Service. Mem. Jamestown Ministerial Assn., Jamestown Ecumenical Ministries. Home: 517 E 5th St Jamestown NY 14701 Office: PO Box 1385 Jamestown NY 14701

FINKENBINDER, PAUL EDWIN, minister; b. Santurce, P.R., Sept. 24, 1921; s. Frank Otto and Aura (Argetsinger) F.; diploma Zion Bible Inst., East Providence, R.I., 1941; postgrad. Central Bible Coll., Springfield, Mo., 1941-42; m. Malinda Swartzentruber, Jan. 25, 1942; children: Paul, Gene, Sharon (Mrs. Jonathan M. Brown), Joan, Ellin (Mrs. Gregory R. Sinsley). Ordained to ministry Assemblies of God, 1948; pastor Spanish Assembly of God Ch., Raton, N.Mex., 1942-43; missionary El Salvador, 1943-64; founder, pres. Hermono Pablo Ministries, Costa Mesa, Calif., 1964—; syndicated newspaper columnist in 30 daily newspapers, Latin Am.; radio broadcaster over 534 stas. Bd. dirs. Latin Am. Mission, Miami, Fla.; bd. dirs. Open Doors, Santa Ana, Calif. Recipient Oscar for film Elijah & Baal, as best Bible story Nat. Evang. Film Found., 1971; certificate of distinction So. Calif. Coll., Costa Mesa, 1971; hon. diploma Orantes Inst., San Salvador, 1971; Angel award for best Spanish broadcast Religion in Media, 1980. Mem. Nat. Religious Broadcasters (Distinguished Service honor citation 1970, Hispanic Program of Yr. 1983), Internat. Christian Broadcasters, Spanish Nat. Religious Broadcasters San Antonio (bd. dirs.), Difuciones Inter Americanas. Home: 2975 Mindanao Dr Costa Mesa CA 92626 Office: 2080 Placentia St Costa Mesa CA 92627 also PO Box 100 Costa Mesa CA 92628

FINLEY, JAMES EDWARD, minister, Pentecostal Holiness Church, Inc.; b. Mobile, Ala., Dec. 20, 1933; s. James Thomas and Printella Elizabeth (Stewart) F.; D.D., Va. Sem., 1976; m. Helen Elizabeth McCoy, June 10, 1953; children—Monica, Mark, James A., Sheila. Ordained to ministry, 1964. Pastor Mt. Zion Apostolic Overcoming Holy Ch. of God, Dayton, Ohio, 1964, Phillips Temple A.OH. Ch. of God, Mobile, 1973—. Dir. Commonwealth Nat. Bank, Mobile. Active Community Devel. Project Mobile County, Cystic Fibrosis Found., Mobile County Alcoholics Prevention Program. Mem. Interracial, Interdonominal; ministers alliances, NAACP, Urban League Am. Home: 711 Elmira St Mobile AL 36603 Office: 2257 St Stephens Rd Mobile AL 36617

FINLEY, ROBERT VAN EATON, missionary executive; b. Charlottesville, Va., May 2, 1922; s. William Walter and Melissa (Hoover) F.; m. Ethel Drummond, Dec. 23, 1949; children: Deborah Ann, Ruth Ellen. B.A., U. Va., 1944; postgrad. U. Chgo. Div. Sch., 1946-47; Litt.D., Houghton (N.Y.) Coll., 1952. Ordained to ministry Baptist Ch., 1957. Evangelist Inter-Varsity Christian Fellowship and Youth for Christ Internat., 1945-46, overseas, 1948-51; pastor Evang. Free Ch., Richmond, Calif., 1952; minister to fgn. students Tenth Presbyn. Ch., Phila., 1952-55; founder Internat. Students, Inc., Washington, 1953, pres., 1953-67, chmn., 1968-70; pastor Temple Bapt. Ch., Washington, 1965-66; founder, gen. dir. Christian Aid Mission, Washington, 1953-70, chmn., pres., 1970—; founder, gen. dir. Overseas Students Mission, Ft. Erie, Ont., Can., 1954-68, pres., 1969—; pastor Beltway Bapt. Ch., Washington, 1971-76; gen. dir. Bharat Evang. Fellowship, Washington, 1971-72, pres., 1973-83. Editor, pub. Conquest for Christ, 1954-73; Christian Mission Mag., 1974—. Bd. dirs. Sino-Am. Cultural Soc., Washington. Mem. Omicron Delta Kappa. Home: 4518 Western Ave Bethesda MD 20816 Office: 555 Broomley Rd Charlottesville VA 22901 also 201 Stanton St Fort Erie ON Canada

FIORENZA, JOSEPH A., bishop, Roman Catholic Church. Bishop of San Angelo, 1979—. Office: 5002 Blue Gramo Trail San Angelo TX 76904*

FIREBAUGH, ROBERT DEAN, minister, United Meth. Ch.; b. Wichita, Feb. 18, 1944; s. Earl Morland and Gladys (Varner) F.; B.A. in Psychology, Southwestern Coll., 1966; M.Th., So. Meth. U., 1969; m. Patricia Merlene Barner, Aug. 21, 1966; children—Deirdre Rae, Jerrod Lee. Ordained to ministry, 1967; minister, Friberg-Codpor, Charlie, Tex., 1968-69, Roundup, Grassrange, Winnett, Mont., 1969-70, Huntley-Ballantine United Parish, Mont., 1970-76, Lonsdale United Meth. Ch., Sidney, Mont., 1976—. Chmn. worship, evangelism Yellowstone Conf., 1975-76, conf. missionary sec., 1975—; mem. task force hunger Mont. Assn. Chs., 1976—; instr. Big Sky Mission Forum, Bozeman, Mont., 1976—. Contbr. articles to religious publs. Home and Office: 205 3d Ave SE Sidney MT 59270

FIRESTONE, MILTON, religious newspaper editor; b. N.Y.C., June 8, 1927; s. Louis and Anna (Fleiderbaum) F.; B.A. in Econs., U. Kan., 1946; m. Bea Blumenthal, May 30, 1954; children—David, Michael, Judith. Editor, pres. Kansas City (Mo.) Jewish Chronicle, 1963—. Bd. dirs. Beth Shalom Synagogue, Jewish Conservative, Kansas City, 1966—; organizing founder, mem. bd. Hebrew Acad. Greater Kansas City. Recipient Community Service award B'nai B'rith Women, 1965. Mem. Am. Jewish Press Assn. (v.p., treas. 1968-72), World Fedn. Jewish Journalists, Phi Beta Kappa, Pi Sigma Alpha. Home: 711 E 80th St Kansas City MO 64131 Office: POB 8709 Kansas City MO 64114

FIRESTONE, RONALD LEE, minister, Church of God (Anderson, Indiana); chiropractor; b. LaPaz, Bolivia, Mar. 12, 1950; s. Homer Leon and Elvira Ruth (Englund) F.; m. Esther Violet Cepoda, Dec. 27, 1969; children: LaMel Ruth, Homer Ezequiel. A.A., Pasadena City Coll., 1968; B.A., Edison State Coll., 1981; M.S., U. Bridgeport, 1982; D.C., Los Angeles Coll. Chiropractic, 1972; M.D., Bolivian Nat. U.; postgrad. Walden U. Ordained to ministry Ch. of God (Anderson), 1966. Assoc. pastor 1st Ch. of Nazarene,

Los Angeles, 1968-70; co-pastor Pasadena Nazarene Ch., 1970-74; pastor El Libertador Ch., Cochabamba, Bolivia, 1974-78; missionary Ch. of God (Anderson, Ind.), 1974-78; pastor 1st Ch. of God, Riverside, Calif., 1978-80, Sky View Chaple Ch. of God, Joshua Tree, Calif., 1982-84; pres. Vacation Samaritans, Yucca Valley, Calif., 1983—; clinic dir., practitioner, clinician Ch. of God Clinic, Bolivia, 1974-78; dist. sec. Assn. Ch. of God So. Calif., 1980-83, mem. missions com., 1983—. From instr. to prof. Los Angeles Coll. Chiropractic, 1972-74, 80; pvt. practice, Riverside and Yucca Valley, Calif., 1978—. Contbr. articles to profl. jours. Am. Chiropractice Assn. research scholar, 1968-72; Chiropractic Heart Found. scholar, 1969. Mem. So. Calif. Ministerial Assembly of Ch. of God, Delta Sigma. Lodge: Rotary. Home: 57610 Crestview Dr Yucca Valley CA 82274 Office: Vacation Samaritan 57610 Crestview Dr. Yucca Valley CA 92284

FISCHER, CARL WILHELM, lay worker, Episcopal Church; b. Wilkes-Barre, Pa., July 14, 1913; s. Ernest Julius Carl and Mary Vesta (Horton) F.; m. Frances Emma Wheeler, Aug. 26, 1939; 1 son, Ernst Jay. B.S. in Chem. Engring., U. Cin., 1935. Chmn. Episcopal Charities Appeal, Garden City, N.Y., 1974-76; vestryman, All Saints' Episc. Ch., Bayside, N.Y., 1962-63, 73-75, 84—, warden, 1963-71. Vice pres. in charge mfg. Pepsi Co., 1938-75. Author: Between The Lakes Cemeteries, 1974; The Wick Family Genealogy, 1973; Descendants of Thomas Horton, 1965; Descendants of Girge Fischer, 1966. Bd. dirs. Family Consultation Service, Jamaica, N.Y., 1976—, pres., 1976-79; bd. dirs. St. Mary's Hosp. for Children, Bayside, 1967—. Served to lt. col. USAAF, 1940-45. Mem. New Eng. Historic Geneal. Soc., DeWitt Hist. Soc., N.Y. Geneal. and Biog. Soc., Interlaken Hist. Soc., Detroit Soc. for Geneal. Research, Central N.Y. Geneal. Soc. Home: 214-57 33d Rd Bayside NY 11361

FISCHER, DONALD LOUIS, priest, Roman Cath. Ch.; b. Cin., Jan. 23, 1940; s. Fred H. and Muriel C. (Hehman) F.; student U. Dallas, 1958-60; B.A. in Philosophy, St. Bernard Sem., 1963, St. John's Sem., Little Rock, 1967. Ordained priest, 1967; asst. pastor St. Monica's Ch., Dallas, 1969-73, St. Thomas Aquinas Ch., Dallas, 1967-69; chaplain U. Dallas 1973—. Dir. vocations Diocese of Dallas, Roman Cath. Ch., 1973-80, mem. commn. on liturgical art and music, 1974—, mem. priest's senate, 1970-72; chaplain Dallas Serra Club, 1973-80; bd. dirs. NCCJ, 1974-79. Address: University of Dallas Irving TX 75061

FISCHER, JAMES ADRIAN See Who's Who in America, 43rd edition.

FISCHER, JOHN DALLAS, ecumenical exec., minister, United Ch. Christ; b. Louisville, Dec. 30, 1933; s. Adams T. and Ethel A. (Simms) F.; A.B., U. Ky., 1955; M.A., Union Theol. Sem., N.Y.C., 1959; M.S., U. Wis.-Milw., 1969; m. Betty Ann Myers, Dec. 27, 1954; children—Thomas, James, Stephen. Ordained to ministry, 1959; pastor, Kansas City, Mo., 1959-64; minister Met. Mission, Minn. Conf. United Ch. Christ, 1964-69; exec. dir. Greater Milw. Conf. Religion and Urban Affairs, 1970-77, Wis. Conf. of Chs., 1981-85. Bd. dirs. Interfaith Housing Found., Second Harvesters of Wis., Conf. Point Camp. Mem. Nat. Assn. Ecumenical Staff, Phi Beta Kappa. Home: 5029 Manitowoc Pkwy Madison WI 53705 Office: 1955 W Broadway Madison WI 53713

FISCHER, MARILYN CAROL, nun, major superior, Roman Catholic Church; b. Quincy, Ill., May 23, 1936; d. Frank Carl and Marie Elizabeth (Mennel) F. B.S. in Nursing, U. Dayton, 1964; M.A. in Edn., Xavier U., Cin., 1974. Joined Franciscan Sisters of Poor, Roman Cath. Ch., 1958. Dir. of formation Sisters of Poor, Cin., 1967-77, mem. leadership bd., Bklyn., 1977-80, major superior, 1980—; chmn. Franciscan Sisters of Poor Health System, Inc., Bklyn., 1982—. Mem. Leadership Conf. Women Religious. Office: Franciscan Sisters of Poor 191 Joralemon St Brooklyn NY 11201

FISH, JANE, lay church worker, Southern Baptist Convention; b. El Reno, Okla., Mar. 29, 1925; d. Josiah Holland and Cassandra (Clements) Rosson. Youth dir. First So. Bapt. Ch., Imperial, Calif., 1970-76, sec., 1970—; youth dir. Trinity So. Bapt. Assn., 1971—; youth specialist Bapt. Sunday Sch. Bd. Pub., author religious tracts, youth Sunday Sch. materials, pupil commentary, teaching procedures and articles for Youth Leadership and Equipping Youth Mags.; also editor ch. newsletter Lighthouse, 1970—. Home: 600 N Imperial Ave Imperial CA 92251 Office: PO Box 147 Imperial CA 92251

FISHER, CONSTANCE LOUISE, lay church worker, liturgical dance director United Methodist Church; b. Spokane, Wash., Oct. 20, 1921; d. William Walter and Rebekah Mary (Lynde) Armfield; m. Charles Wesley Fisher, Aug. 9, 1944; children: Thomas Michael, John Wesley, Mary Beth, Thomas Walter. B.A., Eastern Wash. U., 1944. Soloist Westminster Congregational Ch., Spokane, 1941-44; choir dir. Corbin Park Meth. Ch., Spokane, 1944-46, Ch. of All Nations, Boston, 1946-49, Queen Anne Meth. Ch., Seattle, 1953-59, Wesley Meth. Ch., San Diego, 1960-67; sacred dance dir. Celebrants sacred dance

choir, Denver, 1977—. Sacred dance dir. Sacred Dance Choir of Calif. Western U., San Diego, 1960-67, Altar Choir, Amarillo, Tex., 1967-69, Jubilate Dancers, Denver, 1969-77. Adj. prof. sacred dance Iliff Sch. Theology, Denver, 1975—, Pacific Sch. Religion, Berkeley, Calif., 1983—. Author: Dancing the Old Testament, 1980; Dancing With Early Christians, 1983. Founder Connie Fisher Endowment, Iliff Sch. Theology, 1984. Mem. Sacred Dance Guild (v.p. nat. chpt. 1977-79, bd. dirs. 1979-83). Avocations: music; drama. Home: 2557 S Dover #22 Lakewood CO 80227

FISHER, DONALD WAYNE, minister, ch. ofcl., United Pentecostal Ch., Internat.; b. Bend, Oreg., Feb. 16, 1939; s. Harry Benson and Freda Blanche (Harlan) F.; student Conquerors Bible Coll., 1956-58; B.A., Cascade Coll., 1960; m. Donna Rae Lewis, Aug. 14, 1959; children—Susan, Karissa, Ronna. Ordained to ministry, 1964; pastor chs. in Alaska, Wash., 1960-65; instr. Bible Conquerors Bible Coll., Portland, Oreg., 1964-65; editor Internat. Youth Div., United Pentecostal Ch. Internat., St. Louis, 1966-68, founding editor Word Aflame Publs. Ch. Sch. div., Hazelwood, Mo., 1968-71, coordinator overseas ministries Fgn. Missions div., Hazelwood, Mo. 1971-76; exec. v.p. Jackson (Miss.) Coll. of Ministries, 1976—. Home: 107 Duranville St Jackson MS 39212

FISHER, NEAL FLOYD See Who's Who in America, 43rd edition.

FISHER, RICHARD L., Bishop, African Methodist Episcopal Zion Church. Office: 8015 Sanford St St Louis MO 63130*

FISHER, ROBERT ELWOOD, church official, Church of God, Cleveland, Tenn.; b. Glendale, Cal., Aug. 29, 1931; s. Heman Harold and Anna Elizabeth (Einzig) F.; B.A., Fresno State U., 1964, M.A., 1967; Ph.D., U. Hawaii, 1973; m. Mary Lena Sadler, Aug. 1, 1952; children—Robert Wesley, Cameron Michael, Loretta Lynne. Ordained to ministry Ch. of God, Cleveland, Tenn., 1958; bus. mgr., v.p., supt. West Coast Bible Coll., 1952-60; pastor Church of God Temple, Fresno, Cal., 1960-67; state overseer Chs. of God in Hawaii, 1967-74; dir. Met. Center, Honolulu, 1972-74; pres. Central Pacific Christian Coll., Honolulu, 1970-74; state overseer Md.-Del.-Washington, 1974-76; nat. dir. dept. gen. edn. Ch. of God, 1977-84, state overseer, N. Ga., 1984—, mem. exec. council, 1984, mem. Gen. Bd. Edn., 1968-74. Chmn. bd. dirs. Lee Coll., 1984—. Mem. Am. Psychol. Assn. Republican. Home: 6163 Buford Hwy Doraville GA 30340 Office: Ch of God State Office PO Box 47-400 Doraville GA 30362

FISHER, STEPHEN KENT, minister, Christian Church (Disciples of Christ); b. Anderson, Ind., Mar. 6, 1952; s. Earl Eugene and Pauline Mae (Shafer) F.; m. Patricia Lynn Wolfe, Aug. 4, 1973; children: Jonathan David, Benjamin Earl. B.A., Tex. Christian U., 1974; M.Div., Christian Theol. Sem., 1978. Ordained to ministry Christian Ch., 1978. Student assoc. Univ. Park Christian Ch., Indpls., 1974-76; student pastor New Lisbon Christian Ch., Union City, Ind., 1976-78; pastor Union Ch., Cissna Park, Ill., 1978-80, Ursa Christian Ch., Ill., 1980-85, Marshfield Christian Ch., Mo., 1985—; chmn. Wenois cluster Christian Chs., 1982-85; mem. regional bd. Christian Ch. in Ill., Bloomington, 1982-85; pres. Bear Creek Ministerial Assn., Mendon, Ill., 1983-84; mem. steering com. Blessing Hosp. Vol. Chaplains, Quincy, Ill., 1984-85; chmn. Adams County CROP/Ch. World Service, Quincy, Ill., 1984-85. Author numerous poems. Mem. exec. com. Adams County Red Cross, Quincy, 1984-87; coordinator Ursa Bloodmobile, Ill., 1982-85; mem. dist. nominating com. Saukee Area council, Alqonquin Dist., Boy Scouts Am., 1983. Recipient award Am. Legion, Anderson, Ind., 1967. Mem. Coll. Profl. Christian Ministers, Profl. Assn. Clergy Credit Union, Bear Creek Ministerial Assn. (sec., pres.). Lodge: Lions (coordinator blood drives, chmn. health and social services com.). Office: Marshfield Christian Ch PO Box 222 Marshfield MO 65706

FISHMAN, JOSHUA, Jewish organization executive. Exec. dir. Torah Umesorah—Nat. Soc. for Hebrew Day Schs. Office: 160 Broadway New York NY 10038*

FITTERER, JOHN ANGUS, priest, Episcopal Church. B. Ellensburg, Wash., July 1, 1922; s. Clarence Philip and Violet (MacMillan) F.; m. Barbara Trombley, Dec. 23, 1977. B.A., St. Louis U., 1946, M.A., Ph.L., 1947; S.T.L., Gregorian U., Rome, 1954; D.Hum., Our Lady of Lake U., 1972. Received to ministry Episcopal Ch., 1978. Pres., exec. officer Assn. Jesuit Colls. and Univs., Washington, 1971-77; interim rector Ch. of St. John the Evangelist, Hingham, Mass., 1978-79; dir. devel. Diocese of Calif., San Francisco, 1980-84; vice chmn. Episcopal Homes Found., Lafayette, Calif., 1984—; sec. Nat. Jesuit Ednl. Assn. for Colls. and Univs., Washington, 1966-69; vice chmn. bd. trustees Loyola Coll., Balt., 1970-76. Translator: Thomas Aquinas Commentary on Nichomachean Ethics of Aristotle, 1965. Contbr. articles on higher edn. and religion to various publs., 1956-75. Chmn. Nat. Council on Crime and Delinquency, Wash. council, 1965-70; pres., chmn. bd. trustees Seattle U., 1965-70; vice chmn. Wash. Urban Affairs Council, 1966-69; trustee U.

Detroit, 1976-77. Recipient Disting. Civilian Service medal U.S. Army; Disting. Citizen's award Boy's Clubs Am., N.Y.C., 1971, Outstanding Service award Nat. Council on Crime and Delinquency, 1969. Club: Cosmos (Washington) (house com. 1971-77). Lodge: Rotary (bd. dirs. 1965-76). Home: 114 Barbaree Way Tiburon CA 94920 Office: Episcopal Homes Found 3650 Mt Diablo Blvd Lafayette CA 94549

FITZ, RAYMOND L. See Who's Who in America, 43rd edition.

FITZGERALD, ERNEST ABNER, bishop, United Methodist Ch.; b. Crouse, N.C., July 24, 1925; s. James Boyd and Hattie (Chaffin) F.; A.B. cum laude, Western Carolina Coll., 1947; B.D., Duke, 1951; D.D. (hon.), High Point Coll., 1968; m. Sarah Frances Perry, Aug. 25, 1945; children—James Boyd, Patricia Ann. Ordained to ministry United Methodist Ch., 1946; minister N.C. chs., 1944-59, Purcell Ch., Charlotte, N.C., 1959-64, Grace Ch., Greensboro, N.C., 1964-66, Centenary Ch., Winston-Salem, N.C., 1966-82, West Marked St. Ch., Greensboro, N.C., 1982-84; bishop Atlanta area, 1984—; Staley Christian Scholar lectr. Brevard, Pfeiffer colls., 1973; mem. commn. on Christian social concerns Western N.C. Conf., mem. bd. pensions, mem. com. on Meth. info., vice chmn. com. on conf. structure; mem. Evangelistic Mission to Dominican Republic; ofcl. visitor World Meth. Conf., London, 1966, del., Denver, 1971; del. Jurisdictional Conf., 1968, 72. Dir. Winston-Salem Good Will Industries, 1968-74. Trustee Pfeiffer Coll., 1962—, mem. search com. for new pres.; trustee Inst. for Homiletical Studies, Forsyth County United Way; bd. visitors Duke Divinity Sch. Recipient award for outstanding service Pfeiffer Coll., 1973, Distinguished Alumni award, 1965; Distinguished Alumni award Duke, 1973. Mason. Clubs: Torch (past pres.), Rotary (Winston-Salem). Author: There's No Other Way: the Structures of Inner Peace, 1973; The Upper Room Disciplines, 1972; You Can Believe!, 1975; Living Under Pressure, 1975; A Time to Cross the River, 1977; How to Be a Successful Failure, 1978; God Writes Straight with Crooked Lines, 1980; Diamonds Everywhere, 1983. Contbr. articles religious periodicals. Home: 1921 Virginia Rd Winston Salem NC 27104 Office: United Meth Ch 159 Ralph McGill Blvd NE Atlanta GA 30365

FITZGERALD, THOMAS ROLLINS See Who's Who in America, 43rd edition.

FITZMYER, JOSEPH AUGUSTINE, priest, educator, Roman Catholic Church; b. Phila., Nov. 4, 1920; s. Joseph Augustine and Anna Catherine (Alexy) F.; A.B., Loyola U., Chgo., 1943; A.M., 1945; S.T.L., Facultés St.-Albert de Louvain, Belgium, 1952; Ph.D., Johns Hopkins, 1956; S.S.L., Pontifical Bibl. Inst., 1957. Joined Soc. of Jesus, 1938, ordained priest Roman Catholic Ch., 1951; asst. prof. N.T., Bibl. langs. Woodstock (Md.) Coll., 1958-59, assoc. prof., 1959-64, prof., 1964-69; prof. Aramaic and Hebrew dept. Nr. Eastern langs. and civilizations U. Chgo., Chgo., 1969-71; prof. N.T. and Bibl. lang., dept. theology, Fordham U., Bronx, N.Y., 1971-74, Weston Sch. Theology, Cambridge, Mass., 1974-76; prof. dept. Bibl. Studies, Cath. U. Am., 1976—; Speaker's lectr. Bibl. studies U. Oxford (Eng.), 1974-75; instr. Gonzaga High Sch., Washington, 1945-48. Mem. Cath. Bibl. Assn. (pres. 1970 editor Quar. 1980-84), Soc. Bibl. Lit. (pres. 1979, editor Jour. 1971-76), Studiorum Novi Testamenti Societas. Author: Essays on the Semitic Background of the New Testament, 1971; The Genesis Apocryphon of Qumran Cave I, 1966. Editor: (with R.E. Brown, R.E. Murphy) The Jerome Biblical Commentary, 1968; The Gospel According to Luke (Anchor Bible), vol. 28, 1981, vol. 28A, 1985. Address: Jesuit Community Georgetown U Washington DC 20057

FITZPATRICK, JOHN JOSEPH, bishop, Roman Cath. Ch.; b. Trenton, Ont., Can., Oct. 12, 1918; s. James J. and Lorena (Pelkey) F.; B.A., Niagara U., 1941; postgrad. Collegio de Propaganda Fide, Rome. Ordained priest Roman Catholic Ch., 1942, consecrated bishop, 1968; titular bishop of Cenae and aux. of Miami, Fla., 1968; bishop of Brownsville, Tex., 1971—. Chmn., Com. for Latin Am., U.S. Cath. Conf., 1973. Address: POB 2279 Brownsville TX 78520

FITZSIMOS, GEORGE K., bishop, Roman Catholic Church. Bishop, Salina, Kans. 1984—. Office: 421 Country Club Rd PO Box 999 Salina KS 67401*

FIZER, WILLIAM J., Chief bishop Church of God (Which He Purchased With His Own Blood), Oklahoma City. Office: Ch of God (Which He Purchased With His Own Blood) 1907 NE Grand Blvd Oklahoma City OK 73111*

FJELD, ROGER W., seminary administrator. Pres. Wartburg Theol. Sem. (American Lutheran), Dubuque, Iowa. Office: Wartburg Theol Sem 333 Wartburg Pl Dubuque IA 52001*

FJORDBAK, EVERITT MERLIN, minister, Assemblies of God; b. Storm Lake, Ia., May 2, 1921; s. Bernard Otto and Emma Catherine (Hansen) F.;

student Central Bible Coll., 1943, Dallas Theol. Sem., 1945; m. Mary Annette Tarter, Dec. 26, 1943; children—Edward M., Timothy E., Stephen M. Ordained to ministry, 1947; pastor Iowa, Tex., 1954—, Lakewood Assembly of God, Dallas, until 1977. Pres., Full Gospel Ministers' Assn.; mem. Greater Dallas Charismatic Com.; v.p. Wisdom House Press. Author: The Ministry of the Holy Spirit in Hebrews - a Commentary, 1977; Jonah, A Study in God's Love for Wayward Man; Hezekiah, Judah's Great King; Samson, A Study in the Unfinished Task and Ministry of a Fallen Man; The Sword of the Lord; Goliath; Why Christians Cannot Be Demon-Possessed. Home: 6115 Berwyn Ln Dallas TX 75214 Office: 2707 Abrams Rd Dallas TX 75214

FJORDBOTTEN, ALF LEE, minister, American Lutheran Church. B. Camrose, Alta., Can., Apr. 26, 1952; came to U.S., 1960, naturalized, 1985; s. Alf Lee and Helene Josephine (Hansen) F.; m. Beverly Elaine Lee, Oct. 22, 1983. B.A. in Religion, St. Olaf Coll., 1974; M.Div. Luther/Northwestern Theol. Sem., St. Paul, 1978. Ordained to ministry Am. Luth. Ch., 1978. Intern (vicar) Grace Luth. Ch., Allentown, Pa., 1976-77; pastor St. Mark's Luth. Ch., Ridge, N.Y., 1978-83, Holy Spirit Luth. Ch., Leonia, N.J., 1983—; bd. dirs. Camp Koinonia, Highland Lake, N.Y., 1979-84; mem. campus ministry bd. Stony Brook U. Chaplaincy, N.Y., 1980-81; aux. counselor Luth. Community Services, Hauppauge, N.Y., 1980-83; mem. Luth./Roman Cath. Dialogue of L.I., N.Y., 1981-83; instr. ch. history and liturgics Diakonia N.Y., Huntington, 1981, 83; mem. worship commn. Luths. Cooperating in Met. N.Y., 1981—; continuing edn. coordinator L.I. Conf., 1982-83; mem. planning com., sacristan, 1984 Workshop Conf., N.Y., mem. planning com. 1985 Worship Conf., Lehigh U., Pa.; presenter workshop on bells in the liturgy Muhlenberg Coll., Pa., 1984. Author: (devotional booklet) Light for Today, 1980. editor, contbr. parish newsletters. Bd. dirs. YMCA of L.I., N.Y., 1979-81, Strathmore Ridge Homeowners' Assn., N.Y., 1982; bass Bach Soc. Minn., 1974-78, Bach Choir of Bethlehem, 1976-77, L.I. Symphonic Choral Assn., 1979-83. Mem. Leonia Ecumenical Clergy (convenor 1983—). Home: 580 Gail Ct Teaneck NJ 07666 Office: Holy Spirit Luth Ch 313 Woodland Pl Leonia NJ 07605

FLAHERTY, HELEN JOSEPHINE, nun, religious order executive; Roman Catholic Church. B. Denver, June 22, 1920; d. Daniel J. and Jennie (Dougherty) F.; A.B., Mt. St. Joseph Coll., 1942, (Ph.D.) (hon.), 1984; M.A., Xavier U., 1951. Joined Sisters of Charity, Roman Catholic Ch., 1940. Campus minister Mich. State U., East Lansing, 1965-67; dean students Mt. St. Joseph Coll., Cin., 1967-69; provincial Sisters of Charity, Detroit, 1969-73, pres., Cin., 1979—; vicar for religious Archdiocese of Denver, 1974-79; del. Union Internat. Superior Gens., Rome, 1984—; keynote speaker Nat. Conv. Cath. Women, Fla., 1977; only woman speaker Internat. Assembly Vicars, Rome, 1978. Trustee St. Joseph Hosp., Mt. Clemens, Mich., 1970-73, Penrose Hosp., Colorado Springs, Colo., 1975-81; del. Nat. Woman's Conf., Houston, 1976. Contbr. articles to religious publs. Trustee, mem. exec. com. Sisters of Charity Health Care Systems, Cin., 1979—. Mem. Nat. Leadership Conf. Women Religious (v.p., pres., past pres. 1982-84), Nat. Vicars for Religious (sec. 1976-78). Office: Sisters of Charity of Cin Mount Saint Joseph OH 45051

FLAHERTY, JOHN FRANCIS, priest, Roman Catholic Church; b. Camden, N.J., Feb. 1, 1918; s. Patrick and Margaret-Theresa (Foy) F. B.A., St. Bonaventure U., 1951. Ordained priest Roman Cath. Ch., 1955. Asst. pastor St. James Ch., Ventnor, N.J., 1955-60, Holy Savior Ch., Westmont, N.J., 1960-62, St. Joseph's Ch., Camden, 1962-65; pastor Holy Spirit Ch., Atlantic City, N.J., 1965-74, Our Lady Star of Sea Ch., Atlantic City, 1974—; Episcopal vicar, Atlantic City, 1984—; asst. vocat. dir. Diocese of Camden, 1958-60, mem. social justice commn., 1978-82, mem. Presbyn. council, 1973-78, bd. consultors, 1984. Bd. dirs. Atlantic Human Resources Poverty Program, Atlantic City, 1965-73, Atlantic City Library, 1979—; mem. N.J. State Adv. Bd. on Alcoholism, Trenton, 1983—; chmn. Atlantic County Alcoholic Adv. Bd., Northfield, 1982—. Recipient plaque of appreciation Interfaith Clergy, 1971, 82, Commendation award Detox Ctr., 1982, Man of Yr. award Salvation Army, 1983. Address: 2651 Atlantic Ave Atlantic City NJ 08401

FLAHIFF, GEORGE BERNARD CARDINAL, archbishop, Roman Catholic Church; b. Paris, Ont., Can., Oct. 26, 1905; s. John James and Eleanor Rose (Fleming) F.; B.A., St. Michael's Coll., U. Toronto, 1926; student U. Strasbourg (France) 1930-31; Dipl. Archiviste-Paleographe, Ecole Nat. des Chartes, Paris, France, 1935; hon. degree in law U. Seattle, 1965, U. Notre Dame, 1969, U. Man., 1969, U. Windsor, 1970, U. Winnipeg, 1972, U. Toronto, 1972, U. St. Francis Xavier, 1973, Laval U., 1974. Ordained priest, 1930; prof. medieval history Pontifical Inst. Medieval Studies and U. Toronto, 1935-54, sec. inst., 1943-51; superior-gen. Basilian Fathers, 1954-61; archbishop of Winnipeg Can., 1961-82; named to Coll. Cardinals, 1969; mem. Sacred Congregation for Religious. Decorated companion Order of Can., 1974. Office: 50 Stafford St Winnipeg MB R3M 2V7 Canada

FLAKE, THOMAS RANDAL, minister, United Pentecostal Church International; b. Tupelo, Miss., Jan. 20, 1949; s. Thomas Jefferson and Mildred Alice (Mathis) F.; B.A., Twin Cities U., West Monroe, La., 1981; m. Patricia Dianne Colvin, June 2, 1967; 1 child, Melody Lynn. Ordained to ministry, 1976. Pastor Community United Pentecostal Ch., Walnut, Miss., from 1973. Mem. Nat. Geog. Soc. Home and Office: Route 2 Box 60 Walnut MS 38683

FLAKS, HYMAN, religious organization executive, Orthodox Jew; b. U.S.S.R., Jan. 16, 1915; s. Nehemia and Anna (Levin) F.; came to U.S., 1940, naturalized, 1945; m. Doris Katz, Aug. 24, 1941; children: Norma, Isaac, Ann, Leonard. Ed. Talmudic Acad. Riga, 1928-32, Latvian State U., 1933-37. Chief kashruth inspector Vaad Hoeir United Orthodox Jewish Community, St. Louis, 1941-50, exec. sec., 1950-74, exec. dir., 1974—; midwest regional dir. Union of Orthodox Jewish Congregations, St. Louis, 1958-68; sec. Epstein Hebrew Acad., 1954-62, v.p., 1962-72; bd. dirs. Jewish Community Relations Council, 1968—; trustee St. Louis Jewish Light Newspaper, 1975—, v.p., 1980-82, 84—; bd. dirs. Jewish Fedn. St. Louis. Author: Introduction to Kashruth, a Practical Approach; The History of the St. Louis Orthodox Jewish Community. Editor, Kashruth Bull., Vaad Hoeir. Contbr. articles to Jewish publs. Recipient Disting. Service award Jewish Welfare Bd., 1962; Meritorious Achievement award Nat. Conf. Synagogue Youth, 1968; Nat. Service award Union of Orthodox Jewish Congregations, 1972. Home: 7748 Wild Plum Lane Saint Louis MO 63130 Office: 4 Millstone Campus St Saint Louis MO 63146

FLANAGAN, BERNARD JOSEPH, bishop, Roman Cath. Ch.; b. Proctor, Vt., Mar. 31, 1908; s. John B. and Alice (McGarry) F.; student Holy Cross Coll., N. Am. Coll., Rome, Italy; J.C.D., Catholic U. Am., 1943. Ordained priest Roman Catholic Ch., 1931, consecrated bishop, 1953; sec. to bishop, chancellor of diocese, Burlington, Vt., 1943-53; bishop diocese of Norwich, 1953-59; bishop, diocese of Worcester (Mass.), 1959—. Address: Bishop's House 49 Elm St Worcester MA 01602

FLANDERS, HENRY JACKSON, JR., educator, minister, So. Baptist Conv.; b. Malvern, Ark., Oct. 2, 1921; s. Henry Jackson and Mae (Hargis) F.; B.A., Baylor U., 1943; B.D., So Bapt. Theol. Sem., 1948, Ph.D., 1950; m. Tommie Lou Pardew, Apr. 19, 1944; children—Janet (Ms. Anthony Gilbert Mitchell), Henry Jackson III. Ordained to ministry So. Baptist Conv., 1940; prof. religion, chmn. dept. chaplain Furman U., 1950-62; pastor First Bapt. Ch., Waco, Tex., 1962-69; prof. religion Baylor U., 1969—, chmn. dept., 1980-83; chaplain Tex. Ranger Commn., 1972—. Chmn. bd. trustees Golden Gate Bapt. Theol. Sem., 1971-76; bd. dirs., mem. exec. com. Heart of Tex. chpt. ARC. Mem. Assn. Bapt. Profs. Religion (pres. 1958-59), Waco Bapt. Ministerial Assn. (pres. 1964-65), S.C. Christian Action Council (dir. 1959-62), Baylor Ex-Students Assn. (pres. 1968-69), Am. Acad. Religion, Soc. Bibl. Lit., AAUP (pres. Baylor U. chpt. 1971-72), Sigma Tau Delta. Mason. Rotarian. Author: (with R.W. Crapps and D.A. Smith) People of the Covenant: An Introduction to the Old Testament, 1963, rev. edit., 1973; (with Bruce Cresson): Introduction to the Bible, 1973. Home: 3820 Chateau St Waco TX 76710 Office: Baylor U Waco TX 76703

FLANNERY, LAILON DANIEL, minister, Southern Baptist Convention; b. Hazard, Ky., Jan. 23, 1930; s. Palmer Myrle and Gladys Ann (Reynolds) F.; m. Helen Doris Price, Nov. 27, 1948; children: Dorothy, Mildred Arnold. G.E.D., Danville High Sch., Ky., 1972. Ordained to gospel ministry So. Bapt. Conv., 1968. Pastor New Hope Bapt. Ch., Stanford, Ky., 1968-69, Popular Springs Bapt. Ch., Liberty, Ky., 1969-72, Pleasant Run Bapt. Ch., Danville, 1972-76, Mt. Vernon Bapt. Ch., Ky., 1976-78, So. Ave. Bapt. Ch., Danville, 1978—. Office: So Ave Bapt Ch PO Box 819 Danville KY 40422

FLAVIN, GLENNON P., bishop, Roman Cath. Ch.; b. St. Louis, Mar. 2, 1916. Ordained priest Roman Catholic Ch., 1941, consecrated bishop, 1957; aux. bishop diocese of St. Louis, 1957-67, bishop diocese of Lincoln, Nebr., 1967—. Address: 3400 Sheridan Blvd POB 80328 Lincoln NE 68510

FLEISCHMAN, ALEXANDER, association executive, journalist; b. N.Y.C., Feb. 22, 1921; s. Joseph and Ethel (Schuller) F.; m. Georgette Duval, Apr. 14, 1946. Sec., layreader, instr. Hebrew Assn. of Deaf, N.Y.C., 1941-45; with Washington Post, 1950-84; with Nationwide Flashing Signal System Inc.; pres. Nat. Congress Jewish Deaf, Greenbelt, Md., 1958-72, exec. dir., 1972—, conv. chmn., 1972, 82, speaker at workshops and seminars; presenter papers World Orgn. Jewish Deaf, Tel Aviv, Jersulem, 1971, 77, 81. Columnist: The Silent News, 1970's; sports editor, columnist: The Cavalier/Nat. Observer, 1955-62; editor: Voice of M.A.D., 1955-64, Nat. Congress of Jewish Deaf Jour., 1956-74. Pres. Md. Assn. Deaf, Silver Spring, 1962-64; mem. religious commn. World Fedn. Deaf, Rome; mem. adv. council Internat. Commn. of Deafness Gallaudet Coll., Washington, 1974-83. Recipient diploma for top performance Internat. Games for the Deaf, 1959, 65, 69; named Man of Yr. Washington Div. Nat. Fraternal Soc. of the Deaf, 1969. Mem. Am. Athletic Assn. Deaf (chmn. 1951-54, named to Hall of Fame 1965), World Orgn. Jewish Deaf (pres. 1971—).

FLEMING, CHARLES WOODROW, choir director, lay church worker, Southern Baptist Convention; b. Laurens, S.C., July 31, 1916; m. William and Lula Lillie Lee (McKelley) F.; B.S. cum laude, Miner Tchrs. Coll., Washington, 1939; M.A. in Ednl. Adminstrn., Columbia U., 1962. Usher, tchr., Mt. Jezreel Bapt. Ch., Washington, 1931-47, dir. vacation Bible sch., 1939-42, musical dir. choirs and choruses, 1936-68, chmn. bldg fund program com., 1949-65, chmn. bd. trustees, 1963-66, minister music, 1951-68; dir. sr. choir Shiloh Bapt. Ch., Washington, 1969—; tchr. ch. music Bapt. Ednl. Congress D.C. and Vicinity, 1956-72; founder, dir. Sanctuary Choristers, 1961; dir. one thousand voice pre-conv. mus. choir Nat. Bapt. Conv., Washington, 1984. Asst. prin. Charles R. Drew Elem. Sch., Washington, 1968-74. Named to Afro-Am. Honor Roll, 1970; recipient D.C. Acad. Minister of Music award, 1973. Mem. Am. Choral Dirs. Assn. (life). Home: 726 Quebec Pl NW Washington DC 20010 Office: Shiloh Baptist Ch 9th and P Sts NW Washington DC 2000

FLEMING, DAVID ARNOLD, priest, educational administrator, Roman Catholic Church; b. Topeka, Kans., Apr. 14, 1939; s. Ambrose David and Mildred Eileen (Williams) F. B.A., St. Mary's U., San Antonio, 1959; M.A., U. Chgo., 1963, Ph.D., 1965; S.T.B., U. Fribourg, 1967, S.T.L., 1969. Ordained priest Roman Catholic Ch., 1969. Tchr. secondary sch., Chaminade Prep., St. Louis, 1959-62; prof. St. Mary's U., San Antonio, 1969-76; dir. formation Soc. of Mary, San Antonio, 1971-75; provincial superior Soc. of Mary, St. Louis, 1979—; dir. Conf. of Maj. Superiors of Men, Washington, 1982—; chancellor St. Mary's U., San Antonio, 1984—. Editor: Euphormio's Satyricon, 1973; (anthology) The Fire and the Cloud, 1979. Contbr. articles to profl. jours. Home: 4528 Maryland Saint Louis MO 63108 Office: Soc of Mary PO Box 23130 Saint Louis MO 63156

FLEMING, DAVID LEE, educator, priest, Roman Catholic Church; b. St. Louis, July 4, 1934; s. Clarence C. and Emily A. (O'Brien) F. A.B. in Classics, St. Louis U., 1958, M.A. in Philosophy, 1959; S.T.L., St. Mary's Coll., 1966; S.T.D., Cath. U. Am., 1969. Joined Soc. Jesus, 1952; ordained priest Roman Catholic Ch., 1965; classics tchr. St. Louis U. High Sch., 1959-62; pastoral retreat work in Eng. and Wales, 1966-67; asst. prof. theology Dept. Theology St. Louis U., 1970-71, asst. prof. spirituality Sch. of Div., 1971-75, also co-dir. Inst. Religious Formation, 1971-76; rector Jesuit Theologian Community, St. Louis U., 1972-76; mem. staff Ministry Tng. Services, Denver, 1976-85; provincial superior Soc. of Jesus, 1979-85. Mem. Cath. Theology Soc. Am. Author: The Spiritual Exercises of St. Ignatius, 1978; A Contemporary Reading of the Spiritual Exercises, 1976, 80; Modern Spiritual Exercises, 1983. Editor: Notes on the Spiritual Exercise, 1981. Editorial bd. Am. Assistancy Seminar on Jesuit Spirituality, 1972-78, Human Devel., 1979—; contbr. articles to religious publs. Office: 4511 W Pine Blvd Saint Louis MO 63109

FLEMING, JOHN WESLEY, minister So. Bapt. Conv.; b. Prestonburg, Ky., May 5, 1941; s. Leonard E. and Hannah (Price) F.; B.S. in Edn., Berea Coll., 1957-60; extension courses So. Bapt. Sem.; m. Kay M. Trussell, July 5, 1966; children—Melissa, Stacey. Minister of edn. 1st Bapt. Ch., Pinellas Park, Fla., 1962-64, 71-75, North East Park Bapt. Ch., St. Petersburg, Fla., 1964-66, 1st Bapt. Ch., Belle Glade, Fla., 1967-68, 1st Bapt. Ch., Sebring, Fla., 1968-69, 1st Bapt. Ch., Lake Wales, Fla., 1969-71, Parkwood Bapt. Ch., Jacksonville, Fla., 1976—. Pres. Religious Edn. Assn., Fla. Bapt. Conv., 1976—, spl. instr. youth leadership studies, 1971—; faculty Lake Yale Sch., Leesburg, Fla., 1969, 72, 75; dir. vacation Bible sch. Jacksonville Bapt. Assn., 1976—; chmn. ch. camps and assemblies com. Pinellas County Bapt. Assn., 1975; mem. exec. bd. Jacksonville Bapt. Assn., 1976-76. Home: 1309 Westlawn Dr Jacksonville FL 32211 Office: 7900 Lone Star Rd Jacksonville FL 32211

FLEMING, SAMUEL LAFAYETTE, minister, Christian Church (Disciples of Christ); b. Hot Springs, N.C., Dec. 25, 1916; s. Harvey James and Julia Ann (Parker) F.; m. Willie Irene Thompson, June 26, 1943; children: Helen Elizabeth, Mary Ann, Samuel Lafayette. A.B., Johnson Bible Coll., 1940; B.D., Butler U., 1944; M.Div., Christian Theol. Sem., 1946; Th.D., Washington Profl. Coll., 1951. Ordained to ministry Christian Ch., 1941. Minister Donelson Christian Ch., Nashville, 1964-72, 1st Christian Ch., New Castle, Pa., 1955-64, Asheville, N.C., 1950-55, Crossville, Tenn., 1972-82, Peru, Ind., 1982—; mem. Internat. Recommendations Com. of Christian Chs., 1953-54; pres. Pa. Ministerial Assn., 1962-64; pres. Christ Child Festival, New Castle, Pa., 1956-64; mem. regional bd. Christian Ch., Tenn., 1970-71. Author: What Must I Do To Be Saved, 1944; Debates of Alexander Campbell, 1946. Contbr. articles to religious jours. Mem. Internat.

Platform Assn., Ind. Ministerial Assn., Miami County Ministerial Assn. Democrat. Lodges: Kiwanis, Masons. Home: 185 E Main St Peru IN 46970 Office: First Christian Ch 53 W Main St Peru IN 46970

FLENER, KERMIT EDWARD, minister, United Methodist Ch.; b. Morgantown, Ky., Apr. 6, 1925; s. Gobel B. and Loletuth (Flener) F.; A.A., Lindsey Wilson Coll., 1948; B.A., Evansville U., 1951; B.D., Vanderbilt U., 1954, M.A., 1973, D.D., Union Coll. at Barbourville, 1975; m. Virginia Ruth Alexander, Mar. 14, 1949; children—Kermit Edward, Stephen Ray. Ordained to ministry, 1951; pastor chs. Ky., 1948—, Bethany United Meth. Ch., Louisville, 1963-69, Audubon United Meth. Ch., Louisville, 1969-71, 1st United Meth. Ch., Hopkinsville, Ky., 1971—. Mem. bd. edn. Louisville Conf., 1960-68, bd. ministry, 1964-72, coordinator youth council, 1966-68, chmn. com. on higher edn., 1966-68; pres. Southeastern Jurisdiction Ministers Conf., 1970; bd. mgrs. Ky. United Meth. Pastors Sch., 1968-76, dean, 1972-76; del. World Meth. Conf., Dublin, Ireland, 1976; trustee Meth. Retirement Homes Ky., Inc., 1972—; chaplain Chism Clan Assn. Ky. Col. Home: 2715 Clinton Circle Hopkinsville KY 42240 Office: 1305 S Main St Hopkinsville KY 42240

FLESHER, HUBERT LOUIS, priest, educator, Episcopal Church; b. Elyria, Ohio, Apr. 30, 1933; s. O. Jay and Armide Elizabeth (de Saulles) F.; B.A., Pomona Coll., 1954; B.D., Yale, 1958, M.A., 1961, postgrad., 1961-63; m. Mary June Mosher, Apr. 3, 1965; children: Erika Anne, Jonathan Jay. Ordained priest Episcopal Ch., 1958, deacon, 1958. Asst. to dean of chapel Princeton, 1956-57; asst. minister ch., Lakewood, Ohio, 1958-59, West Haven, Conn., 1959-63; instr. New Haven Coll., 1961-63, Episcopal Theol. Sch., Cambridge, 1963-65; minister ch., Arlington, Mass., 1966; chaplain united campus ministry Millersville State Coll., Pa., 1967-71; lectr. Lancaster Theol. Sem., Pa., 1968-70; chaplain Lehigh U., 1971—, asst. prof. religion, 1971-75, assoc. prof. religion, 1975-80; prof., 1980—; lectr. Cedar Crest Coll., 1980. Chmn. bd. dirs. Lancaster Ind. Press, 1969-71; bd. dirs. Young People's Philharmonic Orch. of Lehigh Valley, Pa., 1985—. Mem. bd. exam. chaplains Diocese of Central Pa., 1969-71, Diocese of Bethlehem, 1984—; mem. Nat. Campus Ministry Assn., 1st pres. Pa. chpt., 1969-71; mem. commn. on ministry Diocese of Bethlehem, Pa., 1972-80, Pa. Commn. of United Ministries in Higher Edn., 1969—. Univ. fellow Yale U., 1961; grantee Nat. Endowment for Humanities, 1985. Mem. Am. Acad. Religion, Soc. Bibl. Lit., Nat. Assn. U. and Coll. Chaplains, Phi Beta Kappa, Omicron Delta Kappa. Home: 224 W Packer Ave Bethlehem PA 18015

FLINT, ROBERT BOYD, minister, United Pentecostal Ch., Internat.; b. Big Springs, Ohio, Nov. 27, 1921; s. Joseph Benson and Nora May (Brammer) F.; came to Can., 1973; B.Th., M.Bible Philosophy, God's Bible Sch. and Coll., Cin., 1950; m. Shirley Virginia Lucas, Oct. 19, 1947; 1 dau., Sharon Kay. Ordained to ministry, 1960; pastor and evangelist, Md., Ohio, So. U.S., Va., W.Va., 1951-70; pastor Apostolic Faith Ch., Hazelton, Pa., 1970-72, United Pentecostal Ch., Prescott, Ont., Can., 1973—; lectr. Writer, Word Aflame Press. Recipient trophies for Youth Week scrapbooks United Pentecostal Ch. Internat., 1971, 72, 73. Mem. Am. Fedn. Police. Contbr. articles to ch. publs. Home: 84 Pearl St W Brockville ON K6V 4C2 Canada Office: PO Box 1890 Prescott ON K0E 1T0 Canada

FLISS, RAPHAEL M., bishop, Roman Catholic Church. Coadjutor bishop of Superior with right of succession, 1979—. Office: Box 969 Superior WI 54880*

FLORENCE, FRANK TILLMAN, JR., minister emeritus, Southern Baptist Convention; b. Cynthia, Ky., Aug. 17, 1921; s. Frank Tillmanaand Effie Mae (Kendall) F.; m. Lelia Elizabeth Vater, Jan. 30, 1943; children: Terry Allen, F.; Linda Lee French, Nancy Ann Whitlock. B.A. magna cum laude, Georgetown Coll., Ky., 1950; B.D., Southern Bapt. Sem., 1955, M.Div., 1968. Ordained to ministry Southern Baptist Convention, 1949. Pastor Kento-Boo Bapt. Ch., Florence, Ky., 1949-55, Ormsby Bapt. Ch., Louisville, 1956-58, Lynn Acres Bapt. Ch., Louisville, 1958-70, First Bapt. Ch. of Tomkinsville, Ky., 1974-76; missionary Bapt. Mission Bd., Bogotá, Columbia, 1970-73; pastor First Bapt. Ch. of Cold Spring, Ky., 1977-82, pastor emeritus, 1982—; interim pastor various chs., 1982—; inspirational speaker numerous orgns. Author: Feet of Clay: The True Story of a Prisoner-of-War's Search for God, 1958. Contbr. poetry and feature articles to mags. Bd. dirs. Holly Hill Orphanage, Cold Springs, 1981—; chaplain North Ky. Seniors, Alexandria, Ky., 1983—. Served to sgt. U.S. Army, 1942-46, ETO; prisoner-of-war. Decorated Purple Heart, Bronze Star. Mem. Ky. Bapt. Conv., Nat. Art Fraternity, VFW (Americanism award 1982), Ex-Prisoners of War Assn. Republican.

FLORENCE, FRANKLIN DELANO WINSTON, minister, Ch. of Christ; b. Cynthiana, Ky., Jan. 15, 1942; s. Robert Newton and Ethel Mae (NaVarre) F.; B.A., Cin. Christian Seminary and Bible Coll., 1965; m. Janet Gaye Freeman, June 21, 1963; children—David, James, Stephen, Daniel, John Mark. Ordained to ministry, 1965; sr. minister Mt. Victory (Ohio) Ch. of Christ, 1973-83; chaplain Hardin County Ohio Home for the Aged, 1974-83; field evangelist Chs. of Christ/Christian Chs., 1983—. Speaker at men's retreats, instr. Christian day camps, hosp. chaplain; sec.-treas. Hardin County Ministerial Assn.; evangelist. Named hon. Ky. Col., 1963. Home: 113 S Sycamore St Lynchburg OH 45142 Office: PO Box 96 Lynchburg OH 45142

FLORES, PATRICK F., archbishop, Roman Catholic Church; b. Ganado, Tex., July 26, 1929. Ed. St. Mary's Sem, Houston. Ordained priest Roman Cath. Ch., 1956. Consecrated titular bishop of Itolica and aux. bishop San Antonio, 1970, bishop of El Paso, Tex., 1978; archbishop of San Antonio, 1979—. Office: Archdiocese of San Antonio Chancery Office 9123 Lorene Ln PO Box 32648 San Antonio TX 78284*

FLORIAN, ROBERT BRUCE, minister, United Meth. Ch.; b. Hartford, Conn., Jan. 17, 1930; s. Franklin Benjamin and Gertrude (Bruce) F.; B.A., Adrian Coll., 1951; B.D., Garrett Theol. Sem., 1956 (converted to M.Div. 1972); M.A., W.Va. U., 1963, Ph.D., 1973; m. Barbara Jean Walker, June 2, 1951; children—Linda Florian Neyhart, Laura Florian Moul, Joseph. Ordained deacon, 1953, elder, 1957; instr. Wesley Coll., Dover, Del., 1956-58, Salem (W.Va.), Coll., 1958—, prof. history and religion, chmn. liberal studies dept., 1974—; pastor in Haywood, W.Va., 1961-62, Jarvisville, W.Va., 1971-73, Pennsboro circuit, 1976-79, Wallace, W.Va., 1979-84; supervising pastor-in-charge, Bristol, W.Va., 1984—; treas. Salem Ministerial Assn., 1969-76; mem. commn. archives and history W.Va. conf. United Meth. Ch., 1973—, treas., 1984—, conf. bd. edn., 1966-69. Chmn. hist. com. Salem Bicentennial Commn., 1976. Mem. W. Va. (past pres.), Hist. Assn., W. Va. Assn. Humanities. Compiler, Bicentennial Hist. Directory of W.Va. United Meth. Chs., 1976; co-author: Melting Times: A History of West Virginia United Metodism, 1984. Home: 51 Moore St Salem WV 26426 Office: Dept Liberal Studies Salem Coll Salem WV 26426

FLOWER, JOSEPH REYNOLDS, administrative executive, Assemblies of God Church; b. Indpls., Mar. 11, 1913; s. J. Roswell and Alice Marie (Reynolds) F.; m. Mary Jane Carpenter, June 6, 1940; children: Joseph Reynolds, Mary Alice, Paul William. Diploma Central Bible Coll., Springfield, Mo., 1934. Ordained to ministry Assemblies of God Ch., 1934; Pastor chs. in Pa., N.Y., Maine, Mass., 1934-54; supt. N.Y. dist. Assemblies of God, 1954-75, mem. gen. presbytery of gen. council, 1953—, mem. exec. presbytery, 1966—, gen. sec. gen. council, Springfield, 1976—; bd. regents, bd. dirs. Valley Forge Christian Coll., Phoenix Valley, Pa.; bd. dirs. Central Bible Coll., 1965-73, Assemblies of God. Grad. Sch., Springfield, 1973—, Evangel Coll., Springfield, 1979—. Mem. Assn. Statisticians Am. Religious Bodies. Office: 1445 Boonville Ave Springfield MO 65802

FLOYD, WINFORD RAY, minister, Free Will Baptist Ch.; b. Belmont, N.C., Apr. 1, 1932; s. Albert Ray and Elsie E. (Gantt) F.; B.A., Milligan Coll., 1956-59; m. Frances Juanita Pittman, July 1, 1949; children—Myra, Rebecca, Elisa, Sherri. Ordained to ministry, 1950; chmn. Appalachian Preaching Mission, 1967; mem. nat. bd. fgn. missions Nat. Assn. Free Will Baptists, 1963-68; pastor Highland Pines Free Will Bapt. Ch., 1952-56, Bethany Christian Sch., Norfolk, Va., 1969-73, First Free Will Bapt. Ch., Elizabethton, Tenn., 1956-69, 73—; evangelist, conf. speaker. Trustee Free Will Bapt. Children's Home, Greenville, Tenn. Home: 1242 Thomas Blvd Elizabethton TN 37643 Office: 706 First St Elizabethton TN 37643

FLYNN, JAMES EMMITT, pastor, Southern Baptist Convention; b. Chillicothe, Tex., May 13, 1930; s. James Emmitt and Gladys Lopez (Wilkinson) F.; m. Norma Jean Rosson, Jan. 24, 1952; 1 child, Danny (dec.). B.A., Howard Payne Coll., 1951; B.Div., Golden Gate Bapt. Theol. Sem., 1960, M.Div., 1972. Ordained to ministry So. Bapt. Conv., 1954. Pastor, First So. Bapt. Ch., Yreka, Calif., 1966-68, Calvary Bapt. Ch., Chico, Calif., 1968-75, Trinity Bapt. Ch., Arcata, Calif., 1975-79, Tabernacle Bapt. Ch., Pickton, Tex., 1979-82, Lake O The Pines Bapt. Ch., Avinger, Tex., 1982—; ethics teaching fellow Golden Gate Theol. Sem., Mill Valley, Calif., 1962-63; pres. Ministerial Alliance, Colusa, Calif., 1963-66. Chmn. Democratic caucus, Jefferson, Tex., 1984. Recipient cert. continuing edn. Golden Gate Bapt. Theol. Seminary, 1979, cert. Sch. of Evangelism, Billy Graham Evangelistic Assn., 1974. Cubmaster, Cub Scouts, Vernon, Tex., 1956-58. Home: Route 2 Box 454 Avinger TX 75630 Office: Lake O' The Pines Bapt Ch Route 2 Box 454 Avinger TX 75630

FLYNN, MICHAEL FRANCIS, priest, counselor, Roman Cath. Ch.; b. Chgo., Dec. 2, 1935; s. Michael Joseph and Mary Ellen (Lydon) F.; B.A., St. Bonaventure U., 1958, B.S., 1960; M.A., De Paul U., 1966; Ph.D. in Clin. Psychology, Loyola U., Chgo., 1974. Ordained priest, 1961; pastoral/marital counselor Carmel High Sch., Mundelein, Ill., 1963-70; pastoral counselor St. Athanasius Parish, Evanston, Ill., 1970-71; dir. Carmelite Inst. of Renewal, Mundelein, 1968-70; condr. workshops and retreats in various states, 1965-70, also counselor, 1968-70; diagnostic cons. to marriage tribunal Chancery Office, Cath. Archdiocese of Chgo., 1975—; pastoral counselor Nativity of Our Lord Parish, Chgo., 1971—; lectr. religion and mental health to religious groups, 1961—. Mem. Am., Ill. psychol. assns., Ill. Group Psychotherapy Soc., Assn. Psychology Internship Ctrs. (exec. com. 1980—), Assn. Chgo. Area Tng. Centers in Clin. Psychology, Am. Soc. Clin. Hypnosis (bd. govs. 1984—), Chgo. Soc. Clin. Hypnosis (exec. bd. 1984—), Internat. Soc. Hypnosis, Soc. Personality Assessment (membership com. 1982—), Internat. Platform Assn. Home: 653 W 37th St Chicago IL 60609 Office: 820 S Damen Ave Chicago IL 60680

FOCHT, ROBERT PATRICK, JR., minister, social worker So. Baptist Conv.; b. Atlanta, May 15, 1947; s. Robert Patrick and Ruby Lee (Adams) F.; B.S., Emory U., 1969; M.R.E., New Orleans Bapt. Theol. Sem., 1973; M5S.W., Tulane U., 1974; m. Judith Anne Adams, Aug. 22, 1969; 1 son, Adam Patrick. Ordained to ministry, 1973; missionary, 1969-71; intern Home Mission Bd., 1971-73; asst. dir. Crisis Clinic, Orleans Parish Prison, New Orleans, 1972-73; dir. Crisis Line, New Orleans, 1973-74; dir. spl. ministries Pulaski County Bapt. Assn., Little Rock, 1975—. Covenor, Consultation on Bapt. Student Concerns, 1969—; mem. planning com. Mission 70, 1969; conf. leader Freedom '76. Bd. dirs. Urban League Greater Little Rock, 1975—, v.p., 1976—; bd. dirs. Prepared Childbirth, Inc., 1975—, pres., 1976—; bd. dirs. Crisis Center Ark., 1976—; bd. dirs. CONTACT, Little Rock, 1976—. William Walker Brookes scholar, 1973-75. Mem. Nat. Assn. Social Workers, Am. Assn. Suicidology, So. Bapt. Social Service Assn. Home: 2022 Center St Little Rock AR 72206 Office: 1522 W 10th St Little Rock AR 72202

FOERSTER, JOHN DALE, minister, Luth. Ch. Am.; b. Johnstown, Pa., Oct. 5, 1907; s. Louis John and Clara Isabelle (Shirey) F.; A.B., Thiel Coll., 1938; B.D., Gettysburg Sem., 1941, S.T.M., 1951; Th.D., Clairmont Sch. Theology, 1967; D.D., U. Redlands, 1973; m. Mary Ellen Straley, June 6, 1942; children-David John, Richard Dale, Robert William (dec.), Barbara Jean, Fredric Charles. Ordained to ministry, 1943; minister, Loganville, Pa., 1939-42, Stoystown, Pa., 1942-50, Redlands, Calif., 1950—; dir. Camp Nawakwa, Bigglersville, Pa., 1941-50; dir. youth and religious edn. Synod of Pacific S.W., 1950-58, dir. Camp Yolijwa, 1950-58; dir. Mt. Cross, Santa Cruze, Calif., 1956-58; dir. summer assemblies, Thiel, Pitts. Synod Coll., Pa., 1939-40; substitute tchr. Bible, U. Redlands, Calif., 1956-59. Chaplain, Redland Community Hosp., 1950—, Redlands Police Force, 1976—; pres. Council of Chs., 1954-58. Chmn. Commn. of Personnel, City of Redlands, 1974—; bd. dirs. Hosp. and Corp. Body, 1960—, Community Chest, 1970; mem. Redlands Scholarship Bd., 1972-75; bd. dirs. Redlands Bowl Music Assn., 1973—. Recipient Grail award Knights of Round Table, 1963. Mem. Soc. Bibl. Lit. and Exigesis, Luth. Acad. for Scholarship, Soc. of Reformation Research, Acad. of Religion, Assn. of Religious Edn. Author: Hand of God, 1943; Abide in the Presence, 1950; contbr. religious articles to mags. Home: 1215 W Cypress Ave Redlands CA 92373 Office: 1207 W Cypress Ave Redlands CA 92373

FOGARTY, GERALD PHILIP, priest, educator, Roman Catholic Church; b. Balt., Jan. 7, 1939; s. Gerald Philip and Ellen Theresa (McHugh) F.; B.A., Fordham U., 1964, M.A., 1966; Ph.L., Woodstock Coll., 1965, M.Div., 1971; S.T.M., Union Theol. Sem., 1972; M.Phil., Yale U., 1967, Ph.D., 1969. Ordained priest, 1970. Assoc. prof. Woodstock Coll., N.Y.C., 1972-74, Fordham U., Bronx, 1974-75 U. Va., Charlottesville, 1975—. Author: The Vatican and the Americanist Crisis, 1974 (Brewer prize of Am. Soc. Ch. History); The Vatican and the American Hierarchy from 1870 to 1965, 1982. Trustee, Loyola Coll., Balt., 1971-77, Fairfield U., Conn., 1983—, Loyola High Sch., Towson, Md., 1983—. Fellow Am. Council Learned Socs.; mem. Cath. Hist. Assn. (exec. council 1977-80), Am. Soc. Ch. History, Am. Hist. Assn., Cath. Com. on Intellectual and Cultural Affairs. Home: 1847 Winston Rd Charlottesville VA 22903 Office: Dept Religious Studies Univ Va Charlottesville VA 22903

FOGGIE, CHARLES HERBERT, bishop, African Methodist Episcopal Zion Ch.; b. Sumter, S.C., Aug. 4, 1912; s. James L. and Mamie Louise (Jefferson) F.; A.B., Livingstone Coll., D.D., 1949; A.M., Boston U., 1938, S.T.B., 1939, S.T.M., 1942; m. Madeline S. Sharpe, Jan. 9, 1952; 1 dau., Charlene M. Ordained elder, 1936, bishop, 1968; pastor Wadsworth St. A.M.E. Zion Ch., Providence, 1936-39, Rush A.M.E. Zion Ch., Cambridge, Mass., 1939-44, Wesley Center A.M.E. Zion Ch., Pitts., 1944-68; bishop 12th Dist. Pa., 1968-72, 5th Dist., 1972—; sec. bd. bishops A.M.E. Zion Ch. Del., World Meth. Conf. Former chmn. Pitts. Housing Authority; bd. dirs. Pitts. Symphony; sec. bd. trustees Livingstone Coll. Recipient Martin Luther King award, Home Mission Evangelistic award A.M.E. Zion Ch. Mem. NAACP (past pres. Pitts. br.), Alpha Phi Alpha. Home: 1200 Windermere Dr Pittsburgh PA 15218

FOLEY, JOHN PATRICK, archbishop Roman Catholic Ch.; b. Darby, Pa., Nov. 11, 1935; s. John Edward and Regina Beatrice (Vogt) F.; B.A. summa cum laude, St. Josephs Coll., Phila., 1957; B.A., St. Charles Borromeo Sem., Phila., 1958; Ph.L., U. St. Thomas Aquinas, Rome, Italy, 1964, Ph.D. cum laude, 1965; M.S. magna cum laude, Columbia, 1966. Ordained priest Roman Catholic Ch., 1962; asst. pastor Sacred Heart Ch., Havertown, Pa., 1962-63; asst. editor Cath. Standard & Times, Phila., 1963, 67-70, student priest, Rome corr., 1963-65, editor, 1970-84; ordained archbishop Roman Catholic Ch., 1984; apptd. pres. Pontifical Commn. for Social Communications, Vatican City; pres. Vatican TV Ctr. student priest Columbia, 1965-66; asst. pastor St. John the Evangelist Ch., Phila., 1966; faculty Cardinal Dougherty High Sch., Phila., 1966-67; asso. prof. philosophy St. Charles Borromeo Sem., Phila., 1967-84; news sec. gen. meetings Nat. Conf. Cath. Bishops, 1969-84; pres. U.S. Cath. Conf. Communications Com., 1949-82; bd. govs. Internat. Eucharistic Congress. Mem. regional bd. dirs. NCCJ, 1969-82. Named hon. prelate Pope Paul VI, 1976. Mem. Am. Cath. Hist. Soc., Am. Cath. Philos. Assn., Cath. Press Assn. Author: Natural Law, Natural Right and the Warren Court, 1965. Home: Villa Stritch via della Noretta 63 00164 Rome Italy Office: Pontifical Commn for Social Communications 00120 Vatican City The Vatican

FOLSOM, PAUL DAVID, priest, Roman Catholic Church; b. St. Cloud, Minn., Dec. 12, 1938; s. Robert E. and Gretchen (Morneau) F.; M.A., Aquinas Inst. Theology, 1964, D. Ministry, 1976; M. Religious Edn., Loyola U., Chgo., 1971. Ordained priest, 1965. Dir. adult edn. St. Cloud Diocese, from 1970; pastor St. Ann's Ch., Kimball, Minn., 1978-85, St. Piers X Ch., Zimmerman, Minn., 1985—. Chmn. continuing edn. for clergy Diocese of St. Cloud, 1976-80; chaplain USAR, 1973—. Recipient St. George's award Boy Scouts Am., 1975. Author: Rural Ministry, 1976. Home: St Piers X Ch Zimmerman MN 55398

FOLWELL, WILLIAM HOPKINS, bishop, Episcopal Ch.; b. Port Washington, N.Y., Oct. 26, 1924; s. Ralph Taylor and Sara (Hopkins) F.; B.C.E., Ga. Inst. Tech., 1947; L.Th., Seabury Western Sem., 1952, B.D., 1953, D.D., 1970; D.D., U. South, 1970; m. Christine Elizabeth Cramp, Apr. 22, 1949; children—Ann Folwell Stanford, Mark, Susan. Ordained priest, 1952; vicar St. Peter's Ch., Plant City, Fla., 1952-55; priest-in-charge St. Luke's Ch., Mulberry, Fla., 1954-55; chaplain St. Martin's Sch., New Orleans, 1955-56; rector St. Gabriel's Ch., Titusville, Fla., 1956-59, All Saints' Ch., Winter Park, Fla., 1959-70; bishop Diocese of Central Fla., 1970—. Office: 324 N Interlachen Ave Winter Park FL 32789

FONG, WILFRED WAI FAI, lay church worker, Wesleyan Methodist Church; librarian; b. Hong Kong, Nov. 28, 1959; s. Wing Kwong and Kor Ngan (Young) F. B.Sc. in Computer Sci., U. Western Ont., London, Can., 1981; postgrad. Regent Coll., Vancouver, B.C., Can., 1981, Moody Bible Inst., 1981-82; M. Library and Info. Sci., U. Wis.-Milw., 1985. Library dir. London Chinese Alliance, Ont., 1979-81, Christian edn. dir., 1981-83; sec. 9th Eastern Can. Chinese Youth Winter Conf., 1980; Bible tchr. Eastbrook Ch. Chinese Ministry, Milw., 1984—. Project asst. Sch. Library and Info. Sci., U. Wis.-Milw., 1984—. Editor-at-large jour. Echo, 1983. Compiler bibliographies. Author computer software. Contbr. articles to profl. publs. Mem. Fellowship of Christian Librarians and Info. Specialists, Assn. Christian Librarians, ALA, Wis. Library Assn., Christian Edn. Fellowship, Western Chinese Christian Fellowship (exec. com.), Am. Soc. Info. Sci. (sec.-treas. 1984—). Club: Christian Reader's (London) (adviser 1982-84). Avocations: music, reading, squash. Office: Sch Library and Info Sci U Wis PO Box 413 Milwaukee WI 53201

FOOCKLE, HARRY FRANCIS, minister, United Meth. Ch.; b. La Salle, Ill., June 29, 1939; s. Robert Fred and Elanore Louise (Urbanski) F.; B.A. cum laude, Mo. Valley Coll., 1969; M.Div., St. Paul Sch. Theology, 1972; D.D., Universal Bible Inst., 1974; m. Rita B. Hale, July 11, 1959; children—Robert Thomas, Christopher Alan, Victoria Lynne. Ordained to ministry, 1970; pastor Wesley United Meth. Ch., Springfield, Mo., 1976—, Goodwill Chapel United Meth. Chs., Sedalia, Mo., 1965-69, New Bethel United Meth. Ch., Sedalia, 1965-69; pastor United Meth. Ch., Humansville, Mo., 1972-76, Corder United Meth. Ch., 1969-72. Mem. com. on nominations Mo. West conf. United Meth. Ch., 1972—; chmn. Nev. Dist. Council on Ministries, 1973-76; mem. Nev. Dist. Bd. of Ministry, 1972-76; chmn. Lake Ministry Com., 1974-76; chmn. Springfield Dist. Council on Ministries, 1976—; mem. Spl. Minister's Mission United Meth. Ch., 1973-76; sec. bd. discipleship Mo. W. Ann. Conf. Chmn. Humansville Area Cystic Fibrosis Fund Dr., 1975; city clk. Humansville, 1974-76; city councilman, Corder, 1971-72. Mem. Humansville C. of C. Home: 3965 S Fairview St Springfield MO 65807 Office: Route 12 PO Box 301-A Springfield MO 65807

FOOR, DENNIS WAYNE, minister, Church of the Nazarene; b. Westerville, Ohio, Jan. 14, 1943; s. Harold Leslie and Ina Mae (Perry) F.; m. Carol Louise Moore, June 24, 1967; children: Matthew Dennis, Marcia Lynn. B.A., Olivet Nazarene Coll., 1965, M.A., 1966, M.Div., Nazarene Theol. Sem., 1969. Ordained to ministry Ch. of the Nazarene, 1971. Minister, Ch. of Nazarene, Mansfield, Ohio, 1969-70, New Lexington, Ohio, 1970-80, Churubusco, Ind., 1980—; sec. dist. youth program Central Ohio Dist., 1974-78; elected del. Gen. Youth Conv., Central Ohio Dist., 1976; bd. dirs. Orders and Relations, Central Ohio Dist., 1979-80; mem. ways and means com. Northeastern Ind. Dist., 1983—. Author: Forsyth: Man and Concept, 1968; (with others) Innovative Ideas For Pastors, 1976. Contbr. articles to profl. mags. Chaplain Young Republicans, Olivet Nazarene Coll., 1964-65; sta. clk. Police Dept., Kansas City, Mo., 1967-69. Mem. Churubusco Ministerial Assn. (pres. 1983-85), New Lexington Ministerial Assn. (pres. 1978-80). Home: 413 N Conway Churubusco IN 46723 Office: Ch Nazarene 1000 W Whitley St Box 85 Churubusco IN 46723

FORBES, DOUGLAS PORTER, JR., minister, Conservative Baptist Association of America; b. Boston, Aug. 18, 1950; s. Douglas Porter and Pauline Ann (Brentlinger) F.; m. Kathleen Ann Coyle; children: Faith Ann, Joy Ann, Hope Ann. B.R.E., Northeastern Bible Coll., Essex Fells, N.J., 1973; cert. in bus. mgmt. Belknap Coll., N.H., 1974; cert. in continuing edn. Internat. Ctr. Learning, Ventura, Calif., 1978; M.R.E., Christian Internat. U., Port Washington, Fla., 1985. Ordained to ministry Bapt. Gen. Conf., 1975; lic. constrn. supr., Mass. Pastor Onset Bapt. Ch., Mass., 1975-77; asst. pastor 1st Bapt. Ch. Duxbury, Mass., 1977-78, West Bridgewater Bapt. Ch., Mass., 1978—; New Eng. dir. Dennis O'Neill Ministries, Rutherford, N.J., 1981—; Bible tchr. Oak Ridge Camp, East Haddam, Conn., 1974-76; chaplain Tobey Hosp., Wareham, Mass., 1975-76, Quincy Aux. Police Dept., 1985; Christian edn. cons. Gospel Light Pubs., Ventura, Calif., 1977—. Editor children's books. Contbr. articles to mags., religious columns to local newspapers. Vol. group leader, drug counselor Mc Cauley Mission, N.Y.C., 1969-73; head tchr. reading program, Newark, 1979-80; pres. PTA, Russell Sch., Brockton, Mass, 1981-83, chmn. parents' adv. council, 1981-83, city-wide rep., 1983-84; sector dir. Area II Civil Def., Bridgewater, Mass., 1984-85; coach Crusaders Ski Team, Canton, Mass. Recipient Cert. of Merit, Russell Sch., 1982. Mem. Conservative Bapt. Assn. New Eng. (asst. to pres. 1982-83), Eastern Mass. Evang. Ministers Fellowship, Christian Service Brigade (capt. 1978-85, recipient plaque). Republican. Home: 53 Milton St Brockton MA 02401 Office: West Bridgewater Bapt Ch 65 N Elm St West Bridgewater MA 02379

FORD, ANNA MAE (MRS. ROBERT L. FORD), ch. ofcl.; b. Lexington, Miss., Aug. 15, 1916; d. Leland Davis and Anna Bell (Banks) Broy; student Am. Conservatory Music, 1935-36; B.A., Eastern Fla. Coll., 1949; A.A., Saints Jr. Coll., 1959; m. Robert L. Ford, Mar. 16, 1962; children by previous marriage—Audrey LaVerne (Mrs. Harold Brown, Jr.), Beverly Antonia, John Leland, Patricia Mae (Mrs. Donald I. Hopkins); Founder music dept. Ch. of God in Christ, Inc., Memphis, Tenn., 1949, pres., 1949-72; founder-mem. God's Vol. Mission, 1968—; dir. music Womens Internat. Conv. Ch. of God in Christ, Inc., 1951—; founder-pres. Pentecostal Singers and Musicians Alliance, Internat.-Ann. Conf., Scholarship Aid, Camp and Retreat; pres. Pentecostal Singers and Musicians Alliance Sch. Music, 1949—. TV and radio actress; profl. model, 1970—. Mem. Civil Liberty League, 1972—, Ethiopian World Fedn., 1971—. Recipient medal of honor City of Wichita, Kan., 1970; licensed missionary evangelist. Mem. AFTRA, Screen Actors Guild. Editor, pub. Pentecostal Alliance Crescendo, 1952. Composer numerous songs, 1947—; 1st recording as gospel singer, 1951, first album, 1973. Home: 1431 S Christiana Ave Chicago IL 60623

FORD, EDDYE BETTY, lay church worker, Church of God in Christ; b. Greenwood, Miss., Aug. 7, 1911; d. Samuel Douglas and Emma Jane (Williams) Chambers; student Moody Bible Inst., 1960-61, U. Detroit, 1964-65; m. Frank Curtis Ford, Sept. 2, 1939; 1 child, Juanita (Mrs. Augustus Martin). Lic. missionary evangelist Ch. of God in Christ, 1937. State pres. Mich. Young Women's Christian Council, Detroit, 1948-73, chmn. internat. adv. bd., 1965—; dist. missionary and supr. women's auxs. North Central Mich. Jurisdiction, Ch. of God in Christ, Detroit, 1972-82, Dist. 11 Gt. Lakes Jurisdiction of Mich., Detroit, 1982—; radio commentator religious news program Sta. WJLB, Detroit, 1959-61; free lance society and religious news reporter, columnist Mich. Chronicle; trainer, dir. various mus. groups and choirs, St. Louis and Detroit. Bookkeeper, acct. U.S. govt., 1949-61; dist. mgr. Avon Products, Inc., 1961-76. Recipient 2d Place award Detroit Favorite Churchwoman Survey, 1956. Mem. Nat. Council Negro Women. Home: 12335 Broadsteet Blvd Detroit MI 48204

FORD, JOHN THOMAS, theology educator, Roman Catholic Church; b. Dallas, Nov. 21, 1932; s. Thomas E. and Lenora Ann (Senn) F. A.B., U. Notre Dame, 1955; M.A., Holy Cross U., 1959; S.T.L., Gregorian U., 1960, S.T.D., 1962. Ordained priest Roman Catholic Ch., 1959. Instr. theology U. Notre Dame, Ind., 1962; prof. Holy Cross Coll., Washington, 1962-68; asst. prof. Cath. U. Am., 1968-71, assoc. prof., 1971—; mem. staff Holy Cross Missions, 1964—; observer cons. Consultation Ch. Union, 1974—; mem. faith and order commn. Nat. Council Chs., 1981—. Contbr. articles to profl. jours. Mem. Am. Acad. Religion, AAUP, Cath. Theol. Soc. Am., Cath. Hist. Assn., N. Am. Acad. Ecumenists. Office: Cath U Am PO Box 236 Washington DC 20064

FORD, L. H., bishop, The Church of God in Christ. Mem. gen. bd., 1st asst. presiding bishop The Church of God in Christ. Office: The Ch of God in Christ 9401 King Dr Chicago IL 60619*

FORD, RICHARD EDWIN, religious orgn. exec.; b. Wabash, Ind., Feb. 27, 1939; s. Wilbur Edwin and Florence Gertrude (Jeup) F.; B.S. in Bus. Adminstrn., Ind. U., 1961. Vice pres., trustee Bauman Bible Telecasts, Inc., Arlington, Va., 1976—; mem. adminstrv. bd. Foundry Meth. Ch., 1974—. Pres., Washington Sanitation Conf., 1975; v.p., bd. dirs. D.C. Met. Police Boys Club; bd. dirs. Eisenhower Meml. Scholarship Found.; chmn. com. Nat. Debutante Cotillion, 1976, 77; mem. com. Internat. Ball, N.Y.C. Mem. Am. Water Works Assn., Am. Def. Preparedness Assn. (life), Navy League (life), U.S. Naval Inst., Smithsonian Assos., Nat. Trust for Historic Preservation, Newport Hist. Soc. (life), Nat. Wildlife Fedn. (life), Wolf Trap Assn., Friends of the Corcoran, Met. Opera Guild, Soc. Friends of Music of Ind. U. (life), Washington Film Council, Washington Performing Arts Soc., U. Md. Charter Council, Dept. State Americana Project, Friends of Kennedy Center. Home: 2000 S Eads St Apt 1125 Arlington VA 22202 Office: 3436 Lee Hwy Arlington VA 22207

FORDHAM, VIRGINIA JEAN, minister, United Church of Christ; b. Marietta, Ohio, Jan. 16, 1926; d. Harlan Arthur and Jean Irene (Hawkins) F. A.B., Marietta Coll., 1949; B.D., Andover Newton Theol. Sch., 1953; S.T.M., Oberlin Grad. Sch. Theology, 1960; D.Ministry, Vanderbilt U., 1974. Ordained to ministry Ohio Baptist Conv. (1st woman), 1952. Asst. pastor Court Street United Bapt. Ch., Auburn, Maine, 1952-53; pastor South Ridge Bapt. Ch., Conneaut, Ohio, 1953-55; minister edn. 1st Congregational Ch., DeKalb, Ill., 1957-59; tchr. weekday religious edn. Washington County Schs., Ohio, 1959-64; pastor Highland Ridge Community Ch., Lowell, Ohio, 1964-83, Zion United Ch. Christ, Thornville, Ohio, 1983—; exec. sec. Washington County Larger Parish, 1961-65; del. Gen. Synod United Ch. Christ, 1979; pres. Marietta Ministerial Assn., 1979-80; chmn. spl. events Inter-Ch. Council, Marietta, 1978-83. Recipient appreciation award Inter-Ch. Council, 1983. Pres., Marietta Retail Mchts. Assn., 1971-72. Republican. Home: 102 St Patrick Dr Somerset OH 43783

FORDHAM, WILLMON ALBERT, minister, Southern Baptist Convention; . b.West Monroe, La., Nov. 13, 1926; s. William Ether and Lura Annie (Hatten) F.; B.A., William Carey Coll., 1956; B.D., New Orleans Bapt. Theol. Sem., 1961, M.Div., 1975; m. Ethel Mae Hover, Dec. 22, 1946; children: Willmon Albert, Gary W. Ordained to ministry, 1952; pastor Napoleon Bapt. Ch., Picayune, Miss., 1952-59; Oak Hill Bapt. Ch., Poplarville, Miss., 1959-61, 1st Bapt. Ch., Petal, Miss., 1961—. Pres., Lebanon Bapt. Pastors' Conf., 1962-63, moderator, 1972-73; mem. assembly com. Miss. Bapt. Conv. Bd., 1966-70, mem. pioneer missions com., 1970-73; pastor-advisor Tom Cox Evang. Assn., 1972. Active Boy Scouts Am., Petal, 1974-76. Recipient certificate of Appreciation, Miss. Bapt. Conv. Bd., 1970, Petal-Harvey Kiwanis Club, 1970. Home: PO Box 318 Petal MS 39465 Office: 201 W Central Ave Petal MS 39465

FORDON, JOHN, minister, Unitarian Universalist Association; b. Chgo., Nov. 21, 1925; s. Walter and Jane (Woods) F.; m. Nancy Doolittle, May 19, 1972; children: (by previous marriage) Nancy, Jeffrey, Karen, Susan); (by present marriage) Kathy, Douglas. B.S. in Chemistry Edn., U. Ill., 1950; B.D., Starr King Sch. Ministry, 1952; Th.D., Central Sch. Theology, 1961. Ordained to ministry, 1952. Minister, Ft. Wayne, Ind., 1952-55, St. Louis, 1955-58; assoc. dir. Jewish Hosp. of St. Louis, 1958-61; assoc. dir. devel. Unitarian Universalist Assn., Boston, 1961-64; pres. Am. Council Exec. in Religion, Huntington, N.Y., 1974—; trustee, v.p., treas. N.Y. Metro Unitarian Universalist Dist., N.Y.C., 1973-82; trustee fin. com. St. Lawrence Theol. Found., Syracuse, N.Y., 1982—; minister Unitarian Universalist Fellowship, E. Norwich, N.Y., 1976—. Chmn., L.I. Women's Coalition, Islip, N.Y., 1983—; pres., treas. Huntington Townwide Fund, 1976-82; pres. Parents for Progress, Montclair, N.J., 1983—. Served to capt. USAR, 1955-61. Mem. N.Y. Acad. Sci., Nat. Soc. Pub. Accts., Nat. Soc. CLU's, Internat. Assn. Fin. Planners. Club: Williams. Office: One Old Country Rd Care Place NY 11514

FORE, WILLIAM FRANK, religious orgn. administr., editor, minister United Meth. Ch.; b. Memphis, Tex., May 30, 1928; s. Frank K. and Willie (Clower) F.; student U. Calif. at Los Angeles, 1947-48; B.A., Am. U. of Cairo, Egypt, 1950; B.A., Occidental Coll., 1951; B.D., Yale, 1955; Ph.D., Columbia, 1972; m. Elizabeth Stauffer, Aug. 12, 1952; children—Christine, Peter Frank, John Arthur, David William. Ordained to ministry, 1956; dir. visual edn. Meth. Bd. Missions, N.Y.C., 1956-61; exec. sec. joint sect. edn. and cultivation Meth. Bd. Missions, N.Y.C., 1961-62; exec. dir. broadcasting and film commn. Nat. Council Chs., N.Y.C., 1964-73, asst. gen. sec., 1973—; pres. World Assn. for Christian Communication, 1983-86. Chmn. nat. adv. council Corp. Pub. Broadcasting, Washington, 1971—; chmn. Nat. Coalition Against Censorship, 1974—; trustee Media Action Research Center, N.Y.C., 1974—. Recipient citation Corp. Pub. Info., 1973, CINE award Com. Internat. Nontheatrical Events, 1963, 65. Mem. Nat. Acad. TV Arts and Scis., Internat. Radio and TV Soc., Nat. Screen Council, World Assn. Christian Communication (v.p. 1971-74). Author: South Americans All, 1961; Image and Impact, 1970. contbg. editor The Christian Century, 1974—. Home: 121 N Van Dien Ave Ridgewood NJ 07450 Office: 475 Riverside Dr New York City NY 10027

FORMAN, CHARLES WILLIAM, minister, United Presbyterian Church in U.S.A.; b. Gwalior, India, Dec. 2, 1916; s. Henry and Sally (Taylor) F.; B.A., M.A., Ohio State U., 1938; Ph.D., U. Wis., 1941; B.D., Union Theol. Sem. N.Y., 1944, S.T.M., 1947; m. Helen Janice Mitchell, Mar. 12, 1944; children—David, Sarah, Harriet. Ordained to ministry, 1944; prof. N. India Theol. Coll., Saharanpur, 1945-50; sec. for program emphasis Nat. Council Chs. U.S.A., N.Y.C., 1951-53; prof. missions Yale Div. Sch., 1953—. Mem. Commn. on Ecumenical Mission and Relations United Presbyn. Ch. in U.S.A., 1961-70, chmn., 1964-70. Mem. Bethany (Conn.) Bd. Edn., 1958-67. Bd. dirs. Theol. Edn. Fund, World Council Chs., from 1965, chmn., 1965-70; bd. dirs. Found. for Theol. Edn. in S.E. Asia, chmn., from 1970. Author: A Faith for the Nations, 1957; The Nation and the Kingdom, 1964; Christianity and the Non-Western World, 1967; The Island Churches of the South Pacific, 1982. Office: Div Sch Yale U New Haven CT 06510

FORRESTER, DONALD DWIGHT, minister, Churches of Christ; b. Haskell, Tex., Oct. 9, 1930; s. George Robert and Bessie Mae (Johnson) F.; m. Jewell Gay Broyles, July 1, 1952; children: Diana Marie, Donald Scott, William Gary. B.A., Johnson Bible Coll., Knoxville, Tenn., 1956; postgrad. Southwest Christian Sem., Phoenix, 1957-59. Ordained to ministry Ch. of Christ, 1955. Evangelist, Ambassadors for Christ, Phoenix, 1957-60; minister 1st Christian Ch., Forest Park, Ga., 1960-63; founding evangelist 1st Christian Ch., Fairburn, Ga., 1963-67, Kings Hiway Christian Ch., Eden, N.C., 1967-75; sr. minister 1st Christian Ch., Harlingen, Tex., 1975-76; with Southwest Christian Ch., Jackson, Miss., 1977-78; pres. Winston-Salem Bible Coll., N.C., 1978—; mem. council Johnson Bible Coll., 1967—; missionary Haiti Ch. of Christ, Port-au-Prince, Haiti, 1970-75; co-dir. Bible Lands Seminar, Charlottesville, Va., 1971—; trustee Internat. Christian Mission Inst., San Juan, P.R., 1974-82. Author: Baptism: What Shall We Do?, 1977; (study guide) Revelation: Another View, 1982. Author weekly newspaper columns: Christian Comments, 1965-73, Words for Living, 1965-73. Contbr. articles to profl. jour. Served with U.S. Army, 1950-52; Korea. Mem. Assn. Christian Coll. Pres. Republican. Club: Optimists. Lodge: Kiwanis. Home: 305 Logan Ct King NC 27021 Office: Winston Salem Bible Coll 4117 Northampton Dr PO Box 73 Winston-Salem NC 27102

FORSBERG, C. ROBERT, minister, Presbyterian Church in the U.S.; b. N.Y.C., Sept. 11, 1924; s. Carl H. and Naomi H. (Sundquist) F.; m. Joan H. Bates, June 7, 1952 (div. July 1979); children: Larry, Babs, Tim. B.A., Coll. Wooster, 1946; B.D., Yale U., 1953; research fellow Hartford Sem., 1961, Urban Tng. Ctr., Chgo., 1968. Ordained to ministry Presbyn. Ch., 1953. Mem. group ministry Oak St. Christian Parish, New Haven, 1950-56; mem. group ministry, dir. Wider City Parish, New Haven, 1957—; sec. hunger work group Presbyn. Synod of N.E., 1976—; mem. edn. in soc. com. Nat. Council Chs., 1976-79; vol. Am. Friends Service Com., Italy, France, Ger., 1946-49; pres., housing chmn. New Haven Human Relations Council, 1956-59; sec. peacemaking task force So. New Eng. Presbytery, 1980—, chmn. social issues com., 1980—. Bd. dirs. New Haven Civil Liberties Union, 1955—, NAACP, C.O.R.E.; pres. Citizens for Humanizing Criminal Justice, New Haven, 1983—. Conscientious objector, World War II, Korean Conflict. Recipient Humanitarian award New Haven B'nai B'rith, 1981. Mem. Witherspoon Soc. (v.p. 1983—). Democrat. Home: 105 Birstol St New Haven CT 06511 Office: 48 Howe St New Haven CT 06511

FORSBERG, MARK, bishop, Orthodox Church in America. Formerly bishop of diocese of Boston, now bishop diocese of Fort Lauderdale, Fla. Office: 1435 Crest Dr Fort Lauderdale FL 33461*

FORSEE, DANIEL ELDRIDGE, minister, Southern Baptist Convention; b. Dayton, Ohio, Apr. 28, 1945; s. Joseph Threckle and Norma Lena (Smith) F.; m. Saundra LaVern Goings, Aug. 14, 1965; children: Daniel Eldridge II, Heather Dawn. B.S., William Carey Coll., 1975; M.Div., New Orleans Bapt. Theol. Sem., 1978; Th.D., Internat. Bible Inst. and Sem., 1981, D.D. (hon.), 1983. Ordained to ministry So. Bapt. Conv., 1975. Dir. edn. Elysian Fields Bapt. Ch., New Orleans, 1975-76; sr. pastor Damascus Bapt. Ch., Hazlehurst, Miss., 1976-78; assoc. pastor Bethany Bapt. Ch., Wilmington, Del., 1978-79; sr. pastor New Hope Bapt. Ch., Camden, Del., 1979—; pres. Forsee Evangelism Assn. (Radio), Wilmington, 1975—, He's Alive Ministries (TV), Wilmington, 1982—, Dover Clergy Assn., Del., 1981-83; lectr., advisor Pastoral Care Assocs., Dover, 1979-83; dir. stewardship Del. Bapt. Assn., 1980-82, dir. tng., 1981—; sec. Del. Bapts. Pastors Conf., 1978—; bd. dirs. Del. Sem. Extension, Dover, 1981—. Com. chmn. Gov./White House Conf. on Families, Wilmington, 1979-80. Served with USAF, 1973-75. Mem. Pi Gamma Mu (v.p. 1975). Republican. Home: 9 Forest Creek Dr Dover DE 19901 Office: He's Alive Ministries PO Box 11525 Wilmington DE 19850

FORST, MARION FRANCIS, bishop, Roman Catholic Ch.; b. St. Louis, Sept. 3, 1910; s. Frank A.J. and Bertha T. (Gulath) F.; student Kenrick Sem., Webster Groves, Mo., 1934. Ordained priest, 1934, consecrated bishop, 1960; asso. pastor, Denver, 1934-36, Glendale, Mo., 1936-42, St. Louis, 1942-43, 46-49; chaplain USNR, 1943-46; pastor St. Mary's Cathedral, Cape Girardeau, Mo., 1949-60; bishop Cath. Diocese Dodge City, Kans., 1960-76; aux. bishop Archdiocese of Kansas City, Kans., 1977—. Mem. Am. Legion. K.C. (past chaplain Mo.). Address: 615 N 7th St Kansas City KS 66101

FORSTMAN, HENRY JACKSON, educator, minister, Christian Ch.; b. Montgomery, Ala., June 15, 1929; s. Joseph Carl and Kate Gertrude (Kelley) F.; B.A., Phillips U., 1949; B.D., Union Theol. Sem., N.Y., 1956, Th.D., 1959; m. Shirley Marie Cronk, June 3, 1950; children: David Jackson, Valerie Marie, Paul Frederick. Ordained to ministry Christian Ch., 1952; minister chs., Ala., 1950-53, N.Y.C., 1953-58; asst. prof. religion Randolph-Macon Woman's Coll., 1958-60, Stanford, 1960-64; assoc. prof. theology Vanderbilt U., 1964-69, prof., 1969—, chmn. grad. dept. religion, 1969-72, acting dean div. sch., 1970. Mem. Soc. Values in Higher Edn., Am. Assn. Theol. Schs., Am. Soc. Ch. History, Am. Acad. Religion, Assn. Disciples for Theol. Discussion. Fulbright fellow, 1973-74, 79-80. Author: Word and Spirit, 1962; Christian Faith and the Church, 1965; A Romantic Triangle, 1977.

FORSYTHE, JAMES EDWARD, minister, prison chaplain, United Church of Christ; b. Weymouth, Mass., Aug. 16, 1942; s. Chester and Elizabeth (Silva) E.; 1 child, Matthew. B.A., Eastern Nazarene Coll., 1965; M.Div., Andover Newton Theol. Sch., 1969, D.Min., 1976; Th.M., Princeton Theol. Sem., 1971. Assoc. minister St. Paul United Ch. Christ, Nutley, N.J., 1969-71; with U.S. Dept. of Justice Fed. Correctional Inst., Danbury, Conn., 1972-79; fed. prison chaplain U.S. Penitentiary, Terre Haute, Ind., 1979-82, Fed. Correctional Inst., Ray Brook, N.Y., 1982—; dir. Yokefellows Prison Ministry, Shamokin Dam., Pa., 1975—. Mem. Assn. Clin. Pastoral Edn. (acting supr.). Republican. Home: 105 Lake Flower Ave Saranac Lake NY 12983 Office: Chaplain's Office Fed Correctional Inst PO Box 300 Ray Brook NY 12977

FORTIER, JEAN-MARIE, archbishop, Roman Catholic Church Canada; b. Que., Can., July 1, 1920; s. Joseph and Alberta (Jobin) F.; student Grand Sem. Que., 1940-45; L.Th., Laval U., Que., 1945; postgrad. U. Louvain, Belgium, 1946-48; Licentiate in Ch. History, Gregorian U., Rome, Italy, 1950. Ordained priest, Roman Catholic Ch., 1944; sec. to bishop of Hearst, Ont., Can., 1945-46; tchr. ch. history Grand Sem. of Que., Can., 1950-60; consecrated bishop of Ste.-Anne-de-la-Pocatiere, Que., 1961-65, Gaspe, Que., 1965-68; elected archbishop of Sherbrooke, Que., 1968—. Vice pres. Can. Cath. Conf., 1971-73, pres. 1973—. Mem. Knights Order of Holy Sepulchre of Jerusalem. Address: 130 Rue Cathedrale Sherbrooke PQ J1H 4M1 Canada

FOSHEE, HOWARD BRYCE, minister, So. Baptist Conv.; b. Birmingham, Ala., May 20, 1925; s. Cornelius Howard and Audie Lucille Foshee; B.A., Samford U., Birmingham, 1950; M.Div., So. Bapt. Theol. Sem., Louisville, 1952; m. Zola Leek, June 7, 1949; children: Zola, Becky, Elizabeth. Ordained to ministry, 1951; pastor, minister edn. chs. in Ind. and N.C., 1950-56; minister edn. First Bapt. Ch., Durham, N.C., 1954-56; sec. ch. adminstrn. dept. Bapt. Sunday Sch. Bd., Nashville, 1958—; lectr. sems., colls. Mem. ch. devel. commn. Bapt. World Alliance. Recipient Distinguished Service award Samford U., 1975. Mem. Soc. Religious Orgn. Mgmt., Nat. Assn. Ch. Bus. Adminstrn. Author: Ministry of Deacon, 1968; Broadman Church Manual, 1973; Now That You Are a Deacon, 1976; also articles. Home: 5629 Highland Way Nashville TN 37211 Office: 127 9th Ave N Nashville TN 37234

FOSS, HARLAN FUNSTON, religion educator, minister, Lutheran Church; b. Canton, S.D., Oct. 10, 1918; s. Hans and Thea (Hokenstad) F.; m. Beatrice Naomi Lindaas, Sept. 2, 1943; children: Richard John, Kristi Marie, Mailyn Jean. B.A., St. Olaf Coll., 1940; B.Th., Luther Theol. Sem., 1944; Th.M., Princeton Theol. Sem., 1945; Ph.D., Drew U., 1956; postgrad. Mansfield Coll., Oxford U., Eng., 1967, Pontifical Inst. and Gregorian U., Rome, 1974. Ordained to ministry Lutheran Ch., 1944. Pastor Mt. Carmel Luth. Ch., Milw., 1944-47; mem. faculty St. Olaf Coll., Northfield, Minn., 1947—, assoc. prof. religion, 1954-56, prof., 1957—, v.p., dean coll., 1979-80, pres., 1980-85. Mem. Northfield Bd. Edn., 1959-66, treas., 1960-61, chmn., 1961-66, Ezra Squire Tipple fellow, 1951-52. Mem. AAUP, Am. Acad. Religion, Norwegian-Am. Hist. Assn., Blue Key. Republican. Lodge: Lions. Home: 216 Manitou St Northfield MN 55057

FOSS, MICHAEL WARREN, minister, American Lutheran Ch.; b. Richland, Wash., Sept. 20, 1948; s. James Albert and Adelaide (Arthur) F.; m. Cynthia Christie Cox, Aug. 30, 1969; children: Sarah Christine, Linnea Mikkel. B.A. in Religion, Pacific Luth. U., 1970; M.Div., Wartburg Theol. Sem., 1974. Ordained to ministry Am. Luth. Ch., 1974. Assoc. pastor Christ Luth. Ch., Opportunity, Wash., 1974-77, Our Savior's Luth. Ch., Spokane, Wash., 1977-79; lead pastor Our Savior's Lutheran Ch., Salem, Oreg., 1979—; mem. dist. council N. Pacific Dist, Am. Luth. Ch., Seattle, 1983—, vision bd. chmn., 1984—, task force on regional design for new Luth. Ch., 1985; participant, Oreg. State Bioethics Commn., Salem, Portland, 1984—; chmn. Luth. Ministerium, Spokane, 1975; co-author Marriage Encounter, Internat., 1976, team presentor, 1976-80, clergy team, 1977-80; advisor Luther League Conv. N. Pacific Dist., 1977-80; nat. del. Singles Ministry, 1978-79; presenter, leader All Alaska Youth Gatherings, Anchorage, 1981, 82; vice dean Mid-Willamette Conf., N. Pacific Dist., 1982-83; preacher Luther League Conv., Spokane, 1983. Author: Created in the Image of God, 1984; editor creative lit. jour.; reviewer Augsburg Pub. House, 1981—. Pastor for tour YMCA Mideast and Scandanavia, 1983; bd. dirs. YMCA, Salem, Oreg., 1984-85; community resource person YMCA Games for Physically Limited, Salem, 1982; chmn. bd. dirs. Mid-Willamette Valley Hospice, Salem, 1983—; mem. task force Friends in Touch, Mental Health Assn. Oreg., Salem, 1982-83. Recipient cert. for beginning and advanced tng. Transactional Analysis and Gestalt Therapy, 1975-77. Included in Outstanding Young Men Am., 1981. Democrat. Lodge: Sertoma Internat. (v.p. Salem 1980-81). Home: 313 Marietta St SE Salem OR 97302 Office: Our Saviours Lutheran Church 1274 Cunningham Ln S Salem OR 97302

FOSSELMAN, ALBERT MICHAEL, priest, Roman Catholic Church. b. Waverly, Iowa, July 21, 1932; s. Bernard Peter and Maria Dolores (Lizama) F. B.A., Pontifical Coll. Josephinum, Worthington, Ohio, 1956, M.Div., 1960; J.C.B., Gregorianum, Rome, 1972; J.C.L., Cath. U., 1973. Ordained priest Roman Cath. Ch., 1960. Vice chancellor, Diocese of Reno-Las Vegas, 1968—, chief justice, 1970—, vicar for religious, 1975—; pastor St. Francis of Assisi Ch., Incline Village, Nev., 1975—; chaplain Nev. State Prison, Carson City, 1962-63. Mem. Canon Law Soc. Am. Home: 755 Mt Rose St Reno NV 89509 Office: Chancery Office 515 Court St Box 1211 Reno NV 89504

FOSTER, DANIEL GEORGE, music director, Lutheran Church-Missouri Synod; cargo company executive; b. South Bend, Ind., Feb. 28, 1958; s. E.D. and Barbara Warlick (Yount) F. A.A., Western Piedmont Coll., N.C., 1978; B.S., U. N.C., 1980. Substitute organist Luth. Ch.-Mo. Synod, Newton and Conover, N.C., 1971-74; organist, choirmaster First Bapt. Ch., Claremont, N.C., 1974-78, Holy Cross Luth. Ch., Newton, N.C., 1979-85; asst. league services chmn. N.C. and S.C. dist. Luth. Laymen's League, 1982-84, sec., Newton, N.C., 1982—; dir. music Concordia Evang. Luth. Ch.-Mo. Synod, 1985—. Asst. mgr. Far East Cargo Inc., Hickory, N.C., 1983—. Conover Service League scholar, 1976. Republican. Avocations: Swimming, racquetball. Home: 210 3d St NE Conover NC 28613 Office: Concordia Evang Luth Ch-Mo Synod 216 5th Ave SE Conover NC 28613

FOSTER, DOUGLAS ALLEN, minister, educator, Churches of Christ. B. Sheffield, Ala., Aug. 30, 1952; s. Ralph Douglas and Lisabeth Allen (Morris) F.; m. Mary Linda Grissom, Dec. 29, 1979; 1 child, Mary Elizabeth. B.A., David Lipscomb Coll., 1974; M.A., Scarritt Coll., 1980; postgrad. Vanderbilt U., 1980—. Youth minister Highland Park Ch. of Christ, Muscle Shoals, Ala., 1970-72; minister edn. Jackson Park Ch. of Christ, Nashville, 1974-83; Bible instr. Goodpasture Ch. Sch., Nashville, 1974-76, Ezell-Harding Ch. Sch., Nashville, 1978-79; instr. ch. history and Am. history David Lipscomb Coll., Nashville, 1984—; mission work, summers 1969-74; missionary lang. instr. Project Italy, Nashville, 1973-75. Sponsor, tchr. Amigos de las Americas, Nashville, 1978. Mayhew fellow Vanderbilt U., 1983-84. Mem. Am. Soc. Ch. History, Am. Acad. Religion, Orgn. Am. Historians, Disciples of Christ Hist. Soc. Home: 713 Baugh Rd Nashville TN 37221 Office: Box 4210 David Lipscomb Coll Granny White Pike Nashville TN 37203

FOSTER, JOHN JOSEPH, priest, Roman Cath. Ch.; b. Coaldale, Pa., Mar. 4, 1925; s. George Washington and Isabel Veronica (Daley) F.; B.A., St. Charles Borromeo Sem., Phila., 1948, M.Div., 1951; grad. in Counseling Psychology, LaSalle Coll., Phila., 1967-68. Ordained priest, 1951; tchr. St. James High Sch., Chester, Pa., 1952-58, Cardinal Dougherty High Sch., Phila., 1956-68, dir. vocations, 1968-71; prin. Bishop

McDevitt High Sch., Wyncote, Pa., 1971—. Mem. Cheltenham Twp. Drug and Alcohol Com., 1971—. Recipient citation Pa. Ho. of Reps., 1976, Cheltenham Twp. Bd. Commrs., 1976. Mem. Nat., Pa. assns. secondary sch. prins., Nat. Cath. Edn. Assn., Pa. Assn. Supervision and Curriculum Devel. Author: History of Presentation B.V.M. Parish, Cheltenham, 1965; The First Fifteen Years: A History of Bishop McDevitt High Sch., 1974; History of Blessed Sacrament Parish, Philadelphia, 1976. Home: St Mary's Villa 701 Bethelehem Pike Ambler PA 19002 Office: Bishop McDevitt High Sch Royal Ave at Mulford Rd Wyncote PA 19095

FOSTER, JOHN KEITH, minister, So. Baptist Conv.; b. Sheridan, Wyo., Feb. 19, 1932; s. John Thomas and Grace Margaret (Kennedy) F.; B.S., Okla. Bapt. U., 1960; M.Div., Midwestern Bapt. Theol. Sem., 1965; m. Dixie Lee Walker, Aug. 19, 1956; children—Sherri Beth, Shay Harvey. Ordained to ministry, 1960; pastor Lebanon Bapt. Ch., Hemple, Mo., 1961-64, Randolph Bapt. Ch., Kansas City, Mo., 1964-66, Calvary Bapt. Ch., Sheridan, Wyo., 1966, Big Horn (Wyo.) Community Ch., 1967, Salcha Bapt. Ch., Fairbanks, Alaska, 1967-70, Univ. Bapt. Ch., Anchorage, Alaska, 1970—. Vice pres. Chugach Bapt. Assn., 1973-74; v.p. Alaska Bapt. Conv., 1974-75. Home and Office: 4313 Wright St Anchorage AK 99504

FOSTER, RICHARD JAMES, religion educator, Society of Friends; b. Albuquerque, May 3, 1942; m. Carolyn Kerr, 1967; children: Joel, Nathan. B.A., George Fox Coll., Newberg, Oreg., 1964; D. Pastoral Theology in Biblical Studies and Social Ethics, Fuller Theol. Sem., 1980. Minister of youth Alamitos Friends Ch., Garden Grove, Calif., 1962-67; counselor Family Counseling and Research Ctr., Garden Grove, 1967-68; asst. pastor Arcadia Friends Ch., Calif., 1968-70; pastor Woodlake Ave Friends Ch., Canoga Park, Calif., 1970-74, Newberg Friends Ch., 1974-79; assoc. prof. theology and writer in residence Friends U., Wichita, Kans., 1979—. Author: Celebration of Discipline: The Path to Spiritual Growth, 1978; Freedom of Simplicity, 1981; Study Guide for Celebration of Discipline, 1982; (booklet) Meditative Prayer, 1983; Money, Sex, and Power, 1985; Study guide to Money, Sex, and Power, 1985. Producer tapes, film. Contbr. articles to mags. Recipient Writer of Yr. award Warner Pacific Coll., 1978, Gold Medallion award Christian Booksellers Assn., 1982, Christy award Christian Life Mag., 1982. Office: Friends Univ 2100 University Wichita KS 67213

FOSTER, RONALD ALBERT, music minister; b. Paterson, N.J., Jan. 8, 1941; s. Harold Doby and Ethel Anne (Hamlin) F.; m. Josephine Narisee Bates, 1960 (div. Feb. 1976); children: Ronald Tramaine, Josharmaine, Landon Lee; m. Elesia Louise Foster, Mar. 20, 1977; 1 child, Loren Michael Blackwell. Student Kean Coll., Union, N.J. Choir dir. Christ Temple Baptist Ch., Paterson, 1957-59, Northside Community Chapel, Paterson, 1963—; dir./founder All God's Children, Washington, N.J., 1976—; minister of music Fountain Bapt Ch., Summit, N.J., 1984—; mem. revision com. for New Psalter Hymnal, Christian Ref. Ch., Grand Rapids, Mich., 1984. Self-employed music tchr., 1964—; record producer/arranger, 1964—; artist, 1964—; enrichment specialist Summit Child Care, 1984—. Composer: So Good To Know Him, 1977; Don't Put Off a Day, 1979. Inventor popcorn visual art, 1977. Mem. audition com. Gateway Talent Search, Hackensack, N.J., 1982—. Served with USN, 1959-64. Black United Fund grantee, 1984. Mem. Broadcast Music, Nat. Found. (charter). Home: 17 Chestnut Ave Summit NJ 07901

FOSTER, STILLMAN ALLEN, JR., minister, United Presbyterian Church in U.S.A.; b. Pitts., Nov. 10, 1939; s. Stillman Allen and Ruth Elizabeth (Sherrard) F.; B.A., Westminster Coll., New Wilmington, Pa., 1961; B.D. (Sr. N.T. fellow), Princeton Theol. Sem., 1964; Ph.D. (Higgins fellow), U. Edinburgh (Scotland), 1976; m. Miriam Marie Morris, Aug. 18, 1962; children: Stillman Allen III, Robin Wallace, Amy Ruth. Ordained to ministry, 1966; instr. Am. U., 1966-67, Westminster Coll., 1970; sr. pastor Highland United Presbyn. Ch., New Castle, Pa., 1967-71, Southminster Presbyn. Ch., Dayton, Ohio, 1973-84; sr. minister Southminster Presbyn. Ch., Pitts., 1984—; chmn. com. ministerial services Miami (Ohio) Presbytery, 1975, com. candidates, 1976; bd. dirs. United Campus Ministry, Miami U., Oxford, Ohio. Mem. exec. bd. NAACP., New Castle, 1968-69; mem. New Castle Human Relations Commn., 1967-71. Mem. Omicron Delta Kappa, Phi Alpha Theta. Home: 739 Pinetree Rd Pittsburgh PA 15241 Office: 799 Washington Rd Pittsburgh PA 15228

FOUIN, DEANNA FRANCES, major superior, Roman Catholic Church; b. New Orleans, Nov. 28, 1937; d. Frank Anthony and Adele (Collins) Fouin. B.A., U. Southwestern La., 1958, M.Ed., 1965; M.A., Duquesne U., 1970. Joined Sisters of the Most Holy Sacrament, Roman Catholic Ch. Pres., Most Holy Sacrament, Lafayette, La., 1977—; vicar for religious Diocese of Lafayette, 1976-77, mem. diocesan pastoral council, 1974-77; pres. LCWR Region Vi, La., 1978-81, v.p., 1978-79; cons. Mgmt. Desing Inc., Cin., 1976—; pres. Nat. Cath. Vocation Council, Chgo., 1983—; del. Union of Superior Gen., Rome, 1979; liaison Nat. Sisters Vocat. Council, 1981—, NCVC, 1981—, New Ways Ministry, 1981—. Mem. La. Women's Network, Baton Rouge, 1983-84; advisor Gov.'s Com. of 1000, Baton Rouge, 1983. NSF grantee, 1960; Outstanding Citizen award, City of Lafayette, 1984. Mem. Women's Ordination Conf. Democrat. Address: Sisters of Most Holy Sacrament PO Box 2429 Lafayette LA 70502

FOUNTAIN, EDWIN BYRD, minister, educator, librarian, Independent Baptist Ch.; b. Manassas, Ga., Mar. 11, 1930; s. David Theodore and Laura Bertha (Phillips) F. B.F.A., U. Ga., 1951; B.R.E., Lexington Bapt. Coll., 1980, Th.B., 1980, M.R.E., 1981; M.S. in L.S., U. Ky., 1984. Ordained to ministry Bapt. Ch., 1982. Library asst. Lexington Bapt. Coll. (Ky.), 1980-81, tchr., librarian, 1981—; pastor Riverview Bapt. Ch., Lexington, 1982—. Compiler indexes for religious books; contbr. articles to religious jours. Served as 1st lt. USAF, 1951-53. Mem. Lexington Bapt. Coll. Alumni Assn. (pres. 1982—), Christian Librarians Assn. Actors Equity Assn., Screen Actors Guild, Beta Phi Mu. Home: 145 Walton Ave Lexington KY 40505 Office: Lexington Baptist Coll 163 N Ashland Ave Lexington KY 40502

FOUST, ELMER JESSE, minister, So. Bapt. Conv.; b. Lake City, Tenn., Jan. 21, 1922; s. Sebra Esker and Sarah Ellen (Holder) F.; B.A., Carson Newman Coll., 1949; B.D., So. Bapt. Sem., 1952, M.Div., 1968; Th.D., Luther Rice Sem., 1972; m. Mary Elizabeth Reed, May 21, 1946; children—Brenda, Reed. Ordained to ministry, 1942; student pastor First Bapt. Ch., Lawnsdowne, Md., 1941-45, Richland Bapt. Ch., Knoxville, Tenn., 1945-49, Bethabara Bapt. Ch., Owensboro, Ky., 1949-52; pastor Meridian Bapt. Ch., Knoxville, 1952-56, White Oak Bapt. Ch., Chattanooga, 1956-66, Olive Springs Bapt. Ch., Marietta, Ga., 1966-72, Spring Creek Rd. Bapt. Ch., Chattanooga, 1972-74, Berney Points Bapt. Ch., Birmingham, Ala., 1974—; mem. exec. bd. Tenn. Bapt. Conv.; past pres. Chattanooga Ministers Conf.; pres. Birmingham Ministers Conf.; speaker on TV for Chattanooga Clergy Assn.; chaplain Masonic Order. Trustee Tenn. Bapt. Found. Author: Doctrine of New Testament Baptism, 1974; Pickings, A Bit of Wit, A Bit of Wisdom, 1977. Home: 894 Velmont Ln Birmingham AL 35226 Office: 1637 Pearson Ave SW Birmingham AL 35211

FOUST, WAYNE, clergyman, moderator General Association of General Baptists, Poplar Bluff, Mo. Office: 100 Stinson Dr Poplar Bluff MO 63901*

FOUTS, STEPHEN WAYNE, minister, Church of God (Anderson, Ind.); b. Ballinger, Tex., Sept. 4, 1951; s. Carl Edward and Mary Tiny (Chapman) F.; m. Karen Ann Atkins, Nov. 3, 1973; children: Jennifer Lynne, Amanda Ellen. B.S.M., Gulf Coast Bible Coll., 1975. Ordained to ministry Ch. of God (Anderson), 1978. Minister of youth and music Redfork Ch. of God, Tulsa, 1975-76, Dayspring Ch., Cin., 1976-79; assoc. pastor Woodstock Ch., Portland, Oreg., 1979-82; sr. pastor Ch. of God, Gordon, Nebr., 1982—; vice chmn. Gen. Assembly of Nebr. Chs. of God, 1983—; mem. Bd. Evangelism, Nebr., 1983—. Mem. Gordon Ministerial Assn. (chmn.), C. of C. Home: 213 N Birch St Gordon NE 69343 Office: Gordon Ch of God PO Box 100 Gordon NE 69343

FOWLER, CHARLES ESTES, JR., minister, Assemblies of God Church; b. McKinney, Tex., June 15, 1955; s. Charles Estes and Wannella (Baxter) F.; m. Jean Marie Scalfri, June 14, 1980. Student, East Tex. State U., Commerce, 1973-74, Oral Roberts U., Tulsa, 1974-75; B. Gen. Studies, U. Tex.-Dallas, 1981; diploma in Ministerial Studies, Berean Bible Sch., Springfield, Mo., 1981. Ordained to ministry Assemblies of God Ch., 1981. Youth pastor 1st Presbyn. Ch., Cushing, Okla., 1974-75; minister of evangelism Southside Assembly, McKinney, Tex., 1975-80; sr. pastor Assembly of God, Las Animas, Colo., 1982—; host religious radio broadcast, Rocky Ford, Colo., 1984—; narrator tapes on N.T., 1985. Mem. Las Animas Bd. Edn., 1984-87. Republican. Avocations: music; writing; cassette tape ministry. Home: 439 Vigil Ave Las Animas CO 81054 Office: Assembly of God Box 580 Las Animas CO 81054

FOWLER, GERALD LEMUEL, church executive, Christian and Missionary Alliance Canada; b. Calgary, Alta., Can., Sept. 5, 1931; s. Lemuel Beryl and Mary Jane (Taylorson) F.; m. Gladys Marilyn Schmick, Aug. 15, 1952; children: David, Sandra. B.S. in Edn., U. Alta., 1959; M.Edn., U. Calgary, 1966. Tchr., prin., dep. chief supt. of schs., Calgary Bd. Edn., 1952-80; exec. v.p. Christian and Missionary Alliance in Canada, Willowdale, Ont., 1981—; chmn. bd. dirs. Can. Bible Coll., Regina, Sask., 1979—, Can. Theol. Sem. Office: Christian and Missionary Alliance in Canada Suite 907 235 Yorkland Blvd Willowdale ON M2J 4Y8 Canada

FOWLER, STEVEN WADE, minister, Southern Baptist Convention. B. Austin, Tex., Jan. 29, 1957; s. Harold Ragan and Eva Mae (Garner) F.; m. Lu Ann Hamilton, Aug. 12, 1978; 1 son, Hamilton Travis. B.A., NE La. U., 1978; M.Div., Southwestern Bapt. Theol. Sem., 1981, M.Ed., 1984. Lic., 1976; ordained, 1980. Pastor Liberty Bapt. Ch., Marion, La., 1977-78, 1st Bapt. Ch., Hebron, Tex., 1980-82, Henderson St. Bapt. Ch., Cleburne, Tex., 1982-85, 1st Bapt. Ch., Frisco, Tex., 1985—; exec. bd. Johnson Bapt. Assn., Cleburne, 1982—, stewardship dir., 1982—, missions com., 1982—; messenger So. Bapt. Conv., 1984-85; mem. Christian Bus. Men's Orgn., Cleburne, So. Bapt. Pastors Conf. Contbg. editor: An Exegetical, Illustrative, and Homiletical Analysis of James, 1984. Mem. com. to rev. and recommend new pub. sch. site, Cleburne, 1983; mem. Univ. Jud. Bd. NE La. U., 1978. Republican. Club: U.S. Golf Assn. Home: PO Box 555 Frisco TX 75034 Office: First Bapt Ch PO Box 307 Frisco TX 75034

FOWLER, W. LERAY, minister, So. Baptist Conv.; b. Hillsboro, Tex., Oct. 30, 1923; s. William Travis and Susie Lorena (Anderson) F.; B.A., Baylor U., 1944, M.A., 1945; B.D., S.W. Bapt. Theol. Sem., 1949; D.D., Howard Payne U., 1955; m. Rosemary Turner, Dec. 15, 1945; children—David Mark, Steve Douglas. Ordained to ministry So. Bapt. Conv., 1942; minister chs., Moody, 1948-50, Brady, 1950-55, Ballinger, 1955-58, Sweetwater, all Tex., 1958-62, West Univ. Bapt. Ch., Houston, 1962-85; dir. Bapt. Standard; mem. Human Welfare Commn., Christian Edn. Commn., So. Bapt. Annuity Bd.; mem. exec. com. So. Bapt. Conv. Trustee Howard Payne U., Houston Bapt. U. Recipient George Washington Freedom Found. award for sermon, 1970, Honor awards Freedom Found. for television programs, 1971-73; Fowler Chapel of West Univ. Bapt. Ch. named in his honor. Contbr. articles to newspapers, mags. Home: 3610 Durness St Houston TX 77025

FOWLKES, NANCY LANETTA, ch. ofcl., United Meth. Ch.; b. Athens, Ga., Aug. 26; d. Amos Malone and Nettie Belle (Barnett) Pinkard; B.A., Bennett Coll., 1946; M.A., Syracuse U., 1952; M.S.W., Smith Coll., 1963; m. Vester Guy Fowlkes, June 4, 1955; 1 dau., Wendy Denise. Chmn. adminstrv. bd. Trinity United Meth. Ch., White Plains, N.Y., 1970-72, lay speaker 1970—, vice chmn. bd. trustees, 1973—, mem. com. on race and religion, 1972—, treas. United Meth. Women, 1969-73, pres., 1974—; pres. Inter Faith Council White Plains, 1972-74; bd. dirs. Bethel Meth. Home, Ossining, N.Y., 1973—; lay del. ann. conf. United Meth. Ch., 1976, Westchester dist. rep. Council on Ministries, 1976. Supr. adoption services Westchester County Dept. Social Services, White Plains, 1967—. Pres., Westchester chpt. Jack and Jill Am., Inc., 1965-67, sec.-treas. Eastern region, 1967-71, recipient Distinguished Service award, 1976; adv. bd. White Plains Adult Edn., 1970—. Bd. dirs. Family Service of Westchester, 1961-71. Recipient Schaefer award for distinguished community service, 1963; Recognition plaque for service Jack and Jill of Am., Inc., 1976. Mem. Acad. Certified Social Workers, Urban League Westchester, Internat. Platform Assn., Theta Sigma Phi, Alpha Kappa Alpha (pres. Zeta Nu Omega chpt. 1958-62). Editor: Va. Edn. Bull., 1948-50. Home: 107 Valley Rd White Plains NY 10604 Office: 85 Court St White Plains NY 10601

FOX, EDGAR LEROY, minister, Christian Ch.; b. Tulsita, Tex., Oct. 8, 1934; s. John B. and Mary (Green) F.; B.A., Tex. Christian U., 1957, B.D., 1960; D.D., Universal Bible Inst., 1975. Ordained to ministry, 1960; pastor First Christian Ch., Gordon, Tex., 1958-59; film librarian Tex. Christian U., Fort Worth, 1958-60; pastor, bus. mgr. Valley Christian Ch., 1960-65; exec. dir. Yakima Indian Nation, 1965-70; pastor 1st Christian Ch., Post, Tex., 1973-77, Quanah, Tex., 1977—. Mem. Ft. Simcoe Job Corp Adv. Council, 1965-69 scoutmaster Troop 57, Boy Scouts Am., 1977—; bd. dirs. Sr. Citizen, 1983—. Mem. Post Ministerial Alliance (pres. 1976-77), Quanah Ministerial Alliance (v.p. 1977—). Author booklets: It Must Be Done, God's Gifts, God's Claims. Address: PO Box 356 Quanah TX 79252

FOX, H. EDDIE, minister, church official, United Methodist Church; b. Sevier County, Tenn., July 26, 1938; m. Mary Nell Leuty, 1959; children: Gaye Nell, Tim, Tom. A.A., Hiwassee Jr. Coll., 1957; B.A. cum laude, Tenn. Wesleyan Coll., 1959; M.Div. magna cum laude, Candler Sch. Theology, Emory U., 1962; D.Min., Vanderbilt U., 1979. Ordained to ministry United Methodist Ch., 1962. Student pastor, 1957-61; pastor Holston View and Prospect Meth. Chs., Weber City, Va., 1962-71, Concord Meth. Ch., Knoxville, Tenn., 1971-73; exec. dir. Preaching, World Evangelization and Congregational Devel., Discipleship, United Meth. Ch., Nashville, 1973—; adj. prof. evangelism and preaching Emory U.; sec. N. Am. region World Evangelism, World Methodist Council; mem. World Meth. Council, 1976—, mem. exec. com., 1983—; trustee Holston Conf., United Meth. Ch., dir. various youth camps and preaching seminars. Author: Living A New Life; Getting The Story Straight; Inherit The Kingdom. Named Pastor of Yr., 1967. Address: PO Box 840 Nashville TN 37202

FOX, MARVIN, rabbi, Conservative, philosophy educator; b. Chgo., Oct. 17, 1922; s. Norman and Sophie (Gershengorn) F.; m. June Elaine Trachtenberg, Feb. 20, 1944; children: Avrom Baruch, Daniel Jonathan, Sheryl Deena. B.A., Northwestern U., 1942, M.A., 1946; Ph.D., U. Chgo., 1950. Ordained conservative rabbi, 1942. Faculty Ohio State U.,

Columbus, 1948—, assoc. prof., 1956-61, prof. philosophy, 1961-73, Leo Yassenoff prof. philosophy and Jewish studies, 1973-74; Philip W. Lown prof. Jewish philosophy, dir. Lown Sch. Nr. Eastern and Judaic Studies, Brandeis U., Waltham, Mass., 1974—; vis. prof. Hebrew Theol. Coll. Chgo., summer 1955, Hebrew U. Jerusalem, 1970-71, Bar-Ilan U., Ramat-Gan, Israel, 1970-71; mem. exec. com. Conf. Jewish Philosophy, 1963-69, Inst. for Judaism and Contemporary Thought, Israel, 1971—; mem. acad. bd. Melton Research Ctr., Jewish Theol. Sem. Am., 1972—. Author: Modern Jewish Ethics - Theory and Practice, 1975. Editor: Kant's Fundamental Principles of the Metaphysic of Morals, 1949; cons. editor jour. History of Philosophy, 1970-76. Mem. editorial bd. Library of Living Philosophers, 1946—, Judaism, 1953—, Tradition, 1956—, AJS Rev., 1976—, Daat, 1978—, Jewish Edn. Yearbook, 1979—. Contbr. articles to profl. jours. Served with USAAF, 1942-46. Fellow Am. Council Learned Socs., 1962-63, NEH, 1980-81, Elizabeth Clay Howard Found., 1956-57. Mem. Nat. Commn. B'nai B'rith Hillel Founds. (exec. com.), Assn. Jewish Studies (bd. dirs. 1970—, v.p. 1973-75, pres. 1975-78), AAUP, Am. Philos. Assn., World Union Jewish Studies (governing council), Medieval Acad. Am., Metaphys. Soc. Am., Am. Acad. Jewish Research, Conf. Jewish Philosophy. Home: 11 Ellison Rd Newton Centre MA 02159 Office: Dept Near Eastern and Judaic Studies Brandeis U Waltham MA 02254

FOXWORTH, JOHN TYLER, minister, Southern Baptist Conv.; b. Florence County, S.C., June 8, 1923; s. Benjamin Franklin and Tula Belle (Collins) F.; A.B. in History, Carson-Newman Coll., Jefferson City, Tenn., 1950; B.D., New Orleans Bapt. Theol. Sem., 1954; m. Jewell Maree Magee, May 3, 1952; children: Jane Foxworth, Benjamin Magee. Ordained to ministry, 1952. Pastor chs. in La. and S.C., 1952-65; pastor Rochelle (Ga.) Bapt. Ch., after 1965, also Pine Grove Bapt. Hosp., to 1986. Associational rep. Christian Index, Ga. Bapt. Index, 1967—; moderator Little River Bapt. Assn., 1968-70; mem. exec. com. Ga. Bapt. Conv., 1969-74; rep. Ga. Bapt. Hosp. Assn., 1967—; vice moderator Tattnal Evang. Assn. Address: PO Box 452 Rochelle GA 31079

FRANCIS, JOSEPH A. See *Who's Who in America,* 43rd edition.

FRANCIS, PAUL RICHARD EMMANUEL, priest, Roman Catholic Church; b. Stann Creek, Belize, June 15, 1915; s. George William Emmanuel and Bernice Leonora (Laidman) F.; came to U.S., 1952, naturalized, 1960; student St. John's Coll., Belize, 1931-33; Ph.B., Urban U., Rome, 1938, S.T.D., 1943, J.C.B., 1944; law student London U.; postgrad. Boston State Coll., 1972-73. Ordained priest, 1941. Parish worker Diocese of Rome, 1941-45; assoc. pastor Diocese of Belize, 1945-52; assoc. pastor St. Charles Borromeo Ch., N.Y.C., 1952-59, St. Francis De Sales Ch., Roxbury, Boston, Mass., 1959-66, Holy Cross Cathedral, Boston, 1966-67, Sacred Heart Ch., Weymouth, Mass., 1967-82; now pastor St. Theresa Parish, Revere, Mass.; chief adv., Met. Tribunal Archdiocese Boston, 1977—. Tchr. Wyndham Sch., Boston, 1964-69. Contbr. articles to religious jours. Home and Office: 500 Revere St Revere MA 02151

FRANCISCO, SYLVESTER ORVILLE, pastor, Seventh-day Adventists; b. Burrton, Kans., Nov. 3, 1920; s. Lamont Jay and Lillie (Arnold) F.; B.A., Loma Linda U., 1949; M.A., Andrews U. Theol Sem., 1950; m. Margie Marie Brown, June 3, 1945; children—Kelly Allen, Patrick Neal. Ordained to ministry, 1955; pastor, chaplain, Calif., Germany, Idaho, 1950—; adj. chaplain to U.S. Army in Europe, Heidelberg, Germany, 1960-66; pastor Seventh-day Adventist Ch., Twin Falls, Idaho, 1969-76, Mira Loma, Calif., 1976—. Chaplain Victorville (Calif.) Civil Def., 1966-68. Mem. adv. bd. USO, 1966-68. Home: 2847 Tropicana Dr Riverside CA 92504 Office: PO Box 5 Mira Loma CA 92502

FRANGELLA, CHARLES RUSSELL, minister, Southern Baptist Convention; counseling center executive; b. Joliet, Ill., Mar. 28, 1946; s. Francis Louis and Olive Adeline (Anderson) F.; m. Jane Snider, June 18, 1966 (div. Mar. 1971); 1 child, Matthew Charles; m. Michele Ranae Matson, Feb. 26, 1977; children: Jessica Trezise, Jordan Davis. A.A., Joliet Jr. Coll., 1967; B.S., Sch. of Ozarks, 1977; cert. Multnomah Sch. of Bible, 1980, M.A. in Bibl. Studies, 1982. Ordained to ministry So. Bapt. Conv. Dir. pub. relations Missions Outreach, Inc., Bethany, Mo., 1977-79; founder, dir. Frangella Ministries, Charleston, W.Va., 1979—; interim pastor Birkenfeld Community Ch., Oreg., 1982; seminar coordinator Grace Fellowship Internat., Denver, 1981—. Exec. v.p. Women's Counseling Ctr., Charleston, 1985—; bd. dirs. Appalachin Women's Cons. Services, Charleston, 1985; pres. Blue Ridge Press, Charleston, 1985. Dir., producer The Great Exchange, 1980. Author poetry. Avocations: horses, travel. Office: Women's Counseling Ctr 1021 Quarrier St Suite 214 Charleston WV 25301

FRANK, CRAIG FRED, minister, Church of God (Anderson, Indiana); b. Milw., Nov. 1, 1950; s. Gerald Harry and Inez Miriam (Buettner) F.; m. Leatha Jane Varvel, Aug. 5, 1973; children: Marla, Kevin. B.A., Anderson Coll., 1972; M.Div., Anderson Sch. Theology, 1978. Ordained to ministry Ch. of God (Anderson), 1975. Youth pastor Chesterfield Christian Ch., Ind., 1972-73; assoc. pastor 1st Ch. of God, Atwater, Calif., 1973-75; pastor 1st Ch. of God, Springfield, Ill., 1978—; bd. mem. Ill. Ch. Action on Alcohol Problems, Springfield, 1978—; chmn. gen. assembly Ch. of God in Ill., Mt. Zion, Ill., 1983-84; mem. Commn. on Social Concerns, Ch. of God (Anderson, Ind.), 1982-84; pres. Evangelical Ministers Assn., Springfield, 1981. Home: 3205 Warner Dr Springfield IL 62703 Office: First Church of God 2800 Stevenson Dr Springfield IL 62703

FRANKLIN, CAROL BERTHA, religious organization executive, American Baptist Churches in the U.S.A.; b. Paris, Tex., Apr. 5, 1947; d. Forrest Treadwell and Bertha Florence (Breazeale) F. B.A., U. Wash., 1969; M.Div., So. Bapt. Sem., 1976; postgrad. U.Hawaii, 1972. Ordained to ministry Baptist Ch., 1982. Tchr., Hawaii Bapt. Acad., Honolulu, 1969-71; journalist Bapt. Press, Washington, 1976-79; minister of edn. First Bapt. Ch., Washington, 1979-82; policy adv. Am. Bapt. Chs., Washington, 1983—. Contbr. articles and feature to religious publs. Democrat. Office: Office of Govtl Relations 110 Maryland Ave NE Washington DC 20002

FRANKLIN, JAMES LORAN, JR., religion writer, editor; b. Boston, Jan. 11, 1947; s. James Loran and Mary Rose (McCarthy) F.; m. Eunice Julia Kellerer, Feb. 14, 1969; children: Eunice D., Mary K., James Loran III, Julia R. A.B., Boston Coll., 1969; student Holy Cross Coll., 1965-66. Religion writer Boston Globe, 1976—, copy-editor, 1971-76. Editor: Religion Newswriters Assn. Newsletter, 1983-84. Mem. Religion Newswriters Assn. (sec. 1984—). Democrat. Office: Boston Globe 135 Morrissey Blvd Boston MA 02107

FRANKLIN, RONALD MONROE, pastor, Southern Baptist Convention; B. Carthage, Mo., Jan. 5, 1953; s. Earl Monroe Franklin and Ruby Frances (Forrester) Burt; stepfather: Leslie Jacob Burt; m. Cheryl Lynne Jennings, May 24, 1975; children: Aaron Monroe, Leslie Lynne. B.A. in Christianity and Sociology, SW Bapt. U., 1975. Lic., 1971; ordained, 1981. Pastor Sheldon Bapt. Ch., Mo., 1976-81, Elm Grove Bapt. Ch., Curryville, Mo., 1981-84, Broadway Bapt. Ch., Oak Grove, Mo., 1984—; cons. brotherhood dept. Mo. Bapt. Conv., 1977—; camp dir. Salt River Bapt. Assn. Youth Camp, Troy, Mo., 1982, 83; youth dir. Nevada Bapt. Assn., Mo., 1978, 79, brotherhood dir., 1980, 81; state royal ambassador, officer, sec., v.p. brotherhood dept. Mo. Bapt. Conv., 1970, 71; mem. Oak Grove Ministerial Alliance. Alderman, City of Sheldon, 1981. Mem. Sheldon Ministerial Alliance (pres. 1974-81). Home: 208 W 21st St Oak Grove MO 64075 Office: Broadway Bapt Ch 600 Maple Ln Oak Grove MO 64075

FRANKS, EDWIN DALE, minister, evangelist, Assemblies of God; construction, real estate and computer consultant; b. Shamrock, Tex., Jan. 28, 1943; s. Raymond Lloyd and Mary Verena (Grubbs) F.; 1 son, Edwin Dale. Student Southwestern Assemblies of God Coll., Waxahachie, Tex., 1960-63; Ordained to ministry Assemblies of God, 1966. Evangelist, 1963-66, 67-75; ednl. dir. Dallas Teen Challenge, 1966-67; sr. pastor Trinity Temple Assembly of God, Albuquerque, 1976-79; assoc. pastor, music dir. First Assembly of God, Farmington, N.Mex., 1982-84; sr. pastor Family Worship Ctr., Reno, Nev., 1985—; dir. campus ministry N.Mex. Dist. council Assemblies of God, 1975-77; sec.-treas. Pentecostal Fellowship Greater Albuquerque, 1974-75, v.p., 1975-76; host Inspirational Nightsongs, KFMK-FM, Houston, 1969. Vice pres., broker Franks & Assocs., Inc., Albuquerque, 1981—; v.p. Christian Communicators, Inc., Albuquerque, 1974—; owner Prestige Data Systems, Reno, 1983—. Address: PO Box 11583 Reno NV 89510-1583

FRANZ, FREDERICK WILLIAM See *Who's Who in America,* 43rd edition.

FRANZ, LOUIS JOSEPH, priest, Roman Catholic Ch.; b. New Orleans, July 27, 1931; s. Valentine Joseph, Jr. and Hilda (Tregre) F.; B.A. in Philosophy, St. Mary's Sem., Perryville, Mo., 1954; M.A. in English, St. Louis U., 1959; Ph.D., U. So. Calif., 1966. Joined Congregation of Mission, Roman Catholic Ch., 1948, ordained priest, 1957; dean students Regina Cleri Sem., Tucson, 1957-58, St. Vincent's Sem., Montebello, Calif., 1958-61; dean St. John's Sem. Coll., Camarillo, Calif., 1961-66, rector, pres., 1966-70; faculty St. Mary's Sem. Coll., Perryville, 1970-73; rector, pres., 1972-73; vice provincial New Orleans vice province Vincentian Community, 1973-75, Provincial So. Province, 1975-82, provincial dir. formation, dir. devel., 1983-85; mem. Ark. Mission Team, 1985—; chmn. priestly formation com. Conf. Maj. Superiors, 1975, 76. Mem. bd. trustees De Paul U., Chgo., 1969—. Mem. Nat. Cath. Edn. Assn., MLA. Address: PO Box 128 Star City AR 71667

FRANZEN, JANICE MARGUERITE GOSNELL, editor, b. LaCrosse, Wis., Sept. 24, 1921; d. Wray Towson and Anna Heldena (Renstrom) Gosnell; B.S. cum laude, Wis. State U. at LaCrosse, 1943; M.R.E., No. Bapt. Theol. Sem., 1947; m. Ralph Oscar Franzen, Feb. 15, 1964. Registrar Christian Writers Inst., Chgo., 1947-49, dir., 1950-63, dir. studies, 1964—; fiction editor Christian Life Mag., 1950-63, woman's editor, 1964-72, exec. editor, 1972—; exec. editor Christian Bookseller mag., 1972—; free-lance writer religious publs.; mem. editorial bd. Creation House Pub. Co., Wheaton, Ill., 1971—; sec., v.p., bd. dirs. Christian Life Missions, Wheaton, 1971—; speaker writers confs. Author: Christian Writers Handbook, 1960, 61. Home: 3N455 Mulberry St West Chicago IL 60185 Office: 396 E St Charles Rd Wheaton IL 60188

FRANZETTA, BENEDICT C., bishop, Roman Catholic Church. Titular bishop of Oderzo, aux. bishop, Youngstown, Ohio, 1980—. Office: St Columba Rectory 159 W Rayen Ave Youngstown OH 44503*

FRASER, RICHARD JOSEPH, minister, United Ch. Christ; b. White County, Ind., Oct. 8, 1927; s. Roscoe Randylle and Eleanor Celia (Veneman) F.; B.P.E., Purdue U., 1948; B.D., McCormick Theol. Sem., 1956; postgrad. Yale, Union Theol. Sem.; m. Esther Louise Koning, Apr. 1, 1948; children—Rebecca, Susan, Ross, Emily. Ordained to ministry, 1956; dir. Ind. Christian Rural Overseas Program, Indpls., 1951-52; program dir. St. Paul's Ch., Chgo., 1952-57; pastor St. John's Ch., Cullman, Ala., 1957-60, St. John's Ch., Niles, Mich., 1960-64, St. James Ch., Louisville, 1964-68, 1st Congl. Ch., DeKalb, Ill., 1968-76, Friedens United Ch. Christ, Indpls., 1976—. Pres. DeKalb County Assn. Chs., 1970-72; chmn. health, edn. and welfare com. Ill. conf. United Ch. Christ, 1972-75; chaplain Ill. Senate, 1971. Mem. adv. com. DeKalb County Home Commn. Bd. Suprs., 1971; bd. dirs. Brooklawn Children's Home, Louisville, 1965-68; trustee Uhlich Children's Home, Chgo., 1974—. Club: Indpls. Athletic. Home: 727 W Ralston Rd Indianapolis IN 46217 Office: 8300 S Meridian St Indianapolis IN 46217

FRASER, THOMAS AUGUSTUS, JR., bishop, Episcopal Church; b. Atlanta, Apr. 17, 1915; s. Thomas Augustus and Lena Lee (Connell) F.; B.A., Hobart Coll., 1938, S.T.D., 1965; B.D., Va. Theol. Sem., 1941, D.D., 1960; spl. student U. Jena (Germany), 1937; D.D., U. of South, 1960; D.D., Wake Forest Coll., 1961; m. Marjorie Louise Rimbach, May 29, 1943; children: Thomas Augustus III, Constance Louise. Ordained deacon, 1941, priest, 1942, bishop, 1960; missionary Diocese L.I., N.Y., 1941-42; sec., chaplain Bishop of L.I., 1942; sr. asst., N.Y.C., 1942-44; rector in Alexandria, Va., 1944-51, Winston-Salem, N.C., 1951-60; bishop coadjutor Diocese of N.C., Raleigh, 1960-65, bishop, 1965—. Mem. editorial com. Anglican Congress, Toronto, Can., 1963; chmn. Joint Commn. on Edn. Holy Orders Episcopal Ch., 1963—. Mem. Community Nursing, Alexandria, 1944-50, Winston-Salem, 1951-60, Alcoholic Rahab., Winston-Salem, 1954-59, United Fund, Winston-Salem, 1957-60, Family and Child Welfare, Winston-Salem, 1955-57, Childrens Psychol. Clinic, Winston-Salem, 1955-57. Trustee U. of South, Va. Theol. Sem., St. Mary's Jr. Coll., Raleigh, N.C., St. Augustine's Coll. Mem. exec. com. Gov.'s Commn. on Piedmont Crescent, 1964—, sec. Commn. Priesthood, 1968; Lambeth Conf., London, Eng. Mem. Tau Kappa Alpha, Sigma Chi. Office: 201 St Albans Dr Raleigh NC 27609

FRAZER, JOE JACKSON, minister, United Methodist Ch.; b. Lafayette, Ala., May 16, 1927; s. Joe Toliver and Maggie Myrtle (Trimble) F.; B.S. cum laude, Birmingham-So. Coll., 1950; B.D., Vanderbilt U., 1952; D.Min., Fuller Theol. Sem., 1977; m. Martha Louise Johnson, Aug. 19, 1956; children—Joe J., Denman Edwin, Emily Ruth, Susan Elizabeth. Ordained to ministry, 1954; pastor chs., Tenn. and Ala., 1949-72; pastor Neely's Bend Ch., Madison, Tenn., 1972—. Pres. Lewis County Ministerial Assn., 1965; bd. missions Tenn. Conf., 1962-66. Chmn. Cancer Drive, Warrior, Tenn., 1961. Home: 1236 Neely's Bend Rd Madison TN 37115 Office: 1605 Neely's Bend Rd Madison TN 37115

FRAZIER, EDWIN RAY, clergyman, Southern Baptist; b. Wake County, N.C., Apr. 6, 1945; s. James Robert and Violet Utoka (Pearce) F.; m. Sandra Gail Echols, June 24, 1967; children: James Blake, Amanda Gail. B.A., Mars Hill Coll., 1967; M.Div., So. Bapt. Sem., 1970, D.Min., 1982. Ordained to ministry So. Bapt., 1968. Pastor, Greenup Fork Bapt. Ch., Owenton, Ky., 1968-70, Bethlehem Bapt. Ch., Ga., 1970-73, Calvary Bapt. Ch., Austell, Ga., 1973-77, Enon Bapt. Ch., Roanoke, Va., 1977—. Author: Matthew, 1981, Luke, 1985. Contbr. devotions in field. Mem. Roanoke Valley Bapt. Ministers Conf. Democrat. Office: Enon Baptist Ch Route 11 Box 4 Roanoke VA 24019

FRAZIER, KENNETH ARNOLD, JR., minister, United Church of Christ and Christian Church (Disciples of Christ); b. Winston-Salem, N.C., Apr. 21, 1943; s. Kenneth Arnold and Mary Alice (Bnikley) F.; m. Emily Susan Figgins, Sept. 6, 1968; children: Jennifer Alane, Leah Eunice, Sara Elizabeth. B.A., Bethany Coll., 1977; M.Div., Yale U., 1980. Ordained to ministry United Ch. Christ and Christian Ch. (Disciples Christ), 1982. Parish assoc. 1st Congl. Ch.,

United Ch. Christ, Cheshire, Conn., 1977-82, pastor Stanley Meml. Ch., New Britain, Conn., 1982—; pres. New Britain Area Clergy Assn., 1982-83; treas. Greater New Britain United Campus Ministries, Central Conn. State U., 1984—; clergy del. New Britain Human Resources Agy., 1983—. Contbr. book revs. to religious jours. Served with USN, 1964-68. Recipient Charles Mersick prize Yale Div. Sch., 1980. Home: 48 Sefton Dr New Britain CT 06053 Office: Stanley Meml Ch 639 East St New Britain CT 06051

FRAZIER, KENNETH ELDRED, lay ch. worker, Christian Ch. (Disciples of Christ); b. Ursa, Ill., Oct. 22, 1912; s. Grover Lee and Jennie Phobe (Daugherty) F.; grad. high sch.; m. Pauline Francis Woodruff, June 20, 1934; children—Ronald, Myrna (Mrs. Darrell Mixer), Gloria (Mrs. Larry Jenkins). Chmn. bd. Ursa (Ill.) Christian Ch., 1947—, Sunday sch. supt., 1959-62, elder, 1944—, deacon, 1936-44, Sunday sch. tchr., 1936-74; pres. Adams County Council Chs., 1953-59; dist. chmn. men's work Christian Ch., 1961-72, chmn. men's work Ill.-Wis., 1972-74; mem. regional bd. Ill.-Wis. Disciples of Christ, 1972—, chmn. clergy-laity task force, 1975-76. Pres. N. Adams County Nursing Home, 1975-76; mem. budget com. United Community Services Adams County, 1976. Address: Rt 2 Quincy IL 62301

FRAZIER, MICHAEL FORD, minister, educator, Presbyterian Church in America; b. Alexandria, La., Jan. 3, 1951; s. Andrew N. and Eldred Maye (Ford) F.; m. Carolyn Sue Ford, Aug. 14, 1973; children: Kristy Michelle, Matthew Thomas. Student La. State U., 1969-72; B.A., Northwestern State U., Natchitoches, La., 1974; M.Div., Reformed Theol. Sem., Jackson, Miss., 1981. Ordained to ministry Presbyterian Ch. Am., 1982. Instr. Whitworth Bible Coll., Brookhaven, Miss., 1981-82; supply pastor Monticello and Wesson Presbyn. Ch., Magee and Wesson, Miss., 1981-82; stated supply pastor Tabb Street Presbyn. Ch., Petersburg, Va., 1983, pastor, 1983—; tchr. West End Christian Sch., Hopewell, Va., 1984—. Chmn. Petersburg Residents Organized to Uphold Decency, 1985—. Avocations: woodworking; piano; trombone; hunting; fishing. Home: 230 Greenwood Dr Petersburg VA 23805 Office: Tabb Street Presbyn Ch 29 W Tabb St Petersburg VA 23803

FRAZIER, RICHARD GLENN, minister, Lutheran Church in America; b. Zanesville, Ohio, Aug. 5, 1931; s. Herbert Llewellan and Vera Zeleth (Stiers) F.; m. Sally Ruth Stockwell, Oct. 1, 1966; children: Anne Elizabeth, Katherine Ruth, Cynthia Mary, Jane Rebekah, Daniel Llewellan. B.A., Wittenberg U., 1953, D.D., 1971; M.Div., Hamma Sch. Theology, 1956; L.H.D., Ind. Inst. Tech., 1983. Ordained to ministry Lutheran Ch., 1956. Asst. pastor Trinity English Luth. Ch., Ft. Wayne, Ind., 1956-67, sr. pastor, 1967—; bd. dirs. Wittenberg U., Springfield, Ohio, 1981—, Luth. Social Services, Ft. Wayne, 1981—. Author: (with Dan Hamlin and Richard Hunt) What's The Good Word, 1979. Club: Quest (Ft. Wayne). Lodge: Rotary (dir. 1984—). Home: 3912 Tarrington Dr Fort Wayne IN 46815 Office: Trinity English Lutheran Ch 405 W Wayne St Fort Wayne IN 46802

FREBURGER, WILLIAM JOSEPH, editor, author, Roman Catholic Church. b. Balt., Oct. 6, 1940; s. William Joseph and Nellie Elizabeth (Bagdonas);F.; m. Mary Elizabeth Algeo, Feb. 23, 1979; 1 son, William Daniel. B.A. in Philosophy, St. Mary Sem., 1962; S.T.L. in Theology, Gregorian U., Italy, 1966. Ordained priest Roman Catholic Ch., 1965. Asst. sec. Diocesan Liturgical Com., Balt., 1968-70; dir. Div. Liturgy, Balt., 1970-76; laicized, 1976; liturgical cons. Ave Maria Press, Notre Dame, Ind., 1984—, Silver Burdett, Morristown, N.J., 1984—; program dir. Time Cons., Severna Pk., Md., 1976-78; editor Celebration Publs., Kans. City, Mo., 1978—. Author: Eucharistic Prayers, 1976; This is the Word of the Lord, 1984; Liturgy: Work of the People, 1984. Mem. N.Am. Acad. Liturgy (assoc. mem.). Home: 11211 Monticello Ave Silver Spring MD 20902 Office: NCR PublCo 115 E Armour Kansas City MO 64111

FREED, PAUL ERNEST, minister, religious broadcasting executive, Southern Baptist Convention; b. Detroit, Aug. 29, 1918; s. Ralph and Mildred (Forsythe) F.; m. Betty Jane Seawell, Oct. 17, 1945; children: Paul David, James, Donna, Stephen, Daniel. B.A., Wheaton Coll., 1940; diploma Nyack Coll., 1943; M.S., Columbia U., 1956; Ph.D., NYU, 1960; L.H.D. (hon.), Immanuel Bible Sem., 1982. Ordained to ministry So. Bapt. Conv., 1949. Pastor chs. in Greenville, S.C., 1943-45; exec. dir. Youth for Christ, Greensboro, N.C., 1946-50; evangelist, 1950-52; founder/pres. Trans World Radio, Chatham, N.J., 1952—. Author: Towers to Eternity, 1968; Let the Earth Hear, 1980. Recipient Alumnus of Yr. award Nyack Coll., 1982; Founders Day award NYU. Fellow Royal Geog. Soc.; mem. Nat. Religious Broadcasters Assn. (bd. dirs. 1956—; Percy award 1960), Kappa Delta Phi. Office: Trans World Radio PO Box 98 Chatham NJ 07928

FREEDMAN, DAVID NOEL, educator, minister Presbyterian Church; b. N.Y.C., May 12, 1922; s. David and Beatrice (Goodman) F.; student Coll. City N.Y., 1935-38; A.B., UCLA, 1939; Th.B. (William H. Green fellow), Princeton Theol. Sem., 1944; Ph.D., Johns Hopkins, 1948; D.Litt., U. Pacific, 1973; D.Sc., Davis and Elkins Coll., 1974; m. Cornelia Anne Pryor, May 16, 1944; children—Meredith Anne (Mrs. Allan LaVoie), Nadezhda, David Micaiah, Jonathan Pryor. Ordained to ministry Presbyn. Ch., 1944. Teaching fellow, asst. instr. Johns Hopkins, Balt., 1946-48; faculty Western Theol. Sem., Pitts., 1948-60, Pitts. Theol. Sem., 1960-64, San Francisco Theol. Sem., 1964-71; faculty Grad. Theol. Union, Berkeley, Calif., 1964-71, dean, 1966-71; prof. Bibl. studies, dir. program on studies in religion U. Mich., Ann Arbor, 1971—; vis. prof. Hebrew U., Jerusalem, 1976—. Vice pres. Am. Schs. Oriental Research, Cambridge, Mass., 1970—; mem. adv. com. acad. study of religion Mich. Dept. Edn., 1972-74; mem. study group situation in Middle East, World Council of Chs., 1972—; chmn. Council on the Study of Religion in Mich. Schs., 1972—. Recipient Carey-Thomas award Pub's Weekly, 1965. William S. Rayner fellow Johns Hopkins U., 1948; Guggenheim fellow, 1958-59; Am. Assn. Theol. Schs. fellow, 1963-64. Mem. Assn. Am. Colls. (mem. commn. on religion in higher edn. 1974—), Am. Oriental Soc., Am. Schs. Oriental Research, Soc. Bibl. Lit. (pres. 1975-76), Bibl. Colloquium (sec., treas. 1958—), Am. Acad. Religion, Soc. Sci. Study Religion, Am. Archeol. Inst. Author: (with J.D. Smart) God Has Spoken, 1949; (with Frank M. Cross) Studies in Ancient Yahwistic Poetry, 1950; (with Frank M. Cross) Early Hebrew Orthography, 1952; (with J.M. Allegro) The People of the Dead Sea Scrolls, 1958; (with R.M. Grant) The Secret Saying of Jesus, 1960; (with M. Dothan) Ashdod I, 1967; The Published Works of W.F. Albright, 1975. Editor or co-editor The Biblical Archaeologist Reader, Vol. I, 1961, Vol. II, 1964, Vol. III, 1970; Anchor Bible Series, 1956—; The Computer Bible, 1971—; New Directions in Biblical Archaeology, 1969; Pictorial Biblical Encyclopedia, 1964; Scrolls from Qumran Cave I, 1972; Jesus, the Four Gospels, 1973; Religion and the Academic Scene, 1975. Home: Box 7434 Liberty Sta Ann Arbor MI 48107 Office: 445 W Engring U of Michigan Ann Arbor MI 48109

FREEHLING, ALLEN ISAAC, rabbi, Reform Jewish Congregations; b. Chgo., Jan. 8, 1932; s. Jerome Edward and Marion Ruth (Wilson) F.; A.B., U. Miami (Fla.), 1953; B.H.L., Hebrew Union Coll., 1965, M.A., 1967; Ph.D., Kensington U., 1977; m. Leonore Weidberg, July 19, 1953 (div. Apr. 1976); children—Shira Kopelnikov, David Matthew, Jonathan Andrew; m. 2d, Tressa Ruslander Miller, Apr. 17, 1976. Rabbi, 1967; asso. rabbi The Temple, Toledo, Ohio, 1967-72; rabbi Univ. Synagogue, Los Angeles, 1972—. Adminstrv. dir. Temple Israel, Miami, Fla., 1957; exec. dir. Temple Emanu-El of Miami Beach (Fla.), 1960-62; exec. com. Los Angeles Bd. Rabbis, 1972—; cons. social action com. Pacific SW Council, Union Am. Hebrew Congregations, 1973—; bd. dirs. Bay Cities Jewish Community Relations Com., 1973—, urban affairs com., 1973—; rabbinic adv. com. Am. Jewish Congress, 1973—, chpt. pres., 1974-75, regional v.p., 1975—; mem. program, pub. relations com. Jewish Fedn. Council, 1974—; residential lectr. occupying Jewish Chautauqua Socs. chair in Judaic Studies, at Loyola-Marymount U., 1974—; nat. interim adv. resolutions com., Union Am. Hebrew Congregations, 1974-75; mem. Pacific SW regional bd. Anti-Defamation League of B'nai B'rith, 1975—. Home: 810 20th St Santa Monica CA 90403 Office: 11960 Sunset Blvd Los Angeles CA 90049

FREEMAN, ARTHUR JAMES, educator, minister, Moravian Church; b. Green Bay, Wis., Oct. 11, 1927; s. Arthur and Ethel A. (Bins) F.; m. Carole Jean Droney, July 21, 1984; 1 child by previous marriage: David Freeman. B.A., Lawrence Coll., 1949; B.D., Moravian Theol. Sem., 1952; Ph.D., Princeton Sem., 1961. Ordained to ministry, 1953. Founding pastor Big Oak Moravian Ch., Yardley, Pa., 1953-61; assoc. prof. Moravian Theol. Sem., Bethlehem, Pa., 1961-66, prof. religion, 1966—; adminstr. Ecumenical Com. for Continuing Edn., Bethlehem, 1974—; dir. Soc. for Advancement of Continuing Edn. in Ministry, 1982-84; del. Faith and Order Commn., Nat. Council Chs., 1982—. Contbr. articles to profl. jours. Mem. Moravian Hist. Soc., Soc. Bibl. Lit., Friends of Photography. Home: 1753 North Blvd Bethlehem PA 18017 Office: Moravian Theol Sem 60 W Locust St Bethlehem PA 18018

FREEMAN, CARROLL BENTON, seminary educator, Southern Baptist Convention; b. Petal, Miss., Sept. 18, 1928; s. Riley L. and Mary Bessford (Reynolds) F.; m. Hellon Elaine Ford, Jan. 26, 1951; children: Carroll B., Robert Bryan. B.A., Miss. Coll., 1951; M.R.E., So. Sem.-Louisville, 1956; Ed.D., New Orleans Bapt. Theol. Sem., 1972. Youth dir. First Bapt. Ch., Memphis, 1952-54; ednl. dir. 23rd and Broadway Bapt. Ch., Louisville, 1954-55, Carlisle Ave. Bapt. Ch., Louisville, 1955-60; dir. ch. activities Parker Meml. Bapt. Ch., Anniston, Ala., 1960-65; prof. psychology and counseling New Orleans Bapt. Theol. Sem., 1974—. Author: Christian Psychology of Aging, 1979. Contbr. articles to profl. jours. Kahn Trust Fund scholar, 1954. Mem. Am. Assn. Marriage and Family Therapists, La. Chaplains Assn. Republican. Club: Faculty (pres. 1979-80). Lodge: Elks. Home: 4321 Seminary Pl New Orleans LA 70126 Office: New Orleans Bapt Theol Sem 3939 Gentilly Blvd New Orleans LA 70126

FREEMAN, HAROLD FRANCIS, ministry, Ind. Fundamental Chs. Am.; b. Swink, Colo., Mar. 1, 1918; s. Harold Fremont and Leona Frances (Powell) F.; Th.B., Midwest Bible Coll., St. Louis, 1950; m. Esther Lucille Lynn, July 14, 1940; 1 son, Harold Philip. Ordained to ministry Independent Fundamental Chs. Am., 1943; pastor, Grace Bapt. Ch., St. Louis, 1948-56, Salina (Kans.) Bible Ch., 1956-64, Vallejo (Calif.) Bible Ch., 1964—. Prof. theology Sacramento Bible Inst., 1968-72; trustee Ind. Fundamental Chs. Am., 1968-75. Mem. National Exec. Dir.-Independent Fundamental Churches of America, 1975— Polar Bear Assn, World War II. Home: 918 Donner Pass Rd Vallejo CA 94590

FREEMAN, JOEL ARTHUR, minister; b. Lewiston, Maine, July 24, 1954; s. Arthur Fickett and Katherine Ann (Schroeder) F.; m. Laurie Ann Caron, May 1, 1976; 1 child, David Joel. Ordained to ministry The Bible Speaks World Outreach, 1975. Pastor The Bible Speaks Ch., Friendship, Maine, 1975-77, Balt., 1977-80, Columbia, Md., 1980—; vol. chaplain Washington Bullets Basketball Team, 1981—; radio talk show host Sta. WJRO, Balt., 1977—; TV host Howard Cable Co., Ellicott City, Md., 1980—; cons. mission ch., Mayaguez, P.R., 1981—. Author: How to Enjoy Being the World's Need, 1979. Author The Doctrine of Fools booklet, 1984. Steering com. mem. County Exec. Prayer Breakfast, Howard County, 1983—, Word Renewal Pastor's Fellowship, Balt. City, 1977-83; area coordinator Washington for Jesus, 1980; instr. chaplain's office Johns Hopkins U., Balt., 1977-79. Mem. Operation Seareach (dir. 1984—), Inst. in Basic Youth Conflicts (coordinator 1979—). Republican. Home: 5720 Stillmeadow Ln Columbia MD 21045 Office: The Bible Speaks Ch PO Box 2757 Columbia MD 21045

FREEMAN, JOSEPH, JR., minister, Baptist Missionary Association of America; b. Birmingham, Ala., Nov. 27, 1932; s. Joseph Freeman and Ruth Etta (Porter) Lowe; m. Mary Lee McDowell, Sept. 12, 1952; children: Theresa Ann, Joseph Freeman. B. Th., So. Bible Sem., Brunswick, Ga., 1978; D.D., New World Bible Inst., 1981. Ordained to ministry Bapt. Missionary Assn. of Am., 1958. Gen. sec. Mt. Calvary Bapt. Assn., Columbus, Ohio, 1961-73, 1st vice moderator, 1972-73, moderator, 1973; pastor East Mt. Olivet Bapt. Ch., 1985—; gen. sec. Ohio Bapt. Conv., 1971-73, 77-80. Democrat. Home: 1463 Watkins Rd Columbus OH 43207 Office: East Mt Olivet Bapt Ch 2940 E 11th St Columbus OH 43219

FREEMAN, LACY WILLARD, minister, So. Bapt. Conv.; b. Kenton, Tenn., Mar. 13, 1917; s. Jess Walker and Elizabeth Mae (Cherry) F.; student Union U., Jackson, Tenn., 1943; Th.B., So. Bapt. Theol. Sem., Louisville, 1951; m. Ima Florine Derryberry, Oct. 4, 1941; children—Reba Jayce (Mrs. David K. Johnson), John Lacy. Ordained to ministry, 1941; pastor chs. in Tenn., 1941-59; asso. Sunday sch. dept. Tenn. Bapt. Conv., 1959-65; supt. missions Robertson County Bapt. Assn., Springfield, Tenn., 1966—. Mem. personnel com. Tenn. Bapt. Conv., 1954, now regional ch. tng. pres.; mem. emphasis planning coordinating com. So. Bapt. Conv., 1974—. Contbr. articles to religious jours. Address: POB 546 Springfield TN 37172

FREEMAN, SIDNEY LEE, minister, Unitarian Universalist Association, communication arts educator; b. Madison, Wis., Jan. 23, 1927; s. Jack and Gertrude (Kaifetz) F.; m. Evelyn Marie Gronberg, Feb. 3, 1950 (div. 1965); children: Lynn Claire, David Eugene, Michael John; m. Gaynell Bradley, Apr. 28, 1967. B.S., U. Wis., 1947; M.A., Bowling Green State U., 1949; Ph.D., Cornell U., 1951. Ordained to ministry, 1957. Minister, Unitarian Ch., Charlotte, N.C., 1957—; pres. So. Unitarian Council, Atlanta, 1953, Thomas Jefferson Unitarian Dist., Charlotte, 1963-64; lectr. Albert Schweitzer Coll., Churwalden, Switzerland, summer 1959, Starr King Sch. for Ministry, Berkeley, Calif., summer 1965. Assoc. prof. communication arts Johnson C. Smith U., Charlotte, 1958—. Pres. Mental Health Assn., Charlotte, 1978-80. Recipient Disting. Service award Mental Health Assn., 1983. Mem. Unitarian Universalist Ministers Assn. (past sec.), Charlotte Area Clergy Assn. (past exec. com.). Home: 4500 Rockford Ct Charlotte NC 28209 Office: Unitarian Ch Charlotte 234 N Sharon-Amity Rd Charlotte NC 28211

FREITAS, GORDON ANTHONY, minister, Southern Baptist Convention; b. Oakland, Calif., July 26, 1950; s. Anthony and Sally (Alberti) F.; m. Cheryl Marie Steele, Nov. 7, 1970; children: Jennifer Lynne, Rebecca Sue, Carrie Elizabeth. Student Calif. State U.-San Jose, 1968-70, Golden Gate Bapt. Theol. Sem., Mill Valley, Calif., 1984—. Licensed to ministry So. Bapt. Conv., 1984. Sunday sch. supt. Fremont Community Ch., Calif., 1974-77, First Bapt. Ch., Vacaville, Calif., 1979-83, minister of edn., 1981—; Sunday sch. growth cons. Redwood Empire Assoc., Vallejo, Calif., 1983—. Recipient Growth Spiral Eagle award So. Bapt. Conv., 1981, 83. Mem. Western Bapt. Religious Educators Assn. Republican. Avocations: stained glass, miniatures. Home: 115 Cavan Ct Vacaville CA 95688

Office: First Bapt Ch of Vacaville 1127 Davis St Vacaville CA 95688

FRENCH, JOHN HENRY, music director, Lutheran Church in America; music educator; b. Knoxville, Tenn., July 17, 1954; s. Sumner Ross and Mary (Penketh) F.; m. Edwina Dunkle, July 27, 1975; children: Rachael Amelia, Lydia Eve. Mus.B., Phila. Coll. of Performing Arts, 1977; Mus.M., Westminster Choir Coll., 1979; postgrad. U. Cinn., 1982—. Cert. lay profl. in ch. music Lutheran Church in America. Music dir. 1st Presbyn. Ch., Malvern, Pa., 1972-75, 1st Presbyn. Ch., Willow Grove, Pa., 1975-78, St. John's Luth. Ch., Melrose Park, Pa., 1978-83; Emmanuel Luth. Ch., Pottstown, Pa., 1983—; mem. profl. leadership service com. Southeast Pa. synod, Phila., 1984—. Asst. prof. music Ursinus Coll., 1979—. Finalist, Stokowski conducting competition, Phila. Orch., 1978; recipient Lindback award for disting. teaching Ursinus Coll., 1982. Mem. Am. Choral Dirs. Assn. (life), Am. Choral Found., Coll. Music Soc., Pa. State Collegiate Choral Assn. Democrat. Office: Ursinus Coll Music Dept Collegeville PA 19426

FRENCH, MICHAEL CHARLES, priest Roman Cath. Ch.; b. N.Y.C., Feb. 27, 1939; s. John Philip and Margaret Bernadette (De Poala) F.; B.A., St. John's U., Jamaica, N.Y., 1960; M.Div., St. Vincent's Coll., Latrobe, Pa., 1964; M.A., Seton Hall U., South Orange, N.J., 1969; Ph.D., Calif. Sch. Profl. Psychology, San Diego, 1976. Ordained priest Roman Cath. Ch., 1964; asso. pastor St. Anselm's Ch., Bklyn., 1964-71; founder Anselm Counseling Center, Bklyn., 1967; chaplain Benedictine Convent of Perpetual Adoration, San Diego, 1973—. Clin. psychologist La Jolla (Calif.) Clinic, 1976—; unit coordinator Marriage Encounter, Unit 6, Calif.-Ariz., 1975—. Pres. Community Sch. Bd. N.Y.C., Dist. 20, 1970-73. Recipient Award for Community Involvement, Assn. Recreation Tchrs., 1971. Mem. Am., Calif. psychol. assns. Home: 1119 Agate St San Diego CA 92109

FRENCH, THOMAS CHARLES, JR., minister, Southern Baptist Convention; b. Flint, Mich., Aug. 10, 1930; s. Thomas Charles and Patty Ree (Murphy) F.; B.A., Baylor U., 1954; B.D., Southwestern Bapt. Theol. Sem., Ft. Worth, 1957, M.Div., 1969; m. Mary Elizabeth Harrell, Aug. 2, 1951; children: Elidia Anne, Carol Ree. Ordained to ministry So. Bapt. Conv., 1953; pastor Harmony Bapt. Ch., Caldwell, 1953-57, 2d Bapt. Ch., Caldwell, 1957; organizer Jefferson Hwy. Mission, Baton Rouge, La., 1958; organizer, pastor Jefferson Bapt. Ch., 1963—; chmn. adminstrv. com. Judson Bapt. Assn., 1969-71, chmn. finance com., 1971-72, mem. properties com., 1983-85; mem. pub. affairs com. La. Bapt. Conv., 1969-72, mem. exec. com., 1972-79, mem. spl. study com. on conv. structure, 1971-72, mem. denomination cooperation com., 1972-75, mem. operating com., 1976-79, chmn. nominating com., 1980-83, mem. program and exec. coms., 1982-85, 1st v.p., 1983-84, internat. evangelist Korean Crusade, 1970; evangelist Alaska Crusade, Home Mission Bd., So. Bapt. Conv., 1973, mem. credentials com., 1983-85. Bd. rev. East Baton Rouge City-Parish Govt., 1973—, vice chmn. liquor law revision com., 1980-81; chmn. reunion com. Thomas Jefferson High Sch., Port Arthur, Tex., 1972—. Republican. Author: Let's Be Realistic, 1965; Double Taxed Citizen, 1969; Where Have All the Pastors Gone?, 1971. Home: 5015 Parkhollow Dr Baton Rouge LA 70816 Office: 9135 Jefferson Hwy Baton Rouge LA 70809

FRENCH, WILLIAM GEORGE, minister, Presbyn. Ch. Can.; b. Owen Sound, Ont., Can., May 25, 1933; s. Alfred Earl and Emily Hazel (Dickie) F.; B.Sc., Dubuque U., 1956; M.Div., Dubuque Theol. Sem., 1963; m. Barbara Jo Couchman, June 5, 1956; children—William George, Susan Ann. Ordained to ministry, 1963; asso. pastor, Montclair, N.J., 1963-66, Ridgefield Park (N.J.) First Presbyn. Ch., 1966-68, Cedar Grove Presbyn. Ch., N.J., 1968-73, St. Andrew's Ch. and St. Paul's Ch., Maple and Vaughan, Ont., 1973—. Parole and aftercare vol. worker Presbyters of W. Toronto, 1973-76, convenor Christian edn. com., 1974-76, mem. bus. com., 1974-76. Capt. Padre Lorne Scots unit Militia, Brampton, 1976—; bd. advisers Iona Camp, Bala, Ont., 1973-76. Mem. Mil. Inst., Inst. Psychiatry and Religion, Adler Inst., So. Christian Leadership Conf. Home: 9846 Keele St Maple ON L0J 1E0 Canada Office: PO Box 91 Maple ON L0J 1E0 Canada

FRENSDORFF, WESLEY, bishop, Episcopal Ch.; b. Hanover, Germany, July 22, 1926; s. Rudolph August and Erma Margarete (Asch) F.; B.A., Columbia U., 1948; S.T.B., Gen. Theol. Sem., N.Y.C., 1951; m. Dolores C. Stoker, Nov. 1, 1953; 5 children. Ordained deacon, 1951, priest, 1951; vicar St. Mary Virgin Ch., Winnemucca, Nev. and St. Andrew's Ch., Battle Mountain, Nev. and St. Anne's Ch., McDermitt, Nev., 1951-54; rector St. Paul's Ch., Elko, Nev. and vicar St. Barnabas and St. Luke Ch., Wells, Nev., 1954-59; vicar Transfiguration Ch., Darrington, Nev. and St. Martin's Ch., Upper Skagit Valley, Nev. and Community Ch., Newhalem, Wash., 1959-62; dean St. Mark's Cathedral, Salt Lake City, 1962-72; bishop Diocese of Nev., Reno, 1972—. Dir., N. Pacific and Western Parish Tng. Program, Episc. Ch., 1959-64; trustee Gen. Theol. Sem., 1965-74; priest-in-charge St. Francis Ch., Managua, Nicaragua, 1968-69. Office: 2930 7th St Reno NV 89503*

FRERKING, JAMES VICTOR, religion educator, Lutheran Church-Missouri Synod; b. Kansas City, Mo., Mar. 10, 1955; s. Melvin J. and Myrtle Anna (Woodrich) F.; m. Christal Elaine Frerking, July 20, 1985; 1 child, Derek Johnson. A.A., St. Paul's Coll.; B.A., Concordia Coll., St. Paul, 1978; postgrad. Calif. State Coll.-Fullerton, 1984—. Youth dir. St. John's Luth. Ch., Long Beach, Calif., 1978-80, day sch. tchr., 1978-80; youth dir., day sch. tchr. Peace Luth. Ch. and Sch., Tustin, Calif., 1980—; bd. dirs. Tustin Young Adults Ch. League, 1981—. Avocations: sports, photography, ceramics, dog breeding, hiking. Home: 15500 Tustin Village Way Apt 70 Tustin CA 92680 Office: Peace Luth Ch 18542 Vanderlip St Santa Ana CA 92705

FREUND, CAROL DARNELL, lay worker, Episcopal Church; b. Mineola, N.Y., Feb. 21, 1933; d. Warren Edwn and Dorothy Geraldine (Gilbrech) Darnell; m. William O.H. Freund, Jr., Sept. 16, 1960; children: Carol Burnam, William O.H. III. B.A., Allegheny Coll., 1954; M.A., John Carroll U., 1982. Trainer, Episcopal Diocese of Ohio, Cleve., 1972—; mem. tng. div. extension edn. dept. Diocese of Ohio, 1979—, mem., chmn. task force on women, 1974-76, 77-81; mem. Nat. Task Force on Women, Episcopal Ch., N.Y.C., 1979—, chmn., 1981—; exec. dir. Hitchcock House, Cleve., 1983—; dep. to Gen. Conv. Episcopal Ch., N.Y.C., 1973, alt. dep., 1976; mem. diocesan council Diocese of Ohio, 1974-76; jr. warden Christ Ch., Shaker Heights, Ohio, 1979. Mem., v.p. Children's Services, Cleve., 1965-75; pres. Shaker Heights PTA Council, 1975-76, Cleve. Internat. Program, 1980-83; 1st v.p. Council Internat. Programs, 1984—. Named Outstanding Vol., Cleve. Internat. Program, 1983; Founding Trustee award Edn. for Freedom of Choice in Ohio, 1982; cert. of recognition Council Internat. Programs, 1981. Home: 2850 Broxton Rd Shaker Heights OH 44120 Office: Hitchcock House 10917 Magnolia Dr Cleveland OH 44106

FREY, GERARD LOUIS, bishop, Roman Cath. Ch.; b. New Orleans, May 10, 1914; s. Andrew and Marie Therese (DeRose) F.; D.D., St. Joseph's Sem. at St. Benedict's, La., 1933; postgrad. Notre Dame Sem., New Orleans. Ordained priest Roman Catholic Ch., 1938, consecrated bishop, 1967; asst. pastor, Taft, La., 1938-46, St. Leo the Great Ch., 1946-47; asst. dir. Confraternity Christian Doctrine, Archdiocese New Orleans, 1946, dir., 1946-47; pastor St. Frances Cabrini Ch., New Orleans, 1952-63, St. Frances De Sales Ch., Houma, La., 1962-67; bishop Diocese of Savannah, Ga., 1967-72, Diocese of Lafayette, La., 1972—; clergy rep. 2d Vatican Council, 1964; dir. Diocesan Friendship Corps, New Orleans, 1966; Episcopal moderator Theresians Am., 1968—. Recipient Bishop Tracy Vocation award St. Joseph's Sem. Alumni Assn., 1959. Address: 515 Cathedral St Lafayette LA 70501

FREY, WILLIAM CARL, bishop, Episcopal Ch.; b. Waco, Tex., Feb. 26, 1930; s. Harry Frederick and Ethel (Oliver) F.; B.A., U. Colo., 1952; B.Th., Phila. Div. Sch., 1955, D.D. (hon.), 1970; m. Barbara Louise Martin, June 12, 1952; 5 children. Ordained deacon, 1955, priest, 1956; vicar Timberline Circuit Missions, Colo., 1955-58; rector Trinity Ch., Los Alamos, 1958-62, Good Shepherd Ch., San Jose, Costa Rica, 1962-64; dir. Spanish Publs. Center, Episc. Ch. in Costa Rica, 1964-67; bishop Diocese of Guatemala, 1967-73, Diocese of Colo., Denver, 1973—. Dean, Santa Fe Convocation, Episc. Ch., 1959-62, chmn. dept. Christian social relations, 1960-62, chmn. exam. chaplains, 1963-67; bishop-in-charge El Salvador, 1967-68. Address: 1313 Clarkson St Denver CO 80210*

FRIEDMAN, MORRIS S., Rabbi; pres. N.Y. Bd. Rabbis (exec. council). Office: New York Bd of Rabbis 10 E 73rd St New York NY 10021*

FRIEND, WILLIAM B., bishop. Roman Catholic Church. Bishop of Alexandria-Shreveport, 1983—. Office: 2127 Cabrini Ave Alexandria LA 71301*

FRIES, ANDRÉ, nun, religious order administrator, Roman Catholic Church; b. Quincy, Ill., Aug. 12, 1941; d. Andrew W. and June (Reilly) F. B.S., Quincy Coll., 1970; M.B.A., So. Ill. U., 1972. Joined Sisters of the Most Precious Blood, Roman Cath. Ch., 1959. Tchr., St. Monica Sch., Creve Coeur, Mo., 1963-66, St. Peter Sch., Quincy, 1966-69; dir. fin. planning St. Mary's Inst., O'Fallon, Mo., 1971-74; gen. councilor Srs. of Most Precious Blood, O'Fallon, 1974-80, superior gen., 1980—; chmn. bd. St. Mary's Inst., Inc., 1980—, St. Mary's Coll., Inc., O'Fallon, 1980—. Co-author: Accounting and Financial Management for Religious Institutes, 1981; Guidelines for Evaluation: Financial Viability and Accountability, 1984. Contbr. articles to profl. jours. Recipient Disting. Alumna award Quincy Coll., 1982. Mem. Leadership Conf. Women Religious (bd. dirs. 1982—, chmn. Region X 1982—), Nat. Conf. Religious, Nat. Assn. Ch. Personnel Adminstrs. (fin. cons.), Soc. for Acad. Achievement (charter). Home and Office: Sisters of the Most Precious Blood 204 N Main St O'Fallon MO 63366

FRIESEN, LOYAL MELVIN, minister; b. Dallas, Oreg., Nov. 5, 1928; s. Daniel K. and Margaret (Ratslaff) F.; student Northwestern Coll., 1949-50; B.S. M., Simpson Coll., 1953; B.A., Seattle Pacific Coll., 1957; M.A., Mennonite Brethren Bibl. Sem., 1980; m. Carol Lombardi, Feb. 24, 1973; children: Dale, Melodie, Kevin, LaRhonda. Ordained to ministry, 1970; minister youth and music Willow Glen Alliance Ch., San Jose, Calif., 1957-59; minister youth First Bapt. Ch., San Jose, 1959-68; Christian edn. cons. David C. Cook Pub. Co., Elgin, Ill., 1968-71; minister Christian edn. First Bapt. Ch., Modesto, Calif., 1971—. Mem. Nat. Assn. Dirs. Christian Edn. (pres.). Home: 22587 S Burwood Ln Escalon CA 95320 Office: 808 Needham St Modesto CA 95354

FRIESEN, RONALD, minister, Conference of Mennonite Brethren Churches; b. Abbotsford, B.C., Can., Oct. 14, 1948; came to U.S., 1980; s. Peter John and Elizabeth (Schmidt) F.; m. June Eileen Sommer, Apr. 3, 1972; children: Shawn, Wendel. B.A., Simon Fraser U., 1973; diploma in Christian studies Regent Coll., Vancouver, 1974; M.Div., Mennonite Brethren Bibl. Sem., Fresno, Calif., 1981. Ordained to ministry, Mennonite Brethren Ch., 1980. Minister, Yorkdale Community Ch., Toronto, 1975-80, Palm Glen Mennonite Brethren Ch., Phoenix, 1981—; chaplain Thunder Bird Samaritan Hosp., 1984-85, pres. 1982-83; bd. dirs. Mennonite House, Inc., Phoenix, 1983—. Editor: Single Spirit, 1984—. Recipient Disting. Service award Glendale Samaritan Hosp., 1983. Mem. Nat. Assn. Evangelicals (chpt. pres. 1984-85), Alban Inst., Greater Phoenix Assn. Evangelicals (pres. 1984—), North West Valley Clergy Assn. (pres. 1983-85). Home: 3736 W Mission Ln Phoenix AZ 85021

FRIESENHENGST, ALFRED RUDOLF, lay ch. worker, United Methodist Ch.; b. Lorain, Ohio, Aug. 27, 1910; s. Rudolf Karl and Wilhelmina Marie (Duldner) F.; A.B. (Ohio scholar), Western Res. U., 1932; m. Helen Marie Horrall, June 6, 1937; children—Mary (Mrs. Steve Glen Rhoads), Nancy (Mrs. Paul O. Yarbrough). Mem. South Ind. Conf. United Meth. Ch., 1943—, mem. bd. lay activities, 1946-49, edn. com., 1952-56, bur. conf. sessions, 1960-64, rep. to South Ind. Ann. Conf., 1956—; mem. Ind. Conf. Council on Ministries, 1969-80; mem. Ind. Found. of United Meth. Ch., 1982—; chmn. South Ind. Conf. Com. Layworker, 1971-73, chmn. conf. com. Interpretation, 1972-80, mem. conf. Task Force Capitol Funds, 1973-74; layleader United Meth. Ch., Shoals, Ind., 1947-57, 60-62, treas., 1967—, supt. ch. sch., 1958-62, chmn. bd. trustees, 1947-56, chmn. bldg. fund, 1947-51, lay leader Vincennes (Ind.) Dist., 1950-56, chmn. ch. extension drive Vincennes Dist., 1952-56, mem. council on ministries, 1969—, exec. com., 1969-76, mem. parsonage trustee com., 1980—, fin. com., 1980—; assoc. conf. layleader Ind. Conf., 1959-66, mem. conf. nominating com., 1952-68, conf. pension com., 1948-56. Pres. A.R. Friesenhengst, Inc., Shoals, 1941—, A.R. Friesenhengst Wholesale Co., Shoals, 1948—. Chmn. Tb Assn., Martin County, Ind., 1950-51; active Boy Scouts Am., 1954-64, chmn. fin. drive ARC, Shoals, 1943-47; chmn. Tri-County Anti-Poverty Community Action Program, 1962, 63; chmn. Martin County Sch. Reorgn. Com., 1958-63; chmn. Overall Econ. Devel. Com., 1962-63; mem. Martin County Welfare Bd., 1975—, Bd. dirs. United Meth. Home for Aged, Franklin, Ind., 1952-68. Mem. Ind., French Lick Chambers Commerce, Ind. Retail Assn., Lambda Chi Alpha. Mason (32 deg., Shriner), Lion. Home: Route 2 Shoals IN 47581 Office: Box 10 Main St Shoals IN 47581

FRITZ, WILLIAM RICHARD, educator, minister, Lutheran Ch. Am.; b. Maywood, Ill., July 31, 1920; s. Charles Everett and Rose Margaret (Stump) F.; A.B., Lenoir Rhyne Coll., Hickory, N.C., 1942, D.D. (hon.), 1966; B.D., Lutheran Theol. So. Sem., Columbia, S.C., 1945; M.S., Columbia, 1955; m. Evelyn Rogers Ackerman, Feb. 1, 1945; children—Kathlyn Ann, William Richard, Charles Everett II, Rebecca Elizabeth. Ordained to ministry Luth. Ch. in Am., 1945; pastor in S.C., 1945-47; mem. faculty Luth. Theol. So. Sem., Columbia, 1947—, librarian, 1951—, prof. bibliography, 1969—, founder, dir. A Capella choir, 1949-69, lectr. ch. music, 1949-54; archivist S.C. synod, 1945-63. Mem. Am. Theol. Library Assn., Am. Ch. History Soc., Luth. Hist. Soc. Democrat. Author: History of Lutheran Church in South Carolina, part I, 1730-1803, 1971. Contbr. articles to rel. jours. Home: 905 Timrod St Columbia SC 29203

FROEHLE, CHARLES LEO, priest Roman Catholic Church; b. St. Cloud, Minn., Apr. 20, 1937; s. Leo J. and Catherine (Leither) F. B.A., St. Paul Sem., Minn., 1959; S.T.L., U. St. Thomas, Rome, Italy, 1966, S.T.D., 1968. Ordained priest, Roman Catholic Ch., 1963; asst. pastor Basilica of St. Mary, Mpls., 1963-65; prof. theology St. Paul (Minn.) Sem., 1968-80, dean of studies, 1974-80, rector-pres., 1980—. Author: The Idea of Sacred Sign According to Anscar Vonier, 1970. Mem. Midwest Assn. Theol. Schs. (pres. 1982-84), Minn. Consortium of Theol. Schs. (v.p. 1980-81), Cath. Theol. Soc. Am.

FRONK, RHONDA BETH, lay church worker, United Methodist Church; accountant; b. Liberal, Kans., Sept. 8, 1956; d. Ronald Solomon and Margaret Belle (Williams) F.; B.A., Oral Roberts U., 1979. Singles leader First Methodist Ch., Tulsa, Okla, 1981-82, 85, choir accompanist, 1982-83; youth worker Higher Dimensions, Tulsa, 1984, singles leader, 1984. Accountant Leming and Thomas, Tulsa, 1981—. Contbr. articles to profl. jours. Republican. Club: Mensa (Tulsa). Home: 7919 E 60th St Tulsa OK 74145 Office: Leming and Thomas CPAs 4815 S Harvard #225 Tulsa OK 74135

FROST, JERRY WILLIAM, educator, Religious Soc. of Friends; b. Muncie, Ind., Mar. 17, 1940; s. J. Thomas and Margaret (Meredith) F.; B.A., DePauw U., 1962; postgrad. Yale Div. Sch., 1962-63; M.A., U. Wis., 1964, Ph.D., 1968; m. Susan Kohler, Sept. 7, 1963; 1 son, James. Mem. Religious Soc. of Friends (Gen. Conf.), 1972—; asst. prof. history Vassar Coll., 1967-73; asso. prof. religion, dir. Friends Hist. Library, Swarthmore Coll., 1973—. John Carter Brown fellow, 1969. Mem. Am., Friends hist. assns., Am. Soc. Ch. History, Columbia Seminars in Early Am. History, Phi Beta Kappa. Author: The Quaker Family in Colonial America, 1973; Connecticut Education in the Revolutionary Era, 1974. Contbr. articles to profl. jours. Home: 601 N Chester Rd Swarthmore PA 19081 Office: Friends Hist Library Swarthmore Coll Swarthmore PA 19081

FRY, CHARLES GEORGE, minister, educator, Lutheran Church-Missouri Synod; b. Piqua, Ohio, Aug. 15, 1936; s. Sylvan and Lena Freda Marie (Ehle) F.; B.A., Capital U., 1958; M.A., Ohio State U., 1961; B.D., Evang. Luth. Theol. Sem., 1962, M.Div., 1977; Ph.D., Ohio State U., 1965; postdoctoral student Ankara U., Istanbul U., Tehran U., Near East Sch. Theology; D.Min., Winebrenner Theol. Sem., 1978. Ordained to ministry, 1963; instr. Wittenberg U., 1962-63; mem. faculty Capital U., Columbus, Ohio, 1963-75, assoc. prof. history and religion, 1971-75; assoc. prof. hist. and systematic theology Concordia Theol. Sem., Springfield, Ill. and Fort Wayne, Ind., 1975-84; vis. prof. Damavand Coll., Tehran, Iran, 1973-74; mem. exec. com. Fellowship of Faith for Muslims, 1970—; mem. Luth.-Jewish Concerns Com., 1974-75; pastor Martin Luther Luth. Ch., Columbus, 1963-66; theologian in residence North Community Luth. Ch., Columbus, 1971-73; protestant chaplain St. Francis Coll., Ft. Wayne, Ind., 1982—. Mem. exec. council Regional Council for Internat. Edn., 1969-74, Lutheran Ch. Bd. Theol. Edn. scholar, 1962; Regional Council Internat. Edn. grantee, 1969. Mem. Am. Acad. Religion, Am. Hist. Assn., Ref. Bible Coll. Assn., Author: The Middle East in Transition, 1970; The Past in Perspective, 1971; The Search for a New Europe, 1971; The Middle East: Crossroads of Civilization, 1973; Ten Contemporary Theologians, 1976; Islam: An Evangelical Perspective, 1976, European Theology, 1648-1914, 1976. Editor: An Anthology of Middle Eastern Literature from the Twentieth Century, 1974; Islam: A Survey of the Muslim Faith, 1980, 82; The Way, The Truth and The Life, 1982; Great Asian Religious, 1984. Contbr. articles to profl. jours. Home: 158 W Union St Circleville OH 43113 Office: Protestant Chaplain St Francis Coll 2701 Spring St Fort Wayne IN 46808

FRY, MALCOLM CRAIG, minister, National Association of Free Will Baptists; b. Detroit, June 6, 1928; s. Dwight Malcolm and Josephine Adrienne (Craig) F.; m. Myrtle Mae Downing, June 5, 1948; children: Pamela Mae, Malcolm Craig, Rebecca Dawn Fry Gwartney, Matthew Dwight. Th.B., Bible Bapt. Sem., 1959; B.S., Austin Peay State U., 1962; M.Ed., U. Ariz., 1969; D.Min., Luther Rice Sem., 1978; D. Laws and Letters (hon.), Clarksville Sch. Theology, 1974. Ordained to ministry Nat. Assn. of Free Will Bapts., 1955. Pastor chs., La., Tex., Tenn., 1955-62; asst. pastor Central Free Will Bapt. Ch., Royal Oak, Mich., 1962-64; pastor First Free Will Bapt. Ch., Tucson, 1964-71; dir. curriculum ch. tng. Nat. Assn. Free Will Bapts., Nashville, 1971-72, gen. dir. ch. tng., 1972-78, asst. dir. Sunday sch. dept., 1978-83, mem. Sunday sch. bd., 1984—; pastor Unity Free Will Bapt. Ch., Smithfield, N.C., 1983—. Author: Precepts for Practice, 1971; Disciplining and Developing, 1971; Ministry of Music, 1974; also study booklets. Served to sgt. USAF, 1951-57. Republican. Lodge: Kiwanis (treas. local chpt. 1972-78). Avocation: bowling. Home: 722 S Second St Smithfield NC 27577 Office: Unity Free Will Bapt Ch 104 W Langdon Ave Smithfield NC 27577

FRYSHMAN, BERNARD, Jewish association executive. Exec. dir. Assn. Advanced Rabbinical and Talmudic Schs. Office: Assn Advanced Rabbinical and Talmudic Schs 175 Fifth Ave New York NY 10010*

FUCHS, PAUL GERHARDT, minister, Am. Luth. Ch.; b. Beulah, N.D., July 30, 1937; s. Emmanuel and Ida B. (Schnell) F.; B.A., Wartburg (Iowa) Coll., 1959; B.D., Wartburg Theol. Sem., 1963; m. Constance Joyce Wiechers, June 4, 1961; children—Beth, Gray, Meg, Phillip. Ordained to ministry, 1963; organizing pastor Living Lord Luth. Ch., Warren, Ohio, 1963-74; sr. pastor Grace Luth. Ch., Fremont, Ohio, 1974—. Chmn. Augustana conf., Ohio dist. Am. Luth. Ch., 1968-72. Bd. dirs. Fremont YMCA, 1974—; chmn. student rights and responsiblities com. Howland (Ohio) Schs., 1973-74. Home: 1205 Croghan St Fremont OH 43420 Office: PO Box 149 Fremont OH 43420

FULCHER, ROBERT VEHIE, minister, Gen. Baptists; b. Union County, Ky., Apr. 1, 1930; s. Guy Thomas and Dovie Lee (Sutton) F.; A.B., Oakland City Coll., 1958; m. Corrine Welborn, July 16, 1956; 1 dau., Christy Ann. Ordained to ministry, 1949; pastor Davies County, Ky., 1948-51, Caldwell County, Ky., 1949-51, Hopkins County, Madisonville, Ky., 1951-54, Shady Grove Gen. Bapt. Ch., Poole, Ky., 1954—. Tchr., Webster County Bd. Edn., 1957—. Mem. NEA, Ky. Edn. Assn. Home: Box 92 Poole KY 42444

FULGHUM, CHARLES BENJAMIN, assistant rector, Episcopal Church; psychiatrist. B. Selma, N.C., July 20, 1926; s. Charles Benjamin and Alice (Kirby) F.; m. Joan Knoch, Aug. 1, 1953 (div. 1974); children: Charles, Tom, Carol, Betty, John; m. Carole McCarson, Apr. 20, 1977. B.S., U. N.C., 1950, M.D., 1954; postgrad. Emory U., 1980-84. Ordained deacon Episcopal Church, 1965, priest, 1984; diplomate Am. Bd. Psychiatry and Neurology. Asst. rector Holy Innocents Ch., Atlanta, 1965-68, Ch. of Atonement, Atlanta, 1968-82, St. Andrews Ch., Hartwell, Ga., 1982-83, St. Bedes Ch., Atlanta, 1983—; mem. med. staff Ctr. for Advancement of Personal and Social Growth (Presbyterian orgn.), 1974-78, med. dir., 1976-78; staff mem. St. Luke's Tng. and Counseling Ctr., 1977—, Dunwoody Counseling Ctr., (Baptist orgn.), 1984—; dir. All Saints Conf. for Medicine and Religion, 1972-73; group leader Columbia Sem. Conf. for Religion and Mental Health, 1961-71. Pvt. practice psychiatry, Atlanta, 1961—. Contbr. articles to profl. jours. Served with USN, 1943-46, PTO. Mem. AMA, Am. Psychiatry Assn., Ga. Psychiatry Assn. (treas. 1963-66), Med. Assn. of Atlanta, Democrat. Club: Cherokee. Home: 759 Loridans Dr Atlanta GA 30342

FULLER, MARY ELIZABETH, minister, Church of God (Anderson, Indiana); b. Dallas, July 27, 1947; d. Walter Elvie and Lois Marie (Lister) Bruce; m. Tommy Wayne Fuller, June 21, 1968; children: Penny Elayne, Matthew Wayne. B.S., Gulf Coast Bible Coll., 1970; M.A., Sch. Theology, Anderson, 1982. Ordained to ministry Ch. of God (Anderson), 1983. Assoc. pastor 1st Ch. of God, Porterville, Calif., 1972-74, College Park Ch. of God, Coalinga, Calif., 1974-78; minister of music 1st Ch. of God, Lima, Ohio, 1980-82; assoc. pastor West Side Ch. of God, Phoenix, 1982—; speaker prayer retreat Women of Ch. of God, Ariz., 1983; conf. leader Ariz. State Campmeeting, 1984. Contbr. articles to profl. jours. Mem. Women of Ch. of God (spiritual life dir.), Assn. Ch. of God in Ariz. (sec.), Band Parents Assn., Delta Epsilon Chi. Home: 5313 W Osborn Rd Phoenix AZ 85031 Office: West Side Church of God 5313 W Osborn Rd Phoenix AZ 85031

FULLINWIDER, CHARLES MILFORD, minister, Presbyterian Church (USA); b. El Dorado, Kans., July 20, 1924; s. Burgess Harrold and Fanny Marie (Eckel) F.; A.B., Sterling Coll., 1953; B.D., Western Theol. Sem., 1956; M.Div., Pitts. Theol. Sem., 1972; m. Margaret Joyce Horn, Aug. 24, 1962; children: John Andrew, Ruth Esther. Ordained to ministry, 1956. Pastor, Hopewell Presbyn. Ch., Anthony, Kans., 1956-58, 1st Presbyn. Chs., Conway Springs, Kans., 1958-66, Viola, Kans., 1965-66, 1st Presbyn. Ch., Dexter, N.Mex., 1966—, Hagerman, N.Mex., 1968—; moderator Wichita Presbytery, 1961, Pecos Valley Presbytery, 1968; mem. Presbytery coms. on stewardship, Christian edn., ministerial relations, 1956—; stated clk. Presbytery of Sierra Blanca, 1979-85. Home: 204 E 3d St Dexter NM 88230 Office: PO Box 367 Dexter NM 88230

FULTON, JAMES WAYTE, JR., minister, Presbyterian Ch. in U.S.A.; b. Stuart, Va., Feb. 23, 1911; s. James Wayte and Mary Ward (King) F.; m. Jerry Liddell, Mar. 9, 1946; children: Alyce Fulton Perkins, Christine Fulton Baldwin, Frances Anne Fulton Barnett, Jerry Virginia Fulton Mink, Kathleen Bell. B.A., Davidson Coll., 1933; M.Div., Union Theol. Sem., 1936; D.D., Belhaven Coll., 1956. Ordained to ministry Presbyn. Ch. U.S.A., 1937. Pastor, First Presbyn. Ch., Gloucester, Va., 1937-39, First Presbyn. Ch., Bishopville, S.C., 1939-41, Royal Oak Ch., Marion, Va., 1946-49; dir. Christian edn. Synod La., New Orleans, 1949-52; pastor Shenandoah Ch., Miami, Fla., 1952-69, Meml. Presbyn. Ch., West Palm Beach, Fla., 1969-82; interim pastor First Presbyn. Ch., New Orleans, 1983, Hope Presbyn. Ch., Winter Haven, Fla., 1983-85, Ind. Presbyn. Ch., Savannah, Ga., 1985—; moderator Synod of Fla., 1978-79; bd. dirs. Columbia Theol. Sem., Christianity Today. Trustee Davidson Coll. Served with Chaplain's Corps USNR, 1941-46; ret. capt. USNR. Mem. U.S. Naval Inst., Sons Am. Revolution. Lodge: Kiwanis. Home: 201 Barcelona Bldg Orchid Springs Villas Winter Haven FL 33880 Office: Ind Presbyn Church 25 W Oglethorpe Ave Savannah GA 31401

FULTON, THOMAS BENJAMIN See *Who's Who in America*, 43rd edition.

FULWILER, ANNE, nun, Roman Cath. Ch.; b. Williamsport, Pa., Oct. 14, 1924; d. Harold J. and Joann E. (White) Fulwiler; A.B., Marywood Coll., 1955; M.A., St. John U., 1963; L.H.D., Scranton U., 1974. Joined Servants of the Immaculate Heart of Mary, 1944; tchr. Mount Holly (N.J.) Regional Sch., 1947-56, St. Leo High Sch., Ashley, Pa., 1956-65, Dunmore Central Cath. High Sch., 1965-68, St. Dominic High Sch., Oyster Bay, N.Y., 1968-70; dir apostolic works Sisters, Servants of Immaculate Heart of Mary, Scranton, Pa., 1970-74, superior gen., 1974—, del. to gen. chpt., 1974. Pres. Scranton Diocesan Sisters' Council, 1970-73; mem. Scranton Diocesan Bd. Edn., 1965-68, pres. diocesan council of math. tchrs., 1964-68. Trustee Marywood Coll., Marian Center Women Prisoners. Mem. Leadership Council of Women Religious (rep. to meeting in Rome 1975). Address: Immaculate Heart Mary Generalte Marywood Scranton PA 18509

FUQUA, THOMAS KENT, minister, Lutheran Church, Missouri Synod; b. Wichita, Kans., Feb. 18, 1949; s. Dexter Thomas and Anita A. (Koch) F.; m. Arlene Ruth Schweer, June 19, 1971; children: Angela Dawn, Jennifer Lynn. B.A., Concordia Sr. Coll., 1971; M.Div., Luth. Sch. Theology (Concordia Sem. in Exile), Chgo., 1975. Ordained, 1975. Pastor Christ the King Luth. Ch., Dighton, Kans., 1975-77, Lake Wales Luth. Ch. (Fla.), 1977—; pres. Ministerial Fellowship, Lakes Wales, 1980-82; mem. devel. com. for Woodlands Luth. Camp, 1984—. Contbr. article to jours. Pres. Ridge Area Red Cross, Lake Wales, 1984—; bd. mem. Lakes Wales Family YMCA, 1978—. Named Clergyman of Yr., Kiwanis Club Lake Wales, 1981; recipient Citizens award for Participation, City Commn. Lake Wales, 1981. Democrat. Club: Kiwanis (pres. Lake Wales 1983-84). Home: 1019 Yarnell Ave Lake Wales FL 33853 Office: Lake Wales Luth Ch 411 Alvina Lake Wales FL 33853

FURCHA, EDWARD J., minister, United Church of Canada, educator; b. Sibiu, Romania, Oct. 26, 1935; arrived in Canada, 1954; s. Julius and Amalia (Schunn) F.; m. Heidi E. Mettler, 1962; children: Heidi Ruth Cornelia J., Rowland E. B.A., McMaster U., 1957; B.D., McGill U., 1963; Ph.D., Hartford Sem., 1966. Ordained to ministry, United Ch. of Can., 1963. Prof. Vancouver Sch. Theology, 1969-73; prof. Serampore Coll., Calcutta, India, 1973-77; parish minister Aylwin Pastoral Charge, 1966-68, Schomberg United, 1977-78, Washington United Ch., Scarborough, 1978-80; prof. Faculty of Religious Studies, McGill U., Montreal, Que., Can., 1980—. Mem. Can. Soc. Can. History (pres. 1984-85), Montreal Presbytery (chmn. 1984-85).

FURLONG, JOHN DARYL, priest, Roman Cath. Ch.; b. Hazel Green, Wis., May 16, 1938; s. Thomas Earl and Lorena Ann (Leglar) F.; student U. Wis. at Platteville, 1956-58; B.A., Loras Coll., 1962; student St. Francis Sem., 1962-66. Ordained priest, 1966; asso. pastor Immaculate Heart of Mary, Madison, Wis., 1966-71; asso. pastor St. Bernard Ch., Middleton, Wis., 1971-75; asso. dir. Office of Marriage and Family Life, Madison Diocese, 1975-76, dir., 1976—. Mem. Office Diocesan Music Commn., 1966-74; Madison Diocesan Liturgy State of Wis. Com. for Rite of Reconciliation, 1975-76; mem. Diocesan Life of the Clergy Commn., 1970-74; mem. Family Life Commn. to establish common policy for pastoral marriage preparation for state of Wis., Wis. Cath. Conf., 1975-77. Home: 3577 High Point Rd Madison WI 53703 Office: 142 W Johnson St Madison WI 53703

FURNISS, JOHN GERARD, priest, Roman Catholic Church; b. Jersey City, June 16, 1913; s. Thomas Benedict and Florence Frances (Beatty) F.; A.B., Georgetown U., 1938; Ph.L. Woodstock Coll., 1939; S.T.L., 1946; M.A., Cath. U., 1940. Ordained priest, 1945; mem. S.J.; dir. Jesuit Sem. and Mission Bur., N.Y.C., 1947-51; dir. Jesuit Sem. Bldg. Fund, N.Y.C., 1951-55; dir. Fordham U. Devel., 1955-58; asst. to Jesuit Provincial, Bronx, N.Y., 1958-62; dir. Colegio San Ignacio Bldg. Fund, 1962, Xavier High Sch. Bldg. Fund, N.Y.C., 1962-64; dir. Jesuit Sem. and Mission Bur., N.Y.C., 1964-76; dir. Xavier High Sch. Devel. Office, 1976—. Mem. K.C., Nat. Cath. Devel. Conf. Editor: The Jesuit, 1967-76. Contbr. articles to religious publs. Home and Office: 30 W 16th St New York City NY 10011

FUTRELL, CHRISTOPHER JEFFERSON, JR., minister, So. Baptist Conv.; b. Savannah, Ga., Nov. 14, 1927; s. Christopher Jefferson and Lois (Wrye) F.; B.A., Furman U., Greenville, S.C., 1948; B.D., M.R.E., Southwestern Baptist Theol. Sem., Ft. Worth, 1951; certificate S.C. Baptist Hosp. Sch. Pastoral Care, 1958; m. Rebecca Gregory, June 5, 1948; children—Christopher, Joel. Ordained minister So. Bapt. Conv., 1948; pastor chs. in S.C., 1951-60; asso. dir. ch. tng. dept. So. Bapt. Conv., Columbia, S.C., 1960—. Pres. pastor's conf. Kershaw Bapt. Assn., 1953, chmn. missions coms., 1952; dir. tng. union Fairfield Bapt. Assn., 1956-60; pres. ministers conf. Central Region, So. Bapt. Conv., 1964, pres. tng. union conv., 1955; chmn. nominating com. for state tng. union conv. S.C. Bapt. Conv., 1958, chmn. reference com. on tng. union, 1959; Home: 158 St Andrews Rd Columbia SC 29210 Office: 907 Richland St Columbia SC 29201

GABLE, DAVID LEE, minister, Episcopal Church; b. Anniston, Ala., Mar. 18, 1943; s. Carl Franklin and Lena Mae (Weems) G. B.A., Jacksonville State U., 1965; M.S., U. Miss., 1967; Ph.D., Memphis State U., 1977; M.Div., Va. Sem., 1980. Ordained priest, 1981. Deacon, St. James' Ch., Knoxville, 1980-81; rector St. Andrew's Ch., Harriman, Tenn., 1980—; del. to Intramont, Appalachian People's Service Orgn., Blacksburg, Va., 1981—; diocesan tutor Diocese of Tenn., Knoxville, 1983—, asst. sec., 1983—, jubilee ministry parish, 1984, bishop and council, 1984—, examining chaplain, 1984—. Lodge: Rotary (chplain Harriman). Address: Rt 6 Box 564 Harriman TN 37748

GABLER, RUSSELL ALLAN, minister, Interdenominational Church; b. Ann Arbor, Mich., Oct. 19, 1922; s. Joseph Walter and Caroline (Souster) G.; m. Marie Trieber, June 15, 1947; children: Grace Marie Gabler Martin, Allan Russell, Daniel Lee. Pastors cert. Moody Bible Inst., 1945; B.B.A., Wheaton Coll., 1948; M.Div., Fuller Theol. Sem., 1956; Ph.D., Calif. Grad. Sch. Theology, 1971. Ordained to ministry Independent Fundamental Churches of America, 1946; lic. Marriage, Family and Child Counselor, Calif. Pastor, Oak Park Christian Ch., Savanna, Ill., 1945-53, First Friends Ch., Los Angeles, 1954-57, Central Bible Ch., Costa Mesa, Calif., 1957-62, Carson Bible Ch., (Calif.), 1963—; instr. in Bible Biola U., La Mirada, Calif., 1961-70; Bible tchr. Cedar Lake Boys Camp (Ind.), 1947-53; trustee Am. Missionary Founc, Camp Wynla, Juliah, Calif., 1965—; mem. ordination com. So. Calif. Independent Fundamental Chs., 1959-62, 82—; chmn. Am. Bd. Hundustan Bible Inst., Madras, India, 1984—. Mem. Human Resources Com., Carson, 1976-79, Carosn Cares Com., 1983—. Mem. Evangel. Theol. Soc., Carson-Wilmington Ministerial Assn. (pres. 1972—). Republican. Home: 23018 Catskill Ave Carson CA 90745 Office: Carson Bible Ch 23601 Main St Carson CA 90745

GABOR, GEORGIA MIRIAM, lay administrator, Conservative Judaism; b. Budapest, Hungary, 1930; 2 children. A.A., Los Angeles City Coll., 1965; B.A., UCLA, 1966, M.A., 1968, postgrad. 1968-69. West Coast dir. Jewish Soc. Americanists, 1965-68; exec. dir. The Jewish Right, Sierra Madres, Calif., 1969-74; lectr. on The Holocaust Founder Students for an Open-minded Soc., UCLA, 1966-68. Author: My Destiny, 1981. Address: The Jewish Right 365 Mariposa Ave Sierra Madre CA 91024

GABRIEL, ANTONY FRANCIS, priest, Antiochian Orthodox Christian Archdiocese of North America. b. Syracuse, N.Y., July 14, 1940; s. William Abraham and Nettie Helen (Sopp) G.; m. Margaret Lynn Georges, Nov. 6, 1960; children: David Abraham, Mark Antony, Tamara Lynn. Student, Syracuse U., 1958-59; M. Div., St. Vladimir's Sem., 1962; postgrad., Dominican House of Studies, 1968-69, Lutheran Sch. Theology, 1970-75. Ordained to ministry Antiochian Orthodox Christian Archdiocese of N. Am. 19—. Chaplain Order of St. Ignatius of Antioch, Internat., 1974-83; chmn. Conv. Planning, Internat., 1970-82, Credentials & Stats., Internat., 1970—; spiritual advisor CAN/AM Youth Movement, Internat., 1983—; v.p. and pres. Eastern Orthodox Clergy Assn., Montreal, Que., 1977-84, Orthodix Clergy Assn., Chgo., 1968-76; mem., del. World and Nat. Council Chs., Chgo., N.Y., 1962—; mem. Mayor's Council on Religion and Race, Chgo., 1966-75; del. Synods of Ch. of Antioch, Damascus, Beirut, 1966—, Ch. Russia, Antiochian Ch., Moscow, 1984. Author: St. Ignatius of Antioch, 1975, 84; St. Ephreme and Ascoticism, 1974; Church of Antioch in North America, 1984; manuel Convention Planning, 1970, 77. Contbr. of articles to The Word Mag., 1962—. Mem. editorial bd. The Word Mag. 1982—. Recipient Knight of the Cross of Cedars Archbishop Elia Karram, 1966, Arrchpriest Archpriest Philip Saliba, 1974. Archdiocese of N. Am. grant 1970-75. Mem. Internat. II Orthodox Theologians, Nat. Assn. Am. Arabs (organizer, founder 1969), Arab Am. U. Grads. (founding mem. 1969), Can. Arab Assn. (founder), St. Valdimir's Alumni Assn., N. Am. Acad. Ecumenist, Inter-faith Com. Montreal, Council Chs. (media com. co-ordinator 1962—). Office: St George Orthodox 575 Jean Talon East Montreal PQ H2R 1T8 Canada

GABRIELSEN, PAUL THOMAS, religious educational administrator, American Lutheran Church; b. Bonners Ferry, Idaho, Aug. 1, 1929; s. Gabriel and Edna (Roen) G.; m. Karen Elaine Johnk, July 18, 1954; children: Virginia, Stephen. B.A., Concordia Coll., Moorhead, Minn., 1952; M.Th., Luther Theol. Sem., St. Paul, 1956; M.A., U. Chgo., 1960; postgrad. U. Minn., 1960-62; Ph.D., U.S. Internat. U., 1975. Ordained to ministry Am. Luth. Ch., 1958. Pastor North Cape Evangel. Luth. Ch., Franksville, Wis., 1958-60; chaplain Augsburg Coll., Mpls., 1960-61; faculty, counselor Luth. Bible Inst., Mpls., 1961-70; dir. advancement Luth. Bible Inst., Seattle, 1976-79, dir. planned giving, Issaquah, Wash., 1979—; owner Kairos Fin., 1970-76; seminar leader estate planning for Christians, 1979—. Author: (curriculum texts) Why Doesn't God?, 1965; (programmed instrn.) Tests of True Christianity, 1966; (pamphlet) How To Write a Will that Works—For Christians, 1980. Mem. Planned Giving Officers Puget Sound (pres. 1980-81), Internat. Assn. Charitable Estate Planners, Am. Assn. Pastoral Counselors. Home: 12414 89th Pl NE Kirkland WA 98034

GADMAN, WAYNE ARNOLD, minister, So. Bapt. Conv.; b. Ripley, Miss., Apr. 20, 1946; s. William Arles and Mary Louise (Thomas) G.; B.S., La. Coll., 1969; M.Ch. Music, Southwestern Bapt. Theol. Sem., Ft. Worth, 1974; m. Sandra Marie Myers, Aug. 4, 1967; children—Wayne Anthony, Jason Clark, Stephanie Marie. Ordained to ministry, 1969; minister music and youth chs. in La., 1966-70; minister music and youth Normandale Bapt. Ch., Ft. Worth, 1970-71; minister music, youth and edn. Crestview Bapt. Ch., Richardson, Tex., 1971-76, Pleasant Grove 1st Bapt. Ch., Dallas, 1977—. Mem. Tex. Bapt. Singing Men, So. Bapt. Ch. Music Conf., Choristers Guild. Home: 8738 Barclay St Dallas TX 75227 Office: 1401 S Buckner Blvd Dallas TX 75217

GAETANO, LEWIS FRANCIS, priest, Roman Catholic Church; b. Canton, Ohio, Sept. 18, 1946; s. Anthony Frank and Gloria Joan (Walthour) G. B.A. in Philosophy, Athenaeum of Ohio, 1968; M.A. in Hist. and Edn., W.Va. U., 1976. Ordained priest Roman Cath. Ch., 1973. Instr., dean students St. Joseph Prep. Sem., Vienna, W.Va., 1974-81; chaplain Bethany Coll., W.Va., 1981—; dir. Office for Diaconate and Ministries Formation, Diocese of Wheeling-Charleston, W.Va., 1984—, mem. Religious Unity Commn., 1981—, co-chmn. Presbyterian-Roman Cath. Dialogue, 1983—. Mem. Nat. Assn. Permanent Diaconate Dirs., Nat. Assn. Vocation Dirs., Nat. Assn. Diocesan Ecumenical Offices, Sigma Nu Epsilon (chpt. advisor 1982—). Lodge: Kiwanis (moderator 1982). Avocations: theater; gardening; classical music. Home: 201 Richardson St Bethany WV 26032 Office: Office for Diaconate and Ministries Formation 1300 Byron St PO Box 230 Wheeling WV 26003

GAGE, ROBERT CLIFFORD, minister, Gen. Assn. Regular Bapt. Chs.; b. Beverly, Mass., Nov. 20, 1941; s. George V. and Elizabeth B. (May) G.; student Tenn. Temple Coll., 1961-62; B.A., Phila. Coll. of Bible, 1964; postgrad. Eastern Bapt. Sem., 1966-67; m. Mary Neefe, June 17, 1961; children—Joanna, Jonathan, Judith, Joshua, Joy. Ordained to ministry, 1964; pastor Whitehall Bapt. Ch., Phila., 1964-65, Glencroft Bapt. Ch., Glenolden, Pa., 1966-68, First Bapt. Chs., Newfield, N.J., 1969-70, Hackensack, N.J., 1971—; radio minister Bible Truth Hour, WWDJ, 1965—. Chattanooga dir. Youth Crusader Mission, 1961-62; mem. adv. bd. Assn. of Bapt. for World Evangelism; mem. Council of Six, Garden State Fellowship of Regular Bapt. Chs.; founder, supt. Hackensack Christian Schs.; pres. Fundamental Bible Inst. Mem. Nat. Assn. Christian Marriage Counselors, Am. Personnel and Guidance Assn., Nat. Vocat. Guidance Assn. Author: The Birthmarks of the Christian Life, 1976. Editor: Sword and Shield, 1969—. Contbr. sermons to ch. publs. Home: 200 Catalpa Ave Hackensack NJ 07601 Office: 15 Conklin Pl Hackensack NJ 07601

GAGNE, CHARLES ROBERT, priest, educator, Roman Catholic Church; b. Senneterre, Que., Can., July 21, 1921; s. Joseph Georges and Lucie Marie (Fortier) G.; 4 adopted children: Daniel P., Kenneth B., Randy, Joseph Wilfrid. B.L., Laval U., 1946; B.Th., St. Augustine's Sem., 1951; B.A., U. Montreal, 1957; M.A., Niagara U., 1958; Litt.D. (hon.), Internat. Bible Inst., Orlando, Fla., 1984. Ordained priest Roman Catholic Ch., 1951. Asst. priest St. Michael's Cathedral, Toronto, Ont., Can., 1951, St. Ann's Penetanguishene, Ont., 1951-54, Star of the Sea Ch., St. Catharines, Ont., 1954-59, St. Mary's, Welland, Ont., 1959-64; parish priest l'immaculee Conception, St. Catharines, Ont., 1964—; prof. Niagara U., Lewiston, N.Y., 1958-84. Lodges: KC (chaplain 1980—), Daus of Isabella (chaplain 1982—). Home and Office: 99 Garnet St St Catharines ON L2M 5G3 Canada

GAINER, MELVIN, minister, Southern Baptist Convention; b. Richwood, W.Va., Mar. 2, 1920; s. Melvin E. and Ethel Mary (Jones) G.; m. Fern Novella Crump, Dec. 24, 1945. D.D., S.W. Bapt. U., 1981, Th.D., 1981; B.A., Alderson-Broadus Coll., 1985. Ordained to ministry So. Bapt. Conv., 1972. Mem. Mo. Bapt. Exec. Bd. Mo. Bapt. Conv., Jefferson City, 1960-64; moderator Bapt. Assn., Dexter, Mo., 1960-66; trustee Southwestern Bapt. U., Bolivar, Mo., 1960-85, Mo. Bapt. Found., Jefferson City, 1984—; owner Gainer Jewelry Co., Dexter, 1946-84. Mayor, Dexter, 1964. Served with AUS, 1940-45; ETO. Decorated Bronze Star. Democrat.

GAINES, WILLIE THOMAS, JR., minister, Southern Baptist Convention; b. St. Louis, Feb. 9, 1942; s. Willie Thomas and Bessie Lee (McCoy) G.; m. Alice Marie Hailey, July 20, 1963; 1 child: Galen Marie. B.A. in Social Sci., Chapman Coll., 1976; postgrad. Golden Gate Bapt. Sem., 1984—; D.D. (hon.), Calif. Sch. Theology, Glendale, 1985. Ordained to ministry So. Bapt. Ch., 1969. Chaplain Almaden Air Force Sta., San Jose, Calif., 1977-78; pastor East Barstow Bapt. Ch., Calif., 1970, Emmanuel Bapt. Ch., San Jose, 1977—; mem. missions com. So. Bapt. Gen. Conv., Fresno, Calif., 1978-80, 83-84 evangelistic com., 1982-84, exec. bd. ops. com., 1983-84, Calif. pres.-elect, 1985; vice chmn. Billy Graham Crusade, 1981. Contbr. articles to religious publs. Active mem. NAACP, Pacific Mgmt. System. Served in USN, 1960-66. Recipient Certs. of Recognition, Emmanuel Bapt. Ch., other chs., 1977, 78, 79, 80, 81-83, Mayoral Commendation for Outstanding Contbn. and Service to Community, Mayor of San Jose 1982, Excellence in Religion award, Mayor of San Jose, 1982; named Father of Yr., Emmanuel Bapt. Ch., 1978. Office: Emmanuel Bapt Ch 467 N White Rd San Jose CA 95152

GAJEWSKI, MARY ELLENE, educator, nun, Roman Cath. Ch.; b. Milw., Jan. 30, 1922; d. Frank E. and Helen J. (Grzona) Gajewski; B.E., Mt. Mary Coll., 1954; certificate in theology, 1962; postgrad. Marquette U., 1967-70, Cardinal Stritch Coll., 1975-76. Joined Sch. Sister of Notre Dame, 1940; tchr. Sts. Cyril and Methodius Sch., Milw., 1943-50, prin., 1967-73; tchr. St. Casimir Sch., Kenosha, Wis., 1950-57, St. Adalbert Sch., Grand Rapids, Mich., 1957-58, St. Hedwig Sch., Milw., 1958-67; prin. St. John De Nepomuc Grade Sch., Milw., 1967—. Recipient certificate of Appreciation, League of Cath. Home and Sch. Assns., 1973, certificate for Outstanding Prin., 1976. Mem. Milw. Archdiocesan, Wis. elementary prins. assns., Nat. Assn. Elementary Sch. Prins., Nat. Cath. Edn. Assn. Home: 3426 N 38th St Milwaukee WI 53216 Office: 3421 N 37th St Milwaukee WI 53216

GALATI, MICHAEL BERNARD, lay ch. worker, United Methodist Ch.; b. Chgo., Sept. 4, 1931; s. Anthony Kenneth and Ingeborg Marie (Flugum) G.; B.S. in Edn., No. Ill. U., DeKalb, 1953, M.S., 1956; m. Mary Jeanne Kelsey, Apr. 19, 1952; children—Anna Marie (Mrs. Gayle Logsdon), Anthony K., Peter M., Joseph S. Mem. bd. Christian social concerns Rock River conf. United Methodist Ch., 1965-67; mem. council ministries No. Ill. conf., 1971-76, 83—; vice chmn. Aurora dist. council ministries, 1974-76. Chmn. dept. lang. arts and social scis., dir. student teaching program Lemont (Ill.) Twp. High Sch., 1956-81, head humanities div., 1981—. Trustee Village of Lemont, 1963-69. Recipient Valley Forge Tchr. medal, 1971; Rosicrucian Humanitarian award, 1973. Mem. Speech Communication Assn., Nat. Council Tchrs. English, Ill. Assn. Tchrs. English, Ill. Speech and Theatre Assn., Assn. Supervision and Curriculum Devel. Democrat. Author: Love Me a Village; contbr. poems, articles to mags. and jours. Home: 21 Norton Ave Lemont IL 60439 Office: 800 Porter St Lemont IL 60439

GALL, DONALD ARTHUR, minister, religious organization executive United Church of Christ; b. Edgely, N.D., Apr. 30, 1936; s. Arthur Fred and Luella (Sarah) G.; m. Shirley Ann Stevenson, Aug. 19, 1956 (div. 1973) children: Debora Sue, Craig Donald, Matthew Allen; m. Patricia Ellen deJong, Dec. 29, 1984. B.A., Yankton Coll., 1958; M.Div., Hartford Sem., 1962, M.A. in Religion 1962; D.Min., Eden Theol. Sem., 1983. Ordained to ministry United Ch. Christ, 1962. Pastor, First Congl. Ch., Whiting, Iowa, 1962-64; assoc. conf. minister Nebr. Conf. United Ch. Christ, Lincoln, 1964-69; master tchr. Presbyn. Ch., Eugene, Oreg., 1970-73, assoc. pastor First Congl. Ch., Eugene, Oreg., 1973-75; assoc. conf. minister Fla. Conf. United Ch. Christ, Miami, 1975-79; program exex. United Ch. Bd. for Homeland Ministries, N.Y.C., 1979—; tchr., instr. Yankton Coll., S.D., 1963-64; interim dir. Fla. Council Chs., Orlando, 1978-79; adj. prof. Lancaster Sem., Pa., 1978-79. Author: The Eleventh Hour, 1979.

GALLAGHER, JOHN ROBERT, priest, Roman Cath. Ch.; b. Mineral Point, Wis., Mar. 21, 1929; s. Raymond Joseph and Bridget Ellen (Ryan) H.; B.A., Loras Coll., Dubuque, Iowa, 1951. Ordained priest, 1955; founder, 1972, now pres. Camp Courage, Monticello, Iowa; pastor St. Joseph's Ch., Marion, 1974—. Mem. bd. regents Loras Coll., 1973—. Address: 967 5th Ave Marion IA 52302

GALLAGHER, THOMAS GEORGE, priest, Roman Catholic Church; b. N.Y.C., Jan. 20, 1941; s. Thomas John and Emma Theresa (Jalek) G. B.A., St. Pius X Coll., 1964; M.Th., St. John Vianney Sem., 1968; M.A. in Edn., St. John U., 1973, profl. diploma in edn., 1973. Ordained priest Roman Catholic Ch. Asst. pastor St. Francis Ch., Wantagh, N.Y., 1968-70; assoc. supt. schs. Diocese of Rockville Centre, N.Y., 1970-75, supt. schs., 1975-79; rep. Cath. schs. U.S. Cath. Conf., Washington, 1979-80, sec. edn., 1980—; chmn. editorial bd. The Living Light, Washington, 1982—. Contbr. articles to profl. jours.; author mo. column The Catechist, 1980—. Mem. Council Am. Pvt. Edn. (bd. dirs.), Am. Assn. Sch. Adminstrs. (del. 1984), Edn. Commn. of the States (adv. commr.), Nat. Cath. Edn. Assn. (dir.), Phi Delta Kappa. Home: 4001 14th St NE Washington DC 20017 Office: US Cath Conf 1312 Massachusetts Ave NW Washington DC 20005

GALLAHER, DAVID JOHN, minister, Presbyterian Church in U.S.A.; b. Calgary, Can., Oct. 7, 1928; came to U.S., 1951; s. David Andrew and Edith Gertrude (McWilliam) G.; m. Shirley Leone Cumberland, May 23, 1950; children: David Kelley, Regan Shawn. B.A., Whitworth Coll., 1955; M.Div., Austin Presbyn. Sem., 1964; postgrad. Presbyn. Sch. Christian Edn., 1969. Ordained as minister in Presbyterian Ch., 1964. Pastor

1st Presbyn. Ch., Ingram, Tex., 1964-67; Harper Presbyn. Ch., Tex., 1964-67; 1st Presbyn. Ch., Edinburg, Tex., 1967-76, Central Presbyn. Ch., Pine Bluff, Ark., 1976—; moderator Presbytery of the Pines, 1984; chmn. dir. pastoral care, 1978-80, div. nurture & leadership, 1981-83; commr. Gen. Assembly. Pres. Hidalgo County Easter Seal Soc., MacAllen, Tex., 1973-76, Salvation Army Ser. Unit, Edinburg, 1969-73, Shepherds Ctr., Pine Bluff, 1984, Pine Bluff Ministerial Assn., 1980. Recipient Disting. Service award Salvation Army, 1975. Mem. Presbyn. Hist. Soc., County Donegal Hist. Soc. Lodge: Rotary (bd. dirs. 1970-76). Office: Central Presbyn Ch 1515 Poplar Pine Bluff AR 71601

GALLAHER, LOYAL RAY, minister, Christian Ch.; b. Plainville, Ill., Jan. 1, 1937; s. Daniel Monroe and Leta Frances (Hull) G.; B.A., St. Louis Christian Coll., 1958; postgrad. Lincoln Christian Coll., 1960-61; m. Beverly Jeanine Gibson, June 9, 1956; children—Debra, Diane, Danette, Darisa. Ordained to ministry, 1955; pastor chs., Ill., Mo., 1954-69; pastor 1st Ch. of Christ Christian, Binghamton, N.Y., 1969—. Dir. Empire State Evangelizing Assn., 1969—; trustee N.Y. Christian Inst.; dean, counselor Lamoine Christian Service Camp, Oil Belt Christian Service Camp; trustee St. Louis Christian Coll.; pres. Eastern Christian Conv., 1973; moderator By The Way, TV program. Mem. St. Louis Christian Coll. Alumni Assn. (pres.). Home: 139 Kennedy Rd Binghamton NY 13901 Office: Upper Fron St and River Rd Binghamton NY 13901

GALLAWAY, IRA, minister, United Methodist Church; b. Coleman, Tex., May 24, 1923; s. W.F. and Julia Gallaway; m. Sally Baxter; children: Jerry, Cynthia, Craig, Timothy. Student Austin Coll., 1944; B.S. in Internat. Law and Polit. Sci. with honors, U. Tex., 1948; Th.M., So. Meth. U., 1960; D.D. (hon.), Asbury Theol. Sem., 1970. Ordained to ministry United Methodist Ch. Student asst. Highland Park Meth. Ch., Dallas, 1956-57; pastor Hutchins Meth. Ch., Dallas County, Tex., 1957-59, Kirkwood Meth. Ch., Irving, Tex., 1959-62, Walnut Hill Meth. Ch., Dallas, 1962-67; dist. supt. Ft. Worth East dist. United Meth. Ch., 1967-72; gen. sec. Bd. Evangelism, gen. sec. Bd. Discipleship, United Meth. Ch., Nashville, 1972-74; directing minister 1st United Meth. Ch., Peoria, Ill., 1974—; served in numerous positions in North Tex. conf., Central Tex. conf., and Central Ill. conf.; pres. Council on Evangelism of United Meth. Ch., 1967-71; del. World Meth. Council, Denver, 1971, Dublin, Ireland, 1976; exec. com. World Meth. Council, 1976, mem. evangelism com., 1972-75; mem. Joint Internat. Bilateral Commn.-Roman Catholic Ch. and World Meth. Council, chmn. bd. Asbury Theol. Sem., Meth. Med. Ctr. of Ill., Peoria; exec. officer Gen. Bd. Evangelism. Author: Drifted Astray, 1982. Contbr. articles to profl. jours. Bd. dirs. Chemical Dependency Unit Proctor Community Hosp., Christian Health Services, Inc., Peoria Urban League, Peoria Young Life Com., Youth Farm Bd., Crittendon Home Bd. Named Outstanding Young Man, Tex. Jaycees, 1952; recipient Philip award Nat. Assn. Evangelists, 1975. Served with USAF, 1941-45. Mem. Phi Beta Kappa, Pi Sigma Alpha, Phi Eta Sigma. Lodges: Rotary, Masons, Shriners. Office: 1st United Meth Ch 116 N E Perry Ave Peoria IL 61603

GALLE, JOSEPH ERNEST, III, minister, So. Baptist Conv.; b. New Orleans, Mar. 1, 1933; s. Joseph Ernest and Eva Mae (Purdue) G.; B.A., Miss. Coll., 1954; M. Div., New Orleans Baptist Theol. Sem., 1961; M.A., L.I. U., 1972; Th.M., Princeton Theol. Sem., 1973; m. Margie Lorraine Lea, Aug. 30, 1952; children—Joseph E., Jeffrey W., Jay Lea, John B., JoAnn R. Ordained to ministry, 1951; pastor chs., Prichard, Ala., Raymond and Pocahontas, Miss., and Larose, La., 1951-61; commd. 1st lt. U.S. Army, 1961, advanced through grades to lt. col., 1973; chaplain stationed at Ft. Bliss, Tex., Stuttgart, Ger., Ft. Polk, La., Vietnam, Ft. Hamilton, N.Y., 1961-76, hdqrs. 2d inf. div., 1977—. Mem. bd. Gen. Commn. of Chaplains, Washington, 1975-76. Decorated Silver Star, 2 Bronze Stars; recipient 1st Place award Nat. Cath. Press, 1976. Mem. Mil. Chaplains Assn. Editor Mil. Rev., 1973-76; mem. advisory council Mil. Chaplains Rev., 1973-76; contbr. articles to religious jours. Home: PO Box 873 Tioga LA 71477 Office: Generals Mess Hdqrs 2d Inf Div APO San Francisco CA 96224

GALLEGOS, ALPHONSE, bishop, Roman Catholic Church. Titular bishop of Sasabe, aux. bishop, Sacramento, Calif., 1984—. Office: PO Box 5037 Oak Park Sta Sacramento CA 95817*

GALLEHER, STEPHEN CARY, minister, Episcopal Church; b. Richmond, Va., Sept. 26, 1942; s. Frank Marion and Dorothy Elizabeth (Grice) G.; m. Lee Marshall Price, Feb. 19, 1971. B.A. with highest honors, U. Va., 1964; M.Div., cum laude, Va. Theol. Sem., 1970. Ordained to ministry Episcopal Ch., 1971. Asst. rector St. John's Episcopal Ch., Lynchburg, Va., 1971-75; rector Piedmont Parish, Marshall, Va., 1975-82; archdeacon Diocese of Newark, 1982—; chmn. Peace Commn., Diocese of Newark, 1982—. Editor The Voice, 1982—. Pres., Planned Parenthood, Lynchburg, 1972-75; bd. dirs. Cancer Soc., Warrenton, Va., 1977-82. Mem. Shalem Inst. for Spiritual Formation, Evang. Edn. Soc. Home: 7000 Blvd E Apt 133 E Guttenberg NJ 07093 Office: Cathedral House 24 Rector St Newark NJ 07102

GALLMAN, LAWRENCE KLETUS, minister, Lutheran Church-Missouri Synod; b. Wellsville, N.Y., Nov. 22, 1902; s. Frederick Carl and Ottilia Marie (Roeske) G.; m. Emma Selma Kruepke, June 30, 1928 (dec. Sept. 1963); children: Lawrence Frederick, Lois Gallman Overn, Judith Gallman Hillman; m. Ethel Stege, June 13, 1965. Diploma Concordia Coll., Bronxville, N.Y., 1922; B.D., Concordia Sem., St. Louis, 1927; D.Litt. (hon.), Concordia Coll., St. Paul, Minn., 1970. Ordained to ministry Lutheran Church-Missouri Synod, 1927. Pastor, St. John Ch., Ladysmith, Wis., 1927-34, St. Matthew Ch., Eau Claire, Wis., 1934-41, Mt. Olive Ch., Duluth, Minn., 1941-48, Peach Ch., Faribault, Minn., 1948-70; assoc. pastor Ch. of Redemption, Bloomington, Minn., 1971—; sec. North Wis. Dist. Luth. Ch. Mo. Synod, Merrill, Wis., 1939-41; dir., lectr. Luth. Youth Camp, Virginia, Minn., 1943-48; counselor Luth. Laymen's League, Mpls., 1953-60; pres. Luth. Children Friend, Mpls., 1960-69. Contbr. The Lutheran Witness, 1953-55. Editor: Minnesota Lutheran, 1957-66. Pres., Youth Coordinating Counsel, Faribault, Minn., 1950; bd. dirs. United Fund, Faribault, 1952; chmn. CROP Appeal, Rice County, Minn., 1952; mem. Curriculum Commn. Faribault Pub. Schs., 1957. Recipient Citation, Spiritual Life Mission, Fairlawn, N.J., 1964; Good Neighbor award WCCO Radio, Mpls., 1970; Cert. of Merit, Concordia Sem., 1982. Mem. Mpls. Pastoral Conf. (counselor 1982—), Am. Guild English Handbell Ringers. Republican. Lodge: Rotary Internat. Home: 7500 York St #929 Edina MN 55435 Office: Luth Ch Redemption 927 E Old Shakopee Rd Bloomington MN 55420

GALLOWAY, ERNESTINE ROYALS, religious organization executive; National Ministries, American Baptist Churches in the U.S.A.; b. Newark, May 7, 1928; d. Seymour Page Galloway and Ethel (Bishop) Galloway Bigham. B.A., NY U, 1957, M.A., 1960, 69, Ed.D., 1981. Dir. edn. Concord Bapt. Ch., Bklyn., 1956-60; adminstrv. asst. United Presbyn. Ch., Los Angeles, 1960-62; social group worker, Los Angeles, 1962-64; adminstrv. asst. various Presbyn. and Meth. chs., N.Y.C., 1973-78; mgr. nat. ministries Am. Bapt. Chs. U.S.A., Valley Forge, Pa., 1978—. Mem. Religious Edn. Assn. NY U. Home: 25 Warman St Montclair NJ 07042 Office: Am Bapt Chs/Nat Ministries PO Box 851 Valley Forge PA 19482

GALVAN, ELIAS G., bishop, United Methodist Church; b. Puebla, Mex., Apr. 9, 1938; came to U.S., 1956. B.A., Calif. State U.; M.A., Sch. of Theology. Pastor City Terr. United Meth. Ch., Los Angeles, 1966-69, All Nations United Meth. Ch., Los Angeles, 1969-71; exec. dir. Ethnic Planning Dept., Los Angeles, 1971-74; council dir. Pacific and S.W. Conf., Calif., Ariz., Nev., and Hawaii, 1980-84; bishop Desert S.W. Conf., Ariz. and Nev., 1984—. Office: Desert Southwest Conf 5510 N Central Ave Phoenix AZ 85012

GAMMON, JAMES EDWIN, minister, Churches of Christ; b. San Diego, Jan. 23, 1944; s. Jack Albert and Thalia (Montgomery) G.; m. Sharon Elaine Head, June 26, 1965; children: John Paul, James Edwin, Jeffrey David. B.A., Tex. Christian U., 1970, postgrad., 1970-72. Ordained to ministry Chs. of Christ, 1966. Minister, Northside Ch., Dallas, 1971-73, Central Ave. Ch. of Christ, pres. So. Bible Inst., Valdosta, Ga., 1973-78; minister Trinity Oakes Ch., Dallas, 1978-80, Parkview Ch. of Christ, Sherman, Tex., 1980-85, Eisenhower Ch. of Christ, Odessa, Tex., 1985—; dir. Texoma Bible Inst., Sherman, 1980-85; chmn. No. Dallas Christian Schs., 1973; trustee Ga. Christian Sch., Valdosta, 1974-75. News editor Gospel Advocate, 1977-78. Author: Bible Notes, 1974-85. Pres. Young Republicans, Abilene, Tex., 1963; del. state conv. Tex. Rep. Party, 1972, 80. Served with U.S. Army, 1963-66. Home: 1707 Laurel Odessa TX 79716 Office: Eisenhower Ch of Christ 807 E 21st St Odessa TX 79761

GAMWELL, FRANKLIN IRVING, minister Presbyterian Church; b. Bayshore, N.Y., Dec. 25, 1937; s. Franklin and Marjorie (White) G.; m. Frances Lorell Ellis, Mar. 14, 1969; children: Christopher Max Snider, Lisa Lorell Snider. B.A., Yale U., 1959; B.Div., Union Theol. Sem., N.Y.C., 1963; M.A., U. Chgo., 1970, Ph.D., 1973. Ordained to ministry, United Presbyterian Church, 1963; pastor West Side Christian Parish, Chgo., 1963-66; dean, assoc. prof. The Divinity Sch., U. Chgo., 1980—. Author: Beyond Preference, 1984; co-editor: Existence and Actuality: Conversations with Charles Hartshorne, 1984. Mem. Am. Acad. Religion, Soc. Christian Ethics. Office: The Divinity Sch Univ Chgo 1025 E 58th St Chicago IL 60637

GANNON, J. TRUETT, minister, Southern Baptist Convention; b. Cordele, Ga., Apr. 5, 1930; s. Clifford G. and Jewell (Rudd) G.; m. Margaret Lewis, Jan. 27, 1951; children: Kenny C., Karen Gannon Griffith. A.B., Mercer U., 1951; B.D., Southeastern Bapt. Theol. Sem., 1956, D.Min., 1975. Ordained to ministry Baptist Ch., 1948. Pastor 1st Bapt. Ch., Eatonton, Ga., 1956-61, Avondale Estates, Ga., 1961-73, New Orleans, 1973-76, Smoke Rise Bapt. Ch., Stone Mountain, Ga., 1976—; mem. exec. com. Ga. Bapt. Hosp. Commn., 1981-84; mem. exec. com. Ga. Bapt. Conv., 1971-73, 81-84. Trustee La. Bapt. Coll., 1973-76, Mercer U., 1979-81; trustee Midwestern Bapt. Theol. Sem., 1980—, chmn. instrn. com. of bd. trustees, 1984-85; instr. New Orleans Bapt. Sem., Marietta, Ga., 1982-84. Home: 5591 Militia Dr Stone Mountain GA 30087 Office: Smoke Rise Baptist Ch 5901 Hugh Howell Rd Stone Mountain GA 30087

GANTER, BERNARD JACQUES, bishop, Roman Catholic Church; b. Galveston, Tex., July 17, 1928; s. Bernard Jacques and Marie (Bozka) G.; student Tex. A. and M. U., 1944; student St. Mary's Sem., LaPorte, Tex., 1945-52; Juris Canonici Doctoris, Cath. U. Am., 1955. Ordained priest Roman Catholic Ch., 1952; asst. pastor Sacred Heart Ch., Conroe, Tex., 1955, Sacred Heart Ch., Houston, 1956; officialis, diocesan matrimonial tribunal, Galveston-Houston, 1958-66; chancellor Diocese of Galveston-Houston, 1966-73; rector Sacred Heart Co-Cathedral, Houston, 1969-73; bishop of Tulsa, 1973-78; apptd. bishop of Beaumont, Tex., 1977—. Mem. Canon Law Soc. Am., Equestrian Order Holy Sepulchre. K.C. (4 deg.). Office: Diocese of Beaumont PO Box 3948 Beaumont TX 77704*

GANZ, VIRGIL ARDEN, pastor, American Lutheran Church; b. Milw., Jan. 18, 1928; s. Emil Richard and Cleaphinea Hazel (Burmeister) G.; m. Dolores Marie Angerer, Aug. 15, 1953; children: Elizabeth Marie, Katherine Ann, Rebecca Sue. B.A., Capital U., 1951; B.D. in Theology, Wartburg Theol. Sem., 1954; M. in Guidance/Counseling, Long Island U., 1972. Ordained to ministry Am. Luth. Church, 1954. Pastor, Trinity Luth. Ch., New London, Wis., and Immanuel Luth. Ch., Zittau, Wis., 1954-59, Trinity Luth. Ch., Loyal, Wis., 1960-62, Lord of Life Luth. Ch., Kirby, Tex., 1977-81; commd. U.S. Army, 1962, advanced through grades to lt. col., 1977, ret., 1977; chaplain, 1962-77; interim pastor So. dist. Am. Luth. Ch., Tex., 1981-83; visitation pastor Grace Luth. Ch., San Antonio, 1983—; mem. youth com. Wis. dist. Am. Luth. Ch., 1960-62; treas. San Antonio Conf., Am. Luth. Ch., 1984—. Contbor articles to Luth. publs., 1965-66. Bd. dirs. Luth. Gen. Hosp., San Antonio, 1984—. Decorated Bronze Star, Army Commendation medal with one oak leaf cluster, Vietnam Service medal, Republic of Vietnam Campaign medal. Republican. Lodge: Rotary. Home: 6719 Oak Lake Dr San Antonio TX 78244 Office: Grace Luth Ch 504 Ave East San Antonio TX 78215

GAON, SOLOMON, rabbi, history educator, Jewish; b. Travnik, Yugoslavia, Dec. 15, 1912; came to U.S., 1965, naturalized, 1982; s. Isaac and Raquel (Pinto) G.; m. Regina Hassan, Nov. 5, 1944; children: Raquel Gaon Cohen, Isaac. B.A., London U., 1940, Ph.D., 1943; minister's diploma Jews' Coll. London, 1944 rabbinic diploma, 1948; D.D. (hon.), Yeshiva U., 1969. Ordained rabbi, 1948. Haham of Sephardi Congregation of Brit. Commonwealth, London, 1949-75; prof. Sephardic studies Yeshiva U., N.Y.C., 1976—, Sephardic rosh yeshiva, 1978—; chief rabbi of congregations affiliated with World Sephardi Fedn., 1978—; bd. dirs. Bar Ilan U., Ben Gurion U., Hebrew U.; v.p. Meml. Found. for Jewish Culture. Author: The Contribution of the Sephardim to Anglo Jewry, 1950; The Sephardi Folklore, 1949; The Meaning of the Synagoguge Ceremonial, 1956; The History of the Jewish Communities on the Mediterranean Coast, 1957; Yehuda Alcalay and Sir Moses Montefiore, 1969; The Character of the Sephardim and Their Outlook, 1967; The Challenge of Israel to Our Religious Life, 1970; The Relationships During the Last Three Centuries Between Shaar Hashamayim of London and Shearith Israel of New York, 1970; The Sephardic Contribution to the Idea of Zionism, 1974; also chpts., articles. Accorded Decoration Alphonso XI (Spain); named hon. life pres. Hebrew U., Jerusalem, 1982. Mem. Rabbinical Council Am., Union Rabbis and Ministers of Brit. Commonwealth, Am. Soc. Sephardic Studies, Union Sephardic Congregations Am. (pres. 1970—). Lodges: Abravanel Lodge (hon. mem.), Halcyon Lodge (paster master), Ajex Lodge (past worshipful master), Gaster Lodge, Masons. Office: Yeshiva U 500 W 185th St New York NY 10033

GARATE, GORKA IREN, priest, Roman Cath. Ch.; b. Guetxo, Basque Country, Spain, July 3, 1936; s. Jose Maria and Maria Mercedes (Bayo) G.; came to U.S., 1968; licentiate humanities Universidad Católica de Quito, Ecuador, 1958, licentiate philosophy, 1961; Th.M, St. Mary's U., Halifax, Can., 1968; postgrad. Fordham U., 1969—. Joined S.J., 1953; ordained priest, 1967; tchr. Seminario San Jose, San Salvador, El Salvador, 1961-64; asst. pastor St. Columba Ch., N.Y.C., 1969-71, St. Aloysius Ch., N.Y.C., 1971-72, St. Jude Ch., N.Y.C., 1972—. Home and Office: 431 W 204th St New York City NY 10034

GARBER, HENRY CHARLES, minister, Presbyterian Church in the U.S. b. Beaver Falls, Pa., Sept. 13, 1920; s. Charles Wesley and Margaret Maude (Nowery) G.; m. Betty Jane Eazor, July 12, 1942; children: Henry Charles II, Ronald Alan. B.A., Howard Payne U., 1949; B.D. (hon.), 1966; B.D., Southwestern Bapt. Theol. Sem., 1953. Ordained to ministry, 1972; ordained to ministry Presbyterian Ch. in the U.S., 1973. Minister, First Bapt. Ch., Mineral Wells, Tex., 1954-60, Denison, Tex., 1960-72, Southminster Presbyn., Garland, Tex., 1973—; dir. home mission bd. Southern Bapt. Conv., 1963-66; pres. Ministerial Alliance, Garland, 1974-75. Trustee, Howard Payne U., Brownwood, Tex., 1958-64; bd. mgmt. YMCA, Garland, 1976-81; adv. council Salvation Army, Garland, 1980-83. Served to staff sgt. USAF, 1942-45. Lodges: Rotary (pres. 1969-70), Masons (32 degree). Home: 8109 Skillman Dallas TX 75231 Office: Southminster Presbyterian Ch 2722 S First St Garland TX 75041

GARBER, REUBEN LEE, minister, church official, Lutheran Church-Missouri Synod; b. Garland, Nebr., June 21, 1929; s. Walter Joseph and Emma Anna (Sieck) G.; m. Arline Lorraine Wolf, Nov. 18, 1951; children: Phillip, David, Leslie, Joel, Kenneth, Wayne, Tamara. A.A., St. John's Coll., 1949; B.A., Concordia Sem., St. Louis, 1951, postgrad. 1956-58; B.S. in Edn., Concordia Tchrs. Coll., 1953. Ordained to ministry Luth. Ch.-Mo. Synod, 1958. Prin., tchr. St. Paul Luth. Sch., Ellsworth, Kans., 1953-58; pastor St. Paul Luth. Ch., Addison, Ill., 1958-62; founder, pastor Trinity Luth. Ch., Columbia, Tenn., 1962-70; pastor Grace Luth. Ch., New Albany, Ind., 1970-83; mission developer Ind. Dist. Luth. Ch.-Mo. Synod, 1983—; sec. bd. evangelism No. Ill. Dist., Chgo., 1959-62; bd. youth ministry Mid-South Dist., Memphis, 1968-70, sec. pastoral conf., 1965-70; mem. bd. evangelism, Ind. Dist., Ft. Wayne, 1972-78, v.p., 1978—. Author: Charting a Course in Christian Doctrine, 1968. Bd. dirs. Family Service Bur., New Albany, Ind., 1978-82; chmn. Maury County Assn. Retarded Children, Columbia, Tenn., 1966-68; chmn. religious nurture com. Tenn. Assn. Retarded Children and Adults, Nashville, 1968-70. Address: Route 2 Box 748 Leitchfield KY 42754

GARCIA, ALBERT LAZARO, minister, educator, Lutheran Church-Missouri Synod. B. Havana, Cuba, May 2, 1947; came to U.S., 1960, naturalized, 1973; s. Antonio and Norma (Giro) Garcia; m. Moraima Aleida Yates, Sept. 8, 1968; children: Yvette Marie, Albert Phillip. B.A., Fla. Atlantic U., 1969; M.Div., Concordia Sem., Springfield, Ill., 1974; Th.M., Luth. Sch. Theology, Chgo., 1978 postgrad., 1979—. Ordained to ministry Luth. Ch.-Mo. Synod, 1974. Pastor, missionary El Buen Pastor Evangelical Luth Ch., Chgo., 1974-79; asst. prof. systematics, Concordia Sem., Fort Wayne, Ind., 1979—; chmn. Hispanic Task Force Luth. Ch.-Mo. Synod, St. Louis, 1975-77, v.p. Nat. Hispanic Conf., St. Louis, 1977-78, pres., 1978-79. Author: Evangilismo En El Contexto Miscanico, 1983; adult edn. course Conozca a Cristo, 1977. Editor: Destellos Teologicos, 1982—; editor, transl. Luther's Sermons, 1983. Bd. dirs. Edocatic orgn. to help minority edn., Fort Wayne, 1982-84, Civil Review Bd. Selective Service, Indpls., 1984. Fellow Aid Assn. for Luths., 1983. Mem. Christian Philosophers Soc., Soc. Sci. Study of Religion. Home: 7128 Kebir Ct Fort Wayne IN 46815 Office: Concordia Theol Sem Fort Wayne IN 46825

GARCIA, RUBEN ALEGRIA, minister, Iglesia Ni Cristo; b. San Jose, Nueva Ecija, Philippines, May 27, 1944; came to U.S., 1978; s. Juan and Eudocia (Alegria) G.; m. Sally Vasquez, Dec. 9, 1972; children: Aliw, Joy. Grad. New Era Evang. Coll., Quezon City, Philippines, 1977. Ordained to ministry Ch. of Christ, 1977. Vol. worker Iglesia Ni Cristo (Ch. of Christ), Bontoc, Mt. Province, Philippines, 1966-68, Baguio City, Philippines, 1969, ch. under probation worker, Manila, 1970, ch. regular worker, 1971-77, pastor, Malabon, Paco, Philippines, 1977-78, resident minister, Virginia Beach, Va., 1979, Guam, 1980, resident minister, supervising minister, Honolulu, 1981—. Author, designer: Minister's Personal Book, 1984. Home and Office: 1021 Valley View Dr Honolulu HI 96819

GARCIA-ACEVEDO, MIGUEL ANGEL, priest, Roman Catholic Church; b. Moca, P.R., Dec. 11, 1945; s. Anselmo and Petra (Acevedo) Garcia. B.A., St. Alphonsus Coll., 1969; M.R.E., Mt. St. Alphonsus, Coll., 1971, M. Div., 1973. Joined Redemptorist Order, Roman Cath. Ch., ordained priest, 1972. Asst. dir. St. Mary's Minor Sem., North East, Pa., 1974-75; parish priest Santa Maria Reina, Ponce, P.R., 1975-77; asst. dir. Seminario Familiar Alfonsiano, Caguas, P.R., 1977-81; youth counselor Notre Dame High Sch., Caguas, 1978-80; pastor Nuestra Señora del Perpetuo Socorro, Caguas, 1981-85; asst. dir. Casa San Alfonso-Teologado, Santo Domingo, R.D., 1985—; sec. formation Redemptorist Fathers, San Juan, 1977-81, 85—; bd. dirs. Conf. of Religious, San Juan, 1982—; vicar pastoral affairs Diocese of Caguas, 1983-84; columnist. Lodge: K.C. Address: Padres Redentoristas PO Box 5447 Puerta de Tierra PR 00906

GARD, RICHARD ABBOTT, religious institute executive, educator, Buddhist Churches; b. Vancouver, B.C., Can., May 29, 1914; came to U.S., 1916; s. Charles Ned and Clara Edna (Abbott) G.; m. Tatiana Ruzena Kristina Moravec, Nov. 1, 1952; children: Alan Moravec, Anita Nadine. B.A., U. Wash., 1937; M.A., U. Hawaii, 1940; postgrad. U. Pa., 1945-47; Ph.D., Claremont Grad. Sch., 1951; postgrad. Otani U., Ryukoky U., 1953-54; D.H.L., Monmouth Coll., 1963. Vice pres. (U.S.A.) World Fellowship of Buddhists, Bangkok, Thailand, 1961-64, asst. sec.-gen., 1971-75; dir. inst. services Inst. for Advanced Studies of World Religions, Stony Brook, N.Y., 1971-84, pres., 1985—; cultural affairs officer U.S. Info. Agy., Washington, 1963-64; Buddhist affairs officer U.S. Dept. State, Washington and Hong Kong, 1964-69. Editor, author: Buddhism, 1961. Editor-in-chief Great Religions of Modern Man, 1961. Editor periodicals: Buddhist Text Information, 1974—, Buddhist Research Information, 1979—. Contbr. articles to profl. jours. Bd. dirs., sec. Three Village Men's Garden Club, Setauket, N.Y., 1980-84. Served to lt. col. USMCR, 1941-46; PTO. Recipient Japanese Buddhist okesa Jodo-shu, 1946, Shingon-shu, 1950; Thai Buddhist Theravada award Mahamakuta Found., 1956, Burmese Buddhist Theravada award Shwedagon, 1957, Korean Buddhist Mahayana award Chogye-jong, 1963; Rockefeller Found. fellow, 1946-47; Ford Found. grantee, 1970. Mem. Mid-Atlantic Region of Assn. for Asian Studies (pres. 1974-75), Tibet Soc. (Ind. U.; bd. dirs. 1978-83), Internat. Assn. Buddhist Studies (bd. dirs. 1982—), Am. Soc. Study of Religion (exec. council 1983—). Home: PO Box 2866 Setauket NY 11733 Office: Inst for Advanced Studies of World Religions SUNY Melville Meml Library Stony Brook NY 11794-3383

GARDNER, ROBERT EVAN, minister, Lutheran Church-Missouri Synod; b. Reedsburg, Wisc., Feb. 22, 1950; s. Edward Burton and Eleanore Eda (Schafer) G.; m. Diane Lynn Dankert, Nov. 25, 1972; children: Sarah Elizabeth, Matthew Robert, Joshua Edward. A.A., Concordia Coll., 1970; B.A., Concordia Sr. Coll., 1972; M.Div., Concordia Theol. Sem., 1976. Ordained to ministry Lutheran Ch., 1976. Pastor, Zion & Trinity Luth. Chs., Presho & Reliance, S.D., 1976-81; head pastor Emanuel Luth. Ch., Milbank, S.D., 1981—; Mem. S.D. Dist. Luth. Ch. - Mo. Synod (sec. Pastors Conf., 1978, nom. com. 1980 convention, parish service commn., 1980-82, chmn. nom. com. 1982 convention, sec. parish service commn. 1983-84). Republican. Home: 701 South Main St Milbank SD 52252 Office: Emanuel Lutheran Church 701 South First St Milbank SD 57252

GARDNER, VICTOR FRANKLIN, minister, district supervisor, Internat. Ch. of the Foursquare Gospel; b. Mansfield, Ohio, Mar. 17, 1927; s. Noble J. and Frieda Mae (Stoner) G.; grad. Life Bible Coll., Los Angeles, 1950; m. Dorothy Koon, Aug. 13, 1949; children—Steven Eugene, Thomas Randall. Ordained to ministry, 1950; pastor chs., Md., Pa., Ohio, 1950-74; pastor Kingsway Foursquare Ch., Vancouver, B.C., Can., 1974—; dist. supr. Western Can. dist.; exec. dir. L.I.F.E. Bible Coll. Can., Burnaby, Vancouver, B.C. Mem. missionary cabinet and home missions com.; bd. dirs. Foursquare Madge Meadwell Found. Chmn., Central Park Sr. Citizens Assn., Vancouver; bd. dirs. Dover (Ohio) YMCA, 1967-70; chmn. Dover Zoning Bd. Appeals, 1972-74. Named Pastor of Year, Eastern dist., 1965. Contbr. articles to religious jours. Office: 4061 Kingsway St Burnaby BC Canada

GARKE, MARY ELAINE, nun, Roman Catholic Church; b. Coldwater, Ohio, Dec. 8, 1935; d. Richard Isidore and Loretta Eleanor (Kothman) G. B.S. in Edn., U. Dayton, 1961; M.P.S., U. Ottawa, Ont., 1971, Ph.D., 1975. Joined Sisters of Precious Blood, 1954. Elem. tchr. Resurrection Sch., Dayton, Ohio, 1954-58, Good Hope Sch., Miamisburg, Ohio, 1958-62, Incarnation Sch., Dayton, 1962-63; secondary tchr. Central Cath. High Sch., Lafayette, Ind., 1963-66; dir. clin. services Dartmouth Hosp., Dayton, 1975-80; regional dir. Sisters of Precious Blood, Dayton, 1980—; clin. psychologist in pvt. practice, Dayton, 1977—; trustee Maria-Joseph Ctr., Dayton, 1980-83, v.p., 1977-80, pres., 1980-83, mem. council Sisters of Precious Blood, 1980—, assembly del., 1972—. Democrat. Address: 4960 Salem Ave Dayton OH 45416

GARLAND, DAVID ELLSWORTH, religious studies educator, Southern Baptist Convention; b. Crisfield, Md., Sept. 24, 1947; d. Edward Ellsworth and Ruth (Grey) G.; m. Diana Sue Richmond, Aug. 22, 1970; children: Sarah, John. B.A., Okla. Bapt. U., 1970; M.Div., So. Bapt. Theol. Sem., Louisville, 1973, Ph.D., 1976; postgrad. Eberhard-Karls Universität, Tübingen, Fed. Republic Germany, 1984-85. Ordained to ministry Bapt. Ch., 1976. Pastor, Immanuel Bapt. Ch., Shepherdsville, Ky., 1973-76; asst. prof. N.T., So. Bapt. Theol. Sem., Louisville, 1977-83, assoc. prof., 1983—. Author: The Intention of Matthew 23, 1979. Contbr. articles to religious publs. Served with USNR, 1965-71. Mem. Soc. Bibl. Lit., Assn. Bapt. Profs. Home: 4400 Rudy Ln Louisville KY 40207 Office: So Bapt Theol Sem 2825 Lexington Rd Louisville KY 40280

GARLAND, JAMES H., bishop, Roman Catholic Church. Titular bishop of Garriana, aux. bishop, Cin., 1984—. Office: 100 E 8th St Cincinnati OH 45202*

GARLAND, PHILIP OWEN, deacon, Episcopal Church; educator; b. Benham, Ky., Jan. 4, 1931; s. Charles Raleigh and Pearl (Finchum) G.; m. Mary Lou Burkhart, Dec. 26, 1960; children: Todd Eben, Candia Ann. A.B. Wofford U., 1957; M.Ed., Rollins Coll., 1970. Ordained to ministry Episc. Ch., as deacon, 1978. Deacon St. Philip Ch. Harrodsburg, Ky., 1978-79, St. John Ch., Versailles, Ky., 1979, Trinity Ch., Danville, Ky., 1979—; vestryman All Saints Episc. Ch., Lakeland, Fla., 1972-74, ch. sch. supt., 1967-68; vestryman Trinity Epis. Ch., Danville, Ky., 1976-78, ch. sch. supt., 1975-76. Tchr. Boyle Pub. Middle Sch., Danville, 1977—. Writer, producer multi-media presentation Workshop for Correctional Edn. Assn., (1st runner-up award) 1982. Served with USAF, 1951-55. Named Ky. Tchr. of Yr., Correctional Edn. Assn., 1982. Mem. NEA. Democrat. Lodge: Lions. Home: 133 Lisa St Danville KY 40422

GARMENDIA, FRANCISCO See *Who's Who in America*, 43rd edition.

GARNER, KENT HOWARD, minister, American Lutheran Church; b. Niagara Falls, N.Y., May 9, 1945; s. T. Howard and Eleanor L. (Milleville) G.; m. Linda L. Baird, July 3, 1971; children: Marc A., Kari L. B.A., Capital U., 1966; D.Min., Luth. Theol. Sem., Columbus, Ohio, 1970; Th.M., Pitts. Theol. Sem., 1976. Ordained to ministry Am. Luth. Ch., 1970. Intern, First Luth. Ch., Fullerton, Calif., 1968-69; minister St. Paul's Luth. Ch., Canonsburg, Pa., 1970-77, Bethlehem Luth. Ch., Fairport, N.Y., 1977—; pres. Ohio River Valley Conf., Pitts., 1974-75; nat. trainer SEARCH Bible Study, 1983—. Bd. regents Capital U., Columbus, Ohio, 1983—. Recipient Osterman scholarship Eastern dist. Am. Luth. Ch., 1970. Home: 19 Winding Brook Dr Fairport NY 14450 Office: Bethlehem Luth Ch 48 Perrin St Fairport NY 14450

GARNER, ROBERT F. See *Who's Who in America*, 43rd edition.

GARNER, SAMUEL LEE, minister, So. Bapt. Conv.; b. Red Oak, Okla., Nov. 20, 1945; s. Lee and Atha Lodell (Wilson) G.; degree Hosp. Adminstrn., Eastern State Coll., Wilburton, Okla., 1964; student Okla. Bapt. U., Shawnee, 1966-68; m. Patricia Ann Lee, May 23, 1969; children—Jason Lee, Kimberli Anne. Ordained to ministry, 1965; Bapt. Student Union dir. Eastern State Coll., 1964-66; pastor chs. in Okla., 1965—, Trinity Bapt. Ch., Vinita, 1972-76; dir. missions Atoka (Okla.) Bapt. Assn., 1976—; chaplain Okla. Ho. of Reps., 1975-76, N.E. Okla. Electric Coop., Vinita, 1972—. Mem. Atoka C. of C. Address: PO Drawer 859 Atoka OK 74525

GARNSWORTHY, LEWIS SAMUEL, archbishop, Anglican Church of Canada; b. Edmonton, Alta., Can., July 18, 1922; m. Jean Valance Allen, Aug. 7, 1954; children: Peter, Katherine. B.A., U. Alta., 1943; L.Th., Wycliffe Coll., Toronto, Ont., Can., 1945, D.D. (hon.), 1968; D.D. (hon.), Trinity Coll., Toronto, 1973, Huron Coll., London, Ont., 1976. Ordained deacon Anglican Ch. Can., 1945, priest, 1946. Curate, then rector chs. in Ont., 1946-68; suffragan bishop Anglican Ch. Can. Diocese of Toronto, 1968-72, bishop, 1972-79, archbishop of Toronto, Met. of Ont., 1979—. Fellow Coll. Preachers. Clubs: Albany, York. Address: 135 Adelaide St E Toronto ON M5C 1L8 Canada

GARRABRANDT, JOHN NEAFIE, JR., minister, United Methodist Church; b. Ocean Grove, N.J., Feb. 15, 1917; s. John Neafie and Viola (Bills) G.; A.B. magna cum laude, DePauw U., 1940; S.T.M., Temple U., 1950; M.Div., Eastern Bapt. Theol. Sem., Phila., 1972; m. Doris Roberson, Nov. 1, 1942; children—Theodore, Deborah, Pamela. Ordained to ministry, 1947. Exec. sec. North Phila. Bapt. Assn., 1944; pres. Camden Bapt. Assn., 1950; founder Bapt. Home for Aged of South Jersey, 1950; prof. O.T. Bapt. Inst., Phila., 1953-54; chmn. nominations, exec. bd. St. Benedicts Found., 1972-75. Chmn., Jerome Housing Authority, Idaho, 1967-68; pres. bd. trustees Coll. So. Idaho, Twin Falls, 1971-73; chmn. Speakers Bur. Twin Falls Mental Health Soc., 1963-65; chmn. bd. Jerome Pub. Library, 1966-68; founder St. Benedict's Hosp. Found.; founder Buhl Emergency Food Pantry, 1982; chmn. Buhl Pub. Library, Idaho, 1983—. Mem. Gold Key, Phi Beta Kappa, Phi Eta Sigma, Pi Sigma Alpha, Lambda Chi Alpha. Lodge: Masons. Home: 504 13th Ave N Buhl ID 83316

GARRELS, DENNIS EARL, minister, Lutheran Church-Missouri Synod; b. Detroit, Aug. 27, 1942; s. Earl Henry Hartwick and Milda Caroline Emma (Diefenbach) G.; m. Dale Patricia Wooliver, Aug. 20, 1966; 1 child, Robin Heather. B.Mus., U. Mich., 1966; M.Div., Concordia Luth. Sem., Ft. Wayne, Ind., 1978. Ordained to ministry Luth. Ch., 1978. Religious musician, organist, mem. choir gospel tour, Detroit, 1974-76; pastor Our Savior Luth. Ch., Fort Madison, Iowa, 1978-81, St. Luke's Luth. Ch., St. Louis, 1982—; sec. S.E. Iowa Pastors Conf., Mount Pleasant, 1979-81; del. Clergy for Life, St. Louis, 1982—. Author: Self Identity: Buddhism and Christianity, 1976. Creator, producer films: Dream and Reality-Nicholas Berdeav, 1962; Nicodemus Reborn, 1972. Lodge: Lions. Mem. Phi Sigma Kappa. Home: 4506 Tennessee Saint Louis MO 63111

GARRETT, CARL WHITLEY, minister, Southern Baptist Convention; b. Duncan, Okla., Feb. 24, 1939; s. Whitley Emory and Wilma Cleo (Eberhart) G.; m. Frances Eulene Person, July 14, 1962; children: Carla Francine, Angela Kay. B.S., Okla. Bapt. U., 1961; M.

Div., Southwestern Bapt. Sem., 1964; M. Religious Edn., 1965; Ph.D., Columbia Pacific U., 1983; D. Sacred Theology, Southwest Bapt. U., 1977. Ordained to ministry Baptist Ch., 1958, Asst. Pastor 1st. Bapt. Ch., Waurika, Okla., 1963; chaplain State Home for Children, Corsicana, Tex., 1964-65; assoc. pastor Immunel Bapt. Ch., Tulsa, Okla., 1965-67; pastor Hamlin Bapt. Ch., Springfield, Mo., 1967-73, 1st. Bapt. Ch., Carthage, Mo., 1973-85, Emmanuel Bapt. Ch., Overland Park, Kans., 1985—; pres.-chmn. Mo. Bapt. Conv., Jefferson City; trustee Southwest Bapt. U., Bolivar, Mo. Composed numerous lyrics for religious songs. Chmn. Bd. of County Jail Visitors, Carthage, 1984; foreman Jasper County Grand Jury, Carthage, 1980; trustee Innovative Inds., Inc., Carthage, 1984. Walter Pope Binns fellow, William Jewel Coll., 1982. Home: 10120 Craig Overland Park KS 66212

GARRETT, CLETIS EUGENE, minister, So. Bapt. Conv.; b. Mangum, Okla., Feb. 4, 1953; s. Whitley Emery and Wilma Cleo (Eberhart) G.; B.A., Mo. Bapt. Coll., 1975; postgrad., Midwestern Theol. Sem., 1976—; m. Saundra Jane Cline, Dec. 31, 1971; children—Vicki Melinda, Andrew Whitley. Ordained to ministry, 1975; minister of music Cherokee Hills Bapt. Ch., Oklahoma City, 1970-71; minister of youth 1st Bapt. Ch., St. Charles, Mo., 1972; minister of music 1st Bapt. Ch., Affton, Mo., 1972-73; minister of music and youth 1st Bapt. Ch., St. Peters, Mo., 1973-75; pastor Higland Prairie Bapt. Ch., Ethlyn, Mo., 1974-75; asso. pastor, minister youth edn. Swope Park Bapt. Ch., Kansas City, Mo., 1976—. Home: 8717 Arlington St Kansas City MO 64138 Office: 2521 E Meyer St Kansas City MO 65132

GARRETT, DAVID, priest, Episcopal Church; b. Memphis, Oct. 9, 1951; s. James Eldon and Edna Angelene (Hall) G.; m. Virginia Ruth Shettlesworth, June 19, 1971; children: Geoffrey Reese, Arwen Eileen. B.A., Southwestern at Memphis, 1973; M.Div., Sch. Theology, U. of South, 1977. Ordained priest Episcopal Ch., 1978. Deacon, St. Martin's Ch., Chattanooga, 1977-78, curate, 1978; vicar Ch. of Annunciation, Newport, Tenn., 1978—; presenting couple Episcopal Marriage Encounter, 1982—; assoc. Community of St. Mary, Sewanee, Tenn., 1977—; mem. dept. of mission Diocese of East Tenn., 1984—, mem. bd. examining chaplains, 1985; mem. Rural Workers Fellowship, 1981—. Contbr. articles to prof. jours. Bd. dirs. Boys Club of Newport, 1981-83; del. bd. to adminstr. fed. grants, East Tenn. region, 1984. Mem. Cocke County Ministerial Assn. (pres.), Mid-South Aquarium Soc., Mid-South Killifish Assn. (pres. 1972-74). Office: Episcopal Church of the Annunciation 502 Cosby Rd PO Box 337 Newport TN 37821

GARRISON, MARVIN LEE, minister, Christian Ch.; b. Iowa City, Iowa, June 15, 1938; s. Jack and Cleo Juanita (Kane) G.; B.Th., Midwest Christian Coll., 1962; M.A., Bethany Nazarene Coll., 1973; m. Vickie Lea Clay, June 12, 1960; 1 son, Douglas Clint. Ordained to ministry, 1961; pastor Westside Christian Ch., Guthrie, Okla., 1959-60, Christian Ch., Ripley, Okla., 1960-62, Ch. of Christ, Glencoe, Okla., 1962-63, 1st Christian Ch., Kiowa, Kans., 1963-68, 1st Christian Ch., Wellington, Tex., 1968-72; Cache (Okla.) Christian Ch., 1972-77, 1st Christian Ch., Shattuck, Okla., 1977—. Prin., Carriage Hills Christian Sch., Lawton, Okla., 1975-76; chaplain George Thomas Boy Scout Camp, Apache, Okla., 1972, 73, 74. Mem. Midwest Christian Coll. Alumni Assn. Home: 416 S Santa Fe Shattuck OK 73858 Office: Box 212 Shattuck OK 73858

GARROW, SHEILA MAY, church school educator, Seventh-day Adventists; b. Calgary, Alta., Can., May 11, 1942; came to U.S., 1961; naturalized, 1966; d. Berthold Rueben and Opal Ruth (Beckthold) Kandt; m. David Ronald Garrow, Sept. 11, 1968; children: Jill Renee, Mark David. B.S., La Sierra Coll. (now Loma Linda U.,), 1965. Cert. elem. tchr., Seventh-day Adventists, Calif. Elem. sch. tchr. Calif. Conf. Seventh-day Adventists, Santa Monica, 1965-68, Bellflower, 1967-68, Lynwood, 1968-69, Newbury Park, 1976-79, Oreg. Conf. Seventh-day Adventists, Roseburg, 1979—; mem. bd. edn. kindergarten - 12th grade So. Calif. Conf. Seventh-day Adventists, Glendale, 1978-79. Vol. multiple sclerosis, Calif., Oreg. Recipient Disting. Service in Curriculum award So. Calif. Conf. Seventh-day Adventists, 1968. Mem. North Pacific Union Conf. Home: 2242 Esquire Dr Roseburg OR 97470 Office: Roseburg Jr Acad 1653 NW Troost St Roseburg OR 97470

GARTMAN, MAX DILLON, minister music So. Bapt. Conv.; b. Mobile, Ala., May 3, 1938; s. Noah Christopher and Edna (Schwartzauer) G.; A.B., Samford U., 1960; M.A., U. Ala., 1962, Ph.D., 1973; m. Marcia Ann Hubbard, Aug. 31, 1962; children—Noel Don, Polly Antoinette, Paul Dillon. Minister of music Hopewell Bapt. Ch., Tuscaloosa, Ala., 1960-64, Vestavia Hills (Ala.) Bapt. Ch., 1964-69, Boyles Bapt. Ch., Tarrant, Ala., 1969-73, Raleigh Ave. Bapt. Ch., Birmingham, Ala., 1973—; head dept. fgn. langs. Samford U., Birmingham, 1973—. Soloist choir Dauphin Way Bapt. Ch., Mobile, Ala., 1953-56, Vesper Hour TV Choir, Mobile, 1953-56, Am. Ch., Nice France, 1955, Southside Bapt. Ch., Birmingham, 1958-59. Mem. So. Conf. on Lang. Teaching (chmn. 1976). Soloist record album. Home: 2368 Farley Rd Birmingham AL 35226 Office: Dept Foreign Languages Samford U Birmingham AL 35209

GARVEY, JOHN D., priest, educator, Roman Catholic Church; b. Buffalo, Dec. 3, 1919; s. John W. and Louise (Dentinger) G. B.A., Georgetown U., 1943; M.A., Woodstock Coll., 1946; S.T.D., Institut Catholique de Paris, 1968. Ordained priest Roman Cath. Ch., 1950. Asst. prof. theology St. Peter's Coll., Jersey City, 1952-60; asst. prof. religion St. Canisius Coll., Buffalo, 1960-69, assoc. prof., 1969—; adviser Buffalo Christian Life Community, 1960—. Contbr. articles to profl. jours. Mem. Coll. Theol. Soc., Cath. Theol. Soc. Am.

GARVEY, THOMAS J., clergyman, educational administrator, Roman Catholic. Pres. Sacred Heart Sch. Theology, Hales Corners, Wis. Office: Sacred Heart Sch Theology 7335 S Lovers Ln Rd Hales Corners WI 53130*

GASS, SYLVESTER FRANCIS, priest, Roman Catholic Church; b. Milw., Dec. 31, 1911; s. Jacob and Julia (Weninger) G.; B.A., St. Francis Major Sem., 1936, M.A., 1939; J.C.D., Cath. U. Am., 1942; ordained priest Roman Catholic Ch., 1939; parish worker, Milw., 1941-45; ecclesiastical notary Milw. Archdiocesan Curia, 1940-56; sec. Tribunal, Milw., 1942-56; prof. canon law and moral theology St. Francis Major Sem., 1945-47; rep. Milw., Wis. Provincial Conf., 1954-72; promoter of justice Archdiocese of Milw., 1955-61, vice-officialis, 1956-61; archiepiscopal vicar Dominican Sisters of the Perpetual Rosary, 1956-83; clergy counsellor St. Michael Hosp. Family Clinic, 1948-71, spiritual dir., 1961-71; speakers' staff Cath. family life program, Milw., 1949-72, officialis, 1961-76, vicar gen., 1969-83; papal chamberlain, 1954, domestic prelate, 1959. Mem. Canon Law Soc. Am. (pres. 1960-61), Can. Canon Law Soc. Author: Ecclesiastical Pensions, 1942. Home: 3501 S Lake Dr Milwaukee WI 53207

GAST, AARON EDWARD, minister, United Presbyterian Ch.; b. Baroda, Mich., July 22, 1927; s. Edward F. and Oral G. (Arend) G.; A.B., Wheaton (Ill.) Coll., 1950; M.Div., Princeton Theol. Sem., 1953; postgrad. Cambridge (Eng.) U., 1954; Ph.D., Edinburgh (Scotland) U., 1956; Litt.D. (hon.), Geneva Coll., Beaver, Pa., 1972; m. Beverly Shaffer, June 16, 1950; children—Gregory, Lisa, Brian. Ordained minister United Presbyn. Ch. in U.S.A., 1953; pastor chs. in Pa., 1950-60; instr. religious thought Temple U., 1960-62; dean, prof. theology Conwell Sch. Theology Temple U., Phila., 1960-68; sr. minister 1st Presbyn. Ch. in Germantown, Phila., 1968—. Moderator Phila. Presbytery, 1974, chairperson gen. council, 1975. Bd. corporators Presbyn. Ministers' Fund, 1966; v.p. Phila. Presbyn. Found., 1970-75, pres., 1976—; bd. dirs. Florence Crittendon Services, 1972—, Phila.-South Jersey chpt. NCCJ, 1962—; alumni trustee Princeton Theol. Sem., 1971-74; bd. visitors Gordon-Conwell Theol. Sem., 1973—. Mem. Alumni Assn. Princeton Theol. Sem. (pres. Phila.-Wilmington chpt. 1974-75), Internat. Platform Assn. (speakers bur. 1968—). Rotarian. Home: 2 Haddon Pl Fort Washington PA 19034 Office: 35 W Chelten Ave Philadelphia PA 19144

GATES, GARY LYNN, minister, religious organization executive, Evangelical Mennonite Church; b. Springfield, Ill., Feb. 6, 1950; s. Harold Ross and Myra Evelyn (Love) G.; m. Rebecca Lynn Zimmerman, June 5, 1971; children: Amy, Joshua, Amber. B.S., Sterling Coll., 1972; M.S., Fort Hays State Coll., 1975; M.C.M., Huntington Sch. of Christian Ministry, 1984. Ordained to ministry, Evang. Mennonite Ch., 1981; bd. dirs. Christian Edn. Evang. Mennonite Ch., Fort Wayne, Ind., 1977-80, dir. ch. extension, 1979—, asst. to pres., 1980-82, pres., 1982—. Mem. Nat. Assn. Evangs. (bd. dirs.), Greater Fort Wayne Assn. Evangs. (sec. 1981-82). Office: Evang Mennonite Ch 1420 Kerrway Ct Fort Wayne IN 46805

GATTA, JULIA MILAN, priest, Episcopal Church; b. N.Y.C., Aug. 20, 1948; s. Thomas George and Margaret Patricia (Arctander) O'B.; m. John Joseph Gatta, Jr., July 11, 1970. B.A., St. Mary's Coll., 1970; M.A., Cornell U., 1973; M.Div., Episcopal Div. Sch., 1979; Ph.D., Cornell U., 1979. Ordained priest Episcopal Ch., 1981. Intern minister Christ Ch. Cathedral, Hartford, Conn., 1979-80; curate St. Paul's Ch., Willimantic, Conn., 1980-82; asst. missioner Middlesex Area Cluster, Diocese of Conn., 1982—; faculty Sch. Deacons, Diocese of R.I., 1982—; Episcopal del. Faith and Order Commn., Nat. Council Chs., 1982—; part-time spiritual dir. Berkeley Div. Sch., Yale U., 1984—. Contbr. articles to profl. jours. Mem. Fellowship of St. John, Cath. Fellowship of Episcopal Ch. Address: 47 Fellen Rd Storrs CT 06268

GAUGER, REUEL CARL WALTER, minister, Lutheran Church-Missouri Synod; b. Milw. Nov. 25, 1931; s. Emil Carl and Ella Martha (Kasten) G.; m. Janice Cheryl Jeske, June 13, 1966; children: Timothy Lee, Benjamin, Amanda Ja'el. B.Th., Concordia Sem., Springfield, Ill., 1963. Ordained to ministry Luth. Ch., 1963. Pastor, St. Luke Ch., Olney, Tex., 1963-68, Holy Cross Ch., Lidgerwood, N.D., 1968-77, Grace-Zion-Trinity Ch., Cooperstown, N.D., 1977—; trustee Luth. Social Services, Fargo, N.D., 1976—; chmn. Div. Social Ministry, Fargo, 1978—. Trustee Lidgerwood Sch. Bd., 1973. Home: 1046 Burrell Coopertown ND 58425 Office: Grace Luth Ch Box 674 Cooperstown ND 58425

GAUGHAN, NORBERT F., bishop, Roman Catholic Church; b. Pitts., May 30, 1921; s. Thomas and Martha (Paczkowska) G. M.A., St. Vincent Coll., 1944; Ph.D., U. Pitts., 1963; LL.D. (hon.), Seton Hill Coll., 1963; D.D. (hon.), Lebanon Valley Coll., 1980. Ordained priest Roman Cath. Ch., 1945. Priest, parishes, Uniontown, Pa., and Greensburg, Pa.; mem. Chancery, 1955—; chaplain Seton Hill Coll., Greensburg, 1958-62, St. Emma Retreat House, Greensburg, 1962-84; lectr. religious studies St. Vincent Coll., 1967-77; lectr. philosophy U. Pitts., Greensburg, 1971-84; chancellor of Diocese, 1960-70, apptd. vicar gen., 1970; aux. bishop Greensburg, 1975, bishop, 1975-84; apptd. bishop Gary, Ind., 1984—; mem. bd. dels. Christian Assocs. Southwest Pa.; trustee Mount St. Mary's Coll., Emmitsburg, Md.; chmn. communication com. U.S. Cath. Conf.; mem. adminstrv. bd. Pa. Cath. Conf. Author: Shepherd's Pie, 1978. Contbr. articles to various publs. Columnist Cath. papers. Office: Diocese of Gary PO Box M-474 975 W 6th Ave Gary IN 46401

GAUTHIER, ROLAND JOSEPH, priest, Roman Catholic Church; b. Montreal, Que., Can., Oct. 2, 1915; s. Hector and Alice (Laberge) G. B.A., U. Montreal, 1936, L.Ph., 1940; diploma Gregorian Chant, Saint Benoit du Lac, Que., 1945; D.Th., U. St. Thomas, Rome, 1948. Ordained priest Roman Cath. Ch., 1940. Prof. theology Holy Cross Sem., Montreal, 1942-54; editor Cahiers Josephol St. Joseph Oratory, Montreal, 1953—, rector pilgrimage, 1956-62; prof. Josephology U. Montreal, 1958-62; gen. dir. Centre of Josephology, Montreal, 1950—. Author: La paternite de St. Joseph, 1958; L'office de St. Joseph, 1970; Ouvrage de Jean Tritheme, 1973; (with others) Joseph et Jesus, 1975. Fellow Can. Soc. Marian Studies (counsellor 1970-76); mem. Pontifical Acad. Mariology (lectr. 1954-84), N.Am. Soc. Josephology (pres. 1962—), Ibero-Am. Soc. Josephology (cons. 1957—), Cath. Theol. Soc. Am. Home: 3800 Queen Mary Rd Montreal PQ H3V 1H6 Canada Office: St Joseph Oratory 3800 Queen Mary Rd Montreal PQ H3V 1H6 Canada

GAVENTA, BEVERLY ROBERTS, religious educator, American Baptist Ch.; b. Humboldt, Tenn., Sept. 14, 1948; s. Harold Edward and Annie Margaret (Headrick) R.; m. William Carter Gaventa Jr., June 8, 1971; 1 child, Matthew. B.A., Phillips U., 1970; M.Div., Union Theol. Sem., 1973; Ph.D., Duke U., 1978; D.D., Kalamazoo Coll., 1983. Teaching asst. Duke Div. Sch., Durham, N.C., 1974-75; vis. asst. prof. Union Theol. Sem., N.Y.C., 1978; asst. prof. Colgate Rochester Div. Sch., Rochester, N.Y., 1976-79, assoc. prof. N.T., 1979—; adj. assoc. prof. U. Rochester, N.Y., 1983-84; mem. Commn. on Theology, Disciples of Christ, 1983—; trustee Union Theol. Sem., N.Y.C., 1973-85, Rochester Ctr. for Theol. Studies, 1976-84. Contbr. articles to numerous jours. Recipient Award for Theol. Scholarship and Research, Assn. Theol. Schs., 1981. Mem. Assn. Disciples Theol. Discussion, Soc. Bibl. Lit., Am. Acad. Religion, Cath. Bibl. Assn. Office: Colgate Rochester Div Sch 1100 S Goodman St Rochester NY 14620

GAVIN, JOHN ROBERT, priest, Roman Catholic Church; b. Chgo., May 3, 1922; s. Thomas Edward and Dorothy Virginia (Kenny) G. Student Chgo. Tchrs. Coll., 1940-41; A.B. Villanova U., 1945; M.A., Cath. U. Am., 1949; postgrad. in Spl. Edn., DePaul U., 1963. Ordained priest Roman Cath. Ch., 1948; cert. guidance dir., Ill. Alumni dir. St. Rita High Sch., Chgo., 1950-54; athletic dir. Mendel Cath. High Sch., Chgo., 1954-64, prin., 1972-81, devel. dir., 1981-82, alumni dir. 1972-82; prin. St. Augustine High Sch., Holland, Mich., 1964-68, Augustinian Acad., St. Louis, 1968-72; pastor Immaculate Conception Ch., St. Louis, 1982—; 1st asst. to provincial, Chgo., 1972-80; del. Internat. Chpt., Rome, 1977. Named to Cath. League Hall of Fame, 1980, Man of Yr., Men of Tolentine, 1983. Mem. Augustinian Secondary Sch. Assn. Home and Office: 3120 Lafayette Ave Saint Louis MO 63104

GAWTHROP, LARRY ALLEN, minister, American Baptist Churches in the U.S.A.; b. Richwood, W.Va., June 24, 1952; s. John Frank Jr. and Freda (Carte) G.; m. Marietta Lea Walker, June 9, 1972; children: Melissa Ann, John Lee. Student Glenville State Coll., 1970-71. Ordained to ministry Bapt. Ch., 1982. Pastor Kenney's Creek Bapt. Ch., Winona, W.Va., 1977-79, Big Union Bapt. Ch., Dille, W.Va., 1980-82, Johnstown Bapt. Ch., Ohio, 1982—. Republican. Home: 450 S Main St Johnstown OH 43031 Office: Johnstown Bapt Ch 450 S Main St Johnstown OH 43031

GAY, GEORGE ARTHUR, religion educator, minister, Associated Gospel Churches of Canada; b. Niagara Falls, Ont., Can., Apr. 13, 1916; s. Robert Marshal and Marie (Copp) G.; m. Mary Thomas Bellah, May 16, 1942; children: Robert Stephen, Lloyd Thomas. B.A., U. Toronto, 1942; B.D., Fuller Theol. Sem., 1952, Th.M., 1958; Ph.D., U. Manchester (Eng.), 1971. Ordained to ministry Associate Gospel Churches of

Can., 1942. Sec., field rep. InterVarsity Christian Fellowship, Alberta, Can., 1942-43; missionary Evang. Union S. Am., Bolivia, 1944-49; sem. prof. Latin Am. Mission, San Jose, Costa Rica, 1953-74, Fuller Theol. Sem., Pasadena, Calif., 1974—, acting dir. Hispanic Ministries, 1974-77, 82-85. Contbr. articles to religious jours. Mem. Soc. Bibl. Lit., Acad. Evangelism, Tyndale Fellowship, Inst. Bibl. Research, Hispanic Assn. for Theol. Edn. (sec.-treas. 1973—), Alberto Mottesi Evangelistic Assn. (bd. dirs.). Active YMCA, Pasadena, 1975—. Home: 1259 N Hill Ave Pasadena CA 91104 Office: Fuller Theol Sem 135 N Oakland Ave Pasadena CA 91101

GAY, RICHARD MARION, minister, Southern Baptist Convention; b. Shawnee, Okla., July 23, 1933; s. Marion Word and Bessie Ellen (Woods) G.; m. Mary Ola Sangster, Aug. 9, 1953; children: Donna Louise Gay Ware, David Loren, Dennis Lynn. B.A., Okla. Bapt. U., 1957; B.Div., Southwestern Bapt. Theol. Sem., 1961, M.Div., 1973. Ordained to gospel ministry Baptist Ch., 1957. Pastor chs. in Colo., 1961-66, Okla., 1966—, Aydelotte Bapt. Ch., Shawnee, 1984—; bd. dirs. Okla. Bapt. Conv., 1979-83; moderator Pott-Lincoln Bapt. Assn., 1978-79, Mesa Verde Bapt. Assn., 1964; mem. exec. bd. Colo. Bapt. Conv., 1965-66. Author: (booklets) Rodeo, America's Number One Sport, 1974; Witness Training Course, 1975; Christian Training Course, 1976; (children's drama) A Mission Turns Missionary. Served with U.S. Army, 1953-55. Home: PO Box 3816 Shawnee OK 74802 Office: Aydelotte Baptist Ch Route 3 Box 113 Shawnee OK 74801

GEANEY, JOHN JOSEPH, priest; Roman Catholic Church; b. Stoneham, Mass., Nov. 8, 1937; s. Denis Patrick and Hannah Mary (Barry) G. B.A., St. Paul's Sem., Washington, 1960, M.A. in Theology, 1964; M.A. in Speech, UCLA, 1968. Ordained priest Roman Catholic Ch., 1964; asst. pastor St. Paul the Apostle Ch., Los Angeles, 1964-66; campus chaplain UCLA, 1966-68; prof. communications St. Paul's Coll., Washington, 1968-75; dir. communications Archdiocese of Balt., 1975-82, dir. intercommunity telecommunications, Silver Spring, Md., 1982—, bd. dirs. com. on evangelization, 1980—. Producer radio programs Sound and Sense, Counter point: An Act of Thanksgiving, 1973; producer TV program Share the Word; producer TV spot: You Only Live Once, 1979 (recipient Clio award 1979.) Mem. N. Am. Regional Assn. World Assn. Christian Communication, Unda-USA (pres. 1978-84), Unda-Internat. (mem. exec. com. 1983—). Office: Intercommunity Telecommunications 818 Roeder Rd Silver Spring MD 20910

GEARHART, EDWIN FRANCIS, priest, Roman Catholic Church; b. Sidney, Ohio, May 25, 1946; s. Robert Milton and Marguerite Alma (Guillozet) G.; A.B., Athenaeum of Ohio, 1968, M.A., 1969, M.A. Theology, 1972, M.Div., 1973; postgrad. in Canon Law Pont. U. of St. Thomas Aquinas, 1985—. Ordained priest, 1973. Deacon Ch. of the Assumption, Mt. Healthy, Ohio, 1972-73; asso. pastor St. Matthias Ch., Forest Park, Ohio, 1973-75; faculty McAuley High Sch., Cin., 1973-75; chaplain Good Samaritan Hosp., Cin., 1975; asso. pastor Ch. of the Guardian Angels, Cin., 1975-80; faculty St. Gregory's Sem., 1976-79; chaplain Good Samaritan Hosp., Cin., 1980-81, Dayton, 1981-85. Home: North Am Coll Casa Santa Maria Via dell' Umilta 30 00187 Rome Italy

GEBHART, KEITH ANSON, minister, Church of God, Anderson, Indiana; b. Dayton, Ohio, Dec. 15, 1956; s. R. Anson and A. Sue (Christian) G.; m. Marsha Kay Williamson, Sept. 15, 1978; 1 child, Amanda Nicole. B.A., Anderson Coll., 1979; M.Div., Anderson Sch. Theology, 1984. Ordained to ministry, 1983. Assoc. pastor Alexandria Ch. of God, Ind., 1977-81; sr, pastor N.E. Ch. of God, Marion, Ind. 1981—; program com. Ind. State Ministers Fellowship, Indpls., 1983-84. Recipient Russ Whalen Christian Life award Anderson Sch. Theology, 1984. Mem. Ind. Ministerial Fellowship. Home: 1007 E Bradford St Marion IN 46952 Office: Northeast Church of God 1007 E Bradford St Marion IN 46952

GEDDE, LARRY ARTHUR, minister, American Lutheran Church; b. Wadena, Minn., Mar. 8, 1944; s. Arthur O. and Alice L. (Olson) G.; m. Evelyn Marie Guttromson, June 12, 1970; children: Erika, Adam, Sonja. B.A., Concordia Coll., Moorhead, Minn., 1970; M.Div., Luth. Theol. Sem., Columbus, Ohio, 1973; D.Min., Luther Theol. Sem., St. Paul, 1982. Ordained to ministry Am. Luth. Ch., 1973. Pastor, Watson Luth. Parish, Minn., 1973-77, Immanuel Luth. Ch., Clara City, Minn., 1979—; assoc. pastor Richland Luth. Ch., Wash., 1977-79; dir. human affairs Good News Today, Richland, 1977-79; area dir. sem. appeal Southwest Minn. dist., Am. Luth. Ch. 1980-81, mem. media ministry task force, 1982—. Publicity coordinator Garden and Pantry Truck, Southwest and Southeast Minn., 1982—. Served as chaplain Minn. Army N.G., 1977-79. Office: Box 236 Clara City MN 56222

GEER, MARY LOU, worship resources administrator, director music, Lutheran Church in America; b. Munich, Fed. Republic Germany, Nov. 12, 1947 (parents Am. citizens); d. Lewis Henry and Edna Muriel (Hall) Ribble; m. John Monroe Geer Jr., May 31, 1969. B.A. magna cum laude, Trinity U., San Antonio, 1969, post grad. 1970-71, postgrad. Old Dominion U., 1983-84; B.A. magna cum laude, Presbyn. Coll., Clinton, S.C., 1978. Cert. lay profl. ch. music Level I, Luth. Ch. in Am., 1979. Organist, Christ the King Luth. Ch., Universal City, Tex., 1966-67; Protestant Chapel, Kwajalein, Marshall Islands, 1981-82; organist St. John's Ch., Bayonne, N.J., 1973-75, organist, choir dir., Clinton, S.C., 1975-78; dir. worship resources Emmanuel Luth. Ch., Virginia Beach, Va., 1978-80, 82—; mem. profl. preparations mng. group Va. Synod, 1979-80, mem. council for ministry, 1983-85, congregation del. conv., 1983, 84; chmn. worship com. Luth. Council Tidewater-Norfolk area, Va., 1984-85. Author hymn text, 1982, instrn. booklet, 1979. Vol. supr. Army Community Services, Fort Story, Va., 1978-80; subscribing mem. Community Orch., Virginia Beach, 1982—. Recipient scholarships Va. Synod Worship Com. Nat. Confs., 1983, 84. Mem. Am. Guild Organists, Choristers Guild, Liturg. Conf., Hymn Soc. Am., Am. Recorder Soc., Mortar Bd., Mu Phi Epsilon, Sigma Delta Pi, Pi Delta Phi, Alpha Chi. Club: Fort Story Women's Club (pres. 1979-80). Home: 509 Boswell Ct Virginia Beach VA 23452 Office: Emmanuel Luth Ch 301 Lynn Shores Dr Virginia Beach VA 23452

GEHANT, MARILYN, minister, Church of God. Convener, Evanston Ecumenical Action Council, Ill. Office: PO Box 1382 Evanston IL 60204*

GEIST, ERNEST EDWARD, minister, Nat. Council Community Chs.; b. Zanesville, Ohio, Dec. 8, 1938; s. Ernest Walter and Erma C. (Shrake) G.; B.B.A., Stanton U., 1969; B. Bible Philosophy, Am. Bible Inst., 1967, M. Bible Philosophy, 1969, D.D., 1972; m. Nancy Mace Simpson, Mar. 27, 1981; 1 son, Daniel; children by previous marriage: Ernest Edwin, Douglas Alan, Michelle Dawn. Ordained to ministry, 1965; pastor Christ Meth. Ch., Tampa, Fla., 1963, Hernando (Fla.) Meth. Ch., 1964-65, Hartford Community Chs., 1966-70, Olive Chapel United Ch. of Christ, 1970-71; sr. pastor New Carlisle (Ind.) Community Ch., 1970—; v.p. United Religious Community St. Joseph County, 1972-74; chaplain Ind. Nat. Guard Res., 1970—; moderator ch. relations commn. Internat. Council Community Chs. Mem. adv. bd. St. Joseph County Planned Parenthood Assn., 1975—; juvenile officer Town of New Carlisle, 1972-76. Recipient award of Merit, Olive Chapel United Ch. Christ, New Carlisle, 1971. Mem. Acad. Parish Clergy, St. Joseph County Clergy Assn. Home: 106 West Chestnut St New Carlisle IN 46552 Office: 201 W Michigan St New Carlisle IN 46552

GELDMACHER, JOAN ELIZABETH, church administrator, Presbyterian Church; b. N.Y.C., Aug. 1, 1931; d. Henry William and Hazel Grace (Longstreet) Meyer; children: Cheryl, Phyllis, Dolores, David, James. B.S. in Edn., Elmira Coll., 1969. Dir. released time religious edn. Council of Chs., Elmira, N.Y., 1963-68, exec. dir., 1979—; nursing asst. St. Joseph's Hosp., Elmira, 1975—. Mem. Elmira City Council, 1975; policy council mem. Head Start Day Care, 1979—; bd. dirs. Family Support Project, Elmira, 1980—; mem. Southern Tier Regional Planning and Devel. Bd., 1975-78; active Meals on Wheels. Home: 621 Newton St Elmira NY 14904 Office: Council of Churches 330 W Church St Elmira NY 14904

GELINEAU, LOUIS EDWARD, bishop, Roman Catholic Church; b. Burlington, Vt., May 3, 1928; s. Leon and Juliette (Baribault) G.; student St. Michael's Coll., 1946-48; B.A., Ph.B., St. Paul's U., Ottawa, Ont., Can., 1950, L.S.T., 1954; Licentiate Canon Law, Catholic U. Am., 1959; D.Religious Edn., Providence Coll., 1972. Ordained priest Roman Catholic Ch., 1954, consecrated bishop, 1971; asst. chancellor diocese of Burlington, 1959-61, chancellor, 1961-71, vicar gen., 1968-71; bishop diocese of Providence, 1971—. Office: Cathedral Sq Providence RI 02903

GEMIGNANI, MICHAEL, priest, Episcopal Church; b. Balt., 1938. A.B., U. Rochester, 1962; M.S., Ph.D., U. Notre Dame, 1965; J.D., Ind. U., 1980. Ordained to priest Episcopal ch., 1973. Vicar, St. Franics-in-the-Fields, Zionsville, Ind., 1974-79; mem. governing council Ind. Office for Campus Ministries, Episcopal Ch., 1974—, pres., 1983—; interim pastor-in-charge Grace Ch., Muncie, Ind., 1983-84; Episcopal chaplain, dean scis. and humanities Ball State U., Muncie, 1981—. Home: 3556 Johnson Circle Muncie IN 47304 Office: Ball State U NQ 112 Muncie IN 47306

GENADER, ANN MARIE, church musician, Roman Catholic; teacher; b. West Milford, N.J., May 28, 1932; d. Arthur John and Verina Agnes (Mathews) G. B.S., Jersey City State Coll., 1954; M.A., William Paterson Coll., 1969. Church organist St. Joseph's Cath. Ch., West Milford, 1947-67, Our lady Queen of Peace Cath. Ch., West Milford, 1960-84, Episcopal Ch. of Incarnation, West Milford, 1977—. Inst. West Milford Bd. Edn., 1963—. Avocation: free-lance writer for newspapers, mags. Home: 1681 Union Valley Rd West Milford NJ 07480

GENDRON, ODORE JOSEPH, bishop, Roman Catholic Church; b. Manchester, N.H., Sept. 13, 1921; s. Francis and Valida (Rouleau) G.; student U. Ottawa, 1942-47. Ordained priest Roman Catholic Ch., 1947; asso. pastor Angel Guardian Ch., Berlin, N.H., 1947-52, Sacred Heart Ch., Lebanon, N.H., 1952-60, St. Louis Ch., Nashua, 1962-65; pastor Our Lady of Lourdes Ch., Pittsfield, 1965-67, St. Augustine Ch., Manchester, 1967-71; became monsignor, Manchester, 1970; episcopal vicar for religious, Manchester, 1972-74, episcopal vicar for clergy, from 1974; bishop Diocese of Manchester, 1975—. Home: 67 William St Manchester NH 03102 Office: Diocese of Manchester 153 Ash St Manchester NH 03105

GENEST, JEAN-BAPTISTE, priest, Roman Catholic Church; b. Montréal, Que., Can., Oct. 2, 1927; s. Theodore and Alice (Leclerc) G.; Lic. in Theology, Grand Séminaire, 1954; D.E.N.S., U. Montréal, 1972. Joined Order of St. Viator, Roman Cath. Ch., 1949, ordained priest Roman Cath. Ch., 1954. Tchr. biology Ecole Paul-Gerin-Lajoie, Outremont, Que., 1954-85; pastoral minister parish youth, Montreal, 1954-85; bd. dirs. Camp DèEcologie St. Viateur, Port-Au-Saumon, Que., 1960-85. Mem. Assn. des Camps du Que., Société de Botanique, Ambulancier St-Jean. Home: 450 Ave Querbes Outremont PQ H2V 3W5 Canada

GENGE, MARK, bishop; b. St. John's Nfld., Can., Mar. 18, 1927; s. Lambert and Lily Beatrice (Hodge) G.; m. Maxine Clara Major, Aug. 5, 1959; children: Angela, Stephanie, Michele, Margot, Christine. L.T.H., Queen's Coll. and Meml. U., 1951; M.A., U. Durham (Eng.), 1955. Ordained deacon, 1951, ordained priest, 1952, ordained bishop, 1976. Vice prin. Queen's Coll., 1955-57; curate St. Mary's Parish, St. John's, 1957-59, other chs., 1959-75; bishop, Gander, Nfld., Can., 1976—. Office: 34 Fraser Rd Gander NF A1V 2E7 Canada

GENOVESI, VINCENT JOSEPH, priest, Roman Catholic Church; b. Phila., Oct. 9, 1938; s. Dominic Vincent and Ruth Lillian (Savarese) G. B.A. in Sociology, Fordham U., 1962, M.A. in Philosophy, 1966; M. Div., Woodstock Coll., 1969; Ph.D. in Christian Ethics, Emory U., 1973. Joined Soc. Jesus; ordained priest Roman Cath. Ch., 1969. Assoc. prof. St. Joseph's U., Phila., 1973—. Author: Expectant Creativity, 1982. Contbr. articles to religious jours. Mem. Soc. Christian Ethics, Hastings Inst. Soc. Ethics and Life Sci., Cath. Theol. Soc. Am. Democrat. Home: St Joseph's U Philadelphia PA 19131

GENTILE, ROBERT JACOB, minister, United Meth. Ch.; b. Buffalo, June 16, 1925; s. Zachariah Michael and Betty A. (Petschke) G.; A.B., Brothers Coll., 1950; M.Div., Drew U., 1953, D.Min., 1977; M.A. in Psychology, Fairleigh Dickinson U., 1975; m. Alice O. Cappuccino, June 12, 1949; children—Kathi, Elizabeth, Carol, Dorothy, David. Ordained to ministry, 1952; pastor Scotch Plains (N.J.) United Meth. Ch., 1947-49, Everittstown-Pattenburg United Meth. Ch., Everittstown, N.J., 1949-53; chaplain USN, 1953-57; pastor Hoboken (N.J.) United Meth. Ch., 1957-60, Orange (N.J.) United Meth. Ch., 1960-63, New Dover United Meth. Ch., Edison, N.J., 1963-67, Rutherford (N.J.) United Meth. Ch., 1967-71, Boonton (N.J.) United Meth. Ch., from 1971; now pastor Colesville United Meth. Ch., Boonton. Exec. dir. Inst. Personal and Family Relations, 1974—; pres., exec. dir. Am. Inst. Human Relations; adj. prof. sociology Fairleigh Dickinson U., Rutherford, N.J., 1967-72. Commr. Housing Authority, Boonton, N.J., 1973—; chmn. pastoral care dept., Riverside Hospice; pres. Boonton Area Council Social Agencies, 1976—. Recipient Liberty Bell award Bergen County Bar Assn., 1971; Meritorious Service award Civil Air Patrol, 1971. Mem. Am. Assn. Marriage and Family Counselors, Nat. Council on Family Relations. Lodge: Boonton Rotary. Home: RD 5 Box 1017 Sussex NJ 07461 Office: 307 Main St Boonton NJ 07005

GENTLE, JIMMIE LYNN, minister, Christian Ch. (Disciples of Christ); b. Prosper, Tex., Mar. 24, 1936; s. Roscoe Colkin and Lucille (Coplen) G.; student Tex. A. and M. Coll., 1954-55; AB, Phillips U., 1959; M.Div., Grad. Sem., Enid, Okla., 1962, Ph.D., 1973; m. Connie Kay Roberts, June 14, 1959; children—Stephen, Donald, David. Ordained to ministry, 1959; asso. minister Crown Heights Christian Ch., Oklahoma City, 1962-63; pastor First Christian Ch., Seminole, Okla., 1963-64, Newkirk, Okla., 1964-66; sr. minister First Christian Ch., Alva, Okla., 1966-74, Phoenix Central Christian Ch., 1974—. Pres. Maricopa Ecumenical Council, 1976—; moderator Christian Ch. in Okla., 1973-74; mem. gen. bd. Christian Ch. (Disciples of Christ), 1973—; bd. dirs. Ariz. Ecumenical Council, 1974—, sec., 1977; sec. bd. mgrs. Christian Ch. in Ariz., 1977; chmn. Central Corridor Chs., 1977. Mem. Alva City Council, 1971-74; mem. central com. Okla. Democratic party, 1970-74, county chmn., 1972-74; mem. adv. bd. Salvation Army, 1962—. Mem. Council Christian Unity. Author: Programmed Guide to Increasing Church Attendance; contbr. articles to religious periodicals. Home: 4140 W Denton Lane Phoenix AZ 85019 Office: 18 E Roanoke St Phoenix AZ 85004

GENTRY, GENE ALLEN, minister, American Baptist Churches in the U.S.A.; b. Twin Falls, Idaho, Dec. 30, 1938; s. Harold Malachai and Rosalyn Ida (Brewer) G.; m. Margaret Ann Crowley, June 11, 1960; children: Patricia Janeen, Suella Ruth, Wayne Thomas, Steven Ward. B.S. in Agr., U. Idaho, 1961; M.S. in Agr., U. Md. Coll., 1966; M.Div., Am. Bapt. Sem. West, 1969. Ordained to the ministry Am. Bapt. Chs. in U.S.A., 1969. Youth minister First Bapt. Ch., South Pasadena, Calif., 1967-69; missionary Bd. Internat. Ministries, Valley Forge, Pa., 1969-83; missionary, pastor Bd. Nat. Ministries, Valley Forge, 1983—; pres. World Mission Support Com., Sierra, Nev., 1983—; v.p. Friends of Citizens Under Stress, Carson City, Nev., 1983—; sec. Ministerial Assn., Carson City, 1984—. Served to 1st lt. U.S. Army, 1961-63. Home: 5340 Snyder Ave Carson City NV 89701 Office: Stewart Community Bapt Ch 5340 Snyder Ave Carson City NV 89701

GENTRY, MICHAEL RAY, minister, Church of the Nazarene; b. El Reno, Okla., Apr. 8, 1951; s. Emmanuel Howard and Leona Drende (Morris) G.; m. Diana Kay Sharp; children: Penelope Kaye, Amy Michelle, Andrew Michael. A.B. in Religion, Bethany Nazarene Coll., 1973; Th.B., Freelandia Inst., 1982, Th.M., 1985. Ordained to ministry Ch. of Nazarene, 1976. Dir. bus. ministry Grace Ch. of Nazarene, Kansas City, Mo., 1973-74; pastor First Ch. of Nazarene, Okemah, Okla., 1974-77, Ch. of Nazarene, Republic, Mo., 1977-79, First Ch. of Nazarene, Centralia, Ill., 1979—; chaplain coordinator Okfuskee County Hosp., Okemah, 1977-79; founder, pres. Def. Ministries, Centralia, 1981-83; Christian life chmn. Mt. Vernon Zone, Springfield, Ill., 1983-85; pres. Centralia Area Ministerial Alliance, 1982-83. Asst. supr. Shaklee, Centralia, 1984—. Author: Christian Holiness Pulpit Digest, 1979, Defender of the Faith, 1981, The Preacher's Mag., 1985. Coordinator Boy Scouts Am., Centralia, 1983—, trainer Crooked Creek Dist., Belleville, Ill., 1984—; sec. Centralia Area PTA Council, 1984—. Mem. Bonnie Holiness Camp Assn. Democrat. Lodge: Lions (dir. Centralia, 1985-86). Avocations: piano and accordian; racquetball; stamps; motivational-entertainment speaker. Home: 1206 W 4th St Centralia IL 62801 Office: First Ch of Nazarene 1206 W 4th St Centralia IL 62801

GEORGE, EWART BALFOUR, assistant minister, Christian Church (Disciples of Christ); b. London, Ont., Can., Apr. 20, 1903; s. Albert James and Frances Eliza (Miller) G.; m. Lillian Margaret Etchells, July 18, 1936 (dec. May 1979). Assoc., Can. Coll. Organists, 1926; D.Th., Chatham Hill U., 1955; LL.D., St. Andrew's U., Eng., 1954; Ph.D. (hon.), 1968. Ordained to ministry Free Protestant Episcopal Ch., 1977. Minister of music United Ch., London, 1930-32, Ch. of Christ, London, 1932-39, asst. pastor, minister music, 1939—; prin. Philathea Sem., London, 1946—, dir., trustee, 1946—. Author: The Steam Age in Western Ontario, 1977. Editor-in-chief Philathea Jour., 1953-72. Fellow Am. Internat. Acad.; mem. High Acad. Letters, Eloy Alfaro Found., Gideons Internat (Can. trustee 1942-46). Club: Can. Progress (London, Ont.) (dir. 1960-84). Home: 777 Central Ave London ON N5W 3R1 Canada Office: Philathea Sem 430 Elizabeth St London ON N5W 3R7 Canada

GEORGE, RICHMOND CALVERT, JR., minister, Christian M.E. Ch.; b. Carlton, Miss., Sept. 10, 1934; s. Richmond Calvert and Irene (Baskin) G.; B.A., Lane Coll., Jackson, Tenn., 1972; m. Eunice Hughlett, Nov. 30, 1958; children—Mary Jean, Irene, Yvette, Adrianne. Ordained to ministry, 1960; pastor chs., Miss. and Tenn., 1960-70; dist. supt., Memphis, 1970—. Del. gen. conf. Christian M.E. Ch.; sec. of staff 1st Episc. Dist. Christian M.E. Ch.; sec. Elders Council. Trustee, Lane Coll.; aide to mayor Shelby County. Named hon. dep. sheriff Shelby County, 1976. Mem. NAACP. Home: 1802 Parkway Terr Memphis TN 38114 Office: PO Box 14843 Memphis TN 38114

GEORGE, ROY KENNETH, minister, Assemblies of God; b. Haskell, Tex., Sept. 23, 1934; s. Roy F. and Jimalee (Scott) G.; m. Patsy Sue George, May 14, 1955; children: Janis Sue, Cheryl Anne. Ordained to ministry Assemblies of God, 1959. Evangelist, U.S., Africa, Europe, Asia, 1954-63; pastor Highland Assembly of God, Bakersfield, Calif., 1964-65, 1st Assembly of God, Carlsbad, N.Mex., 1966-67, Seminary South Ch., Ft. Worth, 1968-73, Christian Center, Ashland, Oreg., 1974-75, First Family Ch., Albuquerque, 1975—. Vice pres. Rogue Valley Nat. Assn. Evangelicals, 1974-75; pres. Pentecostal Fellowship Greater Albuquerque, 1975-76, presbyter West Central Sect., 1976-81; state exec. presbyter Assemblies of God N.Mex., 1976—; asst. dist. supt. N.Mex. Dist. Assemblies of God, 1981—, mem. Gen. Presbytery, 1981—; bd. regents Southwestern Assemblies of God Coll. at Waxahachie, Tex., 1981—; 2d exec. officer N.Mex. Ch. Builders Loan Assn., 1981—; broadcaster religious radio and TV programs, most recent being Moments with the Master, Sta. KKIM, Albuquerque, 1975—; chaplain Civitan Club Fort Worth South, 1969-73. Mem. Albuquerque Ministerial Assn., Greater Albuquerque Pentecostal Fellowship. Lodge: Kiwanis (pres. 1982-83). Contbr. articles to ch. publs. Home: 13321 Tierra Montanosa NE Albuquerque NM 87112 Office: 4701 Wyoming Blvd NE NE Albuquerque NM 87111

GERARD, JOSEPH EUGENE, minister, General Association of Regular Baptist Churches; b. Mishawaka, Ind., July 31, 1944; s. Joseph and Maxine (LaRue) G.; m. Alice Lynn Martindill, Sept. 3, 1964; children: David, Pamela, Cheri, Michael. B.A., Faith Baptist Bible Coll., 1973; postgrad. Oakland Community Coll., Pontiac, Mich., 1968, Grace Theol. Sem., Winona Lake, Ind., 1974, Moody Bible Inst., Chap., 1985. Ordained to ministry Bapt. Ch., 1975. Minister of edn. Urbandale Bapt. Ch., Iowa, 1971-72; pastor Bluffton Bapt. Ch., Ind., 1973-74, Calvary Bapt. Ch., Adrian, Mo., 1974-77, Portage Ave. Bapt. Ch., Ind., 1977—; Sunday sch. tchr., supt., youth sponsor, musical evangelist various chs. Served to capt. U.S. Army, 1962-73, Vietnam. Decorated Bronze Star with oak leaf cluster, Purple Heart, Air medal with two clusters. Home: 6601 Portage Ave Portage IN 46368 Office: Portage Ave Baptist Ch 6605 Portage Ave Portage IN 46368

GERBER, EUGENE J., bishop, Roman Catholic Church. Bishop of Wichita, 1982—. Office: 424 N Broadway Wichita KS 67202*

GERDES, NEIL WAYNE, librarian, Unitarian Universalist Assn.; b. Moline, Ill., Oct. 19, 1943; s. John Edward and Della Marie (Ferguson) G.; A.B., U. Ill., 1965; B.D., Harvard, 1968; M.A., Columbia, 1971; M.A. in L.S., U. Chgo., 1975. Ordained Unitarian Universalist Assn., 1975; copy chief Little, Brown, 1968-69; instr. Tuskegee Inst., 1969-71; library asst., Augustana Coll., 1972-73; editorial asst. Library Quar., 1973-74; librarian Meadville Theol. Sch., Chgo., 1973—; library program dir. Chgo. Cluster Theol. Schs., 1977-80; librarian, prof. Chgo. Theol. Sem., 1980—; v.p. Hyde Park Kenwood Interfaith Council, 1980—. Mem. ALA, Chgo. Area, Am. theol. library assns., Phi Beta Kappa. Office: 5757 S University Ave Chicago IL 60637

GERETY, PETER LEO, archbishop, Roman Catholic Ch.; b. Shelton, Conn., July 19, 1912; s. Peter Leo and Charlotte (Daly) G.; student St. Thomas Sem., Bloomfield, Conn., 1934, Seminaire St. Sulpice, Paris, France, 1939. Ordained priest Roman Catholic Ch., 1939; consecrated bishop, 1966; asst. pastor New Haven, 1939-42; pastor, 1956-66; dir. Blessed Martin dePorres Interracial Center, 1942-56; coadjutor bishop diocese Portland, Me., 1966-69, apostolic adminstr., 1967-74, bishop, 1969-74; archbishop of Newark, 1974—. Address: 31 Mulberry St Newark NJ 07102

GERHARDT, RANDY GENE, religious organization official, Independent Churches of America; b. Quincy, Ill., Aug. 13, 1961; s. Robert Gene and Lucille Irene (Gooding) G.; m. Kathleen Julie Schneider, Aug. 18, 1984. Diploma Pastoral Ministry, Grand Rapids Sch. Bible and Music, 1982, Diploma of Missions, 1982, Tchr.'s diploma, 1982. Dir. inner city boy's camp Mel Trotter Ministries, Grand Rapids, Mich., 1981-82, youth and camp dir., 1982—; interim pastor Huggard Bible Ch., Sand Lake, Mich., summer 1981; camp program dir. Camp Mel Tro Mi, Belding, Mich., 1982, camp dir., 1983—. Advisor Grand Rapids Inner City Youth Task Force Com., 1983-84, Grand Rapids Met. Youth Service Com., 1984—; vol. ARC, Grand Rapids, 1984—. Mem. Internat. Christian Edn. Assn., Christian Camping Internat. Avocations: computer technology; scuba diving; swimming. Home: 6644 Lincoln Lake Ave Belding MI 48809 Office: Mel Trotter Ministries 225 Commerce SW Grand Rapids MI 49503

GERIKE, GERHARDT JOHN CHARLES, pastor, Lutheran Church-Missouri Synod; b. Tripp, S.D., May 1, 1911; s. Henry Fred W. and Clara Wilhelmine (Bornhoeft) G.; grad. St. Paul's Jr. Coll., Concordia, Mo., 1931; B.D., Concordia Sem., St. Louis, 1956, M.Div., 1971; B.A., Valparaiso (Ind.) U., 1947; m. Letta Louise Fulton, May 3, 1936; children: Gloria Gerike Vogel, Paula Gerike Jolley, Carol Gerike Seyfert. Ordained to ministry, 1936. Pastor chs., N.D., Ill. Minn., Iowa, Mo., 1936-41, 44-72; mil. chaplain, 1943-45; pastor dual parish, Flat River, Bonne Terre, Mo., 1972-76; pastor Immanuel Luth. Ch., Lone Rock, Iowa, 1976-80, 1st English Luth. Ch., Spring Valley, Mo., 1981, Redeemer Luth. Ch., Potosi, Mo., 1982—, also St. John Luth. Ch., Bismarck, Mo. Mem. bd. parish edn. N.D.-Mont. Dist.; bd. dirs. Minn. and Iowa Dist. West; mem. mission bd. Mo. Dist.; counselor of Iowa and Mo. circuit, Luth. Laymen's Laymens League, Luth. Women's Missionary League, Youth League. Mem. Nat. Honor Soc. Author sermons and radio sermons. Home and Office: 321 Cedar Dr Potosi MO 63664

GERKEN, ERWIN AUGUST, minister, Lutheran Church-Missouri Synod; b. Monroeville, Ind., June 29, 1921; s. August Carl and Alma Wilhelmina (Kramer) G.; m. Willene Elsie Kerkman, Aug. 17, 1946; children: Norman Paul, Daniel John, Charles Erwin, Douglas James. B.A., Concordia Sem., St. Louis, 1943, B.D., 1945, M.Div., 1971; D.Ministry, Pacific Luth. Coll., Berkeley, Calif., 1982. Ordained to ministry Luth. Ch., 1945. Pastor, Pilgrim Luth. Ch., Beaverton, Oreg., 1945-50; pastor Immanuel Luth. Ch., Puyallup, Wash., 1950—; circuit counselor N.W. dist. Luth. Ch.-Mo. Synod, Puyallup, 1953-67, mem. mission com., Portland, Oreg., 1973—, pres. Puget Sound Pastoral Conf., 1980—; bd. regents Concordia Coll., Portland, 1967-73, 1981—; bd. dirs. Pierce County Luth. Welfare Soc., Tacoma, 1969—. Author: From Professionalism to Enabling, 1982. Founder, chmn. Puyallup Family Counseling Service, 1968-72; bd. dirs. Good Samaritan Hosp., Puyallup, 1972—, chmn., 1974, 75, 80, 81, 82, 84—. Lodge: Rotary (pres. 1964, Rotarian of Yr. 1964). Home: 902 18th St SW Puyallup WA 98371 Office: Immanuel Luth Ch 720 W Main Puyallip WA 98371

GERMOVNIK, FRANCIS, priest, Roman Catholic Ch.; b. Vodice, Slovenija, Sept. 27, 1915; s. Joseph and Frances (Kosec) G.; came to U.S., 1946, naturalized, 1952; J.C.D., Angelicum, Rome, 1945; B.S. in L.S., Our Lady of the Lake Coll., San Antonio, 1950; M.A. in L.S., Rosary Coll., River Forest, Ill., 1967. Joined Vincentians (Congregation of the Missions) Roman Catholic Ch., 1935, ordained priest, 1941; librarian, prof. Canon law St. John's Sem., San Antonio, 1946-52, Assumption Sem., San Antonio, 1952-54, St. Mary's Sem., Perryville, Mo., 1954-64, De Andreis Sem., Lemont, Ill., 1964-84, St. Thomas Theol. Sem., Denver, 1984—. Mem. Canon Law Soc. Am., Cath. Library Assn. Contbr. articles to profl. jours. Address: 1300 S Steele St Denver CO 80210

GERRISH, BRIAN ALBERT See *Who's Who in America*, 43rd edition.

GERVAIS, MARCEL ANDRE See *Who's Who in America*, 43rd edition.

GESCHWINDT, DONALD FREDERICK, minister, United Ch. of Christ; b. Shoemakersville, Pa., Mar. 28, 1924; s. Morris Clayton and Katie Mae (Stitzel) G.; B.A., Franklin and Marshall Coll., Lancaster, Pa., 1952; B.D., Lancaster Theol. Sem., 1955; m. Betty D. Greenawalt, Dec. 27, 1952; children: Deborah Ann, Karl Donald. Mem. Cocalico Area Ministerium. Home: Route 1 Reinholds PA 17569

GESLER, ALBERT URBAN, JR., minister, Lutheran Church in America; b. New Eagle, Pa., Jan. 9, 1935; s. Albert Urban and Nora Jane (Goodman) G.; student Behrend Coll., 1952-54; A.B., Thiel Coll., 1956; B.D., Luth. Theol. Sem. Phila., 1959; m. Edwina Mary Emilia Hem, Feb. 6, 1960; children: Albert, Carol. Ordained to ministry Luth. Ch. in Am., 1959; pastor Christ Luth. Ch., Lawrence Park, Erie, Pa., 1959-74, Our Saviors Luth. Ch. Kearsarge, Erie, 1974—, Trinity Luth. Ch., McKean, Pa., 1979—; dean, Erie dist. Luth. Ch. Am.; pres. bd. Luth. Home for Aged, 1968-74, chmn. bldg. com., 1973—; mem. sch. bd. Luther Meml. Learning Ctr., 1974—; pres. bd. dirs. Holy Trinity Community Ctr., 1979—. Vice pres. East Erie Suburban Recreation Conservation Authority, 1971—; mem. Lawrence Park Recreation Planning Com., 1963—. Mem. Erie Luth Pastors Assn., Luth Soc. Worship, Music and the Arts. Home: 809 Tyndall Ave Erie PA 16511 Office: 5312 Peach St Erie PA 16509

GESNER, LLOYD ROSCOE, priest, religious educator, Anglican Church of Canada, educator; b. Digby, N.S., Can., Jan. 17, 1928; s. DeLancey Sneyden and Marion Margaret (Hersey) G.; m. Muriel May Ferguson, July 11, 1953; children: Stephen Lloyd, Susan Ferguson. Diploma in Edn., N.S. Tchrs. Coll., 1946; B.A., Dalhousie U., 1951; Ed.M. in Ednl. Adminstrn., U. Toronto, 1973, Ed.D. in Ednl. Adminstrn., 1982. Ordained deacon Anglican Ch. of Can., 1961, priest, 1963. Headmaster, King's Coll. Sch., Windsor, N.S., 1954-60; housemaster St. Andrew's Coll., Aurora, Ont., 1961-63; dean students, registrar U. Kings Coll., Halifax, N.S., 1963-64; diocesan univ. chaplain, N.S., 1963-64; asst. headmaster, dir. studies, Breck Sch., Mpls, 1964-66; asst. St. Mary's Episcopal Ch., St. Paul, 1964-66; headmaster St. Mary's Hall, Faribault, Minn., 1966-71; canon residentiary Cathedral of Our Merciful Savior, 1968-71; asst. St. Cuthbert's Anglican Ch., Toronto, 1971-72; headmaster Glen Oak Sch., Gates Mills, Ohio, 1972-77; vestryman St. Christopher's-by-the-River, Gates Mills, 1975-77; headmaster Grace-St. Luke's Episc. Sch., Memphis, 1977-79; locum St. James Anglican Ch., Caldeon East, Ont., 1979-80; hon. asst. St. Theodore's Anglican Ch., Willowdale, Ont., 1981—; exec. dir. Coordinating Com. Theol. Edn. in Can., 1980—; mem. Chaplaincy Com. Diocese of N.S., 1963-64; assoc. chmn. div. community relations, Diocese of Minn., 1966-67; trustee Univ. Episc. Ctr., U. Minn., 1966-67; mem. dept. communications Diocese of Minn., 1970-71, Bishop and council, 1968-72; mem. Diocesan Schs. Commn. Diocese of Tenn., 1977-79; mem. Council for Religion in Ind. Schs., 1974-79, Nat. Assn. Episc. Schs., 1964-76. Active Boy Scouts Assn. Can., 1946-60, Boy Scouts Am., 1977-79, Girl Scouts U.S., 1966-71, Mpls. Art Inst., 1966-71, Walker Art Centre, 1966-71; bd. dirs. Cleve. Ballet Co., 1974-76; trustee Payzant Meml. Hosp. Sch. Nursing, 1955-60; bd. overseers vis. coom. Case Western Res. U., 1972-77, others. Served with Royal Can. Army, 1948-51, capt. Res. ret. Fellow U. Toronto, 1961, 80, Inst. for Devel. Ednl. Activities, 1964, Met. Toronto Schs., 1971-72. Mem. Nat. Assn. Schs., Ind. Schs. Assn. of Central States, Can. Headmasters Assn. Clubs: Chagrin Valley Hunt (Gates Mills); Memphis Country. Lodges: Masons, Gyro, Lions (bd. dirs. Faribault chpt. 1968-70). Home: 63 Risebrough Ave Willowdale ON M2M 2E2 Canada (416) 226-4210 Office: Coordinating Com Theol Edn in Can 60 Saint Clair Ave E Suite 504 Toronto ON M4T 1N5 Canada (416) 921-4860

GETHERS, LEROY, Bishop Reformed Methodist Union Episcopal Church, Charleston, S.C. Office: Reformed Methodist Union Episcopal Ch 1136 Brody Ave Charleston SC 29407*

GEWIRTZ, LEONARD BENJAMIN, rabbi, Orthodox Jewish Congregations; b. N.Y.C., Jan. 25, 1918; s. Henry and Leah Peshe (Greenberg) G.; m. Gladys Sarah Kerstein, Nov. 21, 1948; children: Isaac Meir, Joseph Jacob. B.S. cum laude, CCNY, 1941; grad. Hebrew Theol. Coll., 1945; postgrad. Dropsie Coll., 1952. Ordained rabbi, 1945. Supply rabbi Beth Shalom Congregation, Danville, Ill., 1943-45; rabbi Congregation Oir Chodosh, Chgo., 1945-47; Congregation Adas Kodesh Shel Emeth, Wilmington, Del., 1947—; dir. campus activities Hillel U. Del., Newark, 1960-63; instr. Gratz Hebrew High Sch., Wilmington, 1971-83; founder, speaker WDEL weekly radio program Rabbi Speaks, 1950—; bd. govs. Jewish Community Ctr. Author: Authentic Jew & His Judaism, 1961; Authentic Jewish Living, 1977; Jewish Spirituality: Hope and Redemption, 1985. Pres. Del. Citizens Conf. Social Work, Wilmington, 1954-56; bd. govs. Del. Mental Health Assn., 1967-71. Recipient 40 Years Continuous Service award Phila. Bd. Rabbis, 1984, Cert. Honor B'nai B'rith. Mem. ACLU, Pacem En Terris, Rabbinic Assn. Del. (pres. 1967-69, 75-77, 80-82), Rabbinical Council Am. (chmn. social actions 1966-68, exec. com. 1960-64), Phila. Bd. Rabbis, Jewish Fedn. (bd. govs.). Lodge: B'nai B'rith. Home: 127 W 37th St Wilmington DE 19802 Office: Adas Kodesh Shel Emeth Synagogue Washington Blvd and Torah Way Wilmington DE 19802

GEYER, EDWARD BLAINE, JR., priest, Episcopal Church; b. N.Y.C., Aug. 23, 1929; s. Edward Blaine and Ethyl Frances (Hazleton) G.; m. Laura E. Williams, Apr. 8, 1967; children: Edward Blaine, Ruth Anne. A.B., NYU, 1954; S.T.B. cum laude, Phila. Div. Sch., 1958; D.D. (hon.), St. Paul's Coll., 1983. Ordained priest Episcopal Ch., 1958. Rector, St. Luke's Ch., New Haven, 1960-68, St. Peter's Ch., Bennington, Vt., 1968-72, Good Shepherd Ch., Hartford, Conn., 1972-80; exec. adminstrs. Asst. to Presiding Bishop, The Episcopal Ch., N.Y.C., 1980-83; exec. for nat. mission Episcopal Ch., N.Y.C., 1984—. Lodge: Rotary. Office: Episcopal Church Center 815 2d Ave New York NY 10017

GFELLERS, MAYBREY EVELYN SHELTON, lay ch. worker, Ch. of God-Anderson, Ind.; b. Greene County, Tenn., Aug. 27, 1928; d. Chapelle Robert and Martha Jane (Shelton) Shelton; student E. Tenn. State U., 1968—; m. Charles Doyle Gfellers, June 10, 1946; children—Charles C., Neil Reed. Sunday sch. tchr. Ch. of God-Anderson, Ind., 1957-74; pres. Horse Creek Ch. of God Missionary Soc., Chuckey, Tenn., 1958-68; mem. Tenn. Bd. Kingdom Builders and Home Missions, 1972—; state stewardship dir. E. Tenn. Missionary Soc., 1966-72, pres., 1972—, mem. state exec. council, 1975—; mem. nat. bd. Women's Missionary Soc., 1972—. Supr. partners program Greene Valley Devel. Center, Greeneville, Tenn., 1973—. Mem. First Tenn.-Va. Dist. Adv. Council Aging, 1973—. Home: Route 3 Chuckey TN 37641 Office: Greene Valley Devel Center Greeneville TN 37743

GIAMPETRO, ANITA MARIE, nun, Roman Cath. Ch.; b. Dunbar, Pa., Sept. 27, 1916; d. Peter and Maria (Traficanti) G.; B.S., Fordham U., 1956; M.Ed., St. Louis U., 1958. Joined Apostles of Sacred Heart of Jesus, 1940; tchr. St. Michael Sch., New Haven, 1942-49, prin., 1950-51; prin. and superior St. Vitus Sch., New Castle, Pa., 1951-55, Cor Jesu Acad., St. Louis, 1955-68; provincial Mt. Sacred Heart, New Haven, 1968—. Author: Pray Always, 1976. Home: 265 Benham St Hamden CT 06514

GIBB, CEDRIC EARL, minister, religious organization executive, American Lutheran Church; b. Paraiso, Canal Zone, Sept. 8, 1945; s. Cedric Ivanhoe Gibb and Leonora Alfreda (Barett) Cyrus; m. Katharine Marie O'Brien, July 12, 1969; children: Trina Melisa, Karita Leonora, Vanecia Vida. B.S., Athens State Coll., 1976; B.A., Oakwood Coll., 1977; M.S., Tenn. State U., 1982; M.Div., Vanderbilt Div. Sch., 1982. Ordained to ministry American Baptist Convention, 1979. Exec. dir. Tenn. Assn. Churches, 1978-82; chaplain Riverside Hosp., Nashville, 1977-78; minister of social concerns First Baptist Ch., Capitol Hill, Nashville, 1979-85; pastor Gracious Saviour Lutheran Ch., Detroit, 1985—; exec. dir. Nat. Conf. Black Churchmen, Detroit, 1982—; bd. dirs. Congregational Help Line, Nashville, 1983—, NCCJ, Nashville, 1982—; v.p. Interdenominational Minister's Fellowship, Nashville, 1984—; pres. Interfaith Assns., Nashville, 1981-82. Mem. Mayor's Council on Alcohol and Drug Abuse, Nashville, 1984; moderator Nashville Network for Community Devel., Nashville, 1984—; bd. dirs. Community Housing Resource Bd., Nashville, 1985; trustee So. Hills Hosp., Nashville, 1983. Mem. Am. Assn. Pastoral Counselors, Internatl. Transactional Analysis Assn., Nat. Black Pastor's Conf., Phi Beta Sigma. Office: Gracious Saviour Evang Luth Ch 19484 James Couzens Detroit MI 48235

GIBBS, JOHN GAMBLE, minister, educator, editor, Presbyterian Church in the U.S.A.; b. Asheville, N.C., Aug. 25, 1930; s. Robert Shuford and Isabella Frances (Gamble) G.; m. Karen L. Johnson, Dec. 31, 1972; children: Elizabeth, Suzanne, Ian, Patrick, Anne. A.B., Davidson Coll., 1952; M.Div., Union Theol. Sem., 1955, Th.M., 1958; Ph.D., Princeton Theol. Sem., 1966. Ordained to ministry Presby. Ch. in U.S.A., 1956. Pastor various chs. S.C., W.Va. and N.J., 1956-64;

interim instr. religion Macalester Coll., St. Paul, 1964-65; tchr. Latin, Blake Sch., Mpls., 1965-67, asst. prof. 1967-72, assoc. prof., 1972-77; prof. humanities Moorhead State U., Minn. 1978-82; fellow Inst. Ecumenical and Cultural Research, Collegeville, Minn., 1973-74; acquisitions editor John Knox Press, Atlanta, 1983—; del. to gen. assembly United Presbyn. Ch. U.S.A., Balt., 1976; faculty mem. Charis Ecumenical Inst., Moorhead, 1971-81. Author: Creation and Redemption, 1971. Contbr. articles to profl. jours. Coordinator 7th congl. dist. Minn. McCarthy Presdl. Campaign, 1968; bd. dirs. Inter-Faculty Orgn. for Minn. State U. System, 1979-81. NEH fellow Veshiva U., 1980. Mem. Soc. Bibl. Lit. (sec. upper midwest region 1981-83), Studiorum Novi Testamenti Societas, Inst. Bibl. Research, No. Plains Presbytery. Democrat. Home: 4111 Tahoe Ct Stone Mountain GA 30083 Office: John Knox Press 341 Ponce de Leon Ave NE Atlanta GA 30365

GIBBS, LANETTE SUSAN, religious educator, Roman Catholic Church; b. Bklyn., Apr. 11, 1957. B.A., Fordham U., 1978; postgrad. N.Y. Theol. Sem. Lector St. Matthews Ch., Bklyn., 1981—, eucharistic minister, 1984—; hosp. chaplain intern Luth. Med. Ctr., Bklyn., 1982-83; dir. religious edn. St. Jeromès Roman Cath. Ch., Bklyn., 1983—. Recipient Pope Pius X award for teaching religion, 1976, Woman's Day honor award, 1983. Office: St Jeromès Roman Ch 2900 Newkirk Ave Brooklyn NY 11226

GIBBS, NORMAN WESLEY, minister, Ind. Fundamental Chs. Am.; b. Bellingham, Wash., Mar. 10, 1928; s. Norman W. and Ruth (Wilson) G.; diploma Phila. Coll. Bible, 1952; student Wycliff Inst. Linguistics, 1952; m. Audrey E. Gillan, Nov. 27, 1949; children—Norman Paul, Ruth Elaine. Ordained to ministry, 1953; missionary pastor Am. Mission for Opening Chs., 1958—, pastor Cedar Chapel, Alexander, Maine, 1958-64, Glencliff (N.H.) Community Ch., 1964-69, Wentworth (N.H.) Bapt. Ch., 1964-69; founding pastor Charlestown (N.H.) Bible Ch., 1975-77, Ch. of Open Bible, Ascutney, Vt., 1975-77; co-founder N.Y. region Ind. Fundamental Chs. Am., 1972-73; mem. IFCA New Eng. Regional Ch. Extension team, 1979-84, v.p., 1980-84; chaplain N.H. Tb Sanitorium Glencliff, 1964-69; chaplain CAP, commd. capt., 1980; deputation sec. Am. Mission for Opening Chs., 1969-70, exec. dir., 1970-72, dir. pub. relations, 1972-74, regional dir. Vt. and N.H., 1974—. Mem. nat. exec. council Nat. Home Missions Fellowship, 1970-73; dir. Niagara Bible Conf., 1970, 72. Address: Drawer 262 Ascutney VT 05030

GIBNEY, DELMARIE, nun Roman Catholic Church; educational coordinator; b. Scobey, Mont., Mar. 18, 1935; d. Raymond and Teresa (Killorn) G. R.N., Sacred Heart Sch. Nursing, Spokane, 1956; B.S. in Biology, Viterbo Coll., LaCrosse, Wis., 1964; postgrad. midwifery, U. Costa Rica, 1974. Entered Order Franciscan Sisters of Perpetual Adoration, Roman Catholic Ch., 1956; night supr. Sacred Heart Hosp., Idaho Falls, Ida., 1959-60; med. supr. St. Francis Hosp., LaCrosse, Wis., 1960-63; parish worker health care, Santa Ana, El Salvador, 1964-76; midwifery edn. Maryknoll Parish, Peten, Guatemala, 1976-78; provincial adminstr. Health Care Province, St. Paul, Minn., 1979-83; coordinator Global Edn. Assocs. Upper Midwest, St. Paul, Minn., 1983—. Editor: Focus Newsletter, 1979. Mem. Leadership Conf. of Women Religious. Office: Global Education Associates Upper Midwest 1884 Randolph Ave Saint Paul MN 55105

GIBSON, CHARLES RICHARD (DICK), youth minister, Independent Christian Churches and Churches of Christ; b. Joplin, Mo., Oct. 10, 1956; s. Charles Ray and Barbara Louise (Poor) G.; m. Carrie Lynn Smith, Aug. 26, 1978; children: Julie Janell, Courtney Lynn. B.A., Ozark Bible Coll., 1979; postgrad. Cin. Christian Sem., 1985—. Ordained minister Christian Ch., 1978. Minister to youth Northside Christian Ch., Broken Arrow, Okla., 1978-82, Central Christian Ch., St. Petersburg, Fla., 1982—; pres. Okla. Christian Youth Conv., Oklahoma City, 1980; bd. dirs. Youth Evangelism Service, Tulsa, 1981-82, Lake Aurora Christian Assembly, Lake Wales, Fla., 1984—; chaplain Suncoast Chpt. Am. Marriage Encounter, 1984—. Contbr. articles to religious jours. Del., Am. Legion Boys, Talequah, Okla., 1973. Recipient Outstanding Young Man Am., U.S. Jaycees, 1979, Student of Today award Masonic Grand Lodge, 1974. Mem. Fla. Christian Youth Conv. (officer, adv.), Fla. Christian Ministers Assn., Tulsa Christian Ministers Assn. (sec. 1981), Student Bocy Ozark Bible Coll., (pres. 1978), Athletes for Christ (v.p. 1974-77), Fellowship Christian Athletes. Avocations: basketball; golf; snow-skiing; sailing. Home: 366 54th St N Saint Petersburg FL 33710 Office: Central Christian Ch 4824 2nd Ave S Saint Petersburg FL 33711

GIBSON, CLAUDIA ANN, nun, religious organization executive, Roman Catholic Church; b. New Orleans, Feb. 7, 1931; d. Jesse Moore and Elva Marie (Breavy) G. B.S., Dominican Coll., New Orleans, 1960; postgrad. Peabody Coll., summers 1963-65; M.Ed., Loyola U., New Orleans, 1974. Joined Dominican Sisters of St. Mary, Roman Cath. Ch., 1949. Tchr. various parochial schs., La., 1951-61, prin. elem. parochial schs., 1951-84; superior gen. Dominican Sisters of St. Mary, New Orleans, 1984—. Democrat.

Home: 580 Broadway Ave New Orleans LA 70118 Office: Dominican Sisters 580 Broadway Ave New Orleans LA 70118

GIBSON, DEWEY ELVIN, minister, Southern Baptist Convention; b. Malakoff, Tex., Dec. 24, 1933; s. John Dewey and Margie Louise (Rogers) G.; B.S., Stephen F. Austin State U., 1954; B.D., Southwestern Bapt. Theol. Sem., 1957, M.Div., 1968; Th.D., Luther Rice Sem., 1975; m. Dorothy Jean Ratcliff, June 12, 1954; children—Sherry Jean, Jerry Elvin. Ordained to ministry, 1957. Pastor chs. in Tex., 1957—; pastor Tex. Ave. Bapt. Ch., League City, Tex., 1968-74, Hillcrest Bapt. Ch., Nederland, Tex., 1974—; Bapt. Gen. Conv. of Tex. trustee Bapt. Hosp. Southeast Tex., 1977—. Pres. League City Elementary Sch. PTA, 1969-70. Mem. Sabine Valley Bapt. Assn. (vice moderator 1961-63), Galveston Bapt. Pastors Fellowship (pres. 1970), Clear Creek Ministerial Alliance (pres. 1971), Galveston Bapt. Assn. (clk. 1972-74). Author booklet: Your Church and You; also articles. Home: 3304 Park Dr Nederland TX 77627 Office: 3324 Park Dr Nederland TX 77627

GIBSON, SAMUEL NORRIS, ecumenical church executive, United Methodist Church; b. Troy, Ala., Sept. 2, 1926; s. Clarence Samuel and Annie Pearl (Clark) G.; m. Ella Marie Booth, Oct. 28, 1972; children by previous marriage: Richard Waldo, Christopher Samuel; stepchildren: Curtis David Schurman, Darryl John Schurman. B.S. in Arch., Ga. Inst. Tech., 1947; B.D., Yale U., 1951; S.T.M., 1955; Ph.D., U. Pitts., 1980. Ordained to ministry, 1960. Exec. dir. U. Christian Assn., Pa. State U., State College, 1956-64; research dir. Nat. Study of Wesley Founds., Nashville, 1964-66; exec. minister U. and City Ministries, Pitts., 1968-72; exec. dir. East End Coop. Ministry, Pitts., 1978-82, United Meth. Ch. Union, Pitts., 1982—; pres. Univ. Sch., Pitts., 1981—; trustee Otterbein Coll., 1983—; nat. vice chmn. Meth. for Ch. Renewal, 1965-69; mem. Second Inst. for Meth. Theol. Studies, Oxford U., Eng., 1962, Ethics and Pub. Policy Panel, Pitts., 1984—. Author: The Campus Ministry and the Church's Mission, 1967; Viewpoints on Higher Education, 1973; You and the Community Challenge, 1962. Treas., The Dollar Energy Fund, Pitts., 1984—; exec. com. Pitts. Council on Pub. Edn., 1972-77; publisher Connections newspaper, Pitts., 1974-82. Served with USN, 1944-46. Danforth Found. campus ministry grantee, 1962-63; Ford Found. fellow, 1953-54. Mem. Leadership Pitts., Am. Assn. Homes for Aging, Policy Scis. Orgn., Ctr. for Def. Info. Democrat. Clubs: Harvard-Yale-Princeton, Longue Vue, Rotary. Home: 1094 Devon Rd Pittsburgh PA 15213 Office: United Meth Ch Union 223 Fourth Ave Pittsburgh PA 15222

GIBSON, THEODORE ROOSEVELT, priest, Episcopal Ch.; b. Miami, Fla., Apr. 24, 1915; s. Charles and Effie (Smith) G.; A.B., St. Augustine Coll., 1938, LL.D., 1964; B.D., Bishop Payne Div. Sch., 1943; D.D., Va. Theol. Sem., 1971; m. Thelma V. Anderson, Apr. 2, 1967; 1 son, Theodore Roosevelt. Ordained priest Episcopal Ch., 1944; priest-in-charge St. Thomas Ch., Sladesville, N.C., 1944; minister-in-charge St. Paul, St. Mary, St. Jude chs., Washington, 1943-44; priest-in-charge Cyprus Ch., Homestead, Fla., 1944-45; priest, rector Christ Episcopal Ch., Miami, Fla., 1945—; mem. Bd. Theol. Edn., Episcopal Ch. Commr., City of Miami, 1973—, vice mayor, 1973—. Trustee St. Augustine Coll. Home: 3401 Williams Ave Miami FL 33133 Office: 3481 Hibiscus St Coconut Grove Sta Miami FL 33133

GIES, KENNETH WARD, minister, Lutheran Church; Social worker; b. Galt, Doon, Ont., Can., Oct. 9, 1943; s. Henry Laval and Christa Gertrude Anna (Meuller) G.; m. Susan Elizabeth Cooke, Apr. 22, 1972; children: Benjamin Thomas, Katharine Christa. B.A., Waterloo Luth. U. (now Wilfred Laurier U.), 1967, M.S.W., M.Div., 1972. Ordained to ministry Luth. Ch., 1976. Intern, Augustana Luth. Ch., Saskatoon and Christ Luth. Ch., Young, Sask., Can., 1969-70; part-time Luth. chaplain Queen's U., Kingston, Ont., 1972-78; assoc. pastor St. Mark's Luth. Ch., Kingston, 1976-83, resigned 1983. Social worker Kingston Psychiat. Hosp., 1972-78, social work supr. psychogeriatric unit, 1978—; instr. seminars for local ch. groups, Kingston, 1972—; cons. The Amphetamine Abuse Program for Kingston, 1973-74. Author, editor papers on handling physically and emotionally disturbed elderly patient, 1980. Mem. search and cons. com. Theol. Internship Program for Community of Kingston, Queen's U. and Kingston Psychiat. Hosp., 1979-82; mem. Ad Hoc Com. to Study Aging in Kingston, 1979—. Co-founder, asst. instr. (brown belt) Goju Kai Karate Club, Kingston, 1983—. Mem. Ont. Assn. Profl. Social Workers, Ont. Coll. Cert. Social Workers, Ont. Psychogeriatric Assn., Ont. Assn. Profl. Social Workers (corr. mem., mem. standing com. on aging), Continuing Care Com. Kingston. Home: 785 Haverhill Dr Kingston ON K7M 4V1 Canada

GIESCHEN, ROGER J., Synodical bishop Lutheran Church in America, Overland Park, Kans. Office: Lutheran Ch in Am 9800 Metcalf St Suite 400 Overland Park KS 66212*

GIESE, VINCENT JOSEPH, priest, Roman Catholic Church; b. Ft. Wayne, Ind., Oct. 19, 1923; s. Joseph J.

and Mae Genevieve (Yaste) G. Ph.B., St. Joseph's Coll., 1945; M.A. in Journalism, Marquette U., 1947; M.S. in Edn., Polit. Sci., U. Notre Dame, 1950; S.T.B., Gregorian U., 1966. Ordained priest, Roman Cath. Ch., 1965. Assoc. pastor Blessed Sacrament Ch., Chgo., 1966-72; pastor Our Lady of Perpetual Help, Chgo., 1972-78; assoc. editor Chgo. Cath., 1968-78; editor, Harmonizer, Ft. Wayne/South Bend, Ind., 1978-80; editor-in-chief Our Sunday Visitor, Huntington, Ind., 1980—. Author: Apostolic Itch, 1953; Patterns for Teenagers, 1954; Training for Leadership, 1959; Revolution in the City, 1961; Journal of Late Vocation, 1966; You Got It All, 1980; Youth for Peace, 1984. Named Notre Dame Man of Yr., 1981. Mem. Cath. Press Assn., Ft. Wayne Press Club (v.p. 1982-84). Democrat. Lodge: Rotary. Home: 4525 Arlington Ave Fort Wayne IN 46807 Office: Our Sunday Visitor 200 Noll Plaza Huntington IN 46750

GIESMANN, DONALD JOHN, minister, Evangelical Presbyterian Church; b. Pitts., Apr. 15, 1949; s. John Weber and Harriet Elizabeth (Collingwood) G.; m. Sara Mosher, June 2, 1974; children: Carrie, Alison. B.S., Indiana U. of Pa., 1971; M.R.E., Gordon-Conwell Sem., South Hamilton, Mass., 1974; D.Edn., Columbia Pacific U., 1980. Ordained to ministry Presbyn. Ch. in Am., 1975. Assoc. pastor Westminister Presbyn. Ch., Rock Hill, S.C., 1974-76, South Park Ch., Park Ridge, Ill., 1977-81; pastor Heritage Congregational Ch., Middletown, Conn., 1976-77, Community Ch. at Bristol, Tenn., 1981—; mem. nat. edn. com. Evangelical Presbyn. Ch., Dearborn, Mich., 1982—. Contbr. articles to profl. jours. Del., White House Conf. on Families, Chgo., 1980; rep. Ill Sch. Bd. Caucus Dist. 207, Park Ridge, 1979-80; bd. dirs. Salvation Army, 1985—; mem. adjudication bd. U.S./Ill. Selective Service Bd., Park Ridge, 1981. Recipient 4 Way Test award Christian Workers Found., 1974, Cert. Evangelical Tchr., Tng. Assn., 1974. Mem. Presbyn. Hist. Soc., Ministerial Com. Southeast Presbyn., Freedom House, Inst. Religion and Democracy, Bristol Ministerial Assn. Lodge: Rotary. Avocations: political artifact collection; hiking; geography study. Home: 520 Brookwood Dr Bristol TN 37620 Office: Community Ch Bristol 6320 Old Jonesboro Rd Bristol TN 37620

GIFFORD, HARTLAND HERBERT, church official Lutheran Church Am.; b. Hartford, Conn., Apr. 29, 1934; s. Herbert Cyril and Sallie Vendelia (Nelson) G.; A.B., Upsala Coll., East Orange, N.J., 1956; M.Div., Lutheran Sch. Theol., Chgo., 1959; m. Carol Jean Lincke, June 7, 1959 (dec. Nov. 5, 1983); children—John, Diane. Ordained minister Luth. Ch. in Am., 1960; pastor chs. in Pa. and Mass., 1960-70; pastor Christ Luth. Ch., Middletown, Conn., 1970-72; editor adult parish mission resources, div. parish services Luth. Ch. Am., Phila., 1973-75, sec. for stewardship, 1975-81, editor for interpretation resources, 1981—. Mem. Alpha Phi Omega (pres. chpt. 1956). Author: Isaiah: The Times Observer, 1971; Crucifixion, 1973; Amnesty?, 1973; The Charismatic Movement, 1973; Year-Round Stewardship, 1976; Stewardship as a Way of Life, 1980; Methods for the Every Member Response, 1984. Editor The New Eng. Luth., 1966-70. Home: 1607 Dogwood Rd Flourtown PA 19031 Office: 2900 Queen Ln Philadelphia PA 19129

GILBERT, ARTHUR JOSEPH, bishop, Roman Catholic Ch.; b. Hedley, B.C., Can., Oct. 26, 1915; s. George Miles and Ethel May (Carter) G.; student St. Joseph's Coll., St. Joseph, N.B., 1931-34, St. Francis Xavier U., 1934-38; B.A., postgrad. Holy Heart Sem., Halifax, N.S., 1938-43. Ordained priest, 1943, bishop, 1974; bishop of St. John (N.B.) Diocese, 1974—. Home: 9 Bishops Dr Renforth Saint John NB E2H 2N2 Canada Office: 91 Waterloo St Saint John NB E2L 3P9 Canada

GILBERT, GORDON HICE, lay ch. worker, So. Baptist Conv.; b. Chickamauga, Ga., Oct. 2, 1904; s. Arch J. and Lille Belle (Madaris) G.; student U. Chatannoga, U. Ariz.; m. Lucy Gertrude Aaron, July 17, 1934; children—Gail, Brenda. Supt. Sunday sch. Clifton Hill Bapt. Ch., Chattanooga, 1950-52, 57-59, 62-64, adult dir., 1966-76, chmn. fin., 1961-75, deacon, 1967; vice moderator Hamilton County Bapt. Assn., 1973-74, pres. library orgn., 1969-71, chmn. resolutions com., 1969-73. Ret. U.S. Postal Service ofcl. Address: 200 Hogan Rd Rossville GA 30741

GILDNER, LEO HELWIG, priest, Roman Cath. Ch.; b. Bloomington, Ill., Sept. 21, 1927; s. Leo August and Sylvia Maria (Helwig) G.; student St. Bede Coll., 1945-46; B.A., Loras Coll., 1949; postgrad. St. Paul Sem., 1949-53. Ordained priest Roman Catholic Ch., 1953; asst. pastor Holy Family Ch., Oglesby, Ill., 1953-56; tchr. St. Paul High Sch., Odell, Ill., chaplain Dwight (Ill.) Vets. Hosp., 1956-58; tchr. Schlarman High Sch. and LaSallette Sem., Danville, Ill., 1958-59; tchr., student activities coordinator Alleman High Sch., Rock Island, Ill., 1959-66, mem. bd. edn., 1971—; pastor St. John's Ch., Woodhull, Ill., 1966-71, St. Mary's Ch., Moline, Ill., 1971-76, St. Francis of Assisi Ch., Ottawa, Ill., 1976—. Defender of bond Peoria Diocesan Tribunal, 1969—; Diocesan dir. cemeteries Cath. Dioceses of Peoria, 1973—. Named Outstanding Young Religious Educator, Moline Jr. C. of C., 1971-72. Mem. Am., Nat. Cath. cemetery assns. Address: 820 Sanger St Ottawa IL 61350

GILL, THEODORE ALEXANDER, JR., minister, religious studies educator, Presbyterian Ch.; b. N.Y.C., Sept. 16, 1951; s. Theodore Alexander and Katherine (Yonker) G.; m. Ruth Ann Shriver, May 27, 1972; child: Elizabeth Katherine. B.A., U. Wis.-Madison, 1972; M.Div., Princeton Theol. Sem., 1975; M.Litt., Oxford U., England, 1980. Ordained to ministry Presbyterian Ch., 1975. Asst. minister Brown Meml. Ch., Balt., 1975-76; co-psychotherapist Fairmile Hosp., Cholsey, England, 1976-78; co-pastor Trinity Ch., Abingdon, England, 1978-80; instr. So. Ill. U., Carbondale, 1983-85; dir. Interfaith Center, Carbondale, 1980-85; reporter General Assembly Daily News, N.Y., Atlanta, 1975—; mission design writer Presbyn. Gen. Assembly Council, Princeton, N.J., 1985—. Author numerous sermons, prayers, mag. articles. Co-ordinator Bread for the World, 22nd Congressional Dist., Ill., 1982-85; chmn. So. Illinoisans for Gary Hart 22nd Congl. Dist., Ill., 1983-84; permanent mem. rules com. Democratic Nat. Convention, San Francisco, 1984. New Testament fellow Princeton Theol. Sem., 1975. Mem. Am. Assn. Counseling and Devel., Presbyterian Peace Fellowship. Home: 342 Dodds Ln Princeton NJ 08540 Office: Princeton Theol Sem CN 821 Princeton NJ 08540

GILL, THOMAS JEFFREY, priest, Episcopal Church; b. Savannah, Ga., Mar. 20, 1954; s. Clarence Redmond and Lorraine (Blume) G.; B.A. in History, U. of South, 1975; M.Div., Gen. Theol. Sem., N.Y.C., 1978. Ordained deacon Episcopal Ch., 1978, priest, 1979. Seminarian asst. St. James' Ch., N.Y.C., 1975-76, St. Michael's Ch., N.Y.C., 1976-78; asst. chaplain Columbia U., N.Y.C., 1978-80; asst. minister St. Michael's Ch., N.Y.C., 1978-81, assoc. rector, 1981—; v.p. Inter-parish Council, N.Y.C., 1979-81; chaplain Diocesan Youth Confs., N.Y.C., 1980; mem. Diocesan Council, N.Y.C., 1981; assoc. prelate Knights of the Red Cross of Constantine, N.Y.C., 1983—. Bd. dirs. Concerned Citizens Speak, Inc., N.Y.C., 1982—; life mem. Nat. Trust for Scotland, Edinburgh, 1980—. Recipient Internat. Meritorious Service award Order of DeMolay, Kansas City, 1972; named Demolay of Yr. in Ga., Order of Demolay, Atlanta, 1972. Mem. Scottish Heritage Soc., Scottish Am. Found. Lodge: Masons (grand chaplain 1983—). Home: 225 W 99th St New York NY 10025 Office: St Michael's Ch 225 W 99th St New York NY 10025

GILLESPIE, FREEMAN WILLIAMSON, minister, Baptist Ch.; b. Pleasant Grove, Miss., May 3, 1912; s. Frank Lee and Minnie Ann (Bailey) G.; student Draughn Bus. Coll., 1933; B.A., Miss. Coll., 1938; D.D. (hon.) Ohio Christian Coll., 1968; m. Frances Gilligan, Oct. 18, 1939; children—Jacqueline Ann, Kenneth Lee. Ordained to ministry, 1934; pastor chs., Tenn., 1938—, N. Frayser Bapt. Ch., Memphis, 1971—. Vice pres. Memphis Bapt. Conf., 1962—; mem. exec. com. Shelby Bapt. Assn., 1938-76; mem. Memphis Censory Com., 1964-65. Mem. Memphis Ministerial Assn. Author: Live On, My Boy, 1964. Home: 2924 Overton Crossing Memphis TN 38127 Office: 3735 N Trezevant Memphis TN 38127

GILLESPIE, THOMAS WILLIAM, seminary president, Presbyterian Church U.S.A.; b. Los Angeles, July 18, 1928; s. William A. and Estella (Beers) G.; m. Barbara A. Lugenbill, July 31, 1953; children: Robyn C., William T., Dayle E. B.A., George Pepperdine Coll., 1951; B.D., Princeton Theol. Sem., 1954; PhD., Claremont Grad. Sch., 1971; D.D. (hon.), Grove City Coll., 1984. Ordained to ministry Presbyn. Ch. U.S.A., 1954. Pastor First Presbyn. Ch., Garden Grove, Ca, 1954-66, First Presbyn. Ch., Burlingame, Calif., 1966-83; pres., prof. N.T., Princeton Theol. Sem., N.J., 1983—; trustee Westminster Choir Coll., Princeton, 1984—, Ctr. Theol. Inquiry, Princeton, 1984—; mem. New Brunswick Presbytery, Trenton, 1984—. Served with USMC, 1946-47. Recipient A. A. Hodge prize in systematic theology Princeton Theol. Sem., 1953; Disting. Alumnus award Claremont Grad Sch., 1984. Mem. Soc. Bibl. Lit. Office: Princeton Theol Sem Mercer St Box 552 Princeton NJ 08542

GILLEY, BOBBY LEE, religious educator, Church of God; b. Burlington, N.C., Oct. 31, 1949; s. Lewis Lee and Lillie (Peninger) G.; m. Betty Grace Pierce, May 21, 1971; children: Kimberly Elaine, Pamela Dawn. B.A., Lee Coll., 1972; M.A., Wheaton Coll., Ill., 1973; M.Ed., Winthrop Coll., 1983. Ordained to ministry Ch. of God, 1978. Mem. faculty N.W. Bible Coll., Minot, N.D., 1974-76; dean of students East Coast Bible Coll., Charlotte, N.C., 1976—; bd. dirs. Western N.C. youth and Christian edn. Ch. of God, 1982-84; council mem. Western N.C. Ch. of God, Charlotte, 1984—; writer Sunday sch. lit. Pathway Press, 1984. Author: God's Plan for Man: New Testament Survey, 1982. Contbr. articles to jours. Bd. dirs. Paw Creek Christian Acad., 1978—, Victory Christian Acad., Gastonia, N.C., 1980-83. Mem. Assn. for Christians in Student Devel., Assn. Christian Service Personnel. Home: 9019 Singingpine Rd Charlotte NC 28208 Office: East Coast Bible Coll 6900 Wilkinson Blvd Charlotte NC 28214

GILLIAM, JACKSON EARLE, bishop, Episcopal Church; b. Heppner, Oreg., June 20, 1920; s. Edwin Earle and Mary (Perry) G.; A.B., Whitman Coll., 1942; B.D., Protestant Episcopal Sem. in Va., 1948, S.T.M., 1949, D.D., 1969; m. Margaret Kathleen Hindley, Aug. 11, 1943; children—Anne Meredith (Mrs. Glenn Vanatta), Margaret Carol (Mrs. Gary Lynman), John Howard. Ordained deacon, 1948, priest, 1949; consecrated Bishop, 1968; vicar St. John's Ch., Hermiston, Oreg., 1949-53; canon St. Mark's Cathedral, Mpls., 1953-55; rector Ch. of the Incarnation, Great Falls, Mont., 1955-68; bishop Diocese of Mont., 1968—; mem. Presiding Bishop's Adv. Council; chmn. Council of Devel. of Ministry. Trustee St. Peter's Hosp., Helena, Mont. Home: 1726 Cannon Blvd Helena MT 59601 Office: Diocese of Mont 303 Horsny Block Helena MT 59601

GILLILAND, WILLIAM YOUNG, minister Christian Chs. and Chs. of Christ; b. Clifton Forge, Va., Apr. 7, 1951; s. Walter William and Lillie Frances (Nicely) G.; A.B., Ky. Christian Coll., 1973; m. Susan Jane Roberts, Aug. 2, 1970; children—Susan Lee, Jeri Rae. Ordained to ministry, 1973; pastor Prestonsburg (Ky.) 1st Christian Ch., 1970-74, 1st Christian Ch., Dugger, Ind., 1974—. Instl. rep. Cub Scouts; chmn. Ind. Mental Health Assn., Cystic Fibrosis. Mem. Ministerial Assn., Ky. Christian Coll. Alumni Assn. Home: Box 177 Dugger IN 47848 Office: Third St Dugger IN 47848

GILMORE, JOHN ALEXANDER, minister, Presbyn. Ch. U.S.A.; b. Belfast, No. Ireland, Sept. 12, 1938; s. Samuel and Esther (Campbell) G.; came to U.S., 1938, naturalized, 1956; B.S. in Edn., Temple U., 1961, B.D., 1964; Th.M., Princeton Sem., 1965; m. Sylvia Anne Daugherty, June 13, 1964; children—Gregory William, Brenda Esther, Kevin John. Ordained to ministry, 1964; asst. chaplain Phila. Youth Study Center, summer 1964; pastor 1st Presbyn. Ch., Grenloch, N.J., 1965-69; asso. pastor 1st Presbyn. Ch., Ambler, Pa., 1969-72; pastor Oxford (Pa.) Presbyn. Ch., 1972-79, First Presbyn. Ch., Milford, Del., 1979—; moderator New Castle Presbytery, 1985-86. Home: 435 S Walnut St Milford DE 19963 Office: S Walnut and SE Front Sts Milford DE 19963

GILMORE, MARSHALL, Bishop, Christian Episcopal Church (Fourth Dist.), chair Gen. Bd. Evangelism. Office: 109 Holcomb Dr Shreveport LA 71103*

GILREATH, JUDITH ANNE MORINIERE, lay ch. worker, United Meth. Ch.; b. Houston, Aug. 20, 1938; d. E. Code and Judith Anne (Hamilton) Moriniere; B.S., U. Tex. at Austin, 1960; m. Charles Nelson Gilreath, Apr. 2, 1958; children—Steven Nelson, Michael Brooke, John Lindsay. Tchr. ch. sch., 1st United Meth. Ch., Sulphur Springs, Tex., 1960—; sec. gen. bd. discipleship United Methodist Ch., Nashville, 1972—, mem. exec. com., 1972—, mem. budget com., 1972—, mem. legislative com., 1974-76; del. South Central Jurisdictional Conf., 1972, 76, Gen. Conf., 1976, Mexican Meth. Centennial Celebration, 1973; mem. N. Tex. Conf. Children's Ministry Com., 1968-72; v.p. Paris-Sulphur Springs Dist. Council, 1972—; lay del. First United Meth. Ch. of Sulphur Springs N. Tex. Annual Conf., 1972—. Trustee, Sulphur Springs Ind. Sch. Dist., 1974, pres. Bd. Edn., 1976-77; pres. Austin Sch. PTA, 1967-68; den mother Sulphur Springs Area council Boy Scouts Am., 1967-73; pres. Sulphur Springs Woman's Forum, 1966-67; chmn. Woman's div. Citizens' Com. New Hosp., 1965, co-chmn. bond election campaign for additions to hosp., 1960—. Bd. dirs. Sulphur Springs Pub. Library, 1973—, United Campus Christian Center E. Tex. State U. Mem. D.A.R., Alpha Delta Pi (pres. 1963-65), Alpha Delta Pi N.E. Tex. Alumnae Assn. (parliamentarian 1964-66), Alpha Delta Pi State Alumnae Assn. Home: 516 Oak Ave Box 556 Sulphur Springs TX 75482 Office: Sec Bd Discipleship United Meth Ch Box 840 Nashville TN 37202

GILSTRAP, JAMES CURTIS, minister, Southern Baptist Convention; b. Greenville, S.C., Feb. 6, 1929; s. John Henry and Nancy Katherine (Thompson) G.; A.A., North Greenville Coll., 1965; B.A., Furman U., Greenville, 1967; student Erskine Sem., 1967-68; m. Mary Louise Smith, June 26, 1949; children—Curtis Stanley, Rebecca Louise. Ordained to ministry, 1962. Pastor Blue Ridge Bapt. Ch., Pickens, S.C., 1962-66, King's Grove Bapt. Ch., Central, S.C., 1966-72, Pleasant Grove Bapt. Ch., Lavonia, Ga., 1972-84, Cherryfield Bapt. Ch., Brevard, N.C., 1984—. Moderator Twelve Mile River Bapt. Assn., 1968-69, Picken Twelve Mile Bapt. Assn., 1972; pres. Franklin County Ministers Assn., 1975-76; mem. exec. com. Ga. Bapt. Conv., 1975-79. Address: Route 2 Box 661 Brevard NC 28712

GINDER, HENRY AUCKER, minister, bishop, Brethren in Christ Church, Nov. 22, 1911; s. Jacob T. and Amanda (Aucker) G.; m. Martha N., Nov. 24, 1932; children: Roy, Glenn, Carl, Ruth. D.D. (hon.), Western Evangel. Sem., 1975. Ordained minister Brethren in Christ Ch., 1937. Pastor, Brethren in Christ Ch., Pa., 1938-48, bishop, 1948-78; pres. Christian Holiness Assn., 1972-74; minister at large Messiah Coll., Grantham, Pa., 1978—; nat. rep. Brethren in Christ Missions, Pa., 1978—. Contbr. articles to religious publs. Named Holiness Exponent of Yr. CHA, 1974, disting. alumni award Messiah Coll., 1975. Republican. Home: 611 Messiah Village Mechanicsburg PA 17055 Office: Messiah Coll Grantham PA 17027

GINGERICH, HAROLD DEAN, evangelist, Old Mennonite Church; b. Albany, Oreg., July 6, 1947; s.

Joseph J. and Shirley Maxine (Eicher) G.; student Ind. U., 1968-72, Fort Wayne Bible Coll., 1971-72; m. Janice Louise Peters, Apr. 13, 1968; children: Matthew James, Jason Michael. Ordained to ministry, 1977; youth worker Mennonite Vol. Service, 1966-68; pastor Mennonite Ch., Albuquerque, 1969-70; founder, pres. Whole Life Crusades, Topeka, Ind., 1972—. Recorded gospel music albums. Editor The Vessel, 1981—; editor Empowered Mag., 1983—. Contbr. articles to religious jours. Home: South Main St Topeka IN 46571 Office: South Main Box 426 Topeka IN 46571

GINSBERG, HERSH MAYER, rabbi, Orthodox Jewish; b. Vienna, Austria; s. Lazar Ginsberg and Perl (Roth) G.; m. Fradel Levy; children: Yonah, Meshulom, Rebezin Chana. Dean R.J.J. Sch., N.Y.C., 1955-73; dir. Union Orthodox Rabbis, 1973—. Office: Union of Orthodox Rabbis of the United States and Canada 235 E Broadway New York NY 10002

GIORDANO, ANTHONY DANIEL, SR., minister, Judeo-Christian Alliance; b. Bklyn., Dec. 29, 1948; s. John Daniel and Rose (DiTaranto) G.; m. Renee Toni Schindelheim, July 13, 1975; children: Anthony Daniel, Sara Beth, Rebecca Marie. A.A.S., Coll. S.I., 1967; B.S. in Edn., CCNY, 1970, M.S. in Edn., 1972. Ordained to ministry Judeo-Christian Alliance, 1984. Counseling intern Com. on Community Services, Bklyn., 1966-74; home ministries pastor Ch. of God, Bklyn., 1975-82; supt. schs. Evang. Free Ch., Bklyn., 1983; ministerial intern New Hope Free Ch., Bklyn., 1984, pastor, 1985—, dir. summer inst., 1981—. Editor Transitions mag., 1969. Producer, dir. film: Quest For God, 1981. Pres. Sunset Park Peace Group, Bklyn., 1970, Precinct Community Council, Bklyn., 1972; mem. Bklyn. Community Planning Bd., 1973; founder Sunset Village Council, Bklyn., 1974; v.p. Sunset Park Ind. Democrats, 1971; active Central Bklyn. Ind. Dems. Scholar Coll. S.I., N.Y., 1966; NIMH community grantee, 1972. Mem. Council Judeo-Christian Clergy. Avocation: computer programming.

GIPSON, JOHN DURWOOD, minister, Chs. of Christ; b. Turkey, Tex., Aug. 31, 1932; s. Felix Claude and Mary Del (Butler) G.; B.A., Abilene (Tex.) Christian Coll., 1953; m. Euella Beth Stirman, June 18, 1953; children—Sherri Lynn, Kathy Jo, John David. Ordained minister, 1953; minister chs. in Tex., 1953-68; minister Sixth and Izard Ch. of Christ, Little Rock, 1968—. Mem. med. com. Ark. Kidney Found., 1972-74. Trustee Ft. Worth Christian Coll., 1967-68; adv. bd. Christian Center Psychol. Services, Little Rock, 1974—. Author: Happiness Day and Night, 1968; Paths to Peace, 1969. Contbr. to religious jours. Home: 1500 Northwick Ct Little Rock AR 72207 Office: Box 228 Little Rock AR 72203

GIRARDOT, NORMAN J., religion educator; b. Balt., Apr. 19, 1943; s. Norman Francis and Ruth Miriam (O'Leary) G.; m. S. Kay Singleton, Nov. 15, 1969; children: David M., J. Jacob. B.S. cum laude, Holy Cross Coll., Worcester, Mass., 1965; M.A., U. Chgo., 1968, Ph.D., 1974. Asst. prof. Notre Dame U., South Bend, Ind., 1972-79; asst. prof. Oberlin Coll., Ohio, 1979-80; assoc. prof. religious studies, chmn. dept. Lehigh U., Bethlehem, Pa., 1980—. Author: Myth and Meaning in Early Taoism, 1983. Editor: Imagination and Meaning, 1982, China and Christianity, 1979. Fellow Woodrow Wilson Found., 1967-68, U. Chgo., 1969-71, NEH, 1982-83. Mem. Am. Acad. Religion, Assn. Asian Studies, Soc. Study Chinese Religions (exec. bd. 1985—), Phi Beta Kappa. Office: Lehigh U Maginnes Hall Bethlehem PA 18015

GIROUX, RAYMOND ABEL, priest, Roman Catholic Church; b. Burlington, Vt., Jan. 22, 1934; s. Abel Amedee and Aline Rose (Choiniere) G.; A.B., St. John's Sem., 1956; S.T.B., U. Montreal, 1963; M.A., Cath. U. Am., 1971. Ordained priest, 1963; mem. faculty Mt. St. Joseph's Acad., Rutland, Vt., 1963-65; prin. Marian High Sch., Barre, Vt., 1966-69; dir. guidance Rice Meml. High Sch., South Burlington, Vt., 1969-72; instr. psychology, guidance St. Michael's Coll., Winooski, Vt., 1967-72; pastor St. Luke's Ch., Fairfax, Vt., 1972-77, Holy Angels Ch., St. Alban's, Vt., 1977—. Mem. Vt. Council of Chs. Chmn. Vt. Bd. Parole, 1968-78; bd. dirs. Vt. Cath. Tribune, Franklin-Grand Isle Mental Health; chmn. St. Albans City Housing Authority; mem. Diocesan Tribunal; chmn. Police-Firemen Merit Pay Bd., Barre, Vt.; mem. Gov.'s Pardon Adv. Commn. Mem. Am. Correctional Assn., New Eng., Nat. councils crime and delinquency. Address: 246 Lake St St Alban's VT 05478

GIRZONE, JOSEPH FRANCIS, priest, Roman Catholic Ch.; b. Albany, N.Y., May 15, 1930; s. Peter Joseph and Margaret Rita (Campbell) G.; B.A. in Philosophy, St. Bonaventure U., Olean, N.Y., 1951; grad. in theology Cath. U. Am., 1955; postgrad. Fordham U., Columbia. Joined Carmelite Order, 1948, ordained priest, 1955; tchr. high schs. in N.Y. and Pa., 1955-64; mem. faculty St. Albert's Sem., Middletown, N.Y., 1960-61; pastor chs. in N.Y., 1964—; pastor Our Lady of Mt. Carmel Ch., Amsterdam, 1974—. Dir. Dominican 3d Order Religious Lay People, 1964-76; mem. N.Y. State Bishops' Adv. Com. Criminal Justice, 1973—; mem. Roman Cath. Diocesan Peace and Justice Commn., 1976—. Chmn. Schenectady County Human Rights Commn., 1973-74; vice chmn. Title III adv. bd. N.Y. State Office Aging, 1974-76; co-owner Golden Age Sentinel, newspaper sr. citizens; pres. Amsterdam Community Concerts; past bd. dirs. Joint Com. Christians and Jews, Schenectady. Recipient Liberty Bell award Am. Bar Assn., 1974; Citizen of Age of Enlightenment award Soc. Creative Intelligence, 1976. Address: 39 St John St Amsterdam NY 12010

GITTELSOHN, ROLAND BERTRAM, rabbi; b. Cleve., May 13, 1910; s. Reuben and Anna (Manheim) G.; B.A., Western Res. U., 1931; B.H., Hebrew Union Coll., Cin., 1934, Rabbi, 1936, D.D., 1961; Sc.D., Lowell (Mass.) Tech. Inst., 1961; m. Ruth Freyer, Sept. 25, 1932; children—David, Judith Fales. Rabbi, Central Synagogue Nassau County, N.Y., 1936-53; rabbi Temple Israel, Boston, 1953-77, rabbi emeritus, 1977—. Pres. Mass. Bd. Rabbis, 1958-60, Jewish Community Council Met. Boston, 1961-1963; mem. exec. bd. Central Conf. Am. Rabbis, 1949-51, chmn. placement com., 1949-52, chmn. commn. justice and peace, 1950-54, pres., 1969-71; trustee, chmn. commn. Jewish edn. Union Am. Hebrew Congregations, 1959-68, vice chmn. bd., 1973-75. Mem. Truman Com. Civil Rights, 1947, Gov. Mass. Commn. to Survey Cts., 1955, Mass. Commn. Abolition Death Penalty, 1957-58, Gov. Mass. Com. Migratory Labor, 1960-62, Gov. Mass. Com. to Survey Operations in Prisons, 1961-62. Mem. Phi Beta Kappa. Author: Modern Jewish Problems, 1943; Little Lower Than the Angels, 1954; Man's Best Hope, 1961; Consecrated Unto Me: A Jewish View of Love and Marriage, 1965; My Beloved Is Mine, 1969; Wings of the Morning, 1969; Fire in My Bones, 1969; The Meaning of Judaism, 1970; Love, Sex and Marriage—A Jewish View, 1976; The Extra Dimension, 1983. Home: Jamaicaway Tower Boston MA 02130 Office: Temple Israel Boston MA 02215

GJERNESS, OMAR NORMAN, minister, religious educator, Church of the Lutheran Brethren; b. Mandal, Norway, Mar. 5, 1922; came to U.S., 1922; s. Ove. Oleson and Amalie (Aaneson) G.; m. Joan Elsie Larsen, Dec. 17, 1949; children: David, Melinda, Craig, Peter. Student, Augsburg Coll., 1943-44; B.A., Wagner Coll., 1950; M.A., Pasadena Coll., 1970; M.Div., Luth. Brethren Sem., 1980. Ordained to ministry Ch. of Luth. Brethren, 1949. Pastor, Luth. Brethren Ch., Malta, Mont., 1945-46, N.Y.C., 1946-47, 59th St. Luth. Ch., Bklyn., 1947-54, Yellowstone Luth. Brethren Ch., Billings, Mont., 1954-57, Immanuel Luth. Ch., Pasadena, 1957-62; prof. systematic theology Luth. Brethren Sem., Fergus Falls, Minn., 1962—, pres., 1984—; v.p. Ch. Luth. Brethren, Fergus Falls, 1970—, sec., 1958-69; dist. pres. Central Dist., Ch. Luth. Brethren, 1970—; v.p. Luth. Brethren Schs., 1964—. Author: Baptism and Related Doctrine, 1950; Knowing Good from Evil, 1980. Republican. Home: Route 1 Box 240 Fergus Falls MN 56537 Office: Luth Brethren Schs W Vernon Ave Fergus Falls MN 56537

GLADDEN, RICHARD K., minister. Exec. dir. Am. Bapt. Churches in the U.S.A., Bd. of Ednl. Ministries, Valley Forge, Pa. Office: Bd of Ednl Ministries Valley Forge PA 19481*

GLASER, JOSEPH BERNARD, religious assn. exec.; b. Boston, May 1, 1925; s. Louis James and Dena Sophie (Harris) G.; B.A., UCLA, 1948; J.D., U. San Francisco, 1951; B.H.L., Hebrew Union Coll., 1954, M.H.L., 1956, D.D., 1981; postdoctoral student Hebrew U., 1970; m. Agathe Maier, Sept. 23, 1951; children: Simeon, Meyer, Sara, John. Rabbi Ventura County Jewish Council, Ventura, Calif., 1956-59; registrar, instr. homiletics Hebrew Union Coll., 1956-59; regional dir. Union of Am. Hebrew Congregations, No. Calif., Pacific Northwest, 1959-71; exec. v.p. Central Conf. Am. Rabbis, N.Y.C., 1971—. Vice-chmn. San Francisco Conf. on Religion and Race, 1963-69; vice-chmn. San Francisco Conf. on Religion and Peace, 1965-71; chmn. Clergy Com. Negotiated Agreement with UFWOC-Teamsters-Grape Growers, 1966-67; mem. Calif. State Legislature Panels on Revision of Criminal Code and Teaching of Bill of Rights, 1966-69; chmn. San Francisco Conf. Religion and Drugs, Police and Social Revolution, 1968-69; chmn. Religion in Am. Life, 1978-82; mem. life membership com. NAACP; mem. exec. com. Synagogue Council Am.; bd. dirs. Am. Hebrew Congregations. Office: 21 E 40th St New York NY 10016

GLASGOW, FRANCIS MARION, lay church worker, United Meth. Ch.; b. Akron, Ohio, Dec. 22, 1913; s. John William and Neva Janet (Brown) G.; grad. high sch.; m. Mabel Ethel Felton, Mar. 7, 1936; children—Patricia (Mrs. Rex Walter Dinsmore), Sandra (Mrs. Philip Thomas Robinson). Akron Dist. lay leader Methodist Ch., 1964-67, 82-84; asso. conf. lay leader, N.E. Ohio Conf., 1967-68, lay leader, 1968-72; treas. North Central Jurisdiction Assn. Conf. Lay Leaders, 1969-72, mem. leadership devel., 1971-72; mem. various coms. East Ohio Conf., 1972—; del. Uniting Conf. and Gen. Conf. United Meth. Ch., Dallas, 1968, United Meth. Gen. Conf., St. Louis, 1970, Atlanta, 1972, Portland, Oreg., 1976; del to Jurisdictional Confs., Peoria, Ill., 1968, Indpls., 1972, Sioux Falls, S.D., 1976, Dayton, 1980, Duluth, Minn., 1984. assisted with UN Meth. Seminar to N.Y.C., 1967; del. Ohio Council of Churches, 1969-71; apptd. del. World Meth. Conf., Denver, 1971; chmn. pastor-parish relations com. Faith United Meth. Ch., Brimfield, Ohio, 1965—; mem. N. Central Jurisdictional Council on Fin. and Adminstrn., 1972-80. Technician compound devel. lab. Firestone Tire and Rubber, Akron, 1942—. Pres., Brimfield Lake Assn., 1967-68. Mem. E. Ohio Conf. Assn. Lay Speakers (pres. 1973-80, Episcopacy com. 1985—). Home: 3755 Martha Rd Kent OH 44240

GLASSER, ROBIN BARBARA, librarian, educator, Jewish; b. N.Y.C., Oct. 9, 1935; d. Sam Sacknoff and Lillian Sacknoff; m. Jay H. Glasser; children: Jaime, Carrie, Marck and Tracey (twins). B.A., Bklyn. Coll., 1959; M.L.S. U. N.C.-Chapel Hill, 1970. Head librarian Congregation Beth Yeshurun, Rubin Kaplon Meml. Library, Houston, 1970—. Contbr. articles to profl. jours. Mem. ALA, Tex. Library Assn. Address: 5727 Valkeith Houston TX 77096 Office: Cantor Rubin Kaplan Meml Library of Cong Beth Yeshurun 4525 Beechnut Houston TX 77096

GLAZIER, FREDERICK LEROY, JR., minister, Luth. Ch. in Am.; b. Springfield, Ohio, Dec. 8, 1938; s. Frederick Leroy and Leah Mae (Young) G.; B.A., Newberry (S.C.) Coll., 1960; B.D., M.A., Luther Theol. Sem., Saskatoon, Sask., Can., 1965; m. Donna Louise Apolzon, Aug. 28, 1960; children—Cynthia Louise, Frederick Leroy, III, Erick Albert Lee, Melissa Lynn. Ordained to ministry, 1965; asst. pastor, Cin., summer 1960; dir. group work Luth. Inner Mission, Springfield, Ohio, 1960-61; organizer, pastor Resurrection Luth. Ch., St. Peter's Luth. Ch., Calmar, Alta., Can., 1962-63; pastor chs. in Sask. and No. Alta., Can., 1963-66; asso. pastor St. John's Ch., Russell, Kans., 1966-67, Scherer Meml. Ch., Chapman, Kans., 1967-68; commd. capt. U.S. Army, 1968, advanced to maj., 1976; chaplain U.S. Army Hosp., Ft. Carson, 1968-69, 269th Combat Aviation Bn., Vietnam, 1969-70; group chaplain 11th M.P. Group, Ft. Bragg, N.C., 1970-71; chaplain adviser upper delta area Vietnam, 1971-72; asst. brigade chaplain 4th Combat Support Brigade, Ft. Polk, La., 1972-74; bn. chaplain 4th/23d Inf., temp. brigade chaplain 172d Inf., now asst. post chaplain Ft. Richardson, Alaska, 1974—; supervisory chaplain for dir. religious edn. and Sunday Sch. Program and for sr. high and jr. high Protestant youth of chapel groups, also support Bn. chaplain, stockade chaplain, drug & alcohol chaplain, 1974—; chaplain for Am. Boy Scouts attending Australian Nat. Jamboree, 1976; dist. chmn. for scouting Denali dist. Western Alaska council Boy Scouts Am.; leader Alaska Scouts, Canadian 77th Jamboree, also chaplain; recipient Scout Tng. award Scouter Key, Silver Beaver, Wood Badger awards. Decorated Bronze Star medal with 2 oak leaf cluster, Air medal with 3 oak leaf clusters, Army Commendation medal with oak leaf cluster, Purple Heart, Cross of Gallantry 1st class (Vietnamese); recipient Social Service medal 2d class Civilian Govt. Vietnam, 1970-72. Author numerous pamphlets, tracts and articles. Home: 394-C Kenai Fort Richardson AK 99505 Office: PO Box 5-409 Post Chapel APO Seattle 98749

GLICK, GARLAND WAYNE, minister, educator, Ch. of Brethren; b. Bridgewater, Va., Jan. 27, 1921; s. John Titus and Effie Iwilla (Evers) G.; B.A., Bridgewater Coll., 1941, LL.D., 1970; B.D., Bethany Theol. Sem., 1946; M.A., U. Chgo., 1949, Ph.D., 1957; m. Barbara Roller Zigler, Jan. 1, 1943; children—Martha, John Theodore, Mary Margaret. Ordained to ministry Ch. of Brethren, 1945; minister Ch. Brethren, Richmond, Va., 1942-43; asst. minister Warren Ave. Congl. Ch., Chgo., 1944-45; minister York Center Ch. Brethren, Lombard, Ill., 1945-48; asst. prof. bibl. studies Juniata Coll., Huntingdon, Pa., 1948-53; asst. prof. to prof. religion Franklin and Marshall Coll., Lancaster, Pa., 1955-66; pres. Keuka Coll., Keuka Park, N.Y., 1966-74; dir. Moton Ctr. for Ind. Studies, Phila., 1975-78; pres. Bangor Theol. Sem., Maine, 1978—. Mem. program and budget com. Margaret Woodbury Strong Found., 1968-74; mem. program com. on edn. in soc. Nat. Council Chs., 1966-82, chmn., 1976-82. Mem. Am. Acad. Religion, Am. Soc. Ch. History, Am. Conf. Acad. Deans (treas. 1965-66). Democrat. Author: The Reality of Christianity, 1967. Home: 15 5th St Bangor ME 04401

GLOCK, DELMAR JULIAN, minister, Lutheran Church-Missouri Synod; b. Grangeville, Idaho, Dec. 23, 1926; s. Ernest and Meta (Matulle) G.; m. Jessie Lee Hamm, July 23, 1950; children: Nathan, Delmar Julian, Melanie L., Jacob L., Marie A. B.A., Concordia Theol. Sem., St. Louis, 1947, B.D., 1950. Ordained to ministry Luth. Ch.-Mo. Synod, 1951. Dir., founder Japan Luth. Hour, Tokyo, Japan, 1951-57; missionary Ryukyu Islands, Okinawa, 1958-65; asst. dir. overseas broadcasting Luth. Laymens League, 1965-67; mass communication cons. Luth. Mission, Seoul, Korea, 1969-71; area rep. Far East Broadcasting Co., Korea, 1971-72; pastor Trinity Luth. Ch., Daytona Beach, Fla., 1972—. Served to capt. U.S. Army, 1960-66. Home: 215 Euclid Ave Daytona Beach FL 32018 Office: Trinity Luth Ch 1205 Ridgewood Ave Holly Hill FL 32017

GLOGOWSKI, JOHN JOSEPH, priest, Roman Cath. Ch.; b. Rochester, N.Y., Mar. 11, 1935; s. Joseph Thomas and Rita (Schwarzmeier) G.; B.A., St. Bernard's Sem., 1958; M.S., Syracuse U., 1974. Ordained priest, 1962; asst. pastor St. John The Evangelist Ch., Rochester, N.Y., 1962-65; asso. pastor Holy Family Ch., Auburn, N.Y., 1965-73, Immaculate Conception Ch., Ithaca, N.Y., 1973—. Founder, Christian Edn. Dept. Auburn Region, 1966, dir., 1966-73. Dir., Office of Fam. Life, Auburn, N.Y.,

1966-73; asso. dir., chief of chaplains service Cayuga County (N.Y.) Civil Defense, 1966-73; chaplain Auburn (N.Y.) Police Dept., Auburn Fire Dept., Fleming (N.Y.) Fire Dept., 1966-73, Ithaca Fire Dept., 1975—; dir. Office of Family Life, Ithaca, 1975—. Chmn. bd. dirs. Tompkins County R.C., 1973—. Received Key to City of Auburn (N.Y.), 1973. Mem. The Liturgical Conf. (life mem.), Nat. Alliance for Family Life. Address: 113 N Geneva St Ithaca NY 14850

GLOSSON, HENRY BRIGHT, III, minister, Christian Churches/Churches of Christ; b. Burlington, N.C., May 8, 1945; s. Henry Bright and Virginia Dare (Shepherd) G.; m. Eva Annette Williams, May 29, 1966; 1 child, Nathaniel Henry. A.A.S., Tech. Coll. Alamance, 1967; A.B. in Ministry, Atlanta Christian Coll., 1974; M.Div., Emmanuel Sch. Religion, 1977. Ordained to ministry Christian Chs./Chs. of Christ, 1974. Youth minister chs. Kingsport, Tenn., 1974-75, Decatur, Ga., 1973, Newport News, Va., 1971-73; sr. minister Carter Christian Ch., Elizabethton, Tenn., 1975-76, Burlington Ch. of Christ, N.C., 1977-83, First Ch. of Christ, Altoona, Pa., 1985—; v.p. in west 1000 Club, Williamston, N.C., 1978-83; pres. bd. Campus Christian Fellowship, U. N.C., Chapel Hill, 1982-84; v.p. Piedmont Evangelizing Fellowship, Burlington, 1981-83; state conv. talent chmn. Carolina Christian Youth Conf., Chapel Hill, 1982-83; missionary tchr. World Bible Inst. to Curacao, Netherland Antilles, 1982. Author: The Essentials of Christian Baptism, 1977. Author/editor Carter Christian Caller, 1975-76, Burlington Broadcaster, 1977-83, N.C. Christian Progress, 1977-82, The Caller, 1985—. Contbr. articles to profl. jours.; author of booklets. Vol. and care team Suicide and Crisis Service, Alamance County, 1979-82. Mem. Piedmont Dist. Christian Ministerial Assn. (sec. 1978-83), Altoona Area Clery Assn., Am. Schs. Oriental Research. Republican. Avocations: bibliophile; writer; fisherman. Home: 2907 4th Ave Altoona PA 16602-1931 Office: First Ch of Christ Route 4 Box 167 Altoona PA 16601-9749

GLOVER, NORMAN SPENCER, minister, Baptist Missionary Association of America; b. Clifton, N.J., Apr. 29, 1929; s. Clarence Holton and Daisy Marshal (Newman) G.; m. Joyce Bryant, Jan. 21, 1972; children: Norman Spencer, II, Carnie Holton. B.A., Pierre-Royston Acad., 1950; Th.M., Maranatha Bible Sem., 1966; M.Div., Meth. Theol. Sem., 1978; Th.D., Internat. Bible Inst. and Sem., 1983. Ordained to ministry Bapt. Missionary Assn. Am., 1950. Pastor, Mt. Moriah Bapt. Ch., Linden, N.J., 1950-52, Messiah Bapt. Ch., East Orange, N.J., 1953-70, Christ Meml. Bapt. Ch., Columbus, Ohio, 1971-78, Trinity Missionary Bapt. Ch., Cin., 1978—; moderator Shiloh Bapt. Assn., N.J., 1966-70; pres. Bapt. Ministerial Alliance, Columbus, 1972-74; instr. Ohio Bapt. Congress of Christian Edn., 1972; prof. theology Temple Bible Coll. and Sem., Cin., 1981. Author: Church Music, 1975; The Cults and the Church, 1978; Trilogy of Theological Cognition, 1984. Contbr. articles to mags. Mem. Human Relations Commn., East Orange, 1962; pres. Bd. Police Commrs., East Orange, 1965. Recipient Pres.'s award Temple Bible Coll. and Sem., 1983. Democrat. Home: 6501 Stoll Ln Cincinnati OH 45236 Office: Trinity Missionary Bapt Ch 6320 Chandler St Cincinnati OH 45227

GNAT, THOMAS J., bishop, Polish National Catholic Ch. Am., Eastern Diocese. Office: 635 Union St Manchester NH 03104*

GOAD, DAVID GENOA, minister, Southern Baptist Convention; b. Morrison, Tenn., Nov. 2, 1938; s. James Leonard and Veda May (Pendergraft) G.; B.A., Wayland Bapt. Coll., 1962; M.Div., Bapt. Sem. (Southwestern), 1969; m. Martha Mae Rector, Aug. 25, 1961; children: Rebecca Ranei, Sherri Lyn. Ordained to ministry, 1961; pastor Trinity Bapt. Ch., Dickens, Tex., 1961-63, Friendship Bapt. Ch., Cleburne, Tex., 1964-66, First Bapt. Ch., Goree, Tex., 1966-70, Northside Bapt. Ch., Plainview, Tex., 1970-72, First Bapt. Ch., Vega, Tex., 1972-76, First Bapt. Ch., Stratford, Tex., 1976—. Evangelist, Korea, 1975, Brazil, 1980, 81, Can., 1984; mem. Tex. Bapt. Exec. Bd., 1977—; pres. Pastors and Laymen Conf. Panhandle of Tex., 1985. Home: PO Box 796 Stratford TX 79084 Office: PO Box 390 Stratford TX 79084

GOATES, DONALD RAY, minister, So. Bapt. Conv.; b. Corpus Christi, Tex., Jan. 14, 1943; s. Joe Elbert and Willie Bob (Cochran) G.; Mus.B. in Edn., E.Tex. State U., 1965; M.Div., Southwestern Bapt. Theol. Sem., 1974, postgrad., 1976—; m. Patsy La Netta Owens, June 7, 1963; children—Gretchen Gwyndolyn, Sunnae Millicent, Donald Ray II. Ordained to ministry, 1972; minister of music So. Bapt. Conv., Delta County, Tex., 1962-63; pastor Water St. Bapt. Ch., Waxahachie, Tex., 1972-76, 1st Bapt. Ch. of Forest Hill, Ft. Worth, 1976—. Home: 3451 Cardinal Ridge Fort Worth TX 76119 Office: 3430 Horton Rd Fort Worth TX 76119

GOCKLEY, DAVID WOODROW, ecumenical exec.; b. Ephrata, Pa., Oct. 9, 1918; s. David and Elizabeth (Donner) G.; A.B., Lebanon Valley Coll., 1942; M.Div., United Theol. Sem., 1945; M.A., Temple U., 1955; m. Olive Porter, Apr. 21, 1945; children—Pamela, Charles, David, Sally, Stephanie, Brian. Ordained minister United Methodist Ch., 1945; youth pastor, Dayton, Ohio, 1943-45; dir. pub. relations Lebanon Valley Coll., 1945-48; chaplain Lebanon Valley Coll., 1948-51; pastor United Meth. Ch., Phila., 1951-56; exec. sec. dept. pub. relations Greater Phila. Council Chs., 1956-61; dir. pub. relations Religion in Am. Life, N.Y.C., 1961-69, dir., exec. v.p., 1969—. Mem. Phila. Youth Services Bd., 1958-61; TV commn. Pa. Council Chs., 1959-61; bd. mgrs. broadcasting and film commn. Nat. Council Chs., 1959-62; chmn. Westport office Alcoholism Council Mid-Fairfield County, 1970. Mem. Religious Pub. Relations Council (pres. Phila. 1960-61, nat. pres. 1964-66), Lebanon Valley Coll. Alumni Assn. (citation 1975). Home: 8 Pond Edge Rd Westport CT 06880 Office: 475 Fifth Ave New York City NY 10017

GODFREY, WILLIAM NELSON, minister, Ch. of God in Christ; b. Wallisville, Tex., Oct. 12, 1911; s. John W. and Rose (Raymond) G.; student Career Inst., 1950-52, Prairie View Coll., 1966-68; D.D., Universal Bible Inst., 1972; m. Josie McBride, Sept. 17, 1935. Ordained to ministry, 1939; pastor, Wallisville, 1938-46, Liberty, Tex., 1939-46, Port Arthur, Tex., 1946-57, Houston, 1957—. Dist. supt. Ch. of God in Christ, 1947—, state chmn., 1958-72, adminstrv. asst., 1972—. Recipient citation of spl. commendation Houston Garden Elementary Sch., 1974. Home: 4301 Dabney St Houston TX 77026 Office: 7206 N Main St Houston TX 77022

GODIN, EDGAR, bishop, Roman Catholic Church; b. Neguac, N.B., Can., May 31, 1911; s. Joseph Albany and Marguerite (Breau) G.; B.A., Sacred Heart U., Bathurst, N.B., 1935; Licentiate in Canon Law, Gregorian U., Rome, 1948; Dr. in Canon Law (hon.), U. Bathurst, 1955. Ordained priest, 1941; consecrated bishop, 1969; retreat master St. Josephs Retreat House, Bathurst, 1942-48; chancellor Diocese of Bathurst, 1948-55, vicar gen., 1955-59, bishop of Bathurst, 1959—. Nat. pres. Canadian Assn. Cath. Hosps. Author: Hospital Ethics, 1954. Address: 645 Ave Murray CP 460 Bathurst NB E2A 3Z4 Canada

GODSEY, JOHN DREW, educator, minister, United Methodist Church; b. Bristol, Tenn., Oct. 10, 1922; s. William Clinton and Mary Lynn (Corns) G.; B.S., Va. Poly. Inst. and State U., 1947; B.D., Drew U., 1953; D.Theol., U. Basel (Switzerland), 1960; m. Emalee Caldwell, June 26, 1943; children: Emalee Lynn Godsey Murphy, John Drew, Suzanne Godsey Douglas, Gretchen Godsey Brownley. Ordained to ministry, 1952; instr. systematic theology, asst. dean Drew U., Madison, N.J., 1956-59, asst. prof. systematic theology, 1959-64, asso. prof., 1964-66, prof., 1966-68; prof. systematic theology, asso. dean Wesley Theol. Sem., Washington, 1968-71, prof., 1971—. Mem. Montgomery County (Md.) Fair Housing Assn., 1968—. Fulbright scholar U. Goettingen (Germany), 1964-65. Mem. Karl Barth Soc. N.Am., New Haven Theol. Discussion Group, Am. Acad. Religion, Am. Theol. Soc., AAUP, Bibl. Theologians, Internat. Bonhoeffer Soc., Omicron Delta Kappa, Phi Kappa Phi, Alpha Zeta. Author: The Theology of Dietrich Bonhoeffer, 1960; Karl Barth's Table Talk, 1963; Preface to Bonhoeffer, 1965; Introduction and epilogue to Karl Barth's How I Changed My Mind, 1966; The Promise of H. Richard Niebuhr, 1970; co-editor: Ethical Responsibility: Bonhoeffer's Legacy to the Churches, 1981. Home: 8306 Bryant Dr Bethesda MD 20817 Office: 4500 Massachusetts Ave NW Washington DC 20016

GODWIN, JANIS HILBURN, lay worker, Foursquare Church; elementary educator; b. Monroe, La., June 19, 1940; d. William Baskin and Eva Lenora (Crow) Hilburn; m. Charles B. Godwin, Aug. 16, 1964; 1 child, Aimee Noelle. B.A. in Elementary Edn., U. Northeast La. State, 1962; postgrad. Southwestern Bapt. Theol. Sem., 1962-63, U. North Fla., 1983—. Youth choir dir., soloist First Bapt. Ch., Fernandina Beach, Fla., 1963-64; dir. youth choirs Hyde Park Bapt. Ch., Jacksonville, Fla., 1964-71; pianist, youth leader Jacksonville Foursquare Ch., 1973-83, music worship leader, 1981-83, dir. children's edn., 1983—, dir. youth drama, 1973-80; bible tchr. United Foursquare Women, Jacksonville, 1976-80; bible tchr., intercessor Women's Aglow Fellowship, Orange Park, Fla.; 1980-82, organizer, v.p., bible tchr., speaker, Women's Aglow Fellowship Westside, Jacksonville, 1984—; speaker full gospel groups, Fla., 1982—. Author youth dramas for small chs. Spiritual life chmn. Stonewall Jackson PTA, 1984—. Mem. Duval Tchrs. Assn. (exec. bd. 1965-68), Duval Tchrs. United. Democrat. Avocations: free-lance writing; music; puppets, bible study. Home: 6250 Autlan Dr Jacksonville FL 32210 Office: Jacksonville Foursquare Ch Hyde Grove Ave Jacksonville FL 32210

GOECKNER, MARY MARGE, nun, Benedictine Sisters, Roman Catholic Church; b. Cottonwood, Idaho, Jan. 28, 1937; d. Charles Henry and Margaret Mary (Bosse) G. A.A., Coll. St. Gertrude, 1961; B.A., St. Martin's Coll., 1968; M.A., Seattle U., 1974; postgrad. St. Anselmo Coll., Rome, 1976-77. Tchr., St. Nicholas Sch., Rupert, Idaho, 1959-61; prin., tchr. St. Mary's Sch., Boise, Idaho, 1961-67, St. Anthony's Sch., Pocatello, Idaho, 1967-70; dir. religious edn. Diocese of Boise, 1970-75; prioress of Idaho Corp. Benedictine Sisters, Cottonwood, 1977—; pres. Coll. St. Gertrude, 1977—. Mem. Leadership Conf. Women Religious, N.W. Assn. Bishops and Religious Superiors, Cath. Health Assn. U.S., Conf. Am. Benedictine Prioresses, Fedn. St. Gertrude. Home: Priory of St Gertrude Box 107 Cottonwood ID 83522 Office: Idaho Corp Benedictine Sisters Box 107 Cottonwood ID 83522

GOEHRING, CHARLES NIEBAUM, minister, Lutheran Church-Missouri Synod; b. Pitts., Apr. 17, 1923; s. Harvey John and Grace Emily (Niebaum) G.; m. Elinor Grace Overbeck, Apr. 30, 1955; children: Nancy R., Eunice L., David C. B.S. in Elec. Engring., 1944; B.Th., Concordia Sem., Springfield, Ill., 1954. Ordained to ministry Luth. Ch., 1954. Pastor, St. Paul's Luth. Ch., Long Beach, Calif., 1954-59, Holy Nativity Luth. Ch., Highland Heights, Ohio, 1959-69, Trinity Luth. Ch., Spencerport, N.Y., 1960—; pres., bd. dirs. Greater Cleve. Fedn. Luth. Chs., 1955-58; pres., bd. dirs. Rochester Luth. Mission Soc., N.Y., 1975-84; circuit counselor Rochester West Circuit Luth. Ch.-Mo. Synod, 1980-83; chmn. Luth. Reformation Festival, Rochester, 1984. Mem. bd. ethics Town of Ogden, Spencerport, 1970—, chmn. narcotics guidance council, 1970-77, mem. youth-adult coalition, 1970-72. Served as cpl. U.S. Army, 1949-50. Recipient Cert. Achievement, Greater Cleve. Fedn. Luth. Chs., 1958. Mem. Rochester Luth. Pastoral Conf. (pres. 1971-73), Spencerport Ecumenical Clergy (pres. 1974-77), Bd. for Community Ministry (chmn. bd. 1976-78, 84—). Home: 171 Nichols St Spencerport NY 14559 Office: Trinity Luth Ch 191 Nichols St Spencerport NY 14559

GOERING, LEONARD LOWELL, minister, Presbyterian Church in the U.S.; b. McPherson, Kans., June 22, 1938; s. Ellis Elbert and Esther Elva (Wedel) G.; m. Jane Ellen Kurtz, Dec. 15, 1980; children: David, Jonathan, Rebekah. Ph.B., Northwestern U., 1964; postgrad. Northeastern Ill. U., Chgo., 1969-72; M.Div., McCormick Theol. Sem., 1973; postgrad. Vanderbilt U., 1975-77. Ordained to ministry Presbyn. Ch., 1977. Campus pastor United Ministeries in Higher Edn., Emporia, Kans., 1973-75, Univ. Christian Ministeries, So. Ill. U., Carbondale, 1977-80; pastor United Presbyn. Ch., Trinidad, Colo., 1981—; instr. philosophy Trinidad State Coll., 1983—. Congl. dist. coordinator Bread for the World, Ill. 5, 1981; local bd. chmn. Fed. Emergency Mgmt. Agy., Las Animas County, Colo., 1984. Bernadine Orme Smith fellow McCormick Theol. Sem., Vanderbilt U., 1973. Mem. Assn. Mental Health Clergy, Trinidad Ministerial Assn. (pres. 1981-83). Home: 721 Pine St Trinidad CO 81082 Office: United Presbyn Ch 224 N Commercial St Trinidad CO 81082

GOERING, PETER W., minister, Gen. Conf. Mennonite Ch.; b. Moundridge, Kans., May 23, 1909; s. Andrew C. and Katherine (Flickner) G.; student McPherson Coll., 1928-29; B.A., Bethel Coll., 1932; student U. Chgo., 1937, Kans. U., 1939, Emporia Tchrs. Coll., 1955-60, U. Minn., 1963; M.Div., Hartford Theol. Sem., 1943; m. Mary Elizabeth Henderson, May 22, 1943; children—Deanne (Mrs. Gerald Duerksen), Peter W., Peggy Sue. Ordained to ministry, 1943; pastor, high sch. tchr., Methodist chs., Barnes, Kans., 1943, Linn, Kans., 1944-47; pastor, high sch. tchr. Mennonite Ch., Lehigh, Kans., 1947-61; sch. prin., supply pastor Mennonite Chs., McPherson, Halstead, Inman and Moundridge, Kans., 1961-66; pastor Mennonite Ch., Lehigh, 1967—; dir. Northview Opportunity Center, Newton, Kans., 1970—. Mem. Coms. Western Dist. Gen. Conf. Mennonite Ch., 1951—. Mem. Nat. Edn. Assn., Kans. State Tchrs. Assn., Lehigh C. of C., Assn. Tchrs. Fgn. Langs. Home: Box 116 Lehigh KS 67073

GOETZ, ROGER MELVIN, minister, Lutheran Church-Missouri Synod; b. Chgo., May 17, 1940; s. Charles Albert and Sidonia Helene (Heck) G.; 1 child, Anne-Katharine. B.S. in Chemistry, Iowa State U., 1962, B.S. in Math., 1967; B.D., Concordia Theol. Sem., Springfield, Ill., 1967; S.T.M., Luth. Theol. Sem., 1972. Ordained to ministry Luth. Ch., 1968. Asst. pastor, dir. music Gethsemane Luth. Ch., St. Paul, 1968-80, St. John's Luth. Ch., Topeka, Kans., 1980—; instr. Walther Luth. Jr. High Sch., St. Paul, 1968-80; mem. hymnal introduction com., musician Kans. Dist. Luth. Ch.-Mo. Synod, 1981-82, archivist, 1985—; co-founder, bd. dirs. East St. Paul Kantorei, St. Paul, 1972-76; organ recitalist various Luth. Chs., 1970—. Author: The Descendants of Johann Georg Gotz (1797-1862), 1976; Double Cousins by the Dozens, 1982; (booklet) A Goodly Heritage, 1984. Mem. Am. Guild Organists (chpt. pres. 1983-84), Phi Mu Alpha Sinfonia, Alpha Chi Sigma. Office: St John's Luth Ch 901 Filmore Topeka KS 66606

GOGGIN, CORNELIUS JOHN, priest, Roman Catholic Church; b. Keene, N.H., Apr. 24, 1931; s. Michael John and Margaret Mary (Driscoll) C. Student Holy Cross Coll., 1949-51; B.S.T., Grand Seminaire, St. Brieuc, France, 1956. Ordained priest Roman Cath. Ch., 1956. Assoc. pastor various chs., N.H., 1956-71; pastor St. Christopher's Ch., Nashua, N.H., 1971—; mem., former chmn. adminstrn. com. Diocese of Manchester, N.H., 1967—, del. Diocesan Fiscal Mgmt. Conf., 1974-84, exec. com., 1983-84; bd. dirs. Nashua Cath. Regional Schs., 1973-80, 83—; developer fund raising program for parishes, also bookkeeping system for parishes. Democrat. Address: St Christopher Rectory 62 Manchester St Nashua NH 03060

GOINS, WILLIAM WESLEY, minister, So. Baptist Conv.; b. Clay County, Ga., Oct. 26, 1932; s. Felix and Mary Lou (Peterson) G.; B.A. in Edn., La. Coll.,

Pineville, 1965; M.Th., New Orleans Bapt. Theol. Sem., 1969; m. Helen Maxine Garbett, Sept. 1, 1957; 1 son, William Wesley. Ordained to ministry, 1954; pastor chs. in Ga., Fla., La. and Miss., 1954-72; clin. chaplain Montgomery Correctional Instn., Mt. Vernon, Ga., 1972-74; dir. religious therapy programs Ga. Dept. Corrections, Atlanta, 1974—; dir. counseling First Bapt. Ch., Vidalia, Ga., 1973-74. Pres. Music Parents Assn., Lilburn, Ga., 1975-76; div. dir. United Way campaign, Atlanta, 1974-76. Mem. Internat. Transactional Analysis Assn., Am. Protestant (v.p. Southeastern region), Am. correctional chaplains assns., Ga., Ga. Bapt. (steering com.) chaplains assns. Home: 2161 Jordan Dr Tucker GA 30084 Office: 800 Peachtree St N Atlanta GA 30308

GOKEE, DONALD LEROY, clergyman, Presbyterian Church, U.S.A.; b. Lansing, Mich., Aug. 9, 1933; s. Richard Alden and June Elizabeth (Colenso) G.; m. Maxine Pawlik Adkins, Apr. 21, 1974; children: Douglas Richard, Charles Jeffrey, Mary Beth, Jessica Lynn. B.A., Mich. State U. and Temple U., Chattanooga, 1958; postgrad. (A. Morehouse and William Walker scholar 1962-63) George Washington U., 1960-64, Va. Theol. Sem., Union Theol. Sem., 1964-65, Columbia Theol. Sem., 1968, New Coll., U. Edinburgh, Scotland, 1975, Frankfurt (Germany), 1977, U. Athens, Greece, 1978; M.A. cum laude, Ph.D. magna cum laude, Columbia Pacific U. Ordained to ministry, Presbyn. Ch. U.S.A., 1965. Dir. Christian edn. Central Presbyn. Ch., Chattanooga, 1958-59, Fairlington Presbyn. Ch., Alexandria, Va., 1959-66; assoc. pastor Pine Shores Presbyn. Ch., Sarasota, Fla., 1966-69; pastor Conway Presbyn. Ch., Orlando, Fla., 1969—; frequent conf. speaker at colls., univs.; chaplain Orange County Juvenile Ct., 1969-73; mem. council Synod of Fla., 1972-75; mem. ecumenical coordinator team as Fla. rep. Presbyn. Ch., U.S., 1977-81; 1st ann. Gingerich meml. lectr. Goshen Coll., Ind.; vis. prof. So. Coll. Mem. Nat. Task Force on Criminal Justice and Prison Reform, 1976-82. Author: Rabbits or Pros?, 1972; contbr. articles to profl. jours. Recipient cert. of merit for disting. service to Christ, Ch. and Community, 1970; In-God-We-Trust award Family Found. A., 1980; key to City of Orlando, 1981; Mayoral Proclamation for 15 years dedicated service to young people and community, 1984. Home: 3026 Carmia Dr Orlando FL 32806 Office: 4300 Lake Margaret Dr Orlando FL 32806

GOLD, VICTOR ROLAND, educator, minister, Lutheran Ch. America; b. Garden City, Kans., Sept. 18, 1924; s. Helmuth Hugo Carl and Wilhelmina Johanna (Knake) G.; B.A., Wartburg Coll., Ia., 1944; B.D., Wartburg Theol. Sem., 1946; Ph.D., Johns Hopkins, 1951; postgrad. Am. Sch. Oriental Research, Jerusalem, 1951-52; m. children—Victor Roland II, Stephan Michael, Joanne Elisabeth. Ordained to ministry Am. Lutheran Ch., 1946; pastor chs. in Tex., 1946-47, St. Paul's Evang. Luth Ch., Balt., 1947-49; stated supply pastor Md. Synod, Luth. Ch. Am., 1949-51; pastor Trinity Evang. Luth. Ch., Kalamazoo, 1953-56; asst. prof. O.T., Hamma Div. Sch., Springfield, O., 1952-53; prof. O.T. Pacific Luth. Theol. Sem., Berkeley, Cal., 1956—, Grad. Theol. Union, Berkeley, 1962—. Guest prof. Kirchliche Hochschule, Berlin, Germany, 1959, 68; vis. prof. semitic langs. U. Calif., Berkeley, 1968—. Trustee Albright Inst. Archaeol. Research, 1981—; chmn. inclusive lang. lectionary com. Nat. Council Chs. of Christ in U.S. Hebrew Union Coll. fellow, 1963. Mem. Soc. Bibl. Lit. (sec. Pacific coast region 1961-76), Am. Schs. Oriental Research, Am. Oriental Soc., Archeol. Inst. Am., Pacific Coast Theol. Soc. Editor: Episcopacy in the Lutheran Church?, 1970; Kirchenprasident Oder Bischof?, 1968. The Mosaic Map of Madeba, Biblical Archaeologist Reader III, 1970; A Biblical View of the Secular, Christian Hope and the Secular, 1969; contbr. exegetical notes Oxford Annotated Bible, 1962, 75. Contbr. articles to profl. publs. Home: 775 Alvarado Rd Berkeley CA 94705 Office: 2770 Marin Ave Berkeley CA 94708

GOLDEN, GEORGE BALTON, minister, Ch. of God; b. Shawmut, Ala., Mar. 7, 1936; s. Augusta Lee and Annie Mae (Smith) G.; B. Sacred Music, Gulf Coast Bible Coll., 1968; M.Bible Studies, Universal Bible Inst., 1977; m. Hylance Laverne Sorrell, Sept. 4, 1955; 1 son, David Balton. Ordained to ministry, 1968; counselor, dormitory parent Gulf Coast Bible Coll., Houston, 1964-69; pastor chs., Tex., Kans., 1966-73; pastor 1st Ch. God, Odessa, Tex., 1973—. Mem. nat. music com. Ch. God; evangelist, marriage counselor, youth adviser; chmn. bd. Christian edn., W. Tex. Recipient Merit award Gulf Coast Bible Coll., 1966; named Pastor of Year, Kans., 1970. Contbr. articles to religious jours. Home: 1513 E 11th St Odessa TX 79761

GOLDEN, PAUL LLOYD, priest, Roman Catholic Church; b. San Francisco, Jan. 4, 1939; s. John Henry and Julia Lee (Clements) G. B.A., St. Mary's Sem., Perryville, Mo., 1961; M.Div., De Andreis Sem., Lemont, Ill., 1965; J.C.L., Gregorian U., Rome, 1967; J.C.D., St. Thomas U., Rome, 1971. Ordained priest Roman Cath. Ch., 1965. Prof. canon law Kenrick Sem., St. Louis, 1968-77, St. Louis U. Div. Sch., 1968-71, 75; dir. formation Kenrick Sem., 1970-77; pres./rector St. Thomas Sem., Denver, 1977-84; dir. Inst. Leadership, DePaul U., Chgo., 1984—; bd. dirs. St. Louis Theol. Consortium, 1970-74; mem. steering com., bishop's com. on priestly formation, Nat. Conf. Cath. Bishops, 1978-81; trustee St. Thomas Sem., Denver, 1984—. Contbg. author: The Formation of Clerics, 1984. Mem. Canon Law Soc. Am. (sec. 1973-74), Nat. Cath. Edn. Assn. Home: 2233 N Kenmore Ave Chicago IL 60614 Office: DePaul U 243 S Wabash Ave Chicago IL 60604

GOLDIE, ARCHIBALD R., minister, association executive, Baptist Church. Assoc. sec. Baptist World Alliance, Washington, 1981—. Office: Baptist World Alliance 1628 16th St NW Washington DC 20009*

GOLLEDGE, ROBERT WALTER, vicar, Episcopal Church; b. Worcester, Mass., May 19, 1933; s. Walter Percival and Hazel Vera (Hathaway) G.; A.B., Trinity Coll., 1955; M.Div., Episcopal Theol. Sch., 1958; D.D., Northeastern U., 1975; m. Roberta Naylor Smith, May 21, 1955; children: Susan Joyce, Robert Walter, Stephen John. Ordained to ministry Episcopal Ch., 1958; asst. to rector Ch. of the Atonement, Westfield, Mass., 1958-60; rector Ch. of the Messiah, Auburndale, Mass., 1960-71; summer rector St. Andrews-By-The Sea, Rye, N.H., 1965-70; vicar Christ Ch., (Old North Ch.), Boston, 1971—; Mem. presiding bishop's com. on bicentennial 1972-76; chmn. bicentennial com. Diocese of Mass., 1982-84, chmn. com. on examination of candidates for ministry, 1980—. Mem. Boston Mayor's Commn. on Violence, 1976. Recipient citation, Bryant & Stratton, 1975; Third Lantern award, Boston Rotary, 1975; named hon. chaplain to Bishop of Norwich, Eng., 1974. Mem. Order of the Paul Revere Patriots. Home: 24 N Shore Rd Hampton NH 03842 Office: 193 Salem St Boston MA 02113

GOLTZ, CARL MILTON, clergyman, Berean Fundamental Church Council; b. Falls City, Nebr., Sept. 9, 1923; s. Emil J. and Friederike (Wissman) G.; grad. Moody Bible Inst., Chgo., 1949; m. Doris L. Kent, Sept. 25, 1945; 1 dau., Carolyn Sue. Ordained minister Berean Fundamental Ch. Council, Inc., 1950; pastor, Torrington, Wyo., 1950-56, Scottsbluff, Nebr., 1956-74; pres. Berean Fundamental Chs., 1954—, exec. adviser, 1975—; chmn. four religious book stores, 1962—; pres. Maranatha Bible Camp, Maxwell, Nebr., 1965—. Author articles, booklet. Office: PO Box 397 North Platte NE 69103*

GOMES, ELIAS MANOEL, minister, So. Baptist Conv.; b. Vitoria, Brazil, Oct. 4; s. Tranoelino M. and Margarida Leandra Gomes; came to U.S., 1963; B.S.L., E.S. State Coll., Brazil, 1958; B.Th., Bapt. Sem. S. Brazil, 1962; M.R.E., Southwestern Bapt. Theol. Sem., Ft. Worth, 1964; M.Div., N.Y. Theol. Sem., 1967; M.A., Columbia Tchrs. Coll., 1973; m. Maria Helena Dias Sampaio, Feb. 2, 1963; children—Paulo Sergio, Debbie Helena. Ordained to ministry, 1962; pastor chs. in Brazil, Tex., and N.J., 1963-71; pastor Living Gospel Bapt. Ch., Rutherford, N.J., 1971-76; pastor internat. ministries So. Bapt. Conv., 1976—; evangelist for Portuguese, Spanish and English countries. Mem. gen. council Bapt. World Alliance; exec. bd. N.Y. State Bapt. Conv.; internat. corr., columnist O Jornal Batista, Rio de Janeiro. Author: Church Life, 1976. Home: 12705 Kalnor Ave Norwalk CA 90650 Office: 14000 San Antonio Dr Norwalk CA 90650

GONZALES, LUZ CAMACHO, evangelist Ch. God (Anderson, Ind.); b. Houston, Apr. 4, 1934; s. Bartolo Haro and Santitos Garcia (Camacho) G.; B. Th., Gulf Coast Bible Coll., 1964, Latin Am. Sem., Costa Rica, 1973; m. Carol Jean Troutt, July 17, 1960; children—Ronnie, Randy, Rebecca. Ordained pastor Ch. God, 1962; pastor ch., Houston, 1967-73; missionary, Mexico, Costa Rica; evangelist Spanish Am. Christian Crusades, Springfield, Ohio, city-wide crusades Latin Am. U.S., 1973—; radio speaker Nueva Dimension, daily program Latin Am., Tex., 1975—. Mem. Spanish Council Ch. God, Spanish Am. Christian Crusades (v.p. 1973—). Publ. bd. Warner Press, 1976—; contbr. articles to relgious mags. Home: 519 Moorefield Rd Springfield OH 45502 Office: 256 Linden Ave Springfield OH 45505

GONZALEZ, EDGAR MATEO, minister, American Baptist Association; electronic engineering technician; b. Managua, Nicaragua, Dec. 29, 1955; came to U.S., 1973; s. Mateo and Aura Marina (Leyton) G.; m. Cynthia Elizabeth Garcia, July 11, 1981. A.S., Los Angeles Trade Tech. Sch., 1977. Lic. to ministry Am. Bapt. Assn., 1982. Congl. music dir. Los Angeles City Bapt. Ch., 1974-80, deacon, 1978-80, youth dir., 1980-81; Hispanic pastor First Bapt. Ch., Pomona, Calif., 1982—. Technicial, Reap Inc., Upland, Calif., 1982—. Mem. Am. Bapt. Chs. (minister's council 1985—), Regional Ministerial Alliance, Am. Bapt. Chs. of Pacific Southwest. Office: First Bapt Ch 586 N Main St Pomona CA 91768

GONZALEZ, JOSE GONZALO, priest, Roman Cath. Ch.; b. Havana, Cuba, Dec. 25, 1927; s. Jose and Josefa (Rubio) G.; came to U.S., 1961; B.A. in Theology, Gregoriana U., Rome, 1953; M.A. in Piano, Havana U., 1958; B.A. in Philosophy, B.A. in Latin and Greek, Don Bosco Coll., Newton, N.J., 1962; M.A. in Spanish Lit., Fla. State U., 1970, Ph.D. in Spanish Lit., 1973. Ordained priest, 1954; dir. studies, prof. philosophy Salesian Sem. Havana, 1955-61; prof. Latin and music Don Bosco Coll., Newton, 1962-68; prof. Mary Help of Christians, Tampa, Fla., 1970-74; Newman chaplain Ga. So. Coll., 1974-77; asso. pastor St. Laurence Ch., Tampa, 1977—. Prof. Spanish, Italian, Latin and Greek, Fla. State U., 1968-70, Ga. So. Coll., 1970-74. Chaplain, Cuban Civic Club, Agrupacion Latinoamericana de Tampa. Mem. Phi Kappa Phi. Address: 4606 N Saint Vincent St Tampa FL 33614

GONZALEZ, MARIA DE JESUS CUEVA, nun, Roman Cath. Ch.; b. Esmeralda, Coahuila, Mexicao, Dec. 6, 1913; d. Juan Gonzalez Flores and Petra Cueva (de Gonzalez) F.; came to U.S., 1924, naturalized, 1954; student Robstown Sch., 1925. Joined Sisters of Incarnate Word and Blessed Sacrament, 1932; social worker Our Lady of Good Counsel, Brownsville, Tex., 1971—. Home: 700 W Jefferson St Brownsville TX 78520 Office: Route 2 Box 711A Brownsville TX 78520

GONZALEZ, RAFAEL GARCIA, bishop, Roman Catholic Church; b. Guadalajara, Mex., May 10, 1926; s. Jose Garcia Calderon and Carmen (Gonzalez) Chavez. Lic. Theology, Pio Latino Americano, Rome, 1949; Lic. Canon Law, Gregorian U., Rome, 1952. Ordained priest Roman Catholic Ch., 1949, ordained bishop, 1972. Instr. Sem. Guadalajara, 1952-67; founder, dir. Mex. Nat. Secretariate Priestly Vocations, 1955-67; spiritual dir. Mex. Pontifical Sem., Rome, 1967-70; bishop of Urbisaglia, 1972; residential bishop of Tabasco, Mex., 1974—; pres. Mex. Episcopal Secretariate for Evangelization and Catechetics, 1982; mem. Roman Cath. Bishops Synod in Rome, 1980; mem. Conferencia Episcopal Latino Americana, 1983—. Club: Paul VI. Lodge: KC. Home: Fidencia 502 Villahermosa Tabasco 86000 Mexico Office: Apartado Postal 97 Villahermosa Tabasco 86000 Mexico

GONZÁLEZ, ROMUALDO, lay worker, Episcopal Church; lawyer; b. La Havana, Cuba, Dec. 1, 1947; came to U.S., 1961, naturalized, 1966; s. Romualdo and Nohemi (Díaz) G.; m. Sally Howell, Jan. 22, 1972; children: Romualdo, Pablo. Student U. Madrid, 1967; B.A., U. of South, 1970; J.D., Tulane U., 1973; Bar: La. 1973. Bd. dirs., mem. exec. com. Nat. Commn. on Hispanic Ministries, N.Y.C., 1978-80; mem. Diocesan Refugee Com. of La., New Orleans, chmn. 1980-83; bd. dirs. Presiding Bishop's Fund for World Relief, Episc. Ch. Ctr., N.Y.C., 1980-83, mem. refugee and migration com., 1980-83; mem. responsibility in investments com., Episcopal Ch. Ctr., N.Y.C., 1984—; mem. Hispanic seminarians trust fund com., 1984—. Ptnr., Murray, Murray, Braden, Landry & Gonzalez, New Orleans, 1973—. Bd. dirs. Internat. House, Met. Area com., 1978-81; vice chmn. Central Am. Conf., 1979, mem. Central Am. Conf. Com., 1976-80; trustee Sta. WYES-TV; mem. adv. bd. Hispanic bus. devel. project Nat. Chamber Found., Washington 1982—; co-chmn. Reagan-Bush re-election com. of 2d congl. dist., 1984; chmn. Hispanic Democrats for Reagan, 1984. Mem. ABA, La. Bar Assn., New Orleans Bar Assn., Assn. Trial Lawyers Am., La. Trial Lawyers Assn., New Orleans C. of C. (bd. dirs.), Latin-Am. C. of C. (pres. 1977-78), Cuban Profls. (bd. dirs. 1976—, pres. 1978-79). Clubs: New Orleans Lawn Tennis, Pendennis. Club: Thackeray Soc. Home: 1818 Upperline Rd New Orleans LA 70115 Office: Murray Murray Braden Landry & Gonzalez 612 Gravier St New Orleans LA 70130

GOOCHEY, PEGGY LOUISE, educator, United Methodist Church; b. Tonkawa, Okla., Mar. 17, 1941; d. Jesse Elvin and Minnie Louise (Bushorr) Warren; m. Jimmy Dale Haggard, May 28, 1960 (div. June 1972); children: Tammra Louise, Jay Warren, Justin Wade; m. Jerry Milton Goochey, Feb. 14, 1973. B.A. in Speech and Theater, Okla. City U., 1979; M.R.E., So. Meth. U., 1985. Freelance Christian dramatist, Kans., Okla., Tex., 1974—; student pastor Okla. Conf., United Meth. Ch., Warner/Porum, 1979-81, Kingston/Woodville, 1981-82; dir. edn. Oak Lawn United Meth. Ch., Dallas, 1984—; family ministries coordinator Dallas Central dist. North Tex. Conf., United Meth. Ch., 1984—. Mem. Christian Educator's Fellowship (coordinator profl. resources 1985-86). Republican. Lodge: Soroptomist Internat. Home: 655 Park Blvd Apt 199 Grapevine TX 76051 Office: Oak Lawn United Methodist Ch 3014 Oak Lawn Dallas TX 75219

GOOD, EDWIN MARSHALL, educator; b. Bibia, Cameroon, Apr. 23, 1928; came to U.S., 1933; s. Albert Irwin and Mary Rachel (Middlemiss) G.; m. Janice Sundquist, July 26, 1952; children: Brian, Lawrence, John. B.A., Westminster Coll., 1949; B.D., Union Theol. Sem., 1953; Ph.D., Columbia U., 1958; M.A., Stanford U., 1974. Ordained to ministry, 1953, demittel, 1968. Faculty, Stanford U., Calif., 1956—, prof. religious studies, 1971—. Author: You Shall be My People, 1959; Irony in the Old Testament, 1964; Giraffes, Black Dragons and Other Pianos, 1983; The Eddy Collection of Musical Instruments, 1985. Contbr. articles to profl. jours. Kent fellow, 1955. Mem. Soc. Bibl. Lit., Am. Acad. Religion, Am. Musical Instrument Soc., Am. Musicological Soc. Democrat. Home: 827 Sonoma Ter Stanford CA 94305 Office: Dept Religious Studies Stanford Univ Stanford CA 94305

GOODINGS, ALLEN, bishop, Anglican Church of Canada; b. Barrows-in-Furness, Eng., May 7, 1925; came to Can., 1952; s. Thomas Jackson Goodings and Ada Tate; m. Joanne Talbot, Sept. 26, 1959; children: Suzanne Elizabeth, Thomas. B.A., Sir George Williams U., Montreal, 1958; Licentiate in Theology, Diocesan Theol. Coll., Montreal, 1959; D.D. (hon.), 1978; B.D., McGill U., 1959. Ordained deacon, Anglican Ch. Can., 1959, ordained priest, 1959. Deacon, Diocese Montreal, 1959, priest, 1959-69; dean of cathedral, Diocese of Que., 1969-77, bishop Diocese of Que., 1977—. Served to capt. chaplaincy corps Army of Can., 1966-69. Clubs: Garrison, Çercle Universitaire, Royal 22 Regt. Mess. Office: Anglican Diocese of Quebec 36 Rue Des Jardins Quebec PQ G1R 4L5 Canada

GOODMAN, ARNOLD, rabbi; pres. Rabbinical Assembly (Conservative). Office: The Rabbinical Assembly 3080 Broadway New York NY 10027*

GOODSON, JAMES LENARD, minister, So. Baptist Conv.; b. Augusta, Ga., Sept. 2, 1938; s. James Conrad and Rita Mae (Youngblood) G.; B.A., Grand Canyon Coll., 1962; B.D., Midwestern Bapt. Sem., 1965; Th.D., Southwestern Bapt. Sem., 1970; m. Gail Jacqueline Hartman, Aug. 25, 1961; children—Jacqueline Lenar, James Lenard. Ordained to ministry, 1963; pastor Silver Belle (Ariz.) Bapt. Ch., 1958-59, Yates (Mo.) Bapt. Ch., 1962-65, First Bapt. Ch., Trinidad, Tex., 1965-66; Bible tchr. Bapt. Student Union, U. Tex., Austin, 1968-69; pastor Emmanuel Bapt. Ch., Voorhees, N.J., 1969-72; editor Bapt. Sunday Sch. Bd., Nashville, 1972-73; pastor First Bapt. Ch., Fulton, Mo., 1973-77; dir. missions dept. Mo. Bapt. Conv., 1977—. Conf. leader Glorieta, Ridgecrest, and Windermere bapt. assemblies; mem. Nat. Bible Conf., Memphis, 1973—, Bible Conf. on Holy Spirit, St. Louis, 1975; chmn. com. on coms., Penn-Jersey Bapt. Conv., 1971, exec. bd. mem., 1971-72, chmn. pub. relations com., 1972, conv. rep. to N.J. Council of Alcohol Problems, 1970-72; pub. relations agt. Mo. Bapt. Conv. ann. meeting, Joplin, 1974; spl. worker Mo. Sunday Sch. Dept., 1973-76; mem. tellers com. So. Bapt. Conv., 1970, impact 80's com., 1976—. Recipient Puckett award for attainment in Greek, 1962. Contbr. articles in field to religious jours. Office: Bapt Bldg Jefferson City MO 65101

GOODWIN, EVERETT CARLTON, minister, American Baptist Churches in the U.S.A., Southern Baptist Convention; b. Los Angeles, July 28, 1944; s. Carlton Byron and Pauline (Freeman) G.; m. Jane Gray, Sept. 3, 1966; children: Elizabeth Jane, Leah Grace. B.A. in Polit. Sci., U. Chgo., 1966; M.Div., Andover Newton Theol. Sch., 1969; M.A. in History, Brown U., 1969, Ph.D., 1979. Ordained to ministry Am. Bapt. Chs. in U.S.A., 1971, So. Bapt. Conv., 1981. Asst. chaplain Harvard U. No. Bapt. Edn. Soc., Cambridge, Mass., 1968-69; asst. pastor Quidnick Bapt. Ch., Coventry, R.I., 1969-71; pastor People's Bapt. Ch., Cranston, R.I., 1971-78, First Bapt. Ch., Meriden, Conn., 1978-81, First Bapt. Ch., Washington, 1981—; chmn. United Ministries in Higher Edn., R.I. State Council Chs., 1976-78; bd. dirs. Am. Bapt. Chs. of R.I., Am. Bapt. Chs. of Conn.; mem. exec. council D.C. Bapt. Conv., 1981—. Author: The Magistracy Rediscovered, 1980. Contbr. revs. to profl. jours. Revisions editor: Diary of Isaac Backus, 1974. Mem. budget panel United Way Southeast New Eng., Providence, 1974-76, chmn. appeals com., 1977; trustee Cranston Pub. Library, R.I., 1976-78. Brown U. fellow, 1971; Woodrow Wilson fellow Woodrow Wilson Found., 1971-73; recipient Eastern Star Religious Leadership award, Providence, 1976. Mem. D.C. Bapt. Ministries Assn., Inter-ch. Club of D.C., Am. Bapt. Ministers Assn. Office: 1328 16th St NW Washington DC 20036

GOODWIN, RUSSELL DIXON, JR., minister, United Meth. Ch.; b. Yonkers, N.Y., Feb. 4, 1933; s. Russell Dickson and Agnes Mae (Williams) G.; diploma in theology Zion Bible Inst., 1953; B.A., Dutchess Community Coll., 1964, Berkshire Christian Coll., 1968; M.A., Hartford Sem. Found., 1970, M.Div., 1971; D.Min., Drew U., 1975; m. Jean Carol Ericksen, Apr. 24, 1954; children—David Russell, Debra Jean, Dean Carl. Ordained to ministry, 1956; pastor Beacon (N.Y.) Assembly of God Ch., 1957-67; pastor Bantam (Conn.) United Meth. Ch., 1967-70, South Bethlehem (N.Y.) United Meth. Ch., 1970-74, Aldersgate United Meth. Ch., Dobbs Ferry, N.Y., 1974—; new life missioner, dept. preaching ministries Bd. Discipleship, United Meth. Ch., 1972—. Sectional youth leader, eastern sect. Assemblies of God, N.Y., 1953-54, sectional sec. treas., 1958-60; mem. Hudson N. Dist. Council on Ministries, N.Y. Ann. conf. United Meth. Ch., 1972-74, Met. Dist. Spiritual Life Com., 1975—; mem. spiritual life com. St. Christophers Sch., Dobbs Ferry, N.Y., 1975—. Chairperson Urban Renewal Citizens Study Com., Beacon, N.Y., 1966-67, Beacon City Devel. Com., 1966-67; mem. South Bethlehem Devel. Com., 1973-74. Nominated Outstanding Civic Leader, City of Beacon, 1967; recipient Edward Everett Nourse prize Hartford Sem. Found., 1971. Home: 60 Seneca St Dobbs Ferry NY 10522 Office: 600 Broadway Dobbs Ferry NY 10522

GOODYEAR, CLARENCE JOSEPH, priest, Roman Catholic Church; b. Pitts., May 26, 1913; s. Clarence Joseph and Elizabeth Mary (Sullivan) G. B.A., St. Charles Borromeo Sem., 1934; M.A., Villanova U., 1944. Ordained priest Roman Catholic Ch., 1938. Tchr. St. Thomas More High Sch., Phila., 1938-58, Roman Cath. High Sch., Phila., 1958-66; pastor St. Philip Neri Ch., Lafayette Hill, Pa., 1966-75, St. Gabriel Ch., Phila., 1975-82, Holy Family Ch., Phila., 1982—. Home and Office: Holy Family Ch 234 Hermitage St Philadelphia PA 19127

GORDIS, ROBERT, Biblical scholar, clergyman, educator, author, editor; Jewish; b. Bklyn., Feb. 6, 1908; s. Hyman and Lizzie (Engel) G.; m. Fannie Jacobson, Feb. 5, 1928; children: Enoch, Leon, David. A.B. cum laude, CCNY, 1926; Ph.D., Dropsie Coll., 1929; rabbi (with distinction), Jewish Theol. Sem. Am., 1932, D.D., 1950; D.H.L. (hon.), Spertus Coll., Chgo., 1981. Ordained rabbi. Tchr., Hebrew Tchrs. Tng. Sch. for Girls, 1926-28, Yeshiva Coll., 1929-30, Sem. Coll. of Jewish Studies, 1931; lectr. Rabbinical Sch. Sem., 1937-40, prof. Bibl. exegesis, 1940-60; rabbi Rockaway Park Hebrew Congregation, 1931-69, rabbi emeritus, 1969—; adj. prof. religion Columbia U., 1948-57; cons. and assoc. Ctr. for Study Dem. Instns., Santa Barbara, Calif., 1960-80; vis. prof. O.T., Union Theol. Sem., 1953-54; Sem. prof. Bible, Jewish Theol. Sem., 1961-69, prof. Bible, also Rapaport prof. philosophies of religion, 1974-81, prof. emeritus, 1981—; vis. prof. religion Temple U., 1967-68, prof. 1968-74; vis. prof. Bible, Hewbrew U., Jerusalem, 1970; lectr. and speaker in field. Author books including: Wisdom of Ecclesiates, 1945; Conservative Judaism-An American Philosophy, 1945; Koheleth, The Man and His World, 1951; The Song of Songs, 1954; Judaism for the Modern Age, 1955; A Faith for Moderns, 1960; The Root and The Branch-Judaism and the Free Society, 1962; The Book of God and Man, A Study of Job, 1965; Judaism in a Christian World, 1966; Leave a Little to God, 1967; Sex and the Family in Jewish Tradition, 1967; Poets, Prophets and Sages, Essays in Biblical Interpretation, 1970; The Biblical Text in the Making, augmented edit., 1971. Chmn. bd. editors Rabbinical Assembly and United Synagogue Sabbath and Festival Prayer Book, 1946; Song of Songs-Lamentations, 1973; The Book of Esther, 1974; The Word and the Book: Studies in Biblical Language and Literature, 1976; The Book of Job: Commentary, New Translation and Special Studies, 1978; Love and Sex-A Modern Jewish Perspective, 1978; Understanding Conservative Judaism, 1978; assoc. editor dept. Bible Universal Jewish Ency.; contbg. editor: Jewish Digest, Jewish Quar. Rev., Med. Aspects of Human Sexuality.; bd. editors Judaism, 1942-68, editor, 1969—. Contbr. in field. Chmn. social justice com. Rabbinical Assembly Am., 1935-37, mem. exec. council, 1935, del. Synagogue Council Am., 1937-40, pres., 1940-41, pres. Rabbinical Assembly, 1944-46; founder Bel-El Day Sch. (now Robert Gordis Day Sch.), Belle Harbor, N.Y., 1950; mem. council on religious freedom NCCJ; bd. dirs. Inst. Ch. and State, Villanova U., Overseas mission War-Navy depts., investigating religious condition armed forces Pacific, Asiatic theatres, 1946; mem. exec. com. Nat. Hillel Commn., 1960-80, nat. adminstrv. council United Synagogue Am.; bd. govs. Nat. Acad. Adult Jewish Studies; mem. Nat. Com. on Scouting; pres. Synagogue Council Am., 1948-49, Jewish Book Council Am., 1980—; trustee Ch. Peace Union; assoc. trustee Am. Sch. Oriental Research, 1971-73. Recipient Nat. Jewish Book award, 1979; Centennial award Am. Jewish Congress. Fellow Am. Acad. Jewish Research. Office: 15 E 84th St New York NY 10028

GORDON, BARBARA ANN, religion educator, Roman Catholic Church; public school teacher; b. Cin., Jan. 31, 1950; d. James Joseph and Rosemary Virginia (Kuderer) Papke, m. Robert Steward Gordon, Apr. 1973. A.B., Mt. St. Joseph Coll., 1972; Ed.M., Miami U., Oxford, Ohio, 1982. Dir. religious edn. St. Aloysius Ch., Shandon, Ohio, 1981—, religious edn. instr., 1980—. Tchr., Ross Local Schs., Hamilton, Ohio, 1980—. Author jr. high sch. religious edn. curricula, 1984; sacramental preparation program for confirmation, 1984. Office: St Aloysius Ch PO Box 95 Shandon OH 45063

GORDON, CLEMENT DWIN, minister, Southern Baptist Convention; b. Cleburne, Tex., Feb. 26, 1933; s. Elwood and Marguerite G.; B.A., Baylor U., Waco, Tex., 1956; M.R.E., Southwestern Bapt. Theol. Sem., Ft. Worth, 1961; m. Alma Faye Brown, June 21, 1952; children—Joey Dale, Brenda Carol, Jerry Dwin. Ordained to ministry, 1954; pastor McClanahan Bapt. Ch., Marlin, Tex., 1954-57, First Bapt. Ch., Riesel, Tex., 1958-65; minister edn. First Bapt. Ch., Marlin, 1965-78; minister edn. Trinity Meml. Bapt. Ch., Marlin, 1980—. Sunday sch. dir., Royal Ambassadors; dir., ch. camp leader Falls Bapt. Assn. Tchr., Marlin Ind. Sch., 1956—. Bd. dirs. Central Tex. Horse Show and Rodeo Assn., 1962-64; past pres. Lions Club. Home: 102 Lakeview Dr Marlin TX 76661

GORDON, DAVID WALTER, church administrator, Episcopal Church; b. Oregon City, Oreg., Oct. 30, 1927; s. John Dawes and Dorothy (Wissinger) G.; m. Ann Curiale, Dec. 29, 1974; children by previous marriage: John David, Mary Elizabeth, Anne Catherine, James Charles; stepchildren: Andrew Dennis Miles, Elizabeth Ann Miles. B.S., Oreg. State U., 1948; M.Div., Ch. Div. Sch. Pacific, 1951. Ordained priest Episcopal Ch.; rector, St. Martin's Episcopal Ch., Lebanon, Oreg., 1951-58; vicar St. Francis Episcopal Ch., Sweet Home, Oreg., 1952-58; rector St. James Episcopal Ch., Coquille, Oreg., 1958-60; provincial sec. for coll. work 8th Province, Berkeley, Calif., 1960-63; rector Holy Trinity Episcopal Ch., Richmond, Calif., 1963-73, Ch. of Epiphany, San Carlos, Calif., 1973-82; dir. stewardship Diocese of N.Y., N.Y.C., 1982—; trustee Ch. Divinity Sch. Pacific, Berkeley, 1964-76; chmn. dept. coll. work Diocese of Calif., 1965-67, chmn. dept. edn., 1967-70, dir. vocations, 1968-72, mem. diocesan council, 1965-70, 72-73; past mem. coms. Diocese of Oreg., Province of Pacific; mem. West Contra Costa Council Chs., 1963-73, v.p., 1965; charter mem. Greater Richmond Interfaith program, 1966-73. Bd. dirs. West Contra Costa chpt. ARC, 1965-73; bd. dirs. Richmond Symphony, 1964-65. Lodge: Rotary. Home: 700 Scarsdale Ave Apt 3T Scarsdale NY 10583 Office: Diocese of NY 1047 Amsterdam Ave New York NY 10025

GORMAN, CELINE, nun, administrator, Roman Catholic Church; b. Chgo., June 15, 1908; d. Patrick Phillip and Anna Loretta (Liston) G. B.A. in Edn. and English, Fontbonne Coll., 1945; M.A. in Edn. and History, De Paul U., 1950; M.A. in Lit., Notre Dame U., 1960; M.A. in Theology, Loyola U., Chgo., 1970. Joined Sisters of St. Joseph of Carondelet, Roman Cath. Ch.; cert. high sch. tchr., prin., Ga. Prin. Sacred Heart Sch., Atlanta, 1947-53, Mt. Joseph Sch., Augusta, Ga., 1953-57; chmn. English dept. St. Pius High Sch., Atlanta, 1964-69; religious coordinator St. Joseph Parish, Marietta, Ga., 1969-74; religious coordinator Cathedral of Christ the King, Atlanta, 1975—, also mem. parish council, bd. edn.; dir. cathechetical ctr. Archdiocese of Miami, Fla., 1974-75; ecumenical chmn. Ch. Women United, Marietta, 1969-74; Book reviewer The Voice, 1974-75. Ecumenical chmn., sponsor Neighborhood Youth Corps Group, Chgo., 1972. Recipient Star Tchr. award St. Pius Star Student, 1967, plaque Atlanta Citizen, 1982. Mem. Nat. Cath. Music Assn. Avocations: dancing; dramatics; reading; writing. Home: 2479 Peachtree Rd Apt 712 Atlanta GA 30305 Office: Cathedral of Christ the King 2699 Peachtree Rd Atlanta GA 30305

GORMAN, LEO JOSEPH, priest, Roman Catholic Church; b. Far Rockaway, N.Y., June 11, 1929; s. Joseph J. and Helen Cecilia (Lally) G.; student Holy Cross Sem., Dunkirk, N.Y., 1944-49; Ba. in Philosophy, Passionist Monastic Sem., 1953, M.A. in Theology, 1957. Ordained priest, 1957; itinerant preacher Eastern U.S. and Can., 1957-59, 61-64; asso. pastor St. Mary's Parish, Dunkirk, N.Y., 1959-61; asso. dir. retreats Our Lady of Fla. Monastery, North Palm Beach, Fla., 1964-67, resident retreat preacher, 1967-69; dir. Passionist Retreat House, West Springfield, Mass., 1969-74; vice rector St. Gabriel's Monastery, Brighton, Mass., 1974-76; asso. producer Sunday Mass program WOR-TV, sec. Passionist Communications, Pelham, N.Y., 1976—; v.p., sec. That's the Spirit Prodns., Inc., 1980—; substitute chaplain Kennedy Meml. Hosp. for Children, 1974-76; moderator Cath. Young Adult Club, West Palm Beach, 1963-68; vol. counselor Palm Beach County Juvenile Ct., 1963-69; panelist television program Face to Face on ABC, Palm Beach, 1968-69; mem. Springfield Clergy Task Force on Drugs, 1970-74; mem. Priests Senate, Diocese of Springfield, 1970-74; Co-chmn. West Springfield Clergy Assn., 1971-73. Founding pres. Hope Home of Western Mass., Inc., 1972-74; pres. Community Health Commn., West Springfield, 1971-72; v.p. Big Brothers, 1968-69; bd. dirs. YMCA, Palm Beach County Mental Health Assn. Mem. Nat. Assn. Broadcasters, Fla. Sheriffs Assn. (hon.). Home: 190 Mount Tom Rd Pelham NY 10803 Office: PO Box 440 Pelham NY 10803

GORNEY, FRANCIS LEONARD, priest, Roman Cath. Ch.; b. Natrona, Pa., Aug. 12, 1914; s. George and Helen (Persinski) G.; B.A., Duquesne U., 1936; B.A., St. Francis Sem., Loretto, Pa., 1940, M.Div., 1975. Ordained priest Roman Catholic Ch., 1940; asst. pastor St. John Co-Cathedral, Johnstown, Pa., 1940-48; pastor Holy Family Ch., Hooversville, Pa., 1948-54, St. Joseph Ch., Coupon, Pa., 1954-56, St. Mary Ch., Gallitzin, Pa., 1956-64, Saints Peter and Paul Ch., Altoona, Pa., 1964—. Diocesan Scout chaplain, Diocese of Altoona-Johnstown, 1972-74, mem. exec. bd. Penn's Woods council Boy Scouts Am., 1973-74; chmn. Blair County chpt. ARC; state chaplain Pa. Cath. Com. on Scouting, 1976; exec. bd. Blair County Day Care; chaplain 4 deg. K.C., Altoona, Pa. Recipient St. George Cath. Boy Scout award, 1972, Silver Beaver award, 1973. Mem. St. Francis Sem. Alumni Assn. (pres. 1971-74). Home: 1906 19th St Altoona PA 16601 Office: 1906 19th St Altoona PA 16601

GORTNEY, JOHN TAYLOR, JR., minister, International Church Foursquare Gospel; b. Little Rock, Oct. 24, 1921; s. John Taylor and Julia Ann (Jones) G.; B.Th., Life Bible Coll., 1945; postgrad. Indsl. Coll. Armed Forces, 1959-60, Air U., 1965, Air War Coll., 1972-74; grad. Police Chaplains Sch. FBI, 1984; m. Ruth Ione Lindstrom, Feb. 13, 1943; children: Danny Jay, Anita Rae. Ordained to ministry, 1945;

pastor Hyattsville (Md.) Foursquare Ch., 1945-50, Petersburg (Tex.) Foursquare Ch., 1951-56, Little Rock Foursquare Ch., 1956—. Chaplain, CAP, 1962, Ark. Wing chaplain, 1966-78, now lt. col.; chaplain Little Rock Police Dept., 1977; mem. Foursquare Chaplaincy Commn., 1965-78; chmn. com. on edn. S. Central Dist. Foursquare Chs., 1960—, mem. scholarship com. Dist. Ministerial License Com., 1960—; supt. Ark. div. Foursquare Chs., 1956—, moderator dist. bus. meetings, 1959-75; mem. South Central Dist. Inst. Theol. Studies, 1959-69; bd. dirs. Ark. Prison Ministries, 1984—; bd. advisors Peace Officer Prayer Ptnr. Program, 1985—; mem. exec. council South Central Dist. Foursquare Chs., 1985—; bd. dirs. Police Chaplaincy Program, 1980—; moderator corporate bus. meetings Internat. Foursquare Conv., 1976, 83. Recipient Ministerial Service award Internat Ch. Foursquare Gospel 1970, Meritorious Service award CAP, 1967, 72, 79, Certificate of Proficiency, 1965. Mem. Mil. Chaplains Assn. (sec.-treas. Ark. chpt. 1971-72), Internat. Conf. Police Chaplains, Ark. Police Chaplains (bd. dirs. 1980—), Life Coll. Alumni Assn. (dist. rep.). Home: 10001 Brooks Ln Little Rock AR 72205

GOSS, E. DUANE, minister Southern Baptist Convention; b. Brookfield, Mo., Dec. 12, 1945; s. Elmer L. and Mildred E. (Anderson) G.; B.A., William Jewell Coll., Liberty, Mo., 1967; postgrad. U. Mo., Kansas City, 1976; m. Sandra K. Klingler, June 8, 1968; 1 son, Bret Duane Goss. Ordained deacon, 1975, minister of music, 1976; minister music Wyatt Park Bapt. Ch., St. Joseph, Mo., 1972, First Bapt. Ch., Kearney, Mo., 1972-85. Tchr. vocal and instrumental music Polo (Mo.) High Sch., 1971-79; tchr. Lawson High Sch., Mo., 1979—. Mem. Music Educators Nat. Assn., Mo. Music Educators Assn., Mo., Community (pres. 1976) tchrs. assns., Am. Choral Dirs. Assn., Mo. Bandmasters Assn., Mo. State Tchrs. Assn., Nat. Geog. Soc., Phi Mu Alpha Sinfonia. Home: Route 2 Box 23 Kearney MO 64060 Office: First Baptist Ch Kearney MO 64060

GOSSAGE, ROBERT GENE, minister, So. Baptist Conv.; b. Orient, Ill., July 1, 1932; s. Robert Wilbourn and Nancy Matilda (Ray) G.; Th.B., Berean Coll. and Sem., 1959; LL.B., Blackstone Coll. Law, 1962; B.A., So. Ill. U., 1968, M.S., 1972, postgrad. 1975—; m. Dorothy Lea McGhee, July 31, 1954; children—Charles Eugene, Dorothea Sue, Jonathan Wayne, Barbara Lea. Ordained to ministry, 1962; pastor chs., Ill., 1962-75, Liberty Bapt. Ch., Pekin, Ill., 1975—. Chmn. evangelism Williamson Bapt. Assn., 1968; dir. brotherhood Nine Mile Bapt. Assn., 1974-75; chmn. evangelism, pres. pastor's conf. Metro-Peoria Bapt. Assn., 1975—. Ford Found. fellow, 1968. Contbr. articles to religious jours. Home: 2109 Sheridan Rd Pekin IL 61554 Office: 2105 Sheridan Rd Pekin IL 61554

GOSSAN, ALFRED ANTHONY, JR., religious organization executive, United Pentecostal Church International; b. Chgo., Aug. 8, 1950; s. Alfred Anthony and Virginia Ann (Abraham) G.; m. Janice Beryl Sundman, Nov. 24, 1973; children: Maiya, Shayla, Alayna, Corrina. Grad. high sch., Escanaba, Mich. Ordained to ministry, United Pentecostal Ch., 1983. Itinerant bible tchr. United Pentecostal Chs., U.S., 1978; editor World Evangelism Ctr., St. Louis, 1979; interim pastor Abundant Life Ch., Holland, Mich., 1980; ch. growth cons. United Pentecostal Chs., U.S., 1981—; pres., founder Nat. Pentecostal Ch. Growth Inst., Jackson, Miss., 1983—; guest lectr. Jackson Coll. of Ministries, 1983—; pastor Pentecostal Temple, Midland, Mich., 1984—. Author: Church Growth Principles and Practices, 1982; soulwinning seminar The Fishermens' Workshop, 1978; prayer seminar Adventures in the Supernatural, 1984. Editor convert's course My Father's House, 1979. Home and Office: Nat Pentecostal Ch Growth Inst 5303 N Jefferson St Midland MI 68640

GOSSELIN, JOSEPH PAUL, priest, religious organization executive, Roman Catholic Church; b. Manchester, N.H., May 4, 1940; s. Romeo Arthur and Eva (Marcoux) G. B.A. in Philosophy, La Salette Coll., 1962; B.A. in Theology, U. Ottowa, 1966; M.A. in Counseling Psychology, Boston Coll., 1981. Ordained priest Roman Cath. Ch., 1965. Prefect, treas. La Salette Prep. Sem., 1967-69; dir. La Salette Coll., Baguio City, Philippines, 1969-71, Worcester, Mass., 1971-75; pastor Holy Rosary Ch., Windsor, Ont., Can., 1976-79; dir., superior Grad. House of Students, Cambridge, Mass., 1979-81; pastor Sacred Heart Ch., Lebanon, N.H., 1981—; trustee Corp. of Hosp. Chaplaincy Found., Inc., Mary Hitchcock Hosp., Hanover, N.H., 1982—; chpt. del. La Salette Missionaries, 1982—. Home and Office: Sacred Heart Parish 2 Hough St Lebanon NH 03677

GOSSLEE, DAVID SCOTT, minister, Southern Baptist Convention; b. Ames, Iowa, Mar. 5, 1949; s. David Gilbert and Lela Clair (Berg) G.; m. Francie Loraine Guillermin, Mar. 24, 1979; children: John, Joshua. B.S. with honors in Elec. Engring., U. Tenn., 1975; M.Div., Mid-Am. Bapt. Theol. Sem., 1979. Ordained to ministry Bapt. Ch., 1980. Asst. pastor Byram Bapt. Ch., Jackson, Miss., 1980; pastor Toxish Bapt. Ch., Pontotoc, Miss., 1980-84; chaplain intern Parkview Mem. Hosp., Ft. Wayne, Ind., 1984—; pres. Pontotoc County Bapt. Ministers and Wives Conf., 1983—. Chaplain Yacona Area council Boy Scouts Am., 1978—, Miss. Post #1 Vets. of Vietnam War, 1982—. Served with U.S. Army, 1968-71, Vietnam. Decorated Bronze Star. Mem. Mid-Am. Bapt. Theol. Sem. Alimni Assn. (v.p. Miss. State chpt. 1980-81), Tau Beta Pi, Eta Kappa Nu. Republican. Home: 1748 Hobson Fort Wayne IN 46805

GOSSMAN, FRANCIS JOSEPH, bishop, Roman Catholic Church; b. Balt., Apr. 1, 1930; s. Frank Michael and Mary Genevieve (Steadman) G.; B.A., St. Mary Sem., 1952; S.T.L., North Am. Coll., Rome, Italy, 1955; Juris Canonici D., Catholic U. of Am., 1959. Ordained priest Roman Catholic Ch., 1955; asst. pastor Basilica of the Assumption, Balt., 1959-68; adminstr. Cathedral of Mary Our Queen, Balt., 1968; named aux. bishop of Balt., also titular bishop of Aguntum, vicar gen. Balt., 1968; aux. bishop St. Peter the Apostle, Balt., from 1968, urban vicar, from 1970; bishop Diocese of Raleigh, N.C., 1975. Asst. chancellor Archdiocese of Balt., 1959-65, vice chancellor, 1965; pro-synodal judge Tribunal Archdiocese of Balt., 1961, vice officialis, 1962-65, officialis, 1965; papal chamberlain 1965; mem. Nat. Conf. of Cath. Bishops, 1968—, adminstrv. bd. U.S. Cath. Conf., 1973—; mem. Bd. of Consultors of Archdiocese, Balt., 1969. Mem. Balt. Community Relations Commn., 1969; mem. exec. com. of Md. Food Com., Inc., 1969-75. Bd. dirs. United Fund of Central Md. Mem. Canon Law Soc. Am. Address: Diocese of Raleigh 300 Cardinal Gibbons Dr Raleigh NC 27606*

GOTTSCHALK, ALFRED, educator, rabbi, Jewish religion; b. Oberwesel, Germany, Mar. 7, 1930; s. Max and Erna (Nussbaum) G.; A.B., Bklyn. Coll.; B.H.L., Hebrew Union Coll.-Jewish Inst. Religion, also M.A. with honors; Ph.D., U. So. Calif., 1965, S.T.D. (hon.), 1968, LL.D. (hon.), 1976; D.H.L. (hon.), U. Judaism, 1971; D.Litt. (hon.), Dropsie U., 1974; LL.D., U. Cin., 1976, D.Rel.Ed., Loyola Marymount U., 1977; LL.D., Xavier U., 1981; Litt.D. (hon.), St. Thomas U., 1982; children—Marc Hillel, Rachel Lisa. Rabbi, 1957; instr. Jewish history Hebrew Union Coll.-Jewish Inst. Religion, 1957-59, asst. prof. Bible and Jewish religious thought, 1959-62, asso. prof., 1962-65, dir. Calif. sch., 1957-58, acting dean, 1958-59, dean, 1959-71, pres. sch., 1971—; vis. prof. U. Calif. at Los Angeles, 1965-66, 68, 70, 71; mem. exec. com. Am. Jewish Com., Central Conf. Am. Rabbis; hon. v.p. N.Y. Bd. Rabbis; v.p. World Union Progressive Judaism. Mem. joint com. Master Plan for Higher Edn. in Calif., Pres.'s Com. on Equal Employment Opportunity, 1965-68, Gov.'s Poverty Support Corps Program Calif., Los Angeles Mayor's Community Devel. Adv. Com., Los Angeles Community Redevel. Agy. Adv. Bd., Trustee Albright Inst. Archaeol. Research, Union Am. Hebrew Congregations. U.S. State Dept. research grantee, 1963; Bertha Guggenheimer fellow, 1967, 69; recipient human relations award Am. Jewish Com., 1971; Israel Medallion Jewish Nat. Fund, 1971; Tower of David award Govt. of Israel, 1971; named Alumnus of Year award Bklyn. Coll., 1972; Henrietta Szold award, 1977. Mem. Loyola U. Interreligious Inst., Nat. Assn. Temple Educators (exec. com.), Am. Assn. Pres.'s of Ind. Colls. and Univs., So. Calif. Jewish Hist. Soc. (hon. pres.), Am. Acad. Religion, Am. Assn. Higher Edn., Am. Philos. Soc., Am. Assn. U. Profs., Internat. Conf. Jewish Communal Service, Israel Exploration Soc., N.E.A., Soc. Sci. Study Religion, Soc. Bibl. Lit. and Exegesis, World Union Jewish Studies, So. Calif. Assn. Liberal Rabbis (pres. 1966-67). Author: Your Future as a Rabbi—A Calling that Counts, 1967; The Future of Human Community, 1968; A Jubilee of the Spirit, 1972; many articles. Home: 17 Belsaw Pl Cincinnati OH 45220 Office: 3101 Clifton Ave Cincinnati OH 45220

GOTTWALD, GEORGE J. See *Who's Who in America,* 43rd edition.

GOULDRICK, JOHN WILLIAM, priest; b. Victor, N.Y., May 5, 1941; s. William Patrick and Alden Camilla (Hackett) G. B.A., Mary Immaculate Sem., Northampton, Pa., 1965, M.Div., 1968, Th.M., 1975; B.B.A., Niagara U., 1973; S.T.D., Catholic U., 1979. Joined Congregation of the Mission, Roman Cath. Ch., 1967, ordained priest, 1969. Tchr. St. John's Prep. High Sch., Bklyn., 1969-70; treas. Vincentian Residence, Niagara Falls, N.Y., 1970-74, rector, 1978-79; lectr. Niagara U., N.Y., 1970-74; asst. prof. Mary Immaculate Sem., Northampton, Pa., 1976-78, asst. student dir., 1977-78, prof., 1979—, rector, pres., 1979—; elected del. provincial assembly Congregation of Mission, Phila., 1977, 79, 83; spiritual dir. Daughters of Charity, Buffalo, Rochester, N.Y. and Pottsville, Pa., 1971-72, 81—; med. ethics cons. Good Samaritan Hosp., Pottsville, 1984—. Lectr. on world hunger, war and peace, medical ethics, sem. formation and various other topics. Mem. Cath. Theol. Soc. Am., Nat. Cath. Edn. Assn., East Coast Conf. of Major Sem. Rectors (sec. 1982—). Home: PO Box 27 Northampton PA 18067

GOUVEIA, ANSELM ERNEST, priest, Roman Cath. Ch.; b. Honolulu, Mar. 13, 1919; s. Manuel Vincent and Mary (Enos) G.; M.A. in Theology, Cath. U. Am., 1938-44. Entered Order of Sacred Hearts Fathers, Roman Catholic Ch., 1937; ordained priest, 1943; asso. pastor, organizer Cath. Youth Orgn., St. Anthony Ch., Wailuku, Maui, Hawaii, 1944-48; asso. pastor, Diocesan dir. scouting St. Augustine Ch., Honolulu, 1948-53; pastor St. Ann Ch., Kaneohe, Hawaii, 1953-57; superior Sacred Hearts Sem., Kaneohe, Hawaii, 1957-63; pastor St. Anthony Ch., Honolulu, 1963-73; pastor St. Augustine Ch., Honolulu, 1973—. Organized Cath. Youth Orgn. on island of Maui to serve youth; responsible for building two churches, two schools and two convents. Address: 130 Ohua Ave Honolulu HI 96815

GRABHER, JEAN MARIE POWELL, minister, United Meth. Ch.; b. Paradise, Kans., Nov. 3, 1934; d. Dale Idris and Rosa (Howe) Powell; A.B., Southwestern Coll., 1956; M.A., Scarritt Coll., 1964; M.Div., St. Paul Sch. Theology, 1966; m. Jerald Grabher, Aug. 28, 1964; children—Jasonne Marie, Jocelyn Renee. Ordained to ministry, 1968; missionary, Seoul, Korea and Wonju, Korea, 1958-63, Baguio City, Philippines, 1966-70; dir. Christian edn., asso. pastor Lowman United Meth. Ch., Topeka, 1971—. Chmn. Dist. Council on Ministries, 1973—; mem. bd. ministry Kans. East Conf., 1975—, South Central Jurisdiction Com. on Missionary Personnel, 1975—; trustee St. Paul Sch. Theology. Mem. area council PTA, Topeka, 1974-75. Mem. St. Paul Sch. Theology Alumni Assn. (v.p.). Home: 1828 Village Dr Topeka KS 66604 Office: 4000 Drury Ln Topeka KS 66604

GRACIDA, RENE HENRY, bishop, Roman Catholic Church, Bishop of Corpus Christi, 1983—. Office: 4109 Ocean Dr Corpus Christi TX 78411*

GRADY, ANN MARIE, religion educator, nun, Roman Catholic Church; b. Cambridge, Mass., June 10, 1939; d. John Francis and Mary Josephine (Keane) G.; A.B., Regis Coll., 1963; M.A., U. St. Michael's Coll., Toronto, Ont., Can., 1966; M.Ed., Boston U., 1978. Joined Sisters of St. Joseph, Roman Cath. Ch., 1957. Tchr., Mount St. Joseph Acad., Brighton, Mass., 1967-68, Regis Coll., Weston, Mass., 1966-67, 68—. Mem. Coll. Theology Soc. (adv. bd. 1976-82), Internat. Visual Literacy Assn. Office: Regis Coll 235 Wellesley St Weston MA 02193

GRADY, THOMAS JOSEPH, bishop, Roman Catholic Church; b. Chgo., Oct. 9, 1914; s. Michael Joseph and Rose Buckley (Brown) G.; S.T.L., St. Mary of the Lake Sem., Mundelein, Ill., D.D., 1938; postgrad. Gregorian U., Rome, 1938-39; M.A. in English, Loyola U., Chgo., 1944. Ordained priest, 1938, bishop, 1967; prof. Quigley Prep. Sem., 1939-45; procurator St. Mary of the Lake Sem., 1945-56; dir. Nat. Shrine of Immaculate Conception, Washington, 1956-67; aux. bishop of Chgo., 1967; titular bishop of Vamalia, 1967; pastor St. Hilary Ch.. Chgo., 1968-74, St. Josephs Ch., Libertyville, Ill., 1974; bishop of Orlando, Fla., 1974—; archdiocesan dir. sems. and priestly tng., 1967; chmn. Archdiocesan Liturgical Commn., 1968, dir. permanent diaconate program, 1969; cons. Bishop's Com. on Priestly Formation, 1967-69, 72, chmn., 1969-72; chmn. Ad Hoc Com. on Priestly Life and Ministry, 1973. Home: 952 Leigh Ave Orlando FL 32804 Office: 421 E Robinson PO Box 1800 Orlando FL 32802

GRAEFE, JAMES ARTHUR See *Who's Who in America,* 43rd edition.

GRAF, DAVID FRANK, religious educator, Churches of Christ; history educator; b. Detroit, Dec. 3, 1939; s. Carl Oakley and Rose Lou Graf.; m. Linda Conner, Aug. 31, 1963; children: John David, Jennifer Laurel. B.A., Harding U., 1965; B.D., McCormick Sem., 1970; M.A., U. Mich., 1975, Ph.D., 1979. Lectr. U. Mich., Ann Arbor, 1982-83, research assoc. program on studies in religion, 1984—; asst. prof., Mont. State U., Bozeman, 1983-84. Editor: Palestine in Transition: The Emergence of Ancient Israel, 1983. Contbr. articles to profl. jours. NEH fellow 1979-80. Mem. Am. Schs. Oriental Research. Home: 2481 Lancashire St Apt 1A Ann Arbor MI 48105 Office: U Mich Program Studies in Religion 445 W Engineering Ann Arbor MI 48109

GRAF, RICHARD BYRON, JR., minister, Lutheran Church in America; b. Charlotte, N.C., Sept. 27, 1939; s. Richard B. and Helen (Stilwell) G.; m. Shirley Whitley, June 10, 1961; children: Eric, Kristin. B.A., Lenoir Rhyne Coll., 1961; M.Div., Luth. Theol. Sem., Gettysburg, Pa., 1965; D.Min., Pitts. Theol. Sem., 1980. Ordained to ministry Lutheran Ch., 1965. Pastor, mission developer St. Stephen Luth. Ch., Tallahassee, Fla., 1973-75, St. Thomas Luth. Ch., Miami, 1970-73, Grace Luth. Ch., Boone, N.C., 1965-67; chaplain U. Miami, Coral Gables, Fla., 1967-70; sec. and asst. to bishop Fla. Synod, Luth. Ch. Am., Tampa, Fla., 1975-77; sr. pastor Macedonia Evang. Luth. Ch., Burlington, N.C., 1977-83, St. Pauls Evang. Luth. Ch., Wilmington, N.C., 1983—; founder, bd. dirs. Friendship Ctr., Burlington, N.C., 1979-83, Allied Chs. of Alamance County, 1982-83; chmn. bd. Luth. Retirement Ministries of Alamance County, 1980-81; chmn. social ministry com. N.C. Synod, Luth. Ch. Am., 1982—. Author: Re-Discovering Direction, 1965; A Radio Ministry to the Elderly, 1980. Contbr. sermons, plays and articles to various publs. Pres. Community Council Alamance County, 1982; chmn. Gov.'s

Involvement Council, N.C., 1982; chmn. Coaliation for Needed Services, Burlington, 1982-83; bd. dirs. planning com. N.C. United Way, Raleigh, N.C., 1982-84. Recipient Outstanding Pub. Service award Community Action, Leon County, Fla., 1975; Outstanding Community Service award United Way N.C., 1980; Gov.'s award State of N.C., 1981. Democrat. Lodge: Kiwanis. Office: Saint Paul's Evang Luth Ch 12 N 6th St Wilmington NC 28401

GRAHAM, BILLY, see Graham, William Franklin

GRAHAM, JEWEL FREEMAN, organization executive. Pres. Young Women's Christian Assn. of the United States and Can. Office: YWCA 135 W 50th St New York NY 10020*

GRAHAM, JOHN B. See *Who's Who in America*, 43rd edition.

GRAHAM, MATT PATRICK, minister, religious educator, Church of Christ; b. Colorado City, Tex., Sept. 28, 1950; s. Matt Noe and Mary Edna (Frizell) G.; m. Doris Jean Mickey, Jan. 1, 1971; children: Jennifer, Abigail, Joy, Crystal. B.A. in Greek, Abilene Christian U., 1973, M.A., 1974, M.Div., 1976; Ph.D., Emory U., 1983. Minister, Red Springs Ch. of Christ, Tex., 1970-72, Goree Ch. of Christ, Tex., 1972-76; asst. minister Druid Hills Ch. of Christ, Atlanta, 1976-79, minister, 1979-83; minister East County Ch. of Christ, Portland, Oreg., 1983-85; asst. prof. bible and religion, Columbia Christian Coll., Portland, 1983—. Recipient J.W. Roberts Greek award Abilene Christian U., 1976. Mem. Soc. Bibl. Lit. Home: 685 NE 157th Ave Portland OR 97230 Office: Columbia Christian Coll 200 NE 91st Ave Portland OR 97220

GRAHAM, TECUMSEH XAVIER, minister, A.M.E. Zion Ch.; b. Washington, Mar. 14, 1925; s. James Webster and Marjorie (Reeves) G.; B.A., Livingstone Coll., 1955; M.Div., Hood Theol. Sem., 1958; LL.D., Xavier U., Cin., 1971; Litt.D., Cin. Tech. Coll., 1976; m. Loreda Branch, Sept. 14, 1956; children—Tecumseh Xavier, Marjorie Ella. Ordained to ministry, 1950; pastor chs., N.Y., N.C., and Oreg., 1950-64; pastor St. Mark A.M.E. Zion Ch., Cin., 1964—. Instr. dept. history U. Cin., Xavier U., 1968; mem. nat. adv. bd. Am. Jewish Com.; mem. commn. on regional and local ecumenism Nat. Council Chs.; mem. TV panel Dialogue, NCCJ; exec. dir. Council of Christian Communions of Greater Cin., 1972—. Vice chmn. Save Our Schs. Com., Cin., 1967-68, Cin. Human Relations Commn., 1969-71; pres. Cin. Bd. Edn., 1972-73; trustee Cin. Tech. Coll.; mem. Cin. Com. on Youth; mem. adv. bd. Univ. Without Walls, Cin.; cons. on black history Cin. pub. schs. Recipient citation for service in edn. and religion State of Ohio, 1972; award for religious and community service City of Cin., 1972, Outstanding Citizen of Yr., 1973. Mem. Nat. Acad. Ecumenists, AAUP, Nat. Assn. Ecumenical Staff Persons, Sigma Rho Sigma. Home: 1288 Paddock Hills Ave Cincinnati OH 45229 Office: 1836 Fairmount Ave Cincinnati OH 45214

GRAHAM, W(ILLIAM) FRED, religious studies educator, minister, Presbyterian Church (USA); b. Columbus, Ohio, Oct. 21, 1930; s. William Fred and Serena (Clark) G.; m. Jean Garrett, Aug. 12, 1953; children: Terese, Bonny, Marcy Graham-Murphy, Geneva. B.A., Tarkio Coll., 1952; M.Div., Pitts. Theol. Sem., 1955; Th.M. Louisville Presbyn. Sem., 1958; Ph.D., U. Iowa, 1965. Ordained to ministry Presbyterian Ch. (USA), 1955. Pastor Bethel Presbyn. Ch., Waterloo, Iowa, 1955-61; prof. religious studies Mich. State U., East Lansing, 1963—. Author: The Constructive Revolutionary, 1971; Picking up the Pieces, 1975. Contbr. articles to religious jours. Mem. Am. Soc. Ch. History, Sixteenth Century Studies Soc., Am. Acad. Religion, Calvin Studies Soc. Home: 332 Chesterfield Pkwy East Lansing MI 48823 Office: Dept Religious Studies Mich State U East Lansing MI 48824

GRAHAM, WARREN RALPH, minister, educational administrator; b. Kline, W.Va., Nov. 4, 1920; s. William P. and Lelah G. (Mitchell) G.; B.A., Bridgewater Coll., 1943; B.D., Wartburg Theol. Sem., 1945; M.S., Ind. State U., 1972; m. Betsy B. Powell, June 14, 1969; children—Mark William, Judith Ann, Lynn Ann, Susan Ann. Chaplain intern Elgin (Ill.) State Hosp., 1945-46, Gallanger Municipal Hosp., Washington, 1946; ordained to ministry Am. Luth. Ch., 1947; chaplain with Fed. Bur. of Prisons, Tallahassee, Fla., 1947-48, Ashland, Ky., 1948-50, El Reno, Okla., 1950-52, Denver, 1952-56, Terre Haute, Ind., 1966-73; parish pastor (part-time) St. Paul's Luth. Ch., Denver, 1956-66; individual and family counseling Lakewood (Colo.) Cons. Group, 1962-66; adj. prof. of pastoral care Iliff Sch. of Theology, Denver, 1965-66, Anderson (Ind.) Sch. of Theology, 1970-73; cons. U.S. Army Correctional Tng. Facility, Ft. Riley, Kans., 1970, to Chaplain's Dept., Dept. of Corrections, state of Ga., Atlanta, 1974-76; mem. workshop on corrections U.S. Army 15th Mil. Police Brigade, Kaiserlautern, W.Ger., 1972; adminstr. of religious services SE region, Fed. Bur. of Prisons, Atlanta, 1973-75, adminstr. of recruitment and tng., 1975—. Chmn. Denver Conf., central dist. of Am. Luth. Ch., 1962-65; chmn. com. on pastoral care in pub. institutions, Colo. Council of Chs., 1957-65; mem. Ho. of Dels. of Assn. for Clin. Pastoral Edn., N.Y.C., 1967-68; mem. certification com. Am. Protestant Correctional Chaplains Assn., 1974—, exec. project dir., 1981—. Bd. mgrs. Jour. Pastoral Care Publs. Fellow Am. Assn. of Pastoral Counselors. Home: 5235 Greenpoint Dr Stone Mountain GA 30088 Office: 5135 Memorial Dr Stone Mountain GA 30083

GRAHAM, WILLIAM FRANKLIN, evangelist, Southern Baptist Convention; b. Charlotte, N.C., Nov. 7, 1918; s. William Franklin and Morrow (Coffey) G.; A.B., Wheaton Coll., 1943; Th.B., Fla. Bible Sem., Tampa, 1940; LL.D., Houghton Coll., 1950, Baylor U., The Citadel, William Jewell Coll.; numerous other hon. degrees; m. Ruth McCue Bell, Aug. 13, 1943; children—Virginia Graham Tchividjian, Anne Graham Lotz, Ruth Graham Dienert, William Franklin, Nelson Edman. Ordained to ministry; minister First Bapt. Ch., Western Springs, Ill., 1943-45; 1st v.p. Youth for Christ, Internat., 1945-48; pres. Northwestern Coll., Mpls., 1947-52; founder World Wide Pictures, Inc., Burbank, Calif.; Worldwide evangelistic campaigns, 1949—; speaker weekly Hour of Decision radio program, 1950—, also periodic Crusade Telecast; founder, pres. Billy Graham Evangelistic Assn. Recipient numerous awards including Bernard Baruch award, 1955; Humane Order of African Redemption, 1960; Gold award George Washington Carver Meml. Inst., 1963; Horatio Alger award, 1965; Internat. Brotherhood award N.C.C.J., 1971; Sylvanus Thayer award Assn. Grads. U.S. Mil. Acad., 1972; Franciscan Internat. award, 1972; Man of South award, 1974; Liberty Bell award, 1975. Author: Peace with God, 1953; World Aflame, 1965; The Jesus Generation, 1971; Angels, God's Secret Agents, 1975, How to Be Born Again, 1977; The Holy Spirit, 1978; Till Armageddon, 1981; also writer daily newspaper column. Office: 1300 Harmon Pl Minneapolis MN 55403*

GRAHMANN, CHARLES V., bishop, Roman Catholic Church. Bishop of Victoria, Tex., 1982—. Office: PO Box 4708 Victoria TX 77903*

GRANFIELD, PATRICK RICHARD, priest, theology educator, Roman Catholic Church; b. Springfield, Mass., Mar. 8, 1930; s. Patrick E. and Mabel (Fitzgerald) G. Ph.L., Pontifical Inst. St. Anselm, Rome, 1954, Ph.D., 1958; S.T.L., Cath. U. Am., 1958, S.T.D., 1962; Ordained priest Roman Cath. Ch., 1957. Mem. faculty Cath. U. Am., Washington, 1964—, prof. systematic theology, 1980—. Author: Theologians at Work, 1967; Ecclesial Cybernetics, 1973; Papacy in Transition, 1980; (with A. Dulles) The Church: A Bibliography, 1985; also articles. Editor: (with J. Jungmann) Kyriakon, 1970. Mem. Cath. Theol. Soc. Am. (v.p. 1982-83, pres.-elect 1983-84, pres. 1984-85), Coll. Theology Soc. Office: Catholic U Am Dept Theology Washington DC 20064

GRANSHOFF, MARIE PHILOMENE, nun, religion educator, Roman Catholic Church; b. Brussels, Belgium, Nov. 22, 1901; came to U.S., 1939, naturalized, 1946; d. Isidore Hubert and Alice Martine (Helskens) G. Diploma in Teaching, Ecole Gantomale, Switzerland, 1919; B.A., Cath. Tchrs. Coll., 1950; M.A., Boston Coll., 1956. Joined Sisters of St. Dorothy, Roman Cath. Ch., 1921. Tchr. lang. Sisters of St. Dorothy, Lisbon, Portugal, 1924-25; tchr., prin., Lucerne, Switzerland, 1926-38; prin., coordinator, New Bedford, Mass., Bristol, R.I. and Newport, R.I., 1940-75; missionary, Macau, China, 1964-67; founder mountain mission for sugar plantation workers, Brazil, 1976; coordinator Our Lady of the Rosary Convent, Providence, 1977—. Address: 17 Traverse St Providence RI 02903

GRANT, LOWELL DEAN, minister, General Association Regular Baptist Chs.; b. Mannington, Ky., Oct. 12, 1935; s. William Hershall and Mell Juanita (Hunt) G.; B.R.E., Grand Rapids Bapt. Coll., 1966; M.Div., Grand Rapids Bapt. Sem., 1969; m. Shirley Ann Hughes, Mar. 4, 1955; children: Luann, Sheila, Gary, Rachael, David. Ordained to ministry, 1970. Pastor Moline (Mich.) Bapt. Ch., 1969-73, First Bapt. Ch., Caro, Mich., 1973—. Mem. Conservative Bapt. Youth Com., State of Mich., Detroit, 1970-72; bd. dirs. Bapt. Acad., Grand Rapids, Mich., 1971-73; mem. Saginaw Valley (Mich.) Truth For Youth Bd., 1973—; mem. council of 13, Mich. Assn. Regular Bapt. Chs., 1975—, v.p. council of 10, Eastern Mich. Assn., bd. dirs., 1978-79; mem. exec. bd. Saginaw Valley Truth for Youth, 1974-75, v.p., 1975-76, pres., 1977-81. Recipient Christian Service award Grand Rapids Bapt. Coll., 1965; Pres.'s award Grand Rapids Bapt. Sem., 1969, Leham Strauss Expository Preaching award, 1969, Leon J. Wood Holy Land Tour award Grand Rapids Bapt. Sem., 1969. Mem. Alumni Assn. Grand Rapids Bapt. Coll. (v.p. 1969-71). Home: 112 N Almer St Caro MI 48723

GRANT, ROBERT MCQUEEN, educator, author, Episcopal Ch.; b. Evanston, Ill., Nov. 25, 1917; s. Frederick Clifton and Helen McQueen (Hardie) G.; A.B., Northwestern U., 1938; postgrad. Episcopal Theol. Sch., 1938-39, Columbia, 1939-40; B.D., Union Theol. Sem., 1941; S.T.M., Harvard U., 1942, Th.D., 1944; D.D., Seabury-Western Theol. Sem., 1969, Glasgow U., 1979; L.H.D., Kalamazoo Coll., 1979; m. Margaret Huntington Horton, Dec. 21, 1940; children: Douglas McQueen, Peter Williams, Susan Hardie, James Frederick. Ordained to ministry Episcopal Ch., 1942; minister St. James Ch., South Groveland, Mass., 1942-44, instr. to prof. N.T. U. of South, 1944-53, acting dean, 1947; vis. lectr. U. Chgo., 1945, research assoc., 1952-53, asso. prof., 1953-58, prof., 1958—, Carl Darling Buck prof. humanities, 1973—. Vis. lectr. Vanderbilt U., 1945-47, Seabury-Western Theol. Sem., 1954-55; Fulbright research prof. U. Leiden, 1950-51; lectr. Am. Council Learned Socs., 1957-58; vis. prof. Yale, 1964-65; assoc. editor Vigiliae Christianae. Guggenheim fellow, 1950, 54, 59. Fellow Am. Acad. Arts and Scis.; mem. Soc. Bibl. Lit. and Exegesis (pres. 1959), Am. Soc. Ch. History (pres. 1970, co-editor), Chgo. Soc. Bibl. Research (pres. 1963-64), Phi Beta Kappa, Alpha Delta Phi. Author: Second Century Christianity, 1946; The Bible in the Church, 1948; Miracle and Natural Law, 1952; The Sword and the Cross, 1955; The Letter and the Spirit, 1957; Gnosticism and Early Christianity, 1959; (with D.N. Freeman) The Secret Sayings of Jesus, 1960; Gnosticism: an Anthology; The Earliest Lives of Jesus, 1961; Historical Introduction to the New Testament, 1963; The Apostolic Fathers Vol. I, 1964, Vol. II (with H.H. Graham), 1965, Vol. IV, 1966; U-Boats Destroyed 1914-1918, 1964; The Formation of the New Testament, 1965; History of Early Christian Literature (rev. from Goodspeed), The Early Christian Doctrine of God, 1966; After the New Testament, 1967; U-Boat Intelligence 1914-1918, 1969; Augustus to Constantine; Theophilus of Antioch Ad Autolycum, 1970; Early Christianity and Society, 1977; Eusebius as Church Historian, 1980.

GRANT, WORTH COLLINS, minister, Southern Baptist Convention; b. High Point, N.C., Oct. 26, 1918; s. Lon L. and Elsie May (Warren) G.; m. Kathryn Stephens; children: Donna, Angela, Deborah, Kitty. A.A., Mars Hill Coll., 1939; B.A., Furman U., 1941; Th.M., So. Bapt. Theol. Sem., 1944. Ordained to ministry Baptist Ch., 1940. Pastor, Weldon Bapt. Ch., N.C., 1946-50; missionary, Japan, 1950-71; pres., founder So. Bapts. for Bible Transl., Washington, 1972-78; pastor Temple Bapt. Ch., Washington, 1979—; v.p. Jordan Press, Tokyo, 1960-70; mem. stewardship commn. So. Bapt. Conv., 1980—. Author: A Work Begun, 1966; Japan with Love, 1977; (pamphlet) This is Dynamic Japan, 1966. Columnist, Abbeville Press and Banner, S.C., 1971-75. Served to lt. comdr. USNR, 1944-46. Republican. Club: Fgn. Corrs. of Tokyo. Home: 4333 Verplanck Pl NW Washington DC 20016 Office: Temple Baptist Ch 3850 Nebraska Ave NW Washington DC 20016

GRAPENTHIN, INA SLATER, music director, Lutheran Church of America, music educator; b. Reading, Pa., Nov. 5, 1947; d. Richard Irving and Doris Virginia (Grater) Slater; m. Warren Harold Grapenthin, Feb. 15, 1975; children: Mark Richard, Amelia Lynn. B.M. in Edn., Ithaca Coll., 1969; M.M. in Sacred Music, U. Mich., 1971. Cert. Level II div. profl. leadership Lutheran Church of America, 1982. Minister music Nardin Park Meth. Ch., Farmington, Mich., 1970-77; dir. music St. Thomas United Ch. of Christ, Reading, Pa., 1977-79, Advent Luth. Ch., West Lawn, Pa., 1979—; mem. worship and music com. Northeast Pa. Synod, Wescosville, 1980—; nat. edn. cons. ch. music Baldwin Piano and Organ Co., Cin., 1984—. Prof. music Kutztown U., Pa., 1977—. Composer anthem, 1984. Founder, tchr. class to determine mus. readiness in pre-sch. children Wyomissing Inst. Fine Arts, 1977—; bd. dirs. Muhlenburg Council Arts, Pa., 1983-84. Recipient Outstanding Music award Music Club Reading, 1965, Outstanding Contbn. to Music award Farmington Music Club, 1977. Mem. Music Educators Nat. Conf. Republican. Home: 2074 Elder St Reading PA 19604 Office: Advent Luth Ch Telford and Noble Sts West Lawn PA 19609 also Old Main Room 112 Kutztown U Kutztown PA

GRARUP, KJELD, minister, American Baptist Churches in the U.S.A.; b. Soro, Denmark, Dec. 2, 1944; came to U.S., 1980; s. Orla and Astrid Edel (Petersen) G.; m. Mary Kay Paulse, Aug. 12, 1967; children: Anna-Marie, Mai-Lis. B.D. equivalent, Danish Bapt. Sem., Tollose, 1966; B.D., Bapt. Theol. Sem., Ruschlikon, Switzerland, 1974. Ordained to ministry Danish Baptist Union, 1967. Missionary, Union des Eglises Baptistes, Burundi, Africa, 1967-71; pastor Norresundby Bapt. Ch., Denmark, 1974-80; sr. pastor First Bapt. Ch. of Turner, Kansas City, Kans., 1980—; civilian aux. chaplain USAF, Denmark, 1974-80; charter mem. Christian Community Action Jail Ministry, Kansas City, Kans., 1981—; mem. continued edn. com. Central Bapt. Theol. Sem., Kansas City, Kans., 1982—; mem. adv. bd. United Prayer Movement, Kansas City, 1980—; East Central Area rep. Am. Bapt. Chs. Central Regional Commn. on Ministry, 1984—. Mem. Minister's Council Am. Bapt. Chs. Home: 823 S 57th Terr Kansas City KS 66106 Office: First Bapt Ch of Turner 701 S 55th St Kansas City KS 66106

GRASSELL, ROBERT WARNER, protestant lay worker; life insurance company agent; b. Los Angeles, June 17, 1941; s. Warner Huges and Kathrine (Crow) G.; m. Judith Arline; children: Kirsten, Andrew. Pres.

San Moritz Christian Ctr., Crestline, Calif., 1978—; sales mgr. Franklin Life Ins. Co., Newport Beach, Calif., 1985—. Served with USNG, 1960-65. Mem. Nat. Life Underwriters. Republican. Avocations: golf; boating. Office: 3700 Campus Dr #102 Newport Beach CA 92660

GRASSINGER, TIMOTHY LLOYD, minister, Lutheran Church-Missouri Synod; b. St. Paul, Mar. 1, 1940; s. Lloyd Louis and Caroline Dorothy (Koch) G.; m. Mary Elizabeth Walz, Dec. 29, 1962; children: Lisa Marie, Lori Lee, Scott Timothy. B.S., Concordia Coll., St. Paul, 1961, B.Th., Concordia Sem., Springfield, Ill., 1965. Ordained to ministry Luth. Ch., 1965. Pastor, St. John's Luth. Ch., Columbia, S.D., 1965-71, Peace Luth. Ch., Hecla, S.D., 1965-71, Peace Luth. Ch., Rapid City, S.D., 1971-77; sr. pastor Immanuel Luth. Ch., Colorado Springs, Colo., 1977—; com. mem. Parish Services Commn. S.D. dist. Luth. Ch.-Mo. Synod, 1966-69, circuit counselor, 1967-70, sec. bd. dirs., 1970-77, pastoral advisor Luth. Laymen's League, Columbia, 1975-77; speaker VFW, Columbia, 1967, Sertoma, Bismarck, N.D., 1972; chaplain Nat. Farm Orgn., Columbia, 1969. Contbr. articles to religious publs. Coach Football and Baseball Young Am. League, Colorado Springs, 1977-79. Recipient Service to Ch. and Christ award Concordia Sem., 1977. Mem. Am. Ski Assn. Republican. Home: 5225 N Carefree Circle Colorado Springs CO 80917 Office: Immanuel Luth Ch 846 E Pikes Peak Ave Colorado Springs CO 80903

GRATE, PHILLIP EUGENE, minister, Church of the Nazarene; b. Rutland, Ohio, July 8, 1950; s. Arnold Maxwell and Minnie Mildred (Vance) G.; m. Ronoyce Dianne Barnes, June 6, 1971; children: Gina Marie, Christopher Ryan. A.A., Mt. Vernon Nazarene Coll., 1970; B.A., Bethany Nazarene Coll., 1972, M.A., 1974; M.Div., Nazarene Theol. Sem., 1976. Ordained to ministry, 1978. Pastor Ch. of the Nazarene, Lodi, Mo., 1976-78, St. Charles, Mo., 1978—; pres. St. Louis Nazarene Ministers Assn., St. Louis, 1980-81; sec. Mo. Dist. Bd. Ministerial Studies, 1982; treas. Mo. Dist., Nazarene Youth Internat., St. Louis, 1976-80, pres., 1982—. Office publicity Am. Cancer Soc., Piedmont, Mo., 1977-78. Mem. Phi Delta Lamba. Republican. Avocations: sports; photography. Home: 11 Millbrooke Saint Charles MO 63303 Office: Harvester Ch of the Nazarene 3115 McClay Rd Saint Charles MO 63303

GRATTON, JEAN See *Who's Who in America,* 43rd edition.

GRAVELY, WILLIAM BERNARD, religious educator, United Methodist Ch.; b. Pickens, S.C., Aug. 19, 1939; s. William Marvin and Artie Louise (Hughes) G.; m. Michele Garrison, Dec. 2, 1984; 1 child, Julia Lynn. B.A., Wofford Coll., 1961; B.D. magna cum laude, Drew U. Theol. Sch., 1964; Ph.D., Duke, 1969. Ordained deacon United Meth. Ch., 1962, elder, 1968, lay status, 1975. Mem. faculty U. Denver, 1968—, asst. prof., 1968-72, assoc. prof. dept. religious studies, 1972—; denominational rep. United Ministries High Edn., Denver, 1971-74, 75-76; mem. com. conf. history Rocky Mountain United Meth. Conf., Denver, 1974-77. Author: Gilbert Haven, Methodist Abolitionist, 1973. Contbr. articles and revs. in religious history, black history to Meth. jours. Recipient Jesse Lee prize in Am. Meth. History, Commn. on Archives and History, United Meth. Ch., 1970. Ethnic Minority Studies fellow Nat. Endowment for Humanities, 1974-75; Am. Council Learned Socs. fellow, 1981-82. Mem. Am. Acad. Religion, Am. Soc. Ch. History. Democrat. Home: 4209 S Washington St Englewood CO 80110 Office: Dept Religious Studies U Denver Denver CO 80208

GRAVES, CHARLES ELLIOTT, minister, American Baptist Churches in the U.S.A.; b. Harlan, Iowa, Oct. 12, 1940; s. John Fredrick and Rhoda Velma (Petersen) G.; m. Brenda Lee Woodrick, Aug. 24, 1963; children: Mark, Scott, Julie. B.A., Sioux Falls Coll., 1964; M.Div., Berkeley Bapt. Div. Sch., 1968; D.Min., Drew U., 1984. Ordained to ministry Am. Bapt. Chs. in the U.S.A., 1968. Minister of Christian edn. First Bapt. Ch., Twin Falls, Idaho, 1968-71, First Bapt. Ch., Salt Lake City, 1972-73; minister of camping and Christian edn. Mid-Am. Bapt. Chs., Des Moines, 1974-80; pastor United Ch., Milw., 1980—; curriculum counselor Am. Bapt. Chs. U.S.A., 1978-84; chmn. camp com. Am. Bapt. Chs. of Wis., 1981-84, mem. Christian edn. com., 1982-84; v.p. Milw. Am. Bapt. Assn., 1983-84. Treas. La Casa Housing Project, Milw., 1981-84. Mem. Ministers Council. Democrat. Home: 7916 W Rogers St Wauwatosa WI 53213 Office: United Ch 2906 W Scott St Milwaukee WI 53215

GRAVES, LOWELL BROOK, minister, American Baptist Churches in the U.S.A.; b. Turlock, Calif., Nov. 1, 1946; s. Clem Aaron and Maxine (Murray) G.; m. Linda Lambert, July 16, 1972; children: David Aaron, Joshua Michael Murray. B.S., George Fox Coll., 1968; M.Div., Golden Gate Theol. Sem., 1973. Ordained to ministry Baptist Ch., 1972. Chaplain intern N.D. State Hosp., Jamestown, 1974-75, Bapt. Med. Ctr., Oklahoma City, 1978; chaplain Redfield State Hosp., S.D., 1976-78; pastor Fellowship Bapt. Ch., Portland, Oreg., 1980—; mem. witness and life com. Ecumenical Ministries of Oreg., Portland, 1980—, chmn. chaplaincy, 1982—; chaplain Bess Kaiser Hosp., Portland, 1983—, Portland Meadows Race Track, 1984—. Mem. Coll. of Chaplains (clergy affiliate). Republican. Club: Optimists (chaplain 1983-84) (Portland). Home: 7516 N Columbia Blvd Portland OR 97203 Office: Fellowship Baptist Ch 4737 N Lombard St Portland OR 97203

GRAVES, WILLIAM H., Bishop, Christian Methodist Episcopalian Church (First Dist.), chair Gen. Bd. Publ. Services. Office: 564 Frank Ave Memphis TN 38101*

GRAY, CHARLES AUGUSTUS, lay church worker, Lutheran Church in America; b. Syracuse, N.Y., Sept. 16, 1928; s. Charles William and Elizabeth Marie (Koch) G.; student Am. Inst. Banking, 1958, Sch. for Bank Adminstrn., 1961. Treas., mem. bd. 1st English Luth. Ch. Sch., 1946-66, Luth. Soc. Syracuse and Onondaga County, 1960-66, Luth. Student Found., Syracuse U., 1961-66, Upper N.Y. Synod Luth. Ch. in Am. 1966—, Luth. Found. Upper N.Y., 1972-79. With Mchts. Nat. Bank & Trust Co., Syracuse, 1947-77, v.p., auditor, 1960-77 regional auditor Charter N.Y. Corp., 1977-82; asst. v.p. Irving Bank Corp., 1982—. Mem. Bank Adminstrn. Inst. (pres. Central N.Y. chpt. 1970-72), Inst. Internal Auditors (chpt. treas. 1974-76, pres. 1985—), Phi Gamma Delta. Home: 1321 Westmoreland Ave Syracuse NY 13210

GRAY, CHARLES SAMUEL, non-denominational missions executive; b. Barberton, Ohio, May 18, 1930; s. Samuel K. and Grace (Clemans) G.; m. D. Jean Forquer, July 25, 1953; children: Charles K., Elizabeth A., William S., Rebecca G. A.B., Wheaton Coll., 1952, postgrad., 1952-54; M.B.A., U. Chgo., 1974. Ordained to ministry by ind. council, 1954. Dir. publs. Christian Service Brigade, Wheaton, Ill., 1954-68, dir. of central services, 1968-70, exec. dir., 1970-72, pres., 1972—. Editor: The Stockader's Log, 1955; Brigade Trails, 1958; Boys for Christ, 1962; Builder/Sentinel Trails, 1968. Pres. West Suburban Oratorio Chorus, 1980-83; treas. West Suburban Choral Union, 1983—. Home: 117 S President St Wheaton IL 60187 Office: Christian Service Brigade PO Box 150 Wheaton IL 60189

GRAY, DAVID FRANKLIN, minister, United Pentecostal Ch.; b. Yokohama, Japan, May 6, 1917 (parents Am. citizens); s. Franklin Hoover and Elizabeth May (Heath) G.; student Citrus Coll., 1934, Morse Bible Tng. Inst., 1936; D.Div. (hon.), Colonial Acad., 1958; D.Litt. (hon.), Pioneer Theol. Sem., 1958; B.A. (hon.), Western Apostolic Bible Coll., 1975; m. Emily Belle Butler, Nov. 22, 1936; children—Naomi May (Mrs. John Harvey Burrows), David Samuel, Deborah Sharon. Ordained to ministry United Pentecostal Ch., 1940; founding pastor United Pentecostal Ch. Pasadena, Calif., 1937-39; pastor United Pentecostal Ch., Turlock, Calif., 1939-43; founding pastor Revival Tabernacle San Diego, 1945—, United Pentecostal Ch., Oakland, Calif., 1951; acting pres. Western Apostolic Bible Coll., Stockton, Calif., 1970. Youth pres. Western dist. United Pentecostal Ch., 1940-43, first gen. pres. youth dept. (nat.), 1947-50, dist. presbyter Western dist., 1954—; speaker on Hour of Power nationwide radio broadcast, 1955-67; mem. bd. Christian edn. United Pentecostal Ch., 1955-61, chmn. campus evangelism commn., 1970-74; co-founder Pentecostal Students Fellowship Intl., 1971, Forerunners, 1973; founder chmn. bd. Christian Service Tng. Inst., San Diego, 1973—; mem. bd. publs. United Pentecostal Ch., 1974—. Author: The Way of Victory, 1947, The Light of Truth, 1947, The Seven Men and the Two Natures, 1957, Spiritual Temperature Chart Study, 1957; The Last Will and Testament of the Lord Jesus Christ, 1969; Our Inheritance, 1971. Asso. editor Gospel Tidings, 1972—. Contbr. articles to religious publs. Home: 6390 Lake Shore Dr San Diego CA 92119 Office: 1765 Pentecost Way San Diego CA 92105

GRAY, DUNCAN MONTGOMERY, JR., bishop, Episcopal Ch.; b. Canton, Miss., Sept. 21, 1926; s. Duncan Montgomery and Isabel (McCrady) G.; B.E.E., Tulane U., 1948; M.Div., U. of South, 1953, D.D., 1972; m. Ruth Miller Spivey, Feb. 9, 1948; children—Duncan Montgomery, Anne Gray Finley, Lloyd Spivey, Catherine Gilmer. Ordained priest, 1953, bishop, 1974; priest-in-charge Calvary Ch., Cleveland, Miss. and Grace Episc. Ch., Rosedale, Miss., 1953-57, Holy Innocents Ch., Como, Miss., 1957-60; rector St. Peter's Ch., Oxford, Miss., 1957-65, St. Paul's Ch., Meridian, Miss., 1965-74; bishop coadjutor Diocese of Miss., Jackson, 1974, bishop, 1974—. Chmn. Miss. Religious Leadership Conf.; chmn. bd. trustees All Saints Episc. Sch., Vicksburg; trustee U. of South, Sewanee, Tenn. Active, So. Regional Council, 1967-73, Miss. Mental Health Assn., 1968-73; bd. dirs. Miss. Council on Human Relations, 1962—, pres., 1963-67. Recipient Nat. Speaker of Year award Tau Kappa Alpha, 1962. Contbr. articles to religious publs. Home: 3775 Old Canton Rd Jackson MS 39216 Office: PO Box 1636 Jackson MS 39205

GRAY, ETHEL MCCULLOUGH (MRS. BRUCE GRAY), lay church worker, United Methodist Church; b. Hastings, Fla., July 29, 1912; d. Charles H. and Cuba (Doak) McCullough; grad. Hastings High Sch., 1929; H.H.D., Fla. So. Coll., 1975; m. Bruce Gray, Jan. 30, 1929; children: Donna (Mrs. D. Myhre), Jennie (Mrs. J. Boyer), David, Dale Marie, Alan. Pres. Women's Soc. United Meth. Ch. Fla. Conf., 1966-70, sec. spiritual life of Fla. Conf., 1964-66, del. to World Meth. Conf., London, 1966, Denver, 1971, Dublin, Ireland, 1976; v.p. Ch. Women United in Fla., 1970-73; del. to gen. conf., United Meth. Ch., Dallas, 1968, Atlanta, 1972, Portland, Oreg., 1976, Indpls., 1980, leader Fla. del., Balt., 1984; lay leader Fla. Conf. United Meth. Ch., 1980-84. Propr. Gray Farms, Fla., 1962-82. Mem. Fla. Farm Bur., 1960—; trustee Fla. So. Coll., 1967-71, Paine Coll., 1967-74. Recipient Distinguished Service award Bethune-Cookman Coll., 1968. Mem. Fla. Council Chs. (pres. 1972-74). Home: PO Box 36 Hastings FL 32045 Office: Route 2 Box 183 East Palatka FL 32031

GRAY, FLOYD HASKELL, minister, Church of God (Anderson, Ind.); b. Greeneville, Tenn., Apr. 22, 1948; s. Huvel and Irene (Landers) G.; m. Joyce Lynn Combs, June 5, 1968; children: Jeremy Lance, Kirsten Michelle. Ordained to ministry Church of God (Anderson, Ind.), 1975. Assoc. pastor Flag Br. Ch. of God, Greeneville, 1973-74; pastor First Ch. of God, Baxter, Tenn., 1974-76, Piggott, Ark., 1976-79, Gratis, Ohio, 1979—; vol. chaplain Cookeville Gen. Hosp., Tenn., 1975-76, Middletown Hosp., Ohio, 1983—; treas. Piggott Ministerial Assn., 1976-79; mem. South East Mo. Assembly of Ch. of God, 1976-79; mem. Ark. Assembly of Ch. of God, 1976-79, bd. dirs., 1977-78; mem. Southwest Ohio Assembly of Ch. of God, 1979—, mem. campgrounds bd., 1979—. Co-editor: Preacher's Perspective, 1980—. Contbr. articles to religious publs. Recipient Cert. of Appreciation, Eastern Ark. council Boy Scouts Am., 1979. Mem. Gratis Community of Chs. Home: Box 125 State Route 122 Gratis OH 45330 Office: United First Ch of God State Route 122 Gratis OH 45330

GRAY, GEORGE MCBURNEY, minister, American Baptist Churches in U.S.A.; consulting psychologist; b. Belfest, No. Ireland, Oct. 12, 1941; came to U.S., 1970; s. Charles and Wilhelmina (McBurney) G.; m. Christine Irvine, Aug. 20, 1966; children: George Andrew, Charis Mary. Student Bible Tng. Inst., Glasgow, Scotland, 1963-66; diploma in theology, U. London, 1966; Th.M., Luther Rice Sem., 1973, Th.D., 1974; D.Min. in Psychology, Fuller Theol. Sem., 1979. Ordained to ministry Bapt. Union of Scotland, Gt. Britain and Ireland, 1966. Pastor, Batrick Bapt. Ch., Glasgow, Scotland, 1966-70, United Bapt. Ch., Milo, Maine, 1970-74, First Bapt. Ch., Gloversville, N.Y., 1974-82, Kenwood Bapt. Ch., then Grace Bapt. Ch., Cin., 1982—. Cons. family counselor, mental health. Contbr. articles to psychology, religious jours. Am. Bapt. Chs. scholar Regents Coll., Oxford U., 1981. Mem. Am. Assn. Marriage and Family Therapists, Am. Bapt. Minister's Council, Brit. Psychol. Soc., Am. Psychol. Assn. Home: 4967 Twinbrook Ct Cincinnati OH 45242 Office: Grace Bapt Ch 10620 Montgomery Rd Cincinnati OH 45242

GRAY, HENRY DAVID, minister, National Association of Congregational Christian Churches; b. No. Ireland, Jan. 18, 1908; s. Nathaniel and Margaret (Lawther) G.; came to U.S., 1923, naturalized, 1942; B.A. magna cum laude, Pomona (Calif.) Coll., 1930, D.D., 1952; student Boston U., 1932; B.D. summa cum laude, Hartford (Conn.) Theol. Sem., 1933; Ph.D., Edinburgh (Scotland) U., Tübingen (Germany) U., 1935; D.Litt., Piedmont Coll., 1976; m. Helen Katherine Lorbeer, Aug. 10, 1930; children: Ellen (Mrs. Frederick Spaulding), David Lawther, Betsey (Mrs. Bruce Kenworthy). Ordained to ministry Nat. Assn. Congl. Christian Chs., 1935; dir. youth chs., Calif., Conn., 1928-29, 30-31; asst. minister, Pomona, 1929-30; minister, Edinburgh, 1933-35, South Hadley, Mass., 1935-39; dir. edn., Hartford, 1931-33; nat. sec. young people and student life Congl. Christian Chs., 1939-42; minister, South Pasadena, Calif., 1942-55, Hartford, 1955-70; dean Am. Congl. Ctr., 1970—; Calif., lectr. numerous colls. and univs. U.S. and abroad; moderator, Hampshire Assn. Congl. Chs., 1937-38, So. Calif. Congl. Conf., 1943-55, Los Angeles Assn. Congl. Ch., 1947-48, Conn. Congl. Fellowship, 1957-65, 67-68, Nat. Assn. Congl. Chs., 1958-59; dir. So. Calif. Conf. Congl. Chs., 1946-54, Hartford Assn. Congl. Chs., 1956-60, Greater Hartford Council Chs., 1956-62; publs. com., Nat. Assn. Congl. Christian Chs., 1959-62, exec. com., 1955-59, mem. World Christian relations comnn.; del. internat. and nat. meetings, 1936—; founder, adviser Pilgrim Fellowship for Youth, 1939-42, 59-62, now life counsellor; founder, dir. Youth Odysseys, 1948-77, Youth Pilgrims to Greece and Britain, 1960-70, Caravan U.S.A., 1969-70; chmn. Congl. World Assembly of Youth, Boston, 1985. Mem. Hartford Planning Commn., 1959-70, chmn., 1961-65, 70; mem. Conn. Capitol Region Planning Commn., 1963-65; exec. com. Conn. Govt. Center Commn., 1965, 70; active Boy Scouts, YMCA, numerous other local and nat. orgns. William Thompson fellow, 1933-35. Fellow Am. Anthrop. Assn., Royal Anthrop. Inst.; mem. Am., Calif., Western hist. assns., Southwestern Anthrop. Assn., Am. Ethnol. Soc., Soc. for Am. Archeology, Am. Acad. Religion, Soc. Bibl. Lit. Author, editor books including: Theology for Christian Youth, 1941; Words for Today, 1944; Science and Religion, 1946; Under Orders, 1946; Primacy of God, 1947; Doctrine of Grace, 1948; Christian Marriage,

1950; Symbolism, 1950; Upward Call, 1952; Some Christian Convictions, 1955; South Church Prayers, 1960; Guidebook and Iconography Old South Church, 1960; Service Book, 1963; Blue Book of Congregational Usage 1965; Guidebook to the Holy Land, 1965; Mayflower Pilgrims, 1970; God's Torchbearers, 1970; Congregational Churches and Ministers, 1970; Panorama of Man, 1973; Hollywood Prayers, 1973; Bicentennial Christian Year, 1975; Congregational Usage, 1976; Congregational Worshipbook, 1978, rev. edit., 1984; Soundings, 1980; Pilgrim Fathers Reach the Pacific, 1981; Waymarks, 1983; Plus Ultra, Vol. 1, 1983; The Mediators, 1984; A Theology to Live By, 1984. Editor The Congregationalist, 1964-68; contbg. Editor: The Pilgrim Highroad, 1939-42, Congl. Jour., 1975—. Contbr. numerous articles to profl. jours. Home: 298 Fairfax St Ventura CA 93003 Office: 7065 Hollywood Blvd Hollywood CA 90028

GRAY, KENNETH LEE, minister, Southern Baptist Convention; b. St. Louis, June 7, 1939; s. William and Margaret I. (Martin) G.; m. Helen L. Brown, May 31, 1964; children: Ginger, Derek, Deven. Cert., Southwest Bapt. Jr. Coll., 1959; Th.B., Clarksville Sch. Theology, 1976, Th.M., 1977, Th.D., 1982. Ordained to ministry Bapt. Ch., 1960. Pastor chs. in Mo., 1959-67; evangelist, Hot Springs, Ark., 1967-70; pastor Smithton Bapt. Ch., Mo., 1970-77, New Salem Bapt. Ch., Winfield, Mo., 1977—; dir. evangelism Harmony Bapt. Assn., 1976; chmn. program com. Cuivre Bapt. Assn., 1978, chmn. nominating com., 1979. Author: How to Make Up a Church Budget, 1977; Expository Sermons: Matthew, 1982. First v.p. PTA, Winfield, 1980-81. Republican. Home: Route 1 Box 115 Winfield MO 63389

GRAY, RONALD FRANCIS, priest, Roman Catholic Church; b. Chgo., Mar. 22, 1918; s. Harry W. and Frances (O'Toole) G. M.A. in Philosophy, Cath. U. of Am., 1943. Ordained priest Roman Catholic Ch., 1943. Assoc. pastor St. John's Ch., Leonia, N.J., 1950—; dir. Conf.-a-Month Club, Englewood, N.J., 1950-84. Author: This is the Mass, 1955; Come to Lisieux, 1960; Catholic Living in a Nutshell, 1963. Vice-pres. Westmoor Gardens Project, Englewood, 1980-84. Home and Office: St John's the Evangelists Ch 235 Harrison St Leonia NJ 07605

GRAY, WALLACE GALE, minister, educator, United Methodist Church; b. Palmyra, Mo., May 3, 1927; s. Wallace Gale and Marjorie (Thomas) G.; m. Ina Turner, Dec. 18, 1948; children: Toni Jo, Tara Joy. B.A., Central Meth. Coll., 1948; B.D., Perkins Sch. Theology, 1950; Ph.D., Vanderbilt U., 1953; postgrad. U. Hawaii, 1963-64, U. Japan, 1971-72. Ordained to ministry United Meth. Ch., 1950. Assoc. pastor First Meth. Ch., Lawton, Okla., 1953-54; mem. Kans. West Conf., 1961—; prof. philosophy and religion, Southwestern Coll., Winfield, Kans., 1956—, Kirk chair of philosophy, 1966—; chmn. task force on upgrading human life Kans. Council Chs. and Wesley Med. Ctr., Wichita, 1967—. Author: (with John C. Plott) New Keys to East-West Philosophy, 1979; Global History of Philosophy, Vol. IV, 1984. Inventor diamond profile for studying and comparing Am. and Japanese coll. students. Mem. Am. Acad. Religion (regional chmn. 1960), Am. Philos. Assn. Democrat. Lodge: Rotary. Home: 1701 Winfield St Winfield KS 67156 Office: Southwestern Coll Winfield KS 67156

GREELEY, ANDREW MORAN, sociologist, educator, priest, Roman Catholic Church; b. Oak Park, Ill., Feb. 5, 1928; s. Andrew T. and Grace (McNichols) G.; A.B., St. Mary of Lake Sem., 1950, S.T.L., 1954; M.A., U. Chgo., 1961, Ph.D., 1961. Ordained priest 1954; asst. pastor Ch. of Christ the King, Chgo., 1954-64; program dir. Nat. Opinion Research Center, Chgo., 1961-73; dir. Center for Study Am. Pluralism, Loyola U., Chgo., 1973—; former lectr. sociology U. Chgo.; cons. Hazen Found. Commn.; newspaper columnist. Recipient Cath. Press Assn. award for best book for young people, 1965, Thomas Alva Edison award for radio broadcast, 1963, C. Albert Kobb award Nat. Cath. Edn. Assn., 1977. Mem. Am. Sociol. Assn., Am. Cath. Sociol. Soc. (pres.), Soc. for Sci. Study Religion, Religious Research Assn. Author: The Church and the Suburbs, 1959; Strangers in the House, 1961; Religion and Career, 1963; (with Peter H. Rossi) Education of Catholic Americans, 1966; Why Can't They Be Like Us?, 1969; Come Blow Your Mind With Me, 1971; Friendship Game, 1971; Life for a Wanderer: A New Look at Christian Spirituality, 1971; The Denominational Society: A Sociological Approach to Religion in America, 1972; Priests in the United States: Reflections on A Survey, 1972; The Sinai Myth, 1972; That Most Distressful Nation, 1972; New Agenda, 1973; The Persistence of Religion, 1973; The Devil, You Say!, 1974; Unsecular Man, 1974; The Great Mysteries; An Essential Catechism, 1976; Love and Play, 1975; Death and Beyond, 1976; The American Catholic: A Social Portrait, 1977; The Making of the Pope, 1978, 79; The Cardinal Sins, 1981; Thy Brother's Wife, 1982; Ascent Into Hell, 1983; Lord of the Dance, 1984. Contbr. articles to profl. jours. Home: 1012 E 47th St Chicago IL 60653 Office: Cultural Pluralism Research Ctr 5801 Ellis Ave Chicago IL 60637

GREEN, BARBARA, nun, religion educator, Roman Catholic Church; b. Stockton, Calif., Feb. 20, 1946; d. Robert E. and Barbara Ann (Page) G. M.A., Grad. Theol. Union, 1976; Ph.D., Grad. Theol. Union-U. Calif.-Berkeley, 1980. Joined Order Dominican Religious Women, 1964. Tchr., San Domenico High Sch., San Anselmo, Calif., 1968-73; instr. religious studies Dominican Coll., San Rafael, Calif., 1980—, dir. humanities program, 1982—, chmn. gen. edn., 1983—; worker vol. St. Vincent de Paul dining room, San Rafael, 1983-84. Contbr. article to bibl. book. Mem. Bread for the World, Global Edn. Assocs. (assoc.). Democrat. Home and Office: 1520 Grand Ave San Rafael CA 94901

GREEN, BRUCE, priest, Episcopal Church; b. Tuscaloosa, Ala., Sept. 27, 1936; s. Benjamine Arthur and Alice (Williams) G.; m. Dorothy Allen Cooke, June 19, 1961; children: Alice Elizabeth, Jennifer Cooke, Carolyn Louise. B.A., U. South, 1958; M.Div., Va. Theol. Sem., 1961. Ordained priest Episcopal Ch., 1962. Vicar, St. Mark's Ch., Copperhill, Tenn., 1961-64; rector St. Andrew's Ch., Marianna, Ark., 1964-67; vicar Holy Apostles Ch., Memphis, 1967-69; rector Trinity Ch., Gatlinburg, Tenn., 1969-77, St. Peter's Ch., Amarillo, Tex., 1977—; exec. com. Diocese of N.W. Tex., Lubbock, 1984—; del. synod Province VII, 1984; exec. com. Diocese of Tenn., 1972-77, Appalachian People's Service Orgn., 1969-77. Chmn. allocations United Way, Amarillo, Tex., 1983-84; chmn. bd. Overlook Mental Health Ctr., Knoxville, 1973-77. Mem. C. of C. (dir. 1976). Lodge: Rotary (pres. 1975). Home: 3103 Sunlite Amarillo TX 79106 Office: Saint Peters Episcopal Ch PO Box 3751 Amarillo TX 79116

GREEN, BRUCE WAYNE, minister, So. Bapt. Conv.; b. Nacogdoches, Tex., Sept. 14, 1953; s. Gilmer Delmer and Essie Lee (Johnson) G.; B.A., E. Tex. Bapt. Coll., 1976; m. Debra Jean Brumley, Jan. 10, 1976. Asst. pastor DeBerry (Tex.) Bapt. Ch., 1974-75; minister youth Central Bapt. Ch., Marshall, Tex., 1975-76; pastor County Line Bapt. Ch., Ballard, Tex., 1976—. Chmn. retreat com. Bapt. Student Union, 1975. Recipient Youth Achievement award Optimist Club, 1975. Home: PO Box 58 Oil City LA 71061 Office: Route 1 Box 90 Ballard TX 75757

GREEN, CARROL ROBERT, minister, Disciples of Christ Church; b. Caldwell, Idaho, July 15, 1935; s. Carrol Norton and Rotha Maxine (Hammond) G.; m. Diana Faye Pearson, Dec. 2, 1957; children: Kelly Robert, Forrest Glenn, Jade Alan. B.A. in Sociology, Boise State U., 1979; M.Div., Pacific Sch. Religion, 1982. Ordained, 1982. Interim pastor Ukiah Christian Ch. (Calif.), 1982; adminstr. Christian Ch. Homes N.C., Oakland, Calif., 1982-84; pastor Univ. Christian Ch., Berkeley, Calif., 1984—; regional bd. No. Calif. Regional Office Disciples of Christ, Oakland, 1984. Corporal Idaho State Police, Boise, 1960, 79. Served with USMC, 1954-57. Study grantee, Order Eastern Star, 1980-81, Nat. Office Disciples of Christ, 1980-81. Mem. Pacific Sch. Religion Alumni Assn. (v.p. 1984—). Home: 5017 Santa Rita Rd Richmond CA 94803 Office: Univ Christian Ch 2401 LeConte Berkeley CA 94701

GREEN, DUARD WINDELL, minister, Southern Baptist Convention; b. Bridgeport, Tex., Oct. 20, 1929; s. Cuel Weldon and Minnie Lee (Davidson) G.; student Draughon's Bus. Coll., 1950; diploma in theology Southwestern Theol. Sem., 1966-68; B.A., William Carey Coll., 1970; postgrad. U. So. Miss., 1972-73; D.Min., Luther Rice Sem., Jacksonville, Fla., 1979; m. Ora Maudean Shannon, Feb. 14, 1948; children—Sharon Kay, Patsy Gay, Hope Ray, Leeron. Ordained to ministry, 1966; pastor Balsoria (Tex.) Bapt. Ch., 1966-68, E. Lincoln Bapt. Ch., Brookhaven, Miss., 1968-70, Crooked Creed Bapt. Ch., Monticello, Miss., 1970-72, Calvary Bapt. Ch., Canton, Miss., 1972-73, Edwards (Miss.) Bapt. Ch., 1973—. Sec.-treas. pastor's conf. Lawrence-Marion Bapt. Assn., 1972; mem. exec. com. Hinds-Madison Bapt. Assn., 1972; pres. Edwards Ministerial Assn., 1974; exec. sec. Ch. Community Services, Edwards, 1974-76; vol. chaplain Univ. Med. Center, Jackson, Miss., 1976; bd. dirs. Beginning Again in Christ Corp., 1974—; prison work. Organizer, Carter for Pres., Edwards, 1975-76. Home: 100 Montgomery Dr Edwards MS 39066 Office: Box 138 Edwards MS 39066

GREEN, GARRETT DOUGLAS, educator, Presbyterian Church (USA); b. Oakland, Calif., June 1, 1941; s. Carleton and Lois (Livingston) G.; m. Priscilla Bogard, Apr. 18, 1970; children: Joshua, Abigail. A.B., Stanford U., 1963; M.Div., Union Theol. Sem., 1967; M.Phil., Yale U., 1970, Ph.D., 1971. Asst. prof. religious studies Conn. Coll., New London, Conn., 1970-76, assoc. prof., 1976-82, prof. religious studies, 1982—; ruling elder Presbyn. Ch. (USA), 1972—. Translator: Attempt at a Critique of All Revelation (J.G. Fichte), 1978. Contbr. articles to profl. jours. Fulbright student, 1963-64; Alexander von Humboldt research fellow, 1976-77, 79-80; Sr. Fulbright scholar, 1976-77. Mem. Am. Acad. Religion, Am. Philos. Assn., 19th Century Theology Working Group, AAUP. Democrat. Home: 47 Westomere Terr New London CT 06320 Office: Dept Religious Studies Conn Coll New London CT 06320

GREEN, GERRELL LYNN, minister, Baptist Missionary Assn. Am.; b. Waldo, Ark., Sept. 11, 1937; s. William Grady and Carolyn Irene (Clark) G.; B.S., So. State Coll., Magnolia, Ark., 1962; postgrad. Bapt. Missionary Assn. Sem., Jacksonville, Tex., 1965-66; m. Betty Sue Hairston, Sept. 14, 1963; 1 dau., Betty Renae. Ordained to ministry Bapt. Missionary Assn. Am., 1959; pastor Bodcaw Bapt. Ch., Rosston, Ark., 1959-67; writer publs. com. Bapt. Missionary Assn. Am., 1965-70; sec. bd. trustees Central Bapt. Coll., Conway, Ark., 1966-68, Bapt. Missionary Theol. Sem., 1967-69; pastor Beech St. Bapt. Ch., Crossett, Ark., 1967-71; v.p. Bapt. Missionary Assn. of Ark. 1973-74, pres., 1975-76; vice-moderator Columbia Bapt. Assn., 1973-74, moderator, 1975-76; v.p., instr. Columbia Bapt. Bible Sch., Magnolia, 1974—; pastor College View Bapt. Ch., Magnolia, 1971—; ednl. dir. S.Ark. Bapt. Encampment, 1976-77. Hon. bd. dirs. Magnolia area ARC. Contbr. articles to religious publs. Home: 507 S Carson Dr POB 743 Magnolia AR 71753

GREEN, ISAAC, minister, Nat. Bapt. Conv., U.S.A.; b. Kerens, Tex., Nov. 2, 1919; s. Charlie and Clara (Runnels) G.; B.A., Bishop Coll., 1952; B.D., Bible Bapt. Sem., 1957; D.D. (hon.) Gordon Conwell Sem., 1975; m. Freddie Mae Burton, Aug. 13, 1939; children—Bennie, James L., Isaac. Ordained to ministry, 1949; pastor New Mount Zion Bapt. Ch., Waxahachie, Tex., 1952, Greater Mount Zion Bapt. Ch., Dallas, 1953-59, Mount Olive Bapt. Ch., Fort Worth, 1959-63, Central Bapt. Ch., Pitts., 1963—. Pres. Pitts. Ministers Conf., 1970-71; moderator Allegheny Bapt. Assn. Pitts., 1973-76; treas. Nat. Bapt. Conv., U.S.A., 1976—. Home: 3068 Iowa St Pittsburgh PA 15219 Office: 2200 Wylie Ave Pittsburgh PA 15219

GREEN, JOEL BENNETT, minister, United Methodist Church; b. Lubbock, Tex., May 7, 1956; s. John Wayne and Myrtle Adele (Bennett) G.; m. Pamela Jane Kelley, Feb. 24, 1982; children: Aaron Michael Scott, Heather Allison. B.S., Tex. Tech U., 1978; M.Th., Perkins Sch. Theology, 1982; Ph.D. candidate, U. Aberdeen, Scotland, 1982—. Ordained to ministry United Meth. Ch., as deacon, 1980. Pastor Welch/Wellmann United Meth. Chs., Tex., 1977-78; assoc. pastor First United Meth. Ch., Irving, Tex., 1978-79, Pleasant Mount United Meth. Ch., Dallas, 1979-82; minister North of Scotland Mission Circuit, Aberdeen, 1982—. Author: How to Read Prophecy, 1984. Contbr. articles to profl. jours. Mng. editor Catalyst Mag., 1980—. Fellow John H. Moore Found., 1982-83; John Wesley Found., 1982—. Mem. Soc. Bibl. Lit., Tyndale Fellowship, Wesleyan Theol. Soc. Home: 49 Queen St Peterhead Aberdeenshire Scotland AB4 6TU

GREEN, JOHN EDWARD, minister, Southern Baptist Convention; b. Neches, Tex., Apr. 18, 1930; s. Rubie and Hattie (Wood) G.; m. Annie Joyce Arnett, July 11, 1953; children: Sarah F., John S. A.B., Baylor U., 1952; B.D., Southwestern Bapt. Theol. Sem., 1957; M.A., Stephen F. Austin U., 1965. Ordained to ministry Baptist Ch., 1948. Pastor 1st Bapt. Ch., Ironton, Tex., 1948-52, Lone Pine Bapt. Ch., Palestine, Tex., 1953-57, Trinity Bapt. Ch., Seguin, Tex., 1977-79, Richey St. Bapt. Ch., Pasadena, Tex., 1979—; commd. 1st lt. Chaplains Corps, U.S. Army, 1957, advanced through grades to lt. col., 1968; served in Germany, Korea, Vietnam; pres. Armed Forces Bapt. Euroep, 1974-75, Pasadena Ministerial Alliance, 1982-83; bd. dirs. The Bridge, Houston, 1981-84. Pres. Frankfurt Am. PTA, Fed. Republic Germany, 1975; mem. Family Time, USA, Pasadena, 1983. Decorated Bronze Star, Legion of Merit, others. Mem. Nat. Geog. Soc., Mil. Chaplains Assn. Lodges: Lions, Rotary, Masons. Home: 706 Handell Pasadena TX 77502 Office: 1010 S Richey Pasadena TX 77506

GREEN, LARRY A., minister, college chaplain, United Methodist Church; b. Atlanta, Dec. 26, 1940; s. Archie and Sybil (Nance) G.; m. Melanie Moore, July 15, 1962; children: Gayla Lyn, Gary Layne. A.A., Young Harris Coll., 1960; B.A., LaGrange Coll., 1962; M.Div., Emory U., 1965; D.Min., McCormick Theol. Sem., 1983. Ordained to ministry Meth. Ch. as elder, 1965. Pastor Mizpah-Rush Chapel Chs., Rome, Ga., 1965-66; campus minister, asst. prof. Reinhardt Coll., Waleska, Ga., 1966-71; assoc. minister First United Meth. Ch., Decatur, Ga., 1971-72; chaplain, adj. asst. prof. Berry Coll., Mt. Berry, Ga., 1972—; mem. Bd. Ordained Ministry North Ga. Conf., United Meth. Ch., 1976-84, sec., 1980-84, mem. com. health and welfare, 1984—. Bd. dirs. Floyd County chpt. ARC, Rome, 1976—; bd. dirs. Mental Health Assn. Floyd County, 1980—; cert. ofcl. N.W. Ga. Football Ofcls. Assn., 1972-83. Named Faculty Staff Mem. of Yr., Berry Coll. Student Govt. Assn., 1974; Minister of Yr., Met. Kiwanis Club, 1984. Mem. Nat. Assn. Coll. and Univ. Chaplains (sec. 1979-84, exec. com. 1984-87), Assocs. Religion and Intellectual Life.

GREEN, LOWELL CLARK, pastor, Lutheran Church, Missouri Synod. B. Findlay, Ohio, Nov. 29, 1925; s. Clark Frederick and Gertrude Grace (Kibler) G.; m. Violet Eleanora Handahl, July 29, 1956 (dec. 1980); children: Daniel, Katharine, Sonja, Barbara. B.A., Wartburg Coll., 1946; B.D., Wartburg Sem., 1949; D.S.T., Friedrich and Alexander U., Erlanger,

Germany, 1955. Ordained American Luth. Ch., 1949. Pastor various congregations, Tex., S.D., Minn., Ill., 1949-52, 52-67; prof. history Appalachian State U., Boone, N.C., 1968-80; prof. history and theology Concordia Coll., River Forest, Ill., 1978-80; prof. theology Concordia Sem., St. Catharines, Ont., Can., 1980-83; pastor Gethsemane Luth. Ch., Buffalo, 1984—; dean Concordia Acad., Dubuque, Iowa, 1973—; cons. in ch. music; participant Luther Symposium, Acad. of Sci., Mainz, Germany, 1983; vis. sr. fellow Ctr. for Reformation Research, St. Louis, 1971. Author: How Melanchthon Helped Luther, 1980; editor: Luth. Theol. Rev., 1983; translator, cons. Bach cantatas for Gregorian Inst. Am., 1984—; author 4 books, 60 articles. Mem. Am. Soc. Ch. History, 16th Century Studies Conf. (governing council 1974-78), Am. Soc. for Reformation Research, Concordia Hist. Inst. Home: 95 Rand Ave Buffalo NY 14216 Office: Gethsemane Luth Ch 427 Goodyear Ave Buffalo NY 14211

GREEN, WILLIAM BAILLIE, religious educator, priest, Episcopal Church; b. Mayfield, Ky., Apr. 3, 1927; s. Eben Elmer and Novella (Baillie) G.; m. Donna Harpold, Dec. 29, 1956; children: Stuart David, Ian Baillie. A.B., Baylor U., 1948; B.D., Louisville Sem., 1953; S.T.M., Union Sem., N.Y.C., 1953; Phil.D., U. Edinburgh, Scotland, 1955. Ordained priest Episcopal Ch., 1972. Asst. minister First Presbyn. Ch., Mt. Vernon, N.Y., 1952-54, First Presbyn. Ch., Youngstown, Ohio, 1955-56; priest-in-charge St. Cuthbert's Episcopal Ch., MacMahan, Maine, 1972-73; prof. theology Episcopal Theol. Sem. of Southwest, Austin, Tex., 1973—; mem. Internat. Anglican-Orthodox Theol. Consultation, 1983—; mem. Gen. Bd. Examining Chaplains, 1977—. Editor/contbr.: Spirit and Light, 1982. Author: What is Religion?, 1969. Contbr.: Political Expectations, 1971. Mem. Am. Acad. Religion (chpt. v.p. 1969-70), Conf. Anglican Theologians, Am. Philos. Assn. Club: University (Denver); Capitol (Austin). Address: Episcopal Theol Sem Southwest 606 Rathervue Pl Austin TX 78768

GREENBERG, SIMON See *Who's Who in America,* 43rd edition.

GREENBERG, WILLIAM H., rabbi, Orthodox Jewish congregation; b. Des Moines, Iowa, Mar. 13, 1926; s. Albert Samuel and Ethel (Matlaw) G.; m. Rosa F. Igell, Oct. 13, 1951; children: Sarah, Don, Deena, Aryeh. B.S.E.E., Ill. Inst. Tech., 1948; B. Hebrew Lit., Hebrew Theol. Coll., 1950; M.A., Ariz. State U., 1964; Ph.D., U. Wash., 1973. Ordained rabbi, 1950. Rabbi Beth Israel, Chicago Heights, Ill., 1951-53, Hebrew Theol. Coll., Chgo., 1956-58, Congregation Beth Hebrew, Phoenix, 1958-62, Congregation Ezra Bessaroth, Seattle, 1962—. Served to 1st lt. U.S. Army, 1953-56. Mem. Rabbinical Council Am. Office: Congregation Ezra Bessaroth 5217 S Brandon St Seattle WA 98118

GREENE, CHARLES ROBERT, minister, United Meth. Ch.; b. Liberty, Tex., Aug. 21, 1943; s. Charles Robert and Louise Ann (Partlow) G.; B.S., U. Corpus Christi, 1968; postgrad. Crozer Theol. Sem., 1968-70; M.Div., Wesley Theol. Sem., Washington, 1974; postgrad. Coventry (Eng.) Cathedral, 1975. Ordained to ministry, 1970; youth dir. 1st Presbyn. Ch., Corpus Christi, Tex., 1965-67; interim pastor Hubbard (Tex.) Presbyn. Ch., 1967-68, 1st Congl. Ch., Rhinelander, Wis., 1968; pastor Cookman United Meth. Ch., Phila., 1968-69, Cherry Hill United Meth. Ch., Elkton, Md., 1969-70; ordained deacon, 1970; instr. Am. culture U. Nagasaki (Japan), 1971-72; instr. English, Nagasaki State Coll., 1971-72; advisor UNESCO, Nagasaki, 1971-72; pastor Seaford (Del.) United Meth. Circuit, 1972-73; ordained elder, 1975; pastor Royal Oak (Md.) United Meth. Ch., 1974-75; asso. pastor St. Paul's United Meth. Ch., Wilmington, Del., 1976—. Youth advisor Easton Dist. United Meth. Ch., 1974-75; patron Corrymeela Community, Belfast, No. Ireland, 1975; del. World Meth. Conf., Dublin, Ireland, 1976; bd. dirs. Wilmington Pacem in Terris, 1976, Ireland Children's Fund, 1977—. Reg. Democratic mem. Elkton Welfare Bd., 1969; chmn. CROP dr. Talbot County, Md., 1974-75; chmn. programs Ulster Project, Wilmington, 1976. Mem. Community of the Cross of Nails, Japan-Am. Soc., Wesley Alumni Assn. Home: 2219 Prior Rd Wilmington DE 19809 Office: 1314 Foulk Rd Wilmington DE 19803

GREENE, GLEN LEE, minister, Southern Baptist Convention; b. Clarks, La., Nov. 12, 1915; s. Columbua C. and Roxie S. (Byrd) G.; m. Grace Lois Prince, Nov. 22, 1938; children: Glen Lee, Roxie Green St. Martin, Jerry Prince. B.A., La. Coll., 1939; B.D., New Orleans Bapt. Theol. Sem., 1948, Th.D., 1950. Ordained to ministry So. Bapt. Conv., 1934. Pastor, Pollock Bapt. Ch., La., 1938-40, Long Leaf Bapt. Ch., La., 1940-42, First Bapt. Ch., Paris, Mo., 1942-44, Gonzales, La., 1944-53, Oak Ridge Bapt. Ch., La., 1953—; Protestant chaplain State Colony and Tng. Sch., Pineville, La., 1938-42; ofcl. historian La. Bapt. Conv., 1973—. Author: History of the Baptists of Oak Ridge, 1960; Masonry in Louisiana, 1962; The History of Southern Baptist Hospital, 1969; House Upon a Rock: About Southern Baptists in Louisiana, 1973. Sec., Oak Ridge Democratic Exec. Com.; mem. United Fund Com. Recipient plaque La. Bapt. Hist. Soc., 1969. Lodges: Lions, Masons (worshipful master) (Oak Ridge). Home: PO Box 203 Oak Ridge LA 71264

GREENE, ROBERT THOMAS, ch. ofcl., So. Bapt. Conv.; b. nr. Henderson, N.C., Aug. 28, 1919; s. Edward Jones and Iola (Gooch) G.; B.A., Wake Forest Coll., 1944; B.D., So. Bapt. Theol. Sem., 1948; spl. student Syracuse U., 1963; m. Grace Bailey, Dec. 24, 1939; children—Annette Greene Adams, Robert Thomas. Ordained to ministry, 1942; pastor in N.C., Ind. and Ky., 1942-52; missionary in West Chowan Assn., Ahoskie, 1952-53, Cabarrus Assn., Concord, N.C., 1953-60; sec. retirement plans dept. Bapt. State Conv., Raleigh, N.C., 1960-61, sec. dept. stewardship devel., 1962-70, dir. Office Coop. Program Promotion, 1971-72, dir. dept. stewardship and coop. program promotion, 1973—. Mem. Bapt. Stewardship Devel. Assn. (pres. 1972-73). Author: Leonard E. Hilland R. T. McCartney) How to Write and Use a Few Words for an Effective Harvest, 1967. Contbr. articles to profl. publs. Home: 2700 St Marys St Raleigh NC 27609 Office: 301 Hillsborough St Raleigh NC 27611

GREENFIELD, LARRY LEE, educator, minister, Am. Bapt. Chs. in U.S.A.; b. Sioux Falls, S.D., Sept. 8, 1941; s. LeRoy H. and Isabell M. (Sneiderman) G.; A.B., Sioux Falls Coll., 1963; D.B., U. Chgo., 1966, A.M., 1970, Ph.D., 1978; m. Barbara Jean Shoemaker, Aug. 31, 1963; children—Sarah Elizabeth, Jessica Christine. Ordained to ministry Am. Baptist Chs. in the U.S.A., 1966; chaplain to Baptist students U. Chgo., 1966-67, dir. Baptist Grad. Student Center, 1967-69, asst. dean students Div. Sch., 1971, acting dean students, 1972, dean students, 1972-80, asst. prof. theology, 1975-80; pres. Colgate Rochester Div. Sch./Bexley Hale/Crozer Theol. Sem., Rochester, N.Y., 1980—. Mem. Am. Acad. Religion, Am. Theol. Soc.-Midwest. Home: 1122 S Goodman St Rochester NY 14620 Office: 1100 S Goodman St Rochester NY 14620

GREENGUS, SAMUEL, dean Jewish Institute of Religion; b. Chgo., Mar. 11, 1936; s. Eugene and Thelma (Romirowsky) G.; m. Lesha Bellows, Apr. 30, 1957; children: Deana, Rachel, Judith. M.A., U. Chgo., 1959, Ph.D., 1963. Prof. semitic langs. Hebrew Union Coll., Jewish Inst. Religion, Cin., 1963—, dean, 1979—; chmn. acad. officers Greater Cin. Consortium of Colls. and Univs., 1983—. Author: Old Babylonian Tablets from Ischali and Vicinity, 1979; Studies in Ishchali Documents, 1985. Mem. Am. Oriental Soc., Soc. Bibl. Lit., Assn. Jewish Studies, Phi Beta Kappa. Office: Hebrew Union Coll Jewish Inst Religion 3101 Clifton Ave Cincinnati OH 45220

GREENLEE, JOHN EDWARD, minister Christian Church; b. Fremont, Nebr., Dec. 1, 1929; s. Paul Russell and Zoe Angeline (Morgan) G.; m. Della Jean Sharp, June 15, 1951; children: Suzanne, Allyson, Jeannine. A.B., Manhattan Christian Coll., 1952; A.B., Friends U., 1958; M.Div. cum laude, Christian Theol. Sem., 1963; M.A., Butler U., 1967. Ordained to ministry, Christian Ch., 1951. Pastor Diamond Christian Ch., Mo., 1952-53, West Side Christian Ch., Wichita, Kans., 1952-59, 67-74, Oaklandon Christian Ch., Kans., 1959-67, First Christian Ch., Thousand Oaks, Calif., 1976—; past trustee, lectr. on preaching Manhattan Christian Coll., Pacific Christian Coll.; mem. com. N.Am. Christian Conv., 1955—; bd. dirs. Emmanuel Sch. Religion, Johnson City, Tenn., 1976—; chaplain Ventura County Fire Dept., Calif., 1976—. Contbr. column for periodical Christian Standard, 1965-82. Advisor Ventura County Bd. Commrs., 1980—; bd. dirs. Los Robles Hosp., 1981—. Mem. Mensa, Theta Phi. Home: 1741 Calle Zocalo Thousand Oaks CA 91360 Office: First Christian Ch 301 W Ave de las Flor Thousand Oaks CA 91360

GREENSPOON, LEONARD JAY, religion educator, Jewish; b. Richmond, Va., Dec. 5, 1945; s. Alvin Louis and Rose (Levy) G.; m. Eliska Rebecca Morsel, Aug. 25, 1968; children: Gallit, Talya. B.A., U. Richmond, 1967, M.A., 1970; postgrad. U. Rome, Italy, 1967-68, U. Calif.-Santa Barbara, 1978-79, Jewish Theol. Sem., 1978; Ph.D., Harvard U., 1977. Assoc. prof. history and religion Clemson U., S.C., 1983—; faculty adviser Hillel, 1979-81. Author: Textual Studies in the Book of Joshua, 1983; assoc. editor Ezekiel vols. 1 and 2, 1979, 1983; contbr. book chpts., book revs., jour. articles to Assn. for Jewish Studies Newsletter, Bibl. Archaeologist, Bibl. Theology Bull., Bull. Internat. Orgn. for Septuagint and Cognate Studies, others; also ency. articles. Lodge pres., state sec., del. to internat. conv. B'nai B'rith, Greenville, S.C., 1983—. Fulbright scholar, 1967; Danforth scholar, 1967; Woodrow Wilson scholar, 1967; grantee NEH, 1981, 78, Am. Council Learned Socs., 1984; Clemson U. grantee. Mem. Internat. Orgn. for Septuagint and Cognate Studies (sec. 1980—), Am. Schs. Oriental Research, Assn. Jewish Studies, Cath. Bibl. Assn., Soc. for Values in Higher Edn., Soc. Bibl. Lit, S.C. Acad. Religion. Democrat. Home: 300 Hunting Hill Circle Greer SC 29651 Office: Dept of History Clemson U Clemson SC 29631

GREENWOOD, DILLARD (BILL) WAYNE, religious educator, Seventh-Day Adventist Church; b. Los Angeles, May 18, 1929; s. Thomas Ray Greenwood and Althea Mable (Hampton) Gray; m. Verna B. Cannon, May 4, 1949 (div. 1952); 1 child, Dennis; m. Nova Bardeen Vaught, Sept. 9, 1956; children: Colleen, Jack. G.E.D., Pueblo Coll., 1956; B.A. in Elem. Edn., Pacific Union Coll., 1965. Ordained to ministry Seventh-day Adventist Ch. as local elder, 1966. Prin., tchr. Hawaiian Mission 7th Day Adventist Ch., Molokai, 1966-69; v.p., tchr. So. Bay Jr. Acad., Torrance, Calif., 1969-74; prin., tchr. No. Calif. Conf. 7th Day Adventists Ch., Pleasant Hill, Calif., 1974-77, Colo. Conf., Denver, 1978—; rep. curriculum com. Rocky Mountain Conf. 7th Day Adventists, Denver, 1978-81; bd. dirs. 7th Day Adventists Credit Union, Denver, 1981-82; mem. adminstrv. com. Mile High Acad., Denver, 1984—; faculty rep. 7th Day Adventists Sch. Bd., Denver, 1984—. Home: 1551 E Bates Pkwy Englewood CO 80110 Office: Mile High Acad 711 E Yale Denver CO 80210

GREER, MARTIN LUTHER, minister, United Meth. Ch.; b. Parrottsville, Tenn., July 24, 1918; s. David Hunter and Charity Louise (Wardroup) G.; A.A., Tenn. Wesleyan Coll., 1938; B.A., U. Chgo., 1940; M.Div., Garrett Bibl. Inst., 1944; M.A., State U. Iowa, 1956; m. Martha May Morrison, June 7, 1945; children—Patricia Louise Greer Tharp, David Ray, Susanna Lee Greer Fein, Jane Christine Greer Fultz, James Martin, Martha Joellyn, William Luther. Ordained to ministry as deacon, 1945, elder, 1947; student pastor No. Ind. Conf., Meth. Ch., 1943-44; pastor S. Iowa Meth. Conf., 1944-64, W. Va. United Meth. Conf., 1966—, West Buckhannon United Meth. Circuit, 1975—; instr. Bible, Iowa Wesleyan Coll., Mt. Pleasant, 1956-57; lectr. English, Drake U., Des Moines, 1962-63; instr. English, lit., speech Freeport (Ill.) Community Coll., 1963-64, Canton (Ill.) Community Coll., 1964-65; asst. prof. English, W.Va. Wesleyan Coll., Buckhannon, 1965-70. Sec., v.p. N. Central Jurisdiction Meth. Soc., sec. Iowa Conf. Hist. Soc., 1948-60, pres. 1961-63, mem. conf. bd. missions, 1961-63. Scoutmaster, Boy Scouts Am., Victor, Iowa, 1948-50, cub scout com. chmn., Buckhannon, 1968-70; mem. Buckhannon Community Action Council, 1973, Buckhannon Community Theatre, 1973-75, Community Choir, 1975-76; ration bd. mem. Monroe County, Albia, Iowa, 1944-46; bd. dirs. Upshur County (W.Va.) Homes Corp., 1974-76. Mem. AAUP, Am. Studies Assn., W. Va. Coll. Council, W.Va. Assn. Coll. English Tchrs., Nat. Council Tchrs. English, Freeport Edn. assn., Ill. Assn. Classroom Tchrs. Editor: Proc. N. Central Jurisdiction Meth. Hist. Soc., 1961, 1962; editor with introduction Iowa Conf. M.E.Ch., 1854, 1855, 1856. Contbr. articles to Ency. World Methodism, 1974, also religious jours. Address: 46 College Ave Buckhannon WV 26201

GREEVER, JOHN EADS, minister, So. Baptist Conv.; b. Louisville, Apr. 1, 1953; s. Marshall John and Ruth (Eads) G.; B.A., Howard Payne U., 1975; postgrad. Southwestern Bapt. Theol. Sem., 1975—; m. Irma Vickers, June 16, 1973. Ordained to ministry, 1973; youth evangelist, Ky., 1971-72; asso. pastor First Cumberland Presbyn. Ch., Louisville, 1972; youth minister First Bapt. Ch., Greenville, Tex., 1973; pastor First Bapt. Ch., Cherokee, Tex., 1973-75; young adult minister First Bapt. Ch., Duncan, Okla., 1975—. Mem. Mullins Bapt. Assn., San Saba Bapt. Assn., Assn. Sunday Sch. Dirs. Home: 1809-E J T Luther Dr Fort Worth TX 76115 Office: First Baptist Church 9th at Ash Duncan OK 73533

GREGG, JOHN SHELTON, religious educator, Roman Catholic Church; b. Wichita, Kans., Aug. 2, 1944; s. Donald Bruce Gregg and Nina Marie (Shelton) Neff; m. Mary Jo Wood, June 11, 1966; children: Michael, Teresa, John, Sarah, Stephen. B.S., U.S. Naval Acad., 1966; M.A. in Applied Theology, Sch. Applied Theology Berkeley, Calif., 1972. Ordained as deacon Roman Catholic Ch., 1984. Parish coordinator St. Stephen Indian Mission, Wyo., 1972-76; dir. religious edn., youth minister St. Anthony's Ch., Casper, Wyo., 1976-79; pastoral assoc. Saints Cyril and Methodius Ch., Rock Springs, Wyo., 1979-83; area edn. coordinator Archdiocese of Balt., 1983—; pres. Deo Gratias Photos, Inc., Riverton, Wyo., 1978—. Photographer religious publs., 1978—. Contbr. articles to religious publs. Served to lt. USN, 1966-71. Mem. Nat. Conf. Diocesan Dirs., Nat. Cath. Edn. Assn. Democrat. Clubs: Washington Apple Pi; Frederick Computer (Md.). Home: 1807 Noblewood Ct Frederick MD 21701 Office: Central Md Ctr for Christian Formation 1807 Noblewood Ct Frederick MD 21701

GREGG, MARY JO, religious educator, Roman Catholic Church; b. Balt., Mar. 6, 1944; d. Robert Lukens and Mary (Olys) Wood; m. John Shelton Gregg, June 11, 1966; children: Michael, Teresa, John, Sarah, Stephen. B.A. in Elem. Edn., Mt. St. Agnes, 1965. Mission bookkeeper St. Stephen Indian Mission, Wyo., 1972-76; dir. religious edn., youth minister St. Anthony's Ch., Casper, Wyo, 1976-79; pastoral assoc. Saints Cyril and Methodius Ch., Rock Springs, Wyo., 1979-81; dir. religious edn. Saints Cyril and Methodius Ch. and Our Lady of Sorrows Ch., Rock Springs, 1981-83; area edn. coordinator Archdiocese Balt., Frederick, Md., 1983—. Contbr. articles to religious publs. Mem. Nat. Conf. Diocesan Dirs. Democrat. Home: 1807 Noblewood Ct Frederick MD 21701 Office: Central Md Ctr for Christian Info 1807 Noblewood Ct Frederick MD 21701

GREGOIRE, PAUL, archbishop, Roman Catholic Church; b. Verdun, Oct. 24, 1911; s. Albert and Marie (Lavoie) G.; student, Seminaire de Sainte-Therese, theol. student Grand Sem. Montreal Que., Can.; Ph.D.; S.T.L.; Litt.L., M.A. in History; diploma in pedagogy; hom. doctorate U. Montreal, 1969. Ordained priest, 1937; dir. Seminaire de Sainte-Therese; prof. philosophy of edn. l'Ecole Normale Secondaire, also l'Institut Pedagogique; chaplain of students U. Montreal; consecrated bishop, 1961; aux. to Archbishop of Montreal; vicar gen., dir. Office for Clergy; acting adminstr. diocese; apostolic adminstr. archdiocese of Montreal, 1967-68, archbishop, 1968—. Pres. French sect. Episcopal commn. ecumenism Canadian Cath. Conf. 1965; presided over numerous diocesan commns., 1965—. Address: 2000 Sherbrooke St W Montreal PQ H3H 1G4 Canada

GREGORIEW, DALE IRA, minister, Lutheran Church in America; b. Elmira, N.Y., May 4, 1940; s. Afonosy and Mora Rae (Leavenworth) G.; m. Mary Jo Cannon, Aug. 28, 1965; children: Elisabeth Mary, John Peter. B.A., Drew U., 1962; M.Div., Hamma Sch. Theology, 1965; Th.M., Princeton Theol. Sem., 1966; D.Min., Phillips U., 1974. Ordained to ministry Lutheran Ch., 1966. Pastor St. Luke Ch., Gilbertsville, Pa., 1966-70, Our Lord's Ch., Oklahoma City, 1970-76; sr. pastor First Luth. Ch., Topeka, Kans., 1976—; bd. dirs. Bethany Coll., Lindsborg, Kans., 1970-74; mem. bd. Kans. Outdoor Luth. Ministries, 1984—; mem. permanent panel Your Question Please, WIBW-TV, Topeka, 1977—. Contbr. articles to publs. in field. Div. chmn. United Way Greater Topeka, 1984. Republican. Lodge: Rotary (Topeka). Office: First Lutheran Ch 1234 Fairlawn Rd Topeka KS 66604

GREGORY, (GEORGE ASONSKY), Bishop of Sitka, Alaska, Orthodox Church in America. Office: St Michael's Cathedral Box 697 Sitka AK 99835*

GREGORY, (NICOLA UDICKI), Bishop of Western Diocese, Serbian Eastern Orthodox Church in the U.S.A. and Canada. Office: 2511 W Garvey Ave Alhambra CA 91803*

GREGORY, MILTON D., bishop, Roman Catholic Church. Titular bishop of Oliva, aux. bishop, Chgo., 1983—. Office: PO Box 733 South Holland IL 60473*

GREHL, PAUL F., priest; provincial; b. Newark, Oct. 23, 1931; s. Paul Henry and Minnie Augusta (Haag) G. B. in Commerce Sci., NY U, 1953; M.A., Niagara U., 1959. Ordained priest Roman Catholic Ch., 1960. Tchr. Salesian High Sch., Wilmington, Del., 1955-56, Detroit, 1962-70, prin., 1967-70; tchr. St. Francis High Sch., Toledo, 1956-57; Fr. Judge High Sch., Phila., 1961-62; prin. Aquinas High Sch., Southgate, Mich., 1970-75; provincial Toledo-Detroit Provincial of Oblates of St. Francis de Sales, Toledo, 1977—, pres. Provincial Conf., 1970-73, provincial counselor, 1973-77.

GREIN, RICHARD FRANK, educator, Episcopal Church; b. Bemidji, Minn., Nov. 29, 1932; s. Lester Edward and LaVina Minnie (Frost) G.; B.A. in Geology, Carlton Coll., Northfield, Minn., 1955; M.Div., Hashotah (Wis.) House Sem., 1959, S.T.M., 1970; m. Joan Dunwoody Atkinson, Nov. 25, 1961; children—David, Margaret, Mary Leslie, Sara. Ordained priest, 1959; priest-in-charge Elk River (Minn) mission field, 1959-64; rector St. Mathew's Ch., Mpls., 1964-69, St. David's Ch., Minnetonka, Minn., 1969-73; prof. pastoral theology Nashotah House Theol. Sem., 1973-74, also trustee; rector St. Michael and All Angels Ch., Mission, Kans., 1974-81; bishop of Topeka, 1981—. Priest asso. Order Holy Cross, Pres. Guardian Angels Found., Elk River, 1963-64. Mem. Council Asso. Parishes. Co-author: Preparing Younger Children for First Communion, 1972.

GRELL, DAVID ERIC, minister, Lutheran Church-Missouri Synod; b. N.Y.C., Feb. 27, 1956; s. Matthew and Mary Victoria (Morgan) G. B.A., Concordia Coll., Bronxville, N.Y., 1974-78; M.Div., Concordia Sem., St. Louis, 1982. Ordained to ministry Luth. Ch., 1982. Vicar, Ascension Luth. Ch., Montreal, Que., Can., 1980-81; minister Trinity Luth. Ch., Stamford, N.Y., 1982—; sec. Capital Area Luth. Pastoral Conf., Albany, N.Y., 1983—. Anna Fulling scholar Concordia Coll., 1974. Mem. Nat. Geog. Soc. Republican. Home: 13 Prospect St Stamford NY 12167 Office: Trinity Luth Ch Route 10 Stamford NY 12167

GRELL, MARY ELLEN, lay ch. worker, Assemblies of God; b. Freeport, Ill., May 30, 1930; d. Clayton George and Marietta H. Bast; student Gt. Lakes Bible Inst., Zion, Ill., 1948; m. Dwain Leo Grell, Aug. 30, 1949; 1 son, Denis Lee. Pres. Ill. Women's Ministries, Assemblies of God, 1955—. Home: Rural Route 3 Lake Williamson Carlinville IL 62626 Office: PO Box 225 Carlinville IL 62626

GREMILLION, DOROTHY ANN, organist, choirmaster, Episcopal Church, piano instructor; b. Algiers, La., Sept. 1, 1942; d. Donald Monroe and Marie Belle (Clemons) Risinger; m. O'Keefe John Gremillion, Dec. 21, 1963; children: Elizabeth India, O'Keefe John, Mark Russell. B.A. in Music Theory and Composition, McNesse State U., 1971; diploma Edn. for Ministry, U. South Sewanee Tenn., 1981. Assoc. of Order of Holy Cross, West Park, N.Y., and Order of St. Helena Holy Cross, Vails Gate N.Y., 1978—; cert. lay reader St. Michael's Ch., Lake Charles, La., 1977—, chalice minister, 1981—, Bible tchr., 1981—, organist-choirmaster, adult and children's choirs, 1981—; del. Christian Edn. Leadership Cert. Episcopal Theol. Sem., Lexington, Ky., 1982—; pres., Protestant coordinator Ulster Project-Lake Charles, Lake Charles and Belfast, Northern Ireland, 1977-80. Composer: clarinet, piano, organ, choir anthems, 1969—. Visiting fellow Episcopal Theol. Sem. of Southwest Tex., 1985. Mem. Lake Charles Piano Tchrs. Assn., Royal Sch. of Ch. Music, The Hymn Soc. of Am. Democrat. Office: St Michael and All Angels Episcopal Ch 123 W Sale Rd Lake Charles LA 70605

GRENZ, STANLEY JAMES, minister, religious studies educator, North American Baptist Conference; b. Alpena, Mich., Jan. 7, 1950; s. Richard Albert and Clara Frieda (Ruff) G.; m. Edna Lois Sturhahn, Dec. 29, 1971; children: Joel Richard, Corina Diane. B.A., U. Colo., 1973; M.Div., Conservative Bapt. Theol. Sem., Denver, 1976; Th.D., U. Munich, Feb. Republic Germany, 1980. Ordained to ministry N.Am. Bapt. Conf., 1976. Asst. pastor Northwest Bapt. Ch., Denver, 1972-76; pastor Rowandale Bapt. Ch., Winnipeg, Man., Can., 1978-81; adj. prof. theology U. Winnipeg, 1980-81; asst. prof. theology N.Am. Bapt. Sem., Sioux Falls, S.D., 1981-83, assoc. prof. systematic theology, 1984—; mem. Bapt. Joint Com. on Pub. Affairs, Washington, 1982—. Author: The Baptist Congregation, 1985; Isaac Backus-Puritan and Baptist, 1983; also articles. Recipient Robert G. Kay Scholastic award Conservative Bapt. Theol. Sem., 1976; named Among Outstanding Young Men in Am., U.S. Jaycees, 1982. Mem. World Future Soc., Am. Theol. Soc., Conf. on Faith and History, Am. Acad. Religion (program com. mem.), Phi Beta Kappa. Office: N Am Bapt Seminary 1321 W 22nd St Sioux Falls SD 57105

GRESCHUK, DEMETRIUS MARTIN, bishop, Ukrainian Catholic Church; b. Innisfree, Alta., Can., Nov. 7, 1923; s. Thomas and Sophia (Steblyk) G. Student St. Joseph's Coll., 1941-42, St. Augustines Sem., Toronto, Ont., Can. Ordained priest, Ukrainian Cath. Ch., 1950, subdeacon, 1948-49, deacon, 1949-50, priest, 1950, consecrated bishop, 1974. Sec. Chancery Office, Edmonton, Alta., 1950-59; pastor numerous parishes, 1950-74; apostolic adminstr. Edmonton Eparchy, 1984—. Office: Chancery Office 10825 97th St Edmonton AB T5H 2M4 Canada

GRESHAM, CHARLES RUSSELL, minister, educator, Christian Chs. and Chs. of Christ; b. Erie, Ill., Mar. 20, 1928; s. Fred Earl and Sara Jane (Duncan) G.; A.B., Manhattan Christian Coll., 1949; M.R.E., Southwestern Bapt. Theol. Sem., 1956, D. Religious Edn., 1958, Ed.D., 1970; m. Virginia Ruth Smith, Aug. 3, 1947; children—Michael Ross, Barbara Lynn, Timothy Ward, Janelda Rae. Ordained to ministry, 1947; pastor First Christian Ch., Dighton, Kans., 1950-51; faculty Dallas Christian Coll., 1951-56, Midwest Christian Coll., Oklahoma City, 1956-60, Manhattan (Kans.) Christian Coll., 1960-66, Emmanuel Sch. Religion, Johnson City, Tenn., 1966-73, lectr. religious edn., 1975—; dean Ky. Christian Coll., Grayson, 1973-75; pastor First Christian Ch., Elizabethton, Tenn., 1975—. Exec. sec. Chaplaincy Endorsement Commn., Christian Chs. and Chs. of Christ, 1969—. Mem. Nat. Assn. Evang., Disciples of Christ Hist. Soc. Editor: Christian Educators Jour., 1966—. Contbr. articles to religious jours. Home: Rt 9 Box 182 Elizabethton TN 37643 Office: 513 Hattie St Elizabethton TN 37643

GRESSLE, LLOYD EDWARD, bishop, Episcopal Ch.; b. Cleve., June 13, 1918; s. Edward W. and Olga (Hoppensack) G.; B.A., Oberlin Coll., 1940; B.D., Bexley Hall (Ohio), 1943; postgrad. Fell Coll. Preachers, 1951; D.D., Kenyon Coll. (Ohio), 1958; m. Marguerite Kirkpatrick, July 12, 1943; 3 children. Ordained priest, 1943; rector St. James Ch., Wooster, Ohio, 1943-48, St. John's Ch., Sharon, Pa., 1948-56; dean Cathedral of St. John's, Wilmington, Del., 1956-69; rector St. James Ch., Lancaster, Pa., 1969-70; bishop coadjutor of Bethlehem (Pa.), 1970-72, bishop, 1972—. Mem. exec. council, 1948-56; pres. Wilmington Council Chs., 1963-70; Wates/Seabury exchange priest, Portsmouth, Eng., 1965-66. Contbr. articles to Jour. Pastoral Psychology. Office: 826 Delaware Ave Bethlehem PA 18015*

GREY, JAMES DAVID, minister, Baptist Ch.; b. Princeton, Ky., Dec. 18, 1906; s. George Lindsay and Lucy (Keeney) G.; A.B., Union U., 1929, D.D., 1938; Th.M., Southwestern Bapt. Theol. Sem., 1932; LL.D., La. Coll., 1952; D.D., Baylor U., 1953; m. Lillian Tooke, Sept. 16, 1927; children—Mary Beth (Mrs. Jules Burg), Martha Ann (Mrs. Richard C. Cantrell). Ordained to ministry Bapt. Ch., 1925; pastor First Bapt. Ch., Denton, Tex., 1934-37; pastor First Bapt. Ch., New Orleans, 1937-72, pastor emeritus, 1973—; minister Gospel Hour radio program, New Orleans, 1940-72. Pres. La. Bapt. Conv., 1949-50, So. Bapt. Conv., 1951-52, New Orleans Fedn. Chs., 1957. mem. exec. com. Bapt. World Alliance, 1950-70; chmn. Greater New Orleans Billy Graham Crusade, 1954; mem. Missions Challenge com. So. Bapt. Conv., 1974-76. Mem. La. State Bd. Corrections, 1968—. Founder, pres. La. Moral Civic Found., 1953-56. Bd. dirs. So. Bapt. Hosps., 1967—, World Evangelism Found., 1972—; bd. dirs. Met. Crime Commn., 1960—, pres. 1968-69. Named Distinguished Alumnus Southwestern Bapt. Theol. Sem., 1962, Union U., 1970; recipient Times-Picayune Loving Cup, 1971. Mem. Alpha Tau Omega, Kiwanian. Author: Epitaphs for Eager Preachers, 1972. Home: 4524 S Galvez St New Orleans LA 70125

GRIFFIN, BENJAMIN THEODORE, minister, United Church of Christ; b. Ogbomosho, Nigeria, Sept. 27, 1940 (parents American citizens; s. B.T. and Alice Maude (Latham) G.; m. Gail vanOrmer, Apr. 1, 1977; children: Geoffrey, Jeremy, Jennifer. B.A., Baylor U., 1961; B.D., Andover Newton Sem., 1964; D.Ministry, Lancaster Sem., 1975. Ordained to ministry United Chs. of Christ, 1964. Pastor, 1st United Ch. of Christ, Mt. Pleasant, Pa., 1964-69, St. John's United Ch. of Christ, Orwigsburg, Pa., 1969-75; sr. pastor Trinity United Ch. of Christ, York, Pa., 1975—; pres. York County Council of Chs., 1981—; trustee Lancaster Theol. Sem., 1976—. Author: Pastoral Care of Children, 1975; Americanization of a Congregation, 1984; also articles on ch. renewal and profl. ethics. Pres., Mt. Pleasant Area Sch. Bd., 1968-69; mem. Orwigsburg Borough Council, 1971-75; bd. dirs. York County YMCA, 1984—. Recipient Allan Meck award Lancaster Sem., 1978. Mem. Am. Assn. Pastoral Counselors (cert. pastoral counselor), York Area C. of C. (bd. dirs. 1984—). Democrat. Home: 481 Waters Rd York PA 17401 Office: Trinity United Ch of Christ 32 W Market St York PA 17401

GRIFFIN, DALE E., theology educator, The Lutheran Church-Missouri Synod. b. Strasburg, Ill., Dec. 21, 1920; s. L. Elbert and Anna Charlotte (Schmidt) G.; m. Marjorie Louise Baepler, May 5, 1945; children: Patricia L., Joan L., John E., Cheryl L. B.Th., Concordia, 1944; M.Edn., Temple U., 1961; M.Div., Phila. Luth. Sem., 1962, S.T.M., 1963. Ordained to ministry Lutheran Ch., 1944. Pastor, Zion Luth. Ch., Oklahoma City, 1944-46, Our Savior Luth. Ch., Hillsboro, Ill., Ill., 1946-49, Pilgrim Luth. Ch., Cheltenham, Pa., 1949-61; editor youth materials Luth. Ch.-Mo. Synod, St. Louis, 1961-68, exec. sec. Sunday, Weekday and Summer Schs., 1968—; coordinator 450th reformation anniversary observance Inter-Luth. Consultation, N.Y., 1966-67. Editor: Directors of Christian Education Bulletin, 1969—, Program Resources for Church School Conferences, 1969—. Contbr. articles to profl. jours. Bd. dirs. TEAM. Mem. Religious Edn. Assn., Concordia Hist. Inst., Luth. Edn. Assn. Home: 254 Elm Ave Glendale MO 63122 Office: The Luth Ch Missouri Synod 1333 South Kirkwood Rd Saint Louis MO 63122

GRIFFIN, DANIEL M., minister, Southern Baptist Convention; b. Charleston, S.C., July 26, 1953; s. Francis M. and Mary Louise (Brown) G.; m. Edith Inez Fallaw, May 11, 1975; children: Katie Michelle, Cheryl Macie. B.A., Clemson U., 1975; M.Div., Southwestern Bapt. Theol. Sem., 1978. Ordained to ministry Bapt. Ch., 1978. Youth dir. Ashley River Bapt. Ch., Charleston, summer 1974; counselor Ridgecrest Conf. Ctr., 1978-79; pastor Hankins Bapt. Ch., Marion, N.C., 1979-80, Red Bank Bapt. Ch., Saluda, S.C., 1980—; sec.-treas. Saluda County Ministerial Assn., 1981-82, Ridge Bapt. Assn., 1983-84; teller S.C. Bapt. Conv., 1983. Com. chmn. Helping Hands, Saluda, 1983-84; chmn. task force Chem. People, Saluda, 1984; chmn. Saluda Task Force on Drug Abuse, 1984; mem. adv. bd. Saluda County Alcohol and Drug Abuse Com., 1983-84. Recipient cert. of appreciation Gov. of N.C., 1981, Gov. of S.C., 1984. Home: 608 Waters Ave Saluda SC 29138 Office: 309 E Church St Saluda SC 29138

GRIFFIN, HARRY DEE, minister, So. Bapt. Conv.; b. Kingfisher County, Okla., Jan. 16, 1925; s. Howard Otto and Maude Alice (Scott) G.; B.A., Central State U., Edmond, Okla., 1949; B.D., Southwestern Bapt. Theol. Sem., Ft. Worth, 1953; m. Barbara Jo Terry, May 23, 1948; children—Patricia Deanne, Pamela Diane, Harry Dee. Ordained to ministry, 1943; pastor chs. in Okla., 1943-74; fgn. missionary, Japan, 1962-69; dir. missions Cimarron Bapt. Assn., Cushing, Okla., 1974—. Home: 815 E Broadway St Cushing OK 74023 Office: 112 E Moses St Cushing OK 74023

GRIFFIN, JAMES ANTHONY, priest Roman Catholic Church; b. Fairview Park, Ohio, June 13, 1934; s. Thomas Anthony and Margaret Mary (Hanousek) G.; B.A. magna cum laude, Borromeo Sem., Wickliffe, Ohio, 1956; J.C.L. magna cum laude, Pontifical Lateran U., Rome, Italy, 1963; J.C.L. summa cum laude, Cleve. State U., 1972. Ordained priest, Ch., 1960; asso. pastor St. Jerome Parish, Cleve., 1960; sec. notary Cleve. Diocesan Tribunal, 1963-65; asst. chancellor Diocese of Cleve., 1965-68, vice chancellor, 1968-73, chancellor, 1973-78, vicar gen., 1978-79; pastor St. William Ch., Euclid, Ohio, 1978-79; aux. bishop Diocese of Cleve., vicar western region, Ohio, 1979-83; bishop of Columbus, 1983—. Bd. dirs. Holy Family Cancer Home. Mem. Am. Canon Law Soc., Am., Ohio bar assns. Author: (with A. J. Quinn) Thoughts For Our

Times, 1969, Thoughts For Sowing, 1970, Ashes From the Cathedral, 1973; Sackcloth and Ashes, 1976. Contbr. articles to profl. jours. Home: 1007 Superior St Cleveland OH 44114 Office: 198 E Broad St Columbus OH 43215*

GRIFFIN, ROBERT DALE, minister, So. Bapt. Conv.; b. Borger, Tex., Nov. 30, 1938; s. Robert Franklin and Avil Viola (Taylor) G.; B.A., Wayland Bapt. Coll., 1964; M.Div., Southwestern Bapt. Theol. Sem., 1968; m. Faye LaVerne Jackson, June 6, 1958; children—Michael Dale, Derinda Dee, Ray Neil. Ordained to ministry, 1958; minister Friendship Bapt. Ch., Dickens, Tex., 1961-63, Lakeview Bapt. Ch., 1963-64, Era (Tex.) Bapt. Ch., 1964-67, Eastside Bapt. Ch., Marietta, Okla., 1967-68, First Bapt. Ch., Atoka, Okla., 1968-71, First Bapt. Ch., Post, Tex., 1971-73, Central Bapt. Ch., Carthage, Tex., 1973—. Exec. bd. Bapt. Gen. Conv. of Okla., 1969-71; moderator Rusk-Panola Assn., 1974-76; bd. dirs. E. Tex. Bapt. area, 1976-79. Active Panola County Child Welfare Bd., 1971—; trustee United Fund, 1975-78, chaplain Masonic Lodge 521. Home: 400 Perry Pl Carthage TX 75633 Office: PO Drawer H Carthage TX 75633

GRIFFIN, WILLIAM ARTHUR, clergyman Pentecostal Assemblies of Canada; b. Coboconk, Ont., Can., July 29, 1936; s. Arthur Campbell and Anne (Bradamore) G.; m. Patricia Rose Russell, Aug. 18, 1956; children: Kent, Wendy, Mark, Patti, Becky. Diploma Eastern Pentecostal Bible Coll., Peterborough, Ont., 1957; B.A., U. Toronto, Ont., 1960; M. Div., Lutheran Theol. Sem., Saskatoon, Sask., Can., 1970; M.A., U. Sask., Saskatoon, 1973. Ordained to ministry Pentecostal Assemblies of Can., 1962. Pastor Fergus Pentecostal Ch., Ont., 1960-62; dean of students Central Pentecostal Coll., Saskatoon, 1963-69; lectr. U. Sask., 1970-72; acad. dean Ea. Pentecostal Bible Coll., 1973-79; exec. dir. Pentecostal Assemblies of Can., Toronto, 1980—. Exec. editor Chivalry, 1980—, Source, 1980—, Youth Profile, 1980—; editor Pentecostal Testimony, 1982. Contbr. articles to religious jours. Mem Can. Theol. Soc., Evang. Press Assn. Office: Pentecostal Assemblies of Can 10 Overlea Blvd Toronto ON M4H 1A5 Canada

GRIFFITH, BARBARA ELLEN, youth minister, counselor, Southern Baptist Church; b. Alliance, Ohio, Dec. 4, 1931; d. Harold Jacob Bye and Frances Margaret (Eddleblute) McCune; m. Donald Curtis Griffith, July 1, 1950 (div. 1975); children: Donald Carl, Shelly Jo Linderman, Ronald Troy. A.A., Manatee Community Coll., 1978; B.A., New Coll., 1980; M.A., U. So. Fla., 1981. Lic. minister of youth, 1984. Staff counselor Kensington Park Bapt. Ch., Sarasota, Fla., 1976-84, minister of youth and counseling, 1984—; asst. dir. programs L.I.F.E., Nokomis, Fla., 1980-84; mem. com. representing U. So. Fla., New Coll., Ecumenical Bd. Campus Ministries, 1980-82; mem. com. pastoral counseling Sarasota Ministerial Assn., 1984—. Mem. Phi Kappa Phi. Republican. Avocations: camping, canoeing, bicycling, swimming, walking. Home: 937 Caloosa Dr Sarasota FL 33580 Office: Kensington Park Bapt Ch 3308 E 17th St Sarasota FL 33580

GRIFFITH, MABEL MAXINE, lay church worker; b. Wheeling, W.Va., Dec. 14, 1919; d. Thomas Joseph and Elizabeth Matilda (Reese) Minns; m. George William Griffith, Apr. 17, 1944; children: Terrill Lee, Gerrill Lynn. Sec., United Meth. Supt., Wheeling, W.Va., 1972-75; exec. dir. Greater Wheeling Council Chs., 1975—. Sec., program chmn. Wheeling Child Study Club, 1952—. Democrat. Office: Greater Wheeling Council Chs 110 Methodist Bldg Wheeling WV 26003

GRIFFITH, MARSHALL DEAN, minister, United Church of Christ; b. Ironton, Ohio, Dec. 21, 1945; s. Marshall and Hazel Dean (Poole) G.; m. Barbara J. Smith, Aug. 15, 1970; 1 child, Charista Jean. B.S., U. Cin., 1972, postgrad. 1980-81; M.Div., No. Bapt. Theol. Sem., 1979; postgrad. U. Ariz., 1974-75. Ordained to ministry United Ch. Christ, 1979. Youth coordinator North Shore Baptist Ch., Chgo., 1975-76; asst. pastor First Baptist Ch., Aurora, Ill., 1976-78; assoc. pastor Yorkville Congregational Ch., Yorkville, Ill., 1978-79; pastor United Ch. Christ in Oakley, Cin., 1979—; chaplain Ohio Nat. Guard, Hamilton, Ohio, 1979—; del. Gen. Synod United Ch. Christ, N.Y.C., 1980-83; v.p., dir. project devel. Ecumenical Programs in Info. and Communication, Cleve., 1981—; del. Cin. United Ch. Assembly, 1979—, treas., 1982-83. Founding pres. Oakley Community Urban Redevel. Corp., Cin., 1981-82; bd. dirs. Oakley Residents Assn., Cin., 1979-83. Mem. Cin. Ministerium (v.p. 1980-81), Joint Strategy and Action Com., Mensa. Democrat. Lodge: Masons. Home: 4971 Charlemar Dr Cincinnati OH 45227 Office: United Ch Christ in Oakley 4100 Taylor Ave Cincinnati OH 45209

GRIFFITH, VENCY ENOS, minister, Ch. of the Brethren; b. Woolwine, Va., Mar. 14, 1922; s. William Frank and Lena Mae (Roberson) G.; m. Edith Diana Cosner, Aug. 22, 1954; children—Deborah, Donna, Dianne, Calvin, Grace, Karen, Ruth, Carol Lena. Ordained to ministry, 1956; pastor New Hope Ch., Jonesboro, Tenn., 1955-58, Pleasant View Ch., Fayetteville, W.Va., 1958-62, Selma (Va.) Ch., 1962-63, Mt. Union Ch., Bent Mountain, Va., 1963-64, Copper Hill (Va.) Ch., 1963-67, Pleasant Hill and Pkwy. chs., Willis, Va., 1967-69, Pleasant Hill and Laurel Br. chs., 1967-69, Coulson Ch., Hillsville, Va., 1970—; dist. chaplain Am. Legion. Camp dir., counselor Area Ministers Assn., 1957-76; pres. United Workers for Christ, Caroll-Greyson-Galax dist., 1974-75; mem. standing com. Ann. Conf. of Ch.-Community Action, 1969-70. Chmn., Floyd County (Va.) Heart Assn., 1967-68; active Ruritan Clubs, PTA. Home: Route 1 Box 154 Hillsville VA 24343

GRIFFITTS, F(RANCIS) JOE, minister, Southern Baptist Convention; b. Antioch, Calif., July 23, 1945; s. Martin James and Pauline (Harmon) G.; m. Carole Jean Reader, July 16, 1966; children: Thomas Andrew, William James. B.A., Calif. Bapt. Coll., 1973; M.Div., Golden Gate Bapt. Theol. Sem., 1980. Ordained to ministry So. Bapt. Conv., 1981. Asst. pastor Meml. Bapt. Ch., Willits, Calif., 1974; dir. religious edn. Coddingtown Bapt. Ch., Calif., 1979-80; minister Ione Bapt. Ch., Wash., 1980—; chaplain USAR, 1982—; mem. exec. bd. Inland Empire Bapt. Assn., Spokane, 1980—. Author article. Coordinator Bike-a-Thon, St. Jude's Children's Hosp., Ione, 1983. Served with USAF, 1964-68. Republican. Home and Office: Box 306 Ione WA 99139

GRIMM, ARTHUR GUSTAVE, JR., minister, Lutheran Church America; b. Depew, N.Y., Apr. 28, 1935; s. Arthur Gustave and Hazel Ann (Landgraff) G.; B.A., Midland Luth. Coll., Fremont, Nebr., 1958; M.Div., Luth. Sch. Theology, Chgo., 1962; 1 son, Shane Todd. Ordained to ministry, 1962; pastor Bd. Am. Missions, Shreveport, La., 1962-64, Synder, Tex., 1964-65, St. Johns Luth. Ch., Marquette, Nebr., 1965-69, Berea Luth. Ch., Chappell, Nebr., 1969-76, St. Paul's Luth. Ch., Diller, Nebr., 1977-82; chaplain Good Samaritan Ctr. and State Devel. Ctr., Beatrice, Nebr., 1983—. Chmn. Synodical Stewardship Com.; sec.-treas. Blue Valley Div., 1984-85. Vice pres. Deuel County Republican Party, 1973-76. Recipient Outstanding Leadership award for community improvement, 1975. Participant Interlutheran Parish Leadership Lab., 1976. Address: 1306 S 9th St Beatrice NE 68310

GRIMM, ROBERT ELMER, minister, united Ch. of Christ; b. Chgo., May 1, 1922; s. Norman Albert and Ethel Merle (Wheeler) G.; B.A., Denison U., 1943; B.D., Colgate-Rochester Div. Sch, 1949; m. Roberta P. Johnson, Sept. 24, 1943; children: Carole, Michael, Leslie (Mrs. Craig Archer), Marcia, Nancy, Mark. Ordained to ministry, 1949; student minister, Pittsford, N.Y., 1947-49; minister Pickstown (S.D.) Community Ch., 1949-54; exec. sec. S.D. Council Chs., 1951-54, 54-57; exec. minister Erie (Pa.) Council Chs., 1957-65; gen. sec. Syracuse (N.Y.) Area Council Chs., 1965-71; exec. dir. Met. Ch. Bd., Syracuse Area, 1971-76; exec. dir. Buffalo Area Council Chs., 1976—; mem. governing bd. Nat. Council Chs., 1971-75; mem. Nat. Assn. Ecumenical Staff. Mem. Erie Human Rights Commn., 1963-65, Syracuse Interfaith Housing Corp., 1966-75; mem. adv. bd. County Dept. Mental Health, Cultural Resources Council. Trustee N.E. Regional Office Econ. Opportunity, 1967-69. Office: 1272 Delaware Ave Buffalo NY 14209

GRIMMET, ALEX J., minister, Churches of Christ; b. McVeigh, Ky., July 17, 1928; s. Alex A. and Edna Mae (Boyd) G.; B.S., Ky. Christian Coll., 1949; M.Ed., U. Cin., 1964, postgrad., 1970-72; postgrad. Washburn U., 1967, Georgetown U., 1968; m. Lois Jean Carter, June 24, 1949; children: Larry Bruce, Raven Alexis Grimmet Woods. Ordained to ministry, 1947; minister Choateville Christian Ch., Frankfort, Ky., 1949-51; evangelist, Ky., 1951-52; minister Capella and Jefferson Chs. of Christ, King and Rural Hall, N.C., 1952-57, Danville Ch. of Christ, Hillsboro, Ohio, 1957-62, Loveland (Ohio) Ch. of Christ, 1962-66, Lerado Ch. of Christ, Williamsburg, Ohio, 1966—. Trustee Winston Salem (N.C.) Bible Coll., 1955-57; trustee, treas. Piedmont Christian Service Camp, 1953-57; chaplain Winston-Salem City Hosp., 1955-56. Head, tchr. math. dept. Lebanon (Ohio) City Schs., 1970—. Mem. Southwest Area Ohio Council Tchrs. Math. (bd. dirs. 1981-84), Ohio Council Tchrs. Math. (v.p. secondary edn. 1984—). U. Cin. Alumni Assn. Contbr. articles to religious jours. Home and Office: 848 Kenmar Dr Loveland OH 45140

GRINDEL, JOHN ANTHONY, educator, priest, Roman Catholic Church; b. Kansas City, Mo., Sept. 14, 1937; s. Edward Anthony and Inez Elizabeth (Weber) G.; B.A., St. Mary's Sem., Mo., 1960; S.T.L., Cath. U. Am., 1965, M.A. in Semitic Langs., 1966; S.S.L., Pontifical Bibl. Inst., Rome, 1967. Joined Congregation of the Mission, 1956, ordained priest, 1964; research asso. Am. Sch. Oriental Research, Jersualem, 1967-68; prof. O.T., St. John's Sem., Camarillo, Calif., 1968-78, pres./rector, 1973-78; provincial Province of the West, Vincentian Fathers and Bros., 1978—; chair Region VI, Conf. Major Superiors of Men, 1980—, also nat. bd. dirs., chair formation com. Author: Repentance and Renewal, 1971; Until He Comes, 1972; I and II Chronicles, 1973. Address: 949 W Adams Blvd Los Angeles CA 90007

GRINDER, TOM GEORGE, minister, International Pentecostal Church of Christ; b. Cornel, Wis., Jan. 7, 1927; s. Reuben George and Nellie C. (White) G.; BB.A., Beulah Heights Bible Coll., 1969; m. Hattie Irene Markham, Dec. 19, 1946; children: Barbara (Mrs. Amos Eby), Beverly Jeane (Mrs. Jimmy Sawyer). Ordained to ministry, 1946; gen. overseer Internat. Pentecostal Ch. of Christ, 1982—. Office: PO Box 439 London OH 43140

GRINDLE, LOUIS YOUNG, JR., minister, Southern Baptist Convention; b. Dahlonega, Ga., Jan. 27, 1930; s. Louis Young and Pauline Janie (Edge) G., Sr.; m. Mary Michaleen McCarthy, Dec. 2, 1949; children: Linda Louise, Louis Young III, Daniel David. Ordained to ministry Bapt. Ch., 1979. Minister, Cavenders Creep Bapt. Ch., Dahlonega, Ga., 1951—; pastor Alpha Bapt. Ch., Leesburg, Ga., 1978—; pastor to prisons U.S. and overseas; student dean Ga. Bapt. Extension Ctr., Albany, Ga., 1971-73. Letter carrier U.S. Post Office, Macon, Ga., 1968-70, Albany, Ga., 1970—. Served with USAF, 1948-68. Mem. Albany Hosp. Chaplains Assn., Nat. Assn. Letter Carriers (pres. local chpt. 1973-74). Lodges: Masons, Shriners. Home: 204 Elva St Albany GA 31705 Office: US Postal Service 1501 S Slapey Blvd Albany GA 31706

GRINDSTAFF, ROY ARTHUR, minister, International Church of the Foursquare Gospel; b. Cambridge, Ohio, Jan. 18, 1946; s. William Roy and Hazel Mae (Barrett) G.; m. Loris Marie Caudill, Sept. 3, 1966; children: Roy Arthur II, Yolanda Grace, Benjamin Caudill. B.A., Olivet Nazarene Coll., 1972, M.A., 1973; M.Div., Asbury Theol. Sem., 1977; postgrad. Ohio State U., 1979-86. Ordained to ministry Internat. Ch. of Foursquare Gospel, 1969. Pastor Foursquare Gospel Ch., Bradley, Ill., 1968-73, Royal Oak Community Foursquare Ch., Mich., 1973-74, Sugartree Ridge Circuit, United Meth. Ch., Hillsboro, Ohio, 1974-77; prof. Mt. Vernon Bible Coll., Ohio, 1977-78; adminstrv. chaplain Mt. Vernon Developmental Ctr., Ohio, 1978—, program coordinator, 1983—; mem. task force on ch. and handicapped Ohio Council of Churches, 1980-83; chaplain Country Club Ctr., Mt. Vernon, 198—84. Author: (with D. R. Ohler) Chaplaincy Services, 1982. Parent v.p. Parent Tchr. Orgn., Royal Oak, 1974. Mem. Religious Communication Assn., Speech Communication Assn., Knox County Ministerial Assn. (sec.-treas. 1983-85), Theta Phi. Home: 5021/2 N Main St Mount Vernon OH 43050 Office: Mount Vernon Developmental Ctr PO Box 762 Mount Vernon OH 43050

GRIPE, ALAN GORDON, church official, minister, Presbyterian Church in U.S.A.; b. Indpls., Sept. 8, 1920; s. Otto Herman and Bertha (Anderson) G.; B.A., Lake Forest Coll., 1942; B.D., Princeton Theol. Sem., 1946; S.T.M., Union Theol. Sem., N.Y.C., 1951; m. Elizabeth Howell; Sept. 1951 (div. Aug. 1972); children: Stephen Howell, David Alan. Ordained to ministry, 1946; missionary tchr. Silliman U., Dumaguete, Philippines, 1946-50; chaplain Davidson Coll., Davidson, N.C., 1951-52; asst. chaplain U.S. Mil. Acad., West Point, N.Y., 1952-55; pastor First Presbyn. Ch., Westfield, N.Y., 1955-65; recruiting sec. Commn. on Ecumenical Mission, N.Y.C., 1965-69; asso. sec. Interbd. Personnel Office, Phila., 1969-72; mgr. Information Services for Personnel, Vocation Agy. of United Presbyn. Ch., N.Y.C., 1973-75, coordinator of ministerial relations, 1976-82, coordinator coms. on ministry, 1983—; dean, chmn. Chautauqua Mission Inst., Chautauqua, N.Y., 1958-64. Sec. Ramapo Housing Authority, Suffern, N.Y., 1967-69. Recipient Disting. Service citation Lake Forest Coll., 1967. Home: 205 W Clinton Ave Tenafly NJ 07670 Office: Suite 406 475 Riverside Dr New York NY 10115

GRISHAM, LENDON LEE, minister, United Pentecostal Ch., Internat.; b. Morris Chapel, Tenn., July 30, 1921; s. Lemual Delona and Amanda Eudora Grisham; student pub. schs., Morris Chapel; m. Daisy M. Gibbs, July 13, 1943; children—Sammy L., Donna S., Brenda K., Claude D., Raymond E., Kenneth W. Ordained to ministry, 1973; pastor Palestine Pentecostal Ch., Lexington, Tenn., 1970—. Chaplain, Lexington post DAV. Partner, Pipkin & Grisham Ins. & Real Estate. Mem. VFW (service officer Morris Chapel, Tenn.). Home: Route 1 Box 386 Sardis TN 38371 Office: PO Box 158 Scotts Hill TN 38374

GRISLIS, EGIL, minister, Lutheran Church in America Canada Section, educator; b. Mitau, Latvia, Feb. 19, 1928; came to U.S., 1949, Can., 1976; s. Robert and Lucie Maria (Einfeld) G.; m. E. Lorraine Sommers, June 30, 1956; children: Karen Ann, Kristin Eva, Erik Lauri. B.A., Gettysburg Coll., 1950; B.D., Luth. Theol. Sem., Gettysburg, 1953; Ph.D., Yale U., 1958. Ordained, 1957. Pastor, Emanuel Luth. Ch., Hudson, N.Y., 1957-59; faculty Div. Sch. Duke U., Durham, N.C., 1959-69; with Hartford Sem. Found., Conn., 1969-74; faculty dept. theology Fordham U., Bronx, N.Y., 1974-76; prof. religion U. Man., Winnipeg, Can., 1976—; mem. bd. govs. Luth. Theol. Sem., Saskatoon,

Sask., 1984—. Author books, articles on Luther and other reformers. Faculty leave fellow, Can. Council, 1983. Home: 50 Thatcher Dr Winnipeg MB R3T 2L3 Canada Office: Dept Religion U Manitoba Winnipeg MB R3T 2N2 Canada

GRISLIS, LORRAINE SOMMERS, minister, Lutheran Church in America; b. Republic, Mich., Feb. 21, 1932; came to Can., 1976; d. John Evald and Tyyne Evelyn (Hangas) Sommers; m. Egil Grislis, June 30, 1956; children: Karen Ann, Kristin Eva, Erik Lauri. B.S., No. Mich. U., 1953; M.A., Hartford Sem. Found., 1973, M.Div., 1974. Ordained to ministry Luth. Ch., 1975. Pastor Redeemer Luth. Ch., Yonkers, N.Y., 1975-76, St. Luke's Luth. Ch., Winnipeg, Man., Can. 1976—; bd. dirs. Pacific Luth. Theol. Sem., Berkeley, Calif., 1980—; mem. mgmt. com., div. for profl. leadership Luth. Ch. in Am., 1980—. Mem. adv. council Word and World jour. Luther Northwestern Theol. Sem., St. Paul, 1982—. Contbr. articles to religious publs. Adviser vol. visitors program Seven Oaks Hosp., Winnipeg, 1983—. Mem. Can. Assn. for Pastoral Edn., Can. Luth. Assn. for Worship, Internat. Assn. Women Ministers. Home: 50 Thatcher Dr Winnipeg MN R3T 2L3 Canada

GRIZZLE, RONALD HOWARD, minister, Southern Baptist Convention; b. Gainesville, Ga., Nov. 2, 1952; s. Arthur Howard and Connie Lee (Adams) G.; m. Penny Ann Hoffman, Sept. 21, 1974; children: Amy Rebecca, Ashley Jill, Audrey Beth. B.A., U. Ga., 1974; M.Div., Midwestern Bapt. Theol. Sem., 1980. Lic., ordained to ministry Bapt. Ch., 1978. Pastor Faith Bapt. Chapel, Carrollton, Ga., 1976-77, Hale Bapt. Ch. (Mo.), 1978-81, Dogwood Hills Bapt. Ch., East Point, Ga., 1981—; vice moderator Atlanta Bapt. Assn., 1983-84, moderator, 1984—; v.p. Atlanta Bapt. Ministers' Conf., 1982-83; chmn. Christian Index Com., Ga. Bapt. Conv., 1981-82; co-convenor East Point Ministers' Fellowship, 1982. Adv. com. Fulton County Sch. Supt., Atlanta, 1981—. Burson Meml. scholar, Carrollton, Ga., 1977; recipient award, spl. resolution Fulton County Commn., 1981. Home: 2791 Lancaster Dr East Point GA 30344 Office: Dogwood Hills Bapt Ch 2435 Ben Hill Rd East Point GA 30344

GROENLUND, JOHN LIVINGSTON, minister, Evangelical Free Church of America; b. Seattle, Dec. 20, 1915; s. Wilho Arvid and Saima Johanna (Riekko) G.; m. Vera Fern Waller, Aug. 19, 1939 (dec. Dec. 1960); children: Donna Mae, Ruth Naomi, Jonathan Wilho, David Roy; m. Katherine Lucile Petrie, Apr. 19, 1918. B.A., Lewis and Clark Coll., 1958; M.A., U. Portland, 1963; postgrad. U. So. Calif., 1965-69. Ordained to ministry Evangelical Free Ch. of Am., 1943. Pastor El Sobrante Evang. Free Ch., 1941-49, Portland Evang. Free Ch., 1949-63, Calvary Bapt. Ch., Portland, 1982—; Pacific N.W. dist. chmn. Evang. Free Ch. Am., Wash., Oreg., Idaho, 1952-55, chmn. Black Lake Conf., 1956-60; mem. history faculty Cascade Coll., 1958-60, Judson Bapt. Coll., 1962-63, Warner Pacific Coll., 1964-65, Multnomah Sch. Bible, 1959-82; lectr. creationism Multnomah Sch. Bible, Portland, 1959-82, Inst. Creation Research, El Cayon, Calif., 1982—, Evang. Free Ch. Am. and Bay Cities Bible Inst., Oakland, Calif., 1940-59. Editor: Class Notes in Ancient Mediterranean History, 1962; Class Notes in My Specialty, 1965-67. Recipient Outstanding Educator award, 1973. Home: 8713 SE 91st Ave Portland OR 97266

GROFF, WARREN FREDERICK, educator, pres. seminary, Church of the Brethren; b. Harleysville, Pa., June 27, 1924; s. Reinhart R. and Reba H. (Rupert) G.; B.A., Juniata Coll., 1949; B.D., Yale Div. Sch., 1952; Ph.D., Yale, 1955; m. Ruth Naomi Davidheiser, Aug. 30, 1947; 1 son, David Warren. Ordained to ministry, 1947; prof. Bible and religion Bridgewater (Va.) Coll., 1954-58; prof. theology Bethany Theol. Sem., Oak Brook, Ill., 1958—, dean, 1960-75, pres., 1975—. Mem. World Council Chs. (mem. faith and order commn. 1963—), Am. Assn. Theol. Schs. (mem. commn. on accrediting 1968-74). Author: (with D.E. Miller) The Shaping of Modern Christian Thought, 1968; Christ the Hope of the Future, 1971; Story Time: God's Story and Ours, 1974; Prayer Time: God's Time and Ours, 1984. Office: Bethany Theol Sem Oak Brook IL 60521

GRONER, OSCAR, rabbi, religious organization executive. Internat. dir. B'nai B'rith Hillel Founds., Inc., Washington. Office: B'nai B'rith Hillel Found Inc 1640 Rhode Island Ave NW Washington DC 20036*

GRONHOVD, RICHARD LYNN, minister, United Presbyn. Ch. in U.S.A.; b. Ventura, Calif., Oct. 3, 1936; s. Gilbert Otto and Verna Lucille (Spangler) G.; B.A., U. Calif., Los Angeles, 1958; M.Div., Princeton Theol. Sem., 1961, Th.M., 1962; m. Darlene Joyce Klinckman, Dec. 23, 1960; children—Deborah, David. Ordained to ministry, 1962; asst. pastor, Hanford, Calif., 1962-65; minister to students Lakewood 1st Presbyn. Ch., Long Beach, Calif., 1965-70; sr. pastor La Habra (Calif.) Hills Presbyn. Ch., 1970-75, Whitworth Community Presbyn. Ch., Spokane, Wash., 1975—. Coordinator ongoing ministry to Cocopah Indians, Yuma, Ariz., 1966-70. Chmn. bd. dirs. Gary Center, La Habra, 1971-75. Mem. Presbytery of the Inland Empire, Synod of Alaska-Northwest. Home: N 11706 Madison St

Spokane WA 99218 Office: W 212 Hawthorne Rd Spokane WA 99218

GRONLI, JOHN VICTOR, minister, educational administrator, America Lutheran Church; b. Eshowe, Natal, S. Africa, Sept. 11, 1932; s. John Einar and Marjorie Gellet (Hawker) G.; came to U.S., 1934; naturalized, 1937; B.A., U. Minn., 1953; B.Th., M.Div., Luther Theol. Sem., St. Paul, 1958, D.Min., 1978; M.A., Pacific Luth. U., 1975; m. Jeanne Louise Ellertson, Sept. 15, 1952; children—Cheryl Marie Gronli Mundt, Deborah Rachel, John Timothy, Peter Jonas, Daniel Reubin. Ordained to ministry, 1958; pastor United Luth. Ch., also Lawton Luth. Ch., Brocket, N.D., 1958-61, Am. Luth. Ch., Trinity Luth. Ch. and Grace Luth. Ch., Harlowton, Mont., 1961-66, sr. pastor St. Luke's Luth. Ch., Shelby, Mont., 1966-75; missionary, prof. Paulinum Sem., Otjimbingwe, Karibib, Nambia, 1975-76; prof. religion and philosophy, chmn. dept. philosophy and humanities Golden Valley Luth. Coll., Mpls., 1976—, dean students, 1976-83, dean Summer Inst. Pastoral Ministry, Mpls., 1980-85. Sec. Rocky Mountain dist. Am. Luth. Ch., 1963-70, sec. bd. for communications and mission support, 1973-75; bd. dirs. Mont. Assn. Chs., 1973-75. Editor: Rocky Mountain Views, 1974-75. Contbr. articles to religious jours. Home: 1321 Orkla Dr Minneapolis MN 55427

GROOMS, JAMES TRENTON, minister, Disciples of Christ Church; b. Casstown, Ohio, July 15, 1931; s. Lester Henry and Mary Francis (Gladman) G.; m. Marcia Ann Malmsbury; 1 child, Sherry Norene Grooms Smith. Student Wittenburg U., 1950; B.S.L., Cin. Bible Coll., 1955; M.Div., Christian Theol. Sem., Indpls., 1960; student Inc. U.-Indpls., 1959-60; D.Min., St. Mary's Sem., Cin., 1977. Ordained, 1954. Campus minister State Tchrs. Coll., Emporia, Kans., 1960-62; pastor 1st Christian Ch., Fort Scott, Kans., 1962-66; sr. pastor 1st Christian Ch., Wellington, Kans., 1966-69, 1st Christian Ch., Athens, Ohio, 1969—; bd. dirs. Kans. Christian Chs., 1964-66, Christian Ch. in Ohio, 1980—, clergy advisor, 1973-84; charter mem. Spiritual Life Com., Cleve., 1974—; rep. Ohio Bd. for United Ministries in Higher Edn., 1971-73. Campus instr. Mcpl. Coll./Mercy Sch. Nursing, Fort SCott, 1964-65. Contbg. author: The Young Christian Observes the Law, 1983; contbr. articles to Jour. Christian Ch. Founding pres. Bourbon County Joint Bd. Phys./Mental Health, Fort Scott, 1962-66; bd. dirs. Kans. Mental Health Assn., 1963-66; mem. labor mediation com. O'Bleness Hosp., Athens, 1979. Sweeney grad. scholar, 1955; recipient Commendation for Community Service, 1st Christian Ch., Fort Scott, 1964, Cert. Recognition, Bourbon County Assn. Mental Health, 1966; Italian sabbatical grantee, 1st Christ Ch., Athens, 1983; nominee for gen. minister and pres. Christian Ch. U.S. and Can., Christian Ch., Athens, 1984. Mem. Athens County Ministerial Assn., Found. for Christian Living, Disciples Peace Fellowship. Democrat. Clubs: Kiwanis (Ft. Scott). Rotary (Wellington). Lodges: Masons, Order Eastern Star. Home: 14 Roxbury Dr Athens OH 45701 Office: 1st Christian Ch W State and N Congress Athens OH 45701

GROS, JEFFREY, ecumenical theologian, Roman Catholic Church; b. Memphis, Jan. 7, 1938; s. C. Jefferson and Faye Elizabeth (Dickenson) G. B.A., St. Mary's Coll., 1959, M.Ed., 1962; M.A., Marquette U., 1965; Ph.D., Fordham U., 1973. Tchr. high schs., coll., Chgo., St. Louis, Memphis, 1959-69, Christian Bros. Coll., Memphis, 1972-81, Memphis Sem., 1976-81; dir. faith and order Nat. Council Chs. of Christ in U.S.A., N.Y.C., 1981—. Editor: The Search for Visible Unity, 1984. Contbr. articles to profl. jours. NSF fellow, 1961-64; Hebrew Union Coll. travel grantee, 1968. Mem. Cath. Theology Soc., Coll. Theology Soc., Nat. Assn. Ecumenical Officers (dir. 1979-81), Nat. Assn. Evangelicals. Home: 93 Park Terrace W New York NY 10034 Office: Nat Council Chs Christ 475 Riverside Dr New York NY 10115

GROUNDS, VERNON CARL, minister, sem. pres., Conservative Baptist Assn. Am.; b. Jersey City, July 19, 1914; B.A., Rutgers U., 1937; B.D., Faith Theol. Sem., 1940; D.D., Wheaton (Ill.) Coll., 1956; Ph.D. in Philsophy of Religion, Drew U., 1960. Ordained to ministry; pastor Paterson (N.J.) Gospel Tabernacle, 1934-45; prof. English and philosophy King's Coll., Del., 1943-45; prof. theology, dean Bapt. Bible Sem., N.Y., 1945-51; prof. apologetics Conservative Bapt. Theol. Sem., Denver, 1951—, prof. ethics and counseling, pres., 1956—. Instr., Young Life Inst. 1952—; sec.-treas. Evang. Theol. Soc., 1965—. Author: Evangelical Reason for Our Hope, 1945; Evangelicalism and Social Concern, 1968; Revolution and the Christian Faith; contbg. author: Is God Dead?, 1967. Office: Conservative Bapt Theol Sem PO Box 1000 University Park Sta Denver CO 80220*

GROVE, KATHRYN MOWREY (MRS. D. DWIGHT GROVE, lay church worker, Evangelical United Brethren Church; b. Harrisburg, Pa., Jan. 11, 1914; d. D. Floyd and Eva S. (Shearer) Mowrey; A.B., Lebanon Valley Coll., 1934; postgrad. Millersville State Tchrs. Coll., 1937; m. D. Dwight Grove, July 11, 1939; children—David Dwight, Carol (Mrs. Ronald W. Miller). Missionary Evang. United Brethren Ch., Sierra

Leone, West Africa, 1939-41; pres. East Pa. Women's Soc., Evang. United Brethren Ch., 1957-62, treas. Gen. Women's Soc., 1965-66, pres., 1966-68; v.p. Pa. Council Chs., 1964-68; mem. joint commn. on ch. union Meth. and Evang. United Brethren chs., 1966-68; sec. Jud. Council, United Meth. Ch., 1968-76; v.p. bd. trustees Logan United Meth. Ch., Phila., 1972—, choir dir., 1973-79; trustee Eastern Pa. Conf. United Meth. Ch., 1976-82, mem. Eastern Pa. Conf. Loan Fund, 1976—. Tchr. high sch., New Cumberland, Pa., 1934-39. Pres. Phila. Story League, 1955-57. Trustee Lebanon Valley Coll., 1968—. Mem. AAUW, Hahnemann Hosp. Assn. Phila. Contbr. articles to religious jours. Address: 5025 N Marvine St Philadelphia PA 19141

GROVE, WILLIAM BOYD, bishop, United Methodist Church; b. Johnstown, Pa., Apr. 24, 1929; s. William Morgan and Elizabeth (Boyd) G.; m. Mary Lou Naylor, July 29, 1951; children: Susan Jone Grove-DeJarnett, Rebecca Louise. B.A., Bethany Coll., 1951, D.D. (hon.) 1982; M. Div., Drew U., 1954; D.Min., Pitts. Theol. Sem., 1978; D.D. (hon.), Allegheny Coll., 1965. Ordained to ministry United Meth. Ch., 1952, ordained elder, 1954, consecrated bishop, 1980. Pastor Western Pa. Conf. United Meth. Ch., 1954-80; pres. Bd. of Ch. and Society, United Meth. Ch., Charleston, W.Va., 1984—; trustee W.Va. Wesleyan Coll., Buchhannon, 1974—, Morristown Coll., Tenn., 1980—. Office: United Meth Ch 900 Washington Ct I Charleston WV 25301

GRUBBS, JERRY CORNELIUS, minister, educator, theology school dean, Church of God. b. Lamar, S.C., Sept. 26, 1940; s. J.C. and Ruth (Reagan) G.; m. Janette Smith, Aug. 6, 1961; children: Kimberley, Keith. B.A. in Edn., N.E. La. U., 1966; M.R.E., Anderson Sch. Theology, 1970; M.S., Ind. U., 1977, Ed.D., 1981. Ordained to ministry Ch. of God, 1965. Pastor, 1st Ch. of God, Rayville, La., 1962-66, Pendleton, Ind., 1966-70, Tacoma Ch. of God, Johnson City, Tenn., 1970-73; prof. religious edn. Anderson Sch. Theology, Ind., 1973-83, dean, 1983—; dir. Nat. Bd. Christian Edn., Ch. of God, Anderson, 1973-81. Author: Teaching Doctrine, 1974. Served with U.S. Army, 1958-61, Korea. Mem. Religious Edn. Assn., Adult Edn. Assn., Nat. Interfaith Coalition on Aging, Soc. for Advancement Continuing Edn. for Ministry, Phi Delta Kappa. Home: 25 N Roby Anderson IN 46012 Office: Anderson Sch Theology Anderson IN 46012

GRUBBS, LESTER RAY, minister, Southern Baptist Convention; b. Ft. Worth, Oct. 13, 1923; s. Lee Vanner and Christine (Nelson) G.; B.A., Baylor U., 1949; B.D., M.Div., Southwestern Baptist Theol. Sem., Ft. Worth, 1957, Th.M., 1967; D.Min., Midwestern Bapt. Theol. Sem., 1977; m. Billye Fern Huffman, May 31, 1947; children: Darla, Don, John, Mary. Ordained minister, 1951; pastor chs. in Tex., 1951-64; pastor Emmanuel Bapt. Ch., Cheyenne, Wyo., 1968-71, Trinity Bapt. Ch., Laramie, Wyo., 1971—; Bible chair prof. Sch. Religion, U. Wyo., 1969-70, 71—, chmn., 1978-81; moderator Tarrant Bapt. Assn., 1961-62, Frontier So. Bapt. Assn., 1970-72, 82-84; chmn. Wyo. So. Bapt. Area, 1975-77; pres. Laramie Ministerial Assn., 1976-83; mem. exec. bd. No. Plains Bapt. Conv., 1970-76, 82-83; bd. dirs. No. Plains Bapt. Found., 1974—; chmn. chaplaincy program Ivinson Meml. Hosp., 1978-84; chmn. exec. bd. Wyo. So. Bapt. Conv., 1984, pres., 1984-85. Lester R. Grubbs scholarship fund established in his honor Midwestern Bapt. Theol. Sem., 1983. Mem. Am. Acad. Religion, No. Plains Bapt. Conv. Sem. Alumni Assn. (pres. 1971-73). Home: 711 Gerald Pl Laramie WY 82070 Office: 1270 N 9th St Laramie WY 82070

GRUDEM, WAYNE ARDEN, seminary educator, minister, Baptist General Conference; b. Chippewa Falls, Wis., Feb. 11, 1948; s. Arden Elvin and Jean Calista (Sheady) G.; m. Margaret Ellen White, June 6, 1969; children: Elliot, Oliver, Alexander. B.A., Harvard U., 1970; M.Div., Westminster Sem., 1973; Ph.D., U. Cambridge, Eng., 1979. Ordained to ministry Bapt. Gen. Conf., 1974. Asst. prof. theology Bethel Coll., St. Paul, 1977-81; assoc. prof. N.T., Trinity Evang. Div. Sch., Deerfield, Ill., 1981—; bd. pres. Christian Heritage Acad., Northbrook, Ill., 1983—; sec.-treas. Inst. Advanced Christian Studies, Chgo., 1982—; bd. dirs. Mission: Moving Mountains, Eden Prairie, Minn., 1980-84. Author: The Gift of Prophecy in 1 Corinthians, 1982. Mem. Evang. Theol. Soc., Tyndale Fellowship, Inst. Bibl. Research. Republican. Home: 2 Dukes Ln Lincolnshire IL 60015 Office: Trinity Evang Div Sch 2065 Half Day Rd Deerfield IL 60015

GRUMMER, ROGER HAROLD, minister, Luth. Ch.-Mo. Synod; b. Okarche, Okla., July 28, 1936; s. Norman Henry and Adelia Dora (Bohlmann) G.; B.Th., Concordia Sem., Springfield, Ill., 1961; M.A. in Psychology, Nicholls U., Thibodaux, La., 1976; m. Betty Laverne Bourgeois, Aug. 6, 1960; children—Cheryl, Cynthia, Jonathan. Ordained to ministry, 1961; pastor Holy Trinity Luth. Ch., Statesville, N.C., 1961-65, Grace Luth. Ch., Houma, La., 1965-77, Concordia Luth. Ch., Bedford, Tex., 1977—; mem. evangelism com. So. Dist. Luth. Ch., 1968-70; pastoral adviser Gulf Dist. Luth. Laymen's League, 1969-71; creator, moderator Consensus Eleven religious talk show on KHMA-TV, Channel 11, 1972; Luth. campus contact pastor Nicholls U., 1965—; mem.

planning com. Dulac Community Indian Med. Clinic. Founding sec. Terrebonne Assn. Ministers, 1969-71, pres., 1971-72; pres. Greater New Orleans Luth. Pastors Conf., 1974. Active, Terrebonne Assn. for Retarded Children, 1970—, La. Dist. III Alcoholism Adv. Council, 1973—. Editor: Houma C. of C. Resource Book of Helping Agencies, 1972. Contbr. articles to religious publs. Home: 1400 Fair Oaks Euless TX 76039 Office: Route 1 Box 192 Bedford TX 76021

GRUNDEN, LARRY ALAN, minister, Disciples of Christ Church, pastoral counselor; b. Natrona Heights, Pa., Apr. 16, 1947; s. Kenneth A. and Gertrude J. (Klinkenberg) G.; m. Helen Marie Cogley, Aug. 3, 1968; children: Larry Alan, Lara Marie. B.F.A., Carnegie-Mellon U., 1969; M.Div., Tex. Christian U., 1973; D.Min., Lexington Theol. Sem., 1979. Ordained, 1973. Chaplain, VA Hosp., Chillicothe, Ohio, 1975-78; minister 1st Christian Ch., Chillicothe, 1973-78, Lancaster Christian Ch. (Ky.), 1978-80, Disciples Christian Ch., Hamilton, Ohio, 1980-84, St. Paul's United Ch. of Christ, Middletown, Ohio, 1984—; pastoral counselor, Pastoral Counseling Service, Middletown, 1983—; field dir. Lexington Theol. Sem., 1984; mem. new ch. com. Christian Ch. in Ohio, 1982-84. Chmn. fund raising Wilderness Rd. Council Girl Scouts U.S.A., Garrard County, Ky., 1979-80; mem. Bluegrass Mental Health and Mental Retardation Adv. Bd., Lexington, 1980; mem. citizens adv. com. Ohio Penal System, 1976-78. Mem. Am. Assn. Pastoral Counselors (pastoral affiliate). Democrat. Home: 7641 Vinnedge Rd Hamilton OH 45011 Office: St Paul's United Ch of Christ 114 S Broad St Middletown OH 45044

GUENTHER, ALLEN ROBERT, minister, religious educator, General Conference of Mennonite Brethren Churches; b. Steinbach, Man., Can., Sept. 13, 1938; s. John Allen and Anna (Braun) G.; m. Anne Wall, Aug. 16, 1962; children: Ronald Allen, Barry Mark, Michael Bruce. Th.B., Mennonite Brethren Bible Coll., Man., 1962; B.A., U. B.C., Can., 1963; M.A., Wheaton Grad. Sch. Theology, 1967; M.Div., Gordon-Conwell Sch. Theology, 1969; M.A., U. Toronto, Ont., Can., 1971, Ph.D., 1978. Ordained to ministry Mennonite Brethren Ch. Gen. Conf., 1981. Instr. Mennonite Brethren Bible Inst., Coaldale, Alta., 1962-65; pastor Lakeview Mennonite Brethren Ch., Lethbridge, Alta., 1963-65; instr., dean of students, Mennonite Brethren Bible Coll., Winnipeg, Man., 1967-70, asst. prof. O.T., 1975-81; pastor Mennonite Brethren Ch., Toronto, 1971-74; assoc. prof. O.T., Mennonite Brethren Bibl. Sem., Fresno, Calif., 1981—; mem. editorial council Believer's Ch. Bible Commentary, Scottsdale, Pa., 1980—; chmn. bd. pastoral ministries Butler Mennonite Brethren Ch., Fresno, Calif., 1983-85. Editor Direction, 1981—. Coach Little League, Sunnyside and Fresno, Calif., 1982-83. Fellow Can. Council, 1971-73, Gordon-Conwell Div. Sch. 1967, Govt. Ont. Liberal. Home: 5257 E Madison Ave Fresno CA 93727 Office: Mennonite Brethren Bibl Sem 4824 E Butler Ave Fresno CA 93727

GUENZEL, LAWRENCE MARTIN, minister, Lutheran Church in America; b. Phila., Apr. 18, 1947; s. Rudolph Andrew and Marion Catherine (Williams) G.; m. Virginia Lee Valerio, June 27, 1970; 1 child, Rebecca Christine. Cert. Concordia Jr. Coll., Bronxville, N.Y., 1967; B.A., Concordia Coll., Ft. Wayne, Ind., 1970; M.Div., Concordia Theol. Sem., St. Louis, 1973. Ordained to ministry Luth. Ch.-Mo. Synod, 1973. Pastor, Alpha Luth. Ch. of Deaf, Rochester, N.Y., 1973-77, St. Stephen Luth. Ch., Mifflintown, Pa., 1977-82; assoc. pastor Trinity Luth. Ch., Lansdale, Pa., 1982—; Protestant chaplain N.Y. Sch. for Deaf, Rome, 1973-77, Nat. Tech. Inst. for Deaf, Rochester Sch. for Deaf, 1973-77. Bd. dirs. North Pa. YMCA, 1983—. Office: Trinity Luth Ch 1000 W Main St Lansdale PA 19446

GUEST, PAUL IVINS, lay ch. worker, Methodist Ch.; b. Camden, N.J., May 2, 1916; s. Leon C. and May (Hall) G.; A.B., Ursinus Coll., 1938, LL.D., 1972; J.D., U. Pa., 1941; m. Helen V. Habfast, Oct. 4, 1941 (dec. Feb. 1948); children—Joan Lynn Guest Rothrock, Carol V. Guest Videon; m. 2d, Dorothy M. Dunkin, Apr. 16, 1949; 1 son, Paul Ivins. Trustee Meth. Hosp., Phila., 1952—, pres., 1960; trustee Phila. Conf. United Methodist Ch. 1956-68, Bala Cynwyd United Meth. Ch., 1967—, Meth. Hosp. Found., 1976—. Admitted to Pa. bar, 1942; partner firm Guest and Greene, Phila., 1971—. Bd. dirs. Russell C. Ball Found., Delaware Valley Hosp. Council. Recipient Outstanding Alumnus of the Year award Ursinus Coll., 1964. Mem. Am., Pa., Phila. bar assns. Clubs: Philadelphia Country (gov. 1968). Home: 1316 Colton Rd Gladwyne PA 19035 Office: Fidelity Bldg Philadelphia PA 19109

GUIDO, MICHAEL ANTHONY, minister, religious organization executive, Southern Baptist Convention; b. Lorain, Ohio, Jan. 30, 1915; s. Mike and Julia (DePalma) G.; m. Audrey Forehand, Nov. 25, 1943. Student Moody Bible Inst., 1933-35. Ordained to ministry So. Bapt. Conv., 1939. Minister of youth and music First Presbyn. Ch., Sebring, Fla., 1936-38, First Bapt. Ch., Lake Charles, La., 1939; evangelist Moody Bible Inst., Chgo., 1940-50; founder, pres., speaker Guido Evangelistic Assn., Metter, Ga., 1950—; writer and speaker daily telecast A Seed From the Sower, 1972—, daily broadcaster The Sower, A Seed From the Sower, Seeds from the Sower, Your Favorite Ten, 1957—. Contbr. daily newspaper column Seeds From the Sower, 1957—. Editor Sowing and Reaping mag., 1957—. Named Alumnus of Yr., Moody Bible Inst., 1982, Citizen of Yr., Metter Kiwanis Club, 1982. Home: PO Box 508 Metter GA 30439 Office: Guido Evangelistic Assn 600 N Lewis St Metter GA 30439

GUIDON, PATRICK, clergyman, educational administrator, Roman Catholic. Pres. Oblate Sch. of Theology, San Antonio. Office: Oblate Sch of Theology 285 Oblate Dr San Antonio TX 78216*

GUILARTE, RAUL GONZALO, chaplain, interdenominational, Church of the Nazarene, psychologist; b. Tarata, Cochabamba, Bolivia, Oct. 22, 1945; came to U.S., 1963, naturalized, 1971; s. Raul and Hercilia (Pardo) G.; m. Virginia Perez; children: Gina, Cynthia, Ivana, Aaron. B.A. in Religion, Loma Linda U., 1971; M.A. in Psychology, U. Beverly Hills, 1978, Ph.D., 1980; M.A. in Community Mental Health, Calif. State U.-San Bernardino, 1982. Ordained to ministry Church of the Nazarene, 1979. Pastor, Christian Missionary Alliance, Simi, Calif., 1967-69, Ch. of the Nazarene, Corona, Calif., 1974-82; asst. pastor Spanish Assemblies of God, Corona, 1970-74; chaplain intern Calif. Dept. Youth Authority, Whittier, Calif., 1981-82; chaplain resident St. Joseph Hosp., Orange Calif., 1982—; co-founder Bolivian Christian Evangelical U., 1979-83. Author: Assessment of Mental Health Needs and Services in Hispanic Communities, 1981, Educational Failures and the Chicano Pastoral Management by Objectives, 1981. Commr. community relations City of Riverside, Calif., 1980-82; organizer, dir. ednl. summer schs. for Hispanic children and youth, 1970-80; mem. outreach program Calif. Youth Authority, 1981. Recipient cert. of recognition City of Riverside, 1982. Western Latin Am. Ch. of Nazarene plaque, 1980, others. Mem. Acad. of Parish Clergy, Am. Soc. Internat. Law, Inter-Am. Soc. Psychology, Nat. Honor Soc. of Psychology, Assn. Mental Health Clergy, Hispanic Coalition of Mental Health and Human Services. Democrat. Club: LASO Loma Linda U. (pres.) (Riverside). Home: 18648 Bert Rd Riverside CA 92504 Office: St Joseph Hospital 1100 Stewart Orange CA 92667

GUILFOYLE, GEORGE H., bishop, Roman Catholic Church; b. N.Y.C., Nov. 13, 1913; s. James J. and Johanna (McGrath) G.; A.B. Georgetown U., 1935; postgrad. St. Joseph's Sem., 1939-44, N.Y. U., 1945; J.D., Fordham U., 1939; LL.M., Columbia, 1946; LL.D., St. Francis Coll., 1958, Manhattan Coll., 1962, Iona Coll., 1966; Litt.D., St. Joseph's Coll., Phila., 1968. Ordained priest Roman Catholic Ch., 1944, named papal chamberlain, 1955, domestic prelate, 1958; asst. St. Patrick's Cathedral, 1944-45, St. Andrew's Ch., 1944-46; asst. chancellor, asst. St. Elizabeth's Ch., N.Y.C., 1946-47; with Cath. Charities, N.Y.C., 1947-66, exec. dir., 1956-66; episcopal vicar Richmond County (S.I.), pastor St. Peter's Ch., 1966-68; bishop Diocese of Camden, N.J., 1968—. Asso. moderator coordinating com. Cath. Lay Orgns. Archdiocese of N.Y., 1954-57; archdiocesan consultor, 1960-68; nat. spiritual dir. Soc. St. Vincent De Paul, 1966—. Pres. Nat. Conf. Cath. Charities, 1959-61, bd. dirs., 1959-67; mem. N.Y.C. Adv. Bd. Pub. Welfare, 1960-66; mem. Archdiocesan Commn. for Community Planning, 1964-68. Bd. dirs. Nat. Shrine Immaculate Conception; trustee Seton Hall U. Decorated Knight grand cross equestrian order Holy Sepulchre; recipient John Carroll award Georgetown U., 1963. Address: 1845 Haddon Ave Camden NJ 08101

GUILLORY, ALBINA, nun, Roman Catholic Ch.; b. Ville Platte, La., Feb. 3, 1923; d. Nathan and Avia (LaFleur) G.; M.Ed., Our Lady of Lake Coll., 1959. Joined Marianite of Holy Cross Sisters, 1940; prin. St. Rita Sch., New Orleans, 1965-67, St. Alphonsus Sch., Oceans Springs, Miss.. 1967-68; reading tchr. Vandebilt Cath. High Sch., Houma, La., 1968-70; campus minister Southeastern, 1970-75; guidance counselor Sacred Heart High Sch., Ville Platte, 1975—. Mem. diocesan pastoral council Diocese of Lafayette (La.), 1975—, mem. sisters council, 1975—, extraordinary minister of Eucharist, 1972—; organizer youth group City of Ville Platte, 1975—; rep. sisters council to Nat. Assembly of Women Religious Conf., Ky., 1976. Instr. ARC, New Orleans, 1965-67. Mem. Fedn. Holy Cross, Finally Professed Marianite Holy Cross, La. Sch. Counselor Assn., Am. Personnel and Guidance Assn., Nat. Assn. Women Religious. Home: 532 E Main St Ville Platte LA 70586 Office: 114 Latour St Ville Platte LA 70586

GUINOTTE, HENRY PAUL, minister, United Presbyterian Church in U.S.A.; b. Omaha, June 16, 1930; s. Henry P. and Pearl (Eisele) G.; B.A., Hastings Coll., 1953; B.D., U. Dubuque, 1956; m. Martha Jean Marling, June 7, 1953; children—Diana, Henry. Ordained to ministry, 1956; pastor Divide Center, Lyons, Nebr. and Presbyn. Ch., Craig, Nebr., 1955-60, Neola (Iowa) Presbyn. Ch., 1960-66, Cedar Bluffs (Nebr.) Presbyn. Ch., 1966-72, United Presbyn. Ch., Palmer, Alaska, 1972—. Dir. youth caravans Nebr.-Alaska, 1963-74; mem. Synod of Alaska NW Mission evangelism com., 1975—; mem. Synod of Iowa Camp and Conf. com., 1962-66; dir. Alaska Youth teams wellington Ch. Scotland, Glasgow, 1983-85. Organizer, tchr., dir. vol. rescue squads Neola Fire Dept., 1961-66, Cedar Bluffs Fire Dept., 1967-72. Named Lion of Year, 1976. Address: PO Box 699 Palmer AK 99645

GUIZAR, RICARDO DIAZ, bishop, Roman Catholic Church; b. Mexico City, Feb. 26, 1933; s. Antonio Barragan and Elena Pico (De Guizar) Diaz; Classic Letters and Scis. Bachelor, Instituto Agelo Secchi-Rome, 1951; Philosophy Licentiate, Pontificia Università Gregoriana-Rome, 1954, Div. Licentiate, 1959. Ordained priest, 1958, bishop, 1970. Pvt. sec. The Archbishop, Puebla, Mex., 1960-63; prof., dir. of spirit Seminario Palafoxiano, Puebla, 1963-70; aux. bishop Archdiocese of Puebla, 1970-78, Diocese of Aquascalientes, 1978-84; bishop Diocese of Atlacomulco, Mex., 1984—; pres. liturgy, holy music, and arts Archdiocesan Commn. of Puebla, 1970-78; advisor Cursillos de Cristiandad, Puebla, 1970-78, Diocesan Council for Laical Apostolate, 1971-78; nat. charge Vocat. Pastoral Action, Mexico, 1970—. Contbr. articles to profl. jours. Mem. Comisión Episcopal de Seminarios y Vocaciones. Address: Gabriel Mancera 336 Mexico DF Mexico 03100

GULAS, WILLIAM EDWARD, priest, Roman Catholic Church; b. W. Hazleton, Pa., June 17, 1934; s. Michael Anthony and Helen Antoinette (Yarrosh) G. B.A., St. Francis Coll., 1957; M.A. in Journalism, Marquette U., 1972. Ordained priest, 1961. Editor, Franciscan Pubs., Pulaski, Wis., 1962-69; tchr. St. Mary High Sch., Burlington, Wis., 1969-70; pub. relations staff Franciscan Friars, Pulaski, 1970-72; pastor St. Thomas Aquinas Ch., Saginaw, Mich., 1972-81; minister provincial Franciscan Friars, Pulaski, 1981—; priest senator Diocese of Saginaw, 1975, mem. edn. bd., 1979-81, diocesan vicar, 1979-80; bd. consultors Franciscan Frairs, 1978-81. Editor, Franciscan Message, 1962-69. Mem. Conf. Major Superiors of Men. Democrat. Lodge: K.C. (chaplain 1978-81). Home: Assumption Friary Pulaski WI 54162 Office: Franciscan Friars 143 E Pulaski St Pulaski WI 54162

GULBRANSON, GARY LYNN, minister, Bible Church; b. Sioux Falls, S.D., Nov. 22, 1950; s. Merlyn H. and Dolores (Thomas) G.; m. Jorie Lee Dykstra, June 16, 1973; children: Marci, Marisa. Diploma, Moody Bible Inst., 1972; B.A., Trinity Coll., 1973; M.Div., Denver Conservative Bapt. Sem., 1976; Ed.D., Loyola U., 1983. Ordained to ministry Bible Ch., 1978. Minister of youth Central Bapt. Ch., Sioux Falls, S.D., 1972-73; Christian edn. dir., Grace Missionary Ch., Zion, Ill., 1973-74; ednl. coordinator Rocky Mountain Bapt. Conf., Denver, 1974-75; pres. His Men, Christian Fellowship, South Holland, Ill., 1979—; sr. pastor Glen Ellyn Bible Ch., Ill., 1983—; chmn. bd. Met. Chgo. Youth for Christ, 1979—; trustee Denver Conservative Bapt. Sem., 1979—, vice chmn., 1984—; music ministry WCFC-TV Faith 20, Back to God Hour; nat. speakers bur. Stonecroft Ministries, Kansas City, Kans. Dir. 1st Savs. & Loan, South Holland, Burdyke Co., South Holland. Named An Outstanding Young Man of Am., 1980, 82. Mem. Phi Delta Kappa. Lodge: Rotary. Home: 1160 N Stoddard St Wheaton IL 60187 Office: Glen Ellyn Bible Ch 501 Hillside Glen Ellyn IL 60137

GULLEDGE, MYRA ESTELLA, educational administrator, Southern Baptist Convention; b. Akron, Ohio, Sept. 15, 1924; d. Herbert I. and Lillian E. (Jones) G. B.A., Miss. Coll., 1948; M.R.E., Southwestern Bapt. Theol. Sem., 1950. Ednl. dir. First Bapt. Ch., Arcadia, La., 1950-51; Bapt. student dir. Northwestern State U., Natchitoches, La., 1951—; mem. Fgn. Mission Bd., So. Bapt. Conv., Richmond, Va., 1975-83, rec. sec., 1980-81; pres. Uniting Ministries in Higher Edn., 1983-84. Served with WAC, 1944-46. Recipient awards La. Bapt. Conv., 1972, Bapt. Student Alumni, 1976, First Bapt. Ch., Natchitoches, 1976, Dist. VIII Conv., 1981. Mem. Blue Key. Democrat. Home: 810 College Ave Natchitoches LA 71457 Office: Bapt Student Union Box 4144 Northwestern State U Natchitoches LA 71497

GULLETT, JAMES LLOYD, minister, Am. Bapt. Conv.; b. Tuscumbia, Ala., Jan. 24, 1938; s. Lloyd Gilmore and Christine (Mays) G.; B.S., U. No. Ala., 1960; LL.B., U. Miss., 1963; M.Div., So. Baptist Theol. Sem., 1975; m. Grace Ellen Smith, Apr. 18, 1965; children—Ellen Smith, Emily Melissa. Individual practice law, Corinth, Miss., 1964-71; ordained to ministry, 1972; pastor W Maple St. Bapt. Ch., Jeffersonville, Ind., 1972—. Mem. Ind. Bapt. Conv., Clark County (Ind.) Ministerial Assn., Miss. State Bar Assn. Home: 1236 Gail Dr Apt 160 Jeffersonville IN 47130 Office: 401 W Maple St Jeffersonville IN 47130

GULLEY, FRANK, religion educator, United Methodist Church; b. Lexington, Ky., Jan. 28, 1930; s. Frank and Agnes Opal (Stapp) G.; m. Anne Chastian Hoover, Aug. 24, 1957; children: Frank Stuart, Elizabeth Page. B.A., U. Ky., 1952; B.D., Emory U., 1955; Ph.D., Vanderbilt U., 1961. Ordained to ministry as elder United Meth. Ch., 1956. Instr., asst. to dean Vanderbilt Div. Sch., Nashville, 1960-61, librarian, asst. prof. religion and ch. history, 1966-69, assoc. dean, assoc. prof. ch. history, 1969—; bd. dirs. United

Protestant Edn. Bd., Urbana, Ill., 1961-62; dean, acting pres. Tenn. Wesleyan Coll., Athens, 1962-66; chmn. commn. on archives and history Tenn. Conf. United Meth. Ch., 1980—, chmn. bicentennial com., 1980—. Mem. Am. Soc. Ch. History. Democrat. Home: 904 Robertson Acad Rd Nashville TN 37220 Office: Vanderbilt U Div Sch Nashville TN 37240

GULNAC, JON CRAWFORD, minister, United Methodist Church; b. St. Marys, Pa., Apr. 14, 1948; s. Harry Eugene and Dorothy Ellen (Crawford) G.; B.A. in Sociology, W.Va. Wesleyan Coll., 1970; M.Div., Wesley Theol. Sem., Washington, 1973; m. Kathryn Suzanne Greer, Dec. 30, 1972 (dec. 1982); 1 dau., Rebekah Ellen, Sarah Irene, Daniel Walton; m. Jill Renee Royer, Sept. 17, 1983; 1 son, Nathaniel Eugene. Ordained to ministry, 1973; student asst. minister St. Andrews United Meth. Ch., Bethesda, Md., 1971-72; minister ch., Whitakers, N.C., 1973-74, Sheakleyville, Pa., 1974-78, Centennial-Faith, Johnstown, Pa., 1978-80, Lanes Mills, Brockway, Pa., 1980-84, Thorn Creek, Butler, Pa., 1984—. Participant community interdenominational services, Sheakleyville; substitute tchr. local sch. dist.; mem. Western Pa. Conf. Commn. Ecumenical and Interreligious Affairs, United Meth. Ch. clergy mem. at large Franklin Dist. Council on Ministries. Address: RD 4 Rockdale Rd Butler PA 16001

GUMBLETON, THOMAS J. See *Who's Who in America*, 43rd edition.

GUMS, REUBEN HENRY, minister, religious communication official, United Methodist Church; b. Cleve., N.D., Oct. 16, 1927; s. Fredrick and Kathrine (Vossler) G.; m. Frances Lorene Seifert, Mar. 9, 1956 (dec. 1970). B.A., North Central Coll., Naperville, Ill., 1949; M.Div., Evang. Theol. Sem., 1952; S.T.M., Union Theol. Sem., 1959. Ordained to ministry Evang. United Brethren Ch., 1952. Dir. radio and audio-visual commn. Philippine Fedn. Christian Chs., Manila, 1953-58; dir. radio and TV Ch. Fedn. of Greater Chgo., 1959-68, Council Chs., N.Y.C., 1968-74; exec. dir. Tri-State Media Ministry, N.Y.C., 1974—, Laymen's Nat. Bible Com., Inc., N.Y.C., 1983—; chmn. communications com. N.Y. Conf. United Meth. Ch., 1975-79; dir., exec. com. mem. communications com. Nat. Council Chs., 1960-72; producer TV and radio programs and series on religious themes, 1953—. Mem. alumni bd. Union Theol. Sem., N.Y.C., 1964-74; bd. dirs., acting pres. Exodus House, Inc., N.Y.C., 1984—. Mem. Nat. Acad. TV Arts and Scis. (gov. 1976-80, gov.'s citation 1980), Assn. Regional Religious Communicators (founder, pres. 1965-69). Democrat. Home: 244 W 75th St New York NY 10023 Office: Laymen's Nat Bible Com 815 2d Ave New York NY 10017

GUNCKEL, VERNON FRANKLIN, JR., minister, United Methodist Church; communications educator; b. Galesburg, Ill., June 28, 1939; s. Vernon Franklin and Esther Anna Katherine (Landmeier) G.; B.S., No. Ariz. U., 1961; M.Div. (Estarl fellow 1962-64), Garrett Theol. Sem., 1964; M.A. (Cokesbury fellow in Communication studies 1966), Northwestern U., 1966; m. Shirley Gail Parker, Dec. 18, 1965; 1 child, Coretta Elizabeth. Ordained to ministry, 1964; dir. housing and employment Garrett Theol. Sem., Northwestern U., 1962-67; assoc. pastor River Forest United Meth. Ch., Ill., 1963-65; pastor Roselawn United Meth. Ch., San Jose, Calif., 1967-69; secular employment by spl. appointment Bishop of San Francisco Area United Meth. Ch.; asst. prof., adminstrv. asst. to dean acad. planning San Jose State U., 1969-71; dir. news Sta. KEMO-TV, San Francisco, 1969-71; program coordinator div. lang. and communication Cambrian Coll., North Bay, Ont., Can., 1971-73; course dir. radio-TV, Seneca Coll, Toronto, Ont. Can., 1973-74, chmn. div. creative and communication arts, 1974—, acad. dean, 1975; cons. on religious TV programs; cons. to Can. Royal Commn. on Violence in the Communications Industry. Recipient Pres.'s prize, 1961, Man of Yr. award, 1961, Distinguished Alumni award, 1975 (all No. Ariz. U.); Columbia U. Scholastic Press award, 1961. Mem. Assn. Communication Adminstrs., Ont. Ministry Colls. and Univs. Task Force on TV Broadcasting, Can. Speech Assn., Internat. Platform Assn., Speech Communication Assn. Am. Author: Immortal Longings, 1972; You and Others: An Introduction to Interpersonal Communication, 1975; Your Grief: The First Painful Days, 1983; Impact, series of religious TV programs, 1966-67; also articles. Home: 109 Olde Towne Pl Thornhill ON L3T 4K9 Canada Office: 4164 Sheppard Ave E Toronto ON M1S 1T3 Canada

GUNDRUM, JAMES RICHARD See Who's Who in America, 43rd edition.

GUNNELLS, DREW JEFFERSON, minister, Southern Baptist Convention; b. Shreveport, La., Oct. 17, 1932; s. Drew Jefferson and Dura Lee (Hortman) G.; m. Flora Margery Noble; children: D. Jeffrey, Lisa Gunnells Steed, Susan Lee. B.A., Baylor U., 1953; M.A., U. So. Miss., 1966; M.Div., Southwestern Bapt. Theol. Sem., 1958. Ordained to ministry Bapt. Ch., 1953. Pastor Zion Hill Bapt. Ch., Bluffdale, Tex., 1957-58, 1st Bapt. Ch., Summit, Miss., 1958-62, Eastern Hills Bapt. Ch., Montgomery, Ala., 1962-72, Spring Hill Bapt. Ch., Mobile, Ala., 1972—; trustee, chmn. acad. affairs com. Southwestern Bapt. Theol. Sem., Ft. Worth, 1981—; pres. Ala. Bapt. State Conv., 1979-81, Fgn. Mission Bd. of So. Bapt. Conv., 1970-72; mem. ministerial adv. com. Mobile Infirmary, 1980—. Author: The Christian Family: Mission Possible, 1981. Contbr. articles to denominational publs. Active Beck-Stolz Meml. Fund Com., Mobile. Served to 1st lt. USAF, 1953-55. Mem. Mobile C. of C., Pi Gamma Mu, Phi Alpha Theta. Club: Rotary. Home: 820 Regents Dr W Mobile AL 36609 Office: Spring Hill Bapt Ch 2 S McGregor Ave Mobile AL 36608

GUNTER, EVELYN COLEMAN, minister, Assemblies of God; b. Elbridge, Tenn., Dec. 18, 1919; d. Charlie Lee and Frances (Wakefield) Coleman; B.S. cum laude, Bethel Coll., McKenzie, Tenn., 1965; spl. edn. certificate Memphis State U., 1960; grad. Berean Sch. Bible, Springfield, Mo., 1960; m. John Herbert Gunter, Jan. 16, 1942; 1 son, John Herbert (dec.). Ordained to ministry, 1960; pastor chs. in Tenn., 1960—; pastor Revival Tabernacle Assembly of God, Lane, 1972, evangelist, 1973-75; asso. pastor Evangel Temple Assembly of God, Union City, 1975—. Spl. edn. tchr., 1941-75; marriage and family counselor, 1960—. Mem. Nat., Tenn. edn. assns., PTA, Obion County Ministerial Assn., Student Christian Assn., 4-H Club. Author articles, poetry. Address: 1321 Sun Swept Dr Union City TN 38261

GUNTER, VERL EUGENE, minister, Lutheran Church-Missouri Synod; b. Ewing, Nebr., Mar. 9, 1929; s. Lionel Wilson and Martha Ellen (Cary) G.; m. Betty Jean Shrader, Aug. 28, 1949; children: Judy Ann, Johnny Verl, Jamey Eugene, Janet Jean. B. Theology, Concordia Theol. Sem., 1981. Ordained to ministry Luth. Ch.-Mo. Synod, 1981. Minister, Christ Luth. Ch., Nebraska City, Nebr., 1981-82, St. Paul's Luth. Ch., Chambers, Nebr., 1982-84, Trinity Luth. Ch., Akron, Colo., 1984—. Republican. Address: 762 Date Ave Akron CO 80720

GUSS, JEROME VINCENT, minister, Lutheran Church in America; b. Confluence, Pa., Apr. 10,1951; s. Jerome Vincent Sr. and Kathryn Mary (orne) G.; m. Karen Anne Wright, Aug. 21, 1976. M.A., Gettsburg Coll., 1973; M.Div., Luth. Theol. Sem., Gettysburg, 1977. Ordained to ministry Luth. Ch. in Am., 1977. Intern pastor Moxham Luth. Ch., Johnstown, Pa., 1975-76; pastor Sheperdstown Luth. Parish, W. Va., 1977-81; chaplain Med. Coll. Va. Hosp., Richmond, 1981-82; pastor Petersburg Gen. Hosp., Va., 1982—; mem. Profl. Services Mng. Group, Va. Synod, 1979—. Fellow Richmond Acad. Chaplains, Coll. of Chaplains; mem. Petersburg Area Clergy Assn., Phi Alpha Theta (v.p. 1973). Office: Petersburg Gen Hosp 801 S Adams St Petersburg VA

GUST, CORNELIA MARY, prioress, Roman Catholic Church; b. East Grand Forks, Minn., June 27, 1924; d. George William and Julia Ann (Pribula) G. B.A. in English, Clarke Coll., 1963; postgrad. St. Thomas Coll., St. Paul, summers 1964-66. Joined Sisters of St. Benedict, Roman Cath. Ch., 1946. Local superior St. Elizabeth Convent, Lefor, N.D., 1959-60; dir. aspirants Mt. St. Benedict Acad., Crookston, Minn., 1963-64; dir. initial formation Mt. St. Benedict, 1964-71, prioress (maj. superior), 1977-81; spiritual dir. at retreats, 1964—; organizer Religious Formation Conf., 1969; pres. Mt. St. Benedict sponsored health care facilities, 1977-84; planner for on-going formation Sisters St. Benedict of Crookston, 1977—; mem. Juridic com. Fedn. St. Gertrude, 1983-85; mem. Benedictines for Peace, Crookston, 1981—. Author pamphlets. Promotor peace and social justice programs, aid to poor, refugee sponsorship, aid to migrant workers, Crookston, 1977—. Robert Taft Inst. grantee, 1974. Mem. Crookston Conf. Women Religious (sec. 1974-77), Leadership Conf. Women Religious (nat. and Region XI), Cath. Hosp. Assn. Home and Office: Mt St Benedict Priory Crookston MN 56716

GUSTAFSON, ARTHUR EMIL, minister, Evangelical Covenant Church; b. South Dayton, Iowa, Jan. 1, 1912; s. Joseph Emil and Anna Albertina (Anderson) G. A.A., N. Park Coll., 1948; diploma N. Park Theol. Sem., 1951; postgrad. Div. Sch., U. Chgo., 1951-54. Ordained to ministry, 1953; pastor Emmanuel Covenant Ch., Merrill, Wis., 1947—, Evang. Covenant Ch., Tomahawk, Wis., 1964-81. Mem. Merrill Clergy Assn., Lincoln County Clergy Assn. Home: 400 Superior St Merrill WI 54452 Office: 305 N Genesee St Merrill WI 54452

GUSTAFSON, JAMES MOODY, educator, minister, United Church of Christ; b. Norway, Mich., Dec. 2, 1925; s. John Otto and Edith Anna (Moody) G.; student North Park Coll., 1942-44; B.S., Northwestern U., 1948; B.D., Chgo. Theol. Sem., 1951; Ph.D. (Kent fellow 1953), Yale, 1955; D.H.L., Bloomfield Coll., 1972; D.D., Chgo. Theol. Sem., 1980; D.Litt., Concordia Coll., Minn., 1983; Theol. Dr., Uppsala U., Sweden, 1985; m. Louise Roos, Sept. 3, 1947; children: Karl, Greta, John, Birgitta. Ordained to ministry United Ch. of Christ, 1951; pastor Northford (Conn.) Congl. Ch., 1951-54; asst. dir. Study of Theol. Edn. in Am., New Haven, 1954-55; mem. faculty Yale, 1955-72; prof. theol. ethics Div. Sch. U. Chgo., 1972—. Guggenheim fellow, 1959-60, 67-68. Fellow Inst. Soc., Ethics and Life Scis., Am. Acad. Arts and Scis.; mem. Am. Soc. Christian Ethics (pres. 1969). Author: Treasure in Earthen Vessels, 1961; Christ and the Moral Life, 1968; The Church as Moral Decision Maker, 1970; Christian Ethics and the Community, 1971; Theology and Christian Ethics, 1974; Can Ethics be Christian?, 1975; Contributions of Theology to Medical Ethics, 1975; Protestant and Roman Catholic Ethics, 1978; Ethics From a Theocentric Perspective, 2 vols., 1981, 84; (with others) Advancement of Theological Education, 1957. Office: U Chgo Swift Hall Chicago IL 60637

GUSTASON, REYNOLD AMES, minister; b. Grand Rapids, Minn., Oct. 1, 1921; s. Reynold Adolph and Anna Gunberg (Carlson) G.; B.S. in Edn., Am. U., 1952, M.S., 1961; T.H.D., Germinde Godgest Germany, 1963; children—Janis Lynn, Todd Allan, David John. Ordained to ministry, 1952; prof. Old Testament Theology, Heileron, Germany, 1960-64; dir. youth challenge, Christian Fellowship Ch., Cusseta, Ga., 1970—; chaplain Ga. Prison System, 1975—. Chaplain, vice sec., chmn. local bd. dirs. Cystic Fibrosis Found. Mem. Ga. Assn. Justice of the Peace, Constables Inc., Ga. Sheriffs Assn. Author numerous publs. in field. Home and Office: PO Box 116 Cusseta GA 31805

HAAK, ROBERT DONEL, educator, Association of Evangelical Lutheran Churches; b. Springfield, Ill., Jan. 16, 1949; s. Rudolph Albert and Lenora (Becker) H.; m. G. Diane Albanito, June 7, 1969; children: Michael Andrew, Robert Aaron. B.S., Concordia Coll., Seward, Nebr., 1970; M.T.S., Luth. Sch. Theolgy, 1974; postgrad. Divinity Sch. U., Chgo., 1977-84. Instr. religion Luther North High Sch., Chgo., 1970-77; lectr. Luth. Sch. Theology, Chgo., 1978-80, St. Xavier Coll., Chgo., 1982-83, McCormick Sem., Chgo., 1983; instr. Augustana Coll., Rock Island, Ill., 1983—; youth minister Faith Luth. Ch., Homewood, Ill., 1979-82. Contbr. articles to Jour. Bibl. Lit., Vetus Testamentum, Ency. Britanica. Mem. Soc. Bibl. Lit., Am. Schs. Oriental Research, Chgo. Soc. Bibl. Research, Cath. Bibl. Assn. Democrat. Home: 1515 Highland Pl Streator IL 61364 Office: Augustana Coll Rock Island IL 61201

HAAS, RALPH THEODORE, minister, United Presbyn. Ch. U.S.A.; b. Scranton, Pa., July 20, 1911; s. Theodore John and Katherine (Schanz) H.; B.A., Hamilton Coll., 1937, D.D., 1955; B.D., Union Theol. Sem., 1940; m. Bernadena Elizabeth Bryant, Feb. 12, 1938; children—Sharon Jane, Sandra Ann. Pastor First Presbyn. Ch., Liberty, N.Y., 1940-43, Hickory St. Presbyn. Ch., Scranton, Pa., 1943-48, Crescent Ave. Presbyn. Ch., Plainfield, N.J., 1948-60, First Presbyn. Ch., Buffalo, 1960-62, First Presbyn. Ch., Fullerton, Calif., 1962—. Moderator Presbytery of Lackawanna (Pa.), 1945, Presbytery Elizabeth, 1950, Presbytery of Los Ranchos, 1971, Synod of So. Calif., 1975-76; vice chmn. commn. on ecumenical mission and relations, United Presbyn. Conf., 1952-64. Trustee United Fund, Plainfield, 1952-58, Buffalo, 1960-62, Fullerton, Calif., 1962-68; mem. mayors com. to form human relations commn., Fullerton, 1970; mem. county citizens com. to select tax assessor, 1975. Mem. World Alliance of Presbyn. Chs. (gen. bd. 1967-73), Nat. Council Chs. (gen. bd. 1957-63), Phi Beta Kappa, Pi Delta Epsilon, Chi Alpha. Contbr. articles in field to religious jours. Home: 441 W Sunny Hills Rd Fullerton CA 92635 Office: PO Box 409 Fullerton CA 92635

HABADA, PATRICIA ADELAIDE, school administrator, religion textbook editor, Seventh-day Adventist; b. Flint, Mich., Mar. 17, 1929; d. Robert Wiley and Lillie Savannah (Bowden) Breedlove; m. Joseph Paul Habada, June 5, 1949; children: Shirley Dawn Habada-Harvey, Beverly Kay, Paula Jo. B.S., Kutztown State Coll., 1968; M.Ed., U. Pitts., 1976, Ph.D., 1982. Cert. tchr., Ohio, Pa. Tchr., Pa. Conf. Seventh-day Adventist, prin., 1970-73, assoc. supt. schs., 1975-79; textbook editor Gen. Conf. Seventh-day Adventists, Washington, 1979—; trustee Blue Mountain Acad., Hamburg, Pa., 1971-80; v.p. Pa. Lay Adv. Bd., Reading, 1969-71; dir. family life workshops, Pa. Conf. of Seventh-day Adventists, 1975-80; adj. prof. Andrews U.; instr. Takoma Inst. Author: (with others) Family Life Workshops, 1979; Editor: Life Series Seventh-day Adventists Readers, 1982—; contbr. articles to profl. jours. Mem. Assn. Adventist Women, Assn. for Supervision and Curriculum Devel., Internat. Reading Assn. Republican. Office: Gen Conf Seventh-day Adventists 6840 Eastern Ave NW Washington DC 20012

HABECKER, EUGENE B., college president, United Brethren in Christ; b. Hershey, Pa., June 17, 1946; s. Walter E. and Frances (Miller) E.; m. Marylou Napolitano, July 27, 1968; children: David, Matthew, Marybeth. B.A., Taylor U., 1968; M.A., Ball State U., 1969; J.D., Temple U., 1974; Ph.D., U. Mich., 1981. Asst. dean, fin. aid dir. Eastern Coll., St. Davids, Pa., 1970-74; asst. prof. polit. sci., dean students George Fox Coll., Newberg, Oreg., 1974-78; exec. v.p. Huntington Coll., Ind., 1979-81, pres., 1981—; cons./evaluator North Central Assn., Chgo., 1982—; bd. dirs. Christian Coll. Coalition, 1982—, Associated Colls. Ind., 1982—, Ind. Colls. and Univs. Ind., 1983—. Lodge: Rotary (Huntington). Office: Huntington Coll 2303 College Ave Huntington IN 46750

HABERKORN, KEITH ALBERT, minister, Wis. Evang. Luth. Synod; b. Waukesha, Wis., July 2, 1943; s. Marlowe Albert and Marcella Dorathea (Poetter) H.; B.A., Northwestern Coll., Watertown, Wis., 1965; M.Div., Wis. Luth. Sem., Mequon, 1969; m. Ruth Caroline Schlavensky, June 21, 1970. Ordained to ministry, 1969; vicar King of Kings Ch., Garden Grove, Calif., 1967-68; asst. to librarian Wis. Luth. Sem., 1968-69; pastor Trinity and Immanuel Luth. Chs., Elkton and Ward, S.D., 1969-72, St. John's Evang. Luth. Ch., Manitowoc, Wis., since 1972—. Mem. Bd. Sr. Citizens, Elkton, 1970-72. Contbr. to Meditations, 1976. Home: 7525 English Lake Rd Manitowoc WI 54220

HABIGER, JAMES DAVID, priest, Roman Catholic Church; b. Harvey, N.D., Feb. 6, 1927; s. Joseph John and Edith Elizabeth (Renchin) H. B.A., St. Mary's Coll., Balt., 1947; M.A., Cath. U., Washington, 1951; postgrad. U. Minn., 1955, 56. Ordained priest Roman Cath. Ch., 1951. Assoc. pastor St. Augustine Ch., Austin, Minn., 1951-56; prin. St. Augustine High Sch., Austin, 1952-56; prin. Cotter High Sch., Winona, Minn., 1956-60; supt. edn. Diocese of Winona, 1960-75; pastor St. John's Ch., Winona, 1957-75; exec. dir. Minn. Cath. Conf., St. Paul, 1980—; trustee Coll. St. Teresa, 1980-86; bd. dirs. Derham Hall High Sch., St. Paul, 1984—; mem. Respect Life Bd. Archdiocese of St. Paul, 1983—. Guest editorial writer Minn. Cath. newspapers; mem. Bd. Joint Religious Legis. Coalition, 1980. Co-chmn. Nat. Workshop on Christian and Jewish Relations, 1987; registered lobbyist State of Minn.; Minn. Catholic bishops' rep. to Minn. Council of Chs., Minn. Jewish Community. Papal Chamberlain Vatican City, 1962, Domestic Prelate, 1966. Mem. Nat. Assn. State Catholic Conf. Dirs. (sec. 1984-86). Lodge: K.C. Office: Minn Catholic Conf 296 Chester St Saint Paul MN 55107

HACAULT, ANTOINE JOSEPH LEON, archbishop, Roman Catholic Church; b. Bruxelles, Man., Can., Jan. 17, 1926; s. Francois and Irma (Mangin) H.; B.A., U. Man., 1947; theol. student, St. Boniface Maj. Sem., 1947-51; S.T.D., Angelicum U., Rome, 1954. Ordained priest, 1951; chaplain St. Boniface Sanatorium, 1954; prof. theology St. Boniface Maj. Sem., 1954-64; dir. diocesan rev. Les Cloches de Saint Boniface, 1961; personal theologian toarchbishop of St. Boniface, also council expert 2d Vatican Ecumenical Council, 1962-64; bishop titular of Media, aux. bishop of St. Boniface, 1964-72, coadjutor bishop, 1972-74, archbishop of St. Boniface, 1974—; rector Coll. St. Boniface 1967-69. Address: 151 Ave de la Cathedrale Saint Boniface MB R2H 0H6 Canada*

HACKER, HILARY BAUMANN, bishop, Roman Cath. Ch.; b. New Ulm, Minn., Jan. 10, 1913; s. Emil and Sophia (Baumann) H.; student Nazareth Hall, St. Paul, Minn., 1928-32, St. Paul Sem., 1932-38; J.C.B., Gregorian U., Rome, Italy, 1939. Ordained priest Roman Catholic Ch., 1938, consecrated bishop, 1956; asst. pastor Ch. of Nativity, St. Paul, 1938, Ch. of Most Holy Trinity, Winsted, Minn., 1939-41; vice-chancellor Archdiocese of St. Paul, 1941, chancellor, 1941-45, vicar gen., 1945-56; bishop Diocese of Bismarck, N.D., 1956-82; asst. pastor Ch. of Christ the King, Mandan, N.D., 1982—. Address: 505 10th Ave NW Mandan ND 58554

HACKETT, JOHN FRANCIS See *Who's Who in America*, 43rd edition.

HACKMANN, RONALD EDWARD, minister, Lutheran Church in America; b. St. Louis, Aug. 19, 1939; s. Frank E. and Lee C. (Jackson) H.; m. Miriam Esther Hackmann, Dec. 22, 1968; children: Christina, Analisa, Jonathan, David. B.A., Augustana Coll., 1962; M.Div., Luth. Sch. Theology, 1966; C.P.E., Hazelden Coll., 1979. Ordained to ministry, Luth. Ch. in Am., 1966. Minister, Fish Lake and Spring Lake Luth. chs., North Branch and Harrish, Minn., 1966-70, First Evang. Luth. Ch., Taylors Falls, Minn., 1970-84, Cross Calvary Luth. Ch., Olivia, Minn., 1984—; bd. dirs. Bd. Social Ministry, Minn., 1981-85, Parmly Nursing Home, Chgo., 1981-85, Luther Point Bible Camp, Grantsburg, Wis., 1974-79; chmn. Taylors Falls Pastor Orgn., 1970-84. Adv. bd. St. Croix Falls Hosp., Wis., 1980—; bd. dirs. Family Resource Ctr., Chicago City, Minn., 1978-85. Democrat. Home and Office: 1101 Chestnut W Olivia MN 56277

HACKNEY, HOWARD SMITH, lay church worker, Society of Friends; b. Wilmington, Ohio, May 20, 1910; s. Volcah Mann and Gusta Anna (Smith) H.; B.S., Wilmington Coll., 1932; m. Lucille Morrow, June 28, 1933; children—Albert, Roderick, Katherine. Mem. permanent bd. Wilmington Yearly Meeting, Young Friends Bd., 1927-37; Sunday sch. supt. Chester Friends Meeting, 1933-37, presiding clk. monthly meeting, ministry and council, 1963—; mem. exec. com., pres. Am. Young Friends Fellowship, 1937; yearly meeting rep. Friends Com. on Nat. Legislation. Treas., Clinton County Council Chs., 1966-71. Farmer, Wilmington, 1933—; county exec. dir. Clinton County Agrl. Stblzn. and Conservation Service, 1952—; bd. dirs., treas. Clinton County Community Action Council; trustee Wilmington Coll. Recipient awards Nat. Agrl. Stblzn. Conservation Office Employees, 1970. Mem. Nat. Farmers Union, Farm Bur., Ohio Duroc Breeders Assn. (pres. 1940-45), Clinton County Agrl. Soc. (dir., treas.), Clinton County Hist. Soc. Mason. Home: 2003 Inwood Rd Wilmington OH 45177 Office: 24 Randolph St Wilmington OH 45177

HADLEY, TIMOTHY DAVID, religious educator, Church of Christ; b. Searcy, Ark., Nov. 28, 1949; s. John Paul and Helen Elizabeth (Farris) H.; m. Nancy Dee Coffman, July 9, 1971; children: Matthew Thomas, Mark Ryan, Sarah Elizabeth, A.A., Lubbock Christian Coll., 1969; B.A., Harding Coll., 1971; M.A., Harding Grad. Sch. Religion, 1973. Campus minister Austin St. Church of Christ, Levelland, Tex., 1974-75; minister Arlington Ch. of Christ, Cin., 1975-82; mem. faculty Ohio Valley Coll., Parkersburg, W.Va., 1982—, assoc. prof. Bible and Bibl. lang., 1982—. Contbr. articles to profl. jours. Mem. Nat. Assn. Profs. Hebrew (mem. adv. council 1984—), Evang. Theol. Soc., Swedish Exegetical Soc. Republican. Office: Ohio Valley Coll College Pkwy Parkersburg WV 26101

HADLEY, WAYNE NELSON, retired minister, American Baptist Churches in the U.S.A.; b. Buffalo, May 6, 1919; s. Bert Nelson and Ruth Anna (Oyer) H.; m. Virginia Margaret Jominy, Aug. 15, 1942; children: Lawrence H., Christine Hadley Laquintano, Karen Hadley Dyke, Ronald A. B.S., U. Mich., 1941; M.Div., Eastern Bapt. Theol. Sem., 1948; D.D. (hon), 1970. Ordained to ministry, Am. Bapt. Chs. in U.S.A., 1948. Pastor, Grace Bapt. Ch., Westmont, N.J., 1948-55; sr. pastor First Bapt. Ch., Somerville, N.J., 1955—; exec. com. Am. Bapt. Chs., N.J.; chaplain Somerville Fire Co., 1957—. Pres., bd. dirs. Somerville Sr. Citizens Housing, 1980—. Mem. Eastern Bapt. Theol. Sem. Alumni Assn. (exec. com.). Republican. Home: 130 W High St Somerville NJ 08876 Office: First Bapt Ch 132 W High St Somerville NJ 08876

HAEGER, MARTIN ALBERT, minister, Lutheran Church-Missouri Synod; b. LaSalle-Peru, Ill., Jan. 26, 1953; s. Albert Eugene and Martha Jean (Schwedler) H.; m. Cinthea Ann Baker, Aug. 13, 1983. B.A., No. Ill. U., 1975; M.Div., Concordia Sem., 1981. Ordained to ministry Luth. Ch.-Mo. Synod, 1981. Campus pastor to Luth. students Community Luth. Ch., South Burlington, Vt., 1979-80, vicar, 1979-80; asst. pastor St. John Evang. Luth. Ch., Peru, Ind., 1981-83, sr. pastor, 1983—; circuit chmn. Ind. Dist.-Luth. Ch.-Mo. Synod, 1982—. AID Assn. for Lutherans grantee, 1981. Mem. Alban Inst., Smithsonian Inst. Republican. Lodge: Rotary (Peru). Home: 27 E 2d St Peru IN 46970

HAERTEL, CHARLES WAYNE, minister, American Lutheran Church. B. Stevens Point, Wis., May 20, 1937; s. George Henry and Eva Georgia (Kingsland) H. B.A., St. Olaf Coll., 1960; B.D., Luther Theol. Sem., St. Paul, 1965; S.T.M., Wartburg Sem., 1977; D.Min. candidate, McCormick Sem., Chgo., 1983. Ordained to ministry American Lutheran Church, 1965. Pastor, Our Saviour's Luth. Ch., Almira, Wash., 1965-68, St. Jacob's Luth. Ch., Jackson Center, Ohio, 1969-76, Zion Luth. Ch., Bridgewater, S.D., 1977—; rep. nat. Am. Luth. Ch. conv., Sioux Valley Conf., 1984-85; host refugee families Luth. Soc. Services, Sioux Falls, S.D., 1984. Mem. Peace and Justice Ctr., 1977-83, Better Bridgewater Club, 1977-78; bd. dirs. Wellspring Wholistic Care, Freeman, S.D., 1980—, M-2 State Penitentiary Inmate Visitation Program, 1980—. Recipient scouting scholarship Luth. Brotherhood, St. Olaf Coll., 1956, McCormick scholarship, 1982; grantee Shaloam Continuing Edn. Program, Sioux Falls, 1980—. Mem. McCook County Clergy (pres. 1982-83). Club: Toastmasters ATM (Sioux Falls). Home and Office: Zion Luth Ch PO Box 38 Bridgewater SD 57319

HAGAN, WESLEY DILLARD, minister, Southern Baptist Convention; b. Tompkinsville, Ky., Jan. 16, 1924; s. Bascal and Effie (Carlock) H.; m. Maxine Britt Hagan, Mar. 15, 1951; children: Michael, David, Elizabeth Ann. Student, Clear Creek Bapt. Sch., Pine Valley, Ky., 1943-44, Campbellsville Coll., 1945-46, So. Bapt. Theol. Sem., 1956. Ordained to ministry, 1946. Pastor, First Bapt. Ch., Friendsville, Tenn., 1946-51, Tenn. Ave. Bapt. Ch., Knoxville, 1951-55, McPheeters Bend Bapt. Ch., Church Hill, Tenn., 1965-67, First Bapt. Ch., Kuttawa, Ky., 1967-68, Beaumont Ave. Bapt. Ch., Knoxville, 1968-71, Buffalo Trail Bapt. Ch., Morristown, Tenn., 1971-73, Forest Hill Bapt. Ch., Maryville, Tenn., 1973-76, First Bapt. Ch., Philadelphia, Tenn., 1970-73, North Athens Bapt. Ch., Tenn., 1973-75, White Plains Bapt. Ch., Scottsville, Ky., 1975-78, Indian Creek Bapt. Ch., Flippin, Ky., 1979—; moderator Chillihowee Bapt. Assn., Maryville, 1975-76, Loudon County Bapt. Assn., Philadelphia, Tenn., 1977-78, Allen Bapt. Assn., Scottsville, Ky., 1981-82, Monroe Bapt. Assn., Flippin, 1983-84. Author: Philadelphia History, 1822-1973, 1978; The Joy of Being His, 1980; Looking Upward, 1982; Lord Teach Me to Pray, 1984. Address: Rural Route 4 Flippin KY 42132

HAGAN, WILLIAM REECE, minister, Southern Baptist Convention; b. Larue County, Ky., July 23, 1936; s. William Stuben and Bertha May (Lafollette) H.; B.S., Campbellsville (Ky.) Coll., 1964; m. Rachel Alice Gilpin, Feb. 8, 1957; children—William David, Timothy Wayne. Ordained to ministry, 1960; pastor Dunbar Hill Bapt. Ch., Knifley, Ky., 1960-64; chmn. Knifley Area Revival Crusade, 1963; supply preaching and interim pastorates, 1965-67; pastor Van Buren (Ky.) Bapt. Ch., 1968-70, 73-81, supply preacher, 1971-72. Chmn. Christian lit. com. Russel Creek Bapt. Assn., 1962-63; chmn. stewardship com. Anderson Bapt. Assn., 1973-74, also mem. exec. bd.; moderator Anderson Bapt. Assn., 1979-80; organizer William R. Hagan Evangelistic Ministry, 1981; gospel radio broadcaster, 1982—. Editor, pub. Gospel Voice Newsletter. Tchr. Taylorsville (Ky.) Jr. High Sch. Chmn., Spencer County Educators Pub. Affairs Council, 1976—. Mem. Ky., Fifth Dist. (Pres.'s Plaque award 1971) edn. assns. Contbr. letters to religious publs. Home: Box 528 Washington St Taylorsville KY 40071

HAGEMAN, HOWARD GARBERICH See *Who's Who in America*, 43rd edition.

HAGEMAN, LOUISE, nun, Roman Catholic Church; b. Willowdale, Kans., Nov. 26, 1932; d. Fred and Louise (Schulte) H. Student Sacred Heart Coll., 1950-52, postgrad. 1959-60; B.A. summa cum laude, Marymount Coll., 1961; M.A., Duquesne U., 1972; postgrad. Immaculate Conception Coll., 1956, Notre Dame U., 1964, 65, Aquinas Inst. Theology, 1975, Eastern Christianity Cour, 1975. Joined Dominican Sisters, Roman Catholic Ch., 1948. Tchr. elem. sch., Kans., 1951-66; novice directress Dominican Sisters, Great Bend, Kans., 1966-69, 72-78, formation asst., Nigeria, 1977, prioress, pres., 1978—; chaplain Alcohol Treatment Ctr., Norton, Kans., 1976; presenter workshops, 1974-85; bd. dirs. Sister Formation Conf., 1974-75; mem. task force Ordination Conf., Detroit, 1975; chmn. Nat. Sisters Formation Conf., 1976-77; chmn. Community Days for Dialogue, Great Bend, 1978—; bd. dirs. Study Days in Dominican Life, 1970's; mem. commn. Dominican Leadership Conf., Ecclesial Study of Preaching and Related Ministries, 1976-78. Author: In the Midst of Winter, 1976 (Thomas More Book of Month award 1976). Contbr. articles to mags. Facilitator, Stateside Women's Day, Wichita, Kans., 1975; ex-officio bd. dirs. pres. St. Catherine Hosp., Garden City, Kans., 1978—, St. Joseph Meml. Hosp., Larned, Kans., 1978—, Central Kans. Med. Ctr., Great Bend, 1978—, Cedar Park Place, Great Bend, 1978—, Home Health, Great Bend, 1978—. Recipient Outstanding Service at Time of Flood award City of Great Bend, 1981. Mem. Leadership Conf. of Religious Women (mem. Ecclesial Role of Women Commn. 1978-81, chmn. region XIII 1983-85, mem. nat. bd., mem. nuclear protest com. 1983, sponsor election workshop 1984). Democrat. Home: 3600 Broadway Great Bend KS 67530

HAGEMANN, DAVID ROLAND, minister, American Lutheran Ch. B. Lawton, Okla., Dec. 2, 1954, S. Robert Floyd and Lorraine Ann (Kolczaski) H. B.A. in Psychology, Wartburg Coll., 1977; M.Div., Wartburg Theol. Sem., 1981. Ordained to ministry American Luth. Ch., 1981. Intermin pastor St. Paul's Luth. Ch., Wauzeka, Wis., 1980-81; pastor Revere and Trinity Luth. Chs., Revere, Minn., 1981—; bd. dirs. St. John Luth. Home, Springfield, Minn., 1983—. Author: One Hundred Thirty Years, 1979. Home: Box 66 Revere MN 56166 Office: Revere-Trinity Parish Box 66 Revere MN 56166

HAGEN, JOHN HOLTE, pastor, American Lutheran Church. B. Crookston, Minn., Aug. 7, 1933; s. George Toralf and Evelyn Irene (Holte) H.; m. Diane Louise Reinertson, Dec. 22, 1961; children: Mark Reinertson, Kristin Anne. Student Sophia U., Tokyo, 1951-52; B.A. cum laude, St. Olaf Coll., 1956; J.D. with honors, George Washington U., 1960; B.D. with honors, Trinity Sem., Columbus, Ohio, 1965; M.Phil., Ohio State U., 1967; student U. Edinburgh, 1969-73. Ordained to ministry American Lutheran Church, 1973. Pastor Gol Luth. Ch., Kenyon, Minn., 1973—, Grace Luth. Ch., Nerstrand, Minn., 1973—; chmn. life and mission com. Cannon River Conf., Am. Luth. Ch., 1974-78; sec. life and mission com. Southeastern Minn. dist. Am. Luth. Ch., 1976. Editor Cannon Report newspaper, 1976-81. Chmn. Democratic Farmer Labor party Kenyon Twp., 1974—; mem. Dem. Farmer Labor central com. State of Minn., 1980-84. Mem. Kenyon, Minn. Ministerium (pres. 1974—). Lodge: Lions (pres. 1983-84). Home and Office: Rural Route 2 Box 8 Kenyon MN 55946

HAGEY, WALTER R., lay worker, Lutheran Church in America; banker; b. Hatfield, Pa., July 24, 1909; s. Justus T. and Martha M. (Scheetz) H.; m. Dorothy E. Rosenberger, Oct. 17, 1931; 1 child, Donald C. Student, Pierce Jr. Coll., 1929; cert. proficiency U. Pa., 1936; LL.B., LaSalle Extension U., 1938; S.T.B., Temple U., 1943; postgrad. Rutgers U., Stonier Grad. Sch. of Banking, 1951; LL.D. (hon.), Muhlenberg Coll., 1963. Treas. Eastern Pa. Synod Luth. Ch. Am., 1950-68, Bethesda House, 1950-68, Luth. Children and Family Services Eastern Pa., 1950-68, Luth. Camp Corp. Eastern Pa., 1950-68, Luth. Synod Southeastern Pa. Luth. Ch. Am., 1969-80; gen. supt. Grace Luth. Ch. Sch., Hatfield, Pa., 1930-65; bd. dirs. Pa. Council Chs., 1954-70; treas. Luth. Laymens Movement for Stewardship United Luth. Ch. Am., 1959-63, Luth. Retirement Homes, Inc., 1978-82; councilor Luth. Council U.S.A., 1962-74, exec. com. 1970-74; vice chmn. Office Adminstrn. and Fin., Luth. Ch. Am., 1972-78; v.p. Bd. Am. Missions, 1972-78, mem. com. for investments, 1978-82, bd. pensions, 1978-84; sec. Martin Luther Sch., Silver Springs, Pa., 1976—; registrar Penn Luth. Sch., 1981—. Vice pres. Fidelity Bank, Phila., 1966-74. Bd. dirs. Prosser Found., 1968; mem. Phila. Estate Planning Council. Mem. Luth. Hist. Soc. Eastern Pa. (bd. dirs.), Luth. Social Union Phila. (past pres., bd. dirs.), Pa. Bible Soc. (sec.-treas. 1966-71, pres. 1983—), Men of Mounty Airy Sem. (pres. 1976—). Republican. Club: Anglers of Phila. Lodge: Rotary. Home: 510 E Lawn Ave Lansdale PA 19446 Office: Pa Bible Soc 701 Walnut St Philadelphia PA 19106

HAGLUND, VIRGINIA DAWN, church musician, Seventh-day Adventist; dental hygienist and assistant; b. National City, Calif., Aug. 15, 1948; d. Francis Raleigh Edwards and Marianne Elizabeth (Lindsay) Humphrey; m. Thomas Ernest Haglund, Dec. 22, 1968 (div. 1978); 1 son, Andrew Thomas. A.A., Loma Linda U., 1971, B.S., 1984. Vocalist, soloist La Mesa Seventh-day Adventist Ch. Choir, Calif., 1960-66, Loma Linda U. Freshman Singers, Riverside Calif., 1966-67, Loma Linda U. Chamber Singers, 1967-68, Loma Linda U. Sanctuary Choir, 1977-79, 80—. Registered dental hygienist and dental asst., Palm Springs, Riverside, San Bernardino, Ridgecrest, Calif., 1984—. Calif. Masonic Found. scholar, 1983. Mem. Am. Dental Hygiene Assn., So. Calif. Dental Hygienists Assn., Tri-County Dental Hygiene and Assistants Soc., Am. Dental Assistants Soc., Nat. Assn. Dental Assistants, So. Calif. Dental Assistants Assn. Republican. Club: Loma Linda Lopers (treas. 1981). Office: c/o Donald Reid DDS 128 Silver Ridge Ridgecrest CA 93555

HAGMANN, JAMES JEROME, priest Roman Catholic Church; b. Eau Claire, Wis., May 4, 1932; s. Michael Joseph and Mary Laurentia (Stopfer) H. B.A., St. Francis Sem., 1954. Ordained priest Roman Catholic Church, 1958. Assoc. pastor Diocese of LaCrosse, Wis., 1958-70; pastor St. John the Baptist, Marshfield, Wis., 1970-82, St. Stanislaus, Arcadia, Wis., St. Marys Assumption, Durand, Wis., 1982—; diocesan chaplain KC, Marshfield, Wis., 1971-73; dean Arcadia Deanery, Diocese of LaCrosse, Arcadia, 1978-82. Lodge: KC (chaplain). Address: 911 W Prospect St Durand WI 54736

HAIFLICH, STEVAN RICHARD, minister, United Methodist Church. B. Bluffton, Ind., July 13, 1948; s. Richard Edward and Dorma Mae (Hoppingarner) H.; m. Cynthia Ann Harris, May 29, 1970 (div. 1976); children: Phillip, Andrew; m. Ruby May Wilcott, Dec. 18, 1977; children: Ramona O'Donnell, David O'Donnell. B.A., Taylor U., 1970; M.Div., Asbury Theol. Sem., 1974. Ordained to ministry United Methodist Church, 1977. Dir. Calaski Parish, Science Hill, Ky., 1974-77; asst. supt. Meth. Mountain Missions, Jackson, Ky., 1977-81; pastor Main St. United Meth. Ch., Redkey, Ind., 1981—; pres. Pulaski County Ministerial Assn., Somerset, Ky., 1977; dist. dir. Church and Society Conf., Lexington, 1976-81; dir. Hazard Community Ministers, Ky., 1977-79; town and country rep. North Ind. Conf., Marion, 1984—. Contbr. articles to profl. jours. Vice pres. Lake Cumberland Home Health Assn., Somerset, 1976; pres. Mental Health Assn. of Jay County, Portland, Ind., 1982-84. Republican. Lodges: Lions (pres. 1984-85), Masons. Home: 122 W Main St Redkey IN 47373

HAIG, FRANK RAWLE, priest, educator, Roman Catholic Ch.; b. Phila., Sept. 11, 1928; s. Alexander Meigs and Regina Ann (Murphy) H.; A.B., Woodstock Coll., 1952, S.T.L., 1961; Ph.L., Bellarmine Coll., 1953; Ph.D., Catholic U. Am., 1958. Joined Soc. of Jesus, 1946; ordained priest Roman Catholic Ch., 1960; asst. prof. physics Wheeling (W.Va.) Coll., 1963-66, pres., 1966-72; vis. fellow dept. physics Johns Hopkins, 1972; asst. prof. physics Loyola Coll., Balt., 1972-74, assoc. prof., 1974-81; pres. LeMoyne Coll., Syracuse, N.Y., 1981—. Bd. visitors USAF Acad., 1970-73; pres. Syracuse Opera Co., 1983-85, bd. chair, 1985—; bd. dirs. Syracuse Symphony, 1982—; gen. chair United Way Campaign of Central N.Y., 1985-86. Recipient Harry J. Carman award Middle State Council Social Studies, 1985; NSF fellow, 1962-63. Mem. Wheeling Area C. of C. (pres. 1969-71), W.Va. Assn Colls. and Univs. (pres. 1970-71), Am. Assn. Physics Tchrs., Am. Phys. Soc., AAUP (1st v.p. Md. conf. 1979-81), Theta Chi Beta, Sigma Xi. Contbr. articles to religious and profl. jours. Address: LeMoyne Coll Syracuse NY 13214

HAIGHT, DAVID B., church official. Mem. Quorum of the Twelve, The Church of Jesus Christ of Latter-day Saints. Office: The Church of Jesus Christ of Latter-Day Saints 50 E North Temple St Salt Lake City UT 84150*

HAIGHT, LARRY LEROY, religion educator, librarian, Assemblies of God. b. Alva, Okla., July 13, 1950; s. LeRoy James and Alta Maria (Stallings) H.; m. Rebecca Louise Figuli, Aug. 5, 1972; children: Matthew David, Michael Darin. B.A., Central Bible Coll., Springfield, Mo., 1972; M.A. in Bibl. Langs., Assemblies of God Theol. Sem., 1978; M.A. in Library Sci., U. Mo.-Columbia, 1983. Ordained to ministry Assemblies of God 1972. Asst. pastor Painesville Assembly of God, Ohio, 1972-75; adj. faculty Assemblies of God Theol. Sem., Springfield, Mo., 1978—, librarian, 1980—. Author: Pentecostal Periodicals in the Assemblies of God Libraries and Archives in Springfield, Missouri, 1983. Mem. Am. Theol. Library Assn., Springfield Area Librarians Assn. (pres. 1982-83), Delta Epsilon Chi, Beta Phi Mu. Home: 1400 S Plaza St Springfield MO 65804 Office: Cordas C Burnett Library Assemblies of God Theol Sem 1445 Boonville Ave Springfield MO 65802

HAIL, FRANCINA KERHEVILLE, minister, academic dean, Christian Church (Disciples of Christ); b. Albuquerque, Nov. 12, 1934; d. Frances Monroe and Christina (Johnson) K.; m. Thomas Joseph Hail, Oct. 11, 1956. B.A., U. N.Mex., 1956, M.A., 1959, Ph.D., 1977. Ordained to ministry Evang. Ch. Alliance, 1976, Christian Ch. (Disciples of Christ), 1981. Christian edn. dir. Christian Ctr., Albuquerque, 1975-76; assoc. minister Bible Teaching Ctr., Albuquerque, 1977-78, Los Altos Christian Ch., Albuquerque, 1980-81; pastor Covenant Christian Ch., Albuquerque, 1982—; acad. dean Albuquerque Bibl. Studies Inst., 1979—, pres. bd. dirs., 1985—; vol. chaplain Bernalillo County Detention, Albuquerque, 1979-80. Sec. bd. Vol. Police Chaplain, Albuquerque, 1979-80. Mem. Am. Hist. Soc., Ministers Fellowship of Albuquerque, Bibl. Archaelogy Soc., Albuquerque Ministerial Alliance. Home: 8810 James St NE Albuquerque NM 87111 Office: Covenant Christian Ch Alliance 8516 Trumball St SE Albuquerque NM 87108

HAILE, PETER KENNETH, religious educator, minister Congregational Church; b. Tiger Kloof, South Africa; s. Alfred John and Adelaide Ethel (Palmer) H.; m. Jane Hollingsworth, May 7, 1954; children: John Hollingsworth, Rebecca Jane. B.A., Oxford U., 1950, M.A., 1960; D.D., Eastern Coll., St. Davids, Pa., 1979. Ordained to ministry Congregational Church, 1963. Staff mem. Inter-Varsity Christian Fellowship, Chgo., 1951-61; tchr. Bible, chaplain Stony Brook Sch. (N.Y.), 1961—. Trustee, Latin Am. Mission, Coral Gables, 1969—, chmn., 1976-80; trustee Fellowship Christians in Univs. and Schs., Greenwich, Conn., 1979—, chn., 1982—. Author: The Difference God Makes, 1981; contbr. articles to profl. jours. Served with Brit. Navy, 1943-47. Home: 5 New York Ave Stony Brook NY 11790 Office: Stony Brook Sch Stony Brook NY 11790

HAILES, EDWARD ALEXANDER, minister, American Baptist Churches; b. Petersburg, Va., Mar. 26, 1925; s. Walter Franklin and Maggie Otelia (Pierce) H.; certificate Va. State Coll., 1946; B.A., Va. Union U., 1950; postgrad. Harvard, 1952-54, Boston U., 1961; certificate adminstrn. and mgmt. Howard U., 1965; m. Nettie Drayton, June 23, 1946; children—Edward Alexander, Gregory, Patricia. Ordained to ministry, 1951; assoc. pastor Ebenezer Bapt. Ch., New Brunswick, N.J., 1946-51; pastor Union Bapt. Ch., New Bedford, Mass., 1951-63; assoc. pastor Zion Bapt. Ch., Washington, 1964, now assoc. pastor 19th St. Bapt. Ch., Washington; dir. ops. Opportunities Industrialization Center, Washington, 1966-68, exec. dir., 1968—. Supr. religious edn. Inter-Ch. Council Greater New Bedford, Mass., 1954-61, exec. sec., 1961; chmn. promotion and finance dept. United Bapt. Conv. Mass. and R.I., 1960-63. Vice-chmn. Project Build, Washington, 1969—; mem. Mayor's Adv. Com. on Project Home, Washington, 1973—, D.C. Citizens United for Progress, 1976—; mem. Adv. Panel for Adult Edn. Demonstration Project, Washington, 1974—; mem. Health and Welfare Council, Washington, 1969—; bd. dirs. Housing Devel. Corp., Washington; pres. Charitable Found., United Supreme Council, Scottish Rite, Prince Hall Affiliation, 1984—; bd. dirs. D.C. Street Acad. Recipient award D.C. C. of C., 1963, Certificate of Recognition, Inter-Ch. Council, 1963, Merit award Inter-Denominational Ch. Ushers Assn. Washington, 1964, award Nat. Postal Alliance, 1966, Freedom Fund Com. award NAACP, D.C. br., 1966, Family award Hearts, Inc., Washington, 1966, Distinguished Service award United Supreme Council, Ancient and Accepted Scottist Rite of Fremasonry, Prince Hall Affiliation, 1970. Mem. NAACP (nat. dir. 1969—, nat. v.p. 1980—, pres. D.C. 1978—), Va. Union U. Alumni Assn. (vice-chmn. D.C. chpt. 1976—), D.C. C. of C. (bd. dirs.). Home: 1439 Roxanna Rd NW Washington DC 20012 Office: 3224 16th St NW Washington DC 20010

HAINES, PAUL LOWELL, educational administrator, United Methodist Church; b. Tokyo, Japan, Jan. 10, 1953; s. Paul Whitfield and Florence Alice (Hall) H.; m. Sherryl Ann Karomacher, Aug. 16, 1975. B.A., Taylor U., 1975, M.A., Ball State U., 1977. Residence hall dir. Taylor U., Upland, Ind., 1977-80, dir. student programs, 1980-83, dean of students, 1983—, founder, co-dir., Nat. Student Leadership Conf. for Christian Colls., 1981-84, presenter Christian Artists Music Seminar, Estes Park, Colo., 1982. Mem. Assn. for Christians in Student Devel. (presenter nat. conf. 1983), Nat. Assn. Student Personnel Adminstrs., Am. Personnel and Guidance Assn. Republican. Home: 807 Valhalla Dr Upland IN 46989 Office: Dean of Students Taylor U Upland IN 46989

HAIRE, FRANKLIN, minister, So. Bapt. Conv.; b. Leitchfield, Ky., Oct. 26, 1923; s. Carmel and Laura Bel (Reeves) H.; B.A., Miss. Coll., 1948; Ed.M., 1967 M.A., 1972; m. Nell Yarborough, Jan. 18, 1945 children—Truett, Nan (Mrs. W.H. Boutwell), Cela (Mrs. Anthony Smith), Albert Alan, Timothy Franklin Nola Gail. Ordained to ministry, 1945; pastor Escatawpa Bapt. Ch., Escatawpa, Ala., 1944-45; pastor various chs. in Miss., 1945-53, Providence Bapt. Ch. 1953—. Founder, headmaster Franklin Christian Acad. Roxie, Miss., 1969; guidance counselor Franklin County (Miss.) Schs., 1971—. Chmn. area-wide Evangelistic Crusades, 1960, 63. Mem. Franklin Bapt Assn. (clk. 1954—), Miss. Edn. Assn. (chpt. pres 1967-69). Home: Rt 2 Meadville MS 39653 Office: Rt 2 Box 116 Meadville MS 39653

HAIT, PAUL L., rabbi; exec. dir. New York Bd. of Rabbis, also mem. exec. council. Office: New York Bd Rabbis 10 E 73rd St New York NY 10021*

HAKES, LARRY ALLEN, minister, United Methodist Church. B. Chippewa Falls, Wis., Oct. 24, 1956; s. Lawrence Oliver and Ruby Alice (Taylor) H.; m. Elizabeth Anne Hershaw, Aug. 7, 1982; 1 child, Jessie Anne. A.S., U. Wis.-Barron County, 1977; B.A., U. Wis.-Eau Claire, 1979; M.Div., United Theol. Sem. 1982. Ordained to ministry United Meth. Ch., ordained as deacon, 1981, ordained as elder, 1984. Youth minister First United Meth. Ch., Barron, Wis., 1976-79 South Haven/Kimball United Meth. Chs., South Haven, Minn., 1979-80; sem. intern Parkview United Ch. of Christ, White Bear Lake, Minn., 1980-81; team coordinator vacation Ch. Sch., Wis. Conf. United Meth Ch., 1981; pastor Balsam Lake/Centuria United Meth Chs., Balsam Lake, Centuria, Wis., 1981—; sec Christian Edn. Commn., Wis. Conf., 1981—; young adult coordinator N.W. Dist. Council on Ministries Wis. Conf., 1982—; dist. rep. Commn. Christian Unity and Inter-Relations Concerns, Wis. Conf. United Meth Ch., 1983—. Bd. dirs. Kinship Polk County, Wis. 1983-85, v.p., 1984-85; supr. Unity Tentmaker Project Balsam Lake, Wis., 1982-83. Mem. Polk County Ministerial Assn. Independent. Home and Office: Rural Route 1 Box 105 Balsam Lake WI 54810

HALAAS, DAVID ROLF, pastor, American Lutheran Church. B. Havre, Mont., Oct. 15, 1954; s. Russel Edward and Mary Helen (Brenden) H.; m. Janet Ruth Olson, Jan. 30, 1976; children: Katie, Joseph. B.A. Augsburg Coll., 1976; M.Div., Trinity Luth. Sem. Columbus, Ohio, 1980. Ordained to ministry Am. Luth Ch., 1980. Pastor, Osakis Luth. Ch., Minn., 1980-83 First Luth. Ch., Marshall, Minn., 1983—; dist coordinator hunger appeal S.W. Minn. dist. Am. Luth Ch., 1982—, chmn. ch. in soc. com., 1984—. Mem. Am Revolution Bicentennial Com., Washington, D.C. 1976; com. mem. Douglas County Hosp. Bd. Alexandria, Minn., 1981-83. Minnesota Democratic Farm Labor. Lodge: Kiwanis (bd. dirs. 1983—). Home 500 N High St Marshall MN 56258 Office: First Luth Ch 100 Church St Marshall MN 56258

HALDANE, ROBERT, JR., minister, National Association of Congregational Christian Churches; b. Rumford, Maine, Apr. 12, 1928; s. Robert and Inez Alice (Elwell) H.; m. Marian Jennie Jordan, Aug. 15, 1948; children: Robert, John L., Mark T., Patricia J., Karen I. B.A., U. Maine, 1953; M.Div., Bangor Theol. Sem., 1953; D.D. (hon.), Piedmont Coll., 1982. Ordained to ministry, 1953. Student pastor Federated Ch., Millbridge, Maine, 1948-51; pastor First Congl. Ch., North Anson, Maine, 1951-53; minister Orthodox Congl. Ch., Manchester, Mass., 1953-57, Arbor Grove Congl. Ch., Jackson, Mich., 1957-79, Congl. Ch. of Messiah, Los Angeles, 1979—; moderator Central Mich. Assn. Congl. Christian Chs., 1961, Mich. Conf. 1968, Cal-West Assn., 1984; dir., exec. com. Nat. Assn. Congl. Christian Chs., 1979-84. Editor religious column: The Free Lance, 1954-56. Contbr. articles to profl. jours. Cons. editor The Congl. Jour., 1979—. Chaplain, CAP, Mich., 1958-71; pres. Better Housing Com., Jackson, Mich., 1961-67; founder, exec. couple Mich. Inter-Faith Marriage Encounter, 1976-79. Fellow Am. Congl. Ctr. Clubs: High Twelve, Sertoma. Lodges: KT (chief shepherd), Masons. Home: 7257 W 90th St Los Angeles CA 90045 Office: Congl Ch of Messiah 7300 W Manchester Ave Los Angeles CA 90045

HALE, JOE, church executive, United Methodist Church; b. Texarkana, Tex., Mar. 25, 1935; s. Alfred Clay and Bess (Akin) H.; m. Mary Richey, June 2, 1964; 1 child, Jeffrey Glen. B.A., Asbury Coll., 1957; B.D., So. Meth. U., 1960; D.D. (hon.), Asbury Theol. Sem., 1978 Ordained deacon United Meth. Ch., 1958, elder, 1960 Staff evangelist Bd. Evangelism, United Meth. Ch., Nashville, 1960-66, assoc. dir. dept. evangelism, 1966-68, dir. ecumenical evangelism, 1968-74, dir. evangelization devel. Bd. of Discipleship, 1975; gen. sec. World Meth. Council, Lake Junaluska, N.C. 1976—; mem. exec. com. Key '73, 1970-73; pres Communications Found., Inc., Burbank, Calif., 1974-75; world ambassador Internat. Prayer Fellowship, 1974; trustee Asbury Theol. Sem., Wilmore, Ky., 1981—; chmn. Conf. of Secs. Christian World Communions, Geneva, 1983—. Author: Design for Evangelism, 1970; Christ Matters, 1971; God's Monent, 1972. Producer (films) Roots of Faith, 1979;

The Spirit is Moving, 1981; To Live To God, 1984. Recipient Key to City, Daytona Beach, Fla., 1963, 64, Asbury Alumni award Asbury Coll., 1977. Home: 301 Forest Park Dr Waynesville NC 28786 Office: World Meth Council PO Box 518 39 Lakeshore Dr Lake Junalaska NC

HALEY, MARY JOAN, religious educator, nun, Roman Catholic Church; b. Bklyn., June 22, 1917; d. Patrick Joseph and Helen (Collins) Haley. B.A., Good Counsel Coll., 1941; M.S., Fordham U., 1950, Iona Coll., 1969; D.H.L. (hon.), Pace U., 1983. Tchr., Mt. Carmel Sch., Elmsford, N.Y., 1937-46, Good Counsel High Sch., White Plains, N.Y., 1946-64; formation dir. Sisters of Divine Compassion, White Plains, 1954-70; asst. prof. Pace U., White Plains, 1970-76; gen. superior Sisters of Divine Compassion, White Plains, 1976-84, gen. treas., 1984—; dir. Religious Studies Ctr. of Pace U., 1972-76. Mem. Nat. Orgn. Treas. Religious Insts., Council of Women Religious (exec. com., v.p. 1982-84). Address: 52 N Broadway White Plains NY 10603

HALIVNI, DAVID WEISS, rabbi, theology educator; b. Romania, Dec. 21, 1928; came to U.S., 1947; s. Callel Wiederman and Fanny Weiss; m. Ann Hager, Dec. 9, 1953; children: Bernard, Ephraim, Isaiah. B.A., Bklyn. Coll., 1953; M.A., NY U, 1956; D.H.L., Jewish Theol. Sem., 1957. Prof. The Jewish Theol. Sem. of Am., N.Y.C., 1968—; adj. prof. Columbia U., N.Y.C., 1968—. Guggenheim fellow, 1970; NEH fellow, 1980. Mem. Am. Acad. Jewish Research (v.p.).

HALL, CECIL EDWARD, minister, So. Baptist Conv.; b. Aiken County, S.C., Sept. 15, 1913; s. Carlos Edward and Maggie Cyntia (Wall) H.; student U. S.C., 1938; diploma sacred music, New Orleans Bapt. Theol. Sem., 1946; m. Carolyn Louise Long, Feb. 10, 1940; 1 dau., Sylvia Jean. Licensed to ministry, 1966; minister edn., youth and music chs. in Ga., N.C. and S.C., 1949-68; minister edn., youth and music Grace Bapt. Ch., Sumter, S.C., 1968-75, Bethel Bapt. Ch., Sumter, 1975—. Pres. S.C. Bapt. Tng. Union, 1969. Mem. So., Eastern, S.C. Bapt. religious edn. assns. Author articles. Home: 210 Winn St Sumter SC 29150 Office: Route 2 Box 709 Sumter SC 29150

HALL, DOUGLAS JOHN, minister, United Church of Canada, educator; b. Ingersoll, Ont., Mar. 23, 1928; s. John Darius and Louisa Irene (Sandick) H.; m. Rhoda Catherine Palfrey, May 28, 1960; children: Mary Kate, Christopher, Sara, Lucia. B.A., U. Western Ont., 1953; M.Div., Union Sem., N.Y.C., 1956, S.T.M., 1957, Th.D., 1963. Ordained to ministry United Ch. of Can., 1956. Minister St. Andrew's Ch., Blind River, Ont., 1960-62; prin. St. Paul's Coll., Waterloo, Ont., 1962-65; prof. St. Andrew's Coll., Saskatoon, Sask., 1965-75; prof. Christian theology McGill U., Montreal, Can., 1975—. Author: Hope Against Hope, 1969; The Reality of the Gospel and the Unreality of the Churches, 1975; Lighten Our Darkness: Towards an Indigenous Theology of the Cross, 1976; Has the Church a Future?, 1980; The Canada Crisis, 1981; Ecclesia Crucis, 1979; The Steward: A Biblical Symbol Come of Age, 1982. Mem. Can. Theol. Soc. New Democratic Party Can. Home: 5562 Ave Notre-Dame-de-Grace NDG Montreal Que H3A 1L7 Canada Office: McGill Univ 3520 University St Montreal Que H3A 2A7 Canada

HALL, HAROLD ARTHUR, radio broadcaster, Evangelical Free Church America; b. Chgo., May 13, 1938; s. Wendell Gladstone and Margaret Elisabeth (Asplund) H.; m. Marjorie Alice Neff, Jan. 16, 1960; children: Steven Arthur, Nancy Ruth, Roger Alan, Daniel Craig. A.A., San Jose City Coll., 1958. FCC gen. radio telephone operator license. Announcer, bd. operator Family Stas. Inc., San Francisco, 1959-65; program dir., announcer Air Network, Glendale, Calif., 1965-66; announcer, continuity dir. Family Stas. Inc., Oakland, 1966—; producer, host Christian Home, Life with Meaning, Radio Reading Circle; vol. cons. broadcast media Internat. Council Bibl. Inerrancy, Oakland, 1984—; mem. adv. bd. Star Song Enterprises, San Jose, Calif., 1983-84; ch. officer Evang. Free Ch. San Jose, 1966—, tchr., 1966—, home Bible study leader, 1978—. Served with USCGR, 1956-64. Republican. Avocations: gardening; writing. Office: Family Stas Inc 290 Hegenberger Rd Oakland CA 94621

HALL, JAMES LELAND, minister, Southern Baptist Convention. b. Little Rock, Ark., Dec. 12, 1923; s. James Wesley and Ruth Adelia (Hale) H.; m. Bette Jo Cochran, May 28, 1946; children: Bette Lee, Alma, Jim, Lydia, Hal. B.A., Ouachita U., 1945; B.D., So. Bapt. Sem., 1948, Th.M., 1949, M.Div., 1974; D.Ministry, Luther Rice Sem., 1976. Ordained to ministry So. Bapt. Conv. 1942. Pastor various chs., Ark., Ind., Ky., Okla., Mo., 1941-71, First Bapt. Ch., Melbourne, Fla., 1971—; trustee So. Bapt. Coll., Walnut Ridge, Ark., 1959-66, S.W. Bapt. U., Bolivar, Mo., 1963-70, instr., 1963-70; mem. adminstrv. com. of the exec. com. So. Bapt. Conv. Republican. Lodges: Kiwanis, Rotary. Home: 155 Bry Lynn Dr Melbourne FL 32901 Office: First Bapt Ch PO Box 366 Melbourne FL 32901

HALL, JOSEPH HILL, elder, educator, Presbyterian Church in America; b. Orlando, Fla., June 2, 1933; s. Robert Bryan and Fannie Emmons (Humphreys) H.; A.B., Calvin Coll., 1960; M.Div., Covenant Theol. Sem., 1970; Th.D., Concordia Sem., St. Louis, 1974; m. Hermina Shirley Kempema, Dec. 28, 1960; children—Timothy, Steven. Assoc. prof. ch. history, librarian Covenant Theol. Sem., St. Louis, 1968—; librarian U. Iowa, Iowa City, 1964-68. Mem. Christian sch. bds. Mem. Presbyn. Hist. Soc., Am. Soc. Ch. History, Calvin Studies, Evang. Theol. Sem. Home: 826 Crestland St Ballwin MO 63011 Office: 12330 Conway Rd Saint Louis MO 63141

HALL, LARRY BRUCE, minister, United Methodist Ch. B. Georgetown, Ky., Dec. 11, 1942; s. Bruce Browning and Juanita Ann (Patrick) H.; m. Sara Kay Yarbrough, Mar. 26, 1966; children: Larissa Kathleen, Larry Bruce. B.A., Georgetown Coll., 1964; postgrad., Lexington Theol. Sem., 1974-75; M.Div., Emory U., Atlanta, 1977, postgrad., 1977-78. Ordained elder United Methodist Ch., 1979. Pastor, Centerville United Meth. Ch., Paris, Ky., 1974-75; assoc. pastor Sandy Springs United Meth. Ch., Atlanta, 1975-77, United Meth. Ch., Pampa, Tex., 1977-80; pastor Agape United Meth. Ch., Lubbock, Tex., 1980-82; sr. pastor First United Meth. Ch., Dumas, Tex., 1982—; dir. Wesley Found. West Tex. State U., Canyon, 1978-80; chmn. evangelism Lubbock Dist. United Meth. Ch., 1980-82, ethnic minority religion and race Northwest Tex. Conf. United Meth. Ch., 1982—, leadership devel. Amarillo Dist. United Meth. Ch., Tex., 1983—, chmn. ch. extension and devel., 1982-85. Editor Theol. Thoughts newspaper, Acad. of Faith bible study series, Resource Guide for Services in the Tex. Panhandle. Bd. dirs. County Child Welfare Bd., Dumas, 1983—, Mental Health Workshop, Dumas, 1983—, YMCA, Dumas, 1984—; founding dir. Council on Volunteerism, Dumas, 1984—. Served to capt. U.S. Army, 1965-69. Recipient Ky. Col. award State of Ky., 1972, Youth Leadership award Northwest Tex. Conf. United Meth. Ch., 1980, Evangelism Growth award Northwest Tex. Conf. United Meth. Ch., 1981, 82, 83, Outstanding Service award United Meth. Coll. Assn. of Tex., 1984. Mem. Fellowship for Reconciliation, Christian Educators Fellowship. Democrat. Lodge: Lions. Home: 220 Carson Ave Dumas TX 79029 Office: First United Meth Ch PO Box 395 Dumas TX 79029

HALL, RICHARD CLYDE, JR., religious educational administrator, Southern Baptist Convention; b. Florence, Ala., Apr. 13, 1931; s. Richard Clyde Sr. and Annie Hazel (Darrah) H.; m. Mildred Marie Denham, May 19, 1957; children: Richard Denham, Darralyn Marie, Kevin Clyde, Edward Earnest. A.A., U. Fla., 1950, B.A., 1953; M.R.E., Southwestern Bapt. Theol. Sem., 1958, D.R.E., 1966, Ed.D., 1975, M.A., 1984. Ordained to gospel ministry, 1955. Youth dir. 1st Bapt. Ch., Miami, Fla., 1953; ednl. sec., youth dir. Avenue J Bapt. Ch., Fort Worth, 1953-54; dir. Bapt. Student Union, Fla. Bapt. Conv., Jacksonville, Fla., 1954-57; minister edn. Eastover Bapt. Ch., Fort Worth, 1957-61, 1st Bapt. Ch., Elizabethton, Tenn., 1961-63, Gambrell Street Bapt. Ch., Fort Worth, 1963-65; assoc. ch. tng. dept. Bapt. Gen. Conv. Tex., Dallas, 1965-72, sec. ch. tng. dept., 1972-73; mgmt. cons. Pro, Inc., San Diego, 1973-74; cons. adult work ch. tng. dept. Bapt. Sunday Sch. Bd., Nashville, 1974-75, cons. gen. adminstrn. ch. tng. dept., 1975-76, supr. youth sect. ch. tng. dept., 1976—; teaching fellow religious psychology and drama Southwestern Bapt. Theol. Sem., Fort Worth, 1960-61; instr. youth edn. Sem. Extension, 1981—. Author: Source, 1967-70; Church Training, 1970—; (cassette and workbook) The Work of the Associational Age Group Leader, 1980; (filmstrips) DiscipleLife: Training Youth in Discipleship, 1981; DiscipleLife, 1984. Compiler: Youth Leadership Training Pak, 1982, DiscipleHelps: A DiscipleYouth Daily Quiet Time Guide and Journal, 1985; (with Joe Ford) DiscipleYouth Kit, 1982, DiscipleYouth Notebook, 1982, Disciple Youth II Kit, 1985, DiscipleYouth II Notebook, 1985. Mem. So. Bapt. Religious Edn. Assn. (sec.-treas. 1982-83), Eastern Bapt. Religious Edn. Assn. (sec.-treas. 1975-79, pres. 1980), Southwestern Bapt. Religious Edn. Assn., Internat. Religious Edn. Assn., Am. Soc. Tng. and Devel., Adult Edn. Assn. Office: Sunday Sch Bd of So Bapt Conv 127 9th Ave N Nashville TN 37234

HALL, THOMAS HARTLEY, IV, seminary president, Presbyterian Church, U.S.A.; b. Macon, Ga., July 1, 1929; s. Thomas Hartley and Mildred (Baird) H.; m. Ann Hartzog, May 24, 1957; children: Aurie, Grace, Hartley V, Leigh. B.S., Davidson Coll., 1951, D.D. (hon.), 1981; M.Div., Union Sem., Richmond, Va., 1957; S.T.M., Div. Sch., Yale U., 1958; D.D. (hon.), Austin Coll., 1982. Ordained to ministry Presbyn. Ch., U.S.A., 1957. Chaplain N.C. State U., Raleigh, 1959-61; pastor First Presbyn. Ch., Lenoir, N.C., 1961-66, First Presbyn. Ch., Tyler, Tex., 1966-73, Westminster Ch., Nashville, 1973-81; pres. Union Sem., 1981—; trustee Lees McRae Coll., Banner Elk, N.C., 1962-66, Stillman Coll., Ala., 1973-76, Austin Coll., Sherman, Tex., 1970-82. Served to 1st lt. inf. U.S. Army, 1951-53; Korea. Decorated Silver Star, Bronze Star with oak leaf cluster. Clubs: Forum (Richmond); Cincinnati (Washington). Office: Union Theol Sem 3401 Brook Rd Richmond VA 23227

HALL, THOR, educator, United Methodist Ch.; b. Larvik, Norway, Mar. 15, 1927; s. Jens Martin and Margit Elvira (Petersen) H.; came to U.S., 1957, naturalized, 1973; Dipl.Th., Scandinavian Methodist Sem., 1950; M.R.E., Duke, 1959, Ph.D., 1962; m. Gerd Hellström, July 15, 1950; 1 son, Jan Tore. Ordained deacon United Meth. Ch., 1952, elder, 1954; asst. pastor, then pastor in Norway, 1946-53; exec. sec. youth dept. Meth. Ch. Norway, 1953-57; minister, Ansonville, N.C., 1958-59; asso. minister First Presbyn. Ch., Durham, N.C., 1960-62; asst. prof. preaching and theology Duke Div. Sch., 1962-68, asso. prof., 1968-72; Distinguished prof. religious studies U. Tenn., Chattanooga, 1972—. Mem. gen. bd. evangelism United Meth. Ch., 1968-72, Oxford Inst. Meth. Theol. Studies, 1982—; v.p. Western N.C. Conf. Inst. Homiletical Studies, 1967-72; mem. Holston Conf., United Meth. Ch., 1973—; cons. Ecumenical Prayers Seminars, 1967—. Am. Assn. Theol. Schs. Faculty fellow, 1968-69; Fulbright scholar U. Copenhagen, 1984. Mem. Soc. Sci. Study Religion, Am. Acad. Religion, Soc. Philosophy Religion, Democrat. Author: A Theology of Christian Devotion, 2d edit., 1972; A Framework for Faith, 1970; The Future Shape of Preaching, 1971; Whatever Happened to the Gospel?, 1973; Advent-Christmas, 1975; Anders Nygren, 1978, 2d edit., 1985; Systematic Theology Today, 1978, The Evolution of Christology, 1982. Editor: The Unfinished Pyramid, Sermons by Charles P. Bowles, 1967; Var Ungdom, 1953-57; A Directory of Systematic Theologians in North America, 1975. Home: 1102 Montvale Circle Signal Mountain TN 37377 Office: Dept Philosophy and Religion Univ Tenn Chattanooga TN 37401

HALLANGER, FREDERICK TORVAL, pastor, American Lutheran Church; b. Paris, May 21, 1929 (parents Am. citizens); came to U.S., 1947; s. Fredrick Stang and Alvilde Margrethe (Torvik) H.; m. Lucille Caroline Hansen, Aug. 6, 1952; children: John Frederick, Ann Elsbeth, Carol Marie, Martin Hansen. B.A. cum laude, U. Minn., 1952; M.Div., Luther Theol. Sem., St. Paul, 1956; Ph.D. in Theology candidate, Marquette U., 1980—. Ordained to ministry Lutheran Ch., 1956. Pastor, Fulton Luth. Ch., Moorland, Iowa, 1956-59; sr. pastor Luth. Ch. of Good Shepherd, Des Moines, 1959-69, St. Olaf Luth. Ch., Detroit, 1969-74, Calvary Luth. Ch., Brookfield, Wis., 1974—; protestant chaplain Girls' Tng. Sch., Mitchellville, Iowa, 1963-68; mem. Mich. dist. council Am. Luth. Ch., Detroit, 1973-74; pastoral psychotherapist Calvary Luth. Ch., Brookfield, 1974—. Served to col. USAR, 1954—. Recipient Long Timer award Res. Officers Assn., 1984. Mem. various ecclesiastical orgns. Home: 1785 N 166th St Brookfield WI 53005 Office: Calvary Luth Ch 1750 N Calhoun Rd Brookfield WI 53005

HALPIN, CHARLES AIME, archbishop, Roman Cath. Ch.; b. St. Eustache, Man., Can., Aug. 30, 1930; s. John Stanley and Marie Anne (Gervais) H.; B.A., U. Man., B.Th., U. Montreal, 1956; J.C.L., Gregorian U., Rome, Italy, 1951. Ordained priest, 1956; asst. St. Mary's Cathedral, Winnipeg, Man., 1956-58; vice chancellor Archdiocese of Winnipeg, 1960; sec. to archbishop Winnipeg, 1960-62; officialis Archdiocesan Matrimonial Tribunal, Winnipeg, 1962-73; vice ofcl. Regional Matrimonial Tribunal, Regina, Sask., 1970-73; archbishop of Regina, 1973—; chaplain to Holy Father, given title of Monsignor, 1969. Pres., Can. Canon Law Soc. Home: 2522 Retallack St Regina SK S4T 2L3 Canada Office: 3225 13th Ave Regina SK S4T 1P5 Canada

HALTNER, ROBERT EDWARD, SR., minister, Lutheran Church Missouri Synod; educator, psychologist; b. Milw., Nov. 18, 1926; s. Elroy Charles and Esther Alma (Ehlert) H.; m. Ila Josephine Thompson, May 20, 1950; children: Robert Edward, Jr., Martin, Ruth, Rebecca, Naomi, Charles, Rachel. B.Div. Concordia Sem., Springfield, Ill., 1955; M.S. in Psychology, St. Francis Coll., Ft. Wayne, Ind., 1966; Th.D., Inter Luth. Sem., Golden Valley, Minn., 1970; postgrad. U. No. Iowa, 1975; Ph.D., Trinity Coll., Newburgh, Ind., 1985. Luth. parish pastor Luth. Ch.-Mo. Synod, St. Louis, 1955—; now pastor Christ Luth. Ch., Trego, Wis. Mem. faculty U. Wis.-Stout, 1966-69, U. No. Iowa, 1974, Gogebic Community Coll., Ironwood, Mich., 1979-83; clinical psychologist Wis. Dept. Pub. Instrn., Madison, 1975—; guest lectr. Concordia Coll., St. Paul. Fellow Menninger Psychiat. Found. Author: Moments With Jesus, 1964. Served as sgt. USMC, 1945-49, ETO. Home: Route 1 Box 1119 Trego WI 54888 Office: Christ Luth Ch Route 1 Box 119 Trego WI 54888

HALTOM, MICHAEL FRED, educator, Assemblies of God; b. Dallas, June 22, 1950; s. Aubry Benny and Tressie Margaret (Langley) H.; m. Jean Anne Pressnall, Aug. 20, 1971; children: Michael David, Andrea Christina. B.A., Vennard Coll., 1972; M.Div., Western Evang. Sem., 1977, D.Min., 1984. Ordained to ministry, 1982. Asst. pastor Evang. Meth. Ch., Duncanville, Tex., 1972-74; pastor Viola Community Ch., Estacada, Oreg., 1974-78; prof. N.T. Greek, Eugene Bible Coll., Oreg., 1978—; chaplain U.S. Air Force Res., 1982—. Contbr. articles to profl. jours. Author: An Exegetical Workbook, 1984. Recipient Top Teen award, Dallas Times Herald, Dallas, 1966; Internat. Civitan award,

Rotary, 1967; Model of Merit, SAR, 1968; Service award Boy Scouts Dist. Camporee, 1982. Mem. Evang. Tchr. Tng. Assn., Soc. for Pentecostal Studies, Assemblies of God Heritage Soc., Res. Officers Assn., Air Force Assn. (chaplain). Club: Circle K Internat. (pres. 1970). Office: Eugene Bible Coll 2155 Bailey Hill Rd Eugene OR 97402

HALVORSEN, RICHARD ELLIS, minister; Lutheran Ch. in Am.; b. Chgo., Dec. 12, 1935; s. Eugene and Gertrude Dorothy (Pelz) H.; m. Barbara Ann Bouton, May 20, 1961; children: Christine, Richard, Mark. A.A., Chgo. City Jr. Coll., 1958; B.A., Elmhurst Coll., 1961; B.D., Luth Sch. Theol. Chgo., 1963, M.Div., 1972; M.A., Ball St. U., 1974. Ordained to ministry Lutheran Ch. in Am., 1964. Pastor St. James Luth. Ch., Peoria, Ill., 1964-66; mission developer Luth. Ch. Am., McKinney, Tx., 1966-67; chaplain U.S. Army, U.S., Vietnam, W. Ger., 1967-83; chaplain, counselor Luth. Social Services, Racine, Wis., 1983—. Served to lt. col. U.S. Army, 1967-84. Mem. Assoc. for Clin. Pastoral Edn., Mil. Chaplains Assn., Ret. Officers Assoc., Jaycees. Democrat. Home: 4218 Chekanoff Dr Racine WI 53403

HALVORSEN, ROBERT ANTHONY, minister, Luth. Ch. Am.; b. Chgo., Jan. 31, 1931; s. Anthony and Ragna Louise (Hagensen) H.; B.A., Luther Coll., 1960; M.Div., Northwestern Luth. Theol. Sem., 1964; m. Barbara Clark, Apr. 20, 1963; children—Heidi, Robert Anthony, Kurt, Michael. Ordained to ministry, 1964; pastor St. Stephen's Luth. Ch., Erie, Pa., 1964-66, Christus Victor Luth. Ch., Fort Wayne, Ind., 1967-68, St. Luke's Luth. Ch., Charlotte, N.C., 1968-73, Holy Spirit Luth. Ch., Villas, N.J., 1973-74; dir., counselor Domestic Relations Counseling Service, Cumberland County Ct., Bridgeton, N.J., 1975—. Chaplain, Lower Twp. Police Dept., 1975—; bd. dirs. Ocean View Luth. Home for Aged, 1974—; pres. Cape May Ministerium, 1974-75; sec. Luth. Council Greater Charlotte (N.C.), 1968-69, 72-73. Active Boy Scouts Am.; mem. Cape May County Housing Authority, 1977—. Mem. Am. Assn. Marriage and Family Counselors, Luth. Ch. Hist. Assn., Luth. Soc. Worship, Music and the Arts, Norwegian-Am. Hist. Assn. Home: 18 Mimosa Dr North Cape May NJ 08024 Office: 10 Fayette St Bridgeton NJ 08302

HALVORSON, JOHN V., clergyman, American Lutheran Church. Chairperson, Bd. of Theol. Edn. and Ministry. Office: in care of Am Luth Ch Nat Office 422 S 5th St Minneapolis MN 55415*

HALVORSON, MAYNARD GERHARD, minister, Am. Luth. Ch.; b. Thompson, Iowa, June 25, 1911; s. Conrad Silas and Ida (Hovland) H.; B.A., St. Olaf Coll., Northfield, Minn.; grad. Luth. Theol. Sem., St. Paul; m. Henrietta Marie Hansing, June 4, 1939; children—Richard, Ruth, Janelle. Ordained to ministry; pastor in S.D., Minn., Ill., Hawaii and Utah, 1939-67; pastor First Luth. Ch., Plano, Ill., 1967-74; chaplain Bethesda Homes, Willmar, Minn., 1974—; radio speaker St. Paul's Luth. Hour, 1948-56. Address: 46 Edgebrook Dr Sandwich IL 60548

HAM, JAMES RICHARD See *Who's Who in America*, 43rd edition.

HAMBIDGE, DOUGLAS WALTER, archbishop, Anglican Church of Canada; b. London, Eng., Mar. 6, 1927; s. Douglas and Florence (Driscoll) H.; m. Denise Colvill Lown, June 9, 1956; children: Caryl Denise, Stephen Douglas, Graham Andrew. A.L.C.D., London U., 1953, B.D., 1958, D.D., 1969. Ordained deacon Ch. of Eng., 1953, priest, 1954, consecrated bishop, 1969. Asst. curate St. Mark's Ch., Dalston London, 1953-55, priest-in-charge 1955-56; transferred to Anglican Ch. of Can., 1956; incumbent All Saints, Cassiar, B.C., Can., 1956-58; rector St. James Parish, Smithers, B.C., 1958-64; rector North Peace Parish, Ft. St. John, B.C., 1964-69; canon St. Andrew's Cathedral, 1965; elected Lord Bishop of Caledonia, 1969, consecrated, 1969, enthroned, 1969; elected Lord Bishop of New Westminster, 1980, enthroned, 1980; elected archbishop of New Westminster and metropolitan of the Ecclesiastical Province of B.C., 1981, enthroned, 1981. Office: 814 Richards St #302 Vancouver BC V6B 3A7 Canada

HAMBRICK, BOBBY WAYNE, minister, Church of the Nazarene; b. Madison, Tenn., Aug. 26, 1946; s. Climmie E. Hambrick and Effie O. (Bain) Hambrick Tucker; m. Barbara S. Mays, Aug. 19, 1966; children: Robert Douglas, Roclin Kenneth, Ronald Jason. Student Austin Peay State U., 1966-67; B.A., Trevecca Nazarene Coll., 1968. Ordained to ministry Ch. of the Nazarene, 1969. Pastor Ch. of the Nazarene, Central City, Ky., 1968-70, Ch. of the Nazarene, Glens Fork, Ky., 1970-71, Ch. of the Nazarene, Parsons, W.Va., 1971-74, Ch. of the Nazarene, Logan, W.Va., 1974—; del. Gen. Youth Conv., Dallas, 1976, Kansas City, Mo., 1980, Gen. Ch. Conv., Anaheim, Calif., 1985; dist. sec. W.Va. south dist. Ch. of the Nazarene, Charleston, W.Va., 1984—. Pres. Logan chpt. Easter Seal Soc., 1980-81, Nat. Fedn. Decency, Logan, 1985. Mem. Nat. Coalition for Pornography, Decency and Obscenity, Christian World Affairs Conf. Democrat. Avocations: religious computer applications. Home: 108 Elm St Logan WV 25601 Office: Ch of the Nazarene PO Box 1410 Logan WV 25601

HAMED, NIHAD TALAAT, church official, Muslims; mechanical engineer; b. Damascus, Syria, Dec. 5, 1924; came to U.S., 1970, naturalized, 1975; s. Hamed Youssef Hassanin and Nounira (Talaat) Naimee; divorced; children: Hossam, Nadia, Hazem, Hala, Lina. B.S. in Engring., U. Cairo, 1952; M.S., U. Detroit, 1974. Pres. Am. Muslim Soc., Dearborn, Mich., 1973-76; 2d v.p. Fedn. Islamic Assns., Detroit, 1976-77, 1st v.p., 1977-78, pres., 1978-81. Chief engr. Lapper Mfg. Co., Detroit, 1973—. Chief editor Muslim Star Mag., 1979—. Contbr. articles to profl. jours. and info. to scholarly books. Mem. Am. Welding Soc., Detroit Engring. Soc., Plastic Engring. Soc., Am. Metal Soc. Clubs: Cairo Rowing: Wayandott Boat (Detroit). Office: 25351 Five Mile Rd Redford Twp MI 48239

HAMELIN, JEAN-GUY, bishop, Roman Catholic Church; b. St. Severin, Que., Can., Oct. 8, 1925; s. Bernard and Gertrude (Bordeleau) H.; B.A., U. Laval, 1945; L.Th., Angelicum U., Rome, 1953; Lic. Social Scis., Gregorian U., Rome, 1955. Ordained priest, 1949; consecrated bishop, 1974; pretre Diocese de Trois-Rivieres, 1949-64; dir. dept. d'action sociale Conf. des Eveques Ducanada, 1964-68; sec. gen. L'Assemblee des Eveques du Quebec, 1968-74; bishop of Rouyn-Noranda, 1974—. Aumonier de Mouvements de Travailleurs. Mem. Conf. Aux Semaines Sociales du Can., Conf. Dans Des Sessions de Formation Sociale au Can. Home and office: 515 rue Cuddihy CP 1060 Rouyn PQ J9X 4C5 Canada

HAMER, GEORGE RAYMON, minister, So. Baptist Conv.; b. Carrollton, Tex., Jan. 30, 1931; s. Danial Dalton and Opal Marie (Bridges) H.; diploma in theology Southwestern Bapt. Theol. Sem., 1971; m. Celta La Verne Ward, Aug. 13, 1949; children—Sandra Kay, Lou Nell. Ordained to ministry, 1967; pastor Hillburn Dr. Bapt. Ch., Dallas, 1967-69, Friendship Bapt. Ch., McKinney, Tex., 1970-71, Cedar Springs Bapt. Ch., Ore City, Tex., 1971-73, 1st Bapt. Ch. of Bloomburg (Tex.), 1973-76, N. Side Bapt. Ch., Uvalde, Tex., 1976—. Home: 1812 N Park St Uvalde TX 78801 Office: PO Box 1594 Uvalde TX 78801

HAMILTON-OGDEN, JAMES (R. JAMES OGDEN), minister, American Baptist Churches in the U.S.A.; b. Mt. Vernon, Wash., Jan. 7, 1940; s. Donald James and Grace Wilma MacCarahan) O.; m. Dorene Nina MacArthur, June 10, 1962 (div. 1980); children: Jonquil Dawn, Juliette Dorene; m. Cynthia Hamilton, Apr. 20, 1980; children: Kaija Lynn Comin, Christopher Mac Hamilton-Ogden. A.A., Skagit Valley Coll., 1960; A.B., U. Wash., 1962; B.D. cum laude, Berkeley Bapt. Div. Sch., Calif., 1966; Ph.D., Northwestern U., 1973. Ordained to ministry Am. Bapt. Chs. in U.S.A., 1981. Missionary, First Mesa Bapt. Ch. and Mission, Polacca, Ariz., 1964-65; research asst. Bur. Social and Religious Research, Evanston, Ill., 1966-68; mem. planning and evangelism staff Am. Bapt. Nat. Ministries, Valley Forge, Pa., 1968-76, 79-80, exec. dir. Office of Evangelism, 1977-79; pastor First Bapt. Ch., Batavia, N.Y., 1981—; mem. evangelism working group Nat. Council Chs., N.Y.C., 1976-79, chmn., 1977-79; mem. evangelism and edn. com. Bapt. World Alliance, Washington, 1976-79; moderator Genesee Bapt. Assn., Genesee and Wyoming Counties, N.Y., 1982-84; 1st v.p. Genesee County Council of Chs., 1982—, bd. dirs. housing devel. corp., Batavia, 1981-82, participant jail ministry, 1981—. Co-author: Life Support Systems. Editor: Going Public With One's Faith; To Be A Person of Integrity. Contbr. articles to religious jours. Mem. Am. Bapt. Ministers' Council. Democrat. Lodge: Lions (bd. dirs. Batavia 1983—). Home: 227 East Ave Batavia NY 14020 Office: First Bapt Ch 306 E Main St Batavia NY 14020

HAMLET, WILLIAM ROGER, minister, Church of Christ; b. Detroit, Sept. 20, 1954; s. John William and Minnie Frances (Flatt) H.; m. Sandra Joyce Parnell, July 4, 1975; children: James William, Thomas Wesley. B.S. in Bible, Freed-Hardeman Coll., Tenn., 1976. Ordained minister. Minister, Fort Hill Ch. of Christ, Salem, Ind., 1973, 77-78 Cloverport Ch. of Christ, Mercer, Ind., 1973-76, Paoli Ch. of Christ, Ind., 1979—; lectr. Soul Winning Workshop, Evansville, Ind., 1983. Sec., Paoli Meridian Lions Club, 1983-85. Home and Office: 219 Stucker St Paoli IN 47454

HAMLIN, CURTIS RAY, minister music, So. Baptist Conv.; b. Dallas, Aug. 14, 1952; s. Luther William and Marjorie Katherine (Green) H.; student Hill Jr. Coll., Hillsboro, Tex., 1976-78. Criswell Bible Inst., Dallas, 1975—; m. Belinda Rae Ruff, Mar. 12, 1971; 1 son, Curtis Ray. Called to service, 1971; served Northside Bapt. Ch., Duncanville, Tex., 1971-74; dir. various youth Sunday sch. depts. and Young Musicians choir, Kenwood Bapt. Ch., Dallas, 1974-76, interim minister music, 1974-76; minister music and youth First Bapt. Ch., Milford, Tex., 1976-77; minister music and youth First Bapt. Ch., Campbell, Tex., 1977—. Pres., Bapt. Student Union, Hill Jr. Coll. Tchr. choir Milford Sch. System, 1976—. Author: Music 001-A Layman's Music Theory, 1976.

HAMLIN, WAYLAND, minister, Association of Independent Methodist Churches; b. Chillicothe, Ohio, Sept. 6, 1949; s. Woodrow and Miley (Powers) H.; m. Naomi June Grooms, Oct. 6, 1968; children; Wayland Jay, Elbert Brian, Angela Dawn. B.A. with honors Circleville Bible Coll., 1978; M.Div., Wesley Bibl. Sem. 1981; postgrad. Ref. Theol. Sem., 1984—. Ordained to ministry Churches of Christ in Christian Union, 1975. Missionary fgn. missionary dept. Chs. of Christ in Christian Union, Circleville, Ohio, 1981-84; pastor St. Paul Ind. Meth. Ch., Oxford, Miss., 1984—; prof. Circleville Bible Coll., 1983; pres. Christian Union Bible Sch., Roseau, Dominica, W.I., 1983-84; chaplain Oxford Police Dept., 1984—; asst. coordinator Fellowship Christian Athletes, Oxford, 1984—; group leader On Campus Ministry, Oxford, 1984—; chmn. missions Assn. of Ind. Meth. Chs., Jackson, 1984—; ministerial assoc. Oxford Ministerial Assn., 1984—. Contbr. articles to denominational jours. Relief vol Salvation Army, Jackson, Miss., 1979. Served with U.S Army, 1966-69, Vietnam. Decorated Purple Heart. Bronze Star; named one of Outstanding Young Men Am., U.S. Jaycees, 1984. Mem. Wesleyan Theol. Soc. Avocations: reading; woodworking; tennis and other sports. Home: 913 Chickasaw Rd Oxford MS 38655 Office: St Paul Ind Meth Ch 1740 Jefferson Oxford MS 38655

HAMM, MICHAEL DENNIS, priest, educator, Roman Catholic Church; b. Cin., Jan. 18, 1936; s. Victor Michael and Agnes (Curren) H.; B.A., Marquette U., 1958; M.A., St. Louis U., 1964, Ph.D., 1975. Ordained priest, Roman Cath. Ch., 1970. Instr. N.T., Creighton U., Omaha, Nebr., 1975—; rector Campion House, Soc. of Jesus, Omaha, 1983—. Mem. Cath. Bibl. Assn., Soc. Bibl. Lit. Democrat. Office: Creighton U 24th and California Omaha NE 68178

HAMMER, DOW LLOYD, JR., minister, Southern Baptist Convention; b. Knoxville, Tenn., Oct. 10, 1920; s. Dow L. and Elizabeth (Jollay) H.; B.A. Carson-Newman Coll., 1952; B.D., Southwestern Bapt. Theol. Sem., 1955, now postgrad.; m. Mary Ruth Bean, Aug. 1, 1941; children—Carol (Mrs. G. Arthur), Cindy (Mrs. R. Deaderick), Sondra Gail (Mrs. K. Sparks). Ordained to ministry So. Bapt. Ch., 1946; asso. pastor Deaderick Ave. Bapt. Ch., Knoxville, 1946-47, Gallaher Meml. Bapt. Ch., Knoxville, 1947-52, First Bapt. Ch., Alvord, Tex., 1952-55, Washington Pike Bapt. Ch., Knoxville, 1958-69, York Terr. Ch., Sheffield, Ala., 1969-74, Cedar Grove Bapt. Ch., 1974-76, First Bapt. Ch., Fountain City, Tenn., 1977—; mem. Greater Chgo. Enlargement Preaching Mission, 1967; preaching mission, Jamaica, 1968; vice-moderator St. Clair Baptist Assn. Chaplain Knoxville Tenn. Police dept., 1964-69 hon. chaplain Senate of State of Tenn.; moderator Colbert-Lauderdale Bapt. Assn., 1973-74. Mem. Leeds Ministerial Assn. (pres.). Home: 5220 Lavesta Rd Knoxville TN 37918 Office: Washington Pike Bapt Ch 1700 Washington Pike Knoxville TN 37917

HAMMES, GEORGE ALBERT, bishop, Roman Catholic Church; b. La Crosse, Wis., Sept. 11, 1911; s. August Isidore and Caroline (Schumacher) H.; student St. Lawrence Sem., Mt. Calvary, Wis., 1925-31, St. Louis Prep. Sem., 1931-33, Kenrick Sem., St. Louis 1933-34, Sulpician Sem., Washington, 1934-37; M.A. Cath. U. Am., 1937; L.H.D. (hon.), Mt. Senario Coll. Ladysmith, Wis., 1969. Ordained priest, 1937 consecrated bishop, 1960; sec. to bishop diocese of LaCrosse, 1937-43; instr. Latin and religion Aquinas HIgh Sch., LaCrosse, 1937-42; instr. ethics and religion St. Francis Sch. Nursing, LaCrosse, 1937-46; chancellor diocese of LaCrosse, 1943-60; pastor St. Leo the Great parish, West Salem, Wis., 1957-60; bishop diocese of Superior, Wis., 1960—. Officialis Diocesan Matrimonial Tribunal, LaCrosse, 1943-60; diocesan dir Cath. Lawyers' Guild, LaCrosse, 1956-60; pres Tri-State Interfaith Devel. Enterprise, Superior 1970-84. Adv. bd. Viterbo Coll., LaCrosse, 1954— Cath. Social Service, LaCrosse, 1954-60; trustee Mt Senario Coll., 1969—; bd. dirs. Nat. Tech. Assistance Found., Mpls., 1971—. Home: Gitchinadji Dr Superior WI 54880 Office: 1201 Hughitt Ave Superior WI 54880

HAMMONS, THOMAS LEE, JR., minister, United Methodist Ch.; b. Limestone County, Ala., July 1, 1943 s. Thomas Lee and Annette (Black) H.; B.A., Athens (Ala.) Coll., 1966; B.D., Candler Sch. Theology Atlanta, 1968, M.Div., 1972; m. Linda Jeannette Carter, Feb. 28, 1970; children—Thomas Lee, III Christopher Denton. Ordained to ministry, 1966 pastor, Faith United Meth. Ch., Hartselle, Ala. 1968-69; asso. ministe Tuscumbia (Ala.) First United Ch., 1969-71, Central Heights United Meth. Ch. and Wesley Chapel, 1971-76; pastor Druid Hills United Meth. Ch., Tuscaloosa, Ala., 1976—. Chmn. Commn Ecumenical and Interreligious Concerns N. Ala. conf United Meth. Ch., 1972-76, elementary camp dir. 1972-76, elementary camp dir., 1970-77; bd. dirs Wesley Found., U. Ala.; mem. Clergy Counseling Service, Tuscaloosa. Mem. Ron Kerr Evangelistic Assn Home: 1329 39th Ave E Tuscaloosa AL 35401 Office 1331 39th Ave E Tuscaloosa AL 35401

HAMPTON, TOMMY JAY, minister, Free Will Bapt Ch.; b. Springfield, Mo., July 26, 1950; s. Raymond Charles and Betty Jean (Lunsford) H.; student Hillsdale ree Will Bapt. Coll., 1968-70; B.S., Calif. Christian Coll., 1972; postgrad Mennonite Brethren Bibl. Sem., 973, Calif. Grad. Sch. Theology, 1976—; m. Nora Mae ernigan, Aug. 16, 1969; 1 dau., Nikki Sue Ann. Ordained to ministry, 1971; pastor, 1st Free Will Bapt. Ch., Stockton, Calif., 1971-72, Free Will Bapt. Ch., Concord, Calif., 1973-75, Bell Gardens, Calif., 1975—. Dir. Calif. Christian Coll. So. Extension Sch., 1975-76; mem. mission bd. Calif.; coordinator West Coast Assn. Youth Camps; clk. West Coast Assn. Free Will Baptists. George McLain scholar, 1972. Home: 7231 Granger St Bell Gardens CA 90201 Office: 7235 Granger St Bell Gardens CA 90201

HAND, HAROLD LEROY, JR., minister, Lutheran Church in America. B. Pottsville, Pa., Nov. 18, 1952; s. Harold Leroy Sr. and Eleanore Estella (Purnell) H.; m. Helen Christine Hildenbrand, Oct. 28, 1978; children: Christopher Matthew, Jonathan Martin. B.A. in Religion, Susquehanna U., 1974; M.Div., Luth. Theol. Sem., 1978. Ordained to ministry Lutheran Ch. in Am., 1978. Pastor St. Mark Luth. Ch., Nescopeck, Pa., 1978-84, Prince of Peace Luth. Ch., Balt., 1984—; sec., treas. Nescopeck Ministerium, 1979-81, 84; chmn. community concerns com. Berwick Ministerium, Pa., 1983-84; parish edn. com. Northeastern Pa. Synod, Wescosville, 1979-80. Recipient God and Country award Am. Legion, 1970, award Nescopeck VFW, 1984, award Nescopeck Ambulance Assn., 1984, God & Country award Nescopeck Fire Co., 1984. Mem. Am. Philatelic Soc., Jaycees (Berwick bd. dirs. 1979-83), Phi Sigma Kappa (v.p. 1972-73). Democrat. Club: Franklin D. Roosevelt Philatelic Soc. (St. Augustine Shores, Fla.) (asst. sec. 1984—). Home: 1314 Pine Grove Ave Baltimore MD 21237 Office: Prince of Peace Luth Ch 8212 Philadelphia Ave Baltimore MD 21237

HAND, LAWRENCE L. Bishop, Lutheran Church in America. Office: 2900 Queen Ln Philadelphia PA 19129*

HAND, WILLIAM JOHN, educator, minister, American Baptist Churches; b. Bridgeton, N.J., Dec. 22, 1912; s. Reuben T. and Edith C. (Anderson) H.; B.S., Phila. Coll. Pharmacy and Sci., 1934; M.S., U. Pa., 1936; B.D., Eastern Baptist Theol. Sem., 1943; B.L.S., Drexel U., 1949; S.T.D., Temple U., 1960. Ordained to ministry Am. Baptist Chs. in the U.S.A., 1943; pastor Manayunk Bapt. Ch., Phila., 1943-46; librarian Eastern Bapt. Theol. Sem., Phila., 1946-59, prof. pastoral counseling, 1960-78, adj. prof. Ministry to the Aging, 1978—, sem. pastor, 1984—; cons. Phila. Bapt. Assn., 1978; founder field edn. program Whitley Bapt. Coll., Melbourne, Australia, 1981. Mem. Commn. Human Rights and Religious Liberty, Bapt. World Alliance, 1970-75. Mem. Assn. Profl. Edn. for Ministry, Assn. Clin. Pastoral Edn. (dir. hist. research 1970-75), Assn. Clin. Pastoral Edn., Gerontol. Soc. Am., Nat. Coalition on Aging, Nat. Council Aging, Internat. Fedn. Aging, Episcopal Soc. Ministry on Aging, Cumberland County (N.J.) Hist. Soc., Smithsonian Assos., Beta Phi Mu, Alpha Sigma. Address: Eastern Baptist Theological Seminary Philadelphia PA 19151

HANDKINS, EDWARD E., pastor, Southern Baptist Convention; b. Marion, Ill., Aug. 9, 1942; s. Alva Ray and Mildred Lorene (Miller) H.; m. Donna Childers, Apr. 21, 1963; children: David, Christy. B.A., So. Ill. U., 1964; M.Div., So. Bapt. Theol. Sem., Louisville, 1970, D.Ministry, 1977. Ordained to ministry Southern Baptist Convention, 1963. Pastor, New Hope Bapt. Ch., Buncombe, Ill., 1964-67, Goshen Bapt. Ch., Lawrenceburg, Ky., 1967-69, First So. Bapt. Ch., Cairo, Ill., 1969-73, Brainard Ave. Bapt. Ch., LaGrange, Ill., 1973-79, Roland Manor Bapt. Ch., East Peoria, Ill., 1979—; preacher Evangelistic mission to Eng., North Shields, 1975, 80; sec. State Bapt. Ministers Conf., Ill., 1982-83. Corr., Ill. Bapt. newspaper, 1980—; writer weekly syndicated newspaper column Strength for Living, 1979—; contbr. articles to various periodicals. Mem. Ill. So. Sem. Alumni Assn. (pres. 1984-85), Peoria Met. Bapt. Assn. (moderator 1984), Ill. Bapt. State Assn. (sec. state ministers conf. 1983, nominating com. chmn. 1984-86), Ill. State Sunday Sch. Cons. (gen. officer 1975—), Chgo. Met. Bapt. Assn. (dir. Bible conf. 1978). Home: 306 Lotus Ln Washington IL 61571 Office: Roland Manor Bapt Ch 2433 Washington Rd Washington IL 61571

HANDY, WILLIAM TALBOT, JR., church official, United Methodist Church; b. New Orleans, Mar. 26, 1924; s. William Talbot and Dorothy Pauline (Pleasant) H.; student Tuskegee Inst., 1940-43; A.B., Dillard U., 1948; M.Div., Gammon Theol. Sem., 1951; S.T.M., Boston U., 1952; D.D., Wiley Coll., 1973, Huston-Tilotson Coll., 1973; m. Ruth Odessa Robinson, Aug. 11, 1948; children—William Talbot III (dec.), Dorothy Denise, Stephen Emanuel. Became elder United Meth. Ch., 1951; pastor ch., Alexandria, La., 1952-59, Baton Rouge, 1959-68; pub. rep. The Meth. Pub. House, 1968-70; v.p. personnel United Meth. Pub. House, Nashville, from 1970. Chmn. La. Conf. Bd. Ministry, 1958—. Mem. La. state adv. com. U.S. Commn. Civil Rights, 1959-68; 1974—; trustee Gammon Theol. Sem., Interdenomination Theol. Center, bd. dirs. Nashville Area United Way, Nashville Opportunity Industrialization Center, Urban League. Mem. NAACP (life), Nashville C. of C., Frontiers Internat. Home: 640 Shipp Ln Nashville TN 37207 Office: 201 8th Ave S Nashville TN 37202

HANIFEN, RICHARD CHARLES, bishop, Roman Catholic Church; b. Denver, June 15, 1931; s. Edward Anselm and Dorothy Elizabeth (Ranous) H.; B.S., Regis Coll., 1953; S.T.B., Cath. U., 1959, M.A., 1966; J.C.L., Pontifical Lateran U. (Italy). Ordained priest, 1959, consecrated bishop, 1974; asst. pastor Cathedral Parish, Denver, 1959-66; sec. to archbishop Archdiocese Denver, 1968-69, chancellor, 1969-76; aux. bishop, 1974-84; bishop of Colorado Springs, Colo., 1984—. Office: 29 W Kiowa St Colorado Springs CO 80903

HANN, WILLIAM RAY, minister, So. Baptist Conv.; b. Bessie, Okla., Oct. 29, 1935; s. Louie and Erma Louise (Schenewolf) H.; B.A., Calif. Baptist Coll., Riverside, 1965; student Calif. Bapt. Theol. Sem., Covina, 1969; M.A., Calif. Grad. Sch. Theology, Glendale, 1976; m. Joanne Katheryn DeWatney, Sept. 2, 1961; children—Andrew Keith, Eric Ray. Ordained to ministry, 1962; pastor chs. in Calif., 1962—; pastor Monterey Ave. Bapt. Ch., Baldwin Park, 1965-72, Hillcrest Bapt. Ch., Bakersfield, 1972—. Mem. supervisory com. So. Bapt. Credit Union, 1970-75 mem. com. order bus. So. Bapt. Gen. Conv. Calif., 1972-75, 1st v.p. conv., 1975, pres., 1976. Recipient President's award Calif. Bapt. Coll., 1965, Master Key award, 1965. Home: 963 Chalet Dr Concord CA 94518 Office: 535 Walnut Ave Walnut Creek CA 94598

HANNA, KING WILLIAM, minister, United Methodist Church; b. Detroit, Oct. 6, 1939; s. John Gilmore and Dorothea May (Flood) H.; m. Anne Marie Buss, June 7, 1963. A.Gen. Studies, Jackson Jr. Coll., 1960; B.S., Eastern Mich. U., 1966; M.Div., Meth. Theol. Sch. Ohio, 1970. Ordained to ministry United Meth. Ch., 1970. Lay pastor Wellsville United Meth. Ch., Blissfield, Mich., 1965-67, Maple Grove United Meth. Ch., Columbus, Ohio, 1967-70; assoc. pastor West Side United Meth. Ch., Ann Arbor, Mich., 1970-72; pastor Grace/Skandia United Meth. Ch., Marquette, Mich., 1972-82, Mitchell United Meth. Ch., Negaunee, Mich., 1982—; sec. bd. trustees Wesley Found. No. Mich. U., 1972—; trustee, v.p., pres. Dist. Bd. Mission, Marquette, Mich., 1972—; bd. local ch. ministries Connectional Outreach, Detroit, 1972-84; mem. Bd. Ordained Ministry, Detroit, 1984—; del. 2d Internat. Seminar on World Evangelism, Atlanta, 1984. Bd. dirs. Upper Peninsula Health Systems Agy., Marquette, 1978—; mem. Instl. Rehab. Bd., Marquette Gen. Hosp., 1982—, Irontown Assn. Negaunee, Mich., 1982; chmn. edn. needs com. area pub. schs., Negaunee, 1983; vice comdr. U.S. Coast Guard Aux., 1980-84. Named Outstanding Auxilliarist, U.S. Coast Guard Aux., 1976, Flotilla Achievement award, 1983. Mem. W. Marquette County Clergy Assn. Club: Marquette Yacht (dir.). Home: 1013 Hungerford Negaunee MI 49866 Office: Mitchell United Meth Ch 207 Teal Lake Ave West Case St Negaunee MI 49866

HANNAFORD, PAUL EMERSON, priest, Episcopal Church; b. Hillsboro, Ohio, Dec. 29, 1926; s. Burch and Barbara Emma (Young) H.; A.B./B.E., Wilmington (Ohio) Coll., 1949; M.Div., Bexley Hall, Gambier, Ohio, 1952; m. Claudia Lee Hatch, Sept. 2, 1951; children: Lynn Marie, Pamela Ann, David Carlyle. Ordained priest Episcopal Ch., 1952; rector chs., Ohio, 1952-64; rector Christ Ch., Oil City, Pa., 1965-70, Trinity Ch., Pottsville, Pa., 1976-79, St. Michael's in the Hills, Toledo, Ohio, 1979—; archdeacon Diocese of Erie (Pa.), 1970-75; spl. adminstrv. aide to Bishop of Ecuador, 1975. Dep. gen. conv. Episcopal Ch., 1973; mem. standing com. Diocese of Bethlehem (Pa.), 1976—. Mem. Diocese of Bethlehem Clergy Assn. Home: 4684 Brittany Rd Toledo OH 43615 Office: St Michael's in the Hills 4718 Brittany Rd Toledo OH 43615

HANNAN, PHILIP MATTHEW, archbishop, Roman Catholic Church; b. Washington, May 20, 1913; s. Patrick Francis and Lillian Louise (Keefe) H.; student St. Charles Coll., 1931-33; A.B., Cath. U. Am., 1935, M.A., 1936, J.C.D., 1949; postgrad. N. Am. Coll., Rome, Italy, 1936-40; S.T.B., S.T.L., Gregorian U., Rome, 1940. Ordained priest, 1939, consecrated bishop, 1956; asst. St. Thomas Aquinas Ch., Balt., 1940-42; vice chancellor Cath. U. Am., Washington, 1948-51, chancellor, 1951-62, vicar gen., 1960—, chmn. bd. trustees, 1972—; administr. St. Patrick's Ch., Washington, 1951-56, pastor, 1956-65; aux. bishop Archdiocese Washington, 1965; archibishop Archdiocese of New Orleans, 1965—. Editor-in-chief Catholic Standard, 1956-65; chmn. ad hoc com. Nat. Conf. Cath. Bishops Office Priestly Life and Ministry, 1971—; nat. chaplain Cath. Daus. Am., 1974-78; mem. communications com. U.S. Cath. Conf. Bishops, 1979—. Mem. goals com. Met. Area Com. New Orleans; mem. White House Conf. on Children and Youth, 1970—; mem. bd., chmn. interfaith com. United Funds New Orleans, 1970—; bd. dirs. Met. council Boy Scouts Am., 1975—. Address: 7887 Walmsley Ave New Orleans LA 70125*

HANNEN, J. E., bishop of Caledonia, Anglican Church of Canada. Office: #208-4th Ave W Prince Ruppert BC V8J 1P3 Canada*

HANSEN, CARLTON DEAN, minister, Ch. of the Nazarene; b. Attica, Ind., Dec. 22, 1940; s. Carl Christian and Vivian Hilda (Troxel) H.; ed. Ch. of Nazarene; m. Betty Lou Truesdale, Sept. 25, 1958; children—Randall, Susan, Joseph. Ordained to ministry, 1966; pastor Nazarene Ch., Bainbridge, Ind., 1961-63, Nazarene Ch., Roachdale, Ind., 1963-66, Northside Nazarene Ch., Terre Haute, Ind. 1966-71, Ch. of the Nazarene, Lowell, Ind., 1972—; radio ministry Sta. WLCL-FM, Lowell, 1972—. Mem. Home Missions Bd., Ch. of the Nazarene, 1976—, bd. orders and relations, 1973—, bd. ch. extension, 1976—, dist. ch. sch. bd., 1973-77; adv. book com. Nazarene Pub. House, Kansas City, Mo. Treas. Friends of the Lowell Pub. Library, 1975. Clubs: Rotary (treas. 1976-77, sec. 1977—). Author: So You're Planning a Wedding, 1976; contbr. articles to religious publs.; columnist Post-Tribune, 1976—. Home: 131 S Fremont St Lowell IN 46356 Office: PO Box 201 Lowell IN 46356

HANSEN, FRANCIS EUGENE, bishop, Reorganized Ch. of Jesus Christ of Latter Day Saints; b. Underwood, Iowa, Oct. 30, 1925; s. John Alexander and Annie (Rasmussen) H.; student Biarritz (France) Am. U., 1946; A.A., Graceland Coll., Lamoni, Iowa, 1948; B.S., U. Kans., 1950; m. Wanda Ann Hoss, Aug. 20, 1949; children—Blair, Cheryl. Ordained to ministry, 1943, ordained bishop, 1956; asst. to presiding bishopric, World Hdqrs. Reorganized Ch. Jesus Christ of Latter-day Saints, Independence, Mo., 1954-56, bishop Los Angeles stake and Hawaii dist., Los Angeles, 1956-66, counselor to presiding bishop, 1966-72, presiding bishop, Independence, 1972—. Mem. Good Govt. League, 1969—; mem. community adv. com. to Councilman John Cassidy, Los Angeles, 1966; treas., trustee Independence Sanitarium and Hosp., 1966—; bd. dirs. Mound Grove Cemetery, Social Service Center; mem. bd. Central Devel. Assn., Central Profl. Bldg.; v.p. Truman-Forest Pharmacy Bd.; pres. bd. suprs. Atherton Levy Dist.; mem. bd. publs., v.p. Herald Pub. House; hon. fellow Harry S. Truman Library Inst. Mem. Jackson County Hist. Soc., Jackson County Farm Bur., C. of C. (dir.), Order of Bishops, Lambda Delta Sigma, Beta Gamma Sigma. Home: 3321 S Crane St Independence MO 64055 Office: The Auditorium River at Walnut Sts PO Box 1059 Independence MO 64051

HANSEN, HELEN STILL, lay church worker, Roman Catholic Church; b. Hastings, Nebr., Apr. 3, 1912; d. Peter H. and Rose Mary (Stumpf) Still; m. Wilbur Walvoord Hansen, Dec. 30, 1936; children: Wilbur Walvoord, Thomas Peter. B.A., U. Nebr., 1934, M.S.W., 1938; postgrad. U. Chgo., 1935-36. Lic. clin. social worker, marriage, family and child counselor. Dir. social services St. Elizabeth's Hosp., Chgo., 1934-36, Mercy Hosp., Chgo., 1945-55; dir. clin. services Cath. Social Service Santa Clara County, San Jose, Calif., 1955-70, dir., 1970-83, vol., 1983—; pres. Calif. Cath. Conf. Social Work, 1962; mem. Dirs. Cath. Social Service Archdiocese of San Francisco; mem. adv. com. John XXIII Sr. Ctr. Supr. Crippled Children Services, State of Nebr., 1936-38; supr. admitting Yale Med. Ctr., New Haven, 1938-41; dir. social service and admitting Monmouth Meml. Hosp., Long Branch, N.J., 1941-43; asst. dir. Hennepin County chpt. ARC, Mpls., 1943-45; instr. Loyola U., Chgo., 1948-55, St. Xavier Coll., Chgo., part-time faculty Notre Dame Coll., Belmont, Calif., 1956-60, O'Connor Sch. Nursing, San Jose, 1956-57, Russell Coll., Burlingame, Calif., 1957-58; Head Start asst. prof. home econs. San Jose State Coll., 1968-71; faculty Gavilan Coll., Gilroy, Calif., 1972-79. Mem. adv. com. Santa Clara County Welfare Dept., 1961-73, Hope for Retarded Children, San Jose, Santa Clara County Mental Retardation Commn., 1965-70; mem. Gov.'s adv. bd. Porterville State Hosp., 1970-77; bd. dirs. Legal Aid Soc., San Jose, 1961-70; mem. exec. com. San Jose Downtown Community Mental Health Ctr.; mem. family and children's adv. bd. Santa Clara County Dept. Social Services; past chmn., mem. exec. com. Assn. United Way Agys.; pres., mem. exec. com. Short-Doyle Contract Agys. Mem. Calif. Conf. Cath. Charities Dirs. (pres. 1979-80), Nat. Conf. Cath. Charities (bd. dirs., exec. com. 1975-81, search com. 1981-82). Home: 542 Bay Rd Menlo Park CA 94025

HANSEN, JOHN PATRICK, publisher, minister, Church of God, Anderson, Indiana, b. Bklyn., July 6, 1949; s. John Robert and Patricia (Kane) H.; m. Theresa Carol Tyer, Feb. 2, 1974; children: Candy L., John Paul. Diploma in Bible, Internat. Bible Inst. and Sem., Orlando, Fla., 1981. Ordained to ministry, 1982. Pub., editor The Christian Contender, Hockley, Tex., 1983—The Christian Community News, 1984—; nat. dir. Christian C. of C., Hockley, 1984—; nat. sales mgr. The Christian Yellow Pages, 1981-84; missionary/pastor Atlantic City Christian Ministries, Atlantic City, N.J., 1980-81. Alt. del. Republican Party, Senatorial Dist. Tex., 1984. Mem. Evang. Press Assn., Nat. Chaplains Assn., Moral Majority. Republican.

HANSON, FREDERICK DOUGLAS, minister, Free Will Baptist Church; b. Perth, N.B., Can., Dec. 17, 1948; s. Douglas Aubrey and Mona Evelyn (Hitchcock) H.; m. Lavergne Alice Sullivan, Apr. 6, 1968; children: Darren Daniel, Darcy Elizabeth. Cert. Evang. Tchr. Tng. Assn., 1984; B.A., Trinity Coll., Dunedin, Fla., 1984; postgrad. Luther Rice Sem., Jacksonville, Fla., 1984—. Ordained to ministry Free Will Bapt. Ch., 1970.

Pastor Free Will Bapt. Ch., N.B., 1970—, moderator, 1978—; gen. dir. St. John Valley Bible Camp, N.B., 1973-76, 79-81. Contbr. numerous articles to profl. jours. Mem. Atlantic Can. Assn. Free Will Baptists (exec. com. 1978—, gen. bd. mem., Nashville 1981—), Christian Camping Internat., Can. Camping Assn., N.B. Camping Assn., Free Will Baptists Assn. (promotional sec. 1981—, gen. bd. 1981—). Office: Atlantic Can Assn Free Will Baptists PO Box 355 Hartland NB E0J 1N0 Canada

HANSON, HAROLD GLENN, minister, Southern Baptist Convention; b. Smackover, Ark., June 25, 1931; s. George W. and Katie Lee (Bolton) H.; B.S., Stephen F. Austin U., 1952; M.R.E., Southwestern Bapt. Theol. Sem., Ft. Worth, 1961; m. Naomi Ruth Honeycutt, Feb. 6, 1954; children—Debbie R., Glenda L. Licensed to ministry, 1960; minister edn. Northside Bapt. Ch., Weatherford, Tex., 1960-61, 1st Bapt. Ch., Nederland, Tex., 1961-64; asso. Sunday sch. sec. Tex. Bapt. Conv., 1964-67; minister edn. First Bapt. Ch., Tyler, Tex., 1967-73; dir. ch. tng. dept. Bapt. Gen. Conv. Tex., 1973—. Vice pres. Southwestern Bapt. Religious Edn. Assn., 1966. Author articles. Home: 2700 Biloxi Ln Mesquite TX 75150 Office: 511 N Akard Baptist Bldg Dallas TX 75201

HANSON, JAMES HERBERT, minister, American Lutheran Church; b. Bemidji, Minn., Oct. 1, 1929; s. Arthur Edwin and Marie Rebecca (Hugelen) H.; B.A., St. Olaf Coll., 1950; B.Th., Luther Sem., 1954; m. Ramona Steinun Kompelien, June 16, 1954; children—Nathan, Kathryn, John, Paul, Timothy. Ordained to ministry, 1954; pastor First Am. Luth. Ch., Hardin, Mont., 1954-58, Zion Luth. Ch., Glendive, Mont., 1958-68; sr. pastor Trinity Luth. Ch., Crookston, Minn., 1968-85; senate chaplain State of Minn., 1985; sr. pastor Luth. Ch. of the Risen Lord, Odessa, Tex., 1985—. Served bd. theol. edn. Am. Luth. Ch. Active Gov's. Com. Alcohol and Drugs State Minn., 1972—; chmn. bd. dir. Glenmore Found. Treatment and Research in Chem. Dependency; chmn. Polk County (Minn.) Democratic-Farm Labor Party, 1973. Recipient Distinguished Service award Glendive Jr. C. of C., 1966. Author: Through Temptation, 1959, What Is The Church?, 1961. Office: Luth Ch Risen Lord Odessa TX

HANSON, JOHN DAVID, minister, United Methodist Church; b. Reform, Ala., Aug. 20, 1936; s. Robert Cole and Annie Lou (Godfrey) H.; B.A., Emory U., 1958; B.D., Drew U., Madison, N.J., 1962; m. Kay Brooks Watkins, June 19, 1960; children—Jay David, Jeffrey Brooks. Ordained to ministry, 1960; asso. pastor chs. in Ga. and Fla., 1955-60; pastor Chester (N.Y.) Meth. Ch., 1960-62, Geneva Larger parish United Meth. Ch., Ga., 1962-64; mem. staff S. Ga. conf. United Meth. Ch., St. Simons Island, Ga., 1964—; pastor Christ United Meth. Ch., Warner-Robins, Ga., 1977—; lab. instr. council youth ministries United Meth. Ch. Home: 113 Sandra Ave Warner Robins GA 31093 Office: 511 Russell Pkwy Warner Robins GA 31093

HANSON, MELVIN HUBERT, minister, Open Bible Standard Chs.; b. Klamath Falls, Oreg., Aug. 29, 1931; s. Herbert O. and Mary M. (Hunt) H.; B.A., Eugene Bible Coll., 1953; postgrad. Berkley Coll., 1954, Stockton Coll., 1955; m. Barbara M. Smith, Aug. 7, 1952 (dec. 1976); children—Dan, Deniece, Dorene, Douglas. Ordained to ministry, 1954; asso. pastor, Port Chicago, Calif., 1953-54; pastor Open Bible Ch., Stockton, Calif., 1954-59, First Ch. of Open Bible, Portland, Oreg., 1959-73; U.S. dir. for mission Underground Evangelism Internat., Los Angeles, 1973—. Dist. supt., mem. gen. bd. dirs. Open Bible Standard Chs., 1961-73; asst. dir. Holy Land Seminars Tour Co., 1967-70; founder, dir. Internat. Opportunities Unlimited; bd. dirs. Eugene Bible Coll.; officer Internat. Cultural Exchange Schs., 1968-70. Recipient nat. awards as church builder, 1961, 69. Archtl. designer for seven ch. bldgs.; oil painter. Home: 942 Linda Vista Ave Pasadena CA 91103 Office: 800 W Colorado St Los Angeles CA 90041

HANUS, JEROME GEORGE, ednl. adminstr., Roman Catholic Church; b. Brainard, Nebr., May 26, 1940; s. Leo A. and Kristine A. (Polak) H.; A.B., Conception (Mo.) Sem. Coll., 1963; S.T.L., St. Anselm Coll., Rome, 1967; M.A., Princeton, 1972. Joined Order St. Benedict, 1961; ordained priest, 1966; asst. prof. Sch. Theology, Conception Sem., 1967-69; prof. religion, chmn. dept. Conception Coll., 1973-76; adj. prof. moral theology St. Anselm Coll., Rome, 1974-76; abbot Conception Abbey, also chancellor Conception Sem. Coll., 1977—; pres. Swiss-Am. Benedictine Congregation, 1984—. Mem. Kansas City (Mo.) Soc. Theol. Studies. Author articles. Home: Conception Abbey Conception MO 64433

HANVEY, ROBERT MONROE, minister, So. Bapt. Conv.; b. Fairfield, Ala., Sept. 17, 1939; s. Emmett Monroe and Claudia Mildred (Richardson) H.; B.S., Jacksonville State Coll., 1962; Th.M. with honors, New Orleans Bapt. Theol. Sem., 1972; Th.D., Bapt. Christian U., 1976; m. Mary Katheryn Moore, Nov. 21, 1959; 1 dau., Katheryn Roberta. Ordained to ministry, 1972; asso. pastor 1st Bapt. Ch., McComb, Miss., 1972-74; pastor Easthaven Bapt. Ch., Brookhaven, Miss., 1974—. Dir. Pike County Baptist Sunday Sch. Assn.; mem. exec. com. Lincoln County (Miss.) Baptist Assn. Mem. Brookhaven Ministerial Conf., SW Miss., Lincoln County Bapt. pastors' assns. Contbr. articles in field to religious jours. Home and Office: POB 882 Brookhaven MS 39601

HARASZTI, ALEXANDER SANDOR, minister, Bapt. Ch.; b. Soltvadkert, Hungary, Mar. 2, 1920; s. Joseph and Katalin (Katzenbach) H.; Came to U.S., 1956, naturalized, 1962; B.D., Bapt. Theol. Sem., Budapest, Hungary, 1944; M.A., Royal Hungarian Tchrs. Coll., Budapest, 1943; Ph.D., Royal Hungarian Peter Pazmany U., Budapest, 1944; M.D., Semmelweis U., Budapest, 1951; m. Rozalia Baan, Aug. 9, 1943; children—Joseph S., Rose B., Stella C., Benedict F., Pamela R., Leland B. Ordained to ministry, 1944; pastor Ujpest (Hungary) Bapt. Ch., 1944-52; traveling missionary, Hungary, 1952-55; pastor 1st Bapt. Ch. of Budapest, 1955-56; tchr. Bapt. Theol. Sem., Budapest, 1945-55, v.p., 1955-56; instr. Internat. Bapt. Theol. Sem., Zurich, Switzerland, 1948-49; counseling pastor Hungarian Bethany Bapt. Ch., Cleve., 1971-73, 1st Bapt. Ch., Detroit, 1975-76; med. missionary, Mbeya, Tanzania, 1970. Chmn. missions and lit. com. Hungarian Bapt. Union Am., 1971-77, in charge ministerial exchange program, 1971—. Intern, Mo. Bapt. Hosp., St. Louis, 1957-58, St. Louis County Hosp., 1958-59; resident in gen. surgery Ga. Bapt. Hosp., Atlanta, 1959-60; resident in gen. surgery Emory U. Hosp., Atlanta, 1960-64, Fellow in clin. cancer research Emory U. Sch. Medicine, 1964-65; practice medicine specializing in gen. and gynecol. surgery, College Park, Ga., 1966-71, Jonesboro, Ga., 1971—. Diplomate Hungarian Bd. Obstetrics Gynecology. Fellow Am. Soc. Abdominal Surgeons; mem. AMA, Ga., Atlanta Med. assns. Contbr. articles to religious jours. Home: 6608 Morning Dove Pl Jonesboro GA 30236 Office: 217 Arrowhead Blvd Ct B Jonesboro GA 30236

HARBOUR, WILLIAM RALPH, minister, Seventh-day Adventist Church; b. Glendale, Calif., May 27, 1924; s. William Ralph and Josephine Laura (Patterson) H.; m. LaVerne Benson, May 4, 1984; children: William R., Daniel Lee. B.A., LaSierra Coll., 1946; M.A., Andrews U., 1964, B.D., 1970. Ordained to ministry Seventh-day Adventist Ch., 1950. Pastor Mich. Conf. Seventh-day Adventists, 1946-53; dept. leader S.D. Conf., 1953-54; pastor N.D. Conf., Fargo, 1954-55, Tex. Conf., Rio Grande Valley, 1955-57, So. Calif. Conf., Los Angeles, 1957-75; pastor No. Calif. Conf. Seventh-day Adventists Chs., 1975—. Republican. Home: PO Box 1577 Magalia CA 95954 Office: No Calif Conf Seventh-day Adventists 401 Taylor Blvd Pleasant Hill CA 94523

HARDEMAN, CHERYL LEE, evangelist, Seventh-day Adventist; b. Seoul, Korea, July 25, 1953; d. Doris Anita (Cherry) Hardeman; came to U.S., 1959. B.A. in Sociology, Oakwood Coll., 1975. Evangelist, Seventh-day Adventist, St. Petersburg, Fla., 1979—; coordinator, dir. LEA Lit. Evangelist Assn., St. Petersburg, 1979-80; mem. state bd. State Women's Conv. Seventh-day Adventist chs., 1983—; editor-founder Fla. state How Great Thou Art newsletter, 1983—. Mem. (hon.) Fla. Sherriff's Assn., St. Petersburg, 1983-85; mem. staff (hon.) State Ala. Office of Atty. Gen., 1978—. Named Top Soul Winner in Evangelism, Regional Inst., Orlando, Fla., 1982; elected to Pres.'s Club Ala., 1976; recipient Cert. Merit, ARC Pinellas Country Conf. Mem. South Atlantic Conf. Assn., Southeastern Conf. Assn., Omega Sigma Psi. Home: 2231 14th Ave S St Petersburg FL 33712

HARDENBROOK, KURT O., minister, Ch. of Christ; b. Boise, Idaho, Jan. 19, 1950; s. Donald Orin and Dorothy June (Bartholomew) H.; B.A., Puget Sound Bible Coll., Seattle, 1974; m. Betty Lou Prather, June 26, 1970; children—J. Douglas, Tonya Marie. Ordained to ministry, 1972; minister First Christian Ch., Shelton, Wash., 1972—. Treas. N.W. Schs. of Mission; trustee Christian Evangelistic Assn. Bd. dirs. Tumwater Area council Boy Scouts Am., Mason County chpt. Am. Cancer Soc. Club: Shelton Kiwanis (dir.). Home: 530 E Birch St Shelton WA 98584 Office: PO Box 472 Shelton WA 98584

HARDIN, NEWTON R. N., minister, So. Baptist Conv.; b. Spindale, N.C., Jan. 22, 1926; s. Newton Hunt and Alma Novella (Scoggin) H.; B.A., Carson-Newman Coll., Jefferson City, Tenn., 1950; M.Div., Southeastern Bapt. Theol. Sem., Wake Forest, N.C., 1954; m. Betty Audrey Smith, Nov. 1, 1947; children—Randall, Lonnie. Pastor, Stoner's Grove and Holloways Bapt. Ch. Field, 1954-58; commd. 1st lt. Chaplain Corps, USAF, 1956, advanced through grades to lt. col., 1971; chaplain in U.S., Azore Islands and Thailand, 1958—, Myrtle Beach AFB, S.C., 1975—. Mem. Myrtle Beach Ministerial Assn. (pres. 1976-77), Waccamaw Bapt. Bapt. Pastors Conf. Home: 675 Elder Ave Myrtle Beach SC 29577 Office: 354 CSG/HC Myrtle Beach SC 29577

HARDISON, JESSE PERRY, minister, Southern Baptist Convention. B. Kinston, N.C., Nov. 5, 1956; s. Marcellus Jesse and Estelle (Whaley) H.; m. Mary Robin Stapleford, July 22, 1979. A.A. with honors, Lenoir Community Coll., Kinston, 1977; B.A. magna cum laude, East Carolina U., Greenville, N.C., 1979; M. Divinity, Southeastern Sem., Wake Forest, N.C., 1983, Th.M. candidate, 1983-85. Ordained to ministry So. Bapt. Conv., 1983; minister of youth Dover Missionary Bapt. Ch., N.C., 1976-79, pastor, 1979—; bd. ministers Campbell U., Buies Creek, N.C., 1982—. Fellow Southeastern Bapt. Sem.; mem. So. Bapt. Hist. Soc., Atlantic Bapt. Assn. (exec. council 1979—), Phi Theta Kappa. Democrat. Home: PO Box 546 Knightdale NC 27545 Office: Dover Missionary Bapt Ch PO Box 158 Dover NC 28526

HARDMAN, KEITH JORDAN, philosophy and religion educator, Presbyterian Church in the U.S.A. b. Wellsville, N.Y., May 20, 1931; s. Keith Jordan and Frances Marie (Drumm) H.; m. Jean Ethel Parker, June 22, 1963; children: Carolyn, Keith Jordan III, Colleen. B.A., Haverford Coll., 1954; M.Div., Princeton Theol. Sem., 1957; M.A., Columbia U., 1961; Ph.D., U. Pa., 1970. Ordained to ministry Presbyn. Ch. 1957. Minister Southwestern Presbyn. Ch., Phila., 1957-70; asst. prof. philosophy and religion Ursinus Coll., Collegeville, Pa., 1970-77, assoc. prof., 1977—; v.p. Covenant Prodns., King of Prussia, Pa., 1983—; interim pastor Market Square Presbyn. Ch., Phila., 1981—. Author: Ingredients of the Christian Faith, 1980; The Spiritual Awakeners, 1983; Charles Grandison Finney: Revivalist, Reformer and Radical, 1985. Contbr. articles to profl. jours. Home: 815 Mockingbird Ln Audubon PA 19403 Office: Ursinus Coll Collegeville PA 19426

HARDT, JOHN W., bishop Okla. Conf., United Methodist Ch., Oklahoma City. Office: 2217 NW 18th St Oklahoma City OK 73130*

HARE, PETER HEWITT, philosophy educator, Episcopal Church; b. N.Y.C., Mar. 12, 1935; s. Michael Meredith and Jane Perry (Jopling) H.; m. Daphne Joan Kean, May 30, 1959; children: Clare Kean, Gwendolyn Meigs. B.A. in Philosophy, Yale U., 1957; M.A., Columbia U., 1962, Ph.D., 1965. Prof. philosophy SUNY-Buffalo, 1962—. Co-author: Evil and the Concept of God, 1968; Causing, Perceiving and Believing, 1975; co-editor: Religion, History and Spiritual Democracy, 1980; A Women's Quest for Science: Portrait of Anthropologist Elsie Clews Parsons, 1985; mem. editorial bd. Philosophy Research Archives, 1975—, Am. Philos. Quar., 1978—. NEH younger scholar, 1968-69. Mem. N.Y. State Philos. Assn. (pres. 1975-77), Charles S. Pierce Soc. (pres. 1976, editor quar. 1974—), Soc. for Advancement Am. Philosophy (exec. com. 1977-80). Republican. Home: 219 Depew Ave Buffalo NY 14214 Office: Philosophy Dept Baldy Hall SUNY-Buffalo Buffalo NY 14260

HARE, ROBERT LEE, JR., evangelist, Churches of Christ; b. McKinney, Tex., Jan. 12, 1920; s. Robert Lee and Mary Charlotte (Ingle) H.; m. Ruth Lorene Bradley, June 6, 1949; children: Reggy Lynn Hiller, Mary Lee, Linda Jean. B.A., Harding U., 1950, M.A., 1956; postgrad. Vienna U., 1958. Ordained to ministry Ch. of Christ, 1940. Preacher, Ch. Christ, Olyphant, Ark., 1946-48, Judsonia, Ark., 1949-50; evangelist Ch. Christ, Munich, Fed. Republic Germany, 1950-55, Salzburg, Austria, 1952-55, Vienna, 1956-81, throughout Eastern Europe, 1960—. Contbr. articles to religious jours. Recipient Disting. Alumnus award Harding U., 1981. Served in USN, 1944-46, PTO. Republican. Club: Frater Sodalis Searcy (pres. 1947, 49). Home and Office: 307 S Harding Breckenridge TX 76024

HARGIS, BILLY JAMES, evangelist, Independent Christian Churches (Disciples); foundation executive; b. Texarkana, Tex., Aug. 3, 1925; s. James Earsel and Laura Lucille (Fowler) H.; m. Betty Jane Secrest, Dec. 21, 1951; children: Bonnie Jane Abrego, Billy James II, Becky Jean Killburn, Brenda Jo Davis. B.A., Pikes Peak Bible Sem., 1957; Th.B., Burton Coll., 1958; LL.D. (hon.), Bob Jones U., 1961. Ordained to ministry Ind. Christian Chs. (Disciples), 1944. Pastor, First Christian Ch., Sallisaw, Okla., 1944-46, Granby, Mo., 1946-47, Sapulpa, Okla,, 1947-50; founder, pres. Ch. of Christian Crusade, Tulsa, 1948—, pastor, Tulsa, 1966—, Neosho, Mo., 1982—; pres., founder Billy James Hargis Evangelistic Assn., Tulsa, 1975—, David Livingstone Missionary Found., Tulsa, 1970-80, Am. Christian Coll., Tulsa, 1970-74, Ams. Against Abortion, Tulsa, since 1971—, Good Samaritan Children's Found., Tulsa, 1975—; pub. Christian Crusade Newspaper, 1948—; speaker Christian Crusade Daily Network Broadcast, 1949—, Christian Crusade TV Network, 1964—; pres. Christian Crusade Pub. Co., Tulsa, 1949—. Home: Rose of Sharon Farm Box 279 Neosho MO 64850 Office: Box 977 Tulsa OK 74102

HARGRAVE, CHARLES CLYDE, minister, Ch. of God, Cleveland, Tenn.; b. Mount Vernon, Tex., Sept. 4, 1930; s. Benonie Sparks and Stella Annetti (Ledbetter) H.; student Internat. Prep. Inst., San Antonio, 1948-50; Del Mar Coll., 1953-54, Canal Zone Coll., 1972; m. Erma Joy Brown, May 15, 1948; children—Sandra Kay, Joy Lynn, Kathy Gail, Rose Charlene, John Mark. Ordained to ministry, 1959; evangelist, Tex., 1946-49; pastor chs., Tex., N.Mex., Miss., 1950-58; missionary overseer Ch. of God, Honduras, 1959-61, Guatemala, 1961-64, El Salvador, 1964-66, Panama, 1966-72; pastor Ch. of God, Ada, Okla., 1972-74; supt. N. Central Spanish Chs. of God, Lansing, Ill., 1974—. Pres. Ch. of God Bible Inst. C.Am., Santa Tecla, El Salvador,

1964-66, founder, pres. Panama Bible Inst., 1968-72; builder Internat. Latin Sem., Ciudad Radial, Panama, 1970; exec. sec. Evang. Alliance Panama, 1970; pres. Internat. Bible Inst. Chgo. (Spanish), 1974—. Home: 3341 178th St Lansing IL 60438 Office: Box 512 3554 Ridge Rd Lansing IL 60438

HARGROVE, THURMAN LOUIS, SR., minister, Apostolic Faith; accountant; b. Warren County, N.C., May 16, 1940; s. James Daniel and Lucy (Henderson) H.; m. Birddie Hendorson, Aug. 15, 1959; children: Thurman, Jr., Zelna, Ivan, Immanual. Cert. IBM Tng. Inst., 1966; student computer programming Southside Va. Community Coll., 1972; Doctorate (hon.), New Haven Theol. Sem. Ordained to ministry Church of Our Lord Jesus Christ, 1966. Dist. sec. Ch. of Our Lord Jesus Christ, Va., 1970-80, state sec., 1980—, dist. elder, 1980—; prison minister Brunswick Corrections, Lawrenceville, Va., 1982—; pastor Refuge Ch., Alberta, Va., 1971—; mem. nat. fin. com. Ch. of Our Lord Jesus Christ, N.Y., 1979-82; adminstr. Refuge Day Care, 1976—; acct. St. Paul's Coll., Lawrenceville, Va., 1968—. Bd. dirs. Wellness Com., Brunswick, Colo., 1984, Brunswick Health Care, 1984—. Lodge: Optimist (sec. 1982—, bd. dirs. 1981-82). Democrat. Home: PO Box 44 Alberta VA 23821

HARISTON, CHRISTAL TROYLEE, minister Bible Way Church World Wide Inc.; b. Winston-Salem, May 18, 1924; s. James Theodore and Laura (Florence) H.; m. Mattie O'Neall Taylor, July 21, 1946; children: Barbara Oneall Carter, Christal Hairston. B.Th., Am. Bible Coll., 1967. Ordained to ministry Bible Way Ch. World Wide Inc. Pastor, Bible Way Ch., Richmond, Va., 1962—; gen. sec. Bible Way Ch. World Wide Inc., 1976—, central dist. dir., Richmond, 1967—, exec. bd., 1976—, vice bishop to State of Va., 1974—; trustee Bible Way World Wide, Inc., State of Va., 1980—, Richmond, 1962—. Mem. Commn. on Human Relations, Richmond, 1983; gen. sec. Sr. Citizens, Richmond, 1981; bd. dirs. Social Action for the Ch., Richmond, 1984—. Served with U.S. Army, 1946-47. Address: Bible Way Church World Wide Inc 1630 Rose Ave Richmond VA 23222

HARKINS, JAMES STANLEY, lay church worker, Southern Baptist Convention; educator; b. Blairsville, Ga., Dec. 15, 1932; s. General Pat and Maver Clara (Nix) H.; B.A. in History, U. W.Fla., 1969, B.A. in Edn., 1973; D.D., So. Bible Sem., 1975; M.A. in Counseling, Troy State U., 1977; M.E., U. West. Fla., 1980; m. Leanora Julette Johnson, Dec. 25, 1964; children: James Stanley, Brett Johnson. Minister music Ardsley Park Bapt. Ch., Savannah, Ga., 1953-54, Second Bapt. Ch., Harlingen, Tex., 1960, Ballast Point Bapt. Ch., Tampa, Fla., 1961; asst. minister music First Bapt. Ch., Ft. Walton Beach, Fla., 1962-67; interim minister music Cinco Bapt. Ch., Ft. Walton Beach, 1967-73; minister music First Bapt. Ch., Mary Esther, Fla., 1973-75; founder, pres. Am. Gospel, Inc., Ft. Walton Beach, 1974—, Conservative Majority for Citizens' Rights in Am., 1981; with Nationwide Affiliates, monthly gospel concerts in Civic Auditoriums. Tchr. Bruner Jr. High Sch., 1973—. Author, pub.: The Angry Samaritan; History and Development of Curriculum for the Mentally Retarded; Curriculum Development in the Secondary School; Christian Education vs Secular Education. Home: 302 Briarwood Circle NW Fort Walton Beach FL 32548 Office: Bruner Jr High Sch Fort Walton Beach FL 32548

HARKINS, WARREN WILLIAM, minister, Assemblies of God; b. Miami, Okla., Mar. 3, 1945; s. Virgil D. and Shirley Dean (Buffalo) Baker; diploma, Trinity Bible Coll., 1967; M.Min., Trinity Theol. Sem., 1982; m. Caroline Jane Merit, July 19, 1963; children: Warren David, Stephen Dean. Ordained to ministry, 1971; pastor Assembly of God Ch., Roby, Mo., 1970-71, First Assembly of God Ch., Iola, Kans., 1971-72, First Assembly of God Ch., Bernie, Mo., 1972-74, Skyview Assembly of God Ch., Sand Springs, Okla., from 1974; now sr. pastor First Assembly of God Ch., Comanche, Okla.; chaplain CAP. Mem. Sand Springs Area Pastors Fellowship, Tulsa Area Ministers Fellowship. Contbr. articles to religious publs. Home: 6133 S 126th West Ave Tulsa OK 74107 Office: PO Box 105 Comanche OK 73529

HARKNESS, SHEPHERD GARFIELD, minister, religious organization executive, United Methodist Church. b. Eutaw, Ala., Nov. 15, 1937; s. Marshall and Iola (Colvin) H.; m. Pearleye M. Savage, Dec. 24, 1959; children: Gina Shalon, Shepherd Demetrius. Diploma Chattanooga Bus. Coll., 1964; B.A., Am. Bapt. Coll., 1968; M.Div., Gammon Theol. Sem., 1975. Ordained to ministry United Meth. Ch., 1971. Social worker United Meth. Community Ctr., Chattanooga, 1969-71; coordinator Wesley Brock Community Ctr., Chattanooga, 1971-73; pastor, 1969-81; dist. supt. United Meth. Ch., East Ohio Conf., Painesville, 1981—; del. United Meth. Gen. Conf., Balt., 1984—, North Central Jurisdictional Conf., Duluth, Minn., 1984. Organizer NAACP, Oberlin, 1975, bd. mem., 1975. Served with USAF, 1955-59. Recipient Disting. Service award Chattanooga C. of C., 1970; Outstanding Leadership award Youngstown Interdenominational Ministerial Alliance, Ohio, 1981. Mem. Nat. Urban League, Nat. Black Meths. for Ch. Renewal, Nat. C. of C., Nat. Clergy Assn., NAACP. Republican. Lodge: Masons. Home: 222 Fairfield Rd Painesville OH Office: Painesville Dist Office UMC 1610 Mentor Ave Room 1 Painesville OH 44077

HARLAN, JOHN DENORMANDIE, JR., minister, Am. Bapt. Chs., U.S.A.; b. New Kensington, Pa., Nov. 18, 1946; s. John D. and Nancy E. (Rorabaugh) H.; B.A., U. Miami, 1970; M.Div., Eastern Bapt. Theol. Sem., 1971; m. Patricia Lynne McLendon, Nov. 20, 1971; 1 dau., Courtney Joy. Ordained to ministry, 1971; minister of edn. Univ. Christian Ch., Miami, Fla., 1971-74; pastor 1st Bapt. Ch., Lewistown, Pa., 1974—. Mem. region youth com. Am. Bapt. Chs. of Pa. and Del., 1975—; chmn. bd. Christian edn. Centre Bapt. Assn., 1976—. Bd. dirs. Juniata Valley YMCA, 1976—. Mem. Lewistown Ministerial Assn. Home: 109 E 3d St Lewistown PA 17044 Office: 111 E 3d St Lewistown PA 17044

HARMELINK, HERMAN III, minister, educator; b. Sheldon, Pa., Dec. 26, 1933; s. Herman Andrew and Thyrza (Eringa) H.; m. Barbara Mary Conibear, Aug. 11, 1959; children: Herman Alan, Lindsay Alexandra. B.A. cum laude, Central Coll., Pella, Iowa, 1954; M.A., Columbia U., 1955; M.Div., New Brunswick Sem., 1958; S.T.M. magna cum laude, Union Theol. Sem., 1964, M.Phil., 1978. Ordained to ministry Reformed Ch. Am., 1959. Assoc. minister Community Ch., Glen Rock, N.J., 1959-64; minister Woodcliff Community Ch., Woodcliff-on-Hudson, N.J., 1964-71; minister The Reformed Ch., Poughkeepsie, N.Y., 1971—; adj. faculty philosophy SUNY, Poughkeepsie, 1983—; chmn. interchurch relations Reformed Ch. Am., N.Y.C., 1964-71, pres. Synod N.J., New Brunswick, 1968-69; advisor World Council Chs., Uppsala, Sweden, 1968; vice chmn. Faith & Order Commn. Nat. Council Chs., N.Y.C., 1976-79; pres. Dutchess Interfaith Council, Poughkeepsie, 1977-78. Author: Ecumenism and the Reformed Church, 1968; Another Look at Frelinghuysen & His Awakening, 1968; The Reformed Church in New Jersey, 1969; contbr.: Piety and Patriotism, 1978, Vision from the Hill, 1984. Bd. trustees Dutchess County Hist. Soc., Poughkeepsie, 1974-78; bd. trustees Dutchess County Arts Council, 1976-80, Bardavon 1869 Opera House, Poughkeepsie, 1979-80; bd. trustees, exec. com. St. Francis Hosp., Poughkeepsie, 1979—; pres. bd. Ranfurly Library Services, N.Y.C., 1982—. Served to lt. USNR, 1957-61. Paul Harris fellow Rotary Internat. 1980; Fulbright grantee, 1958-59. Mem. N. Am. Acad. Ecumenists, Am. Soc. Ch. History, Presby. Hist. Soc., Poughkeepsie Area C. of C., New Brunswick Sem. Alumni Assn. (pres. 1967-68). Clubs: Circumnavigators (mem. program com. 1984—), Poughkeepsie Social Reading (pres. 1980-82). Lodge: Rotary (pres. 1977-79, sec. 1979—, dist. gov. 1982-83). Office: 70 Hooker Ave Poughkeepsie NY 12601

HARMER, CATHERINE MARY, nun, consultant psychologist, Roman Catholic Church. b. Phila., Sept. 6, 1932; s. John Thomas and Frances Regina (Keogh) H. B.A. in Philosophy, Chestnut Hill Coll., 1957; M.S., Cath. U. Am., 1962; M.A. in Psychology, Temple U., 1970, Ph.D. in Psychology, 1973. Joined Med. Mission Sisters, Roman Cath. Ch., 1950. Religious formation, librarian Med. Mission Sisters, Phila., Philippines, 1957-62, 62-65, Rawalpind, Pakistan, 1965-68, pvt. practice psychology, 1982—, major superior, 1976-82, religious systems dir. Mng. Design, Inc., Cin., 1972-82; bd. dirs. Div. Overseas Ministries, Nat. Council Chs., N.Y.C., 1976-82; bd. dirs. U.S. Cath. Mission Council, Washington, 1976-79; founding organizer U.S. Cath. Mission Assn., Washington, 1980-83; program com. Leadership Conf. Religious Women, region III, Phila., 1976-82. Author: Books for Religious Sisters, 1964. NDEA Title IV fellow Temple U., Phila., 1971-73. Mem. Am. Psychol. Assn., Assn. Humanistic Psychology, Assn. Women in Psychology, Assn. for Psychol. Type, People's Med. Soc., LWV, Network, Common Cause, Delta Epsilon Sigma, Phi Beta Mu. Democrat. Home: 5617 N Palethorpe St Philadelphia PA 19120 Office: Med Mission Sisters 8400 Pine Rd Philadelphia PA 19111

HARMS, WILLIAM CARL, priest, Roman Catholic Church; b. Bronx, N.Y., Nov. 15, 1939; s. William Carl and Veronica Gertrude (Doyle) H.; B.A., Seton Hall U., South Orange, N.J., 1961; M. in City and Regional Planning, Rutgers U., 1973; M.Div., Immaculate Conception Sem., Darlington, N.J., 1975; M.A., Seton Hall, 1977. Ordained priest, 1965; asst. pastor St. Michael's Ch., Elizabeth, N.J., 1965-71; dir. planning Roman Cath. Archdiocese Newark Sch. Office, 1973-75, planning assoc. Office Research and Planning, 1975-78, dir. pastoral planning, 1978-81; cons. U.S. Army Chaplain Bd., 1981-82; assoc. pastor O.L.P.H., Oakland, N.J., 1982-85; dir. ch. mgmt. program Seton Hall U., South Orange, N.J., 1985—. County dir. Mt. Carmel Guild, Apostolate for Deaf, 1965-75; mem. mission to city Roman Cath. Archdiocese Newark, 1967-69, mem. ednl. planning commn., 1972-74. Adv. bd. Elizabeth Community Adv. Program, 1966-70; mem. Elizabeth Human Relations Commn., 1966-71; bd. dirs. Eastern Union County chpt. ARC, 1966-71; chmn. priority com. Eastern Union County United Way, 1968-70; mem. Tri-State Regional Planning Commn. Contbr. articles on pastoral planning. Recipient various service awards. Mem. Nat. Conf. Pastoral Planning (chairperson 1980-83, coordinating com.), Am. Inst. Planners (asso.), Am. Soc. Planning Ofcls., Internat. Soc. Ednl. Planners, Nat. Career Edn. Assn., Regional Plan Assn., Delta Kappa Psi. Home and Office: Seton Hall U 400 S Orange Ave South Orange NJ 07079

HARP, CHARLES OLIN, lay ch. worker, United Meth. Ch.; b. Haynesville, La., Feb. 7, 1900; s. Charles Willis and Mary Lizzie (Sherman) W.; Ph.G., Atlanta Coll. Pharmacy, 1922; m. Georgina McKinley Paterson, Mar. 17, 1946. Mem. lay witness movement United Methodist Ch., 1966; mem. conf. bd. health and welfare, 1968—; treas. First United Meth. Ch. Prichard, Ala., 1954—, bd. stewards, 1952—, mem. commn. for upkeep of dist. parsonage, 1968—, chmn. ofcl. bd., 1970-72, chmn. pastor-parish relations com., 1958-64, trustee, 1966-75; treas. United Meth. conf. Bd. Health and Welfare, 1970-74. Club: Meth. Men's Club (Prichard). Address: 227 Baratara Dr E Chicksaw AL 36611

HARPER, EDWARD JOHN, bishop, Roman Catholic Church; b. Bklyn., July 23, 1910; s. John Edward and Josephine Theresa (Realander) H.; St. Mary's Coll., North East, Pa., 1928-33, Mt. St. Alphonsus, 1934-40. Joined Congregation of Most Holy Redeemer, 1934, ordained priest, 1939, consecrated bishop, 1960; missionary priest, Mayaguez, P.R., 1941-46; superior First Redemptorist Found. in Republic of Santo Domingo, Las Matas de Farfan, 1946-50; dean of Mayaguez, P.R., 1950-56; provincial Vice Province of San Juan, P.R. of Redemptoris Fathers, 1956-60; bishop of Earclea Pontica and prelate of V.I., 1960-77; 1st residential bishop of Diocese of St. Thomas, V.I., 1977—. Sec. Conf. Cath. Bishops of P.R.; chmn. bd. Interdiocesan Cath. Sem. P.R. Pres. Citizens' Com. for Drug Edn. Bd. dirs. V.I. Econ. Devel. Council, V.I. Council on Alcoholism; trustee Cath. U. P.R., Santa Maria. Address: 9 Estate Elizabeth Box 1825 St Thomas VI 00801

HARPER, GEORGE LEA, retired minister, United Methodist Church; b. Tabor City, N.C., Feb. 10, 1915; s. Matt Cleveland and Cara Wilhelmina (Lea) H.; B.A., U. Richmond, 1937; B.D., Emory U., 1951, M.Div., 1972; m. Mildred Jeannette Surrency, Oct. 24, 1943; children: George Lea, Thomas Edwin, Naina Jean (Mrs. Richard White), Jane Cara (Mrs. Donald Sanborn Lewis), David Hampton, Ada Jo. Ordained to ministry United Methodist Ch. as deacon, 1943, elder, 1943; pastor chs., Trenton-Newberry, 1940-42, Inverness, 1942-43; served to capt., chaplain AUS, 1943-46; pastor, Citra, 1946-47, Venice-Nokomis, 1947-50, Palmetto, 1950-51, Frostproof, 1952-54, Wauchula, 1954-58, Bartow, 1958-62, Tampa, Seminole Heights, 1962-64, Jacksonville, Avondale, Fla., 1964-68, Broadway Ch., Orlando, 1968-70, Mt. Dora, 1970-72, 1st Meth. Ch. Starke, 1972-80, ret., 1980 (all Fla.); mem. Bd. Missions Fla. Conf., 1956-64, sec., 1960-64. Vice pres. Mental Health Bd., 1975-77, pres., 1977-80; pres. Bradford County Children's Com., 1975; mem. ednl. adv. council, 1974; Bd. dirs. North Central Fla. Community Mental Health Ctr., 1976-79. Recipient Humanitarian Service award Starke-Bradford County C. of C., 1979. Mem. Bradford County (pres. 1974), Starke (pres. 1973) ministerial alliances, Phi Beta Kappa, Omicron Delta Kappa, Tau Kappa Alpha, Alpha Mu Omicron, Phi Gamma Delta. Kiwanian (pres. 1970), Rotarian (pres. 1977-78, Paul Harris fellow 1978). Home and Office: 2435 NW 55th Blvd Gainesville FL 32606

HARPER, RAY, JR., minister, Disciples of Christ Church; b. Carroll County, Ind., Nov. 21, 1925; s. Ray and Opal Regina (Lynch) H.; B.A., Canterbury Coll., 1949; postgrad. Butler U., 1949-50, Butler Sch. Religion, 1950-51; m. Elyse E. Long, Dec. 13, 1957; children: Kevin, Lon, Marc. Ordained to ministry, 1951. Youth dir., Danville, Ind., 1949-51; minister of youth and edn., Lincoln, Nebr., 1951-57; minister Christian edn., Fremont, Nebr., 1957-59; minister of Christian edn., Yakima, Wash., 1959-64; minister of Christian Edn., Bellflower, Calif., 1964-81; pastor First Christian Ch., Monrovia, Calif., 1981—. Pres., Bellflower Coordinating Council, 1970-71, 71-72; trustee Bellflower Unified Sch. Dist., 1975; pres. Bellflower Bd. Edn., 1976; bd. dirs. Monrovia ARC, 1985. Mem. Assn. Christian Ch. Educators (nat. pres. 1972-73), Monrovia Ministerial Assn. (pres. 1983, 84). Home: 139 W Palm Ave Monrovia CA 91016 Office: 147 W Palm Ave Monrovia CA 91016

HARPER, RICHARD MUNROE, minister, United Methodist Church; b. St. Paul, Sept. 5, 1930; s. Raymond Benjamin and Minnie Josephine (Docken) H.; m. Shirley Ann Spencer, Nov. 9, 1950; children: Ruth Elise, Emily Ellen, Paul Richard. B.A., Macalester Coll., 1951; B.D., Evang. Theol. Sem., 1954. Ordained to ministry United Meth. Ch., 1954. Pastor, E.U.B. Ch., Le Sueur, Minn., 1954-58, Bethany United Meth. Ch., Rochester, Minn., 1958-61, Messiah United Meth. Ch., Plymouth, Minn., 1971-78, Sunrise United Meth. Ch., Mounds View, Minn., 1984—; dist. supt. United Meth. Ch., Mpls., 1978-84; trustee Meth. Hosp., St. Louis Park, Minn., 1978—; Walker Meth. Residence and Health Services, Inc., Mpls., 1978—; del. to jurisdictional conf. United Meth. Ch., Dayton, Ohio,

1980. Contbr. articles, sermons to religious publs. Mem. Hymn Soc. Am., Mpls. Ministerial Assn. (v.p. 1977-78), Minn. Conf. Hist. Soc., Garrett-Evang. Alumni Assn. (pres. 1973-74). Club: Y's Men's (Rochester, Minn.). Home: 2520 County Rd I Mounds View MN 55432 Office: Sunrise United Meth Ch 2520 County Rd I Mounds View MN 55432

HARPER, RONALD DEAN, religious publishing administrator, Seventh-day Adventists; b. Peculiar, Mo., Mar. 10, 1935; s. Raymond Henry and Mildred Louise (King) H.; m. Phyliss June Zaritz, Mar. 7, 1965; children: David, Monica. Student, Central Mo. State U., 1953-54; Assoc. Sci., Central Tech. Inst., Kansas City, Mo., 1957-59. Lit. evangelist Home Health Edn. Service, Kansas City, Mo., 1975-81, Springfield, Mo., 1981-82; asst. pub. dir. Seventh-day Adventist Ch., Springfield, 1982—. Served with U.S. Army, 1954-56. Home: Route 1 Box 133-7 Ozark MO 65721 Office: PO Box 65665 West Des Moines IA 50265

HARPER, TERRY LAYNE, minister, Southern Baptist Convention; b. Roanoke, Va., May 20, 1948; s. Carl P. and Lottie O. (Cook) H.; m. Cheryl Davis, June 1, 1974; children: Derrick Layne, Carla DeAnn. A.A., Bluefield Coll., 1971; B.S. in Psychology, Averett Coll., 1973; M.Div., Southeastern Bapt. Theol. Sem., 1979. Ordained to ministry Bapt. Ch., 1972. Pastor, White Rock Bapt. Ch., Hardy, Va., 1973-74, Exmore Bapt. Ch., Va., 1974-76, First Bapt. Ch., Alamance, N.C., 1976-79, Waverly Bapt. Ch., Va., 1979-84, Colonial Heights Bapt. Ch., Va., 1984—; dir. evangelism Petersburg Bapt. Assn., Va., 1982-84; mem. faculty Eagle Eyrie Bapt. Assembly, Lynchburg, Va., 1980-83. Vocalist, rec. artist. Mem. Petersburg Human Rights Commn., 1980—. Home: 2010 Snead Ave Colonial Heights VA 23834

HARPUR, THOMAS WILLIAM, writer, broadcaster, Anglican Church; b. Toronto, Apr. 14, 1929; s. William Wallace and Elizabeth (Hoey) H.; m. Mary Clark, June 2, 1956 (div. 1983); children: Elizabeth, Margaret, Mary Catharine; m. Susan Bette Anne Coles, Apr. 7, 1984. B.A., U. Coll., U. Toronto, 1951; B.A., Oriel Coll., Oxford, Eng., 1954, M.A., 1956; M.Div., Wycliffe Coll., Toronto, 1956. Ordained deacon Anglican Ch., 1954, priest, 1956, resigned orders, 1979. Curate St. John's York Mills, Toronto, 1956-57; rector St. Margaret's-in-the-Pines, West Hill, Ont., 1957-64; lectr. introductory philosophy Trinity Coll. and Wycliffe Coll., 1959-63; assoc. prof. N.T., Greek, Wycliffe Coll., 1964-68; prof. Toronto Sch. Theology, 1969-71; religion editor Toronto Star, 1971-83; freelance writer, broadcaster on religious affairs, 1983—; host radio show, 1967-71; host TV show Sta. CFTO-TV, Toronto, 1979-84. Co-editor: Jesus, 1973; author: Road to Bethlehem, 1977; Harpur's Heaven and Hell, 1983. Recipient Gold medal U. Toronto, 1951; Award of Merit Religious Pub. Relations Council, 1974; Rhodes scholar, 1951. Mem. Can. Assn. Rhodes Scholars, Assn. Can. Radio and TV Artists. Home: PO Box 4231 Station C Richmond Hill ON L4E 1B1 Canada

HARRELL, WILHELMINA WINERICH, practitioner, Church of Christ Scientist; b. Houston; d. Charles Henry and Shelma (Sheffield) Winerich; diploma Washington Sem., Atlanta, 1927; diploma in music Finch Jr. Coll., N.Y.C., 1929; m. Robert Ditchler Harrell, Sept. 10, 1929; children—Robert Ditchler, Nancy Harrell Ellison Hellman. Worker, Women's House of Detention, N.Y.C., 1969-71; reader Goldwater Hosp., N.Y.C., 1965-68; mem. exec. bd. for Christian Sci. instnl. services N.Y. State, 1968-71; bd. dirs. Manhattan-Bronx Vis. Nurse Assn. for Christian Scientists, Inc.; trustee 8th Ch. Christian Science, N.Y.C., 1972-74. Home and Office: 1175 York Ave New York NY 10021

HARREN, ROBERT CHARLES, priest, Roman Catholic Church; b. St. Francis, Minn., Aug. 2, 1940; s. Norbert Nicholas and Frances B. (Lange) H.; B.A., St. John's U., Collegeville, Minn., 1962; J.C.L., N. Am. Coll., Rome, Italy, 1970. Ordained priest, 1966; asso. pastor St. John's Ch., Foley, Minn., 1966-68; chancellor Diocese of St. Cloud (Minn.) Roman Cath. Ch., 1970-84, vicar gen. Diocese of St. Cloud, 1984—, vice-officialis tribunal, 1970-78; pastor St. Lawrence Parish, Duelm, Minn., 1971—. Mem. Priest's Senate, Diocese of St. Cloud, 1971-75, mem. Pastoral Council, 1974-76; sec., bd. trustees St. Cloud Hosp., 1975-78. Mem. adv. com. Foley (Minn.) Sch., 1976-78; mem. rev. com. Benton County 4-H and Youth Devel., 1976-79; mem. Benton County Devel. Council, 1975-79. Mem. Canon Law Soc. Am., K. of C. Home: Route 2 Foley MN 56329 Office: 214 3d Ave S St Cloud MN 56301

HARRINGTON, TIMOTHY J., bishop, Roman Catholic Church. Bishop of Worcester, Mass., 1983—. Office: 2 High Ridge Rd Worcester MA 01602*

HARRIS, C. R. Bishop, Apostolic Overcoming Holy Church of God. Office: 7925 Kimbark Ave Chicago IL 60619*

HARRIS, CHARLES UPCHURCH, church official, priest, Episcopal Ch.; b. Raleigh, N.C., May 2, 1914; s. Charles U. and Saidee Westbrook (Robbins) H.; B.A., Wake Forest U., 1935; M.Div., Va. Theol. Sem., 1938, D.D. (hon.), 1957; D.D. (hon.), Union Theol. Sem., 1940; D.Canon Law (hon.), Seabury-Western Sem., 1972; m. Janet Jeffrey Carlile, June 17, 1940; children: John C., Diana (Mrs. S.N. Melvin). Ordained to ministry as deacon, 1938, priest, 1939. Deacon-in-charge, rector All Saints Ch., Roanoke Rapids, N.C., 1938-39; asst. rector St. Bartholomew's Ch., N.Y.C., 1939-40; rector Trinity Ch., Roslyn, N.Y., 1940-46; rector Trinity Ch., Highland Park, Ill., 1946-57; pres., dean Seabury-Western Theol. Sem., Evanston, Ill., 1957-72. Hon. chaplain Archbishop of Canterbury, 1961; chmn. Chgo. Theol. Inst., 1967-72; pres. Inst. Advanced Theol. Studies, Chgo., 1969-72; mem. Drafting Com. Holy Eucharist, Episcopal Ch., 1969-76, sec., 1970-76. Bd. dirs. Anglican Theol. Rev., 1957—, pres., 1968—; trustee Am. Schs. Oriental Research, 1975, treas., 1985; mem. alumni council Wake Forest U., 1975-78, bd. visitors, 1978—; mem. adv. council St. George's Coll., Jerusalem, 1975—; bd. dirs. Div. Sch. U. Chgo.; trustee Cyprus-Am. Archeal. Research Inst., 1979—, pres., 1984—. Consortium dir. Joint archeol. expdn. to Tell el Hesi (Israel), 1972-73, 75. Mem. Acad. Parish Clergy, Am. Acad. Religion, Soc. Colonial Warriors, S.R. Contbr. to Confirmation: History, Doctrine and Practice, 1962; Episcopal Church in Mid-Century, 1965; Preaching About Death, 1975; Harris-LeCroy Report, 1976. Contbr. revs. and articles to secular publs. and religious jours. Home: Flint Hill Farm Delaplane VA 22025 Office: 811 Westerfield Dr Wilmette IL 60091

HARRIS, CHARLOTTE DONA, minister, Christian Church (Disciples of Christ); elementary school educator; b. Los Angeles, Apr. 23, 1946; d. John Henry and Celestal Lula (Riley) H. A.A., Los Angeles City Coll., 1966; B.A., Calif. State U.-Los Angeles, 1968, M.A. in Edn., 1976; M.Div., Am. Bapt. Sem. of West, 1983. Ordained to ministry, Christian Ch. (Disciples of Christ), 1984. Teen post dir. First Congl. Ch., Pasadena, Calif., 1971-72; youth choral dir. Holman United Meth. Ch., Los Angeles, 1971-75; resident counselor Ecumenical summer Service, Los Angeles, 1974; counselor Los Angeles Summer Youth Program, 1978; 50th anniversary historian McCarty Christian Ch., Los Angeles, 1979-81; sem. student intern Pacific Southwest Disciples of Christ, Los Angeles, summer 1982; student pastor Mt. Hollywood Congl. Ch., Los Angeles, 1983; racial/ethnic resource leader Disciples of Christ Homeland Ministries, 1984—. Elem. tchr. Los Angeles sch. dist., 1971—. Vol. sec. Operation Breadbasket, Los Angeles, 1968; active Black Women's Forum, Los Angeles, 1978—; vol. Tom Bradley mayoral campaign, Los Angeles, 1968, Robert Kennedy presdl. campaign, 1968; active Adams-Jefferson Palm Grove Assn., Los Angeles. Recipient Vol. award Calif. Senate, 1984; Acad. Excellence award Ecumenical Ctr. Black Ch. Studies, 1984; Cert. of Recognition, Los Angeles Council Chs., 1979. Mem. United Tchrs. Los Angeles, Calif. Tchrs. Assn., Disciple Women in Ministry. Democrat. Home: Los Angeles CA Office: Mt Hollywood Congl Ch 4607 Prospect Ave Los Angeles CA 90027

HARRIS, DAVID, JR., minister, non-denomination; b. Dallas, Apr. 12, 1931; s. David Harris and Annie M. (Sanford) H. B.S., Wilby Coll., 1957; B.D., Southwestern Sem., 1967, M.R.E., 1968, M.A., 1983; L.H.D. (hon.), Teamer Bible Sch., 1981. Pastor, 2d Corinthian Ch., Dallas, 1968—; lectr. chs., colls., univs. Owner, operator Janitorial Service Bus., Dallas, 1970—. Mem. nat. steering com. Nat. Orgn. Black Colls., Washington, 1984—; chmn. So. Leadership Conf., 1982—. Named by Resolution, Dallas Commrs.; named Outstanding Citizen, Second Corinthian Ch.; recipient award Dallas Times-Herald. Republican. Lodge: Masons (Dallas).

HARRIS, DONNELL RAY, minister, American Baptist Churches U.S.A.; b. St. Louis, June 12, 1936; s. David Pritchard and Jewel (Mitchener) H.; B.A., William Jewell Coll., 1958; B.D., Am. Assn. Theol. Schs. Sr. Honors fellow, Colgate Rochester Div. Sch., 1962, Th.M., 1972; m. Norma Ruth Stacy, June 1, 1959; children—Stacy Lynne, Stephen Donnell. Ordained to ministry, 1962; minister West Shore Bapt. Ch., Rocky River, Ohio, 1962-67, First Bapt. Ch. in Chili, Rochester, N.Y., 1967-75, Montgomery Hills Bapt. Ch., Silver Spring, Md., 1975—. Clk. Am. Bapt. Chs. N.Y., 1973-75; mem. gen. bd. Am. Bapt. Chs. U.S.A., 1977-83, mem. world relief com., 1979-83. Contbr. articles to religious publs. Home: 14305 Myer Terr Rockville MD 20853 Office: 9727 Georgia Ave Silver Spring MD 20910

HARRIS, HINTON HARMON, JR., minister, So. Baptist Conv.; b. Powhatan County, Va., Feb. 8, 1937; s. Hinton Harmon and Alice Harris (Duffer) H.; B.A., Carson-Newman Coll., 1959; Th.M. with honors, New Orleans Bapt. Theol. Sem., 1968, M.R.E., 1970; m. Barbara Jean Ellison, Dec. 23, 1958; 1 son, David Michael. Ordained to ministry, 1961; minister music and edn. Fair Oaks Bapt. Ch., Marietta, Ga., 1959-61; pastor First Bapt. Ch., Centreville, Va., 1961-64; asst. field mission dir. New Orleans Bapt. Theol. Sem., 1966-67; asso. pastor Emmanuel Bapt. Ch., Riverdale, Ga., 1970—. Mem. Clayton Gen. Hosp. Chaplaincy, 1971—; vice moderator S. Metro Bapt. Assn., 1975-76, moderator, 1976-77. Mem. Clayton Ministerial Assn., Atlanta Bapt. Religious Edn. Assn. Home: 8289 Lake View Terr Riverdale GA 30274 Office: 230 Hwy 138 Riverdale GA 30274

HARRIS, JAMES GORDON, minister, So. Bapt Conv.; b. Little Rock, Oct. 27, 1913; s. J. Gordon and Ellen Launice (McManaway) H.; B.A., La. Coll., 1935 Th.M., M.R.E., Southwestern Bapt. Theol. Sem., 1939 D.D., Ouachita Bapt. U., 1956; m. Tunis Johns, Jan. 10 1939; children—James Gordon III, John Charles, Jane Ellen (Mrs. Philip N. Smith). Ordained to ministry 1933; pastor First Bapt. Ch., Bunkic, La., 1940-45 Calvary Bapt. Ch., Birmingham, Ala., 1945-48, First Bapt. Ch., Texarkana, Ark., 1948-54, University Bapt Ch., Ft. Worth, 1954—; preacher CBS Ch. of the Air 1955, NBC Radio Christmas Service, 1963, NBC TV Easter Service, 1975; mem. Radio and TV Commn., So Bapt. Conv., 1953-59; mem. Fgn. Mission Bd., 1971—pres., 1975-77; mem. Christian Life Commn., Bapt Gen. Conv. of Tex., 1959-74, chmn. exec. bd., 1969-71 v.p., 1965-66, 71-72, pres., 1975-77; 1st v.p. So. Bapt Conv., 1973-74. Trustee Baylor U., 1965-73, 75—. Named Distinguished Alumnus, La. Coll., 1974. Mem. Alumni Assn. Southwestern Bapt. Theol. Sem. (pres 1974-75), Ft. Worth C. of C. Contbr. articles to profl publs. Home: 3413 Lawndale St Fort Worth TX 76133 Office: 2720 Wabash Fort Worth TX 76109

HARRIS, JAMES GORDON, III, minister, N.Am. Baptist Conference; b. Bunkie, La., Nov. 1, 1940; s. James Gordon, Jr. and Tunis (Johns) H.; m. Joyce Behm, Mar. 24, 1967; children: Donna Joy, Jami Ruth. B.A., Baylor U., 1962; B.D., Southwestern Bapt. Sem., 1965, Th.M., 1967; Ph.D., So. Bapt. Sem., 1970. Ordained to ministry, 1963. Pastor in Idabel, Okla., 1963-66, Zenas, Ind., 1966-70; missionary to Philippines with Fgn. Mission Bd., So. Bapt. Conv., 1970-75; dir. extension sem. edn., Philippines, 1971-74; tchr. Philippine Bapt. Sem., 1970-74; assoc. prof. O.T., N.Am. Bapt. Sem., Sioux Falls, S.D., 1975-80, prof. 1980—, v.p. for acad. affairs, 1983—; chaplain S.D. State Prison, 1976—. Author numerous book and articles. Former mem. bd. dirs. Sioux Falls Christian High Sch. Cystic Fibrosis Found. Mem. Soc. Bibl. Lit. (regional sec. 1983-85), Nat. Assn. Hebrew Profs, (v.p.). Chaplain, USAR, 1977—. Lodge: Lions (v.p.). Home: 1604 Riverdale Rd Sioux Falls SD 57105 Office: 1605 S Euclid Ave Sioux Falls SD 57105

HARRIS, JAMES HENRY, minister, American Baptist Convention; b. Petersburg, Va., June 6, 1952; s. Richard and Carrie Anna (Jones) H.; m. Demetrius Dianetta Bright, June 21, 1979; 1 child, James Corey Alexander. B.S., Va. State U., 1974; M.Div., Va. Union U., 1976; M.A., Old Dominion U., 1981, postgrad. in urban mgmt. Ordained to ministry Am. Bapt. Conv., 1976. Intern Ebenezer Bapt. Ch., Richmond, Va., 1974-76; pastor Mt. Pleasant Bapt. Ch., Norfolk, Va., 1976—; gen. bd. dirs. Bapt. Gen. Conv. Va., Richmond, 1980—; chmn. edn. com. Tidewater Metro Ministers Conf., 1979. Contbr. to profl. jours. Pres. Norfolk Coalition for Quality Edn., 1984. Old Dominion U. fellow, 1982-84. Mem. Pi Alpha Alpha. Democrat. Office: Mt Pleasant Bapt Ch 934 W Little Creek Rd Norfolk VA 23505

HARRIS, JONATHAN MARK, minister; United Pentecostal Church International; automotive technician; b. Bartow, Fla., Apr. 22, 1958; s. Mary Janice (Chislebrook) H.; m. Michele Ann White, June 9, 1979. B. in Apostolic Studies, Apostolic Bible Inst., 1980; postgrad. Eastern Iowa Community Coll., Sears Tech. Tng. Ctr., 1981. Ordained to ministry United Pentecostal Ch. Internat., 1983. Youth leader United Pentecostal Ch., Ocala, Fla., 1976-77; assoc., youth pastor Midway Tabernacle, Davenport, Iowa, 1980-82; pastor First United Pentecostal Ch., Lake City, Fla., 1982—; home missions dir. sect. 3 Fla. Dist. United Pentecostal Ch., 1982-84, youth dir., 1985—. Owner, operator Mobile Mechanic Repair Service, Lake City, 1984—. Lake City, 1984—. Republican. Home: 400 Lomond St Lake City FL 32055 Office: First United Pentecostal Ch PO Box 2871 Lake City FL 32056

HARRIS, LEENELL, minister, Allen's Evangelical Organization; employment consultant; b. Frankfort, Ky., July 4, 1914; d. William and Cora Lee (Peters) H.; divorced; children: James Bason, Marietta Ryley. Student, N.Y. Bapt. Inst., 1954-59, Brookdale Community Coll., 1971-73. Ordained to ministry Allen's Evang. Orgn., 1960. Missionary, Allen's Evang. Ogn., Fla., Va., 1960-64; dir. Christian Edn. Calvary Bapt. Ch., Red Bank, N.J., 1968-83, asst. pastor, 1982—; sec., treas. Minister's Council, Red Bank, 1969-83; chaplain Riverside Hosp., Red Bank, 1970—, Monmouth County Jail, Freehold, N.J., 1982—; employment cons. Dept. of Aged, Trenton, N.J., 1979—. Bd. dirs. Red Bank Sr. Ctr., 1979—, Freeholder Aging Com., 1982—. Recipient, Increasing Understanding award Interfaith House, Tinton Falls, N.J., 1975; Outstanding Dedicated Service award NAACP, 1982; Cert. of Recognition award Bd. Freeholders, 1982. Mem. Am. Bapt. Women (Faithful Service award 1979, v.p. 1980—). Democrat. Home: 11 River St Red Bank NJ 07701

HARRIS, LOYD CLAY, minister, Church of Christ; b. Homer, La., May 21, 1949; s. Henry Clyde and Myrtle Beatrice (Hill) H.; m. Ora Mae Newsome, June 1, 1969; children: Clay MaLoyd, Dexter Wayne, Orena LaCay. B.S., Stephen F. Austin Coll., 1973; M.Bible Subjects, Internat. Bible Inst. and Sem., 1981; M.A. in Religion, Harding Grad. Sch., 1984. Ordained to ministry Church of Christ, 1960. Minister, Ch. of Christ, Nacogdoches, Tex., 1968-74, Mt. Pleasant, Tex., 1974-77, Greenville, Miss., 1977—; dir. and founder Sch. of Religious Studies, Greenville, Miss., 1978—; founder, treas. Christian Retreat, Hot Springs, Ark., 1975—; chmn. Project Indianola Mission, Miss. Delta Chs. of Christ, 1982—; advisor, co-founder Bible Chain Ch. of Christ, Itta Bean, Miss., 1978—; mem. Common Ministry, Itta Bean, 1983—. Author: Leadership: A Men's Training Course, 1975; Prophetic Significance of Prophecy of Daniel, 1982. Pres. Northgate Lakeview Homeowners Assn., Greenville, Miss., 1983; mem. adv. bd. Malcolm Wall Campaign, Greenville, 1984; del. Pres. Carter's Conf. on Families, Moorehead, Miss., 1979. Home: 1024 Meadow Dr Greenville MS 38703

HARRIS, RALPH EUGENE, minister, United Meth. Ch.; b. Forsyth County, Ga., Sept. 30, 1925; s. Vernie Eugene and Alma Inez (Martin) H.; student U. Ga., 1959-64; m. Kathryn Cowart, Oct. 26, 1946; 1 dau., Martha Ann. Ordained to ministry, 1961; pastor Upper Dawson Charge, United Meth. Ch., Dawsonville, Ga., 1958-63, Mossy Creek Charge, Cleveland, Ga., 1963-72, Gordon's Chapel, Hull, Ga., 1972—. Mem. com. on chaplains N. Ga. Conf., United Meth. Ch. Home and Office: PO Box 85 Lincolnton GA 30817

HARRIS, ROBERT EDWARD, evangelist; b. Asheville, N.C., June 13, 1923; s. Bradly and Mary Edith (Wright) H. Grad. high sch.; D.D. (hon.), Colonial Acad., Rockford, Ill., 1959. Ordained to ministry Baptist Ch., 1941. Pastor/evangelist, Asheville, 1940—; pres. Robert E. Harris Evang. Assn., Inc., Asheville, 1961—, cir. rider, 1979—; founder The Asheville Drive-In Church, 1961; radio personality, 1949—, TV personality, 1956—. Compiler: God's Answers for You, 1983; Bible on Index Cards, 1983, Scofield on Words, 1984; The Character of Christ, 1984, Christ is King, 1984, Christ is God, 1984, Western N.C. History Index, 1984. Office: PO Box 67 Asheville NC 28802

HARRIS, SYDNEY MALCOLM, lay worker, Canadian Jewish Congress; b. Toronto, Ont., Can., June 23, 1917; s. Samuel Aaron and Rose (Geldzaeler) H.; B.A., U. Toronto, 1939; Barrister-at-law, Osgoode Hall, 1942; m. Enid Perlman, 1949; children: Mark, David. Pres., Jewish Vocat. Service, 1947-49, Upper Can. lodge B'nai B'rith, 1951; sec. Holy Blossom Temple, 1965-68; pres. Canadian Council Reform Congregations, 1969; chmn. nat. joint community relations com. Canadian Jewish Congress and B'nai B'rith, Toronto, 1960-67, chmn. Central region Canadian Jewish Congress, 1968-71, nat. v.p., 1971-74, nat. pres., 1974—; mem. governing bd. World Jewish Congress; exec. Canadian Council Christians and Jews. Judge criminal div. Provincial Ct. Ont., 1976—. Recipient Canadian Centennial medal, 1967. Mem. B'nai B'rith, Canadian Friends World Union Progressive Judaism, Canadian Friends Boys' Town Jerusalem. Office: Can Jewish Congress 1590 Ave Docteur Penfield Montreal PQ H3G 1C5 Canada

HARRIS, VINCENT MADELEY, bishop, Roman Cath. Ch.; b. Conroe, Tex., Oct. 14, 1913; s. George Malcolm and Margaret (Madeley) H.; student St. Mary's Sem., La Porte, Tex., 1932-34; S.T.B., N.Am. Coll. and Pontifical Gregorian U., Rome, Italy, 1936, J.C.B., 1939; J.C.L., Cath. U. Am., Washington, 1940. Ordained priest, 1938; consecrated bishop, 1966; prof. St. Mary's Sem., 1940-51; chancellor Diocese of Galveston-Houston, 1948-66; diocesan consultor, 1951-66; domestic prelate, 1956; first bishop of Beaumont, Tex., 1966-71; bishop of Austin, Tex., 1971—. Mem. adminstrv. bd. Nat. Conf. Cath. Bishops, 1973-75; mem. adminstrv. com., mem. bishops com. on liturgy, U.S. Cath. Conf., 1973-75. Decorated knight Grand Cross, Equestrian Order Holy Sepulchre Jerusalem. K.C. Home: 4007 Balcones Dr Austin TX 78731 Office: POB 13327 Austin TX 78711

HARRISON, FRANK J. See *Who's Who in America,* 43rd edition.

HARRISON, GEORGE LOUIS, minister, Disciples of Christ; social worker; b. Moorhead, Iowa, Oct. 28, 1928; s. Hugh and Elizabeth (Whitehead) H.; m. Francel Charlene Oliver, May 14, 1952 (dec. 1965); children: Wayne, Emily. A.B. in Ministerial, Minn. Bible Coll., 1951; B.D. in Old Testament, Lincoln Christian Sem., 1962; M.S. in Counselling, Ft. Hayes State Coll., 1971. Ordained to ministry, 1950. Minister, Ch. of Christ, Sutherland, Iowa, 1952-55, Greenbush Ch., Avon, Ill., 1955-57; sr. minister First Christian Ch., Newport, Tenn., United Ch. of Christ, various locations, 1963-66; ad. interum pastor Faribault Ch. of Christ, Minn., 1966-74; facilitator/tchr. Valley View Christian Ch., Fridley, Minn., 1980—; sec. Newport Ministerial Assn., Tenn., 1960. Soc. worker Minn. Correctional Instn. Lino Lake, Minn., 1963—. Contbr. articles to profl. publs. Leader Smoky Mountain council Boy Scouts Am., 1960-63. Lodge: Kiwanis. Home: 7661 Lake Dr Lino Lakes MN 55014 Office: Minn Correctional Facility 7525 4th Ave Lino Lakes MN 55014

HARRISON, PORTER HARMON, minister, So. Bapt. Conv.; b. Clay County, Ala., Mar. 28, 1909; s. Pinkney Merriman and Rose Bell (Sprayberry) H.; student Samford U., 1938-41, So. Bapt. Theol. Sem., 1949-53, Eastern Bapt. Theol. Sem., 1945, Union Theol. Sem., 1946; m. Rosalie Thornton, Apr. 12, 1941; children—Porter Harmon. Ordained to ministry So. Baptist Conv., 1939; pastor East Thomas Bapt. Ch., Birmingham, Ala., 1939-41, McElwain Bapt. Ch., Birmingham, 1946-49, Youngers Creek Bapt. Ch., Elizabethtown, Ky., 1950-52, Riverside Bapt. Ch., Washington, 1953-65; minister on call for spl. ministries Washington, 1966—; del. Tenth Congress of Bapt. World Alliance, Rio de Janeiro, Brazil, 1960, Eleventh Congress of Bapt. World Alliance, Miami Beach, Fla., 1965; minister Masonic and Eastern Star Home, Washington, 1968—; parish minister Arlington (Va.) Temple Ch. and Community Center in Rosslyn, 1974—; bd. advisers Washington City Bible Soc. Aux. of Am. Bible Soc., 1972-75, bd. dirs., 1976—; mem. pastors conf. D.C. Bapt. Conv., 1953—, v.p., 1954; mem. com. on bds. So. Bapt. Conv., 1959; chaplain St. John's Masonic Lodge, Washington, 1957—; pres. Ministerial Union of Central Union Mission, Washington, 1961-62. Mem. So. Bapt. Theol. Sem. Alumni Assn. (pres. 1962), Alpha Delta Kappa Assn. Address: 3828 17th Pl NE Washington DC 20018

HARRISON, ROLAND KENNETH, minister, Church of England; b. Lancashire, Eng., Aug. 4, 1920; s. William and Hilda Mary (Marsden) H.; B.D., U. London, 1943, M.Th., 1947, Ph.D., 1952; D.D. (hon.), Huron Coll., London, Ont., Can., 1963; m. Kathleen Beattie, Oct. 18, 1945; children: Felicity, Judith, Graham. Ordained to ministry Ch. of Eng., 1943; chaplain Clifton Theol. Coll., Bristol, Eng., 1947-49; prof. Bibl. Greek, Huron Coll., 1949-52, Hellmuth prof. O.T., 1952-60; Bishops Frederick and Heber Wilkinson prof. O.T., Wycliffe Coll., Toronto, Ont., 1960—. Mem. Worshipful Soc. Apothecaries (faculty history of medicine and pharmacy), Canadian Psychiat. Assn. Author: Introduction to the Old Testament, 1969; Old Testament Times, 1970; The Ancient World, 1971. Office: Wycliffe Coll Toronto ON M5S 1H7 Canada

HARROLD, AUSTIN LEROY, minister, Christian Methodist Episcopal Church; b. Omaha, Jan. 28, 1942; s. Walter Wallace and Madeline (Brown) H.; B.A., Lane Coll., 1964; B.D., Interdenominational Theol. Center, 1968, M.Div., 1973; m. Gussie Mae Williams, May 20, 1967; children: Sabrina Latrice, Austin Allen, Sophia Dionne. Ordained to ministry, 1964; pastor Barr's Chapel, Paris, Tenn., 1963-64, St. Mary's Ch., Chattanooga, 1964-66; asst. pastor W. Mitchel Christian M.E. Ch., Atlanta, 1966-67; pastor Holsey Ch., Newton, Kans., 1967, St. John Ch., Hutchinson, Kans., 1967, Lane Chapel, Topeka, 1967-68, Turner Chapel, Mt. Clemens, Mich., 1968-75, Calvary Christian M.E. Ch., Jersey City, 1975-82, Phillips Met. Christian M.E. Ch., Hartford, Conn., 1982-83, Russell Instl. Christian M.E. Ch., Bronx, N.Y., 1983—; del. to gen. conf. Christian M.E. Ch., 1974, rep. to Nat. Council Chs. Christ in U.S.A.; mem. planning com. Nat. Conf. Christian Edn. in Local Chs., exec. com. working group on domestic hunger and poverty; staff Operation Crossroads Africa program, Sierra Leone, West Africa, summer 1973; dean Detroit Leadership Schs., 1971-75; organizer Concerned Clergy of Jersey City, 1981, del. Interdenominational Conf. Clergy, Portugal, 1983. Sec. exec. bd. Macomb County (Mich.) Child Guidance Clinic, 1972-75; sec. adv. bd. Macomb County Drug Abuse Centers, 1974-75; exec. sec. to mayor of Jersey City, from 1981; adv. bd. sr. companion program Jersey City Dept. Dept. Human Resources; bd. dirs. Operation PUSH-Jersey City; founding mem. Ind. Polit. Assocs.; mem. policy council, also social services com. Jersey City Devel. Ctrs.-Project Head Start. Recipient Dept. Sociology award Lane Coll., 1964, Dept. Religion and Philosophy award, 1964. Mem. NAACP (past v.p. Jersey City), Nat. Rehab. Counselors Assn., Jersey City C. of C., Jersey City Interdenomination Ministerial Assn. (past sec.). Lodges: Masons, King Solomon. Home: 25 Oak St Jersey City NJ 07304 Office: 2729 Oak St Jersey City NJ 07304

HARSHAW, ALBERT EDWARD, priest, Roman Catholic Ch.; b. Ventnor, N.J., Feb. 28, 1947; s. Albert Edward and Isabelle Bridget (McGarvey) H. Student Mother of Savior Sem., Blackwood, N.J., 1961-65, St. Charles Coll., Catonsville, Md., 1965-67; B.A., St. Mary's Sem., Balt., 1969, postgrad., 1969-73. Ordained priest Roman Catholic Ch., 1973. Assoc. pastor St. Stephen's Ch., Pennsauken, N.J., 1973-74, St. Aloysius Ch., Oaklyn, N.J., 1974-75, Ch. of Annunciation, Ballmawr, N.J., 1975-79, Ch. of Incarnation, Mantua, N.J., 1979-83, St. Maria Goretti Ch., Runnemede, N.J., 1983—; diocesan chaplain Camden Diocese, Boy Scouts Am., 1974—. Mem. Juvenile Conf. Com., Bellmawr, 1976-79, Mantua, N.J., 1983. Recipient St. George award Diocesan Cath. Com. on Scouting, Camden Diocese, 1979. Avocations: camping; photography; retreat planning for youth. Home: 18 S Newark Ave Ventnor NJ 08406 Office: St Maria Goretti Ch 321 Orchard Ave Runnemede NJ 08078

HART, B. SAM, minister non-denominational church; b. Harlem, N.Y., Apr. 8, 1931; s. Arthur and Doris (Miller) H.; m. Joyce E. Cushnie, June 9, 1951; children: Sharon, Tony, Robert, Bradley, Patrice. Student Jamaica Coll., 1942-48, Gordon Coll., 1949-54; D.Div., Carver Bible Coll., 1968. Ordained to ministry Calvary Gospel Chapel, 1961. Pres. Grand Old Gospel Fellowship, Inc., Phila., 1961—; dir. Grand Old Gospel Hour Worldwide; pastor Montco Bible Fellowship, Ambler, Pa., 1981—, also 12 other chs. on Eastern seaboard; dir. Grand Old Gospel Hour Radio Broadcast, Phila., 1961—; pres. Hart Broadcasting Co., 1976—. Nominee chmn. Civil Rights Commn., Washington, 1982. Mem. Nat. Religious Broadcasters (v.p., award of merit 1976). Republican. Office: Grand Old Gospel Fellowship 610 E Mt Pleasant Ave Philadelphia PA 19119

HART, DANIEL ANTHONY, priest, Roman Cath. Ch.; b. Lawrence, Mass., Aug. 24, 1927; s. John J. and Susan T. (Tierney) H.; B.S.B.A., Boston Coll., 1956; M.Ed., Boston State Coll., 1972; M.Div., St. John's Sem., Brighton, Mass., 1974. Ordained priest, 1953; asst. pastor, Lynnfield, 1953-54, Wellesley, 1954-56, Malden, 1956-64 (all Mass.); vice-chancellor Archdiocese of Boston, 1964-70; asst. pastor, Peabody Mass., 1970-76; titular bishop of Tepelta, aux. bishop of Boston, 1976—; regional bishop Brockton Region, 1976—; pres. Boston Senate of Priests, 1972-74; mem. exec. bd. Nat. Fedn. Priests' Councils, 1973-75. Address: 235 N Pearl St Brockton MA 02401

HART, JOSEPH See *Who's Who in America,* 43rd edition.

HART, KENNETH BRYON, minister, Church of Christ; b. Parkersburg, W.Va., Aug. 8, 1956; s. Kenneth Fletcher and Anna Jean (Mixer) H.; m. Carol Waldon Thom, May 2, 1975; children: Rhiannon Lee, Hillary Andrews. B.A. in Bible, Am. Sch. Religion, 1981; Assoc. in Sacred Lit., White's Ferry Rd. Sch. Bibl. Studies, 1981. Assoc. minister S.W. Ch. of Christ, Ada, Okla., 1982, Derby Ch. of Christ, Kans., 1982-84; minister Kremmling Ch. of Christ, Colo., 1984—; counselor Pettijohn Springs Christian Camp, Madill, Okla., 1982—. Guest editor Middle Park Times, 1984—. Firefighter, Kremmling Vol. Fire Dept., 1984—; counselor juvenile div. Grand County Dist. Atty.'s Office, Hot Sulphur Springs, Colo., 1984—. Served with USAF, 1974-78. Republican. Avocations: reading, outdoor sports. Home: PO Box 795 Kremmling CO 80459 Office: Kremmling Ch of Christ PO Box 558 Kremmling CO 80459

HART, ROBERT, gen. sec.-treas. Church of God, Cleveland, Tenn. Office: Keith St at 25th NW Cleveland TN 37311*

HART, WILLIAM MACDONALD, minister, United Ch. of Religious Science; b. San Francisco, Sept. 18, 1913; s. Ralph Warner and Hilda Wandersford (Macdonald) H.; R.Sc.F., Inst. Religious Sci., 1962; D.Div. (hon.), United Ch. Religious Sci., 1972; m. Madeline Allen Burwell, Aug. 6, 1942. Ordained to ministry, 1965; minister chs. Calif., Bakersfield, 1963-66, Whittier, 1966-73, Beverly Hills, 1973—. Mem. United Clergy Religious Sci. (pres. So. Calif. chpt. 1971), Internat. New Thought Alliance, Beverly Hills C. of C. Contbr. articles to Science of Mind and New Thought Mags. Home: 631 N Wilcox Ave Los Angeles CA 90004 Office: 410 S San Vicente Blvd Los Angeles CA 90048

HARTE, JOSEPH MEAKIN, bishop, Episcopal Church; b. Springfield, Ohio, July 28, 1914; s. Charles Edward and Ruth Elizabeth Harte; m. Alice Eleanor Taylor; children: Victoria Ruth, Joseph M., Jr., Judith Alice. A.B., Washington and Jefferson U., 1936, D.D. (hon.), 1954; M.Div., Gen. Theol. Sem., N.Y.C., 1939, S.T.D. (hon.), 1955; D.Min., Notre Dame U., 1985; D.D. (hon.), U. South, 1955. Ordained priest, Episcopal Ch. Rector All Saints' Ch., Miami, Okla., 1939-40, All Saints Parish, Austin, Tex., 1942-51; curate Trinity Parish, Tulsa, 1940-41; dean St. Paul's Cathedral, Erie, Pa., 1951-54; bishop Diocese of Dallas, Episcopal Ch., 1954-62, Diocese of Ariz., Phoenix, 1962—; mem. Coll. Bishops, 1954—; pres. Pacific Province, 1966-67; dep. Gen. Conv., 1952; trustee Great Western Bank, Phoenix, 1979—. Author monographs on religious topics. Bd. dirs. Human Relations Commn., Phoenix, 1963, Community Chest, Austin, 1945, Community Council, Austin, 1950. Served to maj. USNG, 1945-54. Named Man of Yr., NCCJ, 1965, Anti-Defamation League of B'nai Brith, 1975. Mem. Nat. Orgn. Episcopalians for Life (chmn. 1966—), Soc. King Charles, Martyr (patron 1960—). Republican. Lodges: Shriner, Knights Templar. Home: 815 E Orangewood St Phoenix AZ 85020

HARTFIELD, TURNER S., lay Christian education worker, National Baptist Church U.S.A.; b. Little Rock, Ark., Oct. 15, 1922; s. Frank and Della (Tramble) H.; m. Lavinia M. C. Watkins, Sept. 26, 1954; children: Jerone, Eleanor, LaWanda. A.S., Dunbar Jr. Coll., 1940; student, Wayne State U., 1946; M.R.E., United Theol.

Sem., Flint, Mich., 1982-84. Dir. Christian edn. Macedonia Bapt. Ch., Flint, 1958-70, gen. supt. ch. sch., 1970—; dean Great Lakes Dist. Congress, Flint, 1956—; assoc. dean Wolverine Bapt. Congress of Christian Edn. of Mich., 1972-84; dean's spl. asst. Nat. Bapt. Congress U.S., Inc., 1976—; vice chmn., bd. dirs. Foss Ave. Christian Sch., Flint, 1978—; pres. Greater Flint Council of Chs., 1980-82. Citizen's rep. gifted children selection com. Flint Bd. Edn., 1980—. Served to sgt. U.S. Army, 1942-45. Recipient Mark of Excellence award Gen. Motors Corp., Flint, 1969; New Human Relations Outstanding Achievement award City of Flint, 1982; Layman of Yr. award Great Lakes Dist. Bapt. Assn., Flint, 1984. Democrat. Lodges: Masons (33 deg., grand master 1950-52, imperial potentate 1964—, lectr. 1980-84).

HARTHERN, ROY A., minister, Assemblies of God; b. Staffs, Eng., Oct. 17, 1927; s. Charles Henry and Flori (Bradbury) H.; came to U.S., 1949, naturalized, 1977; L.H.D. So. Coll., Orlando, Fla., 1974; m. Pauline Lilian Skinn, Jan. 14, 1951; children—Charles, Leanne, Suzanne, Elizabeth. Ordained to ministry, 1951; pastor Calvary Assembly, Winter Park, Fla., 1970—. Presbyter, Peninsula Fla. dist. Assemblies of God, 1976—; internat. Bible tchr. Charismatic Movement; bd. dirs. Jesus '77; bd. dirs., tchr. Internat. Ch. Growth Inst., Seoul, Korea. Mem. Nat. Assn. Evangelicals, Nat. Religious Broadcasters Assn., Ionosphere Club. Columnist, Charisma mag. Home: 1911 Willa Vista Trail Maitland FL 32751 Office: 1919 Miller Ave Winter Park FL 32789

HARTMAN, RAY HOWARD, nursing home administrator, Lutheran Church in America; health care services consultant; b. Bethlehem, Pa., Nov. 18, 1928; s. Harry Calvin and Nellie Blanche (Stoops) H.; m. Kathryn M. Horwath, June 21, 1954; children: Kirk D., Gregg S. B.S. in Chem. Engring., Lehigh U., 1950; M.Div., Luth. Theol. Sem., Phila., 1954; S.T.M., Luth. Theol. Sem., Phila., 1958; M.S.S., Bryn Mawr Coll., 1968. Ordained to ministry Lutheran Ch., 1954. Pastor Gloria Dei Luth. Ch., Phila., 1954-56, St. Marks Luth. Ch., Conshohocken, Pa., 1956-68; nat. social welfare cons. Luth. Council, N.Y.C., 1968-78; exec. dir. programs Tressler Luth. Service Assocs., Camp Hill, Pa., 1978-80; pres. Luth. Retirement Homes, Phila., 1980—; chaplain Phila. Jaycees, 1957-67; mem. exec. com. Religion in Am., Phila., 1978. Dir. facilities devel. M. Breines & Assocs., White Plains, N.Y., 1984—. Author: Day By Day, 1969; Mobilizing Children of Light, 1973; Systems for Service, 1978. Bd. dirs., v.p. Family Service Montgomery County, Phila., 1956-64; pres. Children's Aid Soc., Norristown, Pa., 1957-59; mem. exec. com. Phila. United Way, 1958-63; bd. dirs. Montgomery County Planning Commn., 1958, Human Relations Commn., Phila., 1970. Named Outstanding Young Man of Yr., Phila. Jaycees, 1959. Mem. Am. Coll. Nursing Home Adminstrs. (bd. dirs.), Eastern Park and Monument Assn. (bd. dirs.). Republican. Home: 1517 Maple Ave Paoli PA 19301 Office: M Breines & Assocs 202 Tarrytown Rd White Plains NY 10591

HARTSELL, JAMES LEE, minister, Southern Baptist Convention; b. Concord, N.C., June 18, 1938; s. Jonas Calvin and Bertie Lee (Auten) H.; m. Charlott Lee Ross, July 2, 1961; children: Lee Anne, Ross Marie, James Clyde. Student Wingate Jr. Coll., 1959-63, U. N.C.-Charlotte, 1965-66; B.Min., Luther Rice Sem., 1980. Ordained to ministry So. Bapt. Conv., 1969. Pastor, Palmerville Bapt. Ch., Badin, N.C., 1968-71, South China Grove Bapt. Ch., N.C., 1971-76, Immanuel Bapt. Ch., Salisbury, N.C., 1976-80, Island Creek Bapt. Ch., Rose Hill, N.C., 1980—; Sunday sch. approved spl. worker N.C. State Bapt. Conv., Cary, 1977—. Home and Office: Route 2 Box 349 Rose Hill NC 28458

HARTUNIAN, VARTAN, minister, United Church of Christ and American Evangelical Union N. Am.; b. Marash Armenia, Turkey, Feb. 11, 1915; came to U.S., 1922; s. Abraham Harootune and Shushan (Kazanjian) H.; m. Grace Dogramajian, July 3, 1943; children: Nelson Seth, Byron Vartan, Sharon Grace. B.S., Swarthmore Coll., 1938; M.Div., Union Theol. Sem., N.Y.C., 1949. Ordained to ministry United Ch. Christ, 1959. Minister, 1st Armenian Ch., Belmont, Mass., 1959—; moderator Armenian Evangel. Union Eastern States and Can.; pres. Belmont Religious Council; vice moderator Armenian Evangel. Union N. Am.; campaign dir. 50th anniversary Five Million Dollar Fund Drive, Armenian Missionary Assn. Am., 1968. Translator: Neither to Laugh Nor to Weep: A Memoir of the Armenian Genocide, 1968. Mem. Am. Missionary Assn. Am., Phi Beta Kappa. Democrat. Lodge: Masons (master 1981). Home: 392 Concord Ave Belmont MA 02178 Office: 1st Armenian Ch 380 Concord Ave Belmont MA 02178

HARTZLER, MERLE EUGENE, lay ch. worker, Mennonite Ch.; b. Didsbury, Alta., Can., Oct. 9, 1942; s. Willard Joseph and Estella (Erb) H.; student Eastern Mennonite Coll., 1961-62, Prairie Bible Inst., 1964-67; m. Janet Marie Zimmerman, June 17, 1967. Entered Mennonite Vol. Service, 1967; dir. Teen Center, Canton, Ohio, 1967-68; youth worker in ghetto area, nr. west side Chgo., 1968-69; civilian Peace Service coordinator, Chgo., 1969-70; sec. Commn. on Missions and Service, N.W. Conf. Mennonite Ch., Carstairs, Alta., 1970—, co-chmn., 1975-77; chmn. bd. dirs. Reachout Ministries, Inc., Great Falls, Mont., 1975—. Pres., Triple M Farms Ltd., 1973—. Home: RR 2 Carstairs AB Canada

HARVEY, CHARLES E., religious organization executive, minister, Southern Baptist Convention; b. Shreveport, La., Mar. 31, 1926; m. Ethelene Harvey; children: Charles, Ronald. B.A., East Tex. Bapt. Coll., 1950, D.Div., 1975; M.Div., New Orleans Bapt. Theol. Sem., 1945. Ordained to ministry Bapt. Ch., 1947. Pastor, Pilgrim's Home Bapt. Ch., Shreveport, Dixie Garden Bapt. Ch., Shreveport, Sunset Acres Bapt. Ch., Shreveport; dir. evangelism La. Bapt. State Conv., Shreveport; vice pres. La. Bapt. Conv., 1960-61, then nominating com. mem., pres., 1971-72, then mem. exec. bd., v.p. exec. bd., pres. exec. bd.; mem. exec. com. So. Bapt. Conv., vice chmn. exec. com., 1973-74, chmn. 1974-75, 75-76. Trustee, Carver Sch. Missions and Social Work; commencement speaker New Orleans Bapt. Theol. Sem., 1965, East. Tex. Bapt. Coll., 1977; participant Korean Crusade, 1970. Served with USAF, World War II. Recipient Disting. Service award City of Shreveport, 1962, 66, Alumnus of Yr. award East Tex. Bapt. Coll., 1973, New Orleans Bapt. Theol. Sem., 1976. Mem. Alumni of New Orleans Bapt. Theol. Sem. (pres. elect 1982). Lodge: Rotary. Office: La Bapt Conv Box 311 Alexandria LA 71301

HARVEY, DENNIS GLENN, minister, Southern Baptist Convention; b. Shreveport, La., Dec. 17, 1951; s. Boyce and Bobie Louise (Morrison) H.; m. Sheila Kay Nichols, Aug. 9, 1975. B.A., Northeast La. U., 1974; M.Div., Southwestern Bapt. Theol. Sem., 1977. Minister of youth First Bapt. Ch., Monroe, La., 1974-75, Gatesville, Tex., 1978-79; N. Monroe Bapt. Ch., Monroe, La., 1979-82; minister edn. Central Bapt. Ch., Jacksonville, Tex., 1982—; associational youth minister Coryell Bapt. Assn., Gatesville, Tex., 1978-79; bd. dirs. Bapt. Student Union, Monroe, La., 1981-82, United Campus Ministry, Northeast La. U., Oskaloosa Bapt. Camp, W. Monroe, 1981-82; associational youth minister Cherokee Bapt. Assn., Jacksonville, Tex., 1982—. Named one of Outstanding Young Men in Am., U.S. Jaycees, 1980. Mem. Southwestern Bapt. Religious Edn. Assn., So. Bapt. Religious Edn. Assn., Singing Men of East Tex. Republican. Office: Central Bapt Ch 402 S Main Jacksonville TX 75766

HARVEY, THOMAS JEROME, priest, Roman Catholic Ch.; b. Pitts., Jan. 5, 1939; s. James Raymond and Margaret Ellen (Gillen) H.; B.A. in Philosophy, St. Charles Borromeo, 1960; S.T.B., Gregorian U., Rome, 1962, S.T.L., 1964; M.S.W., Columbia U., 1974. Ordained priest, 1963; asso. pastor Our Lady of Grace Parish, Pitts., 1964-69; adminstr. St. Stephen Parish, Pitts., 1969-72; chaplain Marist Bros., Bronx, N.Y., 1972-74; asst. dir. Pitts. Diocesan Dept. for Social and Community Devel., 1974—. Lectr. theology Carlow Coll., Pitts., 1975—; pres. Assn. Pitts. Priests, 1967-68. Bd. dirs. Mini-Corp. of Allegheny County, Pitts., 1970-72, pres. bd., 1972; v.p. Housing and Community Devel. Corp., 1975—; exec. dir. Nat. Conf. Cath. Charities. Mem. Nat. Assn. Social Workers. Office: 1346 Connecticut Ave NW Washington DC 20036

HARVEY, VAN AUSTIN educator; b. Hankow, China, Apr. 23, 1926; s. Earle Ralston and Mary Lee (Mullis) H.; B.A., Occidental Coll., 1948, D.Hum., 1964; Ph.D., Yale, 1957; m. Margaret Lynn, Aug. 31, 1950; children: Jonathan Lynn, Christopher Earle. Asst. prof. religion Princeton U., 1954-58; prof. Perkins Sch. Theology, 1958-68; chmn. dept., prof. religious thought U. Pa., Phila., 1968-77; prof. religious studies Stanford, 1977—. Guggenheim fellow, 1966, 71, Bollingen fellow, 1960. Mem. Am. Theol. Assn., Am. Acad. Religion, Phi Beta Kappa. Author: A Handbook of Theological Terms, 1964; The Historian and the Believer, 1966. Address: Dept Religious Studies Stanford U Stanford CA 94305

HARVEY, WILLIAM CAREY, minister, United Baptist Convention of Atlantic Provinces; b. Dundee, Scotland, July 6, 1922; s. Thomas John and Elizabeth Mary (McBride) H.; came to Can., 1952, naturalized, 1959; Honors diploma Irish Bapt. Coll., Dublin, Ireland, 1950; D.D., Acadia U., Wolfville, N.S., 1968; m. Frances Beatrice Ryder, July 29, 1950; children: Deirdre, Sheila, Rosemary, Marion. Ordained to ministry, 1950; hon. asst. chaplain RAF, India, 1944-46; pastor First Bapt. Ch., Halifax, N.S., 1964—; mem. social service com. Conv., 1956-60, mem. bd. evangelism, 1960-62, conv. exec., 1967-68, 2d v.p., 1967-68, chmn. hosp. chaplaincy com., 1966—; pres., Bible Soc., New Glasgow, 1954-55; Bapt. rep. com. for chaplaincy in armed forces Can. Council Chs., 1984—. Vice chmn. United Appeal, New Glasgow, 1960-61; chmn. Red Cross Soc., New Glasgow, 1961. Home: 1290 Oxford St Halifax NS B3H 3Y8 Canada Office: 1300 Oxford St Halifax NS B3H 3Y8 Canada

HARWELL, ALBERT BRANTLEY, minister, Southern Baptist Convention; b. Jefferson, Ga., Apr. 3, 1935; s. Loy Napoleon and Audrey (Foster) H.; m. Joanne Brindley June 18, 1957; children: Albert Brantley, Jr., Hugh Blake, Loy Barry. B.S. in Acctg., Howard Coll., 1956; M.R.E. and Grad. Specialist in Religious Edn., So. Bapt. Theol. Sem., 1961; D.Ministry, Midwestern Bapt. Theol. Sem., 1982. Ordained to ministry Bapt. Ch., 1965. Youth minister First Bapt. Ch., Charlestown, Ind., 1958-59; minister edn. Bethany Bapt. Ch., Louisville, Ky., 1959-61, Immanuel Bapt. Ch., Paducah, Ky., 1961-64; assoc. pastor First Bapt. Ch., Marietta, Ga., 1964-65, Vineville Bapt. Ch., Macon, Ga., 1965-72; pastor First Bapt. Ch., Barnesville, Ga., 1972-76, First Bapt. Ch., Carrollton, Ga., 1976—; dir. Home Mission Bd., Atlanta, 1975-83, v.p., 1979-80, mem. missions awareness tours, 1976, 82. Contbr. articles, devotionals, study materials to religious publs. Chaplain, Lamar County High Sch. football team, Barnesville, Ga., 1972-75, Carrollton High Sch. football team, 1976—; chmn. United Fund, Barnesville, 1973-74, Bi-Racial Com., Barnesville, 1973-76; trustee West Ga. Mental Hosp., Columbus, Ga., 1978-82. Mem. Carroll County Ministerial Assn. (pres. 1978-81), Carroll County Cancer Soc., Carroll County Assn. For Retarded Citizens, Omicron Delta Kappa, Alpha Phi Omega, Alpha Kappa Psi. Home: 1340 Blandenburg Rd Carrollton GA 30117 Office: First Bapt Ch 102 Dixie St Carrollton GA 30117

HASEL, GERHARD FRANZ, educator, Seventh-day Adventists; b. Vienna, Austria, July 27, 1935; s. Franz Joseph and Helene (Schroeter) H.; B.A., Atlantic Union Coll., 1959; M.A., Andrews U., 1960, M.Div., 1962; Ph.D., Vanderbilt U., 1970; Lic. Theol., Marienhoehe Sem., 1958; m. Hilde Schaefer, June 11, 1961; children: Michael, Marlene, Melissa. Ordained to ministry Seventh-day Adventist Ch., 1966; minister So. New Eng. Conf. Seventh-day Adventist Ch., 1962-63; asst. prof. So. Missionary Coll., 1963-67; asst. prof. O.T. and bibl. theology Andrews U., 1967-72, assoc. prof., 1972-75, prof., 1975—, chmn. dept. O.T., 1974-82, dir. Th.D./Ph.D. program, 1976—, dean Theol. Sem., 1982—. Danforth Tchr. grantee, 1968-70. Mem. Soc. Bibl. Lit., Soc. Scientific Study of O.T., Am. Acad. Religion, Chgo. Soc. Bibl. Studies, Am. Schs. Oriental Research. Author: The Remnant, 1972; Old Testament Theology, 1980; Jonah, Messenger of the Eleventh Hour, 1976; New Testament Theology, 1982; Covenant in Blood, 1982; Understanding the Living Word of God, 1983; Biblical Interpretation Today, 1985. Contbr. numerous articles to scholarly jours., encys., Bible dictionaries. Assoc. editor Andrews U. Sem. Studies. Office: Theol Seminary Andrews U Berrien Springs MI 49104

HASELTINE, ELWIN KEITH, minister, Church of God, Anderson, Indiana; b. Springfield, Mo., July 19, 1929; s. Chester Dorchester and Mable Jenevery (Bowland) H.; m. Marilyn Louise Young, Nov. 24, 1954; children: Timothy Neal, David Keith, Regina Ruth. B.A., Okla. Bapt. U., 1956; M.A., Drake U., 1974; Ph.D., Jackson State U., 1975. Ordained to ministry Ch. of God, Anderson, Ind., 1968. Pastor, First Ch. of God, El Paso, Tex., 1969-71, Des Moines, Iowa, 1971-76, Newton, Tex., 1976-78; prof. Bayridge Coll., Kendleton, Tex., 1978-80; pastor First Ch. of God, Cushing, Okla., 1980—; chaplain SAR, Des Moines, 1971-76, Bayridge Coll., 1978-80; mem. dist. credentials com. N. Central Dist., Ch. of God, Cushing, Okla., 1983-84. Author: Geneological Sketches of the Haseltine Family, 1963; And He Shall Reign, 1983. Contbr. poem anthology: The Clover Collection of Verse, vol. 9, 1975. Served with USN, 1948-52. Home: 1015 E 10th St Cushing OK 74023 Office: First Ch of God 501 N Noble St Cushing OK 74023

HASENSTEIN, STEVEN JOHN, minister, Luth. Ch.-Mo. Synod; b. Sheboygan, Wis., Oct. 28, 1946; s. Edward Herman and Virginia (Valdes) H.; A.A., Concordia Luth. Jr. Coll., 1967; B.A., Concordia Sr. Coll., 1969; M.Div., Concordia Sem., 1977; m. Laurel Jean Ehlke, Mar. 6, 1971; children—Christopher Michael, Shannon Michele. Ordained to ministry, 1973; pastor St. Paul and St. Luke Luth. Chs., Colby, Unity, Wis., 1973-75, Sion Luth. Ch., Chatham, Mich., 1975—. Circuit youth adviser, Circuit 14, North Wis. dist. Luth. Ch.-Mo. Synod, 1974-75, circuit social ministry adviser, 1975—. Home and Office: Box 131 Chatham MI 49816

HASTRICH, JEROME JOSEPH, bishop, Roman Catholic Ch.; b. Milw., Nov. 13, 1914; s. George Peter and Clara (Detlaff) H.; student Marquette U., 1933-35; B.A., St. Francis Sem., Milw., 1940, M.A., 1941; postgrad. Catholic U. Am., 1947. Ordained priest, 1941; consecrated bishop, 1969; chancellor diocese of Madison, Wis., 1952-53, vicar gen., 1953, aux. bishop, 1963-67; pastor St. Raphael Cathedral, Madison, 1967-69; bishop diocese of Gallup, N.M., 1969—. Diocesan dir. Confraternity Christian Doctrine, 1946—, St. Martin Guild, 1946-69; pres. Latin Am. Mission Program; sec. Am. Bd. Cath. Missions; vice chmn. Bishop's Com. for Spanish Speaking; pres. Nat. Blue Army; founder, Episcopal moderator The Queen of the Ams. Guild. Mem. Gov. Wis. Commn. on Migratory Labor. Home: 201 E Wilson St Gallup NM 86301

HATAWAY, LEON BEECHER, minister, So. Bapt. Conv.; b. Kansas City, Kans., July 28, 1935; s. Oscar R. and Mary C. (Beecher) H.; Asso. Sci., Decatur Bapt. Coll., 1956; B.S., Tex. Wesleyan Coll., 1960; M.R.E., So. Bapt. Theol. Sem., 1963; m. Velma Ann Sheppard, June 15, 1956. Ordained to ministry, 1966; minister of youth Bapt. Temple, Oklahoma City, 1963-66; minister, pastor First So. Bapt. Ch., Dove Creek, Colo., 1966-68, Sioux Valley Bapt. Ch., Sioux Falls, S.D., 1968-71, First So. Bapt. Ch., Cortez, Colo., 1971—. Moderator assn., 1968-69; mem. state exec. bd., 1970-75. Home: 740 Birch Dr Cortez CO 81321 Office: Box 376 Cortez CO 81321

HATFIELD, LEONARD FRASER, bishop, Anglican Church Canada; b. Port Greville, N.S., Can., Oct. 1, 1919; s. Otto Albert and Ada (Tower) H. B.A., Dalhousie U., 1940, M.A. in Sociology, 1943; D.D. (hon.), Kings U., 1956. Ordained deacon Anglican Ch. of Can., 1942, priest, 1943. Curate All Saints Cathedral, Halifax, N.S., 1942-46; rector Antigonish, N.S., 1946-51; sec. Council for Social Service, Gen. Synod, 1951-61; rector Christ Ch., Darmouth, N.S., 1961-71, St. John's Ch., Truro, N.S., 1971-76; bishop suffragan Diocese N.S., Halifax, 1976-80, Diocesan bishop, 1980-84. Author: He Cares, 1958. Home: Site 31 PO Box 1 Rural Route 3 Parrsboro NS B0M 1S0 Canada

HATFIELD, WILLIAM KEITH, pastor, Baptist Bible Fellowship; b. Detroit, Dec. 26, 1951; s. William Grant and Marquita (Ratliff) H.; m. Sharon Jean, Aug. 26, 1972; children: Sarah, Elisabeth, Matthew, Charity, Jonathan, Joshua. B.A., Baptist Bible Coll., Springfield, Mo., 1976. Assoc. pastor Brown Ave. Baptist Ch., Springfield, Mo., 1974-76; pastor Bible Baptist Ch., South Haven, Mich., 1976-79, Golden Gate Baptist Ch., Tulsa, 1979-85, Charity Bapt. Ch., Tulsa, 1985; bd. advisors Moral Majority, Tulsa, 1981—. Host; Dynamics for Living, TV show, 1982-83, 1985—; columnist Tulsa Tribune, 1983—. Spokesman Tulsans for Life, 1983-85, Oklahomans for Life, 1983-85. Republican. Home: 5315 E 26th Pl Tulsa OK 74114 Office: Charity Baptist Ch 7301 E 15th St Tulsa OK 74112

HATTON, G. RUSSELL, priest, Anglican Church; b. Springhill, N.S., Can., June 4, 1932; s. George Arthur and Hannah Irene (Langille) H.; m. Barbara Irene Weary, June 11, 1960; children: Brooke, Wendy. B.A., Dalhousie U., 1956; S.T.B., Gen. Sem., N.Y.C., 1958; S.T.M., Yale Div. Sch., 1963; Ph.D., U. Minn., 1971. Ordained priest Anglican Ch., 1958. Rector parish, Lantz, N.S., 1963-64; chaplain U. Minn., Mpls., 1964-72; mem. exec. staff Anglican Ch., Toronto, Ont., 1972-77; dir. Toronto Sch. Theology, 1977-80; pres. Atlantic Sch. Theology, Halifax, N.S., 1980—. Recipient Morris Scholarship King's Coll., Europe, 1960; Danforth Scholarship Danforth Found., Minn., 1969. Mem. Can. Theol. Soc., Study of Religion Soc.

HAUG, DOMINIC, nun, Roman Catholic Ch. B. Seneca, Kans., July 22, 1933; d. Omer Edward and Lucille Mary (Noll) H. R.N., St. Francis Sch. Nursing, 1951; B.S. in Nursing Edn., St. Mary Coll., Leavensworth, Kans., 1964; M.S. in Nursing, Tex. Women's U., 1978. Joined Sisters of St. Dominic, Roman Catholic Ch., 1955. Instr. nursing Dominican Sch. Nursing, Great Bend, Kans., 1958-67; supr. St. Catherine Hosp., Garden City, Kans., 1967-68; evening supr. Central Kans. Med. Ctr., Great Bend, 1968-71, nursing inservice dir., 1971-76; founder, exec. dir. Golden Belt Home Health Service, Great Bend, 1978—; founder, exec. dir. Birthright of Great Bend, 1973-76, bd. dirs., 1973—; mem. adv. com. Serenity Hospice, 1983—. Recipient award Soroptimist Internat., 1984. Mem. Nat. Hospice Orgn., Kans. Assn. Home Health Agys. (bd. dirs. 1981—, v.p. 1981-83). Address: Golden Belt Home Health Service PO Box 937 Great Bend KS 67530

HAUGHNEY, DENIS, priest, Roman Catholic Church; b. Carlow, Ireland, June 3, 1930; s. James and Esther (Walsh) H.; came to U.S., 1969; B.D., Claretian Major Sem., Eng., 1963; postgrad. Bristol (Eng.) U., 1966; S.T.M., N.Y. Theol. Sem., 1976; certificate pastoral counseling Postgrad. Center Mental Health, N.Y., 1976; postgrad. Human Devel. Center, Sparta, N.J., 1976. Ordained priest, 1963; instr. English Lit. and Latin, St. Hugh's Sem., Buckden, Eng., 1957-59, 63-65; vocat. counselor Anglo-Irish Province Claretian Congregation, U.K., 1963-66; officiating chaplain Royal Air Force, Eng., 1964-65; contract chaplain U.S. Air Force, Alconbury, Eng., 1966-69; asso. pastor St. Paul's Ch., Prospect Park, N.J., 1969-74, St. Michael's Ch., Netcong, N.J., 1974-85. Dir. deacon internship Diocese of Paterson, N.J., 1973-74, Counselor, Paterson Family Life Bur., 1973-85. Address: 4 Church St Netcong NJ 07857 Died Feb. 16, 1985.

HAUSMAN, WILLIAM RAY, minister Evangelical Covenant Church; b. Bradford, Pa., Apr. 22, 1941; s. Raymond Harvey and Eleanor Janet (Freeman) H.; m. Rosalyn Mae Schmidt, Aug. 16, 1963; children: Valerie Noelle, Stephanie Carol. A.B., Wheaton Coll., 1963, student Grad. Sch., 1963-64; M.A., Trinity Evang. Div. Sch., Deerfield, Ill., 1966; student North Park Theol. Sem., Chgo., 1968-69; Ed.M., Harvard U., 1977; D.D., Trinity Evang. Div. Sch., 1981. Ordained to ministry, Evang. Covenant Ch., 1971; minister Christian edn. Glen Ellyn (Ill.) Covenant Ch., 1966-69; tregistrar, dir. admissions Trinity Evang. Div. Sch., Deerfield, Ill., 1969-72, dean records and admissions Trinity Coll. and Trinity Evang. Div. Sch., 1972-75, v.p. student affairs Trinity Evang. Div. Sch., 1975-80; pres. North Park Coll. and Theol. Sem., Chgo., 1980—. Mem., Dist. 109 Bd. Edn., Deerfield, Ill., 1979-80; dir. North River Commn., Chgo., 1980—. Trustee, Swedish Covenant Hosp., Chgo., 1983—. Recipient Lilly Endowment presdl. planning grant, 1980-82. Mem. Ministerium Evang. Covenant Ch., Assoc. Colls. Ill. (v.p.), Am. Assn. Higher Edn., Chgo. Assn. Theol. Schs. Office: North Park Coll Theol Sem 3225 W Foster Ave Chicago IL 60625

HAWES, ARIZONA DAPHNE, minister, Internat. Ch. Foursquare Gospel; b. Cochise, Ariz., Dec. 19, 1916; d. Isaac Newton and Nancy Prilee (Johnston) Hawes; grad. Life Bible Coll., Los Angeles, 1941. Ordained to ministry, 1942; pastor, Seligman (Ariz.) Foursquare Gospel Ch., 1954—. Field dir., camp dir. leader, Girl Scouts U.S.A.; bd. dirs. Seligman Health Clinic. Mem. Seligman C. of C. Home: Pine and 3d Sts Seligman AZ 86337 Office: PO Box 267 Seligman AZ 86337

HAWK, CHARLYE MAE, lay church worker, Seventh-Day Adventists; accountant, computer analyst; b. Atlanta, July 30, 1926; d. Charlie Sidney and Nellie Mae (Henderson) Porter; m. Albert H. Bliss, Jr., July 30, 1950 (dec. 1951); 1 child, Albert H. Bliss. B.A., Oakwood Coll., Huntsville, Ala., 1948. Sec., So. Atlantic Conf., Seventh-Day Adventist Ch., Atlanta, 1948-60, sec., acct., 1960-70, adminstrv. sec., 1970-75, adminstrv. sec., acct., computer analyst, 1975-80, adminstrv. sec., computer analyst, 1980—. Clubs: King Daus. (sec. 1975-80), Bus. League (Atlanta). Home: 2720 Lincoln Ct NW Atlanta GA 30318

HAWK, ROBERT CLARE, minister, Lutheran Church in America; b. New Kensington, Pa., May 7, 1942; s. Clare Allen and Fern Virginia (Livengood) H. B.A. in Philsophy, Thiel Coll., 1964; M.Div., Luth. Theol. Sem., Phila., 1967. Ordained to ministry Lutheran Ch., 1968. Asst. pastor Epiphany Luth. Ch., Hempstead, N.Y., 1968-73; pastor St. Barnabas Luth. Ch., Howard Beach, N.Y., 1974-78, Redeemer Luth. Ch., Yonkers, N.Y., 1978-81, Messiah Luth. Ch., Moundsville, W.Va., 1982—, Good Shepherd Luth. Ch., New Martinsville, W.Va., 1982—; mem. council on ecumenical relations Western Pa.-W.Va. Synod, Luth. Ch. Am., 1982—, mem. com. on ch. vocations and examination, 1982—; mem. Luths., Anglicans and Roman Catholics Together Trialog of W.Va., 1982—; Western Pa.-W.Va. Synod rep. W.Va. Council of Chs., 1984—. Hoh fellow Luth. Theol. Sem. Phila., 1967-68. Republican. Lodge: Kiwanis. Home: 22 Glen Dale Manor Glen Dale WV 26038 Office: Messiah Luth Ch 503 Lafayette Ave Moundsville WV 26041

HAWKES, MARY NEWGEON, religious educator, United Church of Christ; b. Thessaloniki, Greece, June 27, 1934 (parents Am. citizens); d. William Emory and Jessie Harriett (Newgeon) H. A.B. in Music, Doane Coll., 1956; M.A. in Religious Edn., Hartford Sem., 1958; Ed.D. in Religious Edn., Columbia U., 1983. Ordained United Ch. of Christ, 1980. Dir. Christian edn. United Chs. of Christ, Conn., 1958-67; specialist in ch. edn., 1963—; ecumenical worker German Ch., Hamburg and Berlin, Conn., 1967-69; dir. Christian edn. United Chs. of Christ, Conn., N.Y. and Mich., 1969-81; sec. edn. program United Ch. Bd. for Homeland Ministries, N.Y.C., 1981—; mem. various teams and coms. Nat. Council Chs. Joint Ednl. Devel., 1981—; past pres. alumni council Hartford Sem. Mem. editorial com. Sing of Life and Faith hymnbook, 1963-67; editor, co-author: Festivals of Christmas, 1983; content editor: Sing to God: Songs and Hymns for Christian Education, 1984. Contbr. articles to religious edn. jours. Recipient Doane Builder award Doane Coll., 1981. Mem. Religious Edn. Assn. (treas. chpt. 1966-67), Assn. Profs. and Researchers in Religious Edn., Assn. United Ch. Educators, Assn. for Supervision and Curriculum Devel., Common Cause, ACLU, NOW, Smithsonian Assocs., Adam Hawkes Family Assn. Democrat. Office: United Church Bd for Homeland Ministries 132 W 31st St New York NY 10001

HAWKINS, BARRY TYLER, minister, Lutheran Church in America; b. Seattle, June 28, 1943; s. Stuart Maxwell and Roberta (Mabry) H.; m. Jane Van Ness, Jan. 24, 1965 (dec. 1974); children: Kelly Anne, Renee Noel; m. Lorraine Joyce Pearson, May 29, 1976; children: Jeremy, Aaron. B.A. with honors, U. Puget Sound, 1965; M.Div., Luth. Sch. Theology, Chgo., 1969; S.T.M., N.Y. Theol. Sem., 1973, postgrad., 1984—. Ordained to ministry Lutheran Ch., 1969; pastoral counseling cert., 1973; alcohol counseling credential, 1980. Team leader Archdiocese of N.Y. Counseling Program, N.Y.C., 1973-76; pastor St. Philips Luth. Ch., Bklyn., 1974-78; chmn. faculty, head dept. Martin Luther High Sch., Maspeth, N.Y., 1976-80; dir. alcohol edn. St. Vincent's Med. Ctr., S.I., N.Y., 1980-82; pastor Christ Luth. Ch., Newburgh, N.Y., 1982—; cons. in alcoholism, 1978—; founder, dir. Luth. Ministry of Alcohol Edn., Newburgh and N.Y.C., 1979—; chmn. commn. on corp. mission Met. N.Y. Synod, Luth. Ch. Am., 1970-75, mem. commn. of social concerns, 1981—; mem. planning bd. N.Y. State Council of Chs., 1972-74; chmn. alcohol task force Met. N.Y. Synod, Luth. Ch. Am., 1981—; mem. adv. bd. Luth. Social Services Agy., Hudson Dist., 1982—; bd. dirs. N.Y. State Alcohol Counselor Credential Bd., Albany, 1984—; lectr. to various ednl. and counseling groups. Samuel Trexler fellow, 1972, 84. Mem. Nat. Clergy Council on Alcoholism, N.Y. Fedn. Alcoholism Counselors, Fellowship of Reconciliation. Club: Powelton (Newburgh). Lodge: Kiwanis (bd. dirs. Newburgh 1982—).

HAWKINS, REGINALD ARMISTICE, ch. ofcl., United Presbyn. Ch. in U.S.A.; b. Beaufort, N.C., Nov. 11, 1923; s. Charles Columbus and Lorena (Smith) H.; B.S., Johnson C. Smith U., 1948, B.D., 1956, LL.D., 1962; D.D.S., Howard U., 1948; M.Div., Johnson C. Smith U., 1973; m. Catherine Elizabeth Richardson, Sept. 8, 1945; children—Pauletta, Reginald Armistice, Wayne, Lorena. Ordained to ministry, 1956; mem., organizer council on ch. and race United Presbyn. Ch. U.S.A., 1963, bd. mem., gen. assembly mission council, 1973—, bd. mem. council adminstrv. services, 1974—. Pvt. practice dentistry, Charlotte, N.C., 1948—; vice chmn. Eastern N.C. Devel. Corp., 1967—; dir. Southeastern Regional Investment Corp., Parker Heights Ltd. Civil rights leader, 1948—; mem. N.C. Good Neighbor Council, 1963-65; mem. Black Econ. Devel. Council, SBA, 1968; precinct chmn. N.C. Democratic com., 1954-65; mem. Dem. Nat. Speakers Bur., 1960-64; del. Dem. Nat. Conv., 1968; candidate for gov. N.C., 1968, 72; trustee N.C. Central U., Durham, 1961-66. Recipient Distinguished Service award Alpha Kappa Alpha, 1969. Fellow Royal Soc. Health; mem. Am., N.C. dental assns., Nat., Old North State (citation of merit 1968) dental socs., Acad. Gen. Dentistry, Internat. Platform Assn., NAACP, Beta Kappa Chi, Kappa Alpha Psi. Home: 1703 Madison Ave Charlotte NC 28216 Office: 951 S Independence Blvd Suite 355 Charlotte NC 28202

HAWKINS, RICHARD THURBER, priest, Episcopal Church; b. Walpole, Mass., Mar. 4, 1933; s. Edward Jackson and Harriet (Sherman) H.; B.S., U.S. Mil. Acad., 1955; B.D., Episcopal Theol. Sch., 1961; m. Michelle Woodhouse, June 30, 1956; children—Charles Sherman, Jeffery Lee, Elizabeth J. Ordained deacon, 1961, priest, 1962; asst. minister, Cin., 1961-63; rector St. Mark's Ch., Fall River, Mass., 1963-68; St. Thomas Ch., Fort Washington, Pa., 1968—. Chmn., Commn. on the Ministry, 1972-78, mem. Bd. Episcopal Community Services, 1974-84; chaplain Vet. Guard 3d Inf., N.G. Pa., 1976. Chmn. service acad. selection bd. U.S. Mil. Acad., 13th Congl. Dist., 1973—; trustee House of Rest for Aged, 1974—; chmn. bd. All Saints Hosp., Springfield, 1979-82; mem. exec. bd. Family Service Phila., 1982—, chmn. personnel com., 1984—. Home: 826 Pine Tree Rd Lafayette Hill PA 19444 Office: St Thomas Ch Fort Washington PA 19034

HAWKINS, ROBERT A., educator, writer, minister; b. Anabelle, W. Va., Aug. 21, 1924; s. Lawrence R. and Grace O. (Glover) H.; B.A., Abilene Christian Coll., 1948, M.A., 1967; Ed.D., Tex. Tech. U., 1974; m. Nina Jo Milton, June 6, 1943; children: Paul Clark, Sheila Ann. Minister chs., N.Mex., Colo., Calif., 1948-65; dir. youth camps and vacation Bible schs., 1948-65; part-time instr. Bible, Abilene Christian Coll., 1965-68; registrar, prof. Bible, Lubbock Christian Coll., 1968-74; now counselor, tchr. Midland (Tex.) Coll. Mem. Tex. Personnel and Guidance Assn., Jr. Coll. Assn. Student Personnel Adminstrs. Tex., Alpha Chi, Phi Kappa Phi. Contbr. articles to religious jours. Transl., pub. Bible Students New Testament, Spiritual Awareness. Home: 3305 Providence Dr Midland TX 79707

HAY, DAVID WILLIAM, minister, Presbyn. Ch. in Can.; b. Capetown, S.Africa, Aug. 18, 1905; s. David Thom and Elizabeth (Hendry) H.; came to Can., 1944, naturalized, 1949; M.A., Edinburgh U., 1929; D.D. (hon.), Queens U., Ont., 1949, Trinity U., Toronto, Ont., 1949; m. Christina Crawford Reid, Apr. 26, 1936; children—Olive Allen Hay Meyer, David Alastair. Ordained to ministry, 1933; minister St. Margarets Ch., Dunfermline, Scotland, 1933-40; Pollok lectr. Pinehill Div. Coll., Halifax, N.S., 1939; chaplain Brit. Forces, 1940-44; prof. systematic theology Knox Coll., U. Toronto, 1944-75, prof. emeritus, 1975—; moderator Gen. Assembly, Presbyn. Ch. in Can. 1975-76; minister-in-charge, Caledon East and Claude, Ont., 1976—. Mem. faith and order com. World Council Chs., 1954-63; pres. Canadian Council Chs., 1962-64, Student Christian Movemen Can., 1965, Canadian Soc. Bibl. Lit., 1954, Canadian Theol. Soc., 1966; Birks lectr. McGill U., Montreal, 1974. Pres. Sir Walter Scott Club of Toronto, 1952-54. Mem. Canadian Liturgical Soc., St. Andrew Soc. Toronto. Asso. editor: Canadian Jour. of Theology, 1956-66; contbr. articles to religious jours. and chpts. to books. Office: Knox Coll U Toronto 59 St George St Toronto ON M5S 2E6 Canada

HAY, IAN MORELAND, missionary, administrator Independent Baptist Church; b. Miango, Nigeria, Dec. 19, 1928; s. John and Sarah Elizabeth (McFarlane) H.; B.A., William Jennings Bryan Coll., Dayton, Tenn., 1950, D.D., 1976; M.A., Columbia (S.C.) Sch. Bible and Mission, 1951; D.Miss., Evangel. Div. Sch., Deerfield, Ill., 1984; m. Sarah June Bell, June 7, 1951; children: Brenda Carol, Robert Ian. Ordained to ministry, 1950; pastor 1st Bapt. Ch., Reevesville, S.C., 1950-51; missionary to Nigeria, 1951-65, N.Am. dir. Sudan Interior Mission, 1965-72, dep. gen. dir., 1972-75, gen.

dir., 1975—. Bd. dirs. Interdenoml. Fgn. Missions Assn., 1965—; past pres. Evang. Missions Info. Service; bd. dirs. William Jennings Bryan Coll., 1968—, Columbia Bible Coll., 1976—. Contbr. chpts. on missions to books. Home: 48 Lynwood Rd Cedar Grove NJ 07009 Office: SIM Internat Cedar Grove NJ 07009

HAY, STANLEY LEE, theology educator, college and seminary president, Baptist General Conference; b. Cananea, Mex., Apr. 3, 1932; came to U.S., 1946; s. Harold L. and Thelma B. (Jones) H.; m. Evelyn Rowdean Gleco, Aug. 27, 1954; children: Jackolin, Deborah, Laura, Lisa. A.S., San Diego Bible Coll., 1976, B.A., 1977; Ph.D., St. John's U., New Orleans, 1981; D.R.E. (hon.), Christian Bible Coll., 1982. Adminstrv. dean San Diego Bible Coll., 1975-79; v.p., acad. dean Spring Valley Bible Coll., Calif., 1979-80; pres. Spring Valley Bible Coll. and Sem., 1980—; deacon Coll. Avenue Bapt. Ch., San Diego, 1980-83; vice chmn. Mt. Miguel Covenant Ch., Spring Valley, 1970-78. Author curriculum: A Five Point Th.D. Program, 1979. Served with U.S. Army, 1949-52, Korea. Mem. Am. Assn. Specialized Colls. (cons. 1979—). Republican. Home: 10767 Jamacha Blvd Apt 219 Spring Valley CA 92077 Office: Spring Valley Bible Coll PO Box 2511 Spring Valley CA 92077

HAYDEN, ROY EDMUND, educator; b. Rockville, Utah, Jan. 20, 1932; s. James Edmund and Gladys (DeMille) H.; A.A., Los Angeles City Coll., 1952; B.A., U. Calif. at Los Angeles, 1953; B.D., Fuller Theol. Sem., 1956, Th.M., 1959; M.A., Brandeis U., 1961, Ph.D., 1962; m. Mary Elizabeth Richardson, June 24, 1951; 1 dau., Helen Olynda. Asso. prof. Bible, Huntington (Ind.) Coll., 1962-67; prof. Bibl. lit. Oral Roberts U., Tulsa, 1967—, pres. faculty senate, 1972-73. Mem. Am. Oriental Soc., Am. Profs. for Peace in the Middle East, Am. Schs. Oriental Research, Evang. Theol. Soc., Gilcrease Inst., Near East Archaeol. Soc., Soc. Bibl. Lit. Contbr. to Wycliffe Bible Ency., Zondervan Pictorial Ency.; contbg. author: The Biblical World, 1966, Internat. Standard Bible Ency. Home: 7805 S College Ave Tulsa OK 74136 Office: 7777 S Lewis St Tulsa OK 74171

HAYES, EDWARD JAMES, priest, Roman Cath. Ch.; b. West Orange, N.J., Dec. 11, 1914; s. James Edward and Teresa Immaculata (Meyers) H.; B.A., Seton Hall Coll., 1938; B.Th., Immaculate Conception Sem., 1941. Ordained priest, 1941; asso. pastor St. Anthony's Ch., East Newark, N.J., 1941-42, St. Anthony's Ch., Union City, 1942-44; chaplain USAF, 1944-46; asso. pastor St. Patrick's Ch., Elizabeth, N.J., 1946-48, St. Charles Borromeo's Ch., Newark, 1948-58, St. Thomas Aquinas Ch., 1958-68; pastor Mount Carmel Ch., Lyndhurst, N.J., 1968—. Asst. chaplain Newark Fire Dept., 1948—; visual aid research dir. Apostolate for the Deaf, Newark, 1945-76; prof. med. ethics St. Michael's Med. Center, Newark, 1959-61, All Souls Hosp., Morristown, N.J., 1961-69; charter mem. Senate of Priests, Newark, 1967-68. Mem. Mil. Chaplains Assn. U.S.A. Author: Three Keys to Happiness, 1952; Love for a Lifetime, 1955; Moral Handbook of Nursing, 1956; Moral Principles of Nursing, 1964; Confession Aid for Children, 1959; Catholicism and Reason, 1973; Catholicism and Society, 1975; Catholicism and Life, 1976. Producer religious instrl. films, 1941-49; co-author med.-moral books. Contbr. articles to religious jours. Address: 1961 Ernst Terr Union NJ 07083

HAYES, GEORGE OLIVER, minister, Evangelical Church North America; b. Coon Rapids, Iowa, May 20, 1924; s. Leonard Leroy and Violet Daisy (Wright) H.; degree Capital City Comml. Coll., Des Moines, 1942; student Kletzing Coll., 1943-45, Cascade Coll., 1947, Western Evang. Sem., 1949-52, Loma Linda U., 1959; m. Ruth Viola Rayl, May 12, 1945; children—Ellen (Mrs. Joe Kunkle), Lois (Mrs. Dennis Stoltenberg), Mark Alvin. Ordained to ministry, 1954; minister Evang. U.B. Ch., Iowa, Oreg., Wash., 1945-68, Evang. Ch. N.Am., Sacramento, 1968—. Dir. pub. relations Peniel Missions, Sacramento, 1963-66, gen. supt., 1966-71, 72-74; exec. dir. Fairhaven Home for Unwed Mothers, Sacramento, 1969-75; regional dir. World Gospel Mission, Portland, Oreg., 1976-84. Home: 18830 S Hwy 99E Sp 20 Oregon City OR 97045

HAYES, JAMES MARTIN, archbishop, Roman Catholic Church; b. Halifax, N.S., Can., May 27, 1924; s. Leonard James and Rita Genevieve (Bates) H.; B.A., St. Marys U., Halifax, 1943; B.D., Holy Heart Sem., Halifax, 1947; J.C.D., Angelicum, Rome, 1957; LL.D., St. Annes Coll., Church Point, N.S., 1965; S.T.D., Kings Coll., Halifax, 1967. Ordained priest, 1947; priest Archdiocese of Halifax, 1947-65; consecrated bishop, 1965; aux. bishop of Halifax, 1965-67, archbishop, 1967—. Pres. liturgical com. Canadian Cath. Bishops' Conf. Bd. dirs. Liturgical Conf. Decorated knight Grand Cross, Order St. Lazarus of Jerusalem. Address: 6541 Coburg Rd PO Box 1527 Halifax NS B37 2Y3 Canada

HAYES, LEROY RONDALL, III, minister, educator, Baptist Church; b. Ridgeland, S.C., Mar. 10, 1954; s. LeRoy Hobby and Lucinda V. (Grant) H.; m. Carolyn Diane Leggett, Jan. 20, 1976. B.Th., World Inst. Religious Edn., Farmington, N.Mex., 1984, M. Religious Edn., 1985. Ordained to ministry Baptist Ch., 1978. Assoc. minister Black's Meml. Bapt. Ch., Austin, Tex., 1976-77, Bapt. Temple, Newburgh, N.Y., 1977-78; youth dir. Friendship Bapt. Ch., El Paso, Tex., 1978-80; pastor Mt. Carmel Bapt. Ch., Las Cruces, N.Mex., 1980—; pres. Christian edn. New Hope Dist. Assn., Las Cruces, 1983—; state evangelist chmn. Mt. Olive Bapt. State Conv., Albuquerque, 1983—. Host weekly radio program: Peoples Gospel, 1981—; producer, host weekly TV program Perspective, 1985—. Mem. adv. bd. Basic Adult Edn. Dona Ana Community Coll., 1985; mem. adv. bd. Salvation Army, Las Cruces, 1985. Served with U.S. Army, 1974-80. Recipient Commanders award White Sands Mil Range, 1984. Mem. S.W. N.Mex. Ministers Assn. (pres. 1983). Democrat. Avocations: traveling; singing; camping; jogging. Home: 9745 Butler Field Blvd Las Cruces NM 88001 Office: Mt Carmel Bapt Ch 955 Walnut St Las Cruces NM 88001

HAYES, NEVIN WILLIAM See *Who's Who in America*, 43rd edition.

HAYES, RICHARD ALAN, minister, college instructor; b. Escondido, Calif., Sept. 3, 1957; s. Guy Herman and Edna Lela (Beck) H.; A.A., Palomar Coll., 1978; B.S., Biola U., 1983; M.Div., Talbot Theol. Sem., 1986. Youth worker First Evangelical Free Ch., Fullerton, Calif., 1981-84; assoc. pastor Bell Gardens Baptist Ch., Calif., 1985—. Author: Handbook for Parents of Young Singles, 1985; The Melchizedek Priesthood: Mormon versus Evangelical Interpretation, in press. Mem. Evangelical Tchr. Training Assn., Theol. Students Fellowship. Republican. Office: Bell Gardens Baptist Ch 7301 Perry Rd Bell Gardens CA 90201

HAYES, WILLIAM JOSEPH, priest, Roman Catholic Church. B. Hartford, Conn., Feb. 17, 1915; s. Anthony Joseph and Katherine Theresa (Tracy) H. B.A., St. Mary Sem. U., 1942. Ordained priest Roman Cath. Ch., 1942. Asst. pastor St. James Ch., Stratford, Conn., 1942-48, St. Joseph Ch., New Britain, Conn., 1948-56; adminstr. St. Cecilia Ch., Waterbury, Conn., 1956-65; pastor St. John The Evangelist, New Britain, 1965—. Chaplain Fire Dept. Waterbury, 1960, New Britain, 1972. Democrat. Home and Office: 655 East St New Britain CT 06051

HAYNES, DOUGLAS EUGENE, minister, Ch. of the Nazarene; b. Terre Haute, Ind., Dec. 31, 1951; s. Theodore and Mildred Vandetta (Waggle) H.; B.S. in Mktg., Ind. State U., Terre Haute, 1973; m. Nina Kay Mays, Oct. 20, 1973. Licensed to ministry, 1973; pastor Northside Ch. of Nazarene, Vincennes, Ind., 1973-75, 1st Ch. of Nazarene, Mt. Carmel, Ill., 1975—. Pres. Vincennes zone Nazarene Young Peoples Soc., 1974-75, Sunday Sch. chmn., 1974-75; speaker Moments of Inspiration radio broadcast, 1976, 79-84; pastor 1st Ch. of Nazarene, Paris, Ill., 1977-79, South Side Ch. of Nazarene, Mishawaka, Ind., 1979-84, Taylorville 1st Ch. of Nazarene, Ill., 1984—. Mem. Taylorville Ministerial Assn. (treas. 1985—). Home: 1217 Brown Ct Taylorville IL 62568 Office: 300 S Shumway Taylorville IL 62568

HAYNES, EMERSON PAUL, bishop, Episcopal Church; b. Marshfield, Ind., May 10, 1918; s. Ora Wilbur and Lydia Pearl (Walsh) H.; m. Helen Charlene Elledge, Nov. 15, 1935; children: Rosaline Elledge Haynes Triano, Emerson Paul II, Roland Lewis (dec.). A.B., Ind. Central U., 1942, L.H.D., 1976; M.Div., United Theol. Sem., 1946; D.D., U. of South, 1975. Ordained as deacon Episcopal Ch., 1948, priest, 1949, bishop, 1974. Rector Holy Trinity Parish, Cin., 1948-53, All Saints Parish, Portsmouth, Ohio, 1953-57, Calvary Parish, Cin., 1957-59; canon chancellor St. Luke's Cathedral, Orlando, Fla., 1959-64; rector St. Luke's Parish, Ft. Myers, Fla., 1964-74; bishop coadjutor Diocese of S.W. Fla., St. Petersburg, 1974—, mem. standing com., 1969-74, del. to provincial synod, 1969-74, dep. to Episcopal Gen. Conv., 1970, 73, chmn. Christian edn. of diocese, 1969-74. Mem. Ft. Myers City Planning Bd., 1968-73; trustee U. of South, Suncoast Manor, Bishop Gray Inn. Mem. County Ministerial Assn. (pres. 1956, 73). Address: 219 4th St N Box 491 Saint Petersburg FL 33731

HAYTER, LONNIE RAY, minister, So. Baptist Conv.; b. Monahans, Tex., Mar. 29, 1947; s. R.L. and Earlene (Williams) H.; B.A. in Religion, Baylor U., Waco, Tex., 1969; m. Karen Bruce Johnson, Aug. 29, 1969. Ordained to ministry, 1969; asso. pastor social ministries Seventh and James Bapt. Ch., Waco, 1970-71; pastor Belfalls (Tex.) Bapt. Ch., 1971-73; asst. dir. Office Religious Activities, Baylor U., 1973-74, dir. religious activities, 1974—. Exec. bd. Waco Bapt. Assn.; Bapt. student missionary to Singapore-Malaysia, 1968. Pres. Tex. Assn. Student Councils, 1965; chmn., Let's Clean Up Waco, 1975; campaign worker Clergy for Carter, 1976. Editor The Vision, 1975—. Home: 212 Lelia St Waco TX 76706 Office: Baylor Univ Waco TX 76703

HEAD, EDWARD DENNIS, bishop, Roman Catholic Church; b. White Plains, N.Y., Aug. 5, 1919; s. Charles and Nellie (O'Donahue) H.; ed. Cathedral Coll., Columbia, St. Joseph's Sem., N.Y. Ordained priest Roman Catholic Ch., 1945, consecrated bishop, 1970; staff N.Y. Cath. Charities, 1947-62; apptd. papal chamberlain, 1962-66, domestic prelate, 1966; sec., exec. dir. N.Y. Cath. Charities, 1966; episcopal vicar for Manhattan, 1970-74; bishop of Buffalo, 1974—. Office: 35 Lincoln Pkwy Buffalo NY 14222

HEAD, KENNETH MAYNARD, minister, author, So. Baptist Conv.; b. Middlesboro, Ky., June 29, 1938; s. Albert Dock and Myrtle May (Morgan) H.; B.S., Cumberland Coll., Williamsburg, Ky., 1968; m. Joyce Earls, Aug. 9, 1960; children—Kenneth David, Michael Steven. Ordained to ministry, 1959; pastor various chs. in Ky., 1959-73; dir. radio prodn. and pub. relations Clear Creek Bapt. Sch., Pineville, Ky., 1973—; moderator Bapt. Assns. Mem. Nat. Thespian Soc., Nat. Beta Club. Author newspaper column Mountain Moments, 1975—; editor: Mountain Voice, producer radio broadcast Clear Creek Chimes. Home: PO Box 83 Cumberland Gap TN 37724 Office: Clear Creek Bapt Sch Pineville KY 40977

HEAD, ROY LEE, minister, Southern Baptist Convention; b. Rutledge, Ga., June 27, 1939; s. Charloe Manuel and Ophelia Florence (Stapp) H.; B.A., Mercer U., 1963; B.D., So. Bapt. Theol. Sem., 1966; M.Div., So. Sem., 1969, postgrad., 1976—; m. Mary Vonceil Smith, Sept. 8, 1962; children: Kevin, Derek, David. Ordained to ministry, 1959; pastor Smithboro Bapt. Ch., Monticello, Ga., 1959-61, Oxford (Ga.) Bapt. Ch., 1961-63, Salem, Ind., 1963-66, Glover Bapt. Ch., Norcross, Ga., 1966-74, 1st Bapt. Ch., Belevedere, S.C., 1974—; mem. gen. bd. S.C. Bapt. Conv. Mem. Aiken Bapt. Assn. (moderator 1981-83), Pastors Conf., Belevedere Community Ministers Council. Club: Optimists (chaplain). Home: 401 Clearwater Rd Belevedere SC 29841 Office: 421 Edgefield Rd Belevedere SC 29841

HEADLEY, HARRIET PAULINE, religious organization executive; b. Philip, S.D., June 25, 1911; d. Clarence M. and Sadye E. (Reynolds) Peirce; m. A. Dean Headley, June 9, 1932; children: Joan, Art, Joel. B.A., Dakota Wesleyan U., 1933. Exec. dir. Arrowhead Council Chs., Duluth, Minn., 1972—. Mem. Arrowhead Regional Devel. Assn., Duluth, 1980—, Minn. Conf. Bd. of Nominations, 1976-84, Minn. Conf. Council on Ministries, 1980—, Minn. Conf. Bd. of Youth Ministry, 1960-68; dir. Twp. Bd. Adjustment, 1980-85. Mem. Democratic Farm Labor Party. Lodge: PEO. Address: Arrowhead Council Chs 230 E Skyline Pkwy Duluth MN 55811

HEADLEY, WILLIAM R., priest, Roman Catholic Church; b. Phila., Apr. 1, 1938; s. George and Gertrude V. (Denney) H. B.A., St. Mary's Sem., Norwalk, Conn., 1961, B.Div., 1965; M.Ed., U. S.C.-Columbia, 1967; M.A. in Sociology, Atlanta U., 1969; Ph.D., NY U, 1974. Ordained priest, Roman Cath. Ch., 1965; asst. pastor St. Patrick Ch., Charleston, S.C., 1965-69; dir., counselor Manhattan Career Ctr., N.Y.C., 1969-74, West Penn Career Ctr., Pitts., 1974-77; coordinator Social Sci. Research, Maryknoll Fathers, Maryknoll, N.Y., 1977-79; provincial USA-East Congregation of Holy Ghost, Bethel Park, Pa., 1979—; chairperson, bd. dirs. African Faith & Justice Network, Washington, 1983—; vis. scholar Harvard Div. Sch., 1976-77. Martin Luther King fellow, NY U, 1970; NY U fellow, 1972. Mem. Nat. Assn. Ch. Personnel Adminstrs., Eastern Sociol. Soc., Conf. Major Superiors of Men (chmn. Region III), Holy Childhood Assn. (dir. 1979—). Clubs: Pittsburgh Runners, South Park Runners. Office: Congregation of Holy Ghost 6230 Brush Run Rd Bethel Park PA 15102

HEADY, MICHAEL ALAN, minister, Church of God, Anderson, Indiana; b. Evansville, Ind., Aug. 14, 1948; s. James T. and Elma Lois (Claycamp) H.; m. Lois Ellen Stewart, Oct. 31, 1970; children: Shannan Rene, Amy Richelle, Nathan Michael. B.A. in Journalism, U. Evansville, 1970; B.A. in Bible and Theology, Gulf Coast Bible Coll., 1974; M.Min., Anderson Coll. Sch. Theology, 1975. Ordained to ministry Ch. of God, 1976. Pastor First Ch. of God, Iowa Falls, Iowa, 1975-78, Flora, Ill., 1978-79, Meadowbrook Ch. of God, Rayland, Ohio, 1979—; chmn. bd. Christian edn. Iowa Ch. of God, 1977-78, chmn. bd. evangelism, 1976-78; v.p. Flora Ministerial Assn., 1978-79, Buckeye Local Ministerial Assn., 1982—; mem. Ohio bd. Christian edn., Ch. of God., 1981—. Contbr. articles to profl. jours. Served with U.S. Army, 1970-72. Home: Rural Route 2 Rt 150 Rayland OH 43943 Office: Meadowbrook Church of God RD 2 Rayland OH 43943

HEAGY, HENRY CYRUS, clergyman, religious administrator, United Christian Ch.; b. Lebanon, Pa., Sept. 27, 1921; s. Forney and Emma Mabel (Smith) H.; m. Dorothy Ann Wenger, June 26, 1943; children: David, Della, Ruth, Elva, Glenn, Edward, Thelma, Lynwood, Nelson, Luke, Samuel, Alice. Ed., high sch. Ordained minister, 1953. Minister, Lebanon County, Pa., 1947—; chmn. ch. conf., 1956, presiding elder, 1965—, mem. mission bd., 1952—. Address: 110 Lebanon PA 17042

HEALAN, CLAUD ALLEN, JR., minister, So. Bapt. Conv.; b. Carl, Ga., Nov. 27, 1933; s. Claud Allen and Ann Lou (Parker) H.; A.A., Truett-McConnell Coll., 1954; student Ga. State U., 1955; m. Mavis Elaine

Nichols, June 26, 1956; children—Gregory Lee, Rebekah Leigh. Ordained to ministry, 1954; missionary, W.Va., 1973-76; leader numerous revival meetings, So. and Northeastern U.S.; pastor chs., Ga., 1952—, Mars Hill Bapt. Ch., Watkinsville, 1969—. Moderator numerous Bapt. assns.; mem. exec. com. Ga. Bapt. Conv., 1972-77, dir. lay evangelism schs., 1972-76; chmn. evangelism Appalachee Bapt. Assn., 1969—; chaplain high sch. football team, Watkinsville, 1976—; featured speaker Ga. Bapt. Conf. on Evangelism, 1976. Mem. Ga. Bapt. (v.p. 1976—), Oconee, Appalachee pastors confs. Address: Route 2 Box 128 Watkinsville GA 30677

HEALY, TIMOTHY STAFFORD See *Who's Who in America*, 43rd edition.

HEANEY, JOHN JOSEPH, religious educator, Roman Catholic Church. B. Arklow, County Wicklow, Ireland, Dec. 7, 1925; came to U.S. 1929, naturalized 1936; s. William and Caroline (Keogh) H.; m. Patricia Bree, June 2, 1971. B.A. Boston Coll., 1949, M.A., 1950; S.T.L., Woodstock Coll., 1957; S.T.D., Cath. Inst., Paris, 1963. Ordained priest Roman Cath. Ch., 1956, laicized, 1970. Assoc. prof. Fordham U., Bronx, N.Y., 1964—. Author: The Modernist Crisis: von Hugel, 1968; The Sacred and the Psychic, 1984. Editor: Faith, Reason and the Gospels, 1962; Psyche and Spirit, (rev.) 1984. Mem. Cath. Theol. Soc., Am. Acad. Religion, Am. Soc. for Psychical Research. Democrat. Home: 9 Heathcote Rd Yonkers NY 10710 Office: Fordham U Bronx NY 10458

HEARD, RALPH DENNIS, ch. ofcl., Pentecostal Ch. of God; b. Coal Hill, Ark., Nov. 10, 1918; s. Grover Cleveland and Emilie Lucinda (Ketcharside) H.; D.D., So. Bible Coll., Houston, 1958; m. Edith Mildred Shaffer, Dec. 5, 1939; children—Alice Christine (Mrs. C. Leon Thacker), Mildred Elizabeth. Ordained minister, 1942; divisional officer Pentecostal Young People's Assn., So. Calif. Dist., 1938-42, internat. pres., 1946-49; pastor chs. in Calif., 1938-43, 44, 48-53; editor P.Y.P.A. Challanger, 1942-46; dist. sec.-treas. So. Calif. dist. Pentecostal Ch. God, 1944-46; chmn. Kern County Inter-Pentecostal Fellowship, 1952; gen. supt. Pentecostal Ch. God Am., Joplin, Mo., 1953-75. Mem. Commn. Chaplains and Service to Mil. Personnel, 1960-75; sec. N.Am. Pentecostal Press Assn., 1973—; pastor-overseer Interstate Temple, Tulsa, 1975—; mem. gen. bd. Pentecostal Ch. of God of Am., 1975—. Bd. dirs. So. Bible Coll., Pentecostal Bible Coll., Livermore, Calif., 1953-75. Hon. lt. col., aide de camp to Gov. Ala.; named Ky. col., 1960. Mem. Nat. Assn. Evangelicals, Joplin C. of C. (dir.), Internat. Platform Assn. Author: Patterns for Abundant Living, 1965. Editor-in-chief Messenger Publs., 1953-75. Home: 5115 S Quincy Ave Tulsa OK 74105 Office: Osborn Found 1400 E Skelly Dr Tulsa OK 74105

HEARN, J(AMES) WOODROW, bishop, United Methodist Church; b. MacIntyre, La., Mar. 7, 1931; s. John Elton and Alta (Fordham) H.; m. Anne Connaughton, Sept. 24, 1952; children: John Mark, Paul Woodrow, Diana Elizabeth Smith, Bruce Charles. A.B., La. Tech. U., 1952; M.S.T., Boston U. Sch. Theol., 1955, D.S.T., 1965; post grad. Harvard U., 1956; D.Div., Nebr. Wesleyan, 1985. Ordained elder United Methodist Ch. 1955. Exec. dir. Ft. Worth Council of Chs., Tex., 1966-69; program council dir. La. Conf., Shreveport, La., 1969-73; dist. supr. United Meth. Ch., Lake Charles, La., 1973-74; sr. pastor First United Meth. Ch., Baton Rouge, 1974-84; bishop United Meth. Ch., Lincoln, Nebr., 1984—; trustee So. Meth. U., Dallas, Nebr. Wesleyan U., Lincoln, St. Paul Sch. Theol., Kansas City, Mo., Bryan Meml. Hosp., Lincoln, Nebr. Mem. Bd. Global Ministries United Meth. Ch., Advance Com., African Ch. Growth and Devel. Com. Home: 1027 Twin Ridge Rd Lincoln NE 68510 Office: NE Conf United Meth Ch 2641 N 49th St Lincoln NE 68504

HEARNE, STEPHEN ZACHARY, minister, religion educator, Southern Baptist Convention; b. Burlington, N.C., Jan. 18, 1952; s. Stephen T. and Diana (Zachary) H.; m. Mary Gay Jaundrill, Dec. 31, 1974; children: Stephen, David. B.A. in Religion, Elon Coll., 1976; M.Div., Southeastern Bapt. Theol. Sem., 1979, Th.M., 1981. Ordained to ministry So. Bapt. Conv., 1978. Student pastor Berea United Ch. of Christ, Elon Coll., N.C., 1975-77; minister of edn. Hocutt Meml. Bapt. Ch., Burlington, 1977-81; asst. prof. religion North Greenville Coll., Tigerville, S.C., 1981—, chaplain, 1981—. Author Th.M. thesis The Messianic Secret in Mark; A Literary and Historical Investigation, 1981. Active Tigerville PTA, 1983-85; chief Tigerville Fire Dept., 1984-85. Mem. S.C. Acad. Religion, Soc. Bibl. Lit., Nat. Assn. Bapt. Profs. of Religion. Democrat. Office: North Greenville Coll Tigerville SC 29688

HEATH, MARK, priest, seminary president, Roman Catholic Church; b. Boston, Apr. 20, 1918; s. Leslie John and Genevieve (Stapleton) H. B.S., U.S. Naval Acad., 1940; A.B., Providence Coll., 1943; S.T.L., Dominican House of Studies, Washington, 1948; Ph.D., St. Thomas U., Rome, 1951; LL.D. (hon.), LaSalle Coll., Phila., 1959. Ordained priest Roman Catholic Ch., 1947. Chaplain, prof., chmn. grad. programs La Salle Coll., Phila., 1952-67; chmn. religious studies Providence Coll., 1967-73; dir. Washington Theol. Consortium, 1973-76, 80-81; pres. Dominican House of Studies, Washington, 1976—; regent of studies Province of St. Joseph Dominican Fathers, Washington; mem. Ofcl. Roman Cath. So. Bapt. Scholars Dialogue, 1979-82; mem. corp. Providence Coll., 1977-83; trustee Acad. Preachers Luth. Theol. Sem. Author articles and book revs. Mem. Assn. Profs. and Researchers in Religious Edn., Religious Edn. Assn. (bd. dirs. 1976-82). Home and Office: 487 Michigan Ave NE Washington DC 20017

HEATON, KENNETH GORDON, minister, United Methodist Church; b. Zephyr, Ont., Can., Jan. 31, 1935; came to U.S., 1960; s. James and Rose Hearty (Rye) H.; m. Sylvia Caroline Matheson, June 27, 1959; children: Kenneth Gordon Jr., Caroline. B.A., Olivet Coll., 1961; B.D., Nazarene Theol. Sem., Kansas City, 1976; Th.M., So. Bapt. Theol. Sem., Louisville, 1970; D.Min., Sch. Theology at Claremont, 1976. Lic. to preach, 1956; ordained to ministry Methodist Ch., 1962. Pastor chs. in Galt, Ont., Can., Tefft, Ind., Temperance, Mich., St. Joseph, Mo., New Salisbury, Ind., 1956-71; assoc. minister U. Meth. Ch. of Lancaster, Calif., 1971-72; sr. minister U. Meth. Ch., Valencia, Calif., 1972-80, First United Meth. Ch., Redondo Beach, Calif., 1980-84, Grace United Meth. Ch., Long Beach, Calif., 1984—; chaplain Ind. Ho. of Reps., Indpls., 1970, Los Angeles Bd. Suprs., 1980, Republican Central Com. Conv., Irvine, Calif., 1980. Pres. Santa Clarita Valley Mental Health Co., Newhall, Calif., 1976; bd. med. ethics Henry Mayo Newhall Hosp., Valencia, 1978-80; pres. Valencia Hills Homeowners Assn., 1978-80; bd. dirs. Toberman Settlement House, San Pedro, Calif., 1983-84. Grad. study grantee Ind. Ann. Conf., United Meth. Ch., 1969-70; in-service doctoral scholar Pacific and Southwest Ann. Conf., United Meth. Ch., 1974-76. Mem. Santa Clarita Valley Ministerial Assn. (pres. 1976-78), East Long Beach Interfaith Council, Long Beach C. of C., Newhall C. of C. (bd. dirs. 1978-80). Republican. Lodge: Rotary. Home: 6228 Vista St Long Beach CA 90803 Office: 2325 E 3rd St Long Beach CA 90814

HECHT, ABRAHAM B., rabbi. Pres. Rabbinical Alliance of America (Orthodox). Office: Rabbinical Alliance of Am 156 Fifth Ave Suite 807 New York NY 10010*

HECHT, HAROLD LOUIS, bishop, Assocіan Evangelical Lutheran Churches; b. St. Louis, Mo., Sept. 15, 1923; s. Louis Carl William and Lillian Adele (Buser) H.; m. Betty Emily Meinzen, Oct. 9, 1949; children: Philip Herbert, Mary Elizabeth Witt, Kathryn Susan Hartz. B.A., Concordia Sem., 1945; D.D., Christ Sem., 1978. Ordained to ministry Luth. Ch., 1949. Pastor Faith Luth. Ch., Milw., 1951-59; asst. pastor Cross Luth. Ch., Milw., 1949-51; mission counselor English Dist., Detroit, 1959-66, exec. sec., 1966-74, pres., 1974-76; bishop English Synod, Detroit, 1976—; dir. Luth. World Relief, N.Y.C., 1978—, Ptnrs. in Mission, St. Louis, 1979—, Assn. Evang. Luth. Chs., St. Louis. Democrat. Club: Detroit Athletic. Home: 17868 Berg Rd Detroit MI 48219 Office: English Synod PO Box 19307 Detroit MI 48219

HECHT, JACOB JUDAH, rabbi, Orthodox Jewish Congregations; b. Bklyn., Nov. 3, 1923; s. Samuel and Sadie (Auster) H.; ed. Tomchei Tmimiim Lubavitch Rabbinical Coll.; m. Elaine Lasker, Jan. 28, 1945; children—Sholom Ber, Basya (Mrs. Ben. Zion Raskin), Fraida (Mrs. David Sabol), Yosef Yitzchak, Yehoshua, Rivka (Mrs. Shlomo Leib Abromowitz), Rachel (Mrs. Mendel Duchman), Levi, Shimon, Chaye Bina (Mrs. Alter Tennenbaum), David, Gershon. Rabbi, 1946; rabbi Congregation Yeshiva Rabbi Meir Simcha HaCohen of East Flatbush, Bklyn., 1947—. Exec. v.p. Nat. Com. Furtherance of Jewish Edn., 1946—; chmn. Nat. Council Mesibos Shabbos, 1946—; pres. Camp Emunah for Girls, Camp Shaloh, Camp Emunah Tiny Tots, Summer Inst. Girls; v.p. Rabbinical Bd. East Flatbush, 1962—; chaplain Kings County Jewish War Vets., 1964; vice chmn. Jewish Polit. Actions Com., 1972; lectr.; columnist Jewish Press. Vice pres. Rugby East Flatbush Community Council, 1972—; mem. pres.'s com. Citizens for Decent Lit., 1968—; chmn. fin. com. Machon Chana Women's Inst. for Higher Learning; exec. mem. Morality in Media, 1968—. Bd. dirs. Hadar Hatorah Rabbinical Coll. Recipient Scroll of Honor, Yeshiva Rabbi Chaim Berlin, 1960, certificate of merit Kings County council Jewish War Vets., 1962, humanitarian award Nat. Com. Furtherance of Jewish Edn., 1950, leadership award Flatbush Women's Charity Soc., 1952, service award Crown Heights Post Jewish War Vets., 1956. Mem. Assn. Orthodox Jewish Scientists, B'nai Zion. Author: 17 vols. of Teachers Guides. Radio and TV personality. Home: 180 E 54th St Brooklyn NY 11203 Office: 824 Eastern Pkwy Brooklyn NY 11213

HECHTMAN, ISAAC LEIB, Orthodox rabbi; b. Rubel, Poland, Feb. 18, 1918; s. Moshe Chaim and Sara (Rips) H.; grad. Mirer Rabbinical Coll., Shanghai, China, 1946; m. Bella Spielman, May 3, 1953; children—Sara, Marsha Leah. Ordained rabbi, 1946; exec. dir. Mizrachi Orgn. of N.Y.C., 1947-55; exec. v.p. Jewish Community Council of Montreal (P.Q.), 1956—; exec. dir. Rabbinical Ct. of Greater Montreal, 1956; founder Torah Youth Council Montreal. Mem. Rabbinical Council U.S. and Can. Author: Jewish Dietary Laws - Their Meaning and Significance, 1962, 2d edit., 1979. Founding editor Voice of the Vaad, 1961. Home: 2615 Soissons St Montreal PQ Canada Office: 5491 Victoria Ave Montreal PQ Canada

HECK, STEPHEN THEODORE, educational administrator, Christian Church and Church of Christ; b. Indpls., June 4, 1949; s. Charles T. and Kathryn M. (Lusk) H.; m. Shirley J. Headrick, July 9, 1971; children: Nathan R., Andrew C. B.S., Ind. U., 1971, M.S., 1976. Chmn. bd. deacons Englewood Ch. of Christ, Indpls., 1972-74, 1978-79, dir. Christian edn., 1978-81, bus. agt., 1980-81; dir. Christian edn. Indian Creek Christian Ch., Indpls., 1982—; bldg. com. chmn. Indian Creek Ch. of Christ, Indpls., 1984—; profl. educator MSD Warren Twp., Indpls., 1971—. Pub. relations dir. Ind. Profl. Educators, Indpls., 1979-83, lobbyist, 1979-84; mem. adv. com. Gov.'s Commn. Edn., Indpls., 1982-84. Mem. Hoosier Orgn. Profl. Educators (pres. 1980-83). Avocation: furniture restoration. Home: 4104 Wayne Dr Greenfield IN 46140 Office: Indian Creek Christian Ch 6430 S Franklin Rd Indianapolis IN 46259

HEDRICK, CHARLES WEBSTER, religion educator; b. Bogalusa, La., Apr. 11, 1934; s. Henry Berry Hedrick and Harriet Eva (Smith) Maki; m. Peggy Margaret Shepherd, Dec. 8, 1955; children: Charles Webster Jr., Janet Lucinda, Lois Kathryn. B.A., Miss. Coll., 1958; B.D., Golden Gate Sem., Mill Valley, Calif., 1962; M.A., U. So. Calif., 1968; Ph.D., Claremont Grad. Sch. (Calif.), 1977. Ordained to ministry So. Bapt. Conv., 1956. Pastor, Mayersville Bapt. Ch., Miss., 1956-58, First Bapt. Ch., Needles, Calif., 1962-65; asst. prof. religion Wagner Coll., Staten Island, N.Y., 1978-80; assoc. prof. Southwest Mo. State U., Springfield, 1980—; dep. probation officer Los Angeles County Probation Dept., 1965-78. Author: The Apocalypse of Adam: A Literary and Source Analysis, 1980. Contbr. articles to profl. jours. Served with U.S. Army, 1954-56; to col. USAR, 1968—. Grantee in field. Mem. Soc. Biblical Lit., Studiorum Novi Testamenti Societas, Egypt Exploration Soc., Internat. Assn. Coptic Studies, Societe d'Archeologie Copte. Home: 963 S Delaware St Springfield MO 65802 Office: Dept Religious Studies Southwest Mo State Univ Springfield MO 65804-0095

HEDRICK, RALPH WESLEY, retired minister, United Methodist Church; b. Fort Spring, W.Va., Jan. 23, 1903; s. William Alfred and Laura (Shepherd) H.; B.A., Marshall U., 1928; B.D., Drew U., 1937, M.Div., 1940; m. Laura Janice Rector, Dec. 26, 1953. Pastor, Meth. Chs., W. Va., 1937-68; ordained to ministry, 1938, ret., 1968. Counselor, tchr. ch. youth camps, 1944-48. Mem. S.A.R., State Hist. Soc. W.Va., West Augusta Hist. and Geneal. Soc. (past pres.), Drew Alumni W.Va. (past pres.). Author: William G. Shepherd Family Story and Genealogy, 1778-1970, 1970; Moses Hedrick - His Ancestors and Descendants 1750-1973, 1973. Home: 3309 Hemlock St Parkersburg WV 26104

HEDSTROM, DOUGLAS PAUL, minister, United Church of Christ; b. Caribou, Maine, Nov. 6, 1953; s. Theodore Carl and Evelyn Claudia (Larsson) H.; m. Jane Ellen MacEwen, Feb. 19, 1984; 1 son, Stuart Gordon. B.A., U. Maine, 1976; M.Div., Andover Newton Theol. Sch., 1981. Ordained to ministry United Ch. Christ, 1977. Student minister 1st Congl. Ch., Milton, Mass., 1978-79, Ch. of Christ, Millis, Mass., 1979-80; minister Trinity United Ch., Seabrook, N.H., 1981—; trustee N.H. Conf. United Ch. Christ, Concord, 1982-84, mem. council, 1984—. Trustee, Dearborn Scholarship Fund, Seabrook, 1981—. Named An Outstanding Young Man Am. U.S. Jr. C. of C., 1982. Mem. Seabrook Clergy Assn. Republican. Lodge: Hampton Rotary (dir. 1984—). Home: 650 Lafayette Rd Seabrook NH 03874 Office: Trinity United Ch 652 Lafayette Rd Seabrook NH 03874

HEFFNER, WILLIAM CLANCY, priest, Episcopal Church; b. Lock Haven, Pa., Nov. 18, 1923; s. Edgar Franklin and Ruth Eleanor (Clancy) H.; m. Naeko Yoshihira, July 25, 1960; children: David, Michael, Paul, Maria. B.A., Coll. of William and Mary, 1947, M.Div., Va. Theol. Sem., 1950; D.D. (hon.), Va. Theol. Sem., 1972. Ordained priest, 1951. Pioneer missionary Episcopal Ch., Okinawa, Ryukyu Islands, 1950-62; vicar St. Barnabas Ch., Garland, Tex., 1962-65, Holy Nativity Ch., Plano, Tex., 1962-64; Asia /Pacific sec. nat. staff Episcopal Ch. Exec. Council, 1965-74; rector St. Mark's Ch., Mt. Kisco, N.Y., 1974—; mem. standing com. Diocese of N.Y., 1979-83, pres., 1982-83, mem. diocesan council, 1982-83, chmn. nominating com., 1983; trustee Cathedral of St. John the Divine, 1982-83. Contbr. articles to profl. jours. Served to lt. (j.g.), USN, 1942-46; PTO. Recipient Disting. Service Cross, Diocese of Hawaii, 1958. Mem. Suburban Clergy Group. Democrat. Lodge: Rectory. Home: 14 Emery St Mount Kisco NY 10549 Office: Saint Marks Episcopal Church East Main St Mount Kisco NY 10549

HEFLIN, KENNETH LEE, minister, United Methodist Church; b. Harlan, Iowa, Mar. 29, 1932; s. Gaillard Ray and Thelma Elizabeth (Cade) H.; m. Nancy Sue Mortensen, Aug. 14, 1955; children: Elizabeth Snider, Travis E., Kenneth Mark, Gregory R. B.A., U. Northern Iowa, Cedar Falls, 1954; student Oslo U., Norway, 1952; S.T.B., Boston U. Sch. Theology, 1957, M.Div., 1957; D. Ministry, San Francisco Theol. Sem., 1977. Ordained deacon United Methodist Ch., 1955, elder, 1959. Student asst. First Congl. Ch., Rockland, Mass., 1956-57; organizing pastor Valley United Meth. Ch., Veneta, Oreg., 1957-61; pastor-in-charge Anchor Park United Methodist Ch., Anchorage, 1961-65; assoc. pastor First United Meth. Ch., Honolulu, 1965-69; sr. pastor Kailua United Meth. Ch., Kailua, Hawaii, 1969-78; pastor Lancaster United Meth. Ch., Calif., Lancaster, 1979—; pres. Anchorage Council Chs., 1964-65; chmn. nurture div. Hawaii Council Chs., 1966-68; chmn. Community Centers Task Force, Windward Citizens' Planning Conf., 1970-71; mem. Hawaii Dist. Children's Com.; mem. exec. com. Windward Coalition Chs.; chmn. planning com. first Easter Sunrise Service Windward Coalition; preacher Easter Sunrise Service, Punchbowl Nat. Cemetery, Honolulu, 1972; dean elem. camps United Meth. Ch. Oreg., Alaska, Hawaii, 1958-72; Hawaii dist. dir. evangelism United Meth. Ch., 1966-67, chmn. Hawaii dist. council adminstrn. and fin., 1972-73. Mem. Castle Hosp. Citizens' Adv. Council; chmn. Pohai Nani Residents' Adv. Bd.; mem. Hawaii Dist. Council Ministries; mem. Ann. Conf. Council Ministries; mem. personnel com. Hawaii Dist. and Supts. Adv. Com. Apportionments; trustee Calif.-Pacific Ann. Conf.; mem. chaplaincy program Antelope Valley Hosp. Club: Rotary (chmn. scholarship com.).

HEGENER, MARK PAUL, publisher, Roman Catholic Ch.; b. Petoskey, Mich., Apr. 6, 1919; s. John and Anna Marie (Mayer) H.; A.B., St. Joseph Sem., 1932-38; postgrad., St. Joseph Sem., Cleve. and Teutopolis, Ill., 1939-46; B.J., Marquette U., 1947-48. Joined Order of Friars Minor, 1938; ordained priest Roman Catholic Ch., 1945; mng. dir. Franciscan Herald Press, Chgo., 1949—; editor Franciscan Herald mag., Chgo., 1955—. Provincial dir. of lay Franciscans, 1949—; pres. Mayslake Village Retirement Complex, 1962—, Chariton Apts. Retirement complex, St. Louis, 1968—. Officer, Back of the Yards Community Council, Chgo. Founder, trustee Cath. Theol. Union at Chgo., 1968—. Mem. Am. Home Builders Assn., Cath. Press Assn., Assn. Am. Publishers, Nat. Council Aging, Nat. Inst. Sr. Centers. Home: 5045 S Laflin St Chicago IL 60609 Office: 1434 W 51st St Chicago IL 60609

HEGLUND, FRANKLIN C. Synodical bishop Lutheran Church in America, Denver. Office: Luth Ch in Am 240 Josephine St PO Box 6820 Denver CO 80206*

HEGMON, OLIVER LOUIS, minister, Nat. Bapt. Conv. Am.; b. Boling, Tex., Feb. 28, 1907; s. John Charles and Martha (Robins) H.; B.Th., Conroe Normal and Indsl. Coll., 1937; D.D., Union Bapt. Theol. Sem., 1950; LL.D., Union Bapt. Sem., 1953; B.A., Bishop Coll., 1970; m. Emma Louise Jones, Apr. 25, 1929; children—Paul E., Beverly Ann. Ordained to ministry, 1932; pastor chs., Houston, 1932-35, Liberty, Tex., 1933-35, Dayton, Tex., 1934-35, Galveston, Tex., 1936-40, Tolivers Chapel Bapt. Ch., Waco, Tex., 1940-59, Calvary Bapt. Ch., Los Angeles, 1948-49, Antioch Missionary Bapt. Ch., Fort Worth, 1959—. Pres., Southwestern Dist. Bapt. Tng. Union Congress, 1938-41, Bapt. Minister Union, Waco, 1951-59, Bapt. Ministers Union, Fort Worth, 1964-71; chmn. civic com. Inter-Denominational Ministers Alliance, Forth Worth, 1963—; mem. ch. relation nat. bd. Bishop Coll., 1973-74; corr. sec. Evang. Bd., Missionary Bapt. Gen. Conv. Tex., 1965—; founder, pres. Truth Seekers Bible Sch., 1964—. Mem. Fort Worth Mayor's Com. on Human Resources, 1972-73; head ch. div. Fort Worth United Fund, 1966. Bd. dirs. Fort Worth Area Council Chs. Mem. NAACP (chmn. ch. work com. Tex. State Conf. brs. 1959-74), Gen. Ministers Assn. Ft. Worth-Tarrant County (pres. 1976). Editor, pub. Truth Seeker mag., 1964-74. Home: 800 E Baltimore Ave Fort Worth TX 76104 Office: 1063 E Rosedale St Fort Worth TX 76104

HEGSTAD, ROLAND REX, minister, church official, Seventh-day Adventists; b. Stayton, Ore., Apr. 7, 1926; s. Phillip Roland and Lydia B. (Prospal); B.Th., Walla Walla Coll., 1949; M.A., Andrews U., 1954; m. Stella Marie Radke, Aug. 22, 1949; children—Douglas Roland, Sheryl Marie (Mrs. John F. Clarke III), Kimberly Marie. Ordained to ministry Seventh-day Adventists, 1955; pastor Upper Columbia Conf., 1949-55; asst. editor These Times, 1955-57, asso. editor, 1957-58; book editor So. Pub. Assn., Nashville, 1958-59; editor Liberty, Washington, 1959—; acting editor Insight, Washington, 1971-72; mem. exec. council Gen. Conf. Seventh-day Adventists, 1959—, mem. bd. higher edn., 1973—, mem. ch.-state study commn., 1970—. Author: Rattling the Gates, 1973; Mind Manipulators, 1974; Tall in the Saddle, 1977; As the Spirit Speaks, 1973; others. Office: 6840 Eastern Ave NW Washington DC 20012

HEIDE, JOHN JOSEPH, religious institute dean, Assemblies of God; b. Hinsdale, Ill., June 18, 1950; s. John Frederick and Jeannie Lois (Kocar) H.; m. Judy Carol Cook, Aug. 31, 1973; 1 child, Juliana Paige. A.A., Crowder Coll., 1978; B. in Bibl. Lit., Ozark Bible Inst., 1981; Th.M., Internat. Bible Inst., 1983. Ordained to ministry Assemblies of God, 1976. Supr. of men Ozark Bible Inst., Neosho, Mo., 1974-76, dean of students, 1977-81, adminstrv. and acad. dean, 1982—. Author: The Veil Rolled Aside, 1973; Sermon Illustrations, 1983. Chmn., Mo. Citizens for Life, Neosho, 1978-83; mem. Neosho City Council, 1981-83; del. Republican Party, Neosho, 1980. Found. for Econ. Edn. scholar, 1982. Mem. Neosho C. of C. (edn. com. 1980—). Home: 509 Morrow Neosho MO 64850 Office: Ozark Bible Inst PO Box 398 Neosho MO 64850

HEIGL, JOHN JOSEPH, missionary, Roman Catholic Church; b. Buffalo, Mar. 14, 1933; s. Joseph and Bertha Katharine (Stang) H. Cert., Little Sem., 1952; B.A. in Philosophy, River Ridge Sem., 1955; B.A. in Theology, St. Louis Scholasticate, 1959; cert. in counseling Mt. St. Mary's Sem., 1964. Ordained priest Roman Catholic Ch., 1959. Vocat. dir. Missionaries of Africa-U.S.A., 1959-65; assoc. pastor Archdiocese of Tabora, Tanzania, 1965-67, lay apostolate dir., 1967-70, assoc. pastor, 1979-82; regional superior Missionaries of Africa, Tanzania, 1970-79; provincial coordinator Soc. Missionaries Africa, Washington, 1982—; v.p. Coordination in Devel., N.Y.C., 1982-83; bd. dirs. Washington Office on Africa, 1984—, U.S. Cath. Mission Assn., 1984—, African Faith and Justice Network, 1983—. Mem. U.S. Cath. Mission Assn., Conf. Maj. Superiors Men. Hine and Office: Soc Missionaries of Africa 1624 21st St NW Washington DC 20009

HEIKKILA, GUNARD WILBERT, minister, Lutheran Church - Missouri Synod; b. Hancock, Mich., Nov. 24, 1941; s. Wilmer Wilho and Bertha Sophie (Kaurala) H.; m. Janice Margaret Koosmann, Aug. 28, 1964; children: Sarah, Thomas, Mark, Kari. Student Concordia Coll., 1959-61; B.Th., Concordia Sem., 1965. Ordained to ministry Lutheran Ch., 1965. Missionary Minn. North Dist. Luth. Ch. - Mo. Synod, Manitouwadge, Ont., 1965-68; pastor Immanuel/Trinity Luth. Ch., Callaway, Minn., 1968-75; missionary, pastor Luth. Ch. Our Savior, Rosemount, Minn., 1975-79; pastor Bethlehem Luth. Ch., Frazee, Minn., 1979—; chmn. Detroit Lakes Ministerium, Minn., 1969-70; Park Region Pastors Conf., Brainerd, Minn., 1982—; del. Luth. Ch. - Mo. Synod Conv., St. Louis, Minn., 1983; cir. councilor Luth. Ch. - Mo. Synod Minn. No. Dist., Brainerd, 1983—; bd. dirs. Frazee Community Club, 1983—. Mem. Manitouwadge (Ont.) Jaycees (various offices), Callaway (Minn.) Jaycees (v.p. 1972), Rosemount (Minn.) Jaycees (v.p. 1975). Club: Nat. Railroad Hist. Soc. Lodge: Lions (bd. dirs. 1982—). Home: 213 Maple Ave E Frazee MN 56544 Office: Bethlehem Luth Ch PO Box 335 Frazee MN 56544

HEIKKILA, RUSSELL GARY, minister, Evangelical Congregational Church; b. Trimountain, Mich., May 21, 1932; s. Wallace Richard and Agnes Charlotte (Carlson) H.; grad. Tenn. Temple U., Chattanooga, 1957. Ordained to ministry, 1956; pastor Mission Evang. Congl. Ch., Maynard, Mass., 1966, Mission St. Congl. Ch., Gardner, Mass., 1962—. Chaplain, Dist. Ct. Central Middlesex, Concord, Mass., Maynard Police Dept.; speaker TV talk shows. Author: Furnace of Affliction, 1976; contbr. articles to religious jours. Recipient Citizenship medal Mass. chpt. VFW, 1977. Home: 7 Great Rd PO Box 340 Maynard MA 01754 Office: 19 Walnut St Maynard MA 01754

HEIL, PAUL SAMUEL, religious radio program producer, Evangelical Congregational Church; b. Reading, Pa., June 8, 1947; s. David Paul and Virginia May (Gaul) H.; m. Shelia Kay Troyer, Dec. 18, 1982; 1 child, Jason David. B.A. in English, Elizabethtown Coll., 1969. Producer, host syndicated Gospel music radio program Heil Enterprises, Lancaster, Pa., 1980—. Recipient Silver Mike award So. Gospel Music Assn., 1984; People's Choice award Gospel Music News, 1984. Home and Office: Heil Enterprises 1519 Springside Dr Lancaster PA 17603

HEIL, WILLIAM THEODORE, JR., minister, Lutheran Church in America. b. N.Y.C., June 11, 1934; s. William Theodore and Elizabeth (Lauenroth) H.; m. Kathleen Gibbons, Aug. 25, 1957 (div. 1982); children: James Christopher, Christine Rose; m. Judith Ann Parsons, Mar. 5, 1983. B.A., Wagner Coll., 1955; M.Div., Luth. Theol. Sem., 1959; S.T.M., Union Theol. Sem., 1964. Ordained to ministry Luth. Church in Am., 1962. Pastor St. John Luth. Ch., Mamaroneck, N.Y., 1962-64; chaplain Wagner Coll., Staten Island, N.Y., 1964-71; pastor Faith Luth. Ch., East Hartford, Conn., 1971-74; project mgr. Luth. Ch. in Am. Div. Profl. Leadership, Phila., 1974-75; pastor Trinity Luth. Ch., Battle Creek, Mich., 1975-79, Immanuel Luth. Ch., Detroit, 1980—; mem. exec. bd. Mich. Synod, Detroit, 1978—; dir. Christian Communication Council, Detroit, 1984—; del. Luth. Ch. in Am. nat. conv., 1968, 74, 82. Contbr. articles to profl. jours. Founder, Clergy and Laity Concerned, Staten Island, 1968. Democrat. Office: 13031 Chandler Park Dr Detroit MI 48213

HEILIGER, ROBERT LEE, minister, Lutheran Church in America. b. Milw., Nov. 14, 1948; s. Robert Bailie and Elayne Violet (Brennan) H.; m. Ethel Leah Waite, Dec. 27, 1970; children: Robert Bailie John Tietjen, Elizabeth Rebecca, Evangeline Marcella, Christopher William Aaron. B.A., Concordia Sr. Coll., 1970; M.Div., Concordia Sem.-in-Exile, 1974; S.T.M., Christ-Sem.-Seminex, 1976; D.Min., Andover Newton Theol. Sch., 1981. Ordained to ministry Lutheran Church in America, 1976. Assoc. dir. Luth. Service Assn. of New Eng., children's services, Framingham, Mass., 1975-82; asst. pastor Peace Luth. Ch., Dedham, Mass., 1977-78; assoc. pastor Trinity Luth. Ch., Springfield, Ohio, 1982-85; pastoral counselor Pastoral Psychotherapy Inst., Cin., 1985—; chaplain Emerson North Psychiat. Hosp., Cin., 1985—; cons. Miami Valley Outdoor Ministries, Cin., 1983—; cert. social worker Mass., 1982-83. Cons. Khmer Cultural Inst., Amherst, Mass., 1981-82. Home: 4227 Oakwood Ave Cincinnati OH 45236 Office: Mental Health Services East 3322 Erie Ave Cincinnati OH 45208

HEIN, ROLLAND NEAL, English educator. b. Cedar Rapids, Iowa, Sept. 12, 1932; s. George Henry and Henrietta Rose (Werner) H.; m. Dorothy Mae Netolicky, Aug. 31, 1954; children: Steven, Christine. B.A., Wheaton Coll., 1954; B.D., Grace Seminary, 1957; M.A., Purdue U., 1963, Ph.D., 1971. Ordained Nat. Fellowship of Brethren Ministers, 1958. Pastor Grace Brethren Ch., Flora, Ind., 1959-62; asst. prof. Bethel Coll., St. Paul, Minn., 1962-67, assoc. prof., 1968-70; assoc. prof. Wheaton Coll., Ill., 1970-78, prof. English, 1979—. Author: The Harmony Within, 1982. Editor: George MacDonald sermons Life Essential, 1974, Creation in Christ, 1976; editor novels George MacDonalds World, 1978; editor essays Miracles of Our Lord, 1980; contbr. articles to various publs. Wade lectr. Wade Collection, Wheaton Coll., 1984. Mem. MLA, George MacDonald Soc. Clubs: Men's Garden Club Villa Park (pres. 1976); Central States Dahlia Society (pres. 1981). Home: 325 W Harrison St Wheaton IL 60187 Office: Wheaton Coll Wheaton IL 60187

HEIN, THEODORE PAUL, pastor, American Lutheran Church. B. Independence, Iowa, Aug. 13, 1951; s. Kenneth Arthur and Ruth D. (Ullerich) H.; m. Nancy Ann Glew, June 4, 1972; children: Jason Peter, Jeremy John Dean. B.A., Luther Coll., 1973; M.Div., Wartburg Sem., 1977. Parish pastor Concordia Parish, Fessenden, N.D., 1977-79; assoc. pastor First Luth. Ch., Fargo, N.D., 1979-81, co-pastor, Morris, Minn., 1981—; mem. dist. com. on coll. and theol. edn., mem. dist. conv. planning com. S.W. Minn. Dist., 1982—. Mem. Agy. Older Adults. Lodge: Kiwanis. Office: First Lutheran Ch 200 E 5th St Morris MN 56267

HEINE, RAYMOND A. Synodical bishop Lutheran Church in America, Detroit. Office: Luth Ch in Am 19711 Greenfield Rd Detroit MI 48235*

HEISER, WALTER CHARLES, librarian, priest, Roman Catholic Church; b. Milw., Mar. 16, 1922; s. Walter Matthew and Lauretta Katherine (Kopmeier) H.; A.B., St. Louis U., 1945, A.M., 1947, S.T.L., 1955; M.S.L.S., Cath. U. Am., 1959. Joined Soc. of Jesus, 1940, ordained priest Roman Catholic Ch., 1953; Latin tchr. St. Louis U. High Sch., 1947-50; librarian St. Louis U. Div. Sch., 1955-75, St. Louis U. Div. Library, 1975—; faculty dogmatic and systematic theology, 1966—. Mem. Cath., Am. Theol. library assns., Cath. Theol. Soc. Am. Book rev. editor Theology Digest, 1963—; cons. Wilson Sr. High Sch. Library Catalog-Cath. supplement, 1968-77. Home: 3601 Lindell Blvd St Louis MO 63108 Office: 3655 W Pine Blvd St Louis MO 63108

HEITZ, WARREN DANIEL, priest, Roman Cath. Ch.; b. Huntingburg, Ind., May 30, 1940; s. Norbert Gerhard and Bertha Louise (Radke) H.; B.S., St. Meinrad Coll., 1963, M.Div., 1967; M.S. in Instl. Adminstrn. U. Notre Dame, 1972. Joined Order of St. Benedict, 1960; ordained priest, 1966; asst. bus. mgr. St. Meinrad (Ind.) Coll., 1966-73, spiritual advisor, 1969-70; asso. pastor St. Mary Ch., Huntingburg, Ind., 1973—. Chaplain Young Men's Inst., Huntingburg, 1973—; mem. Religious Life In Am. Com., Huntingburg, 1973—. Address: 313 Washington St Huntingburg IN 47542

HEITZNRATER, RICHARD PAUL, religion educator; b. Dover, N.J., Nov. 9, 1939; s. H. Clair and Ruth Naomi (Ross) H.; m. Karen Louise Anderson, June 2, 1962; children: Julia Marie, Jeffrey Paul, John Clair. A.B., Duke U., 1961, B.D., 1964, Ph.D., 1972. Ordained elder, United Meth. Ch., 1964. Assoc. minister First United Meth. Ch., Butler, Pa., 1964-66; asst. prof., then assoc. prof. history and religion Centre Coll., Danville, Ky., 1969-77; Albert C. Outler prof. Wesley studies So. Meth. U., Dallas, 1977—; assoc. editor-in-chief Wesley Works Editorial Project, 1980—; mem. Gen. Commn. on Archives and History, United Meth. Ch., 1980—, vice chmn. gen. conf. com. on doctrine, 1984—; pres. faculty senate So. Meth. U., 1984-85. Author: The Elusive Mr. Wesley, 2 vols., 1984. Editor: Diary of an Oxford Methodist, 1985, Oxfordnotes, 1984—. Contbr. articles to profl. jours. Mem. editorial bd. Meth. History Jour., 1976—.

Recipient Disting. Prof. award Centre Coll., 1975. Mem. Am. Council Learned Socs. (fellow 1975-76), Am. Acad. Religion, Am. Soc. Ch. History, Am. Soc. for Eighteenth-Century Studies, United Meth. Hist. Soc., Wesley Hist. Soc., Oxford Inst. Meth. Theol. Studies, Phi Beta Kappa. Clubs: Dallas Masters Track and Field, Dallas Cross Country. Home: 7611 Rolling Acres Dallas TX 75248 Office: Perkins Sch Theology So Meth U Dallas TX 75275

HELLESEN, REGINA MARY, lay church worker, Roman Catholic Ch.; banking official; b. Bklyn., Sept. 23, 1952; d. Clarence Joseph and Helen Frances (De Mott) Black; m. James Cameron Hellesen, Apr. 14, 1973; children: Jennifer Jean, Jamie Lyn. Student Grahm Jr. Coll., Boston, 1970-72; cert. of completion, L.I. Banking Inst., 1973. Confraternity Christian doctrine tchr. St. Joseph's Parish, Kings Park, N.Y., 1964-70; Confraternity Christian doctrine coordinator pre-sch. and 1st grade Holy Angels Parish, Plaistow, N.H., 1984—. Individual retirement account coordinator Family Mut. Savs., Haverhill, Mass. Mem. Bus. and Profl. Women's Club (runner-up Woman of Yr. local chpt. 1980). Democrat. Avocations: tennis, hiking, camping, bicycling, family. Home: 162 Main St Plaistow NH 03865 Office: Family Mut Savs 153 Merrimack St Haverhill MA 01830

HELM, TOMMIE LEE, evangelistic organization director, Southern Baptist Convention, Baptist Missionary Assn. Am.; b. Grapeland, Tex., May 11, 1946; s. Albert Lee and Isabel (Allen) H.; B.S. in Architecture, U. Houston, 1968; M.Div., Bapt. Missionary Theol. Sem., Jacksonville, Tex., 1971; m. Cindy Grace Yawn, Aug. 23, 1968; children: Blake Alden, Chaela Michelle. Ordained to ministry, 1969; chaplain City Prison Farm, Houston, 1967-68; staff evangelist Bethel Bapt. Ch., Pasadena, Tex., 1968-71; founder, organizer, pres. Spirit & Understanding, Inc., Jacksonville, 1973—; mgr. Damascus Road, 1975—; founder, organizer Duo Studios, 1983—. Composer contemporary Christian music and songs; author: Declaration of Dependence. Office: POB 524 Jacksonville TX 75766

HELMAN, ALFRED BLAIR, college president, minister, Church of Brethren; b. Windber, Pa., Dec. 25, 1920; s. Henry E. and Luie (Pritt) H.; A.B., McPherson Coll., 1946, D.D., 1956; M.A., U. Kan., 1947, postgrad. 1948-51; m. Patricia Ann Kennedy, June 22, 1947; children: Harriet Ann, Patricia Dawn. Ordained to ministry, 1942; pastor, Newton, Kans., 1944-46, Ottawa, Kans., 1946-54, First Ch. of Brethren, Wichita, Kans., 1954-56; faculty Ottawa U., 1947-48, 51-54, chmn. div. social scis., 1952-54; instr. extension div. U. Kans., 1951-54; faculty Friends U., 1955-56; pres. Manchester Coll., Ind., 1956—. Chmn. com. higher edn. Ch. of Brethren, 1964-67, nat. moderator, 1975-76. Trustee McPherson Coll., 1951-56, chmn., 1955-56; trustee Kans. Found. Pvt. Colls. and Univs., 1955-56; pres. Ind. Conf. Higher Edn., 1960-61; pres. Ind. Colls. and Univs. of Ind., 1966-67; chmn., interim pres. Council Protestant Colls. and Univs., 1967; chmn. bd. dirs. Central States Coll. Assn., 1968; pres. Asso. Colls. of Ind., 1970-72; mem. commn. on religion in higher edn. Assn. Am. Colls., 1968-71. Mem. Am. Hist. Assn., Soc. Advancement Edn. Inc., Soc. Historians Am. Fgn. Relations, Comparative and Internat. Edn. Soc., Orgn. Am. Historians, Am. Assn. Higher Edn., Am. Acad. Polit. and Social Sci., Nat. Council Chs. Christ Am. (policy bd. dept. higher edn. 1960-71), Ind. Council Chs. (dir., mem exec. com. 1960-62), C. of C Phi Beta Kappa, Phi Alpha Theta, Pi Sigma Alpha, Pi Kappa Delta. Author articles religion and higher edn. Home: 1400 East St North Manchester IN 46962 Office: Manchester Coll 604 College Ave Manchester IN 46962

HELMS, JOHN FRANKLIN, deacon, lay ch. worker, So. Baptist Conv.; b. Charlotte, N.C., Mar. 7, 1929; s. U. Boyce and Elizabeth Faye (Phifer) H.; student U. N.C., 1947-49, Wake Forest U., 1949-50; B.R.E., Southwestern Baptist Theol. Sem., 1956; m. Lucille Virginia Crowe, June 1, 1963. Organist Green Meml. Baptist Ch., Charlotte, N.C., 1954; minister of edn., 1956-58; minister edn. E. Washington Heights Baptist Ch., Washington, 1958-60; home missionary So. Baptist Conv., Johenning Baptist Goodwill Center, Washington, 1960-62; minister of music Clinton (Md.) Baptist Ch., 1965-74, Greenbelt, Md., 1974—; ordained deacon, 1960. Transportation industry analyst Fed. Maritime Commn., Washington, 1962—. Served with AUS, 1951-53. Recipient Achievement certificate Comdg. Gen., Ft. Hood, Tex. Home: 12700 Haskell Ln Bowie MD 20715

HELTON, BOBBY EASON, minister, Southern Baptist Convention; b. Grantville, Ga., June 20, 1933; s. James Monroe and Hannie Susie (Eason) H.; m. Ruth Eveon Williams, Apr. 27, 1952; children: Angela Denise, James Murphy, Charlotte Renee. A.A., Truett-McConnell Jr. Coll., 1958; student Mercer U., 1958-59; B.S. in Edn., Ga. So. Coll., 1961; M.Div., So. Bapt. Theol. Sem., 1972; D.Min., Luther Rice Sem., 1983. Ordained to ministry Southern Baptist Convention, 1957. Pastor Upper Hightower Bapt. Ch., 1957-58, Little Ogeechee Bapt. Ch., 1958-61, Elam-Egypt Bapt. Ch., 1958-61, Friendship Bapt. Ch., Statesboro, Ga., 1961-67, Ridgeland Heights Bapt. Ch., Sandersville, Ga., 1967-69, Ballardsville Bapt. Ch., Ky., 1969-73, Valley Grove Bapt. Ch., Thomaston, Ga., 1973-78, New River Bapt. Ch., Tifton, Ga., 1978—; vice moderator Sulfork Assn., Ballardsville, 1971-72; clk. Ogeechee River Assn., Statesboro, 1964-66; moderator Centennial Assn., Thomaston, 1976-78, Mell Assn., Tifton, 1984—; chaplain Civitan Club, Sandersville, 1968, Explorer Post of N.C., Tifton, 1983. Pres. Tift County Band Booster Club, 1980-82. Home: Rural Route 5 Box 308 Tifton GA 31794 Office: New River Bapt Ch Rural Route 5 Box 308 Tifton GA 31794

HEMMEN, WILLIAM FREDERICK, JR., minister, United Methodist Church; b. Kansas City, Mo., July 11, 1942; s. William Frederick Sr. and Dorothy Hilma (Peterson) H.; m. Marsha Elaine Boyd, Oct. 24, 1970; children: Benjamin Boyd, Adam Gentry. B.A., Baker U., 1964; M. Div., St. Paul Sch. Theology, 1968; M.R.E., 1976. Ordained to ministry United Methodist Ch., 1969. Campus minister U. Mo., Columbia, 1968-74; hosp. chaplain U. Mo. Med. Ctr., Columbia, 1974-75; minister Trinity U. Meth. Ch., Leavenworth, Kans., 1975-77, Centenary United Meth. Ch., Lawrence, Kans., 1977-80, Stilwell United Meth. Ch., Kans., 1980-83, First United Meth. Ch., Hiawatha, 1983—; mem. Bd. Ordained Ministry, Kans. East Conf., 1980—, Bd. Diaconal Ministry, 1976-84; police chaplain, Lawrence, Kans., 1978-80. Active in Human Rights Commn., Columbia, 1973-75, Lawrence, 1978-80. Mem. Order St. Luke, Christian Educators Fellowship, Fellowship United Methodists in Worship, Music, and Other Arts, Alpha Phi Omega. Lodge: Kiwanis. Home: 300 N 6th Hiawatha KS 66434 Office: First United Meth Ch 410 Hiawatha Ave Hiawatha KS 66434

HENCIER, JACK GREGORY, priest, Roman Cath. Ch.; b. St. Paul, July 22, 1925; s. Charles B. and Katherine (Cannon) H.; B.A., St. Thomas Coll., St. Paul, 1949; M.A., San Francisco Theol. Union, Berkeley, Calif., 1971, now postgrad. Joined Claretian Missionary Order, 1967, ordained priest, 1972; team minister St. Anne's Shrine, Denver, 1972-75; mem. priest council, Pueblo, Colo.; alt. to Priests Senate, Pueblo; hosp. chaplain Prowers Med. Center, Lamar, Colo.; faculty Lamar Community Coll.; friar 4th deg. K.C.; active Lamar Ministerial Alliance; mem. Lamar Liturgy Commn., Religious Life Com. for Colo. Bd. dirs. Lamar Meals on Wheels. Mem. Nat. Assn. Cath. Chaplains. Address: 600 E Parmenter St Lamar CO 81052

HENDERSON, HOMER DIMON, minister, United Church of Christ and United Methodist Church; b. Ft. Worth, Jan. 21, 1939; s. Irwin Louis and Sarah Kathryn (Woodruff) H.; m. Rosemary Whiteside, Aug. 18, 1962; children: Mark Andrew, Catherine Claire, Maria Elizabeth. B.A. cum laude, So. Meth. U., 1962; M.Div., Yale U., 1966; D.Ministry, Drew U., 1982. Ordained to ministry United Meth. Ch., 1966. Sr. pastor St. Andrew's United Meth. Ch., New Haven, 1963-66; pastor 1st United Meth. Ch., Ropesville, Tex., 1966-68; sr. pastor St. Matthew United Meth. Ch., Lubbock, Tex., 1968-72, Plymouth Congregational United Ch. of Christ, Lawrence, Kans., 1973—; field instr. Perkins Sch. Theology, Dallas, 1970-71; pres. Lubbock Ministers Assn., 1971; conf. preacher Kans.-Okla. conf. United Ch. Christ, 1980; fellow Interpreters House, Lake Junaluska, N.C., 1975. Bd. dirs. United Fund, Lawrence, 1974-77; pres. Kans. Sch. Religion at Kans. U., Lawrence, 1981-82, chaplain Kans. U. football team, 1983-84. Named as one of Top Five Community Leaders, Kansas U., 1983. Democrat. Club: Rotary (v.p. 1984, pres. 1985) (Lawrence). Home: 1332 Strong Ave Lawrence KS 66044 Office: Plymouth Congl Ch (UCC) 925 Vermont St Lawrence KS 66044

HENDERSON, VERYL FLOYD, minister, So. Bapt. Conv.; b. Shamrock, Tex., Jan. 13, 1943; s. Lonnie Floyd and Laura Mary (Roberts) H.; diploma Mesa Coll., 1963; B.A., Wayland Bapt. Coll., 1965; M.Div., Southwestern Bapt. Theol. Sem., 1969; m. Cheryl Lynn Owen, June 15, 1965; children—Jana Kay, Andrea Mikala. Ordained to ministry, 1967; pastor with Home Mission Bd., So. Bapt. Conv. in resort communities in Colo., summers 1965-66; pastor Mildred Bapt. Ch., Corsicana, Tex., 1967-69; pastoral missionary Lahaina Bapt. Ch. and West Maui Ministries (Hawaii), 1969—. Bible tchr. Teen Challenge Rehab. Center, 1972—; moderator, past missions and evangelism dir., camp dir., religious edn. dir. Maui County Bapt. Assn. Chs. Asst. wrestling coach Lahainaluna High Sch., 1969-76, head wrestling coach, 1977—. Mem. Jaycees (named Jaycee of Year 1971, past pres., sec., treas.). Home: 520 Wainee St PO Box 1093 Lahaina HI 96761 Office: 209 Shaw St PO Box 1093 Lahaina HI 96761

HENDRICK, KENNETH EUGENE, religious educator, chaplain, minister, Church of the Nazarene; b. Ludington, Mich., Sept. 10, 1932; s. Irwin Ray Hendrick and Alma Dorothy (Johnson) Visscher; m. Rosemary McDonald, Sept. 22, 1951; children: Kirt Allen, Jason Paul. A.B., Olivet Nazarene Coll., 1959; M.Div., Nazarene Theol. Sem., 1962; Th.M., Midwestern Bapt. Sem., 1969, D.Min., 1975; postgrad. Command and Gen. Staff Coll., 1978. Ordained to ministry Ch. of the Nazarene, 1962. Pastor, Ch. of Nazarene, Kansas City, Mo., 1960-74; prof. Olivet Nazarene Coll., Kankakee, Ill., 1974—. Contbr. articles to religious jours., chpts. to books. Served with USN, 1951-55, ETO; to col., chaplain, USAR, 1964—. Mem. Am. Sch. Oriental Research, Am. Theol. Soc., Wesleyan Theol. Soc., Res. Officers Assn. (v.p. chpt. 1980). Lodge: Rotary. Home: 1113 Armour Rd Bourbonnais IL 60914 Office: PO Box 89-Religion Div Olivet Nazarene Coll Kankakee IL 60901

HENDRICKS, DAVID GROSS, broadcaster, Independent Fundamental Churches America; b. Hilltown, Pa., June 22, 1924; s. Clarence Smith and Martha Overholt (Gross) H.; student pub. schs., Montgomery County, Pa.; m. Nedra Hosfeld Moser, Aug. 13, 1966. Owner, mgr. WBYO radio, Boyertown, Pa., 1960—; bd. dirs. Faith Mt. Mission Ky. Composer gospel songs. Mem. Boyertown Businessmen's Assn. (pres. 1974-75), Hal Webb Evang. Assn., Nat. Assn. Religious Broadcasters (bd. dirs.), Nat. Assn. Broadcasters. Home and Office: Box 177 Mill St Boyertown PA 19512

HENDRICKS, STANLEY RECTOR, minister, Southern Baptist Convention; b. Ardmore, Okla. Oct. 28, 1933; s. Sam Lee and Lois Caroline (Burnett) H.; m. Mary LaVerne Hartley, May 22, 1952; children: Richard Lee, Cynthia Lynn. Th.B., Th.M., Internat. Sem., Plymouth, Fla., 1980, Th.D., D.D. (hon.), 1981. Ordained to ministry So. Bapt. Conv., 1958; pastor Henderson Bapt. St. (Ga.), 1966-68, Stapleton Bapt. Ch. (Ga.), 1968-72, Oak Dale Bapt. Ch., Moultrie, Ga., 1972-74, Oak Grove Bapt. Ch., Tifton, Ga., 1974-80, 1st Bapt. Ch., Colquitt, Ga., 1980—; moderator Hepzibah-Mell-Bowen Assocs., Ga., 1969-72, 76-79, 82—; mem. nominating com. Ga. Bapt. Conv., 1982, exec. com., 1983-88, ch. Christian index com., 1984. Author: Great Bible Doctrines, 1980. Served with U.S. Army, 1955-56. Recipient Cert. of Honor, Internat. Sem., 1981. Mem. Miller County Ministers Fellowship (pres. 1981-83, treas. 1983—). Democrat. Lodges: Lions, Masons, Order of Eastern Star. Home: 263 E Pine St Colquitt GA 31737 Office: First Bapt Ch 351 E Pine St Colquitt GA 31737

HENLEY, GURDEN FLOYD, minister, Christian and Missionary Alliance; b. Everett, Wash., Nov. 9, 1933; s. Floyd and Ida (Hixson) H.; children: Steven, Vicki. Student, Fla. Bible Inst., 1963-64, Luth. Bible Inst., 1966, Seattle Pacific Coll., 1966, Berean Sch. of the Bible, 1974-75. Musician, Kroeze Evang. Assn., Everett, Wash., 1952-62, Musical Harts, Dallas, 1962-63; asst. pastor Christ Temple, St. Petersburg, Fla., 1963-64, assoc. pastor The Little Chapel, Seattle, 1964-68; pastor Ch. of the Open Bible, Aberdeen, Wash., 1968-73; sr. pastor Victoria Community Ch., Riverside, Calif., 1973—; bd. dirs. B.R.A.S.S., Riverside, Calif., 1979—. Contbr. articles to profl. jours.; composer songs. Served with U.S. Army, 1966-69. Recipient Award of Excellence, So. Calif. Inland Empire Theatre League, 1981. Fellow Broadcast Music Inc. Home: 5632 Carson Rd Riverside CA 92506 Office: Victoria Community Ch 5320 Victoria Ave Riverside CA 92506

HENRITZY, DAVID GEORGE, minister, United Methodist Ch.; b. Hazleton, Pa., Mar. 18, 1944; s. Samuel David and Helen Eleanor (Mowrey) H.; B.A., Moravian Coll., Bethlehem, Pa., 1966; M.Div., Crozer Theol. Sem., Chester, Pa., 1970. Ordained to ministry, 1970; pastor Pomeroy (Pa.) United Meth. Ch., 1970-72; asst. dir., chaplain Meth. Home for Aged, N.Y.C., 1972-75; dir. Bowery Mission, N.Y.C., 1975—. Chaplain, Brotherhood of St. Gregory. Vice chmn. Bowery Planning Task Force; chmn. Creative Arts Center Rockland County. Home: 20 N Broadway White Plains NY 10601 Office: 227 Bowery New York City NY 10002

HENRY, AUGUIE, ch. ofcl., minister, So. Baptist Conv.; b. Howe, Okla., Aug. 1, 1900; s. James and Jane (Tiffee) H.; B.A., Okla. Bapt. U., 1925, D.D., 1941; postgrad. Central Bapt. Theol. Sem., 1942; m. Avo Edmunds, July 24, 1921; children—Auguie, Bette Jane (Mrs. Alan G. Graham), Jeannie (Mrs. Robert C. Palmer). Ordained to ministry So. Baptist Conv., 1920; pastor Okla. chs., 1924-49; exec. sec.-treas. Bapt. Found. Okla., Oklahoma City, 1949-67, exec. sec. emeritus, 1968—; Okla. mem. So. Bapt. Home Mission Bd., 1935-48; pres. Bapt. Gen. Conv. Okla., 1942-43, Assn. Bapt. Found. Execs. U.S.A., 1953-54; mem. at large So. Bapt. Found., 1953-60. Bd. dirs. Bapt. Gen. Conv. Okla., 1934-49; trustee Okla. Bapt. U., 1925-34. Mem. Oklahoma City C. of C. Mason, Kiwanian, Rotarian. Contbr. articles and sermons to periodicals. Home: 208 N W 32d St Oklahoma City OK 73118

HENRY, CHARLES WILLIAM, priest, Roman Catholic Church. B. St. Cloud, Minn., July 22, 1923; s. John Achilles and Rose (Kraker) H. B.A., St. John's U., 1950; S.T.L., Collegio di Sant Anselmo, Rome, 1954; J.C.D., Cath. U. Am., Washington, 1957. Ordained priest Roman Cath. Ch., 1953. Rector, St. Maur Sem., South Union, Ky., 1957-59, 63-67, 74-76, prof. moral theology, 1957-75; prior St. Maur Priory, South Union, 1961-63; chaplain St. Vincent Hosp., Indpls., 1982—; bd. dirs. Cath. Sem. Found., Indpls., 1969-75; pro-synodal judge Diocesan Tribunal, St. Cloud, Minn., 1958-61, Owensboro, Ky., 1963-67; acting dir. Pastoral

Care Dept., Georgetown U. Hosp., Washington, 1981-82. Author: (historical) Canonical Relations Between Bishops and Abbots, 1957. Served with U.S. Army A.C., 1943-46, PTO. Fellow Cambridge U., 1973-74. Mem. Nat. Assn. Cath. Chaplains (supr. 1976—), Instutional Ethics Com. Home: 4615 N Michigan Rd Indianapolis IN 46208

HENRY, JERRY WAYNE, minister, United Methodist Church; b. Holly Hill, S.C., July 24, 1953; s. Otis Purvis Henry and Helen Louise (Shuler) Henry. B.A., Wofford Coll., 1975; M.Div., Yale U., 1980. Ordained to ministry United Meth. Ch. as elder, 1982. Assoc. minister Grace United Meth. Ch., North Augusta, S.C., 1980-84; exec. sec. Fellowship United Meths. in Worship, Music and Other Arts, North Augusta, 1984—; liaison Bd. of Discipleship, Nashville, 1983—, Bd. Higher Edn. of United Meth. Ch., Nashville, 1984—. Editor monthly resource jour. News Notes, 1983—. Mem. Greater North Augusta C. of C., Wofford Nat. Alumni Assn. (bd. dirs. 1985—). Home: 1834 Paris Ave North Augusta SC 29841 Office: Fellowship United Meths in Worship Music and Other Arts PO Box 6867 North Augusta SC 29841

HENRY, PATRICK, institute director; b. Dallas, Apr. 22, 1939; s. Patrick and Jean Shelley (Jennings) H.; m. Patricia Anne Gillespie, June 6, 1972; children: Stephen Marshall, Miranda Gail, Juliet May, Brendan Wilfred. B.A., Harvard U., 1960; B.A., Oxford U.-Eng., 1963, M.A., 1967; Ph.D., Yale U., 1967. Asst. prof. to prof. religion Swarthmore Coll., Pa., 1967-84; exec. dir. Inst. for Ecumenical and Cultural Research, Collegeville, Minn., 1984—; ruling elder Swarthmore Presbyn. Ch., 1977-79. Author: New Directions in New Testament Study, 1979; God on Our Minds, 1982. Editor: Schools of Thought in the Christian Tradition, 1984. Marshall scholar, 1960; Kent fellow, 1963; NEH fellow, 1979. Mem. Am. Acad. Religion, Phi Beta Kappa. Democrat. Home: Rural Route 2 Box 83A Cold Spring MN 56320 Office: Inst for Ecumenical and Cultural Research Collegeville MN 56321

HENRY, PAUL EUGENE, JR., minister, Lutheran Church America; b. Summit, N.J., Jan. 10, 1941; s. Paul Eugene and Arline Anita (Ferns) H.; B.A., Gettysburg Coll., 1963; M.Div., Luth. Theol. Sem., Gettysburg, Pa., 1966; m. Carolyn Sandra Haas, July 16, 1966; children—Susan Beth, Thomas Paul, Carol Lee. Ordained to ministry, 1966; asst. pastor First Luth. Ch., Albany, N.Y., 1966-67; pastor St. John's Luth. Ch., Canajoharie, N.Y., 1967-70, St. John's Luth. Ch., Mamaroneck, N.Y., 1970-77, Faith Luth. Ch., East Hartford, Conn., 1977—. Chmn. lay workers Conf. Met. N.Y. Synod, 1974; sec. Capitol dist. Upper N.Y. State, 1966-67, mem. worship com. Met. N.Y. State, 1975-76; mem. exec. bd. New Eng. Synod, 1979-85, mem. Commn. on budget and fin., 1979-85, chmn., 1980-82; coordinator Area V-No. Conn., 1979-85; chaplain Mamaroneck Volunteer Fire Dept., 1970-77, East Hartford Police Dept., 1982—. Mem. East Hartford Clergy Assn., Greater Hartfort Luth. Chs. (dean 1985—). Home: 22 Dartmouth Dr East Hartford CT 06108 Office: 1120 Silver Ln East Hartford CT 06118

HENRY, TOM GLENN, minister, So. Baptist Conv.; b. Jackson, Tenn., Nov. 2, 1937; s. William Earl and Lessie Virginia (Jenkins) H.; B.A., Georgetown Coll., 1960; M.Div., So. Bapt. Theol. Sem., 1966; m. Anne Baber, July 29, 1961; 1 dau., Amy Paige. Ordained to ministry, 1960; pastor chs. Winchester, Ky., 1960-62, Taylorsville, Ky., 1962-64, Graefenburg Bapt. Ch., Waddy, Ky., 1964-69, Bashford Manor Bapt. Ch., Louisville, 1969-71, 1st Bapt. Ch., Lebanon, Tenn., 1971—. Mem. religion dept. faculty Cumberland Coll.; mem. exec. bd. Tenn. Baptists; chaplain Old Masons Home Ky.; v.p. Ky. Bapt. Pastors Conf.; mem. Wilson County Bicentennial Religious Com. Bd. dirs. YMCA, Boys Club, McFarland Hosp., Lebanontown, March of Dimes, Fellowship Christian Athletes, Welfare Commn.; mem. Tenn. Gov.'s Age Advisory Com. Mem. Tenn. Bapt. Pastors Conf., Wilson County Bapt. Assn. Contbr. articles to denominational periodicals. Home: 1711 Indian Hill Rd Lebanon TN 37087 Office: Box 548 Lebanon TN 37087

HENSGEN, SISTER CAROLEEN, Roman Catholic nun, superintendent of schools; b. St. Louis, Nov. 11, 1914; d. Jules Francis and Louise (Meyer) H. A.B., St. Louis U., 1944, M.A., 1948. Joined Sisters of Notre Dame, Roman Catholic Church, 1932; tchr. Cath. schs., Ill. also Mo., 1933-48, prin. Cath. schs., Ill. also La., 1948-67; supt. schs. Cath. Diocese of Dallas Schs., 1967—. Mem. adv. com. Ednl. Service Ctr., Region 10, Tex., 1981; mem. adv. com. on fed. assistance U.S. Cath. Conf., Washington, 1976. Bd. dirs. Holy Trinity Sem., Irving, Tex. Mem. Common Cause, Nat. Cath. Edn. Assn., Tex. Cath. Conf. Democrat. Office: Catholic Diocese of Dallas Edn Office 3915 Lemmon Ave PO Box 190507 Dallas TX 75219

HENSLEY, JOHN CLARK, church official, Southern Baptist Convention; b. Sullivan County, Mo., June 16, 1912; s. Truman and Ivan (Moddrell) H.; A.B., William Jewell Coll., Mo., 1935; Th.M., Central Bapt. Theol. Sem., Kansas City, Kan., 1943, Th.D., 1946; m. Margaret Sipes, Nov. 24, 1946; children—Gary, Clark, Dana. Ordained minister So. Bapt. Conv., 1930; pastor, Moberly and Kansas City, Mo., 1935-46; asso. prof. Central Bapt. Theol. Sem., 1943-46; pastor, Nashville and Pulaski, Tenn., 1947-58; supt. missions Hinds County Bapt. Assn., Jackson, Miss., 1958-66; exec. dir. Christian Action Commn., Miss. Bapt. Conv., Jackson, 1966-82, exec. dir. emeritus, 1982—, family life cons., 1982—, rec. sec., 1982-85. Pres. bd. CONTACT, 1973—; trustee Radio and TV Commn. So. Bapt. Conv., 1980—; mem. Gov. Miss. Com. Alcohol Abuse and Alcoholism, 1972—; mem. bd. Am. Council Alcohol Problems, 1972—. Trustee Hannibal, Mo. LaGrange Coll., 1939-45. Recipient Distinguished service award for leadership in christian social ethics Christian Life Commn., 1975. Mem. Nat., Southeastern, Miss. councils family problems, Am. Judicature Soc., Am. Acad. Polit. Assn., Am. Assn. Sex Educators and Counselors. Author: The Pastor as Educational Director, rev. edit., 1950; My Father is Rich, 1956; In the Heart of the Young, 1952; Behaving at Home, 1972; Help for Single Parents and Those who Love Them, 1973; Coping With Being Single Again, 1978; Preacher Behave! Pointers on Ministerial Ethics, 1978; Good News for Todays Single, 1985. Home: 6083 Waverly Dr Jackson MS 39206 Office: POB 530 Jackson MS 39205

HENSLEY, KIRBY JAMES, minister, Universal Life Ch.; b. N.C, July 23, 1911; s. John Calvin and Delliah (McPeters) H.; D.D., Williams Coll., Berkeley, Calif., 1964; m. Lida G. Hensley, July 19, 1952; 3 daus., 2 sons. Ordained to ministry Ch. of God, 1939; young peoples leader Okla., 1941-42; ind. minister, 1949-62; founder, pres. Universal Life Ch., Inc., Modesto, Calif., 1962—. Home: 1766 Poland Rd Modesto CA 95351 Office: 601 3d St Modesto CA 95351

HENSON, KENNETH LEON, pastor, So. Bapt. Conv.; b. Wagarville, Ala., May 26, 1928; s. Dan J. and Estelle (Furr) H.; A.B., Samford U., 1954; M.Div., New Orleans Baptist Theol. Sem., 1963; m. Loriene Bailey, Oct. 31, 1947; children—Charlotte, May, Kay. Ordained to ministry, 1950; pastor Marble City Bapt. Ch., Sylacauga, Ala., 1954-59, Mt. Zion Bapt. Ch., Magee, Miss., 1959-61, Crosby (Miss.) Bapt. Ch., 1962-63, Westview Bapt. Ch., Sylacauge, Ala., 1963-69, 1st Bapt. Ch., Ashland, Ala., 1969-74, 1st Bapt. Ch., Grove Hill, Ala., 1974—. Pres., Sylacauga Ministerial Assn.; v.p. Pastors' Conf. Clarke County (Ala.); mem. Clarke County com. Crusade for Christ. Advisor to Sylacauga City Commn., 1970-74. Mem. Clarke County Bapt. Assn., Wild Turkey Nat. Fedn. Contbr. articles to religious jours. Home and office: PO Box 546 Grove Hill AL 36451

HENSON, ROBERT GRANT, minister, United Meth. Ch.; b. Charleston, W. Va., Apr. 5, 1922; s. Robert Hyatte and Martha Ella (Gunnoe) H.; student Asbury Coll., 1939-40, Bob Jones Coll., 1942; A.B., Morris Harvey Coll., 1943; S.T.M., Westminster Theol. Sem. (name now changed to Wesley Theol. Sem.), 1948; m. Orpha Sara Akers, Dec. 26, 1944; 1 dau., Sara Alyene Henson McClure. Ordained to ministry, 1945; student pastor, Charleston, W.Va., 1940-43, Clearville, Pa., 1943-44, Grantsville, Md., 1944-45, Balt., 1945-46; pastor W.Va. Ann. Conf., Meadow Bridge, 1946-49, Rupert, 1949-53, St. Paul Grafton, 1953-56, Milton, 1956-60, St. Paul, South Charleston, 1960-66, Calvary, Moundsville, 1966-69; instl. chaplain W.Va. State Penitentiary, Moundsville, 1969—. Dist. dir. youth work and camping, 1953-63; mem. edn., world service and finance commns. W.Va. Ann. Conf., 1960-68; pres. United Ch. Alcohol Action Program of W.Va., 1966-67. Mem. dist. bd. ARC, 1954; mem. budget com. Ohio Valley United Way, 1971; chmn. finance com. Grafton Centennial, 1956; pres. PTA; mem. bd. Salvation Army, now chmn. Mem. Am. Correctional Assn., Am. Protestant Correctional Chaplain's Assn., Am. Correctional Chaplains Assn. Home: 2016 Meighen Ave Moundsville WV 26041

HENSON, ROBERT THOMAS, minister, evangelist; b. Buffalo, W.Va., Apr. 18, 1929; s. Charles Thomas and Hazel Mirrell (Mitchell) H.; student Marshall Coll., 1948-49, Anderson (Ind.) Coll., 1949-53, Jordon Conservatory, 1954; student voice Dana Sch. Music, 1955, Cin. Conservatory Music, 1958-62, also pvt. study; m. Nancy Lucille Stephens, Aug. 9, 1952; children—Stephen Robert, Marilyn Elizabeth. Unordained minister Ch. of God-Anderson, Ind., 1954—, ordained as evangelist Messiah Bible Fellowship, 1974; minister music, asso. pastor chs. in Ind., Ohio and Tex., 1952-73; founder, pres. Bob Henson Evangelistic Assn., Inc.; singer, preacher, evangelist all-denominational chs., 1967—. Pres. Bob Henson Travel, Alexandria, Ind., 1970—. Recs. include various solos; composer gospel and spirituals. Address: Route 1 Alexandria IN 46001

HENTON, WILLIS RYAN, bishop, Episcopal Church; b. McCook, Nebr., July 5, 1925; s. Burr Milton and Clara Vaire (Godown) H.; B.A., Kearney State Coll., 1949; S.T.B., Gen. Theol. Sem., N.Y., 1952, S.T.D., 1972; D.D., U. of South, 1972; m. Martha Somerville Bishop, June 7, 1952; 1 son, David. Ordained priest Episcopal Ch., 1953, consecrated bishop, 1971; missionary, Mountain Province, P.I., 1952-57; asst. pastor, N.Y.C., 1957-58; rector ch., Mansfield, La., 1958-61, Baton Rouge, 1961-64; archdeacon of La., 1964-71; bishop coadjutor of N.W. Tex., 1971-72, bishop 1972-80; bishop Western La., 1981—. Trustee U. of South. Home: 3202 40 St Lubbock TX 79413 Office: PO Box 4046 Alexandria LA 71301*

HERING, EBERHARD ARNULF, minister, Lutheran Church in America; b. Marburg, Germany, Nov. 1, 1936; came to U.S., 1949, naturalized, 1952; s. Karl Friedrich and Elionore Wilhelmine (Friedrich) H.; m. Deloris Marie Bartling, Dec. 28, 1962; children: Angela Marie, Tyler Bartling. B.A., Midland Coll., 1958; M.Div., Central Sem., Fremont, Nebr., 1963; D.Min., Luth. Sch. Theology at Chgo., 1977. Ordained to ministry Lutheran Ch., 1963. Vicar Heilig Geist Kirche, Mexico City, Mex., 1961-62; pastor Immanuel and Swede Valley Luth. Ch., Ogden, Iowa, 1963-69, St. Paul Luth. Ch., Mason City, Iowa, 1969-73, St. John Luth. Ch., Council Bluffs, Iowa, 1973—; bd. dirs. Bethany Luth. Home, Council Bluffs, 1978-79, 84—, Bethphage Mission, Axtel, Nebr., 1984, Luth. Sch. Theology at Chgo., 1981-82; tchr. yearly nursing classes Death and Dying, 1975—. Mem. Council Bluffs Ministerial Assn. (pres. 1984—). Republican. Home: 110 Sleepy Hollow St Council Bluffs IA 51501 Office: St John Lutheran Ch 633 Willow Ave Council Bluffs IA 51501

HERLONG, BERTRAM NELSON, priest, Episcopal Ch.; b. Lake City, Fla., Oct. 16, 1934; s. Benjamin D. and Ava T. (Phillips) H.; B.A. in Edn., U. Fla., 1956; M.Div., U. of South, 1959, S.T.M., 1970; m. Barbara Ann Vickers, June 28, 1957; children—Mary Angela, Sharon Michele. Ordained deacon Episcopal Ch., 1960, priest, 1961; vicar chs., Fla., 1959-63; canon residentiary St. John's Cathedral, Jacksonville, Fla., 1963-72, canon pastor, 1963-67; chmn. radio-TV dept. communications Diocese of Fla., 1964-67; founding chaplain, asst. headmaster Jacksonville Episcopal High Sch., 1967-72; chmn. planning com. Diocese of Fla., 1969-72, mem. standing com., 1972; asso. rector Parish of Trinity Ch., N.Y.C., 1972-76, vicar Trinity Ch. and St. Paul's Chapel, N.Y.C., 1977—; founder, dir. Cathedral Communications, Inc., 1965-72. Dir. N.Y. Bd. Trade, 1975. Bd. dirs. Assn. Episcopal Colls., 1973—; mem. Manhattan Community Bd. #1, 1976—; bd. dirs. Chinatown Mission, Inc., 1976—. Mem. Sigma Phi Epsilon, Scabbard and Blade. Home: 404 Riverside Dr New York City NY 10025 Office: 74 Trinity Pl New York City NY 10006

HERMAN, (JOSEPH SWAIKO). Bishop of Phila., Orthodox Church in America. Office: St Tikhon's Monastery South Canaan PA 18459*

HERMANIUK, MAXIM, archbishop, Ukrainian Catholic Church; b. Nowe Selo, Ukraine, Oct. 30, 1911; s. Mykyta and Anna (Monczuk) H.; student philosophy, Louvain, Belgium, 1933-35, student Maitre Agrege Theol., 1947, Orient. Philol and History, 1943. Came to Can., 1948, naturalized, 1954. Joined Redemptorist Congregation, 1933, ordained priest, 1938; supr. vice provincial Can. and U.S., 1948-51; aux. biship Winnipeg, Man., Can., 1951, aposteli adminstr. 1956, archbishop met., 1956—. First editor Logos, Ukraine Theol. Rev., 1950-51; mem. Vatican II Council, 1962-65; mem. Secretariat for Promoting Christian Unity, Rome, 1963; prof. moral theology, sociology and Hebrew, Beauplateau, Belgium, 1943-45; prof. moral theology and holy scripture Redemptor Sem. Waterford, Ont. Can., 1949-51. Co-founder, mem. Ikrainian Relief Com., Belgium, 1942-48; co-founder, 1st pres. Ukrainian Cultural Soc., Belgium, 1947; organizer Ukrainian univ. students orgn. Obnova, Belgium, 1946-48, Can., 1953; Mem. joint working group Cath. Ch. and World Council Chs., 1969 Mem. World Congress Free Ukrainians, Taras Shevchenko Sci. Sot., Ukrainian Hist. Assn. Author: La Parabole Evangelique, 1957; Our Duty, 1960. Address: 235 Scotia St Winnipeg MB RV2 1V7 Canada

HERMANUS-RAMPENGAN, ALICE ANNA VICTORIEN, minister, Reformed Church in Indonesia; b. Kumelembuai, Menado, North Celebes, Indonesia; Jan. 25; came to U.S., 1966, naturalized, 1971; d. Manuel Kainde Rampengan and Antoinette Josephine Victorien Motto; m. Reinhold Andrew Hermanus, June 1, 1963; 1 child, Marvela Gratia. B.Div., Sekolah Tinggi Theol. Sem., Jakarta, Indonesia, 1963; Th.M., Princeton Theol. Sem., 1967; M.S.T., N.Y. Theol. Sem., 1971. Ordained to ministry Reformed Ch. in Indonesia, 1963. Instr. Theol. Sch., Tomohon, Menado, Indonesia, 1963-66, 72-76, acting dean, 1976; instr. Sam Ratulangi U., Menado, 1963-66; ecol. asst. and minister various chs. N.J., Indpls., N.Y., 1967-72; part-time teaching and preaching chs. Indonesia, 1963-66, 1972-76; founder, pastor Indonesia Ecumenical Fellowship, Inc. serving Indonesian Americans in N.Y., N.J., Pa., 1967—, coordinator, trustee, 1983-85, also dir.; with service dept. Am. Bible Soc., N.Y.C., 1979-80; with stats. dept. Gen. Assembly, United Presbyn. Ch., 1980-83; trustee Christian U., Tomohon; coordinator sch. and edn. Synod of GMIM, Tomohon, 1973-76; bd. dirs. Victory House, Newark, 1978-79; mem. staff Racial Ethic Clergy-Women, Presbyn. Ch. U.S.A., 1980—; leader spiritual activities Christian Youth Movement, Indonesia, 1956-66; leader, preacher Indonesian Christian Women Unity, Indonesian Chrisian Unity, 1964-65. Editor: (newsletter) Indonesia Ecumenical Fellowship. Contbr.

articles to profl. jours. Ch. scholar, 1956-62, World Council Chs. scholar, 1966-68, Disciple of Christ Mission Bd. scholar, 1971, N.Y. Theol. Sem. scholar, 1967-69; recipient Letters of awards and honors Ch. Women Assn., 1972, 76. Mem. Ch. Women United, Internat. Clergy-Women Assn., East Orange Discipleship Team, Orange Presbyn. Ch. Women Assn., Indonesian Community Club. Avocations: sports; music; book collecting; reading/writing; traveling. Office: care Jan Hus Ch 351 E 74th St New York NY 10021

HERNANDEZ, ALFRED, priest, Roman Catholic Church; b. Los Angeles, Sept. 16, 1926; s. Alfred and Teodolinda (Gatti) H. A.A., Los Angeles Coll., 1949; B.A., St. John's Coll., 1951; postgrad. St. John's Theol. Sem., 1955. Ordained priest, Roman Cath. Ch., 1955. Assoc. St. Ann's Ch., Santa Monica, Calif., 1955-59; chaplain Junenile Hall and U. So. Calif. Med. Ctr., Los Angeles, 1960-62; assoc. Immaculate Heart of Mary Ch., Hollywood, Calif., 1963-69, St. Joseph's Ch., La Puente, Calif., 1969-71, Ressurection Ch., East Los Angeles, 1971-72; pastor San Antonio de Padua Ch., Los Angeles, 1972-78, St. Ignatius of Loyola Ch., Los Angeles, 1978—. Chaplain Cedars of Lebanon Hosp., Hollywood, 1963-69, Hollywood Presbyn. Hosp., 1963-69, Children's Hosp., Hollywood, 1963-69, Los Angeles Fire Dept., 1974—; mem. Los Angeles Priest Senate, 1971-78, chmn. Spanish speaking com., 1972-75; coordinator spanish speaking Apostolate, Los Angeles, 1972-76; supt. schs. of Los Angeles Clergy Adv. Com., 1973-81; mem. Liturgical Commn. Archdiocese Los Angeles, 1974—; mem. bd. Interreligious Council So. Calif., 1977-80. Mem. Model Cities, Los Angeles, 1971-72; bd. dirs. Arroyo Vista Family Health Ctr., Los Angeles, 1982, Charisma in Missions, Los Angeles, 1984; liaison Charisma in Missions, 1983. Named Chaplain of His Holiness Pope VI with title Rev. Monsignor, 1975. Home and Office: St Ignatius Ch 322 N Ave 61 Los Angeles CA 90042-3499

HERNECK, HAROLD VIRGIL, JR., minister, So. Baptist Conv.; b. St. Louis, Jan. 29, 1945; s. Harold Virgil and LaVerne Violit (Falter) H.; B.A., Southwestern Bapt. Coll., Bolivar, Mo., 1967; m. Nancy Fran Sabin, Aug. 20, 1966; children—Gwendolyn Marie, Harold Virgil, III. Ordained to ministry, 1973; minister youth and music choirs, St. Louis, 1969-76; minister youth and music, Overland (Mo.) Bapt. Ch., 1969—. Vice pres. St. Louis Bapt. Youth Ministry, 1975-77; mem. organizing com. Super 76, 1976—; organizer, dir. Overland and Community Choir, 1976. Organizer Overland Community Bicentennial Celebration, 1976. Home: 12064 Charleston Maryland Heights MO 63043 Office: 9303 Midland St Overland MO 63114

HERR, MARK VAN, minister, Moravian Church of America (Unitas Fratrum); b. Lancaster, Pa., Sept. 15, 1952; s. Veryl Robert and Linda May (Musser) H.; m. Susan Amelia Whiteman, May 9, 1976; 1 son, Hans Christian. B.S. in Music Edn., Elizabethtown Coll., 1974; M.Div., Moravian Sem., 1979. Ordained deacon Moravian Ch. of America (Unitas Fratrum), 1979, consecrated presbyter, 1985. Asst. pastor, minister of music Nazareth Moravian Ch., Pa., 1976-83; assoc. pastor, minister of music St. Paul's Moravian Ch., Upper Marlboro, Md., 1983—; founder, dir. Moravian Sem. Vocal Ensemble, Bethlehem, Pa., 1976-79, Moravian Sem. Brass Ensemble, Bethlehem, 1977-79; mem. design team for program and liturgies for The Clown, Mime, Puppet and Dance Ministry Workshop, Lancaster, Pa., 1982-83; sec. Moravian Interprovincial Hymnal Revision Com., Bethlehem, 1984—. Editor, contbr.: Moravian Music Jour., 1985. Composer various choral works, 1977—. Mem. Am. Guild Organists, Pen Mar Moravian Clergy Assn. (pres. 1983—), Moravian Hist. Soc. Democrat. Avocations: gardening; calligraphy; pen and ink designing; puppetry; toymaking. Home: 11600 Tyre St Upper Marlboro MD 20772 Office: St Paul's Moravian Ch 8505 Heathermore Blvd Upper Marlboro MD 20772

HERRICK, LANCE ALAN, minister, United Methodist Church; b. Harvard, Ill., May 10, 1937; s. Robert Loren and Roma Louie (Rawson) H.; m. Mary Anne Estes, Dec. 27, 1964; children: Sara Elizabeth, Kristin Andrea, Robert Vernon. B.A., Carleton Coll., 1959, Drew U., 1960; B.D. with honors, Garrett Theol. Sem., 1966; Ph.D., U. St. Andrews, Scotland, 1971. Ordained to ministry United Meth. Ch., 1969. Pastor Cadahy United Meth. Ch., Cudahy, Wis., 1968-72, Kenwood United Meth. Ch., Milw., 1972-75; supt. Milw. Dist. Wis. Conf. United Meth. Chs., 1975-81; pastor United Meth. Ch., Platteville, Wis., 1981—; instr. N.T., Milw. Theol. Inst., 1971-81; pres., 1972-75; chmn. Health and Welfare Ministries Ctr. Wis. Conf. United Meth. Chs., 1984—. Clergy rep. Coping Inc., Grant County, 1984—; founder, leader Compassionate Friends, S.W. Wis. chpt., Platteville, 1983—. Morava fellow Garrett Theol. Sem., Evanston, Ill., 1966-67, Dempster grad. fellow Meth. Ch., Nashville, 1967-68; recipient Three Month Sabbatical Program United Meth. Found., Sun Prairie, Wis., 1971, First Dist. Leader Exchange award World Meth. Council, Lake Junaluska, N.C., 1978. Mem. Soc. Bibl. Lit., Chgo. Soc. Bibl. Research. Lodge: Kiwanis (pres. 1984—). Office: Platteville United Meth Ch 1065 Lancaster St Platteville WI 53818

HERRING, ROBERT WILBUR, minister, Southern Baptist Convention; b. Little Rock, Ark., June 15, 1911; s. William Jesse and Mae (Gladden) H.; J.D., U. Ark., 1935; postgrad. Stanford U., 1944-45, Southwestern Baptist Theol. Sem., 1952; D.D., John Brown U., 1963; m. Mary Elizabeth Taul, Feb. 27, 1936; children: William Taul, Elizabeth Herring Harrison. Ordained to ministry, 1947; pastor chs., Little Rock, Ark., 1947-52, Jonesboro, Ark., 1952-58, Jacksonville, Fla., 1958-67, Chamblee, Ga., 1967-69; sr. pastor Central Baptist Ch., Jonesboro, 1969-83. Pres. exec. bd. Ark. Baptist Conv., 1973-75, pres., 1975-77; bd. dirs. Affiliated Baptist Hosps., 1975—; mem. radio TV commn. So. Bapt. Conv., 1965-68; gen. chmn. State-wide Life and Liberty Campaign, 1976; mem. adv. com. Ark. Baptist Newsmag. Bd. trustees Fla. Jr. Coll., Jacksonville. Recipient Disting. Service award, Ark. State U., 1975; cert. merit Gov. Ark., 1983; (with wife) citation Ark. Ho. of Reps., 1983. Home: 1100 Wilmar Circle Jonesboro AR 72401 Office: 1010 S Main Jonesboro AR 72401

HERTER, THEOPHILUS JOHN, bishop, Reformed Episcopal Church; b. Kesab, Turkey, Asia Minor, June 5, 1913; s. John Michael and Agnes Barbara (Schuck) H.; came to U.S., 1920, naturalized; B.A., Haverford Coll., 1945, M.A., 1947; B.D., Theol. Sem. of Reformed Episcopal Ch., 1945, D.D. (hon.), 1969; Th.M., Westminster Theol. Sem., 1962, Th.D., 1966; m. Ruth Lillian Birbeck, June 14, 1941; 1 son, Philip John. Ordained deacon Ref. Episcopal Ch., 1943, presbyter, 1944; rector St. Matthews Ch., Havertown, Pa., 1943-60; lectr. Theol. Sem. Ref. Episcopal Ch., Phila., 1948-56, 60-63, prof. N.T., 1960-84, prof. emeritus, 1984—; asst. bishop New York and Phila. Synod, 1965-72, bishop, 1972-84, presiding bishop Reformed Episcopal Ch., 1975—; sec. Gen. Council, Ref. Episcopal Ch., 1948-60; pres. bishop Ref. Episcopal Ch., 1976—. Author: The Abrahamic Covenant in the Gospels, 1966. Home: 26 Strathaven Dr Broomall PA 19008

HERTZBERG, ARTHUR, rabbi; b. Lubaczow, Poland, June 9, 1921; s. Zvi Elimelech and Nehamah (Alstadt) H.; m. Phyllis Cannon, Mar. 19, 1950; children: Linda, Susan. A.B., Johns Hopkins U., 1940; M.H.L., Jewish Theol. Sem., 1943; Ph.D., Columbia U., 1966; D.D., Lafayette Coll., 1970; D.H.L., Balt. Hebrew Coll., 1974. Ordained rabbi, 1943. Hillel dir. Mass. State U. and Amherst Coll., 1943-44; rabbi Congregation Ahavath Israel of Oak Lane, Phila., 1944-47, West End Synagogue, Nashville, 1947-56, Temple Emanu El, Englewood, N.J., 1956—; vis. assoc. prof. Jewish studies Rutgers U., 1966-68; lectr. religion Princeton U., 1968-69; vis. prof. history Hebrew U., Jerusalem, 1970-71; pres. Conf. Jewish Social Studies, 1967-72; mem. exec. com. World Zionist Orgn., 1969-78, Jewish Agy. for Israel, 1969-71, bd. govs., 1971-78; pres. Am. Jewish Congress, 1972-78, Am. Jewish Policy Found., 1978—; v.p. World Jewish Congress, 1975—. Lectr., adj. prof. history Columbia U., N.Y.C., 1959-61. Author: The Zionist Idea, 1959; (with Martin Marty and Joseph Moody) The Outbursts that Await Us, 1963; The French Enlightenment and the Jews, 1968; Being Jewish in America, 1979. Editor: Judaism, 1961. Sr. editor: Ency. Judaica, 1972. Contbr. to Ency. Brit., 1975. Vice pres. bd. dirs. Meml. Found. for Jewish Culture; bd. dirs. Jewish Home and Hosp., Jersey City. Served to 1st. lt., chaplain USAF, 1951-53. Recipient Amram award, 1967. Home: 83 Glenwood Rd Englewood NJ 07631 Office: 147 Tenafly Rd Englewood NJ 07631

HESBURGH, THEODORE MARTIN, univ. pres., priest, Roman Cath. Ch.; b. Syracuse, N.Y., May 25, 1917; s. Theodore Bernard and Anne Marie (Murphy) H.; student U. Notre Dame, 1934-37; Ph.B., Gregorian U., Rome, 1939; postgrad. Holy Cross Coll., Washington, 1940-43; S.T.D., Cath. U. Am., 1945; hon. degrees Bradley U., LeMoyne Coll., U. R.I., Cath. U. Santiago (Chile), Dartmouth Coll., Villanova U., St. Benedict's Coll., Columbia, Princeton, Ind. U., Brandeis U., Gonzaga U., U. Calif. at Los Angeles, Temple U., Northwestern U., U. Ill., Fordham U., Manchester Coll., Atlanta U., Wabash Coll., Valparaiso U., Providence Coll., U. So. Calif., Mich. State U., St. Louis U., Cath. U. Am., Loyola U. at Chgo., Anderson Coll., State U. N.Y. at Albany, Utah State U., Lehigh U., Yale, Lafayette Coll., King's Coll., Stonehill Coll., Alma Coll., Syracuse U., Marymount Coll., Hobart and William Smith Coll., Hebrew Union Coll., Cin., Harvard U. Joined Order of Congregation of Holy Cross, 1934; ordained priest, 1943; chaplain Nat. Tng. Sch. for Boys, Washington, 1943-44; vets. chaplain U. Notre Dame, 1945-47, asst. prof. religion, head dept., 1948-49, exec. v.p., 1949-52, pres., 1952—. Former dir. Woodrow Wilson Nat. Fellowship Corp.; mem. Civil Rights Commn., 1957-72; mem. Carnegie Commn. on Future of Higher Edn.; chmn. U.S. Commn. on Civil Rights, 1969-72; mem. Commn. on an All-Volunteer Armed Force, 1970. Bd. dirs. Am. Council Edn., Freedoms Found. Valley Forge, Adlai Stevenson Inst. Internat. Affairs; trustee Rockefeller Found., Carnegie Found. for Advancement Teaching, Woodrow Wilson Nat. Fellowship Found., Inst. Internat. Edn., Nutrition Found., United Negro Coll. Fund, others. Recipient U.S. Navy's Distinguished Pub. Service award, 1959; Presdl. Medal of Freedom, 1964; Gold medal Nat. Inst. Social Scis., 1969; Cardinal Gibbons medal Cath. U. Am., 1969; Bellarmine medal Bellarmine-Ursuline Coll., 1970; Meiklejohn award AAUP, 1970; Charles Evans Hughes award NCCJ, 1970; Merit award Nat. Cath. Ednl. Assn., 1971; Pres.' Cabinet award U. Detroit, 1971; Am. Liberties medallion Am. Jewish Com., 1971; Liberty Bell award Ind. State Bar Assn., 1971; others. Fellow Am. Acad. Arts and Scis.; mem. Internat. Fedn. Cath. Univs., Freedoms Found. (dir., mem. exec. com.), Nutrition Found., Commn. on Humanities, Inst. Internat. Edn. (pres., dir.), Cath. Theol. Soc. Author: Theology of Catholic Action, 1945; God and the World of Man, 1950; Patterns for Educational Growth, 1958; Thoughts for Our Times, 1962; More Thoughts for Our Times, 1965; Still More Thoughts for Our Times, 1966; Thoughts IV, 1968; Thoughts V, 1969; The Humane Imperative: A Challenge for the Year 2000, 1974. Home: Corby Hall Notre Dame IN 46556

HESCHT, BLAINE EDWARD, minister, Churches of Christ; b. Saint Marys, W.Va., Jan. 17, 1941; s. Glen Kenneth and Marguerite Virginia (Cross) H.; m. Sonya Estrellita Inman, Apr. 12, 1968; 1 child, Jonathan. A.B., Marshall U., 1964; M.A. in Religion with honors, Harding Grad. Sch. Religion, 1981. Ordained to ministry Chs. of Christ, 1982. Missionary ministry Chs. of Christ, Rainelle and Springdale, W.Va., 1982-84; minister Ch. of Christ, Bridgeport, W.Va., 1984—; tchr. Bible class Bridgeport Manor, 1984—. Contbr. articles to Bible Herald, Gospel Adv. Vol. tchr. Literacy Vols. W.Va., Clarksburg, 1985—; counselor, vol. Hope, Inc., Fairmont and Clarksburg, W.Va., 1985—. Avocations: visual arts, gardening, hunting. Home: 135A Forest Dr Bridgeport WV 26330 Office: Ch of Christ Philadelphia Ave and Center St Bridgeport WV 26330

HESS, BARTLETT LEONARD, minister, Evangelical Presbyterian Church; b. Spokane, Wash., Dec. 27, 1910; s. John Leonard and Jessie (Bartlett) H.; B.A., Park Coll., 1931, M.A., 1932, Ph.D., 1934; postgrad. (Univ. fellow), U. Kans., 1931-34; M.Div., McCormick Theol. Sem., 1936; m. M. Margaret Young Johnston, July 31, 1936; children—Daniel Bartlett, John Howard and Janet Elizabeth (twins), Deborah Margaret (Mrs. Hans Morsink). Ordained to ministry, U.P. Ch. U.S.A., 1936; pastor various chs. Kans., Ill., Mich., 1932-68; founder, pastor Ward Evang. Presbyn. Ch., Livonia, Mich., 1968—. Instr. history and Bible, Detroit Bible Coll., 1956—; bd. dirs., founder, chmn. Friendship and Services Com. for Christian Refugees, Chgo., 1940-44; condr. tours Bible Lands, 1965, 67, 73, 74, 76, Far East, 1982, Europe, 1984; missioner Philippines U.P. Ch. U.S.A., 1961; mem. Cicero Ministers Council, 1942-58, pres. 1951; minister radio stas. WHFC, Chgo., 1942-50, WMUZ-FM, Detroit, 1958-68, 80—, WOMC-FM, Detroit, 1971, WBFG-FM, Detroit, 1972-80. Bd. dirs. Beacon House, Chgo., 1945-52, Presbyns. United for Bibl. Concerns, 1975—; pres. bd. dirs. Peniel Community Center, Chgo., 1942-52; exec. com. Evang. Presbyn. Ch., 1980—. Named Pastor of Yr., Mid-Am. Sunday Sch. Assn., 1974; Pastor of Yr., Youth for Christ, Detroit, 1979. Mem. Phi Beta Kappa, Phi Delta Kappa. Contbr. articles to profl. jours. Author: (with Margaret Johnston Hess) How to Have a Giving Church, 1974; Love in the Church, 1977; How Does Your Marriage Grow, 1983; Never Say Old, 1984. Home: 16845 Riverside Dr Livonia MI 48154 Office: 17000 Farmington Rd Livonia MI 48154

HESS, CARL CURTIS, minister, Christian Church; b. Indpls., May 3, 1926; s. Robert Franklin and Freddie Alice (Trotter) H.; B. Sacred Lit., Cin. Bible Sem., 1948; D.D. (hon.), Atlanta Christian Coll., 1964; m. Lynn Joan West, Sept. 1, 1946; children—Timothy Curtis, Tricia Jo, Joy Sue. Ordained to ministry, 1944; pastor ch., Cadiz, Ind., 1944-47, Xenia, Ohio, 1947-48; pastor Sciotoville Christian Ch., Portsmouth, Ohio, 1948-55, Central Christian Ch., St. Petersburg, Fla., 1955—. Pres. So. Christian Conv., 1962-63, Fla. Christian Conf., 1969-70; v.p. N. Am. Christian Conv., 1972-73. Trustee Atlanta Christian Coll., 1957—. Home: 1815 Sailfish Rd S St Petersburg FL 33707 Office: 4824 2d Ave S St Petersburg FL 33711

HESS, KURTIS CLAUDE, minister, Presbyterian Church U.S.A.; b. Dayton, Va., Apr. 29, 1941; s. John Claude and Dorothy (Matheny) H.; m. Jean Agnes Craig, June 11, 1965; children: Karen, Susan, John. B.A., Davidson Coll., 1964; M.Div., Union Theol. Sem., Richmond, Va., 1967; postgrad. New Coll., U. Edinburgh, Scotland, 1965-66; D.Min., McCormick Theol. Sem., 1975. Ordained to ministry, Presbyn. Ch. U.S.A., 1967. Pastor, Faison Presbyn. Ch., N.C., 1967-69, Mt. Horeb Presbyn. Ch., Grottoes, Va., 1969-75; pastor Colonial Heights Presbyn. Ch., Va., 1975-78; exec. presbyter Stated clk. Blue Ridge Presbytery, Lynchburg, Va., 1978-85; dir. Office of Field Edn. and Placement, Union Theol. Sem., Richmond, Va., 1985—; chmn. bd. dirs. Tri-City Area CONTACT, Petersburg, Va., 1974-75; bd. dirs. Westminster-Canterbury, Lynchburg, 1980-84. Editor: A Quick Reference Guide to the Form of Government, Book of Order, 1983; author/ editor: The Clerk of Session: A Guide to Roles and Responsibilities, 1984.

Author: A Guide for Pastor Nominating Coms., 1985. Bd. dirs. WARA Wildwood Area Recreation Assn., Lynchburg, 1980. Mem. Assn. Exec. Presbyters, Middle Judicatory Staff Assn. (dir. 1979-80). Office: Union Theol Sem 3401 Brook Rd Richmond VA 23227

HESSEL, JOHN LEWIS, minister, Southern Baptist Convention; b. Aug. 28, 1947; s. John Frederick and Louise (Kindle) H.; m. Brenda Elaine Dunn, May 27, 1967; children: DaNae, Rebekkah, Katherine. B.A., Okla. Bapt. U., 1970; M.Div., Southwestern Sem., 1974, postgrad., 1977-80. Ordained to ministry, Bapt. Ch., 1967. Pastor, Calvary Bapt. Ch., Wilburton, Okla., 1969-71, Valleyview Bapt. Ch., Pauls Valley, Okla., 1971-72, Pleasant Wood Bapt. Ch., Dallas, 1972-76, Springfield So. Bapt. Ch., Springfield, Ill., 1976-80, First Bapt. Ch., West Frankfort, Ill., 1980—; bd. dirs. Ill. Bapt. State Assn., Springfield, 1978-84, Home Mission Bd., So. Bapt. Conv., Atlanta, 1980—; mem. com. on coms. So. Bapt. Conv., 1979; chaplain West Frankfort Police Dept., 1983—; bd. dirs. UMWA Hosp., West Frankfort, 1984. Mem. West Frankfort Ministerial Assn. (pres. 1984), West Frankfort C. of C. (bd. dirs. 1984), Kappa Delta Pi. Lodges: Lions, Masons, K.T. Home: 609 S Lincoln St West Frankfort IL 62896 Office: First Bapt Ch 106 West Oak St West Frankfort IL 62896

HESSELINK, I. JOHN, seminary adminstrator. Pres. Western Theol. Sem. (Reformed Church in America). Office: Western Theol Sem 85 E 13th St Holland MI 49423*

HESTER, MALCOLM O'NEAL, minister, Southern Baptist Convention; b. Russellville, Ala., Mar. 9, 1949; s. Lonnie C. and Ruby E. (Hester) H.; m. Brenda Gail Jones, Dec. 27, 1970; children: David, Stephen, Emily. B.A., Samford U., 1971; M.Div., So. Bapt. Theol. Sem., 1974, Ph.D., 1981. Ordained to ministry Baptist Ch. Pastor Providence Bapt. Ch., Campbellsburg, Ky., 1971-74, Mt. Hope Bapt. Ch., Crane Hill, Ala., 1974-78, New Salem Bapt. Ch., Cox's Creek, Ky., 1978-82, Spray Bapt. Ch., Eden, N.C., 1982-84; missionary; prof. Korean Bapt. Theol. Sem., 1984—. Chmn. mission com. Dan Valley Bapt. Assn., 1983—, pres. pastors conf., 1984. Lodge: Kiwanis (bd. dirs. 1984) (Eden). Home: Yeo Fui Do PO Box 165 Seoul 150 Korea

HESTERBERG, PAUL ARTHUR, minister, American Lutheran Ch. B. Champaign, Ill., Mar. 14, 1935; s. Arthur Carl Herman and Mareka Christina (Schlueter) H.; m. Ruby May Hinsman, Aug. 24, 1957; children: Doris Ann, Timothy Paul, John Paul, Luther Paul, Judith May. B.A., Wartburg Coll., 1957; postgrad. Emanuel Hosp., 1960; Th.M., Wartburg Sem., 1961; postgrad., Luther-Northwestern Sem., 1967-70. Ordained to ministry American Lutheran Ch., 1961. Intern, Grace Luth. Ch., Anaheim, Calif., 1959-60; pastor Zion Ch., Gillespie, Ill. and St. Paul Luth. Ch., Dorchester, Ill., 1961-66, Immanuel Luth., New Auburn, Minn., 1966-71; sr. pastor St. Paul Luth., Le Center, Minn., 1971-81, Messiah Luth., St. Paul, 1981—; intern supr., Wartburg Sem., Dubuque, Iowa, 1972-80, Luther-Northwestern Sem., St. Paul, 1981-84; bd. dirs. Luth. Social Services, Park Ridge, Ill., 1963-66, Southeast Asian Ministry, St. Paul, 1981-83, Lyngblomsten, Inc., St. Paul, 1981—. Vol. fireman New Auburn Fire Dept., Minn., 1968; vol. Le Center Ambulance, Minn., 1978. Mem. Inter-Luth. Pastors' Group (treas. 1983-84), St. Paul Conf. Pastors. Home: 651 E Nebraska Ave Saint Paul MN 55106 Office: Messiah Luth Ch 1510 Payne Ave Saint Paul MN 55101

HESTON, WILLIAM RAY, minister, So. Bapt. Conv.; b. San Antonio, June 21, 1948; s. Richard Lee and Betty Frank (King) H.; A.A., San Antonio Jr. Coll., 1968; B.A., Howard Payne U., 1970; M.Div., Southwestern Bapt. Theol. Sem., 1973; m. Angela Louise Hooper, Nov. 27, 1976. Ordained to ministry, 1976; asst. minister youth Castle Hills Bapt. Ch., San Antonio, 1967-68; minister youth First Bapt. Ch., Conroe, Tex., 1973-76; minister edn. First Bapt. Ch., Brownwood, Tex., 1977—. Youth ch. conf. leader, 1973-77; asso. youth dir., 1973-76. Resource person Montgomery County Youth Home, Conroe, Tex., 1976. Recipient Philosophy award Howard Payne U., 1970. Mem. Southwestern Religious Edn. Assn., So. Bapt. Religious Edn. Assn. Home: 4317 Woodland Park Brownwood TX 76801 Office: 208 Austin Ave Brownwood TX 76801

HETICO, ROBERT PAUL, minister, Lutheran Church in America; b. Erie, Pa., Mar. 4, 1925; s. John Ephraim and Hilja Matilda (Lahti) H.; m. Rachel Selma Pentinmaki, Aug. 6, 1949; children: John, Timothy, Stephen, Robert Jr., Hope Rachel. B.A. magna cum laude, Wheaton Coll., 1949; B.D. magna cum laude, Suomi Theol. Sem., 1954; M.Div., Luth. Sch. Theology, Chgo., 1956; D.D. (hon.), Carthage Coll., 1975. Ordained to ministry Luth. Ch. in Am., 1947. Pastor Trinity Luth. Ch., Chgo., 1949-52, St. Mark's Luth. Ch., Waukegan, Ill., 1952-64, 4th Luth. Ch., Springfield, Ohio, 1964-72; asst. to bishop Mich. Synod, Detroit, 1972-76; sr. pastor Holy Trinity Luth. Ch., Glenview, Ill., 1976—; pres. bd. of parish edn. Luth. Ch. in Am., Phila., 1962-68, pres. exec. council, 1968-74; Luth. World Ministeries, N.Y.C., 1970-77; mem. exec. com. Luth. World Fedn., Geneva, 1970-77. Pres. Family Service Inc., Springfield, 1968; sec. bd. dirs. Springfield YMCA, 1970. Named Disting. Alumnus, Suomi Coll., 1970, Luth. Sch. Theology, 1975. Democrat. Lodge: Rotary. Office: Holy Trinity Luth Ch 2328 Central Rd Glenview IL 60025

HETZLER, DONALD F., minister, American Lutheran Church; b. Fargo, N.D., Apr. 7, 1923; s. Karl Philip and Rose Elizabeth (Bergeson) H.; m. Marilyn Joyce Jens, June 10, 1950; children: Jens Timothy, John Donald, Paul Thomas. B.A., U. Iowa, 1948, M.F.A., 1960; B.Th., Luther Theol. Sem., 1952; D.Div. (hon.), Wittenberg U., 1976. Ordained to ministry Am. Luth. Ch. (then Evang. Luth. Ch.), 1952. Pastor Concordia Luth. Ch., Kans., 1952-54; campus pastor Luth. student Found., Iowa City, Iowa, 1954-60; regional sec. Div. Coll. and Univ. Work, Nat. Luth. Council, Chgo., 1960-66; asst. exec. dir. Nat. Luth. Campus Ministry, Chgo., 1966-68, dir., 1968-76; exec. sec. Associated Ch. Press, Geneva, Ill., 1976—; dir. pastoral care Luth. Social Services of Ill., Park Ridge, Ill., 1977—; mem. youth student work com. Luth. World Fedn., Geneva, Switzerland, 1966-70, chmn., 1968-70; cons. Ctr. for Study Campus Ministry, Valparaiso, Ind., 1971—; mem. central com. World Assn. Christian Communication, London, 1978-81; pres. Fox Valley Hospice, St. Charles, Ill., 1984—. Chmn. Geneva Human Relations Com., Ill., 1965-68; mem. Community Resources Commn., Geneva, 1977-79. Served with U.S. Army, 1943-46; ETO, PTO. Recipient citation Am. Luth. Ch. Div. Coll. and Univ. Services, 1976, citation Ministry to Blacks in Higher Edn., 1976. Mem. Religious Pub. Relations Council, Phi Beta Kappa. Democrat. Office: Luth Social Services Ill/Associated Ch Press 321 James PO Box 306 Geneva IL 60134

HETZMER, MARK WILLIAM, minister, Lutheran Church-Missouri Synod; b. Saginaw, Mich., Feb. 16, 1953; s. Hugo Henry and Jean Ellen (Hill) H.; m. Monica Marie Bickel, July 31, 1976; children: Matthew William, Joel Mark. A.A., Concordia Tchrs. Coll., Ann Arbor, Mich., 1973; B.A. in Elem. Edn., Concordia Tchrs. Coll., River Forest, Ill., 1975, M.A. in Sch. Adminstrn., 1976. Ordained to ministry Luth. Ch., 1983. Dir. ch. edn., Charity Luth. Ch., Detroit, 1976-81, pastor, 1983—; mem. dist. youth bd. Mich. dist. Luth. Ch.-Mo. Synod, 1982—, counselor coordinator Dist. Youth Gathering, 1984; rep. Luth. Ctr. Book Store Com., Detroit, 1982-84. Office: Charity Luth Ch 17220 Kelly Rd Detroit MI 48224

HEURING, ALVAN PETER, priest, Roman Catholic Church; b. Rogers, Minn., Jan. 23, 1916; s. Matthias and Laura Clara (Eull) H. B.A., Iowa State Tchrs. Coll., 1938; M.S., Notre Dame U., 1939; postgrad. St. John's U., 1939-41, St. John's Sem., 1941-44. Ordained priest, Roman Cath. Ch., 1944. Assoc. pastor St. Joseph Ch., Mason City, Iowa, 1945-50, Sacred Heart Ch., Osage, Iowa, 1950-51; organizer, pastor St. Nicholas Ch., Evansdale, Iowa, 1951-68; pastor, dir. bldg. new parish complex St. Francis Ch., Belmond, Iowa, 1968-81; pastor St. Michael Ch., Belle Plaine, Iowa, 1981-85; mem. St. Raphael Priest Fund Soc., Archdiocese of Dubuque, 1981-85. Named Monsignor Pope Paul VI, 1974. Club: Belle Plaine Country. Lodge: K.C. Home and Office: St Michael Ch 1304 9th Ave Belle Plaine IA 52208

HEUSER, DARWIN HALBERT, minister, Assemblies of God; b. Blue Mounds, Wis., Nov. 19, 1921; s. Otto Henry and Mayme Lucille (Thistle) H.; grad. Great Lakes Bible Inst., Zion, Ill., 1942; m. Ona Anna Campbell, May 21, 1943; children—Rolland Frank, Roger Darwin, Rachel Darona. Ordained to ministry, 1946; minister Assemblies of God, Wis., 1942-66, Calvary Temple Assembly of God, Waukegan, Ill., 1966—. Dist. presbyter, gen. presbyter, dist. supt. Assemblies of God; dir. Youth for Christ. Editor, Full Gospel Tidings, dist. paper Wis. and N. Mich. Assemblies of God, 1957-65; chmn. bd. regents N. Central Bible Coll., 1962-66. Home: 448 Keller Ave Waukegan IL 60085 Office: 450 Keller Ave Waukegan IL 60085

HEWETT, JOHN HARRIS, minister, Southern Baptist Convention; b. St. Augustine, Fla., Sept. 3, 1952; s. Warren Dewey and Evelyn Christine (June) H.; m. June Lillian Martin, June 22, 1974; children: Martin Allen, Joel Pelham. B.A., Stetson U., 1974; M. Div., So. Bapt. Theol. Sem., 1977, Ph.D., 1981. Ordained to ministry Southern Baptist Convention, 1971. Minister of music First Bapt. Ch., Bunnell, Fla., 1970-72; minister of youth, Holly Hill, Fla., 1973-75; pastor Elmburg Bapt. Ch., Ky., 1975-79, Graefenburg Bapt. Ch., Ky., 1979-81; sr. pastor Kirkwood Bapt. Ch., St. Louis, 1982—; trustee Mo. Bapt. Coll., St. Louis, 1982—, Mo. Bapt. Hosp., St. Louis, 1984—; order bus. com. Mo. Bapt. Conv., Jefferson City, 1982—. Author: After Suicide, 1980. Contbr. articles to profl. jours. William Jewell Coll. fellow 1983. Recipient State Missions award Mo. Bapt. Conv., 1985. Home: 1010 Anduin Ct Saint Louis MO 63131 Office: Kirkwood Bapt Ch 211 N Woodlawn Ave Saint Louis MO 63122

HEYMANN, WERNER H., interfaith council executive; b. Oberhausen, Germany, July 10, 1910; came to U.S., 1936; s. Albert and Else (Klestadt) H.; m. Alice A. Sachs, May 26, 1940; 1 child, Ruth Heymann Baker. Abitur, Realgymnasium, Germany, 1929. Trustee Chgo. Sinai Congregation, 1964-72; chmn. Coll. Com. Nat. Fedn. Temple Brotherhoods, 1973—, mem. exec. bd., 1972-84, hon. mem., 1984—; chmn. Coll. Com. Chgo. Fedn. Union Am. Hebrew Congress, 1968—; exec. dir. Hyde Park and Kenwood Interfaith Council, Chgo. (312) 747-3517

HEYNEN, ANTHONY JAMES, religious organization official, business executive; b. Fremont, Mich., July 21, 1945; s. Anthony Heynen and Dena H. (Nibbelink) Brink; m. Marcia Lynn Fisher, Oct. 7, 1966; children: Gregory James, Matthew Joseph, Nicholas Jon, Emily Lynn. A.B., Calvin Coll., 1969; B.D., Calvin Theol. Sem., 1972. Dir. pastor tng., bd. home missions Christian Reformed Ch. in N. Am., Grand Rapids, Mich., 1972, mng. editor edn. dept., 1974-77, dir. and mng. editor, 1977-79, exec. dir. bd. publs., 1979—; trustee, pres. Grand Rapids Christian Schs., 1975-78, 80-83; bd. dirs. The Friendship Found., 1983—; pres. The Greystone Group, Grand Rapids, 1984—. Author: A Time to Keep, 1984. Bd. dirs. Dyer-Ives Found., 1983—; founder ITM Acad.—Sch. for Drop-outs, Grand Rapids, 1966, Switchboard-Crisis Intervention, 1969, The Jellema House, 1971. Recipient Meritorious Service award Stonehedge Found., 1974; Founders award Jellema House, 1982. Mem. Religious Newswriters Assn. Office: Greystone Group PO Box 3277 Grand Rapids MI 49501

HIBBITTS, JOHN BERNARD, religion educator, priest Episcopal Church; b. Halifax, N.S., May 12, 1918; s. John Timothy and Ethel Augusta (Wambolt) H.; m. June Marie Hilchey, May 13, 1958; children: Bernard John, Paul David. B.A. with 1st class honors, Dalhousie U., 1945; M.A., 1946; M.S.L., U. King's Coll., 1948; M.Div. with distinction, Gen. Theol. Sem.-N.Y.C., 1949; M.S.T., 1951; Phil.D., Oxford U.-Eng., 1954; D.D., Pine Hill Div. Hall, 1970, U. King's Coll., 1983. Ordained priest, 1948. Fellow, tutor Gen. Theol. Sem., N.Y.C., 1949-51; acting chaplain U. Coll., Oxford U., Eng., 1952; curate Cowley Parish, Oxford, 1952-54; assoc. prof. divinity U. King's Coll., Halifax, N.S., 1954-59, prof. Bibl. studies, 1954-71, dean div. faculty, 1963-71; prof. scripture Atlantic Sch. Theology, Halifax, 1971-83, prof. scripture, part-time, 1983—; bd. govs. U. King's Coll., 1963—. Contbr. articles to profl. jours. Mem. Soc. Bibl. Lit., Am. Acad. Religion, Cath. Bibl. Assn., Can. Soc. Bibl. Studies, Can. Soc. Ch. History. Home: 1625 Preston St Halifax NS B3H 3V2 Canada Office: Atlantic Sch Theology 640 Franklyn St Halifax NS B3H 3B5 Canada

HICK, ROY H., SR., church official. Gen. supr. Internat. Ch. of the Foursquare Gospel. Office: in care of Angelus Temple 1100 Glendale Blvd Los Angeles CA 90026*

HICKEY, DENNIS H., bishop, Roman Catholic Church. Titular bishop of Rusuccuru, aux. bishop, Rochester, N.Y., 1968—. Office: 415 Ames St Rochester NY 14611*

HICKEY, JAMES ALOYSIUS, archbishop, Roman Catholic Church; b. Midland, Mich., Oct. 11, 1920; s. James P. and Agnes (Ryan) H.; J.C.D., Lateran U. (Italy), 1950; S.T.D., Angelicum U. (Italy), 1951; M.A., Mich. State U., 1962. Ordained priest 1946; sec. to Bishop of Saginaw, 1951-60; rector St. Paul Sem., Saginaw, Mich., 1960-68; aux. bishop Saginaw, 1967-69; chmn. bishops' com. on Priestly Formation, 1968-69; rector N.Am. Coll., Rome, 1969-74; bishop of Cleve., 1974-80; archbishop of Washington, 1980—. Mem. Central Com. for 1975 Holy Year, 1973-75; chmn. Bishop's Com. Pastoral Research and Practices, 1974—. Address: Archdiocese of Washington 1721 Rhode Island Ave NW Washington DC 20036

HICKMAN, CAROLYN BURRELL GRANGER, lay church worker, Episcopal Church; b. Denver, Jan. 30, 1920; d. Frank Rollins and Elizabeth Hall (Slattery) Chedsey Granger; m. John Everette Hickman, Jan. 12, 1943; children: Mary Elizabeth Hickman Golden, Rollins Granger. B.S., U. Utah, 1941. Treas. Women's Aux., Denver, 1947-50, sec., Fort Collins, Colo., 1951-56; directress Altar Guild, Fort Collins, 1956-60; treas. Episcopal Ch. Women, Moscow, Idaho, 1970-72; chmn. bd. Campus Christian Ctr., Moscow, 1972-76, 76-78; diocesan treas. United Thank Offering, Diocese of Spokane, 1976-79, diocesan dir. Ch. Periodical Club, 1980—, synod del. Province 8, 1981-83, triennial province del., 1978-84; diocesan conv. del. St. Mark's, Moscow, 1974-75; triennial del. Mpls., 1976, Denver, 1979, New Orleans, 1982—. Neighborhood chmn. Girl Scouts U.S.A., Greeley, Colo., 1962, leader troop, 1962-69. Mem. Am. Soc. Clin. Pathologists. Republican. Clubs: Faculty Women (Fort Collins) (treas. 1956); Panhellenic (Greeley, Colo.) (sec., pres. 1956-57). Home: 807 Mabelle St Moscow ID 83843

HICKMAN, HOYT LEON, minister, United Methodist Church; b. Pitts., May 22, 1927; s. Leon Edward and Mayme (Hoyt) H.; m. Martha Jean Whitmore, Dec. 16, 1950; children: Peter, John, Stephen, Mary. B.A. magna cum laude, Haverford Coll., 1950; M.Div. cum laude, Yale U., 1953; S.T.M., Union Theol. Sem., 1954; D.D. (hon.), Morningside Coll.,

1978. Ordained to ministry as deacon Methodist Ch., 1952, as elder, 1953. Pastor, First Meth. Ch., Windber, Pa., 1954-57, Claysville and Stony Point Meth. Chs., Pa., 1957-59, Coll. Hill Meth. Ch., Beaver Falls, Pa., 1959-64, Cascade United Meth. Ch., Erie, Pa., 1964-72; dir. office local ch. worship Gen. Bd. Discipleship, United Meth. Ch., Nashville, 1972-78, asst. gen. sec., 1978—; exec. sec. Commn. on Worship, United Meth. Ch., 1968-72; pres. Erie County Council Chs., Pa., 1970-71; mem. com. on worship World Meth. Council, 1971-81; bd. dirs. Liturgical Conf., Washington, 1973-80. Author: Strengthening Our Congregation's Worship, 1981; At the Lord's Table, 1981; United Methodist Altars, 1984; A Primer for Church Worship, 1984. Served to seaman 1st class USN, 1945-46. Mem. North Am. Acad. Liturgy, Liturgical Conf. (bd. dirs. 1973-80), Order of St. Luke (nat. pres. 1965-68), Phi Beta Kappa. Democrat. Home: 2034 Castleman Dr Nashville TN 37215 Office: Gen Bd of Discipleship United Meth Ch PO Box 840 Nashville TN 37202

HICKS, KENNETH W., bishop, the United Methodist Church, Kansas East Conf. and Kansas West Conf., Wichita. Office: The United Meth Ch 151 N Volutsia Wichita KS 67214*

HICKS, LAMORA RAYMOND, minister, Baptist Church; quality control specialist; b. Rogersville, Tenn., June 26, 1930; s. Frank Adams and Martha Jane (Trent) H.; m. Margie Belle Eidson, Dec. 21, 1950; children: Lamora Raymond, Rita Jane, Terri Lynne. M.S., Internat. Inst. and Sem., Orlando, Fla., 1984. Ordained to ministry Bapt. Ch., 1974; pastor Howe's Bapt. Ch., Rogersville, Tenn., 1974-76, Tarpine Bapt. Ch., Rogersville, 1977-83; evangelist Holston Assn., Rogersville, 1983—; pastor Kyles Ford Bapt. Ch., Tenn., 1984—. Quality control mgr. IPC Dennison Co., Rogersville, 1968—. Served with U.S. Army, 1948-68. Decorated Bronze Star. Democrat. Lodge: Masons (32 deg.). Home: RD 2 Box 98 Rogersville TN 37857 Office: PO Box 230 Rogersville TN 37857

HICKS, WILBUR LEE, religious organization executive, American Baptist Chs.; b. Canton, Ohio, Apr. 19, 1933; s. Wilbur Duane and Vera (McLain) H.; A.B., Barrington Coll., 1955; B.D., No. Bapt. Theol. Sem., 1958; m. Arlene Ruth Kober, June 12, 1954; children—Steven, Cathleen. Ordained to ministry Am. Baptist Chs. in U.S.A., 1958; pastor First Bapt. Ch., Cornell, Ill., 1955-59, Auburn (Ill.) Bapt. Ch., 1959-61; asso. pastor First Bapt. Ch., Bloomington, Ill., 1961-63; asso. exec. dir. Council Chs. Met. Kansas City, Mo., 1963-65; asso. dir. Council Chs. Pitts. Area, 1965-68; exec. dir. Christian Assos. S.W. Pa., Pitts., 1968—. Mem. Commn. on Regional and Local Ecumenism, Nat. Council Chs. Bd. dirs. Health and Welfare Assn. Pitts., Pitts. Council for Internat. Visitors; bd. dirs. Pitts. chpt. NCCJ, also nat. trustee; Protestant del. to elevation of Cardinals, Rome, 1969. Mem. Am. Bapt. Ministers Conf., Pitts. Soc. Assn. Execs., Nat. Assn. Ecumenical Staff. Rotarian. Home: 110 Yosmite Dr Pittsburgh PA 15235 Office: 239 4th Ave Pittsburgh PA 15222

HICKS, WOODROW WILSON, ednl. adminstr., minister, Ch. of God in Christ; b. Lexington, Miss., July 14, 1918; s. James and Pearl (Williams) H.; Saints Coll., 1940, Henderson Bus. Coll., 1942; LL.D., Saints Coll., 1969; D.D., Pillar of Fire Wesleyan Sem., York, Eng., 1970; m. Evelyn Green, Oct. 16, 1960; children—Juanita, Juana, Maurice. Ordained to ministry Ch. of God, 1948; pastor, founder Holy Trinity Ch. of God in Christ, Chgo., 1960—. Pres. Nat. Bd. Edn. of Ch. of God in Christ, 1968—, mem. nat. governing bd. colls. and univs. higher learning. Bd. dirs. Charles Harrison Mason Found., 1970; trustee Charles Harrison Mason Theol. Sem. Recipient Gov.'s Citizenship award of Ill., 1946. Mem. Nat. Urban League, NAACP, Nat. Alumni Assn. Saints Coll. (pres. 1948). Home: 5958 W Washington Blvd Chicago IL 60644 Office: 2 W Washington Blvd Oak Park IL 60302

HIGGS, CHARLES EDWARD, minister, So. Baptist Conv.; b. Pueblo, Colo., Jan. 30, 1950; s. Grady L. and Audie L. H.; B.A., Ind. Bapt. Coll., 1972; postgrad. N.Am. Theol. Sem., 1972-74; m. Nancy Lynn Lanham, Dec. 18, 1970; 1 dau., Andrea Lynnette. Ordained to ministry, 1976; minister youth and outreach Grace Temple Bapt. Ch., Dallas, 1972-74; minister youth and edn. 1st Bapt. Ch., Dimmitt, Tex., 1974-76; dir. ch. tng. Llanos Alto Bapt. Assn., S. Plains Area, Tex., 1975-76; pastor Forrest Park Bapt. Ch., Corpus Christi, Tex., 1976—. Vice pres., treas. Castro County (Tex.) Ministerial Alliance, 1975-76. Active United Fund, Castro County, 1975. Home: 4506 Galway St Corpus Christi TX 78413 Office: PO Box 4153 Corpus Christi TX 78408

HIGH, EDWARD GARFIELD, lay church worker, Episcopal Church; biochemistry and nutrition educator; b. Indpls., Jan. 4, 1918; s. Osborn Edward and Meta Louise (Abernathy) H.; m. Kathryn Weston Toole, Oct. 27, 1943; children: Yolanda, Wanda, Sandra, Miranda, Travonda. A.B., Ind. U., 1940, A.M., 1941, Ph.D., 1950. Supt., ch. sch. tchr. Holy Trinity Episcopal Ch., Nashville, 1955-62, chmn. stewardship com., 1959-61, jr. warden, 1961-62, sr. warden, 1962—, lay reader, chalice bearer, 1962—; mem. bd. and organizing com. St. Anslem Episcopal Ch., 1959-61; mem. Com. on Episcupate, Diocese of Middle Tenn., 1984. Faculty Meharry Med. Coll., Nashville, 1953—, prof., chmn. dept. biochemistry and nutrition, 1959-82, instl. dir. nutrition programs, 1982—. Bd. dirs. Episcopal Ministry of Middle Tenn., 1980—. Chmn. adv. com. Tenn. Commn. on Aging, 1973—; mem. Tenn. Bd. Examiners of Nursing Home Adminstrs., 1978—; mem. adv. council Nat. Inst. on Aging, Bethesda, Md., 1983—. Fellow Am. Coll. Nutrition, Am. Inst. Chemists, AAAS; mem. Am. Inst. Nutrition, Am. Soc. Biol. Chemists, Ind. U. Alumni Assn. Home: 333 22nd Ave N Nashville TN 37203 Office: Meharry Med Coll 1005 DB Tood Blvd Nashville TN 37208

HIGHLANDER, DONALD HUGH, JR., minister, Presbyn. Ch. in U.S.; b. Bluefield, W. Va., Oct. 14, 1942; s. Donald Hugh and Genevieve (Bradley) H.; B.A., Columbia Bible Coll. and Grad. Sch. Missions, 1964; M.A. in Christian Edn. and Counseling, Trinity Evang. Div. Sch., 1970; Ed.S. in Counseling and Psychol. Services, Ga. State U., 1977; m. Emilie Wade Apple, June 25, 1966; children—Mary Elizabeth, Jennifer Emilie. Ordained to ministry, 1968; minister of edn. and counseling Winnetka (Ill.) Bible Ch., 1967-68; cons. Christian Edn., David C. Cook Co., Md., Washington, Va., Pa., 1969-72; cons. Christian edn., S.E. regional dir., Gospel Light Pubs., Regal Publs., Internat. Center for Learning, Atlanta, 1972-76; asso. counselor Northside Counseling Center, Atlanta, 1976—; exec. dir. Internat. Family Found., Inc., Atlanta, 1975—. Mem. Am. (co-supr. 1976-77), Ga. assns. marriage and family counselors, Christian Assn. Psychol. Studies, Nat. Council on Family Relations. Author: (with James E. Kilgore) Getting More Family Out of Your Dollar, 1976; editor, author family life curriculum resources Word Pub. Co., 1977—. Home: 504 Fond du Lac Dr Stone Mountain GA 30088 Office: Suite 204 Northside Medical Center 275 Carpenter Dr Atlanta GA 30328

HIGI, WILLIAM L., bishop, Roman Catholic Church. Bishop of Lafayette, Ind., 1984—. Office: PO Box 260 Lafayette IN 47902*

HILCHEY, HARRY ST. CLAIR, priest Anglican Church of Canada; b. N.S., Can., Feb. 12, 1922; s. Stanley Bertram and Loretta Esperance (Lawlor) H.; m. Charlotte Ruth Gibson. B.A., Dalhousie U., 1941; M.A., U. Toronto, 1945; Licentiate in Theology, Wycliffe Coll., 1944; B.Div., Gen. Synod, Anglican Ch. Can., 1951; D.Div. (hon.), Wycliffe Coll., 1972, Montreal Diocesan Theol. Coll., 1979. Ordained deacon, Anglican Ch. Can., 1944; ordained priest, Anglican Ch. Can., 1945; incumbent Stanhope Mission, Diocese of Toronto, 1944-46, St. Elizabeth's Ch., Queensway, Toronto, 1946-55; rector St. Paul's Ch., Halifax, N.S., 1955-64, Ch. St. James the Apostle, Montreal, 1964-79; gen. sec. Anglican Ch. Can., Toronto, 1979—. Address: Anglican Church House 600 Jarvis St Toronto ON M4Y 2J6 Canada

HILDEBRAND, HENRY PETER, educator, minister, Associated Gospel Churches; b. Stonefield, Russia, Nov. 16, 1911; s. Peter and Anna (Froese) H.; came to Can., 1925, naturalized, 1936; B.A., Winona Lake Sch. Theology, 1964, M.A., 1966; D.D., Winnipeg Theol. Sem., 1975; m. Inger Soeyland, Aug. 12, 1937; children—Marcia (Mrs. Phillip Leskewich), Evelyn (Mrs. Robert Moore), David, Paul, Glen. Ordained to ministry Asso. Gospel Chs., 1937; founder, pres. Briercrest Bible Coll., Caronport, Sask., Can., 1935-77, chancellor, 1978—; provincial supt. Canadian Sunday Sch. Mission for Sask., 1937-45, trustee, 1946—. Mem. Christian Educators Assn. (chmn. 1964-66), Assn. Canadian Bible Colls. (pres. 1976—). Address: Box 42 Caronport SK S0M O5O Canada

HILDEBRAND, RICHARD ALLEN See *Who's Who in America*, 43rd edition.

HILGENDORF, MAYNARD DONAVON, clergyman, educator, Lutheran Church-Missouri Synod; b. Gilman, Ill., Mar. 20, 1929; s. Arthur Henry and Clara Marie (Tiarks) H.; m. Adeline Bohlmann, Aug. 8, 1954; children: Stephen, Thomas, Ruth, Mary, Nathan, Daniel, Lois, Rebecca. B.Th., Concordia Theol. Sem., Springfield, Ill., 1955, M.Div., 1975; D.Min., Concordia Theol. Sem., Ft. Wayne, Ind., 1977; M.A., Eastern Ill. U., 1974; postgrad. U. Mich., 1977—. Ordained Luth. Ch.-Mo. Synod, 1955. Pastor St. Paul's Luth. Ch., Park City, Mont., 1955-60, St. John's Luth. Ch., Buhl, Idaho, 1960-64, Bethlehem Luth. Ch., Engadine, Mich., 1964-69, Immanuel Luth. Ch., Tuscola, Ill., 1969-77; prof. Concordia Coll., Ann Arbor, Mich., 1977—; holder various dist. offices. Recipient Servus Ecclesiae Christi, Concordia Theol. Sem., Ft. Wayne, 1980. Home: 2120 Garden Homes Ct Ann Arbor MI 48103 Office: Concordia Coll 4090 Geddes Rd Ann Arbor MI 48103

HILL, DAVID EARL, minister, Baptist Church; b. Dallas, Aug. 25, 1937; s. Robert Lee and Margurite Sally Hill; m. Jackie Lynn Durham, Mar. 20, 1964; children: Michael Lee, Jeffery David, Steven Todd. B.A., Dallas Baptist Coll., 1970; M., Jacksonville Sem., 1982. Ordained to ministry Baptist Ch., 1964. Minister various chs. in Tex. Pleasant Haven Baptist, Mesquite, 1967-72; First Bapt. Ch., Elkhart, 1972-75; West Athens Bapt., Athens, 1975-79; Park Heights Bapt. Ch., Tyler, 1979—; moderator Henderson Bapt. Assn., Athens, 1972; vice moderator Smith County Bapt. Assn., Tyler, 1981—; Bd. trustees Timberline Bapt. Camp, Lindale, Tex., 1981—, Pineywoods Bapt. Camp, Groveton, Tex., 1983-84. Composer religious song, Was It I?, 1978; contbr. articles to newspaper. Pres. Ministerial Alliance, Athens, 1976-79. Home: 3108 Shady Trail Tyler TX 75702

HILL, DOUGLAS WHITTIER, administrator, American Baptist Churches USA; b. Dayton, Ohio, Apr. 11, 1927; s. Eric Leslie and Helen Elizabeth (Metz) H.; m. Helen Kleinhenz, June 14, 1952; children: Linda E., David D., Peter D. B.S. in Edn., Miami U.-Ohio, 1949; M.Div., Colgate Rochester Sem., 1952; D.D. (hon.), Alderson Broaddus Coll., 1978. Ordained to ministry, 1952. Minister Christian edn. Delaware Ave. Bapt. Ch., Buffalo, 1952-57; organizing pastor S. Hills Bapt. Ch., Pitts., 1957-62; assoc. pastor Fifth Ave. Bapt. Ch., Huntington, W.Va., 1962-67; area minister/campus minister W.Va. Bapt. Conv., Charleston, 1967-77, exec. minister, 1978—; trustee Alderson Broaddus Coll., Philippi, W.Va., 1977—; mem. Regional Exec. Min. Council, Valley Forge, Pa., 1978—, mem. gen. staff council, 1978—; dir. W.Va. Council Chs., 1978—. Editor W.Va. Bapt. 1978—. Bd. dirs. Kootaga Area council Boy Scouts Am., Parkersburg, 1980—. Recipient Good Shepherd award, Bapt. Com. on Scouting, 1983. Home: Route 2 35 Bethel Pl Washington WV 26101 Office: W Va Bapt Conv 1019 Juliana St Parkersburg WA 26102

HILL, ELSIE MARGUERITE ISENSEE, minister, Assemblies of God; b. Tolleson, Ariz., Sept. 25, 1919; d. Ezra Ruben and Marguerite Elsie (Houghton) Beedle; student Tchrs. Coll., Lewiston, Idaho, 1940-41, Central Bible Inst., Springfield, Mo., 1944-45, Latin Am. Bible Inst., Tex., 1943-44; m. Frank E. Isensee, Jr., Sept. 16, 1945 (dec.); children: Kenneth Eugene, Marguerite Ethel; m. J.W. Hill, Feb. 14, 1981. Ordained to ministry, 1954; missionary Assemblies of God, Peru and Mex., 1946-59; dir. Bible Sch. Corr. for Latin Am., 1960-65; proofreader, translator Gospel Pub. House, Springfield, Mo., 1966—. Author: Abused But Chosen, 1983. Contbr. articles to various religious publs.; editor devotional book Springs of Refreshing, 1973. Tutor, Spanish-speaking inmates fed. prisons; pres. Springfield chpt. Ladies Aux. Evangel Coll., Springfield, Mo., 1968-72, nat. pres., 1974—. Recipient Golden Shield award Evangel Coll., 1971. Mem. Laubach Literacy Assn. (cert. tutor), Internat. Platform Assn. Home: 1408 N Summit St Springfield MO 65802 Office: 1445 Boonville Ave Springfield MO 65802

HILL, ERIC DALE, pastor, Southern Baptist Convention; b. Beaumont, Tex., Nov. 23, 1952; s. Elvin Levelle Hill and Velma Genevieve (Parfait) Hill Busby; m. Karen Denise McCollum, Aug. 17, 1974; children: Jeremy Dale, Christy Denise. B.A., Baylor U., 1978; M.Div., Southwestern Sem., 1980. Ordained to ministry Baptist Ch., 1973. Pastor Ephesus Bapt. Ch., Marquez, Tex., 1972-74, Cego Baptist Ch., Eddy, Tex., 1974-76, Honey Creek Bapt. Ch., Wolfe City, Tex., 1977-79, First Bapt. Ch., Celeste, Tex., 1979-81, First Bapt. Ch., Alief, Tex., 1981—; dir. Sunday sch. Leon Assn., Marquez, 1972-74; preacher Evangelism Conf., Greenville, Tex., 1980-81, Mission Eng., 1984; pres. Zone J Ministers Conf., Houston, 1984. Recipient Fastest Growing Sunday Sch. award Union Bapt. Assn., 1982, 84; Cert. of Appreciation, Soc. Disting. Am. High Sch. Students, 1983. Mem. Houston C. of C., Community of the Cross of Nails. Lodges: Lions, Kiwanis, Masons. Home: 7235 La Entrada Houston TX 77083 Office: First Baptist Ch PO Box 396 Alief TX 77411

HILL, JOHN HENRY, minister, United Methodist Church; b. N.Y.C., Jan. 4, 1945; s. John Henry and Geraldine Berdella (McGinty) H.; m. Emily Alberta Bohn, June 12, 1965; children: Paul Mark, Deborah Lynn. B.A., CCNY, 1966; M. Div., N.Y. Theol. Sem., 1971; postgrad., Drew Theol. Sem., 1984—. Ordained to ministry United Methodist Ch., 1970. Asst. pastor Farmingdale Meth. Ch., N.Y.C., 1966-68; pastor Kenoza Lake Cir., N.Y., 1968-70, Woodhaven United Meth. Ch., N.Y., 1970-73, Woodhaven and Ozone Park United Meth. Ch., N.Y., 1973-76, Clinton Ave United Meth. Ch., Kingston, N.Y., 1976—; dir. Woodhaven Interfaith Community Council, 1972-76; chmn. bd. dirs. Kingston Emergency Assistance Program, Kingston, 1977-85; conf. statistician N.Y. Ann. Conf., White Plains, N.Y., 1984—; chmn. funding sect. Parish Develop. Commn., N.Y. Ann. Conf., 1982—. Republican. Avocations: hunting; fishing; computers. Home: 1033 Pine Pl Kingston NY 12401 Office: CPO Box 1101 122 Clinton Ave Kingston NY 12401

HILL, JOSEPH ALLEN, minister, Reformed Presbyterian Church North America, theology educator; b. Beaver Falls, Pa., Jan. 29, 1924; s. George Dawson and May (Fullerton) H.; m. Barbara Adams, May 31, 1945; children: Robert A., Linda Hill Hughes, John Timothy. A.B., Geneva Coll., 1947; B.D., Reformed Presby. Theol. Sem., 1950; Th.M., Pitts. Theol. Sem., 1971. Ordained to ministry, 1950. Minister, Reformed Presbyn. Ch. Denver, 1950-52, Reformed Presbyn. Ch., Walton, N.Y., 1952-56; instr.

Unity Christian High Sch., Hudsonville, Mich., 1956-64; assoc. prof. Geneva Coll., Beaver Falls, 1964; interim minister North Br. Presbyn. Ch., Monaca, Pa., 1983-84. Author: A Theology of Praise, 1983; contrbng. author The Book of Books, 1978. Pres. Borough Council, Patterson Heights, 1979-80; mem. adv. bd. Vocat. Tech. Sch., Beaver County, Pa., 1983. Served with USN, 1943-45, PTO. Recipient Edwin F. Wendt award Geneva Coll., 1947. Mem. Evang. Theol. Soc. Republican. Home: 410 4th St Patterson Heights PA 15010 Office: Geneva Coll Beaver Falls PA 15010

HILL, LEON RICHARD, church official United Methodist Church; computer analyst; b. Williamsport, Pa., Apr. 1, 1930; s. Norman Franklin and Hazel Mae (Shafer) H.; B.S., Drexel U., 1953, M.B.A., 1967; M.S., Villanova U., 1981; m. Cheryl Lee Dawson, Mar. 2, 1985; 1 child, Joy (Mrs. Paul Yecker). Assoc. lay leader Eastern Pa. Conf. United Methodist Ch., 1972—, laity rep. council on ministries, 1974-83, assoc. lay leader West Chester (Pa.) Dist. Eastern Pa. Conf., 1971-72, exec. com. Council on Ministries, 1984—; cert. lay speaker, 1968—; pres. bd. trustees Atglen (Pa.) United Meth. Ch., 1973-80, chmn. adminstrv. bd., 1983—, supt. ch. sch., 1969-73, tchr. adult class, 1960—; treas. Atglen Community Vacation Bible Sch., 1960-72; pres. United Meth. Men, Eastern Pa. Conf., 1981—, mem. nat. exec. com., 1984—. Supr. computer applications Lukens Steel Co., Coatesville, Pa., 1975-80, sr. computer analyst, 1981—, dept. rep. to Common, IBM computer users group, 1971-75. Auditor Borough of Atglen, 1969-71, Republican com. rep., 1984—; area capt. United Fund, Atglen, 1964-65; mem. computer installation vol. task force Coatesville Hosp., 1972; chmn. data processing com. Central Chester County Vo-Tech, Coatesville, 1980—. Home: PO Box 273 Atglen PA 19310 Office: Lukens Steel Co ARC Bldg Coatesville PA 19320

HILL, MICHAEL JAMES, minister, Assemblies of God; b. Everett, Wash., Sept. 16, 1948; s. Alexander and Sue Juanita (Kime) H.; B.A., Northwest Coll., Kirkland, Wash., 1970; m. Margie Lee Conger, Sept. 5, 1969; children—Penelope Joy, Julie Anne. Ordained to ministry, 1973; intern pastor Bethel Assembly of God, Sedro-Wooley, Wash., 1969-70; asso. pastor Assembly of God, Jefferson, Oreg., 1970-71; pastor Nestucca Valley Assembly of God, Hebo, Oreg., 1971-73; asso. pastor, then pastor Tillamook (Oreg.) Christian Center, 1973-76; pastor Assembly of God, Sparta, Wis., 1976—. Pres. Tillamook Ministerial Assn., 1976. Named Youth Rep. of Yr., Oreg. Dist. Assemblies of God, 1973. Mem. Laotian Resettlement Com., Sparta. Mem. Sparta Ministerial Assn., Gen. Council Assemblies of God, Wis. and No. Mich. Dist. Assemblies of God. Home: 911 Williams St Sparta WI 54656 Office: 603 N Court St Sparta WI 54656

HILL, RAYMOND DELBERT, minister, Christian Church (Disciples of Christ); b. Detroit; s. Raymond Delbert and Martha Belle (Miracle) H.; m. Sandra Lee Stark, July 29, 1972; 1 son, Christopher Ray. B.A. in Philosophy, U. Cin., 1972; M.Div., No. Bapt. Sem., 1975; postgrad. Presbyn. Sch. Christian Edn., 1978, 85, Wesley Theol. Sem., 1984-85. Ordained to ministry Am. Bapt. Chs. of Mich., 1976, Christian Church (Disciples of Christ), 1977. Youth minister State St. Bapt. Ch., Rockford, Ill., 1974-75; assoc. minister First Bapt. Ch., Mt. Clemens, Mich., 1975-77, First Christian Ch., Falls Church, Va., 1977—; camp dir. Christian Ch.-Capital Area, Chevy Chase, Md., 1978-83, regional CYF advisor, 1979-85; chaplain No. Bapt. Sem., Oak Brook, Ill., 1974-75; editor, sec. Nat. Seminarians' Council, Valley Forge, Pa., 1974-75. Mem. steering com. Christian Emergency Temp. Shelter Bailey's Crossroads, Va., 1984—. No. Bapt. Sem. grantee, scholar, 1972-75. Mem. Falls Ch. Ministerial Assn. (youth softball coordinator 1977-84), Christian Ch.-Capital Area Ministers Assn. Clubs: Mustang of Am. (Lithonia, Ga.); Capital Area Mustang (Washington); Baraca Philathea Union (Mt. Vernon, Va.). Home: 7848 Snead Ln Falls Church VA 22043 Office: First Christian Ch 6165 Leesburg Pike Falls Church VA 22044

HILL, SALLY LOU, minister, Presbyterian Church U.S.A.; b. Mpls., Aug. 14, 1930; s. Harold W. and Ebba A. (Clausen) A.; m. Curtis Stanley Hill, Aug. 17, 1951; children: Steven Alan, Bonnie Kaye. B.A., Macalester Coll., 1951; M. Divinity, United Theol. Seminary, 1976. Ordained to ministry Presbyn. Ch., 1976. Assoc. minister St. Luke Presbyn. Ch., Wayzata, Minn., 1976-81; assoc. exec. dir. Twin Cities Met. Church Commn., Mpls., St. Paul, 1981—. Mem. bd. religious affairs Univ. Minn., 1981—, Clery/Laity Concerned, Minn., 1982, Interreligious Com. Central Am., 1983—; moderator Twin Cities Area Presbytery, Mpls.-St. Paul, 1984—. Mem. bd. Vols. of Am., 1984—; founder, chmn. Minn. Peace Child Project Minn., 1983—. Mem. Nat. Assn. Ecumenical Staff, Weaver's Guild Minn. Democrat. Home: 3719 Larchwood Dr Minnetonka MN 55345 Office: Twin Cities Met Ch Commn 122 Franklin Room 218 Minneapolis MN 55345

HILL, WILLIAM JOSEPH, theology educator, priest, Roman Catholic Church; b. N. Attleboro, Mass., Mar. 30, 1924; s. William Edward and Rita Eugenie (Lanteigne) H. A.B., Providence Coll., 1945; S.T.L., S.T.Lr., Dominical House of Studies, Washington, 1951; S.T.D., U. St. Thomas, Rome, Italy, 1952; D.Rel. Edn. (hon.), Providence Coll., 1976. Ordained priest, Roman Catholic Ch., 1950; prof. theology Dominican Ho. of Studies, Washington, 1953-71; prof. theology Cath. U. Am., Washington, 1971—; bilateral cons. Roman Cath.-Presbyn.-Reformed Chs., 1982—. Editor-in-chief The Thomist, 1975-82; mem. editorial bd. New Cath. Ency., 1972—; author: Knowing the Unknown God, 1971; The Three-Personed God, 1982; contbr. articles to theol. jours. Recipient John Courtney Murray award, Cath. Theol. Soc. Am., 1983. Mem. Cath. Theol. Soc. Am. (past pres.). Democrat. Office: Cath Univ Am Caldwell Hall Washington DC 20064

HILLIARD, DUANE ELWIN, lay worker, Seventh-day Adventist; music educator; b. Los Angeles, Nov. 30, 1948; s. Clarence D. and Ermel LaVonne (Cozad) H.; divorced; children: Tobin, Tanya, Amy. M.A. in Music, Pacific Union Coll., 1972. Cert. elem., secondary tchr., Calif., Colo. Music dir. grades 9-12 Oak Park Acad., Nevada, Iowa, 1972-74; band dir. grades 5-12 Highland View Acad., Hagerstown, Md., 1974-79; music tchr. Greater Balt. Jr. Acad., 1979-80; youth leader Pathfinders, Grand Junction, Colo., 1982—; choir dir. 1st Congl. Ch., Grand Junction, 1982-83, Seventh-day Adventist Ch., Grand Junction, 1984—. Homeroom tchr. grades 5-8, music tchr. Intermountain Jr. Acad., Grand Junction, 1980—. Trombonist, stage mgr. Grand Junction Symphony Orch., 1982-84. Republican. Home: 474 N Sherwood Dr Grand Junction CO 81501 Office: Intermountain Jr Acad 1704 N 8th St Grand Junction CO 81501

HILLMAN, SISTER GLORIA, minister of religious education, Roman Catholic Church; b. Bklyn., Dec. 23, 1934; d. Joseph Edmund and Anna Mae (Jones) H. B.S., Nazareth Coll., 1964; M.M., Catholic U., 1970; M.A., Fairfield U., 1983. Religion tchr. elem. schs., N.J., 1955-66, high sch., Raleigh, N.C., 1966-70; religion and music tchr. high sch., Danbury, Conn., 1970-75; dir. religious edn. total parish, Hawthorne, N.Y., 1975-80, Sarasota, Fla., 1980—; lectr. Black Awareness, Raleigh, 1968-69. Contbr. articles to religious jours.; lectr. in religious edn. Mem. Nat. Cath. Religious Edn. Assn. Republican. Office: Religious Edn Office 2605 Gulf Gate Dr Sarasota FL 33581

HILLMER, MELVYN R., college adminstrator. Prin. McMaster Div. Coll. (Baptist), Hamilton, Ont., Can. Office: McMaster Div Coll Hamilton ON L8S 4K1 Canada*

HILTSLEY, MILTON JAY, minister, Conservative Baptist Assn. Am.; b. Knox, N.Y., Mar. 20, 1911; s. Arthur B. and Edith L. (Dexter) H.; student Prairie Bible Inst., 1944-47; A.B.Th., Gordon Coll. Theology Missions, 1951; M.R.E., Fuller Sem., 1954; m. Ruth Sarah Davidson, Oct. 24, 1942. Ordained to ministry Conservative Baptist Assn. Am., 1947; pastor Calif. and Utah chs., 1954-66, 1st Bapt. Ch. of Holladay, Salt Lake City, 1966-77. Prin. Walnut Creek (Calif.) Christian Acad., 1962-63. Sec. bd. Conservative Bapt. Assn. No. Calif., 1960-63, mem. Christian edn. bd., 1960-63, mem. camping com., 1959-63; initiated Market-Place Ministry, 1966-69; radio minister KFMC-FM, Salt Lake City, 1967-69. Address: 2147 E 4800 S Salt Lake City UT 84117

HIMMELFARB, MILTON, editor, educator, Jewish; b. Bklyn., Oct. 21, 1918; s. Max and Bertha (Lerner) H.; m. Judith Siskind, Nov. 26, 1950; children: Martha, Edward, Miriam, Anne, Sarah, Naomi, Dan. B.A., City Coll. N.Y., 1938, M.S., 1939; B. Hebrew Lit., Jewish Theol. Sem. Coll., 1939; diplôme, U. Paris, 1939; postgrad., Columbia U., 1942-47. Dir. info. and research Am. Jewish Com., N.Y.C., 1955—; editor Am. Jewish Year Book, N.Y.C., 1959—; contbr. editor Commentary Mag., N.Y.C., 1960—; vis. prof. Jewish Theol. Sem., N.Y.C., 1967-68, 71-72, Yale U., 1971, Reconstructionist Rabbinical Coll., Phila., 1972-73. Author: The Jews of Modernity, 1973. Office: 165 E 56th St New York NY 10022

HINCKLEY, GORDON B., church official. Mem. 1st Presidency, The Church of Jesus Christ of Latter-day Saints. Office: The Church of Jesus Christ of Latter-Day Saints 50 E North Temple St Salt Lake City UT 84150*

HINDSON, EDWARD EARL, minister, religion educator, Independent Baptist; b. Detroit, Dec. 21, 1944; s. Edward J. and Helen L. (Snyder) H.; m. Donna Jean Currie, Aug. 6, 1966; children: Linda, Christy, Jonathan. B.A., William Tyndale Coll., Farmington Hills, Mich., 1966; M.A., Trinity Evangelical Div. Sch., Deerfield, Ill., 1967; Th.M., Grace Theol. Sem., Winona Lake, Ind., 1970; Th.D., Trinity Grad. Sch. Theology, Dunedin, Fla., 1971; D.Min., Westminster Theol. Sem., Phila., 1978; D.Litt., D.Phil., U. South Africa, Pretoria, 1984; D.Litt. (hon.), Calif. Grad. Sch. Theology, 1981. Ordained to ministry Bapt. Ch., 1966. Youth minister Youth for Christ, Detroit, 1964-66, Skokie Valley Bapt. Ch., Wilmette, Ill., 1966-67; pastor Fulton Bapt. Ch., Ind., 1967-70; assoc. dir. Life Action Ministries, St. Petersburg, Fla., 1970-74; assoc. pastor Thomas Road Bapt. Ch., Lynchburg, Va., 1974—; prof., assoc. dean Sch. Religion, Liberty Bapt. Coll. and Sem., Lynchburg, 1974—; vis. prof. Grace Theol. Sem., 1980-81; vis. lectr. Harvard Div. Sch., Mass., 1981. Author: Philistines and Old Testament, 1972, Glory in the Church, 1975, Introduction to Puritan Theology, 1976, Isaiah's Immanuel, 1978, The Total Family, 1980, The Fundamentalist Phenomenon, 1981. Editor: Liberty Bible Commentary, 1983. Sr. editor Fundamentalist Jour., 1982—. Mem. transl. com. New King James Version, 1982. Contbr. articles to religious and theol. publs. Va. state del. Republican Conv., Richmond, 1980. Recipient award for creative medium Evang. Press Assn., 1983. Home: 200 Chesterfield Rd Lynchburg VA 24502 Office: Liberty Bapt Coll Lynchburg VA 24506

HINES, LUCILLE BROWN, minister, Upper Kingdom Ch. of the Trinity; b. Grenada, Miss., July 19, 1924; d. Clarence Eugene and Rosa (Sykes) Brown; ed. pub. sch., Moody Bible Inst.; m. Howard Hines, Jan. 18, 1942; children—Ardelia (Mrs. Alfonza Lomax), Mitchell. Ordained to ministry Upper Kingdom Ch. of the Trinity, 1973; missionary, 1950-72; Sunday sch. jr. dept. Ch. God in Christ, 1960-62; dist. missionary, 1973—; founder, pastor Upper Kingdom Ch. of the Trinity, Cleve., 1973—; revivalist. Mem. Rosicrucian Order. Address: 12106 Emery Ave Cleveland OH 44135

HINES, SAMUEL G., chairperson Church of God, Anderson, Ind. Office: 9553 Fort Foote Rd Fort Washington MD 20744*

HINGSON, ROBERT ANDREW, religious organization executive, Baptist Church; b. Anniston, Ala., Apr. 13, 1913; s. Robert Andrew and Elloree Elizabeth (Haynes) H.; A.B., U. Ala., 1935, L.H.D., 1974; M.D., Emory U., 1938; LL.D., William Jewell U., 1963; postgrad. Eastern Bapt. U., 1963; L.H.D., Monrovia Coll., Liberia, West Africa, 1962, U. Ala., 1974; Litt.D., Hardin Simmons U., 1964; D.Sc., Thomas Jefferson U., 1974; m. Gussie Dickson Hingson, Mar. 2, 1940; children—Dickson James, Andrew, Ralph, Luke, Roberta (Mrs. Allan Gates). Pres., Ala. Bapt. Student Union, 1932-33; deacon, First Bapt. Ch., Cleve., 1964-67; dir. Bapt. World Alliance Med. Mission Global Survey, Cleve., 1958—; founder, dir. Bros. Bro. Found., Pitts., 1962—; dir. Bapt. World Alliance Internat. Yr. of the Child Expanded Program of Immunizations in Coop. with WHO. Physician; prof. pub. health U. Pitts., 1968—. Recipient numerous awards U.S., fgn. nations. Mayo Clinic fellow, 1940-41. Fellow Royal Coll. Surgeons (Eng.), Internat. Coll. Surgeons; mem. AMA, Internat. Anesthesiology Research Soc. (v.p. 1947), Am. Coll. Anesthesiology. Inventor midget anesthesiology machine, various types jet injectors for mass immunizations, instruments to control pain, continuous caudal and peridural anesthesia for childbirth. Author books, chpts. in books on anesthesia and pub. health. Home: 816 Grandview Ave Pittsburgh PA 15211 Office: 824 Grandview Ave Pittsburgh PA

HINKLE, CHRIS NELSON, minister, Lutheran Church-Missouri Synod; software editor; b. Ft. Leonard Wood, Mo., Aug. 29, 1954; s. Charles Nelson and Delores Jacquiline (Riemer) H.; m. Carol Ann Cherveny, June 6, 1981; 1 child, Jennifer Marie. B.S. in Indsl. Mgmt. with distinction, Purdue U., 1975; M.Div., Concordia Sem., 1981. Ordained to ministry Lutheran Ch., 1981. Pastor Luth. Ch. of Good Shepherd, Ft. Lauderdale, Fla., 1981-83; computer products mgr. Concordia Pub., St. Louis, 1983—; pub's. rep. Consultation on Congregational Use of Computers, 1983—. Editor, adminstr. (computer software) Lutheran Congregational Information System, 1983—. Counselor St. Louis Jr. Achievement, 1976. Mem. Luth. Ch. - Mo. Synod, Beta Gamma Sigma. Office: Concordia Pub House 3558 S Jefferson Ave St Louis MO 63118

HINOJOSA BERRONES, ALFONSO, bishop, Roman Catholic Church; b. Monterrey, Mex., Oct. 7, 1924; s. Emilio Hinojosa Cantu and Guadalupe Berrones de Hinojosa. Grad. Seminario de Monterrey, 1948, Th.M., 1950; Th.D., Gregorian U., Rome, 1951. Ordained priest Roman Cath. Ch., 1949, consecrated bishop, 1974. Bishop of Diocese of Ciudad Victoria, Tamaulipas, Mex., 1974—. Home: Carretera Naccional KMT.701 Ciudad Victoria Tamaulipas 87000 Mexico Office: 15 Hidalgo y Juarez Ciudad Victoria Tamaulipas 87000 Mexico

HINSON, ARLIS CLARENCE, JR., ch. adminstr., mgr., So. Baptist Conv.; b. Crystal Springs, Miss., May 20, 1931; s. Arlis Clarence and Susie Etta (Joyner) H.; B.A., Miss. Coll., 1955; M.R.E., So. Baptist Theol. Sem., 1963; fellow Ch. Bus. Adminstrn., Nat. Assn. Conservative Bapt. Assns.; m. Georgia Louise Herrin, May 24, 1959. Ordained to ministry So. Baptist Conv., 1955; mgr. Cedarmore Bapt. Assembly, Bagdad, Ky., 1971—; dir. Christian edn. First Bapt. Ch., Elizabethton, Tenn., 1958-59; dir. Rockridge Bapt. Assembly, Franklin, Ga., 1964-68; ch. adminstr. Calvary Bapt. Ch., Washington, 1968-71; mem. So. Bapt. Assembly and Camp Mgrs. Conf., 1966—, pres., 1967, sec.-treas., 1972-77. Mem. Nat. Assn. Ch. Bus. Adminstrs., Christian Camping Internat., Miss. Coll. Alumni Assn. Home: Route 1 Bagdad KY 40003 Mailing address: POB 37 Bagdad KY 40003

HINTON, HOMER EUGENE, lay preacher, Baptist Convention; educational administrator; b. Greenville, S.C., Dec. 17, 1939; s. Homer Woodrow and Clara Belle (DuBose) H.; A.A., N. Greenville Coll., 1965; B.A., Furman U., 1967; M.Ed., Clemson U., 1973; m. Charlotte Ann Ford, Apr. 14, 1968; 1 child, Charlyn Beth. Tchr. Sunday sch. Sans Souci Bapt. Ch., Greenville, S.C., 1961; mission preacher Berea Bapt. Ch., Oakmont, S.C., 1968; tchr. Cross Roads Bapt. Ch., Simpsonville, S.C., 1970; dir. music, assoc. pastor Rockvale Bapt. Ch., Piedmont, S.C., 1972-75; tchr., ch. clk. Five Forks Bapt. Ch., Simpsonville, 1976—; music dir. Rabon Creek Bapt. Ch., Gray Court, S.C., 1977-81, Grove Station Bapt. Ch., Piedmont, S.C., 1981-84. Asst. prin. Hillcrest Middle Sch., Simpsonville, S.C., 1976—; founder, pres. Candid Photo, 1980—. Mem. NEA, Nat. Assn. Elem. Sch. Prins., Greenville County (S.C.) Edn. Assn. Home: Route 1 Box 301 Simpsonville SC Office: Hillcrest Middle School Garrison Rd Simpsonville SC 29681

HIPPLE, ELWOOD BILLET, JR., minister, Lutheran Church in America; b. Lancaster, Pa., Dec. 2, 1941; s. Elwood Billet and Mary Elizabeth (Sourbeer) H.; m. Cheryl Kay Gillilan, Dec. 29, 1974. B.A., Susauehanna U., 1963; postgrad. U. Del., 1963-64; M.Div., Luth. Theol. Sem., Gettysburg, Pa., 1964-68; pastoral clin. tng. Immanuel Med. Ctr., Omaha, 1967. Ordained to ministry Lutheran Ch., 1968. Intern pastor Grace Evang. Luth. Ch., Ft. Dodge, Iowa, 1966-67; pastor Zion Evang. Luth. Ch., Sutton, Nebr., 1968-82, Saron Evang. Luth. Ch., Saronville, Nebr., 1968-82, Trinity Evang. Luth. Ch., Wolbach, Nebr., 1982—; central dist. rep., parish service com. Nebr. Synod, Luth. Ch. Am., Omaha, 1975-77, chmn. social ministry com., 1976-82. Synod rep. Inter-Ch. Ministries of Nebr., Lincoln, 1979-83, v.p. bd., 1981-82, sec. bd., 1983; central dist. corr. The Nebr. Luth., Nebr. Synod, Wahoo, 1982—. Chmn. Clay County Christian Rural Overseas Program Com., 1973-74, sec., 1978-79, vice chmn., 1980-82. Publicity chmn. Sutton Centennial Com., 1971; chmn. Sutton Community Improvement Program, 1972; mem. Sutton Bicentennial Com., 1975-76; mem. Greeley County Adv. Council, Central Nebr. Community Services, Inc., Loup City, 1984-85. Recipient Leadership award Nebr. Community Improvement Program, 1973; named one of Outstanding Young Men in Am., 1975. Mem. Howard County Ministerium (v.p. 1984). Lodge: Lions (sec. Sutton 1982). Republican. Home: Box 37 Wolbach NE 68882 Office: Trinity Evang Luth Ch Ctr at Kearney Sts Wolbach NE 68882

HIRSCH, RICHARD GEORGE See *Who's Who in America,* 43rd edition.

HIRTLE, DAVID CLYDE, minister, National Association of Congregational Christian Churches; b. Rochester, N.H., July 14, 1950; s. Ralph Lincoln and Janice (Bird) H.; m. Wanda Lewis, Jan. 8, 1976; children: Christopher Allen, David Andrew. B.A., U. Ill., 1971; M.A., Am. Bible Inst., 1973; M.A., Wesleyan U., 1974; Ph.D., Yale U., 1983. Ordained to ministry, Congl. Christian Ch., 1976. Sr. minister First Congl. Ch., Frankfort, Mich., 1975-78, Breckenridge, Mich., 1978, Millinocket, Maine, 1978-82, Middletown, Conn., 1982—; chaplain Middletown Police Dept., 1982—; chmn. spiritual resources commn. Nat. Assn. Congl. Christian Chs., 1981—; mem. exec. com. Conn. Fellowship congl. Christian Chs., 1982—. Exec. dir. Dunotas Techs. and Info., Norwich, Conn., 1983—. Commr. Transportation Commn., Millinocket, 1979-82; bd. dirs. Middletown YMCA, 1984—, Middlesex Assn. Retarded Citizens, Portland, Conn., 1982—. Editor Mayflower Devotionals for a Duet, 1982. Recipient FAA Pilot Proficiency award, 1984; named Outstanding Young Am. Men Jaycees, 1982. Mem. Mich. Sheriff's Assn. (chaplain 1976-82), Internat. Conf. Police Chaplains, Am. Legion. Lodges: Kiwanis, Masons. Home: 114 Miner St Middletown CT 06457 Office: Third Congl Ch 94 Miner St Middletown CT 06457

HITCHENS, LAWRENCE RUSSELL, minister, Presbyterian Church (U.S.A.); b. Phila., July 29, 1947; s. Russell Max and Elizabeth Ruth (Claghorn) H.; m. Janis Mary McLeish, Sept. 6, 1969; children: Christian, Cortney, Kathleen. B.S., Geneva Coll., 1969; M.Div., Princeton Theol. Sem., 1972. Ordained to ministry United Presbyn. Ch. in the U.S.A., 1972. Assoc. pastor First Presbyn. Ch., Albuquerque, 1972-74, El Paso, Tex., 1974-77; pastor Bethany Presbyn. Ch., Muskogee, Okla., 1977-82, First Presbyn. Ch., Lewisville, Tex., 1982—; chaplain Lewisville Police Dept., 1982—; pres. Muskogee Co-Op Ministry, 1979-81; del. United Presbyn. Ch. in U.S.A., Detroit, 1980; pres. Presbyn. Council of El Paso/Juarez, 1977. Democrat. Home: 2015 Aspen Lewisville TX 75067 Office: First Presbyn Ch 1002 Fox Ave Lewisville TX 75067

HITTINGER, RAYMOND CLAYTON, minister, Lutheran Church in America; b. White Haven, Pa., July 9, 1942; s. Henry Grant and Grace Catherine (Warg) H.; m. Joyce Alice Herbener, June 10, 1967; children: Tammy Jo, Jeffrey Alan, Matthew David, Jessica Ann. B.A., Gettysburg Coll., 1964; M.Div., Luth. Theol. Sem., Phila., 1968. Ordained to ministry Lutheran Ch., 1968. Pastor, Friedens Luth. Ch., Hegins, Pa., 1968-75, Rosemont Luth. Ch., Bethlehem, Pa., 1975—; mem. justice and social change com. Northeastern Pa. Synod; Luth. Ch. in Am., 1973-76, sec. Bethlehem-Easton dist., 1980—; chmn. migrant ministry com. Pa. Council of Chs., Harrisburg, 1974-78; chmn. com. on seasonal farm workers Pa. Conf. of Interchurch Cooperation, 1974-79; bd. dirs. Bethlehem Area Lutherans in Mission, 1978—; pres. Luth. Manor of Lehigh Valley, Inc., Bethlehem, Pa., 1979-82; pres. Rosemont Wholistic Health Ctr., Bethlehem, 1983—; mem. exec. bd. Northeastern Pa. Synod, 1982—; del. Luth. Ch. in Am. Biennial Conv., 1984. Bd. dirs. Tri-Valley Can Do., Hegins, 1970-75; pres. Hegins Area Ambulance Assn., 1973-75; mem. Schuylkill County Child Welfare Adv. Com., 1972-75; mem. com. on seasonal farm workers Pa. Dept. Environment Resources, 1978-79. Mem. Bethlehem Ministerial Assn., Bethlehem Luth. Pastors Assn. Office: Rosemont Luth Ch 1705 W Broad St Bethlehem PA 18018

HIVELY, NEAL OTTO, minister, Lutheran Church in America; b. Williamsport, Pa., Aug. 19, 1950; s. Otto Ezra and Mildred Ruth (Mizener) H.; m. Lee Codd, Aug. 23, 1975; children: Christopher Stephen, Beth Ellen. B.A. in Classical Greek, Thiel Coll., 1972; M.Div., Gettysburg Sem., 1976, S.T.M., 1984. Ordained to ministry Luth. Ch. in Am., Central Pa. Synod, 1976. Pastor Upper Bermudian Luth. Parish, Gardners, Pa., 1976-82, Bethlehem (Steltz) Coop. Parish, Glen Rock, Pa., 1982—; dir. Luth. Social Services-South Region, Pa., v.p., 1985; chmn. Evangelism to Inactives, Central Pa. Synod, 1977—, Evangelism to Unchurched, 1977-82; Author: History of Upper Bermudian Lutheran Church, 1984. Area chmn. United Way, Upper Adams County, 1978-79. Mem. Upper Adams Ministerium (pres. 1978-80). Home and Office: Rural Route 3 Box 219 Glen Rock PA 17327

HLOND, WACLAW ANDREW, priest, Roman Catholic Church; b. Blachownia, Czestochowa, Poland, July 12, 1929; came to U.S., 1958, naturalized, 1967; s. Stanislaw and Genowefa (Matuszewski) H. Student Jagiellonian U., Cracow, Poland, 1950-51; B.Theology, Vincentian Inst., Cracow, 1951-55. Ordained priest, Roman Catholic Church, 1955. Tchr. Cath. high sch., Pabianice, Poland, 1955-58; asst. pastor St. Joseph Parish, Ansonia, Conn., 1961-64; superior Mission House, Utica, N.Y., 1967-74; pastor St. Stanislaus Parish, New Haven, 1974-81; superior provincial Vincentian Fathers, West Hartford, Conn., 1981—. Co-editor: St. Stanislaus Church, 1976. Chaplain Polish Army Vets. Assn., Dist. IV, Hartford, Conn., 1975. Office: Vincentian Provincial Residence 1109 Prospect Ave West Hartford CT 06105

HOADLEY, WALTER EVANS, lay church worker, United Methodist Church; b. San Francisco, Aug. 16, 1916; s. Walter Evans and Marie Howland (Preece) H.; B.A., U. Cal. at Berkeley, 1938, M.A., 1940, Ph.D., 1946; D.Comml. Sci. (hon.), Franklin and Marshall Coll., Lancaster, Pa., 1963; LL.D., Golden Gate U., San Francisco, 1968; hon. diploma El Instituto Tecnologico Autonomo de Mexico, 1974; m. Virginia Alm, May 20, 1939; children—Richard Alm, Jean (Mrs. Donald A. Peterson). Tchr., Epworth United Meth. Ch., San Francisco, 1934-38; mem. ofcl. bd. 1st Meth. Ch., Evanston, Ill., 1942-46; chmn. finance com., mem. ofcl. and adminstrv. bds., trustee 1st United Meth. Ch., Lancaster, Pa., 1950-66; chmn. investment com., commn. world service and finance Phila. conf. United Meth. Ch., 1958-66, vice chmn. Bishop's Crusade, 1960; chmn. adminstrv. mem. council ministers, mem. com. planning and evaluation Trinity United Meth. Ch., Berkeley, Calif., 1966-84; mem. Lafayette (Calif.) United Meth. Ch., 1984—; mem. investment com., bd. trustees Cal.-Nev. United Meth. Found., 1970—; sr. research Fellow Hoover Instn., 1981—. Evec. v.p., chief economist Bank of Am. NT /& SA, San Francisco, 1966-81. Bd. dirs. U.S. Council Internat. Bus., Internat. Mgmt. and Devel. Inst., U.S. Com. for Pacific Econ. Coop. Trustee Wesley Theol. Sem., Washington, 1963-66, Duke, 1968-73, Grad. Theol. Union, Berkeley, 1968-70, Golden Gate U., 1974—, Conservation Found., 1974—; trustee, mem. finance com. Pacific Sch. Religion, Berkeley, 1971—; corp. dir., sr. econ. specialist Sta. KRON-TV, San Francisco. Fellow Nat. Assn. Bus. Economists, Am. Statis. Assn. (pres. 1958); mem. Am. Finance Assn. (pres. 1969), Conf. Bus. Economists (chmn. 1962-63). Office: PO Box 37000 Bank of Am Center San Francisco CA 94137

HOAGLAND, ALBERT JOSEPH, JR., pastor, Disciples of Christ Church, educator, psychotherapist; b. Clayton, N.J., July 2, 1939; s. Albert Joseph and Elnora Mary (Duncan) H.; m. Tanna Lynn Flaherty, Feb. 14, 1975; children: Jeffrey, Amy Nichole, Joshua. Student Monmouth Med. Ctr. Sch. Nursing, 1959-61; B.S., Monmouth Coll., 1964; M.S.W., Rutgers U., 1966; postgrad. Calif. Grad. Inst., 1973, U. So. Calif., 1975; Ph.D., Pacific Coll., 1976; M.Div., Fuller Theol. Sem., 1978; D.Min., Boston U., 1981; postdoctoral Sch. Law, U. West Los Angeles, 1982, Pacific Sch. Religion, 1983—. Ordained to ministry Disciples of Christ Ch., 1978; lic. clin. social worker, Calif.; lic. marriage, family, child counselor, Calif.; R.N., Calif., N.J.; cert. tchr., Calif., Ariz. Assoc. pastor 1st Christian Ch., San Pedro, Calif., 1978-79; pastor 1st Christian Ch., Lynn, Mass., 1979-81; assoc. pastor 1st Christian Ch., Torrance, Calif., 1981-84; pastor Marana Community Christian Ch., Ariz., 1984—; v.p. Greater Lynn Council Chs., 1979-81; dir. Greater Lynn Council Chs. Counseling Service, 1979-81; v.p. New England Dist. Christian Ch., 1979-81; active Disciples Outreach Program, Disciple Ministers Cluster Group, South Bay Interfaith Fellowship, Torrance Ministerial Group, 1981-84; dir., counselor, lifeguard, nurse various summer ch. camps; bd. dirs. Long Beach State Campus Ministry, 1981-84; mem. social concerns com. Pacific Southwest Region Christian Ch., 1981-84, mem. adult nurture com., 1981-84. Clin. social worker, dist. supr. Jewish Family Service, Boston, 1968; dir. casework Family AID and Counseling Ctr., Palm Springs, Calif., 1969-70; dist. dir. Los Angeles Family Service, 1970-71; exec. dir. Pacific Coast Counseling Ctr., Redondo Beach, 1971-79; instr. Torrance Adult Sch., 1977-79, 81-85, Beverly Hills Adult Sch., 1984-85; cons. Los Angeles County Probation, guest instr., 1972-75; instr. Calif. State U., Dominguez Hills, 1974, Chapman Coll., 1972-74, Calif. Grad. Inst., 1973; exec. dir. Alcoholic Rapp Ctr., Redondo Beach, 1979. Editor: (collection) Professional Papers from the Desert, 1970; Jonestown Collective, 1978. Actor, Fisherman's Players West, 1983-84. Active Regional Mental Health Coordinating Com., 1971-78, Madrona Sch. Site Com., chmn. 1981-83. Recipient Good Citizen award Los Angeles County, 1978. Mem. Nat. Assn. Social Workers, Am. Assn. Marriage and Family Therapists, Am. Orthopsychiat. Assn., Los Angeles Group Psychotherapy Soc., Nat. Assn. Christians in Social Work, Am. Guild Hypnotherapists, Congress of Disciples Clergy, Disciples Peace Fellowship, Disciples of Christ Hist. Soc., Clowns of Am., Calif. Tchrs. Assn., Aircraft Owners and Pilots Assn., Rancho Mirage C. of C. (v.p. 1969), Torrance C. of C. Democrat. Home: 11734 W Grier Rd Marana AZ 85238 Office: Marana Community Christian Ch Corner Grier and Sandario Rds Marana AZ 85238

HOAGLAND, DAVID ADAIR, minister, Southern Baptist Convention; b. Rahway, N.J., Aug. 5, 1946; s. Lester A. and Audrey F. (Williams) H.; m. Mildred Thompson, July 29, 1972; children: D. Wesley (dec.), Scott Lamar, Jessica Ruth. B.A., Davis and Elkins Coll., 1968; M.S.T., Gordon Conwell Theol. Sem., 1971; M.Ed., Kean State U., 1969; Th.D., Covington Theol. Sem., 1981. Ordained to ministry Bapt. Ch., 1976. Assoc. pastor Meml. Bapt. Ch., Arlington, Va., 1972-73, Calvary Rd. Bapt. Ch., Alexandria, Va., 1972-74; prof. Luther Rice Coll., Alexandria, 1974-77; pastor Vansant Bapt. Ch., Va., 1977—; mem. Va. Bapt. Gen. Bd., Richmond, Va., 1983—. Bd. dirs. Buchanan YMCA, Grundy, Va., 1982—. Mem. New Lebanon Bapt. Assn. (moderator). Lodge: Lions. Home and Office: PO Box 649 Vansant VA 24656

HOAR, LEO JAMES, priest, educator, Roman Cath. Ch.; b. Holyoke, Mass., June 22, 1940; s. Thomas Francis and Helen J. (O'Sullivan) H.; A.B. in Philosophy and Sociology, St. Anselm's Coll., 1962; S.T.B., Cath. U. Am., 1966, postgrad. in adminstrn., 1962-66; M.Ed. in Psychology, Springfield Coll., 1970, certificate of advanced studies in rehab. psychology, 1972; Ed.D., U. Mass., 1977. Ordained priest, 1966; chaplain Holy Family Ch., Holyoke, Mass., 1966-68; dir. Confrat. of Christian Doctrine, Cath. Charities, St. Matthew's Ch., Indian Orchard, Mass. and St. Patrick's Ch., Chicopee, Mass., 1970-72; dir. Notre Dame High Sch. and Sacred Heart Elementary Sch., Springfield, Mass., 1972—; lectr. Am. Internat. Coll., summers 1973-76, Springfield Tech. Community Coll., 1974-76, U. Mass., 1975. Chaplain Providence (Mass.) Hosp., 1966-68; aux. mil. chaplain Westover (Mass.) AFB, 1966-68; bd. dirs. Urban Ministry Inc. of Holyoke, Springfield Clergy Assn. Bd. dirs. Chicopee Downeyside Homes, Chicopee Community Center, Recycle for Children, Holyoke Pre-Release Center, Hope Home of Holyoke, Hill Inc. of Chicopee. Mem. Chicopee Clergy Assn. Home: 319 Broadway Chicopee MA 10120 Office: 370 Stafford St Springfield MA 01104

HOARD, STEVEN ED, minister, So. Bapt. Conv.; b. Griffin, Ga., Oct. 11, 1951; s. Dan Bishop and Clyde (Mullis) H.; diploma in electronics engring., Elkins Inst. Radio, 1969; student Middle Ga. Coll., 1969-70; A.S. in E.E., So. Tech. Inst., 1971; M.B.D., Fla. Bible Coll., 1973; postgrad. Luther Rice Sem., 1974—; m. Brenda Evelyn Johnson, Dec. 23, 1972. Ordained to ministry So. Bapt. Conv., 1973; mem. Brotherhood Evangelistic Team, 1973-74; pastor Olivet Bapt. Ch., Dublin, Ga., 1974-75, Sandtown Bapt. Ch., Atlanta, 1975—. Pres. Atlanta Bible Inst., 1976—, also prof.; chaplain Dublin Civitan Club, 1974-75, Sandtown Civitan Club, Atlanta, 1975—; v.p. Pastors Orgn. of Dublin, 1974-75. Dir. Bd. Reference of Laurens County Mental Health Assn., 1974-75. Mem. Atlanta, Dublin, Laurens County Bapt. assns. Home: 608 Upper Riverdale Rd Riverdale GA 30274 Office: 5450 Campbellton Rd SW Atlanta GA 30331

HOBBS, DAVID LIVINGSTON, lay ch. worker, Episcopal Ch.; b. St. Augustine, Fla., Nov. 9, 1938; s. William Henry and Martha Charlotte (Rabb) H.; A.A. in Christian Edn., B.A. in Bibl. Studies, Okla. City Southwestern Coll., 1976; m. Alice Louise Robinson,

Jan. 8, 1966; children—Martha Louise, William David, Thomas Rabb. Sunday Sch. tchr. All Saints Episcopal Ch., Austin, Tex., 1961-67, Ch. of the Resurrection, Austin, 1967-72, lay reader, 1969-72, dir. Brotherhood of St. Andrew, 1970-72, active Episcopal Young Churchman, 1971-72, Austin Convocational coordinator, 1972; lay reader St. Mark's Episcopal Ch., Austin, 1973—; asst. field sec. Brotherhood of St. Andrew, 1971—, bd. dir., 1973—; mem. Dept. of Evangelism Diocese of Tex., 1972. Asso., Data Systems Bur. Tex. Dept. Pub. Welfare. Active, Boy Scouts Am., 1957-67. Home: 7908 Creekmere Ln Austin TX 78745

HOBSON, GEORGE ERNEST, church administrator, Anglican Church of Canada; b. Regina, Sask., Can., Oct. 23, 1920; s. George and Lily (Beddall) H.; m. Edna Hobson, Jan. 27, 1945; children: Daphne Joy, Stuart Kirk. Ordained to ministry, 1962. Curate of Parish of Transfiguration, Toronto, Ont., 1962-64; rector Parish of Uxbridge, Ont., 1964-66; exec. sec. Diocese of Qu'Apple, Regina, Sask., 1966-71; dir. pensions Anglican Ch. of Can., Toronto, 1971—. Served with Canadian Army, 1941-45. Mem. Assn. Canadian Pension Mgmt. (pres. 1978-80), Ch. Pension Conf. (pres. 1981). Home: 5 Dufresne CRT PH8 Don Mills ON M3C 1B7 Canada Office: Anglican Church 600 Jarvis St Toronto ON M4Y 2J6 Canada

HOBUS, ROBERT ALLEN, minister, Lutheran Church-Missouri Synod. B. Milw., Apr. 11, 1924; s. Herbert W. and Clara M. (Haas) H.; m. Alica Olinda Jacobsmeyer, July 10, 1949; children: Paul Alan, David Andrew, Steven Robert, Michael Jon. M. Sacred Theology, Perkins Sch. Theology, So. Meth. U., 1970; M.Div., Concordia Sem., St. Louis, 1971. Ordained to ministry Luth. Ch., 1949. Pastor, Redeemer Luth. Ch., Wichita, Kans., 1973-78, Redeemer Luth. Ch., Arkansas City, Kans., 1980—; exec. dir. Inter-Faith Ministries, Wichita, 1978-79; chaplain Wichita Police Dept., 1974-79. Contbr. articles sermons to religious publs. Home: 312 W Central St Arkansas City KS 67005 Office: Redeemer Luth Ch 318 W Central St Arkansas City KS 67005

HODAPP, LEROY C. Bishop, The United Methodist Church North Ind. Conf. and South Ind. Conf., Bloomington. Office: The United Meth Ch 2427 E 2d St Bloomington IN 47401*

HODGE, ARTHUR WILEY, lay ch. worker, Ch. of God (Cleveland, Tenn.); b. Morgan County, Ala., Sept. 6, 1931; s. Leonard Wiley and Roberta (King) H.; B.S. in Bus. Adminstrn., Miss. Coll., Clinton, 1958; m. Betty Joyce Statum, Nov. 25, 1954; children—Arthur Gregory, Lisa Wilette. Mem. lay study com. Ch. of God, Cleveland, 1964-66, mem. nat. laymens bd., 1966-68, mem. nat. radio and TV bd., 1968-76, chmn. Miss. laymen's bd., 1968-76, chmn. nat. laymen's bd., 1976—. Chmn. bd. Bank of Simpson County, Magee, Miss., 1974-77; pres., owner McAlpin's Dept. Store, Inc., 1970-75. Vice chmn. Strong River dist. Boy Scouts Am., 1970—, mem. exec. bd. Andrew Jackson council, Jackson, Miss., 1974—; bd. dirs. Miss. Coll. Alumni; mem. pres.'s council Lee Coll. Mem. Menswear Retailers Am., Miss. Retail Mchts. Assn. (dir.). Home: 802 S Main Ave Magee MS 39111 Office: 102 S Main Ave Magee MS 39111

HODGE, JOSEPH LONNIE, missionary, Methodist Church; b. Pueblo, Colo., Oct. 12, 1953; s. Joseph and Irene (Curry) H.; m. Peggy Arnold, June 23, 1984. A.A. in Behavioral Sci., U.S. Army, West Wash. State Coll., 1974. Ordained to ministry Meth. Ch., 1985. Co-founder Search, Pueblo, Colo., 1971-74; missionary, actor, various locations, 1974-85; pres. Crossroads, La Veta, Colo., 1983—; pres. Christian Artists League, La Veta, 1984—; owner, operator Your Nickel, La Veta, 1984—. Author: In the Shadow of the Peaks, 1984; Wild Game Handbook, 1983, others. Playwright: Luther, 1984; William Butler Yeats, 1976. Pres. Mesa Merchants Assn., 1978, Miss. Bow and Arrow Assn., 1979, Pueblo Writers Co-op, 1977-78; pres., v.p. Picayune on Stage, Miss., 1978-80. Served to 2d lt. U.S. Army, 1973-81. Tex. Comm. on Arts and Humanities scholar, 1976; So. Colo. U. presdl. scholar, 1973-83. Fellow Am. Fish and Game Assn.; mem. Tex. Child Care Assn. Club: Full Gospel. Avocations: running; poetry. Home: PO Box 609 LaVeta CO 81055 Office: Your Nickel PO Box 252 La Veta CO 81055

HODGE, LARRY DUANE, minister, Assemblies of God; b. Norfolk, Va., Dec. 22, 1943; s. Durward Duane and Martha Ellen (Harris) H.; student Central Bible Coll., Springfield, Mo., 1962; B.A., So. Ill. U., Edwardsville, 1969; m. E. Loudene Mayberry, Dec. 18, 1965; children—Kellie Loudene, Scott Duane. Ordained to ministry, 1967; pastor chs. in Ill., 1966-73; dist. officer, dir. youth and edn. dept. Ill. Assemblies of God, Carlinville, 1973—. Mem. nat. youth com. Assemblies of God, 1977—. Bd. dirs. Boys' Club, Du Quoin, Ill., 1969-70. Home: Rural Route 3 Box 82 Carlinville IL 62626 Office: PO Box 225 Carlinville IL 62626

HODGE, RAYMOND DOUGLAS, minister, Ch. of God; b. Charlotte, N.C., Dec. 5, 1951; s. Billy Nole and Mary Estelene (Allen) Maloy; student Carson-Newman Coll., 1968, Lee Coll., 1970-71, Ch. of God Grad. Sch. Christian Ministries, 1977; m. Gale Lynn Baldwin, Aug. 11, 1972; 1 son, Raymond Douglas. Ordained to ministry; state evangelist Chs. of God, S.C., 1972-73; asst. pastor chs., Laurel Hill, N.C., 1973-74; pastor chs., Statesville, N.C., 1974, Maryville, Tenn., 1974—. Youth and Christian edn. dir. Jonesville, N.C. Dist., 1974. Mem. Greater Knoxville Pentecostal Ministerial Assn., Pentecostal Fellowship N.Am. Home: Route 7 Blockhouse Rd Maryville TN 37801

HODGES, JAMES HAROLD, minister, Baptist Missionary Association of America; b. Wewoka, Okla., May 9, 1932; s. Ivy William and Lillian Francis (White) H.; m. Louise Willie Cornish, June 7, 1953; children: Winona Faye Hodges White, Wendell Lee. B.S., Okla. State U., 1955; M.S., Okla. U., 1962. Ordained to Baptist Ch. as minister, 1962. Pastor, Southgate Bapt. Ch., Moore, Okla., 1962—; v.p. Bapt. Missionary Assn. Am., Little Rock, 1970, 71, 76, 77; sec.-treas. missions Bapt. Missionary Assn. Okla., Moore, 1967-72, 77—, personal com., Little Rock, 1978-82. Served to capt. U.S. Army Signal Corps, 1955-57. Democrat. Home: 717 Eagle Dr Moore OK 73160 Office: Southgate Bapt Ch 809 SW 4th St Moore OK 73160

HODGSON, ROBERT, theology educator, Roman Catholic Church; b. Seattle, July 13, 1943; s. Robert and Eileen (Campbell) H.; m. Mary Timothy Downs, June 26, 1965; children: Robert, Mary, Jennifer. BA., Gonzaga U., 1965; M.A., Marquette U., 1967; Th.D., Heidelberg, 1976. Prof. Bible, St. Andrews Theol. Sem., Manila, 1977-80; assoc. prof. religious studies S.W. Mo. State U., Springfield, 1980—. Editor: Gnosticism and Early Christianity, 1985. Contbr. articles to profl. jours. Mem. Soc. Bibl. Lit., Cath. Bibl. Assn. Home: 1943 E Swallow Springfield MO 65804 Office: SW Mo State U Springfield MO 65802

HOEPFL, MARGARET RINARD, ecumenical commission executive, Roman Catholic Church; b. North Vernon, Ind., Aug. 13, 1928; d. Jasper Newton and Julia Margaret (Horan) Rinard; m. Kenneth J. Hoepfl (div.); children: Michele Thompson, Jon Rinard (dec.), Marie Cecile, Therese Schwind, Mark Joseph. Exec. dir. Ecumenical Communications Commn. of Northwestern Ohio, Inc., Perrysburg, Ohio, 1973—; mem. gen. bd. Ohio Council Chs., Columbus, 1972—, mem. communication commn., 1974—. Mem. Peace Media Task Force. Mem. Assn. Regional Religious Communicators (pres. 1979-80). Club: Press (Toledo). Office: Ecumenical Communications Commn 1011 Sandusky Suite M Perrysburg OH 43551

HOFF, MARVIN DEAN, theology educator; Reformed Church in America; b. Sioux Center, Iowa, Oct. 3, 1936; s. Arend and Nellie Mildred (Dykstra) H.; m. Joanne Beth Rozendaal, June 4, 1958; children: Jean Marie, David John, Mary Elizabeth. B.A., Central Coll., 1958; B.D., Western Sem., 1961; M.Th., Princeton Sem., 1965; Doctorandes, Kampen Sem., 1977. Ordained to ministry Reformed Ch. in Am., 1961. Minister, Rea Ave. Reformed Ch., Hawthorne, N.J., 1961-66; minister Reformed Ch. in Am., Palos Heights, Ill., 1966-69, 81-85, sec. for Asia, N.Y.C., 1969-72, sec. for ops., 1972-77, sec. for fin., 1977-81; pres. Western Sem., Holland, Mich., 1985—; dir. Interch. Ctr., N.Y.C., 1977-81, Found. for Theol. Edn., N.Y.C., 1970—. Author: Structures for Mission, 1985. Contbr. articles to religious publs. Mem. Am. Soc. Missiology, Internat. Assn. Mission Studies, Soc. Bibl. Lit. Home: 2390 Orchard Idlewood Beach Holland MI 49423 Office: Western Sem 86 E 12th St Holland MI 49423

HOFFMAN, DAN CLAYTON, mission executive, Christian Church (Disciples Christ); b. Denver, June 19, 1943; s. Clayton Pershing and Doris Bernice (Adle) H.; B.A., Phillips U., 1966; M.A.R. cum laude, Christian Theol. Sem., 1970, D.Min., 1982; M.Div., Iliff Sch. Theology, 1975; S.T.M., Union Theol. Sem., N.Y., 1976; m. Josenilda Correia de Araujo, July 8, 1971; children: Marcelo Iraja Araujo, Nelia Berenice. Ordained to ministry, 1974; vol. Peace Corps., Timbauba, Pernambuco, Brazil, 1966-68; minister edn. Meadlawn Christian Ch., Indpls., 1968-69; missionary to Evang. Congl. Ch. Brazil, Rio Grande do Sul, 1970-74; missionary to Ref. Ch. France, 1976-81; exec. sec. Dept. Africa, Christian Ch. (Disciples of Christ), 1982—; missionary to Mindolo Ecumenical Found., Kitwe, Zambia, 1981; bd. dirs. Washington Office on Africa; chairperson Africa com. Nat. Council Chs., mem. exec., unit and fin. coms. div. overseas ministries. Contbr. articles to religious jours. Home: 2712 Constellation Dr Indianapolis IN 46229 Office: PO Box 1986 Indianapolis IN 46206

HOFFMAN, DAVID MARK, minister, Lutheran Church America; b. Storm Lake, Iowa, Mar. 2, 1946; s. Harold Alvin and Evelyn Louise (Johnson) H.; B.A., U. Iowa, 1967; M.Div., Luth. Sch. Theology, Chgo., 1971; D.Min., Andover-Newton Theol. Sch., 1974; m. Linda Louise Larsen, Sept. 17, 1966; children: Megan, Jennifer. Ordained to ministry, 1973; pastor Bethany-Bethel Luth. Parish, Olean, N.Y., 1973-76; sr. pastor Luth. Ch. of Incarnate Word, Rochester, N.Y., 1976—. Mem. exec. bd. Upper N.Y. Synod, Luth. Ch. Am., 1974—, mem. town and country task force, 1973, resources mobilization team, 1975—; bd. dirs. Luth. Social Services, 1973-76. Contbr. articles to jours. Chmn. bd. dirs. Cattaraugus County Drug Abuse Council, 1973-75; bd. dirs. Cattaraugus County Mental Health Soc., 1973-76; mem. Pam. Luth. Reformation Com., 1981-84; mem. Monroe County Interfaith Jail Ministry Com., 1980-83; marriage counselor Wormer Med. Center, Portville, N.Y., 1973-76. Mem. Am. Assn. Clin. Pastoral Edn. Office: 597 East Ave Rochester NY 14607

HOFFMAN, JAMES R. See *Who's Who in America*, 43rd edition.

HOFFMAN, JOSIAH OGDEN, JR., priest, Episcopal Ch.; b. Providence, July 2, 1920; s. Josiah Ogden and Anna Hampton (Carson) H.; B.A., U. Calif. at Los Angeles, 1943; M.Div., Episcopal Theol. Sch., 1945; Ph.D., U. So. Calif., 1964; m. Eleanor Jane Cary, Aug. 10, 1945; children—Margaret Cary, Richard Luke, Nancy Carson, Josiah Ogden, Geoffrey Michael. Ordained priest, 1945; vicar, St. Timothy's Ch., Compton, Calif., 1945-47; rector St. Luke's Ch., Monrovia, Calif., 1947-50; vicar St. Dunstan's Chapel and Episcopal chaplain San Diego State Coll., 1950-55; Episcopal chaplain U. So. Calif., 1955-61; exec dir. dept. Christian edn. Episcopal Diocese Los Angeles, 1961-65; dean Trinity Cathedral Ch., Sacramento, 1966-74; instr. philosophy, humanities and world religions Los Rios Community Colls., Sacramento, 1974-81. Dep., Gen. Conv., 1967, 69, 70, 73, mem. Joint Commn. on Ecumenical Relations, 1970-76; mem. Bd. for Clergy Deployment, 1973-76; chaplain Calif. State Senate, 1966. Mem. Alpha Mu Gamma, Blue Key, Phi Mu Alpha. Home and Office: 4072 Cresta Way Sacramento CA 95864

HOFFMAN, MARCIA A., lay minister, Roman Catholic Church; b. Coudersport, Pa., Dec. 4, 1943; d. Veryl Fisher and Marjorie (Falk) Scheibner; m. Donald Joseph Hoffman, Aug. 28, 1965; children: Yetta Marie, Lori Lynn. Student pub. schs. Port Allegany, Pa. Tchr. Ch. Sch. Meth. Ch., Roulette, Pa., 1958-64; chairwoman Commn. of Edn., 1959-60; eucharistic minister St. Casimir Roman Catholic Ch., Endicott, N.Y., 1980—, lector, commentator, 1980—, lay minister, 1985—. Religious edn. tchr. St. Casimir Roman Catholic Ch., 1979—. Address: 703 Univ Ave Endwell NY 13760

HOFFMAN, SISTER MARY LOUISE ANN, nun, Roman Catholic Church; b. Toledo, June 1, 1929; d. George C. and Louise (Comes) H. B.A., Mary Manse Coll., Toledo, 1959; M.A., St. Mary's Coll., Notre Dame, Ind., 1963; Dipl. Magisterii in Scientiis Sacris, Inst. Regina Mundi, Rome, Italy, 1963. Joined Order Sisters of Notre Dame. Dir. Diocesan Religious Edn. Ctr., Fremont, Ohio, 1969-76; provincial superior Sisters of Notre Dame, Toledo, 1976—, del. gen. chpt., Rome, Italy, 1974, 75, ex-officio mem., 1980, pres. Corp. of Sisters of Notre Dame, 1976—. Democrat.

HOFFMAN, ROSE MAE, minister, Church of the Nazarene; b. Gordon, Pa., Mar. 21, 1928; d. Earl G. and Mildred G. (Cresswell) H 1 adopted child, Evangeline Rose. Student Eastern Pilgrim Coll., 1948, Eastern Nazarene Coll., 1950, Th.B., Am. Div. Sch., 1961; postgrad. Pa. State U.-Schuylkill, 1962-67. Ordained to ministry Ch. of the Nazarene, 1953. Youth evangelist various chs. in U.S., 1946-48; assoc. pastor Ch. of the Nazarene, Schuylkill Haven, Pa., 1953-73, pastor, 1974—; chmn. mission reading zone Ch. of the Nazarene, 1971-83; pres. Council of Chs. Schuylkill Haven and vicinity, 1974-76. Trustee-at-large Pa. Council on Alcoholic Problems, Harrisburg, 1976-78. Home: 220 W Main St Schuylkill Haven PA 17972

HOFFMANN, OSWALD CARL JULIUS, association executive, radio speaker, Lutheran Church-Missouri Synod; b. Snyder, Nebr., Dec. 6, 1913; s. Carl John and Bertha (Seidel) H.; m. Marcia Rosalind Linnell, June 23, 1940; children: Peter Carl, Paul George, John Linnell, Katharine Ann. Grad. Concordia Coll., St. Paul, 1932; M.A., U. Minn., 1935; B.D., Concordia Sem., St. Louis, 1936, D.D. (hon.), 1952; LL.D. (hon.), Valparaiso U., 1952; L.H.D. (hon.), Philippine Christian H., 1982. Ordained to ministry Luth. Ch.-Mo. Synod, 1939. Instr. dean of men Bethany Coll., Mankato, Minn., 1936-40; pastor English Luth. Ch., Cottonwood, Minn., 1939; instr. linguistics and classical langs., founder Luth. campus services, U. Minn., 1940-41; prof. Greek and Latin, Concordia Collegiate Inst. (now Concordia Coll.), Bronxville, N.Y., 1941-48, also dir. publicity and promotion; dir. dept. pub. relations Luth. Ch.-Mo. Synod, 1948-63, founder offices, N.Y.C., Washington, St. Louis; apptd. Luth. Hour Speaker, Internat. Luth. Laymen's League, St. Louis, 1955—; asst. pastor St. Matthew Ch., N.Y.C., 1948-63; pres. United Bible Socs., N.Y.C., 1977—; chmn. U.S. Congress on Evangelism, 1969; ofcl. observer for Luth. Ch.-Mo. Synod at Vatican Council, 1964, 65; past pres. Luth. Council U.S.A.; past mem. bd. dirs. Found. for Reformation Research; past pres. Religious Pub. Relations Council; bd. dirs. Aid Assn. for Lutherans, 1962-83. Appeared on various network radio and TV programs including Today, Face the Nation; prodn. asst. films: Martin Luther and Question 7. Author: Hurry Home Where You Belong, God Is No Island, Life Crucified, God's Joyful People—One In the Spirit, Lord, I Pray to You for a Sunny Day, The Lord's

Prayer, 1982, also mag. articles. Hon. bd. mem. Wheat Ridge Found. Recipient Gutenberg award Chgo. Bible Soc., 1980, Sec. of Def. award for Outstanding Service, U.S. Dept. Def., 1980, Gold Angel award as Internat. Media Clergyman of Yr., Religion in Media, 1982; named Clergyman of Yr., Religious Heritage Am., 1973. Mem. Am. Bible Soc. (life, bd. mgrs., chmn. trans. com.), Aid Assn. for Lutherans (bd. dirs. 1962-83), Luth. Film Assocs. (past sec.). Office: Internat Luth Laymen's League 2185 Hampton Ave Saint Louis MO 63139

HOFFMANN, RAIMUND JOSEPH, New Testament studies educator, Roman Catholic Church; b. St. Louis, Dec. 16, 1947; s. R.J. and Nadine (Taylor) H.; m. Leora DeLelys Lucas, Sept. 5, 1970. B.A., M.C.L., Fla. State U., 1969; M.T.S., Harvard U., 1977, Th.M. cum laude, 1978; Ph.D., Oxford U., 1981. Asst. prof. New Testament studies U. Mich., Ann Arbor, 1982—; mem. nat. exec. com. Biblical Criticism Research Project, 1982—. Author: Marcion: On the Restitution of Christianity, 1983; Jesus: Outside the Gospels, 1984; Christianity: The Classical Critiques, 1984. Contbr. articles to profl. jours. Assoc. editor Anchor Bible Dictionary, 1984—. Rockefeller Found. scholar, 1975-77, St. Cross Coll., Oxford U. sr. scholar, 1980-82, NEH grantee, 1984—. Fellow Am. Inst. Patristic and Byzantine Studies; mem. Soc. Biblical Lit., Am. Acad. Religion, U. Mich. Research Club. Home: 555 E William Apt 14-C Ann Arbor MI 48104 Office: Dept Near Eastern Studies U Mich Ann Arbor MI 48109

HOFFMANN, RALPH GEORGE, priest, Roman Catholic Church; b. Hartford City, Ind., Sept. 24, 1911; s. John L. and Marie Theresa (Andre) H.; student St. Joseph Coll., Rensselaer, Ind., 1928-31, St. Gregory Sem., Cin., 1931-33, St. Mary Sem., Norwood, Ohio, 1933-37. Ordained priest Roman Catholic Ch., 1937; asst. pastor Holy Trinity Ch., East Chicago, Ind., 1937-42; asst. pastor St. Mary Ch., Michigan City, Ind., 1942-43; chaplain AUS, 1943-47; pastor St. Dominic Ch., Bremen, Ind., 1947-51, St. Patrick Ch., Chesterton, Ind., 1951-66, St. Mary of the Lake, Gary, Ind., 1966—; Episcopal vicar of Gary Deanery, 1976—. Pro-synodal judge Diocese of Gary, 1971—; mem. Diocesan Senate, 1974—; diocesan coordinator 41st Internat. Eucharistic Congress, 1975. Home: 6060 Miller Ave Gary IN 46403

HOFMAN, LEONARD J. clergyman, stated clk. Christian Reformed Church in North America. Office: 2850 Kalamazoo Ave SE Grand Rapids MI 49560*

HOGAN, JAMES JOHN, bishop, Roman Catholic Church; b. Phila., Oct. 17, 1911; s. James and Mary E. (Molloy) H.; B.A., St. Mary's Sem., Balt., 1934; S.T.L., Gregorian U., Rome, Italy, 1938; J.C.D., Catholic U. Am., 1941. Ordained priest Roman Catholic Ch., 1937; consecrated bishop; from diocesan ofcl. and consultor, to chancellor of diocese, aux. bishop Trenton, N.J.; pastor St. Catherine's Ch., Spring Lake, N.J.; bishop Diocese of Altoona-Johnstown, Pa., 1966—. Office: Box 126 Logan Blvd Hollidaysburg PA 16648

HOGAN, JAMES PHILIP, minister, General Council Assemblies of God; b. Olathe, Colo., Dec. 4, 1915; s. Leslie Irvin and Lucy (Van Trump) H.; grad. Central Bible Coll., 1936; grad. student U. Calif. at Berkeley, 1945-46; D.D., So. Asia Bible Coll. (Bangalore, India), 1970, North Central Bible Coll., 1975; m. Mary Virginia Lewis, Dec. 28, 1937; children: James Richard (dec.), Phyllis Lynne (Mrs. Robert McGlasson). Ordained to ministry, Gen. Council of the Assemblies of God Ch., 1938; evangelist, 1936-40; pastor chs., Plainesville, Ohio, 1941-42, Lincoln Park, Mich., 1942-44; missionary to China, 1947-48, Formosa, 1948-50; pastor ch., Florence, S.C., 1951-52; sec. for promotions, div. Fgn. Missions, Springfield, Mo., 1952-59, asst. gen. supt., exec. dir. fgn. missions, 1959—; mem. exec. presbytery of Gen. Council of Assemblies of God, also mem. gen. presbytery, chmn. fgn. missions bd.; v.p. Evang. Fgn. Missions Assn., 1966-67, 76-78, pres., 1968-70, mem. exec. com. 1971-75, 76—. Trustee Severance Found., Saginaw, Mich. Home: Route 22 Box 2438 Springfield MO 65803 Office: 1445 Boonville Ave Springfield MO 65802

HOGE, JAMES CLEO, priest, Roman Catholic Church; b. Charelston, W.Va., Nov. 28, 1916; s. James Cleo and Theresa (Bohnert) H. B.A., Benedictine Coll., 1940; M.A., St. Leo Coll., 1980. Joined Order St. Benedict, Roman Catholic Ch., 19—, ordained priest 1943. Priest in charge Henando County Missions, Brooksville, Fla., 1944-48, 54-55; pastor Our Lady of Fatima Ch., Inverness, Fla., 1962-65, St. Anthony Ch., Brooksville, 1967-69; pastor St. Benedicts Ch., Crystal River, Fla., 1969—. Trustee, St. Leo Coll., 1965-78. Bd. dirs. Homosassa Area Improvement Assn., 1983—; mem. Sch. Bd. Diocese St. Petersburg, 1983—. Mem. North Suncoast Ministers Assn. (pres. 1974-75, 83-84). Lodge: Rotary (pres. 1982-83), K.C. (chaplain). Democrat. Home: 455 S Suncoast Blvd Crystal River FL 32629 Office: St Benedicts Cath Ch US Hwy 19 S Crystal River FL 32629

HOGGARD, JAMES CLINTON See *Who's Who in America,* 43rd edition.

HOKE, KENNETH OLAN, minister, Brethren in Christ Ch. B. Jamalpur, Bihar, India, Nov. 5, 1949 (parents Am. citizens); s. William Robert and Mary (Hess) H.; m. Carolyn Louise Thuma, Jan. 3, 1970; children: Bryan, Steven, Julie. B.A. in Psychology, Messiah Coll., 1970; M.Div. in Psychology and Pastoral Care, Ashland Theol. Sem., 1973. Ordained minister Brethren in Christ Ch., 1978. Assoc. pastor Sippo Brethren in Christ Ch., Massilon, Ohio, 1971-72; pastor Ashland Brethren in Christ Ch., Ashland, Ohio, 1972-75; assoc. pastor Carlisle Brethren in Christ Ch., Pa., 1975—; pres., sec. Carlisle Ministerial Assn., 1977-83; ministerial tng. com. Brethren in Christ Ch., 1980-84, mem. ministerial credentials bd., 1980-84, mem. commn. ednl. instns., 1984—; lectr. Ch. Edn. Messiah Coll., Grantham, Pa., 1983—. Republican. Lodge: Kiwanis (pres. Carlisle chpt.). Home: 101 Clarindon Pl Carlisle PA 17013 Office: Brethren in Christ Ch 1155 Walnut Bottom Rd Carlisle PA 17013

HOLAND, CLIFFORD BENJAMIN, ret. minister, Luth. Ch. Am.; b. McKinley, Minn., Mar. 23, 1902; s. Peter and Camilla (Berger) H.; B.A., U. N.D., 1923; postgrad. Yale Div. Sch., 1924-25; M.Div., Union Theol. Sem., N.Y.C., 1927; M.A., Tchrs. Coll., Columbia, 1932; D.D., Wesley Coll., Grand Forks, N.D., 1958; postgrad. Sch. Social Welfare U. Calif., Los Angeles, 1952-53; m. Jessie Frances Simpson, Aug. 7, 1929; 1 dau., Frances Carolyn. Ordained to ministry, 1927; asst. pastor Luth. Ch. Advent, N.Y.C., 1927-28; pastor Grace Luth. Ch., Forest Hills, N.Y., 1928-38, St. Pauls Luth. Ch., Santa Monica, Calif., 1938-52, Transfiguration Luth. Ch., Los Angeles, 1952-59, Good Shepherd Luth. Ch., Claremont, Calif., 1960-63, Redeemer Luth. Ch. Leisure World, Seal Beach, Calif., 1963-68; ret., 1968. Ofcl. visitor World Council Chs., Amsterdam, 1948, Evanston, Ill., 1952; chmn. social welfare com. Pacific SW Synod, United Luth. Ch., 1945-57. Author: Good Morning and Other Sermons, 1965; Towhead: Son of a Northman, 1976. Home: 567 Mayflower Rd Claremont CA 91711

HOLBROOK, CLYDE AMOS, theologian, educator, United Church of Christ; b. Greenfield, Mass., Mar. 20, 1911; s. Fred Earl and Adella Sabra (Caswell) H.; A.B., Bates Coll., 1934; B.D., Colgate-Rochester Div. Sch., 1937; Ph.D., Yale, 1945; S.T.D. (hon.), Denison U., 1969; H.H.D. (hon.), Oberlin Coll., 1982; m. Dorothy Bush Wheeler, Dec. 27, 1937; children—Richard, Arthur, Deborah. Ordained to ministry Baptist Ch., 1937; pastor ch., Weston, Conn., 1937-42, New Haven, 1942-45; asst. prof. religion, dean Shove Chapel, Colo. Coll., 1945-49; asso. prof. religion Denison U., 1949-51; prof. religion Oberlin Coll., 1951—, chmn. dept., 1951-75, prof. Christian ethics Sch. Theology, 1951-56, Danforth chair religion, 1957-77. Trustee Oberlin Shansi Meml. Assn. Colgate-Rochester fellow, Yale, 1937-40; sr. fellow Council Humanities Princeton, 1961-62. Mem. Soc. Values in Higher Edn., Am. Acad. Religion, Am. Theol. Soc., Phi Beta Kappa. Author: Faith and Community, 1959; Religion, A Humanistic Field, 1963; Jonathan Edwards' Original Sin, 1970; The Ethics of Jonathan Edwards, 1973, The Iconoclastic Deity: Biblical Images of God, 1984 many articles. Address: 21 Hawthorne Dr Oberlin OH 44074

HOLBROOK, DELMAR DAY, minister Ch. of God (Anderson, Ind.); b. Portsmouth, Ohio, June 10, 1924; s. Daniel Martin and Ida B. (Day) H.; student pub. schs., Melvin, Ill.; m. Ruth E. Crossman, May 5, 1946; children—Janis, James, Jayne, Jeffry, Jeana. Ordained to ministry, 1966; Ill. youth dir., Bloomington, 1956-66; dir. Youth for Christ, Normal, Ill., 1964-66; pastor 1st Ch. of God, Vandalia, Ill., 1966-68, Effingham, Ill., 1968-76; pastor Camrose Ch. of God (Alta., Can.), 1976—; chaplain, tchr. pastoral methods Alta. Bible Inst., Camrose, 1976—. Ill. camping dir., 1970-73; pres. Ministerial Assn., 1974; vice chmn. Ill. State Assembly, 1974-75, chmn., 1976; chmn. Central States Ministers Conf., 1976; chmn. gen. assembly Ch. of God Western Can., 1977. Home: 5509 48th Ave Camrose AB T4V 0J8 Canada Office: 55 St and 48th Ave Camrose AB T4V 0J8 Canada

HOLDEN, DELMA JOHN, pastor, Christian Church (Disciples of Christ); b. Lonoke, Ark., Feb. 14, 1918; s. Odis and Pennia (Mitchell) H.; m. Ola Mae Whitley, Sept. 15, 1940; 1 child, Delores Anne Holden Austin. Student, Phillander Smith Coll., 1950-52. Ordained to ministry Christian Ch. (Disciples of Christ), 1958. Asst. pastor Mt. Beulah Christian Ch., Pine Bluff, Ark., 1954-58, pastor, 1965—; pastor Edwards Chapel Ch., Russellville, Ark., 1958-65; pres. Pearidge Christian Ch. and Cemetery, Lonoke, 1979-85; state youth dir. Ark. Chs., 1954-72, pres. chs., 1958-65; chaplain Post Office Union Br. 35, 1948-52. Served with USN, 1938-45. Mem. Ministers Study Fellowship (sec. 1982-84), Internat. Platform Assn. Home: 3117 Arch St Little Rock AR 72206 Office: Mt Beulah Ch 2305 Main St Pine Bluff AR 71601

HOLDER, MAURICE LEE, minister, So. Bapt. Conv.; b. Laurinburgh, N.C., May 14, 1930; s. Gordon Alexander and Ann Lee (Humphrey) H.; B.S. in Edn., Towson State Coll., 1953; postgrad. Loyola Coll., 1953-54; B.D., Crozer Theol. Sem., 1963; postgrad. Drew U., 1964-65, Am. Jewish Sem., 1966-67; Th.M., Colgate Rochester Div. Sch., 1973; m. Norma Elizabeth Shoemaker, Aug. 30, 1952; children—James Mark, Deborah Lee (Mrs. Robert E. Frank), Carolyn Elizabeth. Ordained to ministry Am. Bapt. Conv., 1962; changed to So. Bapt. Conv., 1969; asst. minister First Bapt. Ch., Phila., 1962-63; minister First Bapt. Community Ch., Parsippany, N.J., 1963-66, Cranston St.-Roger Williams Bapt. Ch., Providence, 1966-69, First Bapt. Ch., Balt., 1969—; chaplain Holiday Inn, Balt., 1973-74. Recipient St. John's Ch. award Phila., 1962; Rebecca Cohen award for Christian Ethics, Crozier Theol. Sem., 1963. Mem. Am. Sci. Found., Christian Ethics Soc., Clergy Brotherhood of Balt., Nat. Edn. Assn., Ecumenical Inst. Washington, Crozer Sem. Alumni Assn., Howard Park Improvement Assn., Ordination Council of Balt., Nat. Ethics Inst., Nat. Chaplaincy Assn., Bapt. Assn. Balt. (cooperation com.), Phi Beta Kappa, Kappa Delta Pi. Contbr. articles, prayers, sermons to various religious jours. Address: 4200 Liberty Heights Ave Baltimore MD 21207

HOLLAAR, LEROY ALAN, educational administrator, Reformed Church; b. Linton, N.D., Jan. 4, 1943; s. Aren A. and Harriet (Haveman) H.; B.S., U. S.D., 1969, M.A., 1971; m. Ilean Van Beek, July 31, 1959; children: Timothy, Gwendolyn, Carmen, Candace. Prin., Volga (S.D.) Christian Sch., 1962-66, Ireton (Iowa) Christian Sch., 1966-71, Mt. Vernon (Wash.) Christian Sch., 1971-73, Edmonton (Alta., Can.) Soc. for Christian Edn., 1973—; mem. various provincial task forces and study coms. on pub. and ind. schs. Nominated Outstanding Young Educator, Volga C. of C., 1965. Mem. Assn. Christian Sch. Adminstrs., Iowa Assn. Ind. Schs., Alta. Ind. Schs. and Colls. Assn. (sec. 1976-79, pres. 1979-84), Edmonton Pastoral Inst. (dir. 1976—, sec. 1976-78), Alta. Prins. Assn., Fedn. Ind. Schs. Can. (founding mem., pres. 1983-85), Alta., Christian tchrs. assns. Helped develop distinctive Christian curriculum for schs. Home: 5711 141 Ave Edmonton AB T5A 1H7 Canada Office: 14304 109th Ave Edmonton AB T5N 1H6 Canada

HOLLADAY, JAMES FRANK, lay church worker, Southern Baptist Convention; b. Birmingham, Ala., Apr. 5, 1922; s. Allen Arthur and Mary Estell (Campbell) H.; B.S.E.E., Ga. Inst. Tech., 1950; m. Anna Wedsworth, July 17, 1948; children: James Frank, David Allen, Cynthia Anne. Ordained deacon So. Baptist Conv., 1956; deacon Tabernacle Baptist Ch., Carrollton, Ga., 1956—, dir., tchr. Sunday sch., 1956—, tng. dir., 1962-65, youth leader, 1967-70; dir. So. Baptist Home Mission Bd., 1973—; bd. dirs. So. Bapt. Found., 1975—. Vice pres. plant engring. Southwire Co., Carrollton, 1963. Mem. Ga. Safety Council, 1967—. Bd. dirs. Ga. Council Moral and Civic Concerns, 1980—; trustee Tift Coll., Forsyth, Ga., 1981-86. Mem. Nat., Ga. socs. profl. engrs., Ga. Bus. and Industry Assn., Am. Inst. Plant Engrs. (pres. 1973-74). Lion. Home: 305 Kramer St Carrollton GA 30117 Office: Box 1000 Fertilla St Carrollton GA 30117

HOLLADAY, JAMES FRANKLIN, JR., minister, Southern Baptist Convention; b. Meridian, Miss., May 23, 1951; s. James Franklin and Anne (Wedsworth) H.; m. Patricia Ann Martin, June 18, 1977; 1 child, Meredith Anne. B.A., Samford U., Birmingham, Ala., 1973; M.Divinity, So. Bapt. Sem., Louisville, 1976, D.Ministries, 1983. Ordained to ministry So. Bapt. Conv., 1976; summer youth minister 1st Bapt. Ch., Chatsworth, Ga., 1972; campus minister Ky. Bapt. Conv., Middletown, 1974-76; program coordinator E. Bapt. Ch., Louisville, 1976-79; pastor, dir. E. Bapt. Ch.-Ctr., Louisville, 1979—; sec. Kentuckiana Interfaith Community, Louisville, 1979-80, v.p., 1980-81, pres., 1981-82. Chmn. Louisville Full-Employment Task Force, 1976-78; mem. Jefferson County Anti-Freeze Com., Louisville, 1980-81; pres. Phoenix Hill Assn., Louisville, 1981-83, now bd. dirs. Mem. Fedn. Ch. Social Agys. (pres. 1979—), Omicron Delta Chi. Democrat. Home: 165 Pennsylvania Ave Louisville KY 40206 Office: E Bapt Ch Ctr 400 E Chestnut St Louisville KY 40202

HOLLAND, DARRELL WENDELL, religion editor; b. Charleston, W.Va., Apr. 30, 1932; s. Ray E. and Esther (Dean) H.; m. Ann Holland, Nov. 25, 1971; 3 children. A.B., Olivet Coll., 1954; B.D., Nazareth Theol. Sch., 1957; M.S. in Journalism, Boston U., 1970. Dir. communications Mass. Conf. United Ch. of Christ, Boston, 1966-74; religion editor Plain Dealer Pub. Co., Cleve., 1974—. Home: 12900 Lake Ave Lakewood OH 44107 Office: The Plain Dealer 1801 Superior St Cleveland OH 44114

HOLLANDER, DAVID B., Jewish organization executive. Pres. Poale Agudath Israel of Am., Inc. Office: Poale Agudath Israel of Am Inc 156 Fifth Ave New York NY 10010*

HOLLE, REGINALD HENRY, bishop, Michigan District American Lutheran Church; b. Burton, Tex., Nov. 21, 1925; s. Alfred William and Lena (Nolte) H.; m. Marla Christianson, June 16, 1949; children: Todd William, Joan Holle Long. A.A., Tex. Luth. Coll., 1944; B.A., Capital U., Columbus, Ohio, 1946; D.Div. (hon.), 1979; M. Div., Trinity Sem., 1949; D. Ministry, Wittenberg U., 1977. Ordained to ministry American Lutheran Ch., 1949. Assoc. pastor Zion Luth. Ch., Sandusky, Ohio, 1949-51; sr. pastor Salem Meml. Luth.

Ch., Detroit, 1951-72, Parma Luth. Ch., Cleve., 1972-78; bishop Mich. dist. Am. Luth. Ch., Detroit, 1978—; chmn. bd. youth activity Am. Luth. Ch., 1968-73, chmn. bd. for life and mission in congregations, 1973-76; chmn. bd. regents Capital U., 1972-78; chmn. Inst. for Mission in U.S.A., Columbus, 1984—. Contbr. chpts. to profl. books. Recipient Exceptional Community Service award Detroit Pub. Schs., 1970; named Alpha Disting. Alumnus, Trinity Sem., 1978, Disting. Alumnus, Tex. Luth. Coll., 1979. Office: Am Luth Ch Mich Dist 21900 Greenfield Rd Detroit MI 48237

HOLLIFIELD, MORRIS SHUFFORD, minister, Southern Baptist Convention; b. Chesnee, S.C., Aug. 4, 1929; s. Carl Shufford and Effie Allie H.; B.A., Wake Forest U., 1955; B.D., Southeastern Bapt. Theol. Sem., 1958, Th. M., 1960; m. Hannah Lou Brown, Nov. 8, 1950; children—Hannah Jeanne, Jeffrey Morris. Pastor chs., N.C., 1957-66, Tenn., 1966-70; pastor Jersey Bapt. Ch., Lexington, N.C., 1970—. Clk., Liberty Bapt. Assn., Lexington, 1971—; moderator Holston Valley (Tenn.) Bapt. Assn., 1967-68; mem. gen. bd. N.C. Bapt. State Conv., 1981-84, chmn. missions com., 1982-84, chmn. relationship study com., 1984; chmn. gen. bd. com. Fruitland Bapt. Bible Inst.; trustee Davidson County Hist. Mus., Lexington, N.C., 1982-84. Bd. dirs. Davidson County (N.C.) Developmental Center, Inc., Lexington. Contbr. articles to denominational jours. Home and Office: Rt 7 Box 45 Lexington NC 27292

HOLLINGER, KENNETH WANDLE, pastor, Church of the Brethren; b. Darke County, Ohio, Aug. 11, 1912; s. E.S. and Sarah (Wandle) H.; B.S. in Secondary Edn., Manchester Coll., 1935; M.Div., Bethany Bible Sem., 1946; m. Helen Louise Darley, June 1, 1938; children: John David, Richard Eugene, James Elvin, Roger William, Elizabeth Marie. Ordained to ministry, 1931; pastor, chs. Ohio, Ind., Ill., 1938—, Olivet Ch., Thornville, Ohio, 1948-57, New Paris, Ind., 1957-62, Lanark, Ill., 1962-73, Cedar Creek Ch., Garrett, Ind., 1973-76, Maple Grove Ch., New Paris, Ind., 1976-80, Little Pine, Goshen, Ind., 1981—. Del. N.Am. Family Life Conf. of All People, 1960, 70. Bd. dirs. Farmers Home Adminstrn. Bd., Perry County, 1951-54. Named Rural Minister Year, Ohio Ch. of the Brethren, 1950. Author: History of the Prices Creek Congregation, 1944; History of the Olivet Congregation, 1954; contbr. articles to mags. Home and Office: 64398 CR 21 Goshen IN 46526

HOLLINGSWORTH, JERRY JACOB, evangelist; Southern Baptist Convention; b. Winfield, Ala., July 10, 1954; s. Wiley Jacob and Zora Mae (Gray) H. Student, Brewer State Jr. Coll., 1972-75, Jacksonville State U., 1974-75, Bapt. Bible Inst., 1976-78. Ordained to ministry, 1980. Pastor, Westside Bapt. Ch., Vernon, Ala., 1979-82; evangelist Jerry Hollingsworth Ministries, Fayette, Ala., 1982—; counselor Ala. Bapt. Boys Camp, Talledega, Ala., summer 1976; lectr. Lamar Bapt. Assn. Ann. meeting, Vernon, 1981; counselor A.G.I. Prison, Snead, Fla., 1977. Author: You Gave Me Love, 1984. Mem. Jaycees. Club: Bapt. State U. Address: 709 3d Way NE Fayette AL 35555

HOLLIS, REGINALD See *Who's Who in America*, 43rd edition.

HOLLYFIELD, WALLACE G., executive presbyter, Presbyterian Church in the U.S.; b. Birmingham, Ala., June 30, 1931; s. Grover Austin and Anna Louise (Register) H.; m. Clara K., Sept. 10, 1950 (div. 1979); children: Wallace G. Jr., Tracy Louise; m. Wendy Eileen, Jan. 18, 1981. B.A., Birmingham So. Coll., 1958; M.Div., Columbia Theol. Sem., 1962; D.Min., McCormick Theol. Sem., 1977. Cert. bus. adminstr. Presbyn. Ch., 1984. Ordained to ministry Presbyterian Church in the U.S. 1962. Pastor various chs. Ala., Ga., Fla., 1962-81; pastoral counselor Mid-Fla. Ctr. Alcoholics, Orlando, Fla., 1971-76; instr., chaplain Lake Highland Prep. Sch., Orlando, 1973-79; exec. presbyter Presbyter of the Everglades, No. Miami, Fla., 1981—; mem. Christian Edn. com. Birmingham Presbytery, 1962-64; mem. Christian Edn. Com., Southwest Ga. Presbytery, 1964-66; chmn. Christian Action Com., 1964-66, Campus Christian Life Com. Synod Ga., 1964-66; chmn. elem. div. Christian Edn. Com. Suwannee Presbytery, 1967-68, chmn. Christian Action Com., 1968-70; mem. New Ch. Devel. com. St. John's Presbytery, 1970-77, chmn. adminstrn. com., 1978-81; chaplain Orlando Police Dept., 1971-75; liason Presbytery Staff person, 1980-81; bd. dirs. Christian Community Service Agency, 1981-83, Mental Health Assn. Orange County, 1976-81; program com. chmn. Christian Community Service Agency, 1983—; vice pres. Metro. Alcoholism Council Central Fla., 1978-80, pres. 1980; pres. Hillcrest House, Orlando, 1971-81; mem. Inter-faith Task Force Fla. Commn. Drug and Alcohol Concerns, 1984. Served to s/sgt. USAF, 1950-52. Mem. Presbyn. Ch. Bus. Adminstrs. Club: Exchange (Orlando). Office: Presbytery of the Everglades PO Box 1605 North Miami FL 33161

HOLMES, EDDIE, clergyman, broadcaster; b. Hopkinsville, Ky., Jan. 21, 1956; s. Roy Edward and Lilly Hyacinth (Long) H.; m. Maria Kane, Apr. 25, 1977; children: Roy, Melisa. Student Fla. State U., 1974-75, Mid-Continent Bible Coll., 1975-78; B.S. in Math., Bethel Coll., McKenzie, Tenn., 1982. Ordained to ministry So. Baptist Conv., 1978. Youth dir. Enon Bapt. Ch., McKenzie, 1977-78, youth minister, 1984—; asst. pastor Long Heights Bapt. Ch., McKenzie, 1978-80; pastor Beech Springs Bapt. Ch., Gleason, Tenn., 1981-83; program dir. Sta. WHDM-AM, McKenzie, 1982—; chmn. pub. relations Weakly County Bapt. Assn., Dresden, Tenn., 1981-82. Mem. Am. Meteorol. Assn. (assoc.). Republican. Office: WHDM Radio 143 S Main St McKenzie TN 38201

HOLMES, EUGENE COVINGTON, minister, United Meth. Ch.; b. Aberdeen, Miss., Dec. 17, 1932; s. Howard Eugene and Emma Maye (Covington) H.; B.A., Milsaps Coll., 1955; B.D., Emory U., 1957, M.Div., 1972; m. Eleanor Leigh Haynes, June 10, 1954; children—David Chrisopher, Marcus Eugene, Jonathan Wesley. Ordained deacon, 1956, elder, 1958; pastor Sallis (Miss.) Charge, 1954-55; organist, choir dir. 1st Meth. Ch., Monroe, Ga., 1955-56; student asso. pastor Inman Park Meth. Ch., Atlanta, 1956-57; pastor Sturgis (Miss.) Charge, 1957-58; asso. pastor Bethel Meth. Ch., Spartanburg, S.C., 1958-60; pastor Nichols (S.C.) Charge, 1960-64, Suber-Marshall Meml. Ch., Columbia, S.C., 1964-68, St. Paul's Ch., Ninety-Six, S.C., 1968-72, Wesley Ch., Hartsville, S.C., 1972-77, Virginia Wingard Ch., Columbia, S.C., 1977—. Mem. bd. Christian social concerns S.C. Conf., Meth. Ch., 1960-64, chmn. commn. on worship, 1964-68, mem. nat. commn. on worship, 1968-72, chmn. com. on creative sources of worship, 1968-72, mem. bd. of discipleship, 1972-76, mem. exec. com., 1972-76, div. on evangelism, worship, and stewardship, 1972-76, chmn. sect. on worship, 1972-76, bd. evangelism, 1977—. Mem. Fellowship United Meth. Musicians, United Meth. Soc. for Worship. Contbg. editor: Sacrament of the Lord's Supper, 1972; A Service of Baptism, Confirmation, and Renewal, 1976, Word and Table, 1976, Ritual in a New Day, 1976. Home: 1376 Railfence Dr Columbia SC 29210 Office: 1500 Broad River Rd Columbia SC 29210

HOLMES, REED M. See *Who's Who in America*, 43rd edition.

HOLMGREN, LATON EARLE, church official, United Methodist Church; b. Mpls., Feb. 20, 1915; s. Frank Albert and Freda Ida (Lindahl) H.; student U. Minn., 1934-35; A.B. cum laude, Asbury Coll., 1936; M.Div. summa cum laude, Drew U., 1941; postgrad. Edinburgh (Scotland) U., 1947; D.D., Ill. Wesleyan U., 1956; D.D., Asbury Theol. Sem., 1972. Ordained to ministry United Methodist Ch., 1942; assoc. minister Calvary Meth. Ch., East Orange, N.J., 1940-42, Christ Ch. Meth., N.Y.C., 1943-48; minister Tokyo (Japan) Union Ch., 1949-52; lectr. internat. dept. Tokyo U. Commerce, 1950-52; adviser Japanese Fgn. Office, Tokyo, 1951; sec. for Asia, Am. Bible Soc., N.Y.C., 1952-54, exec. sec. overseas dept., 1954-62, gen. sec., rec. sec., 1963-78, resident cons., 1978—; mem. exec. com. United Bible Socs., Stuttgart, W. Ger., 1957-78, chmn., 1963-72, spl. cons., 1978—. Trustee, Asbury Theol. Sem. Recipient Gutenberg award, 1975; Disting. Alumni award Asbury Coll., 1981, Baron von Canstein award, 1982. Mem. Japan Soc. Club: Met. Home: 322 W 57th St New York NY 10019 Office: 1865 Broadway New York NY 10023

HOLMGREN, WARNER ELOF, minister, Luth. Ch. in Am.; b. Chgo., June 14, 1912; s. Werner E. and Josephine (Peterson) H.; B.A., Wittenberg U., 1935; B.D., Hamma Sem., Springfield, Ohio, 1936; postgrad. Ohio State U., 1948-52; M.Div., Hamma Sch. Theology, 1970; m. Hazel Madeline Veith, June 25, 1938; children—Mary Josephine Holmgren Henry, Barbara Anne Holmgren Jones, Nancy Ellen Holmgren Hickman. Ordained to ministry, 1936; pastor St. John Luth. Ch., Mt. Vernon, Ohio, 1936-38, Minerva (Ohio) Parish, 1938-42; chaplain U.S. Army, 1942-45; pastor Zion Luth. Ch., Defiance, Ohio, 1945-47, Indianola Luth. Ch., Columbus, Ohio, 1947-54, Trinity Luth. Ch., Dayton, Ohio, 1954-59, St. Luke's Luth. Ch., Youngstown, Ohio, 1959-69, Trinity Luth. Ch., Brookville, Ohio, 1969—. Chmn. social ministry com. Ohio Synod, Luth. Ch. Am., 1967-69, mem. Christian edn. com., 1962-65. Mem. Mental Health Bd., Youngstown, 1962-64; bd. dirs. Wittenberg U., Springfield, Ohio, 1972—, Luth. Social Services, Dayton, Ohio, 1977—. Recipient Chaplain plaque award Luth. Ch. in Am., 1946. Mem. Hamma Alumni Fellowship Assn. (dir. 1970-75). Home: 351 Sycamore St Brookville OH 45309 Office: Trinity Lutheran Ch Westbrook and Wolf Creek Streets Brookville OH 45309

HOLSINGER, JAMES WILSON, JR., lay ch. worker, United Methodist Ch.; b. Kansas City, Kans., May 11, 1939; s. James Wilson and Ruth Leona (Reitz) H.; student Duke, 1957-60, M.D., 1964, Ph.D., 1968; m. Barbara Jenn Craig, Dec. 28, 1963; children—Anna, Ruth, Sarah, Rachel. Chmn. edn. commn. Trinity United Methodist Ch., Gainesville, Fla., 1969-70, adult coordinator, 1970-71, vice chmn. adminstrv. bd., 1971-72; asso. dist. lay leader Gainesville Dist. United Meth. Ch., 1971-72; lay mem. Fla. Ann. Conf., 1971-72, bd. laity, 1971-72; lay mem. Nebr. Ann. Conf., 1972-74, bd. higher edn., 1972-74; chmn. council on ministries Rockbrook (Nebr.) United Meth. Ch., 1972-73, lay leader, 1973-74; adult coordinator West Hartford (Conn.) United Meth. Ch., 1974-76, chmn. adminstrv. bd., 1977—. Chief of staff VA Hosp., Newington, Conn., also asso. dean U. Conn. Sch. Medicine, Farmington, Conn., 1974—. Trustee Capitol Area Health Consortium, Hartford, Conn., 1976—. Recipient Travel fellow Endocrine Soc., 1968; Army Res. Achievement Medal, 1972. Asso. fellow Am. Coll. Cardiology; mem. Am. Assn. Anatomists, Am. Heart Assn. (alt. del. ann. meeting 1973), Am. Physiol. Soc., Nebr. Heart Assn. (dir. 1973-74, pres. Douglas-Sarpy div. 1973-74). Author: Cardiology Board Review; contbr. articles to profl. jours. Home: 555 Willard Ave Newington CT 06111 Office: VA Hosp 555 Willard Ave Newington CT 06111

HOLST, ERNST FREDERICK, minister, Lutheran Church in America; b. Bklyn., Mar. 18, 1934; s. Ernst John and Kathryn Anna (Meyer) H.; m. Barbara Ann Christman, Sept. 7, 1957; children: Diane Marie, Susan Ellen, Beth Anne. B.A., Wagner Coll., 1955; M.Div., Luth. Theol. Sem., 1958; M.A., Union Coll., 1969. Ordained to ministry Luth Ch. Am., 1958. Pastor, mission developer Redeemer Luth. Ch., Orangeburg, N.Y., 1958-61; pastor Our Savior Luth. Ch., Schenectady, 1961-64, Zion Luth. Ch., Cobleskill, N.Y., 1964-69, Prince of Peace Luth. Ch., Brentwood, N.Y., 1969-72, Augustana Luth. Ch., Tonawanda, N.Y., 1972-78; pastor, chaplain Luth. Ch./Cornell U., Ithaca, N.Y., 1978—; sec., v.p. Luth. Theol. Sem. Bd., Phila., 1981—; synodical rep. Continuing Edn. com. Council for Theol. Edn. in N.E., Phila., 1976—; chmn. bd. Cornell United Religious Work, 1979-83; clergy mem. exec. bd. Upper New York Synod, Syracuse, 1979—, v.p., 1984—. Author: Light for Today, 1978; Preaching Helps, 1982. Bd. dirs. Hospicare, Ithaca, N.Y., 1984, Am. Cancer Soc., 1979-82; mem. Collegetown Neighborhood Council, 1983. Trexler scholar, 1983. Mem. Tompkins County Religious Workers Assn. (treas.). Democrat. Home: 185 West Haven Rd Ithaca NY 14850 Office: The Lutheran Ch 109 Oak Ave Ithaca NY 14850

HOLST, WAYNE ALFRED, minister, Lutheran Church in America; b. Kitchener, Ont., Can., June 12, 1942; s. Alfred Carl and Marieta Lillian (Boyd) H.; m. Eleanor Joan Snider, July 11, 1964; children: Jacqueline Ann, Gina Marieta. B.A., Wilfred Laurier U., 1964; M.Div., Waterloo Luth. Sem., 1967; cert. d'Etudes Oikumeniques U., Geneva, Switzerland, 1968; D.Min., St. Stephen's U.-Alberta, Can., 1985. Ordained to ministry Lutheran Ch. in Am., 1968. Missionary Luth. Ch. in Am., Trinidad, W. Indies, 1969-71; asst. to bishop Cen. Can. Synod, Winnepeg, Manitoba, Can., 1971-77; acting bishop Luth. Ch. Am., 1976; dir. cons. Luth. Ch. Am., N.Y.C., 1977-80; pastor Advent Luth. Ch., Calgary, Alberta, Can., 1980—; dir. Pastoral Inst., Calgary, 1982—; mem. exec. com. Christian Festival Cretien, Calgary, Can., 1984—; cons. Luth. Merger Commn., Winnipeg, Can., 1982—; mem. task force Commd. Ministries, Winnipeg, 1983—. Strategist Luth. Ch. Am., 1979; designer N. Can. Mission Models, 1976; staff-developer Can. Ch. Mission Strategy, 1979. World Council of Chs. fellow, 1967, Luth. Brotherhood Sem. grad., 1968, Div. for Mission in N. Am. fellow, 1979. Mem. Can. Assn. Pastoral Edn., 1983—. Liberal party of Can. Home: 7240 Silver Springs Rd NW Calgary Alberta T3B 4A2 Canada Office: Advent Luth Ch 11 Scenic Acres Gate Calgary Alberta T3L 1E4 Canada

HOLT, JOHN ALBERT, minister, United Methodist Church; b. Alamo, Tenn., Sept. 15, 1947; s. Albert Curtis and Syble Marie (Forsythe) H.; m. Robbie Ferguson Blurton, Apr. 20, 1973; children: Michael Blurton, Jan Blurton, David Blurton. B.A., Lambuth Coll., 1977; M.Div., Memphis Theol. Sem., 1980; D. Ministry, St. Paul Sch. Theology, 1984. Ordained to ministry Meth. Ch., 1980, elder, 1982. Minister E. Jackson United Meth. Ch., Tenn., 1974-77, Gates Cir. United Meth. Ch., Tenn., 1977-80, Munford First United Meth. Ch., Tenn., 1980—; sec. Brownsville Dist. Ministers, Tenn., 1982; mem. Equitable Salary Commn., Memphis Ann. Conf., 1980—; mem. Brownsville dist. Council on Ministries, 1980—; mem. small membership ch. com. Memphis Annual Conf., 1982-83; v.p. Brownsville Dist. Ministers, Tenn., 1983, pres., 1984; dir. Coop. Parish Ministries, Memphis Ann. Conf., 1984-88, chmn. Equitable Salary Commn., 1984-88; sec. Munford Ministerial Assn., 1983—; mem. Bd. Ordained Ministry, Brownsville Dist., 1984; mem. Council on Ministries, Brownsville dist., 1984. Mem. adv. bd. Tenn. Dept. Human Services, Tipton County, Covington, 1980-83; mem. Munford Brotherhood, Tenn., 1980-84; chmn. ch. coordinator Celebrate 84 Town Festival, Munford, 1984. Recipient Plaque of Merit, Girl Scouts Am., Munford, 1982-83. Lodge: Masons, Scottish Rite, Order Eastern Star. Home: 216 S Tipton St Munford TN 38058 Office: Munford First United Meth Ch 138 S Tipton St Munford TN 38058

HOLT, JOHN B., educator, minister, educator United Methodist Church; b. Abilene, Tex., June 15, 1915; s. Holland and Emma Cleora (Morriset) H.; B.S., McMurry Coll., 1937, D.D., 1954; postgrad. U. Tex., 1938-39; Th.M., So. Meth. U., 1945; postgrad. U. Chgo., 1958; D.D., Paul Quinn Coll., 1962; m. Margaret Ann Buster, Feb. 14, 1940; children: John Michael, Stephen Lee, Paul Holland. Ordained to ministry, 1944;

youth dir. Central Tex. Conf., 1941-43, exec. sec. Bd. Edn., 1944-46; asso. pastor Austin Ave. Meth. Ch., Waco, Tex., 1946-48; pastor Knox Ch., Manila, 1948-58; assoc. dean Perkins Sch. Theology, So. Meth. U., Dallas, 1958—. Sec., Gen. Conf., United Meth. Ch., 1973—. Trustee Mary Johnston Hosp., Union Theol. Sem., Am. Bible Soc., Philippine Christian Coll. Author: Our Methodist Heritage, 1952; A Study Guide for the Book of Acts, 1956; Financial Aid for Seminarians, 1966; editor: Perkins Perspective, 1958-72; contbr. articles to mags. Office: Perkins Sch Theology So Meth U Dallas TX 75275

HOLT, NOEL CLARK, minister, United Meth. Ch.; b. Cape Girardeau, Mo., Dec. 8, 1935; s. Archie Noel and Dorothy Geraldine (Shaw) H.; B.A., Central Meth. Coll., 1959; M.Div., Garrett-Evang. Theol. Sem., 1963; m. Rosalee Powell, Feb. 27, 1954; children—Sidney Clark, Jennifer Lee, Julie Powell. Ordained to ministry, 1963; pastor Kingswood United Meth. Ch., Buffalo Grove, Ill., 1963-71; sr. pastor Faith United Meth. Ch., Dolton, Ill., 1971—. Mem. No. Ill. Bd. Health and Welfare Ministries, 1968-74; pres. South Suburban Interfaith Clergy Council, 1974-76. Gen. chmn. Sch. Dist. No. 21 Citizen Com., Wheeling, Ill., 1970-71; bd. mem. South Suburban chpt. Am. Heart Assn., 1973—. Mem. ACLU, Inst. Meth. Studies, Pi Gamma Mu, Phi Mu Alpha. Home: 15133 Dante St Dolton IL 60419 Office: 15015 Grant St Dolton IL 60419

HOLTZ, AVRAHAM, seminary educator, Jewish, b. N.Y.C., May 26, 1934; s. Leon and Pauline (Nadel) H.; m. Toby Esther Berger, Dec. 22, 1974; children: Shalom Eliezer, Razelle Devora, Mordecai Yehiel, Miriam Malka. B.A., Bklyn. Coll., 1955; M.H.L., Jewish Theol. Sem., 1959, D.H.L., 1962. Simon H. Fabian prof. Hebrew lit. Jewish Theol. Sem. Am., N.Y.C. Office: Jewish Theol Sem Am 3080 Broadway New York NY 10027

HONEYCUTT, ROY S., JR., seminary adminstrator. Pres. So. Bapt. Theol. Sem., Louisville. Office: So Bapt Theol Sem 2825 Lexington Rd Louisville KY 40206*

HOOD, HULON WOODROW, minister, Assemblies of God; b. Collin County, Tex., Oct. 25, 1918; s. James Jefferson and Evie Eldorado (Foster) H.; student pub. schs., Farmerville, Tex.; m. Eunice Bernice Brummett, Oct. 24, 1936; children: Peggy Jean, Hulon W., Charlotte Ann. Ordained to ministry, 1949; pastor 1st Assembly of God Ch., Mesquite, Tex., 1947-85; now in spl. ministry; speaker Words of Life, sta. KSKY, Dallas, also Mid-Day Devotions, sta. KDTX, Dallas, also TV program Words of Life, sta. KDFW, Dallas. Committeeman North Dallas Sect., Assemblies of God, 1957-69, sec.-treas., 1969-73, presbyter, 1973—; organizational founder Mesquite Ministerial Alliance, 1956, pres., 1969; pres. Greater Dallas Pastors Assn., 1962-66. Mem. adv. com. Mesquite United Fund, 1971-75. Mem. Mesquite C. of C. Home: 1018 Lakeview St Mesquite TX 75149

HOOD, TAYLOR MAC, minister, United Meth. Ch.; b. Longview, Tex., Jan. 27, 1938; s. James Taylor and Hedy (McCoy) H.; B.S., N. Tex. State U., 1960; S.T.B., Wesley Theol. Sem., 1964, Th.M., 1964; S.T.D., Wesley Theol. Sem./Galilean U., 1965; postgrad U. Edinburg (Scotland), 1974; m. Emma Lou Stewart, Aug. 30, 1959; children—Michael Stewart, David Wesley. Ordained to ministry, 1962; asso. pastor Westbury United Meth. Ch., Houston, 1964-66; pastor, Alta Loma, 1966-69, Pleasant Retreat Ch., Tyler, Tex., 1969-72, Holy Trinity Meth. Ch., Houston, 1972—. Missionary, Chile, 1971; mem. Tex. ann. conf. Bd. Evangelism; chmn. bd. disciplineship Tex. ann. conf., treas. bd. ministry. Home: 13102 Corpus Christi St Houston TX 77015 Office: 13207 Orleans St Houston TX 77015

HOOKER, ROBERT LEROY, minister, Luth. Ch. Am.; b. Kanawah, Iowa, Aug. 30, 1921; s. Robert Kelsey and Lavigne Ethyl (Tobias) H.; B.A., Carthage Coll., 1943; Th.M., Chgo. Luth. Sem., 1945; m. Edith Sarah Lambert, Feb. 18, 1945; children—Ronald, Renel. Ordained to ministry, 1945; pastor 1st English Luth. Ch., San Francisco, 1945-46, Mt. Calvary Luth. Ch., DeSoto, Ill., 1946-50; supt. home missions Ill. Synod, Luth. Ch. Am., 1950-53; pastor Grace Luth. Ch., Woodstock, Ill., 1953-63, Epiphany Ch., Elmhurst, Ill., 1963-76, Faith Luth. Ch., Homewood, Ill., 1976—. Home: 18719 Highland Ave Homewood IL 60430 Office: 186th Pl and Dixie Hwy Homewood IL 60430

HOOPER, WILLIAM RALEIGH, minister, United Meth. Ch.; b. Whitewright, Tex., Dec. 15, 1928; s. Walter Raleigh and Mary Pauline (Devenport) H.; A.A., Lon Morris Coll., 1948; B.B.A., U. Tex., 1950; B.D., So. Meth. U., 1961; m. Ruby Nell Kimmons, Feb. 13, 1949; 1 son, William Raleigh. Ordained to ministry, 1961; dir. adult work bd. edn. Tex. conf., Palestine, 1961-63; pastor Holmes Chapel Meth. Ch., Palestine, 1963-66, Elkhart (Tex.) Meth. Ch., 1966-67, Buna (Tex.) United Meth. Ch., 1967-71, First United Meth. Ch., Trinity, Tex., 1971-73, Danville United Meth. Ch., Kilgore, Tex., 1973-74, Asbury United Meth. Ch., Tyler, Tex., 1974-75, Velasco First United Meth. Ch., Freeport, Tex., 1975—. Winning editor of local church communication contest United Meth. Communications Council of Tex., 1975. Home: 515 N Ave B Freeport TX 77541 Office: 320 N Ave A Freeport TX 77541

HOOTEN, LAWRENCE KENNETH, II, minister, Presbyterian Church in the U.S.A.; b. North Charleroi, Pa., Sept. 8, 1946; s. Lawrence Kenneth Sr. and Hazel Virginia (Dolan) H.; m. Judith Ann Hall, Aug. 23, 1969; 1 dau., Errin Elizabeth. B.Music Edn. with honors, Grove City Coll., 1968; M.Div. cum laude, Pitts. Theol. Sem., 1971, D.Min., 1984. Ordained to ministry Presbyn. Ch. (U.S.A.), 1971. Assoc. pastor Union Presbyn. Ch., Endicott, N.Y., 1971-74; pastor Wickliffe Presbyn. Ch., Youngstown, Ohio, 1974-79, Gray Stone Presbyn. Ch., Leechburg, Pa., 1979—; pres. bd. trustees Kiskiminetas Presbytery, Pa., 1984, sec. com. ministry, 1981-84; commr. gen. assembly Presbyn. Ch. in the U.S., 1984; coordinator religious TV spots, Youngstown, 1977-79. Steering com. Leechburg Counseling Ctr., 1979—; bd. dirs. Kiski Valley Y.M.C.A., Vandergrift, Pa., 1984-85, Fish-Samaritan House, Youngstown, 1976-79. Recipient McConkey Prize in Homiletics Pitts. Theol. Sem., 1970. Mem. Kiskiminetas Presbytery, Leechburg Ministerial Assn. (sec., treas. 1981-85). Democrat. Club: Hillcrest Racquet (Lower Burrell, Pa.). Home: 218 First St Leechburg PA 15656 Office: Gray Stone Presbyn Ch First & Main Sts Leechburg PA 15656

HOPKINS, ELLIS ARTHUR, lay worker, United Church of Christ; b. Rensselaer, Ind., Dec. 15, 1912; s. Arthur Herbert and Martha Crowel Alice (Ellis) H.; m. Vera Catherine Schaaf, Apr. 16, 1946; 1 son, Stephen Ellis H. Student U. Chgo., 1930-32; B.E., Ind. U., 1937, M.A., 1950; postgrad. U. Iowa, summer 1953, Purdue U., 1952. Mem. Bd. Homeland Ministries, United Ch. of Christ, 1976-85, div. health and welfare, 1976-78, div. evangelism and ch. devel., 1978—; mem. Commn. on Evangelism and Worship, Ind.-Ky. Conf. United Ch. of Christ, 1979-82, edn. for mission com., 1977-83; v.p. Western Assn., Ind.-Ky. Conf. United Ch. of Christ, 1979-81, pres., 1981-83; deacon Immanuel United Ch. of Christ, Lafayette, Ind., 1961-64, elder, 1966-69, v.p. congregation, 1967-68, pres. congregation, 1968-69, mem. scholarship com., 1971-82, mem. pulpit com. for selection of pastor, 1972, mem. Bd. Christian Edn., 1979-81, Sunday Sch. tchr., 1970-74, 76-77, vol. to shut-ins, 1976-79; active in planning and conducting religious services Westminster Village, Lafayette, 1978—. Bd. dirs. Tippecanoe County Hist. Assn., 1961-68; mem. exec. com. Palatines to Am., 1977-78; mem. absent voter team, dep. registrar, Tippecanoe County, 1974, 76-84; vol. Am. Cancer Soc., 1978-82. Served to capt. U.S. Army, 1942-47; lt. col. USAFR, ret. Recipient Service award Ind. Council for Social Studies, 1949; Service award Ind. State Tchrs. Assn., 1964, Service award and plaque of appreciation Jefferson High Sch., Lafayette, 1973, Meml. Day award City of Lafayette, 1983. Mem. NEA (life), Nat. Ret. Tchrs. Assn. (life), Ind. Ret. Tchrs. Assn., Benton-Tippecanoe Ret. Tchrs. Assn., Res. Officers Assn., Air Force Assn., SAR (Service medal 1946), Am. Legion, Phi Delta Theta, Phi Delta Kappa. Republican. Lodge: Masons. Home: 2741 N Salisbury St Apt 2408 West Lafayette IN 47906

HOPKINS, JESSE EVANS, JR., minister of music, Church of the Brethren; music educator; b. Pulaski, Va., Apr. 24, 1948; s. Jesse Evans and Arbutus (Hamilton) H.; m. Alice Lee Murray, July 9, 1973. . B.S., Bridgewater Coll., 1970; M. Music Edn., James Madison U., 1976; postgrad., U. Ill., Dir. music Dayton United Meth. Ch., Va., 1969-70, Central United Meth. Ch., Staunton, Va., 1970-72, Bridgewater Ch. of the Brethren, Bridgewater, Va., 1973—; deacon, peace com. mem. Bridgewater Ch. of the Brethren, 1975-78, 80-83; sponsor Bridgewater Coll. Brethren Youth Fellowship, 1978—; mem. On Earth Peace, 1981—. Adv. bd. The Brethren Hymnal, 1984—. Mem. Music Educators Nat. Conf., Am. Choral Dirs. Assn. (life), Am. Guild English Handbell Ringers, Phi Delta Kappa. Democrat. Lodge: Rotary Internat. (dir. Bridgewater chpt. 1979—). Home: 118 W College St Bridgewater VA 22812 Office: Bridgewater Coll Bridgewater VA 22812

HOPPE, NEIL W., minister, American Baptist Churches in the U.S.A.; b. Portage, Wis., June 12, 1931; s. Lloyd Jacob and Eunice Evelyn (Noble) H.; m. Ann Rankin Mungo, May 28, 1953; children: Scott Carlton, Pamela Hoppe White, Sharon Hoppe McClung, Lisa. B.A., Bob Jones U., 1953; B.Div., No. Bapt. Theol. Sem., 1956, M.Div., 1973; D.Min., Luther Rice Sem., 1979. Ordained to ministry Baptist Ch., 1955. Pastor Wood Street Bapt. Ch., Aurora, Ill., 1955-57, First Bapt. Ch., Sheboygan, Wis., 1957-64, First Bapt. Ch., Sheboygan Falls, Wis., 1962-64, Lincoln Bapt. Ch., Columbus, Ohio, 1964-71, Twentieth Street Bapt. Ch., Huntington, W.Va., 1971—. Trustee Cabell Huntington Hosp., W.Va., 1974—, chmn.-pres. 1976-80. Mem. W.Va. Bapt. Conv., W.Va. Bapt. Ministerial Assn., Guyandotte Bapt. Assn., Guyandotte Ministers Assn. (pres. 1973-74), Guyandotte Bapt. Ministerial Assn., Huntington Ministerial Assn. (pres. 1976). Home: 3167 Sumner Ave Huntington WV 25705 Office: Twentieth Street Bapt Ch 20th St and 5th Ave Huntington WV 25703

HOPPERT, EARL WILLIAM, chaplain educator, counselor, United Church of Christ; b. Duluth, Minn., Nov. 14, 1939; s. Glenn A. and Margaret J. (Server) H.; m. Candice N. Leuthold, Dec. 26, 1974; children: Lesley, Kelly. A.A. with honors, N.D. State Sch. Sci., 1959; B.A. magna cum laude, Yankton Coll., 1961; M.Div., Andover Newton Theol. Sem., 1965; postgrad. U. Glasgow, Scotland, 1965-68; D.Ministry, Christian Theol. Sem., Indpls., 1982. Ordained to ministry United Ch. of Christ, 1965. Asst. pastor Tron Ch., Balornock, Scotland, 1967-68; pastor First Congl. Ch., Eastlake, Colo., 1968-72, United Ch. of Christ, Westminster, Colo., 1968-72; chaplain resident Meth. Hosp., Rochester, Minn., 1972-73; chaplain intern/resident St. Luke's Hosp., Milw., 1973-75; chaplain educator, head dept. pastoral care Central State Hosp., Indpls., 1975—; staff counselor Pastoral Counseling Service, Christian Theol. Sem., Indpls., 1980—. Contbr. articles to profl. jours. Founder, chmn. patient advocacy com. Central State Hosp., 1979—. Recipient Outstanding DeMolay award Internat. DeMolay Assn., 1960, ESTARL award N.D. Eastern Star, 1961, 63, 65, 66, 67; Edward J. Frost scholar, 1961, scholar United Ch. of Christ, 1965, 66, 67; Turner fellow, 1965; grantee Ind. Dept. Mental Health, 1976-82. Mem. Am. Assn. Pastoral Counselors (cert.), Assn. Clin. Pastoral Edn., Inc. (life, cert. supr., facilitator suprs. group). Democrat. Clubs: DeMolay (Wahpeton, N.D.)(master counselor 1957-59), Central State Hosp. Golf League. Lodges: Masons, Royal Arch (lectr. 1966-68). Home: 9001 Caminito Ct Indianapolis IN 46234 Office: Central State Hosp Dept Pastoral Care 3000 W Washington St Indianapolis IN 46222

HORATH, DONALD EUGENE, minister, Bethel Ministerial Association, Inc.; b. Decatur, Ill., July 2, 1941; s. Floyd Harvey and Madelia Marie (Roberts) H.; m. Vickie Darleane Koontz, Aug. 28, 1960; children: Lorie, Bryan, Kevin. Assoc. degree, Bethel Ministerial Acad., 1984. Ordained to ministry Bethel Ministerial Assn., 1963. Pastor Hillside Bethel Tabernacle, Decatur, 1961—; vice chmn. Bethel Ministerial Assn., Evansville, Ind., 1983—, chmn. credential com., 1983—; pastor and tchr. TV ministry, 1982—; camp speaker Circle J Ranch, Lynnville, Ind., evangelist Central Ill., 1980—. Mem. Full Gospel Minister Fellowship (chmn. 1980-81), Decatur Area Clergy (steering com. 1984-85). Democrat. Home: 4535 Hilltop Blvd Decatur IL 62521 Office: Hillside Bethel Tabernacle 3575 Greenhill Rd Decatur IL 62521

HORDERN, WILLIAM EDWARD, Lutheran minister, religious educator; b. Dundurn, Sask., Can., Sept. 8, 1920; s. Paul Sylvester and Ethyl (Davis) H.; m. Marjorie Edith Joyce, Jan. 28, 1944; children: Richard, Joyce, Davis. B.A., U. Sask., 1941; B.D., St. Andrew's Coll., Sask., 1945; S.T.M., Union Theol. Sem., N.Y.C., 1946, Th.D., 1951; D.D. (hon.), St. Andrew's Coll., 1968. Ordained minister, United Ch. Can., 1943; pastor Marsden-Neilburg Parish, Marsden-Neilburg, Sask., 1943-45; assoc. prof. Swarthmore Coll., 1949-57; prof. theology Garrett Theol. Sem., Evanston, Ill., 1957-66; pres. Luth. Theol. Sem., Sask., Sask., Can., 1966—; dir. Luth. Life Ins. of Can., Waterloo, 1971—. Author: Christianity, Communism and History, 1954; A Layman's Guide to Protestant Theology, 1955, rev. edit., 1968; The Case for a New Reformation Theology, 1959; Speaking of God, 1964; New Directions in Theology Today, 1966; Living by Grace, 1976; Faith and Experience, 1983; co-author: The Holy Spirit Shy Member of the Trinity, 1984. New Democrat. Clubs: Saskatoon Golf, Saskatoon Country. Office: Luth Theol Sem 114 Seminary Crescent Saskatoon SK S7N 0X3 Canada

HORKAN, THOMAS A., JR., religious organization executive, Roman Catholic Church; b. Miami, Fla., Nov. 10, 1927; s. Thomas A. and Agnes (O'Dowd) H.; m. Ann C. Munley, Sept. 2, 1957; children: Thomas, Jacquelyn, Timothy, Louise. A.B., U. Miami, Fla., 1948, LL.B., 1950. Exec. dir. Fla. Cath. Conf., Tallahassee, 1969—. Vice-pres. Casa Calderon Home for Aged, Tallahassee, 1980—; treas. Fla. Assn. Vol. Agys. for Caribbean Action, 1982—. Mem. ABA, Fla. Bar Assn., Nat. Assn. State Cath. Conf. Dirs. (pres. 1978-80), Delta Theta Phi. Lodge: Serra (pres. 1976-78, 82-83) (Tallahassee). Home: 2344 Limerick Dr Tallahassee FL 32308 Office: Fla Cath Conf PO Box 1571 Tallahassee FL 32302

HORN, PAUL ERVIN, minister, Conservative Baptist Assn. Am.; b. Grinnell, Iowa, Mar. 24, 1919; s. Harry Edgar and Florence Henrietta (Bump) H.; m. Elvis Devlin, Dec. 21, 1940; children: Sandra, Larry, Cynthia. B.A., San Jose State U., 1942; M.Div., Berkeley Bapt. Div. Sch., 1945; Ph.D., Calif. Grad. Sch. Theology, 1973. Ordained to ministry Conservative Bapt. Assn. Am., 1945. Pastor, Elmhurst Bapt. Ch., Oakland, Calif., 1945-55, Bell Baptist Ch., Cudahy, Calif., 1955-66, First Bapt. Ch., Montclair, Calif., 1966-77, Calvary Bapt. Ch., Hemet, Calif., 1977-83, First Bapt. Ch., Wrightwood, Calif., 1984—; bd. dirs. Conservative Bapt. Assn. So. Calif., Anaheim, 1956—, pres., 1959-60; bd. dirs. Conservative Bapt. Home Mission Soc., Wheaton, Ill., 1960-66; parlimentarian Conservative Bapt. Assn. Am., Wheaton, 1950—, western v.p., 1967-74. Republican. Avocation: photography. Office: First Bapt Ch PO Box 212 Wrightwood CA 92397

HORN, WILLIAM EVERETT, minister, So. Bapt. Conv.; b. Oak Park, Ill., Dec. 25, 1944; s. David Edward and Valda L. (Johnson) H.; B.S., Mo. Valley Coll., 1967; M.Th., New Orleans Bapt. Theol. Sem., 1972; m. Sarah Lawton Holloway, Mar. 29, 1970; 1 son, Nathan Everett. Ordained to ministry, 1968; pastor Tex. and Mo. chs., 1967-69; pastor Vacherie (La.) Bapt. Mission, 1970-73, Santa Fe Hills Bapt. Ch., Kansas City, Mo., 1973-76, Ch. of Abundant Life, 1976—; chaplain Dinner Playhouse, Inc., 1976—. Mem. Am. Humanics Found., Insts. of Religion and Health, Alpha Phi Omega. Lyricist: On This Day: an Easter Cantata, 1974; My New Song: a Christmas Cantata, 1974. Compiler: Introduction to Deaf Sign Language, 1976; writer Conv. Sunday Sch. lessons: Word and Way, 1977; author weekly newspaper column, 1976—. Home and Office: 809 W 89th St Kansas City MO 64114

HORNER, NORMAN ASTE, minister, Presbyterian Ch. in U.S.A.; b. Denver, Sept. 6, 1913; s. John Willard and Lillian Rose (Aste) H.; B.A., Coll. Emporia (Kans.), 1935; B.D., Louisville Presbyn. Theol. Sem., 1938; M.A., Kennedy Sch. Missions, Hartford, Conn., 1950; Ph.D., Hartford Sem. Found., 1956; m. Esther May Daniels, Dec. 16, 1940. Ordained to ministry, 1938; missionary/tchr., Cameroun, W.Africa, 1938-49; dean, prof. mission and ecumenics Louisville Presbyn. Theol. Sem., 1949-68; cons. ecumenical relationships in Middle East, United Presbyn. Ch. in U.S.A., Beirut, 1968-76; prof. Near East Sch. Theology, Beirut, 1974-76; assoc. dir. Overseas Ministries Study Center, Ventnor, N.J., 1976-82. Mem. Assn. Profs. Missions, Am. Soc. Missiology, Internat. Assn. Mission Studies. Author: Cross and Crucifix in Mission, 1965; Protestant Crosscurrents in Mission, 1968; Rediscovering Christianity Where It Began, 1974. Home: 2520 Glenmary Ave Louisville KY 40204

HORTON, JERRY SMITH, minister, United Methodist Church; b. Columbus, Miss., Oct. 6, 1941; s. William Robert and Sarah Elizabeth (Smith) H.; m. Patricia Jan Taylor, May 30, 1964; children: Thomas Christian, William Andrew. A.A., Wood Jr. Coll., 1963; B.A. in Edn., U. Miss., 1968; M.Div., Emory U., 1972. Ordained to ministry United Meth. Ch., 1973. Minister various chs. in Miss. and Ga., 1962-72; assoc. minister Southaven First United Meth. Ch., Miss., 1972-74; minister Minor Meml. United Meth. Ch., Walls, Miss., 1974-81; parish dir. Iuka First United Meth. Ch., Miss., 1981-84; minister Belzoni First United Meth. Ch., Miss., 1984—; mem. bd. diaconal ministries No. Miss. Conf., United Meth. Ch., 1972-74, mem. commn. on equitable salaries, 1981—. Named one of Outstanding Young Men of Am., 1976, Top Evangelistic Pastor of Conf., 1981; honored with Spl. Proclamation, Mayor of Iuka. Lodge: Rotary. Avocations: hunting, scuba diving, fishing; youth work; writing devotions. Home: 208 Central Ave Belzoni MS 39038 Office: First United Meth Ch 202 Castleman St Belzoni MS 39038

HORTON, O. CHARLES, pastor, Southern Baptist Convention; b. Palatka, Fla., Nov. 18, 1937; s. Alva E. and Estelle (Minton) H.; m. Carolyn DeLoach, Sept. 6, 1957; children: Holli Suzanne, Vincent Charles. B.A., Stetson U., 1959; M.Div., Southwestern Bapt. Theol. Sem., Ft. Worth, 1962; M.Th., New Orleans Bapt. Theol. Sem., 1967, D.Ministry, 1975. Ordained to ministry Southern Baptist, 1956. Student pastor, Oakland, Fla., 1956-59, Whitewright, Tex., 1960-62, Baton Rouge, 1963-64; pastor First Bapt. Ch., Lake Alfred, Fla., 1964-66, Flagami Bapt. Ch., Miami, Fla., 1966-77, Coll. Park Bapt. Ch., Orlando, Fla., 1977—; mem. budget allocations com. State Bd. Missions, Fla. Bapt. Conv., 1969-72, vice chmn. nominating com., 1970-71; chmn. constn. and by-laws com. Miami Bapt. Assn., 1970-72, chmn. fin. com., 1972-74, moderator, 1975-76, chmn. Bapt. campus ministry com., 1970-74, mem. civic righteousness com., 1969-71, credentials com., 1971-73; program chmn. Miami Pastors Conf., 1973-74; mem. fin. com. Greater Orlando Bapt. Assn., 1978-80, mem. personnel com., 1984-85; trustee Bapt. Hosp., Miami, 1975-77; trustee Southeastern Bapt. Theol. Sem., Wake Forest, N.C., 1975—, vice chmn. bd., 1984-85, chmn. instrn. com., 1981-84, chmn. bd. dirs., 1985—; mem. campus ministry proposal com. Fla. Internat. U., Miami, 1968-70; mem. exec. com. Billy Graham Central Fla. Crusade, 1983; pres. Fla. Bapt. Pastors Conf., 1984. Pres., Polk County Mental Health Assn., 1963-65. Democrat. Lodge: Orlando Kiwanis. Home: 3913 Lake Sarah Dr Orlando FL 32804 Office: College Park Bapt Ch 1914 Edgewater Dr Orlando FL 32804

HORTON, THOMAS WALTER, JR., minister Presbyterian Church (U.S.A.); b. Spartanburg, S.C., Sept. 4, 1926; s. Thomas Walter and Mary Hester (Estes) H.; m. Sue Allston Royall, May 23, 1950; children: Mary Courtenay Horton Brown, Susan Allston Horton Willet, Thomas Walter III. A.B., Presbyn. Coll., Clinton, S.C., 1945; B.D., Columbia Sem., 1948, M.Div., 1971; D.Min., McCormick Sem., 1976; D.D., Presbyn. Coll., 1972. Ordained to ministry Presbyterian Church (U.S.A.) 1948. Pastor, Sullivans Island Church (S.C.), 1948-50, Mt. Pleasant Presbyn. Ch. (S.C.), 1948-61; presbytery exec. Charleston Presbytery (S.C.), 1961-74, Bethel Presbytery, Rock Hill, S.C., 1974—. Chmn. bd. William Brearley Home, Montreat, N.C., 1976—; mem. nominating com. Gen. Assembly Presbyn. Ch. USA, 1983—. Democrat. Lodge: Rotary. Home: 843 Milton Ave Rock Hill SC 29730 Office: Bethel Presbytery 515 Oakland Ave Rock Hill SC 29730

HORTON, WADE H., gen. overseer Ch. of God (Cleveland, Tenn.). Address: Keith St at 25th NW Cleveland TN 37311*

HOSE, JOHN HENRY, minister emeritus, Universal Fellowship of Metropolitan Community Churches; b. Massillon, Ohio, June 11, 1914; s. Henry Fred and Augusta Edna (Zerbe) H.; m. Ruth Maxine Schmidt, Nov. 21, 1940 (div.); children: Martha Jane Hose Welti, Mary Maxine Hose Strange. A.B., Elmhurst Coll. (Ill.), 1937; B.D., Eden Theol. Sem., 1940; M.S. in Edn., U. So. Calif., 1971. Ordained to ministry Evangelical and Reformed Ch., 1969. Pastor, Evang. and Reformed Ch., Belleville, Ill., 1937, 40, Trinity Evang. and Reformed Ch., Carrollton, Ohio, 1940-42, Evang. and Reformed St. Paul's Ch., Woodsfield, Ohio, 1942-43, Pilgrim Evang. and Reformed Ch., Zanesville, Ohio, 1943-46, Met. Community Ch., San Diego, 1970-74, Tampa, Fla., 1974-79; pastor emeritus Met. Community Ch., Atlanta, 1979—; elder Universal Fellowship Met. Community Ch., Los Angeles, 1969-81, elder emeritus, 1983; treas., 1980-81; pres. Samaritan Inst. Theology, Los Angeles, 1970-74; prof. religion U. So. Fla., Tampa, 1976-79. Author: Statement of Faith Universal Fellowship of Metropolitan Community Church, 1969; Religion in the Contemporary Scene, 1977. Contbr. articles to religious jours. Bd. dirs. Samaritan Hosp., Zanesville, Ohio, 1944; mem. gov.'s ad hoc com., Tampa, 1978-79. HEW fellow U. So. Calif., 1970-71. Mem. Samaritan Inst. Theology (bd. regents), ACLU (bd. dirs. 1971-74, vice chmn. 1975-79). Lodge: Kiwanis. Home: 459 Euclid Terr NE Atlanta GA 30307 Office: Met Community Ch PO Box 8356 Atlanta GA 30306

HOSEA, ADDISON, bishop, Episcopal Ch.; b. Pikeville, N.C., Sept. 11, 1914; s. Addison and Alma Eugenia (Bowden) H.; student U. N.C., 1930-31; A.B., Atlantic Christian Coll., 1938; M.Div., U. of South, 1949, D.D., 1970; postgrad. student Union Theol. Sem., 1948, Duke, 1950-53; D.D., Episcopal Theol. Sem. Ky., 1968; m. Jane Eubank Marston, June 24, 1944; children—Nancy Jane, Addison III, Anne Cameron. Ordained deacon Episcopal Ch., 1948, priest, 1949, consecrated bishop, 1970; priest-in-charge St. Gabriel's Ch., Faison, N.C., 1949-51; rector St. Paul's Ch., Clinton, N.C., 1949-54; rector St. John's Ch., Versailles, Ky., 1954-70; bishop-coadjutor of the Diocese of Lexington (Ky.), 1970, bishop of Lexington, 1971—; prof. N.T., Lang. and Lit. Episcopal Theol. Sem. Ky., 1954-59, 65-70; mem. exec. council Diocese of East Carolina, 1951-54, Diocese of Lexington, 1954-70, mem. standing com., 1957-58, 1960-64; examining chaplain of Lexington, 1964-70; hon. canon Cathedral of St. George the Martyr, 1964-70; dep. to Epis. Gen. Conv., 1955, 58, 64, 67, 69. Trustee U. of the South, 1949-54, 70—. Mem. Soc. Bibl. Lit. Home: 536 Sayre Ave Lexington KY 40508 Office: 530 Sayre Ave Lexington KY 40508

HOSEA, EARL EDWARD, minister, Southern Baptist Convention; b. Houston, Nov. 3, 1930; s. Lee G. and Winnie (Lee) H.; m. Eleanor Jane White, July 25, 1950; children: Elva Jane, Debra Anne, James David, Michael Walter. Student U. Corpus Christi, 1960-63. Ordained to ministry Baptist Ch., 1961. Pastor chs. in Tex., 1965-73, Nev., 1972-81, Keystone Bapt. Ch., Carson, Calif., 1981—; vice-moderator Long Beach Harbor Bapt. Assn., Calif., 1983—; program chmn. Long Beach Pastors Conf., 1982—. Bd. dirs. Stovall Found., Los Angeles, 1984. Nev. Spl. Olympics 1976 Games dedicated to him. Democrat. Office: Keystone Baptist Ch 435 W 220th St Carson CA 90745

HOSTETTER, HENRY NEFF, bishop, Brethren in Christ Ch.; b. Manor Twp., Pa., Oct. 8, 1902; s. Christian Newcomer and Ella Brubaker (Neff) H.; student Messiah Coll., 1918-20; m. Beula Viola Hess, Jan. 19, 1924; 1 dau., Alice Grace (Mrs. John Zercher). Ordained to ministry, 1929, bishop, 1942; Sunday sch. tchr., supt., youth worker in Lancaster, Manor and Pequea Brethren in Christ Chs., 1918-29; mem. bd. Young Peoples Work, Brethren in Christ Ch., 1931-49; sec. Bd. for Youth Work, Brethren in Christ Ch., 1937-48; commd. to visit Brethren in Christ Missions in Rhodesia, Zambia and India, 1948-49; exec. sec. Bd. Fgn. Missions, 1951-66; exec. dir. Brethren in Christ World Missions, 1966-70; pastor Manor Brethren in Christ Ch., 1970-74; field rep. Commn. Stewardship and Fin., Brethren in Christ Ch., 1974—; chmn. Manor Area Christian Fellowship, 1973—. mem. Council Mission Bd. Secs. (affiliate Mennonite Central Com., Akron, Pa.), 1958-70; assigned to visit all Mennonite Central Com. related missions in Africa, 1960; visited Australian missions, 1961; supr. opening of Brethren in Christ missions in Japan, 1953, Cuba, 1954, Nicaragua, 1964; bd. dirs. Evang. Fgn. Missions Assn., 1964-70, treas. bd., 1966-70. Recipient citation Bd. for Young Peoples Work, 1949, plaque Bd. World Missions, 1970. Contbr. articles to religious publs. Home: Rural Route 1 Washington Borough PA 17582 Office: 49 S Market St Elizabethtown PA 17022

HOTCHKIN, JOHN FRANCIS, ch. ofcl., Roman Cath. Ch.; b. Chgo., Feb. 3, 1935; s. John Edward and Sarah Jane (Cure) H.; B.A., St. Mary of the Lake Sem., Mundelein, Ill., 1954; S.T.L., Pontifical Gregorian U., Rome, 1960, S.T.D. cum laude, 1966. Ordained priest Roman Catholic Ch., 1959; asso. pastor Christ the King Parish, Chgo., 1960-64, St. Therese Parish, Chgo., 1966; asso. dir. Bishop's Com. for Ecumenical and Inter-religious Affairs, Nat. Conf. Cath. Bishops, Washington, 1967-71, exec. dir., 1971—. Consultor, Vatican Secretariat for Promoting Christian Unity, 1972—, Vatican Secretariat for Non-Christians, 1985—. Recipient award Cath. Press Assn., 1969. Mem. Cath. Theol. Soc. Am., N.Am. Acad. Ecumenists, Ecumenical Officers Assn. Office: 1312 Massachusetts Ave NW Washington DC 20005

HOTCHKISS, JOE VAUGHN, minister, denominational exec., Nat. Council Community Chs.; b. Howland Twp., Ohio, Aug. 25, 1926; s. Ray and Frances May (Vaughn) lH.; student Kent State U., 1947-50, Youngstown State U., U. Mich., 1951-52; m. Lillian Newey, May 1953. Ordained to ministry, 1976; pastor 1st Meth. Ch., Jefferson, Ohio, 1951, Ohio, 1952-53; elder Howland Community Ch., Warren, Ohio, 1956-66; exec. dir. Nat. Council Community Chs., Worthington, Ohio, 1966—. Guest chaplain U.S. Senate, 1967; mem. religious council Religion in Am. Life, 1970; dir. agr. missions, 1971-72. Mem. U. Mich. Alumni Assn. Contbr. articles to Christian Community newspaper. Home: 29 Lynette S Westerville OH 43081 Office: 89 E Wilson Bridge Rd Worthington OH 43085

HOUCK, JOHN ROLAND, organization executive, Lutheran Church U.S.A.; b. Balt., Apr. 15, 1923; s. Walter Webb and Wilhelmina Anna (Pfaff) H.; m. Minerva Arline Wiessinger, Nov. 28, 1947; children: John Roland, James Michael, David Walter, Paul Harold. B.A., Capital U., Columbus, Ohio, 1947; D.D. (hon.), 1976; B.D., Evang. Luth. Sem., 1950. Ordained to ministry American Lutheran Church U.S.A., 1950. Pastor St. Michael Luth. Ch., Perry Hall, Md., 1950-60; regional dir. Bd. Am. Missions, Am. Luth. Ch., Washington, 1960-67; assoc. exec. sec. div. mission services Luth. Ch. U.S.A., N.Y.C., 1967-70, gen. sec., 1979—; dir. Bd. Am. Missions, Am. Luth. Ch., Mpls., 1970-73, dir. div. service and mission, 1974-79. Bd. dirs. Religion in Am. Life, N.Y.C., 1984—; trustee Luth. Med. Ctr., Bklyn., 1981—. Democrat. Office: Luth Council USA 360 Park Ave S New York NY 10010

HOUCK, WILLIAM RUSSELL, bishop, Roman Catholic Church. Aux. bishop, Jackson, Mich., 1979-89, bishop, 1984—. Office: 237 E Amite St PO Box 2248 Jackson MI 39205*

HOUSE, ALVIN JUSTUS, JR., minister, religious supply company executive, American Evangelical Christian Churches; b. Canandaigua, N.Y., Jan. 27, 1926; s. Alvin Justus and Wilhelmina Anna (Osgood) H.; m. Dorothy Anne Adamson, Aug. 8, 1947; children: Carolyn, Philip, Esther. A.B. in Religion, NW Nazarene Coll., 1950. Ordained to ministry Church of the Nazarene, 1951. Pastor Ch. of Nazarene, Glasgow and Hashua, Mont., 1950-52, Helena, Mont., 1952-59; pastor Evang. Covenant Ch., Helena, 1960-63; mgr. Christian Supply Ctr., Bozeman, Mont., 1963—; pastor Dry Creek Bible Ch., Belgrade, Mont., 1964-78; Gallatin Gateway Christian Ch., Mont., 1980-84; interim pastor Livingston Bible Ch., Mont., 1984—; sec. Christian Enterprises, Inc., 1968—; sec., treas. Light of Life, Inc.; chmn. various Billy Graham film crusades, 1965. Mem. adv. bd. Salvation Army, Bozeman, 1972—. Served with U.S. Army, 1944-46. ETO. Mem. Nat. Assn. Evangs., Christian Booksellers Assn., Am. Watchmakers Inst., Mont. Assn. Evangs. (past pres., sec. 1983—), Greater Bozeman Assn. Evangs. (pres. 1970—). Republican. Avocations: watchmaking; gardening; reading. Home: 3310 Stucky Rd Bozeman MT 59715 Office: Christian Supply Ctr PO Box 1089 2630 W Main Bozeman MT 59715

HOUSEAL, REUBEN ARTHUR, clergyman, educator, writer, Independent Fundamental Churches America; b. York, Pa., Jan. 6, 1910; s. John Franklin and Beatrice Vervean (Dellinger) H.; grad. Phila. Coll. Bible, 1932; tchrs. diploma Evang. Tchr. Tng. Assn., Glen Ellyn, Ill., 1932; M.A., U. Pa., 1935; postgrad. Ref. Episcopal Theol. Sem., 1934-37; Th.D., Clarksville Sch. Theology, 1973, L.L.D., 1974, Ph.D. in Religion, 1977; m. Jennie Belle Hinkle, June 1, 1929 (dec. Feb. 6, 1964); m. 2d, Marguerite Edna Ruth Arnold, Nov. 26, 1964; children—Reuben John, Elisabeth June (Mrs. James Page Honecker), Lawrence Garrison. Ordained to ministry Ind. Fundamental Chs. Am., 1940; pastor Bethany Community Ch., Dayton, Ohio, 1937-40, Olive Br. Congl. Ch., St. Louis, 1941-45, Central Bapt. Ch., Erie, Pa., 1950-57; cons. ednl. dept. Ency. Brit., 1957-62; exec. bd., faculty Greensburg (Pa.) Bible Inst., 1960-71; co-founder, acad. dean Calvary Sch. Theology, Mercer, Pa., 1974—. Founder, dir. GospeLiteHouse of the Air, Ohio, Ill., Mo., Mich., Pa., 1942-57; instl. chaplain Mercer County, Pa. Bible Conf. Evangelistic Ministry, 1967—; chmn. Nat. Ind. Fundamental Chs. Am. Commn. on Instl. Chaplains, 1972—. Commd. Ky. col., 1977. Author: Enoch's Monumental Masterpiece-The Great Pyramid of Gizeh, 1945; Halloween-Is It Christian or Pagan?, 1964; Why We Are

Not Ecumenists, 1967; What About Faith Healing, 1971; Holiness, Carnality, and Parental Discipline, 1975, others; contbr. articles to numerous religious jours.; writer Weekly Meditation column, 1960—. Home: 132 S Erie St Mercer PA 16137

HOUSER, C. RAYMOND, minister, Church of God, Anderson, Indiana; b. Wichita, Kans., June 20, 1952; s. Veryle Eldon and Wanda Viola (Holloway) H.; m. Christina Marie Hurt, June 18, 1976; 1 child, Jarad Benjamin. B.A., Anderson Coll., 1974; M.Min., Anderson Sch. Theology, 1976. Ordained to ministry, 1979. Asst. pastor Larchmont Ch. of God, Louisville, 1973-75; youth pastor Garden Grove Ch. of God, Calif., 1976-77; assoc. pastor First Ch. of God, Fresno, Calif., 1977-79; pastor Ch. of the Foothills, Pasadena, 1979-83, Central Community Ch., Hanford, Calif., 1983—; bd. dirs. Camp Oakhurst, Calif., 1983—; youth camp dir. Central and No. Calif., Diamond Arrow, 1978, 79, So. Calif., Oakhurst, 1982, Central and So. Calif., 1983, 84. Contbr. articles to profl. jours. Mem. Hanford Ministerial Assn. (co-pres.). Lodge: Kiwanis (1st v.p.). Home: 1093 N Williams St Hanford CA 93230 Office: Central Community Ch 1100 N Redington Hanford CA 93230

HOUSER, KEITH ALLAN, minister, television broadcast consultant, Evangelical Christian Churches; b. Canton, Ohio, Aug. 13, 1948; s. Joseph F. and Vera I. (Newton) H.; m. Barbara E. Kanary, June 6, 1970; 1 child, Kristin E. B.A. in Sociology, Malone Coll., 1970; postgrad. Wittenburg U., 1970, Capital U., 1971. Ordained to ministry Full Gospel Fellowship of Chs. and Ministers International, 1973. Minister of Youth, St. John's United Ch. of Christ, Massillon, Ohio, 1971; pres. Evang. Christian Concern, Canton, Ohio, 1972—, Evang. Ministry of Christian Ch., El Paso, Tex., 1982—; sec., founder Nat. Religious Broadcasters TV Com., Morristown, N.J., 1980-82; sec., treas., founding dir. Christian TV Services, Inc., Pitts., 1981—; pres., dir. Family TV, Inc., Poughkeepsie, N.Y., 1979-84. Editor Family TV Mag., 1980-81. Contbr. articles to The Poughkeepsie Jour. and Forbes Mag. Mem. adv. bd. Marist Coll., Poughkeepsie, 1980-81, Mt. St. Mary's Coll., Poughkeepsie, 1980-81, Dutchess Community Coll., Poughkeepsie, 1980-82. Recipient Minority Opportunity award Ariz. Bus. Resource Ctr., Inc., 1974, Jerry Lewis Muscular Dystrophy Award of Merit, 1981. Mem. Nat. Assn. Evangs. Avocations: travel; photography; tennis; bowling. Office: Evang Ministry Christian Ch PO Box 13100 El Paso TX 79913

HOUSTON, JAMES MICHAEL, minister, Southern Baptist Convention; b. Sulphur Springs, Tex., Nov. 2, 1956; s. James Edgar and Grace Elaine (Plaster) H.; m. Deborah Hanson, July 9, 1977; children: Ashley Dawn, Amber Leigh. B.S., Howard Payne U., 1980; M.R.E., Southwestern Bapt. Theol. Sem., 1983. Lic. minister Southern Baptist Convention, 1975. Minister of youth Eastside Bapt. Ch., Comanche, Tex., 1977-78, minister of edn. 1st Bapt. Ch., Howe, Tex., 1980; minister of edn. and youth 1st Bapt. Ch., Everman, Tex., 1981-83, 1st Bapt. Ch., Cleburne, Tex., 1983—. Contbg. mem. Southern Bapt. Religious Edn. Assn. Lodge: Kiwanis. Avocations: softball; basketball. Home: 1601 Woodside Dr Cleburne TX 76031 Office: 1st Bapt Ch 105 E Willingham St Box 751 Cleburne TX 76031

HOUSTON, WALTER B., minister, Ch. of God in Christ; b. Tyler, Tex., Sept. 21, 1907; s. Alexander and Idonda (Mims) H.; student pub. schs., Smith County, Tex.; m. Ceaugry Scott, Sept. 1, 1926 (dec. May 1969); children—Lola Houston Walter, Dorcas, Gladys, Johnnie, David, Mary, Arthur; m. 2d, Maundie V. Davis, Nov. 14, 1970. Ordained to ministry, 1933; pastor chs., Houston, Temple, Carthage, and Tex.; now pastor, Tex. Supt. Mineola dist. Ch. of God in Christ, 1958, chmn. ordination bd. Tex. N.E. dist., 1950. Named Outstanding Personality of Year in Tyler, Delta Sigma Theta, 1972. Mem. Tyler Ministerial Alliance (organizer), NAACP, Voter's League. Home: 1908 N Tenneha St Tyler TX 75701 Office: 1815 N Palace St Tyler TX 75702

HOUWEN, WINNIE JACKSON, minister, Evangelical Methodist Church; b. Dallas, Aug. 4, 1955; d. Guy Adolphus and Elizabeth (Leach) Jackson; m. Stephen Arthur Houwen, May 30, 1982; 1 child, Jessica Dianne. B.E.D., Tex. A&M U., 1979; postgrad. Southwestern Bapt. Theol. Sem., 1981—. Sunday sch. vol. Grace Bible Ch., College Station, Tex., 1977-79; Sunday sch. tchr. First Ch. of the Nazarene, Bryan, Tex., 1979-81, youth vol., 1979-81; Sunday sch. tchr., youth vol., Evang. Meth. Ch., Irving, Tex., 1981-83; minister of young adults Evang. Meth. Ch., Denton, Tex., 1984—; mem. bd. stewards Univ. Meth. Ch., Denton, 1984—, asst. Sunday sch. supt., 1984—, Sunday sch. tchr. Vacation Bible Sch. dir., 1984—. Contbr. articles to profl jours. Republican campaign vol. College Station, 1976, Hurst, Tex., 1984. Mem. Exec. Christian Women (chpt. leader), Evang. Meth. Women. Avocations: softball, writing for children. Home: 784 Thomas St Hurst TX 76053 Office: Univ Meth Ch 1023 Maple St Denton TX 76201

HOVSEPIAN, VATCHE, archbishop, Armenian Apostolic Ch.; b. Beirut, June 11, 1930; s. Krikor and Ovsanna (Tchakerian) H. Diploma, Armenian Theol. Sem., Lebanon, 1951; postgrad. Coll. Resurrection, York, Eng., 1953-54, U. Edinburgh, Scotland, 1954-56; B.Div., New Brunswick Theol. Sem., 1960. Ordained priest Armenian Apostolic Ch., 1951. Instr. Armenian Theol. Sem., Lebanon; priest Holy Cross Ch., Union City, N.J., 1956-67; bishop of Can., 1967-71; elevated to archbishop, 1976; primate of Armenian Ch. of Western Diocese, Hollywood, Calif., 1971—. Mem. Nat. Council Chs. (past mem. central bd.). Clubs: Riviera Country (Pacific Palisades, Calif.); Knights of Vartan. Address: 1201 N Vine St Hollywood CA 90038*

HOWARD, DAVID MORRIS, missionary, organization executive; b. Phila., Jan. 28, 1928; s. Philip E. Jr. and Katharine (Gillingham) H.; A.B., Wheaton Coll., 1949, M.A. in Theology, 1952; LL.D., Geneva Coll., Beaver Falls, Pa., 1974; m. Phyllis Gibson, July 1, 1950; children—David, Stephen, Karen Elisabeth, Michael. Ordained to ministry, 1952; asst. gen. dir. Latin Am. Mission, Colombia, S.Am., Costa Rica, C.Am., 1953-68; missions dir. Inter Varsity Christian Fellowship, Madison, Wis., 1968-76, asst. to the pres., 1976-82; gen. dir. World Evang. Fellowship, 1982—. Dir. Urbana Student Missionary Convs., 1973, 76. Bd. dirs. Interdenominational Fgn. Missions Assn.; trustee Latin Am. Mission, Wheaton Coll. Author: Hammered as Gold, 1969, reprinted as The Costly Harvest, 1975; Student Power in World Evangelism, 1970; How Come, God? 1972; By the Power of the Holy Spirit, 1973; Words of Fire, Rivers of Tears, 1976; The Great Commission for Today, 1976. Office: PO Box WEF Wheaton IL 60187*

HOWARD, THEODORE KORNER, minister, Pentecostal Free-Will Baptist Ch., Inc.; b. Norfolk, Va., Aug. 20, 1915; s. Willard Mallilau and Eva Dora (Korner) H.; D.Lit., Gramling New Era U., 1944; D.D., Fundamental Christian Coll., 1957; Ph.D. (hon.), Jameson Bible Inst., 1963; m. Marie White, May 28, 1935; children—Norma Jean Howard Warren, Donald Willard. Ordained to ministry, 1946; co-founder Pentecostal Ch. Christ, Virginia Beach, Va., 1950; founder Trinity Pentecostal Holiness Ch., Chesapeake, Va., 1951-54; founder, pastor Faith Temple, Norfolk, Va., 1963—. Chartered King James Bible Sch., Norfolk, 1965; Va. state dir. Assn. Fundamental Ministers and Chs., Kansas City, Mo., 1955-69; pres. Community Counseling Center. Home: 1167 George St Norfolk VA 23502 Office: 1173 George St POB 12226 Norfolk VA 23502

HOWDEN, FRANK NEWTON, priest, Episcopal Ch.; b. Phila., Mar. 23, 1916; S. John George and Sarah (McFarlane) H.; student Berkshire Bus. Sch., 1935-36; A.B., Univ. South, 1940; M.Div., Gen. Theol. Sem., 1943; psotgrad. Div. Sch. McGill U., 1952-55; M.S., Central Conn. State Coll., 1968; m. Cornelia Jane Fenton, Oct. 7, 1943 (dec. Aug. 1981); children—Robert Newton, William John McFarlane, Susan Catherine Victoria, Sarah Jane Fenton, David Stuart (dec.), Stephane Ann Mary (dec.); m. Mary Valerie Clark, Apr. 23, 1983. Ordained deacon Episcopal Ch., 1943, priest, 1943; minister, chs. N.Y., Vt., Conn., N.J., from 1943, including rector St. Luke's Ch., St. Albans, Vt., 1951-56, Trinity Ch., Waterbury, Conn., 1956-67, Trinity Ch., Lime Rock, Lakeville, Conn.; dean Litchfield Deanery of Conn., 1974-85, ret. 1985; chaplain U.S. Army, 1943-51. Archdeacon New Haven County, 1962-66, instr. Waterbury State Tech. Coll., 1970-75, asst. prof. English and pub. speaking, 1975—; pres. Priests' Fellowship, Diocese Conn., 1961-63. Mem. Am. Fedn. Tchrs. Author: A Rule of Life, 1954; Holy Communion for the Sick and Shut-Ins, 1957. Founder St. George's Ch., Middlebury, Conn., 1959. Home: 3 Argyle House Argyle Rd Southborough Turnbridge Wells Kent TN4 0SU England

HOWELL, BILLY R., counselor, minister Am. Baptist Chs.; b. Rocky Mount, N.C., Aug. 21, 1941; s. Ralph M. and Iva Dell (Skinner) H.; A.A. Chowan Coll., 1961; B.A., Wake Forest U., 1963; B.D., Southeastern Bapt. Sem., 1966; m. Mary Ann Mooney, Aug. 3, 1964; children—Kena, Kimberly, Laura, Andrew, Alicia. Ordained pastor Am. Baptist Chs. in U.S.A., 1966; pastor Rileyville (Va.) Bapt. Ch., 1966-69, 1st Bapt. Ch., Hutsonville, Ill., 1969-70, Grandview Bapt. Ch., Quincy, Ill., 1970-75; alcohol counselor Western Ill. Council Alcoholism, 1975-76; coordinator Alcohol and Drug Abuse Services Community Mental Health Center, Bureau, Marshall, Putnam and Stark Counties, Ill., 1976—. Mem. steering com. Blessing Hosp. Chaplaincy, 1971-74. Bd. dirs. Hudelson Childrens Home, Centralia, Ill., Western Ill. Council on Alcoholism. Named One of Outstanding Young Men in Am., 1974. Mem. Quincy Jr. C. of C., Great Rivers Ministers Council (pres. 1972), Quincy Ministerial Assn. (pres. 1973-74). Home: 422 S Church St Princeton IL 61356 Office: #530 Park Ave E Princeton IL 61356

HOWZE, (JOSEPH) LAWSON E., bishop, Roman Catholic Church. Bishop of Biloxi, Miss., 1977—. Office: PO Box 1189 Biloxi MS 39533*

HOY, GEORGE PHILIP, minister, United Church of Christ; b. Indpls., Feb. 5, 1937; s. Clarence Augustus Hoy and Margaret Louise (Etter) Wooley; m. Barbara Jo Turpen, Aug. 11, 1957; children: Rene, Sherri, Matthew. B.A., Ky. Wesleyan U., 1958; M.Div., So. Baptist Theol. Sem., 1962. Ordained to ministry Bapt. Ch., 1958, transferred credentials to United Ch. of Christ, 1962. Pastor Union United Ch. of Christ, Evansville, Ind., 1962-72, Faith United Ch. of Christ, Ft. Wayne, Ind., 1975-80, St. Matthew's United Ch. of Christ, Evansville, Ind., 1981—; chaplain Evansville State Hosp., 1966-72; exec. dir. Youth Service Bur., Evansville, 1972-75; vol. Habitat for Humanity, Americus, Ga., 1980-81; gen. synod del. Ind.-Ky. conf. United Ch. of Christ, 1978-81; pres. United Ch. of Christ Tri-State Assn., Evansville, 1972-75, Pastor's Assn., 1984—; chaplain Fraternal Order Police, Evansville, 1982—. Columnist Evansville Press, 1983—. Commr. Human Relations Commn., Evansville, 1984—. Participant Leadership Evansville, 1983—; pres. Neighborhood Econ. Devel. Ctr., Evansville, 1983—. United Ch. Christ grantee Inst. for Transactional Analysis, 1971-72. Mem. Evansville Tri-State Pastors Circle (pres. 1984), Northside Ministerial Assn., Profl. Clergy Group, Southwestern Ind. Psychol. Assn. Democrat. Home: 217 Cherry St Evansville IN 47713 Office: St Matthew's United Ch of Christ 3007 1st Ave Evansville IN 47710

HOY, WILLIAM IVAN, minister, educator, Presbyterian Church USA; b. Grottoes, Va., Aug. 21, 1915; s. William Isaac and Ileta (Root) H.; m. Wilma J. Lambert, Apr. 29, 1945; children: Doris Lambert Hoy Bezanilla, Martha Virginia. B.A., Hampden-Sydney Coll., 1936; B.D., Union Theol. Sem., 1942; S.T.M., Bibl. Sem. N.Y., 1949; Ph.D., U. Edinburgh, Scotland, 1952. Ordained to ministry Presbyn. Ch. USA, 1942. Asst. prof. Bible, Guilford Coll., N.C., 1947-48; supply minister Asheboro Presbyn. Ch., 1947-48, 52-53; mem. faculty U. Miami, Coral Gables, Fla., 1953—, now prof. religion, chmn. dept. religion, 1960-79; pres. Greater Miami Ministerial Assn.; clergy dialogue moderator Synod of Fla., Orlando, 1984-85, mem. council, 1983—; mem. bd. Christian edn. Presbyn. Ch., 1969-73; mem. gen. assembly, mission bd. Presbyn. Ch. U.S.A., Atlanta, 1978—; v.p. Met. Fellowships of Chs., 1971-73; interim exec. dir., 1974-76; moderator Everglades Presbytery, 1960-61, stated clk., 1968-73, 78-79; mem. Bd. Christian Edn., Presbyn. Ch. U.S., 1963-69; mem. bd. Pastoral Inst., 1972—; host TV show Protestant Worship Hour, 1968-69; originator Religion in the News, 1972-73; mem. Greater Miami Religious Leaders Coalition. Trustee Davidson Coll., 1975—; mem. Miami Citizens against Crime. Served to comdr. USNR ret. Mem. Studiorum Novi Testamenti Societas, Soc. for Sci. Study of Religion, Religious Research Assn., Acad. Religion, Soc. Bibl. Lit., Am. Oriental Assn., Internat. Sociol. Assn., Am. Soc. Ch. History, Scottish Ch. History Soc., Res. Officers Assn. (nat. and state chaplain, pres. Fla.), Coral Gables C. of C., Iron Arrow, Omicron Delta Kappa (province dep., gen. council, service key 1976), Phi Kappa Phi, Alpha Psi Omega, Lambda Chi Alpha (Activity Key), Theta Delta. Club: Tiger Bay. Lodge: Rotary (dir. 1981-83, historian 1983-84). Home: 5881 SW 52nd Ter Miami FL 33155 Office: PO Box 8348 Coral Gables FL 33124

HOYE, DANIEL FRANCIS, priest, Roman Catholic Church; b. Taunton, Mass., Jan. 18, 1946; s. Charles Edward and Virginia Mary (Cleary) H. B.A., St. John's Sem., 1968, M.Th., 1972; J.C.L., Cath. U., 1975. Ordained priest, 1972. Parish assoc. St. John's Parish, Attleboro, Mass., 1972-73; vice officialis Diocese of Fall River, Mass., 1975-77; assoc. gen. sec. Nat. Council Cath. Bishops/U.S. Cath. Conf., Washington, 1977-82, gen. sec., 1982—; bd. dirs. Cath. Relief Services, N.Y.C., 1982—, Cath. Telecommunications Network of Am., 1982—. Mem. Canon Law Soc. Am., Canon Law Soc. of Great Britain and Ireland. Office: Nat Conf Cath Bishops US Cath Conf 1312 Massachusetts Ave NW Washington DC 20005

HOYNG, WILLIAM GERALD, priest, Roman Catholic Church; b. Coldwater, Ohio, Aug. 22, 1934; s. Ernest Joseph and Helen Elizabeth (Losche) H. B.A., U. Dayton, 1957; M.R.E., Loyola U., Chgo., 1968. Ordained priest Roman Cath. Ch., 1961. Tirocinium, Soc. Precious Blood, Detroit, 1961-62; tchr. religion Acad. Our Lady, Chgo., 1962-65, Brunnerdale Sem., Canton, Ohio, 1965-71, vocation recruiter, 1971-74; pastor St. Anthony Ch., Detroit, 1974-80; pastor Holy Name Ch., Cin., 1980—. Spiritual dir. Crusillo and Christian Family Movement, 1968-71; mem. inner city caucus Soc. Precious Blood, Detroit, 1972-80. Mem. Ecumenical Assn. (pres. Canton 1969-71). Democrat. Home: 2448 Auburn Ave Cincinnati OH 45219

HROMATKO, WESLEY VINTON, clergyman, Unitarian Universalist Association; b. Slayton, Minn., Oct. 2, 1947; s. Annel Jay and Maybelle (Moffatt) H.; B.A. cum laude, U. Minn., 1969; M.A., Meadville Theol. Sch., Chgo., 1971, D.Min., 1973. Ordained minister Unitarian Universalist Assn., 1973; asst. minister 3d Unitarian Ch., Chgo., 1972-73, Unity Temple, Oak Park, Ill., 1972-73; minister Abraham Lincoln Fellowship, Springfield, Ill., 1972-73, Oaklandon (Ind.) Universalist Ch., 1973-75, 1st Unitarian Ch., Hobart, Ind., 1975-82, All Souls Ch., Braintree, Mass., 1982-85; assoc. minister Ch. of Larger Fellowship, Boston, 1985—; chaplain Oaklandon Vol. Fire Dept., 1973-74. Mem. Ind. justice project

Unitarian-Universalist Service Com., 1973-74, recipient Entemann Ohanian award, 1975; mem. Ind. Unitarian-Universalist Legislative Conf., 1973-75; mem. adv. council Religious Coalition for Abortion Rights, 1974-75. Mem. Orgn. for Better Austin, Chgo., 1972; bd. dirs. Oaklandon Civic Assn., 1974-75, Eastern Lawrence Twp. Planning Commn., 1974-75; mem. Prairie Group program com. Save the Dunes Council, 1973-82, Hobart Am. Revolutionary Bicentennial Commn. Trustee Chgo. area Unitarian Universalist Council, 1976-78; bd. dirs., religious edn. chmn. Ch. of the Larger Fellowship, 1983—. Mem. Unitarian-Universalist Ministers Assn., Central Midwest Unitarian Universalist Minister's Assn. (sec. 1976—), Meadville Theol. Sch. Alumni Assn. (treas. 1973-75), U. Minn. alumni assns., Hobart Ministerial Assn., ACLU (legal panel 1982-83), Internat. Assn. Religious Freedom, Council World Affairs, Unitarian Universalist Advance (former bd. dirs., v.p.) Universalist Hist. Soc., Indpls. Mental Health Assn., Americans United (treas. Indpls. 1974-75), New Eng. Hist. Geneal. Soc., Unitarian Universalist Geneal. Soc., others. Author book revs. Co-editor: Appeal of the Irreligious, 1980. Address: Rural Route 1 Lake Wilson MN 56151

HSU, HERALD, minister, American Baptist Churches; b. Shatung, China, Sept. 28, 1922; came to U.S., 1973, naturalized, 1979; s. Chung-Hsin and Wang-Shi H.; m. Haun-Yu L. Hsu, Nov. 11, 1952; children: Mary, David, Elizabeth, Joshua. B.S. in Mech. Engring., Nat. Chaio-Tung U., Shanghai, 1949. Ordained to ministry Ch. Assembly Hall of Taipei, Taiwan, 1953. Minister Watchwan Nee's Group, Taipei, 1950-59, Manila, Philippines, 1960-73; minister Christian Testimony Ch., Rutherford, N.J., 1973-76; minister, local missionary First Baptist Peddie M Ch., Newark, 1976—; speaker various ind. chs., confs., retreats. Income maintenance technician Bergen County Bd. Social Service, Paramus, N.J., 1982—. Author: God's Workers and His Church, 1962. Editor Overcomers mag., 1961—. Home: 243 Jay Ave Lyndhurst NJ 07071

HUBBARD, CHARLES SPENCE, minister, United Methodist Church; b. Sanford, N.C., Dec. 12, 1913; s. Archibald Monroe and Mina Amanda (York) H.; A.B., U. N.C. at Chapel Hill, 1936; B.D., Duke, 1939; m. Mercer Reeves, Aug. 26, 1938; children: Martha (Mrs. Robert O. Forrest), Charles Spence, Thomas Edwin, John Spaugh. Ordained to ministry United Methodist Ch., 1940; pastor, Roseboro, N.C., 1939-45, Hillsborough, 1945-51, Trinity Ch., Raleigh, N.C., 1951-53, University Ch. at Chapel Hill, 1953-62, 1st Ch., Wilson, N.C., 1962-71, Duke Meml. Ch., Durham, 1971-75; del. World Meth. Conf., Dublin, Ireland, 1976; bd. dirs. dept. gifts and wills N.C. Meth. Conf., 1976—. Guest chaplain, U.S. Senate and Ho. of Reps. Mem. Kerr Reservoir Commn., 1954-58, Commn. to Study Conservation and Devel. of N.C., 1964-68, Commn. to Reorganized Dept. Natural and Econ. Resources N.C., 1972-73; mem. N.C. Recreation Commn., 1945—, chmn., 1955-75; vice chmn. Park and Recreation Council, N.C. Dept. Natural Resources, 1975—; trustee Louisburg Coll., 1960-64; bd. dirs. N.C. Bot. Gardens Found., 1976—, N.C. Recreator's Found., 1976—, N.C. Natural Resources and Community Devel. Recipient Silver Beaver award Boy Scouts Am., 1956, Nat. Preaching award Freedoms Found. Valley Forge, 1969. Mem. Nat. Recreation and Park Assn. (nat. dir. 1968—; founding trustee 1961-65, nat. commr. award 1975). Home: Box 58 Pittsboro NC 27312 Office: Hackberry Hill Pittsboro NC 27312

HUBBARD, DAVID ALLAN, minister, American Baptist Churches, religion educator; b. Stockton, Calif., Apr. 8, 1928; s. John King and Helena (White) H.; m. Ruth Doyal, Aug. 12, 1949; 1 child, Mary Ruth. B.A., Westmont Coll., 1949; B.D., Fuller Theol. Sem., 1952, Th.M., 1954; Ph.D., St. Andrews U., Scotland, 1957; D.D., John Brown U., 1975; L.H.D. (hon.), Rockford Coll., 1975. Ordained to ministry Conservative Bapt. Assn., 1952, Am. Bapt. Chs., 1984; lectr. O.T., St. Andrews U., 1955-56; asst. prof. bibl. studies Westmont Coll., Calif., 1957, chmn. dept. bibl. studies and philosophy, 1958-63; interim pastor Montecito Community Ch., Calif., 1960-62; pres., prof. O.T., Fuller Theol. Sem., Pasadena, Calif., 1963—; exec. v.p. Fuller Evangelistic Assn., 1969—; Tyndale O.T. lectr., Cambridge, Eng., 1965; Soc. O.T. studies lectr., London, 1971; lectr. numerous U.S. univs., 1973—; speaker internat. radio broadcast Joyful Sound, 1969-80. Author many books including: Thessalonians - Life That's Radically Christian, 1977; Why Do I Have to Die?, 1978; How to Study the Bible, 1978; What We Evangelicals Believe, 1979; Book of James - Wisdom that Works, 1980; Right Living in a World Gone Wrong, 1981; Parables Jesus Told, 1981; (with Bush, LaSor) Old Testament Survey, 1982. Contbg. editor: Eternity mag.; mem. editorial bd. Ministers Permanent Library, 1976—; mem. adv. bd. Evang. Book Club, 1977—. Contbr. articles to dictionaries, mags. Chmn. Pasadena Urban Coalition, 1968-71; mem. Calif. Bd. Edn., 1972-75. Mem. Am. Acad. Religion, Soc. Bibl. Lit., Assn. Theol. Schs. in U.S. and Can. (exec. com. 1972-40, pres. 1976-78). Club: University (Pasadena). Lodge: Rotary. Office: Fuller Theol Sem 135 N Oakland Ave Pasadena CA 91101

HUBBARD, EDWARD WAYNE, pastor, Southern Missionary Baptist Church; teacher; b. Edmonton, Ky., Nov. 14, 1954; s. B.B. and Dorthy D. (Romines) H.; m. Connie G. Durrett, June 3, 1972. A.A., Lindsey Wilson Coll., 1982; B.S. in Teaching Rights, Campbellsville Bapt. Coll., 1984; postgrad. in pastoral counseling Liberty Bapt. Coll., summers 1981-82. Ordained to Bapt. ministry, 1972. Cert. tchr. secondary schs., 1984; cert. pastoral counseling, 1982. Pastor, Pink Ridge Bapt. Ch., Sulpher Well, Ky., 1972-73, New Salem Bapt. Ch., Greensburg, Ky., 1974-76, Russell Creek Bapt. Ch., Greensburg, 1979-80, Macedonia Bapt. Ch., Greensburg, 1977-80, Okalona Bapt. Ch., Nancy, Ky., 1981—. Tchr. Pulaski County Sch., Somerset, Ky., 1984—.

HUBBARD, HOWARD JAMES, bishop, Roman Catholic Church; b. Troy, N.Y., Oct. 31, 1938; s. Howard James and Elizabeth D. (Burke) H.; B.A., St. Joseph's Sem., Yonkers, N.Y.; S.T.L., Gregorian U., Rome; D.D. (hon.), Siena Coll., 1977; L.H.D. (hon.), Coll. St. Rose, 1977. Ordained priest, 1963; bishop of Albany (N.Y.) 1977—; parish priest St. Joseph's Ch., Schenectady, Cathedral Parish, Albany. Asst. dir. Cath. Charities, Schenectady; chaplain Convent of the Sacred Heart, Kenwood, Albany; dir. Providence House, Albany; vicar gen. Diocese of Albany; dir. Cath. Interracial Council; coordinator Urban Apostolate. Pres., Urban League. Office: 465 State St Albany NY 12203*

HUBBARD, L. RON, founder, Scientology; author, explorer, philosopher; b. Tilden, Nebr., Mar. 13, 1911; s. Harry Ross and Dora May (Waterbury De Wolfe) H.; student George Washington U., 1932, Princeton U. Sch. Govt., 1945; m. Mary Sue Whipp; children: Diana Meredith de Wolfe, Mary Suzette Rochelle, Arthur Ronald Conway. Writer aviation, adventure and travel articles, 1930—; leader Caribbean motion picture expdn., 1932, W.I. minerals expdn., 1933, Alaska radio expt. expdn., 1940, others; founder, Scientology, 1951; bd. dirs. humanitarian orgns., including Dianetics and Scientology, 1952-66; research and devel. to improve edn., 1964-71, research, programs to combat drug abuse, 1966—; exptl. works in music and photography, 1974—. Author over 140 novels and short stories, 1934-50; author: (sci. fiction) Battlefield Earth: A Saga of the Year 3000, 1982 (spl. achievement award Acad. Sci. Fiction 1984); non-fiction includes Dianetics: 1950; The Modern Science of Mental Health, Science of Survival, 1951; Scientology: A New Slant on Life, 1966; The Fundamental of Thought, 1956; Self-Analysis, 1968; Dianetics Today, 1975; also articles. Recipient Internat. Social Reform award, 1976, Ingrams West award, 1977, Nat. Life Achievement award Ill. Soc. Psychic Research, 1978, Internat. Profl. Assn. award 1978, numerous other awards for community service and mus. creations; also numerous hon. citizenships and keys to cities in U.S. Home: Saint Hill Manor East Grinstead Sussex England Office: PO Box 39623 Los Angeles CA 90029

HUBBERT, ALLEN MICHAEL, minister, church executive, Church of Scientology Internat. B. Birmingham, Ala., Feb. 8, 1946; s. Ealon Aubrey and Norma Mae Hubbert; m. Debra Lewis, Feb. 18, 1973. A.A., Am. River Coll., 1965; B.A., Calif. State U.-Sacramento, 1967. Ordained to ministry Ch. of Scientology, 1971. Minister-in-tng. Ch. of Scientology of Hawaii, Honolulu, 1968-69; pub. relations officer Ch. of Scientology of Calif., Los Angeles, 1969-74, asst. dir., 1974-80, resident dir., 1980-81, pres., 1981-84; staff Ch. of Scientology Internat., Los Angeles, 1984—. Editor FREEDOM newspaper, 1981-83. Trustee Citizen's Commn. on Human Rights, Los Angeles, 1982—. Mem. Sea Orgn. (officer 1969—). Home: 1404 N Catalina St Los Angeles CA 90027 Office: Church of Scientology Internat 4751 Fountain Ave Los Angeles CA 90029

HUBBLE, DAVID HOWE, minister, General Association of Regular Baptist Churches. B. Crawfordsville, Ind., Mar. 25, 1954; s. Paul Marion and Betty Jane (Neal) H.; m. Susan Leigh Thompson, Dec. 17, 1976; children: Christine, Amy, Michelle. B.R.E., B.Th., Bapt. Bible Coll. of Pa., 1978. Ordained to ministry Gen. Assn. Regular Bapt. Chs., 1979. Pastor, W. Colesville Bapt. Ch., Binghamton, N.Y., 1978-83, Faith Bapt. Ch., Oelwein, Iowa, 1983—; sec.-treas. Rural Bapt. Pastors Fellowship, Binghamton, N.Y., 1981-82; v.p. NE Iowa Regular Bapt. Pastors Fellowship, Oelwein, 1984-85; mem. state youth com. Iowa Assn. Regular Bapt. Chs. Home: 28 7th St NW Oelwein IA 50662 Office: Faith Bapt Ch 305 6th St NW Oelwein IA 50662

HUBERT, BERNARD, bishop, Roman Catholic Church; b. Beloil, Que., Can., June 1, 1929. Ordained priest, 1953; bishop of St. Jerome (Que.), 1971-77; coadjutor bishop of Saint-Jean-de-Quebec (now Saint-Jean-Longueuil), 1977-78, bishop, 1978—. Office: 740 Blvd Ste-Foy CP 580 Saint Jerome PQ J7Z 5V3 Canada*

HUCK, GRACE ELOISE, minister, United Meth. Ch.; b. Harding County, S.D., June 27, 1916; d. William Gladstone and Grace (Kearns) Huck; B.S. in Edn., Black Hills State Coll., 1949; M.S. in Edn., N.D. State U., 1956; M.A. in C.E., Scarritt Coll., Nashville, 1968. Ordained deacon, 1945, elder, 1949, 1st woman to receive full clergy rights in Meth. Ch. in U.S., 1956; pastor chs. in N.D., 1941-43, 45-48; mem. N.D. Interchurch Council, 1949-50; dir. Christian edn., Spearfish, S.D., 1951-52, Navajo Meth. Mission Sch., Farmington, N.Mex., 1952-53; minister Christian edn. First Meth. Ch., Fargo, N.D., 1953-59; missionary-tchr. Harris Meml. Coll., Manila, P.I., 1960-71; pastor Faith-Marcus United Parish, Faith, S.D., 1972—. Mem. com. on nominations, status and role of women Conf. Bd. Ministry, Gen. Conf. Bd. Global Ministries. Author: Songs of the Soul, 1957; When Does it Start?, 1966. Contbr. poems and articles to anthologies and profl. publs. Home and office: Box 215 Faith SD 57626

HUCKABY, JAMES L., JR., lay ch. worker, Baptist Ch.; b. Teague, Tex., Sept. 13, 1922; s. James L. and Sylvann (Peters) H.; B.S. in English, Prairie View Coll., 1945; M.Ed., Tex. State U., 1951, Ph.D., 1962; m. Daisy F. Whitfield, June 13; children—Norman E., Otha Wayne, Gloria, Davis, James L. III. Tchr., Teague, Tex., 1938-45; tchr. Sunday sch. Harmony Bapt. Ch., Sherman, Tex., 1966—; dir. extracurricular activities First Bapt. Ch., Bryan, Tex., 1964—; sch. supt. Missionary Bapt. Ch., Palestine, Tex., 1943-46. Realtor, Sherman, 1969—. Address: 814 Northeast St Sherman TX 75090

HUCLES, HENRY BOYD, III, bishop, Episcopal Church; b. N.Y.C., Sept. 21, 1923; s. Henry Boyd and Alma Leola (Lewis) H.; m. Mamie Dalceda, Sept. 18, 1948; children: Henry B. IV, Michael Edward. B.S., Va. Union U., 1943; B.D., Bishop Payne Divinity Sch., 1946; M.Div., Va. Theol. Sem., 1970, D.D., 1976. Ordained to ministry Episcopal Ch. as deacon, 1946, as priest, 1947. Pastor St. Andrews Upright, Millers Tavern, Va., 1946-49; rector St. George's Ch., Bklyn., 1949-79; archdeacon of Bklyn., Diocese of L.I., Garden City, N.Y., 1976-81, suffragan bishop, 1981—; v.p., dir. Church Charity Found., Hempstead, N.Y., 1954—; v.p. Diocesan Council, Garden City, 1981—; hon. v.p. Family Consultation Service Jamaica, N.Y., 1981—. Bd. dirs. Bedford Stuyvesant Restoration Corp., Bklyn., 1967-81. Named Hon. Conon, Cathedral of the Incarnation, 1975; Man of Yr., Kings County Med. Soc., 1965, Rector Emeritus St. George's Ch., 1983. Mem. Sigma Pi Phi. Democrat. Home: 152 Kilburn Rd Garden City NY 11530 Office: Diocese of L I 36 Cathedral Ave Garden City NY 11530

HUDGENS, RICHARD WAYNE, minister, Wesleyan Church; b. Greensboro, N.C., Feb. 13, 1955; s. Paul Richard and Dora Mae (Cooke) H.; m. Sharron Marie Wiltshire, June 9, 1978; children: Danielle Marie, Stephanie Nicole. B.A. in Bible and Theology, Central Wesleyan Coll., 1977; postgrad. in religious edn. Bethany Sem., 1984—. Ordained to ministry Wesleyan Ch., 1980. Assoc. pastor St. Paul Wesleyan Ch., Charlotte, N.C., 1977-81; minister of youth Christian Fellowship Ch., Vienna, Va., 1981-84, assoc. pastor, 1984—; mem. Clergy Task Force, Charlotte, 1978; dist. pres. Wesleyan Youth, Washington, 1982-83, vice-chmn. Northeast area, 1983—; mem. local steering com. The Winning Way, Washington; mem. exec. com. Christian Ams. for South Africa; youth camp evangelist, rally speaker; workshop speaker Youth Congress, 1985. Author handbook and tng. materials; contbr. to youth discipleship books. Named One of Outstanding Young Men of Am., U.S. Jaycees, 1980, 83. Avocation: reading. Home: 516 Aspen Dr Herndon VA 22070 Office: Christian Fellowship Ch 10237 Leesburg Pike Vienna VA 22180

HUDSON, KIRK ARTHUR, minister, United Presbyterian Church in U.S.A.; b. Penfield, N.Y., May 5, 1929; s. Kirk Davis and Charlotte (Crego) H.; B.A., St. Lawrence U., 1953; B.D., Princeton Theol. Sem., 1957; M.Ed., U. Pitts., 1970; D.Ministry, Pitts. Theol. Sem., 1974; D.D., Lebanon Valley Coll., 1972, Waynesburgh Coll., 1973; Litt.D., Grove City Coll., 1975; m. Carolyn Pruyn, Sept. 6, 1952; children—Carolyn, Elizabeth, Robert, Kirk (dec.). Ordained to ministry, 1956; pastor Fort Dix, Pa., 1957-59, Highland Presbyn. Ch., Lancaster, Pa., 1959-66, Pleasant Hills Community Ch., Pitts., 1966-75, Meml. Presbyn. Ch., Midland, Mich., 1976—. Mem. exec. council program agy. United Presbyn. Ch., 1984—; trustee Alma Coll. (Mich.). Home: 1005 W Park Dr Midland MI 48640 Office: 1310 Ashman St Midland MI 48640

HUDSON, LOREN RICHARD, minister, Disciples of Christ Church; b. Davenport, Iowa, June 11, 1923; s. Loren Richard and Margaret Elizabeth (Adams) H.; m. Mary Ann Harvey, Aug. 12, 1950; children: Loren Thomas, Richard Lewis, Margaret Frances, Harvey Dean. Student, Iowa Wesleyan Coll., 1941-42; A.B., Drake U., 1945; M.Div., Union Theol. Sem., N.Y.C., 1948; postgrad., Christian Theol. Sem., Indpls., 1967-68. Ordained to ministry Disciples of Christ Ch., 1948. Minister Jasper County Pastoral Unity, Newton, Iowa, 1949-50, Jackson Blvd. Christian Ch., Chgo., 1950-53, Marana Community Christian Ch., Ariz., 1953-54; new ch. dir. Ohio Soc. of Christian Chs., Cin., 1954-65; assoc. regional minister Christian Ch. in Ind.,

Indpls., 1965-70, mem. commn. on ch. devel. and evangelism, 1981—, steering com. for Faith United Christian Ch., 1982-84; exec. dir. Community Interfaith Housing, Indpls., 1969—. Recipient Service to Mankind award Sertoma, Indpls., 1984.

HUDSON-KNAPP, MARSHALL RALPH, minister, United Church of Christ; b. Bennington, Vt., July 16, 1949; s. Ronald Ralph and Frances Evelyn (Marshall) Knapp; m. Lucinda Jean Hudson, June 23, 1973; children: Naomi Ruth, Moses James. B.A. cum laude, Lone Mountain Coll., 1973; M.Div., Pacific Sch. Religion, 1975. Ordained to ministry United Ch. of Christ, 1975. Chaplain intern Med. Ctr. Hosp. Vt., Burlington, 1973; asst. pastor Rockland Area Ministry, Roscoe, N.Y., 1974; pastor Orleans Federated Ch., Vt., also Brownington Congregational Ch., Vt., 1975-80, 1st Congl. Ch. United Ch. of Christ, Fair Haven, Vt., 1980—; founding mem. com. on healing ministry Vt. conf. United Ch. Christ, 1976—; alt. del. gen. synod United Ch. Christ, 1985—; cert. trainer Calling and Caring Ministry, Princeton Sem., 1984—. Author: Clothes for Celebrating Good News, 1974. Vice pres. Orleans County Council Social Agys., Newport, Vt., 1975-80; pres. Fair Haven Concerned, Inc., 1983—; bd. dirs. Apple Tree Children's Ctr., Castleton, Vt., 1981-83. Mem. Order St. Luke (chaplain 1982—), Bros. and Sisters of the Way (able bro.), Bibl. Archaeol. Soc., Geneal. Soc. Vt., New Eng. Historic Geneal. Soc. Democrat. Home: 19 West St Fair Haven VT 05743 Office: First Congl Ch United Ch of Christ North Park Pl Fair Haven VT 05743

HUEBSCH, ROBERT WILLIAM, religious literature educator, Roman Catholic; b. Buffalo, Apr. 9, 1947; s. Raymond Albert and Marion Florence H.; m. Patricia Ann Mullins, June 21, 1969. A.B., Canisius Coll., 1968, M.A., 1972; Ph.D., McMaster U., 1981. Tchr. Victory Acad., Lackawanna, N.Y., 1968-72; adminstrv. teaching asst. McMaster U., Hamilton, Ont., Can., 1972-76, research asst., 1976-77, vis. lectr., 1977-78; assoc. prof. early Jewish and early Christian lit. Niagara U., N.Y., 1977—; chmn. dept. religious studies, 1984—. Editor (with others) Proc. Eastern Great Bibl. Soc., 1981-83. Contbr. articles to profl. jours. McMaster U. scholar, 1972-76, research grantee, 1976-77; Ont. Govt. fellow, 1974-75. Mem. Assn. for Jewish Studies, European Assn. for Jewish Studies, Cath. Bibl. Assn., Soc. Bibl. Lit. Home: 619 Morgan Dr Lewiston NY 14092 Office: Dept Religious Studies Niagara U Niagara University NY 14109

HUESCA PACHECO, ROSENDO, archbishop, Roman Catholic Church; b. Ejutla, Méx., Mar. 1, 1932. Ordained priest Roman Catholic Ch., 1956; named bishop, 1970; archbishop of Puebla de los Angeles, 1977—. Address: Calle 2 Sur N 305 Puebla Mexico

HUEY, F. B., JR., minister, theology educator, Southern Baptist Convention; b. Denton, Tex., Jan. 12, 1925; s. F.B. and Alma Gwendolyn (Chambers) H.; m. Nonna Lee Turner, Dec. 22, 1950; children: Mary Anne, Linda Kaye, William David. B.B.A., U. Tex., 1945; M.Div., Southwestern Bapt. Theol. Sem., 1958, Ph.D., 1961. Ordained to ministry So. Bapt. Conv., 1956. Pastor Bolivar Bapt. Ch., Sanger, Tex., 1956-59, Univ. Bapt. Ch., Denton, 1959-61; prof. Old Testament, S. Brazil Bapt. Theol. Sem., Rio de Janeiro, 1961-65; prof. Old Testament, Southwestern Bapt. Theol. Sem., Fort Worth, 1965—, chmn. D.Ministry program, 1978-79, assoc. dean for Ph.D. degree, 1984—; guest prof. Bapt. Theol. Sem., Ruschlikon, Switzerland, 1971-72. Author: Exodus: Bible Study Commentary, 1977, Chinese edit., 1983; Yesterday's Prophets for Todays' World, 1980; Jeremiah: Bible Study Commentary, 1981, Chinese edit., 1982; Numbers: Bible Study Commentary, 1981; Ezekiel-Daniel, 1983; (with others) Student's Dictionary for Biblical and Theological Studies, 1983; Helps for Beginning Hebrew Students, 1981. Translator: (with others) New American Standard Bible, 1971; New International Version Bible, 1978. Contbr. articles to profl. jours. Mem. Soc. Bibl. Lit., Nat. Assn. Profs. Hebrew, Nat. Assn. Bapt. Profs. Religion, Delta Sigma Pi, Beta Gamma Sigma, Theta Xi. Home: 6128 Whitman Ave Fort Worth TX 76133 Office: Southwestern Bapt Theol Sem Box 22000 Fort Worth TX 76122

HUFFAKER, JAMES HARRY, minister, Presbyterian Church, U.S.A.; b. Chattanooga, Nov. 6, 1935; s. Herbert Hughes and Anna Susan (Eisenberg) H.; m. Icie Almeda Shimer, Dec. 28, 1963; children: Michael Hughes, Ellen Carole, Peter James. B.S., East Tenn. Union, 1957; M.Div., Columbia Theol. Sem., 1960, D.Min., 1985; M.Christian Edn., Presbyn. Sch. Christian Edn., 1963. Ordained to ministry Presbyterian Ch., 1960. Assoc. pastor Eastminster Presbyn. Ch., Knoxville, 1960-61, Central Presbyn. Ch., Chattanooga, 1961-62; pastor Sunnyside Presbyn. Ch., Winchester, Va., 1963-66; assoc. pastor First Presbyn. Ch., Danville, Va., 1966-72, Venice-Nokomis Presbyn. Ch., Venice, Fla., 1972-79; pastor Parkway Presbyn. Ch., Panama City, Fla., 1979—; chmn. stewardship and budget com. Presbyn. Ch. of Fla., 1981-83, mem. rev. and evaluation com., 1980-82, chmn. leadership and devel. com. Christian Edn. Div., 1980-83, moderator, adminstrn. div., 1983—; chmn. Christian Edn. Westminster Presbytery, St. Petersburg, 1975-79, vice chmn., 1975-79; mem. rev. and evaluation com. Synod of Fla., 1983—. Adult chmn. Mayors Youth Council, Danville, Va., 1969-72; mem., chmn. Venice Housing Authority, 1973-77; mem., v.p. Venitian Sun Fiesta, 1976-79. Named Most Outstanding Adult Leader of Youth, Mayor's Youth Council, Danville, Va., 1970, Outstanding Leader, Venitian Sun Fiesta, 1978. Mem. Bay County Ministerial Assn. (pres. 1981-82). Democrat. Lodge: Kiwanis (bd. dirs. 1976-78, 83—). Home: 1420 Parkway Dr Panama City FL 32404 Office: Parkway Presbyn Ch 505 S Tyndall Pkwy PO Box 10605 Panama City FL 32040

HUFFMAN, GORDON SETH, retired bishop, American Lutheran Church; b. Hickory, N.C., June 8, 1916; s. Loy Seth and Ruth Edna (Yount) H.; B.A., Lenoir-Rhyne Coll., 1935, S.T.D., 1974; B.D., Luth. Theol. Sem., Columbus, Ohio, 1938; D.D., Capital U., 1955; m. Janet K. Koster, June 14, 1941; children: Gordon Seth, Patricia Huffman Miller (dec.), Jonathan, Stephen. Ordained to ministry Am. Luth. Ch., 1938; asst. pastor St. Johns Luth. Ch., Akron, Ohio, 1938-41; pastor St. Johns Luth. Ch., Mars, Pa., 1941-46; sr. pastor St. Marks Luth. Ch., Butler, Pa., 1946-58; pres. Eastern Dist., Am. Luth. Ch., Washington, 1958-60, bishop, 1960-78, pres. Council of Bishops, 1969-74; mem. Joint Civilian Orientation Conf., 1965; pastor Our Savior Luth. Ch., Freeport, Grand Bahama Island, Bahamas, 1979-84; ret., 1984. trustee Luth. Med. Ctr., Bklyn. Author: (with Marcus Rieke) From Plight to Power, 1951. Columnist ch. periodicals. Mem. Am. Sch. Oriental Research. Lodges: Kiwanis, Rotary. Home: Apt 210 10300 Bushman Dr Oakton VA 22124

HUFFMAN, WILLARD KEITH, minister, Southern Baptist Convention; b. Marquand, Mo., Nov. 16, 1939; s. George Henry and Ruby Alma (Gipson) H.; A.A., SW Bapt. Coll., 1960; B.A., Union U., Tenn., 1962; M.Div., Midwestern Bapt. Theol. Sem., 1965; m. Jacquelyn Zeldara Upchurch, June 2, 1962; 1 dau., Becki Lyn. Ordained to ministry, 1959; student pastor chs. Mo., 1960-65; pastor 1st Bapt. Ch., Clarkton, Mo., 1965-66, Elvins, Mo., 1966-74, Ironton, Mo., 1974—. Moderator, Mineral Area Bapt. Assn., 1968-70; ch. tng. dir. Assn., 1967; mem. exec. bd. Mo. Bapt. Conv., 1974-78; pres. Bates Creek Camp Bd., 1976. Mem. Child Welfare Abuse Com. Iron County, 1975-77. Pres., Mineral Area Bapt. Pastors Conf. Home: Star Route 69 Box 1695 Ironton MO 63650 Office: Madison and Knob Sts Ironton MO 63650

HUGHBANKS, WOODARD MONROE, minister, educator, Evang. Meth. Ch.; b. Attica, Kans., Dec. 20, 1928; s. James Frank and Vivian Esther (Hunt) H.; A.B., Asbury Coll., 1952; postgrad. Asbury Theol. Sem., 1958, Nat. U. of Mexico, Mexico City, 1956; M.S., Emporia (Kans.) State Coll., 1964; Ed.D., U. Nebr., 1971; m. Avis Corinne Neubauer, Sept. 2, 1948; children—Stephen Bryce, Melody Ann, Vincent Monroe. Ordained to ministry, 1953; pastor Crisfield (Kans.) Meth. Ch., 1949-51, Science Hill (Ky.) Meth. Ch. Circuit, 1952-53, Missionary Ch. Assn., Hutchinson, Kans., 1963-64, Monitor Community Ch. of the Brethren, Conway, Kans., 1969-70, 72—; missionary World Gospel Mission, McAllen, Tex., 1953-58, Saltillo, Mexico, 1959-61; prof. edn. McPherson (Kans.) Coll., 1964—. Bd. dirs. Deer Creek Christian Camp, Pine, Colo. Mem. Nat. Assn. Evangs. Contbr. articles to religious publs. Home: 1204 Glendale Rd McPherson KS 67460 Office: McPherson Coll McPherson KS 67460

HUGHES, ALFRED CLIFTON, bishop, Roman Catholic Church; b. Boston, Dec. 2, 1932; s. Alfred Clifton and Ellen C. (Hennessey) H. A.B., St. John's Sem. Coll., Boston, 1954; S.T.L., Gregorian U., Rome, 1958, S.T.D., 1961. Ordained priest Roman Cath. Ch., 1957, consecrated bishop, 1981. Pastor chs. in Mass., 1958-62; lectr. St. John's Sem., Brighton, Mass., 1962-65, spiritual dir., lectr., 1965-81, rector, 1981—; aux. bishop Archdiocese of Boston, 1981—. Author: Preparation for Church Ministry, 1979; also articles. Assn. Theol. Schs. grantee, 1976. Mem. Cath. Theol. Soc. Am., Nat. Fedn. Sem. Dirs. (bd. dirs. 1975-79). Address: Saint John's Sem Brighton MA 02135

HUGHES, EDWARD T. See *Who's Who in America*, 43rd edition.

HUGHES, HUBERT EUGENE, minister, Wesleyan Ch.; b. Randolph County, Ind., May 21, 1928; s. Cleftie Aaron and Rachel Ioma (Todd) H.; student Frankfort Pilgrim Coll., 1945-47, Marion Coll., 1947-50; m. Irma Jean Householder, June 15, 1948; children—Suzanne Louise, Rachel Beth, Michelle Lanette. Ordained to ministry, 1954; pastor Pilgrim Holiness Ch., Benkelman, Nebr., 1951-54, Albuquerque, 1954-56, Imperial, Nebr., 1956-61; pastor Taft Hill Wesleyan Ch., Ft. Collins, Colo., 1961-74, 1st Wesleyan Ch., Nashville, 1974—. Mem. Mayor's Com. against Crime, Nashville, 1976-77. Mem. Christian Holiness Assn., Wesleyan Theol. Soc. Home: 907 Potter Ln Nashville TN 37206 Office: 611 Shelby Ave Nashville TN 37206

HUGHES, ROBERT DAVIS, III, theological educator, Episcopal Church; b. Boston, Feb. 16, 1943; s. Robert Davis and Nancy (Wolfe) H.; m. Barbara Brunn, June 12, 1965; children: Robert David, Thomas Dunstan. B.A., Yale U., New Haven, 1966; M.Divinity, Episcopal Divinity Sch., 1969; M.A., U. St. Michael's Coll., Toronto, Ont., 1973, Ph.D., 1980. Ordained deacon Episcopal Ch., 1969, priest, 1970. Assoc. rector Good Shepherd, Athens, Ohio, 1969-72; vicar Epiphany, Nelsonville, Ohio, 1969-72; asst. curate St. Anne's, Toronto, Ont., 1972-75; instr. Sch. of Theology, Univ. of South, Sewanee, Tenn., 1977—, assoc. prof. systematic theology, 1984—; dir. Anglican Center Christian Family Life, Sewanee, Tenn., 1981—. Mem. Dept. Christian Edn. Ecumenical Commn. Alcohol and Drug Commn., Diocese Tenn., 1981—. Contbr. articles to various publs. Soloist Toronto Chamber Soc., 1975-77; pres., soloist Sewanee Chorale, Sewanee, Tenn., 1977—; vol. Community Chest, Boy Scouts Am., Sewanee, 1979—; pres. Sewanee Chem. Dependency Assn., 1982. Episcopal Ch. Found. fellow, 1972—; Kent fellow Danforth Found., 1975-77; Sabbatical grantee Mercer and Conant funds, 1984. Mem. AAUP (v.p. chpt. 1982-83), Conf. Anglican Theologicans, Phi Beta Kappa. Democrat. Clubs: E.Q.B. (bd. dirs. 1981-83) (Sewanee, Tenn.); Crystal Lake Yacht (Frankfort, Mich.). Office: Sch of Theology Univ of the South Sewanee TN 37375

HUGHES, WILLIAM ANTHONY See *Who's Who in America*, 43rd edition.

HUGUS, JOHN EARL, III, pastor, Lutheran Church in America. B. Danville, Pa., May 16, 1952; s. Howard Shannon and Rachel Snyder (Berstresser) H.; m. Martha Gail Loadholt, May 16, 1976; 1 child, Amelia Shannon. B.A., Newberry Coll., 1974; M.Div., Luth. Theol. Sem. at Phila., 1978. Ordained to ministry Lutheran Church in America, 1979. Pastor Ch. of Holy Spirit, Estate Hope, Sao Tome and Principe, 1979—; assoc. pastor Frederick Evangel. Luth. Ch., Charlotte Amalie, Sao Tome and Principe, 1979—; bd. dirs. Luth. Soc. Services, Caribbean Synod, Virgin Islands dist., 1980—, mem. alcoholism task force, chmn. parish life com., 1982—, synod exec. officer for ecumenical relations, mem. profl. leadership com., 1983—. Mem. (seaman) U.S. Power Squadrons, Naples, Fla., 1971—; v.p. Shaky Acres Alcoholism Halfway House, Charlotte Amalie, 1982—; USO, Charlotte Amalie, 1983—; bd. dirs. Council on Alcoholism St. Thomas/St. John, Charlotte Amalie, 1983—, pres., 1985—. Republican. Home: 41 A Taarneberg Charlotte Amalie Sao Tome and Principe 00802 Office: Frederick Evangelical Luth Ch PO Box 58 Charlotte Amalie Sao Tome and Principe 00801

HUIE, BILL WAYNE, church official, Presbyterian Church U.S.A.; b. Gadsden, Ala., Feb. 11, 1933; s. William Hoyt and Margaret Lois (Noah) H.; B.A., Ga. State U., 1965; M.Div., Columbia Theol. Sem., 1968; D.D., Nebr. Christian Coll., 1972, Southwestern Coll., 1976; m. Marsha K. Hughes, Aug. 28, 1982; 1 dau. by previous marriage, Kathrine Kore. Dir. radio TV, Radio and Audio-Visuals, Presbyn. Ch. U.S., Atlanta, 1968-73, staff dir. electronic media, 1973-75, dir. communications, 1975—. Mem. bd. mgrs. Communication Commn., Nat. Council Chs., 1973—; bd. dirs., mem. exec. com. Intermedia, Nat. Council Chs., 1974—; mem. Cable-TV Com. for Joint Ednl. Devel., 1975-76; bd. dirs. World Assn. Christian Communication, 1973—, Protestant Radio and TV Center, 1970—; mem. ecumenical coordinating team Presbyn. Ch. U.S., 1975—; mem. CBS adv. com. for religious and pub. affairs, 1974-75. Recipient Gabriel awards UNDA, 1973, 74, 76, awards Billboard Mag., 1973, 74, 75, 76, Clio awards Internat. Advt. Assn., 1974, Internat. Broadcasting awards, 1974, 82, 83, 84, citation Nat. Council Chs. of Christ U.S.A., 1975, John Foster Peabody award, 1984. Mem. Broadcast Edn. Assn., Radio Advt. Bur., TV Bur. Advt., Nat. Acad. Recording Arts and Scis. (nat. v.p., nat. trustee; bd. dirs. ednl. inst.; exec. editor quar. jour.). Editor What's It All About?, radio programs broadcast in 14 countries, 1969—; contbr. articles to religious jours. Home: 3619 Autumn Leaves Ln NE Marietta GA 30066 Office: 341 Ponce de Leon Ave NE Atlanta GA 30365

HULBERG, JAMES ARLEN, minister, American Lutheran Church; b. Eau Claire, Wis., Oct. 11, 1938; s. Torval S. and Marie Viola (Aaasgard) H.; m. Esther Thordis Konsterlie, Jan. 5, 1969; children: Paul, John. B.A., St. Olaf Coll., 1960; B.D., Luther Sem., 1964. Ordained to ministry Am. Luth. Ch., 1964. Founding pastor first ecumenical parish involving Am. Luth. Ch., Adrian, Minn., 1964-69; sr. pastor 1st Luth. Ch., Volga, S.D., 1969-82; Am. Luth. Ch., Milbank, S.D., 1982—; religious broadcaster. Home: 912 S Viola Milbank SD

57252 Office: Am Luth Ch 111 W 5th Ave Milbank SD 57252

HULL, J. ROGER, JR., minister, Presbyterian Church U.S.A.; b. Nashville, Mar. 20, 1937; s. J. Roger and Rosalie (Paschal) H.; m. Judy Brown, Nov. 11, 1967; children: Deborah, Hannah and Abigail (twins). B.A., Amherst Coll., 1959; B.D., Princeton Theol. Sem., 1964, Th.M., 1969; D.Min., San Francisco Sem., 1982. Ordained to ministry Presbyn. Ch. U.S.A., 1964. Pastor, United Ch. of Van Ness, Bronx, 1964-68, Broadway Presbyn. Ch., N.Y.C., 1968-77, Old First Presbyn. Ch., San Francisco, 1978—; mem. evangelism com. Presbyn. Ch. U.S.A., 1982-85, candidate for moderator, 1982; trustee Princeton Theol. Sem., 1983—; chmn. long-range planning com. Presbytery of San Francisco, 1983—. Mem., World Affairs Council of No. Calif., 1978—; assoc. class agt. Amherst Coll., 1983—. Served as agt. USMCR, 1956-62. Am. Field Service internat. scholar, 1954. Democrat. Club: Kiwanis (San Francisco). Avocations: Fishing; skiing; golf. Home: 493 Molino Dr San Francisco CA 94127 Office: Old First Presbyn Ch 1751 San Francisco CA 94109

HUMBARD, REX EMANUEL See *Who's Who in America*, 43rd edition.

HUMBER, JOHN FRANK, minister of edn., So. Baptist Conv.; b. Cuthbert, Ga., Mar. 1, 1949; s. Frank and Ruby Mae (Jordan) H.; B.A., Samford U., 1971; M.R.E., New Orleans Sem., 1973; m. Sheila Marie Graham, Dec. 28, 1971. Licensed to ministry, 1968; minister edn. and activities Grove Level Bapt. Ch., Dalton, Ga., 1973-76; minister edn. First Bapt. Ch., Quitman, Ga., 1976—. Mem. joint steering com., nominating com. N.Ga. Assn., Dalton; sec.-treas. Quitman Assn.; associational vocation bible sch. team mem. N.Ga. Assn.; spl. Sunday sch. worker Ga. Bapt. Mem. Eastern, Ga. religious edn. assns. Home: PO Box 653 Quitman GA 31643 Office: PO Box 569 Quitman GA 31643

HUMBERT, JOHN O. Gen. minister, pres., Christian Church (Disciples of Christ) Indpls., 1985—. Office: 222 S Downey Ave Box 1986 Indianapolis IN 46206*

HUME, JESSICA A., church business administrator, Presbyterian Ch.; b. Indpls., Jan. 14, 1945; d. A. Robert and Jessie S. (Reece) Vestal; m. Gary L. Hume, June 18, 1966; children: Gretchen Renee, Christopher Michael. B.A. in Secretarial Sci., Butler U., 1965. Bus. adminstr. Old Bethel United Meth. Ch., Indpls., 1979-83, Second Presbyn. Ch., Indpls., 1983—; del. So. Ind. Conf. United Meth. Ch. Bd. of Missions and Ch. Extension, Bloomington, 1984—. Mem. Nat. Assn. of Ch. Bus. Adminstrs. (regional v.p. 1984—, chmn. pub. relations 1982-83, pres. Indpls. chpt. 1981-83), Presbyn. Ch. Bus. Adminstrn. Assn., United Presbyn. Assn. of Ch. Bus. Adminstrs., Nat. Assn. Ch. Bus. Adminstrs. (Nat. Trail chpt.). Office: Second Presbyn Ch 7700 N Meridian St Indianapolis IN 46260

HUMMEL, GENE MAYWOOD, bishop, Reorganized Church of Jesus Christ of Latter-day Saints; b. Lancaster, Ohio, Nov. 12, 1926; s. Ivan Maywood and Anna Mildred (Black) H.; student Miami U., Oxford, O., 1944, Dartmouth, 1944-45; B.S. in Agr. Ohio State U., 1949, B.S. in Agrl. Engring., 1950; m. R. Jeannine Lane, June 17, 1950; children—Gregory L., G. Michael. Ordained to ministry Reorganized Ch. of Jesus Christ of Latter-day Saints, 1961; ministerial asst. to Center Stake bishop, Independence, Mo., 1961-63; bishop San Francisco Bay stake, 1964-70, Hawaii, 1968-70, Center stake, Independence, 1970-72; bishop, mem. Presiding Bishopric, Internat. Ch., 1972—. Bd. dirs. Independence Sanatarium and Hosp., 1972—, Mound Grove Cemetery, Independence, 1970—, Reorganized Ch. of Jesus Christ of Latter-day Saints Social Service Center, Independence, 1970—. Mem. Independence C. of C. Rotarian. Home: 2024 S Leslie St Independence MO 60455 Office: Box 1059 221 W Lexintgon St Independence MO 64051

HUMPHREY, ARTHUR FRANK, priest, Roman Cath. Ch.; b. Elizabeth, N.J., Dec. 7, 1948; s. Frank Jennings and Ann (Healy) H.; B.A., Seton Hall U., 1971; M.Div., Darlington Sch. Theology, 1975. Ordained priest, 1975; youth minister St. Joseph the Carpenter Parish, Roselle, N.J., 1975—. Chaplain, mem. faculty St. Joseph's Grammar Sch.; chaplain Roselle Police Dept.; mem. social action com. Roselle-Roselle Park Interfaith Council; instr. Permanent Diaconate Program, Archdiocese of Newark; master of ceremonies to Bishop Dominic Marconi; bd. dirs. Cath. Youth Orgn.; faculty Girls High Sch., Roselle. Home: 157 4th Ave Roselle NJ 07203

HUNDIAK, MARK. Archbishop Ukrainian Orthodox Church in the U.S.A. Office: Ukrainian Orthodox Ch in the USA 641 Roosevelt Ave Carteret NJ 07008*

HUNEKE, JOHN GEORGE, minister, Lutheran Church in America; b. N.Y.C., Aug. 6, 1931; s. John Jacob and Adelaide (Peper) H. B.A., Columbia U., 1953; M.Div., Luth. Theol. Sem., Phila., 1956; Th.M., Harvard U., 1958. Ordained to ministry Lutheran Ch., 1958. Asst. pastor Holy Trinity Luth. Ch., Bklyn., 1957-59, Trinity Luth. Ch., Middle Village, N.Y., 1959-60; pastor St. John's Luth. Ch., Bklyn., 1960-73, Luth. Ch. of the Reformation, Bklyn., 1973—; instr. religion dept. Wagner Coll., S.I., N.Y., 1957-58; mem. stewardship com. Met. N.Y. Synod, Luth. Ch. in Am., 1966-73. Author: Our Church 1867-1967, 1967. Bd. govs. Greenpoint br. YMCA, Bklyn., 1963-73. Mem. Timotheans. Home: 6016 Palmetto St Ridgewood NY 11385 Office: Luth Ch of the Reformation 105 Barbey St Brooklyn NY 11207

HUNT, EARL GLADSTONE, JR., bishop, college president, United Methodist Church; b. Johnson City, Tenn., Sept. 14, 1918; s. Earl Gladstone and Tommie Mae (DeVault) H.; m. Mary Ann Kyker, June 15, 1943; 1 child, Earl Stephen. B.S., East Tenn. State U., 1941; M.Div., Emory U., 1946, D.D., 1983; D.D., Tusculum Coll., 1956, Lambuth Coll., 1978; LL.D., U. Chattanooga, 1957; D.C.L., Emory and Henry Coll., 1965; D.D., Duke U., 1969; L.H.D., Belmont Abbey Coll., 1976, Fla. So. Coll., 1981. Ordained to ministry Meth. Ch., 1944. Pastor Sardis Meth. Ch., Atlanta, 1942-44; assoc. pastor Broad Street Meth. Ch., Kingsport, Tenn., 1944-45, Wesley Meml. Meth. Ch., Chattanooga, 1945-50, First Meth. Ch., Morristown, Tenn., 1950-56; pres. Emory and Henry Coll., 1956-64; resident bishop Charlotte Area United Meth. Ch., 1964-76, Nashville area, 1976-80, Fla. area, 1980—; participant Meth. series Protestant Hour, nationwide broadcast, 1956; mem. Meth. Gen. Bd. Edn., 1956-68; bd. fellows Interpreters' House, Inc., 1967-78; del. Meth. Gen. Conf., 1956, 60, 64, S.E. Jurisdictional Conf., 1952, 56, 60, 64; chmn. gen. commn. family life United Meth. Ch., 1968-72, mem. gen. council ministries, 1972-80, chmn. bicentennial planning com., 1978-80; pres. Southeastern Jurisdictional Coll. Bishops, 1973, Southeastern Jurisdictional Conf. Council on Ministries, 1978-80; Gen. Bd. Higher Edn. and Ministry, 1980-84; lectr. numerous religious and ednl. founds.; chmn. Com. to Revise United Meth. Theol. Statement, 1985—. Author: I Have Believed, 1980. Editor: Storms and Starlight, 1974. Contbr. numerous articles to scholarly jours., mags. Trustee Emory U., Fla. So. Coll., Bethune-Cookman Coll., Wesleyan Coll., Lake Junaluska United Meth. Assembly, Found. Theol. Edn.; keynote speaker World Meth. Conf., Dublin, 1976; exec. com. World Meth. Council, 1976—, chmn. N. Am. div., 1981—; mem. governing bd. Nat. Council Chs., 1968-84; mem. Com. One Hundred, Emory U. Mem. Newcomen Soc., Blue Key, Pi Kappa Delta. Address: PO Box 1747 Lakeland FL 33802

HUNT, HARRY BASS, JR., minister, Old Testament educator, Southern Baptist Convention; b. Marshall, Tex., July 16, 1944; s. Harry Bass and Annie Beverly (Ross) H.; m. Patricia Lou Blackwell, Jan. 23, 1965; children: Patrick Douglas, Amy Carol. B.S., Stephen F. Austin State U., 1966; M.Div., Southwestern Bapt. Theol. Sem., 1968, Th.D., 1972, Ph.D., 1978. Ordained to ministry, So. Bapt. Conf., 1965. Pastor Pleasant Valley Bapt. Ch., Jonesboro, Tex., 1965-70, Friendship Bapt. Ch., Gladewater, Tex., 1971-73; asst. prof. Religion Southwest Bapt. Coll., Boliver, Mo., 1973-76; assoc. prof. Old Testament Southwestern Bapt. Theol. Sem., Fort Worth, 1976—; deacon South Hills Bapt. Ch., Fort Worth, 1978—; numerous interim pastorates. Author: (workbook) Old Testament Background Material, 1977. Contbr. articles to profl. jours. Mem. Am. Sch. Oriental Research, Nat. Assn. Profs. of Hebrew, Soc. Bibl. Lit., Assn. Bapt. Profs. of Religion (v.p. 1983-84, pres. 1984-85). Home: 1313 Country Manor Rd Fort Worth TX 76134 Office: Southwestern Bapt Theol Sem 2001 W Seminary Dr Fort Worth TX 76122

HUNTER, CHARLES ALVIN, minister, United Presbyterian Church U.S.A.; b. Longview, Tex., May 7, 1926; s. Wallace Alvin and Ivernia Charlott (Fleming) H.; B.A., Bishop Coll., 1947; B.D., Howard U., 1950; M.Th., Phila. Div. Sch., 1954, Th.D., 1958; M.S. in Sociology, North Tex. State U., 1970; m. Annie Mary Alexander, June 5, 1950; children: Alpha Angela, Rhonda Felming, Rhasell Debra, Byron Charles, Rosalyn A. Ordained to ministry, 1946; pastor chs., Ala., 1950-52, Fla., 1959-61; dir. United Campus Christian Fellowship, Fla. A. and M. U., Tallahassee, 1959-61; minister, Hope Presbyn. Ch., Dallas, 1962-68; assoc. pastor St. Luke Presbyn. Ch., Dallas, 1969-81; moderator Covenant Presbytery, Tex., 1985; prof. sociology Bishop Coll., Dallas, 1961—. Mem. Southwestern Social Sci. Assn., So. Sociol. Assn., AAUP, Amigos, NAACP, Alpha Kappa Delta. Home: 2329 Southwood Dr Dallas TX 75224 Office: 3837 Simpson Stuart Rd Dallas TX 75241

HUNTER, HOWARD WILLIAM, church official, Church of Jesus Christ of Latter-day Saints; b. Boise, Idaho, Nov. 14, 1907; s. John William and Nellie May (Rasmussen) H.; J.D., cum laude, Southwestern U., Los Angeles, 1939; m. Clara May Jeffs, June 10, 1931; children—Howard William, John Jacob, Richard Allen. Ordained apostle Ch. of Jesus Christ of Latter-day Saints, 1959; bishop, Los Angeles, 1941-47, high councilor, 1947-50; stake pres., Pasadena, Cal., 1950-59; mem. Council Twelve Apostles, Salt Lake City, 1959—. Dir. Deseret Fed. Savs. & Loan Assn., Beneficial Life Ins. Co., Utah Home Fire Ins. Co., Weber J. Grant & Co., 1st Security Corp., Beverly Enterprises, Pasadena, Watson Land Co., Los Angeles. Trustee Brigham Young U., Ricks Coll., Ch. Coll. of Hawaii; pres. Polynesian Cultural Center (Laie, Hawaii). Office: 50 E N Temple St Salt Lake City UT 84150

HUNTER, JOHN E. Bishop, African Methodist Episcopal Church (Nineteenth Dist.). Office: 22335 La Garonne Southville MI 48075*

HUNTER, LEA ANNE, nun, Roman Catholic Church; b. Summit, N.J., June 13, 1945; d. Edward Francis and Thelma Henrietta (Baker) H. Joined Little Servant Sisters of the Immaculate Conception, 1964, Sisters for Christian Community, 1980. Dir. religious edn. St. Matthew's Parish, National Park, N.J., 1968-72; missionary Papago Indians, San Solano Missions, Topowa, Ariz., 1972-76; contemplative, Vincentown, N.J., 1976-78; dir. ednl. ministry to poor Diocese of Allentown, Pa., 1979—; founder Montessori sch. for Papago Indians, 1974. Author: Learning Clubs for the Poor, 1984. Contbr. article to profl. jour.

HUNTER, LEWIS EDGAR, minister, Southwide Baptist Fellowship; b. Akron, Ohio, Aug. 11, 1954; s. Lewis Ervin and Inez Alma (Vaught) H.; grad. Tenn. Temple Bible Coll., 1975; m. Pamela Arlene Freer, July 12, 1975. Ordained to ministry, 1976; minister of music and youth Valley Bapt. Ch., Chattanooga, 1974-75, Northgate Bapt. Ch., Knoxville, Tenn., 1975-76; minister of music Faith Bapt. Ch., Avon, Ind., 1976—; interim adminstr. Christian Acad., Inc. Mem. Internat. Thespian Soc. Home: 270 Avon Ave Plainfield IN 46168 Office: Rural Route 1 Box 262 Danville IN 46122

HUNTHAUSEN, RAYMOND GERHARDT, archbishop, Roman Catholic Church; b. Anaconda, Mont., Aug. 21, 1921; s. Anthony G. and Edna Marie (Tuchscherer) H.; B.A., Carroll Coll., 1943; M.Div., St. Edward's Sem., 1946; postgrad. St. Louis U., 1947, Cath. U. Am., 1948-49, Fordham U., 1950; M.S., U. Notre Dame 1953; LL.D., DePaul U., 1960. Ordained priest Roman Catholic Ch., 1946, consecrated bishop, 1962; faculty Carroll Coll., 1946-57, pres., 1957-62; bishop of Helena, Mont., 1962-75; archbishop of Seattle, 1975—; domestic prelate, 1958-62. Office: Archdiocese of Seattle 907 Terry Ave Seattle WA 98104*

HUNTLEY, THOMAS ELLIOTT, minister, Nat. Bapt. Conv., U.S.A., Inc.; b. Wadesboro, N.C., June 28, 1903; s. John Preston and Lula J. (Brewer) H.; B.A., Morehouse Coll., 1934, D.D., 1984; postgrad. Atlanta U., 1937, Union Theol. Sem., 1951; m. Kiffie Elizabeth Esther Maddox, Dec. 21, 1933. Ordained to ministry, 1928. Pastor Hall St. Bapt. Ch., Montgomery, Ala., 1933-38, Mt. Zion Bapt. Ch., Pensacola, Fla., 1938-41, Spruce St. Bapt. Ch., Nashville, Tenn., 1941-42, Central Bapt. Ch., St. Louis, 1942-83. Founder, Mobile Ch. Ministry, Ch.-on-Wheels, 1947; organizer Ministers Prayer March on Washington, 1948; student pastor, treas. Coll. YMCA, 1925-26. Recipient citation St. Louis Met. Ch. Fedn., 1958, award Phi Beta Sigma, 1973, award for lit. achievement Sigma Gamma Rho, 1976. Mem. Americans United for Separation of Ch. and State, NAACP, Soc. Sci. Study Religion, Urban League, Phi Beta Sigma. Author: As I Saw It (Not Communism but Commonism), 1954; Huntley's Manual for Every Baptist, 1963; editor Bharath Social and Cultural Trust of South India, 1957. Home: 4959 Cote Brilliante St Louis MO 63113 Office: 2842 Washington Blvd St Louis MO 63103

HUNTLEY, WILLIAM BARNEY, educator, minister, United Presbyterian Church in U.S.A.; b. Charlotte, N.C., Feb. 19, 1933; s. William Barney and Mary Betts (Reid) H.; B.A., Duke U., 1955, Ph.D., 1964; postgrad. U. Edinburgh, 1959-60; B.D., Yale U., 1961; m. Helen Rank, June 18, 1961; children: Heather, Kim. Ordained minister United Presbyn. Ch. in U.S.A., 1964. Prof. religion, chmn. div. humanities Westminister Coll., Mo., 1964-74; prof. religion U. Redlands, Calif., 1974—, dir. Jameson Ctr., Study Religion and Ethics, 1976-84. Danforth grantee, U. Calif.-Berkeley, 1970-71. Mem. Soc. Study History of Early Am. Republic, Omicron Delta Kappa. Author articles. Home: 1474 Pacific Redlands CA 92373

HURAS, WILLIAM DAVID, bishop, Lutheran Church in America; b. Kitchener, Ont., Can., Sept. 22, 1932; s. William Adam and Frieda Dorothea (Rose) H.; m. Barbara Elizabeth Lotz, Oct. 5, 1957; children: David, Matthew, Andrea. B.A., Waterloo Coll., 1954; M.Th., Knox Coll., 1968; M.Div., Waterloo Luth. U., 1973; D.D. (hon.), Wilfred Laurier Coll., 1980. Ordained to ministry Luth. Ch. in Am., 1957. Pastor, St. James Ch., Renfrew, Ont., 1957-62, Advent Ch., Willowdale, Toronto, Ont., 1962-78; bishop Eastern Can. Synod, Luth. Ch. Am., Kitchener, 1978—; mem. exec. com., cons. Can. sect. Luth. Ch. Am., 1969—, sec., 1975-79; pastoral counselor Toronto Inst. Human Relations, 1970-78; mem. Luth. Merger Commn., 1978—; pres. Luth. Council in Can., Winnipeg, Man., 1985. Mem. Can. Assn. Pastoral Edn. Office: Eastern Can Synod-Luth Ch in Am 2d Floor Commerce House 50 Queen St N Kitchener ON N2A 2X8 Canada

HURLBERT, DONALD EARL, minister, Ind. Fundamental Chs. Am.; b. Oshawa, Ont., Can., Sept. 8, 1924; s. Earl Thomas and Eleanor Gertrude (Root) H.; came to U.S., 1945, naturalized, 1956; diploma Moody Bible Inst., 1949; B.A., S.E. Mo. State Coll., 1954; m. Donna Lovena Liichow, Aug. 6, 1949; children—David, Gary, Phillip, Paul, Richard. Ordained to ministry, 1950; pastor York (Pa.) Gospel Center, 1968—; mem. exec. com. York Bible Inst., 1970—; chmn. bd. Christian Sch. of York, 1972—; bd. dirs. Lancaster Bible Coll., 1973—; nat. pres. Ind. Fundamental Chs. Am., 1975—. Home: 251 Reynolds Mill Rd York PA 17403 Office: Box 1 York PA 17405

HURLEY, FRANCIS T., archbishop, Roman Catholic Church; b. Jan. 12, 1927. Ordained priest Roman Catholic Ch., 1951, consecrated bishop, 1970; titular bishop Daimlaig, 1970-71, bishop Diocese of Juneau, Alaska, 1971-77; ordinary of See, 1971-77; archbishop of Anchorage, 1976—. Address: Archdiocese of Anchorage 2111 Muldoon Rd Anchorage AK 99504*

HURLEY, MARK JOSEPH, bishop, Roman Catholic Church; b. San Francisco, Dec. 13, 1919; s. Mark Joseph and Josephine (Keohane) H.; student St. Joseph Coll., Mountain View, Calif., 1937-39, St. Patricks Coll., Menlo Park, Cal., 1939-44; postgrad. U. Calif. at Berkeley, 1944-45; Ph.D., Cath. U. Am., 1947; J.C.B., Lateran U., Rome, 1963; LL.D., U. Portland (Ore.), 1971. Ordained priest Roman Catholic Ch., 1944; named domestic prelate, 1962; consecrated bishop, 1968; asst. archdiocesan coordinator Campaign of Taxation of Schs. in Calif., 1958; asst. archdiocesan coordinator Rosary Crusade, 1961; adminstr. Cath. Sch. Purchasing Div., 1948-51; adminstr. St. Eugene's Ch., Santa Rosa, Calif., 1959, St. Johns Ch., San Francisco, 1961; chancellor Diocese of Stockton, diocesan consultor, 1962-65; asst. chancellor Archdiocese of San Francisco, 1965-69; aux. bishop of San Francisco, 1967-69; apptd. bishop of Santa Rosa, 1969. Asst. supt. schs. Archdiocese of San Francisco, 1944-51; prin. Bishop O'Dowd High Sch., Oakland, Calif., 1951-58, Marin Cath. High Sch., Marin County, Calif., 1959-61; supt. schs. Diocese of Stockton, Calif., 1962-65; prof. Grad. Schs., Loyola U., Balt., U. San Francisco, San Francisco Coll. for Women, Dominican Coll. of San Rafael, Cath. U. Am. Syndicated columnist San Francisco Monitor, Sacramento Herald, Oakland Voice, Yakima Our Times, Guam Diocesan Press, 1949-66; speaker Faith of Our Fathers TV Weekly Program, 1956-58; TV panelist weekly program Problems Please, San Francisco, 1961-69; mem. U.S.A. Bishops Press Panel, Vatican Council, Rome, 1964; mem. U.S.A. Bishops Com. for Cath. Jewish Relationships, 1965—; chmn. Bishops Com. for Ecumenical and Interreligious Affairs, 1970; mem. Conf. Psychiatry and Religion, San Francisco, 1957; Cath. del. and observer Nat. Council Chs., Columbus, Ohio, 1964; del. Nat. Cath. Edn. Assn. Ednl. Conf. German and Am. Educators, Munich, Germany, 1960, now mem. commn.; papal appointment to Internat. Com. of Secretariat for Non-Believers, 1973; moderator Secretariat Human Values Nat. Conf. Cath. Bishops, Washington, 1974, mem. adminstrv. com., 1976; trustee Cath. U. Am., 1980—. Del. at large State of Calif., White House Conf. on Youth, Washington, 1960. Bd. dirs. Calif. Com. for Study Edn., 1955-60; trustee N.Am. Coll., Rome, 1970. Mem. Nat. Conf. Cath. Bishops. Author: Privacy, An Inalienable Right?, 1974. Contbr. articles to profl. jours. Office: PO Box 1297 Santa Rosa CA 95403

HURT, BILLY GREY, minister, Southern Baptist Convention; b. Hazel, Ky., Sept. 27, 1931; s. Wilburn and Geneva Lawrence H.; m. Verr Scharlyene Harbison, Mar. 15, 1951; children: Billy Grey, Robert Hal, Mark Harbison. A.A., Cumberland Coll., 1951; A.B., Union U., Jackson, Tenn., 1956; M.Div., So. Sem., Louisville, 1959, Ph.D., 1966. Ordained to ministry, So. Bapt. Conv., 1952; pastor Shady Grove Bapt. Ch., Murray, Ky., 1956-60, 1st Bapt. Ch., Benton, Ky., 1960-66, 1st Bapt. Ch., Independence, Mo., 1966-71, Immanuel Bapt. Ch., Paducah, Ky., 1971-77, 1st Bapt. Ch., Frankfort, Ky., 1977—. Trustee, Cumberland Coll. Williamsburg, Ky., 1980—; adj. prof. So. Sem., 1980—; chmn. program com. Christian Life Com., Nashville, 1985; chaplain Ky. Gen. Assembly, 1980, 84. Mem. Blue Grass Area Devel. Council, 1981-84. Vis. prof. N.T., Georgetown Coll. (Ky.), 1980. Fellow So. Sem.; mem. Franklin Bapt. Assn. (pres. 1981; chmn. resolutions com. 1983, chmn. budget com. 1985). Lodge: Rotary. Home: 8 Breckinridge Blvd Frankfort KY 40601 Office: 1st Bapt Ch 201 St Clair St Frankfort KY 40601

HURTER, NOREEN MARGARET, religious superior, former educator, Roman Catholic Church; b. Cranford, N.J., Nov. 22, 1927; d. Henry George and Ruth Ann (Saunderson) H. B.A., Mt. St. Scholastica, 1950; M.S.L.S., Cath. U. Am., 1963; M.S. in Edn., U.So. Calif., 1969. Joined Sisters of Mt. St. Scholastica, 1950. Prioress Mt. St. Scholastica Convent, Atchison, Kans., 1976—.

HUSBAND, J. D., Bishop, mem. gen. bd. The Church of God in Christ. Office: The Church of God in Christ PO Box 824 SW Atlanta GA 30310*

HUSBAND, RICHARD LORIN, lay church worker, Episcopal Church; furniture company executive; b. Spencer, Iowa, July 28, 1931; s. Ross Twetten and Frances Estelle (Hall) H.; A.A., Rochester Community Coll., 1952; B.A., U. Minn., 1955; m. Darlene Joyce Granberg, Mar. 21, 1954; children: Richard, Thomas R., Mark T., Julia L., Susan E. Pres. Rochester Area Council Chs., 1969-70, bd. dirs., 1966-72; mem. ho. of deps. Protestant Episcopal Ch. of Am., 1969-73; lay stewardship speaker Episcopal Ch., Diocese of Minn., 1966—, mem. State Planning Commn., 1970-76, state v.p. State Youth, 1950-51, del. to conv., 1958—, chmn., 1978, chmn. planning and agenda, 1979—; sr. high ch. sch. instr. Calvary Episcopal Ch., Rochester, 1958-68, ch. sch. chmn., 1966, vestryman, clk., jr. warden, 1966-70, sr. warden, 1979-80; mem. Ch. Extension Com., Diocese of Minn.; co-founder Ann. H.D. Mayo meml. lectures on religion. Pres., owner Orlen Ross Furniture, Inc., Rochester, Minn., 1964—. Pres. Rochester Symphony Orch., Chorale, Chamber and Opera, 1974, Rochester Arts Council, 1970-71, Mayowood State Historic Home, 1966-67, Adv. Com. on Rochester Edn., 1968-73; v.p. statewide com. U. Minn.-Rochester, 1968-72; v.p. Minn. Congress of Parents and Teachers, 1967-70; chmn. Am. Revolution Bicentennial Commn. Olmsted County, 1974—; trustee Seabury-Western Theol. Sem., Evanston, Ill., 1974—; chmn. Minn. 125th Anniversary, 1983. Named One of Minn.'s Ten Outstanding Young Men, 1966; Outstanding Young Man of Am., 1967; recipient Disting. Service award Rochester Jr. C. of C., 1965, Disting. Christian Service award Seabury Western Theol. Sem., 1983. Mem. Olmsted County Hist. Soc. (trustee 1964—, pres. 1976—), 1st Dist. Hist. Assn. Minn. (pres. 1970-72), Minn. Retail Fedn. (trustee 1972—), Minn. Home Furnishings Assn. (trustee 1968—, pres. 1976), Soc. Desc. Colonial Clergy, Minn. Mayflower Desc. (jr. dep. gov.), Minn. Hist. Soc. (exec. council 1983—), U. Minn. Alumni Assn. (life), U. Minn. Alumni Club (charter), Rochester Civil War Roundtable (founder), Olmsted County Archeology Soc. (founder). Home: 1820 26th St NW Rochester MN 55901 Office: 105 N Broadway Rochester MN 55904

HUTCHENS, EUGENE GARLINGTON, minister, So. Bapt. Conv.; b. Birmingham, Ala.; s. Wallace Luther and Reydonia (Corry) H.; B.A., Samford U., Birmingham, 1952; B.D., New Orleans Baptist Theol. Sem., 1956; M.Th., 1970; M.S. in Econs. (NSF grantee), U. Mo.-Columbia, 1972; m. Betty Frances Goode, Aug. 26, 1951; children—Dale Eugene, Wayne Goode, Dennis Wade. Ordained minister, 1952; pastor North Brewton Bapt. Ch., Brewton, Ala., 1st Bapt. Ch., Ashland, Ala., Highlands Bapt. Ch., Huntsville, Ala., 1st Bapt. Ch., Toney, Ala.; pastor Elkton Rd. Bapt. Ch., Athens, Ala., 1976—; instr. social sci. N.W. Ala. State Jr. Coll., Phil Campbell, Ala., 1972—. Mem. exec. bd. Ala. Bapt. Conv., 1961-63; v.p. Ala. Bapt. Pastor's Conf., 1966; pres. Madison Bapt. Pastor's Conf., 1966-67. Recipient citation A.R.C. Mem. Nat., Ala. edn. assns., Nat. Council Geog. Edn. Home: 4004 Nelson Dr NW Huntsville AL 35810

HUTCHINSON, CLARK GILBERT, minister So. Bapt. Conv.; b. Hamburg, Iowa, Mar. 10, 1942; s. John Gilbert and Frances Willard (Ewton) H.; B.A., Baylor U., 1964; M.Div., Southwestern Theol. Sem., 1968; D. Ministry, Luther Rice Sem., 1977; m. Josephine Moore, Aug. 8, 1969; children—Joseph, Thomas. Ordained to ministry So. Bapt. Conv., 1966; asst. to pastor 1st. Bapt. Ch., Dallas, 1967-68; asst. pastor, 1968-70; pastor Bapt. Ch., Troy, Ala., 1970-73, Eastside Bapt. Ch., Marietta, Ga., 1973—. Mem. pastors' steering com. Agape Atlanta, 1974-75. Mem. Cobb County C. of C., Noonday Bapt. Pastors Assn., Kenestone Chaplains Assn. Home: 1489 Bollingbrook Rd Marietta GA 30067 Office: 339 Little Rd Marietta GA 30067

HUTHMACHER, HERBERT LEROY, minister, So. Bapt. Conv.; b. Charleston, S.C., Aug. 10, 1931; s. George Wingate and Ruby Elizabeth (Nix) H.; B.A., Furman U., Greenville, S.C., 1961; M.Div., Southeastern Bapt. Theol. Sem., 1968; m. Vivvian Al Bertha Quinby, Jan. 10, 1954; 1 dau., Joyce Lynne. Ordained to ministry, 1957; pastor Pine Pleasant Bapt. Ch., Saluda, S.C., 1957-60, Spring Gulley Bapt. Ch., Andrews, S.C., 1960-62, Front St. Bapt. Ch., Roxboro, N.C., 1963-67; asso. pastor Indian River Bapt. Ch., Chesapeake, Va., 1967-71; pastor Sea Gate Bapt. Ch., Wilmington, N.C., 1971-76, Sandy Run Bapt. Ch., Roxobel, N.C., 1976—. Chaplain Sea Gate Vol. Fire Dept., Wilmington, 1972-76; foster home for N.C. Bapt. Children's Home, 1972—. Treas. Bradley Creek Sch. PTA, Wilmington, 1973-76. Home and Office: PO Box 95 Roxobel NC 27872

HUXFORD, SAMUEL WILDER, III, minister, Christian Churches/Churches of Christ; b. Moncks Corner, S.C., Mar. 28, 1951; s. Samuel Wilder II and Ellen DuBois (Crowder) W.; m. Vicki Lynn Kindt, Aug. 10, 1973; children: Sarah Gayle, Bethany Lynn. A.B., Atlanta Christian Coll., 1973; M.Div., Cin. Christian Sem., 1976. Ordained minister Christian Chs./Chs. of Christ, 1973. Minister, English Christian Ch., Carrollton, Ky., 1973-76; prof. Greek Atlanta Christian Coll., East Point, 1976-84; sr. minister First Christian Ch., College Park, Ga., 1984—; trustee Auburn Christian Fellowship, Ala., 1978—, Pathway Christian Sch., East Point, Ga., 1979—, Christian City, College Park, 1983. Mem. Soc. Biblical Lit., Am. Acad. Religion, Hist. Soc. Disciples of Christ. Republican. Home: 2333 Dabney Terr East Point GA 30344 Office: First Christian Ch 5665 Old National Hwy College Park GA 30349

HUYCK, ALBERT WARREN, JR., pastor, Southern Baptist Convention; b. Maysville, Ky., Oct. 6, 1932; s. Albert Warren and Charlie Mae (Anderson) H.; m. Sydelle Lavenia Gosnell, Aug. 16, 1956; children: Kenneth Warren, Charles David, Thomas Wayne. B.A., Furman U., 1954; M.Div., Southeastern Bapt. Theol. Sem., 1957. Ordained to ministry So. Bapt. Conv., 1955. Pastor, 1st Bapt. Ch., Washington, Ga., 1974—, Royston Bapt. Ch. (Ga.), 1960-68, 1st Bapt. Ch., Swainsboro, Ga., 1968-74; chmn. dirs. Penfield Christian Home (Ga.), 1978—; trustee Tift Coll., Forsyth, Ga., 1970—. Chmn., Augusta Area Mental Health, 1980-81; bd. dirs. Salvation Army, 1976—. Lt. col., aide de camp Staff Gov. Harris Ga., 1984. Mem. Ga. Bapt. Assn. (moderator 1977-78), Ga. Bapt. Assn. Pastors Conf. (pres. 1977-78). Lodge: Rotary (pres. 1977-78). Home: Route 2 Box 222 Washington GA 30673 Office: 1st Bapt Ch PO Box 603 Washington GA 30673

HYATT, G. W., ch. ofcl., Am. Evang. Christian Chs. Grad. Lindlawr Chiropractic Coll.; S.T.D., St. Andrews Sem. Moderator; pres. Am. Bible Coll. Fellow Royal Geog. Soc., Internat. Acad. Address: Waterfront Dr Pineland FL 33945

HYATT, MARVIN EDWIN, minister, Church of God, Anderson, Indiana; b. Saginaw, Mich., Oct. 3, 1951; s. Marvin Raymond and Marguerite Louise (Leach) H.; m. Janette Elaine Bennett, Dec. 18, 1971; children: Rachel Marie, Craig Stephen. A.A., Delta Coll., 1972; B.A., Saginaw Valley Coll., 1973; M.Min., Anderson Sch. Theology, 1975, M.Div., 1976. Ordained to ministry, 1978. Pastor, East Side Ch. of God, Swift Current, Sask., Can., 1976—; mem. nomination com., chmn. Western Can. Ch. of God, Camrose, Alta., 1980—; bd. dirs. pub. bd. Ch. of God, Anderson, 1982—, Western Can. Ch. of God, 1984—, Gardner Bible Coll., 1980-83; Sask. youth advisor Sask. Ch. of God, 1978—. Mem. Refugee Resettlement joint com. of Can. Manpower & Immigration and Community Service Group, 1979-81. Mem. Fellowship of Evang. Chs., Swift Current Ministerial Assn. Democrat. Home: 1144 Winnie St E Swift Current SK Canada S9H 1R1 Office: East Side Church of God 1465 Winnie St E Swift Current SK S9H 1R2 Canada

IAKOVOS, (IAKOVOS GARMATIS), Bishop of Chgo., Greek Orthodox Archdiocese of North and South Am. Office: 40 E Burton Pl Chicago IL 60610*

IAKOVOS, ARCHBISHOP (DEMETRIOS A. COUCOUZIS), bishop, Greek Orthodox Ch.; b. Imvros, Turkey, July 29, 1911; s. Athanasios and Maria Coucouzis; grad. Theol. Sch. of Halki, Ecumenical Patriarchate, 1934; S.T.M., Harvard, 1945; D.D., Boston U, 1960, Bates Coll., 1970, Assumption Coll., 1980; L.H.D., Franklin and Marshall Coll., 1961, Seton Hall U., 1968, Cath. U. Am., 1974, Queens Coll., 1982; LL.D., Brown U., 1964, Notre Dame U., 1979; hon. degrees Holy Cross, Fordham U., 1966; H.H.D., Suffolk U., 1967; D.S.T., Gen. Theol. Sem., 1967, numerous others. Ordained deacon Greek Orthodox Ch., 1934, priest, 1940; archdeacon Met. Derkon, 1934-39, Greek Archdiocese, Pomfret, Conn., 1939; prof. Archdiocese Theol. Sch., Pomfret, 1939; parish priest, Hartford, Conn., 1940-41, St. Louis, 1942; preacher Holy Trinity Cathedral, N.Y.C., 1941-42; dean Cathedral of Annunciation, Boston, 1942-54; dean Holy Cross Orthodox Theol. Sch., Brookline, Mass., 1954; bishop of Melita, 1954-56; rep. Ecumenical Patriarchate, World Council Chs., Geneva, 1955-59, then co-pres. council; elevated to Metropolitan, 1956; archbishop N. and S. Am. Holy Synod of Ecumenical Patriarchate, 1959—; exarch, Ecumenical Patriarchate of Constantinople; leader of delegation of Ecumenical Patriarchate to World Council Chs. Assembly, Vancouver, B.C., Can., 1983; del. various internat. confs. Chmn. Standing Conf. Canonical Orthodox Bishops in the Americas; mem. adv. bd., v.p. Religion in Am. Life; hon. bd. adv. council on Religious Rights in Eastern Europe and the Soviet Union. Pres. St. Basil's Acad., Garrison, N.Y.; chmn. bd. trustees Hellenic Coll., Brookline; trustee Anatolia Coll., Salonika, Greece; internat. chmn. Investment in Children, Children's Heart Fund. Recipient Presidential Medal of Freedom, 1980; Inaugural award NY U, 1981; Patriarchate of Jerusalem, 1982; Silver World award Boy Scouts Am., 1984; Great Cross of the Holy Sepulchre. Mem. Am. Bible Soc. (bd. mgrs.). Author works in Greek, French, English. Address: 10 E 79th St New York City NY 10021

IBRAHIM, IBRAHIM N., clergyman. Chaldean apostolic exarch for the U.S., 1982, also titular bishop of Abnar. Office: Our Lady of Chaldeans Cathedral 25585 Berg Rd Southfield MI 48034*

ICE, RICHARD EUGENE, minister, American Baptist Churches in the U.S.A.; b. Ft. Lewis, Wash., Sept. 25, 1930; s. Shirley M. and Nellie Rebecca (Pedersen) I.; m. Pearl Lucille Daniels, July 17, 1955;

children: Lorinda Susan, Diana Laurene, Julianne Adele. A.A., Centralia Coll., 1950; B.A., Linfield Coll., 1952, L.H.D. (hon.), 1978; M.A., Berkeley Bapt. Div. Sch., 1959. Ordained to ministry Am. Bapt. Chs. in the U.S.A., 1954. Dir. ch. extension Wash. Bapt. Conv., Seattle, 1959-61; dir. loans Nat. Ministries, Am. Bapt. Chs., Valley Forge, Pa., 1961-64, dep. exec. sec., 1967-72, gen. bd., exec. com., 1982—; assoc. exec. minister Am. Bapt. Chs. West, Oakland, Calif., 1964-67; pres. Am. Bapt. Homes West, Oakland, 1972—; dir. Ministers Life Ins. Co., Mpls.; bd. dirs. Bacone Coll., Muskogee, Okla., 1969-77; Ministers and Missionaries Benefit Bd., N.Y.C., 1982—; trustee Linfield Coll., McMinnville, Oreg., 1972—, Grad. Theol. Union, Berkeley, Calif., 1982—; trustee Calif., Nev. Meth. Homes, Oakland, 1975—; mem. Bapt. Joint Commn. on Pub. Affairs, 1984—. Mem. Friends Commn. on Aging, 1983—. Recipient Disting. Baconian award Bacone Coll., 1977, Disting. Alumnus award Centralia Coll., 1981, Meritorious Service award Am. Assn. Homes for Aging, 1982, Merit citation Am. Bapt. Homes and Hosps. Assn., 1985. Democrat. Clubs: Athenian Nile, Lakeview (Oakland). Office: Am Bapt Homes West PO Box 6669 400 Roland Way Oakland CA 94621

ICHIM, DUMITRU, priest, Romanian Orthodox Ch.; writer, poet; b. Darmanesti, Bacau, Romania, Aug. 14, 1944; immigrated to Can., 1973, naturalized, 1978; s. Dumitru and Elena (Camara) I.; m. Florica Batu, May 24, 1974; 5 children. Student Neamtu Theol. Sem., 1959-64; student Theol. Inst. Bucharest, 1964-70, postgrad., 1968-70; student Seabury-Western Theol. Sem., 1970-72, Garrett Meth. Sem., 1970-72, McCormick Presbyn. Sem., 1970-72, Princeton Presbyn. Sem., 1972-73. Ordained priest Romanian Orthodox Ch., 1974. Priest, Romanian Orthodox Episcopate of Am., chs. in Can., 1974-79, St. John the Baptist Romanian Ch., Kitchener, Ont., 1979—. Author: De unde incepe Omul, 1970; Agape, 1983; also poetry and short stories. Editor Romanian Can. Herald. Mem. Am. Romanian Acad. Home: 71 Vanier Dr 201 Kitchener ON N2C 1J4 Canada Office: St John the Baptist Romanian Ch 335 Lancaster St W Kitchener ON N2C 1Y4 Canada

IDERAN, CHARLES MICHAEL, minister, American Lutheran Ch.; b. Brownwood, Tex., Sept. 26, 1946; s. George and Phyllis (Bell) I.; m. Mary Louise Rohr, June 14, 1969; children: David, Trisha, Katherine. B.A., Luther Coll., 1968; M.Div., Wartburg Sem., 1974; D.Min., Luth. Sch. Theology, 1981. Ordained to ministry Luth. Ch., 1974. Minister, Otter Creek Luth. Parish, Highland, Wis., 1974-76, St. John's Luth. Ch., Johnson Creek, Wis., 1976-79, Faith Luth. Ch., Palos Heights, Ill., 1981-83; therapist Ctr. for Life Skills, Chgo., 1980—. Mem. D.Mins. com. Luth. Sch. Theology, Chgo., 1982—; bd. dirs. Christian Care Ctr., South Holland, Ill., 1981—. Mem. Am. Assn. Marriage and Family Therapy, Christian Assn. Psychol. Studies. Home: 516 Buckley Ct University Park IL 60466 Office: Center for Life Skills 300 W Hill St Chicago IL 60610

IDICULLA, MUTTANIYIL EAPEN, deacon, priest, Indian Syrian Orthodox Ch.; b. Kerala, India, May 10, 1930; s. Geevarshese K. and Accamma E. (Chacko) Eapen; came to U.S., 1958, naturalized, 1973; B.A. in Sacred Theology, Leonard Theol. Coll., India, 1957; B.D., Serampore U., Calcutta, India, 1958; M.Th. (Dean Muelders award), Boston U., 1959, M.Ed. (Richard Young award), 1960; M.A., U. N.H., 1962; Ed.D., Brigham Young U., 1964; m. Aug. 15, 1966; children—Saji, Sebu. Ordained to priesthood, 1977; vice chmn. St. Gregorio's Orthodox Ch., Toronto, Ont. Can., 1975-76; chmn. Interfaith Center, State U. N.Y., Geneseo; vestry mem. St. Michael's Episcopal Ch., Geneseo; asso. prof. edn. State U. N.Y., Geneseo, 1968—; Gen. sec. Am. Canadian diocese Indian Syrian Orthodox Ch. India, 1977-80. Mem. Rochester Episcopal Diocese Clergy Assn. Contbr. articles to religious publs. Home: 68 2d St Geneseo NY 14454 Office: State Univ New York Geneseo NY 14454

IHLOFF, ROBERT WILKES, priest, Episcopal Church; b. New Britain, Conn., May 19, 1941; s. Ernest Otto and Mildred Arlene (Schnippel) I.; m. Nancy Virginia Bailey, June 11, 1966; children: Robert Bruce, Erika Christine. B.A., Ursinus Coll., 1964; M.Div., Episcopal Theol. Sem., 1967; M.A., Central Conn. State Coll., 1971; Certificate, Boston Gestalt Inst., 1978; D.Min., Episcopal Div. Sch., 1985. Ordained priest, 1968. Curate, St. Mark's Ch., New Britain, Conn., 1967-69; vicar St. George's Ch., Bolton, Conn., 1969-72; priest-in-charge Trinity Ch., Southport, Conn., 1973-75; presiding minister United Parish of Natick, Mass., 1980-83; rector St. Paul's Ch., Natick, 1976—; field edn. adj. faculty Episcopal Div. Sch., 1979—; stewardship cons. Diocese of Mass., 1978—; coordinator, pres. Manchester Area Conf. Chs., Conn., 1972-73; bd. dirs. Greater Bridgeport Council Chs., 1973-75. Mem. Democratic Town Com., Bolton, Conn., 1970-72; mem. ch. sponsored elderly housing project, Fairfield, Conn., 1973-75. Fellow Coll. of Preachers; mem. Natick Clergy Assn. (pres.), Natick Interfaith Dialogue Group (co-leader). Democrat. Home: 99 Walnut St Natick MA 01760 Office: Saint Paul's Episcopal Church 39 E Central St Natick MA 01760

IHRIE, ARTHUR DALE, JR., minister, United Presbyterian Church, U.S.A., speech and philosophy educator; b. Detroit, Mar. 25, 1917; s. Arthur Dale and Clara Matilda (Atkinson) I.; m. Patricia Ann Green, Dec. 25, 1970; children: Susan, Robert, Arthur Dale, III. B.A., Wayne State U., 1941, Ph.D., 1973; B.D., No. Bapt. Theol. Sem., 1944, Th.D., 1948. Ordained to ministry Bapt. Ch., 1946, Presbyn. Ch., 1974. Teaching fellow No. Bapt. Theol. Sem., Oakbrook, Ill., 1944-49; sr. minister Grosse Pointe Bapt. Ch., Mich., 1949-69; assoc. minister Lakeshore Presbyn. Ch., St. Clair Shores, Mich., 1973—; pres. Grosse Pointe Ministerium, 1964-66, St. Clair Shores Christian Clergy, 1976, 78; moderator N. Am. Bapt. Gen. Conf., Oak Brook, 1965-68; dir. Personal Counseling Services Clinic, St. Clair Shores, 1975—. Instr. speech communications, humanities and philosophy Wayne County Community Coll., Detroit, 1969—. Author: What is the Christian Life?, 1965. Mem. Am. Assn. Marriage and Family Therapy, Mich. Assn. Marriage and Family Therapy. Republican. Avocations: folk music instrumentation; antique cars. Office: Lake Shore Presbyterian Ch 27801 Jefferson Saint Clair Shores MI 48081

IKE, REVEREND See Eikerenkoetter, Frederick Joseph.

IMESCH, JOSEPH LEOPOLD See *Who's Who in America*, 43rd edition.

IMHOFF, ROGER GORDON, minister, Lutheran Church in America; b. Keokuk, Iowa, Nov. 30, 1938; s. Roger Gordon and Virginia (Milner) I.; m. Charlene Sandstrom, July 16, 1964 (div. Jan. 1973); m. Carol Robin Moroz, June 23, 1979. A.B. in Social Sci., Wittenberg U., 1960; M.Div., Trinity Sem., Columbus, Ohio, 1964. Ordained to ministry Lutheran Ch., 1964. Pastor Redeemer Luth. Ch., Elkhart, Ind., 1964-70, Holy Trinity Luth. Ch., New Rochelle, N.Y., 1970-82, Resurrection Luth. Ch., Mt. Kisco, N.Y., 1982—. Tennis instrn, L.I. and Westchester, N.Y., 1975—. Bd. dirs. Mt. Kisco Mental Health Clinic, 1983—; mem. Mayor's Com. on Disabled, 1982—. Recipient Brotherhood award Inter-religious Council New Rochelle, 1982. Mem. Acad. Parish Clergy (bd. dirs. 1982—). Home: Rural Route 2 McLain St Mount Kisco NY 10549 Office: Resurrection Luth Ch 15 S Bedford Rd Mount Kisco NY 10549

IMIG, DUANE ELDON, minister, Lutheran Church-Missouri Synod; b. San Jose, Ill., Nov. 17, 1931; s. Jacob Paul and Anna Iheanen (Jacobs) I.; m. Carol Jean Krestik, Feb. 18, 1961; children: Eunice, Lois, David. B.F.A., Bradley U., 1953; ministry cert. Concordia Sem., Springfield, Ill., 1961. Ordained to ministry Luth. Ch., 1961. Minister, Peace of St. Paul Luth. Ch., Slater, Mo., 1961-63, Trinity Ch., Pekin, Ill., 1963-67, Bethany Luth. Ch., Charlevoix, Mich., 1967-73, St. Matthew Luth. Ch., Marcelona, Mich., 1967-73, Hope Luth. Ch., Ballaire, Mich., 1972-73, Christ Luth. Ch., Jacob, Ill., 1973-79, Olive Branch Luth. Ch., Coon Rapids, Minn., 1979—; vol. chaplain Anoka Police, Minn., 1979, Anoka Jail, 1984, St. John's Hosp., St. Paul, 1983—; sec. Blaine-Coon Rapids Ministry, Coon Rapids, 1984—. Vol. Amicus, Mpls., 1982—; dist. del., caucus convener Ind. Republican Party, Coon Rapids, 1984. Lodge: Rotary (pres. 1983-84). Home: 11328 Bittersweet St NW Coon Rapids MN 55433 Office: Olive Branch Luth Ch 2135 Northdale Blvd Coon Rapids MN 55433

INGERSOLL, DONALD RALPH, minister, Wesleyan Holiness Association of Churches; b. Fredericton, N.B., Can., Mar. 18, 1954; s. Harold Ralph and Kathleen Ire (Wilson) I.; m. Janet Lynn Ryder, May 24, 1975; children: Lindsay Janet, Bradley Donald. B.S. in Bible, Houghton Coll., 1975; B.A. in Religion, Bethany Bible Coll., Sussex, N.B., Can., 1981. Ordained to ministry Wesleyan Ch., 1981. Dir. recruitment Bethany Bible Coll., Sussex, N.B., 1975-78, asst. to pres., 1978-81; minister of music, pastoral adminstr. Moncton Wesleyan Ch., N.B., 1981—; dir. Beulah Youth Camp, N.B., 1978—; mem. 90th Anniversary Com. Beulah, 1983-84; v.p. Atlantic Dist. Wesleyan Youth, N.B., N.J., Maine, 1983—. Home and Office: Moniton Wesleyan Ch Box 1206 St George St Moncton NB E16 8P9 Canada

INGHAM, NANCY JANE, religious educator, massage therapist, Seventh-day Adventist; b. Providence, Aug. 23, 1930; d. Lloyd Tarbell and Ella Mae (Holmes) Coombs; m. Clifford Elton Ingham, Sept. 20, 1953; children: Sandra Jane Ingham Thomas, Karen Jean, Sharie Lynne. Cert. massage therapist, Bancroft Sch. Massage, 1980. Cert. Bible tchr., missionary Seventh-day Adventist Ch., 1976. Tchr. Sabbath Sch., Greater Providence Seventh-day Adventist Ch., 1957-58, supt., 1959-64, chmn. festival com., 1958-66, tchr., 1973-84; tchr. Sabbath Sch., Greater Providence Seventh-day Adventist Ch., Johnston, R.I., 1984-85; region dir. (3 chs.), 1962-65; youth missionary group dir., 1960-65, 68-75; asst. chaplain Fuller Meml. Hosp., South Attleboro, Mass. Massage therapist, asst. to phys. therapist Fuller Meml. Hosp., South Attleboro, 1972-85, acting head phys. therapy dept., 1978-83; instr. home health edn. Outreach Program, 1985. Home: Rural Route 2 PO Box 2020 Plainfield Pike Foster RI 02825 Office: Fuller Meml Hosp 231 Washington St South Attleboro MA 02703

INGIBERGSSON, ASGEIR, minister, Evangelical Lutheran Church of Canada, librarian; b. Alafoss, Iceland, Jan. 17, 1928; immigrated to Can., 1968; s. Ingibergur and Sigridur Olga (Kristjansdottir) Runolfsson; m. Janet Smiley, June 27, 1959; children: David, Ragnar, Elisabet, Margret. Candidatus theologiae, U. Iceland, 1957, teaching diploma, 1967; postgrad. Trinity Coll., Ireland, 1958; M.L.S., U. Alta., 1980. Ordained to ministry Evang. Luth. Ch. Can., 1958. Pastor, Hvamms Parish, Iceland, 1958-66; chaplain, youth dir. Keflavik, Iceland, 1966-68; pastor Grace Luth. Ch., Man., Can., 1968-71, Bawlf Luth. Ch., Alta., 1971-78; head librarian Camrose Luth. Coll., Alta., 1978—. Chmn. bd. trustees Stadarfell Home Econs. Sch., Iceland, 1958-66, Bethany Aux. Hosp., Camrose, 1974-82. Mem. Can. Library Assn., ALA, Assn. Coll. Librarians of Alta., Library Assn. Alta. Home: 6213 42 Ave Camrose AB T4V 2W8 Canada Office: Camrose Luth Coll Camrose AB T4V 2R3 Canada

INGLE, RICK, minister, evangelist, So. Bapt. Conv.; b. Coeburn, Va., Feb. 27, 1930; s. Thomas Melvin and Cora Ethel (Kelly) I.; B.A., Immanuel Bapt. Coll., 1973, D.D., 1973; diploma in theology Southwestern Bapt. Theol. Sem., 1965; m. Betty Lou Bywaters, June 8, 1952; children—Debbie, Stephen, Becky, Bruce. Ordained to ministry, 1959; pastor Patrick Bapt. Ch., Wilmer, Tex., 1959-60, East Side Bapt. Ch., Arlington, Tex., 1960-61; evangelist, 1961-63; pastor Ponder (Tex.) Bapt. Ch., 1963-65, Oak Cliff Bapt. Ch., Ft. Smith, Ark., 1965-69, Market St. Bapt. Ch., Houston, 1969-70; evangelist Highland Park Bapt. Ch., Chattanooga, 1975—; radio ministry program Unshackled, Pacific Garden Missions, 1973; condr. numerous revival campaigns in various states of U.S., 1960—. Chmn. missions com. Concord Bapt. Assn., 1965-69, dir. of evangelism, 1965-69, chmn. youth activities com., 1967-68. Honored for outstanding baptismal records. Clubs: Lion, Optomist. Author: Heavens of Brass; First Experiences After Death for the Christian; You Have Fallen from Grace; Why Do Dedicated Christians Have Troubles?; If I Had My Ministry to Live Over I Would. Address: PO Box 235 Denton TX 76201

INGLES, JAMES DUNCAN, priest, Episcopal Church; personnel data analyst, psychotherapist; b. Bklyn., June 2, 1932; s. James Wesley and Priscilla Glazier (Miles) I.; m. Faith Petra Eyman, Aug. 29, 1959 (div. July 1981); children: Walter James, Peter Benet, Christopher David; m. Elizabeth Louise Boggs, Feb. 20, 1982. B.A., Haverford Coll., 1954; M.Social Service, Bryn Mawr Grad. Sch. Social Work, 1962; M.Theol. Studies, Seabury-Western Theol. Sem., 1975. Ordained priest Episcopal Ch., 1976. Asst. rector Episc. Ministry of Unity, Palmerton, Pa., 1975-78; interim priest various Episc. parishes, Phila., 1979-82; rector St. David's Episc. Ch., Phila., 1982—; bd. dirs. Advance Fund, Diocese of Bethlehem, Pa., 1977-78. Sch. dist. personnel data analyst, Phila., 1978—. Bd. dirs. Carbon-Monroe-Pike Counties Mental Health/Retardation Bd., Stroudsburg, Pa., 1977-78, Sr. Citizens Assn., Palmerton, Pa., 1976-78. Mem. Nat. Assn. Social Workers (pres. Lehigh Valley chpt., del. nat. assembly 1970). Democrat. Home: 2401 Pennsylvania Ave Apt 16-B-25 Philadelphia PA 19130 Office: St David's Episcopal Ch PO Box 29102 Dupont and St David's Sts Philadelphia PA 19127

INGLIS, LAURA LYN, religious educator, Religious Society of Friends; b. Wheatland, Wyo., Sept. 23, 1952; d. Alan Olds and Margaret (Tollefson) I.; m. Peter K. Steinfeld, June 15, 1978; children: Coryn Inglis-Steinfeld, Nathaniel Inglis-Steinfeld. B.A., Earlham Coll., 1974; M.A., U. Chgo. Div. Sch., 1975; Ph.D. cum laude, Princeton Theol. Sem., 1981. Vis. asst. prof. religion Lafayette Coll., Easton, Pa., 1981-83, U. Evansville, Ind., 1983—. Cons., co-founder Alternative Childbirth Taskforce, Evansville, 1983—. Recipient Bertram Morris prize U. Colo., 1984. Mem. Am. Acad. Religion. Home: 623 S Rotherwood Evansville IN 47714 Office: U Evansville PO Box 329 Evansville IN 47702

INGRAHAM, MERRIAN VIRGIL, minister, missions administrator, Brethren Church; b. Merrill, Oreg., Oct. 30, 1916; s. Samuel Merrian and Goldie Athen (Johnson) I.; m. Alice Naomi Larson, June 14, 1941; children: Joann Louise, Evelyn Alice, Daniel Mark, Ruth Elaine. Cert. in Engring., Nat. Schs., Los Angeles, 1939; cert. in Bus., Acctg., Fin., Stockton Coll. Commerce, 1939; student in Theology, Winona Lake Sch. Theology, 1959; D.Div. (hon.) Ashland Theol. Sem., 1985. Ordained minister Brethren Ch., 1945. Pastor Brethren Ch., Stockton, Calif., 1943, 47-48, pastor, asst., Manteca, Calif., 1946-47; Nappanee, Ind., 1956-63, moderator Brethren Ch. Gen. Conf., Ashland, Ohio, 1961-62; pastor Thornton Community Ch., Calif., 1949-56; exec. dir., gen. sec. Missionary Bd. Brethren Ch., Ashland, Ohio, 1963-84, cons., 1984—; trustee Ashland Coll., 1949-58; dir., officer Missionary Bd. Brethren Ch., Ashland, 1957-63; dir. Riverside Christian Tng. Sch., Lost Creek, Ky., 1959-84; treas. Evang. Fgn. Missions Assn., Washington, 1970-84; dir.

Evang. Missions Info. Service, Wheaton, Ill., 1971-82. Author: Brethren Encyclopedia, 1983. Served with USN, 1943-46; PTO. Republican.

INGRAM, CHARLES OWEN, priest, Episcopal Church. B. Lee County, Miss., Oct. 23, 1929; s. Leonard Thaddeus and Elizabeth (Owen) I.; m. Frances Chick Hyde, Jan. 8, 1977. m. Dorothy Ann Latt, Aug. 29, 1952 (dec.); 1 child, Charles Mark Ingram. B.S., Memphis State U., 1950, M.A., 1958; B.D., Southwestern Theol. Sem., 1953; Ph.D., U. Ariz., 1967; postgrad. U. South, 1983—. Ordained priest, 1975. Missionary, Sudan Interior Mission, Addis Ababa, Ethiopia, 1954-57; deacon St. Stephan's House, Oxford, Eng., 1974-75; vicar St. Andrew's Episcopal Ch., Tucson, 1975-81, rector, 1981—; faculty dept. psychology and student counseling service U. Ariz., Tucson, 1962—; pres. standing com. Diocese of Ariz., 1982—, chmn. commn. on ministry, 1976-82; pres. Found. for Campus Ministry, Tucson, 1982—; alt. dep. Gen. Conv., Episcopal Ch., New Orleans, 1982, dep., Los Angeles, 1985. Founder, New Start, program of acad. assistance for minority students, U. Ariz., 1968—; pres. A Place Apart Retreat Ctr., Tucson, 1985. Hon. Alumnus, Ch. Div. Sch. Pacific, 1984. Mem. Phi Alpha Theta. Democrat. Home: 6380 E Printer Udell Tucson AZ 85710 Office: 545 S 5th Ave Tucson AZ 85701

INGRAM, OSMOND KELLY, educator, United Methodist Church; b. Birmingham, Ala., Aug. 22, 1918; s. Ezra Paul and Maude (Montgomery) I.; m. Norma Geraldine Dysart, June 2, 1979; children by previous marriage: Mary Beth, Julia Maude. A.B., Birmingham-So. Coll., 1940; B.D., Duke U. Div. Sch., 1945. Ordained elder United Methodist Ch. Pastor, St. Luke United Meth. Ch., Birmingham, Ala., 1938-40; assoc. pastor Trinity United Meth. Ch., Durham, N.C., 1940-41; pastor Robbins Circuit, N.C., 1941-42, Sunset Park United Meth. Ch., Wilmington, N.C., 1942-46, Erwin Circuit, N.C., 1946-50, Oxford United Meth. Ch., N.C., 1950-54, First United Meth. Ch., Elizabeth City, N.C., 1954-59; dean students Duke U. Div. Sch., Durham, N.C., 1959-68, prof. parish ministry, 1959—. Editor: Methodism Alive in N.C., 1976; Jerusalem, Key to Peace in the Middle East, 1978. Contbr. articles to profl. jours. Mem. Assn. for Creative Change in Religious and Other Systems. Democrat. Home: 302 N Hillsborough St Franklinton NC 27525 Office: Duke U Div Sch Durham NC 27525

INMAN, CHARLES STEPHEN, minister, So. Bapt. Conv.; b. Tuscumbia, Ala., June 9, 1949; s. Charles Richard and Margaret Eloise (Richardson) I.; B.S., U. No. Ala., Florence, 1971; M.Div., Southwestern Bapt. Theol. Sem., Ft. Worth, 1975; m. Barbara Annette Marston, June 19, 1970. Ordained to ministry, 1966; pastor Springfield Bapt. Ch., Rogersville, Ala., 1966-69, First Bapt. Ch., Loretto, Tenn., 1969-72; minister of youth Southcliff Bapt. Ch., Fort Worth, 1974-75; Sunday Sch. resource person Bapt. Gen. Conv. Tex., 1975—, ch. tng. resource person, 1976—; pastor First Bapt. Ch., Monahans, Tex., 1976—. Home: 904 S Leon St Monahans TX 79756 Office: PO Box 385 Monahans TX 79756

INMAN, ROGER CLIFTON, educator, editor, minister, Church of Christ; b. Scroggins, Tex., Dec. 30, 1915; s. Gates Warren and Czar Belle Zora (Sparks) I.; student North Tex. State Tchrs. Coll., 1935-37; B.A., Abilene Christian Coll., 1970, M.A., 1974; m. Pauline Jane Watts, Nov. 9, 1940; children—Sonya (Mrs. B. Hescht), Roger, Michael, Paul, Stanley, Cynthia (Mrs. Paolo DiLuca). Preacher Ch. Christ, 1937; minister various Chs. Christ, W. Va., 1940-41, 45-69, Ky., 1941-43, Pa., 1944-45; minister Sunrise Ch. of Christ, Parkersburg, W.Va., 1969-76; instr. Bible Ohio Valley Coll., Parkersburg, 1970—, dir. devel., 1957-59. Pres. Bible Herald Corp., Parkersburg, 1953-56, 58-82; mgr. Bible Herald Bookstore, Parkersburg, 1959-73. Author: The Hunt-Inman Debate, 1942; Problems of Life and Scriptural Answers, 1952; The Willis-Inman Debate, 1969. Editor For Your Soul, 1944-48; editor Bible Herald, 1953-62, 67-76, 79-82; dir. student affairs Ohio Valley Coll., 1976—. Home: 3316 6th Ave Parkersburg WV 26101 Office: Ohio Valley College College Parkway Parkersburg WV 26101

IPPOLITO, DANIEL, general superintendent Italian Pentecostal Church Canada. Office: 384 Sunnyside Ave Toronto ON M6R 2S1 Canada*

IRANYI, LADISLAUS ANTHONY, bishop, Roman Catholic Church; b. Szeged, Hungary, Apr. 9, 1923; s. Ladislaus I. and Elizabeth J. (Pocker) I.; came to U.S., 1953, naturalized, 1959; B.A., Pazmany U., Budapest, 1944; S.T.D., Gregorianum U., Rome, 1951; Ph.D., Angelicum U., Rome, 1952. Ordained priest, 1948, bishop, 1983; co-founder founder Piarist Fathers in U.S.A., House of Studies, 1953, provincial, 1967-82, provincial asst., 1982—; titular bishop of Castel Mediana for Spiritual Assiatance of all Hungarians living outside Hungary. co-founder, 1st rector House of Studies, Washington, 1954; religious broadcaster Voice of Am. Vice pres. Hungarian Cultural Center; nat. dir. Am. Hungarian Fedn.; chaplain. Recipient Spl. award Am. Hungarian Ref. Fedn. for Ecumenical Cooperation, 1975. Mem. AAUP, Cath. Theol. Soc. Am., Coll. Theology Soc., Cath. Bibl. Assn., Mariological Assn., Cath. Philos. Assn., Philol. Assn. Am. Contbr. articles to New Cath. Ency., Cath. Hungarians Sunday, religious jours. Address: 1339 Monroe St NE Washington DC 20017

IRONS, NEIL L., bishop, United Methodist Church, No. N.J. Conf. Office: PO Box 546 Madison NJ 07940*

IRVIN, FREDRIC BRINKER, ret. coll. pres.; b. Mt. Pleasant, Pa., Oct. 13, 1913; s. Frederick Swisher and Bessie Maud (Brinker) I.; B.A., Temple U., 1936, LL.D., 1956; postgrad. U. Heidelberg (Germany), 1936-37; M.A., U. Pitts., 1942; Ph.D., 1947; D.H.L., Thiel Coll., 1960; m. Ruth M. McElhaney, Dec. 23, 1939; children—Sara (Mrs. John H. Shields), Mary Jane (Mrs. John Pethick), Joseph F. Mem. bd. world missions Luth. Ch. Am., 1952-60; ednl. missionary Andhra Christian Coll., Guntur, India, 1947-52; pres. Thiel Coll., Greenville, Pa., 1952-60; mem. Div. Luth. World Fedn. Affairs, 1957-60; mem. Com. on Theol. and Ch. Exchange, Luth. World Fedn., 1955-60; pres. Newberry (S.C.) Coll., 1971-75, pres. emeritus, 1975—. Recipient Distinguished Alumni awards Geneva Coll., 1956, Thiel Coll., 1958. Mem. Council Luth. Coll. Presidents. Contbr. articles to various publs. Home: Caribbean Gardens-202 1901 E Missouri St Phoenix AZ 85016

IRVIN, HENRY STUART, priest, Episcopal Ch.; b. Augusta, Ga., Apr. 8, 1932; s. Willis and Willye Augustus (Stuart) I.; B.A., U. N.C., 1952; M.Div., Emory U., 1955; M.A. in Religion, Am. U., 1972; D.Min., San Francisco Theol. Sem.; m. Georgia Baxter Kennedy, Dec. 28, 1957; children—Henry Stuart, Kate Kennedy. Ordained to ministry, 1956; rector Trinity Ch., St. Mary's City, Md., and St. George's Ch., Valley Lee, Md., 1956-64; asso. rector All Saints Ch., Chevy Chase, Md., 1964-79, exec. assoc., 1979-80, priest in charge, 1980-81, rector, 1981—. Pres. St. Mary's County Ministerial Assn.; Chevy Chase Clergy, 1975—; mem. Diocesan Council, 1980, fin. com., 1982-83, Diocesan Peace Commn., 1982—. Past mem. St. Mary's County Human Relations Commn., Columbia Heights Community Assn., Washington. Mem. Am. Acad. Polit. and Social Sci., Acad. Religion and Health. Author publs. in theology and psychology of religion. Home: 5507 Center St Chevy Chase MD 20015 Office: 3 Chevy Chase Circle Chevy Chase MD 20015

IRVIN, JOSEPH FREDERICK, minister, Lutheran Church in America; b. Greenville, Pa., Aug. 8, 1953; s. Fredric Brinker and Ruth Mae (McElhaney) I.; m. Tracy Jean Shaffer, July 13, 1980. B.A., Duke U., 1976; M.Div., Luth. Theol. Sem., Phila., 1980. Ordained to ministry Luth. Ch., 1980. Pastor Nativity Luth. Ch., Chester, Pa., 1980—; chaplain Viet Vets. of Am., Chester, 1980-84; pres. Chester Council of Chs., 1983—; mem. exec. bd. S.E. Del. dist. Luth. Parish, 1983—; sec. Luth. Parish, 1984—. Bd. dirs. Chester Community Improvement Project, 1982-83, Bethesda House Corp., Delaware County, 1983—. Recipient civic award Viet Vets Am., 1983. Democrat. Home: 30 E 23d St Chester PA 19013 Office: Nativity Luth Ch 22d and Edgmont Ave Chester PA 19013

IRVINE, DONALD FREDRICK, priest, Anglican Church of Canada; college administrator; b. Vancouver, B.C., Can., July 31, 1934; s. Arthur Donald and Beatrice Margaret (Brown) I.; m. Joyce Jacqueline Reid, Sept. 20, 1958; children: Karl Frederick, Kathryn Elizabeth, Peter Andrew. B.A., U. Western Ont., 1960; B.Th., Huron Coll., London, Ont., Can., 1962; M.A., U. Waterloo, Ont., 1966, Ph.D., 1978. Ordained priest, Anglican Ch. Can., 1963; Clergyman, Anglican Ch., London, Ont., 1962-68; prof. theology Huron Coll., 1968-76, academic dean, 1976—, mem. corp., 1976-84; mem. bd. London Pastoral Inst., 1980-84. Canada Council Doctoral Fellow, 1967-68. Mem. Can. Philos. Assn., Assn. Case Teaching (dir. 1984—), Alban Inst., The Hastings Centre, Soc. Christian Philosophers. Office: Huron Coll 1349 Western Rd London ON N6G 1H3 Canada

IRVINE, JAMES THEODORE, priest, Anglican Church of Canada; b. Fredericton, N.B., Can., Mar. 21, 1945; s. James Theodore and Cora Alice (O'Conner) I.; m. Pansy Hannah Price, Oct. 11, 1973; children: Sarah Elizabeth, Deborah Anne, Mary Rebekah, James Theodore. B.A., Dalhousie U., Halifax, N.S., Can., 1969; S.T.B., King's Coll., Hailfax, 1971. Ordained priest Anglican Ch. Can., 1972. Asst. curate Trinity Ch., St. John, N.B., 1970-71; rector Ludlow-Blissfield Ch., Doaktown, N.B., 1971-74; asst. to rector St. Paul's Ch., St. John, 1974-77; rector St. Jude's Ch., St. John, 1977-83; sr. priest, rector Hammond River Parish, Rothesay, N.B., 1983—; warden layreaders Fredericton Diocese, 1978—; mem. exec. com. Diocesan Synod of Fredericton, 1978—; coordinator Diocesan Primate's World Relief and Devel. Fund, 1978-83; del. Gen. Synod, Anglican Ch. Can., 1983—. Editor: You Will Bear Witness I, 1982, You Will Bear Witness II, 1983. Home: 4 Riverview Dr Gondola Point Rothesay NB E0G 2W0 Canada Office: Parish Hammond River 12 Quispamsis Rd Gondola Point Rothesay NB E0G 2W0 Canada

IRWIN, WILLIAM HENRY, educator, priest, Roman Catholic Church; b. Houston, Oct. 25, 1932; s. William Henry and Marguerite Harriet (Hunsaker) I.; B.A., U. Toronto, 1956, M.A., 1958; S.T.B., St. Basil's Sem., 1960; S.T.L., Angelicum, Rome, 1961; S.S.L., Pontifical Bibl. Inst., 1963, S.S.D., 1974; postgrad. Ecole Biblique, Jerusalem, 1963-64. Joined Order Basilian Fathers, 1951, ordained priest Roman Catholic Ch., 1959; asst. prof. faculty theology U. St. Michael's Coll., Toronto, Ont., Can., 1965-70, asso. prof., 1973—, now dean. Office: 81 St Mary St Toronto ON M5S 1J4 Canada*

ISAACS, FREDERICK WILSON, JR., lay worker, Southern Baptist Convention, athletic industries executive; b. Durham, N.C., Aug. 29, 1926; s. Frederick Wilson and Inez Margaret (Watkins) I.; m. Edith Cornelia Rawls, Jan. 28, 1960; children: Cornelia, Catharine Merritt, Josephine Rowlette, Marianna Watkins, Margaret Inez. Student, Wake Forest U., 1943, B.A., 1950; M.A., M.B.A., Columbia U., 1952. Trustee So. Bapt. Found., Nashville, 1980-84; mem. endowment bd. So. Bapt. Annuity Bd., Dallas, 1980—, exec. bd. Tenn. Bapt. Conv., Nashville, 1982—; chmn. bd. trustees Radio-TV Commn., So. Bapt. Conv., Fort Worth, 1976-84. Chmn. bd., chief exec. officer athletic Industries Internat., Knoxville, Tenn., 1976—. Vice chmn. United Way, Knoxville, 1976; mem. exec. bd. Knoxville Boys Club, 1971-77, Gt. Smoky Mountain council Boy Scouts Am., 1970-76. Served with USMC, 1943-46, PTO. Recipient Disting. Leadership award Radio-TV Commn. So. Bapt. Conv., 1984, Disting. Service award Radio-TV Commn., 1980, Gold Helmet award NFL, 1966; named Number 1 Athletic Goods Mfr. U.S.A., Nat. Sporting Goods Assn., 1970. Mem. Greater Knoxville C. of C. (1st v.p. 1974). Republican. Clubs: Order of Washington (Phila.); Plantagenet Soc. (Lafayette Hills, Pa.). Lodges: Masons, Shriners. Home: PO Box 666 Old English Mountain Cosby TN 37722

ISBELL, CHARLES LESTER, minister, Disciples of Christ Church; b. Galveston, Tex., Oct. 10, 1936; s. Frank Lester and Elba Versilla (Goodyear) I.; m. Carol McBride, Jan. 23, 1958; children: Elizabeth, Ian, Sara. B.A., Tex. Christian U., 1958, M.Div., Brite Div. Sch., 1961, D.Min., 1978. Ordained to ministry Disciples of Christ Ch., 1961. Minister 1st Christian Ch., Marfa, Tex., 1961-62, 1st Christian Ch., Uvalde, Tex., 1962-66, Northwood Christian Ch., Beaumont, Tex., 1966-72, Irving North Christian Ch., Tex., 1972-81; sr. minister 1st Christian Ch., Denton, Tex., 1981—; chmn. ch. devel. dept. Dallas Area Assn. Christian Chs., 1984—; mem. ch. advance task group Christian Ch. (Disciples of Christ) in Southwest, 1982—. Mem. Denton Ministers Assn. (sec. 1982-83). Lodge: Kiwanis (bd. dirs. Denton 1984), Masons. Office: 1st Christian Ch 1203 N Fulton Denton TX 76201

ISOM, DOTSY I., Bishop, Christian Methodist Episcopal Church (Fifth Dist.), also chair Gen. Bd. Lay Activities. Office: 308 10th Ave W Birmingham AL 35204*

ISON, BILLY L., administrator religious school; b. Pittsburg, Kans., May 14, 1926; s. C.W. and Etta (Fintel) I.; m. Bernita M. Kreutzer, June 3, 1952; children: Eloise, Jeanine. B.S., Pittsburg State U., 1949; M.S., Fort Hays State U., 1958. Prin., St. Mary Sch., Garden City, Kans., 1983—. Mem. Kans. Assn. Elem. Sch. Prins. (pres. 1976-77, state rep. 1977-79). Home: 1710 Belmont Pl Garden City KS 67846 Office: St Mary Sch 503 St John St Garden City KS 67846

ISSLER, KLAUS DIETER, Christian ministries educator, minister, Conservative Baptist Association of America. b. Stuttgart, Germany, Mar. 27, 1951; came to Can., 1962; s. William and Ruth (Baresel) I.; m. Beth Morris, Aug. 2, 1975; children: Daniel, Ruth. B.A., Calif. State U.-Long Beach, 1973; Th.M., Dallas Theol. Sem., 1977; M.A. in Edn., U. Calif.-Riverside, 1982; Ph.D. in Edn., Mich. State U., 1984. Ordained to ministry Baptist Ch., 1981. Minister Christian edn. Parma Heights Bapt. Ch., Cleve., 1977-78; minister of coll. S. Bapt. Ch., Lansing, Mich., 1983; assoc. minister Grace Bapt. Ch., San Bernardino, Calif., 1984—; asst. prof. edn. Internat. Sch. Theology, San Bernardino, 1979—. Recipient Scholarship, Martha Schoepe Meml. Found., Anaheim, Calif., 1981-82. Mem. Am. Ednl. Research Assn., Nat. Assn. Profs. Christian Edn., Evangel. Theology Soc., Moral Edn. Assn. Home: 5055 N Citadel Ave San Bernardino CA 92407

IVERSON, GREGORY BLAINE, minister United Methodist Church; b. Mpls., Jan. 10, 1950; s. Jack Dale and Marilyn Jean (Pilgren) I.; m. Rita Jane King, Aug. 18, 1974; children: Emily, Bradley. B.A., Hamline U., 1972; M.Div., Duke U., 1975; D.Min. candidate, McCormick Theol. Sem. Ordained deacon United Meth. Ch., 1973, elder, 1976; assoc. minister Bethany United Meth. Ch., Durham, N.C., 1974-75; minister South Ridge United Meth. Ch., LaCrescent, Minn., 1975-79, Byron United Meth. Ch., Minn., 1979-82; sr. minister Minnetonka United Meth. Ch., Minn., 1982—. Vice chmn. Byron Community Edn. Assn., 1980-82; bd. dirs. Hiawatha Valley Mental Health Assn., 1977-79. Marlen Johnson scholar, 1969-72. Mem. South Shore Ministers Assn. (pres. 1984—), Jaycees. Home: 19155 Maple Leaf Dr Eden Prairie MN 55344 Office: Minnetonka United Meth Ch 17611 Lake St Extension Minnetonka MN 55345

IVES, ROBERT BLACKMAN, minister, Bretheran in Christ Church; b. Bryn Mawr, Pa., Nov. 9, 1936; s. Robert B. and V. Grace (Harpster) I.; m. Nancy Draper, Aug. 4, 1962; children: Karen, Brian Daniel, Jeffrey Nathan. B.S., Drexel U., 1959; B.D., Fuller Sem., 1962; Th.M., Princeton Sem., 1963; Ph.D., U. Manchester, Eng., 1965. Ordained to ministry United Presbyterian Ch. in U.S.A., 1965. Minister to students Park St. Ch., Boston, 1965-69; asst. minister Tenth Presbyn. Ch., Phila., 1969-71; pastor Grantham Ch., Pa., 1971—; coll. pastor, lectr. religion Messiah Coll., Grantham, 1971—; asst. chmn. hymnal com. Brethren in Christ Ch., Grantham, 1980-84, chmn. music and worship com., 1974-84. Co-editor Messiah Coll. Occasional Papers, 1981—. Contbr. articles to profl. jours. Mem. C.S. Lewis Soc. N.Y.C. Home: 604 Wingert Dr Mechanicsburg PA 17055 Office: Grantham Ch Grantham PA 17027

IVEY, ROBERT ALLISON, pastor, Southern Baptist Convention; b. Woodruff, S.C., Jan. 5, 1933; s. Roy Simpson and Fannie Vesta (Godfrey) I.; m. Kathryn Elizabeth Reeves; children: Timothy Reeves, John Brent, Mary Elizabeth. B.A., Furman U., 1955; B.Div., Southeastern Bapt. Theol. Sem., 1958; D.Theology, Pioneer Theol. Sem., 1959. Ordained: Gospel Ministry, First Baptist Ch., Woodruff, 1954. Ednl. dir. David St. Bapt. Ch., Greenville, S.C., 1952; pastor Unity Bapt. Ch., Roebuck, S.C., 1953-58, Cedar Grove Bapt. Ch., Laurens, S.C., 1954-57, Pacolet Mills Bapt. Ch., S.C., 1958-66, First Bapt. Ch., South Hill, Va., 1966-74, Draytonville Bapt. Ch., Gaffney, S.C., 1974—; mem. hist. com. Broad River Bapt. Assn., S.C., 1976-77, 1983-85; mem. gen. bd. S.C. Bapt. Conv., 1980-85. Author: History of First Baptist Church, Woodruff, S.C., 1962; History of Pacolet Mills Baptist Church, 1966; 15 church histories pub. Spartan Baptist Assn. Minutes, 1960-65. Contbr. chpts. to books, articles to encys. and jours. Mem. numerous civic orgns. including pres. Friends of Library, Gaffney, S.C., 1984-85. Recipient numerous awards including Ruritan of Yr., Pacolet Ruritan Club, 1965, South Hill Ruritan Pub, 1971. Mem. Broad River Bapt. Assn., So. Bapt. Hist. Soc., S.C. Bapt. Hist. Soc. Address: Rural Route 8 Box 354 Gaffney SC 29340

IVIE, OPAL LILLIAN HANER, practitioner, Christian Science; b. Knox County, Ill., Nov. 30, 1903; d. George Washington and Emma Evalyn (Dixson) I.; B.A., Western Ill. U., 1926; m. Lloyd Willard Ivie, Dec. 25, 1928; children—Gordon Willis, Donald Lee. Practitioner Christian Sci., Galesburg, Ill., 1958—, chmn. exec. bd., 1974-76, tchr. Sunday Sch.; asst. Christian Sci. Com. on Publs. for Ill., 1952-67. Chaplain Galesburg State Mental Health Center. Home: 1089 Bateman St Galesburg IL 61401 Office: Bank of Galesburg Bldg Suite 310 203 E Main St Galesburg IL 61401

IVORY, ELENORA GIDDINGS, minister, religious organization executive, Presbyterian Church in the U.S.A.; b. Phila., Aug. 15, 1945; d. Edward Littleton and Phoebe (Hill) Giddings; m. Tommie Lee Ivory, Dec. 8, 1962 (div.); children: Cynthia Betty, Tommie Lee Jr. B.A., Douglass-Rutgers U., 1973; M.Div., Harvard U., 1976. Ordained to ministry, Presbyn. Ch. in the U.S.A., 1976. Supply pastor Gloucester Meml. Presbyn. Ch., Boston, 1974-78; assoc. dir. for pub. policy N.Y. State Council Chs., Albany, 1979—; bd. dirs. Nat. Council Chs., N.Y.C., 1981—, Nat. Impact, Washington, 1979—; mem. Albany Presbytery, 1979—, mem. Presbyn. Ch. Com. on Religious Liberty, N.Y.C., 1983—; mem. N.Y. State Clergy Com. on Latch Key Children, 1983; bd. dirs. Ams. United for Separation of Ch. and State, 1983—. Bd. dirs. N.Y. State Civil Liberties Union, 1983—; del. White House Conf. on Families, 1980; mem. N.Y. State Citizens Com. on Child Abuse, 1983. Mem. Assn. Execs. Upstate N.Y., 100 Black Women, Altrusa. Home: 794 Park Ave Albany NY 12208 Office: NY State Council Chs 362 State St Albany NY 12210

IWAI, HIRAKU, minister, United Ch. of Christ in Japan; b. Funabashi, Japan, June 16, 1931; s. Kyozo and Harumi (Mori) I.; B.A., Kwansei Gakuin U., Japan, 1954, Th.M., 1957; postgrad. McGill U., Can., 1968-71; m. Michiru Takeshita, Mar. 22, 1956; 1 dau., Nobuko. Came to Can., 1963. Ordained to ministry United Ch. of Christ in Japan, 1959; minister Narimatsu Ch., Japan, 1956-63, South Alta. Japanese United Ch., Lethbridge, Can., 1963-68, Montreal Japanese United Ch., Montreal, Que., Can., 1968-73, Toronto (Ont.) Japanese United Ch., Can., 1973—. Chmn. Nat. Conf. Japanese United Ch., 1970-73; chmn. Task Force of Ministries of Minorities and Immigration, United Ch. Can., 1972—; sec. Canadian Nat. Inter-faith Immigration Com., 1976—. Adviser Japanese Canadian Citizen's Assn., 1974—. Mem. Toronto Japanese Ministerial Assn. Home: 93 Ridgehill Dr Toronto ON M6C 2J7 Canada Office: 701 Dovercourt Rd Toronto ON M6H 2W7 Canada

IWANSKI, RUTH ANN, nun, school administrator, Roman Catholic Church; b. Wisconsin Rapids, Wis., Aug. 22, 1946; d. Adam John and Mary Elizabeth (McNamee) I. B.A., Alverno Coll., 1969; M.A.T., Webster Coll., 1974; M.A., Tex. Woman's U., 1977. Professed nun Roman Catholic Ch., 1965. Grade sch. tchr. St. Monica Sch., Whitefish Bay, Wis., 1969-70; primary tchr. St. John Nepomuk Sch., Racine, Wis., 1970-74; adapted phys. edn. cons. St. Francis and St. Vincent Schs., Freeport, Ill., 1976-84; adminstr. St. Francis Sch., Freeport, 1984—; pres. Freeport Sacred, 1977—; rep. Liturgy Com., Racine, 1970-72, Freeport Area Ch. Coop., 1977-79. Choreographer liturgical dance. Researcher NAACP, Milw., 1967; advisor Sect. 504 Adv. Com., Freeport, 1984, Northwest Ill. Spl. Olympics, Rockford, 1982—. Named Outstanding Young Woman, Jaycees, 1977. Mem. Internat. Platform Assn., Ill. Park and Recreation Assn., Nat. Recreation and Park Assn., Am. Alliance Health, Phys. Edn., Recreation and Dance. Club: Sacred Dance Guild. Avocations: quilting; landscaping; arts and crafts; bicycling. Home: 1209 S Walnut Ave Freeport IL 61032 Office: St Francis Sch for Exceptional Children 1209 S Walnut Ave Freeport IL 61032

IWICKI, JOHN JEROME, priest, Roman Catholic Ch.; b. Chgo., May 27, 1928; s. Joseph J. and Antoinette E. (Kasprzak) I.; A.B., St. Louis U., 1953, A.M., 1955. Joined Congregation of Resurrection; ordained priest, 1955; asst. dir. novices Resurrection Novitiate, Winnetka, Ill., 1956-60; instr. Weber High Sch., Chgo., 1960-63; superior Resurrection Sem., St. Louis, 1963-65; sec.-gen. Congregation of Resurrection, Rome, Italy, 1965-69; instr. Gordon Tech High. Sch., Chgo., 1969; pastor St. Hedwig Ch., Chgo., 1969—. Provincial consultor Chgo. Province, 1970-73. Mem. Polish Roman Cath. Union, Polish Am. Hist. Assn. Author: 35 Years in St. Louis, 1953; Resurrectionists in Canada, 1957; The Novitiate Story, 1960; The Literary Apostolate of the Founders, 1961; The History of Gordon Tech, 1962; Weber's New Frontier, 1962; The First 100 Years, 1965; The Constitution and Rule of the Congregation of the Resurrection, 1969. Address: 2226 N Hoyne Ave Chicago IL 60647

IZAKSON, JACOB, rabbi, Traditional Jewish Congregations; b. Wiesbaden, Germany, Mar. 24, 1946; came to U.S., 1947, naturalized, 1952; s. Siegmund and Ruth (Pluder) I.; m. Linda Sisk, Sept. 13, 1970 (div. 1977); m. Mania Ferszt, June 18, 1978. B.S., U. Tex., 1968; postgrad. Acad. for Jewish Religious, N.Y.C., 1970-74, Yeshiva Shevet Y'huda, Bklyn., 1974-76. Ordained rabbi, 1976. Youth dir. Hollis Hills Jewish Ctr., Queens, N.Y., 1968-69, Lincoln Park Jewish Ctr., Yonkers, N.Y., 1969-70; rabbi Temple Beth Torah Synagogue, Wethersfield, Conn., 1970-74, B'nai Israel Synagogue, Corpus Christi, Tex., 1976-81, Congregation Ahavath Sholom, Ft. Worth, 1981—; sec.-treas. Kallah of Tex. Rabbis, Ft. Worth, 1980-81. Bd. dirs. Epilepsy Assn., Ft. Worth, 1984—. Mem. NCCJ (bd. dirs. Ft. Worth chpt. 1981—), Nat. Honor Soc. Lodge; Masons, Rotary (deliverer invocation Ft. Worth chpt.). Home: 4801 Barkridge Terr Fort Worth TX 76109 Office: Congregation Ahavath Sholom 4050 S Hulen St Fort Worth TX 76109

JACK, DANNY LEE, minister, American Baptist Churches in the U.S.A.; b. Pittsburg, Kans., Apr. 26, 1953; s. Wayne L. and Georgene (Williamson) J.; m. Arlean Arnice Johnson, June 1, 1975; children: Elizabeth, Rachel, Sarah. B.S. in Psychology, Pittsburg U., 1975; M.Div., Central Sem., Kansas City, Kans., 1978. Ordained to ministry Baptist Ch., 1979; commd. home missionary; cert. birth instr. Pastor, Wolcott Bapt. Mission, Kansas City, Kans., 1975-78; chaplain intern Trinity Luth. Hosp., Kansas City, Mo., 1978; program dir. Bethel Neighborhood Ctr., Kansas City, Kans., 1978—; home missionary Neighborhood Action Program, Kansas City, Kans., 1979—; chaplain Kansas City Police Dept., Kans., 1983—; youth adviser Am. Bapt. Chs. U.S.A., Kansas City, Kans., 1984. Contbr. articles to newsletters and newspapers. Adviser Citizen/Labor Energy Coalition, Kansas City, Mo., 1983-84, Hmong Assn. Named Gardener of Yr., Gardens for All, 1983. Mem. Ministers Assn., Central Sem. Alumni Assn., Am. Bapt. Ch. Men's Assn. (pres. Kansas City, Kans. 1983-84). Lodge: Masons. Office: Bethel Neighborhood Ctr 14 S 7th St Kansas City KS 66101

JACK, HOMER ALEXANDER, church official, Unitarian Universalist Assn.; b. Rochester, N.Y., May 19, 1916; s. Alexander and Cecelia (Davis) J.; B.S., Cornell U., 1936, M.S., 1937, Ph.D., 1940; B.D., Meadville Theol. Sch., 1944; D.D., 1971; m. Ingeborg Kind, June 14, 1972; children—Alexander, Lucy (Mrs. John Williams). Ordained to ministry Unitarian Universalist Assn., 1949; minister Universalist Ch., Litchfield, Ill., 1942, Unitarian Ch., Lawrence, Kans., 1943; exec. dir. Chgo. Council Against Racial and Religious Discrimination, 1944-48; minister Unitarian Ch., Evanston, Ill., 1948-59; asso. dir. Am. Com. on Africa, 1959-60; exec. dir. Nat. Com. for Sane Nuclear Policy, 1960-64, mem. nat. bd., 1965—; dir. Div. Social Responsibility, Unitarian Universalist Assn., 1964-70; sec.-gen. World Conf. Religion and Peace, N.Y.C., 1970—. Pres., Unitarian Fellowship for Social Justice, 1949-50; vice chmn. Ill. div. Am. Civil Liberties Union, 1950-59. Bd. dirs. Albert Schweitzer Fellowship. Recipient Thomas H. Wright award City of Chgo., 1958; Albert Schweitzer award, 1975. Editor: Wit and Wisdom of Gandhi, 1951; The Gandhi Reader, 1956; Religion and Peace, 1967; World Religion and World Peace, 1969; Religion for Peace, 1973. Office: 777 UN Plaza New York City NY 10017

JACK, HUGH NEIL, minister, Presbyterian Church in Canada; b. Tatamagouche, N.S., Can., June 26, 1956; s. Milford Austin and Beatrice Louise (Brown) J. B.A., St. Francis Xavier U., 1977; M.Div., U. Toronto, 1980. Ordained to ministry Presbyn. Ch., 1980. Minister Roxborough Park Presbyn. Ch., Hamilton, Ont., Can., 1980-82, Hopewell Pastoral Charge, N.S., 1982—; spiritual dir. Christopher Leadership Movement, Northeastern N.S. br., 1984—. Home: General Delivery Hopewell NS B0K 1C0 Canada Office: First Presbyn Ch Gen Delivery Hopewell NS B0K 1C0 Canada

JACKSON, DANIEL EDWARD, minister, American Baptist Churches in U.S.A.; b. Joplin, Mo., Sept. 29, 1938; s. George William and Ella Jean (Mack) J.; m. Nelda Elaine Young, Nov. 21, 1958; children: Tamara Leigh, Tanya Lynn, Teri Lynette, Daniel Erin. B.S., Tex. Wesleyan Coll., 1963; postgrad. Fuller Sem., 1978-80; M.Div., Beth Sem., 1983. Ordained to ministry Bapt. Gen. Conf., 1976. Assoc. pastor Peoples Ch., Fresno, Calif., 1966-71; field service mgr. Gospel Light Pub. Co., Ventura, Calif., 1972-76, cons., 1972—; sr. pastor Camarillo Bapt. Ch., Calif., 1976-80, First Bapt. Ch., El Centro, Calif., 1980-85, Northlake Bapt. Ch., Longview, Wash., 1985—; pres. El Centro Ministerium, 1983—; trustee S.W. Bapt. Conf., 1978-80. Mem. Children's Fair Com., El Centro, 1984. Named Minister of Yr., El Centro Kiwanis Club, 1982, 84. Republican. Club: Kiwanis (pres. 1984-85) (El Centro). Office: Northlake Bapt Ch 2614 Ocean Beach Hwy Longview WA 98632

JACKSON, DAVID GORDON, religious union and society official; b. Derby, N.Y., Nov. 5, 1936; s. Peter Thomas and Sarah (Staubitz) J. B.S., SUNY-Buffalo, 1960; M.Div., Huntington Coll. Theol. Sem., 1964. Ordained elder, Church of the United Brethren in Christ, 1969; dir. youth work Ch. United Brethren in Christ, Huntington, Ind., 1966-73, adminstrv. asst. treas., 1973-79; exec. sec.-treas. Internat. Soc. Christian Endeavor, Columbus, Ohio, 1979-84; gen. sec. Internat. Soc. Christian Endeavor and World's Christian Endeavor Union, Columbus, Ohio, 1984—. Office: 1221 E Broad St PO Box 1110 Columbus OH 43216

JACKSON, DONALD EDWARD, minister, Church of Christ; b. Jasper, Ala., Oct. 9, 1954; s. Donald W. and Billie Jean (Myers) J.; m. Donna Jo Dill, May 31, 1973; children: Michael, Mandy, Matthew. A.A., Freed-Hardeman Coll., 1973; B.A., Harding U., 1975; M.A., Harding Grad. Sch. Religion, 1982, M. Theology, 1980, D.Min., 1984. Ordained to ministry Ch. of Christ. Minister Church of Christ, Cuba, Mo., 1976-77, Looxahoma, Miss., 1977-81, Kosciusko, Miss., 1982—; mem. faculty Magnolia Bible Coll., Kosciusko, 1979—, assoc. prof. Bible and ministry, 1984—. Author: Churches of Christ in Mississippi, 1985. Contbr. articles to various publs. Mem. Evang. Theol. Soc., Assn. Christian Service Personnel. Club: Rotary (chmn. pub. relations 1984). Home: 714 Glendale Kosciusko MS 39090 Office: Magnolia Bible Coll PO Box 655 Kosciusko MS 39090

JACKSON, EARL, JR., minister, Missionary Baptist Church; state agency administrator; b. Chattanooga, Mar. 11, 1943; s. James Charlie and Keathryn (Jorner) J.; m. Barbara Faye Anderson, Oct. 12, 1963; children: Earl Darelwin, Roderick Lamar. B.Th., Detroit Bapt. Sem., 1968; B.A., M.Div., M.R.E., Emmanuel Bible Coll., 1978; D.D. (hon.), Detroit Bapt. Sem., 1969. Ordained to ministry Missionary Bapt. Ch., 1963. Pastor New Bethel Bapt. Ch., Bowling Green, Ky., 1969—. Sr. interviewer Ky. Job Service Agy., Bowling Green, 1970—. Bd. dirs. War Meml. Boys Club, Bowling Green, 1978—. Mem. NAACP, People United to Save Humanity, Internat. Assn. People in Employment Service (local office rep. Lake and Cave chpt. 1978-79), Ten-Ure Club, Kappa Alpha Psi (province chaplain 1984—). Lodges: Kiwanis (religious aims com. 1973—), Masons (worshipful master 1982—). Address: 803 Chestnut St Bowling Green KY 42101

JACKSON, EVERETT, minister, Evangelical Covenant Church; b. Phila., Nov. 10, 1933; s. Mamie Stith Barnes; m. Joyce Pelzona Robinson, June 19, 1942. B.G.S., Roosevelt U., 1972; M.S.Ed., No. Ill. U., 1974, C.A.S., 1976; M.Div., Garrett Sem., 1978; D.Min., Chgo. Theol. Sem., 1982. Ordained to ministry, 1970. Dir., exec. Martin Luther King Ctr., Freeport, Ill., 1969-70; pastor First Ch. of God, Freeport, 1969-74; sem. instr. N. Park Sem., Chgo., 1983—; chaplain St. Francis Hosp., Evanston, Ill., 1980—; vol. chaplain Evanston Police Dept., 1982—. Served with U.S. Army, 1954-56. Mem. NAACP, Assn. Clin. Pastoral Edn., Phi Delta Kappa. Lodge: Kiwanis. Home: 9041 N Ewing Ave Skokie IL 60203 Office: Pastoral Care Dept Saint Francis Hosp 355 Ridge Evanston IL 60202

JACKSON, GREGORY LEE, minister, Lutheran Church in America; b. Moline, Ill., Oct. 15, 1948; s. Homer Noel Jackson and Gladys Lucille (Parker) Jackson Meyer; m. Christina Elizabeth Ellenberger, Nov. 22, 1969; children: Martin Henry, Bethany Joan Marie (dec.), Erin Joy. B.A., Augustana Coll., Rock Island, Ill., 1969; M.Div., Waterloo Luth. Sem., 1972; S.T.M., Yale U., 1973; M.A., Notre Dame U., 1978,

Ph.D., 1982. Ordained to ministry Lutheran Ch., 1973. Pastor, St. Thomas Luth. Ch., Cleve., 1973-75, St. Timothy Luth. Ch., Sturgis, Mich., 1975-81, St. Timothy Luth. Ch., Midland, Mich., 1981—; bd. dirs. Midland Christian Sch., 1984—. Contbg. author: Spiritual Well Being of the Elderly, 1980. Contbr. articles to profl. jours. and mags. Mem. protocol com. Midland Hosp., 1984. Ill. State scholar, 1966; Notre Dame U. dissertation fellow, 1978. Republican. Home: 1305 Scott St Midland MI 48640 Office: St Timothy Luth Ch 2417 Abbott Rd PO Box 1005 Midland MI 48641

JACKSON, HERBERT CROSS, educator; b. War, W.Va., May 13, 1917; s. John Henry and Sara Martha (Cross) J.; student U. Nebr., 1935-37; B.A., William Jewell Coll., 1939; Th.M., So. Bapt. Theol. Sem., 1942; M.A., Yale, 1944, Ph.D., 1954; m. Mary Caroline London, Aug. 30, 1941; children: Charlotte, Carolyn (Mrs. Richard Angell), Bruce, Stephen. Prin., Coles Meml. High Sch., Kurnool, Andhra State, India, 1945-47; prof. history Andhra Christian Coll., 1947-49; asst. prof. comparative religion Central Bapt. Theol. Sem., 1950-51; prof. comparative religion Eastern Bapt. Theol. Sem., 1951-54, registrar, 1953-54; asso. prof. comparative religion So. Bapt. Theol. Sem., 1954-59, prof. comparative religion, chmn. hist. div., dean summer sch., 1959-61; dir. Missionary Research Library, N.Y.C., 1961-66; adj. prof. history of religion Union Theol. Sem., N.Y.C., also research sec. div. overseas ministries Nat. Council Chs. of Christ in U.S.A., 1961-66; prof. religious studies Mich. State U., 1966—. Mem. Internat. Assn. History of Religions, Assn. Asian Studies, N.Am. Assn. Profs. Missions, Am. Soc. Missiologists, Deutsche Gesellschaft für Missionswissenschaft, Internat. Assn. Mission Studies, Am. Acad. Ecumenists, Am. Acad. Religion. Author: Man Reaches Out to God, 1963; also articles. Home: 1927 Tomahawk Rd Okemos MI 48864 Office: Dept Religious Studies Mich State U East Lansing MI 48824

JACKSON, HOMER HALE, organist; b. Camden, Ark., May 28, 1938; s. Leonard Patillo and Ruby Imogene (Akins) J.; Mus.B., U. Okla., 1961; postgrad. Union Theol. Sem. Sch. Sacred Music, N.Y.C., 1963, U. Cambridge (Eng.), 1972, Internat. Acad. Organists, Haarlem, Netherlands, summer 1974. Organist, choirmaster (5 singing choirs, 2 English handbell choirs) Mayflower Conglist. Ch., Grand Rapids, Mich., 1973—. Concert organist St. Thomas Ch. and St. Patrick Cathedral, N.Y.C., 1964, 70, Washington Nat. Cathedral, 1972, Rockefeller Chapel, U. Chgo., 1974; coach and accompanist. Bd. dirs. Western Mich. Opera Assn. Congressional page, Washington, 1956. Mem. Am. Guild Organists, Nat. Soc. Lit. and Arts. Clubs: Peninsular (Grand Rapids); Cliffdwellers (Chgo.). Home: 65 Lafayette NE Grand Rapids MI 49503 Office: 2345 Robinson Rd Grand Rapids MI 49506

JACKSON, JAMES LARRY, minister, educator, Southern Baptist Convention; b. California, Mo., Nov. 27, 1940; s. James Taylor and Ruby Catherine (Steenbergen) J.; B.S. in Edn., Lincoln U., 1962; M.S. in Recreation, U. Mo., 1977; Ed.S. in Higher Edn., U. Mo., 1980; Ph.D., 1983; m. Kay Galloway, July 27, 1974; 1 child, Russ. Ordained to ministry So. Baptist Conv., 1965; minister recreation First Bapt. Ch., Jefferson City, Mo., 1960-65, Pompano Beach, Fla., 1965-69; minister of activities Walnut St. Bapt. Ch., Louisville, 1969-74; instr. ch. recreation So. Sem., 1970-73; chmn. dept. recreation, prof. ch. recreation S.W. Bapt. U., Bolivar, Mo., 1974—. Fellow Nat. Recreation and Park Assn.; mem. Soc. Park and Recreation Educators, Mo. Park and Recreation Assn. Contbr. to Ch. Recreation mag., 1960—. Home: 1303 S Oakland Dr PO Box 329 Bolivar MO 65613 Office: Southwest Baptist U Bolivar MO 65613

JACKSON, JEREL LYNN, minister, United Methodist Church; b. Bklyn., Apr. 16, 1946; s. George Frederick and Margaret Eloise (Hooser) J.; m. Eunice Flora Fish, Dec. 21, 1946; children: Chad Alan, Emma Leigh. B.A., Lycoming Coll., 1968; M.Div., Wesley Sem., 1973. Ordained to ministry United Meth. Ch., as deacon, 1969, as elder, 1976. Student assoc. minister Good Shepherd United Meth. Ch., Balt., 1969-72; assoc. minister Central United Meth. Ch., Springfield, Ohio, 1973-78; minister West Union United Meth. Ch., Ohio, 1978-84, Milford Center United Meth. Ch., Ohio, 1984—; v.p. Clark County Council Chs., Springfield, 1975-76; pres. Adams County Ministerial Assn., West Union, 1979-80; clergy team couple Worldwide Marriage Encounter, United Meth. Ch., Ohio, 1981—; co-founder, bd. dirs. Adams County Christian Sch., West Union, 1981—; founder Adams County United Meth. Ministries, West Union, 1984—. Democrat. Home: 52 E State St Milford Center OH 43045 Office: Milford Center United Meth Ch 55 E State Milford Center OH 43045

JACKSON, JOHN EDWARD, minister, Ch. of God in Christ; b. Troy, Ala., July 23, 1950; s. John Thomas Fields and Geraldine (Carter) J.; B.A., Troy State U., 1975; M.A., Charles Harrison Mason System of Bible Colls., 1976; D.D. (hon.), Ch. of Gospel Ministry, 1976; m. Minnie Pearl Hines, Dec. 30, 1969; children—John Michael, JacqueLynne, EveLynne. Ordained to ministry, 1976; pastor Holy Communion Temple, Troy, 1973; asso. pastor Ch. God in Christ, Goshen, Ala., 1976—, Spring Hill Ch. God in Christ, River Falls, Ala., 1976—. Youth dir. Troy dist. Ch. of God in Christ, 1969—, sec. joint fellowship Greenville dist., 1973—; asso. to royal priesthood Holy Ch., Inc., Albany, Ga.; revivalist, evangelist Ala. Ch. God in Christ, 1972—. Sales dir. Nat. Comp Assos., Alabama Jubilee, Ala., 1976—. Mem. S.E. Ala. Community Devel. Corp. Technol. Transfer Center, Troy, 1976—. Recipient Blair Dealer award, 1976, Blair Star Dealer award, 1976. Mem. Ancient Mystical Order Rosea Crusci, Amway Distbrs. U.S., Raleigh Distbrs. Am. Okinawa editor Room 201 News, Ch. of God in Christ youth newspaper, 1972. Home: 305 Hubbard St Troy AL 36081 Office: 123 Lake Ave Troy AL 36081

JACKSON, KENT P., theology educator, Church of Jesus Christ of Latter-day Saints; b. Salt Lake City, Aug. 9, 1949; s. Richard W. and Hazel (Phillips) J.; m. Nancy Porter, June 18, 1975; children: Sarah, Rebecca, Jennifer, Jonathon Edward, Alexander Kent. B.A., Brigham Young U., 1974; M.A., U. Mich., 1976, Ph.D., 1980. Assoc. prof. ancient scripture Brigham Young U., Provo, Utah, 1980—. Author: The Ammonite Language of the Iron Age, 1983. Editor: Studies in Scripture, vols. 1-3, 1984—. Served with U.S. Army, 1970-76. Mem. Am. Oriental Soc., Soc. Biblical Lit., Am. Schs. Oriental Research, Am. Acad. Religion (regional pres. 1985-86). Office: 23 JSB Brigham Young U Provo UT 84602

JACKSON, PAUL HOWARD, religion educator, minister, Lutheran Church-Missouri Synod; b. Topeka, Kans., Nov. 10, 1952; s. Dwight Storer and Janice Ilona (Woeltje) J.; m. Elizabeth Ann McGhghy, July 23, 1977; children: Christopher, Jeremy. B.A. in Music, Washburn U., 1973; M.Librarianship, Emporia State U., 1974; M.Div., Concordia Sem., St. Louis, 1979. Ordained to ministry Luth. Ch.-Mo. Synod, 1979. Pastor, St. Paul's Ch., Wakefield, Nebr., also First Trinity Ch., Altoona, Nebr., 1979-81; librarian, religion instr. Luth. High Sch. of Indpls., 1981-82; librarian, asst. prof. religion St. John's Coll., Winfield, Kans., 1982—; dir. Trinity Luth. Ch. S.E. Asian Mission, Winfield, 1984; zone counselor Luth. Women's Missionary League, 1981; faculty sponsor Jesus Christ at East Central Union, Mo., 1974-76; sponsor, Key Club of Luth. High Sch. Indpls., 1982. Mem. ALA, Kans. Library Assn., Pvt. Acad. Libraries of Kans., Phi Kappa Phi, Mu Alpha Pi. Republican. Club: Trinity Luth. Men's. Home: 1020 E 8th St Winfield KS 67156 Office: St Johns Coll Library 1500 E 7th St Winfield KS 67156

JACKSON, SHELDON GLENN, minister, Calif. Yearly Meeting of Friends Ch.; b. Cherokee, Okla., June 5, 1918; s. Ralph Elmer and Marva (Coppock) J.; A.B., Marion Coll., 1940; Th.B., 1939; A.M., U. Kans., 1944; Ph.D., U. So. Calif., 1970; m. Irene Elizabeth Ballard, Mar. 27, 1942; children—Edward Eldon, Charles Sheldon, Marilyn Ruth. Ordained to ministry, 1940; pastor Bridgeport Friends Ch., Wichita, Kans., 1940-41; instr. history Friends Bible Coll., Haviland, Kans., 1941-46, pres., 1946-64; prof. history Azusa (Calif.) Pacific Coll., 1964—; pastor Azusa Friends Ch., 1971-75. Clk. Calif. Yearly Meeting Friends Ch., 1975—. Mem. Orgn. Am. Historians, Friends Hist. Assn., Phi Beta Kappa. Author: History of Kansas Yearly Meeting of Friends, 1946. Contbr. articles to religious jours. Home: 405 N Valencia St Glendora CA 91740 Office: Citrus and Alosta Sts Azusa CA 91702

JACKSON, WILLIAM EDGAR, minister, So. Baptist Conv.; b. Hattiesburg, Miss., Dec. 23, 1934; s. Albert and Grace (Ryan) J.; B.A., William Carey Coll., 1961; M.R.E., New Orleans Sem., 1967; m. Emma Jean Scruggs, Jan. 31, 1954; children—Jack Edward, Rebecka Ann. Ordained to ministry, 1958; pastor Cedar Grove Bapt. Ch., Leakesville, Miss., 1958-65, Beulah Bapt. Ch., Pensacola, Fla., 1965—. Pres., Pastors Conf.; moderator Bapt. Assn. in Green County. Named Outstanding Young Man, Green County, Miss., 1962. Author: The Glass House, 1966. Home: Box 723 Route 8 Pensacola FL 32506 Office: Box 720 Route 8 Pensacola FL 32506

JACO, JAMES HAROLD, JR., minister, United Pentecostal Church International; b. Warren County, Tenn., June 11, 1941; s. James Harold Sr. and Margaret Louanne (Jaco) m. Frances Juanita Smithson, June 20, 1963; children: James H. III, Jina F., Jeffery Y. Student, Union U., 1959-61, Conquerors Bible Coll., 1961-63; B.Th., Pentecostal Bible Inst., 1975, B.A., 1975. Ordained to ministry United Pentecostal Ch. Internat., 1965. Pastor various chs., Tenn., Ont., Can. and Miss., 1963-75, East Dyersburg Pentacostal Ch., Tenn., 1975—; head counselor Pentecostal Children's Retreat, Perryville, Tenn., 1976—; past pres. Apostolic Missionary Inst. Author: The Tabernacle, 1974. Editor Pentecostal Voice of Tennessee, 1975—, Ont. Dist. News, 1968-73. Contbr. articles to profl. jours. Mem. Dyersburg Ministerial Assn. (v.p. 1982-83). Home: 908 Lewis Ave Dyersburg TN 38024 Office: East Dyersburg Pentecostal Ch 922 Lewis Ave Dyersburg TN 38024

JACOBS, HAROLD MILTON, lay church worker, Orthodox Jewish Congregations; b. Oct. 25, 1912; s. Max and Kate (Fried) J.; B.S. in Econs., Columbia, 1934, M.S., 1936; m. Pearl Schraub, Apr. 11, 1939; children: Vivian, Joseph, Paul. Pres., Union Orthodox Jewish Congregations Am.; chmn. Jewish Bd. Higher Edn., N.Y.C., 1975-76; dir. Shaare Zedek Hosp. Dir., Am. Bank & Trust Co.-N.Y.; fin. cons. to maj. pub. cos. Chmn. adv. bd. U.S. Small Bus. Adminstrn.; dir. ops. U.S. Naval Yard, Bklyn. Recipient Religious award Bklyn. Hall of Fame, 1968; named Man of Year, Nat. Council Young Israel. Office: Nat Council Young Israel 3 W 16th St New York NY 10011

JACOBS, STEVEN LEONARD, rabbi, Reform Jewish Congregations; b. Balt., Jan. 15, 1947; s. Ralph Albert and Ruth Esther (Buchler) J.; m. Judith Irene Gold Jacobs, Sept. 5, 1970; children: Hannah Beth, Naomi Rachel. B.A. with distinction, Pa. State U., 1969; B.H.L., Hebrew Union Coll., Jewish Inst. Religion, 1972, M.A. in Hebrew Lit., 1974. Ordained rabbi, 1974. Asst. rabbi Temple Emanu-El, Birmingham, Ala., 1974-76, sr. rabbi, 1984—; assoc. rabbi Temple Shalom, Dallas, 1976-77; rabbi Spring Hill Ave. Temple, Mobile, Ala., 1977-84; Chautauqua prof. Jewish studies Spring Hill Coll., Mobile, 1977-84; founding sponsor Am. Friends World Bible Ctr. of Jerusalem. Contbr. numerous articles on Jewish edn., Holocaust to profl. jours. Contbr. numerous book revs. to profl. jours. Contract chaplain VA ctrs. Biloxi and Gulfport, Miss., 1977-84, U.S. Naval Retirement Home, Gulfport, 1982-84; treas. Mobile Bay Area Planned Parenthood, 1982-84; mem. numerous adv. councils; chairperson Clergy Conf. on Cancer, Am. Cancer Soc. Named Outstanding Young Religious Leader, Mobile Jaycees, 1978. Mem. Assn. Reform Zionists Am., So. Jewish Hist. Soc., Nat. Inst. Holocaust, Central Conf. Am. Rabbis (exec. bd. 1982-84, treas. Southeast Assn. 1983), NCCJ (state bd. dirs. 1980—), Soc. Bibl. Lit., No. Am. Fedn. Temple Youth (life), Mobile Ministerial Assn. (pres. 1980-81). Lodges: Beth Zur, Rotary. Office: Temple Emanu-El 2100 Highland Ave PO Box 55403 Birmingham AL 35255

JACOBSON, GERALD DUANE, prison chaplain, American Lutheran Church; b. Rothsay, Minn., June 11, 1928; s. Oswald H. and Florence (Rudh) J.; m. Jean Elizabeth Groth, Dec. 27, 1951; children: Timothy, Thomas, Michael, Daniel. B.S. in Mech. Engring., N.D. State U., 1950; M.Div., Luther Theol. Sem., St. Pual, 1966; M.A. in Social Scis., Pacific Luth. U., 1973; M.A. in Criminal Justice, Wash. State U., 1983. Ordained to ministry Am. Luth. Ch., 1958. Pastor, Lemmon Rural Luth. Parish, S.D., 1958-61, missionary to Brazil, Am. Luth. Ch., Mpls., 1961-65; chaplain Luth. Community Services, Tacoma, Wash., 1968-73, Doctors Hosp., Seattle, 1974-75, Wash. State Penitentiary, Walla Walla, Wash., 1975—. Served as staff sgt. USAF, 1950-54. Mem. Am. Protestant Correctional Chaplains Assn. (cert. chaplain, past regional v.p.), Am. Correctional Assn. (profl.), Wash. Correctional Assn. (profl.), Wash. State Chaplains Assn. (past pres.). Home: 109 Rancho Villa Walla Walla WA 99362

JACOBSON, SVERRE THEODORE See *Who's Who in America*, 43rd edition.

JACQUET, CONSTANT HERBERT, JR., religious organization official, Churches of Christ; b. Bridgeport, Conn., Dec. 3, 1925; s. Constant Herbert and Hazel Elizabeth (Herthal) J.; B.S., Columbia, 1949, M.A., 1951, M.Phil., 1973; m. Sally Graham, June 18, 1949; 1 son, Timothy John. Research asso. Union Theol. Sem., 1953-56; with Nat. Council Chs. of Christ in the U.S.A., N.Y.C., 1956—, staff asso. info. services Office of Research, Evaluation and Planning, 1973—. Mem. Religious Research Assn., Religious Research Assn. (pres. 1984—), Assn. Statisticians of Am. Religious Bodies, Am. Polit. Sci. Assn. Editor: Yearbook of American and Canadian Churches, 1967, 70—; contbg. editor Rev. of Religious Research, 1973-78. Home: 150 E 93d St New York NY 10128 Office: 475 Riverside Dr New York NY 10115

JADOT, JEAN, bishop, Roman Cath. Ch.; b. Brussels, Nov. 23, 1909; s. Lambert and Gabrielle (Flanneau) J.; came to U.S., 1973; student Louvain U., 1926-30, Maj. Sem. of Archdiocese of Malines, Brussels, 1930-34; Ph.D., U. Louvain. Ordained priest, 1934, bishop, 1968; asst. pastor St. Gertrude, Brussels, 1934-39; nat. chaplain Young Cath. Students (Belgium), 1939-45; mil. chaplain Royal Mil. Acad. Belgium, 1945-52; chief chaplain Congalese Forces in Belgian Congo, 1952-60; nat. dir. Soc. for Propagation of Faith in Belgium, 1960-68; pro-nuncio in Thailand, apostolic del. in Laos, Malaysia and Singapore, 1968-71; pro-nuncio apostolic in Cameroons and Gabon, apostolic del. in Equatorial Guinea, 1971-73; apostolic del. in Washington, 1973—. Address: 3339 Massachusetts Ave NW Washington DC 20005

JAEGER, VERNON PAUL, minister, church official American Baptist Churches; b. St. Paul, Apr. 17, 1906; s. Paul Harry and Mathilda (Hirt) J.; student Cal. Inst. Tech., 1923-27; A.B., U. Redlands, 1928; B.D., No. Bapt. Theol. Sem., 1931, D.D., 1952; postgrad. U. Chgo.; m. Alice Harriet Cole, July 16, 1928; children: Wendell F., Charles P., Jane L. (Mrs. Leroy E. Randall). Ordained to ministry Am. Baptist Chs. in U.S.A., 1931; pastor ch., Wash., 1931-32; chaplain U.S. Army, 1932-63; state missionary Oreg. Bapt. Conv., 1963-69, interim exec. minister, 1970, state missionary and bus.

mgr., 1971-73; asst. pastor Mountain Park Ch., Lake Oswego, Oreg., 1974—, also research cons. Am. Bapt. Chs. of Oreg., 1974—. Mem. Portland U.S.O. Com., 1969-76; bd. dirs. Portland Campus Christian Ministry, 1968-84; Oreg. state chaplain DAV, 1976-77; adv. com. dept. vets. affairs State of Oreg., 1977—, chmn., 1978-79, 84-85; DAV vol. service rep. to Portland VA Med. Ctr., 1976—. Named hon. rabbi Jewish Welfare Bd., 1962. Mem. Oreg. Council Chs. (treas. 1970-73), Ret. Officers Assn., Am. Bapt. Ministers Council. Home: 6230 S W Wilbard St Portland OR 97219 Office: 40 McNary Pkwy Lake Oswego OR 97034

JAEGER, WILLIAM JOHN, priest, Roman Catholic Ch.; b. Joliet, Ill., Nov. 2, 1949; s. William John and Kathleen Ann (Cusick) J.; B.A., St. Meinrad (Ind.) Coll., 1971, M.Div., 1975. Ordained priest, 1975. Vocation dir. Diocese of Joliet; sec. Presbyterial Council; chaplain K.C.; aux. master of ceremony for bishop of Joliet; mem. subcom. religious history Will County Hist. Soc. Mem. Nat. Cath. Educators Assn. Address: St Charles Borromeo Pastoral Ctr Route 53 and Airport Rd Romeoville IL 60441

JAFFA, LAWRENCE MARVIN, minister, Unitarian Universalist Association, continuing Congregationalist; b. Palo Alto, Calif., Aug. 19, 1923; s. Milton Jerome Katzky and Aileen Raby Jaffa.; m. Jarmila Mikulasova, June 14, 1951; 1 child, Thomas Emerson. B.S. in Bus. Adminstrn., U. Calif.-Berkeley; M.Div., Harvard U., 1949. Ordained to ministry Unitarian Ch., 1949. Minister various parish chs. Mass., Calif., 1949-70; minister United Community Ch. of San Joaquin Valley, Modesto, Calif., 1980—; co-founder Unitarian-Universalist Symposium, Boston, 1969; mem. nat. exec. bd. Spiritual Frontiers Fellowship, Independence, Mo., 1980-83; bd. dirs. Unitarian-Universalist Christian Fellowship, 1961-70; chaplain various councils Boy Scouts Am., 1962-79. Contbr. poems to anthologies, articles to books and mags. Trustee Modesto, Calif., Bd. Edn., 1983—; bd. dirs. Modesto performing Arts Assn., 1983—; pres. Modesto Arts Adv. Council, 1984, YMCA Men's Club, 1977; treas. Calif. State Poetry Soc., 1974-75. Served to lt. (j.g.) USNR, 1943-46. Recipient Silver Beaver award Mt. Whitney Council, Boy Scouts Am., 1958; life membership award Calif. PTA, 1957; retired mem. for life Calif. Tchrs. Assn., 1981; Paul Harris fellow Rotary Found., 1981. Mem. Unitarian Universalist Ministers' Assn., NEA, Inst. Noetic Scis., Assn. for Research and Enlightenment, Modesto C. of C. Republican. Lodges: Rotary (pres. Modesto North chpt. 1976), Masons. Home: 1105 Wellesley Modesto CA 95350 Office: Modesto Bd Edn 426 Locust St Modesto CA 95351

JAFFRY, JOHN HERBERT, minister Association of Evangelical Lutheran Churches; b. N.Y.C., Dec. 29, 1953; s. John and Katharine (Grosch%e() J.; m. Janet Marie Jungk, June 6, 1981. A.A., Concordia Coll., Bronxville, N.Y., 1973; B.A., Concordia Sr. Coll., Ft. Wayne, Ind., 1975; M.Div., Christ Sem., St. Louis, 1979. Ordained to ministry Luth. Ch., 1979. Minister of edn. Trinity Luth. Ch., Alton, Ill., 1979—; mem. youth bd. So. Ill. Conf., 1980—; treas. Alton area Alliance Religious Leaders, Ill., 1982-84; mem. Episc. ecumenical com. Luth. Religious Conf., Alton, 1981—. Contbr. articles to religious publs. Mem. religious com. Piasa Bird council Boy Scouts Am., Wood River, Ill., 1982—, com. mem. Exploring div., 1982-83, v.p. Exploring div., 1984; mem. Alton crop com. Crop Walk, Ch. World Service, Alton, 1983. Recipient award for excellence Boy Scouts Am., 1982. Mem. Alton Area Alliance Religious Leaders, Bibl. Archaeology Soc., Planetary Soc. Republican. Office: Trinity Luth Ch 801 Blair St Alton IL 62002

JAMES, ALMA REBECCA, minister, Assemblies of God; b. Marianna, Fla., Nov. 4, 1912; d. John Reddin and Lurena Elizabeth (Rawls) Porter; student pub. schs., Fla., also corr. courses; m. William Hampton James, Mar. 23, 1929; children—William Leland, Floyce Elaine James Baxter, Ginger Euretha. Ordained to ministry, 1942; pastor ch., Cottondale, Fla., 1938-42, Welcome Assembly, Dellwood, Fla., 1942-54, Bascum (Fla.) Assembly, 1954-62; asst. pastor ch. Alford, Fla., 1962-64, Page Pond Assembly, Altha, Fla., 1964-69, Pilgrims Rest Assembly, Marianna, 1975-76; evangelist; condr. radio ministry. Vacation Bible sch. dir. West Fla. Dist., Assemblies of God., 1942; youth dir. sect. 7 1948. Address: PO Box 343 Old Cottondale Rd Marianne FL 32446

JAMES, FREDERICK C., Bishop, The African Methodist Episcopal Church, 7th dist., Columbia, S.C. Office: 3701 Landmark Dr Suite 400 Columbia SC 29240*

JAMES, GILLETTE ORIEL, minister, American Baptist Churches in the U.S.A.; b. Grand Bay, Dominica, W.I., May 5, 1935; came to U.S., 1955, naturalized, 1966; s. Samuel Emmanuel and Ethlyn James; m. Rosa Vernita Ferguson, June 30, 1961; 1 child, Jennifer. B.A., God's Bible Sch. and Coll., 1959, U. San Francisco, 1968; M.Div. with honors, Am. Bapt. Sem. of West, 1970, D. Min., 1976. Ordained to ministry Bapt. Ch., 1963. Pastor, Newtown Christian Union Ch., Dominica, 1959-60, Grace Bapt. Ch., San Francisco, 1963-69; asst. pastor Beth Eden Bapt. Ch., Oakland, Calif., 1970-71, pastor, 1971—; gen. sec. Calif. State Bapt. Conv., Richmond, 1984—; dean of instrn. Bapt. Ministers Union of Oakland, 1971—. Author: Through Toils and Snares: A Preacher Testifies, 1984. Served with U.S. Army, 1961-63. Mem. St. Luke Soc. (pres. 1984—). Republican. Lodge: Masons. Office: Beth Eden Ch 1183 10th St Oakland CA 94607

JAMES, LEROY, minister, Baptist Church and United Church of Christ. B. Oakfield, Ga., Dec. 24, 1928; s. Perry and Fannie (Grier) J.; m. Clara Alice Price, Mar. 10, 1962; children: Carlton Leroy, Karen Renee. B.A., Morehouse Coll., 1955; B.Div., Andover Newton Theol. Sch., 1960. Ordained Baptist Ch., 1954, United Ch. of Christ, 1961. Commd. 1st lt. U.S. Army, 1961, advanced through grades to col., 1980, ret., 1982; chaplain U.S. Army Dept., Washington, 1961-82; interim pastor First Congregational Ch., Washington, 1982; pastor Second Congregational Ch., Memphis, 1982—; mem. exec. bd. Chs. and Synagogues Serving Families, Memphis, 1983—. Chmn. Mil. Retirees of the Tri-State Area, Memphis, 1983; vol. Shelby County Voter Registration, Memphis, 1984. Decorated Legion of Merit, 1982. Mem. Mil. Chaplains Assn., Met. Interfaith Assn., NAACP, Phi Beta Sigma. Democrat. Home: 1946 Finley Rd Memphis TN 38116 Office: Second Congregational United Ch of Christ 764 Walker Ave Memphis TN 38126

JAMES, RALEIGH MILTON, minister, Southern Baptist Convention; b. Greensboro, N.C., July 22, 1928; s. Porter Clark and Allie Ray (Keen) J.; m. Lora Jane Allen, Sept. 16, 1949; children: Kathi, Dennis, Joni, Lori, David, Jonathan. B.A., Campbell Coll., 1964; Th.M., New Orleans Bapt. Theol. Sem., 1969. Ordained to ministry Southern Baptist Convention, 1961. Pastor, Salem Bapt. Ch., Apex, N.C., 1960-64, Pine Grove Bapt. Ch., Livingston, La., 1966-69, Oakcrest Bapt. Ch., Baton Rouge, 1969-73, Four Mile Creek Bapt. Ch., Richmond, Va., 1973-75, New Life Bapt. Ch., Richmond, Va., 1979—. Chmn. evangelism Judson Assn., 1970-73, Dover Assn., 1973-75. Author: Kinsman Redeemer, 1975, Bible Refreshing, 1979; Healing is for Everybody, 1982. Served to sgt. maj. USMC, 1946-60. Republican. Home: Rural Route 6 Box 318P Richmond VA 23231 Office: New Life Bapt Ch 6229 Osborne Tpk Richmond VA 23231

JAMES, RONALD GENE, minister, American Baptist Churches in the U.S.A.; b. Parkersburg, W.Va., Feb. 5, 1937; s. Archie Quentin and Hazel May (Corbett) J.; m. Annette Louise Cunningham, Dec. 26, 1959; children: Janet Elizabeth, Ronald Eric. B.A., Alderson-Broaddus Coll., 1959; M.Div., Colgate-Rochester Div. Sch., 1963. Ordained to ministry Am. Bapt. Chs. in U.S.A., 1962. Pastor, East End Bapt. Ch., Williamsport, Pa., 1963-68; chaplain, dir. religious activities Alderson-Broaddus Coll., Philippi, W.Va., 1968-75; pastor First Bapt. Ch., Shinnston, W.Va., 1975—. Recipient Parents award Parents-Alumni Council, Alderson-Broaddus Coll., 1974. Mem. Bapt. Theol. Fellowship, Harrison County Ministerial Assn. (pres. 1983—). Republican. Lodges: Kiwanis (pres. Phillipi 1972-73), Lions (pres. Shinnston 1976-77). Home: 72 Rebecca St Shinnston WV 26431 Office: 70 Rebecca St Shinnston WV 26431

JAMES, WILLIAM PAUL, pastor, The Wesleyan Church; b. Muncie, Ind., July 11, 1951; s. William David and Clara Elizabeth (Chizum) J.; m. Susan Lynn Cooke, June 10, 1972; children: David Paul, Elizabeth Ann, Katherine Lynn. Student Ky. Mountain Bible Sch., 1969-72, Central Wesleyan Coll., 1972-74, Wesley Bibl. Sem. Ordained to ministry Wesleyan Ch. Pastor, Tuckaseegee Wesleyan Ch., N.C., 1972-73, Seneca Wesleyan Ch., S.C., 1973-77, Fairview Wesleyan Ch., Cottondale, Ala., 1977-81, Lakeside Wesleyan Ch., Anderson, S.C., 1981—; dir. Sunday schs. S.C. Dist. Wesleyan Ch., 1984—. Chaplain, Fraternal Order of Police, Anderson County, 1984—. Named one of Outstanding Young Men of Am., U.S. Jr. C. of C., 1982; recipient award Top Ten Fastest Growing Chs., Wesleyan Ch., 1982, 84. Avocations: golf; reading. Home: Rural Route 9 Box 309 Anderson SC 29624 Office: Lakeside Wesleyan Ch PO Box 1107 Anderson SC 29622

JAMESON, NORMAN LEE, minister, Southern Baptist Convention; b. Kenosha, Wis., May 10, 1927; s. Lyle Lee and Freda Belle (Smelser) J.; m. Elizabeth Boone, Mar. 22, 1952; children: Larry Joe, Joy B. Jameson Stricklin. B.A., Bob Jones U., 1951. Ordained to ministry Bapt. Ch., 1951. Pastor 1st Bapt. Ch., Clio, Mich., 1964-71, Bethany Bapt. Ch., Godfrey, Ill., 1971-75; dir. missions Alton Indsl. Bapt. Assn., Ill., 1975-80; pastor Whitelaw Ave Bapt. Ch., Wood River, Ill., 1980—; sec. Ill. Bapt. Pastors Conf., 1983-84; emergency chaplain Wood River Twp. Hosp., 1983—. Bd. dirs. Wood River 75th Jubilee, 1984. Lodge: Rotary (dir.).

JAMESON, RICHARD PARKER, minister, United Methodist Church, religious organization executive; b. Akron, Ohio, Oct. 31, 1928; s. Henry Parker and Imogene (Bunnell) J.; m. Ruth Anne Mills, June 13, 1954; children: Lisa, John. B.A., U. Akron, 1950; B.D., Oberlin Coll., 1953; M.Div., Vanderbilt U., 1972; Ph.D., U. Cin., 1974. Ordained to ministry Meth. Ch., 1954. Pastor Brimfield Meth. Ch., Ohio, 1954-60, Groveport Meth. Ch., Ohio, 1960-66, Clifton United Meth. Ch., Cin., 1966-72; dir. communications Council of Christian Communions, Cin., 1972-78, exec. dir., 1978—; v.p. communication Nat. Council Chs., 1982-84; pres. Nat. Assn. Regional Religious Communicators, 1980-82. Author: Human and Community Uses of Cable Television, 1974; co-author curriculum materials. Mem. Model Cities Evaluation Team, Cin., 1970-72; bd. dirs. Emanuel Community Ctr., Cin., 1968-72, Meml. Community Ctr., Cin., 1976-80. Mem. Phi Sigma Kappa. Democrat. Home: 4240 Langland St Cincinnati OH 45223 Office: Council Christian Communions 2439 Auburn Ave Cincinnati OH 45219

JAMISON, LARRY WAYNE, evangelist, minister, Christian Church; b. Clay City, Ill., Sept. 9, 1939; s. Owen L. and Mildred Marie (Evans) J.; student Eastern Ill. U., Charleston, 1957-58; B.A., Cin. Bible Sem., 1961, postgrad., 1961-62; m. Barbara D. Phillips, Nov. 24, 1960; children—Tracy Wayne, Kathryn Lea. Ordained to ministry, 1960; minister Birdseye (Ind.) Christian Ch., 1959-62, Union Ch. of Christ, Mowrystown Ch. of Christ, 1962-65, Parkview Christian Ch., Mt. Carmel, Ill., 1965-68, Princeton (Ind.) Christian Ch., 1968—. Dir. evangelist Go Tell Others Evangelizing Assn., 1968—; printer GTO Soul-Winner; speaker Kiamichi Men's Clinic (Honobia, Okla.); preacher crusades in South Korea, Mex., India, Philippines, Burma, Haiti. Home: 109 S Jefferson St Princeton IN 47670 Office: PO Box 567 Princeton IN 47670

JAMME, ALBERT JOSEPH, Roman Catholic priest, religious educator; b. Senzeilles, Namur, Belgium, June 27, 1916; came to U.S., 1953; s. Alfred and Albine (Roulin) J. S.T.D., Cath. U., Louvain, Belgium, 1946, Ph.D. in Philology and History, 1952; Lic. Bibl. Studies, Vatican City, 1948. Ordained priest, Roman Catholic Ch., 1944. Research prof. semitics Cath. U., Washington, 1954—; v.p. Am. Found. for Study of Man, Yemeni, 1979—. Mem. Cath. Bibl. Assn., Am. Oriental Soc., Am. Inst. Studies. Office: The Cath Univ Washington DC 20064

JANETZKE, DOUGLAS KIRK, minister, Lutheran Church-Missouri Synod; b. Lansing, Mich., Dec. 2, 1948; s. Reinhold Herman and Mary Lou (Jolliff) J.; m. Marguerite Ellen Zerbst, Feb. 28, 1970; children: Joshua Douglas, Andrew William. A.A., Concordia Coll., 1969, B.A., 1970; M.Div., Concordia Theol. Sem.-Springfield, Ill., 1974; D.Min., Concordia Theol. Sem.-Ft. Wayne, Ind., 1983. Ordained to ministry, 1974. Asst. pastor Bethlehem Luth. Ch., Roseville, Mich., 1974-78; pastor Christ Luth. Ch., Boyne City, Mich., 1978-82; sr. pastor St. Paul's Luth. Ch., Fairmont, Minn., 1982—; zone counselor Luth. Women's Missionary League, Roseville and Fairmont, 1974-78, 84—; vice chmn. Mich. Dist. Youth Bd., Ann Arbor, 1978-82; steering com. Minn. So. Dist. Singles Gathering, Burnsville, 1984—. Contbr. articles to profl. jours. Mem. Fairmont Circuit Winkel Conf., Phi Alpha Theta. Republican.

JANKE, ROGER ALVIN, minister, Lutheran Church-Missouri Synod; b. Milw., July 22, 1938; s. Alvin Henry and Ruth Elisa (Plautz) J.; m. Nancy L. Strobel, June 7, 1964 (dec. 1974); children: Paul Janke, Joel, Naomi; m. Marva Lou Fedderson, June 15, 1975; children: Jonathan Kugath, Nathaniel Kugath, Melissa Kugath. B.A., Concordia Sr. Coll. Ft. Wayne, Ind., 1960; B.D., Concordia Sem., St. Louis, 1964, M.Div., 1964, M.S.T., 1965. Ordained to ministry Luth. Ch.-Mo. Synod, 1965. Pastor, Grace Luth. Ch., Hastings, Mich., 1965-68, Grace Luth. Ch., Oberlin, Ohio, 1968-75; asst. pastor St. John's Luth. Ch., West Bend, Wis., 1975-82; sr. pastor Our Father's Luth. Ch., Greenfield, Wis., 1982—; counselor Luth. Women's Missionary League, N.Y.C., 1967; synodical del. Luth. Ch.-Mo. Synod, St. Louis, 1983; nat. chaplain Luth. Rangerettes, 1985—. Mem. Hastings Ministerial Alliance (pres. 1967), Oberlin Ministerial Assn. (pres. 1971). Office: Our Fathers Luth Ch 6025 S 27th St Greenfield WI 53221

JANNE, MAXINE ELIZABETH, lay church worker, Lutheran Church-Missouri Synod; b. Norwich, Kans., Mar. 23, 1920; d. Albert Robert and Amelia (Kunz) J., A.A., St. John's Coll., Winfield, Kans., 1939. Tchr elem. grades Trinity Luth. Sch., Winfield, Kans. 1939-40, Zion Luth. Sch., St. Louis, 1940-42, Immanuel Luth. Sch., Wichita, 1942-44; parish worker Immanuel Luth. Ch., Wichita, 1945—. Mem. Internat. Walther League, St. John's Coll. Alumni Assn., Kans. Luth. Hist. Soc. Home: 1755 Exchange Pl Wichita KS 67213 Office: 909 S Market St Wichita KS 67211

JANNEKE, ALAN W., minister, Lutheran Church-Missouri Synod; b. Willmar, Minn., Feb. 27, 1956; s. Ronald O. and Dorothy A. (Smith) J.; m Donna K. Schwarz, May 31, 1981. Student Concordia Coll., St. Paul, 1974-75; B.A., Concordia Sr. Coll., Ft. Wayne, Ind., 1977; M.Div., Concordia Sem., St. Louis, 1981. Ordained to ministry Luth.-Ch.-Mo. Synod, 1981. Pastor Trinity Luth. Ch., Royal, Iowa and Concordia Luth. Ch., Webb, Iowa, 1981—; bd. dirs. St Luke Luth. Home, Spencer, Iowa, 1983—; del. Synodical Conv., St. Louis, 1983. Home: PO Box 236

502 Church St Royal IA 51357-0236 Office: Trinity Luth Ch PO Box 236 504 Church St Royal IA 51357-0236

JANSEN, E. HAROLD, bishop, American Lutheran Church; b. Bklyn., Aug. 31, 1930; s. Herman Nicholas and Gesine Amalie (Olsen) J.; m. Patricia Hughes, May 29, 1954; children: Daniel, Elizabeth, Nathanael, Mark. B.C.E., CCNY, 1952; C.Th., M.Div., Luther Theol. Sem., 1957; D.D., Capitol U., 1981; D.D., Wagnec Coll., 1983. Pastor Eltingville Luth. Ch., Staten Island, N.Y., 1957-71; ecumenical dir. St. Francis Sch., Staten Island, 1971-72; dean Eastern Dist. Am. Luth. Ch., Washington, 1972-78, bishop, Springfield, Va., 1978—. Home: 4952 Gainsborough Dr Fairfax VA 22032 Office: 6506 Loisdale Rd Suite 308 Springfield VA 22150

JANSSEN, ORVILLE HENRY, priest, Roman Catholic Church; b. Appleton, Wis., Mar. 7, 1926; s. Henry Edward and Rose Marie (O'Barski) J.; B.A., Pontifical Coll. Josephinum, Worthington, Ohio, 1948; M.A., Register Coll. Journalism, Denver, 1957. Ordained priest Roman Catholic Ch., 1952; asso. pastor Holy Innocents Parish, Manitowoc, Wis., 1952-56; founder St. Bernard's Parish, Appleton, Wis., 1966, pastor, 1966—. First chmn. Diocesan Ecumenical Commn., 1968; mem. Priest Senate, 1968-74; mem. Presbyteral Council and Coll. Consultors, Diocese of Green Bay, 1984—, diocesan dir. of evangelization, 1979-84. Pres., Community Alcoholism Services, 1970-73, Family Service Assn., 1974-75. Bd. dirs. United Fund, Vis. Nurses Assn., Epilepsy Found., Fox Valley Sheltered Workshop, Outagamie County Jail Rehab. Com., 1974, St. Elizabeth Hosp., 1979—. Named Man of Yr. U. Notre Dame Club, 1974; recipient Fox Valley Brotherhood award, 1972. Founding editor Green Bay Register, 1957-66. Home: 1600 Orchard Dr Appleton WI 54914 Office: 1617 W Pine St Appleton WI 54914

JANTZ, FRED EWALD, minister, North American Baptist Conference; b. Germany, Jan. 29, 1942; came to U.S., 1949, naturalized, 1957; s. Ewald and Lydia (Hans) J.; m. Kathleen Louise Linke, Feb. 19, 1965; children: Philip Loren, Steven Jonathan, Jennifer Carolyn. B.A. in History, Biola U., 1965; M.Div., N. Am. Bapt. Sem., 1968; postgrad. Portland State U., 1968-69; M.A., U. Pacific, 1974. Ordained to ministry, N. Am. Bapt. Conf., 1968. Dir. youth Magnolia Bapt. Ch., Anaheim, Calif., 1965; dir. youth and Christian edn. Central Bapt. Ch., Sioux Falls, S.D., 1965-68; minister of youth Trinity Bapt. Ch., Portland, Oreg., 1968-70; sr. pastor Quail Lakes Bapt. Ch., Stockton, Calif., 1970—; del. to gen. council N. Am. Bapt. Conf., Chgo., 1974-77, 79-82, bd. dirs. ch. extension/ch. growth bd., 1982—; dir. ch. extension No. Calif. Assn., 1979-83. Bd. dirs. Stockton YMCA, 1979; pres. Lincoln PTA, 1983—. Mem. Stockton Ministerial Assn. (pres. 1974-76). Republican. Home: 8256 Colonial Dr Stockton CA 95209 Office: Quail Lakes Bapt Ch 1904 Quail Lakes Dr Stockton CA 95207

JANUCIK, MARY ANITA, hospital administrator, nun, Roman Catholic Church; b. Reading, Pa., Apr. 4, 1930; d. Joseph Anthony and Cecelia (Erwetowski) Janucik; R.N., St. Joseph's Hosp. Sch. Nursing, 1962; B.S., Temple U., 1969, M.B.A., 1971. Joined Sisters of St. Felix, 1947; tchr. elementary Roman Cath. Schs. of N.J., 1949-50, Pa., 1951-52, 58-59, Md., 1953-54, Del., 1955-57; nursing supr. St. Joseph's Hosp., Phila., 1962-71, asso. adminstr, 1971-72, adminstr., 1972—, religious superior, 1972—, also mem. bd. mgrs., 1971—. Sec., Phila. Conf. Cath. Health Care Facilities, 1972, pres., 1974; mem. exec. com. Pa. Conf. Cath. Health Care Facilities, 1985-88. Mem. exec. com. Del. Valley Hosp. Forum, 1974. Mem. Del. Valley, Cath., Pa. hosp. assns., Am. Coll. Hosp. Adminstrs., Temple Alumni Health Adminstrn. Assn. (treas. 1973-74). Address: St Josephs Hosp 16th St and Girard Ave Philadelphia PA 19130

JANZEN, WALDEMAR, minister, religious educator, Mennonite Church General Conference; b. Ohrloff, Ukraine, USSR, Aug. 7, 1932; s. Wladimir and Helene (Dueck) Janzen; m. Irene Mary Warkentin, June 25, 1960; children: Werner Martin, Hilda Ruth, Edwin Peter. B.A., U. Western Ont., Can., 1953; B.D., Mennonite Bibl. Sem., Chgo., 1956; M.A. in German, U. Man., Winnipeg, Can., 1961; Th.M. in O.T., Harvard U., 1963, Ph.D. in Near Eastern Lang., 1969. Ordained to ministry Mennonite Church Gen. Conf., 1978. Instr. Can. Mennonite Bible Sch., Winnipeg, Man., 1956-68, assoc. prof., 1968-71, prof. O.T., 1971—, registrar, 1958-64, dean, 1968-78; adj. prof. grad. studies U. Man., Winnipeg, 1979—; mem. Commn. on Faith and Order, Nat. Council Chs., 1972-76; bd. dirs. Mennonite Bible Sem., Elkhart, Ind., 1977—. Author: Mourning Cry and Woe Oracle, 1972; Still in the Image, 1982. Contbr. articles to various publs. Mem. adv. bd. to minister edn. Province of Man., 1974-78. Can. Council grantee, Ottawa, 1964-65; Inst. Ecumenical and Cultural Research fellow, 1971-72; Harvard U. scholar, 1964. Mem. Soc. Bibl. Lit., Am. Schs. Oriental Research. Home: 991 Fleet Ave Winnipeg MB R3M 1K5 Canada Office: Can Mennonite Bible Coll 600 Shaftesbury Blvd Winnipeg MB R3P 0M4 Canada

JARMAN, ELDREDE LEROY, family counselor, church financial consultant, minister, Conservative Baptist Assocation of America; b. Aurora, Ill., Sept. 12, 1923; s. Thomas Sidney and Helen Irene (Cave) J.; m. Leone VerDelle, Oct. 13, 1945; children: David LeRoy, James Eldrede. B. Bibl. Studies, Trinity Bible Coll., Newburgh, Ind., 1980; M.Th., Trinity Theol. Sem., Newburgh, 1981, Ph.D. in Religion, 1982, Ph.D. in Counseling, 1983. Ordained to ministry Conservative Baptist Assn. Am., 1963. Pastor Calvary Bapt. Ch., Ossining, N.Y., 1958-64; pres. Elja Group, ch. fin. cons., Glen Ellyn, Ill. and Pompano Beach, Fla., 1964-83; dir. devel. Wycliffe Bible Translators, Huntington Beach, Calif., 1982; minister Mt. Shavano Bible Chapel, Salida, Colo., 1982-83; exec. dir. Mt. Shavano Counseling Ctr., Salida, 1982-83; exec. dir. Family Counseling, Inc., Pompano Beach, Fla., 1983—; chaplain, maj. CAP. Author: Personality Insight, 1967; Christian Counseling, 1984. Served with USAAF, 1941-43. Recipient Most Outstanding Alumnus award Trinity Theol. Sem., 1983. Mem. Pilots Internat. Assn. Republican. Club: Alumnus (Trinity Theol. Sem.). Avocations: swimming; flying; golfing; boating; photography. Home: 1000 S Ocean Blvd Pompano Beach FL 33062 Office: PO Box 2715 Pompano Beach FL 33062

JARVIS, MARGARET MARY, Sister, Roman Catholic Church; b. St. Louis, June 28, 1907; d. William Henry and Mary Rose (Deehan) J.; R.N., St. Louis U., 1932, B.S. in Nursing Edn., 1951, M.Health Adminstrn., 1953. Joined Sisters St. Mary Third Order St. Francis, 1925; staff nurse St. Mary's Hosp., St. Louis, 1932-33; accountant Firmin Desloge Hosp., St. Louis, 1933-36; dir. bus. office St. Louis U. Hosp., 1936-59; treas. St. Mary's Hosp., Kansas City, Mo., 1959-60, asst. adminstr., 1960-66, exec. dir., 1966-68; treas.-gen. Sisters St. Mary, Inc. and Sisters St. Mary Third Order St. Francis, Inc., 1968—; mem. governing bd. of 12, Sisters of St. Mary Hosps., 1968—; treas. St. Louis Archdiocesan Group Women Religious, 1973—; chmn. region X, Nat. Group Religious Treasurers, 1972—; bd. govs. Cardinal Glennon Meml., 1974—. Recipient William C. Follmer award, 1964, Robert Reeves award, 1968, Frederick Muncie award, 1972 (all Hosp. Fin. Mgmt. Assn.); Silver Alumni award St. Louis U., 1976; Gateway award, 1983. Fellow Am. Coll. Hosp. Adminstrs., Am. Acad. Med. Adminstrs.; mem. Hosp. Fin. Mgmt. Assn. (nat. bd. dirs. 1968-70), Am., Mo., Cath. hosp. assns., Nat. Assn. Hosp. Purchasing Mgmt., Am. Assn. Hosp. Accountants, Am. Accountants Assn., Med. Edn. Found. Kansas City (pres. 1972-75). Home and Office: 1100 Bellevue Ave St Louis MO 63117

JAVALERA, ELIZABETH RICO, educator; b. Manila, Philippines, Oct. 8, 1934; d. Ireneo Topacio and Salome Villamina (Rico) Javalera; Elementary Tchrs. certificate with honors, Philippine Normal Coll., 1953; A.B. in Psychology cum laude, Far Eastern U., 1968; M.A. in Christian Edn. cum laude, Trinity Evang. Div. Sch., 1973; Ph.D. in Edn., Mich. State U., 1984. Instr. Far Eastern Bible Inst. and Sem., Bulacan, Philippines, 1960-61; instr. Christian edn. Philippine Missionary Inst., Cavite, 1961-65; Christian edn. editor Crusader Mag., 1966-71; nat. missionary Philippines Crusades, Manila, 1969-76; nat. coordinator Nat. Sunday Sch. Convs., 1969—; instr. Christian edn. Asian Theol. Sem., Quezon City, Philippines, 1974-80; dir. Christian edn. studies Asia Grad. Sch. Theology, Manila, 1984—; dir. tng. Women's Tng. Sessions, Haggai Inst., Singapore, 1984—. Bd. dirs. Philippine Sunday Sch. Publs., 1968—. Named Miss Sunday Sch. of Philippines, 1971. Mem. Philippine Assn. Christian Edn. (bd. chmn. 1967-69, 72-74, publ. editor 1969—, gen. sec. 1974—). Author: National Sunday School Convention...How to Conduct it Successfully, 1971; Training for Competence, 1973; Christian Education and Its Correlated Educational Agencies, 1977. Editor Pace Mag., 1969—. Home: 623 Sto Nino St Mandaluyong Metro Manila Philippines Office: ACPO Box 301 Cubao Quezon City 3001 Philippines

JAY, CHARLES DOUGLAS, educator, minister, United Church Canada; b. Ont., Can., Oct. 10, 1925; s. Charles Arthur and Luella Gertrude (McPherson) J.; B.A., U. Toronto, Can., 1946, M.A., 1947; B.D., Victoria U., Can., 1950; Ph.D., U. Edinburgh (Scotland), 1952; D.D. (hon.), Queen's U., Can., 1971, Wycliffe Coll. U. Toronto, 1976; m. Ruth Helen Crooker, Jan. 31, 1948; children—David, Ian, Garth. Ordained to ministry United Ch. Can., 1950; minister Elk Lake-Matachewan United Ch., Elk Lake, Ont., Can., 1952-54, Trafalgar United Ch., Oakville, Can., 1954-55; asst. prof. philosophy of religion Emmanuel Coll. of Victoria U., 1955-58, asso. prof., 1958-63, prof., 1963—, prin., 1981—; chmn. div. World Outreach United Ch. Can., 1976-82. Bd. dirs. Toronto Sch. Theology. Fellow Am. Assn. Theol. Schs. U.S. and Can. (v.p. 1976); mem. Assn. Theol. Schs. U.S. and Can. (pres. 1984—), Canadian Soc. for Study Religion, Am. Soc. Christian Ethics (dir. 1960-66), World Council Chs. (mem. working group on dialogue with people of living faiths 1972-82), Canadian Theol. Soc. Author: (with R. C. Chalmers and J.A. Irving) The Meaning of Life in Five Great Religions, 1965; Peace, Power, Protest, 1967. Office: 4 St Thomas St Toronto ON M5S 2B8 Canada

JAYNES, MARLIN SANDERS, JR., minister, Church of God, Anderson, Indiana; b. Kingsport, Tenn., Nov. 28, 1942; s. Marlin Sanders and Frances Lee (Dodson) J.; m. Karen Fern Lindsey, June 14, 1963; children: Brenda Lynn, Sandra Marlene. Student, Anderson Coll., 1960-61; B.Th., Gulf Coast Bible Coll., 1964; postgrad. Midwestern Sem., 1966. Ordained to ministry, 1965. Asst. pastor First Ch. of God, Texas City, Tex., 1961-63; pastor First Ch. of God, Farmington, Mo., 1964-66; pastor Narrow Ln. Community Ch. of God, Montgomery, Ala., 1967-69, First Ch. of God, New Boston, Ohio, 1969-73; co-pastor First Ch. of God, Ft. Myers, Fla., 1973-74; pastor Anderson Ch. of God, Bristol, Va., 1974—; mem. bd. conservation and evangelism Ch. of God in Ohio, 1970-73; dir. camping in Ala., Ch. of God, 1968; v.p. evang. Christian Sch., Ft. Myers, Fla., 1973-74; lectr. in field. Contbr. Pathways to God mag., 1969—; speaker daily radio broadcast: IN THE WORD, Bristol, Tenn., 1983—. Exec. dir. Bristol Children's Acad., Va., 1974—; div. advisor Practical Nurses Ohio, 1969-73; pres., v.p. New Boston Kiwanis, 1970-72. Recipient Internat. Kiwanis award, 1972, Ohio Dist. Kiwanis award, 1972. Mem. Farmington Ministerial Assn. (pres. 1965-66), New Boston Ministerial Assn. (pres. 1970-71). Home: 6 Woodway Cir Hartwood Addition Bluff City TN 37618 Office: Anderson Ch of God 1075 Wagner Rd Birstol VA 24201

JEAN, SYLVIO HERVE, priest, Roman Catholic Church; b. Nashua, N.H., Nov. 27, 1926; s. Thomas Noel and Elise (Archambeault) J. B.A., U. Montreal, 1950, B.Th., 1954. Ordained priest Roman Cath. Ch., 1955. Tchr. St. Laurent Coll., Que., 1954-57; missionary in Bangla Desh (East Pakistan), 1958-70; priest, pastor West Island, Dollar Des Ormeaux, Que., 1971—. Home: 48 Westpark Dollard Des Ormeaux PQ H9A 2J6 Canada Office: Diocese of Montreal 2000 Sherbrooke Montreal PQ Canada

JEANE, LAVELLE MILAM, minister, United Pentacostal Ch., Internat.; b. Houston, Apr. 6, 1938; s. Harlice Henry and Margaret (Hanby) J.; student theology Tex. Bible Coll., 1965-68; student Med. Sch., U. Tex.-Galveston, 1972; m. Phyllis Annette Veno, June 22, 1956; children—Kim Reneé, LaVelle Milam Jr., Julie Marie. Ordained to ministry, 1969; evangelist, 1964-65; asst. pastor United Pentecostal Ch., Pasadena, Tex., 1965-67; pastor, founder 1st Pentecostal Ch., Alta Loma, Tex., 1967—. Sec., Santa Fe Ministerial Alliance, 1970—; chmn. Fellowship Bayshore Area. Contbr. articles to denominational periodicals. Home: 12017 24th St Alta Loma TX 77510 Office: PO Box 417 5502 Main St Alta Loma TX 77510

JEANES, SAMUEL ARTHUR, minister, Am. Baptist Conv.; b. Phila., June 16, 1912; s. Arthur H. and Marguerite Pearl (Smyth) J.; A.B., Eastern Bapt. Coll. and Sem., 1940, Th.B., 1938, B.D., 1941; Th.M., 1945, D.D., 1966; postgrad. Temple U., 1945-48; m. Harriette Swope, Dec. 21, 1935. Ordained to ministry Am. Bapt. Conv., 1938; pastor Trinity Bapt. Ch., Phila., 1935-42, 1st Bapt. Ch., Merchantville, N.J., 1942—; pres. Internat. Reform Fedn. Inc., Washington, also editor Progress, monthly pub. Gen. sec. Lord's Day Alliance of N.J., 1951—; exec. sec. Council Chs. Greater Camden, 1957—; chaplain Gen. Assembly of N.J., 1970. Mem. Camden County Com. Aging. Contbr. articles to religious jours. Office: Centre St at Walnut Ave Merchantville NJ 08109

JECKO, STEPHEN HAYS, priest, Episcopal Church; b. Washington, D.C., Jan. 15, 1940; s. Wilbur Hays and Martha Constance (Herrick) J.; m. Joan D. Stever, Aug. 8, 1964; children: Bryan, Sean. B.S.C.E., Syracuse U., 1964; M.Div., Gen. Theol. Sem., N.Y.C., 1967; D.Min., Va. Theol. Sem., 1982. Ordained to ministry Episc. Ch., as deacon, 1967, as priest, 1968. Curate, Christ Episc. Ch., Binghamton, N.Y., 1967-69; vicar St. Margaret's Episc. Ch., Plainview, N.Y., 1969-74; assoc. rector St. James' Ch., Warrenton, Va., 1974-77; rector Zion Episc. Ch., Rome, N.Y., 1977-84, St. Michael's Episc. Ch., Gainesville, Fla., 1984—; priest assoc. Order of Holy Cross, West Park, N.Y., 1967—; bd. dirs. Community Chaplaincy Program, Binghamton, 1967-69; guest 100 Huntley St., Toronto, Ont., Can., 1983. Contbr. articles to religious publs. Bd. dirs. United Way, Rome, N.Y., 1980-84; mem. Mayor's Com. for Human Services, Rome, 1982-84. Recipient Citizenship award City of Rome, 1984. Mem. Fellowship of Witness, Episcopal Renewal Ministries, Rome Clergy Assn. (pres. 1982-84), Sigma Nu (chaplain Syracuse chpt. 1958-64). Office: St Michael's Episcopal Ch 4315 NW 23d Ave Gainesville FL 32606

JEFFCOAT, JAMES ROY, lay ch. worker, United Methodist Ch.; b. Opp, Ala., Oct. 7, 1918; s. Julius Claude and Ruth Hightower (Breedlove) J.; student pub. schs., Opp, Ala.; m. Julia Armilla Bowden, Sept. 10, 1936; children—Marjorie Ann (Mrs. Robert Waller), James Roy. Mem. adminstrv. bd. and council on ministries United Methodist Ch., 1963—, chmn., 1964-68, youth div. coordinator, 1962—, lay leader, 1968-74, Sunday Sch. tchr., 1968—; mem. dist. staff Ala.-W.Fla. Conf., 1968-74; vice-chmn. Equitable Salary Commn., 1973—; vice-chmn. Com. on Interpretation, 1973—, mem. nominating com., 1972-74, mem. conf. council, 1968-74. Purchasing agt.

Opp and Micolas Cotton Mills, Opp, Ala., 1937—. Mem. adv. and craft com., chmn. steering com. MacArthur Tech. Inst., 1964—; recreation dir., Opp, 1964-68; mayor protem, treas., chmn. utility bd., Opp, 1968-72, city councilman, 1976-80, chaplain, 1976-80; mem. exec. bd. Ala.-Fla. council Boy Scouts Am., 1972—, dist. commr., 1971-76, dist. chmn., 1976—. Recipient Dr. G. R. Smith Scouting award Boy Scouts Am., 1972, Silver Beaver award Boy Scouts Am., 1973. Lion. Home: POB 253 Brookside Dr Opp AL 36467 Office: POB 70 Douglas Ave Opp AL 36467

JEFFERSON, RALPH LIVINGSTON, minister, Ch. of God in Christ; b. Southampton, N.Y., Nov. 6, 1932; s. William Lankford and Lillie Mae (Chapman) J.; B.R.E., O.M. Kelly Religious Tng. Sch.; A.A., Suffolk Community Coll., 1976; postgrad. Moody Bible Inst., Chgo.; m. Ada Mae Pyrnell, Dec. 16, 1953; children—Joseph, Theresa, Victoria, Ralph, Loretta. Ordained to ministry, 1963; pastor chs. in Selden, Centereach, and Bellport, N.Y.; dist. sec. Ch. of God in Christ; marriage counselor, community planner, religious social worker. Active PTA. Mem. N. Bellport, S. Bellport, S. Brookhaven, N. Brookhaven councils chs. Address: 126 Miller Rd Southampton NY 11968

JEFFERY, INEZ MCNEILL, practitioner Christian Science; b. Calico Rock, Ark., Jan. 6, 1904; d. Stephen E. and Nora (Smith) McNeill; student pub. schs., Calico Rock; m. Roy N. Jeffery, June 9, 1923 (dec.); children—Royce, Stephen L. Practitioner, Christian Science, Dallas, 1958—. Mem. John M. Tutt Class Assn. Kansas City, Mo.; 1st Ch. of Christ Scientists, Boston, Fifth Ch. of Christ Scientists, Dallas. Home and Office: 5930 Morningside St Dallas TX 75206

JEFFRIES, GENE LAROY, minister, educator, college dean, Southern Baptist Convention. b. Webb City, Mo., July 22, 1935; s. Eugene Harvey and Velma Elizabeth (Anderson) J.; m. Rose Marie Strubelt, May 21, 1955; children: Richard Eugene, Teri Ann Jeffries VerHoeven, Robert Earl. A.A., S.W. Bapt. U., 1955; B.A., Pitts. State U., 1957; M.Div., Midwestern Bapt. Sem., 1961; Th.D., Luther Rice Sem., 1972. Ordained to ministry So. Bapt. Conv., 1953. Pastor, Mary Ann Bapt. Ch., St. Louis, 1973-76; dean Ark. Inst. Theology, Fayetteville, 1977-80; acad. dean Northeastern Bible Coll., Essex Fells, N.J., 1980-82; pastor Grace Bapt. Ch., Cape Coral, Fla., 1982—; prof., dean Gulf Shore Bible Coll., Fort Myers, Fla., 1983—; speaker Evang. Hour Internat., radio program 1964-71; asst. dean Luther Rice Sem., St. Louis, Jacksonville, Fla., 1972-76; founder, pres. St. Louis Inst. Bibl. Studies, 1974-78. Author: The Truth About "Tongues", 1979; Handbook for Pulpit Committees, 1982; Man Alive!, 1985. Mem. Evang. Theol. Soc., Near East Archaeol. Soc., Gene Jeffries Evang. Assn. (pres. 1965—). Republican. Office: Grace Baptist Ch PO Box 764 Cape Coral FL 33910

JEFFRIES, JAMES RICHARD, minister, educator, Baptist Church. B. Glasgow, Ky., Jan. 23, 1940; s. Delmar Clayborn and Annie (Medley) J.; m. Betty Joyce Meece, Apr. 3, 1959; children: Melody L., Timothy, Jamie, Richard, Robert, Philip, Steven. B.A., Lexington Bapt. Coll., 1975, M.R.E., 1978, D.D. (hon.), 1981; M.A., Morehead State U., 1976, M.H.E., 1977. Ordained to gospel ministry Bapt. Ch., 1960. Pastor, Emmanuel Bapt. Ch., Winchester, Ky., 1967-70, Fincastle Bapt. Ch., Ohio, 1970-74; missionary Bryan Station Bapt. Ch., Lexington, Ky., 1974-76; acad. dean Lexington Bapt. Ch., 1976—; bus. dir., new membership dir. Ashland Avenue Bapt. Ch., Lexington, 1976; bd. dirs. Blue Grass Bapt. Sch., Lexington, 1979. Author: A Brief Bible Survey, 1980. Editor: A Study Guide: Term Papers, Reports and Theses, 1981. Advisor Blue Grass council Boy Scouts Am., 1982; asst. Little League, Lexington, 1984. Served with USAF, 1957-59. Recipient Guardsmen award State of Ohio, 1958; named Ky. col. State of Ky., 1969. Mem. Assn. Bus. Adminstrs. of Christian Colls., Ky. Assn. Collegiate Registrars and Admissions Officers (orgn. and adminstrn. com.), Ky. Assn. Coll. Admissions Officers, So. Assn. Collegiate Registrars and Admissions Officers. Republican. Home: 713 Franklin Ave Lexington KY 40508 Office: Lexington Bapt Coll 163 N Ashland Ave Lexington KY 40502

JEGEN, MARY EVELYN, religious peace/justice association official, Roman Catholic Church; b. Chgo., Feb. 15, 1928; d. Julian Aloysius and Evelyn (Bostelman) J. B.A. summa cum laude, Edgecliff Coll., 1957; Ph.D., St. Louis U., 1967; M.A., Mundelein Coll., 1984; D.Litt. (hon.), Wadhams Hall, 1984. Exec. dir. Bread for the World Ednl. Fund, Chgo., 1976-78; nat. coordinator Pax Christi/U.S.A., Chgo., 1979-82; chmn. Fellowship of Reconciliation, Nyack, N.Y., 1982-83; v.p. Pax Christi Internat., Antwerp, Belgium, 1984—; trustee Trinity Coll., Washington, 1981—. Editor: The Earth Is The Lord's, 1977; Growth With Equity, 1978.

JELINEK, BONNIE SCOTT, minister, United Church of Christ; b. N.Y.C., Mar. 15, 1945; d. Robert C.L. and Joan (Keyes) Scott; m. Richard Ulrich Jelinek, Apr. 28, 1985; children: Barton, Jennifer, Joshua. B.A., Lake Forest Coll., 1967; M.A.R., Yale U., 1969; D.Min., Andover-Newton Theol. Sch., 1983. Ordained to ministry United Ch. Christ, 1977. Student pastor

Park Congl. Ch., Norwich, Conn., 1967-68, United Ch.-on-Green, New Haven, 1968-69; co-pastor United Ch. of Chester, Conn., 1973-79; sr. pastor Newton Highlands Congl. Ch., Newton, Mass., 1979—; chaplain Andover Newton Theol. Sch., 1981—, adj. faculty, 1981—; trustee Ctr. Bd. of Laity, Newton, 1982—. Interfaith Counselling Ctr., Newton, 1981—. Trustee com. on acad. affairs Beaver County Day Sch., Newton, 1984—; chmn. psychol. evaluation com. Met. Boston Assn., 1980-83. Mem. Newton Clergy Assn., Newton United Ch. Christ Clergy, DAR (chaplain 1980—), Colonial Dames of R.I. Democrat. Club: Chatham Yacht. Home: 39 Forest St Newton MA 02161 Office: Newton Highlands Congregational Ch 54 Lincoln St Newton MA 02161

JEMISON, T. J., clergyman, Baptist. Former sec. Nat. Baptist Conv., U.S.A., now pres. Address: 915 Spain St Baton Rouge LA 70802*

JEN, SHARON MEILIN, missionary; b. Honolulu, Dec. 28, 1945; d. Francis Fook Leong and Esther Mew Chinn (Lum) Lau; m. Alvin Kim Loy Jen, Aug. 1, 1971; children: Trisha Leolani, Leighton Kamaile, Karee Uilani. B.S., Pacific Union Coll., 1968. Adminstrv. sec. Hawaii Conf. Seventh-day Adventists, Honolulu, 1970—, mem. presch. adv. bd., 1984—. Mem. Nat. Assn. Exec. Secs. Republican. Club: Hawaiian Mission Acad. Alumni Assn. (v.p.). Office: Hawaii Conf Seventh-day Adventists 2728 Pali Hwy Honolulu HI 96817

JENKINS, ERNEST ALFRED, religious educator, minister, American Baptist Church; b. Detroit, Aug. 10, 1926; s. Ernest F. and Zoey (Bramall) J.; m. Katherine Dean Griffin, Aug. 27, 1948; children: Judith Lynn, Sandra Beth, Joan Carol. B.A., Wheaton Coll., Ill., 1948; B.D., No. Bapt. Theol. Sem., 1951; M.A., U. Chgo., 1953, Ph.D., 1967. Ordained to ministry Am. Bapt. Ch., 1951. Minister edn. St. Paul's Union, Chgo., 1951-63, Morgan Park Bapt. Ch., Chgo., 1963-66, 1st Bapt. Ch., Oak Park, Ill., 1966-68; assoc. prof., dir. admissions No. Bapt. Theol. Sem., Lombard, Ill., 1964-75, prof. Christian edn., 1972—; dir. doctoral studies, 1976—; mem. nat. com. Pastor as Tchr., Convocation, Am. Bapt. Assn., Green Lake, Wis., Oct. 1984; pres. Soc. of Profl. Ch. Leaders, Chgo. Bapt. Assn., 1980-81; dir. Chgo. Bapt. Credit Union, 1982—. Author, editor curriculum plan D.Min. Policy Manual, 1978, 83; author study guides. Contbr. articles to religious jours. Served with USAAF, 1944-45. Mem. Religious Edn. Assn., Assn. Profs. and Researchers in Religious Edn., Am. Bapt. Educators, Phi Delta Kappa. Home: 1139 Aurora Way Wheaton IL 60187 Office: No Bapt Theol Sem 660 E Butterfield Rd Lombard IL 60148

JENKINS, FRANKLIN MARSHALL, minister, Seventh-day Adventists; b. Temple, Tex., Dec. 1, 1950; s. Marshall Lee and Winnie Ellen (Whitlow) J.; m. Cathy Euniece Trull, May 27, 1972; child: Jennifer Ellen. A.A., Temple Jr. Coll., 1971; B.A., Southwestern Union Coll., 1977. Ordained to ministry, Seventh-day Adventists, 1981. Minister, Okla. Conf. Seventh-day Adventists, Guthrie, Perry and Edmond, Okla., 1977-79, Ada and Coalgate Madill, Okla., 1979-82, Tahlequah, Wagoner and Stillwell, Okla., 1982—; speaker Revelation for Today Broadcast, Okla., 1980—. Mem. exec. com. Tulsa Adventist Acad. Sch. Bd., Okla., 1983—. Home: Route 1 Box 123 Welling OK 74471

JENKINS, WILLIAM FERRELL, minister, Church of Christ; b. Huntsville, Ala., Jan. 3, 1936; s. B.M. and Vera Elizabeth (Mann) J.; m. Elizabeth Ann Williams, Dec. 16, 1954; children: William Ferrell, Jr., Stanley Eugene. A.A., cert., Fla. Christian Coll., 1957; student Western Ky. U., 1957, 62-63; M.A., Harding Grad. Sch., 1971. Minister, numerous Chs. of Christ, Fla., Ky., Mo., Tenn., Ind., Ohio, 1953-82, Carrollwood Ch. of Christ, Tampa, Fla., 1983—; mem. Bible faculty Fla. Coll., Temple Terrace, 1969-84; dir. study tours to Bible Lands, 1967—; assoc. editor Cogdill Found., Marion, Ind., 1969-76. Author: The Old Testament in Book of Revelation, 1973; The Finger of God, 1984; Studies in Revelation, 1984. Assoc. editor study materials. Contbr. articles to New Smith's Bible Dictionary, 1966. Mem. ednl. staff Lachish Archeol. Expedition to Israel, 1980. Mem. Am. Schs. Oriental Research, Evang. Theol. Soc., Soc. Bibl. Lit., Near East Archaeol. Soc. Republican. Home: 9211 Hollyridge Pl Temple Terrace FL 33617

JENNE, WALTER HAROLD, religious organization executive; b. Elyria, Ohio, Mar. 11, 1943; s. William Henry and Mary Ellen (Gillen) J. B.A., Borromeo Sem., 1966; M.Div., St. Mary Sem., 1970; M.S.W., Cath. U. Am., 1977. Assoc. pastor Our Lady of Guadalupe, Macedonia, Ohio, 1970-75; assoc. dir. Cath. Charities, Cleve., 1974-80, dir., 1980—; sec. for social concerns Diocese of Cleve., 1984—; trustee Nat. Conf. Cath. Charities, Washington, 1982—, Holy Family Cancer Home, 1980—. Mem. Nat. Conf. Cath. Charities, Ohio Cath. Conf. Home: 3547 E 80th St Cleveland OH 44105

JENNINGS, GEORGE JONATHAN, minister, American Baptist Churches in the U.S.A.; b. Parsons, W.Va., Nov. 3, 1949; s. Hervy William and Betty Ruth (Delaney) J.; m. Mildred Florence Huffman, Nov. 30, 1968; children: Elizabeth Dawn, Susie Dianne, Joni

Michelle. B.A. cum laude, U. Charleston, 1976; B.D., Eastern Mennonite Sem., 1980. Ordained to ministry Am. Bapt. Chs. in the U.S.A., 1982. Student pastor United Meth. Ch., Brandywine, W.Va., 1976-79; pastor United Meth. Ch., Lexington, Va., 1979-82, Pererstown Bapt. Ch., Peterstown, WVa., 1982—; v.p. Weekday Religious Edn., Lexington, 1981-82; mem. stewardship, ordination and evangelism coms. Greenbrier Bapt. Assn., 1982—; v.p. Christian Edn. Conv., 1984, pres., 1985. Republican. Lodge: Rotary (sgt. at arms). Home: East Market St Peterstown WV 24963 Office: Peterstown Bapt Ch Market St Peterstown WV 24963

JENSEN, CARL ANDREW, minister, Lutheran Church in America; b. Hudson, N.Y., Aug. 21, 1946; s. David Andrew and Elmeda Barbara (Walton) J.; m. Patricia Ann Torstrick, Sept. 11, 1971; children: Jeffrey Andrew, Stephanie Ann. B.A., Wittenberg U., 1968; M.Div., Luth. Sch. Theology, 1972; M.S. in Edn., Duquesne U., Pitts., 1982. Ordained to ministry Luth. Ch. in Am., 1972. Pastor Baden-Conway Luth. Parish, Pa., 1972-76, Good Shepherd Luth. Ch., McKees Rocks, Pa., 1976-84; dir. counselor Eng., pastoral counselor Pitts. Pastoral Inst., 1984; nat. del. Conv. Luth. Ch. in Am., 1978; congl. cons. Western Pa. and W.Va. Synod, 1975-76, 78-79. Bd. dirs. Meals on Wheels, McKees Pocks, 1978-80. Named Outstanding Young Man of Am., Jaycees, 1976. Fellow Am. Assn of Pastoral Counselors. Office: Pitts Pastoral Inst 6324 Marchand St Pittsburgh PA 15206

JENSEN, GERTRUDE MARIE ROGNESS, lay ch. worker, Am. Lutheran Ch.; b. Astoria, S.D., Oct. 11, 1921; d. Gilbert A. and Anna N. (Trooien) Rogness; B.A. magna cum laude, Augustana Coll., 1943; postgrad. U. Minn., 1945, Union Theol. Sem., N.Y.C., 1946-47, Columbia, 1946-47; postgrad. Chgo. Luth. Theol. Sem., 1948-51, M.Th., 1974; postgrad. Union Sacred Sch. of Music, 1946-47; m. Rodger Jensen, June 12, 1949; children—Mark, Erik, Rolf. Campus counselor U. Oreg., Oreg. State U., adviser to Student Council Religion, campus counselor U. Minn., 1947-51; parish counselor, tchr. Univ. Luth. Ch. of Hope, Mpls., 1951-52; family counselor, 1966—; rep. Luth. Council in U.S.A., 1966-77; cons. Luth. Council U.S.A. div. theol. studies, Jewish-Christian relations, 1976—; participant Luth.-Jewish Colloquium, 1973; mem. com. Luth.-Jewish Concerns Am. Luth. Ch., 1974—; resource person com. ordination of women, 1970, lectr., cons., author consultation on laity, 1966, lectr. dist. pastoral conf., 1964, 66, mem. cons. planning com., 1976-77; lectr. research and social action conf., 1971; lectr., adv. com. Faith in Life Dialog, 1964—; tchr. lay schs. of theology, 1965; mem. dist. com. on nominations, youth and edn., 1955-73, mem. dist. task force on continuing edn. and pastoral, staff congl. relationships, 1975—; mem. planning com. Mpls. Conf., 1966-67; del. Luth. World Fedn., Oslo, Norway, 1975; tchr., youth adviser, choir dir. local Am. Luth. Ch., 1940—; adult edn. lectr., 1974—; mem. planning com. Mpls.-St. Paul Interfaith Symposium, 1977—. Tchr. English and music secondary schs., 1943—. Republican chairwoman Rock County, state conv. del., 1957—. Regent, Augustana Coll., 1956-68, sec. bd. regents, 1956-67; regent United Theol. Sem., 1976—, acad. affairs com., 1977—; patron Minn. Symphony Orch. Women's Aux. Recipient Distinguished Alumni Achievement award Augustana Coll., 1973. Mem. Lawyers Wives Minn. (state projects chmn., dist. pres.), AAUW, P.E.O. Rotary Ann. Author: Parents Manual, 1958; Parent-Teachers Guide, 1958. Poet: Pasque Petals, 1964. Contbr. articles to religious periodicals. Home: 4420 Philbrook Ln Minneapolis MN 55424

JENSEN, HARRY ROBERT, evangelistic singer, Southern Baptist Convention; b. Woonsocket, S.D., Mar. 10, 1921; s. James Peter and Ruby Jane (Gault) J.; B.Mus., Bethany Coll., Lindsborg, Kans.; postgrad. Southwestern Bapt. Theol. Sem., Ft. Worth; m. Jo Ella Pitts, Nov. 26, 1944; children—Betty Lou, Katherine Jo, Bonnie Gay, Harry Robert. Dir. music and/or youth and edn. chs. in Okla. and Tex., 1951-67; dir. music and edn. First Bapt. Ch., Llano, Tex., 1967; evangelistic singer, 1967—; chaplain Vets. Hosp., Spokane. Address: 1603 E Wellesley St Spokane WA 99207

JENSEN, HERLUF MATTHIAS, bishop, Lutheran Church in America; b. Cordova, Nebr., July 12, 1923; s. Alfred and Milda Hannah (Schmidt) J.; m. Dorthea Lund, July 3, 1948; children: Tezanne, Lance, Cynthia, Peter, Roslind. A.B., Harvard U., 1949; M.A., U. Minn., 1951; M.Div., Union Theol. Sem., 1964. Ordained to ministry Lutheran Church in America, 1968. Pres. Luth. Student Assn. in Am., Chgo., 1951-53; exec. sec. U.S. Christian Council, N.Y.C., 1954-59; gen. sec. Nat. Student Christian Council, N.Y.C., 1959-62; staff ofcl. Bd. Social Ministry, Luth. Ch. Am., 1963-68; pastor St. Matthew's Luth. Ch., Moorestown, N.J., 1968-78; bishop N.J. Synod, Luth. Ch. in Am., 1978—; trustee Neighborhood House, New Brunswick, N.J., 1965-68, Luth. Theol. Sem., Phila., 1975—, Upsala Coll., East Orange, N.J., 1978—; pres. Human Relations Council, New Brunswick, 1965-68, Coalition of Religious Leaders, N.J., 1983—. Served with U.S. Army, 1943-46, ETO. Decorated Purple Heart; recipient Disting. Service award Human Relations Council, 1968. Mem. Liturgical Soc. Am., Luth. Human Relations Assn. Am., Luth. Soc. Worship, Music, and Arts.

Democrat. Office: NJ Synod Luth Ch Am 1930 State Hwy 33 Hamilton Square Trenton NJ 08690

JENSEN, JOSEPH (NORMAN), priest, Roman Catholic Church, educator; b. Mannheim, Ill., Nov. 22, 1924; s. Harry and Annette (Gerbing) J. B.A., Cath. U. Am., 1951, S.T.D., 1971; S.T.L., Collegio San Anselmo, Rome, 1955; S.S.L., Pontifical Bibl. Inst., Rome, 1968. Joined Benedictine Order, Roman Cath. Ch., 1948; ordained priest, 1954. Assoc. prof. Cath. U. Am., Washington, 1961—; prior St. Anselm's Abbey, Washington, 1981-85; exec. sec. Cath. Bibl. Assn., Washington, 1970—. Author: The Use of Tora by Isaiah, 1977; God's Word to Israel, 1982; Isaiah 1-39, 1984. Mng. editor O.T. Abstracts, Washington, 1977—. Served to 2d lt. USAAF, 1943-45. Mem. Cath. Bibl. Assn., Soc. Bibl. Lit., Cath. Learned Socs. (sec. joint com. 1977-82, del. 1974—), Council on Study of Religion (treas. Waterloo, Can. 1970-77, del. 1970—). Home: St Anselm's Abbey 4501 S Dakota Ave NE Washington DC 20017 Office: CBA 415 Adminstrn Bldg Cath U Am Washington DC 20064

JENSEN, OLUF CHRISTIAN, minister, religious educator, General Association of Regular Baptist Churches; b. Webster Groves, Mo., July 25, 1903; s. Jens Christian and Bodil Elisabeth (Thorsen) J.; m. Lois Corin, July 8, 1940; children: Susan Jensen Howe, Clifton, Julianne. B.A., Wheaton Coll., Ill., 1933; Th.M., Dallas Theol. Sem., 1940. Ordained to ministry No. Bapt. Conv., 1934. Pastor, Fosterberg Bapt. Ch., Ill., 1934-36, People's Ch., Montreal, Que., Can., 1940-41; assoc. pastor Scofield Meml. Ch., Dallas, 1942-43; pastor 1st Bapt, Ch., Caro, Mich., 1946-73; assoc. prof. Spurgeon Bapt. Bible Coll., Mulberry, Fla., 1973—; treas. Mich. Bapt. Youth Camps, 1950-73; sec. Bapt. Children's Home, St. Louis, Mich., 1963-73. Served as chaplain, served to capt. U.S. Army, 1943-46, PTO. Republican. Home: 4410 Spurgeon Dr Mulberry FL 33860 Office: Spurgeon Bapt Bible Coll 4440 Spurgeon Dr Mulberry FL 33860

JENSEN, STEVEN LOUIS, minister, Lutheran Ch. Am.; b. Albany, N.Y., July 12, 1947; s. Richard Carl and Shirley Jeanette (Elliott) J.; B.A., State U. N.Y., 1969; M.Div., Luth. Theol. Sem., 1973. Ordained to ministry Lutheran Ch. Am., 1973; pastor Kensington Evang. Luth. Ch., Buffalo, 1973-76; lt. chaplain corps USNR, 1971—, assigned U.S.S. Halsey, 1976—. mem. dist. cabinet Luth. Ch. Am., 1974—. Active Neighborhood Civic Action Orgn. Bd. dirs. YMCA, Neighborhood Housing Services, Inc., East Side Coop. Youth Program. Mem. Mil. Chaplains Assn., Naval Res. Assn., Alumni Assn. State U. N.Y. Address: USS Halsey (CG 23) FPO San Francisco CA 96601

JENSEN, WILMA MARY (WESTBURG) (MRS. EMMANUEL T. JENSEN), library official; b. Hopkins, Minn., June 11, 1916; d. Andrew Herman and Ida Sandelia (Anderson) Westburg; B.A., Gustavus Adolphus Coll., 1938; B.S. in L.S., U. Minn., 1940; m. Emmanuel T. Jensen, Aug. 15, 1947. Guest speaker Drexel Ch. Library Confs., Phila., 1963-66, Ch. and Synagogue Library Confs., Phila., 1968, Washington, 1969, Pitts., 1970, St. Paul, 1971, Balt., 1972, Portland, Oreg., 1973, Boston, 1974, Oberlin, Ohio, 1975, Phila., 1976, Dallas, 1977, Luth. Ch. Library Confs. in various univs. and cities, 1962—, Cath. Library Assn. Confs., various cities, 1968-72; nat. del. Luth. Ch. Am., 1966; counselor Luth. students U. Calif. at Berkeley, 1943-47, Iowa State U., Ames, 1947-48; sec. Bd. Am. Missions, Augustana Luth. Ch., Mpls., 1957-62, mem. Bd. Am. Missions, Minn. Synod, 1963-68. Bd. dirs. Minnetonka Music Assn. Recipient Disting. Alumni citation Gustavus Adolphus Coll., 1974. Mem. Ch. and Synagogue Library Assn. (nat. pres. 1971-72), Minn., Luth. Ch. Library Assn. (exec. sec. 1963—, nat. pres. 1963), Council Nat. Library and Info. Assns. (dir. 1983-86), Gustavus Library Assocs. (editorial bd., fin. officer), ALA, Luth. World Fedn. (assembly sec. 1957), Luth. Ch. Women. Contbr. articles to library and religious jours. Republican. Home: 3620 Fairlawn Dr Minnetonka MN 55345 Office: Lutheran Ch Library Assn 122 W Franklin Ave Minneapolis MN 55404

JENSEN, WOLLOM ALLEN, minister, Lutheran Church in America; b. Grafton, N.D., May 18, 1948; s. Wollom Theodore and Alice Louise (Mortensen) J.; m. Rita Joanne Windingland, Dec. 28, 1969; children: Kristin Erika, Erik Einar. B.A. in English, U. N.D., 1972; M.Div., Luth. Theol. Sem., 1976. Ordained to ministry Luth. Ch. in Am., 1976. Pastor St. Matthew Ch., Richmond, Va., 1976-78, Nativity Luth. Ch., Alexandria Va., 1978—; mem. Council for Ministry, Va. Synod, 1978—, Profl. Preparation, 1977—. Author articles and poems. Bd. dirs. Residential Youth Services, 1980—. Served with U.S. Army, 1967-69, Viet Nam, chaplain Res., 1980—. Office: Nativity Luth Ch 1300 Collingwood Rd Alexandria VA 22308

JERAULD, PHILIP ELDREDGE, priest, Episcopal Church; b. Barnstable, Mass., Mar. 18, 1926; s. Bruce Kempton and Jennie Lucile (Thayer) J.; m. Iris Teresa Garcia, Apr. 30, 1960; children: Michael Thayer, Joseph Garcia; m. Nancy Jean Kullman, June 19, 1982; 1 stepchild, William A. Kullman, Jr. Mus.B., Boston U., 1949; M.Div., Ch. Div. Sch. Pacific, 1954; S.T.M., Yale U., 1968. Ordained deacon, 1954, priest, 1955. Asst. priest All Saint's Episcopal Ch., Anchorage, 1954-56; vicar St. Mary's Episcopal Ch., Anchorage, 1956-58; diocesan supply priest Diocese of Hawaii, Honolulu, 1981-82; diocesan supply, interim and cons. Diocese of Mass., Boston, 1982—; team mem. The Beginning Experience, Hawaii, 1980-82, Boston, 1982—. Chaplain U.S. Navy, 1958-81. Home: 7 Lucy St Stoneham MA 01280

JERNIGAN, HOMER LARGE, educator, United Methodist Ch.; b. Longmont, Colo., Mar. 6, 1922; s. Virgil Jackson and Mary Ethel (Large) J.; B.A., U. Denver, 1943; B.D. magna cum laude, Union Theol. Sem., N.Y., 1946; Ph.D., Northwestern U., 1959; postdoctoral studies Harvard U., 1964-65, 78-79; m. Margaret Jane Belinfante, June 19, 1949; children: Daryl Beth, Catherine, Margaret Ann, David, Christopher. Ordained deacon United Methodist Ch., 1947, elder, 1949; layreader St. John's Chapel, Greenwich, Conn., 1944-46; pastor chs., St. Albans, N.Y., 1946-49, Amityville, N.Y., 1949-51; chaplain Cook County Hosp., Chgo., 1951-53, Western State Hosp., Staunton, Va., 1953-57; faculty Boston U. Sch. Theology, 1957—; dir. Danielsen Pastoral Counseling Service, Boston, 1963-71; vis. prof. Trinity Theol. Coll., Singapore, 1971-72. Whiting fellow; diplomate Am. Assn. Pastoral Counselors. Fellow The Pastoral Inst. Washington, Am. Assn. Theol. Schs.; mem. Am. Psychol. Assn., Assn. Clin. Pastoral Edn. (supr.). Office: 745 Commonwealth Ave Boston MA 02215

JESPERSEN, RONALD PETER, minister, Lutheran Ch. America; b. Viborg, S.D., Mar. 25, 1916; s. Niels Christian and Ludevikke (Buck) J.; A.A., Jr. Coll., 1938; B.A., Doane Coll., 1949; student Grand View Sem., 1941; M.Div., Luth. Sch. Theology; m. Delores Holmgaard, June 7, 1941; children—Donna, Diana, Dan. Ordained to ministry, 1941; pastor chs., Nebr., 1941-47, Iowa, 1948-54, Tex., 1954-58, Bethlehem Luth. Ch., Cedar Falls, Iowa, 1958-70, Faith Luth. Ch., Eldridge, Iowa, 1970-81. Prin., Cordova High Sch., 1944-46; dist. pres. and dean; chmn. bd. dirs. Grand View Coll.; pres. Danish Interest Conf., 1984—. Home: 116 N 7th St Eldridge IA 52748

JEWELL, WALTER WILLIAM, minister, Wesleyan Church of Canada; b. Picton, Ont., Can., Aug. 2, 1923; s. John Albert and Mary Emma (Potter) J.; m. Dorothy Pearl Haggarty, Jan. 5, 1943; children: Leslie, Susan. Student Brockville Bible Coll., Ont., 1958-62, Houghton Coll., N.Y., 1961, Marion Coll., Ind., 1973. Ordained to ministry Wesleyan Meth. Ch. of Am. in Can., 1961. Minister, The Wesleyan Ch., Ont., 1958—, dist. sec., 1963—, chmn. dist. camp bd., 1963-81, mem. dist. bd. adminstrn., 1963—, dist. supt., 1981—; pres. Brockville Ministerial, Ont., 1964-66, Can. Holiness Fedn., 1964-68, Oshawa Ministerial, Ont., 1970-72; sec. Can. Holiness Fedn., 1981—. Chmn., bd. dirs. Men's Hostel, Oshawa, 1972-74; pres. Chaplaincy Bd. Oshawa Gen. Hosp., 1976-78. Named Pastor of Yr., Houghton Coll., 1974.

JIMENEZ DE LA SOTA, RAFAEL, priest, Episc. Ch.; b. Seville, Spain, Nov. 12, 1922; s. Rafael Jimenez Carles and Brigida De La Sota Bidou; A.B., Jesuit Coll., 1940; L.Th., Seville Sem., 1948; D.D., Pontificial U., Seville, 1950; m. Regla Garcia Vidal, Sept. 1, 1958; children—George Phelps, Dorothy Virginia. Ordained priest, Roman Cath. Ch., 1948; parish priest and army chaplain in Spain and Morocco, 1950; received priest Episc. Ch., 1960; pastor chs. in Can., Washington and Trinity Ch., N.Y.C., 1961-62; Spanish counsellor Help Line, N.Y.C., 1969—; chaplain to gipsys of N.Am., 1962—. Decorated Order Holy Cross of Jerusalem. Author: Vida del Cardenal Segura; Ministerio de Marina; J.F. Kennedy. Home: 237 Carlton Ave Brooklyn NY 11205 Office: 1 W 29th St New York City NY 10001

JOB, RUEBEN PHILIP, minister, United Methodist Church; b. Jamestown, N.D., Feb. 7, 1928; s. Philip and Emma (Schock) J.; A.B., Westmar Coll., 1954, D.D., 1975; B.D., Evang. Theol. Sem., Naperville, Ill., 1957; m. Beverly Nadine Ellerbeck, Aug. 20, 1953; children—Deborah, Ann, Philip, David. Ordained to ministry, 1957; pastor chs., Tuttle, N.D., 1957-60, Minot, N.D., 1960-61, Fargo, N.D., 1962-65, Calvary Ch., Fargo, 1962-65; chaplain USAF, France, 1961-62; elected asst. sec. evang. United Brethren Bd. Evangelism, Dayton, Ohio, 1965-67; asst. gen. sec. Bd. Evangelism, United Meth. Ch., Nashville, 1967-74, elected asso. gen. sec., div. evangelism, worship and stewardship, Bd. Discipleship, Nashville, 1974-84; bishop, Des Moines, 1984—; tchr. young adult Sunday sch. class. Editor, compiler religious books; co-author student and tchrs.'s books in Living Bible Series, 1974. Office: 1019 Chestnut St Des Moines IA 50309*

JOCHUM, SISTER MARY EMMA, nun, educator, Roman Catholic Church; b. Huntingburg, Ind., July 13, 1940; d. Otto A. and Emma (Brinkman) J. B.S., St. Benedict Coll., Ind., 1961; M.A., Mundelein Coll., Chgo., 1982. Joined Sisters of St. Benedict, Roman Catholic Ch. Tchr., St. Mary Sch., Washington, Ind., 1962-65, St. Thomas Sch., Vincennes, Ind., 1965-68; prin. Holy Cross Elem. Sch., Fort Branch, Ind., 1968-73; parish dir. religious edn. St. Clement Ch., Boonville, Ind., 1973-82, St. Joseph Ch., Evansville, Ind., 1982—. Editor article in religious jour. Bd. dirs. Tri-Cap, pres., 1981, 82. Home and Office: Rural Route 4 Box 469 Evansville IN 47712

JODOCK, DARRELL HARLAND, minister, religion educator, Lutheran Church in America. b. Northwood, N.D., Aug. 15, 1941; s. Harry N. and Grace H. (Hansen) J.; m. Janice Marie Swanson, July 8, 1972; children: Erik Thomas, Aren Kristofer. B.A. summa cum laude, St. Olaf Coll., 1962; B.D. with honors, Luther Theol. Sem., 1966; postgrad. Union Theol. Sem., N.Y.C., 1966-67; Ph.D., Yale U., 1969. Ordained to ministry Am. Luth. Ch., 1973, Luth. Ch. in Am., 1978. Instr., Luther Theol. Sem., St. Paul, 1969-70, asst. prof., 1970-73, 75-78; asst. pastor Grace Luth. Ch., Washington, 1973-75; prof., head dept. religion Muhlenberg Coll., Allentown, Pa., 1978—; mem., chmn. various coms. N.E. Pa. Synod, Luth. Ch. in Am., 1979—. Translator: Luther and the Peasants War (Hubert Kirchner), 1972; contbr. articles to profl. jours. Del., Democratic Farm Labor Party Con., Rochester, Minn., 1972, St. Paul, 1976. Danforth Found. fellow 1962-69; Inst. for Ecumenical and Cultural Research fellow, 1982-83. Mem. Am. Acad. Religion (pres. 19th century theology group 1981—), Am. Soc. Ch. History, Soc. for Values in Higher Edn., Luth. Acad. for Scholarship, Phi Beta Kappa. Home: 2738 Highland St Allentown PA 18104 Office: Muhlenberg Coll Allentown PA 18104

JOHANSEN, JERALD RAY, educator, Church of Jesus Christ of Latter-day Saints; b. Mount Pleasant, Utah, Feb. 3, 1933; s. Ray I. Johansen and VaLene (Stevens) Johansen Watson; m. Lenore Allred, Mar. 9, 1956; children: Diane, Alan, Blake, Valerie, Mark, Laura. B.S., Brigham Young U., 1958, M.R.Ed., 1961; Ed.D., U. So. Calif., 1967. Prin. Tropic Latter-day Saints Sem., Utah, 1958-60; tchr. Pleasant Grove Sem., Utah, 1960-61; dir. Boise Inst. of Religion, Idaho, 1961-63; dir., tchr. So. Calif. Inst., 1963-67; tchr. Ogden Latter-day Saints Inst., Utah, 1967—; bishop Ogden 77th Ward, 1980—; travel study dir. Brigham Young U., Provo, Utah, 1975—. Author: Commentary on the Pearl of Great Price, 1985.

JOHN, GODFREY DAVID CARVAN, educator, writer, practitioner, Church of Christ, Scientist; b. Fonmon, S. Wales, U.K.; s. David Gwilliam and Edythe Mary (Mann) J.; B.A., Cambridge U., Eng. U., 1950, M.A., 1956; C.S.B., Bd. Edn. 1st Ch. Christ Scientist, Boston, 1973; came to Can., 1970, naturalized, 1975; m. Rosalind; children: Kristen Ruth, Stephen Leo. Authorized Christian Sci. tchr. Mem. English faculty Principia Coll., Elsah, Ill., 1958-61, U. Iowa, Iowa City, 1961-63, Boston U., 1963-64; arts critic Christian Sci. Monitor, Boston, 1964-66; vis. chaplain colls. and univs., U.S., Can., Gt. Britain, 1966-69; practitioner, Boston, 1965-70, Toronto, Ont., Can., 1970—; tchr. Christian Sci., Can., 1973—. Vol. probation parole officer Ont. Ministry Correctional Services. Recipient 1st award Am. Acad. Poets, 1962; Mem. Can. Inst. Internat. Affairs. Author: Five Seasons, 1977; contbr. theol. articles to Christian Sci. periodicals, essays and poems to Christian Sci. Monitor and lit. revs. Address: 61 Paperbirch Dr Metropolitan Toronto Don Mills ON M3C 2E6 Canada Office: 123 Edward St Suite 1003 Toronto ON Canada

JOHN, HIS GRACE see Kallos, John

JOHNESSEE, ROBERT LYNN, minister, General Association of Regular Baptist Churches; b. Carlinville, Ill., July 23, 1954; s. Robert Fisher and Juanita (Pettyjohn) J.; m. Heidi Constance Gustenhoven, May 17, 1975; children: Robert Justin, Brian Paul, Bethany Anne. A.A., Bapt. Bible Coll., Clarks Summit, Pa., 1974, B.R.E., 1976. Ordained to ministry Berean Bapt. Ch., 1979. Pastoral apprentice Mt. Top Bapt. Ch., Pa., 1975-76; minister youth and Christian edn. Madison Ave. Bapt. Ch., Cleve., 1976-78; pastor Oreana Bapt. Ch., Ill., 1979—; rep. Camp Manitoumi, Low Point, Ill., 1979—; chmn. Talents for Christ, Ill. and Mo., 1983—; com. mem. Bapt. State Youth Com., Ill. and Mo., 1983—; chmn. Central Ill. Regular Bapt. Youth. Vol. fireman Argenta-Oreana Fire Protection Dist., Ill., 1984; emergency med. technician, 1984. Mem. Central Ill. Pastors' Fellowship (sec. 1983-84), Oreana Emergency Med. Technician Assn. Home and Office: Oreana Bapt Ch PO Box 168 Oreana IL 62554

JOHN PAUL II, His Holiness Pope (Karol Jozef Wojtyla); b. Wadowice, Poland, May 18, 1920; s. Karol and Emilia (Kaczorowska) W. Student Jagiellonian U., Krakow; studied in underground Sem., Krakow, during World War II; Doctorate in ethics, Pontifical Angelicum U., Rome, 1948, Catholic U. of Lublin, Poland; Dr. (hon.), J. Guttenberg U., Mainz, W. Ger., 1977. Ordained priest Roman Cath. Ch., 1946; prof. moral theology Jagiellonian U.; prof. ethics Cath. U. of Lublin, 1954-58, dir. ethics inst., 1956-58; aux. bishop of Krakow, 1958, archbishop of Krakow, 1964-78; great chancellor Pontifical Theol. Faculty, Krakow; created cardinal by Pope Paul VI, 1967; elected Pope, Oct. 16, 1978, installed, Oct. 22, 1978. Author of books, poetry, plays including The Goldsmith's Shop, Play Easter Vigil and Other Poems, 1979, Love and Responsibility, 1960, The Acting Person, 1969, Foundations of Renewal, 1972, Sign of Contradiction, 1976, Redemptor Hominis;

Encyclical Redemptor Hominis, 1979; contbr. articles on philosophy, ethics and theology to jours.

JOHNS, HARRISON HAYNES, minister, Southern Baptist Convention; b. Sardis, Miss., Jan. 7, 1928; s. Walter Mylers and Maude Lee (Youngblood) J.; B.A., Ouachita Bapt. U., Arkadelphia, Ark., 1950; B.D., Southwestern Bapt. Theol. Sem., Ft. Worth, 1954; m. Barbara Vandiver, Dec. 25, 1951; children—Rebecca, Harrison Haynes, II. Ordained to ministry, 1948; pastor chs. in Ark., Tex. and Okla., 1950-62; pastor Calvary Bapt. Ch., Ft. Morgan, Colo., 1962-71, Coll. Heights Bapt. Ch., Alamosa, Colo., 1971-76, Pleasant Grove Bapt. Ch., Conway, Ark., 1976-84; pastor Cherry Valley Bapt. Ch., Ark., 1984—. Exec. com., also chmn. coms. Colo. Bapt. Gen. Conv. Mem. Alamosa Ministerial Assn. Contbr. articles to profl. jours. Address: PO Box 72 Cherry Valley AR 72324

JOHNSON, ARTIS, minister, United Church of Christ; educator; b. Thomsville, Ga., Oct. 3, 1948; s. Moses Cecil and Lillie Ruth (Ross) J.; m. Myrtle Elizabeth Woodruff, Sept. 16, 1969; children: Latoya, Michael Shon, Artis II, Lisa. B.S.Ed., Albany State Coll., 1970; A.A.Ed., Birdwood Jr. Bapt. Coll., 1968; M.Ed., Valdosta State Coll., 1971; postgrad. Moody Bible Inst., Lancaster Theol. Sem. (Pa.), U. Ala., Fla. State U., U. Ga. Ordained to ministry United Ch. of Christ, 1973. Pastor, Bethany Congl. Ch., Thomasville, Ga., 1972-81, Evergreen Congl. Ch., Beachton, Ga., 1974—. Tchr., Howard Middle Sch., Monticello, Fla., 1982—. Author: Oliver Wants a Pony, 1978. Mem. Nat. Tchrs. Assn., Fla. Tchrs. Assn., Ga. S.C. Assn. Christian Ministry. Lodge: Masons. Home: 110 Florida Ave Thomasville GA 31792

JOHNSON, BEN ARLEN, minister, educator, Luth. Ch. Am.; b. Melby, Minn., June 29, 1937; s. Ben Arvid and Ruth Ulrika (Werner) J.; B.A., Gustavus Adolphus Coll., 1959; M.Div., Luth. Sch. Theology, Chgo., 1961; Th.D., Harvard, 1966; postgrad. Oxford, 1971-72; m. Suzanne Frances Wasgatt, May 13, 1960; children—Samuel, Jennie Ruth, Krister, Jesse. Ordained to ministry, 1965; asst. prof. Hamma Sch. Theology, Wittenberg U., Springfield, Ohio, 1965-68, asso. prof., 1968-72, dean, prof., 1972—; pastor St. Paul's Luth. Ch., Springfield, Ohio, 1975—. Danforth fellow, 1959-65, Soc. for Religion in Higher Edn. Cross-Disciplinary fellow, 1971-72. Mem. Soc. Bibl. Lit., Soc. Values in Higher Edn. Author: Holy Week, 1973; The Mark of the Christian Community, 1975; editor: The Maturing of American Luthernism, 1968. Home: 264 S Broadmoor St Springfield OH 45504 Office: Hamma Sch of Theology Springfield OH 45501

JOHNSON, BENJAMIN EDGAR See *Who's Who in America*, 43rd edition.

JOHNSON, CHARLES EARL, minister, Luth. Ch.-Mo. Synod; b. Watseka, Ill., Jan. 22, 1948; s. Earl F. and Vera Evadell (Higgins) J.; A.A., Concordia Coll., Milw., 1968; B.A., Concordia Sr. Coll., Ft. Wayne, Ind., 1970; Div.M., Concordia Sem., St. Louis, 1974; m. Kathleen Diana Krypciak, Aug. 12, 1972; 1 son, Matthew Thomas. Ordained to ministry, 1974; pastor Trinity Luth. Ch., Roanoke, Ill., 1974—; sec. Bloomington (Ill.) Circuit Pastoral Conf., 1975-77; Christian edn. rep. Bloomington Circuit, 1975—. Sec., Roanoke (Ill.) Bicentennial Assn., 1975-77. Home: 704 N Jefferson St Roanoke IL 61561 Office: 202 W Lincoln St Roanoke IL 61561

JOHNSON, CHARLIE JAMES, minister, United Presbyterian Church U.S.A.; b. Barnesville, Ga., Sept. 24, 1923; s. Emory Moses and Ruth Belle (Traylor) J.; B.A., Morehouse Coll., 1956; B.D., Morehouse Sch. Religion, 1960, M.Div., 1973; Th.D., Trinity Coll. Bible and Theol. Sem., 1980; D.Min. in Pastoral Counseling summa cum laude, Trinity Theol. Sem., 1982; m. Mary Ellen Upton, June 7, 1957; children: Marcus Anthony, Michael A. (dec.). Ordained to ministry Bapt. Ch., 1949; pastor New Hope Bapt. Ch., Dalton, Ga., 1950-61; pastor Presbytery, Holston, Johnson City, Kingsport, Greeneville, Tenn., 1961-66, Union, Sweetwater, Athens, Tenn., 1966-82; instr. Cedine Bible Inst., Spring City, Tenn. Treas., Sweetwater Ministerial Assn., 1975-76; writer weekly column Daily Post-Athenian, 1967—. Mem. Mayor's Com. on Human Relations, Athens, 1967-69; bd. dirs. McMinn County Vocat. Edn., Athens, 1968-70; mem. Mental Health Com., Athens, 1967-69. Recipient Mathalathian award Morehouse Coll., 1956, 60, citation Athens Kiwanis Club, 1968. Home and Office: Rt 3 Pond Creek Rd Sweetwater TN 37874

JOHNSON, DOUGLAS WAYNE, church organization official, United Methodist Church; b. nr. Carlyle, Ill., Aug. 21, 1934; s. Noel Douglas and Laura Margaret (Crocker) J.; student So. Ill. U., 1952-53; B.A., McKendree Coll., 1956; S.T.B., Boston U., 1959, M.A., 1963; Ph.D., Northwestern U., 1968; m. Phyllis Ann Heinzmann, June 8, 1956; children—Kirk Wayne, Heather Renee, Kirsten Joy, Tara Carlynne. Ordained to ministry as elder United Meth. Ch., 1959; pastor Pullman Meth. Ch., Chgo., 1960-64; dir. research No. Ill. Conf. of United Meth. Ch., Chgo., 1964-66; teaching fellow Garrett Theol. Sem., Evanston, Ill., 1967-68, research asst., 1966-68; asso. for planning and research Nat. Council Chs. of Christ in the U.S.A., N.Y.C., 1968-75; exec. dir. Inst. Ch. Devel., 1976—; faculty Western Conn. State Coll., Danbury, 1969-73. Mem. research adv. com. United Meth. Ch. Recipient Service award Nat. Council Chs., 1973. Mem. Soc. Sci. Study of Religion, Religious Research Assn. (dir.), Am. Sociol. Assn. Author: Managing Change in the Church, 1974; (with George Cornell) Punctured Preconceptions, 1972; The Care and Feeding of Volunteers, 1978; The Challenge of Single Adult Ministry, 1982; Computer Ethics, 1984; Growing Up Christian in the Twenty-First Century, 1984. Contbr. articles to periodicals. Home and Office: 420 Cambridge Rd Ridgewood NJ 07450

JOHNSON, EARLE E., clergyman. Gen. sec.-auditor, African Methodist Episcopal Zion Church. Office: African Meth Episcopal Zion Ch PO Box 32843 Charlotte NC 28232*

JOHNSON, ENGRUM LEE, JR., minister, Southern Baptist Convention; b. Kingstree, S.C., Sept. 18, 1944; s. Engrum Lee and Eloise Rebecca (Caulder) J.; m. Ruth Senn, June 16, 1968; 1 child, William Engrum. B.A., Furman U., 1966; M.Div., Southeastern Bapt. Theol. Sem., 1970. Ordained to ministry So. Bapt. Conv., 1969; minister to youth First Bapt. Ch., Laurens, S.C., 1966, 1st Bapt. Ch., Anderson, S.C., summers 1967-68; pastor McDuffie Meml. Bapt. Ch., Chapel Hill, N.C., 1968-70, Black Creek Bapt. Ch., Dovesville, S.C., 1970-75, Rocky Creek Bapt. Ch., Greenville, S.C., 1975—; pres. Ministerial Assn., Furman U., 1965-66, student body Southeastern Bapt. Sem., 1969. Patron, Community Concert, Florence, S.C., 1973-74; bd. dirs. Hotline, Florence, S.C., 1973-75. Mem. Greenville Ministers Conf. (pres.), Greenville Bapt. Assn. Home: 101 Brown Dr Simpsonville SC 29681 Office: Rocky Creek Bapt Ch Greenville SC 29607

JOHNSON, FRANCIS WILLARD, minister, Lutheran Church America; b. Haxtun, Colo., Mar. 13, 1920; s. Aaron William and Lettie Victoria (Lindgren) J.; B.A., Augustana Coll., 1943, M.Div., Augustana Theol. Sem., 1946; D.Ministry, Luth. Sch. Theology, Chgo., 1977; m. Ruth Marian Palm, Sept. 11, 1945; children: Christine Louise (Mrs. Thomas A Sleight), Roland Wayne. Ordained to ministry, 1946; pastor Bethany Luth. Ch., Laurens, Iowa, 1946-50, Mamrelund Luth. Ch., Stanton, Iowa, 1950-59; sr. pastor St. Mark's Luth. Ch., Washington, Ill., 1969—. Mem. evangelism commn. Augustana Luth. Ch., 1958-62, council stewardship dirs., 1956-62; mem. exec. bd. Iowa synod Luth. Ch. Am., 1962-68, dean S.W. dist., 1965-69, mem. exec. bd. Ill. Synod, 1974-77, dean Peoria dist., 1973-83; Montgomery County (Iowa) Ministerial Assn., 1952-69; pres. Washington (Ill.) Ministerial Assn., 1971-72; mem. Luth. Ch. Am. Manifesto Commn., 1966-68; mem. evangelism commn. Joint Commn. Luth. Unity, 1960-62; stewardship dir. Iowa synod Luth. Ch. Am., 1962-69; chmn. SW Iowa Inter-Luth. Forum, 1967-69; pres. Greater Peoria Luth. Ministerial Assn., 1973-74; mem. task force on profl. support systems Ill. synod Luth. Ch. Am., 1975-78. Chmn. bldg. com. Bd. Edn., Stanton, Iowa, 1967-69; co-chmn. Stanton Community Centennial, 1968-69; pres. Youth Guidance Council, Washington, Ill., 1973-75; chmn. bd. dirs. Hovenden Meml. Hosp., Laurens, Iowa, Laurens Community Library, 1947-50, Luth. Home, Peoria, 1977-83,85—, Luth. Social Services Ill., 1971-73; chaplain Iowa Legislature, 1956-58; mem. Washington (Ill.) Bicentennial Commn., 1976; bd. dirs. Luth. Home, Peoria, Ill., 1977-82, 85—, Luth. Social Services Ill., 1971-73. Mem. Washington Ministerial Assn., Luth. Clergy Greater Peoria Area, Peoria Dist. Clergy, Ill. Synod Ministerium. Home: 606 Yorkshire Dr Washington IL 61571 Office: 101 Burton St Washington IL 61571

JOHNSON, FRANK ARTHUR, minister, Seventh-day Adventists; b. Salmon Arm, B.C., Can., Oct. 29, 1938; s. Frank Alba and Ada Florence (Astleford) J.; m. Muriel Yvonne Critchley, June 27, 1960; children: Richard Frank Alfred, Rosalie Ann. B.Sc. in Edn., Atlantic Union Coll., 1970. Ordained to ministry Seventh-day Adventists, 1978. Tchr., prin. Seventh-day Adventist Ch. Schs., various locations, Can., 1960-74; pastor Seventh-day Adventist Ch., Bonavista, Nfld., Can., 1969, 70-73; ship missionary Seventh-day Adventist Ch., B.C. Coast, 1974-75; pastor, evangelist Seventh-day Adventist Ch., B.C. and Alta., 1975-84, Edson, Alta., Can., 1982-85, Edmonton, Alta., 1985—; operator, announcer Voice of Adventist Radio, St. John's, Nfld., 1961-63; dir., speaker Profiles of Faith TV program, Revelstoke, B.C., 1980-82; speaker Sounds of Praise, radio program, Edson, 1984—. Pres., Clarenbridge br. Nfld. Tchrs. Assn., 1971-74. Mem. Ministerial Assn. Home: 117 Oak St Sherwood Park AB T8A 0V8 Canada Office: Seventh-day Adventist Church 11036 96th St Edmonton AB T5K 2K9 Canada also 2110 137th Ave Edmonton AB T5B 4K6 Canada

JOHNSON, GORDON GILBERT, educator, minister, Baptist Gen. Conf.; b. St. Paul, Nov. 19, 1919; s. Gilbert and Myrtle (Bjorklund) J.; A.A., Bethel Coll., 1943; student Harvard, 1944-45; B.A., U. Minn., 1945; B.D., Bethel Theol. Sem., 1946; Th.M., Princeton, 1950; Th.D., No. Bapt. Theol. Sem., 1960; m. Alta Fern Borden, May 21, 1945; children—Gregg, Gayle. Ordained to ministry, 1946; pastor chs., Milltown, Wis., 1946-48, Montclair, N.J., 1948-51, Chgo., 1951-59; prof. preaching Bethel Theol. Sem., 1959-64, v.p., dean, 1964-84; minister of Pastoral Care, San Diego, 1984—. Mem. gen. council Bapt. World Alliance, 1965-85; moderator Bapt. Gen. Conf., 1957-58, 85-86. Mem. Am. Acad. Homileticians, Assn. for Profl. Edn. for Ministry, Religious Speech Communication Assn. Author: My Church, 1957, 2d edit., 1973 (17 printings). Home: 6944 Camino Degrazia San Diego CA 92111

JOHNSON, HARMON ALDEN, minister, Independent Charismatic Church; b. McGregor, Minn., May 22, 1933; s. Arthur Milvin and Alma Josephine (Peterson) J.; m. Carol Elaine Porter, Oct. 17, 1959; children: Ayn, Desiree, Harmon Jr., Lynell. M.A., Fuller Theol. Sem., 1969. Ordained to ministry Lake View Gospel Ch., 1955. Pastor Sioux Mission, Granite Falls, Minn., 1952-53, Calvary Gospel Ch., Montpelier, Vt., 1957-59, Christian Fellowship, Midland Park, N.J., 1981—; missionary Assembleia De Deus, Aracaju, Brazil, 1961-73; dean Salem Sch. of the Bible, Bklyn., 1977-79. Author: The Growing Church in Haiti, 1970; Missoes, 1973. Co-author (with Read and Monterroso): Latin American Church Growth, 1969. Mem. Soc. for Pentecostal Studies. Home: 1510 Jefferson St Teaneck NJ 07666 Office: Christian Fellowship 225 Franklin Ave Midland Park NJ 07432

JOHNSON, HAROLD STEPHENS, minister, Seventh-Day Adventists; b. Newport, Ky., Feb. 11, 1928; s. Oren Glessner and Loretta (Stephens) J.; m. Marjorie Ethel Connell, Aug. 17, 1953 (dec. 1976); children: Stephen Walten, Karen Winetta; m. Harriet Elsie Dinsmore, Aug. 8, 1976. Diploma in Edn., So. Missionary Coll., Collegedale, Tenn., 1952, B.S. in Elem. Edn. and Religion, 1958; B.D., Immanuel Bapt. Coll., 1965, M.A. in Edn., 1969, D.D. (hon.), 1975. Ordained to ministry Seventh-Day Adventist, 1969; cert. tchr., Ky., Tenn. Pastor, tchr., prin. Seventh-Day Adventist Ch. Schs., Fla., Tenn., Ky., Ga., 1953-60; missionary pastor/tchr. Middle East div. Seventh-Day Adventists, Beirut and Iran, 1960-70; chaplain, tchr., v.p. Laurelbrook Sanitarium and Sch., Dayton, Tenn., 1970-77; missionary South East Africa Union Seventh-Day Adventists, Blantyre, Malawi, 1977-83; assoc. chaplain Meml. Hosp., Manchester, Ky., 1984—. Editor SEAU Tidings, 1981-83. Served as sgt. AAF, 1945-51. Mem. Seventh-Day Adventist Chaplains' Assn. (instl. chaplain 1983-84), Ky. Chaplains' Assn., Malawi Bible Soc. (life), Maranatha Flights Internat. Home: Route 5 Box 423 Manchester KY 40962 Office: Meml Hosp 401 Memorial Dr Manchester KY 40962

JOHNSON, JACK BERNHARDT, minister, So. Baptist Conv.; b. Clovis, N.Mex., Aug. 29, 1934; s. Walter B. and Mable W. (Walls) J.; A.B. in Sociology, Okla. Bapt. U., 1957; B.D., Golden Gate Sem., 1962; Ph.D., Calif. Grad. Sch. Theology, Glendale, 1973; m. Mary Ruth Giger, Aug. 8, 1954; children—Joyce Elaine, Jack Stephen. Ordained to ministry, 1956; pastor Olive (Okla.) Bapt. Ch., 1956-57, La Puente (Calif.) First So. Bapt. Ch., 1962-64, Anaheim (Calif.) Bapt. Ch., 1964-67, First Bapt. Ch., Fairfield, Calif., 1967-69, Crescent Park Ch., Odessa, Tex., 1969-70, First So. Bapt. Ch., El Monte, Calif., 1970-71, First Bapt. Ch., Ponca City, Okla., 1976—; prof. homiletics Calif. Grad. Sch. Theology, Glendale, 1974-76; mem. adj. faculty Golden Gate Bapt. Theol. Sem., 1974-76; tchr. Bible, Fall Retreat Coll. Student Ministry, 1974. Vice chmn. exec. bd. So. Bapt. Gen. Conv. of Calif., 1969, chmn. com. on coms., 1972-74; moderator N. Bay Assn., 1969; parliamentarian State Conv., So. Bapt. Gen. Conv. of Calif., 1974; chmn. evangelism Los Angeles So. Bapt. Assn., 1971-73; pres. Los Angeles So. Bapt. Ministerial Assn., 1971-73, Los Angeles Met. Missions Com., 1971-74. Chmn. Citizens Adv. Devel. Bd., El Monte, 1974-75; chmn. City Image Com., El Monte, 1974-75; chmn. cdnl. goals com. El Monte Elementary Sch. Dist., 1973-74. Mem. Golden Gate Sem. Alumni Assn. (dir. 1970-72, pres. 1969). Home: 1515 E Grand St Ponca City OK 74601 Office: 218 S 6th St Ponca City OK 74601

JOHNSON, KATHY J., minister, American Baptist Churches U.S.A. B. Kansas City, Mo., Jan. 3, 1950; d. Don M. and Reba P. (Cooper) J. B.A., Ottawa U., 1972; M.Div., Am. Bapt. Sem. of West, 1976. Ordained, 1978. Sem. intern Bd. Nat. Ministries, Am. Bapt. Chs. U.S.A., Valley Forge, Pa., 1974-75; minister pub. ministries Am. Bapt. Chs. of West, Oakland, Calif., 1976-81; assoc. exec. dir. No. Calif. Ecumenical Council, San Francisco, 1982—; bd. mem. Interfaith Council on Econ. Justice and Work, Oakland, 1983—; del. World Council Chs., Nairobi, Kenya, 1975, Consultation on Women and Men in the Ch., Sheffield, Eng., 1981; bd. and exec. Nat. Council Chs., N.Y.C., 1972-81. Mem. adv. com. Women's Econ. Agenda, No. Calif., 1984. Mem. Nat. Assn. Ecumenical Staff (program com. 1984—), Ministers Council Am. Bapt. Chs. Office: No Calif Ecumenical Council 942 Market St Room 702 San Francisco CA 94102

JOHNSON, KENNETH MARSHALL, minister, United Meth. Ch.; b. Randolph County, N.C., Feb. 11, 1928; s. Jesse Deverin and Lydia (Craven) J.; B.S., Davidson Coll., 1952; M.Div., Duke, 1955; m. Evelyn

Guyton, Nov. 22, 1951; children—Martha Lynn, Kenneth Jr., Robin Brent, Wesley Craig, Christopher Mark. Ordained to ministry, 1952; pastor, chs. N.C., 1951—, including West Bend Ch., Asheboro, 1955-60, St. Andrew's Ch., Charlotte, 1971-74, Central Ch., Mooresville, 1974-77, Leaksville Ch., Eden, 1977—. Del. World Meth. Conf., 1966, 1971; mem. Mission to Brit. Methodism team, 1962; chmn. conf. commn. communications, interpretation, 1976—; Recipient Hickman Preaching award Duke, 1955. Mem. Sinfonia, Phi Delta Theta. Contbr. articles religious jours. Home: 222 Farrell St Eden NC 27288 Office: PO Box 663 Eden NC 27288

JOHNSON, KENNETH RAY, radio station executive; b. Oakland, Calif., Oct. 24, 1956; s. Milton Arthur and Evelyn Bernita (Reid) J.; m. Karen Marie Bumpus, Nov. 24, 1979; children: William Ray, Calvin Reid. Student, Chabot Coll. Pub. affairs dir. Sta. KEAR, San Francisco, 1975-79, Sta. KVIP, Redding, Calif., 1979-81; ops. mgr. Sta. KWBI Religious Radio, Denver, 1981-85, sta. mgr., 1985—; pres. Harvest Helper Ministries, Inc., Littleton, Colo., 1984—. Mem., deacon Littleton Bible Chapel, 1981—. Republican. Avocations: photography; family camping. Address: KWBI-FM 16075 W Belleview Ave Morrison CO 80465

JOHNSON, KENT L., minister, religious educator, American Lutheran Church; b. Rockford, Ill., Nov. 18, 1934; s. Earl Alfred and Geneva Marie (Quist) J.; m. Shirley Constance Breen, Aug. 27, 1955; children: Karen Marie, Steven Kent. B.A., Luther Coll., 1955; B.D., Luther Sem., 1961; M.A., U. Wyo., 1965, Ed.D., 1970. Ordained to ministry Am. Luth. Ch., 1961. Dean of men Augustana Coll., Sioux Falls, S.D., 1966-70, campus pastor, 1974-76; pastor St. Pauli Luth., Lynwood, Calif., 1970-74; assoc. prof. Luther Northwestern Sem., St. Paul, Minn., 1976—. Author: Called To Teach, 1984. Served to maj. U.S. Army, 1961-64. Mem. Religious Edn. Assn., Phi Kappa Phi. Home: 354 W Charlotte River Falls WI 54022 Office: Luther Northwestern Sem 2481 Como St Paul MN 55108

JOHNSON, LANEY LESTER, minister, So. Bapt. Conv.; b. Linden, Tex., July 30, 1935; s. Laney Elmer and Lydia Christine (O'Rand) J.; B.A., Baylor U., 1957; B.D., Southwestern Bapt. Theol. Sem., 1961, M.R.E., 1964; Th.D., Luther Rice Sem., 1970; m. Emily Jane Spurlock, Sept. 5, 1960; children—Laney Alan, John Lester. Ordained to ministry, 1955; asst. pastor Cockrell Hill Bapt. Ch., Dallas, 1962-66; pastor First Bapt. Ch., Throckmorton, Tex., 1966-68; pastor N. Temple Bapt. Ch., Dallas, 1968-70, Mobberly Ave. Bapt. Ch., Longview, Tex., 1970—. Moderator, So. Assn., 1968, Gregg Assn., 1972-74; preaching missions to Eng. and Scotland; del. Conf. on Prophecy, Jerusalem, 1971. Chmn. United Fund campaign, Throckmorton County, 1968—; trustee E. Tex. Bapt. Coll., Marshall, 1970. Home: 2206 Buccaneer Longview TX 75601 Office: 1400 S Mobberly Ave Longview TX 75601

JOHNSON, LARRY DEAN, minister, Am. Lutheran Church; b. Alexandria, Minn., Jan. 4, 1943; s. Olaf M. and Marilynn Elizabeth (Nelson) J.; B.A., Concordia Coll., 1965; M.Div., Luther Theol. Sem., 1969; Th.M., Princeton, 1970; Ordained to ministry, 1971; intern campus pastor S.W. Minn. State Coll., Marshall, 1967-68; youth evangelist commn. evangelism Am. Luth. Ch., Mpls., 1968-70; asso. pastor First Luth. Ch., Columbia Heights, Minn., 1971-72; pres. Luth. Youth Encounter, St. Paul, 1973—; exec. com., bd. dirs. Tentmakers, 1978—, Friends for Biblical Lutheranism, 1983—, Affiliation of Luth. Movements, 1980—. Editor, contbr. Encounter paper, 1973—. Contbg. author: Mission, '77, 1976; Institutions and Movements, 1983. Home: 2901 NE 31st Ave Minneapolis MN 55418 Office: 2500 39th Ave NE Minneapolis MN 55421

JOHNSON, LOWELL BERTHEN, minister, United Methodist Ch.; b. Foley, Minn., Dec. 12, 1928; s. Oscar Berthen and Amanda (Johnson) J.; A.A., North Park Jr. Coll., 1947; B.A., U. Minn., 1951; M.A., Trinity Coll. (Hartford), 1964; M.Div., Hartford Theol. Sem., 1956; D.Ministry, Drew U., 1975; m. Janet M. Christianson, Sept. 4, 1954; children—Cynthia, Randall, Kent, Lynn. Ordained to ministry; pastor Queen Street Congregational Ch., Bristol, Conn., 1953-57, United Meth. Ch., Pleasant Valley, Conn., 1957-61, United Meth. Ch., Seynour, Conn., 1961-70, United Meth. Ch., Riverhead, N.Y., 1970-74, Faith United Meth. Ch., Staten Island, N.Y., 1974—. Supervising pastor Yale Divinity Sch., New Haven, Conn., 1961-70. Mem. Conn. com. McCarthy for Pres., 1967-68. Mem. Appreciation award Seymour C. of C., 1970. Mem. NAACP (life), N.Y. Annual Conf. United Meth. Ch. Home: 582 Delafield Ave Staten Island NY 10310 Office: 213 Heberton Ave Staten Island NY 10302

JOHNSON, ODIS RAY, minister, Ch. of God (Cleveland, Tenn.); b. Henegar, Ala., Oct. 28, 1938; s. Jesse Reese and Mary Helen (Wilborn) J.; grad. Bible Inst. Ministerial Enrichment, 1974; student N.E. State Jr. Coll., 1969, 75; m. Wanda Lee Lassetter, Nov. 2, 1957; children—Sandy Ray, Madonna Lynn. Ordained to ministry, 1969; pastor Fyffe (Ala.) Ch. of God, 1964-69, 71—, Barrytown Ch. of God, Gilvertown, Ala., 1969-71, Dist. overseer Ch. of God, Barrytown Dist., Gilbertown, 1969-71, dist. youth dir., 1962-65, 74, 75; sec. N. Ala. Ministerial Fellowship, 1971-73. Address: Box 124 Fyffe AL 35971

JOHNSON, ORA J., minister, Gen. Baptists; b. Oakland City, Ind., Aug. 31, 1932; s. Ora F. and Thelma P. (Julian) J.; B.S., Oakland City Coll., 1971; m. Wanda Mae Lockamy, Aug. 11, 1952; children—David Russell, Kent Alan, Vicki Jeanne. Ordained to ministry, 1966; pastor chs., Ind., Ky., 1964-76; dir. evangelism and ch. growth Gen. Baptists, Poplar Bluff, Mo., 1976—; producer, speaker TV series Moments of Worship, Evansville, Ind., 1973-76. Pres. home missions bd. Gen. Baptists, 1972-73, pres. gen. bd., 1973; pres. Greater Evansville Clergy Assn., 1974-75; exec. com. Gen. Bapt. Hist. Soc., 1974—. Recipient Brotherhood award Oakland City Coll., 1971. Mem. Evangelization Forum, Christian Resource Assos., Nat. Assn. Evangs. Home: 2021 N 14th St Poplar Bluff MO 63901 Office: PO Box 912 Poplar Bluff MO 63901

JOHNSON, ROBERT ROSS, minister, United Church of Christ; b. Spokane, June 26, 1920; s. John J. and Metta (Nickleberry) J.; m. Ernestine Norwood, June 3, 1943; children: Michelle Johnson Tompkins, Stephen, John E. B.A., Whitworth Coll., 1943; M.Div., Colgate Rochester Sem., 1946. Ordained to ministry United Ch. Christ, 1945. Pastor 2d Bapt. Ch., LeRoy, N.Y., 1947-48, South Congl. Ch., Chgo., 1948-52; Bklyn. Nazarene Congl. Ch., 1952-56; St. Albans Congl. Ch., N.Y., 1953— (also founder); moderator State Conf. United Ch. Christ, 1968-69, conf. chaplain, chmn. ch. extension; bd. dirs. Queens Fedn. Chs.; bd. cooperators, founder, past bd. dirs. Queens Interfaith Clergy Council. Bd. dirs. YMCA; chmn. Arthur Ashe Vols. com. United Negro Coll. Fund; mem. N.Y.C. Bd. Higher Edn., 1968-73; bd. dirs. NAACP; mem. Jamaica Queens Dist. 15 Sch. Bd.; bd. dirs. Neighbors Houses. Named Clergy of Yr. NCCJ, 1973; Outstanding Churchman of Yr., Queens Fedn. Chs., 1981; recipient Disting. and Exceptional award Friends of Sr. Citizens; Religion award NAACP, 1981. Club: The Fellas (pres. 1975-80). Lodge: Rotary. Office: St Albans Congl Ch 172-17 Linden Blvd St Albans NY 11434

JOHNSON, ROY WOOTEN, minister, Southern Baptist Convention; b. Ochlocknee, Ga., Jan. 19, 1934; s. Roy and Lozie (Wooten) J.; m. Helen Hamrick, June 30, 1956; children: Roy H., Elizabeth A., Susan L., Sandra L. B.A., Stetson U., 1973; M.Div., New Orleans Bapt. Theol. Sem., 1976, M.R.E., 1977; M.S. in History, La. State U., 1976. Ordained to ministry Baptist Ch., 1970. Pastor, Forist City Bapt. Ch., Fla., 1970-73, West Shady Grove Ch., Waynesboro, Miss., 1973-77, Ivey Bapt. Ch., Ga., 1977-79, Worthville Bapt. Ch., Jackson, Ga., 1979-81, New Bethel Bapt. Ch., Moultrie, Ga., 1981—; mem. exec. com. Ga. Bapt. Conv., 1980-81, faculty tchr. edn. extension, 1978—; moderator Colquitt County Bapt. Assn., 1984. Bd. dirs. Heart Fund, Jackson, 1980. Served with USMC, 1953-55. Democrat. Home: Route 1 Box 246 Meigs GA 31765

JOHNSON, SUSANNE, religion educator, Christian Church (Disciples of Christ); b. Poplar Bluff, Mo., July 15, 1950; d. Cecil Robert and Clara Elizabeth (Boyd) J. A.A., Three Rivers Community Coll., 1970; B.S., Phillips U., 1972, M.Div., 1977; Ph.D., Princeton Theol. Sem., 1984. Ordained to ministry Christian Ch. (Disciples of Christ), 1977. Minister to youth First Christian Ch., Poplar Bluff, Mo., 1969, 70, 71, minister edn., 1972-73; summer minister to youth First Christian Ch., Cherokee, Okla., 1974, First Christian Ch., Perryton, Tex., 1975; assoc. minister Christian Ch. of Covenant, Enid, Okla., 1975-77; adj. faculty mem. Phillips U., Enid, 1977, Princeton Theol. Sem. (N.J.), 1981; asst. prof. Christian Edn., Perkins Sch. Theology, So. Meth. U., Dallas, 1982—; mem. Yokefellow Prison Ministry Met. Correctional Ctr., N.Y.C., 1977-78; del. Gen. Assembly Christian Ch. (Disciples of Christ), San Antonio, Tex., 1979. Mem. U.S. out of Central Am., Women's Caucus/Religious Studies, Assn. Profs. and Researchers in Religious Edn., United Meth. Assn. Profs. Christian Edn., Religious Edn. Assn., Am. Acad. Religion, Internat. Assn. Women Ministers. Democrat. Home: 3848 Turtle Creek Dr Dallas TX 75219 Office: Perkins Sch Theology So Meth U Dallas TX 75275

JOHNSON, TERENCE ELWYN, minister, United Church of Christ; b. Miami, Fla., Dec. 24, 1938; s. Elwyn Merton and Gathary Louise (DeVane) J.; B. Mus. Edn., Fla. State U., 1960; postgrad. David Lipscomb Coll., 1960-61; M.A., George Peabody Coll., 1964; postgrad. Crozer Theol. Sem., 1968-69, United Theol. Sem. of Twin Cities, 1970-73; D.D., Olivet Coll., 1982, Oxford U., 1984; m. Joan Carolyn Davis, Aug. 15, 1959; children—Kimberly Gay, Kenneth Armand. Ordained to ministry 1966; minister Valley Forge Ch. of Christ, King of Prussia, Pa., 1966-69; asso. minister Plymouth Congl. Ch., Mpls., 1969-74; sr. minister 1st Congl. Ch., Royal Oak, Mich., 1974-85; sr. minister Margate Community Ch., N.J., 1985—. Nat. adviser Heritage of Pilgrim Endeavor of Congl. Coll. Group, 1972-74; speaker Mich. Congl. Conf., 1973; mem. commn. ministry Nat. Assn. Congl. Christian Chs., 1975—, Keynote speaker, 1976—. ecumenical leader. Mem. Phi Mu Alpha Sinfonia. Sermons editor The Congegationalist, 1973, columnist, 1975—. Contbr. articles and sermons to religious publs. Office: 8900 Ventnor Pkwy Margate NJ 08402

JOHNSON, THOMAS KENNEDY, minister, Independent Baptist; b. Raleigh, N.C., Feb. 15, 1932; s. Atlas Thomas and Iris Elizabeth (Kennedy) J.; B.A., Bob Jones U., 1960; postgrad. U. N.C., 1970-72; m. Ada Marjorie Harris, Sept. 8, 1950; children—Thomas Kennedy, Timothy Clyde, Archie Eugene. Ordained to ministry, 1960; tchr., coordinator Coop. Distributive Edn.. New Hanover County Schs., 1969-72; missionary-pastor Brookwood Free Will Bapt. Ch., Fayetteville, N.C., 1960-62; pastor Ahoskie (N.C.) Free Will Bapt. Ch., 1963-65; founder, missionary-pastor Friendship Free Will Bapt. Ch., Wilmington, N.C., 1966-75, Grace Free Will Bapt. Ch., DeQueen, Ark., 1975-82; founder, pastor Grace Bapt. Ch., DeQueen, 1983—. Sec.-treas. Cape Fear Evangel. Ministers Assn., 1974-75; pres. Cape Fear Minister's Conf., 1960-61; moderator Northeastern Assn. of Free Will Bapts., 1964-65; asst. moderator Costal Assn. of Free Will Bapts., 1968-69, 74-75, Little Mo. River Assn. Free Will Bapts., 1976-78. Mem. Nat. Assn. Free Will Bapts., N.C. Assn. Free Will Bapts., Little Missouri River and Ark. State Assn. Free Will Bapts. Coordinator migrant edn. DeQueen Pub. Schs., 1979—. Home: RFD 3 Box 520 DeQueen AR 71832 Office: RFD 3 Box 520 DeQueen AR 71832

JOHNSON, WILLIAM ALEXANDER, priest, Episcopal Ch.; b. Bklyn., Aug. 20, 1934; s. Charles Raphael and Ruth Augusta (Anderson) J.; B.A., City U. N.Y., 1953; B.D., Drew Theol. Sem., 1956; Teol.Kand., U. Lund (Sweden), 1957, Teol.Lic., 1958, Teol.Dr., 1962; M.A., Columbia, 1958, Ph.D., 1959; m. Carol Genevieve Lundquist, June 11, 1955; children—Karin Ruth, Karl William, Krister Frederick. Ordained to ministry, 1958; pastor Teabo (N.J.) Meth. Ch., 1954-56, Immanuel Meth. Ch., Bklyn., 1957-59; asst. prof. religion Trinity Coll., Hartford, Conn., 1959-63; asso. prof. religion, chmn. dept. religion Drew U., Madison, N.J., 1963-66; prof., chmn. dept. religion Manhattanville Coll., Purchase, N.Y., 1967-71; Albert V. Danielsen prof. Christian thought, prof. philosophy and history of ideas Brandeis U., Waltham, Mass., 1971—, canon residentiary, dir. Inst. Theology, Cathedral Ch. of St. John the Divine, N.Y.C., 1973—. Lectr. in field to colls. and univs. Danforth Assos. award, 1964; Soc. Religion in Higher Edn. postdoctoral fellow, 1970; recipient Roian Flect prize Bryn Mawr Coll., 1976. Mem. New Haven Theol. Discussion Group, Author's Guild, Soc. for Religion in Higher Edn., Am. Acad. Religion, Episc. Churchmen for S. Africa. Author: Nature and the Supernatural in the Theology of Horace Bushnell, 1963; On Religion: A Study of the Theological Method in Schleiermacher and Nygren, 1964; The Search for Transcendence, 1974; Invitation to Theology, 1976; (with Nels Ferre) Swedish Contributions to Modern Theology, 1966. Home: 27 Fox Meadow Rd Scarsdale NY 10583 Office: 1047 Amsterdam Ave New York City NY 10025

JOHNSON, WILLIAM CAMPBELL, minister, United Wesleyan Methodist Church America; b. Miami, Fla., July 4, 1925; s. Nathaniel and Annie J.; m. Margaret K. Johnson; children—Mervin C., Brenda J., Hammuel P., Hiram N., Mary E. B.S., M.Div. Ordained to ministry, 1959; pastor St. Marys Wesleyan Meth. Ch., N.Y.C., 1960—. Worker, E. Side Community Corp.; chmn. United Wesleyan Meth. Conf. Am.; worker N.Y. Council Smaller Chs. Mem. Council Chs. N.Y.C., United Wesleyan Meth. Ministerial Instl. Fellowship, Harlem Ministerial Interfaith Assn. Home: 109-60 141st St Jamaica NY 11435

JOHNSON, WILLIAM DECKER, elder, African Methodist Episcopal Church; b. Albany, Ga., Jan. 31, 1900; s. William Decker and Winnifred (Simon) J.; student Payne Coll., Wilberforce Coll.; B.S. cum laude, Paul Quinn Coll., 1923; B.D., Campbell Coll., 1929, D.D., 1932; Ph.D. (hon.), Monrovia, Liberia, 1956; m. Beatrice Evelyn Denson, Sept. 14, 1926. Ordained elder, 1923; pastor, Ga., Miss., Okla., 1923-29, 33-36; presiding elder chs., Okla., Ga.; gen. officer A.M.E. Ch., 1948-51; pres. Campbell Coll., Jackson, Miss., 1928-32, Flipper-Key-Davis, Davis, Okla., 1932-36; dean theol. sem. Shorter Coll., 1936-37; mgr. A.M.E. Book Concern, 1948—. Mem. NAACP, World Council Chs. Editor A.M.E. Ch. Rev., 1971—. Address: 468 Lincoln Dr NW Atlanta GA 30318

JOHNSON, WILLIAM R., bishop, Roman Catholic Church; b. Tonopah, Nev., Nov. 19, 1918; ed. St. Patrick's Sem., Menlo Park, Calif., St. John's Sem., Camarillo Calif.; B.S. in Social Work, Cath. U. Am. Ordained priest, 1944; staff Cath. Welfare Bur., Archdiocese of Los Angeles, 1948-76, dir., 1956-76; pastor Holy Name of Jesus Ch., Los Angeles, 1962-68, Am. Martyrs Ch., Manhattan Beach, Calif., 1968-70; parochial vicar St. Vibiana's Cathedral, Los Angeles, 1970-76; consecrated titular bishop of Blear and aux. bishop of Los Angeles, 1971; bishop of Orange (Calif.), 1976—. Office: 2811 Villa Real Dr Orange CA 92667*

JOHNSON, WINFRED VAN, minister, chapel dean, United Methodist Church; b. Norfolk, Va., Aug. 21, 1926; s. Molden and Gracie Marie (Portor) J.; B.A.,

Livingstone Coll., 1949; B.D., Capital Theol. Sem., 1958; m. Shirley Mae Alfred, July 7, 1973. Ordained to ministry, 1958; pastor Caldwell A.M.E. Ch., Houston, 1958—. Mem. local Meth. Bd.; dir. Tex. Minister's Conf.; asso. prof. social studies, dir. sociology Prairie View A. and M. U., dean of chapel, 1958—, also dir. student activities; mem. bd. of commn./social concerns Tex. So. Bapt. Conv., 1982—. Named Minister of Year, 1968, Omega Man of Year, 1953. Mem. Social Studies Soc., Soc. Social Workers, NAACP, Urban League, Tex. Tchrs. Assn. Home: 14743 Perthshire Rd Houston TX 77079

JOHNSRUD, LEROY A., clergyman, American Lutheran Church. Chmn. Bd. for World Mission and Inter-Ch. Cooperation, Mpls. Office: Am Luth Ch Gen Orgn 422 S 5th St Minneapolis MN 55415*

JOHNSTON, DANIEL EVANDA, minister, Southern Baptist Convention; b. Sumter, S.C., July 20, 1935; s. Arthur O'Donald and Edith Estelle (Rodgers) J.; m. Virginia Carol Evans, May 30, 1959; children: Daniel, Stephen, Paul. A.A., North Greenville Coll., 1960; B.A., Carson-Newman Coll., 1962; M.Div., Southeastern Bapt. Theol. Sem., 1965. Ordained, 1962. Pastor Calvary Bapt. Ch., Virgilina, Va., 1962-64, Parksville and Modoc Chs., Parksville, S.C., 1964-65, New Market Ch., Greenwood, S.C., 1965-70, Shiloh Bapt. Ch., Aiken, S.C., 1970-80, 1st Bapt. Ch., Mount Pleasant, S.C., 1980—; supt. 1st Bapt. Day Sch., Mount Pleasant, 1980—; view poll panel mem. Bapt. Sunday Sch. Bd., Nashville, 1978—; mem. pastors adv. bd. Bapt. Coll., Charleston, S.C., 1982—; mem. clergy staff Univ. Hosp., Augusta, Ga., 1975—; chaplain Center Fire Dept., Aiken, 1970-75; chaplain Aiken Youth Correction Ctr., Aiken, 1976-80. Trustee Connie Maxwell Children's Home, Greenwood, 1974-76, North Greenville Coll., Tigerville, S.C., 1985—. Home: 1149 Elizabeth Circle Mount Pleasant SC 29464 Office: First Bapt Ch 681 McCants Dr Mount Pleasant SC 29464

JOHNSTON, GEORGE, educator, minister, Church of Scotland, b. Clydebank, Scotland, June 9, 1913; s. William George and Jenny Connolly (McKeown) J.; M.A., Glasgow U., 1935, B.D., 1938, D.D. (hon.), 1960; Ph.D., Cambridge U., 1941; LL.D., (hon.), Mt. Allison U., 1974; D.D. (hon.), United Theol. Coll., Montreal, 1974; D.D. (hon.), Montreal Diocesan Theol. Coll. 1975; m. Alexandra Gardner, Aug. 6, 1941; children—Christine, Ronald, Janet (Mrs. John Campbell). Came to Can., 1952. Ordained to ministry Ch. of Scotland, 1940; minister Martyrs' Ch., St. Andrews, Scotland, 1940-47; asso. prof. Hartford Theol. Sem., 1947-52; prof. N.T., Emmanuel Coll., Toronto, 1952-59, McGill U., 1959—, also prin. United Theol. Coll., 1959-70; dean Faculty of Religious Studies of McGill U., 1970-75; commr. United Ch. Gen. Council, 1958, 66, 68; acting chaplain 7th Black Watch 51st Div., Germany, 1945; mem. New Delhi World Council Chs. Assembly, 1961, Humanities Research Council, Can., 1974-75. Mem. Port Credit (Ont.) Pub. Library Commn., 1958-59; gov. McGill U., 1971-75. Decorated France-Germany Star, U.K. Def. Medal. Black Theol. fellow, Glasgow, 1938; Brown Downie fellow, 1937; Am. Assn. Theol. Schs. fellow, 1967; Can. Council fellow, 1975. Mem. Canadian Bibl. Soc. (pres. 1963), Canadian Theol. Soc. (pres. 1966), Soc. Bibl. Lit. (mem. council). Author: The Church in the New Testament, 1943; The Secrets of the Kingdom, 1954; The Church in the Modern World, 1967; The Spirit-Paraclete in the Gospel of John, 1970; contbr. to New Century Bible, Peake's Commentary, The Interpreter's Dictionary of the Bible. Office: McGill U Faculty of Religious Studies 3520 University St Montreal PQ H3A 2A7 Canada*

JOHNSTON, JAMES SINCLAIR, priest, Episcopal Ch.; b. Cleve., Apr. 1, 1924; s. Gail Arnold and Eva Mae (Crooks) J.; B.A., Baldwin-Wallace Coll., 1950; M.Div., Kenyon Coll., 1953; M.A., Case Western Res. U., 1970; children—James Sinclair, Beth Macdonald, Geoffrey Sinclair. Ordained priest, 1953; curate St. Paul's Ch., Akron, Ohio, 1953-55; rector Grace Ch., Willoughby, Ohio, 1955-70; vicar St. Hubert's Chapel, Kirtland Hills, Ohio, 1970—; staff counselor Univ. Sch., Cleve., 1970—; counselor alcohol rehab. Woodruff Meml. Hosp., Cleve., 1975—. Nat. chaplain Naval Res. Assn., 1974-76, mem. nat. adv. bd., 1975—; staff chaplain Naval Res. Readiness Command Region 5, 1977—. Mem. bd. Republican Century Club of Lake County, 1975—; active Lake County Mental Health Assn., 1970-75; mem. adv. bd. Lake County Family Health Assn., 1970—. Office: Saint Hubert Chapel Baldwin Rd Kirtland Hills OH 44060

JOHNSTON, JIM, minister, So. Bapt. Conv.; b. Lampasas, Tex., July 29, 1947; s. Joe Edward and Ida Mae (Smith) J.; B.A., Howard Payne U., 1969; postgrad. Southwestern Bapt. Theol. Sem., 1970; m. Mary Sims, June 6, 1970; children—Jeremy, Jill. Ordained to ministry, 1971; dir. Bapt. student work Sul Ross State U., Alpine, Tex., 1970-71; minister to youth Sherwood Bapt. Ch., Odessa, Tex., 1971-73, 1st Bapt. Ch., Plainview, Tex., 1973—; dean Youth Sch. Evangelism, Tex., 1976—; guest speaker youth evangelism confs., revivals, clinics and youth camps. Home: 2609 W 20th St Plainview TX 79072 Office: 205 W 8th St Plainview TX 79072

JOHNSTON, JOHN ALEXANDER, minister, Presbyterian Church in Canada; b. Edmonton, Alta., Can., Nov. 3, 1927; s. Joseph Samuel and Marian Halley (Leslie) J.; m. Erika Heather Elizabeth Heppe, Feb. 20, 1957; children: Andrew, Ian, Mary. B.A., U. Western Ont. (Can.), 1950; M.A., McGill U. (Can.), 1951, Ph.D., 1955; B.D., Presbyn. Coll. (Que.), 1954, D.D. (hon.), 1980; Th.M., Princeton Theol. Coll., 1956. With St. Timothy's, Ottawa, Can., 1956-64, Lagos Ch., Nigeria, 1964-66; sr. minister MacNab St. Presbyn. Ch., Hamilton, Ont., 1966—; chmn. archives com. Presbyn. Ch. in Can., Toronto, 1979—, history com., 1968-78, Christian edn. com., 1961-64. Author: Strong Winds Blowing, 1979; Church Union, 1956; PYPS Thru the Keyhole, 1954; (with others) Reformed & Reforming, 1964. Pres. Leprosy Mission of Can., 1981-85; chmn. Boys Brigade of Can., 1962-64, Planned Parenthood, Hamilton, 1972-73; dir. Hamilton Dictionary of Biography, 1982—, EH Johnson Trust, Toronto, 1982—; exec. Social Planning and Research Council of Hamilton, 1984—. Mem. Presbyn. Ch. History Soc. (sec. 1961-63). Lodges: Masons (grand chaplain 1981-82, past master 1975). Home: 147 Chedoke Ave Hamilton ON L8P 4P2 Canada Office: MacNab St Ch Presbyn Ch Canada 116 MacNab St S Hamilton ON L8P 3C3 Canada

JOHNSTON, KENNETH CAROL, minister, United Methodist Church; b. Cape Girardeau, Mo., Jan. 16, 1923; s. Martin Paul and Anna Virginia (Henson) J.; A.B., S.E. Mo. State U., 1947; M.Div., Yale, 1950; D.D., Central Meth. Coll., 1965; m. Joy Hahs, Sept. 1, 1948; children—Donald Kenneth, Susanna Joy. Ordained to ministry, 1950; pastor United Meth. Ch., California, Mo., 1950-55, Neosho, Mo., 1955-60; sr. pastor First United Meth. Ch., Joplin, Mo., 1960-64; supt. Kansas City N. Dist., 1964-66; v.p. Central Meth. Coll., Fayette, Mo., 1966-68; sr. pastor Plate Woods (Mo.) United Meth. Ch., 1968-74, Webster Hills United Meth. Ch., Webster Groves, Mo., 1974-84; supt. Cape Girardeau-Farmington Dist., 1984—. Mem. jurisdictional and gen. confs., 1970-72; mem. gen. bd. higher edn., ministry United Meth. Ch., 1972-76, minority scholarship com., 1972-76. Vol. ARC, Mo., 1946-84, water safety instr. trainer, 1957-84. Home and Office: 810 Alta Vista Dr Cape Girardeau MO 63701

JOHNSTON, ROBERT KENT, minister, educator, Evangelical Covenant Church of America; b. Pasadena, June 9, 1945; s. Roy G. and Naomi (Harmon) J.; m. Anne R. Johnston, Dec. 14, 1968: children: Elizabeth, Margaret. A.B., Stanford U., 1967; B.D., Fuller Theol. Sem., 1970; postgrad. North Park Sem., 1970-71; Ph.D., Duke U., 1974. Ordained to ministry, Evang. Covenant Ch. of Am. Asst. prof. religion Western Ky. U., Bowling Green, 1974-78, assoc. prof., 1978-82; vis. prof. theology New Coll., Berkeley, Calif., 1980-81; dean, assoc. prof. theology and culture North Park Sem., Chgo., 1982—. Author: Evangelicals at an Impasse, 1979, Psalms for God's People, 1982, The Christian at Play, 1983, The Use of the Bible in Theology: Evangelical Options, 1985. Mem. Am. Acad. Religion, Phi Beta Kappa. Democrat. Home: 613 Central Ave Wilmette IL 60091 Office: North Park Theol Sem 5125 N Spaulding Ave Chicago IL 60625

JOHNSTONE, DOUGLAS VERNON, minister, missionary, Lutheran Church-Missouri Synod; b. Oakland, Calif., Sept. 28, 1944; s. Ross Vernon and Margaret (Ness) J.; m. Phyllis Louise Wulferdingen, July 1, 1967; children: Rebecca, Amy, Michael. B.A., Concordia Sr. Coll., 1966; M.Div., Corcordia Sem., 1970. Ordained to ministry Luth. Ch., 1970. Evangelist pastor La Ascension Cong., San Felix, Venezuela, 1970-71; instr. Juande Frias Extension Sem., Caripe, Venezuela, 1971-74; assoc. dir. Cristo Paratodas las Naciones, Caracas, Venezuela, 1974-78; field mission dir. Luth. Mission, Luth. Ch., Mo. Synod, Caracas, 1978—; v.p. Luth. Ch. Venezuela, 1973, 80, pres., 1975-79; dir. Colegio la Concordia, Caracas; 1978. Cristo Para Todas las Naciones, Caracas, 1979—. Mem. NCCJ (bd. dirs. 1983—). Avocations: music; tennis. Home: Aptd 60.387 Caracas 1060A Venezuela. Office: Iglesia Luterana de Venuezuela care Jet Cargo Internat M-182 PO Box 020010 Miami FL 33102

JONES, A. J., SR., clergyman, Church of God in Christ, also Internat. second vice presiding bishop. Office: 638 W 35th St Norfolk VA 23508*

JONES, ADRIAN LESLIE, minister, So. Baptist Conv.; b. Los Angeles, Apr. 30, 1941; s. Adrian Terry and Carrie Louise (Todd) J.; B.B.A., N. Tex. State U., 1963; M.R.E., Southwestern Bapt. Theol. Sem., Ft. Worth, 1965; m. Nona Sue Cossey, Nov. 15, 1969. Ordained to ministry, 1974; minister youth, edn. and music First Bapt. Ch., Rotan, Tex., 1965-67; minister youth First Bapt. Ch., Shawnee, Okla., 1967-70, Southwood Bapt. Ch., Oklahoma City, 1970—. Conf. tchr. Glorieta (N.Mex.) Bapt. Tng. Center; adv. bd. Bapt. Student Union, U. Okla., also Okla. Bapt. U.; youth dir. Capital Bapt. Assn., 1972—. Dir. activities Okla. High Sch. Student Council Clinics. Author curriculum materials. Home: 7900 S Hillcrest Dr Oklahoma City OK 73159 Office: 911 SW 59th St Oklahoma City OK 73109

JONES, AMOS, JR., minister, Nat. Baptist Ch.; b. Giles County, Tenn., Sept. 18, 1938; s. Amos and Roberta (Payne) J.; B.A., Am. Bapt. Theol. Sem., Nashville, Tenn., 1968; M.Div., Vanderbilt U., 1971, D.Min., 1975; m. Grace Elaine Mimms, July 27, 1957; 1 dau., Sabrina Gayle. Ordained to ministry, 1964; pastor Mt. Olivet Bapt. Ch., Hendersonville, Tenn., 1966-69, Westwood Bapt. Ch., Nashville, 1969—. Chmn. Tenn. Bapt. Pastors Conf., 1974—. Bd. dirs. Nashville chpt. NAACP, 1971-74; chmn. bd. Nashville Opportunities Industrialization Center, 1973-76; co-organizer Black Churchmen Econ. Devel., 1974; chmn. strategy Black Community Conf., 1971. Named Minister of Year, Sta. WVOL, 1971; recipient Religious Leadership award Middle Tenn. Bus. Assn., 1975; Pathfinder award Nashville Opportunities Industrialization Center, 1976; Man of Year award Nashville chpt. Nat. Negro Bus. and Profl. Women. Mem. NAACP, Stones River Dist. Bapt. Assn., Interdenominational Ministers Fellowship, Tenn. Bapt. Ednl. and Missionary Conv. Home: 939 Seymour Ave Nashville TN 37206 Office: 2510 Albion St Nashville TN 37208

JONES, BOB, JR. See *Who's Who in America*, 43rd edition.

JONES, BRIAN KEITH, minister, Lutheran Church America; b. Gary, Ind., Apr. 21, 1943; s. Cleo Herbert and Marion Esther (Braatz) J.; B.S. in Edn., N.E. Mo. State Coll., 1965; M.Div., Wartburg Theol. Sem., Dubuque, Iowa, 1970; postgrad. State U. Tenn.; m. Emily Scott Borst, May 2, 1980; children: Rita Faye, Thomas F., William N. Ordained to ministry, 1970; pastor Emmanuel Luth. Ch., LaOtto, Ind., 1970-72, Grace Luth. Ch., Elkhart, Ind., 1972-74, Our Savior Luth. Ch., Gatlinburg, Tenn., 1974—; mem. synod operational com. The Lutheran; mem. appalachian concerns com., dean Tenn. Valley Area, 1984—. Pres., Gatlinburg Ministerial Assn., 1974—; pres., host family Am. Field Service; supr. for summer chaplain in Gatlinburg and chaplains in Christian ministries to Nat. Parks. Active, Knoxville Area Internat. Council. Mem. Gatlinburg C. of C., COSERV. Home: Route 1 Box 338 Gatlinburg TN 37738 Office: PO Box 511 Gatlinburg TN 37738

JONES, CHRISTOPHER, JR., priest, Episcopal Church; dean; b. Del Rio, Tex., Sept. 30, 1921; s. Christopher and Abbe Bell (Landrum) J.; Asso. Sci., N. Tex. Agrl. Coll., 1942; B.A., U. Tex., Austin, 1947; M.Ed., Trinity U., 1965; M.Div., Protestant Episc. Theol. Sem., 1957; m. Elizabeth Lewis Root, Sept. 1, 1950; children: Elizabeth, Caroline. Ordained priest, 1958; asst. rector All Saints Episc. Ch., Corpus Christi, Tex., 1957-59; rector, headmaster Redeemer Episc. Ch. and Sch., Eagle Pass, Tex., 1959-62; headmaster St. Luke's Episc. Sch., 1962-84; asst. rector St. Luke's Episc. Ch., San Antonio, 1962—; dean admissions Tex. Mil. Inst., San Antonio, 1984—. Mem. exec. bd. Southwestern Assn. Episc. Schs., 1969—, treas., 1979-80, pres., 1980. Bd. dirs. Community Guidance Center Bexar County, 1973-76. Mem. Nat. Assn. Elementary Prins., Assn. Childhood Edn., Nat. Assn. Episc. Schs., Ind. Schs. Assn. S.W., Clergy Assn. Diocese W. Tex., Tex. Assn. Elementary Prins. Home: 215 College Blvd San Antonio TX 78209 Office: Tex Mil Inst 800 College Blvd San Antonio TX 78209

JONES, CLARENCE VICTOR, ch. ofcl., minister, Am. Baptist Chs.; b. Indpls., Nov. 19, 1911; s. Robert Victor and Nannie Belle (Shelton) J.; B.A., Franklin Coll., 1936; B.D., So. Bapt. Theol. Sem., 1944; grad. Nat. Center Housing Resident Mgmt., Washington, 1976; m. Daisy Cathryn Lynch, Oct. 8, 1936; 1 dau., Nancy (Mrs. Robert Boyce Doran). Ordained to ministry Am. Baptist Chs. U.S.A., 1939; pastor various chs., Ind., Iowa, 1937-47, 1st Bapt. Ch., Newton, Iowa, 1947-53; dir. Christian edn. and camping Ariz. Conv. Am. Bapt. Chs., 1953-70; asso. exec. sec. S.D. Bapt. Conv., 1970-72; asso. minister Christian edn. First Bapt. Ch. Phoenix, 1972-73; adminstr. Vista Tower Residences of Bapt. Service Corp. of First Bapt. Ch. Los Angeles, 1973—. Builder camp Tonto Rim Am. Bapt. Camp, Payson, Ariz.; mem. gov.'s com. dropouts, Ariz., 1968-70; pres. State Com. Juvenile and Adult Problems, Ariz., 1968. Bd. dirs. Cook Christian Tng. Sch., Tempe, Ariz., 1969-71. Recipient Distinguished Service placques, Lions, 1948, 66. Mem. Inst. Real Estate Mgmt. (accredited resident mgr.). Lion (chaplain, pres. Newton 1950). Contbr. articles to profl. jours. Address: 3000 Leeward Ave Apt A Los Angeles CA 90005

JONES, CLIFFORD ANTHONY, minister, Missionary Baptist Ch.; b. Phila., Sept. 1, 1943; s. Loston Riley and Cora (Harris) J.; B.S., U. Md., 1967; M.Div., Southeastern Theol. Sem., 1972, Th.M., 1976; m. Carolyn Brenda Reynolds, June 10, 1967; children—Michelle Antoinette, Clifford Anthony. Ordained to ministry, 1969; pastor First Bapt. Ch., Clinton, N.C., 1972—. Vice moderator Western Union Assn., 1974—; pres. bd. dirs. James A. Ezzell Sr. Outreach Day Care Center, Clinton, 1972—; chmn. commn. united ministries higher edn. Am. Bapt. Chs. of South, 1975—; Sampson County rep. Black Activist Com. for 3d Dist. N.C. Mem. Voters League, NAACP. Home: 820 College St Clinton NC 28328 Office: 900 College St Clinton NC 28328

JONES, CLIFFORD EARL, minister, Pentecostal Church; b. Whitley County, Ky., Sept. 22, 1918; s. Cleveland and Mildred Jane (Lynch) J.; student pub. schs., Cin.; m. Jean Clark, May 1, 1948; children—Deborah Jean, Denise Lynn, Clifford Mark, Rebecca Ruth, Rachel Yvonne. Ordained to ministry, 1969; pastor Apostolic Lighthouse, Pompano Beach, Fla., 1969—. Active rest home, hosp. and jail ministries; chaplain Juvenile Detention Center, Pompano Beach. Dir. rehab. program for delinquent youths, Pompano Beach; mem. community appearance com., Pompano Beach. Recipient certificate of appreciation Health Rehab. Services of Broward County, 1976; Minister of Yr. Fla. Ho. of Reps., 1984. Author: Doctrine of the Scriptures, 1975. Home: 2242 SE 10th St Pompano Beach FL 33064

JONES, CORNELIUS J., minister, denominational ofcl., Ch. of God in Christ; b. Dallas, Mar. 15, 1915; s. Cornelius and Adelia (Grieffeth) J.; B.A., Southwestern U., 1938, M.B.A., 1942; D.D., Trinity Hall Coll. and Sem., Springfield, Ill., 1973, D.B.A., 1974; postgrad. Blackstone Coll. Law, 1951; m. Annie May Richards, Feb. 12, 1940. Ordained to ministry, 1938; instr. Anderson County (Tex.) Vocat. Sch., Palestine, 1948-65; pastor Greater Love Chapel Ch. God in Christ, Ft. Worth, 1967—; dist. supt. Ch. God in Christ, Palestine, 1956—, state sec. fin., 1956—, exec. sec. fin. Tex. NE Jurisdiction, 1956, chmn. bd. elders, 1960, chmn. Tex. NE project com., 1965; pres. Dallas Ministerial Alliance, 1968—. Pres. Tex. Cultural Enrichment Found., Inc. Home: 3609 Alhambra Dr Fort Worth TX 76119 Office: 1149 E Rosedale St Fort Worth TX 76104

JONES, DONALD B., minister, United Methodist Church; b. Suffern, N.Y., Apr. 20, 1939; s. Donald E. and Lillian C. (Jones) J.; m. Kathleen Rigolosi, Nov. 17, 1962; children: Donald Ellsworth, Matthew Paul, Holly Michelle, Anthony Timothy. B.A., Tenn. Wesleyan U., 1961; M.Div., Drew U., Madison, N.J., 1965. Ordained to ministry United Meth. Ch., 1965. Pastor, Wesley Chapel Circuit, United Meth. Ch., Suffern, N.Y., 1962-65, Madison Park Simpson United Methodist Ch., Paterson, N.J., 1965-69; urban pastor Grace United Methodist Ch., Wyckoff, N.J., 1969-72; pastor Pearl River United Meth. Ch., N.Y., 1972-77; pastor Trinity United Meth. Ch., Rahway, N.J., 1977—; chaplain Tallman Fire Dept., N.Y., 1962—, Rahway Geriatric Ctr., N.J., 1983—; radio ministry Prayer Time Pastor, In His Presence, WFME-Christian Family Radio, West Orange, N.J., 1977—. Author: (guidebooks) Drug Abuse: Action Guide for Churches, Drug Abuse: Action Guide for Synagogues; contbr. articles to profl. jours. Police chaplain, Bergen County, Rahway, N.J., 1977—; trustee Union County ARC, N.J., 1977—; counselor Hospice program dept. psychiatry Rahway Hosp., 1977—; adv. com. Adult Basic Edn., Rahway, 1980—; cons Rahway Pub. Schs., 1980—. Recipient numerous awards for pub. service. Mem. Internat. Narcotic Enforcement Officers Assn., N.J. Council on Alcohol Problems (trustee exec. com.), Gerontol. Soc. N.J., N.J. Pub. Health Assn., Sigma Phi Epsilon. Home: 790 Bryant St Rahway NJ 07065 Office: Trinity United Methodist Ch 1428 Main St Rahway NJ 07065

JONES, DWAIN WAID, minister, Assemblies of God; b. Campbell, Tex., Oct. 2, 1958; s. Mylus Moody and Bess Leona (Waid) J.; m. Jeanne Beth Phipps, Apr. 25, 1959; children: Tamera D. Jones Czermak, Stephen W. Student East Tex. State U., 1957-61; B.Th., Internat. Bible Inst., Orlando, Fla., 1980, M.Th., 1981. Ordained to ministry Assemblies of God, 1967. Pastor, various chs., Tenn., Ark., Tex., Okla., First Assembly of God, Chickasha, Okla., 1985—; missionary, gen. supt. Tonga Islands, 1971-75; speaker for youth camps, convs., retreats, dist. councils, coll. ministries; bd. dirs. South Pacific Bible Sch., Fiji Islands, 1972-75; nat. bd. dirs. Light for the Lost, Springfield, MO., 1979-84, for men Ministries Assemblies of God, Springfield, 1983-85; now vice chmn. Inter-Cities Ministry of Bklyn.; Chaplain Okla. Ho. of Reps., June 1985. Contbr. to Advance, 1979; Spotlight; Evangel; founding editor Today's Man; Lodge: Rotary. Home: 105 Elmview Dr Chickasha OK 73018

JONES, FRANKLIN ALLAN, minister, Luth. Ch. Am.; b. Mason City, Iowa, July 25, 1932; s. Randall Franklin and Lydia (Moen) J.; B.A. cum laude, Augustana Coll., Sioux Falls, S.D., 1954; M.Div., Luth. Sch. Theology, Maywood, Ill., 1959; m. Carol Sue Silverman, Nov. 30, 1974; 1 dau., Rachel Sarah; children by previous marriage—Eric Hodges, Lydia Jo, Keith Fairbanks, Ingrid Sonia. Ordained to ministry, 1959; vicar ch., Phila., 1957-58; founding pastor St. Philip Luth. Ch., Trenton, Mich., 1959-64; pastor Advent Luth. Ch., Arlington, Va., 1964—. Founder, coordinator CREW (Christianity-Recreation-Edn.-Worship), Washington, 1967-71. Vol. exec. sec. Arlington Community Action Program, 1965-66. Fulbright scholar, Eberhard-Karls U., Tubingen, W.Ger., 1954-55. Home: 515 N George Mason Dr Arlington VA 22203 Office: 2222 S Arlington Ridge Rd Arlington VA 22202

JONES, FRED ELMER, minister, Rocky Mountain Yearly Meeting of Friends; b. Perry, Iowa, Feb. 20, 1951; s. Claire Eugene and Marjorie Beulah (Smith) J.; student Friends Bible Coll., 1969-71; B.A., Friends U., 1973; postgrad. Moody Aviation Sch., 1973-74, Nazarene Theol. Sem., 1975; student Navajo lang., Penrose, Colo., 1983—; m. Sharon Kay Binford, Dec. 27, 1971; children: Michelle Kay, Michael Allen, Melissa Sue. Ordained to ministry, 1976; minister of youth Grace United Meth. Ch., Wichita, Kans., 1972-73; pastor Willow Creek Friends Ch., Kansas City, Mo., 1974-78, Salem Friends Ch., Iowa, 1979-83, Beaver Park Friends Ch., Penrose, 1983—; missionary under appt. Rough Rock Friends Navajo Mission, Ariz., 1983—. Sec. social concerns commn. Evang. Friends Alliance, 1976-78, mem. missions bd., 1981-83; mem. Kans. Yearly Meeting Outreach Bd., 1975-78, mem. ministers fellowship com., 1975-78; mem. missions bd. Iowa Yearly Meeting, 1980-83, chmn., 1981-83. Recipient Order of the Tower, Friends U., 1973. Mem. Evangelization Forum. Home: 120 Illinois St Penrose CO 81240 Office: 140 Illinois St Penrose CO 81240

JONES, G. DANIEL, minister, American Baptist Churches in U.S.A.; b. Norfolk, Va.; s. George Raymond and Estelle Ruth (Campbell) J.; m. Geraldine Estelle Saunder, Nov. 27, 1965; 1 child, Bryant Daniel. B.S., Va. Union U., 1962; M.Div., Andover Newton Theol. Sch., 1966; D.Min., Howard U., 1978. Ordained to ministry Baptist Ch., 1964. Pastor St. Johns Bapt. Ch., Woburn, Mass., 1965-67, Messiah Bapt. Ch., Brockton, Mass., 1967-73, Zion Bapt. Ch., Portsmouth, Va., 1973-82, Grace Bapt. Ch. of Germantown, Phila., 1982—; adj. prof. Sch. of Religion, Va. Union U., Norfolk, 1979-81; bd. dirs. Am. Bapt. Chs. of the South, 1974-76, 81, 82, Am. Bd. Chs. of Mass., 1969-73; mem. exec. bd. Lott Carey Bapt. Fgn. Mission Conv., 1973—. Mem. sch. bd. Portsmouth City Schs., Va., 1974-80; bd. dirs. Effingham Street YMCA, Portsmouth, 1978-82, Germantown YMCA, Phila., 1984—; pres. bd. Family Service Personal Counseling, Brockton, Mass., 1969-73. Recipient Key to City, Brockton, 1983. Mem. Minister's Council Am. Bapt. Chs. U.S.A. (nat. v.p. 1974-82), Omega Psi Phi, Mu Omega. Democrat. Club: Links (Phila.). Lodge: Masons. Office: Grace Bapt Ch of Germantown 25 W Johnson St Philadelphia PA 19144

JONES, HUGH R., chancellor, Episcopal Church; lawyer, former judge; b. New Hartford, N.Y., Mar. 19, 1914; s. Hugh Richard and Anna Gwendolyn (Jones) J.; m. Jean McMillen, July 3, 1937; children: Hugh Richard, Anne E., Thomas McM., Jean C., David B. A.B., Hamilton Coll., 1935, LL.D. (hon.), 1974; J.D., Harvard U., 1939; LL.D. (hon.), Albany Law Sch., 1981. Bar: N.Y., U.S. dist. ct. (no. dist.) N.Y., U.S. Ct. Appeals (2d cir.), U.S. Treas. Dept., U.S. Tax Ct., U.S. Supreme Ct. Chancellor, Diocese Central N.Y., Episcopal Ch., 1957—; lay dep. Gen. Conv., 1952, 58, 61, 64, 67, 70, 73, 76, 79, 85, Spl. Gen., Conv. II, 1969; del. Anglican Congress, Toronto, 1963. Ptnr. firm Evans, Burdick, Severn & Jones and predecessor firms, Utica, N.Y., 1949-72; assoc. judge N.Y. State Ct. Appeals, Utica, 1973-84; chmn. N.Y. state select com. correctional instns. and programs, 1971-72; dir. Security Mut. Life Ins. Co. Am., 1970-72, Utica Radiator Corp., 1964-71. Trustee Hamilton Coll., 1967-84, emeritus, 1984—, SUNY 1969-72; co-chmn. N.Y. State Citizens Com. for Revenue Sharing, 1971-72; mem. N.Y. State Bd. Social Welfare, 1959-69, chmn., 1964-69; pres. Family Service Assn. Am., 1955-57, N.Y. State Assn. Councils and Chests, 1950-52, N.Y. State Welfare Conf., 1959; exec. com. Nat. Social Welfare Conf., 1958-61; bd. dirs. Am. Pub. Welfare Assn., 1967; former dir. and officer various health and welfare agys.; chmn. alumni fund Hamilton Coll., 1957-58, alumni council, 1962-63. Served to lt. comdr. USN, 1942-45. Decorated Bronze Star; recipient William R. Hopkins Bronze Medal, St. David's Soc. State of N.Y., 1974, Civic award, Colgate U., 1970, Humanitarian award for services to Spanisk speaking community N.Y. State, 1969. Fellow Am. Coll. Probate Counsel, Am. Bar Found.; mem. ABA (ho. of dels. 1971-72), N.Y. State Bar Assn. (pres. 1971-72, Root-Stimson award 1978, Gold medal 1985) exec. com. 1961-72, ho. of dels. 1972—, chmn. com. profl. ethics 1959-62, chmn. tax sect. 1967), Oneida County Bar Assn. (pres. 1962), Assn. Bar City of N.Y., Am. Law Inst. (adviser restatement, restitution 2d 1981—), Am. Judicature Soc. (bd. dirs. 1965-69). Republican. Clubs: Ft. Schuyler, Sadaquada Golf, Century Assn. Home: 111 Paris Rd New Hartford NY 13413

JONES, HYWEL JAMES See *Who's Who in America,* 43rd edition.

JONES, JACK MONTE, priest, Episcopal Church; b. San Angelo, Tex., July 15, 1936; s. Arvid Arthur and Christine (Montgomery) J.; m. Virginia Inabinet, Feb. 2, 1962; children: John Robinson, Julie Christine. B.A., Sul Ross State U., 1961, M.A., 1967; M.Div., U. South, 1977. Ordained priest, Episcopal Ch., 1978. Vicar, St. John's Snyder and All Saints Ch., Colorado City, Tex., 1977—; mem. com. of Christian Living and edn., Diocese of N.W. Tex., 1978-80, chmn., 1980. Trustee, Colorado City Ind. Sch. Dist. Bd. Edn., 1981-84, U. South, 1978-84; bd. dirs. Colorado City Playhouse, 1984; chaplain Colorado City Vol. Fire Dept., 1980-84. Named Outstanding Citizen Colorado City C. of C., 1983. Lodge: Lions (pres. 1982). Home: 123 Castle Hills Rd Sonora TX 76950 Office: St John's Episcopal Ch PO Box 1103 Sonora TX 76950

JONES, JOHN ALBERT, JR., minister, Ch. of God in Christ; b. Greenwood, Miss., Feb. 25, 1929; s. John Albert and Fannie (Mason) J.; student Cameral Coll., 1944; D.D., Trinity Coll., 1974; m. Mary Louise Hawthone, July 3, 1949. Ordained minister Ch. of God in Christ, 1949; founder, organizer, pastor Rehoboth Ch. of God in Christ, Chgo., 1955—. Dist. supt., 1956-72; organizer Rehoboth Day Care Center, 1973—. Home: 8543 S Dante Ave Chicago IL 60619 Office: 11032 S Indiana Ave Chicago IL 60628

JONES, KEITH EDWARD, minister, Presbyterian Church U.S.A.; b. Los Alamos, N.Mex., July 27, 1945; s. Martin Cunningham and Eleanor Emma (Swede) J.; m. Nancy Sue Vann, Sept. 8, 1966 (div. 1968); 1 child, Heather Anne; m. Brenna Marie McGee, Dec. 27, 1969; children: Dylan McGee, Eron William, Kaysey Noelle. B.A., Maryville Coll., 1967; M.Div., Louisville Presbyn. Theol. Sem., 1970; D.Min., McCormick Theol. Sem., 1986. Ordained to ministry Presbyn. Ch. U.S.A., 1970. Co-pastor Pioneer Parish, Superior, Wis., 1970-72; asst. pastor Glen Avon Presbyn. Ch., Duluth, Minn., 1972-74; pastor Lisbon United Presbyn. Ch., Sussex, Wis., 1974-79; parish assoc., Brookfield United Presbyn. Ch., Wis.; chaplain Tudor Oaks Retirement Community, Hales Corners, Wis., 1980-84; pastor Cleveland Ave. United Presbyn. Ch., West Allis, Wis., 1982—; counselor Gordon State Camp, Wis., 1970-72; bd. dirs. Lighthouse for Blind, Duluth, Minn., 1973-74, C.H.A.R.T.S., Duluth, 1973-74; initiator, coordinator, moderator Evergreen Parish area, Minn., 1973-74. Active F.I.S.H., Inc., Duluth, 1973-74. Mem. West Allis Clergy Assn. Democrat. Clubs: Civic, Model A Restorers, Early Day Gas Engine. Lodge: Lions. Home: 8706 W Cleveland Ave West Allis WI 53227 Office: Cleveland Ave United Presbyn Ch 8716 W Cleveland Ave West Allis WI 53227

JONES, KELSEY A., minister, educator, Christian Methodist Episcopal Church; b. Holly Springs, Miss., July 15, 1933; s. Duria and Erma (Turner) J.; B.A. summa cum laude in English, Miss. Indsl. Coll., 1955, D.D., 1969; M.Div., Garrett Theol. Sem., Northwestern U., 1959; certificate in clin. pastoral care Wesley Med. Center, 1967; m. Virginia Bethel Ford, May 30, 1954; children: Kelsey A., Cheryl Darlene Jones Campbell, Eric Andre, Claude Anthony. Ordained to ministry, 1956. Pastor Walls Meml. Ch., Chgo., 1956, Lane Meml. Ch., Jackson, Mich., 1959-62, Cleaves Temple, Omaha, 1962-65, St. Matthew Ch., Wichita, Kans., 1965-70; acad. preceptor for community change Inter/Met. Sem., Washington, 1973—; vis. chaplain to Cook County Jail, Chgo., 1956-58. Assoc. prof. behavioral sci. U. D.C., 1972-84, prof., chmn. dept. criminal justice, spl. asst. to pres., 1984—. Sec., Kans.-Mo. ann. conf. Christian M.E. Ch., 1962-70, del. to gen. conf., 1966, 70; pres. Ministerial Alliance, Christian M.E. Ch., 1966—; bd. dirs. Wichita (Kans.) Council Chs., 1968, Greater Washington Area Council Chs., 1969. Pres. Citizen's Co-ordinating Com. for Civil Liberties, Omaha, 1963; mem. Kans. State Bd. Probation and Parole, 1966-70, vice chmn., 1966-67, chmn., 1967-70; bd. dirs. Phyllis Wheatley Children's Home, Brother, Inc. Mem. Alpha Phi Alpha. Contbr. articles to newspapers and scholarly jours. Home: 5427 Kansas Ave NW Washington DC 20011 Office: U DC 4200 Connecticut Ave NW Div Interdisciplinary Studies Washington DC 20011

JONES, L. BEVEL, bishop, United Methodist Church, Western N.C. Conf. Office: PO Box 18005 Charlotte NC 28218*

JONES, LAWRENCE NEALE See *Who's Who in America,* 43rd edition.

JONES, O. WYNDELL, minister, Southern Baptist Convention; b. Philadelphia, Miss., June 29, 1933; s. John O. and Erna L. (Coker) J.; m. Audie M. Jenkins, Sept. 16, 1951; children: Kathy Lynn, Karen Elisabeth. B.A., Miss. Coll., 1958; M.Div., New Orleans Bapt. Theol. Sem., 1961; D.D. (hon.), Samford U., 1979. Ordained to ministry Bapt. Ch., 1955. Pastor, Trinity Bapt. Ch., Oakdale, La., 1961-64, First Bapt. Ch., Trenton, Tenn., 1964-72, Highland Bapt. Ch., Florence, Ala., 1972-77; denominational adminstr. Ala. Bapt. Conv., 1977—; dir. So. Bapt. Home Missions Bd., 1976-85. Author articles. Home: 107 Coosada Dr Montgomery AL 36117 Office: PO Box 11870 Montgomery AL 36198

JONES, OSCAR CALVIN, minister, American Baptist Churches in the U.S.A.; b. San Antonio, Tex., Sept. 1, 1932; s. Oscar C. and Nonnie Lee (Cunningham) Simpson; m. Peggy Ann Helm, June 12, 1967; children: Dennis Ray, Shawntelle Janora. B.A., Tex. So. U., 1954; Th.M., Am. Evang. Div. Sch., 1972, Th.B., 1968; Ph.D., Trinity Theol. Sem., 1981, D.Min., 1982. Ordained to ministry Am. Bapt. Chs. U.S.A., 1952. Pastor, Greater Mt. Olive Bapt. Ch., Los Angeles, 1958-62; dir. Christian edn. Treevine Bapt. Ch., Hawthorne, Calif., 1962-65; pastor St. John Bapt. Ch., Long Beach, Calif., 1965-69; exec. dir. Mut. Assistance Team Endeavors, Inc., Los Angeles, 1969-71; rep. Ministers and Missionaries Bd. Am. Bapt. Chs., N.Y.C., 1971-83; pastor Shiloh Bapt. Ch., Sacramento, 1983—; bd. dirs. Black Caucus Am. Bapt. Chs. U.S.A., Valley Forge, Pa., 1968—, Western Commn. Ministry, 1972—;

mem. adv. com. Interfaith Service Bur., Sacramento, 1984—; mem. at large gen. bd. Am. Bapt. Chs. U.S.A.; trustee Am. Bapt. Sem. West, Oakland, Calif., 1984—, Am. Bapt. Homes of the West. Author: Emancipating the Emancipated, 1970. Bd. dirs. Sacramento Urban League, 1984; mem. Nat. Caucus Ctr. Black Aged, Inc., 1983; mem. adv. com. Vol. Caregivers Interfaith Service Bur., Sacramento, 1984. Mem. Assn. Clin. Pastoral Edn. (adv. com. 1981-84), Greater Faith Bapt. Ch. Assn. (counselor 1983-83). Democrat. Home: 6760 Riverside Blvd Sacramento CA 95831 Office: Shiloh Bapt Ch 3565 9th Ave Sacramento CA 95817

JONES, OTIS C(ECIL), minister, National Baptist Convention U.S.A.; b. North Little Rock, Ark., Jan. 19, 1927; s. Otis and Aldonia (Ridgel) J.; B.S., Ark. Bapt. Coll., 1972; D.D., Morris-Booker Meml. Coll., Dermott, Ark., 1972; m. Tabitha McCoy, Aug. 21, 1949. Ordained to ministry, 1957; pastor Mt. Pleasant Bapt. Ch., North Little Rock, 1957—. Past pres. Greater Little Rock Bapt. Pastors' Conf.; pres. Middle Western Dist. Sunday Sch. and Bapt. Tng. Union Congress, 1958-80; pres. Regular Am. Bapt. Conv., 1984; assoc. dir. gen. Nat. Bapt. Congress, 1984. Bd. dirs. Urban League of Little Rock. Mem. NAACP, YMCA. Home: 820 Vine St North Little Rock AR 72114 Office: 2200 Willow St North Little Rock AR 72114

JONES, PAUL GRAY, minister, Internat. Ch. of Foursquare Gospel; b. Pomona, Calif., June 23, 1937; s. Benjamin Gray and Martha Ellen (Hastings) J.; diploma Life Bible Coll., 1961; m. Dorothy May Beber, Feb. 17, 1962; children—Mark Gregory, Cathleen Renee. Ordained to ministry, 1956; co-pastor San Gabrial Valley Revival Center, Covina, Calif., 1956-57; gospel evangelist, Mo., 1961; asst. pastor Cape Girardeau, Mo.., 1961; pastor, Grant, Nebr., 1962-63; dist. youth dir. Midwest Dist., 1963-66; nat. youth dir. Internat. Ch. of Foursquare Gospel, Los Angeles, 1966-71; pastor First Foursquare Gospel Ch., Omaha, 1971—. Charter mem. Nebr. Meth. Hosp. Dept. Pastoral Services, Omaha, 1972; supt. Eastern Nebr. Foursquare Chs., 1973; charter mem. Childrens Meml. Hosp., Dept. Pastoral Services, Omaha, 1973-75; pastoral adviser Womens Aglow Fellowship, 1975. Mem. Met. Assn. Evangelicals (pres. 1976—). Home: 10930 Hascall St Omaha NE 68144 Office: 4423 Bancroft St Omaha NE 68105

JONES, RAYMOND JACKSON, minister, Southern Baptist Convention; b. Birmingham, Ala., Nov. 10, 1959; s. Raymond J. and Dessie (Wineman) J.; m. Alison Lea Payne, Dec. 27, 1981. B.A., Dallas Bapt. U., 1982. Ordained to ministry Southern Baptist Convention, 1981. Mem. vol. staff Campus Crusade Christ, Birmingham, 1977-78; minister to youth Glenview Bapt. Ch., Fort Worth, 1980-82; minister to students First Bapt. Ch., Dothan, Ala., 1981-85, Calvary Bapt. Ch., Clearwater, Fla., 1985—; dir. Bapt. Student Union, Wallace Community Coll., Dothan, 1982-83; sec./treas. Fellowship Ala. Youth Ministers, Montgomery, 1984-85; speaker in field. Author numerous Insight Bible Study Lessons, 1981—; author workbooks: Insight Discipleship Notebook, 1982; author (manual); S.M.A.R.T., 1983. Named to Outstanding Young Men Am., U.S. Jaycees, 1982. Lodge: Kiwanis. Office: Calvary Bapt Ch 331 Cleveland St Clearwater FL 33515

JONES, RUFUS, minister, Conservative Baptist; b. Stewart, Tenn., Jan. 20, 1915; s. Marvin and Rosa (Dunning) J.; m. Ruth Justine Renswick, Mar. 10, 1937; children: Judith, Carol, David, Ralph. Student Am. Inst. Banking Wayne State U., 1934-35; D.Div., Linda Vista Bapt. Coll. and Sem., Pasadena, Calif., 1953, Conservative Bapt. Sem., Denver, 1977. Ordained to ministry Conservative Baptist Ch., 1942. Pastor, Westwood Bapt. Ch., Inkster, Mich., 1940-43, Livernois Ave. Bapt. Ch., Detroit, 1943-50; asst. treas. Conservative Bapt. Fgn. Mission Soc., Chgo., 1950-52; gen. dir. Conservative Bapt. Home Mission, Wheaton, Ill., 1953-80; bd. dirs. Nat. Assn. Evangelicals, Wheaton, 1950—, pres., 1966-68, dir. social action com., 1980. Author: If I Were in My Thirties, 1978. Recognized for service So. Poverty Law Ctr., Atlanta, 1984. Mem. Nat. Black Evang. Assn. (bd. dirs.). Home: 2091 Creekside Dr Wheaton IL 60187 Office: Social Action Commn Nat Assn Evang PO Box 28 Wheaton IL 60189

JONES, SHUFORD MARKS, JR., minister, So. Bapt. Conv.; b. Atlanta, Jan. 27, 1939; s. Shuford Marks and Katherine Elizabeth (Nix) J.; B.A., Mercer U., 1976; student So. Bapt. Theol. Sem., 1973-74, Southwestern Bapt. Theol. Sem., 1976; m. Ann Margurite Head, Aug. 30, 1959; children—Shuford Marks, Elizabeth Ann, Michael Ernest, Teresa Ruth. Ordained to ministry, 1958; pastor Mount Yonah Bapt. Ch., Cleve., 1957-58, New Hope Bapt. Ch., Madison, Ga., 1958-60, Clear Springs Bapt. Ch., Alpharetta, Ga., 1958-60, Immanuel Bapt. Ch., Macon, Ga., 1960-62, Ruth Bapt. Ch., Cochran, Ga., 1962-64, Wolf Fork Bapt. Ch., Rabun Gap, Ga., 1964-65, Franklin (Ga.) Bapt. Ch., 1965-68, Sargent (Ga.) Bapt. Ch., 1969—. Mem. exec. com. Ga. Bapt. Conv., 1973—, mem. state missions com., 1973—, mem. budget com., 1975; chmn. exec. com. Western Bapt. Assn., 1972, moderator, 1973-75. Mem. Coweta County Fire Commn., 1973-75; fire chief County of Coweta, Ga., 1973-75, asst. fire chief, 1975—; pres. Arnco-Sargent PTA, 1972-74. Recipient award for Community Service, Newnan Civitan Club, 1975. Columnist Newnan Times-Herald, 1973—. Home: Route 5 Box 434 Wagers Mill Rd Newnan GA 30263 Office: PO Box 177 Sargent GA 30275

JONES, STEPHEN RICHARD MAURICE, minister, Baptist Convention of Ontario and Quebec; b. St. Thomas, Ont., Can., Aug. 20, 1950; s. Maurice Baldwin and June Mae (Williams) J.; m. Kim Colleen Stemmler, Oct. 2, 1976; children: Mark Douglas, Erin Leigh, Robyn Lynn. B.R.E., Ont. Bible Coll., 1973; B.A., U. Windsor, Ont., 1975. Ordained to ministry Bapt. Conv. of Ont. and Que., 1976. Pastor Brooker Bapt. Ch., Cottam, Ont., 1973-77, Mimico Bapt. Ch., Toronto, 1977-83, Lakefield Bapt. Ch., Ont., 1983—; mem. Assembly program com. Bapt. Conv. of Ont. and Quebec, 1983—. Mem. Bapt. Minister's Fellowship (Ont.-Quebec chpt., v.p. 1984-85, pres. 1985-86). Home: 111 Albert St Lakefield ON K0L 2H0 Canada Office: Lakefield Bapt Ch Regent St Lakefield ON K0L 2H0 Canada

JONES, SUZANNE, lay church worker, Evangelical Free Ch.; b. Kansas City, Mo., Sept. 28, 1947; d. John Seth and Lucretta M. (Thompson) Chaney; m. Tommy Kent Jones, Feb. 24, 1968; children: Jennifer Anne, Rodney Craig, Kimberly Walker. Student Emporia State Tchrs. Coll., 1966-68. Dir. children's ch. program Westbrooke Bapt. Ch., Overland Park, Kans., 1972-73; tchr. Evang. Free Ch., Columbia, Mo., 1973-81, dir. Vacation Bible Sch., 1982, chmn. edn. com., 1983-85, leader Potter's Clay program, 1983-85, sec., 1979-85. Club: Christian Women's (nursery chmn. 1977, bd. dirs. 1977-80). Avocation: calligraphy. Home: 21855 SE Lagene Boring OR 97009

JONES, THOMAS DALE, minister, So. Bapt. Conv.; b. Underwood, Md., July 28, 1940; s. Carl Henry and Dorothy Claribel (Cathell) J.; B.A., Carson Newman Coll., 1963; M.Div., So. Bapt. Theol. Sem., 1967; m. Rita Brooks, June 8, 1963; children—Keith Alan, Christina Deanne, Adonna Janine. Ordained to ministry, 1965; asst. pastor Riverside Bapt. Ch., Balt., 1962; pastor Center Square Bapt. Ch., Vevay, Ind., 1965-67, Westview Bapt. Ch., Martinsburg, W.Va., 1967-76, Ft. Lewish Bapt. Ch., Salem, Va., 1976—. Moderator Shenandoah Bapt. Assn. Va., 1972-74; mem. Bapt. extension bd. Va. Bapt. Gen. Assn., 1974-76; chmn. worship and evangelism com. Martinsburg Berkeley County Ministerial Assn., 1974-76; counselor Religious Edn. class for Handicapped; chaplain Eastern Panhandle Tng. Center for Mentally and Physically Handicapped. Mem. recreation com. Assn. Handicapped Citizens. Home and Office: Rt 1 Box 371 Salem VA 24153

JONES, TOMMIE LEE, minister, Southern Baptist Convention; b. Spray, N.C., Sept. 17, 1917; s. Ulrich Bradley and Teresa (Shockley) J.; m. Louise Rice, Feb. 14, 1952. Student Campbell U., 1941; B.A., Wake Forest U., 1943; B.Div., So. Bapt. Sem., 1946, M.Div., 1973; master cert. counseling, social studies U. Ga., 1974. Ordained to ministry Southern Baptist Convention, 1947. Camp Pinnacle mgr. Ga. Bapt. Women's Mission Union, Clayton, 1946-51; pastor Battle Branch Ch., Tiger Ch., Pleasant Hill Ch., all Clayton, 1947-51, Preston Bapt. Ch., Ga., 1951-53; Plains Bapt. Ch., Ga., 1951-55, Winterville Bapt. Ch., Ga., 1955-64, Radium Springs Bapt. Ch., Albany, Ga., 1964-69, Center Hill Bapt. Ch., Loganville, Ga., 1969-70, Corinth Bapt. Ch., Athens, Ga., 1970-83; mem. Ga. Bapt. exec. com., Ga. Bapt. Conv., 1983—. Home: 853 Ivywood Dr Athens GA 30606

JONES, WARREN, JR., minister, National Baptist Convention U.S.A.; b. New Orlens, Sept. 22, 1947; s. Warren and Dorothy (Daggs) J.; m. Yvonne Marie Bibbins; children: Warren III, Lisa, Jemel. B.A., So. U., New Orleans, 1972; M.Div., New Orleans Bapt. Theol. Sem., 1975; D.Div. (hon.), United Theol. Sem., Monroe, La., 1980. Ordained to ministry Nat. Bapt. Conv. U.S.A., 1967. Tchr., Union Bapt. Theol. Sem., New Orleans, 1973-76; chaplain Charity Hosp. New Orleans, 1974-79; pastor New Salem Bapt. Ch., New Orleans, 1977-80, 1st Israel Bapt. Ch., Belle Rose, La., 1981—. Fellow Coll. Chaplains; mem. Seven Seals Dist. Assn. (pres. 1977—), 9th Ward Minister Conf. (bible lectr. 1980-84). Home: 7624 Primrose Dr New Orleans LA 70126

JONES, WILLIAM AUGUSTUS, JR., bishop, Episcopal Ch.; b. Memphis, Jan. 24, 1927; s. William Augustus and Martha (Wharton) J.; B.A., Memphis Coll., 1948; B.D., Yale U., 1951; m. Margaret Loearing-Clark, Aug. 26, 1949; 4 children. Ordained priest, 1952; minister-in-charge Ch. of the Messiah, Pulaski, Tenn., 1952-57; curate Christ Ch., Nashville, 1957-58; rector St. Mark's Ch., LaGrange, Ga., 1958-65; asso. rector St. Luke's Ch., Mountainbrook, Ala., 1965-66; dir. research So. Regional Assn. for Christian Tng. and Service, 1966-67; exec. dir. Assn. for Christian Tng. and Service, 1968; now bishop Diocese of Mo., St. Louis. Office: 1210 Locust St Saint Louis MO 63103*

JORDAN, EDWARD LYNN, minister, Southern Baptist Convention; b. Winnemucca, Nev., Feb. 22, 1953; s. Carl Donald and Armelda (Puryear) J.; m. Eniko Judith Margit Danilowicz, July 7, 1979. B.A., U. Nev., 1975; M.Div., Golden Gate Theol. Sem., 1979. Ordained to ministry So. Bapt. Conv., 1978. Assoc. pastor Sunrise So. Bapt. Ch., Las Vegas, Nev., 1975-80; pastor First Bapt. Ch., Gardnerville, Nev., 1980—. Mem. Spooner Bapt. Assn., U. Nev. Alumni Assn., Golden Gate Bapt. Theol. Sem. Alumni Assn. Democrat. Club: Sertoma. Home: PO Box 576 Gardnerville NV 89410

JORDAN, IRA SAMUEL, minister, United Meth. Ch.; b. Darlington, S.C., Oct. 28, 1918; s. Jimmy J. and Addie (Dixon) J.; B.A., Claflin U., 1945; m. Ruth Ellen Cox, Dec. 21, 1960. Ordained to ministry, 1945; pastor Rock Mill charge, 1947-48, Belton charge, 1949-53, Minus Chapel charge, 1953-59, St. James charge, 1960-62, North Greenville, S.C., 1963-66, Cowpens-Spartanburg, S.C., 1967-69, Rock Hill, S.C., 1968-73, Pickens and Landrum, S.C., 1973-74, Chesnee (S.C.) Circuit, 1974—. Mem. Ecumenical Commn., 1974—. Mem. Mental Health Assn., NAACP. Home: 509 Jacob Rd Greenville SC 29605

JORDAN, PHILIP DEAN, religious educator, lay church worker; b. Copaigue, L.I., Nov. 23, 1940; s. Arthur Mason and Emily (Denton) J.; m. Kay Irene Kirkpatrick, June 22, 1968; children: Anne Katherine, Mead Mason. B.A., Alfred U., 1963; M.A., U. Rochester, 1965; Ph.D., U. Iowa, 1971. Elder, Mt. Calvary Luth. Ch., Gunnison, Colo., 1977-79, v.p., 1979-80, pres., 1980-81; mem. Episcopal Diocesan Ecumenical Council, Colo., 1985—. Assoc. prof. history Hastings Coll., Nebr., 1985—; vis. assoc. prof. dept. history and Sch. Religion, U. Iowa, summer 1979. Author: Evangelical Alliance for the U.S.A., 1983; contbg. author: The Social Gospel: Religion and Reform in Changing America, 1976. Contbr. articles to profl. jours. Trustee Campus Ministry, Western State Coll., Gunnison, 1971-73; county coordinator George McGovern campaign, Gunnison, 1972; del. State Dem. Conv., Colo., 1972, 74. N.Y. State Regents scholar, 1959-63; N.Y. State Coll. Teaching fellow, 1963-65; U. Rochester tuition scholar, 1963-65; U. Iowa teaching assistantship, 1966; All Univ. Teaching Research fellow, 1968-69; NEH fellow, summer 1980; Western State Coll. Found. grantee, 1984. Mem. Am. Acad. Religion (Rocky Mt.-Great Plains regional conf. 1979-85), Colo. Assn. Univ. Press (trustee), Orgn. Am. Historians, Am. Hist. Soc., Am. Soc. Ch. History, Am. Acad. Religion, Phi Alpha Theta. Democrat. Office: Dept History Hastings Coll Hastings NE 68901

JORGENSON, WAYNE JAMES, priest, Orthodox Church in America; b. Evanston, Ill., Sept. 1, 1943; s. Wayne W. and Kathleen J. (Conroyd) J.; m. Patricia Ellen Guzy, June 7, 1969; children: Daria, Michael. B.A., St. Meinrad Coll., 1966; M.Div., St. Vladimir Sem., 1969; Ph.D., Boston U., 1979. Ordained priest Orthodox Ch. in Am., 1969. Pastor, Holy Assumption Ch., Lublin, Wis., 1969-71, Nativity of Virgin Mary Ch., Chelsea, Mass., 1974-79, St. Seraphim Ch., Dallas, 1979-81, All Saints Ch., Detroit, 1981—; asst. pastor St. Mary's Ch., Mpls., 1971-74; prof. ch. history St. John Provincial Sem., Plymouth, Mich., 1983—. Mem. Orthodox Theology Soc. Am. Home: 35655 Dover Livonia MI 48150 Office: All Saints Ch 2918 E Hendrie Detroit MI 48211

JOSLIN, DAVID ARTHUR, minister, National Association Free Will Baptists; b. Van Buren, Ark., Mar. 10, 1937; s. Joel Arthur and Clara Edna Flossie (Jones) J.; B.A., Free Will Bapt. Bible Coll., 1960; m. Mary Kay Kelley, Aug. 20, 1958; children—David Arthur, Kelley Kristen. Ordained to ministry, 1957; pastor, Pleasant View, Tenn., 1960-61, Batesville, Ark., 1962-63, Mt. Carmal, Sharon and Liberty Hill Free Will Bapt. Ch., White County, Ark., 1965-67, 1st Free Will Bapt. Ch., Searcy, Ark., 1967-69, 71-73, Pochahontas, Ark., 1970; promotional dir. Ark. Assn. Free Will Bapts., Conway, 1973—, editor state paper Vision, 1973—; rep. gen. bd. Nat. Assn. Free Will Bapts., 1974—, mem. exec. com., 1979-81, 83—. Home: 122 Oaklawn Dr Conway AR 72032 Office: PO Box 1404 Conway AR 72032

JOVANOVIC, ROBERT PAUL, priest, Roman Catholic Church; b. St. Louis, July 18, 1935; s. Paul Gregory and Agatha Valentine (Durbin) J.; B.A., Kenrick Sem., 1957; M.Ed. in Adminstrn., St. Louis U., 1971. Ordained priest, 1961. Assoc. pastor various parishes Archdiocese of St. Louis, 1961-83; tchr. St. Pius X High Sch., Festus, Mo., 1961-67; tchr., asst. adminstr. Bishop DuBourg High Sch., St. Louis, 1967-75; adminstr. Duchesne High Sch., St. Charles, Mo., 1975-83; pastor Sacred Heart Ch., Crystal City, Mo., 1983—. Mem. support group Dealing with Feelings Club, Barnes Hosp., St. Louis, 1982. Mem. Nat. Cath. Edn. Assn. Lodge: Optimists. Address: 555 Bailey Rd Crystal City MO 63019

JUDA, ALLEN ISRAEL, rabbi, Conservative Jewish; b. Fall River, Mass., Aug. 12, 1948; s. Erwin Julius and Rose (Feder) J.; m. Toby Keller, Aug. 24, 1975; children: Adam Isaac, Aaron Jacob, Tamar Sara. B.A., Columbia U., 1971; B.H.L., Jewish Theol. Sem., N.Y.C., 1971, M.A., 1972. Ordained rabbi Conservative Jewish,

1975. Rabbi, Brith Sholom, Bethlehem, Pa., 1975—; chaplain Allentown State Hosp., Pa., 1982—, mem. Jewish student adv. council Lehigh U., 1981—, Jewish nursing home com. Beth Tikvah Leader II, 1979—; mentor United Jewish Appeal, 1979. Bd. dirs. Lehigh Valley Hospice, Allentown, 1979-81; bd. dirs., chmn. dept. pastoral care St. Lukes Hosp., Bethlehem, 1976-83; co-chmn. Operation Ricebowl, Lehigh Valley, 1978-79. Mem. Rabbinical Assembly (nat. conv. com. 1982, exec. council 1980-81, pres. 1979-81), Greater Phila. Bd. Rabbis. Home: 1320 Stonewood Dr Bethlehem PA 18017 Office: Brith Sholom PO Box 5323 Bethlehem PA 18015

JUDD, RAYMOND EARL, university chaplain, Presbyterian Church; b. Sherman, Tex., Aug. 27, 1934; s. Raymond Earl and Glenna Charlyn (Robinson) J.; B.A. magna cum laude, Trinity U., 1956; M.Div., Princeton Sem., 1959; m. Mary Jane Grafton, Sept. 12, 1959; 1 child, Jan Charlyn. Ordained to ministry Presbyn. Ch., 1959; minister First Presbyn. Ch., Clarksville, Tex., 1959-64, Hemphill Presbyn. Ch., Ft. Worth, 1965-67; univ. chaplain Trinity U., San Antonio, 1967—, instr. Latin, 1970—. Founder, chmn. Red River County Pub. Library, Clarksville, 1960-64. Bd. dirs. San Antonio Council Chs. Mem. Nat. Assn. Coll. and U. Chaplains. Home: 139 Oakmont Ct San Antonio TX 78212

JUERGENSMEYER, JOHN ELI, lay church worker, United Methodist Church; b. Stewardson, Ill., May 14, 1934; s. Irvin Karl and Clara Augusta (Johannaber) J.; B.A., U. Ill., 1955, J.D., 1963; M.A. (Merrill Found., Univ. fellow), Princeton U., 1957, Ph.D., 1960; m. Elizabeth Ann Bogart, Sept. 10, 1963; children—Margaret Ann, Frances Elizabeth. Lay leader Grace United Meth. Ch., Elgin, Ill., 1967-68; mem. bd. edn. No. Ill. Conf., United Meth. Ch., Elgin, 1966-74; chmn. adminstrv. bd. Wesley United Meth. Ch., Elgin, Ill., 1981-84; Mem. firm Juergensmeyer & Assocs., Elgin, Ill., 1964—; prof. constl. law and polit. sci. Judson Bapt. Coll., Elgin, Ill., 1963—. Sec. Republican Central com., Elgin Precinct, 1973—, chmn. Kane County, 1978-80; mem. adv. bd. Salvation Army, 1965—; trustee Elgin Family Service Assn., 1965-76; mem. bd. dirs. Judson Bapt., Coll., 1964—, Elgin Jr. C. of C., 1965-70, Wesley Found., 1971-75; chmn. No. Kane County Right-to-Life Adv. Bd., 1982—; mem. Nat. Commn. on Libraries and Scis., 1982—. Recipient Outstanding Young Man award Elgin Jr. C. of C., 1967; Echo award Defenders of the Fox River, Inc., 1971; certificate of merit Heart Fund, 1971. Mem. ABA (mem. spl. taxing dist. com.), Fed. Bar Assn., Ill. Bar Assn. (past chmn. mcpl. law com.), Elgin, Kane County (past chmn. legis. com.), Chgo. (past chmn. local govt. com.), Seventh Circuit (mem. membership com.) bar assns., Am. Polit. Sci. Assn., Elgin Bd. Realtors, Union League of Chgo., Phi Beta Kappa, Phi Alpha Delta, Alpha Kappa Lambda. Home: 401 Hazel Dr Elgin IL 60120 Office: 707A Davis Rd Elgin IL 60120

JUERGENSMEYER, MARK KARL, minister, United Methodist Church, religion educator; b. Carlinville, Ill., Nov. 13, 1940; s. Irvin Karl and Clara J.; m. Sucheng Chan, Sept. 21, 1969. B.A., U. Ill., 1962; M.Div., Union Theol. Sem., 1965; M.A., U. Calif.-Berkeley, 1968, Ph.D., 1974. Ordained to ministry United Meth. Ch., 1965. Project dir. Ctr. for South/Southeast Asia Studies, U. Calif.-Berkeley, 1970-74, assoc. dir. Ctr. for Ethics and Social Policy, Grad. Theol. Union, 1974-80, coordinator religious studies program, vis. prof. religious studies program, 1976—, prof. ethics and phenomenology of religions, 1974—, prof., 1985—, dir. programs in comparative religion, 1984—; chmn. selection com. Fulbright Grants in Religion, Washington, 1982—; advisor on religion and ethics Sta. KQED-TV, PBS, San Francisco, various corp. media, govtl. orgns. Co-author: Ethics in the Policy Process, 1976. Author and editor: Sikh Studies, 1979. Author: Religion as Social Vision, 1982; Fighting with Gandhi, 1984. Contbr. sects. to encys., books, articles to profl. jours. Internat. fellow Columbia U. Sch. Internat. Affairs, 1963-65, research fellow Am. Inst. Indian Studies, 1978, 79, 85-86, Fulbright Indo-Am. fellow, 1982, Wilson Ctr. fellow Smithsonian Inst., 1986. Mem. Am. Acad. Religion (pres. Western region 1984-85), chmn. nominating com. 1982—), Assn. for Asian Studies (exec. com., research com. on Punjab), Soc. Christian Ethics. Democrat. Office: Grad Theol Union U Calif 2465 Le Conte Ave Berkeley CA 94709

JUNG, JAY JOSEPH, priest, campus minister, Roman Catholic Church; b. Evanston, Ill., May 31, 1950; s. John Peter and Dorothy Rose (May) J. B.A., St. Mary's Sem., 1973; M.A., Southeast Mo. State U., 1976; M.Div., DeAndreis Inst. Theology, 1977. Dir. vocations Vincentian Fathers and Brothers, Chgo., 1977-83; dir. campus ministry DePaul U., Chgo., 1983—. Mem. Catholic Campus Ministry Assn., Assn. Vincentians (chmn. 1984—). Home: 2233 N Kenmore Chicago IL 60614 Office: DePaul U 25 E Jackson Chicago IL 60604

JUNG, L. SHANNON, minister, Presbyterian Church in U.S., religion educator; b. Baton Rouge, July 23, 1943; s. Jean Baptiste and Frances Ellen (Shannon) J.; m. Patricia Jeanne Beattie, June 1, 1974; children: Michael, Robbie. B.A., Washington and Lee U., 1965; B.D., Union Theol. Sem., Richmond, Va., 1968; S.T.M., Yale U., 1969; Ph.D., Vanderbilt U., 1973. Ordained to ministry Presbyn. Ch. in U.S., 1973. Interim pastor Thomas Meml. Presbyn. Ch., Bluff City, Tenn., 1977-79, Dilworth Presbyn. Ch., Minn., 1982—; assoc. prof. Concordia Coll., Moorhead, Minn., 1979—; coordinator Agrl. Symposium, Moorhead, 1984-85. Author: Identity and Community, 1980; also articles. Chmn. bd. dirs. Offender Aid and Restoration, Bristol, Va., 1974-79, Ret. Sr. Vol. Program, Bristol, 1977-79; coach soccer team, Moorhead, 1983-85. Recipient Outstanding Faculty award Va. Intermont Coll., Bristol, 1977; fellow NEH, Northwest Area Found.; Bush scholar, 1984-85. Mem. Am. Acad. Religion (pres. Upper Midwest 1985-86), Soc. Christian Ethics, Am. Sociol. Assn. Democrat. Home: 224 7th Ave S Moorhead MN 56560 Office: Dept Religion Concordia Coll Moorhead MN 56560

JUNGKUNTZ, RICHARD PAUL, minister, educator, Association of Evangelical Lutheran Churches; b. Cleve., Oct. 1, 1918; s. Otto William and Clara Magdalen (Lange) J.; B.A., Northwestern Coll., 1939; postgrad. Concordia Sem., 1939-40, Wis. Lutheran Sem., 1940-42, Ind. U., 1951; M.A., U. Wis., 1955, Ph.D., 1961; m. Grace Elisabeth Kowalke, Aug. 16, 1943; children: Gay (Mrs. Jeffrey Osborn), Paula (Mrs. Thomas Warren III), Richard, Lisa (Mrs. Richard Campbell), Andrea, William, Laura. Ordained to ministry Luth. Ch., 1942; pastor chs., Janesville, Wis., 1942-46, Ft. Atkinson, Wis., 1946-49; prof. classical lit. Northwestern Coll., Watertown, Wis., 1949-61; prof. exegetical theology Concordia Theol. Sem., Springfield, Ill., 1961-65; exec. sec. Commn. Theology and Ch. Relations, Luth. Ch.-Mo. Synod, St. Louis, 1965-69; vis. prof. Eden Theol. Sem., St. Louis, 1970; provost Pacific Luth. U., Tacoma, Wash., 1970—, acting pres., 1974-75; chmn. bd. dirs. Christ Seminary-Seminex, 1974-80; mem. Commn. on Faith and Order, World Council Chs., 1968-76. Mem. Soc. Bibl. Lit., Am. Assn. Higher Edn., Am. Conf. Acad. Deans, Luth. Acad. Scholarship (pres. 1981—), Luth. Human Relations Assn. Author: Lectures on Galatians, 1964; The Gospel of Baptism, 1968; A Project in Bibl. Hermeneutics, 1969. Home: 6310 Hillcrest Dr SW Tacoma WA 98499

JURKAT, KATHRYN ELIZABETH, lay ch. worker, United Ch. of Christ; b. Dayton, Ohio, Jan. 28, 1915; d. Ernest Henry and Mary Louise (Myers) Finke; B.S. in Edn., Cedarville (O.) Coll., 1943; m. Elmer C. Jurkat, Sept, 23, 1944; children—Edward W., Susan Ann (Mrs. William C. Staker). Speaker, tchr., specialist in nursery and kindergarten religious edn., 1960—; speaker, tchr. arts and crafts, 1950—; tchr. lab. sch., 1960—; program coordinator Pilgrim Hills Summer Camp, Brinkhaven, Ohio, 1968, Temple Hills Camp, Bellville, Ohio, 1970-71; chmn. lay leadership devel. dept. S.W. Assn. United Ch. Christ, 1971-74, mem. council, 1972—; trustee Ohio Conf. United Ch. Christ, 1974—. Mem. Children's Petting Zoo Commn. Springfield, 1973-74; acting dir. Springfield Union Settlement, 1961-62; pres. Wittenberg Wives, 1962, Jefferson Sch. P.T.A., 1956. Mem. Springfield Art Assn., Urban League, League of Women Voters (chmn. com. parks and recreation Springfield chpt. 1964-72). Address: 45 E Ward St Springfield OH 45504

KAELBER, WALTER OTTO, religion educator, United Church of Christ; b. Irvington, N.J., July 3, 1943; s. Otto Emil and Louise (Voelker) K.; m. Sally Ann Ventura, May 15, 1983. B.A., Bucknell U., 1965; M.A., U. Chgo., 1968, Ph.D., 1971. Prof. religious studies, chmn. dept. Wagner Coll. Staten Island, N.Y., 1981—. Contbr. articles, conf. papers to profl. jours. and ency. Recipient numerous grants Wagner Coll., 1961—, U. Chgo., 1983. Mem. Am. Acad. Religion, Phi Beta Kappa, Phi Alpha Theta.

KAELKE, LINDA KAY, church educator, Lutheran Church in America; b. Elgin, Ill., Sept. 13, 1947; d. Martin Frank and Kathryn Leone (Andresen) Kaelke. Student Queens Coll., Charlotte, N.C., 1965-68. Cert. lay profl. leader Level I, Lutheran Ch. in Am., 1982. Edn. dir. Bethany Luth. Ch., Burlington, Iowa, 1968-71, Emmanuel Luth. Ch., Lincolnton, N.C., 1971-73, Resurrection Luth. Ch., Augusta, Ga., 1975-78, First Luth. Ch., Greensboro, N.C., 1978—; asst. to Bishop youth ministry Ill. Synod, Luth. Ch. in Am., Chgo., 1974-75; chmn. youth ministry leadership devel. N.C. Synod, Luth. Ch. in Am., Salisbury, 1981—, chmn. profl. preparation com., 1983—. Author: Genesis to Revelation: 50 Ways to Teach the Bible, 1976; (curriculum) Following Jesus, 1984. Braille transcriber Assn. for Blind, Charlotte, N.C., 1966-67; bd. dirs. YWCA, Augusta, Ga., 1977. Mem. Religious Educators Assn. (pres. 1983-84). Club: Rainbow (worthy advisor 1965). Home: 134-F British Lake Dr Greensboro NC 27410 Office: First Luth Ch 3600 W Friendly Ave Greensboro NC 27410

KAETZEL, REKA LOIS, minister, United ch. Christ; b. Van Houten, N.Mex., Apr. 7, 1922; d. Karl William and Reka (Owensby) Black; B.S. in Edn., U. N.Mex., 1943; B.D., Hartford Theol. Seminary, 1947; D.Min., Andover Newton Theol. Sch., 1974; m. Samuel Timothy Kaetzel, Aug. 11, 1945; children—Carol Ruth Kaetzel Booth, Marcia Aldyth. Ordained to ministry, 1948; missionary United Ch. Bd. for World Ministries, S. Africa, 1947-64, Ghana, 1964-69; supt. Walker Missionary Homes, Inc., Auburndale, Mass., 1969-75; chaplain Westborough State Hosp., Westborough, Mass., 1974-75; missionary United Ch. Bd. for World Ministries in S. Africa, Plessislaer, Natal, Republic of S. Africa, 1976—; trainer for lifeline counselors, ch. sch. tchrs. Supr., Assn. for Clin. Pastoral Edn. sec., S. Africa, 1976—. Nat. tng. team Boy Scouts S. Africa, 1976—; guide advisor Natal Inland Province Girl Guides Assn. of S. Africa, 1976—. Recipient Medal of Merit African Boy Scouts, S. Africa, 1959, Silver Stool Girl Guides of Ghana, 1969. Mem. Am. Assn. for Pastoral Counselors, Coll. of Chaplains, Am. Protestant Hosp. Assn. Author: Healing and Counseling, 1977. Home: 46 Winthrop St Hallowell ME 04347 Office: Fed Theol Seminary Pvt Bag X505 Plessislaer Natal 4500 Republic South Africa

KAETZEL, SAMUEL TIMOTHY, minister, United Ch. of Christ; b. Clarington, Ohio, Feb. 27, 1915; s. Samuel Edward and Agnes Viola (Schierbaum) K.; B.A. magna cum laude Baldwin-Wallace Coll., 1936; B.D. cum laude Garrett Bibl. Inst., 1939; M.A., Yale, 1946; D.Min., Andover Newton Theol. Sch., 1972; postgrad. Hartford Sem. Found., 1946-47, 53-54; m. Reka Lois Black, Aug. 11, 1945; children—Carol (Mrs. Harold W. Booth), Marcia. Ordained to ministry, 1946; asst. prof. sociology Alfred (N.Y.) U., 1945-46; missionary Am. Bd. Commrs. for Fgn. Missions, South Africa, 1946-64, United Ch. Bd. for World Ministries, Accra, Ghana, 1965-69; supt. Walker Missionary Homes, Auburndale, Mass., 1969-76, prof. pastoral studies Fed. Theol. Sem., 1976—; chmn. com. for liturgy Ghana Ch. Union, 1968-69. Dep. camp chief internat. tng. team Boy Scouts Assn., South Africa, 1958-64, Ghana, 1967-69, leader trainer, South Africa, 1976—. Chmn. Lincoln Community Sch. Bd., Accra, 1969. Fellow Am. Assn. Pastoral Counselors, Assn. for Clin. Pastoral Edn. (acting chaplain supr.). Mem. editorial com. Amagama okuhlabelela (Zulu hymnal), 1956; editor Incwadi yezinkonzo (Zulu book of services of worship), 1964. Home: Federal Theol Seminary Pte Bag X505 Plessislaer 4500 Republic of South Africa

KAHAN, NORMAN, rabbi, Jewish (Reform); b. Mozyr, USSR, Jan. 2, 1922; came to Can., 1923; s. Shaia and Fannie (Grand) Kahanowitch; m. Shirley Segal; children: Sylvia, Judith Kahan Rowland, Eric. Student Hebrew Theol. Coll., 1936-38, Coll. Jewish Studies, 1938, Western Res. U., 1943, Telshe Yeshiva, 1943, Hebrew U., 1950-51; B.H.L., Hebrew Union Coll., 1950, D.D., 1977; M.A. in Hebrew Lit., Jewish Inst. Religion, 1952. Ordained rabbi, 1952. Rabbi Temple Beth Israel, Lima, Ohio, 1952-55; Jewish chaplain U.S. Mil. Acad., West Point, N.Y., 1956-61; rabbi Temple Beth Jacob, Newburgh, N.Y., 1955-68; sr. rabbi Temple Sinai, Roslyn Heights, N.Y., 1968—; chmn. bd. dirs. N.Y. Bd. Rabbis; bd. govs. Hebrew Union Coll.-Jewish Inst. of Religion; United Israel Appeal; mem. nat. rabbinic cabinet Israel Bonds; trustee Fedn. Jewish Philanthropies of N.Y.; del. Jewish Agy. Assembly; past v.p. commn. on synagogue relations; mem. various coms. Central Conf. of Am. Rabbis, rep. Synagogue Council of Am.; past. pres. Newburgh Ministerial Assn. Host Sta. WOR-TV program Point of View, (several nat. and internat. awards). Past v.p. Orange County (N.Y.) Mental Health Assn.; past mem. City of Newburgh Human Relations Commn. Served as acting chaplain and ednl. cons. USAAF, 1946. Recipient Hon. Palatine award Newburgh City Council, 1967; Tzedakah award Commn. on Synagogue Relations of Fedn. Jewish Philanthropies; awards and honors United Jewish Appeal, State of Israel Bonds Orgns.; awards from Jewish, Christian, cultural and civic orgns.; Hebrew U. fellow, 1950. Mem. Hebrew Union Coll.-Jewish Inst. Religion Rabbinic Alumni Assn. (past pres.). Lodge: Rotary (past pres. Newburgh chpt., dist. gov. 1966-67). Home: 157 High St East Williston NY 11596 Office: Temple Sinai 425 Roslyn Rd Roslyn Heights NY 11577

KAINER, GORDON ADAM, religious educator, Seventh-day Adventist Church; b. Regina, Sask., Can., Oct. 20, 1937; came to U.S., 1940; s. Adam and Madeline (Forkel) K.; m. Janette Joy Harchenko, June 19, 1957; children: Judy Irene, Perry Michael. B.A., Union Coll., 1960; M.A., Andrews U., 1961. Ordained to ministry, 1966. Religion educator Blue Mt. Acad., Hamburg, Pa., 1961-71, Platte Valley Acad., Shelton, Nebr., 1971-74, Rio Lindo Acad., Healdsburg, Calif., 1974-83, Loma Linda Acad., Calif., 1983—, campus chaplain, 1983-84; ch. pastor Platte Valley Acad., Shelton, 1971-74. Contbr. articles to profl. jours. Author: Faith, Hope and Clarity, 1978; 4 vol. study guide: God's Church, 1982, God's Word, 1984. Mem. Assn. Adventist Forums, others. Democrat. Home: 10674 Elm Ave Loma Linda CA 92354 Office: Loma Linda Acad 10656 Anderson Loma Linda CA 92354

KAISER, PAUL S., orgn. exec., Salvation Army; b. London, Eng., Oct. 21, 1911; s. Paul W. and Elizabeth (Barnet) K.; came to U.S., 1914, naturalized, 1942; student Case Western Res. U., 1950-51; B.S. magna cum laude, N.Y. U., 1954; m. Louise Duerr, June 27,

1934. Commd. officer Salvation Army, 1930, divisonal youth sec., N.Y.C., 1941-49, N.E. Ohio, 1949-52, territorial youth and edn. sec., 1952-58, divisional comdr., 1958-65, chief sec., Switzerland, 1965-66, territorial comdr., Germany, 1966-68, internat. sec., London, 1968-71, commr. Western Ty., San Francisco, 1971-74, commr. Central Ty., Chgo., 1974—. Trustee, Booth Meml. Hosps. USO Corp., U.S. Commrs. Conf. Mem. Internat. Platform Assn., Nat. Assn. Social Workers. Home: 1445 N State Pkwy Chicago IL 60610 Office: 860 N Dearborn St Chicago IL 60610

KAISER, WALTER CHRISTIAN, JR., educator, minister, Evangelical Free Church America; b. Folcroft, Pa., Apr. 11, 1933; s. Walter Christian and Estelle Evelyn (Jaworsky) K.; B.A., Wheaton Coll., 1955, B.D., 1958; M.A., Brandeis U., 1962, Ph.D, 1973; m. Margaret Ruth Burk, Aug. 24, 1957; children—Walter Christian, Brian Addison, Kathleen Elise, Jonathan Kevin. Ordained to ministry Evang. Free Ch., 1966; asst. pastor, Geneva, Ill., 1957-58; instr. Bible, Wheaton (Ill.) Coll., 1958-61, asst. prof., 1961-65, acting dir. archaeology and Nr. Eastern studies, 1965-66; asso. prof. O.T., Trinity Evang. Div. Sch., Deerfield, Ill., 1966-73, prof., chmn. dept. Semitics and O.T., 1973-80, acad. dean, v.p. edn., 1980—. Trustee Wheaton Coll. (Ill.), 1983—. Danforth grantee, 1961-63. Mem. Nr. East Archaeol. Soc. (dir.), Soc. Bibl. Lit., Evang. Theol. Soc. (nat. pres. 1977—), Inst. Bibl. Research. Editor: Classical Evangelical Essays in Old Testament Interpretation, 1972; The Old Testament in Contemporary Preaching, 1973; Towards a New Old Testament Theology, 1977; Ecclesiastes: Total Life, 1979; Toward an Exceptional Theology, 1981; Toward Old Testament Ethics, 1983; The Uses of the Old Testament in the New, 1985. co-editor O.T., Expositor's Bible Commentary; transl. New Internat. Version, 1968—. Contbr. articles to religious jours. Home: 1150 Linden Ave Deerfield IL 60015

KAISER, WARD LOUIS, minister, church official, Evangelical United Brethren Ch.; b. Kitchener, Ont., Can., July 1, 1923; s. Lorne Herman and Freda Dorothy (Reuber) K.; came to U.S., 1957; B.A., U. Western Ont., 1945; postgrad. Emmanuel Coll., Toronto, 1945-46; M.Div., Union Theol. Sem., 1949; postgrad. Rutgers U., 1966, Columbia, 1969-70; m. Lorraine Eva Macke, June 25, 1949; children—Margaret Susan, Gary, Christopher, Jacqueline. Ordained to ministry, 1949, United Ch. of Can., 1968; pastor Evang. United Brethren Ch., Kitchener, also Milverton, Stratford, Ont., 1949-57; asso. editor, dir. youth publs. Friendship Press, Nat. Council Chs. of Christ in U.S.A., N.Y.C., 1957-59, editor, dir. youth publs., 1960-69, sr. editor, 1969—, asso. exec. dir., 1976—. Dir. Christian edn. Can. conf. Evang. United Brethren Ch., 1953-57. Pres. Fair Housing Council of Bergen County (N.J.), 1962-65; pres., ch. commn. on scouting Nat. council Boy Scouts Am., 1972—. Recipient citation of year Waterloo Luth. U. (now Wilfrid Laurier U.), 1968. Mem. Nat. Assn. Ecumenical Staff, Internat. Platform Assn. Author: Intersection: Where School and Faith Meet, 1969; (with C.P. Lutz) You and the Nation's Priorities, 1971; Living the Liturgy, 1975. Contbg. author Forum: Religious Faith Speaks to American Issues, 1975. Contbr. articles to religious periodicals, mags. Office: 475 Riverside Dr New York NY 10027

KAKAC, CARROLL CONRAD, minister, Christian Church; b. Cresco, Iowa, July 24, 1929; s. Victor Otto and Blanche (Frazier) K.; B.A., Lincoln Bible Inst., 1955; m. Karen Joyce Corbin, Sept. 22, 1961; children: Kim Annette, Kevin Carroll, Kyle Douglas. Ordained to ministry, 1952; pastor chs., Benton City, Mo., 1952-55, Novelty, Mo., 1955-61, Shelbina, Mo., 1961-69, Fairfield, Ill., 1970—; bd. dirs. Central Christian Coll. Bible, Moberly, Mo., 1956-57; pres., So. Ill. Christian Conv., 1974; prayer chmn. Nat. Missionary Convs., 1975; bd. dirs. Fellowship of Assocs. of Med. Evangelists, 1975—, South India Ch. of Christ Mission, Christian Hosp. of South India; mem. Slavic Mission Bd., Bel Air, Md.; mem. continuation com. Nat. Missionary Conv. Chmn. Shelby County (Mo.) chpt. ARC, 1968-69. Home: 18 Park Ln Fairfield IL 62837 Office: Center at 1st St Fairfield IL 62837

KALAU, EDMUND, minister, missionary Evangelical Lutheran Church; b. Slawicken, Germany, July 9, 1928; came to U.S., 1954, naturalized, 1963; s. Josef and Minna (Lackner) K.; m. Elizabeth Ruth Grunewald, Oct. 16, 1954; children: Esther, Norbert, Dieter. Student Bad Liebenzel Sem., W. Ger., 1950-54. Ordained to ministry, Luth. Ch., 1954. Missionary, Liebenzell Mission to Yap, Micronesia, 1950-75; founder, pres., missionary Pacific Missionary Aviation to Micronesia, East and West Carolines, 1975—, also dir. Republican. Avocations: flying; filming documentaries. Home: PO Box 517 Pohnpei East Caroline islands Fed States of Micronesia 96941 Office: Pacific Missionary Aviation PO Box 3209 Agana Guam 96910

KALIR, JOSEPH, rabbi, religion educator, Jewish; b. Stettin, Germany, Dec. 2, 1914; came to U.S., 1957; s. Herman and Regina (Stegman) K.; m. Hilda Ostfeld, Nov. 8, 1938; children: Shulamith, Jeanette. B.A., U. Berlin, 1933, M.A., 1934; Ph.D., U. Wuerzburg, Fed. Republic Germany, 1936; rabbi Hochschule fuer die Wissenschaft des Judentums, 1936. Ordained rabbi, 1936. Rabbi, Jewish Community, Bochum, Fed. Republic Germany, 1936-38; religious educator Jewish Nat. Fund, Jerusalem, 1939-55; rabbi Jewish Community, Gothenburg, Sweden, 1955-57; religious educator Jewish Community, Orange County, Calif., 1965-70; asst. prof. Hebrew Coll., Boston, 1958-65; prof. Calif. State U.-Fullerton, 1970—, also chmn. dept. religious studies; advisor Bur. Jewish Edn., Orange County, 1965—, Methodology of Teaching Judaism, Los Angeles, 1985—; del. Am. Jewish Com., Los Angeles. Author 4 books in Hebrew; Introduction to Judaism, 1980, also editor other books; mem. editorial bd. Jewish Quar. Rev.; editor Israel Today. Contbr. articles to religious jours. Mem. Nat. Council for Jewish Edn., Orange County Bd. Rabbis, So. Calif. Bd. Rabbis, Central Conf. Am. Rabbis, AAUP. Home: 17902 Orange Tree Ln Tustin CA 92680 Office: Calif State U Fullerton CA 92634

KALLAND, LLOYD AUSTIN, theology educator American Baptist Churches U.S.A.; b. Superior, Wis., Aug. 8, 1914; s. Jean Ann Williams, July 20, 1945; children: Doris Jean Kalland McDowell. A.B., Gordon Coll., 1942; B.S., Reformed Episcopal Sem., 1945; M.A., U. Pa., 1945; Th.M., Westminster Theol. Sem., 1946; Th.D., No. Bapt. Sem., Chgo., 1955. Ordained to ministry Am. Bapt. Chs. U.S.A., 1947. Minister, 1st Bapt. Ch., Slatington, Pa., 1946-49, Calvary Bapt. Ch., Chgo. 1949-55; mem. faculty Gordon Conwell Theol. Sem., Hamilton, Mass., 1955—. Mem. Evangel. Theol. Soc. Home: 102 Chebacco Rd South Hamilton MA 01982 Office: Gordon Conwell Theol Sem 130 Essex St South Hamilton MA 01982

KALLAS, ENDEL, minister, Lutheran Church in America; b. Phila., June 7, 1947; s. Endel and Estelle (Wiss) K.; m. Nancy Schmit, Jan. 7, 1978; children: Leif, Joel. B.S., Calif. State Poly. U., 1969; M.A., Grad. Theol. Union, Berkeley, Calif., 1972, Ph.D., 1979; M.Div., Pacific Luth. Theol. Sem., Berkeley, 1973. Ordained to ministry Lutheran Ch., 1978. Lab. asst. Ecole Federale, Lausanne, Switzerland, 1970; teaching asst. Pacific Sch. of Religion, Berkeley, 1976-77, faculty lectr., 1977-78; pastor First Luth. Ch., Watsonville, Calif., 1978-81, Grace Luth. Ch., Santa Barbara, Calif., 1981—; Luth. lectr. Calif. Luth. Coll., Thousand Oaks, 1983; council pres. Luth. Campus Ministry, U. Calif.-Santa Barbara, 1982-83; mem. regional bd. Luth. Campus Ministry So. Calif., 1983—. Contbr. articles to religious publs. Luth. Brotherhood Sem. grad. scholar, 1973. Mem. Sigma Pi Sigma. Democrat. Home: 2955 Calle Noguera Santa Barbara CA 93105 Office: Grace Luth Ch 3869 State St Santa Barbara CA 93105

KALLOS, JOHN, bishop, Greek Orthodox Ch.; b. Chgo., Mar. 29, 1928; s. James Michael and Kalliope (Bratsos) K. B.S. in Edn., Boston Coll., 1955; B.D., Holy Cross Sem., Brookline, Mass., 1957; Lic. Theol. Div., U. Athens, 1963; postgrad., Harvard U., 1967-69. Ordained priest Greek Orthodox Ch., 1956, bishop, 1971. Pastor St. Demetrios Ch., Fall River, Mass., 1956-59; dean of students Holy Cross Sem., Brookline, 1959-60; pastor Annunciation Ch., Montgomery, Ala., 1963-65; dean Holy Trinity Ch., Charlotte, N.C., 1965-66; asst. dean, instr. Holy Cross Theol. Sch., Brookline, 1966-67; pastor Dormition Ch., Somerville, Mass., 1967-71; diocesan bishop, Houston Dist. VIII, 1971-74, Denver Dist. VIII, 1974-78, Charlotte, 1978-79; bishop Diocese of Charlotte, 1979-80, Diocese of Atlanta, 1980—; pres. St. Photios Shrine, St. Augustine, Fla.; bd. dirs. Tex. Conf. of Chs., Austin, 1971-77, Okla. Conf. Chs., Oklahoma City, 1972-77, Colo. Council of Chs., Denver, 1974-77. Contbr. articles to various religious mags. Decorated comdr. Holy Lamb, Kuopio, Finland, Finnish Orthodox Ch., knight of Holy Sepulchre Patriarch of Jerusalem; recipient Excellence in Religion award Boston Coll., 1980. Mem. Armed Forces Chaplaincy (endorsing agt.), Ga. Christian Council (bd. dirs.). Office: Greek Orthodox Diocese of Atlanta 2801 Buford Hwy Suite 365 Atlanta GA 30329

KALSHOVEN, THOMAS N., minister, Presbyterian Church USA; b. N.Y.C., Apr. 12, 1931; s. William T. and Elizabeth B. (Csokany) K.; m. Mary E. Rienbeck, Sept. 17, 1955; children: David W., Karen E., Peter J. A.B., Cornell U., 1951; M.Div., Union Theol. Sem., 1954; postgrad. Syracuse U., 1958-62. Ordained to ministry, 1954. Asst. pastor First Presbyn. Ch., Watertown, N.Y., 1954-56; pastor Jamesville Federated Ch., N.Y., 1956-61; dir. research Syracuse Area Council Chs., N.Y., 1961-62; dir. research/planning Ohio Council Chs., 1962-69; pastor Bethany Presbyn. Ch., Memands, N.Y., 1969-73; exec. dir. Chs. United of Scott and Rock Island Counties, Rock Island, Ill., 1973—; treas. Nat. Assn. Ecumenical Staff, 1983—; del. Synod of Lincoln Trails, Indpls., 1984—. Pres., Council on Community Services, Rock Island, 1980-82; bd. dirs. Health Systems Agy., Davenport, Iowa, 1974-80, Iowa State Health Coordinating Council, 1975-80. Fellow Religious Research Assn. (program chmn. 1968). Lodge: Rotary (pres. 1972). Home: 1130 Kirkwood Blvd Davenport IA 52803 Office: Churches United of Scott and Rock Island Counties 630 9th St Rock Island IL 61201

KALWEIT, DENMORE CLIFFORD, minister, Lutheran Church in America; b. Cleve., June 16, 1926; s. August and Aleene (Peterson) K.; m. Nancy Nylen, Oct. 24, 1953; children: Karin Marie Kalweit Haxton, Linda Mari, Lisa Aleene. B.A. in Edn., Seattle U., 1950; ordination cert. Augustana Sem., 1954; M.Div., Luth. Sch. Theology, 1975. Ordained to ministry Luth. Ch. in Am., 1954. Pastor Bethelehem Luth. Ch., Rockford, Ill., 1954-59, Messiah Luth. Ch., Racine, Wis., 1959-65; sr. pastor Messiah Luth. Ch., Marquette, Mich., 1965-84; chmn. Hosp. Chaplaincy Com., Marquette, 1972-84; dean Lake Superior Dist., Marquette, 1982-84. Author: Devotional Book, 1984. Editor: New Member Book, 1978. Recipient Pres.'s Disting. Service award No. Mich. U., 1974. Club: Kiwanis. Home: 438 W Michigan St Marquette MI 49855 Office: Messiah Luth Ch 305 W Magnetic Marquette MI 49855

KAMIN, BENJAMIN ALON, rabbi, Reform Jewish; b. Kfar-Saba, Israel, Jan. 11, 1953; came to U.S., 1962; s. Jeff Israel and Ruth (Flek) K.; m. Cathy Jill Rosen, June 8, 1975; children: Sari, Debra. B.A. with honors, U. Cin., 1974; M.A. in Hebrew Letters, Hebrew Union Coll., 1977. Ordained rabbi, 1978. Asst. rabbi Temple Sinai Congregation, Toronto, Can., 1978-81; rabbi Sinai Reform Temple, Bay Shore, N.Y., 1981-82; N. Am. dir. World Union for Progressive Judaism, N.Y.C., 1982—; gov. World Union for Progressive Judaism, N.Y.C., Jerusalem, 1982—; dir. Assn. Reform Zionists Am., N.Y.C., 1982—; faculty Hebrew Union Coll., N.Y.C., 1983, 84, Eisner Camp Inst., Great Barrington, Mass., 1983, 84; mem. Nat. Com. Rabbis for Mondale, Mpls., 1984. Contbr. articles to profl. jours. Mem. Central Conf. Am. Rabbis (com. mem. 1984), Phi Alpha Theta, Omnicron Delta Kappa. Democrat. Home: 475 Lenox Ave South Orange NJ 07079 Office: World Union Progressive Judaism 838 Fifth Ave New York NY 10021

KAMMAN, HAROLD WILLIAM, minister, Lutheran Ch.-Missouri Synod; b. Cin., Nov. 8, 1924; s. Louis William and Bertha Elizabeth (Miller) K.; m. Thelma Dorothea Dittmer, Apr. 21, 1957; children: Ruth Elizabeth, Lois Margaret. A.A., Concordia Jr. Coll., Ft. Wayne, Ind., 1945; A.B., Concordia Sem., St. Louis, 1948, diploma, 1950. Ordained to ministry Luth. Ch.-Mo. Synod, 1950. Pastor, Faith Luth. Ch., Abilene, Kans., 1950-57, St. Paul Luth. Ch., Texhoma, Okla., 1957-64, Hope Luth. Ch., Boise City, Okla., 1957-64, Trinity Luth. Ch., El Reno, Okla., 1964-75, Good Shepherd Luth., Duncan, Okla. 1975—; del. nat. convs. Luth. Ch.-Mo. Synod, 1962, pub. relations staff 1967, 69, 71, 73, 77, 79, 83; circuit counselor Luth. Ch.-Mo. Synod, Kans., 1955-57. Okla., 1963-74, 77-82; dist. dir. pub. relations, Okla., 1967-70, 76—; mem. Dist. Commn. on Adjudication, Okla., 1974-78. Editor Luth. Witness, Okla. edit., 1959—. Bd. dirs. Duncan Community Residence, 1979-82. Mem. C. of C. Republican. Office: Good Shepherd Luth Ch 2401 Country Club Rd Duncan OK 73533

KAMSLER, HAROLD MILTON, rabbi, Conservative Jewish; b. N.Y.C., Dec. 10, 1911; s. Samuel S. and Annie (Levy) K.; m. Etta M. Seymans; children: Joel, David (dec.). B.A., NY U, 1932, M.A., 1935; M.H.L., Jewish Inst. Religion, 1936; D.D. (hon.), Jewish Theol. Sem., 1975. Ordained rabbi, 1936. Rabbi Hillside Hollis Hebrew Ctr., Jamaica, N.Y., 1936-43; rabbi, exec. dir. Jewish Community Ctr., Norristown, Pa., 1943-80, rabbi emeritus, 1980—; rabbi Oyster Bay Jewish Ctr., N.Y., 1980—; exec. com. Rabbinical Assembly, N.Y.C., 1958-61; chmn. youth commn. United Synagogue Am., N.Y.C., 1963-68. Contbr. articles to profl. jours. Pres. bd. dirs. Norristown Pub. Library, Pa., 1960-65; v.p., bd. dirs. Montgomery County Library, Norristown, 1965-68; bd. dirs. Sacred Heart Hosp., Norristown, 1974-80; chmn. Human Relations Com., Norristown, 1965-75. Mem. Rabbinical Assembly, N.Y. Bd. Rabbis, Phila. Bd. Rabbis. Lodges: Kiwanis, Masons (pres. 1965). Home: 1 Temple Ln Oyster Bay NY 11771 Office: Oyster Bay Jewish Ctr Berry Hill Rd Oyster Bay NY 11771

KANGAS, HENRY RUBEN, minister, Luth. Ch. in Am.; b Mass City, Mich., Nov. 20, 1924; s. Samuel and Hilda (Parkkila) K.; A.A., Suomi Coll., 1944; grad. Suomi Luth. Theol. Sem., 1947; B.A., Kent State U., 1949; M.A., Western Res. U., 1952. Ordained to ministry, 1947; pastor in Warren, Ohio, 1947-57, 74—; pastor Gethsemane Luth. Ch., San Francisco, 1957-62, Cleve., 1962-63, St. Francis Luth. Ch., San Francisco, 1964-74. Chaplain constituting conv. Luth. Ch. Am., 1962; pres. Lake Erie chpt. Suomi Free Conf., Luth. Ch. Am., 1976—. Active, United for Life, San Francisco, 1971-74, Noe-Henry Community Assn., San Francisco, 1964-74. Mem. Am. Soc. Ch. History. Home: 363 Parkman Rd SW Warren OH 44485 Office: 551 Parkman Rd SW Warren OH 44485

KANIECKI, MICHAEL JOSEP, bishop, Roman Catholic Church. Coadjutor bishop, Fairbanks, Alaska, 1984-85, bishop, 1985—. Office: 1316 Peger Rd Fairbanks AK 99701*

KANIPE, JOE CARSON, minister, So. Bapt. Conv.; b. Shelby, N.C., Dec. 29, 1923; s. Zephaniah Lester and Jessie Belle (Laughridge) K.; A.A., Gardner-Webb Coll., 1961; B.A., Limestone Coll., 1963; postgrad. New Orleans Bapt. Sem., 1963-66; m. Naomi Helen Bright, Feb. 8, 1941; children—Harold, Jerry, Linda. Ordained to ministry, 1959; pastor Mt. Paran Bapt. Ch., Grover, N.C., 1959-64, Rehoboth Bapt. Ch., Gaffney, S.C., 1964-66, Gaston Bapt. Ch., Dallas, N.C., 1966-67, Thompson's Chapel Bapt. Ch., Spartanburg, S.C., 1967-68, Buffalo Bapt. Ch., Blacksburg, S.C., 1968-70, 2d Bapt. Ch., Clifton, S.C., 1970-72, Cumberland Drive Bapt. Ch., Clarksville, Tenn., 1972—. Chaplain, Montgomery County Civil Def., 1975—. Bd. dirs. Youth Challenge Internat., Clarksville, Tenn., 1975. Home: 1018 Davidson Dr Clarksville TN 37040 Office: 1101 New Ashland City Rd Clarksville TN 37040

KANOUSE, MERRILL WAYNE, minister, United Methodist Church; b. Jackson, Ohio, Dec. 19, 1944; s. Ernest Harry and Geneva May (Leedy) K.; B.A., Asbury Coll., 1966; M.Div., Asbury Theol. Sem., 1970; S.T.M., N.Y. Theol. Sem., 1973; postgrad. San Francisco Sch. Theology, 1973-74, Blanton Peale Inst. Psychiatry and Religion, 1976-77. Ordained to ministry, 1970; pastor chs. in Ky., 1966-69, Ohio, 1969-70, Met. Community United Meth. Ch., N.Y.C., 1970-73, Oceanside (N.Y.) United Meth. Ch., 1973—; sec. Oceanside Clergy Assn., 1974—; sec. United Methodists for ch. renewal N.Y. Ann. Conf., 1973-77, mem. com. on family care and pastoral counseling, 1975-78, chmn. Good News Forum for Scriptural Christianity, 1982—, mem. camping com., 1979-81, 83—. Lectr. Salvation Army Tng. Sch., 1971-76; mem. N.Y. State Commn. Human Rights, 1971-72; chmn. Voter Registration N.E. Harlem, 1972; mem. Democratic Com., 1973—; bd. dirs. Oceanside chpt. ARC, 1974-79, disaster chmn., 1976; trustee Dem. Club, 1976-80; chmn. Runaway Youth Coordinating Council, 1976-77; organizer, founder, chmn. bd. Onward to Excellence, 1977-78; organizer, exec. dir. People Involved in Mission, 1978—; camp dir., 1977—. Mem. Editor: History of Oceanside, 1975. Home: 2825 Davison St Oceanside NY 11572 Office: Davison St and Atlantic Ave Oceanside NY 11572

KANTNER, ROBERT OBURN, minister, Presbyterian Church (U.S.A.); b. Altoona, Pa., Apr. 15, 1934; s. Robert Clifford and Ruth Hamilton (Irwin) K.; B.A., Wheaton Coll., 1956, M.A., 1960; M.Div., Gordon-Conwell Theol. Sem., 1959; D.Min., Fuller Sem., 1980. m. Helen Dorothy Johnson, Aug. 22, 1959; children—Sheryl Lynn, Robert Oburn. Ordained to ministry, 1959; pastor Countryside Chapel, Glen Ellyn, Ill., 1960-70; minister of edn. Meml. Presbyn. Ch., West Palm Beach, Fla., 1970-72; sr. minister 1st Presbyn. Ch., North Palm Beach, Fla., 1972-73; sr. pastor Champion Presbyn. Ch., Warren, Ohio, 1976—. Mem. bd. Fox Valley Youth for Christ, 1964-69. Counselor div. youth services State of Fla., 1974-76; mem. Glen Ellyn Human Relations Bd., 1964-70; mem. Glen Ellyn United Fund Com., 1966-70; mem. Clergy Task Force Violent Crime, Warren, 1976—; mem. Trumbull County Children's Services Bd., 1977-84. Recipient 5 awards Freedoms Found., Valley Forge, Pa., 1968, 69, 70, 77, 81. Mem. Evang. Theol. Soc., Nat. Assn. Evangs. Home: 1086 Center St NW Warren OH 44483 Office: 4997 Mahoning Ave NW Warren OH 44483

KAPLAN, ALINE, organization official, Jewish; lawyer; b. N.Y.C., June 23, 1923; d. Morris and Dora (Zeresky) K. B.A., Hunter Coll., 1943; LL.B., Columbia U., 1946; postgrad. Sch. Edn., Yeshiva U., 1959-62. Bar: N.Y. 1946. Pvt. practice law, N.Y.C., 1946-52; dir. Nat. Jr. Hadassah, 1952-64; asst. dir. Hadassah, Zionist Women's Orgn. Am., 1964-81, exec. dir., 1971—; Hadassah rep. Am. Israel Pub. Affairs Com., 1971—; Hadassah del. World Zionist Congress in Jerusalem, 1956, 64, 72, 78, Convs. of World Fedn. United Zionists, 1956, 64, 72, 78; mem. tribunal World Zionist Orgn., 1978. Contbr. articles to Zionist ency. Bd. dirs. United Israel Appeal, 1971—. Mem. Am. Zionist Fedn. (nat. bd. 1970—), Delta Phi Epsilon. Office: 50 W 58th St New York NY 10019

KAPLAN, ALLEN STANFORD, rabbi, Reform Jewish Congregations; b. Chgo., Mar. 26, 1939; s. Nathan and Sarah Belle (Levin) K.; B.A., U. Cin., 1960; B.H.L., Hebrew Union Coll., 1963, M.A., 1965; m. Jane Rochelle Gruber, July 23, 1967; children—Walter Haim, Sarah Nes, David Jeremy. Ordained rabbi, 1965; chaplain USAF, Hdqrs. SAC, 1965-67, W.Ger., 1967-70; rabbi Temple Beth Sholom, N.Y.C., 1970-78. Pres., Rockland County Bd. Rabbis, 1975—; bd. govs. N.Y. Bd. Rabbis, 1977, assoc. dir., 1978-82; exec. bd. N.Y. Assn. Reform Rabbis, 1977; assoc. dir. N.Y. Fedn. Reform Synagogues, Union of Am. Hebrew Congregations, 1982-84; dir. Union Am. Hebrew Congregations Fund for Reform Judaism, 1984—. Founder, chmn. Rockland County Fair Campaign Practices Commn., 1971-72; bd. dirs. Planned Parenthood, 1975-76, Vol. Counseling Service, 1973-76, Family Counseling Service, Archdiocese N.Y., 1975-76, Romic Center, Rise West Sch., 1977. Recipient Outstanding Religious Edn. award USAF, 1966; named Man of Year, Israel Bonds, 1973. Mem. Am. Jewish Hist. Soc., Central Conf. Am. Rabbis, Phi Alpha Theta. Home: 555 E 78th St New York NY 10021 Office: Union Am Hebrew Congregations 838 Fifth Ave New York NY 10021

KAPLAN, BERNARD LOUIS, lay church worker; b. New Orleans, Aug. 19, 1931; s. Meyer and Lena (Wellan) K.; m. Jean Lowentritt, June 9, 1957; children: Deborah, Meyer, Rachel, Miriam, David, Judith, Jonathan. B.S., La. State U., 1952; M.D., La. State U. Med. Ctr., 1956. Pres., Bnai Israel Synagogue, Alexandria, Va., 1963—; bd. dirs. Central La. Jewish Welfare, Alexandria, 1967—, campaign chmn., 1983-84. Practice medicine specializing in surgery, Alexandria, La., 1963—. Served to lt. comdr., USN, 1961-63. Fellow ACS, Am. Coll. Chest Physicians; mem. Am. Bd. Surgery (diplomate), La. Med. Soc. (exec. com. 1981—), Rapides Parish Med. Soc. (pres. 1982). Lodge: Kiwanis. Home: 100 Park Pl Alexandria LA 71301 Office: PO Box 5086 Alexandria LA 71301

KAPPELMANN, GLENN MARTIN, minister, American Lutheran Ch.; b. Lohman, Mo., May 13, 1937; s. Emil Ernst and Bertha Margareta (Soell) K.; m. Mary Elizabeth Ritland, Sept. 6, 1968; children: Jennifer, Mark. B.A., Capital U., 1959; M.Div., Wartburg Sem., 1962; postgrad. U. Hamburg, 1962-65, U. Munich, 1969-70. Ordained to ministry Am. Luth. Ch., 1965. Asst. pastor 1st Luth. Ch., Decorah, Iowa, 1965-69; pastor Grace Luth. Ch., Tripoli, Iowa, 1970-75; pastor for family life Nazareth Luth. Ch., Cedar Falls, Iowa, 1975-79, pastor for evangelism, 1980—; chmn. spiritual growth com. Internat. Luther League, Am. Luth. Ch., Columbus, Ohio, 1958-60, parish mission builder, 1958; sec. Iowa Dist. Am. Luth. Ch., Des Moines, 1978-84; preacher Sta. WCAL, Northfield, Minn., 1973—; assoc. clin. tchr. Evangelism Explosion, Ft. Lauderdale, Fla., 1983—. Editor Spectator mag., 1957-59. Gen. chmn. Family Affair, Waterloo, 1977; sec., bd. dirs. Bethesda Counseling Ctr., Cedar Falls, 1978-84; mem. religious symbol com. Allen Meml. Hosp., Waterloo, 1983-84. Recipient Appreciation letter U.S. Army Security Agy., 1969. Mem. Cedar Falls Ministers Assn. (chmn. 1979-80). Republican. Home: 335 Bonita Blvd Cedar Falls IA 50613 Office: Nazareth Luth Ch University and Main Sts Cedar Falls IA 50613

KARAMPELAS, NAPOLEON DEMETRIOS, archpriest, Greek Orthodox Archdiocese of N. and S.Am.; b. Varympope, Menastereon Messeneas, Dec. 31, 1904; s. Demetrios Panteles and Georgia (Kalampokes) K.; came to U.S., 1938, naturalized, 1944; diploma in theology Coll. of Corinthos, Greece, 1932; m. Panagoula Lontos, July 20, 1929; children: Angelos, Panagiotis. Ordained deacon, 1934, priest, 1934; pastor ch., Greece, 1934-38, Calif., 1938-39, Colo., 1939-41, Little Rock, 1941-42, Ill., 1942-45, Kans., 1945-49, Mich., 1949-52, Nebr., 1952-55, Wyo., 1955-56, Idaho, 1956-59, Nebr., 1959-63; archpriest of upper peninsula, Mich., 1963—. Mem. Marquette Ecumenical Council, 1963, Clergy Assn. Marquette. Mem. Hellenic Profl. Assn. Am. Contbr. articles on theology and Greek history to Jour. of Hellenic Am. Soc., Am. Rev. of Eastern Orthodox Ch. and various newspapers. Home: 237 W Ridge Marquette MI 49855

KARCH, JOHN DONALD, JR., minister, Lutheran Church-Missouri Synod; b. Passaic, N.J., Mar. 4, 1954; s. John Donald and Joan Carol (Figlyar) K.; m. Susan Beth Schroeder, Aug. 20, 1977; children: Justin, Alison, Erin. A.A., Concordia Jr. Coll., 1974; B.A., Concordia Sr. Coll., 1976; M.Div., Concordia Theol. Sem., 1980. Ordained to ministry, 1980. Pastor, St. Paul's Luth. Ch., Ellsworth, Kans., 1980—; chmn. Circuit #12 Conf., Great Bend, Kans., 1980—, youth coordinator, 1982—; chmn. Ellsworth County Pastoral Assn., 1983—. CPR instr. ARC, Salina, Kans., 1984; ambulance driver Ellsworth County Ambulance Service, 1984; coach Ellsworth Law Enforcement softball team, 1983-84. Address: Rural Route 1 Ellsworth KS 67439

KARFF, SAMUEL EGAL, rabbi, educator, Jewish; b. Phila., Sept. 19, 1931; s. Louis and Reba (Margalit) K.; m. Joan Gabrielle Mag, June 29, 1959; children: Rachel Karff Weissenstein, Amy, Elizabeth. A.B., Gratz Coll., 1949; A.B. magna cum laude, Harvard U., 1953; M. Hebrew Letters, Hebrew Union Coll., 1956, D.H.L., 1961. Ordained rabbi, 1968. Rabbi, Congregation Beth Israel, Hartford, Conn., 1958-60, Temple Beth El, Flint, Mich., 1960-62, Chgo. Sinai, 1962-75; sr. rabbi Congregation Beth Israel, Houston, 1975—; lectr. Rice U., Houston, 1976—; mem. exec. com. Houston Met. Ministries, 1980. Author: Agada: The Language of Jewish Faith, 1979; (with others) Religions of the World, 1982. Editor Jour. of Reform Judiasm, 1981-84. Bd. dirs. ARC, Houston, 1980—. Served as 1st lt., chaplain USAF, 1956-58. Mem. Houston Rabbinic Assn. (pres. 1982-84), Central Conf. Am. Rabbis, Union Am. Hebrew Congregations (rabbinic chmn. task force on religious commitment 1984), Hebrew Union Coll. Alumni Assn. (pres. 1971-72). Home: 5343 Paisley Houston TX 77096 Office: Congregation Beth Israel 5600 N Braeswood Houston TX 77096

KAROUB, IMAM MUHAMMAD, religious organization executive, editor, Muslims; b. Highland Park, Mich., Nov. 9, 1924; s. Hussien and Maryam Karoub; married Aug. 3, 1951; children: Carl, Lila, Susan, Richard, Frederick. B.A., Wayne State U.; student in Theology, Cairo U. Dir. Am. Moslem Soc., Dearborn, Mich.; dir. religion Fed. Islamic Assns., Detroit; religious editor: Muslim Star; American-Arab Message; Fedn. Islamic Assns., U.S. and Can. Jour. Lectr. on Islamic and Arab affairs. Mem. Round Table of Christians and Jews, American-Arabic Council. Office: PO Box 2544 Farmington Hills MI 48018-0544

KARPF, TED, educator, minister, United Methodist Ch.; b. Peekskill, N.Y., Sept. 18, 1948; s. William and Joan (Shepherd) K.; B.A., Tex. Wesleyan Coll., 1974; Th.M., Boston U., 1974; m. Kaye Margaret Blanche Reynolds, Sept. 21, 1975. Ordained to ministry, 1971; researcher communication div. Ecumenical Center, World Council Chs., Geneva, 1972; field edn. staff Boston Theol. Inst., 1973-74; campus minister, problems analyst Bath circuit Brit. Meth. Ch., 1974-75; pastor Sadler-Gainesville (Tex.) Mission United Meth. chs., 1975-76; tchr. religion, campus minister, dir. United Ministry Center, North Tex. State U., Denton, 1976—. Counselor, Alcoholics Anonymous, Gainesville, Tex., 1975-76, Cook County Mental Health Center, 1975-76. Mem. Am. Assn. Theol. Sch. Field Educators, Alpha Phi Omega. Home: 103 B Heritage Ln Denton TX 76201 Office: POB 13765 Denton TX 76203

KARRES, GEORGE RANDALL, minister, Lutheran Church in America; b. Tonawanda, N.Y., May 31, 1952; s. George Edward and Jean Audrey (Clemens) K.; m. Elizabeth Harris, May 3, 1980; children: Jeffrey, Matthew. Student Albion Coll., 1970-72, Am. U. of Beirut, Lebanon, 1972-73; B.A. in Polit. Sci., U. Central Fla., 1975; M.Div., Luth. Theol. So. Sem., Columbia, S.C., 1979. Ordained to ministry Lutheran Ch., 1979. Pastor Christ's Luth. Ch., Columbia, S.C., 1979-83, St. Peter Luth. Ch., Ft. Pierce, Fla., 1983—. Home: 805 Hickory St Fort Pierce FL 33450 Office: St Peter Luth Ch 2501 Virginia Ave Fort Pierce FL 33482

KARSTEN, CHARLES EMIL, JR., minister, Episcopal Church; b. N.Y.C., May 30, 1924; s. Charles Emil and Elizabeth Adeline (Scovil) K.; B.A., U. of the South, 1945; M.A., Oxford (Eng.) U., 1952; m. Daphne Eileen Wootton; children—Wendy Daphne, Charles Christopher. Ordained priest, 1948; asst. minister St. Stephen's Ch., Wilkes-Barre, Pa., 1948-51, Trinity Ch., New Haven, 1951-53; minister-in-charge Olivet Ch., Alexandria, Va., 1953-57; rector Christ Ch., Gardiner, Maine, 1957—. Mem. standing com. Episcopal Diocese of Maine, 1968, 76-82; canon St. Luke's Cathedral, Portland, Maine, 1968; vis. scholar Cambridge (Eng.) U., 1972-73; del. Episc. Gen. Conv., 1976, 79, 82. Home: 15 Pleasant St Gardiner ME 04345 Office: 1 Pleasant St Gardiner ME 04345

KASTNER, MARK STEVEN, minister, Lutheran Ch.-Missouri Synod; b. Oshkosh, Wis., June 18, 1951; s. Wilfred Martin and Arline Mae (Procknow) K.; m. Deborah Ann Bandurski, Nov. 26, 1977; children: Jeremiah David, Jennifer Marie. B.A., U. Wis.-Milw., 1978; M.Div., Concordia Theol. Sem., 1982. Ordained to ministry Lutheran Ch., 1982. Minister Mt. Calvary Luth. Ch., Eagle Grove, Iowa, Immanuel Luth. Ch., Rowan, Iowa, 1982—; co-founder Christian Apologetics Research and Info. Service-Midwest, Milw., 1975-78; lectr. on religious cults in Am., 1981—. Mem. Eagle Grove Ministerial Assn. (v.p. 1983-84, pres. 1984—). Office: Mount Calvary and Immanuel Luth Chs 400 W Broadway Eagle Grove IA 50533

KASZYNSKI, ROBERT STEPHEN, priest, Roman Cath. Ch.; b. New Bedford, Mass., Oct. 28, 1933; s. Chester Stanislaus and Genevieve Bernice (Kalisz) K.; B.A., St. John's Sem., Boston, 1954; M.Div., Ss. Cyril and Methodius Sem., Mich., 1975. Ordained priest, 1960; pastor retreats and parish missions various locations, 1961—; Bishop's liaison to Charismatic Renewal, Diocese of Fall River (Mass.), 1976—. Pres., Senate of Priests, Diocese of Fall River, 1976—. Address: 36 Rockland St Fall River MA 02724

KATHMAN, MARY ANN CHRISTINE, religious orphanage administrator, nun, Roman Catholic Church; b. Cin., Apr. 27, 1936; d. Gervase George and Christine (Kaelble) K. A.B., Villa Madonna Coll., 1966; M.Ed., Xavier U., 1972; M.S.W., U. Louisville, 1982. Joined Sisters of Notre Dame, Roman Catholic Ch., 1954. Elem. sch. prin. St. Augustine Sch., Covington, Ky., 1967-73, St. Agnes Sch., Ft. Wright, Ky., 1976-80; adminstr. St. Aloysius Orphanage, Cin., 1982—. Mem. Nat. Assn. Social Workers. Office: St Aloysius Orphanage 4721 Reading Rd Cincinnati OH 45237

KATZ, LEON, rabbi, Jewish Congregations; b. Poland, Aug. 12, 1913; s. Reuven and Reichel (Maskilleitan) K.; came to U.S., 1930, naturalized, 1934; B.A., Yeshiva Coll., 1937, M.A., 1939, Ph.D., 1948, hon. degree, 1979; m. Rhea S. Herzog, Feb. 17, 1946; children: Varda (dec.), Shimon, Mayer (dec.), Avram. Ordained rabbi, 1935; rabbi Congregation Adas Israel, Passaic, N.J., 1938—. Instr. Jewish tradition and philosophy N.Y. U.,

1962-65; instr. history Yeshiva U., 1950-59; prof. Stern Coll. for Women, 1967-69. Recipient Peace award City of Jerusalem, 1971. Established Rabbi Dr. and Mrs. Leon Katz vis. professorship in rabbinics Rabbi Isaac Elchanan Theol. Sem., N.Y.C., 1984. Mem. Rabbinical Council N.J. (past pres.), Rabbinical Council Am., Religious Zionists Am. (v.p.), Soc. Profs. Hebrew Culture, Hist. Soc. Am., World Acad. Jerusalem, Rabbinical Alumni Yeshiva U. (past pres.). Author: The Life, Times, Works of Rabbi Moshe Sofer, 1960. Home: 32 Laurel Ave Clifton NJ 07012 Office: 565 Broadway Passaic NJ 07055

KATZ, NATHAN, religious studies educator; b. Phila., Aug. 11, 1948; s. Charles and Frances (Gelb) K.; m. Ellen S. Goldberg, Aug. 7, 1982. B.A., Temple U., 1970, M.A., 1975, Ph.D., 1979. Asst. religious studies prof. U. South Fla., Tampa, 1984—; asst. prof. religion Williams Coll., Williamstown, Mass., 1979-84; vis. core faculty Naropa Inst., Boulder, 1978-79. Author: Buddhist Images of Human Perfection, 1982. Home: 7501 Camarina Calle Tampa FL 33615 Office: U South Fla Dept Religious Studies Tampa FL 33620

KAUFFMAN, LUKE EDWARD, minister, Fellowship of Grace Brethren Churches; b. Hummelstown, Pa., Dec. 19, 1941; s. Jeremiah M. and Mary E. (Kreider) K.; m. Sandra Jean Garber, Aug. 1, 1964; children: Kurt Alan, Kent David, Kristen Lyn. A.A., Hershey Jr. Coll., 1961; B.A., Grace Coll., Winona Lake, Ind., 1963; M.Div., Grace Theol. Sem., 1966. Ordained to ministry Fellowship of Grace Brethren Chs., 1968. Pastor, Grace Brethren Ch., Beaverton, Oreg., 1966-69; founder/pastoral advisor Grace Christian Sch., Myerstown, Pa., 1974—; sr. pastor Myerstown Grace Brethren Ch., 1969—; trustee Brethren Missionary Herald Co., Winona Lake, 1974-77; pres. Grace Brethren Home Missions Council, Inc., 1982—, Grace Brethren Investment Found., Inc., 1982—, No. Atlantic Dist. mission bd. Fellowship of Grace Brethren Chs., 1971—; speaker radio show The Grace Brethren Hour, 1976—, TV show The Message of Grace, 1983—; chaplain Pa. State Senate, Dec. 1983. Vice-pres., Pa. Counseling Ctr., 1970-76. Named Alumnus of Yr., Grace Coll. Alumni, 1979. Mem. Internat. Fellowship of Grace Brethren Ministers (pres. 1978-79), Conf. of Fellowship of Grace Brethren Chs. (vice-moderator 1980-81, moderator 1981-82). Republican. Home: 613 Hilltop Rd Myerstown PA 17067 Office: 430 E Lincoln Ave Myerstown PA 17067

KAUFFMANN, IVAN JOHN See *Who's Who in America*, 43rd edition.

KAUFFROTH, JOHN ANDREW, minister, Presbyterian Ch. in U.S.A.; b. Gap, Pa., July 14, 1909; s. George Sylvester Martin and Lydia (Sensenig) K.; student Franklin and Marshall Coll.; B.S., Ursinus Coll., 1931; M.Div., Westminster Theol. Sem., 1934, Th.M., 1935; m. Marguerite Davis, Aug. 28, 1933 (dec. Aug. 1984). Ordained to ministry, 1934; pastor chs. in Ill., 1935-42, West Grove Presbyn. Ch., Pa., 1942-49, Westminster Presbyn. Ch., Bridgeport, Conn., 1949-62, United Presbyn. Ch. Good Shepherd, Phila., 1962-66, Forks of Brandywine Ch., Glen Moore, Pa., 1966-77, pastor emeritus, 1977—. Commr., Presbyn. Gen. Assembly, 1948, 50, 55, 69. Mem. Presbyn. Hist. Soc. Home and Office: Box 190 Honey Brook PA 19344

KAUFMAN, GORDON D., religion educator, General Conference Mennonite Church; b. Newton, Kans., June 22, 1925; s. Edmund George and Hazel (Dester) K.; m. Dorothy Wedel, June 11, 1947; children: David W., Gretchen E., Anne L., Edmund G. A.B., Bethel Coll., Kans., 1947; M.A., Northwestern U., 1948; B.D., Yale Div. Sch., 1951; Ph.D., Yale U., 1955; M.A. (hon.), Harvard U., 1963; L.H.D. (hon.), Bethel Coll., 1973. Ordained to ministry, 1951. Pastor part-time Mennonite Congregation of Boston; prof. theology Harvard Div. Sch., Cambridge, Mass., 1963—, Mallinckrodt prof. of div., 1969—; trustee Mennonite Bibl. Sem., Elkhart, Ind., 1977-80; bd. dirs. Bethel Coll., Kans., 1964-76. Author: Theology for a Nuclear Age, 1985; Relativism, Knowledge and Faith, 1960; The Context of Decision, 1961; Systematic Theology: A Historical Perspective, 1968, 2d edit., 1978; God the Problem, 1972; An Essay on Theological Method, 1975, rev. edit., 1979; Nonresistance and Responsibility and Other Mennonite Essays, 1979; The Theological Imagination: Constructing the Concept of God, 1981; Theology for a Nuclear Age, 1985. Contbr. articles to profl. jours. Fulbright fellow, 1961-62; Guggenheim fellow, 1969-70; Japan Found. fellow, 1983. Mem. Am. Acad. Religion (pres. 1981-82), Am. Theol. Soc. (pres. 1979-80), Metaphys. Soc. Am., Soc. for Values in Higher Edn. Democrat. Home: 6 Longfellow Rd Cambridge MA 02138 Office: Harvard Div Sch 45 Francis Ave Cambridge MA 02138

KAUFMAN, MONTY LEE, minister, American Lutheran Church; b. Sandusky, Ohio, Nov. 24, 1946; s. Vincent Earl and Janet Louise (Dalton) K.; m. Suzanne Craig Boyd, Aug. 2, 1969; children: Jeremy, Nathan. B.A., Capital U., 1969; M.Div., Evang. Luth. Theol. Sem., Columbus, Ohio, 1973. Ordained to ministry Am. Luth. Ch., 1973. Intern Faith Luth. Ch., Massillon, Ohio, 1970-71; pastor St. John's Luth. Ch., Sidney, Ohio, 1969-73, St. Paul's Luth. Ch., 1973—; camp chaplain Boy Scouts Am., Marion and Morrow Counties, 1978, 79, 80; mem. chaplain Prospect Vol. Fire Dept., Ohio, 1979—; mem. environ. edn. com. Luth. Meml. Camp, Fulton, Ohio, 1980—; mem., chaplain, technician Emergency Med. Services, Prospect, Ohio, 1982—; mem. council N. Central Conf., Ohio Dist., Am. Luth. Ch., 1983—; mem. life and mission in the congregation com. Ohio Dist., Am. Luth. Ch., 1983—. Cub master, dist. chmn. Evergreen dist. Harding Area council Boy Scouts Am., 1977-81. Recipient Dist. award Merit, Boy Scouts Am., 1975, Silver Beaver award, 1981. Mem. Marion Area Luth. Pastors (pres. 1982-84), Marion County Ministerial Assn. (treas. 1983-84), Prospect Ministerial Assn. (chmn. 1979—). Democrat. Lodge: Lions (trustee 1980—). Home: 406 Water St Prospect OH 43342 Office: St Paul's Luth Ch E Water and Elm Sts Prospect OH 43342

KAVANAGH, AIDAN JOSEPH, educator, priest, Roman Catholic Church; b. Mexia, Tex., Apr. 20, 1929; s. Joseph Gerard and Guarrel Dee (Mullens) K.; student U. South, 1947-49; B.A., St. Meinrad Sem., 1956; S.T.L., U. Ottawa, 1958; postgrad. Oxford U., 1960-61; S.T.D., U. Trier, 1963. Joined Order of St. Benedict, 1952, ordained priest Roman Catholic Ch., 1957; prof. St. Meinrad Sem., Ind., 1962-66; prof., dir. Grad. Program in Liturgical Studies, U. Notre Dame, 1966-74, dir. grad. studies in theology, 1970-73; prof. liturgics Div. Sch., Yale, 1974—, acting dir. Yale Inst. Sacred Music, 1974-76, 82-83; corp. mem. Anglican Theol. Rev., 1973-84; dir. Liturg. Conf., 1973-74; asso. editor Worship, 1966—, Studia Liturgica, 1974—; mem. editorial bd. Concilium, 1969—; founder Murphy Center for Liturg. Research U. Notre Dame, 1971. Mem. Am. Benedictine Acad., N.Am. Acad. Liturgy (Berakah award 1976), Guild Religious Architecture (hon.). Author: The Canon Revisions of Thomas Cranmer, 1964; The Shape of Baptism, 1978; Elements of Rite, 1982; On Liturgical Theology, 1984; also essays and articles. Home: 208 Carmalt Rd Hamden CT 06517 Office: 409 Prospect St New Haven CT 06510

KAWASHIMA, MAS, minister, United Methodist Church; b. Yokosuka, Japan, Mar. 12; s. Hideshiro and Tsuma; came to U.S., 1959, naturalized, 1976; B.D., Fuller Theol. Sem., Pasadena, Calif., 1962; Th.M., San Francisco Theol. Sem., 1965; Ph.D., Claremont (Calif.) Grad. Sch., 1974; m. Hope Omachi, June 14, 1964; children—Mariya, Rebekah. Ordained teaching elder, 1964, elder, 1971; pastor Altadena (Calif.) 1st United Presbyn. Ch., 1964-71, Ontario (Oreg.) Community United Meth. Ch., 1972-80; pastor Japanese Am. United Ch. of N.Y., N.Y.C., 1980—. Exec. officer So. Calif. Ministerial Assn., 1966-71; vice chmn. commn. race and religion conf. United Meth. Ch., 1973, chmn. bd. ch. and society, 1974-76, chmn. div. religion and race, 1976; pres. Ministerial Assn. Ontario, 1976; mem. coordinating com. Asian Am. caucus Western Jurisdictional caucus United Meth. Ch., 1974—; chmn. Northeastern jurisdictional caucus United Meth. Asian-Am. Caucus; bd. dirs. Nat. United Meth. Ch. Asian Am. Fedn. Office: 255 7th Ave New York NY 10001

KAY, JIMMY LAMAR, minister, Southern Baptist Convention; b. Jasper, Tex., Sept. 14, 1953; s. Homer L. and Evelyn (Martin) K.; m. Darlene Faye Harrington, July 15, 1972; children: Jason Lamar, Angela Raye. B.S., Lamar U., 1980; M.R.E., Luther Rice Sem., 1982, Ph.D. in Bible Philosophy, 1984. Ordained to ministry Baptist Ch., 1975. Pastor chs. in Tex., 1976—, Mt. Olivet Bapt. Ch., Fred, 1981—; missions devel. dir. New Bethel Bapt. Assn., 1982—, del. to exec. bd., 1981—; chmn. resort mission Sabine Neches Bapt. Area, 1982—. Chaplain, Am. Legion, Jasper, Tex., 1982—, DAV, 1979, Jasper Convalescent Home, 1974-76. Served with USMC, 1972-76; Vietnam. Mem. U.S. Parachute Assn., Harley Owners Group. Republican. Home: PO Box 120 Fred TX 77616

KAY, THOMAS OBED, history educator; b. Geneva, Ill., Dec. 20, 1932; s. Obed S. and Margaret A. (Brown) K.; m. Janice Cave, Apr. 25, 1959; children: Catherine, Robert, John. A.B., Wheaton Coll., 1953; M.A., U. Chgo., 1954, Ph.D., 1974. Prof. history, chmn. dept. Wheaton Coll., Ill., 1978—. Contbr. articles to religious publs. Leader, treas., counsellor, com. mem. Boy Scouts Am., 1980—; chmn., v.p. City Council Nominating Assembly, 1974-78; chmn. Ch. Centennial Program, 1977-78. Mem. Ill. Assn. Advancement of History (pres. 1984), Conf. on Faith and History (bd. dirs. 1984—). Republican. Home: 1319 Irving Wheaton IL 60187 Office: Wheaton Coll Wheaton IL 60187

KAYS, JOHN WESLEY, JR., chaplain, United Meth. Ch.; b. Harrodsburg, Ky., Oct. 9, 1932; s. John Wesley and Lida (Vaught) K.; A.B., Asbury Coll., 1954; M.Div., Louisville Presbyn. Sem., 1961; m. Audra Marie Cooper, Dec. 20, 1953; 1 son, Michael Alan. Ordained to ministry, 1961; pastor Glendale Meth. Ch., 1961-62; chaplain U.S. Army, 1962—, Tex., 1962-64, Europe, 1964-67, Md., 1967-69, Vietnam, 1969-70, N.Y., 1970-71, Ga., 1971-74, Europe, 1974—. Decorated Bronze Star medal, Army commendation medal. Writer, composer hymns Long Ago When Stars of Wonder, 1974, God of Our Nation, 1975. Home: 2619 Meadow Dr Louisville KY 40220 Office: HHC 2nd Bde 3rd Armored Div APO NY 09091

KEALY, ROBERT LOUIS, priest, Roman Cath. Ch.; b. Chgo., Nov. 15, 1946; s. J. Arthur and G. Genevieve (Harris) K.; M.Div., St. Mary of the Lake Sem., 1972, S.T.L., 1971; J.D., DePaul U., 1976. Ordained priest, 1972; asso. pastor St. Germaine Parish, Oak Lawn, Ill., 1972—. Advocate Archdiocesan Met. Tribunal, 1976—; pres. Oak Lawn Cath. Parish Cluster. Mem. Am., Ill. bar assns., Canon Law Soc. Am. Contbr. articles to religious edn. jours. Home: 4240 W 98th St Oak Lawn IL 60453

KEANE, PATRICK JOSEPH, priest, Roman Cath. Ch.; b. Kildysart, County Clare, Ireland, Feb. 7, 1948; s. Patrick John and Margaret Mary (Canny) K.; came to U.S., 1973; student St. Flannan's Coll., Ennis, Ireland, 1962-67, St. Patrick's Coll., Carlow, Ireland, 1967-73. Ordained priest, 1973; asso. pastor St. Edward the Confessor Ch., Metairie, La., 1973—; dir. Cath. Youth Orgn. Archdiocese of New Orleans, 1975—, dir. Office Youth Retreats, 1977—, also youth ministry adviser Office Religious Edn. Chaplain East Jefferson (La.) Fire Dept. Home: 4940 Park Dr Metairie LA 70001 Office: 7887 Walmsley Ave New Orleans LA 70125

KEARNS, WILLIAM PATRICK, minister, Am. Bapt. Chs., U.S.A.; b. Winchester, Ky., Feb. 4, 1934; s. William and Mary Margaret (Ganley) K.; B.A., Bob Jones U., 1956, M.A., 1957, Ph.D., 1960; Th.M., Pitts. Theol. Sem., 1969; postgrad. Eastern Bapt. Theol. Sem., 1976—; m. Janice Evelyn Bolt, Aug. 19, 1955; children—Barbara Lois, Thomas William. Ordained to ministry, 1960; pastor Zion Bapt. Ch., Slippery Rock, Pa., 1960-62, 1st Bapt. Ch., Oil City, Pa., 1962-65, West Newton, Pa., 1965-70; sr. pastor 1st Bapt. Ch., Massillon, Ohio, 1970-75, Van Riper-Ellis Meml. Bapt. Ch., Fair Lawn, N.J., 1975—. Trustee Ohio Bapt. Conv., 1973-74, program chmn., 1974; sec. bd. dirs. Laurel Higlands Camp, Pitts., 1966-69; v.p. ministers council Am. Bapt. Ch. N.J., 1976—, mem. nat. ministers council Am. Bapt. Chs., U.S.A., 1960—. Home: 358 Owen Ave Fair Lawn NJ 07410 Office: River Rd and Morlot Ave Fair Lawn NJ 07410

KEATHLEY, NAYMOND HASKINS, minister, religion educator, Southern Baptist Convention; b. Memphis, Sept. 25, 1940; s. Maurice Franklin and Rubye Geneva (Haskins) K.; m. Carolyn Jeannine Griffin, Aug. 4, 1962; children: Kevin, Craig, Kristen. B.A. cum laude Baylor U., 1962; B.D., So. Bapt. Theol. Sem., 1966, Ph.D., 1971. Ordained to ministry So. Bapt. Conv., 1966. Mgr. Bapt. Book Store, Louisville, 1969-72; asst. prof. religion Palm Beach Atlantic Coll., West Palm Beach, Fla., 1972-76; asst. prof. N.T. Golden Gate Bapt. Theol. Sem., Mill Valley, Calif., 1976-79, assoc. prof. N.T., 1979-81; assoc. prof. Religion Baylor U., Waco, Tex., 1981—. Author Sunday sch. curriculum So. Bapt. Conv., 1976—. Contbr. book revs. to profl. jours. Mem. Soc. Bibl. Lit. and Exegesis, Nat. Assn. Bapt. Profs. of Religion, Alpha Chi. Democrat. Home: 310 Trailwood Dr Waco TX 76710 Office: Baylor U CSB 216 Waco TX 76798

KEATING, JOHN RICHARD, priest, Roman Catholic Church; s. Robert James and Gertrude Helen (Degen) K.; B.A., St. Mary of the Lake Sem., 1955; S.T.L., Gregorian U., Rome, 1959, J.C.D., 1963. Ordained priest, 1958; asst. chancellor Archdiocese of Chgo., 1963-70, co-chancellor, 1970—, mem. clergy personnel bd., 1971—, bd. consultors, 1975—; judge Chgo. Met. Tribunal, 1968—; ordained bishop of Arlington, 1983. Cons. canon law com. Nat. Conf. Cath. Bishops, 1969—; mem. Chgo. Presbyteral Senate, 1972—. Mem. com. on human subjects ADA, 1976—. Mem. Am., Canadian canon law socs. Author: The Bearing of Mental Impairment on the Validity of Marriage, 1964, 2d edit., 1973; also articles. Office: 200 Glebe Rd Suite 704 Arlington VA 22203*

KECK, BENNY EDSEL, minister, Southern Baptist Convention; b. Knoxville, Tenn., Oct. 16, 1953; s. Troy Edsel and Ruby Helen (Johnson) K.; m. Melody Ann Allsup, Aug. 4, 1979; children: John Mark, Elissa Hope. A.S., Walters State Community Coll., Morristown, Tenn., 1973; B.S., Carson-Newman Coll., Jefferson City, Tenn., 1976; M.Div., So. Bapt. Theol. Sem., Louisville, 1982. Ordained to ministry So. Bapt. Conv., 1977; pastor Leadvale Bapt. Ch., White Pine, Tenn., 1976-79, Lynn Acres Bapt. Ch., Louisville, 1980-84, Nat. Ave. Bapt. Ch., Memphis, 1984—. Home: 3637

Hazelwood Memphis TN 38122 Office: 1348 National St Memphis TN 38122

KECK, LEANDER EARL, educator, minister; b. Washburn, N.D., Mar. 3, 1928; s. Jacob J. and Elizabeth E. (Klein) K.; B.A., Linfield Coll., 1945; B.D., Andover Newton Theol. Sch., 1953; postgrad. U. Kiel (Germany), 1955-56, U. Göttingen (Germany), 1956; Ph.D., Yale, 1957; post-doctoral studies U. Tübingen (Germany), 1964-65, U. Cambridge (Eng.), 1971, 76; m. Janice Lee Osburn, Sept. 7, 1956; children—Stephen, David. Ordained to ministry Christian Ch., 1952; instr. Bibl. history Wellesley Coll., 1957-59; from asst. prof. to prof. Vanderbilt Div. Sch., 1959-72; prof. N.T., Emory U., Atlanta, 1972, chmn. div. religion Grad. Sch.; now prof., dean Yale U. Div. Sch.; vis. prof. Union Theol. Sem., Manila, P.I., 1971. Author: Taking the Bible Seriously, 1962; Mandate to Witness, 1964; A Future for the Historical Jesus, 1971; editor, transl.: David Friedrich Strauss: The Christ of Faith and The Jesus of History, 1976; editor: (with J.L. Martyn) Studies in Luke-Acts (Paul S. Festschrift), 1966; monograph series Soc. Bibl. Lit.; series editor Lives of Jesus; contbr. articles to profl. jours. Office: Yale U Div Sch 409 Prospect St New Haven CT 06510*

KECKLEY, E. WELDON, minister, Christian Church (Disciples Christ); b. Licking County, Ohio, Jan. 8, 1921; s. Arthur Carl and Mae Deborah (Hoover) K.; A.B., Bethany Coll., W.Va., 1943; M.Div., Yale, 1946; M.A., Washington U., St. Louis, 1951; D.Div., Piedmont Coll., Demorest, Ga., 1977; m. Betty Marion McIntyre, Aug. 27, 1944; 1 son, Thomas Weldon. Ordained to ministry, 1942; minister edn. Union Ave. Christian Ch., St. Louis, 1946-49, Country Club Christian Ch., Kansas City, Mo., 1949-53; sr. minister 1st Community Ch., Joplin, Mo., 1953-60, Bethany Union Ch., Chgo., 1960-85. Mem. adj. faculty Bethany Theol. Sem., Oak Brook, Ill.; co-founder, dir. Beverly Hills/Morgan Park Protestant Cluster, Chgo.; observer, mem. exec. com., del. Consultation Ch. Union; rep. Nat. Council Community Chs. to Vatican Ecumenical Council II, Rome, 1963; pres. Nat. Council Community Chs., 1962-64. Mem. Inst. Humane Studies (Midwest dir. 1985—), Phi Delta Kappa, Kappa Delta Pi. Author: The Church School Superintendant, 1961. Home: PO Box 1822 Tabor Woods Joplin MO 64802

KEE, HOWARD CLARK, religion educator; b. Beverly, N.J., July 28, 1920; s. Walter Leslie and Regina (Corcoran) K.; m. Janet Burrell, Dec. 15, 1951; children: Howard Clark III, Christopher Andrew, Sarah Leslie. A.B., Bryan Coll., 1940; Th.M., Dallas Theol. Sem., 1944; postgrad. Am. Sch. Oriental Research, Jerusalem, 1949-50; Ph.D., Yale U., 1951. Instr. religion, classics U. Pa., 1951-53; from asst. prof. to prof. N.T. Drew U., 1953-68; Rufus Jones prof. history of religion, chmn. dept. Bryn Mawr Coll., Pa., 1968-77; William Goodwin Aurelio prof. bibl. studies, chmn. grad. div. religious studies Boston U., 1977—; vis. prof. religion Princeton U., 1954-55; mem. archaeol. teams, Roman Jericho, 1950, Shechem, 1957, Mt. Gerizim, 1966, Pella, Jordan, 1967, Ashdod, Israel, 1968; chmn. Council on Grad. Studies in Religion. Author: Understanding the New Testament, 4th edit., 1983; Making Ethical Decisions, 1958; The Renewal of Hope, 1959; Jesus and God's New People, 1959; Jesus in History, 1970, 2d edit., 1977; The Origins of Christianity - Sources and Documents, 1973; Christianity - An Historical Approach, 1979; Miracles in the Early Christian World, 1983; The New Testament in Context - Sources and Documents, 1984; others. Editor: Biblical Perspectives on Current Issues, 1976—. Librettist: New Land, New Covenant (Howard Hanson), 1976. Contbr.: Interpreter's Dictionary of the Bible, 1962, supplement, 1976. Bd. dirs. Mohawk Trail Concerts, Charlemont, Mass.; mem. adv. bd. Yale U. Inst. Sacred Music. Fellow Am. Assn. Theol. Schs., W. Ger., 1960, Two Bros., Guggenheim Found., Israel, 1966-67; NEH grantee, Eng., 1984. Mem. Am. Bible Soc. (bd. mgrs. 1956, chmn. transls. com.), Soc. Values in Higher Edn., Am. Acad. Religion, Soc. Bibl. Lit., Bibl. Theologians, Studiorum Novi Testamenti Societas, New Haven Theol. Discussion Group. Presbyterian. Office: Dept Religion Boston U 745 Commonwealth Ave Boston MA 02215*

KEEFE, ALLEN ELIAS, church music administrator, minister, Church of God; b. Everett, Wash., Sept. 5, 1926; s. James and Margaret Viola (Ferdon) K.; student Warner Pacific Coll., 1945-48, 55-56; m. Charlotte Ann Corey, May 27, 1955; 1 child, Jeffrey Allen. Ordained to ministry Ch. of God, 1964; music dir. Ch. of God, Portland, Oreg., 1948; pastor First Ch. of God, Aberdeen, S.D., 1963-68; secular employment, 1968-73; music dir. Ch. of God., Everett, Wash., 1970—; pastor 1st Ch. of God, Grants Pass, Oreg., 1976—; minister of music Medford Ch. of God, Oreg., 1983—. Performer Rogue Valley Opera; mem. Rogue Valley Opera Assn. Mem. Western Wash. Assn. Ch. of God, Assn. Chs. of God of Oreg. Home: 1401 NE Ridge Rd Grants Pass OR 97526

KEELER, CHARLES JOHN, minister, Evangelical Lutheran Synod; b. Graceville, Minn., July 21, 1947; s. John Vernon and Lois Dorothea (Meers) K.; m. Yvonne Ardelle Peterson, Feb. 11, 1973. B.A., U. Minn. Mpls., 1970; M.A., Bethany Theol. Sem., 1977. Ordained to ministry, 1977. Pastor, Oklee Trail Parish, Minn., 1977-82, Immanuel Luth. Ch., Audubon, Minn., 1982—; sec. Bd. Edn. and Youth, 1982-84; seminar leader Youth Leadership Seminar, Mankato, 1984; camp chaplain Camp Indianhead, Brainerd, Minn., 1978—. Del. Republican Party County Conv., 1978. Served with U.S. Army, 1970-73. Home: Rural Route 1 Audubon MN 56511

KEELER, JACK EDWARD, clergyman, Lutheran Church in America; b. Bethlehem, Pa., Apr. 15, 1944; s. George Harold and Elizabeth Jenny (Fuge) K.; m. Marilyn Llewellyn Pritchard, May 23, 1967; children: Jonathan David, Erin Elizabeth, Stephanie Ann. B.A., Kutztown U., 1967; M.Div., Gettysburg Sem., 1971; M.A., Marywood Coll., 1978. Ordained to ministry, 1971. Asst. pastor Our Saviour Luth. Ch., Temple Hills, Md., 1971-72; pastor St. John Luth. Ch., Nanticoke, Pa., 1972-78, Christ's United Luth. Ch., Millmont, Pa., 1980—; musician Buffalo Valley Singers, Mifflinburg, 1980—; clin. pastor edn. com. Lancaster Gen. Hosp., Pa., summer 1969; chaplain Leader Nursing Rehab. Ctr., Sunbury, Pa., 1983-84; mem. Mifflinburg Ministerium, 1980-84; evangelism cons. Central Pa. Synod, 1984—. Recipient Silver Cross, Trinity Episcopal Ch., 1956; Order of Arrow, Boy Scouts Am., 1984. Mem. Nat. Music Frat., Smithsonian Assocs. Republican. Home: Rural Route 1 Box 277 Mifflinburg PA 17844 Office: Christs United Luth Ch Rural Route 1 Millmont PA 17845

KEELER, WILLIAM HENRY, church official, Roman Catholic Church; b. San Antonio, Mar. 4, 1931; s. Thomas Love and Margaret Theresa (Conway) K.; A.B., St. Charles Sem., Phila., 1952; S.T.L., Gregorian U., Rome, 1956, J.C.D., 1961. Ordained priest Roman Catholic Ch., 1955, named papal chamberlain, 1965, prelate of honor, 1970; sec. to tribunal Diocese of Harrisburg, 1956-58, defender of the bond, 1961-66, also peritus 2d Vatican Council, 1962-65; pastor Our Lady of Good Counsel Ch., Marysville, Pa., 1964-65; vice chancellor Diocese of Harrisburg, 1965-69, chancellor, 1969—; exec. sec. Diocesan Ecumenical Commn., 1966-70. Mem. Diocesan Consultors of Diocese of Harrisburg, 1969—, council adminstrn., 1969—; mission bd., 1969—, planning adv. bd., 1973—, ecumenical commn., 1966—; mem. Pa. Conf. Inter-Ch. Cooperation, 1973—; mem. adminstrv. bd. Pa. Cath. Conf., 1970—. Bd. dirs. Holy Spirit Hosp., Camp Hill, Pa., 1975—, Harrisburg chpt. ARC, 1969—. Mem. Canon Law Soc. Am., Am. Cath. Hist. Assn. Office: 4800 Union Deposit Rd PO Box 2153 Harrisburg PA 17105

KEELER, WILLIAM OSBORNE, minister, United Church of Christ; b. Canton, Ohio, Apr. 22, 1917; s. Lawrence Cleator and Lena Frances (Reichenbaugh) K.; m. Geraldine K. Kennedy, Sept. 16, 1942; 1 child, Nancy Ellen Carney. B.A. summa cum laude, Mt. Union Coll., 1939; B.D., M.Div., Eden Theol. Sem., 1942; M.A. in Guidance and Counseling, Bowling Green State U., 1956; D.Min., Eden Theol. Sem., 1982. Ordained to ministry United Ch. of Christ, 1942. Asst. pastor Trinity United Ch. Christ, Canton, Ohio, 1942-45; pastor Grace United Ch. Christ, Massillon, Ohio, 1945-53, 1st Grace United Ch. Christ, Fostoria, Ohio, 1953-57, St. John's United Ch. Christ, Coshocton, Ohio, 1957-65, Mt. Olivet United Ch. Christ, North Lima, Ohio, 1965-82; interim pastor Coshocton, 1982-83, St. John's United Ch. Christ, Strasburg, Ohio, 1984—; v.p. East Ohio Classis, Canton, 1960-61; moderator E. Ohio assn. United Ch. Christ, 1971, trustee Ohio conf., 1969-71, del. to gen. synod, 5 times. Formerly active YMCA, Am. Cancer Soc., mental health and social work areas. Mem. Acad. Parish Clergy. Home: 12682 Freedom Rd Kimbolton OH 43749

KEENEY, WILLIAM ECHARD, minister, General Conference Mennonite Church; b. Fayette County, Pa., July 17, 1922; s. William Leroy and Kathryn Olive (Echard) K.; m. Willadene Hartzler, Oct. 12, 1947; children: Lois Ruth, Carol Louise, William Leroy, Richard Lowell. A.B., Bluffton Coll., 1948; B.D., Bethany and Mennonite Bibl. Sem., 1953; S.T.M., Hartford Theol. Sem., 1957, Ph.D., 1959. Ordained to ministry, 1953. Asst. to pres. Bluffton Coll., Ohio, 1953-56, prof. Bible, 1956-68; acad. dean Bethel Coll., North Newton, Kans., 1968-71, provost, 1972-73, prof. Bible/Peace studies, 1968-80; interim and/or part-time pastor various chs., Kans. and Ohio, 1965-67, 73-75; vis. prof. integrative change Kent State U., Ctr. for Peaceful Change, Ohio, 1980—; relief worker Mennonite Central Conf., Ger., 1948-49, dir. Netherlands program, 1949-50, rep., 1961-63, peace sect. study sec. 1973-74; mem. Gen. Conf. Mennonite Ch. com. on peace and social concerns, 1963-69, mem. reference council for peace social concerns, 1969-71, chmn. peace sect., 1963-73; chmn. Assoc. Colls. Central Kans. Acad. Deans, 1969-73; bd. dirs. Leadership Inc., Newton, Kans., 1971-73. Author: The Development of Dutch Anabaptist Thought and Practice from 1539-1564, 1968; Lordship as Servanthood, 1975; contbr. articles to profl. jours., chpts. to books. Chmn., Harvey County Edn. Action Council, 1976-80; adv. council Self-Directed Profl. Devel. Program, Prairie View Mental Health Ct., 1976-80; mem. del. in dialogue for reconciliation to Teheran, Iran, 1980; co-chmn. Kent Ecumenical Peace Group, 1983—. Hartzler fellow Hartford Theol. Sem., 1956-58. Mem. Consortium on Peace Research, Edn. and Devel. (exec. dir. 1978-84), Internat. Studies Assn., Faith and History Soc. Democrat. Home: 826 Mae St Kent OH 44240 Office: Center for Peaceful Change Kent State U Kent OH 44242

KEES, JOHN CARL, minister, United Methodist Church. B. Nanty-Glo, Pa., Dec. 14, 1940; s. Francis McClure and Lorna Blanche (Sykes) K.; m. Pamela Helene Southerland, Nov. 28, 1964; children: Cheri, Jeffrey, Peter, Linda. A.B., Dartmouth Coll., 1962; M.Div., Meth. Theol. Sch. Ohio, 1969; D.Min., Drew Coll., 1981. Ordained to ministry United Meth. Ch., 1970. Pastor Grace United Meth. Ch., Tacoma, Wash., 1969-71; assoc. pastor Homestead Park United Meth. Ch., Munhall, Pa., 1971-78; pastor Center Ave. United Meth. Ch., Pitcaim, Pa., 1978-83; Crafton United Meth. Ch., Pa., 1983—; chmn. nominating com. Western Pa. Conf. United Meth. Ch., Pitts., 1983—; chaplain Munhall Fire Dept., Pa., 1975-78. Fireman Munhall Vol. Fire Dept., 1972-78, Pitcairn Vol. Fire Dept., 1978-83. Served to lt. (j.g.) USN, 1962-66. Mem. Crafton/Ingram Ministerial Assn. Lodge: Rotary. Home: 85 Belvidere St Pittsburgh PA 15205 Office: Crafton United Meth Ch 43 Belvidere St Pittsburgh PA 15205

KEFFER, DOUGLAS FOSTER CLARK, minister, Independent Church of Christ; b. Connellsville, Pa., July 12, 1951; s. Joseph Louis and Iola Pearl (Welling) K.; m. Dana Louise Butterworth, Mar. 20, 1972; children: Robert Douglas, Matthew Louis. B.S., Roanoke Bible Coll., N.C., 1973. Ordained minister Independent Church of Christ. Minister, Central Point Christian Ch., Waynesboro, Va., 1973-75, Gt. Bridge Christian Ch., Va., 1975-78, Falls Mills Christian Ch., Va., 1978-81, West Side Ch. of Christ, South Bend, Ind., 1981—; sec. Michiana Ministers Assn., South Bend, 1982-84, pres., 1984-85; marriage prep. com. United Religious Community, South Bend, 1983—. Parent rep. South Bend Sch. Corp., 1984—. Avocations: reading; biking; swimming; softball; basketball. Home: 22959 W Edison Rd South Bend IN 46628 Office: West Side Ch of Christ 22987 W Edison Rd South Bend IN 46628

KEGLER, MAYNARD CLEMENS, priest, Roman Cath. Ch.; b. Glencoe, Minn., Nov. 26, 1924; s. Louis Ferdinand and Elizabeth Frances (Artmann) K.; student St. Henry's Sem., 1938-44, U. Ottawa (Can.), 1945-51. Novitiate Oblate Mary Immaculate, 1944-45; ordained priest, 1951; tchr. St. Henry's Sem., Belleville, Ill., 1951-55; pastor Veblen, S.D., 1955-56, Orient, S.D., 1956-57; preacher Oblate Mission Band, through U.S., Can., Europe, 1957-67; dir. King's House of Retreats, Austin, Minn., 1967-69, Buffalo, Minn., 1969—. Dir., pastoral tng. program, St. Paul, 1963-67; promoter Cause Dr. Thomas Dooley, 1974—. Pres., Wright County (Minn.) Arts Assn., 1974, 75. Recipient Palladin Cross, Cath. Mission Crusade, 1953, Gold Cross Jerusalem, Protectorate of Holy Land, 1972. Home and Office: 621 S 1st Ave Buffalo MN 55313

KEHRES, DONALD WAYNE, minister, Lutheran Church in America; b. Homestead, Pa., Oct. 17, 1951; s. Paul William and Dorothy Virginia (Pesch) K.; m. Ruth Ellen Dumroese, June 24, 1972; 1 dau., Jennifer Collette. B.A., Concordia Tchrs. Coll., River Forest, Ill., 1973; M.Div., Luth. Sch. Theology, 1980. Ordained to ministry Lutheran Church in America, 1980. Pastor Prince of Peace Luth. Ch., Grandview, Mo., 1980—; pres. Grandview Ch. Alliance, 1981-83. Bd. dirs. Community Services League, Independence, Mo., 1983—. Democrat. Lodge: Kiwanis (pres. 1984-85). Home: 13001 Crystal St Grandview MO 64030 Office: Prince of Peace Luth Ch 13031 Winchester Ave Grandview MO 64030

KEILLER, JAMES BRUCE, minister, educator, International Pentecostal Church of Christ; b. Racine, Wis., Nov. 21, 1938; s. James Allen and Grace (Modder) K.; diploma in Bible, Beulah Heights Bible Coll., Atlanta, 1957; B.A., William Carter Coll., Goldsboro, N.C., 1963, Ed.D. (hon.), 1973; LL.B., Blackstone Sch. Law, 1964; M.A., Evang. Theol. Sem., Goldsboro, 1965, B.D., 1966, Th.D., 1968; M.A. in Ednl. Adminstrn., Atlanta U., 1977; postgrad. Ga. State U.; m. Darsel Lee Bundy, Feb. 8, 1959; 1 child, Susanne Elizabeth. Ordained to ministry, 1957; pastor chs. in Mass. and Mich., 1957-64; nat. youth and Sunday sch. dir. Internat. Pentecostal Assemblies, 1958-64, dir. world missions, 1964-77; global missions dir. Internat. Pentecostal Ch. of Christ, 1976—, mem. exec. com., 1976—. v.p., acad. dean Beulah Heights Bible Coll., 1964—, also trustee. Mem. exec. bd. Mt. Paran

Christian Sch.; exec. sec. So. Accrediting Assn. Bible Colls.; mem. Republican Presdl. Task Force, Nat. Rep. Senatorial Com.; mem. pubs. com. Moral Majority Found. Named Alumnus of Year, William Carter Coll., 1965. Mem. Evang. Theol. Soc., Acad. Polit. Sci., So. Ctr. Internat. Studies, Ga. Council Notaries Pub., Am. Tax Reduction Movement, Ind. Order Foresters, Woodmen of World. Address: 892 Berne St SE PO Box 18145 Atlanta GA 30316

KEIPER, ALLEN STEWART, minister, Methodist Ch.; b. Phila., Apr. 10, 1930; s. Stewart Ben and Alice Dorothy (Raws) K.; B.A. in Bible, Phila. Coll. Bible, 1954-58; S.T.B., Boston U., 1959-62; B.A. in History, Houghton Coll., 1965; M.Div., Colgate Rochester U., 1971; m. Nancy Jane Jones, June 15, 1957; children—Allen Stewart, James W. Ordained to ministry Meth. Ch., as deacon, 1960, elder, 1963; minister chs., Locke, N.Y., 1958-62, Angelica, N.Y., 1962-65, Warren's Corners United Meth. Ch., 1965-71, United Meth. Ch., Attica, N.Y., 1971—. Chmn. Western N.Y. Bd. Evangelism, Attica, 1971-74; dist. sec. Batavia Dist., 1971—, dist. treas. program council, 1972—; dist. registrar Bd. Ministry, 1972—. Pres., Chmn. Area Interfaith Ministry, 1972—, Letcheworth Area Ministerial Assn., 1973-74; sec.-treas. Attica Clergy Assn., 1972—. Home: 19 North View Park Attica NY 14011 Office: 75 Main St Attica NY 14011

KEISER, JON NOBLE, minister, Lutheran Church in America; b. Syracuse, N.Y., May 5, 1948; s. Victor Noble and Florence Marguerite (Reussow) K.; m. Dorothy Jean Hayes, Aug. 24, 1975; children: Sonja Lee, Richard Noble, Jodi Lorraine. A.A. in Physics, U. Fla., 1968; B.A. in History, U. Central Fla., 1970; M.Div., Luth. Theol. Sem., 1979. Ordained to ministry, 1979. Pastor, First Luth. Ch., Brooksville, Fla., 1979-83, Gethesemane Luth. Ch., Gainesville, 1983—; mem. task force clergy compensation Fla. Synod, Luth. Ch. Am., Tampa, Fla., 1982—, chmn. peace task force, 1984—, dist. dean, Gainesville, 1984—. Contbr. articles to profl. jours. Lodge: Kiwanis. Democrat. Home: 6512 NW 31st Ter Gainesville FL 32606 Office: Gethesemane Luth Ch 1220 NE 23d Ave Gainesville FL 32609

KEITH, CURTIS LLOYD, JR., minister, Disciples of Christ Church; b. Houston, May 29, 1939; s. Curtis Lloyd and Mary Lee (McBrayer) K.; m. Barbara Jeanne Arneson, July 31, 1958; children: Matthew Dwayne, Deborah Layne, Timothy Wayne, Curtis Lloyd III. B.A., Tex. Christian U., 1961, B.Div., 1963, M.Th., 1968, D.Min., 1978. Ordained to ministry Disciples of Christ Ch., 1963. Minister, Central Christian Ch., Childress, Tex., 1963-66, 1st Christian Ch., Lancaster, Tex., 1966-69, 1st Christian Ch., Brownwood, Tex., 1969-75; sr. minister 1st Christian Ch., Lufkin, Tex., 1975—; bd. dirs. Christian Ch. in Southwest, 1972-75; mem. ch. adv. bd. Tex. Dept. Human Resources, 1982-85; chaplain Lufkin High Sch. Panthers, 1983-85. Founder, Lifeline of Lufkin, 1982 (commendation 1983); chmn. Child Welfare Bd., Brownwood, 1972; pres. Workshop and Opportunity Ctr., Lufkin, 1982-83; mem. exec. bd. United Way, Lufkin, 1984-85. Named Most Outstanding Man under 35, Brownwood C. of C., 1974; recipient commendation for ministry with elderly, Tex. Dept. Human Resources, 1983. Mem. Angelina County Ministerial Alliance (pres. Lufkin 1978-79), Angelina County C. of C. Lodge: Kiwanis (pres. Brownwood 1972-73, lt. gov. Tex.-Okla. Dist. 1974-75, dist. chmn. 1975-78, Disting. Community Service award 1973). Home: 210 Lavan Lufkin TX 75901 Office: 1st Christian Ch 1300 S First St Lufkin TX 75901

KELEHER, JAMES P., bishop, Roman Catholic Church. Bishop of Bellerville, Ill., 1984—. Office: 220 Lincoln St Bellerville IL 62221*

KELLAWAY, JAMES LOWELL, priest, Episcopal Church; b. Amityville, N.Y., July 26, 1950; s. James Frederick and Helen (Resch) K.; m. Genevieve Doran, Nov. 24, 1979; 1 child, Molly McNeill. B.A., Colgate U., 1972; M.Div., Episcopal Div. Sch., 1977. Ordained to ministry Episcopal Ch., 1978. Asst. chaplain UCLA, Los Angeles, 1975-76; asst. Christ Ch., Greenwich, Conn., 1977-81, dir. lay ministries, 1982-83; rector Christ Ch., Fairmont, W.Va., 1983—; mem. commn. lay ministry Diocese W.Va., Charleston, 1983—; staff counselor Fairmont Family Practice, 1984—. Bd. dirs. Stepping Home For Boys, Fairmont, 1983—; community adv. bd. Jr. League, Fairmont, 1983—. Mem. Internat. Transactional Analysis Assn., Episcopal Div. Sch. Alumni Assn. (exec. com. 1977-80). Democrat. Lodges: Kiwanis (bd. dirs. 1979-83), Rotary. Office: Christ Episcopal Ch 405 Fairmont Ave Fairmont WV 26554

KELLEHER, SISTER MARY ANNUNCIATA, nun, hospital adminstr., Roman Cath. Ch.; b. Buffalo, Apr. 4, 1926; d. James and Julia Marie (Hyde) Kelleher; R.N., Mercy Hosp. Sch. Nursing, 1948; B.S., D'Youville Coll., 1958. Entered Religious Sisters of Mercy, Roman Catholic Ch., 1949; sch. tchr., Buffalo, 1949-51; mem. staff St. Jerome Hosp., Buffalo, 1952-54, Kenmore (N.Y.) Mercy Hosp., 1954-66; mem. staff Mercy Hosp., Buffalo, 1966-68, adminstr., 1968-76. Gen. Council Congregation, Buffalo, 1972-76; superior gen. Sisters of Mercy, Buffalo, 1976-84; pres. Mercy Health Systems of Western N.Y., Kenmore, 1984—. Bd. dirs. Kenmore Mercy Hosp., 1970—, St. Jerome Hosp., 1970—, Mercy Hosp., Buffalo, 1967—, Trocaire Coll., Buffalo, 1967-84; mem. adv. com. nursing curriculum Erie (N.Y.) Community Coll., 1969-82. Mem. Am. Coll. Hosp. Adminstrs., Western N.Y. Hosp. Assn. (dir. 1972-74), Cath. Health Assn. Address: Mercy Health Systems 2950 Elmwood Ave Kenmore NY 14217

KELLER, JOHN EUGENE, minister, American Lutheran Church; b. Jamestown, N.D., Apr. 23, 1924; s. Walter William and Bertha (Sackman) K.; m. Doris Weltha Kumpf, Sept. 7, 1946; children: David John, Phillip James, Joel Thomas. B.A., Wartburg Coll., 1945; M.Div., Wartburg Sem., 1947. Ordained to ministry Lutheran Ch., 1947. Minister, parishes, Medina, N.D., Sioux Falls, S.D., Palatine, Ill., 1947-55; specialized ministry in alcoholism, 1955—; chaplain, counselor Luth. Social Services Minn., 1955-63; chaplain Luth. Gen. Hosp. Alcoholism Services, Park Ridge, Ill., 1963-69, adminstrv. dir. Alcoholism Treatment Ctr., 1969-77; pres. Operation Cork, The Kroc Found., San Diego, 1977-80; pres. Luth. Ctr. for Substance Abuse, Park Ridge, 1980-82; chmn., chief clin. officer Parkside Med. Services, Park Ridge, 1982—; pres. Parkside Alcoholism Research Found., 1984—; mem. faculty Rutgers Summer Sch. Alcohol Studies, 1958-73, Internat. Summer Sch. Alcohol Studies, Univ. N.D., 1957-83; lectr. in field; chmn. ethics com. Nat. Assn. Alcoholism Treatment Programs, Los Angeles, 1984—. Author: Ministering to Alcoholics, 1966; Drinking Problem?, 1971; Alcohol: A Family Affair, 1977; Let Go, Let God, 1985. Mem. Citizens Adv. Council on Alcoholism, Ill., 1979-80, bd. regents Wartburg Coll., Waverly, Ia., 1977—. Recipient Alumni Citation Wartburg Coll. Alumni Assn., 1968, Loehe award Wartburg Sem., 1979. Fellow Coll. of Alcoholism Treatment Adminstrs. (charter mem.). Home: 2 Wiscasset on Auburn Rolling Meadows IL 60008 Office: Parkside Med Services 205 W Touhy St Park Ridge IL 60068

KELLER, JOHN FREDERICK, minister, Southern Baptist Convention; b. Marianna, Fla., Mar. 23, 1949; s. William Fred and Ruth Elizabeth (Cox) K.; m. Beverly Ann Leonard, June 1, 1969; children: Kimberly, Gray. B.S., U. Tenn.-Knoxville, 1971; Th.M., Mid Am. Bapt. Theol. Sem., 1976. Ordained to ministry, 1971. Pastor, Sylvan Hill Bapt. Ch., Little Rock, 1972-74, Calvary Bapt. Ch., Bristol, Tenn., 1974-78, Delaney St. Bapt. Ch., Orlando, Fla., 1978-81, First Bapt. Ch., Texarkana, Tex., 1981—. Home: 6013 Pleasant Ln Texarkana TX 75503 Office: First Bapt Ch 401 Pine St Texarkana TX 75501

KELLER, STEPHEN ANDERSON, minister, American Baptist Churches in the U.S.A.; b. Oak Park, Ill., Jan. 26, 1948; s. Arthur Bernheart and Mary Ann (Ballard) K.; m. Lynise Eileen Millican, May 25; children: Seth Millican, Mara LyAnn, Kirstie Denise. B.A., Ottawa U., 1972; M.R.E., Central Bapt. Theol. Sem., 1978, M.Div., 1981. Ordained to ministry American Baptist Churches in the U.S.A., 1981. Asst. to dir. Henry Croes Youth Camp, Clark, Colo., 1981; home missionary Pueblo Bapt. Union, Colo., 1981-82; pastor, organizer Porter-Lake Am. Bapt. Fellowship, Valparaiso, Ind., 1982—; tchr. prison fellowship Westville Corrections Facility, Ind., 1982-84. An organizer Parents Anonymous Porter County, 1983; vol. worker Contact Cares, Merrillville, Ind., 1983—. Mem. Minister Council Am. Baptist Chs. Republican. Club: Lions (Valparaiso). Home and Office: 2208 Flemming Rd Valparaiso IN 46383

KELLER, WILLIAM CAREY, minister, Independent Evangelical Ch., b. Muncie, Ind., Feb. 21, 1918; s. Charles Willard and Wilda May (Crow) K.; m. E. Irene Kaster, Feb. 13, 1938; children: Martha Sue, Harold Lloyd, David Earl, Paul Louis, Donald Eugene, William Carey Jr. B.Th., Olivet Nazarene Coll., 1953. Pastor Ch. of Nazarene, Kankakee, Ill., 1944-46, Momence, Ill., 1946-52, evangelist, Muncie, 1952-69; pres. Delaware County Evangelistic Assn., Muncie, 1969—; treas. Christian Ministries, Muncie, 1978-80; participant Amsterdam Conf., 1983, exec. dir. World Wide Pictures, Delaware County, 1972—; voting mem. Nat. Assn. Evangelicals, 1978—. Charter mem. Republican Presdl. Task Force, 1985; treas. Action Inc., Muncie, 1982—; vol. probation officer, Delaware County, 1981—. Avocation: gardening. Home: 5001 W Hessler Rd Muncie IN 47302 Office: Delaware County Evangelistic Assn 5101 W Hessler PO 2564 Muncie IN 47302

KELLEY, ALOYSIUS PAUL See *Who's Who in America*, 43rd edition.

KELLEY, CHARLES S., JR., minister, religious educator, Southern Baptist Convention; b. Beaumont, Tex., July 27, 1952; s. Charles S. and Doris W. Kelley; m. Rhonda Joyce Harrington, June 21, 1974. B.A. Baylor U., 1974; M.Div., New Orleans Bapt. Theol. Sem., 1978, Th.D., 1983. Ordained to ministry, 1972. Asst. dir. Bapt. Student Union, Baylor U., Waco, Tex. 1972-75; outreach minister Ministry of Bob Harrington Inc., New Orleans, 1975-76; pres. Innovative Evangelism, New Orleans, 1977—; asst. prof evangelism New Orleans Bapt. Theol. Sem., 1983—; mem. Conf. So. Bapt. Evangelists. Office: New Orleans Bapt Theol Sem 3939 Gentilly Blvd New Orleans LA 70126

KELLEY, CURTIS AMON, JR., minister, Southern Baptist Convention, religious organization executive; b. Aliceville, Ala., Feb. 11, 1933; s. Curtis Amon and Ruth Catherine (Sellers) K.; B.A., Tenn. Temple Coll., 1959; m. Barbara Louise Duke, Aug. 7, 1955; children—Curtis Mark, Krista Louise, Matthew James. Ordained to ministry, 1951; pres., Evangelists Club, Temple Coll. Chattanooga, Tenn., 1953-54; pres. Tuscaloosa (Ala.) Bapt. Pastors Conf., 1961-62, Tuscaloosa Evang. Ministers Assn., 1971-72; participant overseas mission projects; chmn. missions com. Tuscaloosa County Bapt. Assn. Home: 118 Hargrove Rd Tuscaloosa AL 35401 Office: Suite 2 Princeton Heights Tuscaloosa AL 35401

KELLEY, ELDRED LEE, minister, Evangelical Free Church of America; b. Cass City, Mich., Aug. 25, 1944; s. Warren Arthur and Ruth Marion (Tuckey) K.; m. Luanne Vanderkarr, June 11, 1965; children: Douglas Warren, Michael Wayne. Diploma Am Floral Art Chgo., 1962; B.A., Spring Arbor Coll., 1966; M.Div. Asbury Theol. Sem., 1973, now postgrad. Ordained to ministry Evangelical Free Ch. of America, 1983. Pastor Ames United Meth. Ch., Saginaw, Mich., 1971-74 Salem United Meth. Ch., Cass City, Mich., 1974-83 founding pastor Evang. Free Ch., Cass City, 1983—; v.p., trustee Romeo Camps, Mich., 1971—; founder Area Men's Prayer Breakfast, Cass City, 1977—; trustee Bay Shore Camp, Sebewaing, Mich., 1981-83, Century House Found., Elizabethtown, Ky., 1981—. Founder Grief Recovery Program, Cass City, 1985; trustee Allen Home Care, Cass City, 1984—. Mem. Nat. Ministerial Assn., Area Ministerial Assn. (pres. and treas. 1974-85) Mich. Farm Bur. Republican. Avocations: fishing; hunting; woodworking. Home: 6317 Houghton St Cass City MI 48726 Office: Evang Free Ch 4533 Weaver Cass City MI 48726

KELLEY, FRANCIS H., priest, Roman Catholic Church. b. Boston, Sept. 9, 1941; s. Francis James and Margaret Elizabeth (Reid) K. A.B. in History, Holy Cross Coll., 1963; student St. John's Sem., 1963-68 M.A. in Pastoral Theology, Notre Dame U., 1976 Ordained priest Roman Catholic Ch., 1968. Assoc pastor St. Ambrose Parish, Dorchester, Mass., 1968-75 St. John's Parish, Peabody, Mass., 1976-83; team ministry St. Boniface Parish, Quincy, Mass., 1983—; cons. Ctr. Pastoral and Social Ministry U. Notre Dame South Bend, Ind., 1976-82; participant Yr. of Learning Archdiocese of Boston, 1977-78; pres. Pine St. Inn, Inc. Boston, 1970—. Contbr. articles to religious jours Chmn. Dorchester House Health Ctr., 1973-74 Address: St Boniface Parish 26 Shed St Quincy MA 02169

KELLEY, FRANK, priest, Episcopal Ch.; b. Bingham Canyon, Utah, Sept. 9, 1914; s. Franklin Thomas and Juanita (Vorhees) K.; A.B., U. Calif. at Berkeley, 1938 postgrad. Bloy House Sem., Los Angeles, 1957-60; m. Doris Patricia Hampton, Sept. 17, 1937 children—Donald Lawrence, Patrick Clark, Jean Arlene (Mrs. Richard Billheimer). Ordained priest 1960; vicar, Chapel St. Francis, Los Angeles, 1960—; rector St. Athanasius' Episcopal Ch., Los Angeles 1968—. Dir. stewardship Los Angeles, 1962-65 chaplain Monte Sano Hosp., Diocese Los Angeles, and Glendale Meml. Hosp., 1961—; adminstr. St. Francis' Chaplaincy Guild, 1962—; protestant chaplain Los Angeles Children's Hosp., Barlow San., Kaiser Permanente Hosp., Los Angeles, Cedars of Lebanon Hosp., Los Angeles, 1964—; chaplain rampart div. Los Angeles Police Dept., 1974—; dir. social services dept. Monte Sano Hosp., Los Angeles, 1970—, Park View Hosp. and Met. Hosp., Los Angeles, 1975—; dir. City Mission Soc. Diocese of Los Angeles, 1977—; columnist The Ch. Speaks, Hick's Deal Weekly Publs. Los Angeles, 1960—. Chmn. Los Angeles Mayor's Adv Bd., 1962-64; commr. Los Angeles Social Services Commn., 1964-65; commr. Bd. Zoning Adjustments 1965-73, pres. bd., 1967-73; sec. Los Angeles Comprehensive Health Planning Council, 1972—, pres 1975; pres. Monte Sano Hosp. Found., 1964—; chmn adv. bd. Gateways Mental Hosp., Los Angeles 1969-72; mem. Los Angeles County Crime and Juvenile Delinquency Planning Council, 1963-65; pres. Coordinating Council of Echo Park, 1976—; bd. dirs Comprehensive Health Planning Council So. Calif., 1971, East Valley Mental Health Dist., 1968—, NOVA Mental Health Assn., 1972—. Recipient Man of Year award C. of C., 1968. Mem. Episcopal Hosp. Chaplain's

Assn., Griffith Park C. of C., Echo Park C. of C., Harp and Shamrock Irish Assn., Irish-Israeli Soc. So. Calif. Home: 4198 Sunswept Dr Studio City CA 91604 Office: 3621 Brunswick Ave Los Angeles CA 90039

KELLEY, RANDY C., minister, Southern Baptist Convention; b. Andalusia, Ala., Dec. 17, 1950; s. Jack and Martha Nobie (Barton) K.; m. Sherry Lynn Parker, Aug. 17, 1974; children: Jason, Scotty, Julie, Timothy. Diploma sacred music Bapt. Bible Inst., 1980, B.Min., 1980. Ordained to ministry Southern Baptist Convention, 1981. Minister music Hopewell Bapt. Ch., Andalusia, Ala., 1975-78; minister music and youth Hillcrest Bapt. Ch., Ozark, Ala., 1978-80; assoc. pastor Carmel Bapt. Ch., Meridian, Miss., 1980-81; interim pastor Hopewell Bapt. Ch., Andalusia, 1981-82; pastor Pigeon Creek Bapt. Ch., Red Level, Ala., 1982-84, North Creek Bapt. Ch., Florala, Ala., 1985—. Carpenter, Andalusia, 1965-85. Pres., Andalusia Midget League Baseball, 1983; mem. River Falls Fire Dept., Ala., 1984-85; mem. Rescue Squad, Red Level, Ala., 1984, chaplain, 1985. Mem. Covington County Bapt. Assn. (assoc. ch. tng. dir. youth 1981-82). Home: Route 4 Box 181B Andalusia AL 36420

KELLEY, WILLIAM JOSEPH, priest, Roman Catholic Church; b. Attleboro, Mass., May 26, 1940; s. John Spencer and Ethel Mary (Holt) K.; B.A., State U. N.Y. at Albany, 1963; postgrad. Spring Hill Coll., summer 1964, Loyola U., Chgo., summer 1965, Divine Word Sem., Bay St. Louis, Miss., 1963-67. Joined Soc. of Divine Word, 1962; ordained priest Roman Catholic Ch., 1967; editor Divine Word Messenger, Bay St. Louis, Miss., 1967-69; co-dir. vocations Divine Word Missionaries So. Province, Bay St. Louis, 1967-69; assoc. pastor Assumption Ch., Braithwaite, La., 1967, Our Lady of Lourdes Ch., New Orleans, 1984-85; rector Divine Word Sem., Bay St. Louis, Miss., 1985—; dir. vocations Divine Word Missionaries So. Province, Bay St. Louis, 1969-76, dir. pub. relations and communications, 1976-82, provincial treas., 1976—; mem. Priests Senate, 1972-74; organizer ann. Hancock County Fleet blessing fishing vessels, 1969-73; chaplain Bay St. Louis Fire Dept., 1971-75, Hancock County Sheriff's Office, 1968—. Mem. Bay St. Louis Jr. C. of C. (bd. dirs. 1969-70). Mem. Nat. Geog. Soc., Knights of Peter Claver. Editor: Divine Word Messenger, 1975—. Home and Office: Divine Word Seminary Bay Saint Louis MS 39520

KELLOUGH, DOUGLAS ROBERT, minister, United Baptist Convention; b. Edmonton, Alta., Can., Mar. 6, 1951; s. Gordon Vincent and Sarah Jane (Cheshire) K.; m. Laura Lee MacFarlane, Aug. 16, 1975; children: Christopher, James, Kevin. Honours Cert. Bapt. Leadership Tng. Sch., Calgary, Alta., 1970; B.S., U. Alta., Edmonton, 1973; M.Div., So. Bapt. Theol. Sem., 1976; M.Theology, Acadia Div. Coll., 1985. Ordained to ministry Bapt. Ch., 1977. Student pastor Lavoy Bapt. Ch., Alta., 1972-73; pastoral intern Highland Bapt. Ch., Louisville, 1973-74, Beechwood Bapt. Ch., Louisville, 1975-76; pastor Bethel First Bapt. Ch., Prince Rupert, B.C., 1976-79, South Rawdon Bapt. Ch., South Rawdon, N.S., 1979-85; chaplain Halifax Hosps., N.S., 1985—; active Bapt. Youth Fellowship, Western Can., 1967-70; publicity dir. Gull Lake Bapt. Camp Lacombe, Alta., 1970-73; del. People's Law Conf., Ottawa, Ont., 1984; commr. Eastern Valley Assn. United Baptists, 1984—; ministerial rep. Inter-Agy. Council, Prince Rupert, B.C., 1977-79. Contbr. articles to various publs. Mem. Can. Assn. Pastoral Edn. Office: Pastoral Services Dept Victoria Gen Hosp 1278 Tower Rd Halifax NS B3H 2Y9 Canada

KELLY, DOROTHY ANN See *Who's Who in America*, 43rd edition.

KELLY, JESSE THOMAS, priest, Episcopal Church in the U.S.A., history educator; b. Louisville, Sept. 19, 1923; s. Giles Thomas and Elsie (Wooden) K.; m. Shirley Mae Assavedo, Dec. 30, 1945; children: Michael Thomas, Theresa Marie, David Thomas. B.A., U. Louisville, 1951; M.A., U. Chgo., 1952; M.Div., Ch. Div. Sch. of Pacific, 1960; Ph.D., U. Ky., 1972. Ordained priest Episcopal Church in the U.S.A., 1960. Priest (missionary) Episcopal Ch., Rio de Janiero, Brazil, 1960-61; priest Grace Episcopal Ch., Elkins, W.Va., 1961-63, Redeemer Episcopal Ch., Louisville, 1963-66, St. Mary's Episcopal Ch., Vicksburg, Miss., 1971-78; supply priest Episcopal Diocese of Miss., Jackson, 1978—. Prof. history Jackson State U., Miss., 1970—. Author: Thorns on the Tudor Rose: Monks, Rogues, Vagabonds and Sturdy Beggars, 1977. Served with USN, 1943-45. Recipient sr. honors scholarship Am. Assn. Theol. Schs., Knights Templar Ednl. Found. Calif., 1959; NDEA fellow U. Ky., 1968. Mem. Celtic Cross, Kappa Delta Pi, Phi Alpha Theta, Phi Delta Kappa. Democrat. Home: 176 Cooper Rd Jackson MS 39212 Office: Jackson State U History Dept Jackson MS 39212

KELLY, KENNETH WILLIAM, minister, Southern Baptist Convention; b. Anderson, S.C., June 17, 1953; s. John Butler and Doris Jane (Madden) K.; m. Sara Anita Bishop, July 10, 1976; children: Kenneth William Jr., Kevin Bishop. B.S. in Math., Clemson U., 1975; M. Div., Southwestern Bapt. Theol. Sem., 1979, now postgrad. Ordained to ministry Southern Baptist Convention, 1980. Asst. to dir. activities First Bapt. Ch., Anderson, S.C., 1975-76, summer intern, 1976; pastor First Bapt. Ch., Melissa, Tex., 1980—; instr. Collin Bapt. Tng. Ctr., McKinney, Tex., 1981-82, dir., 1982—; chmn. Christian life com. Collin Bapt. Assn., McKinney, 1982-84, mem. Christian helping ministries com., 1984—. Advisor Mothers against Drunk Drivers, Collin County, 1983—. Recipient Stella P. Ross Meml. award Southwestern Sem., 1977, T.B. Maston scholarship, 1984, Avocations: jogging; moral issues; dog training. Address: PO Box 188 Melissa TX 75071

KELLY, LEONTINE, bishop, United Methodist Church, Calif.-Nev. Conf., 1984—. Office: PO Box 467 San Francisco CA 94101*

KELLY, MARY CELESTE, nun, Roman Catholic Church; b. Bloomingdale, N.Y., Nov. 26, 1922; d. William John and Mary Margaret (Keese) K. B.A., Manhattan Coll., 1957. Joined Religious Sisters of Mercy, Roman Catholic Ch., 1940. Elem. tchr. St. John's Sch., Plattsburgh, N.Y., 1943-45, 62-64, St. Bernard's Sch., Saranac Lake, N.Y., 1945-51, 60-62, 64-79, St. Patrick's Sch., Rouses Point, N.Y., 1951-54, St. Patrick's Sch., Brasher Falls, N.Y., 1954-60; mem. parish ministry St. Patrick's Ch., Brasher Falls, 1980—. Dir. Head Start Program, Saranac Lake, 1975-80, bd. dirs. 1975-78; vol. Saranac Lake Gen. Hosp., 1975-79. Mercy Action Found. grantee, 1977. Club: Catholic Daus. of Am. (Saranac Lake) (pres. 1977-79). Address: St Patrick's Convent Brasher Falls NY 13613

KELLY, THOMAS CAJETAN, archbishop, Roman Catholic Church; b. Rochester, N.Y., July 14, 1931; s. Thomas A. and Katherine Eleanor (Fisher) K.; A.B., Providence Coll., 1953; S.T.L., Dominican House Studies, Washington, 1959; J.C.D., U. St. Thomas, Rome, 1962. Joined Dominican Order Preachers, 1951, ordained priest Roman Catholic Ch., 1958; sec. Dominican Provincial, N.Y.C., 1962-65; sec. to apostolic del., Washington, 1965-71; asso. gen. sec. Nat. Conf. Cath. Bishops, Washington, 1971-77; gen. sec. Nat. Conf. Cath. Bishops and U.S. Cath. Conf., 1977-81; aux. bishop Archdiocese of Washington, 1977-81; apptd. archbishop of Louisville, 1981—. Recipient Benemerenti medal, 1971. Mem. Canon Law Soc. Am. Office: Archdiocese of Louisville 212 E College St Louisville KY 40203

KELMAN, WOLFE, rabbi, Jewish religion; b. Vienna, Austria, Nov. 27, 1923; s. Hersh Leib and Mirl (Fish) K.; B.A., U. Toronto (Ont., Can.), 1946; M.H.L., Jewish Theol. Sem. Am., 1950; m. Jacqueline Levy, Mar. 2, 1952; children—Levi Yehuda, Naama Kathrine, Abigail Tobie. Came to U.S., 1946, naturalized, 1962. Rabbi various congregations; vis. rabbi West London Congregation Brit. Jews, 1957-58; exec. v.p. Rabbinical Assembly, 1951—, rep. to U.S. com. for UN, 1951—; dir. joint placement commn. Rabbinical Assembly, United Synagogue Am. and Jewish Theol. Sem. Am., 1951-66; vis. prof. homiletics Jewish Theol. Sem. Am., 1966-73, adj. asst. prof. Jewish history, 1973—; mem. gov. bd. World Jewish Congress, 1968—, chmn. cultural commn., 1975—. Office: 3080 Broadway New York NY 10027

KELSEY, DAVID HUGH, educator, United Presbyterian Church in U.S.A.; b. Tanta, Egypt, Apr. 10, 1932; s. Hugh Espy and Mildred (Allison) K.; A.B., Haverford Coll., 1954; B.D., Yale, 1958, M.A., 1960, Ph.D., 1964. Teaching elder, 1958; prof. theology Yale Div. Sch., 1965—. Kent fellow, 1960, Rockefeller grad. fellow, 1960. Mem. Soc. Religion in Higher Edn., Am. Acad. Religion. Author: The Fabric of Paul Tillich's Theology, 1967; The Uses of Scripture in Recent Theology, 1975. Address: 409 Prospect St New Haven CT 06510

KELSOE, ARTHUR HUBERT, minister, Am. Baptist Assn.; b. Cloud Chief, Okla., Mar. 20, 1901; s. Henry Thomas and Maggie Donie (Steward) K.; teaching certificate S.W. State Coll., Weatherford, Okla., 1926; m. Lydia E. Ridenour, Dec. 4, 1921 (dec. Dec. 1959); children—Arthur Leroy, Ozella; m. 2d, Bessie May Sharpe, July 29, 1963. Ordained to ministry, 1924; pastor chs., Okla.; mem. bd. Okla. Bapt. Assn., 1963-72; real estate broker for ministers and chs.; trustee Christian Workers Sch., 1963—; treas. Peniel Ch., 1956—. Address: 3723 NW 49th St Oklahoma City OK 73112

KEMBER, JANE CATHERINE, ch. ofcl., Ch. of Scientology; b. Nairobi, Kenya, Sept. 26, 1936; d. Arthur and Bliss Nielsen-Wood; grad. St. Hill Coll. Scientology, Sussex, Eng., 1962; m. Henry Kevin Kember, Sept. 2, 1961; children—Peter and Charles (twins). Qualified as counselor, 1961, appointed minister, 1963; ch. ofcl. dept. social affairs, Africa, 1963-65; mem. exec. bd. Ch. of Scientology world hdqrs., Sussex, Eng., 1965—, dep. guardian, 1968-69, guardian (sr. exec.), 1969—. Speaker numerous ch. confs., Europe, Africa, and U.S. Author religious pamphlets. Home: Craiglath Courtlands Sharpthorne England Office: Saint Hill Manor East Grinstead Sussex England

KEMMERER, CURTIS GALE, minister, United Church of Christ; therapist; b. Bethlehem, Pa., Mar. 27, 1954; s. Stanley Oscar and Eleanor Mary (Stauffer) K.; m. Sandra Jean Yoder, Aug. 21, 1976; children: Lisa, Laura. B.A. in History, Lebanon Valley Coll., 1976; M.Div., Lancaster Theol. Sem., 1979. Ordained to ministry United Ch. of Christ, 1979. Chaplain Tobyhanna State Park, Pa. Northeast Conf. United Ch. Christ, Mt. Pocono, Pa., 1976; assoc. minister Congregational Ch., New Canaan, Conn., 1979—; bd. dirs. Westchester Inst. Tng. in Psychotherapy, Mt. Kisco, N.Y., 1983—, New Canaan Hospice, 1984—, Person to Person, Darien, Conn., 1984—. Staff therapist So. Conn. Counseling Ctr., Norwalk, 1982—. Adult supr. Safe Rides of New Canaan, 1983—. Recipient YMCA Service award YMCA New Canaan, 1982, Service award Soc. to Advance Retarded, 1982; named to Outstanding Young Men Am. Jaycees, 1984. Mem. Am. Assn. Marriage and Family Therapy, Nat. Assn. Advancement Psychoanalysis, Pi Gamma Mu, Phi Alpha Epsilon. Lodge: Kiwanis (pres. 1982-83). Office: Congl Ch 23 Park St New Canaan CT 06840

KEMP, ARTHUR EDWARD, minister, housing executive, American Baptist Association; b. Hickory, N.C., Nov. 21, 1929; s. James and Rosa Margaret (Hill) K.; m. E. Francene Palmer, Dec. 30, 1962; 1 child, Douglas Arthur. B.A. in Religion, Capital U., 1974; M.Div., Ashland Theol. Sem., 1981, D.Min., 1984. Lectr. Ohio Bapt. Gen. Conv., Columbus, Ohio, 1968-75, sec., 1974-78; pres. Mt. Olive Met. Housing, Inc., Akron, Ohio, 1983-85; trustee Interfaith Council, Akron, 1984—. Author: Black Theology, Black Evangelicals, 1983; Development of Black Hermeneutic, 1984. Local staff mem. for Senator John Glenn for Ohio, 1974, Pres. Jimmy Carter, 1976; coordinator minority affairs Gov. James Rhode, Ohio, 1976; trustee Akron Urban League, 1978-82, Community Action Agy., Akron, 1984—; pres. Human Relations Community, 1983—; chmn. Human Rights Commn., Akron, 1984-85. Named Outstanding Black Minister, Black Muslim Soc., 1983, Minister of Yr., Sigma Beta, 1984, Man of Yr., Alpha Phi Alpha, 1984. Mem. Frontiers Internat. (minister), NAACP, Ohio Bapt. Gen. Conv. (chmn. dept. devel. 1981-83). Club: Sertoma. Avocations: bowling; fishing; hiking; photography. Home: 1135 Stoner St Akron OH 44320

KEMP, RONALD NUBURN, minister, Am. Baptist Assn., Southern Bapt. Convention; psychologist; b. Cyril, Okla., July 23, 1936; s. Luther N. and Lois Mary (Scoggins) K.; m. Lou Thelen Peterson, Aug. 3, 1957; children: Ronald, Hal, Wesley. B.A., Okla. Bapt. U., 1958; B.D., M.Div., Southwest Theol. Sem., 1962; M.A., Sam Houston State U., 1970; D.Min., Midwestern Bapt. Theol. Sem., 1981. Ordained to ministry Baptist Ch., 1956. Lic. psychologist, Mo. Pastor 2d Bapt. Ch., Huntsville, Tex., 1962-67; specialist on alcohol Tex. Commn. Alcoholism, Huntsville, 1967-69; coll. chaplain Southwest Bapt. U., Bolivar, Mo., 1969-76; ctr. dir. Mo. Bapt. Children's Home, Bolivar, 1976-79; pastoral counselor Assocs. for Counseling, Springfield, Mo., 1980—. Mem. Am. Assn. Pastoral Counselors, Am. Assn. for Marriage and Family Therapy (bd. dirs.), Mo. Psychol. Assn. Lodge: Bolivar Optimist Club. Democrat. Office: Assocs for Counseling & Consultation 315 Professional Bldg Springfield MO 65806

KEMP, WILLIAM VANCE, minister, United Meth. Ch.; b. Corinth, Miss., Mar. 30, 1926; s. Charles O'Dell and Annie (Moore) K.; student N.E. Miss. Jr. Coll., 1953-54; B.A., Blue Mountain Coll., 1956; M.Div., Emory U., 1958; m. Sybal Geraldine Fowler, June 6, 1943; children—William, Michael, Susan, Timothy. Ordained to ministry, 1957; pastor in Ashland, Miss., 1958-62, Marks, Miss., 1962-66, Wesley Ch., Columbus, Miss., 1966-71, Winona, Miss., 1971-77; dist. supt. Greenwood dist. No. Miss. Conf., 1977—. Mem. council on fin. and adminstrn. No. Miss. conf. United Meth. Ch., 1973-76, mem. conf. council on ministries, 1976—, conf. personnel com., 1976, council com. on nominations, 1976; mem. Greenwood dist. council on ministries, 1976. Trustee Millsaps Coll., 1976—. Mem. Montgomery County Ministerial Assn. Home: 606 Emerson Ave Greenwood MS 38930

KEMPER, ROBERT GRAHAM, minister, United Church of Christ; b. Alton, Ill., Mar. 31, 1935; s. Robert Chatfield and Virginia (Owens) K.; m. Margery Klontz, Mar. 30, 1959; children: Edward, Virginia, Mary Elizabeth. A.B., Cornell Coll., 1957; B.Div., U. Chgo., 1961; M.Div., Chgo. Theol. Sem., 1961, D.D., 1981. Ordained to ministry United Ch. Christ, 1961. Minister 1st Congl. Ch., Newton Falls, Ohio, 1961-65, Watchung Congl. Ch., Upper Montclair, N.J., 1965-69; editor Christian Ministry, Chgo., 1969-73; minister 1st Congl. Ch., Western Springs, Ill., 1973—. Author: An Elephant's Ballet, 1976; Beginning a New Pastorate, 1977; The New Shape of Ministry, 1979; What Every Church Member Should Know About Clergy, 1985. Mem. Assn. Parish Clergy, Profl. Assn. Clergy (founder). Home: 4325 Grand Ave Western Springs IL

60558 Office: First Congl Ch 1106 Chestnut St Western Springs IL 60558

KEMPSKI, RALPH ALOISIUS, minister, Lutheran Church in America; b. Milw., July 16, 1934; s. Sigmund J. and Cecilia J. (Chojnacki) K.; B.A., Augsburg Coll., 1960; M.Div., Northwestern Luth. Theol. Sem., 1963; m. Mary Jane Roth, July 30, 1955; children: Richard, Joan, John. Ordained to ministry, 1963; pastor Epiphany Luth. Ch., Mpls., 1963-68, St. Stephen Luth. Ch., Louisville, 1968-71, Our Saviour Luth. Ch., W. Lafayette, Ind., 1971—. Sec. S.W. dist. Ind.-Ky. Synod, Luth. Ch. Am., 1968-70, exec. bd., 1970-72, 73—, dean, 1970-71; dean Lafayette Dist., 1973—. Mem. W. Lafayette Human Relations Commn., 1976—; exec. bd. Family Service Agy., Lafayette, 1975—. Mem. Purdue U. Ministers Orgn. (pres. 1974), Louisville Area Council Chs. (exec. bd. 1970-71), Tippecanoe County Fedn. Chs. (exec. bd. 1974-75), Greater Lafayette LWV (adv. bd. 1974—). Home: 924 N Chauncey St West Lafayette IN 47906 Office: 300 W Fowler St West Lafayette IN 47906

KENDALL, GARY LYNN, pastor, Church of God (Anderson, Ind.); b. Houston, May 18, 1957; s. Paul Edwin and Mary Ruth (Collins) K.; m. Belinda Beryl Barker, June 22, 1979; children: Kristen Janee', Jeremiah Lynn. B.A. cum laude, Gulf Coast Bible Coll., 1979; postgrad. Nazarene Theol. Sem., 1980—. Ordained to ministry First Ch. of God, 1982. Assoc. pastor First Ch. of God, Kansas City, Kans., 1979-81, sr. pastor, 1982—; asst. dir. Kans. State Youth Fellowship, Wichita, 1980-82; sec. State Exec. Council of Ch. of God, Wichita, 1981-82; vice-chmn. State Minister's Steering Com., Wichita, 1981—; mem. State Ministers Credentials and Adv., Wichita, 1984—; pres. Mid-West Minister's Fellowship, Kansas City, Mo., 1983—. Contbr. articles to religious mags. Asst. adv. Pierson Jr. High Fellowship of Christian Athletes, Kansas City, Kans., 1979-81; asst. adv. Turner High Sch. Fellowship of Christian Athletes, Kansas City, Kans., 1980-81; sec. Camp Fellowship Bd. Trustees, Wichita, 1981-82, mem., 1984. Recipient Homoletical Preaching award Gulf Coast Bible Coll., 1979. Mem. Kans. State Ministerial Fellowship, Midwest Ministerial Fellowship, Greater Kansas City Area Ministerial Fellowship. Republican. Home: 2933 South 53rd Terr Kansas City KS 66106 Office: 4835 Shawnee Dr Kansas City KS 66106

KENNAMER, PLEASANT DECATUR, III (PETE), minister, church official, Christian Ch. (Disciples of Christ); alcohol education instructor, drug abuse counselor; b. Brownsville, Tex., June 27, 1941; s. Pleasant Decatur Kennamer and Helen Lucille (Minton) Kennamer Jackson; m. Patsy Kate Weeks, Apr. 8, 1974; 1 child, Amber Leigh. A.A., Tarrant County Jr. Coll., 1973; B.A., Howard Payne U., 1975; postgrad Brite Div. Sch., Tex. Christian U. Ordained to ministry, Christian Ch.; cert. alcohol edn. instr., drug abuse counselor. Supply preacher Central Tex. Conf., United Meth. Ch., Brownwood, 1982-83; pastor First United Meth. Ch., Cross Plains, Tex., Burkett United Meth. Ch., Burkett, Tex., 1983-84; interim pastor First Christian Ch., Sweetwater, Tex., 1984; exec. dir. Christian Ministries of Westcentral Tex., Cross Plains, 1984—. Author hist. papers, poems. Lobbyist Tex. Jr. Coll. Assn., Austin, 1972-73; polit. liaison Callahan County Child Welfare Bd., Baird, Tex., 1984—. Served to 2d lt. USMC, 1959-68, Vietnam. Decoated Purple Heart; recipient scholarship medal Pi Gamma Mu, Howard Payne U., 1975; Dean's Book award Brite Div. Sch., 1983. Mem. Tex. Assn. of Alcohol and Traffic Safety Edn. Instrs. Lodge: Kiwanis (Cross Plains, Tex.). Avocations: creative writing, gardening, fishing, visiting historical sites. Home: PO Box 307 Bangs TX 76823 Office: Christian Ministries of West Central Tex PO Box 777 Cross Plains TX 76443

KENNEDY, ARTHUR LEO, priest, educator, Roman Catholic Ch.; b. Boston, Jan. 9, 1942; s. Arthur L. and Helen I. (O'Rourke) K. B.A., St. John's Coll., 1963; S.T.M., Gregorian U., 1967; Ph.D., Boston U., 1978. Ordained priest Roman Cath. Ch., 1966. Assoc. pastor St. Monica's Ch., Methuen, Mass., 1967-69, St. Joseph's Ch., East Boston, Mass., 1969-74, Holy Trinity Ch., South St. Paul, Minn., 1974-82, Assumption Ch., St. Paul, 1982—; asst. prof. St. Thomas Coll., St. Paul, 1974-84, assoc. prof., 1984—, chmn. dept. theology, 1985—; councillor Lonergan Trust Fund, Toronto, Ont., Can., 1981—. Author jour. Lonergan Workshop, 1984. Mem. Am. Acad. Religion, Cath. Theol. Soc. Am., Am. Philos. Assn., Boston Theol. Inst., Jaspers Soc. N.Am. Home: 47 Crehore Rd Chestnut Hill MA 02167 Office: St Thomas Coll 2115 Summit Ave Saint Paul MN 55105

KENNEDY, DODRIDGE ROBERT, minister, Seventh-day Adventist Church; b. Jamaica, W.I., Aug. 24, 1946; came to U.S., 1979; s. Robert and Mary (Williamson) K.; m. Seslie E. Barham, Sept. 13, 1970; children: Robert, Leighton, Sheldon. B.Th., W.I. Coll., 1969; M.A. in Religion, Andrews U., 1971; M.S.T., McGill U.-Montreal, 1980; M.Edn., Columbia U., 1983, Ed.D., 1984. Ordained to ministry, 1974. Pastor, Seventh-day Adventist Ch., Jamaica, 1971-76, edn. supr., 1976-79; pastor Seventh-day Adventist Ch., Manhasset, L.I., 1980—; lectr., panelist ethics seminars Greater N.Y. Conf., 1983, chmn. devel., 1983-84. Mem. Religious Broadcaster Group W Cable, 1984-85. Home: 4392 Carpenter Ave Bronx NY 10466 Office: Greater NY Conf Seventh-day Adventists 7 Shelter Rock Rd Manhasset LI NY 11030

KENNEDY, FRANCIS BARRETT, priest, Roman Catholic Church; b. Cin., Aug. 10, 1915; s. Joseph James and Helen Marie (Taylor Barrett) K. B.A., Atheneum Ohio, 1936; S.T.L., Pontifical Gregorian U., Rome, 1940. Ordained priest Roman Catholic Ch. 1939; monsignor, 1957. Asst. pastor Archdiocese Cin., 1940-52; tchr., librarian Elder High Sch., Cin., 1946-52; asst. nat. sec. Cath. Nr. East Welfare Assn., N.Y.C., 1952-57; asst. dir. Papal mission to Palestinians, Beirut, Lebanon, 1954-56; rector St. Peter in Chains Cathedral, Cin., 1957-70; pastor St. William Ch., Cin., 1970—. Sec., Archdiocesan Priest Senate, 1966-72; dean St. Lawrence Deanery, Cin., 1972-75. Pres., HOPE Cin., 1967-72; chmn. trustees Sr. Chateau on the Hill, Cin., 1972—; mem. West End Task Force, 1967; mem. Cin. Restoration, 1974-76. Served to lt. comdr. USNR, 1944-57. Named domestic prelate by Pope Paul VI, 1967; decorated knight comdr. with star Order Knights Holy Sepulchre, 1957. Democrat. Lodge: K.C. Address: 4107 W 8th St Cincinnati OH 45205

KENNEY, PATRICIA DIANE, minister, Christian Ch.; b. Glendale, Calif., Nov. 25, 1941; d. Thomas Lawrence and Patricia Lillus (East) K.; B.A., Chapman Coll., 1964; B.D., Pacific Sch. Religion, 1969, postgrad., 1974-76. Ordained to ministry, 1969; asst. dean of chapel Stanford U., 1969-74; chaplain Mills Coll., 1975—. Liturgist profl. seminars; mem. exec. com. Nat. Assn. Coll. and U. Chaplains, 1971-76. Active United Farm Workers, Women's Internat. League for Peace and Freedom. Underwood fellow, Danforth Found., 1974-75. Mem. Liturg. Conf. Home: 438 Addison Ave Palo Alto CA 94301

KENNY, LAWRENCE J., bishop, Roman Catholic Church. Titular bishop of Holar; aux. bishop of Mil. Vicariate, 1983—. Office: Chancery of Military Vicarate 452 Madison Ave New York NY 10022*

KENNY, MICHAEL H. See *Who's Who in America,* 43rd edition.

KENSETH, ARNOLD MARTINIUS, minister, United Church of Christ; English educator; b. Milton, Mass., Dec. 19, 1915; s. Arnold Martinius and Anna Charlotte (Wahl) K.; m. Betty Josephine Amey; Aug. 17, 1940; children: Elaine Dagmar Kenseth Abel, Arnold Geoffrey, Evan Warren. B.A., Bates Coll., 1937; S.T.B., Harvard U., 1944, M.A. in English, 1950. Ordained to ministry Congl. Christian Ch., 1944. Pastor Union Congl. Ch., Ballardvale, Mass., 1943-47; chaplain U. Mass., Amherst, 1947-51; pastor South Congl. Ch., Amherst, 1949—; mem. commn. Worship United Ch. Christ, N.Y.C., 1964-66. Mem. English faculty U. Mass., Amherst, 1960-72. Author: A Cycle of Praise, 1952; The Holy Merriment, 1963; Sabbaths, Sacraments, and Seasons, 1969; (with Richard Unsworth) Prayers for Worship Leaders, 1978. Editor: Poems of Protest, Old and New, 1968; poetry editor Ministers Quar., Boston, 1950-59, United Ch. Herald, N.Y.C., 1968-71. Bd. dirs. Hampshire County chapter ACLU, 1952-67; ann. UNICEF drive, Amherst, 1954—; mem. exec. com. UN Assn., Amherst, 1975—. Democrat. Home: 1067 S East St Amherst MA 01002 Office: South Congl Ch S East St Amherst MA 01002

KENSKY, ALLAN DAVID, rabbi, Conservative Jewish; b. Bronx, N.Y., July 17, 1946; s. Samuel R. and Ada (Leinwand) K.; m. Tikva Simone Frymer, Oct. 20, 1974; children: Meira, Eitan. B.A., Queens Coll., 1967; M.A., NYU, 1971; M. Hebrew Lit., Jewish Theol. Sem. Am., 1969. Ordained rabbi, 1971. Rabbi Beth Israel Congregation, Ann Arbor, Mich., 1971—; mem. exec. bd. Interfaith Council of Congregations, Ann Arbor, 1983—; chmn. Soviet Jewish absorption com. Jewish Community Council Washtenaw County, Ann Arbor, 1980—; chmn. scholarship com. Hebrew Day Sch., Ann Arbor, 1976—. Bd. dirs. Vis. Nurse Assn. Huron Valley, Ann Arbor, 1980-83; mem. Citizens Adv. Bd. Sex Edn. In Pub. Schs., Ann Arbor, 1979-80. Mem. Rabinical Assembly. Home: 1304 Wells St Ann Arbor MI 48104 Office: Beth Israel Congregation 2000 Washtenaw Ave Ann Arbor MI 48104

KENT, CLIFFORD EUGENE, priest, Episcopal Church; b. Agusta, Kans., Oct. 11, 1920; s. Oris Glee and Lucy (Sillin) K.; m. Elizabeth Rue Kent, Oct. 3, 1942; children: Jane Kent, Peter Reeves, Richard Dennis. B.S. in Chem. Engring., Purdue U., 1942; Cert. Theology, Diocesan Sch. Ministry, 1980. Ordained priest, 1984. Lay leader First Meth. Ch., Scnenectady, 1964-66; warden, vestry St. Andrew's Ch., Saratoga, Calif., 1972-75; deacon assoc. St. Andrew's Ch., 1982-84, priest assoc., 1984—; camp dir. St. Andrew's Ch., 1978—; conv. process Diocese of El Camino Real, 1983—, mem. world mission com., 1984—. Contbr. articles to profl. jours. Mgr. symphony Richmond Symphony Orch., 1950; chmn. local chpt. Am. Inst. Chem. Engrs., 1950. Mem. Am. Chem. Soc. Republican. Lodge: Kiwanis. Office: Saint Andrews Episcopal Church 13601 Saratoga Ave Saratoga CA 95070

KENYON, WALTER WYNN, Bible and philosophy educator, Presbyterian Church in the U.S.A.; b. Mckeesport, Pa., Feb. 12, 1948; s. Walter Russell and Mary Lillian (Gethin) K.; m. Virginia Stulen, June 11, 1976; children: Amy Lyn, Stephen Wynn. B.A., Marietta Coll., 1970; M.Div., Pitts. Theol. Sem., 1974; M.A. in Philosophy, U. Miami, Fla., 1978, Ph.D. in Philosophy, 1981. Dir. community youth recreation program, West Deer Twp., Pa., 1967-75; student pastor Harmarville United Presbyn. Ch., Pitts., 1971-75; youth dir. First United Presbyn. Ch., Miami, Fla., 1976-81; assoc. prof. Bible and philosophy Belhaven Coll., Jackson, Miss., 1981—; mem. steering com. Concerned United Presbyns., 1978-81; bd. mem. Beginning Again in Christ, Jackson, 1984—. Author: The Concept of God, 1981; Christian World and Life View, 1984. Mem. Soc. Christian Philosophers, Miss. Philos. Assn., Phi Kappa Phi. Republican. Home: 1846 Howard St Jackson MS 39202 Office: Belhaven Coll 1500 Peachtree St Jackson MS 39202

KEOWN, WILLIAM ARVEL, minister, Church of God-Anderson, Ind.; b. Clinton, Ind., June 4, 1920; s. James and Lula (Jackson) K.; Th.B., God's Bible Sch., Cin., 1949; M.A., Butler U., 1956; certificate Ind. State U., 1961; m. Jewel Cook, Mar. 25, 1950; children: Evelyn, Deborah, William, Duane, Wayne. Ordained to ministry Ch. of God-Anderson, Ind., 1957; pastor ch., Evansville, Ind., 1950-51, Clinton, Ind., 1952; dean of men God's Bible Sch. and Coll., Cin., 1948-49; tchr. Frankfort Coll., 1954-57, dean of men, 1954-55; tchr. jr. high sch., Clinton, Ind., 1957-79; pastor 1st Ch. of God, Terre Haute, Ind., 1970-80; interim pastor, 1980—; instr. Ind. State Dept. Corrections, Anderson, 1979-82. Fellow Internat. Platform Assn.; mem. Nat. Ret. Tchrs. Assn., Ind. Ret. Tchrs. Assn., Ind. Ministerial Assembly. Home: Route 2 Box 26 Clinton IN 47842

KERINS, JOSEPH LEO, priest, college president; b. N.Y.C., June 28, 1917; s. John and Ellen (Rooney) K. M.Div., Mt. St. Alphonsus, 1943; M.A., Catholic U. Am., 1944, M.L.S., 1948, Ph.D., 1963. Ordained priest Roman Catholic Ch., 1943. Librarian, Mt. St. Alphonsus, Esopus, N.Y., 1949-63; pres. St. Alphonsus Coll., Suffield, Conn., 1963-67, Mt. St. Alphonsus, 1967-69, 85—, Holy Redeemer Coll., Washington, 1980-85; provincial Redemptorist Order, 1969-78. Home and Office: Mount Saint Alphonsus Esopus NY 12429

KERLEY, OTTIE RAY, minister, American Baptist Churches in the U.S.A.; b. Burlington, Iowa, May 30, 1949; s. Loren Clarence and Betty Lou (Timberlake) K.; m. Erlene Grace Shoesmith, Dec. 18, 1971; children: Elizabeth Grace, Deborah Rae, Clara Eilene, Ottie Ray III. B.S., Ottawa U., 1971; M.A., Eastern Bapt. Theol. Sem., 1974, M.Div., 1975. Ordained to ministry Baptist Ch., 1976. Student supr. Am. Bapt. Chs. U.S.A., Valley Forge, Pa., 1971-75; youth pastor Manoa Bapt. Ch., Havertown, Pa., 1972-73; asst. pastor Oaklyn Bapt. Ch., N.J., 1973-75; pastor First Bapt. Ch., McKees Rocks, Pa., 1975-82, Bethel Bapt. Ch., Powers Lake, N.D., 1982—; chmn. nominating com. Pitts. Bapt. Assn., 1973-75; v.p. South Hills Bapt. Chs., Pitts., 1973-74; del. gen. bd. Am. Bapt. Chs. U.S.A., 1984—, bd. nat. ministries, 1984—; bd. dirs. N.D. Bapt. Conv., 1984—. Mem. Flood/Disaster Preparedness Com., McKees Rocks, Pa., 1973, McKees Rocks Community Center Citizens Com., 1974-75; bd. dirs. Sto-Ken-Rox Meals-On-Wheels, 1973-75. Mem. N.D. Bapt. Ministers Council (sec.-treas. 1984—). Home: Box 377 Powers Lake ND 58773 Office: Bethel Baptist Ch Box 377 Powers Lake ND 58773

KERR, HUGH THOMSON See *Who's Who in America,* 43rd edition.

KERR, JAMES MILTON, minister, United Methodist Church; b. Buckhannon, W.Va., Aug. 28, 1937; s. William James and Tocie Nile (Morris) K.; m. Carolyn Grace DeVault, Dec. 23, 1962; children: Elizabeth Ann, Jon Wesley, Laura Lee. A.B., W.Va. Wesleyan Coll., 1960; M.Div., Garrett-Evang. Theol. Sem., 1963. Asst. pastor Kingsley Meth. Ch., Milw., 1960-62; assoc. pastor Spruce St. Meth. Ch., Morgantown, W.Va., 1962-65; pastor Marlinton Meth. Ch., W.Va., 1965-68, Barrackville United Meth. Ch., W.Va., 1968-80, Mannington First United Meth. Ch., W.Va., 1980-82; assoc. pastor Bridgeport United Meth. Ch., W.Va., 1982—; chmn. Commn. on Christian Unity United Meth. Ch. W.Va., 1980—; sec. council on ministries W.Va. Ann Conf., 1980-84; bd. dirs. W.Va. Council Chs., 1982—; bishop's rep. to Roman Cath. Diocese of Wheeling-Charleston and Presbyn. Ch. U.S.A. Synod of the Virginias, 1984—. Author: (with others) Critical issues for Fairmont, 1971; contbr. to book Religion In Appalachia, 1978. Fellow Soc. Religious Orgn. Mgrs. (bd. dirs. 1984—); mem. Bridgeport Ministerial Assn. (treas. 1984—), Harrison County Ministerial Assn. Home: 217 W Philadelphia Ave Bridgeport WV 26330 Office: Bridgeport United Meth Ch 251 Worthington Dr Bridgeport WV 26330

KERR, JOHN EDWARD, minister, American Lutheran Church; b. Marion, Ohio, Sept. 10, 1939; s. Judson Edward and Rowena Marie (Wagner) K.; m. Diane Ross, Aug. 26, 1961; children: Stephen, Thomas, Kristin. B.A., Capital U., 1961; B.D., Trinity Luth.

Seminary, 1965, S.T.M., 1972, D. Ministry, 1983. Ordained to Luth. Ch., 1965. Pastor Zion Luth. Ch., Clifton, Ill., 1965-68, St. John Luth. Ch., Lithopolis, Ohio, 1968-72; assoc. pastor Good Hope Luth. Ch., Bucyrus, Ohio, 1972-73, sr. pastor, 1973—; pres. Lithopolis Ministerial Assn., Lithopolis, Ohio; 1970; del. Am. Luth. Ch. Nat. Conv., Washington, 1976; mem. bd. service and mission in Am., Am. Luth. Ch., Mpls., 1982—. Mem. Harding Area Council Boy Scouts Am., Marion, Ohio, 1973—; pres. Bucyrus Family Service Bd., Bucyrus, Ohio, 1976-78; v.p. Bucyrus City Sch. Bd., 1980—. Recipient Dist. Award of Merit, Tarhe Dist., Boy Scouts Am., Bucyrus, 1979. Mem. Acad. Parish Clergy, Religious Edn. Assn. Republican. Home: 111 Crescent Ct Bucyrus OH 44820 Office: Good Hope Luth Ch South Poplar and West Charles St Bucyrus OH 44820

KERR, WILLIAM FULTON, minister, educator, Conservative Baptist Assn. Am.; b. Pitman, N.J., Sept. 6, 1915; s. William James and Jeannie Camac (Stuart) K.; student Wheaton Coll., 1934-37; B.A., Bryan Coll., 1939, LL.D., 1960; M.Div., Grace Theol. Sem., 1942, D.D., 1961; postgrad. Garrett Theol. Sem., 1948-50, Harvard, 1952-54; m. Ruth Eleanor Braddock, Nov. 16, 1941; children—William James, David Alfred, Thomas Hugh, Paul Robert, Matthew Terrelle, Kathleen Ann. Ordained to ministry, 1943; pastor chs., Ind., 1941-47; prof. theology No. Bapt. Theol. Sem., Chgo., 1945-50; dean, prof. theology Conservative Bapt. Theol. Sem., Denver, 1950-51; prof. theology, chmn. dept. Barrington (R.I.) Coll., 1951-54; pastor chs., Calif., Oreg. and N.Y., 1954-72; prof. theology Los Angeles Bapt. Sem., 1970-72, Calif. Grad. Sch. Theology, Glendale, 1970-72, Western Conservative Bapt. Sem., Portland, Oreg., 1972—; vis. prof. theology Internat. Coll., Honolulu, 1972—; editorial and theol. cons. Tyndale Ho. Pubs. Mem. bd. Am. Assn. for Jewish Evangelism, 1955; rec. sec. Conservative Bapt. Home Mission Soc., 1955-58, mem. bd., 1959-63. Mem. Soc. Bibl. Lit. and Exegesis, Am. Acad. Religion, Evang. Theol. Soc., Internat. Platform Assn. Author: A Christology for Our Day, 1954; Rediscovering the New Testament, 1957; God's Holiness, 1970; many others. Revision editor Dickson Bible, 1950, Good Leader Bible, 1951. Home: 15342 SE Hawthorne Ct Portland OR 97233 Office: 5511 SE Hawthorne Blvd Portland OR 97215

KERSEY, RODDY LEE, evangelist, So. Bapt. Conv.; b. Canton, Okla., Feb. 11, 1936; s. Hosea Martin and Dell Ionia (Jones) K.; B.A. in Edn., Northeastern Okla. State U., 1961; M.R.E., Southwestern Bapt. Theol. Sem., 1964; m. Barbara Ann Brown, Oct. 27, 1957; 1 dau., Kimberly Kay. Ordained to ministry, 1959; pastor Boudinot Bapt. Ch., Tahlequah, Okla., 1958-59, First Bapt. Ch., Panola, Okla., 1959-62, Elm Grove Bapt. Ch., Fort Worth, 1962-64, Bethel Bapt. Ch., Adrian, Mich., 1964-68, Bethel Bapt. Ch., Niles, Mich., 1968-70; pastoral missionary Quad Cities for Ill. Bapt. State Assn., Springfield, Ill., 1970-72; pastor Sooner Bapt. Ch., Midwest City, Okla., 1972-75; crusade coordinator Larry Jones Evangelism Assn., Oklahoma City, 1976; evangelist Roddy Kersey Evangelism Orgn., Del City, Okla., 1976—. Dir. area-wide crusades (inter-denominational); dir. ch. bus evangelism confs.; survey specialist for home mission bd. for So. Baptist Conv., 1965—; exec. bd. Mich. Bapt. State Conv.; pres. Lenawee County Ministerial Assn., Adrian; evangelism com. chmn. Huron Assn. & Southwestern Assn. of Mich.; mem. evangelism com. for Capital Baptist Assn., Oklahoma City. Commd. home missionary Home Mission Bd., 1970; diplomas Billy Graham Sch. Evangelism, 1973, 75. Contbr. articles to religious jours. Home and Office: 3433 Royalwood Circle Del City OK 73115

KERSEY, STUART ASHBY, minister, So. Baptist Conv.; b. Richmond, Va.; s. Stuart Ashby and Alene (Childress) K.; B.A., Ouachita Bapt. U., 1950; B.Th., So. Bapt. Theol. Sem., 1955; postgrad. U. Ind., 1954-55, U. Va. Hosp., 1955; m. Margaret Jean Coons, Dec. 21, 1951; children—Ruth Nanette, Stuart Harrod. Ordained to ministry, 1948; pastor Cherokee Ave. Bapt. Ch., Gaffney, S.C., 1974—. Pres. ministers confs., Harrodsburg, Ky., 1954-55, Orange, Va., 1959-60, Goshen Bapt. Assn., Va., 1958-59, Roanoke, Va., 1966-67; moderator Concord Bapt. Assn., Va., 1956-57, Goshen Bapt. Assn., 1963-64; chmn. time, place, preacher com., Christian life com. Gen. Assn. Va. Baptists; mem. exec. com., exec. bd., chmn. evangelism D.C. Bapt. Conv.; mem. coms. on bds. and annuity bd. So. Bapt. Conv.; mem. radio and TV commn. S.C. Bapt. Conv.; pres. Greater Caffney Ministers Fellowship. Cherokee County rep. Title 20 Appalachian Council Govts.; bd. dirs. Cherokee Health Found., Gaffney. Home: 108 Avondale Dr Gaffney SC 29340 Office: 805 Cherokee Ave Gaffney SC 29340

KERSHNER, WAYNE ALLEN, minister, American Baptist Churches in the U.S.A.; b. Ridley Park, Pa., Aug. 17, 1940; s. Earl Oscar and Lillian Mae (Guyer) K.; m. Mary June Hurd, May 21, 1966; children: Jonathan W., Carol Beth, David D. A.B., Wheaton Coll., 1962; M.Div., Eastern Bapt. Theol. Sch., 1968; A.B. (hon.), Orlinda Childs Pierce Meml. Sch. Theology, 1962. Ordained to ministry Baptist Ch., 1968. Pastor, Gesthsemane Bapt. Ch., Woodbine, N.J.,

---

1966-68, Dalton Bapt. Ch., Pa., 1968-72, First Bapt. Ch., St. Marys, W.Va., 1972-77, Sabraton Bapt. Ch., Morgantown, W.Va., 1977—; mem. exec. bd. W.Va. Bapt. Chs., 1983—, mem. local ch. commn., 1983—, mem. com. on ministerial standing, 1983—, exec. chmn. prodigal com., Morgantown, 1984; moderator Goshen Bapt. Assn., 1981-82. Served to 1st lt. U.S. Army, 1962-64. Mem. Ministers Council Am. Bapt. Chs., Ministers Council W.Va. Bapt. Chs., Goshen Bapt. Ministerials Assn. (pres. 1982-83). Republican. Club: Lions (treas. 1979-81, 84—, 1st v.p. 1982, Pres.'s plaque 1983). Home: 192 Dug Hill Rd PO Box 3040 Morgantown WV 26503 Office: Sabraton Bapt Ch 1641 Sabraton St PO Box 3040 Morgantown WV 26503

KESLER, JAY LEWIS, association official, Youth for Christ Internat.; b. Barnes, Wis., Sept. 15, 1935; s. Herbert E. and Elsie (Campbell) K.; student Ball State U., 1953-54; B.A., Taylor U., 1957; m. Helen Jane Smith, June 7, 1957; children—Laura, Bruce, Terri. Dir. Youth for Christ, Marion, Ind., 1955-58, crusade staff evangelist, 1959-60, dir. Ill.-Ind. region, 1960-62, dir. coll. recruitment, 1962-63, v.p. personnel, 1963-68, v.p. field coordination, 1968-73, pres., 1973—; pastor First Bapt. Ch., Geneva, Ill., 1971—. Bd. dirs. Bethel Coll., Mishawaka, Ind., 1967-75. Recipient Chamber of Achievement award Alumni Assn. Taylor U., 1972. Mem. Sigma Tau. Author: Let's Succeed with our Teenagers, 1973. Office: 360 S Main Pl Carol Stream IL 60187

KESSEL, WILLIAM BURKHARDT, minister, religious organization executive, Evangelical Lutheran Synod; b. McNary, Ariz., Dec. 9, 1947; s. George Herbert and Ruth Emma (Guenther) K.; m. Lynne Ann Timmerman, June 2, 1973; children: Melissa Ann, Amanda Christine, Kendra Dawn, Thomas William. B.A., U. Ariz., 1969, M.A., 1972, Ph.D., 1976; M.Div., Bethany Luth. Sem., 1978. Ordained to ministry, Luth. Ch., 1978. Pastor Our Savior Luth. Ch., Bishop, Calif., 1978-80, Our Saviour Luth. Ch., Lake Havasu City, Ariz., 1980-84, Good Shepherd Luth. Ch., Blythe, Calif., 1982-84, Christ the Cornerstone Luth. Ch., Phoenix, 1984—; area mission developer Evang. Luth. Synod, Ariz., Calif., 1984—; circuit visitor, 1983—; pres. pastoral Conf., 1981—; mem. doctrine com. Evang. Luth. Synod, Mankato, Minn., 1984—. Author: The Life of Christ, 1984; The Living Church-The New Testament, 1985. Asst. to editor Western Apache Raiding and Warfare, 1971. Contbr. articles to profl. jours. Instr. Mohave Community Coll., Lake Havasu City, 1982-83; lectr. Nat. Forest Service, Whiteriver, Ariz., 1984—; rotational chaplain Havasu Regional Hosp., 1982-84. Recipient Meritorious Performance in Teaching award U. Ariz., 1973; George Lillegard Meml. scholar, 1977-80. Mem. U. Ariz. Alumni Assn., Navy League of U.S., Luth. Pioneers Youth Orgn., Phi Beta Kappa, Phi Kappa Phi. Home: 4614 E Sharon Dr Phoenix AZ 85032

KESSLER, GLENN DANIEL, minister, American Baptist Churches U.S.A.; b. Utica, N.Y., Dec. 7, 1926; s. Vernon A. and Myrtle (Moyer) K.; m. Mary Elizabeth Wynne, Nov. 11, 1950; children: Ruth Jane, Ann Elizabeth. B.A., Stetson U., 1969. Ordained to ministry Baptist Ch., 1964. Minister Altay/Reading Bapt. Chs., Reading Ctr., N.Y., 1969-71, Calvary Bapt. Ch., Schenectady, 1971-73, First Bapt. Ch., Middletown, N.Y., 1973-79, Poland/Newport Bapt. Chs., N.Y., 1979—; chaplain Broadacres Skilled Nursing Facility, Utica, 1982—; bd. mgrs. Am. Bapt. Chs. N.Y. State, Syracuse, 1980—; pres. Council of Chs. of Mohawk Valley Area, Utica, 1984—. Chaplain Monhagen Hose Co. No. 1, Middletown, 1974-79; mem. adv. bd. Salvation Army Middletown, 1974-79, Herkimer, N.Y., 1982. Served with USN, 1944-46, PTO. Mem. Ministers Council Am. Bapt. Chs. Home: PO Box 143 Poland NY 13431

KESTLER, RICHARD, provincial, Roman Catholic Church; b. Phila., Jan. 8, 1943; s. John Bernard and Alice (Oest) K. M.A., LaSalle U., 1973, B.A., 1965; M.A., Villanova U., 1979. Cert. secondary sch. adminstr., N.J. Tchr., Hudson Catholic High Sch., Jersey City, 1965-73; community superior Hudson 1968-73; prin. West Catholic Boys High Sch., Phila., 1973-79; provincial Christian Bros. Balt. Province, Adamstown, Md., 1979—; chmn. Calvert Hall Coll. High Sch., Towson, Md., 1979—, St. John's Coll. High Sch., Washington, 1979—, LaSalle Coll. High Sch., 1983—; bd. dirs. LaSalle U., 1979—; bd. edn. Archdioceses of Phila., 1979—, also bd. dirs. Catholic Charities. Recipient Pres.'s medal St. John's Coll. High Sch., 1983. Mem. Nat. Cath. Edn. Assn., Christian Bros. Regional Conf. (trustee). Democrat.

KETCHIE, WILLIAM STEWART, minister, Lutheran Church in America; educator; b. Salisbury, N.C., Feb. 1, 1949; s. William Wesley and Mary Frances (Roseman) K.; m. Kathy Marlene Brown, Aug. 30, 1970; children: Christine Michelle, William Christopher. B.A., Lenoir-Rhyne Coll., 1971; M.Div., Luth. Theol. So. Sem., 1975. Ordained to ministry Lutheran Ch., 1975. Intern, St. Paul Luth. Ch., Postville, Iowa, 1973-74; team pastor Reformation Luth. Ch., Columbia, S.C., 1975-77; pastor St. John Luth. Ch., Asheboro, N.C., 1977—; chmn. parish life and ministry devel. com. N.C. Synod, Luth. Ch. Am.,

---

1982-84, chmn. profession services subcom., 1981-83; chmn. hosp. chaplaincy com., Asheboro, 1982-84. Instr. Randolph Tech. Coll., Asheboro, 1984—. Bd. dirs. Randolph County Women's Aid, Asheboro, 1982-84, treas., 1984; bd. dirs. Hospice of Randolph County, Asheboro, 1982—, pres. bd., 1984. Recipient Disting. Work award Randolph County Women's Aid, 1982; Clergy Recognition award Civitans of Randolph County, 1984. Mem. Asheboro Ministerial Assn. (sec. 1982-83). Office: St John Luth Ch 505 S Park St Asheboro NC 27203

KEYES, KENNETH SCOFIELD, lay church worker, Presbyterian Church in America; b. Morenci, Mich., Sept. 29, 1896; s. Minor Ellery and Blanche (Scofield) K.; m. Lucile Thomas, Oct. 21, 1919 (div. 1948); m. Pauline Sprinkle, Aug. 4, 1949. A.B., U. Mich., 1917; LL.D., Houghton Coll., 1949. Ruling elder Shenandoah Presbyn. Ch., Miami, Fla., 1935-77; elder emeritus Seacrest Presbyn. Ch., Delray Beach, Fla., 1978-84; chmn. fin. com. Nat. Assn. Evangelicals, 1941-75, bd. adminstrn., 1941-75; mem. World Relief Commn., 1943-75; head Concerned Presbyterians, 1964-72; mem. steering com. to form Presbyn. Ch. in Am., 1972-73; mem. Com. on Mission to the World, 1974-76; mem. com. on stewardship ministries Presbyn. Ch. in Am., 1976-78. Lecturer in field. Trustee Ridge Haven Conf. Ctr., 1978-85. Served to 1st lt. inf. U.S. Army, 1918-19. Mem. Nat. Assn. Realtors (pres. 1957), Brokers Inst. (pres. 1937). Republican. Club: Sweetwater Country (Longwood, Fla.). Home: 1316 Majestic Oaks Dr Apopka FL 32703 also Wildcat Ridge RD US 64 PO Box 40 Highlands NC 28741

KEYS, ARTHUR BOYD, SR., minister, Christian Ch. (Disciples of Christ); b. Graysville, Pa., Aug. 9, 1917; s. Arthur and Nettie Edna (Meek) K.; student Washington and Jefferson Coll., 1935-36; B.S., Waynesburg Coll., 1939; postgrad. Bethany Coll., 1954-56, Lexington Theol. Sem., 1961, 62, 63, 65, Christian Theol. Sem., 1964; M.Div., Pitts. Theol. Sem., 1970; m. Esther Romayne Bayne, Aug. 3, 1940; 1 son, Arthur Boyd. Tchr., youth dir., deacon, elder Lone Pine Christian Ch., Washington, Pa., 1940-56; ordained to ministry, 1956; minister Claysville (Pa.) Christian Ch., 1956-66, 1st Christian Ch., New Kensington, Pa., 1966-72; pastor Bellaire (Ohio) Christian Ch., 1972—. Vice pres. Pitts. dist. Christian Ch. in Pa., 1968-70, pres., 1970-72, mem. state bd., 1970-72; rep. Christian Assos. Pa., 1970-72; pres. Bellaire Area Clergy Assn., 1974-75, Ohio Valley Christian Ministers Assn., 1975-76; adviser men's work dist. 11 Christian Ch. in Ohio, 1975—; mem. evangelism com. State Ohio Christian Ch., 1974—; chaplain Bellaire City Hosp., Christians Without Spouses. Pres., Big Bros. and Sisters Bd. Belmont County (Ohio), 1975—; asso. Bethany Coll., 1973. Home: RD 3 Box 45 Bellaire OH 43906 Office: 3565 Belmont St Bellaire OH 43906

KHALSA, SARDARNI PREMKA KAUR, minister, Sikh Dharma; b. Seattle, July 1, 1943; d. Marc L. and G. Josephine (Skarpness) Venable; student pub. schs., Seattle. Sec. gen. Khalsa Council of Sikh Dharma; adminstv. dir. nat. hdqrs. Sikh Dharma, Los Angeles 1974—; adminstrv. sec. to Secretariat of Siri Singh Sahib, 1976—; editor Beads of Truth mag. Mem. Interreligious Council So. Calif., Women's Interfaith Com., Interfaith Coalition on Aging. Author: Peace Lagoon, 1971; Guru for the Aquarian Age, 1973. Home: 1905 Preuss Rd Los Angeles CA 90034 Office: 1620 Preuss Rd Los Angeles CA 90035

KHAMIS, MAR APRIM, bishop, Holy Apostolic Catholic Assyrian Church of East; b. Habbaniya, Iraq, Jan. 7, 1943; s. K. and J.D. Khamis. Ed. Tchrs. Instn., Rabadi, Iraq, Sem., Baghdad, Iraq. Bishop Apostolic Cath. Assyrian Ch. of East, Baghdad, 1973-75, U.S. and Can., 1975—. Home: 8908 Birch Ave Morton Grove IL 60053

KHAN, ABRAHIM HABIBULLA, religion educator, Lutheran Church in America; b. Albion, British Guiana, Apr. 13, 1943; came to Can., 1968; s. Habibulla and Delasia Khan; m. Pamela Anne O'Neill, Oct. 11, 1969; children: Tariq, Roshan, Laith. B.S., Howard U., 1965; B.Div., Yale U., 1968; M.A., McGill U., Montreal, Can., 1971, Ph.D., 1973. Researcher, lectr. Trinity Coll., U. Toronto, 1984—; lectr. McMaster U., Hamilton, Ont., Can., 1985—. Author: Salighed As Happiness? Kierkegaard on the Concept of Salighed, 1985. Contbr. articles to theol. jours. Fellow McGill U., summer 1971, summer 1972; grantee Que. Govt., 1973, Can. Fedn. Humanities, 1982. Mem. Am. Acad. Religion (chmn. Kierkegaard Seminar 1985—), Can. Theol. Soc. (newsletter editor 1985—), Can. Soc. Study of Religion, Soren Kierkegaard Soc. in Denmark, Can. Philos. Assn. Office: Trinity Coll Univ Toronto 6 Hoskins Ave Toronto ON M5S 1H8 Canada

KHANJIAN, JOHN, religion educator, Armenian Evangelical Church; b. Aleppo, Syria, Dec. 3, 1932; came to U.S., 1966; s. Gergis and Sayoud Zevart (Karigian) Khanji Ekmeji; m. Pauline Lucy Alexanian, July 28, 1966; children: Tanya Joy, Jonathan-Alex. B.A., Am. U. Beirut, Lebanon, 1962, M.A., 1968; B.D., Near East Sch. Theology, 1963; Ph.D., Claremont Grad. Sch., 1974. Ordained to ministry, 1971. Tchr., Aleppo Coll., Syria, 1963-66; assoc. prof. religion, librarian Near East Sch. Theology, Beirut, Lebanon, 1971-76; assoc. prof., chmn. dept. religion Kans. Wesleyan Coll., Salina, 1977—. Author: Wisdom in Ugarit & ANE, 1973; (in Arabic) The Relationship of ANE Thought to the Old Testament. Contbr. articles to profl. jours. Fellow Soc. Bibl. Lit. Home: 739 E Leslie St Salina KS 67401 Office: Kansas Wesleyan U 100 E Claflin St Salina KS 67401

KHOURY, GEORGE FARID, pastor, Seventh-day Adventists; b. Beirut, Lebanon, June 18, 1934; came to U.S., 1976, naturalized, 1982; s. Farid N. and Nabeeha (Karim) K.; m. Venice Simon, Jan. 4, 1959; children: Nina, Vicky, Ruby. B.S. in Theology, Middle East Coll., Beirut, 1957; M.A. in N.T., Andrews U., 1963, M.Div., 1971. Ordained to ministry Seventh-day Adventists. Pres., Lebanon Seventh-day Adventist, Beirut, 1963-67; evangelist Middle East div., Beirut, 1967-70; tchr. Middle East Coll., 1971-76; pastor Seventh-day Adventist Ch., Elyria, Ohio, 1976-84, Defiance, Bryan and Hicksville, Ohio, 1984—. Home and Office: 201 E Smith St Hicksville OH 43526

KIBBLE, HARVEY WARD, elder, Seventh-day Adventists; b. Huntsville, Ala., Jan. 28, 1908; s. Edward and Mittie (Livingston) K.; student Oakwood Jr. Coll., 1928; m. Thelma Lois Winston, June 4, 1929; children—Harvey W., Herman Loris, William Harold, Marie L., Ann L., Alvin M. Ordained to ministry, 1934; pastor, evangelist, Houston, Tyler, San Antonio, Tex., 1929-35, Newark, 1935-42, Chgo., 1942-48, Bklyn., 1948-51; weekly radio broadcaster Sta. WAIT, Chgo., 1943-45; pres. Lake Region conf. Seventh-day Adventists, Chgo., 1951-61; lay activities sec. Northeastern Conf. N.Y.C., 1962-70. Mem. hosp. bd., Hinsdale, Ill., 1951-61; bd. dirs. Andrews U., Berrien Springs, Mich., 1951-61, Oakwood Coll., Huntsville, Ala., 1951-61; mem. Newark Mayor's Interracial Com., 1938-40; mem. com. Essex County council Boy Scouts Am., 1938-40; bd. dirs. Urban League, 1936-40. Contbg. editor Message mag., 1951-61. Home: 3611 Reynolds Circle Huntsville AL 35810

KIDWELL, GARY WAYNE, minister, Christian Church (Disciples of Christ); b. Madison, Ind., July 10, 1955; s. Charles Edward and Mary Frances (Galusha) K.; m. Judy Hubbard, Dec. 22, 1979; children: Joseph Marion, Amy Marie. B.S., Campbellsville Coll., 1977; M.Div., Lexington Theol. Sem., 1980. Ordained to ministry, 1981. Student pastor Sparta Christian Ch., Ky., 1978-80; pastor Walton Christian Ch., Ky., 1980—; v.p. Christian Chs. of No. Ky., 1982-84; del. No. Ky. Interfaith Commn., 1983-84; pres. Christian Chs. No. Ky., 1984—; alumni fund coordinator Lexington Theol. Sem., 1983—; com. for young adult ministry Christian Ch. in Ky., 1984—, enabler for stewardship programming, 1983—. Contbr. articles to profl. jours. Chaplain Walton Vol. Fire Dept., 1982—; sponsor Soc. of Disting. Am. High Sch. Students, Walton, 1983. Recipient A.J. Whitehouse award, Lexington Theol. Sem., 1981, George V. Moore award, 1979. Mem. Disciples Peace Fellowship. Democrat. Home: 33 Bedinger Ave Walton KY 41094 Office: Walton Christian Ch 33 Bedinger Ave Walton KY 41094

KIDWELL, HAROLD LABAN, minister, American Baptist Convention; b. Lyndon, Kans., Jan. 30, 1927; s. Laban Edward and Ora Frances (Whitney) K.; m. Sylvia Murlene Cook, Jan. 27, 1945; children: James Harold, Richard Lee. Student Tulsa U., 1961, Central Bapt. Sem., 1956. Ordained to ministry Am. Bapt. Conv., 1955. Pastor, First Bapt. Ch., Newcomerstown, Ohio, 1965-69, First Bapt. Ch., Jefferson, Ohio, 1969-76, First Bapt. Ch., Sterling, Colo., 1976-78, Grove City Bapt. Ch., Ohio, 1978—; trustee Ohio Bapt. and Columbus Assn., Columbus, Ohio, 1979—; chmn. com. World Mission Support, Granville, Ohio, 1982—. Served with USN, 1944-46. Mem. Columbus Bapt. Assn. (pres. 1984—), Grove City Ministerial Assn. (v.p. 1984—), Am. Bapt. Minister's Council, Ohio Bapt. Minister's Council. Home: 2666 Kenny Ln Grove City OH 43123

KIESER, ELLWOOD EUGENE, religious television program producer, priest, Roman Catholic Ch.; b. Phila., Mar. 27, 1929; s. Ellwood Eugene and Helen Marie (Kleinsmith) K. B.A., LaSalle Coll., 1950; M.A., St. Paul's Coll., 1953; Ph.D., Grad. Theol. Union, Berkeley, Calif., 1973. Ordained priest Roman Catholic Ch., 1956. Pres./exec. producer Paulist Prodns., Pacific Palisades, Calif., 1960—; pres. Humanitas Prize, Los Angeles. Instr. philosophy UCLA. Creator (TV series) Insight, 1960—; contbr. articles to various publs. Recipient Emmy awards, 1980, 81, 82, 83, 84. Mem. Writers Guild Am. West, Am. Acad. TV Artists. Office: Paulist Prodns Inc 17575 Pacific Coast Hwy Pacific Palisades CA 90272

KIEWE, BERNHARD, religious organization executive. Orthodox Jewish Congregations; b. Koenigsberg, Germany, Nov. 4, 1929; s. Leser and Etl (Marvit) K.; came to U.S., 1948, naturalized, 1953; student Mirrer Rabbinical Sem., Shanghai, China, 1941-46, Southeastern U., Washington, 1955; m. Marlene Rosella Schulman, Dec. 27, 1953; children—Roy, Ronald, Jerome, Robert, Michael. Acting chaplain U.S. Air Force, 1950-54; pres. Adath Yesgurunm Synagogue, Balt., 1976—, Adath Yeshurun-Mogen Abraham Synagogue, Balt., 1976—; chaplain Md. sect. Jewish War Vets., 1974-75; pres. Farband Labor Zionist Council, 1970-71; pres. Pinski br. Labor Zionist Council Am., 1968-69; exec. dir. Jewish Nat. Fund of Md., 1967-84; nat. dir. devel. Jewish War Vets. U.S.A. Nat. Meml., Inc. Mem. Labor Zionist Alliance, Union Orthodox Congregations. Home: 1010 Scotts Hill Dr Baltimore MD 21208 Office: 1811 R NW Washington DC 20009

KIK, FRANK NICHOLAS, minister United Presbyterian Church in U.S.A.; b. Dalhousie, N.B., Can., Nov. 17, 1935; s. Jacob Marcellus and Evelyn Winona (Reid) K.; came to U.S., 1952, naturalized, 1957; B.A., Gordon Coll., 1959; M.Div., Gordon Conwell Sem., 1963, D.D., 1976; m. Phyllis Ann Savage, June 1, 1957; children: Scott Douglas, Heather Jean, Daryl Andrew. Ordained to ministry, 1963; pastor Queens Village Presbyn. Ch., N.Y.C., 1963-68; sr. pastor Knox Presbyn. Ch., Buffalo, 1968-73, Eastminster United Presbyn. Ch., Wichita, 1973—; lectr. Gordon-Conwell Sem., Mass., Wichita State U.; founder, Ellicott Ministry, Inc., Buffalo; chmn. adv. bd. World Impact Inc., Wichita; founder Wichita Christian Counseling Center; v.p. Presbyterians United for Bibl. Concerns, 1974—; chmn. bd. Sterling (Kans.) Coll., 1974—. Club: Wichita Downtown Kiwanis (past pres.). Home: 232 Lochinvar Wichita KS 67207 Office: 7202 E 9th St Wichita KS 67206

KIKER, HENRY ROGER, minister, Southern Baptist Convention; b. Monroe, N.C., Jan. 5, 1949; s. John Henry and Ruby Jane (Rushing) K.; m. Sheila Gail Helms, Jan. 18, 1969; children: Thomas Henry, Rhonda Lynn, Donna Marie. Student, Central Piedmont Coll., Wingate Coll.; Assoc. Div., Southeastern Sem., 1981. Ordained to ministry Southern Baptist Convention, 1981. Pastor Eureka Bapt. Ch., Keysville, Va., 1981-83, Reedy Creek Bapt. Ch., Freeman, Va., 1983—; mem. Concord Ministers Conf., South Hill, Va., 1984—, Greensville Ministers Conf., Emporia, Va., 1984—. Active in Charlotte County Rescue Squad, Keysville, 1982-83. Served with U.S. Army, Vietnam. Mem. Va. Bapt. Pastors Conf. (sec., treas., 1984—), Am. Christian TV System Concord Bapt. Assn. (cons. 1984—). Republican. Avocations: golf; fishing; hunting. Home: Rural Route 1 Box 220 Freeman VA 23856 Office: Reedy Creek Bapt Ch Rural Route 1 Box 220 Freeman VA 23856

KILGO, BENNY LARUE, minister, So. Bapt. Conv.; b. West Point, N.Y., Aug. 3, 1945; s. Louis Eugene and Audery Maud (Torbett) K.; B.S. in Religious Edn., Hardin-Simmons U., Abilene, Tex., 1968; postgrad. Southwestern Sem., Ft. Worth, 1969-70, Luther Rice Sem., Jacksonville, Fla., 1975—; m. Patricia Anita Woodard, June 12, 1971. Youth dir. First Bapt. Ch., Carrollton, Tex., 1969-70; youth and music dir. Calvary Bapt. Ch., Dumas, Tex., 1970-74; asso. pastor First Bapt. Ch., Wellington, Tex., 1974-76; youth minister First Bapt. Ch., Dalhart, Tex., 1976—. Associational youth and music dir.; youth camp personality; Glorieta staff tchr. Sunday Sch. Bd. Dir., Community Patriotic Musical, Wellington, 1975-76. Home: 708 E 16th St Dalhart TX 79022 Office: PO Box 951 Dalhart TX 79022

KILGORE, LEROY WILSON, minister, Presbyterian Ch. U.S.A.; b. Elmira, N.Y., Feb. 25, 1917; s. Roy Dunning and Bertha Pearl (Bush) K.; m. Ursula Dunbar, Aug. 27, 1940 (dec. 1960); children: Keith, Sharon, Paul, Debra; m. Lois Bell Kilgore, Feb. 14, 1961; children: Richard, Nancy, Douglas, Cynthia, Kristie. B.A., Colgate U., 1939; M.Div., Colgate Rochester Div. Sch., 1942; D.Div. Lincoln Coll., 1955, Colgate U., 1964. Ordained to ministry, 1942. Minister, First Presbyn. Ch., Hartford, Conn., 1943-53; sr. minister Lakewood Presbyn. Ch., Cleve., 1953-64, Cherry Hill Presbyn. Ch., Dearborn, Mich., 1964-72, Valley Presbyn. Ch., Scottsdale, Ariz., 1972—; clk. of Presbytery, moderator Presbytery of Conn. Valley, 1947-55; chmn. bd. trustees Cleve. Presbytery, 1955-59; chmn. budget and ministerial relations Presbytery of Detroit, 1967-72; mem. gen. council Presbytery of Grand Canyon, Phoenix, 1973-79; chmn. major mission fund Synod of Southwest, Phoenix, 1978; trustee San Francisco Theol. Sem., others. Author: What A Way to Live, 1978; When the River Runs Backward, 1984. Author sermons, series of meditations. Mem. Support Agy. of Presbyn. Ch. Lodge: Rotary. Home: 7800 N 65th St Scottsdale AZ 85253 Office: Valley Presbyn Ch 6947 E Macdonald Dr Scottsdale AZ 85253

KILLMAN, JOHN RUSSELL, broadcaster, American Baptist Church; b. Chgo., Mar. 8, 1921; s. David and Gertrude (Anderson) K.; m. Virginia M. Killman, Nov. 20, 1982; children by previous marriage: Candace Lee, Cheryl Lynn. B.A., Calif. Bapt. Sem., 1950; Th.B., Biola Coll., 1949; D.D. (hon.), Hindustan Bible Inst.-India, 1976; Ph.D. (hon.), Fla. Research Inst., 1972. Youth dir. First Bapt. Ch., Lynwood, Calif., 1946-48; assoc. pastor First Bapt. Ch., Paramount, Calif., 1949-50, asst. pastor, Torrance, Calif., 1950-51; missionary Hong Kong, 1954-58; dir. Heaven and Home Hour, Glendale, Calif., 1958—. Author: Meet the Authors of the Bible, 1982; Steps to the Abundant Life, 1976. Served with USN, 1942-45. Recipient award Nat. Religious Broadcasters, 1983. Mem. Western Religious Broadcasters (v.p. 1979-80). Republican. Home: 3922 Community Ave La Crescenta CA 91214 Offic Heaven and Home Hour 1520 W Glenoaks Blv Glendale CA 91201

KILPATRICK, DAVID MAURER, ministe American Baptist Churches U.S.A.; b. Port Huror Mich., Oct. 12, 1939; s. Miller C. and Doris Laver (Maurer) K.; B.S.E., U. Mich., 1962; M.Div., Colgat Rochester Div. Sch., 1965; D.Min., Andover Newto Theol. Sch., 1975; m. Sandra Jean Smith, Aug. 11, 196 children—Stephen, Scott, Daniel, David. Ordained t ministry, Am. Baptist Chs. U.S.A., 1965; asso. pasto First Bapt. Ch., Fairport, N.Y., 1962-65; pastor Firs Bapt. Ch., Macedon, N.Y., 1965-68, Wickford Firs Bapt. Ch., North Kingstown, R.I., 1968-76; sr. pasto Greenville (R.I.) Bapt. Ch., 1976-84; sr. pastor Firs Bapt. Ch., Malden, Mass., 1984—. Mem. exec. com. bd. mgrs. Am. Bapt. Chs. N.Y., 1967-68, Am. Bapt. Chs R.I., 1968-84; v.p. Bapt. Camps R.I., 1968-75, pres. 1975-77; mem. gen. bd. Am. Bapt. Chs./U.S.A. 1976—. Bd. dirs. Washington County Mental Healt Clinic, 1973-76. Mem. Am. Bapt. Ministers R.I. (treas 1971-82). Rotarian (charter mem., treas. 1970-75) Home: 166 Hawthorne St Malden RI 02148 Office: 49 Main St Malden MA 02148

KIM, CHAN-HIE, minister, United Methodis Church; b. Hoeryong, Korea, June 7, 1935; came t U.S., 1961, naturalized, 1973; s. Chongjin and Kansun (Moon) K.; m. Sook-Chung Kim, Sept. 9, 1962; 1 child Alexis H. B.A., Yonsei U., Seoul, Korea, 1958; postgrad U. Heidelberg, Germany, 1960-61; B.D., Vanderbilt U. 1964, Ph.D., 1970. Ordained to ministry United Meth Ch., 1965. Staff mem. Bd. of Discipleship United Meth Ch., Nashville, 1974-77; assoc. prof. N.T., Sch. o Theology at Claremont, Calif., 1977—; exec. dir. Ctr for Asian-Am. Ministries, 1977—. Author: Form and Structure of Familiar Greek Letter of Recommendation 1974. Served to 1st lt. Korean Air Force, 1958-60 Mem. Soc. of Bibl. Lit., Soc. of Korean Studies (pres. 1983—), Am. Acad. Religion. Home: 189 E Limestone Rd Claremont CA 91711 Office: Sch of Theology a Claremont 1325 N College Ave Claremont CA 91711

KIM, HEE-JIN, religious educator; b. Masan, S. Kyongsang-do, Korea, Apr. 8, 1927; came to U.S., 1952; s. Young-Ho and Um-Chon (Kim) K.; m. Kyue-In Lee, June 4, 1957 (dec. 1963); children: Sun-Chul, Hae-Sil; m. Jung-Sun Kim, Feb. 7, 1965; 1 child, Yeong-Jue. B.A., U. Calif.-Berkeley, 1957, M.A., 1958; Ph.D., Claremont Grad. Sch., 1966. Faculty, U. Oreg., Eugene, 1973—, prof. religious studies, 1983—. Author: Dogen Kigen-Mystical Realist, 1975. Mem. Assn. for Asian Studies, Soc. for Asian and Comparative Philosophy, Am. Acad. Religion, Internat. Assn. Buddhist Studies. Home: 570 Ful Vue Dr Eugene OR 97405 Office: Univ Oreg Eugene OR 97403

KIM, RICHARD, priest, Episcopal Church; b. Seoul, Korea, June 29, 1927; came to U.S., 1946; s. Chang Sei and Chung (Sil) K.; m. Catharine Rikert, Apr. 2, 1949 (div. 1984); children: Carroll, Theresa, Margaret, Richard, Dorothy Babson, Camilla, Matthew, Peter. Student, Dickinson Coll., 1948-50, U. South, Sewannee, Tenn., 1971-72. Ordained priest, 1974. Asst. chaplain Canterbury Chapel, U. Ala., Tuscaloosa, 1972-74; rector Grace Episcopal Ch., Sheffield, Ala., 1974-77, Good Shepherd Ch., Maui, Hawaii, 1977-81, Trinity Episcopal Ch., Lexington, Mich., 1981—; founder, pres. Blue Water Hospice, Inc., Port Huron, Mich., 1981-84; founder Project Blessing, Lexington, 1981—; dean Blue Water Convocation, 1982-83. Bd. dirs. Salvation Army, Port Huron, 1982-83. Served to lt. col. U.S. Army, 1950-71. Recipient Citizen of the Yr. award Social Workers Assn. U.S.A., 1976; Joint Resolution, Mich. State Legislature, 1983. Address: Trinity Episcopal Ch PO Box 315 Hubbard and Main Lexington MI 48450

KIM, SANG-BOK DAVID, minister, educator, Presbyterian Church U.S.A.; b. Pyong Yang, Korea, Jan. 11, 1939; came to U.S., 1965; s. Chan-Yong and Sool-E (Chang) K.; m. Young-Ja Helen Kim, June 12, 1965; children: Grace, Eunice, Christine. B.A., Seoul Nat. U., 1963; M.Div., Faith Theol. Sem., 1968, S.T.M., 1972; Th.D., Grace Theol. Sem., 1977. Ordained to ministry, 1971. Pastor, Calvary Presbyn. Ch., Trenton, N.J., 1968-69, Sheridan Presbyn. Ch., Ind., 1970-76; instr. Grace Coll., Winona Lake, Ind., 1972-75; prof. Ind. Christian U., Indpls., 1972-77; prof. Washington Bible Coll., Lanham, Md., 1977—; sr. pastor Bethel Presbyn. Ch., Randallstown, Md., 1980—; chmn. bd. Washington Christian Broadcasting System, 1978-85; pres. N.Am. Council Youth Leaders, Balt., 1980-85. Author: The Wave of the Future, 1977; Affirmation of Woman, 1977. Publisher: Our Daily Bread mag., 1980. Recipient Sr. award Faith Theol. Sem., 1968. Home: 6522 Jodie St New Carrollton MD 20784 Office: Washington Bible Coll 6511 Princess Garden Pkwy Lanham MD 20801

KIMBALL, SPENCER WOOLEY, church official, Church of Jesus Christ of Latter Day Saints; b. Salt Lake City, Mar. 28, 1895; s. Andrew and Olive (Wooley) K.; ed. Eastern Ariz. Jr. Coll., U. Ariz.; LL.D. (hon.) Brigham Young U., 1969; m. Camilla Eyring, Nov., 1917; children—Olive Beth (Mrs. Grant M. Mack), Spencer L., Andrew, Edward. Missionary, Ch. of Jesus Christ of Latter-Day Saints, Switzerland and Germany,

914, Central States Mission, 1914-1916; pres. deacon's quorum; former clerk St. Joseph Stake, also counselor in stake presidency; past pres. Mt. Graham Stake; mem. Council of the Twelve Apostles Ch. of Jesus Christ of Latter-Day Saints, 1943—, ordained apostle, 1943, now pres., also chmn. exec. com. of Missionary Com., chmn. budget com.; mem. expenditure com. and correlation com. Lectr. Latter-day Saints Insts.; pub. speaker. Dir., v.p. council Boy Scouts Am.; sec. Gila Valley Irrigation Dist.; active Indian Student Placement Program, AYUDA. Chmn. bd., trustee Brigham Young U., Bd. Edn. Ch. Schs. Mem. C. of C. Rotarian. Author: The Miracle of Forgiveness; also numerous pamphlets. Address: 50 E N Temple St Salt Lake City UT 84150*

KIMBLE, MARCUS ALLEN, minister, United Presbyn. Ch. in U.S.A.; b. Sussex, N.J., Oct. 30, 1920; s. Marcus Lynn and Wilhelmina (McConnell) K.; B.A., Wheaton (Ill.) Coll., 1942; B.D., Princeton Theol. Sem., 1946, M.Div., 1972; D.D. (hon.), Lake Forest (Ill.) Coll., 1976; L.H.D., Nat. Coll. Edn., Evanston, Ill., 1976; m. Sara Elizabeth Rogers, Aug. 28, 1945; children—Carolyn, Beverly. Ordained to ministry, 1946; asst. minister First Presbyn. Ch., Westfield, N.J., 1946-47; minister Presbyn. Ch. of Lawrenceville, N.J., 1947-59; master of religion Lawrenceville Boys Sch., 1947-52; minister Calvary Presbyn. Ch., Wyncote, Pa., 1959-72; dir. devel. Presbyn. Home, Evanston, Ill., 1972—. Trustee, Presbytery of Chgo.; mem. div. fin. and resource devel. Synod of Lincoln Trails. Home: 865 Hiawatha Ln Riverwoods IL 60015 Office: 3200 Grant St Evanston IL 60201

KIMBLE, MELVIN ARNOLD, educator, Luth. Ch. in Am.; b. Toledo, Ohio, Mar. 20, 1926; s. Avery Dean and Frieda A. (Manthey) K.; A.B., Wittenberg U., 1947; M.Div., Hamma Sch. Theology, 1950; Th.M., So. Bapt. Theol. Sem., 1960; Ph.D., U.S. Internat. U., 1974; postgrad. U. Vienna (Austria) (Luth. World Fedn. scholar), 1960-61, (Aid Assn. fellow) King's Coll. and Westminster Pastoral Found. (both London, Eng.), 1975; m. JoAnne Trew, Dec. 30, 1950; children—Cynthia Kay, Marsha Ann. Ordained to ministry, 1950; pastor Grace Luth. Ch., Steubenville, Ohio, 1950-54, Calvary Luth. Ch., Chillicothe, Ohio, 1954-58; chaplain Miss. State Hosp., Whitfield, 1959-60; pastor Am. Protestant Ch., Bad Godesberg, West Germany, 1961-65; prof. pastoral care Northwestern Luth. Theol. Sem., St. Paul, Minn., 1965—, chmn. dept. pastoral theology and ministry, 1976—. Adv. bd. Inst. Logotherapy. Tressler Univ. scholar, 1958-59, Bd. Theol. Edn. fellow, 1970-71. Mem. Insts. Religion and Health, Soc. Sci. Study Religion, Assn. Clin. Pastoral Edn., Assn. Humanistic Psychology, Soc. Study Med. Ethics (asso. mem.; Gt. Britain). Contbr. articles, book revs. to jours. Home: 2200 Chalet Dr Minneapolis MN 55421 Office: 1501 Fulham St St Paul MN 55108

KIMMEL, EDITH MAY, lay church worker, Churches of Christ; b. Johnstown, Pa.; d. John Ira and Rosa Pearl (Zimmerman) Bowman; B.A. magna cum laude, U. Pitts., 1980; postgrad. Lancaster Theol. Sem., 1984—; m. Charles E. Kimmel, May 22, 1937; 1 son, Lawrence Winfred. Mem. steering com. Council of Chs. of Christ in Greater Johnstown, Pa., 1958, mem. bd. dirs., 1958-63, exec. sec., 1963-76; pres. St. Paul's United Ch. of Christ, Johnstown, 1976—; pres. Johnstown Council of Ch. Women, 1959, 60; mem. bd. mgrs. dept. United Ch. Women, Pa. Council Chs., 1959-61; pres. Johnstown aux. Am. Bible Soc., 1964, 65; bd. dirs. Penn West Conf., United Ch. of Christ, 1976-80, pres. Somerset Assn., 1980-81; bd. dirs. Found. Campus Ministry, U. Pitts.-Johnstown, 1979-81. Mem. Am. Bible Soc. (life), Nat. Assn. Ecumenical Staff, Internat. Platform Assn. Address: RD 7 Box 516 Johnstown PA 15905

KINCL, RICH LOUIS, minister, Southern Baptist Convention; b. Sacramento, Jan. 31, 1953; s. Jerry J. and Vinola R. (Hunziker) K.; m. Kay G. Owens, May 14, 1978; children: Sarah Vi, Barry Richard. B.A., U. Ark., 1975; M.Div., Southwestern Bapt. Theol. Sem., 1978; D.Min., Midwestern Bapt. Theol. Sem., 1986. Ordained to ministry, 1978. Minister of youth 1st Bapt. Ch., North Little Rock, 1975-76, 1st Bapt. Ch., Mineola, Tex., 1977-78; assoc. pastor Watson Chapel Bapt. Ch., Pine Bluff, Ark., 1978-80; pastor 1st Bapt. Ch., Berryville, Ark., 1980—; exec. bd. Ark. Bapt. State Conv., 1984—; stewardship cons. Stewardship Commn. So. Bapt. Conv., 1983—; mem. Associational Sunday Sch. Improvement Support Team, No. Ark. Bapt. Assn., 1980-84. Dir. Citizens United Against Gambling, Berryville, 1984; mem. Health Bd., Berryville. Mem. Pastors Conf. Ark. Bapt. State Conv. (2d v.p. 1985), Berryville C. of C. (v.p. 1983), Sigma Pi (assoc.). Club: Rotary (bd. dirs.). Home: 502 E Madison Berryville AR 72616 Office: First Bapt Ch PO Box 347 Berryville AR 72616

KINDRICK, LARRY EUGENE, minister, Southern Baptist Convention; b. Houston, Oct. 5, 1945; s. Gerald K. and Sybil Alene (Frazier) K.; m. Pamela Nanette Dickens, Aug. 20, 1966; children: Pamela Ann, Patricia Nanette. BA., U. Corpus Christi, 1969; M.Div., Southwestern Bapt. Theol. Sem., Ft. Worth, 1972, D.Min., 1977, postgrad., 1978—. Ordained to ministry Southern Baptist Convention, 1971. Assoc. pastor Molina Bapt. Mission, Corpus Christi, Tex., 1965; assoc. pastor, minister of youth Calvary Bapt. Ch., Corpus Christi, 1966-68; pastor Little River Bapt. Ch., Cameron, Tex., 1970-72, Poynor Bapt. Ch., Tex., 1973-74, Second Bapt. Ch., Marshall, Tex., 1974-76, Greggton First Bapt. Ch., Longview, Tex., 1976—; chmn. area com. Gregg-Soda Lake Area, Longview, 1981-83; mem. Gene Williams Evangelistic Assn. Crusade, Philippines, 1985. Founding bd. dirs. Food Box, Longview, 1982—. Mem. Gregg County Bapt. Assn. (moderator 1978-81), Longview Area Ministerial Alliance (pres. 1981-83). Democrat. Lodge: Lions. Avocations: golf; fishing; hunting; camping; sports. Home: 1315 Trailwood Ln Longview TX 75605 Office: Greggton Frist Bapt Ch 4520 W Marshall Ave Longview TX 75604

KING, AUSTIN BRYANT, lay ch. worker, So. Bapt. Conv.; b. Marion, S.C., Aug. 20, 1939; s. Austin McCoy and Ileen (Bryant) K.; certificate music U.S. Naval Sch. Music, 1961; Mus.B., Peabody Conservatory Music, 1967; Mus.M., Vandercook Coll. Music, 1976. Minister music and youth Pleasant Grove Bapt. Ch., Dillon, S.C., 1972-73, College Park Bapt. Ch., Florence, S.C., 1973-75, Union Bapt. Ch., Marion, S.C., 1976—. Dir. bands Marion (S.C.) Pub. Schs., 1972—. Mem. Music Educators Nat. Assn., NEA, S.C. Music Educators Assn., S.C. Nat. Educators Assn. Home: Route 1 Marion SC 29571 Office: Conway Hwy Marion SC 29571

KING, BERNARD PAUL, rabbi, Reform Jewish Congregations; b. Tucson, Apr. 21, 1938; s. Jake Sandusky and Florence Ruth (Rothberger) K.; B.A., U. Calif. at Los Angeles, 1963; B.H.L., Hebrew Union Coll.-Jewish Inst. Religion, 1965, M.A.H.L., 1969; m. Barbara Lynn Plotkin, June 26, 1980; children: David Jeffrey, Neil Michael, Stephen Haim, Adeena Rochelle. Rabbi, 1969; student rabbi Temple Beth Solomon of Deaf, 1961-64, Temple Beth Tikvah, Fullerton, Calif., 1964-65, Mattoon Jewish Ctr., Ill., 1966-68, Beth Israel, Hamilton, Ohio, 1968-69; rabbi Shir Ha-Ma'a lot-Harbor Reform Temple, Newport Beach, Calif., 1969—; adviser to Jewish students U. Calif.-Irvine, 1969-72; rabbinic adviser to bd. trustees Hebrew Union Coll.-Jewish Inst. Religion; v.p. U. Calif. Interfaith Found. Irvine, 1976-77; founding pres. Newport-Mesa-Irvine Interfaith Council, 1978. Mem. Central Conf. Am. Rabbis, Pacific Assn. Reform Rabbis (exec. bd.), Orange County Bd. Rabbis (pres. 1982-83). Home: 1910 Lanai Dr Costa Mesa CA 92626 Office: 1400 W Balboa Newport Beach CA 92663

KING, CHARLES BERNARD, priest, Roman Catholic Church; b. Wichita Falls, Tex., Nov. 5, 1931; s. Charles Bernard and Jean Hilda (Leahey) K. B.S. in Econs., Georgetown U., 1953; S.T.L., Gregorian U., Rome, 1957. Ordained priest Roman Cath. Ch., 1956. Assoc. pastor St. Pius X Ch., Dallas, 1957-66; sem. rector Holy Trinity Sem., U. Dallas, 1967-69; pastor St. Andrews Ch., Ft. Worth, 1969-79, Sacred Heart Ch., Wichita Falls, 1979—; past pres. InterFaith Ministries, Inc., Wichita Falls; bd. dirs. Samaritan Counseling Ctr., Wichita Falls. Lodge: Rotary (chaplain Wichita Falls, Paul Harris fellow 1983). Home and Office: Sacred Heart Ch 1505 9th St Wichita Falls TX 76301

KING, CORETTA SCOTT (MRS. MARTIN LUTHER KING, JR.), religious organization executive, concert singer, lecturer, author, Baptist Church; b. Marion, Ala., Apr. 27, 1927; B.A., Antioch Coll., Yellow Springs, Ohio; Mus.B., New Eng. Conservatory Music, Boston, 1954, Mus.D. (hon.), 1971; L.H.D. (hon.), Boston U., 1969, Marymount-Manhattan Coll., 1969, Morehouse Coll., 1970; H.H.D. (hon.), Brandeis U., 1969, Wilberforce U., 1970, Bethune-Cookman Coll., 1970, Princeton, 1970; LL.D. (hon.), Bates Coll., 1971; m. Martin Luther King, Jr., June 18, 1953 (dec. Apr. 1968); children—Yolanda Denise, Martin Luther, Dexter Scott, Bernice Albertine. Singer, Chorus Antioch Coll., 1945-51; mem. Conservatory Chorus, New Eng. Conservatory Music, 1951-54, premiered song cycle Motivos de Son, 1953; performed first ofcl. Freedom Concert at Town Hall, N.Y.C., 1964; performed Freedom Concerts in Amsterdam, Holland, 1970, also in Cin. and Newark; pres. Martin Luther King, Jr. Center for Social Change, Atlanta, 1968—; numerous lectures abroad and throughout U.S., 1968—, including Parliament House, New Delhi, India, Womens U., Bombay, India, Boston U., Brandeis U., Harvard and Yale, also St. Pauls Cathedral and Central Hall, Westminster Abbey, London, Bethune-Cookman and Morehouse colls.; del. 17 Nation Disarmament Conf., Women Strike for Peace, Geneva, 1962; trustee Ebenezer Bapt. Ch.; bd. dirs. SCLC; appeared on numerous TV and radio shows. Co-chairperson Nat. Com. for Full Employment; pres. Martin Luther King, Jr. Found., Martin Luther King, Jr. Center for Social Change; trustee Robert F. Kennedy Meml. Center; mem. exec. bd. Nat. Health Ins. Com.; active Nat. Union Hosp. and Health Care Employees Dist. 1199, So. Rural Action, Inc. Recipient Distinguished Achievement award Nat. Assn. Colored Women's Clubs, 1962, award of excellence in field of human relations Soc. for Family of May, 1968, Universal Love award Premio San Valentine Com., Verona, Italy, 1968, Wateler Peace prize, 1968, Pacem in Terris award Internat. Overseas Service Found., 1969, award World Orgn. Diplomatic Press, 1969, Martin Luther King Meml. medal City Coll. N.Y., 1971. Mem. Nat. Council Negro Women (Ann. Brotherhood award 1957), Womens Internat. League for Peace and Freedom, NAACP, Alpha Kappa Alpha. Author: My Life With Martin Luther King, Jr. (Internat. Viareggio award 1971), 1969; conbg. author: Exploring Mental Health Perameters; Trumpet of Conscience; Where Do We Go From Here: Choas or Community?; contbr. articles to popular mags. and ch. publs. First woman to deliver Class Day Address at Harvard, 1968, first woman to preach at Statutory Service, St. Paul's Cathedral, London, 1969. Home: 234 Sunset Ave NW Atlanta GA 30314 Office: 671 Beckwith St SW Atlanta GA 30314

KING, DONALD REX, minister, Southern Baptist Convention; industrial engineer; b. Thomaston, Ga., Jan. 1, 1951; s. Julius O. and Norma B. (Ford) K.; m. Vicki Coogler, Apr. 14, 1974; children: Brent, Brooke. B.Engring., So. Tech. U., 1973; M.Bible Theology, Internat. Bible Inst. and Sem., 1984, D.Bible Theology, 1984. Ordained to ministry, 1975. Youth minister Mountain View Bapt. Ch., Thomaston, 1975-76, pastor, 1978—; assoc. pastor Clark's Chapel Bapt. Ch., Thomaston, 1976-78; del. Centennial Assn., 1978—, So. Bapt. Conv., 1978—, Ga. Bapt. Conv., 1978—. Indsl. engr. Thomaston Mills, Inc., 1976—. Author: Baptist Doctrine, 1984; Bible Characters, 1984; What the Future Holds, 1981. Asst. chmn. Anti-Liquor League, Thomaston, 1982. Recipient Cert. of Merit, U.S. Rep. Jack Brinkley, 1979, Cert. of Appreciation, Thomaston Sertoma Club, 1981. Club: Thomaston Youth Football Assn. (coach 1974-78). Home: 19 Ave D Thomaston GA 30286 Office: Mountain View Bapt Ch 2569 Jefferson David Rd Thomaston GA 30286

KING, FRANCIS EDWARD, priest, religion educator, Roman Catholic Church; b. San Francisco, Nov. 19, 1931; s. Francis A. and Helene B. (Johnson) K. B.A., Gonzaga U., 1955, M.A., 1956; S.T.L., Alma Coll., 1963; S.T.M., Santa Clara U., 1963; S.T.D., Pontifical Gregorian U., Rome, 1972. Ordained priest, Roman Cath. Ch., 1962. Asst. prof. theology U. San Francisco, 1964-66, 69—. Author: The Institutional Aspects of the Church According to William Law (1686-1761), 1971. Contbr. articles to profl. jours. Democrat. Home and Office: U San Francisco San Francisco CA 94117

KING, LOUIS BLAIR, minister, General Church of the New Jerusalem; b. Glenview, Ill., Dec. 31, 1925; s. Louis Blair and Dorothy (Cole) K.; m. Freya Synnestvedt, Aug. 15, 1945; children: Khary, Steven, Alan, Janna, Cedric, Bronwin, Aileen, Blair, Wendy, Kristin, Dag, Bradley, John, Tamar. Secondary Sch. Diploma, Acad. of New Ch., Bryn Athyn, Pa., 1944; student U. Pa., 1944; B.A., Acad. New Church Coll., Bryn Athyn, 1948, B.T., 1951. Ordained to ministry Gen. Ch. of the New Jerusalem, 1951. Tchr. in Acad. Schs., 1951; minister Sharon Ch., 1952-54; pastor Pitts. Soc., 1955-63; princ. Pitts. New Ch. Sch., 1955-63; pastor Immanuel Ch., 1963-72, also princ.; ordained into the 3d degree of priesthood, 1972, becoming the asst. bishop of Gen. Ch.; dean Bryn Athyn Ch., 1973, exec. v.p., 1974, pres., 1975-76; exec. bishop Gen. Ch., chancellor acad., Pastor of Bryn Athyn Ch., pres. Gen Ch. in Can., Inc., 1977-79; gen. pastor Gen. Church, Bryn Athyn, 1980—; exec. bishop, pres. Gen. Ch. of the New Jerusalem, Bryn Athyn, 1976—. Address: Gen Church of the New Jerusalem PO Box 278 Bryn Athyn PA 19009

KING, LOUIS LADNER, church organization executive, Christian and Missionary Alliance Church; b. Hurffville, N.J., Nov. 30, 1915; s. Raymond R. and Lydia C. (Dennis) K.; m. Esther Lillian Mertz, Apr. 14, 1939; children: Paul, David, Stephen, Mark. Student Missionary Tng. Inst., Nyack, N.Y., 1936-38; D.D. (hon.), Wheaton Coll., Ill., 1967, Asbury Theol. Sem., 1980. Ordained to ministry Christian and Missionary Alliance Ch., 1938; pastor chs. N.Y., Ill., Nebr., 1938-46; missionary to India, 1947-53; area sec. for India and Far East, Christian and Missionary Alliance Ch., Nyack, 1954-56, fgn. sec., 1957-74, v.p. overseas ministries, 1974-78, pres., 1978—; trustee Nyack Coll., M.E. Found., Balt.; bd. dirs. Christian Publs., Inc., Harrisburg, Pa., World Relief Corp., Christ's Mission, Hackensack, N.J.; sec. bd. adminstrn. Nat. Assn. Evangelicals. Author articles in field. Office: 350 N Highland Ave Nyack NY 09160

KING, MACK STRICKLIN, minister, So. Baptist Conv.; b. Elba, Ala., Aug. 10, 1941; s. Clyde Agustus and Mary Emma (Stricklin) K.; B.S. in Edn., Troy (Ala.) State U., 1964, M.S. in Edn., 1973; Ednl. Specialist, Auburn U., 1974; m. Sue Griffin, Mar. 12, 1977. Ordained to ministry, 1962; pastor chs., Ala., 1961—, Bethlehem Bapt. Ch., Brundidge, 1964-74, Shiloh Bapt. Ch., Banks, 1974—. Tchr. Elba City Schs., 1967-74, 77—. Chmn. com. on coms. Salem-Troy Bapt. Assn., 1973-74. Recipient Voice of Democracy award V.F.W., Enterprise, Ala., 1972. Mem. Nat., Ala., Elba edn. assns., Phi Delta Kappa. Address: Route 1 Box 128 Elba AL 36323

KING, MARTIN LUTHER, SR., minister, Baptist Ch.; b. Stockbridge, Ga., Dec. 19, 1899; B.Th., Morehouse Coll., D.D., 1969; D.D. (hon.), Morris

Brown Coll., 1945, U. Haiti; LL.H.D. (hon.), Wilberforce U., 1965; m. Alberta (dec.); children—Christine, Martin Luther (dec.), Alfred D. Williams (dec.). Pastor, Ebenezer Bapt. Ch., Atlanta, 1932—. Past moderator Atlanta Missionary Bapt. Assn. Bd. dirs. SCLC, Carrie-Steele-Pitts Children's Home; trustee Atlanta U., Morehouse Coll., Interdenoml. Theol. Center. Named Clergyman of Year, Ga. region NCCJ, 1972. Office: 413 Auburn Ave NE Atlanta GA 30312*

KING, NOEL QUINTON, comparative religion educator; b. Rawalpindi, Pakistan, Dec. 25, 1922; came to U.S., 1968; s. William Henry and Mary (McCarthy) K.; m. Evelyn Collard, Dec. 9, 1946 (dec. 1972); children: Francis, Clare, Naomi, Jeremy; m. Laurie Richardson, Nov. 22, 1978; children: Zoe Quinton, Nathan Wayland. B.A., U. Oxford, Eng., 1947, M.A., 1949; Ph.D., U. Nottingham, Eng., 1954. Prof. history and comparative religion U. Calif.-Santa Cruz, 1968—. Author: Theodosius and Establishment of Christianity, 1961; African Religions, 1970; Christianity and Islam in Africa, 1971. Editor: Customs of Swahili, 1981. Served to lt. Brit. Army, 1941-46. Home: 823 Green Valley Rd Watsonville CA 95076 Office: Merrill Coll Univ Calif Santa Cruz CA 95076

KING, RACHEL HADLEY, religious educator, Presbyterian Church (U.S.A.); b. Leavenworth, Kans., Apr. 27, 1904; d. Frank Campbell and Georgianna May (Brackett) King; B.A. Smith Coll., 1926; M.A., Chgo. U., 1927, U. Colo., 1931; Ph.D., Yale U., 1937. Adj. prof. bibl. studies, Barrington Coll., R.I., 1972—; vol. tchr. underprivileged children, N.Y.C. pub. schs. summers, 1969-71; tchr. Kobe Coll., Japan 1937-38; adj. prof. bibl. studies, Barrington Coll., 1972-85; chmn. curriculum com. Nat. Assn. Bibl. Instrs., 1946-64; mem. Alumni Council Yale Div. Sch., 1968-74. Author: George Fox and the Light Within 1650-1660, 1940; God's Boycott of Sin, 1946; Theology you can Understand, 1956; The Ommission of the Holy Spirit from Reinhold Niebuhr's Theology, 1964; The Creation of Death and Life, 1970; contbr. articles to religious jours. Recipient citation 70th anniversary of the Council for Religion in Independent Schs., 1967. Mem. Am. Schs. Oriental Research, Am. Acad. Religion, Soc. Bibl. Lit. Republican. Home: 60 Broadway 905 Providence RI 02903

KING, ROBERT HARLEN, college dean, religion educator, United Methodist Church. b. McCook, Nebr., Feb. 2, 1935; s. Floyd E. and Lola M. (Banta) K.; m. Sandra Lee Cooney, May 27, 1961; children: Paul Daniel, Jennifer Ann. B.A., Harvard U., 1957; postgrad. Edinburgh U., Scotland, 1957-58, Oxford U., Eng., 1967-68; B.D., Yale U., 1960, Ph.D., 1965. Ordained elder United Methodist Church, 1964. Prof. philosophy and religion DePauw U., Greencastle, Ind., 1963-80; prof., v.p., dean Millsaps Coll., Jackson, Miss., 1980—; mem. bd. ministry South Ind. Conf., 1978-80; pres. Ind. Acad. Religion, 1979-80. Author: The Meaning of God, 1973. Editor: Christian Theology, 1982. Contbr. articles and revs. to religious publs. Danforth fellow, 1957; NEH jr. fellow, 1967. Mem. Am. Acad. Religion, Am. Assn. Higher Edn. Soc. Values in Higher Edn., Phi Beta Kappa. Home and Office: Millsaps Coll Jackson MS 39210

KING, ROSALIE M., nun, Roman Catholic Church; b. Davenport, Iowa, Apr. 29, 1924; d. William Jerome and Edna Mary (McCormick) K. B.S. in Edn., Alverno Coll., 1951; M.A., Loyola U.-Chgo., 1959. Joined Sisters of Saint Francis, Roman Catholic Ch. Tchr. elem. parochial schs., Ill., Nebr., 1944-51, secondary parochial schs., Ill., S.D., Nebr., 1951-76; dir. communications School Sisters of St. Francis, Wis., 1978-81, provincial of Omaha, 1981-84, U.S. provincial, Milw., 1984—; bd. dirs. Peace and Justice Ctr., Omaha, 1981—. Contbr. articles to profl. jours. Mem. Leadership Conf. of Women Religious. Office: School Sisters of Saint Francis 1515 S Layton Blvd Milwaukee WI 53215

KING, ROY D., church official. Pres., gen. supt. Pentecostal Assemblies of Nfld., St. Johns. Office: Pentecostal Assemblies of Nfld 10 Symonds Ave St Johns NF A1E 3A2 Canada*

KING, WILLIAM MCGUIRE, minister, religion educator, United Methodist Church; b. Chgo., Mar. 27, 1947; s. Edward Ernst and Ione Dorothy (McGuire) K.; m. Janet Lynn Schulz, Aug. 31, 1968; children: Jeremy, Eleanor, Gregory. B.A. summa cum laude, Cornell Coll., 1968; B.D. cum laude, Harvard Div. Sch., 1971, Ph.D., 1978. Ordained to ministry, United Meth. Ch., 1980. Asst. prof. religious studies U. Va., Charlottesville, 1976-83; asst. prof. religion Albright Coll., Reading, Pa., 1983—; mem. bd. higher edn. and campus ministry, Va. Ann. Conf., United Meth. Ch., Richmond, 1981-83; sesquicentennial assoc. Ctr. for Advanced Study, U. Va., 1982. Contbr. articles to profl. jours. Mem. Am. Soc. Ch. History, Am. Hist. Assn., Am. Acad. Religion, Phi Beta Kappa. Home: 1610 N 15th St Reading PA 19604 Office: Albright Coll PO Box 516 Reading PA 19603

KINGMAN, PERRY ALDEN, priest, Episcopal Ch.; b. Orange, N.J., Sept. 23, 1941; s. Barclay Alden and Eleanora Balch (Blood) K.; B.A., Williams Coll., 1963; B.D., Episcopal Theol. Sch., Cambridge, Mass., 1966; m. Donna Cheryl Watkins, Oct. 14, 1967; children: Elizabeth Alden, Virginia Anne. Ordained priest, 1966; with Grace Ch., Madison, N.J., 1966-69; rector All Saints Ch., Valley City, N.D. and Holy Trinity Ch., Lisbon, N.D., 1969-76, Holy Trinity Ch., International Falls, Minn., 1976-85, Christ Ch., North Conway, N.H., 1985—. Mem. fin. com. Diocesan Council, Diocesan Planning Group, dir. youth; dep. Gen. Conv., Louisville, 1973. Bd. dirs. N.D. Mental Health Assn., 1970-75. Rural Workers fellow, 1976. Home: Pine St North Conway NH Office: Box 382 North Conway NH 03860

KINLAW, DENNIS CHARLES, minister, chaplain, United Meth. Ch.; b. Jacksonville, Fla., June 13, 1929; s. James Edward and Christine (Oehler) K.; B.S., Fla. So. U., 1951; B.D., Garrett Theol. Sem., 1954; S.T.M., Wesley Theol. Sem., 1965; Ed.D., George Washington U., 1973; m. Beatrice S. Davidson, June 16, 1955; 1 dau., Claire Siobban. Ordained to ministry, 1956; chaplain U.S. Navy, 1956-76; mem. adj. faculty McCormick Theol. Sem., Chgo., 1973—, George Washington U., Washington, 1973—. Licensed personnel guidance counselor, Va. Author: Helping Skills for Developing Human Resources, 1967; Helping Skills Training: Design and Exercise Book, 1967. Contbr. articles to religious jours. Home: 711 Stockley Gardens Norfolk VA 23507

KINNEY, JOHN F., bishop, Roman Catholic Church; b. Oelwein, Iowa, June 11, 1937; s. John Francis and Marie B. (McCarty) K. B.A., St. Paul Sem.; J.C.E., Lateran U., Rome, 1971. Ordained priest, Roman Cath. Ch. Asst. pastor St. Thomas Parish, Mpls., 1963-66; vice chancellor Chancery, St. Paul, 1966-68, 71-73, chancellor, 1973-78; pastor St. Leonard of Port Maurice, Mpls., 1973-82; vicar for parishes Chancery, St. Paul, 1979-82; aux. bishop St. Paul and Mpls. and Titular Bishop of Caorle, 1976—. Author: The Juridic Condition of the People of God, 1972. Office: Chancery Office PO Box 1575 420 Raymond St Bismarck ND 58502-1575

KINTNER, DWIGHT LAMAR, minister, United Methodist Church; b. Defiance, Ohio, May 5, 1925; s. Charles Lincoln and Edith (Sellers) K.; B.S. in Chem. Engring., U. Tex., 1949; Th.M., So. Meth. U., 1952; M.A. in India Missions, Hartford Sem. Found., 1960; Ph.D. in Ecumenics, Boston U., 1980; m. Katherine Eloise Barr, Sept. 12, 1948; children: Thomas, Russell, Avery. Ordained to ministry, 1950; pastor, central Tex., 1950-53; missionary tchr., India, 1953-57; pastor, N.Y., also dist. missionary sec., exec. program com. Conf. Council on Ministries, United Meth. Ch., 1957-69; dir. spl. ministires Conn. Council Chs., 1969-72, gen. sec., 1972-76; exec. minister Santa Clara County (Calif.) Council Chs., 1976—. Founder Smithtown (N.Y.) Clergy Assn., 1958-59, Newington (Conn.) Clergy Assn., 1961-63; pres. N. Shore Clergy Assn., Queens, N.Y., 1966-67. Bd. dirs. New Eng. Farm Workers' Council, 1970-72. Mem. Nat. Assn. Ecumenical Staff, N.Am. Acad. Ecumenists. Office: 1229 Naglee Ave Box 26308 San Jose CA 95159

KIPNIS, JUDITH ROBISON, lay church worker, religion educator; Episcopal Church; writer, editor; b. Bklyn., July 14, 1931; d. Richard Porteous and Doris (Turney) Robison; m. Igor Kipnis, Jan. 6, 1953; 1 son, Jeremy Robison. B.A., Radcliffe Coll., 1952; M.A., Columbia U., 1953; M.A. in Religion, Yale Div. Sch., 1983. Intern retreat conductor Mercy Ctr., Madison, Conn., 1982-83; lay reader Christ Ch. Parish, West Redding, Conn., 1979—, chalice bearer, 1980—, also lector, 1976-79, vestry mem., 1981-84, staff sec., 1978-79, parish del. Danbury Deanery, 1977-78, 79—, subdean, 1981-83, guest preacher, 1982—; del. exec. council, 1983—; conv. del. Diocese of Conn., 1977-78, 83—, exec. council, 1983—, various coms. Free-lance writer, educator, counselor, West Redding, 1954—. Asst. editor: The Encyclopedia of Twentieth-Century Music, 1974. Mem. Redding Bd. of Edn., 1973—, chairmn. 1977-81. Recipient William E. Downes prize Yale U., 1983; Grammy awards nominee Nat. Acad. Recording Arts and Scis., 1976; grantee Martha Baird Rockefeller, 1969-70, Ford Found., 1970-71. Mem. Religious Edn. Assn., Am. Acad. Religion (assoc.), Nat. Ctr. for Diaconate, Associated Parishes. Democrat. Home: 20 Drummer Ln West Redding CT 06896

KIRALY, CLEMENT FRANK, priest, Roman Cath. Ch.; b. Szentfulop, Hungary, Apr. 24, 1893; s. Josef and Anna (Pertschi) König; came to U.S., 1947, naturalized, 1953. Joined Franciscan Order, 1908; ordained priest, 1916; pastor for Cath. Hungarians in Berlin and Germany, 1934-37; asst. pastor and pastor chs. in U.S. and Can., 1947—, Holy Cross Ch., Detroit, 1974—. Former catechet, folksmissionary, master novices and theologians, guardian, definitor of Province, visitator gen. Province St. John Capistran, Hungary; pres. Cath. Hungarian Ecumenical Commn., 1964-69. Recipient Nat. Hungarian Defense Cross, 1941. Author: Lord Send Laborers: Priesthood, 1923; Introduction in Spiritual Life, Introduction in Religious Life, 1927-28; Six Hundred Years History of the Franciscans in Szecseny, 1932; Union of the Christian Churches, 1942; Hitlerism and Christianity; the Struggle of the Lutheran Church Against National-Socialism, 1946; History of Ecumenism in Hungary, 1965; My Diary, 1974. Home: 8423 South St Detroit MI 48209

KIRBY, CHARLES DELMAS, II, minister, So. Bapt. Conv.; b. West Monroe, La., June 27, 1930; s. Charles Delmas and Rubye O'Dell (Arrington) K.; O.D., So. Coll. of Optometry, 1949; B. of Sacred Music, New Orleans Bapt. Theol. Sem., 1955, M. of Sacred Music, 1956; m. Barbara Grey Leake, Mar. 11, 1949; children—Lyle David, Kenneth Wayne. Ordained to ministry, 1963; minister of music and edn. 1st Bapt. Ch., Houma, La., 1953-54, Plateau, Ala., 1956, E. Lake Bapt. Ch., Chattanooga, 1957-58; minister of music Central Bapt. Ch., Johnson City, Tenn., 1958-60, 1st Bapt. Ch., Rockwood, Tenn., 1960-67, Avondale Bapt. Ch., Jacksonville, Fla., 1967-70, 1st Bapt. Ch., Dawson, Ga., 1970-75; minister of music and youth 1st Bapt. Ch., Lynn Haven, Fla., 1975—. Dir. music Big Emory Bapt. Assn., 1961-67. Mem. ASCAP, Fla. Bapt. Singing Men, Fla. Bapt. Ch. Music Conf. Composer numerous anthems and cantatas. Home: 1006 Iowa Ave Lynn Haven FL 32444 Office: 102 E 10th St Lynn Haven FL 32444

KIRBY, LAWRENCE LEE, minister, National Baptist Convention U.S.A.; b. Atwood, Tenn., Aug. 1, 1953; a. Alex and Ida Mae (Greer) K.; m. Renee Marie Sartin, June 30, 1979; 1 son, Larence Lee II. B.A., Am. Bapt. Coll., 1976; M.A., Scarriot Coll., 1978; M.Div., Memphis Theol. Sem., 1980; D.Min. candidate Trinity Evang. Sem. Ordained to ministry Nat. Bapt. Conv. U.S.A., 1970. Pastor St. Paul Bapt. Ch., Racine, Wis., 1981—; trustee Am. Bapt. Coll., Nashville, 1983—; 1st v.p. Wis. Bapt. Conv., Milw., 1984. Bd. dirs. George Bray Community Ctr., Racine, Wis., 1983—, Big Bros., Racine, 1983—, Ctr. Community Concerns, Racine, 1983—; v.p. NAACP, Racine, 1982—. Mem. Interdenominational Ministers Alliance, Evang. Ministers Fellowship. Lodge: Masons. Home: 1145 Russet St Racine WI 53405 Office: 1120 Grand Ave Racine WI

KIRBY, PAUL ARNOLD, minister, Church of God, Anderson, Indiana; b. Anderson, Ind., Oct. 4, 1940; s. Lawrence and Linnie Belle (Girt) K.; m. Sharon Kay Pyles, Mar. 19, 1966; children: Sherry, David, Jonathan. A.Gen.Edn., North Wood Coll., 1976; postgrad. Okla. State U., 1979. Ordained to ministry, Pastor, Huron Ch. of God, Ind., 1972-77, Yale Ch. of God, Okla., 1977-80, Parogould Ch. of God, Ark., 1980-81, Willshire Ch. of God, Ohio, 1981—; credentials chmn. S.E. Dist. Ch. of God, Okla., 1978-80; youth evangelist Ark. State. Youth Camp, Ark., 1981; pres. Ministerial Assn. Wilshire, Ohio, 1983-84. Served with U.S. Army, 1963-65; PTO. Home and Office: Rural Route 4 Box 268 Mitchell IN 47446

KIRCHOFF, GARY RAY, minister, American Baptist Churches U.S.A.; b. Edwardsport, Ind., Dec. 15, 1947; s. Foster Lee and Lorene Elsie W.; m. Bonnie M. Coates, Mar. 11, 1967; children: Aaron, Amelia, Andrew. B.S. in Social Studies, Ind. State U., 1971; Th.M., Am. Bible Inst., 1975. Ordained to ministry Bapt. Ch., 1971. Pastor New Hope Bapt. Ch., Clay City, Ind., 1967-72, First Bapt. Ch., Amo, Ind., 1972-74; assoc. pastor North Terre Haute Bapt. Ch., Ind., 1974-75; pastor First Bapt. Ch., Centerville, Ind., 1975-79; sr. pastor First Bapt. Ch., Rushville, Ind., 1979—; dir. Ind. Bapt. Ch., 1982—; v.p. Rush County Ministerial Assn., Rushville, 1984—. Home: Route 6 Box 16 Rushville IN 46173 Office: First Baptist Ch R6 Box 16 Rushville IN 46173

KIRK, ALSTON SHEPHERD, minister, Lutheran Church-Missouri Synod; b. Little Rock, Sept. 3, 1938; s. Chester Alston and Bernice Amelia (Shepherd) K.; m. Susan Jane Dodson, June 7, 1964; children: Brigette, Rachel, Brian. B.A., Concordia Sr. Coll., Ft. Wayne, Ind., 1960; B.D., Concordia Sem., St. Louis, 1964; Th.M., Union Theol. Sem., Richmond, Va., 1974. Ordained to ministry Lutheran Ch.-Mo. Synod, 1964. Pastor, Good Shepherd Ch., Olney, Md., 1964-66; chaplain U.S. Navy, 1966—, dir. Chaplain Resource Bd., Norfolk, Va., 1984—; mem., sec. Southwestern dist. Dept. Mission Service, Washington, 1974-77. Author: Curriculum Outline for Chaplains Advanced Course, 1981. Contbr. articles to profl. jours. Fellow Am. Acad. Religion; mem. Internat. Bonhoeffer Soc., Naval Inst. Democrat. Lodge: Kiwanis (pres.). Home: 106 Coachman Dr Tabb VA 23602 Office: Chaplain Resource Bd 6500 Hampton Blvd Norfolk VA 23508

KIRK, CLYDE EARL, minister, United Pentecostal Ch., Internat.; b. Call, Tex., Apr. 8, 1937; s. Allen Lafayette and Lucille (Bass) K.; m. Barbara Ann Sapp, July 25, 1953; children—Clyde Earl, Melba Lucille, Allen Ray, Lisa Ann, Julie Ellen. Ordained to ministry, 1966; pastor, adult Sunday Sch. tchr. Saratoga (Tex.) 1st United Pentecostal Ch., 1969-72, Hemphill (Tex.) 1st United Pentecostal Ch., 1973—. Circle Wide youth leader, 1970-71; tent revival evangelist, 1972-73; speaker Tex. Dist. Camp Meeting, Lufkin, 1974. Home and office : POB 844 Hemphill TX 75948

KIRK, WARREN GERALD, minister, evangelist, Missionary Bapt. Ch.; b. Charleston, W.Va., July 26, 1933; s. Warren Clifton and Eula Grey (Westfall) K.; B.S., Morris Harvey U., 1960; Th.D., Southwestern Sem., 1966; m. Carolyn June Moore, Dec. 20, 1952; children—Nancy Charlene, Kathryn Karol, Teri Lynn. Ordained to ministry, 1974; clk. Bapt. missionary Assn. Fla., Melbourne, 1975—; founder True Gospel Evang. Assn., Cocoa, Fla., 1975; full-time evangelist. Home: 2447 Ricky Rd Melbourne FL 32935 Office: Box 22 Rockledge FL

KIRKENDOLL, C. A., Bishop Christian Methodist Episcopal Church, 3d dist., St. Louis, also patron bishop Women's Missionary Council. Office: Christian Meth Episcopal Ch 11470 Northway Saint Louis MO 63136*

KIRKLAND, BRYANT MAYS, minister, United Presbyterian Ch. in U.S.A.; b. Essex, Conn., May 2, 1914; s. Henry Burnham and Helen Josephine (Mays) K.; A.B., Wheaton (Ill.) Coll., 1935; Th.B., Princeton Theol. Sem., 1938; Th.M., Eastern Bapt. Theol. Sem., Phila., 1946; D.D. (hon.), Beaver Coll., 1949, Lafayette Coll., 1962, Dennison U., 1964; LL.D., U. Tulsa, 1962; S.T.D., Parsons Coll., 1966; Litt.D., Washington and Jefferson Coll., 1968; m. Bernice Eleanor Tanis, Aug. 19, 1937; children—Nancy Tanis Kirkland Thompson, Elinor Ann Kirkland Hite, Virginia Lee Kirkland Stuart. Ordained to ministry, 1938; pastor, Pa., 1938-46, N.J., 1946-57, Tulsa, 1957-62, Fifth Ave. Presbyn. Ch., N.Y.C., 1962—; vis. lectr. homiletics Princeton Theol. Sem., 1951-56, 64-75; instr. Bible, Buckley Sch. for Boys, N.Y.C., 1964—; overseas lectr. U.S. Armed Forces, 1965, 68, 72, 74, also U.S. Army Chaplain Sch.; spl. lectr. preaching including Finch lectrs., 1964, Berger lectrs., 1968, Swartley lectrs., 1969, also lectr. on Bible including T.J. and Inez Raney lectrs., 1969, Logan lectrs., 1974, Royster lectrs., 1976. Mem. commn. ecumenical mission and relations United Presbyn. Ch., 1949-62, commn. continuing edn., 1967-69; mem. council Nat. Presbyn. Ch. Center, Washington, 1962-65; participant Pentagon preaching series, 1973, 75. Bd. dirs. Tulsa Community Chest, 1958-61; trustee Beaver Coll., U. Tulsa; pres. trustees Princeton Theol. Sem. Named Clergyman of Year, Am. Heritage of Religion, 1975. Mem. Am. Bible Soc. (trustee). Author: Growing in Christian Faith, 1963; Home Before Dark, 1965; Living in a Zigzag Age, 1972. Contbr. to Evang. Sermons of Our Day, 1959; Year of Evangelism in Local Church, 1960. Home: 1158 Fifth Ave New York City NY 10029 Office: 7 W 55th St New York City NY 10019

KIRKSEY, FLOYD THOMAS, minister, So. Baptist Conv.; b. Newbery, Fla., Apr. 6, 1928; s. Victor Thompkins and Viola (Holt) K.; degree in theology Fruitland Bapt. Inst., 1964; m. Dorothy Agnes Lynch, Apr. 6, 1945; 1 dau., Carol Ann. Ordained to ministry, 1958; missionary, So. Fla., 1960-61; pastor Massapoag Bapt. Ch., Lincolnton, N.C., 1961—. Mem. Interdenoml. Pastors' Conf., S. Fork Bapt. Assn. Home and Office: Route 6 Box 525 Lincolnton NC 28092

KISCHEL, IRVING, cantor; b. N.Y.C., Mar. 10, 1916; s. Hyman and Ida (Weinstein) K.; student Coll. City N.Y., 1933-35; grad. Rabbi Israel Salanter Yeshivah; student Hertzliah Acad; m. Evelyn Licker, June 23, 1940; children—Aaron, Ellen. Cantor, Temple Shalom, Milton, Mass., 1950—, adminstr. congregation, 1974-77; youth dir. Young Israel Movement, Bronx, N.Y.; cantor, youth dir. Mattapan Young Israel, 1967—. Honored fellow Jewish Theol. Sem., Am., 1962; mem. Cantors Assembly, 1953—, rep. to nat. youth commn. United Synagogue Am., 1965-75. Mem. New Eng. Cantors Assn. (pres. 1969-77). Home: 30 Summit St Hyde Park MA 02136 Office: 180 Blue Hill Ave Milton MA 02187

KISHINO, YUTAKA, minister, Lutheran Church in America; b. Tokyo, Jan. 3, 1952; came to U.S., 1975; s. Hiroshi and Ikuko (Goto) K.; m. Nancy Daubert, Mar. 19, 1957. B.A., St. Paul's Episcopal U., Tokyo, 1975; M.Div., Luth. Theol. Sem., 1979. Ordained to ministry Lutheran Church in America, 1979. Asst. pastor Zion Luth. Ch., Phila., 1979-83; assoc. pastor Resurrection Luth. Ch., Plano, Tex., 1983—; mem. mgmt. com. Div. of World Mission and Ecumenism, 1984—; exec. com. Asian Luth. Caucus, 1979—. Home: 4444 Odissa Dr Plano TX 75075 Office Resurrection Luth Ch 1919 Independence Pkwy Plano TX 75075

KISSINGER, GEORGE MEADE, III, church official, Southern Baptist Convention; b. Williamsport, Pa., Aug. 29, 1912; s. George Meade and Elizabeth Weaver (Yoder) K.; (student or grad.) Moody Bible Inst., 1934; B.A., Hampden Sydney Coll. of Va., 1938; chaplains sch. U.S. Army, 1942; B.D., So. Bapt. Theol. Sem., 1948; m. Margaret Elizabeth Hollis, Feb. 18, 1949; children: George Meade IV, John Walter, Judith Maffet. Ordained to ministry So. Baptist Conv., 1936; pastor Ivor Field of Chs., Ivor, Va., 1938-43; chaplain U.S. Army, 1943-45; pastor Union Bapt. Ch., Achilles, Va., 1949-60; exec. dir. missions Peninsula Bapt. Assn., Newport News, Va., 1960—. Pres. Pastor's Conf. Blackwater and Peninsula Assns., 1963—; moderator Peninsula Bapt. Assn., 1958; preacher ann. sermon for Va. Bapt. Gen. Assn., 1957; exec. com. So. Bapt. Conv., 1981—. Bd. dirs. High Tide Camp for High Sch. Youths, 1949-53; bd. dir., mgr. Camp Woodcliff for Boys, Middlesex County, Va., 1953-60. Recipient Carnegie award, 1935. Home: 527 Lucas Creek Rd Newport News VA 23602 Office: 863 Cloverleaf Ln Newport News VA 23601

KITAGAWA, JOHN ELLIOTT, minister, Episcopal Church; b. Mpls., May 10, 1950. s. Daisuke and Fujiko (Sugimoto) K.; m. Kathleen Ann Stack, July 10, 1982; B.A., Hobart Coll., 1972; M.Div., Union Theol. Sem., 1978. Ordained to ministry Episcopal Ch. as deacon, 1978, priest, 1978. Coffeehouse mgr. Trinity Parish, N.Y.C., 1972-74; student asst. St. Alban's Parish, Washington, 1974-77; asst. to rector Calvary/St. George, N.Y.C., 1978-80; coordinator Downtown Coop. Ministry, New Haven, 1980-84; canon for mission devel. Diocese Md., Balt., 1984—; del. Episcopal Ch. U.S. to World Council Chs. 5th Assembly, Nairobi, Kenya, 1975, 6th Assembly, Vancouver, B.C., Can., 1983, mem. standing com. on ecumenical relations, 1976-85, renewal/congl. life, 1976-83, Women in Ch. and Soc., 1984—. Contbr. articles to profl. jours. Assoc. Order of St. Helena.

KITAGAWA, JOSEPH MITSUO, educator; b. Osaka, Japan, Mar. 8, 1915; s. Chiyokichi and Kumi (Nozaki) K.; B.A., Rikkyo U., 1937; Ph.D., U. Chgo., 1951; m. Anne Rose Kitagawa, July 22, 1946. Assoc. prof. history of religion U. Chgo., 1959-64, prof., 1964—, dean div. sch., 1970—. Mem. Am. Council Learned Socs., Am. Soc. Study of Religions (pres. 1969-72), Am. Acad. Religion, Internat. Assn. History of Religions (v.p. 1975—), Assn. Religious Studies in Japan, Fund for Theol. Edn. Author: Religions of the East; Religion in Japanese History; (with others) The Great Asian Religions. Editor: The Comparative Study of Religions; Understanding Modern China; (with others) Myths and Symbols: Studies in Honor & Mircea Eliade. Home: 5512 Woodlawn Ave Chicago IL 60637

KITCHENS, RANDALL ERIC, minister, Southern Baptist Convention; b. Macon, Ga., Jan. 24, 1960; s. Walter Stephen and Betty Juanita (NeSmith) K.; m. Sherri Lee Stricklen. B.A. in Christianity, Mercer U., 1983. Ordained to ministry So. Bapt. Conv., 1983. Minister of music Wheeler Heights Bapt. Ch., Macon, 1974-77, Shurlington Bapt. Ch., Macon, 1977-78, Walkerville Bapt. Ch., Macon, 1978-81; minister of music and youth Bethel Bapt. Ch., Lizella, Ga., 1981-83; bible tchr., coach Cross Keys Christian Acad., Macon, 1982-83; pastor Big Coppitt First Bapt. Ch., Key West, Fla., 1983—; ch. tng. dir. Fla. Keys Bapt. Assn., Marathon, 1983—; chaplain Seaside Resort Park, Key West, 1985—. Bd. dirs. Key West Helpline, 1984—. Named Outstanding Young Man of Am., U.S. Jaycees, 1984; Star Tchr. Ga. C. of C., 1983. Mem. Lower Keys Ministerial Assn. (community action com. chmn. 1984—). Lodge: Kiwanis (treas. 1984—) (Key West). Home: 720 Ave G Big Coppitt Key West FL 33040 Office: Big Coppitt First Bapt Ch Ave F PO Box 2555 Key West FL 33045-2555

KITCHINGS, HAROLD TRIBBLE, minister, So. Bapt. Conv.; b. Eminence, Ky., Mar. 13, 1927; s. Atley Asher and Marion Beulah (Mudd) K.; B.A. with distinction, Miss. Coll., 1948; M.Div., So. Bapt. Theol. Sem., 1951; postgrad. New Orleans Bapt. Theol. Sem., 1956-59; D.D., Miss. Coll., 1972; m. Patricia Ann Overstreet, Dec. 20, 1949; children—Kathy (Mrs. Gary Nowell), Karen (Mrs. Neil Hitchcock), Harold. Ordained to ministry So. Baptist Conv., 1951; asso. pastor Daniel Meml. Bapt. Ch., Jackson, Miss., 1951-53, Calvary Bapt. Ch., Jackson, Miss., 1953-54, Gaston Av. Bapt. Ch., Dallas, 1954-56; pastor Holmesville Bapt. Ch., McComb, Miss., 1956-59, Univ. Bapt. Ch., Hattiesburg, Miss., 1959-65, First Bapt. Ch., Kosciusko, Miss., 1965-76; exec. sec. Miss. Bapt. Found., 1977—. Mem. bd. Miss. Bapt. Conv., 1973-76, chmn. resolutions com., 1966, sec. edn. commn., 1965-70, chmn. commn., 1970-71, pres. conv. bd., 1974-76; faculty and resource person State Assembly and Family Life Conf., 1960-65; chmn. evangelism Attala Bapt. Assn., 1967-68, moderator, 1971-73. Recipient Jackson Exchange Club plaque for Outstanding Service with Youth, 1952; Eagle Scouts award, 1953; Meritorious Service plaque Miss. Christian Edn. Commn., 1971; Service to Humanity award Miss. Coll., Clinton, 1976. Mem. Kosciusko Ministerial Assn. (pres. 1967). Rotarian. Contbr. to So. Bapt. Edn. Family Life Bulletin. Home: 216 Simmons Pl Clinton MS 39056 Office: Miss Bapt Found Jackson MS

KITE, JOSEPH HIRAM, JR., lay church worker, United Methodist Church; b. Decatur, Ga., Nov. 11, 1926; s. Joseph Hiram and Lulie (Hatch) K.; A.B., Emory U., 1948; M.S., U. Tenn., 1954; Ph.D., U. Mich., 1959; m. Jane Fay Pascale, Aug. 6, 1970. Mem. work area on edn. Trinity United Meth. Ch., Amherst, N.Y., 1965-68, ch. sch. supt., 1968-70, lay speaker, 1965—, lay leader, 1970-74; chmn. Wesley Found. Bd., United Meth. Ch., Buffalo, 1966-68, 72-74, Buffalo dist. lay leader, 1971-75, Buffalo dist. dir. lay speaking, 1971-76, dist. rep. to conf. Council on Ministries, 1972-74; mem. Western N.Y. Conf., Long Range Planning Com., 1973-74; mem. Conf. Com. for Restructuring, 1973-74, conf. lay leader, 1975-77, mem. exec. com. Conf. Council, 1975-77, chmn. Conf. sect. on lay life and work, 1975-77, co-chmn. Conf. Human Resources Forum, 1975-77, del. Gen. and Jurisdictional Confs., 1976, mem. Commn. Central Conf. Affairs, 1976-79; mem. Northeastern Jurisdictional Com. Episcopacy, 1976-79; bd. dirs. Niagara Frontier Meth. Home, Niagara Frontier Nursing Home Co., Blocher Homes, Beechwood-Blocher Found., 1980—, sec., 1983—. Prof. microbiology State U. N.Y. at Buffalo, 1972—. Mem. Am. Assn. Immunologists, Am. Soc. Microbiology, Tissue Culture Assn., AAAS, Reticuloendothelial Soc., AAUP, N.Y. Acad. Scis., Sigma Xi. Contbg. author manual lay speakers; contbr. articles to profl. jours. Home: 108 Chasewood Ln East Amherst NY 14051 Office: Dept Microbiology Med Sch State U NY Buffalo NY 14214

KITTS, ELBERT WALKER, minister, Grace Missionary Baptist Church; b. Knoxville, Tenn., Apr. 12, 1939; s. Robert Theodore and Armanda (Van DeGriff) K.; m. Ellen Abner, May 11, 1956; children: David, Donna, Timothy, Ronald, Daniel, Paul, Jonathan, Angela. Ordained to ministry Bapt. Ch., 1965. Evangelist, Texas Valley Ch., Knoxville, 1961-65; pastor Centerview Bapt. Ch., Knoxville, 1965-68, Valley Grove Bapt. Ch., Maynardville, Tenn., 1968-70, Emory Valley Bapt. Ch., Knoxville, 1970-74, Pleasant Hill Bapt. Ch., Powell, Tenn., 1974-84; founder, dir. TV and radio ministry Old Time Bapt. Hour, Knoxville, 1976—; exec. dir. Bapt. United in Missions, Knoxville, 1982—; founder, dir. Proclaiming Jesus to the World, St. Kitts, W.I., 1982—; chmn. Midland Assn. for Endowment, Jefferson City, 1983—. Editor-pub. BUIM Mission News jour., 1982. Mem. bd. advisors Nat. Home Health, Inc., Knoxville, 1983. Republican. Home: Route 11 Texas Valley Rd Knoxville TN 37938 Office: Bapt United in Missions PO Box 5873 Knoxville TN 37918

KJOLLER, JOHN KAI, minister, Association of Evangelical Lutheran Churches; b. Holyoke, Mass., June 2, 1936; s. Kai Emil and Ruth Olga (Zaumseil) K.; m. Elizabeth Mehrtens, Dec. 27, 1959; children: John Kai Jr., Catherine Elizabeth, Maria Louise, Andrew Charles. B.A., Valparaiso U., 1958; M.Div., Concordia Sem., 1973. Ordained to ministry Assn. Evang. Luth. Chs., 1962. Minister Trinity Ch., St. Francis, Kans., 1962-64, Resurrection Ch., Cairo, N.Y., 1964-68; sr. minister St. Andrew's Ch., Ridgefield, Conn., 1968—; coordinator pastoral care Ridgefield Hospice, 1983—; commr. Christian Conf. of Conn., 1979—. Contbr. articles to religious periodicals. Bd. dirs. Mid-Fairfield Hospice, Inc., Norwalk, Conn. Mem. Ridgefield Clergy Assn. (pres. 1977-82), Toastmasters. Lodge: Lions. Home: 40 Ivy Hill Rd Ridgefield CT 06877 Office: St Andrews Ch 6 Ivy Hill Rd Ridgefield CT 06877

KLAAREN, EUGENE MARION, lay theologian, United Church of Christ; college educator; b. Coopersville, Mich., Aug. 9, 1937; s. Marion Ernest and Cornelia Gertrude (DeKock) K.; m. Mary Lynn Decker, Aug. 18, 1961; children: Jonathan, Kristen, Joshua. A.B., Hope Coll., 1959; M.A., Emory U., 1960; B.D., Western Theological Seminary, 1963; Ph.D., Harvard U., 1970; student Harvard Divinity Sch., 1960-62. Teaching fellow in theology Harvard U., 1965-67; lectr., asst. prof. Wesleyan U., Middletown, Conn., 1968-75, assoc. prof. religion, 1976—; vis. lectr. theology Fuller Theol. Sem., Pasadena, Calif., 1976; critic S. Congregational Ch.; chmn. religion dept. Wesleyan Univ., 1981-83. Author: Religions Origins of Modern Science, 1977. Contbr. articles to profl. jours Rockefeller doctoral fellow, 1970, NEH fellow, 1973. Mem. Am. Acad. Religion, Soc. Values in Higher Edn., Soc. Philosophy and Tech. Office: Dept Religion Wesleyan Univ Middletown CT 06457

KLAM, NORMAN WAYNE, religious organization executive, Seventh-day Adventists; b. Outlook, Sask., Can., Jan. 19, 1945; s. John Harvey and Martha (Bodrug) K.; m. Marlene Gail Skula, Mar. 22, 1970; children: Cheri, Nicole, Jeffrey, John. B.A. in Bus., Walla Walla Coll., 1968. Ordained to ministry Seventh-day Adventists, 1981. Tchr. Bermuda Inst., 1971-74; asst. auditor Seventh-day Adventist Ch. Can., Oshawa, Ont., Can., 1974-76, treas., 1981—; treas. Alberta Conf. of Seventh-day Adventist Chs., Red Deer, 1976-81. Bd. dirs. Sherwood Park Nursing Home, Alta., Can., 1976-81, Can. Union Coll., College Heights, Alta., 1976—, Kingsway Coll., Oshawa, 1981—, Branson Hosp., Toronto, Ont., 1981—. Office: Seventh-day Adventist Ch in Can 1148 King St E Oshawa ON L1H 1H8 Canada

KLAPERMAN, GILBERT, Jewish organization executive. Pres. Rabbinical Council Am., Inc. Office: Rabbinical Council Am Inc 1250 Broadway Suite 801 New York NY 10001*

KLASSEN, JACOB M., retired administrator, Mennonite Church; b. Steinfeld, Sagradowka, Ukraine, USSR, Feb. 12, 1929; came to Can., 1930; s. Jacob and Aganetha (Martens) K.; m. Katherine Thiessen, July 2, 1950; children: Martha, Lorna. B.A., U. Man., 1969. B.Ed., 1970. Dir., Mennonite Central Com., Taegu, Republic of Korea, 1958-61; asst. overseas services dir., Akron, Pa., 1961-63; exec. dir. Mennonite Central Com. Can., Winnipeg, Man., Can., 1963-70, exec. dir.,

1976-84; moderator River E. Mennonite Brethren Ch., Winnipeg, 1966-75; moderator Man. Mennonite Brethren Conf., 1972-74, asst. moderator, 1970-72, 80-81. Home: 106 Cameo Crescent Winnipeg MB R2K 2W4 Canada

KLASSEN, JOHN, religious educator, United Church of Canada; b. Herbert, Sask., Can., May 4, 1929; married, July 28, 1954; children: Daphne, Gregory. B.A., U. Man., Can., 1951; M.Div., Union Coll., N.Y., 1954; D.Min., Toronto Sch. Theol., 1982. Ordained to ministry United Ch. of Can., 1954. Minister various chs., Ont. and Man., 1954-77; assoc. prof. Queen's Theol. Coll., Kingston, Ont., 1977—. Home: 102 Barrie St Kingston ON K7L 3J9 Canada Office: Queen's Theol Coll Kingston ON K7L 3N6 Canada

KLEIN, JERRY LEE, theology educator, bible chair director, Churches of Christ; b. Walters, Okla., Oct. 25, 1947; s. Rudolf Anton and Mable Eula (Elliott) K.; m. Jane Ellen Keeth, Apr. 20, 1969; children: Jerry, John. A.A., Cameron Coll., 1967; B.A., Okla. Christian Coll., 1969; M.A., Harding U., 1974. Instr. in Bible Henderson State Coll., Arkadelphia, Ark., 1970-71; pulpit minister Ch. of Christ, Comanche, Okla., 1971-75, Main St. Ch. of Christ, Lockney, Tex., 1975-82; instr. in Greek, Prairie Hill Sch. of Bible, Comanche, 1974-75; prof. religion Amarillo Coll., Tex., 1982—; dir. Amarillo Bible Chair, 1982—. Author: Leadership in Christ, 1976. Contbr. articles to profl. jours. Dir. of vols. Ark. Childrens Colony, Arkadelphia, 1970-71; city chmn. Heart Fund and Kidney Found., Comanche, 1974-75; cubmaster Cubscouts, Lockney, 1978-82; bd. dir. VICA Tascosa High Sch., Amarillo, 1983—. Recipient citation Ark. Childrens Colony, 1971, Cert. of Appreciation, Tex. Dept. Health, 1982, Tex. Dept. Human Resources, 1983. Mem. The Bibl. Archaelogy Soc., Am. Soc. Ch. History. Club: Road Runners Am. Lodge: Lions (pres. 1974-75). Home: 5614 Purdue St Amarillo TX 79109 Office: Amarillo Bible Chair 2107 S Washington St Amarillo TX 79109

KLEIN, RICHARD EDWARD, minister, Lutheran Church-Missouri Synod; b. Marshfield, Wis., Nov. 1, 1945; s. Herman Olaf Klein and Arlene Caroline (Zophia) Gauger; m. Carol Louise Dean, Aug. 12, 1967 (div. 1979); children: Kevin, Timothy; m. Rosemarie Freda Rath, June 30, 1979); children: Matthew, Sarah, Christina. B.A., Concordia Sr. Coll., Ft. Wayne, Ind., 1967, postgrad., 1978-83; B.D., Concordia Theol. Sem., Springfield, Ill., 1971. Ordained to ministry Luth. Ch.-Mo. Synod, 1971. Pastor, Klondike Trail Parish, Mellowdale, Vega and Swan Hills, Alta., Can., 1971-73, St. Peter Luth. Ch., Castleger-St. John-Nelson, B.C., Can., 1973-78, Immanuel Luth. Ch., Nipigon, Ont., Can., 1979—; circuit mission rep. Ont. circuit Luth. Ch.-Mo. Synod, 1982—. Town counselor Nipigon Twp., 1982—; mem. Mcpl. Adv. Com. N.W. Ont., Thunder Bay, 1982—; chmn. health concerns com., 1984; v.p. North of Superior Community Mental Health Program, Terrace Bay, 1971—. Progressive-Conservative. Club: Royal Can. Legion (Nipigon). Home: Box 520 116 5th St Nipigon ON P0T 2J0 Canada Office: Immanuel Luth Ch Box 520 164 5th St Nipigon ON P0T 2J0 Canada

KLEIN, WILLIAM WADE, theology educator, Conservative Baptist Association America; b. Weehawken, N.J., Feb. 11, 1946; s. William Carl and Eleanor (Kinkel) K.; m. Phyllis Gail Merritt, June 29, 1968; children: Alison, Sarah. B.S., Wheaton Coll., 1967; M.Div., Denver Sem., 1970; Ph.D., U. Aberdeen, 1978. Ordained to ministry Conservative Bapt. Assn. Am., 1973. Assoc. pastor Calvary Bapt. Ch., Los Gatos, Calif., 1970-74; instr. Columbia Bible Coll., S.C., 1977-78; assoc. prof. Denver Sem., 1978—; researcher Tyndale House, Cambridge, Eng., 1985. Contbr. articles to religious jours. King William scholar, 1976. Fellow Inst. Bibl. Research; mem. Soc. Bibl. Lit., Evangel. Theol. Soc. Democrat. Home: 1231 W Radcliff Ave Englewood CO 80110 Office: Denver Sem PO Box 10 000 Denver CO 80210

KLEINERT, HENRY BERNHARD, minister, Luth. Ch. Am.; b. Keyeser, Wis., Mar. 5, 1917; s. Bernhard Haakon and Olena Rokne (Anfinson) K.; B.A., Midland Coll., 1952; B.D., Central Luth. Theol. Sem., 1953; m. Helen Rose Peck, Aug. 2, 1940; children—Gary Bernhard, Linda Marlene Kleinert Cole. Ordained to ministry Luth. Ch. Am., 1953; asst. pastor Luth. Meml. Ch., Madison, Wis., 1953-55; pastor Luth. chs., Black Earth, Wis., 1955-57, West Middleton, Wis., 1955-57; sr. pastor Mt. Carmel Luth. Ch., Mpls., 1961-68, First Luth. Ch., Ottumwa, Iowa, 1968-70, Grace Luth. Ch., Deephaven, Minn., 1971—. Adviser to Luth. Student Assn., U. Wis., Eau Claire, 1957; chaplain Midland Coll., Fremont, Nebr., 1957-61; mem. exec. bd. parish edn. com. Minn. Synod, Luth. Ch. Am., 1962-65; pres. Mpls. Ch. Athletic Assn., 1965-66; bd. dirs. Greater Mpls. Council Chs., sec., 1968; chmn. Bd. Social Ministry, Iowa Synod, Luth. Ch. Am., 1968-70; bd. dirs. United Prayer Tower, Mpls., 1976—. Pres. Am. Bethesda Found., 1970-71; mem. Capital Long Range Improvements Com. Mpls., 1970-74; bd. dirs. YMCA, Mpls., 1963-67, YMCA, Ottumwa, Iowa, 1968-70, Vols. of Am., Mpls., Wis., 1973-75; mem. Mpls. Bd. Ethics, 1967; bd. dirs. Minn. Group Homes, chmn., 1974-75. Home: 18140 Fairhomes Ln Wayzata MN 55391 Office: 18360 Minnetonka Blvd Wayzata MN 55391

KLEINHANS, ROBERT G., theology educator, Orthodox Ch. in Am.; b. Rochester, N.Y., May 16, 1936; s. Eugene B. and Naomi (Hoff) K.; m. Joyce L. Richardson, Aug. 5, 1961 (div. Aug. 1974); children: Martha Mary, David Jonathan. B.A., St. John Fisher Coll., Rochester, 1963; M.A., St. Michael's Coll., Toronto, Can., 1966; Th.D., Princeton Sem., 1968. Assoc. prof. theology St. Xavier Coll., Chgo., 1968—. Contbr. articles to profl. jours. NEH summer fellow, 1983, 84. Mem. Am. Acad. Religion, Soc. Values in Higher Edn., Orthodox Theology Soc. Home: 536 Addison St Apt 381 Chicago IL 60613 Office: St Xavier Coll 3700 W 103d St Chicago IL 60655

KLEINHANS, THEODORE JOHN, editor, writer, minister, Lutheran Church-Missouri Synod; b. Oswego, Kans., Mar. 29, 1924; s. Theodore and Marie Margaret (Hellwig) K.; m. Leona E. Eisele, Dec. 22, 1956; children: Christopher Allen, Kathryn Ann. B.A., Div.M., Concordia Sem., St. Louis, 1950; M.A., U. Mich., 1946, Calif. State U.-Fresno, 1975. Ordained to ministry Luth. Ch.-Mo. Synod, 1950. Asst. to dir. Luth. World Fedn., Geneva, Switzerland, 1950-52; pastor Luther/Tyndale Ch., London, 1952-53; chaplain U.S. Air Force, 1953-73; sr. editor Aid Assn. for Luths., Appleton, Wis., 1975—. Author: The Year of the Lord, 1967; Cantor of Leipzig: J.S. Bach, 1968, others. Contbr. articles to profl. jours. Recipient medal Freedoms Found., 1964-71. Mem. Luth. Soc. Scholarship, Authors Guild, Authors League. Republican. Home: 1710 S Bluemound Rd Appleton WI 54914 Office: Aid Assn for Luths Appleton WI 54919

KLEINSTEUBER, RONALD WAYNE, minister, Free Methodist Church in Canada. b. Belleville, Ont., Can., Jan. 17, 1949; s. Ronald Leon and Marjorie Beryl (Elmy) K.; m. Nancy Alice VanDruff, Feb. 7, 1970; children: Laura Marie, Lynnette Michelle, Alexandra Francis. B.A. with honors, Queen's U., 1978; diploma theology, Berean Sch. of the Bible, Springfield, Mo., 1973; diploma journalism, Conestoga Coll., 1973; postgrad. Queen's Theol. Coll., 1978-79. Ordained elder Free Meth. Ch., 1983, deacon, 1981. Inner city worker, pastor Assemblies of God, Springfield, Mo., Rochester, N.Y., 1968-72; pastor United Pentecostal Ch., Pembroke, Ont., 1972-73, United Ch. of Can., Belleville, Ont., 1975-79, Free Meth. Ch., Westport, Ont., 1979-81, Harrowsmith, Ont., 1981—; chmn. conf. hist. com. Free Meth. Ch., 1980—; pres. Central Frontenac Ministerial, 1983-84. Author: Coming of Age: The Making of a Canadian Free Methodist Church, 1980; More Than a Memory: The Renewal of Methodism in Canada, 1984. Contbr. articles to profl. jours. Tchr. religious edn. Loughborough Pub. Sch., Sydenham, Ont., 1983—. Urquhart Kay Gray scholar Queen's Theol. Coll., Kingston, Ont., 1979. Mem. Can. Wesleyan Theol. Soc. (sec.-treas. 1981-84), Can. Meth. Hist. Soc. (exec. mem. 1981—, lectr. 1980), Can. Holiness Fedn. (lectr. 1983), Wesleyan Theol. Soc. Progressive Conservative. Home: Box 201 Harrowsmith ON K0H 1V0 Canada Office: Harrowsmith Free Methodist Ch Box 201 Harrowsmith ON K0H 1V0 Canada

KLEISER, WILLIAM JOSEPH, priest, Roman Catholic Ch.; b. Nashville, Sept. 24, 1925; s. William Joseph and Rose Anna (Martin) K.; student St. Ambrose Coll., Davenport, Ia., 1943; B.S., Cardinal Glennon Coll., St. Louis, 1946; M.A., George Peabody Coll., 1955; postgrad. N.Am. Coll. Rome, 1973. Ordained priest Roman Catholic Ch., 1950; asso. pastor Immaculate Conception Cathedral, Memphis, 1950-57, also instr. Latin, Cath. High Sch. for Boys; asso. pastor St. Louis Ch., Memphis, 1957-60; pastor chs., Cookeville, Tenn., 1960-62, Humboldt, Tenn., 1962-64, St. James Ch., Memphis, 1964-66, St. Joseph Ch., Memphis, 1966-75; first pastor Holy Spirit Ch., Memphis, 1975; rector Cathedral of the Immaculate Conception, Memphis, 1975—. Chaplain, Serra Club, 1966-70, Cenacle Retreat League, 1967-69; chmn. Priests Council, 1971-72; chmn. Personnel Bd., 1971-73; dir. vocations Diocese, 1974-76; synodal judge, Memphis, 1973—. Recipient Recognition certificate Right To Life, 1974. Mem. Memphis Priests Assn. (pres. 1969-70). Home: 1695 Central Ave Memphis TN 38104 Office: 1695 Central Ave Memphis TN 38104

KLEM, HERBERT V., theology educator, Baptist General Conference; b. N.Y.C., Jan. 9, 1937; s. Arthur Christian and Jessie Mable (Fisher) K.; m. Barbara Hellen Gustavson, June 10, 1961; children: Johnathan H., Daan Allen, Carolyn Kristin. B.A., Gordon Coll., 1959; M.S., Hofstra U., 1963; M.Div., Gordon-Conwell Theol. Sem., 1971; D. Missiology, Fuller Sem., 1977. Ordained to ministry Bapt. Ch., 1971. Lectr. Igbaja Sem., Nigeria, 1966-72; project dir. Daystar Communications, Nairobi, Kenya, 1973-78; vis. prof. Wheaton Grad. Sch., Ill., 1978-80; prof. Bethel Sem., St. Paul, 1980—; del., speaker African Christian Leadership Conf., Nairobi, 1980; cons. communications Lausanne Com. on World Evangelism Conf., Pattaya, Thailand, 1981; bd. dirs. Mission Moving Mountains, Mpls., 1983, Bd. of World Missions, Bapt. Gen. Conf., Arlington Heights, Ill., 1984—, chmn. task force on evangelism, 1985—. Author: Toward Ora Communication and Scripture, 1982. Contbr. articles to profl. publs. Mem. Am. Soc. Missiology, Evang. Theol Soc., Christian Speech Assn. Assn., Club: Nairobi Home: 1370 Skiles Ln Arden Hills MN 55112 Office: Bethel Sem Bethal Dr St Paul MN 55112

KLEMT, CALVIN CARL, librarian, minister Presbyterian Church in U.S.; b. Louisville, Aug. 19, 1925; s. William Walter and Emma (Bach) K.; m. Bette Mae Bartlett, June 7, 1951; children: Kristin Elizabeth, Paul William. Student U. Ky., 1946-49; B.A., Heidelberg Coll., 1950; M.Div., Union Theol. Sem., N.Y.C., 1953; A.M. in Library Sci., U. Mich., 1962. Ordained to ministry Evang. and Ref. Ch. Pastor Evang. and Reformed Ch., Suffield, Ohio, 1953-58, United Ch. Christ, Big Rapids, Mich., 1958-61; librarian Central Luth. Theol. Sem., Fremont, Nebr., 1962-66, Austin Presbyn. Theol. Sem., Tex., 1966—; candidates chair Tres Rios Prebytery, Midland, Tex., 1981-83. Served with AUS, 1943-46. Mem. Am. Theol. Library Assn. Democrat. Home: 4804 Broken Bow Pass Austin TX 78745 Office: Stitt Library Austin Theol Sem 106 W 27th St Austin TX 78705

KLENICKI, LEON, rabbi, Reform Jewish Congregations; b. Buenos Aires, Argentina, Sept. 7, 1930; s. Isaias and Inda (Kuzewicka) K.; came to U.S., 1973; B.A., U. Cin., 1963; B.Hebrew Letters, Hebrew Union Coll.-Jewish Inst. Religion, 1965, M.H.L., 1967; m. Ana Raquel Dimsitz, Aug. 16, 1959; children—Ruth Sharon, Daniel Raphael. Ordained rabbi, 1967; dir. World Union for Progressive Judaism, Latin Am. Office, Buenos Aires, 1967-73; dir. dept. Jewish-Cath. relations Anti-Defamation League, N.Y.C., 1973—. Rabbi, Congregation Emanu-El, Buenos Aires, 1970-73; editor Teshuvah mag., 1968-70; co-editor Face to Face: An Interreligious Bulletin, 1975. Mem. Central Conf. Am. Rabbis, N.Y. Bd. Rabbis, Am. Acad. Religion. Home: 13 Stonicker St Lawrenceville NJ 08648 Office: 315 Lexington Ave New York City NY 10016

KLIETZ, SHELDON HENRY, minister, Lutheran Church-Missouri Synod; b. Chgo., Feb. 26, 1935; s. George Henry and Edna Bertha (Neumann) K.; m. JoAnne Marie Thomas, June 7, 1959; children: Mark Thomas, Beth Jeannine, Todd Stephen. A.A., Concordia Coll., 1954; B.A., Concordia Theol. Sem., 1960. Ordained to ministry Luth. Ch., 1960. Pastor St. Paul's Luth. Chs., Campbell-Nashua, Minn., 1960-65, Grace Evang. Luth. Ch., Hazel Crest, Ill., 1965-74, Trinity Evang. Luth. Ch., Marseilles, Ill., 1974-83, Faith Evang. Luth. Ch., Oak Lawn, Ill., 1983—; part-time chaplain Tinley Park Mental Health Ctr., Ill., 1965—, Howe Devel. Ctr., Tinley Park, 1974—; dist. bd. dirs. Standing Comm. for the Retarded, Hillside, Ill., 1978—; contact campus pastor Morraine Valley Community Coll., Palos Hills, Ill., 1983—. Bd. dirs. Marseilles Nursing Service, 1975-78, 82-83. Mem. Marseilles Ministerial Assn. (sec. 1978-82). Office: Faith Evang Luth Ch 9701 S Melvina Ave Oak Lawn IL 60453

KLIMES, RUDOLF EMANUEL, minister, Seventh-day Adventist Church; health administrator; b. Sternberk, Czechoslovakia, Jan. 9, 1932; came to Can., 1948; s. John and Marianna (Friedman) K.; m. Anna Homenchuk, July 14, 1954; children: Anita, Bonnie, Randall. Ph.D., Ind. U., 1964; M.A., Andrews U., 1977; D.Min., McCormick Theol. Sem., 1981; M.P.H., Johns Hopkins U., 1984. Ordained to ministry Seventh-day Adventist Ch., 1961. Tchr., Seventh-day Adventist schs., Can., 1951-64; pres. Korean Union Coll., Seoul, 1964-69, Saniku Gakuin Coll., Chiba, Japan, 1969-73; prof. Andrews U., Berrien Springs, Mich., 1973-79; exec. dir. Adventist Health Network, Washington, 1979—; mem. N. Am. div. Seventh-day Adventists, Washington, 1979—, Gen. Conf. Com., 1979—; sec. Pub. Ministries Com., 1982—; dir., spl. asst. Adventist Health System/U.S., Washington, 1982—. Exec. dir. Am. Health and Temperance Soc., Washington, 1979—. Contbr. articles to research jours. Mem. United Way Com., Benton Harbor, Mich., 1978. Recipient Outstanding Service award Minister of Health, Republic of Korea, 1969, Dongbaeg medal pres. Republic of Korea, 1969. Fellow Nat. Ctr. for Health Educators; mem. Am. Pub. Health Assn., Soc. for Pub. Health Educators, Nat. Assn. Drug Abuse Counselors, Phi Beta Kappa. Home: 3332 Greencastle Rd Burtonsville MD 20833

KLINE, ROBERT, clergyman, Churches of Christ in Christian Union; b. Champaign County, Ohio, Oct. 11, 1925; s. George Ira and Clarabelle (Humble) K.; m. Lediabelle Wolf, Mar. 29, 1947; children: Karen Sue, Connie Rae, Barbara Lynn. Ed. pub. schs., London, Ohio. Ordained to ministry Chs. of Christ in Christian Union. Pastor chs., Tucson, 1959-64, Columbus, Ohio, 1964-67; Washington Ch., Ohio, 1973-75; dist. supt. Chs. of Christ in Christian Union, 1967-73, adminstrv. sec. Circleville, Ohio, 1975-78, gen. supt., 1978—; trustee World Gospel Missions, Marion, Ind., 1978—, Wesley Bibl. Sem., Jackson, Miss., 1979—. Editor Advocate, 1978—. Mem. Christian Holiness Assn. (v.p. 1982-84, pres. 1984-86). Republican. Office: Chs of Christ in Christian Union PO Box 30 Circleville OH 43113

KLINK, CHARLES ELMER, minister, United Methodist Church; b. Oelwein, Iowa, Dec. 31, 1953; s. Norman Elmer and Martha Anne (Schutz) K.; m. Margaret Louise Ernst, Jan. 10, 1976; children: Kiersten Brown, Ian Ernst. B.A., Upper Iowa U., 1975; M.Div., U. Dubuque Theol. Sem., 1978. Ordained to ministry United Methodist Ch., 1978. Minister Bussey-Tracy-Harvey United Meth. Ch., Bussey, Iowa, 1978-81, St. Mark's United Meth. Ch., Camanche, Iowa, 1981-85, Summer United Meth. Ch., Summer, Iowa, 1985—; Ch. Soc. Bd. Mem. Iowa Conf. United Meth. Ch., 1978-81, 1982-85; Massed Choir Festival organizer, St. Mark's United Meth. Ch., Camanche, Iowa, 1983-85; chmn. Reach Out, Muscatine Dist., Iowa Conf., 1984-85. Mem. Health Care Com., Gov.'s Council On Ageing, Clinton, Iowa, 1984-85. Democrat. Home: 209 Chicago St Sumner IA 50674

KLOEPFER, JOHN WARNER, minister, United Presbyterian Church U.S.A.; b. Emporia, Kans., July 12, 1947; s. Henry Warner and Ruth Elizabeth (McCoy) K.; B.A., U. Ill., Chgo., 1969; M.Div., Colgate Rochester Div. Sch., 1976; postgrad. Duquesne U., 1984—; m. Margery Lucille Coon, Aug. 9, 1975; children: Karen Jean, Kristen Elizabeth, Kendra Grace. Ordained to ministry, 1976; religious edn. cons. Ecumenical Inst., Chgo., 1966-70; dir. religious studies Ecumenical Inst., Denver, 1970-71; exec. dir. Ecumenical Inst., Cin., 1971-73; program dir. Univ. Presby. Ch., Buffalo, 1973; asst. pastor Eastside Meml. Presby. Ch., Rochester, N.Y., 1974-75; interim pastor West Ave. Presby. Ch., Buffalo, 1975-76; pastor Bovina Center Presby. Ch., Bovina Center, N.Y., 1976-84, McGinnis Presbyn. Ch., Pitcairn, Pa., 1984—. Mem. nat. faculty Ecumenical Inst. Home: 410 3d St Pitcairn PA 15140 Office: McGinnis Presbyterian Ch Pitcairn PA 15140

KLOESE, BRUCE GERALD, minister, developer, Lutheran Church in America; b. Milw., Dec. 30, 1928; s. William Carl and Betty Elizabeth (Suchinski) K.; m. Dorla Rae Chadd, 1952; children: Linda, Karen. B.A., Carthage Coll., 1950; M.Div., Luther Northwestern, 1953; M.S.W., U. Wis.-Milw., 1969, M.Ed., 1974; D.Min., Luth. Sch. Theology, Chgo., 1981. Ordained to ministry United Lutheran Church in America, 1953. Asst. pastor St. Matthew's Ch., Wauwatosa, Wis., 1953-54; pastor Resurrection Luth. Ch., Green Bay, Wis., 1954-60, St. Stephen's Luth. Ch., Madison, Wis., 1960-67, King of Glory Luth. Ch., Milw., 1967-73; pastor, developer Tex. Twp., Kalamazoo, 1974—; mem. various coms. Northwest Synod and Wis./Upper Mich. Synod, 1954-74, Mich. Synod, 1974—; bd. dirs. Oakwood Luth. Home, Madison, 1964-67. Home and Office: 7426 Thrasher Ln Kalamazoo MI 49002

KLOHN, FRANKLIN JAMES, priest, Episc. Ch.; b. Sandusky, Ohio, Sept. 13, 1923; s. Frank Jacob and Marguerite (Anders) K.; A.B., Ohio U., 1944; M.Div., Bexley Hall, 1947; S.T.M. summa cum laude, U. Dubuque, 1972; D.Ministry, Aquinas Inst., 1975; m. Ruth E. Dorchester, June 25, 1947; children—Darlene, Franklin James, Melanie, Jonathan, Mark. Ordained to ministry, 1947; rector Grace Ch., Galion, Ohio, 1947-51, St. Andrew's Ch., Akron, Ohio, 1951-63, St. John's Ch., Mason City, Iowa, 1963-70, St. John's Ch., Dubuque, Iowa, 1970—. Chmn. Ecumenical Commn., Diocese Iowa, 1972—, chmn. ch. architecture and allied arts, 1966—, ecumenical officer, 1972— pres. Ecumenical Council, Dubuque, 1976—; pres. Dubuque Ministerial Assn., 1975, Council Chs., Mason City, 1968; grand chaplain Grand chpt. Royal Arch Masons, State of Iowa, 1977-78. Chmn. fin. NE Iowa council Boy Scouts Am., 1976, v.p., 1977, recipient Silver Beaver award, 1976. Author: Pre-Marital Counseling, 1975. Home: 1819 Norland Dr Dubuque IA 52001 Office: PO Box 874 Dubuque IA 52001

KLOS, FRANK WILLIAM, JR., minister, church official, Lutheran Church in America; b. Wheeling, W.Va., July 20, 1924; s. Frank William and Irma Kathryn (Bayha) K.; m. Sarah Eleanor Wolfe, May 24, 1946; children: Kathryn Klos Reehl, Eric, Beverly Klos Perry, Thomas. A.B., Gettysburg Coll., 1946; B.D., Gettysburg Sem., 1949, S.T.M., 1961; M.Ed., Temple U., 1969, Ed.D., 1979. Ordained, 1949. Pastor St. Johns Luth. Ch., Martinsburg, W.Va., 1949-55; mem. field staff bd. parish edn. Luth. Ch. Am., Phila., 1955-58, audio visual editor, catechetics editor, 1958-69, sr. editor youth and adult resources, div. parish services, 1969-79, dir. dept. program resources, 1980—. Author: Four Pictures of Christ, 1965; Confirmation and First Communion, 1968; A Companion for Reading and Understanding the Good News, 1972. Editor: Here Comes the Future, 1981. Pres., v.p., treas. Upper Dublin Sch. Bd., Pa., 1966-77; mem. Upper Dublin Park and Recreation Bd., 1966-68. Mem. Adult Edn. Assn., Assn. Ednl. Communications and Tech., Phi Beta Kappa. Republican. Home: 18 S Wendover Rd Marlton NJ 08053 Office: Div Parish Services Lutheran Ch Am 2900 Queen Ln Philadelphia PA 19129

KLOS, SARAH WOLFE, religious educator, Lutheran Church in America; b. Boston, Dec. 16, 1925; d. G. Edgar and Jane Taylor (Miller) Wolfe; m. Frank William Klos, May 24, 1946; children: Kathryn Klos Reehl, Erie Gilbert, Beverly Klos Perry, Thomas Andrew. B.A., Gettysburg Coll., 1948; M.A.R., Luth. Theol. Sem., 1974. Cert. lay profl. leader Luth. Ch. in Am. Dir. Christian edn. St. Peter's Luth. Ch., Phila., 1965-67, Christ's Luth. Ch., Oreland, Pa., 1967-80, St. Paul's Luth. Ch., Ardmore, Pa., 1980—; mem. exec. com. Div. for World Mission and Ecumenism, Luth. Ch. Am., N.Y.C., 1978—; mem. Commn. for Edn. in Mission, Nat. Council Chs., N.Y.C., 1978—. Author: Prayers: Alone/Together, 1970. Columnist Partners Mag., 1980—. Bd. dirs. Montgomery County Head Start, 1978—. Republican. Home: 18 S Wendover Rd Marlton NJ 08053 Office: St Paul's Luth Ch 415 E Athens Ave Ardmore PA 19003

KLOSTERBOER, JAMES EDWARD, minister, American Lutheran Church; b. Waterloo, Iowa, Sept. 15, 1949; s. Edward John and Florene Ellen (Walter) K.; m. Laurel Sue Pautsch, Aug. 3, 1974; children: Jesse Paul, Sara Marie. B.A., Luther Coll., 1971; M.Div., Luther Theol. Sem., 1978. Ordained to ministry Am. Luth. Ch., 1978. Pastor, Nazareth Luth. Ch., Cambridge, Iowa, 1978-82; assoc. pastor 1st Luth. Ch., Waterloo, 1982-85, co-pastor, 1985—; chmn. Iowa Dist. Leadership Tng. Sch., 1980—; mem. pastoral care adv. com. Allen Hosp., Waterloo, 1982—. Mem. Waterloo Ministerial Assn. (sec.-treas. 1983). Office: 1st Luth Ch 118 High St Waterloo IA 50703

KLOTZ, JOHN WILLIAM, seminary educator, author, minister, Lutheran Ch.-Mo. Synod; b. Pitts., Jan. 10, 1918; s. John William and Anna Mathilde (Kauffmann) K.; M.Div., Concordia Sem., 1941; Ph.D., U. Pitts., 1947; m. Florence Marie Succop, Oct. 17, 1942; children: Frederick, Kenneth, Richard, Martin, Barbara, Alan, Nancy, Marilyn. Ordained to ministry, 1943; instr. Concordia Coll., Bronxville, N.Y., 1941-43, Bethany Luth. Coll., Mankato, Minn., 1943-45; prof. Concordia Tchrs. Coll., River Forest, Ill., 1945-59; prof. and academic dean Concordia Sr. Coll., Ft. Wayne, Ind., 1959-74; prof. practical theology, dean academic affairs, Concordia Sem., St. Louis, 1974-78, dir. grad. studies, 1978—. Sec. Com. Research Luth. Ch.-Mo. Synod, 1955—, mem. Commn. Constl. Matters, 1974-81. Pres. Friends of Our Native Landscape, Chgo., 1954-59, ACRES, Inc., Ft. Wayne, 1960-70; bd. dirs. Merry Lea Environ. Center, Wolf Lake, Ind., 1970-74. Mem. AAAS, Am. Inst. Biol. Sci., Izaak Walton League, Nature Conservancy. Author: Genes, Genesis and Evolution, 1955; The Challenge of the Space Age, 1961; Modern Science in the Christian Life, 1961; Abortion, 1973; Ecology Crisis, 1973; Studies in Creation, 1985. Office: 801 De Mun Ave Saint Louis MO 63105

KLUG, RAYMOND FREDERICK, pastor, American Lutheran Church; b. Blackduck, Minn., Dec. 16, 1930; s. Frederick Carl Henrick and Lora Vivian (DeFrang) K.; m. Elaine Shirley Jacobson, Apr. 21, 1957; children: Rebekah, Luther, Daniel, Deborah. B.S., U. Minn., 1952; theology candidate Luther Theol. Sem., St. Paul, 1957-60. Ordained to ministry American Lutheran Church, 1960. Pastor Edmore Parish, N.D., 1960-64, First Luth. Ch., Valley City, N.D., 1964-68, Zion Luth. Ch., Blackduck, 1974-80, Glyndon Luth. Ch., Minn., 1980-85, Am. Luth. Ch., Fairbury, Nebr., 1985—; exec. dir. Red Willow Bible Camp, Binford, N.D., 1968-74; dist. coordinator for bible camping Am. Luth. Ch. (ea. N.D. dist.), Fargo, 1964-74; chmn. Luth. Camping Retarded Citizens, Valley City, 1967-80; founder, organizer Christian Nurture Camps, N.D.; chaplain, Emergency Med Technician, Blackduck Ambulance Service, Minn., 1975-80; chaplain Glyndon Fire Dept., 1983-85. Leader No. Lights council Boy Scouts Am., 1964-74; chmn. Youth Summer Baseball Program, Blackduck, 1975-79. Served to sgt. U.S. Army, 1953-55. Recipient Am. Farmers degree Future Farmers Am., 1950, Mr. and Mrs. Non Eagle award Eagle Club (N.D. chpt.), 1973; named Man Yr., Boy Scouts Am., Troop 114, 1962, Mr. and Mrs. Non Eagle of Yr., Eagles Club, Valley City, N.D., 1972. Mem. Glyndon Ministerium (chmn. 1980-85). Democrat. Clubs: Exchange (Valley City, N.D.) (youth chmn. 1966-68), Civic, Commerce (Blackduck). Home: Route 2 Box 40 D Glyndon MN 56547 Office: Glyndon Luth Ch 414 Parke Ave S PO Box 38 Glyndon MN 56547

KLUMPP, DAVID JOHN, minister, Lutheran Church-Missouri Synod; b. Buffalo, Apr. 9, 1934; s. Elmer John and Alice Emma (Winter) K.; m. Marian Phyllis Maerten, Aug. 29, 1959; children: Nathan, Karen, Joel. A.A., Concordia Coll., Ft. Wayne, Ind., 1954; B.D., Concordia Sem., St. Louis, 1959, S.T.M., 1965; M.A., Okla. U., 1977. Ordained to ministry Luth. Ch., 1960. Pastor, St. Paul Luth. Ch., Hammond, La., 1960-63, St. Stephen Luth. Ch., New Orleans, 1963-68; pastor, campus pastor Univ. Luth. Chapel, U. Okla., Norman, 1968—; mem. bd. Christian edn. so. dist. Luth. Ch.-Mo. Synod, New Orleans, 1965-67, circuit counselor, 1965-67, coordinator for univ. ministries Okla. dist., 1968-78; pres. Luth. Council Central Okla., Oklahoma City, 1982—. Contbr. sermons, papers to religious publs. Mem. Norman Mental Health Adv. Council, 1979. Mem. Assn. Univ. Ministries, Luth. Campus Ministries Assn. (sec.). Democrat. Lodge: Civitan (chaplain 1983). Office: Univ Luth Chapel 914 Elm Ave Norman OK 73069

KMIEC, EDWARD V., bishop, Roman Catholic Church. Titular bishop of Simidicca, aux. bishop, Trenton, N.J., 1983—. Office: 215 Essex Ave Spring Lake NJ 07762*

KNAPPE, WOLF DIETRICH, minister, Lutheran Church in America; b. Hohegrethe, Germany, Mar. 30, 1926; came to U.S., 1951, naturalized, 1955; s. Wilhelm E.M. and Jula Karolina (von Thuengen) K.; m. Inga Helen Korte, Aug. 29, 1950; children: Mark William, Jane Helen. Cand. Theol., Erlangen U., Germany, 1948; S.T.M., Chgo. Luth. Sem., 1949; S.T.D., Luth. Sch. Theology, 1977. Ordained to ministry Luth. Ch. of Bavaria, 1949. Asst. pastor Epiphany Luth. Ch., Munich, Germany, 1949-51; pastor St. Peter's - Wine Hill, Steeleville, Ill., 1951-55; instr. Trinity Sem., Blair, Nebr., 1955-56; mission developer Wartburg Synod, Belleville, Ill., 1956-57; pastor St. Paul's Luth. Ch., Lyons Wis., also Trinity Luth. Ch., Pell Lakes, Wis., 1957-61, St. Paul's Luth. Ch., Chgo., 1961-70, Tabor Luth. Ch., Phila., 1970—; trustee Phila. Protestant Home, 1973—; bd. dirs. Southeast Pa. Synod, Phila., 1982—. Contbg. editor Kirchliches Monatsblatt Jour., 1972—. Served as sgt. German Army, 1943-45. Home: 4860 N Howard St Philadelphia PA 19120 Office: Tabor Luth Ch Roosevelt Blvd and Mascher St Philadelphia PA 19120

KNAUER, PAUL FRANCIS, priest, Roman Catholic Church; b. Passaic, N.J., Aug. 11, 1938; s. Lawrence Ryan and Loretta (Trainor) K. B.A., Seton Hall U., 1960; postgrad., Immaculate Conception Sem., Darlington, N.J., 1964. Ordained priest Roman Catholic Ch., 1964. Assoc. pastor St. Vincent Ch., Madison, N.J., 1964-67, St. Christopher's Ch., Parsippany, N.J., 1967-68; dir. Cath. Community Ctr., Paterson, N.J., 1969-73; pastor Our Lady of Victories Ch., Paterson, 1973—; mem. Paterson Vicarate, 1979—, bd. dirs. urban study, 1982-84. Bd. dirs. Inner City Community Action for Housing, Paterson, 1975—, pres., 1982—. bd. dirs. summer program, 1978-84. Recipient Polit. Action award Paterson chpt. NAACP, 1974.

KNAUFF, LUTHER LEVERN, minister, American Lutheran Church; b. Venus, Pa., July 23, 1922; s. George Martin and Luella E. (Wagner) K.; m. Mildred R. Albrecht, May 25, 1946; children: Karen, Mark, Philip, Lois, Craig. B.A., Capital U., 1943; cert. Trinity Sem., Columbus, Ohio, 1946. Ordained to ministry Am. Luth. Ch., 1946. Pastor Gethsemane Luth. Ch., Warren, Mich., 1946-48, Nazareth Luth. Ch., Chatfield, Ohio, 1948-57, Perry Hwy. Luth. Ch., Wexford, Pa., 1957-59, St. Martin Luth. Ch., North Tonawanda, N.Y., 1959-71, Old St. Paul Luth. Ch., Newton, N.C., 1971—; chmn. North Amherst Coop. Ministery, Tonawanda, 1967-71, Catawba Valley Luth. Fellowship, Hickory, N.C., 1978-84; v.p. Eastern dist. Am. Luth. Ch., Washington, 1967-69; trustee Council of Chs. of Buffalo, 1968-71. Chmn. Crawford County chpt. Am. Cancer Soc., Bucyrus, Ohio, 1955. Mem. Catawba County Hist. Assn. (treas. 1984). Lodge: Optimists. Home: Route 3 Box 110 Newton NC 28658 Office: Old St Paul Luth Ch Newton NC 28658

KNEAFSEY, CORNELIUS THOMAS, priest, community organizer, Roman Cath. Ch.; b. N.Y.C., Mar. 1, 1933; s. John James and Helen Theresa (Moran) K.; B.A., Cathedral Coll., 1954; M.Ed., St. John's U., 1962, profl. diploma in psychology, 1975, M.Div., 1977. Ordained priest, 1958; community organizer involved in parish youth work, religious edn. programs, mental health, human resources devel., N.Y.C., 1960—; founder, chmn. Community Service Council of College Point, Inc., 1969—; profl. marriage counselor Diocese of Bklyn., 1974—. Recipient Brotherhood award NCCJ, 1972; Community Service award Flushing Drug Council, 1974. Home and Office: 136-06 87th Ave Richmond Hill NY 11418

KNIFFEN, ARVAL WAYNE, minister, Southern Baptist Convention; b. Tyler, Tex., Jan. 10, 1949; s. Arval Dale and Betty Lou (Wroten) K.; m. Nancy Ann Peterbaugh, Jan. 2, 1970; children: Melanie, Paige, Justin. A.A., Tyler Jr. Coll., 1975; Th.B., Albany Coll.-Sem., 1978, Th.M., 1980, Th.D., 1984. Ordained to ministry Baptist Ch., 1974. Pastor Hopewell Bapt. Ch., Tyler, Tex., 1976-77, Prairie Creek Bapt. Ch., Lindale, Tex., 1977-80; assoc. pastor evangelism Trinity Bapt. Ch., Tyler, 1980-81; pastor Eastside Bapt. Ch., Henderson, Tex., 1981—; trustee Pineywoods Bapt. Encampment, Groveton, Tex., 1982-83; evangelism chmn. Rusk-Panola Bapt. Assn., Henderson, Tex., 1982—; bd. dirs. Tex. Prisoners Bible Inst., Houston, 1984—. Author: Does Anybody Care, 1984; They Married and Lived Miserably Everafter, 1984. Served with U.S. Army, 1967-70, Vietnam. Decorated Purple Heart. Office: Eastside Bapt Ch 2300 E Main St Henderson TX 75652

KNIGHT, CAROLYN ANN, minister, Progressive National Baptist Convention; b. Denver, Aug. 7, 1956; d. Edd and Dorothy (Green) K. B.A., Bishop Coll., 1977; M.Div., Union Theol. Sem., 1980, S.T.M., 1983; postgrad. Drew U., 1983—. Ordained to ministry Bapt. Ch., 1978. Asst. pastor Canaan Bapt. Ch., N.Y.C., 1977—; adj. prof. N.Y. Theol. Sem., N.Y.C., 1981-82; bd. dirs. Black Theology Project, N.Y.C., 1980—. Bd.

dirs. Breast Examination Ctr. of Harlem, N.Y.C., 1980—; mem. steering com. Black Conv. '82-'83, N.Y.C., 1982-83; mem. Jesse Jackson for Pres. Com., 1983-84. Recipient Youth Community Service award Milbank Community Ctr., N.Y.C., 1983; United Negro Coll. Fund Colo. scholar, 1977; Benjamin E. Mays fellow Fund for Theol. Edn., 1978-80. Mem. Orgn. of African-Am. Clergy, Black Women in Ministry. Democrat. Home: 427 W 154th St Apt 6 New York NY 10032 Office: Canaan Bapt Ch 132 W 116th St New York NY 10026

KNIGHT, KEITH, elder, Christian Reformed Ch.; b. Delft, Netherlands, Dec. 18, 1949; s. John Jan and Grace (Weeda) K.; came to U.S., 1950; grad. secondary sch.; m. Marian Los, Sept. 18, 1971; 1 dau., Erika Kristin. Ordained elder, 1972; elder Welland (Ont.) Christian Ref. Ch., 1971-76; editor/pub. Calvinist Contact, St. Catharines, Ont., 1976—. Edn. reporter, city editor Welland Tribune, 1969-76. Mem. Evang. Press Assn. Home: 725 S Pelham St Welland ON L3C 3C9 Canada Office: 99 Niagara St Saint Catharines ON L2R 4L3 Canada

KNILL, KEITH RODERICK, minister, United Church of Canada; b. Hamilton, Ont., Can., Nov. 17, 1944; s. Gordon Lyall and Gwenyth Marion (Pryce) K.; m. Nancy Leigh Passmore, Aug. 3, 1968; children: David Roderick, Graham Kenneth. B.A., McMaster U., 1967; B.D., U. Toronto, 1970, D.Min., 1982; M.S., Cambridge U., Eng., 1971, M.Litt., 1973. Ordained to ministry Hamilton Conf., 1970. Chaplain, Donjail Cts., Toronto, 1968; minister Turner Valley United Ch., Alta., 1973-76, St. Paul's United Ch., Richmond Hill, Ont., 1976-83, St. Andrews United Ch., Niagara Falls, Ont., 1983—; mem. nat. div. mission United Ch. Can., 1978-82; mem. Christian Edn. Project Planning Group, 1982—; chmn. chaplaincy com. York Central Hosp., Richmond Hill, 1980-82. Author: Liturgical and Psychotherapeutic Healing, 1973; Explorations in Lay Ministry, 1982; also articles and sermons. Chmn. adv. com. Emmanuel Coll., 1980-82, mem. council, 1978-84; bd. regents Victoria U., 1982—; bd. dirs. YM-YWCA, Richmond Hill, 1979-81, Social Planning Council, Niagara Falls, 1983-84, chmn. Inter-Profl. Agy., Richmond Hill, 1977-80. Elsie Watt fellow Victoria U., 1970; recipient Laidlaw Found. award, 1971-72. Home: 5952 Stevens St Niagara Falls ON L2E 3A3 Canada Office: St Andrews United Ch 5645 Morrison St Niagara Falls ON L2E 2E8 Canada

KNISELEY, KARL EUGENE II, minister, Lutheran Church in America; b. Pitts., June 2, 1940; s. Karl Eugene and Margaret Helen (Dunkle) K.; m. Sally Ann Hurd, July 27, 1962; Karen, Karl Eugene III, Michael, Ann. B.A., Calif. State U.-Los Angeles, 1962; M.Div., Pacific Luth. Theol. Sem., 1966; D.Min., Fuller Theol. Sem., 1974. Ordained to ministry, Luth. Ch. in Am., 1966. Pastor Bethlehem Luth. Ch., Sanger, Calif., 1966-69, First Luth. Ch. of Glendale, Calif., 1969-74; sr. pastor Immanuel Luth. Ch. of San Jose, Calif., 1974-79, First Luth. Ch. of Los Angeles, 1979—; past pres. Luth. Social Services No. Calif. and Nev., 1977-79; bd. dirs. Benevolence Funding Luth. Chs. Am., Pacific Southwest Synod, Los Angeles, 1979-82, Luth. Hosp. Soc., Los Angeles, 1979—; instr. campus ministry Loyola U. Sch. of Law, Los Angeles, 1983—; radio commentator St. KIEV Glendale, Calif., 1979—, religious newscaster Sta. KFAC-AM-FM, Los Angeles, 1979—. Served as chaplain USAR. Lodge: Kiwanis. Office: 3119 W 6th St Los Angeles CA 90020

KNITTER, PAUL FRANCIS, educator, theology Roman Catholic Church; b. Chgo., Feb. 25, 1939; s. Paul Lewis and Rose (Dolezal) K.; m. Catherine Mary Cornell, Dec. 31, 1982; children: John, Moira. B.A., Divine World Sem., 1962; Licentiate Theology, Pontifical Gregorian U., Rome, 1966; Th.D., U. Marburg, Fed. Republic Germany, 1972. Faculty, Cath. Theol. Union, Chgo., 1972-75; assoc. prof. Xavier U., Cin., 1975-78, prof. theology, 1978—. Author: No Other Name?, 1984. Contbr. articles to profl. jours. Mem. Am. Acad. Religion, Cath. Theol. Soc. Am., Coll. Theology Soc. (bd. dirs.), Am. Soc. Missiology. Democrat. Home: 2636 Marlington St Cincinnati OH 45208 Office: Xavier U Dept Theology Cincinnati OH 45207

KNOX, JAMES LLOYD, bishop, United Methodist Church, Ala.-W. Fla. Conf., N. Ala. Conf. Office: PO Box 700 Andalusia AL 36420*

KNOX, THOMAS STEPHEN, priest, Episc. Ch.; b. St. John, N.B., Can., May 4, 1924; s. John Samuel and Edith Pearl (Stephens) K.; B.A., Bishops U., 1950, licentiate theology, 1952; postgrad. Theol. Coll. Chichester, Sussex, 1975-76. Ordained priest, 1952; curate, Quebec City, Que., Can., 1951-54; rector, Port Daniel, Que., 1954-57, Trinity Ch., Saco, Maine, 1957-64; curate St. Philips Ch., Coral Gables, Fla., 1964-65; rector St. Lukes Ch., Caribou, Maine, 1965—. Commissary to Bishop Antiqua, W.I.; mgr. architecture Diocese Maine. Mem. Aroostock Arts Council. Mem. Coll. Preachers Washington, Am. Ch. Union, Asso. Order of Holy Cross. Home and Office: 365 Main St Caribou ME 04736

KNUDSON, ARTHUR JOSEPH, minister, radio moderator, So. Bapt. Conv.; b. Madison, Wis., Sept. 19, 1908; s. Hans and Anna Marie (Tobiason) K.; B.A., Trinity Coll. and Sem., Deerfield, Ill., 1930; postgrad. Winona State U., 1942-43, Eastern N.Mex. U., 1962-63, U. Wyo., 1964-65, Utah State U., 1966-67; m. Doris Elaine Christiansen, Aug. 6, 1953; children—Doris Anne, Rebecca Ruth, William Arthur, David Paul. Ordained to ministry, 1944; evangelist, 1930-36; campaign coordinator; tchr. Trinity Coll., 1937-38; dir. Christ for Am. Crusades, Winona Lake, Ind., 1944-50, Billy Sunday Jubilee, Garner, Iowa, 1946-47; pastor evangelist, N.Mex., Colo., Wyo., 1962—; moderator Green River (Wyo.) Assn., 1974-76; dir. radio program Singing Knudsons, Kemmerer, Wyo., 1963—; tchr. Lincoln County (Wyo.) Sch. Dist., 1963-73, dir. accelerated reading lab., jr. and sr. high schs., 1970-73; Bd. dirs. S. Lincoln County Mental Health Assn. Composer religious songs. Home: PO Box 308 LaBarge WY 83123

KNUDSON, ROGER LEROY, minister, American Lutheran Ch.; b. Inwood, Iowa, Apr. 9, 1931; s. Howard Tegnor and Anna Marie (Bankson) K.; m. Nancy Ann Foster, July 3, 1952; children: Kimberly Ann, David Roger, Sheryl Marie. B.A., Augustana Coll., 1955; B.Th., Luther Sem., 1959. Ordained to ministry Am. Luth. Ch., 1959. Pastor, 1st East KoshKoning, Cambridge, Wis., 1959-60; sr. pastor Luth. Ch. of Resurrection, Racine, Wis., 1961-83, Central Luth. Ch., Winona, Minn., 1983—; mem. council So. Wis. dist. Am. Luth. Ch., Madison, 1964-70, del. gen. conv., 1978, mem. bd. social services, Mpls., 1972-73, mem. ch. council, 1980-83. Mem. adv. com. on family life and human sexuality Racine Sch. Bd., Wis., 1981-83. Home: 1342 Crocus Circle Winona MN 55987 Office: Central Luth Ch 259 Wabasha Winona MN 55987

KNUDSON, STANLEY GEORGE, minister, administrator, American Lutheran Church; b. Rolette, N.D., Dec. 31, 1916; s. Peder Johan and Malene Marie (Riise) K.; m. Mildred A. Swedberg, June 11, 1949; children: Naomi, Ruth, Miriam. B.A., Luther Coll., 1943; C.T., Luther Sem., 1949. Ordained to ministry Am. Luth. Ch., 1949. Pastor, Evang. Luth. Ch., Lignite, N.D., 1949-53, Evang. Luth. Ch., Harlem, Mont., 1953-58, Am. Luth. Ch., Scobey-Peerless, Mont., 1958-71; pastor-in-residence Trinity Luth. Sem., Columbus, Ohio, 1984; exec. asst. to bishop Am. Luth. Ch., Western N.D., Bismarck, 1972-84, dir. United Mission Appeal Western Dist., 1974-75, dir. sem. appeal, 1980-81. Recipient Pres.' award, 1969, Regents award, 1977 (both Concordia Coll., Moorhead, Minn.). Club: C-400. Home: 1009 N 1st St Bismarck ND 58501

KNUTH, JAMES ALLAN, pastor, Lutheran Church-Missouri Synod; b. St. Joseph, Mich., June 7, 1941; s. Fernest Ludwig and Martha (Gallert) K.; m. Constance Lydia Rueter, Aug. 20, 1966; children: Christa Renee, James Christian, Catherine Joy, Corrie Celeste. Diploma Concordia Jr. Coll., Milw., 1961; B.A., Concordia Sr. Coll., Fort Wayne, Ind., 1963; B.Div., M.Div., Concordia Sem., St. Louis, 1967. Ordained to ministry Lutheran Ch., 1967. Pastor, Trinity & Grace Luth. Ch., Bear Creek, Wis., 1967-70, Good Shepherd Luth. Ch., Two Rivers, Wis., 1970-74, Mt. Olive Luth. Ch., Madison, Wis., 1984—; sr. pastor Calvary Luth. Ch., U. Wis.-Madison, Madison, 1974-84; staff chaplain 127th Tactical Fort Wing, Wis. Air Nat. Guard, 1981—; mem. dist. bd. evangelism, Southern Wis. Dist. Luth. Ch.-Mo. Synod, 1975-78, mem. dist. recruitment com., 1982—; mem. campus ministry com. Luth. Ch.-Mo. Synod, 1982-84; dist. pastoral adv. Luth. Laymen's League, Wis., 1984—; elected circuit pastoral counsellor Madison area Luth. Ch.-Mo. Synod Chs.; resource leader Campus Ministry Conf. and Great Commn. Convocation; served on task force Luther's 500th Anniversary, U. Wis.-Madison, 1983, Book and Spade, U. Wis.-Madison, 1978; lectr. pastoral and sch. principle confs. Bd. dirs. United Way, Two Rivers, 1972-73. Served to maj. U.S. Army Reserve, 1967. Home: 1526 Comanche Glen Madison WI 53704 Office: Mt Olive Luth Ch 4018 Mineral Pt Rd Madison WI 53705

KNUTSON, LANNY DEAN, minister, Evangelical Lutheran Church of Canada; b. Canby, Minn., July 6, 1943; s. Lloyd Cecil and Mabel Marie (Peterson) K.; m. Anna Lee Lucas, July 10, 1972; children: Robert Aaron, Mandy Elizabeth, Signe Kathryn. B.A., Augustana Coll., 1965; M.Div., Luther Theol. Sem., St. Paul, 1969. Ordained to ministry Am. Luth. Ch., 1969. Intern pastor First Luth. Ch., Onalaska, Wis., 1967-68; assoc. pastor First Luth. Ch., Bottineau, N.D., 1969-71; mission pastor Glasgow Air Base Ministry, Mont., 1971-72; asst. pastor Christ Luth. Ch., Regina, Sask., Can., 1973-77; pastor Christ Luth. Ch., Calgary, Alta., Can., 1978—; sec., v.p. Regina conf. Evang. Luth. Ch. Can., 1974-77, vice chmn. bd. communication, Saskatoon, Sask., 1976-80, chmn. bd. communication, 1980-84; sec., pres. Regina Ministerial Assn., 1974-77; chmn., advisor Concord Can. Bookstore Com., Calgary, 1982—; mem. Luth. Merger Task Force on Communication, Winnipeg, Man., Can., 1984-85. Contbr. articles to mags. Chmn. Ten Days for World Devel., Calgary, 1980-83. Mem. Alta. Pioneer Auto Club. Home: 4407 Richmond Rd SW Calgary Alta T3E 4P5 Canada Office: Christ Luth Ch 4211 Richmond Rd SW Calgary AB T3E 4P4 Canada

KOCH, GLENN ALAN, seminary educator and administrator, American Baptist Churches U.S.A.; b. Quinton, N.J., Feb. 23, 1932; s. Garth Colet and Pearl Louise (Storm) K.; m. Peggy Ann Barber, June 5, 1954; children: Cheryl Ann, David Alan, Julie Alyson. B.A., Marshall U., 1953; B.D., Eastern Bapt. Theol. Sem., 1956, Th.M., 1959; M.A., U. Pa., 1962, Ph.D., 1976. Ordained to ministry Am. Bapt. Chs. U.S.A., 1957. Pastor, 1st Community Bapt. Ch., West Collingswood Heights, N.J., 1956-59; interim pastor Kings Community Bapt. Ch., Cherry Hill, N.J., 1959, Bapt. Chs., Camden, N.J., Phila., Dividing Creek, N.J., Kennett Sq., Pa., 1956-84; prof. N.T. studies Eastern Bapt. Theol. Sem., Phila., 1957-61, assoc. prof., 1969-76, prof., 1976—, assoc. dean, 1984—, acting dean, 1980-83, dir. evening courses for Christian workers, 1960-63; asst. prof. Greek and religion Eastern Coll., St. Davids, Pa., 1961-69; mem. pres.' cabinet Eastern Bapt. Sem., Phila. Seminar on Christian Origins; instr. N.T. and religion courses adult evening schs., Phila., 1960-63; sponsor Holy Land tours, 1973—; ednl. cons. for colls. Collaborator with Centre d'Analyse et de Documentation Patristiques, 1972-75; co-author: Learning to Read New Testament Greek, 1983. Contbr. articles to United Presbyn. and Am. Bapt. publs., uniform lecture series The Bapt. Leader, book revs. to Christianity Today and Mission mags. Mem. Soc. Bibl. Lit. Home: 1401 Fairview Ave Havertown PA 19083 Office: Eastern Bapt Theol Sem Lancaster and City Aves Philadelphia PA 19151

KOCH, KARL WILLIAM, minister, Lutheran Church-Missouri Synod; management analyst; b. Seattle, May 21, 1933; s. William Henry and Dora Martha (Vorwerk) K.; m. Dorothea Ruth Bellmann, Aug. 23, 1958; children: Kristen Martha, Douglas William. B.A., Concordia Sem., St. Louis, 1956, M.Div., 1959, M.S.T., 1960; M.A. in Sociology, U. Cin., 1974. Ordained to ministry Luth. Ch.-Mo. Synod, 1960. Pastor Trinity Luth. Ch., Coal Valley, Ill., 1960-63, Concordia Luth. Ch., Pullman, Wash., 1963-69; Luth. campus pastor U. Cin., 1969-74; pastor King of Kings Luth. Ch., Westerville, Ohio, 1982—; adj. faculty Franklin U., Columbus, Ohio, 1980—; especially assigned vacancy pastor Chs. Ohio Dist., Luth. Ch.-Mo. Synod, 1976—. Mgmt. analyst, dir. tng. programs State of Ohio, 1976-83; mgmt. analysis cons. Karl William Koch, Assocs., Columbus, 1983—. Editor, mgr. police tng. Systems Series, 1974-79; author devotions, tng., research writings. First v.p. Mental Health Assn., Rock Island, Ill., 1963; mem. Human Relations Commn., Pullman, 1969; bd. dirs., treas. Mt. Airy Community Council, Cin., 1974. Recipient award Exemplary Model Client Computer System, Home Energy Assistance Program, HHS, 1982. Home: 5445 Aqua St Columbus OH 43229 Office: Karl William Koch Assocs PO Box 29682 Columbus OH 43229

KOCH, THERESE, nun, Eucharistic minister, Roman Catholic Church; administrator health care facility; b. Petersburg, Nebr., Oct. 28, 1924; d. Frank Joseph and Elizabeth (Brachle) K. Student Chadron State Tchrs. Coll., 1942, Creighton U., 1944, St. Mary's Coll., 1944-45, St. Louis U., 1957, Columbia U., 1960-61. Joined Religious of the Fedn. of St. Scholastica, Roman Cath. Ch., 1977. Mem. Missionary Benedictine Sisters, Norfolk, Nebr., 1944-77; sec./treas. Benedictine Sisters, Liberty, Mo., 1977—, transferred vows Fedn. of St. Scholastica Priory, Tulsa, Okla., 1980—; adminstr. Immacolata Manor, Liberty, 1981—, pres. bd., 1981-84, treas., 1981—, spiritual leader aux., 1982—; editor Immacolata newsletter. Recipient Charles Pfizer Co. award U.S. Civil Def., 1970; award of Merit Mid-Am. Council Boy Scouts Am., 1975. Home: 2101 Hughes Rd RFD 4 Box 450 Liberty MO 64068

KOCISKO, STEPHEN JOHN, archbishop, Roman Catholic Church; b. Mpls., June 11, 1915; s. John Z. and Anna (Somosz) K.; Ph.B., Propaganda Fide U., 1937, S.T.L., 1941. Ordained priest Roman Cath. Ch., 1941, consecrated bishop, 1956; chancellor Byzantine Cath. Diocese of Pitts., 1956; rector Byzantine Cath. Sem., Pitts., 1958-63; 1st bishop Byzantine Eparchy (diocese) of Passaic, 1963-69; met. archbishop of Munhall (title of see changed to Pitts. 1977), 1969—. Address: 50 Riverview Ave Pittsburgh PA 15214

KOEHLER, ARTHUR HAROLD, ch. ofcl., Bapt. Ch.; b. Sailor Springs, Ill., Jan. 12, 1925; s. John George and Mary Ann (Williams) K.; student U. Mich., 1942-43; m. Marjorie Lucille Jones, Apr. 21, 1946; children—John A., Beverly Sue (Mrs. Jack A. Bennett). Ordained deacon Baptist Ch., 1954; now serving First Bapt. Ch., Camdenton, Mo.; pres. brotherhood, 1952, dir. tng. union, 1955, chmn. budget com., 1960-70, chmn. bldg. com., 1971; mgr. Windermere Bapt. Assembly, Roach, Mo., 1958—; an organizer So. Bapt. Assembly, Camp Mgrs. Conf., 1963, pres., 1968. Address: Windermere Bapt Assembly Roach MO 65787

KOEHLER, FREDERIC FRANK, minister, Lutheran Church-Missouri Synod; b. Nipawin, Sask., Can., Apr. 14, 1932; s. Leonard Wilbur and Fannie Mathilda (Mehlbrech) K.; m. Gloria Louis Roschke, Nov. 8, 1958; children: Denise Leslie, Koehler Manweiler,

Kathryn Kim Koehler Griewisch, David Frederick John. A.A., Concordia Coll., St. Paul, 1952; B.A., Concordia Sem., St. Louis, 1957, M.Div., 1962, S.T.M., 1977. Ordained to ministry Luth. Ch.-Mo. Synod, 1957. Minister, First Luth. Ch., Lloydminster, Sask., 1957-64, Christ Luth. Ch., Waterloo, Iowa, 1964-67, Luth. Ch. of Good Shepherd, Winnipeg, Man., Can., 1967—; chmn. Dept. Social Ministries, Lloydminster-Waterloo, 1959-67, Dept. Parish Services, Winnipeg, 1972-74; counselor Red River Circuit, Luth. Ch.-Mo. Synod, Winnipeg, 1979—. Bd. dirs. Allen Meml. Hosp., Waterloo, 1966. Mem. Luth. Welfare Assn (pres. 1959-64). Home: 406 Kildare Ave W Winnipeg MB R2C 2B5 Canada Office: Luth Ch of Good Shepherd 401 Kildare Ave W Winnipeg MB R2C 2B4 Canada

KOEHNEKE, DALE ALAN, minister, Lutheran Church-Missouri Synod; b. Lawrenceville, Ill., Mar. 7, 1951; s. Paul Alvin Carl and Edna Louise (Woodard) K.; m. Donna Mae Secord, June 9, 1973; children: Andrew, Nathaniel, Rachel. A.A., Concordia Luth. Jr. Coll., Ann Arbor, Mich., 1971; B.A., Concordia Sr. Coll., Ft. Wayne, Ind., 1973; M.Div., Christ Sem.-Seminex, St. Louis, 1977. Ordained to ministry Luth. Ch.-Mo. Synod, 1977. Pastor of evangelism St. John Luth. Ch., Salem, Oreg., 1977—; regional coordinator Luth. Parish Sec.'s Seminars, St. Joseph, Mich., 1978-82; del. Luth. Ch.-Mo. Synod Conv., St. Louis, 1983. Mem. Circuit Pastoral Conf. (sec. 1978-80), Oreg. Pastoral Conf. (vice chmn. 1978-80), Salem Luth. Ministerial Assn. (chmn. 1983-84). Office: St John Luth Ch 1350 Court St NE Salem OR 97301

KOELEMAY, RALPH LAWRENCE, family consultant, retired minister, chaplain, United Methodist Church; b. Beaumont, Tex., Feb. 10, 1926; s. Martin and Anna (Westerterp) K.; A.A., Lon Morris Coll., 1948; B.A., Vanderbilt U., 1951, B.D., 1954, M.Div., 1973; M.A. in Teaching Social Scis., U. Wis., 1972; m. Ann Watkins, Sept. 12, 1951; children: LuAnn Koelemay Bearman, R. Larry, Mary Lynne Koelemay Strickland, Donna Koelemay Berg. Ordained to ministry, 1951; pastor chs., Tenn. Conf., 1951-55; chaplain SAC, USAF, 1955-58, res. chaplain, 1958-72, sr. staff chaplain, spl. assignments, 1972-77, ret., 1977; pastor chs., W. Wis. and Wis. confs., 1958-71; now marriage and family consultant. Co-dir. Wis. Conf. Marriage Family; conductor courses seminars on faith, human relations, sexuality, ethics; counselor and dir. youth camps. Home: 702 Opportunity Ln Plover WI 54467

KOENIG, DARYL DUANE, religious organization executive, American Lutheran Church; B. Kingsville, Tex., Nov. 16, 1947; s. Walter William and Esther Emilie (Franke) K. B.A., Tex. Luth. Coll., 1970; M.Div., Luther Theol. Sem., St. Paul, 1974. Ordained to ministry Am. Luth. Ch., 1975. Clergyman St. Timothy Luth. Ch., Lakewood, Calif., 1975-78; event coordinator nat. youth gatherings Am. Luth. Ch. Nat. Office, Mpls., 1978—, exec. dir. Luther League, 1980—; coordinator inner-city advocacy program Central Luth. Ch., Mpls., 1974-75; chmn. South Pacific dist. youth com. Am. Luth. Ch., Lakewood, Calif., 1976-78; featured conv. speaker, 1978—. Mem. Long Beach Child Trauma Council, Calif., 1976-78. Recipient Disting. Alumni award Tex. Luth. Coll., 1981. Home: 4014 15th Ave S Apt 8B Minneapolis MN 55407 Office: Luther League Am Luth Ch 422 S 5th St Minneapolis MN 55415

KOENIG, ROBERT AUGUST, minister, Presbyterian Church (U.S.A.); b. Red Wing, Minn., July 14, 1933; s. William C. and Florence Ellen (Tebbe) K.; B.S. cum laude, U. Wis., 1955; M.A., U. Minn., 1965, Ph.D. in Ednl. Adminstrn., 1973; M.Div. magna cum laude, San Francisco Theol. Sem., 1969; m. Pauline Louise Olson, June 21, 1962. Ordained to ministry, 1970; minister Sawyer County (Wis.) Larger Parish, Presbyn. Chs. Couderay, Wis., 1969-74, Radisson, Wis., 1969-74, Winter, Wis., 1969-74, First Presbyn. Ch., Chippewa Falls, Wis., 1974-85, Grove Presbyn. Ch., Danville, Pa., 1985—; adj. prof. dept. ednl. adminstrn. U. Minn., Mpls., 1976-77. Chairperson Synod of Lakes and Prairies standing com. on ch. related colls., 1975, mem. vocation dept., 1977-81; sec., treas. of Chippewa Area Clergy Conf., 1974-75, pres., 1976—; mem. com. on ministry Presbytery of No. Waters, 1977-82, chmn., 1981-83. Recipient Good Neighbor award Radio Sta. WCCO, Mpls., 1974, WEAQ and WIAL, Eau Claire, Wis., 1975-76. Mem. Am. Assn. for Higher Edn. Contbr. articles on edn. to profl. jours., also chpt. in yearbook. Home: 42 Timberwood Dr Danville PA 17821 Office: 332 Bloom St Danville PA 17821

KOENIG, ROBERT EMIL, retired minister, United Church of Christ; b. St. Louis, Aug. 31, 1919; s. Hermann Emil and Martha Ida Johanna (Baur) K.; m. Norma Caroline Evans, July 18, 1943; children: Elsa Weber, Robert, Richard, Martha, Thea Burton, Laura. S.B., U. Chgo., 1941; postgrad. Eden Theol. Sem., 1942-43; B.D., Chgo. Theol. Sem., 1945; Ph.D., U. Chgo., 1953. Ordained to ministry United Ch. of Christ, 1945. Pastor St. John's Ch., Fullersburg, Ill., 1943-46; instr. Elmhurst Coll., Ill., 1946-53, assoc. prof., 1953-54; dir. curriculum Bd. Ch. Edn., Phils., 1954-61; editor-in-chief United Ch. Bd. Homeland Ministry, N.Y.C., 1961-84; dir. Coop. Pub. Assn., St. Louis, 1968-84, Protestant Ch. Pub. Assn., Nashville, 1978-84. Author: The Use of the Bible with Adults, 1959, Jesus Christ, the Basis of Our Faith, Parts I, II, 1960, Man's Use of God's Power, 1965; (with other) Tell Me the Stories of Jesus, 1957. Mem. U. Chgo. Alumni Cabinet. Democrat. Club: Glee (Phila.) (bd. mem.). Home: 566 Haverford Rd Havertown PA 19083

KOENIG, TIMOTHY WILBERT, minister, Lutheran Church-Missouri Synod; b. St. Louis, May 7, 1938; s. Wilbert Henry and Viola Anna (Haag) K.; m. Neloise Nadine Geihsler, Aug. 9, 1959; children: Lisa Morgan, Lori Rebarchik, Timothy Jr., Jennifer. B.S., Concordia Coll., 1960; B.D., Concordia Theol. Sem., 1967; M.Div., 1973. Ordained to ministry Luth. Ch., 1967. Cert. elem. tchr., Iowa. Prin., tchr. Christ Luth. Sch., Juniata, Nebr., 1960-63; pastor St. John's Luth. Ch., Chatham, Ill., 1967-70, St. Paul Luth. Ch., Carroll, Iowa, 1970-74, Zion Luth. Ch., Pampa, Tex., 1974-80, Trinity Luth. Ch., Brownsville, Tex., 1980—; circuit youth facilitator Tex. Dist. Luth. Ch.-Mo. Synod, Rio Grande Valley, 1980-83, area dir. hymnal introductory team, So. Tex., 1981-82, dir. dist. ch. extension, Austin, Tex., 1983—. Lodge: Rotary (pres. elect 1984—, club services dir., 1983—). Home: 1134 Cypress St Brownsville TX 78520 Office: Trinity Luth Ch 901 Boca Chica Blvd Brownsville TX 78520

KOENIGSBERG, SOL, association executive, Jewish; b. Detroit, Dec. 11, 1924; s. Charles Phillip and Pearl (Fine) K.; m. Rosette Ostrowiecki, Apr. 12, 1951; children: Michael, Beth. B.A., Wayne State U., 1949; M.S.W., U. Pa., 1952. Exec. dir. Jewish Fedn. of Greater Kansas City, Mo., 1968—; sec. Jewish Community Found., Kansas City, 1968—; mem. Nat. Conf. Jewish Communal Service; mem. publ. com. Jour. Jewish Communal Service, 1981—. Vice pres. United Way Execs. Assn., 1970-72. Mem. Nat. Conf. Social Welfare, Nat. assn. Social Workers, Assn. Jewish Community Orgn. Profls. (chmn. personal standards com. 1979, chmn. nominating com. 1981-83, v.p. 1978-79, pres. 1979-81). Home: 640 W 69th Terr Kansas City MO 64119 Office: Jewish Fedn Greater Kansas City 25 E 12th St Kansas City MO 64119

KOEPPEL, JOSEPHINE, nun, Roman Catholic Church; b. Widnau, St. Gallen, Switzerland, Mar. 24, 1921; d. Frank Sales and Emma Barbara (Frei) Koeppel. A.A., Felician Coll., 1979; postgrad. Creighton U., 1980—. Professed nun in Discalced Carmelite Order, 19—. Dir. Edith Stein Ctr., Elysburg, Pa., 1975—. Editor (booklet) Ways to Know God (Edith Stein), 1980. Translator Edith Stein, 1985. Democrat. Home: Carmelite Monastery Elysburg PA 17824 Office: Edith Stein Ctr Thornbrow Elysburg PA 17824

KOEPPEN, ROBERT DUANE, minister Lutheran Church-Missouri Synod; b. Saginaw, Mich., Aug. 11, 1939; s. Herman William and Selma M. (Tessin) K.; m. Theodora Justine Poehler, Aug. 20, 1961; children: John, Justine, Stephanie, Katherine. B.S. in Edn., Concordia Coll., River Forest, Ill., 1961; B.D., Concordia Theol. Sem., Ft. Wayne, Ind., 1968, M.Div., 1984. Ordained to ministry Luth. Ch., 1968. Tchr., prin. Immanuel Luth. Sch., Murphysboro, Ill., 1961-63; tchr. Luth. High Sch. East, Harper Woods, Mich., 1963-65; pastor St. John's Luth. Ch., St. Johns, Mich., 1968-74, Zion Luth. Ch., Ninsdale, Ill., 1974—; chmn. commn. on worship Luth. Ch.-Mo. Synod, 1978-80. Republican. Home: 116 S Grant St Hinsdale IL 61521 Office: Zion Luth Ch Grant and 2d Sts Hinsdale IL 60521

KOESTER, CHARLES R., bishop, Roman Catholic Church. Titular bishop of Suacia, aux. bishop, St. Louis, 1971—. Office: 15 Plaza Sq St Louis MO 63103*

KOESTER, HELMUT HEINRICH, educator, minister, German Luth. Ch.; b. Hamburg, Germany, Dec. 18, 1926; s. Karl and Marie-Luise (Eitz) K.; came to U.S., 1958; Th.D. magna cum laude, U. Marburg, 1954; m. Gisela G. Harrassowitz, July 8, 1953; children: Reinhild, Almut, Ulrich, Heiko. Ordained to ministry, 1954; asst. pastor, Hannover, Germany, 1951-54; teaching asst. to asst. prof. U. Heidelberg, 1954-59; mem. faculty Harvard Div. Sch., 1958—, John H. Morison prof. N.T. studies, 1964—, Winn prof. eccles. history, 1968—; vis. prof. U. Heidelberg, 1963, Drew U., 1966. Trustee, Albright Inst. Archaeol. Research, 1975-81. Guggenheim fellow, 1964-65; Am. Council Learned Socs. fellow, 1971-72, 78-79. Fellow Am. Acad. Arts and Scis.; mem. Am. Schs. Oriental Research (asso. trustee), Soc. Bibl. Literature, Soc. Novi Testamenti Studiorum. Author: Synoptische Ueberlieferung bei den Apostolischen Vaetern, in Texte and Untersuchungen, 1957; (with James M. Robinson) Trajectories Through Early Christianity, 1971; Einfuehrung in das Neue Testament, 1981; Introduction to the New Testament, 2 vols., 1983. Editor: Harvard Theol. Rev., 1974—. Office: 45 Francis Ave Cambridge MA 02138

KOFINK, WAYNE ALAN, minister, Lutheran Church in America; b. Chgo., Apr. 21, 1949; s. Lawrence Howard and Catherine Elizabeth (Szlavik) K.; B. Music, Chgo. Mus. Coll., 1971; B.A., Fla. Internat. U., 1981, M.S., 1985; M.Div., Luth. Sch. Theology, Chgo., 1976; postgrad. Westminster Choir Coll., 1982, St. Thomas U., 1984. Ordained to ministry Luth. Ch. in Am., 1977. Choir dir. Ascension Luth. Ch., Chgo., 1971-73; pastor Messiah Evang. Luth. Ch., Miami, Fla., 1977—; dir. Luth. Campus Ministry, Miami, 1979—, v.p., 1983—; mem. exec. com. Luth. Parish Dade County, 1982-84; sec. com. Worship Fla. Synod, Tampa, 1982—; rep. dialogues with Dade County Roman Cath. and Episc. Chs., 1984—. Contbr. articles to profl. jours. Composer: (hymn) Promise, 1970. Mem. Am. Guild Organists (chaplain 1982—), Liturgical Conf., Hymn Soc. Am. Democrat. Home: 3840 SW 102d Ave Miami FL 33165 Office: Messiah Luth Ch 9850 Coral Way Miami FL 33165

KOHLHEPP, GLENN BRUCE, minister, United Methodist Church; b. Pitts., Oct. 10, 1941; s. Bruce Cook and Martha Eunice (Myers) K.; m. Janet Irene Clark, June 12, 1965; children: Gregg, Mark, Brian. A.B., West Va. Wesleyan Coll., 1963; M.Div., Drew Theol. Sch., 1966, D.Min., 1984. Ordained to ministry United Meth. Ch. as deacon, 1964, as elder, 1966. Minister Chicora-Karns City Chs., 1967-72, Mars United Meth. Ch., Pa., 1972-79, Whitaker United Meth. Ch., Pa., 1979-81, McKnight United Meth. Ch., Pitts., 1981—; sec. Western Pa. Conf. United Meth. Ch., Pitts., 1974—; del. Gen. Conf. United Meth. Ch., Balt., 1984, Jurisdictional Conf. United Meth. Ch., Annville, Pa., 1984. Editor Western Pa. Conf. Jour., 1974—. Bd. dirs. Karns City Area Schs., Pa., 1970-72, Rural Leadership, Inc., Pa. State U., State College, 1984. Recipient Rural Leadership award Pa. State U., 1973. Republican. Home: 511 Hunter Dr Pittsburgh PA 15237 Office: McKnight United Meth Ch 600 Fox Dr Pittsburgh PA 15237

KOHLMEIER, KEITH EDWARD, minister, Lutheran Church-Missouri Synod; b. Linn, Kans., July 12, 1952; s. Delmar Edward and Viola Clara (Dittmer) K.; m. Marlene Kay Blaske, June 17, 1972; children: Jacob, Jeremy, Emily. A.A., St. John's Coll., 1972; B.A., Concordia Sr. Coll., 1974; M.Div., Concordia Sem., Ft. Wayne, Ind., 1978. Ordained to ministry Luth. Ch.-Mo. Synod, 1978. Pastor, Holy Trinity Luth. Ch., Farnhamville, Iowa, 1978-83, First English Luth. Ch., Spencer, Iowa, 1983—; chmn. youth ministry Iowa West Dist., 1982—; dist. pastoral advisor Luth. Laymen's League, 1982—; circuit pastoral advisor Humboldt circuit Iowa-West, 1980-82, bd. dirs., 1982—; bd. dirs. Iowa Luth. Home for Aged Assn., 1981; trustee Perry Luth. Home, 1981. Contbr. articles to profl. jours. Office: First English Luth Ch 23 E 10th St Spencer IA 51301

KOHLS, EUGENE CLARENCE, priest, Roman Catholic Church; b. Ottawa, Ohio, Dec. 23, 1931; s. Neil John and Mary Rose (Recker) K. M.Div., Josephinum Coll., 1967; J.C.D., Lateran U., Rome, 1964. Ordained priest Roman Cath. Ch., 1957. Chancellor, Diocese of St. Augustine, Jacksonville, Fla., 1966—; pastor Assumption Parish, Jacksonville, 1977—; prothonotary apostolic Holy See, Vatican City, 1974. Author: An Interpretation of Canon 1500, 1966. Address: 2403 Atlantic Blvd Jacksonville FL 32207

KOHN, WILLIAM HENRY, minister, Lutheran Ch.-Mo. Synod; b. Winnipeg, Man., Can., Sept. 27, 1915; s. William Lewis and Christine (Obermowe) K.; student Concordia Coll., Milw., 1929-35; D.D. (hon.), Concordia Sem., St. Louis, 1964; postgrad. Johns Hopkins, 1946-48; m. Marian Ruth Luenser, June 1, 1941; children—Kathy (Mrs. Ralph Landry), Carol (Mrs. Arthur Agostinho), Marian (Mrs. John Hunken). Ordained to ministry Lutheran Ch.-Mo. Synod, 1940; asst. pastor ch., Merrill, Wis., 1939-40, Balt., 1940-43; chaplain AUS, 1943-46; pastor, Balt., 1946-54, Mt. Rainier, Md., 1954-56, Hyattsville, Md., 1956-63; dist. pres. Southeastern dist. Lutheran Ch.-Mo. Synod, 1963-67, exec. sec. Bd. for Missions, 1967-74; mem. Lutheran Immigration Service Com., 1960-67, chmn., 1964-67; chmn. Council of Pres.'s, Lutheran Ch., 1965-67; mem. bd. dirs. Lutheran World Relief, 1967—; chmn. coordinating com. parish services, 1967-74, div. missions and spl. ministries, 1967-74; pastor Capitol Dr. Luth. Ch., Milw., 1974—. Bd. dirs. Good Samaritan Med. Ctr., Milw. Mem. Assn. Evang. Luth. Chs. (pres. 1976-84). Home and Office: 2707 N 67th St Milwaukee WI 53210

KOLB, JOHN CARL, minister, Lutheran Church-Missouri Synod; b. Bay City, Mich., Apr. 6, 1943; s. Carl Henry Edwin and Reneate Margaret Johanna (Krieger) K.; m. Malinda Marie Hartman, June 5, 1966; children: Rebecca Marie, Debra Rene', Charles Walter. B.A., Concordia Sr. Coll., 1964; M.Div., Concordia Sem., 1968; M.S.T., Christian Theol. Sem., 1972; student Garrett Sem., 1974-75, McCormick Sem., 1975-76. Ordained to ministry, 1968. Asst. chaplain Luth. Med. Ctr., St. Louis, 1967-68; pastor Emanuel Luth. Ch., Arcadia, Ind., 1968-72; chaplain resident Luth. Gen. Hosp., Park Ridge, Ill., 1972-73; chaplain fellow Evanston Hosp., Ill., 1974-75; pastor Hosanna Luth. Ch., Oaklandon, Ind., 1980—; vis. prof. Concordia Theol. Sem., Ft. Wayne, Ind., 1984—; family counselor Luth. Child and Family Services, Indpls., 1978—; pastoral advisor Luth. Laymen's League, Indpls., 1981—; chmn. worship com. 1985 Internat. Luth. Laymen's League Conv., 1983-85; mem. Luth. Ch.-Mo. Synod, Ind. Dist. Adult Christian Edn. Family Life Com., 1980—; program chmn. Indpls. Circuit Pastors, 1982-84; mem. spl. services com. Indpls. Fedn.

Luth. Ch.-Mo. synod Chs., 1983-84, mem. chaplains com., 1984—. Contbr. articles to profl. jours. Mem. Mental Health Assn. Ind., Parion County, 1979—; pres. Trinity Luth. Sch. PTL, 1982-84; pres. Hamilton County Mental Health Assn., 1971-72. Mem. Am. Assn. Pastoral Counselors. Home: 2613 Sheffield Dr Indianapolis IN 46229 Office: Luth Child and Family Services 1525 N Ritter St Indianapolis IN 46219

KOLBELL, ERIK, university protestant chaplain, religious educator, United Ch. of Christ; b. Hempstead, N.Y., Dec. 17, 1952; s. Edward Maurice and Edna May (Calamia) K.; m. Nancy Lee Combs, July 29, 1978. B.S. in Religious Studies, Brown U., 1975; M.Div., Yale U., 1978; postgrad. U. Mich., 1984—. Ordained to ministry United Ch. of Christ, 1978. Assoc. chaplain Central Conn. U., New Britain, Conn., 1977-81; chaplain, instr. dept. religious studies Oakland U., Rochester, Mich., 1981—, co-founder Com. for Study of Nat. Security, 1982—; chmn., co-founder Mich. Educators for Social Responsibility, 1983—. Contbr. articles to profl. jours. Chmn., co-founder Rochester Peace task force, 1981—; co-founder Focus: Hope, Oakland County chpt., Pontiac, Mich., 1983; mem. Save the Children Fedn., Wilton, Conn., 1983, Oakland U. Hunger Relief Task Force, Rochester, 1983. Peace Edn. grantee United Meth. div. Higher Edn., Nashville, 1984; recipient univ./community relations award Oakland U., 1982. Mem. Nat. Inst. Campus Ministry, Rochester Ministerium (program coordinator 1982—), NOW. Home: 539 West 4th St Rochester MI 48063 Office: Campus Ministry 3665 Walton Blvd Rochest MI 48063

KOLCH, VICTOR FREDERICK, hospital chaplain, Association of Evangelical Lutheran Churches; b. Stillwater, Okla., May 5, 1951; s. Frederick Luther and Anne Louise (Meisner) K.; m. Diane Virginia Laux, Aug. 25, 1973; children: Peter Matthew, Amy Lauren. A.A., St. John's Coll., 1972; B.S., Concordia Sr. Coll., 1973; M.Div., Concordia Sem. in Exile. 1977. Ordained to ministry, 1977. Shared pastor Bristol Area Luth. Chs., Conn., 1977-79; chaplain Lutheran Hosp., Ft. Wayne, Ind., 1979—. Bd. dirs. Washington House Treatment Ctr., 1980—. Republican. Office: Lutheran Hospital 3024 Fairfield Ave Fort Wayne IN 46807

KOLLMANN, ALVIN VICTOR, religious organization executive, Lutheran Church-Missouri Synod; b. Royal, Iowa, Nov. 7, 1929; s. Victor J. and Elda M. (Schneider) K.; m. Jacquelin Dee Briggenhorst, Aug. 29, 1953; children: Victor J., Sue C., Kenneth S., Richard A., David E. A.A., Concordia Coll., St. Paul, 1949, Litt.D. (hon.), 1981; B.A., Concordia Sem., St. Louis, 1951, B.D., 1954, M.S.T., 1958. Ordained to ministry Lutheran Church-Missouri Synod, 1954. Pastor St. Paul Luth. Ch., West Frankfort, Ill., 1954-59, Good Shepherd Luth Ch., Collinsville, Ill., 1959-78; pres. So. Ill. Dist. Luth. Ch.-Mo. Synod, Belleville, Ill., 1976—; pastoral counselor Luth. Women's Missionary League So. Ill. Dist., 1955-62; chmn. So. Ill. Dist. Pastoral Conf., 1968-70; 2d v.p. So. Ill. Dist. Lutheran Ch.-Mo. Synod, 1970-74, 1st v.p., 1974-76. Contbr. articles to profl. jours. Lodge: Lions (bd. dirs. 1971-73). Office: So Ill Dist Luth Ch-Mo Synod 2408 Lebanon Ave Belleville IL 62221

KOLLMANN, VICTOR JOHN, minister, Lutheran Church-Missouri Synod; b. Christopher, Ill., Dec. 19, 1954; s. Alvin Victor and Jacquelin Dee (Briggenhorst) K.; m. Angela Kay Bentley, July 29, 1978; children: Jonathan, Kristen. A.A., St. Paul's Coll., 1975; B.A., Concordia Tchr.'s Coll., 1977; M.Div., Concordia Sem., 1981. Ordained to ministry Luth. Ch., 1981. Pastor Our Shepherd Luth. Ch., Searcy, Ark., 1981—; mem. bd. of youth Mid-South Dist. of Luth. Ch.-Mo. Synod, Memphis, Tenn., 1983—. Mem. Searcy Ministerial Alliance. Republican. Home: 116 Liles Dr Searcy AR 72143 Office: Our Shepherd Luth Ch 110 N Main St Searcy AR 72143

KOLP, ALAN LEE, educator, Religious Society of Friends; b. Winchester, Ind., Sept. 10, 1944; s. Richard Lee and Mildred Ann (Talley) K.; m. Letitia Ann Milner, Jan. 23, 1966; children: Felicity, Christina. B.A., Guilford Coll., 1967; B.D., Harvard Div. Sch., 1970; Ph.D., Harvard U., 1976. Asst. prof. religion Earlham Sch. Religion, Richmond, Ind., 1974-78, assoc. prof., 1978—, dean, 1978-84. Author: Participation Is Not a Spectator Sport, 1976. Contbr. articles to profl. jours. Mem. Am. Acad. Religion, Soc. Bibl. Lit., N. Am. Patristic Soc. Home: 234 College Ave Richmond IN 47374 Office: Earlham Sch Religion National Rd W Richmond IN 47374

KONKOWSKI, CALVIN B., minister, Lutheran Church in America; b. Chgo., Oct. 28, 1933; s. Adolph Edward and Emily Agnes (Erickson) K. B.A., Augustana Coll., Rock Island, Ill., 1958, M.Div., 1962. Ordained to ministry Luth. Ch. in Am., 1963. Pastor Shiloh Luth. Ch., Walton, Ind., 1963-67; assoc. dir. Repertory Theatre Christian Theol. Sem., Indpls., 1967-81; pastor Bethlehem Luth. Ch., Gary, Ind., 1981—. Address: 601 Fillmore St Gary IN 46402

KONSTANTINOW, DIMITRY VASSILIEVICH, archpriest, Orthodox Ch. in Am.; b. St. Petersburg, Russia, Mar. 21, 1908; s. Basil and Claudia (Ossipow) K.; B.A. Edn., Ushinsky Pedagogical Technicum, Leningrad, 1927; B.D., Theol. Sch. in Leningrad, 1928; M.A. Journalism, Leningrad Editorial and Pub. Inst., 1930; postgrad. Leningrad Research Inst. Bibliology, 1933; m. Anna Paramonowa, July 16, 1944. Came to U.S., 1960, naturalized, 1965. Ordained to ministry Russian Orthodox Ch. Outside Russia as priest, 1944; priest various chs. in Germany, 1944-49; joined Orthodox Ch. in Am., 1950; priest Russian Orthodox Cathedral, Buenos Aires, Argentina, 1949-55; rector St. Mary's Ch., Buenos Aires, 1955-60; priest Holy Trinity Cathedral, San Francisco, 1960-61, Saints Peter and Paul Ch., Syracuse, N.Y., 1961-64; rector Holy Annunciation Ch., Maynard, Mass., 1964-68, St. Mary's Ch., Chelsea, Mass., 1968-71, Chapel of our Lady of Kazan, West Hyannis Port, Mass., 1972—. Recipient 7 ecclesiastical awards. Mem. Assn. Russian-Am. Scholars in U.S.A. Author 9 books on religion pub. in Russian, English, German, French and Spanish, 1950-74. Editor: Nueva Palabra newspaper, Buenos Aires, 1949-60. Contbr. numerous religious and non-religious articles to various publs. Home: 35 Patricia St West Hyannis Port MA 02672 Office: POB 212 West Hyannis Port MA 02672

KONSTANTOPOULOS, BILL CONSTANTINE, minister, Church of God, Anderson, Indiana; b. Agridi, Arcadia, Greece, Mar. 16, 1938; came to U.S., 1962; s. Constantine A. and Constantina (Georgacopoulou) K.; m. Leona Kay Matney, Aug. 27, 1966; children: Jonathan, David, Daniel. B.A., Gulf Coast Bible Coll., 1966; postgrad. Asbury Theol. Sem., 1968, Fuller Sem., 1976, East Tenn. State U., 1983—; diploma Instituto de Idiomas, San Jose, Costa Rica, 1976-77. Ordained to ministry, 1967. Pastor, First Ch. of God, Kankakee, Ill., 1966-67; evangelist Ch. of God, various locations, 1968; sr. minister First Ch. of God, Saltville, Va., 1968-76; missionary Missionary Bd. of Ch. of God, Central & S. Am., 1976-80; evangelist, 1980-81; sr. minister Tacoma Ch. of God, Johnson City, Tenn., 1981—; chmn. Bd. Ch. Extension, Ch. of God, Va., 1972-76, credentials com., 1973-76, pres. bd. ch. found., 1973-76; exec. council Ch. of God, Tenn., 1982—. Contbr. articles to profl. jours. Served with Greek Army, 1960-62. Recipient Merit award, Gulf Coast Bible Coll., 1963, Max R. Guacke award, 1976; Academia Cristiana Mission and Edn. award, 1978. Republican. Lodge: Ruritan. Home: 614 Wendover Dr Johnson City TN 37601 Office: Tacoma Ch of God 1005 John Exum Pkwy Johnson City TN 37601

KONTOGIORGIS, MICHAEL THEODORE, priest, Greek Orthodox Church; b. Boston, May 15, 1948; s. Theodore Michael and Panagiota (Andriopoulos) K.; m. Vicki Betty George, Aug. 27, 1972; children: Kristen, Patricia, Megan. B.A., Hellenic Coll., 1970; M.Div., Holy Cross Greek Orthodox Sch. Theology, 1973, S.T.M., 1974. Ordained priest, 1973. Asst. to dean Annunciation Greek Orthodox Cathedral of New Eng., Boston, 1973-75; priest Holy Trinity Greek Orthodox Ch., Orlando, Fla., 1975—; dir. Greek Orthodox Youth Actionline, Orlando, 1981, Altar Boy's Workshop, Brooksville, 1981—; mem. Presbyters Conf., Greek Orthodox Archdiocese of N. and S. Am., N.Y.C., 1983, mem. Presbyters council, 1983-84. Editor newsletter The Harbinger, 1975—. Author: The Altar Boy's Guidebook, 1981, rev. 1984. Contbr. articles to newspapers. Co-producer, dir. Grecian Echoes Radio program, Orlando, 1978; chaplain Orlando Police Dept., 1978-79. Elevated to Sakellarios, Greek Orthodox Archdiocese of N. and S. Am., 1980. Mem. Greek Orthodox Clergy Assn. Diocese of Atlanta (pres.), Orthodox Clergy Fellowship N. and Central Fla. (sec.), Holy Cross Alumni Assn. Home: 106 Valencia Loop Altamonte Springs FL 32714 Office: Holy Trinity Greek Orthodox Ch 1217 Trinity Woods Ln Maitland FL 32751

KONYA, ALEX WILLIAM, JR., minister, General Association of Regular Baptist Churches; b. Cleve., Oct. 9, 1952; s. Alex William Sr. and Evelyn (Barath) K.; m. Pamela Joy Stallard, Aug. 19, 1972; children: Ann, Alex William III, Philip. B.A., Cedarville Coll., 1974; M.Div., Grace Sem., Winona Lake, Ind., 1976, Th.M. candidate, 1985—; student Inst. Holy Land Studies, Jerusalem, 1984. Ordained to ministry Gen. Assn. Regular Bapt. Chs., 1976. Pastor, Honeycreek Bapt. Ch., Christiansburg, Ohio, 1972-74; asst. pastor Mayflower Bapt. Ch., South Bend, Ind., 1976, pastor, 1977—; v.p. Michiana Pastors' Fellowship, South Bend, 1978; sec.-treas. Crystal Lake Area Fellowship Regular Bapt. Chs., Mentone, Ind., 1982-84. Republican. Office: Mayflower Bapt Ch 23624 Lynn St South Bend IN 46628

KOOISTRA, PAUL DAVID, religious educator, seminary president, Presbyterian Church in America; b. Duluth, Minn., Oct. 11, 1942; s. David and Laura M. (Bowman) K.; m. Janet Marie Carlson, June 27, 1964; children: Paul David, Shary Malin, Jennifer Elizabeth. B.A., U. Minn., 1964; M.Div., Columbia Sem., Ga., 1967; Ph.D., U. Ala., 1980. Ordained to ministry Presbyn. Ch., 1967. Asst. pastor Pinelands Presbyn. Ch. in Am., Miami, Fla., 1967-69; assoc. pastor Seminole Presbyn. Ch., Tampa, Fla., 1969-73; asst. prof. Christian edn. Belhaven Coll., Jackson, Miss., 1973-75; prof. practical theology Ref. Theol. Sem., Jackson, 1975-84; pres. Covenant Theol. Sem., St. Louis, 1985—; mem. Christian edn. com. Presbyn. Ch. Am., 1979-83. Mem. Assn. Researchers in Christian Edn., Menninger Found., Phi Delta Kappa, Delta Kappa Pi. Office Covenant Theol Sem 12330 Conway Rd Saint Louis MO 63141

KOOPMAN, JOHN JACOB, minister, American Baptist Churches in the U.S.A.; b. Elizabeth, N.J., Mar 28, 1948; s. John Jacob and Doris (Riehl) K.; m. Leslie Kitsz, May 27, 1972; children: Heather Lynn, Dawn Renee. B.A., Blackburn Coll., 1970; M.Div., Eastern Bapt. Sem., 1973. Ordained to ministry Am. Bapt. Chs in U.S.A., 1973. Racetrack minister Am. Bapt. Ch., Monmouth, N.J., 1971-72; assoc. minister First Bapt. Ch., Lockport, N.Y., 1973-74; minister First Bapt. Ch., Lancaster, N.Y., 1974-76; chaplain U.S. Army, Ft. Bragg, N.C., 1977-79; minister Central Bapt. Ch., Greene, N.Y., 1979—, Brisben Bapt., N.Y., 1979—; del. Nat. Am. Bapt. Conv., 1983, Fransego Assn., N.Y., 1979—; youth coordinator Niagara Frontier Assn., Buffalo, 1974-76; pres. Ministerium, Greene, 1981—. Author: Marriage Enrichment ME in Small Churches, 1982. Exec. bd. County Headstart, Norwich, N.Y., 1979-81. Served to capt. U.S. Army, 1977-79. Club: Jaycees (Lancaster N.Y.) (bd. dirs. 1975). Lodge: Rotary (bd. dirs. 1982, pres. 1984). Republican. Home and Office: Route 1 Box 262B Greene NY 13778

KOPATZ, PERRY ALLEN, minister, Lutheran Church-Missouri Synod. B. Springfield, Ill., Feb. 5, 1955; s. Carl Walter and Betty (Aderman) K.; m. Cindy Lynn Schumacher, Aug. 5, 1978; children: Christine, Jeremy. A.A., Springfield Coll. in Ill., 1974-75; B.S., Ill. State U., 1976; M.Div., Concordia Theol. Sem., Fort Wayne, Ind., 1980. Ordained to ministry Luth. Ch., 1980. Pastor, Christ Luth. Ch., Winchester, Ill., 1980-84, mem. Adult-Youth Bible Class Com., 1981-83; missionary at large assigned Abiding Savior Luth. Ch., St. Louis, 1985—. sec.-treas. Jacksonville Cir. Pastors Conf., 1982—; speaker workshops, radio stations. Recipient Nat. Appreciation Soc. Disting. High Sch. Students, 1984. Home: 5268 Camelot Estates Dr Saint Louis MO 63129

KOPLITZ, RONALD GENE, chaplain, American Lutheran Church; b. Oshkosh, Wis., Mar. 8, 1943; s. Norman Albert and Ruth Nora (Abraham) K.; m. Mary Ellen Norma Garbisch, Aug. 6, 1966; B.A., Wartburg Coll., 1965; M.Div., Wartburg Theol. Sem., 1969. Ordained to ministry Am. Luth. Ch., 1969. Pastor Otter Creek Luth. Ch., Highland, Wis., 1969-73, Fairview Luth. Ch., Avoca, Wis., 1969-73, Trinity and Immanuel Luth. Ch., Cashton, Wis., 1973-78, Bethany Luth. Ch., LaFarge, Wis., 1973-78; instl. chaplain. Ariz. State Prison, Florence, 1980-83; sr. instl. chaplain Maricopa County Jail System, Phoenix, 1983—; mem. clergy roster South Pacific dist. Am. Luth. Ch. Mem. Ariz. Ecumenical Council, Am. Protestant Correctional Chaplain's Assn., Am. Correctional Assn. Home: 907 E Broadmor Dr Tempe AZ 85282 Office: Maricopa County Jail System 225 W Madison St Phoenix AZ 85003

KOPP, GEORGE PHILIP, JR., minister, United Church of Christ; b. Cin., July 17, 1927; s. George Philip and Ann Elizabeth (Suffield) K.; m. Janet Marie Thompson Shultz, Oct. 13, 1956. B.A., Heidelberg Coll., 1950; B.D., Eden Sem., 1955, M.Div., 1969. Ordained to ministry United Ch. of Christ, 1955. Pastor St. John Ch., Middlebrook, Va., 1955-60; commd. ensign U.S. Navy, 1954, advanced through grades to lt. comdr., 1976, served as chaplain; ret., 1976; pastor St. John's Ch., Middlebrook, 1983—; dir. Central Atlantic Conf. United Ch. Christ, 1983—. Home and Office: 308 Valley View Dr Staunton VA 24401

KOPP, LAMAR WARNER, minister United Methodist Church; b. York, Pa., Nov. 22, 1925; s. Howard John and Dora May (Warner) K.; m. Naomi Jean McClintock, June 3, 1950; children: Steven, Bruce, Katharine. B.S., Albright Coll., 1949; M.Div., United Theol. Sem., Dayton, 1952. Ordained to ministry United Meth. Ch., 1952; pastor St. John's Evang. United Brethren Ch., Balt., 1947-54, Salem United Meth. Ch., Baltimore County, 1954-76; sr. pastor Otterbein United Meth. Ch., Hagerstown, Md., 1976—. Del., jurisdictional conf. Balt. Conf. United Meth. Ch., 1972, 76, bd. ordained ministry, 1972-80; sec. Hagerstown Dist. Com. on Ordained Ministry, 1976—. Mem. Human Relations Commn., Hagerstown, 1981-84. Served as sgt. USAAF, 1943-46. Lodge: Lions (chaplain 1960-70, 79-84). Home: 1131 Oak Hill Ave Hagerstown MD 21740 Office: Otterbein United Meth Ch 108 E Franklin St Hagerstown MD 21740

KOPSAHILIS, PETROS, priest, Greek Orthodox Archdiocese of North and South America; b. Lithboron, Greece, May 5, 1938; came to U.S., 1961, naturalized, 1979; s. Ioannis and Poulheria (Voulgaropoulos) K.; m. Christine Pliakas, Aug. 25, 1968. B.Th., Hellenic Coll., 1967; M.Div., Holy Cross Sch. Theology, 1968; S.T.M., Boston U., Sch. Theology, 1973, postgrad., 1973-77. Ordained priest Greek Orthodox Ch., 1968. Pastor, Holy Trinity Ch., Casper, Wyo., 1968-70, St. Vasilios Ch., Newport, N.H., 1975-76, St. George Ch., Oklahoma City, Okla., 1977—; dir. registrar, admissions Hellenic Coll., Brookline, Mass., 1973-76, asst. to pres., 1976-77; treas. Denver Diocese Clergy Orgn., 1982—; mem. Diocese Mixed Council, Denver,

979—, Diocese Spiritual Ct., Denver, 1982—; bd. dirs. Athenageras Nat. Inst., Cheyenne, Wyo., 1983. Author: The Word of God in Our Church, 1974; Taylor Found. scholar Greek Archdiocese, 1971-77; named Oikonomos, Greek Archdiocese, 1983. Mem. Hellenic Coll. Alumni Assn., Boston U. Alumni Assn. Home: 717 Tilman Dr Oklahoma City OK 73138

KORBMAN, MEYER HYMAN, rabbi, Conservative Jewish Congregation; public school administrator. b. Newark, Oct. 30, 1925; s. Abraham and Celia Korbman; married, Dec. 17, 1950; children: Marc, Riva, David. B.A., Yeshiva U., 1949; M.A., Seton Hall U., 1954. Ordained rabbi. Rabbi Congregation Beth El, Hightstown, N.J., 1951-70, Temple Israel, Union, N.J., 1970—; trustee Jewish Fedn., Union, 1970—; trustee exec. bd. Grad. Inst. Talmudical Studies, 1954, Rabbinical Coll. N.J., 1952-54; mem. Council Congregations and Chs., Union, 1970—; v.p. pub. schs., Newark, 1974—. Mayoral appointee Sr. Citizens Adv. Commn., Union, 1976—. Served with U.S. Army, 1944-46. Recipient Cert. Merit Newark Bd. Edn., 1978. Mem. Union County Bd. Rabbis, Essex County Bd. Rabbis, Newark Reading Resource Assn. (pres. 1969-72), Right to Read (N.J. bldg. dir. 1970-72), City Adminstrs. and Suprs. Assn., Nat. Edn. Assn., Internat. Reading Assn. Home: 2454 Ogden Rd Union NJ 07083 Office: Temple Israel of Union 2372 Morris Ave Union NJ 07083

KORFF, IRA A., rabbi, Orthodox Jewish; b. Boston, Aug. 30, 1949; s. Nathan and Helen (Pfeffer) K.; m. Shari E. Redstone, 1980; children: Kimberlee A., Brandon J. B.J.E., Hebrew Coll., 1968; postgrad. Chaim Berlin Rabbinical Acad., Rabbinical Acad. Israel, 1968-71; B.A., Columbia, 1969; J.D., Bklyn. Law Sch., 1972; M.A., Fletcher Sch. Law and Diplomacy (Tufts-Harvard), 1973, M.A.L.D., 1975, Ph.D., 1976; postgrad. Harvard Div. Sch., 1975-76; LL.M., Boston U., 1981. Ordained rabbi, 1971; admitted to Mass. and U.S. Supreme Ct. bar, 1978, D.C. bar, 1981; fed. ct. bars, 1974, 75, rabbi Charles River Park Synagogue, 1969-70, Temple Israel of Nantasket, Hull, Mass., 1970-74, Temple Beth Sholom, Providence, 1974-75, Temple Aliyah, Needham, Mass., 1975-83; chaplain U. R.I., 1974-75; chaplain City of Boston, 1974—; rabbi B'nai Jacob Synagogue, Dover, Mass., 1983—; columnist Boston Jewish Times, 1984—; mem. Rabbinical Ct. of Justice, Boston. Pvt. practice law, cons. internat. law and relations, 1974—; cons. Norfolk County Dist. Atty., 1975-79. Bd. dirs. Friends of Fletcher Sch. of Law and Diplomacy, 1974—, Council on Religion and Law. Mem. Rabbinical Alliance Am., New Eng. Rabbinical Council, Am. Arbitration Assn. (panel arbitrators), Am., Internat., Mass., Boston bar assns., Am. Soc. Internat. Law. Home: 90 Beacon St Boston MA 02116 Office: 211 Congress St Boston MA 02110

KORNEGAY, ROY AUBRY, JR., minister, Southern Baptist Convention; b. Shreveport, La., Aug. 15, 1937; s. Roy Aubry and Clara Agnes (Gray) K.; B.A., Howard Payne Coll., 1959; M.R.E., Southwestern Bapt. Theol. Sem., 1961; m. Bertha Janette Sewell, Dec. 27, 1958; children: Kari Lynn, Karla Jan, Kathryn Ann. Ordained to ministry, 1968; minister edn. First Bapt. Ch., Dumas, Tex., 1961-64, Texas City, Tex., 1964-67, Pampa, Tex., 1967-70, North Phoenix Bapt. Ch., Phoenix, 1970-71, First Bapt. Ch., Amarillo, Tex., 1971—. Mem. Tex. Bapt. Exec. Bd., 1975—. Mem. Southwestern Religious Edn. Assn., Metro Religious Edn. Assn. Curriculum writer So. Bapt. Sunday Sch. Bd., 1970—. Home: Route 7 Box 32-4 Amarillo TX 79118 Office: 218 W 13th St Amarillo TX 79101

KORPUSIK, HENRY BERNARD, priest, Roman Cath. Ch.; b. Duryea, Pa., Aug. 28, 1919; s. Peter Paul and Angela Mary (Grudzinski) K.; A.B., St. Mary's U. and Sem., Balt., 1941, S.T.B., 1943. Ordained priest, 1945; asst. pastor chs. in Pa., 1945-62; pastor St. Mary's Ch., Blossburg, Pa., 1962-66, St. Mary's Ch., Mocanaqua, Pa., 1966—; dir. pastoral care Retreat State Hosp., Hunlock Creek, Pa., 1966—. Coordinator drive for community ambulance, Dickson City, Pa., 1960; coordinator Conyngham Twp. Bicentennial, 1976; dir. recreational program, Mocanaqua, 1976. Named Outstanding Citizen, Lions Club, 1949, 64. Mem. Nat. Cath. Chaplains Assn., Assn. Mental Health Clergy. Address: 150 Main St Mocanaqua PA 18655

KORSTJENS, KEITH ALLEN, minister, American Baptist Churches in the U.S.A.; b. Los Angeles, Apr. 19, 1929; s. John Edward and Roberta (Crabb) K.; m. Mary Jeanette Calvin, June 10, 1951; children: Kenneth, Karen. A.B., Calif. Bapt. Theol. Coll., 1951; M.A., Claremont Grad. Sch., 1968; Ph.D., Calif. Sch. Theology, 1977. Ordained to ministry Am. Bapt. Chs. in U.S.A., 1954. Dir. Christian edn. First Bapt. Ch., West Los Angeles, Calif., 1949-50; dir. Christian edn. and youth Fountain Ave. Bapt. Ch., Hollywood, Calif., 1951-53; minister Christian edn. Calvary Bapt. Ch., Sacramento, Calif., 1953-54, First Bapt. Ch., San Bernardino, Calif., 1955-57, First Bapt. Ch., Modesto, Calif., 1957-59; minister pastoral care and family life First Bapt. Ch., Pomona, Calif., 1959—. Author: Not A Sometimes Love, 1981. Mem. Christian Camping Assn., Christian Assn. Psychol. Studies, Pomona Valley Ministerial Assn. (pres. 1973), Phi Delta Kappa. Home: 721 Ridgefield Dr Claremont CA 91711 Office: First Bapt Ch 586 N Main St Pomona CA 91767

KOSINSKI, STEPHEN DOMINIC, priest, Roman Catholic Church; b. Chgo., Aug. 22, 1952; s. Florian and Cecilia (Wolowiec) K. B. in Theology, St. Mary's Coll., Orchard Lake, Mich., 1980. Curate, St. Bridget's, Hobart, Ind., 1981-82; assoc. St. Casimir's, Hammond, Ind., 1982-83; assoc. St. Stanislaus, Michigan City, Ind., 1983—. Avocations: scuba diving; skiing; biking. Home and Office: 109 Ann St Michigan City IN 46360

KOSOVSKE, HOWARD ARNOLD, rabbi, reform Jewish; college lecturer; b. Chgo., Jan. 29, 1941; s. Abe and Ethel (Bartow) K.; m. Barbara Karen Falk, Dec. 22, 1963; children: Raquel Shira, Joelle Lea. A.B. cum laude, U. Ill., 1962; B.H.L. with honors, Hebrew Union Coll., Cin., 1964, M.A. in Hebrew Letters with honors, 1967. Ordained rabbi, 1967. Rabbi Temple Beth Israel, Sharon, Pa., 1971-74, Temple Beth Elohim, Wellesley, Mass., 1974-76, Tree of Life Congregation, Columbia, S.C., 1976—; pres. Christian-Jewish Congress S.C., Columbia, 1981-82, 83-84; lectr. history U. S.C., Columbia, 1979—. Author: Jewish Ethics and the Aged, 1983. Served as chaplain U.S. Army, 1967-71. Mem. Central Conf. Am. Rabbis. Democrat. Office: Tree of Life Congregation PO Box 5632 Columbia SC 29250

KOUTH, WILLIAM JOHN, minister, United Methodist Ch.; b. Massillon, Ohio, May 26, 1939; s. Louis Leroy and Mary Eunice (Harmon) K.; A.B., Ohio U., 1961; M.Div., United Theol. Sem., Ohio, 1964; postgrad. Evang. Luth. Theol. Sem., 1965-67, Crozer Theol. Sem., 1967-68; m. Linda F. Warstler, Aug. 25, 1961; children—Thomas Christian, Tamara Christiann, Timothy Christopher, Tobin Christen. Ordained to ministry, 1964; youth minister ch., Kettering, Ohio, 1961-63; pastor Calvary Evang. United Brethren Ch., W.Salem, Ohio, 1963-66, Ch. at the Lake, Chippewa Lake, Ohio, 1966-67; asso. chaplain Parkview Meml. Hosp., Ft. Wayne, Ind., 1970-72; chaplain/clin. pastoral edn. supr. Nebr. Meth. Hosps., Omaha, 1972—. Mem. task force on spl. appointments Nebr. conf. United Meth. Ch., 1974-75, clin. pastoral edn. positions, 1967-70. Fellow Coll. Chaplains, Am. Protestant Hosp. Assn.; mem. Assn. Clin. Pastoral Edn. (certified supr.), Omaha Chaplain's Assn. (pres. 1977—). Home: 2717 Country Club Ave Omaha NE 61804 Office: 8303 Dodge St Omaha NE 68114

KRABBE, ALAN ROBERT, minister, Lutheran Church in America; b. Appleton, Wis., Mar. 2, 1945; s. Alvin Arthur and Florence Esther (Roate) K.; m. Sandy Kathleen Bade, May 31, 1969; children: Jill, Jennifer, Kelly. B.S., Carthage Coll., 1967; M.Div., Northwestern Sem., 1971. Ordained to ministry Luth. Ch. in Am., 1971. Pastor, St. Marks Luth. Ch., Batesville, Ind., 1971-74, Bethel Luth. Ch., Great Falls, Mont., 1974-78; asst. pastor Central Luth. Ch., Yakima, Wash., 1978-82; pastor Bethany Luth. Ch., Spanaway, Wash., 1982—; youth ministry coordinator Pacific Northwest Synod, 1984—; chaplain Pierce County Fire Dist., Spanaway, 1983—. Emergency coordinator ARC, Spanaway, 1984—. Mem. Graham Ministerial Assn. Lodge: Kiwanis (Spanaway). Home: 1618 158th Ct E Spanaway WA 98445 Office: Bethany Luth Ch 26418 Mountain Hwy Spanaway WA 98387

KRAFT, CAROL JOYCE, lay church worker; b. Jackson, Mich., Dec. 8, 1935; d. Lester Christian and Grace Florence (Amstutz) Kraft. B.A., Wheaton Coll., 1957; M.A., Columbia U., 1958; M.A., U. Mich., 1960; postgrad Middlebury Coll., summers 1963, 64, 72, Goethe Inst., Munich, summers 1976, 77. Mem. vestry, treas. St. Barnabas Episcopal Ch., Glen Ellyn, Ill., 1982—. Assoc. prof. German, Wheaton Coll., Ill., 1960—. Mem. Am. Assn. Tchrs. German, Ill. Fgn. Lang. Tchrs. Assn., Delta Kappa Gamma. Home: 124 W Prairie St Wheaton IL 60187 Office: Wheaton Coll Dept German Wheaton IL 60187

KRAHN, JOHN HENRY, minister, Lutheran Ch. - Missouri Synod; b. Balt., Nov. 1, 1943; s. Ferdinand Charles and Lillian Mae (Trader) K.; m. Doris Eleanor Peylo, Aug. 6, 1966; children: Andrea, Lisa. M.Div., Concordia Sem., 1969; M.A., Union Sem., 1972, Columbia U., 1974; D.Min., N.Y. Theol. Sem., 1979. Ordained to ministry Lutheran Ch., 1969. Asst. pastor Trinity Luth. Ch., N.Y.C., 1969-74, sr. pastor, 1974—; del. Luth. High Sch. Assn., L.I., N.Y., 1974—; seminar leader Parish Sec. Seminar, N.Y.C., 1975—; dir. A Call to Make a Difference, N.Y.C., 1983—. Author: Ministry Ideabank, 1982, Reaching the Inactive Member, 1983, Seasonings for Sermons, 1983. Editor (newsletter) Ministry Ideabank. Contbr. articles to profl. jours. Mem. Hicksville Community Council, N.Y., 1984—. Served to 2nd lt. U.S. Army chaplain, 1969-74. Mem. Luths. Cooperating in Metropolitan N.Y., Luth. Business & Profl. Assn. (program dir. 1975—). Home: 35 Coachman Ln Levittown NY 11756 Office: Trinity Lutheran Ch 40 W Nicholai St Hicksville NY 11801

KRAMER, HEROLD GOTTHILF, minister, Lutheran Church-Missouri Synod; b. New Orleans, Mar. 23, 1908: s. Gotthilf Mathias and Antoinetta (Smrcka) K.; m. Helen Mary Kruse, June 18, 1932; 1 son, Harold Arthur. B.A., Concordia Sem., St. Louis, 1931; B.D., Chgo. Lutheran Sch. Theology, 1950, M.S.T., 1965. Ordained to ministry Lutheran Church-Missouri Synod, 1931. Asst. pastor Trinity Luth. Ch., Port Arthur, Tex., 1931-33; missionary-at-large Redeemer Mt. Calvary, Harlingen-Raymondsville, Tex., 1933-35; pastor Emmanuel-Redeemer Ch., Van Wert-Convoy, Ohio, 1935-42, St. John Ch., LaGrange, Ill., 1942-53; founding pastor Lake Wales Luth. Ch., Fla., 1953-77; chaplain Lake Wales Hosp., 1977—, trustee, 1979-82, cir. counsel Fla.-Ga. Dist. Luth. Ch.-Mo. Synod, 1954-64, chmn. bd. appeals, 1960-66, chmn. bd. adjudication, 1966-69. Contbr. in field. Chaplain Fedhaven Vespers Fellowship, Fla., 1962-77, Nalcrest Vesper Fellowship, Fla., 1968-77; bd. dirs. Vis. Nurses Assn., Polk County, Fla., 1967-82; bd. dirs. Black Hills Passion Play, Lake Wales, Fla., 1975—. Recipient 50-Yr. award Lutheran Ch.-Mo. Synod, 1981; 50-Yr. award Fla.-Ga. Dist. Luth. Ch.-Mo. Synod, 1982. Mem. Am. Coll. Chaplains Assn. Republican. Home: 1040 Sunset Dr Lake Wales FL 33853 Office: Lake Wales Hosp 410 S 11th St Lake Wales FL 33853

KRAUS, CLYDE NORMAN, minister, educator, Mennonite Church; b. Newport News, Va., Feb. 20, 1924; s. Clyde Henry and Phebe (Shenk) K.; B.D., Goshen Bibl. Sem., 1951; Th.M., Princeton Theol. Sem., 1954; Ph.D., Duke, 1961; m. Ruth Elizabeth Smith, May 16, 1945; children: Yvonne, JoAnn, John Norman, Bonnie and Robert (twins). Ordained to ministry, 1950; tchr. Eastern Mennonite Sch., Harrisonburg, Va., 1946-49; mem. faculty Goshen Coll. (Ind.), 1951—, prof. religion, 1962-80, adj. prof., 1980—; vis. prof. N.T., Serampore Theol. Coll., India, 1966-67. Conducted Spl. Asian-African Teaching Mission, 1974-75; mem. health and welfare com. Mennonite Bd. Missions, 1967-74, mem. overseas com., 1976-80; leadership trainer Japan Mennonite Ch., Hokkaido, 1980—. James B. Duke fellow, 1958-59; Rockefeller fellow, 1959-61. Mem. Am. Soc. Ch. History, Am. Acad. Religion, Mennonite Hist. Soc., Phi Beta Kappa. Author: Dispensationalism in America, Its Rise and Development, 1958; Integration, Who's Prejudiced, 1958, 3d edit., 1964; The Healing Christ, 1972; The Community of the Spirit, 1974, 76; The Authentic Witness, 1979. Editor, contbr. Bible Survey Course, 5 vols., 1956; Evangelicalism and Anabaptism, 1979; Missions, Evangelism and Church Growth, 1980. Contbr. articles, book revs. to jours. Home: 615 College Ave Goshen IN 46526 Office: Azabu Cho 3 chome 2-6 Kita-Ku Sapporo 001 Japan

KRAUS, MICHAEL, clergyman, president New Apostolic Church of N.Am. Address: 267 Lincoln Rd Waterloo ON Canada

KRAUSE, HILMER CHARLES, minister, American Lutheran Ch. B. San Antonio, Nov. 21, 1932; s. Hilmer Charles and Irene (Mamme) K.; m. Laura Eckhardt, Dec. 22, 1954; children: Mark, Deborah, John, Laura. B.A., Tex. Luth. Coll., 1954; B.D., Wartburg Sem., 1958, D.D. (hon.), 1984; S.T.M., Episcopal S.W., 1967. Ordained to ministry Am. Luth. Ch., 1958. Rector, prof. Augsburg Sem., Mexico, D.F., Mexico, 1967-72; pastor Martin Luther Ch., Carmine, Tex., 1972-76; prof. Hispanic ministry Wartburg Sem., Dubuque, Iowa, 1974—; prof. homiletics and Hispanic ministry Episcopal Seminary Southwest, Austin, Tex., 1983—; mem. refugee task force So. Dist., Am. Luth. Ch., Austin, Tex., 1983—; trustee Hispanic Ministry Ctr., 7th Episcopal Province, Austin, 1981—. Editor: Liturgia Luterana, 1983. Served to lt. USNR, 1957-64. Mem. Acad. Himiletics. Home: 3003 Pin Oak Ct Austin TX 78704 Office: Wartburg House 605 Rathervue Pl Austin TX 78705

KRAUSS, HERBERT MAX, retirement village dir., Presbyn. Ch.; b. Chgo., Mar. 28, 1915; s. Willy Arno and Elizabeth Minna (Winkler) K.; B.A. with honors, Beloit Coll., 1937; M.A., Oberlin Coll., 1941; M.B.A., U. Chgo., 1948; m. Ethelyn Mary Rasmussen, July 5, 1948; children—Stephen Herbert, Kirsten Elizabeth, Keary Richard, Herbert Andrew. Adminstr. Burlington (Iowa) Hosp., 1948-54; adminstr. Latrobe (Pa.) Hosp., 1954-63; asso. dir. Genesee Hosp., Rochester, N.Y., 1963-67, dir., 1967-72; exec. dir. The Presbyn. Home, Evanston, Ill., 1973—. Bd. dirs. Genesee Valley Planning Council, 1971-73. Decorated Silver Star, Purple Heart. Fellow Am. Coll. Hosp. Adminstrs.; mem. Am. Hosp. Assn., U. Chgo. Hosp. Adminstrs. Alumni Assn. (pres. 1960-61). Contbr. articles to profl. jours. Home: 1105 Longmeadow Rd Northbrook IL 60062 Office: 3200 Grant St Evanston IL 60201

KRAWCZAK, ARTHUR HENRY See *Who's Who in America*, 43rd edition.

KRAYBILL, JOHN HENRY, bishop, Mennonite Ch.; b. Elizabethtown, Pa., July 24, 1931; s. John Rutt and Esther Garber (Nissley) K.; student Ontario Mennonite Bible Inst., 1951-53, U. Pitts.-Johnstown, 1966-67, Eastern Mennonite Coll. extension, 1963-64; clin. pastoral tng. Bellevue Hosp., N.Y.C., 1979; m. Thelma Mumma Snyder, Jan. 2, 1954; children: Charles, Fred, Janet, Rose. Ordained to ministry, 1954; pastor Seventh Ave. Mennonite Ch., N.Y.C., 1954-66, 1st Mennonite Ch., Johnstown, Pa., 1966-71, Springs (Pa.) Mennonite Ch., 1971-81; bishop Harrisburg dist. Lancaster Conf.,

Mennonite Ch., 1981—. Sec., Allegheny Mennonite Conf., 1970-76, moderator, 1977-80. Office: 100 N 44th St Harrisburg PA 17111

KREITMAN, BENJAMIN ZVI, rabbi, United Synagogue of American Conservative Jewish; b. Warsaw, Poland, Dec. 25, 1920; came to U.S., 1925, naturalized, 1926; s. Jacob and Anna (Grabower) K.; m. Joyce Beth Krinsky, Aug. 7, 1956; children: Jamie Lauren, Jill Allyn. B.A., Yeshiva U., 1939; M.A., Yale U., 1950; M. Hebrew Lit., Jewish Theol. Sem., 1943, D. Hebrew Lit., 1952, D.D. (hon.), 1972. Rabbi, Temple Bethel, New London, Conn., 1948-52, Bklyn. Jewish Ctr., Bklyn., 1952-68, Shaare Torah, Bklyn., 1968-76; rabbi emeritus Shaare Torah Flatbush Jewish Ctr., 1976—; exec. v.p. United Synagogue, N.Y.C., 1976—; cons. World Council Synagogues, N.Y.C., 1976—. Editor: Illustrated History of Jews, 1962. Chmn. Bklyn. Commn. Human Rights, 1963, Bklyn. Small Bus. Opportunities Corp., 1965. Served to lt. (s.g.) USN, 1943-46. Mem. Rabbinical Assembly (com. on Jewish law). Office: United Synagogue Am 155 Fifth Ave New York NY 10010

KREKELBERG, RICHARD GEORGE, priest, Roman Catholic Ch.; b. Hutchinson, Minn., June 6, 1947; s. Edward Henry and Liberty Bell (Woodard) K.; B.A. in Philosophy, St. Johns Sem. Coll., Camarillo, Calif., 1969; M.Div., 1973; postgrad. psychology Loyola-Marmount U., Los Angeles, 1968-69, Mt. St. Mary's Coll., 1977—. Ordained priest, 1973; asso. pastor St. Pauls Ch., Los Angeles, 1973-76; trainer, elementary and secondary catechetical tchrs., 1973—; exec. sec. Los Angeles Priests Senate, 1974-76; mem. exec. com. S. Central Priests and Religious Assn. Black Community Los Angeles, 1974, 75, 76; chaplain Jr. Legion Mary, Our Lady Queen Angeles Curia, Archdiocese Los Angeles, 1974-76; dean students Our Lady of the Angels High Sch. Sem., San Fernando, Calif., 1977—. Chmn., archdiocesan area dir., S. Central Coordinating Com. Minority Vocations to Religious Life, 1974—; has done sermonettes and pub. prayer for CBS and KTTV Metromedia. Res. officer police chaplain, 1977—. Office: POB 1071 San Fernando CA 91341

KRESHTOOL, CONSTANCE SAVAT, religious organization executive, Reform Jewish; b. Worcester, Mass., May 15, 1927; d. Samuel and Tillie (Lederman) S.; m. Bernard Kreshtool, May 31, 1953; children: Jeffrey, Daniel, Richard. B.S. in Chemistry, U. Ill., 1949; M.S., Cornell U., 1950. Pres., Nat. Fedn. of Temple Sisterhoods, N.Y.C., 1981—; trustee Union of Am. Hebrew Congl., 1981—; gov. Hebrew Union Coll., Cin., 1981—; mem. exec. bd. Progressive Judaism, Jerusalem, 1981—; bd. dirs. Jewish Fedn. Del., Jewish Community Ctr., Wilmington. Bd. dirs. United Way of Del.; mem. Del. Today. Office: Nat Fedn of Temple Sisterhoods 838 Fifth Ave New York NY 10021

KREUTZER, MARY FIDELIS, nun, Roman Cath. Ch.; b. Sheridan, Oreg., Oct. 4, 1925; d. George Peter and Helen Elizabeth (Dunser) K.; B.S., Maryhurst Coll., 1952; M.Ed., Gonzaga U., 1958; Ph.D. in Edn., Loyola U., Chgo., 1964. Joined Sisters of St. Mary of Oreg., 1941; sec. Diocesan Bd. Edn., Portland, Oreg., 1969-76; superior gen., 1976—. Home and Office: 4440 SW 148th Ave Beaverton OR 97005

KREUTZER, ROBERT ALAN, brother, Roman Cath. Ch.; b. Hays, Kans., Nov. 9, 1940; s. Otto Adolph and Scholastica Elizabeth (Gerstner) K.; B.A., St. Joseph's Coll., Ind., 1969. Joined Soc. Precious Blood, 1961; asst. dean students, tchr. English, Brunnerdale High Sch. Sem., Canton, Ohio, 1963-73; engr. Communications Center, Calumet Coll., Whiting, Ind., 1973—. Corr. sec. Internat. Mission Radio Assn., 1972-76; pres., bd. dirs. Cath. Interracial Council Stark County, 1965-73. Mem. Am. Radio Relay League Nat. Assn. Ednl. Broadcasters, Soc. Broadcast Engrs. Home and Office: 2400 New York Ave Whiting IN 46394

KRIEG, HUGH JOHN, minister, Lutheran Church - Missouri Synod; b. Alpena, Mich., Feb. 2, 1914; s. Hugo Adolph and Augusta Anna (Ziemann) K.; m. Emmie Emilie Krieg, Aug. 10, 1940; children: Carl Hugh, Donn Fred, Ronald John. B.A., Concordia Coll., 1935; B.Div., Concordia Sem., 1939. Ordained to ministry Lutheran Ch., 1940. Pastor St. Paul's Luth. Ch., Eden Valley, Mich., 1940-47, Eastern Hts., Luth. Ch., St. Paul, 1947-54, Grace Luth. Ch., Long Beach, Calif., 1954-57, Lynwood Luth. Ch., Calif., 1957-75; chaplain Redwood Terr. Luth. Ch., Escondido, Calif., 1981—; pastoral adv. Luth. Laymen's League, Los Angeles, 1957-65; mem. constitution com. Minn. Dist., St. Paul, 1952-54, chmn. comm. on Luth. union So. Calif. Dist., Los Angeles, 1958-74, sec. So. Calif. Dist., Los Angeles, Luth. Ch. - Mo. Synod, 1959-60. Chmn. St. Paul City Transportation Com., Minn., 1948. Home: 2100 S Escondido Blvd #8 Escondido CA 92025 Office: Redwood Terr Luth Home 710 W 13th Ave Escondido CA 92025

KRINER, CHARLES FREDERICK, minister, United Presbyterian Ch. and Presbyterian Ch.; b. Mt. Vernon, Ohio, June 7, 1937; s. Charles M. and Phyllis (Tucker) K.; student Grove City Coll., 1955-56; B.S., Duquesne U., 1961; M.Div., Louisville Presbyn. Theol. Sem., 1965; postgrad. W. Tex. State U., 1971-72; M.A., Vaparaiso U., 1972; D.Min., McCormick Theol. Sem., 1976; m. Shirley Ann Beham, Jan. 25, 1956; children—Mary Lynette, Charles Jeffrey, John Mark. Ordained to ministry U.P. Ch. U.S.A., 1965; pastor, Newark, Ohio, 1965-67, 1st U.P. Ch., Portage, Ind., 1967-70; asso. pastor 1st Presbyn. Ch., Amarillo, Tex., 1970-. Mem. bd. nat. missions U.P. Ch., 1970-73; mem. joint com./task force on union presbyteries U.P. Ch.-Presbyn. Ch. U.S., 1975—. Bd. dirs. Ret. Sr. Vol. Program, Amarillo, Amarillo Sr. Citizens Assn. Home: 3608 Doris Dr Amarillo TX 79109 Office: 1100 Harrison St Amarillo TX 79101

KROENING, ROBERT WILLIAM, minister, United Ch. Christ; b. St. Louis, June 21, 1925; s. Henry William and Jean Elizabeth (Jackson) K.; student Westminster Coll., Fulton, Mo., 1943-44; J.D., Washington U., St. Louis, 1946; m. Patricia Lee Bixby, Nov. 6, 1948; children—Marjorie, Cynthia, Richard. Ordained to ministry, 1977; lay supply preacher, 1971-74; pastor Ebenezer United Ch. Christ and St. James United Ch. Christ, New Haven, Mo., 1974—. Pres., Churchmen of Greater St. Louis, 1970-71, Churchmen of Mo., 1972-73; sec.-treas. Hermann Area Pastors Circle, 1977; trustee Deaconess Hosp., St. Louis, 1957-65, Evang. Childrens Home, St. Louis, 1957—. Vice chmn. Nat. Fedn. Young Republicans, 1949-53; pres. Mo. Fedn. Young Reps., 1951; asst. to U.S. Sen. James P. Kem, Washington, 1951-52. Mem. Delta Tau Delta (Distinguished Service award St. Louis Alumni chpt. 1968, Distinguished Alumni award Westminster Coll. 1958). Home and office: Route 1 Box 301 New Haven MO 63068

KROKER, BRUNO ERNEST KURT, ch. ofcl.; b. Berlin, Germany; s. George Edward and Anna Adelheid (Winkler) K.; student Berlin U., 1933-34, Copenhagen U., 1934-35; student Keijo U., Japan, 1935-36, Peita U., China, 1936, Ind. U., 1954-56; m. Linda Kirstein, May 13, 1961; 1 son, Kevin Olaf. Came to U.S., 1949, naturalized, 1955. Nat. pub. relations dir. Christian Rural Overseas Program, Elkhart, Ind., 1950-61; chmn. merit awards com. Nat. Religious Pub. Relations Council, 1972-73; asso. dir. dept. information Nat. Council Chs., N.Y.C., 1961-70, United Presbyn. Ch. U.S.A., N.Y.C., 1970-74; sr. press officer World Council Chs., Geneva, Switzerland, 1974—. Mem. Royal Asiatic Soc (England). Club: Overseas Press (N.Y.C.). Author: Border Tribes of Southwest China, 1940; The Chinese Jews of Kaifeng, 1940; Chinese Civilization, 1942. Home: 158 Magnolia Ave Tenafly NJ 07670 Office: 150 Route de Ferney Geneva Switzerland

KROL, JOHN JOSEPH CARDINAL, archbishop, Roman Catholic Church; b. Cleve., Oct. 26, 1910; s. John and Anne (Pietruszka) K.; student St. Mary's Coll., Orchard Lake, Mich., 1929-31, St. Mary's Sem., Cleve., 1931-37; J.C.L., Pontifical Gregorian U., Rome, 1940; J.C.D., Pontifical Catholic U. Am., 1942; LL.D. (hon.), John Carroll U., Cleve., 1955, St. Joseph Coll., Phila., 1961, Temple U., 1964, St. John U., N.Y.C., 1964, Lycoming Coll., Williamsport, Pa., 1966, Coll. of Steubenville (Ohio), 1967, Drexel U., Phila., 1970; D. Pedagogy (hon.), La Salle Coll., Phila., 1961; D.S.T. (hon.), Villanova (Pa.) U., 1961; D.H.L. (hon.), Alliance Coll., Cambridge Springs, Pa., 1967, Chestnut Hill Coll., 1975; Litt.D. (hon.), Bellarmine-Ursuline, Louisville, 1968; D.D. (hon.), Susquehanna U., Selinsgrove, Pa., 1970. Ordained priest Roman Cath. Ch., 1937; asst. pastor Immaculate Heart of Mary Ch., Cleve., 1937-38; prof. canon law St. Marys Sem., Cleve., 1942-43; defender of bond Matrimonial Tribunal, 1943; vice chancellor Diocese of Cleve., 1943-51; pres. Canon Law Soc. Am., 1948-49; promoter of Justice, 1950; chancellor Diocese of Cleve., 1951-53; titular bishop of Cadi and aux. to bishop of Cleve., 1953; vicar gen. Diocese of Cleve., 1953-60; named by Pope John XXIII as mem. Preparatory Commn. on Bishops and Diocesan Govt., 1960; apptd. tenth Ordinary, Archdiocese of Phila., 1961; archbishop of Phila., 1961—; chmn. Pa. Cath. Conf., 1961; mem. adminstrv. bd., chmn. youth dept., dept edn., com. on motion pictures, radio and television Nat. Cath. Welfare Conf., 1961-66; named undersec. II Vatican Council, 1962; mem. Pontifical Commn. for Mass Media Communications, 1964-69; v.p. Nat. Conf. Cath. Bishops and U.S. Cath. Conf., 1966-72, pres., 1972-74; chmn. com. for study life and ministry of priest Nat. Conf. Cath. Bishops, 1967; elected to Internat. Council, Secretariate of Synod of Bishops, Rome, 1971; elevated to Sacred Coll. of Cardinals by Pope Paul VI, 1967. Mem. Sacred Congregation for Oriental Ch., 1967—, Sacred Congregation for Evangelization of Nations, 1967-72, Sacred Congregation for Doctrine of Faith, 1973—, Pontifical Commn. for Revision Code of Canon Law, 1973—. Hon. chmn. Pulaski Day Observance, Phila., 1961-71; mem. Commn. for Cath. Negro and Indian Missions, Com. for N.Am. Coll., Rome, 1965-70; chmn. bd. govs., host Internat. Eucharistic Congress, Phila., 1976. Bd. dirs. Cath. Standard and Times; trustee Cath. U. Am., 1961-71, Nat. Shrine of Immaculate Conception, Washington, St. Mary Coll., Orchard Lake, Cath. League for Religious Assistance to Poland, St. Charles Borromeo Sem., Phila., Roman Cath. High Sch., Phila., Cath. Relief Services, Cath. Community Services; bd. advisers Fu-Jen U., Taiwan. Decorated comdr. Republic of Italy, 1958, knight grand cross, Order of Merit Italian Republic, 1971; recipient award Temple Adath Israel, Phila., 1970, Pub. Relations award, Phila., 1970, Man of our Quarter Century award Am. Council Polish Cultural Clubs, Phila., 1973, Heritage award Polish Am. Congress, Chgo., 1973, Ohio Gov.'s award, 1976, others; named comdr. l'Ordre Nat. du Tchad, Pres. Republic of Tchad, 1970, Am. Prelate of Year, Ariz. chpt. Polish Am. Congress, Phoenix, 1973. Office: 222 N 17th St Philadelphia PA 19103

KRUEGER, WILLIAM EDWARD, priest, Episcopal Church; b. Green Bay, Wis., Nov. 28, 1919; s. Edward Henry and Mable (Thorn) K.; Ph.B., Carroll Coll., 1942; grad. Nashotah House, 1950; 1 child, James Francis. Ordained priest Episcopal Ch., 1950; pastor Holy Trinity Ch., Platteville, Wis., 1950-53, St. Michael's Ch., Shullsberg, Wis., 1950-53, Kemper Meml. Ch., Darlington, Wis., 1951-53, St. Paul's Ch., Watertown, Wis., 1953-62, Good Shepherd Mission, Ft. Defiance, Ariz., 1962-63, St. Luke's Ch., Springfield, Ill., 1963—; priest-in-charge St. Paul's, St. Anne's and St. Andrews Chs., Bermuda, 1955, St. Mary's Ch., Jefferson, Wis., 1957-61, St. Joseph's Ch., Clinton, Ill., 1963-70; assoc. pastor St. John's Ch., Decatur, Ill., 1963; chaplain 79th Gen. Assembly, Ill. Hos. of Reps., 1975-76; convocation dean Diocese of Milw., 1952-53; rural dean Diocese of Springfield, 1970-75, pub. relations dir., 1965—, diocesan sec., 1968-71; co-chmn. Anglican-Roman Cath. Dialogue, 1969—. Mem. Springfield Fair Housing Bd., 1968—; bd. dirs. Family Service Center, Springfield, 1965—, Luth. Family Service, Springfield, 1975—, Sr. Citizens Sangamon County, 1965—. Recipient Internat. Pres.'s award Lions Internat., 1969, 71, 75, 79; named Ambassador Extraordinary, City of Springfield, 1969; Melvin Jones fellow, 1975. Mem. Ch. Hist. Soc., Churchmen United, Confraternity of Blessed Sacrament (assoc.), Soc. of Mary (assoc.), NAACP, ACLU, VFW, Oshkosh Alumni Assn., Nashotah House Alumni Assn., Am. Ch. Union, Soc. St. John the Evangelist. Club: Lions Internat. (trustee found. 1978-79, pres. stamp club 1984-85). Editor Springfield Churchmen, 1965-71. Home: PO Box 3101 Springfield IL 62708 Office: PO Box 3103 Springfield IL 62708

KRUMM, JOHN MCGILL, bishop, Episcopal Church; b. South Bend, Ind., Mar. 15, 1913; s. William Frederick and Harriet Vincent (McGill) K.; B.A., U. Calif., at Los Angeles, 1935; B.D., Va. Theol. Sem., Alexandria, 1938, D.D. (hon.), 1973; Ph.D., Yale, 1948; S.T.D. (hon.) Kenyon Coll., 1962; D.D. (hon.), Berkeley Div. Sch., 1971, Gen. Theol. Sem., 1975. Ordained deacon Episcopal Ch., 1938, priest, 1938, consecrated bishop, 1971; vicar, Compton, Lynwood and Hawthorne, Calif., 1938-41; asst., New Haven, 1941-43; rector, San Mateo, Calif., 1943-48; dean St. Paul's Cathedral, Los Angeles, 1948-52; chaplain Columbia, 1952-65; rector Ascension Ch., N.Y.C., 1965-71; bishop of So. Ohio, Episcopal Ch., Cin., 1971-80; Suffragan bishop in Europe, Paris, 1980-83; assisting bishop, Los Angeles, 1983—, St. Paul's Ch., Tustin, Calif., 1983—. Bd. dirs. Children's Hosp., Cin., Kenyon Coll., Gambier, Ohio, Bexley Hall, Rochester, N.Y. Clubs: Century (N.Y.C.); University, Cin. Country, Bankers (Cin.). Author: Why I Am An Episcopalian, 1956; Modern Heresies, 1962; The Art of Being a Sinner, 1968; also articles, revs. Office: 1221 Wass Ave Tustin CA 92680*

KRUMPE, WILLIAM FRANCIS, priest, Roman Catholic Church; b. Cin., Nov. 23, 1940; s. William Frederick and Gladys Mary (Torry) K.; A.B., Athenaeum Ohio, 1962; postgrad. Xavier U., 1962-65, Mt. St. Joseph Coll., 1977-79, U. Dayton, 1977, U. Cin., 1977, N. Am. Coll., Rome, 1981, U. Notre Dame, 1982, 83, 85. Ordained priest, 1966. Assoc. pastor St. Margaret Mary Parish, N. Coll. Hill, Ohio, 1966-71, St. Cecilia Parish, Cin., 1971-73, St. Monica Parish, Cin., 1973-75, St. Jude Parish, Mack, Ohio, 1975-79, St. William Parish, Cin., 1979-82; pastor Our Lady of Perpetual Help, Cin., 1982—. Asst. youth dir. Archdiocese of Cin., 1972-75, adv. bd. youth council, 1969-76, moderator Gregorian program, 1967-77, mem. vocation council, 1973-77; chaplain Camp Fire Girls, Cin., 1972-76; active Oakley Ecumenical Youth Ministry, 1971-73. Recipient Archbishop Paul F. Leibold award Archdiocese Cin., 1972, 79-80; Outstanding Young Clergy Western Hills Jaycees, 1978. Mem. N. Coll. Hill, Oakley, Western Hills ministerial assns. Contbr. monthly comments Archdiocesan Youth Bull. Home and Office: 639 Steiner Ave Cincinnati OH 45204

KUCERA, DANIEL WILLIAM, college president, priest, Roman Catholic Church; b. Chgo., May 7, 1923; s. Joseph F. and Lillian C. (Petrzelka) K.; B.A., St. Procopius Coll., 1945; M.A., Cath. U. Am., 1950, Ph.D., 1954. Joined Order of St. Benedict, 1944, ordained priest, 1949; registrar St. Procopius Coll. and Acad., Lisle, Ill., 1945-49; registrar St. Procopius Coll., Lisle, 1954-56, acad. dean, head. dept. edn., 1956-59, pres., 1959-65; abbot St. Procopius Abbey, Lisle, 1964-71; pres. Ill. Benedictine Coll. (formerly St.

Procopius Coll.), Lisle, 1971-76, chmn. bd. trustees, 1976—; titular bishop of Natchez and aux. bishop of Joliet, 1977; apptd. bishop of Salina, 1980-84; archbishop of Dubuque, 1984—; chmn. devel. council Collegio Sant' Anselmo, Rome. Chaplain, Chgo. council Navy League U.S., 1974—, Czech Cath. Union; nat. adv. bd. Holy Cross Abbey and Sch., Canon City, Ill. bd. dirs. Rice Found., Ill. Cath. Conf. Mem. Am. Benedictine Acad., Nat. Cath. Edn. Assn., Am. Assn. for Higher Edn., Fedn. Ind. Ill. Colls. and Univs., North Central Assn. Colls. and Secondary Schs., Assn. Am. Colls., Am. Council Edn., Contbr. articles to religious publs. Address: 1229 Mt Loretta Ave Dubuque IA 52201*

KUCHARSKY, DAVID EUGENE, editor; b. Pitts., Aug. 3, 1931; s. Leon and Marie (Dachko) K.; B.A., Duquesne U., 1953; M.A., Am. U., 1961; postgrad. Cath. U. Am., 1969-74; m. Patricia Eleanor Patterson, Aug. 31, 1957; children—Brenda Lee, Deborah Lynn, Sandra Lou, David John. News editor Christianity Today, Washington, 1958-67, asso. editor, 1967-71, mng. editor, 1971-76, sr. editor, 1976—. Bd. dirs. Asso. Ch. Press. Mem. Nat. Press Club. Author: The Man from Plains-The Mind and Spirit of Jimmy Carter, 1976. Office: 1014 Washington Bldg Washington DC 20005

KUDER, RALPH HARRY, brother, Roman Catholic Ch.; b. Wauwatosa, Wis., Mar. 26, 1928; s. Harry Jack and Marie Bertha (Goetzke) K.; B.B.A., Spencerian Coll., 1949; M.B.A. U. Notre Dame, 1958. Joined Bros. of Holy Cross, Roman Cath. Ch., 1950; tchr. Cathedral High Sch., Indpls., 1951-54; tchr. St. Edward's U., Austin, Tex., 1954-65, asst. to pres., 1963-65, dir. student fin. aid, 1962-64, v.p. fin. affairs, 1965-69; provincial treas. Bros. Holy Cross, SW Province, Austin, 1969-. Mem. Estate Planning Council Central Tex., 1962-65; vol. counselor Hotline, 1972-73. Trustee vice-chmn. St. Edward's U. Recipient Certificate of Achievement, Travis County Probation Dept., 1973. Address: Provincial Residence St Edward's U Austin TX 78704

KUEHN, ARTHUR HARRY, minister, American Baptist Churches; b. Cin., Oct. 31, 1936; s. Harry H. and Dorothy I. (Kellogg) K.; B.A., Wilmington Coll., 1958; M.Div., Colgate Rochester Div. Sch., 1961; m. Gladys Marlene George, June 12, 1959; children: Cynthia Ann, Krista Marie. Ordained to ministry Am. Bapt. Ch., 1961; asso. minister First Bapt. Ch., Columbus, Ohio, 1961-63; pastor First Bapt. Ch., Hudson, Wis., 1963-67; asso. minister Central Bapt. Ch., Hartford, Conn., 1967-76, also dir. visitation and counseling, 1967-76; sr. minister United Bapt. Ch., Lewiston, Maine, 1977—. Mem. exec. com. Center City Chs. of Hartford, Inc., 1974; pres. Center City Chs. for Aging, Inc., 1971-74; v.p. bd. dirs. Sarah Frye Home, 1982—. Chmn. Services Performed with Aging Council, Hartford, 1974; v.p. Conn. League for Abortion Law Repeal, 1969-74; mem. cons. group Dept. Children and Youth Services, State of Conn., 1974. Bd. dirs. Planned Parenthood League of Conn., 1974—, chmn. nominating com., 1976-77; trustee Lewiston Pub. Library, 1983—; bd. dirs. Pathways, 1983—; bd. dirs. United Way of Androscoggin County, 1978—, pres., 1984; cons./planner Wrap Around Services for Older Persons Project, 1976. Mem. Ministers Council, Interfaith Clergy Assn. (pres. 1978-79), Alpha Phi Gamma, Alpha Psi Omega, Phi Alpha Theta. Editor: The Wilmingtonian, 1958; contbr. articles to mags. and profl. jours. Home: 336 College St Lewiston ME 04240 Office: 250 Main St Lewiston ME 04240

KUHLMANN, MARVIN EARL, minister, Lutheran Church-Missouri Synod. B. Chester, Nebr., Sept. 15, 1931; s. Walter Oscar and Hulda Meta (Grabau) K.; m. Donna Mae Schneller, Oct. 17, 1953; children: Brent, Karen. A.A., St. John's Coll., 1952; B.A. in Edn., Concordia Sem., St. Louis, 1954, B.D., 1963, M.Div., 1971. Ordained to ministry Luth. Ch., 1963. Pastor, St. Peter Luth. Ch., Westgate, Iowa, 1963-65, St. Stephen Luth. Ch., Liberty, Mo., 1965-71, St. Mark Luth. Ch., Flint, Mich., 1971-78, Holy Trinity Luth. Ch., Grandview, Mo., 1978—; counselor Luth. Women's League, Flint, 1976-78; cir. counselor Kans. City s. cir. Luth. Ch.-Mo. Synod, Kansas City, 1978—. Com. mem. Clay County Home, Liberty, Mo., 1968; mem. spiritual life com. Ozanam Home for Boys, Kansas City, 1980—. Recipient Freedom award Freedoms Found., 1966. Home: 204 Johnston Pkwy Raymore MO 64083 Office: Holy Trinity Luth Ch 5901 E 135th St Grandview MO 64030

KULPINSKI, STANLEY ALOYSIUS, priest, Roman Cath. Ch.; b. Poland, Mar. 24, 1909; s. Stanislaus and Theresa (Urbanski) K.; came to U.S., 1910, naturalized, 1922; B.A., Canisius Coll., 1930; M.A., St. Bonaventure U., 1932; postgrad. Christ the King Sem., Alleghany, N.Y., 1933-34, Cath. U. Am., 1936-37. Ordained priest, 1934; prof. social philosophy and papal social encyclicals, various univs. and schs., 1939—; arbitrator, 1946—; adminstr. St. Stanislaus Parish, 1945; pastor St. Mary's Parish, E.Eden, 1953-55, Queen of Martyrs Ch., Buffalo, 1955—. Mem. founding com., asso. dir. Labor Mgmt. Coll., 1939, diocesan dir., Diocese of Buffalo and 10 dist. schs., 1953—, chmn. Nat. Cath. Indsl. Conf., 1955-60; participant Canisius Coll. Television Indsl. Seminars, Indsl. Relations Workshops; cons. various labor union orgns. Western N.Y. and nationally; condr. seminars for labor and indsl. groups throughout Western N.Y.; guest lectr. State U. Coll. of Buffalo, State U. N.Y. at Buffalo, Niagara U., St. Bonaventure U.; chaplain, religious celebrant Westinghouse Electric Corp.; chaplain Erie County Penitentiary, Erie County Home and Infirmary, 1945-52, Steelworkers Unions at Bethlehem Steel Corp., United Rubber Workers of Am. AFL-CIO Western N.Y., Internat. Union Elec. Workers, Am. Fedn. Grain Millers; internat. chaplain Bakery and Confectionery Workers; pres. Priests Clerical Mut. Benefit Soc.; four year priest senator; asst. editor Labor Observor; radio commentator Church in the News, WWOL-AM, FM; del. Nat. Cath. Social Welfare Conf., Rome, Italy, 1961; bd. dirs., permanent chair Polish Culture and lit. Canisius Coll.; mem. founding com. St. Joseph the Worker Shrine at St. Ignatius Retreat House, Clarence, N.Y.; co-founder, charter mem. St. Rita's Home, Getzville, N.Y. Chmn., Buffalo Indsl. Progress Council; mem. Pres. Johnson's Equal Opportunity Employment Commn., Gov. Rockefeller Com. for Erection Ashford Nuclear Project, Pub. Employees Relations Bd., City of Buffalo. Recipient Gold Lifetime membership Internat. Bakery and Confectionery Workers Union of Am., 1969, Communication and Leadership award Toastmasters Internat., 1972, Plaque award Faculty Labor Mgmt. Coll. Diocese of Buffalo, 1974, Americanization award Adam Plewacki post Am. Legion, i945, Buffalo Bison awards Mayor Frank A. Sedita, 1970, Mayor Stanley Makowski, 1973, Key to City, Mayor Sedita, 1972. Mem. Am. Arbitration Assn., Buffalo C. of C., Am. Sociol. Assn., Am. Mgmt. Assn., Cath. Econ. Assn., Indsl. Relations Research Assn. Western N.Y. (exec. council), Polish Lit. Assn. Home and office: 180 George Urban Blvd Cheektowaga NY 14225

KUMONTIS, FRANCIS MICHAEL, church administrator, Roman Catholic Church; b. York, Pa., July 26, 1947; s. John Joseph and Ethel Marie (Kecsey) K. B.A., St. Mary's Sem., 1969; B.S., St. Vincent Coll., 1973; M.Div., St. Vincent Sem., 1973; M.S.W., Columbia U., 1980, M.B.A., 1980. Ordained to ministry, 1973. Asst. pastor St. Theresa Ch., New Cumberland, Pa., 1973-76; dir. family life Cath. Diocese, Harrisburg, Pa., 1976-78; exec. dir. Cath. Charities, Harrisburg Diocese, 1981—; vicar, Cath. Social Service and Social Justice, Harrisburg Diocese, 1981—; bd. dirs. Villa Teresa Nursing Home, Harrisburg, Camp New Dawn, Gettysburg, Pa., 1981—; adminstrv. bd. Pa. Cath. Conf., 1983—. Mem. Gov.'s Council on Human Service, State of Pa., Harrisburg, 1983—. Mem. Nat. Assn. Social Workers, Pa. Assn. Social Workers, Nat. Conf. Cath. Charities, Assn. Mgrs. Bus. Democrat. Address: Catholic Social Services 4800 Union Deposit Rd Harrisburg PA 17105

KUNTZ, JOHN KENNETH, educator, minister, United Methodist Church; b. St. Louis, Jan 20, 1934; s. John Frederick and Zula Belle (Reed) K.; B.A., Grinnell Coll., 1956; B.D., Yale U., 1959; Ph.D., Union Theol. Sem., 1963; m. Ruth Marie Stanley, July 7, 1962; children: David, Nancy. Ordained to ministry, 1961; instr. religion Wellesley Coll., 1963-65, asst. prof., 1965-67; asst. prof. religion U. Iowa, 1967-70, asso. prof., 1970-76, prof., 1976—. Mem. Am. Acad. Religion, Am. Schs. Oriental Research, Soc. Bibl. Lit., Chgo. Soc. Bibl. Research, Phi Beta Kappa. Author: The Self-revelation of God, 1967; The People of Ancient Israel: An Introduction to Old Testament Literature, History, and Thought, 1974.

KUNZ, MELVIN ROY, minister, coll. dean, Ind. Fundamental Chs. Am.; b. Springfield, Ill., Feb. 10, 1932; s. Roy Russel and Mildred Louise (Williamson) K.; B.A., Wheaton (Ill.) Coll., 1954; student No. Bapt. Sem., 1955-56; M.A. cum laude, Trinity Evang. Div. Sch., 1968; m. Marian Mildred Shinneman, Apr. 10, 1954; children—James, John, Janna, Jonathan, Joel. Ordained to ministry, 1956; minister Village Bible Ch., Park Forest, Ill., 1955-66, Dubuque (Iowa) Bible Ch., 1966-73, Grace Evang. Ch., Elgin, Ill., 1973-76; dean students Southeastern Bible Coll., Birmingham, Ala., 1976—. Dir. Family Counseling Service Dubuque, 1968-73; chmn. youth com. Ind. Fundamental Chs. Am., 1966-72; pres. Lake Waubesa Bible Camp Bd., Madison, Wis., 1966—; chmn. Greater Elgin Evang. Ministers Fellowship, 1974-76; chaplain Sherman Hosp., Elgin. Mem. bd. reference St. Josephs Hosp., Dubuque, 1971-72, Mayors Com. Edn., Dubuque, 1970-73. Contbr. book revs. and articles to religious mags. Home: 5244 Beacon Circle Irondale AL 35210 Office: 2901 Pawnee Ave Birmingham AL 35205

KUPPE, PAUL MICHAEL, priest, Roman Catholic Church; b. Balt., Aug. 9, 1944; s. Joseph John and Mary (Skembo) K. B.A., St. Fidelis Coll., 1967; M.A., Capuchin Coll., 1970; M.A., Loyola U., Chgo., 1972. Ordained priest, Capuchin Franciscan Order, Roman Cath. Ch., 1970. Asst. pastor Presentation Ch., Chgo., 1970-72, St. Augustine Ch., Pitts., 1972-77; pastor St. Martin Ch., Balt., 1977-80, Our Lady of Peace Ch., Conway, Pa., 1980—; dir. Christian Housing Inc., Pitts., 1972-77; del. Quigley High Sch. Bd. Dirs., Baden, Pa., 1984—. Democrat. Home and Office: Our Lady of Peace Ch 1001 2d Ave Conway PA 15027

KURZ, ALBERT LESLIE, minister, Conservative Bapt. Assn. Am.; b. Ashton, Ill., Jan. 6, 1933; s. Walter Carl and Bertha Chapman (Bothe) K.; student Moody Bible Inst., 1956, Trinity Evang. Div. Sch., 1964, Winona Lake Sch. Theology, 1966, U. Denver, 1968; B.A., Wheaton Coll., 1958; D.D., Inst. Evangelism, India, 1969; m. Donna Marie Frost, Sept. 9, 1951 (dec. 1963); m. 2d, Karla Lynn Kelsay, Dec. 17, 1966; children—David, Robert, Peggy, Cathy, Jonathan. Ordained to ministry, 1959; founding pastor Addison (Ill.) Bible Ch., 1954-67, Calvary Evang. Free Ch., Roselle, Ill., 1959; sr. pastor Belcaro Evang. Free Ch., Denver, 1967-73, 1st Bapt. Ch., Pekin, Ill., 1973—. Pres., W.Suburban Evang. Fellowship, Chgo., 1959-60; sec. Gt. Lakes dist. Evang. Free Ch. Am., 1962-67, chmn. Rocky Mountain dist., 1968-70; mem. assn. gen. bd., 1968-73, sec. Christian edn. bd., 1968-73; pres. Colo. Assn. Evangelicals, 1969-71; pres. Fellowship of Ill. Conservative Baptists, 1975-76; bd. dirs. Conservative Bapt. Assn. Am., 1975—; trustee Judson Coll., 1976—. Mem. Nat. Assn. Evangelicals, Evang. Free Ch. Ministerial Assn. Author: Beyond Discouragement, 1975; also articles and pamphlets. Home: 9 Burning Tree Ln Pekin IL 61554 Office: 701 S 4th St Pekin IL 61554

KURZAWA, RONALD, priest, Roman Catholic Church. B. Detroit, Nov. 17, 1938; s. Sigmund Stephen and Helen (Kopas) K. B.A., St. Mary's Coll., 1960; M.A., Notre Dame U., 1973. Ordained priest, Roman Cath. Ch., 1964. Asst. pastor St. Cunegunda Parish, Detroit, 1964-68, St. Bartholomew Parish, Detroit, 1968-73; pastor St. Clement of Rome, Mich., 1973-82, Precious Blood Ch., Detroit, 1982—; adj. faculty mem. Saints Cyril and Methodius Sem., Orchard Lake, Mich., 1976-82, Sacred Heart Sem. Ministries Program, Detroit, 1985—. Home and Office: Ch of the Precious Blood 13305 Grove Detroit MI 48235

KUSCHAK, ANDREI, primate, Ukrainian Orthodox Church in America (Ecumenical Patriarchate). Address: St Andrews Ukrainian Orthodox Diocese 90-34 139th St Jamaica NY 11435

KUSIK, VICTOR, priest, Episcopal Ch.; b. Vladivostok, Russia, Sept. 18, 1926; s. Harry Alexander and Emma (Abol) K.; came to U.S., 1949, naturalized, 1955; student German Coll., Tsingtao, China, 1945; M.Div., Va. Theol. Sem., 1952; fellow Coll. of Preachers, Washington, 1958; D.D., Berkeley Div. Sch., New Haven, 1968; m. Ellen S. Babcock, June 2, 1951; children—Barbara, Victor, Richard, Christopher, Nancy. Ordained priest, 1952; vicar St. Mary's Ch., Bridgeville, Del., 1952-53; rector St. Mary's Ch., 1953-72, Immanuel Ch., Highlands, Wilmington, Del., 1972—. Mem. exec. council Diocese of Del., 1958-60; dep. to Gen. Conv., 1961-73; canon missioner Diocese of Del., 1964-71, pres. standing com., 1964-71; chmn. spl. ministry task force Delmarva Ecumenical Agy., 1971. Mem. Del. Human Relations Commn., 1965-73; vol. probation officer Family Ct. State of Del. for Sussex County, 1971. Recipient conservation award Del. Fedn. Sportsmen and Conservation Clubs, 1964. Home: 2404 W 16th St Wilmington DE 19806 Office: 2400 W 17th St Wilmington DE 19806

KUTZ, LEROY MARSHALL, JR., minister, United Ch. of Christ; b. Phila., May 1, 1922; s. LeRoy Marshall and Clara Mae (Kulp) K.; A.B., Franklin and Marshall Coll., 1943; B.D., Lancaster Theol. Sem., 1945; m. Marie Ethel Brooks, July 3, 1943; children—LeRoy Marshall III, Rebecca Marie. Ordained to ministry, 1945; pastor, Allentown and Lock Haven, Pa., 1945-57, Buffalo, 1957-59; dir. member relations Heifer Project Internat., 1959-63; sr. pastor St. Johns Evang. Protestant Ch., Columbus, Ohio, 1963-73; sr. minister 1st Congl. Ch., Port Huron, Mich., 1973—. Founder, Met. Area Ch. Bd. Columbus; founder radio program Bible Biography Broadcast, Pa., also TV program Search, N.Y. Active United Way, Boy Scouts Am., Family Service Bd. Mem. Sci. Study Religion Soc. Author: The Chancel, 1960; contbr. sermons and articles to various profl. jours. Home: 3455 Gratiot St Port Huron MI 48060 Office: 723 Court St Port Huron MI 48060

KUZY, PAULITA, nun, Roman Catholic Church, educator; b. North Braddock, Pa., June 19, 1939; d. George and Anne Frances (Sanigna) K. B.A., La Roche Coll., 1968; M.Edn., Duquesne U., 1971; Ed. Adminstrn., U. of Pitts., 1979; postgrad. Notre Dame U., 1975, 76. Joined Sisters of Divine Providence, Roman Cath. Ch., 1957; cert. advanced religious Diocese of Pitts. Tchr., Alpha Sch., Allison Park, Pa., 1968-69; prin. St. Mary Sch., Herman, Pa., 1969-71; tchr. St. Isaac Joques, St. Clair Shores, Mich., 1971-72; prin. St. Bonaventure Sch., Glenshaw, Pa., 1972-79, St. Martin Sch., Pitts., 1979—; mem. forum Sisters of Divine Providence, Pitts., 1978-82, com. long range planning, 1982; coordinator St. Martin's Youth Group, 1982-83, Food Bank, 1983. Contbr. articles to profl. jours. Liaison, Easter Seal Soc., 1980-83, Div. Courts, Family Courts, Pitts., 1982-84; coordinator Systematic Trng. for Parents, Pitts., 1980. Recipient Jr.

Achievement award, 1981, 82, Parents Adv. Council award Pitts. Pub. Schs., 1980. Mem. Nat. Cath. Ednl. Assn., Assn. Supervision and Curriculum Devel., Smithsonian Instn., Duquesne Alumni Assn., Assn. La Roche Alumni. Democrat. Office: St Martin Sch 1000 Logue St Pittsburgh PA 15220

KWOCK, CHARLES MAIN CHIN, minister, United Ch. of Christ; b. Fatshan, Kwang-Tung, China, Feb. 2, 1911; s. Mon Yew and Shee (Chun) K.; came to U.S., 1915, naturalized, 1947; B.A., U. Hawaii, 1933; M.A., U. Chgo., 1936; B.D., Chgo. Theol. Sem., 1936; postgrad. (Jacobus fellow) Hartford Sem. Found., 1944-46; D.D., Pacific Sch. Religion, 1971; m. Annie Yuk Lin Tom, July 25, 1936; children—Lynette Lin Jun Kwock Chung, Dennis Wing Tuck Kwock. Ordained to ministry Waimea Chinese Ch., Kauai, Hawaii, 1937; pastor Waimea Chinese Ch., 1936-38, United Ch. of Christ, Honolulu, 1938-44; pastor 1st Chinese Ch. of Christ, Honolulu, 1946-76, pastor emeritus, 1976—; exec. dir. Pacific Christian Missions Found., 1976—. Instr. Hawaii Sch. Religion, Honolulu Christian Coll.; moderator Oahu Evang. Assn., 1948, 68; pres. Honolulu Ministerial Fellowship, 1949; pres. Oahu Evang. Ministers Assn., 1954; chaplain Palolo Chinese Home, Honolulu, 1965—. Recipient Sermon awards Freedoms Found., 1956, 67, 69, Outstanding Alumnus, U. Hawaii, 1971. Mem. Peng Hui frat. Author: A Hawaii Chinese Looks at America. Home and Office: 2893 Oahu Ave Honolulu HI 96822

KYLE, ULYSSES CURTIS, minister, Baptist Missionary Assn. Am.; b. nr. Rusk, Tex., Nov. 16, 1912; s. Henry Leonard and Victoria (Brown) K.; student Va. State Coll., 1943; student Howard U., 1947, 63, Litt.D. (hon.), 1976; student U. Md., 1948-50, Am. U., 1961, Wesleyan Sem., 1962; Th.B., Bapt. Sem., Washington, 1959; postgrad. Northwestern Coll. and Sem., Washinton, 1967-70, D.D. (hon.), 1973; postgrad. U. Israel, 1972; D.D. (hon.) Balt. Coll. Bible, 1976; m. Eula M. Powell, Oct. 15, 1944; children—Cynthia, Elaine (Mrs. Robert Crouch). Ordained minister Baptist Missionary Assn. Am., 1956; asst. pastor Shiloh Bapt. Ch., Washington, 1959-61; pastor 16th St. Bapt. Ch., Washington, 1964—. Mem. exec. ednl. com. Progressive Nat. Bapt. Conv., 1970—; mem. exec. bd. Ednl. Congress D.C. and vicinity; mem. adv. council, dean religious edn. Washington Saturday Coll., Howard U., 1975—. Chaplain, funeral dir. John T. Rhines Co., Washington, 1970-74; mem. adv. council for study on Black Chs. of Am., 1976—. Bd. dirs. Phyliss Wheatley YWCA, Inc. Recipient Excellence award Hebrew U. Jerusalem, 1972; Outstanding Service in Community award WOL radio, 1974, Father of Year award, 1974. Mem. Ministers Conf. Washington and vicinity, Upper 16th St. Ministerial Group. Toastmaster (pres. 1969). Author: Defence of the Gospel, 1976. Home: 1419 Longfellow St NW Washington DC 20011 Office: 5800 16th St Washington DC 20011

KYRILL (ELIA YONCHEV), Bishop of Pitts., Orthodox Church in America. Office: PO Box R Wexford PA 15090*

LABARGE, JOSEPH ALBERT, religious educator, Roman Catholic Church; b. St. Louis, Dec. 11, 1937; s. Joseph Albert and Bonita June (Tillison) LaB.; m. Maureen Murphy, May 30, 1970; children: Joseph W., Michelle A., William M. Ph.B., Pontifical Gregorian U.-Rome, 1959, S.T.L., 1963; Ph.D., Cath. U. Am. 1971. Ordained priest, Roman Catholic Ch., 1963, laicized, 1970. Assoc. pastor Christ the King Cath. Ch., Oklahoma City, 1963-66; assoc. prof. religion Bucknell U., Lewisburg, Pa., 1970—, chmn. dept. religion, 1985—. Assoc. editor Horizons, 1977-82. Mem. Coll. Theology Soc. (bd. dirs.), Am. Acad. Religion, Soc. Christian Ethics. Home: RD 1 Box 487 Lewisburg PA 17837 Office: Dept Religion Bucknell U Coleman Hall 207A Lewisburg PA 17837

LABIANCA, ØYSTEIN SAKALA, religion educator, Seventh-day Adventist Church, archaeologist; b. Kristiansand, Norway, Sept. 10, 1949; came to U.S., 1962; s. Olav Michele and Kirsten (Olsen) LaB.; m. Asta Sakala, Sept. 3, 1972; children: Erik, Aren. B.A. with honors in Religion and Behavioral Scis., Andrews U., 1971; M.A. in Anthropology, Loma Linda U., 1972; spl. student in anthropology Harvard U., 1972-73; postgrad. in anthropology Brandeis U., 1974—. Chief anthropologist Andrews U.-ASOR Heshbon Expdn., Jordan, 1971-76; core staff mem. U. Toronto-ASOR Wadi Tumilat Project, Egypt, 1976—; assoc. project dir. Andrews U.-ASOR Madaba Plains Project, Jordan, 1980—; chmn. dept. behavioral scis., Andrews U., Berrien Springs, Mich., 1983—; guest lectr. on bibl. archaeology, 1973—; organizer Asor Symposie on Ancient Mediterranean Food Systems, 1982, 83, 84; mem. Evangelicals for Social Action, Balt., 1983—. Author articles in univ. and anthropol. publs. Active, Educators for Social Responsibility, 1982—; Reach Internat., 1983—. Albright fellow, Am. Schs. Oriental Research, 1980-81; research fellow NEH, 1978-79, Zion Research Found., 1973, 76. Mem. Am. Schs. Oriental Research, Am. Anthrop. Assn., Soc. for Am. Archaeology, Soc. for Med. Anthropology, Assn. Adventist Forums. Home: Rural Route 2 Box 159A Berrien Springs MI 49103 Office: Inst of Archaeology Andrews Univ Berrien Springs MI 49104

LABRECHE, LAURIER ANDREW, priest, Roman Cath. Ch.; b. Stafford Springs, Conn., July 18, 1926; s. William John and Armandine Marguerite (Perras) L.; B.A., State U. N.Y., 1952. Ordained priest, 1959; asst. pastor St. Therese of the Infant Jesus Shrine, Albuquerque, 1959-62; pastor St. Eleanors Ch., Ruidoso, N.Mex., 1962-68, Old San Miguel Mission, Socorro, N.Mex., 1968-75, Ch. of the Ascension, Albuquerque, 1975—. Pres., Ruidoso Ministerial Alliance, 1968; dean, senator Roswell Deanery, 1966-67, Socorro Deanery, 1970-74; dean Albuquerque Deanery, priest senator-at-large; mem. archdiocesan fin. com., 1976. Home and Office: 2150 Raymac Rd SW Albuquerque NM 87105

LABRIE, JEAN-PAUL, bishop, Roman Catholic Church. Titular bishop of Urci, aux. bishop, Quebec, 1977—. Office: 1073 rue St Cyrille Ouest Quebec PQ G1S 4R5 Canada*

LACHINA, VINCENT JOSEPH, minister, So. Bapt. Conv.; b. Memphis, July 3, 1945; s. Frank Joseph and Beverly (Aldridge) L.; A.B. in Religious Edn., Samford U., 1968; M.R.E., Southwestern Bapt. Theol. Sem., 1973; m. Carole Anne Caton, Jan. 26, 1974; 1 son, Joshua Caton. Ordained to ministry, 1973; minister for deaf, Gadsden, Ala., 1966-68; missionary journeyman Fgn. Mission Bd., So. Bapt. Conv., Nairobi, Kenya, 1970-72; minister of edn. and youth Shearer Hills Bapt. Ch., San Antonio, 1973-74; minister of youth 1st Bapt. Ch., Ardmore, Okla., 1974-75; design editor So. Bapt. Sunday Sch. Bd., Nashville, 1975—. Mem. Fellowship Christian Athletes, Conf. Editors Ch. Mags. for Children and Youth. Home: 5510 Country Dr 95 Nashville TN 37211 Office: 127 9th Ave N Nashville TN 37234

LACKEY, EDWIN KEITH, bishop, Anglican Church of Canada; b. Ottawa, Ont., Can. June 10, 1930; s. Elmer Vaughan and Marguerite Hannah (Hawes) L.; m. Judith Helen Doak, Sept. 11, 1954; children: Peter James, Janet Mary, John Andrew, Antony Stephen Cyprian. B.A. in Theology, Bishop's U., 1953. Ordained to ministry Anglican Ch. of Can. as deacon 1953, priest, 1954. Asst. curate of Cornwall, 1953-55; incumbent of Russell, 1955-60, Vankleek Hill, 1960-63; rector of St. Michael and All Angels Ch., Ottawa, 1963-71; dep. dir. program Diocese of Ottawa, 1971-73, dir. of program, 1973-78; hon. canon, 1973-78, archdeacon of Diocese, 1978-81, bishop of Diocese, 1981—.

LACROIX, FERNAND, bishop, Roman Cath. Ch.; b. Quebec City, Que., Can., Oct. 16, 1919; s. Jean-Charles and Cécile x (Doré) L.; B.A., Coll. de Bathurst, N.B., 1941; J.C.L., U. Angelicum, Rome, 1949. Ordained priest, 1946; consecrated bishop, 1970; dir. House of Studies for Eudists, Rome, 1950-53; prof. canon law Holy Heart Sem., Halifax, N.S., 1953-61; superior Eudist Sem., Limbour, Que., 1961-66; superior gen. of Eudists, Rome, 1966-70; bishop of Edmunston (N.B., Can.), 1970—. Home and office: Centre diocésain Edmundston NB E3V 3K1 Canada

LACY, CLEOPATRICK, minister, Progressive National Convention and American Baptist Churches, U.S.A.; b. Bladenboro, N.C., Mar. 10, 1950; s. Benjamin and Annie Julia (Ruffin) L.; m. Portia Denise Hewlett, Dec. 29, 1973; children: Patrice Nicole, Patrick Benjamin Willis. B.A., Shaw U., 1972; M.Div., Morehouse Sch. Religion, 1975. Ordained to ministry Lumber River Assn., 1968. Student minister Friendship Bapt. Ch., Atlanta, 1973-74; interim pastor Ben Hill Presbyterian Ch., Atlanta, 1974-75; co-pastor Wheeler Ave. Bapt. Ch., Houston, 1975-77; pastor Mt. Zion Bapt. Ch., Griffin, Ga., 1977—; mem. bd. edn. and publ. Progressive National Bapt. Conv., Inc., 1983-85; bd. dirs. New Era Congress Christian Edn., State of Ga., 1984—; pres. Cabin Creek Christian Edn. Atlanta, 1984—. Editor: The Informed and Growing Trustee, 1984, Holding Up Arms of Pastor, 1983, When We Pray, 1983. Pres. Citizens Improvement League, Griffin, 1979; bd. dirs. Griffin Voter Edn. Project, 1984—. Recipient Outstanding Leadership award Ft. Valley Griffin Alumni chapt., 1980; named to Outstanding Young Men in Am. U.S. Jaycees, 1977, 79. Mem. Griffin Spalding Ministerial Assn. (Minister of Yr. award 1979); Alpha Phi Alpha. Democrat. Home: 123 S 4th St Griffin GA 30223 Office: Mt Zion Bapt Ch 321 E Taylor St Griffin GA 30223

LACY, CREIGHTON BOUTELLE, educator, minister, United Meth. Ch.; b. Kuling, Kiangsi, China, May 31, 1919; s. George Carleton and Harriet Lang (Boutelle) L.; A.B., Swarthmore Coll., 1941; B.D., Yale, 1944, Ph.D., 1953; m. Frances McGuire Thompson, June 20, 1944; 1 dau., Linda Marie. Ordained elder, 1948; pastor chs., New Haven, 1944-46, Waterbury, Conn., 1951-53; missionary to China, United Meth. Bd. missions 1946-51; prof., Duke Div. Sch., 1953—, assoc. dean, 1975-80. Danforth vis. prof. philosophy Internat. Christian U. Tokyo, 1973-74. Fulbright grantee, 1966-67. Mem. Assn. Profs. Missions (pres. 1964-66), Am. Soc. Missiology, Soc. Values in Higher Edn., Phi Beta Kappa, Phi Tau Phi. Author: Is China a Democracy?, 1943; The Conscience of India, 1965; Frank Mason North, 1967; Indian Insights, 1972; Coming Home-to China, 1978. Office: Duke Divinity School Durham NC 27706

LADE, CHARLES WILLIAM, minister, Lutheran Church-Missouri Synod; b. Oxford, Nebr., Dec. 17, 1941; s. Alvin Richard and Florence (Brestel) L.; m. Charmaine Pamela Adams, Dec. 29, 1966; children: Rebecca Ann, Jennifer Louise. B.A., Concordia Sr. Coll.-Ft. Wayne, Ind., 1964; M.Div., Concordia Sem.-St. Louis, 1968. Ordained to ministry Lutheran Church-Missouri Synod. Minister, St. John's Luth. Ch., Britton, S.D., 1968-71, Reynolds, Ind., 1971-73, Zion/First English Luth. Ch., White/Aurora, S.D., 1973-77, St. John's/St. Paul's Luth. Ch., Aberdeen, S.D., 1977-80, St. John Luth. Ch., Sherwood, Ohio, 1980—; Luth. Ch.-Mo. Synod rep. to campus ministry S.D. State U., Brookings, 1974-77; N.W. cir. conf. pres., Sherwood, 1981-82, zone counselor, 1982-84. Pres., White Community Devel. Corp., S.D., 1976-77; scoutmaster Boy Scouts Am., White, 1976-77; EMT/vol. fire fighter, 1976-77. Democrat. Address: Route 1 Sherwood OH 43556

LADERER, JOHN EDWARD, minister, Presbyterian Church in the U.S.A. B. Columbus, Ohio, Jan. 11, 1941; s. Frank Edward and Anna Belle (Schrock) L.; m. Patricia Mae Pancoast, June 8, 1968; children: Lisa Mae, James Pancoast. B.A. in Psychology, Park Coll., 1965; M.Div., Louisville Presbyn. Sem., 1977; Ph.D., Oxford Grad. Sch., Dayton, Tenn., 1984. Ordained to ministry, Presbyn. Ch. in the U.S.A., 1978. Youth dir. Calvin Presbyn. Ch., Louisville, 1975-76; student pastor Henryville Presbyn. Ch., Henryville, Ind., 1976-77; minister Bell Larger Parish, Wren, Miss., 1977-78, First Presbyn. Ch., Spring City, Tenn., 1978—; moderator Presbytery of Union, 1982-83; chmn. Gen. Council of Union, Knoxville, Tenn., 1983-84; mem. reunion com., 1984—; dir., treas. North Rhea County Cooperative Ministries Assn. Pantry Program, Spring City, Tenn., 1982—. Scholar, Oxford Grad. Sch., Dayton, Tenn., 1984. Lodge: Kiwanis (bd. dirs. Spring City 1981-84). Home and Office: Box 455 Spring City TX 37381-0455

LAGHI, PIO See Who's Who in America, 43rd edition.

LAGRAND, JAMES, minister, Christian Reformed Church in North America; b. Grand Rapids, Mich., Apr. 24, 1941; came to Can., 1977; s. James and Katherine (Tornga) LaG.; m. Virginia Ann Vandermeer, June 5, 1963; children: David Martin, John Patrick, Paul Damien, Peter Lambert. A.B., Calvin Coll. and Theol. Sch., 1962, postgrad., 1968-69, Th.M., 1976; postgrad. U. Mich., 1962-63, A.M., 1968; B.D., Yale U., 1968; diploma in Urban Theology, Sheffield U., Eng., 1975. Missionary tchr. St. Paul's Coll., Zaria, Nigeria, 1963-65; pastor Garfield Christian Reformed Ch., Chgo., 1969-74; ecumenical scholar Brit. Council Chs., Sheffield, 1974-75; pastor All Nations Christian Reformed Ch., Halifax, N.S., Can., 1977—; mem. Latin Am. Com., Christian Reformed World Missions Bd., Grand Rapids, 1982—; chmn. Faith and Order Commn., Halifax, 1979—; del. Classis Eastern Can., 1977—; trustee Can. Bible Soc. Dist. Bd., Halifax, 1981-84. Critic book revs.; author jour. articles. Community organizer East Garfield, Chgo., 1969-74. Ecumenical scholar, Brit. Council Chs., Sheffield, 1974; Centennial Missions scholar Christian Reformed Ch., 1975; Tyndale fellow for bibl. research, Cambridge, Eng., 1976. Mem. Soc. Bibl. Lit., Am. Ch. History Soc., Calvin Alumni Assn. (pres. 1980-82). Home: 1010 Lucknow St Halifax NS B3H 2T4 Canada Office: All Nations Christian Reformed Ch 5651 Inglis St Halifax NS B3H 1K2 Canada

LAI, WHALEN WAI-LUN, religious educator; b. Canton, China, July 8, 1944; came to U.S., 1968; s. Koon-chee and Kit-ming (Tsui) L.; m. Esther Chi-Ning Wan, May 15, 1971. B.A., Internat. Christian U., Tokyo, 1968; postgrad., U. Calif.-Berkeley, 1968, Vrije U., Amsterdam, 1969; Ph.D., Harvard U., 1975. Assoc. prof. U. Calif.-Davis, 1977—. Editor: (with Lancaster) Early Ch'an in China and Tibet, 1983. Contbr. articles to various jours. United Bd. Xian Higher Edn. scholar, 1964-68; fellow: Harvard, Yenching, Kent Univs., 1969-74. Mem. Soc. Study Chinese Religions (exec. com. 1982—), Harvard Ctr. Study World Religions. Office: 912 Sproul Hall U Calif Davis CA 95616

LAIRD, DAVID CHARLES, JR., minister, So. Bapt. Conv.; b. McComb, Miss., Oct. 27, 1953; s. David Charles and Katherin (Simmons) L.; B.A., Ouachita Bapt. U., 1976. Ordained to ministry, 1973; pastor Boughton Bapt. Ch., Prescott, Ark., 1973-75; youth dir., asso. pastor Harmony Bapt. Ch., Baton Rouge, 1975—. Mem. Seminarians mens choir New Orleans Bapt. Sem. Home: 7388 Prescott Rd Baton Rouge LA 70801

LAKEY, OTHAL H. Bishop, Christian Methodist Episcopal Church (Second Dist.), chair Gen. Bd. Christian Edn. Office: 6322 Elwynne Dr Cincinnati OH 45236*

LALLY, FRANCIS JOSEPH, priest, Roman Cath. Ch.; b. Swampscott, Mass., June 11, 1918; s. Frank and Catherine (Farragher) L.; A.B., Boston Coll., 1940; L.Sci. Soc., Laval U., Quebec, Can., 1948; LL.D., Stonehill Coll., 1958, Marquette U., 1960, Manhattan Coll., 1961, Boston Coll., 1962; D.D. (hon.), Northeastern U., 1966; D.H.L. Rivier Coll., 1969. Ordained priest, 1944; asso. pastor ch., Wellesley, Mass., 1944-46; editor Pilot (ofcl. organ Archdiocese

Boston), 1952-72; pastor Sacred Heart Parish, Roslindale, Mass., 1971-75. Chaplain to His Holiness, 1952; prelate of Honor to His Holiness, 1959; spiritual dir. League Cath. Women, Boston Archdiocese, 1961-75; sec. dept. social devel. and world peace U.S. Cath. Conf., Washington, 1975-84. Chmn., Boston Redevel. Authority, 1961-70; mem. Boston Com. on Fgn. Relations, 1953—, Com. for Permanent Charity Fund, Boston, 1970-86. Bd. dirs. Retina Found., Boston, Fund for the Republic, Archbishop's Stewardship Appeal, 1971-75; trustee St. Elizabeth's Hosp., Civic Edn. Found., Boston, Tufts U., Medford, Mass., Boston Athenaeum, Edn. Devel. Center, Newton, Mass.; vis. com. Harvard-Radcliffe. Fellow Am. Acad. Arts and Scis.; mem. Mass. Hist. Soc. Author: The Catholic Church in a Changing America, 1962. Home: 75 Union Park St Boston MA 02118 Office: Cathedral of Holy Cross Boston MA

LALLY, MARTIN, JOSEPH, JR., priest, Roman Catholic Church. B. Denver, Dec. 10, 1949; s. Martin Joseph and Margaret Ann (Lovelace) L. B.A., St. Thomas Sem., 1974, M.A., 1976, M.Div., 1978. Ordained priest Roman Catholic Ch., 1978; co-mem. Sisters of Loretto, 1982—. Asst. pastor Presentation Ch., Denver, 1978-80, St. Catherine Ch., Denver, 1980-81; pastor Cure d'Ars Ch., Denver, 1981—; field edn. supr. St. Thomas Sem., Denver, 1978—; regional coordinator Teens Encounter Christ, Denver, 1980—; mem. Denver Cath. Community Services Bd., Bldg. Commn. Archdiocese of Denver, 1983—. Mem. Gove Community Sch. Bd., Denver, 1981; bds. dirs. East Denver YMCA, 19—. Mem. Denver Priests' Council (v.p. 1979-80), Nat. Conf. Cath. Charities. Democrat. Home: 3075 Dahlia St Denver CO 80207 Office: Cure d'Ars Ch 3050 Dahlia St Denver CO 80207

LAMAR, PHILLIP, minister, United Ch. of Christ; b. Kenosha, Wis., July 29, 1936; s. George Clinton and Ena (Roe) L.; A.A., Santa Ana Jr. Coll., 1960; B.A., Chapman Coll., 1962; S.T.B., Boston U., 1966; postgrad. San Francisco Theol. Sem.; m. Carolyn Sue Medearis, Sept. 9, 1969; children—Douglas, Steven, David, Daniel, Denyse. Ordained to ministry, 1968; youth adviser Meth. Ch., Orange, Calif., 1958-62; asso. pastor Whitinsville (Mass.) Community Ch., 1963-64; pastor Ponkapoag Christian Chapel, Canton, Mass., 1964-66; asso. pastor Meth. Ch., San Luis Obispo, Calif., 1966-69, Country Club United Ch. of Christ, Kansas City, Mo., 1970-71, St. John's United Ch. of Christ, Granite City, Ill., 1971-72; pastor 1st Congl. United Ch. of Christ, Rock Falls, Ill., 1972-76, Trinity United Ch. of Christ, Newton, Kans., 1976—. Chaplain, Community Gen. Hosp., Sterling, Ill.; chaplain to nusing homes. Mem. San Luis Obispo Human Relations Comm., 1968-69; mem. Sterling/Rock Falls Drug Abuse Council, 1972-76; mem. adv. bd. Whiteside County Vocational Bd., Sterling, 1973-76. Recipient Wrangler award United Fund, 1975. Mem. No. Assn. United Ch. of Christ, Sterling Rock Falls Mission Council, Sterling Rock Falls Ministerial Assn., Hosp. Chaplains Assn. Contbr. articles to Power Mag., These Days. Home: 409 Rolling Hills Dr Newton KS 67114 Office: 210 E 4th St Newton KS 67114

LAMB, CHARLES F., minister, Christian Church (Disciples of Christ); b. Maryville, Tenn., Dec. 18, 1934; s. C. Fred and Sadie Ellen (Tedder) L.; m. Betty Jane Simmerman, Dec. 29, 1979; children by previous marriage: Elizabeth Susan, Linda Louise, Jennifer Janet. B.A., Maryville Coll., 1956; M.Div., Grad. Sem. of Phillips U., 1961. Ordained to ministry Christian Ch., 1961. Pastor East Aurora Christian Ch., N.Y., 1961-71; assoc. regional minister Christian Ch. (Disciples of Christ), Northeastern Region, Buffalo, 1971-75, regional minister, 1975—; mem. orgns. clergy and councils of chs. Trustee Village of East Aurora, 1968-73; active environ. groups, Conf. Mayors and Village Ofcls. N.Y., 1968-73. Mem. Conf. Regional Ministers and Moderators. Democrat. Club: Kiwanis. Address: 1272 Delaware Ave Buffalo NY 14209

LAMBERT, DONALD WEST, minister, American Baptist Churches in the U.S.A.; b. Danville, Ind., July 14, 1935; s. Harry Oscar and Geneva Jeanette (West) L.; m. Frances Ann Edgar, Aug. 26, 1955; children: Douglas E., Dennis G., Donna L. B.A., Franklin Coll., 1957; M.Div., So. Bapt. Theol. Sem., 1960; D.Min., San Francisco Theol. Sem., 1975. Ordained to ministry American Baptist Churches in the U.S.A., 1960. Minister, Am. Bapt. Ch., Ft. Collins, Colo., 1972-85; bd. dirs. United Campus Ministries, Ft. Collins, 1972-84; election dist. rep. Am. Bapt. Chs. in U.S.A., 1980-83, mem. gen. bd. exec. com., 1980-83; pres. Am. Bapt. Chs. of Rocky Mountains, 1981-83. Mem. Ft. Collins Human Relations Commn., 1976; bd. dirs. Ret. Sr. Vols. Program, Ft. Collins, 1976-78; mem. No. Colo. Employment Bur., Ft. Collins, 1975; bd. dirs. Commn. for Handicapped Persons, Ft. Collins, 1976-78. Recipient Ch. of Yr. award Ind. Bapt. Conv., 1964, 68, 72. Mem. Colo. Ministers Council Am. Bapt. Chs., Univ. Religious Dirs. Assn. (mem. bd. Ft. Collins 1972-84), Interfaith (mem. exec. com. Ft. Collins 1983-84). Democrat. Home: 1216 W Prospect St Fort Collins CO 80526 Office: American Baptist Church 600 S Shields St Fort Collins CO 80521

LAMBERT, E. ALEXANDER, minister, American Baptist Churches in the U.S.A.; b. Seattle, Sept. 5, 1927; s. Earl M. and Grace May (Skaggs) L.; m. Edith Hilma Lovegrenn, June 10, 1949; children: Mark A., Faith M., Johathan D., Charity S. B.A., Bethel Coll., 1950; M. Religious Edn., Central Bapt. Theol. Sem., 1953; D.D. (hon.), Judson Coll., 1980. Ordained to ministry, Am. Bapt. Chs. in U.S.A., 1953. Pastor Immanuel Bapt. Ch., Minot, N.D., 1954-59; sr. pastor North Bapt. Ch., Topeka, Kans., 1959-63, First Bapt. Ch. Overland Park, Kans., 1963-70, First Baptist Ch., Bellflower, Calif., 1970-78; minister of missions Am. Bapt. Chs., Pacific Southwest, Covina, Calif., 1978-84; sr. minister Judson Bapt. Ch., San Bernardino, Calif., 1984—; held 16 elective positions in Am. Bapt. Chs. and ecumenical orgns. Served with USCG, 1945-47, PTO. Recipient Community Service award Cerritos Coll., 1974. Mem. So. Calif. Ministers Council, Am. Bapt. Ch. Ministers Council. Republican. Office: Judson Baptist Church 1406 E Pacific San Bernardino CA 92404

LAMBERT, LLOYD LAVERNE, minister, administrator Christian organization, Church of God (Anderson, Ind.); b. Augusta, Ill., June 5, 1925; s. Charles N. and Lena (Johnson) L.; m. Dorothy Mae Spaar, June 22, 1946; children: Rebecca, Toby, Michael, Corey. Student Millikin U.; grad. Anderson Coll. Theol. Sem. Ordained to ministry Church of God (Anderson, Ind.), 1955. Founder, exec. dir. The Christian Ctr., Anderson, 1956—; past chmn. Nursing Home Ministries; chaplain Madison County Police Dept. Chmn. Human Relations commn., City of Anderson, 1981-84; mem. drug abuse adv. bd. St. John's Hosp.; Madison County Services Council; dep. sheriff Madison County Sheriff's Dept., Friend of the Ct., Anderson City Ct.; support worker telephone contact service. Internat. Paul Harris fellow Rotary Internat., 1983, Outstanding Citizenship award Ind. Elks, 1973-74; Liberty Bell award ABA, 1973; Community Image award Rotary Internat., 1973, 80, Service to Mankind award Sertoma Club, 1980; Service Recognition award Ind. Dept. Corrections, 1972; Service Recognition award Exchange Club, 1971; Spl. Recognition award ARC, 1965. Mem. Anderson Ministerial Assn., Internat. Union of Gospel Missions (past pres. mid-western dist.). Lodge: Rotary (pres. 1975-76). Home: 6914 Jackson St Anderson IN 46013 Office: The Christian Ctr 625 Main St PO Box 743 Anderson IN 46015

LAMM, MAURICE rabbi, Orthodox Jewish; b. Bronx, N.Y., Mar. 20, 1930; s. Samuel and Pearl (Baumol) L.; m. Shirley Friedman, June 7, 1955; children: David Jay, Judith Lynne, Dodi Lee. B.A., Yeshiva Coll., 1951; M.A., Yeshiva U., 1961, D.D., 1982. Ordained rabbi, 1954. Sr. rabbi Hebrew Inst. University Heights, N.Y.C., 1965-72; field dir. Commn. Jewish Chaplaincy, Jewish Welfare Bd., N.Y.C., 1969-72; sr. rabbi Beth Jacob Congregation, Beverly Hills, Calif., 1972—; lectr. Stern Coll. for Women, N.Y.C., 1970-72; prof. Yeshiva U., N.Y.C., 1985—; pres. Bd. Rabbis So. Calif., Los Angeles, 1976-78; v.p. Rabbinical Council Am., 1978-80, 81-83; founder, chmn. Jewish Hospice Commn., Los Angeles, 1982—. Author: Jewish Way in Death and Mourning, 1969; Love and Marriage, 1981. Mem. editorial bd. Tradition, Jewish Digest, 1969—. Founder, Bet Zedek Legal Assn. for the Poor, 1976, Jewish TV Network, 1978. Recipient Weinberg award Jewish Fedn. Council, Los Angeles, 1984. Mem. Commn. for Bio-Med. Ethics. Office: Beth Jacob Congregation 9030 Olympic Blvd Beverly Hills CA 90211

LAMM, NORMAN, rabbi, educator, author, Jewish religion; b. Bklyn., Dec. 19, 1927; s. Samuel and Pearl (Baumol) L.; B.A. summa cum laude, Yeshiva Coll., 1949, Ph.D., 1966; m. Mindella Mehler, Feb. 23, 1954; children—Chaye, Joshua B., Shalom E., Sara Rebecca. Rabbi, 1951; rabbinic asst. Congregation Kehilath Jeshurun, N.Y.C., 1951-52; rabbi West Side Jewish Center, N.Y.C., 1952-53; Congregation Kodimoh, Springfield, Mass., 1954-59, Jewish Center, N.Y.C., 1959—; Jakob and Erna Michael prof. Jewish philosophy Yeshiva U., N.Y.C., 1961—, pres., 1976—; vis. prof. Judaic studies Bklyn. Coll., 1974-75. Chmn., N.Y. Conf. on Soviet Jewry, 1970. Trustee Rabbi Isaac Elchanan Theol. Sem., Am. Zionist Youth Found. Recipient Abramowitz Zeitlin Found. award, 1972. Mem. Assn. Orthodox Jewish Scientists. Author: A Hedge of Roses, 1966; The Royal Reach, 1970; Faith and Doubt, 1971; Torah Lishmah, 1972; The Good Society, 1974. Editor: The Leo Jung Jubilee Volume, 1962; A Treasury of Tradition, 1967. Office: Yeshiva U 500 W 185th St New York NY 10033*

LANCASTER, HERMAN JACOB, minister, So. Baptist Conv.; b. Cairo, Ga., Nov. 25, 1920; s. Gilbert and Mamie Z. (Robinson) L.; B.S., Ga. State Coll., 1941; B.Th., Selma (Ala.) U., 1959, D.D., 1972; Th.D., Tex. Theol. U., 1961; m. Emma Quarker, Dec. 29, 1957; children—Jacquelyn, Frederick, Hermastine. Ordained to ministry, 1956; pastor chs. in Ala., 1956—, Hartsville Bapt. Ch., 1966-67, Second St. Siloam Bapt. Ch., Brewton, 1967—. Vice moderator Evergreen Bapt. Assn., 1969—; trustee Selma U. Pres. Escambia County Democratic Conf., 1972; 1st v.p. Ala. chpt. NAACP, 1969, pres. Brewton br., 1968. Home: 126 N East St Brewton AL 36426 Office: PO Box 323 Brewton AL 36426

LANCASTER, JAMES WAYNE, evangelist, missionary, Gen. Assn. Regular Bapt. Chs.; b. Kalamazoo, Feb. 17, 1936; s. Lindon Wade and Maida Irene (Hopkins) L.; student Moody Bible Inst., 1954-55; B.A., Trinity Coll., Dunedin, Fla., 1958, D.Sacred Music (hon.), 1967; postgrad. Western Mich. U., summers 1956-57; m. Irma F. Sanabia, Aug. 31, 1957; children—James Wayne, Valerie Sue, Mark Stephen. Ordained to ministry, 1960; dir. Youth for Christ Internat., Kalamazoo and Grand Rapids, Mich., 1958-63; asso. pastor Seminole Heights Bapt. Ch., Tampa, Fla., 1964, Palm Ave. Bapt. Ch., Tampa, 1965; evangelist, missionary statesman, founder, dir. His Glory, Inc., Tampa, 1967—; pastor Carol Estates Bapt. Ch., Gainesville, Fla., 1983—. Dir. Mission Discoveries, 1969—; Nat. High Sch. Assembly speaker, 1969-71; founder Youth Involvement, service and work mission, 1969—; pres. Santa Fe River Bapt. Ministerial Assn., 1984-85; preaching trips to Nigeria, Brazil, Can., Guatemala, Jamaica, Trinidad and Tobago, Haiti, India. Bd. dirs. New Horizons for Youth, Grand Rapids, 1974—. Recipient commendation Gov. S. Korea, 1974. Daily gospel broadcaster His Glory Hour, 1973—; composer book Choir Hymn Arrangements, 1967; rec. artist, 1965—. Home and office: 2818 Springdell Circle Valrico FL 33594

LANCASTER, PARK EUGENE, minister, Conservative Baptist Assn. Am.; b. Somerfield, Pa., May 31, 1936; s. Park Wilbur and Dorothy Irene (Moyers) L.; diploma Moody Bible Inst., 1957; B.A., No. Bapt. Coll., 1959, Th.B., 1961; m. Nancy Jo Doolen, Aug. 22, 1959; children—Kimberly Sue, Pamela Joy, Kevin Eugene, Paula Ann, Kerry Park. Ordained to ministry, 1962; pastor N. Baptist Ch., Flint, Mich., 1973—; cons. Christian edn. Gospel Light Publs., Glendale, Calif., 1971-76. Mem. reference bd. Flint Area Family Radio, 1973-76; pres. Flint Area Moody Alumni Fellowship, 1973-75. Active parent-tchr. orgns. Home: 1408 Ox Yoke Dr Flint MI 48504 Office: 2001 N Saginaw St Flint MI 48505

LAND, RICHARD DALE, minister, educator, So. Bapt. Conv.; b. Houston, Nov. 6, 1946; s. Leggette and Marylee Ethel (Welch) L.; A.B. magna cum laude, Princeton U., 1969; Th.M., New Orleans Bapt. Theol. Sem., 1972; postgrad. Oxford U., 1972—; m. Rebekah Ruth Van Hooser, May 29, 1971; 1 dau., Jennifer. Ordained to ministry, 1969; asst. pastor Bethany Bapt. Ch., New Orleans, 1969-70; pastor Vieux Carre Bapt. Ch., New Orleans, 1970-72; pastor S. Oxford (Eng.) Bapt. Ch., 1972-75; academic dean Criswell Center for Bibl. Studies, Dallas, 1975—; asso. pastor 1st Bapt. Ch., Dallas, 1975—; vis. prof. ch. history Southwestern Bapt. Theol. Sem., Fort Worth, 1976. Dist. conv. del. Dallas County Republican Party, 1976. Mem. Conf. Faith and History, Am. Soc. Ch. History, Brit., So. Bapt. hist. socs. Contbr. to religious publs. Home: 10808 Apt 2123 Audelia St Dallas TX 75238 Office: 525 N Ervay St Dallas TX 75201

LANDAU, SOL, rabbi; b. Berlin, Germany, June 21, 1920; s. Ezekiel and Helene (Grynberg) L.; came to U.S., 1940, naturalized, 1942; B.A., Bklyn. Coll., 1949; M.H.L., Rabbi, Jewish Theol. Sem. of Am., 1951, D.D., 1977; M.A., N.Y. U., 1958; Ph.D., Fla. State U., 1975; m. Gabriela Mayer, Jan. 14, 1951; children: Ezra M., Tamara A. Rabbi, 1951; rabbi Whitestone Hebrew Centre, Whitestone, N.Y., 1952-56; co-rabbi Park Synagogue, Cleveland Heights, Ohio, 1956-60, 63-65; rabbi Beth Hillel, Wilmette, Ill., 1960-63, Beth David, Miami, Fla., 1965—; adj. prof. Fla. Internat. U., 1974—; lectr. Miami-Dade County Coll., 1975; adj. prof. U. Miami, 1980-85. Chmn. Dade County Youth Adv. Bd., 1970-71; pres. Dade County Mental Health Assn., 1971-73. Bd. overseers Dropsie U., Phila. Recipient Jerusalem Liberation award State of Israel Bonds, 1968, Community Rabbinical award, 1976. Fellow Jewish Acad. Sci.; mem. Greater Miami Rabbinical Assn. (pres. 1970-71), Am. Am. Assn. of Adult Edn., AAUP. Author: Christian-Jewish Relations, 1958; Judaism and the Personal Life, 1960; Bridging Two Worlds, 1969. Home: 3 Grove Isle Dr Miami FL 33133 Office: 9200 S Dadeland St Miami FL 33156

LANDES, MORRIS ALEX, rabbi, Jewish Orthodox Church; b. Vashilishok, Vilna, Russia, Oct. 28, 1917; came to U.S., 1920; s. Henry A. and Henna Hiya (Nyman) L.; m. Naomi Borkon, Mar. 4, 1945; children: Nina Ann, Sharon Fredelle, Marc Aaron. B.A. magna cum laude, Yeshiva U., 1939; Ph.D., U. Pitts., 1954. Ordained rabbi, 1941. Rabbi, Cong. Ahavath Shalom, Lynn, Mass., 1941-43, Cong. Radef Shalom, Johnstown, Pa., 1943-45, Cong. Degel Israel, Lancaster, Pa., 1945-48, Cong. Adath Jeshurum, Pitts., 1948—, Cong. Cheseth Israel, Pitts., 1978—; chaplain Pa. State Correctional Instn., Pitts., 1971—; mem. nat. adminstrv. com. Am. Jewish Congress, N.Y.C., 1952, pres. Pitts. chpt., 1950-52; pres. Western Pa. Zionist Region, 1954-56, Tri-State Zionist Region, 1961-63, Pitts. Zionist Council, 1955-66, Pitts. Zionist Dist., 1959-61; chmn. synogogue Council for Israel Bonds, 1965-80; founding pres. Pitts. Zionist Fedn., 1970-72. Book rev. editor Horizon mag., 1950-52. Author: Trends in American Jewish Thought, 1954. Recipient Herzl Anniversary award Zionist Orgn. Am., 1954; Man of Year award Pitts. Zionist Dist. and Pitts. Israel Bond Orgn., 1961; Leadership award Tri-State Zionist

Region, 1963, Justice Brandeis award, 1971; Service award Israel Bond Orgn., 1973; Israel Service award Pitts. Zionist Dist., 1974; Service award United Bessarabians, 1974; Rabbi Ashinsky award, Hebrew Inst. Pitts., 1976. Mem. Zionist Orgn. Am. (nat. v.p. 1970-77, judge of ct. of honor 1980—), Rabbinical Council Am. (v.p. 1956-58), Rabbinical Alumni of Yeshiva U. (past v.p.). Lodge: B'nai B'rith (chmn. adult edn. 1950-52). Home: 5520 Wellesley Ave Pittsburgh PA 15206 Office: Cong Adath Jeshurum 5643 E Liberty Blvd Pittsburgh PA 15206

LANDON, JOHN WILLIAM, minister, educator, United Methodist Church; b. Marlette, Mich., Mar. 24, 1937; s. Norman A. and Merle (Lawrason) L.; B.A. in Sociology, Taylor U., 1959; M.Div., Christian Theol. Sem. and Northwestern U., 1962; M.S.W., Ind. U., 1966; Ph.D., Ball State U., 1972. Ordained to ministry, 1962; pastor chs. in Iowa, 1962-64; pastor Victory Chapel Community Ch., Noblesville, Ind., 1964-66, 67—. Adj. prof. Lexington (Ky.) Theol. Sem., 1974—, Ashbury Theol. Sem., 1980—; organist various chs. in Ind. Chmn. dept. sociology and social work Marion (Ind.) Coll., 1967-69; asst. prof. sociology and social work Ball State U., Municie, Ind., 1969-71; asso. prof., coordinator undergrad. program in social work U. Ky., Lexington, 1971—. Mem. Am. Theatre Organ Soc., Am. Guild Organists, AAUP, Am. Sociol. Assn., Nat. Assn. Social Workers, Nat. Assn. Christians in Social Work. Author: From these Men, 1966; Jesse Crawford-Poet of the Organ, 1974; The History of the Theatre Pipe Organ, 1983; The Development of Social Welfare, 1984. Home: 809 Celia Ln Lexington KY 40504 Office: Coll Social Professions U Ky Lexington KY 40506

LANDRIAULT, JACQUES, bishop, Roman Catholic Church; b. Alfred, Ont., Can., Sept. 23, 1921; s. Amedee and Marie-Louise (Brisebois) L.; B.A., U. Ottawa; Licence on Theology, St. Paul U. Sem., Ottawa. Ordained priest Roman Cath. Ch., 1947; curate in Noranda, Que.; chancellor Diocese Timmins, Ont., 1953; bishop of Cadi, aux. to bishop of Alexandria, Ont., 1962-64; bishop of Hearst, Ont., 1964-71, of Timmins, 1971—; provincial chaplain Cath. Boy Scouts Assn. Ont. Mem. Cath. Conf. Ont. Address: 65 Ave Jubilee est Timmons ON P4N 5W4 Canada

LANDRY, MARY LOUISE, nun, Roman Catholic Church; registered pharmacist. b. Old Town, Maine, Aug. 17, 1911; d. Herbert Albert and Caroline (Tardif) Landry. B.S. in Pharmacy, Fordham Coll., 1945; B.A. in French, St. Joseph's Coll., North Windham, Maine, 1951. Joined Sisters of Mercy, Roman Cath. Ch., 1929. Elem. tchr. parochial schs., Portland, Maine, 1929-42; chief pharmacist Mercy Hosp., Portland, 1945-68, instr. pharmacology Mercy Hosp. Sch. Nursing, 1950-68, asst. adminstr. Mercy Hosp., 1968-76; mem. gen. council Sisters of Mercy, Portland, 1968-74; rep. Sisters of Mercy, Portland West Ch. Alliance, 1965-76; mem. parish council St. Mary's Ch., Eagle Lake, Maine, 1976—, chmn. worship and spiritual commn., 1976—, lectr., eucharistic minister, 1976—. Chief pharmacist, mgr. Eagle Lake Pharmacy, Maine, 1976—. Author: Landry Family Tree, 1978. Trustee St. Joseph's Coll., North Windham, Maine, Blind Resource Children's Ctr. Bd., Healey Found. Fund. Mem. Maine Pharm. Assn. Democrat. Home: St Mary's Convent Church St Eagle Lake ME 04739

LANDSBERG, ULF FREDRIK, minister, American Lutheran Church; b. Sundsvall, Sweden, May 26, 1949; came to U.S., 1953; s. Ake Fredrik and Karin Nancy (Jansson) L.; m. Linda Louise Meacham, June 21, 1975; children: Filip Robson, Nils Fredrik. B.S. in Zoology, San Diego State U., 1972; M.Div., Luther Sem., 1976. Ordained to ministry American Lutheran Ch., 1976. Pastor, St. Stephen's Luth. Ch., Granada Hills, Calif., 1976-79, Mt. Calvary Luth. Ch., La Puente, Calif., 1979-81, Mt. Calvary-Faith Luth. Ch., La Puente, 1981—; del. nat. conv. Am. Luth. Ch., Moorhead, Minn., 1978; pres. San Gabriel Valley Luth. Social Services, Pasadena, Calif., 1982; dean East San Gabriel Valley Conf. Am. Luth. Ch., La Puente, 1983—. Mem. Transition Waste Mgmt. Commn., West Covina, Calif., 1984; bd. dirs. Delhaven Community Ctr., La Puente, 1984. Recipient Outstanding Civic Service award West Covina C. of C., 1983. Mem. East San Gabriel Valley Ministerial Assn., South Pacific Dist. Council Am. Luth. Ch. Democrat. Home: 1121 S Coronado Ave West Covina CA 91790 Office: Mt Calvary-Faith Luth Ch 14422 Francisquito La Puente CA 91746

LANDWEHR, ARTHUR JOHN, JR., minister, United Methodist Church; b. Northbrook, Ill., Mar. 8, 1934; s. Arthur John Sr. and Alice Eleanor (Borchardt) L.; m. Avonna Lee Mitchell Landwehr (Sept. 19, 1953); children: Arthur John III, Andrea Lea. B.A., Drake U., 1956; B.D., Carrett Theol. Sem., 1959; D.D., (hon.), North Central Coll., 1980. Ordained to ministry Methodist Ch. as elder, 1959. Minister, Commerce United Meth. Ch., Iowa, 1954-56, Lyndon Meth. Ch., Ill., 1956-59, Marseilles Meth. Ch., Ill., 1959-65, First Meth. Ch., Elmhurst, Ill., 1965-75; sr. minister First United Meth. Ch. of Evanston, Ill., 1975—; founder Ecumenical Insights, Marseilles, Ill. 1964; vice-chmn. acad. affairs, trustee Garrett Evang. Theol. Sem., Evanston, 1975—; mem. exec. com. Chgo. Conf. on Religion and Race, 1976-82; del. Consultation on Ch. Union, Lexington, Ky., 1981, Balt., 1985, World Council Chs., Vancouver, B.C., Can., 1983; keynote speaker Notre Dame Coll., 1982; mem. World Council Chs. visitation team to Sri Lanka, 1983. Author: In the Third Place, 1972. Contbr. articles and book revs. to religious publs. Charter mem. comprehensive planning commn. DuPage County, Ill., 1971. Recipient Recognition award for efforts in civil rights Trustees Lisle, Ill., 1969. Mem. AAAS, Am. Acad. Religion, Chgo. Council Fgn. Relations. Club: University (Evanston) (v.p. 1985). Home: 310 Church St Evanston IL 60201 Office: First United Meth Ch Evanston 1630 Hinman St Evanston IL 60201

LANE, JOHN HENRY, minister, American Baptist Churches in U.S.A.; b. Brookfield, Ga., Apr. 7, 1924; s. Theodore and Lou Ellen (Hill) L.; student Albany State Coll., Ga., 1941, San Francisco U., 1954, San Francisco State Coll., 1963, San Francisco Theol. Sem. Grad. Theol. Union, Berkeley, Calif., 1972; m. Donneter Elizabeth Dean, Feb. 14, 1959; children: DeEtta Patricia, Gwendolyn Tempie. Deacon, Cosmopolitan Bapt. Ch., 1959-70; ordained to ministry Am. Bapt. Chs. in U.S.A., 1972; pastor Grace Bapt. Ch., San Francisco, 1973—. Pres., Am. Bapt. Chs./West, 1965; Western area v.p. Am. Bapt. Conv./Home Mission Soc., 1971; pres. No. Calif. Ecumenical Council, 1971; pres. Calif. Ch. Council, No. Calif. Council for Ch. and Social Action, 1984; chaplain Nat. Civil Rights Assn., 1976. Pres., San Francisco Negro Hist. and Cultural Soc., 1965-66, 83; v.p. Ocean View, Merced Heights, Ingleside Neighborhood Orgn., 1966-67; chmn. Bayview-Hunters Point Coordinating Council, 1969-70, SSS Bd. 39, 1968-75; equal opportunity officer HUD, 1971—. Mem. Am. Personnel and Guidance Assn., Franklin Mint, Roger Williams Fellowship, NAACP, Ecumenical Inst., Bayview Hunters Point Ecumenical Fellowship (pres. 1976), Bapt. Ministers Conf., Assn. Fed. Investigators. Club: Calif. Commonwealth. Home: 92 Ashton Av San Francisco CA 94112 Office: 800 Innes Ave San Francisco CA 94124

LANE, STEPHEN SCOTT, minister, Lutheran Ch. - Missouri Synod; b. Evansville, Ind., Aug. 14, 1956; s. Ferman Frederick and Marjorie Elizabeth (Kuester) L.; B.A. in Psychology, Indiana U., 1979; M.Div., Concordia Theol. Sem., 1983. Ordained to ministry Lutheran Ch.-Missouri Synod, 1983. Pastor, St. Paul Luth. Ch., Hollandale, Minn., Christ the Redeemer Luth. Ch., Wells, Minn., 1983—. Home and Office: Box 205 Hollandale MN 56045

LANES, T. A., minister, General Baptist Conference. Ordained to ministry Gen. Bapt. Conf., 1940; sec. asso. Independent Assemblies of God Internat. Owner-founder radio sta. WLBK, DeKalb, Ill.; founder, pres. Calvary Bible Coll., Superior, Wis., 1956-59; dir. Harbor Lights Telecast, also Emphasis The Golden Years. Author several books; editor Herald of Faith, Evangelistic Herald, Herald of Pentecost, The Mantle. Address: 3840 5th Ave San Diego CA 92103

LANEY, JAMES THOMAS, minister, Methodist Church, religion educator; university president; b. Wilson, Ark., Dec. 24, 1927; s. Thomas Mann and Mary (Hughey) L.; m. Berta Joan Radford, Dec. 20, 1949; children: Berta Joan, James T., Arthur Radford, Mary Ruth Laney Reilly, Susan Elizabeth. B.A., Yale U., 1950, B.D., 1954, Ph.D., 1966; D.D. (hon.), Fla. So. Coll., 1977; L.H.D., Southwestern U., 1979; H.H.D. (hon.), Mercer U., 1980. Ordained to ministry Methodist Ch., 1955. Chaplain, Choate Sch., Wallingford, Conn., 1953-55; asst. lectr. Yale U. Div. Sch., 1954-55; pastor St. Paul Meth. Ch., Cin., 1955-58; sec. student Christian movement, prof. Yonsei U., Seoul, South Korea, 1959-64; asst. prof. Christian ethics Vanderbilt U. Div. Sch., Nashville, 1966-69; dean Candler Sch. Theology, Emory U., Atlanta, 1969-77, pres. univ., 1977—; vis. prof. Harvard U. Div. Sch., Cambridge, Mass., 1974; dir. Trust Co. of Ga. Author: (with J.M. Gustafson) On Being Responsible, 1968; also essays. Pres. Nashville Community Relations Council, 1968-69; bd. dirs. Fund for Theol. Edn., Christian Higher Edn. in Asia, Atlanta Symphony; chmn. overseers com. Harvard U. Div. Sch., 1980—. Served with AUS, 1946-48. Selected for Leadership award, Atlanta, 1970-71; recipient Disting. Alumnus award Yale U. Div. Sch., 1979; Kellogg Leadership in Higher Edn. award, 1983; D.C. Macintosh fellow, 1965-66. Fellow Soc. Religion in Higher Edn.; mem. Am. Soc. Christian Ethics, Atlanta C. of C. (bd. dirs.), Phi Beta Kappa, Omicron Delta Kappa. Office: Office of Pres Emory U Atlanta GA 30322*

LANEY, JOHN CARL, minister, educator, Conservative Baptist Association of America; b. Dublin, Ga., Apr. 18, 1948; s. Carl Eugene and Clyde Black (Chivers) L.; m. Nancy Sue Lilly, June 5, 1971; children: John, Elisabeth, Laura. B.S., U. Oreg., 1970; M.Div., Western Bapt. Sem., 1973, Th.M., 1974; Th.D., Dallas Theol. Sem., 1978. Ordained to ministry, 1975. Instr. Dallas Theol. Sem., 1975-76; assoc. prof. Western Conservative Bapt. Sem., Portland, Oreg., 1977—. Author: The Divorce Myth, 1981; (Bible commentary) First and Second Samuel, 1981, Ezra-Nehemiah, 1982; Marching Orders, 1983. Contbr. articles to religious publs. Recipient Warner award Writer of Yr. Warner Christian Writer's Conf., 1983. Mem. Evang. Theol. Soc. Republican. Home: 123 SE 63d St Portland OR 97215 Office: Western Conservative Bapt Sem 5511 SE Hawthorne Portland OR 97215

LANG, EMANUEL, minister, Holiness Ch. of God in Christ, Inc.; b. Newton, Miss., Mar. 21, 1940; s. Emanuel W. and Mattie L. (Lewis) L.; B.S., Alcorn A. and M. Coll., 1963; postgrad. Jackson State U., 1976—; m. Katherine Freeman, Oct. 17, 1971; 1 dau., Nea. Ordained to ministry, 1970; sec. fin., bd. regents Charles Harrison Bible Coll., Memphis, 1973—, dean of coll.; evangelist, dist. 1, Holiness Ch. of God, Jackson, Miss., sec. bd. elders, 1973—; pastor chs., Miss., 1975-76. Chmn., Miss. state youth dept. Holiness Ch. of God, Jackson, 1974—, pres. dist. youth dept., 1971—. Mem. Miss. Tchrs. Assn., NAACP. Address: 1546 Weeks St Jackson MS 39213

LANG, FRANCIS HAROVER, lay church worker, United Methodist Church; b. Manchester, Ohio, June 4, 1907; s. James Walter and Mary (Harover) L.; A.B., Ohio Wesleyan U., 1929; J.D., Ohio State U., 1932; m. Rachel Louise Boyce, Oct. 20, 1934; children: Mary Sue, Charles Boyce, James Richard. Trustee First United Methodist Ch., East Liverpool, Ohio, 1936-65, Sunday sch. supt., 1937-41, mem. ofcl. bd., 1934-68, mem. adminstrv. bd., 1968, del. to East Ohio Ann. Conf., 1964-84, mem. conf. planning com., 1972, 74-84, chmn. ann. conf. program com., 1973-74; lay del. to Gen. Confs., 1968, 70, 72, 76, Jurisdictional Confs., 1968, 72, 76, 80; mem. gen. bd. missions United Meth. Ch., 1968-72, mem. gen. bd. global ministries, 1972—; bd. dirs. United Meth. Devel. Fund, 1976-82. Lawyer East Liverpool, 1932—. Pres., chmn. First Fed. Savs. Loan Assn., East Liverpool, 1958-82. Active Boy Scouts Am. Recipient Silver Beaver award Boy Scouts Am., 1955, Silver Antelope award, 1960. Mem. East Liverpool C. of C. (pres. 1950-52), Ohio State Bar Assn., Am. Bar Assn., Sigma Phi Epsilon, Delta Theta Phi. Home: Highland Colony East Liverpool OH 43920 Office: 517 Broadway POB 103 East Liverpool OH 43920

LANG, JOVIAN PETER, priest, Roman Catholic; educator. b. Sioux City, Iowa, June 2, 1919; s. Peter and Margaret (Horvath) L. A.B., Our Lady of Angels Sem., Cleve., 1942; M.S. in Library Sci., Case Western Res. U., 1950, M.A., 1955. Ordained priest Roman Catholic Ch., 1946. Librarian, assoc. prof. Quincy Coll., Ill., 1947-55, 1960-71; asst. prof. St. Joseph Sem., Westmont, Ill., 1955-57; archivist, asst. prof. Provincialate, St. Louis, 1957-60; asst. prof. U. So. Fla., Tampa, 1971-74; mem. faculty St. Johns U., Jamaica, N.Y., 1974—, assoc. prof. library and info. sci., moderator conf. Library-Coll. Assocs., Jamaica, N.Y., 1976; presentor workshop Mary Coll., Bismarck, N.D., 1976, Library-College Assocs., Caldwell, N.J., 1978; chmn. Panel on Handicapped, Met. Cath. Coll. Librarians, Tarrytown, N.Y., 1980; dir. workshop on handicapped Cath. Library Assn., N.Y.C., 1981; chaplain Teams of Our Lady, Massapequa, N.Y., 1978—. Author: Guide for the Liturgy, 1958; Cath. Library Association Profiles, 1967; Ordo for the Celebration of Divine Office and the Mass, 1971; Your Search Key to Library of Congress Classification, 1979; editor Liturgy of Vatican, II (2 vols.), 1966; monthly Pray Together, 1970—; St. Joseph Missal Guide, 1975—; St. Joseph Guide for the Liturgy of the Hours, 1974—; St. Joseph Guide for Christian Prayer, 1975—; Reference Sources: A Systematic Approach, 1976; Reference Sources for Small and Medium-sized Libraries, 1984; contbr. numerous articles to various publs. Mem. Liturgical Commn. Sacred Heart Province (chmn. 1964-68), Pierian Press (mem. editorial bd. 1969—), Learning Today (mem. editorial bd. 1981—). Home: 45 Mayfair Rd New Hyde Park NY 11040 Office: Div Library and Info Sci St John's U Grand Central and Utopia Pkwys Jamaica NY 11499

LANG, MARCUS TITUS, minister, Lutheran Church-Missouri Synod; b. Omaha, Oct. 1, 1920; s. Victor Cornelius and Martha (Kathe) L.; m. Elaine Esther Franzmeier, Nov. 18, 1951; children: Marcus Paul, Deborah Louise, Diana Elaine, Cynthia Ann. B.A., Concordia Theol. Sem., St. Louis, 1941, M.Div., 1947; M.A., Washington U., St. Louis, 1945; postgrad. Heidelberg Universitat, Germany. Ordained to ministry Lutheran Church-Missouri Synod, 1945. Pastor, St. John's Luth. Ch., Fayetteville, Ark., 1945-51, Grace Luth. Ch., Denison-Sherman, Tex., 1954-56, Our Savior Luth. Ch., Abilene, Tex., 1956-60, St. James Luth. Ch., Lafayette, Ind., 1960-76, Messiah Luth. Ch., Grand Junction Luth. Ch., Grand Junction, Colo., 1976-81, Prince of Peace Luth. Ch., Grand Junction, 1981—; chmn. Continuation Com. (Informal Internat. Orthodox Movement), 1969-81; trustee Balance, Inc. Pub. Found., 1970—. Contbr. articles to mags. Served to 1st lt. USAF, 1951-53. Fulbright scholar Heidelberg Universitat, 1953-54. Home: 1708 Hall Ave Grand Junction CO 81501 Office: Prince of Peace Luth Ch 2510 Interstate 70 Grand Junction CO 81505

LANG, THOMAS MICHAEL, minister, Lutheran Church in America; b. Phila., Dec. 28, 1954; s. William Richard and Anna Doris (Forscht) L.; m. Susan Marie Cook, May 30, 1981. Student Eastman Sch. Music, Rochester, N.Y., 1972-73; A.B. in Sociology,

Gettysburg Coll., 1976; M.Div., Luth. Theol. Sem., Gettysburg, Pa., 1980. Ordained to ministry Lutheran Ch., 1980. Asst. pastor St. John's Luth. Ch., Martinsburg, W.Va., 1980-83; co-pastor Manor Luth. Parish, Adamstown, Md., 1983—; mem. com. on agys. and instns. Md. Synod, Luth. Ch. Am. Contact person Nat. Peace Acad. Campaign, Washington, 1984. Republican. Home and Office: 5136 Doubs Rd Adamstown MD 21710

LANGEVIN, LOUIS DE GONZAQUE, bishop, Roman Cath. Ch.; b. Oka, Que., Can., Oct. 31, 1921; s. Eugene and Irene Langevin; B.A., Coll. of Montreal; licence en theologie, U. Gregorienne, Rome; licence en Ecuture Sainte, Inst. Biblique, Rome. Ordained priest, 1950; joined White Fathers; missionary in Uganda, 1957-60; provincial White Fathers of Can., 1961-71; dir. missions Bishop's Conf. of Can. Cath. Conf., 1971-74; bishop (aux.) St. Hyacinthe, Que., 1974-79, bishop, 1979—. Address: Eveché de St Hyacinthe 1900 rue Girouard St Hyacinthe PQ Canada

LANGFORD, N.B., minister, Southern Baptist Convention; b. Jackson, Miss., May 19, 1929; s. N.B. and Margaret (Fuller) L.; m. Nancy Underwood, Sept. 7, 1953; children: Nathan Buell, Nancy Elizabeth. B.S., Miss. Coll., 1957; M.Div., So. Bapt. Sem., 1960; D.Min., Luther Rice Sem., 1975. Ordained to ministry Southern Baptist Convention, 1955. Sr. minister Kirkwood Bapt. Ch., Bondville, Ky., 1957-60, First Bapt. Ch., Union Springs, Ala., 1960-63, North Central Bapt. Ch., Gainesville, Fla., 1963-78, First Bapt. Ch., Panama City, Fla., 1978—; trustee Radio and TV Commn., Ft. Worth, 1977—; chmn. bd. trustees Bapt. Bible Inst., 1974—; pres. Fla. Bapt. Conv., Jacksonville, 1979. Mem. Human Relations Adv. Bd., Gainesville. Democrat. Lodge: Kiwanis. Home: 512 S Bonita Ave Panama City FL 32401 Office: First Bapt Ch 601 Harrison Ave PO Box 1200 Panama City FL 32402

LANGFORD, SIDNEY, minister, Conservative Baptist Association America; b. Phila., May 1, 1912; s. Chris and Alice Muriel (Burns) L.; diploma Phila. Coll. Bible, 1933, Shelton Coll., 1934; m. Jennie Catherine Long, Jan. 22, 1938; children: Lois Langford Wing, Virginia Langford Stonehouse, David, Ronald. Ordained to ministry, 1934; missionary Aba Sta., Republic of Zaire, 1935-38, supt., 1939-52; mem. Zaire Field Council, 1946-52; field dir. Africa Inland Mission, So. Sudan, 1953-56, mem. internat. council, 1955-77, U.S. dir., Pearl River, N.Y., 1956-77, mem. urban outreach com., 1960—, U.S. dir. emeritus, minister-at-large, 1977—; mem. ofcl. bd. Interdenominational Fgn. Mission Assn. N.Am., 1964-72, v.p.; chmn. U.S. coordinating com. African Com. for Rehab. So. Sudan, 1972—; bd. reference Israel's Hope, 1965—. Recipient Phila. Coll. Bible Alumnus award for outstanding Christian service, 1970; Ordre of Cheval (Belgian Govt. in Congo). Editor: Inland Africa, Africa Inland Mission periodical, 1956-77. Home: 21 Roxbury Pl Glen Rock NJ 07452 Office: PO Box 178 Pearl River NY 10965

LANGFORD, THOMAS ANDERSON, educator, minister, United Methodist Ch.; b. Winston-Salem, N.C., Feb. 22, 1929; s. Thomas Anderson and Louie Mae (Hughes) L.; A.B., Davidson Coll., 1951, D.D., 1975; B.D., Duke, 1954, Ph.D. (Gurney Harris Kearns fellow, Dempster fellow), 1958; m. Ann Marie Daniel, Dec. 27, 1951; children: Thomas Anderson III, James Howard, Timothy Daniel, Stephen Hughes. Ordained to ministry United Methodist Ch., 1952; asst. pastor ch., Mebane, N.C., 1954-55; faculty dept. religion Duke U., 1956-71, chmn. dept., 1965-71, dean Div. Sch., prof. systematic theology, 1971—. Named Outstanding Tchr. Undergrads., Duke Student Govt., 1965; recipient E. Harris Harbison Distinguished Teaching award Danforth Found., 1965-66. Am. Council Learned Socs. study fellow, 1965-66; Soc. for Religion in Higher Edn. fellow, 1969. Mem. Am. Theol. Soc., Am. United Meth. Theol. Schs. (pres. 1976-78). Author: (with G.L. Abernathy) Introduction to Western Philosophy: Pre-Socratics to Mill, 1970; In Search of Foundations: English Theology 1900-1920, 1969. Editor: (with G.L. Abernathy) Philosophy of Religion, 1968, History of Philosophy, 1965. Contbr. articles to religious jours. Address: Duke Div Sch Durham NC 27706

LANGHORNE, GEORGE ARMSTEAD JR., minister, American Baptist Churches in the U.S.A.; b. Richmond, Va., Mar. 13, 1940; s. George Armstead and Bessie LaVerne (Holman) L.; m. Shirley Ann Haskins, Sept. 21, 1956 (div. Nov. 1977); children: Deborah, Gregory, Sharon, Gail, Marsha, Anthony, Kevin; m. Joanne Lewis, Dec. 19, 1978; children: Kyna D., Ashleigh E. M.Div., Pitts. Theol. Sem., 1972; B.A., Va. Union U., 1969; M.A., Pepperdine U., 1979; D.Ed., U.S. Internat. U., 1982. Ordained to ministry American Baptist Churches in the U.S.A., 1965. Pastor, Macedonia Bapt. Ch., Heathsville, Va., 1965-69, Antioch Bapt. Ch., Sewickley, Pa., 1969-71; First Bapt. Ch., St. Petersburg, Fla., 1973-75; chaplain USN, Newport, R.I., 1975—; bd. dirs. trustee Pitts. Theol. Sem., 1972-75. Vice pres. bd. dirs. Martin Luther King Community Ctr., Newport, 1984—. Served to lt. comdr. USN, 1975—. Fellow Rockefeller Found., 1969-72. Home: T-1 Coddington Park NETC Newport RI 02840 Office: Naval Chaplains Sch Bldg 114 Naval Trng Ctr Newport RI 02841

LANGLEY, PAUL THOMAS, JR., minister, United Methodist Church; social service agency executive; b. Brookhaven, Pa., Jan. 6, 1953; s. Paul Thomas and Margaretta Edna (Carroll) L.; 1 child, Larry. B.A., Lebanon Valley Coll., 1976; M.A.R., Eastern Bapt. Sem., 1981. Lic. minister Methodist Ch., 1978. Pastor Kemblesville United Meth. Ch., Pa., 1978-81, Fremont United Meth. Ch., Oxford, Pa., 1981-83, Gradyville United Meth. Ch., Pa., 1983-85, Avondale United Meth. Ch., Pa., 1985—; founder So. Chester County Youth Rally Program, West Grove, Pa., 1979, dir., 1979-83; chaplain Brookhaven Fire Co., Pa., 1976-77. Pres., exec. dir. Open Door CYS, Inc., West Grove, Pa., 1982—. Founder Open Door Children and Youth Services, West Grove, 1982. Mem. Alpha Phi Omega (chaplain Annville 1975, Outstanding Service award Nu Delta chpt. Annville 1976). Republican. Avocations: fishing; racquetball; woodworking. Home: 318 Chatham Rd West Grove PA 19390 Office: Open Door CYS Inc PO Box 127 West Grove PA 19390

LANGMADE, OLIVER WENDELL, minister, Ind. Fundamental Chs. Am.; b. St. Paul, July 1, 1931; s. Nye and Lillibelle (Clayson) L.; degree Brown Mackie Sch. Bus., Salina, Kans., 1950; Th.B., Midwest Bible and Missionary Inst., 1954; m. Mary Katherine Stoops, June 17, 1953; children—Calvin, Sharon, Vivian. Ordained to ministry, 1953; pastor chs., Iowa and Wis., 1953-62; pastor Grace Bible Ch., Columbia, Mo., 1962—. Mem. bd. Mid-Am. Mission, 1965-75, Rural Bible Crusade, 1965—; trustee Calvary Bible Coll., Kansas City, Mo. Mem. Evang. Tchr. Tng. Assn. Radio preacher, 1967—. Home: Rt 5 Columbia MO 65201 Office: 1322 Paris Rd Columbia MO 65201

LANGNER, ALLAN MUNISH, rabbi, b. Boberick, Poland, Mar. 14, 1921; s. Marcus and Anne Sarah (Safrin) L.; B.A., U. Toronto, 1944; M.H.L., Jewish Theol. Sem., 1948; m. Nancy Stipelmar, June 14, 1950; children—Nema, Gilah. Rabbi, 1948; rabbi B'Nai Israel Congregation, London, Ont., Can., 1948-52, Temple Israel, Upper Darby, Pa., 1952-59, Congregation Beth-El, Town of Mt. Royal, Que., Can., 1959—. Pres. Bd. Jewish Ministers Greater Montreal, 1969-71; co-chmn. Cath.-Jewish Com. Montreal, 1971—; mem. eastern region exec. Can. Jewish Congress, 1969; Montreal chmn. Rabbinic Cabinet; chmn. religious affairs Can. Jewish Congress, 1974. Commr. Protestant Sch. Bd., Mt. Royal, 1972-73. Home: 632 Kenastoral St Mount Royal PQ Canada Office: 1000 Lucerne Rd Mount Royal PQ H3R 2H9 Canada

LANGSTON, LARRY GENE, pastor, nondenominational; b. Osceola, Ark., Feb. 3, 1952; s. Rev. Jackie and Ruth Marie (Tidwell) L.; m. Diann French, July 28, 1970; children: Jesse, John, Daniel, Carissa, Carrie. B.Theology, Moody Theol. Sem., 1985. Ordained to ministry United Pentecostal Church, 1982. Evangelist Apostolic Ministers Fellowship, S.E., U.S.A., 1972-74; asst. pastor Ch. of the Lord Jesus Christ, Grovetown, Ga., 1974-78; pastor Urania Pentecostal Ch., La., 1978-81, New Life Pentecostal Ch., Grovetown, 1981-84, Christian Life Fellowship, Evans, Ga., 1984—; pres. Christian Life Fellowship Inc. of C.S.R.A., Evans, 1985; mem. bd. of faculty Moody Theol. Sem., Locust Grove, Ga., 1985; state youth dir. Assemblies of Lord Jesus Christ, Ga., 1976; sect. III sec. United Pentecostal Ch., Ga., 1983-84; sect. III youth dir. Assembly of Lord Jesus Christ, La., 1980-81. Author: Self Esteem and the Christian, 1985. Mem. clergy staff Univ. Hosp., Augusta, Ga., 1981—. Named to Outstanding Young Men of Am., 1985. Mem. Toastmasters Internat. (pres. Ga.-Carolina 1985, ednl. v.p. 1984, sargeant-at-arms 1983, named Toastmaster of Yr. 1984, speech contest winner 1984). Republican. Avocations: golf, fishing, bowling, horseback riding, water sports. Home: 987 Reynolds Farm Rd Grovetown GA 30813 Office: Christian Life Fellowship Inc 562 Old Evans Rd Evans GA 30809

LANSFORD, THERON GEORGE, priest, Episcopal Church; b. Denton, Tex., June 13, 1931; s. Marcus L. and Lucile (Wallis) L.; m. Mary Cook, Sept. 1, 1959; children: Marcella, Thomas Leslie. B.A., U. Tex.-Austin, 1957, M.A., 1959. Ordained priest, 1972. Asst., Holy Family Ch., Angola, Ind., 1971-74, priest-in-charge, 1974-80; diocesan missioner Diocese of No. Ind., S. Bend, 1980—; dean students Tri-State U., Angola, Ind., 1965—; mem. com. on marriage and family Diocese of No. Ind., 1983—; dep. to gen. conv. Episcopal Ch., 1970. Mem. Am. Psychol. Assn., Ind. Coll. Personnel Assn. (dir. 1970-72), Nat. Assn. Coll. Personnel Adminstrs., U.S. Fencing Coaches Assn. (v.p.), Sigma Xi. Home: 403 Inglenook Pl Angola IN 46703 Office: Tri-State Univ Angola IN 46703

LANTIS, ANNA JANE, minister, American Lutheran Church; b. Columbus, Ohio, Oct. 14, 1913; d. Clarence Delno and Mabel Eleanor (Crouse) Reed; m. C. Emerson Lantis, Jan. 1, 1954 (dec. 1961). Student, Capital U., 1932-33; B.A., Antioch Coll., 1976; B.D., Luth. Theol. Sem., 1976. Ordained to ministry Luth. Ch., 1976. Social worker and office mgr. Luth. Social Service, Dayton, Ohio, 1941-53; field staff Bd. Am. Missions, various states, 1962-69; lay assoc. pastor Our Saviours Luth. Ch., Rocky River, Ohio, 1969-75; chaplain Lincoln Luth. of Racine, Wis., 1976—. Author Christmas plays for children, 1972. Office: Lincoln Luth 1700 C A Becker Dr Racine WI 53406

LANTZ, ROBERT BRYAN, minister, Lutheran Church in America; health care facilities consultant; b. Mansfield, Ohio, Jan. 11, 1936; s. William Bryan and Dorothy Mae (Weatherbie) L.; A.B., Wittenburg U., 1958; postgrad. Hamma Sch. Theology, 1958-61; m. Katherine L. Isenhour, Aug. 10, 1958. Ordained to ministry, 1961; pastor Holy Trinity Luth. Ch., Akron, Ohio, 1961-63; chief resident, asst. supr. Med. Coll. Va., 1963-64; chmn. chaplain's dept. Balt. City Hosp., 1964-67; dir. Memphis Inst. Medicine and Religion, asso. prof. pastoral care and counseling Memphis Theol. Sem., 1967-69; clin. prof. psychiatry U. Tenn. Med. Units, Memphis; dir. pastoral counseling and field edn. St. Paul's Coll., Washington, 1969-73; cons. Washington Hosp. Center and Crownsville (Md.) Psychiat. Hosp., 1969-76; chmn. bd., dir. Md. Inst. Pastoral Counseling, Annapolis, 1977—. Diplomate Am. Assn. Pastoral Counselors. Mem. Assn. Clin. Pastoral Edn. (mem., chmn. fin. com.), Am. Protestant Hosp. Assn., Nat. Alliance for Family Life. Home: 257 Providence Rd Annapolis MD 21401 Office: 104 Forbes St Annapolis MD 21401

LAPATI, AMERICO DOMENICO, priest, religious educator, Roman Catholic Ch. B. Providence, Nov. 2, 1924; s. Antonio and Civita (DiClemente) L. A.B., St. Mary's Sem., Balt., 1945, S.T.B., 1947; M.A., Boston Coll., 1951, Ph.D., 1958. Ordained priest Roman Catholic Ch., 1949. Prof. Cath. Tchrs. Coll., Providence, 1951-70; guidance dir. St. Raphael Acad., Pawtucket, R.I., 1958-70; prof. edn. Cath. U. of Am., Washington, 1970-76; pastor St. Mary's Ch., Cranston, R.I., 1976—. Author: High School Curriculum for Leadership, 1961; Orestes A. Brownson, 1965; John Henry Newman, 1972; Education and Federal Government, 1975. Recipient UNITAM award United Italo-Amers., 1979; Fulbright scholar, 1964. Mem. Cath. Tchrs. Inst. of R.I. (pres. 1964-65). Home and Office: St Mary's Ch 1525 Cranston St Cranston RI 02920

LAPOINTE, ROGER LUCIEN, educator, Roman Catholic Church; b. Kénogami, Que., Can. July 28, 1929; s. Pierre Antonio and Diana (Olsen) L.; Licentiate in Philosophy and Theology, Rome, 1951, Angelicum, 1955; doctorate Pontificum Inst. Biblicum, Rome, 1966. Assoc. prof. systematic theology St. Paul U., Ottawa, Ont., Can., 1970-75; assoc. prof. sociology of religion Ottawa U., 1976—. Mem. Canadian Soc. Theology (pres. 1971-74), Can. Soc. Study Religion (pres. 1984-86). Author: Les Trois dimensions de l' herméeneutique, 1967; Consultation internationale sur le non-être, 1969; Dialogues bibliques et dialectique interpersonelle, 1971; Regard sur la société de consommation, 1973; Módèle dialectique du Christianisme, 1981. Editor: SR (Studies in Religion/Sci. of religieuses, 1976-81; co-editor Le divorce, 1973; Pluralism-Its Meaning Today, 1974. Contbr. articles to profl. publs. Home: 285 Laurier St Hull PQ J8X 3W9 Canada Office: 177 Waller St Ottawa ON K1N 6N5 Canada

LAPORTE, JEAN-MARC, religious educator; b. Edmundston, N.B., Can., July 5, 1937; s. Jean-Murillo and Laurente (Levesque) L. B.A., Loyola Coll., Montreal, Que., Can., 1957; M.A., U. Montreal, 1958; S.T.L., Regis Coll., 1968; Dr.es.Sc.Rel. Universite de Strasbourg, France, 1971. Ordained Jesuit priest, Roman Catholic Ch., 1967. Prof., Regis Coll., Toronto, Ont., Can., 1971—, pres., 1975-82; mem. accrediting commn. Assn. Theol. Schs. of U.S. & Can., Dayton, Ohio, 1978-84, chmn., 1982-84. Author: Les Structures dynamiques de la grace, 1971. Editor: The Trinification of the World, 1978. Mem. Can. Theol. Soc., Cath. Theol. Soc. Office: Regis Coll 15 Saint Mary St Toronto ON M4Y 2R5 Canada

LAPSLEY, JAMES NORVELL, JR., educator, minister, Presbyn. Ch. U.S.; b. Clarksville, Tenn., Mar. 16, 1930; s. James Norvell and Evangeline (Winn) L.; B.A., Southwestern U., Memphis, 1952; B.D., Union Sem., 1955; Ph.D., U. Chgo., 1961; m. Brenda Ann Weakley, June 4, 1953; children—Joseph W., Jacqueline E. Ordained to ministry, 1955; asst. minister Gentilly Presbyn. Ch., New Orleans, 1955-57; instr. Princeton (N.J.) Theol. Sem., 1961-63, asst. prof., 1963-67, asso. prof. pastoral theology, 1967-76, prof. pastoral theology, 1976—. Mem. Bd. Govs. Council for Clin. Tng., Inc., 1966-67; trustee Westminster Found., Princeton, 1970—. Div. Sch. fellow, 1958-59, Rockefeller fellow, 1959-61, Danforth fellow, Menninger Found. fellow, 1960-61. Mem. A.A.U.P. Author: The Concept of Willing, 1967; Salvation and Health, 1972. Mem. editorial com. Jour. Pastoral Care, 1966-69; chmn. editorial bd. Pastoral Psychology, 1975—. Office: Princeton Theol Sem Princeton NJ 08540

LARGEN, FREDRICK JAMES, minister, American Baptist Churches in the U.S.A.; merchant, consultant; b. Newark, Aug. 1, 1937; s. Frederick Jonathan and Wilma Inez (McElroy) L.; m. Donna Jean Schuetz, May 31, 1957 (div. Feb. 1978); children: Gail Jean Largen

Weeks, Peter John, Sandra Ruth; m. Jennifer K. Caughey, May 20, 1978; children: Daniel Fredrick, Erica Jane. B.A., Elmhurst Coll., 1959; B.D., Lancaster Sem., 1962, Th.M., 1962; postgrad. Union Theol. Sem., 1962-64. Ordained to ministry Baptist Churches in the U.S.A., 1964. Youth pastor, asst. pastor, pastor Christ Ch., St. Marks, Wapwallopen Charge, Pa., 1959-63; research asst. N.T., Union Theol. Sem., N.Y.C., 1962-64; tutorial asst. Greek and N.T., Lancaster Sem., Pa., 1961-62; pastor Foster Park Bapt. Ch., Chgo., 1964-66, Valley Community Ch., Burnsville, Minn., 1966—; bd. dirs. Mpls. Council Chs., 1968-69. Owner, sec.-treas. The Kitchen Store, Inc., Burnsville, 1979—; pres. FJL Assocs., med. cons., Burnsville, 1975—. Author: Source of Gospel of Mark, 1962; The Christian Faith in the Modern World, 1981. Inventor self-contained med. surg. units. Mem. Lebanon Twp. Planning Commn., Apple Valley, Minn., 1967-68; moderator Lebannon Twp., 1967-68; mayor City of Apple Valley, 1968-76; vice chmn., chmn. Dakota County Criminal Justice Council, 1974-75. Recipient Minn. Valley Man of Yr. award Sun Newspapers, Mpls., 1970; Outstanding Community Service award City of Apple Valley, 1976; sr. scholar Lancaster Theol. Sem., 1962; Fred J. Largen Park named in his honor City of Apple Valley, 1982. Independent Republican. Home: 13140 Thomas Ave S Burnsville MN 55337

LARKIN, KENNETH DEAN, minister, Lutheran Church in America. B. Davenport, Iowa, Apr. 19, 1929; s. Robert Joseph and Marie (Moeller) L.; m. Beverley JoAnn Geisler, Sept. 26, 1954; children: Kevin Timothy, Natalie Nadine, Joel Andrew. B.A., Augustana Coll., 1951; B.D., Chgo. Luth. Sem., 1954; M.Div., Luth. Sch. Theol., 1972. Ordained to ministry United Lutheran Ch. in Am., 1954. Mission developer Christ the King Luth. Ch., Livonia, Mich., 1954-55, pastor, 1955-66; asst. to bishop Ohio Synod, Mansfield, Ohio, 1966-81; pastor Shepherd of the Valley Luth. Ch., Phoenix, 1981—; dir. Camp Mowana/Luther, Mansfield, 1966-81; conflict mgmt. counselor Ohio Synod, Mansfield, 1978-81, youth ministry dir., 1966-81; profl. leadership commn. Pacific S.W. Synod, Los Angeles, 1982—. Author: Tinkertoy Church, 1978; The Praying Monk, 1984; The Desert Experience, 1982. Active in The Heard Mus., Phoenix, 1984. Recipient cert. Rutgers U., 1974; citation St. Peters Luth. Ch., 1982; plaque Ohio Synod, 1975; plaque Shepherd of the Valley Ch., 1984. Mem. Ariz. Dist. Luth. Ch. in Am. Home: 3007 W Cactus Wren Dr Phoenix AZ 85021 Office: Shepherd of the Valley Luth Ch 1500 W Maryland Ave Phoenix AZ 85015

LARKIN, WILLIAM THOMAS, bishop, Roman Catholic Church; b. Mt. Morris, N.Y., Mar. 31, 1923; s. William Thomas and Julia A. (Beuerlein) L. D.S.T., Angelicum U., Rome, 1949. Ordained bishop Roman Cath. Ch., 1979. Sec. to bishop Diocese of St. Augustine, Fla., 1949-51; assoc. pastor Holy Family Ch., North Miami, Fla., 1951-54; pastor Christ the King Ch., Jacksonville, Fla., 1954-67, St. Cecelia Ch., Clearwater, Fla., 1967-79; officialis, vicar gen. Diocese of St. Petersburg, Fla., 1968-79, bishop of St. Petersburg, 1979—; trustee St. Vincent de Paul Sem., Boynton Beach, Fla.; com. mem. priestly life and ministry Nat. Conf. of Cath. Bishops, Washington. Office: Diocese of St Petersburg 6363 9th Ave N Saint Petersburg FL 33710

LAROCHELLE, ANDRE LESTER, lay eucharistic minister, Roman Catholic Ch.; b. Hartford, Conn., Feb. 2, 1937; s. Raymond Albini and Leanne Marie (LeBlanc) LaR.; B.A., Trinity Coll., Hartford, 1959; M.S.W., La. State U., Baton Rouge, 1970; m. Constance Maire Cicardo, May 29, 1965; 1 dau., Barbara Joan. Appointed lay minister of holy communion, 1973; mem. pastoral council Shreveport (La.) Deanery, 1976—; dir. Cath. Family Services, Shreveport, 1974—. Mem. La. State Bd. Certified Social Work Examiners. Recipient Alcohol/Drug Abuse Edn. award, 1976. Fellow Acad. Certified Social Workers; mem. Nat. Assn. Social Workers (v.p. La. chpt. 1976-78), Nat. Cath. Conf., Nat. Assn. Christians in Social Work, La. Soc. Clin. Social Work, Air Force Assn., Res. Officers Assn. (chpt. pres.). Home: 221 Charles Ave Shreveport LA 71105 Office: 3109 Alexander Ave Suite 120 Shreveport LA 71104

LAROCQUE, EUGENE PHILIPPE, bishop, Roman Catholic Church; b. Windsor, Ont., Can., Mar. 27, 1927; s. Eugene Joseph and Angeline (Monforton) LaR. B.A., U. Western Ont., 1948; M.A. in French, U. Laval, 1956. Ordained priest Roman Cath. Ch., 1952, bishop, 1974. Asst. Ste. Therese Parish, Windsor, Ont., 1952-54; registrar, dean of men, prin. King's Coll., U. Western Ont., London, 1956-68; pastor St. Joseph's Parish, River Canard, Ont., 1968-70; team leader St. Anne's Parish, Tecumseh, Ont., 1970-74; bishop Diocese of Alexandria-Cornwall, Ont., 1974—; mem., exec. Ont. Conf. Cath. Bishops, Toronto, 1974—; mem. ecumenical commn. Can. Conf. Cath. Bishops, Ottawa, 1974—; mem., past chmn. Nat. Tripartite Liaison Com., Montreal, 1977—; spiritual dir. Cath. Women's League of Ont., 1974-75. Recipient Isaiah award Can. Jewish Congress, Montreal, 1980. Lodge: K.C. (state chaplain 1977—).

LARSEN, DONALD H., religious organization executive, Association of Evangelical Lutheran Churches; b. Detroit, Feb. 17, 1925; s. Harold C. and Minna M. (Koppit) L.; m. Rhoda V. (Birner), June 11, 1947; children: Kristen Ann Dusenbery, Dan Jonathan, Donald Paul, Timothy Peter, Sue Ruth. B.A., Concordia Sem., St. Louis, 1944, M.D., 1947; D.Div., Christ Sem., St. Louis, 1983. Pastor various Luth. Chs. 1947-64; sec. urban ch. planning, Nat. Luth. Council, Chgo., 1964-67; sec. ch. and community planning, Luth. Council in the U.S.A., N.Y.C., 1967-73, exec. dir. research planning, devel., 1973-77, exec. dir. div. mission and ministry, 1977-85; dir. Luth. Immigration and Refugee Service, N.Y.C., 1985—; dir. Nat. Assembly Nat. Vol. Health and Social Welfare Orgns., N.Y.-Washington; bd. dirs.-pres. Joint Strategy and Action Com.; vice-chmn. Com. on Migration, Refugee Affairs, Interaction, N.Y.C. Contbr. articles to religious publs. Active Human Relations Commn. Democrat. Office: Luth Immigration and Refugee Service 360 Park Ave S New York NY 10010

LARSEN, LAWRENCE BERNARD, JR., priest, Episcopal Church, psychotherapist; b. Yonkers, N.Y., Jan. 24, 1937; s. Lawrence Bernard and Astrid Charlotte (Bjorkgren) Larsen; m. Marion Davidson Hines, Nov. 29, 1968; children: Lawrence Bernard III, Hannah Hines, Sarah Astrid. B.A., Trinity Coll., Hartford, Conn., 1958; M.Div., Gen. Theol. Sem., N.Y.C., 1961; diploma candidate G.G. Jung Inst., Zurich, Switzerland, 1972-75. Ordained deacon Episc. Ch. 1961, priest, 1961. Curate, Christ Ch., Poughkeepsie, N.Y., 1961-63; asst. Episcopal chaplain Vassar Coll., Poughkeepsie, 1961-63; vicar All Saints Ch., East Hartford, Conn., 1963-66; asst. to rector Trinity Ch., Southport, Conn., 1966-69; chaplain Bible, ancient history tchr. Chatham Hall Sch., 1969-72; assoc. priest Good Shepherd Ch., Lookout Mountain, Tenn., 1978—. Psychotherapist, Chattanooga, 1975—. Mem. OEO, East Hartford, Conn., 1965. Affiliate mem. Am. Assn. Pastoral Counselors. Republican. Club: Fairyland (Lookout Mountain, Tenn.).

LARSON, JAMES NATHAN, minister, United Pentecostal Church International; b. St. Paul, July 1, 1953; s. James Arvid and Grace Suzanna (Urshan) L.; m. Joleane Rachel Haney, Sept. 22, 1973; 1 child, James Vincent. B.Th., Christian Life Coll., 1973. Ordained to ministry United Pentecostal Ch. Evangelist, United Pentecostal Ch. Internat., nationwide, 1972-77; assoc. pastor Revival Tabernacle, San Diego, 1978-79; pastor Calvary Tabernacle, Indpls., 1979—; founder Calvary Christian High Sch., 1980; radio speaker Voice of Calvary Broadcast, 1979—. Republican. Club: Indpls. Athletic. Lodge: Rotary. Office: Calvary Tabernacle Ch 902 Fletcher Ave Indianapolis IN 46203

LARSON, ROY, religion editor; b. Moline, Ill., July 27, 1929; s. Roy W. and Jane (Beall) L.; B.A., Augustana Coll., 1951; M.Div., Garrett Theol. Sem., 1955; m. Dorothy Jennisch, June 7, 1950; children—Mark, Bruce, Jodie Ann, Bradley. Ordained to ministry United Methodist Ch., 1956; pastor ch., Park Ridge, Ill., 1959-62, Evanston, Ill., 1963-68, Elmhurst, Ill., 1968-69; laicized, 1969; religion editor Chgo. Sun Times, 1969—. Recipient Nat. Headliner award, 1976. Mem. Sigma Delta Chi. Home: 9410 Lincolnwood Dr Evanston IL 60203 Office: 401 N Wabash Ave Chicago IL 60611

LARSON, THORE, president, Evangelical Lutheran Church in America (Eielsen Synod). Address: Jackson MN 56143

LARUE, JOHN HARPER, minister, Southern Baptist Convention; b. Grayson, Va., Mar. 29, 1928; s. Harvey Jehu and Thelma Alma (Funk) L.; m. Marlene Wainwright, Nov. 17, 1954 (div. 1980); children: Loretta, Linda. B.A., Wake Forest U., 1958; M.Div., Southeastern Bapt. Theol. Sem., 1962, M.Theology, 1975, D.M., 1980. Ordained to ministry Southern Baptist Church, 1962. Pastor Spring Road Bapt. Ch., Gretna, Va., 1962-65, Summersett Bapt. Ch., Gretna, 1962-65, West View Bapt. Ch., Madison Heights, Va., 1965-72, Schoolfield Bapt. Ch., Danville, Va., 1978—; interim pastor Forest Lawn Bapt. Ch., Danville, 1972, Vandola Bapt. Ch., Danville, 1973; dir. Pittsylvania Bapt. Assn., Danville; sem. extension tchr. So. Bapt. Conv., Nashville, 1983—; chmn. time, place, preacher com. Pittsylvania Bapt. Assn., 1983—; mem. meml. com. Bapt. Gen. Assn., Richmond, Va., 1982-84; in-service guidance supr. Averett Coll., Danville, 1984—. Bd. dirs. Amherst-Monroe Ruritan Club, 1968-70, chaplain, 1968-70; mem. Grayson County Hist. Com., Independence, Va., 1979—; sec., v.p., pres. Monroe-Parent-Teachers Assn., 1969-71; sec., v.p., pres. Amherst County Ministerial Assn., 1969-71; advisor Explorers, Post 185 Boy Scouts Am., 1969-71. Recipient Citizenship award WBTM Radio, 1980; Anglo-Am. Acad. fellow, London, 1981. Mem. Dan River Retired Club (hon.). Democrat. Home: 534 River Oak Dr Danville VA 24541

LASOR, WILLIAM SANFORD, educator, minister United Presbyterian Ch. in U.S.A.; b. Phila., Oct. 25 1911; s. William Allan and Sara (Lewis) LaS.; A.B., U Pa., 1931; Th.B., Princeton Sem., 1934, Th.M., 1943 M.A., Princeton U., 1934; Ph.D., Dropsie U., 1949 Th.D., U. So. Calif., 1956; m. Elizabeth Grange Vaughan, June 16, 1934; children: William Sanford Elizabeth Ann LaSor Kirkpatrick, Frederick, Susanne LaSor Whyte. Ordained to ministry, 1934; pastor 1st Presbyn. Ch., Ocean City, N.J., 1934-38, Green Ridge Presbyn. Ch., Scranton, Pa., 1938-43; chaplain USNR 1943-46; head dept. religion Lafayette Coll., Easton, Pa., 1946-49; prof. O.T., Fuller Theol. Sem., 1949-77, sr. prof. O.T., 1977-80, emeritus prof., 1980—. Chmn. bd. dirs. Tokyo Evangelistic Center, 1959—; mem. bd. dirs. World-Wide Missions, 1970-75. Mem. Soc. O.T. Scholars (Gt. Britain), Internat. Orgn. O.T. Scholars, Soc. Bibl. Lit., Am. Schs. Oriental Research, Alpha Sigma Phi. Author: Dead Sea Scrolls and the New Testament, 1972; Church Alive! (An Exposition of Acts), 1972; Handbook of New Testament Greek, 2 vols., 1973; Israel, A Biblical View, 1976; Handbook of Biblical Hebrew, 2 vols., 1977; many others. Office: 135 N Oakland Ave Pasadena CA 91101

LASSANSKE, PAUL ALBERT, minister, Lutheran Church, Missouri Synod; b. Milw., May 12, 1912; s. Otto and Amanda L.; m. Ruth Babetta Konemann, Sept. 1, 1934; children: Ruth Joan Lassanske Strubel, Paul Wayne. B.S. in Edn., Concordia Coll., River Forest, Ill., 1942; M.A., Western Res. U., 1945, Ph.D., 1963. Ordained, 1954; cert. tchr., Ill., Ohio. Minister of edn. Luth. Ch., Mo. Synod, various congregations, 1933-54, minister of music, 1933-54; prof. Christian edn. Concordia Coll., St. Paul, 1965-77; pastoral ministry Luth. Ch., Mo. Synod, various congregations, 1954—; pastor Resurrection Evang. Luth. Ch., River Forest, Ill., 1983—; pres. Met. Luth. Tchrs. Conf., N.Y.C., 1951-53; chmn. Tex. Dist. Com. on Fraternal Orgns., Tyler, 1961-64; mem. No. Ill. Dist. Com. on Fraternal Orgns., Chgo., 1964-65; del. Luth. Ch., Mo. Synod Conv., Cleve., 1963; mem. Luth. Edn. Assn., Luth. Acad. for Scholarships. Author: Moral and Spiritual Development of Children, 1967. Tng. officer Chgo. Civilian Def., 1941-43; aux. police Civilian Def., Cleve., 1943-47; instr. first aid ARC, Chgo., 1941-47. Recipient Luth. Choirmasters Guild Key, Walther League, River Forest, 1940. Mem. NEA (life). Republican. Club: Lake Placid Yachting (Fla.). Home: 121 Cumquat Rd NE Lake Placid FL 33852 Office: Resurrection Evang Luth Ch Concordia College Box 44G River Forest IL 60305

LATHAM, DONALD CONWAY, priest, Episcopal Ch.; b. Hempstead, N.Y., Dec. 24, 1933; s. Walter Arlington and Agnes (Weaver) L.; B.A., Hobart Coll., 1955; M.Div., Berkeley Div. Sch., 1958; postgrad. Adelphi U. Sch. Social Work, 1960-61; m. Margaret Audrey Thomas, Oct. 10, 1959; 1 dau., Victoria Anne. Ordained priest, 1958; vicar All Souls Ch., Stony Brook, N.Y., 1958-66; instr. N.T., Knox Sch., St. James, N.Y., 1959-60; chaplain USNR, Viet Nam, 1966-67; Canon to Ordinary, Diocese L.I. (N.Y.), 1967-72; rector Ch. of Ascension, Rockville Centre, N.Y., 1972—. Chaplain to Episc. students State U. N.Y., Stony Brook; mem. dept. youth coll. work, mem. Armed Forces commn., Nassau County chmn., Episc. Charities Appeal, Diocese L.I.; mem. interfaith pastoral care com. Mercy Hosp., Rockville Centre. Chmn. Suffolk County (N.Y.) Prisoners Aid Soc., 1961-64. Contbr. articles to ch. jours. Home: 98 Plymouth Rd Rockville Centre NY 11570

LAUBACH, EUGENE E., minister, United Methodist Church; b. Finesville, N.J., Mar. 20, 1926; s. Elmer Eugene and Ruth (Vanderbilt) L.; m. Patricia Ann Coleman, July 7, 1948; children: Mary Elizabeth, William Bennett, Nancy Ann. A.B., Lafayette Coll., 1946; S.T.B., Boston U., 1949; Ed.D., Columbia U., 1964. Ordained elder United Methodist Church, 1950. Pastor, Junction City Meth. Ch., Oreg., 1950-52; assoc. exec. bd. edn. Oreg. Conf. Meth. Ch., Portland, 1952-53; exec. sec., 1953-56; minister edn. First Meth. Ch., Westfield, N.J., 1956-61; minister parish life Riverside Ch., N.Y.C., 1961—; lectr. Union Theol. Sem., N.Y.C. Author curriculum units for United Meth. Ch. Pres. Morningside Area Alliance, N.Y.C.; chmn. Remedco Found., N.Y.C. Mem. Religious Edn. Assn., Christian Educators Fellowship. Home: 90 La Salle St #9G New York NY 10027 Office: Riverside Ch 490 Riverside Dr New York NY 10027

LAUER, BARBARA ESTELLE, church organization executive; b. Brinkley, Ark., Mar. 17; d. Richard and Cocab (Mahfouz) Ashy; m. John H. Lauer, Aug. 30, 1974. B.A. in Adminstrn. of Human Services, N.Y. State Coll., 1974; Montessori Edn. Cert., Springhill Coll., 1973; Religious Edn. Theology Cert., Cath. U., 1960; student Dominican Coll., 1953. Creative/exec. dir. Tuscarawas County Council for Ch. and Community, New Phila., Ohio, 1975—; cons. Sacred Heart Ch., New Phila., 1983—, religious educator, 1976-80. Recipient Nat. Ecumenical award Nat. Council Chs., 1978; 10 Yrs. Ecumenical Recognition, 1984. Democrat. Home: Route 1 Box 1001 New Philadelphia OH 44163 Office: Tuscarawas County Council for Church and Community 120 First Dr SE New Philadelphia OH 44663

AUGHLIN, THOMAS BERNARD, priest, Roman 'atholic Ch.; b. Omaha, July 26, 1925; s. David Edward nd Marie (Killila) L.; A.B. magna cum laude, Loras 'oll., 1945; S.T.L., St. Mary's Sem., 1948; M.A., 'reighton U., 1955; postgrad Cath. U. Am., 1950-51, U. ortland, 1949-50, Inst. Theol. Continuing Edn., Rome, 973. Ordained priest, 1948; tchr. Central Cath. High ch., Portland, Oreg., 1948-65, chmn. dept. fgn. langs., 952-65, asst. prin., 1955-65; lectr. theology, prof. latin laryhurst (Oreg.) Coll., 1962-64; pastor St. Frederick's h., St. Helens, Oreg., 1965-66, St. Mary's Ch., orvallis, Oreg., 1966-72, All Sts. Ch., Portland, Oreg., 972—. Head chaplain Oreg. State Univ. Newman enter, 1966-72; pres. Corvallis Ministerial Assn., eligious Dirs. Assn. Oreg. State Univ.; v.p. Priests enate Archdiocese Portland, also pres., mem. bd. edn., 967—; mem. Cath. Charities Advisory Bd., 1975—. lem. Classical Assn. Oreg. (co-founder). Founder pectrum, fgn. lang. jour. Home and Office: Foundation louse Jemez Springs NM 87025

AURSEN, CHRIS ANDREW, minister, Lutheran 'hurch in America; b. Warrens, Wis., Sept. 9, 1930; s. 'hristian and Catherine (Sorensen) L.; B.S., U. Wis., lilw., 1952; M.Div., Northwestern Lutheran Theol. em., 1958; m. Margaret Lennox Atkins, Aug. 1, 1953; hildren: Andrew Leslie, Scott Christian. Ordained to inistry Lutheran Ch. Am., 1958; pastor Calvary utheran Ch., Southfield, Mich., 1958-61, St. Peter utheran Ch., Battle Creek, Mich., 1961-70, Good hepherd Lutheran Ch., Manistee, Mich., 1970—. hmn. Parish Life Devel. Com., 1972—; mem. exec. bd. lich. Synod, 1969-71; Pres. Manistee Bd. Edn., 974—; trustee Manistee County Intermediate Sch. ist.; bd. dirs. West Shore Community Coll. Found.; bd. irs., dir. fund drive United Fund, 1972-73; mem. egional Substance Abuse Coordinating Agy., 1976—; em. adv. bd. County Health Dept., 1973-75. Recipient istinguished Service award Jaycees, 1974, utstanding Citizen award VFW, 1976. Mem. St. James cad. Parish Clergy, Manistee Ministerial Assn., lanistee County C. of C. (bd. dirs.). Club: Rotary. lome: 325 5th St Manistee MI 49660 Office: 521 'ypress St Manistee MI 49660

AVEY, BENJAMIN VERDIER, priest, Episc. Ch.; b. 'aynesboro, Pa., July 13, 1927; s. James and Anna lizabeth (Verdier) L.; B.A., Juninta Coll., 1948; B.D., ashotah House Sem., 1952, M.Div., 1971; m. largaret Anne Hoffman, July 30, 1955; 1 dau., atherine Anne. Ordained priest, 1952; asst. youth ork St. Matthew's Ch., Penosha, Wis., 1950-52; asst. h. St. Mary-the-Virgin, N.Y.C., 1952-54; rector rinity Ch., Chambersburg, Pa., 1954-59, St. John's Ch., turgis, Mich., 1959-68; dean Cathedral, Kalamazoo, lich., 1968-74; rector Ch. St. James-by-the Sea, La olla, Calif., 1974—. Chaplain, U.S. Army Res., 958-64; chmn. St. Joseph County Migrant Ministry, 965; dep. Gen. Conv. Episc. Ch., 1964-73; pres. Sturgis linisterial Assn., 1966; mem. Labor Mgmt. Relations 'onf. Bd., 1960-68. Active Am. Cancer Soc., United und, Boy Scouts Am. Recipient citations of Merit, TB oc., 1954-64, Cancer Soc., 1956-73, Mich. linuteman, 1965. Club: Rotary (dist. gov. 1973-74). ffice: 743 Prospect St La Jolla CA 92037

AW, BERNARD F. CARDINAL, archbishop, Roman atholic Ch. Ordained priest Roman Cath. Ch., 1961, onsecrated bishop, 1973; bishop of Diocese of oringfield-Cape Girardeau, Mo., 1973-84; archbishop iocese of Boston, 1984—; elevated to Coll. of ardinals, 1985. mem. administrv. com. Nat. Conf. ath. Bishops, adminstrv. bd. U.S. Cath. Conf.; mem. atican Secretariat for Promoting Christian Unity, 976-81. Home and Office: The Cardinal's Residence 101 Commonwealth Ave Brighton MA 02135

AWRENCE, ARLENE WHITE, ch. ofcl., Pillar of ire Ch.; children: Arthur N.J., Nov. 11, 1916; d. rthur Kent and Kathleen Merrill (Staats) White; A.A., elleview Coll., Westminster, Colo., 1936; postgrad. elleview Bible Sem., 1937; B.A., Alma White Coll., arephath, 1941; M.A., Columbia, 1963; m. E. Jerry awrence, Sept. 10, 1941; children—Arthur Evan, erona Kathleen. Ordained minister Pillar of Fire Ch., 936; bishop Pillar of Fire Soc. Inc., 1974; minister, arephath, 1941—, 1st v.p., 1972—; asst. dir. radio rograms for ch., 1965—; trustee Pillar of Fire, Cin., 969—, Pillar of Fire, Bklyn., 1969—; v.p. Pillar of Fire oc., London, Eng., 1971—. Mem. Internat. Platform ssn., Friends of Alma White Coll., Nat. Trust Historic reservation. Author: Come Along (travelogue), 1956; ady Blue Bell's Forest Banquet (juvenile), 1973; also rmon articles for ch. Office: Weston Canal Rd arephath NJ 08890

AWRENCE, BERNARD PAUL, religion educator, eventh-Day Adventists; b. Kimberley, South Africa, eb. 14, 1937; came to Can., 1977; s. Joseph Bernard id Dorothy L.; m. Pauline Alice Neethling, Dec. 11, 966; children: Ruth, Anne, David. B.S., U. Western apetown, 1962; M.S., Walla Walla Coll. (Wash.), 973, M.Ed., 1981. Instr. religion Good Hope Coll., ape Town, South Africa, 1963-66; instr. religion and i. Solusi Mission Coll., Bulawayo, Zimbabwe, 966-71; instr. religion Rusangu Mission Sch., Monze, ambia, 1975-77; adminstr., counselor Maidstone cad., Windsor, Ont.,Can.,1977-79; adminstr., tchr. Chatham Adventist Sch., Ont., 1980-82, Parkesville Adventist Sch., B.C., 1983—. Home: 94 Wedgewood Ave Chatham ON N7M 5T5 Canada Office: Chatham Adventist Sch 102 Taylor Ave Chatham ON N7M 5T5 Canada

LAWRENCE, CALEB JAMES, bishop, Anglican Church of Canada; b. Lattie's Brook, N.S., Can., May 26, 1941; s. James Otis and Mildred Viola (Burton) L.; m. Maureen Patricia Cuddy, July 18, 1966; children: Fiona Ruth, Karen Roisin, Sean Kevin. B.A., Dalhousie U., Halifax, N.S., 1962; B.S.T., U. King's Coll., Halifax, 1964, D.D. (hon.), 1980. Ordained priest Anglican Ch. of Can., consecrated bishop, 1980. Missionary priest Anglican Ch. of Can., Great Whale River, Que., 1965-74, rector, 1974-79, archdeacon, 1975-79, mem. Council of North, 1980—, nat. exec. council, 1980—, gen. and provincial synod, 1980—; bishop coadjutor Diocese of Moosonee, Schumacher, Ont., 1980, diocesan bishop, 1980—.

LAWRENCE, CHARLES RADFORD, II, religious convention official, Episcopal Church; emeritus educator; b. Boston, May 2, 1915; s. Charles Radford and Letitia Burnett (Harris) L.; m. Margaret Morgan Lawrence, June 5, 1938; children: Charles Radford 3d, Sara Lawrence Lightfoot, Paula Lawrence Wehmiller. B.A., Morehouse Coll., 1936, D.H.L. (hon.), 1977; M.A., Atlanta U., 1938; Ph.D., Columbia U., 1952; D.D. (hon.), Gen. Theol. Sem., 1976; D.C.L. (hon.), Seabury-Western Sem., 1978; D.H.L. (hon.), St. Paul's Coll., Lawrenceville, Va., 1983. Pres. ho. of deps. Gen. Conv., vice chmn. exec. council Episcopal Ch., N.Y.C., 1976—; meh. ch. world service com. Nat. Council Chs. Prof. sociology emeritus Bklyn. Coll., CUNY, 1977—. Pres. Spring Valley chpt. NAACP, N.Y., 1952-53; v.p. East Ramapa Bd. Edn., Spring Valley, 1955-62; nat. chmn. Fellowship of Reconciliation, 1955-63. Recipient Bishop's Cross, Diocese N.Y., 1963. Fellow Am. Sociol. Assn., Soc. for Values in Higher Edn. (past bd. dirs.), Soc. Study Social Problems. Democrat. Club: Ch. of N.Y. Office: Gen Conv Episcopal Ch 815 2d Ave New York NY 10017

LAWRENCE, DENNIS LEE, minister, Ch. of God (Anderson, Ind.); b. Distant, Pa., Nov. 11, 1938; s. Richard W. and Miriam P. (Kunselman) L.; B.A. in Psychology and Religion, U. So. Miss., 1976; m. Glee F. Lash, Sept. 21, 1959; children—Dennis M., Jennifer J. Ordained to ministry, 1969; pastor First Ch. of God chs., Warren, Ohio, 1969-71, Ottumwa, Iowa, 1971-74, Hattiesburg, Miss., 1974—. Pres. Greater Warren Evang. Ministers Fellowship, 1970; chmn. Mahoning Valley Ministerial Assn., 1971; youth dir. Iowa conf. Ch. of God, 1974; sec.-treas. Evang. Minister's Fellowship, Ottumwa, 1974; vice chmn. Hattiesburg Ministerial Assn., 1976; pres., co-founder Assn. Christian Counselors and Psychotherapists, 1975. Pres. United Cerebral Palsy Assn. S.E. Iowa, 1973. Home: 2903 Laramie Circle Hattiesburg MS 39401 Office: 310 Cahal St Hattiesburg MS 39401

LAWRENCE, JOHN ELSON, priest, Episcopal Church; b. Bklyn., Dec. 1, 1945; s. Edward Arthur and Gladys Bates (Jackson) L.; m. Rodney Maxwell Monaghan, Sept. 7, 1968; children: Jeffrey Gowan, Christopher Elson, Nancy Catherine. B.A., George Washington U., 1967; M.Div., Gen. Theol. Sem., 1970. Ordained priest Episcopal Church, 1970. Seminarian asst. St. James Ch., N.Y.C., 1969-70; curate All Saints Ch., Great Neck, N.Y., 1970-71; asst. rector Grace Ch., Nyack, N.Y., 1971-75; rector All Saints Ch., Bayside, N.Y., 1975-80, St. Ann's Ch., Sayville, N.Y., 1980—; sec. Diocese of L.I., Garden City, 1979—; dean Great South Bay Deanery, Suffolk County, N.Y., 1981—; dep. Synod of Province II, 1980—; provisional dep. Gen. Conv. Episc. Ch., 1982—; vicar St. Andrew's Summer Chapel, Saltaire, N.Y., 1980—. Editor newsletter Leaven, 1980—; columnist Diocesan Newspaper, Tidings, 1984—. Mem. The Cathedral Chapter, Nat. Network Episcopal Clergy Assns. (dir.). Lodges: Rotary, Kiwanis (pres. 1978-79). Home: 101 Revelyn Ct Sayville NY 11782 Office: Saint Anns Church 262 S Main St Sayville NY 11782

LAWRENCE, LARRY ALLEN, minister, So. Baptist Conv.; b. Jackson, Miss., July 22, 1951; s. James Bennett, Jr. and Mae Nell (Stevens) L.; A.A., Clarke Coll., Newton, Miss., 1971; B.S., Miss. Coll., Clinton, 1974; m. Anna Elizabeth Sewell, June 22, 1974; 1 dau., Emily Judson. Ordained to ministry, 1974; minister youth, asso. pastor Highland Bapt. Ch., Jackson, Miss., 1971-74, W.Jackson Bapt. Ch., Jackson, 1974-76; minister youth and Christian activities First Bapt. Ch., Jonesboro, Ga., 1976—. Dir., Campus Life Club, Youth for Christ, Jackson, 1971-73; chmn. South Metro Bapt. Recreational Ministry for Camp Clayton (Ga.). Mem. Hinds-Madison Bapt., South Metro Bapt. assns., Fellowship Christian Athletes. (chpt. v.p.), Ga. Mental Health Assn. Home: 106 Evenview Dr Jonesboro GA 30236 Office: PO Box 773 Jonesboro GA 30236

LAWRENCE, RAYMOND EUGENE, minister, college president, Southern Baptist Church; b. Elliston, Ky., Nov. 14, 1921; s. Ray and Mary (Sams) L.; m. Eula Whiteker, Sept. 8, 1948; children: Deborah, Dora. B.A., Georgetown Coll., 1949; M.Div., So. Bapt. Sem., 1973. Ordained to ministry, 1947. Pastor 1st Bapt. Ch., Mt. Vernon, Ky., 1958-62, Shelbyville, Ky., 1957-62, Central Bapt. Ch., Corbin, Ky., 1962-72; asst. to pres. Cumberland Coll., Williamsburg, Ky., 1972-80; pres. Mid-Continent Bapt. Coll., Mayfield, Ky., 1981—; trustee Southeastern Bapt. Hosp., 1962-82, Cumberland Coll., 1970-72; bd. dirs. Western Recorder, 1965-70. Author: History of Ten Mile Association, 1948; Don't Give Up the Ship, 1972; Whiteker Dunn, 1976. Served with U.S. Army, 1943-45. Home: 1311 Fairway Circle Mayfield KY 42066 Office: Mid-Continent Coll Mayfield KY 42066

LAWRENZ, RICHARD GLEN, minister, Church of God (Anderson, Ind.); real estate broker; b. Racine, Wis., June 15, 1943; s. Leonard B. Lawrenz and Marion L. (Langdon) Rampello; m. Sharon K. Burchett, Aug. 17, 1968; children: Roderick J., Jared N. B.A. in Psychology, Azusa Pacific Coll., 1966; M.Div., Anderson Sch. Theology, 1969; postgrad. in psychology U. Alaska, 1969-71, 73-75. Ordained to ministry Church of God (Anderson, Ind.), 1970. Pastor Strawtown Community Ch., Ind., 1966-69, First Ch. of God, Juneau, 1969-71, First Ch. of God, Franklin, Ohio, 1971-73; military chaplain Alaska Air N.G., Anchorage, 1974—; credentials chmn. Ch. of God of Alaska, Anchorage, 1975—. Real estate salesman VR Bus. Brokers, Anchorage, 1984—. Named Counselor of Yr., Vocat. Rehab., Juneau, 1971. Mem. Aircraft Owners and Pilots Assn., Alaska Nat. Guard Officers Assn. Club: Aero. Home: 5226 E 42nd St Anchorage AK 99508 Office: Alaska Air Nat Guard 6000 Air Guard Rd Anchorage AK 99508

LAWSON, CARROLL MCKINLEY, JR., minister, Seventh-day Adventists; b. Honolulu, June 24, 1925; s. Carroll McKinley and Kathryn Chritine (Clanton) L.; m. Elaine Rosalie Ennis, May 6, 1945; children: Carroll III, Richard Keith. B.A., Loma Linda U., 1953; postgrad. Andrews U., 1959-62. Ordained to ministry Seventh-day Adventists, 1966. Pastor, Nev. Utah Conf., Reno, 1953-58, S.E. Calif. Conf., Riverside, 1959-69, Chadron and Scottsbluff, Nebr., 1969-74, Cleve. First Seventh-day Adventist, 1974-77, Brownsburg and Evansville, Seventh-day Adventist, 1977-83; pastor Indpls. Southside Seventh-day Adventist, Indpls., 1983—. Republican. Home: 4555 Blackstone Dr Indianapolis IN 46237 Office: Ind Conf Seventh-day Adventist PO Box 1950 Carmel IN 46032

LAWSON, DAVID A., bishop, United Methodist Church. Bishop, Wis. Conf., United Meth. Ch., Sun Prairie, Wis. Office: PO Box 28 Sun Prairie WI 53590*

LAWSON, JAMES EDWARD, minister, Baptist; b. Grambling, La., Mar. 6, 1936; s. Taylor and Lucille (Allen) L.; m. Omega Ford, May 4, 1958; children: Sylvia Lawson Ross, James E. II, Kenneth, Glorieta, Angela, Lesia, Gregory, Martin. B.Th., United Theol. Sem., 1967, B.R.E., 1971, M.R.E., 1974; D.Divinity (hon.), 1979; Ph.D., Universal Bible Inst., 1977. Pastor Alexander Bapt. Ch., 1960-72, St. John Bapt. Ch., Bastrop, La., 1972-79, Saint's Rest Bapt. Ch., Oakland, Calif., 1979—; del. Nat. Bapt. Conv., Baton Rouge, 1961—, Progressive Dist. Assn., San Francisco, 1981—, So. Bapt. Conv., Atlanta, 1980—; dir. East Bay Bapt. Assn.

LAWTON, LEON REDFORD, minister, Seventh Day Baptist General Conference; b. Battle Creek, Mich., May 21, 1924; s. Stephen Redford Lawton and Ethel (Chapin) Scanlon; m. Dorothy Glee Brannon, Sept. 1, 1946; children: Duane Eugene, Gordon Paul, Patricia Glee Lawton Tauscher, Jeffrey Glen. Student Western Mich. U., 1942, 43, 46; B.A., Salem Coll. (W.Va.), 1947; postgrad. No. Bapt. Theol. Sem., Lombard, Ill., 1947-50; M.Div., Am. Bapt. Sem., West Covina, Calif., 1951. Ordained to ministry Seventh Day Bapt. Ch., 1951; pastor Seventh Day Bapt. Ch., Los Angeles, 1950-56, Denver, 1969-70; missionary Seventh Day Bapt. Missionary Soc., Kingston, Jamaica, 1956-64, dir. evangelism, Westerly, R.I., 1964-68; exec. v.p., 1970—; bd. dirs. Ch. World Service, N.Y.C., 1971—; mem. gen. council Seventh Day Bapt. Gen. Conf., Janesville, Wis., 1978—. Served to sgt. U.S. Army, 1943-46; ETO. Recipient Gold medal of Honor, Govt. of Netherlands, 1945. Office: Seventh Day Bapt Missionary Soc 401 Washington Trust Bldg W Broad St Westerly RI 02891

LAY, ANDY WILLIAM, minister, Nat. Assn. Free Will Baptists; b. Shuyler County, Mo., June 1, 1941; s. Harlan H. and Juanita (Billington) L.; B.A., Free Will Bapt. Bible Coll., 1963; m. Kathy Jo Ratliff, Aug. 9, 1961; children—Marty Kevin, Heidi Lynnette, Jamie Bryan. Ordained to ministry, 1958; pastor Free Will Bapt. chs., Pleasant View, Tenn., 1962-65, Kirksville, Mo., 1965-70, Joplin, Mo., 1970-73, Webb City, Mo., 1973—. Editor GEM mag. Free Will Bapt. Ch., 1972-75. Trustee Hillsdale Coll., Moore, Okla. Mem. Nat. Assn. Free Will Baptists (gen. bd.), Mo. Assn. Free Will Baptists (chmn. bd. Christian edn.), Ministerial Alliance (past pres.), Nat. Assn. Evangelicals (stewardship commn.). Home: 13 Tanglewood Dr Carl Junction MO 64834 Office: 221 S Liberty St Webb City MO 64870

LAY, MICHAEL, minister, Seventh-day Adventist Church. B. Wilmington, Del., Nov. 27, 1937; s. Robert Jeffers and Elizabeth Crary (Jamieson) Kaufmann; m. Marilyn Elizabeth Farley, June 12, 1960; children: David Alan, Brian Patrick, Andrew Sean. B.A., Atlantic Union Coll., 1961; cert. Andrews U., 1963. Ordained to ministry 7th Day Adventist, Ch., 1966. Singing evangelist, intern pastor Potomac Conf. 7th Day Adventists, Md., Va., 1962-64; pastor, assoc. pastor Potomac Conf., Va., 1964-70; pastor N.Y. Conf., 1970-79, No. New Eng. Conf., Maine, 1979-83, N.H./Vt., 1983—; mem. conf. exec. com. No. New Eng. Conf., Maine, N.H., Vt., 1982—. Contbr. articles to religious publs. Republican. Home: PO Box 51 Streeter Hill Rd West Chesterfield NH 03466

LAYMAN, WILLIAM ANTHONY, minister, United Methodist Church; b. Crozet, Va., Aug. 21, 1939; s. William Samuel and Mary Virginia (Tomlin) L.; m. Elsie Elaine Funkhouser, Apr. 3, 1959; children: Tracey Lynn Layman Webb, Julie Ann, Jennifer Leah, Suzanne Kimberly. B.A., Lynchburg Coll., 1966; M.Div., Wesley Theol. Sem., 1970. Minister, deacon Little Fork United Meth. Ch., Jeffersonton, Va., 1966-71; traveling elder, Tappahannock, Va., 1971-74; minister West Point United Meth. Ch., Va., 1974-79, Leesburg United Meth. Ch., Va., 1979-82, Braddock St. United Meth. Ch., Winchester, Va., 1982—; pres. Va. Conf. Fellowship, 1977—; student supply pastor, 1963-67; registrar Minister's Convocation, 1972-76; v.p. Commn. on Enlistment, 1972-76; mem. exec. com. Div. on the Ordained Ministry, 1976-84, local pastor registrar, 1976-84, coordinator local pastors, 1980-84; mem. dist. com. Ordained Ministry, 1973-79; chmn., Winchester, 1982—; mem. Dist. Council on Ministries, Winchester, 1984—. Served with USAF, 1956-59. Decorated Good Conduct medal. Mem. Va. Conf. Brotherhood (sec. 1973-77, pres. 1977—. Ordained deacon United Meth. Ch., 1967, elder, 1970. Democrat. Lodge: Lions (pres. Leesburg sect. 1981-82, 1st, 2d v.p. Tappahannock sect. 1970-71). Avocations: golf; softball; bowling; hiking; movies. Home: 409 Briarmont Dr Winchester VA 26601 Office: Braddock St United Meth Ch 115 Wolfe St Winchester VA 22601

LEACH, NORMAN EDWARD, minister, Presbyterian Church in the U.S.; b. Framingdale, N.Y., May 17, 1940; s. George Alezander and Irene Alice (Bowen) L. A.B., U. Mo., 1962; postgrad. Mo. U. Sch. Social Work, 1962-63; M.Div., San Francisco Theol. Sem., 1970, D. Ministry, 1973. Ordained to ministry Presbyn. Ch., 1971. Mgr., Third Rail Coffee House, First Presbyn. Ch., San Anselmo, Calif., 1968-70; adj. staff cons. Golden Gate Mission Area Ch. and World Com., United Presbyn. Ch. in the U.S.A., San Francisco, 1970-72; dir. San Francisco Bay Area Healing Community Program, 1975—; program adminstr. San Francisco Council Chs., 1976-82, interim acting exec. dir., 1982-84, acting exec. dir., 1984, exec. dir., 1984—; chmn. Presbytery Program Coordinating Council; mem. Presbytery Gen. Council; mem. Presbytery Long-Range Planning Com., Presbytery Nominations Com., Presbytery Permanent Judicial Commn.; founding mem., pres. Presbyterian Disabilities Concerns Caucus, 1981; bd. dirs. World Conf. on Religion and Peace West, 1975-77; mem. Interfaith BiCentennial Com. San Francisco, 1975-76; founding mem. Archdiocese of San Francisco Task Force on Disabilities, 1975—; mem. No. Calif. Ecumenical Council, 1975-78; mem. World Council Chs., Vancouver, B.C., Can., 1983. Editor, pub. Heritage and Hope, 1978, To Free Mankind newspaper. Mem. editorial bd. Caring Congregation Mag. Contbr. columns to mag., chpt. to book. Mem. Congress on Racial Equality, U. Mo.-Columbia, 1958-63; mem. Coalition on Nat. Priorities and Mil. Policy, Washington, 1967-71; bd. dirs. Cambodian-Am. Benevolent Assn., 1975-78, Independent Living Exposition, San Francisco, 1983—, Am.-Israel Friendship League, 1984—; assoc. United Way Execs., San Francisco, 1982—; founding mem. San Francisco Clearinghouse, 1982—; founder, pres. San Francisco Mayor's Council on Disabilities Concerns, 1982—. Recipient Vigil honor Boy Scouts Am., 1974, Nat. Council Chs. award, 1977. Mem. Am. Acad. Polit. and Social Scis., Alpha Sigma Phi, Alpha Phi Omega, Pi Omicron Sigma. Home: 1471 B 46th Ave San Francisco CA 94122 Office: San Francisco Council of Chs 942 Market St Suite 408 San Francisco CA 94102

LEAMAN, PAUL GROFF, minister, Mennonite Ch.; b. Lancaster, Pa., Aug. 29, 1932; s. Sanford D. and Mary (Groff) L.; B.A., Eastern Mennonite Coll., 1972, M.Div., 1976; m. Erma Lois Groff, Sept. 5, 1953; children—Jay Mark, Carl Edward, Stephen Ray, Naomi Jean, Paul Glen. Ordained to ministry, 1953; minister Oakwood Mennonite Ch., Conowingo, Md., 1953-66, Creek Indian Mennonite Ch., Atmore, Ala., 1966-70; dir. devel. Eastern Mennonite High Sch., Harrisonburg, Va., 1970—. Mem. Interdenominational Ministerial Council, 1966-74; chaplain Atmore Meml. Hosp., 1966-70. Home: 444 Biscayne Rd Lancaster PA 17601 Office: 1520 Harrisburg Pike Lancaster PA 17601

LEAR, WILBUR LOUIS, priest, Episcopal Ch.; b. Reno, Nov. 25, 1925; s. Wilbur Clinton and Verne Belle (Wedekind) L.; student theol. studies Ch. Div. Sch. of the Pacific, 1953; A.B., San Francisco State Coll., 1959. Ordained priest, 1953; vicar Ch. of the Good Shepherd, Cloverdale, Calif., 1953-55; rector Ch. of Our Savior, Placerville, Calif., 1955-60; asst. to dir. Bishop Anderson Found., Chgo., 1960-66; rector Ch. of St. Bartholomew, Granite City, Ill., 1967—; vicar St. Thomas Mission, Glen Carbon, Ill., 1967—. Dir. Disaster Relief, Cloverdale, 1953-55; pres. El Dorado County Cancer Soc., 1955-60. Mem. Am. Hosp. Nurses Assn., Episc. Hosp. Chaplains, priest assns. Order of Holy Cross, Guild of All Souls. Contbr. articles to ch. publs. Home: 2604 Delmar St Granite City IL 62040 Office: 22nd St and Grand Ave Granite City IL 62040

LEASE, GARY, religion educator; b. Hollywood, Calif., Sept. 27, 1940; s. Rex Lloyd Lease and Isabelle (Riehle) Reynolds; m. Patricia Ann Metkovich, Sept. 10, 1966; 1 child, Dylan. B.A., Loyola U., Los Angeles, 1962; Ph.D., U. Munich, 1968. Prof. history of consciousness U. Calif.-Santa Cruz, 1973—; investigator various archaeol. excavations, 1974, 76, 80, 81. Author: Witness to The Faith, 1971. Contbr. articles to profl. jours. Instr. hunter safety Calif. Dept. Fish and Game, 1971—. Fellow Nat. Def. Found., 1962, Danforth Found., 1967, NEH, 1971-72, Fulbright Commn., 1984. Mem. Am. Acad. Religion, Am. Schs. Oriental Research, Am. Research Ctr. in Egypt, Am. Hist. Assn. Democrat. Office: History of Consciousness U Calif Santa Cruz CA 95064

LEASURE, CLARA ELIZABETH, lay church worker, United Methodist Church; social worker; b. Wellston, Ohio, Nov. 14, 1914; d. Robert Earl and Hazel Frances (Price) L. B.S. in Edn., Ohio U., 1940, M.A., 1948; D.Edn., Columbia U., 1957. Sunday sch. tchr. Hope United Meth. Ch., Wellston, 1933—, v.p. Hope United Meth. Women, 1966—, chmn. Telecare Com., 1979—, chmn. Church and Society com., 1980—, mem. council of ministries, edn. council, adminstrv. bd., pastor-parish relations commn.; del. West Ohio conf. United Meth. Ch., 1980—. Social worker HHS, Jackson, Ohio, 1962—. Contbr. articles to profl. jours. Leader 4-H Club, 1940-44, Ohio State U. grad. scholar, 1945; asst. professorship Ohio U., 1948. Mem. Ohio Library Assn., Ohio Poetry Assn., Local Poetry Club, Kappa Delta Pi, Pi Lambda Theta. Republican. Avocations: organ; piano; reading; painting; speaking. Home: 214 W Broadway Wellston OH 45692

LEAVELL, LANDRUM PINSON, II, seminary president, Southern Baptist Convention; b. Ripley, Tenn., Nov. 26, 1926; s. Leonard O. and Annie Glenn (Elias) L.; A.B., Mercer U., 1948; B.D., New Orleans Bapt. Theol. Sem., 1951, Th.D., 1954; D.D., Miss. Coll., 1981; m. JoAnn Paris, July 28, 1953; children: Landrum Pinson III, Ann Paris, Roland Q., II, David Earl. Ordained minister So. Baptist Conv., 1948; pastor chs. in Miss., 1948-63, First Bapt. Ch., Wichita Falls, Tex., 1963-74; pres. New Orleans Bapt. Theol. Sem., 1974—. Pres., Bapt. Gen. Conv. Tex., 1971-73. Mem. Wichita County Child Welfare Bd., 1969-74, Baylor U. Devel. Council, 1972-75. Author: John's Letters: Light for Living, 1970; For Prodigals and Other Sinners, 1972; Angels, Angels, Angels, 1973; God's Spirit in You, 1974; Twelve Who Followed Jesus, 1975; Harvest of the Spirit, 1976; Sermons for Celebrating, 1978; The Doctrine of the Holy Spirit, 1983. Lodge: Rotary (pres. Gulfport, Miss. 1961-62). Office: 3939 Gentilly Blvd New Orleans LA 70126

LEAVER, VINCENT WAYNE, minister, United Meth. Ch.; b. Birmingham, Ala., Aug. 21, 1947; s. Vincent Hill and Doris (Eddins) L.; B.A., Birmingham-So. Coll., 1969; M.Div., Wesley Theol. Sem., 1973, D.Min., 1974; m. Shirley Diane Florence, May 19, 1971; 1 dau., Meredith Diane. Ordained to ministry, 1971; clin. pastoral tng. Sibley Hosp., Washington, 1972-73; pastor chs., Ala., Md. and Fla., 1966-75, Miami, Fla., 1975—; Meth. chaplain U. Tampa (Fla.), 1971. Teaching del. U.S. Congress on Evangelism, Mpls., 1969; bd. dirs. Miami Urban Ministries, 1975-76, chmn. task force on mental health, 1976; faculty Miami Lay Sch. Theology, 1975; mem. Miami dist. council on ministries, 1976—. Mem., Atlanta Mayor's Council on Children, 1969; mem. nat. bd. Ams. for Democratic Action, 1974, 75; co-nat. coordinator Religious Leaders for McGovern-Shriver, 1972; chmn. task force on criminal justice Dade County Dem. Exec. Com., 1974-75; mem. Brevard County Dem. Exec. Com., 1974-75. Mem. Acad. Polit. Sci., Am. Acad. Polit. and Social Sci., Assn. Clin. Pastoral Edn., ACLU, Common Cause. Home: 1426 NW 83d Terr Miami FL 33147 Office: 8350 NW 14th Ave Miami FL 33147

LEAVITT, ROBERT F., clergyman, seminary administrator, Roman Catholic. Pres., rector St. Mary's Sem. and Univ. Sch. Theology, Balt. Office: 5400 Roland Ave Baltimore MD 21210*

LEBEL, ROBERT, bishop, Roman Cath. Ch.; b. Trois-Pistoles, Que., Can., Aug. 11, 1924; s. Wilfrid and Alexina (Belanger) L.; B.A., U. Laval, 1946; Lic. Theology, U. St. Paul, Ottawa, Ont., 1950; Th.D., Angelicum U., Rome, 1951. Ordained priest, 1950; consecrated bishop, 1974; bishop of Valleyfield, Que., 1976—. Mem. bd. Canadian Cath. Conf. Bishops; pres. theology com. Assemblee des Eveques du Que. Home and office: 31 Fabrique St Valleyfield PQ J6T 4G Canada

LEBER, CHARLES TUDOR, JR., minister, Unite Presbyterian Church in the U.S.A.; b. Trenton, Feb. 21 1924; s. Charles Tudor and Elizabeth Louise (Heath) L. m. Marian Louise Mattson, June 9, 1948; children Charles Tudor III, Matthew, Irene, Eric. B.A., Hamilto Coll., 1945, D.Div. (hon.), 1960; M.Div., Princeto Theol. Sem., 1949. Ordained to ministry Presbyn. Ch 1949. Pastor, Wolff Meml. Ch., Newark, 1949-53; exec dir. Dodge Community House, Detroit, 1953-57 co-pastor First Presbyn. Ch., Chgo., 1957-63; dir. urba mission N.Y.C. Presbytery, 1963-66; dir. interpretatio Bd. Nat. Missions (Presbyn.), N.Y.C., 1966-72; exec presbyter Presbytery of Newark, East Orange, N.J 1972—; trustee Princeton Theol. Sem., 1968-7 commr. Presbyn. Gen. Assembly, Mpls., 1952; de World Council Chs. conf., Geneva, 1951; truste Detroit Council Chs., 1954-57. Contbr. articles to prof jours. Co-chmn. Newark Citizens Housing Counci 1952; trustee, chaplain Theta Delta Chi, Mich., 196 S.A.R. scholar, 1941. Mem. Met. Ecumenica Ministries (trustee, bd. dirs.), Campus Christian Found (bd. dirs.). Lodge: Lions. Office: Presbytery of Newar 9 S Munn Ave East Orange NJ 07018

LEDFORD, AMOS ANDREW, minister, Ch. of God b. Marked Tree, Ark., Oct. 24, 1930; s. William Arthu and Luttie Ann Laura (Raynor) L.; m. Vivian D Tankersley, July 9, 1949; children—Sharmin Gail (Mrs David Lee Waters), Darla Jennine, Joel D., Mar Randall. Ordained to ministry Ch. of God, Cleveland Tenn., 1956; minister chs., Tex., Ark., Kans., Ill., Ohi 1948-70; apptd. overseer Ch. of God, State of Iowa 1970—. Bd. dirs. N.W. Bible Coll., Minot, N.D. Autho When The Pillars Were Shaking, 1956; Profits fro Prophets and Prophecies, 1971; Manna, 1973; Fait 1974. Home: 6641 Timberline Dr Des Moines IA 5031 Office: Box BB Des Moines IA 50304

LEE, ANTHONY A., publisher, Baha'i Faith; b Tuskegee Institute, Ala., Aug. 5, 1947; s. Asa Penn an Manila Hudlin (Smith) L.; m. Flor Geola, Apr. 29, 197 children: Faizi Geola, Taraz Geola. B.A., UCLA, 196 M.A., 1974, C.Phil., 1976. Asst. dir. nat. youth activitie Baha'i Nat. Ctr., Wilmette, Ill., 1969-71; sec. Baha Assembly of Los Angeles, 1971-83; mem. Baha Assembly of Manhattan Beach, Calif., 1984—; owne mng. editor Kalimat Press, Los Angeles, 1978—; rep South Bay Interfaith Peace Com., 1984-85. Autho children's books on Baha'i Faith. Editor: Circle o Unity: Baha'i Approaches to Current Social Issue 1984. Mem. Am. Acad. Religion, African Studies Ass Office: Kalimat Press 10889 Wilshire Blvd Suite 70 Los Angeles CA 90024

LEE, ARTHUR PATERSON, minister, Baptis Federation of Canada; b. Edinburgh, Scotland, Oct. 2 1926; came to Can., 1958; s. Alexander and Mar (Flockhart) L.; m. Eunice Heraldine Near, Sept. 1949; children: Eunice R., Rosemary F. M.A Edinburgh U. (Scotland), 1951; B.D., New Col (Scotland), 1955; D.D. (hon.), Gordon Coll., 196 Minister various Chs., Scotland, Ont., Mass., 1954-7 First Bapt. Ch., Moncton, N.B., 1979—; co-founde sec. Evang. Fellowship of Can., Toronto, Ont., 1965-6 founder Boston Christian Counselling Ctr., 1972-7 chmn. chaplains com. New Eng. Bapt. Hosp., Bosto 1972-76. Bd. dirs. Gordon Coll., Wenham, Mass 1967-76. Served to sgt. Royal Corps Signals, 1944-4 Mem. World Vision Can. (corp. mem.), Ontario Bib Coll. (corp. mem.), Ontario Theol Sem. (corp. mem. Evang. Fellowship Can. Lodge: Rotary. Home: 5 Hollywood Dr Moncton NB E1E 2R6 Canada Offic First Bapt Ch 157 Queen St Moncton NB E1C 1K Canada

LEE, BYUNG HEE, minister, United Meth. Ch.; b Seoul, Korea, July 29, 1938; s. Chung An and Man Soo (Chung) L.; came to U.S., 1964, naturalized, 197 B.Th., Yon Sei U., Seoul, 1961; M.Div., Meth. Theo Sch., Delaware, Ohio, 1968; m. Hee Sook Kim, Nov. 3 1968; children—Joyce, Robert. Ordained to ministr 1967; asso. minister Mentor (Ohio) United Meth. Ch 1968-73; pastor Cleve. Korean Ch., 1973—. Me religion and race commn. East Ohio Conf. United Met Ch., 1976—, rep. Fellowship of Asian-Am. Unite Methodists, 1976—. Dir. Mentor Human Relatio Council, 1968-71, Greater Cleve. Area Korean Assn 1973—. Home: 4928 Hartley Dr Lyndhurst OH 4412

LEE, DALE WAYNE, minister, So. Bapt. Conv.; Artesia, N.Mex., Oct. 25, 1943; s. Dulen Elmo an Bertha Lee (Thompson) L.; B.A., Wayland Bapt. Col 1975; m. Rosella Jones, July 30, 196 children—Valorie Ann, Wade Allen. Ordained deaco 1971, minister, 1972; pastor Challis Bapt. Ch Brownfield, Tex., 1972-74, Mountain View Bapt. Ch Alamogorodo, N.Mex., 1974—. Chmn. evanglism co Otoero County, 1975-76; v.p. Terry County Ministeri Alliance, Brownfield, 1974-75. Asst. coach Litt League Baseball, Brownfield, 1975. Mem. Mountai Valley Bapt. Assn. Home: 603 Adams Rd Alamogord NM 88310 Office: PO Box 1039 Alamogordo N 88310

LEE, HI YOUNG, lay church worker, Presbyterian Church U.S.A.; physician; b. Seoul, Korea, Oct. 18, 1941; came to U.S., 1965, naturalized, 1976; s. Jung Sup Lee and Hwa (Jung) Kim; m. Sun Myung Lee, June 4, 1965; children: Sandra, Grace, David. M.D., Yon Sei U. Med. Sch., Seoul, 1965. Mem. Self Devel. People Presbyn. of Island Empire, 1981—; co-organizer Korean New Life Presbyn. Ch., Spokane, Wash., 1977, Byeo Grain Korean Christian Group, Spokane, 1970—. Pres. Lee & Leeps Empire Med Clinic, Spokane, 1974—. Contbr. articles to profl. jours. Recipient McDermont award VA, 1970. Fellow Am. Acad. Family Practice; mem. Christian Med. Soc., Gideons Internat. Avocations: golf; music. Office: Empire Med Office E17 Empire St Spokane WA 99207

LEE, JANET ARLENE, diaconal minister, United Methodist Church; b. Detroit, Dec. 8, 1931; d. Homer Brown and Mary Elizabeth (Saettel) Leisenring; m. William Richard Lee, July 4, 1953; children: Janet Susan, William David, Patricia Annette, Douglas Andrew, Richard Allan. B.Mus. Edn., U. Mich., 1953. Organist Hudson Meth. Ch., Mich., 1948-49; organist, choir dir. Southfield Meth. Ch., Mich., 1955-57; asst. in music 1st Meth. Ch., Royal Oak, Mich., 1957-62; minister of music Clawson Meth. Ch., Mich., 1962-77, minister to youth, 1971—, diaconal minister, 1977—; cons. for workshops, choir festivals; v.p. Bd. of Local Ministries, Detroit Conf. United Meth. Ch., 1984-86. Dir. women's chorus Royal Oak Musicale, 1965-76, 83—; dir. Detroit Children's Choir-Detroit Community Music Sch., 1979—. Contbr. articles to religious and musical publs. Vice pres. bd. Art Ctr. Music Sch., Detroit, 1981-85; chmn. pub. relations Clawson Youth Assistance, 1982-85. Recipient Service award East Hills Jr. High Sch., Bloomfield Hills, Mich., 1981, Recognition of 20 Yr. Service award Clawson United Meth. Ch., 1982. Mem. Choristers Guild (pres. Detroit chpt. 1975-76), Fellowship United Methodists in Worship Music and Other Arts (nat. pres. 1981-83, pres. Detroit chpt. 1971-73), Am. Guild Organists, Sacred Dance Guild Am. (bd. dirs. 1974-77), Am. Guild English Handbell Ringers, Royal Oak Musicale (pres. 1972-74), Birmingham Musicale. Home: 958 Lampwick Ct Bloomfield Hills MI 48013 Office: Clawson United Meth Ch 205 N Main St Clawson MI 48013

LEE, JUNG NAM, minister, American Baptist Churches U.S.A.; educator; b. Korea, Oct. 24, 1941; s. Dong Sup and Mae Ye (Lee) L.; m. Hyun Soo Kim, Jan. 20, 1973; children: Chris Youngbin, James Younguk, John Younghoon. B.A., Yonsei U., 1965; M.Div., Am. Bapt. Theol. Sem. of the West, 1975; postgrad. Claremont Grad. Sch., 1975-77. Ordained, 1977. Asst. pastor First Bapt. Ch. Los Angeles, 1975—. Prof. O.T., Calif. Internat. U., Los Angeles, 1983—. Translator into Korean: Studies in Genesis One, 1982. Recipient honors Kor-Am Sr. Citizens, Los Angeles, 1983, Kor-Am Econ. Weekly, 1984. Home: 1265 S Highland Ave Los Angeles CA 90019 Office: First Bapt Ch Los Angeles 760 Westmoreland Ave Los Angeles CA 90005

LEE, JUNG YOUNG, minister, religious studies educator, United Methodist Church; b. Chasan, Sunchon, Korea, Aug. 20, 1935; s. Dong Hi and In Duck (Cho) L.; m. Gy Whang Cho, June 6, 1965; children: Sue, Jonathan. B.S., Findlay Coll., 1957; B.D., Garrett-Evang. Theol. Sem., 1961; M.S., Case Western Res. U., 1962; Th.D., Boston U., 1968. Ordained elder Ohio Conf., United Meth. Ch., 1961. Minister Oeheloff United Meth. Ch., Cleve., 1961-63; assoc. minister Ohmer Park United Meth. Ch., Dayton, Ohio, 1965-66; asst. prof. Otterbein Coll., Westerville, Ohio, 1968-72; assoc. prof. religious studies U. N.D., Grand Forks, 1972-78, prof., 1978—; founder, past pres. Fund for Korean Ministers, Washington, 1963-67; founder, minister Korean Ch., Columbus, Ohio, 1969-72, Grand Forks, N.D., 1983—. Author: The I: A Christian Concept of Man, 1971; Cosmic Religion, 1973; God Suffers for Us, 1974; Theology of Change, 1979. Mem. editorial adv. bd. Jour. Dharma, 1977—. Contbg. editor Korea Jour., 1979—. Sr. Fulbright-Hays scholar, Washington, 1977. Mem. Am. Acad. Religion (chmn. consultation on Korean religions 1981—), Assn. Asian Studies (council on East Asian studies 1977), West Ohio Conf. United Meth. Ch., Fedn. Asian-Am. United Meths. Home: 1624 8th Ave S Grand Forks ND 58201 Office: U ND Grand Forks ND 58202

LEE, MAX, minister, Southern Baptist Convention; b. El Dorado, Ark., July 5, 1931; s. O. Roy and Mattie Lee (Giddens) L.; m. Martha Elizabeth Perritt, Aug. 16, 1957; children: Alvis Robert, Jeffrey Max. B.A., La. Tech. U., 1955; B.Div., So. Bapt. Theol. Sem., 1959, Th.M., 1963; D.Ministry New Orleans Bapt. Theol. Sem., 1976. Ordained to ministry Baptist Ch., 1955. Assoc. pastor Emmanuel Bapt. Ch., Houston, 1960-63; pastor East Pineville Bapt. Ch., La., 1963-66, First Bapt. Ch., Port Allen, La., 1966-71, Winnsboro, La., 1972—; trustee So. Bapt. Theol. Sem., 1984—, Alexandria, La., 1976-82; exec. bd. mem. La. Bapt. Conv., Alexandria, 1982—; exec. bd. chmn. Northeast La. U. Bapt. Student Union, Monroe, 1981-83. Mem. adv. bd. Northeastern La. Vocat. Sch., Winnsboro, 1981—; pres. Ministerial Alliance, Winnsboro, 1980; exec. bd. mem. Mental Health Assn., Columbia, La., 1981—. Mem. Sigma Tau Delta, Omicron Delta Kappa. Democrat. Lodge: Lions (pres. Port Allen 1970-71). Home: 804 Nell Winnsboro LA 71295 Office: First Bapt Ch 502 Highland Winnsboro LA 71295

LEE, RALPH BARRETT, lay ch. worker; b. San Antonio, Aug. 18, 1912; s. Willis Walter and Lina (Coffey) L.; B.A., Baylor U., 1934, LL.B., 1935; m. Jeanette Burress, Oct. 2, 1938; children—Barbara (Mrs. Sam J. Brown), Ralph Barrett, Betty (Mrs. Julian M. Moss), Randolph B. Chmn. bd. deacons South Main Bapt. Ch., Houston, 1964-66. Admitted to Tex. bar, 1935, since practiced in Houston; pres. Am. Savs. & Loan Assn. Houston, 1959—; chmn. exec. com., dir. First Bank Houston, 1970—; chmn. trustees Ch. Loan Corp., Tex. Bapt. Gen. Conv., 1969-72. Trustee Baylor U., So. Bapt. Conv. Annuity Bd. Home: 8840 Memorial Dr Houston TX 77024 Office: POB 27338 Houston TX 77027

LEE, RICHARD KUO-YUAN, minister, United Presbyn. Ch. U.S.A.; b. Peking, China, Jan. 2, 1923; s. Sujan and Senfan (Shaw) L.; came to U.S., 1925, naturalized, 1967; M.D., Peking U., 1949; M.Div., Pitts. Theol. Sem., 1965; m. Joice Yuan Chiaying, June 1, 1944; children—Li-Chung, Fifi, Li-Lin, Li-Young, Li-Eng. Ordained to ministry, 1966; minister Trinity United Presbyn. Ch., Vandergrift, Pa., 1968—. Vice-pres. Gamaliel U., Indonesia, 1955-60; lectr. Westmoreland Coll., 1973; mem. acupuncture med. research program, Pitts., 1973—. Dir. Jamis Medicine Corp., 1959—. Home: 266 Franklin Ave Vandergrift PA 15690 Office: 262 Franklin Ave Vandergrift PA 15690

LEE, ROBERT EDWARD ALEXANDER, church organization official, Evangelical Lutheran Synod; b. Spring Grove, Minn., Nov. 9, 1921; s. Knute A. and Mathilda Clara (Glasrud) L.; B.A., Luther Coll., 1942; D.F.A. (hon.), Susquehanna U., 1979; m. Elaine E. Naeseth, July 29, 1944; children: Margaret Lee Barth, Barbara Lee Greenfeldt, Sigrid, Richard, Sylvia Lee-Thompson, Paul. Dir. Evang. Luth. Ch. films, producer Children's Chapel for radio, asst. dir. pub. relations Evang. Luth. Ch., Mpls., 1947-54; exec. sec. Luth. Film Assn., N.Y.C., 1954—; sec., dept. films, Luth. Council U.S.A, 1967-70, exec. dir. communications, 1970—; v.p. communication commn. Nat. Council Chs., 1973—; radio commentator Cinema Sound for radio, 1973-84; film critic The Luth., 1976—; instr. Adelphi U., 1974, 75. Recipient Disting. Alumni award Luther Coll., 1967. Mem. Overseas Press Club, Religious Pub. Relations Council. Author: Question 7, 1961; Behind the Wall, 1964; Martin Luther: the Reformation Years, 1967; (with Roger Kahle) Popcorn and Parable, 1971; The Joy of Bach, 1979. Producer films: Question 7, 1961; Viewpoint Helsinki, 1963; A Time for Burning, 1966; Before the Cock Crows, 1967; Acts, 1969; Celebration of Learning, 1971; Housing—More Than a Roof, 1973; The Joy of Bach, 1979; Sounds of Summer, 1982; A Parade of Witnesses, 1983; Burchfield's Vision, 1984. Office: 360 Park Ave S New York NY 10010

LEE, THURLO WILLIAM, minister, So. Baptist Conv.; b. Onia, Ark., Nov. 13, 1921; s. A.R. and Malissa (Balentine) L.; A.A., So. Baptist Coll., 1950; B.S., Ark. State U., 1960; m. Hazel Marie Moore, Dec. 19, 1938; children—Jason, Jimmy, Shirley (Mrs. Richard Lewis), Mary (Mrs. Mark Gammill). Ordained to ministry So. Bapt. Conv., 1940; pastor Brown's Chapel Bapt. Ch., 1950-53; missionary Stone, Van Buren, Searcy Assn., 1953-56; pastor Oden (Ark.) Bapt. Ch., 1956-58, Westside Bapt. Ch., Manila, Ark., 1958-67, Martindale Bapt. Ch., Little Rock, 1967-71, Calvary Bapt. Ch., Timbo, Ark., 1972—. Coordinator Mountain View (Ark.) Sch., 1971—. Home: Gen Delivery Onia AR 72663 Office: Mountain View AR 72560

LEE, TIMOTHY FRANK, minister, Southern Baptist Convention; b. Greenville, S.C., Sept. 4, 1944; s. Henry G.B. and Hazel Madeline (Duncan) L.; m. Judith Ann Crain, Aug. 6, 1963; children: Timothy Mark, April Denise. Diploma Fruitland Bible Inst., 1971; A.A., Mars Hill Coll., 1978; B.D., Luther Rice Sem., 1979, M.Ministry, 1980. Ordained to ministry Baptist Ch., 1970. Pastor, Milford Bapt. Ch., Greer, S.C., 1970-73, First Bapt. Ch., DeLeon Springs, Fla., 1973-74, Cherry Springs Bapt. Ch., Old Fort, N.C., 1974-80, Neals Creek Bapt. Ch., Anderson, S.C., 1980—. Pres., Old Fort Ministerial Assn., 1976, Blue Ridge Pastors Conf., Marion, N.C., 1976; moderator Saluda Bapt. Assn., Anderson, 1984-85. Mem. Tri-County Bapt. Pastors Conf. (pres. camp meeting, 1981-82), S.C. Bapt. Pastor's Conf. (v.p. 1985). Home: Route 8 Box 307 Anderson SC 29621 Office: Neals Creek Bapt Ch Route 8 Box 307 Anderson SC 29621

LEE-BEVIER, KIP CLIFFORD, lay ch. worker, Episcopal Ch.; b. N.Y.C., Apr. 16, 1927; s. Clifford and Katherine (Hostettler) L.-B.; student U. Louisville, 1946-48, N.Y.U., 1954-56. Spl. promotions officer Exec. Council Episcopal Ch., N.Y.C., 1963-75; vestryman Episcopal Ch. du Saint Esprit, N.Y.C., 1963—; mem. Pa. Diocesan Com. for World Relief, 1976—; mem. One Great Hour of Sharing and Service com. Ch. World Service, 1967-75, also nat. com. for CROP community hunger appeal, Nat. Council Chs., 1968-75. Sponsor Pa. Ballet Assn., 1976—; trustee Am. Friends of LaFayette, 1970-74. Fellow Royal Soc. of St. George; mem. Huguenot Soc. Am. (v.p., 1967-72), Soc. Colonial Wars (former officer), St. Nicholas Soc. City N.Y., Huguenot Hist. Soc. of New Paltz (past officer), English-Speaking Union, Friends of Am. Mus. in Britain, Phila. Soc. for Preservation of Landmarks, Newport (R.I.) Hist. Soc., Nob Hill Preservation Soc. (2d v.p.). Contbr. articles to Episcopalian mag. Address: 2125 Green St Philadelphia PA 19130

LEGARE, HENRI FRANCIS, archbishop, Roman Cath. Ch.; b. Willow-Bunch, Sask., Can., Feb. 20, 1918; s. Philippe and Amanda (Douville) L.; B.A., Gravelbourg Coll., Sask., Can., 1940; M.A. in Social Scis., Laval U., Que., Can., 1946; D. in Social Scis., Cath. U., Lille, France, 1950; LL.D., Carleton U., Ottawa, 1959, Assumption U., Ont., 1960, Queens U., Ont., 1961, Sask. U., 1963, Waterloo Luth. U., Ont., 1965, U. Ottawa, 1984. Joined Order Oblates of Mary Immaculate, 1937; ordained priest, 1943, consecrated bishop, 1967; prof. sociology Laval U., Quebec, 1947; bursar Grand Sem., St. Norbert, Man., Can., 1947-48; prof. sociology and med. ethics Ottawa (Ont.) U., 1951, 55-58, dean faculty of Social Scis., 1954-58, vice-rector, 1955-58, rector, 1958-64; provincial superior Oblates, Winnipeg, Man., 1966-67; bishop, Labrador, Can., 1967-72; archbishop, Grouard-McLennan, Alta., Can., 1972—. Chmn. steering com. Oblate gen. chpt., Rome, Italy, 1966; pres. Western Conf. Cath. Bishops, 1974-80, Can. Conf. Cath. Bishops, 1981-83; Can. del. to Synods in Rome, 1974, 80. Chmn. Canadian Univs. Found., 1960-62. Mem. Cath. Hosp. Assn. Can. (dir. 1952-57), Internat. Polit. Acad., French Lang. Assn. Ont., Order of Malta. Address: PO Box 388 McLennan AB T0H 2L0 Canada

LEGGE, RUSSEL DONALD, religious educator, minister, United Church of Canada; b. Milton, N.S., Can., Jan. 31, 1935; s. James Farish and Shirley Evelyn (McNutt) L.; m. Elma Gertrude Dingwell, Aug. 20, 1960; children: Cheryl Lee, Scott Douglas, Suzanne Rae, James Earl. B.A., Transylvania Coll., 1962; S.T.B., Harvard U., 1965; Ph.D., McMaster U., 1972. Ordained to ministry, 1965. Pastor, Guelph Christian Ch., Ont., Can., 1965-67, Winger Christian Ch., Wainfleet, Ont., 1967-70; lectr. religious studies U. Waterloo, Ont., 1970-72, asst. prof., 1972-82, assoc. prof. 1982—; dir. studies St. Paul's United Coll., U. Waterloo, 1978—. Mem. Can. Council Chs. (pres. 1982-85), Can. Soc. for Study of Religion. Home: 259 Lourdes St Waterloo ON N2L 1P2 Canada Office: Saint Paul's United Coll Univ Waterloo Waterloo ON N2L 3G5 Canada

LEGGETT, PAUL ARTHUR, minister, Presbyterian Church in the U.S.; b. Montclair, N.J., July 3, 1946; s. Joseph Hoyt and Jane (Stenstrom) L.; 1 child, Elisabeth; m. Beth Petrie, Nov. 28, 1981. Ordained to ministry Presbyn. Ch., 1971. Interim pastor Disston Meml. Presbyn. Ch., Phila., 1971-72; asst. pastor Huntingdon Valley Presbyn. Ch., Pa., 1972-73; prof. theology Latin Am. Bibl. Sem., San Jose, Costa Rica, 1974-80; pastor Grace Presbyn. Ch., Montclair, N.J., 1981—; spl. cons. Gen. Assembly Mission Council, 1980-81; chmn. Hispanic Com. Newark Presbytery, 1982, Ch. and Soc. Com., 1983—; vis. lectr. Vassar Coll., Poughkeepsie, N.Y., 1979-80, 82-83. Co-editor: Lectura Teologica del Tiempo LatinoAmericano, 1979; contbr. articles to profl. jours. Recipient Religion award Syracuse U., 1968; Margot M. Studer award Montclair State Coll., 1984. Home: 63 Tuxedo Rd Montclair NJ 07042 Office: Grace Presbyn Ch 153 Tuxedo Rd Montclair NJ 07042

LEGREE, JOSEPH CLEMENT, priest, Roman Catholic Ch. B. Pembroke, Ont., Can., Aug. 20, 1930; s. Austin and Mary Ellen (Coughlin) L. B.A., St. Patrick's Coll., 1952; B.Th., U. Montreal, 1956. Ordained priest Roman Catholic Ch., 1956. Asst. chs. Pembroke Diocese, Ont. and Que., Can., 1956-69, Ottawa, Ont., summer 1968; pastor ch., Sheenborough, Que., 1969-72, Combermere, Ont., 1972—. Govt. Ont. scholar, 1948. Lodge: K.C.

LEGROW, ALFRED BUTT, orgn. adminstr., United Ch. of Can.; b. Broad Cove, Nfld., Can., May 8, 1918; s. Thomas Parsons and Elizabeth (Butt) LeG.; student Meml. U. Tchr. Tng. Coll., 1943-44; B.A., Dalhousie U., 1957; B.D., Pine Hill Div. Hall, 1958; postgrad. Boston Sch. Theology, 1968; M.Div., Atlantic Sch. Theology, 1973; m. Mildred Butt, Dec. 5, 1944. Ordained to ministry, 1957; sec. Twillingate Presbytery, Lewisporte, Npld., 1960-62, chmn., 1962-64; field sec. Christian edn. Nfld. Conf., St. John's, 1965-70, sec., 1965-67, pres., 1967-68, chmn. Conf. Staff Com., 1973—; exec. officer Denominational Edn. Com. (Anglican, Presbyn., Salvation, United Chs.), St. John's 1970—. chmn. conf. staff com. Gen Council Staff, 1973—. Mem., vice chmn. Cerebral Palsy Sch., St. John's; mem. research com. Meml. U., St. John's; mem. adult edn. com. Agnes Pratt Sr. Citizens Home, St. John's. Author: The Old Testament: Its History, Culture and Themes, 1976. Editor: the Bible as Literature, 1970; History of Methodism, 1973. Home: 4 Argyle St St John's NF A1A 1V3 Canada Office: PO Box 6116 Royal Trust Bldg St John's NF A1C 5X8 Canada

LEGUERRIER, JULES, bishop, Roman Catholic Church; b. Clarence Creek, Ont., Can., Feb. 18, 1915. Ordained priest, 1943; ordained titular bishop of Bavagaliana and vicar apostolic of James Bay, 1964; first bishop of Moosonee (Ont.), 1967—. Office: CP 40 Moosonee ON P0L 1Y0 Canada*

LEHENBAUER, ALBERT WILLIAM, minister, Luth. Ch.-Mo. Synod; b. Linn, Kans., Jan. 17, 1918; s. Carl Frederick and Hedwig (Knoernshild) L.; A.A., St. John's Coll., Kans., 1938; B.A., Concordia Sem., 1943; M.R.E., New Orleans Bapt. Theol. Sem., 1966, grad. specialist in religious edn., 1967, Ed.D., 1977; m. Virginia Marie Hashagen, May 8, 1948; children—Barbara Ellen, Janet Gail, James Michael. Ordained to ministry, 1943; pastor chs. S.C., Md. and La., 1943-61; exec. instl. chaplain So. dist. Luth. Ch.-Mo. Synod, New Orleans, 1961-71; exec. chaplain No. Ill. dist., Chgo., 1971—; v.p. Ill. State Consortium on Pastoral Care, 1975-77, chmn., 1977—. Mem. Am. Protestant Hosp. Assn., Assn. Clin. Pastoral Educators, Res. Officers Assn., Luth. Hosp. Assn. Contbr. articles to religious jours. Composer hymns. Home: 91 Erie St Maywood IL 60153 Office: 77 W Washington St Chicago IL 60602

LEHENBAUER, OSMAR OTTO, minister, Lutheran Ch. - Mo. Synod; b. Arroio do Meio, Lageado, Rio Grande do Sul, Brazil, Sept. 2, 1929; came to U.S., Aug. 1930, naturalized, 1930; s. Conrad Ferdinand and Magdalene Augusta (Wallner) L.; m. Shirlee Eileen Rieck, Feb. 12, 1955; children: Rebecca Ann Boyd, Joel David, Daniel Jon, Eric James. B.Th., Concordia Sem., 1954. Ordained to ministry Lutheran Ch., 1954. Sr. pastor Concordia Luth. Ch., Ft. Wayne, Ind., 1954-67; pastor Trinity Luth. Ch., St. Louis, 1967-69; sr. pastor St. Paul's Luth. Ch., Chicago Heights, Ill., 1969—; v.p. No. Ill. Dist. Luth. Ch. - Mo. Synod, Hillside, Ill., 1978—. Home: 837 Luther Ln Chicago Heights IL 60411 Office: St Paul's Lutheran Church 330 Highland Dr Chicago Heights IL 60411

LEHMAN, EDWIN GERHARD, minister, church official, Lutheran Church-Missouri Synod; b. Edmonton, Alta., Can., Jan. 6, 1932; s. Adolph and Wanda (Rendfleisch) L.; m. Marjorie Evelyn Huber, Aug. 4, 1956; children: Rodney, Barbara, Katherine. B.A., Concordia Sem., 1956, M.Div., 1956. Ordained to ministry Luth. Ch., 1956. Pastor, St. Peter Luth. Ch., Margo, Sask., Can., 1956-58; Mt. Calvary Luth. Ch., Red Deer, Alta., 1958-67; Trinity Luth. Ch., Richmond, B.C., Can., 1967-78; pres. Alta.-B.C. Dist. Luth. Ch.-Mo. Synod, Edmonton, 1978—; pres. Luth. Bible Translators-Can., Kitchener, Ont., 1979-83; sec. Luth. Ch.-Can., Edmonton, 1981-85; chmn. bd. regents Concordia Coll., Edmonton, 1981—, Concordia Luth. Sem., 1983—. Pres. Red Deer Family Service Bur., 1962-66. Home: 686 Lee Ridge Rd Edmonton AB T6K 0P2 Canada Office: Alta-BC Dist Luth Ch-Mo Synod 9912 106th St Room 35 Edmonton AB T5K 1C5 Canada

LEHN, MATTHEW BENEDICT, priest, Roman Cath. Ch.; b. St. Louis, Mar. 21, 1926; s. Joseph and Magdalena (Queiser) L.; B.A., Cardinal Glennon Coll., 1948; A.M. in Religious Studies, St. Louis U., 1976; postgrad. Pontifical Coll. Josephinum, Ohio, 1940-45, St. Henry Sem., Belleville, Ill., 1945, St. Thomas Sem., Denver, 1948-52. Ordained priest, 1952; asso. pastor St. Adalbert Ch., East St. Louis, Ill., 1952-55, St. Francis de Sales Ch., Aviston, Ill., 1955-58, St. Philip Ch., East St. Louis, 1958-59; pastor St. Joseph Ch., Equality, Ill., 1959-65, St. Michael Ch., Paderborn, Ill., 1965-69, St. Lawrence Ch., Lawrenceville, Ill., 1969-76 and Immaculate Conception Mission, Bridgeport, Ill., St. Vincent Ch., Basalt, Colo., 1976—, St. Mary of Crown Mission, Carbondale, Colo., 1976—, Sacred Heart Ch. Mission, Redstone, Colo., 1976—, Cath. Mission at Snowmass Village, Aspen, Colo., 1976—. Deanery moderator Cath. Youth Council, 1959-65, Council Cath. Women, 1959-72; adviser, coordinator, lectr. religious studies of Western Parishes and Area, Roman Cath. Ch.; religion tchr. Central Cath. High Sch., East St. Louis, 1952-53, St. Theresa Acad., 1953-59; mem. Western Parishes services bd. Archdiocese of Denver. Home and Office: Saint Vincent Rectory 240 Midland St Basalt CO 81621

LEHNHOFF, ROLAND ALBERT, minister, Seventh-day Adventist Church; b. Cin., Feb. 23, 1942; s. Siegfried Kurt and Mary Anna (Hafner) L.; m. Janice Sue Wright, June 5, 1966. B.A., Andrews U., 1964, M.A., 1965. Pastor, evangelist Seventh-day Adventist Ch., Ill., 1965-72, evangelist, N.Y., 1972-75, Europe, 1976-81; TV speaker, U.S., Can., Australia, 1981—, assoc. speaker It Is Written Telecast, 1981—. Home: 798 Green Valley Dr Newbury Park CA 91320 Office: It Is Written TV 1100 Rancho-Conejo Blvd Newbury Park CA 91320

LEHRMAN, IRVING, rabbi, Jewish Congregations; b. Poland, June 15, 1911; came to U.S., 1920; s. Abraham and Minnie (Dinowitz) L.; m. Bella Goldfarb, May 21, 1935; children: David, Rosalind. M.H.L., Jewish Inst. Religion, 1930; D.H.L., Jewish Theol. Sem. Am., 1942, D.D. (hon.), 1958. Rabbi, Temple Emanu-El, Miami Beach, Fla., 1943—; former vis. prof. homiletics Jewish Theol. Sem. Am.; mem. rabbinic cabinet and bd. rabbinic visitors; bd. dirs. Internat. Synagogue, Kennedy Airport; pres. Synagogue Council Am., 1971-73, hon. pres., 1973—; fellow Hebrew U.; bd. dirs. Greater Miami Jewish Fedn.; chmn. religious task force White

House Conf. Food, Nutrition and Health, 1969; trustee Ency. Judaica Research Found.; pres. council Bradeis U.; nat. bd. dirs. NCCJ, Jewish Nat. Fund; nat. commr. Hillel Found.; chmn. bd. govs. Israel Bonds of Greater Miami; past chmn. rabbinic cabinet United Jewish Appeal. Mem. Pres.'s Commn. on Obscenity and Pornography, Pres.'s Commn. on Aging; mem. nat. council Boy Scouts Am.; bd. dirs. Dade County chpt. ARC, United Fund Dade County; pres. Travelers Aid, 1958; past mem. exec. com. Am. sect. UNESCO; mem. Community Relations Bd. Greater Miami. Recipient Silver Medallion award NCCJ, 1972, Prime Minister's Medallion, State of Israel, 1969. Mem. Zionist Orgn. Am. (v.p.), Rabbinical Assn. S.W. Region (hon. pres.), Rabbinical Assn. Greater Miami (past pres.), Rabbinical Assembly Am. (past sec.), Am. Technion Soc. (nat. bd. dirs., Albert Einstein brotherhood award 1973). Lodge: Kiwanis. Home: 2925 Flamingo Dr Miami Beach FL 33140 Office: 1701 Washington Ave Miami Beach FL 33139

LEIALOHA, LEMUEL KEALA, lay worker, Seventh-day Adventist Church; educational administrator; b. Schofield, Hawaii, Sept. 24, 1939; s. Benjamin P. and Eleanor (Bailey) L.; m. Sue Brooks, Apr. 1, 1963; children: Terry, Michael Li. B.S., Riverside U., 1967, B.B.A., 1968; postgrad. U. Hawaii, 1972-74, Charmanide U., 1977. Cert. tchr., adminstr. Youth worker Seventh-day Adventist chs., 1958—, lay worker, 1961—, deacon, 1967, elder, 1968—; bd. dirs. Campus Hill Ch., Loma Linda, Calif., 1979—; trustee Hawaiian Mission Acad., Honolulu, 1974-79, Hawaiian Mission Acad. Alumni, 1967—. Treas., bus. adminstr. Loma Linda Acad., 1979—. Housing dir. City and County of Honolulu, 1968-74; mem., chmn. Honolulu Redevel. Commn., 1968-74; mem. Model Cities Commn., Honolulu, 1968-70; trustee Hawaiian Civic Club, Waianae, 1968-74. Served with U.S. Army, 1958-63. Recipient Service award Am. Heart Assn., 1969; Outstanding Service award, Pathfinder Club, Hawaii, 1958-75, 12 mil. awards. Mem. Hawaii Heart Assn. (dir. 1968-69), Nat. Multiple Sclerosis Soc. (dir. 1967-70). Republican. Club: Kiwanis (treas. Loma Linda 1979—). Office: Loma Linda Acad 10656 Anderson St Loma Linda CA 92354

LEIBRECHT, JOHN J., bishop, Roman Catholic Church. Ordained priest Roman Cath. Ch. Bishop, Springfield, Mo., 1984—. Address: 200 McDaniel Springfield MO 65806

LEIFERT, ROBERT JOSHUA, lay ch. worker, Jewish Congregations; b. N.Y.C., June 14, 1945; s. Benjamin L. and Lillian (Wechsler) L.; B.A., Temple U., 1966; M.A., Columbia U., 1969; M.A., Yeshiva U., 1977; m. Jaclyn Kirschenbaum, May 20, 1973. Nat. program dir. dept. youth activities United Synagogue of Am., N.Y.C., 1969—, nat. dir. United Synagogue Youth on Wheels program, 1970—, internat. dir. Kadima, 1974—; mem. area council Greater N.Y. Conf. on Soviet Jewry, 1976—. Mem. Educators Assembly, Jewish Youth Dirs. Assn., Phi Delta Kappa. Contbr. articles to religious jours. Home: 388 Winthrop Rd Teaneck NJ 07666 Office: 155 5th Ave New York City NY 10010

LEIGHTON, DAVID KELLER, SR., clergyman, Episcopal Ch.; b. Edgewood, Pa., June 22, 1922; s. Frank Kingsley and Irene (Keller) L.; B.S., Northwestern U., 1947; D.D., Va. Theol. Sem., 1969; m. Carolyn Ruth Smith, Jan. 18, 1945; children—Charlotte (Mrs. Lawrence Andrew Savin, Jr.), David Keller, Nancy Elizabeth (Mrs. Harold Otto Koenig). Personnel interviewer Ohio Rubber Co., Willoughby, O., 1947-50; asst. supr. employment Fisher Body div. Gen. Motors Corp., Pitts. plant, 1950-54; ordained priest Episcopal Ch., 1955; curate Calvary Episcopal Ch., Pitts., 1955-56; rector St. Andrews Episcopal Ch., Pitts., 1956-59; rector Ch. of Holy Nativity, Balt., 1959-63; tchr. sacred studies St. Paul Schs., Brooklandville, Md., 1960-63; archdeacon Episcopal Diocese Md., Balt., 1964-68, bishop coadjutor, 1968-72, bishop, 1972—. Vice pres. Diocesan Council Md., 1964-72, pres., 1972—; v.p. Cathedral chpt. Md., 1968—. Chmn. bd. Hannah More Acad., Reisterstown, Md., 1968-74; bd. dirs. Md. Council Chs., Heart House, Pitts., Ch. Mission of Help, Balt.; bd. dirs. Ch. Home and Hosp., Balt., v.p., 1972—; bd. mem. U. Balt. Served with USAAF, 1942-45; ETO. Mem. Engring. Soc. Balt., Cum Laude Soc. Balt., St. Andrews Soc. Clubs: Center, University (Balt.). Home: 3601 N Charles St Baltimore MD 21218 Office: 105 W Monument St Baltimore MD 21201

LEIGHTY, DORIS LEE, lay church worker, United Methodist Church; b. Caldwell, Kans., Nov. 3, 1924; d. Elmer Howard and Lovenia Marie (Camerrer) Cook; B.S., Kans. State Coll., 1953; M.S., 1955; ednl. specialist George Peabody Coll. for Tchrs. 1958, D.Ed., 1968; m. Ellis E. Leighty, May 31, 1959; 1 child, Ronald James. Mem., chmn. bd. trustees Wesley United Meth. Ch., Macomb, Ill., 1967-69; pres. Galesburg Dist. Guild, 1965-68; chmn. Central Ill. Guild Weekend, 1969-73; mem., chmn. pastor parish relations com. Wesley United Meth. Ch., Macomb, 1970-72; mem. Galesburg Council on Ministries, United Meth. Ch., 1974—, pres. Galesburg dist. United Meth. Women, 1974-78, mem. council on ministries Central Ill. Conf., 1976—, chmn. bd. discipleship, 1976-80, chmn. commn. on camping,

1980—, treas. conf. found., 1981—, mem. conf. adminstrv. council, 1983—; bd. mgrs. East Bay Camp, 1977—. Assoc. prof. Western Ill. U., Macomb, 1957—. Chmn. admissions com. Wesley Village, 1975-81, treas. 1981—. Mem. Internat. Reading Assn., NEA, Phi Delta Kappa. Home: 104 Oakland Ln Macomb IL 61455 Office: Western Ill U Macomb IL 61455

LEINER, CARL ELTON, minister, Southern Baptist Convention; psychotherapist; b. East St. Louis, Ill., May 16, 1952; s. Carl Garnett and Doris Lavern (Schmidt) L.; m. Janet Louise Pybas, Aug. 11, 1973; children—Cassandra Noelle, Carl Nikolas. Student Southwest Bapt. Coll., 1970-74; B.A., European div. U. Md., 1980; M.Div., New Orleans Bapt. Theol. Sem., 1982, postgrad., 1983—. Ordained to ministry So. Bapt. Conv., 1982. Minister of music and youth Pontoon Bapt. Ch., Granite City, Ill., 1971, Tabernacle Bapt. Ch., St. Louis, 1974, First South Bapt. Ch., Mattoon, Ill., 1975; minister of youth First South Bapt. Ch., Salinas, Calif., 1976; music dir. McNair Chapel, Berlin, Fed. Republic Germany, 1978-80; minister of music and youth Lee's Creek Bapt. Ch., Bogalusa, La., 1980-81; chaplain Bethany Home, New Orleans, 1981-82; assoc. pastor West Marrero Bapt. Ch., La., 1983-84; pastor First Bapt. Ch., Fisher, La., 1984; clin. pastoral edn. intern Presbyn. Hosp., Oklahoma City, 1984; staff counselor So. Hills Bapt. Ch., Oklahoma City, 1984—; program dir. Sta. WBSN-FM, New Orleans, 1981-83; dir. media ctr. New Orleans Bapt. Theol. Sem., 1980-84. Pvt. practice psychotherapy, Oklahoma City, 1984—. Area bd. dirs. Cystic Fibrosis Found., Fisher, La., 1984; vol. therapist Many Mental Health Clinic, La., 1984. Served with U.S. Army, 1975-80, chaplain 1985—. Democrat. Avocations: computers, photography, running, golf. Home: 1413 Circle Tree Loop Killeen TX 76542

LEMAT, JAMES EDWARD, minister, American Baptist Churches in the U.S.A.; educator; b. Saginaw, Mich., Jan. 5, 1949; s. Lee Elijah and Dorothy Anne (Hemingway) LeM.; m. Lynda Kay Langworthy, June 3, 1972; children: Leslie Anne, David Lee. A.A., Delta Coll., 1969, Lincolnland Coll., 1984; B.A., Saginaw Valley Coll., 1972; M.Div., No. Sem., 1976. Ordained to ministry American Baptist Churches in the U.S.A., 1976. Pastor First Bapt. Ch., Sullivan, Ill., 1976-77, First Bapt. Ch., Traverse City, Mich., 1977-80, First Bapt. Ch., Girard, Ill., 1980—; mem. Evangelism Com., Centralia, Ill., 1976-77; del. Billy Graham Crusade Sch. of Evangelism, South Bend, Ind., 1977, Small Ch. Planning, Kansas City, Kans., 1980. Substitute tchr. Unit 4 Schs., Virden, Ill., 1983—. Bd. dirs. Girard Samaritan Corp., 1983-84, Girard Festival Days Assn., 1983-84; vol. worker Muscular Dystrophy Assn., Virden, Ill., 1984; chmn. Chem. People Task Force, Girard, 1984. Recipient Cert. of Achievement Robert H. Schuller Inst. for Successful Ch. leadership, 1985. Mem. Am. Bapt. Ministers. Democrat. Home: 315 W Madison St Girard IL 62640 Office: First Bapt Ch 3d and W Madison St Girard IL 62640

LEMKE, STEVE WARNER, religion educator, minister, Southern Baptist Convention; b. Waco, Tex., Aug. 31, 1951; s. Calvin Aubrey and Wanda (Wilkes) L.; m. Carol Clapp, June 3, 1978. B.A., La. Tech. U., 1971; M.Div., Southwestern Bapt. Theol. Sem., 1976, M.R.E., 1978, Ph.D., 1984. Ordained to ministry So. Bapt. Conv., 1978. Assoc. pastor Ardmore Bapt. Ch., Winston-Salem, N.C., summer 1977; pastor 1st Bapt. Ch., Santo, Tex., 1979-83; chmn. dept. religion So. Bapt. Coll., Walnut Ridge, Ark., 1984—; associational moderator Palo Pinto Bapt. Assn., Tex., 1980-82; mem. area com. Parker-Palo Pinto Capt. Area, 1980-83; exec. bd. dirs. Palo Pinto Bapt. Assn., 1979-84; dir. Camp Copass, Denton, Tex., 1979-82. Author: Home Bible Study Guide, 1979-84; Joy in Christ; Studies in Philippians, 1982; Living Hope: Studies in I Peter, 1983. Project chmn. Santo Booster Club, 1979-84; judge Univ. Inter-scholastic League, Weatherford, Tex., 1982. Southwestern Bapt. Theol. Sem. teaching fellow, 1980, 83. Mem. North Tex. Philos. Assn., Mineral Wells Ministerial Assn., Phi Kappa Phi. Democrat. Club: Louisiana. Home: 307 Ridge Pocahontas AR 72455 Office: So Bapt Coll College Station Walnut Ridge AR 92476

LEMME, RALPH DAVID, minister, United Presbyn. Ch. in U.S.A.; b. Cozad, Nebr., Nov. 20, 1934; s. David Elmer and Anita Johanna (Benson) L.; B.A., Sacramento State Coll., 1956; M.Div., San Francisco Theol. Sem., 1960; m. Patricia Rose Nielson, June 21, 1953; children—David, Susan, Mary, Thomas. Ordained to ministry, 1960; pastor Spalding-Akron (Nebr.) Presbyn. Chs., 1960-61, First Presbyn. Ch. Wood River, Nebr., 1961-65, Presbyn. Ch., Tekamah, Nebr., 1965-71, Ch. of The Master, Mesa, Ariz., 1971—. Chmn. protestant relations com. Overland Trails council Boy Scouts Am., 1964-65; moderator Niobrara Presbytery, 1971; chmn. commn. local ch. mission Presbytery Grand Canyon, 1973, 1974, ch. sch. tchr. tng. com. Nat. Tchr. Edn. Project. Chmn. Burt County (Nebr.) March of Dimes, 1970-71; neighborhood commnr. Mid-Am. council Boy Scouts Am., 1969-71, recipient Award of Merit, 1969. Mem. Tekamah C. of C. (former sec.). Home: 7144 E Azalea Circle Mesa AZ 85208

LEMMONS, MARY LOU, minister music, So. Baptist Conv.; b. Van Buren, Mo., Mar. 2, 1926; d. Monte Howard and Margery (Sheets) Hill; grad. St. Louis Coll. Music, 1945; B.A., U. Ark., 1975; m. Darrel R. Lemmons, Aug. 11, 1946; children—Thomas R., Joseph D., Rochelle M. Licensed to ministry, 1967; minister music Tabernacle Bapt. Ch., St. Louis, Mary Ann Bapt. Ch., St. Ann, Mo., First Bapt. Ch., Berkeley, Mo.; state approved childrens choir worker, 1960-74; adjudicator Ch. Music Festivals for State of Mo.; conf. leader childrens choir work at State Bapt. Assemblies. Mem. Music Educators Assn., Am. Guild Organists, Music Educators Nat. Conf., Mo. Music Women. Home: 9205 Meadowbrook Ln Overland MO 63114

LEMONS, GEORGE ALLEN, minister, Original Free Will Bapt. Ch.; b. Lockhart, S.C., June 16, 1926; s. James Marshall and Daisy Louise (Dickerson) L.; certificate Beaver Creek Bible Inst., 1972, student, 1976; Asso. degree in theology Free Will Bapt. Sch. Theology, Lancaster, S.C., 1974, grad. in theology, 1976; m. Susie Mae Vanderford, June 26, 1948; children—Edna Sue, Stephen A., Phillip A. Ordained to ministry, 1967; pastor Enoree (S.C.) Free Will Bapt. Ch., 1969-72, Grace Free Will Bapt. Ch., Fort Mill, S.C., 1972-76, Calvary Free Will Bapt. Ch., Union, S.C., 1976—. Sec. Beaver Creek Ministers Conf., 1970—; chmn. bd. Beaver Creek Bible Inst., also sec.-treas., 1971—. Postmaster, Lockhart, S.C., 1967—. Mem. Nat., S.C. assns. free will bapts., Beaver Creek Ministers Conf. S.C. Home: Box 100 Summit Dr Lockhart SC 29364

L'ENGLE, MADELEINE, writer; b. N.Y.C., Nov. 29, 1918; d. Charles Wadsworth and Madeleine Hall (Barnett) Camp; m. Hugh Franklin, Jan. 26, 1956; children: Josephine, Maria, Bion. B.A. with honors, Smith Coll., 1941; D.H.L. (hon.), Gordon Coll., 1981, Christian Theol. Sem., Indpls., 1982; Litt.D. (hon.), Miami U., Oxford, Ohio, 1982; D.Litt. (hon.), Wheaton Coll. (Ill.), 1984, Wilson Coll., 1984, Yale Div. Sch., 1984. Writer in residence Cathedral Ch. of St. John the Divine, N.Y.C., 1965—; bd. dirs. St. John of Jerusalem, N.Y.C., 1970—; mem. standing com. Episcopalian Diocese of N.Y., 1978-82. Author books including: A Wrinkle in Time, 1962 (Newbery award 1963); The Moon by Night, 1963 (Austrian State award 1970); A Swiftly Tilting Planet, 1980 (Am. Book award 1981); A Ring of Endless Light, 1981 (Newbery Honor award 1982). Recipient Bishop's Cross, Bishop of N.Y., 1967; medalian U. So. Miss., 1979; Smith medal Smith Coll., 1980; Sophie award Smith Student Body, 1984; Regina medal Catholic Library Assn., 1984. Mem. Authors League Am. (bd. dirs. 1972—), Authors Guild Am. (v.p. 1982—), Authors League Fund (bd. dirs. 1975—). Home: Crosswicks West St Goshen CT 06756 Office: The Cathedral Ch of St. John the Divine 1047 Amsterdam Ave New York NY 10025

LEON, RONALD EDWARD, minister, Gen. Assn. Regular Baptist Chs.; b. Birmingham, Ala., Nov. 4, 1938; s. Edward George and Marie (Olsafsky) L.; B.S. in Chem. Engring., Carnegie Inst. Tech., 1961; B.D. magna cum laude (Fellow), Grand Rapids (Mich.) Bapt. Sem., 1965; m. Carlous Patricia Betts, June 11, 1960; children—Mary Beth, Rachel Celeste, Nathan Edward. Ordained to ministry, 1965; pastor Franklin (Mich.) Bapt. Ch., 1965—. Home missionary Galilean Bapt. Mission, Inc., Grand Rapids, 1965—. Combustion engr. Indsl. Burner Systems Co., Inc., Detroit, 1966—. Home: 4645 Franklin Rd Bloomfield Hills MI 48013 Office: 26109 German Mill Rd Franklin MI 48025

LEONARD, EARL STANLEY, religious educator, minister, Missionary Church; b. Boston, Sept. 22, 1932; s. Earl Beuford and Gladys Bertha (Amstutz) L.; m. Donna Jean Neuenschwander, Aug. 7, 1954. B.A., Ft. Wayne Bible Coll., 1954, Th.B., 1955; M.R.E., Bibl. Sem. N.Y., 1959; M.A. in Edn., NYU, 1960; D.Min., Talbot Theol. Sem., 1985. Ordained to ministry, 1957. Assoc. prof. Christian edn. Biola U., La Mirada, Calif., 1966—; missionary/pastor Missionary Ch., Koloa, Kauai, Hawaii, 1962-66; instr. Christian edn. Ft. Wayne Bible Coll., Ind., 1960-62; cons. Scripture Press, Wheaton, Ill., 1967—. Author: Games to Grow on, 1976; Leader's Guide to Lord, I'm Listening, 1979; The Bible: God's Word in My Life, 1980. Biola U. grantee, 1980; Inst. of Holy Land Studies, Mt. Zion, Jerusalem vis. prof., 1980. Mem. Nat. Assn. Profs. Christian Edn., Evang. Tchr. Tng. Assn., So. Calif. Dirs. Christian Edn. Republican. Home: 14515 Biola Ave La Mirada CA 90638 Office: Biola Univ 13800 Biola Ave La Mirada CA 90639

LEONARD, FRANCIS XAVIER, priest, Roman Cath. Ch.; b. Bronx, N.Y., May 24, 1914; s. Francis B. and Irene (Sharkey) L.; B.A., Fordham U., 1935; postgrad., N.Y. U., Syracuse U. Ordained priest, 1945; parish priest, N.Y.C., 1945-50; chaplain U.S. Army, 1951-71; country parish priest, 1971—; priest St. Staninlaus Ch., Pine Island, N.Y., 1975—. Chaplain, Polish Am. Legion, Am. Vets., Pine Island. Club: N.Y. Athletic. Address: Saint Stanislaus Ch Pine Island NY 10969

LEONARD, VINCENT M., bishop, Roman Cath. Ch. Ordained priest Roman Catholic Ch., 1935, consecrated bishop, 1964; aux. bishop Diocese of Pitts., 1964-69, bishop, 1969—. Address: 111 Blvd of Allies Pittsburgh PA 15222

LEPAIN, MARC ALBERT, religion educator, Roman Catholic Church. B. Southbridge, Mass., Nov. 1, 1942; s. Albert N. and Pauline H. (Dufault) LeP.; m. Patricia Ann Casavant, Jan. 8, 1983; children: Maria, Julie, Joseph. A.B., Assumption Coll., 1965; M.A. U. Pa., 1967; Ph.D., Fordham U., 1978. Assoc. prof. Assumption Coll., Worcester, Mass., 1971—. Bd. dirs. Icon Mus., Sturbridge, Mass., 1983—. Mem. Am. Acad. Religion, Coll. Theology Soc. (nominations com. 1982—), Classical Assn. of New England, Vergilian Soc. Am. Home: 6 Nipmuc Rd Paxton MA 01612 Office: Assumption Coll 500 Salisbury St Worcester MA 01609

LERNER, BARRY DOV, rabbi, publs. exec., Conservative Jewish Congregations; b. Sharon, Pa., July 18, 1942; s. David and Sarah (Jesano) L.; B.A. with honors, Ariz. State U., 1964; M. Hebrew Lit., Jewish Theol. Sem. Am., 1969; m. Barbara Mollin, June 11, 1967; children—Reuven Moshe, Shulamit Esther, Avi Barak. Ordained rabbi, 1970; asst. rabbi Temple Israel, Great Neck, N.Y., 1970-72; rabbi Temple Beth Ahm, Matawan, N.J., 1972—; bus. mgr. Conservative Judaism, N.Y.C., 1975—. Mem. Kadima Commn. United Synagogue Am., 1973—, mem. Solomon Schechter Awards Com., 1975, mem. Central Youth Commn., 1975—; mem. edn. steering com. No. N.J. United Synagogue, rabbi in residence Youth Encampment, 1973—; pres. Ministers Assn. Bayshore Area (N.J.), 1975—; sec.-treas. Shore Area Bd. Rabbis, 1976—; study sessions chmn. Rabbinical Assembly Conv., 1977—. Mem. adv. com. Brookdale Coll., Monmouth County, N.J.; mem. Mayors Human Relations Commn., Matawan, N.J., 1973—; mem. chergy adv. bd. Planned Parenthood Monmouth County, 1976—; mem. No. N.J. Regional Youth Commn., 1977—. Recipient award Nat. Council Jewish Women, 1973, United Jewish Appeal, 1975. Editor: Procs. of Rabbinical Assembly, 1977—; contbg. editor Beinenu, 1975—; contbr. articles to religious jours. Office: Temple Beth Ahm 550 Lloyd Rd Matawan NJ 07747

LERNER, LEIGH DAVID, rabbi, Reform Jewish; b. Rebecca, Alexandra Stelle. Mar. 3, 1945; s. David and Edith Marian (Goldman) L.; B.A., Duke, 1966; B.H.L., Hebrew Union Coll., 1971; M.H.L., 1972; m. Rokelle Elaine Weisberg, June 18, 1970; children: Meredith Rebecca, Alexandra Stelle. Rabbi, 1972; asst. rabbi Mt. Zion Hebrew Congregation, St. Paul, 1972-75, rabbi, 1975—. Pres., Minn. Rabbinical Assn., 1976—; exec. bd. Central Conf. Am. Rabbis, 1982-84; bd. dirs. United Jewish Fund. Bd. dirs. Neighborhood House, United Way Emergency Care Fund, 1984—; Convenor, vice chmn. Ramsey County Blue Ribbon Commn. on Human Needs, 1983. Mem. Midwest Assn. Reform Rabbis (pres. 1982-84. Home: 701 Roundhill Rd St Paul MN 55118 Office: 1300 Summit Ave St Paul MN 55105

LESCH, GOMER RUPERT, telecommunication consultant, Southern Baptist Convention; b. Buffalo, Nov. 26, 1922; s. Gomer George and Ann Elizabeth (Guth) L.; m. Marie Simpson, Aug. 31, 1944; children: Constance Lesch Foster, Nancy Lesch Casson. B.S. in Edn., SUNY-Buffalo, 1944. Ch. pub. relations cons. Sunday Sch. Bd., So. Bapt. Conv., Nashville, 1959-61, dir. Office Pub. Relations, 1961-77, spl. asst. to exec. office, 1977-84, sr. cons. Bapt. Telecommunication Network, 1984—; pres. Nashville chpt. Religious Pub. Relations Council. Author: Church Public Relations at Work, 1962, Creative Christian Communication, 1965. Compiler: Memos for Christian Living, 1966, Reach Out, 1970. Served to maj. USAF, 1943-46. Named Disting. Citizen Jr. C. of C., Greensboro, N.C., 1957. Mem. Pub. Relations Soc. Am. (accredited, pres. Mid. Tenn. chpt. 1964-65), Bapt. Pub. Relations Assn. (pres. 1963-64). Office: 127 9th Ave N Nashville TN 27234

LESHER, WILLIAM ELTON, seminary president, educator, Lutheran Church in America; b. Pitts., May 24, 1932; s. Royal E. Lesher and Ruth Wageman; m. A. Jean Olson, Aug. 31, 1957; children: David, Gregory. B.A., Wittenburg U., 1954; M.Div., Luth. Sch. of Theology at Chgo., 1958; D.D. (hon.), Calif. Luth. Coll., 1976, Pacific Luth. U., 1977. Ordained to ministry Luth. Ch. in Am., 1958. Pastor Reen Meml. Luth. Ch., St. Louis, 1958-64, St. Luke Luth. Ch., Chgo., 1964-70; asst. prof. Luth. Sch. Theol., Chgo., 1970-72, assoc. prof. of parish renewal, 1973; pres. Pacific Luth. Theol. Sem., Berkeley, Calif., 1973-78, Luth. Sch. of Theology, Chgo., 1978—. Author: It Will Be Your Duty, 1973. Pres. Community Renewal Orgn.-St. Luke's, Chgo.; pres. Logan Sq. Citizens for Milw. Mall, Chgo., 1969-70; bd. dirs. Augustana Hosp., Chgo., 1970-73; mem. steering com. Ctr. for Ethics and Social Policy, Berkeley, 1974-78. Mem. Assn. Theol. Schs., Am. Acad. Religion, Inst. Theol. Edn. Mgmt. Office: Luth Sch Theology Chgo 1100 E 55th St Chicago IL 60615

LESKE, ADRIAN MAX, minister, educator, Lutheran Church-Missouri Synod; b. Gumeracha, S. Australia, Apr. 14, 1936; s. Wilhelm Theodor and Leonora Viola (Zacker) L.; M.Div., Concordia Sem., St. Louis, 1960, S.T.M., 1967, Th.D., 1971; m. Patricia Claire Kowald, May 5, 1961; children—Kylie Anne, Jane Patricia, Andrew Christopher. Ordained to ministry, 1960; parish minister, Wellington, N.Z., 1960-65, Waikerie, S. Australia, 1966-69; asst. prof. religion, dean students Concordia Coll., Edmonton, Alta., Can., 1971-75, asso. prof. religion, head of religion dept., acad. dean, 1976-80, prof. religion, 1980—, chmn., 1978-81. Mem. div. theology Luth. Council Can., 1978-81. Mem. Canadian Soc. Study Religion, Canadian Soc. Bibl. Studies, Soc. Bibl. Lit. Contbr. articles to theol. jours. Home: 10323 134th St Edmonton AB Canada Office: Concordia Coll 7128 Ada Blvd Edmonton AB Canada

LESPERANCE, JAMES BROCK, religious television station executive, clergyman; b. Newton, Mass., Sept. 13, 1955; s. Robert James and Mary Geo (Hill) L.; m. Jane Alice Harvey, Mar. 11, 1978. B.S. in Broadcasting, U. Fla., 1976; postgrad. Rollins Coll., 1980—. Ordained to ministry Gospel Crusade. Ops. mgr., Sta. WAJL, Winter Park, Fla., 1976-77; media ministry dir. Calvary Assembly, Winter Park, 1978-82; gen. mgr. Sta. WTGL-TV, Cocoa/Orlando, Fla., 1982—; dir. adminstr. Ch. TV Network, Clearwater, Fla., 1984—. Mem. Assn. Ch. TV (bd. dirs. 1977-83), S.E. Nat. Religious Broadcasters, Omicron Delta Kappa. Republican. Office: Good Life Broadcasting Inc WTGL TV 1205 29th St Orlando FL 32805

LESSARD, RAYMOND W., bishop, Roman Catholic Ch. Ordained priest, 1956, consecrated bishop, 1973; bishop diocese of Savannah, Ga., 1973—. Office: 225 Abercorn POB 8789 Savannah GA 31402

LESSMANN, RICHARD PAUL, minister, Lutheran Ch.-Missouri Synod; b. Milw., Feb. 19, 1936; s. Martin Walter Lessmann and Elizabeth Marie (Busacker) Wallace; m. Judith Gertrude Schumacher, Nov. 24, 1962; children: Steven, Kurt, Erik. A.A., Concordia Coll., 1956; B.A., Concordia Sem., 1958; theol. dip., 1961; M.A., Miss. Coll., 1975; postgrad., Drew U., 1982—. Ordained to ministry Lutheran Ch., 1961. Pastor Good Shepherd Luth. Ch., Marrero, La., 1961-65, Our Redeemer Luth. Ch., Jackson, Miss., 1965-73, Grace Luth. Ch., Huntsville, Ala., 1973—; sec. Miss. religious leaders conf., 1973; mem. Luth. Ch.-Mo. Synod So. Dist. (circuit counselor 1966-69, dir. lay tng. program, 1969-73, chmn. parish edn. comm., 1970-75, 1st v.p., 1970-78, circuit counselor, 1981-82). Bd. dirs. Pathfinders Home for Recovering Alcoholics, Huntsville, 1981-83, The Key-Ctr. for Creative Living, Huntsville, 1982—. Democrat. Lodge: Kiwanis. Home: 8008 Randall Rd SW Huntsville AL 35802 Office: Grace Lutheran Church 3321 S Memorial Parkway Huntsville AL 35801

LESSTEN, FRED IRVIN, minister, Assemblies of God Church; b. Rochester, N.Y., Jan. 2, 1916; s. Fred and Mabel (Boulter) L.; student North Central Bible Coll., 1940-42; B.Th., Los Angeles Bapt. Sem., 1943; B.A., Central Bible Coll., 1951; m. Marjorie E. Chittim, May 22, 1945; 1 dau., Suzanne Kay (Mrs. Robert De Long). Ordained to ministry Assemblies of God Ch., 1944; evangelist, 1944; chaplain Nebr. State Prison, 1944-47; assoc. pastor Central Assembly of God, Springfield, Mo., 1947-49; dean of men Central Bible Coll., 1950-55, bus. mgr., 1955-64; bus. mgr. Evangel Coll., 1959-63; regional dist. sec. Am. Bible Soc., Chgo., 1964-67, exec. sec. Eastern region, N.Y.C., 1967-76, spl. sec. ch. relations, Lincoln, Nebr., 1976-82; assoc. pastor Immanuel Ch., Lincoln, Nebr., 1982—. Home: 6700 Tanglewood Ln Lincoln NE 68516

LESTER, ANDREW DOUGLAS, religion educator; b. Coral Gables, Fla., Aug. 8, 1939; s. Andrew and Dorothy (Atkinson) L.; m. Judith Laesser, Sept. 8, 1960; children: Scott Wayne, Denise Leanne. B.A., Miss. Coll., 1961; B.D., So. Bapt. Theol. Sem., 1964, Ph.D., 1968. Ordained to ministry, 1961. Prof.'s asst. in psychology and religion, 1964-66; minister to youth First Bapt. Ch., Memphis, 1960, Washington Bapt. Ch., Miss., 1960-61, Broadmoor Bapt. Ch., Jackson, Miss., 1961-62; pastor Buena Vista Bapt. Ch., Bryantsville, Ky., 1962-66; pastoral counselor Personal Counseling Service, Jeffersonville, Ind., 1965-69; minister to youth Immanuel Bapt. Ch., Louisville, 1966-67; spl. instr. psychology and religion So. Bapt. Theol. Sem., Louisville, 1967-69, prof. psychology of religion, 1976—; asst. dir. dept. pastoral care N.C. Bapt. Hosp., 1969-70; dir. counseling services, 1970-71; marriage and family therapist Personal Counseling Service, Inc., Clarkesville, Ind., 1965-69, 77—; vis. prof. pastoral care Southeastern Bapt. Theol. Sem., 1972-77; vis. lectr. religion Grad. Sch., Wake Forest U., 1972-77. Contbr. articles to profl. jours. Author: Sex is More Than a Word, 1973; It Hurts So Bad, Lord, The Christian Encounters Crisis, 1976; Understanding Aging Parents (with Judith L. Lester), 1980; Coping with Your Anger: A Christian Guide, 1983; Pastoral Care for Children in Crisis, 1985, others. Fellow Coll. Chaplains of Am. Protestant Hosp. Assn.; mem. Am. Assn. Pastoral Counselors (diplomate), Am. Assn. Marriage and Family Therapists. Democrat. Home: 1907 Lonlipman Ct Louisville KY 40207 Office: Bapt Theol Sem 2825 Lexington Rd Louisville KY 40207

LESTER, DONALD GEORGE, minister, Presbyterian Church USA; b. Youngstown, Ohio, Apr. 17, 1925; s. George William and Lauretta Hilda (Scheutz) L.; m.

Elaine Gertrude Sluiter, June 23, 1973; children by previous marriage: David Scott, Dawnette Elizabeth, Debra Lauretta, Delight Annette, Diane Carol. Student Brown U., 1943-45; M.Div., Yale U., 1948; Th.M., Pitts. Theol. Sem., 1960; D.D. (hon.), Muskingum Coll., 1959. Ordained to ministry, 1948. Asst. pastor Covenant Presbyn. Ch., Sharon, Pa., 1948-50; pastor First United Presbyn. Ch., Canton, Ohio, 1950-55; staff dept. evangelism Presbyn. Ch. USA, N.Y.C., 1955-62; sr. pastor Vance Meml. Ch., Wheeling, W.Va., 1962-67, Westminster Presbyn. Ch., Grand Rapids, Mich., 1967-73; exec. presbyter Presbytery of Detroit, 1973—; trustee Davis & Elkins Coll., 1963-67, McCormick Theol. Sem., Chgo., 1968-76; chmn. dept. evangelism Nat. Council Chs., 1962. Contbr. articles to profl. jours. Bd. dirs. Community Action program, Grand Rapids, 1972; chmn. Community Counseling Ctr., Grand Rapids, 1971, Bridge for Runaways, Grand Rapids, 1979. Served with USN, 1943-46. Lodge: Rotary. Home: 4831 Ballantrae Birmingham MI 48010 Office: Presbytery of Detroit 17575 Hubbell Detroit MI 48235

LESWING, JAMES BARTHOLOMEW, priest, The Episcopal Church. B. Phila., Aug. 24, 1948; s. Herbert and Gladys Irene (MacFarlane) L.; m. Muriel Louise Amadon, Aug. 21, 1971; children: Philip Drayton, Elizabeth Amadon. B.A., Dickinson Coll., 1970; M.Div., Yale U., 1973. Ordained to ministry, Episc. Ch., as deacon, 1973, as priest, 1973. Dir. Christian edn. St. Thomas' Ch., New Haven, Conn., 1971-73, staff asst. Episc. Ch. at Yale U., New Haven, 1971-72; asst. rector St. Paul's Ch., Chatham, N.J., 1973-75, canon precentor St. Paul's Cathedral, Burlington, Vt., 1975-79; rector St. Peter's on-the-green, Monroe, Conn., 1979—; mem. liturgical commn. Diocese of Conn., Hartford, 1979—; evaluator Bridgeport Deanery, Conn., 1982—; pres. Monroe Clergy Assn., 1981—. Designer theatrical scenery. Coordinator Surplus Food Distribution, Monroe, 1983, ARC Blood Bank, Monroe, 1983. Named Outstanding Young Men of Am U.S. Jaycees, 1979. Mem. Country Coll. Players, Omicron Delta Kappa. Home and Office: St Peters on the Green 175 Old Tannery Rd Monroe CT 06468

LETSON, LARRY WILMER, minister, So. Baptist Conv.; b. Jackson, Ga., Jan. 19, 1948; s. Samuel Lamar and Julia LaDelle (Smith) L.; B.S. in Music Edn., Jacksonville (Ala.) State U., 1970; m. Sharon Esleta Stephens, Aug. 11, 1968; 1 son, Stephen Lamar. Ordained to ministry, 1976; minister music Parkway Bapt. Ch., Macon, Ga., 1975—. Mem. Macon Bapt. Assn. Home: 3488 Warpath Rd Macon GA 31201 Office: 5049 Log Cabin Dr Macon GA 31204

LETZRING, DONALD CLIFFORD, pastor, Southern Baptist Convention; b. St. Petersburg, Fla., May 15, 1944; s. Ralph Carlyle and Lillian (Helveston) L.; m. Gail Reba Maley, June 13, 1964; children: Timothy David, Deborah Jean, Susan Gail. B.A., Mars Hill Coll., 1966; M.Div., Southern Bapt. Theol. Sem., 1972; M.A., U. South Fla., 1985. Ordination to ministry Southern Baptist Convention. Pastor Medulla Bapt. Ch., Lakeland, Fla., 1972-74, Fern Creek Bapt. Ch., Louisville, 1975-77, First Bapt. Ch. of Palm River, Tampa, Fla., 1980—; assoc. pastor First Bapt. Ch., Bunnell, Fla., 1978-79; coordinator mission trip to Brazil, 1984-85. Trustee Palm River Christian Sch., 1984. Mem. Phi Kappa Phi. Democrat. Home: 703 S Pearl Circle Brandon FL 33511 Office: 5300 Palm River Rd Tampa FL 33619

LEVADA, WILLIAM J., bishop, Roman Catholic Church. Titular bishop of Capri, aux. bishop, Los Angeles, 1983—. Office: 1531 W 9th St Los Angeles CA 90015*

LEVELL, DORSEY EUGENE, religious orgn. ofcl., Evang. United Brethren Ch.; b. Salisbury, Mo., July 22, 1933; s. Mose Clifford and Norma Nancy (Drew) L.; B.A., Central Mo. State U., 1955; Th.M., United Theol. Sem., 1960; m. Mary Ann Spradling, June 8, 1952; children—Rocky Ray, Marcia. Ordained to ministry Evang. United Brethren Ch., 1960; pastor Brentwood Evang. United Brethren Ch., Springfield, Mo., 1960-68; exec. dir. Springfield Area Council Chs., 1968—, also project dir. Community Treatment Center, 1973. Chaplain, AUS Res. Sect. Chmn. United Way, 1967-68; dir. A.R.C. Mem. Springfield Ministerial Alliance (pres.), Mo. Assn. Social Welfare, Council Clin. Tng. Clubs: Rotary, Exchange (Springfield). Home: 1858 Shamrock Circle Springfield MO 65804 Office: P O Box 3686 Glenstone Station Springfield MO 65804

LEVESQUE, CHARLES-HENRI, bishop, Roman Cath. Ch.; b. St. André de Kamouraska, Que., Can., Dec. 29, 1921; s. Alexis and Atala (Garneau) L.; B.A., Coll. Ste-Anne-de-la-Pocatière, 1944; B.Ph., U. Laval, Que., 1945, L.Th., 1949; D.D.C., Angelicum U., Rome, 1955. Ordained priest, 1948; consecrated bishop, 1965; préfet de discipline et professeur d'histoire et de lettres Coll. de Ste-Anne-de-la-Pocatière (Que., Can.), 1949-51; sec. maître de cérémonies l'Évêché de Ste-Anne, 1951, 55; chancelier Diocese Ste-Anne, 1956; chanoine honoraire, 1956; chanoine titulaire, 1957; camerier secret, 1960; aux. bishop S. Exc. Mgr Bruno Desrochers de Ste-Anne-de-la-Pocatière, 1965-68; bishop of Ste-Anne-de-la-Pocatiè, 1968—. Mem. Comité épiscopal l'Office Catéchèse du Québec, Comité Nature et Fonctionnement; pres. Com. de diffusion des célébrations liturgices; co-pres. Commn. épiscopale de Liturgie; mem. Commn. internationale francophone pour les traductions liturgiques. Mem. Chevelier de Colomb, Chevalier de L'Ordre équestre du St. Sépulcre. Home and office: 1200 4e Ave La Pocatière PQ G0R 1Z0 Canada

LEVESQUE, GEORGES HENRI, priest, Roman Catholic Church. b. Roberval, Que., Can., Feb. 16, 1903. B.A., Coll. de Chicoutimi, Laval U., 1923; Lecteur en Theologie, Dominican Coll. Ottawa, 1930; Diplome supeieur en Scis. Sociales, Ecole des Scis. sociales de l'Universite catholoque de Lille, France, 1933. Joined Order of St. Dominic, 1926, ordained priest Roman Catholic Ch., 1928. Prof. Dominican's Coll. in Ottawa, 1933-38; prof. faculty social scis. U. Montreal, 1935-38; prof. social philosophy Laval U., 1936-62, founder, dean faculty social scis., 1938-55; founder, rector La Maison Montmorency, 1955-63; mem. L'Union Internationale d'Etudes sociales, Malines, Belgium, 1949—; mem. World Brotherhood, Geneva, 1951—; com. mem. Internat. Assn. Non-Govtl. Orgns., Brussels, 1955—; hon. v.p. Can. U. Service Overseas, 1961-62; founder, rector U. Nationale du Rwanda, Butare, 1963-71; mem. Polish Inst. Arts and Scis., 1963—; mem. Inst. of Man and Sci., NYU, 1966—; pres., founder La Cooperation Nord-Sud en education, Montreal, 1982—. Contbr. articles to profl. jours. Mem. Societe des Ecrivains, 1945—; v.p. Can. Council, 1957-62; hon. pres., advisor U. Nationale du Rwanda, 1971—. Recipient medal Les Anciens de l'Universite Laval, 1973, award Le conseil Canadien de la Cooperation, 1978, medal L'Assn. d'Education du Que., 1978, award Assembly of the Bishops, Province of Que., 1979, Chevalier de l'Ordre internat. de la Pleiade, Ottawa, 1980, Royal Bank award, Montreal, 1982, Pearson medal for peace Can. Assn. for U.N., Ottawa, 1983; named Comdr. Ordre Nat. des Mille Collines, Rwanda, 1977, Officer Co. des Cent Associes, Charlottetown, 1981. Fellow Royal Soc. Can. (v.p. 1962-63). Home: 2715 Ch Ste Catherine Montreal PQ H3T 1B6 Canada

LEVINE, ARTHUR J., lay ch. worker, Conservative Jewish Congregations; b. Bklyn., July 2, 1916; s. Louis L. and Esther (Goodman) L.; B.S., N.Y. U., 1939; postgrad. New Sch. Social Research, 1949-62; m. Rosalind E. Kopman, June 22, 1941; children—Nancy Deborah, Helen Susan, Betty Ann. Mem. exec. bd. United Synagogues of Am., 1962—, pres. N.Y. met. region, 1964-66, v.p., 1961-64, nat. treas., 1967-69, nat. v.p., 1967, nat. pres., 1973—; pres. Merrick Jewish Center, 1952-54, Jewish Community Relations Council N.Y., 1967-69; exec. com. Synagogue Council Am., 1971—, Nat. Conf. on Soviet Jewry, 1976—; mem. nat. Jewish com. on scouting Boy Scouts Am., 1973—; exec. World Zionist Orgn., 1977—; Individual practice as C.P.A., N.Y.C., 1952—. Recipient Good Scout award Boy Scouts Am., 1975; named Hon. Citizen State of Tex., 1975. Mem. Am. Inst. C.P.A.'s, Conf. Presidents Maj. Jewish Orgns., Phi Alpha. Contbr. articles to jours. Home: 27 Wooleys Ln E Great Neck NY 11021 Office: 192 Lexington Ave New York City NY 10016

LEVITT, JOY, rabbi; sec. Reconstructionist Rabbinical Assn. Office: Reconstructionist Rabbinical Assn Wyncote PA 19095*

LEVY, EUGENE HENRY, rabbi, Reform Jew; b. El Paso, Tex., July 9, 1945; s. Rene Henry and Betty (Heil) L.; m. Bobbye Nan Waltzer, June 15, 1969; children: Jeremy Marc, Ari David. A.A., San Antonio Coll., 1965; B.A., U. Tex., 1967; M.A., Hebrew Union Coll., 1972. Ordained rabbi, 1972. Dir. B'nai Brith Hillel Found., Norman, Okla., 1972-75; rabbi Temple Beth El, Tyler, Tex., 1975—; cons. Rusk State Hosp., Tex., 1976—; pres. Kallah of Tex. Rabbis, 1983-84; chmn. small cities com. Central Conf. Am. Rabbis, N.Y.C., 1982—. Author Sunday Sch. curriculum How We Celebrate, 1984. Seminar coordinator Tyler Mental Health Assn., and Smith County family Living Com., 1979-81; bd. dirs. Hospice of East Tex., 1980—. Recipient appreciation plaque Tex.-Okla. Fedn. of Temple Youth, 1983. Mem. Tyler Ministerial Alliance (pres. 1983-84), Southwest Assn. Reform Rabbis (justice and peace chmn.), Union Am. Hebrew Congregations (mem. small cities com.). Democrat. Lodges: Rotary (bd. dirs. 1982-84), B'nai Brith. Home: 3016 S Cameron St Tyler TX 75701 Office: Temple Beth El 1102 S Augusta St Tyler TX 75701

LEWIS, CHARLES BADY, church association official, Southern Baptist Convention; b. Pain Courtville, La., Sept. 20, 1913; s. Irving J. and Lizzie Beth (Gilfore) L.; A.B., Leland Coll., 1944; B.D., Am. Bapt. Sem., 1947, Th.M., 1948; now postgrad. Miss. Bapt. Sem. Ordained to ministry, 1946; tchr., missionary, mem. home missions bd. So. Bapt. Conv., 1951-76; dir. Natchez Sem. Center (Miss.), 1962-76; dean religion Natchez Coll., 1948-76. Dir. Bapt. Student Union, 1953-76. Recipient citation Bapt. Student Union, 1960. Mem. Assn. Bapt. Profs. Religion, Miss. Philosophy Assn., Natchez Civic and Profl. League. Author: Jesus, The Christian Religion, 1950. Home: 1006 N Union St Natchez MS 39120 Office: PO Box 53 Natchez MS 39120

LEWIS, CRAIG JOHN, minister, Lutheran Church in America; b. Oneonta, N.Y., Feb. 25, 1947; s. Craig Charles and Naomi Emma (Vining) L.; m. Gloria Jean Chapman, Sept. 9, 1972; children: Craig Khary, Sekov Robert. Grad., Phillips Exeter Acad., N.H., 1965; B.A., Harvard U., 1969, M.Div., 1972; S.T.M., Luth. Theol. Sem., Phila., 1984. Ordained to ministry Lutheran Church in America, 1972. Dir. Luth. Campus Council Ministry, St. Albans, N.Y., 1978-81; assoc. dir. theol. edn. Luth. Ch. in Am., Phila., 1981-84, dir., 1984—; evangelist Pastor Evangelist Program, Phila., 1980-82; cons. Assn. Black Luths., N.Y.C., 1980—; dir. Ken-Crest Ctrs., Phila., 1981—, Luth. Children and Family Services, Phila., 1981—; founder, dir. Queens Christian Devel. Corp., N.Y.C., 1978—. Author: Ministry and Blacks in Higher Education, 1976. Contbr. articles to religious publs. Dir. Karamu House, Cleve., 1975—; dir.-founder Friends of Culture, Inc., Cleve., 1977—. Rockefeller fellow Fund for Theol. Edn., 1970-72. Mem. Alpha Phi Alpha. Office: Div Profl Leadership 2900 Queen Ln Philadelphia PA 19129

LEWIS, GILES FLOYD, JR., priest, Episcopal Church; b. Orlando, Fla., Sept. 22, 1927; s. Giles Floyd and Florence Meriam (Baldwin) L.; B.S., Clemson Coll., 1949; M.Div., U. of South, 1957; m. Dorothy Jane Tauber, Oct. 3, 1957; children: Henrietta, Giles, Celia, Nathaniel. Ordained deacon, 1957, priest, 1958; minister in charge All St's. Ch., Clinton, S.C., 1957-60, Epiphany Ch., Laurens, S.C., 1957-60, priest-in-charge, 1960-63; asst. Christ Ch., Greenville, S.C., 1964; assoc. rector Christ Ch., Lexington, Ky., 1965-67; rector St. Bartholomew's Ch., Nashville, 1967-71; assoc. rector Ch. St. John the Divine, Houston, 1972—; chaplain Tex. chpt. Soc. Companions of Holy Cross. Bd. dirs. Epilepsy Assn. Houston and Gulf Coast. Home: 6127 Longmont St Houston TX 77057 Office: 2450 River Oaks Blvd Houston TX 77019

LEWIS, GLADYS SHERMAN, lay church worker, Southern Baptist Convention; b. Wynnewood, Okla., Mar. 20, 1933; d. Andrew and Minnie (Halsey) Sherman; m. Wilbur Curtis Lewis, Jan. 28, 1955; children: Karen, David, Leanne, Cristen. R.N., St. Anthony's Hosp., 1953; B.A., Tex. Christian U., 1956; M.A., Central State U., 1985. Campus nurse Okla. Bapt. U., Shawnee, Okla., 1953-55; med. missionary So. Bapt. Conv., Asuncion, Paraguay, S.Am., 1959-70; writer, columnist So. Bapt. Periodicals, various, 1960—; author Broadman, Nashville, 1983—; instr. English, Central State U., Edmond, Okla., 1984—; trustee Southwestern Bapt. Theol. Sem., Ft. Worth, 1974—; mem. com. on order ob bus. So. Bapt. Conv., Nashville, 1979-82, conf. leader/speaker, 1975—; mem. Christian life com. Okla. Bapt. Conv., 1983—. Author: Esther Buys a Bible, 1968; On Earth As It Is, 1983; Two Dreams and a Promise, 1984. Co-campaign dir. Democratic Party, Midwest City, Okla., 1974-80; mem. Mental Health Assn. Okla. County, 1978-81. Named Outstanding Woman of the Year, Pilot Club, 1979. Mem. Okla. County Med. Aux., Okla. Med. Aux., Aux. of Am. Coll. Surgeons. Address: 14501 N Western Ave Edmond OK 73034

LEWIS, GRANVILLE DOUGLASS, seminary president, minister, United Meth. Ch.; b. Bolivar, Tenn., Aug. 2, 1934; s. Marion Hollis and Susan Alton (Douglass) L.; B.S., U. Tenn., 1957; B.D., Vanderbilt U., 1960; postgrad. U. Hamburg, Germany, 1960-61; Ph.D., Duke, 1965; m. Shirley Savage, Aug. 11, 1957; children: Laura, Douglass. Ordained to ministry United Methodist Ch., 1966; youth dir. Glendale Meth. Ch., Nashville, 1957-59; asst. in Christian edn. First Presbyn. Ch., Durham, N.C., 1962-64; chaplain, assoc. prof. religion, philosophy Tenn. Wesleyan Coll., Athens, 1964-67; dir. Nat. Co-op. Enlistment Project, Nat. Council Chs. Dept. Ministry, Chgo., 1967-70, dir. ministry in 70's project, 1970-71; adminstrv. coordinator Inst. for Ministry Devel., Chgo., 1971-74; coordinator for parish devel. Hartford (Conn.) Sem. Found., 1974-82; pres. Wesley Theol. Sem., Washington, 1982—. Mem. Religious Research Assn., Organizational Devel. Network, Assn. for Creative Change. Author: The Church Reaching Out-Interpreting Ministry as a Career, 1970. Editor: Explorations in Ministry, 1972; Resolving Church Conflicts, 1981. Office: 4500 Massachusetts Ave NW Washington DC 20016

LEWIS, HAROLD CARTER, minister, Southern Baptist Convention; b. Pittsylvania County, Va., Mar. 31, 1936; s. Leslie Carter and Rena Mae (Shelton) L.; m. Nancy Carolyn Jones, June 9, 1956; children: Donna Lewis Overstreet, Harold Carter, Katherine Denise, Robert Kevin. Student U. Va. Extension, 1955-56, Averett Coll., 1958-59; B.A., U. Richmond, 1962; M.Div., Southeastern Bapt. Theol. Sem., 1967. Ordained to ministry Southern Baptist Convention, 1964. Student asst. Sunset Hill Bapt. Ch., Richmond, Va., 1956-58; pastor Antioch Bapt. Ch., Roxboro, N.C., 1963-69, Courtland Bapt. Ch., Va., 1969-72, New Prospect Bapt. Ch., Hurt, Va., 1972-79, Villa Heights Bapt. Ch., Roanoke, Va., 1980—; chaplain CAP, Franklin, Va., 1969-72; mem. Altaviste-Hurt Area Ministers Conf., 1972-79; mem. Staunton River Bapt. Ministers Conf., 1972-79, pres., 1974-75, moderator, 1975-76; mem. Roanoke Valley Bapt. and Ministers Conf., 1980—, mem. com. on coms., 1984—. Chmn., Bloodmobile, Southampton County, Va., 1970; mem.

Va. Council on Social Welfare, 1970-72; pres. Combined Primary and Elem. PTA, Courtland, 1970-72. Lodges: Ruritan (chaplain Courtland 1969-72), Villa Heights Lions (pres. Roanoke 1983-84). Home: 4329 Cordell Dr SW Roanoke VA 24018 Office: Villa Heights Bapt Ch 1020 Lafayette Blvd NW Roanoke VA 24017

LEWIS, HARRY GARRETT, minister, United Methodist Church; b. Welch, W.Va., Apr. 19, 1931; s. Holbert Garrett and Eddith Mae (Armendtrout) L.; B.A., Ky. Wesleyan Coll., 1964; B.D., Chandler Sch. Theology, 1967; m. Sadie Mae Webb, Nov. 10, 1955; children: Joe Noel, Harry Russell. Ordained deacon, 1964, elder, 1967; pastor, Horse Branch Circuit, Ky., 1963-64, Highland Meth. Ch., Griffin, Ga., 1964-67, Kirk Meml. United Meth. Ch., 1967-70, Cairo United Meth. Ch., Henderson, Ky., 1970-75, Breckenridge Stanley United Meth. Ch., 1982—; asst. chaplain Lady Mercy Hosp.; sec. Owensboro Dist. Council on Ministries, also mem. dist. supt. com.; sec. treas. McLean County Ministerial Assn., 1975-76. Mem. Island Community Devel. Council, 1975-76; chaplain, counselor Ret. Sr. Vol. Program (RSVP), 1975-76; mem. Josephine and Rudy Smith Founds. Mem. Owensboro-Daviess County Ministerial Assn. Ky. Cols., Airbone Assn. Home and office: 907 Dixiana Dr Owensboro KY 42301

LEWIS, HARVEY DELLMOND, JR., minister, Southern Baptist Convention; b. Florence, Tex., Jan. 29, 1918; s. Harvey Dellmond and Roselle Hawkins (Whittenberg) L.; B.A., Baylor U., 1939; D.Div. Mary Hardin Baylor U., 1980; Th.M., Southwestern Bapt. Theol. Sem., 1942; m. Marie Frances Fuscia, Feb. 19, 1945; children: Olan Harvey, Rosell (Mrs. Paul Carr), Frances Ann (Mrs. Norman Smith). Ordained to ministry So. Baptist Conv., 1937; chaplain USAAF, 1942-46; pastor Calvary Bapt. Ch., Port Acres, Tex., 1946-48, First Bapt. Ch., Cleve., 1948-51, First Bapt. Ch., Kerrville, Tex., 1951-55, Harlandale Bapt. Ch., San Antonio, 1955-58, First Bapt. Ch., Mt. Pleasant, Tex., 1958-63, Central Bapt. Ch., Marshall, 1963-76; v.p. devel. East Tex. Bapt. Coll., 1976—, dir. planned giving, 1984. Moderator Tryon Evergreen Assn., Bapt. Gen. Conv. Tex., 1949-51, Medina River Assn., 1953-54, Pittsburg Assn., 1962; moderator Soda Lake Assn., 1967-68, mem. exec. bd., 1969-75. Trustee San Marcos Bapt. Acad., 1955-60, East Tex. Bapt. Coll., Marshall, 1959-68, 70—; bd. trustees Mexican Bapt. Bible Inst., San Antonio, 1955-58. Mem. Marshall C. of C. Home: 3401 Indian Springs Marshall TX 75670 Office: 1209 N Grove St Marshall TX 75670

LEWIS, HENRY SIMPSON, JR., minister, Baptist Church; b. Chester County, S.C., Sept. 26, 1935; s. Henry Simpson and Marie (Sanders) L.; B.S., Winston-Salem State U., 1957; M.Div., Andover Newton Theol. Sch., 1961; postgrad. in sociology Wake Forest U., 1969-70; m. Savannah D. Winstead, Sept. 6, 1958; children: Robin Anita, Kenneth Winstead, Jonathan Henry, Karen Elizabeth. Ordained to ministry, 1961; student chaplain Boston City Hosp., 1959-60; pastor Zion Bapt. Ch., Lynn, Mass., 1959-60, Mt. Pleasant Bapt. Ch., Winston-Salem, N.C., 1966-77; univ. chaplain/asst. prof. religion Winston-Salem State U., 1960-77; vis. lectr. Wake Forest U., 1970, 71; pastoral counselor R.J. Reynolds Industries, 1977—. Mem. bd. Ministries to Blacks in Higher Edn., 1975—. Bd. dirs. Experiment in Self-Reliance, 1965-68, Forsyth Mental Health Assn., 1964-68, Boy Scouts Am., 1971, Girl Scouts U.S.A., 1970-71. Danforth Found. Underwood fellow, 1974-75. Mem. Forsyth Clergyman's Assn., Am. Assn. Marital and Family Therapy, Nat. Inst. Bus. and Indsl. Chaplains. Home: 3400 Jeketer Dr Winston-Salem NC 27105 Office: 110 Reynolds Bldg Winston-Salem NC 27102

LEWIS, JOHN CLIFFORD, minister, Independent Baptist Churches; b. Red Level, Ala., Mar. 27, 1909; s. Elbert Alonza and Zeddie (Jones) L.; A.B., Bob Jones U., 1931, L.H.D., 1942; m. Helen A. Kline, Aug. 12, 1940; children: Carolyn (Mrs. Calvin Richert), David. Ordained to ministry, 1943; evangelist, U.S., Can., 100 fgn. countries, 1931—; pres. Living Faith Fellowship, Inc., Overland Park, Kans., 1955—. Dir. broadcasts Christ for Everyone, 1931—. Author: Youth on the March, 1953; Thrills of Christian Youth, 1936; Japan Needs Jesus, 1938; God's Ideal Woman, 1944. Editor Living Faith News, 1950—. Address: 8344 Foster St Overland Park KS 66212

LEWIS, KEVIN, religion educator, Presbyterian Church in America; b. Asheville, N.C., July 13, 1943; s. Burdett Gibson and Phebe Ann (Clarke) L.; m. Harriet Kirby, Aug. 9, 1969 (div. 1976); m. 2d Becky Wingard, Dec. 23, 1976; children: Jacob, Helen. B.A., Harvard U., 1965; B.A., St. John's Coll., Cambridge, Eng., 1967, M.A., 1971; M.A., U. Chgo., 1969, Ph.D., 1980. Asst. prof. religious studies U. S.C., Columbia, 1973—. Contbr. articles, reviews, poetry to profl. publs. Presbyn. grad. fellow Presbyn. Ch., 1970-72; named Outstanding Educator Am., U. S.C., 1975. Mem. Am. Acad. Religion, Brit. Conf. on Lit. and Religion, MLA, AAUP, S.C. Acad. Religion (pres. 1983-84). Club: Harvard of S.C. (sec.-treas. 1979-83). Home: 4109 Parkman Dr Columbia SC 29206 Office: Dept Religious Studies U SC Columbia SC 29208

LEWIS, LEMOINE GAUNCE, educator, minister, Church of Christ; b. Midlothian, Tex., Feb. 9, 1916; s. Pearl Gaunce and Anna Elizabeth (Holland) L.; m. Shirley Harrell, Aug. 30, 1945; children: LeMoine Gaunce, Stephanie, Claudia. B.A., Abilene Christian U., 1936; S.T.B., Harvard Div. Sch., 1944; Ph.D., Harvard U., 1959. Minister, Ch. of Christ, Ardmore, Okla., 1937-39, Snyder, Tex., 1939-41, Brookline, Mass., 1945-49, Hamlin, Tex., 1951-52; prof. religion, Bible and ch. history Abilene Christian U., Tex., 1949—; dir. Ann. Bible Tchrs. Workshop, 1959-66; minister edn. Highland Ch. of Christ, Abilene, 1954-66. Paul Harris fellow, 1978; named Tchr. of Year, Abilene Christian Coll., 1956, 77; Sweet Award for disting. service Ch. Bible sch., 1963; 20th Century Christian Edn. award, 1964. Mem. Soc. Bibl. Lit., Am. Acad. Religion, Am. Sch. Oriental Research, Am. Soc. Ch. History, Evang. Theol. Soc. Democrat. Lodge: Rotary (dir.). Home: 902 E North 12th Abilene TX 76901 Office: Abilene Christian U ACU Sta Box 7543 Abilene TX 79699

LEWIS, ROBERT DOUGLAS, minister, Southern Baptist Convention; b. Fort Worth, Tex., Jan. 22, 1949; s. William Douglas and Maggie Marie (Golden) L.; m. Deborah Anne Paden, Aug. 26, 1972; children: Robert Trent, Kimberly Anne, Tiffany Marie. A.A., Hannibal LaGrange Coll., 1969; B.A., Okla. Bapt. U., 1971; M.Div., Golden Gate Sem., 1974, D.Min., 1982. Ordained to ministry Southern Baptist Convention, 1974. Pastor 24th St Bapt. Ch., Sacramento, 1973-75; assoc. dir. evangelism So. Bapt. Gen. Conv. Calif., Fresno, 1975-78; pastor Lodi Ave. Bapt. Ch., Lodi, Calif., 1978-85; pastor Rose Dr. Bapt. Ch., Yorba Linda, Calif., 1985—; moderator Delta Valley So. Bapt. Assn., 1982-84; adj. prof. Golden Gate Bapt. Sem., Mill Valley, Calif., 1982—; dir. Stockton Bible Center, Delta Valley So. Bapt. Assn., 1983-85. Mem. Lodi Assn. Evangelicals (sec. 1982-83). Republican. Home: 2044 Gillilan Placentia CA 92670 Office: Rose Dr Bapt Ch 4572 Rose Dr Yorba Linda CA 92686

LEWIS, ROD R., minister, Chs. of Christ; b. Taft, Calif., July 28, 1932; s. William O. and Medora H. (Harper) L.; B.A., Pacific Christian Coll., 1976; m. Beryl Anita Moore, Feb. 14, 1971. Ordained to ministry, 1973; pastor Fellows Ch. of Christ, 1971-73, Central Christian Ch., South Gate, Calif., 1973-74; preaching minister and evangelist Cassettes for Christ, Pacific Christian Coll., Fullerton, Calif., 1972—, founder, exec. dir. Home: 11728 State St Lynwood CA 90262 Office: 2500 E Nutwood St Suite 330 Fullerton CA

LEWIS, TONY LLOYD, minister, American Baptist Convention; b. Lake Charles, La., Sept. 4, 1951; s. Gloria Mae (Lewis) S.; B.A., Bishop Coll., 1979; M.A., Pitts. Theol. Sem., 1981. Ordained to ministry American Baptist Convention. Young adult minister Prosperity Bapt. Ch., Los Angeles, 1976-77; minister Concord Bapt. Ch., Dallas, 1977-79; exec. bd. Ministers' Lyceum, Dallas, 1978-79; assoc. minister Central Bapt. Ch., Pitts., 1979-81; pastor Morning Star Ch., Portland, Oreg., 1982—; del. L.K. Williams Inst., Dallas, 1977—, Gen. Bapt. Conv., Oreg./Wash., 1982—; mem. ch. devel. bd. Am. Bapt. of Oreg.; lectr. in field. Author published sermons. Contbr. article to profl. jour. Mem. Bapt. Ministers' Union, Albina Ministerial Alliance of Portland. Office: Morning Star Mission 106 NE Ivy Portland OR 97212

LEWIS, WILLIE JOSEPH, minister, church official, Seventh-day Adventist Church. b. Gainsville, Fla., July 29, 1939; s. Willie and Marguerite (Walters) L.; m. Barbara Ann Stokes; children: William, Zachary. B.A., Oakwood Coll., 1960; M.A., Andrews U., 1962; L.L.D. (hon.), Faith Coll., 1975. Ordained to ministry Seventh-day Adventist Ch., 1966. Pastor Seventh-day Adventist Ephesus Ch., Columbia, S.C., 1962-65, Elim Ch., St. Petersburg, Fla., 1965-68, Hamilton Ch., Hamilton, 1968-73, Shiloh Ch., Cin., 1973-76; exec. sec. Allegheny West Conf., Seventh-day Adventist Ch., Columbus, Ohio, 1976—; dir. edn. Allegheny West Conf., Columbus, 1976-79, dir. stewardship, 1976—, exec. sec., 1981—; chaplain CAP, U.S. Air Force Aux., Columbus, 1984—. Contbr. articles to profl. jours. Bd. dirs. Pine Forge Acad., Pa., 1981—, YMCA Eastside, Columbus, 1982-83; bd. sec. Allegheny West Exec. Com., Columbus, 1981. Recipient Pastor of Yr. award Allegheny West Conf., 1974. Democrat. Home: 4500 Scissortail Loop Westerville OH 43081 Office: Allegheny West Conf of Seventh-Day Adventists 1339 E Broad St Columbus OH

LEWISON, NORMAN JOEL, rabbi, Conservative Jewish; b. Chgo., Mar. 8, 1940; s. Matthew Michael and Mildred Paula (Eckhaus) L.; m. Linda Salomon, July 3, 1966; 1 child, Laura Rose. B.S., U. Chgo., 1961; M.H.L., Jewish Theol. Sem. of Am., 1966. Ordained rabbi, 1968. Hillel Found. dir. B'nai B'rith Hillel Found., Athens, Ohio, Phila., 1970-74, 74-76; rabbi, edn. dir. Ohave Shalom Synagogue, Rockford, Ill., 1976-80; commn. dir. Am. Jewish Congress, Chgo., 1980—; chaplain Hines VA Hosp., Ill., 1983—, Loyola U. Med. Ctr., 1984—. Pres. Chgo. Area Jewish Hospice Assn., 1983-84, No. Ill. Hospice Assn., Rockford, 1979-80; bd. dirs. Planned Parenthood, Chgo., 1984—; del. Chgo. Conf. on Religion and Race, 1984. Served to capt., USAF, 1968-70. Recipient Service award Am. Cancer Soc., 1979. Mem. Rabbinical Assembly, Chgo. Bd. Rabbis, Assn. Jewish Chaplains. Home: 5401 S East View Park Chicago IL 60615 Office: Am Jewish Congress 22 W Monroe Chicago IL 60603

LEXAU, HENRY See *Who's Who in America*, 43rd edition.

L'HEUREUX, N(ESTOR) J(OSEPH), JR., church official, United Methodist Church; b. Meriden, Conn., Dec. 28, 1945; s. Nestor Joseph and Elsie Jane (Bourne) L'H.; B.A., Ohio Wesleyan U., 1967; Th.M., Boston U., 1971; Ordained to ministry, 1969; asso. pastor St. Paul's United Meth. Ch., Northport, N.Y., 1970-73; pastor Maspeth (N.Y.) United Meth. Ch., 1973-78; exec. dir. Queens Fedn. Chs., Richmond Hill, N.Y., 1978—. Sec. Ecumenical Life Council of Northport-East Northport, 1971-73; internat. ritualist Kappa Sigma, 1975-83. Coordinator United Orgns. of Maspeth, 1976-78. Mem. Order of St. Luke, Soc. Am. Magicians. Home: 66-29 58th Ave Maspeth NY 11378 Office: 86-17 105th St Richmond Hill NY 11418-1597

L'HUILLIER, PETER, bishop, Orthodox Church in America; b. Paris, Dec. 3, 1926; came to U.S., 1980; s. Eugene Henri and Emilienne (Haslin) L'H. Licentiate in Theology, Institut Theologique Saint-Denys-Paris, 1949. Ordained priest, 1954. Priest, Russian Ch., Paris, 1954-68, bishop, 1968-79; bishop Orthodox Ch. in Am., N.Y.-N.J., N.Y.C., 1980—. Home: 33 Hewitt Ave Bronxville NY 10708 Office: Diocese of New York-New Jersey 33 Hewitt Ave Bronxville NY 10708

LI, PETER JOSEPH TA See *Who's Who in America*, 43rd edition.

LIBEN, ZIPPORAH, religious organization executive, Jewish. Exec. dir. World Council of Synagogues, N.Y.C. Office: World Council of Synagogues 155 Fifth Ave New York NY 10010*

LIBERTY, JAMES LEON, priest, counselor, retreat director, Roman Catholic Church; b. Plattsburgh, N.Y., May 22, 1931; s. Leon Dennis and Cecilia Cleo (Brunelle) L.; B.A. in Philosophy, Oblate Coll. Sem., Natick, Mass., Cath. U., Washington, 1954; M.A., in Counseling Psychology, U. Conn. 1979. Ordained priest, 1957; mem. Congregation Oblates of Mary Immaculate; lectr., retreat master, counselor, superior, dir. Immaculata Retreat House, Willimantic, Conn., 1961-76; counselor individuals, families, marriage; lectr. religious renewal and the retreat movement; chaplain Eastern U.S. lieutenancy Knights Jerusalem, 1976—; staff psychotherapist Cath. Family Services, Diocese of Norwich, Conn., 1979—. Home: 3 Oxford Dr Norwich CT 06360 Office: 201 Hickory St Norwich CT 06360

LIBERTY-JONES, PATRICIA LOUISE, minister, Am. Baptist Chs., U.S.A.; b. Springfield, Mass., July 31, 1957; d. George Arthur and Judith Sandra (Hartwick) L.; m. Larry Addison Jones, Aug. 31, 1984. B.S. cum laude, Springfield Coll., 1978; M.Div., Andover Newton Theol. Sem., 1982. Ordained to ministry Baptist Ch., 1982. Asst. pastor First Bapt. Ch., Agawam, Mass., 1978-79; pastor Enfield Am. Bapt. Ch., Conn., 1979—; minister of visitation Central Bapt. Ch., Hartford, Conn., 1984—; bd. mgrs. commn. on ministry Am. Bapt. Chs. Conn., 1982—; pres. Conn. Am. Bapt. Ministers Council, 1984—. Mem. Ministers Council of Am. Bapt. Chs. U.S.A. Home: 351 South Rd Somers CT 06071 Office: Enfield American Baptist Ch 129 Post Office Rd Enfield CT 06071

LICKTEIG, BERNARD FABIAN, priest, Roman Catholic Church; b. Greeley, Kans., Jan. 6, 1921; s. Frank Joseph and Elizabeth Helena (Wolken) L. Ph.B., Mt. Carmel Coll., 1943; M.A., Chgo. U., 1952. Ordained to ministry, 1946. Tchr., retreat master Carmelite Sem., Hamilton, Mass., 1951-60; superior Mt. Carmel High Sch., Houston, 1960-63; pastor St. Cecilia Parish, Englewood, N.J., 1963-72; parish coordinator Carmelite Fathers, Barrington, Ill., 1972-78; pastor St. Raphael Parish, Glendale, Ariz., 1980—; mem. Carmelite Provincial Council, Barrington, 1963-66, dir., goals, 1975-78, dir. apostolate, 1975-78. Editor: Steps for Goal Setting, 1976. Author booklet: Use of Film in Science Education, 1952. Mem. Englewood Housing Authority, N.J., 1966-72; founder Interracial Council, Englewood, 1963. Mem. Valley Friends of the Farm Worker, Bergen County Priest Assn. (pres. 1967-69). Home: 5504 W Acoma Rd Glendale AZ 85306

LICKTEIG, NORBERT, priest, Roman Catholic Church. B. Welda, Kans., Feb. 27, 1934; s. Greg and Veronica (Bowman) L. B.A., St. Thomas, 1957, M.A., 1961, S.T.B., 1961. Ordained to ministry Roman Catholic Ch. 1961. Chaplain Kans. U. Hosp., Kansas City, 1961-67; tchr. Bishop Miege, Shawnee Mission, Kans., 1961-67; pastor Cath. Ch., Kansas City, Kans., 1967—; dir. soc. propagation of faith Archdiocese, Kansas City, Kans., 1971—; Mem. Canon Law Soc., Ministerial Assn. (pres. Wyandotte County 1983, 84). Lodge: K.C. (chaplain 1961—). Home: 1086 N 94th St PO Box 12445 Kansas City KS 66112 Office: Soc Propagation Faith 2220 Central Ave Kansas City KS 66160

LIDERBACH, DANIEL PATRICK, priest, Roman Catholic Church. B. Cleve., Mar. 17, 1941; s. Anthony Alfred and Margaret Mary (Quinlan) L. B.A., Loyola U., Chgo., 1964, Licentiate in Philosophy, 1965; M.A., St. Michael's Coll., Toronto, Ont., Can., 1974, Ph.D., 1979; S.T.L., Regis Coll., 1983. Ordained priest Roman Catholic Ch., 1973. Tchr. theology John Carroll U., Cleve., 1978-83; Canisius Coll., Buffalo, 1983—. Author: The Theology of Grace and the American Mind, 1984. Home and Office: 2001 Main St Buffalo NY 14208

LIEBER, CHARLES DONALD See Who's Who in America, 43rd edition.

LIEBERMAN, SIDNEY ZVULUN, rabbi, educator, Orthodox Jewish; b. N.Y.C., Aug. 5, 1930; s. Henry Hillel and Julia (Chesler) L.; m. Joyce Brocha Friedman, June 13, 1955; children: Tehila, Elyorah Chaya, Hillel Eliyahu. B.A., Yeshiva Coll., 1951; B.R.E., Erna Michael Coll., 1952; M.S., Ferkauf Grad. Sch., Yeshiva U., 1957, Ph.D., 1959. Rabbi, 1954. Rabbi, Congregation Beth Torah, Bklyn., 1959—; prin. gen. studies Yeshiva of Flatbush High Sch., Bklyn., 1954-66; headmaster Ramaz Upper Sch., N.Y.C., 1966-70; prin. Hillel High Sch., Lawrence, N.Y., 1970-79; asst. prof. Ferkauf Grad. Sch., Yeshiva U., N.Y.C., 1977—; ednl. dir. Massad Camps, N.Y.; ednl. cons. Anti Defamation League. Editor Chemed, 1976—. Recipient Bernard Revel award Yeshiva Coll. Alumni Assn., 1970, Service award, 1978. Mem. Am. Soc. Sephardic Studies (pres. 1970-72), Yeshiva Coll. Alumni Assn. (exec. com.), Educators Council Am., Rabbinical Council Am., United Jewish Appeal (Rabbinical adv. council). Home: 854 E 9th St Brooklyn NY 11230 Office: Congregation Beth Torah 1061 Ocean Pkwy Brooklyn NY 11230

LIEBRECHT, MARCILLE, nun, Roman Catholic Church; b. Continental, Ohio, Apr. 25, 1936; d. Sylvester Joseph and Clara Mary (Kahle) L. B.A., Coll. of St. Francis, Joliet, Ill., 1966; postgrad. Eastern Ky. U., 1968, Norfolk State U., 1969; M.A., U. Toledo, 1974. Joined Order of St. Francis, Roman Catholic Ch., 1956. Tchr. various pub. and parochial schs. in Ohio and N.D., 1957-59, 61-76; tchr. religion Our Lady of Consolation, Carey, Ohio, 1976—; adminstr. St. Anthony Pilgrim House, Carey, 1980—. Mem. Northwestern Ohio Retreat Ctrs. Home and Office: St Anthony Pilgrim House 321 Clay St Carey OH 43316

LIESKE, HENRY LOUIS, minister, Association of Evangelical Lutheran Churches; b. Yenderson, Minn., Oct. 21, 1911; s. Henry Froedrich and Clara Margaretha (Blaesing) L.; m. Marguerite Virginia Jones, June 7, 1939; children: Jeanne Lieske Kirkpatrick, Jay, Joy Lieske Skelton, Janice (dec.), Jacquelyn Lieske Copeland, Judy Lieske Wabrek. Student Concordia Jr. Coll., St. Paul, 1925-31; B.D., Concordia Sem., St. Louis, 1935, M.Div., 1971; postgrad. Grad. Sch. Theology, Oberlin Coll., 1950-53, Cleve. Coll. of Western Res. U., 1947-49, Portland State Coll., 1956-61. Ordained to ministry, 1938. Sec., asst. to sec. Luth. Ch.-Mo. Synod, Kendallville, Ind., 1935-38; pastor, mission developer new Luth. congregations, Warsaw and Plymouth, Ind., 1938-43; pastor St. John's Luth. Ch., Elyria, Ohio, 1943-55; founder, pastor, mission developer St. Timothy Luth. Ch., Portland, Oreg., 1955-67; pastor Redeemer Luth. Ch., Burnsville, Minn., 1967-76, Prairie Luth. Ch., Eden Prairie, Minn., 1979; chmn. bd. regents Concordia Coll., Portland, 1958-67; chmn., co-founder All-Luth. Welfare Assn. Oreg. (now Luth. Family Service), Portland, 1957-61. Researcher, compiler, contbr. manuscript collection: The Moderate Movement in the Lutheran Church - Missouri Synod, Oberlin Coll. Archives, 1977-80, supplemental placement, 1980—; author articles, conf. presentations. Chmn. East Portland chpt. Am. Field Service student exchange program, East Portland and Gresham, Oreg., 1960-62; mem., chmn. Elyria Community Welfare Council, 1951-55, del. nat. conf., 1955. Clubs: Am. Philatelic Soc. (life mem.), Postal History Soc. Minn. (writer, distbr. postal history resource books). Home: 55 Idaho Ave N Golden Valley MN 55427

LIFER, CHARLES LAMAR, minister, Southern Baptist Convention; b. Jackson, Miss., June 16, 1938; s. Charles Rudolph and Evelyn (Bell) L.; B.A., William Carey Coll., 1961; postgrad. New Orleans Bapt. Theol. Sem., 1961-63, Memphis Cumberland Presbyn. Sem., 1969; m. Janie Lou Beard, June 3, 1962; children: Andy, Lamarcia. Ordained to ministry So. Baptist Conv., 1958; minister Wayside Bapt. Mission, Hattiesburg, Miss., 1957-61, McCullough (Ala.) Bapt. Ch., 1961-62, Eureka Bapt. Ch., Finchburg, Ala., 1962-64, Bouie St. Bapt. Ch., Hattiesburg, Miss., 1964-66, Emmanuel Bapt. Ch., Forrest City, Ark., 1966-68, Ingram Blvd. Bapt. Ch., West Memphis, Ark., 1968-71, Westhaven Bapt. Ch., Memphis, 1971-73, First Bapt. Ch., Nesbit, Miss., 1973-76, Olivet Bapt. Ch., Little Rock, 1977—; pres. Ark. State Bapt. Pastor's Conf., 1983-84. Chaplain Rowsey's Furniture Co., 1974-75, Indsl. Sales, Memphis, 1974-75; clk., Bethlehem Bapt. Assn., Monroeville, Ala., 1963-64; pres., Bapt. Pastors Conf., Hattiesburg, Miss., 1966. Bd. dirs. Campus Life Mem. Christian Businessmen Fellowship (dir. 1974-75). Club: Civic (Nesbit, Miss.). Home: 2400 Dorchester Little Rock AR 72204

LIFSHEN, LEONARD H., rabbi, Conservative Jewish Congregations; b. N.Y.C., June 29, 1941; s. Maurice and Doris (Gorenstein) L.; B.S., Coll. City N.Y., 1963; M.Hebrew Letters, Jewish Theol. Sem. Am., 1970; m. Faith Epstein, Sept. 12, 1965; children—Michele, Moshe, Eli. Ordained rabbi, 1970; rabbi B'nai Jacob Synagogue, Phoenixville, Pa., 1970-72, Emanuel Synagogue, Oklahoma City, 1972—. Rabbinic adviser Jewish Marriage Encounter, 1976—; chaplain municipal govt. Phoenixville, 1971. Recipient Ba'al Shem Tov citation Little Synagogue, N.Y.C., 1971; Conscientious Service certificate Oklahoma City Sch. Vol. Program, 1973, 74, 75, 76; Merit certificate municipal govt. Phoenixville, 1971. Mem. Rabbinical Assembly, N.Y. Bd. Rabbis, Kallah of Tex. Rabbis (pres. 1975-76). Home: 415 NW 43d St Oklahoma City OK 73118 Office: 900 NW 47th St Oklahoma City OK 73118

LIGGETT, THOMAS JACKSON, theological seminary president, Christian Ch. (Disciples of Christ); b. Nashville, May 27, 1919; s. Thomas Jackson and Lola Cleveland (Ballentine) L.; A.B., Transylvania Coll., 1940, D.Hum., 1969; M.Div., Lexington Theol. Sem., 1944; LL.D., Interam. U., 1965, Culver-Stockton Coll., 1959, Butler U., 1975; D.D., Eureka Coll., 1971; m. Virginia Corine Moore, Aug. 12, 1941; children: Thomas Milton, Margaret Ann (Mrs. William D. Herod). Ordained to ministry Christian Ch., 1940; pastor Ky. chs., 1940-45; missionary, pastor, Argentina, 1946-57, also prof. Union Sem., Buenos Aires, 1949-56; pres. Evang. Sem. of P.R., San Juan, 1957-65; Latin Am. sec. United Christian Missionary Soc., 1965-68, chmn. overseas div., pres., Indpls., 1967-69, pres. Christian Theol. Sem., Indpls., 1974—. Del. World Council Chs., Uppsala, 1968, adviser, Nairobi, 1975. Chmn. Latin Am. task force for George McGovern, 1972. Mem. Nat. Council Chs. (governing bd.), United Christian Missionary Soc. (pres. 1968-74). Author: Where Tomorrow Struggles to Be Born, 1970. Office: 1000 W 42d St Indianapolis IN 46208

LIGHT, ARTHUR HEATH, bishop, Episcopal Church; b. Lynchburg, Va., July 7, 1929; s. Alexander H. and Mary W. (Nelson) L.; m. Sarah Ann Jones, June 12, 1953; children: William A., Philip N., John P., Sarah H. B.A., Hampden-Sydney Coll., 1951; M.Div., Va. Theol. Sem., 1954, D.D. (hon.), 1979; D.D. (hon.), St. Paul's Coll., Lawrenceville, Va., 1979. Ordained priest Episcopal Ch., 1955, consecrated bishop, 1979. Rector chs. in Va., 1954-58, N.C., 1958-79, Christ and St. Luke's Ch., Norfolk, Va., 1967-79; bishop Diocese of Southwestern Va., Roanoke, 1979—. Democrat. Home: 2524 Wycliffe Ave SW Roanoke VA 24014 Office: 1000 1st St Roanoke VA 24009

LIGHTSEY, RALPH, minister, Nat. Assn. Free Will Baptists; b. Bristol, Ga., Nov. 27, 1918; s. Willis and Mamie Leon (Bryson) L.; B.A., Mercer U., 1945; B.D. Emory U., 1951; Th.M., Columbia Theol. Sem., 1955; Ed.D., U. Ga., 1965; m. Velma Wavine Reeves, Feb. 25, 1945; children—June Elizabeth, Ralph Nelson. Ordained to ministry, 1940; pastor chs. Ga., 1941-59, St. Mary's Ch., New Bern, N.C., 1959-63, New Light Ch., Morgan, Ga., 1964—. Dean, Free Will Bapt. Bible Coll., 1951-53; moderator S. Ga. Assn., 1947-51, Ga. Assn., 1957-59; pres. South Ga. Sunday Sch. Conv., 1954-57. Contbr. articles to ch. publs. Home: 119 Woodlawn Dr Statesboro GA 30458 Office: PO Box 731 Statesboro GA 30458

LIKNESS, LAWRENCE RICHARD, pastor, Evangelical Lutheran Church of Canada; b. Consort, Alta., Can., Sept. 30, 1929; s. Oscar and Doris Rose (Gourlie) L.; m. Doreen Ellen Anderson, June 21, 1952; children: Mark Lawrence, Steven Richard. B.A., U. Sask., Saskatoon, Can., 1951; B.D., Luther Sem., Saskatoon, 1952; M.Th., Luther Theol. Sem., St. Paul, 1971. Ordained to ministry Evangelical Lutheran Church of Canada, 1952. Pastor Our Saviour's Luth. Ch., Thunder Bay, Ont., Can., 1952-57, Mt. Zion Luth. Ch., Edmonton, Alta., Can., 1957-62, Sherwood Park Luth. Ch., Winnipeg, Man., 1962-68, Zion Luth. Ch., Saskatoon, 1968-77, Christ Luth. Ch., Toronto, Ont., Can., 1979—; interim dir. div. Congl. Life, Evangelical Luth. Ch. Can., Saskatoon, 1977-79; commr. Inter-Luth. Commn. on Worship, 1967-78; bd. dirs. div. congl. life Evangelical Luth. Ch. Can., 1967-77; pres. Ea. Conf. Evangelical Luth. Ch. Can., 1982—. Author: Our Christian Faith, 1974; (booklet) With Your Promises, 1980; contbg. author: Luth. Book Worship, 1978. Mem. Can. Liturgical Soc. (sec. 1981—). Office: Christ Luth Ch 2850 Midland Ave Agincourt ON M1S 1S4 Canada

LILLICROPP, ARTHUR REGINALD, III, priest, Episc. Ch.; b. Rockville Center, N.Y., June 7, 1947; s. Arthur Reginald and Irene Nora (Yerger) L.; B.A., Lafayette Coll., 1969; M.Div., Gen. Theol. Sem., 1974. Ordained priest, 1974; asst. Christ and St. Stephen's Ch., N.Y.C., 1974-76, Trinity Episc. Ch., Towson, Md., 1976—. Mem. N.Y. Diocesan Ecumenical Commn., 1975-76; mem. clergy conf. com. N.Y. Diocese, 1975-76; chaplain Roosevelt and Meml. hosps., N.Y.C., 1975—, Towson State Coll., 1976—, Goucher Coll., Towson, Md., 1976—. Mem. Md. Diocesan Liturgical Com., also mem. Youth and Young Adult Com. Dir. mem. Lincoln Square Community Coll., 1974-76. Mem.

Nat. Council Chs., Religious Edn. Assn. Office: 120 Allegheny Ave Towson MD 21204

LILLY, LAWRENCE MELVIN, minister, Independent Baptist Church; b. Harve De Grace, Md., Sept. 13, 1941; s. George Melvin Lilly and Virginia Agnes (Lawrence) Lilly Holmes; m. Joyce Dorine Gore, Aug. 29, 1964; children: Dawn Mechael, Jonathan Daniel. Diploma Bible, Md. Bible Inst., 1965; D.D. (hon.) Faith Sem., 1971. Ordained to ministry Baptist Ch., 1967. Visitation dir. Bapt. Bible Ch., Elkton, Md., 1965-66; assoc. pastor Kingston Park Bapt., Balt., 1966-67; pastor Fellowship Bapt. Ch., Wytheville, Va., 1967-74, Meml. Bapt. Ch., Havre De Grace, 1974-75, Faith Bapt. Ch. of Avon, Danville, Ind., 1975—; pres. Spirtual Dynamics, Plainfield, Ind., 1976—, Christian Acad., Inc., Indpls., 1978-82, Internat. fellowship Bapts., Averyville, Ill., 1980-81; adv. Ind. Bapt. Coll., Greenwood, Ind., 1978—, Bapt. Internat. Missions, Inc., Chattanooga, 1982—. Editor Newsletter Spiritual Dynamics Counselor, 1982; contbr. articles to religious pamphlets. Recipient Ky. Col. award Commonwealth of Ky., 1981. Mem. Nat. Speakers Assn. Home: Rural Route 1 Box 445 Danville IN 46122 Office: Faith Bapt Ch of Avon Rural Route 1 Box 262 Danville IN 46122

LIMA, SHARON KUNKEL, religion educator, Evangelical Christian Church. B. Oakland, Calif., July 29, 1956; d. Glenn Everett and Jacqueline (Lemm) K.; m. Samuel Mendonca Lima, Jan. 11, 1981. B.A., Patten Coll., 1978; M.A. in Theology, Fuller Sem., 1980; tchr. credential U. Calif.-Berkeley, 1980. Instr., Patten Coll., Oakland, Calif., 1980-82, asst. prof. religion, 1982-84, chmn. Bibl. div., 1983—; chmn. Christian Service Com., 1980—. Musician, Patten Symphonette, Oakland, 1970—. Mem. Am. Acad. Religion, Soc. Bibl. Lit. Democrat. Home: 2240 Coolidge Ave #4 Oakland CA 94601 Office: Patten Coll 2433 Coolidge Ave Oakland CA 94601

LIN, LARRY KUENTSAI, minister, Presbyn. Ch. in Can.; b. Taiwan, July 5, 1945; s. Tswan Hseng and Sue (Shey) L.; B.A., Tung-Hai U., 1964; B.D., Tainan Theol. Coll., 1969; M.A., McGill U., 1973; m. Sandra Mei-Ai Shen, June 27, 1974; children—Tobi Chongbi, Daniel Chong-Tiat. Ordained to ministry, 1969; pastor Feng-Ku Presbyn. Ch. Taiwan, 1969-70; dir. med. social service St. Paul's Clinic, Taiwan, 1969; tchr. Southshore Cath. High Sch., Montreal, Que., Can., 1972-73; pres. Alin Enterprise Co. Ltd., Montreal, 1972-73; minister Killam (Alta., Can.) Galahad Presbyn. Ch., 1974—. Moderator, Edmonton Presbytery, 1976-77. Mem. Flagstaff Ministerial Assn. Home and Office: POB 386 Killam AB T0B 2L0 Canada

LINCOLN, C. ERIC, educator, minister, United Methodist Ch.; b. Athens, Ala., June 23, 1924; s. Less and M. (Sowell) L.; A.B., LeMoyne Coll., 1947; A.M., Fisk U., 1954; B.D., U. Chgo., 1957; Ph.D., Boston U., 1960; LL.D., Carleton Coll., 1968; D.H.L., St. Michael's Coll., 1971; m. Lucy Alma Cook, July 1, 1961; children—Cecil Eric, Joyce Elaine (by previous marriage), Hilary Anne, Less Charles II. Ordained to ministry United Methodist Ch., 1957; pastor John Calvin Presbyn. Ch., Nashville, 1953-55; prof. sociology of religion Union Theol. Sem., N.Y.C., 1967-73; head. dept. religious and philos. studies Fisk U., Nashville, 1973-76; prof. religion Duke, 1976—. Founding pres. Black Acad. Arts and Letters, 1969-72. Trustee Martin Luther King Found., Atlanta, Boston U. Recipient Creative Communications award Art Inst. Boston, 1970. Fellow Am. Acad. Arts and Scis.; mem. Soc. for Study Black Religion, Am. Psychol. Assn., Am. Sociol. Assn. Author: The Black Muslims in America, 1961; The Negro Pilgrimage, 1967; Profile of Martin Luther King, 1968; The Black Church since Frazier, 1974; The Black Experience in Religion, 1974. Home: Route 1 Box 271-N Hillsboro NC 27278 Office: Dept Religion Duke U Durham NC

LINCOLN, EUGENE, religious newspaper editor, religious organization executive, Seventh-day Adventists, editor. B. Marion, Ind., Oct. 5, 1923; s. Albert and Glenora Agnes (Townsend) L.; m. Darlene Jacqueline Boatwright, July 4, 1947; children: David Lee, Michael Eugene, Angelita Karolene, Jonathan Wayne. B.S., Marion Coll., 1948; M.A., Andrews U., 1973. Credentialed missionary Seventh-day Adventists, 1979. Editor, Bible Sabbath Assn., Fairview, Okla., 1960—, first v.p., 1976—, also dir.; mem. adv. bd. Seventh-day Adventist Missionary Found., Phoenix, 1980—. Copy editor Rev. and Herald Pub. Assn., Hagerstown, Md., 1974—. Author: Right Face, 1976; The High Cost of Loving, 1979; Understanding the Power of Prayer, 1984. Editor The Sabbath Sentinel, 1960—. Contbr. articles to various publs. Democrat. Home: 1228 Wayne Ave Hagerstown MD 21740 Office: Rev and Herald Pub Assn 55 W Oak Ridge Dr Hagerstown MD 21740

LIND, DOUGLASS THEODORE, minister, United Presbyterian Church U.S.A.; b. St. Paul, Dec. 27, 1939; s. Olaf Milton and Jennie Theresa (Skoglund) L.; A.B. cum laude, Harvard, 1961; M.Div., Union Theol. Sem., 1964; certificate Westchester Inst. Counseling and Psychotherapy, 1970; m. Penelope Dougall, July 31, 1965. Ordained to ministry, 1967. Diplomate Am. Assn. Pastoral Counselors. Area counsellor The Fifty

Million Fund, United Presbyn. Ch. U.S.A., 1964-67; asst. pastor, North Ave. Presbyn. Ch., New Rochelle, N.Y., 1967-69; sr. minister, 1969-73; assoc. pastor Wilton (Conn.) Presbyn. Ch., 1973—; pastoral counselor Hudson River Counseling Service, Mt. Kisco, N.Y., 1973—. Dir. tng. Reed and Di Salvo Assos., Inc., N.Y.C., 1973-79. Vice-pres. Charter League, New Rochelle, N.Y., 1970-73; v.p. New Rochelle Council Chs., 1970-73; mem. Westchester area com. Nat. Council on Crime and Delinquency, 1971-73. Past mem. bd. ch. visitors Warren Wilson Coll.; past pres. bd. trustees Hudson River Counseling Service; trustee Johnson C. Smith Sem., Atlanta; faculty Westchester Inst. Counseling and Psychotherapy. Mem. Am. Assn. Marriage and Family Counselors, Acad. Parish Clergy (chmn. profl. responsibilities and standards com. 1972, past pres. dir. 1975-81). Address: 17 Edgewater Hillside Westport CT 06880

LINDAHL, LEROY CHARLES, missionary, Evangelical Methodist Church; b. Waukesha, Wis., June 21, 1924; s. Gustave Adolf and Mabel Louise (Zietlow) L.; m. Mary Jane Weber, June 21, 1948; children: Lawrence LeRoy, Stephen Daniel. B.A., Taylor U., 1951; M.Div., Western Evang. Sem., 1955. Ordained to ministry Evangelical Methodist Ch. as missionary, 1958. Pastor, Proebstel Community Ch., Vancouver, Wash., 1953-57; missionary World Gospel Mission, Ind., 1957—. Contbr. articles to profl. jours. Mem. Rep. Presdl. Task Force, Washington, 1983-84; chaplain CAP, Los Angeles, 1981-83. Served with USN, 1942-45. Republican. Avocations: computers; woodworking; reading. Home: 2312 E 2d St Apt 7 Los Angeles CA 90033 Office: Community House of God 2302 E 2d St Los Angeles CA 90033 also Box WGM Marion IN 46952

LINDBERG, CARTER HARRY, educator, Lutheran Church in America; b. Berwyn, Ill., Nov. 23, 1937; s. Gustaf Harry and Esther (Bell) L.; m. Alice Knudsen, June 4, 1960; children: Anne, Erika, Matthew. B.A., Augustana Coll., 1959; M.Div., Luth. Sch. Theology, 1962; Ph.D., U. Iowa, 1965. Assoc. prof. ch. history and theology Sch. Theology, Boston U., 1972—; research prof. Inst. Ecumenical Research, Strasbourg, France, 1979-82; pres. 16th Century Studies Conf., 1978-79; mem. continuation com. Internat. Congress for Luther Research, 1983—. Author: The Third Reformation?, 1983. Editor: Piety, Politics and Ethics, 1984; (with others: Luther's Ecumenical Significance, 1984. Contbr. articles to profl. jours. Mem. Am. Soc. Reformation Research, Am. Soc. Ch. History, 16th Century Studies Conf., Luther Gesellschaft. Home: 113 Whitney St Northboro MA 01532 Office: Sch Theology Boston Univ 745 Commonwealth Boston MA 02215

LINDBERG, HAROLD ALBERT, minister, American Lutheran Church; b. Chgo., Sept. 8, 1927; s. Harold Emil and Augusta Bessie (Mundt) L.; m. Charisma Hedvig Madson, Sept. 8, 1949 (div. Sept. 1979); children: Christopher, Lisa, Nora, Kari, Sara; m. Barbara Jean Meyer, May 17, 1980; 1 child, Aaron. A.A., North Park Coll., 1947; B.A., St. Olaf Coll., 1949; postgrad. in theology Luth. Theol. Sem., St. Paul, 1956. Ordained to ministry Evangelical Lutheran Church, 1956. Pastor DeSoto Luth. Parish, Wis., 1956-60; chaplain Huntingdon, Pa. State Correctional Inst., 1961-62, Ohio State Penitentiary, Columbus, 1962-67; dir. com. on instl. ministries Ohio Council Chs., Columbus, 1967-72; dir. pastoral care Med. Coll. Ohio at Toledo, 1973—. Contbr. articles to profl. jours. Mem. Ohio citizens Com. on Corrections, Columbus, 1970-71. Fellow Am. Protestant Hosp. Assn. (Coll. Chaplains); mem. Assn. Clin. Pastoral Edn. (supr. 1965—). Democrat. Home: 11236 Neapolis-Waterville Rd Whitehouse OH 43571 Office: Med Coll Ohio C S 10008 Toledo OH 43699

LINDE, RICHARD B.L., minister, United Church of Christ; b. Lima, Ohio, May 5, 1923; s. Elmer Calvin and Mary Mae (Lindamood) Lugabill; m. Loraine Ogden, June 29, 1949; children: Richard Edwards, Thomas Hooker, Robert Downing. M.Div., Drew U., 1945; M.B.A., Harvard U., 1949; D.Div., Christian Theol. Sem., 1972. Ordained to ministry Methodist Ch., 1945. Assoc. minister, Epworth-Euclid Meth. Ch., Cleve., 1949-54; minister Edwards Congl. Ch., Northampton, Mass., 1954-60; sr. minister 1st Congl. Ch., Elyria, Ohio, 1960-73; sr. minister, Countryside Community Ch., Omaha, Nebr., 1973—; chmn. bd. dirs., mem. exec. com. Bd. Homeland Ministries, United Ch. Christ; chmn. bd. dirs. Nebr. Conf., United Ch. Christ. Producer film documentaries for nat. TV Dir. Together, Inc.; pres. Lorain County Family Ser. Assn. Served as chaplain USN, 1945-46. Recipient Disting. Service award U.S. Com. UN. Mem. Harvard Bus. Sch. Assn. Mem. Explorers Club of N.Y. Lodge: Rotary. Home: 9825 Grover St Omaha NE 68124

LINDER, LYLE DEAN, minister, United Methodist; b. Oakland, Nebr., June 9, 1940; s. John Emil and Ethel Hartha (Nelson) L.; m. Mary Ann Brinson, June 18, 1976; children: Harry Kyle, Daniel, Jason, Leslie. A.B., Western Reserve U., Cleve., 1964; M.A., U. Tex., 1968; Ph.D., Duke, 1974; M.Div., Candler U., 1980; postgrad. Kearney State Coll., 1983-85. Ordained to elder Nebr. Conf. United Meth. Ch., 1983. Chaplaincy intern Grady Meml. Hosp., Atlanta, 1980-81; pastor Trinity United Meth. Ch., Renaitre Parish, Omaha, 1981-82, Pleasanton-Zion United Meth. Ch., Pleasanton, Nebr., 1982—; pastor Nebr. Farm Families Crisis Response, 1985—; facilitator Cansurmount Support Team, Am. Cancer Soc., Kearney, Nebr., 1983—; mem. Hospice Steering Com., Good Samaritan Hosp., Kearney, 1983—; mem. Buffalo County Cancer Soc., Kearney, 1984—. Sponsoring editor Sociology Anthropology, Polit. Sci., Social Work, Criminal Justice, 1974-77; asst. editor Jour. Bibl. Lit., Emory U., Atlanta, 1977-80; contbr. articles to various publs. Mem. Nebr. Annual Conf. Club: Lyons (Pleasanton, Nebr.). Home: 103 N Spruce St Pleasanton NE 68866 Office: United Methodist Ch Box 104 Pleasanton NE 68866

LINDSAY, FREDA THERESA, religious organization executive, minister Church of Foursquare Gospel; b. Burstall, Sask., Can., Apr. 18, 1914; d. Gottfred and Kaity (Saklofsky) Schimpf; brought to U.S., 1919; naturalized, 1940; student Life Internat. Foursquare Bible Coll., Portland, Ore., 1933-36, Los Angeles, 1938; m. Gordon James Lindsay, Nov. 14, 1937 (dec.); children: Carole Ann, Gilbert Livingston, Dennis Gordon. Ordained to ministry Internat. Ch. of Foursquare Gospel, 1940; v.p. Full Gospel Fellowship Chs. and Ministers Internat., 1976—; pres. Christ for the Nations, Dallas, 1973—; pres. Christ for the Nations Inst., Dallas, 1973—; editor, pub. Christ for the Nations mag.; founder numerous chs., missions and Bible schs. in numerous countries. Author: My Diary Secrets, 1976; Freda, 1984; speaker at ch. confs. also radio and TV appearances. Home: 441 Fawn Ridge Dr Apt 201 Dallas TX 75224 Office: 3404 Conway St Dallas TX 75224

LINDSELL, HAROLD, minister, educator, editor, Southern Baptist Convention; b. N.Y.C., Dec. 22, 1913; s. Leonard Anthony and Ella Briggs (Harris) L.; B.S., Wheaton Coll., 1938; A.M., U. Cal. at Berkeley, 1939; Ph.D., N.Y. U., 1942; D.D. (hon.), Fuller Theol. Sem., 1964; m. Marion Joanne Bolinder, June 12, 1943; children—Judith (Mrs. William C. Wood), Joanne (Mrs. Robert Webber), Nancy (Mrs. Daniel Sharp), John. Ordained to ministry, 1944; prof. ch. history and missions Columbia Bible Coll., 1942-44; prof. missions, asso. prof. ch. history No. Bapt. Theol. Sem., 1944-47; v.p., dean faculty, prof. missions Fuller Theol. Sem., 1947-64; asso. editor Christianity Today, 1964-67, editor, 1968-78; editor emeritus, 1979—; prof. Bible, Wheaton Coll., 1967-68. Trustee Wheaton Coll., Gordon-Conwell Theol. Sem., Christianity Today, Outreach. Mem. Am. Hist. Assn., Am. Soc. Ch. History, Am. Acad. Polit. and Social Scis., Nat. Assn. Evangs., Pi Gamma Mu, Pi Kappa Delta. Author: An Evangelical Theology of Missions, 1970; The World, the Flesh and the Devil, 1973; When You Pray, 1969; The Battle for the Bible, 1976; many others. Home: 5395 A Paseo del Lago Laguna Hills CA 92653 Office: 430 Gundersen Dr Carol Stream IL 60187

LINDSEY, EDWARD EDWIN, minister, Wesleyan Ch.; b. Towanda, Pa., Oct. 18, 1945; s. Edwin U. and Margaret Mary (MacNamara) L.; B.Edn., Clinton U., 1968, M.S.W., 1970; B.Th., Clarksville Sch. Theology, 1975; M. Psychology, Pacific So. U., 1976; m. Alberta Mae Cole, July 18, 1964; children—Richard, Stephen, Brenda. Ordained to ministry, 1968; pastor Donora (Pa.) Wesleyan Ch., 1967-73, Wesleyan Ch., Julian, Pa., 1973—. Sec. Western Pa. dist. Wesleyan Ch., mem. bd. ministerial standing, mem. dist. Sunday sch. and conf. action coms.; del. Gen. Conf. Wesleyan Ch., 1976. Mem. Christian Marriage Counselors Am., Christian Social Workers Am. Author: The Holy Spirit at Work in the Life of an Individual, 1976. Home and Office: RD 1 Julian PA 16844

LINDSEY, JIMMY, minister, Church of God (Cleveland, Tenn.); b. Brownsville, Tenn., Jan. 17, 1950; s. Marshall and Eva (Roberts) L.; m. Betty Colleen Morgan, May 29, 1976; children: Melanie Gean, Brian James. B.S. in Bible, Lee Coll., 1977; M.S. in Biblical Edn., Ch. of God Sch. of Theology, 1978. Ordained to ministry Ch. of God, Cleveland, Tenn., 1984. Pastor Ch. of God, Selmer, Tenn., 1978-81, Union City, Tenn., 1981—; dist. youth dir. Ch. of God, Union City, 1983—. Served to E-4 U.S. Army, 1969-71. Mem. Union City Ministerial Assn. Republican. Home: 505 S Taylor Union City TN 38261

LINEN, ELMER EDWARD, minister, Lutheran Ch.-Missouri Synod, community organization executive; b. Tichfield, Sask., Canada, May 30, 1927; came to U.S., 1952, naturalized, 1958; s. Albert and Sylvia (Liimatainen) Y.; m. Ann Elizabeth Wiinikka, June 20, 1954; children: Mark Edward, Deborah Ann Linen Foster. B.Th., Concordia Sem., 1952; M.R.E., Gordon Divinity Sch., 1967; M.Div., Concordia Sem., 1975. Ordained to ministry Lutheran Ch., 1952. Pastor Christ Luth. Ch., Troy, N.H., 1952-62, Zion Luth. Ch., Plymouth, Mass., 1962-68, Our Savior Luth. Ch., Westminster, Mass., 1968-73, Redeemer Luth. Ch., Joliet, Ill., 1973-78, St. Luke's Luth. Ch., Croydon, Pa., 1978—; pres. North Atlantic Area Nat. Evang. Luth. Ch., 1952-58; conv. del. Luth. Ch. - Mo. Synod, Milw., 1971; cir. counselor eastern dist. Luth. Ch. - Mo. Synod, Phila., 1981. Dir., Community Day Care, Croydon, 1982—. Republican. Lodges: Rotary, Lions. Home: 322 Wilson Dr Fairless Hills PA 19030 Office: St Lukes Lutheran Church 1305 State Rd Croydon PA 19030

LING, FRANK S. C., minister, Southern Baptist Convention; b. Hankow, China, Dec. 24, 1920; s. Tsoerun L. and Florence S. (Chow) L.; came to U.S., 1949, naturalized, 1962; B.S., U. Shanghai (China), 1942; B.D., New Orleans Bapt. Theol. Sem., 1952, M.Div., 1974, M.R.E., 1953; m. Edith Elaine Long, Dec. 11, 1954; children—Harriet Elaine, David Harrison, Edward Eugene. Ordained to ministry, 1954; pastor Nixville Bapt. Ch., Estill, S.C., 1954-65; asso. pastor Park Bapt. Ch., Rock Hill, S.C., 1965-67, 1st Bapt. Ch., Hampton, S.C., 1967-70, Moncks Corner, S.C., 1970—. Trustee, Connie Maxwell Children's Home, 1977—. Mem. adv. bd. Berkely County (S.C.) Home Health Service, 1976—; active Boys Scouts Am.; ombudsman Berkeley Convalescent Ctr., Moncks Corner, 1982—, Trident Area Agy. on Aging, 1982. Named Rural Minister of Year for S.C., Progressive Farmer Mag. and Candler Sch. Theology, 1963; recipient citation for meritorious service Am. Legion, 1964; Silver Beaver award Boy Scouts Am., 1984. Mem. Screvan Bapt. Assn. (music dir.). Office: 112 E Main St Moncks Corner SC 29461

LING, PHILIP HARMON, minister, Chs. of Christ; b. Matewan, W.Va., Sept. 8, 1931; s. Harmon Riddle and Willa Burgiss (Alley) L.; student Marshall U., 1949-50; A.B., Ky. Christian Coll., 1953; postgrad. Capital U., 1957; m. Ruth Elizabeth Leonard, July 15, 1953; children—Philip Harmon, William Rolland, Kristina Ruth. Ordained to ministry Chs. of Christ, 1953; minister Mowrystown (Ohio) Ch. of Christ, Union Ch. of Christ, Hillsboro, Ohio, 1953-56, Norton Ch. of Christ, Columbus, Ohio, 1957-65, Eastland Ch. of Christ, Columbus, 1966—. Mem. bd. mgmt. Suburban East br. YMCA, 1964—. Trustee Ky. Christian Coll., Grayson, Ky.; bd. advisers Kiamichi Mountain Christian Mission, Okla.; bd. dirs. Mt. Healthy Christian Home, 1959-66. Home: 3261 Noe-Bixby Rd Columbus OH 43227 Office: 3317 Noe Bixby Rd Columbus OH 43227

LINK, CLARICE PRITCHARD, lay ch. worker, So. Bapt. Conv.; b. Elizabeth City, N.C., Feb. 6, 1920; d. Lonnie Baxter and Grace Jacobs (Norris) Pritchard; student Wake Forest U., 1937-38, Meredith Coll., 1938-39, Mars Hill Coll., 1946-49, Westminster Choir Coll., 1953-54; m. John Reinhardt Link, Aug. 31, 1937; children—Jane Elizabeth Link Fleming, John Pritchard. Dir. adult and youth choirs 1st Bapt. Ch., Mount Gilead, N.C., 1950-55; dir. children's choirs Warrenton (N.C.) Bapt. Ch., 1955-68; music dir. Cullom Bapt. Assn., 1957-58; mem. N.C. Bapt. Chorale, 1963; mem. N.C. Bapt. Gen. Bd., 1963-67, exec. com., 1967; dir. choir 1st Bapt. Ch., Spring Hope, N.C., 1968—. Mem. Nash County Mental Health Assn. Address: 221 2d St Spring Hope NC 27882

LINNAN, JOHN EDWARD, theology educator, Roman Catholic Church; b. Springfield, Ill., Apr. 3, 1934; s. John Edward and Mary Ellen (Radigan) L. B.A., Georgetown U., 1956; S.T.B., U. Louvain, Belgium, 1961, M.A., 1962, S.T.L., 1964, S.T.D., 1966. Ordained priest Roman Cath. Ch., 1961. Assoc. prof., dean Viatorian Sem., Washington, 1965-68; assoc. prof. Washington Theol. Union, 1968-72; lectr. theology Carlow Coll., Pitts., 1970, 71, 72; diocesan dir. Univ. Apostolate, Reno, 1972-74; dir. spiritual devel. Clerics of St. Viator, Chgo., 1974-79; assoc. prof. Cath. Theol. Union, Chgo., 1979—, pres., 1981—; pres. central commn. of intersession Clerics of St. Viator, Rome, 1968-69, mem. provincial chpt., Chgo., 1967—, del. gen. chpt., Rome, 1978, 84; bd. dirs. St. Francis Sem., Milw., 1984—; exec. com. Nat. Cath. Edn. Assn., Washington, 1982—. Contbr. articles to profl. jours. Bd. dirs. Southeast Chgo. Commn., 1982—, Hyde Park and Kenwood Interfaith Council, 1982—, Ctr. for Religion and Psychotherapy, 1984—. Mem. Cluster of Theol. Schs. (chairperson common council 1983—), Chgo. Archdiocesan Presbyteral Senate, N. Am. Theology Group. Club: Quadrangle. Office: Cath Theol Union 5401 S Cornell Ave Chicago IL 60615

LINSEY, NATHANIEL L. Bishop, chmn. gen. bd. fin. Christian Methodist Episcopal Church, 9th dist., Los Angeles. Office: Christian Meth Episcopal Ch 5577 W 63d St Los Angeles CA 90056*

LINTON, CALVIN DARLINGTON, lay church worker, Presbyterian Church U.S.; b. Kensington, Md., June 11, 1914; s. Irwin H. and Helen Pauline (Grier) L.; student Erskine Coll., 1931-32; A.B., George Washington U., 1935; M.A., Johns Hopkins, 1939, Ph.D., 1940; m. Jean Elting LeFevre, Aug. 1, 1951. Tchr. Bible, 6th Presbyn. Ch., Washington, 1948-78; bd. dirs. Inst. Advanced Christian Studies, 1983—, pres., 1985—. Prof. English lit. George Washington U., Washington, 1947-84, emeritus, 1984—, dean Coll. Arts and Scis., 1956-84, emeritus, 1984—. Mem. Internat. Assn. U. Profs. English, Modern Lang. Assn., Am., Eastern (pres. 1966-67) confs. acad. deans, Lit. Soc., Washington (pres. 1973-75), Middle States Assn., Modern Humanities Research Assn. (Am. sec. 1963—), Conf. on Christianity and Lit. (pres. 1964-66, dir.). Editor: The Bicentennial Almanac, 1975; editorial cons. New Internat. Version of Bible, 1972—; editor-at-large

Christianity Today, 1973-78, also contbr.; contbr. to Basic Christian Doctrines, 1961; Fundamentals of Faith, 1969; Baker's Dictionary of Christian Ethics, 1973; Internat. Standard Bible Ency., 1978—. Home: 5216 Farrington Rd Bethesda MD 20816

LINZEY, STANFORD EUGENE, JR., minister, Assemblies of God Church; b. Houston, Oct. 13, 1920; s. Stanford and Eva Faye (Wesfphal) L.; m. Verna May Hall, July 13, 1941; children: Gena May Linzey English, Janice Ellen Linzey Drake, Stanford Eugene III, Virginia Darnelle Linzey Lemons, Sharon Faye Linzey Georgianna, George William, Vera Evelyn Linzey Waisanen, Paul Edward, David Leon, James Franklin. B.A., Linda Vista Bapt. Coll., 1952; Th.B., Linda Vista Bapt. Sem., 1954, D.D. (hon.), 1974; M.Div., Bapt. Sem., Berkeley, Calif., 1955; D.Min., Fuller Theol. Sem., 1980. Ordained to ministry Assemblies of God Ch., 1947. Pastor, Assembly of God, El Cajon, Calif., 1947-54; capt. Chaplain Corps, U.S. Navy, 1955; chaplain various assignments, 1955-74; ret., 1974; pastor Assembly of God, Vista, Calif., 1974-75; evangelist, Escondido, Calif., 1975—; advisor Ret. Mil. Full Gospel Fellowship, Macon, Ga., 1985—. Author: Pentecost in the Pentagon, 1975; also pamphlets. Mem. Ret. Officers Assn. Republican. Avocations: photography; tennis. Home: 1641 Kenora Dr Escondido CA

LIOLIN, ARTHUR EVANS, minister, church official, Albanian Orthodox Archdiocese in America. B. N.Y.C., June 19, 1943; s. Evans John and Helena Patricia (Peter) L.; m. Margaret Ann Becker, Aug. 16, 1970; children: Evans, Elena, Emily. A.A., Albert Sweitzer Coll., Chur, Switzerland, 1965; A.B., Princeton U., 1967. Ordained to ministry Albanian Orthodox Archdiocese in Am., 1970. Assoc. pastor St. George Cathedral, Boston, 1970-74, dean, 1975—; chancellor Albanian Archdiocese, Boston, 1975—; gen. sec. Albanian Orthodox Archdiocese in Am., Boston; mem. exec. com. Nat. Council Chs., N.Y.C., 1973-78; mem. external affairs dept. Orthodox Ch. in Am., 1972-79; dir. F.S. Noli Library of Albanian Studies, Boston. Editor Vineyard Mag., 1969-74. Scholar Fulbright, 1967, Robert Woods Bliss, 1968; Woodrow Wilson fellow, 1967. Office: Albanian Orthodox Archdiocese 529 E Broadway South Boston MA 02127

LIPE, MICHAEL ALEXANDER, minister, United Baptist Convention. b. Mooresville, N.C., Aug. 10, 1944; s. Harold Cloe and Lucille Eva (Beam) L.; m. Jeanette Ann Mitchell, June 10, 1967; children: Heather Michelle, Jeremy Aaron, Damon Chandler. B.S., Appalachian State U., 1966; M.Div., Southeastern Bapt. Theol. Sem., 1981; M. Religious Edn., 1981. Ordained to ministry Baptist Ch., 1978. Minister edn. and adminstrn. Westside Bapt. Ch., Titusville, Fla., 1978, First United Bapt. Ch., Charlottetown, P.E.I., Can., 1981-85; chaplain Eric M. Found Meml. Hosp., Charlottetown, 1981-85; editor, pub. Leadership Lines, Charlottetown, 1983-85; chmn. Christian Tng. Commn., P.E.I., 1982—; mem. exec. council Atlantic Bapt. Conv., 1983—; chmn. bd. dirs. Christian Communications, Charlottetown, 1984; mem. council for ordination Atlantic Bapt. Conv., 1982—; editor: Atlantic Baptist, 1985—. Contbr. articles and book reviews to religious jours. Mem. Can. Assn. Pastoral Edn., Queens County Ministerial Assn. Lodge: Rotary. Home: 4 Winjoe Dr Southport PE C1A 7W9 Canada Office: PO Box 756 Kentville NS B4N 3X9 Canada

LIPMAN, EUGENE JAY, rabbi, Reform Judaism; b. Pitts., Oct. 13, 1919; s. Joshua and Bess (Neaman) L.; m. Esther Marcuson, July 4, 1943; children: Michael (dec.), Jonathan, David. B.A., U. Cin., 1941; student U. Pitts., 1936-38; M.H.L., Hebrew Union Coll., 1943, D.D. (hon.), 1968; postgrad. U. Wash., Inst. for Individual Psychology, Am. U. Ordained rabbi, 1943. Rabbi, Temple Bethel, Ft. Worth, 1943-44; dir. Synogogue activities and Commn. on Social Action, Union of Am. Hebrew Congs., N.Y.C., 1951-61; rabbi Temple Sinai, Washington, 1961-85, rabbi emeritus, 1985—; lectr. Columbia U., Harvard U., Am. U., Cath. U., 1951-79; fin. sec. Central Conf. Am. Rabbis, 1983—, v.p., 1985; pres. Interfaith Conf., Washington, 1982-84, Washington Bd. Rabbis, 1970-71. Co-author: Justice and Judaism The Work of Social Action, 1956; A Tale of Ten Cities, 1962; The Mishnah Oral Teaching of Judaism, 1970. Pres., Nat. Capital Area ACLU, 1974-76. Served with U.S. Army, 1944-46, 50-51; ETO. Recipient Georte Brussel Meml. award Stephen S. Wise Free Synoaguge, 1979. Home: 3512 Woodbine St Chevy Chase MD 20815

LIPPY, CHARLES HOWARD, religion educator, United Methodist Church. B. Binghamton, N.Y., Dec. 2, 1943; s. Charles Augustus and Natalie Grace (Selzer) L. B.A. magna cum laude, Dickinson Coll., 1965; M.Div. magna cum laude, Union Theol. Sem., 1968; M.A., Princeton U., 1970, Ph.D., 1972. Ordained to ministry as elder United Meth. Ch., 1968. Interim pastor Litchfield Meth. Ch. (Pa.), 1962, Hornbrook Meth. Ch. (Pa.), 1966; assoc. prof. religion Clemson U., S.C., 1980—. Author: Seasonable Revolutionary, 1981. Editor: Religious Periodicals of the U.S., 1986. Contbr. articles to religious publs. Recipient research awards Clemson U., 1977, 79, 81, 83; Nat. Endowment Humanities grantee, 1975, 78, 83; vis. scholar U. N.C., 1984. Mem. Am. Acad. Religion, Orgn. Am. Historians, Am. Soc. Ch. History, S.C. Acad. Religion (pres. 1981-82), Popular Culture Assn. Democrat. Club: Clemson Bridge (pres. 1979). Home: Dogwood Heights Route 3 Box 90 Pendleton SC 29670 Office: Dept History Hardin Hall Clemson U Clemson SC 29631

LIPSCOMB, OSCAR HUGH, archbishop, Roman Catholic Ch.; b. Mobile, Ala., Sept. 21, 1931; s. Oscar Hugh and Margaret (Saunders) L. S.T.L., Gregorian U., Rome, 1957; Ph.D., Cath. U. Am., 1963. Ordained priest, Roman Catholic Ch., 1956. Asst. pastor ch., Mobile, 1959-65; tchr. McGill Inst., Mobile, 1959-60, 61-62; vice chancellor Diocese of Mobile-Birmingham, 1963-66, chancellor, 1966-80; pastor St. Patrick Parish, Mobile, 1966-71; lectr. in history Spring Hill Coll., Mobile, 1971-72; asst. pastor St. Matthew Parish, Mobile, 1971-79, Cathedral Immaculate Conception, 1979-80; adminstr. sede vacante Diocese of Mobile, 1980, consecrated archbishop, 1980—; chmn. bd. govs. N. Am. Coll. Rome; pres. Cath. Housing Mobile, Mobile Senate Priests, 1978-80; mem. coms. on doctrine and liturgy Nat. Conf. Cath. Bishops-U.S. Cath. Conf. Contbr. articles, papers to profl. publs. Pres. bd. dirs. Mobile Mus., 1966-67; bd. dirs. Met. YMCA Mobile; trustee Ala. dept. Archives and History, Cath. U. Am., 1983—. Mem. Am. Cath. Hist. Assn., So. Hist. Assn., Ala. Hist. Assn. (pres. 1971-72, exec. com. 1981), Hist. Mobile Preservation Soc. Lodge: Lions. Office: Archdiocese of Mobile Chancery Office 400 Government St PO Box 1966 Mobile AL 36601

LIPSITZ, JEROME SAMUEL, rabbi, Orthodox Judaism; b. Chgo., June 10, 1927; s. Ike and Sara (Margolis) L.; m. Rachel Kranz, June 21, 1977; children: William, David, Josua. B.A., Yeshiva U., 1952. Ordained rabbi Orthodox Jewish, 1952. Rabbi, Beth Israel, Lebanon, Pa., Temple Beth El, Margate, N.J., Beth Joseph, Denver. Served to 1st lt. AUS, 1952-54; Korea. Home: 401 Monaco Pky Denver CO 80220 Office: Beth Joseph 825 Ivanhoe St Denver CO 80220

LIPTOCK, EDWARD RICHARD, priest, Roman Catholic Church. B. Scranton, Pa., Nov. 15, 1929; s. Andrew Joseph and Mary Elizabeth (Palko) L. A.B., Mount St. Mary's Coll. Adn Sem., 1951. Ordained priest Roman Cath. Ch., 1955. Catechist, Bishop O'Reilly High Sch., Kingston, Pa., 1963-67, Bishop O'Hara High Sch., Dunmore, Pa., 1967-68; pre cana dir. Mid-Valley Area, 1967-68; pastor Our Lady of Lourdes Ch., Montoursville, Pa., 1979—; defender of the bond, pro-synodal judge marriage tribunal Diocese Scranton, 1967—; regional coordinator religious edn., Susquehanna and Wyoming Counties, 1969-71; v.p. bd. pastors Bishop Neumann High Sch., Williamsport, Pa., 1980—. Contbg. editor: The Catholic Light, 1967-71. Mem. Canon Law Soc. Am. (sec.-treas. 1971-73). Home: 800 Mulberry St Montoursville PA 17754 Office: Chancery Bldg 300 Wyoming Ave Scranton PA 18503

LISCHER, RICHARD ALAN, minister, theology educator, Lutheran Church in America; b. St. Louis, Nov. 12, 1943; s. Herbert Friedrich and Edna (Alsbrook) L.; m. Tracy Ruth Kenyon, June 4, 1966; children: Richard Adam, Sarah Kenyon. B.A. with highest honors, Concordia Sr. Coll., 1965; M.A. in English, Washington U., St. Louis, 1967; B.D., Concordia Sem., 1969; Ph.D. in Theology, U. London, 1971. Ordained to ministry Luth. Ch. in Am., 1972. Pastor Emmaus Luth. Ch., Dorsey, Ill., 1972-74, Prince of Peace Luth. Ch., Virginia Beach, Va., 1974-79; asst. prof. homiletics Duke U. Div. Sch., Durham, N.C., 1979-84, assoc. prof., 1984—; bd. dirs. Contact telephone counseling, Virginia Beach, 1978-79; cons. Luth. World Ministries, N.Y.C., 1979. Author: Marx and Teilhard, 1979; A Theology of Preaching, 1981; Speaking of Jesus, 1982. Editor: Theologies of Preaching, 1985. Contbr. articles to religious jours. Chmn. United Way, Duke Div. Sch., 1983. Recipient Younger Scholar's award Assn. Theol. Schs., 1983; scholar Aid Assn. for Luths., 1965-69, Leathersellers Guild, London, 1970-71; fellow Luth. World Fedn., 1969-71; research grantee Duke U., 1983. Mem. Acad. Homiletics. Democrat. Home: 2212 Thunder Rd Durham NC 27712 Office: Div Sch Duke U Durham NC 27706

LITTLE, THELMA FORTUNE, lay ch. worker, United Methodist Ch.; b. Florence, S.C., Dec. 11, 1927; d. Herbert and Thelma (Cooper) Fortune; B.S., S.C. State Coll., 1947; M.S.W., Fordham U., 1972; m. 2d, Van Crawford Little, Oct. 1, 1955; 1 son by previous marriage—James C. Sec., Womens Soc. Christian Service, Bklyn., 1967-68; fin. sec. Bethany United Meth. Ch., 1968-72, 74, mem. adminstrv. bd., 1968—, chairperson commn. on social concerns, 1976; sec. N.Y. Conf. Commn. on Religion and Race, United Interfaith Action Council, 1970—. Dir. supportive services, dept. social services Bur. Purchased Social Services for Adults, N.Y.C., 1974—. Bd. dirs. Citywide Interfaith, 1973—; United Meth. City Soc., 1974. Mem. ACLU, NAACP (life), Nat. Assn. Social Workers, Nat. Council on Aging, Am. Pub. Welfare Assn., Acad. Polit. Sci., Alpha Kappa Alpha. Home: 666 Linden Blvd Brooklyn NY 11203 Office: 60 Hudson St New York City NY 10013

LITTLETON, DOLORES EVELYN, minister, Lutheran Church in America; b. Phila., May 20, 1955; d. Otis Wilmur and Dolores (Schingen) Littleton. B.A. in Social Work, Eastern Coll., 1978; M.A., Eastern Bapt. Theol. Sem., 1980, M.R.E., 1980; M.Div., Luth. Theol. Sem., 1983. Ordained to ministry Lutheran Ch. in Am., 1983. Vicar Christ Luth. Ch., Wantagh, N.Y., 1981-82; pastor St. Paul Luth. Ch., Lansdowne, Pa., 1983—. Democrat. Home: 268 N Highland Ave Lansdowne PA 19050 Office: St Paul Luth Ch Plumstead and Congress Ave Lansdowne PA 19050

LITTON, JAMES HOWARD, organist, Episcopal Church; b. Charleston, W.Va., Dec. 31, 1934; s. James Howard and Bessie Blue (Binford) L.; m. Lou Ann Hall, Dec. 27, 1957; children: Bruce Edward, Deborah Ann, David Allan, James Richard. B.Mus., Westminster Choir Coll., 1956, M.Mus., 1958. Organist, St. Paul's Luth. Ch., Charleston, W.Va., 1950-52; organist, dir. First Meth. Ch., Plainfield, N.J., 1954-58; organist/choirmaster Trinity Ch., Southport, Conn., 1958-58, Christ Ch., Indpls., 1964-68; organist, dir. music Trinity Ch., Princeton, N.J., 1968-82, St. Bartholomew's Ch., N.Y.C., 1982—; cons. mem. Standing Commn. on Ch. Music, Nat. Episcopal Ch., 1970—, chmn. service music com., 1976—; mem. nat. council Assoc. Parishes, Alexandria, Va., 1980—; mem. exec. edn. com. The Hymnal, 1982. Editor canticle series: Hinshaw Music, 1976—. Am. editor: Duty and Delight, 1983—. Trustee, Princeton U. Concerts, 1970-74, Am. Boychoir Sch., Princeton, 1974-78. Recipient Alumni award, Westminster Choir Coll., 1981. Fellow Royal Sch. Ch. Music; mem. Assn. Anglican Musicians (nat. pres. 1966-67), Am. Guild Organists, Royal Coll. Organists, Am. Choral Dirs. Assn. Democrat. Home: 8 Carnation Pl Lawrenceville NJ 08648 Office: Saint Bartholomew's Ch 109 E 50th St New York NY 10022

LIU, CHARLES MARTIN, minister, Seventh-day Adventist; b. Moscow, Idaho, July 15, 1954; s. Sunny Wing Chun and Bernice (Lee) L.; m. Maryann Lynn Dasher, Aug. 24, 1975; children: Jennifer Lynn, Jonathan Brian, Jenell Marie. B.A., Walla Walla Coll., 1976; M.Div., Andrews U., 1979, D.Min., 1983. Ordained to ministry, 1982. Extern pastor Gold Beach Seventh-day Adventist Ch., Oreg., summer 1975; intern pastor Roseburg Seventh-day Adventist Ch., Roseburg, Oreg., 1976-77; pastor Brookings Seventh-day Adventist Ch., Oreg., 1979-82, The Dalles Seventh-day Adventist Ch., Oreg., 1982—; bd. dirs. K-12 Bd. Edn., Seventh-day Adventist Ch., Portland, 1983—; chmn. Young Adult Ministries, 1982—; producer radio program ThoughtSpots, 1979—, Lifeline, 1978. Mem. The Dalles Ministerial Assn. (pres. 1984), Assn. Adventist Ministers (pres. 1983). Home: 1824 Montana St The Dalles OR 97058 Office: Seventh-day Adventist Ch 1100 Pentland The Dalles OR 97058

LIU, I. HSIN, minister, United Meth. Ch.; b. T'ung P'ing, Shantung, China, Dec. 24, 1896; s. P'an Lin and Liu Chae (Shih) L.; B.A., Yen Ching U., 1920; M.A., Boston U., 1925, M.R.E., U. Calif., Los Angeles, 1952; m. Mei Lin, July 3, 1920; children—Julia, Florence, Lucy. Ordained to ministry, 1937; pastor Morristown and Elysian Meth. Chs., 1956-60, Dodge Center Meth. Ch., 1960-63, Blooming Prairie Meth. Ch., 1963-65, St. Paul Central Park Meth. Ch., 1965-66, Stanton and Randolph Meth. Chs., 1966-70, Wood Lake Meth. Ch., 1970— (all Minn.). Sec. religious edn. North China Meth. Conf., 1926-47; treas., controller North China and Shantung Conf., World War II; treas. relief fund UNRA; del. World Meth. Gen. Conf., 1924, 36, 40, World Missionary Conv., India, 1938, World Christian Ednl. Conv., Toronto, 1950. Clubs: Masons, Shriners. Home: care Mrs Roger Lynn 275 Thomas Dr King of Prussia PA 19406 Office: PO Box 56 Wood Lake MN 56297

LIVINGSTON, F. L. Elder, pres. National Primitive Baptist Convention, Inc., Dallas. Office: Nat Primitive Bapt Conv Inc 1334 Carson St Dallas TX 75216*

LIVINGSTON, IRENE ALICE, church school principal, Seventh-day Adventists; b. Alton, Mo., July 13, 1931; d. Clarence Edward and Dorothy (Helen Feaster) Martin; m. Richard Arden Livingston, Jan. 9, 1975; children by previous marriage: Brenda J., Nancy A., Dale A., Paul E. B.S. in Edn., Union Coll., 1971. Tchr., Mo. Conf. Seventh-day Adventists, Kansas City, 1960-63, 65-67; prin., tchr. Ark-La. Conf. Seventh-day Adventists, Shreveport, 1976—, Bonnerdale, Ark. Republican. Address: Route 1 Box 42 Bonnerdale AR 71933

LIWAG, RICARDO DEL ROSARIO, minister, Seventh-day Adventists; b. Gapan, Philippines, Oct. 20, 1923; s. Estanislao Beltran and Rustica (del Rosario) L.; came to U.S., 1964, naturalized, 1972; B.A., Sacramento Bapt. Coll., 1973; D.D., Faith Coll., 1976; m. Maria Natividad Cayanan, Nov. 24, 1943; children—Charity Liwag Curameng, Galileo Cayanan. Ordained to ministry, 1958; pastor Central Luzon Mission, Manila, 1951-57, So. Central Luzon Mission, Lucena, Philippines, 1957-58; missionary, Saigon, Vietnam, 1958-61; pastor-evangelist Central Luzon Mission, Manila, 1961-64, Central Calif. conf. Seventh-day Adventists, San Jose, 1969—. Chaplain,

Pacifica (Calif.) Police Dept., 1974—. Mem. Nat. Travel Club, Nat. Geog. Soc. Home: 2 Dover Ct Daly City CA 90415 Office: 533 Hickey Blvd Pacifica CA 90444

LIZZI, PHILIP JAMES, minister, Seventh-day Adventist Church; b. Angwin, Calif., Sept. 11, 1948; s. Dominic and Mary Jean (Munfrada) L.; m. Judy Kathleen Cuccia, June 14, 1970; children: Philip Alexander, Carrera Marie. B.A. in Theology, Pacific Union Coll., 1970; M.Div., Andrews U., 1973. Ordained to ministry, 1975. Pastor, Southwestern Calif. Conf., Seventh-day Adventists, San Diego, 1973-74, Needles, Calif., 1974-76, Palm Springs, Calif., 1976-78, Upper Columbia Conf., Sandpoint, Idaho, 1978-81, Hawaii Conf., Kaui and Maui, Hawaii, 1981—. Address: 35 Kupuna St Kihei HI 96753

LLOYD, KERMIT LEWIS, priest, Episcopal Church; b. Kingston, Pa., June 22, 1929; s. Kermit Roosevelt and Rheba Frances (Lewis) L.; A.B., Dickinson Coll., 1952; M.Div., Phila. Div. Sch. Ordained to ministry, 1955; rector All Saints Episc. Ch., Hershey, Pa., 1955-56, St. Paul's Episc. Ch., Bloomsburg, Pa., 1966-69; exec. officer Diocese Central Pa., Harrisburg, 1969-80, dir. Office State Chaplaincy, 1980-82; rector St. John Episc. Ch., York, Pa., 1982—; mem. exec. council Episc. Ch., 1982—, mem. standing com. constns. and canons, 1982—. Exec. com. Province Washington, Episc. Ch., chmn. com. Nat.-Internat. Problems, participant nat., gen. conv. Chmn. Coalition for Human Need, 1982—. Named Citizen of Yr., City Hershey, 1960. Mem. Kappa Kappa (founder), Phi Delta Theta (advisor). Home: 157 Peyton Rd York PA 17403 Office: 143 N Beaver St York PA 17403

LLOYD, ROY THOMAS, communications executive, minister, Lutheran Church in America; b. Wilkensburg, Pa., Mar. 9, 1943; s. Henry George and Lois Evelyn (Thornberg) L.; m. Janet Roberta Stammer, Oct. 4, 1969; 1 child, Rebecca Ann. B.A., Thiel Coll., 1965; M.Div., Luth. Theol. Sem., Phila., 1969; M.Edn., U. Pitts., 1972. Ordained to ministry Lutheran Ch., 1969. Tchr. Schneller Sch., Khirbet Kanafar, Lebanon, 1966-67; asst. pastor Zion Luth. Ch., Penn Hills, Pa., 1969-72; asst. dir. communications Christian Assocs. of Southwest Pa., Pitts., 1972-75; dir. broadcast news Nat. Council of Chs., N.Y.C., 1975-78; dir. Ecumedia News Service, N.Y.C., 1975-78; asst. dir. telecommunications, Luth. Ch. in Am., N.Y.C., 1978-84; dir. communications, pub. relations Council of Chs., N.Y.C., 1984—; pres. Via Media Communications. Composer: Power Up, 1972; Producer (TV program): Perspectives (Gold award 1983), 1983; (cable TV series) Lutherans in Person, 1982. Trustee Thiel Coll., Greenville, Pa., 1972-76; participant Ridgefield Environ. Action Program, Conn., 1975—; mem. Conn. Chamber Choir, Trumbell, 1982—. Mem. Radio & TV News Dirs. Assn. (assoc.); Nat. Fedn. Local Cable Programmers, Assn. Regional Religious Communicators, World Assn. for Christian Communications (steering com. N. Am. broadcasting sect. 1979-81). Office: Via Media Communications 398 Bennetts Farm Rd Ridgefield CT 06877

LOCKHART, GEORGE RICHARD, minister, American Baptist Churches in the U.S.A.; b. Buckhannon, W.Va., July 28, 1953; s. Richard Leslie and Neva Faye (Jordan) L.; m. Beverly Lynn Bird, Aug. 16, 1975; children: James Richard, Rachel Marie. B.S. in Bus. Mgmt., W.Va. Inst. Tech., 1976; M.Div., Southeastern Bapt. Theol. Sem., 1979. Ordained to ministry Baptist Ch., 1979. Pastor, Dorcas-Maysville Bapt. Parish, Arthur, W.Va., 1978-81, Albright Bapt. Parish, W.Va., 1981-85, First Bapt. Ch., Oil City, Pa., 1985—. Mem. ordination com. Goshen Bapt. Assn., Morgantown, W.Va., 1984—. Mem. W.Va. Bapt. Ministers (area v.p. 1985—). Goshen Bapt. Ministers Assn. (pres. 1984), Preston County Ministers Assn. (v.p. 1984). Democrat. Home and Office: 407 E 1st St Oil City PA 16301

LOCKHART, VERDREE, deacon, Baptist Missionary Association of America; dean; b. Louisville, Ga., Oct. 21, 1924; s. Fred and Minnie Bell (Roberson) L.; B.S., Tuskegee Inst., 1949; M.A. in History, Atlanta U., 1957, Ph.D. in Adminstrn. of Pupil Services, 1975; m. Louise Howard, Aug. 5, 1950; children: Verdree II, Vera Louise, Fernandez, Abigail. Ordained deacon, 1952; dir. Bapt. Tng. Union, Eden Bapt. Ch., 1952-63; tchr. Sunday Sch., 1952-63; deacon Union Missionary Bapt. Ch., Atlanta, 1965—, chmn. Youth Leadership Devel. Council, 1974—. Edn. program adviser Ga. Dept. Edn., Atlanta, 1963-80; v.p. Atlanta U., 1981-82; dean edn. Phillips Coll., Atlanta, 1984—. Asst. council commr. Atlanta Area council Boy Scouts Am., 1971—; mem. advisory bd. Southeast Regional Office, Nat. Scholarship Service and Fund for Negro Students, 1970—; trustee Atlanta U., 1975-81. Recipient Leadership award Union Missionary Bapt. Ch.; Silver Beaver award Boy Scouts Am., 1969; Gov.'s Medallion, State of Ga., 1966-67. Mem. Am., Ga. (pres. 1976-77) personnel and guidance assns., Am., Ga. vocat. assns., Nat., Ga. vocat. guidance assns., Ga. Assn. Educators, NAACP (treas. 1971—), Assn. of Counselor Edn. and Supervision, Am. Sch. Counselor Assn., Ga. Tchr. and Edn. Assn. (Distinguished Service award dept. guidance 1969, Achievement award region V 1963, 64), Ga. Adult Edn. Assn. (mem. exec. bd. 1972-80), Tuskegee Inst., Atlanta U. Nat. (Distinguished Service award 1971) alumni assns., Alpha Phi Alpha (award of merit Eta Lambda chpt. 1976, Alumni of Yr. 1980), Phi Delta Kappa. Home: 2964 Peek Rd NW Atlanta GA 30318 Office: Phillips Coll 1340 Spring St Atlanta GA 30309

LODDIGS, HERBERT GEORGE, religious educator, American Lutheran Church; b. Bklyn., June 27, 1913; s. John William and Anna Catherina (Von Thun) L.; m. Edna Berthine Thompson, Sept. 26, 1912; 1 son, Paul Allen. B.A., Wagner Coll., 1936; postgrad. Hartwick Seminary, 1936-37, C.T., Luther Seminary, 1940; postgrad. Princeton Seminary, 1945-46. Ordained pastor Am. Luth. Ch., 1940. Missionary, Am. Luth. Ch., Mpls., 1940-49; pastor Highland Luth. Ch., Brandt, S.D., 1949-51, Concordia Luth. Ch., Los Angeles, 1952-57; mem. faculty Golden Valley Luth. Coll., Mpls., 1957—, instr. Greek, 1983—. Contbr. lessons to various books, daily devotions, and articles to various publs. Mem. Luth. Brotherhood Fraternal Br. (chmn. service counselor), Luth. Lit. for Chinese (bd. dirs.). Home: 5809 34th Ave North Minneapolis MN 55422

LODGE, JOHN GERALD, priest, Roman Catholic Ch.; b. Oak Park, Ill., Aug. 7, 1947; s. Edward James and Helen Louise (McIsaac) L.; B.A., Loyola U., Chgo., 1969; M.Div., S.T.L., St. Mary of the Lake Sem., Mundelein, Ill., 1973; M.A. in English, U. Ill., Chgo. Circle, 1975. Ordained to ministry, 1973; asso. pastor St. Edna's Ch., Arlington Heights, Ill., 1973-76, St. Denis Ch., Chgo., 1976—. Bd. dirs. The Well, An Inst. for Religious Edn., 1975-76; sem. tchr. Quigley Prep. Sem. S., 1976—; coordinator workshops for clergy. Mem. Nat. Council Tchrs. English, U. Ill. Alumni Assn. Contbr. articles, poems to various mags. Home: 8301 S St Louis Ave Chicago IL 60652 Office: Quigley South 7740 S Western Ave Chicago IL 60620

LOEHR, JUDY LEE, church music administrator, United Methodist Church; b. Fort Smith, Ark., Oct. 10, 1942; d. James Robert and Letha Ophelia (Duckworth) Wheeler; m. Klaus Friedrich Loehr, Mar. 28, 1964; 1 child, Elise Adrienne. B.Mus., Baylor U., 1964; M.Mus. in Vocal Performance, Peabody Conservatory, Johns Hopkins U., 1979; diploma in voice and opera Mozarteum (Austria), 1972, 76. Dir., organist Bad Aibling Army Chapel, Germany, 1972-73; dir. 3d century singers Profl. Group, Bonn, Germany, 1974-77; dir. music Severna Pk. United Meth. Ch., Md., 1978-81; dir. ch. music and worship resources Bd. Discipleship, Nashville, 1981—; music cons. Hymnal Revision Com., United Meth. Ch., United Meth. Pub. House, Nashville, 1985—; soloist, choral clinician United Meth. Chs.; liaison Fellowship of United Methodists in Worship, Music and Other Arts, 1981. Editor: Psalms for Singing, 1984; editor, project dir. Service Music Booklet, 1985, Korean-English Hymnal, 1985. Recipient Presdl. scholarship Baylor U., 1960-64; finalist Met. Opera Auditions, 1963; Outstanding Sr. Woman award Baylor U., 1964; finalist San Francisco Opera Auditions, 1965; Best Actress award Fresno Community Theater, 1971. Mem. Nat. Assn. Tchrs. Singing, Am. Choral Dirs. Assn. Avocations: collecting pewter and antiques; reading. Office: Gen Bd Discipleship 1908 Grand Ave Nashville TN 37202

LOEW, EDMUND ALFRED, JR., minister, United Presbyn. Ch. in U.S.A.; b. Clinton, Iowa, Dec. 6, 1932; s. Edmund Alfred and Nell Alice (Crispe) L.; B.A., U. Ariz., 1955; B.D., McCormick Theol. Sem., 1959; m. E. Joyce Wilson, Aug. 16, 1957; children-Edmund Alfred, III, Barbara Joyce, Donald Wilson, Gregory Matthias. Ordained to ministry, 1959; minister 1st Presbyn. Ch., Florence, Ariz., 1959-65, 1st Presbyn. Ch., Globe, Ariz., 1965—. Asst. chaplain Ariz. State Prison, 1959-64; mem. gen. council Presbytery de Cristo, 1975-80; mem. gen. assembly United Presbyn. Ch. in U.S.A., 1972: pres. Gila County (Ariz.) Ministerial Assn., 1967-68, 76-77, 85-86. Active Boy Scouts Am., Girl Scouts U.S.A.; mem. Globe Sch. Bd., 1970-76, pres., 1975; bd. dirs. Am. Field Service Com., 1966—. Mem. Permanent Jud. Commn., Synod of S.W., 1982—; mem. Ariz. Ecumenical Council, 1984—. Co-host weekly religious radio program, 1969-73. Home: 1280 Skyline Dr Globe AZ 85501 Office: 318 S Hill St Globe AZ 85501

LOFFER, ROBERT LEON, minister, United Church of Christ; b. Grand Island, Nebr., June 14, 1948; s. Lloyd Lavern and Lorna Jean (Freel) L.; m. Audrey Lee Sietsema, Dec. 21, 1968; children: Michelle, Markus, Matthew, Michael, Melanie, Merissa. Student Kearney State Coll., 1966-67, Bellevue Coll., 1970-72; B.A. cum laude, Buena Vista Coll., 1974; M.Div., Dubuque Theol. Sem., 1976. Ordained to ministry United Church of Christ. Student pastor Congregational United Ch. of Christ, Aurelia, Iowa, 1972-74, United Methodist and United Ch. of Christ, Sherrill, Iowa, 1974-75; pastor Trinity United Ch. of Christ, Marengo, Iowa, 1975—; sec. Ctr. for Growth, Clear Lake, Iowa, 1973-77; bd. dirs. Family Services of Iowa County, Marengo, 1982—, exec. dir., 1982-84; chmn. Iowa Conf., United Ch. of Christ summer events com., 1978-80; resource person Dept. Human Services, Iowa, Linn and Johnson Counties, 1978—; mem. religious activities com. Iowa Med. Facility, Oakdale, 1984—; sec.-treas. Eastern Iowa Assn., 1984—. Author: Christian Education Camp Design, 1979; Camp Design and Training for Iowa Conference Camping Program, 1978, 79, 80. Chmn. Iowa County Food Bank, Marengo, 1981—; v.p. Iowa Valley Sch. Bd., Marengo, 1977-79; treas., fin. chmn. Iowa County Democrats, Williamsburg, 1980-84; actor, stage hand Cobblestone Theater, Marengo, 1977—. Mem. Iowa Conf. Rural Life Task Force, Marengo Ministerial Assn. (chmn. 1980-84), Ea. Assn. Adv. Com. Lodge: Masons (jr. deacon 1982, sr. deacon 1983), Order Eastern Star (assoc. patron 1983, worthy patron 1984). Home: Route 1 Box 36 Marengo IA 52301

LOGAN, CLIFFORD WAYNE, musician, educator, So. Bapt. Conv.; b. Merced, Calif., May 6, 1942; s. Marion Clifford and Katherine Marine (Thompson) L.; B.A., Wayland Bapt. Coll., 1971; Mus.M. in Edn., Tex. Tech. U., 1972; m. Linda Sue Stuart, June 14, 1968; 1 son, Stuart Wayne. Music dir. 1st Bapt. Ch., Matador, Tex., 1967-68, Silverton, Tex., 1968-69, Happy, Tex., 1969-71, Wilshire Park Bapt. Ch., Midland, Tex., 1971-73, Kennewick (Wash.) Bapt. Ch., 1973—; tchr. music Park Middle Sch., Kennewick, 1975—. Youth dir. Columbia Basin Bapt. Assn., Kennewick, 1973-75. Activities cons. Benton-Franklin Counties Juvenile Ct., Kennewick, 1974-75; dir. Sweet Adeline Barbershop Chorus, Kennewick, 1975-77; organizer, dir. Christmas performances various choirs. Mem. Wash. Edn. Assn., Phi Mu Alpha. Home: 2436 W Albany St Kennewick WA 99336 Office: 1011 W 10th St Kennewick WA 99336

LOGAN, THOMAS WILSON STEARLY, SR., priest, Episcopal Ch.; b. Phila., Mar. 19, 1912; s. John Richard and Mary (Harbison) L.; A.B., Lincoln U., 1935; certificate Gen. Theol. Sem., 1938; S.T.M., Phila. Divinity Sch., 1941; m. Hermione Hill, Sept. 3, 1938; 1 son, Thomas Wilson Stearly. Ordained priest, 1938; vicar St. Philip Ch., N.Y.C., 1938-40, St. Michael's and All Angels Chs., Phila., 1940-45; rector Calvary Ch., Phila., 1945—. Pres. Episc. Ch. Workers Conf., 1951-61; canon St. Mary's Cathedral, Phila.; dean Schykill (Pa.) Deanery; former pres. Hampton (Va.) Ministers Conf.; mem. Diocesan Council; police chaplain; chaplain Phila. Gen. Hosp. Mem. bd. YMCA; trustee Haverford State Hosp.; pres. Downington (Pa.) Sch.; bd. Black Mus., Phila.; life mem. Lincoln (Pa.) U. Mem. NAACP (life), Alpha Phi Alpha (life). Club: Masons (past grand master Pa.), Shrine. Home: 46 Lincoln Ave Yeadon PA 19050 Office: 814 N 41st St Philadelphia PA 19104

LOGAN, WILLIAM STEVENSON, archdeacon, Episcopal Church; b. Detroit, Mar. 10, 1920; s. William Stevenson and Evelyn Lucille (Castle) L.; m. Mary Adelaide Siddall, Dec. 1, 1951; children: Mary Shore, Margaret Elizabeth, William Stevenson. B.S. in Chem. Engring., U. Pa., 1941; M.A.E., Chrysler Inst. Engring., 1943; M.Div., Episcopal Theol. Sch., 1951; M.A., U. Mich., 1980. Ordained priest, 1951. Vicar, Our Savior Ch., Saugus, Mass., 1949-51; curate Christ Ch., Detroit, 1951-52; rector St. Martin's Ch., Detroit, 1952-63; dir. program Diocese of Mich., Detroit, 1963-73, archdeacon, 1973—; v.p. Mich. Council Chs., Lansing, 1968-70; nat. chmn. Conf. Diocesan Execs., 1980-81. Contbr. articles to profl. jours. Chmn. Gov.'s Fair Campaign Practices com., Detroit, 1977—; subcom. chmn. Mayor's Com. on Human Resources Devel., Detroit, 1964-73. Served to lt. (j.g.), USNR, 1945-46. Mem. Engring. Soc. Detroit, United Ministries in Higher Edn. (pres. 1971-73, 80-82). Clubs: Detroit Boat, Prismatic. Home: 1514 Chateaufort Pl Detroit MI 48207 Office: Diocese of Mich 4800 Woodward Ave Detroit MI 48201

LOHMEYER, JAMES ARTHUR, minister, Lutheran Church in America. b. Clay Center, Kans., Feb. 7, 1947; s. Arthur Henry and Mildred Elizabeth (Loges) L.; m. Elizabeth Ana Segerhammar, June 20, 1984; children: Joseph James, Scott Arthur. B.A., Bethany Coll., 1969; M.Div., Luth. Sch. Theology, 1973. Ordained to ministry Lutheran Ch. in Am., 1974. Pastor, Faith Luth. Ch., Junction City, Kans., 1974-81, Scherer Meml. Luth. Ch., Chapman, Kans., 1974-82; chaplain, counselor Hoisington Luth. Hosp., Hoisington, Kans., 1982—; mem. com. Evangelism Central States Synod, 1975-78, Synod Task Force Alcohol and Drugs, 1983—. Mem. Chem. People com., Hoisington, 1984—, Child Advocate Team, Great Bend, Kans., 1983-84, Dickinson Council on Alcohol and Drugs, Abilene, Kans., 1980-82. Mem. Kans. Alcohol and Drug Abuse Counselors Assn. Democrat. Office: Hoisington Lutheran Hospital 250 W 9th St Hoisington KS 67544

LOHMULLER, MARTIN NICHOLAS, bishop, Roman Catholic Ch.; b. Phila., Aug. 21, 1919; s. Martin Nicholas and Mary Frances (Doser) L.; B.A., St. Charles Borromeo Sem., Phila., 1942; D.Canon Law, Cath. U. Am., 1947. Ordained priest Roman Catholic Ch., 1944; officialis Diocese Harrisburg, Pa., 1948-63, vicar for religious Diocese of Harrisburg, 1958-70; pastor Our Lady of Good Counsel parish, Marysville, Pa., 1954-64, St. Catherine Laboure parish, Harrisburg, 1964-68; consecrated bishop, 1970; vicar gen. Archdiocese Phila., 1970—; pastor Old St. Mary's Parish, Phila., Holy Trinity Parish, Phila. Office: 222 N 17 Philadelphia PA 19103

LOHR, HAROLD RUSSELL, bishop, Lutheran Church in America; b. Gary, S.D., Aug. 31, 1922; s. Lester A. and Nora H. (Fossum) L.; m. Theola Marie Kottke, June 21, 1947 (div. Dec. 1973); children: Philip Kyle, David Scott, Michael John; m. Edith Mary Morgan, Dec. 31, 1973. B.S. Summa cum laude, S.D. State U., 1947; Ph.D., U. Calif.-Berkeley, 1950; M.Div. summa cum laude, Augustana Theol. Sem., Ill., 1958. Ordained to ministry Augustana Luth. Ch., 1958. Pastor Ascension Luth. Ch., Northfield, Ill., 1958-70; assoc. exec. sec. Bd. Coll. Edn., Luth. Ch. in Am., N.Y.C., 1970-72, dir. research and planning, div. profl. leadership, Phila., 1973-77, assoc. exec. dir. div., 1977-80; bishop Red River Valley Synod, Luth. Ch. Am., Fargo, N.D., 1980—; bd. dirs. Gustavus Adolphus Coll., St. Peter, Minn., 1980—, Luther Northwestern Sem., St. Paul, 1980—; mem. exec. council Luth. Ch. Am., 1982—, mem. commn. on peace and war, 1983—. Author: Growth in Ministry, 1980; also articles. Served as 1st lt., inf. U.S. Army, 1943-46, ETO. Recipient award Suomi Coll., 1983. Democrat. Home: Rural Route 4 South Acres Fargo ND 58103 Office: Red River Valley Synod 1351 Page Dr S Fargo ND 58103

LOKENSGARD, KEITH HENRY, minister, United Presbyn. Ch. in U.S.A.; b. Spokane, Wash., Apr. 4, 1938; s. Kenov Hayes and Josephine (Clack) L.; B.A., Mont. State U., 1960; B.D., San Francisco Theol. Sem., 1963; m. Janet Lee Brandt, Aug. 29, 1959; children—Kristin Marie, Karin Jo, Kenneth Hayes. Ordained to ministry, 19—; pastor chs., Great Falls, Mont., 1963-66, South Pasadena, Calif., 1966-70, Dillon, Mont., 1970-76; sr. pastor 1st Presbyn. Ch., Helena, Mont., 1976—. Home: 1940 Hauser Helena MT 59601 Office: 535 N Ewing Helena MT 59601

LOKKEN, JAMES ARNOLD, minister, American Lutheran Church, data processing company administrator; b. Pasadena, Calif., Apr. 15, 1933; s. Martin O. and Agnes (Trano) L. B.A., Pacific Luth. Coll., Tacoma, Wash., 1955; M.Div., Luth. Sem., St. Paul, 1959. Ordained to ministry Evangel. Luth. Ch., 1959. Youth pastor First Luth. Ch., Brookings, S.D., 1964-66; asst. editor Luth. Forum, N.Y.C., 1966-68; prodn. dir. Liturgical Conf., Washington, D.C., 1968-78; asst. pastor St. Francis Luth. Ch., San Francisco, 1983—. Data processing mgr. Electrographic Corp., San Francisco, 1979—. Editor/author: Now the Silence Breaks, 1980; asst. editor col., articles in Luth. Forum, 1966-68; editor Luth. New Yorker, 1975-76. Office: St Francis Luth Ch 152 Church St San Francisco CA 94114

LOLIO, JOHN WILLIAM, priest, Roman Catholic Church; b. Providence, Jan. 28, 1944; s. Anthony and Theresa Marie (Di Cenzo) L. B.A., Our Lady of Providence Sem. Coll., 1966; S.T.B., St. Mary's Sem., 1968, M.Div., 1970; postgrad. Boston U., 1979—. Ordained priest, Roman Cath. Ch., 1970. Tchr., chmn. English dept. Our Lady of Providence Sem., R.I., 1970-77; chaplain, counsellor Bryant Coll., Smithfield, R.I., 1977-80; pastor Our Lady of Mt. Carmel Ch., Bristol, R.I., 1980—; bd. advisors Cath. Charity Budget Rev. Panel, Providence, 1980—, Cath. Social Services, Providence, 1980-82. Recipient Citation R.I. State Legislature, 1980. Mem. Priests Personnel Bd., Nat. Assn. Ch. Personnel, Nat. Assn. Campus Ministries, New England Assn. Schs. and Colls., Nat. Council Tchrs. of English, Delta Omega (chaplain Bryant Coll. Chpt. 1977-80). Lodge: Sons of Italy (chapiain 1980—). Home and Office: Our Lady of Mt Carmel Ch 141 State St Bristol RI 02809

LONG, EDWARD LEROY, JR., minister, religion educator, Presbyterian Church in the U.S.A.; b. Saratoga Springs, N.Y., Mar. 4, 1924; m. Dorothy L. Whitney, 1947 (dec. Aug. 1980); children: Roger, Charles, Douglas; m. Grace Darling Cumming, June 5, 1982. B.C.E., Rensselaer Poly. Inst., 1945; B.D., Union Theol. Sem., N.Y., 1948; Ph.D., Columbia U., 1951; postgrad. in law Harvard U., 1969-70; L.H.D., Maryville Coll., 1980. Ordained to ministry Presbyn. Ch. in U.S.A., 1948. Instr. physics Rensselaer Poly. Inst., Troy, N.Y., 1945; minister to students Blacksburg Presbyn. Ch., Va., 1951-54; assoc. prof. philosophy and ethics Va. Poly. Inst., Blacksburg, 1951-54, assoc. prof., head dept. philosophy and religion, 1955-67; assoc. prof. religion Oberlin Coll., Ohio, 1957-65, prof., 1965-76; Eli Lilly vis. prof. sci., theology, and human values, Purdue U., West Lafayette, Ind., 1975-76; prof. Christian ethics Drew U., Madison, N.J., 1976-82, prof. Christian ethics and theology of culture, 1982-84, James W. Pearsall Prof. Christian ethics and theology of culture, 1984—; tutor in Christian ethics Union Theol. Sem., 1950-51; mem. summer session faculty, 1956, 67, 71; Danforth lectr. Pa. State U., summer 1953; mem. com. on relationship philosophy to theology Faculty Christian Fellowship, 1957; lectr. Oberlin Grad. Sch. Theology, 1958-59; mem. leadership team Conf. on Teaching Religion to Undergrads., Soc. Religion in Higher Edn., 1962; invited Protestant observer annual meetings Cath. Theol. Soc. Am., 1967, 68; mem. spl. study and discussion group younger scholars Council on Religion and Internat. Affairs, 1968-74; mem. summer session faculty dept. philosophy and religion Va. Poly. Inst., 1969; mem. summer session faculty advanced pastoral studies program San Francisco Theol. Sem., 1972; mem. task force on conscription, conscientious objection, and the ch.'s response Office Ch. and Soc., United Presbyn. Ch., 1968-69, mem. task force on legal services for the poor, 1972-73, cons. task force on ministry to persons in armed services, adv. com. on ch. and soc., 1975-76, mem. task force on peace making and foreign policy, 1977-80; commr. Gen. Assembly of United Presbyn. Ch., Louisville, 1974; mem. Council for Study Religion, 1973-76; summer faculty Doctor of Ministry Program, Drew U., 1976, 78, 80, 85; vis. prof. Christian ethics Gen. Theol. Sem., 1977-78; vis. lectr. Christian ethics Union Theol. Sem., N.Y., 1978-79, Princeton Theol. Sem., 1980-81, 84-85; mem. faculty Inst. Theology, Cathedral Ch. of St. John the Divine, N.Y.C., 1981-83, mem. adv. com.; lectr. preacher Lafayette Coll., U. Va., Swarthmore Coll., Maryville Coll., U.S. Mil. Acad., St. Lawrence U. Author: Science and Christian Faith, 1950, The Christian Response to the Atomic Crisis, 1950, Religious Beliefs of American Scientists, 1952, reprinted, 1971, Conscience and Compromise: An Approach to Protestant Casuistry, 1954, The Role of the Self in Conflicts and Struggle, 1962, A Survey of Christian Ethics, 1967, War and Conscience in America, 1968, A Survey of Recent Christian Ethics, 1982, Peace Thinking in a Warring World, 1983, Academic Bonding and Social Concern: The History of the Society of Christian Ethics: 1959-83, 1984; (with James T. Stephens) The Christian as a Doctor, 1960. Editor: (with Robert T. Handy) Theology and Church in Times of Change: Essays in Honor of John Coleman Bennett, 1970; (series editor) Haddam House Series on the Christian in His Vocation, 1960-64. Contbr. articles, book chpts. and book revs. to various publs. Mem. interview team Kent Fellowship Selection Com., N.Y. area, 1963-65, Boston area, 1969-70; mem. Oberlin Coll. group, Danforth Workshop on the Liberal Arts, Colo. Coll., 1964; mem. steering and planning com. Central States Faculty Colloquium, 1966-69; mem. interview team U. Iowa Campus Governance Study of Am. Council on Higher Edn.; mem. leadership conf. on medicine, law and ethics VA Hosp., Little Rock, 1978; mem. selection com. Charlotte W. Newcombe Fellowships, Woodrow Wilson Nat. Fellowship Found., 1981. Recipient Herberg Disting. Teaching award Drew Grad. Sch., 1981; Guggenheim fellow, 1963, post-doctoral fellow Soc. Religion in Higher Edn., 1969-70, Underwood fellow Danforth Found., 1973-74. Mem. Am. Acad. Religion (bd. cons. Jour. 1970-77), Am. Soc. Christian Ethics (v.p. 1971, pres. 1972), Soc. Sci. Study Religion, Am. Theol. Soc. (exec. com. 1983-84, sec. 1984—), Sigma Xi, Chi Epsilon, Tau Beta Pi. Office: Drew U Box 15 Seminary Hall Madison NJ 07940

LONG, FREDDRICK LEE, minister, United Methodist Church; b. Kingsport, Tenn., May 2, 1940; s. Hubert Aruilee and Mattie Faye (Lane) L.; m. Judith Ann Walker, May 25, 1959; children: Kristi Suzanne, Freddrick Walker. B.S. in Math., East Tenn. State U., 1965; M.Div., Chandler Sch. Theology, 1978. Ordained to ministry United Methodist Ch. as deacon, 1977, as elder, 1980. Organizing pastor Faith United Meth. Ch., New Port Richy, Fla., 1978-83; pastor Lockhart United Meth. Ch., Orlando, Fla., 1983-84, Grundy United Meth. Ch., Va., 1985—; dir. Children's Advs., New Port Richey, 1983; bd. dirs. Hospice, Hudson, Fla., 1983, Day Care Ctr., Orlando, 1984, Pre-Sch. Ctr., Grundy, 1985, counseling elder, 1985. Mem. New Mountain Playhouse, Grundy, 1985. Mem. Holston Conf. United Meth. Ch., Dist. Bd. of Ordained Ministry. Democrat. Lodge: Rotary. Home and Office: PO Box 715 Grundy VA 24614

LONG, JAY EDWARDS, educator, minister, General Association of Regular Baptist Churches; b. Sweet Valley, Pa., June 18, 1938; s. McKinley and Sarah Hazel (Edwards) L.; m. Mary Ruth Shoop, Aug. 15, 1959; children: Brent, Brenda. B.S., Bloomsburg U., 1959, M.Ed., 1964; postgrad. U. Scranton, Temple U., 1971-72, Bapt. Bible Coll., 1970-73. Ordained to ministry, 1974. Tchr. pub. schs., Pa., 1959-70; instr., Bapt. Bible Coll., Clarks Summit, Pa., 1970-73; pastor Mehoopany Bapt. Ch., Pa., 1972-82; assoc. prof. Bapt. Bible Coll., Clarks Summit, Pa., 1982—. Author: Personal Bible Study, 1983; The Bible's Answers to Teen's Dilemmas, 1984. Contbr. articles to profl. jours. Pres., PTA, Mehoopany, Pa., 1976; sec. Citizen's Adv. Council, Tunkhannock, Pa., 1976-80; sec. Endless Mt. Pastors Fellowship, 1975-81. Mem. Nat. Council Tchrs. English, Nat. Bus. Edn. Assn., Eastern Bus. Edn. Assn., Pa. Bus. Edn. Assn. Republican. Home: 17 Hunts Ct Clarks Summit PA 18411 Office: Bapt Bible Coll 538 Venard Rd Clarks Summit PA 18411

LONG, JOHNNIE JERREL, minister, Southern Baptist Conference, educator. B. Prim, Ark., Jan. 19, 1936; s. Robert and Dora Isalee (Sullivan) L.; m. Dessie Clotine Moody, Sept. 2, 1955; children: Juanita, Darrell. B.S.E., Ark. State U., 1973, M.S.E., 1978. Ordained to ministry So. Bapt. Conf., 1978. Pastor, Tomato Bapt. Ch., Ark., 1978-79; interim pastor Armorel Baptist Ch., Ark., 1979-80; pastor Mary's Chapel Bapt. Ch., Huffman, Ark., 1980—; assoc. youth dir. Miss. County Bapt. Assn., Blytheville, Ark., 1981-82; bus ministry Mary's Chapel Baptist Ch., Huffman, 1982—. Tchr. Armorel Sch., Ark., 1974—. Served with USAF, 1955-63. Democrat. Home: PO Box 22 Armorel AR 72310 Office: Mary's Chapel Bapt Ch PO Box 295 Armorel AR 72310

LONG, PAUL ROBERT, minister, United Presbyn. Ch. in U.S.A.; b. Wilkes-Barre, Pa., Sept. 5, 1932; s. Paul Robert and Dorothy Kershaw L.; A.B., Union Coll., 1954; B.D., Yale, 1957; m. Janice McHugh, Aug. 14, 1954; children—Andrew Porter, Matthew Carr. Ordained to ministry, 1957; asst. pastor State St. Presbyn. Ch., Schenectady, 1957-59; pastor Lakeside Presbyn. Ch., Rochester, N.Y., 1959-64; minister adult edn. Third Presbyn. Ch., Rochester, 1964-67; pastor Indian Hill Episc. Presbyn. Ch., Cin., 1967—. Pres., Met. Area Religious Coalition Cin., 1975—; mem. Presbytery Cin. Mem. Com. Human Investigation Childrens' Hosp. Med. Center, Cin., 1972—; bd. dirs. ARC, 1973—; trustee Cin. Country Day Sch., 1973—. Home: 9845 Cunningham Rd Cincinnati OH 45243 Office: 6000 Drake Rd Cincinnati OH 45243

LONGMAN, TREMPER, III, educator; b. Princeton, N.J., Sept. 8, 1952; s. Tremper and Mary Jane (Stevenson) L.; m. Alice Linda Scheetz, June 23, 1973; children: Tremper, Timothy Schettz, Andrew Eastwick. B.A., Ohio Wesleyan U., 1974; M.Div., Westminster Theol. Sem., 1974-77; M.Phil., Yale U., 1980, Ph.D., 1983. Lectr. O.T., Westminster Theol. Sem., Phila., 1980. asst. prof., 1980-82, assoc. prof. O.T., 1982—; bd. dirs. Phila. Christian Action Council, 1983—. Contbr. articles to profl. jours. NEH summer stipend, 1984. Mem. Evang. Theol. Soc., Inst. Bibl. Research, Soc. Bibl. Lit., Am. Oriental Soc. Republican. Club: Phila. Cricket. Home: 7803 Froebel Rd Philadelphia PA 19118 Office: Westminster Theol Sem Church and Willow Grove Aves Philadelphia PA 19118

LOOKSTEIN, HASKEL, rabbi, Orthodox Jewish Congregations; b. N.Y.C., Mar. 21, 1932; s. Joseph H. and Gertrude (Schlang) L.; B.A., Columbia, 1953; rabbi Yeshiva U., 1958, M.A., 1963; m. Audrey Katz, June 21, 1959; children—Mindy, Debra, Shira, Joshua. Ordained rabbi, 1958; rabbi Congregation Kehilath Jeshurum, N.Y.C., 1958—; prin. Ramaz Sch., N.Y.C., 1968—. Vice chmn. Greater N.Y. Conf. Soviet Jewry, 1976—; sec. N.Y. Bd. Rabbis, 1974—; mem. exec. bd. Nat. Conf. Soviet Jewry, 1973-76; v.p. Yeshiva U. Rabbinic Alumni, 1970-76; co-chmn. edn. com. Massad Camps, Inc., 1969-76; instr. Bible, Yeshiva U., 1968—; mem. rabbinic adv. bd. United Jewish Appeal, 1974-76, mem. synagogue adv. commn., 1975-76. Contbr. articles to religious jours. Home: 993 Park Ave New York City NY 10028 Office: 125 E 85th St New York City NY 10028

LOOMER, FENWICK DANE See *Who's Who in America,* 43rd edition.

LOPEZ, CHARLES JOSEPH, JR., minister, American Lutheran Church. B. Chgo., Oct. 17, 1948; s. Charles Joseph Sr. and Wilma Pauline (Steinhauer) L. A.A., Concordia Coll., St. Paul, 1968; B.A. in Psychology, U. Ill.-Chgo., 1971; M.Div., Christ Sem.-Seminex, Chgo., 1975, S.T.M., 1978; Ph.D. candidate, Drew U., 1976. Ordained to ministry Am. Luth. Ch., 1975. Asst. chaplain St. Louis St. Sch., 1974-76; dir. Spanish ministries Luth. Family and Children's Services, St. Louis, 1975-76; pastoral counselor Clergy Cons., Summit, N.J., 1976—; pastor Holy Trinity Luth. Ch., Rockaway, N.J., 1978—; mem. softball team Holy Trinity Angeles, Rockaway, 1978—; faculty Am. Luth. Ch. (ea. dist.), 1983—; bd. dirs. Luther Northwestern Sem., St. Paul, 1984—. Contbr. Pastoral Care and Counseling Abstracts and revs. to religious publs. Trustee Eger Home, Staten Island, N.Y., 1984—. Recipient scholarship Luth. World Fedn., Colombia, 1973-74. Mem. Am. Assn. Pastoral Counselors, Assn. Mental Health Clergy, Am. Psychol. Assn. Office: 508 Green Pond Rd Rockaway NJ 07866

LOPEZ AVINA, ANTONIO, archbishop, Roman Catholic Church; b. Chalchihuites, Mex., Aug. 20, 1915. Ordained priest Roman Cath. Ch., 1939. Named Bishop of Zacatecas, 1955, named archbishop of Durango, 1961. Office: Arzobispado Apartado Postal 116 Durango Durango Mexico*

LOPEZ DE VICTORIA, JUAN DE DIOS See *Who's Who in America,* 43rd edition.

LORD, CHARLES HARVEY, minister, United Church of Christ; b. Little Rock, Feb. 2, 1924; s. Jethro Dean and Martha Magdelene (Wetterau) L.; m. Lena May Sweet, May 27, 1947; children: Charles Timothy, Stephen Edward, Marilyn Christi. B.A., Phillips U., 1945; M.Div., Union Sem., 1952; M.A., U. Chgo., Ph.D., 1973. Ordained to ministry United Ch. of Christ, 1947. Pastor First Christian Ch., Edmond, Okla., 1952-57; organizing pastor Christian Ch. of Villa Park, Ill., 1957-62; dean of students Christian Theol. Sem., Indpls., 1967-70; campus minister Univ. Ch., Chgo., 1970—, also minister; chmn. Ecumenical Relations Com. Chgo. Met. Assn. of the United Ch. of Christ, Chgo., 1985—; mem. ecumenical relations dept. Christian Ch. in Ill. and Wis., Bloomington, Ill., 1980—; editor Pewbook, Univ. Ch., 1985. Bd. dirs. Blue Gargoyle Youth Service Ctr., Chgo., 1970—. Recipient Youth Service award Blue Gargoyle Youth Service Ctr., 1982. Mem. Coll. Profl. Christian Clergy (pres. Chgo. chpt. 1980-82), Interfaith Council Hyde Park and Kenwood (pres. council 1980-82), Ministers Racial and Social Justice. Home: 4733 S Woodlawn Ave Chicago

IL 60615 Office: Univ Ch 5655 S University Ave Chicago IL 60637

LORD, CLARE, religious organization administrator, Roman Catholic Church; b. N.Y.C., Aug. 26, 1947; d. Penny (Macaluso) L.; m. Leo Cree Ziminsky, Jan. 8, 1966 (div. 1971); 1 child, Robert Lee Ziminsky. A.A. in Early Childhood Edn., Glendale Coll., 1984. Catechist, Archdiocese Los Angeles, 1970-84, Interdiocesan Tribal Council, San Bernardino, Calif., 1984—; adminstr. Our Lady of Guadalupe Preschool, San Bernardino, 1984-85, Bethlehem House, Highland, Calif., 1985—; br. leader Secular Franciscan Order, Los Angeles, 1978-83; founder Consolation Sisters, Highland, Calif., 1981—; mem. Nat. Sisters Vocation Conf., 1983—, Franciscan Fedn. Bros. and Sisters of U.S., 1983—. Active So. Calif. Coalition for Battered Women, San Bernardino, 1985, Task Force Domestic Violence, San Bernardino, 1985, Interdiocesan Tribal Council, San Bernardino, 1984—. Recipient Pius X award Archdiocese of Los Angeles, 1980. Mem. Nat. Assn. Edn. of Young Children. Home: 29803 Canal St Highland CA 92346 Office: Bethlehem House 29803 Canal St Highland CA 92346

LORD, JAMES RAYMOND, priest, Episcopal Church; b. Dublin, Ga., Nov. 8, 1934; s. James Leonard and Susie Elizabeth (Scarborough) L. A.B., Presbyn. Coll., 1956; B.D., Princeton Theol. Sem., 1961; Th.M., Duke U., 1964, Ph.D., 1964. Ordained priest, 1973. Instr., Duke U., Durham, N.C., 1967-69; prof. Coll. of Idaho, Caldwell, 1969-74; vicar St. Martin's Episcopal Ch., Mayfield, Ky., 1974-78; rector Grace Episcopal Ch., Hopkinsville, Ky., 1978—; chmn. Diocesan Commn. on Ministry, Ky., 1983-84, Standing Com. of Diocese, Ky., 1982-84; trustee, council Diocese of Ky., 1977-80; trustee U. South, 1975-80. Translator: Jesus by Hans Conzelmann), 1974. Editor: All About the Bible, 1980. Bd. dirs. Aaron McNeill House, Hopkinsville, 1978—, Regional Mental Health Bd., 1978-81, Community Arts Council, 1979-81; trustee U. Hts. Acad., 1981. Rockefeller Theol. fellow, 1956, doctoral fellow, 1967. Mem. Cath. Bibl. Assn. Democrat. Club: Hopkinsville County (bd. dirs. 1985—). Home: 214 Beaumont Ct Hopkinsville KY 42240 Office: Grace Episcopal Ch 216 E 6th St Hopkinsville KY 42240

LORENZ, LYALL JOHN, minister, American Lutheran Church; b. Castle Shannon, Pa., Jan. 10, 1944; s. Leo Thomas and Barbara (Prokupek) L. A.A., Community Coll. Allegheny County, 1968; B.A., U. Pitts., 1969, M.A., 1972; M.Div., Trinity Sem., 1979. Ordained to ministry, 1979. Pastor, Bethlehem Luth. Ch., Pitts., 1979—. Pres., Lutheran Urban Coalition, Pitts., 1979-80. Author (hymns:) At The Lord's Call, 1975, Dearest Lord, 1978. Mem. Phi Beta Kappa. Democrat. Home: 208 Hargrove Pittsburgh PA 15226 Office: Bethlehem Luth Ch 731 Excelsior St Pittsburgh PA 15210

LORING, RICHARD TUTTLE, minister, Episcopal Church; b. Boston, Oct. 23, 1929; s. Richard Tuttle and Helen (Dexter) L. B.A. cum laude, Harvard U., 1951; S.T.B., Gen. Theol. Sem., 1957; D.Th., 1968. Ordained priest, 1958. Jr. curate All Saints Episcopal Ch., Dorchester, Boston, 1957-59; fellow, tutor Gen. Theol. Sem., N.Y.C., 1959-63; assoc. priest St. John's Lattingtown, Locust Valley, N.Y., 1959-63; asst. Grace Episcopal Ch., Elmira, N.Y., 1963-67; rector St. Luke's Episcopal Ch., Chelsea, Mass., 1968—; exec. sec. Gen. Bd. of Examining Chaplains of Episcopal Ch., Boston, 1983—. Nash fellow, 1977. Mem. Chelsea Ecumenical Council (treas. 1981-82), Margaret Coffin Prayer Book Soc. Clubs: Clerical of Boston (sec-treas.), Parsons. Home: Saint Lukes Church 201 Washington Ave Chelsea MA 02150

LOSHUERTOS, ROBERT HERMAN, minister; b. San Francisco, Apr. 28, 1937; s. Jose Guillermo and Ruth Margarethe (Erdmann) L.; A.A., City Coll. San Francisco, 1957; B.A., Wittenberg U., 1959; M.Div., Luth. Theol. So. Sem., 1963; m. Carolyn Angela Reinartz, Aug. 6, 1960; children—William Frederick, John Martin. Ordained to ministry Luth. Ch. in Am., 1963; asst. pastor, Harrisburg, Pa., 1963-64, Riverside, Calif., 1964-66; pastor Our Saviours Luth. Ch., Oxnard, Calif., 1966-71; asso. pastor Luth. Ch. of the Good Shepherd, Buena Park, Calif., 1971-73; pastor St. Marks Luth. Ch., Huntsville, Ala., 1973—. Bd. dirs. Key Center for Creative Living, Huntsville. Mem. Greater Huntsville Ministerial Assn. Home: 11202 Dellecrest Dr Huntsville AL 35803 Office: 200 Longwood Dr Huntsville AL 35801

LOSTEN, BASIL HARRY, bishop, Ukrainian Cath. Ch.; b. Chesapeake City, Md., May 11, 1930; s. John and Julia (Petryshyn) L.; B.A., St. Basil's Coll., 1954; M.A. in Theology, Cath. U., 1957. Ordained priest Ukrainian Catholic Ch., 1957; pastor St. Mary's Ch., Bristol, Pa., 1962-63, St. Michael's Ch., Camden, N.J., 1964-65; archdiocesan controller Ukrainian Archeparchy, Phila., 1966-74, vicar gen., 1971—; papal chaplain to Pope Paul VI, Byzantine-Ukrainian Rite, Roman Catholic Ch., 1968-71; consecrated bishop, 1971; aux. bishop to Archeparch of Phila. for Ukrainians, 1971-77; bishop of Stamford, Conn., 1977—. Titular Bishop of Arcadiopolis in Asia Minor; appointed apostolic adminstr. of Ukrainian Cath. Archeparchy, 1976—; mem. Nat. Conf. Cath. Bishops U.S. Club: Union League of Phila. Office: Chancery Office 161 Glenbrook Rd Stamford CT 06902

LOTOCKY, INNOCENT HILARIUS, bishop, Ukrainian Catholic Church. Bishop of St. Nicholas of Chgo. for the Ukrainians, 1981—. Office: 2245 W Rice St Chicago IL 60622*

LOUDEN, JEFFREY DEAN, minister; Lutheran Ch. of Am.; b. Denver, Nov. 19, 1954; s. Robert Dean and Suzanne Kay (Ford) L.; B.A. in journalism, Colo. St. U., 1975; M.Div., Luther Northwestern, 1982. Ordained to ministry Luth. Ch. in Am., 1982. Chaplain, Amarillo Hosp. Dist., Amarillo Tx., 1980-81; instr. Greek Luther Northwestern Sem., St. Paul, Minn., 1982; assoc. pastor St. Paul Luth. Ch., Albuquerque, 1982—; educator Karishohe Evangelische Landeskirene, Ludwigsburg, W. Ger., 1976-78. Contbr. articles to profl. jours. Club: Sierra (Albuquerque). Home: 1827 Dartmouth NE #207 Albuquerque NM 87106 Office: St Paul Luth Ch PO Box 25001 Albuquerque NM 87215

LOUDEN, KENNETH HAROLD, psychologist; b. Calgary, Alta., Can., May 27, 1928; came to U.S., 1979; s. Charles Harold and Margaret Emma (Mackay) L.; m. Pamela Joan Havell, June 7, 1958; children: Carol Anne, David Charles. B.A., U. Alta., 1950; M.Div., Fuller Theol. Sem., 1954, Ph.D., 1974. Ordained to ministry, 1948. Student pastor Bapt. Union of W. Can., Edmonton, Alta., 1948-50; staff Inter Varsity Christian Fellowship of Can., S.W. Ont., 1954-58; dir. Ont. Pioneer Jr. Camp, Pioneer Camps of Can., London, Ont., 1954-58; regional dir. Inter Varsity Christian Fellowship of Can., Winnipeg, and regional gen. dir. Man. Pioneer Camps, 1958-64; regional dir. Pacific region Inter Varsity Christian Fellowship of Can., B.C., 1964-66; gen. dir. Pioneer Pacific Camps, Vancouver, 1964-66; psychologist in pvt. practice, Fremont, Calif., 1978—; prof., cons. Arbutus Youth Assn., San Jose, 1977—; profl. cons. Trans World Radio, Newark, 1981—, Narramore Christian Found., 1980—; lectr. in field. Mem. Am. Psychol. Assn., Can. Psychol. Assn., Christian Assn. Psychol. Studies, Psychology and Law Soc., Calif. Psychol. Assn., Am. Sci. Affiliation, Psychologists Interested in Religious Issues. Address: 1047 Vuelta Olivos Fremont CA 94539

LOUGHRAN, JAMES NEWMAN, priest, university president, Roman Catholic Church; b. Bklyn., Mar. 22, 1940; s. John Farley and Ethel Margaret (Newman) L. A.B., Fordham U., 1964, M.A., 1965, Ph.D., 1975. Ordained priest Roman Cath. Ch., 1970. Instr., St. Peter's Coll., 1965-67; from asst. prof. to assoc. prof. Fordham U., Bronx, N.Y., 1974-84, dean, 1979-82; pres. Loyola Marymount U., Los Angeles, 1984—. Contbr. articles to profl. jours. Trustee St. Peter's Coll., 1972-78, Xavier U., Cin., 1981-84. Mem. Am. Philos. Assn.

LOUSBERG, MARY CLARICE, hospital administrator, nurse, nun; Roman Catholic Ch.; b. Fleming, Colo., Aug. 21, 1929; d. Edward P. and M. Irene (Berg) L. R.N., St. Joseph Hosp. Sch. Nursing, Denver, 1952; B.S. in Nursing Edn., St. Mary Coll., 1969; M. in Pub. Adminstrn. (specialty Health Care Adminstrn.), U. So. Calif., 1971. Joined the Sisters of Charity of Leavenworth, 1949. Nursing supr. St. John's Hosp., Helena, Mont., 1954-59; supr. obstetrics St. John's Hosp., Santa Monica, Calif., 1959-63; operating room supr. Providence Hosp., Kansas City, Kans., 1963-66; dir. nursing service DePaul Hosp., Cheyenne, Wyo., 1966-68, pres., 1979—, sec.-treas. bd. dirs., 1979—; adminstr. St. James Community Hosp., Butte, Mont., 1972-79; bd. dirs. St. Joseph Hosp., 1980—, Laramie County Health Planning Com., 1980-84. Mem. Wyo. State Cert. of Need Rev. Bd., 1982-83, Cheyenne MX Impact Com., 1982—. Named Boss of Yr., Am. Bus. Women's Assn., Cheyenne, 1980. Fellow Am. Coll. Hosp. Adminstrs. (regent from Wyo. 1982—); mem. Wyo. Hosp. Assn., (bd. dirs 1983—, chmn.-elect 1984), Cath. Hosp. Assn., Montana Hosp. Assn. (pres. 1976-77). Office: DePaul Hosp 2600 E 18th St Cheyenne WY 82001

LOUX, GORDON DALE, minister, North American Baptist General Conference; b. Souderton, Pa., June 21, 1938; s. Curtis L. and Ruth N. (Derstine) L.; diploma Moody Bible Inst., 1960; B.A., Gordon Coll., 1962; B.D., No. Bapt. Sem., 1965, M.Div., 1971; postgrad. U. Pa., 1967-69; M.S., Nat. Coll. Edn., 1984; m. Elizabeth Ann Nordland, June 18, 1960; children: Mark, Alan, Jonathan. Ordained to ministry, 1965; dir. pub. relations Moody Bible Inst., Chgo., 1972-76; pres. Prison Fellowship Internat., 1979—, Justice Fellowship, 1983—; exec. v.p. Prison Fellowship Ministries Washington, 1977-84, pres., 1984—; asst. pastor Forest Park Bapt. Ch. (Ill.), 1962-65; field dir. Moody Alumni Assn., Chgo., 1965-66; dir. devel. Phila. Coll. Bible, 1966-69; dir. devel. Nat. Sunday Sch. Assn., Wheaton, Ill., 1969; pres. Stewardship Services, Wheaton, 1970-72. Bd. sec. Evang. Lit. Overseas, 1970; v.p. Religious Pub. Relations Council, Chgo., 1975; elder Wheaton Bible Ch., 1974-76; vice chmn. Evang. Council Fin. Accountability, 1984—. Mem. devel. council Salem Children's Home, Flanigan, Ill., 1972; bd. dirs. John Perkin Found. Reconciliation and Devel., 1983—; adv. bd. Nat. Coll. Edn., 1984—. Recipient Baker award No. Bapt. Sem., 1965. Mem. Nat. Assn. Evangelicals (exec. com. social action commn.), Evang. Press Assn. Contbr. articles to religious jours. Home: 813 Carrie Ct McLean VA 22101 Office: 2817 Woodland Dr NW Washington DC

LOVELAND, GEORGE WILLIAM, minister, United Meth. Ch.; b. Indpls., Oct. 7, 1944; s. Clarence Howard and Bonnie (Bell) L.; B.A., Manchester Coll., 1965; M.Div. in Christian Edn. and Psychology, Iliff Sch. Theology, 1968. Ordained to ministry, 1968; pastor chs., Ind. and Wyo., 1964-67, Denver, 1967-68; minister Christian edn. 1st United Meth. Ch., Paris, Ill., 1968-71; asso. pastor 1st United Meth. Ch., Moline, Ill., 1971—; partner Brite Games (prodn. simulation experiences for ch. instns.), 1974—. Mem. Moline Bicentennial Commn.; adj. faculty dept. speech Black Hawk Coll., 1974—. Mem. Christian Educators' Fellowship United Meth. Ch., Am. Religious Edn. Assn. Author: Catacombs Communion, 1974. Home: 3815 15th St Moline IL 61265 Office: 712 16th St Moline IL 61265

LOVELESS, ALTON EARL, magazine editor, religious organization executive, minister, Free Will Baptist Church; b. Greenbrier, Ark., Aug. 10, 1937; s. William Daniel and Mildred (Blair) L.; student Hendrix Coll., 1955-58; B.A. in Theology, Hillsdale Free Will Bapt. Coll., 1980; B.R.E., M.R.E., Covington Theol. Sem., 1981; Ph.D., Columbia Pacific U., 1984; m. Ellen Delois Draby, Aug. 18, 1958; children: Randall Scott, Steven Lynn. Ordained to ministry, 1956; pastor chs., Ark., Mo., 1955-70, Monticello, Ark., 1961-66, Joplin, Mo., 1966-70; editor Gem Mag., ofcl. Free Will Bapt. mag. State of Mo., 1969; cons. Christian edn. Scripture Press, Wheaton, Ill., 1970-74, regional sales mgr., 1974; exec. sec., editor Ambassador Mag., Ohio Assn. Free Will Baptists, Columbus, 1974—, also overseer insts., state historian, 1974—; editor Free Will Bapt. Link, newsletter for denominational bookstores, 1975. Mem. nat. Sunday Sch. Bd., Nat. Assn. Free Will Baptists, 1978; pres. Nat. Free Will Bapt. Bookstore Assn., 1985. Chmn. Nat. Hist. Commn., 1976—. Contbr. articles to religious jours. Home: 4970 Botsford Dr Columbus OH 43232 Office: 3501 Parsons Ave PO Box 07401 Columbus OH 43207

LOVSETH, PERCIVAL CLEMENS, minister, American Lutheran Church; b. Astoria, S.D., July 3, 1921; s. Peter Olson and Cornelia Josephine (Sabe) L.; m. Anne Ludmila Zima, Aug. 23, 1947; children: Mark S., Timothy P. B.A., Augustana Coll., 1945; M.Div., Luther Sem., 1949; M.A. in Alcohol Studies, Pacific Sch. Religion, 1976; student U. Mich., 1944-45. Ordained to ministry, 1949. Pastor, Luth. Ch., Bigfork, Minn., 1949-50; mil. chaplain U.S. Army, 1951-68; field service pastor Luth. Council, U.S.A., Tex., Philippines, Calif., 1969-74; alcohol program dir. Salvation Army, Oakland, Calif., 1976-78; exec. dir. Vols. of Am., Sacramento 1979—; nat. religious activities sec. Vols. of Am., 1983—. Served to lt. col., U.S. Army, 1950-68. Decorated Bronze Star, Army Commendation medal, Legion of Merit; named Citizen of the Day, Kiwanis, Battle Creek, Mich., 1967. Lodge: Kiwanis. Home: 5129 Vista Del Oro Way Fair Oaks CA 95628 Office: Volunteers of America 510 Bercut Dr Ste F Sacramento CA 95814

LOWE, CONRAD LEE, minister, American Baptist Association; b. Charleston, W.Va., Aug. 1, 1945; s. Edgar Earl and Ruth Madeline (Nelson) L.; m. Vivian June Biggers, July 15, 1969; 1 child, Melissa; m. Sharon Carol Sturm, Aug. 14, 1982; children: Rachel, Jamie. B.A. in Psychology, Wheaton Coll., 1967; M.Div., So. Bapt. Theol. Sem., 1970. Ordained to ministry Baptist Ch., 1970. Assoc. minister First Bapt. Ch., St. Albans, W.Va., 1970-72; sr. minister North Parkersburg Bapt. Ch., Parkersburg, W.Va., 1972-77, 79—; Mountview Bapt. Ch., Columbus, Ohio, 1977-79; sec. State Ordination Com. W.Va., 1973-76; mem. minister's adv. council Alderson-Braoddus Coll., Philippi, W.Va., 1980-83, assoc. prof.; chaplain Parkersburg City Police Force, 1980-83. Republican. Lodge: Kiwanis. Home: 3702 River Rd Vienna WV 26105 Office: North Parkersburg Bapt Ch 3109 Emerson Ave Parkersburg WV 26104

LOWE, WILLIAM CARROLL, minister, ch. ofcl., So. Baptist Conv.; b. Lawton, Okla., Aug. 27, 1930; s. William Edward and Jennie Ethel (Benson) L.; B. Music Edn., Howard Payne U., 1953; M. Sacred Music, New Orleans Baptist Theol. Sem., 1955; m. Wanelle Adams, Aug. 25, 1952; children—Carole Annette, Jeri Laureen. Ordained to ministry, 1951; dir. music Calvary Bapt. Ch., Brownwood, Tex., 1950-53, 1st Bapt. Ch., Bay St. Louis, Miss., 1953-55; minister of music 1st Bapt. Ch., Pineville, La., 1955-66; state ch. music dir. La. Bapt. Conv., Alexandria, 1966—. Pres. La. Baptist Ch. Music Conf.; dir. Singing Ministers of La. Baptist Conv.; denominational rep. So. Baptist Ch. Music Conf., 1968-70. Mem. Hymn Soc. Am., Am. Choral Dirs. Assn. (life). Office: 1250 MacArthur Dr PO Box 311 Alexandria LA 71301

LOWERY, DANIEL LORNE, priest, Roman Catholic Church; publisher; b. St. Louis, Mo., Sept. 17, 1929; s. James Michael and Josephine Marie (McCarthy) L. B.A., Immaculate Conception Coll., Oconomowoc,

Wis., 1956; M.A., Catholic U., 1960; S.T.D., Lateran U., Rome, 1967. Ordained priest Roman Cath. Ch., 1955. Asst. prof. Cath. U., Washington, 1960-63; asst. editor Liguorian, Mo., 1963-68, pub., 1981—; provincial superior Redemptorists, Glenview, Ill., 1969-75; pastor St. Alphonsus, Mpls., 1976-81. Author: Life and Love, 1963; Following Christ, 1982; Day by Day thru Lent, 1983. Contbr. articles to Liguorian mag. Mem. Cath. Press Assn., Cath. Theol. Soc. Democrat.

LOWERY, DELMA ODENE, minister, Baptist Ch.; b. Copperhill, Tenn., June 9, 1934; s. James Elmer and Fairl (Bice) L.; m. Edna Lee Barger, Sept. 29, 1957. B.A., Tenn. Temple, 1962; Th.M., Trinity Coll., 1972, Th.D., 1973. Ordained to ministry, Baptist Ch., 1960. Pastor First Bapt. Ch., Kennesburg, Colo., 1962-65, Southside Bapt. Ch., Millington, Tenn., 1965-67, Cumberland Community Ch., Augusta, Kans., 1969-71; conf. speaker various chs., U.S. and Can., 1973—; instr. Memphis Bapt. Coll., Tenn., 1965-67; dean of men, instr. Trinity Coll., Dunedin, Fla., 1971-73; instr. summer master's program in Bible Pensacola Christian Coll., Fla., 1980—. Author: Building Steadfast Christians, 1975. Contbr. articles to periodicals and newspapers. Served with U.S. Army, 1955-57. Home and Office: Route 6 Box 336 Harriman TN 37748

LOWIG, EVAN HENRY FRANCIS, priest, Orthodox Church in America; b. Hobart, Tasmania, Australia, Oct. 7, 1954; came to Can., 1957; s. Henry Francis Joseph and Libuse Barbara (Ottova) L. B.A., U. Man., Winnipeg, Can., 1977; B.D., St. Andrew's Coll., Winnipeg, 1977; M.Div., St. Vladimir's Sem., 1979, postgrad. Ordained priest Orthodox Ch. in Am., 1982. Instr. St. Herman's Sem., Kodiak, Alaska, 1980-81, fall 1981; rector rural Man. Diocese of Can., Winnipeg, 1982; dean central Can. Diocese of Can., Orthodox Ch. in Am., Man., Sask., 1983—; sec. Orthodox Clergy of Winnipeg, 1984—; del. Ecumenical Com. of Man., Winnipeg, 1982—; chmn. program com. Chs. Networking for Winnipeg, 1984—; community advisor Phoenix Centre Inc., Winnipeg, 1983—. Contbr. articles to profl. jours. Mem. Social Planning Council, Winnipeg, 1984, Winnipeg Coordinating Com. for Disarmament, Winnipeg, 1983—, Humane Soc., Winnipeg, 1984—; participant Coalition for Aid to Nicaragua, Winnipeg, 1984. Decorated Cross of St. Herman, Diocese of Alaska, 1981. Home and Office: 643 Manitoba Ave Winnipeg MB R2W 1H1 Canada

LOWRY, EUGENE LAVERNE, educator, minister, United Methodist Church; b. Meade, Kans., Sept. 6, 1933; s. Austin Lynn and Myrtle Louise (Jordan) L.; m. Sarah Cheatum, Oct. 3, 1976; children: Mark Diane, Jill. B.A., Southwestern Coll., 1955; B.D., Drew Theol. Sem., 1958; M.A., Columbia U., 1958; Ed.D., U. Kans., 1972. Ordained to ministry, 1956. Pastor, St. Paul Meth. Ch., West New York, N.J., 1955-59; assoc. pastor 1st Meth. Ch., Wichita, Kans., 1959-62, Country Club United Meth. Ch., Kansas City, Mo., 1962-63; pastor Coll. Heights United Meth. Ch., Kansas City, 1964-68; lectr. St. Paul Sch. Theology, Kansas City, 1962-68, asst. prof., 1968-73, assoc. prof., 1973-79, dir. doctoral studies, 1974-81, prof. preaching/communication, 1979—, interim acad. dean, 1984—. Author: Doing Time in the Pulpit, 1985; The Homiletical Plot: The Sermon as Narrative Art Form, 1980. Contbr. articles to profl. jours. Recipient Masterbuilder award Southwestern Coll., 1955. Mem. Internat. Communication Assn., Am. Acad. Homiletics, Kansas City Soc. Theol. Studies, Religious Speech Communication Assn., Am. Fedn. Musicians, Internat. Soc. Gen. Semantics. Office: Saint Paul Sch Theology 5123 Truman Rd Kansas City MO 64127

LOWRY, WAYNE MITCHELL, minister, United Presbyterian Ch. in U.S.A.; b. Princeton, Ky., Nov. 28, 1934; s. Mitchell J. and Lula Ethlyn (Small) L.; B.S., Bethel Coll., Tenn., 1956; postgrad. Scarritt Coll., 1958-59, U. Dubuque Theol. Sch., 1963-65; m. Annette Freeman, July 7, 1956; children—Mark Freeman, Mitchell Elvin. Ordained to ministry, 1956; pastor chs., Ind., Tenn., Okla. and Iowa, 1956-70; sr. pastor Harvard, 1970-71, 2d Presbyn. Ch., Portsmouth, Ohio, 1971—. Mem. mission council Synod of the Covenant, 1973—, Presbytery of Scioto Valley, 1973—; trustee Nat. Ch. Residences, Waverly, Ohio. Merrill fellow, Harvard Div. Sch., 1970-71. Home: POB 1282 Portsmouth OH 45662 Office: 8th and Waller Sts Portsmouth OH 45662

LOWRY, WILLIAM RONALD, minister, So. Bapt. Conv.; b. Seminole, Okla., Apr. 11, 1934; s. Oscar Newton and Robbie Mae (Pesnell) L.; B.A., Grand Canyon Coll., 1956; M.R.E., Southwestern Bapt. Theol. Sem., 1963; m. Barbara Jane Swafford, Jan. 6, 1956; children—Robin Elizabeth, Ronald Mark, Rebecca Lynne, Barbara Anne. Ordained to ministry, 1968; minister of music Love Bapt. Ch., Phoenix, 1959-60, Wichita Bapt. Ch., Ft. Worth, 1960-63, Westbury Bapt. Ch., Houston, 1963-68, 1st Bapt. Ch., Lubbock, Tex., 1968—. Music dir. So. Bapt. Pastors Conf., Dallas, 1974, So. Bapt. Conv., Miami, 1975, Norfolk, Va., 1976, Glorieta Ch. Conf. Center, 1970, 71, 76; music chmn. Billy Graham Crusade, W. Tex., 1975; chaplain Am. Bus. Club, Lubbock, 1968-74; mem. Lubbock Bicentennial Music Com., 1976. Mem. Met. Ministers of Music Conf., So. Bapt. Ch. Music Conf. Home: 6201 Louisville Dr Lubbock TX 79413 Office: 2201 Broadway Lubbock TX 79401

LOY, CARL, minister, Southern Baptist Convention; b. Fairplay, Ky., Apr. 19, 1908; s. Larue and Margret (Turner) L.; m. Jessie Grimsley, Apr. 15, 1934. A.A., Campbellsville Coll.-Ky., 1948; student, So. Bapt. Theol. Sem., 1950. Ordained to ministry, 1931. Pastor various chs., Ky., 1927-85; pastor Mt. Vernon Bapt. Ch., Jamestown, Ky. and Pierces Chapel Bapt. Ch., Fairplay, Ky., 1972-85. Author: They Followed the Christ, 1984. Contbr. articles to profl. jours. Publisher songs 1937-79. Active PTA. Mem. Ministerial Alliance Williamsburg (pres. 1955-72). Lodges: Lions, Rotary. Address: 502 Jamestown St Columbia KY 42728

LOZANO, JOHN MANUEL, priest, Roman Catholic Church; b. Lora del Rio, Spain, June 18, 1930; s. Antonio and Rosario (Nieto) L.; came to U.S., 1976; B.A. Licentia in Theology, Universite Catholique, Angers, France, 1956; Licentia in Bibl. Scis., Bibl. Inst., Rome, 1958; Th.D., Angelicum U., Rome, 1959. Joined Clarentians (C.M.F.), 1948, ordained priest, 1956; prof. spirituality, Claretianum, Rome, 1962-67, dir. studium, 1961-68; prof. theology and history of spirituality Instituto della Vita Religiosa, Lateran U., Rome, 1971—; prof. spirituality CTU, Chgo., 1979—. Consultor Roman Congregation for Causes of the Saints, 1970—. Mem. Cath. Theol. Soc. Am., Soc. for Sci. Study Religion. Author: Mysic and Man of Action, 1977; Discipleship, 1981, 83; Life as a Parable, 1985. Contbg. author: I Mondi dell'Uomo, 1977; Together Before the Lord, 1983; Ency. of Religion, 1985. Address: 5540 S Everett Ave Chicago IL 60637

LOZANO BARRAGAN, JAVIER, bishop, Roman Catholic Church; b. Toluca, Mex., Jan. 27, 1933; s. Lozano Villanueva Vicente and Maria Dolores Camorlinga Barragan. D.D., Gregorian U., Rome, 1967. Ordained priest Roman Cath. Ch., 1955, consecrated bishop, 1979. Theology tchr. Priests' Sem., Zamora, Michoacan, Mex., 1958-78; dir. CELAM Inst., Medellin, Colombia, 1977-79; pres. Theol. Soc. Mex., 1973-75; spl. sec. Bishops' Synod, Rome, 1980. Author: Puebla, 1980; Cristo Alianza de la Familia, 1982; Iglesia del Pueblo, 1983. Editor: Teologia Moral Hoy, 1984. Mem. Equipo Teologico-Pastoral del CELAM, Consejo Superior de Universidad Pontificia de Mex. Home: Juande Tolosa 306 Sierra de Alica Zacatecas Mexico Office: Miguel Auza 219 Zacatecas Mexico 98000

LUBBA, DAVID PETER, minister, United Meth. Ch.; b. Attica, N.Y., Apr. 12, 1935; s. Chester Burr and Mildred Amelia (Merle) L.; B.A., Albright Coll., 1956; B.D., Evang. Theol. Sem., Naperville, Ill., 1959; S.T.M., McCormick Theol. Sem., 1970; m. Marian Jane Nevinger, June 30, 1956; children—Kim Marie, Nathan David, Debra Sue. Ordained to ministry, 1959; pastor, Naperville, 1957-59, 1st United Meth. Ch., Tonawanda, N.Y., 1959-65; missionary, Philippines, 1965-74; pastor 1st United Meth. Ch., Westfield, N.Y., 1974—. Chmn. council Western N.Y. Conf., United Meth. Ch., mem. exec. com., 1976, asst. sec., 1977—. Co-chmn. Com. for Decent Lit., Tonawanda, 1963-65; coordinator Westfield Town Meeting '76. Home: 160 E Main St Westfield NY 14787 Office: 101 E Main St Westfield NY 14787

LUBBEN, HENRY C., minister, Lutheran Church-Missouri Synod; b. Teaneck, N.J., Sept. 20, 1938; s. Henry C. and Ida G. (Templin) L.; m. Sally J. Brown, May 31, 1964; children: Suzanne E., Steven M. B.Th., Concordia Theol. Sem., Springfield, Ill., 1964. Ordained to ministry Luth. Ch., 1964. Pastor, Messiah Luth. Ch., Grand Rapids, Mich., 1964-67, Mount Calvary Luth. Ch., Greenville, Mich., 1968-70, Trinity Luth. Ch., Taylorsville, Ill., 1976-81; English speaking pastor True Light Luth. Ch., N.Y.C., 1967-68; dir. pub. relations Bethesda Luth. Home, Watertown, Wis., 1970-72, exec. dir. Ceour Lake Lodge, LaGrange, Ill., 1972-76; sr. pastor Immanuel Luth. Ch., Rock Island, Ill., 1981—; chmn. bd. communications services Luth. Ch.-Mo. Synod, St. Louis, 1973-83. Editor: (study guide) Are You Joking Jeremiah, 1969; Luth. Witness Supplement for Central Ill. Recipient Jericho Friend award Cedar Lake Lodge, 1980, Servus Esslesiaste award Concordia Theol. Sem., 1983. Mem. Pastoral Conf. Central Ill. Dist., Cir. Pastoral Conf. Rock Island. Lodges: Optimist. Home: 1820 22d St Rock Island IL 61201 Office: Immanuel Luth Ch 1923 5th Ave Rock Island IL 61201

LUBENOW, MARVIN LOWELL, minister, Conservative Baptist Association America; b. Fargo, N.D., Sept. 25, 1926; s. August Carl and Nettie Wilhelmena (Gaulke) L.; B.A., Bob Jones U., 1949; Th.M., Dallas Theol. Sem., 1954; M.S., Eastern Mich. U., 1976; m. Enid Arlene Hoover, Aug. 19, 1950; children: Mark S., Jean M. (Mrs. Richard Laribee, Jr.), Gary H., David M. Ordained to ministry, 1953; pastor Cambridge Bapt. Ch., Cambridge, Maine, 1954-57, First Bapt. Ch., Foxboro, Mass., 1957-63; sr. pastor First Bapt. Ch., Wayne, Mich., 1963-76, First Bapt. Ch., Ft. Collins, Colo., 1976—. Pres. Conservative Bapt. Assn. Maine, 1956-57; pres. Conservative Bapt. Assn. Mass., 1961-63. Trustee Denver Conservative Bapt. Sem., 1981—; bd. dirs. Conservative Bapt. Home Mission Soc., 1963-68, Conservative Bapt. Fgn. Mission Soc., 1981—. Mem. Evang. Theol. Soc., Bible-Sci. Assn., Am. Sci. Affiliation, Creation Research Soc. Author: Bones of Contention-The Bible and The Human Fossils, 1976; From Fish to Gish. The Creation/Evolution Debates, 1984. Home: 1204 Stover Fort Collins CO 80524 Office: 901 E Lake St Fort Collins CO 80524

LUCAS, CALVIN GLENN, minister, United Church of Canada; b. Carp, Ont., Can., May 24, 1929; s. Robert and Jessie Verna (Ireland) L.; B.A., Queen's U., Kingston, Ont., 1950; postgrad. Queen's Theol. Coll., 1954; M.A., Carleton U., Ottawa, Ont., 1973; m. Phyllis Barbara Napier, Oct. 12, 1968; 1 son, Robert Shaun. Ordained to ministry United Ch. of Can., 1954; parish minister, Bethune, Sask., 1954-55, Fitzroy Harbour, Ont., 1956-59, Montreal, Que., 1959-63; collection historian Fortress of Louisbourg Restoration Project, 1963-66; archivist-historian United Ch. of Can., Victoria U., Toronto, Ont., 1966—. Mem. World Meth. Hist. Soc. (pres. 1981-86). Home: 426 Abington Ave Mississauga ON Canada Office: United Ch Archives Victoria U Queens Park Toronto ON Canada

LUCAS, EDWARD LEE, minister, United Pentecostal Church International. B. Crawfordsville, Ind., Sept. 22, 1943; s. James Spurgeon and D. Ruth (McCoy) L.; m. Mary Frances Sexton, Aug. 26, 1972; children: Jonathan Edward, Jeremy Lee, Jordan Francis. Student U. Louisville, 1961-62, Apostolic Bible Inst., 1962-63, Greenville Coll., 1970-71; B.A., Kent Christian Coll., 1983. Ordained to ministry, United Pentecostal Ch. Internat., 1965. Pastor, First Pentecostal Ch., Savannah, Tenn., 1965-66; youth pres. United Pentecostal Ch., State of Ill., 1970-81; pastor First Pentecostal Ch., Vandalia, Ill., 1969—; supt. of Christian edn. Fayette Christian Acad., Vandalia, 1983—; guest lectr. Kent Christian Coll., Dover, Del., 1982-83; Gateway Coll. of Evangelism, St. Louis, 1973—; presbyter, bd. dirs. United Pentecostal Ch., State of Ill., 1981—. Republican. Home: 127 W Madison St Vandalia IL 62471 Office: First Pentecostal Ch 1009 W Gallatin St Vandalia IL 62471

LUCKER, RAYMOND ALPHONSE, bishop, Roman Catholic Church; b. St. Paul, Feb. 24, 1927; s. Alphonse J. and Josephine T. (Schiltgen) Lucker Mayer. B.A., St. Paul Sem., 1948, M.A., 1952; S.T.D., U. St. Thomas, Rome, 1966; Ph.D., U. Minn., 1969; D.D. (hon.), Vatican, 1971. Ordained priest Roman Cath. Ch., 1952, as bishop, 1971. Dir. Confraternity of Christian Doctrine, St. Paul, 1957-68; prof. religious edn. St. Paul Sem., 1957-68, trustee, 1971—; dir. dept. edn. U.S. Catholic Conf., Washington, 1969-71; aux. bishop Archdiocese St. Paul and Mpls., 1971-76; bishop Diocese of New Ulm, Minn., 1976—; bd. dirs. Human Life Ctr., Collegeville, Minn., 1978-84; mem. adminstrv. bd. Nat. Conf. Cath. Bishops, Washington, 1982-84; pres. Minn. Pax Christi, St. Paul, 1982-84. Author: Aims of Religious Education, 1966; History of Released Time Movement, 1969. Mem. Minn. Cath. Conf. (treas. 1971-83). Home: 1400 Chancery Dr New Ulm MN 56073

LUDWIG, GLENN EDWARD, minister, Lutheran Church in America; b. Lancaster, Pa., Aug. 19, 1946; s. George E. and Betty Jane (Rapp) L.; m. K. Estella Weiser, Aug. 19, 1983; children: Matthew S., Melissa M. B.A., in Psychology, Susquehanna U., 1969; M.Div., Lancaster Theol. Sem., 1973. Ordained to ministry Lutheran Ch. in Am., 1973. Pastor Washingtonville Luth. Ch., Pa., 1973-75; assoc. pastor St. Paul's Luth. Ch., Hanover, Pa., 1976-80; chaplain Susquehanna U., Selinsgrove, Pa., 1980—; dir. Luth. Youth Encounter, St. Paul, 1978—; cons. Commn. Higher Edn., Central Pa. Synod, 1980-84. Author: Building an Effective Youth Ministry, 1979. Sec., treas. Selinsgrove Area Ministerium, 1984—; sec. Gettysburg Sem. Extension Center, 1984—. Named Outstanding Young Men of Am., U.S. Jaycees, 1982. Mem. Luth. Acad. for Scholarship. Democrat. Home: 307 Broad St Selinsgrove PA 17870 Office: Susquehanna U Selinsgrove PA 17870

LUETKEHOELTER, GOTTLIEB WERNER, bishop, Luth. Ch. Am.; b. Markinch, Sask., Can., Nov. 16, 1929; s. Henry Wilhelm and Maria (Schlepper) L.; B.A., U. Sask., 1952; B.D., Luth. Theol. Sem., 1955; Th.M., Vancouver Sch. Theology, 1975; m. Betty Edwards, July 25, 1959; children—David, Jonathan. Ordained to ministry, 1955; pastor, Markinch, Sask., Can., 1955-57, St. Mark's Luth. Ch., Regina, Sask., Can., 1957-61, Erloeser Luth. Ch., Phila., 1961-64, Faith Luth. Ch., Barnaby, B.C., Can., 1964-69, Trinity Luth. Ch., Edmonton, Alta., Can., 1969-76. Mem. exec. bd. Synod Western Can., 1967-76, synod sec., 1971-75; bishop Central Can. Synod, Luth. Ch. Am., 1976-85, Man./N.W. Ont. Synod, Evangelical Luth. Ch. in Can., 1986—. Home: 10 Shakespeare Bay Winnipeg MB R3K 0M6 Canada Office: 2231 Portage Ave Winnipeg MB Canada

LUMBSDEN, SAMUEL, missionary, educational administrator, Seventh-day Adventists. B. Balboa, Republic of Panama; Dec. 17, 1929; came to U.S., 1967, naturalized, 1978; s. Cecil Eugene and Margaret Violet

(Cornwall) L.; m. Violet Isidora Knight, Apr. 11, 1955 (div. 1972); children: Samuel, Annette, Pablo, Braulio, Nellie, Ardyth; m. Estela Redman, July 8, 1974. B.A., Antillian Coll., Mayaguez, P.R., 1970; M.Ed., Antioch U., 1973. Cert. elder Seventh-day Adventists. Youth leader, missionary soc., Represso, Republic of Panama, 1945-46; supt. Sabbath sch., Represso, 1946-47; deacon Panama Indsl. Acad., Republic of Panama, 1947-49; youth leader Third St. Seventh-day Adventist Ch., Colon, Republic of Panama, 1949-52; ch. elder, adminstr. Rio Abajo Seventh-day Adventist Ch., Republic of Panama, 1957-64; youth evangelist, med. cadet chaplain Antillian Coll., Mayaguez, P.R., 1968-70; dean men Bella Vista Hosp., Mayaguez, 1968-70; asst. ch. pastor Ch. Three Angels, Bronx, N.Y., 1971-73; ch. elder/prin. Berean Seventh-day Adventist Ch., Baton Rouge, 1980-84; bilingual prof. Jefferson Sch., Oakland, Calif., 1984—; elder, personal ministry team dir. East Oakland Seventh-day Adventist Ch., Calif. Recipient Ednl. plaque Men of Bethel Seventh-day Adventist Ch., Jersey City, 1973, plaque, Berean Ch. Sch. Bd., 1984. Democrat. Home: 12775 San Pablo Ave Richmond CA 94805 Office: PO Box 5313 Richmond CA 94801

LUMPKINS, JULIUS SMITH, minister, Ch. of God in Christ; b. White Oak, S.C., Oct. 3, 1895; s. William and Patsy (Hartem) L.; m. Elizabeth Hall, Aug. 17, 1917; children—Alleen, Emma, Fanny, James, John, William, Mable, Alice, Ann, Joe. Ordained to ministry, 1932; pastor 2d Bapt. Ch., Harrisburg, Pa., 1932-40, Carlisle (Pa.) Ch. of God in Christ, 1940-44, Lumpkin Temple Ch. of God in Christ, Harrisburg, 1944—. Supt. Eastern jurisdiction Ch. of God in Christ, 1968-71. Mem. Nat. Police Res. Officers Assn. Home: 1250 Bailey St Harrisburg PA 17103 Office: 13th and Herr St Harrisburg PA 17103

LUND, GORDON C., minister, Lutheran Church in America; b. Fremont, Nebr., Apr. 1, 1921; s. Clarence Larsen and Lenora (Laaker) L.; m. Doris Martha Blessing, Apr. 17, 1949; children: Valerie Kay, Debora Ann, Gordon C. B.A., Midland Luth. Coll., 1942; M.Div., Hamma Sch. Theology, 1954. Ordained to ministry Lutheran Ch., 1954. Pastor, Holy Trinity Luth. Ch., Lynchburg, Va., 1961-66; dir. ch. relations Roanoke Coll., Salem, Va., 1966-71; sr. pastor Luth. Ch. of the Holy Comforter, Balt., 1971-76; pastor Christ Luth. Ch., Cambridge, Ohio, 1979—; dean southeast dist. Ohio Synod, Luth. Ch. Am., 1981—, worship chmn. Va. Synod, 1966-71, edn. chmn., 1961-66; dir. pub. relations Luth. Evangelism Mission, N.Y.C., 1956-57. Served with USAAF, 1942-45; CBI. Home: 8 Coventry Dr Cambridge OH 43725 Office: Christ Lutheran Ch 1101 Steubenville Ave Cambridge OH 43725

LUND, NANCY ELIZABETH, minister, American Lutheran Church. B. International Falls, Minn., May 28, 1954; d. Benhard Eugene and Mildred Elizabeth (Carroll) Niemi; m. Richard Eric Lund, Dec. 27, 1975; children: Elizabeth, Christopher. B.A. summa cum laude, U. Minn., 1975; M.Div., Luther Northwestern Sem., St. Paul, 1979. Ordained to ministry American Lutheran Church, 1979. Leisure minister Olivet Luth. Ch., LaCrosse, Wis., 1978; co-pastor Holt Am. Luth. Ch. Parish, Minn., 1979—; chairperson Conf. Pastors, Thief River Falls, Minn., 1982-84; chmn. Thief River Falls Conf. life and mission com., 1982-84. Cellist, Masterworks prodn. Messiah, Thief River Falls, 1983. Alt. del., mem. resolutions com. Democratic Farmer-Labor Dist. Conv., Thief River Falls, 1982; mem. eval. com. Quin County Pub. Nursing, Newfolden, Minn., 1982. Mem. AAUW (editor Thief River Falls chpt. 1983—, honored for contbns. to religion Thief River Falls Br. 1983, named Best of Class Newsletter state div. 1984). Home and Office: Route 1 Box 132 Newfolden MN 56738

LUND, RICHARD ERIC, pastor, American Lutheran Church. B. Sioux Falls, S.D., Jan. 11, 1952; s. Herbert Arthur and Evelyn Marie (Granskou) L.; m. Nancy Elizabeth Niemi, Dec. 27, 1975; children: Elizabeth, Christopher. B.A., St. Olaf Coll., 1974; M.Div., Luther Northwestern Sem., St. Paul, 1978. Ordained to ministry American Lutheran Church, 1979. Leisure minister Olivet Luth. Ch., LaCrosse, Wis., 1978; co-pastor Holt Am. Luth. Ch. Parish, Minn., 1979—. Contbr. articles to religious publs. Home: Rural Route 1 Box 132 Newfolden MN 56738

LUNDE, CLIFFORD ROLF, minister, American Lutheran Church; b. Grand Forks, N.D., Jan. 15, 1930; s. Clifford Madel and Ida Walfrida (Loyd) L.; m. Gillian Beatrice Chapman, Sept. 6, 1956; children: Rolf Lewis, Christopher Madel, Ian David. B.A., Pacific Luth. Coll., 1951, D.D. (hon.), 1985; B.D., Luther Theol. Sem., 1962; D.D. (hon.), Wartburg Theol. Sem., 1985. Pastor, Zion Luth. Ch., Newberg, Oreg., 1962-70, Emmanuel Luth. Ch., Spokane, Wash., 1970-76; exec. asst. to bishop North Pacific Dist. Am. Luth. Ch., Seattle, 1976-81, bishop, 1981—. Bd. dirs. Pacific Luth. Theol. Sem., Berkeley, Calif., 1981—; bd. regents Pacific Luth. U., Tacoma, 1981—; bd. dirs. Luth. Social Service Wash., Seattle, Luth. Family Service Oreg., Portland. Served to 1st lt. USAF, 1952-59. Named Disting. Alumnus, Pacific Luth. U., 1981. Home: 21734 NE 18th Way Redmond WA 98053 Office: North Pacific Dist Am Luth Ch 766-B John St Seattle WA 98109

LUNDGREN, ROBERT G., minister, Lutheran Church in America. b. Wichita, Kans., Mar. 1, 1943; s. Vincent T. and Erlanne A. (Carlson) L.; m. Sonja Sears, June 10, 1969 (div. 1981); children: Erik B., Lisa M., David K. B.S., Bethany Coll., 1965; M.Div., Luth. Sch. Theology, 1969; D. Ministry, North Am. Baptist Sem., 1980. Ordained to ministry Lutheran Church in America, 1969. Pastor, All Saints Luth. Ch., Kansas City, Kans., 1969-71, Our Saviours Luth. Ch., Durant, Okla., 1971-73, Dalesburg Luth. Ch., Vermillion, S.D., 1973-80, Advent Luth. Ch., Overland Park, Kans., 1980-81, Ada Luth. Ch., Courtland, Kans., 1981—; developer Luth. Parish, Overland Park, 1980-81. Author: Dalesburg's Midsummer, 1976; Decade of Renewal, 1979; Centennial Sermons, 1981; Lillies of the Field, 1984. Chmn., Community Devel., Vermillion, 1975-80; bd. dirs. Community Renewal, Courtland, 1981—.

LUNDIN, JOHN OLAF, minister, Am. Luth. Ch.; b. Yankton, S.D., Jan. 2, 1941; s. James M. and Cornelia J. (DeRoos) L.; B.A., Augustana Coll., 1964; B.D., Luther Theol. Sem., 1968; m. Ruth Ellen Hickenbotham, Aug. 10, 1963; children—Christina Anna, Nathan Eric, Kathleen Jennifer, Page Lundin. Ordained to ministry, 1968; pastor West Nidaros Luth. Ch., Crooks, S.D., 1968-76; chaplain USAF, George AFB, Victorville, Calif., 1976—. Mem. Tri-Valley Dist. Sch. Bd., Colton, S.D., 1970-75; bd. dirs. Sioux Falls (S.D.) Boys' Club, 1974-76. Mem. Augustana Fellows. Home: 9 Carolina Ave S Victorville CA 92392 Office: 35th Cmbt Spt Gp/HC George AFB CA 92392

LUNDSTAD-VOGT, BARBARA I., pastor, American Lutheran Church. B. Grinnell, Iowa, Apr. 7, 1951; d. Raymond Fredick and Gail Yvonne (Patten) Vogt; m. Craig S. Lundstad, May 29, 1978; children: Kari Lynn, Amy Anne. B.S., Iowa State U., 1973; M.Div., Luther Theol. Sem., St. Paul, 1978. Ordained to ministry Am. Luth. Ch., 1978. Pastor youth and edn. Trinity Luth. Ch., Yankton, S.D., 1978-81, First Luth. Ch., Mitchell, S.D., 1981—; bd. dirs. Lutherans Outdoors, Sioux Falls, S.D., 1979-81; advisor Dist. Youth Com., Sioux Falls, 1981—; dist. faculty Search Bible Studies, Am. Luth. Ch., Sioux Falls, 1983-84.

LUNSFORD, GERALD D., minister, Southern Baptist Convention; b. Carnegie, Okla., June 20, 1939; s. Alton Ray and Allie May (Treadaway) L.; m. Darla Nan Dabney, Sept. 27, 1957; children: Kevin Dee, Kathleen Diane, Steven Kent. B.A., Okla. Bapt. U., 1966; postgrad. Southwestern Bapt. Theol. Sem., 1975. Ordained to ministry Baptist Ch., 1962. Pastor, Bapt. chs. in Okla., 1961—, Howard Meml. Bapt. Ch., Del City, 1971-73, First Bapt. Ch., Choctaw, 1973—; clk. Pottowatomie-Lincoln Bapt. Assn., Shawnee, Okla., 1965; moderator Concord-Kiowa Bapt. Assn., Cordell, Okla., 1967-69, Capital Bapt. Assn., Oklahoma City, 1982-84; chaplain Okla. Ho. of Reps., 1976, 85. Served with U.S. Army, 1958-59. Recipient commendation Choctaw Police Dept., 1978, 81, 84. Chaplain, Choctaw Police Dept., 1977-84. Republican. Home: PO Box 947 Choctaw OK 73020 Office: PO Box 947 Choctaw OK 73020

LUNSFORD, WALTER B., pastor, United Methodist Church; b. Pueblo, Colo., Feb. 24, 1934; s. John D. and Mary L. (Simmons) L.; m. Alta Mae Neil, July 14, 1952; children: Dorothy Mae, Walter David, Mark Neil, John Paul. Student Bethany Nazarene Coll., 1953-56; B.A., Denver U., 1959; M.Div., Iliff Sch., Denver, 1962. Ordained, 1962. Pastor Elsdon United Meth. Ch., Chgo., 1962-66, Bethany United Meth. Ch., Highland Park, Ill., 1966-72, First United Meth. Ch., Mendota, Ill., 1972-75, Epworth United Meth. Ch., Elgin, Ill., 1976—; pres. Elgin Clergy Assn., 1983; evangelist, bd. discipleship United Meth. Ch., Nashville, 1975—. Ch. builder, new bldgs. 1967, 81 (Elgin Beautification Com. award 1982). Chmn. Bethany Nursery Sch., Highland Park, 1965-68, New Creations Nursery Sch., Elgin, 1981—; Republican candidate for Congress 15th Dist. Ill., 1975; committeeman Elgin Rep. Party 15th Precinct, 1980—; com. mem. Gov.'s Conf. on Children, 1980—. Recipient ARC award Elgin Flood Relief, 1982; City of Elgin award, 1983; Outstanding Parents award Cigo, PTA, 1966; Stiles fellow U. Denver, 1959. Mem. Mendota Clergy Assn. (pres. 1974). Club: Kiwanis. Lodge: Masons. Home: 1940 Murcer Ln Elgin IL 60120 Office: Epworth United Meth Ch 370W040 Highland Ave Elgin IL 60120

LUOMA, JOHN KENNETH REYNOLD, minister, Lutheran Church in America; b. June 19, 1942; s. John Herman and Florence June (Meyer) L.; m. Gracia Anne Nydahl, Aug. 7, 1965; children: Aaron Sean, Jason Brian. B.A. summa cum laude, Augsburg Coll., 1965; M.A. in History, U. Minn., 1968; M.A. in Religion, Hartford Sem., 1970, Ph.D. in Theology, 1974. Ordained to ministry Lutheran Ch., 1978. Instr., Augsburg Coll., Mpls., 1974-75; asst. prof. Hamma Sem., Springfield, Ohio, 1975-77; pastor Our Saviour Luth. Ch., Hinckley, Ohio, 1977-84, Bethlehem Lutheran Ch., Youngstown, Ohio, 1984—; chmn. Luth. Peace Task Force of Ohio, 1983—; mem. Peace and Justice Commn., Ohio Council of Chs., 1983—. Contbr. articles to profl. publs. Bd. dirs. Wittenberg U., Springfield, 1983—. Tozer Found. scholar, 1964; Hartford Sem. scholar, 1968; Case Study Inst. grantee, 1974; recipient grad. award State of Conn., 1973. Mem. Ch. History Soc. Home: 4129 Nottingham St Austintown OH 44515 Office: Bethlehem Luth Ch 388 E Midlothian St Youngstown OH 44507

LUTHER, DAVID ALAN, minister music Baptist Ch.; b. Chgo., Jan. 24, 1947; s. James Henry and Rita Thelma (Chapman) L.; B.A., Bob Jones U., 1970; M. in Ch. Music, New Orleans Bapt. Theol. Sem., 1976; m. Sigrid Skogstad, Dec. 30, 1969; children—Kelly Lynn, Tara Joy. Instr. music Pillsbury Bapt. Bible Coll., Owatonna, Minn., 1971-73, tchr., dir. choirs Jackson Christian Sch., Marianna, Fla., 1973-74; adj. instr. New Orleans Bapt. Theol. Sem., 1974-76; minister of music Grace Bapt. Ch., Owatonna, Minn., 1972-73, Bridgedale Bapt. Ch., New Orleans, 1974-76, Park Forest Bapt. Ch., Baton Rouge, La., 1976—. Home: 1855 Brightside Dr Apt 245 Baton Rouge LA 70808 Office: 3791 Aletha Dr Baton Rouge LA 70808

LUTTRELL, OSCAR EDWYN, JR., minister, Southern Baptist Convention; b. Farnham, Va., June 14, 1919; s. Oscar Edwyn and Vivian Harriett (Heathman) L.; B.A., U. Richmond, 1943, M.A., 1950, D.D., 1972; M.Div., Crozer Theol. Sem., 1946; m. Constance Powell, June 10, 1944; children—Mark Edwyn, Thomas Powell, Carolyn Lee, Elizabeth. Ordained to ministry, 1946; asst. minister 1st Bapt. Ch., Phila., 1944-46; asso. minister 2d Bapt. Ch., Richmond, Va., 1946-48; minister Main St. Bapt. Ch., Emporia, Va., 1948-51, 1st Bapt. Ch., Balt., 1951-54, Larchmont Bapt. Ch., 1954-66, 1st Bapt. Ch., Columbia, Mo., 1966-84, pastor emeritus, 1984—. Mem. faculty U. Richmond Sch. Christian Edn., 1953-65; lectr. philosophy Christopher Newport Coll. of Coll. William and Mary, 1963-66; mem. faculty Mo. Sch. Religion, 1970; pres. Columbia Ministerial Alliance, 1968-69, Norfolk Ministers Assn., 1961-62; trustee Religious Herald Pub. Corp., 1956-66, pres., 1966; trustee Crozer Theol. Sem., 1956-63; mem. bd. mgrs. Great Rivers Region Am. Bapts., 1975—. Mem. Mayor's Tax Commn., Columbia, 1973, 76; mem. bd. Columbia Art League, 1970-72; del. Boone County Democratic Conv., 1976; mem. Bd. Review on Research Involving Human Subjects, U. Mo., 1974—. Mem. Pi Kappa Alpha. Religious book reviewer Crozer Quar., 1946-53, Balt. Sunday Sun, 1952-54. Contbr. articles religious periodicals. Home: 901 Bourn Ave Columbia MO 65201 Office: 1st Baptist Church Broadway and Waugh St Columbia MO 65201

LUTZ, BERNHARD WILLIAM, minister, Lutheran Church. B. Denison, Iowa, May 28, 1934; s. Edward Carl Lutz and Ida Granzmann; M. Roberta Frances Will, June 23, 1956; children: Lori, Robert, David, Rebecca Anne. A.A., Concordia Coll., St. Paul, 1954; B.S. in Edn., Concordia Tchrs. Coll., River Forest, Ill., 1956; B.D., Concordia Sem., Springfield, Mo., 1967, M.Div., 1968. Ordained to ministry Luth. Ch., 1967; tchr. cert. Ill., 1956, Alta., Can., 1961. Tchr. Luth. Ch., Milw., 1956-59, Chgo., 1959-61; athletic dir. Luth. Ch., Edmonton, Alta., 1961-64; missionary Luth. Ch.-Mo. Synod, Papua, New Guinea, 1964-75; parish pastor Fulda, Minn., 1975-80, First Luth. Ch., Boseman, Mt., 1980—; cir. counsellor Divide cir.; counsellor Missionary League, So. Minn. dist., 1976-80; del. Luth. Ch.-Mo. Synod, Dallas, 1977, bd. for missions, Nat. Body, 1977-81, chmn. Muslim ad hoc, 1978-81, mem. bd. missions, 1983—. Pres. No. Alta. Athletic Assn., 1962, 64. Author: (self govt. in Melanesian lang.) Papua New Guinea, 1969. Mem. Sheriff's Search and Rescue Posse, Bozeman, 1980—. Recipient Independence medal Nat. Govt. New Guinea, 1975, Successful Pastor's award Minn. S. Dist., 1976. Lodges: Lions, Ducks Unltd. Home: 16 Sun Dance Trail Bozeman MT 59715 Office: 225 S Black Bozeman MT 59715

LUTZER, ERWIN WESLEY, minister, educator, Christian and Missionary Alliance; b. Colfax, Sask., Can., Oct. 3, 1941; s. Gustav and Wanda (Lutke) L.; came to U.S., 1970; Th.B., Winnipeg Bible Coll., 1962; Th.M., Dallas Theol. Sem., 1967; M.A., Chgo. Grad. Sch. Theology, 1970; M.A., Loyola U., Chgo., 1973, postgrad., 1973—; m. Rebecca Anne Hickman, Aug. 30, 1969; children—Lorisa Beth, Lynette Marie, Lisa Christine. Ordained to ministry Christian and Missionary Alliance, 1971; prof. Briercrest Bible Inst., Sask., 1967-70; pastor Edgewater Baptist Ch., Chgo., 1972-77; prof. Moody Bible Inst., Chgo., 1977-79; sr. pastor Moody Ch., Chgo., 1980—. Mem. Evang. Theol. Soc. Author: The Morality Gap, 1972; How in This World Can I Be Holy?, 1974; Failure: The Backdoor to Success, 1975; Flames of Freedom, 1976; You're Richer Than You Think, 1978; How to Say No to a Stubborn Habit, 1979; Managing Your Emotions, 1981; Living With Your Passions, 1983; When a Good Man Falls, 1985. Home: 5833 N Odell Chicago IL 60631

LYBRAND, RUFUS EDWARD JR., minister, Lutheran Church in America; b. Johnston, S.C., Apr. 23, 1949; s. Rufus Edward and Lucy Rose (Friar) L.; m. Jacquelyn Maurice Wilson, June 3, 1973; children: Jennifer Mauri, Brett Edward. B.A., Newberry Coll., 1967-71; M.Div., Luth. Sem., 1975. Ordained to ministry Luth. Ch. in Am., 1975, Intern Faith Luth. Ch., Phoenex, 1973-74; pastor Trinity Luth. Ch.,

Georgetown, S.C., 1975-78, Resurrection Luth. Ch., Columbia, S.C., 1978-82, Grace Luth. Ch., Rock Hill, S.C., 1982—; cabinet mem. Central Dist. of Ch., Columbia, 1979-82; mem. Christian Edn. Com., S.C. Synod Luth. Ch. Am., 1979-82, Pastoral Support Com., 1976-82. Author: Home is a Four-Letter Word, 1985. Contbr. articles and sermons to profl. jours. Bd. dirs. Mental Health Assn. Mem. Rock Hill Ministerial Assn. (v.p. 1977-78). Lodge: Optimists. Home: 1889 Huntington Pl Rock Hill SC 29730 Office: Grace Luth Ch 508 Aiken Ave Rock Hill SC 29730

LYLE, WILBUR WATSON, minister, Reformed Episcopal Church Canada; b. Wetskiwin, Alta., Can., Oct. 8, 1907; s. John Henry and Ada Lorna (Wooldridge) L.; m. Marie Schneider, Aug. 18, 1984; children by previous marriage: John Clayton, Beverlee Jane, Cameron Wilbur, Wayne William, Fraser. Ordained to ministry, 1945. Assoc. minister St. Paul's Reformed Episcopal Ch., New Westminster, B.C., Can., 1945-48; minister Blue Mt. Union Ch., New Westminster, 1949-56; minister-in-charge Mt. Lehman Presbyn. Ch., B.C., 1957-68; rector St. Paul's Ref. Episcopal Ch., New Westminster, 1970-81, assoc. minister, 1982—. Commr., Boy Scouts of Can., New Westminster, 1962-67. Mem. Social Credit of B.C. Home and Office: 1544 Broadview Ct Coquitlam BC V3J 5X9 Canada

LYNCH, GEORGE EDWARD, bishop, Roman Catholic Church; b. N.Y.C., Mar. 4, 1917; s. Timothy John and Margaret Mary (O'Donnell) L. A.B., Fordham U., 1938; S.T.L., Cath. U. Am., 1943, J.C.D., 1946; LL.D. (hon.), Mt. St. Mary's Coll., 1979. Ordained priest, Roman Cath. Ch. Chancellor Diocese of Raleigh, N.C., 1953-62, consecrated bishop, 1970, aux. bishop, 1970—. Pastor Southport Parish, N.C., 1981—. Author canon law: Auxiliary Bishops, 1946. Mem. Fellowship of Cath. Scholars. Office: Sacred Heart Ch 220 N Caswell St Southport NC 28461

LYNCH, MARY DENNIS, nun, religious educator, librarian, Roman Catholic Church; b. Phila., Apr. 23, 1920; d. J. Raymond and Ida A. (Teal) L. B.A., Temple U., 1941; M.S.L.S., Catholic U., 1956; M.A., Villanova U., 1970; M.A., St. Charles Sem., 1980. Joined Soc. Holy Child of Jesus, 1945. Tchr., librarian Sch. of Holy Child, Sharon Hill, Pa., 1942-45; tchr. Oak Knoll, Summit, N.J., 1945-47, West Phila. Cath. High Sch. for Girls, 1947-53; tchr., librarian Sch. of Holy Child, 1953-62; dir. library services Rosemont Coll., Pa., 1962—; mem. edn. adv. com. St. Charles Sem., Phila., 1968, 76, 78—. Contbr. articles to profl. jours. Mem. ALA, Pa. Library Assn. (parliamentarian 1977-83), Cath. Library Assn. (exec. bd. 1981—, pres. 1983-85), Palinet and Union Library Catalog Pa. (trustee), Tri-State Coll. Library Coop. (bd. dirs. 1967—, pres. 1980-81). Office: Rosemont Coll Library Rosemont PA 19010

LYNCH, MARY ELLEN, nun, Roman Catholic Church; b. N.Y.C., May 6, 1931; d. Thomas Francis and Sarah Margaret (Barlow) L. B.A., Ohio Dominican Coll., 1953; Theology Cert., Providence Coll., 1961; M.A., Fairfield U., 1969. Entered Dominican Sisters of Third Order, 1952. Tchr., various parochial schs., 1956-66, 71-74, 79-82; vice prin. St. Thomas High Sch., Braddock, Pa., 1966-67; novce dir. St. Mary Congregation, Columbus, Ohio, 1967-71, 78-79, mem. council, 1974-78, major superior, 1982—; del. mem., pres. Sister's Council, Diocese of Columbus, 1968-70; del. mem. LCWR, Reg. I and VI, New Haven, 1974-75, Cin., 1982—; trustee Ohio Dominican Coll., 1974-80, 82—, Albertus Magnus Coll., New Haven, 1982—. Trustee St. George Hosp., Cin., 1974; co-sponsor St. Francis-St. George Hosp., Cin., 1982. Mem. Am. Chem. Soc.

LYNE, TIMOTHY JOSEPH, bishop, Roman Catholic Church; b. Chgo., Mar. 21, 1919; s. Michael F. and Mary Therese (Lynch) L. M.A., St. Mary of the Lake Sem., Mundelein, Ill., 1942, S.T.L., 1943. Ordained priest Roman Cath. Ch., 1943, consecrated bishop, 1983. Pastor St. Mary Ch., Riverside, Ill., 1943-62, St. Edmund Ch., Oak Park, Ill., 1962-66, Holy Name Cathedral, Chgo., 1966—; aux. bishop of Chgo., 1983—. Office: Holy Name Cathedral 730 N Wabash Ave Chicago IL 60611

LYONS, CHARLES DAVID, minister, Southern Baptist Convention; b. Olive Hill, Ky., June 12, 1932; s. Mike A. and Maudie Lee (Campbell) L.; diploma Clear Creek Bapt. Sch., 1956; student So. Sem., 1974, Samford U., 1982; m. Sue K. Hanna, Aug. 1, 1951; children: Michael David, Norman Dean. Ordained to ministry, 1955; pastor chs. in Ky., 1955—, Macedonia Bapt. Ch., Burning Springs, 1962-67, 1st Bapt. Ch., East Bernstadt, 1967-72, Fleming Bapt. Ch., 1972—; moderator Boonville Bapt. Assn., 1965-66, Pine Mountain Assn., 1973-74; mem. bd. counsellors Calvery Coll.; assoc. home mission bd. So. Bapt. Conv., 1975—; chaplain Neon Fire and Rescue Orgn., 1976—; dir. missions LynnCamp and North Concord Bapt. Assns., 1985—. Named Ky. col. Home and Office: PO Box 1060 Barbourville KY 40906

LYONS, DWIGHT KEITH, minister, So. Baptist Conv.; b. Elizabethton, Tenn., Jan. 11, 1933; s. James R. and Golda A. (Grindstaff) L.; B.S., East Tenn. State U., 1954; Th.B., So. Bapt. Theol. Sem., 1957, M.R.E., 1961; postgrad. Princeton Theol. Sem., 1974; m. Louise Booth, Aug. 15, 1959. Ordained to ministry So. Bapt. Conv., 1954; minister Vincennes Bapt. Chapel, New Albany, Ind., 1956-57, Cherokee Bapt. Ch., Jonesboro, Tenn., 1957-59; campus minister Eastern Ky. U., Richmond, 1961-69, U. Louisville, 1969—. Chmn. Ky. Bapt. Worship Seminar, 1972-74. Mem. Religious Edn. Assn., Richmond Ministerial Assn. (pres. 1965-66), Nat. Campus Ministry Assn., English-Speaking Union, Eastern Ky. U. Assn. Religious Workers (chmn. 1965-68), Pi Tau Chi, Sigma Phi Epsilon, Alpha Psi Omega. Kiwanian (pres. 1966, dist. lt. gov. 1967). Clubs: Filson, Arts, Executives. Contbr. revs. and articles to various lit. and religious publs. Home: The 800 800 S 4th Louisville KY 40203 Office: University of Louisville Louisville KY 40208

LYONS, EARLE VAUGHAN, JR., minister, United Church of Christ; b. Phila., Oct. 18, 1917; s. Earle Vaughan and Marie Meta (Anderson) L.; m. Eleanor Jean Morris, Sept. 6, 1946; children: Earle Vaughan III, William Morris, Jean Eleanor. B.A., Maryville Coll., Tenn., 1940; Th.M., Princeton U., 1943; M.A., U. Pa., 1952, Chapman Coll., 1977. Ordained to ministry United Presbyterian Ch. USA, 1943. Asst. pastor West Presbyn. Ch., Wilmington, Del., 1943-44; commd. lt. (j.g.) U.S. Navy, 1944, advanced through grades to capt., 1963, ret., 1974, served as chaplain in World War II, Korea, Vietnam; assoc. pastor Mission Hills Ch., San Diego, 1974-78, sr. pastor, 1978-85; officer in charge Chaplain Corps research team, Washington, 1963-64, U.S. Navy Chaplains Sch., Newport, R.I., 1967-71; chmn. planned giving So. Calif. conf. United Ch. of Christ, 1982-84; pres. San Diego Ecumenical Conf., 1980-82, bd. dirs., 1975—; team mem. Focus Five Daily TV program, 1976—, 1976—; mem. ch. and ministry com. San Diego Assn. United Ch. of Christ, 1984—; mem. honor roll NCCJ, 1982-83. Contbr. articles to USN Chaplains Bull. Mem. Calif. Congressman Bates' Polit. Action Com., 1983-84; chmn. Vet.'s Conf. San Diego, 1975-76; bd. dirs. St. Paul's Manor, Green Manor, 1st Congl. Tower, San Diego, 1979-84. Decorated Legion of Merit with combat V, Commendation medal; Honor medal 1st class Govt. of Vietnam; recipient Honor cert. Freedoms Found. at Valley Forge, 1974. Club: Rotary (program chmn. 1982) (San Diego). Home: 2727 Azalea Dr San Diego CA 92106

LYONS, RALPH ORVAL, lay church worker, Assemblies of God Church; b. Halifax, N.S., Can., July 21, 1932; s. James Orval and Edna Mae (MacLeod) L.; came to U.S., 1969; diploma Eastern Pentecostal Bible Coll., Peterborough, Ont., Can., 1957; B.A. in History, Wilfrid Laurier U., Waterloo, Ont., 1968; M.A. in Christian Edn., Wheaton (Ill.) Coll., 1969; Ed.D. in Sch. Adminstrn., No. Ariz. U., 1983; m. Ruth Elizabeth Martin, Aug. 9, 1952; children—Sheryll, Janet, Jacqueline. Ordained to ministry, 1959; deacon Chula Vista (Calif.) Assembly of God Ch., 1976—; prin. Chula Vista Christian Sch., 1974-79; pres. Southland Christian Schs., Inc., 1974—. Home: 838 Floyd Ave Chula Vista CA 92010 Office: 355 K St Suite E Chula Vista CA 92011

LYONS, THOMAS WILLIAM, bishop, Roman Cath. Ch.; b. Washington, Sept. 26, 1923; s. Thomas William and Nora (Bagley) L.; student St. Charles Coll., 1937-43; A.B., St. Mary's Sem., 1945, S.T.B., 1946. Ordained priest, 1948; asst. pastor St. John the Evangelist Ch., Silver Spring, Md., 1948-49, St. Matthew's Cathedral, Washington, 1949-53; dir. Mackin High Sch., Washington, 1953-57; asst. dir. edn. Archdiocese Washington, 1954-64, dir. edn., 1964-73; pastor, St. Francis de Sales Ch., Washington, 1963-66, St. Thomas Apostle Ch., Washington, 1966-76 sec. Christian Edn., Archdiocese Washington, 1972-75, aux. bishop, 1974—. Home: 2665 Woodley Rd NW Washington DC 20008 Office: 1721 Rhode Island Ave NW Washington DC 20036

MAASE, ROBERT LEE, minister, American Baptist Churches in the U.S.A.; b. Gresham, Nebr., Jan. 18, 1923; s. Clyde Fredrick and Nellie (Hannon) M.; m. Elda Ocea, Mar. 6, 1943; children: David, Philip, Karen. Th.B., Judson Coll., 1949; B.A., Roosevelt U., 1950; M.Div., Northern Sem., 1950. Ordained to ministry American Baptist Churches in the U.S.A., 1951. Pastor Bapt. Ch., Muncie, Ill., 1950-52; chaplain U.S. Air Force, 1952-70; dir. ch. relations and alumni services No. Bapt. Sem., Lombard, Ill., 1970-82; asst. adminstr., dir. devel. Atherton Bapt. Homes, Altadena, Calif., 1982—. Served to lt. col. USAF, 1952-70. Decorated Air Force Commendation Medal, Meritorious Service Medal, Bronze Star. Mem. Nursing Home Adminstrs. Assn. Home: 2631 Homepark Ave Altadena CA 91001 Office: Atherton Bapt Homes 214 S Atlantic Blvd Altadena CA 91801

MACDONALD, COLIN ALOYSIUS, priest, Roman Catholic Church; b. Heatherton, N.S., Can., June 21, 1920; came to U.S., 1926; s. Colin Peter and Emma Rachel (Keefe) M. A.B., St. Mary's U., Balt., 1945. Ordained priest Roman Cath. Ch., 1945. Assoc. pastor Diocese of Manchester, N.H., 1945-66, pastor, 1966-71, youth dir., 1950-67; exec. dir. com. on priestly life and ministry Nat. Conf. of Cath. Bishops, Washington, 1971—. Contbr. articles to profl. jours. Recipient Prelate of Honor, Roman Catholic Ch., Rome, 1962. Office: Nat Conf of Cath Bishops 1312 Massachusetts Ave NW Washington DC 20005

MACDONALD, DENNIS RONALD, theology educator, The Mennonite Church; b. Chgo., July 1, 1946; s. James Ronald and Mildred (Friend) MacD.; m. Diane Louise Prosser, June 9, 1973; children: Katya Louise, Julian Peter. B.A., Bob Jones U., 1968; M.Div., McCormick Theol. Sem., 1974; Ph.D., Harvard U., 1978. Asst. prof. Goshen Coll., Ind., 1977-80; asst. prof. theology Iliff Sch. Theology, Denver, 1980-83, assoc. prof. theology, 1983—. Author: The Legend and the Apostle, 1983. Contbr. articles to profl. jours. Grantee Assn. Theol. Schs., 1983, NEH, 1983; vis. assoc. The Folklore Inst. of Ind. U., 1983. Mem. Soc. Bibl. Lit. (pres. Rocky Mountain region chpt.), Am. Acad. Religion (pres. Rocky Mountain chpt.). Democrat. Office: Iliff Sch Theology 2201 S University Blvd Denver CO 80210

MACDONALD, JAMES HECTOR See *Who's Who in America*, 43rd edition.

MACDONALD, JOEL BRIAN, minister, Conservative Baptist Association of America; b. Redmond, Oreg., Mar. 26, 1946; s. Fred Earl and Sheila Jean (Bowman) MacD.; m. Dorothy Eileen Carlson, Dec. 2, 1972; children: Kristin Elise, Kara Ranae. B.S. in Math., Oreg. State U., 1968; M.Div., Western Conservative Bapt. Sem., 1976. Ordained to ministry Conservative Baptist Assn. Am., 1977. Minister of evangelism and discipleship Hinson Meml. Bapt. Ch., Portland, Oreg., 1974—; bd. dirs. Christ Alongside, Bremerton, Wash., 1980—. Active in Happy Valley PTA, Oreg., 1980—. Served as lt. USN, 1968-72. Republican.

MACDONALD, JOSEPH FABER See *Who's Who in America*, 43rd edition.

MACDOUGALL, GOODWILL, minister, Presbyterian Church in Canada; b. Belle River, P.E.I., Can., Oct. 12, 1919; s. Findley John Goodwill and Margaret (MacKenzie) MacD.; m. Margaret Ross, Aug. 21, 1946; 1 child, Marilyn Anne. B.A., McGill U. (Can.), 1957, M.A., 1960, M. Sacred Theology, 1972; B.D., Presbyn. Coll. (Can.), 1960; Ph.D., Edinburgh U. (Scotland), 1964. Ordained to ministry Presbyterian Church in Canada 1960. Student minister Asbestos-Danville Congregation, Que., Can., 1955-60, minister, 1960-61; grad. student, supply minister, Scotland, 1961-64; minister Baie d'Urfe, Que., 1964-74; sec. Univ. Ministries, 1974—; sec. mission personnel, 1981—; chmn. Interfaith Com. Chaplaincy, 1981—; Fed. Correctional Services, Can., 1980-82; dir. Can. Bur. Internat. Edn., Can., 1980—; interim moderator, 1974—; lectr. McGill Faculty Div., 1973-74, Ewart Coll., Toronto, 1975-77, 1978-79. Author: History of St. Giles Church, Baie d'Urfe, Quebec, 1967; Let's Do More than Say 'Good-bye'!, 1980; Steps to Ordination to the Ministry of Word and Sacrament in the P.C.C., 1985. Presbyn. Coll. scholar, 1960. Home: 315-10 Edgecliffe Golfway Don Mills ON M3C 3A3 Canada Office: Presbyn Ch Can 50 Wynford Dr Don Mills ON M3C 1J7 Canada

MACE, WILLIAM MELVIN, JR., minister, United Meth. Ch.; b. Indpls., Jan. 9, 1935; s. William Melvin and Mary Catherine (Brandt) M.; B.S., Ind. U., 1957; M.Div., Boston U., 1960; m. Janet Marion Dean, Aug. 22, 1959; children—David Andrew, Rebecca Diane, William Bradley, Holly Michele. Ordained to ministry, 1959; pastor Hope (Ind.) United Meth. Ch., 1960-62, Southfield United Meth. Ch., Chgo., 1963-67, Community United Meth. Ch., Brookfield, Ill., 1967-71, Tinley Park (Ill.) United Meth. Ch., 1971—. Pres. Tinley Park Pastors Assn.; sec., mem. bd. ecumenical affairs, bd. missions, bd. evangelism, bd. worship and arts United Meth. Ch. Bd. dirs. S. Shore Commn., Chgo., 1963-67. Home: 17342 68th Ct Tinley Park IL 60477 Office: 6875 W 173d Pl Tinley Park IL 60477

MACHADO, GERARD ANTONIO, priest, Orthodox Church in America; b. Santa Clara, Las Villas, Cuba, Jan. 17, 1942; came to U.S., 1961; s. Gerard and Clara (Meléndez) M.; m. Kety C. Gonzalez-del-Valle, Sept. 9, 1967; children: Elizabeth, Katherine, Margaret. B.A., Hobart Coll., 1965; M.Div., Gen. Theol. Sem., 1968; M.S. in Edn., Iona Coll., 1974; Psy.D., Rutgers U., 1982. Ordained priest, 1979. Curate, Grace Ch., Newark, 1968-69; rector Trinity Ch. Bklyn., 1969-77; pastor St. Gregory Palamas Ch., Flemington, N.J., 1981—; prin. clin. psychologist, unit discipline head for transitional services Marlboro Psychiatric Hosp., N.J., 1984—; adj. prof. pastoral theology Gen. Theol. Sem., N.Y.C., 1982—; cons. Ctr. for Alcohol Studies, Rutgers U., 1984—; lectr. in field. Mem. Am. Psychol. Assn. Address: 1102 Hanover St Piscataway NJ 08854

MACK, FRANK JUNIOR, minister, Full Gospel Fellowship International; b. Leuders, Tex., May 14, 1922; s. Frank W. and Malinda Elizabeth (George) M.; m. A. Inez Pearson, June 10, 1944; 1 child, Ranelda Inez. Student Southwestern Assembly of God Bible Sch., 1942-43, Central Bible Inst., 1944-46; Th.D., Trinity So. Bible Sem., 1963, D.D. (hon.), 1963; D.D. (hon.), Belin Meml. U., 1959; D. Counseling (hon.), Mid-States Bible Coll., 1974. Pres. Christ's Ambassadors, West Tex. dist. Assembly of God, 1944-47; pastor Central Assembly of God, Lubbock, Tex., First Assembly of God, Yuma, Ariz., Christian Ctr., Fort Worth, 1966-67; pastoral counselor Fort Worth and Gadsden, Ala., 1973-80; pastor, counselor, tchr. The Lord's Ch., Bellflower, Calif., 1980—; dir. Keys for Charismatic Living Radio Ministry, Fort Worth, 1973-74; founder, pres. Upper-Room Christian Fellowship, Inc., 1961—; speaker weekly TV Counseling Corner, P.T.L. TV Network, 1974-79. Author booklets Doom's Day Weapon, Eleventh Hour Reaper, The Holy Spirit in the Life and Ministry of Jesus, The Pentecostals' Ten Commandments. Mem. Internat. Assn. Christian Clin. Counselors. Home: 619 S Orange Ave Fullerton CA 92633 Office: The Lord's Ch 9740 Flower St Bellflower CA 90706

MACK, GALE ELMER, minister, American Baptist Churches in the U.S.A.; b. Mt. Vernon, Ill., Oct. 11, 1943; s. John Marshall and Nora Belle (Riley) M.; m. Janet Kay Morgan, May 13, 1964; children: Deborah Christine, Robert Gale, Cynthia Lynn. B.M.E., Am. Conservatory Music, 1968, M.M.E., 1976; postgrad. St. Paul Sch. Theology, Kansas City, Mo., 1978; M.Min. Inter Bible Inst. and Sem., 1981, D.D. (hon.), 1982. Ordained to ministry United Methodist Church, 1976. Minister, United Meth. Ch., So. Ill., 1972-77, United Meth. Ch., Lewisburg and Stilwell, Kans., 1976-78, Kincaid 1st Bapt. Ch., Kans., 1980-82; minister Calvary Bapt. Ch., La Cygne, Kans., 1982—. Music tchr. Waltonville Sch. System, Ill., 1968-74. Named Tchr. of Yr., Egyptian High Sch., Tamms, Ill., 1977. Club: Lions (v.p. 1984) (La Cygne). Home: PO Box 520 512 N 4th St La Cygne KS 66040

MACK, JAMES WALTER, minister, Lutheran Church-Missouri Synod; b. Jolley, Iowa, Apr. 5, 1926; s. Ernest Frederick and Ida Elizabeth (Meyer) M.; m. Lois Leona Neuendorf, June 17, 1950; children: Timothy J., David P., Karen L., Rachel A. B.A., Concordia Sem., St. Louis, 1947. Ordained to ministry Lutheran Church-Missouri Synod, 1950. Pastor, Bethel Luth. Ch., Lander, Wyo., 1950-57, St. Paul's Luth. Ch., Ft. Dodge, Iowa, 1957-62, Salem Luth. Ch., Florissant, Mo., 1962-65, First Luth. Ch., Spencer, Iowa, 1965-69, St. Peter Luth. Ch., Belle Glade, Fla., 1969-72,5 St. Andrew's Luth. Ch., Hialeah, Fla., 1972-77, Holy Trinity Luth. Ch., Rome, Ga., 1977—; dist. dir. youth ministry Walther League, Ft. Dodge, Iowa, 1960-62; pastoral advisor Nat. Luth. Parent-Tchrs. League, St. Louis, 1963-67; cir. counselor Fla.-Ga. Dist. Luth. Ch. Mo. Synod, Rome, Ga., 1984—; vol. chaplain N.W. Ga. Regional Hosp., Rome, 1979-84. Author: Mission of the Family, 1964, Money in the Family, 1964, Discipline in the Family, 1964, Forgiveness in the Family, 1964, Communication in the Family, 1964, Patience in the Family, 1964, Worship in the Family, 1964. Chmn. Floyd County Citizens Rev. Panel for Juvenile Ct., Rome, 1983—. Republican. Home: 113 Echota Circle Rome GA 30161 Office: Holy Trinity Luth Ch 3000 Garden Lakes Blvd Rome GA 30161

MACK, JOSEPH C., minister, Baptist Federation of Canada; b. Murfreesboro, Tenn., Dec. 8, 1919; came to Can., 1950; s. Joe and Mary Alice (Henry) M.; m. Ollie Bell Murray, Nov. 2, 1940; children: Bobby Joe, Gerald Kennedy, Carolyn Dianne, Cheryl Lynn. B.Th., Am. Bapt. Theol. Sem., 1948; postgrad. McMaster U., 1963, Acadia Div. Coll., 1970-84; D.D. (hon.), Acadia U., 1983. Ordained to ministry Bapt. Ch. 1939. Pastor, Herricane Creek and Mt. Zion Bapt. chs., Rutherford County, Tenn., 1939-46, Mt. Zion Bapt. Ch., Tullahoma, Tenn., 1946-50, Pilgrim Bapt. Ch., Winnipeg, Man., 1950-66, First Bapt. Ch., Neepawa, Man., 1966-69, Cornwallis St. Bapt. Ch., Halifax, N.S., Can., 1969—; organizer, dir. Christian Social Action, Halifax, 1971, Age and Opportunity Sr. Citizens Activity Centre, 1972, Hot Lunch Program, 1971—; organizer, supr. Opportunities for Youth Programs, 1974-75. Organizer, co-editor, mgr. Black Symposium Choir, 1973. Decorated Order of Can. Lodges: Kiwanis, Masons, Shriners, Victoria Lodge of Perfection. Home: 6696 Chebucto Rd Halifax NS B3L 1M1 Canada

MACKAY, LINDA SCHUTT, church musician, Lutheran Church in America; music teacher; b. Wilmington, N.C., Apr. 20, 1947; d. William Louis and Gertrude Elizabeth (Daniels) Schutt; m. William Henry MacKay, Jan. 2, 1982; children: Kristin, Gary. B.A. in Music, U. N.C.-Wilmington, 1979. Cert. lay profl. musician Lutheran Church in America. Dir. music Wrightsville Beach Meth. Ch., N.C., 1971-72; Christ Episc. Ch., New Bern, N.C., 1972, St. Paul's Luth. Ch., Wilmington, 1977—; organist Pearsall Presbyn. Ch., Wilmington, 1973-76. Piano and organ tchr. Glisson Music Mart, Wilmington, 1973—. Mem. Am. Guild of Organists, Nat. Music Tchrs. Assn. (cert. 1984), N.C. Music Tchrs. Assn. (cert. 1984), Nat. Guild Piano Tchrs. (audition chmn. 1977—), Fed. of Women's Club, Thursday Morning Music Club (scholarship adjudicator). Republican. Home: 1105 Browning Dr Wilmington NC 28405 Office: St Paul's Lutheran Ch 12 N 6th St Wilmington NC 28405

MACKELLAR, JAMES MARSH, minister, Presbyterian Church (U.S.A.); b. Wilkes-Barre, Pa., June 23, 1931; s. Gordon and Anita Ferous (Cornelius) MacK.; m. A. Eugenia Orthey, Aug. 20, 1955; children: Ian James, Margaret Alice, Bruce William. B.A., Cornell U., 1952; M.Div., Princeton Theol. Sem., 1955. Ordained to ministry Presbyn. Ch., 1955. Pastor 1st Presbyn. Ch., Dryden, N.Y., 1955-59, Waverly, N.Y., 1959-65, Stirling, N.J., 1965-76; stated clk. Presbytery of Newton, N.J., 1970-75, Synod of the N.E., 1975—; pastor Forest Presbyn. Ch., Lyons Falls, N.Y., 1976-85. Mem. Nat. Assn. Parliamentarians. Home: RD 1 Box 229 Newport Center VT 05857 Office: 3049 E Genesee St Syracuse NY 13224

MACKENZIE, JAMES DONALD, minister, Presbyterian Church in the U.S.; b. Detroit, Nov. 17, 1924; s. James and Ida Catherine (Conklin) M.; m. Elsie Joan Kerr, May 7, 1960; children: Janet Eileen, Kayly Kathleen, Christy Carol, Kenneth Kerr. Student, Moody Bible Inst., Chgo., 1946-49; Union Theol. Sem., Richmond, Va., 1951-52. Ordained to ministry Presbyterian Ch. in the U.S., 1953. Pastor, Calvary Presbyn. Ch., Swan Quarter, N.C., 1952-60, Kirkwood Presbyn. Ch., Kannapolis, N.C., 1960-64, Barbecue and Olivia Presbyn. Chs., Olivia, N.C., 1964-71, Elise Presbyn. Ch., Robbins, N.C., 1971—; pres. N.C. Presbyn. Hist. Soc., 1972-74; historian Fayette Presbytery, N.C., 1975—, moderator, 1978, chmn. hist. com., 1983—. Author: Colorful Heritage, 1970. Editor Villeann Piper Jour., 1974. Contbr. articles to religious publs. Pres., Hist. Soc., Harnette County, N.C., 1968-71; founder Conf. on Scottish Studies, N.C., 1972, councillor, Can., 1968-75. Served to pfc. U.S. Army, 1943-45, ETO. Recipient Disting. Service award Harnett Hist. Soc., 1970, Disting. Citizens award Robbins Area Civic Orgn., 1983. Home and Office: Elise Presbyn Ch PO Box 867 Robbins NC 27325

MACKENZIE, ROY SHELDON, minister, religion educator, Presbyterian Church in Canada; b. New Glasgow, N.S., Can., July 26, 1930; s. Harold Sheldon and Gladys (MacKenzie) M.; m. Jenipher Isobel Butcher, July 25, 1962; children: Mark Sheldon, Clare Isobel. B.A., Acadia U., Wolfville, N.S., Can., 1955, B.D., Presbyn. Coll., Montreal, Que., Can., 1958; Ph.D., St. Andrew's U., Scotland, 1962; D.D. (hon.), Knox Coll., Toronto, Ont., Can., 1980. Ordained to ministry Presbyn. Ch. in Can., 1958. Minister, St. Paul's Ch., Eckville, Alta., Can., 1958-59, First Presbyn. Ch., Montreal, 1962-69, St. Andrew's Ch., St. John's, Nfld., Can.; prof. religious studies Meml. U., of Nfld., St. John's, 1972—; guest speaker Presbyn. Nat. Congress, 1979; moderator Presbytery of Nfld., 1979-81; mem. senate Meml. U. of Nfld., 1984—. Contbr. articles and book revs. to religious publs. Served to capt. USAFR, 1951-62. Recipient Ind. Order Daus. of Empire travelling fellowship Presbyn. Coll., Montreal, 1958; Can. Council Leave fellowship, 1981; D.M. Baillie scholarship, St. Mary's Coll., Scotland, 1959, 60. Mem. Can. Bible Soc., Soc. Bibl. Studies. Home: 95 Logy Bay Rd St Johns NF A1A 1J5 Canada Office: Meml Univ Nfld Elizabeth Ave St Johns NF A1C 5S7 Canada

MACKEY, JEFFREY ALLEN, minister, Christian and Missionary Alliance; b. Kingston, N.Y., July 12, 1952; s. Allen William and Vivian Mathilda (Hornbeck) M.; m. Martha LaVonne Webster, Dec. 18, 1971; children: Guy Linwood, Kenyon Paul, Geoffrey Joel. B.S., Nyack Coll., 1974; M. Ministry, Trinity Grad. Sch., 1976; D. Ministry, Mansfield Div. Sch. (London), 1982, D. Sci. of Theology, 1982; D. Sacred Lit. (hon.), Ridgedale Theol. Sem., 1976. Ordained to ministry Christian and Missionary Alliance, 1974. Pastor Ponckhockie Cong. Ch., Kingston, N.Y., 1971-74, Christian and Missionary Alliance Ch., Andover, N.Y., 1974-76; acad. dean Macon Bible Inst., Ga., 1976-78; sr. minister Oak Grove Gospel Tabernacle, Williamsport, Pa., 1977-80, 69th St. Alliance Ch., Phila., 1980-83, Vestavia Alliance Ch., Birmingham, Ala., 1983—; dir. Christian edn. So. Dist. Christian and Missionary Alliance, Birmingham, 1984—; adv. bd. Ravi Zacharias Internat. Ministries, Atlanta, 1985—. Author, pub. monthly newsletter 1983—. Contbr. articles to profl. jours. Mem. Am. Assn. Christian Schs., Evang. Tchr. Tng. Assn., Ala. Christian Edn. Assn., Epsilon Delta Chi. Republican. Avocations: organist; pianist; conductor; song writer; book and art collector. Home: 2424 Rocky Ridge Rd Birmingham AL 35243 Office: Vestavia Alliance Ch 1285 Montgomery Hwy Birmingham AL 35216

MACKIE, ARTHUR JAMES, ret. priest, Episc. Ch.; b. Renovo, Pa., June 1, 1896; s. Robert Alexander and Katherine Elizabeth (Bissett) M.; B.A., Pa. State U., 1920; B.A., Va. Theol. Sem., 1923; m. Mabel Helen McConnell, Mar. 20, 1924; children—Arthur James, Edward Alexander, Mabel Helen, Thomas McConell, William Vigourd. Ordained priest, 1923; rector All Saints Ch., Guantanamo, Cuba, 1923-24, St. Thomas Ch., Windsor, N.C., 1923-35, St. James Ch. including missions in Yeatesville and Sladesville, Belhaven, N.C., 1935-56, Christ Ch. including mission in Columbia, Creswell, N.C., 1956-64; ret., 1964; supply priest St. John Evangelist Ch., Edenton, N.C., 1968—. Chaplain, Am. Legion; mem. Provincial Bd. Missions; bd. mgrs. Thompson Orphanage. Recipient numerous awards for working with boys in scouting, clubs and baseball. Home: 107 E Carroll St Windsor NC 27983

MACKIN, KEVIN E., clergyman, seminary administrator, Roman Catholic. Pres., rector Christ the King Sem., East Aurora, N.Y. Office: Christ the King Sem 711 Knox Rd PO Box 160 East Aurora NY 14052*

MACKINNON, DONALD BURR, priest, Roman Catholic Church; b. San Diego, Jan. 20, 1934; s. Burr Marshall and Marie Elizabeth (O'Keefe) MacK. B.Div., Redemptorist Sem., 1960; M.A., Catholic U., 1961; postgrad., Fordham U., 1968; D.Min., Jesuit Sch. Theology, 1978. Ordained priest Roman Catholic Ch., 1959. Instr. Holy Redeemer Coll., Oakland, Calif., 1961-64; missionary Redemptorists, Livermore, Calif., 1964-65; chaplain Hosp. Joint Diseases, N.Y.C., 1966-68; pastor Our Lady of Lourdes, San Francisco, 1968-80; supr., dir. Center Parish Missions, Oakland, 1980—; bd. dirs. Council Civic Unity, San Francisco, 1970—, Conf. Race, Religion, Social Concern, San Francisco, 1970—, Council of Chs., San Francisco, 1974, Calif. Coalition Against Death Penalty, 1975—, Redemptorist Overseas Missions, 1978—, North Calif. Social Justice Coordinators, San Francisco, 1979—, Elmhurst Community Bd., Oakland, 1981—; coordinator Black Catholic Apostolate, San Francisco, 1977. Contbr. articles to profl. jours. Founding pres. Bayview/Hunters Point Coll., San Francisco, 1968; mem. Bayview/Hunters Point Coordinating Council, 1968-75. Recipient St. Thomas More award Univ. San Francisco, 1975, Liberty Bell award San Francisco Bar Assn., 1975, San Francisco Found. award, 1978, resolution Calif. State Assembly, 1975. Mem. Priests' Senate, Redemptorist Provincial Chpt. Home: 8945 Golf Links Rd Oakland CA 94605 Office: Redemptorist Center for Parish Missions 8945 Golf Links Rd Oakland CA 94605

MACKINTOSH, DONALD, minister, Seventh-day Adventist. b. Monte Vista, Colo., Dec. 25, 1902; s. Malcolm and May (Rathbun) M.; m. Helen Louise Metcalf, Dec. 25, 1924; 1 son, Donald Charles. Pre-med. cert. Oshowa Missionary Coll. and Toronto U., 1924. Ordained to ministry Seventh-day Adventists, 1931. Minister, Ontario, Can., Newfoundland, Maritime Conf., 1931-40, Alta. Conf., 1940-45; pastor, Kans. and Okla., 1945-51, Balt., 1951-54, Mpls., 1954-55, Holly, Mich., 1955-61, College Place, Wash., 1968—. Author: Tongues Are For Real (Gen. Conf. Book Com. award 1978), 1973. Mem. Ret. Clergy of Seventh-day Adventist Ch. Republican. Home and Office: 35 Tremont Dr PO Box 36 College Place WA 99324

MACKY, PETER WALLACE, religion educator, Presbyterian Church in the U.S.; b. Auckland, N.Z., July 22, 1937; came to U.S., 1939; s. Wallace Armstrong and Mary Maclean (Whitfield) M.; m. Nancy Ann Space, Sept. 9, 1961; children: Cameron, Christopher. A.B., Harvard U., 1957; B.A., Oxford U., Eng., 1962, M.A., 1966, D.Phil., 1967; B.D., Princeton Sem., 1963, Th.D., 1970. Ordained to ministry, 1967. Asst. minister Pacific Palisades Presbyn. Ch., Calif., 1967-70; asst. prof. Westminster Coll., New Wilmington, Pa., 1970-74, assoc. prof., 1974-83, prof. religion, 1983—, chmn. dept. religion and philosophy, 1983—. Author: The Bible in Dialogue with Modern Man, 1970; Violence: Right or Wrong:, 1973; The Pursuit of the Divine Snowman, 1977. Contbr. articles to profl. jours. Rhodes scholar, 1960; Rockefeller fellow, 1965. Home: RD 1 Susan Trace New Wilmington PA 16142 Office: Westminster Coll New Wilmington PA 16172

MACLEAN, CHARLES WALDO, bishop, Episcopal Church; b. Lincoln, N.H., June 28, 1903; s. Howard Douglas and Ethel (Holmes) MacL.; B.A., St. Stephens Coll., 1925; S.T.D., Gen. Theol. Sem., 1928; D.D., Bard Coll., 1962; m. Paula Feathergill, Jan. 16, 1981; children: Peter Duncan, Judith Ann (Mrs. George Curtis Webber). Ordained priest Episcopal Ch., 1928, bishop, 1962; curate Ch. of Epiphany, N.Y.C., 1928-30; vicar St. John's Chapel, Dunton, L.I., 1930-32; rector Grace Ch., Riverhead, L.I., 1933-49; archdeacon Suffolk Diocese L.I., 1942-50; hon. canon Cathedral of Incarnation, Garden City, L.I., 1947; adminstr. Diocese of L.I., 1950-62, also asst. treas., trustee estate belonging to Diocese of L.I.; suffragan bishop of L.I., 1962-76. Sub-prelate, chaplain Order St. John of Jerusalem, 1972—; dir. diocesan dept. promotion; treas., v.p. George Mercer Jr. Meml. Sch. Theology; exec. adminstr. Mercer scholarship fund. Pres. Suffolk County Social Agys., 1937-43; pres. Suffolk Central Hosp., 1944-50; dir. Episcopal Charities, 1951—. Pres. Anglican Found.; trustee ch. army Am. Ch. Bldg. Fund. Mem. St. Andrews Soc. N.Y., New Eng. Soc. N.Y. Clubs: Brooklyn; Garden City Golf. Home: 191 Kensington Rd Garden City NY 11530 Office: 65 4th St Garden City NY 11530

MACLEAN, DONALD ISIDORE See *Who's Who in America*, 43rd edition.

MACLEOD, DONALD, minister, educator, United Presbyn. Ch. U.S.A.; b. Broughton, N.S., Can., Dec. 31, 1913; s. Donald Archibald and Anne (MacKenzie) M.; A.B., Dalhousie U. (Can.), 1934, M.A., 1935; B.D. (E.F. Grant scholar), Pine Hill Div. Hall (Can.), 1938, D.D., 1970; Th.D., U. Toronto, 1947; m. Norma Harper, Jan. 5, 1948 (dec. Mar. 1972); children—Fraser, David, Anne, Leslie. Ordained to ministry, 1938; minister 1st Ch., Louisburg, N.S., 1938-41; asso. minister Bloor St. Ch., Toronto, 1941-45; sr. tutor Victoria Coll., Toronto, 1943-45; teaching fellow Princeton Theol. Sem., 1946-47, asst. prof. homiletics, 1947-53, asso. prof., 1953-61, prof. preaching and worship, 1961—; chaplain's seminars U.S. Air Force, 1967-68; Oliver lectr. Nazarene Theol. Sem., 1984. Recipient Christian Research Found. award, 1967, George Washington Honor medal Freedoms Found. Valley Forge, 1973. Am. Assn. Theol. Schs. fellow, 1958-59. Mem. Ch. Service Soc. (v.p., mem. council) Am. Acad. Homiletics (founder, 1st pres.), Am. Assn. Profs. in Practical Fields (exec. council), Speech Assn. Am., Hymn Soc. Am. Author: Here Is My Method, 1952, Word and Sacrament, 1961, Presbyterian Worship, 1965, Dynamics of Worship, 1967, Higher Reaches, 1971, Proclamation (Series A), 1975, also articles. Home: 48 Mercer St Princeton NJ 08540 Office: Princeton Theol Sem Princeton NJ 08540

MACLEOD, JOHN DANIEL, JR., minister, church official Presbyterian Church in the U.S.; b. Robbins, N.C., Mar. 16, 1922; s. John Daniel and Sarah Cranor (McKay) MacL.; m. Helen Frances Boggs, Sept. 18, 1945; children: Sarah Martha, Mary Marget, John Daniel, III, William Boggs. Student Pfeiffer Coll., 1938-40; A.B., Davidson Coll., 1942; M.Divinity, Union Theol. Seminary, 1945, Th.M., 1949, Th.D., 1952. Ordained to ministry Presbyterian Ch., 1945. Pastor Carolina Beach Presbyn. Ch., N.C., 1945-48, Brett-Reed Presbyn. Ch., Sweet Hall, Va., 1949-53, Keyser Presbyn. Ch., W.Va., 1953-63; exec. sec. Appomattox Presbytery, Lynchburg, Va., 1963-67, Norfolk Presbytery, Va., 1967-76, Westminster Presbytery, St. Petersburg, Fla., 1976-81; exec. Presbyn. Synod of N.C., Raleigh, 1981—; moderator Presbyn. Synod of Va., Richmond, 1967; mem. program resourcing council Presbyn. Ch., Atlanta, N.Y.C., 1981—; bd. visitors Davidson Coll., N.C., 1981—; adv. trustee Queens Coll., Charlotte, N.C., 1982—; mem. ch. council Montreat-Anderson Coll., Montreat, N.C., 1982—. Editor: Presbyterian News, 1981. Trustee Warren Wilson Coll., Swannanoa, N.C.; mem. Govs. Adv. Council Citizen Affairs, Raleigh, N.C., 1982-85. Moses D. Hoge fellow Union Theol. Seminary Va., 1945. Democrat. Mem. St. Andrews Soc. Fla. (bd. dirs. 1979-81), St. Andrews Soc. N.C., Clan MacLeod Soc. U.S.A. (regional coordinator 1977-81). Home: 809 Davidson St Raleigh NC 27619 Office: Presbyn Synod of North Carolina 1015 Wade Ave Raleigh NC 27605

MACLIN, HARRY TRACY, JR., minister, United Methodist Church; b. Oklahoma City, Nov. 27, 1925; s. Harry Tracy and Winnie Grace (Nelson) M.; B.A., So. Meth. U., 1949, Th.M., 1952; certificat de L'Enseignement, Ecole Colonial, Brussells, 1954; m. Alice Marie Nystrom, Aug. 30, 1947; children: Susan Carol, Catherine Marie, Gregory Paul, Ruth Ellen. Ordained to ministry, 1953; asso. pastor, youth dir. Lakewood Meth. Ch., Dallas, 1950-52; dir. tchr. tng. inst. Central Zaire Ann. Conf., Lodja, 1954-59, founder, dir. Central Zaire Ann. Conf. Sch. for Christian Lay Workers, Lodja, 1955-59, dist. missionary, dir. rural schs. Lodja/Lomela dists. Central Zaire Ann. Conf., 1957-59; asso. prof. Kayeka-Kimbulu Sch. Theol. So. Zaire Ann. Conf., Mulungwishi, 1959-60; dir. broadcasting and audio visual services All Africa Conf. Chs., Nairobi, Kenya, 1962-71; founder/dir. All Africa Christian Communications Inst., Nairobi, 1964-70; liason officer Radio Voice of the Gospel, Addis Ababa, Ethiopia, 1962-71; program counselor Southeastern Jurisdictional Council on Ministries, United Meth. Chs., Atlanta, 1972-74; dir. joint communications com. United Meth. Ch., Atlanta, 1972-74; field rep. for cultivation, div. edn. and cultivation Bd. Global Ministries, Southeastern jurisdiction, United Meth. Ch., Atlanta, 1974-84; pres. Mission for United Methodists, Atlanta, 1984—. Mem. Dept. church-related communications World Assn. for Christian Communication, mem. central com., 1968-71; vis. lectr. Internat. Inst. Christian Communication, Salisbury, Rhodesia, 1971, Chandler Sch. Theology, Emory U., 1974-75. Mem. Nat. Religious Broadcasters. Recipient Knight Grand Comdr. of the Humane Order of African Redemption, Republic Liberia, 1964; Contbr. articles to religious jours. Home: 556 Winley Dr Stone Mountain GA 30083 Office: 159 Forrest Ave NE Atlanta GA 30308

MACNAIR, DONALD J., minister, church growth consultant, Presbyterian Church in America; b. Union City, N.J., June 28, 1922; s. Roy Edwin and Gertrude (Heitmann) MacN.; m. Evelyn MacNair, July 22, 1944; children: Bruce, Miriam, Gregory, Marjory. B.S., Rutgers U., 1944; B.Div., Faith Theol. Sem., 1949; D.D. (hon.), Geneva Coll., 1982. Ordained to ministry, 1947. Pastor, Coatesville Bible Ch., Pa., 1947-53; Covenant Presbyn. Ch., St. Louis, 1953-64; exec. dir. Nat. Presbyn. Mission, St. Louis, 1964-82; adj. prof. Covenant Theol. Sch., St. Louis, 1978—; pres. Churches Vitalized, Inc., St. Louis, 1983—; coordinator theol. edn. Christian Edn. and Pub., Decatur, Ga., 1984—; chmn. fraternal relations com. Reformed Presbyn. Ch. Evang. Synod, St. Louis, 1978-82. Author: Birth Care and Feeding of a Local Church, 1971; The Growing Local Church, 1975; The Living Church, 1980; The Challenge of Eldership, 1984. Bd. dirs. Friendship Villages, West County/South County, St. Louis, 1974—, Life Care Retirement Communities, Des Moines, 1978—. Republican. Home: 480 Brightspur Ln Ballwin MO 63011 Office: Churches Vitalized Inc 480 Brightspur Ln Ballwin MO 63011

MACNAUGHTON, DAVID NEIL, minister, United Church of Canada; b. Glace Bay, N.S., Can., Jan. 28, 1935; s. Alexander John and Dorthy (MacPherson) MacN.; m. Nancy Munro, Sept. 20, 1958; children: David Scott, Munro, John Alexander, Peter Neil. B.A., Mt. Allison U., Sackville, N.B., Can., 1956; M.Div., Pine Hill Div. Hall, Halifax, N.S., Can., 1958, postgrad., 1968-70, Princeton Theol. Sem., 1979, 81. Ordained to ministry United Ch. Can., 1958. Pastor, Escuminac Pastoral Charge, Gaspe Coast, Que., Can., 1959-60; assoc. minister St. Andrews United Ch., Halifax, 1960-66; minister Lunenburg Pastoral Charge, Lunenberg, N.S., 1966-74; srt minister First United Ch., Truro, N.S., 1974—; dir. Pine Hill Div. Hall, Halifax, 1983—; leader Action Cluster Chs. Mission Program, Truron, 1983—. Contbr. articles to profl. jours. Bd. dirs. Jobs Unlimited, Truro, Can., 1984—, Colchester Boy Scouts Orgn.; chaplain Truro Fire Dept., 1974—, Truro Air Cadet Squadron, 1977—; mem. Maritime Conf. Task Force Human Rights, Halifax, 1984—. Served with Royal Can. Navy, 1962-64. Travelling fellow Second Mile Soc., 1984. Lodges: Masons, Scottish Rite, Rotary. Home: 170 Pleasant St Truro NS B2N 3S6 Canada

MACNEIL, JOSEPH NEIL, archbishop, Roman Catholic Ch.; b. Sydney, N.S., Can., Apr. 15, 1924; s. John Martin and Kate (MacLean) MacN.; B.A., St. Francis Xavier U., Antigonish, N.S., 1944; postgrad. Holy Heart Sem., Halifax, N.S., 1944-48, U. Perugia, 1956, U. Chgo., 1964; J.C.D., U. St. Thomas, Rome, 1958. Ordained priest Roman Catholic Ch., 1948; pastor parishes N.S., 1948-55; officialis Chancery Office, Antigonish, N.S., 1958-59; adminstrn. Diocese of Antigonish, 1959-60; rector Cathedral Antigonish, 1961; dir. extension dept. St. Francis Xavier U., Antigonish, 1961-69, v.p., 1962-69; bishop, St. John, N.B., Can., 1969-74; archbishop of Edmonton (Alta.), 1974—. Vice chmn. N.S. Voluntary Econ. Planning Bd., 1965-69; exec. Atlantic Provinces Econ. Council, 1968-73, Canadian Council Rural Devel., 1965-75; dir. Program and Planning Agy. N.S. Govt., 1969. Chancellor U. St. Thomas, Fredericton, N.B., from 1969. Mem. Canadian Assn. Adult Edn. (past pres. N.S.), Canadian Assn. Dirs. U. Extension and Summer Schs. (past pres.), Inst. Research on Pub. Policy (founding), Can. Conf. Cath. Bishops (pres. 1979-81). Address: 10044 113th St Edmonton AB T5K 1N8 Canada

MACRAE, ANDREW DONALD, theology educator; Atlantic Baptist Convention; b. Edinburgh, Scotland, Jan. 3, 1933; s. James and Harriet (Munro) M.; m. Jean Alison Findlay, June 15, 1957; children: Findlay, Fiona. M.A., Edinburgh U., 1954; B.D., New College, Edinburgh, 1957; Ph.D., St. Andrews U., Scotland, 1984; D.D. (hon.), Campbellsville Coll., 1979. Ordained to ministry Bapt. Union of Scotland, 1957. Minister Larbert Bapt. Ch., Stirlingshire, Scotland, 1957-61, Ward Rd. Bapt. Ch., Dundee, Scotland, 1961-66; gen. sec. and supt. Bapt. Union of Scotland, Glasgow, 1966-80; prof. evangelism and missions Acadia Div. Coll., Wolfville, N.S., Can., 1980—, prin., 1985—, dean theology, 1985—; pres. European Bapt. Fedn., 1970-72; chmn. Christian edn. Bapt. World Alliance, Washington, 1970-75; religious advisor BBC Scotland, Glasgow, Scottish TV, Ltd., 1968-80; J. Clyde Turner prof. preaching So. Bapt. Sem., Louisville, 1976; Broady lectr. Swedish Bapt. Sem., Stockholm, 1979; J. Willox Duncan lectr. Regent-Carey Coll., 1980. Author: Christian Baptism, 1967; Listen To Jesus, 1975; God Within Us, 1975; Your Church Must Choose, 1982. Contbr. articles to religious jours., manuals and monographs. Mem. Soc. Advancement Continuing Edn. for Ministry, Assn. Theol. Field Edn. Home: Box 1426 52 Kent Ave Wolfville NS B0P 1X0 Canada Office: Acadia Divinity Coll Wolfville NS B0P 1X0 Canada

MACRAE, GEORGE WINSOR, educator, priest, Roman Catholic Ch.; b. Lynn, Mass., July 27, 1928; s. George Roy and Katherine (MacDonald) MacR.; B.A., Boston Coll., 1953; M.A., Johns Hopkins, 1957; S.T.L., Weston Coll., 1961; Ph.D., Cambridge U., 1966. Joined Soc. Jesus, 1948, ordained priest Roman Catholic Ch., 1960; instr. Fairfield (Conn.) Coll. Prep. Sch., 1954-56; prof. N.T., Weston Coll., Cambridge, Mass., 1965-73; vis. prof. Harvard Div. Sch., Cambridge, 1968-69, Stillman prof. Roman Catholic studies, 1973—; rector Ecumenical Inst. for Theol. Research, Tantur, Jerusalem, 1979-80. Trustee Fordham U., 1968-71, Coll. Holy Cross, 1978—. Fellow Am. Council Learned Socs.; mem. Soc. Bibl. Lit. (exec. sec. 1973-76), Council on Study Religion (chmn. 1977-82), Internat. Soc. N.T. Studies (mem. editorial bd. 1973—); Mass. Bible Soc. (trustee 1977—). Editor N.T. Abstracts, 1967-72; editorial bd. Hermeneia, 1970—. Contbr. articles to profl. jours.; editor, contbr. to books in field. Office: Harvard Div Sch Cambridge MA 02138

MADDEN, LORETTO ANNE, nun, administrator, Roman Catholic Church; b. Denver, Aug. 21, 1922; d. Edward Joseph and Mary Agnes (Kelly) Madden. A.B., Loretto Hts. Coll., 1943; M.A., Cath. U. Am., 1955, Ph.D., 1960. Joined Sisters of Loretto, Roman Catholic Ch., 1946. Tchr., Immaculate Conception High Sch., Las Vegas, N.Mex., 1946-54; instr. to prof. Loretto Hts. Coll., Denver, 1954-73; exec. dir. Colo. Cath. Conf., Denver, 1974—; mem. com. on legislation for social justice Nat. Conf. Cath. Charities, Washington, 1976—; mem. communications com. U.S. Cath. Conf., Washington, 1978-81; columnist polit. commentary Denver Cath. Register, "Capitol Comment", 1974-82. Chmn., Colo. Social Legislation Com., Denver, 1974-80, vice chmn. programs, 1982-83, legis. liaison, 1984. Bonfils scholar Denver Post, 1939; J.K. Mullen scholar, 1955; recipient St. Vincent dePaul award St. Thomas Theol. Sem., 1982. Mem. Personal Care/Boarding Home Coalition (co-chmn.). Home: 1075 Corona St #311 Denver CO 80218 Office: Colo Cath Conf 200 Josephine St Denver CO 80206

MADDOX, LARRY G., minister, Southern Baptist Convention; b. Centertown, Ky., July 11, 1934; s. Joseph Glenn and Fleeta (Faught) M.; m. Betty Roeder, Aug. 16, 1952; children: Perijo, Joi, Shari, Joseph, Juli, James. A.B. with honors, Samford U., 1956; B.D., Southern Bapt. Seminary, 1959, M. Divinity, 1974; D. Ministry, Midwestern Bapt. Seminary, 1978. Ordained to ministry Bapt. Ch., 1952. Pastor Parrish Ave. Bapt. Ch., Owensboro, Ky., 1956-64, Reidland Bapt. Ch., Paducah, Ky., 1964-68, Maywood Bapt. Ch., Independence, Mo., 1968-78, Second Bapt. Ch., Little Rock, 1978-83; assoc. minister First Bapt. Ch., Longview, Tex., 1983—; adj. prof. Midwestern Bapt. Seminary, Kansas City, Mo., 1981—, Boyce Bible Center, Little Rock, 1981-83; mem. Christian Life Commn., So. Bapt. Conv. Missouri, 1971-78, mem. credentials com., 1977, chmn. registration com., 1978; trustee Southwest Bapt. Univ., Mo. Bapt. Conv., Bolivar, Mo., 1978—; founder, pres. Lord's Day Alliance Arkansas, Little Rock, 1981-83. Author: God's Laws for Man, 1973; author sermon series Proclaim, 1982; contbg. author book The Power of the Word, 1981; contbr. numerous articles to various publs. Chmn. Fair Housing Commn., Independence, 1970-74, Human Relations Commn., Independence, 1972-78; trustee Meml. Bapt. Hosp., Kansas City, Mo., 1978. Lodge: Rotary. Home: 1814 Northwood Ct Longview TX 75604 Office: First Bapt Ch 209 E South St Longview TX 75601

MADDOX, RANDY LYNN, religious educator, Church of the Nazarene; b. Jerome, Idaho, Sept. 3, 1953; s. Thane Eugene and Velma Lou (Lewis) M.; m. Aileen Francis Chadwick, May 24, 1975; children: Erin, Jared. B.A. in Religion, Northwest Nazarene Coll., 1975; M.Div., Nazarene Theol. Sem., 1978; Ph.D., Emory U., 1982. Ordained to ministry Ch. of Nazarene. Lectr. in Bible, Nazarene Sem., Kansas City, Mo., 1976-79; adj. faculty Luther-Northwestern Sem., St. Paul, 1983—; asst. prof. religion Sioux Falls Coll., S.D., 1982—; trustee Ch. of Nazarene, Sioux Falls, 1983—; lectr. Shalom Ctr., 1983—. Author: Toward an Ecumenical Fundamental Theology, 1984. Contbr. articles to profl. jours. Mem. Wesley Theology Soc., Am. Acad. Religion. Home: Glidden Hall Sioux Falls Coll Sioux Falls SD 57105 Office: Sioux Falls Coll 1501 S Prairie Sioux Falls SD 57105

MADDOX, ROBERT LEE, JR., minister, religious organization executive, Southern Baptist Convention; b. Atlanta, Apr. 14, 1937; s. Robert Lee and Virginia (Causey) M.; m. Linda Elaine Cook, June 14, 1959; children: Andrew, Benjamin, Elizabeth. B.A., Baylor U., 1959; B.D., Southwest Bapt. Theol. Sem., Ft. Worth, 1963; D.S.T., Emory U., 1975; LL.D. (hon.), Southwest Bapt. U., Bolivar, Mo., 1980. Ordained to ministry So. Bapt. Conv., 1962. Youth minister 1st Bapt. Ch., Arlington, Tex., 1960-63; asst. pastor North Jacksonville Bible Ch. Fla., 1963-64; pastor 1st Bapt. Ch., Vienna, Ga., 1964-68, Calhoun, Ga., 1971-79, Mayfield Rd. Bapt. Ch., Arlington, Tex., 1983-84; assoc. pastor Druid Hills Bible Ch., Atlanta, 1968-71; religious liaison White House, Washington, 1979-81; exec. dir. Ams. United for Separation of Ch. and State, Silver Spring, Md., 1984—; trustee Mercy Corp. Internat., Seattle, 1983. Mem. White House staff Carter Adminstrn., Washington, 1979-81. Author: Preacher at the White House, 1984; also Bible Study books. Recipient Presdl. citation White House Conf. on Families, 1980. Mem. Arlington Initiative, Soc. Assn. Execs. Democrat. Office: Ams United for Separation of Ch and State 8120 Fenton St Silver Spring MD 20910

MADERA, JOSEPH J. See *Who's Who in America,* 43rd edition.

MAES, JOHN L., theology educator, United Church of Christ; psychology educator; b. Watertown, Mich., Aug. 6, 1923; s. John and Mary (Cornwell) M.; m. Mary J. Johnson, Aug. 28, 1942; 1 son, John David. B.Theol., Owosso Coll., 1948; A.B., Mich. State U., 1954; M.A.,

1957, Ph.D., 1963. Ordained to ministry United Methodist Ch., 1963, United Ch. Christ, 1976; lic. psychologist, Mass., N.H.; lic. pastoral counselor, N.H. Assoc. prof. Sch. Theology Boston U., 1963-72, prof., 1972-82, adj. prof., 1982—, exec. dir., Danielsen Inst., Boston U., 1982—, bd. govs., 1967—; pastor Community Ch., Houghton Lake, Mich., 1948-52, Framestown Community Ch. (N.H.), 1977-80; cons. Monadnock Area Pastoral Counseling Service, 1973-81. Dean acad. affairs Franklin Pierce Coll., 1972-75; pvt. practice psychotherapy, 1975-82; cons. Contbr. articles to profl. jours. Mem. Am. Assn. Pastoral Counselors (diplomate; bd. govs. 1966-71, chmn. centers and tng. com. 1967-71), Am. Psychol. Assn. Democrat. Home: 75 Bay State Rd Boston MA 02215 Office: Danielsen Inst 185 Bay State Rd Boston U Boston MA 02215

MAESEN, WILLIAM AUGUST, church program consultant; state psychiatric institute official; b. Albertson, N.Y., May 18, 1939; s. August Peterus and Wilhelmina (Gaska) M.; m. Sherry Lee Jaeger, Aug. 13, 1971 (div. Jan. 11, 1985); children: Ryan and Betsy (twins), Steven. B.A., Oklahoma City U., 1961, B.S.B., 1961; M.A., Ind. State U., 1968; Ph.D. in Social Work, U. Ill.-Chgo., 1979; postgrad. Mich. State U., 1980-81, Seabury-Western Theol. Sem., 1984—. Cert. social worker, Ill. Chmn. dept. Christian social relations, Diocese of Western Mich., Kalamazoo, 1979-81, mem. bishop's council, 1979-81; program cons., fund raiser Villa Maria, Grand Rapids, Mich., 1980-82; dir. residential care Cathedral Shelter, Chgo., 1981-83; vestryman, seminarian, Christ Ch., Joliet, Ill., 1982—; chmn. adv. council RSVP, Cath. Charities, Joliet, 1983—; mem. coadjutor caucus, diocese of Chgo., 1984—. Admissions examiner Ill. State Psychiat. Inst., Chgo., 1984—. Contbr. articles, revs. various jours. City editor Czech. Daily Herald, Berwyn, Ill., 1984; mem. exec. council Captive Nations Council, Chgo., 1984. Served chaplain services, USAFR, 1962-68. Fellow Nat. Assn. Social Workers; mem. Clin. Sociology Assn. (exec. bd. 1978-82, founding editor Clin. Sociology Rev.), ABA, Community Devel. Soc. (jour. and editorial com. 1976-80), Beta Gamma, Alpha Kappa Delta. Club: Lupus Erythematosa Soc. Ill. Home: PO Box 4380 Chicago IL 60680 Office: Ill State Psychiatric Inst 1601 W Taylor Chicago IL 60612

MAGARY, DENNIS ROBERT, religious educator, minister, Missionary Church; b. Peoria, Ill., June 19, 1951; s. George Robert and Marian Louise (Anderson) M.; m. Pamela Kay Miller, Aug. 25, 1973; children: Adam James, Brooke Elizabeth. B.A. cum laude, Ft. Wayne Bible Coll., 1973; M.Div. magna cum laude, Trinity Evang. Div. Sch., 1977, postgrad. 1977—; M.A., U. Wis.-Madison, 1983, postgrad. 1983—. Ordained to ministry Missionary Ch., 1985. Asst. pastor Indian Lakes Community Ch., Bloomingdale, Ill., 1975-77; vis. instr. Old Testament and Semitic langs. Trinity Evang. Div. Sch., Deerfield, Ill., 1979-84; instr. Bible, Trinity Coll., Deerfield, 1978-84; teaching asst. Bibl. Hebrew, U. Wis., Madison, 1981-84; instr. Bible, Bethel Coll., Mishawaka, Ind., 1982; instr. Old Testament, Inst. Christian Studies, Madison, 1983-84; instr. Old Testament and Semitic langs. Trinity Evang. Div. Sch. Deerfield, 1984—. Recipient Excellence in Teaching award U. Wis., Madison, 1983. Mem. Evang. Theol. Soc., Soc. Bibl. Lit., Nat. Assn. Profs. of Hebrew in Insts. of Higher Learning, Evang. Tchr. Tng. Assn., Delta Epsilon Chi. Home: 405 Westmoreland Dr Vernon Hills IL 60061 Office: Trinity Evang Div Sch 2065 Half Day Rd Deerfield IL 60015

MAGEE, PHILIP RODGERS, minister, Presbyterian Church (U.S.A.); b. Seattle, Nov. 14, 1926; s. William Officer and Lina Etta (Treglown) M.; B.A., U. Mont., 1949; M.Div., Princeton Theol. Sem., 1952; m. Dorothy Fuchs, June 29, 1963. Ordained to ministry, 1952; pastor chs. in Pa. and N.Y., 1952-63; minister First Presbyn. Ch., Balt., 1963-72, First Presbyn. Ch., Plymouth, Mich., 1972—; chapel preacher colls. A founder, past pres. Balt. Central Chs. Trustee W. Nottingham (Md.) Acad. Mem. Theta Chi. Author: Several Sermons and a Few Prayers, 1977; also articles. Home: 1029 Roosevelt St Plymouth MI 48170 Office: 701 Church St Plymouth MI 48170

MAGEE, THOMAS ESTON, JR., minister, United Pentecostal Church International; b. DeRidder, La., Aug. 9, 1947; s. Thomas Eston and Doris Maxine (Gallion) M., Sr.; m. Linda Ruth Lewis, Nov. 9, 1967. Student Mc Neese State U., 1966-69; Th.B., Tex. Bible Coll., 1972. Ordained United Pentecostal Ch., 1973. Asst. pastor United Pentecostal Ch., Pasadena, Tex., 1969-72; instr. Tex. Bible Coll., Houston, 1970-72, dean of women, 1970-71; evangelist United Pentecostal Ch., throughout U.S., 1972-77; pastor First United Pentecostal Ch., Ragley, La., 1977—; sect. youth dir. La. Dist. United Pentecostal Ch., Ragley, 1979-83. Named col. La. Gov., 1975. Democrat. Home: Route 1 Box 90-A Longville LA 70652 Office: First United Pentecostal Ch PO Box 44 Ragley LA 70657

MAGGAL, MOSHE MORRIS, rabbi, educator, writer; b. Nagyecsed, Hungary, Mar. 16, 1908; came to U.S., 1950; s. David and Ester (Fulop) Gelberman; m. Rachel Delia Diamond, July 8, 1951; children: Davida Elizabeth DeMonte, Michelle Judith, Elana Ilene. Grad. Nat. Rabbinical Sem., Budapest, Hungary, 1934; postgrad. U. Zurich, 1935, Hebrew U., Jerusalem, Israel, 1936; Ph.D. (hon.), Ben Franklin Acad. Inst. Advanced Studies, 1979. Ordained rabbi, 1934. Rabbi, Temple Meyer-David, Claremont, N.H., 1951-52, Temple Beth Aaron, Billings, Mont., 1952-54, Alhambra Jewish Ct., Calif., 1955-57, Temple Beth Kodesh, Canoga Park, Calif., 1959-61, Congregation Ahavath Israel, Hollywood, Calif., 1966-73, Congregation B'nai Emunah, Burbank, Calif., 1982—; founder, pres. Nat. Jewish Info. Service, Los Angeles, 1960—. Author: Acres of Happiness, 1967; The Secret of Israel's Victories—Past, Present and Future, 1982. Editor: (newspaper) The Voice of Judaism, 1960—. Contbr. articles to mags., newspapers and profl. jours. Mem. Los Angeles World Affairs Council and Internat. Visitors Program, Los Angeles-Eilat (Israel) Sister City Com. (Mayor's citation for Sister-City People-to-People Program); state chmn. Spirit of '76 Found.; state advisor U.S. Congressional Adv. Bd., Calif.; pres. Beverly Hills dist. Zionist Orgn. Am., 1973-76, exec. v.p. So. Pacific Region, 1973—. Served with Israel Def. Army, 1948-49. Recipient citation Crusade for Freedom, 1952; Spirtual Mobilization Nat. Sermon Contest award, 1952; named hon. sheriff Yellowstone County, Mont., 1954; Ben Franklin Soc. fellow, 1984. Democrat. Clubs: Greater Los Angeles Press, Town Hall of Calif. (Los Angeles).

MAGI, EDUARD, minister, editor, Seventh-day Adventists; b. Tartu, Estonia, Sept. 6, 1897; s. Hendrik and Kadri (Josep) M.; came to U.S., 1946, naturalized 1952; B.A., Newbold Coll., Eng., 1938; m. Liisa Bloom, May 20, 1918; children—Eino, Kaljo, Tarmu. Ordained to ministry, 1928; pastor in Estonia, 1920-44, Sweden, 1944-46, N.Y.C., 1946-65; dir. fgn. work N.Y. Evang. Center, 1956-62; editor Estonia Book and Bible House, Riverside, Calif., 1946—, Estonian Bible Quar., 1946—. Conf. pres. Estonian Seventh-day Advent. Conf., 1938-44; sec. Estonian Conf., 1928-38, 44; missionary dir. Adventist Conf., 1930-38. Recipient Successful Work button Estonian Red Cross, 1935. Mem. Estonian Aid in N.Y.C. (treas.), Estonian Male Chorus (life). Home and office: 11472 Flower St Riverside CA 92505

MAGLER, RUTHANN HANSON, minister, United Church of Christ/Baptist; b. St. Paul, Jan. 9, 1942; d. Carl August and Winnifred Mae (Pittman) Hanson; m. David Herbert Magler, Dec. 16, 1961 (div. 1975); children: David Richard, Eric John (dec. 1981), Genelle Elizabeth, Michael Erin. B.A., U. Minn., 1974; postgrad. United Theol. Sem., 1976-78; M.Div., Va. Union Sem., 1980. Ordained to ministry Nat. Bapt. and Am. Bapt., 1980. Assoc. minister Mt. Olivet Bapt. Ch., St. Paul, 1978-82; pastor St. Paul and St. Luke United Ch. Christ, Alma, Wis., Hope United Ch. Christ, Cochrane, Wis., 1982—; active Wis. Conf. Social Concerns Commn., United Ch. Christ, Madison, Wis., 1983—. Pub. poet, singer, Facilitator Alateen Group, Alma, 1983—; polit. activist through ch./community groups, Alma, Cochrane, 1982—. Mem. AAUW. Democrat. Home: 604 2d St South Alma WI 54610

MAGNESS, PAUL DAVID, minister, Am. Baptist Assn.; b. Coalgate, Okla., Mar. 30, 1929; s. Charles Arthur and Jessie (Height) M.; grad. Bible langs., Missionary Bapt. Inst., Marlow, Okla., 1959, B.Th., 1969, M.Th., D.D., 1972; m. Lovada Marie Williams, July 2, 1947; children—James Ronald, Paula Marie, Kale David. Ordained to ministry, 1955; pastor County Ave. Bapt. Ch., Texarkana, Ark., 1976—; prof. Okla. Missionary Bapt. Inst., 1961-64. Moderator, Red River Missionary Bapt. Assn., 1963, Coastal Coop. Bapt. Assn., 1968; asst. moderator Ark. Bapt. Assn., 1975—; dir. Calif. Youth Camp, 1964-68; adv. council nat. ladies aux. Am. Bapt. Assn., 1968-76, dir. nat. youth camp, 1975—; adv. council Missionary Bapt. Inst. Costa Rica; trustee Korea Missionary Bapt. Inst., Seoul. Address: 3524 Locust St Texarkana AR 75502

MAGNUSON, WARREN ROGER, ch. ofcl., Bapt. Gen. Conf.; b. Mpls., Dec. 5, 1921; s. Edwin John and Hulda Marie (Smith) M.; B.A., U. Minn., 1946; B.D., Bethel Theol. Sem., 1946; D.D., Judson Coll., 1973; m. Margaret L.E. Johnson, June 9, 1944. Ordained to ministry Baptist Gen. Conf., 1946; pastor Minn. and Mich. chs., 1943-54, Central Bapt. Ch., St. Paul, 1954-69; gen. sec. Bapt. Gen. Conf., Arlington Heights, Ill., 1969—. Exec. com. Bapt. World Alliance, Bapt. Joint Com. on Pub. Affairs; chmn. program com. Bapt. World Congress, 1980; adminstrv. com. Nat. Assn. Evangelicals. Trustee Minn. Bapt. Conf., Bapt. Gen. Conf.; moderator Bapt. Gen. Conf., 1965, Minn. Bapt. Conf., 1959. Trustee, bd. regents Bethel Coll. and Sem. Office: 2002 Arlington Heights Rd Arlington Heights IL 60005

MAGNUSON-FORD, DAVID, minister, Lutheran Church in America; b. Northfield, Minn., Apr. 26, 1952; came to Can., 1977, naturalized, 1984; s. Martin Marvin and Barbara Claire (Sanderson) Ford; m. Heidi Marie Magnuson, May 29, 1984; children: Julie Heidi, Karen Elizabeth. B.A., U. Minn., 1975; M.Div., Luth. Theol. Sem., Saskatoon, Sask., 1981. Ordained to ministry Lutheran Ch., 1981. Intern, Montney Luth. Ch., Ft. St. John, B.C., Can., 1978-79; student chaplain Health Scis., Centre, Winnipeg, Man., Can., 1981; pastor Cross of Faith Ch., Leaf Rapids, Man., 1981—. Home and Office: Box 637 Leaf Rapids MN R0B 1W0 Canada

MAGOULIAS, NICHOLAS JOHN, priest, Greek Orthodox Archdiocese of North and South America; b. Cin., Oct. 11, 1931; s. John Efstratios and Constantina (Dounias) M.; m. Marilyn Contas, Jan. 16, 1960; children: Jonathan, Carolyn. B.Div., Holy Cross Sem., Brookline, Mass., 1957. Ordained deacon Greek Orthodox Ch., 1960, priest, 1960. Rector St. Paul's Greek Orthodox Ch., Hempstead, N.Y., 1960—; pres. Nassau-Suffolk Greek Orthodox Clergy Fedn., 1981-85; trustee Dion Found., Inc., Hempstead, N.Y., 1981—; mem. 1st Diocesan Bd., Astoria, N.Y., 1982—; mem. spiritual ct. Greek Orthodox Archdiocese-Diocese N.Y., Astoria, 1977-80, 82-83; project and research dir. Installation of extensive 13th Century Byzantine Mosaics. Editor The Epistle 1963. Recipient Heritage award J. F. K. Library of Minorities, N.Y.C., 1972. Office: St Paul's Greek Orthodox Ch 110 Cathedral Ave Hempstead NY 11550

MAGUIRE, ALBAN ANTHONY, priest, administrator, Roman Catholic Church. b. Meriden, Conn., Sept. 28, 1915; s. John Patrick and Edna Frances (Cashen) M. B.A., St. Bonaventure U., 1938; S.T.L., Cath. U., 1945, S.T.D., 1958. Ordained priest Roman Cath. Ch., 1941. Rector, Holy Name Coll., Washington, 1964-68; definitor Holy Name Province, N.Y.C., 1967-73, vicar provincial, 1976-80, minister provincial, 1980—; rector Christ the King Sem., St. Bonaventure, N.Y., 1973-76, trustee, 1976—; trustee St. Bonaventure U., 1967—, Siena Coll., Loudonville, N.Y., 1967-77, 81—. Contbr. articles to profl. jours. Mem. Cath. Theol. Soc. (bd. dirs. 1962-64), Mariological Soc. Am. (bd. dirs. 1964-69, pres. 1968-69), Nat. Franciscan Marian Commn. Office: Holy Name Province 135 W 31st St New York NY 10001

MAGUIRE, CRISPIN MICHAEL, priest, Roman Catholic Church; b. New Britain, Conn., Oct. 13, 1928; s. John Patrick and Edna (Cashen) M. B.A., St. Bonaventure U., 1951, M.A., 1955; postgrad. Holy Name Coll., 1956; M.F.A., Yale U., 1966. Ordained priest Roman Catholic Ch., 1955. Instr. St. Bonaventure U., Allegany, N.Y., 1956-59; asst. chaplain Yale U., New Haven, 1960-64; asst. prof. St. Francis Coll., Rye Beach, N.Y., 1964-67, St. Bonaventure U., 1967-78; pastor Our Lady of Holy Angels Ch., Little Falls, N.J., 1978—; chaplain Knights of Columbus, Little Falls, 1980—. Cand. U.S. Ho. of Reps., 39th Dist., N.Y., 1978-79; active Council on Aging, Little Falls, 1981—. Republican. Club: N.Y. Athletic. Address: Our Lady of Holy Angels Ch 473 Main St Little Falls NJ 07424

MAGUIRE, JOSEPH F. See *Who's Who in America*, 43rd edition.

MAGUIRE, MAX RAYMOND, chaplain, Presbyterian Church in U.S.A.; b. Dwight, Kans., June 12, 1928; s. Ray Thomas and Helen Olive (Paulson) M.; A.B., Wichita State U., 1955; M.Div., San Francisco Theol. Sem., 1958; m. Martha Ellen Berndt, Dec. 27, 1958; children: Kimberly, Kenton. Ordained to ministry United Presbyn. Ch. in the U.S.A., 1958; pastor chs., Lawrence, Kans., 1958-61; chaplain Big Spring (Tex.) State Hosp., 1961-65, Presbyn. Hosp. Ministry, Rochester, Minn., 1965-71, Abbott-Northwestern Hosp., Mpls., 1971—, dir. chaplaincy services, 1971—. Moderator Presbytery of Sheldon Jackson, 1970-71. Mem. Assn. Clin. Pastoral Edn. (chmn. N. Central region 1975—), Coll. Chaplains (past pres.). Author papers in clin. pastoral psychology. Home: 4744 10th Ave S Minneapolis MN 55407 Office: 810 E 27th St Minneapolis MN 55407

MAHAFFEY, JAMES OWEN, minister, United Meth. Ch.; b. Memphis, Aug. 29, 1940; s. William Eldred and Annie Jane (Thomas) M.; B.A., Georgetown (Ky.) Coll., 1963; M.Div., So. Bapt. Theol. Sem., 1969; m. Betty Sue Chatman, June 13, 1964; children—Kenneth Allen, Jonathan Michael, Christopher Lynn. Ordained to ministry, 1962; student missionary So. Bapt. Home. Mission Bd., Tucson, 1962; pastor chs., Ky., Ill., 1962-73; pastor Bethany United Meth. Ch., Chgo., 1973—; chaplain United Meth. Home, Chgo., 1976—. Supr. field edn. Garrett Evang. Theol. Sem., Evanston, Ill., 1971-72, 74-75; mem. dept. attending clergy Swedish Covenant Hosp., Chgo. Mem. Acad. Parish Clergy, Irving Park (Chgo.) Ministerial Assn., N. Ill. Ann. Conf. Home: 3901 N Richmond St Chicago IL 60618 Office: 3900 N Albany Ave Chicago IL 60618

MAHAN, RICHARD GABRIEL, minister, American Lutheran Church; b. Charleston, W.Va., Sept. 29, 1939; s. Albert and Angie (Skaff) M.; B.A., Pacific Luth. U., 1962; M.Div., Evang. Luth. Sem., 1968; postgrad. Morris Harvey Coll., 1973-76; m. Donna Jean Ellis, June 12, 1965; children: Kristi Ellis, Brent Richard. Ordained to ministry, 1968; pastor Trinity Luth. Ch., Jersey City, 1968-72, St. Timothy Luth. Ch., South Charleston, W.Va., 1972—. Mem. Dept. Met. Ministry, Eastern Dist. Conf. on Inner City Ministries, 1968-72; del. Nat. Conv. Am. Luth. Ch., 1970; mem. N.J. Pan Luth. Com. on Ch. Relationship. Mem. Police-Community Relations Bd., 1968-72; fire commr., South Charleston, 1973-76; hosp. bldg. commr., South

Charleston, 1976—; trustee Thomas Meml. Hosp., 1977—, chmn. bd., 1980-82. Named Citizen of Yr., Lion's Club, 1982. Mem. Jersey City Council Chs., South Charleston Ministerial Assn., Jersey City Luth. Parochial Sch. Assn. Home: 809 Whispering Way South Charleston WV 25303 Office: PO Box 9155 South Charleston WV 25309 Charleston WV 25309

MAHER, LEO THOMAS, bishop, Roman Catholic Ch.; b. Mt. Union, Iowa, July 1, 1915; s. Thomas and Mary (Teberg) M.; ed. St. Joseph's Coll., Mountain View, Calif., also St. Patrick's Sem., Menlo Park, Calif. Ordained priest Roman Catholic Ch., consecrated bishop, 1962; asst. pastor in San Francisco, 1944-47; sec. to archbishop of San Francisco, 1947-61; chancellor Archdiocese of San Francisco, 1956-62, dir. vocations, 1957-62, archdiocesan consultor, 1959-62; apptd. domestic prelate, 1954; bishop Santa Rosa, Calif., 1962-69, San Diego, 1969—; prior Western Lieutenancy of Knights and Ladies of Holy Sepulchre. Bd. dirs. Soc. Propagation of Faith, Youth's Director, Cath. Youth Orgn.; chmn. bd. trustees U. San Diego. Del. Ecumenical Council, Rome, Italy, 1962, 63, 64, 65. Home: 2031 Sunset Blvd San Diego CA 92103 Office: Diocesan Office Alcala Park San Diego CA 92110

MAHONEY, GERARD MICHAEL, seminary executive, Roman Catholic Church; b. Bklyn., Feb. 23, 1933; s. Michael and Barbara (Schmitt) M. B.A., Mary Immaculate Sem. and Coll., Northampton, Pa., 1957, postgrad., 1957-61; J.C.B., Cath. U. Am., 1962, M.C.L., 1963, J.C.D., 1964. Joined Congregation of Mission, Roman Cath. Ch., 1947, ordained priest, 1961. Spiritual dir., prof. theology and canon law Sem. Our Lady of Angels, Albany, N.Y., 1964-66; dir. scholastics, prof. theology and canon law Mary Immaculate Sem. and Coll., 1966-69, part-time lectr., 1969-75; dir. novices St. Vincent's Sem., Phila., 1969-75; superior Vicentian Residence, Niagara Falls, N.Y., 1975-76; part-time lectr. Niagara U., N.Y., 1975-76, pres., 1976-81, chmn., 1975-79, trustee, 1976—, chmn. bd. trustees, 1981—; provincial superior Eastern Province of Congregation of Mission, Phila., 1981—, chmn. commn. formation and membership gen. assembly, 1974, superior gen. preparatory commn. gen. assembly, 1974; trustee Congregation of Mission of St. Vincent de Paul, Germantown, Pa., St. John's U., N.Y.C. Mem. Sigma Alpha Sigma, Delta Epsilon Sigma. Lodge: K.C. Address: St Vincent's Sem 500 E Chelten Ave Philadelphia PA 19144

MAHONEY, JAMES P., bishop, Roman Cath. Ch.; b. Saskatoon, Sask., Can., Dec. 7, 1927. Ordained priest, 1952; bishop of Saskatoon, 1967—. Office: 106 5th Ave N Saskatoon SK S7K 2N7 Canada*

MAHONEY, JAMES PATRICK, bishop, Roman Catholic Church; b. Kingston, N.Y., Aug. 16, 1925. Grad. St. Joseph's Sem., 1951. Ordained priest, Roman Cath. Ch., 1951, elevated to bishop, 1972. Pastor various chs., until 1972; titular bishop of Ipagro and aux. bishop of N.Y., Mahopac, N.Y., 1972—; Episcopal Vicar, North Westchester, N.Y., 1978—. Address: 235 Msgr O'Brien Blvd Mahopac NY 10541

MAHONEY, JOSEPH MARY, religious administrator; Dominican Sisters of Blauvelt, N.Y.; b. N.Y.C., Sept. 29, 1937; d. Cornelius Michael and Mary Veronica (Neenan) Mahoney. B.S. in Edn., Dominican Coll., 1963; M.S. in Edn., Fordham U., 1974. Religion educator St. Dominic's, 1955-59, dir. edn., 1971-77; tchr. St. Luke's, N.Y.C., 1959-62, St. Martin de Porres, Poughkeepsie, N.Y., 1965-70, Transfiguration, West Collingswood, N.J., 1962-65; exec. dir. St. Dominic's Home, 1978—. Bd. dirs. Rockland County Youth Bur., N.Y.; v.p. Assn. for Rockland County Mentally Retarded and Developmentally Disabled; active mem. Rockland County Adv. Council, Family Court Adv. Com. Recipient Outstanding Service to Youth award N.Y. State Assembly, 1981, Myrtle Wreath award L.N.Y.S. Hadassah, 1983. Mem. Nat. Cath. Edn. Assn., Nat. Conf. of Catholic Charities. Office: St Dominic's Home Western Hwy Blauvelt NY 10913

MAHONY, ROGER MICHAEL, bishop elect Los Angeles 1985—. See *Who's Who in America,* 43rd Edition.

MAIDA, ADAM J., bishop, Roman Catholic Church. Bishop of Green Bay, Wis., 1984—. Office: PO Box 66 Green Bay WI 54305*

MAIER, RAYMOND HAROLD, minister, United Church of Christ; b. Portland, Oreg., July 22, 1931; s. Jacob J. and Mary (Martin) M.; A.B., Cascade Coll., 1956; m. Mirriam Rae Targgart, Aug. 21, 1953; children: Andrea, David, Clarolyn, Joel. Ordained to ministry, 1958; minister Univ. Park Congregational Ch., Portland, 1953-57; mem. faculty, adminstrn. Cascade Coll., Portland, 1956-62; dir. admissions Seattle Pacific Coll., 1962-64; minister Lake Oswego (Oreg.) United Ch. Christ, 1964—. Chmn. mission and outreach dept. Central Pacific Conf., 1974—, mem. exec. bd. Conf., 1972—; chaplain Meridian Park Hosp., Tualatin, Oreg., 1974—. Mem. Tri-County Local Govt. Commn., 1976—; pres. Lake Oswego Jr. High Parent-Tchrs. Club, 1975—, Housing Options of Clackamas County, 1980—; mem. Lake Oswego Bicentennial Commn., 1976—; bd. dirs. Clackamas County Mental Health Program, Lake Oswego Adult Community Ctr., Highland Community Services, 1969—. Mem. Lake Oswego C. of C. (pres. 1977), Seattle Pacific Alumni Assn., Parishes of Oswego. Home: 14138 SW Knaus Rd Lake Oswego OR 97034 Office: 1111 SW Country Club Rd Lake Oswego OR 97034

MAIKOWSKI, THOMAS ROBERT, priest, Roman Catholic Ch.; b. Milw., Oct. 20, 1947; s. Thomas Robert and Eugenia Antoinette (Rogowski) M.; B.A., St. Francis de Sales Coll., 1970, Notre Dame Coll., 1976; M.S., St. Francis Coll., 1972; M.A., Cardinal Stritch Coll., 1974; M.Div., Kenrick Sem., 1976; postgrad. Marquette U., 1973—. Ordained priest, 1976; prin. St. James Sch., Rising Sun, Wis., 1969-70, St. Luke Sch., Gary, Ind., 1969-70, Queen of Angeles Sch., Ft. Wayne, Ind., 1971-72; tchr. St. Stanislaus High Sch., Chgo., 1970-71, St. Vincent de Paul Sch., Ft. Wayne, 1971-72, Cathedral High Sch., Gallup, N.Mex., 1976—; instr. spl. edn. Cardinal Stritch Coll., Milw. and Silver Lake Coll., Manitowoc, Wis., 1973-74; asso. prin. academic affairs Cath. High Sch., 1976—; chaplain St. Joseph Hosp., Milw., 1970-76, Sacred Heart Convent, Gallup, 1976—; cons. in field. Mem. Religious, Nat. Cath. edn. assns., Am. Assn. Mental Deficiency, Nat. Council Tchrs. English, Religious Certification Agy. for Retardation, Nat. Apostolate for Mentally Retarded, Council Exceptional Children, Nat. Assn. Cath. Chaplains, Quill and Scroll. Home and Office: 4th St at Park Ave Gallup NM 87301

MAIN, N. JAMES, educator, administrator, Church of the Nazarene. B. Moravia, Iowa, Dec. 27, 1929; s. R. Forrest and Doris Thelma (Darby) M.; m. Elaine K. Medrud, Jan. 26, 1951; children: Jolaine Kay, James Daniel, Douglas Martin. B.A., Central Coll., Pella, Iowa, 1952; M.A., No. Iowa U., 1959; D.Ed., U. Okla., 1969. Music supr. Iowa pub. schs., 1952-63; assoc. prof. Bethany Nazarene Coll. (Okla.), 1963-68; prof. Mid-Am. Nazarene Coll., Olathe, Kans., 1968—; minister of music Marshalltown Ch. of Nazarene (Iowa), 1954-58, First Ch. of Nazarene, Oskaloosa, Iowa, 1959-63, First Ch. of Nazarene, Oklahoma City, 1963-65; presenter music workshops, 1969—. Arranger choral anthems and hymns. Mem. Music Educators Nat. Conf., Phi Delta Kappa, Phi Delta Lambda (pres. 1983-84). Office: Mid-Am Nazarene Coll Box 1776 Olathe KS 66061

MAJOR, ELBERT FRANKLIN, minister, educational administrator, Southern Baptist Convention; b. Cumming, Ga., June 4, 1938; s. Elbert Andrew and Myrtle Allene (Williams) M.; B.B.A., Ga. State U., Atlanta, 1964; M.Div., So. Bapt. Theol. Sem., Louisville, 1970, D.Min., 1982; m. Peggy Elizabeth Barnette, June 24, 1962; children: Sally Jean, John Mark. Ordained to ministry, 1961; minister chs. in Ga. and Ky., 1961-67; pastor New Highland Bapt. Ch., Brandenburg, Ky., 1967-70, First Bapt. Ch., Pooler, Ga., 1970-83; assoc. dir. edn. extension program Edn. div. So. Bapt. Conv., 1983—; pres. Savannah (Ga.) Bapt. Ministers Conf., 1973-74; moderator Savannah Bapt. Assn., 1975-77, chaplain Lions Club, Pooler, 1973-77; chaplain, emergency room vol. Meml. Med. Center, Savannah, 1973-78. Hon. mem. Pooler Packers. Home: 221 Manning Dr Alpharetta GA 30201 Office: 2930 Flowers Rd S Atlanta GA 30341

MAJORS, CLYDE ROLSTON, minister, educator, So. Bapt. Conv.; b. Akron, Ohio, Apr. 24, 1926; s. Clyde Emerson and Verlie Pauline (Rolston) M.; B.A., Howard Payne Coll., 1951; B.D.(M.Div.), Southwestern Bapt. Theol. Sem., 1963, Th.M., 1966, Th.D., 1973; m. Dora Belle Ellis, July 31, 1947; children—Joseph Benjamin, Melinda. Ordained to ministry, 1950; pastor chs., Tex., Ohio, 1949-68; pastor Community Bapt. Ch., Waco, Tex., 1968-70, Union Bapt. Ch., Thorndale, Tex., 1971-73, 1st Bapt. Ch., Buffalo, Tex., 1973-75; asst. prof. religion Howard Payne U., Brownwood, Tex., 1975—. Mem. Am. Acad. Religion. Home: 2001 1st St Brownwood TX 76801 Office: Box 405 Howard Payne Univ Brownwood TX 76801

MAKI, PENTTI J., minister; Lutheran Church in America; b. Painesville, Ohio, Apr. 10, 1954; s. John August and Martta Elisabet (Malaska) M.; m. Leena Elizabeth Westerholm, June 6, 1981; B.A., Ashland Coll., 1976; M.Div., Luth. Sch. Theol., 1981; postgrad. U. Helsinki, Finland, 1980-81. Ordained to ministry Lutheran Ch. Am., 1981. Pastor Trinity Luth. Ch., Versailles, Ohio, 1981—; mem. Ednl. Ministry Resourse Team, Dayton dist., Ohio synod, 1984. Lodge: Lions (editor 1984). Home: 222 E Wood St Versailles OH 45380 Office: Trinity Luth Ch 204 E Wood St Versailles OH 45380

MALCHOW, BRUCE VIRGIL, minister, Lutheran Church in America, professor of religion; b. Chgo., Jan. 7, 1940; s. Virgil George and Ruth Dorothy (Sylvester) M.; m. Roberta Jeannine Hawkins, June 22, 1963; children: Timothy, Laura. B.A., Concordia Coll., 1961; M.Div., Concordia Sem., 1965, S.T.M., 1966; Ph.D., in Old Testament, Marquette U., 1972. Ordained to ministry, Lutheran Ch. in Am., 1966. Mission developer Lamb of God Ch., Balt., 1966-68; asst. prof. Concordia Coll., Milw., 1968-74; assoc. pastor Lake Park Ch., Milw., 1974-76; assoc. prof. Sacred Heart Sch. of Theology, Hales Corners, Wis., 1975—; lectr. Marquette U., Milw., 1974-75; coordinator Luth. Cath. Dialogue for Wis., Upper Mich. Synod, 1979-80, chmn., 1979-80; mem. Luth.-Cath. Dialogue Milw., 1979-82; mem. Metropolitan Milw. Dist. Cabinet, 1982-83, Ecumenical Relations Com., Wis. Upper Mich. Synod, 1980—. Author: Because He First Loved Us, 1982. Contbr. articles to profl. jours. Mem. Soc. Bibl. Lit., Milw. Assn. Interfaith Relations. Home: 4500 N Bartlett Shorewood WI 53211 Office: Sacred Heart Sch Theology 7335 S Lovers Lane Rd Hales Corners WI 53130

MALDONADO, EMILIO, priest, educator, Roman Cath. Ch.; b. Panindicuaro, Mex., Oct. 20, 1925; s. Bernabe and Paulina (Viveros) M.; came to U.S., 1973; Licentiate in Sociology, Philosophy faculty Pontifica Studiorum, Rome, 1963. Ordained priest, 1954; instr. music, Greek, history and philosophy La Paz Sem., Guadalajara, Mexico, 1954-73; asso. pastor Our Lady of Guadalupe Ch., Calexico, Calif., 1973—. Home: Parral 445 Frac Chapultepec Tijuana Baja California Office: 124 E 5th St Calexico CA 92231

MALESKI, MICHAEL MATTHEW, minister, American Baptist Churches U.S.A.; b. Collinsburg, Pa., June 26, 1949; s. Stanley Michael and Mary Magdaline (Tokar) M.; m. Peggy Garalene Tuck, July 28, 1973; children: Jason Michael, Janelle Geralene. Tchrs. diploma, Wash. Bible Coll., 1976, B.A., 1976; M.Div. cum laude, Eastern Bapt. Sem., 1978. Ordained to ministry Baptist Ch., 1979. Youth dir. First Bapt. Ch., Norristown, Pa., 1976-77; student pastor Community Bapt. Ch., Milmay, N.Y., 1977-89; pastor Washington Ave. Ch., Johnston City, Ill., 1978-80, First Bapt. Ch., Apollo, Pa., 1980-83, Indian Creek Bapt. Ch., Mill Run, Pa., 1983—; dir. Pitts. Bapt. Youth Bd., 1982-83; mission chairperson Monongahela Bapt. Assn., Mill Run, 1983—; cons. Am. Bapt. Evangelistic Team, Valley Forge, Pa., 1983—; dir. Ch. Growth of Pa. and Del., Valley Forge, 1984—. Founder Missions Newsletter, 1984. Contbr. articles to profl. jours. Author (booklet) Pastoral Care for Church Growth, 1984; (book) Kaleidoscope of Prayer, 1985. Bd. dirs. Mill Run Youth Baseball League, 1983—, Citizens for Mill Run Interest, 1983—, Pitts. Pirates Capt.'s Club, 1983—; mem. Springfield Volunteer Co., Mill Run, 1984—. Served as sgt. USAF, 1968-72, Vietnam. Recipient Church Growth award Pitts. Bapt. Assn., 1981; named Volunteer of Yr. USAF, 1970; recipient commendation medal USAF, 1972. Mem. Indian Creek Ministerium, Am. Bapt. Ministers Council, Monogahela Bapt. Ministerium (v.p. 1983—). Democrat. Home and Office: Rd #1 Box 191-A-1 Mill Run PA 15464

MALEWITZ, JOSEPH MCCURRY, priest, Roman Cath. Ch.; b. Grand Rapids, Mich., Aug. 24, 1929; s. Joseph Leon and Mary Ann (McCurry) M.; B.S., Seminaire de Philosophie, Montreal, 1951; B.S., St. John's Sem., Plymouth, Mich., 1955; M.Ed., Mich. State U., 1966. Ordained priest, 1955; instr., athletic dir. St. Simon Sch., Ludington, Mich., 1955-57; instr., curriculum dir. St. Patrick's Sch., Portland, Mich., 1957-60; instr. Sacred Heart High Sch., Mt. Pleasant, Mich., 1960-61, also instr., chaplain Mt. Pleasant Tng. Home Mentally Retarded Children; asst. prin., faculty mgr. Cath. Central High Sch., Grand Rapids, 1961-66; supt. Cheboygan (Mich.) Cath. Schs., 1966-70; pastor St. Patrick's Parish, Portland, also supt. parish schs., 1970-74; pastor, supt. St. Mary's Grade Sch., Spring Lake, Mich., 1974—. Mem. Nat., Mich., Cath. edn. assns., Nat. Curriculum Developers Assn. Address: 406 E Savidge St Spring Lake MI 49456

MALHERBE, ABRAHAM JOHANNES, minister, religion educator, Church of Christ; b. Pretoria, South Africa, May 15, 1950; s. Abraham J. and Cornelia Aletta (Meyer) M.; m. Phyllis Melton, May 28, 1933; children: Selina, Cornelia, Abraham J. B.A., Abilene Christian U., 1954; S.T.B., Harvard U., U. Utrecht, 1957, Netherlands, 1961; Th.D., Harvard U., 1963; LL.D.(hon.), Pepperdine U., 1980. Ordained to ministry Ch. of Christ, 1954. Minister Ch. of Christ, Lexington, Mass., 1956-62; from asst. to assoc. prof. Abilene Christian U., Tex., 1963-69; assoc. prof. Dartmouth Coll., Hanover, N.H., 1969-70; assoc. prof. N.T., Yale U., New Haven, 1970-77, prof., 1977-, Buckingham prof. N.T., 1981—; chmn. bd. trustees Ch. of Christ, Hamden, Conn., 1978-. Author: Social Aspects of Early Christ, 1979, 2d, revised edit.,1983; co-author: Gregory of Nyssa: Life of Moses, 1977. Editor, contbg. author: The Cynic Epistles, 1977; editorial bd. Jour. Biblical Lit., 1976-82, Second Century, 1981—, Bible Rev., 1983-. Contbr. numerous articles to jours., encys., collections. Recipient Outstanding Teaching qward Abilene Christian U., 1965, 67; NEH grantee, 1973. Mem. Soc. Bibl. Lit., N. Am. Patristic Soc., Studiorum Novi Testamenti Societas. Office: Yale U Div Sch 409 Prospect St New Haven CT 06510 Conv 601 50th St NE Washington DC 20019

MALINOWSKI, MARY NORBERTA, hospital administrator, nun, Roman Catholic Church; b. Boston, Apr. 7, 1936; d. Adam and Jane (Kapusta) Malinowski. R.N., St. Elizabeth's Hosp., 1956; B.S., Elms Coll., 1966; M.S., Tufts U., 1972; S.M., MIT, 1980. Joined

Felician Sisters, Roman Catholic Ch., 1959. Coordinator pediatrics Nazareth Child Ctr., Jamaica Plain, Mass., 1973-77; mem. faculty Boston Coll. Sch. Nursing, Chestnut Hill, Mass., 1977-79; assoc. exec. dir. St. Joseph Hosp., Bangor, Maine, 1980-82, exec. dir., 1982—, bd. trustees, 1982—; bd. trustees St. Joseph Healthcare Found., 1983—; bd. dirs. Maine Cancer Research and Edn. Found., Portland, 1984. Contbr. articles to nursing jours. Mem. Gov.'s Commn. on Edn., 1983-84, Cath. Health Assn., St. Louis, 1980. Mem. Am. Pub. Health Assn., Am. Coll. Hosp. Adminstrs., Sloan Fellows (MIT), Bangor Bus. and Profl. Women's Club, Sigma Theta Tau. Democrat. Office: St Joseph Hosp 297 Center St Bangor ME 04401

MALINSKY, MICHAEL ARTHUR, minister, Lutheran Church-Missouri Synod; b. Burlington, Ohio, Mar. 26, 1950; s. Walter Gustav and Leona Eleanor (Reister) M.; m. Teresa Marie Harrison, Oct. 6, 1979; children: Jonathan Michael, Rachel Marie. A.A., Concordia Jr. Coll., 1970; B.A., Concordia Sr. Coll., 1972; M.Div., Concordia Sem., 1977. Ordained to ministry Lutheran Ch., 1978. Assoc. pastor St. Paul Luth. Ch., Trenton, Mich., 1978-84; pastor Resurrection Luth. Ch., Statesville, N.C., 1985—. Republican. Home: 2507 Scalybark Rd Statesville NC 28677 Office: Resurrection Lutheran Church City Center Statesville NC 28677

MALLORY, RUPERT TALMAGE, minister, United Methodist Church; b. Spring Hill, W.Va., Jan. 18, 1915; s. Rupert George and Allie (Fleck) M.; A.B., Morris Harvey Coll., 1936, D.D., 1962; M.Div., Duke U., 1939; M.A., W.Va. Coll. Grad. Studies, 1976; m. Ernestine Sims, Aug. 26, 1941; 1 son, Rupert Talmage. Ordained to ministry, 1939; pastor Fayetteville (W.Va.) circuit, 1939-42; chaplain U.S. Army, 1942-46; pastor chs. Mt. Hope, W.Va., 1946-48, St. Johns Ch., Spencer, W.Va., 1948-53, St. Andrew Ch., St. Albans, W.Va., 1953-60; dist. supt. Wheeling, W.Va., 1960-65; pastor Bland St. Ch., Bluefield, W.Va., 1965-67; exec. sec. Bd. Edn., W.Va. Annual Conf., 1967-72; exec. dir. W.Va. Rehab. Center Found. Inc. and chaplain W.Va. Rehab. Center, Institute, 1972—; chaplain W.Va. N.G.-U.S. Army Res., 1946-75; sec. bd. Christian edn. W.Va. Ann. Conf., 1958-60; mem. world service fin. commn. W.Va. Ann. Conf.; mem. Gen. Bd. Christian Social Concerns, Meth. Ch., 1962-66. Bd. dirs. A.R.C., 1951; trustee W.Va. Wesleyan Coll., 1967-78, emeritus, 1979. Served to col. USAR. Decorated Bronze Star, Purple Heart. Mem. Ret. Officers Assn., Nat., W.Va. rehab. assns., Sigma Epsilon. Home: 1815 Rosewood Rd Charleston WV 25314 Office: West Virginia Rehabilitation Center Institute WV 25112

MALLOY, C(ULBERTH) J(EROME), JR., religious organization administrator, Progressive National Baptist Convention Inc.; b. Charlotte, N.C., Dec. 30, 1936; s. C.J. and Annie Goler (Enloe) M.; m. Phyllis Jean Goodson, June 11, 1966; children: Phyllis Athena, C.J. III. B.A., Va. State U., 1962; M.Div., Va. Union, 1965; D.Div. (hon.), Va. Sem. and Coll., 1982. Ordained to ministry Baptist Ch., 1965. Outreach minister Reformed Ch., N.Y.C., 1965-67; missionary Am. Bapt. Ch., Valley Forge, Pa., 1968-70; minister 1st Bapt. Ch., Williamsburg, Pa., 1970-72; assoc. sec. Progressive Bapt. Nat. Conv., Washington, 1973-79, gen. sec., 1980—; dir. Morehouse Sch. Religion, Atlanta, 1981—. Activities chmn. Manhattan Borough council Boy Scouts Am., 1967. Served with USAF, 1955-59. Mem. Nat. Council Chs. (bd. dirs. 1980—), Bapt. World Alliance (bd. dirs. 1980), Bapt. Joint Com. on Pub. Affairs (bd. dirs. 1980). Democrat. Home: 11002 Trafton Ct Upper Marlboro MD 20772 Office: Progressive Nat Bapt Conv 601 50th St NE Washington DC 20019

MALLOY, PETER VINCENT, JR., priest, Roman Catholic Church; b. Phila., Jan. 31, 1942; s. Peter Vincent and Helen Marie (Turney) M. B.A., Don Bosco Coll., 1966; M.Div., Pontifical Coll. Josephinum, 1974. Joined Salesians of Don Bosco, Roman Catholic Ch., 1962, ordained priest, 1974. Tchr. Don Bosco Tech. Inst., W. Haverstraw, N.Y., 1966-68, Salesian High Sch., New Rochelle, N.Y., 1968-69, 1974-75, Salesian Boys Club, Columbus, Ohio, 1969-73, Don Bosco Tech. High Sch., Boston, 1973-74, Salesian Prep. Sch., Cedar Lake, Ind., 1975-77; chaplain St. Dominic Savio Club, W. Haverstraw, 1977-80, dir., 1981—; chaplain Rockland Council Cath. Commn. on Scouting, N.Y., 1977—; mem. Archdiocese N.Y. Cath. Commn. on Scouting, 1977—. Recipient Bronze Pelican, Archdiocese N.Y., 1981, St. Ellizabeth Ann Seton award, 1982, St. George award, 1983; Shatemuc Dist. award Rockland County Council Boy Scouts Am., 1983. Home: Marian Shrine Filors Ln West Haverstraw NY 10993 Office: Savio Club Internat Headquarters Filors Ln West Haverstraw NY 10993

MALMQUIST, RICHARD CARL, minister, American Baptist Churches in the U.S.A.; b. New Rochelle, N.Y., June 13, 1944; s. Carl Louis and Winifred (VanRaalte) M.; m. Margaret Christine Watson, June 12, 1966; children: Anne Elizabeth, Mark Andrew. B.A., U. Denver, 1966; M.Div., Colgate Rochester Div. Sch., 1969; D. Ministry, Andover Newton Theol. Sch., 1983. Ordained to ministry Am. Bapt. Chs. U.S.A., 1969. Pastor, First Bapt. Ch., Akron, N.Y., 1969-73, Brockton, Mass., 1973-81, Wollaston, Mass., 1981—; adj. faculty Andover Newton Theol. Sch., Newton, Mass., 1981—. Democrat. Lodge: Kiwanis (chaplain). Office: First Bapt Ch 81 Prospect Ave Wollaston MA 02170

MALONE, JAMES WILLIAM, bishop, Roman Cath. Ch.; b. Youngstown, Ohio, Mar. 8, 1920; s. James Patrick and Katherine (McGuire) M.; B.A., St. Mary's Sem., 1945; M.A., Cath. U., 1952, Ph.D., 1957; LL.D., Walsh Coll., 1970; L.H.D., Youngstown State U., 1969. Ordained priest Roman Catholic Ch., 1945; asst. pastor St. Columba Cathedral, 1945-50; supt. schs. Diocese of Youngstown, 1952-65; consecrated bishop, 1960; bishop Diocese of Youngstown, 1968—. Mem. Com. Ecumenical and Interreligious Affairs, Nat. Conf. Cath. Bishops, 1972—, v.p. Nat. Conf. Cath. Bishops, 1980-83, pres., 1983—; co-chmn. Roman Cath./United Meth. Dialogue, 1972—; mem. adminstrv. bd. U.S. Cath. Conf., 1974—, mem. exec. com., 1975—.

MALONEY, CHARLES GARRETT See *Who's Who in America*, 43rd edition.

MALONEY, DAVID M., bishop, Roman Cath. Ch.; b. Littleton, Colo., Mar. 15, 1912. Ed. Gregorian U. and Apollinare U., Rome. Ordained priest Roman Catholic Ch., 1936, consecrated bishop, 1961; titular bishop Ruspae, aux. bishop Diocese of Denver, 1960-67; bishop Diocese of Wichita, Kans., 1967—. Address: 424 N Broadway Wichita KS 67202

MANAFO, JOSEPH, minister, Italian Pentecostal Church of Canada, distribution company executive; b. Gasperina, Italy, Feb. 2, 1939; came to Can., 1957; s. Joseph and Elisabeth (Barbale) M.; m. Maria Fiorenza, Sept. 12, 1958; children: Richard, Elisabeth, David, Jonathan. Student correspondence bible sch., Italy and Can., 1956-82, music student Italy and Can., 1950-57, 1970-80. Evangelist, tchr. Assemblee di Dio in Italia, Italy, 1954-57; radio speaker Pentecostal Ch., Can., 1958-62, 1980—; organist and choirmaster Howard Park Ch., Toronto, Can., 1970-82, asst. pastor, 1979-82; pastor Febre St. Ch., Montreal, Que., Can., 1982—; gen. treas. Italian Pentecostal Ch. of Can., 1980—. Pres. Miore Distbg. Co. Ltd., 1975—. Author: (hymn book) Cantiamo Insieme, 1975. Editor: Evangel Voice Mag., 1962—. Ordained to ministry Italian Pentecostal Ch. of Can., 1982. Home: 1165 Montmartre Laval Montreal PQ H7E 3P2 Canada Office: Italian Pentecostal Ch 6724 Fabre St Montreal PQ H2G 2Z6 Canada

MANCINI, JAMES EDWARD, priest, Roman Cath. Ch.; b. North Little Rock, Ark., Dec. 31, 1940; s. Giusto and Annunziata Lucy (Franceschini) M.; B.A., St. John's Sem., 1962; postgrad U. Ark., Fayetteville, 1963, Cath. U. Am., 1963-65. Ordained priest, 1966; tchr. Cath. High Sch. for Boys, Little Rock, 1966-68; asst. pastor Immaculate Conception Parish, Fort Smith, Ark., 1968-69; asso. pastor St. Joseph Parish, Pine Bluff, Ark., 1969-71, Our Lady of Good Counsel Parish, Little Rock, 1971-76; pastor St. Anthony's Parish, Weiner, Ark., 1976—. Chmn., Clergy Welfare Bd.; Bishop's liaison Charismatic Movement; prison ministry, 1969-71; Bd. dirs. Sebastian County Mental Health Assn., 1968-69. Recipient, For God and Youth nat. award Cath. Youth Orgn. Home and Office: Route 2 Box 19 Weiner AR 72479

MANDEL, GEORGE EDWARD, JR., minister, Assemblies of God; b. Bloomington, Ill., July 28, 1915; s. George Edward and Emma Jane (Crawford) M.; student Shield of Faith Sem., Amarillo, Tex., 1934; m. Mary Marguerite Turner, Sept. 25, 1964. Ordained to ministry; pastor Assembly of God Ch., Washington Park, Ill., 1935-52, 1st Assembly of God Ch., Springfield, Ill., 1952-68, Joliet, Ill., 1968-70, sec.-treas. Ill. Dist. Council, Assemblies of God, Carlinville, 1971-76; evangelist, Carlinville, 1976—; speaker in field. Presbyter Central Ill. sect. Assemblies of God, 1952-65, asst. supt. Ill. Dist. Council, 1965-70, named hon. presbyter, 1976. Contbr. articles to religious jours. Address: PO Box 225 Carlinville IL 62626

MANDEL, MORTON LEON, lay worker, Jewish religion; b. Cleve., Sept. 19, 1921; s. Simon and Rose (Nussbaum) M.; student Western Res. U., 1940-42; m. Barbara Abrams, Feb. 22, 1949; children—Amy, Thomas, Stacy. Mem. campaign cabinet Found. Adv. Council, Jewish Community Fedn., 1949—, chmn., 1967-74, v.p. fedn., 1970-74, pres., 1974-76; v.p. Nat. Jewish Welfare Bd., Cleve., 1964-70, pres., 1970-74; pres. Bur. for Careers in Jewish Service, 1968-71; v.p. Council for Jewish Fedns. and Welfare Funds, 1972-74; mem. exec. com. Meml. Found. for Jewish Culture, 1973—. Chmn. bd., chief exec. officer Premier Indsl. Corp., Cleve.; dir. Central Nat. Bank of Cleve., Cleve. Electric Illuminating Co. Group chmn. United Torch Services, 1962-65, asst. chmn., 1966-67, chmn. Div. A, 1968-69, v.p. fund raising, 1971-76; chmn. Task Force on Community Orgn. Structure, Cleve. Commn. on Health and Social Sci., 1970-71; mem. adv. council Jr. Achievement of Cleve., 1966-75; mem. Businessmens Inter-racial Com., 1968-74. Hon. life trustee Jewish Community Center of Cleve., pres., 1952-55; hon. trustee Cleve. Community Chest, from 1968; trustee Mt. Sinai Hosp. of Cleve.; trustee Cleve. Zool. Soc.; bd. overseers Western Res. U., 1969—, mem. vis. com. Sch. Applied Scis., 1968-72; mem. Meml. Found. Jewish Culture, 1973—; pres. World Confedn. Jewish Community Cts., 1977—; bd. govs. Jewish Agy., 1979—; trustee United Israel Appeal, 1978—; mem. exec. com. Am. Jewish Joint Distbn. Com., 1978—; former pres. Council of Jewish Fedns. and Welfare Funds. Recipient Frank L. Weil award Nat. Jewish Welfare Bd., 1974; named Outstanding Young Man of Year, Cleve. Jr. C. of C., 1956, Businessman of Year, Urban League of Cleve. and Cleve. Area Bd. Realtors, 1973; Charles Eisenman award Cleve. Jewish Community Fedn., 1977; named Man of Yr., B'nai B'rith, 1980. Clubs: Harmonie (N.Y.C.); Standard (Chgo.); Palm Beach (Fla.) Country; Oakwood, Union (Cleve.). Home: 17250 Parkland Dr Shaker Heights OH 44120 Office: 4415 Euclid Ave Cleveland OH 44103

MANEIKIS, VICTOR STANLEY, priest, Episcopal Ch.; b. Battle Creek, Mich., May 3, 1940; s. Victor and Margaret Maxine (Hammond) M.; A.A., Flint Jr. Coll., 1960; B.A., Mich. State U., 1962; M.Div., Seabury-Western Theol. Sem., 1966; m. Mary Elizabeth Schueller, Sept. 8, 1962; children—James, Edward, Steven. Ordained priest Episcopal Ch., 1966; curate St. John's Ch., Mt. Prospect, Ill., 1966, All Saints Ch., Fort Worth, Tex., 1967; canon pastor St. Matthew's Cathedral, Dallas, 1971-76; Episcopal Diocese of Dallas, 1976; rector St. Andrew's Episcopal Ch., 1976—. Home: 805 Sharpshire Dr Grand Prairie TX 75050 Office: POB 958 Grand Prairie TX 75051

MANGER, WILLIAM FREDERICK, priest, Roman Catholic Church; b. Orange, N.J., Jan. 29, 1934; s. William Frederick and Lillian Mae (Marsh) M. B.A., Rice U., 1956; M.Ed., Stephen F. Austin U., 1970. Ordained priest Roman Catholic Church, 1962. Asst. pastor, churches, Houston, Orange, Port Arthur and Beaumont, Tex., 1962-67; chaplain Stephen F. Austin State U., Nacogdoches, Tex., 1967-74; dir. family life Diocese of Beaumont, 1975-78; pastor St. Mary's Ch., Orange, Tex., 1978—. Liaison, Charismatic Catholics Diocese Beaumont, 1981—; pro life dir. Diocese Beaumont, 1967—. Bd. dirs. Southeast Tex. Hospice, Orange, 1978—. Mem. Diocesan Council Priests. Address: 905 W Cherry Ave Orange TX 77630

MANLEY, JOHN STEVAN, minister, Wesleyan Holiness Association of Churches; b. Quincy, Ill., Oct. 11, 1949; s. Harry Russell and Mary Ella (Balzer) M.; m. Helen Jean Denniston, June 7, 1969; children: Brenda Jean, John Russell, Andrew Jay. B.A., Kansas City Coll. & Bible Sch., 1971; B.A. in Missions, 1975; postgrad. Eastern Mich. U., 1977-78. Ordained to ministry, 1973. Pastor, Wesleyan Holiness Ch., Peoria, Ill., 1971-75, Ann Arbor, Mich., 1975-78; prin. Wesleyan Holiness Acad., Portage, Pa., 1978-81; pastor Wesleyan Holiness Ch., Portage, 1981—; gen. sec., treas. Wesleyan Holiness Assn., Dayton, Ohio, 1979-84; bd. dirs. Evangelistic Faith Missions, Bedford, Ind., 1980-84. Republican.

MANN, GARY ALLEN, minister, Lutheran Church in America; b. Burlington, Wis., Apr. 2, 1954; s. George Kendig and Pauline Delores (Lenox) M.; m. Valerie Nudd, Jan. 22, 1975; 1 child, Michelle Marie. B.A. in Theology, Theatre, Luther Coll., 1976; M.Div., Wartburg Theol. Sem., 1980; M.Phil., Drew U., 1983, Ph.D. Ordained to ministry Lutheran Ch. in Am., 1981. Vicar Zion Luth. Ch., W. Union, Iowa, 1978-79; assoc. pastor Good Shepherd Luth. Ch., Somerville, N.J., 1981-82; pastor Holy Trinity Luth. Ch., Wildwood, N.J., 1982—; pastoral rep. Synodical Evangelism Task Force, Trenton, N.J., 1981—; v.p. Wildwood Pastoral Assn., 1983-84, pres., 1984—. Del. Cape May County Child Abuse and Neglect Study Team, N.J., 1982—. Recipient Graduate Academic grant Drew U. Grad. Sch., 1980-84. Democrat. Home: 9 Shadow Lane Cape May Court House NJ 08210 Office: Holy Trinity Luth Ch 2810 Atlantic Ave Wildwood NJ 08260

MANN, JOHN MARTIN, minister, Lutheran Church in America. b. McKeesport, Pa., Nov. 18, 1946; s. Glenn Grant and Mary Dorothy (Flaherty) M. B.A., Clarion State Coll., 1967; M.Div., Duke U., 1970, M. Theology, 1972; D. Ministry, Wittenburg U., 1976. Ordained to ministry Luth. Ch. in Am.. Pastor, First Luth. Ch., Edinboro, Pa., 1971-82; Edinboro State Coll., 1971-82; adj. prof. religion Theil Coll., Greenville, Pa., 1980-82, baccalaureate preacher, 1980, 84; sr. pastor St. John's Luth. Ch., Erie, 1982—; trustee Theil Coll., Greenville, 1974-80, 82-85; dir. Luth. Home, Erie, 1976-79, 82—, Holy Trinity Community Ctr., Erie, 1984—, Interchurch Ministeries Northwest Pa., 1979-84; chmn. Synod Vocations Examining, West Pa.-West Va. Synod, 1984—; chaplain Erie Yacht Club, 1984—. Contbr. articles to profl. jours. Bd. dirs. South Erie Hillside Community Orgn., 1982—. Recipient Outstanding Young Men of Am. award Jaycees, 1982. Mem. Luth. Assn. Larger Chs., Am. Assn. Pastoral Counselors, Luth. Campus Ministry Assn. Club: Erie Yacht. Home: 3910 Trask Ave Erie PA 16508 Office: St Johns Lutheran Church Peach at 23d Erie PA 16502

MANNERS, ROGER EDWIN, minister, United Church of Christ; b. Wahoo, Nebr., Oct. 13, 1919; s. John Raymond and Edna (Bell) M.; m. Elizabeth Ann Roby, Feb. 12, 1949; children: Mary Elizabeth Mullen, John Sheldon, Roger Scot, Julia Roby Wenker. A.B.,

Doane Coll., 1942; M.Div., Yale U., 1945, S.T.M., 1974; postgrad. Ecumenical Inst., Celigny, Switzerland, 1967. Ordained to ministry Congregational Christian Ch., 1945. Minister Congl. Chs., Curtis, Stockville, Nebr., 1945-49; founding minister Countryside Community Ch., Omaha, 1949-59; sr. minister First Congl. Ch., Branford, Conn., 1959—; bd. dirs. United Ch. Bd. World Ministries, 1975-79; supervising pastor Yale Div. Sch. field educ. program, 1961—; chmn. nominating com. Conn. Conf., United Ch. Christ, 1984—, moderator, 1981-82; moderator Nebr. Congl. Conf., Hastings, 1955-56; founder Killam's Point Conf. Ctr., Branford, 1969—; pres., treas. Am. Friends of Asian Rural Inst., Inc., Nishinasuno, Tochigi-Ken, Japan, 1982—; del. World Conf. Christian Youth Nat. Council Pilgrim Fellowship, Oslo, 1947; instr. U. Omaha Coll. Adult Educ., 1952-53, 56-59. Mem. Commn. for Services Elderly, Branford, 1966—; chaplain Branford Fire and Police Depts., Branford, 1966—; pres. Davenport Village, Inc., Hamden, Conn., 1972-74. Recipient trip to Israel First Ecclesiastical Soc., Branford, 1978. Mem. Iona Community, Scotland. Lodge: Rotary. Home: 79 Cedar St Branford CT 06405 Office: First Congregational Ch 1009 Main St Branford CT 06405

MANNEY, RUSSELL FIELD, JR., priest, Episcopal Church; b. Detroit, Oct. 11, 1933; s. Russell F. and Mildred A. (Lamb) M.; m. M. Janet Fairbanks, June 9, 1955; children: Russell Field III, Timothy, Thomas. B.B.A., U. Detroit, 1957; postgrad. Whitaker Sch. Theology, Detroit, 1972-81, Seabury-Western Theol. Sem., 1981-82. Ordained priest Episcopal Ch., 1983. Lic. lay reader St. James Episcopal Ch., Birmingham, Mich., 1959-62; tchr., treas. Cathedral Ch. of St. Paul, Detroit, 1962-75, 78-83, dir. religious edn., 1976-81; vicar St. Mathew's Episcopal Ch., Flat Rock, Mich., 1982-84; chpt. provost Cathedral Ch. of St. Paul, Detroit, 1984—; bd. dirs., treas. Cathedral Found., Detroit, 1981—; counselor New Beginnings, Ann Arbor, Mich., 1982—; alumni chmn. Whitaker Sch. Theology, Detroit, 1982-83, bd. dirs., 1984—. Bd. dirs. Citizens for Good Govt., Harper Woods, Mich., 1969-70; leader Boy Scouts Am., Harper Woods, 1973-76; chmn. Civic Affairs Action Com., Flat Rock, 1982-84. Avocations: tennis; home improvements. Home: 18987 Huntington St Harper Woods MI 48225 Office: Cathedral Church of St Paul 4800 Woodward Ave Detroit MI 48201

MANNING, BRUCE EDWIN, minister, Assemblies of God; b. Portland, Oreg., Apr. 19, 1934; s. Ralph George and Ethel Corina (Speakman) M.; B.A., Bethany Bible Coll., 1957; postgrad. in Spanish, Goshen Coll., 1974; m. Audrey Gay Delp, June 7, 1955; children—Rebecca Jean, David Edwin, Teresa Gray. Ordained to ministry, 1961; pastor chs., Caldwell, Idaho and Glendale, Oreg., 1957-62; nat. dir. Christian edn., missionary, 1962—; founder, pastor chs., Chile, 1965—. Nat. dir. Assemblies of God Internat. Corr. Inst. Pres. Glendale Grade Sch. PTA, 1961. Contbr. articles to denominational jours. Address: Casilla 5021 Santiago 3 Chile

MANNING, CHARLES THOMAS, priest, Roman Cath. Ch.; b. Rochester, N.Y., Sept. 25, 1947; s. Albert Thomas and Anne Catherine (Marino) M.; B.A., St. John Fisher Coll., 1969; M.Div., St. Bernard's Sem., 1974. Ordained priest, 1975; intern deacon Holy Ghost Ch., Rochester, 1974-75; asst. pastor St. Mary's Parish, Waterloo, N.Y., 1975—. Chaplain, Cath. Daus. Am., Finger Lakes council Boy Scouts Am., Mem. Waterloo Council Chs., Clin. Pastoral Experience Assn., Charismatic Movement. Home and Office: 25 Center St Waterloo NY 13165

MANNING, LINDA CAMPBELL, minister, Lutheran Church in America; b. St. Paul, Nov. 7, 1955; d. Kenneth Charles and Doris Eunice (Peterman) C.; m. Gordon Conant Manning, June 28, 1980. B.A. cum laude, St. Olaf Coll., 1976; M.Div., Vanderbilt U., 1980. Ordained to ministry Lutheran Ch., 1981. Intern, Grace Luth. Ch., Oak Ridge, 1978-79; youth dir. Chapel on the Hill, Oak Ridge, 1980-81; asst. pastor St. Mark's Luth. Ch., Jefferson, Wis., 1981-83; chaplain resident St. Luke's Hosp., Milw., 1983-84; campus pastor U. Wis., Whitewater, 1985—; leader edn. com. Wis.-Upper Mich. Synod, Luth. Ch. Am., 1982-83, stewardship rep., 1982-85. Mem. adv. bd. Planned Parenthood of Walworth County. Mem. Jefferson Clergy Assn., Whitewater Ministerial Assn. Office: Shalom Ctr for All Faiths 344 N Prairie St Whitewater WI 53190

MANNING, TIMOTHY CARDINAL, cardinal, Roman Cath. Ch.; b. Cork, Ireland, Oct. 15, 1909; came to U.S., 1928, naturalized, 1945; s. Cornelius and Margaret (Cronin) M. Student St. Patrick's Sem., Menlo Park, Calif., 1928-34; D.C.L., Gregorian U., Rome, 1938. Ordained priest Roman Catholic Ch., 1934, consecrated bishop, 1946, elevated to cardinal, 1973; titular bishop Lesvi, aux. bishop Diocese of Los Angeles, 1946-67; bishop Diocese of Fresno, Calif., 1967-69; titular bishop Capri, coadjutor archbishop Diocese of Los Angeles, 1969-70, archbishop of Los Angeles, 1970-85, elevated to Sacred College of Cardinals, 1973. Office: Archdiocese of Los Angeles 1531 W 9th St Los Angeles CA 90015

MANOOGIAN, TORKOM, archbishop, Armenian Church N.Am. Primate, Armenian Ch. of Am. including Diocese of Calif. Address: 630 2d Ave New York NY 10016

MANROSS, WILLIAM WILSON, priest, Epsicopal Church; b. Syracuse, N.Y., Feb. 21, 1905; s. William Doane and Martha Elizabeth (Wilson) M.; B.A., Hobart Coll., 1926, D.D., 1982; M.A., Columbia, 1930; Ph.D., 1938; M.Div., Gen. Theol. Sem., 1931; D.D., Phila. Div. Sch., 1973; m. Catherine Amelia Wisner, Jan. 26, 1936. Ordained to ministry, 1929; fellow, tutor Gen. Theol. Sem., N.Y.C., 1929-39, research fellow, 1960-62; librarian, treas. Ch. Hist. Soc., Phila., 1948-56; librarian Phila. Div. Sch., 1956-73, lectr., 1956-59, prof. ch. history, 1959-73, prof. emeritus, 1973—; adj. prof. Temple U., Phila., 1964. Mem. Am. Hist. Assn., Am. Soc. Ch. History, Ch. Hist. Soc., Nat. Hist. Soc. Author: History of the American Episcopal Church, 1935, 2d edit., 1950, 3d edit., 1959; The Episcopal Church in the U.S., 1800-1840, 1938, 2d edit., 1967; The Fulham Papers in Lambeth Palace Library, 1965; The S.P.G. Papers in Lambeth Palace Library, 1974. Address: Room 318 Kearsley Home 49th St and Monument Ave Philadelphia PA

MANSFIELD, ROBERT DEAN, pastor, teacher, Church of the Nazarene; b. Peoria, Ill., June 27, 1958; s. Harold Dean and Dorothy Helen (Scholl) M. B.S. in Math., Olivet Nazarene Coll., 1980; J.D., Washington U., St. Louis, 1983. Lic. pastor, 1984. Youth pastor, teen dir. Peoria 1st Nazarene Ch., 1979-84; youth pastor East Peoria 1st Ch. Nazarene, 1984—; substitute tchr. Peoria Christian Sch., 1984—; chmn. Peoria-Pekin zone Nazarene Youth Internat., 1983—, del. from Northwestern Ill. dist. to 1985 gen. conv.; dir. evangelism and missions Northwestern Ill. dist., Ch. Nazarene, 1984—. Mem. Tri-County Holiness Assn. Avocations: sports; music. Home: 2002 N Bigelow St Peoria IL 61604 Office: East Peoria 1st Ch Nazarene 1325 Meadows St East Peoria IL 61611

MANSON, JOYCE LAVERNE, minister, educator, Presbyterian Church (U.S.A.); b. Kansas City, Mo., Sept. 15, 1937; d. Nellis Emmanuel and Alice Winifred (Olson) M. B.A. in Elem. Edn., Wheaton Coll. (Ill.), 1959; M.A. in Eng. Lit., Stanford U., 1963; B.D., San Francisco Theol. Sem., 1966; diploma Renewal of the Ch. and Soc. Grad. Sch. of Ecumenical Studies, U. Geneva, 1967; M.A. in Urban Policy, New Sch. for Social Research, 1976. Ordained to ministry Presbyn. Ch. (U.S.A.), 1966; cert. elem. and jr. high sch. tchr., Calif.; substitute cert. K-12, Wash.; cert. lower secondary dept. edn. and sci., Eng. and Wales. Asst. pastor, postgrad. urban intern Howard Presbyn. Ch., San Francisco, 1966-67; mem. internat. staff COEMAR, UPCUSA/Brit. SCM., London, 1968-71; coordinator Southwest Interchurch Ministry, Pitts., 1972-73; liaison for Europe Assoc. for Mission Devel., Program Agy., UPCUSA, N.Y.C., 1973-74; dean staff, program staff Madison Campus Ministry (Wis.), 1976-80; pastor Madrona Presbyn. Ch., Seattle, 1981-85; mem. gen. com. Christians Assn. for Relations with Eastern Europe, N.Y.C., 1973—, nat. council Ams. for Middle East Understanding, N.Y.C., 1980—, placement com. Com. on Ministry, Presbytery of Seattle, 1982—, task force on human relations Synod of Alaska-Northwest, Seattle, 1983—; moderator Gen. Assembly Provisional Com. on Representation, Presbyn. Ch. in U.S., 1984—; mem. urban task force Ch. Council of Greater Seattle, 1983—. San Francisco Theol. Sem. fellow, 1966. Mem. Internat. Assn. Women Ministers (asst. to internat. dir. 1980—, reporter 1983—). Home: 611 32d Ave Seattle WA 98122

MANTELLO, MARIA CONSILIA, nun, Roman Catholic Church; b. N.Y.C., Oct. 24, 1932; d. Salvatore and Elizabeth (Docimele) Mantello. B.S., St. Louis U., 1958; M.A., Manhattanville Coll., 1968. Joined Apostles of Sacred Heart of Jesus, Roman Cath. Ch., 1954. Tchr., Cor Jesu Acad., St. Louis, 1956-60, Sacred Heart Acad. and Mt. Sacred Heart Coll., Hamden, Conn., 1960-74; directress of aspirants Mt. Sacred Heart Coll., Hamden, 1960-65, directress of postulants, 1965-74, provincial superior, 1977—, pres., 1977--; prin. Rev. Daniel J. Barry Jr. High Sch., Hamden, Conn., 1974-77. Mem. Leadership Conf. of Religious Women, Consortium Perfectae Caritatis, Inst. Religious Life, Nat. Cath. Edn. Assn., Conn. Council Higher Edn. Home: 265 Benham St Hamden CT 06514 Office: Apostles of the Sacred Heart of Jesus 265 Benham St Hamden CT 06514

MANWORREN, DONALD BERWIN, minister, Christian Ch. (Disciples of Christ); b. Galesburg, Ill., Jan. 25, 1937; s. Berwin E. and Annise Matilla (Hadden) M.; m. Elaine Karen Jensen, June 15, 1957; children: Julia Lynn Manworren Biskowski, Susan Annette Manworren Sinclair, John Franklin. B.A., Drake U., 1957, M.Div., 1961; S.T.M., Yale U., 1962; D.D. (hon.) Drake U., 1981. Ordained to ministry Christian Ch. (Disciples of Christ), 1961. Pastor, First Christian Ch., Keota, Iowa, 1962-64, Covenant Christian Ch., Des Moines, 1965-71, Central Christian Ch., Waterloo, Iowa, 1972-77; exec. coordinator Iowa Inter-Church Forum, Des Moines, 1977—; mem. exec. com. Christian Ch. (Disciples of Christ), Indpls., 1976-82; trustee Christian Theol. Sem., Indpls., 1976—; mem. governing bd. Nat. Council Chrs. of Christ in U.S.A., N.Y.C., 1978-84, v.p. 1985-88. Commr. Urbandale Park Commn., Iowa, 1966-71, Iowa Commn. on Aging, Iowa, 1978-82; pres. Northeast Iowa Council on Aging, Waterloo, 1974-77. Mem. Nat. Council Chs. (bd. dirs. commn. on regional & local ecumenism 1978—, chmn. 1985-88), Phi Beta Kappa. Home: 2708 Watrous St Des Moines IA 50321 Office: Iowa Inter-Church Forum 317 E 5th St Des Moines IA 50309

MANZO, MARCELLUS PERES, priest, Roman Cath. Ch.; b. Monte Maggiore, Italy, Mar. 1, 1900; s. Valentine Calogero and Rose (D'Angelo) M.; came to U.S., 1905, naturalized, 1924; B.A., St. Lawrence Coll., Mt. Calvary, Wis., 1925; M.A., Fordham U., 1933, Ph.D., 1941; postgrad. Cath. U. Am., Gregorian U., Rome, Angelico U., Rome. Ordained priest, 1926; pastor chs. in Va., 1967—, Shrine of Sacred Heart, Hot Springs, 1967—; port chaplain, Norfolk, Va., 1960-64; tchr., N.Y., Va. and N.J. Author: The Philosophy of Joseph McCabe, 1933; The Seraphic Castle, 1949; Do You Know St. Francis of Assisi?, 1944; Recalling St. Anthony of Padua, 1946; also articles, poems. Address: Box B Hot Springs VA 24445

MAPPES, MARTIN LOUIS, minister, Lutheran Church-Missouri Synod; b. Norman, Okla., Feb. 23. 1926; s. Henry Peter and Minnie Louise (Hansmeyer) M.; m. Doris Marie Awe, July 26, 1964; children: Brian, Teresa, Martin. Student, St. John's Coll., 1947-49; B.A., Concordia Sem., 1954. Ordained to ministry Luth. Ch.-Mo. Synod, 1954. Pastor, Trinity Luth. Ch., Ramona, Kans., 1954-57, Hoyleton, Ill., 1957-60, Salina, Kans., 1960-72, Cristus Victor Luth. Ch., Knoxville, 1972-76, Shepherd of the Hills Luth. Ch., Georgetown, Ind., 1976—; circuit counselor Herington Circuit, Salina, 1965-67, Nashville circuit, 1959. Served with U.S. Army, 1945-46. Republican. Address: Route 4 Box 132 Georgetown IN 47122

MARAMAN, CHARLES REGINALD, minister, So. Bapt. Conv.; b. Sturgis, Ky., May 18, 1928; s. Charle William and Ruth Lillian (Collins) M.; A.B., Union U., Jackson, Tenn., 1956, B.D., 1960; M.Div., Golden Gate Bapt. Theol. Sem., 1975; M.S., U. Tenn., 1973; m. Lois Daun Adkins, Dec. 16, 1951; children—Charles Alan, Virginia Ann, Keith Anderson. Ordained to ministry, 1953; pastor chs. in Tenn. and Calif., 1953-68; pastor First Bapt. Ch., Morgan Hill, Calif., 1968-70, Natchez Trace Bapt. Ch., Camden, Tenn., 1970—; chaplain CAP. Pres. Benton County Ministerial Assn., 1976. Address: Rt 1 Box 9BG Mountain View MO 65548

MARCANTUONO, DANIEL LOUIS, hospital administrator, Roman Catholic Church; b. Newark, Sept. 27, 1941; s. Daniel and Liberta (Francescone) M.; m. Joanne Molinaro, Nov. 14, 1964; children: David, Lisa, Cheryl. B.S., Seton Hall U., 1963; M.B.A., George Washington U., 1966. Vice pres. ops. Cooper Med. Ctr., Camden, N.J., 1975-77, sr. v.p. adminstrv. affairs, 1977-79; v.p. profl. affairs St. Michael's Med. Ctr., Newark, 1979-80, 1st v.p., 1980-82; pres. St. James Hosp., Newark, 1981—; chmn. bd. Sparta (N.J.) Bd. Health; dir. Ironbound Mfrs. Assn., Newark. Bd. advisors East Side High Sch., Newark. Mem. Am. Coll. Hosp. Adminstrs., Am. Mgmt. Assn. (pres.), Am. Hosp. Assn., N.J. Hosp. Assn., Essex County Hosp. Adminstrv. Council, N.J. Cath. Health Assn. (treas. 1983-84). Home: 10 Deer Run Sparta NJ 07871 Office: St James Hosp 155 Jefferson St Newark NJ 07105

MARCELLE, CHARLES EMANUEL, minister, Church of God; b. Orlando, Fla., Nov. 2, 1931; s. Bishop Norbert Soloman and Melissa (Evans) M.; m. Edith Gertrude Barrow, Oct. 1953 (dec. 1973); children: Linda, Deborah, Gwendolyn, Edythe, Karen, Esther; m. Celia Arnet Thurston, July 7, 1973; 1 child, Rene Michelle. Cert. Bethel Bible Inst., 1954; student NY U, 1955-56. Ordained to ministry Ch. of God, 1976. Evangelist, pastor Ch. of God, Bklyn., 1965-74, state youth and Christian edn. dir., met. N.Y.C., 1974-78, Cocoa, Fla., 1978-82; state coordinator black chs. Ch. of God, Birmingham, Ala., 1983—; pastor Ch. of God, Brighton, Ala., 1984—; mem. Bessemer Prayer Group, Ala., 1984—; chaplain Arthur C. Logan Hosp., N.Y.C., 1975-78, East 93d St. Block Assn., Bklyn., 1974-78. Mem. exec. bd. N.Y.C. Police Dept. 44th precinct, Bronx, 1977-78; active Cocoa/Rockledge Civic Assn., Fla., 1983. Served with U.S. Army, 1950-53, Korea. Recipient Citation of Achievement, Ch. of God, 1980, 82; Citation of Recognition Ch. of God, 1982; Leadership award Ch. of God, 1978, 82; Spl. Honors award Faith Temple Youth Camp, 1980, 82. Home: 271 Westlake Lodge Bessemer AL 35020 Office: Ch of God Ala State Exec Offices State Hwy 11 Birmingham AL 35228

MARCONI, DOMINIC ANTHONY See *Who's Who in America*, 43rd edition.

MARINO, EUGENE ANTONIO See *Who's Who in America*, 43rd edition.

MARINO, VINCENT JOSEPH, priest, Roman Catholic Ch.; b. Pitts., Nov. 22, 1947; s. Vincent Joseph and Helen Catherine (Agnich) M.; B.A. cum laude in Classics, Duquesne U., 1969; S.T.B. cum laude, Pontifical Gregorian U., Rome, 1972; certificate of study Pontifical Inst. Christian Archaeology, Rome, 1972. Ordained priest, 1974; tchr. Hilltop Cath. High Sch., Pitts., 1973—; asso. pastor St. George Ch., Pitts., 1974-77, St. Pius X Ch., Pitts., 1977—. Chaplain, Naim Guild for Catholic Widows and Widowers Diocese of Pitts., 1973-76, Rosalia Manor, Pitts., 1975-76; instr. Continuing Christian Devel. Program Diocese of Pitts., 1975—; lectr. in field. Home and Office: St Pius X Church 3040 Pioneer Ave Pittsburgh PA 15226

MARIOTTINI, CLAUDE FRANCISCO, minister, religion educator, Southern Baptist Convention; b. Rio de Janeiro, Brazil, Dec. 24, 1942; came to U.S., 1963, naturalized, 1972; s. Waldemiro and Palmyra (Neves) M.; m. Donna Sue Anderson, Oct. 27, 1967; children: Claude Francisco, Christopher Matthew, James Andrew. B.A., Calif. Bapt. Coll., 1968; M.Div., Golden Gate Bapt. Sem., 1971; postgrad. Grad. Theol. Union, 1971-73; Ph.D., So. Bapt. Sem., 1983. Ordained to ministry Bapt. Ch., 1967. Missionary, Home Mission Bd., So. Bapt. Conv., San Francisco, 1968-72; coordinator ethnic chs. San Jose Association (Calif.), 1972-73; pastor Meml. Bapt. Ch., San Jose, 1973-76, Spanish Bapt. Ch., Radcliff, Ky., 1977-83; assoc. prof. Old Testament, Southwest Bapt. U., Bolivar, Mo., 1983—; radio speaker Portuguese Bapt. Hour, San Francisco, 1968-72; advisor Confraternity of Spanish Chs., Calif., 1972-74; bd. dirs. Evang. Release Time, Inc., San Jose, Calif., 1973-76; mem. Multi-Ethnic Adv. Com., Calif., 1974-75. Contbr. articles, book reviews, religious study materials to profl. publs. Mem. Soc. Bibl. Lit., Bibl. Archeol. Soc. Republican. Home: Route 1 Box 322 Bolivar MO 65613 Office: Southwest Bapt U 1601 S Springfield Bolivar MO 65613

MARJANCZYK, JOSEPH ANICETUS, priest, Roman Catholic Church; b. Elizabeth, N.J., Apr. 17, 1921; s. Joseph John and Catherine Frances (Cwik) M.; B.A., Seton Hall U., 1941; M.Div., Darlington Sem., 1975. Ordained priest, 1945, named monsignor, 1979; asst. pastor St. Valentine's Ch., Bloomfield, N.J., 1945-72; prof. Polish, Master Sch. Fgn. Langs., Seton Hall U., 1948-60; pastor St. Adalbert's Ch., Elizabeth, N.J., 1972-83, Our Lady of Mt. Carmel Ch., Bayonne, N.J., 1983—; chmn. personnel bd. Archdiocese of Newark, 1972-74, mem. pastoral council, 1972-83; chmn. adminstrv. com., mem. exec. bd. Archdiocesan Pastoral Council, 1972—; dean Union County East Deanery, 1975-83; trustee Roman Cath. Archdiocese of Newark, 1975—, Immaculate Conception Sem., South Orange, N.J., 1979—; hon. pres. Archdiocesan Polish Clergy Soc., 1979—. Chmn. bd. dirs. Polish Cultural Found., 1974—; nat chaplain Polish Army Vets. Assn. Am., 1980—; trustee Seton Hall U., 1978—; commr. bd. edn. City of Elizabeth, N.J., 1979-83. Mem. Polish Am. Hist. Assn., N.J. Hist. Soc., Polish Am. Congress, Order Alhambra, Polish Am. Numis. Assn., Polonians. Lodge: K.C. Home: PO Box 456 Point Pleasant NJ 08742 Office: 39 E 22d St Bayonne NJ 07002

MARKHAM, ALEXANDER SYLVESTER, bishop, British Methodist Episcopal Church; b. Bethel, Montserrat, W.I., Dec. 2, 1908; came to Can., 1941; s. Henry W. and Rebecca (Williams) M.; m. Linda Ann Elisa Lee, 1931 (div. 1970); children: William, Norman, Juliet, Archibald; m. Jean Joyce Burke, Nov. 28, 1970. Th.M., Am. Div. Sch., Chgo., 1956, D.D. (hon.), 1957. Ordained priest Episcopal Ch., 1952, consecrated bishop, 1977. Elder, Afro Community Ch., Toronto, Ont., Can., 1950-52; elder Brit. Meth. Episc. Ch., Toronto, 1952—, gen. supt., 1962-77, bishop, 1977-82; mem. Interfaith Soc. Toronto, 1974-82, Can. Council Christians and Jews, 1970-82; trustee United Appeal Greater Toronto, 1975-78; chaplain 182d Boy Scouts Greater Toronto, 1955-82; mem.-honoree Toronto Evang. Ministerial Fellowship, 1984. Author hymns. Founder/owner, Greenwood Children's Camp, 1957-83. Served with Engrs., Royal Can. Army, 1941-45; ETO. Recipient Queen's Jubilee medal, 1977; recipient Disting. Service award Black Media, Toronto, 1975; Disting. Pub. Service award City of Toronto, 1977; Exceptional Service award Summer Rendezvous for Srs., Toronto, 1980; Disting. Service award Brit. Meth. Episc. Ch. Conf., 1984; Good Servant medal Can. Council Christians and Jews, 1985. Mem. Meth. Hist. Soc., Lodges: Masons (grand master 1949-51), Lions (plaque 1973). Home: 205 Locksley Ave Toronto ON M6B 3P1 Canada

MARKS, FREDERICK AUGUST, minister, Lutheran Church in America. b. Racine, Wis., Dec. 7, 1926; s. Otto F.A. and Martha Minnie (Patzke) M.; m. Jewel Elinore Beres, May 7, 1948; children: John Frederick, Joel Peter. B.A., Carthage Coll., 1948, D.D. (hon.), 1981; M.Div., Northwestern Luth. Theol. Sem., 1951. Ordained to ministry Lutheran Ch. in Am. 1951. Pastor Calvary Lutheran, Two Rivers, Wis., 1951-56, Holy Cross Luth., Menonomee Falls, Wis., 1956-65; regional sec. Bd. Am. Missions Luth. Ch. Am., Mich., Ohio, 1965-72; assoc. dir. Div. Mission, Chgo., 1973-76, regional dir., Wis., Minn., Upper Mich., Ill., 1976—; program dir. Pine Lake Camp, Waupaca, Wis., 1959-62; chmn. Mission Bd., Wis. Upper Mich. Synod, 1963-65; dir. Luther Manor Program for Aging, Milw., 1963-65; mem. Joint Strategy and Action Com., N.Y.C., 1972-76. Mem. Interfaith Forum on Religion, Art and Architecture. Home: W305 N2561 Ravine Ct Pewaukee WI 53072

MARKS, JOSEPH ALBERT, minister, school administrator, non-denominational church; b. Chgo., Mar. 22, 1950; s. Albert Charles and Rose Felicia (DeFronzo) M.; m. Karen Lynn Murra, Oct. 27, 1973; children: Robert, Marina, Darren. A.A., L.A. Pierce Coll., Woodland Hills, Calif., 1969; B.B.A., U. So. Calif., Los Angeles, 1972. Ordained to ministry Ind. Bapt. Ch., 1981, transferred credentials to Ch. of Christ, 1982. Asst. children's dir. 1st Bapt. Ch., Van Nuys, Calif., 1969-71; children's dir., 1st Bapt. Ch., Lakewood, Calif., 1971-76; minister to children 1st Bapt. Ch., Modesto, Calif., 1976-81, Crossroads Christian Ch., Corona, Calif., 1982-83; pastor ch. programming and adminstrn. Community Christian Ch., Sunnyvale, Calif., 1984—; adminstr. Sunnyvale Christian Sch., 1984—; mem. tng. task force Bapt. Gen. Conf., West Covina, Calif., 1971-76; mem. bd. Christian Edn., Southwest Bapt. Gen. Conf., West Covina, 1971-76; chmn. Inst. for Child Edn., Modesto, 1976-81; cons. Gospel Light Publs., 1976-85; mem. exec. com. Los Angeles Sunday Sch. Conv., 1982-84; program chmn. Bay Area Sunday Sch. Conv., San Jose, Calif., 1984—. Author child edn. manuals, stewardship curriculum. Vol. Inglewood Bapt. Children's Home, Calif., 1974-76, Intercommunity Exceptional Child Home, Long Beach, Calif., 1975-76. Mem. Creative Evangelism Inc. (bd. dirs. 1976-85). Republican. Avocations: music, interior design, puppetry, writing and directing children's musicals. Home: 670 San Antonio Rd Apt 10 Palo Alto CA 94306 Office: Community Christian Ch 397 S Mary Ave Sunnyvale CA 94086

MARKSTROM, PAUL RAGNVALD, minister, Assemblies of God Church; b. Skanninge, Sweden, May 30, 1921; s. Gustaf Eric and Elsa (Markstrom) M.; brought to U.S., 1922, naturalized, 1970; student Zion Bible Inst., 1940-41; student Central Bible Coll. Sem., 1941-44, So. Methodist U., 1948, Southwestern State Coll., 1961-62; m. Berniece Elva Hoehn, June 1, 1944; children: Paul Eugene, Sandra Kay (Mrs. John Marion Todd). Ordained to ministry, Assemblies of God Ch., 1947; pastor Assembly of God Ch., Ely, Nev., 1944-46; pastor First Assembly of God Ch., Newburgh, N.Y., 1946-49; pastor Assembly of God Ch., Bucklin, Kan., 1950-57; pastor Assembly of God Ch., Coldwater, Kan., 1958-63; dir. chaplains Assemblies of God Ch., Springfield, Mo., 1963—, dir. spl. ministries, 1974—; instr. Central Bible Coll., 1966—. Bd. dirs. Am. Indian Bible Inst., Phoenix. Mem. Am. Protestant Correctional Chaplains Assn. (dir. 1963, pres. Central region 1974—), Correctional Assn., Am. Correctional Chaplains Assn., Nat. Assn. Evangs. (mem. com. on pastoral care in instns., 1970, chmn. instnl. chaplaincy commn., 1967—, chmn. spl. ministries 1973—. Home: 1520 Devon St Springfield MO 65802 Office: 1445 Boonville Ave Springfield MO 65802

MAROT, ROGER LEO, priest, Roman Catholic Church; b. Pawtucket, R.I., Nov. 7, 1925; s. Armand Joseph and Alice Mary (Cote) M.; B. Philosophy, U. St. Paul, Ottawa, 1946, B.A., 1946, S.T.L., 1950. Ordained priest, 1950; asso. pastor St. James Ch., Manville, R.I., 1950-68, St. Agatha Ch., Woonsocket, R.I., 1968-69; regional dir. youth ministry, No. R.I., parttime, 1951-69, full time, 1969—, diocesan dir. youth ministry, 1977—; coordinator Youth Ministries New Eng., 1979-81; pastor St. Aloysius Parish, 1984—. Founder Youth Council R.I., 1952, Cath. Youth Orgn. Adult Council New Eng., 1957. Mem. Youth Commn. Dept. Atty. Gen. R.I., 1961-63; chmn. Clasp anti proverty program; mem. Council Community Services R.I., 1973—. Named Citizen of Yr., City Woonsocket, 1975; Father Marot youth center named in his honor. Club: Kiwanis. Home and Office: 53 Federal St Woonsocket RI 02895

MARQUIS, WILLIAM HARRISON, minister, Presbyterian Church (U.S.A.); b. South Charleston, W.Va., June 23, 1920; s. Harold Edwin and Margaret Mabel (Jackson) M.; m. Gwendolyn Gail Bevis, Apr. 10, 1948; 1 child, William Samuel. B.S., Morris Harvey Coll., 1953; B.D., Columbia Theol. Sem., 1955, M.Div., 1971; D.Min., Trinity Evang. Div. Sch., 1980. Ordained to ministry, Presbyterian Ch. (U.S.A.), 1955. Pastor Hazelwood Presbyn. Ch., N.C., 1955-64, Northshore Presbyn. Ch., Jacksonville, Fla., 1964-72, First Presbyn. Ch., Soddy Daisy, Tenn., 1972-81; evangelist Presbytery of Giddings/Lovejoy, St. Louis, 1981—. Author: Our Zion, 1978. Served with USN, 1940-46. Clubs: Kiwanis (Fla.); Rotary (Mo.). Home: PO Box 444 Arnold MO 63010

MARRON, PATRICK LEO, priest, Roman Cath. Ch.; b. Dublin, Ireland, Feb. 4, 1939; s. Michael J. and Teresa M. (McClory) M.; came to U.S., 1967, naturalized, 1974; student Trinity Coll., Dublin, 1959-60; M.Ed., Our Lady of the Lake Coll., 1971; M. Div., Oblate Coll. of S.W., 1974. Ordained priest, 1967; asst. pastor St. John's Ch., San Antonio, 1967-68, Assumption Ch., Ganado, Tex., 1968, Sts. Cyril and Methodius Ch., Shiner, Tex., 1968-72; asso. pastor St. Michael's Ch., Weimar, Tex., 1972, St. Mary's Ch., Fredericksburg, Tex., 1972-74, Our Lady of Victory Ch., Victoria, Tex., 1974—. Youth moderator Victoria Deanery, 1977. Contbr. to radio program Interchange, 1976-77. Address: 1309 E Mesquite Ln PO Box 3687 Victoria TX 77901

MARRS, KENT DAVIS, minister, United Methodist Church. B. Dawson, Tex., June 12, 1940; s. Olen Bert and Leola (Davis) M.; m. Mary Diane Morris, July 20, 1963; children: Darin, Cory. B.A., McMurry Coll., 1965; M.Div., Tex. Christian U., 1968, Doctor of Ministry, 1976. Ordained to ministry United Methodist Ch., 1968. Pastor, First United Meth. Ch., Gorman, Tex., 1972-73, Diamond Hill United Meth. Ch., Fort Worth, 1973-76, First United Meth. Ch., Grandview, Tex., 1976-79, First United Meth. Ch., Harker Heights, Tex., 1979-81, St. Stephen's United Methodist Ch., Arlington, Tex., 1981—; del. World Meth. Conf., Honolulu, 1981; adj. prof. Tex. Christian U., 1982—. Bd. dirs. Nat. Fedn. for Decency, Arlington, 1983; chaplain, res. officer Southlake Police Dept., Tex., 1983; emergency care attendant Grandview Fire Dept., 1976-79. Recipient Outstanding Service to Ch. and Community award Tex. Meth. Coll. Assn., 1984, Community Service award Harker Heights City Council, 1981. Mem. Internat. Soc. of Theta Phi, Bibl. Archeology Soc., Nat. Bd. Dirs. Inst. of Indsl. and Comml. Ministries, Law Enforcement Officers Assn. of Tex., Arlington C. of C. Democrat. Lodges: Kiwanis (bd. dirs.), Rotary. Home: 1707 Park Ridge Terr Arlington TX 76012 Office: St Stephen United Meth Ch 1800 W Randol Mill Rd Arlington TX 76012

MARSHALL, ALLEN ST. CLAIR, minister; b. Dover, N.H., Sept. 19, 1921; s. Robert William and Alice Maud (Carter) M.; B.Th., Aurora Coll., 1944, B.A., 1951; B.D., No. Bapt. Theol. Sem., 1954, M.Div., 1973; M.A., Olivet Nazarene Coll., 1969; Th.D., S.W. Internat. Coll., San Antonio; m. Thelma Irene Barnett, Oct. 27, 1944; 1 dau., Carol. Ordained to ministry, 1944; pastor Advent Christian Ch., Watertown, Wis., 1944-47, Galesburg, Ill., 1947-50, Plank Road Bapt. Ch., Naperville, Ill., 1952-53, First Bapt. Ch., Highland, Ill., 1954-59, First Bapt. Ch., Chatsworth, Ill., 1959-66, Fairmont Meth. Ch., Lockport, Ill., 1966-72, Summit (Ill.) Bible Ch., 1972—. Sec. Alton (Ill.) Assn., Am. Bapt. Conv., 1955-57, moderator, 1957-58; mem. Order Barnabas, No. Ill. Meth. Conf., 1970-72; pres. Joliet (Ill.) Regional Ministerial Assn., 1970-72; pres. Evang. Ch. Alliance, Bradley, Ill., 1973-75. Pres., Band Parents, Highland, 1955-57; active ARC, Salvation Army. Home: 7332 W 55th Pl Summit IL 60501 Office: 7400 W 55th Pl Summit IL 60501

MARSHALL, ARTHUR, JR., bishop, A.M.E. Zion Ch.; b. High Point, N.C., Mar. 2, 1914; s. Arthur and Nellie (Kindle) M.; A.B., Livingstone Coll., 1937, D.D., 1962; S.T.B., Boston U., Am., 1941; m. Mary Ann Stotts, May 3, 1952; 1 son, Arthur Clifford. Ordained deacon A.M.E. Zion Ch., 1934, elder, 1936, consecrated bishop, 1972; now bishop 9th Episcopal area, Atlanta. Mem. council Meth. World Conf.; chmn. bd. publs. A.M.E. Zion Ch. Pres., Kansas City (Mo.) Ministerial Alliance, 1956; mem. exec. com. Mo. Council Chs., 1961, mem. gen. bd. Nat. Council Chs., 1963; mem. exec. council St. Louis Interfaith Council, 1966. Chmn. bd. trustees Clinton Coll.; trustee Livingstone Coll.; mem. nat. council Minority Bus. Enterprise; v.p. bd. dirs. NAACP. Recipient Meritorious service award Kansas City Coll., St. Louis Citizens award St. Louis Argus. Mem. Alpha Phi Alpha. Home: 3141 Pyrite Circle Atlanta GA 30331 Office: Ben Hill Station POB 41138 Atlanta GA 30331

MARSHALL, JOE D., hospital chaplain, Seventh-Day Adventists. B. McGregor, Tex., Sept. 14, 1902; s. Cy and Stella (Rayburn) M.; m. Glenda Merle Johnson, Sept. 1, 1927; children: Joseph Donald, Janice Dell Marshall Younker. Student, Walla Walla Coll., 1925-28; B.A., Pacific Union Coll., 1930; M.A., Andrews U., 1957. Ordained to ministry Seventh-day Adventists, 1940; cert. tchr. Bible history, Spanish. Tchr., Seventh-day Adventists, Cottagegrove, Oreg., 1923-24, Spanish pastor, Calexico, Calif., 1940, pastor, supt., Kauai, Hawaii, 1940-43, tchr., pastor, Honolulu, 1943-51, pastor, Hanford, Calif., 1961-65, San Francisco, 1965-69; tchr., prin. Sanitarium Ten Grade Sch., St. Helena, Calif., 1930-33; tchr. Bible history, Spanish, San Diego Acad., tchr. pastor San Pasqual Acad., Escondido, Calif., 1951-56, Monterey Bay Acad., Watsonville, Calif., 1956-61; chaplain San Joaquin Community Hosp., Bakersfield, Calif., 1969-. Republican. Home: 4209 Cambridge Dr Bakersfield CA 93306 Office: San Joaquin Community Hosp 2615 Eye St Bakersfield CA 93301

MARSHALL, JOHN ALOYSIUS, bishop, Roman Catholic Ch.; b. Worcester, Mass., Apr. 26, 1928; s. John A. and Katherine T. (Redican) M.; A.B., Holy Cross Coll., Worcester, student Sem. de Philosophie, Montreal, Can.; S.T.L., Pontifical Gregorian U., Rome, 1954; M.A. in Guidance and Psychology, Assumption Coll., Worcester, 1964. Ordained priest, 1953, consecrated bishop, 1972; assigned Our Lady Lake Ch., Leominster, 1954-56, St. Paul's Ch., Blackstone, 1956, St. Mary's Ch., Southbridge, 1956-57; asst. vice rector and repetitor Pontifical N. Am. Coll., Rome, 1957-61, spiritual dir., 1968-69, bus. mgr., 1969-71; faculty Acad. Sacred Heart, St. Stephen's Central High Sch., St. Vincent's Hosp. Sch. Nursing, Worcester, 1961-62; headmaster St. Stephen's High Sch., 1962-68; bishop of Burlington, Vt., 1972—. Chmn. high sch. religion com. Diocese of Worcester, 1964-68. Address: 351 North Ave Burlington VT 05401*

MARSHALL, NORMAN STEPHEN, JR., minister, Salvation Army; b. Chgo., Apr. 30, 1920; s. Norman Stephen and Marjorie E. (Miles) M.; m. Marjorie Mae Kimball, Sept. 19, 1944; children: Norman S., John F., Anne K., Evelyn T. Grad. Salvation Army Tng. Coll., 1942; D.D. (hon.), Houghton Coll., N.Y., 1984. Commd. officer Salvation Army, 1942. Asst. officer Salvation Army, 1942-43, comdg. officer, New Eng., 1943-53, divisional young people's sec., Portland, Maine, 1953-55, Pitts., 1955-60, field tng. and intelligence officer, Bronx, N.Y., 1960, divisional sec., Cin., 1960-63, divisional comdr., Met. N.Y., 1963-66, tng. prin. Sch. Officers Tng., Chgo., 1966-72, field sec., Chgo., 1972-73, N.Y.C., 1973-76, chief sec. Eastern ter., N.Y.C., 1976-78, internat. sec. for Ams. and Caribbean, London, 1978-82, territorial comdr., N.Y.C., 1982-83, nat. comdr., Verona, N.J., 1983—. Office: Salvation Army 799 Bloomfield Ave Verona NJ 07044

MARSHALL, ROBERT JAMES, church official, Luth. Ch. Am.; b. Burlington, Iowa, Aug. 26, 1918; s. Robert McCrae and Margaret Emma (Gysin) M.; A.B., Wittenberg Coll., Springfield, O., 1941, D.D., 1963, LL.D., 1969; B.D., Chgo. Lutheran Sem., 1944; D.D., Carthage Coll., 1961, Waterloo U., 1970, N.W., Sem., 1969; S.T.D., Thiel Coll., 1971; LL.D., Upsala Coll., 1969, Augustana Coll., 1968, Wagner Coll., 1968, Muhlenberg (Pa.) Coll., 1969; Litt.D., Roanoke Coll., 1970, Newberry Coll., 1972; L.H.D., Gettysburg Coll., 1965; J.C.D., Susquehanna U., 1969; Th.D., St. Olaf Coll., 1974; m. Alice Johanna Hepner, Feb. 6, 1943; children—Robert Edward, Margaret Alice (Mrs. Wilhelm Niederer). Ordained minister Lutheran Ch. Am., 1944; pastor, Alhambra, Calif., 1944-47; instr. religion Muhlenberg Coll., 1947-49, head dept., 1952-53; prof. O.T. interpretation Chgo. Luth. Sem., 1953-62; pres. Ill. Synod, Luth. Ch. Am., 1962-68, Luth. Ch. Am., N.Y.C., 1968-78; dir. Mission Service and Devel., Luth. World Ministries, 1978-80; prof. O.T., Luth. Theol. So. Sem., 1980—. Vice pres. Luth. World Fedn., 1970-77, mem. exec. com., 1968-78; mem. exec. and central coms. World Council Chs., 1968-80; gov. bd. and exec. com. Nat. Council Chs. Christ, 1968-78; exec. com. Luth. Council U.S.A., 1968-78; bd. mgrs. Am. Bible Soc., 1969-80; exec. council Luth. Ch. Am., 1964-78, chmn. evangelism., 1963-64; ann. prof. Am. Sch. Oriental Research, Jerusalem, Jordan, 1958-59; mem. exec. bd. Chgo. Conf. Race and Religion, 1964-68; pres. Luth. World Relief, 1978—. Vice chmn. adv. com. on voluntary fgn. aid, AID, U.S. Dept. State, 1979—; mem. Commn. for a New Luth. Ch., 1982—; fin. moderator Commn. on Interchurch Aid, Refugees and World Service, World Council of Chs., 1984—; chmn. Ch. World Service, 1985—. Bd. dirs. Grand View Coll., 1966-68, Augustana Coll., 1963-68, Luth. Sch. Theology, 1963-68, Chgo. Augustana Hosp., 1963-68, Luth. Hosp., Moline, Ill., 1963-68. Mem. Chgo. Soc. Bibl. Research (sec. 1962-68), Nat. Assn. Profs. Hebrew, Soc. Bibl. Lit. and Exegesis, Religion in Am. Life (religious adv. council). Author: The Mighty Acts of God, 1964. Home: 1005 Wildwood Ave Columbia SC 29203 Office: 4201 N Main St Columbia SC 29203

MARSHALL, ROGER ALLEN, minister, So. Baptist Conv.; b. Kansas City, Mo., Sept. 21, 1947; s. James Edward and Margaret Lillian (Leach) M.; B.A., S.W. Bapt. Coll., 1969; M.Div., Southwestern Bapt. Theol. Sem., 1972; m. Dee Ann Riley, Aug. 25, 1968; children—Karen Michelle, Rebekah Gayle. Ordained to ministry, 1969; pastor First Bapt. Ch., Urbana, Mo., 1968-69, Central Bapt. Ch., Ft. Dodge, Iowa, 1972—. Active Ft. Dodge YMCA, 1972—; v.p. Ft. Dodge Ministerial Assn., 1973, sec.-treas., 1976; pres. Miller County Bapt. Youth Assn., 1966. Mem. N. Central Iowa So. Bapt. Assn. Home: 1027 N 3rd St Fort Dodge IA 50501 Office: 2891 N 15th St Fort Dodge IA 50501

MARSLAND, IRVING A., JR., religious organization executive; United Methodist Church. B. Port Chester, N.Y., Feb. 4, 1919; s. Irving A. and Elizabeth Anne (Brewer) M.; m. Roberta Helen Many, Feb. 16, 1946; children: Lyn Marsland O'Brien, Ann Marsland Millet, Melissa. A.B., Lafayette Coll., 1940; M.Div., Union Theol. Sem., 1943. Ordained deacon United Methodist Church, 1943, elder, 1945. Asst. pastor St. Luke's Meth. Ch., Bronx, N.Y., 1944-45; pastor Grahamsville-Sundown, N.Y., 1945-48, Bedford Hills Meth. Ch., N.Y., 1948-57, Cornwall Meth. Ch., N.Y., 1957-59, Dobbs Ferry United Meth. Ch., N.Y., 1959-65, Grace United Meth. Ch., Newburgh, N.Y., 1965-70, Hempstead United Meth. Ch., N.Y., 1970-77; supt. L.I. Eastern Dist., United Meth. Ch., N.Y., 1977-83; ret., 1983; minister Outreach Met. Community United Meth. Ch., N.Y.C., 1983—; chmn. Council of Fin. and Adminstrn., N.Y. Ann. Conf., 1971-74; pres. bd. trustees, 1978-82; del. Gen. Conf. United Meth. Ch., Portland, Oreg., 1976, Jurisdiction Conf. United Meth. Ch., 1960-80. Case worker Big Brother Movement, N.Y.C., 1943-44; chmn. Newburgh Human Relations Council, N.Y., 1967-68. Mem. Monday Club (pres. 1950-51). Democrat. Lodges: Lions (Bedford Hills, N.Y. pres. 1955-56), Rotary. Home: 153 Grand Ave Rockville Centre New York NY 11570 Office: Met Community United Meth Ch 1975 Madison Ave New York NY 10035

MARSTON, JOSEPH GEORGE LANAUX, JR., lay church worker, Roman Catholic Church; b. Mobile, Ala., July 13, 1919; s. Joseph George Lanaux and Emily Page (Hereford) M.; student McGill Inst., 1936, Spring Hill Coll., 1936-37, U. Ala., 1942, Auburn U., 1974; m. Rose Marie Smith, Sept. 28, 1940; children: Leila Marguerite (Mrs. Gordon U. Sanford), Rose Marie (Mrs. Bernard A. Fogarty, Jr.), Joseph George Lanaux, III, C. Henry, Christopher A., Patrick J., Nicholas S., Hereford F. Mem. orgn. com. Nat. Assn. Holy Name Soc., 1968-69, chmn. youth com., 1970-75, v.p. region III, 1971-73, treas., 1973-75; pres., 1975-77, chmn. nat. adv. bd,, 1977-78; v.p. Mobile-Birmingham Diocesan Holy Name Union, 1965-67, treas, 1966-67; pres. Mobile Diocesan Holy Name Union, 1970-71; dir. Cath. Cemetery of Mobile, 1963-77; adminstr. Cath. Housing of Mobile, Inc., 1974-77; pres. Diocesan Pastoral Council, 1974-75; mem. Nat. Cath. Disaster Relief Com., 1972-76. Pres. Mobile Dist. Cath. Sch. Bd., 1971-72, Mobile dist. Bd. Cath. Edn., 1973-74. Chmn. adv. bd. Cath. Housing Mobile, Inc., 1972-77. Mem. Corpus Christi Parish Council (pres. 1969-71). Internat. Platform Assn. Contbr. articles to profl. and religious jours. Home: 339 Park Ave Mobile AL 36609 Office: 1700 Stone St Mobile AL 36617

MARTENS, ELMER ARTHUR, educator, minister, seminary administrator, Gen. Conf. Mennonite Brethren Chs.; b. Main Centre, Sask., Can., Aug. 12, 1930; s. Jacob Henry and Susie (Nickel) M.; B.A., U. Sask., 1954; B.Ed., U. Man. (Can.), 1956; B.D., Mennonite Brethren Bibl. Sem., 1958; Ph.D., Claremont Grad. Sch., 1972; m. Phyllis Hiebert, Aug. 24, 1956; children—Lauren, Frances, Vernon, Karen. Came to U.S., 1955. Ordained to ministry Gen. Conf. Mennonite Brethren Chs., 1959; pastor Butler Ave. Mennonite Brethren Ch., Fresno, Calif., 1958-66; dir. Christian edn. Brethren in Christ Ch., Upland, Calif., 1967, chmn. bd. Christian lit., from 1966; asso. prof. O.T. Mennonite Brethren Bibl. Sem., Fresno, 1970-73, registrar and prof., 1973-76, pres., 1977—. Participant archaeol. excavation, Israel, 1968, 73, 75; mem. Mennonite World Conf., Brazil, 1972. Recipient First award Nat. Assn. Evangs., 1962. Mem. Soc. Bibl. Lit., Soc. Antiquity and Christianity, Inst. Bibl. Research. Mem. transl. team New Am. Standard Bible, 1969-70; contbr. articles to religious jours. Office: Mennonite Brethren Bibl Sem 4824 E Butler St Fresno CA 93727

MARTI, RAMON TIMONEDA, religious educator, Roman Catholic Church; b. Vallbona de las Monjas, Spain, Nov. 26, 1928; came to U.S., 1978; s. Jose Amenos Marti and Maria Figueras Timoneda. Grad. Philosophy and Theology Sem., Tarragona, Spain, 1951; postgrad. U. Barcelona, Spain, 1964; M.S., Normal Superior, Oaxaca, Mexico, 1972. Pastor Santa Teresita Ch., Los Angeles; chaplain K.C., Los Angeles, 1980-84; moderator asst. Holy Name Soc., Los Angeles, 1984; bd. dirs. Instituto Carlos Pereyra, Puebla, Mexico, 1973-76, Escuelas Dias, Morella, Spain, 1964-70. Author: Dios en las Trincheras, 1964; Quienes el Padre Yermo?, 1974; Las Aventuras del Padre Yermo, 1975; Fantasticos Cuentos del Padre Yermo, 1976; Un Gigante de la Caridad, 1978; Mi Amor, Es Para Ti, 1984; author booklet: A Mi Madre Con Todo Mi Amor, 1982. Recipient 1st prize Spanish Contest, City's Bicentennial, Los Angeles, 1982. Home: 2645 Zonal Ave Los Angeles CA 90033 Office: Santa Teresita Parish 2645 Zonal Ave Los Angeles CA 90033

MARTI, ROBERT WAYNE, minister, So. Bapt. Conv.; b. Springfield, Mo., June 10, 1944; s. Jesse Wayne and Vivian (Elsey) M.; A.A., S.W. Bapt. Coll., 1964; B.A., Ouachita Bapt. U., 1966; M.Div., Southwestern Bapt. Theol. Sem., 1970; m. Judith Joan Welch, Aug. 6, 1966; children—Angela, Robert II, Shannon. Ordained to ministry, 1964; pastor Mt. Moriah Bapt. Ch., Murfreesboro, Ark., 1965, New Home Ch., Nashville, Ark., 1965, Nashville Mission Bapt. Ch., 1966-68, Newport (Tex.) Bapt. Ch., 1968-69, First Bapt. Ch., Lamar, Mo., 1970—. Mem. nominating com. Mo. Bapt. Conv., 1973—, bd. curators S.W. Bapt. Coll., Bolivar, Mo., 1973—. Mem. Lamar Ministerial Alliance, Barton County Bapt. Assn. Home: Route 3 Box 2 Lamar MO 64759 Office: 1108 Gulf St Lamar MO 64759

MARTIN, ALBERTUS See *Who's Who in America*, 43rd edition.

MARTIN, ALVIN, minister, religion educator, Christian and Missionary Alliance; b. nr. Magnolia, Minn., Oct. 25, 1919; s. Oscar and Hanna (Thu) M.; m. Ruth Mildred Pierce, Aug. 12, 1942; children: Daniel, Keith, Shirley, Nathan, Darrell. B.Theology, NY U, 1947; M.A. in Theology, Winona Lake Sch. Theology, 1955, B.D., 1958, Th.M., 1962; D.Missiology, Fuller Theol. Sem., 1974; postdoctoral NY U, 1956, Hebrew U., Jerusalem, 1965. Ordained to ministry Christian and Missionary Alliance Ch., 1944. Missionary, Christian and Missionary Alliance, Jerusalem and Beersheba, Israel, 1947-54, 1973; founding pastor Fourth Ave. Alliance Ch. (now Rosewood Park Alliance Ch.), Regina, Sask., Can., 1957-58; pres. Can. Bible Coll., Regina, 1958-72; founding pres. Can. Theol. Coll. and Sem., Regina, 1970-72; dir. in-service program Fuller Theol. Sem., Pasadena, Calif., 1974-84; pastor Christian and Missionary Alliance Ch., Pasadena, 1982—; founding pres. Assn. Can. Bible Colls., Regina, 1967-68; vis. prof. Hebrew Chgo. Grad. Sch. Theology, 1969; first dir., dean Summer Inst. Internat. Studies, Wheaton, Ill., 1974. Author: Fulfilled Prophecy in Israel Today, 1956; (sound film prodn.) Jerusalem, the Divided City, 1955; (with others) Can. transl. team and cons. for New Internat. Version of Bible, 1972-79. Named Alumnus of Yr., Winona Lake Sch. Theology, 1968. Mem. Nat. Assn. Profs. Hebrew, Am. Soc. Missiology, Nat. Assn. Evangs. Republican. Avocations: photography; collecting books on Jerusalem and Bible lands. Home: 1636 N Allen Ave Pasadena CA 91104 Office: Pasadena Alliance Ch 2113 E Villa St Pasadena CA 91107

MARTIN, ANTHONY GENE, minister, So. Bapt. Conv.; b. Spartanburg, S.C., Sept. 17, 1955; s. Bobby Gene and Jerolyn Alva (Dial) M.; student U. S.C., 1973-77. Ordained to ministry, 1975; asso. pastor Rock Hill Bapt. Ch., Inman, S.C., 1974-76, Arcadia 1st Bapt. Ch., Spartanburg, 1976—. Vice pres. S.C. Royal Ambassadors, 1973; mgr. Royals Quartet, 1971-74. Mem. Am. Council Alcohol Problems, Washington. Mem. N. Spartan Bapt. Assn., Found. for Christian Living. Home: 726 Farley Ave Spartanburg SC 29301 Office: Box 25 Arcadia SC 29320

MARTIN, CHARLES WADE, minister, religious organization administrator, educator, Southern Baptist Convention; b. Athens, Ga., June 7, 1952; s. William Edward and Winifred Louise (Maxwell) M.; m. Rebecca Lynn Hankins, May 26, 1973; children: John Wade, Elizabeth Lynn. B.A. in Bible, Asbury Coll., 1974; M.Div., Asbury Theol. Sem., 1977, M.A.R. in Bibl. Lit., 1977; postgrad. Inst. Holy Land Studies, Jerusalem, 1977, Wheaton Coll., 1981, 82-83; D.Ministry in Preaching, Fuller Theol. Sem., 1982. Ordained to ministry Baptist Ch., Sylvania, Ga., 1983. Pastor, Mt. Moriah UMC, Matthews, Ga., 1977-80; founder, dir. Evang. Ministries of Sylvania, Inc., Ga., 1980—. Editor Bull. of Evang. Ministries, 1978—; contbr. articles to profl. jours. Fellow Case Method Inst.; mem. Israel Exploration Soc., Religious Speech Communication Assn., Wesleyan Theol. Soc., Bibl. Archeol. Soc. Lodge: Lions (chaplain 1983—). Avocations: archaeology; linguistics. Home: 206 Pinecrest Dr Sylvania GA 30467 Office: PO Box 1664 Sylvania GA 30467

MARTIN, FRANCIS AUSTIN, minister, So. Baptist Conv.; b. Louisiana, Mo., Dec. 3, 1941; s. Frances Mae (Davis) M.; A.A., Hannibal LaGrange Coll., 1961; B.A., Okla. Baptist U., 1963; M.Div., So. Bapt. Theol. Sem., 1969, Ed.D., 1973; m. Martha Virginia Woolf, June 2, 1964; 1 dau., Susan Yvonne. Ordained to ministry, 1971; minister of youth 1st Bapt. Ch., Bowling Green, Ky., 1969-70; minister of edn. Lyndon Bapt. Ch., Louisville, Ky., 1970-73; editor pastoral ministries products Bapt. Sunday Sch. Bd., Nashville, 1973-75; asst. prof. psychology Belmont Coll., Nashville, 1975—. Chmn. edn. div. Glendale Bapt. Ch., Nashville, 1975-76, deacon, 1976—. Adj. prof. psychology Tenn. State U., Nashville, 1976—. Author 4 books. Home: 314 Eulala Ct Nashville TN 37211 Office: Belmont Coll Nashville TN 37203

MARTIN, FRED LEE, minister, Southern Baptist Convention; b. Covington, Ky., Oct. 11, 1928; s. William Samuel and Nannie Juanita (Bates) M.; m. Carol Ann Mullins, Dec. 22, 1950; 1 child, Carey Lee. B.A., Georgetown Coll., 1950; B.D., So. Bapt. Sem., 1955, M.Div., 1970, D.Ministry, 1977. Ordained to ministry Baptist Ch., 1948. Assoc. and mission pastor Citadel Square Bapt. Ch., Charleston, S.C., 1955-59; pastor Norway Baptist Ch., S.C., 1959-63, Calvary Bapt. Ch., Meggett, S.C., 1963-73, St. Johns Bapt. Ch., Ehrhardt, S.C., 1973-76, Marion St. Bapt. Ch., Aiken, S.C., 1976-80, 1st Bapt. Ch., Murrells Inlet, S.C., 1980-85, Brentwood Bapt. Ch., Charleston Heights, S.C., 1985—. Pres. Puritan Nat., Norway, 1962. Democrat. Lodge: Lions.

MARTIN, IRVIN HURST, minister, Ind. Fundamental Chs. Am.; b. Blue Ball, Pa., Dec. 27, 1928; s. Clarence and Anna Mary (Hurst) M.; student Lancaster Bible Coll., 1963-68; m. Ruth Irene Smoker, June 2, 1949; children—Wayne, James, Michael. Ordained to ministry, 1971; pastor, founder The Christian Fellowship Ch., Lancaster County, Pa., 1971—. Organizes religious tours to Israel and Europe. Mem. Lancaster Republican Com.; nat. adv. bd. Am. Security Council; chmn., mem. Octorara Area (Pa.) Christian Businessmen Com. Exec. com. Guidelines for Today Mag., 1967-74. Home: 3476 Beacon Hill Dr Ronks PA 17572 Office: Box 61 New Holland PA 17557

MARTIN, ISAAC, minister, So. Baptist Conv.; b. Bainbridge, Ga., Sept. 30, 1930; s. Isaac and Bessie Mae (Joyce) M.; A.B., Ft. Valley State Coll., 1953; M.A., Rutgers U., 1958; M.A., Seton Hall U., 1961; m. Bernice McKinnon, Apr. 14, 1957; 1 son, Cornelius. Ordained to ministry, 1966; prof. history Ala. State Coll., Mobile, 1964-65; pastor Newborn Bapt. Ch., Newark, 1967-71; pastor and founder Unity Freedom Bapt. Ch., Newark, 1971—. Chaplain, Newark Housing Police, 1966-72, Sr. Citizens Assn., 1972-76. Adminstrv. asst. Montgomery Sch., Newark, 1970-76. Bd. dirs. Girls' Club Am., Central Ward Newark, 1973—; active Boy Scouts Am.;

pres. S. 20th St. Day Care Center, 1974—. Mem. Met. Assn. So. Bapt. Conv., Newark Ministerial Alliance, Met. Pastors Assn., NAACP, Urban League. Editor Unity Freedom Bapt. Ch. Monthly News. Home: 355 Keer Ave Newark NJ 07112 Office: 739 S 20th St Newark NJ 07112

MARTIN, JAMES H., minister, Congregational Holiness Church; b. Jacksonville, Ala., Aug. 15, 1930; s. Joe H. and Lilliam (Snider) M.; m. Sara L. Martin, Mar. 10, 1948; children: Debra, James. Student, Jacksonville State U., 1956-60; T.H.B., Internat. Bible Inst., Plymouth, Fla., 1983, T.H.M., 1984. Ordained to ministry Congregational Holiness Ch. Pastor, Congl. Holiness Ch., Inc., Jacksonville, Ala., 1959-69, Griffin, Ga., 1970-71, Weaver, Ala., 1972-73; pastor, conf. supt., Lincolnon, Ga., 1974-73; gen. supt. Congl. Holiness Ch., Griffin, 1977—; treas. Pentecostal Fellowship of N. Am., 1980-83. Served with USN, 1952-56. Office: Congl Holiness Ch Inc 3888 Fayetteville Hwy Griffin GA 30223

MARTIN, JOHN GOVERNOR, minister, American Baptist Convention, Southern Baptist Convention, National Baptist Convention, U.S.A.; b. Aiken, S.C., Jan. 4, 1929; s. Booker T. and Essie (Thompson) M.; m. Ruth Collins, Feb., 1965; children: Walter John, Devadia M. B.S., S.C. State Coll., 1950; M.S., Howard U., 1956; student Christian Theol. Sem., 1965; M.Div., Howard U., 1972. Ordained to ministry Central Baptist Ch., 1966. Statistician, Bapt. Ministers Conf., Washington, 1968—; pastor Holy Comforter Bapt. Ch., Washington, 1972—; host and moderator WYCB-AM radio, Washington, 1981—; founder, exec. dir. Third World Assembly and Political Party, Washington, 1979—, presdl. candidate, 1980, 84; debit mgmt. staff Supreme Life Ins., Washington, 1978—. Contbr. med. articles to profl. jours. Mem. Washington, D.C., Mayors Budget Adv. Com., 1982—. Mem. D.C. Bapt. Convention (bd. dirs. 1972—), Am. Bapt.Convention, So. Bapt. Convention, Nat. Bapt. Convention U.S.A., Alpha Theta Nu Omega (nat. pres. 1971—). Office: Holy Comforter Bapt Ch PO Box 29101 Washington DC 20017

MARTIN, JOHN RAYMOND, bishop, Orthodox Christian Church; b. Pitts., Jan. 5, 1931; s. John and Veronica Helen (Mihach) M. A.A., St. Fidelis Coll., 1950; B.A., Duquesne U., 1953; postgrad. Sts. Cyril & Methodius Sem., 1950-55, Stanford U., 1965-66. Ordained priest Orthodox Christian Ch., 1955, consecrated bishop, 1966. Pastor, St. John the Baptist Ch., Avella, Pa., 1955-59; vice chancellor and sec. to bishop Byzantine Cath. Diocese, Pitts., 1955-62, chancellor, 1962-64; bishop Am. Carpatho-Russian Orthodox Diocese, Johnstown, Pa., 1966—; head coll. dept. Sts. Cyril & Methodius Sem., Pitts., 1955-56; rector, prof. philosophy Christ the Saviour Sem., Johnstown, Pa., 1966-77, pres., 1966—; pres. The Ch. Messenger, 1966—, author feature column, 1966—. Founder, Camp Nazareth Youth Camp, Mercer, Pa., 1976, Monastery of the Annunciation, Tuxedo Park, N.Y., 1979, Bethany: Retirement Home for Elderly, Phila., 1982. Designated Very Reverend, Byzantine Cath. Diocese, Pitts., 1959; Archimandrite, Am. Carpatho-Russian Orthodox Diocese, 1966; Knight of Holy Sepulchre, Greek Orthodox Patriachate, Jerusalem, 1982. Mem. Cannonical Orthodox Bishops in the Ams. (standing conf. vice chmn. 1969, 70). Club: Byzantine Serra (chaplain 1959-64). Address: Am Carpatho-Russian Orthodox Greek Catholic Diocese of USA 312 Garfield St Johnstown PA 15906

MARTIN, JOSEPH ALBERTUS, bishop, Roman Catholic Church; b. Southbridge, Mass., Oct. 4, 1913; s. Arthur and Parmelie (Beaudoin) M.; came to Can., 1920, naturalized, 1935; B.A., Nicolet Sem., Laval U., 1935, S.T.L., 1939, S.T.D., 1942. Ordained priest, 1939, consecrated bishop, 1950; prof. philosophy, history and Greek, Nicolet Sem., 1939-46, rector, 1946-49; vicar gen. Diocese of Nicolet, 1949-50, coadjuter bishop, 1950, bishop of Nicolet, 1950—. Home and Office: Bishop House PO Box 820 Nicolet PQ J0G 1E0 Canada

MARTIN, LEWIS GLENN, minister, United Methodist Church; b. Albany, Ga., Jan. 13, 1958; s. Frederick Lewis and Martha Jane (Akridge) M.; m. Nancy Elizabeth Bagwell, Sept. 6, 1980. Student Ga. State U., 1977-80, Ga. So. Coll., 1983, Valdosta State Coll., 1984-85. Ordained to ministry United Methodist Ch., 1982. Youth dir. First United Meth. Ch., Camilla, Ga., 1976-77; minister to youth and children Wesley Chapel United Meth. Ch., Decatur, Ga., 1979-82; pastor Rocky Ford United Meth. Ch., Ga., 1982-84; minister of edn. and youth First United Meth. Ch., Bainbridge, Ga., 1984—; mem. South Ga. Conf. Council on Youth Ministries, 1983-86; coordinator Statesboro Dist. Council on Youth Ministries, 1983-84; coordinator Thomasville Dist. Council Youth Ministries, 1985-86; mem. Statesboro Dist. Council on Ministries. Tchr. sex edn., pub. schs., Sylvania, Ga., 1982. Author: An Expression of Love, 1979; author study book and leader's guide: I Am . . . God's Creation, 1984. Mem. Christian Educator's Fellowship, South Ga. Fellowship of Profls. in Youth Ministry, Holy Fools Clown Ministry Orgn. Office: First United Meth Ch 300 W Shotwell St Bainbridge GA 31717

MARTIN, SAMUEL JOSEPH, ret. priest, Episc. Ch.; b. Huntsville, Ala., June 5, 1905; s. John Thomas and Dorrence (Hubbard) M.; B.S., Ill. Inst. Tech., 1933; B.D., Va. Episc. Sem., 1939; S.T.M., Seabury Western Sem., 1935, D.D., 1954; postgrad. Boston U., Tufts U., U. Chgo., m. Clarice White, Apr. 6, 1931; children—Annette (Mrs. Jon Craighead), Samuel Joseph. Ordained priest, 1929; rector St. Edmund's Ch., Chgo., 1928-70; founder St. Edmund's Parochial Day Sch., Chgo. Pres. Standing Com., Diocese Chgo., 1957-59, mem. diocesan council, 1959, 60; dean Chgo. South Deanery, 1962-70; dep. gen. convs. Episc. Ch., 1957-70; hon. canon Cathedral St. James, Chgo., 1970. Recipient Bishop's Distinguished Service Cross, 1936. Mem. NAACP. Contbr. articles to religious jours. Home: Lake Shore Dr Cassopolis MI 49031

MARTIN, SELBY RAY, minister, Assemblies of God; b. Arditta, Mo., Oct. 2, 1937; s. Thomas Elbert and Stella Bell (Adams) M.; student N.W. Bible Coll., Minot, N.D., 1965-66; m. Shirley Ann Bevans, Dec. 28, 1957; children—Lennie Ray, Anita Sue. Licensed to ministry Ch. of God-Cleveland, Tenn.; transferred to Assemblies of God, 1973; pastor chs., Wichita and Arkansas City, Kans., 1963-68, Mount Pleasant, Pa., 1968-70; pastor 1st Assembly of God Ch., Swifton, Ark., 1970-76, Hopewell Assembly of God, Alicia, Ark., 1976—. Chaplain St. Joseph's Hosp., Mount Pleasant; sectional Sunday Sch. dir. Ark. dist. council Assemblies of God, 1972-76. Recipient Christian Service award Ark. Dist. Assembly of God, 1976. Mem. Swifton Ministers Fellowship. Home and Office: PO Box 405 Swifton AR 72471

MARTIN, WALTER RALSTON, minister, religious editor, Southern Baptist Convention; b. N.Y.C., Sept. 10, 1928; s. George Washington and Maud (Ainsworth) M.; B.A., Shelton Coll., 1951, B.R.E., 1952; M.A., NY U, 1956; Ph.D., Calif. Western U., 1976; m. Darlene E. Nesland, Nov. 17, 1973; children: Bryan, Jill, Daniel, Cindy, Elaine, Deborah. Ordained to ministry, 1951; founder dir. Christian Research Inst., El Toro, Calif., 1960; founder pres. Dover (N.J.) Christian Nursing Home Retirement Center, 1969; asso. prof. Bibl. Studies, Kings Coll., Briarcliff, N.Y., 1960-66; spl. editor Zondervan Pub. House, Grand Rapids, Mich., 1955-65; editorial assoc. Action Mag., 1960-62; editor Vision House Pubs., Santa Ana, Calif., 1974—; prof. comparative religions and apologetics, M.A. program Simon Greenleaf Sch. Law: pastor Bibl. studies Capistrano Valley Bapt. Ch., San Juan Capistrano, Calif.; founding bd. mem. Gordon-Conwell Theol. Sem.; co-founder Christian Cassette Club, Santa Ana, Calif. Contbg. editor Eternity Mag., 1954-60; author; Jehovah of the Watch Tower; The Kingdom of the Cults; The Maze of Mormonism; Screwtape Writes Again; The New Cults, The Cults Reference Bible; also numerous articles and video tapes. Address: Box 500 San Juan Capistrano CA 92675

MARTINEZ, ARMANDO, minister, American Baptist Churches in the U.S.A.; sheriff; b. Los Angeles, Jan. 11, 1928; s. Octaviano and Ysidra (Espinoza) M.; m. Cherubina Proffitt; children: George, Alexander. Diploma, Evangel. Bible Inst., La Puente, Calif., 1972. Ordained to ministry Interdenominational Christian Assn. Incorp., 1972. Asst. pastor Spanish Mission Ch., La Habra, Calif., 1970-72; asst. pastor Evangelistic Assocs., Elkhart, Ind., 1972-73; youth minister Mexican Missionary Ch., Phoenix, 1973-74; missionary pastor Stamford Bapt. Ch., Conn., 1975-84; evangelist, 1974-84. Sheriff Fairfield County Ct. System, Stamford, 1984—. Vol. worker Stamford Social Services, 1975-84. Served with USAAF, 1946-48. Democrat. Office: PO Box 3044 Stamford CT 06905

MARTINEZ, DANIEL, minister, So. Baptist Conv.; b. Tex., Sept. 30, 1937; s. Ynocencio P. and Sue (Rogers) M.; B.A., Calif. Bapt. Coll., 1966; M.R.E., New Orleans Bapt. Theol. Sem., 1969; m. Janice Carol Bobe, Aug. 23, 1963; children—Andrea, Renea, Douglas, Scott. Ordained to ministry, 1974; music dir. State Youth Assembly, 1974; music dir. Minister Conf., Calif. So. Bapt. Conv., Upland, 1974-76, Calvary-Arrowhead Assn., 1974-76, 1st Bapt. Ch., Anchorage, 1977—. Pres., Calif. Bapt. Coll. Alumni Assn., 1971-73. Bd. dirs. West End Opera Assn., 1975—. Named Outstanding Young Man Am., 1973. Address: 1100 10th Ave Anchorage AK 99501

MARTINEZ, ISABEL, missionary, Missionary Church; b. Sugarland, Tex., Aug. 24, 1944; d. Luis Martinez and Ascension (Hipolito) M. Misionera Biblica Dip., Sociedad Biblica Nacional, Naucalpan, Mex., 1967; A.A., Wharton County Jr. Coll., 1981; Formacion en Ciencias Religiosas Dip., Universidad Iberoamericana, Mex., 1982. Local superior Our Lady of Sorrows Convent, Victoria, Tex., 1973-75, local superior, dir., 1978-79, 81-82, promoter vocations, 1984—, also Victoria Diocese; mistress of postulants Our Lady of Mt. Carmel Convent, Wharton, 1982-83; local sec. Immaculate Heart of Mary, Ft. Worth, 1983-84; promoter for vocations Missionary Catechists of the Sacred Hearts, 1984—. Club: Neuman (sec. 1980-81).

MARTY, MARTIN EMIL, religion educator, editor; b. West Point, Nebr., Feb. 5, 1928; s. Emil A. and Anne Louise (Wuerdemann) M.; m. Elsa Schumacher, June 21, 1952 (dec. 1981); children: Frances, Joel, John, Peter, James, Micah.; m. Harriet Lindemann, 1982. M.Div., Concordia Sem., 1952; S.T.M., Luth. Sch. Theology, Chgo., 1954; Ph.D. in Am. Religious and Intellectual History, U. Chgo., 1956; Litt.D., Thiel Coll., Thomas More Coll.; L.H.D., Marian Coll.; W.Va. Wesleyan Coll., Colo. Coll., Providence Coll., Willamette U., St. Olaf Coll., DePaul U.; D.D., Bethany Sem., Wabash Coll., Muhlenberg Coll., Capital U., U. So. Calif., Valparaiso U., Christ Sem.-Seminex, Maryville Coll., North Park Coll.; LL.D., Keuka Coll. Ordained to ministry Luth. Ch., 1952; pastor, Washington, 1950-51, Elk Grove Village, Ill., 1956-63, asst. pastor, River Forest, Ill., 1952-56; prof. history of modern Christianity Div. Sch. U. Chgo., 1963—, Fairfax M. Cone disting. service prof., 1978—; asso. editor Christian Century, Chgo., 1956—; co-editor Ch. History, 1963—. Author: A Short History of Christianity, 1959, The New Shape of American Religion, 1959, The Improper Opinion, 1961, The Infidel, 1961, Baptism, 1962, The Hidden Discipline, 1963, Second Chance for America Protestants, 1963, Church Unity and Church Mission, 1964, Varieties of Unbelief, 1964, The Search for a Usable Future, 1969, The Modern Schism, 1969, Righteous Empire, 1970 (Nat. Book award 1971), Protestantism, 1972, You Are Promise, 1973, The Fire We Can Light, 1973, The Pro and Con Book of Religious America, 1975, A Nation of Behavers, 1976, Religion, Awakening and Revolution, 1978, Friendship, 1980, By Way of Response, 1981, The Public Church, 1981, A Cry of Absence, 1983, Health and Medicine in the Lutheran Tradition, 1983; contbr. articles to religious publs.; editor: Context, 1969—. Fellow Am. Acad. Arts and Scis., Soc. Am. Historians; mem. Am. Soc. Ch. History (pres. 1971), Am. Cath. Hist. Assn. (pres. 1981), Am. Antiquarian Soc. Home: 239 Scottswood Rd Riverside IL 60546 Office: Swift Hall Univ Chicago Chicago IL 60637

MARTZ, WILLARD JAMES, minister, Gen. Assn. Regular Baptists; b. Chgo., Feb. 16, 1911; s. William and Myrle Lillian (Ostrander) M.; diploma Moody Bible Inst., 1937; A.B., Wheaton Coll., 1947, M.A., 1952; Ph.D., Calif. Grad. Sch. Theology, 1975; m. Arlene Jean Sawallisch, June 4, 1938; children—Lois Jean, William David. Ordained to ministry, 1940; pastor Christian and Missionary Alliance, Maywood, Dixon and Peoria, Ill., 1939-49; pastor ch., Plainfield, Ill., 1949-52; campus pastor, Ames, Iowa, 1952-55; pastor Calvary Bapt. Ch., Burbank, Calif., 1955-60, 1st Bapt. Ch., Walnut Creek, Calif., 1970—. Dean, Bible Inst., Los Angeles Bapt. Coll. and Sem., 1955-59; active Christian Day Sch. Movement, 1955—; chmn. bd. Regular Bapt. High Sch., Martinez, Calif., 1971-73, 76—. Home: 2348 Buena Vista Ave Walnut Creek CA 94596 Office: 2336 Buena Vista Ave Walnut Creek CA 94596

MARVIN, FRANK CLYDE, JR., minister, United Presbyterian Church in U.S.A.; b. Edgewood, Pa., May 1, 1924; s. Frank Clyde and Edna Elizabeth (Goldinger) M.; B.A., U. Pitts., 1948; B.D., Princeton, 1951; M.A., U. Mich., 1967, Ph.D., 1976; m. Virginia Elizabeth Showalter, Jan. 7, 1956; children: Elizabeth (Mrs. John C. Stewart), Paul, David. Ordained to ministry, 1951; asst. minister East Liberty Presbyn. Ch., Pitts., 1951-54; pastor 1st Presbyn. Ch., Fairmont, W.Va., 1954-67, Cherry Hill United Presbyn. Ch., Dearborn, Mich., 1970—. Home: 24420 Winona St Dearborn MI 48124 Office: 24110 Cherry Hill Rd Dearborn MI 48124

MARVIN, JOHN GEORGE, minister, Presbyterian Church in the U.S.A.; b. Summit, N.J., May 8, 1912; s. George and Caroline (Whitman) M.; m. Elizabeth Anne Wheater, June 30, 1944; children: Caroline Marvin Dorney, Elizabeth Marvin West, Martha, Alice Marvin Heidel. B.S., Davidson Coll., 1933; Th.B., Princeton Theol. Sem., 1936; D.D. (hon.), Coll. Emporia, 1964; LL.D. (hon.), Tarkio Coll., 1964. Ordained to ministry Presbyn. Ch., 1936. Sr. pastor St. Andrew Ch., Denton, Tex., 1952-61, First Presbyn. Ch., Bartlesville, Okla., 1965-69, Sr. pastor Chevy Chase Presbyn Ch., Washington, 1969-77, pastor emeritus, 1977—; minister at large Inter-Faith Chapel; Leisure World; Washington, 1984——. interim pastor Pine Shores Presbyn. Ch., Sarasota, Fla., 1984; mem. nominating com. Presbyn. Gen. Assembly, Phila., 1950's; mem. Brit. Am. Mission, Brit. Council Chs., London, 1973; bd. visitors Warren Wilson Coll., N.C., 1974-84; leader, lectr. Religious Heritage Tours, 1973—; mem. long range planning com. Council Chs., Kansas City, Mo., 1965, exec. com., Washington, 1972. Author study materials, conf. and devotional guides. Bd. dirs. Found.

for Blind, Pa., 1946, Univ. Campus Found., 1960. Named Disting. Citizen Denton C. of C., 1955,Bd. visitors Warren Wilson Coll. Mem. Nat. Capital Presbytery, Am. Philatelic Soc. (life) Beta Theta Pi. Club: Kenwood Country (Bethesda; Md.). Lodge: Rotary. Home: 14500 Elmhan Ct Silver Spring MD 20906 Office: Inter-Faith Chapel 3680 S Leisure World Blvd Silver Spring Md 20906

MARXHAUSEN, VICTOR HERSCHEL, minister, Lutheran Church—Missouri Synod; b. Waltham, Minn., May 27, 1926; s. Ernst John August and Aurelia Marie (Schaefer) M.; B.Th., Concordia Theol. Sem., Springfield, Ill., 1949; m. Evelyn Bertha Rengstorf, June 18, 1950; children: Timothy John, Mary Beth, Martha Jane, Jonathan James. Ordained to ministry; pastor Immanuel Luth. Ch., Roseau, Minn., 1949-53, Bethlehem Luth. Ch., Morristown, Minn., 1953-58, Our Savior Luth. Ch., Hutchinson, Minn., 1958-67, Trinity Luth. Ch., White Bear Lake, Minn., 1967—. Mem. commn. on ch. lit. Mo. Synod, 1972—; bd. dirs. Minn. dist. Mo. Synod, 1969—, dist. sec., 1969-74, exec. com., 1969-74, chmn. dist. fin. com., 1974—, mem. synod bd. pub. relations, 1981, bd. dirs. synod, 1983—; chmn. Ch. Extension Fund, 1974; dist. v.p., 1974, 78; counselor Luth. Women's Missionary League, Minn. South dist., 1966-72; toured Seven Chs. of Asia Minor, 1972. Recipient Servus Ecclesiae Christi award, 1978. Home: 4154 Hillaire Rd White Bear Lake MN 55110 Office: 2480 S Shore Blvd White Bear Lake MN 55110

MASCARELLA, PATRICK JOSEPH, priest, Roman Catholic Ch.; b. Baton Rouge, Apr. 12, 1941; s. Charles Vincent and Lucy (Territo) M. A.A., St. Joseph Sem., 1961; B.A. in History, Notre Dame Sem., 1963, postgrad., 1963-67, U. of St. Thomas, 1980-81. Ordained priest, Roman Catholic Church, 1966. Assoc. pastor Lady of Mercy Parish, Baton Rouge, 1981-74; pastor St. Isidore Parish, Baton Rouge, 1974-78; assoc. chaplain La. State U. Student Ctr., Baton Rouge, 1979-80; in-residence St. George Parish, Baton Rouge, 1981-83; adminstr. St. John the Bapt. Parish, Brusly, La., 1983; pastor Immaculate Conception, Denham Springs, La., 1983—; dir. Clergy Continuing Edn., Baton Rouge, 1984—; sec. Pastoral Ministries Diocese of Baton Rouge, 1984—; judge Tribunal, 1983—; dir. Religious Studies Instrn., Baton Rouge, 1982—. Mem. Common Cause, 1983—. Mem. St. Joseph Sem. Alumni, Notre Dame Sem. Alumni, Canon Law Soc. Am. (assoc.), Nat. Orgn. for Continuing Edn. Roman Cath. Clergy, Denham Springs C. of C. Democrat. Club: Grandsons of Italy (Baton Rouge). Avocations: reading; traveling; snow skiing. Office: Immaculate Conception Church PO Box 308 Denham Springs LA 70727-0308

MASCARI, SALVATORE JOHN, director of religious education, Roman Catholic Church; b. Pitts., May 16, 1935; s. Salvatore August and Mary Jane (Spracale) M.; m. Rose Marie Marchese, June 27, 1959; children: Natalie Marie, Salvatore Martin, Lisa Ann. B.S., LaRoche Coll., 1971; Th.M., Pitts. Theol. Sem., 1975; M.A. in Spirituality, Duquesne U., 1982, postgrad. doctoral studies, 1983—. Tchr., Nativity Sch., Pitts., 1960-62; tchr., prin. Holy Ghost Byzantine Cath. Sch., McKeesrocks, Pa., 1962-70; tchr. Resurrection Sch., Pitts., 1970-71, North Cath. High Sch., Pitts., 1971-84; mem. campus ministry team, 1974-84; dir. religious edn., pastoral asst. St. Teresa of Avila, Pitts., 1984—; tchr. adult edn. program Diocese of Pitts., 1974—; speaker Teen Speakers Bur., Diocese of Pitts., 1980—, Adult Speakers Bur., 1974—; tchr. Confrat. Christian Doctrine, Diocese of Pitts., 1960—. Author high sch. course of study History of the Early Church, 1975. Editor: History of the Early Church, 1977. Served to cpl. U.S. Army, 1957-59. Avocations: golf; painting; reading; stamp collecting; writing. Office: St Teresa of Avila 1000 Avila St Pittsburgh PA 15237

MASCHKE, TIMOTHY HARVEY, minister, educator, Lutheran Church-Missouri Synod; b. Decatur, Ala., Dec. 24, 1947; s. Robert Otto and Ruth Hildegard (Schuchardt) M.; m. Sharon Louise Kettelhut, June 17, 1972; children: Jedidiah, Benjamin. B.A., Concordia Sr. Coll., Fort Wayne, Ind., 1970; M.Div., Concordia Sem., St. Louis, 1974; M.S.T., 1981; D.Min., Trinity Evang. Div. Sch., Deerfield, Ill., 1984. Ordained to ministry Lutheran Ch.-Missouri Synod, 1974. Asst. pastor St. John's Luth. Ch., Elgin, Ill., 1974-75, assoc. pastor, 1975-80; pastor Luth. Ch. of St. Luke, Itasca, Ill., 1980-82; campus pastor, prof. Concordia Coll., Mequon, Wis., 1982—; sec. Circuit Pastoral Conf., Elgin, Ill., 1974-80; mem., coordinator Itasca Ministerium, 1980-82. Mem. Luth. Edn. Assn., Internat. Luth. Layman's League. Clubs: Kiwanis, Lions. Home: 1041 7th Ave Grafton WI 53024 Office: Concordia Coll Wis 12800 N Lake Shore Dr Mequon WI 53092

MASEK, JAMES JOSEPH, priest, Roman Cath. Ch.; b. Cleve., Apr. 23, 1948; s. Raymond Clement and Rita Ann (Kalous) M.; B.A., Borromeo Sem. Coll., 1970; M.Div., St. Mary Sem., 1974. Ordained priest, 1974; asso. pastor St. James Parish, Lakewood, Ohio, 1974—. Asso. defender of the bond, procurator-adv. Cleve. Diocesan Tribunal, 1975; program dir. Suburban West Deanery, 1975—. Mem. Lakewood Commn. on Community Action, 1975. Mem. Lakewood Ministerial Assn. Home and Office: 17514 Detroit Ave Lakewood OH 44107

MASON, DAVID ERNEST, religious orgn. ofcl., minister, So. Baptist Conv.; b. Natchitoches, La., Jan. 3, 1928; s. Charles C. and Marjorie (O'Bannon) M.; B.A., La. State U., 1949; B.D., So. Bapt. Theol. Sem., 1952, M.Div., 1973; D.D., U. Corpus Christi, 1958; M.A., Syracuse U., 1954; m. Betty D. Oxford, Aug. 11, 1950 (div.); m. 2d, Alberta Martin, July 2, 1964; children—David Ernest, Paul Alexander; stepchildren—Hobart, Jeffrey, William, Suzanne. Ordained to ministry So. Baptist Conv., 1950; asst. to pastor Ga. chs., 1952-55; pastor 1st Bapt. Ch., Jonesboro, La., 1955-60, Alice, Tex., 1960-62; exec. dir. Laubach Literacy, Inc., 1962-69; pres. Supportive Services, Inc., 1969-72; exec. dir. Greater New Orleans Fedn. Chs., 1972—; mem. exec. com. Here's Life Am. Dir. Am. Council Vol. Agys. for Fgn. Service, 1967-68. Trustee So. Bapt. Theol. Sem., 1959-60; bd. dirs. Koinonia Found., 1967-68 chmn. adv. bd. overseers Dag Hammaroskold Coll., 1970—; bd. dirs. Inst. Human Understanding, 1973-78; mem. New Orleans Mayor's Human Relations Com., 1973—; state chmn. La. Renaissance-Religion and the Arts, 1976-77, pres., after 1977; bd. dirs. La. Council Music and Performing Arts, from 1977; v.p. Community Access Corp., 1981-84; exec. chmn. Greater New Orleans 1984 World's Fair Com. Mem. So. Bapt. Theol. Sem. Alumni Assn. La. (past pres.), Assn. Internat. Vol. Orgns. (chmn. 1966-69), Adult Edn. Assn., Jonesboro-Hodge Ministerial Assn. (past pres.), Bapt. Writers Assn. (past chmn.), Fellowship Religious Journalists (pres.), Soc. Internat. Devel., Religious Pub. Relations Assn., Assn. Edn. Journalism. Rotarian. Author: Now Then, 1957; The Charley Matthews Story, 1958; Eight Steps Toward Maturity, 1962; The Vacant Hearted, 1963; Apostle to the Illiterates, 1965; Frank C. Laubach, Teacher of Millions, 1967; Reaching the Silent Billion, 1967; The Compulsive Christian, 1968. Contbr. numerous articles to periodicals. Office: Greater New Orleans Fedn of Chs 301 Camp St New Orleans LA 70130

MASON, PAUL HENRY, minister, So. Bapt. Conv.; b. Iron City, Tenn., Aug. 24, 1938; s. Floyd Henry and Eula (Wilson) M.; B.A., Union U., Jackson, Tenn., 1967; M.Div., Southwestern Bapt. Sem., 1970, Th.D., 1974; m. Barbara June Mashburn, May 29, 1959; children—Missy, Lisa, Micah, Matthew, Amanda. Ordained to ministry, 1964; pastor Tenn., 1963-67, 1st Bapt. Ch., Maypearl, Tex., 1967-72, Sweetwater Bapt. Ch., Thomson, Ga., 1972-74, 1st Bapt. Ch., Sylvester, Ga., 1974-76, Second Bapt. Ch., College Park, Ga., 1976—. Exec. mem. Ga. Bapt. Conv., mem. budget com.; mem. Worth County Ministerial Assn., Worth County Bapt. Pastors Fellowship; chaplain USAR, 1968—. Columnist, Sylvester Local, McDuffie Progress. Home: 1667 Cheryl Terr Riverdale GA 30296

MASON, WILLIAM CLIFFORD, JR., minister, religion educator, administrator, United Methodist Church; b. Athens, Tenn., Aug. 8, 1925; s. William Clifford and Myrtle Elizabeth (Allen) M.; m. Laura Lee Frederick, July 9, 1946; children: William, Linda, Ann. A.A., Tenn. Wesleyan Coll., 1944; B.A., Emory and Henry Coll., 1946; M.Div., Emory U., 1949; Ed.D., NY U, 1973. Ordained elder, 1949. Pastor, S. Bristol Meth. Ch., Tenn., 1949-53, State St. Meth. Ch., Bristol, Va., 1953-56; chaplain Emory and Henry Coll., Emory, Va., 1956-67, dean students, 1967-79, dir. religious life, prof. religious edn., 1979—; del. World Meth. Conf., Lake Junaluska, N.C., 1966-81; supr. Holston Counseling Ctr., Knoxville, Tenn., 1972-82; trustee Holston Conf. Cemetery, Emory, 1980—; dir. Va. Council Chs., Richmond, 1983—. Author: Church School Worker's Handbook, 1955. Bd. dirs. Mental Health Ctr., Bristol, Va., 1956-66, Highlands Children's Home, Abingdon, 1973—, Crisis Ctr., Bristol, 1978—, William King Arts Found., Abingdon, 1980-84. Recipient civic leadership award Bristol Newspapers, 1956; named Disting. Univ. Scholar, NY U, 1974, Outstanding Educator of Yr., Washington, 1975, Counselor of Yr., Va. Counselors Assn., 1976. Mem. Va. Council on Family Relations (sec. 1971—), SW Counselors Assn. (pres. 1983—), Southeastern Council on Family Relations (v.p. 1983—), Religious Edn. Assn., Christian Educators Fellowship. Home: PO Box 13 Emory VA 24327 Office: Emory and Henry Coll Emory VA 24327

MASSEY, JAMES EARL, minister, educator, Church of God (Anderson, Ind.); b. Ferndale, Mich., Jan. 4, 1930; s. George Wilson and Elizabeth (Shelton) M.; m. Gwendolyn Inez Kilpatrick, Aug. 4, 1951. B.R.E., B.Th., Detroit Bible Coll., 1961; M.A., Oberlin Grad. Sch. Theology, 1964; D.D. (hon.), Asbury Theol. Sem., 1972. Ordained to ministry Ch. of God (Anderson, Ind.), 1951. Assoc. pastor Ch. of God, Detroit, 1950-53; pastor Met. Ch. of God, Detroit, 1954-76; pres. Jamaica Sch. Theology, Kingston, 1963-66; campus minister Anderson Coll., Ind., 1969-77; radio preacher Ch. of God, Anderson, 1977-82; dean chapel Tuskegee Inst., Ala., 1984—; guest prof. Princeton Theol. Sem.; vice-chmn. N. Am. sect.; Lausanne Com. on World Evangelization; del. World Congress on Evangelism, Berlin, Fed. Republic Germany, 1966, Internat. Congress on World Evangelization, Lausanne, Switzerland, 1974, World Congress on Evangelization, Pattaya, Thailand, 1980; mem. theol. study commn., bd. dirs. Detroit Council Chs.; corp. mem. Inter-Varsity Christian Fellowship; editorial adviser Tyndale House Pubs., 1968-69; vice-chmn. publ. bd. Ch. of God, chmn. com. on christian unity; Gautschi lectr. Fuller Theol. Sem., 1975; Freitas lectr. Asbury Theol. Sem., 1977; Rall co-lectr. Garrett-Evang. Theol. Sem., 1980; Mullins lectr. So. Bapt. Theol. Sem., 1981; Swartley lectr. Eastern Bapt. Theol. Sem., 1982; Jameson Jones lectr. Iliff Sch. Theology, 1983. Dir. Warner Press, Inc. Author: Designing the Sermon, 1980; Educating for Service: Essays in HMA of Robert H. Reardon, 1984. Editor: (with Wayne McCown) Interpreting God's Word for Today, 1982; mem. editorial bd. Christian Scholar's Rev., Leadership mag.; author, editor eleven additional books. Contbr. articles to religious publs. Sec., pres. Anderson Civil Service Merit Commn. Served as cpl. U.S. Army, 1951-53. Named Preacher of Yr., Nazarene Theol. Sem., 1984; Underwood fellow Danforth Found., 1972; Staley Disting. scholar, 1977; Christianity Today Inst. resource scholar, 1985—. Mem. Nat. Black Evang. Assn. (bd. dirs.), NAACP (life), Nat. Com. Black Churchmen, Nat. Assn. Coll. and Univ. Chaplains, Wesleyan Theol. Soc., Nat. Assn. of Ch. of God (historian), Lausanne Continuation Com. Democrat. Home: 1006 Chris Circle Tuskegee AL 36083

MASSEY, WILLIAM ALBERT, JR., minister, So. Baptist Conv.; b. Vinita, Okla., May 23, 1929; s. William Albert and Normal (Dixon) M.; B.A. in Social Studies Edn., N.E. La. U., 1957, M.Ed. in Guidance, 1972; M.Div., New Orleans Bapt. Theol. Sem., 1963, M.R.E., 1967; m. Billie Griggs Massey, Dec. 30, 1946; children—Larry Wayne, John Kenneth. Ordained to ministry; pastor First Bapt. Ch., Urania, La., 1958-66; chaplain La. Tng. Inst., Monroe, 1966—. Named Pastor of Year, La. Bapt. Conv., 1965. Mem. La. Chaplains Assn., Coll. Chaplains of Am. Hosp. Assn., Phi Delta Kappa. Address: Box 1631 Monroe LA 71202

MAST, EDWIN STEWART, minister, Ch. of United Brethren in Christ; b. Lockport, N.Y., Oct. 22, 1931; s. Amos J. and Carrie (Reigsecker) M.; A.B., Huntington Coll., 1963; M.Div., Fuller Theol. Sem., 1966; postgrad. Ind. U., 1964-65, Calif. Grad. Sch. Theology, 1972-73; m. Mary Lucille Deepe, Apr. 13, 1952; children—Randy, Susan (Mrs. Vernon Copp), Sandra (Mrs. Timothy McMahan). Ordained to ministry Church of United Brethren in Christ, 1967; pastor South Scipio U.B. Ch., Antwerp, Ohio, 1957-63, Lakewood (Calif.) U.B. Ch., 1965-66, First U.B. Ch., Montpelier, Ohio, 1967, First U.B. Ch., Glendale, Calif., 1967-73, First U.B. Ch., Fountain Hills, Ariz., 1973—. Mem. bd. Christian edn. and evangelism North Ohio conf. Ch. of United Brethren in Christ, 1967; v.p. N. Ohio Camp Meeting Assn., 1967; mem. council Orgn. of Protestant Chs. of William County, 1967; mem. Youth For Christ Bd., Williams County, 1967; conf. supt. Pacific Conf. United Brethren In Christ, 1968—, asst. tour dir. to Holy Land, 1968, mem. Calif. council on alcoholic problems, 1969-70, organizer stewardship bd. Pacific conf., 1974, developer, organizer Christos Corps, Pacific conf., 1972-73, mem. Gen. Bd., 1968—; asst. chmn. Pacific Conf. Council Adminstrn., 1971-74, chmn., 1974—. chmn. churches Billy Graham film, Glendale and Burbank, 1973; asst. chmn. finance com. Glendale Council Christian Chs., 1971-72. Chmn. coordinating Council Fountain Hills, Ariz., 1974—; chmn. Fountain Hills Bicentennial Com., 1976—; bd. dirs. Fountain Hills 4th of July; mem. Transitional Study Com. Fountain Hills, 1977. Mem. Fountain Hills C. of C. Contbr. articles to profl. jours. Home: 14830 Alamosa Circle Fountain Hills AZ 85268 Office: Box 177 Fountain Hills AZ 85268

MASTERS, MICHAEL RAY, minister, So. Baptist Conv.; b. Wharton, Tex., July 9, 1948; s. George Ralph and Dorothy Faye (Taylor) M.; B.Music Edn., E. Tex. Bapt. Coll., Marshall, 1972; postgrad. Southwestern Bapt. Theol. Sem., Ft. Worth; m. Patricia Margaret Roberts, July 25, 1970; 1 son, Michael Blakley. Founder Soda Lake Bapt. Youth Assn., Marshall, Tex., 1972; mem. Singing Churchmen Miss., 1975-76; music specialist Miss. Bapt. Conv., 1975-76; dir. New Life Singers, Lake Jackson, Tex., 1976—. Recipient award leadership Am. Legion, 1966. Mem. Singing Men Tex., Phi Mu Alpha. Home: 132 Tulip Trail Lake Jackson TX 77566 Office: 401 Yaupon St Lake Jackson TX 77566

MATE, MARTIN See *Who's Who in America,* 43rd edition.

MATHENY, RUTH ANN (MRS. CHARLES EDWARD MATHENY), editor; b. Fargo, N.D., Jan. 17, 1918; d. Jasper Gordon and Mary Elizabeth (Carey)

Wheelock; B.E., Mankato State Coll., 1938; M.A., U. Minn., 1955; postgrad. Georgetown U., summer 1960, Universidad Autónoma de Guadalajara (Mexico), summer 1956; m. Charles Edward Matheny, Oct. 24, 1960. Tchr., Confraternity Christian Doctrine, Washington Court House, O., 1969-70. Asso. editor Jr. Cath. Messenger, 1966-68; editor Witness Intermediate, 1968-70, Today's Cath. Tchr., 1970—, Ednl. Dealer, Dayton, 1976-80; editor-in-chief Catechist, 1976—; editorial collaborator Dimensions of Personality series, 1969—. Mem. EDPRESS, Cath. Press Assn., Nat. Cath. Ednl. Assn., 3d Order St. Francis. Roman Catholic. Co-author: At Ease in the Classroom. Office: 2451 E River Rd Dayton OH 45439

MATHENY, TOM HARRELL, church official, United Methodist Church; b. Houston; s. Whitman and Lorene (Harrell) M.; B.A., Southeastern La. U., 1954; J.D., Tulane U., 1957. Conf. lay leader La. Ann. Conf., United Meth. Ch., 1966—, del. Gen. Conf., 1968, 70, 72, pres. Jud. Council, 1976—, pres. Nat. Assn. Conf. Lay Leaders, bd. trustees La. Ann. Conf.; del. World Meth. Conf., London, 1966, Denver, 1971, Dublin, 1976; trustee Scarritt Coll.; hon. sec. U.S. Com. for Audenshaw Found.; chmn. bd. Wesley Found. Partner firm Pittman & Matheny, Hammond, La., 1957—. Mem. dist. council Boy Scouts Am., 1957-66, chmn. advancement com., Hammond, 1960-64, mem. exec. bd. Istrouma Area council, 1966—; area campaign mgr. for Democratic candidate for gov. La., 1959-60, 63-64; bd. dirs. Tangipahoa Parish chpt. ARC, 1957-67, Hammond United Givers Fund, 1957-68, La. Council Chs., La. Interchurch Conf.; trustee Centenary Coll.; hon. trustee John F. Kennedy Coll. Recipient Distinguished Service award Hammond Jr. C. of C., 1960, 64; named One of Three Outstanding Men of La., 1964, Layman of Year, La. Ann. Conf., United Meth. Ch., 1966, 73. Mem. Am., La. (chmn. com. on legal aid), 21st Jud. Dist. (v.p. 1967-68, 71—) bar assns., Comml. Law League Am., La. Alumni Council (pres. 1963-65), Acad. Religion and Mental Health, Internat. Platform Assn., La. Assn. Claimants Compensation Attys., Southeastern La. Coll. (dir., pres. 1961-62), Tulane alumni assns., UN Assn., Am. Trial Lawyers Assn., Am. Judicature Soc., Law-Sci. Inst., World Peace Through Law Acad., Am. Acad. Polit. and Social Sci., Am. Acad. Law and Sci., Hammond Assn. Commerce (dir. 1960-65), Phi Delta Phi, Phi Delta, Phi Alpha Delta. Home: PO Box 221 Hammond LA 70404 Office: Guaranty Bank Bldg Hammond LA 70401

MATHER, GEORGE ROSS, minister, Presbyterian Church, U.S.A.; b. Trenton, N.J., June 1, 1930; s. Samuel Wooley and Henrietta (Deardorff) M.; m. Doris Christine Anderson, June 28, 1958; children: Catherine Anne, Geoffrey Thomas. A.B., Princeton U., 1952; M.Div., Princeton Theol. Sem., 1955. Ordained to ministry, Presbyn. Ch. U.S.A., 1955. Asst. pastor Abington Presbyn. Ch., Pa., 1955-58; pastor Ewing Presbyn. Ch., Trenton, N.J., 1958-71; sr. pastor First Ch., Ft. Wayne, Ind., 1971—; trustee Hanover Coll., 1983—. Mem. Allen County Pub. Library Bd., pres., 1980-82. Mem. Clergy United (pres.). Club: Quest (pres.). Office: First Presbyn Ch 300 W Wayne St Fort Wayne IN 46802

MATHER, THOMAS LYNN, pastor, General Association of Regular Baptist Churches; b. Vestal, N.Y., Mar. 12, 1948; s. Walter Thomas and Agnes Irene (Mills) M.; m. Janet Naomi Kemmerer, June 4, 1971; children: Elizabeth, Joshua, Kristen, Benjamin. B.Th., Baptist Bible Coll., Clark Summit, Pa., 1972; tchrs. cert. Winston-Salem State Coll., 1976. Ordained to ministry General Association of Regular Baptist Churches, 1977. Pastor, S. Auburn Bapt. Ch., Meshoppen, Pa., 1971-72, First Bapt. Ch. Evans, Angola, N.Y., 1979—; asst. pastor Maranatha Bapt. Ch., Buffalo, 1972-74; asst. pastor, tchr. Greendale Bapt. Ch., Wis., 1974-76; sch. adminstr. Covenant Bapt. Ch., Matthews, N.C., 1976-79; chmn. Grace Fellowship Independent Bapt. Chs., Western, N.Y., 1982—. Author: Study of Irridology in Bible, 1983. Mem. Bapt. Bible Coll. Alumni Assn. (1st v.p. northwestern N.Y. sect. 1983-84). Republican. Home and Office: 985 Church Rd Angola NY 14006

MATHEWS, JAMES LEONARD, minister, Ch. of the Nazarene; b. Charleston, W.Va., Nov. 14, 1935; s. Clarence Everett and Lillian Ruth (Cox) M.; B.A., Trevecca Nazarene Coll., 1958; M.A., N.E. Mo. State U., 1970; m. Wanda Jean Phillips, June 23, 1956; children—Jeanie Lynn, Sharon Kay. Ordained to ministry, 1961; pastor Ch. of the Nazarene, W.Va., Minn., Ga., Fla., Iowa, Tenn., Okla., 1958—, Dunbar (W.Va.) Ch. of the Nazarene, 1974—. Mem. Phi Delta Kappa. Home: 518 21st St Dunbar WV 25064 Office: 16th and Lightner Sts Dunbar WV 25064

MATHEWS, JAMES ROBERT, minister, So. Baptist Conv.; b. Deweyville, Tex., Nov. 8, 1942; s. Jesse J. and Abbie (Hill) M.; B.S., E. Tex. Bapt. Coll., 1965; M.Div., Southwestern Bapt. Theol. Sem., 1974; m. Gloria Jean Langford, Aug. 29, 1964; children—Jeffrey Douglas, Tonya Annette. Ordained to ministry, 1964; pastor First Bapt. Ch., Big Sandy, Tex., 1964-69, Myrtle Springs Bapt. Ch., Hooks, Tex., 1969-71, First Bapt. Ch., Aledo, Tex., 1973-75, Pinecrest Bapt. Ch., Silsbee, Tex., 1975—. Moderator Parker Assn., 1973-74; trustee Heart O' Texas Bapt. Encampment. Home and Office: POB 778 4 1/2 Mile Glacier Hwy Juneau AK 99802

MATTEI, RAÚ HERMINIO, minister, Episcopal Church; b. Ponce, P.R., Nov. 22, 1922; s. Geronimo C. and Carmen M. (Sanchez) M.; m. Antonia Castillo, Dec. 29, 1949; children: Raul A., Peter L., Carmen L., Michael D., Cruzie A., Alvar J. B.A., Poly. Inst. of P.R., 1951; B.D., M.Div., U. of the South, 1957, S.T.M., 1976. Ordained to ministry Episcopal Ch., 1957. Pastor, Episc. Ch., Ponce, 1957-58, Vicksburg, Miss., 1958-68, Corinth, Miss., 1968-77, Trenton, N.J., 1977—; dir. Nat. Hispanic Dep. Episc. Ch., 1977-82, v.p. Trenton Clericus, 1980-81; chmn. Hispanic Commn., Diocese of N.J., Trenton, 1977-82, bd. dirs. urban dept., 1977-82; bd. dirs. TEAM, Ecumenical Assn., Trenton-Mercer County, 1977-82. Author poems: Passover Poems, 1960; contbr. articles to religious jours.; pub., editor Hispanic Srs. Newspaper "La Sirena", 1984. Bd. dirs. Sr. Citizens' Legal Aid, Trenton, 1980-84; sec. Old Trenton Neighborhood Corp., 1978-81; bd. dirs. Vis. Nurses Assn. of Mercer County, Trenton, 1978-84, Helene Fould Med. Rev. Bd., Trenton, 1983-84, St. Michael's Hispanic Srs. Program, Trenton, 1979-84, Mercer County Comprehensive Planning Bd.; trustee Trenton Art Mus. Home: 836 Berkeley Ave Trenton NJ 08618 Office: Parish of St Michaels Episcopal Ch 140 N Warren St Trenton NJ 08608

MATTER, EDITH ANN, educator; b. Ft. Smith, Ark., Dec. 29, 1949; d. Robert Allen and Faye Bert (Overton) Matter. A.B., Oberlin Coll., 1971; M.A., M.Phil., Yale U., 1975, Ph.D., 1976. Assoc. prof. religious studies U. Pa., Phila., 1976—. Editor: De partu Virginis. Faculty fellow Van Pelt Coll. House, Phila., 1982—; tchr., lectr. Pa. Humanities Council, 1984. ACLS summer research fellow, 1978; NEH research fellow, 1979; Am. Philos. Soc. grantee, 1977, 81, 84; Lindback award for disting. teaching U. Pa., 1981. Mem. Medieval Acad. Am., Am. Acad. Religion, Delaware Valley Medieval Assn. Democrat. Home: 3909 Spruce St Box 200 Philadelphia PA 19104 Office: Religious Studies Univ Pa Box 36CH Philadelphia PA 19104

MATTER, GLENN EDWARD, minister, United Methodist Church; b. Millersburg, Pa., May 28, 1914; s. William Edgar and Hattie Eve (Burrell) M.; m. Margaret Louise Johns, July 14, 1935; children: Jon William, Paul Eugene. B.S., Albright Coll., 1944; M.Div., United Theol. Luth. Sem., 1947; postgrad. Luth. Sem., Gettysburg, Pa., 1955, 56, 57. Ordained deacon United Methodist Ch., 1941, elder, 1943. Mem. Conf. Relations, 1952-63; trustee Albright Coll., 1959-65; mem. bd. missions United Meth. Ch., 1959-65; mem. Mission and Ch. Extension Meeting, 1970-80; spiritual dir. Lykens Valley Camp, Pa., 1982—; chaplain Montgomery Hosp., Sacred Heart Hosp., Suburban Gen. Hosp., Norristown, Pa., 1969-79. Trustee Sacred Heart Hosp., Norristown, 1979; pres. Day Care Assn., Norristown; chmn. Emergency Relief Com., Norristown, 1979. Recipient Spl. Recognition award Albright Alumni, 1969, Legion of Honor award Chapel of Four Chaplains, Phila., 1978, Cert. of Appreciation, Eastern Pa. Conf. United Meth. Ch., 1979. Republican. Lodges: Lions (past pres.), Kiwanis (chmn.), Charles M. Howell Harrisburg Consistory (pres. 1957).

MATTERN, ALEXANDER WATSON, emeritus minister, Independent Fundamental Churches in America; b. Lindenwold, N.J., Aug. 8, 1916; s. Joseph and Mae (Watson) M.; student Moody Inst., 1942, Phila. Coll. Bible, 1956; Th.B., Th.M., Th.D., Clarksville Sch. Theology, 1978; m. Bernice Hannah Huntington, June 15, 1945; children: Alexander, William. Ordained to ministry, 1958; founder, pastor East Berlin (N.J.) Community Ch., 1958-84, pastor emeritus, 1984—; tchr., Grace Bible Inst.; pres. Lower Camden County Fellowship Fundamental Chs.; adv. bd. child evangelism Camden County, 1982—; past sec. Christian Tng. Missionary Fellowship. Home: 316 S Berlin Rd Lindenwold NJ 08021

MATTHEWS, CHRISTIAN WILLIAM, JR., minister, Presbyterian Church U.S.A.; b. Jersey City, Oct. 12, 1934; s. Christian William and Lydia Louise (Weller) M.; B.A., King's Coll., 1956; M.R.E., Eastern Theol. Sem., 1960; M.Ed., U. Del., 1961; B.D., Eastern Theol., 1962; Th.M., Princeton Theol. Sem., 1965, postgrad., 1973—; m. Elaine Louise Ochs, June 18, 1955; children—Christian William III, Patricia Louise, Judith Ann, Barbara Jean. Ordained to ministry, 1962; dir. Christian edn. United Presbyn. Ch., Manoa, Havertown, Pa., 1959-62; asst. minister First Presbyn. Ch., Norristown, Pa., 1962-65; assoc. minister Marble Collegiate Ch., N.Y.C., 1965-68; sr. minister Fox Chapel Presbyn. Ch., Pitts., 1968-79, Christ Presbyn. Ch., Toledo, 1979—. Mem. The Fellowship, Washington, Synod Gen. Council Presbyn. Ch. in U.S.A.; chmn. Synod Evangelism; leader marriage and family seminars; mem. alumni fund bd. Princeton Theol. Sem., cons. program agy. Presbyn. Ch. in U.S.A., Nat. Com. for Prison Reform, County Human Service Commn.; chmn. Com. for Ecol. Instruction; founding pres. Samaritan Counseling Ctr.; bd. dirs. Toledo Soc. Handicapped, Met. Toledo Chs. United, AASK-Mid Am.; mem. Council for Religion and Psychiatry. A developer Risk Evangelism (nat. program for Presbyn. Ch. U.S.A.); signer Lausanne Covenant of Internat. Congress on World Evangelization; author: Lingering With Luke—A Study of the Life of Christ, 1976; Marriage and Family Study Course, 1983. Office: 4835 Turnbridge Rd Toledo OH 43623

MATTHEWS, DAVID, clergyman, Nat. Bapt. Conv. U.S.A.; b. Indianola, Miss., Jan. 29, 1920; s. Albert and Bertha (Young) M.; A.B., Morehouse Coll., Atlanta, 1950; summer student Atlanta U., 1950, Memphis Theol. Sem., 1965, Delta State U., Cleveland, Miss., 1969, 71, 72; D.D. (hon.), Natchez (Miss.) Jr. Coll., 1973; m. Lillian Pearl Banks, Aug. 28, 1951; 1 dau., Denise. Ordained minister Nat. Baptist Conv. U.S.A., 1946; pastor chs. in Miss., 1951—, Bell Grove Bapt. Ch., Indianola, 1951—, Strangers Home, Greenwood, 1958—; instr. social sci., chmn. dept. Gentry High Sch., Indianola, 1958—. Vice moderator Sunflower Bapt. Assn., 1957—; v.p. Gen. Bapt. Conv. Miss., 1958-76, pres., 1976—, lectr, convs. congress religious edn., 1958—; v.p. Nat. Bapt. Conv. U.S.A., 1971—, del. to Nat. Council Chs., 1960. Mem. Sunflower County Anti-Proverty Bd., 1965-71, Indianola Bi-Racial Com., 1965—; hon. dep. Sheriff Sunflower County, 1972—; part-time dep. chancery clk., 1972—; col. Gov. Finch's staff, 1976—; mem. budget com. Indianola United Fund, 1971—; chmn. bd. Indianola FHA, 1971—. Trustee Natchez Jr. Coll. Served with AUS, 1942-45; PTO. Recipient citation Morehouse Coll., 1950, Miss. Valley State Coll., 1956; J.H. Jackson Preaching award Midwestern Bapt. Laymen Fellowship, 1974. Mem. N.E.A., Miss., Indianola tchrs. assns. Home: PO Box 627 Indianola MS 38751 Office: Baptist Ch Corner Hannah and Chandler Sts Indianola MS 38751

MATTHEWS, JOHN, bishop, Apostolic Overcoming Holy Church of God. Office: 12 College St Dayton OH 45407*

MATTHEWS, RICHARD DAVID, minister, Independent Baptist Church; b. Van Wert, Ohio, May 16, 1933; s. Dale T. Matthews and Evelyn (Riley) Kear; m. Marie Elvira Manera, Feb. 13, 1954; children: Evi, David, Thomas, John. Diploma, Moody Bible Inst., Chgo., 1958, Spanish Lang. Inst., San Jose, Costa Rica, 1969; Th.B., Luther Rice Sem., Fla., 1980; Th.D., Clarksville Sch. Theology, Tenn., 1976. Ordained to ministry, 1962. Pastor chs. in Wis. and Minn., 1958-67; missionary, 1967-70; gen. dir. Mission Outreach Soc., Oregon, Wis., 1970-82; exec. dir. Assoc. N. Am. Missions, Madison, Wis., 1982—. Author: From Whence Cometh My Help?, 1978; also articles. Editor Roundtable mag., 1982—. Served with USAF, 1952-56. Recipient Disting. Achievement award Am. Legion, 1947. Republican. Club: Optimists (Oregon). (608) 835-5489

MATTHEWS, WILLIE W., bishop, Church of God By Faith. Address: 125 Holman St Ozark AL 36360*

MATTHIESEN, LEROY THOEDORE See *Who's Who in America*, 43rd edition.

MATTSON, SHERRY RAE, priest, Episcopal Church; b. Detroit, Feb. 11, 1949; d. Raymond Lionel and Ella Anne (Miller) M. B.A., Simmons Coll., 1971; M.Div., Episcopal Theol. Sem. of the S.W., 1979. Ordained deacon Episcopal Ch., 1979, priest, 1980. Ecumenical chaplain Oakland U., Rochester, Mich., 1979-81; asst. priest St. Stephen's Episcopal Ch., Troy, Mich., 1979-81; Episcopal chaplain Western Carolina U., Cullowhee, N.C., 1981—; rector St. David's Episcopal Ch., Cullowhee, 1981—; province IV rep. to steering com. Episcopal Soc. for Ministry in Higher Edn., 1984—; mem. planning com. Nat. Episcopal Student Gathering, Estes Park, Colo., 1983-85; mem. liturgical commn. Diocese Western N.C., 1982—, chmn. dept. college work, 1982—. Mem. Jackson County Nursing and Domicilary Home Adv. Com., N.C., 1982—. Mem. Episcopal Soc. for Ministry in Higher Edn. Episcopal Women's Caucus, Epis. Peace Fellowship. Democrat. Home: PO Box 43 Cullowhee NC 28723 Office: St David's Episcopal Ch PO Box 152 Cullowhee NC 28723

MATUSZEWSKI, STANLEY, priest, Roman Catholic Church; b. Morris Run, Pa., May 4, 1915; s. Andrew and Mary (Czekalski) M.; student LaSalette Coll., Hartford, Conn., 1933-37, Scholastic Sem., Altamont, N.Y. Ordained priest Roman Catholic Ch., 1942; disciplinarian, prof. classics LaSalette Sem., Olivet, Ill., 1942-46, dir., 1948—; superior Midwest province LaSalette Fathers, 1967—; founding editor Our Lady's Digest, 1946—. Mem. exec. bd. Nat. Cath. Decency in

Reading Program, 1964—; faculty adviser Midwest Conf. Internat. Relations Clubs, 1944. Trustee Nat. Shrine Immaculate Conception, Washington, 1973—. Named Monroe County (N.Y.) Orator, Rochester Centennial Com., 1934. Mem. Mariological Soc. Am. (award 1954), Missionaries of Our Lady of LaSalette, Cath. Press Assn., Canon Law Soc., Cath. Broadcasters Assn., Religious Edn. Assn., Polish-Hungarian World Fedn. (trustee). Author: Rochester Centennial Oration, 1934; Youth Marches On, 1934. Address: Box 777 Twin Lakes WI 53181

MATZ, MILTON, rabbi, pastoral counselor, clinical psychologist; b. N.Y.C., June 30, 1927; s. Joshua E. and Sonja (Kviat) M.; B.A., Yeshiva U., 1947; B.H.L., Hebrew Union Coll., Cin., 1949, M.H.L., 1952; Ph.D., U. Chgo., 1966; m. Anne L. Jaburg, July 5, 1952; children: Deborah, David. Ordained rabbi, 1952; chaplain USAF, 1952-54; asst. rabbi K.A.M. Temple, Chgo., 1954-57; rabbi Temple B'nai Jehoshua, Chgo., 1957-59; asso. rabbi The Temple, Cleve., 1959-66; sr. staff psychologist Fairhill Hosp., Cleve., 1966-70; pvt. practice clin. psychology, Cleveland Heights, Ohio, 1966—; dir. pastoral psychology Service Inst., Case Western Res. U. Med. Sch., Cleve., 1973—. Chmn. central conf. Am. Rabbis Com. Judaism and Health; chmn. Cuyahoga County (Ohio) Mental Health Retardation Bd. Recipient Distinguished Service to Mental Health award Cuyahoga County (Ohio), 1972. Diplomate Am. Assn. Pastoral Counselors. Mem. Am. Psychol. Assn., Author articles on preventive psychology and psychology of religion. Home: 3346 Stockholm Rd Cleveland OH 44120 Office: 3609 Park St E Beachwood OH 44122

MAURER, KENNETH ROBERT, minister, Evang. Congl. Ch.; b. Pitman, Pa., Oct. 21, 1918; s. Raymond L. and Rae F. (Snyder) M.; A.B., Muhlenberg Coll., 1942; M.Div., United Theol. Sem., 1944; S.T.M., Luth. Theol. Sem., Phila., 1947; S.T.D., Temple U., 1956; m. Margaret E. Miller, Nov. 28, 1940; children—Daniel, Allen, Ordained deacon, 1943, ordained elder, 1945; pastor St. John's Evang. Congl. Ch., Allentown, Pa., 1939-47, Trinity Evang. Congl. Ch., Frackville, Pa., 1947-53; prof. ch. history Evang. Sch. Theology, Myerstown, Pa., 1953—, dean, 1953-71. Sec. exec. com. Pa. Temperance League, 1956-68, Pa. Council on Alcohol Problems, 1956-68. Mem. Am. Soc. Ch. History, Conf. On Faith and History, Pa. State Edn. Assn., NEA, Nat. Assn. Evangelicals, Pa. Alcohol Edn. Found. Contbr. articles to religious jours. Home: 5 Werni Dr Lebanon PA 17042 Office: 121 S College St Myerstown PA 17067

MAXELL, CHARLES ALEXANDER, minister, United Presbyn. Ch. in U.S.A.; Sycamore, Ga., Sept. 11, 1934; s. James and Otha Lee (Hunt) M.; B.S., Fort Valley State Coll., 1960; M.S., Johnson C. Smith U., 1963; m. Bernese Shaw, July 7, 1968; children—Charles A., Carlynda Atha. Ordained to ministry, 1963; pastor 1st Presbyn. Ch., Midway, Ga., 1963—. Pres., adminstr. Midway Nursing Inn, 1972—; pres. CAM Pharmacy, 1977—; dir. Liberty County Community Service Center, 1966-71; moderator Knox-Hodge Presbytery; ministerial commr. Gen. Assembly United Presbyn. Ch. in U.S.A., 1966; mem. ministerial relations com., 1967-70. Home: PO Box 64 Midway GA 31320 Office: PO Box 108 Midway GA 31320

MAXIMOS, HIS GRACE AGHIORGOUSSIS, bishop, Greek Orthodox Church; b. Chios, Greece. Licentiate in Orthodox Theology and Patristic Studies, Patriarchal Sem. of Halki, Istanbul; Baccalaureate in Philosophy, Cath. U. Louvain, Belgium; D. Systematic Tyeology, Louvain Advanced Inst. Philosophy. Ordained Patriarchal deacon Greek Orthodox Ch., 1957, ordained priest, 1959, consecrated titular aux. bishop, 1978, elected bishop of Pitts., 1979, enthroned Diocesan Shepherd, 1979. Resident observer, Roman Cath. Ch. worldwide Vatican II Council, Rome; prof. systematic theology Holy Cross Sem., Boston, 1966-79, v.p., acad. dean, until 1979; bishop of Pitts., 1979—; v.p. Nat. Council of Chs.; founder Orthodox Caucus; chmn. ecumenical commn. Am. Greek Orthodox Synod, 1979—, presider dialogues with Nat. Conf. Bishops Am. Roman Cath. Ch., Anglican/Episcopal and Luth. communions, So. Bapt. Conv., Faith and Order Commn. of Nat. Council Chs., Orthodox Evangelicals movement; rep. Ecumenical Patriarchate and Am. archdiocese at World Council Chs. dels. to Middle East, 1983, internat. assembly of Protestant, Old Cath., Orthodox chs., Vancouver, B.C., Can.; founder summer youth camps, retreats, confs. Address: 5201 Ellsworth Ave Pittsburgh PA 15062

MAXSON, MARGARET ETHEL, practitioner, Ch. of Christ Scientist; b. Philipsburg, Mont., Sept. 2, 1897; d. Marshall Edwin and Jennie (Crable) Doe; student Mont. State U., Bozeman, 1917-18, U. Wis., Madison, 1919; tchr. certificate, Wis. Sch. Music and Dramatic Art, Madison, 1920; C.S. pupil of James G. Rowell; m. Lloyd Westley Maxson, Sept. 7, 1927; children—William Westley, John David. C.S. practitioner, 1953—; Sunday sch. tchr. 1st Ch. of Christ Scientist, Butte, Mont., 1946-50, 2d reader, 1950-53, practitioner, 1953—, pres. ch., 1977—; mem. Christian Science Ch., Boston. Mem. James G. Rowells C.S. Assn. Address: 305 W Granite St Butte MT 59701

MAXWELL, JAMES PAUL, church official, Southern Baptist Convention; b. Douglas, Ariz., Apr. 14, 1928; s. Glenn William and Gertrude Inez (Thornton) M.; B.A. cum laude, Okla. Bapt. U., 1950; B.D., Golden Gate Bapt. Theol. Sem., 1953, M.Div., 1972; m. Evelyn LeVoe George, Aug. 30, 1953; children: Paula, Daniel. Ordained to ministry So. Baptist Conv., 1949; asso. pastor First Mexican Bapt. Ch., Oklahoma City, 1948-50; minister music and edn., asso. pastor various chs. in Calif., 1950-53; minister music and edn. Millwood Ch., Oklahoma City, 1953-54; pastor First Bapt. Ch., Helena, Okla. 1954-56; dir. Bapt. Mission Center, Oklahoma City, 1956-58; supt. missions Salt Fork Bapt. Assn., Alva, Okla., 1958-67; dir. associational missions Pottawatomie-Lincoln Bapt. Assn., Shawnee, Okla., 1967—. Instr. bible and religion Northwestern State U., Alva, 1960-69; evangelistic chalk artist. Dir. missions Bapt. Student Union, Alva, 1958-67. Chmn. gov.'s council juvenile corrections State Okla., 1971-73; active Boy Scouts Am.; active Little League, Shawnee, 1969-72. Recipient 25 yr. service award Bapt. Gen. Conv. Okla., 1973. Mem. Nat. Orgn. Dirs. Associations Missions So. Bapt. Conv., Internat. Platform Assn. Home: 3914 N Kickapoo St Shawnee OK 74801 Office: PO Box 2016 Shawnee OK 74802

MAXWELL, KAY MANESS, lay ch. worker, So. Bapt. Conv.; b. Bristol, Va., Aug. 22, 1955; d. Hiram Fulton and Juanita Laura (Johnson) Maness; B.A., Judson Coll., 1977; m. Roland Lee Maxwell, Jan. 1, 1976. Youth and children's dir. Siloam Bapt. Ch., Marion, Ala., 1973-75, youth interim music dir., 1973-74; unit leader Girls in Action-Acteens Camp, Shocco Springs, Ala., 1975; resource person for retreats and camps, 1975-76; gospel ventriloquist, Marion, Ala., 1975—; mem. faculty Children's State Music Camp, 1976. Admissions counselor Judson Coll., Marion, Ala., 1975—. Office: Admissions Office Judson Coll Marion AL 36756

MAXWELL, SPENCER LAWRENCE, minister, Seventh-day Adventist Church; b. Watford, Hertfordshire, Eng., Jan. 13, 1925; came to U.S., 1936; s. Arthur S. and Rachel E. (Joyce) M.; m. Rebecca M. Singer, Oct. 3, 1971; children: Heidi Maye, Heather Maureen. B.A. in Theology, Pacific Union Coll., 1946, M.A., 1950. Ordained to ministry Seventh-day Adventist Ch., 1941. Pastor Seventh-day Adventist Ch., No. Calif., 1946-53; editor Guide, Washington, 1953-70; editor Signs of the Times, Pacific Press, Mountain View, Calif., 1970-84, assoc. book editor, Boise, Idaho, 1984—; dir. Pacific Press Pub. Assn., 1970-84. Author: Pathfinder Field Guide, 1962; What Stopped the Music? (Spanish translator), 1966; Bedtime Stories, 1972; God's Plan for Our Planet, 1973. Republican. Office: PO Box 7000 Boise ID 83707

MAY, ALBERT CARL, JR., minister, United Presbyn. Ch. U.S.A.; b. Cleve., July 21, 1934; s. Albert Carl and Elizabeth Ann (Goehring) M.; student Hamilton Coll., 1952-54; A.B., Case Western Res. U., 1956; M.Div., Princeton Theol. Sem., 1960; m. Frances Grace Simon, June 29, 1957; children—Edith Frances, Carl Webster. Ordained to ministry, 1960; asst. pastor 1st Presbyn. Ch., Canfield, Ohio, 1960-62; pastor 1st Presbyn. Ch., Highland, N.Y., 1962-67; chaplain Highland (N.Y.) Tng. Sch. for Children, 1963-67; pastor 1st Presbyn Ch., New Kensington, Pa., 1967-72, Buffalo Presbyn. Ch., Sarver, Pa., 1972-74; chaplain Sunnyview Home, Butler, Pa., 1977-81. Dir. Peaceful Valley Ministries, Sarver; chaplain Order St. Luke the Physician; literacy cons. Christian Literacy Assocs., Pitts., 1979-85, bd. dirs. overseas projects, 1985; vol. chaplain Allegheny Valley Hosp., Natroma Heights, Pa., 1972-85; bd. dirs. World Salt Found., Newnan, Ga., 1982—; sec. bd. dirs. Logos Translators, Gibsonia, Pa., 1982—; bd. dirs. Greater Pitts. Area Nat. Marriage Encounter. Home: 240 Harbison Rd Sarver PA 16055

MAY, CECIL RICHARD, JR., minister, college president, Church of Christ. b. Martin, Tenn., June 13, 1932; s. Cecil Richard May and Mary Monette (Crain) May Tindall; m. Winnie Agnes Williamson, Apr. 15, 1954; children: Betty, Cecil, Roslyn, Richard. B.A. in Bibl. Langs. magna cum laude, Harding Coll., 1954, M.A. in New Testament, 1967, M.Th., 1984; LL.D., Freed-Hardeman Coll., 1984. Ordained to ministry Ch. of Christ, 19—. Preacher various chs. (Miss.), 1954-57, Eastside Ch. of Christ, Portland, Oreg., 1967-69, Vicksburg Ch. of Christ (Miss.), 1969-76; Bible tchr. Columbia Christian Coll., Portland, 1967-69; dean Internat. Bible Coll., Florence, Ala., 1977-80; pres. Magnolia Bible Coll., Kosciusko, Miss., 1980—. Assoc. editor Magnolia Messenger, 1980; contbr. articles to profl. jours. Dist. exec. Yocona Area Council Boy Scouts Am., Oxford, Miss., 1959-60; campaign chmn. Am. Cancer Soc., Vicksburg, 1971-74; bd. dirs. Miss. Econ. Council, 1985—. Mem. Evang. Theol. Soc. Lodges: Kiwanis, Rotary. Home: Route 2 Box 115-D 307 Woodland Dr Kosciusko MS 39090 Office: Magnolia Bible Coll PO Box 1109 820 S Huntington St Kosciusko MS 39090

MAY, CHARLES SCOTT, priest, Episcopal Church; b. Little Rock, Mar. 4, 1931; s. Guy Noel and Louise (Scott) M. A.B., Washington & Lee U., 1953; B.D., U. South, 1957. Curate Christ Ch., Little Rock, 1957-58; rector St. Paul's Ch., Newport, Ark., 1958-66; asst. rector Trinity Ch., Columbia, S.C., 1966-71; chaplain Mass. Gen. Hosp., Boston, 1971-72; assoc. rector Trinity Cathedral, Columbia, S.C., 1972-73; rector St. James Ch., Marietta, Ga., 1973—; dep. Gen. Conv., St. Louis, 1964; trustee All Saints Sch., Vicksburg, Miss., 1962-64; exec. council Diocese of Ark., 1963-65; bishop and council Diocese of Upper S.C., 1969-71; mem. chaplains assn. Kennestone Hosp., Marietta, 1973—. Trustee Cobb Community Symphony, Marietta, 1975-78. Rotary Internat. fellow 1953-54. Democrat. Office: St James Ch 161 Church St Marietta GA 30060

MAY, EDWARD JAMES, minister, outreach director, Southern Baptist Convention; b. Houston, Dec. 1, 1929; s. Levi John and Edith Mary (Pynn) M.; B.A., Baylor U., 1961; diploma Southwestern Sem., Ft. Worth, 1963; m. Shirley Estelle Horn, June 15, 1956; 1 child, Allen Kyle. Ordained to ministry, 1949; dir. Christian Outreach Ministries, Montgomery County, Tex., 1972—, past pres. Montgomery County Ministerial Assn. Mem. Tex. Hosp. Auxs. Home: 99 Yupon Circle PO Box 677 Montgomery TX 77356

MAY, FELTON E., bishop, United Methodist Church, Wyo. Conf. Office: 3 Orchard Rd Binghampton NY 13905*

MAY, JOHN L., archbishop, Roman Cath. Ch.; b. Evanston, Ill., Mar. 31, 1922; s. Peter Michael and Catherine (Allare) M. M.A., St. Mary of Lake Sem., Mundelein, Ill., 1945, S.T.L., 1947. Ordained priest Roman Catholic Ch., 1947. Asst. pastor St. Gregory Ch., Chgo., 1947-56; chaplain Mercy Hosp., Chgo., 1956-59; v.p., gen. sec. Cath. Ch. Extension Soc. U.S., 1959-67, pres., from 1967; consecrated bishop, 1967; aux. bishop Archdiocese of Chgo., 1967-69; pastor Christ the King Parish, Chgo., 1968-69; bishop Diocese of Mobile, Ala., 1969-80; archbishop of St. Louis, 1980—. Office: Archdiocese of Saint Louis 4445 Lindell Blvd Saint Louis MO 63108

MAY, KENNETH R. Synodical bishop Lutheran Church in America, Pitts. Office: Luth Ch in Am 9625 Perry Hwy Pittsburgh PA 15237*

MAY, WILLIAM EUGENE, theology educator, Roman Catholic Church; b. St. Louis, May 27, 1928; s. Robert W. and Katherine Ann (Armstrong) M.; m. Patricia Ann Keck, Oct. 4, 1958; children: Michael, Mary, Thomas, Timothy, Patrick, Susan, Kathleen. B.A., Cath. U., 1950, M.A., 1951; Ph.D., Marquette U., 1968. Assoc. editor Newman Press, Westminster, Md., 1954-55; editor Bruce Pub., Milw., 1955-68, Corpus Books, Washington and N.Y., 1969-70; assoc. prof. theology Cath. U., Washington, 1971—. Author: Christ in Contemporary Thought, 1971 (best book award Coll. Theology Soc.); Becoming Human, 1974; Human Existance, Medicine and Ethics, 1977; Sex, Marriage and Chastity, 1981; Sex and Sanctity of Life, 1984; Catholic Sexual Ethics, 1985. Recipient Thomas Linacre award Nat. Fedn. Cath. Physicians Guilds, 1983. Mem. Fellowship Cath. Scholars (Cardinal Wright award, 1980), Soc. Christian Ethics, Cath. Theol. Soc. Am., Am. Cath. Philos. Assn. Home: 4412 Saul Rd Kensington MD 20895 Office: Cath U Am Dept Theology Washington DC 20064

MAYBECK, SUSAN STORING, minister, American Baptist Churches in the U.S.A.; b. Ames, Iowa, July 2, 1936; d. James A. and Edith (Ryg) Storing; m. Edward Merrell Maybeck, Sept. 7, 1957; children: Cynthia, Stephen. B.A., U. Rochester, 1958; M.Div., Colgate Rochester-Bexley Hall-Crozer, 1979. Ordained to ministry Am. Baptist Ch. U.S.A., 1979. Interim minister Hilton Bapt. Ch., N.Y., 1980, First Bapt. Ch., Weedsport, N.Y., 1979-80; minister of congl. devel. Calvary Bapt. Ch., Washington, 1980-84; minister United Ch. of Pittsford, N.Y., 1985—; mem. adv. team Women in Ministry project Am. Bapt. Chs. N.Y., 1982—, mem. bd. mgr. Ministers and Missionaries Benefit Bd., 1984—. Editor newsletter Claiming Our Gifts, 1983—. Mem. Ministers Council Am. Bapt. Chs. Office: United Ch of Pittsford PO Box 28 123 S Main St Pittsford NY 14534

MAYHEW, THOMAS CHARLES, priest, Roman Catholic Church; b. Starks, Maine, July 3, 1931; s. James Franklin and Mary Margaret (Higgins) M.; B.A., Maryknoll Coll., Glen Ellyn, Ill., 1953; M.R.E., Maryknoll (N.Y.) Sem., 1958. Ordained priest, 1959; assoc. pastor St. Peters Ch., Provincetown, Mass., 1959-67, St. Josephs Ch., North Dighton, Mass., 1967-76, St. Anthonys Ch., East Falmouth, Mass., 1976-77; pastor Mt. Carmel Ch., Seekonk, Mass., 1977—. Dir. Confraternity of Christian Doctrine, Taunton Area, 1967-71; active in Cursillo and Charismatic movements; founder Echo, exptl. program in religious edn. for coll. students and high sch. seniors, 1968. Bd. dirs. Plymouth Bay Girl Scouts, 1974--. Home: 55 Nauset Rd West Yarmouth MA 02673 Office: 984 Taunton Ave Seekonk MA 02771

MAYNARD, CLAUDE RAY, bishop, minister, Ch. of God of Prophecy; b. New Boston, Ohio, Aug. 18, 1935; s. Kennie and Myrtle Marie (Spradlin) M.; student Ch. of God of Prophecy Bible Tng. Inst., 1964-67; m. Barbara Jean Dodds, Feb. 7, 1953; children—Debra Sue, Cheryl Ann, Brenda Gale, Kenneth Ray. Ordained to ministry, 1964, bishop, 1973; police officer, Portsmouth, Ohio, 1957-70; pastor Ch. of God of

Prophecy, Tronton, Ohio, 1965-70, Painesville, Ohio, 1970-72, Medina, Ohio, 1972-73, Elyria, Ohio, 1973—. Dist. overseer No. Ohio, Ch. of God of Prophecy, 1974—. Mem. Ch. Benefit Assn., Ch. of Prophecy Marker Assn. Address: 244 E 9th St Elyria OH 44035

MAYO, GEORGE ROBERT, lay ch. worker, So. Baptist Conv.; b. Lebanon, Va., July 21, 1936; s. Fletcher Lynn and Bertha Ruth (Farmer) M.; student music Lee Coll., Cleveland, Tenn., 1972-73. Minister music First Bapt. Ch., Benton, Tenn., 1965-76, Big Springs United Methodist Ch., Cleveland, 1962-64; Royal Ambassador dir. First Bapt. Ch., Benton, 1972-74; tchr. 8th grade boys First Bapt. Ch., Cleveland, Tenn., 1976, mem. adult choir, 1977—. Quality control insp. Magic Chef Inc., Cleveland, 1957-77. Mem. Cleveland Civic Choral Soc., 1965-70, officer, 1967-70. Recipient appreciation plaque First Bapt. Ch., Benton, 1974. Mem. Cleveland Community Concert Assn. Home: 2355 Bates Pike Cleveland TN 37311 Office: 740 King Edward Ave Cleveland TN 37311

MAYO, JAMES. Bishop, African Methodist Episcopal Church (Sixteenth Dist.). Office: 115-04 Merrick Blvd Jamaica NY 11433*

MAYS, LOWELL H., minister, educator, American Lutheran Church; b. Toledo, Aug. 15, 1937; s. David P. and Veleta M. (Hoel) M.; B.A., Capital U., Columbus, O., 1958; M.Div., Luth. Theol. Sem., Columbus, 1962; m. Barbara Ann Zimmermann, June 12, 1960; children: Kristen Ann, David Lowell, Stephen Eric. Ordained to ministry Am. Luth. Ch., 1962. Pastor chs., Md., Ohio, Mich., Wis., 1958-67; assoc. prof. theology Edgewood Coll. Sacred Heart, Madison, Wis., 1965-69, dir. ecumenical studies, 1968-69; assoc. campus pastor Luth. campus ministry U. Wis., Madison, 1967-69, sr. campus pastor, 1969-72, dir. campus ministry, 1969-72, vis., assoc. prof. program social and human medicine Med. Sch., 1972-74, lectr. medicine Center Health Scis., staff U. Health Service, 1972—; also clin. assoc. prof. medicine and human ecology Med. Sch. and Clin. Cancer Ctr.; dir. dept. human ecology Madison Gen. Hosp. 1974—; cons. theology VA Hosp., Madison, 1973-75; sr. chaplain Dane County Sheriff's Dept., 1970—; exec. dir. Inst. Human Values of Gen. Health Services, 1985—. Chmn. bd. for 1st offenders Dane County, 1971—; bd. dirs. Vis. Nurse Service of Dane County, 1977, Wis. div. Am. Cancer Soc., Wis. area ARC, Family Service Dane County. Danforth fellow, 1966-69. Named Outstanding Young Man of Year, Brodhead (Wis.) Jr. C. of C., 1965; recipient Nat. Honor citation Am. Cancer Soc., 1976. Mem. Soc. Health and Human Values, Soc. Adolescent medicine, Coll. Chaplains, Fellowship St. Augustine. Clubs: Madison; Blackhawk Country (Shorewood Hills, Wis.). Contbr. numerous articles to profl. jours. Home: 106 Ozark Trail Madison WI 53705 Office: 202 S Park St Madison WI 53715

MAYSE, PRESTON THOMAS, minister, denominational exec., Free Meth. Ch.; b. Durango, Colo., Jan. 23, 1941; s. Preston Thomas and Fern LaDean (Smith) M.; B.A., Greenville (Ill.) Coll., 1963; m. Karen Sue Woods, June 30, 1963; children—Melanie Linn, Melissa Sue. Ordained to ministry, 1966; pastor Free Meth. Ch., Shenandoah, Iowa, 1963-69, Free Meth. Ch., Sioux City, Iowa, 1969-73; denominational dir. Children's Ministries and Camping, Winona Lake, Ind., 1973—; exec. dir. Free Spirit Ministries, 1977—. Pres., Shenandoah Ministerial Assn., 1963-69; regional rep. Christian edn. Free Meth. Ch., 1967-73; v.p. Sioux City Evang. Ministerial Fellowship, 1969-73. Dir. steering com. Self Help Center, Shenandoah, 1968-69. Mem. Nat. Assn. Evangelicals, Christian Holiness Assn., Christian Edn.-Aldersgate Pubs. Assn., Christian Camping Internat., Denominational Execs. in Christian Edn. Exec. editor jours. Accenton Children's Ministries, Pine Knots, Pine Knots News; contbr. articles in field to various denominational publs. Home: 619 N Johnson St Warsaw IN 46580 Office: 901 College St Winona Lake IN 46590

MAZZA, BIAGIO, religion educator, Roman Catholic Church; b. Gioia del Colle, Bari, Italy, Oct. 2, 1946; came to U.S., 1956; naturalized, 1965; s. Ulderico and Mildred (Giannone) M.; m. Dorothy Elizabeth Collins, Aug. 7, 1976; children: Biagio Dominic, Mary Carol. B.A. in English, Marist Coll., 1968; M.A. in English, Fordham U., 1973, M.A. in Religious Edn., 1979. Cert. dir. religious edn., Archdiocese of N.Y. Dir. religious edn. St. Mary's Parish, Poughkeepsie, N.Y., 1976-81, Fishkill, N.Y., 1981—; cons. religious edn. Archdiocese of N.Y., 1985—; co-dir. Crop Walk for Hungry, Poughkeepsie, 1978-80; adj. Bible instr. Dutchess Community Coll., Poughkeepsie, 1978—; workshop presenter N.Y. Archdiocese Cathechetical Inst., Bronx, N.Y., 1980, 82, 84. Fordham U. scholar, 1977. Mem. Cath. Bibl. Assn., Soc. Bibl. Lit., Religious Edn. Assn., Am. Acad. Religion. Democrat. Home: 7 College Ave Poughkeepsie NY 12603 Office: St Mary's Religious Edn Program Jackson St Fishkill NY 12524

MCALLISTER, ROBERT JOSEPH, priest, publisher, Roman Catholic Church; b. Balt., Aug. 29, 1918; s. Robert Emory and Ann Gertrude (Doran) McA. B.A., Loyola Coll., 1940; Ph.L., Gregorian U., Rome, 1945, S.T.L., 1952. Joined Society of Jesus, Roman Cath. Ch., 1940, ordained priest, 1951. Asst. pastor, pastor St. Ignatius Ch., Hill Top, Md., 1954-58; student counselor Gonzaga High Sch., Washington, 1958-64; asst. to nat. dir. Apostleship of Prayer, N.Y.C., 1964-70, nat. dir., 1970—; mem. adv. council Internat. Inst. of Heart of Jesus, 1972—, Apostolate for Family Consecration, 1975—; mem. bd. sponsors Priestly Heart Program, 1976—. Editor monthly leaflets Apostleship of Prayer for High Schools and Colls., 1964-70, Apostleship of Prayer for U.S. Cath. Laity, 1970-82. Home: 3 Stephen Ave New Hyde Park NY 11040 Office: Apostleship of Prayer Inc 3 Stephen Ave New Hyde Park NY 11040

MCARTHUR, JOE EDD, minister, Baptist Ch.; b. Baytown, Tex., Apr. 11, 1948; s. Beemer Harold and Dorothy Louise (DeTuttle) McA.; B.A., Houston Bapt. Coll., 1971; student Luther Rice Sem. Fla., 1971-76; m. Janet Glynn Bellomy, Jan. 25, 1969; 1 dau., Julie Kay. Ordained to ministry, 1969; youth dir. 2d Bapt. Ch., Baytown, Tex., 1968-69; pastor 1st Bapt. Ch., Hockley, Tex., 1969-72, 1st Bapt. Ch., Rosharon, Tex., 1972-74, Dodge, Tex., 1975—. Held many revivals; dir. youth work Gulf Coast Bapt. Assn. Tex., 1974—. Home and Office: Route 13 Box 1648 Conroe TX 77302

MC ASHAN, EUGENE EARL, minister, A.M.E. Ch.; b. Leonard, Okla., July 19, 1932; s. Simon Alexander and Lillian Josephine (Reeves) McA.; B.A., Goddard Coll., 1973; B.Th., Okla. Sch. Religion, 1960; D.D., Monrovia Coll., Liberia, West Africa, 1970; m. Jewel Delores Davis, Sept. 2, 1956; children—Debra Kay, Sherri Lynn, Angela Carla, Craig Eugene. Ordained to ministry, 1949; pastor Bethel A.M.E. Ch., Haskell, Okla., 1949-52, Conners Chapel A.M.E. Ch., Ponca City, Okla., 1953-54, St. Paul A.M.E. Ch., Tulsa, 1955-57, Vernon A.M.E. Ch., Tulsa, 1958-59, First A.M.E. Ch., Oklahoma City, 1959-65, Mt. Zion A.M.E. Ch., Norristown, Pa., 1965-67, People's Instl. A.M.E. Ch., Bklyn., 1967—. Pres., Interdenoml. Ministers Alliance, Bklyn., 1973—. Home: 480 E 24th St Brooklyn NY 11210 Office: 244 Stuyvesant Ave Brooklyn NY 11221

MCAULEY, FRANK MARION, JR., minister, Am. Baptist Chs., U.S.A.; b. Galesburg, Ill., Oct. 20; s. Frank Marion and Dorothy Louise (Thurlby) McA.; B.A. in English Lit., Western Ill. U., Macomb, 1970; M.A. in Communication, Am. Bapt. Sem. of West, Covina, Calif., 1976; postgrad. Christian Internat. U.; m. Sharon Elaine Mick, Mar. 13, 1971. Ordained to ministry; drug crisis counselor Shalom House, 1970-71; minister religious edn. First Bapt. Ch., Olean, N.Y., 1973-75; ednl. cons. Released Time Program, Olean, 1974-75; dir. counselor-in-tng. program Am. Bapt. Chs. Oreg., summer 1975; pastor First Bapt. Ch., Churdan, Iowa, 1976—. Home: PO Box 175 Churdan IA 50050 Office: First Baptist Ch Churdan IA 50050

MCAULIFFE, MICHAEL F., bishop, Roman Cath. Ch.; b. Kansas City, Mo., Nov. 22, 1920. Student St. Louis Preparatory Sem. and Cath. U. Ordained priest Roman Catholic Ch., 1945; consecrated bishop, 1969; bishop Diocese of Jefferson City, Mo., 1969—. Address: Diocese of Jefferson City 605 Clark Ave POB 417 Jefferson City MO 65101

MCBAIN, LEROY DOWARD See *Who's Who in America*, 43rd edition.

MCBETH, PAUL W., minister, Brethren in Christ Church; b. Springfield, Ohio, Aug. 14, 1908; s. William John and Marguerite (Pfeiffer) McB.; m. S. Esther McCulloh, Aug. 31, 1930; children: David Paul, Rachel Esther McBeth Brand, Joseph William, Ethan Ray, John Henry. Grad. Messiah Coll. Acad., 1929, Willis Bus. Sch. Ordained to ministry Brethren in Christ Ch., 1932. Pastor, Brethren in Christ Ch., Arcadia, Fla., 1931-33; assoc. pastor Locke Brethren in Christ Ch., Nappanee, Ind., 1935-42, Conoy Brethren in Christ Ch., nr. Elizabethtown, Pa., 1942-44; pastor, 1944-48; pastor Elizabethtown Brethren in Christ Ch., 1948-51, Hollowell Brethren in Christ Ch., nr. Waynesboro, Pa., 1970-73; mem. mgmt. staff Evang. Visitor Pub. House, Brethren in Christ Publ. Bd., 1935-42, mgr. Christian Light Bookstores chain, 1942-47, sec. Ch. Tract Ministries, 1935-43, supr. traveling library, 1936-46; asst. sec. Gen. Sunday Sch. Bd., 1942-51; mem. Bd. Christian Edn., 1951-64; mem. Gen. Conf. Program, 1967-80; mem. exec. bd. Allegheny Regional Conf., 1968-77; program dir. Roxbury Holiness Camp, Pa., 1950-53; bd. dirs. Nat. Sunday Sch. Assn., 1950-60, sec., treas., initiator Nat. Family Week, 1952; Brethren in Christ Ch. rep. to bd. dirs. Pa. Assns. Evangs., 1975-80; co-founder, Evang. Fellowship Cumberland Valley, 1963-80, pres.; mem. Released Time Bible Program Com. Franklin County, Pa., 1965-80, chmn.; resource person Christian Writers Inst., Wheaton, Ill.; pres. McBeth Corp., 1970-78. Author booklets: Enlarge the Place of Thy Tents, 1955; Men Reach Men for Christ, 1961; Family Prayer Call, 1959; also articles. Mem. editorial com. Aldersgate Bibl. Series, 1961—. Recipient numerous awards for religious activities. Office: Messiah Village 613 Hemlock Hill Mechanicsburg PA 17055

MCBIRNIE, WILLIAM STEUART, JR., minister, educator, independent Baptist; b. Toronto, Ont., Can., Feb. 8, 1920; s. William Steuart and Ethel Betty (Potter) Mc.; m. June M. McBirnie; 1 child, William Steuart III. B.Div., Bethel Theol. Sem., 1945; D. Religious Edn., Southwestern Baptist Sem., 1952; Ph.D., Calif. Grad. Sch. Theol., 1972, D. Theology, 1976; Ph.D. (hon.), Daegu U., Korea, 1982; D. Humanities (hon.), Calif. Grad. Sch. Theology, 1977; D.Div. (hon.), Trinity Coll., 1958. Ordained to ministry Independent Baptist Ch., 1939. Pastor South Ft. Worth Bapt. Ch., 1948-49, Trinity Bapt. Ch., San Antonio, 1949-59; sr. pastor United Community Ch., Glendale, Calif., 1961—; prof. Calif. Grad. Sch. Theology, Glendale, 1968—. Author: Search for the 12 Apostles; The Tomb of Christ; How Comminism Can Be Destroyed; Weapons Which Can Prevent a Soviet Victory, others. Pres. World Emergency Relief, Glendale, 1970—. Recipient George Washington Honor medal Freedoms Found., 1978, Pilgrims medal State of Israel, 1966, Outstanding Young Texan award Tex. Jaycees, 1965. Mem. Order of La Fayette Croix Francais (medal 1965), Ky. Cols. (Cert. award 1966). Republican. Lodge: Knights of Malta. Office: United Community Ch 333 E Colorado Glendale CA 91205

MC BRIDE, C.A., minister, Assemblies of God; b. Travis, Tex., June 2, 1934; s. William Allen and Dessle Zereda (Wiggington) McB.; grad. Southwestern Assemblies of God Coll., Waxahachie, Tex., 1953; m. Carol Ann Allen, June 4, 1954; 1 dau., Mary Ann. Ordained to ministry, 1958; pastor Westside Assembly of God Ch., Carlsbad, N.Mex., 1957-62; dir. christian edn. N. Dallas sect. Assemblies of God., 1966-72; pastor 1st Assembly of God, Coppell, Tex., 1964—. Dir. youth S.E. Sect. of N. Mex.; sec. Carlsbad Ministerial Alliance, also v.p. Pres. Coppell PTA; mem. Coppell Ind. Sch. Bd.; chmn. United Fund, Coppell. Mem. Greater Dallas Pastor's Assn. (pres. 1971-73). Home and Office: PO Box 405 Coppell TX 75019

MCBRIDE, JAMES LEBRON, minister, Seventh-day Adventist Ch.; b. Chattanooga, Sept. 12, 1952; s. James Doyle and Mona Ophelia (Guest) McB.; m. Cathy Lynn Parker, Apr. 14, 1972. B.A. in Sociology, Carrollton, Ga., 1970-73; M.Div., Andrews U., 1978; M.P.H., Loma Linda U., 1980. Ordained to ministry, 1984. Lay vol. Wildwood Inst., Ga., 1975-77; minister Ill. Conf. Seventh-Day Adventists, Brookfield, Ill., 1980—, mem. exec. com., 1983—, mem. acad. bd., 1983—. Contbr. articles to profl. jours. Health educator community programs Lakeview Seventh-Day Adventist Ch., Chgo., 1980-82. Recipient Citizenship award Chattanooga Valley High Sch., 1969, 70; named Christian Athlete of Yr., Chattanooga Valley High, 1970. Mem. Pi Gamma Nu. Home: 59 Bellevue Dr Apt 2 Collinsville IL 62234 Office: Collinsville Seventh-Day Adventist Ch 10 Chapel Ct Collinsville IL 62234

MCBRIEN, RICHARD PETER, priest, Roman Cath. Ch.; b. Hartford, Conn., Aug. 19, 1936; s. Thomas Henry and Catherine Ann (Botticelli) McB.; A.A., St. Thomas Sem., 1956; M.A., St. John Sem., 1962; S.T.L., Pontifical Gregorian U., Rome, 1964, S.T.D., 1967. Ordained priest Roman Catholic Ch., 1962; asso. pastor Our Lady of Victory Ch., West Haven, Conn., 1962-63; chaplain So. Conn. State Coll., New Haven, 1962-63; prof. theology, dean studies Pope John XXIII Nat. Sem., Weston, Mass., 1965-70; asso. prof. theology Boston Coll., 1970-72, prof., 1972-80, dir. Inst. of Religious Edn. and Personal Ministry, 1975-80; Crowley-O'Brien-Walter prof. theology U. Notre Dame, Ind., 1980—, chmn. dept. theology, 1980—. Trustee Boston Theol. Inst. Recipient Best Theology column in Cath. press award Cath. Press Assn., 1974, 75, 78. Mem. Cath. Theol. Soc. Am. (dir. 1970-76, pres. 1973-74, John Courtney Murray award 1976), Am. Acad. Religion, Coll. Theology Soc., AAUP, Authors League Am. Author: The Church in the Thought of Bishop John Robinson, 1966; What Do We Really Believe, 1969; Do We Need the Church, 1969; Church: The Continuing Quest, 1970; Who Is A Catholic? 1971; For The Inquiring Catholic, 1973; The Remaking of the Church, 1973; Has the Church Surrendered, 1974; Roman Catholicism, 1975; Basic Questions for Christian Educators, 1977; Catholocism (2 vols.), 1980 (Christopher award 1981). Office: Dept Theology U Notre Dame Notre Dame IN 46556

MCCAFFREY, MARY PATRICIA, nun, religious organization administrator, Roman Catholic Church; b. Bronx, Apr. 16, 1930; d. Cornelius Thomas and Anastasia Frances (Waterman) McC. B.S. in Edn., Fordham U., 1959, M.A. in English, 1964; M.A. in Hosp. Adminstrn., Columbia U., 1974. Joined Sisters of St. Francis, Roman Cath. Ch., 1947. Tchr., Immaculate Conception Sch., Tuckahoe, N.Y., 1950-59, St. Eugene Sch., Yonkers, N.Y., 1959-61; tchr., prin. St. Clare High Sch., Hastings, N.Y., 1961-72; vocation dir. Sisters of St. Francis, Hastings, 1963-71, 1st councilor, 1971-77, 83—, asst. superior gen., 1974-77, 83—, superior gen., 1977-83, sponsorship coordinator health services, 1983—; adminstr. St. Francis Hosp., Poughkeepsie, N.Y., 1974-77; sponsorship coordinator St. Agnes Hosp., White Plains, N.Y., 1983—, St. Francis Hosp., 1983—. Author Hosp. Progress Mag., 1974. Bd. dirs. Dutchess County Heart Assn., 1976-77. Mem. Am. Coll. Hosp. Adminstrs., Cath. Health Assn. Conservative.

MC CAHON, JOSEPH FRANCIS XAVIER, priest, Roman Catholic Ch.; b. Phila., Aug. 8, 1943; s. Joseph Francis and Martha Mary (McNichol) McC.; B.S. in Social Studies, Villanova U., 1965; M.B.A., U. Pa.,

1967; M. Div., Pope John XXIII Nat. Sem., 1975. Ordained priest, 1975; commd. chaplain U.S. Air Force Res., MacDill AFB, Fla., 1975—; asso. pastor Corpus Christi Ch., Temple Terrace, Fla., 1975—. Mem. Bishop's Fin. Advisory Bd., Diocese of St. Petersburg, Fla.; bd. dirs. Tampa (Fla.) Cath. High. Sch. Mem. Canon Law Soc. Am. (asso.). Home and Office: PO Box 16397 Temple Terrace FL 33687

MCCALL, DUKE KIMBROUGH, clergyman, Southern Baptist Convention; b. Meridian, Miss., Sept. 1, 1914; s. John William and Lizette (Kimbrough) McC.; m. Marguerite Mullinnix, Sept. 1, 1936 (dec. Apr. 1983); children: Duke Kimbrough, Douglas H., John Richard, Michael W. B.A., Furman U., 1936, D.D. (hon.); M.Div., So. Sem., 1938, Ph.D., 1943; LL.D. (hon.), Baylor U.; D.D. (hon.), U. Richmond, Stetson U. Ordained to ministry So. Bapt. Conv., 1937. Pastor Broadway Bapt. Ch., Louisville; pres. New Orleans Bapt. Theol. Sem., 1943-46; exec. sec. So. Bapt. Exec. Com., Nashville, 1946-51; pres. So. Bapt. Theol. Sem., Louisville, 1951-82, chancellor, 1982—; pres. Bapt. World Alliance, Washington, 1980-85, mem. gen. council, 1946—; past chmn. Kentuckiana Metroversity. Author: God's Hurry, 1948; co-author: Passport to the World, 1951; co-author ann. Broadman Comments, 1957, 58. Editor: What Is The Church? Past pres. Nat. Temperance League; mem. nat. council Boy Scouts Am.; bd. dirs. Louisville Fund. Recipient E. Y. Mullins Denominational Service award Bd. Trustees of So. Bapt. Theol. Sem. Mem. Theol. Edn. Assn. Am. (past pres.), N. Am. Bapt. Fellowship (past chmn.), Louisville C. of C. (bd. dirs.). Democrat. Lodge: Rotary. Office: So Bapt Theol Sem 2825 Lexington Rd Louisville KY 40280

MCCALL, EMMANUEL L., religious organization executive, Southern Baptist Convention and Progressive National Baptist Convention; b. Sharon, Pa., Feb. 4, 1936; s. George and Myra Mae (Preston) McC.; m. Emma Marie Johnson, Aug. 23, 1958; children: Emmanuel L., Evalya Lynette. B.A., U. Louisville, 1958; B.D., So. Bapt. Sem., Louisville, 1962, M.R.E., 1963. M.Divinity, 1967; D.Ministry, Emory U., 1976; D.D. (hon.), Simmons Bible Coll., Louisville, 1965, United Theol. Sem., Monroe, La., 1972. Ordained to ministry Bapt. Ch., 1959; assoc. pastor Joshua Tabernacle Bapt. Ch., Louisville, 1954-60; pastor 28th St. Bapt. Ch., Louisville, 1960-68; assoc. dir. home mission bd. So. Bapt. Conv., Atlanta, 1968-74, dept. dir., 1974—; vis. prof. So. Bapt. Sem., Louisville, 1970—; trustee Morehouse Sch. Religion, Atlanta, 1971—, Interdenominational Theol. Ctr., Atlanta, 1978—. Author: Simmons: Past and Present, 1963. Editor: Black Christian Experience, 1973; Centennial Story, 1968. Mem. Bapt. World Alliance (commn. mem., Washington, 1980-85). Home: 3280 Hazelwood Dr SW Atlanta GA 30311 Office: Home Mission Bd So Bapt Conv 1350 Spring St NW Atlanta GA 30311

MCCALL, JOHN KEITH WILLIAM, priest, Episcopal Church; b. Rochester, Ind., May 24, 1948; s. Jack Keith and Mildred Alyce (Cutting) McC. B.A., U. Maine, 1970; M.Div., Gen. Theol. Sem., 1976. Ordained to ministry, 1976. Vicar, St. Giles Ch., Jefferson, Maine, 1976-78; asst. to Bishop of Maine, Episcopal Diocese of Maine, Portland, 1978—; tchr. meditation, Portland, 1983—; assoc. priest St. Gregory's Abbey, Three Rivers, Mich., 1976—. Mem. Insight Meditation Soc., Assn. for Pastoral Care. Democrat. Home: 180 High St #30 Portland ME 04101 Office: Episcopal Diocese of Maine 143 State St Portland ME 04101

MC CALLION, WILLIAM JOHN, priest, Roman Cath. Ch.; b. N.Y.C., July 8, 1923; s. Edward Joseph and Rose Ann (Smith) McC.; student Marist Sem., Langhorn, Pa., 1939-41, St. Joseph's Coll., Covington, La., 1941-43; A.A., Coll. Notre Dame, New Orleans, 1943-48; postgrad. La. State U., 1963-64. Ordained priest, 1948; asso. pastor ch., New Orleans, 1948-55, Baton Rouge, 1955-56; athletic dir. St. Raphael Ch., New Orleans, 1956-61; chaplain La. State Penitentiary, Angola, 1961-65; pastor St. Ann's Ch., Morganza, La., 1965-69, St. Agnes Ch., New Orleans, 1969, Annunziata Ch., Houma, La., 1969, St. Gertrude Ch., Des Allemands, La., 1973—. Chmn. St. Charles Parish Recreation, 1977; asst. chaplain Camp Leroy Johnson, Milne Boys' Home; asst. dir. Archdiocesan Cath. Youth Orgn., 1971. Mem. Sacred Heart Athletic Assn. (life), St. Raphael Athletic Assn. (life). Address: PO Drawer G Des Allemands LA 70030

MCCALLISTER, RAYMOND FORREST, JR., minister, Christian Church (Disciples of Christ); b. Decatur, Ill., Oct. 4, 1934; s. Raymond Forrest and Pauline Bernice (DeBruler) McC.; B.A., DePauw U., Greencastle, Ind., 1956; B.D., Yale U., 1959; D.D., William Woods Coll., Fulton, Mo., 1971; m. Marilee Lidikay, Aug. 10, 1957; children: Lynn Ann, Brian Forrest. Ordained to ministry Christian Ch. (Disciples of Christ). 1959; minister First Christian Ch., Metropolis, Ill., 1959-61, First Christian Ch., Fulton, 1961—; chaplain William Woods Coll., 1974—; mem. exec. com. World Conv. Chs. Christ, 1971-75; pres. Fulton Council Chs., 1970-72; chmn. budget com. Christian Ch. Mo., 1973-76, bd. dirs., 1973-76; bd. dirs. div. higher edn. Christian Ch., 1983—. Pres. Campbell Inst., 1968; Chmn. Mayor Fulton Adv. Com., 1975; bd. assocs. Fulton Colls.; mem. Fulton Sch. Bd., 1978—; mem. alumni bd. dirs. DePauw U., 1977-81; bd. dirs. Mo. Edn./Bus. Ptnrs., 1984—; chmn. Callaway County United Way, 1985-86. Recipient Bordeau Beau award William Woods Coll., 1974. Mem. Mo. Sch. Bds. Assn. (pres. 1983-84). Alpha Phi Omega. Lodge: Fulton Rotary (pres. 1971). Author book revs. Home: 1017 West Ave Fulton MO 65251 Office: Christian Church 7th and Court Sts Fulton MO 65251

MCCAMMON, SAMUEL DOUGLAS, JR., minister, church administrator, Presbyterian Church U.S.A.; b. Richmond, Va., Feb. 3, 1920; s. Samuel Douglas and Annie (Richardson) McC.; m. Jean Williams Bowers, Aug. 31, 1943; children: Anne Reu, John Bowers. B.A., U. Richmond, 1943; M.Div., Union Theol. Sem., 1946. Ordained to ministry, 1946. Pastor, Elk Hills Presbyn. Ch. and South Park Presbyn. Ch., Charleston, W.Va., 1946-48, Fairfield Presbyn. Ch., Richmond, Va., 1948-58, Green Acres Presbyn. Ch., Portsmouth, Va., 1958-63; presbytery exec. Norfolk Presbytery, Va., 1963-67, Westminster Presbytery, St. Petersburg, Fla., 1967-75, Hanover Presbytery, Richmond, Va., 1975—. Democrat. Home: 1310 Whitby Rd Richmond VA 23227 Office: Hanover Presbytery 1205 Palmyra Ave Richmond VA 23227

MCCANDLESS, J(ANE) BARDARAH, religious educator, Presbyterian Church in the U.S.A.; b. Dayton, Ohio, Apr. 16, 1925; d. J(ohn) Bard and Sarah Catharine (Shuey) M.; A.B., Oberlin Coll., 1951; M.R.E., Biblical Sem. in N.Y. (now N.Y. Theol. Sem.), 1953; Ph.D., U. Pitts., 1968. Dir. Christian edn. Wallace Meml. United Presbyn. Ch., Greentree, Pa., 1953-54, Beverly Heights United Presbyn. Ch., Mt. Lebanon, Pa., 1956-61; instr. religion Westminster Coll., New Wilmington, Pa., 1961-65, asst. prof., 1965-71, assoc. prof., 1971-83, prof., 1983—; leader numerous workshops Presbyn. Ch. U.S., Western Pa., 1961—; leader Christian edn. workshops Synod of Trinity, Presbyn. Ch., Pa., 1972, 76; mem. session New Wilmington United Presbyn. Ch., 1977-79. Author: An Untainted Saint . . . Ain't, 1978. Contbr. articles to profl. publs., chpt. to book. Soprano soloist Youngstown Philharmonic Chorus, 1965, Westminster Coll. Orchestra, 1971, New Castle Messiah Chorus, 1975. Mack grantee Westminster Coll., 1962, 63, faculty research grantee Westminster Coll., 1972, 78. Mem. Assn. Profs. and Researchers in Religious Edn. (exec. com. 1978-80), Religious Edn. Assn., Soc. Sci. Study Religion, Phi Beta Kappa, Pi Lambda Theta. Republican.

MCCANT, JERRY WALTER, clergyman, educator. B. Dexter, Ga., Feb. 8, 1942; s. Walter Alan and Maxie Fidella (Bryant) McC.; m. Rosemary Ann Peery, June 7, 1963 (div. June 1980); children: LaDonna Marie, Jonathan Kevin; m. Beverley Ann Morgan, June 19, 1981. A.B., Trevecca Nazarene Coll., Nashville, 1964; M.Div., Nazarene Theol. Sem., Kansas City, Mo., 1967; Ph.D., Emory U., 1978. Ordained to ministry Ch. of the Nazarene, 1968. Pastor, Ch. of the Nazarene, Graham, N.C., 1967-69, Paducah, Ky., 1969-71, Decatur, Ga., 1971-74, Macon, Ga., 1974-76; prof. religion Point Loma Nazarene Coll., San Diego, Calif., 1976—. Author: The Meaning of Church Membership, 1973; Teens and Self Esteem, 1985. Contbr. numerous articles to profl. jours. Vol., Vista Grande Elementary Sch., San Diego, 1983-84. Mem. Soc. Biblical Lit., Soc. New Testament Studies, NEA, Calif. Tchrs. Assn., Phi Delta Lambda (pres. 1974-76, 81-83). Home: 8304 Whelan Dr San Diego CA 92119 Office: Point Loma Nazarene Coll 3900 Lomaland Dr San Diego CA 92106

MCCANTS, ELDER, minister, Lutheran Church-Missouri Synod; b. Sedan, Ala., Mar. 11, 1950; s. James and Willie Mae (Cannon) McC.; m. Gail LaGette Davis, June 24, 1978. A.A., Concordia Jr. Coll.-Selma, Ala., 1971; B.S., Concordia Tchrs. Coll.-Seward, Nebr., 1973; M.Div., Concordia Sem.-Fort Wayne, Ind., 1977; postgrad. Auburn U., 1981-82, Chgo. State U., 1979-81, Our Lady of the Lake U., 1982-83. Ordained to ministry Luth. Ch., 1977. Pastor Resurrection Luth. Ch., Chgo., 1977-81; dean of students Concordia Jr. Coll., Selma, Ala., 1981-82; missionary-at-large Community Luth. Ch., San Antonio, 1982—. Contbr. articles in field. Mem. Luth. Social Service for Adoption. Democrat. Office: Community Luth Ch 5063 Rigsby San Antonio TX 78222

MCCARNEY, HOWARD JOHN See *Who's Who in America,* 43rd edition.

MCCARRICK, THEODORE EDGAR See *Who's Who in America,* 43rd edition.

MCCARTER, NEELY DIXON, minister, school administrator, Presbyn. Ch. in U.S., educator; b. Gastonia, N.C., Oct. 4, 1929; s. Robert William and Nell (Dixon) McC.; A.B., Presbyn. Coll., 1950; B.D., Columbia Theol. Sem., 1953, postgrad., 1968; Th.M., Union Theol. Sem., 1958; M.A., Yale, 1959, Ph.D., 1961; m. Jean Maxwell, May 28, 1954; children—Robert Sidney, Robin, Jeanette, Shirley Jean. Ordained to ministry Presbyn. Ch. U.S., 1953; Presbyn. univ. pastor U. Fla., Gainesville, 1953-58; prof. Christian edn. Columbia Theol. Sem., Decatur, Ga., 1961-66; Robert and Lucy Reynolds Critz prof. Christian edn. Union Theol. Sem. Va., from 1966, dean after 1973; now pres. Pacific Sch. of Religion, Berkeley, Calif.; guest prof. Christian edn. Grad. Theol. Union, Berkeley, Calif., 1969. Mem. Assn. Profs. and Researchers Religious Edn., Am. Ednl. Studies Assn. Author: Hear the Word of the Lord, 1964; (with Charles McCoy) The Gospel on Campus, 1959. Office: Office of Pres Pacific Sch of Religion 1798 Scenic Ave Berkeley CA 94709

MCCARTER, PETE KYLE, JR., religious studies educator, Presbyterian; b. Oxford, Miss., July 9, 1945; s. Pete Kyle and Mary Ann (Hudson) McC.; m. Sherry Ann Martin, June 5, 1971; children: Robert Kyle, David Kyle, Mary Kyle. B.A., U. Okla., 1967; M.Div., McCormick Theol. Sem., 1970; Ph.D., Harvard U., 1974. Asst. prof. U. Va., Charlottesville, 1974-79, assoc. prof., 1980-81, prof. religious studies, 1981—; vis. lectr. Harvard U., Cambridge, Mass., 1978-79; vis. assoc. prof. Dartmouth Coll., Hanover, N.H., 1979. Author: Antiquity of the Greek Alphabet, 1975; I Samuel (Phi Beta Kappa award 1981), 1980; II Samuel, 1984; also numerous articles. Coach Soccer Orgn. of Charlottesville-Albemarle, 1982—; del. Charlottesville Dist. Democratic Com., Albemarle County, 1982—. U. Va. Sesquicentennial fellow, 1981; NEH summer stipendee, 1982; U. Va. Ctr. Advanced Studies grantee, 1982-84. Mem. Soc. Bibl. Lit. (program chmn. S.E. region 1983-84, pres. region 1984-85), Bibl. Colloquium, Am. Schs. Oriental Research, Colloquium for Biblical Research, Trout Unltd. Office: U Va Dept Religious Studies Cocke Hall Charlottesville VA 22903

MCCARTHY, EDWARD ANTHONY, archbishop, Roman Cath. Ch.; b. Cin., Apr. 10, 1918; s. Edward E. and Catherine (Otte) McC.; M.A., Mt. St. Mary Sem. of West, Norwood, Ohio, 1944; Licentiate Canon Law, Cath. U. Am., 1946; J.C.D., Lateran U., Rome, Italy, 1947; S.T.D., Angelicum, Rome, 1948. Ordained priest, 1943; sec. to archbishop of Cin., 1944-65; aux. bishop of Cin., 1965-69; bishop of Phoenix, 1969-76; coadjutor archbishop, Miami, 1976-77, archbishop of Miami, 1977—. Office: Archdiocese of Miami 6301 Biscayne Blvd Miami FL 33138

MCCARTHY, JOHN EDWARD See *Who's Who in America,* 43rd edition.

MCCARTHY, THOMAS BERTRAND, priest, Roman Cath. Ch.; b. Columbus, Ohio, Jan. 16, 1933; s. James Joseph and Olive Elizabeth (McCauley) McC.; A.B., Providence Coll., 1955; S.T.B., Immaculate Conception Coll., 1959; M.A., Cath. U. Am., 1965, Ph.D., 1975. Ordained priest, 1960; pastor St. Dominic Ch., 1961-63, Holy Rosary Ch., Hawthorne, N.Y., 1963-64; chaplain Washington Dept. Corrections, 1964-66; founder, pres. Bros. Ednl. Consortium, 1966-68; adminstr. Notre Dame Sch., West Haven, Conn., 1968-71, St. Dominic Sch., Youngstown, Ohio, 1971—. Adminstr., Christian Edn. and Formation Commn., Youngstown, 1976; provincial research coordinator, 1975-76; provincial promoter of studies, 1976—. Mem. Youngstown Clergy Assn., Nat. Council Family Relations, Nat. Conf. Alcoholism, Am. Assn. Higher Edn., Am. Sch. Counselor Assn., Am. Personnel and Guidance Assn., Soc. for Advancement of Continuing Edn. for Ministry, Nat. Orgn. for Continuing Edn. of Roman Cath. Clergy. Home: 77 E Lucius Ave Youngstown OH 44507 Office: 3403 Southern Blvd Youngstown OH 44507

MCCARTHY, (ROBERT) TIMOTHY, religious organization executive, Roman Catholic Church; b. Milw., June 16, 1929; s. Frank Joseph and Amy Martha (Knospe) M.; m. Geraldine Edith Wilson, Dec. 27, 1951; children: Denise M., Patricia J., Kathleen A., Timothy F. B.S., Marquette U., 1951; J.D., Iowa Law Sch., 1954. Exec. dir. Iowa Cath. Conf., Des Moines. Solicitor gen. State of Iowa, Des Moines, 1965-66. Office: Iowa Catholic Conf 818 Ins Exchange Bldg Des Moines IA 50309

MC CARTY, HARVEY DWIGHT, minister, Southern Baptist Convention; b. Oklahoma City, Nov. 4, 1932; s. Johnny Wendell and Vera Aloma (Whitley) McC.; B.A., So. Meth. U., 1955; Div. M., Southwestern Bapt. Theol. Sem., 1964, postgrad., 1964-65; postgrad. Mid-Am. Bapt. Sem., 1974; D.Min., Calif. Grad. Sch. Theology, 1983; D.Div., Hindustan Bible Coll., Madras, India, 1981; m. Shirley Ann DeBerry, Oct. 5, 1957; children—Karen Diana, Kevin Dwight. Ordained to ministry, 1963; minister of youth Trinity Bapt. Ch., Lake Charles, La., 1958-60; asso. pastor Univ. Bapt. Ch., Ft. Worth, 1960-65; sr. pastor Univ. Bapt. Ch., Fayetteville, Ark., 1965—. Mem. exec. bd. Ark. Bapt. Conv., Little Rock, 1971—; chmn. bd. Ark. Inst. Theology; pres. Ventures for Christ, Inc.; bd. dirs., state chaplain Fellowship Christian Athletes; mem. bd. reference Mid-Am. Bapt. Theol. Sem.; chaplain U. Ark. Razorbacks, Ark. Air N.G., now state chaplain, col.; speaker weekly TV program statewide; tour host to Holy Land, 1971, 72, 73, 77; guest instr. N.T., John Brown U., 1968-69; guest instr. evangelism Southwestern Bapt. Sem., 1972. Bd. govs. Washington Regional Med. Center, Fayetteville, 1973—. Served with USAF, 1955-63. Mem. Fayetteville C. of C. (dir. 1970-73). Club: Kiwanis (past pres. Fayetteville). Author weekly newspaper column Live It Up, 1974—. Home: 1932 Wheeler St Fayetteville AR 72701 Office: 315 W Maple St Fayetteville AR 72701

MC CHESNEY, STEWART REID, JR., minister, So. Bapt. Conv.; b. Oklahoma City, Nov. 14, 1937; s. Stewart Reid and Juanita (Austin) McC.; B.A. cum laude, Howard Payne Coll., 1969; M.Div., Southwestern Bapt. Theol. Sem., 1973, postgrad., 1974-77; m. Dorothy Jean Atwood, Nov. 18, 1954; children—Steward Reid, Elizabeth Ann. Ordained to ministry, 1967; pastor chs., Tex., 1966-74; pastor Ward Rd. Bapt. Ch., Arvada, Colo., 1974—. Mem. Radio TV Commn., So. Bapt. Conv.; pres. Ministerial Alliance, Howard Payne Coll. participant overseas crusades, Korea, 1975, Sweden, 1976. Mem. honor socs. Howard Payne Coll., 1966-69; recipient Letters Howard Payne Coll. golf team. Home: 11418 W 59th Pl Arvada CO 80004

MCCLAIN, HOWARD GORDON, minister, Southern Baptist Convention; b. Cooper, Tex., May 25, 1918; s. Ray G. and Thelma Beatrice (Pratt) McC.; m. Barbara Behrman, Dec. 23, 1941; children: Ray Pratt, Margy, Anna Beatrice. B.A., Vanderbilt U., 1939; B.D., Southern Bapt. Theol. Seminary, 1943; D. Humanities, Wofford Coll., 1977. Ordained to ministry Bapt. Ch., 1953. Dir. CROP, Columbia, S.C., 1949; exec. minister Christian Action Council, Columbia, 1950-85; sec. Columbia Ministers Assn., 1953-68; asst. prof. sociology Campbell Coll., Buie's Creek, N.C., 1945-46, Mercer U., Macon, Ga., 1946-49; research fellow in ch. history Inst. So. Studies, U. S.C., 1985—. Mem. Columbia Urban League, S.C., 1965—. Recipient E. A. McDowell award S.C. Bapt. Conv. Christian Life and Pub. Affairs Com., 1983; Order of Palmetto, Gov. of S.C., 1985. Mem. Nat. Council on Values in Higher Edn., Nat. Assn. Ecumenical Staff, S.C. Acad. Religion. Democrat. Home: 2519 Stratford Rd Columbia SC 29204

MCCLAIN, JAMES OLIN, minister, So. Bapt. Conv.; b. Troup County, Ga., Sept. 24, 1925; s. James Joseph and Tiny Juette (Bales) McC.; student pub. schs., Tatum, Ga.; m. Reba Lois Yates, Mar. 29, 1946; children—David Olin, Rebecca Lynn. Ordained to ministry, 1972; pastor Pineview Bapt. Ch., LaGrange, Ga., 1972—; deacon 2d Bapt. Ch., La Grange, 1963-70, lay preacher, 1970-72. Sales mgr. Fling Ford Co., LaGrange, 1961—. Mem. Troup Bapt. Assn. (chmn. coop. program), Soc. Profl. Sales Mgrs. Ford Motors Co. Home: 203 N Dawson St LaGrange GA 30240 Office: 315 Franklin Rd LaGrange GA 30240

MCCLAIN, WILLIAM BOBBY, religious educator, elder, United Methodist Church; b. Gadsden, Ala., May 19, 1938; s. Frank Bural and Malinda (Williams) McC.; children: William B., David Wilson. A.B., Clark Coll., 1960; M.Div., Boston U., 1962, Th.D., 1977. Ordained elder United Meth. Ch., 1964. Pastor, Haven Meth. Ch., Anniston, Ala., 1962-64; dir. guidance and counseling Gadsden State Coll., Ala., 1962-64; dir. Urban Tng. Ctr., Action for Boston Community Devel., 1966-68; pastor Union United Meth. Ch., Boston, 1968-78; exec. dir. Multi-Ethnic Ctr., Drew U., 1978-80; prof. homiletics and worship Wesley Theol. Sem., Washington, 1980—; dir. Black Theology Project of the Americas, 1980—; lectr. in field. Author: Soul of Black Worship, 1980; Travelling Light, 1981; Black People in the Methodist Church, 1984; contbr. articles to religious jours. Rockefeller Found. fellow, 1961-62; Walker Found. fellow, 1960; Boston U. Human Relations Ctr. fellow, 1960; Crusade scholar United Meth. Ch., 1960-62. Mem. Acad. Homiletics, Nat. Fellowship of Meth. Musicians, Artists and Worship Leaders, Soc. for Study of Black Religion (bd. dirs. 1983—), Soc. for Sci. Study of Religion, Nat. Conf. Liturgists. Home: 500 Round Table Dr Oxon Hill MD 20744 Office: Wesley Theol Sem 4500 Massachusetts Ave Washington DC 20016

MCCLEARY, PAUL FREDERICK, minister, religious organization official, United Methodist Church; b. Bradley, Ill., May 2, 1930; s. Hal C. and Pearl E. (Aeicher) McC.; A.B., Olivet Nazarene Coll., 1952; M.Div., Garrett Sem., 1956; M.A., Northwestern U., 1972; D.D., MacMurray Coll., 1970; m. Rachel Pauline Timm, Jan. 26, 1951; children: Leslie Ann, Rachel Mary, John Wesley, Timothy Paul. Ordained to ministry United Meth. Ch., 1956. Pastor Meth. chs., Reddicks and Essex, Ill., 1950-53, McDowell-Center, Ill., 1953-56, Ch. of the Saviour, Cochabamba, Bolivia, 1957-59, Trinity Ch., Santa Cruz, Bolivia, 1959-61; dist. supt. eastern dist. United Meth. Ch., 1959-61; exec. sec. Bolivia Ann. Conf., United Meth. Ch., 1961-68; exec. sec. structure study commn., United Meth. Ch., Evanston, Ill., 1969-72, asst. gen. sec. Latin Am. Affairs world div. Bd. Global Ministries, N.Y.C., 1972-75; assoc. sec. div. overseas ministries, exec. dir. ch. world Service Nat. Council Chs., N.Y.C., 1975-84; assoc. gen. sec. for research Gen. Council on Ministries, United Meth. Ch., 1984—. Mem. Latin Am. Studies Assn., Alpha Kappa Lambda. Mason. Home: 2001 Tiara Ct Dayton OH 45459 Office: 601 W Riverview Ave Dayton OH 45406

MC CLENDON, PHILLIP WILEY, minister, So. Bapt. Conv.; b. Carthage, Mo., July 16, 1946; s. John Wiley and Opal Arlene (Lewis) McC.; B.A., Cumberland Coll., 1969; M.Div., Midwestern Bapt. Theol. Sem., 1973; m. Jacqueline Roszell, Dec. 18, 1966; children—Raymond Scott, Gwendolyn Nevelle. Ordained to ministry, 1965; pastor Greenland Bapt. Ch., Corbin, Ky., 1967-69, 1st Bapt. Ch., Taos, New Mex., 1973—; dir. religious activities Crowder Coll., 1972-73; chaplain Holiday Inn, 1974—. Sec. Taos Ministerial Assn., 1973-74, pres., 1974-75; supr., counselor Billy Graham Crusade, Albuquerque, 1975; pastor Hillcrest Bapt. Ch., Big Spring, Tex., 1977—. Mem. organizing bd. Taos Alcoholism Program, 1973; mem. adv. bd. Holy Cross Hosp., Taos, N.Mex., 1976-77. Home and Office: PO Box Drawer PP Taos NM 87571

MCCLINTOCK, JOHN DEWITT, priest, Anglican Ch. Can.; b. Toronto, Ont., Can., Sept. 1, 1930; s. John James and Fern Susan (Whitehead) McC.; D.Th., Wycliffe Coll., Toronto, 1961, L.Th., 1970; B.Th., Queen's U., Kingston, Ont., 1970; m. Gertrude Emily Kemp, Sept. 13, 1958; children—Shaun, Shannah. Ordained priest Anglican Ch. Can., 1961; rector St. Aldhelm's Ch., Vulcan, Alta., 1961-63; chaplain Canadian Army, 1963-67; chaplain Kingston Gen. Hosp., 1967-70, Hôtel Dieu, Kingston, 1967-70; rector St. Paul's Ch., Brockville, Ont., 1970—; dir. marriage counseling courses, Brockville, 1970—; chaplain Brockville Fire Dept., 1970—. Bd govs. Brockville Gen. Hosp., 1971—; chmn. bd. govs. Brockville Regional Sch. Nursing, 1971—; chmn. sch. com. St. Lawrence Coll., 1973—; chaplain St. Vincent de Paul Hosp., Brockville, 1973—, mem. fin. com., 1975—; bd. dirs. Family Services Kingston, 1968-72. Mem. Canadian Legion. Mason. Home: 37 Victoria Ave Brockville ON K6V 2B3 Canada Office: St Paul's Ch Pine St Brockville ON K6V 2B3 Canada

MCCLOSKEY, MICHAEL, church official Roman Catholic Church; b. New Orleans, July 13, 1941; s. Hugh and Dorothy (Cook) McC.; A.B. with honors magna cum laude, U. Scranton, 1965; M.A., Loyola U., Chgo., 1969, Ph.D. (Arthur J. Schmitt scholar), 1974; postgrad. Catholic Theol. Union; m. Deborah C. Moloney, Sept. 5, 1970; children: Joel, Mara. Mem. Scranton (Pa.) Swordsmen Sodality, 1961-65, pres., 1964-65; mem. Scranton Confrat. Christian Doctrine, 1962-64, pres., 1963-64; permanent deacon Chgo. Holy Name Cathedral, 1978—. Mng. editor Rev. Religious Research, 1972-79; editor Assn. Sociology Religion News and Announcements, 1974-77. Prof. social sci. Chgo. City Coll., 1974—. Recipient Founders medal Loyola U., 1969, Centennial medallion, 1970. Mem. Religious Research Assn., Assn. Sociology Religion, Soc. Sci. Study Religion, Am., Ill. sociol. assns., Midwest Sociol. Soc. Home: 5956 N Neva Ave Chicago IL 60631 Office: 1145 W Wilson Ave Chicago IL 60640

MCCLOUD, J. OSCAR, ch. exec., United Presbyn. Ch. in U.S.A.; b. Waynesboro, Ga., Apr. 10, 1936; s. George and Sophronia (Foley) McC.; A.A., Warren Wilson Coll., Swannanoa, N.C., 1956; B.A., Berea Coll., 1958; B.D., Union Theol. Sem., N.Y., 1961; D.D. (hon.), Mary Holmes Coll., West Point, Miss., 1974; D.H.L., Whitworth Coll., Spokane, Wash., 1975; m. Robbie Juanita Foster, Sept. 13, 1960; children—Ann Michelle, Cassandra Anita, Tony Delancy. Ordained to ministry, 1961; pastor Davis St. U.P. Ch., Raleigh, N.C., 1961-64; field rep. Bd. Christian Edn. U.P. Ch. U.S.A., Atlanta, 1964-67, asso. div. ch. and race of Bd. Nat. Missions, 1968-69, asso. chmn. operations, N.Y.C., 1969-71, asso. gen. sec. Commn. Ecumenical Mission and Relations, 1971-72, gen. dir. program agy., N.Y.C., 1972—. Bd. dirs. So. Christian Leadership Conf. Nat. pres. Project Equality; vice. chmn. Delta Ministry Commn., Greenville, Miss.; mem. central com., mem. exec. com. World Council of Chs. Office: 475 Riverside Dr New York City NY 10027

MC CLURE, JACK ANDREW, minister, Ch. of God (Cleveland, Tenn.); b. Greenville, S.C., Sept. 15, 1928; s. Raymond Boyd and Buena Mace (Bagwell) McC.; student ann. tng. schs., seminars Ch. of God, 1956—; m. Jewel Ruby Key, Dec. 22, 1945; children—Raymond B., Jackie M., Dennis L. Ordained to ministry, 1956; pastor chs., Fork Shoals, S.C., 1956-59, McCrory, Ark., 1960-62, Norris City, Ill., 1963, Rockford, Ill., 1964-66, Peoria, Ill., 1966-71, Somerset, Pa., 1972, Rock Hill, S.C., 1973, Greenville, S.C., 1974—. Chaplain Greenville Hosp. System; dist. youth dir. Ch. of God, 1960-66, dist. overseer, Rockford, 1964-66, chmn. Ill. ministerial examining com., 1966-71, dist. evangelism dir., Greenville, 1973—. Author: One Nation Under God; A Comprehensive Study of Prayer; author religious tracts. Home: 13 Ackley Rd Greenville SC 29607 Office: 1200 Laurens Rd Greenville SC 29607

MCCLURG, PATRICIA ANN, minister, Presbyterian Church U.S.A.; b. Bay City, Tex., Mar. 14, 1939; d. Tildon H. and Margaret B. (Smith) McC. B.D., Austin Presbyn. Theol. Sem., 1967; M.C.E., Presbyn. Sch. Christian Edn., Richmond, Va., 1963; V.A., Austin Coll., 1961, D.D. (hon.), 1977. Ordained to ministry Presbyn. Ch. U.S.A., 1967. Dir. Christian edn. Second Presbyn. Ch., Newport News, Va., 1963-65; asst. pastor Westminster Presbyn. Ch., Beaumont, Tex., 1967-69; assoc. pastor First Presbyn. Ch., Pasadena, Tex., 1969-71; assoc. exec. Synod of Red River, Denton, Tex., 1973-75; adminstrv. dir. Mission Bd., Atlanta, 1975—; v.p. Nat. Council Chs., N.Y.C., 1985—; bd. dirs. Presbyn. Ministers Fund, Phila., 1983—. Contbr. writings to Presbyn. Survey, 1975. Named Disting. Alumna, Austin Coll., 1979; scholarship grantee, 1957-73. Democrat. Office: Gen Assembly Mission Bd 341 Ponde de Leon Ave NE Atlanta GA 30365

MCCLUSKEY, GARY NORMAN, minister, Lutheran Church in America; b. Hazleton, Pa., Aug. 28, 1954; s. William Edward and Lois Helen (Boughner) McC.; m. Mary Beth Havrilla, Aug. 19, 1978; 1 son, Randall Jay. B.S., Pa. State U.-Middletown, 1976; M.Div., Luth. Theol. Sem., Gettysburg, Pa., 1980. Ordained to ministry Lutheran Ch., 1980. Asst. adminstr. Council of Churches, Harrisburg, Pa., 1975-76; vicar Bethlehem Luth. Ch., Los Alamos, N.Mex., 1978-79; pastor St. Peter Luth. Ch., Carlsbad, N.Mex., 1980-83, First Luth. Ch., Colorado Springs, Colo., 1983—; mem. youth com. Rocky Mountain Synod, Luth. Ch. Am., 1981—, mem. parish services com., 1981—; chmn. chaplain com. Ministerial Alliance, Carlsbad, N.Mex., 1982-83, pres., 1981-82. Bd. dirs. Girl Scouts Am., Artesia, N.Mex., 1981-83, mem. exec. bd., 1981-83; mem. Nat. Council on Alcoholism, 1984; bd. dirs. Martin Luther Homes, Colorado Springs, 1984—. Mem. Am. Soc. Ch. History, Concordia Hist. Inst. Republican. Home: 821 N 31st St Colorado Springs CO 80904 Office: First Luth Ch 1515 N Cascade St Colorado Springs CO 80907

MCCOLLIAN, WILLIAM J., minister, Church of God (Anderson, Ind.); b. Princeton, W.Va., Nov. 20, 1956; s. William Joseph and Thelma Jean (Wimmer) McC.; m. Sonya Gay Mozingo, Dec. 22, 1978; children: Tara Lee, Aubrey Elizabeth. B.A., Warner So. Coll., 1980. Pastor, Chatham Hill Ch. of God, Chatham Hill, Va., 1978-80; pastor Broadford Ch. of God, Saltville, Va., 1981-82; sr. pastor Heritage Ch. of God, Hermitage, Tenn., 1983—; mem. bd. ch. extension and home missions Hope Hill Children's Home, 1984—. Republican. Address: Hope Hill Children's Home Hope KY 40334

MCCOLLUM, ODELL, religious organization executive, United Holy Church of America; b. Reidsville, N.C., Feb. 16, 1927; s. Roy and Carrie Lee (Hodge) McC.; m. Margaret Mae Akins, Aug. 7, 1948; children: Larry Odell, Tresa Lynette. D.D. (hon.), United Christian Coll., Goldsboro, N.C., 1974; S.T.D. (hon.), United Christian Coll., Bklyn., 1979. Ordained to ministry United Holy Church America, 1953. Pastor House of Prayer United Holy Ch. Am., Warren, Ohio, 1957-64, Gospel Tabernacle United Holy Ch. Am., Columbus, Ohio, 1964—; bishop United Holy Ch. Am., 1972—, 2nd v.p., 1980—; pres. Northwestern Dist. United Holy Ch. Am., 1980—, Western Dist., 1980-84. Served to Pfc. U.S. Army, 1944-46, PTO.

MC COMAS, ROBERT FRANCIS, minister, United Meth. Ch.; b. Spencer, Mass., Oct. 23, 1917; s. Ralph and Bessie Beatrice (Wheeler) McC.; A.B., Clark U., 1939; M.Div., Boston U., 1942; S.T.M., Harvard U., 1956; m. Margaret Cameron Farquhar Jackson, Sept. 10, 1945; children—Elizabeth Pugh, Janet MacNeill, Robert J., David C., Joanne Dale. Ordained to ministry, 1942; chaplain USNR, 1942-74; sr. chaplain U.S. Naval Acad., 1967-70; pastor Christ United Meth. Ch., Groton, Conn., 1974—. Pres. Groton Clergy Assn.; pres. Mil. Chaplains Assn., Chgo. chpt., 1965-67, N.Y.C. chpt., 1972-74. Recipient Distinguished Alumnus award Boston U. Sch. Theology, 1969. Home: 160 Laurelwood Rd Groton CT 06340

MCCOMMON, PAUL CLINTON, JR., minister, religious organization executive, Southern Baptist Convention; b. Memphis, Dec. 28, 1920; s. Paul Clinton and Agnes Laverne (Bledsoe) McC.; A.B., Baylor U., 1942; Th.M., So. Baptist Theol. Sem., 1945, Ph.D., 1948; m. Frances C. Larkin, June 16, 1945; children: Erin (Mrs. Harold Barnett), Paul Clinton III. Ordained to ministry So. Bapt. Conv., 1941. Assoc. pastor, Atlanta, 1946-48, pastor, 1948-51; dir. dept. ch. music Ga. Bapt. Conv., Atlanta, 1951—; pres., So. Bapt. Ch. Music Conf., 1957-58. Author: Music in The Bible, 1956 (Portugese and Arabic edits.); Great Hymns of Evangelism, 1978; co-author: Music in the Worship Experience, 1984. Mem. editorial com. Baptist Hymnal, 1956, mem. revision com., 1974. Contbr. numerous articles to denominational periodicals. Mem. Am. Guild Organists, Hymn Soc. Am., Phi Mu Alpha Sinfonia (life). Home: Box 2364 Peachtree City GA 30269 Office: Baptist Center Flowers Rds Atlanta GA 30341

MCCONKIE, BRUCE R., ch. ofcl., Ch. of Jesus Christ of Latter-day Saints; b. Ann Arbor, Mich., July 29, 1915; s. Oscar W. and Vivian (Redd) McC.; B.A., U. Utah, 1937, LL.B., J.D., 1939. Missionary Ch. of Jesus Christ of Latter-day Saints, 1934-36; tchr. ch. classes; pres. 340th Quorum of Seventy, Bonneville Stake; apptd. mem. First Council Seventy, 1946; ch. coordinator for servicemen; pres. South Australian Mission, Melbourne, 1961-64; mem. Council of Twelve, 1972—. Admitted to Utah bar, practiced in Salt Lake City. Asst. city atty., city prosecutor, Salt Lake City, 1940-42. Author: Mormon Doctrine; Doctrinal New Testament Commentary, 3 vols.; The Mortal Messiah—From Bethlehem to Calvary, Book I, 1979, Book II, 1980, Book III, 1980, Book IV, 1981; The Millennial Messiah—The Second Coming of the Son of Man. Trustee Brigham Young U., Provo, Utah, 1972—, Ricks Coll., Rexburg, Idaho, 1973—, Ch. Coll. Hawaii, Laie, Oahu, 1973—. Served to lt. col. M.I., AUS, 1942-46. Editor 3 vols. Doctrines of Salvation. Address: care of Council of Twelve Salt Lake City UT 84101

MCCONNELL, CALVIN DALE See *Who's Who in America,* 43rd edition.

MCCONNELL, RONALD DOUGLAS, minister, Episcopal Church; b. Fort Worth, Feb. 2, 1932; s. Elbert E. and Maude Elizabeth (O'Toole) McC.; m. Marjorie Jane Hassler, June 13, 1961; children: Kelly, Mark, Peter. B.S., Fla. State U., 1953; B.D., Southwestern Theol. Sem., 1956; Th.M., Christian Theol. Sem., 1960; Ph.D., U. Glasgow, Scotland, 1968. Ordained priest, Episcopal Ch., 1976. Pastor, ch. exec. Assembly of God, Tipton, Ind., 1957-59; pastor First Assembly of God, Waco, Tex., 1966-69; founder, pastor The Christian Ctr., Albuquerque, 1970-81; exec. v.p. KFCB, Concord, Calif., 1981-83; exec. dir. Found. for Christian Ministries, 1983—; observer Roman Catholic/Pentecostal Dialogue, 1981, 82, The Secretariat on Christian Unity, Vatican; dir. KLYT-FM Radio, Albuquerque, 1979-81; pres., bd. regents Mellodyland Sch. Theology, Anaheim, Calif., 1979-80; dir., exec. v.p. KFCB, Concord, Calif., 1981-83. Contbr. articles to profl. jours. Bd. dirs. N.Mex. Interch. Agy., Albuquerque, 1981-82. Served to maj. as chaplain USAF, 1959-66. Named Pastor at Large, Albuquerque Christian Ctr., 1981, Hon. Pastor, Ch. of the Highlands, San Bruno, Calif., 1983. Mem. John 17:21 Fellowship (exec. v.p. 1978—), Ch. Renewal Leadership Group, Theta Phi. Republican. Home: 1255 Church St Benicia CA 94510

MCCORD, JAMES ILEY, seminary chancellor, United Presbyn. Ch. in U.S.A.; b. Rusk, Tex., Nov. 24, 1919; s. Marshal Edward and Jimmie Oleta (Decherd) McC.; B.A., Austin (Tex.) Coll., 1938, D.D. (hon.), 1949; student Union Theol. Sem., Richmond, Va., 1938-39; B.Div., Austin Presbyn. Theol. Sem., 1942; postgrad. Harvard, 1942-43, New Coll., U. Edinburgh, 1950-51; M.A., U. Tex., 1942; D.D., Austin Coll., 1949; Th.D. (hon.), U. Geneva, 1958, Reformed Theol. Acad., Debrecren, Hungary, 1967; D.D. (hon.), Knox Coll., Toronto, Can., 1958, Princeton, 1960, Victoria U., Toronto, 1963, Westminster Coll., New Wilmington, Pa., 1969, U. Edinburgh, 1970, United Protestant Theol. Inst., Cluj, Rumania, 1974, Presbyn. Coll., Montreal, Que., Can., 1975; LL.D. (hon.), Maryville (Tenn.) Coll., 1959, Lafayette Coll., Easton, Pa., 1962, Tusculum (Ala.) Coll., 1964, Bloomfield (N.J.) Coll., 1966—, Park Coll., Mo., 1969; Litt.D. (hon.), Davidson (N.C.) Coll., 1959, Washington and Jefferson Coll., 1970; L.H.D., Ursinus Coll., 1962; m. Hazel Gertrude Thompson, Aug. 29, 1939; children—Vincent, Alison (Mrs. James Zimmerman), Marcia. Ordained minister Presbyn. Ch. in U.S., 1942; pastor, Austin, 1944-45, 52-54; instr. philosophy, prof. Bible, U. Tex., 1954-58; dean, prof. systematic theology Austin Presbyn. Theol. Sem., 1944-59; pres., prof. theology Princeton Theol. Sem., 1959-83, chancellor, 1983—; chmn. North Am. Area World Alliance Ref. Chs., 1958-60, North Am. sec. Alliance, 1959-77; former mem. common faith and order World Council of Chs., pres. World Alliance Ref. Chs., 1977-82. Mem. Assn. Theol. Schs. in U.S. and Can., 1978-80. Office: Princeton Theol Sem Princeton NJ 08540

MCCORD, JOHN DAVID, minister, United Church of Canada; b. Montreal, Que., Can., Sept. 22, 1933; s. Robert D. and Irene D. (MacLaren) McC.; m. Norma E. Archer, June 13, 1964; children: Ian Andrew, Kenneth Graham. B.A., U. Toronto, 1954; B.D., U. Edinburgh, 1957; D.D. (hon.), United Theol.-McGill U., 1981. Ordained to ministry United Ch. of Can., 1958. Pastor chs. in Que. and Ont., 1958-74; chaplain Cowansville Penitentiary, Que., 1964-74; exec. dir. Ch. Council on Justice and Corrections, Ottawa, Ont., Can., 1974—. Office: 151 Slater St Suite 305 Ottawa ON K1P 5H3 Canada

MC CORKLE, WILLIAM FRANKLIN, minister, missionary, Assemblies of God; b. Mecca, Mo., May 28, 1922; s. Ernest Estil and Beulah (Rice) McC.; grad. Central Bible Coll., 1943; postgrad. in linguistics U. Okla., 1950; m. Robbie Aneice Smitherman, Apr. 8, 1945; children—Amonna Su McCorkle Goodwin, William Andrew (dec.). Ordained to ministry, 1945; missionary, Ghana, W. Africa, 1947—; prin. No. Ghana Bible Inst., 1961-76. Gen. treas. Assemblies of God, Ghana, past. supt.; bd. govs. W. Ghana Advanced Sch. Theology, Lome, Togo. Mem. Ghana Govt. Bur. Langs. Translator of scriptures into Mampruli and Dagbani langs. Home: 205 N 4th St Baytown TX 77520 Office: PO Box 43 Tamale NR Ghana West Africa

MCCORMICK, J(OSEPH) CARROLL, bishop, Roman Cath. Ch.; b. Phila., 1907; student St. Charles Sem., Phila., Pontifical Roman Sem., Rome. Ordained priest Roman Cath. Ch., 1932, consecrated bishop, 1947; vice chancellor, later chancellor, Archdiocese of Phila., 1936-44; pastor St. Stephen's Ch., Phila., from 1944; titular bishop of Ruspe, aux. bishop of Phila., 1947-60; bishop of Altoona-Johnstown, Pa., 1960-67; bishop of Scranton, Pa., 1967—. Address: 315 Wyoming Ave Scranton PA 18503

MCCORMICK, MARGO, nun, religious school administrator, Roman Catholic Church; b. Scranton, Pa., Apr. 5, 1940; d. Austin Patrick and Irene (Ferrick) McC. B.A., Marywood Coll., 1965; M.S. in Edn., U. Dayton, 1973, cert. adminstr., 1979. Joined Sisters, Servants of the Immaculate Heart of Mary, 1960. Elementary tchr. St. Mary's Sch., Manhasset, L.I., N.Y., 1960-67; math. tchr. W. Gaston High Sch., Newbern, N.C., 1967-68, Archbishop Neale High Sch., LaPlata, Md., 1968-69, Bishop Hannan High Sch.,

Scranton, Pa., 1969-76; secondary prin., Notre Dame High Sch., East Stroudsburg, Pa., 1976-80, Seton Cath. High Sch., Pittston, Pa., 1980-84; asst. supt. Diocese of Trenton, N.J., 1984—. NSF grantee, 1969-72. Mem. Diocesan Council Math. Tchrs. (pres. 1974), Middle States Assn. (chmn. 1980), Assn. for Supervision and Curriculum Devel., Nat. Assn. Secondary Sch. Prins., Nat. Cath. Edn. Assn. Home: Holy Cross Convent Route 130 Riverside NJ 08075 Office: Cath Schs Diocese of Trenton 1931 Brunswick Ave Trenton NJ 08648

MCCORMICK, RICHARD ARTHUR, priest, educator, Roman Catholic Church; b. Toledo, Ohio, Oct. 3, 1922; s. Edward James and Josephine (Beck) McC. A.B., Loyola U.-Chgo., 1945, M.A., 1950; S.T.D., Gregorian Coll.-Rome, 1957; D.H.L. (hon.), Scranton U., 1975, Wheeling Coll., 1976. Joined Soc. Jesus, ordained priest. Prof. moral theology Jesuit Sch. Theology, Chgo., 1957-74; Rose F. Kennedy prof. Christian ethics Georgetown U., Washington, 1974—. Author: How Brave a New World?; Notes on Moral Theology; Health and Medicine in the Catholic Tradition. Editor: Doing Evil to Achieve Good. Mem. Cath. Theol. Soc. Am. (recipient Cardinal Spellman award 1969, pres. 1970). Home: 1419 35th St NW Washington DC 20057 Office: Kennedy Inst Ethics 37th and P Sts Washington DC 20057

MCCOURT, ROBERT R., priest, Roman Catholic Ch.; b. Bklyn., Feb. 15, 1935; s. Robert Ann and Ann Teresa (Reilly) McC. B.A., Cathedral Coll., Bklyn., 1957; S.T.B., Immaculate Conception Sem., Huntington, N.Y., 1961; M.Div., Cathedral Grad. Coll., Douglaston, N.Y., 1981. Ordained priest Roman Catholic Ch., 1961. Asst. pastor Holy Rosary Parish, Bklyn., 1961-70; pastor St. Clement Pope Parish, South Ozone Park, N.Y., 1970-82, St. Pascal Baylon Ch., St. Albans, N.Y., 1982—. Mem. Nat. Council Cath. Chs. Home and Office: St Pascal Baylon Ch 112-43 198th St Saint Albans NY 11412

MCCOURY, DAWNATH GALE, minister, Southern Baptist Convention; b. Lampasas, Tex., Jan. 7, 1936; s. Joseph Cecil and Vera Georgia (Russell) M.; student Hardin Simmons U., 1954, Baylor U., 1954-58; postgrad. Southwestern Bapt. Theol. Sem., 1959-61; D.D. (hon.), Evangelica Sem., 1969; m. Berlee Ann Kuhn, June 28, 1958; children—John Mark, Paul Daaron. Ordained to ministry So. Baptist Conv., 1956; pastor chs., Thorndale, Chilton and Waco, Tex., Rangely, Colo., Denver, Colorado Springs, Colo., Kansas City, Mo.; dir. dept. ch. tng. dept. student ministries and ch. program services No. Plains Bapt. Conv., Rapid City, S.D., 1971-75; dept. dir. Sunday sch., ch. adminstrn. and family ministries Colo. Bapt. Gen. Conv., Denver, 1975-79, dir. ch. services div., 1979-81, assoc. exec. dir. and dir. pastoral ministries, 1981—. Recipient Outstanding Debator award Baylor U., 1958, Ch. State Speakers award, 1957. Mem. Nat. Forensic League, So. Bapt. Religious Edn. Assn., Assn. Couples for Marriage Enrichment, Phi Kappa Delta (pres. Baylor chpt. 1957-58). Mason, Lion. Contbr. articles and sermons to profl. jours., Sunday sch. lessons to Rocky Mt. Bapt., 1968—. Home: 7373 S Franklin St Littleton CO 80122 Office: 7393 S Acton Way Englewood CO 80112

MC COWAN, GEORGE FRANKLIN, priest, Episcopal Ch.; b. Gem County, Idaho, May 13, 1925; s. Ivan Burgess and Lavina Teddy (Sillivan) McC.; A.B., Washington U., St. Louis, 1957; M.Div., Episc. Theol. Sem. S.W., Austin, Tex., 1957; m. Elizabeth Garland Davis, Mar. 4, 1951; 1 son, Dennis Franklin. Ordained to ministry, 1957; vicar Episcopal Ch. of Advent, Crestwood, Mo., 1957-66, rector, 1966; vicar Trinity Episc. Ch., DeSoto, Mo., 1957-59; mem. dept. mission and strategy Diocese Mo., 1961-64, bishop's examining chaplain, 1967-71; mem. Commn. on Ministry, 1971—, mem. Commn. on Architecture and Allied Arts, 1967—; chmn. St. Louis County Bd. Research and Planning, 1965-66; vis. fellow Episc. Theol. Sem. S.W., 1965. Mem. Washington U., Episc. Sem. S.W. alumni assns. Home: 666 Selma Ave St Louis MO 63119

MCCOY, ADAM DUNBAR, priest, Episcopal Church; b. Chgo., Dec. 19, 1946; s. Duncan Redfield and Morna Jean (Marshall) McC. B.A., Mich. State U., 1969; M.A., Cornell U., 1972, Ph.D., 1973; M.Div., Ch. Div. Sch. of Pacific, 1979. Joined Order Holy Cross, Episcopal Ch., life profession, 1978, ordained priest, 1979. Guest master Mt. Calvary Retreat House, Santa Barbara, Calif., 1979-81, prior, 1981—; novice master Order of the Holy Cross, Santa Barbara, 1984—; regional coordinator evangelism Nat. Episcopal Ch., S.W. U.S., 1981—. Address: Mount Calvary Retreat House Box 1296 Santa Barbara CA 93102

MCCOY, ANDREW, minister, Ch. of God in Christ; b. Sibley, La., Dec. 15, 1910; s. Mose and Maria (Jackson) M.; student pub. schs., Sibley; m. Ira Odom Luke, June 12, 1933; 1 dau., Eura Lee Luke Owens. Ordained to ministry, 1940; pastor chs., La., 1940—, pastor Homer, Jamestown and Bossier City. Mem. nat. registration dept. Ch. of God in Christ, Memphis, 1970—, state exec. bd., La. W., supt. Shreveport dist. Recipient Best Pastor award Holmes M. Chapel, 1973; hon. certificate State of Tex. Home: 500 Woodard Minden LA 71055 Office: 715 Butter St Bossier LA 71055

MC COY, DON BURCHARD, minister, educator, Southern Baptist Convention; b. Dresden, Tenn., Apr. 22, 1928; s. Albert Austin and Celia Edith (Bass) McC.; B.A., Cumberland U., 1949; B.D., Golden Gate Bapt. Theol. Sem., 1951, Th.D., 1954; M.A., George Peabody Coll., 1958, Ed.S., 1970; Ph.D., St. Louis U. (Philippines), 1979; m. E. Sterline White, Dec. 28, 1951; children—Don David, James Austin, Sterling Mark, Thomas Jefferson. Ordained to ministry, 1949; pastor Wrigley (Tenn.) Bapt. Ch., Cross Rds. Bapt. Ch., Centerville, Tenn., 1949, Calwa Bapt. Ch., Fresno, Calif., 1950-54; missionary Fgn. Mission Bd. So. Bapt. Conv., Brazil, S.Am., 1954-59; pastor Tusculum Hills Bapt. Ch., Nashville, 1959-65; acad. dean Philippine Bapt. Theol. Sem., Baguio, 1965-72; pastor First Bapt. Ch., Dickson, Tenn., 1972—; adj. prof., dept. philosophy and edn. Am. Bapt. Coll., Nashville, 1964, 1969, 1972—. Lectr. in field; pres. Dickson County (Tenn.) Fellowship Ministers, 1972-74. Trustee Belmont Coll., Nashville; mem. Dickson Recreation Com., 1974—, Mayor's Adv. Com., Dickson, 1975—. Recipient meritorious Citation award Am. Bapt. Coll., 1970. Mem. Missions Advanced Research and Communication Center, AAUP. Contbr. articles to edn. jours., mission mags. Home: 110 Lee Rd Dickson TN 37055 Office: Box 519 Dickson TN 37055

MCCOY, GLENN WESLEY, minister, religious educator, Southern Baptist Convention; b. Hatfield, Ark., July 4, 1933; s. Raymond Wesley and Irene Elizabeth (McDonald) McCoy; m. Dorla Deane Medford, Aug. 29, 1957; children: Annette Kathleen, John Wesley, Stanley Glenn. B.A., Ouachita U., 1956; B.D., Southwestern Sem., 1958, Th.M., 1962; M.A., Eastern N.Mex. U., 1971; D.Min., Southwestern Sem., 1980. Ordained minister Bapt. Ch., 1958. Pastor First Bapt. Ch., Ruidoso Downs, N.Mex., 1959-61, Mountain View Bapt. Ch., Roswell, N.Mex., 1961-63; campus minister Highlands U., Las Vegas, N.Mex., 1963-71; tchr. Eastern N.Mex. U., Portales, 1971—, assoc. prof., chmn. dept. religion. Contbr. articles to religious jours. Pres. Kiwanis Club, Portales, 1980, Babe Ruth Baseball, Portales, 1973-79. Mem. Soc. Biblical Lit. Home: 141 Yucca Dr Portales NM 88130 Office: PO Box 2005 Portales NM 88130

MCCOY, SAMUEL LEE, minister, Presbyterian Church (U.S.A.); b. Morgantown, W.Va., Oct. 2, 1942; s. John Frank and Dorene Elizabeth (Ross) McC.; m. Dorothy M. Storey, May 13, 1984. B.A., King Coll., 1964; M.Div., Union Theol. Sem., Va., 1968. Ordained to ministry, 1969; chaplain Memphis Med. Center, 1968-69; pastoral counselor Memphis Inst. Medicine and Religion, 1968-69; asst. pastor Old Presbyn. Meeting House, Alexandria, Va., 1970-71; chaplain D.C. Children's Center, Laurel, Md., 1971-72; asst. chaplain supr. Spring Grove State Hosp., Balt., 1972-73; psychiatric chaplain supr. Crownsville (Md.) Hosp. Center, 1973—; pastoral counselor Pastoral Counseling and Consultation Centers of Greater Balt., 1973-77; pastoral counselor Md. Inst. Pastoral Counseling, 1977—; asst. pastor Woods Meml. Presbyn. Ch., Severna Park, Md., 1982-85. Interim pastor Nat. Capitol Presbytery, Washington and Presbytery of Balt., 1973—; pres. Dutch Glen Condominium Assn., 1983-84. Mem. Greater Annapolis Ministerium (pres. 1983—), Assn. for Clin. Pastoral Edn. (acting supr. 1974-78), Chesapeake Bay Found., Coll. Chaplains (fellow), Profl. Assn. Chaplains Md. Dept. Health and Mental Hygiene (chmn. 1982—), Chesapeake Bay Maritime Mus. Address: Crownsville Hosp Center Crownsville MD 21032

MCCRARY, LORAN BRENT, minister, So. Bapt. Conv.; b. Hamilton, Mo., June 7, 1941; s. Herbert R. and Anna H. (McCauley) McC.; B.R.E., Zion Theol. Sem., 1974; B.A., Faith Evangelistic Christian Coll., 1975; M.Th., D.Ch. Edn., Faith Bapt. Theol. Sem., 1976, D.Th., 1977; m. Sharon Rose Roberts, Dec. 24, 1961; children—Elizabeth, Joy, Jan, Lonnie, Stacy. Ordained to ministry, 1970; pastor First Bapt. Ch., Nettleton, Mo., 1969-71, First Bapt. Ch. Elmira, Mo. 1971-73, First Bapt. Ch., Glasgow, Mo., 1973-74, Varner River Bapt. Ch., Kennett, Mo., 1974-75, First Bapt. Ch., Morehouse, Mo., 1975—. Chaplain, Fayette (Mo.) City Hosp., 1973-74. Home and office: Box 227 Morehouse MO 63868

MC CRAY, ROBERT DEWEY, minister, So. Bapt. Conv.; b. Bristol, Tenn., July 5, 1932; s. Ross Dewey and Ona Mae (Davis) McC.; B.A. magna cum laude, Carson-Newman Coll., 1954; M.Div., So. Bapt. Theol. Sem., 1957; m. Rebekah Anne McKay, June 15, 1956; 1 dau., Angela Denise. Ordained to ministry, 1955; mission pastor 1st Bapt. Ch., Crossville, Tenn., 1954-57, Pond Grove Bapt. Ch., Rockwood, Tenn., 1957-59, 1st Bapt. Ch., Dandridge, Tenn., 1959—. Mem. exec. bd. Tenn. Bapt. Conv., 1963-69, chmn. com. on coms., 1975—; mem. adv. bd. Carson-Newman Coll., 1971-74, trustee, 1974—; moderator Jefferson County Bapt. Assn., 1975—; pres. Rockwood Ministerial Assn., 1958-59, Dandridge Ministerial Assn., 1971—; chaplain Dandridge Jaycees, 1967-68. mem. Jefferson County Humanities Council, 1974; mem. Jefferson County Welfare Adv. Bd.; dir. Jefferson County Health and Ednl. Facilities Bd. Mem. E. Tenn. Hist. Soc. Club: Lions (1st v.p. 1974-75). Contbr. devotionals to Bapt. and Reflector. Home: Oakwood Dr Dandridge TN 37725 Office: POB 246 Dandridge TN 37725

MC CULLOH, GERALD OTHO, minister, United Methodist Church; b. Auburn, Kans., Sept. 10, 1912; s. Otho John and Eva Floretta (Skaggs) McC.; B.A., Baker U., 1932, D.D., 1954; M.A., Boston U., 1934, S.T.B., 1935; Ph.D., U. Edinburgh (Scotland), 1938; D.D., Hamline U., 1946; L.H.D., Ohio No. U., 1966; m. Evelyn Belle Butler, June 8, 1939; children: Gerald William, Donita Margaret. Ordained to ministry Meth. Ch., 1934. Prof. philosophy Hamline U., St. Paul, 1938-42; pastor Hamline United Meth. Ch., 1942-46; Henry Pfeiffer prof. systematic theology Garrett Theol. Sem., Evanston, Ill., 1946-53; dir. ministerial edn. United Meth. Ch. Bd. Edn., Nashville, 1953-72, assoc. gen. sec. Bd. Higher Edn. and Ministry, 1972-77; vis. prof. Candler Sch. Theology, Emory U., Atlanta, 1974, 77, Meth. Theol. Sch. in Ohio, Delaware, Ohio, 1974, Claremont Sch. Theology, 1975, Drew U. Theol. Sch., 1976, So. Meth. U. Perkins Sch. Theology, 1976; sec. Meth. Commn. Ministerial Tng., 1944-52; chmn. World Meth. Com. Theol. Edn., 1961-80; mem. World Meth. Com. on Oxford Inst., 1956—; mem. gen. bd. Nat. Council Chs., 1962-70; del. World Meth. Conf., 1951, 56, 61, 66, 71, 76, Oberlin Conf. Faith and Order, 1957, World Council Chs. Assembly, New Delhi, 1961, Uppsala, 1968. Lucinda Bidwell Beebe fellow, 1935; recipient Distinguished Alumnus award Boston U., 1964. Editor: The Ministry in the Methodist Heritage, 1960; Man's Faith and Freedom, 1962; (with W. Thomas Smith) Heralds of Christ, 1963; My Call to Preach, 1962; Upper Room Companion, 1959; Upper Room Disciplines, 1962; Ministerial Education in the American Methodist Movement, 1980; interviewer Living History Archives, 1972—. Home: 2110 Ashwood Ave Nashville TN 37212

MC CULLOUGH, FREDERICK DOUGLAS, minister, Nat. Bapt. Conv. Am.; b. Magnolia, Ark., Mar. 17, 1897; s. Henry and Jenie (Brown) McC.; diploma Chgo. Bapt. Inst., 1947, B.Th., 1955; m. Octavia Anderson, Dec. 13, 1922; children—Elsiree Octavia McCullough Robinson (dec.), Frederick Marcus, Anna McCullough McKendall, Josephine R. McCullough Murphy, Anderson Thurn, Henry Glenn. Ordained to ministry, 1945; asso. pastor Shiloh Bapt. Ch., Waukegan, Ill., 1938-45, supt. Sunday Sch., 1924-39; pastor Candle Light Bapt. Ch., Waukegan. Vice pres. New Dist. Sunday Sch. Dept., Little Rock, 1917-22. Recipient Certificate of Recognition, Chgo. Bapt. Inst. Alumni Assn., 1972. Address: PO Box 926 Waukegan IL 60085

MC CULLOUGH, RUSSELL LELAND, ret. minister, Luth. Ch. Am.; b. Chicora, Pa., Dec. 6, 1905; s. John Lorenzo and Martha Florence (Smith) McC.; A.B., Thiel Coll., 1928; M.Div., Luth. Theol. Sem., 1934; D.D., Thiel Coll., 1972; m. Isabel Elizabeth Brod, Nov. 17, 1934; children—Helen Ann, Russell Leland, Alyce Mae, Frederic Charles. Ordained to ministry, 1931; asst. pastor Trinity Luth. Ch., Pottsville, Pa., 1931-34, Epiphany Luth. Ch., Pleasantville, N.J., 1934-37, Gethseman Luth. Ch., Keyport, N.J., Ch. of Reformation, Long Branch, N.J., 1937-43, Trinity-St. John's Luth. Parish, Mount Pleasant, Pa., 1943-53, Brush Creek Evang. Luth. Ch., Irwin, Pa., 1953-71. Mem. nat. adv. bd. Am. Security Council. Recipient Paul Harris fellow award Rotary Internat., 1973. Author: Poems and Prose, 1974; Opening the Files, 1976. Home and Office: 3400 Sweetbriar Dr Apt C-203 Irwin PA 15642 Died Dec 3 1976

MCCULLUM, HUGH BRECKEN, religious publication editor and publisher, television show host, author; b. Toronto, Ont., Can., Nov. 20, 1931; s. Arthur Creighton and Jean (Nicholson) McC. Student Sir George Williams Coll., 1955-56, U. Western Ont., 1960-61, Columbia U., 1963; D.D. (hon.) United Theol. Coll., 1983. Editor, gen. mgr. Can. Churchman, Toronto, Ont., Can., 1967-75; staff coordinator Project North (interchurch coalition working on no. devel. and native land claims), Toronto, 1975-80; editor, publisher The United Ch. Observer, Toronto, 1980—; host Meeting Place Can. Broadcasting Co., Toronto, 1984—; adj. prof. journalism U. Western Ont., 1973—. Co-author: Ordination of Women, 1973; This Land is Not For Sale, 1975, Moratorium, 1976, Caledonia, 1978, Ted Scott, 1979; The Least of These, 1982. Contbr. articles to profl. jours. Recipient award of Excellence Associated Ch. Press, 1968-75, 80-82; Silver award Mags. Can., 1981, 82; Southam fellow Massey Coll., 1972. Mem. Inter Pares (bd. dirs. 1980—). Mem. United Ch. Can. Office: United Ch Observer 85 Saint Clair Ave E Toronto ON M4T 1M8 Canada

MCDANIEL, MICHAEL C.D. Bishop, Lutheran Church in America. Office: PO Box 2049 Salisbury NC 28145*

MC DILL, THOMAS ALLISON, minister, Evang. Free Ch. Am.; b. Cicero, Ill., June 4, 1926; s. Samuel and Agnes (Lindsay) McD.; Th.B., No. Bapt. Theol. Sem., 1949; B.A., Trinity Coll., 1953; M.Div., Trinity Evang. Div. Sch., 1954; D.Ministry, Bethel Theol. Sem., 1975; m. Ruth Catherine Starr, June 4, 1949; children—Karen Joyce, Jane Alison, Steven Thomas. Ordained to ministry, 1949; pastor Grace Evang. Free Ch., Chgo., 1951-59, Liberty Bible Ch., Valparaiso, Ind., 1959-67, Crystal Evang. Free Ch., Minnea, Minn., 1967-76; pres. Evang. Free Ch. Am., 1976—, v.p./moderator, 1974-75, chmn. home missions bd., 1968-73. Chmn. bd. dirs. Trinity Coll., 1974-76. Mem. Greater Mpls. Assn. Evangelicals. Contbr. articles to religious jours. Address: 4356 Florida Ave N Minneapolis MN 55428

MCDILL, THOMAS HALDANE, educator, Asso. Reformed Presbyn. Ch.; b. Little Rock, June 9, 1917; s. Thomas Hemphill and Emmie Gardner (Moody) McD.; A.B., Erskine Coll., 1938, B.D., 1940; postgrad. Princeton Theol. Sem., 1946; M.Div., Columbia Theol. Sem., 1947; M.A., U. Chgo., 1964; Litt.D., Presbyn. Coll., 1968; m. Lila Williams Bost, Dec. 26, 1938; 1 son, Thomas Calvin. Ordained to ministry Asso. R.P. Ch., 1940; pastor Asso. Ref. Presbyn. Ch., Russellville, Ark., 1940-42; moderator Miss. Valley Presbytery, 1942; chaplain AUS, 1942-46; sr. pastor Highlands Presbyn. Ch., Atlanta, 1946-51; moderator 2d Presbytery, 1950; mem. Presbytery Atlanta Presbyn. Ch. U.S., 1951-54, 72—, Presbytery of Central Miss., 1954-72; prof. pastoral care and counseling Columbia Theol. Sem., 1951—; sr. group psychotherapist Georgian Clinic, Dept. Pub. Health, Atlanta, 1953-69; sec. bd., chmn. dept. human relations Exec. Edn. Inc., Decatur, Ga., 1970—. Mem. permanent com. on Christianity and health Presbyn. Ch. U.S., 1956-66, chmn., 1960-66; mem. Joint Office Instnl. Chaplaincies, Council on Ch. Union, 1968-70. Mem. Pres.'s Adv. Com. on Alcoholism, HEW, 1966-67; mem. DeKalb County (Ga.) Mental Health Council, 1962-71, chmn., 1965-71. Bd. dirs. Atlanta Mental Health Found.; bd. dirs., mem. staff Center for Advancement Personal Growth, Atlanta. Mem. Council for Clin. Tng. (nat. accreditation com. 1962-68), Inst. for Pastoral Care, Ga. Assn. Pastoral Care (dir.), Am. Assn. Pastoral Counselors (nat. membership com. 1966-71, chmn. nat. nominating com. 1970-75), Assn. Clin. Pastoral Edn. (mem. house of dels. 1968-69), Alcohol and Drug Problems Assn. N.Am. Mem. editorial adv. bd. Pastoral Psychology mag., 1963-73. Home: 1083 Oakdale Rd NE Atlanta GA 30307 Office: Columbia Theol Sem Decatur GA 30031

MCDONALD, ANDREW J., bishop, Roman Cath. Ch. b. Savannah, Ga., Oct. 24, 1923; s. James Bernard and Theresa (McGrace) McD. A.B., St. Mary's Sem., Balt., 1945, S.T.L., 1948; J.C.B., Cath. U. Am., 1949; J.C.D., Lateran U., Rome, 1951. Ordained priest Roman Catholic Ch., 1948. Curate, Port Wentworth, Ga., 1952-57; chancellor of Diocese of Savannah, 1952-68, vicar gen., 1968—, vice officialis, 1952-57, officialis, 1957; pastor Blessed Sacrament Ch., 1963; named papal chamberlain, 1956, domestic prelate, 1959; apptd. bishop Diocese of Little Rock, 1972. Address: 2415 N Tyler St Little Rock AR 72207

MCDONALD, ERWIN LAWRENCE, clergyman, editor, Southern Baptist Convention; b. London, Ark., Oct. 31, 1907; s. Frank Floyd and Rebecca Geneva (Powell) McD.; A.S., Ark. Poly. Coll., 1933; B.A., Ouachita Bapt. U., 1943; M.Div., So. Bapt. Theol. Sem., 1947; Litt.D., Georgetown Coll., 1958; m. Mary Elsie Price, Mar. 1, 1930; children: Avis Jeannine (Mrs. Sam H. Jones, Jr.), Judy Carole (Mrs. Jay W. Lucas). Ordained to ministry So. Bapt. Conv., 1938. Pastor chs., London, Ark., 1941-42, Washington, Ark., 1942-44, Pendleton, Ky., 1944-47; dir. pub. relations So. Bapt. Theol. Sem., Louisville, 1944-51, editor Tie, 1947-51; dir. pub. relations Furman U., founder-editor Univ. mag., 1951-54; exec. sec. Christian edn. Ky. Bapt. State Conv., Louisville, 1954-57; editor Ark. Bapt. News Mag., Little Rock, 1957-72; religion editor Ark. Democrat, Little Rock, 1972-73; vis. prof. religious journalism Southeastern Bapt. Theol. Sem., summer 1975; tchr. English Composition Boyce Bible Sch. So. Bapt. Theol. Sem., Little Rock, 1975-76; chmn. Greater Little Rock Conf. on Religion and Race, 1966-67; bd. dirs. Aldersgate United Meth. Camp, Little Rock. Mem. Ark. adv. com. U.S. Commn. on Civil Rights, 1965-74. Recipient Disting. Alumnus award Ouachita Bapt. U., 1960; Disting. Bapt. Minister award So. Bapt. Coll., 1963; named Alumnus of Year, So. Bapt. Theol. Sem., 1972. Mem. So. Bapt. Press Assn. (pres. 1965), Greater Little Rock Ministerial Assn. (pres. 1964-65), Am. Assn. for UN (Ark. state pres. 1963-64), Asso. Ch. Press. Author: The Church Using the Newspaper, 1958; 75 Stories and Illustrations from Everyday Life, 1964; (with Ralph Creger) A Look Down the Lonesome Road, 1964; Across the Editor's Desk, 1966; Stories for Speakers and Writers, 1970; History of the Rotary Club of Little Rock, 1974. Address: 1419 Garland Ave North Little Rock AR 72116

MCDONALD, THERESA BEATRICE (PIERCE) (MRS. OLLIE MCDONALD), church official, Progressive National Baptist Convention Inc.; b. Vicksburg, Miss., Apr. 11, 1929; d. Leonard C. and Ernestine Morris (Pierce) Templeton; m. Ollie McDonald, Apr. 23, 1966. Student, Tougaloo Coll., Miss., 1946-47, Roosevelt U., Chgo., 1954-56, 59-62, 64, U. Chgo. Indsl. Relations Ctr., 1963-64. Vol. rep. Liberty Bapt. Ch., Am. Legion Aux., VA West Side Hosp., Chgo., 1971-73; nat. instr. ushers dept. Progressive Nat. Bapt. Conv. Inc., Washington, 1973-75, nat. sec. ushers dept., 1975—, v.p. at-large, 1980-82, chmn. personnel com., 1982—, mem. faculty Congress of Christian Edn., 1978—; mem. pub. relations staff Liberty Baptist Ch., Chgo., 1973—; cons. and lectr. in field. Guest lectr. TV and radio programs. Participant White House Regional Confs., 1961. Recipient Outstanding Service award Am. Legion, 1972, 73. Mem. Bethlehem Baptist Dist. Assn. of Chgo. (asst. sec. 1982-84), Ch. Women United in Greater Chgo. (Ecumenical Actions com. 1981—), Am. Legion, Order of Eastern Star. Address: 9810 S Calumet Ave Chicago IL 60628

MCDONALD, TIMOTHY, III, minister, Progressive National Baptist Church; b. Brunswick, Ga., June 17, 1954; s. Timothy Jr. and Johnnie Mae (King) McD.; m. Shirley Ann Neal, Jan. 3, 1976; children: Nikisha Lynette, Timothy IV. B.A., Berry Coll., 1975; M.Div., Emory U., 1978. Ordained to ministry Nat. Bapt. Ch., 1975. Pastor Shiloh Bapt. Ch., Dalton, Ga., 1976-78; asst. pastor Ebenezer Bapt. Ch., Atlanta, 1978-83; pastor First Iconium Bapt., Atlanta, 1984—; nat. dir. operation breadbasket So. Christian Leadership Conf., Atlanta, 1984—; bd. dirs. Urban Tng. Orgn., Atlanta, 1980—; program chmn. Concerned Black Clergy of Atlanta, 1982—; adv. bd. Clergy and Laity Concerned, Atlanta, 1981—. Chmn. Ga. Pub. Assistance Coalition, Atlanta, 1980—, Christman Against Hunger in Ga., Atlanta, 1982—; alt. del. Democratic Nat. Conv., 1980. Recipient Bill of Rights award Ga. ACLU, 1983; named Minister of Yr., Ga. Citizens' Coalition on Hunger 1982. Home: 2801 Knollview Dr Decatur GA 30034 Office: SCLC 334 Auburn Ave Atlanta GA 30312

MC DONNELL, JAMES, brother, sch. adminstr., Roman Cath. Ch.; b. Marquette, Mich., Nov. 4, 1928; s. Donald Francis and Julia (Burt) McD.; B.A., St. Edward's U., 1955; M.A., U. Notre Dame, 1962; grad. Inst. Spirituality, 1968. Joined Bros. of Holy Cross, 1950; dir. student activities St. Anthony High Sch., Long Beach, Calif., 1956-59, prin., 1967-69; dean of men, vice prin. Archbishop Curley High Sch., Miami, Fla., 1959-62; dir. upper sch. Holy Cross Sch., New Orleans, 1963-65; prin. Notre Dame High Sch., Sherman Oaks, Calif., 1973—. Vocat. counselor Brothers Holy Cross, 1969-73. Mem. San Fernando Valley (Calif.) Nat. Football Found. and Hall of Fame. Mem. Nat. Assn. Secondary Sch. Prins., Assn. for Supervision and Curriculum Devel., Valley Assn. Sch. Prins., Cath. Athletic Assn. Home and Office: 13645 Riverside Dr Sherman Oaks CA 91423

MC DOW, MALCOLM RAY, minister, So. Bapt. Conv.; b. Honey Grove, Tex., Jan. 28, 1936; s. James Luther and Josephine Ivodell (Webb) McD.; B.A., Baylor U., 1958; B.D., Southwestern Bapt. Sem., 1962; Th.M., New Orleans Bapt. Sem., 1965, Th.D., 1968; postgrad. U. Edinburgh (Scotland), 1966; m. Melba Lee Justice, Dec. 22, 1962; children—Melissa Lee, Melody Lyn. Ordained to ministry, 1958; pastor chs., Tex., La., 1957-61; youth minister 1st Bapt. Ch., Houston, 1962-63; pastor Cherry Rd Bapt. Ch., Memphis, 1969—; supr. Dr. of Ministry students New Orleans Bapt. Sem., 1975-76. Trustee, mem. religious adv. bd. Union U., Jackson, Tenn.; pastor advisor Tenn. Brotherhood Dept.; speaker So. Bapt. Conv.; chmn. fin. com. Shelby Bapt. Assn., Memphis, chmn. evangelism com. Home: 1837 S Dearing St Memphis TN 38117 Office: 1421 Cherry Rd Memphis TN 38117

MC DOWELL, CHARLES LENWOOD, minister, So. Bapt. Conv.; b. Conway, S.C., Mar. 17, 1937; s. George W. and Ruby Mae (Holt) McD.; B.A., Columbia Coll., 1971; M.Div., Southeastern Bapt. Theol. Sem., 1975; D.Ministry, Universal Bible Inst., 1976; m. Betty Sue Hucks, Jan. 12, 1957; children—Amy Charlene, Gregory Lynn. Ordained to ministry, 1968; pastor New Hope Bapt. Ch., Pelion, S.C., 1967-71, King Grove Bapt. Ch., Swansea, S.C., 1971-72, New Bethel Bapt. Ch., Garner, N.C., 1972-76, Ravenwood Bapt. Ch., Columbia, S.C., 1976—. Pres., Ministers of Garner Area, 1976; chaplain U.S. Army Res. Bd. dirs. Garner Tar Heel Little League, 1974-75. Mem. Columbia Ministerial Assn., Columbia Met. Bapt. Ministerial Assn. Home: 304 Folkestone Rd Columbia SC 29204 Office: 3545 Raven Hill Rd Columbia SC 29204

MCDOWELL, JOHN B. See *Who's Who in America,* 43rd edition.

MCEACHRAN, JAMES NOEL, minister, Lutheran Church in America; b. Spokane, Wash., July 16, 1946; s. John Robert and Doris Alice (Hedrick) McE.; m. Nancy Elizabeth Schaefer, July 6, 1979; 1 child, Erin Elizabeth. B.A., Whitworth Coll., 1968; M.Div., Pacific Luth. Theol. Sem., 1972; postgrad. Grad. Theol. Union, Berkeley, Calif., 1972-75. Ordained to ministry Luth. Ch., 1975. Asst. pastor Messiah Luth. Ch., Spokane, Wash., 1975-77; assoc. pastor, 1977-83; pastor St. Andrew's Luth. Ch., Bellevue, Wash., 1983—; bd. dirs. Luth. Outdoor Ministry, Coeur d'Alene, Idaho, 1976-80, Luth. Council, Spokane, Wash., 1980-82, Luth. Social Services Wash. State, 1983—; del. biennial conv. Luth. Ch. Am., 1982. Named Outstanding Young Religious Leader, Jaycees, Spokane, 1975. Mem. Liturgical Conf., Alban Inst. Democrat. Club: Alcuin. Home: 4555 165th St SE Issaquah WA 98027 Office: Saint Andrew's Lutheran Church 2650 148th St SE Bellevue WA 98007

MCELHINNEY, JOHN FLAVELL, educator; b. Brighton, N.B., Can., Mar. 16, 1929; s. John Flavell and Hazel Mae (Parsons) McE.; m. Audrey Hildred Bubar, Aug. 29, 1951; children: David John, Cheryl Ann. B.A. in Religion, Bethany Bible Coll., 1971; M.A.R., Asbury Theol. Sem., 1974; postgrad. Tel-Aviv U., 1978; postgrad. Trinity Evang. Sem., 1980. Ordained to ministry, 1959. Minister, Wesleyan Ch., Can. and

U.S.A., 1958-73; prof., librarian Bethany Bible Coll., Sussex, N.B., 1973-83, prof., dir. Christian Service Tng., 1976—; dist. dir. leadership Wesleyan Ch., Atlantic dist., 1975—, bd. Christian Edn., 1975-84. Mem. Wesleyan Theol. Soc., Assn. Can. Bible Colls., Nat. Assn. Profs. Christian Edn., Evang. Tchr. Tng. Assn., Phi Alpha Mu. Home: 48 Western St Sussex NB E0E 1P0 Canada Office: Bethany Bible Coll Sussex NB E0E 1P0 Canada

MCELVANEY, WILLIAM R., educational administrator. Pres. St. Paul Sch. Theology Methodist (United Methodist), Kansas City, Mo. Office: St Paul Sch Theology Methodist 5123 Truman Rd Kansas City MO 64127*

MCEVER, RICHARD DAVID, minister, Southern Baptist Convention; b. San Antonio, May 15, 1954; s. Bobbie Joe McEver and Frances Leona (Barnes) Baugh. B.A., Grand Canyon Coll., 1976; M.Div., Golden Gate Sem., 1981. Ordained to ministry Southern Baptist Convention, 1977. Assoc. pastor Grace Bapt. Ch., Phoenix, 1974-75; pastor 1st Bapt. Ch., Congress, Ariz., 1977-79; counselor Open Door Ministries, Sausalito, Calif., 1979-81; pastor, 1st So. Bapt. Ch., Mayer, Ariz., 1981—. Del., Internat. Congress on the Bible, San Diego, 1982. Dir. public relations People Against Chem. Abuse, 1983-84; mem. Mayer Vol. Fire Dept., 1982—. Kiwanis religion scholar, 1972. Mem. Yavapai Bapt. Assn. (trustee 1982-84), Precott Ministerial Assn., Golden Gate Alumni Assn. (v.p. Ariz. chpt. 1984-85), Grand Canyon Coll. Alumni Assn., Bibl. Archeology Soc. Democrat. Lodge: Lions (sec. 1982-84). Home: 12971 Central Ave Mayer AZ 86333 Office: 1st Southern Bapt Ch PO Box 36 Mayer AZ 86333

MC FADDEN, ARTHUR BILLIE, minister, Presbyterian Church (USA); b. Jacksonville, Fla., Jan. 5, 1940; s. Eugene and Louise (Simmons) McF.; A.B., Stillman Coll., 1962; B.D., Johnson C. Smith Theol. Sem., 1965; S.T.M., Eden Theol. Sem., 1970, D.Min., 1973; m. Marjesta Sanders, June 17, 1962; children: Anntoinette, Renee. Ordained to ministry, 1965; pastor Calvary Presbyn. Ch., Detroit, 1965-66, Butler Meml. Presbyn. Ch., Youngstown, Ohio, 1966-68, 3d Presbyn. Ch., St. Louis, 1968—; mem. com. on evangelism Presbytery of Elijah Parish Lovejoy, United Presbyn. Ch. in U.S.A., 1974-77; mem. adv. council on ch. and soc. Synod of Mid-Am., 1974-77; adj. prof. humanities St. Louis U., 1976-83; dean Black Presbyn. Pastors Conf., Austin Theol. Sem., 1980; nominating com. Synod of Mid-Am., 1984—, Presbytery of Gliddings-Lovejoy, 1984—; bd. cons. for edn. of Black clergy Eden Sem., 1973-76. Bd. dirs. Stillman Coll., 1972-76. Recipient award for service Stillman Coll., 1973, Community Service award St. Louis U., 1982. Mem. Black Presbyns. United, Nat. Com. Black Clergy, Home: 7112 Forest Hill Dr Saint Louis MO 63121 Office: 2426 Union Blvd Saint Louis MO 63113

MC FARLAND, NORMAN F., bishop, Roman Catholic Church; b. Martinez, Calif., Feb. 21, 1922; ed. St. Patrick's Sem., Menlo Park, Calif.; J.C.D., Cath. U. Am., Washington. Ordained priest, 1946, titular bishop of Bida and aux. bishop of San Francisco, 1970; apostolic adminstrn. Diocese of Reno, 1974-76; bishop of Reno, 1976—. Office: 515 Court St Reno NV 98501*

MC FARLAND, WILLIAM DALE, minister, So. Bapt. Conv.; b. Wewoka, Okla., Sept. 10, 1937; s. Robert G. and Lenora Mae (Morrison) M.; A.A., Jacksonville Coll., 1962; B.S., Stephen F. Austin U., 1965; M.Div., Southwestern Bapt. Theol. Sem., 1972; m. Linda Lucille Derrick, Nov. 27, 1964; children—William Dale, Paul Judson. Ordained to minstry, 1960; minister Tundra Bapt. Ch., Canton, Tex., 1961-63, Springhill Bapt. Ch., Martinsville, Tex., 1964-65, Meml. Bapt. Ch., Fremont, Calif., 1965-66, First So. Bapt. Ch., Willcox, Ariz., 1972—. Pres., Western Bapt. Youth Encampment, 1959-60; gen. chmn. area-wide religious crusade, Aug., 1975; moderator Cochise Bapt. Assn., 1976-77; dir. Cochise Assn. Sem. Extension Center, 1974—; pres. Jacksonville Coll. Ministerial Assn., 1962. Mem. Willcox Ministerial Assn. (pres. 1975), Alpha Chi. Contbr. poems to religious jours.; editor Sparks of Youth supplement of Golden State Bapt. paper, 1959-60. Home: 521 N Cochise Ave Willcox AZ 85643 Office: S Cochise at Wasson St Willcox AZ 85643

MCFEE, EVERETT LACOSTA, JR., minister, United Methodist Church; b. Lipcomb, Ala., Mar. 23, 1920; s. Everett LaCosta and Lessie Belle (Cargile) McF.; m. Mabel Viola Williams, Nov. 19, 1941; children: Rebecca Hope, Beverly Anne, Bryan Everett. B.A., Birmingham So. Coll., 1943; D.D., Athens Coll., 1958. Ordained to ministry United Meth. Ch., 1943. Minister, Morgan Meth. Ch., Bessemer, Ala., 1941-43, Courtland Meth. Ch., 1943-47, Goodwater Meth. Ch., Ala., 1948-52, Roanoke First Meth. Ch., Ala., 1952-56, Athens First Meth. Ch., Ala., 1956-63, Anniston First Meth. Ch., Ala., 1966-70, Trinity Meth. Ch., Birmingham, Ala., 1970-82; v.p. Athens Coll., Ala., 1947-48; dist. supt. Tuscaloosa Dist., 1963-66, Anniston Dist. 1982—. Trustee, Athens Coll., 1956-69, Birmingham So. Coll., 1979—. Mem. Limestone Minister's Assn. (pres. 1959-60), Calhoun County Minister's Assn. (pres. 1967-68), Birmingham Minister's Assn. (pres. 1978-79, 81-82). Lodge: Rotary (pres. 1955-56), Masons. Home: 2108 Henry Rd Anniston AL 36201 Office: Dist Supt United Meth Ch 2108 Henry Rd Anniston AL 36201

MCGANN, JOHN RAYMOND, bishop, Roman Catholic Church; b. Bklyn., Dec. 2, 1924; s. Thomas Joseph and Mary (Ryan) McG.; student Cathedral Coll. Immaculate Conception, 1944, Sem. Immaculate Conception, Huntington, 1950; LL.D., St. Johns U., 1971. Ordained priest Roman Catholic Ch.; asst. priest St. Anne's, Brentwood, 1950-57; asso. Cath. chaplain Pilgrim State Hosp., 1950-57; asst. chancellor Diocese of Rockville Centre, 1957-67; asst. sec. to Bishop Kellenberg, 1957-59; elevated to papal chamberlain, 1959; sec. to Bishop Kellenberg, 1959-70; titular bishop of Morosbisdus and aux. bishop of Rockville Centre, 1970-76; bishop of Rockville Centre, 1976—; Episcopal ordination, 1971. Del. Sacred Congregation for Religious to Marianists, 1973, Nat. Conf. Cath. Bishops, Rome, 1974; mem. adv. council U.S. Cath. Conf., 1969-70, mem. bishops' com. on health affairs, 1972-75; vicar gen. Diocese Rockville Centre, 1971—, episcopal vicar Suffolk County, 1971—; mem. U.S. Bishops' Com. for Apostolate of Laity, 1972—; mem. Rockville Centre Diocesan Bd. Consultors, 1969—; episcopal mem. N.Y. State Cath. Com., 1974— chmn. N.Y. State Bishops' Com. on Elective Process, 1974—, Com. Religious Studies in Pub. Edn., 1974—. Bd. dirs. Good Samaritan Hosp., West Islip, N.Y., 1972—, St. Charles Hosp., Port Jefferson, N.Y., 1972—. Address: 50 N Park Ave Rockville Centre NY 11570

MC GARITY, GEORGE HUBERT, JR., minister, Ch. of God (Cleveland, Tenn.); b. Knoxville, Tenn., Sept. 27, 1949; s. George Hubert and Anna Vivian (Cox) McG.; B.A. in Bibl. Edn., Lee Coll., 1972; m. Brenda Ann Lemaster, June 4, 1971. Ordained to ministry, 1977; Tenn. state evangelist Ch. of God, 1972-74; dir. youth and Christian edn. Shelbyville (Tenn.) dist. Ch. of God, 1974—; pastor Ch. of God, Columbia, Tenn., 1974—. Founder, speaker Truth for Our Times program Radio Sta. WMCP, Columbia, 1974-76; instr. Bible Inst., Jackson (Tenn.) Ch. of God, 1977—. Mem. Tenn. Pub. Service Consumer Panel, 1976—. Mem. Maury County Ministerial Assn. Named an Outstanding Young Man Am., 1975. Home: 2112 Highland Ave Columbia TN 38401 Office: 2110 Highland Ave Columbia TN 38401

MC GEE, ARTHUR MARION, minister, Luth. Ch. Am.; b. Lake Stevens, Wash., May 23, 1934; s. William Walter and Frances Bernice (Marquardt) McG.; B.A., Pacific Luth. U., 1956; M.Div., Luth. Sch. Theology, 1961. Ordained to ministry, 1961; pastor Troy (Idaho) Luth. Ch., 1961-65, Central Luth. Ch., Morton, Wash., 1965-68, Gloria Dei Luth. Ch., Kelso, Wash., 1968—. Sec. mission commn. So. dist. Pacific N.W. conf. Luth. Ch. Am., 1975—; rep. Nat. Indian Luth. Bd., 1975-76; pres. Cowlitz County Ministerial Assn., 1975-76, Kelso Ministerial Assn., 1970-71. Pres. bd. local drug abuse prevention center, 1976—; chmn. Cowlitz County Democratic Central Com., 1975-76; mem. Dem. State Platform Com., 1976—, precinct committeeman, 1972-76; county co-coordinator Carter/Mondale campaign, 1976. Home: 407 N 5th St Kelso WA 98626 Office: 402 Crawford St Kelso WA 98626

MCGEE, DENNIS MORGAN, minister, Bible educator, United Pentecostal Church International; b. Winchester, Tenn., Aug. 14, 1950; s. Robert Franklin and Rena Mae (Gifford) McG.; m. Frances Kay Layton, May 12, 1968; children: Lisa, Melanie, Lori. Grad. high sch., Gary, Ind. Ordained to ministry United Pentecostal Ch. Internat. 1982. Assoc. minister United Pentecostal Ch. Internat., Lake Station, Ind., 1979-82; pastor, Gary, Ind., 1982-83, pastor, bible tchr., Stuart, Va., 1983—. Served to E-4 U.S. Army, 1969-71, Vietnam. Home: Blue Ridge St PO Box 1048 Stuart VA 24171 Office: United Pentecostal Ch PO Box 1048 Stuart VA 24171

MCGEE, EUGENE QUINN, minister, Christian and Missionary Alliance; b. Duluth, Ga., Oct. 19, 1916; s. Ernest Hector and Evie Lou (Quinn) McG.; m. Dorothy Virginia Coleman, Oct. 16, 1936; children: Sarah E., Miriam J., Rebecca A., Timothy E., John R., James N. Diploma, Missionary Tng. Inst., Nyack, N.Y., 1941; B.A., Emory U., 1952. Ordained to ministry Christian and Missionary Alliance, 1942. Pastor chs., Ft. Myers, Fla. and Bklyn., 1941-45; dir. Youth for Christ Internat., Atlanta, Chgo. and Paris, 1948-66; pastor Christian and Missionary Alliance Ch., Indpls., 1966-72, N.Y.C., 1972—; bd. mgrs. Christian and Missionary Alliance, Nyack, N.Y., 1974-80. Author commentaries. Bd. trustees Nyack Coll., 1975-76, Toccoa Falls Coll., Ga., 1978—. Served to capt. U.S. Army, 1945-48; Japan; chaplain USAF, 1951. Republican. Home and Office: 355 E 68th St New York NY 10021

MCGEHEE, (H.) COLEMAN, JR., bishop, Episcopal Ch.; b. Richmond, Va., July 7, 1923; s. Harry C. and Annie Lee (Cheatwood) McG.; B.S., Va. Poly. Inst., 1947; J.D., U. Richmond, 1949; M.Div., Va. Theol. Sem., 1957, D.D., 1973; m. June C. Stewart, Feb 1, 1946; children: Lesley (Mrs. Thomas Casey), Alexander, Coleman, Donald, Cary. Ordained priest Protestant Episcopal Ch. in U.S.A., 1958; consecrated bishop, 1971; vicar St. John's Episcopal Ch., Arlington, Va., 1957-60; rector Immanuel Church-on-the-Hill, Alexandria, Va., 1960-71; bishop coadjutor Diocese of Mich., Detroit, 1971-73; VIII Bishop of Mich., Detroit, 1973—; pres. Episcopal Ch. Pub. Co., 1978—; trustee Va. Theol. Sem. Asst. atty. gen. of Va., 1951-54. Mem. Gov.'s Com. on Status of Women, Commonwealth of Va., 1965-66; dir. No. Va. Fairhousing Corp., 1963-67; pres. Alexandria (Va.) Legal Aid Soc., 1969-71, trustee, 1966-71; pres. Mich. Coalition for Human Rights, 1980—; chair Mich. Citizens Com. for Justice, 1983—. Recipient Feminist of Yr. award Detroit chpt. NOW, 1978; Humanitarian award Metro-Detroit chpt. ACLU, 1984; Philip Hart medal Mich. Women's Studies Assn., 1985. Mem. Detroit Econ. Club (bd. dirs. 1973—). Columnist Detroit News, 1979—; commentator Sta. WDET, Detroit Pub. Radio, 1984—. Office: 4800 Woodward Ave Detroit MI 48201

MC GEHEE, DONALD EDWARD, counselor, American Baptist Churches U.S.A.; b. Bagnell, Mo., Oct. 10, 1931; s. LeRoy Edward and Lula M. (Racy) McG.; A.S., Arlington State Coll., 1956; B.R.E., Southwestern Bapt. Theol. Sem., 1959; M.Ed., Central State U., 1972; Ed.D., U. Ark., 1977; m. Mary Carolyn Routh, Apr. 27, 1952; 1 child, Mary Teresa. Ordained to ministry Am. Bapt. Chs. U.S.A., 1958; lic. psychologist, Mo. Minister of edn. and music Parkland Bapt. Ch., Tulsa, 1959-62; minister of edn. and adminstrn. First Bapt. Ch., Paris, Tex., 1961-63; minister of edn. First Bapt. Ch., Miami, Okla., 1963-66; ednl. adminstr. Putnam City Bapt. Ch., Oklahoma City, 1966-71; minister of edn. and adminstrn. Univ. Heights Bapt. Ch., Springfield, Mo., 1971-78; dir./counselor Ozark Christian Counseling Service, Springfield, 1978—; dir. ednl. seminars and confs. various Bapt. chs., 1959-84. Bd. dirs. Greene County Mental Health Assn. Mem. Am. Assn. for Marriage and Family Therapy (clin. mem.), Am. Assn. Sex Educators, Counselors and Therapists (cert. sex counselor), Am. Psychol. Assn., Am. Assn. for Counseling and Devel. Home: 3618 S Broadway Springfield MO 65807 Office: 1500 E Sunshine Suite B Springfield MO 65804

MCGILL, KENNETH ALAN, minister, United Methodist Church. B. Jefferson City, Mo., Oct. 15, 1955; s. Jess Herbert McGill and Carolyn Ann (Butts) Laughlin; m. Laura L. Powell, Sept. 29, 1984; children: Jamie Kay, Kristopher Alan, Travis Michael, Megan Elizabeth. B.S. in Psychology, Southwest Mo. State U., 1977; M.Div., St. Paul Sch. Theol., 1981. Ordained to ministry United Methodist Ch., 1979, ordained deacon, 1979, ordained elder 1982. Pastor, Fordland-Pleasant Hill United Meth. Ch., Mo., 1977, Centerview United Meth. Ch., Mo., 1978-79, Crandall, Grundy Ctr., Spickard United Meth. Ch's., Trenton, Mo., 1979-82, Ozark United Meth. Ch., Mo., 1982-84, King's Way United Meth. Ch., Springfield, Mo., 1985—; dir. United Meth. Camp, El Dorado Springs, Mo., 1 week each summer; trustee United Meth. Camps Inc., Mo., 1984—; treas. Ozark Ministerial Alliance, 1982-84, mem. Bd. Ch. & Soc., Mo. West Annual Conf., 1980-84. Active in Christian County Ambulance, Ozark, 1982—. Mem. Jaycees (pres. Trenton, 1981-82, Disting. Service award, 1982, Outstanding Young Man, 1982, Mo. Outstanding Young Religious Leader, 1981). Lodge: Rotary. Office: King's Way United Meth Ch 2400 Feirts Ln Springfield MO 65804

MC GRATH, JAMES, priest, Roman Cath. Ch.; b. Phila., Apr. 13, 1917; s. James and Lena (Neiss) McG.; J.C.D., Cath. U. Am., 1946. Ordained priest, 1943, monsignor, 1973; faculty St. Joseph Hosp., Phila., 1955—, mem. exec. bd., 1970—; presiding judge Tribunal of Archdiocese of Phila., 1972—. Contbr. to New Cath. Ency. Home: 3667 Midvale Ave Philadelphia PA 19129 Office: 222 N 17th St Philadelphia PA 19103

MCGRATH, JOHN ANTHONY, provincial superior, Roman Catholic Church; b. Bklyn., Jan. 17, 1935; s. Francis Patrick and Theresa Helen (Wilson) McG. B.A., U. Dayton, 1957; M.A., Ohio State U., 1962; S.T.L., U. Fribourg (Switzerland), 1966; Drs., U. Nijmegen (Holland), 1968; Ph.D., St. Michael's U., Toronto, Ont., Can., 1979. Ordained priest Roman Catholic Ch., 1966. Tchr., Chaminade High Sch., Mineola, N.Y., 1957-62; asst. provincial Soc. of Mary (Marianists), Balt., 1969-74; councillor Soc. of Mary, Toronto, 1974-77; provincial superior Soc. of Mary, Balt., 1977—; trustee U. Dayton, 1980—; mem. U.S. Bishop's Nat. Adv. Council, Washington, 1983—, Nat. Bd. Maj. Superiors, Washington, 1983—, exec. com. of Balt. Forum, 1983—. Home and Office: 4301 Roland Ave Baltimore MD 21210

MC GRATH, PATRICK JOSEPH, priest, Roman Cath. Ch.; b. Ireland, Sept. 1, 1940; s. Michael Victor and Josephine (O'Brien) McG.; came to U.S., 1965, naturalized, 1973; B.A. in Philosophy, St. Patrick Coll., Thurles, Ireland, 1965; M.R.E., U. San Francisco, 1973, M.A. in Counseling, 1976, postgrad. in ednl. psychology, 1977—; Ordained priest, 1965; asso. pastor St. Mels Ch., Fair Oaks, Calif., 1966-69, Holy Spirit Parish, Fairfield, Calif., 1969-73; asso. dir. religious edn. Diocese of Sacramento, 1974—, dir. marriage preparation, 1977—, dir. clergy edn., retreats coordinator. Coordinator, Region 11 U.S. Cath. Conf. for Clergy Edn.; mem. Nat. Commn. for Clergy Edn., Nat. Adv. Com. Family Life; dir. Del Paso Heights (Calif.) CYO. Co-chmn. sewerage com. for Robla, Del Paso Heights, Sacramento. Recipient certificate of appreciation U. San Francisco, 1974, Edn. award, 1975.

249 WHO'S WHO IN RELIGION

Mem. Nat. Cath. Edn. Assn., Nat. Orgn. Continuing Edn. Cath. Clergy. Author 3 M.A. programs for U. San Francisco. Home: 1951 North Ave Sacramento CA 95838 Office: 5900 Newman Ct Sacramento CA 95819

MC GRATH, RICHARD T., bishop, Roman Cath. Ch.; b. Oderin, Placentia Bay, Nfld., Can., June 17, 1912. Ordained priest, 1936; bishop of St. George's (Nfld.), 1970—. Office: 16 Hammond Dr Corner Brook NF A2H 2W2 Canada*

MCGRATH, THERESA, nun, Roman Catholic Church; b. Galway, Ireland, June 4, 1934; came to U.S., 1950, naturalized, 1956; d. John and Mary Josephine (Bane) McG. B.A. magna cum luade, Incarnate Word Coll., 1959, M.A., 1978; M.A., U. Ill., 1961; postgrad. Cath. U. Am., 1959-60; cert. in religious edn. East Asian Pastoral Inst., Manila, 1976. Joined Sisters of Charity of Incarnate Word, Roman Cath. Ch., 1950. Asst. registrar, asst. acad. dean, instr. Incarnate Word Coll., San Antonio, 1961-81, trustee, 1981—; dir. Pastoral Inst., 1975-81; provincial superior Sisters of Charity of Incarnate Word, San Antonio, Tex., 1981—; parish religious edn. tchr., 1970-80; trustee Santa Rosa Med. Ctr., San Antonio, 1981-84, Incarnate Word Hosp., St. Louis, 1985-88. NSF grantee, 1960. Mem. Leadership Conf. of Maj. Superiors, Tex. Cath. Conf.

MCGREGOR, DON ALLEN minister, Church of God (Anderson, Indiana); b. Mattoon, Ill., Feb. 16, 1954; s. Don Mervyn and E. Merle (Tuttle) McG.; m. Jeana Star Ervin, Mar. 28, 1981. A.A., Tyler Jr. Coll., 1973; B.S., Gulf Coast Bible Coll., 1976; M.Div., Anderson Sch. Theology, 1985. Ordained to ministry, 1980. Pastor, Highland Ch. of God, Austin, Tex., 1976, Community Ch. of God, Longview, Tex., 1976-81, Shiloh Friends Ch., Alexandria, Ind., 1982-85, First Ch. of God, Seminole, Okla., 1985—; chaplain Longview Police Dept., Tex., 1979-81; treas. exec. council Ch. of God, E. Tex. Dist., 1977-81. Mem. Am. Philatelic Soc., Collectors of Religion on Stamps. Republican. Address: Route 8 Lot 76 Royal Oaks MHP Anderson IN 46011

MC GREGOR, KERMIT DALE, minister, So. Baptist Conv.; b. Pontotoc, Miss., Dec. 25, 1938; s. Lesley Guy and Opal Inez (Ard) McG.; B.A., Blue Mountain Coll., 1960; B.D., New Orleans Bapt. Theol. Sem., 1963; m. Phyllis Lane McCoy, June 18, 1955; children—Lisa Lane, Kermit Dale. Ordained to ministry, 1955; pastor chs., Miss., 1955—, Hattiesburg, 1971—. Mem. nominating com. Miss. Bapt. Conv., 1969; trustee Bapt. Children's Village, Jackson, Miss., 1969-75, vice-chmn. bd., 1974-75, chmn. exec. com., 1974-75; mem. Edn. Commn. Miss. Bapt. Conv. Second v.p. Traveler's Aid Services, 1972-73; bd. dirs. United Way of Forrest-Lamar, 1971-74. Named Hattiesburg's Most Outstanding Young Man, 1972. Mem. Hattiesburg Ministerial Assn., Hattiesburg Area C. of C., Hattiesburg Community Concert Assn. Home: 2604 Clayton Pl Hattiesburg MS 39401 Office: Temple Baptist Ch Hardy at 16th Ave Hattiesburg MS 39401

MCGUGAN, DAVID BROWN, minister, Southern Baptist Convention; b. Hoke County, N.C., Apr. 30, 1938; s. Locke Archie and Mary Gladys (Gibson) McG.; A.A., Campbell Coll., 1959; B.A., Pfeiffer Coll., 1961; B.D., Southeastern Bapt. Theol. Sem., 1965; m. Mary Carolyn Fisher, Apr. 6, 1963; 1 child, Deborah Lynn. Ordained to ministry So. Bapt. Conv., 1961. Pastor chs., N.C., 1958—, Pleasant Hope Bapt. Ch., Fairmont, 1968—, Back Swamp Bapt. Ch., Lumberton, 1981—; correctional chaplain Robeson County Sheriff's Dept. Funeral dir., Red Springs, N.C., 1971—. Home and office: PO Box 686 Red Springs NC 28377

MCGUIGAN, PATRICK JOHN, priest, Roman Catholic Church; b. Harrison, N.J., Sept. 3, 1949; s. Patrick John and Margaret Mary (Hoffman) McG. B.S., U. Md., 1974; postgrad. Wash. Theol. Union, 1975-79. Ordained priest Order of Carmelites, Roman Catholic Ch., 1979. Assoc. pastor St. Simon Stock Ch., Bronx, N.Y., 1980-83, adminstr., 1983-84, pastor, 1984—; religious prior Carmelite Friars, Bronx, 1980—; chaplain N.Y. Yankees Stadium, 1980—. Editor, creator, newsletter The Stockade Revisited, 1983. Lodge: Mordecai (chaplain 1984—). Home and Office: St Simon Stock Priory 2191 Valentine Ave Bronx NY 10457

MC HAN, ALFRED DONALD, minister, So. Baptist Conv.; b. Bryson City, N.C., July 11, 1933; s. Emlis and Emily (Davis) McH.; student Valdosta (Ga.) State Coll., 1958-61, So. Bapt. Sem. Extension, 1973-76; m. Shirley Leah Arvey, Apr. 27, 1957; children—Marvin Mitchell, Theresa Sabra. Ordained to ministry, 1970; minister of music Gordon St. Bapt. Ch., Valdosta, Ga., 1958-60; pastor Mt. Zion and Alarka Bapt. chs., Bryson City, N.C., 1969-71, Dan Springs Bapt. Ch., Bryson City, 1973—. Composer gospel songs. Home: Route 3 Box 118 Bryson City NC 28713

MCILVAIN, TERRY MARK, minister, So. Baptist Conv.; b. Enid, Okla., Apr. 14, 1950; s. Thornton James and Virginia Maxine (Brown) McI.; student Okla. State U., 1968-70, Okla. Bapt. U., 1970-71, Wichita State U., 1976—; m. Virginia Lea Blackburn, Aug. 11, 1972. Ordained to ministry, 1973; youth and music dir. chs. in Hennessey, Okla., 1970-73, Nogales Ave. Bapt. Ch., Tulsa, 1973-75; youth minister Immanuel Bapt. Ch., Wichita, Kans., 1975—; mem. faculty Okla. Youth Evangelism Conf., Ridgecrest Bapt. Assembly, Mo. Youth Evangelism Leadership Conf. Founder, adult leader Hennessey chpt. Fellowship Christian Athletes, 1972-73; mem. Singing Churchmen Okla., 1975; youth music dir. Central Bapt. Assn. Okla., 1969-72, Tulsa Bapt. Assn., 1974-75; mem. youth edn. and Bapt. Student Union com. Sedgwick (Kans.) Bapt. Assn., 1975—; mem. youth evangelism staff Kans./Nebr. Conv. So. Bapts., 1977—. Contbr. articles to religious jours. Home: 8044 E Gilbert St Wichita KS 67207 Office: 1415 S Topeka St Wichita KS 67211

MC ILVAINE, WILLIAM LINCOLN, lay church worker, Southern Baptist Convention; b. Knoxville, Tenn., Apr. 24, 1935; s. Victor Caryl and Eleanor (Dickinson) McI.; B.M.E., N.E. La. State U., 1962; M.Ch. Music, New Orleans Bapt. Theol. Sem., 1968; m. Ruby Christine Smith, June 11, 1960; children: Ruby Celeste, Joanna Noelle. Minister music and youth ch., Statesville, N.C., 1963-66, New Orleans, 1966-68, Charlotte, N.C., 1968-70; interim music dir. 1st Bapt. Ch., Charlotte, 1972-73; minister music Greystone Bapt. Ch., Asheboro, N.C., 1973-82; royal ambassador dir. 1st Bapt. Ch., Asheboro, 1983—, deacon, 1984—, also mem. adult choir and instrumental ensemble. Dir. choral music Randolph Tech. Inst., Asheboro, 1974-84. Mem. NEA, N.C. Music Edn. Assn. N.C. Assn., Educators, Music Educators Nat. Conf. Home: Route 8 Box 39 Asheboro NC 27203

MC ILVEENE, CHARLES STEELE, minister, Southern Baptist Convention; b. McNeil, Ark., Feb. 11, 1928; s. Bonnie Leonard and Lillian Irene (Owen) McI.; B.A., Hardin-Simmons U., 1949; B.D., Southwestern Bapt. Theol. Sem., 1953, M.R.E., 1954, D.Min., 1980; m. Betty Marie Fahlberg, Aug. 12, 1952; children: Carol Ann, Mary Elizabeth, Charles Scott. Ordained to ministry So. Bapt. Conv., 1948. Asst. pastor Broadmoor Bapt. Ch., Shreveport, La., 1954-57; pastor Lakeshore Bapt. Ch., Shreveport, 1957-61, Trinity Bapt. Ch., Lake Charles, La., 1961-71, 1st Bapt. Ch., Lufkin, Tex., 1971—. Mem. exec. bd. La. Bapt. Conv., 1961-67, 70-71; evangelist, S.Am., 1960, Philippines, 1968, S. Korea, 1970; pres., Shreveport Ministerial Assn., 1959, Calcasieu Parish Ministerial Assn. 1961-63, Angelina County Ministerial Assn., 1982-83; moderator Carey Bapt. Assn. 1963-65, 1st v.p. La. Bapt. Conv. 1964; bd. dirs. Bapt. Gen. Conv. Tex., 1971-84, 1st v.p., 1984—, bd. dirs. human welfare coordinating bd., 1984—; trustee La. Coll., 1965-71, East Tex. Bapt. Coll., 1971—. Bd. dirs. local chpts. Am. Cancer Soc., Am. Heart Assn., Angelina County United Way. Contbr. articles to religious jours. Home: 1305 Woodland St Lufkin TX 75901 Office: PO Box 1448 Lufkin TX 75901

MCILVENNA, ROBERT THEODORE, minister, United Meth. Ch.; b. Epping, N.H., Mar. 15, 1932; s. Robert and Lorena Amy (Smith) McI.; B.A., Willamette U., 1954; M.A., U. Edinburgh (Scotland), 1956; M.Div., Pacific Sch. Religion, 1958; Ph.D., Inst. for Advanced Study of Human Sexuality, 1975; m. Winnie Ostergaard Sorensen, May 1, 1956; children—Rand, Lise. Ordained to ministry, 1956; pastor Wesley Meth. Ch., Hayward, Calif., 1956-63; dir. Young Adult Project, San Francisco, 1963-67; mem. Nat. Bd. Edn., Nashville, 1967-68; with Glide Found., San Francisco, 1968-72; pres. Genesis Ch. and Ecumenical Center, dir. Nat. Sex. Forum and pres. Cambium Fund, San Francisco, 1972-75; pres. Exodus Trust and pres. Inst. for Advanced Study of Human Sexuality, San Francisco, 1975—. Recipient Prospero award, Jake Gimbel award Calif. Med. Sch., 1974. Contbr. articles in field to religious jours; author 11 books, including: You Can Last Longer, 1972; When You Don't Make It, 1974; Mission By Penetration-Missionary Methodology, 1965; Meditations on the Gift of Sexuality, 1977; producer 61 films, including: If Ever Two Were One, 1974; Reflections, 1976; Closing the Circle, 1975; Ripple, 1975; Quiet Afternoon, 1976, Going Down to Bimini, 1977. Home: 215 Kenwood Way San Francisco CA 94127 Office: 1523 Franklin St San Francisco CA 94109

MCINNES, VAL AMBROSE GORDON, priest, Roman Catholic Church; b. London, Ont., Can., Apr. 21, 1929; s. Angus and Genevieve (Rodgers) McI.; B.A., U. Western Ont., 1952; student U. Leyden, 1953; diploma in Law, Internat. Ct., The Hague, 1953; M.A., U. Windsor, 1954; Ph.B., Aquinas Inst., 1957, Ph.L., 1958, Ph.D., 1966. Ordained priest, 1961, joined Order of Preachers, 1954; instr. moral theology St. Thomas Coll., St. Paul, 1962-65; head dept. philosophy and theology King's Coll., U. Western Ont., 1965-66; dir. Tulane U. Cath. Center, 1967-70, pastor univ. community of St. Thomas More, 1970-79; prior St. Anthony of Padua Priory, 1976-83; sr. chaplain Knights of St. Lazarus, 1978—. Del. First World Conf. Religion and Peace, Kyoto, Japan, 1970, 2d Conf., Louvain, Belgium, 1974. Mem. bd. La. Council for Music and the Performing Arts, 1967—, chmn. fine arts, 1969-78, pres., 1978—; founding mem., v.p. La. Renaissance, Religion and the Arts, 1976—, pres., 1977-78, founder chair for Judeo-Christian studies, 1979, dir., exec. sec. for the chair, 1979—. UNESCO scholar, 1953; Can. Council grantee, 1966. Mem. Omicron Delta Kappa. Home: 775 Harrison Ave New Orleans LA 70184 Office: Univ Chapel Newcomb Coll 1229 Broadway New Orleans LA 70118

MC INTYRE, DAVID HARVEY, priest, Roman Catholic Church; b. Vancouver, B.C., Can., Dec. 29, 1932; s. Robert Leo and Mary (Blyth) Mc I.; came to U.S., 1946; naturalized, 1955; B.A., St. Edward Sem., 1955; M.Div., St. Thomas Sem., 1959; J.C.L., Cath. U. Am., 1963. Ordained priest Roman Cath. Ch., 1959. Assoc. pastor Our Lady of Fatima Ch., Seattle, 1959-61; asst. chancellor Archdiocese of Seattle, Roman Cath. Ch., 1963-68; pastor Immaculate Conception Ch., Seattle, 1968-73, St. Edward's Ch., Seattle, 1973-76; exec. dir. Wash. State Cath. Conf., 1976—; pres. Seattle Council of Priests, 1975-76; del. Nat. Fedn. Priest Council Assembly, 1975-79. Dir., St. Peter Claver Interracial Center, Seattle, 1964-75; dir. Project Equality, 1966-70, mem. nat. exec. com., 1967-70; Mem. Seattle Human Rights Commn., 1967-77; mem. Seattle-King County Econ. Opportunity Bd., 1966-70; bd. dirs. King County ARC, 1975-78, Seattle Opportunities Industrialization Center, 1967-71. Home: PO Box 70344 Seattle WA 98107 Office: 1402 3d Ave Seattle WA 98101

MC INTYRE, GLENN MICHAEL, former minister, United Methodist Church; b. Jackson County, Ill., July 4, 1942; s. Earl Lester and Mary Margaret (Allen) McI.; B.A., Ill. Wesleyan U., 1965; M.Div., Drew Theol. Sch., 1970; D.Min., Wesley Theol. Sem., Washington, 1978; m. Carolyn Louise Dickerson, Feb. 16, 1974 (div. 1982); 1 child, Andrew Allen. Ordained to ministry Meth. Ch., 1970; staff asst. in dean's office Theol. Sch., Drew U., Madison, N.J., 1970-72; nat. coordinator Religious Leaders for McGovern/Shriver, Washington, 1972; asso. coordinator Bishops' Call for Peace and Self-Devel. of Peoples, United Meth. Ch., N.Y.C., 1973-76; dir. Coalition for Whole Gospel, Washington, 1979-80; founding exec. dir., then religious liaison People for Am. Way, Washington, 1980-82. Pres. bd. dirs. Christianity and Crisis, 1976—. Named Outstanding Young Alumnus, Ill. Wesleyan U., 1975-76. Author: (with Sister Luke Tobin, Hazel T. Johns) Peaceworld, 1976. Contbr. articles to prof. jours. Home: 3818 N Fairfax Dr Arlington VA 22203

MCINTYRE, ROBERT WALTER, ch. ofcl., The Wesleyan Ch.; b. Bethlehem, Pa., June 20, 1922; s. Simon Jesse and Ruth (Young) McI.; student Miltonvale Wesleyan Coll., 1939-43; B.Rel., Marion Coll., 1944, B.A., 1959, Litt.D., 1980; postgrad. Ball State U., 1960-61; D.D., Eastern Pilgrim Coll., 1969; LL.D., Houghton Coll., 1976; m. Elizabeth Norman, Nov. 6, 1953; children: Judith (Mrs. James Keilholtz), Joy (Mrs. Charles McCallum), John, James, June (Mrs. Randall Brannon). Ordained to ministry, 1945—; pastor, Marengo, O., 1944-47, Columbus, Ohio, 1947-52, Coshocton, Ohio, 1952-55, exec. sec. Dept. Youth, The Wesleyan Ch., Marion, Ind., 1955-68; editor The Wesleyan Youth, Marion, 1959-68; gen. editor The Wesleyan Ch., editor The Wesleyan Adv., 1968-73; asso. editor The Preacher's Mag., Marion, 1973; gen. supt. The Wesleyan Ch., Marion, 1973—, mem. gen. bd. adminstrn., 1955—, mem. Commn. Christian Edn., 1959-73, mem. exec. bd., 1968—, chmn. Commn. on World Missions, 1973-76, chmn. Commn. on Ednl. Instns., 1976-80, Commn. on Publs., 1980-84, Commn. on Extension and Evangelism, 1984—; denominational rep. Nat. Assn. Evangelicals. Mem. Christian Holiness Assn. (chmn. social action commn. 1971-73, sec. 1973-76), Nat. Assn. Evangelicals (v.p. 1982-84, pres. 1984-86). Author: Ten Commandments for Teen-Agers, 1965. Editor: Program Pathways for Young Adults, 1964. Contbr. to Strength for Service, Abingdon, 1969, Arnold's Commentary, 1971, 74-75. Office: PO Box 2000 Marion IN 46952

MCKAUGHAN, PAUL EDWARD, minister, Presbyterian Church in America; b. Alhambra, Calif., Sept. 14, 1938; s. Donald and Pauline (Massey) McK.; m. Joanne Repetto, Sept. 13, 1958; children: Don, Douglas, Debbie. Grad. Bethany Inst., Mpls., 1961. Ordained to ministry, 1961. Foreign missionary Co-Laborers Inc., Brazil, 1962-64; dir. Crusade Billy Graham Assn., Brazil, 1965-67; coordinator planning Overseas Crusades Inc., Brazil, 1967-75, asst. to pres. Calif., 1975-76; cons., coordinator Mission to the World, Decatur, Ga., 1977—; dir. Latin Am. Evang. Projects, Orange, Calif. Mem. Free China Christian Coll. Assn. (bd. dirs. 1980—), Evang. Foreign Missions Assn. (bd. dirs. 1980—). Home: 1066 Forest Heights Rd Stone Mountain GA 30083 Office: Mission to the World PO Box 1744 4319 Memorial Dr Suite A Decatur GA 30031

MCKAY, SAMUEL LEROY, minister, Presbyterian Church in the U.S. b. Charlotte, N.C., Oct. 15, 1913; s. Elmer Ranson and Mary Arlena (Benfield) McK.; m. Martha Elizabeth Caldwell, Apr. 29, 1939; children: Samuel LeRoy, Mary Louise, William Ranson. A.B. cum laude, Erskine Coll., 1937; B.D. cum laude, Erskine Theol. Sem., 1939; postgrad. U. Ga., 1941-42, Union Theol. Sem., 1957. Ordained to ministry Presbyn. Ch., 1940. Pastor Prosperity Presbyn. Ch., Fayetteville, Tenn., 1942-46, Bethel Presbyn. Ch., Oak Hill, Ala., 1946-50, Maupin Ave. Presbyn. Ch., Salisbury, N.C., 1950-53, First Presbyn. Ch., Dallas, N.C., 1953-60; organizer, pastor First Presbyn. Ch., Kernersville, N.C., 1960-67; supr. chaplaincy program Dawie County Hosp., 1968-69; pastor Broadway Presbyn. Ch., N.C., 1969-80; pastor Cape Fear Presbyn. Ch., Lillington, N.C., 1983—; stated clk. Gen. Synod Assoc. Reformed Presbyn. Ch., 1950-53; com. gen. assembly Presbyn. Ch.

U.S., 1960, 69; chmn. Christian edn. com. Winston-Salem Presbytery, 1967-68; permanent clk. Winston-Salem Presbytery, 1961-69, chmn. leadership edn. com., 1962-66. Editor: Ann. Award-Winning Poems, 1972-86. Contbr. sermons, articles, poems to jours. Organizer, first pres. Clan Mackay Soc. N. Am., 1971-75, chmn. council, 1984—, chaplain, 1976—; treas. Kernersville Area YMCA, N.C., 1963-64, pres., 1964-66; pres. Dallas PTA, N.C., 1955-56; hon. guest, prin. speaker Clan Mackay Internat. Gathering, Glasgow, Scotland. Mem. N.C. Poetry Soc. (pres. 1963-64). Home: 12 Knollwood Dr Broadway NC 27505 Office: PO Box 160 Broadway NC 27505

MCKEE, PETER KILLEEN, priest, Roman Catholic Church; b. St. John, N.B., Can., Apr. 2, 1936; s. Killeen John and Juliette Marie (Michaud) McK. B.A., St. Thomas U., 1957; Divinitatis Baccalaureus, Holy Heart Sem., Halifax, 1961. Ordained priest Roman Cath. Ch., 1961. Assoc. pastor St. Augustine Parish, Moncton, N.B., 1961-64, St. Bernard's Parish, Moncton, 1964-72; pastor St. Lawrence Parish, Irishtown, N.B., 1972-76, St. Joseph Parish, Shediac, N.B., 1976-81, St. Augustine Parish, Moncton, 1981—; dean Roman Cath. English Deanery, Moncton, 1982—; chaplain, maj. Eastern N.B. Militia, Moncton, 1967—. Bd. dirs. East End Boys Club, Moncton, 1964, St. Pats Family Centre, Moncton, 1964, Big Bros.-Big Sisters, Moncton, 1982, N.B. Cancer Soc., 1982—. Mem. Moncton Council Chs. Club: Flying Fathers Hockey. Lodge: K.C. (chaplain 1967—). Home: 340 Dominion St Moncton NB E1C 6H8 Canada Office: 340 Dominion St Moncton NB E1C 6H5 Canada

MCKEEMAN, GORDON B., educational administrator. Pres. Starr Kings Sch. for the Ministry (Unitarian Universalist), Berkeley, Calif. Office: Starr Kings Sch for the Ministry 2441 Le Conte Ave Berkeley CA 94709*

MCKEEVER, WILLIAM JOSEPH, minister, Independent Pentecostal; b. Fayetteville, N.C., Oct. 2, 1955; s. William Joseph McKeever and Barbara Jean (Byrd) Lanphere; m. Tamar Sue Palermo, Aug. 23, 1975; children: Kristen, Kendra, Jamin. Student pub. schs. El Cajon, Calif. Ordained to ministry Pentecostal Ch., 1979. Founder 1979, since dir., Mormonism Research Ministry, El Cajon, Calif. Author: Answering Mormons' Questions, 1981; Joseph Smith-Prophet True or Prophet False, 1982. Producer film: The Latter-day Facade, 1984. Contbr. articles to religious publs. Republican. Office: Mormonism Research Ministry PO Box 20705 El Cajon CA 92021

MCKENNA, DAVID LOREN, minister, seminary president, Free Methodist Church of North America; b. Detroit, May 5, 1929; s. William Loren and Ilmi E. (Matson) McK.; m. Janet Voorheis, June 9, 1950; children: David Douglas, Debra Lynn, Suzanne Marie, Robert Bruce. A.A., Spring Arbor Jr. Coll., 1949; B.A. magna cum laude in History, Western Mich. U., 1951; M.Div., Asbury Theol. Sem., 1953; M.A., U. Mich., 1955; Ph.D. (Clifford Woody scholar), U. Mich., 1958; LL.D. (hon.), Houghton Coll., 1974, Spring Arbor Coll., 1976, Lewis and Clark Coll., 1978. Ordained to ministry Free Meth. Ch. N. Am., 1950. Dean of men Spring Arbor Jr. Coll., 1953-55, instr. psychology, 1955-60, acad. dean, 1955-57, v.p., 1958-60, pres., 1961-68; lectr. higher edn. U. Mich., 1958-60; asst. prof., coordinator Ctr. for Study of Higher Edn. Ohio State U., Columbus, 1960-61; pres. Seattle Pacific U., 1968-82, Asbury Theol. Sem., 1982—; del. World Meth. Council, London, 1966; chmn. Mich. Commn. Coll. Accrediting, 1966-68; bd. dirs. Council Advancement Small Colls., 1964-67; pres. Assn. Free Meth. Colls., 1968-70; chmn. Christian Consortium, 1970-74; participant Internat. Congress World Evangelization, 1974; cons. World Evangelization, Pattaya, Thailand, 1980; mem. bd. adminstrn., exec. com. Nat. Assn. Evangelicals, 2d v.p., 1975-81; bd. reference Black Evangelistic Enterprise, Evangelicals for Social Action, Ugandan Relief, Youth for Christ Internat. Author: The Jesus Model, 1976, Awake My Conscience, 1977, The Communicator's Commentary-Mark, 1982. Editor: The Urban Crisis, 1969; nat. radio commentator: This is Our World, 1983—. Contbr. articles to profl. jours. Pres. United Community Services, Jackson, Mich., 1968, Wash. Coll. Assn., 1970, 76; trustee United Way, Pacific Sci. Ctr., Seattle Found., Spring Arbor Coll., 1983—; bd. dirs. Bread for the World, 1980—, Jerry Lorentson Found., Crippled Children's Soc., 1965-67, Jr. Achievement, 1966-68, Land O'Lakes council Boy Scouts Am., 1965-68; mem. Wash. State Council Post-secondary Edn., 1969-74, Seattle Found., 1975—. Named One of Outstanding Men of Yr., Jr. C. of C., 1965, Seattle and Puget Sound Outstanding Citizen of Yr., 1976. Mem. Assn. Am. Colls. (dir. 1974-77), Ind. Colls. Wash. (pres. 1969-71), Wash. State Council Econ. Edn. (dir. 1980), N.W. Assn. Schs. and Colls. (commr. 1975-79), North Central Assn. Colls. and Schs. (chmn., dir. 1966-68), Nat. Assn. Ind. Colls. and Univs. (dir. 1976-80, sec. 1978), Council Postsecondary Accreditation (dir. 1979—), Phi Kappa Phi. Clubs: Wash. Athletic (bd. govs.), Rainier (Seattle). Lodge: Rotary (pres. Jackson chpt. 1966-67). Home: 203 Asbury Dr Wilmore KY 40390 Office: Asbury Theol Sem Wilmore KY 40390

MCKINLEY, GEORGE ORLAND ALLSPAUGH, minister, United Church of Christ; b. Correctionville, Iowa, Nov. 2, 1913; s. George Alonzo and Cora Adella (Lindsay) McK.; m. Barbara Edith Kozelka, June 21, 1938; children: Mary Louise McKinley Parrott, Charles Morris. B.A., Grinnell Coll., 1936; B.D., Chgo. Theol. Sem., 1940, M.Div., 1972. Ordained to ministry Aurora Assn. Congl. Christian Conf., 1940. Pastor First Congl. Ch., Algonquin, Ill., 1938-40, Sandwich, Ill., 1940-43, Prophetstown, Ill., 1945-51, South Milwaukee, Wis., 1953-58, Charles City, Iowa, 1959-63, Plymouth Congl. Ch., Eau Claire, Wis., 1963-65, Encanto Community Ch., Phoenix, Ariz., 1965-82, Visitation First Congl. Ch., Phoenix, 1983—. Served to capt. Chaplains Corps, U.S. Army, 1943-45, 51-53, ETO. Decorated Bronze Star. Democrat. Club: Civitan (chaplain 1968—). Home: 2839 N 43rd Ave Phoenix AZ 85009

MCKINLEY, STEVEN LIND, pastor, Lutheran Church in America; b. Burlington, Iowa, Aug. 18, 1942; s. William Steven and Dorothy Clara (Lind) M.; m. Patricia Ann Heinly, July 6, 1968; children: Jill, Kirk, Meg. B.A., Augustana Coll., 1964; B.D., Yale U., 1967. Ordained to ministry Lutheran Church in America, 1967. Asst. pastor Trinity Luth. Ch., New Haven, 1967-70; pastor Bethel Luth. Ch., Auburn, Mass., 1970-73, Christ the King Luth. Ch., Windsor, Conn., 1973-82, Grace Luth. Ch., Anoka, Minn., 1982—. Editor New England Luth. Jour., 1970-82; columnist LCA Partners mag., 1979—, cons. com., 1978—, chmn., 1983—. Mem. Windsor Clergy Assn. (pres. 1974-82). Home: 3701 153d Ln NW Anoka MN 55303 Office: Grace Luth Ch 13655 Round Lake Blvd Anoka MN 55303

MCKINNEY, B., bishop, pres. The Holiness Church of God, Inc. Address: 602 E Elm St Graham NC 27253

MCKINNEY, JOSEPH CRESCENT See *Who's Who in America*, 43rd edition.

MCKIVER, WILLARD, JR., minister, American Lutheran Church; b. Greensboro, N.C., Nov. 2, 1943; s. Willard Jr. and Willie Marie (Anderson) M.; m. Annie Mae Hester, Feb. 6, 1966 (div. June 1974); children: La'Bonni Bionka, Willard III; m. Patricia Anne Williams Roberts, Dec. 28, 1974; children: Michelle Renee, Asim Sinclair, Patrick Hashim. B.S., N.C. Central U., 1970; M.Div., Trinity Luth. Sem., Columbus, Ohio, 1978. Ordained to ministry Am. Luth. Ch., 1978. Intern, St. John Luth. Ch., Waukesha, Wis., 1976-77, pastor, Dallas, 1978-83; pastor Trinity Evangel. Luth. Ch., Chgo., 1983—; tchr. El Centro Jr. Coll., Dallas, 1980-81, campus minister, 1981-83; bd. dirs. div. life and mission in congregation Am. Luth. Ch., Mpls., 1984. Contbr. articles to religious newspapers and mags. Mem. NAACP, Durham, N.C., 1960. Mem. Protestant Cluster of Beverly, Ministerial Alliance, Coalition Black Mems. in Am. Luth. Ch. (pastor in residence 1978—, organizers award 1982). Democrat. Home: 1430 W 100th Pl Chicago IL 60643 Office: Trinity Evangelical Luth Ch 9995 S Beverly Ave Chicago IL 60643

MCLAREN, ROSS HOWLETT, religious educator, Southern Baptist Convention; b. Neptune, N.J., Mar. 25, 1952; s. Robert John and Lorraine (Howlett) McL.; m. Lois Barbara Steenland, Aug. 9, 1975; children: Doris Lorraine, Jeremy Caleb, Stephen Ezra. Diploma Emmaus Bible Coll., 1973; B.A., Trinity Coll., Deerfield, Ill., 1975; M. Divinity, Vanderbilt Divinity Sch., 1978, M.A., 1982, D. Ministry, 1985. Ordained to ministry, 1979. Mem. faculty American Bapt. Coll., Nashville, 1979—, assoc. prof., Bible & theology, 1979—, dir. div. bib. and theol. studies, 1983—. Recipient Elliott F. Shepard prize Vanderbilt Divinity Sch., Nashville, 1978; Instr. of Year award, Am. Bapt. Coll., 1981. Vis. scholar So. Bapt. Theol. Seminary, Louisville, 1983. Mem. Am. Soc. Ch. History, Soc. Bibl. Lit. Democrat. Home: 1409 Ordway Pl Nashville TN 37206 Office: American Bapt Coll 1800 Whites Creek Pike Nashville TN 37207

MCLAUGHLIN, BERNARD J., bishop, Roman Catholic Church. Titular bishop of Mottola, aux. bishop, Buffalo, 1969—. Office: 1085 Englewood Ave Kenmore NY 14223*

MC LAUGHLIN, JAY BRUCE, priest, Episcopal Ch.; b. New Castle, Pa., May 30, 1934; s. William H. and Mae (Rodgers) McL.; A.B., Emory U., 1954; B.S./B.A., U. Fla., 1956; M.Div., Va. Theol. Sem., 1961; fellow Coll. of Preachers, 1966, Seabury Western Theol. Sem., 1968; m. Marliynne Jean Searight, June 1, 1957; children—William Douglas, James Bruce. Ordained priest, 1961; asst. rector Trinity Ch., Columbia, S.C., 1961-65; rector Piedmont and Whittle parishes, The Plains and Marshall, Va., 1965-69; diocesan service officer, exec. council Episcopal Ch., N.Y.C., 1969-70; rector St. Stephens Ch., Milledgeville, Ga., 1970—; chaplain, adj. prof. social scis. Ga. Mil. Coll., Millegeville; chaplain Columbia (S.C.) Coll. Chmn. Greater Columbia Stop Polio Campaign, 1962; organizer County-Wide Youth Program, Fauquier County, Va., 1965-69. Recipient commendation Joint Houses of S.C. Legislature for mass polio immunization program chairmanship, 1962. Home: 224 Lakeside Dr Millegeville GA 31061 Office: Box 309 Millegeville GA 31061

MCLAUGHLIN, KAREN LOUISE, religious education director, Roman Catholic Church; b. Stoneham, Mass., Mar. 28, 1944; d. Edward and Marguerite Lillian (Avery) Muccio; m. Thomas Patrick McLaughlin, July 18, 1965; children: Deborah, Patrick, Jill, Heath, Jared. Student Mass. Bay Community Coll., 1962-63, Harvard U., 1963-64, U. Ariz., 1965-66, St. Mary's U., 1982-83, U. St. Thomas, 1984. Tchr. First Congregation Ch., Tucson, 1965-66; tchr. Immaculate Heart of Mary Parish, Los Alamos, 1973—, dir. religious edn., 1980—; region mem. diocesan religious edn. bd., Albuquerque, 1984—. Mem. Nat. Cath. Religious Edn. Assn. Club: Los Alamos Aquatomics. Office: Immaculate Heart of Mary Parish 3700 Canyon Rd Los Alamos NM 87544

MCLAURIN, ANCE ELMO, minister, So. Baptist Conv.; b. Hattiesburg, Miss., Nov. 20, 1935; s. Virgil L. and Maudie Lee (Sweeney) McL.; B.A., William Carey Coll., Hattiesburg, 1958; M.R.E., New Orleans Bapt. Theol. Sem., 1967; m. Sandra Mondell Pryor, Nov. 11, 1962; children—Tanya Leigh, Stuart Elmo, Julie Elizabeth, Tiffany Anne. Minister music and edn. chs. in Tex. and Miss., 1967-71; minister edn. Highland Bapt. Ch., Meridian, Miss., 1971—. Sunday sch. dir. Lauderdale Bapt. Assn., 1972—. Active United Way Lauderdale County. Mem. Miss. Assn. Children Under Six, Southeastern, Miss. Bapt. religious edn. assns., Miss. Alumni Assn. New Orleans Bapt. Theol. Sem. (sec.-treas.). Author articles. Home: 3517 35th Ave Meridian MS 39301 Office: 3400 27th St Meridian MS 39301

MCLEAN, RALPH DONALD, minister, Chs. of Christ; b. Sault Ste. Marie, Mich., June 30, 1917; s. Donald T.R. and Nettie Viola (Thompson) McL.; A.B. in Th., Cin. Bible Sem., 1944; A.B., Milligan Coll. (Tenn.), 1948; m. Zella Marie Linn Cormeny, July 18, 1953; 1 step-dau., Judith Lee (Mrs. Conrad Noll III). Ordained to ministry Chs. of Christ, 1943; pres. Jr. Class, Cin. Bible Sem., 1942-43; editor ann. The Nautilus, 1943-44; minister Christian edn. and youth Madisonville Christian Ch., Cin., 1943-45, West Side Christian Ch., Wichita, Kans., 1945-47; preacher Council Hill Christian Ch., Peck, Kans., 1947; minister Christian edn. and youth Hopwood Meml. Christian Ch., Milligan Coll., Tenn., 1947-48, minister, 1948; minister Christian edn. and youth Broadway Christian Ch., Lexington, Ky., 1948-51, West Side Christian Ch., Springfield, Ill., 1951-53; founder, dir. Christian Youth Services, 1954-70, Specialized Christian Services, Springfield, 1970—; minister Rochester (Ill.) Christian Ch., 1954-60. Pres., Sedgwick County Christian Endeavor Union, Wichita, 1946-47, Ky. Christian Endeavor Union, Lexington, 1950-51, Central Ill. Christian Ministers Fellowship, 1955-56; sec.-treas. exec. com. Nat. Missionary Conv., 1955-62; dir. Nat. Teen Conv., 1962—. Asst. scoutmaster, scoutmaster Boy Scouts Am., Cin., 1936-40; Boys Club leader Central YMCA, Cin., 1942-43. Sunday Sch. lesson writer Standard Intermediate Class and Standard Intermediate Tchr., 1947, 50. Editor: Highway For Youth sect. Preach mag., 1948-50, Christian Youth Hour dept. Horizons mag., 1951-55, Christian Youth Hour Program packets, 1955-69, Directory of the Ministry, 1960—. Address: 1525 Cherry Rd Springfield IL 62704

MCLELLAND, JOSEPH CUMMING See *Who's Who in America,* 43rd edition.

MC LEMORE, WILLIAM PEARMAN, minister, Episcopal Church; b. West Point, N.Y., Oct. 14, 1937; s. Ephraim Hester and Edith Adeline (Pearman) McL.; B.A., Fla. State U., 1962; M.Div., Va. Theol. Sem., 1965; m. Jacqueline Ruth Spinks, Dec. 14, 1963; children: Mary Kathryn, William Tomlin, Christopher Michael Martin. Ordained to ministry Episcopal Ch., 1965. Regional missioner, Cedar Key, Fla., 1965-68; asst. rector Christ Ch., Pensacola, Fla., 1969; rector St. Paul's Episcopal Ch., Jesup, Ga., 1970-73, Holy Trinity Episcopal Ch., Auburn, Ala., 1974—; pres. Auburn Ministerial Assn., 1975-76, 84-85. Pres. East Ala. Services for Elderly, 1976-78. Mem. Rural Workers Fellowship. Author: An Introduction to New Testament Greek, 1975. Home and Office: Church Dr Auburn AL 36830

MCMANUS, FREDERICK RICHARD, priest, university administrator, Roman Catholic Church; b. Lynn, Mass., Feb. 8, 1923; s. Frederick Raymond and Mary Magdalene (Twomey) McM.; A.B., St. John's Sem., Brighton, Mass., 1947; J.C.D., Cath. U. Am., 1954; LL.D (hon.), St. Anselm's Coll., Manchester, N.H., 1964, Stonehill Coll., North Easton, Mass., 1965. Ordained priest, 1947; assoc. pastor chs. in Mass., 1947-50; master ceremonies Archdiocese Boston, 1948-50, sec. to met. tribunal, 1950-51; prof. canon law and moral theology St. John's Sem., 1954-58; dir. secretariat Bishop's Com. on Liturgy, Nat. Conf. Cath. Bishops, Washington, 1965-75; prof. canon law Cath. U. Am., 1958—, vice provost, dean grad. studies, 1974-83, acad. v.p., 1983—. Pres. Liturgical Conf., 1959-62, 64-65; treas. Internat. Commn. English in liturgy, 1964—. Bd. dirs. Inst. Medieval Canon Law, Am. Council on Edn., 1980—; trustee St. John's Sem. Recipient Pax Christi award St. John's U., Collegeville, Minn., 1964; Michael Mathis award U. Notre Dame, 1978; Presdl. award Nat. Cath. Edn. Assn., 1983. Mem. Canon Law Soc. Am. (Role of Law award 1973), Cath. Theol. Soc. Am., N. Am. Acad. Liturgy, Cath. Commn. Cultural and Intellectual Affairs, Assn. Cath. Colls. and Univs. (bd. dirs. 1979-80, chmn. 1980-82), Joint Com. Cath. Learned Socs. and Scholars (chmn. 1981—), AAUP. Author: Congregation of Sacred Rites, 1954;

Rites of Holy Week, 1956; Revival of the Liturgy, 1963; Sacramental Liturgy, 1967; (with Ralph Keifer) The Rite of Penance, 1975; also articles. Editor The Jurist, 1959—. Address: Cath Univ Am Washington DC 20064

MCMANUS, WILLIAM EDWARD, clergyman, Roman Catholic Church; b. Chgo., Jan. 27, 1914; s. Bernard A. and Marie T. (Kennedy) M.; S.T.L., St. Mary Sem., Mundelein, Ill., 1939; M.A., Cath. U. Am., 1942. Ordained priest Roman Cath. Ch., 1939; asst. dir. dept. edn. Nat. Cath. Welfare Conf., 1945-57; supt. schs. Chgo. archdiocese, 1957-68; aux. bishop Chgo., 1967 bishop of Fort-Wayne-South Bend, 1976—. Address: 1103 S Calhaun St PO Box 390 Fort Wayne IN 46801

MC MILLAN, ALFRED NORMAN, minister, Presbyterian Church Canada; b. Toronto, Ont., Can., Apr. 12, 1906; s. Thomas and Mary (Gowans) McM.; diploma Knox Coll., Toronto, 1934; m. Ida Kathleen McKane, June 27, 1942; children: John David, Ian Keith, Murray Dale. Ordained to ministry Presbyn. Ch. Can., 1934. Pastor Norval Union Presbyn. Chs., Georgetown, Ont., 1935-38, Caledonia, Ont., 1938—; padre Royal Can. Sea Cadets, br. 154 Royal Can. Legion. Scout master Haldimand dist. council Boy Scouts Can., recipient Medal of Merit, 1955; pres. local br. Can. Red Cross Soc. Decorated Can. Armed Forces Decoration, recipient Centennial medal Can. 1967, Queen's Silver Jubilee medal, 1977. Author: Thoughts on Friendship, 1941; Woodsmoke at Twilight, 1955. Home: 129 Argyle St N Caledonia ON N0A 1A0 Canada

MCMILLAN, EMANUEL MURRAY, JR., minister, American Baptist Churches in the U.S.A.; b. Greensboro, N.C., June 19, 1942; s. Emanuel M. and Lucille (Barbour) McM.; m. Donna Lorraine Beam, June 6, 1965; children: William, Jonathan, David. B.S., Guilford Coll., 1966; M.Div., So. Bapt. Theol. Sem., 1968. Ordained to ministry Baptist Ch., 1966. Sr. minister Sand Creek Bapt. Ch., Greensburg, Ind., 1968-70, Franklin Road Bapt. Ch., Indpls., 1970-78, Lewis Creek Bapt. Ch., Shelbyville, Ind., 1978-79, Rosalind Hills Bapt. Ch., Roanoke, Va., 1979-80, Calvary Bapt. Ch., Charleston, W.Va., 1981—; chmn. of evangelism Kawawha Valley Bapt. Assn., 1982-83, moderator, 1983-85; fellow mem. adv. council to pres. Alderson-Broaddus Coll., Philippi, W.Va., 1982-84. Fellow Greater Charleston Ministerial Assn. (sec.-treas. 1984-85). Home: 840 Lower Chester Rd Charleston WV 25302 Office: Calvary Bapt Ch Maryland St and Lee St W Charleston WV 25302

MC MILLAN, ROBERT MCKENZIE, minister, So. Bapt. Conv.; b. Glasgow, Scotland, Feb. 13, 1922; s. David Torrance and Isabella (McKenzie) McM.; grad. Skerrys Coll., 1942; student Glasgow U., 1942-47; diploma theology London U. Div. Sch., 1948; M.A., Trinity Coll., 1955, D.D., 1956; M.S., St. Louis U., 1959; m. Jane Hughes Smith, Dec. 20, 1921; children—Christine Ruth, Pauline Jane. Ordained to ministry, 1943; pastor City Rd. Bapt. Ch., Birmingham, Eng., 1945-48, Peoples Ch., Montreal, Que., Can., 1948-52, Bethel Bapt. Ch., Erie, Pa., 1952-56, Hope Ch., St. Louis, 1956-61, Faith Bapt. Ch., Wichita Falls, Tex., 1961-64, 1st Bapt. Ch., South Miami, Fla., 1964-71, 1st Ch., Tallahassee, 1971—. Chaplain, Fla. Senate, 1972—; trustee Sunday Sch. Bd., So. Bapt. Conv., 1976—. Mem. Fla. Com. Aging, 1974-76; trustee Stetson U., 1976—; mem. Religious Heritage Commn., 1976—. Recipient TV Gold medal award DuPont Found., 1973, Citation of Honor, Fla. Senate, 1976. Fellow Royal Geog. Soc.; mem. Internat. Platform Assn. Author: Beside the Still Waters, 1960; Happiness is God's Gift, 1970; I'm Human - Thank God, 1974. Home: 2010 Amboise Ct Tallahassee FL 32303 Office: PO Box 1017 Tallahassee FL 32302

MCNAIL, STANLEY DUANE, minister, ch. ofcl.; b. Centralia, Ill., Mar. 14, 1918; s. Karl Hicks and Constance Kathleen (Poyner) McN.; Th.B., Northwestern Coll. (Okla.), 1967, Th.M., 1969; D.D., Trinity Hall Coll., 1970, LL.D., 1972. Ordained to ministry Am. Ministerial Assn., 1969; dir. ministry St. Alban's Ch. of the Way, San Francisco, 1973—; exec. v.p. Am. Ministerial Assn., 1974—. Mem. Am. Bd. Nat. Missions, 1972—. Mem. Internat. Platform Assn., Am. Parapsychol. Research Found., Order St. Luke the Physician Am., Trinity Hall Alumni Soc., Epsilon Delta Chi. Mason. Author: (poetry) Footsteps in the Attic, 1956, Something Breathing, 1965, The Black Hawk Country, 1967. Poetry editor Renaissance, San Francisco Bay Guardian, 1962-69; editor-pub. Galley Sail Rev., 1958-73. Contbr. to religious and lit. jours. Home: 525 Hyde St San Francisco CA 94109 Office: PO Box 4842 San Francisco CA 94101

MCNAIR, GAINES D., minister, Assemblies of God; b. Philadelphia, Miss., Apr. 7, 1910; s. Baker and Ruby McNair; B.D., Lee Coll., Cleveland, Tenn., 1928; student Vaughan's Music Conservatory, Laurenceburg, Tenn., 1934-36; m. Myrtuce Long, Dec. 24, 1936; children—Gaines D., Ruby McNair Cook. Ordained to ministry, 1949; pastor chs., Miss., 1948—; pastor 1st Assembly God Ch., Yazoo City, Miss., 1961—. Mem. Yazoo Ministerial Assn. Club: Woodmen of World (chpt. pres. 1961-77). Author numerous gospel songs; asso. editor Lighted Pathway. Address: 1304 Lamar St Yazoo City MS 39194

MCNALLY, JEANNE MARGARET, superior general, nun, Roman Catholic Church; b. N.Y.C., Nov. 22, 1931; d. Edward J. and Margaret E. (Weyland) McNally. Diploma Mercy Sch. Nursing, 1956; A.D., Sacred Heart Coll., 1956, L.H.D., 1981; B.S., Cath. U. Am., 1958, M.S., 1963, Ph.D., 1969. Joined Sisters of Mercy, Roman Cath. Ch., 1949. Tchr. elem. schs., N.C., 1949-53; instr. med.-surg. nursing Mercy Sch. Nursing, Charlotte, N.C., 1958-61, med. supr., 1958-61, dir. nursing edn., 1963-71; assoc. prof. psychology Belmont Abbey Coll., N.C., summer 1970, Sacred Heart Coll., Belmont, 1969-71; vis. lectr. Fordham U. at Lincoln Ctr., N.Y.C., 1972; dir. formation and continuing edn., Sisters of Mercy, N.C., 1972-74, asst. superior gen., Belmont, 1972-76, gen. councilor, 1969-72, dir. formation, 1972-74, dir. ministry, 1976-80, superior gen., 1980—; assoc. prof. ednl. psychology Sacred Heart Coll., Belmont, 1972-74; vis. prof. N.C. Central U., 1978-79; adj. prof. nursing Sch. Nursing U. N.C. at Chapel Hill, 1974-78, assoc. v.p. acad. affairs, gen. adminstrn., 1978-80, adj. prof., 1974-84, research assoc. Health Services Research Ctr., 1979-84, cons., 1980-84; cons. in field; mem. Task Force on the Role of Nursing in High Blood Pressure Control, Nat. Heart, Lung and Blood Inst., Gov.'s Task Force on Maldistribution and Supply of Health Care Personnel; adj. prof. nursing U. N.C. at Greensboro, 1974—; bd. dirs. Mercy Hosp., Charlotte, 1980—, St. Joseph Hosp., Asheville, N.C., 1980—, Holy Angels, Belmont, 1981—; trustee Sacred Heart Coll., 1969—; mem. com. on social devel. and internat. peace Nat. Conf. Cath. Bishops; adv. bd. St. Louis U. Med. Ctr.; liaison Leadership Conf. of Women Religious to Nat. Assn. Treas. of Religious Insts. Author monographs. Contbr. numerous articles to profl. jours., chpts. to books. Harvard U. fellow, 1977; Yale U. fellow, 1980; nurse scientist fellow, 1967. Fellow Am. Acad. Nursing; mem. Leadership Conf. of Women Religious, Fedn. Sisters of Mercy of the Ams., Am. Nurses Assn. (chmn. med.-surg. div. practice, Congress on nursing practice, com. on inter-relationships, chmn. ad hoc com. position paper clin. nurse specialist, ad hoc com. certification of advanced practitioners, vice chmn. med.-surg. div. practice), Nat. Assembly of Women Religious, N.C. Nurses Assn. (task force for revision of nurse practice act, joint practice com. with N.C. Med. Soc., ad hoc com. on entry into profl. nursing practice, chmn. nominating com. baccalureate and higher degree forum), Pi Gamma Mu, Sigma Theta Tau. Republican. Home: Sacred Heart Convent Belmont NC 28012

MCNAMARA, EUGENE P(ETER), priest, Roman Catholic Church; b. Waltham, Mass., Jan. 24, 1929; s. James R. and Mary (Walsh) M. A.B., St. John Sem., Boston, 1953; M.S.W., Boston Coll., 1965; H.H.D. (hon.), Northeastern Sch. of Law, Boston, 1984. Ordained priest Roman Cath. Ch., 1953. Assoc. pastor St. Albert's Ch., Weymouth, Mass., 1953-56, St. Patrick Ch., Lawrence, Mass., 1956-62; asst. dir. Catholic Charitable Bur., Boston, 1962-66, exec. dir., 1966—; archdiocesan dir. Catholic Relief Services. Bd. dirs. Mass. State Dept. Pub. Welfare, St. Margaret's Hosp., Laboure Ctr., Boston, Nazareth, Inc., Citizenship Tng. Ctr.-Boston Juvenile Ct. Office: Catholic Charitable Bur of Boston 10 Derne St Boston MA 02114

MCNAMARA, LAWRENCE J. See *Who's Who in America*, 43rd edition.

MCNAMEE, CATHERINE See *Who's Who in America*, 43rd edition.

MCNAUGHT, JOHN BRADLEY, minister, National Association of Congregational Churches.; b. Mpls., Oct. 25, 1950; s. Charles Eugene McNaught and Edyth Mae (Rediger) Peifer; m. Jane Kay Cahoon, Aug. 5, 1972 (div. July 15, 1981); 1 child, Heather Christel McNaught. B.A., Bethel Coll., 1972; M.Div., Bethel Sem., 1975; postgrad., Luther Sem., 1983—. Ordained to ministry Congl. Christian Chs., 1975. Youth minister Excelsior Congl. Ch., Minn., 1972-74; asst. minister Colonial Ch., Edina, Minn., 1974-75; sr. minister People's Congl. Ch., Bayport, Minn., 1975—; del. St. Paul Council Chs., 1978-80; chmn. St. Croix Valley Inter-Church Event, Stillwater, Minn., 1981; chaplain Oak Park Heights State Prison, Minn., 1982-83. Contbr. poems to Alive Now. Contbg. editor Congregationalist, 1982. Chmn. Sexual Abuse Task Force, Oakdale, Minn., 1976-79, Community Volunteer Service, Stillwater, 1982, Youth Services Bureau, Stillwater, 1978-80; pres. St. Croix Valley United Way, Stillwater, 1979-81; mem. Drug Awareness Program, Maplewood, Minn., 1979-80, Minn. Spl. Olympics, Duluth, 1984. Recipient Award of Merit United Way, 1977, Distinguished Service award Stillwater Jaycees, 1979, Cert. Appreciation Minn. Corrections Commn., 1983; named one of 10 Outstanding Young Minnesotans Minn. Jaycees, 1980. Mem. Nat. Assn. Congl. Christian Chs. (chmn. spiritual resources commn. 1976-80, editorial adv. com., 1980-84, communications commn., 1980-84), Minn. Fellowship Congl. Chs., St. Croix Valley Ministerial Assn. (chmn. 1979). Home: 8989 Lake Jane Trail Lake Elmo MN 55042 Office: Peoples Congregational Ch 309 N 3rd St Bayport MN 55003

MCNAUGHTON, HAROLD D., lay ch. worker; b. Nebr., July 14, 1926; s. Fred Archie and Murriel Joy (Cole) McN.; student So. Calif. Coll., Pasadena, 1944-46; m. Helen Mattie Rush, June 20, 1946; children—Harold D., Riva Lee (Mrs. Joel Colombo), Dwight Fred, Bradford Lyle, Stanley Todd. Vice pres. Christ for India, 1963—, Religious Heritage of Am., 1968—. Youth Crusades of Am., 1974—; mem. bd. Layman's Nat. Bible Com., 1969—. Pres., McNaughton Enterprises, Palmdale, Calif., 1963—. Mem. Calif. Republican Central Com. Bd. dirs. Melodyland Drug Prevention; bd. regents Melodyland Sch. Theology, Anaheim, 1974—. Named Alumni of Year, So. Calif. Coll. Mem. C. of C. Club: Stockdale (Cal.) Country. Office: PO Box 9908 Bakersfield CA 93309

MCNEILL, BOBBY EARL, minister, Ch. of God in Christ; b. Fayetteville, N.C., July 2, 1934; s. Clinton Dixon and Carrie (White) McN.; student Allen Bible Coll., 1968; m. Bertha Louise Dawson, Mar. 3, 1969; children—Bobby Clinton, Bertham Earl. Ordained to ministry, 1955; pastor, Mount Olive-Thomasville, N.C., 1970—; exec. sec. Greater N.C., 1973—. Home and Office: 312 Frances Pl Kinston NC 28501

MC NEILL, RONALD LEWIS, minister, Christian Church (Disciples of Christ); b. Independence, Mo., Aug. 1, 1949; s. Lewis A. and Hazel L. (Wilkins) McN.; B.A., Culver-Stockton Coll., 1971; M.Div., St. Paul Sch. Theol., 1974; D.Min., Drew U., 1980. Ordained to ministry Christian Ch. (Disciples of Christ), 1974. Pastor Covenant Larger Parish, Clarksville, Mo., 1974—; pastor religious program Sta. KPCR-AM-FM, Bowling Green, Mo.; chmn. Dist. III small ch. com. Christian Ch., 1976—, chmn. small ch. com. Mid-Am. region, 1982-84, also mem. council on Christian unity. Treas., Pike County (Mo.) Mental Health Assn., 1975—; chmn. Bicentennial Commn. Clarksville, 1975-76; mem. ch. adv. com. Culver-Stockton Coll., Canton, Mo., 1976—; mem. Raintree Arts Guild, Raintree Theatre Guild. Recipient Community Youth Program award Mo. Community Betterment Program, 1975. Mem. Disciples Peace Fellowship, Fellowship of Reconciliation, ACLU, Clarksville C. of C. Home: Box 82 Clarksville MO 63336 Office: Box 175 Clarksville MO 63336

MC NICHOLAS, JOSEPH A., bishop, Roman Cath. Ch.; b. St. Louis, Jan. 13, 1923; ed. Cardinal Glennon Coll., St. Louis, Kenrick Sem., St. Louis, St. Louis U. Ordained priest, 1949; ordained titular bishop of Scala and aux. bishop of St. Louis, 1969; bishop of Springfield (Ill.), 1975—. Office: 524 E Lawrence Ave Springfield IL 62705*

MC NULTY, EDWARD JOHN, priest, Roman Cath. Ch.; b. Belmond, Iowa, Dec. 13, 1914; s. Thomas Phillip and Julia Ann (McLaughlin) McN.; B.C.S., State U. Iowa, 1937; certificate in exec. tng. Gen. Motors Inst. Tech., 1938; certificate St. Mary's Sem., Balt., 1956. Ordained priest, 1956; chaplain Mercy Hosp., Cedar Rapids, Iowa, 1956-61; asso. pastor St. Matthew's Ch., Cedar Rapids, 1961-65; dir. Am. Martyrs Retreat House, Cedar Falls, Iowa, 1965-70; pastor St. Joseph's Ch., Earlville, Iowa, 1970-71, New Hampton, Iowa, 1971—. Home and Office: 202 N Broadway New Hampton IA 50659

MCNUTT, CHARLIE FULLER, JR., bishop, Episcopal Church; b. Charleston, W.Va., Feb. 27, 1931; s. Charlie Fuller and Mary (Ford) McN.; m. Alice Turnbull, Mar. 3, 1962; children: Thomas Ford, Charlie Fuller, Alson Turnbull. A.B., Washington and Lee U., 1953; M.Div., Va. Theol. Sem., 1956, D.D. (hon.), 1981; M.S., Fla. State U., 1970. Ordained priest Episcopal Ch., 1956, consecrated bishop, 1980. Vicar, Christ Ch., Williamston, W.Va., 1956-60; asst. rector St. John's Episcopal Ch., Tallahassee, 1960-62; rector St. Luke's Ch., Jacksonville, Fla., 1962-68; archdeacon Diocese of Fla., 1968-74; rector Trinity Episcopal Ch., Martinsburg, W.Va., 1974-80; bishop Episcopal Diocese of Central Pa., Harrisburg, 1980—; bd. dirs. Pa. Council Chs., 1982, chmn. dept. social ministry, 1983. Bd. dirs. Boy Scouts Am., Harrisburg, 1981. Mem. Clergy Assn. Diocese of Central Pa. Home: 2428 Lincoln St Camp Hill PA 17011 Office: PO Box 11937 Harrisburg PA 17108

MC NUTT, SANDRA KAY, lay ch. worker, So. Baptist Conv.; b. Avon, Ill., Nov. 20, 1945; d. Cleo Herman and Edna Marie (Kreps) Amos; B.S. in Music Edn., Western Ill. U., 1967; m. Kenneth George McNutt, Feb. 11, 1967; children—Robert Anthony, Renee Marie, Aaron Clee. Music dir. South Side Bapt. Ch., Hannibal, Mo., 1972—. Bapt. day care worker, 1973; tchr. music Hannibal LaGrange Coll., 1975—; family concert Immanuel Bapt. Ch., Monmouth, Ill. Mem. Gideon Aux. Compiler, producer, dir. Easter Pagaent, A Portrayal of Christ, 1975, 76. Home: 2303 Palmyra Rd Hannibal MO 63401

MCPHERSON, ROLF KENNEDY, ch. ofcl., Internat. Ch. Foursquare Gospel; b. Providence, Mar. 23, 1913; s. Harold S. and Aimee Semple (Kennedy) McP.; student So. Cal. Radio Inst.; student L.I.F.E. Bible Coll., then D.D. (hon.); m. Lorna De Smith, July 21, 1931; children—Marleen (dec.), Kay. Pres., Internat. Ch. of Foursquare Gospel, Los Angeles, 1944—, L.I.F.E. Bible Coll., 1944—, Echo Park Evangelistic Assn., Los Angeles, 1944—, Ch. of the Forsquare Gospel, Los Angeles, 1944—. Office: 1100 Glendale Blvd Los Angeles CA 90026

MCRAITH, JOHN JEREMIAH, bishop, Roman Cath. Ch.; b. Hutchinson, Minn., Dec. 6, 1934; s. Arthur Luke and Marie (Hanley) McR.; B.A. cum laude, Loras Coll., Dubuque, Ia., 1956. Ordained priest Roman

Catholic Ch., 1960; asst. pastor, Sleepy Eye, Minn., 1960-64; pastor, Milroy, Minn., 1964-67, St. Leo, Minn., 1967-68; pastor St. Mary's Parish, Sleepy Eye, 1968-72, prin. high sch., 1968-72; exec. dir. Nat. Cath. Rural Life Conf., Des Moines, 1972-78; ordained bishop of Owensboro, Ky., 1982—. Pres. Minn. Cath. Edn. Assn., 1971. Home and office: 2200 Mayfair Dr Owensboro KY 42301

MCREE, EDWARD BARXDALE, lay church worker, United Methodist Church; b. Pauls Valley, Okla., Oct. 20, 1931; s. Henry Barxdale and Mary Elizabeth (Shumate) McR.; B.A., Oklahoma City U., 1957; m. Jan Bryant, Aug. 23, 1957; children: Scott, Kent, Chad. Chmn. bldg. com., First United Meth. Ch., Eaton Rapids, Mich., 1968, lay leader, 1968-82, chmn. council on ministries, 1970, lay speaker, 1971—, bd. stewards, 1959-70, ch. trustee, 1969-72; pres. United Meth. Found. West Mich. Conf., 1981—; lay leader Lansing Dist. United Meth. Ch., 1983, chmn. com. on superintendency, 1979—; mem. Council on Finance and Adminstrn. West Mich. Conf., United Meth. Ch., 1971-79, dist. del., 1976, 77, 78, 79, 80, 81-84. Pres., Ingham Med. Center, Lansing, Mich., 1961—. Mem. Bd. Edn. Eaton Rapids, 1964-72. Bd. dirs. Jarvis Acres Retirement Community, 1972-74, Blus Cross of Mich.; bd. dirs. Hosp. Purchasing Service Mich., 1972—, chmn. bd., 1976; bd. dirs. Tri-County Emergency Med. Services Council, 1972—, pres., 1974—. Recipient Boss of Year award Lansing Jr. C. of C., 1976. Fellow Am. Coll. Hosp. Adminstrs.; mem. Am., Mich. (Homminga award 1974) hosp. assns., Greater Lansing Vis. Nurse Assn. (pres. 1967-69). Home: 201 S Center St Eaton Rapids MI 48827 Office: 401 W Greenlawn Ave Lansing MI 48910

MCTIGHE, SIMON, priest, Roman Catholic Church; b. N.Y.C., Oct. 5, 1917; s. Michael and Ellen (Reapy) McT.; A.B., St. Meinrad (Ind.) Coll., 1950; Th.M., St. Meinrad Sch. Theology, 1954. Ordained priest Roman Catholic Ch., 1953. Assoc. pastor chs. in Ind., 1954-70; pastor Mary, Help of Christians Ch., Mariah Hill, Ind., 1970-79, St. Martin Ch., Sabaria, Ind., 1979-82; asst. archivist St. Meinrad Archives, 1982—; missionary St. Meinrad Archabbey, 1982—; tchr. St. Ferdinand High Sch., Ferdinand, Ind., 1958-64; ecumenical minister North Spencer County, Ind. Bd. dirs. Maria Hilf Found. Mem. North Spencer Clergy Assn. Address: Esser Rd Saint Meinrad IN 47577

MCVEY, WILLIAM LEE, minister, religion educator, General Association Regular Baptist Churches; b. Springfield, Mo., Mar. 8, 1946; s. William C. McVey and Virginia (Oldfield) Putnam; m. Cynthia Ann Eckart, June 14, 1969; children: Diana Joy, William Jason. B.A., Cedarville Coll., 1968; M.Div., Grace Theol. Sem., 1972. Ordained to ministry General Association Regular Baptist Churches. Religion educator Emmanual Bapt. Ch., Clarksburg, W.Va., 1972-73; assoc. pastor First Bapt. Ch., LaGrange, Ohio, 1973-74; pastor Carmel Bapt. Ch., New Straitsville, Ohio, 1974-84; religion educator People's Bapt. Ch., Brunswick, Ohio, 1984—. Republican. Home: 409 Pearl Rd Brunswick OH 44212 Office: Box 0817 3840 Center Rd Brunswick OH 44212

MCWHIRTER, FRANK CARSWELL, minister, Southern Baptist Convention; b. Birmingham, Ala., Sept. 27, 1926; s. Frank E. and LaVada (Payne) McW.; m. Lydia Myrtle Smith, Dec. 17, 1948; children: Deborah, Carol, Sharon. B.A., Samford U., 1952; B.D., Southwestern Bapt. Theol. Sem., 1955. Ordained to ministry Baptist Ch., 1951. Pastor, Calvary Bapt. Ch., Andalusia, Ala., 1980—; mem. exec. bd. Ala. Bapt. Conv., 1963-67, 74-76. Served with USN, 1945-46. Lodges: Lions, Kiwanis, Masons. Home: 1500 Lindsey Bridge Rd Andalusia AL 36420 Office: Calvary Baptist Ch 1500 Lindsey Bridge Rd Andalusia AL 36420

MCWHORTER, DONALD RICHARD, minister, Churches of Christ; b. Chickamauga, Ga., Nov. 17, 1932; s. Gordon Richard and Ellan Beatrice (Madaris) McW.; m. Jane Elizabeth Shannon, Aug. 21, 1956; children: Kathryn, Gregory. B.A., David Lipscomb Coll., 1955; postgrad. U. Tenn., 1956. Ordained to ministry Churches of Christ, 1950. Minister Ch. of Christ, Chattanooga, Tenn., 1957-72, Ch. of Christ, Fayette, Ala., 1972—; TV speaker Know Your Bible, Chattanooga, 1957-72, Herald of Truth, Abilene, Tex., 1960, Bible Talk, Columbus, Miss., 1972—; internat. traveling missionary Ch. of Christ, 1972—. Author: (with others) Plea for Fundamentals, 1978, Eternal Truths, 1980; Getting a Handle on Life, 1984. Editor Truth, 1957—. Avocation: photography. Home: 2336 6th Way NW Route 3 Fayette AL 35555 Office: Church of Christ PO Box 24 Fayette AL 35555

MEACHAM, JAMES HOWARD, minister; b. Newark, Ohio, Feb. 23, 1944; s. Howard Ancil and Alma (Morriss) M.; B.S. in Music Edn., Ohio State U., 1966; postgrad. U. Utah, 1966-67, Xavier U., 1967-70; M.Min., Internat. Bible Inst. and Sem., 1983; m. Sandra Kay Burger, Mar. 27, 1966; 1 child, James Douglas. Ordained to ministry Nat. Council Community Chs. (inter-denominational), 1972; sr. pastor Grace Chapel Community Ch., Westerville, Ohio, 1966—, evangelist, 1983—; chaplain, Genoa Twp. Fire Dept., 1972—, Westerville Police Dept., 1972—; conf. speaker and singer, 1981—; co-chmn. Ohio Conf. on Holy Spirit, 1983-84. Organizer, dir. 3 softball leagues, 1972-74; chmn. Westerville Fund, 1984—; bd. dirs. Happy Canine Helpers, 1984—, Westerville Ctr. for Arts, 1984—; dist. coordinator Freedom Council, 1984—; dist. chmn. Come Alive '85, 1984-85. Recipient bravery commendation City of Westerville, 1973. Mem. Westerville Area Ministerial Assn., Columbus Full-Gospel Pastors, Westerville Full Gospel Pastors, Ohio State Univ. Band Alumni Assn. Lodge: Rotary (pres. Westerville 1976). Home: 7720 Big Walnut Rd Westerville OH 43081 Office: 7798 Big Walnut Rd Westerville OH 43081

MEAD, BRIAN EDWIN, priest, Roman Catholic Church; b. Port Chester, N.Y., June 15, 1942; s. Robert Edwin and Catherine Marie (Geilhard) M.; B.A., St. Joseph Coll. and Sem., Yonkers, N.Y., 1965; M.S.W., Adelphi U., 1979. Ordained priest Roman Cath. Ch., 1969. Asso. pastor chs. in Vt., 1969—; asso. pastor St. Mary's Ch., Springfield, 1974-76; asso. dir. Vt. Cath. Charities, dir. Rutland office, 1976—. Mem. Acad. Cert. Social Workers. Home: St Bridget Rectory West Rutland VT 05777 Office: 24 1/2 Center St Rutland VT 05701

MEAD, MILLARD WILMER, minister, United Methodist Church; b. Cherry Valley, Ohio, May 27, 1930; s. Myrlen Lomas and Winifred Irene (Mills) M.; B.S., Kent State U., 1970; M.Div., Methodist Sch. Theology, 1973; m. Janet Wilma Hummell, Aug. 7, 1948; children—Jacqueline Doyle, David, Susan Dyer. Ordained to ministry, 1974; pastor Johnston Federated United Meth. Ch., Cortland, Ohio, 1963-75, Grace United Meth. Ch., Bucyrus, Ohio, 1975-84, St. Mark United Meth. Ch., Galion, Ohio, 1984—. Dist. sec. United Meth. Ch., 1974-75, mem. conf. council on ministry, 1973-76, 80-84, mem. dist. council of ministry, 1974; E. Ohio Conf. del. United Meth. Conf., Hawaii, 1981, World Meth. Camp Meeting, Ocean Grove, N.J., 1984; E. Ohio Conf. Historian, 1984—; service unit chmn. Salvation Army, Cortland, 1973-75; mem. adv. bd., 1976-84; sec. E. Ohio Conf. Town and Country Fellowship, 1975—, E. Ohio Conf. Archives and History Commn., 1976-84; pres. Gen. Conf. Commn. Archives and History, 1984—, North Central Jurisdiction Archives and History, 1984—. Mem. Commn. on Aging, Trumbull County, Ohio, 1973-75; mem. adv. council agr. Trumbull County, 1968-75. Trustee, v.p. Flat Rock Children's Home. Recipient Young Farmers award Dairyman's Coop. Sales Assn., 1962; Nat. Hwy. Safety award, 1975. Mem. Grange (master 1955-65). Address: 950 N Market St Galion OH 44833

MEADE, ELLEN PATRICIA, nun, hosp. adminstr., Roman Catholic Ch.; b. N.Y.C.; d. Patrick and Ellen (Sullivan) Meade; B.S., Coll. of St. Elizabeth, Convent, N.J., 1953; M.H.A., St. Louis U., 1958. Joined Sisters of Charity of St. Elizabeth, 1937; adminstrv. asst. Office of Mother Gen., Sisters of Charity of St. Elizabeth, Convent, 1946-54; asst. adminstr. St. Elizabeths Hosp., Elizabeth, N.J., 1954-57, adminstr., 1957—. Adj. prof. dept. health care Bernard Baruch Coll., N.Y.C., 1975—. Mem. Union County Charter Study Commn., 1973—, Union County Adv. Com. Hosp. and Health Planning Council Met. N.J., Inc. Trustee, Mental Health Assn. of Union County, Tri-Hosp. Fund of Elizabeth, St. Elizabeth Coll., Convent Station, N.J. Fellow Am. Coll. Hosp. Adminstrs.; mem. St. Louis U. Alumni Assn. (past pres., treas.), Union County Urban League, Cath. Hosp. Assn., Am., N.J. (council on govt. relations) hosp. assns., Nat. League Nursing, N.J. Pub. Health Assn., Union County Hosp. Soc. (pres.), Eastern Union County C. of C. Address: 225 Williamson St Elizabeth NJ 07207

MEADOWS, JOHN FOY, minister, Southern Baptist Convention. b. Columbus, Ga., Sept. 10, 1942; s. Foy Cratus and Geneva (Green) M.; m. Norma Katherine Ward, Nov. 22, 1946; children: Scarlet Kay Meadows Bailey, John F., Jr., Christian Lanier. A.A., Pasco-Hernando Coll., 1977; B.A., in Religion, U. N.C.-Charlotte, 1979; M.Div., Luther-Rice Sem., 1985. Ordained to ministry Baptist Ch., 1974. Pastor, Altman Meml. Bapt. Ch., Columbus, Ga., 1974-75, First Bapt. Ch., Lacoochee, Fla., 1976-78; Concord Bapt Ch., Bostic, N.C., 1979-80; New Georgia Bapt. Ch., Villa Rica, Ga., 1980—; Assn. moderator, Tallapoosa Assn., Dallas, Ga., 1981—, missions chmn., 1981-83, nominating com. chmn., 1981-83; Ga. Bapt. exec. com. Ga. Bapt. Conv., 1984-89. Author: (tape albums) Six Steps to Happiness, 1983. Radio pastor New Ga. Bapt. Ch., 1983. Album rec. by John and Norma, Our Favorites, 1983. Contbr. articles to religious publs. Mem. John Meadows Evangelism Assn. Lodge: Columbian Lodge #7. Home: Rev John F Meadows Route 2 Seals Rd Dallas GA 30132 Office: New Georgia Baptist Ch Route 2 Box 529 Villa Rica GA 30180

MEERSON, MICHAEL AXIONOV, priest, Orthodox Church in America; writer; b. Moscow, Aug. 14, 1944; came to U.S., 1973, naturalized, 1980; s. George Solomon Meerson and Valentina Vasilievna Axionov; m. Olga Anatol Schnittke, Aug. 1, 1977; children: Ilia, Elijah. M. in History, Moscow U., 1968; M.Div., St. Vladimir Orthodox Theol. Sem., 1984. Ordained priest Orthodox Church in America, 1978. Rector, Christ the Savior Orthodox Church, N.Y.C., 1978—; adj. prof. Hunter Coll., 1985—. Free-lance writer Radio Liberty, N.Y.C., 1981—. Author: (with Boris Shragin) The Political, Social and Religious Thought of Russian 'Samizdat', An Anthology, 1977. Editor: (Orthodox Almanac) Put, 1983—; (with others) Samosoznanie, 1976. Contbr. articles pub. in Russian, English, French, Italian, Greek and German to jours. Recipient Nabedrenik, Diocese of N.Y., Orthodox Church in America, 1980, Kamilavka, Diocese of N.Y., Orthodox Church in America, 1983. Home: 730 Fort Washington Ave Apt 4H New York NY 10040 Office: Christ the Savior Orthodox Ch 340 E 71st St New York NY 10021

MEGILL, VIRGIL GLEN, JR., minister, media adminstr., United Methodist Ch.; b. Lyons, Kans., Feb. 28, 1924; s. V. Glen and Rosie Madge (Olney) M.; A.B., Coll. Emporia (Kans.), 1946; M.Div., United Theol. Sem., Dayton, Ohio, 1949; M.A., N.Y. U., 1969; postgrad. Union Theol. Sem.-Columbia, 1949-57, Union Theol. Sem. Tchrs. Coll., 1974-75; m. Ruth Elizabeth Armstrong, Nov. 2, 1951; children—V. Glenn III, Margaret Faith, Caroline Beth. Ordained to ministry, 1945; pastor chs., N.J., N.Y.C., Pa., 1949-62; pastor ch., Ephrata, Pa., 1962-71, Drexel Hill, Pa., 1971-74; dir. nat. mass media, Key 73, Madison, N.J., 1972-73; pastor ch., Paterson, N.J., 1974-75, E. Stroudsburg, Pa., 1975—. Organizer, host weekly TV program Open Door, 1975—; bd. dirs. Evang. Deaconess Hosp., Bklyn., 1953-58; v.p. Lower Bucks County (Pa.) Council Chs., 1958-60, pres., 1961-62. Editor, Northeastern Conf. News, 1959-63; editorial asso. Eastern Conf. Herald, 1963-70; editor NRB Daily News, 1972—; chmn. U.S. media office Internat. Congress World Evangelization, 1974; contbg. editor Religious Broadcasting mag., 1976—; contbr. articles to religious jours. Home: 83 S Courtland St East Stroudsburg PA 18301

MEGLI, ROGER VERNON, minister, American Baptist Churches in the U.S.A.; b. Newton, Kans., Nov. 3, 1953; s. Vernon Edgar and Ruth Edith (Pritchett) M.; m. Sandra Ann Daniels, June 17, 1978; children: Kristine Anne, Kathleen Amy. B.A. in Bible, John Brown U., 1975; M.Div., Western Conservative Bapt. Theol. Sem., 1979. Ordained to ministry Baptist Ch., 1983. Assoc. pastor Arbor Lakes Bapt. Ch., Wichita, Kans., 1980; pastor First Bapt. Ch., Peabody, Kans., 1981—; mem. family life com. Am. Bapt. Chs. of South Central Kans., 1984—. Mem. adv. bd. Peabody Meml. Nursing Home, 1983—. Home: 113 W 3d St Peabody KS 66866 Office: First Bapt Ch 3d and Vine Sts Peabody KS 66866

MEIGHEN, DONALD DAVID, minister, United Meth. Ch.; b. San Francisco, Dec. 31, 1944; s. Harry David and Helen Katherine (Morris) M.; B.S., Fairmont State Coll., 1967; M.Div., Meth. Theol. Sch., 1971; m. Mary Miller Gwinn, Aug. 1, 1970; children—Christopher David, Andrew Gwinn. Ordained to ministry, 1970; pastor Meadowdale Ch., Winfield, 1970-74; asso. pastor 1st United Meth. Ch., Fairmont, W.Va., 1974—. Radio announcer, sta. WMMN, 1971, WFGM, 1975— (both Fairmont); modern music column Fairmont Times West-Virginian, 1973—. Named Soil Conservation Minister of Year, Marion County Ministerial Assn., 1974. Mem. N.Am. Council Religious Broadcasters, Greater Fairmont, W.Va. councils chs., Marion County Ministerial Assn., W.Va. United Meth. Communications Commn. Home: 1650 Beverly Rd Fairmont WV 26554 Office: 322 Fairmont Ave Fairmont WV 26554

MEIN, PETER SIMON, priest, Episcopal Ch.; b. Eastwood, England, Jan. 5, 1927; s. John Boddy and Edith Gwendoline (Widdows) M.; came to U.S., 1971; grad. Kelham Theol. Coll., 1948; B.A., Nottingham U., 1955, M.A., 1958; m. Nancy Ann McCleery, May 29, 1971; 1 child, Andrew St. John. Mem. Soc. Sacred Mission, 1954-70, tutor N.T., Kelham Theol. Coll., 1955-61, dean, 1962-70; ordained priest, 1956; prior House of Sacred Mission, Nottingham, 1964-70; chaplain St. Andrews Sch., Middletown, Del., 1971, chaplain, housemaster, 1972—; vis. preacher Westminster Abbey, 1968, 84; Dean Sage speaker, Cornell U., 1972; mem. standing com. Diocese Del., 1975, 80, 85. Mem. Soc. Study Theology (U.K.). Contbr. revs. to Theology, Living Ch. Home and office: St Andrews Sch Middletown DE 19709

MEITZEN, MANFRED OTTO, religious studies educator, columnist; b. Houston, Tex., Dec. 12, 1930; s. Otto Hugo and Laura Emma (Munsch) M.; m. Fredrica Haden Kilmer, May 16, 1970. B.A., Rice U., 1952; M.Div., Wartburg Theol. Sem., Dubuque, Iowa, 1956; Ph.D., Harvard U., 1961. Vicar, Peace Luth. Ch., Menomonie, Wis., 1955, Sharon Luth. Ch., Pasadena, Tex., 1959, Zion Luth. Ch., Houston, 1960; assoc. prof. religious studies Rocky Mt. Coll., Billings, Mont., 1961-65; prof., chmn. dept. religious studies W.Va. U., Morgantown, 1965—. Columnist: Dominion-Post, Morgantown, W.Va., 1975—. Contbr. chpts. books and articles to profl. jours. Harvard Divinity Sch. fellow, 1958; Rockefeller Found. fellow, 1959-60; Sheldon Travelling fellow, 1961. Mem. Am. Acad. Religion, Univ. Profs. for Academic Order (v.p. 1977-79, pres.

1979, dir. 1980-83). Republican. Office: W Va Univ 324 Stansbury Hall Morgantown WV 26506

MELAMED, MEIR MATZLIAH, rabbi, Jewish; b. Izmir, Turkey, Nov. 7, 1919; came to U.S., 1971, naturalized, 1976; s. Yuda and Oro (Melamed) Masliah; m. Noemi Haim, 1952 (div. 1957); children: Leo, Laura; m. 2d Miriam Nelly Levy; children: Orieta-Becky, Lilian-Regina, Lucy. Grad. Yeshivah, Izmir, 1940, Istanbul, Turkey, 1941; diploma of Rabbinate, Izmir, 1944, Israel, 1954, Istanbul, 1954, Ankara, Turkey, 1952. Rabbi, dir. sch. Communedad Sefardi de Montevideo, Montevideo, Uruguay, 1952-57; rabbi, prof. Jewish High Sch., Centro Hebraico Riograndeuse, Porto Alegre, Brazil, 1957-58; rabbi Centro Israelita Brasileiro, Rio de Janeiro, 1958-66, Union Sefaradi, Mexico City, 1966-71, Cuban Sephardic Hebrew Congregation Miami (Fla.), 1971-79; rabbi Rabbinical Assn. Greater Miami, 1971—; pres. Frat. Christians and Jew, Rio de Janeiro, 1958-66; v.p. ecumenical sect. 19th Olympiad, Mexico City, 1968. Author: A Lei de Moises e as Haftarot, 4th edit., 1962; Le Ley de Moises, 1970; Sidur Masliah, 4th edit., 1966; Sidur Matzliah Hashalem y Manual de Judaismo Practico, 1974; Majzor Leyom Kipur, 4th edit., 1968; Majzor Lerosh Hashana, 2d edit., 1981; Meguilat Esther, 1979; Pirke Avot, 1979; Religiones Sectas y Cultos, Vol I, 1981, Vol. II, 1982. Contbr. numerous articles to profl. jours. Recipient diploma Tribuna Israelita, Mexico, 1969; diploma State of Israel; Masada award State of Israel Bonds, 1973. Home: 4578 Royal Palm Ave Miami Beach FL 33140

MELCZEK, DALE JOSEPH, bishop, Roman Catholic Ch.; b. Dearborn, Mich., Nov. 9, 1938; s. Aloysius and Geraldine (Katus) M. A.B., St. Mary Coll., Orchard Lake, Mich., 1960; M.Div., St. John Sem., Plymouth, Mich., 1982; M.A., U. Detroit, 1969; S.T.B., Cath. U. Am., 1964; D.D. (hon.), 1982. Ordained priest Roman Cath. Ch., 1964, consecrated bishop, 1982. Pastor, assoc. pastor various chs., 1964-72; pastor, vicar St. Christine Ch., Detroit, 1972-75; asst. vicar for parishes Archdiocese of Detroit, 1975-77; sec. to archbishop, vicar gen. and consultor, 1977-82, aux. bishop of Detroit, 1982—. Office: Archdiocese of Detroit 1234 Washington Blvd Detroit MI 48226

MELLIN, WILLARD COLBY, JR., minister, Presbyterian Church (U.S.A.); b. Oakmont, Pa., Apr. 11, 1930; s. Willard Colby and Hazel Naomi (Wylie) M.; B.A., Coll. of Wooster, 1952; M.Div. cum laude, Union Theol. Sem., N.Y.C., 1955, Ph.D., 1975; m. Sarah Ketron Spahr, June 22, 1955; children: Stephen Spahr, Thomas Colby, Lilace Ann. Ordained to ministry Presbyn. Ch. (U.S.A.), 1955. Asst. pastor Lake Forest (Ill.) Presbyn. Ch., 1955-59, assoc. pastor, 1959-61; dean's asst. fgn. students Union Sem., N.Y.C., 1961-62, 63-65, asst. dean students, 1962-63; pastor 1st Presbyn. Ch., Akron, Ohio, 1965-70; pastor Riverdale Presbyn. Ch., University Park, Md., 1970—; chmn. united campus ministries bd. U. Md.; mem. exec. com. Prince George's County Community Ministry. Pres. Robert P. Johnson Housing Devel. Corp. Mem. Acad. Parish Clergy, Nat. Capital Presbytery. Lodge: Rotary. Home: 6216 Carrollton Terr Hyattsville MD 20782 Office: 6513 Queens Chapel Rd Hyattsville MD 20782

MELLON, DAVID DUANE, minister, Presbyterian Church USA; b. Duquesne, Pa., Dec. 14, 1931; s. David Duane and Mary Jane (Bennett) M.; m. Nancy Orahood, June 11, 1955; children: Jeffrey David, Janet Marie. B.A., Coll. of Wooster, 1953; M.Div., Pitts. Theol. Sem., 1956; M.Ed., U. Pitts., 1960; D.D. (hon.), Union Bapt. Sem., 1972. Ordained to ministry, 1956. Pastor, First Presbyn. Ch., Brilliant, Ohio, 1956-60, asst. pastor, Akron, Ohio, 1960-63; assoc. pastor West Side Presbyn. Ch., Ridgewood, N.J., 1963-67; exec. dir. Council of Chs. Greater Trenton, N.J., 1967-72, Capitol Region Conf. Chs., Hartford, Conn., 1972-81; rep. Presbyn. Ministers Fund, 1981-84; exec. dir. New Britain Area Conf. Chs., Conn., 1984—. Author: Christian Education in the Church School, 1968. Mem. governing bd. Nat. Council Chs., 1975-81; pres. Consumer Credit Counseling Service of Conn., 1978-81; founding mem., later treas. N. Central Conn. Health Maint. Orgn., 1973-81; mem. gov.'s energy task force State of Conn., 1979-81; mem. Channel 3, WFSB-TV program adv. com., 1977-81, others; bd. dir. Human Relations Agy. of New Britain, 1985—; corporator YMCA, New Britain/Berlin, 1985—; chmn. policy com. Friendship Ctr. Recipient citation Hartford Common Council, 1975; Nat. Merit award in religion Pi Lambda Sigma, 1972. Address: New Britain Area Conf Churches 19 Chestnut St New Britain CT 06051

MELVIN, BILLY ALFRED, clergyman; b. Macon, Ga., Nov. 25, 1929; s. Daniel Henry and Leola Dale (Seidell) M.; student Free Will Baptist Bible Coll., Nashville, 1947-49; B.A., Taylor U., Upland, Ind., 1951; postgrad. Asbury Theol. Sem., Wilmore, Ky., 1951-53; B.D., Union Theol. Sem., Richmond, Va., 1956; D.D., Azusa (Cal.) Coll., 1968; m. Marcia Darlene Eby, Oct. 26, 1952; children—Deborah Ruth, Daniel Henry II. Ordained to ministry Free Will Baptist Ch., 1951; pastor First Free Will Baptist Chs., Newport, Tenn., 1951-53, Richmond, 1953-57, Bethany Ch., Norfolk, Va., 1957-69; exec. sec. Nat. Assn. Free Will Baptists 1957-67; exec. dir. Nat. Assn. Evangelicals, 1967--, Nat. Assn. Christian Schs., 1976—. Home: 420 E Bridle Ln Wheaton IL 60187

MENCHACA, JOEL HUERTA, minister, Centro de Amistad Cristiana; b. Edna, Tex., Sept. 14, 1937; s. Feliciano DelBosque and Catalina (Huerta) M.; m. Maria De Jesus Adame, June 9, 1968; children: Manuela, Catalina, JoElda, Evangelina. Th.B., Latin Am. Theol. Sem., 1978. Pastor, Assembly of God, Henderson, Nev., 1979-83, Echoes of Faith Ministry, Las Vegas, Nev., 1983-85, Centro De Amistad Cristiana, Las Vegas, 1985—. Author: Diario de Oracion, 1984; Desde La Cruz, 1985. Democrat. Home: 3342 Cape Cod Dr Las Vegas NM 89122 Office: Centro De Amistad Cristiana 900 E Karen #A-220 Las Vegas NV 89101

MENCHHOFER, RAYMOND EDGAR, minister, chaplain American Lutheran Church; b. Wooster, Ohio, July 1, 1941; s. Paul Edgar and Vera Spreng (Hall) M.; m. Diane Clayre Gebbhard, Nov. 26, 1964; children: Mark, John, Paul. B.A. cum laude, Capital U., 1964; M.Div., Trinity Luth. Sem., 1967. Ordained to ministry, 1967. Assoc. pastor Good Hope Luth. Ch., Bucyrus, Ohio, 1967-71; pastor St. John's Luth. Ch., Petersburg, Ohio, 1971-73; resident U. Va. Med. Ctr., Charlottesville, 1973-74; chaplain Pauline Warfield Lewis Ctr., Cin., 1974—. Fellow Coll. Chaplains; mem. Am. Protestant Hosp. Assn., Ohio Chaplains Assn. (treas.). Home: 101 Junedale St Cincinnati OH 45218 Office: Pauline Warfield Lewis Ctr 1101 Summit Rd Cincinnati OH 45237

MENDOZA, MARY JULIETTA, provincial adminstrator, Sisters of the Sorrowful Mother; b. Wichita, Kans., July 31, 1930; d. Julio and Maria (Macias) M. Diploma Nursing, St. Francis Sch., Wichita, Kans., 1955; B.S. in Nursing, Marquette U., 1963; M.S. in Community Health, U. Colo., 1973. Missionary, Sagrado Cura&c;ao, Neropolis, Gois, Brazil, 1967-69; local coordinator St. Ann Convent, Truth or Consequence, N.Mex., 1973-75; provincial councilor Tulsa Province, Sisters of the Sorrowful Mother, Broken Arrow, Okla., 1974-78, provincial adminstr., 1978—, del. Rome, 1975, 79, 83. Bd. dirs. St. Mary's Hosp., Roswell, N.Mex., 1978—, St. John Med. Ctr., Tulsa, Okla., 1970, 75-79; trustee Cath. Charities, 1983—. Democrat. Address: 17600 E 51st St S Broken Arrow OK 74012

MENDOZA, SHIRLEY, children's home administrator, Mennonite Brethren Church; b. Flint, Mich., Oct. 4, 1938; d. Lyle and Thelma Juanita (Reed) Haight; m. Overli Mendoza; children: Cleverie Jean, Kimberly Sue, Benjamin Eric, Jonathan, Patricia. B.A. in Bibl. Edn., Columbia Bible Coll., S.C., 1962; diploma in Spanish lang. Rio Grande Bible Inst., Tex., 1964; cert. in missionary internship, Farmington, Mich., 1963. Missionary, Mexican Indian Mission, La Capilla, Hidalgo, Mex., 1964-69; co-dir. for Latin Am., World Missionary Evangelism, Pharr, Tex., 1970-72; co-founder, dir. Children's Haven Internat., Pharr, 1972—. Recipient cert. of recognition System for Integral Devel. of the Family, 1983, 84. Office: Children's Haven Internat Inc 514 S Cage Blvd Pharr TX 78577

MENNICKE, VICTOR OTTOMAR, minister, Lutheran Church-Missouri Synod, fund raiser; b. Reeseville, Wis., Mar. 1, 1927; s. Victor August Walter and Elsie Louise (Reutlinger) M.; m. Geraldine Ellen Patrick, Aug. 23, 1947; children: Ellen Suzanne Mennicke Barnes, Victoria Marie Mennicke Merwin, Patricia Lynn Mennicke Lavine. M.Div., Christ Sem., St. Louis, 1974. Ordained, 1974; charitable estate planner. Exec. staff Concordia Sem., St. Louis, 1969-72, exec. dir. Luth. Ch. Mo. Synod, St. Louis, 1969-74, cons. in devel., 1975-77; dir. plans and programs Concordia Coll., Austin, Tex., 1974-75; dir. Luth. Ch. Am. Found., N.Y.C., 1978-82; pastor Good Shepherd Luth. Ch., Sarasota, Fla., 1982—; adv. dir. Luth. Music Program, Lincoln, Nebr., 1983—; chmn. chaplaincy program Sarasota Ministerial Assn., 1983—; adv. dir. Luth. Ministries Fla., Tampa, 1983—; treas. Luth. Pastoral Conf. Fla. and Ga., Orlando, Fla., 1982—; pres. Bach Found., Holy Trinity Luth. Ch., N.Y.C., 1979-82; mem. Assn. Luth. Devel. Execs. Commd. 2d lt. U.S. Army, 1945, advanced through grades to lt. col., 1967, ret., 1969. Author manuals, booklet. Decorated Legion of Merit, Bronze Star; recipient Bronze medal Concordia Hist. Inst., 1971. Mem. Assn. U.S. Army, Ret. Officers Assn. (Sarasota chaplain 1983—). Republican. Clubs: Cruisemaster (Los Angeles); Sunrise Country (Sarasota). Home: 6325 Approach Rd Sarasota FL 33583 Office: Good Shepherd Luth Ch 5659 Honore Ave Sarasota FL 33583

MENO, JOHN PETER, chorepiscopus Syrian Orthodox Church of Antioch; b. Carlinville, Ill., Aug. 22, 1942; s. John Victor and Margaret Mary (Cena) M.; m. Rolanda A. Abyad, Sept. 14, 1968; 1 child, Peter James. M.A., Am. U. of Beirut, 1969; S.T.M., Union Theol. Sem., 1972. Ordained priest Syrian Orthodox Ch. of Antioch, 1972, elevated to chorepiscopus, 1983. Gen. sec. Archdiocese of Syrian Orthodox Ch. in U.S. and Can., Lodi, N.J., 1972—; cathedral rector St. Mary's Syrian Orthodox Cathedral, Hackensack, N.J., 1975—; co-sec. Standing Conf. of Oriental Orthodox Chs. in Am., N.Y.C., 1973—. Editor: Hymns of the Syrian Orthodox Church of Antioch, 1976. Home: 45 Fairmount Ave Hackensack NJ 07601 Office: Syrian Orthodox Archdiocese 49 Kipp Ave Lodi NJ 07644

MERCER, HERSHEL RAY, minister, Seventh-day Adventist Church; b. Stillwater, Okla., Aug. 24, 1941; s. Wade Haskell and Hazel Irene (Harris) M.; m. Sandra Lee Brown, Sept. 28, 1968; children: John Mitchell, Patricia Kay. B.A., Pacific Union Coll., 1971; M.Div., Andrews U., 1975. Ordained to ministry Seventh-day Adventist Ch., 1977. Pastor Wis. Conf. Seventh-day Adventists, Madison, 1972-79, Okla. Conf., Oklahoma City, 1979-80; pastor Dade City Seventh-day Adventist Ch., Orlando, Fla., 1981—; v.p. bd. trustees E. Pasco Med. Ctr., Zephryhills, Fla., 1981—; mem. sch. bd. E. Pasco Adventist Ednl. Ctr., 19—. Vice pres. Sunrise Spouse Abuser Shelter, Dade City, 1982—; chaplain Pasco County Sheriff's Dept., 1981—, Dade City Police Dept., 1983—. Mem. N.E. Pasco County Ministerial Assn. (pres. 1984). Republican. Lodge: Kiwanis (chmn. 1984). Home: 2114 Moore Dr Dade City FL 33525 Office: Dade City Seventh-day Adventist Ch 901 W Meridian Dade City FL 33525

MERCURIO, ROGER JOHN, priest, Roman Catholic Church; b. St. Louis, Feb. 14, 1918; s. Peter and Cecilia Marie (Stroehle) M. St.L., Cath. U. Am., 1947; S.S.L., Biblicum Institutum, Rome, 1949. Joined Passionist Order, Roman Cath. Ch., 1938, ordained priest, 1944. Prof. scripture Passionist Sem., Louisville, 1949-59, rector, 1959-62, 65-68; rector Passionist Sem., Warrenton, Mo., 1962-65; pastor Immaculate Conception Ch., Chgo., 1968-71; provincial superior Holy Cross Province, Chgo., 1976-83; dir. Passionist Missions, Chgo., 1983—; mem. faculty Maryville Coll., St. Louis, 1965, St. Meinrad Sem., Ind., 1967; mem. priests senate Louisville Archdiocese, 1966-68, Chgo. Archdiocese, 1983—. Contbr. articles to Worship, Cath. Bibl. Quar., Cath. Ency. Mem. Cath. Bibl. Assn. Office: 5700 N Harlem Ave Chicago IL 60631

MERRELL, JAMES LEE, minister, religious journalist, Christian Church (Disciples of Christ); b. Indpls., Oct. 24, 1930; s. Mark W. and Pauline F. (Tucker) M.; m. Barbara Jean Burch, Dec. 21, 1951; children: Deborah Merrell Griffin, Cynthia Merrell Schrader, Staurt. A.B., Ind. U., 1952; M.Div., Christian Theol. Sem., 1956; Litt.D. (hon.), Culver-Stockton Coll., 1972. Ordained to ministry Christian Ch. (Disciples of Christ), 1956. Assoc. editor World Call, Indpls., 1956-66, editor, 1971-73; pastor Crestview Christian Ch., Indpls., 1966-71; editor The Disciple, St. Louis, 1974—. Author: They Live Their Faith, 1958; The Power of One, 1976; Discover the Word in Print, 1979; Finding Faith in the Headlines, 1985. Recipient Faith and Freedom award Religious Heritage of Am., 1983, Hinkhouse-DeRose award Religious Pub. Relations Council, 1979, 83, 84. Mem. Assoc. Ch. Press (1st v.p. 1983-85), Religious Pub. Relations Council, Sigma Delta Chi. Club: St. Louis Press. Home: 5347 Warmwinds Ct Saint Louis MO 63129 Office: Box 179 2721 Pine St Saint Louis MO 63166

MERRILL, EUGENE HAINES, religion educator, Southern Baptist Convention; b. Anson, Maine, Sept. 12, 1934; s. Orrin H. and Ruby M. (Haines) M. m. Janet Louise Hippensteel, Dec. 18, 1960; 1 child, Sonya Leigh. B.A., Bob Jones U., 1957, M.A., 1960, Ph.D., 1963; M.A., NYU, 1970; M.Phil., Columbia U., 1977, Ph.D., 1985. Grad. asst. Bob Jones U., Greenville, S.C., 1958-60, prof. 1963-66; asst. prof. Northeastern Bible Coll., Essex Falls, N.J., 1966-68; prof. Berkshire Christian Coll., Lenox, Mass., 1968-75; assoc. prof. Dallas Theol. Sem., 1975—. Author: An Historical Survey of the Old Testament, 1966; Qumran and Predestination, 1975. Editor: The Bible Knowledge Commentary, 1983; translator New King James Bible, Jeremiah, 1979. Mem. Am. Oriental Soc., Am. Schs. Oriental Research, Evang. Theol. Soc., Near East Archeol. Soc., Soc. Bibl. Lit. Republican. Home: 9314 Waterview Rd Dallas TX 75218 Office: Dallas Theol Sem 3909 Swiss Ave Dallas TX 75204

MERRILL, JOSEPH HARTWELL See *Who's Who in America*, 43rd edition.

MERTENS, MARY SUE, nun, educational administrator, Roman Catholic Church; b. Jefferson City, Mo., June 27, 1944; d. Edward Theodore and Dorothy Catherine (Rackers) M. B.S. in Edn., U. Mo., 1972; M.S. in Ednl. Adminstrn., U. Dayton, 1980. Joined Sisters of Divine Providence, Roman Cath. Ch., 1961; cert. elem. tchr., Mo., 1972. Primary tchr. St. John's Sch., St. Louis, 1964-65, St. Elizabeth Sch., Granite City, Ill., 1965-68, St. Andrew Sch., Tipton, Mo., 1968-69; primary tchr. Ascension Sch., Normandy, Mo., 1969-80, prin., 1980—. Home: 3810 Colonial Normandy MO 63121 Office: Ascension Sch 3801 Nelson Dr Normandy MO 63121

MERZ, JACQUELINE MARIE, religious order administrator, Roman Catholic Church; b. Effingham, Ill., Feb. 18, 1936; d. Cletus Lawrence and Isabel Johanna (Wessel) Merz. B.A. in Econs., Notre Dame Coll., St. Louis, 1961; M.A. in Theology, St. Mary's U., 1973. Joined Sisters of Notre Dame, Roman Catholic Ch., 1956. Asst. religious edn. supr. Diocese of Dallas,

1969-73; provincial councillor Sch. Sisters of Notre Dame, Irving, Tex., 1974-77, provincial leader, 1977—. Mem. Leadership Conf. of Religious Women, Tex. Cath. Conf. (maj. superiors div.). Democrat. Home and Office: 1451 E Northgate Irving TX 75062

MESSER, DONALD EDWARD, minister, educational administrator United Meth. Ch.; b. Kimball, S.D., Mar. 5, 1941; s. Mr. and Mrs. George Messer; student Madras (India) Christian Coll., 1961-62; B.A., Dakota Wesleyan U., 1963, D.H.L. (hon.), 1977; postgrad. Garrett Theol. Sem., summer 1965; M.Div. magna cum laude, Boston U., 1966, Ph.D. (Jacob Sleeper and Alumni fellow 1966-67, Dempster fellow 1967-68, Rockefeller fellow 1968-69), 1969; postgrad. Harvard, 1966-67; m. Bonnie Jeanne Nagel, Aug. 30, 1964; children: Christine Marie, Kent Donald. Ordained to ministry, 1966; teaching asst. behavioral scis. Boston U. Coll. Bus. Adminstrn., 1967-68; adminstrv. asst. to Commr. Gilbert H. Caldwell, Mass. Commn. Against Discrimination, Boston, 1968-69; asst. prof. sociology Augustana Coll., Sioux Falls, S.D., 1969-71; asso. pastor First United Meth. Ch., Sioux Falls, 1969-71; pres. Dakota Wesleyan U., Mitchell, 1971-81, Iliff Sch. Theology, Denver, 1981—. Mem. steering com. Rosebud Christian Relief Drive; mem. bd. ministry S.D. Conf.; bd. mgrs. Pastors Sch., N. and S.D. S.D. commr. Edn. Commn. of States, 1973—; co-chairperson S.D. Citizens Com. on Corrections, 1975-76; pres. S.D. Found. Pvt. Colls., 1973-75; chmn. bd. trsutees Colls. of Mid-Am., Inc., 1975. Recipient Oxnam-Liebman award for advancement interracial understanding Boston U., 1965, Outstanding Young Man in S.D. award S.D. Jaycees, 1974, Distinguished Service award Mitchell Jaycees, 1974, Key to City of Mitchell, 1975; named one of Ten Outstanding Young Men Am., U.S. Jaycees, 1975. Mem. S.D. Assn. Pvt. Colls (pres. 1976—), Phi Kappa Phi, Sigma Tau Delta, Phi Kappa Delta. Author: Christian Ethics and Political Action, 1983. Contbr. articles to religious jours. Office: Iliff Sch Theology 2201 S University Blvd Denver CO 80210

MESTICE, ANTHONY F. See *Who's Who in America*, 43rd edition.

METTAYER, ARTHUR, religious educator, priest, Roman Catholic Church; b. Drummondville, Que., Can., Nov. 11, 1929; s. Joseph Alexandre and Marguerite (Houle) M. B.A., Universite Laval (Nicolet, Que.), 1951; Th.M., Universite Gregorienne, Rome, 1956; Dr. Religious Scis., Universite de Strasbourg, 1976. Ordained priest Roman Cath. Ch., 1954. Prof. theology, Nicolet Sem., 1956-69; dean of theology Universite du Quebec, Trois-Rivieres, Que., Can., 1969-74, 76-81, prof. theology, 1981—. Author numerous religious books; contbr. articles to religious jours. Mem. Assn. Canadienne for the Advancement of Sci., Can. Soc. Theology (treas. 1972-74, pres. 1983—). Office: Universite du Quebec 3350 Blvd des Forges Trois-Rivieres PQ G9A 5H7 Canada

METTLER, KENNETH GLEN, minister, Evangelical Free Church America; b. Amery, Wis., Nov. 27, 1948; s. Glen Joseph and Ruth Magdalene (Eliason) M.; B.Th., St. Paul Bible Coll., 1971; M.Div., So. Sem., 1976, D.Div., 1978; m. Barbara Jean Litzkow, June 16, 1972; children: David Allen, Laura Ruth. Ordained to ministry Evang. Free Ch. Am., 1976; lic. counselor Am. Assn. Cert. Counsellors. Pastor Calvary Bible Ch., Viper, Ky., 1971—, Cody Bible Ch., Red Fox, Ky., 1973-74; sec. Ky. Dist. Assn. Evangel. Free Ch., 1972, vice chmn., 1973-75, chmn., 1976—, dist. supt. East-Central dist. conf., 1975—; speaker morning devotional radio program, 1974—; dir. Twin Rocks Bible Camp, 1975-82, Perry County Sr. Citizens Devotional Program. chaplain Appalachian Hosp., Hazard, Ky. Named Ky. col., 1976. Mem. Hazard-Perry County Ministerial Assn. (pres. 1983—). Home: General Delivery Viper KY 41774

METZGER, BRUCE MANNING, minister, former educator, Presbyn. Ch. U.S.; b. Middletown, Pa., Feb. 9, 1914; s. Maurice R. and Anna (Manning) M.; B.A., Lebanon Valley Coll., 1935; Th.B., Princeton Theol. Sem., 1938, Th.M., 1939; M.A., Princeton U., 1940, Ph.D., 1942; D.D., Lebanon Valley Coll., 1951, St. Andrews U., 1964; L.H.D., Findlay Coll., 1962; D.Theol., U. Munster, 1970; m. Isobel E. Mackay, July 7, 1944; children: John Mackay, James Bruce. Ordained to ministry, 1939; mem. faculty Princeton (N.J.) Theol. Sem. 1940—, prof. N.T., 1954-64, George L. Collord prof. N.T. lang. and lit., 1964-84, emeritus prof., 1984—. Vis. lectr. Presbyn. Sem. of the South, Campinas, Brazil, 1952; vis. scholar Tyndale House, Cambridge (Eng.) U., 1969; distinguished vis. prof. Fuller Theol. Sem., 1970; mem. Inst. for Advanced Study, Princeton, 1964, 74; vis. fellow Wolfson Coll., Oxford U., 1979; mem. adv. com. Thesaurus Linguae Graecae, 1972-78; chmn. Revised Standard Version Bible Com., 1975—; mem. Kuratorium, Vetus Latina Inst., Monastery of Beuron (Germany), 1961—; mem. mng. com. Am. Sch. Classical Studies, Athens, Greece. Vis. fellow, Clare Hall U. Cambridge (England), 1974; hon. fellow Higher Inst. Coptic Studies, Cairo, 1955—. Fellow Brit. Acad. (corr.); mem. Soc. Bibl. Lit. (pres., 1971), Studiorum Novi Testamenti Societas (pres. 1972), N. Am. Patristic Soc. (pres., 1972). Author: Historical and Literary Studies, Pagan, Jewish and Christian, 1968; Index to Periodical Literature on the Apostle Paul, rev. edit., 1970; A Textual Commentary on the Greek New Testament, 1971; The Early Versions of the New Testament, their Origin, Transmission, and Limitations, 1977; numerous others. Editor: New Testament Tools and Studies, vols. I - X. Contbr. articles to profl. jours. Office: Princeton Theological Seminary Princeton NJ 08542

METZGER, CHARLES LEE, minister, Gen. Assn. Regular Bapt. Chs.; b. Mishawaka, Ind., Apr. 19, 1933; s. John C. and Pearl (Whisman) M.; student Taylor U., 1957-58; Th.B., Bapt. Bible Sem., 1962; M.R.E., Grace Theol. Sem., 1972; postgrad. Toledo Bible Coll., 1974—; m. Barbara M. Hall, Mar. 23, 1957; children—Cindy, Donna, David, Cheryl. Ordained to ministry, 1964; pastor Thurman (N.Y.) Bapt. Ch., 1964-69, Knowlhurst Bapt. Ch., Stony Creek, N.Y., 1965-69, Paul's Chapel, Winamac, Ind., 1970-71, 1st Bapt. Ch., Portage, Ind., 1972—. Mem. and chmn. extension com. Council of Nine Calumet Fellowship of Regular Bapt. Chs.; mem. Calumet Bapt. Sch. Bd.; mem. Com. Concerned Regular Bapts.; established Portage Bapt. Bible Inst., 1974. Home: 2780 Vivian St Portage IN 46368 Office: PO Box 34 Portage IN 46368

METZGER, KURT LEO, rabbi, Reform Jewish Congregations; b. Nuernberg, Germany, Dec. 10, 1909; came to U.S., 1939; s. Nathan and Sali (Habermann) M.; m. Lore Ruth Scharff, Dec. 30, 1942; 1 child, Ralph Bernard. Rabbi, Juedisch-Theologisches Seminar, 1929-34; Ph.D., Universitaet Breslau, 1935; D.H.L., Hebrew Union Coll., 1966. Ordained rabbi, 1934. Rabbi, Congregation Landau/Pfalz, Germany, 1935-38, Nuernberg, 1938-39, Congregation B'nai Israel, Connellsville, Pa., 1940-41, Congregation Temple of Israel, Amsterdam, N.Y., 1941-42, Congregation Temple Beth-El, Glens Falls, N.Y., 1942-62, Bradford, Pa., 1962-70, Congregation Temple B'nai Israel, Olean, N.Y., 1963-70, Beth Am Temple, Pearl River, N.Y., 1970-72, Temple Beth-El, Monroe, N.Y., 1973—; prof. Bibl. antiquities Christ the King Sem., St. Bonaventure U., N.Y., 1967-70; chaplain Great Meadow Correctional Facility, Comstock, N.Y., 1946-62, N.Y. Vets. Camp, Mt. McGregor, 1946-60, Vets. Hosp., Saratoga Springs, N.Y., 1948-51, Warren State Hosp., Pa., 1968-70, Camp LaGuardia, Chester, N.Y., 1973-76, Wallkill Correctional Facility, N.Y., 1973—, Mid-Orange Correctional Facility, 1977—; v.p. Capital Dist. Bd. Rabbis, 1960-62; rabbinical advisor Central N.Y. Fedn. Temple Youth, 1971-72. Editor Das Juedische Nachrichtenblatt fuer die Rheinpfalz, 1936-38; Students Prayer Book, 1950; Syllabus of Jewish Holidays, 1960; Manual for Jewish Correctional chaplains, 1962; Manual for Chaplains in Correctional Institutions, 1961. Recipient citation N.Y. region Anti-Defamation League of B'nai B'rith, 1955; J.X. Cohen Chaplain of Yr. award, 1981; named hon. rabbi Jewish Congregation of Nuernberg, W. Ger., 1977. Mem. Adriondack Ministerial Fellowship (pres. 1945-46, 55-56), Am. Jewish Correctional Chaplains Assn. (pres. 1960-62), Central Conf. Am. Rabbis, N.Y. Bd. Rabbis, Rockland County Bd. Rabbis, Monroe Clergy Assn. Lodge: B'nai B'rith, Rotary, Masons. Home: 32 Amy Todt Dr Monroe NY 10950 Office: Monroe Temple Liberal Judaism 314 N Main St Monroe NY 10950

MEUSCHKE, PAUL JOHN, minister, United Methodist Church; b. Castle Shannon, Pa., Dec. 11, 1927; s. John and Flora Ann (Voigtmann) M.; m. I. Lucille Lewis, May 17, 1956; children: David Paul, Eric Lewis. B.A., U. Pitts., 1950; B.Div., Drew U., 1953; S.T.M., Drew U., 1954; D.Div. (hon.), Ohio No. U., 1973. Ordained to ministry, 1953. Pastor, Creighton Ctr. United Meth. Ch., Pa., 1954-59, Dormont United Meth. Ch., Pa., 1959-64; sr. pastor Franklin St. United Meth. Ch., Johnstown, Pa., 1964-70; Pitts. dist. supt. W. Pa. United Meth. Ch., 1970-72; sr. pastor Baldwin Community United Meth. Ch., Pitts., 1972-78; Butler dist. supt. W. Pa. United Meth. Ch., 1978-84; sr. pastor South Ave. United Meth. Ch., Wilkinsburg, Pa., 1984—; del. N.E. Jurisdiction Conf., 1966, 72, 76, 80, 84, Gen. Conf., 1972, 80, 84. Trustee Albright Coll., 1974—; incorporator Johnstown Day Ctr., Pa., 1968; bd. incorporators Lee Hosp., Johnstown, 1968-70; pres. Zoar Home for Mothers and Children, Allison Park, Pa., 1976-78; bd. dirs. United Way, Johnstown, 1967-70. Served with U.S. Army, 1946-47. Lodges: Lions (dir. 1966-68), Kiwanis, Rotary. Home: 1074 Old Gate Rd Pittsburgh PA 15235 Office: South Ave United Meth Ch 733 South Ave Pittsburgh PA 15221

MEUSER, FREDERICK WILLIAM See *Who's Who in America*, 43rd edition.

MEWBORN, JAMES THOMAS, minister, Southern Baptist Convention; b. Athens, Ga., Dec. 14, 1946; s. Clifford E. and Pauline E. (James) M.; m. Barbara Frances Head, Dec. 16, 1970. B.F.A., U. Ga., 1969; M.Div., Southeastern Bapt. Theol. Sem., 1980; D.Min. candidate Emory U., since 19—. Ordained to ministry Baptist Ch., 1980. Pastor, Demorest Bapt. Ch., Ga., 1980—; moderator Habersham Bapt. Assn., 1981-84, pres. Pastors Conf., 1980-83; instr. Ga. Bapt. Edn. Extension Ctr., Clarkesville, 1983-84, dean, Demorest, 1984-85. Served with U.S. Army, 1969-72. Mem. Phi Kappa Phi. Democrat. Home: PO Box 65 Demorest GA 30535 Office: Demorest Baptist Ch 196 Central Ave Demorest GA 30535

MEYER, CHARLES ROBERT, minister, United Presbyn. Ch. in U.S.A.; b. Jefferson County, Ohio, June 19, 1934; s. Charles Herman and Ethel Lucy (Coulter) M.; B.S., Waynesburg Coll., 1960; B.D., Dubuque U. Theol. Sem., 1964, M.Div., 1967; m. June 21, 1969; children—Christa Jo, Lottie Ann. Ordained to ministry, 1965; pastor chs., Beech Creek and Mill Hall, Pa., 1965-66; chaplain U.S. Army, 1966-69; pastor Bellwood (Pa.) Logan Valley Presbyn. Ch., 1969-73, 1st Presbyn. Ch., Ridgway, Pa., 1973—. Mem. Blair County (Pa.) Mental Health Bd., 1970-73, mem. advisory bd. retardation and tng. program, 1970-73; mem. Bellwood System Sch. Bd., Blair County, 1971-73; trustee Elk County (Pa.) Gen. Hosp., 1975-76; mem. Ridgway Borough Council, 1976-80, pres., 1976-77. Decorated Bronze Star medal. Mem. Assn. Presbyn. Christian Educators, United Presbyn. Ch. Hist. Soc., Nat. Geog. Soc. Contbr. articles to newspapers. Home: 132 Center St Ridgway PA 15853 Office: 119 Center St Ridgway PA 15853

MEYER, DENNIS ALFRED, clergyman, American Lutheran Church; b. Harvey, Ill., Jan. 14, 1949; s. Alfred E. and Minnie B. (Stricker) M.; m. Sally Marie Schmidt, May 25, 1980; children: Kimberly K. Simmons, Barbara Anne Simmons, Maren Marie Elise. A.B., Stanford U., 1971; M.Div., Yale U., 1975. Ordained to ministry American Lutheran Ch., 1975. Asst. pastor Am. Luth. Ch., Rantoul, Ill., 1976-80; pastor Medill Ave. Luth. Ch., Chgo., 1980—; del. Am. Luth. Ch. gen. conv., Moorhead, Minn., 1978; vice chmn. E. Central Conf., Ill., 1979-80; mem. Ill. Dist. Div. for Service and Mission in Am. Com., 1981—, chmn. W. Chgo. Conf., 1981—. Mem. Liturg. Conf. Club: Exchange (bd. dirs. 1978-80). Home: 4907 W Medill Ave Chicago IL 60639 Office: Medill Ave Luth Ch 4917 W Medill Ave Chicago IL 60639

MEYER, DOUGLAS LEROY, clergyman, American Lutheran Church; b. Albert Lea, Minn., July 13, 1951; s. Donald LeRoy and Ona (Knudson) M.; m. Christine Ann Nelson, June 22, 1975; children: Andrew Martin, Timothy Paul. B.A., Augustana Coll., 1973; M.Div., Luther Theol. Sem., 1977. Ordained to ministry Luth. Ch., 1977. Pastor, Trinity Luth. Ch., Chgo., 1977-82, Cross of Glory Luth. Ch., Lockport, Ill., 1982—; chmn. conf. Service and Mission Com., Am. Luth. Ch., 1978—, del. nat. conv., Mpls., 1980; dir. S. Area Luth. Social Services Ill., Chgo., 1980—; adv. mem. Luth. Family Mission, Chgo., 1979—. Bd. dirs. Mid-Am. Assn. Deaf-Blind, Chgo., 1980—. Mem. Am. Acad. Religion, Soc. Bibl. Lit. Club: Kiwanis. Home: 15550 Badger Ln Lockport IL 60441 Office: Cross of Glory Luth Ch 15625 Bell Rd Lockport IL 60441

MEYER, JOHN CHARLES, religious studies educator, Roman Catholic Church. b. Dubuque, Iowa, Aug. 12, 1934; s. George Walter and Mary Helen (Schmitt) M.; m. Mary Claire Wesenberg, July 22, 1970; 1 child, John David. B.A., Loras Coll., 1956; M.A., S.T.G., Louvain U. (Belgium), 1960; Ph.D., Cath. U. Am., 1968. Staff Roman Cath. univs., Iowa and Md., 1960-69; assoc. prof. religious studies Bradley U., Peoria, Ill., 1969—; asst. pastor St. Edward Ch., Waterloo, Iowa, 1960-62. Author: Christian Beliefs and Teachings, 1981; contbr. articles to religious jours. Pres. Peoria Assn. Retarded Citizens, 1984-85; bd. dirs. Heart of Ill. Infant Devel. Ctr., 1984-85; pres. bd. dirs. Resource Assistance Found., 1985; v.p. bd. dirs. PARC Devel. Homes, 1983-85; mem. Care Decisions Com., St. Francis Med. Ctr., Peoria, 1984-85. Mem. Am. Acad. Religion, Coll. Theology Soc., Am. Assn. Mental Deficiency, Cath. Theol. Soc. Am. Home: 3026 W Greenbriar Ln Peoria IL 61614 Office: Bradley U Peoria IL 61625

MEYER, JON CLEMENT, religious organization executive, American Lutheran Church; b. Manitowoc, Wis., Dec. 8, 1952; s. Conrad W. and Clementine J. (Revolinsky) M.; m. Cheryl L. Boyum, Aug. 25, 1973; children: Sarah E., Erik J. B.Music, U. Wis.-Madison, 1975; M.Music, Northwestern U., 1976. Cert. ch. bus. adminstr., Am. Luth. Ch. Bus. adminstr. First English Luth. Ch., Appleton, Wis., 1979—; del. Am. Luth. Ch. Gen. Conv., San Diego, 1982. Lodge: Kiwanis (sec. Appleton chpt. 1981-83, v.p. 1984). Home and Office: 326 E North St Appleton WI 54911

MEYER, KENNETH M., divinity school president, Evangelical Church; b. Chgo., Nov. 27, 1932; s. Kenneth and Lorraine B. (Reiff) M.; m. Carol Ebner, June 12, 1953; children: Keith, Kevin, Caryn. Student Greenville Coll., 1950, No. Bapt. Sem., 1951-53; M.Div., Trinity Evang. Div. Sch., 1956; postgrad. Wheaton Coll., 1957-59; D.Min., Luther Rice Sem., 1978. Ordained to ministry Evang. Free Ch. Sr. pastor Glenview Evang. Free Ch., 1955-60, Crystal Ch., Mpls., 1960-66, First Ch., Rockford, Ill., 1969-74; now pres. Trinity Evang. Div. Sch., Deerfield, Ill. Author: Turning Point Psalms, Clear Trumpets; Homeletical Patterns of Apostle Paul. Mem. Nat. Assn. Evangs., Evang. Theol. Soc., Assn. Evang. Sems., Assn. Theol. Schs.

MEYER, LAURENCE LOUIS, minister, Lutheran Church-Missouri Synod. B. Rockford, Ill., Jan. 26, 1940; s. Louis John Herman and Leona Anna (Lorenz) M.; m. Ona Ruth Klema, July 31, 1965; children: Michael Laurence, David John, Jonathan Louis Rudolph. A.A., Concordia Coll., 1960; B.A., Concordia Coll., 1962; M.Div., Concordia Sem., 1966. Ordained to ministry, Luth. Ch.-Mo. Synod, 1966. Pastor St. Peter's Ch., Bethlehem Luth. Ch., Waterville and Elysien, Minn., 1966-70, Emanuel Luth. Ch., Hamburg, Minn., 1970-82, Redeemer Luth. Ch., Richland, Wash., 1982—; editor Minn. South Luth. Dist. Luth. Ch. Mo. Synod, Mpls., 1974-82, chmn. pub. relations, 1979-82, pastoral advisor, 1979-82, mem. stewardship com. and communications com. Northwest Dist., Portland, Oreg., 1984—. Contbr. articles to profl. jours. Mem. Bi-Centennial Celebration Com., Norwood, Minn., 1976. Home: 518 Thayer Dr Richland WA 99352 Office: Redeemer Luth Ch 520 Thayer Dr Richland WA 99352

MEYER, LESTER ALLEN, minister, religious organization executive, United Methodist Church; b. Beaver, Okla., Apr. 26, 1923; s. James Lester and Leah Rachel (Fox) M.; m. Mattie Ada Cozart, June 17, 1944; children: Carol, Richard, Annette. B.A., Phillips U., 1948; postgrad. Perkins Sch. Theology; B.D., So. Meth. U., 1950; D.D. (hon.), Oklahoma City U., 1970. Ordained to ministry United Meth. Ch., 1950. Minister Linwood United Meth. Ch., Oklahoma City, 1965-70; dir. conf. council on ministries United Meth. Ch., Oklahoma City, 1970-73; supt. Stillwater dist. United Meth. Ch., Okla., 1973-76, Tulsa dist., 1976-79; minister United Meth. Ch. of Nichols Hills, Oklahoma City, 1979—. Trustee Oklahoma City U., 1970—, Philander Smith Coll., Little Rock, 1976—. Served with USN, 1942-45. Democrat. Home: 1707 Huntington Oklahoma City OK 73116 Office: United Meth Ch of Nichols Hills 6517 NW Grand Blvd Oklahoma City OK 73116

MEYER, NELSON CRAIG, minister, social service administrator, American Lutheran Church; b. Lincoln, Nebr., Oct. 2, 1942; s. Elmer Herman and Maria Johanna (Folken) M.; m. Shirley Charlotte Friederich, June 5, 1965; children: Kimberle Lynne, Jonathan Craig. B.A., Wartburg Coll., 1964, M.Div., 1968. Ordained to ministry Am. Luth. Ch., 1968. Pastor, Luth. Ch. of Cross, Cin., 1968-74; dir. family life edn. Luth. Social Service/Miami Valley, Dayton, Ohio, 1974-79; dir. family life enrichment Luth. Social Service Mich., Detroit, 1979-83; pres. Luth. Social Services Central Ohio, Columbus, 1983—. Contbr. articles to religious publs. Home: 1375 Sherbrooke Pl Columbus OH 43209 Office: Luth Social Services Central Ohio 57 E Main St Columbus OH 43215

MEYER, PAUL WILLIAM, New Testament educator; b. Raipur, India, May 31, 1924 (parents Am. citizens); s. Armin Frederick and Hulda Dorothea (Klein) M.; B.A., Elmhurst Coll., 1945; B.D., Union Theol. Sem., 1949, Th.D., 1955; m. Mary Louise Yonker, Sept. 3, 1948; children: Katherine Priode, Elizabeth Cooper. Lectr., Union Theol. Sem., N.Y.C., 1951-52, instr., 1952-54; asst. prof. Div. Sch., Yale U., 1954-62, assoc. prof., 1962-64; prof. Colgate Rochester (N.Y.) Div. Sch., 1964-70, prof. N.T., Div. Sch., Vanderbilt U., Nashville, 1970-78; Helen H.P. Manson prof. N.T. lit. and exegisis Princeton Theol. Sem., 1978—. Morse fellow and Fulbright Research grantee, 1961-62. Mem. Soc. Bibl. Lit., Studiorum Novi Testamenti Societas, Am. Theol. Soc. Address: Princeton Theological Seminary CN821 Princeton NJ 08542

MEYER, SAMUEL DAVID, minister, Seventh-day Adventists; b. N.Y.C., Nov. 26, 1925; s. Theodore and Louvenia (Troupe) M.; B.A., Emmanuel Missionary Coll. (name later changed to Andrews U.), 1947; m. Gloria Lee Vaughn, Dec. 28, 1947; children—Anthony, Pamela, Charles, Donna, Sibyl. Ordained to ministry, 1952; pastor chs., Dallas, 1948-49, Ft. Worth, 1949-51, Baton Rouge, 1951-53, Kansas City, Kans., 1953-59, Omaha, 1959-62, Chgo., 1962-69, Los Angeles, 1969-74; pres. Central States conf. Seventh-day Adventists, Kansas City, Mo., 1974—. Mem. adv. coms. Gen. conf. Seventh-day Adventists. Trustee Oakwood Coll., Huntsville, Ala., Union Coll., Lincoln, Nebr., Shawnee Mission (Kans.) Med. Center, Christian Record Braille Found., Lincoln; bd. dirs. Pacific Press Publ. Assn., Mountain View, Calif. Home: 7924 Pennsylvania Ave Kansas City MO 64114 Office: 5737 Swope Pkwy Kansas City MO 64130

MEYERS, CAROL L., theology educator, Conservative Reconstructionist Jewish; b. Wilkes Barre, Pa., Nov. 26, 1942; d. Harry J. and Irene R. (Winkler) Lyons; m. Eric Mark Meyers, June 25, 1964; children: Julie Kate, Dina Elisa. A.B. with honors, Wellesley Coll., 1964; M.A. in Near Eastern and Judaic Studies, Brandeis U., 1966, Ph.D., 1975. Area supr. Joint Expdn. to Tell Gezer, Israel, 1964-67; editorial asst., asst. to registrar, Ashdod Excavation Project, Israel, 1963, 64-65; quadrangle dir. Brandeis U., Waltham, Mass., 1965-67; teaching asst. Boston Area Seminar Internat. Students, 1965; area supr., lectr. Joint Expdn. to Khirbet Shema, Israel, 1970-71; area supr., 1971, field supr., 1972, assoc. dir. Joint Expdn. to Meiron, Israel, 1978; instr. Bible, Acad. Jewish Studies Without Walls, N.Y.C., 1974-78; instr. Ctr. Continuing Edn., Duke U., Durham, N.C., 1978-79, asst. prof. religion, Duke U., 1977-84, assoc. prof., 1984—; cons., lectr. in field. Author: The Tabernacle Menorah, 1976, Excavations at Ancient Meiron, Upper Galilee, Israel, 1971-72, 74-75, 77, 81, The Word of the Lord Shall Go Forth, 1983. Contbr. articles to profl. jours. Bd. dirs. Bethel Community, Durham, 1980. Wellesley Coll. scholar, 1962-64; Brandeis U. fellow, 1967-69; Meml. Found. Jewish Culture fellow, 1968-69; Thayer fellow Albright Inst. Archeol. Research, Jerusalem, 1975-76; NEH fellow, 1982-83; grantee Ednl. Found. Girls, 1963, 64, Brandeis U., 1966, Undergrad. Tchng. Council Duke U., 1978-79, Coop. Program in Judaic Studies, 1981. Mem. Jewish Fedn., Am. Acad. Religion, Am. Sch. Oriental Research (fellowship com. 1979-82, editorial com. 1978—), Archaeol. Inst. Am. (v.p. 1976, sec. treas. 1984—), Assn. Jewish Studies, Brit. Sch. Archaeology Jerusalem, Cath. Bibl. Assn., Albright Inst. Archaeol. Research (v.p. 1982—), Israel Exploration Soc., Soc. Bibl. Lit. (steering com. seminar on monarchy 1982, chmn. seminar 1981), Soc. for Values Higher Edn. Club: Hadassah (edn. chmn. 1970-71). Home: 3202 Waterbury Dr Durham NC 27707 Office: Duke U Dept Religion PO Box 4735 Durham NC 27706

MEYERS, JOHN FRANCIS, educational association executive; b. Altoona, Pa., July 26, 1930; s. George and Magdalene (Keller) M. A.B., Pontifical Coll. Josephinum, Columbus, Ohio, 1952, M.Div., 1975, D.Litt. (hon.), 1976; M.A., Cath. U. Am., 1959; postgrad. NYU, summers 1961-62; Ed.D., N. Tex. State U., 1964. Ordained priest, Roman Cath. Ch., 1956. Asst. pastor Holy Name Parish, Ft. Worth, 1956-58; dean students, lectr. U. Dallas, 1959-61; asst. supt. schs. Diocesan Schs. Dallas, 1960-61, diocesan supt. schs., 1961-67; pastor Immaculate Conception Parish, Tyler, Tex., 1967-68; exec. sec. dept. chief adminstrs. Cath. edn. Nat. Cath. Ednl. Assn., Washington, 1968-74, v.p. div. fundamental edn., 1970-74, acting pres., 1972-74, pres., 1974—; pres. Council Am. Pvt. Edn., Inc., 1981—; trustee Pontifical Coll. Josephinum, 1973—; bd. dirs. Internat. Cath. Ednl. Assn., 1978—, Confederacion Interamericana de Education Catolica, 1977—. Served to lt. USNR, 1963-69. Mem. Am. Assn. Sch. Adminstrs., Religious Edn. Assn., Phi Delta Kappa. Author: (with Thomas Sullivan) Focus on American Catechetics: A Commentary on the General Catechetical Directory, 1972; exec. editor: Criteria for the Evaluation of Religious Education Programs, 1970; A Curriculum Guide for Continuous Progress in Religious Education, 1973; The Qualities and Competencies of the Religion Teacher, 1973; co-editor: Boards of Education: A Primer, 1972. Contbr. articles to profl. jours. Office: Nat Cath Ednl Assn 1077 30th St NW Suite 100 Washington DC 20007

MICHAEL, DARREN LLOYD, ch. ofcl., Seventh-day Adventist Ch. in Can.; b. Simla, U.P., India, Aug. 15, 1923; s. Thomas John and Phyllis Clare (Campbell) M.; B.Th., Atlantic Union Coll., 1946; M.A., Andrews U., 1947; LL.B., Osgoode Hall Law Sch., 1964; m. Marilyn Ruth West, June 27, 1943; children—John Collin, Charlotte Joan (Mrs. William B. Skwarchuk), Janice Cheryl (Mrs. Barry N. Fenton), Carole Jeannine, Christopher James. Ordained to ministry, 1950; minister Ont. chs., 1945-52; exec. sec. dept. pub. affairs Seventh-day Adventist Ch. in Can., Oshawa, Ont., 1952—, lawyer, gen. counsel, 1966—. Trustee Kingsway Coll., Oshawa, 1952-76. Home: 314 Labrador Dr Oshawa ON L1H 3E9 Canada Office: 181 University Ave Toronto ON M5H 2X7 Canada also 11 Simcoe St N Oshawa ON L1G 3R7 Canada

MICHAELS, MURIEL MADELINE, minister, American Baptist Churches in the U.S.A.; b. McAlester, Okla., June 8, 1926; d. Albert Kouri and Beatrice Hays; m. Bernard Ross Michaels, June 19, 1948; children: Ross Edward, Danny Linn, Cynthia Sue. B.A., U. Denver, 1968, M.S.W., 1978; M.Div., Iliff Sch. Theology, 1980. Ordained to ministry Am. Bapt. Chs. in the U.S.A., 1980; lic. social worker, Colo. Chaplain, Bapt. Home Assn., Wheatridge, Colo., 1981—. Mem. Ministers Council Am. Bapt. Chs., Rocky Mountain Ministers Council Am. Bapt. Chs. (v.p. area II East 1983—). Democrat. Office: Bapt Home Assn 4790 Tabor St Wheat Ridge CO 80033

MICHAELSON, ANN MARIE, director of religious education, Roman Catholic Church; b. Johnstown, N.Y., June 20, 1939; d. Henry John and Margaret Catherine (Mylott) M. A.A., Maria Coll., Albany, 1961; B.E., Coll. St. Rose, Albany, 1969; M.R.E., St. Michaels Coll., Winooski, Vt., 1978. Joined Sisters of Mercy, Roman Cath. Ch., 1957. Tchr. elem. sch. Diocese of Albany, N.Y., 1961-74; dir. religious edn. Holy Family Cathedral Parish, Anchorage, 1974-78; tchr. religion Mercy High Sch., Albany, 1978-82; dir. religious edn. St. Margaret Mary Parish, Albany, 1982—; expert, lectr. Monarch Butterfly/Spiritual, 1969—. Mem. Religious Edn. Assn. of U.S. and Can., Nat. Assn. Parish Coordinators/Dirs. Religious Edn. Avocation: gardening. Office: St Margaret Mary Parish 1168 Western Ave Albany NY 12203

MICHEL, DAVID LAMAR, minister, Lutheran Church in America; b. Springfield, Ohio, Dec. 22, 1926; s. Arthur Paul and Ella Mae (Wagner) M.; m. Jeannine Ilo Wright, Mar. 17, 1951; children: Susan, Rebecca, Jonathan, Joan. B.A., Valparaiso U., 1951; M.Div., Hamma Sch. Theol., 1966; postgrad. Wright State Coll., 1971-72. Ordained to ministry Lutheran Ch. in Am., 1966. Asst. pastor First Luth. Ch., Springfield, 1966-67; asst. to pres. Hamma Sch. of Theol. Springfield, 1966-74; pastor Casstown Luth. Ch., Casstown, Ohio, 1967-71; dir. devel. Luth. Social Services, Balt., 1974-79; exec. dir., chaplain Md. Homes for Handicapped Inc., Balt., 1977—; organized corporation Md. Homes for Handicapped, Balt., 1976. Author: (survey) Historic Old Salem Restoration, 1976. Editor mag. Hamma Digest, 1965-74, newspaper Venture in Services, 1974-79. Museum organizor Historical Old Salem, Catonsville, Md., 1976. Served to pfc USMC, 1944-46; PTO. Recipient Distinguished Service award Hamma Sch. of Theol., 1974. Mem. Am. Assn. for Mental Deficiency, 1981—, Directorate, Balt. City Health Dept. 1980—, Md. of Dirs., 1981—. Home: 832 Glen Allen Dr Baltimore MD 21229 Office: Maryland Homes for Handicapped Inc 35 E 25th St Baltimore MD 21218

MICHELMAN, HENRY D. Rabbi, exec. v.p. Synagogue Council of Am., N.Y.C. Office: Synagogue Council of Am 237 Lexington Ave New York NY 10016*

MICKE, PAULINE GERTRUDE, nun, educator, Roman Catholic Church; b. Cloquet, Minn., Apr. 27, 1940; d. Theodore William and Albena Marie (Demers) M.; B.A. in History, Coll. of St. Scholastica, 1963; Th.M., St. John's U., 1975. Joined Order of St. Benedict, 1958; tchr. Our Lady of Victory Jr. High Sch., Mpls., 1963-68, Duluth Cathedral High Sch., Minn., 1968-73, head religion dept., 1973-74; religious edn. coordinator St. Michael's Ch., Duluth, 1973-78; dir. Shalom Ctr., Coll. of St. Scholastica, Duluth, 1979—; dir. workshops on pastoral ministry, Superior, Wis., Duluth, 1974-76. Chairwoman Outreach Com. for Mayor's Drug Com., 1969-70; advisor area bd. on chem. dependency, 1970-73. Mem. Minn. (v.p.), Nat., Cath. Edn. assns., Minn. Coalition Tchrs. Edn. Home: St Scholastica Priory Duluth MN 55811 Office: Coll of St Scholastica Duluth MN 55811

MICKLE, MARLIN HOMER, lay church worker, United Methodist Church; electrical engineering educator; b. Windber, Pa., July 5, 1936; s. Howard T. and Ruth Elma (Corle) M.; B.S. in E.E., 1961, M.S. in E.E., 1963, Ph.D., 1967. Chmn. adminstrv. bd. Albright United Meth. Ch., 1968-73; dist. dir. United Meth. Men, 1970-71; dist. lay leader Pitts. dist. Western Pa. Conf., United Meth. Ch., 1971-73; mem. adv. com. bd. laity Western Pa. Conf., U. Meth. Ch., 1973-74; chmn. dynamic ch. modeling group Pitts. dist. West Pa. Conf., United Meth. Ch., 1973-. Asso. prof. elec. engring. U. Pitts., 1968-75, prof., 1975—; program dir. system theory and applications NSF, Washington, 1974-75. Mem. IEEE, Eta Kappa Nu, Sigma Tau, Phi Theta Kappa, Sigma Xi. Home: 1376 Simona Dr Pittsburgh PA 15201

MIDDLEBROOK, HAROLD ALBERT, minister, Prog. Nat. Baptist Conv., Inc.; b. Memphis, July 4, 1942; s. Willie T. Waters and Mary Frances (Middlebrook) Jeffries; student Morehouse Coll., 1960-63; B.A., LeMoyne-Owen Coll., 1976; postgrad. Memphis Theol. Sem., 1976—; m. Betty Mock, Feb. 6, 1965; children—Arlene ReSherra, Harold. Ordained to ministry, 1966; asso. minister Greater Middle Bapt. Ch., Memphis, 1966-70; pastor Greater Springfield Bapt. Ch., Bolivar, Tenn., 1970-77, Mt. Calvary Bapt. Ch., Knoxville, Tenn., 1977—. Dir. Christian edn. W. Tenn. Central Bapt. Assn.; past pres. Hardeman County Ministerial Assn. Pres. Bdlivar Human Devel. Corp.; advisor Hardeman County Bi-Racial Commn.; co-ordinator Hardeman County Polit. Action Com.; mem. adv. bd. Tenn. Pub. Service Commn. Mem. Progressive Nat. Bapt. Conv., Nat. Conf. Black Churchmen. Home: 1945 Dandridge Ave SE Knoxville TN 37915 Office: 1807 Dandridge Ave SE Knoxville TN 37915

MIDTHUN, MAYNARD VERNELL, minister, American Lutheran Church; b. Blanchardville, Wis., Feb. 2, 1921; s. Carl Albert and Alma Ovidia (Ankultrud) M.; m. Mary Ellen Mandt, Oct. 21, 1945; children: Darla, Gail, Kevin. Student U. Wis.-Oshkosh, 1939-41; B.S., St. Olaf Coll., 1945-47; postgrad. U. Minn., 1948, 49. Ordained to ministry Am. Luth. Ch., 1950. Pastor, First Luth. Ch., Onalaska, Wis., 1950-55, Christ the King Ch., Torrance, Calif., 1955-64; sr. pastor First Luth. Ch., Eau Claire, Wis., 1964-79, St. Peter Luth. Ch., Mesa, Ariz., 1979—; pres. Ea. Dist. Luther League, Evangel. Luth. Ch., Mpls., 1953-55, Los Angeles Pastoral Conf., 1959, Calif. Ministorim, Torrance, 1980; mem. Nat. Youth Bd., Evangel. Luth. Ch., Mpls., 1953-55, S. Pacific Dist. Council, Los Angeles, 1959, Dist. Family Life Commn., Eau Claire, Wis., 1970-74; convocator Calif. Luth. Coll., Thousand Oaks, 1959-64; sec. Am. Luth. Ch. (S. Pacific dist.), Los Angeles, 1962-64; mem. edn. bd. No. Wis. Dist. Parish, Eau Claire, 1966-72; state chaplain Disabled Vets., Eau Claire, 1974. Mem. Mental Retardation Com., Eau

Claire, 1965-79, Chem. Dependency Council, Eau Claire, 1970-79. Served to t./sgt. U.S. Army, 1941-45, ETO, prisoner of war, Germany. Decorated Four Battle Stars, Purple Heart with Oak Leaf Cluster. Mem. PTA Honorary Life Membership (life), VFW (chaplain 1964—), DAV (chaplain). Republican. Lodge: Kiwanis (Torrance) (chaplain 1961-64). Home and office: St Peter Luth Ch 1844 E Dana Ave Mesa AZ 85204

MIETHE, TERRY LEE, educator, Christian Church; b. Clinton, Ind., Aug. 26, 1948; s. Billy and Rosemary (Procarione) M.; A.B. with honors, Lincoln Christian Coll., 1970; M.A. with honors, Trinity Evang. Div. Sch., 1973; M.Div., McCormick Theol. Sem., 1973; Ph.D., St. Louis U., 1976; A.M., U. So. Calif., 1981, Ph.D., 1984; m. Beverly Jo Deck, June 1, 1969; 1 son, John Hayden. Ordained to ministry Christian Ch., 1970. Asst. minister Lockport (Ill.) Christian Ch., 1968-69; sr. minister Mellott (Ind.) United Ch. Christ, 1969-71; minister Woodburn (Ill.) Congl. Ch., 1973-74; assoc. minister 1st Christian Ch., Pomona, Calif., 1979-83; lectr. philosophy St. Louis U., 1975-76, asst. prof. theol. studies, 1976-77, asst. dir. honors program, 1975-76; prof. philosophy Liberty U., 1984—. Author: The Metaphysics of L.J. Eslick: His Philosophy of God, 1976; Thomistic Bibliography: 1940-78, 1980; Augustinian Bibliography, 1970-1980; With Essays on the Fundamentals of Augustinian Scholarship, 1982; Letters of New Christians, 1982; Reflections, Vol. I, 1980, Vol. II, 1983; The New Christians Guide to Following Jesus, 1984; The Philosophy and Ethics of Alexander Campbell, 1984; Aristotelian Bibliography: 1960-1984, 1986. Contbr. articles to religious jours. Mem. Am. Philos. Assn., Am. Acad. Religion, Soc. Bibl. Lit., Evang. Theol. Soc., Phi Beta Kappa, Phi Alpha Theta, Psi Chi, Eta Sigma Phi, Alpha Sigma Nu. Home: 1407 Lockewood Dr Lynchburg VA 24502

MIHALY, EUGENE, rabbi, coll. dean, Reform Jewish Congregations; b. Hungary, Sept. 29, 1918; s. Hillel and Ida Judith (Kahn) M.; came to U.S., 1930, naturalized, 1935; B.A. magna cum laude, Yeshiva U., 1940; M.A. (Seinsheimer grad. teaching fellow), Hebrew Union Coll., 1949, Ph.D., 1952; m. Cecile Bramer, June 25, 1945; children: Eugene Bramer, Marc Bramer. Ordained rabbi, 1941; prof. rabbinic lit. and homiletics Hebrew Union Coll., Cin., 1951—, acad. coordinator, 1974-75, exec. dean acad. affairs, 1976—; chmn. Assn. Progressive Reform Judaism, Cin., 1975—. Chmn. coms. Central Conf. Am. Rabbis. Mem. Acad. Jewish Research. Author: Jewish Religious Experience, 1958; A Song to Creation, 1975; contbr. studies to periodicals in field. Office: Hebrew Union College 3101 Clifton St Cincinnati OH 45220

MILAM, DON JAMES, minister, So. Bapt. Conv.; b. Memphis, Aug. 28, 1910; s. Don James and Maude Muller (McGee) M.; B.A., William Jewell Coll., 1932; M.Th., So. Bapt. Theol. Sem., 1935; m. Ettie Marie Cross, June 14, 1936; children—Marilyn Milam Fine, Heather Milam Maedgen, Donna Milam Cooper. Ordained to ministry, 1931; pastor Britton Bapt. Ch., 1936-38, 1st Bapt. Ch., Paul's Valley, Okla., 1938-42, Guthrie, Okla., 1942-47; evangelist Oklahoma City, Okla., 1947-57; pastor Ysleta Bapt. Ch., El Paso, Tex., 1957-62, Park Ave. Bapt. Ch., Memphis, 1962—; evangelist, revivalist U.S., Asia, Africa, Middle East. Mem. exec. bd. Tenn. Bapt. Conv., So. Bapt. Conv., 1970-77; pres. Bapt. Pastors Conf. Memphis, 1971-72; moderator Banner and Central Assns. in Okla., 1941-46. Contbr. articles to religious jours. Home: 3245 Estes St Memphis TN 38118 Office: Park Ave Baptist Church 3372 Park Ave Memphis TN 38111

MILBRATH, EARL (BILL) WILLIAM, minister, American Lutheran Church; educator; b. Cashmere, Wash., June 13, 1924; s. Earl Edwin and Rachel Metha (Weber) M.; m. Annie Odine Mann, June 16, 1946; children: Earl, Cynthia Milbrath Stigall, Timothy O. B.A., Pacific Luth. U., 1948; M.Div., Trinity Sem., 1952; tchr. cert. St. Mary's U., San Antonio, 1983. Ordained to ministry American Lutheran Ch., 1952. Pastor, Faith Luth. Ch., Toppenish, Wash., 1952-55; commd. 1st lt. U.S. Air Force, 1955, advanced through grades to lt. col., 19—; chaplain, worldwide, 1955-80; ret., 1980; vis. pastor Zion Luth. Ch. of Helotes, San Antonio, 1983—; chaplain VA Hosp., San Antonio, 1984—; dir. religious edn. Yokota AFB, Japan, 1969-71; vis. flightline chaplain Dover AFB, Del., 1971-75; br. chief Basic Tng. Chapel, Lackland AFB, San Antonio, 1979-80; del. So. Dist. conf. Am. Luth. Ch., 1984. Part time tchr. Northside Ind. Sch. Dist., San Antonio, 1982-84. Chaplain, CAP, Dover, 1973-74, Lackland Area Ministerial Assn., San Antonio, 1979-80; mayor RAF Upper Heyford Mil. Community, Eng., 1975-78; bd. dirs. Halfway House for Alcoholics, Dover, 1973-75. Mem. Air Force Assn., Zool. Soc. San Antonio. Club: Lackland Officers. Home: 9501 Little Geronimo San Antonio TX 78254 Office: Zion Luth Ch Helotes Leslie-Braun Loop 1604 San Antonio TX 78228

MILES, MOSES GENERAL, minister, educator, Primitive Baptists; b. Lakeland, Fla., Jan. 31, 1918; s. Carey and Mariah (Littleton) M.; B.A., Fla. A. and M. Coll., 1941; M.A., Ohio State U., 1948; m. Willie Mae Danford, June 5, 1943; children—Andrea, Keth. Ordained to ministry, 1943; pastor ch., Tallahassee, 1948; pres. Fla. State Primitive Bapt. Conv., 1961—; sec. bd. dirs. Nat. Primitive Bapt. Conv., 1958—, editor-in-chief sch. lit., 1960—; chmn. Fla. Black Leaders Summit Conf., 1974. Bd. dirs. Tallahassee Meml. Hosp.; adminstr. Miracle Hill Nursing and Convalescent Home, Inc., 1969-78. Mem. Tallahassee Ministerial Assn., Alpha Phi Alpha. Author: Walking with God; The Minister's Reminder; The Call to Christian Leadership; An Alpha Man in Action: Guidelines for Deacons and Deaconesses of the Primitive Baptist Church; Musts and Must Nots for God's Minister; The Best Way to Say It and To Do It; Learning to Read and to Write: The Sphinxman Handman. Home: 1525 S Bronough St Tallahassee FL 32301 Office: 1329 Abraham St Tallahassee FL 32304

MILETIC, STEPHEN FRANCIS, theology educator, Roman Catholic Church; b. Windsor, Ont., Can., Nov. 23, 1952; s. Mate Miletic and Ann (Filetic) Miletic Skific.; m. Joyce Elaine Bachmeier, Apr. 19, 1975; children: Isaac Francis, Heather Ann. B.A. (hon.), U. Windsor, 1976, M.A., 1977, B.E., 1978; Ph.D., Marquette U., 1985. Lectr. religious studies U. Lethbridge, Alta., 1984—; vis. asst. prof. U. St. Thomas, Houston, 1983-84; guest lectr. various Roman Cath. and ecumenical contexts, 1975—; leader, tchr., counselor, adminstr., Cath. rep. Lethbridge InterFaith group, 1984—. Translator New Testament and Targums, 1982. Scholar London, Ont. Diocese, 1981, Marquette U., 1979-82, U. Windsor, 1977-78. Mem. Soc. Bibl. Lit., Cath. Bibl. Assn., Can. Soc. Bibl. Studies. Home: 281 7th Ave S Lethbridge AB T1J 1H6 Canada Office: Religious Studies U Lethbridge 4401 University Dr Lethbridge AB T1K 3M4 Canada

MILEY, JAMES EDWARD, minister, Lutheran Ch. Am.; b. Mpls., Feb. 18, 1936; s. Charles Arthur and Amy Elizabeth (Ridenour) M.; A.A., Sacramento Jr. Coll., 1956; B.A., Wittenburg U., 1959; B.D., Pacific Luth. Theol Sem., 1962; M.Div., 1972; m. Avis Marlene Olson, Apr. 15, 1973; children—Jeffrey Charles, James Scott, Stephen Matthew; stepchildren—Robert Vernon, Kari Ann. Ordained to ministry Lutheran Ch. Am., 1962; pastor Our Redeemer Luth. Ch., Simi, Calif., 1962-64, Christ The Shepherd Luth. Ch., Capistrano Beach, Calif., 1964-69, St. James Luth. Ch., Redding, Calif., 1969-72; mgr. Chase Bros. Dairy, Oxnard, Calif., 1972-73; pastor St. Stephen's of the Valley Luth. Ch., Palmdale, Calif., 1973-76, St. Michael Luth. Ch., Sun Valley, Calif., 1976—. Sec. Ministerial Assn., 1965-69; sec. Redding Ministerial Assn., 1969-72; mem. Mission Bd. Pacific SW Synod, 1964-69; pres. Pacific SW Synod Luther League, 1954-56. Mem. Wittenberg, Pacific Luth. Theol. Sem. alumni assns., Phi Mu Delta (Mu Delta chpt.). Home: 8862 Bluffdale Dr Sun Valley CA 91352 Office: 8040 Glenoaks Blvd Sun Valley CA 91352

MILHOUSE, PAUL WILLIAM, bishop, United Meth. Ch.; b. St. Francisville, Ill., Aug. 31, 1910; s. Willis Cleveland and Carrie (Pence) M.; A.B., Ind. Central Coll., 1932, D.D., 1950; S.T.D., Oklahoma City U., 1969; B.D., Am. Theol. Sem., 1937; L.H.D., Westmar Coll., 1965; D.D., So. Meth. U., 1969; m. Mary Frances Noblitt, June 29, 1932; children—Mary (Mrs. Ronald L. Hauswald), Pauline (Mrs. Arthur Vermillion), Paul David. Ordained to ministry as elder, 1931, bishop, 1960; pastor Ill. chs., 1928-51; asso. editor Telescope-Messenger, Harrisburg, Pa., 1951-59; exec. sec. Gen. Council Adminstrn. of United Meth. Ch., Dayton, Ohio, 1959-60; bishop, Kansas City, Mo., 1960-68, Oklahoma City, 1968-80, bishop in residence Oklahoma City U., 1980—. Pres., Council of Bishops, United Meth. Ch., after 1977, v.p. Gen. Council on Fin. and Adminstrn., 1976—. Trustee Oklahoma City U., So. Meth. U., Meth. Home, Meth. Manor. Author: Enlisting and Developing Church Leaders, 1946; Come Unto Me, 1947; Doorways to Spiritual Living, 1950; Except the Lord Build the House, 1949; Christian Worship in Symbol and Ritual, 1953; Laymen in the Church, 1957; At Life's Crossroads, 1959; Lift Up Your Eyes, 1955; Philip William Otterbein, Pioneer Preacher, 1968; Nineteen Bishops of the Evangelical United Brethren Church, 1974; Theological and Historical Roots of United Methodists, 1980; Organizing for Effective Ministry, 1980; Detours into Yesterday, 1984; Miracle at 23rd and Blackwelder, 1984. Recipient Disting. Alumnus award Ind. Central U., 1978, Disting. Service award Oklahoma City U., 1980, Top Hand award Oklahoma City C. of C., 1980. Mem. Alpha Chi. Home: 2213 NW 56th Terr Oklahoma City OK 73112 Office: Oklahoma City Univ 1501 N Blackwelder Oklahoma City OK 73106

MILLARD, JACK HENRY, minister, Reformed Church in America; b. Plainfield, N.J., Mar. 22, 1938; s. Arthur Colin and Dorothy Bird (Van Winkle) M.; m. Donna M. Burggraaff, June 23, 1962; 1 child, Alan C. B.A., Hope Coll., 1961; B.D., M.A., New Brunswick Sem., 1964. Ordained to ministry, Reformed Ch. in Am., 1964. Minister, Fonda Reformed Ch., N.Y., 1964-76, Johnstown Reformed Ch., N.Y., 1976—; v.p., pres. Particular Synod of Albany, 1976-78; pres. Classis of Scholarie, 1971-72; del. Gen. Synod Reformed Ch., 1968, 73, 76, 80; chmn., mem. Commn. on Evangelism, Reformed Ch., 1981-85. Pres., Johnstown Band Support Group, 1982—, Little League, Johnstown, 1978; v.p. Babe Ruth, Johnston, 1979—; mem. Johnstown Area Vol. Ambulance Corp., 1977—. Recipient Service award Johnstown PTA, 1983. Home: 6 W 2d Ave Johnstown NY 12095 Office: Johnstown Reformed Ch 351 N Perry St Johnstown NY 12095

MILLER, CHARLES E., clergyman, seminary administrator, Roman Catholic. Rector St. John's Sem., Camarillo, Calif. Office: St John's Sem 5012 E Seminary Rd Camarillo CA 93010*

MILLER, CHARLES EDWARD (EDDIE), clergyman, Southern Baptist Convention; b. Morristown, Tenn., Sept. 28, 1953; s. Charles Edward and Wanda Faye (Canter) M.; m. Kathy Regina Hurst, June 30, 1972; children: Christopher Edward, Timothy Charles, Angela Denice. A.S., Walters State Community Coll., 1973; B.A., Carson-Newman Coll., 1975; M.Div., Southwestern Bapt. Theol. Sem., 1978. Ordained to ministry So. Bapt. Conv., 1974. Assoc. pastor Wilsonville Bapt. Ch., Newport, Tenn., 1974-75; pastor 1st Bapt. Ch., Lavon, Tex., 1975-78, Flat Gap Bapt. Ch., New Market, Tenn., 1978-80, 1st Bapt. Ch., Mulberry Grove, Ill., 1980—; moderator Kaskaskia Bapt. Assn., Salem, Ill., 1984—. Home and Office: PO Box 57 Mulberry Grove IL 62262

MILLER, CHARLES RAY, bishop, United Brethren in Christ Ch., missionary adminstr.; b. Waynesboro, Pa., Apr. 13, 1928; s. Charles W. and Mary S. (Knepper) M.; B.A., Huntington Coll., 1951; B.D., Huntington Coll. Theol. Sem., 1955, D.D., 1974; m. Elaine M. Bingaman, Nov. 30, 1946; children—Dennis Ray, Pamela Kay. Ordained to ministry United Brethren in Christ Ch., 1955; pastor United Brethren in Christ Chs., Huntington, Ind., 1952-57, Chambersburg, Pa., 1957-59, Shippensburg, Pa., 1959-73; elected bishop, 1973; bishop Ch. of the United Brethren in Christ, east dist., 1973—, now also chmn. Mem. Bd. Missions Ch. of United Brethren in Christ, from 1961, pres., after 1965; mem. gen. bd. Adminstrn. United Brethren in Christ Ch., 1963—, gen. bd. Christian edn., 1973—, gen. bd. Publ., 1973—. Mem. Nat. Assn. Evangs. (bd. adminstrn.). Office: care of United Brethren in Christ Ch 302 Lake St POB 650 Huntington IN 46750

MILLER, CLYDE ALBERT, minister, Am. Luth. Ch.; b. Butler, Pa., Apr. 13, 1919; s. Albert George and Lydia Elizabeth (Frederick) M.; B.A., Capital U., Columbus, Ohio, 1941; B.D., Evang. Luth. Sem., Columbus, 1943; m. Jean Evelyn Baker, July 11, 1944; children—Shirley Ann, Karen Jean. Ordained to ministry, 1943; pastor St. Paul's Luth. Ch., Maumee, Ohio, 1943-48, Faith Luth. Ch., Massillon, Ohio, 1948-56, Hope Luth. Ch., Cleve., 1957-62, Zion Luth. Ch., Lima, Ohio, 1962—. Asst. to pres. Eastern dist. Am. Luth. Ch., 1956, 57; v.p. Ohio dist. Am. Luth. Ch., 1962-68, interim pres., 1964; radio minister, Stas. WIMA and WCIT, 1962—; pres. Augustana Conf. Am. Luth. Ch. Dist., 1950-52, Lake Erie Conf., 1959-60, Western Conf., 1964-68. Home: 1673 Patton Ave Lima OH 45805 Office: 1300 Edgewood Dr Lima OH 45805

MILLER, DALE R., minister, American Baptist Church U.S.A.; b. Pt. Pleasant, N.J., Oct. 15, 1955; s. Robert T. and Joyce Helen (Pasko) M.; m. Deborah Ann Steeb, Jan. 7, 1978; 1 child, Beverly Ann. B.A., Eastern Coll., 1978; postgrad., U. Pa., 1979; M.Div., Eastern Bapt. Theol. Sem., 1982. Ordained to ministry Baptist Ch. Youth pastor, Christ United Meth. Ch., Broomall, Pa., 1977-80; pastor Upland Bapt. Ch., Pa., 1980—; v.p. Chester Council of Chs., Pa., 1982—, Morgan Edwards Group, Valley Forge, Pa., 1984—; adminstr. Upland Emergency Food Ctr., Upland, 1984—. Mem. Am. Bapt. Minister's Council. Lodge: Kiwanis (Chester) (bd. dirs. 1984—). Home: 3744 Clearwater Ln Upland PA 19015 Office: Upland Bapt Ch 3d and Main Sts Upland PA 19015

MILLER, DONALD EARL, religion educator, Episcopal Church; b. Whittier, Calif., Mar. 12, 1946; s. Glenn E. and R. Elizabeth (Haag) M.; m. Lorna Touryan, Mar. 29, 1969; children: Shont E., Arpi M. M.A., U. So. Calif., 1972, Ph.D., 1975. Asst. prof. religion U. So. Calif., Los Angeles, 1972-81, assoc. prof., 1981—. Author: The Case for Liberal Christianity, 1981. Contbr. articles to Christian Century, Religious Studies Rev., Religious Edn., Change. Mem. Soc. Christian Ethics, Soc. for Sci. Study of Religion. Home: 1654 Woodglen Ln Altadena CA 91001 Office: School of Religion 328 THH U So Calif Los Angeles CA 90089-0355

MILLER, DONALD LORNE, minister, Lutheran Church-Missouri Synod; b. Swift Current, Sask., Can., Aug. 28, 1941; came to U.S., 1949, naturalized, 1962; s. Herbert R. and Elsa (Goebel) M.; m. Diane Lee Braley, Aug. 21, 1966; children: Jeffrey Alan, Kristi Michele. A.A., St. Paul's Jr. Coll., 1961; B.A., Concordia Sr. Coll., Ft. Wayne, Ind., 1963; B.D., Concordia Sem., St. Louis, 1967, M.Div., 1971; B.S. in Acctg., Southwestern U., 1983. Ordained to ministry Luth. Ch., 1967. Pastor, First Luth. Ch., Mt. Ayr, Iowa, 1967-69, St. Timothy Luth. Ch., Bedford, Iowa, 1967-69, Zion Luth. Ch., Fairmont, Okla., 1969-73, Our Savior Luth. Ch., Weatherford, Okla., 1973—, Christ Luth. Ch., Elk City, Okla., 1973—; pastoral advisor Luth. Women's Missionary League, Okla., 1972-76; pres. Ministerial Alliance, Weatherford, Okla., 1975-76, sec., 1974-75;

campus coordinator Okla. Dist., 1980-81. Pres. New Horizons Mental Health Bd., Weatherford, 1981-83. Lodge: Kiwanis (bd. dirs. 1981-82). Office: Our Savior Luth Ch 1121 N 7th St Weatherford OK 73096

MILLER, ERIC J., minister, Presbyterian Church in U.S.A.; b. Sherman, Tex., Oct. 6, 1943; s. Max M. and Harriet A. (Foster) M.; A.S., Jr. Coll. Broward County, 1963; B.S., Fla. State U., 1965; M.Div., Fuller Theol. Sem., 1971. Ordained to ministry, 1975; campus staff mem. Inter-Varsity Christian Fellowship, Pasadena, Calif., 1966-68; missionary intern, Nairobi, Kenya, 1968-69; dir. Twentyone hundred Prodns. (multi-media ministries of Inter-Varsity Christian Fellowship), Pasadena, 1969-75 Madison, Wis., 1975-82, dir. internat. devel., 1982—. Recipient B. K. Carrol Meml. Award, 1965; named Outstanding Young Man Am., 1977. Home: 1813 Lynndale Madison WI 53711 Office: 233 Langdon St Madison WI 53703

MILLER, EVERETT GEORGE, SR., minister, United Methodist Ch.; labor studies educator; b. Pumphrey, Md., June 27, 1921; s. Everett Caldwell and Anna (Frederick) M.; m. Ruth Elizabeth Dressel, Feb. 21, 1938 (dec. 1947); m. Eleanor Mae Schaeffer, Aug. 26, 1950 (div. Aug. 1975); children: Everett, Charles F., Marc A., Paul J.; 1 foster child, Heidi; m. Mary Estelle Landry, June 27, 1981. A.A., Towson State U., 1950; B.A., Western Md. Coll., 1952; S.T.B., Westminster Sem., 1955; M.Div., Wesley Sem., 1971; M.A., U. Md.-College Park, 1968; D.D. (hon.) Dundalk Sch. Religion, 1968. Ordained to ministry Methodist Ch., 1955; lic. psychologist, Md. Various appointments Balt. Ann. Conf., Washington, 1948-63; pastor Dundalk United Meth. Ch., Md., 1963-73, Orangeville Meth. Ch., Balt., 1981-84, Rohrersville Charge, Md., 1984—; conf. sec. Christian Social Concerns, Balt., 1955-59; dir. camping Meth. Bd. Edn., Balt., 1959-63; pres. Dundalk Sch. Religion, 1966-78. Prof. labor studies, lobbying Dundalk Community Coll., 1973—; project dir. various research grants, 1976-80. Author: Freeborn, A Life, 1955 (Earp Award). Del. Met. Balt. Council of AFL/CIO Unions, 1973-84; lobbyist Am. Fedn. Tchrs., Balt. County, 1981-83. Recipient award citation VFW, 1977, community service award Balt. United Way, 1978, 79, citation for community service Operating Engineers, 1981. Mem. Md. Univ. and Coll. Labor Edn. Assn., Md. Labor Edn. Assn. (pres. 1973—), Labor Edn. Alumni Assn. (sec. 1976—), Balt. County Community Coll. Employees (sec. 1980—), Md. Religion and Labor Inst. (pres. 1980—). Democrat. Home: Rohrersville United Meth Charge Drawer B Rohrersville MD 21779 Office: Dundalk Community Coll 7200 Sollers Point Rd Dundalk MD 21222

MILLER, HERBERT DONELL, minister, United Methodist Church, educator; b. McKeesport, Pa., Oct. 1, 1926; s. Herbert Charles and Elsabeth Catherine (Donnelly) M.; M.Div., Yale Div. Sch., 1952; M.A., Trinity Coll., 1952; B.S., U. Wash., 1947; Ph.D., La. State U., 1956; m. Marjorie Orea Singer, May 30, 1950; children: Harvey, Beth (Mrs. Johnny Spoon), William, Ted, Mark, Don, Jan, Chantel. Ordained to ministry The United Methodist Ch., 1954; supply preacher, Western Pa., 1941-44; pastor evangelistic campaigns, Pa., 1942-44, La., 1944-46, 52-55, Miss., 1953, Ind., 1958-61, Ill., 1960; pastor chs., Gonzales, La., 1945, Slaughter, La. 1946, Sedro-Woolley, Wash. 1948; Seattle, 1945-46; asst. psychologist, jr. clin. psychologist Conn. Sch. for Boys, pastor Trinity Meth. Ch., Meriden, Conn., 1950-52; clin. psychology fellow S.E. La. Hosp., Mandeville, 1953-55; pastor LaCombe (La.) Meth. Ch., 1954-56; Wesley Found. minister Ohio U., 1956-57; pastor Zion Evang. and Ref. Ch., Henderson, Ky., 1960-62; head psychology dept. Evansville U., 1957-63; pvt. practice clin. psychology, pastoral counseling, cons. group process, 1964-69; adj. prof. Wash. U., 1965-69; adj. prof. Eden Theol. Sem., Webster Groves, Mo., 1963-69; tng. dir. Pastoral Counseling Inst. St. Louis, 1963-69; chief clin. psychology unit St. Louis State Hosp., 1963-67; chief psychologist Youth Center, St. Louis, 1967-69; pastor Winchester (Calif.) Meth. Ch., 1969-71; pastoral counselor, adj. prof. San Francisco Theol. Sem., 1973-74; pvt. practice marriage, family and child counseling, Redlands, Calif., 1971—; prof. social and clin. psychology Johnston Coll., U. Redlands, 1969-81; pastor Ottawa Ave. United Meth. Ch., Riverside, Calif., 1970-80; psychodramatist Patton State Hosp., 1970—; tng. dir. Inst. for Creative Living and Pastoral Counseling of Rialto (Calif.), 1972-76. Mem. Am. Assn. Group Psychotherapy and Psychodrama, Fedn. Trainers, Educators and Practitioners of Psychodrama, Sociometry and Group Psychotherapy, Calif.-Nev. Conf. Meth. Ch. Author: Make-A-Sentence-Test, 1968. Columnist: Slidell Times series Time for Truth, 1953-55. Home: 1610 Helena Ln Redlands CA 92373

MILLER, JAIME POTTER, minister, United Methodist Church; b. Johnstown, Pa., Nov. 18, 1949; d. James Jacob and Gloria Ardell (Williams) Potter; m. Jeffery Alan Miller, Dec. 27, 1970; children: Janna Christine, Jordan Jacob. B.A., Albright Coll., 1971; M.Div., United Theol. Sem., 1975. Ordained to ministry, United Meth. Ch. Youth pastor Holy Cross United Meth. Ch., Reading, Pa., 1969-71; co-pastor Abbottsville/Coefr Chapel/Nashville United Meth. Chs., Greenville, Ohio, 1972-75, Sidman/St. Michael United Meth. Chs., Sidman, Pa., 1975-78; pastor Galloway-Nicklin United Meth. Chs., Franklin, Pa., 1978-80, Galloway United Meth. Ch., 1980—; exec. dir. Summer Pastors Acad. W. Pa. Conf., United Meth. Ch., 1982—; dir. Music W. Pa. Christian Ashram, 1977—; mem. staff Start-Up/Transition Symposium, 1981—; dean sr. high Summer Camp, 1975—; del. N.E. Jurisdictional Conf., United Meth. Ch., 1980, 84; lectr. bibl. women, contemporary music interpretation. Author: (curriculum) Let Go and Let God, 1981; Celebration of Discipline, 1983. Bd. dirs. Franklin Regional Med. Ctr., Pa., 1983—; mem. adv. bd. Compassionate Friends, Oil City, Pa., 1983—. Democrat. Home: RD 4 Box 162 Franklin PA 16322

MILLER, JEFFREY ALLAN, youth administrator Church of the Nazarene; b. Detroit, Mar. 19, 1961; s. Edward Clements Miller and Emilie Donna (LaFave) Golden. B.A., Point Loma Coll., 1984, cert. youth ministry, 1984. Minister of youth Ch. of the Nazarene, Placentia, Calif., 1981, 82-83, Presbyn. Ch., San Diego, 1983—. Campaign worker Congressman Jim Bates, San Diego, 1984, mem. subcom., 1984. Mem. Gamma Pi Epsilon (pres. 1983-84). Democrat. Office: East San Diego Presbyterian Ch 5202 Orange Ave San Diego CA 92115

MILLER, JOHN HENRY See *Who's Who in America*, 43rd edition.

MILLER, JOHN RONALD, minister, United Church of Christ; b. Los Angeles, Jan. 4, 1938; s. Clarence Raymond and Yolanda Sarah (Capenaro) M.; m. Madelon Louise Tetaz, Mar. 26, 1966; children: Sarah Louise, John Ronald. B.A., Southwestern Coll., 1960; M.Div., Drew U., 1963; M.A., Rutgers U., 1966. Ordained to ministry United Ch. of Christ, 1963. Pastor, Burden Meth. Ch., (Kans.), 1958-60; minister Wilson Meml. Union Ch., Watchung, N.J., 1961—; mem. Consultation on Ch. Union, Princeton, N.J., 1982—, com. on disabled United Ch. of Christ, Montclair, N.J., 1982—. Vice pres. Trenton Psychiat. Hosp.-State of N.J.; chmn. Dorthea Dix Chapel Bldg. Program. Southwestern Coll. scholar, 1960; Tipple scholar, 1960. Mem. Internat. Council Community Chs. (moderator ecumenical commn. 1984—), Nat. Council Chs. of Jesus Christ (governing bd. 1985—). Lodge: Optimists (Watchung). Home: 9 Stony Brook Dr Warren NJ 07060 Office: Mary E Wilson Meml Union Ch 7 Valley Rd Watchung NJ 07060

MILLER, JUDEA BENNETT, rabbi; b. N.Y.C., Dec. 10, 1930; s. David and Yetta (Holzberg) M.; m. Anita C. Kaufman, Nov. 11, 1932; children: Jonathan A., Rebecca E. Gottesman. B.A., NYU, 1952; B.H.L., Jewish Inst. Religion, 1954; M.A.H.L., Hebrew Union Coll., 1957, D.D. (hon.), 1982. Ordained rabbi, 1957. Rabbi, Temple Emmanuel, Wichita, Kans., 1959-65, Temple Tifereth Israel, Malden, Mass., 1965-73; sr. rabbi Temple B'rith Kodesh, Rochester, N.Y., 1973—; chaplain VA Hosp., Bedford, Mass., 1965-73, Canandaigna, N.Y., 1973—; faculty Tufts U., Medford, Mass., 1966-73. Served to capt. U.S. Army, 1957-59. Mem. Assn. Mental Health Chaplains, Central Conf. Am. Rabbis. Home: 1615 Clover St Rochester NY 14618 Office: Temple B'rith Kodesh 2131 Elmwood Ave Rochester NY 14618

MILLER, KEITH MICHAEL, minister, Southern Baptist Convention; b. Olney, Md., July 2, 1950; s. Kenneth Marvin and Naomi Elizabeth (Blucher) M.; m. Emily Kay Pickett, Aug. 8, 1970; children: Matthew Keith, Christopher Kevin. B.M. cum laude in Music, Okla. Bapt. U., 1972. Ordained to ministry So. Bapt. Conv., 1972. Minister of youth, music Waldorf Bapt. Ch., Md., 1972-73; minister of music, youth edn. Colesville Bapt. Ch., Silver Spring, Md., 1973-75; minister music, dir. arts First Bapt. Ch., Silver Springs, 1976—; music dir. Potomac Bapt. Assn. Chs., Waldorf, 1972-73. Composer: O Give Thanks Unto the Lord, 1972. Mem. Am. Guild English Handbell Ringers (clinician), So. Bapt. Ch. Music Conf., Am. Guild Organists. Republican. Home: 12004 Cook Ct Wheaton MD 20902 Office: First Bapt Ch 8415 Fenton St Silver Spring MD 20910

MILLER, LLOYD LAWRENCE, pastor, American Lutheran Church. B. Melvina, Wis., Aug. 13, 1938; s. Lawrence Lloyd and Irene Marie (Ornes) M.; m. Janet Joanne Winterfield, Aug. 20, 1960. B.A., Luther Coll., 1961; B.D., Wartburg Sem., 1965. Ordained to ministry Am. Luth. Ch., 1965. Pastor Salem-Emmanuel Luth. Ch., Long Lake, S.D., 1965-69, Emmanuel Luth. Ch., Gackle, N.D., 1969-75, Zion Luth. Ch., Eureka, S.D., 1975—; del. Nat. Am. Luth. Ch. Conv., Mpls., 1972, San Diego, 1982; internship supr. Wartburg Sem., Dubuque, Iowa, 1976-84; chmn. N. Central Conf., Am. Luth. Ch. (S.D. dist.), 1979-84. Republican. Club: Lions (pres. 1981-82). Home: 314 11th St Eureka SD 57437 Office: Zion Luth Ch 909 G Ave Eureka SD 57437

MILLER, MARLIN E., seminary administrator. Pres. Goshen Bibl. Sem. (Mennonite Church), Elkhart, Ind. Office: Goshen Bibl Sem 3003 Benham Ave Elkhart IN 46517*

MILLER, MARY LOU, minister, Christian Church (Disciples of Christ); music educator; b. Miami, Fla., May 26, 1927; d. Robert Miller and Lucy Mae (Barnes) Thomson; m. James Earl Miller, June 11, 1949 (dec. 1981); children: Adele L. Miller Dees, J. Loren, Wendell, Vinson. B.Mus., U. Miami, 1949; M.R.E., Grad. Sem. Phillips U., 1964. Ordained, 1975. Co-pastor Christian Ch., Marion, Ill., 1976-80; interim pastor, Mineral, Va., 1980-81; dir. music and cantor St. Joseph's Cath. Ch., Marion, 1979-80; assoc. minister Middletown Christian Ch., Ky., 1981—; chmn. Christian Edn. Commn., 1972; mem. Youth Commn., Ill.-Wis. Region, 1976-78, Christian Edn. Task Force, Oreg., 1967-68; tchr. Weekday Released Time, Oreg. Council Chs., Eugene, 1966-67; pres. Ch. Woman United Cayuga County, N.Y., 1971-73, chmn., mem. state bd. Central N.Y. Area, 1974-76; 2d v.p. Auburn Interfaith Ministries, N.Y., exec. bd. 1975-76; Disciples mem. exec. bd. Egyptian Mission Council, So. Ill., 1977-79; sec. Marion Ministerial Alliance, 1979-80; mem. Com. on Ministry, Ky., 1982-84; co-chmn. Metro Disciples Clergy, 1983-84; mem. Kentuckiana Disciples Area Cabinet, 1983-84, chaplains adv. com. Christian Ch. Home, 1983-84; mem. Assn. of Disciple Musicians. Tchr. pub. sch. music, N.C. and N.Y., 1968-74; music instr. Auburn Community Coll., N.Y., 1971-73. Contbg. author: Communion Thoughts and Prayers, 1976. Recipient Worship award Christian Bd. Publ., Bethany Press, St. Louis, 1964. Mem. Am. Guild of English Handbell Ringers, Sigma Alpha Iota, Delta Zeta. Democrat. Clubs: Bus. and Profl. Women, Women's Club (v.p. Marion 1979-80). Home: 9818 Vieux Carre Dr Apt 20 Louisville KY 40223 Office: 11508 Main St PO Box 43266 Middletown Christian Ch Middletown KY 40243

MILLER, RANDALL LEE, minister, Southern Baptist Convention; b. Granite City, Ill., June 22, 1950; s. Floyd Leo and Jardena Loraine (Hoover) M.; m. Joy Louise Mallory, Mar. 17, 1973; children: Robert Christopher, James Theodore. B.A., Mo. Bapt. Coll., 1977; M.Div., Southwestern Bapt. Theol. Sem., 1980. Ordained to ministry Baptist Ch., 1979. Part-time pastor Ida Bapt. Ch., Sherman, Tex., 1979-80; pastor Marquette Heights Bapt. Ch., Ill., 1980—; cons. Ill. Bapt. State Assn., 1981—; assoc. ch. tng. dir. Metro-Peoria Bapt. Assn., 1981, mem. exec. com., 1980. Democrat. Home: 109 Lincoln Rd Marquette Heights IL 61554

MILLER, RANDOLPH CRUMP, priest, religious organization executive, Episcopal Church; b. Fresno, Calif., Oct. 1, 1910; s. Ray Oakley and Laura Belle (Crump) M.; m. Muriel Phyllis Hallett, June 9, 1938 (dec. 1948); m. Elizabeth Williams Fowlkes, June 16, 1950; children: Barbara Hallett, Frank Fowlkes, Phyllis Muriel (Mrs. Victor A.B. Symonds), Carol Christine (Mrs. Laurance B. Rand II), Elizabeth Rives (Mrs. Richard Carroll, Jr.), Muriel Randolph (Mrs. James Leahy). A.B., Pomona Coll., 1931; Ph.D., Yale U., 1936; D.D., pacific Sch. of Religion, 1952; S.T.D., Ch. Div. Sch. of Pacific, 1952; D.D. (hon.) Episc. Theol. Sch., 1961, Berkeley/Yale Div. Sch., 1981. Ordained to ministry, Episc. ch., as deacon, 1935, as priest, 1937. Instr., asst. prof., prof. Ch. Div. Sch. of Pacific, Berkeley, Calif., 1936-52; vicar, rector St. Alban's Ch., Albany, Calif., 1940-52; prof. Yale U., New Haven, Conn., 1952-81; exec. sec. Religious Edn. Assn., New Haven, 1982-85, editor religious edn., 1958-78; curriculum com. Episc. Ch., N.Y.C., 1946-56. Author: What We Can Believe, 1941; A Guide for Church School Teachers, 1943; Religion Makes Sense, 1950; Clue to Christian Education, 1950; Biblical Theology and Christian Education, 1954; Christian Nurture and the Church, 1960; Education for Christian Living, (rev.) 1963; The Language Gap and God, 1970, Living With Anxiety, 1971; Live Until You Die, 1973; The American Spirit in Theology, 1974; This We Can Believe, 1976; The Theory of Christian Education Practice, 1980. Editor: Church and Organized Movements, 1946; (with others) Christianity and the Contemporary Scene, 1943. Home: 15 Edgehill Rd New Haven CT 06511 Office: Religious Edn Assn 409 Prospect St New Haven CT 06510

MILLER, RAYMOND ALLEN, JR., minister, Lutheran Church in America; b. Darby, Pa., Feb. 27, 1953; s. Raymond Allen and Helen Irene (White) M. B.A., Upsala Coll., 1975; M.Div., Luth. Theol. Sem., Phila., 1979, postgrad., 1980—. Ordained to ministry Luth. Ch., 1979. Pastor, Trinity Luth. Ch., Fairless Hills, Pa., 1979—; mem. profl. leadership service com. S.E. Pa. Synod, Luth. Ch. Am., 1980—; sec. Ministerium, Levittown-Fairless Hills, Pa., 1980-81; convener Liturgical Interest Group, Eastern Pa. and N.J., 1981-84, Luth. Pastors Cluster, Lower Bucks County, Pa., 1984—. Mem. Concordia Hist. Inst. Democrat. Home: 148 Fairfax Rd Fairless Hills PA 19030 Office: Trinity Evangelical Lutheran Church Hood Blvd Fairless Hills PA 19030

MILLER, RAYMOND SYLVESTER, minister, administrator, Church of God-Anderson, Indiana; b. Salina, Kans., Mar. 31, 1917; s. Calvary Raymond and Pearl Mae (Parman) M.; student Anderson Coll., 1935-38, Kans. U., 1949-50, East Tenn. State U., 1958-60; m. Nelda Nuree Settlemryre, Sept. 4, 1937; children: Joyce (Mrs. Jesse D. Elliott), Carol (Mrs. Lonnie E. Hefner), Marian (Mrs. William P. Mossman).

Ordained to ministry, 1943, part time chaplain N.C. Central Prison, Raleigh, 1943-44; pastor chs., N.C., 1939-46, S.C., 1946-48, Kans., 1948-50, Mo., 1950-57, Tenn., 1957-60, Ill., 1960-66; chmn. Mo. State Ministers Assembly, 1955-57, Tenn. State Ministerial Assembly, 1959-60, Ill, Ministerial Assembly, 1964-65; exec. sec. Gen. Assembly Ch. of God in Ill., 1967-80, Ill. State treas., 1968-80, dir. evangelism and mission, 1970—; dir. devel. Ill. Ch. of God, 1980-85; mem. Div. World Service, chmn. 1973-75; chmn. Central States Ministers Conv. of Ch. of God, 1971, 72, 75, 76; editor Ill. LINK, Ch. of God, 1968—; corr. Vital Christanity, 1971-76. Home: 935 Mintler Dr Mount Zion IL 62549

MILLER, ROBERT ROYCE, priest Roman Catholic Church; b. Chgo., Jan. 5, 1944; s. George James and Genevieve Mary (Royce) M. B.A., Loras Coll., 1965; M.Div., St. Paul Sem., 1975. Ordained priest Roman Catholic Ch., 1969. Assoc. pastor Good Counsel Ch., Aurora, Ill., 1969-71, St. Patrick Ch., St. Charles, Ill., 1971-79; pastor St. James Cath. Ch., Belvidere, 1979—; mem. faculty St. Edward High Sch., Elgin, Ill., 1971-76. Vice pres. Priests Senate, Rockford, Ill., 1982-84; chmn. Rockford Diocese Presbyteral Council, 1985—. Author: That All May Be One, 1976. Bd. dirs. local food pantry Salvation Army, 1983; pres. Boone County Ministerial Assn., 1982-84. Mem. Canon Law Soc. Address: 514 Cawell St Belvidere IL 61008

MILLER, RONALD CLAIR, JR., minister, Lutheran Church in America; b. Bedford, Pa., Nov. 26, 1956; s. Ronald Clair and Louisa Jane (Bowers) M. B.A. in Criminology, Ind. U. Pa., 1978; M.Div., Luth. Theol. Sem., 1982. Ordained to ministry Lutheran Ch. Am., 1982. Pastor St. James Luth. Ch., Jersey Shore, Pa., 1982—; chmn. Central Pa. Synod - Youth Gathering, Shippensburg, Pa., 1984. Chmn. Williamsport Dist. Youth Cabinet, Pa., 1982-84. Democrat.

MILLER, RONALD EARL, minister, Luth. Ch. Am.; b. Savannah, Ga., Aug. 30, 1935; s. Harold Burton and Frances (Blake) M.; A.B., Newberry Coll., 1957; M.Div., Luth. Theol. So. Sem., 1960; grad. Command and Gen. Staff Coll. U.S. Army, 1975; m. Elizabeth Jane Barker, June 4, 1960; 1 son, Burton Ronald. Ordained to ministry, 1960; minister Lutheran chs., Ga., 1960-61, Fla., 1961-63, S.C., 1963—, including St. Luke Luth. Ch., Columbia, 1967-69, Mt. Pleasant Luth. Ch., Ehrhardt, 1969—. Chaplain S.C. Army N.G., 1965—; group chaplain 151st Field Arty. Group, 1972—; condr. WWBD Radio Devotions, Bamberg, S.C., 1970—. Mem. S.C. Army N.G. Assn. Club: Lions (pres. 1975, Ehrhardt). Home and Office: PO Box 37 Ehrhardt SC 29081

MILLER, RUSSELL EDMUND, lay worker, Baptist Church, energy investment analyst; b. Schenectady, N.Y., Mar. 23, 1942; s. L. Russell and Arline (Wooden) M.; m. Nancy Steeble, June 6, 1964; children: Laura, Ted, Sarah, Andrew. A.B., Bowdoin Coll., 1964; M.B.A., Columbia Bus. Sch., 1966. Metro chmn. Christian Bus. Men's Com., Balt., 1976-84; deacon Timonium Presbyn. Ch., Balt., 1978-83; dir. Balt. Billy Graham Crusade, Balt., 1982; trustee Washington Bible Coll., Lanham, Md., 1982—, Arlington Bapt. Ch., Balt., 1985—; v.p. Alex Brown & Sons, Inc., Balt., 1981—. Chmn. Energy Conservation Com., Balt., 1983-85. Served to 1st lt. U.S. Army, 1967-74. Mem. Nat. Assn. Petroleum Investment Analysts, Ind. Producers Assn. Am. Republican. Lodge: Kiwanis. Home: 315 Broxton Rd Baltimore MD 21212 Office: Alex Brown & Sons Inc 135 E Baltimore St Baltimore MD 21202

MILLER, SHOFNER CLEOPHUS, clergyman, Southern Baptist Convention; b. Athens, Tex., Mar. 10, 1916; s. Gus and Maggie (Shofner) M.; m. Vivian Burns, June 1948 (div. 1955); m. Edna M. Hallum, May 21, 1955; 1 child, Charles Le'Von. B.Th., Stanton U., Tampa, Fla., 1975; D.Div., Gramling U., 1969. Ordained to ministry, 1952. Pastor, Mt. Zion Bapt. Ch., Graham, Tex., 1956-60, Solomon Temple, Stanford, Tex., 1960-64, New Mickle Bapt. Ch., Camden, N.J., 1964-71, Manchester Bapt. Ch., Los Angeles, 1971—; pres., dean, dir. Amity Community Bible Sch., Los Angeles, 1979—. Served with U.S. Army, 1942-44. Recipient award Occupational Indsl. Ctr., Phila., 1968; award Pacific Dist. Assn. Jr. Women, Los Angeles, 1982. Mem. NAACP. Democrat. Lodge: Masons. Office: Manchester Bapt Ch 7926 S Vermont Ave Los Angeles CA 90044

MILLER, TIMOTHY ALAN, minister, religion educator, National Association of Congregational Christian Churches; b. Wichita, Kans., Aug. 23, 1944; s. Paul Alfred and Margaret Jean (Thompson) M.; m. Tamara Lea Dutton, Aug. 11, 1982; 1 child, Jesse Emerson. B.A., U. Kans., 1966; M.Div., Crozer Theol. Sem., 1968; M.A., U. Kans., 1969, Ph.D., 1973. Ordained to ministry, Congl. Ch., 1968. Asst. minister Plymouth Congl. Ch., Wichita, 1968; minister Bethany Park Christian Ch., Lawrence, Kans., 1968-71; lectr. religious studies U. Kans., Lawrence, 1969—. Author: (with others) The Sauna Book, 1977; Editor (newsletter) Plumber's Friend, 1981—, Am. Studies Jour., 1982—. Contbr. articles to profl. jours. Chmn. city commn. campaign, Lawrence, 1981, 1983; vice chmn. Traffic Safety Commn., Lawrence, 1982—; bd. dirs. Citizens' Com. on Alcoholism, Lawrence, 1982-84, Oread Neighborhood Assn., Lawrence, 1982-83; Democratic precinct committeeman, 1984—. Grantee Kans. Com. on Humanities, 1981, Kans. Sch. Religion, 1981-82; recipient various scholarships, fellowships. Mem. Am. Acad. Religion (sect. chmn. 1982—), Nat. Hist. Communal Socs. Assn., Midcontinent Am. Studies Assn. Home: 936 Ohio St Lawrence KS 66044 Office: Dept Religious Studies U Kans 103 Smith Hall Lawrence KS 66045

MILLER, WILL LANDON, minister, So. Baptist Conv.; b. Chattanooga, May 6, 1917; s. Will Landon and Evelyn (Sherrill) M.; B.A., Carson-Newman Coll., 1940; Th.M., So. Bapt. Theol. Sem., 1943; Th.D., Southwestern Bapt. Theol. Sem., 1948; postgrad. Princeton Theol. Sem., 1946; m. Katherine Rankin, May 27, 1941; children—Marshall Lee, Lofton Sherill. Ordained to ministry, 1939; pastor Parker's Gap, Chattanooga, 1939-40, White Mills (Ky.) Bapt. Ch., 1940-43, White Oak Bapt. Ch., Chattanooga, 1943-46, Broadway Bapt. Ch., Ft. Worth, 1946-47, First Bapt. Ch., Brookhaven, Miss., 1947-51, First Bapt. Ch., Sherman, Tex., 1951-57, Ruhama Bapt. Ch., Birmingham, Ala., 1957-65, Northminster Bapt. Ch., Richmond, Va., 1965—; chaplain Richmond Bur. Police, 1974—; pres. State Tng. Union Conv. of Tex., 1954-55, guest prof. Southwestern Bapt. Theol. Sem., 1957; Sunday Sch. Bd. So. Bapt. Conv., 1955-58; preacher conv. sermon Ala. Bap. State Conv., 1960; guest speaker USAF, Aerospace Def. Commd. Chaplains' Conf., Colorado Springs, 1970; preacher ann. conv. sermon Bapt. Gen. Assn. Va., 1976; exec. bd. state convs. of Miss., Tex., Ala., Va. Pres. Ministers Assn. Greater Birmingham, 1963. Mem. Birmingham Civic Commn. to Pres. Kennedy, 1963; trustee New Orleans Theol. Sem., 1949-51. Recipient Distinguished Clergymen's award U.S. Navy, 1971. Author: Bible Studies of Difficult Doctrines, 1951; Making a Go of Marriage, 1956; A Baptist Primer, 1959. Office: Westwood and Moss Side Aves Richmond VA 23222

MILLER, WILLIAM ALVIN, minister, American Lutheran Church; b. Pitts., Jan. 1, 1931; s. Christ William and Anna Ernestine (Wilhelm) M.; m. Marilyn Mae Miller, Aug. 8, 1953; children: Mark William, Eric Michael. A.B., Capital U., 1953; M.Div., Luth. Theol. Sem., 1957; M.S.T., Andover Newton Theol. Sch., 1958, D.Ministry, 1974. Ordained to ministry Lutheran Ch., 1958. Pastor St. James Lutheran Ch., Balt., 1958-66; chaplain Fairview Hosp., Mpls., 1966-73; dir. dept. religion and health Fairview Hosp., Mpls., 1973—; instr. Fairview Sch. Nursing, Mpls., 1967-75, Luther Northwestern Theol. Sem., St. Paul, 1973—; chmn. bd. di's. Luth. Social Services Md., Balt., 1963-65; trustee Am. Protestant Health Assn., Schaumburg, Ill., 1984—. Author: Why Do Christians Break Down?, 1973; Big Kids' Mother Goose, 1976; When Going to Pieces Holds You Together, 1976; You Count, You Really Do!, 1976; Mid Life: New Life, 1978; Conversations, 1980; Make Friends With Your Shadow, 1981; Prayers at Mid Point, 1983. Assoc. editor Jour. Pastoral Care, 1984—. Contbr. articles to profl. jours. Chaplain, Randallstown Jr. C. of C., Md., 1962-64. Fellow Coll. Chaplains Am. Protestant Health Assn. (pres. 1985-87), Assn. Mental Health Clergy (regional cert. chmn. 1978—); mem. Assn. Clin. Pastoral Edn. (cert. supr., asst. treas. 1981-82), Minn. C.G. Jung Assn. (pres. 1976-77). Home: 2005 Xanthus Ln Plymouth MN 55447 Office: Fairview Hosp 2312 S 6th St Minneapolis MN 55454

MILLER, WILLIAM BAYARD, religious organization executive, Presbyterian Church (U.S.A.); b. Latrobe, Pa., Mar. 17, 1924; s. Charles Spurgeon and Ethel (Bayard) M.; m. Jean Eisler Keck, Mar. 28, 1948; children: William, Marjorie Keck. B.A., Allegheny Coll., 1947; M.A., U. Pa., 1951. Asst. research historian Presbyn. Hist. Soc., Phila., 1957-59, dir. dept. history, 1968—; sec.-treas. Am. Soc. Ch. History, Wallingford, Pa., 1972—. Assoc. editor Jour. Presbyn. History, 1957—. Bd. dirs. Tullytown Sch. Dist., Pa. 1955-61. Served to lt. (j.g.) USNR, 1945-46. Recipient Disting. Service award Presby. Hist. Soc., 1982; named Profl. Mem. of Yr., Assn. Records Mgmt. Adminstrn., 1982. Mem. Am. Hist. Assn., Pa. Hist. Assn., Phila. Hist. Assn., Soc. Am. Archivists (M. Claude Lane award 1978), Geneal. Soc. Pa. (bd. dirs. 1968-75). Republican. Home: 305 E Country Club Ln Wallingford PA 19086 Office: Presbyn Hist Soc 425 Lombard Philadelphia PA 19147

MILLER, WILLIAM CHARLES, theological librarian, Church of the Nazarene; b. Mpls., Oct. 26, 1947; s. Robert Charles and Cleithra Mae (Johnson) M.; m. Brenda Kathleen Barnes, July 24, 1969; children: Amy Renee, Jared. A.B., Marion Coll., 1968; M.L.S., Kent State U., 1974, Ph.D., 1983; postgrad. U. Kans., 1984-85. Librarian Nazarene Theol. Sem., Kansas City, Mo., 1978—; chmn. OCLC Theol. Users Group, 1984—. Editor TUG Newsletter, 1984—. Contbr. articles to profl. jours. Served with U.S. Army, 1968-72. Mem. Wesleyan Theol. Soc., Am. Theol. Library Assn. (bd. dirs. 1985—), Assn. Study Higher Edn., ALA, Kansas City Theol. Library Assn. (pres. 1979-80, 1983—), Beta Phi Mu. Office: Nazarene Theol Sem 1700 E Meyer Blvd Kansas City MO 64131

MILLER, WILLIAM HOPKINS, minister, Presbyterian Church in the U.S.; b. Lewisburg, Pa., Feb. 1, 1931; s. J. Hillis and Nell Martin (Critzer) M.; m. Gloria Diane Burfeind, Dec. 19, 1953; children: William, Catherine, Ellen, J. Mark. B.A., Swarthmore Coll., 1951; M.Div., Princeton Theol. Sem., 1954. Ordained minister Presbyn. Ch., 1954. Asst. pastor Westminster Presbyn. Ch., Ft. Lauderdale, Fla., 1956-61; dir. Vol. Service Bd. of Nat. Missions, N.Y.C., 1961-72; dir. People in Mission Program Agy., Presbyn. Ch., N.Y.C., 1972—. Democrat. Office: Program Agy 475 Riverside Dr New York NY 10115

MILLER, WILLIAM LEE, JR., minister Christian Church (Disciples of Christ); b. Mammoth Spring, Ark., Dec. 27, 1926; s. William L. and Janie Katherine (Murrell) M.; m. Marion Evelyn O'Neal, Mar. 23, 1947 (div. 1976); children: Georgia Katherine Miller Phelps, William Lee III; m. Judith Ann Bell, Nov. 28, 1977. A.B., Phillips U., 1950; B.D., Lexington Theol. Sem., 1961; postgrad. U. Ark., 1951-52, Tex. Christian U., 1958, U. Ky., 1961. Litt.D., Phillips U., 1968. Ordained to ministry Christian Church (Disciples of Christ), 1950. Pastor, 1st Christian Ch., Rogers, Ark., 1952-59; v.p. Bd. Higher Edn. Indpls., 1962-68; pres. Bd. Higher Edn., Christian Ch. (Disciples of Christ), 1968-77; v.p. devel. Nat. City Christian Ch. Corp., Washington, 1977-82; upper Midwest regional minister, pres. Christian Ch. (Disciples of Christ), Des Moines, 1982—; dir. Christian Ch. Found., Indpls., 1968-77, 84; trustee Bethany Coll. (W.Va.), 1972—, Culver Stockton Coll., 1970—, Tougaloo Coll., Jackson, Miss., 1970-76. Precinct committeeman Democratic Party, Indpls., 1968-72; bd. dirs. St. Louis Christian Home, 1956-68; chmn. Coop. Coll. Registry, Washington, 1963-70. Served with USCG, 1945-47. Mem. Nat. Soc. Fund Raising Execs., Disciples of Christ Hist. Soc., Council Christian Unity (exec. com. 1961), Nat. Evangelitic Assn. (bd. dirs. 1983—), Am. Assn. Higher Edn., Sigma Chi. Lodges: Masons, KT. Home: 1207 21st St West Des Moines IA 50265 Office: Christian Ch Disciples of Christ PO Box 1024 Des Moines IA 50311

MILLER, WILLIAM SHANNON, deacon, Episcopal Church; b. N. Kansas City, Mo., Dec. 3, 1926; s. John Shannon and Eunice Millicent (Barrington) M.; m. Clara Anne D'Orazio, Nov. 21, 1945; children: Cynthia Jeanne, Cheryl Anne, Carolyn Sue, Christine Marie. Student, Ashland Coll., 1975-76, St. Paul Sch. Theology, 1976-77, Rockhurst Coll., 1977-79; Ordained deacon, 1979. Assisting deacon St. Michael's Ch., Independence, Mo., 1979-83; bishop's deacon Diocese of W. Mo., Kansas City, 1979—; assisting deacon All Saints Ch., Kansas City, 1984—; del. Diocese of Huron, London, Ont., 1962-66, Diocese of Ohio, Cleve., 1969-75, Diocese of W. Mo., 1976-78, chmn. VIM, Metro Deanery, 1978-80, coordinator Venture in Mission, 1978—. Contbr. articles to profl. jours. Editor, founder deacon's newsletter, Deacons Doin's, 1983—. Vol., mem. Speakers Bur., Hospice Care, Inc., Pinellas Park, Fla., 1983-84. Served with USCG, 1944-46. Recipient Export Mktg. award U.S. CSC, 1973; Meritorious Service award, Warren Rupp Co., 1976; Year's Spl. Commendation award, Hospice Care, Inc., 1984, others. Mem. Harry S. Truman Library Inst. (hon. fellow), Am. Mental Health Fund. Home: 402 Point Dr Lee's Summit MO 64063 Office: All Saints Episcopal Church 9201 Wornall Rd Kansas City MO 64114

MILLEVILLE, NANCY BETH ANDERSON, minister, Lutheran Church in America; b. Stuttgart, Fed. Republic Germany, Dec. 21, 1952; d. Leonard Wersell and Barbara Anne (Shelton) Anderson; m. Randy Philip Milleville, Sept. 5, 1982; 1 child, Philip Andrew. B.A., Upsala Coll., 1976; M.Div., Luth. Theol. Sem., 1980. Ordained to ministry Lutheran Ch. in Am., 1980. Youth staffer Luth. Ch. in Am., New Eng. Synod, 1973-74; youth coordinator Calvary Luth. Ch., Cranford, N.J., 1975-76; pastor St. John's Luth. Ch., Elma, N.Y., 1980—; sec. Dist. Cabinet, Niagara Frontier Dist., N.Y., 1981—; sem. candidate rev. team Upper N.Y. Synod, 1983—; conv. coordinator Upper N.Y. Synod, 1983—. Sec. Lighten It for These counseling service, Elma, 1981—. Mem. Assn. Women Ministers. Republican. Club: Zonta (East Aurora N.Y.).

MILLS, CHARLES MICHAEL, minister, Presbyterian Church in the U.S.; b. Evansville, Ind., Nov. 7, 1947; s. Charles Willard and Beytte Lorraine (Purtle) M.; m. Dalinda Constable, Jan. 25, 1980. B.A. cum laude in English Lit., U. Louisville, 1970; M.Div. with honors, Louisville Presbyn. Sem., 1973; D.Min., Covington Sem., 1984. Ordained to ministry Presbyn. Ch., 1974. Student asst. Midland Pk. Presbyn. Ch., Louisville, 1970-73; asst. pastor First Presbyn. Ch., Covington, Ky., 1975-77; pastor Grace Ch., Clarksville, Ind., 1977—; coordinating council mem. Ohio Valley Presbytery, So. Ind., 1982—. Author: Dirty Hands, Pure Hearts, 1985; also articles. Recipient Flexner scholarship U. Louisville, 1972; Anderson fellow Louisville Presbyn. Sem., 1973; Woodcock Acad. Soc. award, 1973. Democrat. Lodges: Masons, Shriners, Scottish Rite, York Rite. Home: 606 Harvard Dr Apt 9 Clarksville IN 47130 Office: Grace Presbyn Ch USA 555 Eastern Blvd Clarksville IN 47130

MILLS, EARLE MICHAEL, church youth administrator; American Baptist Church; b. Santa Cruz, Calif., June 7, 1957; s. Earle Harding and Dorothy Ruth (Phillips) M.; m. Janet Marie Hanekamp, Jan. 1, 1983. Youth dir. First Bapt. Ch., Santa Cruz, 1976-78, 83—; actor, dir. Covenant Players, Woodland Hills, Calif., 1981-83; chmn. co-founder Christian Youth Workers Assn., Santa Cruz, 1984—. Editor, pub.: Youth Adventures, 1983—. Republican. Avocations: cross-country bicycling. Office: First Bapt Ch 411 Roxas St Santa Cruz CA 95062

MILLS, HOWARD M., seminary administrator. Pres. United Theol. Sem. of the Twin Cities (United Church of Christ), New Brighton, Minn. Office: United Theol Sem of the Twin Cities 300 5th St New Brighton MN 55112*

MILLS, JON FELTON, minister of music, So. Baptist Conv.; b. Gainesville, Fla., June 11, 1938; s. Felton Graves and Myrtle Adelia (Bassett) M.; Mus.B., U. Chattanooga, 1969; M.Ch. Music, New Orleans Bapt. Theol. Sem., 1971; m. Elsie Kaye Linhart, Jan. 15, 1962; children—Caron Elisabeth, Julia Anne, Jon Felton. Ordained to ministry, 1969; minister music chs. in Ga., 1967-71; minister music S. Harriman (Tenn.) Bapt. Ch., 1972-73; minister music, asso. pastor Parkview Bapt. Ch., Greenville, Miss., 1973—. Mem. Am. Choral Dirs. Assn., Choristers Guild, Phi Mu Alpha. Home: 727 Golf St Greenville MS 38701 Office: 712 McAllister St Greenville MS 38701

MILLS, ROBERT JACKSON, minister, Southern Baptist Convention; b. Atlanta, Nov. 15, 1955; s. Flavel Jackson and Jacqueline (Chlidres) M.; m. Angela Marie Acree, Aug. 5, 1978; 1 son, John Robert. B.S., Ga. State U., 1978; M.Div., So. Bapt. Theol. Sem., 1981. Ordained to ministry, 1979. Assoc. pastor First Bapt. Ch., Pekin, Ind., 1979-80, pastor, 1980-82; pastor Mansfield Bapt. Ch., Ga., 1982—; steering com. Stone Mt. Bapt. Assn., Conyers, Ga., 1984—, dir. V.B.S., 1984-85, chmn. com. on coms., 1983-84, chmn. resolutions com., 1982-84. Active Big Bros., Louisville, 1979-81. Democrat. Office: Mansfield Bapt Ch Hwy 11 Mansfield GA 30255

MILLS, TALMADGE STEVEN, minister, Independent Charismatic Church; b. Elizabeth City, N.C., Aug. 7, 1948; s. Talmadge Dewitt and Doriene (Vinyard) M.; m. Kathleen M. Andruczk, May 2, 1970; children: Talmadge Steven, Jr., Aaron Robert. Lic. broadcasting, Creative Ednl. Media Sch., 1983; student Ministry, Rhema Bible Coll., 1983; B.A. in Bible, Sun Grove Bible Coll., 1984. Ordained to ministry Independent Charismatic Ch., 1980. Youth pastor So. Bapt. Ch., St. Louis, 1978, 79; assoc. pastor Ch. of the Carpender, Toms River, N.J., 1979, 80-81; asst. to chaplain State of Okla., Tulsa, 1981, 83; pastor Victory Christian Fellowship, Odessa, Tex., 1983-84, Morning Star Fellowship, 1984—. Served with U.S. Army, 1966-69, Vietnam. Mem. United Assn. Christian Counselors, Assn. Christian Broadcaster. Home: 50 Gary Pl Odessa TX 79762 Office: Morning Star Fellowship 325 W County Rd Odessa TX 79763

MILONE, ANTHONY M. See *Who's Who in America*, 43rd edition.

MILTON, HENRY, minister, Baptist Ch.; b. Arcadia, Okla., Apr. 13, 1918; s. Sam Emma (Sanders) M.; diploma San Francisco Bapt. Coll., 1949-53; m. Corine Snowden, Jan. 26, 1946; children—Leon, Antonette. Ordained to ministry, 1954; pastor St. Paul Bapt. Ch., Calif., 1956-57; pastor Macedonia Bapt. Ch., Menlo Park, Calif., 1958—. Pres. Peninsula Bapt. Ministers Union, 1969-75; mem. minister's council, finance dir. Bay Area Bapt. Dist. Assn. Mem. bd. Self-Help project, Menlo Park, 1975. Recipient community service awards, Mothers of Edn. Home: 38 N Claremont St San Mateo CA 94401 Office: 1110 Berkeley Ave Menlo Park CA 94025

MIMS, BILLY BURNS, JR., minister, Lutheran Church in America; b. Greensboro, N.C., June 18, 1946; s. Billy Burns Mims and Virginia Lucille (Umbaugh) Mims Calhoun; m. Sherry Lynne Foust, Dec. 21, 1968; children: John Thomas, Stephen Frederick. B.A., U. N.C., 1968; M.Div., Luth. Theol. So. Sem., 1972; D.Min., Union Theol. Sem., Richmond, Va., 1983. Ordained to ministry Lutheran Ch., 1972. Vicar, Trinity Luth. Ch., Jacksonville, Fla., 1970-71; pastor Wittenberg Luth. Ch., Granite Quarry, N.C., 1972-74, Incarnation Luth. Ch., Columbia, S.C., 1974-79, Orangeburg Luth. Ch., S.C., 1979—; trustee Lutheridge, Arden, N.C., 1980—; dean Amelia dist. S.C. Synod, Luth. Ch. in Am., 1983—, chmn. profl. leadership service com. S.C. Synod, 1982-84. Contbr. articles to religious jour. Recipient award cert. Am. Assn. Blood Banks, 1983. Mem. Orangeburg Regional Hosp. Vol. Chaplains Assn. (pres. 1981-83). Office: Orangeburg Luth Ch 610 Ellis Ave NE Orangeburg SC 29115

MINER, MALCOLM HUBBARD, priest, Episcopal Church; charitable organization executive; b. Holyoke, Mass., Nov. 15, 1920; s. Harold Edson and Blanche Barton (Temple) M.; m. Joan Alward Eddy, May 20, 1943 (dec. Mar. 1967); children: Linda Miner Spannagel, Donna Miner Anderson; b. Marga Ruth Hass, Sept. 20, 1968; 1 child, Philip Carl. Student Am. Internat. Coll., 1939; B.A., U. Maine, 1947; postgrad. Bangor Theol. Sem., 1940-47, Berkely Div. Sch., Yale U., 1949. Ordained to ministry Methodist Ch., 1948, Episcopal Ch., 1950. Vicar Episcopal Chs., South Barre and North Brookfield, Mass., 1949-51; rector Saint Andrews Ch., Oakland, Calif., 1952-56, All Saints Ch., Anchorage, 1956-62; vicar Saint Matthias Ch., Seaside, Calif., 1962-68; assoc. rector Saint Barnabas Ch., Warwick, R.I., 1968-69; dir. Greater Anchorage Ministries, 1969—; Pacific N.W. warden Order of St. Luke, 1975-81, Alaska warden, 1983—, dir. nat. bd. dirs., 1983—; mem. standing com. Episcopal Diocese Alaska, Fairbanks, 1982—. Exec. dir. United Way Anchorage, 1969—. Author: Healing is for Real, 1972; Healing and the Abundant Life, 1979. Mem. editorial bd. Sharing, 1984. Contbr. articles to religious jours. Councilman, City Council, Seaside, Calif., 1966-68; mem. Monterey County Anti-Poverty Council, Monterey, Calif., 1965-68; chmn. No. TV Adv. Bd., Anchorage, 1980-82; mem. Crime Stoppers of Anchorage, 1981—. Named Man of Yr., YMCA, Anchorage, 1961; recipient Community Service award C. of C., Anchorage, 1974; Paul Harris fellow Anchorage Rotary, 1982. Lodges: Lions (chaplain 1956-68), Rotary. Home: 1841 Falcon Circle Anchorage AK 99504 Office: United Way of Anchorage 109 W 6th Ave Anchorage AK 99501

MING, DONALD GEORGE, bishop, African Methodist Episcopal Church; b. Devonshire, Bermuda, July 6, 1930; s. C.E. and Mable D. (Woolridge) M.; came to U.S., 1949, naturalized, 1962; B.S., Wilberforce U., 1954, LL.D., 1976; B.D., Payne Theol. Sem., 1955, M.Div., 1974; D.D., Payne Coll., 1975; dip. Edward Waters Coll., 1971; m. Edith White, July 6, 1957. Ordained to ministry, 1952; pastor Bethel A.M.E. Ch., Beverly, N.J., 1955-57, Mt. Zion A.M.E. Ch., Dover, Del., 1957-60, Murphy A.M.E. Ch., Chester, Pa., 1960-64, Allen A.M.E. Ch., Jamaica, N.Y., 1964-76; bishop 15th Dist. embracing Republic of S. Africa and S.W. Africa, 1976—. Organizer Allen Community Day Care Center, 1971-76, Allen Community Sr. Citizens Center, 1974—; vice chmn. sch. bd., Dist. 29, Queens, N.Y., 1971—; program chmn. Jamaica Center for Older Adults, 1973—; mem. Jamaica Anti-Poverty Bd., 1965-71; bd. dirs. Queen Shelter, 1966—, Payne Theology Sem., 1972—, Turner Theol. Sem., 1972—. Recipient Queens Interfaith Clergy award, 1967; African Meth. Spl. Achievement award, 1970; Bd. Edn. award for spl. dedication, City of N.Y., 1973, 75; Allen African Meth. Ch. awards, 1968, 76. Mem. NAACP, Wilberforce U. Alumni Assn., Payne Theol. Sem. Alumni Assn., Queens Fedn. Chs., Protestant Welfare Orgn., Alpha Phi Alpha. Contbr. articles to religious jours. Home: 146-24 223d St Rosedale NY 11413 Office: 28 Walmer Rd Woodstock Capetown Republic South Africa 8001

MING, JAMES MELVYN, religious educator, minister, Assemblies of God; b. Lynwood, Calif., Aug. 8, 1947; s. James Manzell and Mabel Allene (Colby) M.; m. Martha Ann York, June 25, 1971; children: Hannah Marie, Rebekah Ann. B.A., So. Calif. Coll., 1969; M.R.E., Southwestern Bapt. Theol. Sem., 1973; D.Min., Drew U., 1981. Ordained to ministry, 1973. Campus pastor Monte Vista High Sch., Watsonville, CAlif., 1969-70; minister youth Assembly of God, Dallas, 1971-73, minister of edn., Oklahoma City, and Grand Junction, Colo., 1973-76; assoc. prof. N.W. Coll. of Assemblies of God, Kirkland, Wash., 1976-83, acad. dean, 1984—; chmn. ministerial devel. com. N.W. Dist. of Assemblies of God, 1980-84; lectr. in field. Author: A Time Management Training Module for Ministerial Students, 1981. So. Calif. Coll. Pres.'s scholar, 1967-69. Mem. Nat. Assn. Profs. Christian Edn., Nat. Assn. Dirs. Christian Edn., Christian Educators Fellowship, Delta Kappa. Office: Northwest Coll Assemblies of God Kirkland WA 98033

MINGLEDORFF, CHARLES GLENN, minister, United Methodist Ch.; b. Daytona Beach, Fla., Dec. 10, 1925; s. Charles Robert and Nell Estelle (Roberson) M.; A.B., Fla. So. Coll., 1947, D.D., 1971; M.Div., Vanderbilt U., 1950; m. Laura Lee Frame, June 28, 1949; children—Glenna Lee, Laura Lisa, Dana Lynne. Ordained deacon, 1949, elder, 1951; youth dir. and pastor chs., Tenn., 1947-50; dir. youth work Tenn. Conf., 1950-51; adminstrv. dean Martin Coll., Pulaski, Tenn., 1951-53; mem. youth dept. local ch. div. Gen. Bd. Edn., Nashville, 1954-59; pastor chs., Tenn., 1959-69; pastor Belmont United Meth. Ch., Nashville, 1969-70; pres. Emory and Henry Coll., Emory, Va., 1971-73; pastor Central United Meth. Ch., Utica, N.Y., 1973—. Del. to World Meth. Conf., London, 1968; alt. del. to Uniting Conf., Dallas, to United Meth. Conf., St. Louis. Contbr. articles to ch. sch. publs. Home: 2227 Douglas Crescent Utica NY 13501

MINIFIE, CHARLES JACKSON, priest, Episcopal Church; b. Providence, Apr. 1, 1941; s. Benjamin and Frances Turner (Jackson) M.; B.A., Trinity Coll., 1963; M.Div., Episc. Theol. Sch., 1966; m. Elizabeth Horner, June 15, 1963; children: Rachel, Sarah, Rebecca, Jessica. Ordained priest Episc. Ch., 1966. Asst. to rector St. Thomas Ch., N.Y.C., 1966-69; assoc. rector Trinity Ch., Portland, Oreg., 1969-73; rector St. Andrew's by-the-Sea (summer chapel), Hyannis Port, Mass., 1967-73, Trinity Ch., Newport, R.I., 1973-78; v.p. Hartford Sem. Found., Conn., 1979-80; dir. capital giving and asst. chaplain Mt. Holyoke Coll., South Hadley, Mass., 1981-83; pres. Coll. of Preachers, Washington Cathedral, Washington, 1983—; canon Washington Cathedral, 1984—. Home: 3504 Woodley Rd NW Washington DC 20016 Office: 3510 Woodley Rd NW Washington DC 20016

MINK, DONALD EWING, home missionary, Church of God, Anderson, Indiana; b. St. Joseph, Mo., July 14, 1935; s. David Ewing and Alma Helen (Harned) M.; m. Patricia Louise Lymer, Aug. 15, 1954; children: Debra Ann, Melody Dawn, Nathan Abraham. B.A., Gulf Coast Bible Coll., 1964. Ordained to ministry, 1966. Pastor, Old Town Ch. of God, Thayer, Mo., 1964-70; home missionary Ch. of God, Alliance, Nebr., 1970—; field rep. Ch. of God Home Missions, Anderson, Ind., 1980-83; chmn. Alliance Task Force on Domestic Violence, Nebr., 1984. Named Missionary of Yr., Gulf Coast Bible Coll., 1984. Lodge: Rotary (pres. 1974-75). Home: H C 33 Box 1B Alliance NE 69301 Office: Indian Mission Ch of God HC 33 Box 1B Alliance NE 69301

MINNEY, BRUCE KEVIN, evangelist, Church of Christ and Christian Churches; refrigeration executive; b. Cleve., Dec. 22, 1958; s. Leonard Clavel Minney and Wilma Catherine (Elliott) Minney Sage; m. Penelope Sue Pertuset, May 20, 1983. Religious educator Andover Ch. of Christ, Ohio, 1978, youth worker, 1978; evangelist Northeast Crusaders for Christ, Cin., 1979; youth leader Milford Ch. of Christ, Ohio, 1984—. Parts dept. mgr. Otis Refrigeration Service, Inc., Cin., 1984—. Emergency med. tech. Milford-Miami Twp. Emergency Med. Services, 1980-83. Avocations: softball; frisbee; golf. Home: 14 Gateway Loveland OH 45140 Office: Otis Refrigeration Service Inc 4489 Eastern Ave Cincinnati OH 45226

MINNICH, MARTHA JEAN, minister, Christian Church; b. Thayer, Kans., June 4, 1921; d. Harrison Melborn and Ola Edith (Breuer) M. Student jr. coll., Chanute, Kans., 1944-45, Nat. Bible Coll., Wichita, Kans., 1947. Ordained to ministry Christian Ch., 1950. Minister chs., Hepler, Kans., 1950- 56, Savonburg, Kans., 1951-55, Moran, Kans., 1955—; counselor Hidden Haven Christian Camp, 1950-74, mem. bd. dirs.; producer, speaker weekly radio program Moments with the Master, 1960—. Bd. dirs. Marmaton Housing Inc., Moran, Kans.; mem. adv. bd. Moran Manor Nursing Home, 1972-75; pres. Bus. Profl. Womens Club, 1964-65, Woman of Yr., 1966. Home: Box 487 Moran KS 66755

MINNICK, C.P., JR. Bishop The United Methodist Church, N.C. Conf., Raleigh. Office: The United Meth Ch PO Box 10955 Raleigh NC 27605*

MINNICK, MARK ALAN, religion educator, non-denominational; b. Ridgeway, Pa., May 27, 1953; s. Dallas Eugene and Phyllis Lee (Schmidt) M.; m. Linda Anne Largent, May 30, 1976; 1 dau., Abigail Phyllis. B.A. in Bible, Bob Jones U., 1975, M.A. in Bible, 1977, Ph.D. in N.T. Interpretation, 1983. Grad. asst. Bob Jones U., Greenville, S.C., 1975-80, prof. N.T., 1980—; pastor Marsh-Win Bapt. Ch., Marshville, N.C., 1976-80; assoc. pastor Mt. Calvary Bapt. Ch., Greenville, 1980—. Author: Bob Jones University, 1977-80; Bible Curriculum for Christian Schools; contbg. author: Biblical Viewpoint, Faith for the Family. Del., Republican County Conv., Greenville, 1980. Named Outstanding Master's Student in Bible and Theology Baker Book House, 1977. Mem. Bibl. Archaeology Soc. Republican. Home: 16 Faculty Row Greenville SC 29609 Office: Bob Jones U PO Box 34559 Greenville SC 29614

MINOR, ROBERT NEIL, religion educator, Christian Ch. (Disciples of Christ). B. Milw., Oct. 2, 1945; s. Carl Frederick and Alice Charolette (Bates) M.; m. Kristin Ann Boyenga, Aug. 8, 1970 (div. July 1984); 1 child, Matthew Robert. B.A., Trinity Coll., Deerfield, Ill., 1967, M.A., 1969; Ph.D., U. Iowa, 1975. Assoc. prof. religious studies U. Kans., Lawrence, 1977—, acting dir. Ctr. East Asian Studies, 1984-85. Author: Sri Aurobindo: The Perfect and the Good, 1978; Bhagavadgita: An Exegetical Commentary, 1982. Contbr. chptrs. in books and articles to profl. jours. NEH grantee, 1984; Am. Inst. of Indian Studies fellow, 1981; recipient numerous research grants. Mem. Am. Acad. Religion, Assn. for Asian Studies. Democrat. Home: 3709 W 24th St Lawrence KS 66046 Office: U Kans Dept Religious Studies Smith Hall Lawrence KS 66045

MINOR, RONALD R. Clergyman, gen. sec.-treas., Pentacostal Church of God. Office: Pentecostal Church of God 602 Main St PO Box 850 Joplin MO 64802*

MINUS, PAUL MURRAY, religious educator, minister, United Methodist Church; b. Columbia, S.C., July 26, 1935; s. Paul and Mildred M.; m. Carolyn Dickerson, Apr. 15, 1984; children by previous marriage, David, Stephen. B.A., Yale U., 1955, B.D., 1958, M.A., 1960, Ph.D., 1962. Ordained to ministry, 1964. Univ. chaplain Fla. State U., Tallahassee, 1962-64; faculty Meth. Theol. Sch., Delaware, Ohio,

1964—, prof. ch. history, 1972—; del. World Council Chs. 5th Assembly, 1975; del. United Meth. Gen. Conf., 1976, 84. Author: The Catholic Rediscovery of Protestantism, 1976; Christian Responsibility in a Hungry World, 1976. Editor: Methodism's Destiny in an Ecumenical Age, 1969. Fulbright awardee, 1960-61; Ford Found. scholar, 1951-53; NEH fellow, 1980-81. Mem. N.Am. Acad. Ecuminists (exec. com.). Office: Methodist Theol Sch Box 1204 Delaware OH 43015

MIQUELON, JOSEPH PIERRE, lay worker, Episcopal Church, lithograph company executive; b. Sioux City, Iowa, June 29, 1936; s. Joseph Lee and Jean O. (Stewart) M.; m. Julie Ann Bradford, Dec. 7, 1957 (div. 1980); children: Joseph P., Bradford L., Matthew S.; m. 2d Mary Ruth Geiger, Apr. 11, 1981. Student Oberlin Coll., 1952-55; B.S. in Bus. Adminstrn., U. Mo., 1961, M.B.A., 1969. Vestryman, Ch. of Good Shepherd, Kansas City, Mo., 1970-73, treas., 1973—; assoc. treas. Diocese of West Missouri, Kansas City, 1978-80, treas., 1980—. Sec.-treas. Midland Lithographing Co., North Kansas City, Mo., 1967—. Treas. Clay County Sheltered Facilities Bd., Liberty, Mo., 1971—; bd. dirs. Jr. Achievement Greater Kansas City, 1976-79; campaign mgr., Clay County, 1970. Served with U.S. Army, 1957-60. Mem. Printing Industries Fin. Execs., Beta Sigma Phi. Republican. Home: 10098A N Locust Kansas City MO 64155 Office: Midland Lithographing Co 1841 Vernon St North Kansas City MO 64116

MIRANDA, JESSE, JR., minister, Assemblies of God; b. Albuquerque, Apr. 9, 1937; s. Jesus B. Barrios and Emma (Fajardo) M.; B.A., So. Calif. Coll., Costa Mesa, 1966; M.R.E., Talbot Sem., La Mirada, Calif., 1967; M.S. in Edn., U. Calif., Fullerton, 1970; D.Min., Fuller Theol. Sem., Pasadena, Calif., 1975; m. Susan T. Benavidez, Dec. 23, 1956; children—Jesse Rubel, Michael Roland, Cydelia Ines. Ordained to ministry, 1962; instr. Latin Am. Bible Coll., La Puente, Calif., 1959-70; prin. Norwalk (Calif.) Christian Sch., 1970-73; sec.-treas. Pacific Latin Am. Dist. Council, Assemblies of God, La Habra, Calif., 1973—; pres. Latin Am. Theol. Sem., La Puente, 1975—. Gen. presbyter Gen. Council Assemblies of God; treas. regional Hispanic adv. com. Assn. Theol. Sch.; mem. Hispanic adv. com. Fuller Theol. Sem.; Bible translator Lockman Found; bd. dirs. Greater Los Angeles Sunday Sch. Assn.; exec. dir. Mexican Am. Sunday Sch. Addn. Home: 3257 Thaxton Ave Hacienda Heights CA 91745 Office: 850 E La Habra Blvd La Habra CA 90631

MIRITZ, MELVIN AUGUST, minister, American Lutheran Church; b. Fond du Lac, Wis., October 30, 1926; s. Alpha C. and Lina V. (Bock) M.; m. Linda Winter, Aug. 10, 1947; children: Mark, Debra. B.A., Wartburg Coll., 1947; M.Div., Wartburg Sem., 1950; S.T.M., Nashotah House, 1970; D.Min., Luth. Sch. Theology at Chgo., 1978. Ordained to ministry Am. Luth. Ch., 1950. Pastor, First Luth. Ch., Ohio, Ill., 1950-52, St. John's Luth. Ch., Johnson Creek, Wis., 1952-56, Luth. Ch. of Redeemer, Racine, Wis., 1956-79; dir. pastoral care A-Ctr., Racine, 1979—; trustee Lincoln Luth. Home Bd., Racine, 1958-70; pres. State Campus Ministry Bd., Milw., 1960-64; dir. Inner-City Ministry Bd., Racine, 1965; sec. bd. trustees Carthage Coll., Kenosha, Wis., 1969-84; presentor Evang. Ch. Bavaria, Munich, Fed. Republic Germany, 1977; trustee A-Ctr., 1971-79, project dir., 1980; project dir. clergy seminar on alcoholism, Racine, 1979. Author: (book) Conscious Contact, 1981; (tracts) Preparation for Holy Communion, 1955; Preparation for Holy Baptism, 1959. Editor: (book) Alcohol/Drug Dependency, 1983. Bd. dirs. Alliance for Mentally Ill, Racine, 1982. Recipient award Lincoln Luth. Home, 1970, cert. Effectiveness Tng. Found., Kenosha, 1976. Mem. Coll. Chaplains, Racine/Kenosha Pastors Conf. (pres.), Racine Clergy Assn., S. Wis. Dist. Pastor's Assn. Republican. Club: Doctoral Assocs. (Chgo.). Lodge: Kiwanis (pres. 1981-82). Home: 3240 Wheelock Dr Racine WI 53405 Office: A-Ctr 2000 Domanik Dr Racine WI 53404

MIRSKY, NORMAN BARRY, rabbi, Reform Jewish Congregations; b. Toledo, Jan. 5, 1937; s. Joseph H. and Florence Jane (Poneman) M.; B.A., U. Cin., 1959; B.H.L., Hebrew Union Coll., 1960, M.H.L., 1963; Ph.D. in Sociology, Brandeis U., 1971; m. Elaine Torp, June 1, 1958; children—Rebekah, Aaron. Rabbi, 1963; asst. to exec. v.p. Central Conf. Am. Rabbis, 1963-64; Hillel dir. Northeastern U., Boston, 1964-67, also rabbi Temple Beth David, Canton, Mass; faculty Hebrew Union Coll., Cin., 1967-76, asso. prof. human relations, 1967-76; faculty Hebrew Union Coll., Los Angeles, 1976—. Sr. research asso. religion and sociology, dept. psychiatry U. Cin., 1968-76; facilitator Nat. Council Jewish Women, 1976—; lectr. sociology Tufts U., Medford, Mass., 1964-70, evening div. U. Cin., 1967-76. Zizkind fellow, 1964-67; Merril Found. fellow, 1964-67. Mem. Central Conf. Am. Rabbis, Soc. Sci. Study Religion, Am. Sociol. Assn., AAUP, Contbr. articles to religious and profl. jours. Home: 1442 Yale St Santa Monica CA 90040 Office: 3700 University Ave Los Angeles CA 90007

MISCHKE, CARL HERBERT, clergyman, president Wisconsin Evangelical Lutheran Synod; b. Hazel, S.D., Oct. 27, 1922; s. Emil Gustav and Pauline (Alvina) Polzin; m. Gladys Lindloff, July 6, 1947; children: Joel, Susan Blahnik, Philip, Steven. Student Northwestern Coll., Watertown, Wis., 1940-44, Wis. Luth. Sem., 1944-47. Ordained to ministry Wis. Evang. Luth. Synod, 1947. Asst. pastor 1st Luth. Ch., La Crosse, Wis., 1947-49; pastor St. Peter-St. John Ch., Goodhue, Minn., 1949-54; pastor St. John Ch., Junea, Wis., 1954-79; pres. Western Wis. dist. Wis. Luth. Synod, 1964-79, pres. Wis. Luth. Synod, Milw., 1979—. Office: Wis Evang Luth Synod 2929 N Mayfair Rd Milwaukee WI 53222

MITCHEL, LARRY ARTHUR, religious educator, Seventh-day Adventists; b. Deer Park, Calif., Dec. 30, 1944; s. Arthur Earl and Carmelita Esther (Parks) M.; m. Carola Echo Stevens, Aug. 21, 1966; children: Carmelita Echo, Jason Todd. B.A. in Theology, Pacific Union Coll., 1967; B.D., Andrews U., 1969, Th.D., 1980. Ordained to ministry Seventh-day Adventists 1973. Pastor and assoc. evangelist So. Calif. Conf. Seventh-day Adventists, Glendale, Calif., 1967-73; secondary religious tchr. Oreg. Conf. Seventh-day Adventists, Portland, 1973-75; assoc. prof. religion Pacific Union Coll., Angwin, Calif., 1978—; sec., treas. Andrews Soc. Religious Studies, 1980—. Author: A Student's Vocabulary for Biblical Hebrew & Aramaic, 1984. Author of abstracts Old Testament Abstracts, 1977—. Named Outstanding Young Men of Am. 1978. Mem. Soc. Bibl. Lit. Office: Pacific Union Coll Angwin CA 94508

MITCHELL, CARLTON TURNER, educator, minister, Southern Baptist Convention; b. Richmond, Va., Sept. 27, 1920; s. Lester Hall and Annie (Merritt) M.; m. Miriam Grace Sexton, Jan. 31, 1921; children: Grace Mitchell, Betty Mitchell Morgan. A.A., Campbell U., 1941; A.B., Wake Forest U., 1943; B.D., Yale U., 1945; S.T.M., Union Theol. Sem., 1956; Ph.D., NY U, 1962. Ordained to ministry Southern Baptist Convention, 1944. Assoc. pastor First Bapt. Ch., St. Joseph, Mo., 1946-47; pastor Zebulon Bapt. Ch., N.C., 1947-62, First Bapt. Ch., Ridgefield Park, N.J., 1955-61; prof. religion Wake Forest U., Winston-Salem, 1961—, chmn. dept. religion, 1981—; clk. Raleigh Bapt. Assn., 1948-52; pres. Ministers Conf., Ridgefield Park, 1959-60; editorial advisor Studia Liturgia, Amsterdam, Netherlands, 1961-69; bd. dirs. Sch. Pastoral Care, Winston-Salem, 1973-79. Mem. editorial bd. Perspectives in Religion, 1973-80. Contbr. articles to profl. jours. Chmn. Community Council, Zebulon, 1950-52; bd. dirs. YMCA, Ridgefield Park, 1956-61. Served to comdr., USN, 1945-46, 52-54. Named Man of Yr., Zebulon Record, 1951; Disting. Alumnus, Campbell U., 1975. Mem. AAUP (pres. 1969-71), Am. Acad. Religion, Am. Soc. Ch. History, Soc. for Sci. Study of Religion, Am. Cath. Hist. Assn., Am. Assn. for Sociology of Religion, Phi Kappa Phi, Phi Delta Kappa. Home: 3121 Shannon Dr Winston-Salem NC 27106 Office: Wake Forest U PO Box 7363 Winston-Salem NC 27109

MITCHELL, GARY DON, minister, Southern Baptist Convention; b. House, N.Mex., Feb. 18, 1948; s. W.Y. and Della Marie (Franklin) M.; m. Judy Lynn Thomas, Dec. 28, 1969; 1 dau., Mara Sue. B.A., North Tex. State U., 1970; M.Div., S.W. Bapt. Sem., 1973, D.Min., 1984. Ordained to ministry Calvary Bapt. Ch., 1980. Pub. relations newswriter S.W. Bapt. Sem., Fort Worth, 1971-73; tv continuity dir. Sta. KXTX-TV, Dallas, 1973-78; pastor Calvary Bapt. Ch., Clovis, N.M., 1979—; vol. chaplain Clovis Hosp., 1980—; vice moderator Plains Bapt. Assn., 1983—. Mem. Clovis Ministerial Alliance. Lodge: Kiwanis. Home: 2705 Gidding St Clovis NM 88101 Office: Calvary Bapt Ch 720 Davis St Clovis NM 88101

MITCHELL, JULIA BENTON, religious studies educator; b. Richmond, Ind., Oct. 12, 1945; d. Joseph Benton and Dorothy Elizabeth (Mulnix) Sheridan; 1 child, Hinda Diane. B.A., Ohio State U., 1970; M.Div., Meth. Theol. Sch., 1974; M.A., Vanderbilt U., 1978, Ph.D., 1982. Asst. prof. religious studies Ball State U., Muncie, Ind., 1980—. Contbr. articles to profl. jours. Dir., producer Multi-media: Religion in Indiana: Through a Wide Lens, 1984. Mem. Am. Acad. Religion (chmn. Midwest sect. 1985—, v.p., pres. elect 1985-87), Soc. for Sci. Study Religion. Office: Ball State U Dept Philosophy Muncie IN 47306

MITCHELL, TIMOTHY CHARLES, minister, United Pentecostal Church International; b. Baton Rouge, La., Jan. 25, 1950; s. Charles Preston and Gertrude (Artigue) M.; m. Shirley Ann Herrington, Dec. 18, 1971; children: Joel Lynn, Marchele Renee, Sharla Ann. B.Th. with honors, Tex. Bible Coll., 1972. Ordained to ministry United Pentecostal Ch. Internat. 1973. Pastor First Pentecostal Ch., Donaldsonville, La., 1972-75; evangelist, various pastorates United Pentecostal Internat., 1975-80; founder and pastor New Testament Christian Ctr., Montgomery, Ala., 1981—; harvestine dir. Ala. Dist. United Pentecostal Ch., 1984—, youth dir. section 6, 1984—, mem. property com., 1984—. Recipient Pres. Club Membership award Ind. Life Ins., Jacksonville, Fla., 1982. Republican. Home: 365 Eagerton Rd Montgomery AL 36116 Office: New Testament Christian Ctr 4560 Narrow Ln Rd Montgomery AL 36116

MITCHELL, VIRGIL ALLEN, ch. ofcl., Wesleyan Ch.; b. Six Mile, S.C., Apr. 21, 1914; s. Elbert Allen and Annie Mozelle (Davis) M.; Th.B., Central Wesleyan Coll., 1943; postgrad. High Point (N.C.) Coll., 1946; D.D., Houghton Coll., 1964; m. Mary Parks, Mar. 24, 1937; children—Walter Allen, Marilyn (Mrs. Alton C. Hollingsworth), Martha Theresa (Mrs. James Funnell). Ordained to ministry, 1939; pastor in Walhalla, S.C., 1937-39, Westminster, S.C., 1937-40, Oakway, S.C., 1939-40, Cateeche and Central, S.C., 1940-46, Glenwood, S.C., 1946-49; tchr. bible Central Wesleyan Coll., 1943-44, 46-48; pres. S.C. conf. Wesleyan Ch., 1949-57; nat. asst. sec. home missions and ch. extension and evangelism Wesleyan Meth. Ch., 1957-59, nat. sec. ch. extension and evangelism, 1959-63; gen. supt. Wesleyan Meth. Ch. Am., 1963-68; gen. supt. Wesleyan Ch. (merger Wesleyan Meth. and Pilgrim Holiness Chs.), 1968-84. Ofcl. visitor 9th World Meth. Conf., 1956; mem. S.C. Bd. Christian Action, 1949-57; pres. S.C. Wesleyan Youth Soc., 1943-45, 47-49, So. Area Youth, 1945-47. Bd. dirs. Central Wesleyan Coll., 1950-57, vice chmn., 1954-57. Mem. Nat. Assn. Evangs., Nat. Holiness Assn. (dir). Home: Rt 2 Box 453-C Central SC 29630 Office: Box 2000 Marion IN 46952

MITTS, PAUL ELDEN, minister, So. Bapt. Conv.; b. Hominy, Okla., Nov. 10, 1930; s. William Adam and Susan Rodella (Wilson) M.; D.Th., Southwestern Sem., 1960; Th.D., Fla. U., 1971; postgrad. Luther Rice Sem., 1976—; m. Berniece Tommie Echols, Nov. 12, 1949; children—Pauline Ellen, Danny Lee, Jonie Kay, Tommy Paul, Kelly Jane. Ordained to ministry, 1954; pastor Oakwood Bapt. Ch., Ft. Worth, 1960-61, Calvary Bapt. Ch., San Marcos, Tex., 1961-63, First Bapt. Ch., Turpin, Okla., 1963-64, Morris, Okla., 1964-68, Immanuel Baptist Ch., Skiatook, Okla., 1968—. Pres., Family Marriage Counsel Assos., Tulsa; v.p. Bible Speaks, Skiatook; exec. bd. Tulsa Bapt. Assn.; chaplin Christian Athelete OUTREACH, Tulsa, local huddle group Fellowship Christian Athletes. Skiatook. Bd. dirs., chmn. credit com. Skiatook Credit Union; bd. dirs. Skiatook Hist. Soc. Recipient Hon. Farmer award Future Farmers Am., 1967, Hon. mem. Nat. Hwy Patrol, Sheriffs and Peace Officers Assn., 1970. Author: Bible Doctrines, 1962; contbr. articles to Bible Speaks to Today's World, others. Home: 824 Locust St Skiatook OK 74070 Office: 625 S Broadway St Skiatook OK 74070

MOBLEY, CLIFTON DARRELL, religious educator Southern Baptist Convention; b. Oklahoma City, Oct. 23, 1948; s. Clifton Arvil and Marie (Beckes) M.; B.A., Wichita State U., 1970; M.Div., Southwestern Bapt. Theol. Sem., Ft. Worth, 1973; Licensed to ministry, 1970; instr. Bible classes Falls Creek Bapt. Assembly, Davis, Okla., summers 1974, 75; instr. Sem. Extension Center, Oklahoma City, 1975-77; minister edn. Agnew Ave. Bapt. Ch., Oklahoma City, 1974-76; educator, Oklahoma City, 1977-78; educator, Tulsa, 1979-85. Mem. Bapt. Religious Edn. Assn., Southwestern Sem. Alumni Assn. Author articles. Home: 5421 E 71st Pl Tulsa OK 74136

MOBLEY, FORREST CAUSEY, JR., priest, Episcopal Church; b. Atlanta, Aug. 2, 1941; s. Forrest Causey and Jeannette (Apffel) M.; m. Nancy Joyce Mister, Sept. 1, 1961; children: Alison Leigh, Mark Forrest, Andrew Stephen. Student U. Fla., Gainesville, 1959-60; B.B.A., U. Miami, Coral Gables, Fla., 1961; S.T.B., Gen. Theol. Sem., N.Y.C., 1966; postgrad. U. South Fla., 1976. Ordained deacon Episcopal Ch., 1966, priest, 1967. Curate St. Andrew's Ch., Ft. Pierce, Fla., 1966-69; rector St. Andrew's By-the-Sea Ch., Destin, Fla., 1969-76; canon evangelist Cathedral of St. Philip, Atlanta, 1976-80; dean St. Matthew's Cathedral, Laramie, Wyo., 1980—; pres. standing com. Diocese of Wyo., Laramie, 1983—; mem. standing com. Diocese of Central Gulf Coast, Mobile, Ala., 1972-75. Bd. dirs. Cathedral Home for Children, Laramie, Wyo., 1980—, United Way of Albany County, Laramie, 1983; chmn. Good Samaritan Fund, Laramie, 1983. Mem. Am. Assn. Sex Edn. Counselors and Therapists, Christian Assn. Psychol. Services. Republican. Lodge: Rotary. Home: 819 Ivinson Laramie WY 82070 Office: St Matthew's Cathedral 104 S 4th St Laramie WY 82070

MOCKABEE, MARION EUGENE, pastor, Disciples of Christ Church; b. Concordia, Kans., June 17, 1940; s. Henry Carlton and Velda Evon (Cherington) M.; m. Sondra Sue Stanton, June 8, 1963; 1 dau., Tabitha Joy. B.S. E.E., Kans. State U., 1963; M.Div., Lexington Theol. Sem., 1967, D.Min., 1977; postgrad. Pacific Sch. Religion, 1967-68. Ordained to ministry Christian Ch., 1967. Pastor 1st Christian Ch., Dos Palos, Calif., 1967-71, 1st Christian Ch., Plattsmouth, Nebr., 1971-80; sr. pastor Central Christian Ch., Kalispell, Mont., 1980—; chmn. local ch. devel., Christian Ch. in Nebr., 1972-76, mem. adminstrv. bd., 1972-80; chmn. commn. on World Outreach, Christian Ch. in Mont., 1980-84, moderator elect, 1984; mem. dept. pastoral services Nebr. Meth. Hosp., Omaha, 1974-80, chmn., 1976. Contbr. articles to mags. Bd. dirs. Child Saving Inst., Omaha, 1976-80, v.p., 1979-80. Mem. Kalispell Ministerial Assn. (pres. 1980-82). Clubs: Rotary, Toastmasters. Lodge: Masons. Home: 645 7th Ave E Kalispell MT 59901 Office: Central Christian Ch PO Box 955 Kalispell MT 59901

MOCKO, GEORGE PAUL, minister, Luth. Church in America; b. Little Falls, N.Y., Feb. 15, 1934; s. George and Anna (Swancara) M.; m. Elizabeth Carol Davidson, Sept. 2, 1956; children: David, Paul, Kristopger, Elisa. B.A., Hartwick Coll., 1956; B.D., Phila. Sem., 1959, S.D.M., 1972; D.D. (hon.), Gettysburg Coll., 1978. Ordained to ministry Lutheran Ch. in Am., 1959. Pastor Jacob's and Outwood Chs., Pine Grove, Pa., 1959-62; assoc. pastor St. Mark's, Wilmington, Del., 1962-65, sr. pastor, 1965-78; sr. pastor Ascension Ch., Balt., 1978—; coordinator Balt. Council for Mission, 1980—; co-chmn. Balt. Com. for the New Luth. Ch., 1980—. Contbr. articles to profl. jours. Democrat. Home: 501 Sussex Rd Baltimore MD 21204 Office: Ascension Luth Ch 7601 York Rd Baltimore MD 21204

MODSCHIEDLER, JOHN CHRISTIAN, minister, educator, United Church of Christ; b. Seguin, Tex., Apr. 23, 1938; s. Lorenz Franz and Helena (Emigholz) M.; m. Christa Maria Ferckel, Aug. 2, 1965; children: Christina, Michelle. B.A. with high honors, Elmhurst Coll., 1959; B.D., Eden Theol. Sem., 1962; postgrad. Berlin Theol. Sem. (W.Ger.), 1962-65, Free U. Berlin, 1962-65; M.A., Div. Sch., U. Chgo., 1970, Ph.D., 1980. Ordained, 1962. Interim minister, St. John United Ch. of Christ, Lincoln, Ill., summer 1962; part time program dir. St. Paul United Ch. of Christ, Chgo., 1965-66; interim minister Salem United Ch. of Christ, New Orleans, summer 1972; assoc. prof. Coll. of DuPage, Glen Ellyn, Ill., 1977—; bd. mem. University Ch., Chgo., 1976, vice moderator, 1977-78, moderator, 1979-80, trustee, 1984—. Author, translator articles. Bd. dirs. Sem. Coop. Bookstore, Inc., Chgo., 1972-75, pres. bd., 1973-75. World Council Chs. Ecumenical Exchange scholar, 1962-65; Fulbright travel grantee, 1962-65. Mem. Am. Acad. Religion, Soc. Christian Ethics, Am. Philos. Assn., Am. Assn. Philosophy Tchrs., Assn. for Devel. of Philosophy Teaching (pres. 1984—). Democrat. Home: 5477 S Hyde Park Blvd Chicago IL 60615 Office: College of DuPage 22d St and Lambert Rd Glen Ellyn IL 60137

MOEDE, GERALD FRANK See *Who's Who in America,* 43rd edition.

MOFFATT, FRED T., JR., pastor, Southern Baptist Convention; b. Horse Cave, Ky., July 27, 1927; s. Fred T. and Mary L. (Martin) M.; m. Jane Morrison, Dec. 22, 1950; children: Mary Jane Moffatt Snipes, Bruce L. B.A. summa cum laude, Washington and Lee U., 1950; M.Div., So. Bapt. Theol. Sem., 1954, D.Min., 1973; M.A., U. Ky., 1958. Ordained to ministry, 1952. Pastor, No. Benson Bapt. Ch., Frankfort, Ky., 1951-54; asst. pastor Broadway Bapt. Ch., Louisville, 1954-56; pastor 1st Bapt. Ch., Paris, Ky., 1956-63, 1st Bapt. Ch., Shelbyville, Ky., 1963-74, Heritage Bapt. Ch., Annapolis, Md., 1974—; trustee New Orleans Bapt. Theol. Sem., 1979—; 1st v.p. Bapt. Conv. Md., 1982-83. Mem. Bd. Edn., Shelbyville, 1968-72. Served with USN, 1945-46, Philippines. Mem. Phi Beta Kappa, Omicron Delta Kappa. Democrat. Home: 3053 Mimon Rd Annapolis MN 21403 Office: 1740 Forest Dr Annapolis MD 21401

MOHLER, JAMES WILLIAM, minister, American Baptist Churches in the U.S.A.; b. Lynwood, Calif., Nov. 8, 1955; s. Lionel Louis and Sheila (Howard) M.; m. Miriam Ruth Moses, Aug. 23, 1980. Mus.B. cum laude, Biola Coll., 1979; M.A. in Christian Edn., Talbot Theol. Sem., 1984, postgrad., 1984—. Licensed to ministry Baptist Ch., 1977. Club asst. dir. Campus/Life/Youth for Christ, Downey, Calif., 1973-74; intern First Bapt. Ch. of Downey, Calif., 1974-77, minister to jrs., 1977-79, minister to jrs. and jr. highers, 1979—; adj. prof. Biola U., 1985—. Mem. project area com. City of Downey Redevel. Commn., 1983-85. Recipient Nat. Assn. Profs. Christian Edn. award, 1984. Ralph Burnight Music scholar Cerritos Coll., Norwalk, Calif., 1974. Home: 8331 3d St Downey CA 90241 Office: First Baptist Ch of Downey 8348 E 3d St Downey CA 90241

MOKRZYCKI, M. JOSEPH, priest, Roman Catholic Church; b. Sayreville, N.J., May 26, 1940; s. Milton Joseph and Mary Jennie (Rohal) M. A.A., St. Charles Coll., 1959; A.B., St. Mary's Sem., 1961, S.T.B., 1963; M.A., Seton Hall U., 1970; M.A. in History, NYU, 1972. Ordained priest, Roman Cath. Ch., 1965. Asst. pastor St. Hedwig's Ch., Trenton, N.J., 1965-66, Our Lady Star of the Sea Ch., Long Branch, N.J., 1966-68; chaplain Monmouth Coll., founder Bethlehem, Cath. Ctr. for Monmouth Coll., West Long Branch, N.J., 1971-78; dir. campus ministry Diocese of Trenton, N.J., 1974-78; pastor Our Lady Star of the Sea Ch., Long Branch, 1977—; rep. for Province of Newark Nat. Campus Ministry Adv. Bd. U.S. Cath. Conf., 1977-78; mem. commn. N.J. Cath. Hist. Records Assn., 1978—. Author various pamphlets for Our Lady Star of Sea parish. Moderator Monmouth-Ocean region PTO, 1982—; active Juvenile Conf., Long Branch, 1981—. Lodge: K.C. (chaplain Long Branch chpt. 1980—, Monmouth chpt. 1980—). Home and Office: Our Lady Star of the Sea Ch 101 Chelsea Ave Long Branch NJ 07740

MOLE, DOLORES SONNTAG, lay church worker, Seventh-day Adventists; health care administrator; b. Lavaca County, Tex., Sept. 26, 1931; d. Leonary August Ernest and Clara B. (Haltom) Sonntag; m. William Ray Spangler, Sept. 17, 1948 (div. May 1969); children: Robin Spangler Daro, Jana, Mark William; m. Robert Lee Mole, Aug. 3, 1972. Assoc. in Liberal Arts, San Bernardino Valley Coll., 1981; B.A. in Bus. Adminstrn., Calif. State Coll.-San Bernardino, 1983; M.B.A., Calif. State U.-San Bernardino, 1985. Deaconess, Richwood Seventh-day Adventist Ch., Clute, Tex., 1962-64; treas. Houston Central Seventh-day Adventist Ch., 1964-68, clk., 1964-68, missionary vol. leader, 1965-66; treas. Houston Jr. Acad., 1964-68; ch. elder Azure Hills Seventh-day Adventist Ch., Grand Terrace, Calif., 1984—. Adminstrv. coordinator Loma Linda U. Med. Ctr., Calif., 1977—. Mem. LWV, Nat. Assn. Med. Staff Coordinators, Assn. Adventist Women, Phi Kappa Phi, Alpha Gamma Sigma. Republican. Home: 1800 Valle Vista Redlands CA 92373 Office: Loma Linda U Med Ctr PO Box 2000 Loma Linda CA 92354

MOLER, JOHN WARNER, minister, United Meth. Ch.; b. Atlanta, Mar. 28, 1934; s. Bernard Gwynn and Dorothy Blanche (Edmunds) M.; A.B., Emory U., 1955, M.Div., 1958; m. Martha Rochelle McGhee, Sept. 16, 1955; children—John Warner, Darryl Gwynn. Ordained to ministry, 1957; pastor chs., Ga., 1956—, Decatur, 1974—. Mem. Jurisdictional Commn. on Appalachia, 1964-68, Conf. Bd. of Edn., 1965-67; field edn. supr. Emory U., 1965-67; pres. Franklin County Ministerial Assn., 1972-73. Writer, DeKalb News/Sun, 1963—. Pres., Am. Cancer Soc. Fannin County, 1966-67, Franklin County, 70-71; Fannin County rep. Ga. Mountains Area Planning and Devel. Commn., 1967; sec. Fanni County Commn. for Better Tomorrow, 1965-67. Home: 3956 June Apple Ct Decatur GA 30034 Office: 2828 Wesley Chapel Rd Decatur GA 30034

MOLLDREM, MARK JEROME, minister, American Lutheran Church; b. Chgo., July 22, 1947; s. Ariel Robert and Esther Luella (Grindland) M.; m. Shirley Jean Bennett, Aug. 29, 1969; children: Jeffrey Hanson, Jennifer Lynn. A.A., Luther Bible Inst., Mpls., 1967; B.A., Concordia Coll., Moorhead, Minn., 1971; M.Div., Luther Theol. Sem., St. Paul, 1975. Ordained to ministry Am. Luth. Ch., 1975. Pastor, Peace-Bethlehem Luth. Ch., Cobb-Edmund, Wis., 1975-80; assoc. pastor First Luth. Ch., Beaver Dam, Wis., 1981—; mem. Fond du Lac Conf. Ministerium, 1980-84; group leader ENCORE: Marriage Enrichment, 1982—; leader Spiritual Life Group, Dodge County United Services-chem. dependency unit, Juneau, 1983—. Author Lutheran Adult Instruction Manual, 1979. Contbr. articles to religious publs. Actor Tell-A-Tale Theater, Beaver Dam, 1982—; coordinator Singles United, Dodge County, 1982—; advisor Community Supportive Care, Chronic Mentally Ill, Juneau, 1983—; treas. Childbirth/Parenting Edn. Assn., Dodge County, 1984; coordinator Jr. Players, Community Theater, Beaver Dam, 1984-85. Recipient Outstanding Support award People Against a Violent Environment, Dodge County, 1983, cert. Appreciation Beaver Dam Martial Arts Ctr., 1983. Mem. Beaver Dam Ministerium. Home: 425 N Lincoln Ave Beaver Dam WI 53916 Office: First Evangelical Luth Ch 311 W Mackie St Beaver Dam WI 53916

MOLLEGEN, ALBERT THEODORE, JR., lay church worker, Episcopal Church; engineering executive; b. Meridian, Miss., Aug. 13, 1937; s. Albert Theodore Sr. and Harriette Ione (Rush) M.; m. Glenis Ruth Gralton, Feb. 16, 1962; children: Glenis Ione, Marion Anne. Chmn. Mystic Area Ecumenical Council, Conn., 1970-72, Diocese Stewardship Com., Hartford, Conn., 1983—; councilman Seabury Deanery, New London, Conn., 1974—, Diocesan Exec. Council, Hartford, 1982—; del. Conn. Diocesan Conv., 1974—; alt. dep. Episcopal Gen. Conv., New Orleans, 1982, Anaheim, Calif., 1985. Pres., chief exec. officer Analysis & Tech., North Stonington, Conn., 1971—. Contbr. articles, papers and client reports to various publs. Corporator Lawrence and Meml. Hosp., New London, 1982—, bd. dirs. Profl. Services Council, Washington, 1983. Home: 28 Pearl St Mystic CT 06355 Office: Analysis & Tech PO Box 220 North Stonington CT 06359

MOLNAR, ENRICO SELLEY, priest, monk, Episcopal Ch.; b. Frankfurt-am-Main, Germany, Nov. 16, 1913; s. Bede John and Anita Benvenuta (Selley) M.; came to U.S., 1939, naturalized, 1956; diploma in Oriental studies Prague U., 1938; B.D. magna cum laude, Pacific Sch. Religion, 1947; Th.D., Iliff Sch. Theology, Denver, 1953; m. Patricia Ann Hamilton, July 28, 1973. Ordained priest, 1954; vicar St. Mary's Episc. Ch., Ramona, Calif., rector St. Timothy's Epis. Ch., Compton, Calif., 1955-58; warden Bloy Epis. Sch. Theology, Claremont, Calif., 1958-72, warden emeritus, 1972—; prior Order of Agape and Reconciliation, St. Michael's Forest Valley Priory, Tajique, N.Mex., 1972—. Canon theologian to the Ordinary, 1958-72; examining chaplain, 1960-72, mem. Provincial Bd. Examining Chaplains, 1962-72; mem. Joint Commn. on Ecumenical Relations, 1964-70; dir. Continuing Edn. Diocese of San Joaquin, 1972-74. Mem. Am. Soc. Bookplate Collectors and Designers. Author: Athos, Republic Without Women, 1935; The Ethiopian Orthodox Church, 1969; The Rhaeto-Romansch Canton of the Grisons, 1970; Three Christian Kingdoms of Nubia, 1975; Discipline of Devotion, 1975; The Liturgical Reforms of John Hus, 1975. Home and Office: Saint Michael's Forest Valley Priory Tajique NM 87057

MONAN, JAMES DONALD See *Who's Who in America,* 43rd edition.

MONDRAGON, LORENZO, ch. ofcl., Ch. of God; b. Corpus Christi, Tex., Aug. 14, 1940; s. Antonio and Belia (Garcia) M.; student Gulf Coast Bible Coll., 1964-67; B.A. cum laude, Bethany Nazarene Coll., 1969; M.Ed. magna cum laude, Central State U., Okla., 1970; m. Margaretha Penner, May 28, 1966. Pastor, Ch. of God, Houston, 1966-67; youth dir. South Agnew Ch. of God, Oklahoma City, 1968-69; pastor Central Park Ch. of God, Houston, 1970-73; historian Spanish-Am. Council of Ch. of God in U.S.A., 1971-76, pres., 1975—; instr. Gulf Coast Bible Coll., 1976—. Program dir. State Welfare Dept. of Tex., Houston, 1970-76. Mem. Am. Hist. Soc. Home: 1034 Lawrence Houston TX 77008 Office: 911 N 11th St Houston TX 77008

MONET, JACQUES, priest, educational administrator, Roman Catholic Church; b. Saint-Jean, Que., Can., Jan. 26, 1930. B.A., U. Montreal, 1955; Ph.L., Immaculee-Conception, 1956, Th.L., in Theology, 1967; M.A., U. Toronto, 1961, Ph.D. in History, 1964. Joined S.J., Roman Catholic Ch., 1949, ordained priest, 1966. Tchr. history St. Mary's U. High Sch., Halifax, N.S., Can., 1956-58; sessional lectr. Loyola Coll., Montreal, Que., Can., 1964-67; asst. prof. U. Toronto, Ont., Can., 1968-69; assoc. prof. U. Ottawa, Ont., Can., 1969-81, chmn. dept. history, prof., 1981-82, adj. prof., 1982—; pres. Regis Coll., Toronto, 1982—; mem. Formation Council of Upper Can. Province of S.J., 1979—, Huronia Hist. Adv. Council, 1981—, Queen Elizabeth II Scholarship Selection Com., 1981, Stamp Adv. Council Can. Post, 1978—; bd. govs. St. Paul's Coll., U. Man., Can., 1982—, selection com., Killam Research Fellowships, Can. Council, 1982—; spl. advisor on cultural policy to Sec. State, Can., 1978-79; mem. numerous ednl. and hist. coms.; lectr. in field. Editor: Historical Papers. Spl. asst. to gen. editor Dictionary of Can. Biography, 1959-63. Asst. editor Social History/Histoire Sociale. Mem. editorial bd. Jour. Can. Studies, 1970—. Conbr. numerous articles to profl. jours., chpts. to books. Author: The Last Cannon Shot: A Study of French Canadian Nationalism, 1969; Canadian Crown, 1979. Hist. advisor and narrator films by CBC, CTV, and NFB. Recipient Jubilee medal, 1977, Gov. Gen.'s Gold medal, 1978. Mem. Can. Hist. Assn. (council 1969-72, French lang. sec. 1969-74, pres. 1975-76), Social Scis. Fedn. of Can. (research policy com. 1976-81), Can. Cath. Hist. Assn. (council 1977-79), Royal Soc. of Can. (Centenary medal 1982, sec. Academie des Lettres et des Sciences Humaines (1979-80), chmn. centenary com. 1979-82), Assn. of Profs. of U. Ottawa (bd. dirs. 1977-78). Office: Office of Pres Regis Coll 15 St Mary St Toronto ON M4Y 2R5 Canada

MONEY, H(ENRY) THOMAS, minister, Christian Church (Disciples of Christ); b. Louisville, Apr. 13, 1933; s. Milton Thomas and Ethel Mae (Heft) M.; m. Suzanne Lewis Silverman, June 15, 1956 (div. Aug. 1975); children: Terri, Tom; m. Sarah Hubbs Cromartie, Jan. 15, 1977; children: Caroline, Christine. Student, Northwestern U., 1950-51; A.B., Transylvania U., 1955; M.Div., Lexington Theol. Sem., 1958; M.A., East Carolina U., 1962. Ordained to ministry Christian Ch., 1957. Student minister Ewing Christian Ch., Ky., 1952-55, 1st Christian Ch., New Castle, Ky., 1955-58; minister Hooker Meml. Christian Ch., Greenville, N.C., 1958-64; assoc. minister Peachtree Christian Ch., Atlanta, 1964-67, sr. minister, 1967—; mem. Week of Compassion, Indpls., 1969-75; v.p. Pension Fund Bd., Indpls., 1979-85; pres. Christian Ch. in Ga., Macon, 1974-75; trustee Lexington Theol. Sem., 1975—. Mem. Christian Council of Met. Atlanta (vice chmn. 1972-73). Democrat. Lodges: Optimists (pres. 1962-63), Rotary (sec. 1978-79), Masons. Home: 3991 Whittington Dr NW Atlanta GA 30342 Office: Peachtree Christian Ch 1580 Peachtree St NW Atlanta GA 30309

MONJAR, HARVEY, general overseer Christian Nation Church in the U.S.A. Address: Box 142 South Lebanon OH 45065

MONROE, JOHN ROGER, minister, Presbyterian Church in the U.S.A.; b. Johnson City, Tenn., Feb. 15, 1949; s. John Roberts and Helen (Kirkpatrick) M.; m. Susan Kilgore, June 15, 1974; children: Sarah Roberts, Miles Kirkpatrick. B.A. in History, Hampden-Sydney Coll., 1971; D. Ministry, Union Theol. Sem., 1976. Ordained to ministry Presbyn. Ch. in the U.S.A., 1977. Assoc. minister First United Presbyn. Ch., Fayetteville, Ark., 1976-81; minister Forest Hills Presbyn. Ch., Martinsville, Va., 1981—; commr. 196th gen. assembly Blue Ridge Presbytery, 1984, chmn. candidates com., 1982—; chmn. youthwork com. Ark. Presbytery, 1977-81. Chmn. Citizens for Peace, Martinsville, 1984; bd. dirs. Mental Health Assn., Martinsville, 1984, W.C. Ham Ctr., Martinsville, 1984. Named Outstanding Young Men in Am., Jaycees, 1980. Democrat. Lodge: Rotary. Home: 724 Corn Tassel Trail Martinsville VA

24112 Office: Forest Hills Presbyn Ch 725 Beechnut Ln Martinsville VA 24112

MONSON, PAUL ODEAN, pastor, American Lutheran Church. B. Mizpah, Minn., July 24, 1937; s. Odean Cornell and Christie Elvira (Hermanson) M.; m. Margaret Fitch, July 8, 1961; children: Todd Erik, Lisa Kirsten. Student, U. Oslo, 1957, Wis. State U., 1969-70; B.A. summa cum laude, Concordia Coll., Moorhead, Minn., 1959; B.D., Luther Sem., St. Paul, 1963, postgrad., 1984—. Ordained to ministry American Lutheran Church, 1963. Pastor, Trinity-Thompson Valley Ch., Mondovi, Wis., 1963-65, Faith-New Hope Ch., Rosholt, Wis., 1966-70; campus pastor Wis. State U., Stevens Point, 1966-69; assoc. pastor First English Luth. Ch., Faribault, Minn., 1971-79, adminstrv. pastor, 1980—; nat. conv. del. Am. Luth. Ch., 1970, 76, 78, conf. dean, Faribault, Minn., 1975-79, mem. exec. com. SE Minn. dist., St. Paul, 1975-79; creator/adminstr. pastoral sabbatical plan Southeast Minn. dist., 1978-84; designer/leader various clergy retreats, 1975-83. Author/presentor slide-tape media show (hon. mention 1980), 1980; contbr. articles to religious publs. Pres., Citizen's Action Council, Minn., 1972-74, Buckham Meml. Library Bd., Faribault, 1983—; founder/organizer Faribault Big Brother's Program, 1975-76; patron Wilson Ctr. and Psychiatric Hosp. for Adolescents, Faribault, 1978; bd. dirs. YMCA, Faribault, 1978-81, River Bend Nature Ctr., Faribault, 1979-83; v.p. River Bend Art Inst., Faribault, 1981-83. Recipient Spl. Service award Future Farmers Am., Rosholt, Wis., 1969, Outstanding Service award Faribault Area YMCA, 1979, Outstanding Citizen award City of Faribault, 1983. Mem. Pastoral Seminar Group (pres. 1974-76). Home: 216 Hillcrest Dr Faribault MN 55021 Office: First English Luth Ch 216 NW 2nd Ave Faribault MN 55021

MONSON, THOMAS S., church official. Mem. Quorum of the Twelve, The Church of Jesus Christ of Latter-Day Saints. Office: The Church of Jesus Christ of Latter-Day Saints 50 E North Temple St Salt Lake City UT 84150*

MONTGOMERY, DANIEL BINNEY, archhriest, Orthodox Church in America. B. Byrn Mawr, Pa., Feb. 25, 1924; s. Horace Binney and Louise Blake (Tyler) M.; m. Maria Luisa Tamborrel, Nov. 18, 1947; children: Sylvia Binney Montgomery Shaw, Mary Louise Montgomery Snyder, Robert A. B.A., Mexico City Coll., 1949; lic. in theology Ukrainian Orthodox Sem., N.Y.C., 1953; M.A., U. Ibero-Americana, Mexico City, 1972. Ordained priest Ukranian Orthodox Church of America, 1953. Pastor St. John Orthodox Ch., Cedar Rapids, Iowa, 1954-55, St. Michael Orthodox Ch., Beaumont, Tex., 1955-59, St. George Orthodox Ch., Mexico City, 1959-61, Trumbull, Conn., 1976—; chaplain, chmn. lang. dept. Valley Forge Mil. Acad., Wayne, Pa., 1962-76; chaplain House of Stuart, Greenwich, Conn., 1982—, Civil Air Patrol, Pa., 1964-75, SAR (Conn. soc.), 1980—, St. Vincent's Med. Ctr., Bridgeport, Conn., 1984—. Author: The Eye of the Sutra, 1974; The Dynamic Buddhism of Nichiren, 1984. Translator: The Blue Sutra, 1975; El Sutra Azul, 1976. Councillor Order Founders and Patriots, (Conn. soc.), 1980, 83. Served to sgt. U.S. Army, 1943-45, ETO. Recipient Order of Anthony Wayne, Valley Forge Mil. Acad., 1967; named spl. lectr. Reiyukai, Mirokusan, Japan, 1973; grantee Nat. Edn. Devel. Act, Colgate U., 1965. Republican. Club: Col. Clergy (Arlington, Va.). Home and Office: St George Orthodox Ch 5490 Main St Trumbull CT 06611

MONTGOMERY, FELIX EDWARD, minister, Southern Baptist Convention; b. Birmingham, Ala., May 14, 1934; s. William Hayden and Anne (Wilson) M.; B.A., Birmingham-So. Coll., 1955; M.Div., So. Bapt. Theol. Sem., 1959, D.Min., 1977; m. Shirley Lou Ennis, Oct. 4, 1960. Ordained to ministry So. Bapt. Conv., 1959. Pastor Frankfort Ave. Bapt. Ch., Russellville, Ark., 1956-57, Muldraugh (Ky.) Bapt. Ch., 1957-64, 1st Bapt. Ch., Clay, Ky., 1964-68, Lakeview Bapt. Ch., Auburn, Ala., 1973-78; co-pastor South Avondale Bapt. Ch., Birmingham, Ala., 1968-73; cons. on personal and profl. growth Bapt. Sunday Sch. Bd., Nashville, 1978—; moderator Tuskegee-Lee Bapt. Assn. Author: God's People: From One to a Nation, 1974; Pursuing God's Call: Choosing a Vocation in Ministry; writer tchr. and pupil material Youth in Action, Bapt. Sunday Sch. Bd., Nashville, summers 1972, 76. Office: 127 9th Ave N Nashville TN 37234

MONTGOMERY, JAMES WINCHESTER, bishop, Episcopal Ch.; b. Chgo., May 21, 1929; s. James Edward and Evelyn Lee (Winchester) M.; B.A., Northwestern U., 1943; S.T.B., Gen. Theol. Sem., 1949, S.T.D., 1963; D.D., Nashotah House, 1963; D.D. (hon.), Seabury-Western Theol. Sem.; LL.D. (hon.), Shimer Coll., 1969. Ordained deacon, 1949, priest, 1949; suffragan bishop of Chgo., 1962-65; bishop of Chgo., 1965—; bishop coadjutor of Chgo., 1965-71. Address: 65 E Huron St Chicago IL 60611*

MONTGOMERY, WILLIAM FRANKLIN, JR., minister, Southern Baptist Convention; b. Knoxville, Tenn., Jan. 6, 1943; s. William Franklin and Minnie Love (Greer) M.; m. Elaine Boyette, June 20, 1964; children: Katherine, Julia. B.S., Miss. Coll., 1965; Th.M., New Orleans Bapt. Theol. Sem., 1968, D.Min., 1980. Ordained to ministry, 1966. Pastor, 1st Bapt. Ch., Chalvette, La., 1966-70, St. Andrew Bapt. Ch., Panama City, Fla., 1970-80, 1st Bapt. Ch., Enterprise, Ala., 1980—. Club: Rotary.

MONTMIGNY, GASTON JOSEPH, priest, Roman Catholic Church; b. Sherbrooke, Que., Can., Dec. 30, 1928; s. Aime Joseph and Blanche Rose Alma (Laporte) M.; B.A., U. Ottawa, 1956, B.P.T., 1977; B.Ed., Gonzaga U., Spokane, 1958; M.Ed., Seattle U., 1961; Ph.D., Pacific Western U., 1984. Ordained priest, 1955; tchr. Notre Dame Coll., Falher, Alta., Can., 1956-57; prin., adminstr. Assumption (Alta.) Indian Residential Sch., Dept. Indian Affairs, 1957-70; founder, pastor parish, Rainbow Lake, Alta., 1970-71; dir., adminstr. Star of North Retreat House, St. Albert, Alta., 1971-82. Fin. adviser Provincial Council of Oblate Fathers, Alta.-Sask. Province. Postmaster, radio operator, airport mgr., Climatol. Sta. operator, vital statistics ofcl., marriage license issuer, Assumption, 1957-70. Recipient award for services of weather observation Dept. of Transport, 1965. Mem. Alta. Aviation Council, Ft. Edmonton Voyageurs, Guild Indsl., Comml. and Instl. Accts. Can., Assn. Canadienne Française de l'Alta., Franklin Mint, Royal Philatelic Soc. Can. Address: PO Box 270 Saint Albert AB T8N 1N3 Canada

MONTROSE, DONALD, bishop, Roman Catholic Church. Titular bishop of Forum Novum, aux. bishop, Los Angeles, 1983—. Office: 3324 Opal St Los Angeles CA 90023*

MONTZ, FLORENCE STOLTE, church official, Lutheran Church-Missouri Synod; b. Lowden, Iowa, June 7, 1924; d. Emil L. and Emma Marie (Meier) Stolte; B.S., U. Iowa, 1947, R.N., 1947; D.D., Concordia Coll., Bronxville, N.Y., 1984; m. C.R. Montz, June 15, 1947; children: Jennifer (Mrs. Paul Rechlin), Fredrick John. Vice pres. to pres. N.D. dist. Lutheran Women's Missionary League of Luth. Ch.-Mo. Synod, 1960-68, 1st v.p. internat., 1967-71, pres., 1971-75; bd. dirs. Luth. Ch.-Mo. Synod, 1983—. Mem. Sigma Theta Tau. Home: Box 1293 Bismarck ND 58502

MOODY, JOHN HENRY, minister, Am. Luth. Ch.; b. Seattle, Aug. 10, 1945; s. Henry Thornton and Ruby Fern (Johnson) M.; B.A., Pacific Luth. U., 1967; M.Div., Luther Theol. Sem., 1971; D.Min., San Francisco Theol. Sem., 1977; m. Melody Ann Henriksen, Aug. 5, 1967; 1 son, Eric John. Ordained to ministry, 1972; pastor Richland (Wash.) Luth. Ch., 1971-72; dir., founder Tri-Cities Chaplaincy, Kennewich, Wash., 1972—; Chaplain cons. div. Am. Missions Am. Luth. Ch., 1971-72; nat. del. com. inner-cities ministries Am. Luth. Ch. Mem. exec. com. Bi-County Council on Alcoholism, Kennewick, 1971-76; v.p. Social Agencies Coordinating Com., 1972—. Mem. Assn. Mental Health Clergy, N.W. Conf. of the Widowed, Insts. of Religion and Health, Tri-Cities Ministerial Assn. Contbr. article to religious jour. Home: 1821 Alder Ave Richland WA 99352 Office: 1149 N Edison Kennewick WA 99336

MOODY, WILLIAM RALPH, lay religious worker, So. Bapt. Conv.; b. Columbus, Ga., Dec. 27, 1919; s. Bert Squares and Savannah Ostella (Dorough) M.; B.B.A., Emory U., 1947; m. Ruth Addaleene Barker, Mar. 3, 1946; children—Margaret Ruth, William Ralph. Dir. music, Woodlawn Bapt. Ch., Decatur, Ga., 1956-62, Cresthill Bapt. Ch., Decatur, 1962-64, Clairmont Bapt. Ch., Atlanta, 1964—. Asst. chief accountant Grady Meml. Hosp., Atlanta, 1969—. Treas. Hosp. Authority Employees Credit Union, Atlanta, 1976—. Mem. Sons of Jubal. Home: 2785 D Shallowford Rd Chamblee GA 30341 Office: 3542 Clairmont Rd NE Atlanta GA 30319

MOON, MARVIN DENNIS, JR., minister, Am. Luth. Ch.; b. Los Angeles, Nov. 27, 1932; s. Marvin Dennis and Agnes (McLean) M.; B.A., Capital U., 1955; B.D., Evang. Luth. Theol. Sem., 1958; Ph.D., Calif. Grad. Sch. Theology, 1974; postgrad. Sacramento State Coll., U. So. Calif., Adult Christian Edn. Found., Center for Theol. Study; m. Charlotte Marguerite Martel, June 1, 1953; children—Marvin Dennis, Marguerite Charlotte. Ordained to ministry, 1958; pastor Calvary Luth. Ch., Rio Linda, Calif., 1958-64, Faith Luth. Ch., La Puente, Calif., 1964-66; prin. Trinity Luth. Sch., Hawthorne, Calif., 1966-70; pastor Trinity Luth. Ch., Phoenix, 1970—. Chmn. Calif. dist. youth com. Am. Luth. Ch., 1958-64; chaplain Phoenix Fire Dept., 1971—; adviser Luth. layman assn. Boy Scouts Am., 1971—; mem. faculty Calif. Grad. Sch. Theology 1974; Congl. life counselor Am. Luth. Ch., 1975—. Unit and council positions Boy Scouts Am., 1959—, recipient Cross and Crown Distinguished Service award, 1975. Mem. Am. Luth. Ednl. Assn., Phoenix Assn. Evangelicals. Home: 524 W Harmont Dr Phoenix AZ 85021 Office: 9424 N 7th Ave Phoenix AZ 85021

MOON, SUN MYUNG, leader, Unification Ch.; b. Chongju-Gun, Korea, 1920. Founder, Holy Spirit Assn. for Unification of World Christianity, S. Korea, 1954. Author: Divine Principle. Office: 4 W 43d St New York City NY 10036*

MOORE, ARTHUR JAMES, editor, ch. ofcl. United Methodist Ch.; b. San Antonio, May 7, 1922; s. Arthur James and Martha Tabitha (McDonald) M.; student U. Tex., 1939-40; B.A., Emory U., 1946. Staff Bd. Global Ministries United Methodist Ch., 1953—; assoc. editor World Outlook (name now New World Outlook), 1953-64, editor, 1964—, assoc. dir. editorial dept., 1953-64, dir., 1980—; mem. press staff World Council Chs. Assemblies, 1954-60; contbg. editor Christianity and Crisis; corr. Vatican Council, 1965, World Conf. Ch. and Soc., 1966. Mem. Alpha Tau Omega. Contbr. articles to periodicals. Office: 475 Riverside Dr New York NY 10027

MOORE, CHARLES WILSON, minister, American Baptist Churches in the U.S.A.; b. Bath, Maine, Sept. 27, 1920; s. Wilson and Lily Maude (Adams) M.; m. Letitia Katherine Watrous, June 12, 1941; children: James, Kenneth, Karen, Keith. B.A., Eastern Bapt. Coll., 1947, B.Th., 1947, B.D., 1953; D.D. (hon.), Linfield Coll., 1964. Ordained to ministry Baptist Ch., 1947. Pastor First Bapt. Ch., Lebanon Springs, N.Y., 1941-42, Alpha Community Bapt. Ch., Camden, N.J., 1942-49, Allegheny Ave Bapt. Ch., Phila., 1949-54, various chs., Portland and Eugene, Oreg., 1954-68, Bethlehem Ch., Oake Oswego, Oreg., 1968—; mem. gen. counsel Am. Bapt. Chs. U.S.A., 1962-68; bd. dirs. Portland Council of Chs., 1964-69; chmn. Central Lane Council of Chs., Eugene, Oreg., 1959. Mem. Assn. of Christian Therapists, Parish Renewal Council. Republican. Home: 17979 Stafford Rd Lake Oswego OR 97034

MOORE, DONALD BRUCE, minister, Southern Baptist Convention; b. Tyler, Tex., Apr. 14, 1941; s. Bruce Hill and Evelyn Faris (Brown) M.; m. Janice Lorraine Monk, Aug. 13, 1966; children: Melanie, Matthew, Jonathan. B.A., Baylor U., 1963; B.D., Southwestern Bapt. Theol. Sem., 1966, M.Div., 1967, D.Min., 1977. Ordained to ministry Baptist Ch., 1966. Pastor 1st Bapt. Ch., Hanover, Pa., 1967-71; dir. Child Evang. Fellowship, Phila., 1971-75; pastor Monroeville Bapt. Ch., Pa., 1977—; assoc. chmn. Inst. Basic Youth Conflicts, Pitts., 1981—; bd. govs. Am. Coalition for Traditional Values, Pitts., 1984—; mem. exec. bd. Greater Pitts. Bapt. Assn., 1978—; moderator Greater Pitts. Bapt. Assn., 1982-83. Mem. People Concerned for the Unborn Child, Nat. Fedn. for Decency. Republican. Office: Monroeville Baptist Ch 2517 Haymaker Rd Monroeville PA 15146

MOORE, DOUGLAS ROSS See *Who's Who in America,* 43rd edition.

MOORE, E. D., bishop, Apostolic Overcoming Holy Church of God. Office: 1540 E 70th St Cleveland OH 44103*

MOORE, EMERSON JOHN See *Who's Who in America,* 43rd edition.

MOORE, H(ERBERT) RANDOLPH, priest, Episcopal Ch.; b. Darien, Ga., Dec. 19, 1898; s. Jacob and Elizabeth Millege (Thorpe) M.; Ph.B., Valparaiso U., 1920; grad. Payne Div. Sch., 1925; B.D., Oberlin Coll., 1930; Th.M., U. So. Calif., 1939; D.D., Cuttington Coll. and Div. Sch., Liberia, W.Africa, 1966; m. Iona Mae Alethia Buggs, July 28, 1927; children—Leonora Elizabeth, Herbert Randolph. Ordained priest, 1925; lifetime hon. canon St. Pauls Cathedral, Los Angeles, 1963-76; priest-in-charge Mt. Calvary Episc. Ch., Los Angeles, 1976—. Mem. exec. council Episcopal Diocese Los Angeles, 1964-67, mem. Long Range Commn. on Reconstrn., 1965; alternate dep. Gen. Conv. Episc. Ch.; rep. Provincial Synod; lectr. ch. history and theology Laymens Sch. Theology, Bloy Episc. Sch.; trustee Bloy Episc. Sch. Theology, 1965—. Active, Town Hall, Los Angeles YMCA, YWCA, Ch. Fedn. Recipient certificate of appreciation for priesthood and as alumnus Bishop Payne Div. Sch., 1973. Contbr. articles to ch. publs. Home: 14114 Foster Rd La Mirada CA 90638 Office: PO Box 241 La Mirada CA 90637

MOORE, HERSHELL EDWARD, minister, Assemblies of God; b. Belleville, Ark., Nov. 17, 1941; s. Dewey and Gracie Emaline (Yandell) M.; B.A., Tex. Tech. U., 1967; m. Olevia Sue Williams, Dec. 20, 1964. Ordained to ministry, 1969; pastor Needmore Assembly of God, Waldron, Ark., 1962-64, 68-69, evangelist, 1964-65, 69-75; pastor Sudan (Tex.) Assembly of God, 1966-67; coordinator Assemblies of God ministry to the blind and Braille Library, Springfield, Mo., 1975—. Mem. Nat. Fedn. of the Blind (pres. Springfield chpt.). Author: Must I Walk Alone?, 1962. Home: 1409-B N Campbell St Springfield MO 65802 Office: 1409-A N Campbell St Springfield MO 65802

MOORE, IRENE VIOLA, lay worker, Church of God; b. Wisner, Pa., Jan. 29, 1929; d. Mervin W. and Goldie Viola (Shick) Kennedy; m. Ralph Donald Moore, Sept. 1, 1951; children: Ralph Donald Jr., W. Viola, J. Lonnie, David R., T. Renee. Grad. high sch. Erie, Pa. Sec. First Ch. of God, Eric, 1977—, Sunday sch. supt., 1978-82, mem. council, 1977-85, mem. bd. Christian edn., 1982-83, trustee, 1985—. Democrat. Home: 5149

Henderson Rd #43 Erie PA 16509 Office: First Ch of God 3510 Pine Ave Erie PA 16504

MOORE, JEFFREY THOMAS, minister, Christian Church (Disciples of Christ); b. Warren, Pa., Apr. 30, 1956; s. Merton Edward and Betty Lou (Clendening) M.; m. Cherie Jane Allen, May 28, 1978; children: Jeffrey T., II, Michael Allen. Student, Waynesburg Coll., 1974-75; B.A., Eckerd Coll., 1978; M.Div., Brite Div. Sch., 1981. Ordained to ministry Christian Ch. (Disciples of Christ) 1981. Youth dir. Mirror Lake Christian Ch., St. Petersburg, Fla., 1975-78; student minister First Christian Ch., Olney, Tex., 1978-81, Archer City, Tex., 1978-81, minister, Wagoner, Okla., 1981-84, El Campo, Tex., 1984—; pres. Wagoner Ministerial Alliance, 1983-84; bd. dirs. Christian Ch., Okla. City, Okla., 1982-84; chaplain Boy Scouts Am., El Campo, 1984. Chmn. Wagoner County Community Resource Group, 1983-84, Community Walk for World Hunger, Wagoner, 1983; active in Wagoner Playhouse Assn., 1983-84. Ruby Marsh Eldred Fund scholar, 1974-77, Waynesburg Coll. scholar 1974. Mem. El Campo Ministerial Assn. (treas. 1984—), Wagoner C. of C. (ministerial rep.). Democrat. Lodge: Lions. Home: 202 W West St El Campo TX 77437 Office: First Christian Ch Box 748 205 W West St El Campo TX 77437

MOORE, JOHN STERLING, JR., minister, Southern Baptist Convention; b. Memphis, Aug. 25, 1918; s. John Sterling and Lorena (Bounds) M.; student Auburn U., 1936-37; A.B., Samford U., 1940; Th.M., So. Baptist Theol. Sem., 1944; m. Martha Louise Paulette, July 6, 1944; children—Sterling Hale, John Marshall, Carolyn Paulette. Ordained to ministry So. Bapt. Conv., 1942; pastor in Pamplin, Va., 1944-48, Amherst, Va., 1949-57; pastor Manly Meml. Bapt. Ch., Lexington, Va., 1957-84, pastor emeritus, 1984—. Mem. Hist. Commn., So. Bapt. Conv., 1968-75; pres. Va. Bapt. Pastor's Conf., 1963. Chmn., Lexington Mayor's Com. on Race Relations, 1962-65; treas. Rockbridge Mental Health Clinic, 1971-84. Bd. dirs. Stonewall Jackson Hosp., 1967-72, pres., 1969-71; bd. dirs. Oak Hill Acad., 1958-61. Mem. So. Bapt. (dir. 1972—, pres. 1975-76, sec. 1977-85), Va. Bapt. (exec. com. 1963—, pres. 1984—) hist. socs. Mason. Co-author: Meaningful Moments in Virginia Baptist Life, 1715-1972, 1973. Editor: Va. Bapt. Register, 1972—. Contbr. articles to profl. and hist. jours. Home: 8709 Gayton Rd Richmond VA 23229

MOORE, KENNETH WILSON, minister, Christian Church (Disciples of Christ); b. Collingswood, N.J., Mar. 10, 1945; s. Charles Wilson and Letitia Katherine Mae (Watrous) M.; m. Mary Ilene Smith, Oct. 18, 1966 (div. Jan. 1982); m. Susan Jayne Kehrli, Mar. 27, 1982; children: Kristine Joy, James Kehrli. B.A., Linfield Coll., 1967; M.A., Pacific Sch. of Religion, Berkeley, Calif., 1970, M.Div., 1970; Ph.D., U. Calif.-Davis, 1976. Ordained to ministry Am. Bapt. Chs. in U.S.A., 1979. Pastor, Grimes Community Ch., Calif., 1967-74; assoc. pastor Fellowship of Disciples, Davis, 1974-76; interim minister Christian Ch. of No. Calif., 1976-80; deployed staff Christian Ch. (Disciples of Christ), Indpls., 1980-83; pastor First Christian Ch., Manteca, Calif., 1980—; convenor So. San Joaquin Geog. Area, Fresno, Calif., 1978-80, No. San Joaquin Geog. Area, Manteca, 1984—; chmn. evangelism Christian Ch. No. Calif., Oakland, 1980-84; at-large mem. Order of Ministry Commn. Oakland, Calif., 1981—. Editor denominational newsletter Western Witness, 1980-83. Newspaper columnist The Brighter Side, 1984. Producer/writer slide program Asians in Agr., 1984. Founder, Manteca Brown Bag (Sr. Gleaners), 1982, Manteca Surplus Distbn., 1983; pres. Manteca Advs. for Ind. Living, 1984, Manteca Sr. Activities Ctr., 1984; mem. edn. com. Planned Parenthood, Stockton, Calif., 1984. Christian Ministry grantee K.T. Edn. Found., Oakland, 1968. Mem. Inst. for Hist. Study, Manteca Ministerial Assn. (pres. 1983-85), San Joaquin Area Ministers Fellowship (convenor 1984-85). Lodge: Kiwanis (v.p. Manteca 1984-85). Home: 1124 Lexington Ave Manteca CA 95336 Office: First Christian Ch 1125 N Union Rd Manteca CA 95336

MOORE, M. JOANNE, church-related school principal, Episcopal Church; b. Phila., July 31, 1945; d. William Carl and Mary Josephine (Fuss) Mostertz; m. Earle M. Moore Jr., June 15, 1974; children: Jennifer Lynne, Jessica Lee. Student U. Heidelberg, Fed. Republic Germany, 1965-66, U. Pa., 1982—; B.A., Westminster Coll., 1967. Cert. tchr., Pa. Adminstr., St. Barnabas Episcopal Sch., Phila., 1974-78, prin., 1978—; del. to Diocesan Conv., Phila., 1974—; mem. council Episcopal Diocese Pa., Phila., 1976-82, mem. strategy com., 1976-82, chairperson conv. planning com., 1984. Bd. dirs. Germantown YMCA, Phila., 1984—. Mem. Pa. Assn. Pvt. Acad. Schs. (bd. dirs. 1978-81), Council for Religion in Ind. Schs. Home: 627 Glen Echo Rd Philadelphia PA 19119 Office: St Barnabas Episcopal Sch 5421 Germantown Ave Philadelphia PA 19144

MOORE, MARILYN ADAMS, minister, United Church of Christ; b. N.Y.C., Jan. 30, 1933; d. Clarence Lancelot and Ernesta Clarisa (Larrier) A.; m. Gerald L. Moore, Oct. 30, 1960 (div. 1972); children: Sharon-Frances, Meredith Adams. B.A., L.I. U., 1977; Cert. Min., N.Y. Theol. Sem., 1981; B.D., New Brunswick Sem., 1981; postgrad. N.Y. Theol. Sem. Ordained to ministry United Ch. Christ, 1982. Elder, Ch. of the Master, N.Y.C., 1976-80; asst. to editor Ch. Women United, N.Y.C., 1957-61; mem. support staff United Ch. Christ Commn. for Christian Social Action, 1961-64; office mgr. United Ch. Christ Commn. for Racial Justice, 1969-75, asst. to exec. dir., 1975-78, assoc. dir., 1978—; v.p. Nat. Council Chs.; pres. Commn. Justice and Liberation, N.Y.C., 1981—, Interreligious Found. for Community Orgns., 1981-85; del. United Ch. Christ Conf. Racism in the 80's, Netherlands, 1981; accredited vis. and del. to United Council Chs. Assembly, 1983. Contbr. articles to profl. jours. Bd. dirs. Health Crisis, N.Y.C.; chaplain CAP; vol. chaplain Bayview Women's Correctional Facility; mem. Concerned Black Parents, South Brunswick, N.J., 1979—; bd. dirs. NAACP, South Brunswick. Democrat.

MOORE, MELVIN LAWAYNE, minister, United Pentecostal Church International; b. Anacoco, La., Dec. 28, 1934; s. Charles Ira and Ethel Maude (Erwin) M.; m. Glenda Faye Bingaman, Mar. 19, 1959; children: James Lynn, Terry D'Wayne. Grad. high sch., Lake Charles, La. Pastor Faith Tabernacle United Pentecostal Ch., La Marque, Tex., 1981—. Served with USAF, 1954-57. Democrat. Home: 3806 McKinney Ext LaMarque TX 77568 Office: Faith Tabernacle United Pentecostal Ch 701 Delany Rd LaMarque TX 77568

MOORE, PAUL, JR., bishop, Episcopal Ch.; b. Morristown, N.J., Nov. 15, 1919; s. Paul and Fanny Weber (Hanna) M.; grad. St. Paul's Sch., Concord, N.H., 1937; B.A., Yale, 1941; S.T.B., Gen. Theol. Sem., N.Y.C., 1949, S.T.D. (hon.), 1960, D.D. (hon.), 1964; m. Jenny McKean, Nov. 26, 1944; children—Honor, Paul III, Adelia, Rosemary, George Mead, Marian Shaw, Daniel Sargent, Susanna McKean, Patience; m. Brenda Hughes Eagle, May 16, 1975. Ordained to ministry P.E. Ch., 1949; mem. team ministry Grace Ch., Jersey City, 1949-57; dean Christ Ch. Cathedral, Indpls., 1957-64; suffragan bishop, Washington, 1964-70; bishop coadjuter Diocese N.Y., 1970-72, bishop, 1972—; lectr. St. Augustine's Coll., Canterbury, Eng., 1960. Mem. Commn. Delta Ministry, Nat. Council Chs., 1964-67; mem. urban div., nat. exec. council Episcopal Ch., 1952-68; dep. to Gen. Conv., 1961, Anglican Congress, 1963. chmn. com. 100, legal def. fund N.A.A.C.P.; mem. nat. bd. Nat. Recreation Bd.; chmn. Met. Ecumenical Tng. Center, 1968. Trustee Gen. Theol. Sem.; fellow Yale Corp.; trustee Bard Coll., Trinity Sch., N.Y.C. Served to capt. USMCR, 1941-45; PTO. Decorated Navy Cross, Silver Star, Purple Heart. Mem. Urban League Washington (dir.). Club: Century (N.Y.C.). Author: The Church Reclaims the City, 2d edit., 1970; Take A Bishop Like Me, 1979. Office: 1047 Amsterdam Ave New York City NY 10025

MOORE, RAYMOND WARREN ALFRED (RONNIE), minister, Southern Baptist Convention; b. Comanche, Tex., Jan. 21, 1945; s. Seth Edward and Lois Kathern (Gaines) M.; m. Bonnie Joyce Gordon, Sept. 11, 1964; children: Cheri, Yvonne, Ronnie, Paul. B.A., Howard Payne U., 1967; M.Ed. Counseling, S.W. Tex. State U., 1981. Ordained to ministry Southern Baptist Convention, 1969. Mission pastor Hilltop Bapt. Ch., Menard, Tex., 1966-67; pastor Cedar Creek Bapt. Ch. (Ky.), 1967-68, Wickland Bapt. Ch., Bardstown, Ky., 1968-70, Velasco Bapt. Ch., Freeport, Tex., 1976-78; home missionary pastor Bapt. Chapel, Beulah, N.D., 1978-80; counselor Hyde Park Bapt. Ch., Austin, Tex., 1981; pastor Trinity Bapt. Ch., Missoula, Mont., 1982—. Chmn., Western Mont. Crusade, 1984—. Served with USMC, 1970-74. Mem. Evang. Ministerial Alliance (pres. 1984-85), Galcier Bapt. Assn. (moderator 1982-84). Lodge: Masons. Office: Trinity Bapt Ch 3020 S Ave W Missoula MT 59801

MOORE, RICHARD EARL, religious organization executive, Presbyterian Church in the U.S.A.; b. St. Louis, Jan. 21, 1925; s. William McHenry and Annabelle (White) M.; m. C. Evelyn Christian, Apr. 5, 1947; children: Carol, Wayne, Karen. B.A., Westminster Coll., 1945; B.D., Yale U., 1948; S.T.D. (hon.), Lewis and Clark Coll., 1980. Ordained to ministry, Presbyn. Ch., 1948. Pastor Oakland Presbyn. Ch., Middletown, Ohio, 1948-51, Greenhills Community Presbyn. Ch., Ohio, 1951-61; urban dir. Cleve. Presbytery, 1961-67; assoc. exec. Synod of Ohio, Columbus, 1967-72; exec. Synod of the Pacific, San Francisco, 1972—. Author: Urban Church Breakthrough, 1966; Myth America 2001, 1970. Contbr. articles to profl. jours. Home: 618 36th Ave San Mateo CA 94403 Office: Synod of the Pacific 1525 Post St San Francisco CA 94109

MOORE, ROBERT ROOD, religion educator, United Methodist Church. B. Kittanning, Pa., Apr. 6, 1937; s. Howard Mason and Tirza (Rood) M.; m. Dora Lucille Dunmire, Aug. 6, 1956; children: Robert Rodney, Tania Lynn. B.A., Emory and Henry Coll., 1969; M.Div., Asbury Theol. Sem., 1972; Ph.D., Emory U., 1982. Ordained to ministry United Meth. Ch., 1976. Pastor, United Meth. chs., Tenn., Ky., Ga., 1965-75; assoc. prof. religion Asbury Coll., Wilmore, Ky., 1975—; v.p. Disciplined Order of Christ, Nashville, 1979—; mem. Holston Conf. Bd. Ministry United Meth. Ch., Knoxville, Tenn., 1984. Served with USAF, 1955-59. Mem. Soc. Bibl. Lit., Evang. Theol. Soc., Nat. Assn. Evangelicals, Sigma Mu, Theta Phi. Home: 439 Edgewood Dr Nicholasville KY 40356 Office: Asbury Coll Lexington Ave Wilmore KY 40390

MOORE, WALKER PITMAN, JR., minister, So. Baptist Conv.; b. San Antonio, Tex., May 19, 1946; s. Walker Pitman and Evelyn Marie (Jones) M.; B.A., Carson-Newman Coll., Jefferson City, Tenn., 1968; M.R.E., So. Bapt. Theol. Sem., Louisville, 1970; m. Natalie Nations, June 8, 1968; children—Walker Scott, Stephanie Marie. Ordained to ministry, 1970; minister edn. First Bapt. Ch., N. Charleston, S.C., 1970-74; prin. Bapt. Acad. of ch., 1971-73; minister edn. and youth Lake Carroll Bapt. Ch., Tampa, Fla., 1974—. Sunday sch. dir. Charleston Bapt. Assn., 1973-74, mem. pub. relations com. Tampa Bay Bapt. Assn., 1976-77. Mem. Fla. Bapt. Religious Edn. Assn. Home: 12403 Marjory Ave Tampa FL 33612 Office: 1902 Pine Lake Dr Tampa FL 33612

MOORE, WALTER LEVON, minister, Southern Baptist Convention; b. Carthage, Miss., Dec. 5, 1920; s. Elisha Walter and Mary Augusta (Roberts) M.; A.B., Miss. Coll., Clinton, 1942; Th.M., So. Bapt. Theol. Sem., Louisville, 1947, Ph.D., 1950; m. Lonnie Pauline Rone, May 31, 1942. Ordained to ministry So. Bapt. Conv., 1940. Pastor chs. in Ky. and Miss., 1944-60; pastor First Bapt. Ch., Pontotoc, Miss., 1960-74; dir. missions Attala Bapt. Assn., Kosciusko, Miss., 1974—. Pres. bd. Miss. Bapt. Conv., 1968, 1st v.p., 1969-70; trustee So. Bapt. Conv. Sunday Sch. Bd., 1966-73; chmn. edn. commn. Miss. Bapt. Conv., 1971-73; chmn. devel. com. Central Hills Bapt. Retreat, 1975—; trustee So. Bapt. Theol. Sem., Louisville, 1978—. Author articles. Home: Golf Course Rd at Parkway Dr Kosciusko MS 39090 Office: PO Box 188 Kosciusko MS 39090

MOORES, PHILIP, minister, Seventh-day Adventists; b. North Sydney, N.S., Can., Apr. 18, 1914; s. William and Lillian (Amey) M.; B.A., Andrews U., 1938; m. Doris Eliene Bancroft, Dec. 21, 1938; children—Marilyn, Jeanne, Kathie, Anita. Ordained to ministry, 1943; pastor chs., Montreal, Que., Hamilton, Ont., St. John's, Nfld., 1939-49; pres. Newfound Mission Seventh-day Adventist, St. John's, 1949-57; pres. Maritime Conf., Moncton, N.B., 1957-60; pres. Man.-Sask. Conf., 1960-64, Alta. Conf., 1964-66, Ont. Conf., 1966-74; mgr. TV ops. Seventh-day Adventist Television Film Center, Newbury Park, Calif., 1975—. Chmn. bd. dirs. Branson Hosp., Oshawa, Ont., Can., 1967-74. Office: 1100 Rancho Conejo Blvd Newbury Park CA 91320

MORACE, MELVIN EARL, minister, religious edn. dir., Ch. of God (Anderson, Ind.); b. Deville, La., May 27, 1923; s. Oscar and Dorothy M.; B.S. in Psychology and Edn., Centenary Coll., La., 1954; M. in Adult Edn., U. Ind., 1971; m. Doris Carroll Brazzell, Aug. 15, 1947; children—Larry Dale, Melvin Ferrell. Pastor chs., La., 1947-66; chmn. La. Ministerial Assembly, 1955-60; chmn. evangelism com. Ch. God. La., 1960-62; chmn. Bd. Ch. Extension and Home Missions, La., 1962-66; pastor 1st Ch. of God, Eustis, Fla., 1966-68, 1st Ch. God, Bloomington, Ind., 1968-71; dir. adult edn. Ch. of God., Ind., 1969-72; pastor Ch. of God, Kokomo, Ind., also asso. faculty Kokomo continuing edn. div. Ind. U., 1972-73; pastor Westlake (La.) Ch. of God, 1973—; dir. dept. Christian edn. Ch. of God. La., 1973—. Vice chmn. La. Assembly Ch. of God., 1975—, chmn. exec. council, 1976; vis. lectr. adult edn. dept. curriculum and instrn. McNeese State U., Lake Charles; edn. counselor USAF, 1971-72. Bd. dirs. Gulf Assistance Program, Health Services Center, Lake Charles, La. Curriculum writer internat. Sunday Sch. materials; contbg. editor La. Messenger; writer on religious edn. Home and Office: 140 Maddox Rd Westlake LA 70669

MORDEN, JOHN GRANT, priest, Anglican Ch. Can.; b. London, Eng., Aug. 17, 1925; s. Walter Grant and Doris (Henshaw) M.; B.A., U. Toronto, 1949, L.Th., 1952, B.D., 1953; D.D., Wycliffe Coll., Toronto, 1963; S.T.M., Union Theol. Sem., N.Y.C., 1954; D.Th., Gen. Episcopal Sem., N.Y.C., 1963; D.D., Huron Coll., London, 1985; m. Elizabeth Grace Tannahill, Sept. 7, 1949; children—Ann, Margaret, James (dec.), Peter, Mary. Ordained deacon, 1951, priest, 1952; asst. curate Toronto, Ont., Can., and White Plains, N.Y., chs., 1951-56; rector St. Matthews Ch., Toronto, 1956-57, Chapel of Huron Coll., 1957—; archdeacon Diocese of Huron, 1967—. Prof. theology and religious studies Huron Coll., 1962—, prin., 1962-84, prin. emeritus, 1984—; mem. Gen. Synod of Anglican Ch. of Can., 1961—, mem. nat. exec. com. Gen. Synod, 1973-76; mem. Provincial Synod of Province of Ont., 1961-85. chmn. Bd. Examiners of Anglican Ch. of Can., 1969-74. Mem. senate U. Western Ont., 1959-84. Home and Office: Huron College London ON N6G 1H3 Canada

MOREE, CHRISTOPHER CORNELIUS, editor, minister, Church of God; b. Riviera Beach, Fla., June 1, 1932; s. James Alexander and Iva Delphima (Fox) M.; m. Sarah Fae Danehower, Feb. 26, 1955; children: Ronald Fenton, Keith Edward, Stephen James, Melinda Fae. A.A., Lee Coll., 1954; Th.B., London Bible Sem., 1964; B.A., Wayne State U., 1974. Ordained to ministry, Ch. of God, 1960. State youth dir. Ch. of God, Flat River, Mo., 1954-58, Indpls., 1958-60; pastor Ch. of God, various cities, 1960-81; world mission editor Ch. of God, Cleveland, Tenn., 1981—; bd. dirs. Ch. of God Sch. Theology, Cleveland, 1978-82; chmn. dept. edn. Ch. of God in Mich., Troy, 1976-81, mem. state council, 1972-81. Editor Pastor's Resource Manual, 1982; Save Our World. Contbr. articles to profl. jours. Mem. Evang. Press Assn., Internat. Pentecostal Press. Home: 5133 Creekbend Cir NW Cleveland TN 37311 Office: Church of God World Missions Keith at 25th St NW Cleveland TN 37311

MORELAND, F. ELWOOD, minister, Lutheran Church in America; b. Perry County, Pa., Mar. 10, 1921; s. John F. and Ellen M. (Moyer) M.; m. Mary E. Depfer, Aug. 18, 1945; children: David E., John E., Anne E. B.A., Gettysburg Coll., 1943; B.D., Luth. Theol. Sem., 1945. Ordained to ministry Luth. Ch. in Am., 1945. Pastor Calvary Parish, Hampstead, Md., 1945-49, Shrewsbury Parish, Pa., 1949-56, St. Paul's Luth. Ch., Spring Grove, Pa., 1956-65, Our Saviour's Luth. Ch., Orange, Calif., 1965-75, Ch. of Cross, Laguna Hills, Calif., 1975—; dean So. Dist. Pacific S.W. Synod, Luth. Ch. in Am., 1975-79; mem. synodical coms. on Edn., Stewardship, Capital Funding, Nominations. Mem. Religious Council of Chs., York, Pa., 1950-60, Laguna Hills, 1979; pres., sec., Film Com., Laguna Hills, 1975—. Home: 26822 Morena Dr Mission Viejo CA 92691 Office: Luth Ch of the Cross 24231 El Toro Rd Laguna Hills CA 92653

MOREN, ORVAL KENNETH, minister, American Lutheran Church; b. Polk County, Minn., Apr. 29, 1929; s. Albert Anton and Jenny Caroline (Christianson) M.; m. Bernell Elvera Westman, June 5, 1954; children: Jonathan, Rebecca, Deborah, Mary. B.A., Augsburg Coll., 1957; M.Div., Luther Sem., St. Paul, 1960; D.Min., Jesuit Sch. Theology, Berkeley, Calif., 1982; D.D. (hon.), U. Minn.-Duluth, 1983. Ordained to ministry Evang. Luth. Ch., 1960. Minister Dunseith Luth. Ch., N.D., 1960-63, Our Saviors Luth. Ch., Warren, Minn., 1963-71, Duluth, Minn., 1971-77; minister pastoral care Faith Luth. Ch., Albuquerque, 1977—; area clergy contact Luth. Marriage Encounter, Albuquerque, 1984; counselor, cons. N.Mex. Christian Conciliation Service, 1982—. Served with U.S. Army, 1950-53. Mem. Good Samaritan Soc. (pres. 1973-76, treas. 1976-77). Democrat. Home: 9700 Avenida de la Luna NE Albuquerque NM 87111 Office: Faith Luth Ch 10000 Spain Rd NE Albuquerque NM 87111

MORENO, MANUEL DURAN, bishop, Roman Catholic Church; b. Placentia, Calif., Nov. 27, 1930; s. Antonio (dec.) and Enedina (Duran) M. A.A., Fullerton Jr. Coll., 1949-51; B.S.B.A., UCLA, 1953; postgrad., Our Lady Queen of Angels Sem., San Fernando, Calif., 1953-55; B.A., St. John's Sem., Camarillo, Calif., 1961; post-ordination student N. Am. Coll., Rome, 1961. Ordained priest Roman Cath. Ch., 1961. Assoc. pastor St. Thomas Parish, Los Angeles, 1961-66, St. Vibiana Cathedral, Los Angeles, 1966-76; named monsignor, 1974, parochial vicar, 1976, consecrated bishop, 1977, aux. bishop Archdiocese of Los Angeles, 1977-81; episcopal vicar Ventura County Residence, San Buenaventura Mission, Ventura, Calif., 1981-82; named bishop of Tucson, 1982—. Office: Diocese of Tucson PO Box 31 Tucson AZ 85702

MORETON, THOMAS HUGH, minister, British Baptist Church; b. Shanghai, China, Dec. 2, 1917; s. Hugh and Tsuru Moreton; LL.B., 1939, B.D., 1942, Ph.D., 1946, Th.D., Trinity Sem., 1948, Litt.D., 1949; m. Olive Mae Rives, Apr. 1, 1947; children: Ann Rives (Mrs. Dennis Smith), Andrew Hugh, Margaret Evelyn (Mrs. James Hamar). Came to U.S., 1946, naturalized, 1950. Ordained to ministry Brit. Bapt. Ch., 1942. Minister various chs., Eng., 1945-46, also tchr. Seaford Coll.; tchr. coll. and sem. level div. courses, Atlanta, Oklahoma City, 1946-51; chaplain AUS, Tokyo, 1952-63; founder Tokyo Gospel Mission, Inc., also House of Hope, Inc., Tokyo, Japan, 1951—; founder World Gospel Fellowship, Inc., Norman, Okla., 1967—; pastor, Moore, Oklahoma City, Shawnee, Ada, Del City, Okla., 1968-74; preacher numerous fgn. countries; internat. tour dir. Contbr. articles to religious jours. Recipient various awards Japanese govt. Fellow Royal Geog. Soc., Philos. Soc.; mem. Royal Soc. Lit. (all U.K.), Am.-Japan Com. for Assisting Japanese-Am. Orphans (charter), Am.-Japan Soc. (Tokyo), Israel-Japan Soc. (Tokyo).

MORGAN, JOHN HANLY, minister, Unitarian Universalist Assn.; b. New Albany, Ind., Nov. 28, 1918; s. John Sidney and Vada Elizabeth (Dorn) M.; m. M. Jeannette Mutzfeld, 1942; children: Lois, David, Lee, Ann. B.A., Ball State U., 1943; S.T.B., Harvard U., 1946; M.A. in Philosophy, U. Mich., 1955; Ph.D. in English, U. South Fla., 1979. Ordained to ministry Unitarian Universalist Assn., 1946. Minister Unitarian Ch., Flint, Mich., 1952-56, South Bend, Ind., 1956-59; sr. minister 1st Unitarian Congregation, Toronto, Ont., Can., 1959—, now pastor emeritus; mem. exec. com. Metro Toronto Unitarian Council, 1960-70, Can. Unitarian Council, 1960-70. Author: (poetry) Lifetime, 1957, Kangaroo City, 1980; (poetry and prose) Hands of Friends, 1977, Receive These Hands, 1984. Vice pres. Flint chpt. NAACP, 1954, South Bend chpt. NAACP, 1958, World Peace Council, 1983—; pres. Can. Peace Congress, 1972—. Recipient Joliot-Curie Gold Medal for Peace, 1984; Lenin Peace Laureate, 1983. Mem. Unitarian Universalist Assn., Unitarian Universalist Ministers Assn., Fellowship Religious Humanists.

MORGAN, MARGERY LAWRENCE, religion educator, administrator, Seventh-day Adventist; b. Nabaclis, Guyana, June 1, 1941; came to U.S., 1968; d. Frederick Winston and Clarabelle (Trotman) Lawrence; m. Theodore Edward Morgan, Nov. 28, 1978. B.S., Oakwood Coll., 1971; M.S., Johns Hopkins U., 1974. Lic. missionary Seventh-day Adventist Ch.; cert. tchr., Ala., Md. Tchr., prin. Guyana Mission Seventh-day Adventist Ch., 1964-68; tchr., vice prin. Balt. Jr. Acad., 1971-80; prin. Trinity Temple Acad., Hillside, N.J., 1980—; leader Missionary Vol. Soc., Balt., 1975-77; mem. Allegheny East Conf. Bd. Edn., Pine Forge, Pa., 1983—. Mem. Am. Soc. Curriculum Devel. Mem. Sanctuary Choir, Newark, 1980—. Home: 636 Grove St Irvington NJ 07111

MORGAN, MARY HOLLIDAY, minister, Church of God. b. Summerton, S.C., Mar. 11, 1912; d. Washington and Elmira (Bradford) Holliday; m. Clifton M. Morgan, Sept. 7, 1940; 1 child, Carolyn Marie Morgan Brown. B.A., S.C. State Coll., 1951; M.A. in Edn., Ball State U., 1975; M.A. in Religion, Anderson Coll., 1979. Ordained to ministry Ch. of God, 1984. Co-minister Ch. of God, Fla., Ohio, Pa., 1948-60; missionary Ch. of God, Cuttack, India, 1960-70; co-minister Ch. of God, Anderson, Ind., 1970-80; pastor Ind. Ministries, Terre Haute, Ind., 1980—; active Ch. of God, Anderson, Ind. Republican.

MORGAN, NORMAN KENNETH, minister, Presbyterian Church in U.S.; b. Albermarle, N.C., Dec. 10, 1925; s. Eben Clemon and Mamie Estelle (Herrin) M.; A.A., Pfeiffer Coll., 1945; A.B., Duke, 1947; B.D., Union Theol. Sem., 1951, M.Div., 1970; m. Betsy Adeline Lippard, Aug. 27, 1948; children: Martha Ann, Norman Kenneth. Ordained to ministry Presbyn. Ch. in U.S., 1951. Pastor Pineville (W.Va.) Presbyn. Ch., 1951-61, First Presbyn. Ch., Logan, W.Va., 1961—. Moderator, Bluestone Presbytery, 1956; chmn. Christian teaching Synod W.Va., 1962-65; bd. mem. David Stuart Home, Lewisburg, W.Va., 1964-67; chmn. Synod Camp and Conf. Com., 1962-65; bd. dirs. Bluestone Conf. Center, 1962-65; chmn. Synod Stewardship Com., 1966-69; moderator Synod W.Va., 1967. Dir. Am. Nat. Bank, Logan, W.Va. Sec.-treas. Logan (W.Va.) Med. Found., 1969—, pres., 1983—; mem. bd. Logan-Mingo Mental Health Council, 1967—. Mem. Logan Ministerial Assn. (pres. 1964-65), Logan Council Chs. (pres. 1967-68). Home: 209 Nighbert Ave Logan WV 25601 Office: 622 Stratton St Logan WV 25601

MORGAN, ROBERT C., bishop, United Methodist Church, Miss. Conf., N. Miss. Conf. Office: 4724 Kings Hgwy Jackson MS 39206*

MORGAN, ROBERT CHARLES, minister, counselor, Southern Baptist Convention; b. Fulton, Ala., May 1, 1948; s. John Charles and Barbara Jean (Hudson) M.; m. Linda Williams, May 13, 1972; children: John Todd, Kelly Lauren, Robert Patton. B.A., Mobile Coll., 1971; M.Div., So. Bapt. Theol. Sem., 1975; M.S., Troy State U., 1982. Ordained to ministry So. Bapt. Ch., 1975. Pastor, Lisman Bapt. Ch., Ala., 1975-76, Bethel Bapt. Ch., Robertsdale, Ala., 1976-84; counselor Ctr. For Pastoral Counseling and Creative Living, Robertsdale, 1982—. Asst. editor Clarke County Democrat, Grove Hill, Ala., 1971-72. Named to Outstanding Young Men Am. U.S. Jaycees, 1980, 82, Community Leaders Am., Am. Biol. Inst. Fellow Internat. Council Sex Edn. and Parenthood; mem. Am. Inst. Counseling and Psychotherapy (clin. mem.), Am. Mental Health Counselors Assn., Am. Assn. Counseling and Devel., Kappa Delta Pi. Democrat. Office: Ctr for Pastoral Counseling and Creative Living PO Box 3774 Robertsdale AL 36567

MORIN, LAURENT, bishop, Roman Catholic Church; b. Montreal, Que., Can., Feb. 14, 1908. Ordained priest, 1934; ordained titular bishop of Arsamosata and aux. bishop of Montreal, 1955; bishop of Prince Albert (Sask., Can.), 1959—. Office: 1415-Ouest 4e Ave Prince Albert SK S6V 5H1 Canada*

MORITA, TIMOTHY TADAYOSHI, minister, So. Baptist Conv.; b. Hakalau, Hawaii, Feb. 15, 1947; s. Jack Tadatsugu and Margaret Umeyo (Kubo) M.; B.S., U. Hawaii, 1969; M.Div., Golden Gate Bapt. Theol. Sem., 1974; postgrad. San Francisco Theol. Sem., 1975—; m. Janice Ann Keating, Dec. 28, 1968; children—Laura Harumi, LeAnn Natsumi. Ordained to ministry, 1973; pastor Haleiwa Bapt. Ch. (Hawaii), 1973—. Chaplain, Hawaii Army Nat. Guard, 1972—; vice chmn. bd. ops., personnel com. Hawaii Bapt. Conv., also mem. exec. bd.; chmn. missions com. Central Leeward Oahu Bapt. Assn. Chmn. welcoming com. Haleiwa Elementary Sch. PTA, 1975; mem. Haleiwa Waialua Mental Health Adv. Bd., 1975; v.p. Central Oahu Mental Health Adv. Bd., 1975. Hawaii Bapt. Conv. scholar, 1970-73; Hawaii Vets. Meml. scholar, 1975-76; Juliet Atherton Meml. scholar, 1976-77; ARC community outstanding vol., 1974. Home: 66-415 Haleiwa Rd Haleiwa HI 96712 Office: Box 111 Haleiwa HI 96712

MORKOVSKY, JOHN LOUIS, bishop, Roman Cath. Ch.; b. Moulton, Tex., Aug. 16, 1909; s. Alois Joseph and Marie Theresa (Raska) M.; S.T.D., Gregorian U., Rome, 1936; M.Ed., Cath. U. Am., 1943; LL.D. (hon.), St. Edwards U., Austin, Tex., 1958. Ordained priest, 1933; parochial assignments, Weimar, Tex., 1936-40, San Antonio, 1940-56; archdiocesan supt. schs., 1943-56; consecrated aux. bishop of Amarillo, Tex., 1956; named bishop of Amarillo, 1958; coadjutor bishop and apostolic adminstr. of Galveston-Houston, 1963-75, bishop of Galveston-Houston, 1975—. Pres., Nat. Cath. Rural Life Conf., 1960, Tex. Conf. Chs., 1970-71. Named papal chamberlain, 1945, domestic prelate, 1954. Home: 9845 Memorial Dr Houston TX 77024 Office: 1700 San Jacinto Houston TX 77002

MORNEAU, ROBERT FEALEY, bishop, Roman Cath. Ch.; b. New London, Wis., Sept. 10, 1938; s. LeRoy F. and Catherine M. (Fealey) M.; B.S., Cath. U. Am., 1961, M.A. in Philosophy, 1962. Ordained priest, 1966; instr. philosophy Holy Family Coll., Manitowoc, Wis., 1966—; vicar for religious edn. Diocese of Green Bay (Wis.), from 1970; titular bishop of Massa Lubrense and aux. bishop of Green Bay, 1979—; chaplain Park Lawn Nursing Home, 1966—. Contbr. articles to religious jours. Address: St Norbert Abbey De Pere WI 54115

MORREL, GEORGE WILLIAM, minister, educator, EPiscopal Ch.; b. Austin, Tex., Aug. 26, 1917; s. George and Elaine Chilton (Lewis) M.; B.A., U. of South, 1937; M.Div., Ch. Div. Sch. of Pacific, 1940; S.T.M., Pacific Sch. Religion, 1964, Th.D. 1969; m. Grayce Neubauer, Dec. 31, 1939 (dec., 1975); children—Alene, Stephanie, Gracia. Ordained to ministry, 1941; instr. Ch. Div. Sch. of Pacific, Berkeley, Calif., 1940-64; rector Ch. St. Mary The Virgin, San Francisco, 1944-47; prof. systematic theol. Bloy Episc. Sch. Theol., Claremont, Calif., 1964—; vis. prof. hist. theology Fuller Sem. Pasadena (Calif.) Sch. Theol., 1975—; lectr. Patristics Inst., Oxford, Eng. Mem. Am. Acad. Religion, Conf. Anglican Theolgians. Author: Contemporary Continental Theology, 1943, La Ensenanza de San Pablo Acerca de la Santa Communion, 1950, The Theology of Vladimir Lossky, 1959. Home: 701 Hagar St San Fernando CA 91340 Office: 1325 N College Ave Claremont CA 91711

MORRIS, CLIFFORD RAY, minister, educator, Southern Baptist Convention; b. Knox County, Ky., Feb. 7, 1937; s. Cecil and Sarah M.; B.S. in Biology, Cumberland Coll., 1964; M.Ed. in Biology, Eastern Ky. U., 1969; Th.D., Berean Christian Theol. Sem., 1977; Ph.D. in Edn. Adminstrn. and Health Services Adminstrn., Columbia Pacific U., 1983; m. June Girdner Morris, Dec. 21, 1957; 1 child, Carlos Ray. Ordained to ministry So. Bapt. Conv., 1974. Pastor 20th St. Bapt Ch., Corbin, Ky., 1982—, evangelist; researcher evolution and creation. Tchr. biology, anatomy and physiology Knox Central High Sch., Barbourville, Ky., 1962—; med. technologist, respiratory therapist, Knox County Gen. Hosp., Barbourville, 1968—; Mem. AAAS, Am. Soc. Zoologists, Ky. Thoracic Soc., Am. Soc. Med. Tech., Internat. Soc. Clin. Lab. Technologists, NEA, Ky. Edn. Assn., Ky. Soc. Med. Technologists. Contbr. Berean Messenger, 1974—. Home: Route 3 Box 11 Barbourville KY 40906 Office: Biology Dept Knox Central High School Barbourville KY 40906

MORRIS, GEORGE EWING, theology educator, United Methodist Church; b. Inman, Va., Oct. 27, 1935; s. James Walker and Martha Virginia (Ireson) M.; m. Barbara Jean Murphy, Sept. 1, 1956; children: Tonya, David, George Ewing, Serendee. B.A., Asbury Coll., 1957; M.Div., Vanderbilt U., 1963, D.Div., 1970. Ordained pastor United Meth. Ch., 1964. Pastor, Reinzi Circuit, Miss., 1957-59, Pembroke United Meth. Ch., Ky., 1959-63, Emmanuel United Meth. Ch., Menomonee Falls, Wis., 1969-72, 1st United Meth. Ch., Kenosha, Wis., 1975-77; assoc. dir. dept. new life ministries Gen. Bd. Evangelism, 1963-69; dir. dept. new life ministries Bd. of Discipleship, 1972-75; prof. Candler Sch. Theology, Emory U., Atlanta, 1977—, Arthur J. Moore prof., 1977—; trustee Appalachia Service Project, Johnson City, Tenn., 1977—; del. Australia-Asian Congress, 1974; dir. Inst. for World Evangelism, Atlanta, 1982—. Mem. World Meth. Council, Acad. for Evangelism, Internat. Assn. Mission Studies. Office: Chandler Sch of Theology Emory Univ Atlanta GA 30322

MORRIS, GERALD DEAN, minister, American Baptist Churches U.S.A.; b. Wichita, Kan., Oct. 25, 1942; s. Donald Kenneth and Ruby Evelyn (Lewis) M.; m. Mary Jane Coddington, June 13, 1965; children: Jeffrey, Teresa, Brian. B.A., Friends U., 1974. Ordained to ministry Baptist Ch., 1971. Pastor, Minneha Bapt. Ch., Wichita, 1966-69; minister edn. First Baptist Ch., El Dorado, Kan., 1969-70; pastor Central Bapt. Ch., Augusta, Kan., 1970-77, Grant Ave. Bapt. Ch., Chanute, Kan., 1977-82, First Bapt. Ch., Lyons, Kan.,

1982—. Republican. Lodge: Kiwanis (Lyons) (chmn. Spiritual Aims 1983-85). Home: 400 S Clark Lyons KS 67554 Office: First Bapt Ch 803 S Dinsmore Lyons KS 67554

MORRIS, HARRY JACK, minister, Christian Church (Disciples of Christ); marriage and family therapist; b. Dickerson Run, Pa., Jan. 2, 1936; s. Harry Elroy and Etheleen (Carpenter) M.; m. Corin Fuller, June 12, 1954; children: Rebecca, Jack II. B.A., Central Bible Coll., 1963; postgrad. U. Md., 1963; M.A., NYU, 1967; D.Min., Luther Rice Sem., 1978; cert. Family Counseling, Bowie State Coll., 1982; D.Min., McCormick Theol. Sem., 1982. Ordained to ministry Disciples of Christ Ch., 1960. Pastor, Ebony Assembly of God, Va., 1957-59, Assembly of God Ch., Elizabeth City, N.C., 1960, Bethel Tabernacle, Balt., 1963-67, Evang. Assembly of God Ch., Temple Hills, Md., 1967-72, Largo Community Ch., Mitchellville, Md., 1972—; mem. dept. ch. extension Christian Ch., Chevy Chase, Md., 1980—, mem. exec. com. Ministerial Assn., 1981—, dept. evangelism, 1979-80; faculty Luther Rice Coll., Franconia, Va., 1968; guest philosophy lectr., chapel speaker Far East Advanced Sch. Theology, Manila, 1971; gave opening prayer U.S. Ho. of Reps., 1977; marriage and family therapist Christian Counselling Service, Mitchellville, 1982—. Founder, Largo Community Ch., 1972, Christian Counselling Services, 1980. Active Kettering Civic Assn., Upper Marlboro, Md., 1972-82, Kettering Community Assn., 1972-82. Mem. Am. Assn. Marriage and Family Therapists (clin., Middle Atlantic div.), Largo Ministerial Assn., North Am. Soc. Adlerian Psychology, Potomac Dist. Council Assemblies of God (dist. youth dept. com. 1958-59, dist. fin. and edn. coms. 1968-70, elected presbyter of capitol sect. 1972). Republican. Home: 1274 Lavall Dr Gambrills MD 21054 Office: Largo Community Ch 1701 Enterprise Rd Mitchellville MD 20716

MORRIS, MARLIN BLAIR, minister, military chaplain, denominational administrator, Southern Baptist Convention; b. Lampasas, Tex., Nov. 18, 1912; s. Roy Harvey and Bird (Salter) M.; B.A., Howard Payne U., 1935; B.D., Southwestern Bapt. Theol. Sem., 1952; postgrad. counseling U. Tex., 1961; m. Guindola Jones, Jan. 20, 1935; children: Katherine Ann, Mason Kenneth. Ordained to ministry So. Bapt. Conv., 1935. Pastor chs., Tex., 1935-43, 48-51; clk., treas. Big Spring Bapt. Assn., Tex., 1941-42; chaplain, U.S. Army, 1943-48, USAF, 1951-72; adminstr. relief, displaced persons, Bremen, Germany, 1947; mission pastor, low income sect., Brownwood, Tex., 1973-74; stewardship dir. Brown Bapt. Assn., Tex., 1973-82; mem. budget adv. service Bapt. Gen. Conv. Tex., 1974-82; Home Mission Bd. speaker World Mission Conf., 1977, 84; lectr. Bibl. archaeology, historic and prehistoric archaeology; treas. Heart of Tex. Bapt. Area, 1978-85; pres. Pastors Assn., Brownwood, 1975—. Flood relief dir., USAF, Korea, 1966; bd. dirs. Brown County Mus. History, 1982-84. Recipient letter of appreciation for Meritorious Service, South Korean Air Force, 1966. Contbr. articles to religious and archaeol. jours.; recorder archaeol. sites, Tex. Home and Office: 4101 4th St Brownwood TX 76801

MORRIS, PHILIP CROCKETT, minister, Ch. of God; b. Crisfield, Md., Apr. 3, 1941; s. Ralph Leon and Sadie Bond (Crockett) M.; student Lee Coll., 1959-63, Tenn. Wesleyan Coll., 1963-64, U. Tenn., 1964-65; m. Mary Louise Smith, Aug. 20, 1962; children—Philip Crockett, Ralph Ashley. Ordained to ministry, 1976; instr. English, Lee Coll., Cleveland, Tenn., 1965-68, Salisbury (Md.) State Coll., 1968-71; founding pastor Walker Meml. Ch. of God, Princess Anne, Md., 1969—. Mem. chancellor's adv. com. U. Md.; chmn. Somerset County Bicentennial Publs. Com. Home: 129 Prince William St Princess Anne MD 21853

MORRIS, RALPH EDWIN, minister, Church of God; b. Charleston, S.C., June 30, 1941; s. Stephen Uriel and Chub Louise (Bradley) M.; B.Th., Life Tabernacle Bible Inst., 1975; B.A., Am. Christian Bible Coll., 1977; M.Th., New World Bible Sem., 1982, D.D., 1984; B.S. Lee Coll., 1985; m. Elsie LaVoylyn Christopher, Dec. 24, 1964; children: Marla Lyn, Ralph Edwin. Ordained to ministry Ch. of God, 1971. Pastor Cateechee (S.C.) Ch., 1966-68, Ft. Inn (S.C.) Ch., 1968-70; founder, pres. Life Tabernacle Pentecostal Bible Inst., Greenville, S.C., 1972-79; pastor Life Tabernacle Ch., Greenville, 1970-79, Westwood Ch., Simpsonville, S.C., 1979-80, Marshall Road Ch., Greenwood, S.C., 1981-82, Cedar Rock Ch., Easley, S.C., 1982-83; prin. Park Place Christian Acad., Greenville, 1980-81; tchr. pub. and Christian schs., 1975-84; evangelist, 1983—; hosp. chaplain, 1981-82; Christian counselor, 1982—; v.p. Atonement Ministries, Evangelistic Outreach Greenville. Del. Democratic County Conv., S.C., 1976. Mem. Pentecostal Fellowship of N.Am., West Greenville Community Action, Order of Broom, Phi Epislon Phi. Home: Route 8 108 Davis Dr Greenville SC 29611 Office: 108 Davis Dr Greenville SC 29611

MORRIS, SAMUEL S., JR., bishop, African Methodist Episcopal Church. Office: African Methodist Episcopal Ch 4448 S Michigan Ave PO Box 53539 Chicago IL 60653*

MORRISON, FRANCINE REESE, minister, vocalist, Pentecostal Ch.; b. Paris, Tex., Aug. 16, 1935; d. Louvenia Eugenia Flemmings; student Bakersfield (Calif.) Jr. Coll., 1953-54; D. Sacred Music, Union Bapt. Theol. Sem., Houston, 1966; D.D., Internat. Deliverance Ch., Dallas, 1975; m. Jury Morrison, Sept. 17, 1956; 1 dau., LuWilda Diane. Ordained to ministry, 1969; vocalist with Mahalia Jackson, Dallas, 1961, with James Cleveland, Dallas, 1964; guest artist civic and polit. affairs. Home: 928 E Bowie St Fort Worth TX 76104

MORRISON, JIMMIE AARON, minister, American Baptist Churches; b. Parkersburg, W.Va., June 12, 1935; s. Cecil Bayard and Clancie Mae (Ball) M.; B.A., Alderson-Broaddus Coll., Philippi, W.Va., 1958; M.Div., Colgate-Rochester Div. Sch., N.Y., 1962, grad. cert. in pastoral counseling, Found. Religion and Mental Health, 1973; m. Janet June Wilson, Aug. 26, 1956; children: Janene Lea, Jody Lynn, James Bryce. Ordained to ministry Am. Bapt. Churches, 1962. Pastor chs. in N.Y., 1961—; pastor First Bapt. Ch., Central Square, N.Y., 1965-69, Ossining, 1969-74, Brighton Community Ch., Tonawanda, 1974—. Rec. sec. N.Y. State, Am. Bapt. Churches, 1967-69; mem. exec. com. United Ministries Higher Edn. N.Y. State, 1969-74; chmn. community witness dept., 1974-79; bd. dirs. Ecumenical Found. N.Y.C., 1970-74; pres. Council of Chs. Buffalo and Erie County, 1981-84; chmn. dept. ednl. ministries Am. Bapt. Chs., 1979-84. Cons., Town of Tonawanda, 1975—; chmn. Ossining (N.Y.) Narcotics Guidance Council, 1972-74; bd. dirs. Erie County Mental Health, 1977—, planned Parenthood Buffalo and Erie County, 1983—. Recipient Spl. Recognition award Ossining Jaycees, 1973. Address: 211 N Wrexham Ct Tonawanda NY 14150

MORRISON, TIMOTHY ARTHUR, minister, United Church of Christ; b. Greenville, Pa., July 18, 1949; s. Emery Lee and Helen Myra (MacDonald) M.; m. Ann Ruth Eumurian, May 18, 1974; children: Joel Emery, Sean Charles. B.A. with honors, Lehigh U., 1971; M.Div., United Theol. Sem. Twin Cities, 1974; D.Min., Andover-Newton Theol. Sch., 1980. Ordained to ministry United Ch. of Christ, 1974. Assoc. pastor for Christian edn. and youth ministry, Christ United Ch. of Christ, Bethlehem, Pa., 1974-75, High St. United Ch. of Christ, Auburn, Maine, 1975-78; missionary United Ch. of Christ Bd. for World Ministries, N.Y.C., 1978-81; Christian edn. specialist Evang. Presbyn. Ch., Peki, Ghana, West Africa, 1981; organizing pastor United Ch. Fox Valley, Aurora, Ill., 1981-84; pastor Suffield United Ch. of Christ, Ohio, 1984—; leader clown workshops for United Ch. Christ, No. Ill. Contbr. articles to religious newsletters, mags., books. Vice chmn. Auburn Housing Authority, 1977-78; v.p. Western Regional Council on Alcohol Abuse and Alcoholism, Lewiston, Maine, 1976-78; mem. Aurora Revenue Sharing Com., 1982—. Democrat. Lodges: Tranquil, Perfection. Home: 2091 Pontius Rd Suffield OH 44260

MORSCH, JAMES VERNON, minister, administrator, Church of the Nazarene; b. Leland, Ill., Oct. 21, 1927; s. Vernon Joseph and Ruby (Ugland) M.; m. Patricia Estelle Plikerd, Aug. 19, 1950; children: Gary, Rebecca, Mark, Lori, James Kyle. B.S. in Edn., Olivet Nazarene Coll., 1951, Th.B., 1952; Th.M., Luther Rice Sem., 1978, D.Ministry, 1979; L.H.D. (hon.), Union Theol. Sem., N.J., 1982. Ordained to ministry Ch. of Nazarene, 1954. Sr. pastor Ch. of Nazarene, Lomax and Pekin, Ill., also Oklahoma City, Nashville, 1952-74; dist. supt. Central Fla. dist. Ch. of Nazarene, Orlando, 1974—; children's dir. NW Ill. dist. Ch. of Nazarene, 1952-56, evangelism dir., 1956-66, mem. bd. pensions, internat. hdqrs., Kansas City, Mo., 1966-74, mem. gen. bd., internat., 1968-74; chmn. bd. trustees Trevecca Nazarene Coll., Nashville, 1978—, recipient Pres.'s award, 1977, 81; trustee Nazarene Bible Coll., Colorado Springs, Colo., 1980—; chmn. Ill. Prayer in Sch. Com., 1960; chaplain Tenn. Legislature, 1973; mem. exec. com. Christian Counseling Services, Nashville, 1973—; chmn. Sea World Ministries, Orlando, 1976—; pres. Christian Life World, Inc., 1976—; mem. exec. com. Yr. of the Bible, 1983. Author: The Whole Church Evangelizing, 1972; Church Growth as It Relates to the New Testament, 1979; also contbns. to periodicals and films. Served with U.S. Army, 1945-47, Korea. Recipient Nat. Youth award S. Korean Govt., 1946; Internat. Red Cross award, 1954; Community Leadership award State of Tenn., 1973; Christian Leadership award Philippine Govt., 1974; Gt. Commn. medallion, internat. hdqrs. Ch. of Nazarene, 1984; numerous others. Fellow Nat. Assn. Evangelicals; mem. Orlando Downtown Chs. Assn. (exec. com.), Fla. Assn. Evangelicals (exec. com.), Orlando C. of C. Home: 8715 Lansmere Ln Orlando FL 32811 Office: Central Fla Dist Ch of Nazarene 10900 Turkey Lake Rd Orlando FL 32819

MORSE, JONATHAN KENT, deacon, religious educator, Ukrainian Catholic Church; b. Teaneck, N.J., Dec. 10, 1951; s. Alfred George and Agnes Marie (Lagatol) M.; m. Kathleen Zylinsky, May 10, 1980. B.A., Cath. U., 1973; M.R.E., 1976; M.A., John XXIII Inst., 1978; postgrad. Fordham U., 1980—. Ordained deacon Ukrainian Cath. Ch., 1981. Instr., Manor Jr. Coll., Jenkintown, Pa., 1977-83, Holy Family Coll., Phila., 1978—, Gwynedd-Mercy Coll., Pa., 1983—; pastoral assoc. Sacred Heart Ch., Phila., 1981—; dir. religious edn. Maternity BVM Ch., Phila., 1983—; regional coordinator Ukrainian Cath. Archdiocese, Phila., 1984—. Editor: Rich in Compassion, 1984; co-author: The Jesus Prayer, 1985; contbr. articles to religious jours. Mem. Eastern Cath. Dirs. Religious Edn., Phi Alpha Theta, Pi Gamma Mu. Club: Serra (chaplain 1982—) (northeast Phila.). Lodge: K.C. (chaplain N.E. Phila.). Home and Office: 2072 Red Lion Rd Philadelphia PA 19115

MORSE, RUSSELL LAVERNE, theology educator, Christian Churches, (Churches of Christ); b. Los Angeles, Jan. 4, 1929; s. Justin Russell and Gertrude Erma (Howe) M.; m. Lois Carol Elliott, Mar. 27, 1953; children: Marcia, Mark, Cynthia, Beth, Shirley. B.A., Cin. Bible Sem., 1954, B.Th., 1960; student Minn. Bible Coll., 1947-49. Ordained to ministry Chs. of Christ, 1946. Missionary Yunnan-Tibetan Christian Mission, China, 1949-50; missionary educator North Burma Christian Mission, Putao, Kachin State, Burma, 1950-64; missions prof. Cin. Bible Sem., 1965—; missionary coordinator S.E. Asia Evang. Mission, Cin., 1966—; vice chmn. Internat. Disaster Emergency Services, Marion, Ind., 1971—; dir. Christian Arabic Services, Cin., 1982—; editor South East Asia Challenge, Cin., 1967-79, South East Asia Update, Cin., 1979—; trustee Cambodian Evang. Mission Internat., Long Beach, Calif., 1984—. Contbr. articles to jours. Mem. Nat. Assn. Fgn. Student Affairs (fgn. student adv.). Republican. Office: Cincinnati Bible Sem South East Asia Evangelizing Mission 2700 Glenway Ave Cincinnati OH 45204

MORSE, TERRY WAYNE, minister, United Presbyn. Ch. in U.S.A.; b. Grand Rapids, Mich., Aug. 6, 1946; s. Fred Myron and Elizabeth Ida (Cheney) M.; B.A., Houghton (N.Y.) Coll., 1968; M.Div., Union Theol. Sem., Richmond, Va., 1971; m. Martha Ellen Hale, Aug. 11, 1968; children—Charles Eric, Alyssa Marie. Ordained to ministry, 1972; student pastor Zion Evang. Community Ch., Ellicottville, N.Y., 1967-68, Zion Nat. Park, Utah, 1969; intern Yosemite Nat. Park, Calif., 1971; pastor Englishtown (N.J.) Presbyn. Ch., 1972—. Mem. coms. Monmouth (N.J.) Presbytery, moderator, 1976—, del. to synod, 1975. Mem. counseling bd. Monmouth County Action Program, 1974-75. Recipient Service award Monmouth County Action Program, 1975. Home: 60 Main St Englishtown NJ 07726 Office: 50 Main St Englishtown NJ 07726

MORTENSEN, HANS BIRGER, minister, Ind. Fundamental Chs. Am.; b. Skoger, Norway, May 21, 1913; s. Morten M. and Helen (Eriksen) M.; grad. Norwegian Missionary Free Ch. Bible Sch., 1935, Norwegian Practical Pastoral Sem., 1942; B.Th., Am. Bible Sch., 1960; Th.M., Am. Div. Sch., 1965, Th.D., 1969; came to U.S., 1963; m. Wilhelmina Sjemmedal, Sept. 19, 1936; children—Frank Samuel, Svenin Victor, Hans Willy, Laila Cecelie. Ordained to ministry, 1935; evangelist, 1935-39; pastor chs., Norway, 1939-50, Sweden, 1950-56; pastor Seaman mission, Toronto, Ont., Can., 1957-61; gen. dir. Am. Mission to India, Lombard, Ill., 1964—; pastor Woodbin Bible Ch., Stockton, Ill., 1969-72, Faith Bible Ch., Lombard, 1973—. Chaplain, DuPage Area council Boy Scouts Am., 1973. Home and Office: 51 E Hickory St Lombard IL 60148

MORTON, THOMAS WILSON, minister, So. Baptist Conv.; b. Jackson, Ga., Sept. 16, 1941; s. Wellborn Carter and Ethel Louise (Wilson) M.; A.A., Truett-McConnell Jr. Coll., Cleveland, Ga., 1961; B.A. in English, Mercer U., Macon, Ga., 1963; M.Div., New Orleans Bapt. Theol. Sem., 1976, M.R.E., 1977. Ordained to ministry, 1972; pastor, youth dir., ednl. dir., student summer missionary Home Mission Bd., Columbus, Ohio, 1963, Okla., 1964, Nev., 1965; pastor Adgateville Bapt. Ch., Monticello, Ga., 1972-73; asso. pastor, youth dir., ednl. dir. First Bapt. Ch., St. Rose, La., 1974-76. Vice pres. Ga. Club at New Orleans Sem., 1973-74. Mem. Bapt. Hist. Soc. Address: 3939 Gentilly Blvd Box 643 New Orleans LA 70126 also Route 5 Box 60 Jackson GA 30233

MOSELEY, SARA BERNICE, lay church worker, Presbyterian Church in the U.S.; b. Anson, Tex., Aug. 9, 1917; m. John D. Moseley; 3 children. B.A., Tex. Women's U.; postgrad. U. Mich., U. Tex. Mem. Provisional Gen. Exec. Bd. Presbyn. Ch. in the U.S., 1973-74, chmn. Bd. Women's Work, moderator Gen. Assembly, 1978, commr. Gen. Assembly, 1981; chmn. div. Ministers Covenant Presbytery, Tex.; vice chmn. bd., chmn. Div. Internat. Mission of Gen. Exec. Bd.; ruling elder First Presbyn. Ch., Sherman, Tex. Bd. dirs. Sherman's Campfire Girls, City Charity Bd., Musical Arts Bd. Home: 921 N Grand St Sherman TX 75090 Office: Presbyn News Service 341 Ponce de Leon Ave NE Atlanta GA 30308

MOSER, MAURICE LEROY, JR., minister, editor, Independent Baptist Church; b. Pine Bluff, Ark., Nov. 23, 1925; s. Maurice Leroy Sr. and Minnie Juanita (Ashcraft) M.; m. Edith Louise Fryer, Feb. 23, 1947; children: Billy Maurice, Michael David. A.A., Central Bapt. Coll., 1948; B.R.E., New Orleans Bapt. Sem., 1952; B.A., U. Central Ark., 1953; D.D. (hon.), Ind. Bapt. Coll., 1977. Ordained to ministry Baptist Ch.,

1948. Pres. Latin Am. Bapt. Theol. Sem., Morelia, Michioacan, Mex., 1952-65; pastor Central Bapt. Ch., Little Rock, 1965—; mem. council advs. Ind. Bapt. Coll., Dallas, 1970—; pres. Challenge Press, Little Rock, 1970—. Author: The Devil's Masterpiece (Silver medal 1971), 1970; numerous other books. Editor: Bapt. Challenge, 1962—. Served with USMC, 1944-47, PTO. Recipient Bob Jones Meml. award Bob Jones U., 1971. Avocation: flying. Home: PO Box 5567 Little Rock AR 72215 Office: Central Bapt Ch 5722 W 12th St Little Rock AR 72204

MOSES, DONALD HARWOOD, priest, Episcopal Church; b. Fort Wayne, Ind., Nov. 26, 1933; s. Horace Smith Moses and Harriet (Harwood) Moses Kinney; m. Shirley Rae Garrison, Sept. 9, 1956; children: Cynthia Rae, John Garrison, Donald James. B.B.A., Kans. State U., 1956; M.Div., Nashotah House, 1968. Ordained to ministry Episcopal Ch. as deacon, 1968, priest, 1968; cert. drug educator, Wis. Vicar, Holy Trinity Ch., Platteville, Wis., and Trinity Ch., Mineral Point, Wis., 1969-71; chaplain U. Wis.-Platteville, 1969-71; rector St. Francis Episcopal Ch., Menomonee Falls, Wis., 1971-78, St. Peter's Episcopal Ch., Harrisonville, Mo., 1978-82; vicar St. Paul's Ch., Claremore, Okla., 1982—; regional rep. Diocesan Council on Missions, Okla., 1982—; diocesan spiritual dir. Happening Youth Renewal, western Mo., 1979-82; cons. stewardship dept. Diocese of Milw., 1975-78, chmn. coll. dept., 1970-73; clergy coordinator Diocesan Stewardship Commn., 1985. Dir. 1st Fed. Savs. Bank of Okla., Claremore, 1985. Author: (with others) Mission Strategy, 1977. Developer seminarian tng. program, 1973. Bd. dirs. Community Concert, Claremore, Okla., 1984, Tri-County YMCA, Menomonee Falls, 1978; treas. Chem. People Task Force, Claremore, 1983; screening coordinator Am. Field Service, Menomonee Falls, 1977. Recipient Letter of Recognition, Visitation Program, 1984, Letter of Recognition, Cass County Mental Health, 1982. Mem. Soc. St. John the Evangelist, Rural Workers Fellowship. Democrat. Lodges: Rotary (Claremore pres.-elect 1984, sec. 1983-84); Masons, Elks. Home: 1728 Aspen Dr Claremore OK 74017 Office: St Paul's Episcopal Ch PO Box 1165 Claremore OK 74018

MOSES, WAYNE ALAN, youth director, chaplain, Free Methodist Church in North America; counselor; b. Oakland, Calif., Aug. 14, 1954; s. Lowell Bernis and Dolores Adalyn (Hull) M.; m. Karen Deanna Chadwell, July 10, 1976; children: Wendy Elizabeth, Steven Richard. B.A., San Jose Bible Coll., 1979; M.A., Azusa Pacific U., 1982. Area dir. Youth for Christ, San Jose, Calif., 1977-80; pastor to youth Free Meth. Ch., Corralitos, 1981-82; dir. family concern Youth for Christ, San Jose, 1983—; marriage, family, child counselor Family Services, Watsonville, Calif., 1985—; bd. youth dirs. Free Meth. Ch., Modesto, Calif., 1984—; rep. youth Free Meth. Ch., Corralitos, 1984—. Bd. dirs. Kids in Distress Sta., San Jose, 1985. Mem. Christian Assn. Psychol.-Studies, Calif. Assn. Marital Family Therapists (cert.), Nat. Chaplain Assn. (cert., Hall of Fame Nat. Merit award, 1984, Good Samaritan award 1985). Republican. Avocations: backpacking; magician; musician; writing. Office: Youth for Christ 2150 The Alameda San Jose CA 95126

MOSIMAN, MICHAEL DOUGLAS, youth minister, non-denominational; b. St. Joseph, Mo.; s. Robert Michel Mosiman and Amelia Louise (Kost) Mosiman-Hess; m. Mildred Irene Schrader, Sept. 7, 1974; children: Sarah Michelle, John Michael. Diploma in computer sci. Platte Tech. Inst., 1971; student Christ Unlimited Bible Inst., 1980-81, Covington Theol. Sem. Ordained to ministry Kans. City Youth for Christ, 1983; lic. for ministry World Bible Way Fellowship, 1985. Dean students Christ Unltd. Bible Inst., Shawnee Mission, Kans., 1981-84, dir. staff devel., 1984—. Republican. Avocation: woodworking. Office: Kansas City Youth for Christ 4715 Rainbow Blvd Shawnee Mission KS 66205

MOSKAL, ROBERT M. See *Who's Who in America*, 43rd edition.

MOSLEY, CHARLES RONALD, minister, Baptist Missionary Assn. Am.; b. Passaic, N.J., Apr. 9, 1938; s. Frank and Ruthe Lane (Parker) M.; A.B., Shaw U., 1961, B.D., 1964, M.Div., 1974; m. Lue Alvia Riddick, June 2, 1962; children—Charles Ronald, Sybrennah Antanette. Pastor, Eastern Star Bapt. Ch., Tarboro, N.C., 1960-63, Sycamore Hill Bapt. Ch., Greenville, N.C., 1963-67, Mt. Pleasant Bapt. Ch., Belmont, N.C., 1967-75, Nazareth First Bapt. Ch., Asheville, N.C., 1975—. Mem. exec., adminstrn. coms., asso. sec. bd. missions, dir. music Gen. Bapt. State Conv. N.C., Inc.; asso. sec. exec. com., dir. Lott Carey Fgn. Mission, 1974—; asso. trustee Shaw Div. Sch., 1975—; toured Holy Land, 1973. State adv. com. Agr. Stabilization Conservation Service, U.S. Dept. Agr.; U.S. Chmn. Belmont Human Relations Com., 1972-74; bd. dirs. Asheville-Buncombe Christian Community Ministry, 1976-79. Mem. Gaston County Bapt. Assn. (moderator), Shaw Theol. Alumni Assn. (pres. 1976—), Gaston Ministerial Alliance, Belmont Ministers Assn., NAACP (pres. Asheville-Buncombe chpt. 1976—). Home: 144 Pine St Asheville NC 28801 Office: 146 Pine St Asheville NC 28801

MOSS, CHARLES EDWARD, minister, So. Baptist Conv.; b. Gaffney, S.C., Apr. 5, 1933; s. Forest Brown and Agnes Elizabeth (Lanier) M.; B.A., Limeston Coll., 1968; Th.M., New Orleans Bapt. Theol. Sem., 1971; m. Sybil Irene Jones, July 26, 1954; children—Kimberly Jayne, Scott Edward. Ordained to ministry, 1964; pastor 1st Bapt. Ch., Maringouin, La., 1969-71, Camps Creek Bapt. Ch., Gaffney, 1971. Mem. missions and fin. coms. Sandy Run Bapt. Assn. Bd. dirs. Boiling Springs (N.C.) Rescue Squad. Home and Office: Route 2 PO Box 303 Gaffney SC 29340

MOSS, ELZA, pres., Primitive Advent Christian Church. Address: Sissonville WV 25185

MOSS, OTIS, JR., minister, Baptist; b. LaGrange, Ga.; s. Otis and Magnolia Moss; m. Edwina Hudson Smith; children: Kevin, Daphne, Otis III. B.A., Morehouse Coll., 1956; M.Div., Morehouse Sch. Religion, 1959; postgrad. Inter-Denominational Theol. Ctr., 1960-61. Ordained to ministry. Pastor, Mt. Olive Bapt. Ch., LaGrange, Ga., 1956-59, Providence Bapt. Ch., Atlanta, 1956-61, Mt. Zion Bapt. Ch., Lockland, 1961-75; co-pastor Ebenezer Bapt. Ch., Atlanta, 1971; pastor Olivet Instl. Bapt. Ch., Cleve., 1975—; cons. in field; del. World Bapt. Conf., Beirut, 1963; mem. rev. com. Harvard Div. Sch., 1975-82; trustee Morehouse Coll., 1979—, Morehouse Sch. Religion, 1974—; nat. bd., trustee Martin Luther King Jr. Ctr. of Social Change, 1971—; bd. dirs. Operation PUSH, 1971—, acting nat. pres., 1971—; lectr. in field. Columnist Atlanta Inquirer, 1970-75. Contbr. articles to profl. jours. Recipient Human Relations award Bethune Cookman Coll., 1976; Gov's Award in Civil Rights, Ohio, 1983; Black Profl. of Yr., Black Profl. Assn. Cleve., 1983. Mem. NAACP, Alpha Phi Alpha. Home: 22850 Shaker Blvd Shaker Heights OH 44122 Office: Olivet Instl Bapt Ch 8712 Quincy Ave Cleveland OH 44106

MOSS, STEVEN ALAN, rabbi, Reform Jewish; b. Bklyn., Mar. 7, 1948; s. Ira Lloyd and Doris (Fitzer) M.; m. Judy S. Mirrer, Mar. 30, 1969. B.A., NYU, 1969, B.H.L., Hebrew Union Coll., 1972, M.A.H.L., 1974. Rabbi, 1974. Rabbi, B'nai Israel Reform Temple, Oakdale, N.Y., 1972—; chaplain Meml. Sloan Kettering Cancer Ctr., N.Y.C., 1971—, Southside Hosp., Bay Shore, N.Y., 1974—, Suffolk County Police Dept., 1985—; chaplaincy supr. N.Y. Bd. Rabbis, 1981—. Contbr. articles to jours., chpts. to books. Mem. Suffolk Jewish Community Planning Council, 1984—, Islip Youth Bd., 1978-79, 82-83, Fedn. YMHA Bd., 1984—, Islip Town Bd. Ethics, 1984—. Named Chaplain of Yr., N.Y. Bd. Rabbis, 1983; recipient Community Service award United Jewish Fedn., 1979. Mem. Sayville Ecumenical Clergy Group (pres. 1981-84), Islip Clergy Group. Lodge: B'nai B'rith. Office: B'nai Israel Reform Temple 67 Oakdale-Bohemia Rd Oakdale NY 11769

MOSSMAN, GEORGE ALBERT, minister, United Church of Canada; b. Rose Bay, N.S., Can., Dec. 12, 1932; s. Titus Milton and Helen Viola (Spindler) M.; B.A. summa cum laude, Mt. Allison U., 1952; M.Div. with honours, Union Theol. Sem., 1956, Pine Hill Div. Hall, 1956; postgrad. New Coll., Edinburgh (Scotland) U., 1956-59; M.A., U. Chgo., 1970; D.Religion, Chgo. Theol. Sem., 1971; m. Carolyn Lu Schurman, July 2, 1956; children: Catherine, Charlotte, Frederick, John. Ordained to ministry United Ch. Can., 1956. Minister chs., Coldstream, N.S., 1959-62, Fredericton, N.B., 1962-64; gen. sec. Student Christian Movement, U. N.B., Fredericton, 1965-69; chaplain U. Alta., Edmonton, 1971-79; minister Mill Woods, 1981-83; exec. dir. Bissell Centre, Edmonton, 1983-85. Home: 3512 117-B St Edmonton AB T6H 1W2 Canada

MOULDEN, DONOVAN EDWARD FAULKNER, minister, Episc. Ch.; b. Winnipeg, Man., Can., Nov. 10, 1936; s. Leonard William and Dorothy Eveline (Faulkner) M.; diploma theology Anglican Theol. Coll., 1971; m. Helen May Blundell, July 6, 1959; children—Elizabeth Mary, Clive Heubert. Ordained to ministry, 1972; curate St. Barnabas Anglican Ch., Calgary, Alta., Can., 1971-73; asst. priest St. Mary the Virgin, Oak Bay, Victoria, B.C., 1973—. Chaplain Alta. Inst. Tech., 1971-73. Mem. Monarchist League Can. (life), Vancouver Aquarium Soc. (life), B.C. Crickett Assn. (life), Vancouver Sch. Theology Alumni Assn. (pres. 1972-74), Soc. Prevention Cruelty to Animals (life). Home: 1164 Roslyn Rd Oak Bay BC V8S 4R6 Canada Office: 1701 Elgin Rd Oak Bay Victoria BC V8S 4R6 Canada

MOUNCE, WILLIAM DOUGLAS, religious educator, Christian and Missionary Alliance; b. Pasadena, Calif., Feb. 17, 1953; s. Robert Hayden and Jean (McTavish) M.; m. Robin Elaine Brown, July 2, 1983. B.A., Bethel Coll., 1975; M.A., Fuller Sem., 1977; Ph.D., U. Aberdeen, Scotland, 1981. Lectr. Rockmont Coll., Denver, 1981-82; prof. religion Azusa Pacific U., Calif., 1982—. Author: Profiles in Faith, 1984. Contbr. articles to profl. jours. Mem. Evang. Theol. Soc. Republican.

MOUNT, MARGARET ELIZABETH DOYLE (MRS. LEWIS F. MOUNT), minister, Open Bible Standard Chs., educator; b. Franklin, Pa., Sept. 1, 1926; d. James A. and Cynthia A. (Adams) Doyle; B.A. in

Bible, Fla. Beacon Coll., 1964, M.A. in Religious Edn., 1951, Th.B., 1969; Th.D., Trinity Coll. and Sem., 1970; m. Lewis F. Mount, Sept. 1, 1948; children—Martin Fillmore, Arnold Adams, Cynthia Mary (Mrs. Ronald Richard Boffoli). Ordained to ministry Open Bible Standard Chs., Inc., 1969; tchr. Fla. Beacon Coll. and Sem., Largo, Fla., 1959-69; head secretarial sci. dept. Trinity Coll. and Sem., Dunedin, Fla., 1969-73; tchr. ednl. services St. Leo (Fla.) Coll. Home: 4601 18th Ave N St Petersburg FL 33713 Office: St Leo Coll POB 2248 St Leo FL 33574

MOURSUND, CLAUDIA FRANCES, lay worker, Episcopal Church, real estate associate; b. Houston, Jan. 16, 1941; d. Alexander Francis and Louie Elizabeth (Rogers) Reifel; m. Kenneth Carroll Moursund, Dec. 21, 1963; 1 son, Kenneth Carroll. Student U. Tex., 1959-61; grad. Southwestern Bus. U., Houston, 1963. Lic. real estate sales. Del. Diocesan Episc. Ch. Women ann. meetings, 1973-81, Daus. of the King Triennial, 1970, Episc. Ch. Women Triennial, Denver, 1979; v.p. Diocesan Daus. of King, 1972-75; pres. Episc. Ch. Women, Trinity Episc. Ch., Houston, 1978-80; mem., chmn. continuing edn. com. and bd. Episc. Ch. Women, Diocese of Tex., 1978-80; chmn. Episcopal Ch. Women, Diocesan Quilt Project, 1979-82, Annual Meeting, 1981; trustee Autry House (Episc. Ctr. for Rice U. and Tex. Med. Ctr.), Houston, 1980-83; sec. St. James House, trustee, Baytown, Tex., 1981-83, v.p., 1983-84; founding bd. trustees Episc. High Sch., Houston, 1983, sec. bd. trustees, 1984—; mem. Ch. of St. John the Divine, Houston, 1982—. vol. Guild Shop, 1984. Assoc., Mary Wood Glover, Realtors, Houston, 1983—. Editor Episcopal Church Women Continuing Education Workbook, 1980. Life mem. Houston Livestock Show and Rodeo, mem. internat. com., 1981—; pres. Meadowbriar Home for Children Aux., Houston, 1972-74; v.p., sec. bd. trustees Harris County Heritage Soc., 1974-79; pres. Am. Mus. Soc. Houston Bapt. U., 1980-82; provisional docent Bayou Bend Collection Mus. Fine Arts, Houston, 1984-85; bd. dirs. Houston Symphony League, 1981-85. Mem. Houston Bd. Realtors, U. Tex. Ex-Students Assn. (life). Clubs: Pine Forest Country Club Ladies Assn. (bd. dirs. 1984), Pine Forest Country Club Ladies Tennis Assn. (charter mem., founding sec.-treas. 1974). Office: Mary Wood Glover Realtors 1736 Sunset Blvd Houston TX 77005

MOWERY, JOHN AUSTIN, minister, Church of God, Anderson, Indiana; b. Bradenton, Fla., Dec. 15, 1925; s. Leonard Stewart and Alpha May (Houston) M.; m. Margaret May Williamson, Oct. 28, 1951; children: John Michael, Cheryl. Student Emory U., 1948; B.Th., Anderson Coll. and Theol. Sem., 1950. Ordained to ministry Ch. of God, 1948. Mem. Ch. State Council, Fla., 1965-67, Ala., 1968-70, Fla., 1971-74; chmn. Ch. of God Camp Grounds, Fla., 1971-74; chmn. Gen. Assembly of Ch. of God, Miss., 1980-82; pastor First Ch. of God, Beaumont, Tex., 1982—; vice chmn. Ministerial Assembly of Ch. of God, Tex., 1982—, E. Tex. Dist. Ch. of God, 1982—; mem. Tex. Revolving Loan Fund, 1982—. Contbr. to the Sermon Builder, 1983, Idea-Kit, 1984. Served with U.S. Army, 1944-46; ATO. Democrat. Home: 2705 W Lucas Beaumont TX 77706 Office: First Ch of God 4450 Crow Rd Beaumont TX 77706

MOYER, JAMES CARROLL, religion educator, American Baptist Church; b. Norristown, Pa., Nov. 30, 1941; s. Raymond Carroll and Mary Letitia (Bishop) M.; m. Roberta Helen Goff, Aug. 28, 1965; children: Brenda, Marsha, Becky. B.A., Wheaton Coll., 1963; M.Div., Gordon Div. Sch., 1966; M.A., Brandeis U., 1968, Ph.D., 1969. Assoc. prof. religious studies Southwest Mo. State U., Springfield, 1978-79, prof., 1979—; elder First and Calvary Presbyn Ch., Springfield, 1974-76; deacon Univ. Heights Bapt. Ch., Springfield, 1983-85. Editor: (with others) Scripture in Context II, 1983. Contbr. articles to religious publs. Recipient Burlington-No. Tchr. Year award, 1984. Grantee NEH, 1980, 84; archael. fellow Hebrew Union Coll., Jerusalem, 1969-70, Sachar Internat. fellow Brandeis U., Hebrew U., Jerusalem, 1969-70. Mem. Soc. Biblical Lit. (regional sec. Central States 1983-86), Am. Schs. Oriental Research (assoc. trustee 1985—, com. publs. 1984—); Am. Oriental Soc., Cath. Bibl. Assn. Home: 634 E Cardinal Springfield MO 65807 Office: Southwest Mo State U Dept Religious Studies Springfield MO 65804

MOYER, JOHN CLARENCE, minister, Presbyterian Church USA; b. Jackson, Mich., Jan. 22, 1940; s. Glen Ernest and Esther Lee (Hamilton) M.; m. Linda Lancione, June 15, 1963; children: John David, Jason. B.A., U. So. Calif., 1962; B.D., San Francisco Theol. Sem., 1966. Ordained to ministry, 1966. Fronteir intern United Presbyn. Ch., Paris, 1966-69; campus minister United Ministries in Higher Edn., Fullerton, Calif., 1969-71; univ. pastor Berkeley, Calif., 1972-75; gen. sec. European Contact Group, Amsterdam, The Netherlands, 1976-80; gen. sec. Nat. Ecumenical Student Conf., Berkeley, 1980-82; dir. No. Calif. Interfaith Council on Econ. Justice, Oakland, 1983—; exec. dir. No. Calif. Ecumenical Council, San Francisco, 1984—. Co-author: Augustine City, 1965. Layne Found. scholar, 1960; Danforth Found. fellow, 1964; World Council Chs. scholar, 1969. Mem. Nat. Assn.

Ecumenical Staffs. Democrat. Office: NCEC 942 Market St Suite 702 San Francisco CA 94102

MOYER, JOHN EDWARD, clergyman, Evangelical Congregational Church; b. Allentown, Pa., May, 1, 1932; s. Howard Edward and Esther (Waltz) M.; m. Dorothy Agnes Berger, Sept. 11, 1954; children: John Peter, David Lane, Timothy Allen. B.A., Moravian Coll., 1954, D.Div. (hon.), 1980; S.T.B., Temple U., 1957. Ordained itinerant elder Evang. Congregational Ch., 1959. Pastor Grace Evang. Congl. Ch., Columbia, Pa., 1955-60, Trinity Evang. Congl. Ch., Pottstown, Pa., 1960-64, St. Matthew's Evang. Congl. Ch., Emmaus, Pa., 1964-73; dist. supt. Eastern Conf., Evang. Congl. Ch., Reading, Pa., 1973-79; bishop Evang. Congl. Ch., Myerstown, Pa., 1979—; trustee Evang. Sch. Theology, Myerstown, 1972—, chmn. bd., 1974-82; trustee Evang. Congl. Ch. Retirement Village, Myerstown, 1979—. Republican. Office: Evang Congl Ch PO Box 186 Myerstown PA 17067

MOYER, VIRGIL A., JR. Synodical bishop Lutheran Church in America, Salem, Va. Office: Luth Ch in Am Bittle Hall Roanoke Coll Salem VA 24153*

MOZOS, SEBASTIAN, priest, Roman Cath. Ch.; b. Hinojosas de Calatrava, Spain, Jan. 20, 1909; s. Leandro and Angeles (Castellanos) Mozos; came to U.S., 1940, naturalized, 1950. Ordained priest, 1933; Oblate missionary, Pastor Sacred Heart Ch., Hidalgo, Tex., 1973—. Address: 308 E Camelia St PO Box 742 Hidalgo TX 78557

MUDIE, CHARLES ROBERT, lay ch. worker, United Meth. Ch.; b. Eddington, Pa., Sept. 3, 1922; s. Robert P. and Elizabeth (Kester) M.; Chem. Engr., Drexel Inst. Tech., 1943; Organic Chemist, Mich. Normal Coll., 1946; m. Lillian A. Grupp, Mar. 30, 1946; children—Carol (Mrs. William J. Gilliford), Ronald R. Sunday sch. supt. Cornwells United Meth. Ch., Cornwells Heights, Pa., 1946-66, lay leader, 1960-65, chmn. Council of Ministries, 1972-75, leader Agape Bible Study class, 1972—; mem. Lay Witness Mission Team, 1973—; lay disciple, 1975—. Eastern dist. sales mgr. Rohm & Haas Co., 1971—. Mem. Com. Neshaminy Bucks County council Boy Scouts Am., 1953-72. Named Man of Year, Croydon A.C., 1971. Mem. Am. Leather Chemists Assn., Del. Valley Tanners Assn. Mason. Home: 6409 Radcliffe St Bristol PA 19007 Office: Independence Mall Philadelphia PA 19105

MUDRY, MICHAEL, pension and benefit consultant to religious denominations; b. Lucina, Czechoslovakia, Dec. 5, 1926; (father Am. citizen); s. John Zaleta and Helen (Molchan) M.; m. Kendall Archer, June 17, 1960; children: F. Goodrich Archer, Benjamin Kendall. B.A., U. Conn., 1951. Sr. v.p., sec. Hay/Huggins Co. Inc., Phila., 1956—; actuary Ch. Pensions Conf. Active on Com. Gift Annuities, N.Y.C., 1978—. Served to T/5 U.S. Army, 1945-46. Recipient Enrolled Actuary status U.S. Treas. Dept., 1976. Fellow Soc. Actuaries, Conf. Actuaries Pub. Practice; mem. Am. Acad. Actuaries, Internat. Acturial Assn., Internat. Assn. Cons. Actuaries. Democrat. Club: Union League (Phila.). Office: Hay/Huggins Co Inc 229 S 18th St Philadelphia PA 19103

MUELLER, HERBERT A., minister, ch. ofcl., Lutheran Ch.-Mo. Synod; b. Lone Elm, Mo., June 2, 1914; s. John Henry and Anna (Vetter) M.; grad. Concordia Coll., Milw., 1934; grad. Concordia Sem., St. 1938, D.D., 1976; LL.D., Concordia Coll., Seward, Nebr., 1966; m. Elfrieda Rische, May 20, 1939; children: Susanne (Mrs. Les Engstrom), Thomas, Joanne. Ordained to ministry, 1940; pastor Trinity Luth., Ch., Lombard, Ill., 1940-43, Bethlehem Luth. Ch., Dundee, Ill., 1943-69; sec. No. Ill. Dist. of Luth. Ch.-Mo. Synod, 1957-65, mem. Bd. Higher Edn., 1960-65; sec. Luth. Ch.-Mo. Synod, St. Louis, 1965-83, Commn. on Constl. Matters, 1965-83; chaplain Internat. Ctr., Luth. Ch.-Mo. Synod, 1983—; v.p. Luth. Council U.S.A., 1973-76, sec., 1976-79, pres., 1979-82. Editor conv. manuals and ch. body constn. and bylaws. Office: 1333 S Kirkwood St Saint Louis MO 63122

MUELLER, MARY DONALD, nun, educator, Roman Cath. Ch.; b. Milw., Dec. 14, 1912; d. Joseph Donald and Marie Magdelan (Salb) Mueller; B.S. in Edn., Cardinal Stritch Coll., 1938; M.S. in Edn., Purdue U., 1973. Joined Sisters St. Francis of Assisi, 1930; tchr. and prin. elementary schs., Ill., S.D., Wis., N.C., 1934—; instr. religious edn., summers, 1936-50, remedial reading, summers 1943-65. Extraordinary minister Holy Eucharist, Eagle River, Wis. Mem. Nat. Cath. Educators Assn., Assn. for Supervision and Curriculum Devel. Home and Office: 306 Butler St Random Lake WI 53075

MUELLERLEILE, ERNEST HAMMES, priest, Roman Catholic Church; b. St. Paul, June 23, 1919; s. Albert James and Anne Pia (Hammes) M. Student St. Paul Sem., 1945. Ordained priest, Roman Cath. Ch., 1944. Asst., St. Mary's Parish, Bird Island, Minn., 1945-49, adminstr. St. Peter's Parish, Medota, Minn., 1949-57; pastor St. Catherine's Parish, Redwood Falls, Minn., 1957-66, St. Mary's Parish, New Ulm, Minn., 1966-69, St. Gregory's Parish, Sitka, Alaska, 1970-72, St. Michael's Parish, Palmer, Alaska, 1972-74, St. Elizabeth Ann Seton Parish, Anchorage, 1975-84; pastor, founder Holy Cross Parish, Anchorage, (founded parish), 1984—; advisor Women's Aglow, 1977—; team priest Marriage Encounter, 1976—, Beginning Experience, 1978—; mem. coms. on liturgy and edn., Redwood Falls and New Ulm, 1964-69; dir. com. on ecumenism, Sitka, 1970-72. Dir. com. on scouting Redwood Falls, 1960-65, campaign for human devel., Palmer, Anchorage, 1973—. Author: (booklets) At the Cradle of Folk Liturgy, 1953; A Full Life, 1981; A Church for St. Mary, 1968. Contbr. articles to profl. jours. Recipient Eagle Scout award Boy Scouts Am., 1939; adopted into Tlinget Indians, Eagle Tribe, Killer Whale Clan, Sitka, 1973. Mem. Archdiocesan Priests' Senate. Lodge: K.C. Home and Office: 8536 Hartzell Rd #80 Anchorage AK 99507

MUENICH, GEORGE RAYNOR, pastor, Lutheran Ch. in America; b. Michigan City, Ind., Aug. 31, 1939; s. George Rudolph and Beatrice Edythe Ann (Dominick) M.; m. Erika Katharina Bieber, June 24, 1978; children: Renate Marie Louise, Margaret Elise Gabrielle. B.S. in Physics, Calif. Inst. Tech., Pasadena, 1961; D. Theology, Friedrich-Alexander Universitat, Erlangen, Germany, 1975. Ordained to ministry Luth. Ch. America, 1976. Pastor Grace Luth. Ch., Gas City, Ind., 1976-78, St. Mark Luth. Ch., Grandview, Ind., 1980-81, Trinity Luth. Ch., Rockport, Ind., 1981, Redeemer Luth. Ch., Jasper, Ind., 1981—; interim pastor Wittenberg U., Springfield, Ohio, 1978-79; regional worship leader Ind.-Ky. Synod, Indpls., 1982—; chmn. Worship, Music Task Force, Ind.-Ky. Synod, Indpls., 1984—. Author: Der Hauptgottesdienst der Lutherischen Kirche Amerikas, 1973; The Victory of Restorationism, 1984. Served to 1st lt., USAF, 1962-65. Recipient Gen. Motors Nat. Scholarship, Gen. Motors Found., 1957; Nat. Merit Scholarship, Nat. Merit Found., 1957; Humanities Award, State of Ind., 1984. Mem. Hymn Soc. Am., Dubois County Ministerial Assn. (sec., treas. 1982-83). Republican. Clubs: Deutscherverein Wingolf (bd. dirs. 1971-83) (Jasper, Ind.). Home: 1611 Newton St Jasper IN 47546 Office: Redeemer Luth Ch 140 E 32nd St Jasper IN 47546

MUGAVERO, FRANCIS J., bishop, Roman Cath. Ch. b. June 8, 1914, Bklyn. Ed. Cathedral Coll., Bklyn., Immaculate Conception Sem., Huntington, N.Y., Fordham U. Ordained priest, 1940; apptd. bishop Bklyn., 1968, consecrated, installed, 1968. Address: 75 Greene Ave Box C Brooklyn NY 11238

MUHAMMAD, WALLACE D., Islamic leader; b. Hamtrack, Mich., Oct. 30, 1933; s. Elijiah M.; ed. Muhammed U. of Islam; m. Shirley; children: Leila, N'Gina, Wallace, Sadru-Din. Now Imam, Masjid Elijah Muhammad, Chicago. Recipient Pioneer award Black Press; Freedom award (4); numerous Humanitarian awards. Office: 7351 S Stony Island Ave Chicago IL 60649*

MULCAHY, JOHN J. See *Who's Who in America*, 43rd edition.

MULDER, JOHN M., seminary administrator. Pres. Louisville Presbyterian Theol. Sem. Office: Louisville Presbyn Theol Sem 1044 Alta Vista Rd Louisville KY 40205*

MULKERRIN, CATHERINE E., nun, religious order executive, Roman Catholic Church; b. Medford, Mass., Dec. 19, 1935; d. Martin and Catherine Mary (O'Connor) M. B.A., Regis Coll., 1963; M.L.S., Simmons Coll., 1966. Joined Sisters of St. Joseph, Roman Cath. Ch. Tchr. elem. sch. Archdiocese of Boston, 1957-66; librarian Regis Coll., Framingham, Mass., 1966-69; area councillor Sisters of St. Joseph, Brighton, Mass., 1969-78, pres., 1978—; dir. Bridge, Inc., Boston, Bethany Hosp., Framingham. Pres. bd. trustees Aquinas Jr. Coll., Milton, Mass., Aquinas Jr. Coll., Newton, Mass., Fontbonne Acad., Milton, Mt. St. Joseph Acad., Brighton, Bethany Hill Sch., Framingham, Boston Sch.; trustee Regis Coll.; active Network, Bread for World, Common Cause, Nat. Right to Life, Mass. Citizens for Life, Project Equality. Recipient Magnificat award Our Lady of Victories, Boston, 1983. Mem. Nat. Cath. Ednl. Assn., New Eng. Coalition for Responsible Investments, Cath. Hosp. Assn., Nat. Black Sisters Conf., Nat. Conf. for Interracial Justice, Leadership Conf. for Women Religious (bd. dirs. 1978—, chmn. regional chpt. 1980-84). Home and Office: 637 Cambridge St Brighton MA 02135

MULLAY, CAMILLA, history educator, Roman Catholic Church; b. Columbus, Ohio, May 29, 1927; d. Maurice Lawrence and Eulalia Agnes (Cox) M. B.A., Ohio Dominican Coll., 1957; M.A., Cath. U. Am., Washington, 1962, Ph.D., 1966; L.H.D. (hon.), Albertus Magnus Coll., 1982. Gen. councilor Dominican Sisters of St. Mary of the Springs, Columbus, Ohio, 1968-74, sec. gen., 1968-74, mother gen., 1974-82; assoc. prof. history Ohio Dominican Coll., Columbus, 1984—; adv. bd. Washington Inst. for Ethics and Spirituality, Washington, 1984—. Author: The Barren Fig Tree, 1984. Contbr. articles to profl. jours. Trustee Albertus Magnus Coll., 1968-82, St. Francis-St. George Hosp., Cin., 1968-72; mem. Diocesan Bd. of Edn., Columbus, 1970-74; incorporator Legal Assistance Project for Cheyenne-Arapaho Tribes, Okla., 1977; observer Salvadoran Nat. Elections, El Salvador, 1984. Recipient medal of Recognition, Archdiocese of Cin., 1980.

MULLEN, FRANK ALBERT, minister, university director, Christian Church (Disciples of Christ); b. Lafayette, Ind., Apr. 7, 1931; s. Albert Edwin and Bernice Elizabeth (Weidlich) M.; widowed. B.A., Wabash Coll., 1953; M.Div., Yale U., 1956. Ordained to ministry Christian Ch. (Disciples of Christ), 1956. Minister, St. Marks Ch., Ridgewood, N.Y., 1974—; pastor Elmhurst Community Ch., N.Y., 1974—; dir. devel. Div. Sch., Yale U., New Haven, 1984—; trustee Park Ave. Christian Ch., N.Y.C., 1981—; nat. dir. planned giving Guideposts, Carmel, N.Y., 1984—; dir. devel. Bapt. Med. Ctr., N.Y.C., 1980-83; radio speaker. Pres. alumni council Yale Div. Sch., 1967-76; chmn. grad. and profl. schs. com. Yale U., 1977-79; assoc. dir. N.Y. region Campaign for Yale, 1975-79; mem. nat. council YMCA. Recipient Liberty Bell award Queens County Bar Assn., 1968, Award of Merit, Wabash Coll. Alumni Assn., 1969. Republican. Club: Yale (N.Y.C.). Lodges: Rotary, Lions, Masons. Home: 178-33 Croydon Rd Jamaica Estates NY 11432 Office: Yale U Div Sch 409 Prospect St New Haven CT 06510

MULLER, BART ROBERT, pastor, American Lutheran Church; b. Springfield, Mass., July 13, 1950; s. Alwin Daniel and Audrey Paula (Sandhop) M.; m. Jennifer Lynn Hoffman, June 10, 1973; children: Carl Daniel, Kevin Paul, Eric Michael. B.A., Capital U., 1972; M.Div., Luth. Theol. Sem., Columbus, Ohio, 1976. Ordained to ministry American Lutheran Church, 1976. Pastor, Pembina Luth. Ch., N.D., 1976-79, Calvary Luth. Ch., Angola, Ind., 1982—; asst. pastor St. Paul Luth. Ch., Streator, Ill., 1979-82; chaplain Fountain Lake Treatment Ctr., Angola, 1984—; mem. Luth. Soc. Services Bd. Indian Affairs, Fargo, N.D., 1977-79; TV awareness leader Am. Luth. Ch. (Ill. dist.), Park Ridge, 1980—; bd. sec. Lake Luther Bible Camp, Angola, 1982—. Contbr. articles to popular mags. Founder, Pembina Hist. Soc., N.D., 1977; pres. Pembina Community Club, 1978; bd. dirs. Girl Scouts U.S., 1981, Well Child Clinic, Angola, 1983—; bd. dirs., sec. Concerned Citizens for Youth, Streator, Ill., 1981-82. Named Outstanding Young Man, Jaycees, 1981. Mem. Steuben County Ministerium. Democrat. Clubs: Miniature Soldier Soc. Ill. (Chgo.), Victorian Mil. Soc. (London). Home: Route 2 Box 232 Angola IN 46703 Office: Calvary Luth Ch Route 2 Box 7 Angola IN 46703

MULLINS, TERENCE YOOS, minister, editor, Lutheran Church in America; b. Washington; s. Eber Helton and Beulah (Yoos) M.; m. Beverly Schultz, Apr. 4, 1964 (dec.); 1 dau., Joanna Lee. B.A., U. Va., 1943, M.A., 1954; B.D., Luth. Theol. Sem., 1945. Ordained to ministry, 1946. Pastor, Augusta County Luth. Parish, Waynesboro, Va., 1945-59; editor Lutheran Ch. in America, Phila., 1960—. Author: God's Word and Contemporary Ethics, 1970. Contbr. articles to profl. jours. Mem. Soc. Bibl. Lit., Am. Schs. Oriental Research. Office: Div for Parish Services 2900 Queen Ln Philadelphia PA 19129-1094

MULVEE, ROBERT EDWARD See *Who's Who in America*, 43rd edition.

MUNCIE, MARGARET ANN, priest, Episcopal Church; b. N.Y.C., Feb. 4, 1948; d. James Ernest and Doris A. (Schuck) M.; m. Stephen M. Bolle, July 27, 1974; children: Victoria Ann Muncie, Caroline Ann Muncie. A.B. in Religion, Hood Coll., 1970; postgrad. Adelphi U., 1971; M.Div., Gen. Theol. Sem., 1974; Cert. in Aging, U. Mich., 1984. Chaplain, Vassar Coll., 1974-77; asst. minister St. Matthew's Ch., Bedford, N.Y., 1978-80; clin. pastoral edn. Gaylord Hosp., Wallingford, Conn., 1980-81, Bellevue Hosp., N.Y.C., 1981; chaplain Greenwich Chaplaincy Services, Conn., 1982—; mem. bd. assocs. Hood Coll., Frederick, Md., 1977—. Bd. dirs. Country Children's Ctr., Katonah, N.Y., 1979—, past pres. Fellow Coll. Chaplains; mem. Am. Clin. Pastoral Assocs., Greenwich Clergy Fellowship (pres. 1985); Gen. Theol. Sem. Alumni Assn. (exec. com.). Office: Greenwich Chaplaincy Service PO Box 1679 Greenwich CT 06836

MUNNIK, GERRIT, bishop, Liberal Cath. Ch.; b. Middelburg, Netherlands, Feb. 10, 1906; s. Andries Hendrik and Neeltje Johanna (van Riet) M.; M.A., Royal Acad. (The Hague, Netherlands), 1929; D.Litt., U. Amsterdam, 1943. Ordained priest, 1930; consecrated bishop, 1971; priest Netherlands Province, 1930-52; asst. priest St. Michael's Ch., N.Y.C., 1952-54; asst. priest St. Raphael's Ch., Oakland, Calif., 1954-64; asst. priest Our Lady & All Angels Ch., Ojai, Calif., 1964-70; rector, 1970—; bishop Southwestern States, 1971—; regionary bishop Province of U.S.A., 1974—; apptd. chancellor Liberal Cath. Inst. of Studies, 1985. Lectr. arts Hilversum Lyceum and Jr. Coll., Hilversum, Netherlands, 1934-51; lectr. Krotona Sch. Theosophy, Ojai, 1967—. Ex-officio trustee Rogers-Cooper Meml. Found., Ojai. Mem. Theosophical Soc. Am., Am. Fedn. Human Right (co-freemasonry 1931). Home: 16

Krotona Ojai CA 93023 Office: Pro Cathedral Ch of Our Lady & All Angels 1502 E Ojai Ave Ojai CA 93023

MUNOZ NUNEZ, RAFAEL, bishop, Roman Catholic Church; b. Vista Hermosa, Michoacan, Mex., Jan. 14, 1925; s. Francisco Munoz and Sara Nunez Pacheco. Humanities degree, Seminario Dioc., Guadalajara, 1944; philosophy degree, Guadalajara, 1947. Ordained priest, Roman Cath. Ch., 1951. Sec., Apostolic Del., Mex., 1968-71; nat. asst. ACM, 1969-72; pres. Com. Epis. for Laity, 1972-75; bishop of Zacatecas, 1972-84, of Aguacalientes, Mex., 1984—. Home: Allende 238 Pte Aguascalientes Ags Aguascalientes Mexico 2000 Office: Oficinas Catedral Galeana 102 Apartado Postal 167 Aguascalientes Mexico 2000

MUNSEY, FRANK MATHIS, JR., minister, United Pentecostal Ch.; b. Tulsa, Aug. 11, 1930; s. Frank Mathis and Eva (Lindsey) M.; Apostolic Coll., 1947-49; m. Ruth Mae McConley, Oct. 20, 1951; children—Stephan, Joe, Phillip, Sheila. Ordained to ministry United Pentecostal Ch., 1952; pastor, Oshkosh, Wis., 1952-53; founder Evangelistic Temple-United Pentecostal Ch., Hammond, Ind., 1954, pastor, trustee, 1954—, pres., 1962-70; mem. fgn. missionary com. United Pentecostal Ch., Inc., St. Louis, 1969-74, mem. evangelism commn. home missionary dept., 1970-74; trustee, pres. bd. United Pentecostal Ch. P.R., 1964-74; sec. United Pentecostal Ch. Japan, 1971; founder, pres. Hammond (Ind.) Christian Acad., 1971—. Home: 5590 Marshall Pl Merrillville IN 46410 Office: 1300 N Broad St Griffith IN 46410 also PO Box 2218 Hammond IN 46323

MUNSEY, FRANK TORRANCE, minister, Seventh-day Adventists; b. Caldwell, Idaho, Oct. 29, 1922; s. Cassius Marcellus and Hazel Pearl (Torrance) M.; B.Th., Walla Walla Coll., 1946; postgrad. U. Mont., 1956-59, Seventh-day Adventist Theol. Sem., summer 1957; m. Deloris Mildred Beach, Sept. 8, 1943; children—Marilyn Lee Munsey Kreuder, Michael Frank. Ordained to ministry, 1950; pastor Upper Columbia Conf., Wash., 1946-49, Fairbanks and Anchorage, 1950-53, Mont. Conf., 1953-62, Nev.-Utah Conf., 1962-65, Reno Seventh-day Adventist Ch., Santa Cruz, Calif., 1965-74, Ceres, Calif., 1974—. Mem. exec. com. Alaska Mission, 1952-53; exec. com. Nev.-Utah Conf., 1962-65, Central Calif. Conf., 1974—. Contbr. articles to religious jours. Home: 1828 Manassas Ct Ceres CA 95307 Office: 1633 N Central Ave Ceres CA 95307

MURK, LYNDON KEITH, minister, Lutheran Church in America; b. Amor, Minn., June 12, 1926; s. Gilbert Gabriel and Mabel (Lien) M. B.A., Augustana Coll., Rock Island, Ill., 1947; B.D., Austustana Sem., Rock Island, 1951; M.A., Pacific Luth. U., 1971. Ordained to ministry Lutheran Ch., 1951. Pastor Beth. Luth. Ch., Gt. Falls, Mont., 1951-64, Bethel Luth. Ch., Tacoma, Wash.. 1964—; chaplain Boy Scouts Am., 1960, 73, 77, Am. Guild Organists, Tacoma, 1979—; pres., dir. Assoc. Ministries, Tacoma, 1974-78. Author: The Influence of Martin Bucer, 1971. Recipient Silver Beaver award Boy Scouts Am., Gt. Falls, 1960, Vigil Honor, Order of Arrow, Boy Scouts Am., 1960; Lamb award Luth. Council U.S.A., Tacoma, 1975. Mem. Hymn Soc. Am., Soc. for Preservation and Encouragement of Barber Shop Quartet Singing in Am. (treas. Tacoma 1975—). Lodges: Kiwanis (dir. Gt. Falls 1957-61, pres. 1960; dir. Tacoma 1984—), Order of Runeberg (pres. 1980-82). Home: 7240 S Bell St Tacoma WA 98408 Office: Bethel Lutheran Ch 905 S 54th St Tacoma WA 98408

MURPH, HENRY W., bishop, African Methodist Episcopal Ch., Los Angeles. Office: 4625 Crenshaw Blvd Los Angeles CA 90043*

MURPHEY, JOHN WARFORD, minister, So. Baptist Conv.; b. Murray, Ky., Oct. 26, 1934; s. Garland Alexander and Elizabeth (Warford) M.; B.A., Wayland Bapt. Coll., 1956; M.Div., Southwestern Bapt. Theol. Sem., 1967; m. Alta Mae Johnston, Dec. 28, 1954; children-John W., Mark Johnston, Ordained to ministry, 1957; pastor Mambrino Bapt. Ch., Granbury, Tex., 1960-63, Walker Ave. Bapt. Ch., Oklahoma City, 1963-70; fgn. missionary So. Bapt. Fgn. Mission Bd., Richmond, Va., 1970; pastor Boyd Ave. Bapt. Ch., Casper, Wyo., 1970-71, First So. Bapt. Ch., Mesa, Ariz., 1971-72, Palo Verde Bapt. Ch., Tempe, Ariz., 1973, first Bapt. Ch., Heavener, Okla., 1974-76, Shields Blvd. Bapt. Ch., Oklahoma City, 1976-84; minister of personal evangelism and outreach First So. Bapt. Ch., Del City, Okla., 1984—. Presently minister of personal evangelism and outreach, First Southern Baptist Church, Del City, Oklahoma. While at Shields Blvd. Baptist Church, Pastor Morphey led his church to be second in baptisms 1982-1983 and fourth in baptisms 1983-1984 amoung Southern Baptist churches in Okla. Chmn. missions com. LaFlore Bapt. Assn., 1975-76; mem. exec. bd. Okla. County Bapt. Assn., 1965-68, v.p. pastor's conf., 1968-69; state com. mem. for child care for Okla. Bapt. work, 1968-69; chmn. evangelism com. Capital Baptist Assn. Mem. Vols. in Corrections, Okla., 1976—. Presently Chmn. Evangelism Committee of the Capital Baptist Assoc. Mem. Heavener Ministerial Alliance (pres. 1976—). Address: PO Box 25517 Oklahoma City OK 73125

MURPHEY, PAUL WARREN, educator, minister, Christian Ch.; b. Augusta, Ga., Jan. 15, 1932; s. James Evans and Margaret Roberta (Norvell) M.; B.A. cum laude, Tex. Christian U., 1953; B.D., Vanderbilt Div. Sch., 1956, M.Div., 1973; Ph.D., Vanderbilt U., 1964; M.S. in L.S., U. Ky., 1975; m. Marilyn Miller Shipp, May 25, 1951; children—Margaret Lucretia (dec.), Paul Andrew, Frank Warren, John Vinson Evans, Marilyn Amelia. Ordained to ministry Christian Ch., 1955; minister First Christian Ch., Hutchins, Tex., 1951-52; asso. minister Central Christian Ch., Shreveport, La., 1952-53; youth minister Riverside Christian Ch., Fort Worth, 1953; acting librarian religious sect. JUL, Nashville, 1954-55; minister edn. Woodmont Christian Ch., Nashville, 1955-59; coll. chaplain, asst. prof. Eureka (Ill.) Coll., 1960-65; lectr. Bradley U., 1963-65; asso. prof. religion Transylvania U., Lexington, Ky., 1965-72, dir. summer session, 1966-71, prof. religion, dir. humanities program, 1971-76; lectr. U. Ky., 1976—; chaplain U.S. Navy, Yokosuka, Japan, 1976—. Named Faculty Mem. of Year, Eureka Coll., 1965, Transylvania U., 1968. Mem. Soc. Sci. Study Religion, Am. Acad. Religion, Am. Soc. Christian Ethics, AAUP (pres. Transylvania chpt. 1968-69), Beta Phi Mu. Author: Decide - Act!, 1970; also articles and revs. Home: 171 Romany Rd Lexington KY 40502

MURPHY, DENNIS J., priest, Roman Catholic Church; gen. sec. Can. Conf. Catholic Bishops (English sector). Office: 90 Parent Ave Ottawa ON K1N 7B1 Canada*

MURPHY, GEORGE ROBERT, priest, Roman Catholic Church; b. Bridgeport, Conn., May 3, 1941; s. George Henry and Jessica Leona (Irving) M. A.B., Boston Coll., 1965, M.A., 1966; M.Div., Weston Coll., 1971. Ordained priest, Roman Cath. Ch., 1971. Tchr., Fairfield Prep Sch., Conn., 1966-68; chaplain Boston Coll., 1972-78; asst. rector Jesuit Sch. Theology, Berkeley, Calif., 1978-79; dir. novices Soc. of Jesus, Boston, 1980—. Mem. Religious Formation Conf. Address: 300 Newbury St Boston MA 02115

MURPHY, JOHN FRANCIS, priest, religious organization executive, Roman Catholic Church; b. Lexington, Ky., Feb. 25, 1923; s. John Francis and Elizabeth (Geary) M.; A.B., St. Meinrad Coll., 1944; postgrad. St. Meinrad Sem., 1944-46; S.T.L., Theol. Coll., Cath. U., 1947, S.T.D., 1958; hon. degrees Bellarmine Coll., 1971, St. Thomas Inst., Cin., Mt. St. Mary's Coll. Md., 1975. Ordained priest Roman Catholic Ch., 1947, became monsignor, 1961; pastor chs., Ky., 1947, 49-51; instr. scripture Villa Madonna Coll. (now Thomas More Coll.), Covington, Ky., summer 1948, instr. theology, 1949-51, acting dean, 1951-52, dean, 1952-53, pres., 1953-71; v.p. univ. relations Cath. U. Am., Washington, 1971-74; chaplain St. Elizabeth Hosp., Covington, summer 1950, Our Lady of Highlands Sch., Ft. Thomas, Ky., 1951-54; mem. exec. com. coll. and univ. dept., chmn. So. regional unit Nat. Cath. Ednl. Assn., Washington, 1968-72, exec. sec., 1974—. Nat. hdqrs. chaplain High Sch. Young Christian Students, 1953-58; chaplain Family Relations Club, Cath. Colls. Greater Cin., 1949-51; family life dir. Diocese Covington, (Ky.), 1954-64. Charter mem., chmn. Kenton County Human Rights Commn., Covington, 1964-70; mem. Commn. on Higher Edn. Ky., 1963-66. Founder, trustee No. Ky. Mental Health Assn.; founder, trustee Ky. Ind. Coll. Found., 1952-71, Council Ind. Ky. Colls. and Univs., 1965-71; trustee St. Meinrad Coll., St. Meinrad Sch. Theology. Mem. So. Assn. Colls. and Schs. (commn. mem.). Office: Nat Cath Ednl Assn 1 Dupont Circle Washington DC 20036

MURPHY, MICHAEL J. Bishop of Erie, Roman Catholic Church, 1982—. Office: 205 W 9th St Erie PA 16501*

MURPHY, PHILIP FRANCES, bishop, Roman Catholic Church. Ordained priest Roman Cath. Ch. Titular bishop of Tacarata, aux. bishop of Balt., 1976—. Office: 320 Cathedral St Baltimore MD 21201

MURPHY, ROBERT GLENN, minister, Independent Christian Churches; b. East St. Louis, Ill., Nov. 6, 1928; s. Charles Robert and Eva Earl (Wilson) M.; B.S., U. Mo., 1954; B.A., St. Louis Christian Coll., 1967; M.A., Eastern N.Mex. U., 1977; m. Shirley Mae Egan, Sept. 10, 1949; children: Gary Glenn, Janet Lynn, Gail Elaine. Ordained to ministry Ind. Christian Chs., 1967. Pastor Keyesport (Ill.) Christian Ch., 1964-66, Kingshighway Ch. of Christ, East St. Louis, Ill., 1966-70, Christian Ch., Los Alamos, N.Mex., 1970—. Pres. Los Alamos Ministerial Fellowship, 1973; chm. El Porvenir Christian Camp, Montezuma, N.Mex., 1974-76; pres. N.Mex. Christian Conf., 1973, 80; speaker N.Am. Christian Conv. on Ch. Adminstrn., 1973, 74. Bd. dirs., past pres. Los Alamos YMCA; bd. dirs. Los Alamos Family Council, 1980—; mem. instnl. rev. bd. Los Alamos Med. Ctr., 1981—. Home: 104 Azure Dr Los Alamos NM 87544 Office: PO Box 1223 Alamos NM 87544

MURPHY, ROLAND EDMUND, educator, priest, Roman Cath. Ch.; b. Chgo., July 19, 1917; s. John and Marian (Haugh) M.; M.A. in Philosophy, Cath. U. Am., 1943; S.T.D., 1948, M.A. in Semitics, 1949; S.S.L., Rome Bibl. Inst., 1958; LL.D., St. Francis Coll., 1967. Joined Order of Carmelites, 1935; ordained priest, 1942; prof. O.T., Cath. U. Am., 1948-70; George Washington Ivey prof. O.T., Duke Div. Sch., 1971—. Mem. Cath. Bibl. Assn., Soc. Bibl. Lit. Author: Wisdom Literature, 1981. Contbr. articles to profl. jours. Co-editor The Jerome Biblical Commentary, 1968. Office: Duke Div Sch Durham NC 27706

MURPHY, TERRENCE JOHN, coll. pres., priest, Roman Catholic Ch.; b. Watkins, Minn., Dec. 21, 1920; s. Frank and Mary (Lee) M.; B.A., St. Paul Sem., 1946; M.A., U. Minn., 1956; Ph.D., Georgetown U., 1959. Ordained priest Roman Catholic Ch., 1946, became monsignor, 1966; asst. pastor various parishes, 1946-49; chaplain USAF, 1949-54; mem. Coll. St. Thomas faculty, 1954-61, dean of students, 1961-62, exec. v.p., 1962-66, pres., 1966—. Mem. pastoral council Archdiocese of St. Paul and Mpls., del. Congress Cath. Edn., Rome, Italy, 1972. Mem. Minn. Pvt. Coll. Council and Minn. Pvt. Coll. Fund. Bd. dirs. KTCA-TV/KTCI-TV (Twin Cities Ednl. TV Corp.), Mt. St. Mary's Coll. of Md. Mem. Nat. Cath. Ednl. Assn., Assn. Post-Secondary Ednl. Instns. Minn., Assn. Am. Colls., Ministers Life and Casualty Union, Internat. Fedn. Cath. Univs. (dir.). Author: Censorship: Government and Obscenity, 1963. Address: Office of the President 2115 Summit Ave St Paul MN 55105

MURPHY, THOMAS AUSTIN See *Who's Who in America*, 43rd edition.

MURPHY, THOMAS JOSEPH See *Who's Who in America*, 43rd edition.

MURRAY, DONALD WILBIRT, college administrator, Seventh-day Adventists; b. Wallace, Idaho, Apr. 26, 1942; s. Joseph Wilbirt and Beth Alberta (Devereaux) M.; m. Susan Elizabeth Murray, Aug. 18, 1963; children: Marcia Jo, Ryan Matthew. B.A., Walla Walla Coll., 1964, M.Ed., 1970. Ordained elder Seventh-day Adventists, 1979, credentialed missionary, 1967. Assoc. dean boys Laurelwood Acad., Gaston, Oreg., 1964-67; dean boys Columbia Acad., Battle Ground, Wash., 1967-70, Blue Mountain Acad., Hamburg, Pa., 1970-77; assoc. dean men Andrews U., Berrien Springs, Mich., 1977-84, dean men, 1984—; co-founder Adventist Engaged Encounter, Berrien Springs, 1978—. Assoc. editor The Deans Window, 1983-84, editor, 1984—. Mem. Adventist Student Personnel Assn. (pres. 1982-84), Assn. Coll. and Univ. Housing Officers, Am. Coll. Personnel Assn., Am. Assn. Counseling and Devel. Republican. Home: 396 Westwood Dr Berrien Springs MI 49103 Office: Andrews U Berrien Springs MI 49104

MURRAY, JEAN CAROLYN, college administrator, Roman Catholic Church; b. Broadview, Ill., May 30, 1927; d. Meredith C. and Marie (Ryan) M. B.A. in French, Rosary Coll., 1949; Ph.D. in French, U. Fribourg, Switzerland, 1963. From instr. to assoc. prof. Rosary Coll., River Forest, Ill., 1966-80, pres., 1981—, also dir.; provincial councilor Sinsinawa Dominicans, Wis., 1976-78. Author: Georges Bernanos: Correspondence Inedite, 1971 (Les Palmes Academiques award French Govt. 1978). Chairperson West Cook County Heart Assn., Westchester, Ill., 1983—; chairperson pub. relations Fedn. of Ind. Ill. Colls. and Univs., Springfield, Ill., 1983—; exec. com. Assn. Colls. of Ill., Chgo., 1983—. Office: Rosary Coll 7900 W Division St River Forest IL 60305

MURRAY, RALPH LAVERN, minister, So. Baptist Conv.; b. Waterloo, Iowa, May 28, 1921; s. Harry N. and Elsie M. (Huber) M.; B.A., Carson Newman Coll., 1943; B.D., So. Bapt. Theol. Sem., 1947, Th.M., 1948; postgrad. Princeton U., 1963-64, Union Theol. Sem. N.Y., 1966, 67, 73, Mansfield Coll., Oxford (Eng.) U., 1968; m. Beulah Bertha Blunt, Dec. 19, 1942; children—Joseph Paul, Kathryn Elizabeth. Ordained to ministry, 1942; asso. pastor ch., Knoxville, Tenn., 1942-44; pastor chs., Ky., 1944-48, Tenn., 1948-69; editor adult materials Bapt. Sunday Sch. Bd., Nashville, 1969-71, editor Bible study materials, Sunday Sch. dept., 1971-76. Moderator, Knox County Bapt. Assn., 1953-54; mem. exec. com. Tenn. Bapt. Conv., 1960-68, chmn. edn. com., 1965-68; trustee Harrison Chilhowee Bapt. Acad., 1954-59; Mid-South Bapt. Hosp., 1950-54; pres. Tenn. Bapt. Press, 1953-59; pres. Knoxville Ministerial Assn., 1953-54; mem. stewardship commn. So. Bapt. Conv., 1976—; asso. prof. U. Tenn. Sch. Religion, 1964-68. Author: From the Beginning, 1964; The Other Dimension, 1966; Can I Believe in Miracles?, 1967; Christ and the City, 1970; The Biblical Shape of Hope, 1971; Signs of the Savior, 1977; contbg. author: Five Minute a Day, 1969; Light for Lifes' Dark Shadows, 1968; also articles and Bible study materials. D.D. (hon.), Carson Newman Coll., 1967. Home: 113 Skyview Dr Hendersonville TN 37075 Office: 127 9th Ave N 422 North Wing Nashville TN 37234

MURRELL, HERBERT CONRAD, minister, So. Bapt. Conv.; b. Bentley, La., Dec. 15, 1928; s. Alvin Carrol and Era Jane (Thompson) M.; student U. Houston, 1963-65; m. Eunice Vada Phillips, Dec. 22, 1945; children—Timothy Alvin, James Edwin, Kenneth Conrad, Pamela Diane, William Carlton. Ordained to ministry, 1955; pastor Greenlee Bapt. Ch., Humble,

Tex., 1955-63, Unity Bapt. Ch., Houston, 1963-66, Ball (La.) Bapt. Ch., 1966-67; staff evangelist, Bible Conf. preacher Gene Williams Evangelistic Assn., 1967—. Founder, pres., dir. Bible camps, retreats and seminars Grace and Truth Enterprises, 1974; spl. counsel in realm supernatural religious phenomenam. Mem. Conf. So. Bapt. Evangelists. Author: The Roman Road, 1968; To Profit Withal, 1969; Take Heed Brethren, Lest, 1970; and False Tongues, 1973; My Dear Charismatics, 1972; Salvation,....When?, 1971; Practical Demonology, 1973; Faith Cometh, 1976; Spiritual Baptisms and Gifts, 1975; contbr. articles to religious jours.; editor The Gatepost, religious Quar. Home: RT 1 Box 65-B Bentley LA 71407 Office: PO Box 98 Bentley LA 71407

MURTHA, JOHN FRANCIS, priest, Roman Catholic Church; history educator; b. Mount Pleasant, Pa., May 28, 1930; s. Francis Regis and Margaret Ellen (Kearns) M. B.A. cum laude, St. Vincent Coll., 1953; M.A., Columbia U., 1960; Ph.D., Cath. U. Am., 1964; M.Div., St. Vincent Sem., 1985. Ordained priest Roman Cath. Ch., 1957. Assoc. prof. history St. Vincent Coll., Latrobe, Pa., 1977—, bd. dirs., 1977-82, 84—, pres., 1985—; prior St. Vincent Archabbey, Latrobe, 1981-85, mem. council srs., 1977—. Editor: America 200, Essays in American History, 1976. Contbr. articles to New Cath. Ency., 1963. Mem. Am. Benedictine Acad. Democrat. Club: YMCA (Greensburg, Pa.). Lodge: Elks. Office: St Vincent Archabbey Latrobe PA 15650

MUTHERSBAUGH, HADLEY PHILLIP, minister, Seventh-day Adventist; b. Portland, Oreg., May 14, 1947; s. Wallace Phillip and Cecile Theresa (Roberson) M.; m. Debbie Renee Smick, July 26, 1980; 1 child, Amy Renee. A.A., Portland Community Coll., 1972; B.A., Walla Walla Coll., 1980; M.Div., Andrews U., 1983. Pastor Oreg. Conf. Seventh-day Adventists, Portland, 1980-81, pastoral assoc., Springfield, 1984—, pastor, Fall Creek, Oreg., 1984; dir. Campus Ministry Walla Walla Coll., College Place, Wash., 1978-79, sem. student religious affairs Andrews U., 1982. Author articles. Vice pres. ASB-Portland Community Coll., 1966-67. Served with USN, 1967-70. Jackson Found. scholar Portland Community Coll., 1972. Mem. Ministerial Assn. of Springfield, Acad. Adventist Ministers (local sec. 1984-85), Assn. for Clin. Pastoral Edn. Republican. Lodge: Kiwanis. Home: 358 N 69th Pl Springfield OR 97478 Office: Oreg Conf of Seventh-day Adventists 13400 S E 97th Clackamas OR 97015

MYERS, ALBERT EDWIN, minister, Lutheran Church in America, religious organization executive; b. Akron, Ohio, Sept. 18, 1931; s. Forrest D. and Marian H. (Conner) M.; m. Naomi Ann Paullin, Aug. 9, 1953; children: Paul T., Kathryn I., Deborah H., Forrest C. B.A., Akron U., 1954; M.Div., Trinity Luth. Theol. Sem., 1955; S.T.M., Oberlin Coll., 1959; D.Min., Vanderbilt U., 1974. Ordained to ministry Lutheran Ch. in Am., 1955. Pastor chs. in Ohio, Wyo., Ont., Can., and Pa., 1955-74; exec. dir. Pa. Council of Chs., Harrisburg, 1974—; bd. mgrs. Pa. Bible Soc., 1979—; trustee Thiel Coll., Greenville, Pa., 1976—; mem. Commn. on Religion in Appalachia, Nashville, 1974—; mem. governing bd. Nat. Council Chs., 1976-81. Author: The Pastoral Epistles, 1970; A Family of the Bagaduce, 1976; Asa Williams and Direxa Dunn, 1976. Trustee United Way Pa., 1974-76; mem. exec. com. planning div. Tri-County United Way, 1974-78; mem. dist. com. Keystone Area council Boy Scouts Am., 1974-78; moderator radio show Face the Issue, Harrisburg, 1974-82. Named hon. canon St. Stephen's Episcopal Cathedral, 1984; recipient leadership citation Pa. State Senate, 1984. Mem. Nat. Assn. Ecumenical Staff, Soc. Descs. of Colonial Clergy. Democrat. Home: 5341 Windsor Rd Harrisburg PA 17112 Office: Pa Council of Churches 900 S Arlington Ave Harrisburg PA 17109

MYERS, CHARLES WAYNE, minister, Southern Baptist Convention; b. Harrodsburg, Ky., Dec. 20, 1953; s. Russell and Dorothy (Rivers) M.; m. Barbara Ann Carpenter, Dec. 21, 1974. B.A., Cumberland Coll., 1977; M.Div., So. Bapt. Theol. Sem., Louisville, 1981. Lic. preacher Southern Baptist Convention, 1974, ordained to ministry, 1979. Minister music and youth 20th St. Bapt. Ch., Corbin, Ky., 1977; assoc. pastor, minister music and youth Dover Bapt. Ch., Shelbyville, Ky., 1978-81; pastor Mt. Pleasant Bapt. Ch., Shelbyville, 1981-83; assoc. pastor, minister music and youth Dover Bapt. Ch., Shelbyville, 1984-85; pastor Amity Bapt. Ch., Franklin, Ind., 1985—; chmn. recreation com. Shelby County Bapt. Assn., 1982-83, adult leader associational Sunday Sch. improvement support team, 1983-84. Recipient Adult Leadership, Christian Devel. diplomas Sunday Sch. Bd., Nashville, 1983; Nat. Appreciation awards Soc. Disting. Am. High Sch. Students, 1983. Democrat. Home: Route 5 Box 112 Franklin IN 46131

MYERS, DONALD, lay ch. worker, Conservative Jewish Congregations; b. Bklyn., June 9, 1930; s. Lewis Gene and Claire Vivian (Meyerowitz) M.; B.S., Seton Hall U., S. Orange, N.J., 1952, LL.B., J.D., 1955; m. Elaine Kesselhaut, Feb. 20, 1955; children—Jeffrey, Amy Sue. Pres., Temple Mekor Chayim, Linden, N.J., 1970-76, pres. men's club, 1966-68; pres. Elizabeth (N.J.) B'nai B'rith, 1958-60, No. N.J. council, 1969, 3d v.p. dist. 3, 1976—; nat. commr. Anti-Defamation League, 1971-76; chmn. Israel Bond campaign, Linden-Roselle, N.J., 1970—; bd. dirs. Jewish Nat. Fund, United Jewish Appeal; treas. No. N.J. region United Synagogues Am., 1976—. Practice law, Elizabeth, 1955—. Vice chmn. Union County Welfare Bd., 1972; chmn. Union County United Fund, 1962-63; dist. commr. Union council Boy Scouts Am., 1957-62. Recipient Israel Bond award, 1975; Citizenship award B'nai B'rith, 1976, Shofar award Boy Scouts Am., 1976. Mem. N.Am. Judges Assn., Am. Judicature Soc., Am., N.J., Union County bar assns., Smithsonian Assos., Museum Natural History Assos. Home: 237 W 7th Ave Roselle NJ 07203 Office: 1143 E Jersey St Elizabeth NJ 07201

MYERS, HOWARD WARFIELD, chaplain, Lutheran Church in America; b. Washington, June 3, 1937; s. Howard Mills and Marian Parmele (Bates) M.; B.A., George Washington U., 1961; M.Div., Luth. Theol. Sem., Gettysburg, Pa., 1965; M.S., Xavier U., Cin., 1973; m. Elizabeth Jewell Kuether, Aug. 29, 1964 (div. 1974); children: Joel Landon, Kristin Elizabeth; m. Mary Jo Adams, Dec. 12, 1983. Ordained to ministry Luth. Ch. in Am., 1965. Pastor Our Savior's Luth. Ch., Naperville, Ill., 1965-67; chaplain U.S. Navy, 1967-70; clin. trainee Norwich (Conn.) State Hosp., 1970-71; Protestant chaplain Chillicothe (Ohio) Correctional Inst., 1971-73; coordinator reception and diagnostic center Ohio Dept. Rehab. and Correction, Chillicothe, 1973-75; protestant chaplain London (Ohio) Correctional Instn., 1975—. Mem. task force on penal reform Ohio Synod, Luth. Ch. Am., 1976—. Named Co-Chaplain of Year, 1971-72. Mem. Order of Holy Cross (priest asso.), Am. Correctional Assn., Assn. Clin. Pastoral Edn., Am. Protestant Correctional Chaplains Assn., Madison County Ministerial Assn., Ohio State Chaplains Assn., U.S. Naval Inst. Columnist, Chaplain's Chatter, The Booster. Contbr. articles to religious jours. Home and Office: London Correctional Instn Box 69 London OH 43140

MYLET, PAMELA ANN MULAC, priest, pastoral counselor, Episcopal Church; b. Salem, Ohio, Dec. 6, 1944; d. Elmer John and Dorothy Adelaide (McGee) Mulac. Student Bryn Mawr Coll., Pa., 1962-64; A.B., U. Chgo., 1966; M.Div., Seabury-Western Theol. Sem., 1974; postgrad. Garrett Evang. Theol. Sem./Northwestern U., 1977—, Ph.D. candidate, 1981. Ordained priest Episcopal Ch., 1978. Pastoral counselor Swedish Covenant Hosp., Chgo., 1975-84; asst. deacon, priest St. Luke's Ch., Evanston, Ill., 1974-84; adj. lectr. Seabury-Western Theol. Sem., Evanston, 1981-82, trustee, 1981-84; asst. priest St. Mark's Ch., Upland, Calif., 1984—; pastoral counselor Walnut Valley Counseling Ctr., Walnut, Calif., 1984—; bd. dirs. Cathedral Shelter of Chgo., 1980-84; co-chairperson Leader's Sch. Cursillo, Chgo., 1981-83; mem. Commn. on Alcoholism, Diocese of Los Angeles, 1985—. Episcopal Ch. Found fellow, 1978-81. Mem. Am. Assn. Pastoral Counselors (sec. Pacific region 1984—), Am. Assn. Clin. Pastoral Edn. Office: Walnut Valley Counseling Ctr 1210 S Brea Canyon Rd Walnut CA 91789

MYLONAS, EFSTATHIOS VASILIOS, priest, Greek Orthodox Church; b. Thessaloniki, Greece, Mar. 27, 1937; came to U.S., 1965, naturalized, 1972; s. Vasilios Efstathios and Anastasia (Dalkidis) M.; m. Maria Vomvolakis, Aug. 19, 1962; children: Anastasia, Vasilios George. S.T.B., Patriarchal Theol. Sch. of Halki, Turkey, 1962; S.T.M., Boston U. Sch. Theology, 1971; M.A., Boston Coll., 1974; Ph.D., Boston U., 1985. Ordained priest Greek Orthodox Ch., 1962. Pastor Holy Archangels Michael and Gabriel, Istanbul, Turkey, 1962-63, St. George Ch., Toronto, Ont., Can., 1963-65, Assumption Ch., Port Jefferson Station, N.Y., 1965-69, Holy Trinity Ch., Concord, N.H., 1969-71, Annunciation Ch., Brockton, Mass., 1971-80, Modesto Calif., 1980—; guest speaker various orgns.; lectr. U. Pacific, Stockton, Calif., fall 1984; rep. Greek Orthodox Archdiocese of North and South Am. to Mass. Commn. on Christian Unity, 1973-80, biennial clergy-laity Congresses of Greek Orthodox Archdiocese of North and South Am., 1968-84; instr. St. John the Divine Orthodox Theol. Inst., Grad. Theol. Union, Berkeley, Calif., spring 1985. Contbr. articles to newspapers. Apptd. by Congressman Tony Coelho to Congl. Award Council of 15th Congl. Dist. Calif. Recipient Commonwealth of Mass. State Senate Official citation, 1980; named Paul Revere Patriot of the Commonwealth of Mass., 1976; Boston U. Sch. Theology grantee, 1969-75; Taylor scholar Greek Orthodox Archdiocese of North and South Am., 1969-84. Mem. Orthodox Theol. Soc. Am., Am. Hellenic Progressive Assn. Home: 1437 Maplehill Rd Modesto CA 95350

MYRA, HAROLD LAWRENCE, editor; b. Camden, N.J., July 19, 1939; s. John Samuel and Esther (Christensen) M.; B.S. in Edn., East Stroudsburg State Coll., 1961; m. Jeanette Ann Austin, May 7, 1966; children—Michelle Leigh, Todd Stephen, Gregory David. Lay leader in high sch. work Youth for Christ, Stroudsburg, Pa., 1957-61; v.p., editor Campus Life, Youth for Christ Internat., Wheaton, Ill., 1961-75; pres., pub. Christianity Today, Inc., Carol Stream, Ill., 1975—. Mem. Sigma Delta Chi, Sigma Tau Delta. Author: No Man in Eden, 1969; The Carpenter, 1971; Should a Christian Go to War?, 1971; The New You, 1972; Michelle, You Scallawag, I Love You, 1972; What an Ugly, Beautiful World, 1972; Is There a Place I Can Scream?, 1975, Elsbeth, 1975; The Choice, 1980. Office: 465 Gunderson Dr Carol Stream IL 60188

NAAS, JOLINDA, educational administrator, nun, Roman Catholic Church; b. Haubstadt, Ind., May 14, 1937; d. Joseph Paul and Elizabeth Bertha (Brenner) N. B.S., St. Benedict Coll., 1967; M.A., Ball State U., 1976, cert. adminstrn. and supervision, 1982. Joined Sisters of St. Benedict, Roman Cath. Ch., 1953. Tchr., schs. Diocese Evansville, Ind., 1956-69; tchr., prin. Archdiocese Los Angeles, Huntington Beach, Calif., 1969-72; prin. Diocese Evansville, 1972—, Holy Family Sch., Jasper, Ind., 1976-85. Mem. Sisters Senate, Evansville, 1974-76. Nat. Assn. Elem. Sch. Prins. grantee, 1983. Mem. Nat. Assn. Elem. Sch. Prins., Ind. Assn. Elem. Sch. Prins., Assn. Supervision and Curriculum Devel., Ind. Assn. Supervision and Curriculum Devel. Home: 990 Church Ave Jasper IN 47546 Office: Holy Family Sch 990 Church Ave Jasper IN 47546

NADICH, JUDAH, rabbi; b. Balt., May 13, 1912; s. Isaac J. and Lena (Nathanson) N.; B.A., Coll. City N.Y., 1932; M.A., Columbia, 1936; Rabbi, Jewish Theol. Sem., 1936, M.H.L., 1947, D.H.L., 1953, D.D. (hon.), 1966; m. Martha Hadassah Ribalow, Jan. 26, 1947; children: Leah Nessa (Mrs. Aryeh Meir), Shira Adina (Mrs. James L. Levin), Nahma Meira (Mrs. David Belcourt). Ordained rabbi, 1936; rabbi Temple Beth David, Buffalo, 1936-40; co-rabbi Anshe Emet Synagogue, Chgo., 1940-42; chaplain AUS, 1942-46; rabbi Kehillath Israel Synagogue, Brookline, Mass., 1947-57, Park Ave. Synagogue, N.Y.C., 1957—. Conducted retreats U.S. Armed Forces, Japan and Vietnam, 1971, Germany, 1974; pres. Rabbinical Assembly, 1972-74. Adviser to Gen. Eisenhower on Jewish affairs, ETO, 1945; pres. Jewish Book Council Am., 1968-72. Bd. dirs. Jewish Theol. Sem. Am., N.Y. Fedn. Jewish Philanthropies, 1979-85; chmn. Commn. on Jewish Chaplaincy, 1978-81, Nat. Jewish Welfare Bd. Mem. Assn. Jewish Chaplains of Armed Forces (pres. 1971-73), Mil. Chaplains Assn., N.Y. Bd. Rabbis, Phi Beta Kappa. Author: Eisenhower and the Jews, 1953. Editor, translator The Flowering of Modern Hebrew Literature, 1959; Jewish Legends of the Second Commonwealth, 1983. Editor: Al Halakhah v'Aggadah, 1960. Contbr. to Ency. Judaica, 1970. Contbr. articles to religious jours. Home: 993 Park Ave New York City NY 10028 Office: 50 E 87th St New York City NY 10128

NADLER, ALLAN LAWRENCE, rabbi, educator, Orthodox Jewish Congregations; b. Montreal, Que., Can., May 8, 1954; came to U.S., 1976; s. Joseph Y. and Doris (Joselevsky) N. B.A., McGill U., 1976; M.A., Harvard U., 1982. Rabbi, 1976. Rabbi, Charles River Synagogue, Boston, 1980-84, Shaar Hashomayim, Montreal, 1984—; lectr. McGill U., Montreal, 1982-84; exec. dir. Religious Zionists of Toronto, 1978-79; columnist Tanu Rabanan in Boston Jewish Times, 1984. Contbr. articles to profl. jours. Que. Govt. grad. fellow, 1976-78; Harvard U. Solomon fellow, 1980; recipient Berman award, McGill U., 1974, Greenblatt History award, 1975. Mem. Rabbinical Council Am. Home: 2121 Tupper St Apt 1206 Montreal PQ H2H 1P1 Canada Office: Shaar Hashomayim Congregation 450 Kensington Ave Westmount PQ Canada

NAGASHIMA, GLENN JUGI, minister, American Lutheran Church; b. Chgo., Jan. 10, 1949; s. Tom Jugiro and Kay (Tanniguchi) N.; m. Wilma Faye Nagashima, June 17, 1978; children: Christina Kayte, Nathan Jugiro. B.A. in Psychology, Calif. State U.-Long Beach, 1973; M.Div., Luther Northwestern Sem., 1977. Ordained to ministry, Am. Luth. Ch., 1977. Asst. pastor Grace Luth. Ch., Austin, Minn., 1977-82; assoc. pastor St. John Redeemer Ch., Belle Plaine/Henderson, Minn., 1982—. Bd. dirs. Alliance for Battered Women, 1982. Address: 14226 W 280th St Henderson MN 56044

NAGLE, ROBERT SHEARD, priest Roman Catholic Church; b. Astoria, N.Y., May 8, 1934; s. Robert Patrick and Mary (Sorahan) N. B.A., Boston Coll., 1958; M.A., St. Vincent Coll., 1966; Ph.D., U. Md., 1977. Ordained priest Roman Cath. Ch., 1963. Asst. pastor St. Peters Parish, Olney, Md., 1963-70; asst. supt. of schs. Archdiocese of Washington, 1970-78, dir. elem. schs., 1978-82; pastor St. Mary's Parish of Piscataway, Clinton, Md., 1982—. Trustee, St. John Coll. High Sch., Washington, 1980-84. Address: St Marys Ch 13401 Piscataway Rd Clinton MD 20735

NAHMAN, RICHARD M., priest, Roman Catholic Church; b. N.Y.C., June 13, 1938; s. Louis and Anne Josephine (Nolan/Dowdall) N. B.A., Villanova U., 1962, M.A., 1966; S.T.L., Cath. U., 1966; S.T.D., St. Paul U., U. Ottawa, 1970. Ordained priest Roman Cath. Ch., 1965. Tchr. Carroll High Sch., Washington, 1966-69; assoc. St. Augustine Parish, Ottawa, Ont., 1969-71; assoc. pastor Our Mother of Consolation, Phila., 1971-74; assoc. dir. communications, dir. province peace and justice commn., provincial staff mem., sem. staff mem., editor province publ. The Augustinians, Villanova, Pa., 1974-79; pastor, prior St. John's Parish, Schaghticoke, N.Y., 1979—; senator Albany Priest Senate, 1981—; mem. exec. bd.

Washington Archdiocesan Council High Sch. Religion Tchrs., 1967-69; bd. dirs. Chestnut Hill Community Religion Com., Phila., 1972-74, Northwest Interfaith Movement, 1973-74, Phila. Interfaith Task Force on Aging, 1973-74. Chmn. Chestnut Hill Community Assn. Mem. Cath. Theol. Soc. Am. Home and Office: St John's Rectory 6 S Main St PO Box 300 Schaghticoke NY 12154

NAIL, BILLY DEERING, minister, So. Baptist Conv.; b. Kennett, Mo., Apr. 29, 1925; s. Willie Dixon and Harriet Elizabeth (Owen) N.; student Mich. Bapt. Inst., 1955-57, Golden Gate Bapt. Theol. Sem., 1970-71; m. Dorothy Ora Green, Nov. 1, 1928; children—Rudy C., Randy M., Redgy W., Ricky A., Rodney D. Ordained to ministry, 1952; pastor Providence Bapt. Ch., Flint, Mich., 1954-60, First Bapt. Ch., Bettendorf, Iowa, 1960-68, Lakeview Bapt. Ch., Ypsilanti, Mich., 1968-70, Pacifica (Calif.) Bapt. Ch., 1970-72, First Bapt. Ch., Fredericktown, Mo., 1972-74, Normandy Rd. Bapt. Ch., Royal Oak, Mich., 1974—. Mem. exec. bd. Bapt. State Conv. Mich., 1958-60, also mem. state missions com., 1962; chmn. missions com. Iowa So. Bapt. Assn., 1962-63; sec., treas. Bettendorf (Iowa) Ministerial Assn., 1964-67; chmn. missions com. Huron River Valley Assn., Ypsilanti, 1968-69; moderator Huron Valley Bapt. Assn., 1969-70, Oakland County Bapt. Assn., Pontiac, Mich., 1974—, mem. missions com., 1974—; trustee Golden Gate Bapt. Theol. Sem., Mill Valley, Calif., 1974-76. Home: 1450 Normandy Rd Royal Oak MI 48073 Office: 1400 Normandy Rd Royal Oak MI 48073

NAIL, CHARLES LYNN, minister, So. Baptist Conv.; b. Grenada, Miss., Mar. 28, 1937; s. William Lamar and Nannie Beatrice (Lott) N.; B.A., Miss. Coll., 1961; M.Div., So. Bapt. Theol. Sem., 1974; D.D., Am. Sch. Bible, 1972; m. Sonja Jean Strohm, Dec. 27, 1956; children—Charles Lynn, Michael Anthony, Phyllis Lynnette. Ordained to ministry, 1959; pastor chs., Miss., 1959-63, 1st Bapt. Ch., Madisonville, La., 1963-67, Little Bahala Bapt. Ch., Wesson, Miss., 1967-71, Woodburn (Ky.) Bapt. Ch., 1971-74, Capitol Heights Bapt. Ch., Pierre, S.D., 1974—. Chaplain, S.D. Legislature, 1974; moderator East River Bapt. Assn.; chmn. bd. Tri County Christian Schs., Wesson, Miss., 1968-69; revival preacher, Miss., La., Ky., Tenn., S.D. vice chmn. steering com. S.D. conf. Mem. Woodburn Vol. Fire Dept., 1971-74. Home and Office: PO Box 692 Pierre SD 57501

NALLO, LARRY THOMAS, minister, American Baptist Churches U.S.A.; b. Wilkes-Barre, Pa., Dec. 2, 1947; s. Merlin Carl and Marion Ruth (Miller) N.; m. Kathleen Elizabeth Pilgram, June 25, 1967; children: Greggor Thomas, Ann Elizabeth. B.S., Bloomsburg State U., 1969; M.Div., Colgate Rochester Div. Sch., 1973; postgrad. Princeton Theol. Sem., 1980—. Ordained to ministry Baptist Ch., 1973. Chaplain's asst. U. Rochester, N.Y., 1971-73; assoc. pastor Hilton Bapt. Ch., N.Y., 1974-77; pastor Trinity Ch., Nunda, N.Y., 1977-82, First Bapt. Ch., Meriden, Conn., 1982—; mem. Parish Ministries com. Am. Bapt. Chs. Conn., Hartford, 1982—; v.p. Meriden Clergy Assn., Conn., 1984—. Mem. Operation Pantry (emergency food shelf), Meriden, 1983—. Democrat. Home: 600 Yale Ave Meriden CT 06450 Office: First Bapt Ch 460 Broad St Meriden CT 06450

NAPIER, DAVIE See *Who's Who in America,* 43rd edition.

NARBERES, FREDERICK WILLIAM, superintendent diocese, Roman Catholic Church; b. Martinez, Calif., Apr. 30, 1937; s. Rene Joseph and Catherine Eileen (Lane) N.; B.Degree, St. Martin's Coll., 1971; M.Degree, Loyola-Marymount, 1974; Doctorate, Pepperdine U., 1981. Postulant, Dominican Order, Kentfield, Calif., 1959, novice, Oakland, Calif., 1960-61, 1st profession, 1961-67, solemn profession, San Francisco, 1967; supt. Diocese of Phoenix, 1981—; mem. Chief Adminstr.'s of Cath. Edn., Washington, 1981; bd. dirs. Cath. Social Service, Phoenix, 1984. Mem. Assn. Supervision and Curriculum Devel., Am. Assn. Counseling and Devel., Nat. Cath. Edn. Assn. Democrat.

NAROWITZ, CATHLEEN RAE, minister, American Baptist Churches in the U.S.A.; b. Seattle, Sept. 7, 1932; d. Oscar Mitchell and Agatha Bernice (Brugger) N. B.A., U. Wash., 1954; B.D., Crozer Theol. Sem., 1957; M.R.E., Andover Newton Theol. Sem., 1962, D.Min., 1974. Ordained to ministry Baptist Ch., 1957. Pastor, Passumpsic Comminity Bapt. Ch., Vt., 1963-68, Danville Bapt. Ch., N.H., 1969-74; interim pastor Congl. Christian Ch., Toppenish, Wash., 1975-76, First Bapt. Ch., Lewiston, Idaho, 1976; pastor Ch. of Good Shepherd, Newport, N.H., 1977-79; minister at large Am. Bapt. Chs. in U.S.A., 1979—. Mem. Internat. Assn. Women Ministers. Democrat. Home: PO Box 418 Grantham NH 03753

NATHANIEL (NATHANIEL POPP). Bishop of Dearborn, Mich., The Orthodox Church in America. Office: 2522 Gray Tower Rd Jackson MI 49201*

NATIONS, O. LYN, minister, Southern Baptist Convention; b. Carson, Miss., Apr. 27, 1946; s. Homer O. and Alma Lorane (King) N.; m. Virginia Rogers, June 25, 1966; children: Richard Lyn, Regina Elizabeth, Tina Romona. Grad., Copiah-Lincoln Jr. Coll., 1966; B.S., Miss. Coll., 1977; M. Ministry, Luther Rice Sem., 1982. Ordained to ministry Southern Baptist Conv., 1969. Pastor Antioch Bapt. Ch., Lexington, Miss., 1970-72, Bethesda Bapt. Ch., Terry, Miss., 1972-75, Trinity Bapt. Ch., Pearl, Miss., 1977—; assoc. pastor West Jackson Bapt. Ch., Miss., 1975-77; sec., treas. Pearl Ministerial Assn., 1983, pres., 1984-85; chaplain Baldwin Lee & Barnes, Jackson, 1977-84. Republican. Home: 2611 Jennifer Dr Pearl MS 39208

NAUGLE, DAVID KEITH, JR., religion educator; b. Ft. Worth, Tex., Dec. 2, 1952; s. David Keith and Beverly Jane (Chambers) N. B.A. in History, U. Tex.-Arlington, 1975; Th.M., Dallas Theol. Sem., 1979, Th.D., 1982—. Ordained to ministry, 1977. Club leader Young Life Campaign, Ft. Worth, Tex., 1974-75; assoc. pastor Ft. Worth Bible Ch., 1979-80; campus minister Panteo Bible Ch., Arlington, Tex., 1980—; instr. U. Tex., Arlington, 1980—. Contbr. articles to profl. jours. Fellow Evang. Theol. Soc., Am. Acad. Religion, Soc. Bibl. Lit. Republican. Home: 2700 Trinity Bend Circle #515 Arlington TX 76011 Office: U Tex Arlington UTA Sta Box 191080 Arlington TX 76010

NAYLOR, KENT ELDON, minister, Church of the Brethren; b. Harlan, Kans., Feb. 21, 1926; s. Lewis Earl and Virginia (Friend) N.; m. Elva J. Harbaugh, June 5, 1947; children: Janice E. Naylor Yeager, Ronald K. Max E. B.A., McPherson Coll., 1947; B.D., Bethany Theol. Sem., 1952. Ordained to ministry Ch. of the Brethren, 1954. Pastor Ch. of the Brethren, Lebanon, Pa., 1974-81, dir. ch. devel., Elgin, Ill., 1971-74; chaplain Wesley Med. Ctr., Wichita, Kans., 1981-84; indsl. chaplain Copeland Corp., Sidney, Ohio, 1984—; mem. bd. of alumni, McPherson Coll, 1983—; mem. pastoral cabinet Ch. of the Brethren, Wichita, 1981—. Sec. Village Bd., Octavia, Nebr., 1952-54; chmn. Blackhawk Mental Health Bd., Waterloo, Iowa, 1970. Recipient Alumni Citation of Merit McPherson Coll., 1981; Ambassadors award Wesley Med. Ctr., Wichita, 1982; named Employee of the Month, Wesley Med. Ctr., 1982. Mem. Assn. Clin. Pastoral Edn., Nat. Inst. Indsl. Chaplains, Ch. of Brethren Pastors Assn. Home: 116 Queen St Sidney OH 45365 Office: Copeland Corp Sidney OH 45365

NEAL, VANCE LAVERNE, minister, Church of God, Anderson, Indiana; b. Dec. 2, 1951, Anderson, Ind.; s. Guy LaVerne and Norma Jean (Greggs) N.; m. Susan Theresa Bernosky, Jan. 16, 1971; children: Barbara, Kevin. B.A., Anderson Coll., 1973; postgrad. Duquesne U., 1980-81. Ordained to ministry, 1975. Assoc. pastor First Ch. of God, Cambridge Springs, Pa., 1973, First Ch. of God, St. Louis, 1973-76, N. Main St. Ch. of God, Butler, Pa., 1976-84, sr. assoc. pastor, 1984—; chmn. Gen. Assembly, program com. Ch. of God in Western Pa., 1983-84, interim office mgr., 1984—; vice chmn. Christian Edn. Agy., Ch. of God, 1982-83; lectr. in field. Republican. Home: 283 Holyoke Rd Butler PA 16001

NEAL, WILEY CLEVEN, minister, ch. ofcl., Ch. of God in Christ; b. Dothan, Ala., Nov. 4, 1929; s. Cleveland Buster and Leavie Jane (Dawsey) N.; Bible teaching certificate Ala. A. and M. U., 1949, B.S., 1955; M.Ed., Tuskegee Inst., 1967; m. Rosanna Springer, Aug. 19, 1951; children—Rosa Wylene, Mark Anthony. Asst. and jr. pastor, and pastor chs., Kans. and Ala., 1953-59; pastor Chs. of God in Christ, Andalusia, Ala., 1960—, Brundidge, Ala., 1962—, Mobile, Ala., 1966—; pastor Faith Temple Ch. of God in Christ, Fairhope, Ala., 1966—; regent dir., dean Charles Harrison Mason System Bible Colls., Ala., Ga. and Fla., 1974—. Dean Christian edn. Ala. Ch. of God in Christ, 1972; supt. Mobile dist. Ch. of God in Christ, 1973—. Exec. dir. Hawk-Houston Boy's Club, Dothan, Ala., 1966-72. Mem. Houston County Tchrs. Assn. (pres. 1967-68). Home: 1118 Dellwood Ave Dothan AL 36301

NEALL, BEATRICE SHORT, religion educator, Seventh-day Adventists; b. N.Y.C., Feb. 12, 1929; d. James J. and Ruth (Gordon) Short; m. Ralph E. Neall, Aug. 11, 1949; children: Randolph E., Cheryl C. B.A., Loma Linda U., 1949; M.A., Andrews U., 1971, Ph.D., 1982. Lic. missionary Southeast Asia Union of Seventh-day Adventists, Cambodia, 1957-64, Vietnam, 1964-69, Singapore, 1969-74; asst. prof. religion Union Coll., Lincoln, Nebr., 1977-83, assoc. prof., 1983—; elder Coll. View Ch., Lincoln, 1981—. Author: Concept of Character in the Apocalypse, 1983; Outside The Gate, 1976; The Prince & the Rebel, 1960. Mem. Soc. of Bibl. Lit., Evang. Theol. Soc., Andrews Soc. Religious Scholars, Gen. Conf. Seventh-day Adventists (bibl. research inst. com., Daniel and revelation com., commn. on ordination of women). Republican. Office: Union Coll 3800 S 48th St Lincoln NE 68506

NEATHERY, JOHN MARSHALL, minister, Southern Baptist Convention; b. Henderson, N.C., Oct. 2, 1943; s. William Thomas and Mary Frances (Norwood) N.; B.A., Campbell Coll., 1965; degree in clin. pastoral edn. N.C. Bapt. Hosp., 1969; M.Div., Southeastern Bapt. Theol. Sem., 1969; m. Kaye Frances Currrin, Nov. 9, 1969; children: John Marshall, Julie Kaye, Joanna Currin, Justin Thomas. Ordained to ministry So. Bapt. Conv., 1967. Pastor Browns Bapt. Ch., Norlina, N.C., 1966-70, Middleburg (N.C.) Bapt. Ch., 1968-70, New Sandy Creek Bapt. Ch., Henderson, N.C., 1970-74, Rolesville (N.C.) Bapt. Ch., 1974—; radio devotional spots Sta. WIZS, Henderson, 1973-74; sec.-treas. Wake Forest Area Ministers Conf.; mem. exec. council ministers' conf. Raleigh Bapt. Assn., pres. minister's conf., 1980-81, mem. plans and program commn., migrant ministries council. chief exec. officer Cullom Bapt. Assn., 1971-73; trustee Christian Action League N.C., 1971-83; mem. bd. ministers Campbell Coll.; mem. exec. com., chmn. ethics and credentials com. Chaplain Assos. Wake County Hosp. System, pres., 1976-77. Home: PO Box 37 Rolesville NC 27571 Office: PO Box 185 Rolesville NC 27571

NEBLETT, MILTON ELMER, minister, administrator, Seventh-day Adventist; b. La Ceiba, Honduras, Jan. 21, 1924; came to U.S., 1946; s. Edwin Egbert and Lea Alberta (Douglin) N.; m. Ivy Someillan Tynes, Aug. 20, 1950; children: Edwin E., Marina E., Judith L., Milton E. Jr. B.A., Oakwood Coll., 1950; M.A., Andrews U., 1952. Ordained to ministry Seventh-day Adventist Ch., 1958. Dir. youth activities Seventh-day Adventist Conf. Guyana, S. Am., 1953-56; dir. youth and edn. Caribbean Union of Seventh-day Adventist Chs., Trinidad, W. I., 1959-62; pres. Seventh-day Adventist Conf., Guyana, 1963-66; minister Seventh-day Adventist Ch., Fontana, Calif., 1966-69; bur. dir. Adventist Devel. and Relief Agy. Internat., Washington, 1980—; rehab. counselor Los Angeles County, 1966-68; refugee relief advisor U.S. AID, Vietnam, 1969-74. Recipient medal for Disting. Social Service, Vietnam, 1973, Social Service medal, 1974. Mem. Am. Council Vol. Agys., CARE. Democrat. Home: 9904 Grant St PO Box 809 Lanham MD 20706 Office: Adventist Devel and Relief Agy 6840 Eastern Ave Takoma Park Washington DC 20012

NEDELKA, JEROME JOSEPH, priest, Episcopal Ch.; b. Flushing, N.Y., Feb. 27, 1938; s. Frank Josef and Marie (Grolich) N.; B.A., Wagner Coll., 1959; S.T.B., Phila. Div. Sch., 1965, M.Div., 1971; m. Ruth Ann Falbee, Oct. 9, 1960; children—Andrew Jerome, Nicholas Jan. Ordained priest Episcopal Ch., 1965; curate All Saints' Ch., Bayside, N.Y., 1965-67; priest-in-charge Christ the King Ch., East Meadow, N.Y., 1968—. Chmn. Commn. on Environment and Ecology, Diocese of L.I., 1970—, sec. Diocesan Council, 1974—, mem. dept. missions, 1974—, chmn. ann. Clerg. Conf., 1973-77, mem. Diocesan Planning Com., 1977—; coordinator East Meadow Clergy Fellowship, 1969—; delivered opening prayer N.Y. State Senate, 1968, Ho. of Reps., 1973. Bd. mgrs. Camp DeWolfe, 1975—. Recipient Service award East Meadow C. of C., 1976, certificate of merit for services to community K.C., 1977. Mem. L.I. Clerical League (pres. 1969-70). Home and office: 2408 5th St East Meadow NY 11554

NEE, MARY COLEMAN, coll. pres., Roman Cath. Ch.; b. Taylor, Pa., Nov. 14, 1917; d. Coleman James and Nora Ann (Hopkins) Nee; A.B., Marywood Coll., 1939, M.A., 1943; M.S., U. Notre Dame, 1959. Joined Sisters Servants of Immaculate Heart of Mary, 1941; asso. prof. mathematics Marywood Coll., 1959-68, pres. 1970—. NSF fellow, 1957-59. Mem. Am. Assn. Colls., Am. Council Edn., Nat. Cath. Edn. Assn., Pa. Assn. Colls. and Univs. Address: Marywood College Scranton PA 18509

NEECE, WILLIAM CURTIS, minister, Church of God, Anderson, Indiana; b. National City, Calif., Feb. 2, 1925; s. Andrew Walter and Mabel (Hodges) N.; m. Leta June Henrichs, May 25, 1946; children: Debra Lyn, Rene Suzette, Joletta Faye. B.A., Anderson Coll., 1950; D.D. (hon.), Gulf Coast Bible Coll., 1979. Ordained to ministry, 1948. Evangelist, Ch. of God, 1946-51; pastor First Ch. of God, Madera, Calif., 1951-53, First Ch. of God, Hutchinson, Kans., 1954-59, Sixth Ave Ch. of God, Decatur, Ala., 1959-61, First Ch. of God, Mishawaka, Ind., 1961-72, Eastland Ch. of God, Lexington, Ky., 1972-74, First Ch. of God, Kingsport, Tenn., 1975-79, Trinity Ch. of God, Huntington, W.Va., 1980—. Served with U.S. Army, 1943-46. Republican. Home: 2668 3d Ave Huntington WV 25702 Office: Trinity Church of God 2688 3d Ave Huntington WV 25702

NEELEY, MARK E., minister, Southern Baptist Convention; b. Tyler, Tex., Sept. 7, 1952; s. Morris Earl and Margaret Ann (Maynor) N.; m. Peggy Jean Matthews, Dec. 8, 1979; 1 dau., Sarah Ann. B.A., Baylor U., 1974; M.Div., Southwestern Bapt. Theol. Sem., 1977. Ordained to ministry So. Bapt. Conv., 1977. Minister of youth 1st Bapt. Ch., Hitchcock, Tex., 1974-75, assoc. pastor, 1977-80, pastor, 1980—; vice moderator Galveston Bapt. Assn., 1982-84; trustee Tex. Bapt. Encampment, 1981-83. Mem. Hitchcock Community Welfare Bd., 1980-84. Home: 707 Temple Dr Hitchcock TX 77563 Office: First Bapt Ch 6601 FM 2004 Hitchcock TX 77563

NEELY, TAYLOR DALMAINE, minister, American Baptist Association; b. Mulberry Grove, Ill., Oct. 7, 1926; s. George Lewis and Lessie Myrtle (Taylor) N.; m. Catherine Eloise Gibbs, May 28, 1948; children:

Shirley, Stephen, Timothy, Mary. B.A., So. Ill. U., 1949; M.Div., So. Bapt. Sem., 1952; S.T.M., Andover Newton Theol. Sch., 1957, D. Ministry, 1974. Ordained to ministry Am. Bapt. Assn., 1947. Missionary Am. Bapt. Fgn. Missions, Valley Forge, Pa., 1952-59; pastor Spinning Road Bapt. Ch., Dayton, Ohio, 1959-63, Rapid City Am. Bapt. Ch., S.D., 1963-71; chaplain NIMH, VA, Washington, 1971-78; chief chaplain VA, Danville, Ill., 1978—. Served with U.S. Army, 1944-46. Mem. Assn. Mental Health Clergy (cert.), Coll. Chaplains. Home: 215 Orchard Danville IL 61832 Office: VA Hosp 1900 E Main Danville IL 61832

NEELY, WILLIAM KRESWELL, campus minister, So. Baptist Conv.; b. Spartanburg, S.C., Dec. 24, 1947; s. Kirk and Louise Annah (Hudson) N.; B.A., Gardner-Webb Coll., Boiling Springs, N.C., 1971; M.Div., Southeastern Bapt. Theol. Sem., Wake Forest, N.C., 1974; m. Wanda Ellen Suddreth, Dec. 31, 1970; children—Susan Louise, William Suddreth. Ordained to ministry, 1974; youth dir. Fallston (N.C.) Bapt. Ch., 1966-67; chaplain, then chaplain coordinator Myrtle Beach (S.C.) Campground Ministry, summers 1971-72; chaplain N.C. Meml. Hosp., Chapel Hill, summer 1973; intern chaplain Bapt. Campus Ministry, U. N.C., Chapel Hill, 1973-74; staff counselor, residence hall dir. Ridgecrest (N.C.) Bapt. Conf. Center, summer 1974; asso. pastor youth and edn. First Bapt. Ch., Radford, Va., 1974-76; Bapt. campus minister Pembroke (N.C.) State U., 1976—; mem. chaplaincy service Radford Community Hosp., 1974-76. Active local Heart Fund, United Fund, Am. Cancer Soc. Recipient Bible award Gardner-Webb Coll., 1971; also awards of appreciation. Contbr. newspapers. Address: 1307 Charles Dr Laurinburg NC 28352

NEES, LAWRENCE GUY, minister, coll. pres., Ch. of Nazarene; b. Douglas, N.D., Oct. 19, 1916; s. Lawrence Gifford and Emma Myrtle (Ferguson) N.; A.B., NW Nazarene Coll., 1942; D.D., Olivet Nazarene Coll., 1955; m. Doretta Balding Wagner, Sept. 11, 1936; children—Thomas G., Ronald G., Lois Elaine, Carol Joy. Ordained to ministry, 1942; pastor chs., 1937-46, 49-64; pres. Can. Nazarene Coll., Red Deer, Alta., 1946-49; dist. supt., Los Angeles, 1964-75; pres. Mt. Vernon (Ohio) Nazarene Coll., 1975—. Contbr. articles to denominational periodicals. Home and Office: Mt Vernon Nazarene Coll Mt Vernon OH 43050

NEFF, ROBERT WILBUR See *Who's Who in America*, 43rd edition.

NEIDERHISER, FREDERICK GERALD, minister, Lutheran Church in America; b. Greensburg, Pa., Mar. 4, 1951; s. Charles Frederick and Lida Geraldine (Kabernick) N.; m. Debra Ann Jacobs, Aug. 18, 1973; children: Jonathan, Joel. B.A. in Psychology, Thiel Coll., 1973; M.Div., Luth. Theol. Sem., Gettysburg, Pa., 1977. Ordained as minister Luth. Ch. in Am., 1977. Pastor Holy Trinity Luth. Ch., Pitts., 1977-81, St. James Evang. Luth. Ch., Pitts., 1977-81, First Evang. Luth. Ch., New Kensington, Pa., 1981—; mem. Pitts. Area Mission Strategy Team, 1979-81; del. Luth. Ch. in Am. Conv., Toronto, Ont., Can., 1984. Bd. dirs. Beechview Meals on Wheels, Pitts., 1977-81, Arlington Meals on Wheels, Pitts., 1977-81. Mem. Greater New Kensington Clergy Assn., Beechview C. of C. (charter, 1st pres. 1979-81). Republican. Office: First Evang Luth Ch 221 Ridge Ave New Kensington PA 15068

NEIGHBOUR, RALPH WEBSTER, minister, Bible school president, evangelist, Baptist Ch.; b. Salisbury, N.C., July 21, 1906; s. Robert Edward and Nellie Gertrude (Planck) N.; m. Ruth May Zimmerman, June 29, 1928; children: Ralph W., David Eugene, Carol Jane Neighbour Voss. B.A., Wheaton Coll.; D.D. (hon.), Piedmonet Bible Coll., 1968. Ordained to ministry Baptist Ch., 1927. Minister First Bapt. Ch., Paw Paw, Mich., 1929-30, First Bapt. Ch., Northumberland, Pa., 1930-35, First Bapt. Ch., Elyria, Ohio, 1935-40, Ft. Wayne Gospel Temple, Ind., 1946-50, Ch. of the Open Door, Elyria, 1950-72; assoc. dir. Letourneau Evangelistic Ctr., N.Y.C., 1940-46; pres., broadcaster Ralph Neighbour Evangelistic Assn., Houston, 1949—; chaplain Northeastern Penitentiary, Lewisburg, Pa., 1930-35; radio evangelist, 1922—. Author books, novels, short stories. Editor Jour. Christian Conservative, Bapt. News. Mem. Nat. Religious Broadcasters (exec. bd. dirs., hon., Milestone award 1982), Internat. Religious Broadcasters (organizer). Republican. Home: 13851 Hollowgreen Dr Houston TX 77082 Office: Ralph Neighbour Evangelistic Assn Inc PO Box 19888 Houston TX 77224

NELSON, CHRISTOPHER PAUL, minister, Lutheran Church in America; b. Balt., Nov. 4, 1952; s. Lawrence Ernest and Mary Jane (Ostrem) N.; m. Deborah Mae Garbaugh, Aug. 23, 1980; 1 son, James Michael. B.A., Ithaca Coll., 1974; M.Div., Luth. Sem., 1981; postgrad. Christ Sem., Chgo., 1983—. Ordained to ministry, 1981. Assoc. pastor Incarnate Word Ch., Rochester, N.Y., 1981—; advisor, dir. Fellowship Luth. Youth, Rochester, 1981—; sec. bd. Luth. Campus Ministry, Rochester, 1983—; steering com. Pan Luth. Youth Gathering, Buffalo, 1983—; exec. bd. S.E. Ecumenical Ministries, Rochester, 1982-83. Contbr. articles to profl. jours. Mem. 19th Ward Community Assn., Rochester, 1984—, League Women Voters. Recipient Pres.'s award, Ithaca Coll. 1974; Hoh scholar Faculty, Luth. Sem., 1980. Democrat. Home: 105 Flanders St Rochester NY 14619 Office: The Luth Ch of Incarnate Word 597 East Ave Rochester NY 14607

NELSON, DALE CLIFFORD, minister, United Church of Christ; philosophy educator; b. Chgo., Sept. 9, 1933; s. Henry E. and Inga Marie (Rydberg) N.; m. Diana Williams, June 19, 1955 (div. 1971); m. Cynthia Dewees, Aug. 20, 1972; children: Glen Eric, Laurel Ann, Eric James, G. Keith. A.A., North Park Coll., Chgo., 1952; student North Park Theol. Sem., Chgo., 1953; B.A., Trinity Coll., Hartford, Conn., 1956; M.Div., Garrett Sch. Theology, Evanston, Ill., 1960. Ordained minister, United Meth. Ch., 1960, transferred credentials to United Ch. of Christ, 1973. Sr. minister Hinsdale Meth. Ch., Ill., 1960-68, Covenant Meth. Ch., Evanston, 1968-72; co-minister 1st Congl. Ch., Topeka, Kans., 1973-76; sr. minister Flossmoor Community Ch., Ill., 1976—; dist. dir. social concerns No. Ill. Conf. United Meth. Ch., 1963-65, chmn. com. on theology, 1968-71; adj. prof. philosophy Thornton Community Coll., South Holland, Ill., 1978—; scriptwriter nat. broadcast The Word and Music, 1962-66. Broadcaster sta. WTAQ, LaGrange, Ill., 1964-68. Author worship liturgies for adult curriculum publs., 1968, sermons for United Meth. Ch. jour., 1969. Chmn. Hinsdale Conf. on Values, 1965, Hinsdale Festival of Arts and Music, 1967. Recipient Service award Los Amigos de Las Americas, Chgo., 1983, Community Service award St. Bethel Bapt. Ch., Chicago Heights, Ill., 1984, 85. Mem. Homewood-Flossmoor Ministerial Assn. (pres. 1982), Evanston Ministerial Assn. (treas. 1970). Avocations: singing, travel, languages, gardening. Home: 2201 Travers Ln Flossmoor IL 60422 Office: Flossmoor Community Ch 2220 Carroll Pkwy Flossmoor IL 60422

NELSON, DANNY, minister, So. Bapt. Conv.; b. Mobile, Ala., May 20, 1943; s. Harold Maxie and Effie Louise (Rivers) N.; B.A., William Carey Coll., 1965; postgrad. New Orleans Bapt. Theol. Sem., 1968; m. Ann Reid, June 2, 1974; 1 dau., Kristie Marie. Ordained to ministry, 1968; pastor Mt. Sterling Bapt. Ch., Butler, Ala., 1968-71, Elam Bapt. Ch., Thomasville, Ala., 1971—. Chaplain Thomasville Adjustment Center; chmn. associational missions com. Home: Star Rt Thomasville AL 36784

NELSON, FREDERIC JUL, priest, Roman Catholic Church; b. Portland, Oreg., May 18, 1923; s. Fredrik J. and Frances Anne (Plant) N.; B.A., St. Paul Sem., 1946; Ph.D., U. Oreg., 1950. Ordained priest Roman Cath. Ch., 1950. Founder-dir. Marian Hour Radio Rosary Broadcast, 1954, Nat. Shrine of Our Lady of the Prairies, Powers Lake, N.D., 1955; supt., founder St. Olaf's Guest-Retirement Home, Powers Lake, 1962; founder, headmaster Notre Dame Acad., Powers Lake, 1960; founder, editor The Maryfaithful, bi-monthly paper, 1968, Marycords Rec. Co., 1951; singer, condr., lectr., writer. Composer: Lovely Lady Dressed in Blue, 1945; also Masses. Address: Notre Dame Acad Powers Lake ND 58773

NELSON, HARRIET, lay church worker, organist, Presbyterian Church (U.S.A.); b. Arcata, Calif., Aug. 27, 1933; d. Milton Mossler and Ernestine Mae (Colby) Abbott; m. John R. Nelson, Nov. 21, 1954; children: Kristi, Eric, Alex. A.A., Napa Coll., 1952; B.A., U. of Pacific, 1954. Active in First Presbyterian Ch., Napa, Calif., leader Bible Studies, 1976—, church organist, 1974—; active in Presbytery of the Redwoods; co-chmn. Presbytery Capitol Funds Campaign Com., 1982—; active in Synod of the Pacific, mem. council 1973-76, commn. 1972-74, mem. personnel task force 1973-76, chmn. 1975-76; active nat. level Presbyn. Ch. U.S., mem. Program Agy. Bd., 1976-79, mem. Support Agy. Tng. Resource Task Force, 1981—, mem. Nat. Exec. Com. of United Presbyn. Women, 1975-78; served under Commn. on Ecumenical Mission and Relations as a Fraternal Worker, Cameroun, West Africa, 1963-66; travelled to Japan, Korea, and Taiwan as a rep. of United Presbyn. Women and the Program Agy.; participant P.R. Listening Team sponsored by nat. exec. com. of United Presbyn. Women, 1979; moderator 196th Gen. Assembly, Presbyn. Ch. (U.S.A.). Leader English tutoring program for Hispanic women, Napa Valley; active in Meals on Wheels program, Napa/Solano area; active in Church Women United Clothing Ctr., PTA, 4-H, Scouting and community health campaigns. Office: First Presbyterian Ch 1333 3d St Napa CA 94558

NELSON, JAMES FRANK, official, Bah'i Faith, judge; b. Los Angeles, May 19, 1927; s. Franklin D. and Gertrude A. (Younkin) N.; m. Dorothy Jean Wright, Dec. 27, 1950; children: Franklin W., Lorna J. B,S., UCLA, 1950; J.D., Loyola U., Los Angeles, 1953. Bar: Calif. Mem. local assembly Baha'i Faith, Los Angeles, 1955-56, mem., chmn. Citrus Jud. Dist., 1957-69, mem., chmn., Pasadena, 1969—, mem. nat. assembly, Wilmette, Ill., 1977—, chmn., 1978—. Judge Los Angeles Mcpl. Ct., 1968—. Author: The New Comparative Religion, 1968. Referee, Los Angeles Juvenile Ct., 1965,; commr. Los Angeles Superior Ct., 1967. Served as ensign USNR, 1945-46. Mem. Am. Judicature Soc., Calif. Judges Assn. Home: 725 Arden Rd Pasadena CA 91106 Office: Los Angeles Mcpl Ct 110 N Grand Ave Los Angeles CA 90012

NELSON, LAURENCE CLYDE, minister, pastoral psychotherapist, American Baptist/Disciples of Christ; b. Milford, Del., Feb. 5, 1947; s. Leon Claire and Myrtle (Wing) N.; m. Deborah Ruth Trout, Apr. 15, 1977; children: Robert Laurence, Ryan Brooks. B.A., Ottawa U., 1970; M.Div., Central Bapt. Sem., 1972; D.Min., Eden Sem., 1979. Ordained to ministry, 1972. Pastoral assoc. Village Presbyn. Ch., Prairie Village, Kans., 1972-73; minister edn. Central Bapt. Ch., Springfield, Ill., 1973-75; minister youth and adult counseling First Bapt. Ch., Columbia, Mo., 1975-77; minister youth/counseling Webster Groves Presbyn. Ch., Mo., 1977-80; dir. dept. counseling Presbyn. Hosp., Oklahoma City, 1981—. Fellow Am. Assn. Pastoral Counselors. Club: The Courts. Home: 1909 Walking Sky Edmond OK 73034 Office: Dept Counseling 5500 N Western Suite 200 Oklahoma City OK 73118

NELSON, NORMAN AUGUSTINE, pastor, Lutheran Church in America; b. Chgo., Feb. 11, 1926; s. Olof H. and Anna Victoria (Dahlquist) N.; m. Joan Lenore Thorp, June 18, 1955; children: Beth Lenore Smayda, Ruth Deborah, Karen Eileen, Donald Lars, Karl Erik. A.B., Gustavus Adolphus Coll., 1949; M.Div., Luth. Sch. Theology, Chgo., 1953, D.Min., 1977. Pastor, Saron Luth. Ch., Chgo., 1953-61, Salem Luth. Ch., Chgo., 1961-70; sr. pastor Gloria Dei Luth. Ch., Downers Grove, Ill., 1970—; bd. dirs. Com. of Religious Leaders, Chgo. Urban League, 1962-68, Ill. Synod of Luth. Ch. in Am., 1968-74, 83—; dean western Chgo. dist. Luth. Ch. in Am., 1960-61; chairperson Synod Social Ministry Com., Chgo., 1965-68; cons. on stewardship Luth. Ch. in Am., Phila., 1982—. Bd. dirs. Augustana Coll., Rock Island, Ill., 1980-83, ARC, DuPage-Kane Counties, Ill., 1983-85. Mem. Doctoral Assocs. Chgo. Home: 1005 Grant St Downers Grove IL 60515

NELSON, PHILIP LOWELL, minister, Lutheran Church in America; b. Chgo., July 10, 1921; s. Olof H. and Anna Victoria (Dahlquist) N.; m. Eleanor Grace Danielson, Sept. 10, 1955; children: Peter Alan, John Philip, James Lowell, Mary Christine, Paul Laurence. B.Ed., Chgo. Tchrs. Coll., 1942; J.D., Northwestern U., 1949; M.Div., Augustana Theol. Sem., Rock Island, Ill., 1953. Bar: Ill. 1949; ordained to ministry Luth. Ch., 1953. Pastor Messiah Luth. Ch., Bay City, Mich., 1953-62, First Luth. Ch., Rockford, Ill., 1962-69, Faith Luth. Ch., Moline, Ill., 1969-81, Messiah Luth. Ch., Wauconda, Ill., 1981—; sec. central conf. Augustana Luth. Ch., Chgo., 1956-62; sec. Augustana Pension and Aid Fund, Mpls., 1960-61, mem. bd. 1958-61; bd. dirs. Luth. Sch. Theology at Chgo., 1961-63; sec. Ill. Synod, Luth. Ch. Am., 1962—; pres. Chs. United of Scott and Rock Island Counties, 1975; del. Luth. Ch. Am. Conv., 1984. Author: The Home Altar, 1960. Bd. dirs. Marriage and Family Counseling Service, Rockford and Moline, Ill. pres. S.W. Lake County unit Am. Cancer Soc., 1982; bd. dirs., Waukegan, Ill., 1982—. Served to 1st lt. USAAF, 1943-46; PTO. Mem. Wauconda Ministerial Assn. (pres. 1982—). Democrat. Home: 523 E Ivanhoe Rd Wauconda IL 60084 Office: Messiah Luth Ch 25225 W Ivanhoe Rd PO Box 23 Wauconda IL 60084

NELSON, RICHARD DONALD, theology educator, American Lutheran Church; b. Ft. Sill, Okla., Oct. 27, 1945; s. Donald Theodore and Ruth Elizabeth (Cornelius) N.; m. Karen Jean Frye, Aug. 13, 1967; children: Daniel, Gretchen, Erica, Johanna. B.A., Capital U., 1966; M.Div., Trinity Luth. Sem., Columbus, Ohio, 1970; Th.M., Union Theol. Sem., Richmond, Va., 1971, Ph.D., 1973. Ordained to ministry Am. Luth. Ch., 1974. Pastor Good Shepherd Ch., Pitts., 1973-77; asst. prof. Ferrum Coll., Va., 1977-81; assoc. prof. Gettysburg Sem., Pa., 1981—. Author: The Double Redaction of the Deuteronomistic History, 1981. Contbr. articles to religious mags. Mem. Soc. Bibl. Lit. Republican. Home: 145 Woodcrest Dr Gettysburg PA 17325 Office: Luth Theol Sem 66 W Confederate Gettysburg PA 17325

NELSON, RUSSELL MARION, lay church worker, Church of Jesus Christ of Latter-day Saints; surgeon; b. Salt Lake City, Sept. 9, 1924; s. Marion C. and Edna (Anderson) N.; B.A., U. Utah, 1945, M.D., 1947; Ph.D., U. Minn., 1954; Sc.D. (hon.), Brigham Young U., 1970; m. Dantzel White, Aug. 31, 1945; children: Marsha (Mrs. H. Christopher McKellar), Wendy (Mrs. Norman A. Maxfield), Gloria (Mrs. Richard A. Irion), Brenda (Mrs. Richard L. Miles), Sylvia (Mrs. David R. Webster), Emily (Mrs. Bradley E. Wittwer), Laurie (Mrs. Richard M. Marsh), Rosalie (Mrs. Michael T. Ringwood), Marjorie, Russell Marion, Jr. Mem. bishopric of Washington (D.C.) Ward, Ch. of Jesus Christ of Latter-day Saints, 1951-53, Garden Park Ward, Salt Lake City, 1957-63; mem. high council Bonneville Stake, Salt Lake City, 1963-64, pres., 1964-71; gen. pres. Sunday Sch., Ch. of Jesus Christ of Latter-day Saints 1971-79, regional rep., 1979-84, mem. Quorum of 12 Apostles, 1984—. Thoracic and cardiovascular surgeon, Salt Lake City, 1955—; mem. surg. staff LDS Hosp., U. Utah Hosp.; attending surgeon VA Hosp.; mem. courtesy staff St. Marks Hosp., Holy Cross Hosp.; dir. cardiovascular-thoracic tng. U. Utah Coll. Medicine, 1967-84, research prof. surgery, 1970—; cons. in surgery Inter-Soc. Commn. for Heart Disease Resources, 1969-72; regional chmn. Mountain

States, manpower com. on thoracic surgery Am. Assn. for Thoracic Surgery and Soc. Thoracic Surgeons, 1972-79. Bd. dirs. Internat. Cardiology Found., Promised Valley Playhouse; bd. govs., vice chmn. LDS Hosp. Recipient Distinguished Service award State of Utah, 1956, Distinguished Alumni award U. Utah, 1967, Merit award Republic of Argentina, 1974; postdoctoral research fellow Nat. Heart Inst., USPHS, 1949-50, cancer trainee Nat. Cancer Inst., 1953-55; Markle scholar in med. scis., 1957-59; Medici Publici fellow U. Utah Coll. Medicine, 1966. Diplomate Nat. Bd. Med. Examiners, Am. Bd. Surgery, Am. Bd. Thoracic Surgery (dir. 1972-78). Mem. Am. Assn. Thoracic Surgery, Am. Coll. Cardiology, Am. Coll. Chest Physicians, A.C.S. (pres. Utah chpt. 1967-68), Am. (chmn. council cardiovascular surgery 1977-79), Utah (pres. 1964-65) heart assns., AMA, Am. Soc. Artificial Internal Organs, Am., Pan Pacific, Salt Lake, Western surg. assns., Dirs. Thoracic Residencies (sec. 1967-70, pres. 1971-72), Salt Lake County Med. Soc., Societe Internationale de Chirurgie, Soc. Thoracic Surgeons, Soc. Univ. Surgeons, Soc. Vascular Surgery (sec. 1968-72, pres. 1974), Utah Med. Assn. (sec. 1964-67, pres. 1970-71), Utah Thoracic Soc., Western Soc. Clin. Research, Phi Beta Kappa, Sigma Xi, Alpha Omega Alpha, Phi Kappa Phi. Contbr. articles to profl. jours. Home: 1347 Normandie Circle Salt Lake City UT 84105 Office: 47 E South Temple Salt Lake City UT 84150

NELSON, THURLOW CHRISTIAN, priest, Episcopal Church; b. New Brunswick, N.J., June 20, 1922; s. Thurlow Christian and Dorothy (Lewis) N.; m. Joann Louise Staats, June 27, 1946; children: David, Margaret, Douglas, Anne, Dorothy, Thomas, Andrew. B.S., U. Wyo., 1947; M.S., Cornell U., 1950; M.Div., Phila. Div. Sch., 1956. Ordained to ministry, 1956. Seminarian-in-charge All Saints Ch., Wenonah, N.J. and St. Barnabas Ch., Mantua, N.J., 1954-56; vicar St. Matthew Ch. and Associated Missions, Glendive, Mont., 1956-60; asst. rector St. Luke's Episcopal Ch., Billings, Mont., 1960-66; rector Christ Episcopal Ch., Mandan, N.D., 1967—; project engr. Amoco Oil Co. Refinery, Mandan, 1968-84; mem. Diocesan Council, Diocese of Mont., 1964-66, Diocese of N.D., 1969-84; dep. Gen. Conv. Episcopal Ch., Denver, 1979; pres. Standing Com. Diocese of N.D., 1977-80, 81-84. Served with U.S. Army, 1942-46. Democrat. Lodges: Kiwanis, Lions. Home: 1103 Sunset Dr Mandan ND 58554 Office: Christ Episcopal Ch 1705 Sunset Dr Mandan ND 58554

NELSON, WAYNE FRANKLIN, minister, Church of God, Anderson, Indiana; b. Balt., June 25, 1946; s. Jimmie and Gladys Estelle (Stevens) N.; m. Fay Marie Lowry. B.A., Anderson Coll., 1969; M.R.E., Sch. Theology Anderson, 1971. Ordained to ministry, Ch. of God. Interim adminstr. Good Shepherd Sch., Barrington, N.H., 1983-84; pastor Ch. of God, Rochester, N.H., 1971—; exec. council Ch. of God, Anderson, Ind., 1983—. Mem. Evangelical Ministers Fellowship, Ministers Council of Ch. of God. N.E. Home: 2 Howe St Rochester NH 03867 Office: Church of God South Main and Howe Sts Rochester NH 03867

NEMBHARD, HAROLD EDISON, minister, director, Seventh-day Adventists; b. Siquieres, Costa Rica, Dec. 5, 1917; s. George Henry Nembhard and Ann Taylor; m. Valda A. Greene, July 28, 1943; children: Joy E. Nembhard Peters, Audre E. Nembhard Parker, Valrie A. Nembhard White. M.A., Andrews U., 1958. Pastor Seventh-day Adventists Ch., Palo Alto, Calif., 1970-73, East Oakland, Calif., 1973-76, Oakland, 1976-81; dir. black ministries Seventh-day Adventists, Pleasant Hill, Calif., 1981—; mem. minority com. Pacific Union of Seventh-day Adventists, Thousand Oaks, 1978—. Mem. N. Calif. Conf. Seventh-day Adventists (personnel com. 1979). Avocations: golf; music; swimming. Home: 2320 Lafayette Dr Antioch CA 94509 Office: Seventh-day Adventists Ch 401 Taylor Rd Pleasant Hill CA 94523

NESHEIM, OBED JOHN, minister, American Lutheran Church; b. Vernon County, Wis., Mar. 5, 1929; s. Ole John and Vera Josepha (Snartemo) N.; B.A., Luther Coll., 1950; C.T., Luther Sem., St. Paul, 1954; postgrad. Calif. Grad. Sch. Theology, Glendale, 1971-73; m. Donna Lou Hanson, Aug. 22, 1959; children: Paul, Mark. Ordained to ministry Am. Luth. Ch., 1954. Pastor, Burr Oak, Iowa 1954-57; instr. Luther Coll., Decorah, Iowa, 1957-61; sr. pastor Christ Luth. Ch., Preston, Minn., 1961-65, St. Mark's Luth. Ch., Hacienda Heights, Calif., 1965—; dean East San Gabriel conf. Am. Luth. Ch., 1971-74; founder, bd. dirs. Heights Luth. Schs., 1972—, Luth. Credit Union, 1975—. Chmn. human resources San Gabriel Valley council Boy Scouts Am., 1973-76. Home: 2130 Las Lomitas Dr Hacienda Heights CA 91745 Office: 2323 Las Lomitas Dr Hacienda Heights CA 91745

NESMITH, RICHARD DUEY See *Who's Who in America*, 43rd edition.

NESTI, DONALD SILVIO, university president, theology educator, administrator, Congregation of the Holy Ghost; b. Pitts., Jan. 3, 1936; s. Silvio and Edith Lenore (Paterra) N. B.A., St. Mary's Sem., Norwalk, Conn., 1959, B.D., 1964; S.T.L., Gregorian U., Rome, 1966, S.T.D. magna cum laude, 1970; M.A., U. Pitts., 1976. Assoc. prof. theology Duquesne U., Pitts., 1970-76, pres., 1980—; dir. planning Congregation of the Holy Ghost (U.S.A.-East), Bethel Park, Pa., 1976-77, Provincial del., 1977-80; coll. dir. Immaculate Heart of Mary, Bethel Park, 1976-80; speaker to civic and religious groups. Co-editor: Catholic and Quaker Series, 1972—. Contbr. articles to profl. jours. Mem. Consortium Council of Western Pa. Advanced Tech. Ctr., Pitts., 1983—; chmn. Pitts. Council Higher Edn., 1983-84; adv. mem. INROADS, Inc., 1983-85, People Concerned for Unborn Children, 1984-85. Named Man of Yr., Cath. War Vets., 1984. Mem. Assn. Cath. Colls. and Univs., Coll. Theol. Soc., Cath. Theol. Soc. Am., Conf. Religious Planners. Office: Duquesne U 600 Forbes Ave Pittsburgh PA 15282

NETTIFEE, THOMAS HAROLD, minister, Chs. of Christ; b. Mason City, Iowa, Dec. 7, 1948; s. Orville Dean and Audrey Lucille (Calvert) N.; B. Sacred Lit., B.Th., Ozark Bible Coll., Joplin, Mo., 1972; m. Lynne Marie Cocklin, June 19, 1971. Ordained to ministry, 1972; intern minister West Side Ch. of Christ, Des Moines, summers 1969, 70; youth minister E. Tulsa (Okla.) Christian Ch., 1969-70; minister Bronaugh (Mo.) Christian Ch., 1970-73; instr. Ozark Bible Coll., Joplin, 1971-73; minister Christ's Ch., W. Des Moines, 1973—. Chmn. bd. dirs. Christian Fellowship Iowa State U., 1974—; chmn. Iowa Christian Conv., 1975; instr. Iowa Christian Coll., Des Moines, 1975—; cons. and lectr. in field. Contbr. articles in field to religious jours. Home: 1116 Maplenol Dr West Des Moines IA 50265 Office: Box 313 West Des Moines IA 50265

NEU, MELVIN GENE, minister, Church of God, Anderson, Indiana; b. Twin Falls, Idaho, Apr. 21, 1939; s. Carl and Florence (Rudolph) N.; m. Marilyn Sharon Arnbrister, Oct. 28, 1961; children: Calvin Gene, Debra Renee. B.A., Warner Pacific Coll., 1969, postgrad. in religion, 1980—. Ordained to ministry, 1972. Youth minister Oak Park Ch. of God, Salem, Oreg., 1967-69; pastor Springfield Ch. of God, Oreg., 1969-78, First Ch. of God, Klamath Falls, Oreg., 1978-80; supt. bldg. and grounds Warner Pacific Coll., Portland, Oreg., 1980—. Republican. Address: 13836 NE Beech Ct Portland OR 97230

NEUFELD, DON FRANK, minister, Seventh-day Adventist; b. Waldheim, Sask., Can., Dec. 5, 1914; s. Jacob Diedrich and Anna (Spenst) N.; came to U.S., 1953; naturalized, 1961; B.Th., Walla Walla Coll., 1939; M.A., Seventh-day Theol. Sem., Washington, 1948; postgrad. U. Chgo., 1952, Johns Hopkins, 1966-68; D.D., Andrews U., 1972; m. Maxine Marie Berney, July 2, 1939; children—Berney Roy, Timothy Eldon, Karen Marguerite, Gwynne Kenric, Lolita Anne, Donn Ernest. Ordained to ministry, 1943; pastor, evangelist Man.-Sask. Conf., Seventh-day Adventists, 1939-46; tchr. Bibl. langs. and theology, Canadian Union Coll., Lacombe, Alta., 1946-53; asso. editor Seventh-day Adventist Bible Commentary, Review and Herald Pub. Assn., Washington, 1953-57, editor Seventh-day Adventist Bible Dictionary, Seventh-day Adventist Bible Students' Sourcebook, Seventh-day Adventist Encyclopedia, 1957-66, asso. editor Review and Herald, 1967—. Mem. Soc. Bibl. Lit. Home: 705 Langley Dr Silver Spring MD 20901 Office: 6856 Eastern Ave Washington DC 20012

NEUHAUS, RICHARD JOHN, minister, religious organization administrator, Association of Evangelical Lutheran Churches; b. Pembroke, Ont., Can., May 14, 1936; came to U.S., 1950; naturalized, s. Clemens Henry and Ella Wilhelmina Carolina (Prange) N. M.Div., Concordia Sem., St. Louis, 1960. Ordained to ministry Luth. Ch., 1960. Sr. pastor St. John the Evangelist Ch., Bklyn., 1961-78; editor Council on Religion and Internat. Affairs, N.Y.C., 1972-83; dir. Ctr. on Religion and Society, N.Y.C., 1984—. Author: Christian Faith and Public Policy, 1976; Time Toward Home, 1975; Freedom for Ministry, 1978; Naked Public Square, 1984. Recipient Journalism award Catholic Press Assn., 1967, John Paul II Religious Freedom award Catholic League for Civil Rights, 1983. Office: 152 Madison Ave New York NY 10016

NEUMAN, MATTHIAS LAURENCE, religion educator, priest, Roman Catholic Church; b. Huntingburg, Ind., Dec. 2, 1941; s. Henry Edward and Rose (Sanders) N. S.T.L., U. San Anselmo, 1969, S.T.D., 1976. Ordained priest Roman Cath. Ch., 1967. Prof. theology St. Meinrad Sch. Theology (Ind.), 1969-80; pastoral resource theologian Diocese of Nashville, 1980-82; dir. pre-theology program St. Meinrad Coll., 1982—; pres. Am. Benedictine Acad., 1984—. Contbr. articles to religious publs. Mem. Cath. Theology Soc. Am., Coll. Theology Soc. Office: St Meinrad Coll St Meinrad IN 47577

NEUSNER, JACOB, educator; b. Hartford, Conn., July 28, 1932; s. Samuel and Lee (Green) N.; A.B. magna cum laude (Coll. scholar), Harvard, 1954; postgrad. (Henry fellow) Oxford U., 1953-54; postgrad. (Sem. scholar) Jewish Theol. Sem., 1954-57; Fulbright scholar Hebrew U., Jerusalem, 1957-58; M.H.L., Jewish Theol. Sem., 1960; Ph.D., Columbia, 1960; m. Suzanne Richter, Mar. 15, 1964; children—Samuel Aaron, Eli Ephraim, Noam Mordecai Menahem, Margalit Leah Berakhah. Asst. prof. Hebrew, U. Wis., Milw., 1961-62; research asso. Brandeis U., Waltham, Mass., 1962-64; asst. prof. religion Dartmouth Coll., Hanover, N.H., 1964-66, asso. prof., 1966-68; prof. religious studies Brown U., Providence, 1968—; pres. Am. Acad. Religion, 1968-69; mem. founding com. of bd. dirs. Assn. for Jewish Studies, 1968-72. Recipient fellowships and grants from various orgns. and agys., including Am. Council Learned Socs., 1966-67, 70-71; medal for excellence Columbia U., 1974; Guggenheim fellow, 1974. Fellow Am. Acad. Jewish Research, Royal Asiatic Soc. (London); mem. Am. Soc. for Study Religion, Am. Oriental Soc. Author: A Life of Yohanan ben Zakkai (Abraham Berliner prize in Jewish history Jewish Theol. Sem. Am., 1962), 1963, rev. edit., 1970; A History of the Jews in Babylonia, I-V, 1965-70; Development of a Legend: Studies on the Traditions concerning Yohanan ben Zakkai, 1970; Way of Torah: An Introduction to Judaism, 1970, rev. edit., 1973; Aphrahat and Judaism: The Christian-Jewish Argument in Fourth Century Iran, 1971; The Rabbinic Traditions about the Pharisees before 70, I-III, 1971; There We Sat Down: Talmudic Judaism in the Making, 1972; American Judaism: Adventure in Modernity, 1972; Eliezer ben Hyrcanus: The Tradition and the Man, I-II, 1973; From Politics to Piety: The Emergence of Pharisaic Judaism, 1973; A History of the Mishnaic Law of Purities, I-XXII, 1974-77. Editor: Religions in Antiquity: Essays in Memory of Erwin Ramsdell Goodenough, 1968; Formation of the Babylonian Talmud: Studies in the Achievements of Late Nineteenth and Twentieth Century Historical and Literary-Critical Research, 1970; Contemporary Judaic Fellowship, in Theory and in Practice, 1972; The Modern Study of the Mishnah, 1973; Understanding Jewish Theology: Classical Themes and Modern Perspectives, 1973; Understanding Rabbinic Judaism: From Talmudic to Modern Times, 1974. Contbr. to publs. in field. Home: 70 Vassar Ave Providence RI 02906

NEVINS, JOHN J., bishop, Roman Catholic Church. Aux. bishop, Miami, Fla., first bishop, Venice, Fla., 1984—. Office: Archdiocese of Miami 6301 Biscayne Blvd Miami FL 33138*

NEWELL, BRYCE FRANKLIN, minister, Seventh-Day Adventist Ch.; b. Hope, N.D., Nov. 15, 1922; s. Ira Thomas and Ruby C. (Cross) N.; m. Nellie J. Stewart, Dec. 28, 1947; children: Anita D. Newell Mayberry, Judy P. Newell Anderson. B.A., Walla Walla Coll., 1950; B.D., Andrews U., 1968; M.P.H., Loma Linda U., 1980. Ordained to ministry Seventh-Day Adventist Ch., 1964. Bible tchr. Hawaiian Mission Acad., Honolulu, 1968-69; prin. Tacoma Jr. Acad., Wash., 1969-72, Beacon Jr. Acad., Lewiston, Idaho, 1972-75; pastor Coville Seventh-Day Adventist Ch., Wash., 1975-78; assoc. pastor Pendleton Seventh-Day Adventist Ch., Oreg., 1978—. Served with U.S. Army, 1942-45; ETO. Home: 4218 SW Vista Ave Pendleton OR 98701

NEWELL, LUTHER CALHOUN, JR., minister, So. Bapt. Conv.; b. Brookhaven, Miss., May 10, 1945; s. Luther Calhoun and Mildred Alene (Bankston) N.; A.A., Gulf Coast Jr. Coll., 1965; B.S., U. So. Miss., 1967; Th.M., New Orleans Bapt. Theol. Sem., 1971; m. Mary Jane Weathersby, Sept. 13, 1969; children—Laura Jane, Mary Jodie. Ordained to ministry, 1971; pastor chs., Miss., Tex., 1970-73; pastor 1st Bapt. Ch., New Augusta, Miss., 1973-76; Sunday sch. dir. Perry County Bapt. Assn., 1975-76, pastor Richland (Miss.) Bapt. Ch., 1976— Liaison, Christian social ministries dep., home mission bd. So. Bapt., Conv., 1974. Home: Florence MS 39073 Office: Richland Baptist Church Richland MS 39218

NEWELL, PHILIP RUTHERFORD, minister, nondenominational; b. Chgo., June 13, 1902; s. William Reed and Millicent Medora (Woodworth) N.; m. Frances Evelyn Furst, Oct. 11, 1924 (dec. Feb. 1964); children: Martha Newell Coleman, Philip Rutherford, Richard Furst; m. Florine Danielly, Dec. 27, 1969. B.A., U. Mich., 1924. Ordained to ministry Ind. Chs. Am., 1943. Assoc. pastor Berkley Community Ch., Mich., 1943-46; sales mgr. Moody Press, Chgo., 1946-47; dir. Corr. Sch., Moody Bible Inst., Chgo., 1947-51, dean student affairs, 1951-56, mem. extension dept. staff, 1956-70; gen. dir. Gt. Commn. Prayer League, Leesburg, Fla., 1971-85, gen. dir. emeritus, 1971—. Author: Light Out Of Darkness, 1948; Daniel And His Prophecies, 1950; Revival On God's Terms, 1954. Mem. Berkley City Council, 1944-46. Republican. Avocations: antique automobiles; railroads. Home: 100 E Oak Terrace Dr Apt F-1 Leesburg FL 32748 Office: Gt Commn Prayer League PO Box 360 Leesburg FL 32748

NEWELL, WILLIAM JAMES, religious organization executive, Christian and Missionary Alliance in Canada; b. Belfast, No. Ireland, July 9, 1922; came to Can., 1930; s. James Alexander and Catharine (Small) N.; m. Pearl Ferguson, July 8, 1944; children: Darlane Jesperson, Heather Killgore, Philip, Japhia Cowling. Grad. studies in pastoral theology, Nyack Coll., 1949; D.D. (hon.), Coronation Coll. (Ont.), 1982. Ordained to ministry Christian and Missionary Alliance in Can., 1949. Minister Christian and Missionary Alliance,

Oshawa and Toronto, Ont., 1949-60, eastern and central Can. dist. supt., Toronto, 1960-73; exec. dir. World Vision Can., Mississauga, Ont., 1973—; founder, co-chmn. Can. Assn. Christian Humanitarian Agys., Toronto; council mem. Evang. Fellowship Can., Toronto; corp. mem. Ont. Bible Coll./Ont. Theol. Sem., Toronto; bd. dirs. Africa Emergency Aid Com., Ottawa. Author: O God, Won't Somebody Help?, 1982. Editor: Reaching Canada's Unreached, 1983. Served with Royal Can. Navy, 1942-45. Office: World Vision Canada 6630 Turner Valley Rd Mississauga ON L5N 2S4 Canada

NEWENHUYSE, FREDERICK JACOB, minister, United Church of Christ; b. Kenosha, Wis., Apr. 12, 1947; s. Jacob Francis and Beatrice Holmquist (Congdon) N.; m. Elizabeth Lee Cody, Nov. 25, 1978. B.A., Harvard U., 1969; M.Div., North Park Theol. Sem., 1980. Ordained to ministry United Ch. of Christ, 1980. Asst. minister St. Paul's United Ch. Christ, Elgin, Ill., 1978-80; minister St. Paul's United Ch. Christ, Franklin Park, Ill., 1980—; vol. chaplain Westlake Hosp., Melrose Park, Ill., 1984—; mem. Franklin Park Ministerium, 1980—; chaplain Clin. Pastoral Edn. Program Luth. Gen. Hosp., Park Ridge, Ill., 1978. Mem. Community Renewal Soc. Democrat. Club: Harvard (Chgo.). Office: St Pauls United Ch Christ 3342 Calwagner Franklin Park IL 60131

NEWHALL, JEFFREY ROBERT, minister, American Baptist Churches in the U.S.A.; b. Washington, July 14, 1946; s. Robert Moody and Shirley Emily (Raw) N.; m. Sarah Elisabeth Studenmund, Sept. 27, 1971; children: Sarah Elisabeth, Jeremiah Robert. B.A., George Washington U., 1969; M.A., Hartford Sem., 1972, M.Div., 1972; D.Min., Andover Newton Theol. Sch., 1975. Ordained to ministry Baptist Ch., 1972. Sem. assoc. Central Bapt. Ch., Hartford, Conn., 1969-72, assoc. minister, 1972-73; assoc. pastor First Calvary Bapt. Ch., Lawrence, Mass., 1974-78; chaplain Lawrence Gen. Hosp., Mass., 1976-78; sr. minister Palisades Ch., Washington, 1978—; mem. theology commn. Consultation on Ch. Union, Princeton, N.J., 1981—; mem. faith and order commn. Nat. Council Community Churches, 1982—. Wells fellow Hartford Sem., 1972. Mem. Coll. of Chaplains. Democrat. Office: Palisades Community Ch 5200 Cathedral Ave NW Washington DC 20016

NEWKIRK, SHELDON LOWELL, minister, Religious Society of Friends; b. Pond Creek, Okla., Mar. 26, 1912; s. Fred Raymond and Maymie Ann (Pierson) N.; B.A., Friends U., 1933; postgrad Sem., Hunting Park, Calif., 1934-35, Western Evang. Sem., 1960, 67, 68; m. Gladys Melba Norman, July 2, 1933 (dec. Mar. 1975); children: Fred Howard, Charles Sheldon, Jonathan Raymond; m. Marjorie Otis Hadley, July 17, 1977. Ordained to ministry Calif. Yearly Meeting Religious Soc. Friends, 1936. Minister Yorba Linda (Calif.) Friends Ch., 1935-42, Long Beach (Calif.) Bethel Friends Ch., 1942-47, Orland (Calif.) Capay Rancho Friends Ch., 1948-52, Melba (Idaho) Friends Ch., 1952-57, Fowler (Kans.) Friends Ch, 1957-60, Yorba Linda, 1961-67, Portland (Oreg.) Piedmont Friends InterCities Ministry, 1969-80; minister visitation 1st Friends Ch., Vancouver, Wash., 1982—; supt. S.W. Wash. area Religious Soc. Friends, 1982—, Grace Collins Inner City Ministries, Portland, 1981—; dir. Reedwood Soc. Friends 50 Plus Club, 1980—. Mem. adminstrv. staff George Fox Coll., Newberg, Oreg., 1969-72. Mem. Friends Action Bd., 1970-76; mem. social concerns bd. NW Yearly Meeting Soc. of Friends, 1976-82. Mem. Minority People Ministries (v.p. 1970-71). Home: 1501 N Hayden Island Dr Apt 104E Portland OR 97217 Office: 2710 NE 65th Ave Vancouver WA 98661

NEWMAN, ERNEST W., bishop, United Methodist Church, Memphis and Tenn. Conf. Office: 575 Lambuth Blvd Jackson TN 38301*

NEWMAN, LARRY VERN, minister, Assemblies of God; b. Wenatchee, Wash., Aug. 11, 1937; s. Winfred Vern and Ethel May (Morgan) N.; B.A., N.W. Coll., 1962; M.Div., U. Dubuque, 1974; D.Min., Fuller Theol. Sem., 1983; m. Bertha Marlena Green, Dec. 31, 1956; children: Rilla, Michael, Karl, Kurt, Scott, Karen. Ordained to ministry Assemblies of God, 1966. Asst. pastor Beacon Assembly of Good, Seattle, 1961-62; pastor The Neighborhood Ch., Scottsbluff, Nebr., 1962-64; dir. Maranatha Ministries, Inc., Kirkland, Wash., 1969-74; pastor Harmony United Ch. of Christ, Zwingle, Iowa, 1972-74, Peace Ch., Monticello, Iowa, 1974-76, Community Ch., Brewster, Wash., 1978-80; exec. dir. Maranatha Ministries, Wenatchee, Wash., 1974—; prof. pastoral ministries and apologetics Open Bible Coll., Des Moines, 1984—. Dir. Teenanymous Youth Crisis Clinic, Kirkland, Wash., 1971-72; mem. coop. parish council, Monticello, 1974-76; mem. Jones County (Iowa) Food Bank, 1974-76; mem. Meals On Wheels Com., Monticello, 1975-76. Mem. Monticello Ministerial Assn., Soc. for Pentecostal Studies. Author: The Ultimate Evidence, forthcoming. Contbr. articles to religious jours. Office: 2633 Fleur Dr Des Moines IA 50321

NEWMAN, LOUIS ELIOT, Judaic Studies and religion educator; b. St. Paul, July 10, 1956; s. Marion Eliot and Annette Donna (Shedorsky) N.; m. Rosanne Gail Zaidenweber, Sept. 3, 1978. B.A. in Hebrew and Philosophy magna cum laude, U. Minn., 1976, M.A. in Philosophy, 1979; Ph.D. in Judaic Studies, Brown U., 1983. Asst. prof. religion, Carleton Coll., Northfield, Minn., 1983—. Author: The Sanctity of the Seventh Year, 1983. Contbr. articles in field. Brown U. fellow, 1980. Mem. Am. Acad. Religion, Soc. Bibl. Lit., Acad. Jewish Philosophy, Assn. for Jewish Studies, European Assn. Jewish Studies, Phi Beta Kappa, Phi Kappa Phi. Home: 4833 Dupont Ave S Minneapolis MN 55409 Office: Carleton Coll Dept Religion Northfield MN 55057

NEWMAN, ROBERT CARL, minister, General Association of Regular Baptist Churches; b. Hornell, N.Y., Jan. 3, 1936; s. Charles Pomeroy and Leola (Ebersole) N.; m. Betty Jane Rigby, June 15, 1957; children: Barbara, Charles, Donna, Roberta. B.Th., Bapt. Bible Sem., 1959; B.A., Houghton Coll., 1963; M.A., Wheaton Coll., 1971. Ordained to ministry, 1959. Pastor Bapt. chs., N.Y., 1959-69, First Bapt. Ch., Ticonderoga, N.Y., 1965-69, Faith Bapt. Ch., Winfield, Ill., 1969-80, Tabernacle Bapt. Ch., Ithaca, N.Y., 1980—; sec. Council of Ten, Empire State Fellowship of Regular Bapt. Chs., Owego, 1982-84. Contbg. author: The New International Dictionary of the Christian Church, 1974, rev. edit., 1978. Author: Baptists and the American Tradition, 1976. Home: 260 Westwood Knoll Ithaca NY 14850 Office: Tabernacle Bapt Ch 1019 N Cayuga St Ithaca NY 14850

NEWMAN, ROBERT CHAPMAN, educator, Bible Fellowship Church; b. Washington, Apr. 2, 1941; s. Allan L.C. and Lois May (Gardner) N. B.S. in Physics, Duke U., 1963; Ph.D. in Astrophysics, Cornell U., 1967; M.Div., Faith Theol. Sem., 1970; S.T.M. in Old Testament, Bibl. Theol. Sem., 1975. Assoc. prof. math. and sci. Shelton Coll., Cape May, N.J., 1968-71; assoc. prof. N.T., Bibl. Theol. Sem., Hatfield, Pa., 1971-77, prof. N.T., 1977—; dir. Interdisciplinary Bibl. Research Inst., Hatfield, 1981—; bd. dirs. Windward Ministries, Hatfield, 1977—. Co-author: Science Speaks, 3d edit., 1969, 4th edit., 1976; Genesis One to the Origin of the Earth, 1977, 2d edit., 1981; contbr. articles to sci. and religious publs. Bd. dirs. Pinebrook Jr. Coll., Coopersburg, Pa., 1984—. Woodrow Wilson hon. fellow, 1963-64; NSF fellow, 1963-67; A.D. White hon. fellow, 1963-64; A.B. Duke regional scholar, 1959-63. Fellow Am. Sci. Affiliation; mem. Evang. Theol. Soc. Republican. Home: 115 S Main St Hatfield PA 19440 Office: Bibl Theol Sem 200 N Main St Hatfield PA 19440

NEWMAN, WILLIAM C., bishop, Roman Catholic Church. Titular bishop of Numluli, aux. bishop, Balt., 1984—. Office: 320 Cathedral St Baltimore MD 21201*

NEWPORT, JOHN PAUL, educator, minister, So. Bapt. Conv.; b. Buffalo, Mo., June 16, 1917; s. Marvin Jackson and Mildred Dupont (Morrow) N.; B.A., William Jewell Coll., 1938, Litt.D., 1967; Th.M., So. Bapt. Theol. Sem., 1941, Th.D., 1946; M.A., Tex. Christian U., 1968; Ph.D., U. Edinburgh, 1953; m. Eddie Belle Leavell, Nov. 14, 1941; children—Martha (Mrs. Nicholas Bailey), Frank Marvin, John Paul. Ordained to ministry, 1939; minister Miss. and Okla. chs., 1943-49; asst. prof. religion, dir. grad. studies in religion Baylor U., 1949-51; prof. N.T. and philosophy of religion New Orleans Bapt. Theol. Sem., 1951-52; prof. philosophy of religion Southwestern Bapt. Theol. Sem., Ft. Worth, 1952-76; prof. religious studies Rice U., 1976-79, v.p. acad. affairs, provost, 1979—; dir. field work Boston U. Sch. Theology, 1958-59. Postdoctoral vis. fellow Harvard, 1958-59, Union Theol. Sem., N.Y.C., 1965; Seatlantic fellow Rockefeller Found., 1958-59. Mem. Am. Acad. Religion (pres. southwestern region 1964), Southwestern Philos. Assn., Am. Soc. Ch. History. Author: Theology and Contemporary Art Forms, 1971; Demons, Demons, Demons, 1972; Why Christians Fight Over the Bible, 1974; Christ and the New Consciousness, 1979; Paul Tillich, 1984; What Is Christian Doctrine, 1984; The Lion and the Lamb, 1985. Home: 4421 Dunwick Fort Worth TX 76109

NEWSOME, JAMES MARION, JR., minister, Southern Baptist Convention; b. Augusta, Ga., Mar. 1, 1944; s. James Marion and Jenelle (Cofer) N.; B.A., Mercer U., Macon, Ga., 1967; M.R.E., So. Baptist Theol. Sem., Louisville, 1970, grad. specialist in religious edn., 1971; m. Karan Ann Huddleston, Dec. 28, 1968; children—James Marion, Mindy Kathryn, Carolyn Elizabeth. Youth dir. chs. in Ga. and Ky., 1966, 69-71; ordained to ministry, 1972; minister edn. and youth Hartwell (Ga.) First Bapt. Ch., 1971-76; minister edn. First Bapt. Ch., Vero Beach, Fla., 1976—; spl. worker Fla. Bapt. Conv., 1978—. Pres. Ga. Bapt. Religious Edn. Assn., 1975-76. Recipient Outstanding Religions Leader award Vero Beach Jaycees, 1979-80. Address: 2235 16th Ave Vero Beach FL 32960

NEYLON, MARTIN JOSEPH See *Who's Who in America*, 43rd edition.

NG, DAVID, minister, Presbyterian Church USA; b. San Francisco, Sept. 1, 1934; s. Hing and Chin Shee (Chin) N.; m. Irene Young, June 15, 1958; children: Stephen Paul, Andrew Peter. B.A., Westminster Coll., 1956; M.Div., San Francisco Theol. Sem., 1959; D.D. (hon.), Westminster Coll., 1966. Ordained to ministry, 1959. Collegiate pastor Presbyn. Ch. in Chinatown, San Francisco, 1959-62; pastor Mendocino Presbyn. Ch., Calif., 1962-66; sec. for youth resources Bd. Christian Edn., Presbyn. Ch. USA, 1966-75; assoc. prof. ch. program and nurture, Austin Presbyn. Theol. Sem., Tex., 1975-81; assoc. gen. sec. for edn. and ministry Nat. Council Chs. of Christ in U.S.A., N.Y.C., 1981—; bd. dirs., exec. com. Geneva Point Ctr., Centre Harbor, N.H., 1981—, Conf. Point Camp, Williams Bay, Wis., 1981—. Author: Developing Leaders in Youth Ministry, 1984; Youth in the Community of Disciples, 1984; (with V. Thomas) Children in the Worshipping Community, 1981. Contbr. articles to profl. jours. Mem. Mendocino County Grand Jury, Ukiah, Calif., 1966. Mem. Assn. Profs. and Researchers in Religious Edn., Religious Edn. Assn. (dir., exec. com.), Soc. Profs. of Ch. Adminstrn. Democrat. Office: Div Edn and Ministry Nat Council Chs of Christ USA 475 Riverside Dr Rm 704 New York NY 10115-0050

NICHOLAS, DAVID ROBERT, minister, educator, General Association of Regular Baptists; b. Los Angeles, May 10, 1941; s. Robert Grant and Pearl Elizabeth (Pickard) N.; m. Donna Lynn Roberts, June 28, 1969; children: Joy Lynn, Faith Elizabeth. B.A., Los Angeles Pacific Coll., 1963; M.S., U. So. Calif., 1967; M.Div., Los Angeles Bapt. Theol. Sem., 1966; Th.M., Talbot Theol. Sem., 1971; Th.D., Grace Theol. Sem., 1982. Ordained to ministry General Association Regular Baptists, 1970. Faculty, dir. admissions Los Angeles Bapt. Coll., Newhall, Calif., 1966-71; pres., dean Van Nuys Christian Coll. of First Bapt. Ch., Van Nuys, Calif., 1972-76; pastor Tri-Lakes Bapt. Ch., Columbia City, Ind., 1977-78; dean, assoc. prof. Southwestern Bapt. Bible Coll., Phoenix, 1978-80; sr. pastor, acad. supt. Grace Bapt. Ch., Yuba City, Calif., 1980-82; sr. pastor Placerita Bapt. Ch., Newhall, 1982—; trustee Christian Heritage Coll., El Cajon, Calif., 1981—, Regular Bapt. Conf. of So. Calif., 1983—; bd. dirs. Bapt. Youth Assn. of So. Calif., 1969-71; Broadcaster Family Life Radio Network, Phoenix, 1978-80. Author: What's A Woman to Do . . . In the Church?, 1979; Foundations of Biblical Inerrancy, 1978. Contbr. articles to religious publs. Gov. Am. Coalition for Traditional Values, Washington, and San Diego, 1984; chaplain Los Angeles County Bd. Suprs., 1983. Mem. Evang. Theol. Soc., Assn. Governing Bds. of Univs. and Colls., Calif. Scholarship Fedn. (gold seal mem. 1959), Internat. Council for Bibl. Inerrancy, Kappa Tau Epsilon. Republican. Home: 22020 W Placerita Canyon Rd Newhall CA 91321

NICHOLLS, CHARLES GEOFFREY WILLIAM, educator; b. Hitchin, England, Oct. 10, 1921; s. Albert Charles and Kathleen (Thornton) N.; B.A., Cambridge U., 1947, M.A., 1949; m. Hilary McCallum, July 15, 1950; children—Elizabeth Helen, Paul Charles Alexander, Felicity Kathleen Mary. Ordained to ministry Ch. of England, 1953; asst. curate, Ch. of England, Wendover, Bucks, Eng., 1952-54; chaplain to Anglican students Edinburgh Episcopal Ch., Scotland, 1955-60; traveling sec. World's Student Christian Fedn., Geneva, 1949-51; faculty U.B.C., Vancouver, B.C., Can. since 1961—, prof. religious studies 1961—, head. dept. religious studies since 1964—. Mem. Canadian Soc. for the Study of Religion, Am. Acad. Religion, Soc. for the Scientific Study of Religion. Author: Ecumenism and Catholicity, 1952; Systematic and Philosophical Theology, 1969; (with Ian Kent) I AMness: The Discovery of the Self beyond the Ego, 1972. Editor: Conflicting Images of Man, 1966; editor-in-chief Studies in Religion, 1970-73. Home: 3670 W 34th Ave Vancouver BC V6N 2L1 Canada Office: Dept Religious Studies University British Columbia Vancouver BC V6T 1W5 Canada

NICHOLS, ALBERT MYRON, minister, United Presbyterian Church in U.S.A.; b. Creston, Iowa, Oct. 17, 1914; s. Albert Maurice and Lou (Myers) N.; A.B., U. Calif., Los Angeles, 1936; B.S., San Francisco Theol. Sem., 1940; D.D., Occidental Coll., 1952; m. Phyllis Cochran, June 28, 1939; children: Byron Albert, Phillip Garrett. Ordained to ministry, 1940; pastor, North Hollywood, Calif., 1940-43; assoc. pastor Pasadena (Calif.) Presbyn. Ch., 1943-57; pastor 1st Presbyn. Ch., Pendleton, Oreg., 1957-82. Moderator, Oreg. Synod, 1968,69; stated clk. Eastern Oreg. Presbytery, 1975—; chmn. gen. assembly com. on responsible marriage and parenthood United Presbyn. Ch. in U.S.A., 1959-62, mem. Bd. Christian Edn., 1969-72; mem. mission council Synod of Pacific; founding bd. dirs. Presbyn. Intercommunity Hosp., Whittier, Calif., 1969-76; trustee San Francisco Theol. Sem., 1963-84. Mem. Pendleton City Recreation Commn., 1965—; pres. Pasadena Child Guidance Clinic, 1955-57. Life trustee Lewis & Clark Coll., Portland; chmn. capital improvements commn., Pendleton, 1983—. Editor/publisher, Clarion, Pasadena, 1943-57, Pendleton Circuit Rider, 1957—. Named First Citizen of Pendleton, 1984. Home: 1013 NW 12th St Pendleton OR 97801

NICHOLS, DOROTHY LORRINE, minister, Assemblies of God; b. Mobile County, Ala., Nov. 9, 1939; d. William Franklin and Erma Ruth (Cabler) N.; student Lee Coll., Cleve., 1962, Spring Hill Coll., Mobile, Ala., 1963. Ordained to ministry, 1973; youth minister Krafton Ch. of God, Mobile, 1964-66; pastor Norton Ave. Assembly of God, Saraland, Mobile, 1970-76; monthly speaker Golden Age Clubs, Chickasaw, Saraland, Ala., Oakridge Nursing Home, Mobile; apptd. Registrar's com. Dist. council of Ala. Assemblies of God. Contbr. articles to religious jours. Home: 310 Bryant Ct Saraland AL 36571 Office: 611 Norton Ave Saraland AL 36571

NICHOLS, EDWARD K., JR., minister; lawyer; b. Atlanta, Aug. 10, 1918; s. Edward K. and Laura (Drake) N.; m. Kathryn Bough, Aug. 9, 1943 (div. 1948); 1 dau., Charlotte A.; m. Ethel Williams, Jan. 30, 1955; children: Carolyn H., Eloise M., Laura L. A.B., Lincoln U., 1941; J.D., Howard U., 1950. Student Temple U. Sch. of Theology, 1957-58. Ordained to ministry African Meth. Episcopal Ch., 1960. Assoc. minister Greater St. Matthew Ind. Ch., Phila., 1956-74, pastor, 1975—. Ptnr. Nichols & Nichols, Phila., 1951—. Vice pres. Council of Black Clergy, Phila., 1980-84; treas. Stewart Scholarship Found., Phila., 1978—. Served to 1st lt. USAF, 1942-45. Democrat. Home: 6115 Cobbs Creek Pkwy Philadelphia PA 19143 Office: Greater St Matthew Ch Race and Vodges Sts Philadelphia PA 19139 also: Nichols & Nichols 1600 Robinson Bldg Philadelphia PA 19102

NICHOLS, FRANCIS WILLIAM, theology educator, Roman Catholic Church; b. St. Paul, Aug. 3, 1930; s. Francis Wilber and Genevieve C. (Hoffmann) N.; m. Jane Therese Gillespie, June 19, 1969; children: Gregory, Matthew, Genevieve. M.A., St. Mary's Coll., 1955; M.A., Loyola U., Chgo., 1959; L.S.R., Lateran U., Rome, 1964; D.es Th., Strasbourg, France, 1969. Tchr., Christian Bros. Schs., Chgo., Memphis, 1952-61; asst. prof. Christian Bros. Coll., Memphis, 1964-67; asst. prof., assoc. prof. St. Louis U., 1969—. Author: What Puzzled Parents Can Do About Kids and Confession, 1981, Make Mass Mean More for Your Family, 1982. Contbr. articles to profl. jours. Mem. Cath. Theol. Soc. Am., Am. Acad. Religion. Home: 7194 Delmar Blvd University City MO 63160 Office: St Louis Univ 3634 Lindell Blvd Saint Louis MO 63108

NICHOLS, R(ODNEY) RALPH, minister, United Church Christ; b. Pratt, Kans., Apr. 26, 1935; s. Ralph McClard and Lois Elizabeth (Briggs) N.; A.B., U. Mo., 1957, M.A., 1969, Ph.D., 1974; B.D., Andover Newton Theol. Sem., 1963, m. Edith Louise Andrews, July 22, 1956; children: Anita A., Timothy A. Ordained to ministry United Ch. Christ, 1963. Pastor chs. in Minn. and Mo., 1962-74; pastor First Congl. United Ch. Christ, Ft. Worth, 1974—; adj. asst. prof. philosophy Tex. Christian U., 1976—; field supr. Brite Div. Sch., Ft. Worth, 1976—; denominational rep. Tex. United Campus Christian Life Com., 1975—; pres. South Central Conf., United Ch. of Christ, 1979-81. Mem. Southwestern Philos. Soc., Delta Sigma Rho. Author articles, sermons. Home: 5658 Woodway St Fort Worth TX 76133 Office: 3563 Manderly Pl Fort Worth TX 76109

NICHOLS, RICHARD GAY, lay worker Church of God and United Methodist Church; b. Kendleville, Ind., Feb. 27, 1934; s. Audley George and Dorothy Mae (Dingman) N.; m. Carol Ann Jacob, Aug. 22, 1953; children: Christine, Ricky, Martin, Gordon. Youth leader Ch. of God, Colon, Mich., 1971-75, minister, Three Rivers, Mich., 1975-79; lay minister United Meth. Ch., Colon, Mich., 1980—, lay leader, 1980—; lay del. Ch. of God, Colon, 1970-75, treas., 1971-73, trustee, 1972-74. Served with U.S. Army, 1955-57, Korea. Mem. Nat. Campers and Hikers Assn. (pres. Colon 1968-69). Home: 59502 Long Lake Rd #43 Colon MI 49040

NICHOLS, ROBERT CLARENCE, lay church worker, United Methodist Church; b. Akron, Ohio, Nov. 10, 1906; s. Robert Thomas and Zady Dell (Cox) N.; B.S., U. Akron, 1928; m. Gladys Viola Atwell, June 11, 1931; children: Marjorie (Mrs. John W. Baxter), Robert H., John. Lay leader First United Meth. Ch., Cuyahoga Falls, Ohio, 1951-57, 64-67, 72-79, chmn. ch. bldg. fund drive, 1951, chmn. pastor-parish com., 1958-62, 71-72; lay leader Akron Dist. United Meth. Ch., 1973-78, Conf. disaster coordinator, 1973-77; del. World Meth. Conf., 1976; pres. Akron dist. United Meth. Men, 1978—; trustee Meth. Theol. Sch. Ohio, 1965—, Vice chmn. bd. dirs. and sec. Falls Savs. & Loan Assn., Cuyahoga Falls, 1968-78. Active Boy Scouts Am., 1955-56, 61-63; pres. Izaak Walton League, 1959-62; pres. Friends of Library Cuyahoga Falls, 1970—; sec.-treas. Ohio Friends of Library, 1974-79. pres. Goodwill Industries Greater Akron, 1974-75; hon. sec.-treas. Ohio Friends of Library, 1979—; trustee Taylor Meml. Pub. Library, 1980—; bd. dirs. Ohio Library Found., 1980—. Recipient Silver Beaver award Boy Scouts Am., 1963, Community Service award Ohio Bell Tel., 1965, Council Service Clubs, 1969, Citizen's award Ohio Library Assn., 1977. Mem. Tau Delta Beta. Home: 2337 17th St Cuyahoga Falls OH 44223

NICHOLSON, CHRIS EDWARD, minister of music, Independent Baptist Church; b. Everett, Wa., Aug. 9, 1949; s. George Edward and Shirley June (Milner) N.; m. Debra Margene Hill, Dec. 16, 1972. Student Western Baptist Coll., 1967-72. Minister of music, tchr. Grace Bapt. Ch. and Schs., Redding, Calif., 1973-77, North Valley Bapt. Ch., 1980—; music dir. Light Ministries, Redding, 1978-80. Condr. civic concerts, 1973-80; dir. record albums, 1978-84. Avocations: fishing; electronics; sound reinforcement; gardening. Office: North Valley Bapt Ch 2960 Hartnell Ave Redding CA 96002

NICHOLSON, ROBERT ARTHUR, religious educator, college president, Church of God (Anderson, Ind.); b. Pepin, Wis., Oct. 13, 1923; s. Arthur W. and Ethel E. (Weeden) N.; m. Dorothy June Nelis, June 17, 1944; children: Paul M., Gary A. B.S., Anderson Coll., 1944; M.A., NYU, 1946, Ph.D., 1953. Ordained to ministry Ch. of God, 1952. From instr. to prof. Anderson Coll., Ind., 1945-58, v.p. and dean, 1958-83, pres., 1983—; mem./officer publ. bd. Ch. of God, 1954-79; chmn. commn. on Christian higher edn., 1963-84. Author: Handbook to the Hymnal of the Church of God, 1953. Editor: Hymnal of the Church of God, 1953, 2d edit., 1971. Bd. dirs. Anderson Symphony Orch., 1975—. Mem. Assoc. Colls. Ind. (bd. dirs. 1983—), Fellowship of Evang. Sem. Pres., Christian Coll. Coalition (pres.'s council). Republican. Club: Anderson Country. Lodge: Rotary (Anderson). Home: 1240 E 3d St Anderson IN 46012 Office: Anderson College Anderson IN 46012

NICKEL, JAMES RICHARD, priest, Roman Catholic Ch.; b. Bklyn., Nov. 8, 1943; s. Irwin Martin and Jeanette Eugenia (Bucher) N.; B.A. in Philosophy, Queen of Peace Sem., Jaffrey, N.H., 1966; degree theology Washington Theol. Coalition, 1969. Ordained deacon, 1969, priest, 1970; deacon chs. in Tex. and Mass., 1969-70; dir. missionary coop. program Sacred Hearts Community, Fairhaven, Mass., 1970; prof. theology, Latin Bishop Amat High Sch., LaPuente, Calif., 1970-71; dir. Office Vocations, Winona, Minn., 1971-72; asso. pastor Holy Trinity Parish, W. Harwich, Mass., 1972—; chaplain Harwich Fire Dept., 1973. Mem. senate of priests Roman Cath. Diocese Fall River, Mass., 1973-75, sec. senate, 1974-75; mem. formation commn. Sacred Hearts Sem., Washington, 1974; advisory bd. communication office Sacred Hearts Community, Wareham, Mass., 1976. Bd. dirs. Harwich Youth Center, Harwich Meals on Wheels. Address: Holy Trinity Ch West Harwich MA 02671

NICKELSBURG, GEORGE WILLIAM ELMER, JR., religion educator, minister, Association of Evangelical Lutheran Churches; b. San Jose, Calif., Mar. 15, 1934; s. George William Elmer and Elsie Louise (Schwab) N.; m. Marilyn Luce Miertschin, Aug. 28, 1965; children: Jeanne Marie, Michael John. Student Concordia Jr. Coll., Bronxville, N.Y., 1951-53; B.A., Valparaiso U., 1955; postgrad. Washington U., St. Louis, 1956-57; B.D., Concordia Sem., St. Louis, 1960, S.T.M., 1962; postgrad. Am. Sch. Oriental Research, Jerusalem, 1963-64; Th.D., Harvard, 1968. Ordained to ministry Luth. Ch.-Mo. Synod, 1966. Pastor Good Shepherd Luth. Ch., Akron, Ohio, 1966-69; asst. prof., assoc. prof., then prof. Sch. Religion, U. Iowa, Iowa City, 1969—; vis. scholar Institum Judaicum Delitzschianum, Munster, Fed. Republic Germany, 1974; chmn. pseudepigrapha group Soc. Bibl. Lit., 1973-80. Author: Resurrection, Immortality and Eternal Life in Intertestamental Judaism, 1972; Jewish Literature Between the Bible and the Mishnah, 1981. Contbr. articles to profl. jours. Fellow John Simon Guggenheim Meml. Found., 1977-78, NEH, 1984-85, Netherlands Inst. Advanced Study, 1980-81. Mem. Soc. N.T. Studies, Cath. Bibl. Assn. Home: 1713 E Court St Iowa City IA 52240 Office: Sch Religion U Iowa Iowa City IA 52242

NICULESCU, GEORGE MIRCEA PAUL, priest, Eastern Orthodox Church (Romanian); writer; b. Bucharest, Romania, Feb. 14, 1939; came to U.S., 1980; s. Mande Andrei and Niculina (Florea) N.; m. Gabriela Doina Velicu, Aug. 14, 1970; children: Oana Andreea, Ieronim Petru. Th.M., Theol. Inst. Sibiu, Romania, 1969. Ordained priest Eastern Orthodox Ch., 1982. Theologian Bibl. Inst. of Romanian Patriarchate, Bucharest, 1974-79; rector St. John the Bapt. Romanian Orthodox Ch., Los Angeles, 1982—. Author books of poetry: Existenta Si Cuvintele, 1971 (Romanian Writers' award 1971), Asta Seara, 1976, other writings. Named to Biog. Roll of Honor, Hist. Preservations of Am., Inc., 1984. Home: 1209 N Mansfield Ave #6 Hollywood CA 90038 Office: St John the Baptist Romanian Orthodox Ch 6301 W Olympic Blvd Los Angeles CA 90038

NIEBUHR, RICHARD R., educator, minister, United Ch. of Christ; b. Chgo., Mar. 9, 1926; s. H. Richard and Florence Marie (Mittendorf) N.; A.B., Harvard, 1947; B.D., Union Theol. Sem., 1950; Ph.D., Yale, 1955; m. Nancy Mullican, Oct. 14, 1950; children—Richard Gustav, Sarah Louise. Ordained to ministry United Ch. Christ, 1950; minister First Ch. Christ, Cornwall, Conn., 1950-52; lectr. religion Vassar Coll., Poughkeepsie, N.Y., 1954-56; asst. prof. theology, 1956-59, asso. prof., 1959-63, prof., 1963—, chmn. of study of religion, 1966—. Fulbright research scholar, 1958-59. Mem. Am. Acad. Arts and Scis., Phi Beta Kappa. Author: Resurrection and Historical Reason, 1957; Schleiermacher on Christ and Religion, 1964; Experiential Religion, 1972. Editorial com. The Works of Jonathan Edwards, 1965—. Office: Study of Religion Harvard Union Harvard Univ Cambridge MA 02138

NIEDERGESES, JAMES D., bishop, Roman Catholic Church; b. Lawrenceburg, Tenn., Feb. 2, 1917; ed. St. Bernard Coll., St. Ambrose Coll., Mt. St. Mary Sem. of the West, Athenaeum of Ohio. Ordained priest, 1944; pastor Our Lady of Perpetual Help, Chattanooga, 1962-73, Sts. Peter and Paul Parish, 1973-75; bishop of Nashville, 1975—. Mem. personnel bd. Diocese of Nashville. Office: 2400 21st Ave S Nashville TN 37219*

NIEMAN, FRANK BERNARD, educational administrator, Roman Catholic Church. B. Cin., Oct. 16, 1932; s. Frank August and Marie Bernadine (Schoenfeld) N.; m. Mary Margaret Moore, Aug. 6, 1955; children: William, Francis, Ann, Matthew, Peter, Mary, John, Catherine. Lay evangelist Roman Catholic Ch., Fresno, Calif., 1962-66; acad. dean Sch. Applied Theology/Grad. Theol. Union, Berkeley, Calif., 1970—; dir. Inst. Lay Theology, San Francisco, 1972—; sec. Clergy Edn. Adv. Bd., Oakland, Calif., 1979—; trainer Edn. for Ministry Program, Sewanee, Tenn., 1981—; exec. dir. Formation for Christian Ministry, Berkeley, 1981—. Author: (study books) Christian Awareness Program, 1980. Contbr. articles to profl. publs. Mem. Soc. for Advancement of Continuing Edn. in Ministry, Nat. Orgn. Continuing Edn. of Roman Catholic Clergy. Home: 3022 Vessing Rd Pleasant Hill CA 94523 Office: Sch Applied Theology Grad Theol Union 5890 Birch Ct PO Box 20479 Oakland CA 94620

NIEMINSKI, JOSEPH IGNATIUS, bishop, Polish Nat. Catholic Ch. Can.; b. Hazleton, Pa., May 22, 1926; s. Ignatius and Mary (Pekala) N.; diploma in Theology, Savonarola Theol. Sem., Scranton, Pa., 1946; B.A., U. Toronto (Ont., Can.), 1959; Th.M., Christian Acad. Theology, Warsaw, Poland, 1977, Th.D., 1981; m. Marie Remian, Jan. 28, 1953; children—Robin, Renee Ann. Ordained priest, 1946; asst. priest Holy Mother of Rosary Cathedral, Buffalo, 1946-47; rector St. Johns Parish, Toronto, 1947—; sec. Supreme Council, Polish Nat. Cath. Ch., 1962-78; bishop Polish Nat. Cath. Ch. in Can., 1968—. Address: 186 Cowan Ave Toronto ON M6K 2N6 Canada

NIES, WILLIAM LUTHER, minister, American Lutheran Church. B. Detroit, Apr. 13, 1927; s. William Henry and Naomi Louise (Emch) N.; m. Trudi Priddy, June 14, 1949; children: Kathleen Louise Nies-Hepner, William Martin. B.A., Capital U., 1946, D.D. (hon.), 1982; B.D., Trinity Sem., Columbus, Ohio, 1949, M.Div., 1950. Ordained to ministry American Lutheran Church, 1950. Pastor Mt. Zion Luth. Ch., Detroit, 1950-63, Holy Trinity Luth. Ch., Falls Church, Va., 1963-74, S. Miami Luth. Ch., Fla., 1974-80, St. Armands Key Luth. Ch., Sarasota, Fla., 1980—; del. Merging Conv., Am. Luth. Ch., Mpls., 1960; chmn. radio/TV bd. Washington, D.C. Council Chs., 1964-68; protestant preacher CIA, Langley, Va., 1965-73; vis. instr. Holy Trinity Sem., Washington, D.C., 1970-71. Bd. govs. Northeastern YMCA, Detroit, 1950-60; trustee Capital U., Columbus, Ohio, 1966-80, Fair Havens Home for Elderly, Miami Springs, Fla., 1975-81, Southwest Fla. Retirement-Health Ctr., Venice, 1984; vis. instr. U.S. Army War Coll., Carlisle, Pa., 1973. Recipient Lamb award Boy Scouts Am., Nat. Luth. Youth Agy., N.Y., 1961; named Outstanding Religious Leader City of Miami, 1978. Republican. Lodge: Kiwanis (chmn. spiritual aims 1983). Home: 130 N Adams Dr Sarasota FL 33577 Office: St Armands Key Luth Ch 40 N Adams Dr Sarasota FL 33577

NIESSEN, RICHARD, minister, educator, Independent Baptist Church; b. Elizabeth, N.J., Oct. 10, 1941; s. John and Erna (Gutbier) N.; m. Carole Elaine Sheaf, July 11, 1970; children: Jonathan, Sarah. B.A., Northeastern Bible Coll., 1970, Th.B., 1970; M.A., Trinity Evang. Div. Sch., 1974; postgrad. Aquinas Inst. Theology, 1972-76. Ordained to ministry Bapt. Ch., 1980. Interim pastor Grace Evang. Free Ch., Lancaster, Wis., 1975-76; instr. Moody Bible Inst., Chgo., 1976-78; assoc. prof. Christian Heritage Coll., El Cajon, Calif., 1978—. Editor: UFO's and Evolution, 1981. Contbr. articles to various jours., 1978-84. Served with U.S. Army, 1960-63. Mem. Evang. Theol. Soc. (pres. Far-West div. 1984-85), Creation Research Soc., Assocs. for Bibl. Research, Mensa, Delta Epsilon Chi. Republican. Home: 10457 Ken Ln Santee CA 92071 Office: Christian Heritage Coll 2100 Greenfield Dr El Cajon CA 92021

NILLES, ROGER GABRIEL, priest, Roman Catholic Ch.; b. Madison, Wis., June 9, 1933; s. Mathias John and Anna Marie (Ormson) N.; B.A., Loras Coll., 1955; M.A. in Ednl. Adminstrn., Cath. U., Washington, 1959; Ph.D. in Counseling Guidance, U. Wis., Madison, 1974.

Ordained priest, 1959; chaplain Univ. Cath. Center, U. Wis., Madison, 1967—; pres. priest senate, Diocese of Madison (Wis.), 1976—. Home and office: 723 State St Madison WI 53703

NILSON, JON, theology educator, Roman Catholic Church; b. Chgo., Sept. 3, 1943; s. John Edward Nilson and Rosemary Therese (Murnighan) Nilson Daniels; m. Kathryn Mary Hogan, Aug. 24, 1968; children: Julie, Amy, Daniel. A.B., St. Mary of Lake Sem., 1965, S.T.B., 1967; M.A., U. Notre Dame, 1968, Ph.D., 1975. Assoc. prof. theology Loyola U., Chgo., 1975—. Author: Hegel and Lonergan, 1979; From This Day Forward, 1983; contbr. articles to religious jours. Recipient Publ. Subvention award Lonergan Trust Fund, 1978; Loyola-Mellon Fund grantee, 1980; Inst. Advanced Study Religion fellow U. Chgo., 1983. Mem. Cath. Theol. Soc. Am. Home: 2312 W Estes Ave Chicago IL 60645 Office: Loyola U of Chgo 6525 N Sheridan Rd Chicago IL 60626

NISBET, JAMES ALEXANDER, minister, church official, Presbyterian Church (U.S.A.); b. Sanford, N.C., June 20, 1923; s. William Leonidas and Alice Iola (Williams) N.; m. Shirley Ruffner Burnside, May 20, 1948; children: Elizabeth Lynn, Nancy Reid, Ann Ruffner, Virginia Alice, Mary Crockett. B.A., Davidson Coll., 1946; B.D., Union Sem., Richmond, Va., 1949. Ordained to ministry Presbyn. Ch. in U.S., 1949. Pastor Presbyn. Ch., Olivia, N.C., 1949-51, Wallace, N.C., 1951-54; mem. staff Bd. Christian Edn., Richmond, 1954-73; exec. Synod of Southeast, Augusta, Ga., 1973—; past div. chmn. Nat. Council of Chs., N.Y.C., 1971-73; pres. Ga. Christian Council, Atlanta, 1973-74. Trustee Queens Coll., Charlotte, N.C., 1976—. Recipient Service award Office Chief of Chaplains, 1977. Mem. Presbytery of Piedmont (moderator 1973), Assn. Ch. Educators. Democrat. Lodge: Rotary. Home: 3612 Barbados Dr Augusta GA 30909 Office: Synod of the Southeast 509 Executive Park Augusta GA 30907

NITSCH, GABOR GEORGE, minister, Hungarian Reformed Church in America; b. Ianosda, Romania, Mar. 31, 1949; came to U.S., 1974, naturalized, 1979; s. George Daniel and Elizabeth (Dono) N.; m. Helen Y. Grof-Tisza, Apr. 16, 1977; children: Andrew Peter, Daniel Anthony, Martha, Aniko. B.A., Hebrew U., Jerusalem, 1974, B.A. in Art History, 1974; M.Div., Theol. U. Cluj, Romania, 1971; M.Div., New Brunswick Theol. Sem., 1976; postgrad. Union Theol. Sem., 1974-75; cert. theology Leiden Theol. Sem., Netherlands, 1976. Ordained to ministry Hungarian Ref. Ch. in Am., 1977. Pastor, Hungarian Ref. Ch., Roebling, N.J., part-time 1974-76, First Hungarian United Ch. of Christ, Miami, Fla., 1977-81, Hungarian Ref. Ch., Carteret, N.J., 1981—; co-editor, mgr. Magyar Ch. of Hungarian Ref. Ch. in Am., 1983—; del. Hungarian Ref. Fedn. Am., Washington, 1984; v.p. Greater Miami Ministerial Assn., 1978-79, pres., 1979-80. Contbr. articles to profl. jours. Chaplain, Hon. Police Benevolent Assn. and Police Benevolent Assn., Carteret, N.J., 1983-84. Hebrew U. Jerusalem scholar, 1971-74, Union Theol. Sem. scholar, 1974-75, Leiden Theol. Sem. scholar, 1976. (Johanniter Order hon. knight 1980). Republican. Home: 175 Pershing Ave Carteret NJ 07008 Office: Hungarian Ref Ch 175 Pershing Ave Carteret NJ 07008

NITZ, ARTHUR CARL, minister, Lutheran Church-Missouri Synod; b. North Bellingham, Wash., Dec. 4, 1905; s. Frederick Maximillian Leopold and Carolina (Heitmueller) N.; m. Dorothy Louise Kahm, Sept. 15, 1938; children: Faith, Hope, Frederic, Charity, Joy, Felicity. B.A. summa cum laude, Concordia Coll., Ft. Wayne, 1927; C.R.M., Concordia Sem., St. Louis, 1930, D.D.(hon.), 1960; postgrad. Western Wash. State U., 1926, 27, Washington U., St. Louis, 1931, 32. Ordained to ministry Lutheran Ch.-Missouri Synod, 1930. Pastor, St. Stephen Ch., St. Louis, 1930-48, St. Paulus Ch., San Francisco, 1948-66, Trinity Ch., San Rafael, Calif., 1966-76; interim pastor: Resurrection Ch., Terra Linda, Calif., 1968-74, First Redeemer Ch., Vallejo, Calif., 1976-77, St. John Ch., Petaluma, Calif., 1977-78, Shepherd of the Hills, San Francisco, 1978-83; chmn. Luth. City Missions, St. Louis, 1944-48; v.p. worldwide Luth. Ch.-Mo. Synod, 1959-65; v.p. Calif. Nev., Hawaii Dist., 1951-54, pres., 1954-59; chmn. Commn. on Missions and Ministry, St. Louis, 1965-68; bd. mem. Commn. on Theology and Ch. Relations, St. Louis, 1969-75; organizer, bd. dirs., temporary exec. dir. Luth. Care for the Aging, 1961—. Co-founder, chmn. bd. Ella M. Rohlffs Found., San Francisco, 1974—. Frederic Wenchel lectr. in preaching, Concordia Sem., St. Louis and Springfield, Mo., 1960; recipient Disting. Service award Luth. Ch.-Mo. Synod, 1978. Republican. Home: 117 Covent Ct San Rafael CA 94901

NIX, CLARA MARGARET, media resources consultant, United Church of Canada; b. Edmonton, Alta., Aug. 1, 1923; d. George Arthur and Clare O.T. (Clarke) Latter; m. James Ernest Nix, Mar. 16, 1946; children: Margaret, James, Suzanne, Douglas. Student pub. schs., Can. Program and resource officer Montreal Presbytery United Ch. Can., 1976-78; media resources cons. Nat. Office, United Ch. Can., Toronto, 1978—. Mem. Ont. Film Assn. (publ. chmn.). Address: United Ch of Can 85 St Clair Ave E Toronto ON M4T 1M8 Canada

NIX, WILLIAM DALE, JR., priest, Episcopal Church; b. Amarillo, Tex., June 9, 1941; s. William Dale and Mary Alice (Quattlebaum) N.; m. Nelwyn Merle Hermann, Aug. 3, 1963; children: William Dale Todd, Colin Moore, Emilie Christine. B.A., Tex. A&M U., 1963; M.Div., Episcopal Theol. Sem. S.W., Austin, 1975. Ordained priest, Episcopal Ch., 1976. Curate, St. John's Ch., Odessa, Tex., 1975-77; rector St. Stephen's Ch., Lubbock, Tex., 1977-81; canon to the ordinary Diocese of N.W. Tex., Lubbock, 1981—; trustee Episcopal Sem., Austin, 1983—; dep. Gen. Conv., 1982, 85; trustee All Saints Episcopal Sch., Lubbock, 1983—; exec. council Diocese of N.W. Tex., 1981—; chmn. Conf. Ctr. Governing Bd. Contbr. articles to profl. jours. Bd. dirs. Women's Protective Services, Lubbock, 1979-80, Contact Crisis Ministry, 1981—. Served to 1st lt. U.S. Army, 1964-66. Mem. Conf. of Diocesan Execs., Order of St. Benedict (confrator). Office: Diocese of Northwest Tex PO Box 1067 Lubbock TX 79408

NOBUHARA, TOKIYUKI, theology educator, minister, United Church of Christ-Japan; educational administrator; b. Itami, Japan, July 23, 1937; came to U.S., 1976; s. Takami and Kiyono (Yuhki) N.; m. Sasaki Nobuko, May 18, 1969. B.D., Doshisha U., Kyoto, Japan, 1960, M.Div., 1962; D.Min., Sch. Theology at Claremont, 1978; Ph.D., Claremont Grad. Sch., 1981. Ordained to ministry Kyodan, (United Ch. of Christ-Japan). Asst. minister Itami Ch., Japan, 1962-64; minister Kamo Brethren Ch., Kawanishi, Japan, 1964-76; lang. minister Sage-North Gardena United Meth. Ch., Calif., 1976-81; prof. theology Brite Div. Sch., Ft. Worth, 1982-83; lectr. theology Sch. Theology at Claremont and Claremont Grad. Sch., Calif., 1984—; rep. World Ch. Christ Cardiff Consultation, 1972; vis. prof. Katholieke Universiteit, Belgium, 1981-82. Project dir. Ctr. Process Studies, Claremont, 1985—. Co-author: Dharma and Gospel, 1984. Contbr. articles to profl. jours. Doshisha scholar, 1960-62; Japan-North Am. Commn. Coop. Mission scholar, 1976-78; fellow Claremont Grad. Sch., 1980, The Disciples Found., 1977, Katholieke U., 1981-82. Mem. Am. Acad. Religion (co-chmn. com. 1985—).

NOEL, KEITH WAYNE, minister, Christian Church; b. Indpls., Apr. 6, 1948; s. John Edward and Sylvia Nadine (Gregg) N.; m. Donna Toumey, Sept. 5, 1971; children: Cynthia Dawn, Christine Carrie. B.A. in Theology, Johnson Bible Coll., 1971. Ordained to ministry Christian Ch., 1971. Minister Christian Ch., Braddock, Pa., 1971-73, Titusville, Fla., 1973-74, East Peoria, Ill., 1974-75, Fairland, Ind., 1976-81, Woodside Christian Ch., Frankfort, Ind., 1981—. Home: 1355 W Barner St Frankfort IN 46041 Office: Woodside Christian Ch 1359 W Barner St Frankfort IN 46041

NOEL, LAURENT, bishop, Roman Cath. Ch.; b. St. Just de Bretenieres, Que., Can., Mar. 19, 1920; s. Remi and Albertine (Nadeau) N.; student Coll. de Levis, 1940; L.Th., Laval U., 1944, L.Ph., 1948; D.Th., Inst. Angelicum, Rome, 1951. Ordained priest, 1944; consecrated bishop, 1963; prof. theology Laval U., 1946-48, prof. ethics Med. Sch., 1952-63, vice rector Grand Sem., Sch. Theology, 1961-63; aux. bishop Que., 1963-75; bishop Trois-Rivieres, Que., 1975—. Provincial chaplain Assn. des Infirmières Catholiques, 1958-75; chaplain Syndicat Prof. des Infirmières Catholiques, 1958-63; apostolic adminstr. Diocese of Hauterive, 1974-75. Author: Precis. de morale medicale, 1962. Home and Office: 362 Rue Bonaventure CP 879 Trois-Rivieres PQ G9A 5J9 Canada

NOELLISTE, GLORIA JEAN, lay worker, educator, Church of God in Christ, gas company official; b. Detroit, Nov. 1, 1953; d. Clyde and Ella (Charleston) Tingle; m. Dieumeme Exima Noelliste, May 26, 1979; 1 child, Joseph Daniel. B.A. in Acctg., Mich. State U., 1975; postgrad. Moody Bible Inst., 1983, Tyndale Coll., 1977-79, Wheaton Grad. Sch., Ill., 1982—. Founder, pres. Haitian Children Edn. Fund, Chgo., 1979—, Pastor's Wives Fellowship, Chgo., 1982—, pres. Quest II Women's Group, Lombard, Ill., 1980—; free lance writer Exec. Christian Women, Chgo., 1983—; trustee Haitian Evang. Ch., Chgo., 1982—, v.p. women's dept., 1981—; Christian edn. dir. Evangel. Ch. of God in Christ, Detroit, 1976-79; dir. Phoebe (Women's Group), Chgo., 1984—; data adminstr. Natural Gas Pipeline Co., Lombard, 1982—. Contbr. articles to profl. jours. Vol., St. Francis Hosp., Evanston, Ill., 1980, Harper Hosp. Rehab. Ctr., Detroit, 1976-79. Gibson Ednl. Found. scholar, 1971; Cass Tech. High Sch. scholar, 1971-75; Nat. Assn. Black Accts. scholar, 1975; named Outstanding Worker, COGIC Bus. and Profl. Women, Detroit, 1979. Mem. Nat. Black Evang. Assn., Nat. Assn. Black Accts., Bus. and Profl. Women. Democrat. Clubs: Women's Econ., Mich. State U. Alumni, Natural Gas Pipeline Women Bible/Prayer Group. Home: 7362 N Winchester Chicago IL 60626 Office: 701 E 22d St Lombard IL 60148

NOFER, HERMAN FREDRICK, JR., minister, educator, Evang. Free Ch. Am.; b. Columbus, Ohio, July 4, 1930; s. Herman Frederick and Dorothy Margaret (Calvert) N.; B.A., Augsburg Coll., Mpls., 1953; Th.M., Dallas Theol. Sem., 1957, Th.D., 1960; D.D., Los Angeles Bible Coll. and Sem., 1973; m. Carolyn Joyce Heerdt, Dec. 20, 1969; children—Rebecca Lynn, Theodore William. Ordained to ministry, 1976; instr. Luth. Brethren Sem., Fergus Falls, Minn., 1959-62; dean faculty Winnipeg (Man., Can.) Bible Coll., 1962-67; registrar Calif. Grad. Sch. Theology, Glendale, 1972-73; founder, exec. dir. South Coast Bible Sch., Laguna Hills, Calif., 1973-75; registrar, dir. admissions Christian Heritage Coll., El Cajon, Calif., 1975-76, instr. N.T. Greek, 1975—; pastor-tchr. Lake Murray Evang. Free Ch., La Mesa, Calif., 1976—. Mem. Evang. Theol. Soc. Author: New Testament Greek Made Functional, 1972. Home: 6551 Cowles Mountain Blvd San Diego CA 92119 Office: 5777 Lake Murray Blvd La Mesa CA 92041

NOGGLER, BERNICE MARIE, religious order administrator; b. Hereford, Tex., Dec. 13, 1933; d. John Henry and Marie Mary (Koelzer) N. B.A. in Elementary Edn., Our Lady of the Lake Coll., San Antonio, 1965. Joined Franciscan Sisters of Mary Immaculate, 1951. Tchr., St. Mary's Sch., Holman, N.Mex., 1951-53, Resurrection Sch., Los Angeles, 1953-54, St. Laurence Sch., Amarillo, Tex., 1954-62; tchr., prin. St. Mary's Sch., Odessa, Tex., 1962-72; parish worker Holy Family Ch., Sweetwater, Tex., 1972-74; tchr. St. Athansius Sch., Long Beach, lalif., 1974-75; tchr., prin. St. Laurence Sch., Amarillo, 1975-78; Confrat. Christian Doctrine coordinator St. Thomas the Apostle, Amarillo, 1983—; provincial superior Franciscan Sisters of Mary Immaculate, Amarillo, 1981—; with Agape Community (peace movement). Democrat. Home and Office: 4301 NE 18th St Amarillo TX 97107

NOIA, LARREY CATON, minister of music, Southern Baptist Convention; b. Bakersfield, Calif., Feb. 8, 1944; s. Manuel Caton and Betty Gladys (Brewer) N.; m. Rebecca Sue Smith, Aug. 6, 1966; 1 child, Jaime Caton. B.A., Calif. Bapt. Coll., 1966; M.R.E., Golden Gate Bapt. Theol. Sem., 1968, M. Ch. Music, 1969. Ordained to ministry Southern Baptist Convention, 1969. Minister of music, sch. adminstr. First So. Bapt. Ch., Fountain Valley, Calif., 1970—; trustee Christian Life Commn., So. Bapt. Conv., Nashville, 1982—, Calif. Bapt. Coll., Riverside, 1984—. Mem. Calif. Singing Churchmen, So. Bapt. Assn. Christian Schs. (pres. 1981-84), Calif. Bapt. Coll. Alumni Assn. (pres. 1981-83, alumni of yr. 1984). Democrat. Home: 9183 Otter River Circle Fountain Valley CA 92708 Office: First So Bapt Ch 10350 Ellis Fountain Valley CA 92708

NOLAN, RICHARD THOMAS, educator, priest, Episcopal Church; b. Waltham, Mass., May 30, 1937; s. Thomas Michael and Elizabeth Louise (Leishman) N.; B.A., Trinity Coll., 1960; M.Div., Hartford Sem. Found., 1963; M.A. in Religion, yale U., 1967; Ph.D., NYU., 1973; research fellow med. ethics Yale U., 1975-76. Ordained deacon Episcopal Ch., 1963, priest, 1965. With various parishes and colls. of N.Y. and Conn., 1963-74; pastor (part-time) St. Paul's Ch., Bantam, Conn., 1974—; pres. Litchfield Inst., Conn., 1984—. Prof. philosophy Mattatuck Community Coll., Waterbury, Conn., 1969—; guest speaker, lectr. in chs., colls., hosps., and on radio-TV. Mem. Am. Acad. Religion, Am. Philos. Assn. Author: (with H. Titus and M. Smith) Living Issues in Philosophy, 7th edit., 1979, 8th edit., 1986; (with F. Kirkpatrick) Living Issues in Ethics, 1982. Editor, contbr. The Diaconate Now, 1968. Home: 1150 NW 30th Ct Wilton Manors FL 33311 Office: PO Box 483 Bristol CT 06010

NOLEN, MILTON WAYNE, minister, So. Baptist Conv.; b. Carbon Hill, Ala., Apr. 11, 1937; s. Grover Cleveland and Beulah (McAlpin) N.; B.A., Calif. Bapt. Coll., 1967; M.Div., Golden Gate Bapt. Sem., 1970; m. Jacqueline Bowden, Sept. 19, 1959; children—Michael Wayne, Kimberly Ann, Jeffrey Craig, Kristen Leigh. Ordained to ministry, 1966; pastor Bapt. chs., Calif., 1966—, First Bapt. Ch., Prunedale, Salinas, Calif., 1969-72, Temple Bapt. Ch., Redlands, Calif., 1972—. Bd. dirs. United Fund, Redlands, 1973-74. Mem. Nat. Assn. Evangelicals (pres.). Home: 1070 Coronado Dr Redlands CA 92373 Office: 611 E Cypress Ave Redlands CA 92373

NOMMIK, TONIS, minister, Luth. Ch. Am.; b. Tallinn, Estonia, Apr. 29, 1933; s. August and Rita Ludmilla (Leesmaa) N.; came to Can., 1955, naturalized, 1960; B.A., Waterloo Luth. U. (Can.), 1964, B.D., 1967; postgrad. Concordia Sem. (Mo.), 1967; m. Juta Saaret, Sept. 2, 1971; children—Maimu Liis, Kadri Merike, Hendrik Toomas, Vello Andres, Tiiu Viive. Ordained to ministry, 1967; missionary, Argentina, 1967-70; pastor Estonian Congregations No. Ont., 1970-75, Toronto St. James Estonian and Toronto Swedish Chs., Toronto, Ont., 1975—. Chaplain Can. Armed Forces Res., 1967—, Boy Scouts in Sweden, S.Am. and Can., 1953—. Del. Estonian Central Council Can., 1971—. Bd. dirs. Estonian Relief com., Can., 1971—. Mem. Royal Canadian Mil. Inst. Author: Estonian Ecclesiastical History: An Annotated Bibliography, 1964; A Guide to the Baltic Collection at Waterloo Luth. U., 1967; contbr. articles in field to religious jours. Home: 501 Davisville Ave Toronto ON M4S 1J2 Canada Office: 1691 Bloor St W Toronto ON M6T 1B1 Canada

NOON, ROBERT L., priest, missionary, Roman Catholic Church; b. Zanesville, Ohio, May 15, 1923; s. Charles Leo and Elizabeth (Schreiber) N. B.A., St. Charles Coll., 1947. Ordained priest Roman Cath. Ch., 1951. Assoc. pastor St. Peter Ch., Columbus, Ohio, 1951-54, St. Mary Ch., Marion, Ohio, 1954-59; missionary Sicuani, Peru, 1960-65; pastor St. Elizabeth Ch., Columbus, 1966-77; pastor in residence North Am. Coll., Vatican City, 1977-78; pastor St. Bernadette Ch., Lancaster, Ohio, 1983—; mem. Liturgical Commn., Diocese of Columbus, 1984—. Bd. dirs. Fairfield County ARC, Lancaster, 1984—. Democrat. Home and Office: St Bernadette Ch 1343 Wheeling Rd Lancaster OH 43130

NOON, THOMAS ROGER, minister, Lutheran Church-Missouri Synod; b. St. Louis, Oct. 20, 1944; s. Thomas Ray and Virginia Mary (Jiles) N.; m. Laura Martha Peter, Aug. 26, 1973; children: Thomas Michael, Jessica Laura, Nathaniel Peter. B.A., Valparaiso U., 1967; B.D., Concordia Sem., Springfield, Ill., 1971. Ordained to ministry Luth. Ch., 1971. Pastor, St. Paul Luth. Ch., Mansura, La., 1971-76, Augustana Luth. Ch., Alexandria, La., 1971-76, St. Paul Luth. Ch., Birmingham, Ala., 1976—; vacancy pastor Prince of Peace Luth. Ch., Birmingham, 1982—; mem. Clergy That Care, Birmingham, 1980-83. Mem. Concordia Hist. Inst. (Recognition award for jour. articles). Home: 1409 67th St W Birmingham AL 35228 Office: St Paul Luth Ch 132 6th Ave S Birmingham AL 35205

NOREEN, DAVID SHELDON, religious organization executive, Evangelical Covenant Church; b. Gresham, Oreg., Mar. 31, 1930; s. Oscar E. and Floella M. (Jacobs) N.; m. Marilyn G. Larson, Aug. 23, 1952; children: Jerald, Kenneth, Julie. B.S., Purdue U., 1954; B.D., North Park Theol. Sem., 1956; M.A. in Adult Edn., Ind. U., 1966. Ordained to ministry Evangelical Covenant Church, 1957. Sr. pastor Northwest Covenant Ch., Mt. Prospect, Ill., 1955-61, Evang. Covenant Ch., South Bend, Ind., 1961-66; assoc. pastor First Covenant Ch., St. Paul, 1966-70; exec. sec. dept. Christian edn. Evang. Covenant Ch. Am., Chgo., 1970—; bd. dirs. Edn. for Christian Life and Mission, Nat. Council Churches, N.Y.C., 1976—; mem. exec. com. Internatl. Fed. Free Evang. Churches, Stockholm, 1976-80, del., 1971—. Editor: Confirmation Resources, 1970-71, 85. Workshop leader in Church Leadership Devel. Contbr. articles to profl. jours. Mem. Joint Ednl. Devel. (exec. com. 1972—), Adult Edn. Assn., Denominational Execs. of Christian Edn. (officer 1971—). Office: Evangelical Covenant Ch 5101 N Francisco St Chicago IL 60625

NORFOLK, GLENN DALE, minister, So. Baptist Conv.; b. New London, Mo., Oct. 22, 1932; s. Herman Everett and Edna Alice (Hirst) N.; B.A., Culver Stokton Coll., 1945; B.D., Mo. Sch. Religion, 1960; M.Ed., Lincoln U., 1973; m. Barbara Jean Damron, May 15, 1954; children—Dennis Dale, Lori Lyn. Ordained to ministry, 1951; pastor chs., Grand Prairie Bapt. Ch., Auxvasse, Mo., 1956-61; pastor Union Hill Summit Baptist Ch., Holts Summit, Mo., 1961—; chaplain Mo. Senate, 1972-76; moderator Callaway County Baptist Assn., 1965-68; dir. Evangelism Callaway County Baptist Assn., 1969-74; mem. Central Mo. Mission Bd., 1966—; pres. Central Mo. Bapt. Ch. Conf., 1966—; tchr. Sem. Ext. Center, 1966—; speaker Union Hill Gospel Hour, KFAL, Fulton, Mo., 1963—. Trustee Hannibal LaGrange Coll., 1972-76; regional dir. Americans United, 1965—. Home and office: Gen Delivery Holts Summit MO 65043

NORGREN, WILLIAM ANDREW, priest, Episcopal Church; b. Frostburg, Md., May 5, 1927; s. William Andrew and Martha Elizabeth (Richardson) N. A.B., Coll. of William and Mary, 1948; M.Div., Gen. Theol. Sem., 1953; B.Litt., Oxford U.-Eng., 1959; D.D. (hon.), Gen. Theol. Sem., 1984. Ordained priest, 1953. Exec. dir. Nat. Council Chs. Dept., N.Y.C., 1959-71; pastoral asst. Trinity Ch., N.Y.C., 1972-74; asst. ecumenical officer Episcopal Ch., N.Y.C., 1975-79, assoc. ecumenical officer, 1979-81, ecumenical officer, 1981—; bd. dirs. Joint Stragety & Action Com., N.Y.C., 1975—; governing bd. Nat. Council Chs., 1979—. Editor: Living Room Dialogues, 1965; Meanings and Practices of Conversion, 1966; Evangelism in a Pluralistic Society, 1967; Religious Faith Speaks to American Issues, 1975. Contbr. articles to profl. jours. Home: 120 E 79 St New York NY 10021 Office: Exec Council Episcopal Ch 815 Second Ave New York NY 10017

NORMAN, GEORGE SIGURD, minister, Luth. Ch. Am.; b. Bklyn., Sept. 16, 1914; s. George Sigurd and Anna Sofia (Andersen) N.; B.A., Calif. State U., 1973; M.Div., Pacific Luth. Theol. Sem., 1973; m. Dorothy Kathryn Zabler, Apr. 11, 1942; children—Rosanne Norman Fells, David G. Ordained to ministry, 1965; dir. religious edn. Trinity Luth. Ch., Fresno, Calif., 1960-62; pastor Mt. Olivet Luth. Ch., Lakewood, Calif., 1965—. Treas. Fresno Area Council Chs., 1961; sec. Long Beach dist. Pacific S.W. Synod, Luth. Ch. Am., 1969-72; chaplain Los Angeles County Sheriff Dept., 1975; chaplain asso. Meml. Hosp. of Long Beach, 1976—; instr. Cerritos Coll., Norwalk, Calif., 1973; pres. Long Beach Luth. Ministerial Assn., 1970-71. Contbr. articles in field to religious jours. Home: 5960 Sunfield Ave Lakewood CA 90712 Office: 4405 E South St Lakewood CA 90712

NORRIS, FREDERICK WALTER, seminary educator, minister, Christian Church; b. Chillicothe, Ohio, Mar. 13, 1941; s. William Orlan and Julia Helen (Dowdy) N.; m. Carol Jean Brooks, Aug. 30, 1963; children: Lisa Carol, Mark Frederick. B.A., Milligan Coll., 1963; B.D., Th.M., Phillips U., 1967; M.Phil., Ph.D., Yale U., 1970. Ordained to ministry Christian Ch., 1963. Asst. prof. Milligan Coll., Johnson City, Tenn., 1970-72; assoc. dir., dir. Inst. Erforsh. Urchr., Tuebingen, Fed. Republic Germany, 1972-77; lehrbeauftragte Protestant Faculty, U. Tuebingen, 1974-77; prof. Emmanuel Sch. Religion, Johnson City, 1977—. Editor, Patristics, 1981—; assoc. editor Ency. of Early Christianity. Contbr. articles to profl. jours. Honors scholar Milligan Coll., Phillips U., Yale U.; Andrew W. Mellon Found. postdoctoral research fellow, 1981-82. Mem. Am. Soc. Ch. History, Am. Acad. Religion, N. Am. Patristic Soc. Democrat. Home: Route 6 Box 544 Johnson City TN 37601 Office: Emmanuel Sch Religion Route 6 Box 500 Johnson City TN 37601

NORRIS, GARY ANDREW, minister, General Association of Regular Baptist Churches; b. Wheelersburg, Ohio, Dec. 9, 1939; s. Albert Oney and Velma Iren (Gose) N.; m. Wanda Faye Jenkins, Aug. 18, 1961; children: Joseph Mark, Kimberly Dawn. B.R.E., Piedmont Bible Coll., 1962; M.Min., Covington Theol. Sem., 1983, D.Min., 1984. Ordained to ministry Baptist Ch., 1962. Minister, Twin Valley Bapt. Ch., Ohio, 1962-63, Chamblissburg Bapt. Ch., Va., 1963-65, Mt. Carmel Regular Bapt. Ch., Luray, Va., 1965-71, Free Grace Bapt. Ch., Luray, 1971-75, Calvary Bapt. Ch., Chillicothe, Ohio, 1975—; trustee Regular Bapt. Missionary Fund, Luray, 1968-71, Scioto Hills Bapt. Camp, Wheelersburg, Ohio, 1975-76. Substitute mail carrier U.S. P.O., Chillicothe, 1983—. Vice pres. Luray PTA, 1974-75. Home: 410 Chestnut St Chillicothe OH 45601 Office: Calvary Bapt Ch 1530 Western Ave Chillicothe OH 45601

NORRIS, KENDRICK LYDDON, minister, pastoral counselor; United Church of Christ; b. N.Y.C., Feb. 14, 1950; s. Donald Leroy and Carol Elizabeth N.; m. Susan Lott, May 17, 1975; children: Soren, Evan. B.A., Wagner coll., 1973; M.Div., Yale U., 1977; D.Min. Andover-Newton Theol. Sch., 1984. Dir. Sessions Woods Camp, Bristol, Conn., summers 1973, 74; retreat dir. N.Y. Conf. Meth. Ch., Rye, N.Y., 1973-75; student minister First Ch., New Canaan, Conn., 1975-76, Cheshire, Conn., 1976-77; assoc. minister First Ch., Guilford, Conn., 1977—; counselor Pastoral Ctr., St. Raphael's Hosp., New Haven, 1983—; therapist Family Counseling Services of Greater New Haven, 1984—; treas. Conn. Assn. for Jungian Psychology, Guilford, 1984—; mem. Com. on Ministry, 1984, chmn. Com. on Youth, 1980-83. Coordinator Host Homes, Guilford, 1977-80, Task Force on Needs for Children, Guilford, 1979, Human Services Council, Guilford, 1979-81. Mem. Am. Assn. Pastoral Counselors, Omicron Delta Kappa. Republican. Office: First Ch 122 Broad St Guilford CT 06437

NORRIS, RUSSELL BRADNER, JR., minister, educator, Lutheran Church in America; b. Hackensack, N.J., Mar. 3, 1942; s. Russell Bradner and Ann May (Dubanowitz) N.; m. Dixie Darlene Krouse, June 1, 1974; 1 child, Claire Ann Battistella. B.S. in Engring., MIT, 1964; M.Div., Luth. Sch. Theology at Chgo., 1969; Th.D., U. Strasbourg, France, 1972. Ordained to ministry Luth. Ch., 1972. Editorial asst. Centre d'etudes Oecumenique, Strasbourg, 1970-72; pastor Mt. Union Luth. Parish, Pa., 1972-78; sr. pastor Zion Luth. Ch., Hollidaysburg, Pa., 1978—; instr. ethics St. Francis Coll., Loretto, Pa., 1981—; bd. dirs. Camp Sequanota, Jennerstown, Pa., 1980-84; mem. bishop's task force on peace and justice Central Pa. Synod, Luth. Ch. Am., Harrisburg, 1983-84; mem. task force on Marxism, Luth. World Ministries, 1980-84. Author: God, Marx, and the Future, 1974; contbg. author: The Many Faces of Marxism, 1984. Mem. Am. Acad. Religion, Soc. for Christian Ethics. Democrat. Lodge: Rotary. Home: 308 Union St Hollidaysburg PA 16648 Office: Zion Lutheran Ch Allegheny and Union Sts Hollidaysburg PA 16648

NORTHCOTE, L. ANN, religious organization executive. Pres. World Young Women's Christian Assn. Office: 37 Quai Wilson 1201 Geneva Switzerland*

NORTHCOTT, JOHN EDWARD, minister, Luth. Ch. Am.; b. Toledo, Aug. 15, 1939; s. John William and Adele Katharine (Kieper) N.; A.B., Gustavus Adolphus Coll., 1962; M.Div., Northwestern Luth. Theol. Sem., 1965; D.Min., Consortium Higher Edn. Religious Studies, Hamma Sch. Theology, 1975; m. Mary Anne Kern, June 22, 1962; children—John Christian, Lisa Marie. Ordained to ministry, 1965; student asst. Bethesda Luth. Ch., South St. Paul, Minn., 1962-64; asst. chaplain Bethesda Luth. Hosp., St. Paul, 1964-65; pastor Arborg (Man., Can.) Luth. Parish, 1965-68; mission pastor St. Paul's Luth. Ch., Grandville, Mich., 1968-72; pastor Gethsemane Luth. Ch., Berkley, Mich., 1972—. Clergy advisor Youth Assistance Council, Berkley-Huntington Woods. Recipient Canadian Centennial medal Central Can. Youth Convocation, 1966. Home: 1978 Earlmont Rd Berkley MI 48072 Office: 2119 Catalpa Dr Berkley MI 48072

NORTHCUTT, FRANK PAUL, minister, Southern Baptist Convention; b. Houston, Tex., Feb. 26, 1952; s. Marshall Glenn and Dorothy Jane (Weed) N.; m. Tonie Geneva Terry, June 1, 1972; children: Rebekah Leigh, Marshall Frank. A.A., North Greenville Coll., 1973; B.A., Gardner-Webb Coll., 1976; M.Div., So. Bapt. Theol. Sem., 1979. Ordained to ministry Southern Baptist Conv., 1973. Pastor West Florence Bapt., S.C., 1973-74, Harrod's Creek Bapt., Crestwood, Ky., 1978-79, Poplar Springs Bapt., Ware Shoals, S.C., 1979—; interim pastor Mt. Hebron Bapt., Connelly Springs, N.C., 1975, New Buffalo Bapt., Grover, N.C., 1976; pres. J.D. Crain Ministerial Assn., North Greenville Coll., Tigerville, S.C., 1973; Sunday Sch. dir. Laurens Bapt. Assn., S.C., 1980-84, mem. missions com., 1983-86; mem. ministerial bd. of assocs. Gardner-Webb Coll., Boiling Springs, N.C., 1984—. Home and Office: Rt 1 Box 141 Ware Shoals SC 29692

NORTHUP, DAVID H., religious organization executive. Exec. v.p. Advent Christian Ch. Office: Advent Christian Ch PO Box 23152 Charlotte NC 28212*

NORUSIS, NICHOLAS MARY, priest, Roman Cath. Ch.; b. Chgo., Nov. 10, 1915; s. Matthew B. and Mary M. (Krupinskas) N.; B.A., Loyola U., Chgo., 1940; Th.M., Grad. Theol. Union, 1972. Ordained priest, 1944; tchr. St. Philip High Sch., Chgo., 1944-47; asst. pastor St. Joseph's Ch., Cartaret, N.J., 1947-51, Annunciata Ch., Chgo., 1951-61; pastor St. Rita Ch., Portland, Oreg., 1961-67; dir. Mt. Carmel Jr. High Sch., 1968-70; prior, dir. Sanctuary of Our Sorrowful Mother, Portland, 1973—. Mem. Internat. Transactional Assn.; dir., co-founder Marriage Enrichment Encounter Program; active visitors service com. Portland C. of C. Home and Office: 8840 NE Skidmore St Portland OR 97220

NOVAK, DAVID, rabbi, Conservative Jewish Congregations; b. Chgo., Aug. 19, 1941; s. Syd and Sylvia (Wien) N.; B.A., U. Chgo., 1961; M.H.L., Jewish Theol. Sem. Am., 1964; Ph.D., Georgetown U., 1971; m. Melva Ziman, July 3, 1963; children—Marianne, Jacob. Ordained rabbi, 1966; rabbi Shaare Tikvah Congregation, Washington, 1966-68; Jewish chaplain St. Elizabeths Hosp., Washington, 1967-69; rabbi Emanuel Synagogue, Oklahoma City, 1969-72, Beth Tfiloh Congregation, Balt., 1972—. Mem. com. on Jewish law and standards Rabbinical Assembly. Bd. dirs. Am. Citizens Concerned for Life, Jewish Family and Childrens Service, Balt. Recipient Hyman G. Enelow prize essay award Jewish Theol. Sem. Am., 1975. Mem. Balt. Bd. Rabbis. Author: Law and Theology in Judaism, 1st series, 1974, 2d series, 1976; Suicide and Morality, 1975. Home: 3308 Old Forest Rd Baltimore MD 21208 Office: 3300 Old Court Rd Baltimore MD 21208

NOVAK, EDWARD LEROY, minister, American Lutheran Church; b. Omaha, Dec. 17, 1933; s. Edward John and Sena (Mandsager) N.; m. Lorene Joy Olson, Aug. 27, 1955; children: Heidi, Nathan, Karin. B.A., St. Olaf Coll., 1955; B.Div., Luther Theol. Sem., 1959. Ordained to ministry Evang. Luth. Ch., 1959. Pastor, Flaxville Luth. Parish, Mont., 1959-63, Atonement Luth. Ch., Billings, Mont., 1963-68; sr. pastor First Luth. Ch., Sioux Falls, S.D., 1968-75; pastor First Luth. Ch., Glasgow, Mont., 1975-80, St. Peter Luth. Ch., Dubuque, Iowa, 1980—; chmn. Dist. Evangelism Commn., Des Moines, 1983-84; bd. dirs. Kogodus Renewal Movement, Dubuque, 1981-84; nat. del. Am. Luth. Ch., Mpls., 1984; dist. dir. World Hunger, Great Falls, Mont., 1973-75. Bd. dirs. Dubuque Hospice, 1982-84, Milk River Developmentally Disabled Bd., Glasgow, Mont., 1977-80, Luth. Social Service S.D., 1971-75, St. John's Luth. Home, Billings, Mont., 1964-68. Mem. Dubuque Area Christians United. Republican. Lodge: Kiwanis (dir. 1983-84). Home: 3170 Asbury Rd Dubuque IA 52201

NOVAK, PATRICK R., minister, United Church of Christ; b. Seattle, June 21, 1947; s. Rudolph and Pauline Virginia (Lyons) Troxel; m. Norma Yarbrough, Mar. 23, 1936; 1 child, Christine. B.A., Calif. State U.-Long Beach, 1973; M.Div., Gordon-Conwell Theol. Sem., 1976; D. Min., Andover Newton Theol. Sch., 1980. Ordained to ministry American Baptist Assn., 1975. Pastor First Bapt. Ch., Fair Haven, Vt., 1976-78, First Christian Ch., Newton, N.H., 1978-82, Sherman Congl. Ch., Conn., 1982—; dir. pastoral care Rockingham County, Brentwood, N.H., 1979-82; registrar, treas. Litchfield South Assn., Sherman, Conn., 1983—. Chmn. spiritual needs com. White House Conf. on Aging, Concord, N.H., 1979; mem. Council on Aging, Sherman, Conn., 1982—. Served to sgt. USMC, 1965-70, Vietnam. Mem. Gerontol. Soc. Am., Nat. Alliance for Family Life (clin.), Assn. Clin. Pastoral Edn. Republican. Home: RR 1 Box 193 Gelston Rd Sherman CT 06784 Office: Box E Church Rd Sherman CT 06784

OVICK, IVAN J., real estate executive, religious rganization executive, Jewish; b. Butler, Pa., Apr. 5, 927; s. Harry Novick and Sadye Breman; m. Natalie ger, Aug. 27, 1950 (dec. July 1982); children: Howard lan, William Eger, Phyllis Susan Novick Silverman. tudent Johns Hopkins U., 1944, Va. Poly. Inst., 1945; rad. in econs. and polit. sci., U. Pitts., 1949. Ptnr., John Whiteman Real Estate, Pitts., 1950-54; gen. ptnr. Whiteman Ins. Agy., Pitts., 1954-57; pres. SanToy Mining Co., Pitts., 1957-58; exec. v.p. Apollo Industries nc., Pitts., 1958-64; pres. J.J. Gumberg Devel. Co., itts., 1961-64; ptnr. West Penn Realty Co., Pitts., 965—; mng. gen. ptnr. Nobil Novick Assocs., Boca Raton, Fla., 1978—, chmn. affiliate cos. TMI Realty of Fla., TMI Realty Inc. Contbr. articles to profl. jours. Campaign chmn. young adult div. United Jewish Fedn., 959, chmn. exec. com., 1960, assoc. chmn. mfg. div., 961, mem. central planning and budgeting com., 960-65, mem. nat. and overseas com., 1960-65, chmn. net. div., 1964, bd. dirs., Pitts., 1963-66, co-chmn. bldg. nd real estate div., 1966, mem. nat. com. and exec. om., 1967-68, bd. dirs., 1967-70, 74-77, mem. health nd edn. com., 1969-70, mem. leadership devel. com. 978, mem. nat. cabinet, 1966-78; 1st v.p. Pitts. dist. Zionist Orgn. Am., 1972, chmn. bd., 1978, pres. Tri-State region, 1978, vice chmn. nat. adminstrv. bd., 978, chmn. nat. exec. com., 1976-78, chmn. Israel cholarship program Pitts. dist., 1978, pres., 1978-83, hmn. bd., 1983—; bd. govs. Israel Bonds, 1962-64, bd. dirs., 1978, 80—; bd. govs. United Israel Appeal, 1978, d. trustees, 1980—; bd. dirs. Jewish Home & Hosp. for Aged, 1978, 80—; mem. campaign cabinet United Jewish Fedn. Pitts., 1978; bd. dirs. Jewish Nat. Fund, 1980—; mem. nat. bd. Am. Zionist Fedn., 1980—; vice chmn. Nat. Conf. on Soviet Jewry, 1983—; bd. govs. Tel Aviv U., 1983—; mem. internat. com. Hebrew U., Jerusalem, 1983—; mem. bd. Wurzweiler Sch. Social Work, Yeshiva U., 1983—. Served to lt. USAF, 1946-47. Recipient Israel Service award Zionist Orgn. Am., 1975, Justice Louis D. Brandeis award, 1978, award Jabotinsky Found., 1980, Israel Knesset medal Govt. of Israel, 1982. Mem. Internat. Coucnil Shopping Ctrs., Phi Epislon Pi. Republican. Jewish. Clubs: Concordia (Pitts.); Westmoreland Country, Standard, Press, Highridge Country, Three Rivers (Palm Beach, Fla.). Office: West Penn Realty Co 6315 Forbes Ave Pittsburgh PA 15217 or Nobil-Novick & Assocs 2200 N Federal Hwy Suite 204 Boca Raton FL 33432

NOVITSKY, ABRAHAM, rabbi, Orthodox Jewish; b. N.Y.C., May 29, 1930; s. Alex and Tillie (Mordichowitz) N.; M. Florence Doris Budnick, Feb. 15, 1953; children: Deena, Miriam, David, Mitchell, Gila. M.A., Villanova U., 1959. Ordained rabbi, 1953. Rabbi, Brith Sholom Community Ctr., Phila., 1953-58, Rhawnhurst Jewish Ctr., 1958-60, Aitz Chaim Synagogue, 1964—; state chaplain Commonwealth of Pa., 1960—. Kashruth adminstr. Orthodox Rabbinical Council Phila., 1955-81. Mem. Rabbinical Council Am., Phila. Bd. Rabbis. Home: 7601 Langdon St Philadelphia PA 19111 Office: Aitz Chaim Synagogue 7600 Summerdale Ave Philadelphia PA 19111

NOVOSELLER, MAURICE E., rabbi, Orthodox Jewish Congregations; b. Phila., Sept. 29, 1930; s. David Solomon and Reba Maryam (Twersky) N.; B.A., Yeshiva U., 1953; Smicha, 1958; postgrad. Temple U., 1963-66; m. Shirley Dowben, Jan. 29, 1956; children: Zachary J., Joseph A., Zena R., David S., Rachel R., Hya N. Ordained rabbi, 1958; rabbi Congregation Beth Chaim, Feasterville, Pa., 1958—; chaplain Commonwealth of Pa., 1966—; mem. Yeshiva U. Synagogue Council. Pres. Bucks County Rabbinical Bd., KO Kosher Service; founder Bucks County Jewish Community Chaplaincy Service; bd. dirs. Phila. Vaad Hakashrus, 1976. Pres. Tri-County Y; charter mem. Bucks County Planned Parenthood, Big Bros.; Charter, bd. dirs. Jewish Y's and Centers, Phila., others. Active Lower Southampton Twp. Morals Commn. Mem. B'nai B'rith. Home: 800 David Dr Trevose PA 19047 Office: 350 E Street Rd Feasterville PA 19047

NOVOTNY, DANIEL, minister, educator, United Church of Christ; b. Prague, Czechoslovakia, June 11, 1926; came to U.S., 1928; s. Joseph and Dagmar (Mladejovska) N.; m. Jean Anne Schultz, Aug. 20, 1949; children: Mark, Rebecca, Rachel, Benjamin. Student Bates Coll., 1944-45; B.S., Springfield Coll., Mass., 1947; B.D., Union Theol. Sem., 1949; postgrad. Hartford Sem., 1949-51; Ph.D., Fremont Grad. Sch., 1953; D.H.L. (hon.), U. N.H., 1969. Ordained to ministry Baptist Ch., 1949, transferred to Congregational Christian Ch. Minister, Congregational Ch., Goshen, Conn., 1949-51; prof. religion So. Union Coll., Wadley, Ala., 1952-53; minister Congl. Ch., Gorham, N.H., 1953-58, Community Ch., Durham, N.H., 1958-69, Plymouth Congl. Ch., Belmont, Mass., 1969-78, Central Sq. Congl. Ch., Bridgewater, Mass., 1978-83; lectr. Andover Newton Theol. Sch., Newton Centre, Mass., 1983—; co-dir. North Am. Study Sessions, Mansfield Coll., Oxford U., Eng., 1976—. Author: Stirrings, 1979. No. New England corrs. Christian Century, 1958-69. Bd. dirs. Gen. Theol. Library, Boston. Democrat. Avocations: fly fishing; rowing. Home: PO Box 133 West Chatham MA 02669 Office: Andover Newton Theol Sch 210 Herrick Rd Newton Centre MA 02159

NOYCE, GAYLORD BREWSTER, minister, United Church of Christ; b. Burlington, Iowa, July 8, 1926; s. Ralph Brewster and Harriet (Norton) N.; m. Dorothy Caldwell, May 25, 1949; children: Elizabeth, Karen, Timothy. B.A., Miami U., 1947; M.Div., Yale U., 1952. Ordained minister United Ch. of Christ, 1952. Asst. minister Hancock Congregational Ch., Lexington, Mass., 1952-54; minister United Ch., Raleigh, N.C., 1954-60; mem. faculty Yale Divinity Sch., 1960—; sec.-treas. Assn. for Case Teaching, 1984—; mem. steering com., past pres. Assn. for Profl. Edn. in Ministry, 1983—; mem. steering com. Ch. Union Conversations, United Ch. of Christ and Christian Ch. Author: The Church is not Expendable, 1969; The Responsible Suburban Church, 1970; Survival and Mission for The City Church, 1975; The Art of Pastoral Conversation, 1981; New Perspectives On Parish Ministry, 1981. Chairperson Conn. Commn. on Race and Religion, 1965-68. Served with USN, 1944-46. Mem. Assn. Theol. Field Edn. (sec.-treas. 1971-73), Assn. Profl. Edn. for Ministry (pres. 1980-82). Democrat. Office: Yale Div Sch 363 St Ronan St New Haven CT 06511

NOYES, DOROTHY RAE, missionary, American Baptist Association, educator. B. San Francisco, Feb. 18, 1927; d. Raymond Edward and Marjorie E. (Smith) Stannard; m. Alfred Frederic Noyes, Aug. 23, 1952 (dec.); children: Russell Edward, Alfred Frederic Jr., Kathryn Louise, James Duncan. B.A., U. Redlands, 1946-49; cert. in social work, U. Calif., 1967-68. Commd. to ministry American Baptist Fgn. Missionary Soc., 1978. Dir. religious edn. First Bapt. Ch., Yakima, Wash., 1950-51; administrv. clk. Am. Bapt. Assembly, Green Lake, Wis., 1976-78; missionary, tchr. Am. Bapt. Foreign Mission Soc., Yokohama, Japan, 1978—. Republican. Home: 77 Kuritaya Kanagawa-ku Yokohama Japan 221 Office: Soshin Girls Sch 8 Nakamaru Kanagawa-ku Yokohama Japan 221

NUCKOLS, THOMAS WHEELER, religion educator, Southern Baptist Convention; b. Louise, Tex., Sept. 21, 1933; s. Rero Jerald and Floy (Brazzel) N.; m. Pat Mealor, July 3, 1957; children: Ruth E., Thomas M. B.A., Tulane U., 1956; B.D., So. Bapt. Theol. Sem., 1962; Ph.D., Duke U., 1968. Ordained to ministry Baptist Ch., 1960. Pastor, Brush Grove Bapt. Ch., Willisburg, Ky., 1960-62; from asst. prof. to prof. religion Austin Coll., Sherman, Tex., 1965—, dir. Heritage of Western Culture Program, 1980-82, chmn. dept. religion and philosophy, 1971-75. Author articles on Christian ethics. Served to lt. (j.g.) USN, 1956-59, USNR, 1959-62, as chaplain USNR, 1962-65. Recipient Hillel award Tulane U., 1956; Rockefeller Found. fellow, 1959; Woodrow Wilson fellow, 1962-63, 64-65. Mem. Am. Acad. Religion (pres. Southwest region 1983-84), coordinator med. ethics working group 1981-83), Phi Beta Kappa, Omicron Delta Kappa. Democrat. Home: 914 Starlight Dr Sherman TX 75090 Office: Box 1637 Sherman TX 75090

NULMAN, SEYMOUR SHLOMO, rabbi, educator, Orthodox Judaism, author. b. Newark, June 9, 1921; s. Samuel and Nellie (Feder) N.; m. Miriam Weinberg, May 24, 1942; children: Shifra Nulman Zwick, Basheva Nulman Schriber; m. Hilda Chill Leiter, Mar. 10, 1983. A.A., Isaac Elchanon Theol. Sem., 1942; B.A., Yeshiva U., 1942; M.A., Columbia U., 1944, postgrad., 1945. Ordained rabbi, 1943. Rabbi East Side Torah Ctr., N.Y.C., 1943—; dean Yeshiva Konvitz; N.Y.C., 1945—, Talmud Torah Jacob David, 1941—; chaplain Slutzker Landsmanshaft Orgn. Am., 1960—, N.Y. Infirmary-Beekman Downtown Hosp., N.Y.C., 1973—, Bellevue Hosp. Ctr., 1974, Meltzer Sr. Citizens' Tower, N.Y.C. Housing Authority, 1974—; pres. Yehudah Wolf Inst., N.Y.C., 1939-45, Jacob David Assn., 1948—; founder, dir. East Side Jewish Adult Studies Program, 1950—, Mobilization for Youth, Lower East Side, N.Y.C., 1950-54, Youth Commn. East Side C. of C., 1959-70, Nat. Day Schs. Tchrs. Licensing Commn., Nat. Assn. Hebrew Day Schs., 1964—, Religious Instn. Commn., N.Y.C., 1964-70, Essex Delancey Neighborhood Assn., 1970—, Lower East Side Neighborhoods Assn., 1972—, Multi-Service Ctr., N.Y.C., 1973—; dir. Rabbanit Miriam Nulman Free Adult Inst. of Jewish Studies, 1955, Massaryk Towers, N.Y.C., N.Y.C. Com. on Inter-Racial Conflicts; v.p. United Jewish Council of Eastside N.Y.; judge Jewish Conciliation Bd. Am. Author: Syllabus and Techniques for Hebrew Day SChool, 1953; Holiday Customs and Ceremonies, 1959; Torah Journal, 1959; The Memorial Book, 1965; Handbook for Jewish Parents, 1965; The Year of Jewish Holidays, Festivals and Ceremonies, 1982; editor monthly letter, 1958—; contbr. articles to profl. jours. Del. White House Conf. Children and Youth, 1970; state supt. ch.-related schs. com. HEW, 1960-64; mem. planning bd. Borough Manhattan, 1960—, New Gov. Hosp., N.Y.C., 1972-74; mem. Jewish com. Manhattan council Boy Scouts Am., 1955—; mem. adv. council Joint Legis Commn. Pub. Health, Medicine, Medicaid and Compulsory Health and Hosp. Inst. State of N.Y., 1968—; mem. Met. Com. on Talmud Torah Edn., 1969—, Health Systems Agy., N.Y. Recipient numerous merit awards, Service Internat. Torah Schs., 1966, Outstanding Educator Parents Assn., 1968, Shofar Boy Scouts Am., 1969, Community Fedn. Jewish Philanthropies, 1971, Torah Leadership O'eylim, 1972, Community Lower East Side Neighborhoods Assn. Assns,, 1973, Disting. Service Jewish Counciliation Bd. Am., 1974, Pastoral Care Chaplaincy Sch., N.Y. Bd. Rabbis, 1975, State of Israel Bonds, 1982, Negev State of Israel, 1983. Mem. Religious Instn. Assn. (pres. 1958-70), Nat. Conf. Day Schs Prins. and Deans (chmn.), Rabbinical Bd. East Side (founder, v.p.), Union Orthodox Rabbis U.S. and Can. (exec. mem. adminstrv. bd.), Assn. Torah Edn., Rabbinical Alumni Yeshiva U., Orthodox Jewish Congregations Am., Nat. Assn. Orthodox Jewish Scientists (mem. planning bd.), Rabbinical Sem. Am. Alumni Assn. (sec.), Nat. English Prins. Assn. (sec. 1960-70), Nat. Assn. Hebrew Day Schs.-Yeshivas (chmn. bd. 1967-69), Nat. Yeshiva Sch. Prins. (v.p.), N.Y.C. C. of C. (bd. dirs.), NEA. Club: B'nai B'rith. Home: 268 E Broadway New York NY 10002 Office: East Side Torah Ctr 313 Henry St New York NY 10002

NUNN, GEORGE HARRY, minister, college president, religious organization executive, Pentecostal Holiness Church of Canada; b. Noranda, Que., Can., Nov. 29, 1935; s. George Harry and Shiela (Darwin) N.; m. Ruth Naomi Bohrer, Nov. 24, 1954; children: Ruth Ann, Harry, Timothy, Stephen. D.Min., Can. Christian Coll., 1979; D.D. (hon.), Christianview Bible Coll., 1977. Ordained to ministry Pentecostal Holiness Ch. of Can. Pastor Bethel Assembly, Tacoma, Wash., 1962-69, Ch. By The Side of the Road, Seattle, 1969-71; pres. Christianview Bible Coll., Ailsa Craig, Ont., 1975—; gen. supt. Pentecostal Holiness Ch. of Can., Waterloo, Ont., 1971—. Home: 86 E McDougall Rd Waterloo ON N2L 5C5 Canada Office: Pentecostal Holiness Ch of Can PO Box 442 Waterloo ON N2J 4A9 Canada

NUSCHER, MAX EDWIN, minister, United Church of Christ; b. Johnson City, N.Y., Nov. 14, 1929; s. Max Edward Herman and Florence Ellen (Ward) N.; student Central City Bus. Inst., 1948-50; B.A., Albright Coll., 1954; M.Div., United Theol. Sem., 1957; M.Th., Princeton U., 1970; D.Min., Lancaster Theol. Sem.; m. Jean Marian Hook, June 12, 1954; children: Karen Sue, Mark Edwin, Martin Edmund. Ordained to ministry United Ch. of Christ, 1957. Minister in Syracuse, N.Y., 1957-60, Binghamton, N.Y., 1960-61, Washington Mills, N.Y., 1961-63, Havertown, Pa., 1963-66, Pine Grove (Pa.) United Ch. of Christ, 1966-70, St. John's United Ch. of Christ, Pottstown, Pa., 1970—; chaplain Oneida County Prison, 1962-63, 28th Inf. Div., Pa. N.G., 1962-74, Ursinus Coll., 1974—; moderator Ursinus Assn., Pa. S.E. Conf. United Ch. of Christ, 1973; state chaplain Pa. Dept. Mil. Affairs, 1974-81. Pres., Pine Grove Little League, 1968-70; committeeman Boy Scouts Am., 1957-74. Bd. dirs. No. br. ARC, 1971-74; chmn. adv. bd. Pottstown Meml. Hosp. Ctr., 1978-81. Mem. Mil. Chaplains Assn., N.G. Assn., Pottstown Hist. Soc. (dir. 1971-74), Nat. Sojourners (pres. Valley Forge chpt.), Camp Heroes of '76 (comdr.). Mason (32 deg.). Composer: (hymns) To Be Set Free, 1970, God Who Is Father, 1972. Home: Manatawny Rd Pottstown PA 19464 Office: 11 S Price St Pottstown PA 19464

NUSSBAUM, STAN WAYNE, religion educator, Evangelical Mennonite Church; b. Decatur, Ind., Dec. 26, 1949; s. Milo David and Violet Mae (Yoder) N.; m. Lorri Sue Berends, Aug. 22, 1970; children: Anjila, Adam. B.A., Taylor U., 1971; M.A., Trinity Evang. Div. Sch., 1973, M.Div., 1974; postgrad. U. So. Africa, 1979—. Lic. to ministry Evang. Mennonite Ch., 1974. Dir. Christian edn. Evang. Mennonite Hdqrs., Fort Wayne, 1974-76; missionary Africa Inter-Mennonite Mission, Maseru, Lesotho, 1977-83; dir. world mission program Fort Wayne Bible Coll., 1984—. Author: A Historical Sketch of the Evangelical Mennonite Church, 1978. Designer ednl. game, 1976. Mem. So. African Missiological Soc. Home: 1415 Dinnamon Rd Fort Wayne IN 46825 Office: Fort Wayne Bible Coll 1025 W Rudisill Fort Wayne IN 46807

NUTTER, HAROLD LEE, archbishop, Anglican Church of Canada; b. Welsford, N.B., Can., Dec. 29, 1923; s. William Lawton and Lillian Agnes (Joyce) N.; m. Edith Maud Carew, Sept. 21, 1946; children: Patricia Nutter Hunsley, Bruce. B.A., Mt. Allison U., Sackville, N.B., 1944, LL.D., 1972; M.S.Litt., King's Coll., Halifax, N.S., Can., 1947, D.D., 1960; M.A., Dalhousie U., Halifax, 1947; D.D., Montreal Diocesan Theol. Coll., 1982, Wycliffe Coll., Toronto, 1983, Trinity Coll., Toronto, 1985. Ordained priest Anglican Ch. of Can., 1947, consecrated bishop, 1971. Rector, Parish of Simonds and Upham, N.B., 1947-51, Parish of Woodstock, 1951-57, Parish of St. Mark, St. John, N.B., 1957-60; dean of Fredericton, N.B., 1960-71, bishop, 1971-80; archbishop of Fredericton, met. of Eccles. Province of Can., 1980—; co-chmn. N.B. Task Force on Social Devel., 1970-71; mem. Com. on Multiculturism of Can., 1973—. Home: 791 Brunswick St Fredericton NB E3B 1H8 Canada

NUWER, HEROLD MICHAEL, priest, Roman Catholic Church; b. East Aurora, N.Y., Jan. 4, 1934; s. Michael Aloysius and Irene (Herold) N. B.B.A., Canisius Coll., 1956; postgrad. Diocese Prep. Sem., 1956-57, St. Bonaventure U., 1957-61. Ordained priest Roman Cath. Ch., 1961. Adminstr. St. Brendan's Ch., Almond, N.Y., 1961-62, Sacred Heart Ch., Buffalo, 1964-67, St. Nicholas Ch., Buffalo, 1967-77; pastoral asst. St. Nicholas Ch., Buffalo, 1962-63; pastor Our

Lady of Loretto Ch., Buffalo, 1979—. Rep. for Diocese Buffalo to March on Washington, 1963. Mem. NAACP (Human Relations award 1979). Home and Office: 172 15th St Buffalo NY 14213

NUYUJUKIAN, SOGHOMON DAWLAT, minister, United Church of Christ - Armenian Evangelical; b. Aleppo, Syria, Mar. 1, 1923; came to U.S. 1974, naturalized 1980; s. Dawlat and Lucia (Kouyoumjian) N.; m. Mathilda Cholakian, July 1, 1950 (dec. Jan. 10, 1959); children: Jessy Nuyujukian Hagopian, Hratch Nuyujukian; m. Hilda Cholakian, June 5, 1959; children: Ara, Christine. B.A., Am. U. Beirut, 1948; Diploma in Theology, Near East Sch. Theol., Beirut, 1948; M.Div., Andover-Newton Theol. Sch., 1976, D.Min., 1979. Ordained to ministry United Ch. Christ, 1954. Minister Armenian Evang. Ch., Aleppo, Syria, 1948-59, Alexandria, Egypt, 1959-62, Armenian Evang. Ch., Beirut, 1968-74, Ararat Armenian Congl. Ch., Salem, N.H., 1974-80, Armenian Martyrs' Congl. Ch., Havertown, Pa., 1980—; exec. sec. Armenian Evang. Union, Beirut, 1962-67; mem. Phila. Assn. ch. and ministry com. United Ch. Christ, 1982—; synod del. Pa. S.E. Conf. United Ch. Christ, 1984—; gov. rep. Armenian Protestant Community, Aleppo, Syria, 1948-59, Beirut, 1968-74; pres. Religious Court of 1st Instance, Aleppo, 1952-59, Religious Ct. Appeal, Beirut, 1968-74. Mem. Am. Assn. Pastoral Counselors. Home: 830 Blythe Ave Drexel Hill PA 19026 Office: Armenian Martyrs' Congregational Ch 100 N Edmonds Ave Havertown PA 19083

NYCKLEMOE, GLENN WINSTIN, minister, American Lutheran Church; b. Fergus Falls, Minn., Dec. 8, 1936; s. Melvin and Bertha (Sumstad) N.; m. Ann Elizabeth Olson, May 28, 1960; children: Peter, John, Daniel. B.A., St. Olaf Coll., 1958; M.Div., Luther Theol. Sem., St. Paul, 1962; D.Min., Luth. Sch. Theology, Chgo., 1977. Ordained to ministry Am. Luth. Ch., 1962. Asst. pastor Our Savior's Luth. Ch., Valley City, N.D., 1962-64; asst. pastor Our Savior's Luth. Ch., Milw., 1964-67, co-pastor, 1967-73; sr. pastor, Beloit, Wis., 1973-82; sr. pastor St. Olaf Luth. Ch., Austin, Minn., 1982—; mem. Bd. for Theology Edn. and Ministry, Am. Luth. Ch., 1982—; dir. St. Mark's Luth. Home, Austin, 1982—. Author (with others) Parish Team Ministry Manual, 1968. Chmn. bd. dirs. Citizens Adv. Com., Beloit, 1981, Desegregation Bd., Beloit, 1981; mem. Bus. Devel. Bd., Austin, 1982. Named Disting. Citizen, Beloit City Council, 1982. Lodge: Rotary. Office: St Olaf Luth Ch 301 1st St NW Austin MN 55912

NYE, MIRIAM MAURINE HAWTHORN BAKER, lay church worker, United Methodist Church; b. Castana, Iowa, June 14, 1918; d. Horace Boies and Hazel Dean (Waples) Hawthorn; B.A., Morningside Coll., 1939, postgrad., 1957-58; postgrad. U. Ariz., 1973, U. S.D., 1975-76; m. Carl Baker, June 21, 1941 (dec. May 1970); children: Kent A., Dale H.; m. John Arthur Nye, Dec. 25, 1973. Mem. United Meth. Ch. Commn. on Edn., Moville, Iowa, 1955-71, chmn., 1960-64; mem. Iowa Conf. Commn. on Archives-History, 1972-76. Counselor, Iowa State U., 1972—; lay del. Iowa United Meth. Conf., 1981-84. Woodbury County reading chmn., 1956; mem. Woodbury County Extension Council, 1969-72; mem. Siouxland Health Planning Council, 1971-73. Recipient Alumni award Morningside Coll., 1969; Friend of Extension award Iowa State U., 1981. Mem. Common Cause, AAUW, Farm Bur. (county pub. relations com. 1968-72), Iowa Fedn. Women's Clubs, Alpha Kappa Delta, Sigma Tau Delta. Author: Recipes and Ideas from the Kitchen Window, 1973; But I Never Thought He'd Die: Practical Help for Widows, 1978. Columnist, Sioux City Jour. Farm Weekly, 1953-81. Home and office: Route 2 Moville IA 51039

NYGREN, ELLIS HERBERT, religion educator, minister United Methodist Church; b. Bklyn., June 27, 1928; s. Erik Helge and Jenny (Walaas) N.; m. Louise Whitton, June 9, 1951; children: Herbert, Steven. B.A., Taylor U., 1951; M.A., NY U, 1954, Ph.D., 1960; S.T.B., Bibl. Sem., N.Y.C., 1954. Ordained to ministry United Meth. Ch., 1952. Pastor, United Meth. Chs., N.Y., Conn., 1951-60; prof. Emory and Henry Coll., Va., 1960-69, prof. religion Taylor U., Upland, Ind., 1969—. Contbr. to Biblical Errancy, 1983, also articles to profl. jours. Mem. Am. Soc. Ch. History, Evang. Theol. Soc. Office: Taylor Univ Upland IN 46987

NYLINE, KARL FREDRIC, minister, Am. Lutheran Ch.; b. Danbury, Conn., Jan. 10, 1934; s. Wilbert Walter and Greta Esther (Ekberg) N.; A.A., North Park Jr. Coll., 1953; B.A., Augustana Coll. (Ill.), 1955; M.Div. North Park Theol. Sem., 1960; postgrad. Luther Sem., St. Paul, 1963, 64; m. Signie Linnea Gilberg, June 20, 1959; children—Kari Linnea, Maria Kim. Ordained to ministry, 1960; pastor Community Covenant, Mpls., 1960-64, Trinity Luth. Ch., Mpls., 1964-68, Bethany Luth. Ch., St. Paul, 1968-72, Crown of Glory Luth. Ch., Chaska, Minn., 1972—. Chmn. Dist. Urban Ch. Commn.; chmn. Dist. Minn. Task Force. Active Eagle Scouts; chmn. Cedar Riverside Assn., Mpls., 1966-68; chmn. Pahlen Area Community Council, St. Paul, 1971-72; pres. council Mpls. Community Council, 1967-68; del. Carver County Republican Conv., ward chmn., 1974, 76. Mem. Norske Torske Klubben (St.

Paul), Am. Swedish Inst. (Mpls.), Christ and Culture Touching Unfolding Socs., Mexican Youth Encounter. Editor The Crownicle (local ch. periodical). Home: 1260 Stephan Ln Chaska MN 55318 Office: 1141 Cardinal St Chaska MN 55318

OAKLEY, VERNON LEBERT, minister, Christian Ch.; b. Woodbury, Ill., Sept. 15, 1936; s. Francis Warren and Mary Ellen (Berry) O.; B.A., Ky. Christian Coll., 1962; m. Kathryn Ann Baynes, Nov. 13, 1954; children—Cheri Lynn, Cynthia Ann, Douglas Vernon. Ordained to ministry, 1960; missionary, Zambia, Africa, 1967-70; pastor Heyworth (Ill.) Christian Ch., 1971—. Trustee, Zambia Christian Mission, 1971—, Coll. of the Scriptures, 1972—, Ill. State U., Ill. Wesleyan U. Christian Campus Ministry, 1972-74. Mem. Council of Fifty, Ky. Christian Coll., 1971-75; chmn. Heyworth Cancer Crusade, 1973. Home: 307 W Randolph St Heyworth IL 61745 Office: Route 51 N Heyworth IL 61745

OAKLEY, WILLIAM PAUL, minister, So. Bapt. Conv.; b. Dyersburg, Tenn., Sept. 5, 1931; s. Willie B. and Dorothy Lee (Lambert) O.; A.B., William Carey Coll., 1967; Th.M., Luther Rice Sem., 1974, D. Min., 1976; m. Pattye Lavine Norman, June 1, 1950; children—Patricia Elizabeth Oakley George, Dianna Lynn Oakley Clement, Joseph, Paul, Michelle. Ordained to ministry, 1950; pastor chs., Tenn., Mich., Fla., Miss., Calif., Colo., Tex., 1950—, S. Park Bapt. Ch., Beaumont, Tex. Active local Bapt. assns. Mem. Beaumont Ministerial Assn., Golden Triangle Bapt. Assn., Gen. Bapt. Conv. Tex. Author: Exegesis of the Revelation, 1972; Manifesting Victory in the Christian Life, 1976. Home: 685 Zavalla St Beaumont TX 77705 Office: 795 Woodrow St Beaumont TX 77705

OAKS, DALLIN HARRIS, church official, Ch. of Jesus Christ of Latter-day Saints; b. Provo, Utah, Aug. 12, 1932; s. Lloyd E. and Stella (Harris) O.; B.A., Brigham Young U., 1954; J.D. cum laude, U. Chgo., 1957; m. Verda June Dixon, June 24, 1952; children—Sharmon (Mrs. Jack Donald Ward), Cheri (Mrs. Louis Eugen Ringger), Lloyd Dixon, Dallin Dixon, TruAnn Oaks Boulter, Jenny June. Stake mission pres. Chgo. Stake, Ch. of Jesus Christ of Latter-day Saints, 1962-63; second counselor Chgo. South Stake, 1963-70, first counselor, 1970-71; regional rep. Quorum of 12, 1974-80; pres. Brigham Young U., Provo, 1971-80; justice Utah Supreme Ct., 1981-84; mem. Quorum of the Twelve, 1984—. Mem. adv. council Woodrow Wilson Internat. Center for Scholars. Mem. Am. Assn. Presidents Colls. and Univs. (pres. 1975-80), Am. Bar Assn., Order of Coif. Author: (with G.G. Bogert) Cases on Trusts, 1967; (with W. Lehman) A Criminal Justice System and the Indigent, 1968; (with M. Hill) Carthage Conspiracy: The Trial of the Accused Assassins of Joseph Smith, 1975; Trust Doctrines in Church Controversies, 1984. Editor: The Wall Between Church and State, 1963. Editor-in-chief U. Chgo. Law Rev., 1956-57. Office: 47 E South Temple St Salt Lake City UT 84150

OAS, JOHN KENNETH, minister, Assemblies of God; b. Tacoma, Oct. 11, 1946; s. Kenneth Arthur and Esther Carolyn (Anderson) O.; B.A. in Religion/Philosophy, Seattle Pacific Coll., 1969; postgrad. Northwest Coll., 1970; M.A. in Religious Research, Northgate Grad. Sch., 1973; m. Kathleen Alice Swanson, Aug. 15, 1969; children—Jason, Andrea. Ordained to ministry, 1973; traveling evangelist, 1970-73; youth pastor Westgate Chapel and White Center Assembly, 1973-75; mem. N.W. Dist. Choir Com. and Youth Exec. Coms., 1974-76; chaplain Seattle-Tacoma Internat. Airport, 1975—, Seattle Police Dept., 1978; Mem. Airport Emergency Team; area bd. advisor Woman's Aglow Internat.; Mem. Washington State Disaster Assistance Council, 1984, Pacific N.W. Christian Singles Council, 1984; savs. officer Equitable Savs. & Loan Assn., 1975—. Mem. White Center C. of C., Civil Aviation Chaplains Internat., Nat, Inst. Bus. and Indsl. Chaplains (editor Focus 1982, v.p. 1983). Home 17751 10th Ave S Seattle WA 98158 Office: Seattle-Tacoma Internat Airport Room 213 Seattle WA 98158

OATES, CALEB EUGENE, minister, Bapt. Ch.; b. Shelby, N.C., Apr. 5, 1917; s. David Pilgrim and Emma Ethel O.; student pub. schs., Asbury Park, N.J.; m. Authella R. Walker, Jan. 6, 1939; children—Bernard D., David Charles. Ordained to ministry, 1947; pastor Bethany Bapt. Ch., Farmingdale, N.J., 1948—. Corr. sec. Seacoast Missionary Bapt. Assn., 1948-54, treas., 1954-58, sec., 1958-62, vice moderator, 1962-66, moderator, 1966-72, fin. sec., 1974—; fin. sec. Gen. Bapt. State Conv. N.J., 1969-73, 1974—, sec., 1973-74, fin. sec., 1974—, 2d v.p., 1977-81, 1st v.p., 1981-85, pres., 1985—. Mem. Republican Presdl. Task Force, 1979—. Named Pastor of Yr., N.J., 1956; recipient Outstanding Community Work award Kiwanis Club, 1967; Community Service award Asbury Park chpt. NAACP, 1982. Author: The Deacon and His Office, 1957. Home and Office: RD 1 Box 116A Farmingdale NJ 07727

OBAYASHI, HIROSHI, religion educator, United Church of Christ; b. Osaka, Japan, Dec. 3, 1934; came to U.S., 1962; s. Ichiro and Miyuki (Hotehama) O.; m.

Kimiko Fujisawa, Nov. 3, 1960; children: Hal Naoya Seiya John, Anna Jane. B.A., Doshisha U., 1957 B.Div., 1959; S.T.M., Andover Newton Theol. Sch. 1963; Ph.D., U. Pa., 1967. Licentiate United Ch. o Christ in Japan. Minister United Ch. Christ, Osaka 1959-60, Nishinomiya, Japan, 1960-62, Phila., 1963-67 prof. religion Rutgers U., New Brunswick, N.J., 1967— Author: Ernst Troeltsch and Theology Today, 1972 Agape and History, 1981. Mem. Am. Acad. Religion (bd. dirs. 1982-85, pres. Mid-Atlanta region 1980-81) Office: Dept Religion Rutgers U New Brunswick N. 08903

OBESO RIVERA, SERGIO, archbishop, Roman Catholic Church; b. Jalapa, Mex., Oct. 31, 1931 Ordained priest Roman Cath. Ch., 1954. Named bishop of Papantla, 1971, named titular bishop of Uppenna with personal title of archbishop, 1974, now archbishop of Jalapa, Mex., 1979—. Office: Arzobispado Ave Revolucion 2 Apartado 359 Jalapa Mexico*

O'BRIEN, ELMER JOHN, librarian, United Methodist Church; b. Kemmerer, Wyo., Apr. 8, 1932; s Ernest and Emily Catherine (Reinhart) O'B.; m. Betty Alice Peterson, July 2, 1966. B.A., Birmingham So. Coll., 1954; M.Th., Iliff Sch. Theology, 1957; M.A., U. Denver, 1961. Ordained to ministry, 1957. Pastor, Meth. Ch., Papoga Springs, Colo., 1957-60; circulation reference librarian Boston U. Sch. Theology, 1961-65; asst. librarian Garrett Evang. Theol. Sem., Evanston, Ill., 1965-69; librarian, prof. United Theol. Sem., Dayton, Ohio, 1969—. Editor: Bibliography of Festschriften in Religion Published Since 1960, 1972; Religion Index Two: Festschriften 1960-1969, 1980. United Meth. Ch. faculty research grantee, 1985. Mem. ALA, Am. Theol. Library Assn. (pres. 1978-79). Democrat. Club: Dayton Torch (pres. 1982-83). Home: 7818 Lockport Blvd Dayton OH 45459 Office: United Theol Sem 1810 Harvard Blvd Dayton OH 45406

O'BRIEN, JOHN GERARD, priest, Roman Catholic Ch.; b. Limerick, Ireland, Dec. 16, 1912; s. Patrick Joseph and Mary Ann (Guerin) O'B.; came to U.S., 1942, naturalized, 1951; diploma in philosophy Mungret Coll., Ireland, 1935. Ordained priest, 1940; asst. pastor St. Aloysius and Blessed Sacrament, Birmingham, Ala., 1940-49; pastor St. Joseph Ch., Elk City, Okla., and St. Rose of Lima Ch., Perry, Okla., 1949-67; chaplain Lexington Treatment Center. Bd. dirs. USO in Ala., 1943-46. Recipient Chaplain citation Okla. Legislature, 1974. Mem. U. Louvain Alumni Assn. Contbr. articles to religious mags. Home: 316 Jefferson St Purcell OK 73080

O'BRIEN, JOSEPH VINCENT, priest, Roman Catholic Church; b. Coggon, Iowa, Apr. 12, 1931; s. Louis Joseph and Rosemarie (Burke) O'B. B.A., Conception Coll., 1953. Ordained priest Roman Cath. Ch., 1957. Assoc. pastor Dubuque Archdiocese, 1957-66, dir. vocations, 1966-76; pastor St. Donatus Ch., 1976-77, St. Patrick's Ch., Anamosa, 1977-82, St. Pius X Ch., Cedar Rapids, Iowa, 1982—. Spiritual dir. Cursillo Movement, Dubuque, 1967-77; dir. Propagation of Faith, 1967-76. Democrat. Clubs: Serra, Rotary. Office: St Pius X Ch Council and Collins Rd NE Cedar Rapids IA 52402

O'BRIEN, ROGER GERARD, priest, Roman Catholic Church; b. Seattle, Aug. 3, 1935; s. Francis Thomas and Susan Elizabeth (Jurich) O'B. B.A., Sulpician Sem. of Northwest, 1957, M.Div., 1961; M.L.S., U. Wash., 1961; Licentiate in Theology, St. Mary's Sem., 1964; Th.D., Cath. U., Louvain, Belgium, 1969. Ordained priest Roman Cath. Ch., 1961. Prof. systematic theology St. Patrick's Sem., Menlo Park, Calif., 1968-69, St. Thomas Sem., Kenmore, Wash., 1969-76; ecumenical and interfaith officer Archdiocese of Seattle, 1976-80, dir. office of worship, 1977-82; pastor St. Luke Parish, Seattle, 1982—; bd. dirs. Ch. Council Greater Seattle, 1976-82, Wash. Assn. Chs., 1976-82; mem. Jewish/Christian Dialogue, Seattle, 1976—; bd. dirs. Archdiocese of Seattle Faith and Community Devel. Dept., 1982—. Contbr. articles to profl. jours. Mem. Nat. Assn. Diocesan Ecumenical Officers (bd. dirs. 1980-82). Democrat. Home and Office: St Luke's Ch 322 N 175th St Seattle WA 98133

O'BRIEN, THOMAS JOSEPH See *Who's Who in America*, 43rd edition.

O'BRYANT, L.D., JR., elder, Ch. of God in Christ; b. Grenada, Miss., Apr. 2, 1942; s. L. D. and Onnie Mae (Goins) O'B.; student Sts. Coll., 1960-61; m. Mary Louise O'Banion, Aug. 31, 1963; children—Vivion Louise, Eric Lee, Victor Wade, Tiffany LaShell. Ordained to ministry, 1963; pastor-founder Pilgrim Rest Ch. of God in Christ, Oakland, Miss., 1965—, East Batesville Ch. of God in Christ, Batesville, Miss., 1966-70; pastor Rose of Sharon Ch. of God in Christ, Amory, Miss., 1970—. Dist. 8 evangelist, No. Miss. Bd. mem. Delta Area council Boy Scouts Am., 1975-76; mem. state bd. elders no. jurisdiction hdqrs. St. James Temple, Clarksdale, Miss., 1963-76. Home: PO Box 84 Grenada MS 38901 Office: Route 1 Mill St Oakland MS 38948

OBST, MARTIN HERMAN, minister, Am. Luth. Ch.; b. Alamo, Tex., Aug. 1, 1928; s. Bruno Oswald and Gertrude Margaret C. (Eisen) O.; B.A., Wartburg Coll., 1948; certificate of grad., Wartburg Theol. Sem., 1951. Ordained to ministry, 1951; pastor Linton, N.D., 1951-54, Zion-Emmanuel Luth. Ch., Lane, S.D., 1954-57, Peace Luth. Ch., Beeville, Tex., 1958-63, Bethlehem Luth. Ch., Round Top, Tex., 1963-67, St. John Luth. Ch., Boerne, Tex., 1967-73, Salem Luth. Ch., Austin, Tex. and Grace Luth. Ch., Lockhart, Tex., 1973—. Sec.-treas. Central Dakota Conf., 1952-54; v.p. So. Conf., So. Dist., 1961-63; Nat. Luth. Council contact pastor U.S. Navy Aux. Air Sta., Chase Field, Beeville, Tex., 1958-63; v.p. E. Central Conf., So. Dist., 1965-67; chmn. All Luth. Pastors, Austin, Tex., 1974-75. Del. to Tex. Republican State Conv., 1964, 66, 70, 72, 74; Fayette County Rep. vice chmn., 1964-67; Rep. precinct chmn., 1964-67, Kendall County, Tex., 1967-73, Travis County, Tex., 1973—. Recipient Citizenship award Boerne Lions Club, 1973. Mem. Boerne C. of C. (pres. 1969-71). Author: Our God Is Marching On, 1966. Home and Office: 6701 Lockhart Hwy Austin TX 78743

O'BYRNE, PAUL J., bishop, Roman Catholic Church; b. Calgary, Alta., Can., Dec. 21, 1922. Ordained priest, 1948; bishop of Calgary, 1968—. Office: 1916 2d Ave SW Calgary AB T2S 1S3 Canada*

O'CALLAGHAN, JOHN JOSEPH, priest, Roman Catholic Church; b. New Rochelle, N.Y., Oct. 20, 1931; s. Francis Eugene and Marion Helen (O'Reilly) O'C. A.B., Loyola U., Chgo., 1954, M.A. in Classical Langs., 1960; Ph.D. in Theology, Gregorian U., Rome, 1967. Joined S.J.; ordained priest Roman Cath. Ch., 1962. Prof., rector Jesuit Sch. Theology, Chgo., 1967-76; sec. personnel Jesuit Conf., Washington, 1976-80, pres., 1980-83; gen. asst. Soc. of Jesus, Rome, 1983—. Contbr. articles to profl. jours. Mem. Cath. Theol. Soc., Soc. Christian Ethics. Home: Borgo Santo Spirito 5 Rome 00195 Italy Office: Curia Generalizia Compagnia di Gesu Borgo Santo Spirito 5 Rome Italy 00195

OCHS, PETER WARREN, chaplain, religion educator, Conservative Jews; b. Boston, Jan. 26, 1950; s. Sidney and Ruth (Adelman) O.; m. Vanessa Lynn Yablin, June 16, 1974; children: Juliana, Elizabeth. B.A. summa cum laude, Yale Coll., 1971; M.A., Jewish Theol. Sem., 1974; Ph.D., Yale U., 1979. Dir. Jewish Theol. Sem. Pre-High Sch., N.Y.C., 1972-74; counselor to Jewish students Colgate U., Hamilton, N.Y., 1979—, asst. prof. religion, 1979—; dir., advisor Colgate-Hamilton Jewish Community, 1979—. Author: Learning Sea Lore on Puluwat Atoll, 1975. Contbr. articles to profl. jours. Mem. Nitivot Shalom, Jerusalem, 1981—; mem. Labor Zionist Alliance, Israel, 1981—. NEH grantee, 1971, 73, 74, Smithsonian Inst. fellow, 1969, Kent fellow, 1974, Yale U. fellow, 1977, Colgate U. research grantee, 1980, 81, 82. Mem. Soc. for Values in Higher Edn., Am. Acad. Religion, Am. Philos. Assn., Charles S. Peirce Soc., Assocs. for Religion and Intellectual Life. Republican. Lodge: B'nai B'rith. Office: Colgate U Hamilton NY 13346

OCOKOLJICH, FIRMILIAN, bishop, Serbian Eastern Orthodox Church; b. Kaona, Serbia, Yugoslavia, Jan. 7, 1909; came to U.S., 1940; s. Uros and Darinka (Plazinich) O.; m. Nadezda Markovich, 1930 (dec. 1931). Diploma, Theol. Sem.-Yugoslavia, 1930; Licenciate, Belgrade U., 1938; Ph.D., U. Chgo., 1952. Ordained priest, 1931, consecrated bishop Serbian Eastern Orthodox Ch., 1963. Prof., Theol. Sem., Cetinje, Yugoslavia, 1938-40; priest various chs., Detroit, Chgo., Pitts. and N.Y.C., 1940-63; instr. St. Sava Sem., Libertyville, Ill., 1945-50; prof. St. Vladimir's Sem., Crestwood, N.Y., 1956-60; diocesan bishop Serbian Midwestern Diocese, Libertyville, 1963—, sec., 1940-46; dir. Diocesan Estate, Springboro, Pa., 1952-60; del. World Council Chs., N.Y.C., 1956-60; sec. Standing Conf. of Orthodox Bishops, N.Y.C., 1956-60. Home: 32377 N Milwaukee Ave Libertyville IL 60048 Office: Serbian Orthodox Midwestern Am Diocese PO Box 519 Libertyville IL 60048

O'CONNELL, JEROME DAVID, minister, Churches of Christ; b. Bridgeport, Conn., Aug. 24, 1951; s. George Vincent and Ethal Estelle (Moore) O'C.; m. Melba Rose Moss, Aug. 19, 1971; children: Colleen Elizabeth, Erin Rebecca. A.A., Freed-Hardeman Coll., 1971; B.A., Harding U., 1973, M.A., 1975, M.Th., 1978. Ordained to ministry Ch. of Christ, 1971. Minister, Liberty Ch. of Christ, Scotts Hill, Tenn., 1971-72, Maxville Ch. of Christ, Cave City, Ark., 1972-73, Marianna Ch. of Christ, Ark., 1973-74, South Rd. Ch. of Christ, Farmington, Conn., 1978—; assoc. minister Macon Rd. Ch. of Christ, Memphis, 1974-78. Dir. Harvest Northeast Campaign, Clifton Park, N.Y., 1983—. Contbr. articles to religious publs. Mem. Collegiate Civitans, Henderson, Tenn., 1970-72, Tenn. Vols. for Life, Memphis, 1976-78; mem. adv. bd. dirs. Pro-Life Council Conn., Wallingford, 1978—; mem. Civil War Round Table, 1980—, dist. speaker, 1984. Mem. Inst. for Advancement of Christian Theism. Avocations: golf; book collecting; Irish-Am. history. Home: 28 Westview Terr Farmington CT 06085 Office: South Rd Ch of Christ 69 South Rd Farmington CT 06032

O'CONNOR, BRIAN PATRICK, priest, Roman Cath. Ch.; b. N.Y.C., Jan. 16, 1946; s. Bernard and Elizabeth Ann (Herrity) O'C.; A.B., St. Joseph's Coll. and Sem., Yonkers, N.Y., 1967, M.Div., 1970; M.P.H., Columbia, 1976. Ordained priest, 1971; asso. pastor Incarnation Ch., N.Y.C., 1971—. Leader Hispanic Youth Retreats; pres. bd. Washington Heights Sr. Citizens Center. Participant symposia, co-chmn. profl. adv. bd. Found. of Thanatology Columbia Med. Center. Mem. Am. Geriatrics Soc., Ministry Symposium (co-chmn. sect. theology). Home and office: Incarnation Ch 1290 Saint Nicholas Ave New York NY 10033

O'CONNOR, CHARLES E., religious organization executive, Grace Gospel Fellowship; b. Chgo., Dec. 21, 1926; s. Charles E. and Margaret (Love) O'C.; m. Doris Joanne Spalding, Sept. 15, 1950; children: William, Mrs. Tom Hartman, Robert. B.S., Northwestern U., 1951. Exec. dir. Grace Gospel Fellowship, Grand Rapids, Mich., 1971—; dir. Grace Bible Coll., Grand Rapids, 1972—, Grace Ministries Internat., Grand Rapids, 1972—, Grace Youth Camp, Mears, Mich., 1962—, Grace Publs., Grand Rapids, 1982—. Served with AUS, 1944-45. Home: 2651 Doncaster SW Grand Rapids MI 49509 Office: Grace Gospel Fellowship 1011 Aldon St SW Grand Rapids MI 49509

O'CONNOR, DANIEL WILLIAM, educator, United Church of Christ; b. Jersey City, Mar. 17, 1925; s. Daniel William and Emma Pauline (Ritz) O'C.; B.A., Dartmouth, 1945; M.Div., Union Theol. Sem., 1950; M.A., Columbia, 1956, Ph.D., 1960; m. Carolyn Mary Lockwood, June 26, 1954; children—Kathy, Daniel William III. Ordained to ministry United Ch. of Christ, 1950; asso. sec. Student Christian Movement in N.Y. State, 1947-48; exec. sec. Earl Hall of Columbia, 1948-50; pastor Paramus (N.J.) Congl. Ch., 1950-55; mem. exec. com., dir. Bd. Home Missions of Congl-Christian Chs., 1946-51; tutor asst. dept. N.T., Union Theol. Sem., 1957-59; asst. prof. religion St. Lawrence U., 1959-63, asso. prof., 1963-67, asso. dean coll., 1967-68, prof., 1967—, Charles A. Dana prof., chmn. dept., 1973—. Supr., Joint Archaeol. Expdn., Israel, 1969, 71; sec. Northeastern region Am. Acad. Religion, 1968-70, v.p., 1984-85, pres., 1985-86. Mem. Soc. Bibl. Lit., AAUP, U.S. Power Squadron (dir. St. Lawrence squadron 1966-68), Silver Bay Assn. (trustee 1976—). Author: Peter in Rome: the Residence, Martyrdom and Burial of Peter in Rome, 1969. Contbr. articles and book reviews to periodicals, Ency. Britannica. Home: 3 Hillside Circle Canton NY 13617 Office: Dept Religious Studies St Lawrence U Canton NY 13617

O'CONNOR, HUBERT P., bishop, Roman Cath. Ch.; b. Huntingdon, Que., Can., Feb. 17, 1928. Ordained priest, 1954; bishop of Whitehorse (Y.T., Can.), 1971—. Office: 5119 Fifth Ave Whitehorse YT Y1A 1L5 Canada*

O'CONNOR, JOHN JOSEPH CARDINAL, archbishop, Roman Catholic Church; b. Phila., Jan. 15, 1920; s. Thomas Joseph and Dorothy Magdalene (Gomple) O'C. M.A., St. Charles Coll., 1949, Cath. U. Am., 1954; Ph.D., Georgetown U., 1970; D.R.E., Villanova U., 1976. Ordained priest Roman Cath. Ch., 1945, elevated to monsignor, 1966, consecrated bishop, 1979. Served in Chaplain Corps, U.S. Navy, 1952, advanced through grades to rear adm., assigned to Atlantic, Pacific fleets, Okinawa and Vietnam; sr. chaplain U.S. Naval Acad.; chief of chaplains U.S. Navy, Washington; aux. bishop, vicar gen. Mil. Vicarate, 1979-84; archbishop Archdiocese of N.Y., N.Y.C., 1984—; elevated to Sacred College of Cardinals, 1985—. Author: Principles and Problems of Naval Leadership, 1958; A Chaplain Looks at Vietnam, 1969; In Defense of Life, 1981. Mem. exec. bd. Nat. USO, Georgetown Ctr. Strategic and Internat. Studies, Marine Corps Found. Decorated Legion of Merit (3). Mem. Am. Polit. Sci. Assn. Office: Archdiocese of New York 452 Madison Ave New York NY 10022*

O'CULL, JOE FRANK, minister, Christian Churches and Churches of Christ; b. Maysville, Ky., Dec. 3, 1940; s. George and Grace (Thomas) O'C.; m. Phyllis Jean Newsome, Sept. 1, 1963. A.B., Ky. Christian Coll., 1977; M.A., Morehead State U., 1978. Ordained to ministry Church of Christ, 1973. Pastor, Concord Christian Ch., Ky., 1972-76, Bluebank Christian Ch., Flemingsburg, Ky., 1977-78, Antioch Christian Ch., Mt. Sterling, Ky., 1978-80, Glendale Christian Ch., Minford, Ohio, 1980-82, So. Ohio Correctional Facility, Lucasville, Ohio, 1982—. Served to sgt. U.S. Army, 1966-68. Mem. Ohio State Chaplain's Assn., Am. Protestant Correctional Chaplain's Assn., Disciples of Christ Hist. Soc., Morehead U. Alumni Assn., Phi Kappa Phi. Lodge: Am. Legion (Minford) (post chaplain 1981-82). Home: 1816 Vinton Ave Portsmouth OH 45662

O'DELL, JERRY DEAN, minister, Christian Church/Churches of Christ; b. Bristol, Tenn., Apr. 25, 1953; s. Ernest Lee and Mildred Louise (Stout) O'D.; m. Michele Marie King, July 21, 1973; children: Jennifer Michele, Ryan Marie, Jason Dunett. A.B., Atlanta Christian Coll., 1975. Ordained to ministry, 1974. Youth minister Westside Christian Ch., East Point, Ga., 1973-75, Northside Ch. of Christ, Newport News, 1975-78, Westwood Cheviot Ch. of Christ, Cin., 1978-80; youth minister East Point Christian Ch., Ga., 1980-81, sr. minister, 1981—; mem. continuation com. So. Christian Youth Conv., 1977—; conv. dir. So. Christian Youth Conv., Atlanta, 1983; v.p. Minister Council Christian City, College Park, Ga., 1983-84; advisor Christian Key TV; v.p. Atlanta Christian TV Ministries. Republican. Address: East Point Christian Ch 1706 Washington East Point GA 30344

ODOM, C.B., minister, Baptist Ch.; b. Covington County, Ala., Oct. 23, 1926; s. B.G. and Lizzie (Worley) O.; student Howard U., 1952-60, Bapt. Bible Inst., 1963-65; m. Alene M. Morgan, July 14, 1945; children—Mickey David, Danny Paul. Ordained to ministry, 1952; pastor chs., Fla., Ala., 1952—, Bethlehem Bapt. Ch., Headland, Ala., 1970-84, Center Bapt. Ch., Dothan, Ala., 1984—. Home and Office: Rte 3 Headland AL 36345

ODOM, NASH ANDREW, minister, Southern Baptist Convention; b. Robeson County, N.C., Apr. 16, 1933; s. Bernice Mathuel and Emma Winnifred (Johnson) O.; A.A., Campbell Coll., 1954; B.A., Wake Forest U., 1956; B.Div., Southeastern Bapt. Theol. Sem., 1960; M.A. in Edn., East Carolina U., 1971; m. Helen McCray Allen, June 16, 1960; children—Olivia Penny, Andrea Alexis, Mary Christy. Ordained to ministry, 1956; minister West Lumberton Bapt. Ch., Lumberton, N.C., 1956-61, Back Swamp Bapt. Ch., Robeson County, 1957-60, Proctorville (N.C.) Bapt. Ch., 1961-66, 1st Bapt. Ch., Dublin, N.C., 1966-80, 1st Bapt. Ch., Lake Park, Fla., 1980—; clk. Lake Park Bapt. Assn., 1980—. Pres. ministers conf. Wake Forest U., 1956, Bapt. Ministers Conf., Bladen County, N.C., 1967; moderator Bladen Bapt. Assn., 1971-72; mem. Gen. Bd. Bapt. State Conv., N.C., 1974, mem. state hist. com., 1971-76. Tchr. history Fayetteville Tech. Inst., 1974, Bladen Tech. Inst., Dublin, 1975-76. Vice pres. Robeson County Hist. Soc., 1964-66; pres. Bladen County Hist. Soc., 1967—; mem. bd. assos., Gardner Webb Coll., 1972-77. Mem. Bladen County Bapt. Pastors Conf. Contbr. articles to hist. jours. Home: 915 Northern Dr Lake Park FL 33403 Office: 625 Park Ave Lake Park FL 33403

O'DONNELL, CLETUS F., bishop, Roman Cath. Ch. Ordained priest Roman Catholic Ch., 1941; apptd. titular bishop Abrittum, aux. bishop Chgo., 1960, consecrated, 1960; bishop Madison, Wis., 1967—. Address: 15 E Wilson St Madison WI 53701

O'DONNELL, EDWARD JOSEPH, ch. ofcl., Roman Catholic Ch.; b. St. Louis, July 4, 1931; s. Edward Joseph and Ruth Mary (Carr) O'D.; ed. Kenrick Sem., St. Louis, 1953-57. Ordained priest Roman Catholic Ch., 1957; v.p. Vocation Council of St. Louis, 1960-62; exec. sec. Commn. on Human Rights, 1964-68, chmn., 1972—; dir. Radio-TV office, 1966-68; editor St. Louis Rev., 1968-81; ordained titular bishop of Britania and aux. bishop of St. Louis, 1984; coordinator Respect Life Com., St. Louis, 1972—. Chmn. Interfaith Clergy Council of Greater St. Louis, 1965-69; mem. exec. com. NAACP, St. Louis br., 1970—; bd. dirs. Nat. Cath. Conf. Interracial Justice, 1980—. Bd. dirs. Urban League of St. Louis. Mem. Nat. Cath. Conf. on Interracial Justice, Cath. Press Assn., Nat. Acad. TV Arts and Scis., St. Louis Catholics for Peace with Justice. Home: 6052 Waterman St St Louis MO 63112 Office: 4445 Lindell St St Louis MO 63108

O'DONNELL, HUGH FRANCIS, priest, Roman Catholic Church; b. Chgo., Oct. 30, 1934; s. Daniel and Margaret (Gallagher) O'D. B.A. in Scholastic Philosophy, St. Mary's Sem., Perryville, Mo., 1957; student House of Studies, Washington, 1961-62; M.A. in Latin, DePaul U., 1962; M.S. in Library Sci., Cath. U. Am., 1963; S.T.L., U. Fribourg, Switzerland, 1964, S.T.D., 1966. Joined Congregation of the Mission, Roman Cath. Ch., ordained priest. Tchr. Latin, St. Mary's Sem., 1962-63; mem. faculty, formation St. Thomas Sem., Denver, 1966-75; rector/pres. Kenrick Sem., St. Louis, 1975-78; provincial superior Congregation of the Mission, St. Louis, 1978—; trustee DePaul U.; chmn. bd. trustees St. Thomas Sem.; mem. adv. bd. St. Joseph Hosp., St. Louis. Mem. Conf. Maj. Superiors of Men, Nat. Assn. Ch. Personnel Adminstrs. Office: Congregation of the Mission 1723 Pennsylvania Ave St Louis MO 63104

O'DONNELL, WILLIAM MARK, priest, Roman Catholic Church; b. Buffalo, June 14, 1943; s. Philip A. and Kathleen (Maloney) O'D. B.A. in History, Le Moyne Coll., 1965; B.Phil., Pontifical Gregorian U., Italy, 1967, Licentiate Sacred Theology, 1971. Ordained priest Roman Cath. Ch., 1970. Assoc. pastor Sacred Heart Ch., Lowell, Mass., 1971-77; co-pastor Sacred Heart Ch., Princeton, W.Va., 1977-81; mission dir. Oblate Fathers, Tewksbury, Mass., 1981-82; pastor St. Paul's Ch., Douglas, Ga., 1982-84; personnel dir. Oblate Fathers, Boston, 1984—, councillor Eastern Province, 1980—. Mem. Nat. Orgn. for Continuing Edn. Roman Cath. Clergy. Home: 350 Jamaica Way Boston MA 02130 Office: Oblate Fathers PO Box 280 Boston MA 02130

OERTH, FRANZ EDWARD, minister, American Baptist Churches in the U.S.A.; b. Phila., Dec. 10, 1918; s. Franz Edward and Marie Elizabeth (McClellan) O.; m. Bea Kirk, Sept. 4, 1941; children: Douglas K., Deborah A. Oerth Rodgers, Donna Lee Oerth Johnson. B.A., Wheaton Coll., 1940; B.D., Eastern Bapt. Theol. Sem., 1944, M.Div., 1973, D.D. (hon.), 1962; S.T.M., Temple U., 1949. Ordained to ministry Baptist Ch., 1942. Pastor, Olney Bapt. Ch., Phila., 1944-52, First Bapt. Ch., Endicott, N.Y., 1952-58, First Bapt. Ch., Waterloo, Iowa, 1958-65, First Bapt. Ch., Muncie, Ind., 1965-73, First Bapt. Ch., Needham, Mass., 1973-84; asst. to pres., dir. ch. relations Gordon Conwell Theol. Sem., South Hamilton, Mass., 1984—; bd. dirs. Pa. Bapt. Chs., 1949-52, N.Y. Bapt. Conv., 1953-58, Am. Bapt. Chs. of Iowa, 1960-65, Ind. Bapt. Conv.; mem. commn. on ministry Am. Bapt. Chs., 1960-73; bd. dirs. Am. Bapt. Chs. Mass., 1977-83, Central Bapt. Theol. Sem., Kansas City, Kans., 1960-75. Pres. Olney Community Council, Phila., 1951-52; chmn. Civil Rights Commn. of Muncie, 1967-73, Needham Civic Coalition, 1967-70, Needham Commn. on Discrimination, 1971-76; bd. dirs. Judson Coll., Elgin, Ill., 1968-83. Recipient Alumni Achievement award Eastern Bapt. Theol. Sem., Phila., 1955, Key to City, Muncie, 1973. Mem. Ministers Conf. Mass. (bd. dirs. 1983—), Needham Clergy Assn. (pres. 1980-83). Home: 247 South St Needham MA 02192

OESTERREICHER, JOHN M., priest, Roman Catholic Church; educational administrator; b. Stadt Liebau, Austria, Feb. 2, 1904; s. Nathan and Ida (Zelenka) O.; student U. Vienna Med. Sch., 1922-24; student U. Graz, also U. Vienna, 1924-28; lic. theology, U. Vienna, 1928; state certificate for teaching theology higher schs., Vienna, 1935; LL.D., Incarnate Word Coll., San Antonio, 1967; D.H.L., Canisius Coll., 1968; Came to U.S., 1940, naturalized, 1948. Ordained priest Roman Catholic Ch., 1927; became monsignor, 1963, hon. prelate, 1966; pastor chs. Vienna, 1928-38, N.Y.C., 1941-53; prof. religion, Vienna, 1935-38; research prof. Sacred theology Manhattanville Coll., 1944-53; dir. Inst. Judaeo-Christian Studies, Seton Hall U., South Orange, N.J., 1953—, dir. grad. program, 1975-79, disting. prof. emeritus, 1978, scholar in residence, 1979. Recipient Brotherhood award Cong. Achudath Achim, Taunton, Mass., 1964; award L.I. chpt. Cath. League for Religions and Civil Rights, 1984, others. Mem. Cath. Theol. Soc., Cath. Bibl. Assn. (acting pres. 1968), Soc. Bibl. Lit., Am. Acad. Religion, Cath. Com. on Intellectual and Cultural Affairs, Nat. Com. Fgn. Policy, Am. Profs. Peace in Middle East (vice chmn.). Author several books, including Racisme, Anti-Sémitisme, Anti-Christianism, 1939, 43; Walls Are Crumbling, Dutch, French, Japanese, Spanish edits., 1952; Israel of God, French and German edits., 1963; Auschwitz, The Christian and the Council, 1965; The Rediscovery of Judaism, German edit., 1971; Under the Vault of One Covenant, 1974; Jesus' Prayer in the Garden of Olives as Sign of His Humanity, 1974; Anatomy of Contempt, Critique of Rosemary Ruether's Faith and Fratricide, 1975; Martyrs of the Decalogue, 1980; A Witness to God's Triumph, 1981; contbr. articles to profl. jours., chpts. to books. Editor: The Bridge, vols. I-V, 1955-70, Quest (series of monographs), 1965, Jerusalem, 1974; Teshuvah Papers: Jerusalem the Free, Internationalization of Jerusalem?, Salute to Israel. Office: Inst Judaeo-Christian Studies Seton Hall U South Orange NJ 07079

OESTMANN, VERNON ERNEST, minister, Lutheran Church-Mo. Synod; b. Arkansas City, Kans., Jan. 2, 1948; s. Ernest Dietrich and Martha Amanda (Plumer) O.; m. Deborah Ann Richard, Aug. 19, 1972; children: Andrew Vernon, David Richard, Philip Ernest. A.A., St. Paul's Coll., Concordia, Mo., 1968; B.Div., Concordia Sr. Coll., Ft. Wayne, Ind., 1970; M.Div., Christ Sem. in Exile, Concordia Theol. Sem., St. Louis, 1974. Ordained to ministry Lutheran Ch., 1974. Vicar Bethlehem Luth. Ch., Vancouver, B.C., 1972-73; asst. pastor St. John's Luth. Ch., Hannibal, Mo., 1974-75, sr. pastor, 1975-83, Trinity Luth. Ch., Garden City, Kans., 1983—; chaplain Luther Manor Nursing Home, Hannibal, 1975-83, circuit counselor, 1985; mem. social ministry com. English Dist., Hannibal, 1978-82. Pres. bd. dirs. Mobile Agy. for Southwest Health, Garden City, 1983—. Mem. Ministerial Alliance. Club: Lions (chaplain 1975-83). Office: Trinity Luth Ch 1010 Fleming Garden City KS 67846

OFSTEDAL, PAUL ESTREM, minister, American Lutheran Church; b. Fergus Falls, Minn., May 18, 1932; s. Rudolph A. and Edith Evangeline (Estrem) O.; m. Dorothea Ann Jerdee, June 22, 1957; children: Anne, Daniel, Joseph, Ruth. B.A., Luther Coll., 1954; M.Div., Luther Sem., 1958. Ordained to ministry Evang. Luth. Ch., 1958. Pastor, Our Savior's Luth. Ch., Park Falls, Wis., 1958-64, St. Paul's Luth. Ch., Lakota, Iowa, 1964-70, Riverside Luth. Ch., Sioux City, Iowa, 1970-75; asst. to dist. pres. Iowa Dist., Am. Luth. Ch., 1975-81; sr. pastor First Luth. Ch., Williston, N.D., 1982—; bd. dirs. N. Iowa Mental Health Assn., 1968-70; instr. Waldorf Coll., Forest City, Iowa, 1969-70; bd. dirs. Okoboji Bible Camp, 1972-75. Contbr. articles to profl. jours. Chmn., Heart Fund Dr., Lakota, 1968-69, Sioux City Ministers Assn., 1974; bd. regents Concordia Coll., Moorhead, Minn., 1985—.

OGAN, ROBERT FRANCIS, minister, Christian Ch. (Ind.); b. Indpls., May 7, 1925; s. Ralph Burton and Cora Frances (Yancy) O.; B.A., Southwest Christian Sem., 1950; M.A., Ariz. State U., 1961; D.D. (hon.), London U., 1972; m. Hazel Ruth Smith, May 22, 1967; children—Pamela Sue, Cynthia Ann, Wendy Louise, Lizabeth Ann. Ordained to ministry, 1944; founder, minister Mountain View Ch. of Christ, Phoenix, 1948-49, Paradise Valley Christian Ch., Phoenix, 1960-62; headmaster Windsor Hall Sch., Phoenix, 1953-62; asso. pastor 1st Christian Ch., Phoenix, 1963-70; founder, minister 1st Christian Ch., Sun City, Ariz., 1971—. Pres. Ariz. Christian Conv., 1974; bd. regents El Paso Christian Coll., 1975—. Contbr. articles to religious jours. Home: 3015 W Cactus Wren Dr Phoenix AZ 85021 Office: 14001 Thunderbird Blvd Sun City AZ 85351

OGILBY, LYMAN CUNNINGHAM, bishop, Episcopal Ch.; b. Hartford, Conn., Jan. 25, 1922; s. Remsen Brinckerhoff and Lois Manley (Cunningham) O.; B.S., Hamilton Coll., 1943, D.D., 1963; B.D., Episcopal Theol. Sch., 1949; D.D., Trinity Coll., 1954; m. Ruth Dale, Nov. 4, 1953; children—Peter, Lois, Henry. Ordained deacon Episcopal Ch., 1949, priest, 1950; consecrated bishop, 1953; chaplain, tchr. Brent Sch., Philippines, 1949-53; suffragan bishop, Philippines, 1953-57, bishop, 1957-67; bishop coadjutor, S.D., 1967-70; Procter fellow Episcopal Theol. Sch., 1970-71; asst. bishop of Pa., 1971-73, bishop coadjutor, 1973, bishop, 1974—; chmn. bd. council Epis. Community Services, Diocese of Pa., 1974—; trustee Gen. Theol. Sem., N.Y.C., 1973-79. Contbr. articles and essays to profl. publs. Office: Suite 1600 1700 Market St Philadelphia PA 19103

OGILVIE, LLOYD JOHN, minister, United Presbyn. Ch. in U.S.A.; b. Kenosha, Wis., Sept. 2, 1930; s. Varde Spencer and Katherine (Jacobson) O.; B.A., Lake Forest Coll., 1952; B.D., Northwestern U., 1956; D.D. (hon.), Whitworth Coll., Spokane, Wash., 1973; L.H.D., U. Redlands, 1974; H.H.D., Moravian Theol. Sem., Bethlehem, Pa., 1975; m. Mary Jane Jenkins, Mar. 25, 1951; children—Heather, Scott, Andrew. Ordained to ministry, 1956; pastor First Presbyn. Ch., Hollywood, Calif., 1972—; radio and television preacher; conf. leader. Recipient Distinguished Service award Lake Forest Coll. Author: Let God Love You, 1974; Life Without Limits, 1975; Life Full of Suprises, 1969; You've Got Charisma, 1975; Cup of Wonder, 1976; If I Should Wake Before I Die, 1974; Lord of the Ups and Downs, 1974; Drumbeat of Love, 1976; Loved and Forgiven, 1977. Office: 1760 N Gower St Hollywood CA 90028

OGLETREE, THOMAS, educator, minister, United Methodist Ch.; b. Marshall County, Ala., June 17, 1933; s. John Warren and Carrie Elizabeth (Brown) O.; B.A., Birmingham-So. Coll., 1955; M.Div., Garrett Theol. Sem., 1959; Ph.D., Vanderbilt U., 1963; m. Mary-Lynn Rimbey, May 26, 1973; children: Thomas Rimbey, Kathryn Marie; children by previous marriage: David Franklin, Ann Lauren, Julia Brittain. Ordained elder United Methodist Ch., 1960; asst. prof. philosophy and religion Birmingham-So. Coll., 1962-65; from asst. to assoc. prof. constructive theology Chgo. Theol. Sem., 1965-70; from assoc. prof. to prof. theol. ethics Vanderbilt U., 1970-81; prof. theol. ethics, dean Theology Sch. Drew U., Madison, N.J., 1981—; sr. research assoc. Vanderbilt Inst. Pub. Policy Studies, 1977—. Mem. steering com. Operation Breadbasket, Chgo., 1967-68; program coordinator Concerned Citizens for Improved Schs., 1972-73. Guggenheim fellow, 1968-69. Fellow Soc. Values in Higher Edn.; mem. Am. Acad. Religion, Am. Soc. Christian Ethics (pres. 1983-84), Phi Beta Kappa. Author: Christian Faith and History, 1965; The Death of God Controversy, 1966; Openings for Marxist-Christian Dialogue, 1968; (with others) From Hope to Liberation: Towards a New Marxist-Christian Dialogue, 1974; The Use of the Bible in Christian Ethics, 1983. Editor Soundings: An Interdisciplinary Jour.; contbr. articles to theol. jours. Office: Drew U Theol 36 Madison Ave Madison NJ 07940

O'GORMAN, ROBERT THOMAS, religious educator, Roman Catholic Church; b. St. Louis, Mar. 7, 1941; s. John E. and M. Lucile (Carpentier) O'G.; m. Mary Lou Matteuzzi, June 19, 1965; children: Daniel, John, Mark (dec.), Timothy. B.A., St. Louis U., 1963; Diploma Lumen Vitae, Brussels, 1966; M.R.E., Loyola U., Chgo., 1970; Ph.D., Notre Dame U., 1975. Tchr. Vianney High Sch., St. Louis, 1963-69; instr. St. Louis U., 1964-73; asst. prof. St. Thomas Sem., Denver, 1975-81; mem. faculty Scarritt Grad. Sch., Nashville, 1981—, assoc. prof. religious edn., 1981—. Author: Man Comes of Age, 1967; The Church in the Education of the Public, 1984. Mem. Religious Edn. Assn., Assn. Profs. and Researchers in Religious Edn., Assn. Theol. Field Educators. Democrat. Home: 1617 18th Ave S Nashville TN 37212 Office: Scarritt Grad Sch 19th Ave S Nashville TN 37203

O'GRADY, JOHN FERGUS, bishop, Roman Catholic Church; b. Macton, Ont., Can., July 27, 1908; s. Edward and Helen (Frith) O'G.; student St. John's Coll., Edmonton, Alta., Can., 1922-27, Oblate Sem., Ottawa, Ont., 1931-35. Ordained priest Roman Catholic Ch., 1934; asst. pastor St. Augustine's Parish, Vancouver, B.C., Can., 1935-36; superior, prin. St. Mary's Indian Reservation Sch., Mission, B.C., 1936-39, Kamloops (B.C.) Indian Reservation Sch., 1939-52, Cariboc Indian Reservation Sch., Williams Laake, B.C., 1952-53; provincial English oblates Can., 1953-56; bishop of Prince George, B.C., Can., 1956—. A founder integrated Indian schs.; founder Prince George Coll., 1962, Frontier apostolate, 1958. Address: College Rd Prince George BC V2N 2K6 Canada

OH, MARK EDWARD, minister; b. Pohang, Kyung-book, Korea, Dec. 20, 1933; came to U.S., 1960, naturalized, 1971; s. Kap Soo and Boon Hak (Park) O.; m. Rosemary McGuire, Aug. 20, 1965; children: Christopher, Jonathan. B.A., Keimyung U., Republic of Korea, 1958; M.A., San Francisco Theol. Sem., 1963; M.R.E., New Orleans Bapt. Theol. Sem., 1964, postgrad., 1965; M.Div., Western Conservative Bapt. Theol. Sem., 1968; Ph.D., Calif. Grad. Sch. Theology, 1971. Ordained to ministry San Fernando-Crescent Bay So. Bapt. Assn., 1968. Assoc. pastor Berendo St. Bapt. Ch., Los Angeles, 1968-72; pastor Internat. Bible Ch., Los Angeles, 1972—. Mem. San Fernando-Crescent Bay So. Bapt. Assns., Calif. So. Bapt. Conv., Korean Ministers Assn. of So. Calif. Home: 1264 S Lucerne Blvd Los Angeles CA 90019 Office: Internat Bible Ch 3434 W First St Los Angeles CA 90004

O'HALLORAN, JOHN DENNIS, priest, Episcopal Ch.; b. Bay Ridge, N.Y., Sept. 8, 1928; s. William Harold and Katherine Frances (Herlinger) O'H.; diploma George Mercer Sch. Theology, 1962. Ordained to ministry, 1962; mgr. ins. St. Paul Ins. Co., N.Y.C., 1953-62; curate St. Ann's Pro-Cathedral, Brooklyn Heights, N.Y., 1962-65; rector Holy Cross Parish Ch., Ridgewood, L.I., 1965—. Ofcl. historian Village of Island Park (N.Y.), 1949-62, Town of Gravesend (N.Y.), 1949-62; Historian, Parishes of Vernon, Sabine, Beauregard, Louisiana, 1950-53, chmn. publicity bicentennial Greater Ridgewood Hist. Soc., 1976-77; active Boy Scouts Am. Mem. L.I. Anglican-Orthodox Fellowship, Smithsonian Asso. Author: Our Community, 1976. Home: 399A Himrod St Ridgewood LI NY 11237 Office: 176 St Nicholas Ave Ridgewood LI NY 11237

O'HARA, ELIZABETH MARY, nun, religious organization administrator, Roman Catholic Ch.; b. Nov. 11, 1935; d. Michael Andrew and Catharine Margaret (Callahan) O'H. B.A., Georgian Court Coll., 1965; M.S., U. Pa., 1967; Ph.D., Rutgers U., 1973. Joined Sisters of Mercy of N.J., 1953. Tchr. St. Mary's Sch., Camden, N.J., 1956-58; tchr. chemistry Camden Cath. High Sch., Cherry Hill, N.J., 1958-67; prof. chemistry Georgian Court Coll., Lakewood, N.J., 1967-76; pastoral assoc. Immaculate Heart Ch., Blackstone, Va., 1976-77, St. Robert's Ch., Freehold, N.J., 1977-83; dir. religious edn. St. Peter's Ch., Riverside, N.J., 1983—; peace/disarmament issue leader Sisters of Mercy of N.J., Plainfield, 1983—; founding mem. Monmouth County chpt. Pax Christi U.S.A., 1982. Editor: Mercy Coalition CONNECTIONS newsletter; contbr. articles to Contemplative Rev., Jour. Organic Chemistry, Jour. Am. Chem. Soc. Founding mem. Western Monmouth/Lakewood Concerned Citizens for Nuclear Disarmament, Freehold, 1982; del. Witness for Peace, Nicaragua, 1984. Mem. Trenton Religious Edn. Dirs., Guild for Spiritual Guidance. Democrat. Home: 201 Wayne Dr Cinnaminson NJ 08077 Office: St Peter's Ch 101 Middleton St Riverside NJ 08075

O'HARE, JOSEPH ALOYSIUS, priest, university president, Roman Catholic Church; b. N.Y.C., Feb. 12, 1931; s. Joseph Aloysius and Marie Angela (Enright) O'H. A.B., Berchman Coll., 1954, M.A., 1955; S.T.L., Woodstock Coll., 1962; Ph.D., Fordham U., 1968; L.H.D. (hon.), Fairfield U., 1980; Litt.D. (hon.), Coll. of New Rochelle, 1984. Ordained priest Roman Catholic Ch., 1961. Novice Jesuit Order, Poughkeepsie, N.Y., 1948-50, scholastic Cebu City, Philippines, Woodstock, Md., 1950-61; priest, N.Y., Manila, 1961—; pres. Fordham U., Bronx, N.Y., 1984—; prof. Ateneo De Manila, 1968-72. Editor Am. Mag., 1972-84. Home and Office: Fordham U Bronx NY 10058

O'KEEFE, FREDRICK REA, bishop, United Anglican Communion; consultant; b. Washington, Mar. 26, 1944; s. Roy Fox; James Michael (stepfather) and Kathryn Isabelle (Rea) O'K. Cert. U.S. Armed Forces Inst., 1969; student Oberlin Conservatory, 1962-63, Fordham U., 1970-72; S.T.D. (hon.), Star Reach Inst., 1973; postgrad., St. Augustine Sch. Theology, 1984—; consecrated bishop Old Cath. Ch. in N. Am. and United Anglican Communion, 1982. Deacon Old Cath. Ch. in N. Am., Peekskill, N.Y., 1975-77, priest, Laguna Beach, Calif., 1977-82; bishop, vicar gen. Lomita, Calif., 1982-83; presiding bishop United Anglican Communion, Redondo Beach, Calif., 1983—; tchr. Confrat. of Christian Doctrine, Myrtle Beach, S.C., 1967-68; dir. Conlegium Spiriti Refulgentis, Redondo Beach, 1975—; exec. dir. Am. Council on Schs. and Colls., Washington, 1982—; sec., treas. Am. Bd. of Examiners in Pastoral Counseling, Washington, 1982—; chmn. Grad. Coll. of Theology (now Acadia U.), Redondo Beach, 1983—. Editor, pub. Mag. Anchor, 1981—. Mem. Beach Cities Christian ssistance Clearinghouse, Redondo Beach, 1982—; iem. South Bay Ecumenical Council, Long Beach, 982—; chaplain vol. Los Angeles Sheriff Dept., 983—. Served with USAF, 1965-71. Mem. Am. ministerial Assn. (bd. dirs., sec. 1981—), Anglican Soc. '. Am., The Confrat. of the Blessed Sacrament, The iternat. Order St. Luke Physician, Patrons of Iusbandry, Soc. Christian Letters, Small Press and /riters Organ. Libertarian. Club: Planetary Group Dana Point) (founder 1980-81). Address: PO Box 219 omita CA 90717 Home and Office: All Saints Chapel 23 S Catalina Ave Redondo Beach CA 90277

'KEEFE, GERALD FRANCIS, bishop, Roman 'atholic Ch.; b. St. Paul, Mar. 30, 1918; s. Frank Patrick nd Lucille Mary (McDonald) O'K.; student St. 'homas Coll., St. Paul, 1936-38, St. Paul Sem., 1938-44; L.D., St. Ambrose Coll., Davenport, Ia., 1967, Loras 'oll., Dubuque, Ia., 1967; L.H.D., Marycrest Coll., Davenport, 1967. Ordained priest Roman Cath. Ch., 944; consecrated bishop, 1961; asst. pastor St. Paul 'athedral, 1944; instr. St. Thomas Acad., 1944-45; hancellor Archdiocese of St. Paul, 1945-66; rector St. 'aul Cathedral, 1961-66; aux. bishop of St. Paul, 961-66; bishop of Davenport, 1967—. Trustee St. mbrose Coll. Home: 1430 Clay St Davenport IA 2804 Office: 2706 Gaines St Davenport IA 52804

'KEEFE, JOSEPH THOMAS, bishop, Roman 'atholic Church. Titular bishop of Tre Taverne, aux. ishop, N.Y.C., 1982—. Office: 348 55th St New York IY 10030*

KHOLM, DENNIS LEROY, minister, Presbyterian 'hurch in U.S.A., religious educator; b. San Francisco, ug. 22, 1952; s. Huntley Beck and Barbara Jean Ballard) O.; m. Trevecca Annita Newsom, Aug. 24, 973; children: Ryan Beck, Emily Kristen. B.A. in 'hilosophy magna cum laude, Wheaton Coll., 1973; I.A. in Ch. History magna cum laude, Trinity Evang. Div. Sch., 1977, M.Div. summa cum laude, 1977; Th.M. Doctrinal Theology, Princeton Sem., 1978. Ordained ministry Presbyn. Ch. U.S.A., 1984. Sem. asst. Hopewell Presbyn. Ch., N.J., 1980-82; parish assoc. resbyn. Ch., Bowling Green, Ky., 1984—; instr. Vestern Ky. U., Bowling Green, 1982—. Bd. dirs. Crisis regnancy Ctr. Christian Action Council, Bowling reen, 1984. Princeton Theol. Sem. fellow, 1979. Mem. m. Acad. Religion, Am. Soc. Ch. Hist., Soc. Christian hilosophers. Democrat. Home: 823 E 10th St Bowling reen KY 42101 Office: Western Ky U Dept 'hilosophy and Religion Bowling Green KY 42101

LAS, JOSEPH, priest, Antiochian Orthodox 'hristian Archdiocese; b. Newark, Nov. 2, 1940; s. oseph and Maria (Berziner) O.; m. Jean Kowalchuk, une 9, 1974; children: Joseph, Stephen, Mark. B.A., ona Coll., 1966. Ordained priest Eastern Orthodox 'h., 1974. Pastor St. Michael Orthodox Ch., Beaumont, 'ex., 1975-82; now pastor St. George Orthodox Ch., idpls.; spiritual advisor S.W. Region Soyo Teen, 976-78, S.W. Region Sr. Soyo, 1979-82; dir. Conv. and 'onf. Planning Antiochian Orthodox Christian rchdiocese, U.S. and Can., 1979—; pres. Eastern Orthodox Council Chs., 1984—. Home: 3824 Kessler lvd E Dr Indianapolis IN 46220 Office: St George Orthodox Christian Ch 4020 N Sherman Dr ndianapolis IN 46226

LBRICHT, THOMAS HENRY, minister, theology ducator, administrator, Church of Christ; b. Thayer, Io., Nov. 3, 1929; s. Benjamin Joseph and Agnes Iartha (Taylor) O.; m. Dorothy Jetta Kiel, June 8, 951; children: Suzanne M., Eloise J., Joel C., Adele L. Olbricht Foster, Erica M. B.S., No. Ill. U., 1951; M.A., J. Iowa, 1953, Ph.D., 1959; S.T.B., Harvard U., 1962. Ordained to ministry Ch. of Christ, 1949. Minister, Ch. f Christ, DeKalb, Ill., 1949-51, Iowa City, 1951-54, Dubuque, Iowa, 1956-58, Natick, Mass., 1959-62; dean oll. liberal and fine arts Abilene (Tex.) Christian U., 981—, prof. Bibl. theology, 1967—; elder Minter Ln. 'h. of Christ, Abilene, 1974—. Author: Informative peaking, 1968; Power To Be, 1979; He Loves Forever, 980; The Message of Ephesians and Colossians, 1983. Iem. Am. Acad. Religion (pres. SW region 1976-77), outhwest Commn. on Religious Studies (pres. 978-79), 2d Century Bd. (pres. 1981). Democrat. odge: Kiwanis. Office: Abilene Christian U ACU Sta ox 8227 Abilene TX 79699

LCOTT, THOMAS WINCHELL, religious rganization executive, minister, American Baptist 'hurches in U.S.A.; b. Hartford, Conn., 1941; s. Arthur V. and Priscilla V. (Manchester) O.; m. Lois Bennett, Iay 22, 1965; 1 child, Brenda. A.A., Dean Jr. Coll., 961; B.A., Clark U., 1964; B.D., Andover Newton 'heol. Sch., 1968. Ordained to ministry Bapt. Ch., 968. Dir. neighborhood ministry Calvary Bapt. Ch., 'rovidence, 1967-71; dir. urban ministry R.I. Council of 'hs., Providence, 1971-75; pastor First Bapt. Ch., Roselle, N.J., 1975-78; exec. dir. Council of Chs., pringfield, Mass., 1977-83, Interchurch Council Greater Cleve., 1983—; bd. dirs. Mass. State Council of 'hs., 1978-82. Bd. dirs. Goodwil Industries, Iartford-Springfield, Mass., 1978-83, Vis. Nurse Assn., 'leve., 1984—, Innercity Renewal Soc., Cleve., 1984—. Editor newsletter Council Reporter, 1977-83; founder, ditor Interchurch Newsletter, 1983. Recipient Community Service award Springfield Action Com., 1982; Service Recognition award Visitor-Ombudsman Program, Springfield, 1983; Disting. Service award Alumni Assn. Dean Jr. Coll., Franklin, Mass., 1983. Mem. Am. Bapt. Ministers Assn., Nat. Assn. of Ecumenical Staff, Interdenominational Ministers Alliance. Office: Interchurch Council of Greater Cleve 2230 Euclid Ave Cleveland OH 44115

OLCZAK, JOSEPH MARIAN, priest, Roman Catholic Ch.; b. Rudnik, Lublin, Poland, Mar. 19, 1940; came to U.S., 1970, naturalized, 1976; s. John and Maria (Kedra) O. S.T.L., Cath. U., Lublin, 1970. Ordained priest Roman Catholic Ch., 1965. Sub-prior Pauline Fathers, Doylestown, Pa., 1971-75, prior, 1984—; pastor St. Lawrence Parish, Cadogan, Pa., 1975-84. Mem. Assn. Polish Priests (pres. 1984). Home: PO Box 151 Doylestown PA 18901 Office: Pauline Fathers PO Box 151 Doylestown PA 18901

OLDHAM, HAZEL VAFLOR, minister, American Baptist Churches in U.S.A.; b. Iloilo, Philippines, June 27, 1950; came to U.S., 1970, naturalized, 1979; d. Jesus T. Vaflor; m. James T. Oldham, June 14, 1975; 1 child, Violet Ann. B.A., Central Philippine U., 1970; M.Min., Christian Theol. Sem., 1973; M.Div., Eastern Theol. Sem., 1975. Ordained to ministry Bapt. Ch., 1975; instl. chaplain Mountain View Facility, Lockport, N.Y., 1975-78; pastor Jeddo Community Ch., N.Y., 1976-78; minister of Christan edn. Clearfield Community Ch., Utah, 1978-80; minister of pub. ministries Am. Bapt. Chs. of West, Oakland, Calif., 1981—; chaplain USAFR, 1981—.

OLDHAM, JAMES TODD, minister, American Baptist Churches in U.S.A.; b. S.I., N.Y., May 25, 1947; s. Stanley James and Martha Jane (Todd) O.; m. Hazel Grace Vaflor, June 14, 1975; 1 child, Violet. B.A. in History, Wagner Coll., 1968; M.S. in Edn., U. So. Miss., 1970; M.Div., Eastern Bapt. Sem., 1975. Ordained to ministry Am. Bapt. Chs. in U.S.A., 1975. Assoc. pastor First Bapt. Ch., Lockport, N.Y., 1975-77; pastor First Bapt. Ch., Alameda, Calif., 1980-84; minister pub. ministry Am. Bapt. Churches of West, Oakland, Calif., 1984—. Served to maj., chaplain USAF, 1968-72, 77-80; chaplain Res. Republican. Club: Kiwanis (bd. dirs. 1981—) (Alameda). Home: 970 Post St Alameda CA 94501 Office: Am Bapt Chs/West 268 Grand Ave Oakland CA 94610

OLDS, BILLY LEON, minister, Ch. of God; b. Commerce, Okla., Mar. 22, 1930; s. Ole Preston and Sadie E. (Vandyke) O.; student pub. schs., Okla.; m. Peggy Ann Fromm, Aug. 21, 1949; children—Steven Leon, Rebecca Ann, Jerry Allen. Ordained to ministry, 1960; pastor Ch. of God, Pasco, Wash., 1954-70, Graham, Tex., 1970-73, Powell Blvd. Ch. of God, Portland, Oreg., 1973—. Dist. overseer, councilman Wash. Chs. of God, 1962-70, Tex., 1970-73, Oreg., 1973—; pres. Tri-City Evang. Ministerial Alliance, 1968-69. Named Pastor of Year, Chs. of God in Wash., 1964. Home: 4720 SE 111th St Portland OR 97266 Office: 7411 SE Powell Blvd Portland OR 97206

OLDSHUE, JAMES YOUNG, lay church worker, Reformed Church America; b. Chgo., Apr. 18, 1925; s. James and Louise (Young) O.; B.S. in Chem. Engring., Ill. Inst. Tech., 1947, M.S., 1949, Ph D., 1951; m. Betty A. Wiersema, June 14, 1947; children—Paul F., Richard J., Robert W. Mem. gen. program council Ref. Ch. Am., 1967-75, exec. com., 1972-75, mem. bd. world missions, 1966-67; mem. N. Am. Alliance of Ref. Chs., 1969-77; del. World Alliance Ref. Chs., Nairobi, Kenya, 1970; mem. exec. forum Genesee Ecumenical Ministries, 1976—. Vice pres. Mixing Equipment Co., Rochester, N.Y., 1970—. Pres., Rochester Council Sci. Socs., 1963. Chmn. mgmt. com. Bayview YMCA, Rochester, 1960-62, 70-73; chmn. internat. com. Nat. Bd. YMCA's. Pres. Parents' Forum, Irondequoit High Sch., Rochester, 1968; budget chmn. internat. div. Nat. Council YMCAs-U.S. Registered profl. engr., N.Y. Fellow Am. Inst. Chem. Engrs.; mem. Am. Chem. Soc., Nat. Acad. Engring., Internat. Platform Assn. Contbr. articles to profl. jours. Home: 141 Tyringham Rd Rochester NY 14617 Office: 135 Mount Read Blvd Rochester NY 14611

O'LEARY, EDWARD CORNELIUS, bishop, Roman Catholic Church; b. Bangor, Maine, Aug. 21, 1920; s. Cornelius J. and Annabel Cecilia (McManus) O'L.; B.A., Holy Cross Coll., 1942; Licentiate in Sacred Theology, St. Pauls Sem., Ottawa, Ont., 1946. Ordained priest, 1946; consecrated bishop, 1971; curate Sacred Heart Ch., Portland, Maine, 1946, Cathedral, 1946; vice chancellor Diocese of Portland, 1950-52, chancellor, 1952-65; pastor Old Orchard Beach Ch., 1963-67, St. Charles Borromeo Ch., Brunswick, Maine, 1967-70; aux. bishop of Portland, 1970-74, bishop, 1974—. Named papal chamberlain, 1954, domestic prelate, 1959. Address: 510 Ocean Ave PO Box H Woodford Sta Portland ME 04103

OLEKSA, MICHAEL JAMES, priest, Eastern Orthodox Cath. Ch. Am.; b. Allentown, Pa., Mar. 16, 1947; s. Michael and Doris Mae (Conrad) O.; B.A., Georgetown U., 1969; M.Div., St. Vladimir's Orthodox Theol. Sem., 1973; m. Xenia P. Angellan, Apr. 26, 1974; 1 dau., Anastasia Pokrova. Ordained priest, 1974; parish priest various orthodox communities, Western Alaska, 1974-76; pastor St. Seraphim Orthodox Ch., Dillingham, Alaska, 1974—; lectr. pastoral theology St. Herman's Pastoral Sch., Kodiak, Alaska, 1973—; lectr. Yup'ik lang., U. Alaska, Dillingham, 1976—. Chmn. Diocesan Commn. on Children and Child Abuse, 1975—, mem. commn. on alcoholism, 1975-76. Dir. Bristol Bay Council on Alcoholism and Drug Abuse, 1975-76; mem. Nat. Council on Alcoholism, 1975-76. Recipient Kamilavka, for service to Eskimo People, Bishop Gregory, 1975. Author; Orthodox Hymnal, 1973; The Life of Missionary Priests Veniamenov and Netsvetov (in Kup'ik Eskimo), 1975. Address: PO Box 155 Dillingham AK 99576

OLIPHINT, BENJAMIN R., Bishop The United Methodist Church, Tex. Conf., Houston. Office: The United Meth Ch 5215 S Shain St Houston TX 77002*

OLIVER, HAROLD HUNTER, educator, Am. Baptist Conv.; b. Mobile, Ala., Oct. 9, 1930; s. Alonzo Edward and Amelee (Dunaway) O.; A.B., Samford U., 1952; B.D., So. Bapt. Theol. Sem., 1954; Th.M., Princeton Theol. Sem., 1955; Ph.D., Emory U., 1961; m. Martha Anne Maddox, Aug. 12, 1951; 1 dau., Daphne Ann. Ordained to ministry Am. Bapt. Conv., 1950; instr. N.T., Southeastern Bapt. Theol. Sem., 1957-61, asst. prof., 1961-62, asso. prof., 1961-65; asso. prof. N.T., Boston U. Sch. Theology, 1965-70, prof. N.T. and theology, 1970—; acting assoc. dean, 1984; Chavanne vis. prof. Rice U., 1980-81. Mem. Am. Theol. Soc., Am. Acad. Religion, Soc. Bibl. Lit., Royal Astron. Soc., Soc. Religion in Higher Edn., Am. Philos. Assn., Metaphys. Soc. Am., Internat. Soc. Metaphysics. Author: A Relational Metaphysics, 1981; Relatedness: Essays in Metaphysics and Theology, 1984. Editorial bd. The Personalist Forum; editorial adv. bd. ZYGON: Jour. of Religion and Sci.; research editor Jour. of Am. Acad. Religion, 1966-69. Home: 7 Marshall Rd Winchester MA 01890 Office: Boston U 745 Commonwealth Ave Boston MA 02215

OLIVER, JOHN WILLIAM POSEGATE, minister, Presbyterian Church in America; b. Vincennes, Ind., Apr. 9, 1935; s. Dwight L. and Elizabeth (Posegate) O.; B.A., Wheaton Coll., 1956, B.D., Fuller Theol. Sem., 1959; Th.M., So. Bapt. Theol. Sem., 1963; m. Cristina Shepard Hope, Oct. 19, 1968; children—John William Posegate, Sloan Christian Shepard. Ordained to ministry, 1962; asst. pastor Covenant United Presbyn. Ch., Hammond, Ind., 1964-66, Trinity Presbyn. Ch., Montgomery, Ala., 1966-69; pastor 1st Presbyn. Ch., Augusta, Ga., 1969—. Moderator Central Ga. Presbytery, Presbyn. Ch. in Am., 1976. Chmn. clergy Augusta United Way Campaign, 1974; mem. exec. bd. clergy staff Univ. Hosp., Augusta, 1975-76; trustee Westminster Sch., Augusta, 1972—; trustee, chmn. bd. The Cove (Ben Lippen), 1977—; trustee, vice chmn. bd. Columbia Bible Coll., 1978—; mem. ministerial adv. bd. Reformed Theol. Sem., 1978-85; bd. dirs. Mission to the World, Presbyn. Ch. in Am., 1984—; mem. bd. commrs. Augusta Housing Authority, 1976—. Mem. Evang. Theol. Soc., Augusta Clergy, Nat. Assn. Evangelicals. Home: 3205 Huxley Dr Augusta GA 30909 Office: 642 Telfair St Augusta GA 30901

OLIVIERI, LUIS ARTURO, religion educator, American Baptist Churches; b. Guayanilla, P.R., Apr. 21, 1937; s. Arturo and Rosa Maria (Gomez) O.; m. Evelyn Robert, June 30, 1961; children: Luis Fernando, Emanuel. B.A., Interamerican U. of P.R., San German, 1958; Th.M., Evang. Sem., San Juan, P.R., 1962; Mus.B., Conservatory of P.R., San Juan, 1972; M.Sacred Music, Boston U., 1977; postdoctoral Fla. State U., 1982—. Ordained to ministry Baptist Ch., 1967. Pastor, Bapt. Ch., Rio Grande, P.R., 1960-67, First Bapt. Ch., San Juan, 1967-72; organist Episcopal Ch., Hato Rey, P.R., 1972-81; music dir. Episcopal Cathedral, San Juan, 1982—; faculty Evang. Sem., San Juan, 1965—, prof. ch. music and liturgy, 1965—; prof. humanities Interamerican U. P.R., San Juan, 1979—; dir., pres. Interdenominational Chorale of P.R.; mem. ch. music com. Episcopal Ch. Diocesis, San Juan, 1982—. Editor: (hymnal) Himnos y Cantos Puertorriquenos, 1980; Liturgical Anthology, 1981. Editor Coral jour. Contbr. articles to profl. jours. Mem. Am. Guild Organists, Hymn Soc. Am., P.R. Choral Dirs. Assn., Liturgical Conf. Home and Office: 776 Ponce de Leon Ave San Juan PR 00918

OLSON, ELDON LEROY, minister, American Lutheran Ch.; b. Milltown, Wis., Oct. 24, 1938; s. Olaf H. and Alvida U. (Jensen) O.; m. Marcia Jean Humphrey, July 18, 1964; children: Clifford, Ellen, Per, Lucia, Erin. B.A., Willamette U., 1961; M.A., Garrett Inst., 1962; B.D., Luther Sem., 1966; Ph.D., Durham U., 1984. Ordained to ministry Am. Luth. Ch., 1966. Pastor, Calvary Luth. Ch., Minong, Wis., 1966-71, Atonement Luth. Ch., Green Bay, Wis., 1971-79; vis. prof. St. John's Coll., Durham, Eng., 1979-81; asst. prof. Carroll Coll., Helena, Mont., 1982-84; dir. No. Rockies Inst. Theology, Helena, 1981—. Author: Theology of Creation, 1973, also articles. Chmn., Brown County Community Service Ctr., Green Bay, 1977-79. Democrat. Home: 112 Fairway Dr Helena MT 59601 Office: Box 213 Helena MT 59624

OLSON, LYNETTE JEAN, family life educator, Christian Church; b. Wakefield, Nebr., Apr. 10, 1950; d. J. Maurice and Ivadell T. (Gray) O. B. Christian Edn., Ozark Bible Coll., 1972; M.S., Okla. State U., 1973; Ph.D., Kans. State U., 1985. Assoc. prof. Manhattan Christian Coll., Kans., 1974—; cons. family life N. Am. Christian Conv., Cin., 1984. Heaton scholar Kans. State U., 1984. Mem. Nat. Council Family Relations, Kans. Council Family Relations. Republican. Club: MCC Women (Manhattan) (pres. 1981-82). Office: Manhattan Christian Coll 1407 Anderson Manhattan KS 66502

OLSON, STANLEY EDWARD, bishop, Lutheran Church in America; b. Omaha, Sept. 4, 1926; s. Gilbert Edward and Hedwig (Melander) O.; m. Mary Lou Grunow, July 7, 1949; children: Louise, Ann, Sara, Mary. B.A., Wittenberg U., 1949; B.D., Northwestern Luth. Theol. Sem., 1952; D.D. (hon.), Calif. Luth. Coll., 1969. Ordained to ministry Luth. Ch. in Am., 1952. Pastor Faith Luth. Ch., Yuna, Ariz., 1952-57; asst. to pres. Pacific Southwest Synod, Los Angeles, 1957-62, 75-79; pastor St. Andrews Ch., Van Nuys, Calif., 1963-74; bishop Pacific Southwest Synod Luth. Ch. in Am., Los Angeles, 1979—; bd. dirs. Pacific Luth. Theol. Sem., Berkeley, Calif., 1979—; bd. regents Calif. Luth. Coll., Thousand Oaks, Calif., 1979—. Bd. dirs. Lakeview Hosp., Pacoima, Calif., 1965—. Office: Pacific Southwest Synod Luth Ch Am 1340 S Bonnie Brae Los Angeles CA 90006

OLSON, WAYNE CORLIN, minister, United Church of Christ; b. Gary, Ind., Oct. 6, 1943; s. Arnold D. and Gladys V. (Stewart) O.; m. Rosemary Morrison, Sept. 10, 1955; children: Kevin, Kerry, Kendra, Kerwin. A.B. cum laude, Hope Coll., 1955; B.D., Western Theol. Sem., 1958; Ed.D., Columbia U., 1980. Ordained to ministry United Ch. Christ, 1958. Pastor Dutch Reformed Ch., Woodstock, N.Y., 1958-62, First Reformed Ch., Jamaica, N.Y., 1962-69, Bethel Reformed Ch., Passaic, N.J., 1969-71, Brighton Heights Reformed Ch., S.I., N.Y., 1971-73; dir. Met. Indpls. Campus Ministry, Ind., 1980—; instr. Free U., Indpls., 1981-83; pres. Riley-Lockerbie Ministerial Assn., Indpls., 1983—; Gt. Lakes rep. Nat. Campus Ministers Assn., 1983—; mem. exec. com. Ind. Office Campus Ministry, 1982—; chmn. Warwick Youth Conf., N.Y., 1964-69; com. mem. Ch. Planning/Strategy Protestant Council N.Y.C., 1962-68. Author: Emerson, Thoreau, Fuller: Transcendentalist Insights, 1980; Thoreau for Thoughtful Christians, 1983; columnist in Christian jours., newspapers. Pres. br. council YMCA, Jamaica, N.Y., 1966-68; Recipient Pastoral Service award Ind.-Ky. Conf. United Ch. Christ, 1983. Mem. Ind. and Midwest Acad. Religion, Nat. Campus Ministers Assn., Ind. Commn. United Ministers in Higher Edn. Home: 2058 Picadilly Pl Indianapolis IN 46260 Office: Met Indpls Campus Ministry 1226 W Michigan St Indianapolis IN 46202

OLSZEWSKI, BERNARD M., priest, religion educator, Roman Catholic Church; b. Trenton, N.J., Mar. 7, 1951; s. Bernard Joseph and Leona (Grabowska) O. B.A. in Philosophy, St. Hyacinth Coll., 1974; S.T.L., Collegio Internazionale Seraphicum, Italy, 1978; J.C.L., Pontifical U. Gregoriana, Italy, 1980, J.C.D., 1982. Ordained priest Roman Cath. Ch., 1979. Campus minister St. Mary's Coll., Rome, 1979-82; advocate judge Marriage Tribunal, Trenton, 1980; judge Marriage Tribunal, Buffalo, 1982—; campus minister, instr. Hilbert Coll., Hamburg, N.Y., 1982—, chmn. dept. philosophy and religious studies, 1982—. Recipient Pope John Paul II Silver medal for Acad. Excellence, 1982. Mem. Canon Law Soc. Am., Cath. Campus Ministry Assn. Address: 5200 S Park Ave Hamburg NY 14075

O'MALLEY, JOHN MATTHEW, minister; b. Weehawken, N.J., May 20, 1938; s. John M. and Grace Virginia (Bohland) O'M.; B.S., Susquehanna U., 1960; B.Th., Ridgedale Theol. Sem., 1971, D.D., 1972; Ph.D., Clarksville Sch. Theology, 1974; Th.D., Northgate Theol. Sem., 1976; m. Barbara E. Sharpe, July 28, 1960; children—Bonny Lynn, John Matthew, Laurie Sue, Mark Paul, Charie Joy, David Peter. Ordained to ministry, 1970; pastor, Ridgeway, Colo., 1970-71, Green River, Utah, 1971-73, First Bapt. Ch., Loxahatchee, Fla., 1974—. Editor: Son Dial Mag., 1974—; author: Positional Mental Attitude, 1972. Home: 141-99 Tangerine Dr Loxahatchee FL 33470 Office: 517 Folsom Rd Loxahatchee FL 33470

OMAN, SANDRA FAYE, lay church worker, United Presbyterian Church in the U.S.A.; educator; b. Fergus Falls, Minn., July 11, 1946; d. Sanford Raymond and Iona (Leeman) Saunders; children: Amie Marie, Andrew Sanford, Jon Chester. B.S., Bemidji State U., 1968; certificate in learning disability Moorhead State U., 1971. Cert. elem. tchr., Minn. Deacon, Presbyn. Ch., 1978-80, supt. Sunday Sch., 1982—, supt., tchr. Vacation Bible Sch., 1983-84, elder, 1982—, Christian edn. com., 1982—; dir. Teens Encounter Christ Retreats, Fertile, Minn., 1983—. Learning disability, emotionally disturbed tchr. Crookston Pub. Sch., 1984-85. Alternate del. Republican Party, 1979-80. Named Woman of Yr., Beta Sigma Phi, 1973. Mem. Assn. for Learning Disabilities, Beta Sigma Phi. Clubs: Swim (Crookston) (pres. 1984—), Ken Study (Crookston) (treas. 1984—). Avocations: running; cross-country skiing; reading. Home and Office: 103 Golf Terrace Dr Crookston MN 56537

O'MARA, JOHN ALOYSIUS, bishop, Roman Cath. Ch.; b. Buffalo, Nov. 17, 1924; s. John Aloysius and Anna Theresa (Schenck) O'M; licentiate in canon law J.C.L. Angelicum U., Rome. Ordained priest, 1951; sec. to Cardinal McGuigan, Archdiocese of Toronto, 1953-69; pastor St. Margaret Mary Parish, Woodbridge, 1957-69; rector St. Augustine's Sem., Toronto, 1969-75; pastor St. Lawrence Parish, Scarborough, Ont., 1975-76; consecrated bishop, 1976; bishop Thunder Bay Ont., 1976—. Office: PO Box 756 Thunder Bay ON P7C 4V5 Canada

O'MEARA, EDWARD THOMAS, archbishop, Roman Catholic Church; b. St. Louis, Aug. 3, 1921; s. John and Mary (Fogarty) O'M. Student Kenrick Sem., 1943-46; S.T.D., Angelicum U., Rome, 1953. Ordained priest Roman Catholic Ch. Asst. pastor St. Louis Cathedral, 1952-55; asst. nat. dir. Soc. for Propagation of Faith, 1956-60, dir., 1960-67, nat. dir., N.Y.C., 1967-79; became monseignor, consecrated bishop, 1972; archbishop Archdiocese of Indpls., 1979—. Editor World Mission mag. Office: Archdiocese Indpls Chancery Office 1350 N Pennsylvania St Indianapolis IN 46202

ONARECKER, HAYES RICHARD, minister, So. Baptist Conv.; b. Houston, June 6, 1944; s. Hayes Richard and Ruth (Snyder) O.; B.A. in Psychology, William Carey Coll., 1976; student Bapt. Bible Inst., Graceville, Fla., 1972-74; postgrad. U. So. Miss., 1976; m. Helen Anita Lowrey, June 24, 1963; children—Terri Lynn, Richard Kevin. Ordained to ministry, 1972; lay minister youth Westheimer Bapt. Ch., Houston, 1972; pastor Eldorendo (Ga.) Bapt. Ch., 1973; minister evangelism First Bapt. Ch., Chipley, Fla., 1974; pastor Macedonia Bapt. Ch., Hattiesburg, Miss., 1975-76, Oak Forest Bapt. Ch., Houston, 1976—; co-chmn. counselors for James Robison Crusade, 1976. Mem. com. on evangelism Lebanon Bapt. Assn. Author: Seven Days a Week-A Fisherman for God, 1974. Home: 5056 Lido Ln Houston TX 77092 Office: 1700 W 4d St Houston TX

O'NEAL, ERNEST JOE, minister, Ch. of God in Christ; b. Raleigh, N.C., Jan. 10, 1924; s. Ernest Joe and Martha Helen (Penny) O'N.; M. Bible Philosophy, Am. Bible Inst., 1976; m. Lula Mae Knight, Apr. 3, 1948. Ordained to ministry, 1955; pastor, pres. Little Flock Ch. God in Christ, Redwood City, Calif., 1955—; state supt. Sunday Schs., No. Calif., 1958-61; exec. sec. of mission, No. Calif., 1962-70, fin. sec., 1970-74; asst. supt. San Jose Dist., 1960-73; gen. supt. New Horizon Dist., Redwood City, 1973—; clk. in nat. dept. fin. Chs. of God in Christ, Memphis, 1974. Realtor-asso. Dory Realty, Inc., Redwood City. Treas., mem. bd., chmn. com. Citizens Against Racism, Redwood City, 1968-71. Recipient Distinguished Services award Chs. of God in Christ, 1975; Inter-Continental Spl. Achievement award Dickerson Bros. Christian Alliance Am., 1976. Home: 447 Sequoia Ave Redwood City CA 94061

O'NEIL, LEO E., bishop, Roman Catholic Church. Titular bishop of Bencenna, aux. bishop, Springfield, Mass., 1980—. Office: Eden Hill PO Box 798 Stockbridge MA 01262*

O'NEILL, ARTHUR J., bishop, Roman Cath. Ch. Ordained priest Roman Catholic Ch., 1943; appt. bishop Rockford, Ill., 1968, consecrated, installed, 1968. Address: 1245 N Court St Rockford IL 61101

ONG, WALTER JACKSON, priest, educator, author, Roman Catholic Ch.; b. Kansas City, Mo., Nov. 30, 1912; s. Walter Jackson and Blanche Eugenia (Mense) O.; A.B., Rockhurst Coll., 1933; Ph.L., St. Louis U., 1940, A.M., 1941, S.T.L., 1948; Ph.D., Harvard U., 1955; various hon. degrees. Joined S.J., 1935, ordained priest Roman Catholic Ch., 1946; instr. English and French, Regis Coll., Denver, 1941-43; asst. in English, St. Louis U., 1944-47, instr., 1953-54, asst. prof., 1954-57, assoc. prof., 1957-59, prof., 1959—, univ. prof. humanities, 1981—, prof. humanities in psychiatry Sch. Medicine, 1970—. Mem. Fulbright nat. selection com., France, 1957-58, chmn., 1958; regional asso. Am. Council Learned Socs., 1957-66; mem. White House Task Force on Edn., 1966-67; mem. Nat. Council on Humanities, 1968-74, vice chmn., 1971-74; co-chmn. adv. com. sci., tech. and human values Nat. Endowment for the Humanities, 1974-78; mem. Rockefeller Found. Commn. on Humanities, 1978-80. Guggenheim fellow, 1949-50, 51-52; fellow Center Advanced Studies, Wesleyan U., Middletown, Conn., 1961-62, Sch. Letters, Ind. U., 1965—, Center for Advanced Study in Behavioral Scis., Stanford, Calif., 1973-74; vis. prof. U. Calif., 1960; Terry lectr. Yale, 1963-64; vis. lectr. U. Poitiers, 1962, Berg prof. English, N.Y. U., 1966-67; McDonald lectr. McGill U., 1967-68; Willett vis. prof. humanities U. Chgo., 1968-69; nat. Phi Beta Kappa vis. scholar, 1969-70; Lincoln lectr., Central and West Africa, 1973-74; Messenger lectr. Cornell U., 1979-80; Wolfson Coll. lectr. Oxford U., 1985; vis. prof. comparative lit. Washington U., St. Louis, 1983-84. Adv. bd. John Simon Guggenheim Meml. Found.; trustee Nat. Humanities Faculty, 1968-76, chmn., 1974-76. Decorated chevalier l'Ordre des Palm Academiques (France). Fellow Am. Acad. Arts an Scis.; mem. AAUP, Renaissance Soc. Am. (adv. counc 1957-59), Modern Lang. Assn. (pres. 1978), Moder Humanities Research Assn., Nat. Council Tchr English, Cambridge Bibliog. Soc. (Eng.), Cath. Comm Intellectual and Cultural Affairs (exec. com. 1962-63 Milton Soc. Am. (pres. 1967), Phi Beta Kappa, Alph Sigma Nu. Author: Frontiers in American Catholicism 1957; Ramus, Method and the Decay of Dialogu 1958; Ramus and Talon Inventory, 1958; America Catholic Crossroads, 1959; The Barbarian Within, 196 In the Human Grain, 1967; The Presence of the Wor 1967; Rhetoric, Romance and Technology, 1971; Wh Talk, 1973; Interfaces of the Word, 1977; Fighting fo Life: Contest, Sexuality, and Consciousness, 198 Orality and Literature, 1982. Co-author, edito Darwin's Vision and Christian Perspectives, 196 Knowledge and the Future of Man, 1968. Editor: Petru Ramus and Audomarus Talaeus, Collectanea praefationes epistolae, orationes, 1969; Petrus Ramus Scholae in liberales artes, 1970, co-editor, co-tran Logic (John Milton), 1982. Editorial bd. Studies i English Lit., 1962—, Philosophy and Rhetoric, 1967— Abstracts of English Studies, 1964—, English Li Renaissance, 1969—, Manuscripta, 1957—, other Contbr. articles, chpts. to learned and popular publ Address: St Louis University Saint Louis MO 63103

ONOFREY, ROBERT EARL, priest, educato Roman Catholic Church; b. Cleve., Dec. 18, 1932; s John Edward and Olga (Zukovic) O.; Mus. B., U. Mich 1954, Mus. M. in Woodwinds, 1973, Mus. D., 197 Ordained to priesthood Soc. Precious Blood, 1963; tch instrumental and vocal music, speech, radio, dram Brunnerdale Sem. High Sch., Canton, Ohio, 1964-7 instr. clarinet U. Mich., Ann Arbor, 1973-76; asst. pro music St. Joseph's Coll., Collegeville, Ind., 1976— artist-in-residence, 1983—. Mem. Internat. Clarin Soc., Nat. Assn. Pastoral Musicians, Pi Kappa Lambda Composer, performer contemporary clarinet music reviewer instrumental music jour. Pastoral Music 1976—. Home and Office: St Joseph's Coll Box 83 Collegeville IN 47978

OPALINSKI, FRED STANLEY, pastor, Luthera Church in America; b. North Charleroi, Pa., Aug. 1 1948; s. Fred and Margaret Jean (Milhovich) O.; m Janet Ruth Kepple, Sept. 4, 1971; children: Mega Ruth, Kristen Lucille. B.A., Thiel Coll., 1970; M.Div Luth. Theol. Sem., 1974. Ordained to ministry, 197 Pastor, Williamson-Upton Parish, Mercersburg, Pa 1974-80, Trinity Luth. Ch., Latrobe, Pa., 1980—; bd dirs. Luth. Social Services, York, Pa., 1975-80, Thie Coll., 1982—; chmn. Worship W. Pa.-W.Va. Synod Pitts.; sec. Latrobe Ministerium, 1981—. Contbg editor: Synod devotional book: The Church Is . . ., 1979 Recipient Augustana award, Luth. Sem., 1970. Home 606 Weldon St Latrobe PA 15650 Office: Trinity Evan Luth Ch 331 Weldon St Latrobe PA 15650

OPSAHL, PAUL DAVID, minister, America Lutheran Church; b. Story City, Iowa, June 20, 1934; s Carl and Olina Bernice (Trontvet) O.; m. Geraldin Ann Ness, June 9, 1957; children: Kathryn Ann Stephen Paul, LeAnn Marie. B.A., Concordia Coll Moorhead, Minn., 1956; M.Div., Luther Theol. Sem St. Paul, 1960; Th.D., U. Heidelberg, Fed. Republi Germany, 1963. Ordained to ministry Am. Luth. Ch. 1964. Pastor Lakota Luth Ch., N.D., 1964-67; dir theology and worship Luth. World Ministries, N.Y.C. 1967-71; exec. dir. div. theol. studies Luth. Council i U.S.A., N.Y.C., 1967-79; sr. pastor Meml. Dr. Luth Ch., Houston, 1979—; chmn. task force on ministry Am. Luth. Ch., Mpls., 1979-82, pres. SE conf., Houston 1983—; pres. West Meml. Interfaith Community Houston, 1980—; commr. Christian/Jewish relation Tex. Conf. Chs., Austin, 1983—. Editor: Speaking o God Today, Lutherans and Jews in Conversation, 1974 The Holy Spirit in the Life of the Church, 1978 Recipient Service Appreciation award Anti-Defamatio League of B'nai B'rith, N.Y.C., 1979. Home: 1381 Perthshire Houston TX 77079 Office: Meml Dr Luth Ch 12211 Memorial Dr Houston TX 77024

ORENTLICHER, WILLIAM A., rabbi, Orthodox Jewish; b. N.Y.C., Oct. 10, 1920; s. Abraham Marshall Orentlicher and Sophie (Rosenthal) Orentliche Kessler; m. Jeanne Blass, Nov. 3, 1944; children: Allen Harriet, Gary, Paul, Rona. D.D., Yeshiva U., 1943 B.A., CCNY, 1946; J.D., St. John's U., 1949; LL.M. NY U, 1956; D. Hebrew Lit., Hebrew Theol. Coll. 1959. Ordained rabbi Yeshiva U., 1943. Rabbi, Bayside Jewish Ctr., N.Y., 1952—; assoc. prof. theology St. John's U., N.Y.C., 1972—; assoc. prof. law Pace U. Pleasantville, N.Y., 1983—; pres. Brotherhood Counci of Queens, N.Y., 1976-78, Bayside Council Chs. and Synagogues, 1972-76, Rabbinic Assn. North Queens 1970-82. Author Rabbinical Council manuals Le Taliones, 1956, There Are No Shortcuts, 1970, Mora Power, 1982. Mem. Rabbinical Council Am., Yeshiva U. Rabbinic Alumni Assn. (v.p. 1979—), N.Y. Bd. Rabbis (bd. dirs. 1974-80). Office: Bayside Jewish Ct 203 05 32d Ave Bayside NY 11361

ORME, ALAN DAN, minister, educator, Presbyterian Church in America; b. Elmira, N.Y., July 5, 1933; s. Clifton Nelson and Mabel (Rose) O.; B.A., Columbia

Bible Coll., 1959; B.D., Covenant Theol. Sem., 1962, Th.M., 1963; postgrad. Near East Sch. Archaeology, Jerusalem, Jordan, 1962; M.A., U. Ga., 1970, Ph.D., 1974. Ordained to ministry Presbyn. Ch. Am., 1960. Pres. Carver Bible Inst. and Coll., Atlanta, 1963-64, acad. dean, 1963-69; minister Univ. Ch., Athens, Ga., 1970—; teaching fellow U. Ga., Athens, 1970-74. Author: When You Commune, 1980; God's Appointments With Men, 1983. Contbr. articles to religious publs. Mem. Evang. Theol. Soc., Campus Ministry Assn. Home and Office: 397 S Church St Athens GA 30605

ORME, JOHN HOWARD, minister, educator, Conservative Baptist Association of America; b. Pitts., Oct. 7, 1937; s. Glenn Howard and Dorothy Louise (Smith) O.; m. Janet Truax, Aug. 6, 1960; children: Lisa Anne, Laura Lynn. B.S., Phila. Coll. Bible, 1961; Th.M., Dallas Theol. Sem., 1965, Th.D., 1975. Ordained to ministry Grace Bible Ch., 1965. Missionary, prof. CAM Internat., Dallas, 1965-79; prof., dept. chmn. William Tyndale Coll., Farmington Hills, Mich., 1979-84; assoc. pastor Highland Park Bapt., Southfield, Mich., 1984—; mem. U.S. council SEND Internat., Farmington Hills, 1979-82; cons. Interdenominational Fgn. Missions Soc.; instr., cons. various fgn. mission bodies. Author: Dios-Quién Eres Tu? (in Spanish), 1976; contbr. articles to Diccionario Ilustrado, others. Served with USAFR, 1955-60. Recipient William Anderson Scholastic Achievement award Dallas Theol. Sem., 1975. Mem. Am. Missiological Soc., Assn. Evang. Profs. Missions, Evang. Theol. Soc. Office: Highland Park Bapt Ch 28600 Lahser Rd Southfield MI 48034

O'ROURKE, EDWARD WILLIAM, bishop, Roman Cath. Ch.; b. Downs, Ill., Oct. 31, 1917; s. Martin and Mary (Hickey) O'R.; student St. Henry's Coll., Belleville, Ill., 1935-38; B.A., St. Mary of Lake Sem., Mundelein, Ill., 1940, M.A., 1942, S.T.L., 1944; Licentiate of Philosophy, Aquinas Inst., River Forest, Ill., 1960. Ordained priest Roman Catholic Ch., 1944; consecrated bishop, 1971; asst. chaplain Newman Found., U. Ill., priest St. Johns Cath. Chapel, 1944-59; dir. Rural Life Conf., Peoria Diocese, 1945-59; exec. dir. Nat. Cath. Rural Life Conf., Des Moines, 1960-71; bishop of Peoria, 1971—. Chmn. priorities com. United Fund and Human Resources Council, Greater Peoria Area, 1972-73. Recipient John Henry Newman award Newman Found., 1958; Distinguished Service award Nat. Cath. Rural Life Conf., 1960. Author: Marriage and Family Life, 1955; Fundamentals of Philosophy, 1958. Office: Chancery Office PO Box 1406 Peoria IL 61656

O'ROURKE, THOMAS JOSEPH, priest, Roman Cath. Ch.; b. Bklyn., Dec. 12, 1937; s. James J. and Mildred (Cooney) O'R.; B.A., Cathedral Coll., 1959; S.T.B., Cath. U., 1963; M.A., N.Y. U., 1971; Ordained priest, 1963; asst. pastor Corpus Christi Ch., Woodside, N.Y., 1963-69, Am. Martyrs Ch., Bayside, N.Y., 1969-76; counselor Mary Louis Acad., Jamaica, N.Y., 1976—. Mem. Music Commn., 1966-74; exec. team priest Marriage Encounter, Queens County; dir. music Our Lady Skies Cath. Chapel, J.F. Kennedy Internat. Airport. Treas., Sch. Bd. 26, N.Y.C., 1975-76. Mem. NCCJ, Nat. Cath. Music Educators Assn., Nat. Cath. Educators Assn., Cons. Council Bd. Edn. City N.Y. Home: 7200 Douglaston Pkwy Douglaston NY 11362 Office: 175-01 Wexford Terr Jamaica NY 11432

ORR, ALAN GODFREY, minister; chemical company technician; b. Rock Hill, S.C., Nov. 18, 1941; s. Odell and Mildred Harriet (Roberts) O.; m. Charlotte Ann Blue; children: Kenneth Alan, Terri Lynn. A.A., Pensacola Jr. Coll., 1974; B. Ministry, Gulf Coast Sem., 1982. Pastor Pine Forest Bapt. Ch., Pensacola, Fla., 1967-68; asst. pastor Burgess Rd. Bapt. Ch., Pensacola, 1969-73, Amazing Grace Tabernacle, Pensacola, 1974-81; founder, pastor Living Word of Faith Tabernacle, Pensacola, 1981—. Devel. technician Monsanto, Pensacola, 1962—. Contbr. articles to profl. jours. Fellow Living Word Internat. Ministries, (vice bishop 1983—). Republican. Home: 8301 Whitmire Rd Pensacola FL 32514 Office: Living Word of Faith 9201 N Davis Hwy Pensacola FL 32514

ORSY, LADISLAS M., educator, priest, Roman Catholic Ch.; b. Egres, Hungary, July 30, 1921; s. Joseph and Maria (Bujka) O.; came to U.S., 1966, naturalized, 1972; Licentiate in Philosophy, Gregorian U., Rome, Italy, 1948; S.T.L., Jesuit Sch. Theology, Louvain, Belgium, 1952; J.C.D., Gregorian U., 1957; M.A., Oxford U., Eng., 1960. Joined S.J., 1943, ordained priest Roman Cath. Ch., 1951; asst. pastor Sacred Heart Ch., Wimbledon, London, Eng., 1953-54; prof. canon law, Gregorian U., Rome, Italy, 1960-66; vis. prof. canon law Cath. U. Am., Washington, 1966-67; prof. pastoral theology Fordham U., N.Y.C., 1967-74; vis. scholar Grad. Theol. Union, Jesuit Sch. Theology, Berkeley, Cal., 1971-72; prof. canon law Cath. U., Washington, 1974—. Vis. lectr. Boston Coll., summer, 1968, St. Louis U., summer, 1974, Pastoral Inst., Archdiocese of Boston, 1974; vis. prof. Georgetown U. Law Ctr., 1981-82, Université de Fribourg, Switzerland, 1982. Trustee Marquette U., 1968—, LeMoyne Coll., Syracuse, 1975-81. Recipient Cath. Book award, 1968, Des Nat. Lectr. award Nat. Cath. Ednl. Assn., 1974. Mem. Cath. Theol. Soc. Am., Canon Law Soc. Am. (bd. govs. 1968-70), Canadian Canon Law Soc., Internat. Assn. Canon Lawyers, Canon Law Soc. Gt. Britain and Ireland, Canon Law Soc. Australia and N.Z. (hon.). Author: Open to the Spirit, 1968; Lord of Confusion, 1970; Probing the Spirit, 1976; Blessed are those who have Questions, 1976; The Evolving Church and the Sacrament of Penance, 1978; co-author: The Code of Canon Law: Commentary, 1985. Contbr. numerous articles to theol. and legal jours. Asso. editor The Way, 1968—; The Jurist, 1974—. Home: Curley Hall The Catholic Univ Washington DC 20064 Office: Dept Canon Law The Catholic Univ Washington DC 20064

ORTHMANN, JAMES EDWARD, minister, Southern Baptist Convention; nurse; b. Milw., June 26, 1953; s. William Francis and Mary Carol (Goodspeed) O.; m. Patricia Margaret Kennedy, Oct. 5, 1979; children: Maria Carol, Sara Kennedy. A.A. in Nursing, Milw. Area Tech. Coll., 1979; B.A., Toccoa Falls Bible Coll., 1984, Th.B., 1985. Planting lay minister Ch. of Open Door, Milw., 1980; 1980; dir. Youth Bible Sch., Ebenezer Bapt. Ch., Toccoa, Ga., 1982-83, dir. and tchr. ch. tng., 1983-84; minister Homer Alliance Ch., Ga., 1984—. Chief health officer Toccoa Falls Coll., Ga., 1983—. Contbr. articles to various mags. Chmn. blood drive ARC, Toccoa Falls, 1983-84. Mem. Am. Nurses Assn., Banks County Ministerial Assn., Phi Theta Kappa. Republican. Home: Route 5 Box 32 Toccoa GA 30577

ORTOLF, F. WILLIAM, minister, American Baptist Churches in U.S.A., educator; b. Bridgeton, N.J., Apr. 20, 1926; s. Franz and Helen (MacCadden) O.; m. Alice R. Platt, Nov. 26, 1953; 1 child, Ruth Ellen. B.A., Alderson-Broaddus Coll., 1952; B.D., Crozer Sem., 1956; M.Div., Rochester Ctr., 1972; D.Th., Trinity Sem., Evansville, Ind., 1983. Ordained to ministry Am. Bapt. Chs. in U.S.A., 1956. Minister of youth First Bapt. Temple, Youngstown, Ohio, 1955-59; state dir. Christian edn. Conn. Bapt. Conv., Hartford, 1959-67; minister youth and camping N.J. Bapt. Conv., East Orange, 1967-69, interim pastor, 1971-81; bi-vocat. pastor First Bapt. Community Ch., Parsippany, N.J., 1981—; tchr. English, Deerfield Sch., Mountainside, N.J., 1969—. Served with USN, 1944-45. Mem. Am. Bapt. Ministers Council, Parsippany Area Pastors Assn. Lodge: Masons. Home: 278 Ravenswood St Mountainside NJ 07092

ORVICK, GEORGE MYRON, minister, Evang. Luth. Synod Church; b. Hanlontown, Iowa, Jan. 9, 1929; s. George and Mabel Olina (Mandsager) O.; m. Ruth Elaine Hoel, Aug. 25, 1951; children: Daniel, Emily, Mark, Kirsten. A.A., Bethany Luth. Coll., Mankato, Minn., 1948; B.A., Northwestern Coll., Watertown, Wis., 1950; postgrad. Bethany Luth. Sem., Mankato, 1950-53, U. Wis., 1958-61. Ordained to ministry Evang. Luth. Synod, 1953. Pastor Our Savior's Luth. Ch., Amherst Junction, Wis., 1953-54, Holy Cross Luth. Ch., Madison, Wis., 1954—. Editor: Our Great Heritage, 1968. Bd. regents Bethany Luth. Coll., 1957-69; pres. Evang. Luth. Synod, 1970-76, 80—, chmn. doctrine com., 1978-80. Office: 2670 Milwaukee St Madison WI 53704

OSBORNE, GRANT RICHARD, religion educator, minister, Evangelical Free Church; b. N.Y.C., July 7, 1942; s. Thomas William and Clare Evelyn (Burkett) O.; m. Nancy I. Hardy, July 1, 1967; children: Amber, Susanne. B.A., Ft. Wayne Bible Coll., 1966; M.A., Trinity Evang. Div. Sch., 1971; Ph.D., U. Aberdeen, Scotland, 1974. Ordained to ministry, 1984. Pastor, Christian Union Ch., Newark, Ohio, 1966-69; prof. N.T., Winnipeg Theol. Sem., Man., 1974-77; assoc. prof. N.T., Trinity Evang. Div. Sch., Deerfield, Ill., 1977—. Author: Handbook for Bible Study, 1979; The Resurrection Narratives: A Reductional Study, 1984; The Bible in the Churchs, 1985. Assn. Theol. Schs. research grantee, 1979-80. Mem. Soc. Bibl. Lit., Tyndale Fellowship, Inst. Bibl. Research, Evang. Theol. Soc. Address: Trinity Evang Div Sch 2065 Half Day Rd Deerfield IL 60015

OSBORNE, JAMES ALFRED, Salvation Army officer; b. Toledo, July 3, 1927; s. Alfred James and Gladys Irene (Gaugh) O.; grad. Salvation Army Sch. for Officers Tng., 1947; student U. Chattanooga, 1954-55; m. Ruth Glenrose Campbell, Nov. 26, 1945; 1 dau., Constance Jean (Mrs. Donald William Canning). Corps officer Salvation Army, Magness, Nashville, 1947, Southside, Memphis, 1948, Owensboro, Ky., 1949-54, comdg. officer, Chattanooga, 1954-61, city comdr., Miami, Fla., 1961-65, divisional sec. Ky.-Tenn. Div., 1965-68, gen. sec. N. and S.C. Div., 1968-70, pub. relations sec. 15 so. states, D.C. and Mexico, 1970-71, divisional comdr. Md. and No. W.Va. Div., 1971-73, Nat. Capital and Virginias Div., Washington, 1973-78, Fla. Div., 1978-80; chief sec. Western Ter., 1980-84, nat. chief sec. 13 western states, 1984—; chmn. Salvation Army Nat. Planning and Devel. Commn., 1974-76, 84—. Sec., Tenn. Conf. on Social Welfare, 1959, v.p., 1960; pres. Fla. Conf. on Social Welfare, 1965; pres. Ky. Welfare Assn., 1970. Mem. Chattanooga Pastors Assn. (pres. 1958), Va. and W.Va. Welfare Confs. Lodge: Rotary. Home: 131 Christopher St Montclair NJ 07042 Office: 799 Bloomfield Ave Verona NJ 07044

OSBORNE, KENAN BERNARD, theol. sch. pres.; b. Santa Barbara, Cal., May 29, 1930; s. Fredric Earle and Ida Louise (Lerg) O.; B.A., San Luis Rey Coll., 1952; S.T.B., Old Mission Theol. Sem., 1956; S.T.L., Catholic U. Am., 1965; Dr. Theol., Ludwig Maximilians Universitat, Munich, Germany, 1967. Ordained priest Roman Catholic Ch., 1955; instr. Greek and history St. Anthonys Sem. High Sch., Santa Barbara, 1956-57; asst. dir. Franciscan Communication Center, Los Angeles, 1957-58; dir. admissions, dir. missions Franciscan Province of St. Barbara, Oakland, Cal., 1958-64; prof., dean Franciscan Sch. Theology, Berkeley, Cal., 1968—, acting pres., 1969-71, pres., 1971—; prof. systematic theology Grad. Theol. Union, Berkeley, 1968—. Summer faculty Anglican Theol. Coll. and Union Coll. of B.C., Vancouver, 1969, Anglican Diocese, Calgary, 1971, St. Marys Coll., Moraga, Cal., 1971, 74, 77, U. San Francisco, 1972, 76, U. Seattle, 1974. Mem. Am. Acad. Religion (exec. sec. western region, nat. bd. dirs.), Cath. Theol. Soc. Am. (nat. bd. dirs.), Pacific Coast Theol. Conf., Kreis der Freunden Paul Tillich E.V. Author: New Being, 1969. Asso. editor Jour. Ecumenical Studies, 1973—. Contbr. articles to profl. publs. Address: 1712 Euclid Ave Berkeley CA 94709

O'SHEA, WILLIAM JOHN, priest, Roman Catholic Ch.; b. Evanston, Ill., Sept. 8, 1937; s. William Michael and Mary Rita (O'Brien) O'S.; B.A. in Philosophy, St. Mary of the Lake Sem., 1959, S.T.B., 1961, M.A. in Religion, 1962, Licentiate Sacred Theology, 1963. Ordained priest, 1963; tchr. Immaculate Conception High Sch., Elmhurst, Ill., 1963-67; lectr. theology Rosary Coll., River Forest, Ill., 1969-71; asso. pastor chs., Ill., 1963-76; pastor St. Patrick's Ch., Momence, Ill., 1976—. Asso. dir. Chgo. Summer Bibl. Insts., 1960-72. Mem. DuPage Citizens Orgn. Author liturgical-hist. filmstrips. Office: 119 N Market St Momence IL 60954

OSINSKI, HENRY JOSEPH, lay ch. worker, Roman Catholic Ch.; b. Buffalo, Sept. 9, 1911; s. Stanislaus and Amelia (Goniszewski) O.; B.S., Canisius Coll., 1935, D.H.L., 1962; postgrad. U. Buffalo Sch. Social Work, 1937-43, Fordham U. Sch. Social Work, 1935-36; m. Antoinette Lopian, Sept. 5, 1938; children—Elizabeth Louise, Paul, Peter. Treas.-sec. St. Stanislaus and St. Mark Roman Catholic Chs., Buffalo, 1938-40, pres. Holy Name Soc.; an organizer Cath. League for Poland, 1943; chief U.S. Relief Mission in Poland, 1945-48; assisted in organizing Caritas, other Cath. instns. in Poland, 1943-48; chmn. Cath. Charities drive, 1952, mem. budget com., 1952—; mem. financial steering com. Diocese of Buffalo, 1956-61, peace and justice commn.; mem. Nat. Cath. Resettlement Council, 1947-51; adviser numerous Cath. schs., instns. Buffalo Diocese, 1938—. Vice-pres., officer-in-charge community affairs dept. Mfrs. Traders Trust Co., Buffalo, 1969—. Chmn., Nat. Youth Adminstrn. of Western N.Y., 1936-41; mem. State Youth Council, 1956—, Dept. Commerce Adv. Com. on E.-W. Trade; chmn. intra-faith com. United Fund, 1956-59; chmn. fund drive Villa Maria Coll., 1962; sec. fund drive St. Joseph's Intercommunity Hosp. 1955-56; an organizer, treas. chair of Polish culture Canisius Coll., 1953; pres. Community Welfare Council, 1968-70; mem. council SEEK program, 1966-68; mem. Pres.'s Adv. Council on Vol. ACTION, 1974; Pres. Nixon rep. opening Trade Info. Center in Poland, 1972. Named knight St. Gregory, Pope Pius VI. Mem. Polish, German and Italian Fedns. (treas. Supreme council 1938-42). K.C. Home: 175 Parkside Buffalo NY 14214 Office: 1 M & T Plaza Buffalo NY 14240

OST, MILTON FLOYD, minister, Am. Luth. Ch.; b. Beulah, N.D., Nov. 12, 1935; s. Gottfried Peter and Bertha Katherine (Wolf) O.; B.A., Wartburg Coll., 1957; B.D., Wartburg Theol. Sem., 1961; m. Delores Ruth Huber, June 10, 1956; children—Sabrina Marie, Catherine Rose, Deborah Leonne. Ordained to ministry Am. Luth. Ch., 1961; pastor Trinity Luth. Ch. and Glueckstal Lut. Ch., Napoleon, N.D., 1961-65, Atonement Luth. Ch., Jamestown, N.D., 1965-71, Grace Luth. Ch., Albert Lea, Minn. 1971—. Dist. youth com. chmn. Western N.D. Dist. of Am. Luth. Ch., 1963-65, Eastern N.D. Dist., 1966-70; pres. Jamestown (N.D.) Ministerial Assn., 1970-71, Albert Lea Ministerial Assn., 1974-75; bd. dirs. St. John's Luth. Home, Albert Lea. Mem. Gov.'s Task Force for Regional Planning, N.D., 1963-65, Gov.'s Com. for Vocat. Rehab. of the Handicapped, N.D., 1968-70; bd. dirs. United Way, Albert Lea, Trades and Labor Sr. Citizen Housing Center, Albert Lea. Mem. N.D. Mental Health Assn. (dir. 1968-70). Contbr. articles to religious jours. Home: 1204 Kent Ave Albert Lea MN 56007 Office: 918 Garfield Ave Albert Lea MN 56007

OST, WARREN WILLIAM, clergyman, Presbyterian Church, U.S.A.; b. Mankato, Minn., June 24, 1926; s. William Frederick and Margaret (Denison) O.; m. Nancy Nesbitt, May 15, 1954; 1 child, Laura Margaret. B.A., U. Minn., 1948; M.Div., Princeton Theol. Sem., 1951. D.D. (hon.), Moravian Theol. Sem., 1971. Ordained to ministry Presbyn. Ch., U.S.A., 1951. In sem. field positions in parishes in N.J., Pa., 1948-51; resident minister Yellowstone Nat. Park, Wyo., 1950-52; dir. A Christian Ministry in the Nat. Parks, N.Y.C., 1951—; bd. dirs. Ring Lake Ranch, Dubois, Wyo., 1964—; charter mem. Tourisme-Oecumenique,

1967—; cons. Pontifical Commn. on Migration and Tourism, The Vatican, Rome, 1967—. Author devotional booklet: God in My Leisure, 1966. Pres. E. 49th St. Assn., N.Y.C., 1961-62; bd. dirs. Prescott Neighborhood House, N.Y.C., 1961—. Recipient Pub. Service award Dept. Interior, Washington, 1977; named hon. park ranger Nat. Park Service, 1977. Mem. Assn. Theol. Field Educators, Les Amis du Chemin St. Jacques, Nat. Park Service Employees and Alumni Assn. (life), Conf. Nat. Park Concessioners (life), Denison Soc., Phi Mu Alpha. Clubs: Union League, Princeton (N.Y.C.). Office: A Christian Ministry in the Nat Parks 222 1/2 E 49 St New York NY 10017

O'SULLIVAN, SEAN PATRICK, priest, Roman Cath. Ch.; b. Bantry, Ireland, May 19, 1940; s. Stephen Anthony and Mary Margaret (Healy) O'S.; came to U.S., 1964, naturalized, 1972; M.A., Barry Coll., 1972; M.S.W., Fla. State U., 1973; postgrad. Columbia U., 1973—. Ordained priest, 1964; asso. pastor Archdiocese of Miami (Fla.), 1967-71; residence at Ch. of Notre Dame, N.Y.C., 1973—. Home: 400 E 57th St Apt 8F New York City NY 10022

OSWALT, JOHN MACON, minister, Southern Baptist Convention; b. Fayette, Ala., Mar. 19, 1921; s. Andrew Curtis and Ida Pearl (Patterson) O.; m. Lois Elaine Thornton, June 16, 1943; children: Lynn Thornton, Lonn Macon, Lewis Earle, Lori Elaine. B.A., U. Ala., 1943; M.Th., Southwestern Bapt. Theol. Sem., 1945. Ordained to ministry, So. Bapt. Conv., 1942. Student pastor Grace Bapt. Ch., Palestine, Tex., 1943-45, Munson Bapt. Ch., Royce City, Tex., 1943-45; pastor First Bapt. Ch., Blanchard, La., 1945-50, Main St. Bapt. Ch., Bolalusa, La., 1950-54, First Bapt. Ch., Hammond, La., 1954—; trustee La. Moral and Civic Found., Baton Rouge, 1957-64, 65-77, Baton Rouge Gen. Hosp., 1957-64; exec. bd. La. Bapt. Conv., 1956-63, 71-77; trustee So. Bapt. Annuity Bd., Dallas, 1962-68, So. Bapt. Sunday Sch. Bd., Nashville, 1978—. Contbr. articles to profl. jours. Charter mem. Hammond United Way; pres. Tangipalog chpt. ARC, Hammond, 1976—; charter mem. Hammond Hospice Bd., 1982. Mem. Hammond Ministerial Assn. (pres. 1959, 66, 78). Lodge: Kiwanis (pres. 1956-57). Home: 232 Puma Dr Hammond LA 70401 Office: First Bapt Ch PO Box 609 Hammond LA 70404

OSWALT, LAWRENCE EDWARD, minister, American Baptist Churches U.S.A.; b. Wabash, Ind., Sept. 27, 1936; s. Cecil Eugene and Carrie Blanche (Trent) O.; m. Lois Ellen Brown, Aug. 16, 1958; children: Denise, David, Carrie Lynn. B.A. magna cum laude, Colo. Coll., 1958; M.Div., Pacific Sch. Religion, 1970; postgrad. U. Calif.-Berkeley, 1958-62, Ind. U., 1984—. Ordained to ministry Baptist Ch. and Christian Ch., 1970. Ednl. asst. First Methodist Ch., Santa Rosa, Calif., 1966-68; pastor Golden Gate Christian Ch., San Francisco, 1968-70; minister of music and youth First Bapt. Ch., Colorado Springs, Colo., 1970-73; pastor First Bapt. Ch., Palisade, Colo., 1973-80, Bethel Bapt. Ch., Casper, Wyo., 1980-84; sec. bd. dirs. Wyo. Ministries in Higher Edn., Laramie, 1980-84; guest condr. Western Colo. Meth. Choir Clinic, Palisade, 1983. Grad. asst. Ind. U., Bloomington, 1984—. Weekly religious columnist Palisade Tribune, 1978-84. Author numerous adult ch. sch. study books, teaching guides. Composer Centennial Hymn for First Bapt. Ch. Colorado Springs, 1972. Chmn. bd. dirs., sub-area Western Colo. Health Systems Agy., Grand Junction, 1978-80; bd. dirs. Community Services Colo. West, Grand Junction, 1975-80; mem., soloist Casper Civic Chorale, 1980-84. Woodrow Wilson fellow, 1958. Mem. Ministers Council Am. Bapt. Chs. U.S.A. (senator 1977, 82-83); Ministers Council Am. Bapt. Ch. of Rocky Mountains (v.p. 1974-76, pres. 1977, continuing edn. team mem. 1979-82), Phi Beta Kappa. Home: 3622 Parkview Dr Bloomington IN 47401

OTIS, GERTRUDE ANNE, educator, nun, Roman Catholic Church; b. Wesley, Iowa, July 10, 1922; d. Joseph Henry and Mary Martha (Schwiderski) O. B.A., St. Mary's Coll., Notre Dame, Ind., 1952, M.A., 1955, Ph.D., 1960. Entered Congregation Sisters of Holy Cross, 1946. Registrar, dir. admissions, dean St. Mary's Coll., Notre Dame, 1950-67; assoc. prof. religious studies Cardinal Cushing Coll., Boston, 1968-72; asst. dean sch. religious studies Cath. U., Washington, 1974-76; dir. pastoral care dept. St. Joseph Hosp., South Bend, Ind., 1976-78; chmn., prof. religious studies Barry U., Miami, Fla., 1978—. Served with USN, 1943-45. Mem. Coll. Theology Soc. (sec. 1972-74), Cath. Bibl. Assn., Nat. Assn. Cath. Chaplains, Nat. Assembly Religious Women. Democrat. Office: Barry Univ 11300 NE 2d Ave Miami Shores FL 33161

OTIS, HAROLD FRED, JR., minister, Seventh-day Adventists; b. Hinsdale, Ill., Sept. 13, 1938; s. Harold Fred and Bernice (Miller) O.; B.B.A., Andrews U., 1965; m. Rose Marie Niesen, Mar. 1, 1959; children—Harold Todd, Heidi Lynn. Ordained to ministry, 1974; asso. dir. pub. dept. Potomac conf., Staunton, Va., 1965-67; dir. pub. dept. Pa. conf., Reading, 1967-72; asso. dir. pub. dept. Columbia Union conf. (Va., Md., N.J., Del., Pa., W. Va., Ohio), Takoma Park, Md., 1973-75; dir. pub. dept. Southwestern Union conf. (Tex., Okla., N.Mex., La., Ark.), Richardson, Tex., 1975—. Bd. dirs. So. Pub. House, Nashville. Recipient Wall Street Jour. award Andrews U., 1965. Contbr. articles in field to religious jours. Home: Route 4 Box 410 Cleburne TX 76031 Office: 600 S Central Expressway Richardson TX 75080

OTT, STANLEY JOSEPH See *Who's Who in America*, 43rd edition.

OTTENWELLER, ALBERT HENRY, bishop, Roman Catholic Ch.; b. Stanford, Mont., Apr. 5, 1916; s. Charles and Mary (Hake) O.; S.T.L., Cath. U. Am., 1943. Ordained priest, Roman Catholic Ch., 1943, consecrated Auxiliary Bishop, 1974; asso. pastor St. John's Parish, Delphos, Ohio, 1943-59; asso. pastor St. Richard's Parish, Swanton, Ohio, 1959-61; pastor St. Joseph's Parish, Blakeslee, Ohio, also mission Sacred Heart, Montpelier, Ohio, 1961-62; pastor Our Lady of Mt. Carmel Parish, Bono, Ohio, 1962-68, St. John's Parish, Delphos, Ohio, 1968-74, St. Michael's Parish, Findlay, Ohio, 1974-77; Bishop of Steubenville, 1977—. Apptd. Vicar Gen., 1968. Mem. Ohio Gov.'s Com. on Migrant Labor, 1955-75. Home: 422 Western Ave Findlay OH 45840 Office: Chancery Office 422 Washington St PO Box 969 Steubenville OH 43952

OTTO, A. STUART, theology educator, Church of the Trinity; b. Mt. Vernon, N.Y., Apr. 20, 1915; s. Albert Stuart and Verna Howarth (Wilkens) O.; m. Catherine Ruth Gale, Dec. 14, 1968. D.Div., Trinity Sch. Theology, San Marcos, Calif., 1967. Dir. the Invisible Ministry, San Marcos, 1963—; chmn. Trinity Sch. Theology, San Marcos, 1972—; mgr. Dominion Press, 1968—. Author (under name Friend Stuart) 18 books in field; contbr. articles to profl. jours. Chmn., Com. for an Extended Lifespan, 1978-81; founder, exec. The Philos. Library, 1964. Served to 2d lt. AUS, 1943-46. Mem. San Marcos C. of C., San Marcos Ministerial Assn. (chmn. 1971), San Marcos Hist. Soc. Lodge: Rotary. Office: The Invisible Ministry PO Box 37 San Marcos CA 92069

OTTO, EDGAR JOHN, minister, Lutheran Church-Missouri Synod; b. Guthrie, Okla., Oct. 7, 1926; s. Edgar and Anna Hattie (Wendel) O.; m. Rosemarie Naig, July 23, 1949; children: Vicki, Deborah, Bunnie, Ole. B.A., Macalester Coll., 1947; B.Th., Concordia Sem., Springfield, Ill., 1951, B.D., 1969, M.Div., 1971; M.A.D., Concordia Sem., St. Louis, 1973. Ordained to ministry, 1951. Pastor, Grace/Christ Luth. Ch., Pequot Lakes, Minn., 1951-54, Eastern Heights Luth. Ch., St. Paul, 1954-66, Immanuel Luth. Ch., Springfield, 1966-75, St. John's Luth. Ch., East Moline, Ill., 1975-80; adminstrv. asst.-mission South Wis. dist. Luth. Ch.-Mo. Synod, Milw., 1980—. Recipient Servus Ecclesiae Christi, Concordia Theol. Sem., Ft. Wayne, 1978. Republican. Home: 10144 W Vienna Ave Milwaukee WI 53222 Office: South Wis Dist Luth Ch Mo Synod 8100 W Capital Dr Milwaukee WI 53222

OTWAY, HENRY EDWARD, minister, United Ch. of Christ; b. Brighton, Eng., Mar. 26, 1915; came to U.S., 1924; naturalized, 1932; s. Henry Thomas and Eva (Mitton) O.; m. Mildred Emily Barnes, Sept. 29, 1934; children: Harry J., E. William, Thomas R. B.A., Mo. State Tchrs. Coll., Kirksville, 1940; B.D., William Booth Sem., Chgo., 1937. Ordained to ministry Salvation Army, 1937, recognized by Congregational Chs., 1961, United Ch. of Christ, 1963. Mgr. Salvation Army Social Ctr., Fargo, N.D., 1948-55; pastor Congl. Ch., Granite Falls, Minn., 1959-65, Community United Ch. of Christ, Biwabik, Minn., 1965-71, Congl. Ch., Detroit Lakes, Minn., 1965—; registrar NE assn. Minn. conf. United Ch. of Christ, 1966-71, mem. chmn. conf. Indian concerns com., 1972-82, mem. conf. ch. and ministry com., 1981-84; bd. dirs. Minn. Council Chs., 1975-76; pres. Detroit Lakes Ministerial Assn., 1972-73, sec., 1976-84. Author: 10 Years Indian Advocacy, 1982. Pres. United Fund, Granite Falls, 1962-65; del. Minn. Democratic Conv., 1970; bd. dirs. East Range Human Rights Com., Biwabik, 1968-71. Mem. Dem.-Farmer-Labor Party. Club: Exchange; Lodges: Rotary (bd. dirs. 1978-80) (Detroit Lakes); Masons, Elks (chmn. welfare com. 1953). Office: Congregational Ch 900 Lake Ave Detroit Lakes MN 56501

OUELLET, GILLES, archbishop, Roman Catholic Ch.; b. Bromptonville, Que., Can., Aug. 14, 1922; s. Joseph Adelard and Armande (Biron) O.; B.A., Sherbrooke Sem. Ordained priest Roman Catholic Ch., 1946; archbishop of Rimouski, Que., 1973—. Address: PO Box 730 Rimouski PQ G5L 7C7 Canada

OUELLETTE, ANDRE, bishop, Roman Catholic Ch.; b. Salem, Mass., Feb. 4, 1913; s. Amedee and Celina (Ouellette) O.; B.A., Laval U., 1934, L.Th., 1946. Ordained priest Roman Cath. Ch., 1938; prof. philosophy and theology Sem. Trois-Rivieres, Que., 1938-56; rector Major Sem., Trois-Rivieres, 1948-53, Minor Sem., Trois-Rivieres, 1953-57; pres. La Fedn. des Colls. Classiques, 1956; aux. bishop Diocese Mont Laurier, Que., 1957-63, adminstr., 1963-65, bishop, 1965—. Mem. central commn. Canadian Cath. Conf., 1967-69, pres. theology commn. 1967-70, mem. social action and liturgy commn., 1965-69, co-pres. family com., 1969-71; pres. social action commn. Assembly of Bishops of Province of Que., 1969-71. Address: 435 dela Madone Mont-Laurier PQ J9L 1S1 Canada

OUELLETTE, PHILIP R., brother, Roman Catholic Church; b. Daigle, Maine, June 6, 1930; s. Ned and Leda M. (Marquis) O. B.A. in Spanish, St. John's U., M.S. in Spanish, 1960, B.S. in Counseling, M.S. in Counseling, 1973; B.S., Marist Coll., 1953. Vice-provincial Marist Brothers of the Schools, Esopus Province, N.J., 1977-80, provincial, 1980—; sec. treas. Eastern Religious Vocation Dirs. Assn., 1973, chmn. 1975; vice-pres. Nat. Conf. Religious Vocation Dirs. of Men, 1975-76. Mem. Conf. Major Superiors of Men, Nat. Cath. Vocation Council (bd. dirs. 1984—).

OUTKA, GENE HAROLD, philosophy and Christian ethics educator; b. Sioux Falls, S.D., Feb. 24, 1937; s. Harold Irvin O. and Gertrude Anne (Elliot) Finch Outka; m. Susan Owen, Dec. 29, 1984; children (by previous marriage): Paul Harold, Elizabeth Noelle. B.A., U. Redlands, 1959; B.D., Yale U., 1962, M.A., 1964, Ph.D., 1967; L.H.D., U. Redlands, 1978. Instr. Princeton U., N.J., 1965-66, lectr., 1966-67, asst. prof., 1967-73, assoc. prof., 1973-75; assoc. prof. Yale U., New Haven, 1975-81, Dwight prof. philosophy and Christian ethics, 1981—; dir. resdl. seminar for coll. tchrs. NEH, New Haven, 1977-78; Mary Farnum Brown lectr. Haverford Coll., Pa., 1977; mem. faculty workshop on teaching of ethics Hastings Inst. Soc., Ethics and Life Scis., Princeton, 1979; Merrick lectr. Ohio Wesleyan U., Delaware, Ohio, 1983. Author: Agape: An Ethical Analysis, 1972. Co-editor and contbr.: Norm and Context in Christian Ethics, 1968, Religion and Morality, 1973. Service fellow Office of Spl. Projects, Health Services and Mental Health Adminstrn., HEW, Washington, 1972-73; mem. adv. com. social ethics Inst. Medicine, Nat. Acad. Scis., Washington, 1975-77. Fellow Am. Council Learned Socs., 1968-69, NEH, 1979-80, Woodrow Wilson Internat. Ctr. for Scholars, 1983; vis. scholar Kennedy Inst. Ethics, Georgetown U., 1972-73. Mem. Soc. for Values in Higher Edn., Am. Acad. Religion, Soc. Christian Ethics, Am. Theol. Soc., Jour. Religious Ethics (bd. dirs., editorial bd.), New Haven Theol. Discussion Group. Office: Dept Religious Studies Yale U 320 Temple St New Haven CT 06520

OVERGAARD, ROBERT MILTON, missionary adminstr., minister, Ch. of Lutheran Brethren Am.; b. Ashby, Minn., Nov. 6, 1929; s. Gust and Ella (Johnson) O.; certificate Luth. Brethren Sem., 1954; B.S., Mayville State U., 1959; M.S., U. Ore., 1970; m. Sally Lee Stephenson, Dec. 29, 1949; children—Catherine Jean (Mrs. David Thuleen), Robert Milton, Elizabeth Dianne (Mrs. Sean Bearly), Barbara, Craig, David, Lori. Ordained to ministry Ch. Luth. Brethren Am., 1954; pastor Elim Luth. Ch., Frontier, Sask., Can., 1954-57, Ebenezer Luth. Ch., Mayville, N.D., 1957-60, Immanuel Luth. Ch., Eugene, Oreg., 1960-63, 59th St. Luth. Ch., Bklyn., 1963-68, Immanuel Luth. Ch., Pasadena, Calif., 1969-73; exec. sec. Fgn. Missions, Ch. Luth. Brethren Am., Fergus Falls, Minn., 1973—. Mem. Pasadena Assn. Evangelicals (chmn. 1972-73). Editor: Faith and Fellowship, 1967-75. Home: Box 742 Fergus Falls MN 56537 Office: Box 655 Fergus Falls MN 56537

OVERLUND, ERVIN KENNETH, minister, American Lutheran Church; b. Silverton, Oreg., May 6, 1928; s. Oscar R. and Emma (Johnsson) O.; m. Sylvia Adrene Moe, Nov. 25, 1954; children: Ruth Linnea, Mary C. Sluke, Timothy E., Joel K., Rachel J. B.A., Augsburg Coll., 1956; B.D., Luther Sem.-St. Paul, 1961. Ordained to ministry, 1961. Pastor, Coulee-Lostwood Am. Luth. Parish, Coulee, N.D., 1961-65; pastor Benedict Am. Luth. Parish, Benedict, N.D., 1965-68, Fordville, N.D., 1969-78; chaplain Lake Region Nursing Home and Good Samaritan Ctr., Devils Lake, N.D., 1978—; dean Am. Luth. Ch. Conf., 1972—; me. Eastern N.D. Dist. Council, Fargo, 1973; del. Gen. Conv., Detroit, 1974. Vice pres. Devils Lake United Way, 1983. Mem. N.D. Chaplains Assn. (treas. 1978-79), Assn. Clin. Pastoral Edn., Devils Lake Ministerial Assn. (treas.). Democrat. Lodge: Rotary (sec. 1981—). Home: 1213 5th Ave N Devils Lake ND 58301 Office: Lake Region Luth Home Inc E 14th Ave Devils Lake ND 58301

OVERSTREET, R(EGINALD) LARRY, minister, Independent Baptist; b. Owosso, Mich., Aug. 17, 1941; s. Reignald and Nancy Ruth (Clifton) O.; m. Linda Darlene Sunday, Aug. 17, 1962; children: Lori Lea, Lois Ann, Reginald Lloyd. B.A., Bob Jones U., 1963; M.Div., San Francisco Bapt. Theol. Sem., 1968; M.A., Wayne State U., 1974, Ph.D., 1979. Ordained to ministry Bapt. Ch., 1963. Pastor, Beulah Bapt. Ch., Roseville, Mich., 1968-72, Springwells Ave. Bapt. Ch., Detroit, 1972-74, First Bapt. Ch., Warsaw, Ind., 1980—; asst. prof. Midwestern Bapt. Coll., Pontiac, Mich., 1974-75, Detroit Bapt. Theol. Sem., Allen Park, Mich., 1975-79; assoc. prof. Grace Theol. Sem., Winona Lake, Ind., 1979—. Contbr. articles to religious mags. and jours. Mem. Speech Communication Assn., Religious Speech Communication Assn., Central States Speech Assn., Ind. Speech Assn. Republican. Club: Optimist (chaplain 1983-84). Home: Rural Route 3 Box 103 Warsaw IN 46580 Office: Grace Theol Sem 200 Seminary Dr Winona Lake IN 46590

OVERTON, EDWIN DEAN, minister, Christian Church; b. Beaver, Okla., Dec. 2, 1939; s. William Edward and Georgia Beryl (Fronk) O.; B.Th., Midwest Christian Coll., 1963; M.A., Eastern N.M. U., 1969. Ordained to ministry Christian Ch. (Okla.), 1963; student minister Christian Ch., Englewood, Kans., 1961-63; youth minister Christian Ch., Beaver, Okla., 1963-67; campus minister Christian Campus House Eastern N.Mex. U., 1967—, instr. religion, 1970—, dir., 1980—. Chmn. March of Dimes Drive, Beaver County, 1966; mem. com. originating and continuing Community Forum, Portales; Univ. Coordinator Lord of Life Festival, Portales, 1977. Named Mr. Midwest, 1959, 63. Mem. Jaycees (state dir. 1964-65, chmn. com. to select outstanding young teacher in Beaver County 1966), Portales Tennis Assn. (pres. 1977-78), Psi Chi. Home and Office: 223 S Ave K Portales NM 88130

OVERTON, KENNETH WAYNE, pastor, Southern Baptist Convention; b. Star City, Ark., Feb. 20, 1951; s. Carl McKinley and Clara Lou (Hollon) O.; m. Carletta Hope Wadley, May 13, 1978; children: Christina Ruth, Adam Carl. B.A., Ouachita Bapt. U., 1973; M.Div., Southwestern Bapt. Theol. Sem., 1976. Ordained to gospel ministry Bapt. Ch., 1970. Pastor Pleasant Grove Bapt. Ch., Warren, Ark., 1970-73; asst. dir. Bapt. Good Will Ctr., Ft. Worth, 1974-76; pastor Norman Bapt. Ch., Ark., 1977-80; assoc. pastor Dallas Ave Bapt. Ch., Mena, Ark., 1980-81; pastor Wilmot Bapt. Ch., Ark., 1981-84, Arkansas City Bapt. Ch., Ark., 1984—; hosp. chaplain Bapt. Med. Ctr., Little Rock, summer 1973, Baylor Med. Ctr., Dallas, summer 1976; assn. clk. Delta Bapt. Assn., 1982—; chaplain Wilmot Police Dept., 1984-84. Fellow mem. Civil Def., Wilmot, 1982-84, Vol. Fire Dept., Wilmot, 1983-84. Home: PO Box 459 Arkansas City AR 71630 Office: Arkansas City Bapt Ch PO Box 459 Arkansas City AR 71630

OVERTON, THOMAS WESLEY, minister, Chs. of Christ; b. Gibson County, Ind., Feb. 1, 1920; s. Virgil and Della Ruth (Brown) O.; student Johnson Bible Coll., 1939-40, Cin. Bible Sem., 1940-41; A.B., Lincoln Christian Coll., 1942-46, M.A., 1947; D.D., Ky. Christian Coll., 1974; D.Litt. Calif. Grad. Sch. Theology, 1974, Ph.D., 1975; m. Nedra Maxine Wilson, July 4, 1940; children—Linda, Thomas, Randall, Faith. Ordained to ministry Churches of Christ, 1940; minister Emden (Ill.) Christian Ch., 1948-50, First Ch. Christ, Catlin, Ill., 1950-52; sr. minister Blvd. Ch. of Christ, Toledo, 1952-58, Englewood Christian Ch., Indpls., 1958-59, First Christian Ch., Huntington Beach, Calif., 1959—; prof., spl. lectr. Calif. Grad. Sch. Theology, Glendale, Pacific Christian Coll., Fullerton, Calif., Midwest Christian Coll., Oklahoma City. Pres. N.Am. Christian Conv., Cin., 1973-74. Sec. to publ. com. Standard Pub. Co., Cin., 1949—. Recipient Restoration award Lincoln Christian Coll., 1966. Home: 502 Crest St Huntington Beach CA 92648 Office: 1207 Main St Huntington Beach CA 92648

OWEN, JOHN EDWARD, minister, educator, Am. Bapt. Assn.; b. Duncan, Okla., Sept. 20, 1937; s. Lavanda Harlen and Okneta Genevieve (Medley) O.; B.S. in Civil Engring., Tex. Tech. Coll., 1960; Th.M., Missionary Bapt. Sem., 1969, Th.D., 1972; m. Ima Jean Milam, Apr. 15, 1961; children—Karla Denise, John Edward. Ordained to ministry, 1962; pastor chs., Ark., 1962-71; instr. Missionary Bapt. Sem., 1967-70, adminstrv. v.p., 1971-73, pres., 1973—; chmn. missionary com. Ark. Bapt. Assn., 1968-73; pastor 1st Bapt. Ch., Bryant, Ark., 1976—. Asso. editor Missionary Bapt. Searchlight, 1971—; v.p. Am. Bapt. Assn., 1973. Author: (with L.D. Capell) Special Services Manual, 1973. Home: PO Box 547 Bryant AR 72022 Office: 1st Baptist Church Bryant AR 72022

OWENS, C.D., Bishop, Church of God in Christ. Office: 14 Van Velsor Pl Newark NJ 07112*

OWENS, CHARLES LEWIS, minister, Southern Baptist Convention. B. Gadsden, Ala., July 4, 1951; s. Simeon Paul and Anna Geneva (Collins) W.; m. Patricia Lee Ann Pendley, Feb. 28, 1975; children: Amanda Lee Ann, Jessica Simonne, Charles Lewis II, Harrel Harding. B.S., Jacksonville State U., 1972, M.B.A., 1973; M.Div., Luther Rice Sem., 1976, D.Ministry, 1981. Licensed minister, Southern Baptist Convention, 1977, ordained to ministry, 1978. Music evangelist, Gadsden, Ala., 1972-76; minister music Goodyear Heights Bapt. Ch., Gadsden, 1976-78; pastor Central Ave. Bapt. Ch., Gadsden, 1978-80, First Bapt. Ch. Southside, Gadsden, 1980—; Author-preacher (sermon series radio broadcasts), 1983, 84; author-speaker (lecture series) Martial Artists in the Bible, 1984. Named Outstanding Young Man Am., Jaycees, 1978. Mem. Etowah Bapt. Assn. (exec. bd. 1978—, fin. and budget com. 1980—), Christian Black Belt Assn. (evangelist-exhibitor 1980—). Home: Route 14 Box 31 Gadsden AL 35903 Office: First Bapt Ch Southside Route 14 Box 32 Gadsden AL 35903

OWENS, ROBERT JESSEN, minister, religion educator, Christian Church; b. Springfield, Ill., Oct. 20, 1947; s. Robert Jessen and Betty June (Taylor) O.; m. Mary Ann Johnson, Aug. 23, 1969; children: Monica, Michele, Owens. A.B. magna cum laude, U. Ill., 1969; M.A., Lincoln Christian Sem., 1973, M.Div., 1973; Ph.D., Johns Hopkins U., 1982. Ordained to ministry Christian Ch., 1972; cert. secondary tchr., Ill. Minister Christian Ch., Elkhart, Ill., 1970-72; asst. prof. Bible, Manhattan Christian Coll., Kans., 1974-77; instr. Bible, Milligan Coll., Joppa, Md., 1978-79; adj. faculty of sacred scripture St. Mary's Sem., Balt., 1978-83; assoc. prof. Old Testament, Emmanuel Sch. Religion, Johnson City, Tenn., 1980—. Author: Genesis and Exodus Citations of Aphrahat the Persian Sage, 1983. Editor: (with others) Increase in Learning, 1979. Mem. Soc. Bibl. Lit., Cath. Bibl. Assn. Home: 149 E Highland Rd Johnson City TN 37601 Office: Emmanuel Sch Religion Route 6 Box 500 Johnson City TN 37601

OWENS, RONNIE TYLER, minister, Southern Baptist Convention; b. Middlesboro, Ky., Mar. 14, 1952; s. Tyler and Beatrice (Brown) O.; m. Judy Faye Burchett, May 9, 1975; 1 child, Rhonda Faye. B.A., Lincoln Meml. U., 1974; M.A., Union Coll., Barbourville, Ky., 1979; postgrad. Pensacola Christian Coll., 1983—. Ordained to ministry Southern Baptist Convention, 1972. Pastor, Wolfenbarger Chapel, Tazewell, Tenn., 1972-73, Alanthus Hill Bapt. Ch., Ewing, Va., 1973-74, Silver Leaf Bapt. Ch., Rose Hill, Va., 1975-80, First Bapt. Ch., Artemus, Ky., 1981—; pres. Knox County Christian Sch., Artemus, 1982—, Jubilee Camp Meeting, Artemus, 1982—, Heritage Bible Inst., Artemus, 1983—; bd. dirs. Laurel Lake Bapt. Camp, Corbin, Ky., 1982-83; chmn. Knox County Christian Services, Barbourville, 1983-84. Named to Outstanding Young Men of Am., Jaycees, 1979, 80, 83. Mem. Barbourville-Knox County Ministerial Assn. (pres. 1983-85), North Concord Assn. Bapts. (moderator 1982-83), Nat. Christian Educators Assn., So. Bapt. Assn. Christian Schs. Address: Box 128 Artemus KY 40903

OXENDINE, SAMMY RAY, religion educator, minister, Church of God; b. Asheville, N.C., Apr. 7, 1944; s. Sam and Tilda (Anders) O.; m. Helen Beaver, Aug. 22, 1970; children: April, Alison, Amy. B.A. in English, Belmont Abbey, 1966; M.A. in English, Appalachian State U., 1969; Ed.D., U. N.C.-Greensboro, 1984. Ordained to ministry Ch. of God, 1974. Program dir. Ch. of God Orphanage, Kannapolis, N.C., 1969-72; assoc. pastor Eastway Ch. of God, Charlotte, N.C., 1972-73, Cramerton Ch. of God, N.C., 1973-74; asst. supt. Ch. of God Orphanage, Kannapolis, 1974-76; v.p. East Coast Bible Coll., Charlotte, 1977—; chmn. State Bd. Edn. of Chs. of God, N.C., 1982—. Mem. Am. Assn. Higher Edn. Home: 400 Glen Arbor Dr Belmont NC 28012 Office: East Coast Bible Coll 6900 Wilkinson Blvd Charlotte NC 28214

OZBUN, T.J., minister, Southern Baptist Convention, social services agency executive; b. Austin, Tex., July 4, 1930; s. T.J. and Ruby May (Perninor) O.; m. Laquetta Faye Coffey, July 17, 1949; 1 child, T.J. III. B.A., East Tex. State Coll., 1958, M.A., 1960; Th.D., Zion Theol. Sem., Winchester, Ky., 1971; D.Litt., Eastern Nebr. Christian Coll. (hon.), 1971; D.S.L. (hon.), Berean Christian Coll., 1972; D.Ministry, So. Bapt. Ctr., Folkston, Ga., 1984. Ordained to ministry Bapt. Missionary Assn., 1948. Pastor, First Bapt. Ch., Hale Center, Tex., 1966-71, Emmanuel Bapt. Ch., Pittsburg, Tex., 1971-75, Oakcrest Bapt. Ch., Baton Rouge, 1975-78, First Bapt. Ch., Gonzales, La., 1978-84; chaplain Gonzales Police Dept., 1978—; chaplain, counselor United Social Services, Gonzales, 1984—. Author: Security of the Believer, 1982. Inductee, Nat. Chaplains Assn. Hall of Fame, 1983. Mem. La. Chaplains Assn., Am. Chem. Dependency Soc., Assn. Christian Marriage Counselors, U.S. Counseling Assn., Internat. Conf. Police Chaplains. Lodge: Masons.

OZOLINS, KARL LOTARS, college administrator, American Lutheran Church; b. Riga, Latvia, Mar. 11, 1923; came to U.S., 1949; s. Karl and Alma (Cukste) O.; m. Sulamit I. Ivask, Nov. 10, 1945; children: Dina Ruth, Andrew Lynn, Peter Charles. B.A., Augsburg Coll., 1951; B.Th., Augsburg Theol. Sem., 1952; M.A. in L.S., U. Minn., 1961, M.A. in Edn., 1966; M.Div., U. Luther Northwestern Sem., 1970; Ph.D., U. Mich., 1972. Pastor, Luth. Free Ch., Barronett, Wis., 1951-55; instr. Augsburg Coll., Mpls., 1955-59, librarian, 1959-61; asst. prof. U. Minn., Mpls., 1961-69, U. Mich., Ann Arbor, 1966-67; Fulbright prof. Nat. Taiwan U., Taipei, 1963-64; dept. head library sci. Ill. State U., Normal, 1971-73; dir. library Gustavus Adolphus Coll., St. Peter, Minn., 1973-80; dir. library Coll. St. Thomas, St. Paul, 1980—; bd. deacons Latvian Evang. Luth. Ch., Mpls., 1980—. Assoc. editor Jour. Baltic Studies, 1970—; contbg. writer: Akcadimiska Dzive, 1969—. Author: Ticibas Speka, 1983. Bd. dirs. Cooperating Libraries in Consortium, St. Paul, 1980—; mem. adv. bd. Metronet, St. Paul, 1984—. Office Higher Edn. grantee, 1967, 68. Mem. ALA, Minn. Library Assn., Am. Latvian Assn., Hist. Luth. Conf., Spl. Libraries Assn., Am. Soc. Info. Sci., Beta Phi Mu. Home: 1905 N Fairview Ave Saint Paul MN 55113 Office: Coll of Saint Thomas O'Shaughnessy Library 2115 Summit Ave Saint Paul MN 55105

PACE, A.J., minister, So. Baptist Conv.; b. Lamar County, Miss., Oct. 28, 1933; s. Andrew Jackson and Arnie (Kendrick) P.; B.A., Blue Mountain Coll., 1963; B.D., New Orleans Bapt. Theol. Sem. 1966; m. Lottie Jean Fillingame, Aug. 3, 1956; children—Roxanne, Galen, Kelton, Jill. Ordained to ministry, 1959; pastor New Hope Bapt. Ch., Vardaman, Miss., 1959, Pittsboro Bapt. Ch., Pittsboro, Miss., 1959-60, Bethel Bapt. Ch., Houston, Miss., 1960-61, Potts Camp Ch., Potts, Miss., 1961-63, W. Poplarville (Miss.) Ch., 1963-65, County Line Ch., Mendenhall, Miss., 1965-68, Star (Miss.) Ch., 1968-74, E. Moss Point (Miss.) Bapt. Ch., 1974—. Camp dir. Royal Ambassador and Girls' Aux.; chaplain Masons, 1975-76, Order of Eastern Star, 1974-76. Mem. Moss Point Ministerial Assn., Jackson County Pastors Conf. Contbr. articles to religious jours. Home: 1433 Third St Moss Point MS 39563 Office: 1326 Grierson St Moss Point MS 39563

PACHECANO, OMAR H., minister, Southern Baptist Convention; b. San Antonio, Tex., Nov. 25, 1934; s. Natividad Sanchez and Rafaela (Herrera) P.; m. Toni Gloria Huriega, Aug. 24, 1956; children: Debra Rose, Lisa Annette, Omar N., Roy Ralph. B. Career Arts, Dallas Bapt. U., 1976. Ordained to ministry Bapt. Ch., 1979. Adminstr. of ministry and edn. S. San Mexico Bapt. Ch., San Antonio, 1972-75; dir. ethnic missionaries First Bapt. Ch., Plano, Tex., 1975-77; pastor Pruitt Ave Bapt. Ch., San Antonio, 1977-79; assoc. dir. El Paso Bapt. Assn. (Tex.), 1979—; mem. Centennial Com., Bapt. Gen. Conv. Tex., Dallas, 1982—, mem. exec. bd., 1971-75; chmn. Hispanic Bapt. Theol. Sem., San Antonio, 1972-78; mem., 1st vice chmn. So. Bapt. Conv. Home Mission Bd., Atlanta, 1975—. Served with U.S. Army, 1954-56. Mem. Mex. Am. Adv. Orgn. (pres.). Republican. Home: 1936 Septiembre El Paso TX 79935 Office: El Paso Bapt Assn 2012 Grant Ave El Paso TX 79930

PACHOW, WANG, educator; b. Chungking, China, June 1, 1918; s. Wang High-shan and Mashih; came to U.S., 1968, naturalized, 1975; B.A., Mengtsang Coll., Shanghai, China, 1936; M.A., Visva-Bharati U., Santiniketan, India, 1941; Ph.D., U. Bombay (India), 1948; m. Mavis de Silva, June 2, 1956; 1 son, Hsuan. Prof. religion U. Iowa, 1975—. Mem. Am. Acad. Religion, Maha-bodhi Soc., Am. Oriental Soc., Assn. Asian Studies, Soc. Study Chinese Religions, Visva-Bharati Soc. (India). Author: A Comparative Study of the Pratimoksha, 1955. Contbr. to Ency. Britannica, profl. jours. Home: 821 Iowa Ave Iowa City IA 52240 Office: Sch Religion Univ Iowa Iowa City IA 52240

PACK, WALTER FRANK, minister, Churches of Christ; b. Memphis, Mar. 27, 1916; s. Joseph Walter and Mary Elizabeth (Gibson) P.; A.A., David Lipscomb Coll., 1935; B.A., U. Chattanooga, 1937; M.A., Vanderbilt U., 1939; Ph.D., U. So. Calif., 1948; m. Della Carlton, June 22, 1947. Ordained to ministry, 1932; minister St. Elmo Ch. of Christ, Chattanooga, 1936-40; minister Grace Ave. Ch. of Christ, Nashville, 1940-44; instr. bible and sociology David Lipscomb Coll., Nashville, 1940-44; minister Burbank (Calif.) Ch., 1945-49; prof. religion Pepperdine Coll., Los Angeles, 1947-49; minister Northside Ch., Abilene, Tex., 1950-58, Graham St. Ch., Abilene, Tex., 1959-61; prof. bible Abilene Christian Coll., 1949-63; minister Culver Palms Ch., Los Angeles, 1964—; chmn. dept. religion Pepperdine U., Los Angeles, 1963-76, disting. prof., 1979——, dean grad. sch., 1967-78. Mem. Soc. Bibl. Lit., Am. Acad. Religion, Evang. Theol. Soc., Phi Beta Kappa, Phi Kappa Phi, Pi Gamma Mu, Alpha Chi. Author: Great Preachers of Today, 1963; (with Prentice Meador) Preaching to Modern Man, 1969; Tongues and the Holy Spirit, 1973; Living Word Commentary on the Gospel of John, 1977; editor Our Bible, 1951; The Message of the New Testament: the Revelation, I and II, 1984; Mem. editorial bd. Restoration Quar., 1963——. Home: 10858 Wagner St Culver City CA 90230 Office: 24255 Pacific Coast Hwy Malibu CA 90265

PACKARD, GEORGE ALLEN, minister, Southern Baptist Convention; b. Richmond, Maine, Apr. 6, 1933; s. LeRoy Edward and Mildred Aletha (Patten) P.; diploma in theology Southwestern Bapt. Theol. Sem., 1974; B.S. in Sociology, So. Ark. U., 1978; m. Joyce LaJuan Carter, July 2, 1955; children: Joylene Packard Jacoby, Anita Louise Packard Miller. Ordained deacon, 1964, ordained to ministry, 1972; Sunday sch. supt. Midvale Bapt. Ch., Madison, Wis., 1961-62, Immanuel Bapt. Ch., Wiesbaden, W.Ger., 1964-65; minister of edn. Carter Park Bapt. Ch., Del City, Okla., 1972; pastor 1st Bapt. Ch., Carey, Tex., 1974-75, Village (Ark.) Bapt. Ch., 1975-78, 1st Bapt. Ch., Calion, Ark., 1978-79, Taylorville (Ill.) Bapt. Ch., 1980—. Served in U.S. Air Force, 1951-71. Mem. Capital City Bapt. Assn. (Sunday sch. dir. 1981—), Taylorville Ministerial Assn. (incorporating dir., treas. 1982-84, pres. 1985—), Air Force Sgts. Assn. Home: 120 E Pleasant St Taylorville IL 62568 Office: 1121 N Webster St Taylorville IL 62568

PACKER, BOYD K., church official. Mem. Quorum of the Twelve, The Church of Jesus Christ of Latter-day Saints (mem. Quorum of the Twelve). Office: The Church of Jesus Christ of Latter-Day Saints 50 E North Temple St Salt Lake City UT 84150*

PADBERG, JOHN WILLIAM, priest, educator, theology school president, Roman Catholic Church; b. St. Louis, May 22, 1926; s. John Francis and Emily C. (Albrecht) P. A.B., St. Louis U., 1949, Ph.L., 1951,

M.A., 1954; S.T.L., St. Mary's Coll., 1959; Ph.D., Harvard U., 1965. Ordained priest Roman Cath. Ch., 1957. Prof. history St. Louis U., 1964-75, acad. v.p., 1969-73; research assoc. Jesuit Conf., Washington, 1973-75; bd. dirs., pres., prof. history Weston Sch. of Theology, Cambridge, Mass., 1975—; trustee Regis Coll., Denver, Loyola U., New Orleans, Boston Theol. Inst., 1975—; mem. exec. com. Internat. Conf. of Cath. Theol. Inst., 1978—, pres., 1984—. Author: Colleges in Controversy: The Jesuit Schools in France From Revival to Suppression, 1815-80, 1969. Author: Studies in the Spirituality of Jesuits: Personal Experience and the Spiritual Exercises: The Example of St. Ignatius, vol. X, No. 5, The Society True to Itself: A Brief History of the 32d General Congregation of the Society of Jesus, vol. XV, nos. 3, 4, 1974-75. Recipient E. Harris Harbison award Danforth Found., 1969. Mem. Cath. Theol. Soc. Am., Am. Hist. Assn., Am. Soc. Ch. History, Am. Cath. Hist. Assn., Am. Acad. Religion, Soc. French Hist. Studies, Soc. Values in Higher Edn. Home: 15 Hawthorn St Cambridge MA 02138 Office: Weston Sch of Theology 3 Phillips Pl Cambridge MA 02138

PADGETT, ALAN GREGORY, minister, religion educator, United Methodist Church; b. Washington, Sept. 23, 1955; s. Clarence Padgett and Mary Louise Cavalier; m. Sally Victoria Bruyneel, Apr. 30, 1977; 1 son, Luke. B.A. with honors, So. Calif. Coll., 1977; M.Div. with honors, Drew U., 1981. Ordained to ministry United Methodist Church, 1979. Assoc. pastor San Dieguito United Meth. Ch., Encinitas, Calif., 1981-82; pastor Highlands United Meth. Ch. and Sea Bright United Meth. Ch., N.J., 1979-81, United Meth. Ch., San Jacinto, Calif., 1982—; adj. prof. religion So. Calif. Coll., Costa Mesa, 1984—. Contbr. articles, abstracts and book revs. to bibl. and theol. jours. Mem. Theol. Students Fellowship (contbr. 1981—), Am. Acad. Religion, Soc. Christian Philosophers, Philosophy of Religion Soc. Democrat. Avocations: hiking; racquetball; camping; computers. Home: 325 S Wateka St San Jacinto CA 92383 Office: San Jacinto United Meth Ch PO Box 123 San Jacinto CA 92383

PAGÁN, ANTONIO-MARÍA, priest, Roman Catholic Ch.; b. Fortuna, Spain, Aug. 29, 1923; s. Juan Jerónimo and María (Lopez) P.; student St. Ignatius Coll., Ecuador, 1942-45; B.A., Pontificia Universidad Javeriana, Colombia, 1947; postgrad. Facultad de Teología, Spain, 1951-55, St. Stanislaus Coll., Cleve., 1958-59. Joined Soc. of Jesus, 1940; ordained priest Roman Catholic Ch., 1954; mem. Jesuit Missionary Band in Spain, 1955-57; prof., choir dir. St. Gabriel Jesuit High Sch., Ecuador, 1957-58, 59-60, 67-70, Loyola High Sch., Ecuador, 1965-67; prin. Borja Jesuit Sch., Ecuador, 1960-65; exec. sec. clergy and vocational com. Nat. Conf. Bishops of Ecuador, 1968-70; asst. Spanish Mission, Cleve., 1971-72; diocesan dir. Spanish Apostolate, also spiritual dir. Spanish Cursillo Movement, Diocese of Cleve., 1972—; pastor-adminstr., founder San Juan Bautista Hispanic Parish, 1975—. Mem. adv. com. Cleve. Pub. Schs., 1972—, La Raza Unida of Ohio, 1972—; mem. censorship com. City of Cuenca (Ecuador), 1960-68; dir. radio program Ecos Hispanicos, 1973—. Author: Jesus Misionero, 1949; Botánica, 1950; Canticos, 1950, Misas Participadas, 1960, 65; Química, 1951. Contbr. poetry and articles to periodicals. Home and Office: 1946 W 32d St Cleveland OH 44113

PAGE, JEAN-GUY, priest, educator, Roman Catholic Church; b. Montreal, Jan. 17, 1926; s. Almanzor and Alice (Gauvin) P. B.A., Laval U., 1948; License in Theology, Laval U., 1964; Diploma in Pastoral, Lumen Vitae-Belgium, 1965; Ph.D., Gregorianum-Rome, 1967. Ordained priest, 1952. Priest, St. Anselm Parish, Que., Can., 1952-55, Our Lady Parish, 1955-59; chaplain Young Christian Students, Que., 1959-63; prof. theology Laval U., Que., 1967—; dir. Major Sem., 1969-72; mem. Diocesan Pastoral Council, Que., 1967-68, 73-74, diocesan priests council, 1968-72. Author: Reflections Sur Leglise du Quebec, 1976; Foi du Liberte?, 1977; Qui Est L'Eglise?, 1977-79, 3 vols.; Une Eglise Sans Laics?, 1980; Le Nautonier de Dieu, 1984; La Source, 1984. Contbr. articles to profl. jours. Mem. Can. Soc. Religious Studies, Societe Canadienne de Theologie. Home: 4710 Des Jardins Saint Antoine de Tilly G0S 2G0 Canada Office: F A Savard Bldg 736 Laval Univ Ste Foy Quebec PQ G1K 7P4 Canada

PAGE, RUSSELL BRIAN, priest, religious organization executive, Roman Catholic Church. B. Providence, R.I., Oct. 12, 1945; s. Frederick Lloyd and Mary (Landers) P. A.B., Providence Coll., 1968; M. Ch. Adminstrn., Cath. U., 1976. Ordained priest, Roman Cath. Ch., 1973. Assoc. pastor St. Paul Ch., Cranston, R.I., 1973-74; asst. chancellor, sec. to Bishop of Providence, 1974-84; dir. Office of Worship and Liturgy, Diocese of Providence, 1984—; moderator Diocesan Council Cath. Women, Providence, 1975—. Author weekly column in Cath. newspaper The Visitor. Artist liturgical art and calligraphy. Mem. Canon Law Soc. Am., Diocesan Bldg. Commn., Fedn. Diocesan Liturgical Commns., Nat. Pastoral Musicians. Lodge: K.C. (chaplain). Home: Mt Carmel Ch 12 Spruce St Providence RI 02903 Office: Diocese of Providence Office of Worship 1 Cathedral Square Providence RI 02903

PAGE, SYDNEY HARRY THOMAS, minister, religion educator, North American Baptist Conference; b. London, Ont., Can., Nov. 27, 1944; s. Sydney Frederick Walter and Audrey Maria (Hull) P.; m. Faith Evangeline Warman, June 21, 1968; children: Jonathan, Mark, Kathryn Elizabeth. B.Th., London Coll. Bible and Missions, Ont., 1967; M.Div., Westminster Theol. Sem., 1970; Th.M., Princeton Theol. Sem., 1971; Ph.D., U. Manchester, U.K., 1974. Pastor Heaton Moor Evangelical Ch., Stockport, Cheshire, U.K., 1972-77; asst. prof. N. Am. Bapt. Coll., Edmonton, Alta., 1977-82; assoc. prof., acad. v.p. N. Am. Bapt. Div. Sch., Edmonton, 1982—. Contbr. articles to profl. jours. Fellow Inst. Bibl. Research; mem. Evang. Theol. Soc., Soc. Bibl. Lit., Can. Soc. Bibl. Studies. Home: 1291 Millbourne Rd E Edmonton AB T6K 0W5 Canada Office: North Am Bapt Div Sch 11525 23d Ave Edmonton AB T6J 4T3 Canada

PALLMEYER, PAUL HENRY, minister, American Lutheran Church; b. Huntington, N.Y., Oct. 27, 1924; s. Paul Henry and Mamie M. (Mueller) P.; m. Ruth Marie Schrieber, June 2, 1951; children: Barbara Pallmeyer Miller, Thomas, Rebecca, Dwight, Sara Nelson-Pallmeyer, Lois. B.A., Concordia Sem., 1949, B.D., 1951, S.T.M., 1963. Ordained to ministry Luth. Ch., 1951. Missionary to Japan, Luth. Ch.-Mo. Synod, Hokkaido, 1951-57; pastor Christ Luth. Ch., Hartford, Conn., 1958-59; editorial assoc. Bd. Parish Edn., Luth. Ch. Mo. Synod, St. Louis, 1959-75; dir. interpretation Div. for Life and Mission in Congregation, Am. Luth. Ch., Mpls., 1975-81, dir. evangelism ministries, 1981—. Editor: Christian Faith and Life, 1984, also articles; editor Interaction Mag., 1970-75. Served with U.S. Army, 1943-46, ETO, PTO. Home: 6736 Kingston Dr Eden Prairie MN 55344 Office: Am Lutheran Ch 422 S 5th St Minneapolis MN 55415

PALMAS, ANGELO, apostolic nuncio, Roman Catholic Church; b. Villanova, Mont., Sassari, Italy, Dec. 21, 1914; came to Can., 1975; s. Angelo and Emanuela (Calaresu) P. Th.D., Pontifical Theol. Sem., 1939; Ph.L., Gregorian U., Rome, 1942; D.C.L., Lateran Pontifical U., Rome, 1945. Ordained priest Roman Cath. Ch., 1938, consecrated archbishop, 1964. Secretariat of state Holy See, Vatican City, 1946-47; sec. to apostolic nuncio, Brussels, 1947-51; sec. Apostolic Nunciature, Berne, Switzerland, 1951-54, auditor and counsellor, Beirut, Lebanon, 1954-60, apostolic del., Saigon, Vietnam, 1964-69, apostolic nuncio, Bogota, Colombia, 1969-75, Ottawa, Ont., Can., 1975—. Address: 724 Manor Ave Ottawa ON K1M 0E3 Canada

PALMER, DALE EUGENE, minister, So. Baptist Conv.; b. New Augusta, Miss., Apr. 22, 1930; s. Wallace Stephen and Eva Marie Palmer; B.S., Memphis State U., 1952; B.D., Southwestern Bapt. Theol. Sem., Ft. Worth, 1955; D.D., Immanuel Bapt. Coll., Atlanta, 1973; m. Betty Lou Gregory, June 1, 1954; children—Cathy Lou, Dale Eugene. Ordained to ministry, 1953; pastor Ferris (Tex.) Bapt. Ch., 1954-55; founder White Station Bapt. Ch., Memphis, 1955-63; pastor Longview Heights Bapt. Ch., Memphis, 1963-67; asso. pastor Bellevue Bapt. Ch., Memphis, 1967—. Mem. Nat. Woodcarvers Assn. Club: Shrine. Author: Accepting Jesus Christ, then Joining the Church, 1968. Home: 5225 Knight Arnold Rd Memphis TN 38118 Office: 70 N Bellevue St Memphis TN 38104

PALMER, ELLSWORTH LEVI, minister, Ch. of God-Anderson, Ind.; b. Portland, Oreg., Mar. 19, 1910; s. Levi Ellsworth and Lydia Clara (Shuinard) P.; student Western Bapt. Theol. Sem., 1933-34; B.A., Anderson Coll. and Theol. Sem., 1946; D.D., East Nebr. Christian Coll., 1971; student U. Miami, 1968-72; m. Ursula Hilaria Castillo, Nov. 19, 1949; 1 son, Paul Henry. Ordained to ministry Church of God-Anderson, Ind., 1946; asst. to pastor Belvedere Spanish Ch. of God, Los Angeles, 1935-43; pastor Prospect Hill Spanish Ch. of God, San Antonio, 1946-50; missionary-dir. Chs. of God, Cuba, 1950-60; active Cuban Refugee work, Miami, Fla., 1960-72; pastor Spanish Ch. of God, Miami, 1965—; pres. radio and TV com. Inter Am. Conf. Ch. of God, 1973—; v.p. Spanish Am. Conf. Ch. of God, 1972-74, pres., 1974-75. Tchr.-coordinator, Dade County (Fla.) Pub. Schs., 1963—. Home: 940 NW 105th St Miami FL 33150 Office: 4180 SW 5th Terr Miami FL 33150

PALMER, JACK HORACE, minister, Lutheran Ch. in Am. B. Hanover, Pa., Aug. 28, 1939; s. Horace William and Bessie Irene (Peters) P.; m. Helen Margaret Biesecker, Sept. 19, 1964; children: Audrey Dale, Melinda Irene, Sean Douglas. Student Gettysburg Coll., 1957-59, Rutgers State U., 1966-69; B.A., Shippensburg State U., 1977; M. Div., Luth. Theol. Sem., 1981. Ordained to ministry Lutheran Ch. in Am., 1981. Supply pastor Garrett Cooperative Parish, Garrett, Pa., 1980-81; pastor Liberty Valley Luth. Ch., Liberty, Pa., 1981—; mem. Pa. Christians in Coalition, 1980—. Author: (book of poems) Cave Wall Shadows, 1979. Editor Jour. Mountain Light. Composer: Resurrection Cantata, 1982-83, Canticle of the Spirit, 1983, Requiem, 1984, Mass for Peace, 1983-84. Recipient award N.J. Society for Retarded Children, 1979, also numerous literary awards. Fellow Intl. Acad. Poets; mem. Sierra Club. Democrat. Home: PO Box 111 Liberty PA 16930 Office: Liberty Valley Luth Ch PO Box 111 Liberty PA 16930

PALMER, LESTER DAVIS, minister, Christian Church (Disciples of Christ); b. Augusta, Ga., Oct. 6, 1929; s. Lawton Evans and Gwendolyn (Ramsbotham) P.; m. Janelle Griffin, May 6, 1951; children: Gwen Chandler, Kathy, Sandra, Leslie. B.A., Johnson Bible Coll., 1952; M.Div., Lexington Theol. Sem., 1958; postgrad. Boston U. Sch. Theology, 1961-63. Ordained to ministry, 1951. Assoc. gen. minister Christian Ch. Ky., Lexington, 1958-61; assoc. prof. ch. adminstrn. Lexington Theol. Sem., 1963-66; v.p. Pension Fund of Christian Ch., Indpls., 1966-83, pres., 1984—. Contbr. articles to profl. jours. Editor Promotional and Interpretive Bull., Pension Fund Bull., 1984—. Mem. Theta Phi. Home: 5953 Manning Rd Indianapolis IN 46208 Office: Pension Fund of Christian Church 155 E Market Indianapolis IN 46204

PALS, DANIEL L., religion educator, Presbyterian Church U.S.A.; b. South Holland, Ill., Oct. 28, 1946; s. Herbert H. and Margaret B. (Vanderaa) P.; m. Phyllis Ross Balzer, Aug. 11, 1973. A.B., Calvin Coll., 1968; B.D., Calvin Theol. Sem., 1971; M.A., U. Chgo., 1973, Ph.D., 1975. Chmn. dept. religion U. Miami, Coral Gables, Fla., 1980—. Author: The Victorian Lives of Jesus, 1982. Editorial asst. Church History, 1973-76. Contbr. articles to religious jours. Recipient Max Orovitz award U. Miami, 1980, 84; named Outstanding Honors Prof., U. Miami, 1983. Mem. Am. Soc. Ch. History, Am. Acad. Religion. Home: 11116 SW 70 Terr Miami FL 33173 Office: Univ Miami Dept Religion PO Box 248264 Coral Gables FL 33124

PANNENBERG, WOLFHART U., theology educator, writer, Lutheran Church; b. Stettin, Germany, Oct. 2, 1928; s. Kurt B.S. and Tomgard Emma (Kersten) P.; m. Hilke Sabine Schütte, Mar. 5, 1954. Abitur, Gymnasium, Germany, 1947; Dr.Theol., Heidelberg U., Germany, 1953, Habilitation, 1955. Ordained to ministry, 1955. Prof. religion U. Munich, Fed. Republic Germany, 1967—; mem. Ecumenical Working Group of Luth. and Roman Cath. Theologians in Germany, 1956—, chmn., 1979—. Author: Jesus God and Man; Basic Questions in Theology (5 vols.); Theology and Philosophy of Science; Anthropology in Theological Perspective, 1985. Mem. Bavarian Acad. Scis., Academie Internationale des Sciences Religieuses. Office: U Munich Gesslewestrasse-Scholl-Plak 1 Munich Bavaria 8000 Fed Republic Germany

PANUSKA, JOSEPH ALLAN, educator, priest, Roman Catholic Ch.; b. Balt., July 3, 1927; s. Joseph William and Barbara Agnes (Preller) P.; B.S., Loyola Coll., Balt., 1948; Ph.D., St. Louis U., 1958; S.T.L., Woodstock Coll., 1961; LL.D., Scranton U., 1974. Joined Soc. of Jesus, 1948; ordained priest Roman Catholic Ch., 1960; instr. physiology Emory U. Sch. Medicine, 1962-63; asst. prof. biology Georgetown U., 1963-66, asso. prof., 1966-72, asso. chmn. dept., 1970-73, prof., 1972-82; pres. U. Scranton, 1982—; rector Jesuit Community, Georgetown U., 1971-73; provincial Md. Province Soc. Jesus, Balt., 1973—. Vis. fellow St. Edmund's House, Cambridge, 1969-70 cons. Nat. Conf. Cath. Bishops' Liturgy Com., 1974—. Mem. corp. Am. Found. Biol. Research, 1967—, pres. bd. dirs., 1974—; bd. dirs. Cambridge Center Social Studies; pres. bd. dirs. Woodstock Center Theol. Reflection, Corp. Roman Cath. Clergyman Md., 1973—. Fellow AAAS; mem. Am. Physiol. Soc., Am. Soc. Zoologists, Soc. Cryobiology (charter), Soc. Exptl. Biology and Medicine. Editor-in-chief Cryobiology, 1970-74, mem. editorial bd., 1968—. Contbr. articles to profl. lit. Address: Office of President Univ Scranton Linden at Munro Scranton PA 18510

PAPA, FRANK M., priest, Roman Cath. Ch.; b. Tocco Caudio, Italy, Jan. 1, 1941; s. Giuseppe and Filomena (Saccomanno) P.; came to U.S., 1964, naturalized, 1974; S.T.L., Cath. U., Washington, 1967. Joined Order Barnabite Fathers, 1958; ordained priest, 1966; chaplain Sisters of Charity Hosp., Buffalo, 1967-71; provincial vocation dir. St. Anthony Zaccaria Sem., Youngstown, N.Y., 1971-76, superior, 1976—. Asst. dir. Our Lady of Fatima Shrine, Youngstown, 1971—; moderator Crusaders Community Youth Group, 1975—. Home and office: 1023 Swan Rd Youngstown NY 14174

PAPADEMETRIOU, GEORGE CONSTANTINE, theology educator, library administrator, Greek Orthodox Christian Church. b. Saint George, Thasos, Greece, Apr. 11, 1932; came to U.S., 1947; s. Constantine George and Ourania (Katsifas) P.; m. Athanasia Antoniou, June 26, 1960; children: Constantine, Jane, Anastasios. B.A. in Theology, Hellenic Coll., 1959; M.Th., Tex. Christian U., 1966; Ph.D., Temple U., 1977; M.L.S., Simmons Coll., 1983. Pastor, St. Demetrios Ch., Fort Worth, 1960-65, Annunciation Ch., Elkins Park, Pa., 1965-68, Sts. Constantine and Helen Ch., Annapolis, Md., 1968-77, St. Nicholas Ch., Lexington, Mass., 1977-81; prof. systematic theology Hellenic Coll., Brookline, Mass., 1978—, librarian, 1981—; bd. govs. Nat. Council Chs., N.Y.C., 1980—. Author: Introduction to St. Gregory Palamas, 1973; contbr. articles to profl. publs. Mem. Orthodox Theologica Soc. Am. (sec. 1974-76, v.p. 1976-78, pres. 1978-80), New Eng. Greek Orthodox

Clergy Assn. (sec. 1977-78, pres. 1979-81), Soc. Christian Philosophers, Online Computer Library Ctr. (alt. del. User's Council 1983—). Home: 1 Oxbow Rd Lexington MA 02173 Office: Hellenic Coll 50 Goddard Ave Brookline MA 02146

PAPANIKOLAOU, BASIL, priest, Greek Orthodox Church; b. Peloponnese, Greece, Feb. 17, 1934; came to U.S., 1962; s. Constantine and Joanna (Christon) P.; m. Antoinette Vakalakis, May 13, 1962; children: Dean, Lambros, Telly. M.A. in Theology, U. Athens, 1958; Diploma in Social Work, Panteios Sch.-Athens, 1959; M.A. in Classical Philology, U. Ill., 1969; M.A. in Sci. of Edn., Western Ill. U., 1980. Ordained priest, Greek Orthodox Ch., 1962. Priest, Greek Orthodox Ch., Kankakee, Ill., 1962-65, Champaign, Ill., 1966-72, Rock Island, Ill., 1972—. Columnist, Religious Box, The Orthodox Observer, 1976; translator: Greatest Salesman in the World, 1977. Instr. U. Ill., 1967-72, Augustana Coll., 1973-77. Address: 2930 31st Ave Rock Island IL 61201

PAPPIN, BERNARD F., bishop, Roman Catholic Church. Titular bishop of Aradi, aux. bishop, Sault Ste. Marie, Can., 1975—. Office: PO Box 510 North Bay ON P1B 8J1 Canada*

PAPROCKI, JOHN LADISLAUS, priest, Roman Cath. Ch., ednl. adminstr.; b. East Newark, N.J., Jan. 2, 1934; s. James and Anna (Dawidowski) P.; B.A., Seton Hall U., 1955, M.A., 1964; postgrad. Immaculate Conception Sem., 1955-59. Ordained priest Roman Catholic Ch., 1959; asst. pastor St. Casimir's Ch., Newark, 1959-65; sch. chaplain, counselor Essex Cath. High Sch., Newark, 1965—; dir. Inst. Social Relations, Office Social Devel. Archdiocese of Newark, 1965-75; dir. Guild of St. Joseph the Worker, 1965—. Mem. Cath. Commn. on Urban Ministry, Notre Dame, Ind., 1970—. Mem. Nat. Cath. Edn. Assn., Am., N.J. personnel and guidance assns., Nat. Cath. Guidance Conf., Assn. Pastoral Counselors, Polish Nat. Alliance. Home: 335 N 2d St Harrison NJ 07029 Office: Essex Cath High Sch 300 Broadway Newark NJ 07104

PAPROCKI, THOMAS JOHN, priest, educator, religious organization executive, Roman Catholic Church; lawyer. B. Chgo., Aug. 5, 1952; s. John H. and Veronica M. (Bonat) P. B.A., Loyola U., Chgo., 1974; M.Div., St. Mary of the Lake Sem., 1978, S.T.L., 1979; J.D., DePaul U., 1981; Spanish lang. study Archdiocesan Latin Am. Com., Chgo., 1972-74, Middlebury Coll., Vt., summer 1976, Instituto Cuaunnahuac, Cuernavaca, Mexico, summer 1978. Ordained priest, 1978; Bar: Ill. 1981, U.S. Dist. Ct. (no. dist.) Ill. 1981. Assoc. pastor St. Michael Ch., Chgo., 1978-83; faculty mem. Loyola U., Chgo., 1981-82; faculty mem. St. Mary of the Lake Sem., Mundelein, Ill., 1983—; adminstr. St. Joseph's Ch., Chgo., 1983—; bd. dirs. Interfaith Coalition for Justice to Immigrants, 1981-82; guest speaker various schs. and parishes, 1970—. Founder, exec. dir., pres. South Chgo. Legal Clinic, 1981—. Editorial adv. bd. Chgo. Cath. Newspaper, 1984—. Contbr. articles to profl. jours. Treas. United Neighborhood Orgn., Southeast Chgo., 1984—, bd. dirs., 1982—; active Inter-Community Legal Conf., 1982—; vol. Sta. WIND Ask A Lawyer Program, 1982; mem. coordinating bd. Amate House, 1985—. Mem. ABA, Ill. State Bar Assn., Chgo. Bar Assn., Hispanic Caucus of Priests, Advocates Soc. of Lawyers, DePaul Alumni Assn., Quigley South Alumni Assn., Assn. Chgo. Priests, Blue Key, Pi Sigma Alpha. Home: PO Box 589 Chicago IL 60617 Office: South Chgo Legal Clinic 3005 E 92nd St Chicago IL 60617

PAQUETTE, MARIO, priest, Roman Catholic Church; b. Montreal, Que., Can., Apr. 9, 1938; s. Rynaldo and Antoinette (Venne) P. B.A., U. Montreal, 1959, S.T.L., 1963; J.C.D., Gregorian U., Rome, 1971. Ordained priest Roman Cath. Ch., 1963. Sec. to archbishop of Montreal, 1963-68; asst. Office for Ethnic Communities, Montreal, 1971-72; advocate Eccles. Regional Tribunal, Montreal, 1971-75, judge, 1975—; vice chancellor Archdiocese of Montreal, 1975-84, episcopal vicar and dir. Office for Ethnic Communities, 1984—; rep. of Cath. Bishops to Internat. Cath. Migration Commn., Geneva, 1977-80; pres. Standing Conf. Can. Orgns. Concerned for Refugees, 1978-80, Cath. Immigration Services, Montreal, 1982—, Can. Found. for Refugees, Ottawa, 1982—; mem. consultative bd. Minister of Immigration, Que., 1979-82. Author: Priests' Senates in Quebec (in French), 1973. Contbr. articles to periodicals and newspapers. Mem. Can. Canon Law Soc. Home: 1071 rue Cathedrale Montreal PQ H3B 2V4 Canada Office: Roman Catholic Archdiocese Montreal 2000 Sherbrooke St W Montreal PQ H3H 1G4 Canada

PARCHER, ADRIAN JAMES, abbot, administrator, Roman Catholic; b. Oakland, Calif., July 24, 1933; s. George Gerrett and Francis Marie (Hansen) P. B.A., St. Martin's Coll., 1955; B.Ed., Seattle U., 1957; postgrad. Mt. Angel Sem., 1955-59, U. Conn., 1965-67; M.A., U. Notre Dame, 1962; postgrad. Cambridge U. (Eng.), Oxford U. (Eng.), 1967-68, Vandebilt Divinity Sch., Nashville, 1977-78. Ordained priest Roman Catholic Ch., 1959. Registrar, St. Martin's Coll., Lacey, Wash., 1959-61, 62-65, acad. v.p., 1980-81; novice master St. Martin's Abbey, Lacey, 1969-74, abbot-chancellor St. Martin's Abbey-Coll., 1980—; prior-rector Sr. Mark's Priory/Sem., South Union, Ky., 1980-81; trustee St. Martin's Coll., 1968-70, 80—, chancellor, 1980—. Commr., Wash. State Arts Commn., Olympia, 1982—; mem. Pacific Northwest Art Council, 1980—. Mem. Soc. Bibl. Lit. Home and office: St Martins Abbey Lacey WA 98503

PARE, MARIUS, bishop, Roman Cath. Ch.; b. Montmagny, Que., Can., May 22, 1903; s. Joseph and Lucie (Boulet) P.; B.A., Laval U. Ordained priest, 1927; tchr.-dir. Coll. Sainte Anne de la Pocatieère, 1927-52, rector, 1952-56; aux. bishop, 1956; coadjutor bishop, 1960; bishop, Chicoutimi, Que., 1961—. Mem. commn. for clergy Canadian Conf. Catholics; mem. commn. edn. 2d Vatican Council; mem.-cons. Sacred Congregation Cath. Edn., Rome. Decorated knight grand cross Order Equestre du St.-Sepulcre de Jerusalem. Home: 602E Racine St Chicoutimi PQ G7H 5C3 Canada

PARIS, PETER J., religious educator, minister, Am. Baptist Convention; b. New Glasgow, N.S., Can., May 30, 1933; came to U.S., 1965, naturalized, 1982; s. Freeman Archibald and Violet Agatha (Jewell) P.; m. Shirley Ann McMillen, May 13, 1961; children: Valerie Lynn, Peter Brett. B.A., Acadia U., 1956, B.D., 1958; M.A., U. Chgo., 1969, Ph.D., 1975. Ordained to ministry Baptist Ch., 1959. Gen. sec. Student Christian Movement, Alta., Can., 1958-61, nat. traveling sec., Nigeria, 1961-64, Toronto, Ont., Can., 1964-65; asst. prof. Howard U. Sch. Religion, Washington, 1970-72; prof. Vanderbilt Div. Sch., Nashville, 1972—; bd. dirs. Soc. Christian Ethics, 1979—, Am. Acad. Religion, 1983—; exec. council Soc. for Study Black Religion, 1983—; bd. trustees Nat. Council Black Christians, First Baptist Ch., Capitol Hill Homes, Inc., 1980. Author, Black Leaders in Conflict, 1978; The Social Teaching of the Black Churches, 1985. Contbr. articles to profl. jours, chpts. to books. Research grantee Vanderbilt U., 1983-84. Office: Vanderbilt Div Sch Nashville TN 37240

PARISH, FREDERICK LOUIS, minister, United Methodist Church; b. Washington, Sept. 5, 1941; s. Leslie Jessie and Georgie Lou (Smith) P.; m. Sandra Lynn Farley, Dec. 20, 1960; children: Jacquelyn Anne, Keith Douglas. B.A., George Mason U., 1970; M.Div., Wesley Theol. Sem., 1974. Ordained to ministry, 1969. Assoc. minister Groveton Bapt. Ch., Alexandria, Va., 1969-70; minister Round Hill Bapt. Ch., Va., 1970-72, Trinity Bapt. Ch., Arlington, Va., 1972-74; minister Bethel United Meth. Ch., Woodbridge, Va., 1974—; laity div. mem. Va. Conf. Bd. Discipleship, 1982—; exec. com. Alexandria Dist. Bd. Mission, 1976—; discipleship rep. Alexandria Dist. Council Ministries, 1978—; spiritual dir. Upper Room Emmaus, Washington, 1982-84. Sec., Mental Health/Mental Retardation Service Bd., Manassas, Va., 1983—; bd. dirs. N. Va. Tng. Sch., 1981, Didlake Occupational Ctr., 1982. Decorated Legion of Honor, Internat. Order Demolay. Home: 4617 Kenwood Dr Woodbridge VA 22193 Office: Bethel United Meth Ch 3130 Davis Ford Rd Woodbridge VA 22192

PARKE, CLIFFORD THOMAS, minister, Disciples of Christ Church, marriage and family counselor; b. Kansas City, Mo., Jan. 24, 1936; s. Edgar Lloyd and Lula (Cox) P.; m. Alma Nell Logsdon, June 26, 1955; children: Susan Nell Parke Meyer, Janice Lynn, Deborah Ruth, Sarah Kay. B.A., Eureka Coll., 1958; B.Div., Christian Theol. Sem., Indpls., 1963, M.Div., 1972; M.A., St. Mary's U., San Antonio, 1985; postgrad. Brite Div. Sch., Tex. Christian U., 1985—. Ordained, 1963; lic. family counselor. Minister 1st Christian Ch., Benton, Ill., 1963-64, Bellflower Christian Ch. (Ill.), 1964-72, 1st Christian Ch., Knoxville, Ill., 1972-78; sr. minister 1st Christian Ch., Gt. Bend, Kans., 1978-81, Woodlawn Christian Ch., San Antonio, 1981—. Pvt. practice as marriage counselor, San Antonio, 1983—. Columnist Galesburg Post (Ill.) and Knoxville Jour., 1974-78; contbr. articles to The Christian mag. Canfield Found. scholar, 1962; recipient Koinonia Edit. award Christian Theol. Sem., 1963; Pen and Mike award Radio Advt. Bur., Chgo., 1978. Mem. Profl. Assn. Clergy, Congress of Disciple Clergy, San Antonio Community of Chs. (bd.), Bluebonnet Area of Christian Ch. (bd.), Coop. Ministries in Higher Edn. (bd.). Republican. Home: 731 McNeel Rd San Antonio TX 78228 Office: Woodlawn Christian Ch 1744 W Gramercy Pl San Antonio TX 78201

PARKER, CHARLES AVERY, JR., minister, Southern Baptist Convention; b. Birmingham, Ala., Aug. 30, 1948; s. Charles Avery and Nora Pauline (McDanal) P.; m. Barbara Jean McQuillen, June 9, 1973; children: Charles Scott, Timothy Andrew, Joy Carol. B.A. with honors, Samford U., 1970; M.Div., So. Bapt. Theol. Sem., 1973, D.Min., 1978. Ordained to ministry Bapt. Ch., 1971. Pastor, New Hope Bapt. Ch., Elizabethtown, Ky., 1971-74, East Frankfort Bapt. Ch., Frankfort, Ky., 1974-79, Oak Park Bapt. Ch., Jeffersonville, Ind., 1979—; pres. So. Bapt. Sem. Alumni Ind., 1983-84; exec. bd. State Conv. of Baptists in Ind., 1984—; pres. Suburban Assn. Chs., Jeffersonville, 1982-83; Sunday Sch. dir. Southeastern Ind. Bapt. Assn., 1980—; mem. religious adv. bd. Ind. U. Southeast, New Albany, 1980-84; chmn. Ministerial Jail Visitation Com., Jeffersonville, 1983—; mem. Clark County Ministerial Assn. Contbr. articles to jours. Luther Rice scholar So. Bapt. Theol. Sem., 1970-71; recipient John R. Mott award Samford U., 1970, Herman Rice Arnold Meml. award, 1970. Life mem. Alpha Phi Omega. Democrat. Home: 43 Sycamore Rd Jeffersonville IN 47130 Office: Oak Park Bapt Ch 1111 Allison Ln Jeffersonville IN 47130

PARKER, DONNIE VERNON, minister, Southern Baptist Convention; b. Hattiesburg, Miss., June 12, 1947; s. James Elmer and Mildred Inez (Perkins) P.; m. Kathryn Mae MacKenroth, Dec. 23, 1972; children: Amy, Wendy. B.A., William Carey Coll., 1969; Th.M. with honors, New Orleans Bapt. Theol. Sem., 1972. Ordained to ministry So. Bapt. Conv., 1969. Pastor, Leaf Bapt. Ch. (Miss.), 1969-71; assoc. pastor, minister of youth Calvary Bapt. Ch., Slidell, La., 1971-74; minister edn. and youth FBC Glendale, Hattiesburg, 1974-75; pastor Barton Bapt. Ch., Lucedale, Miss., 1975-81, First Bapt. Ch. East Brewton (Ala.), 1981—; pres. Escambia Bapts. Ministerial Conf. (Ala.), 1982-84. Named Minister of Yr., Kiwanis Club, Brewton, 1983. Mem. Brewton Ministerial Assn. (pres. 1983-84, v.p. 1981-83). Republican. Home: 1203 Shoffner St East Brewton AL 36426 Office: First Bapt Ch PO Box 2276 East Brewton AL 36427

PARKER, EFFIE TAYLOR, author, lay ch. worker, Ch. of God (Anderson, Ind.); b. Ziff, Ill., Jan. 16, 1893; d. William Howard and Mary Elizabeth (Meeks) Taylor; student pub. schs., Clay City, Ill.; m. James Arand Parker, May 2, 1933 (dec. 1942). Lay witness, revival worker, 1919; speaker Chs. God, Monticello, Ill., Homer, Ill., 1924; supt. Sunday Sch., Lost Grove Meth. Ch., Homer, 1933; speaker Chs. of Christ, Homer and Longview, Ill., 1934; owner, operator Homer Christian Rest Home, 1945-74. Author: Miracle of Faith, 1971, More Miracles of Faith, 1976; contbr. poems to religious and secular jours. Home: 205 W South St Homer IL 61849 also 308 W 3d St Homer IL 61849

PARKER, GEORGE C., lay ch. worker, Yearly Meeting of Friends; b. George, N.C., Feb. 2, 1912; s. William Edgar and Ruth Eva (Peele) P.; m. Elizabeth Hunter Gilliam, Mar. 20, 1938; children—William Conrad, Elwood Gilliam, George Edgar, John Gurney, Elizabeth LeMay. Treas. Rich Sq. Monthly Meeting of Friends, 1936—, recorded minister, 1968—; clk. N.C. Yearly Meeting of Friends, 1961—. Mem. Roanoke-Chowan Mental Health Area Bd., Ahoskie, N.C. Trustee Roanoke-Chowan Hosp., Ahoskie. Address Woodland NC 27897

PARKER, HAROLD M(ARION), JR., minister, Presbyterian Church in the U.S.A., history educator. B. Oklahoma City, Feb. 9, 1923; s. H.M. and Fredonia Angie (Nash) P.; m. Barbara Ann Malin, May 31, 1967; children: Howard Mikel, Harold Malin. A.B., Park Coll., 1944; B.D., Louisville Presbyn. Sem., 1946, Th.M., 1952; Th.D., Iliff Sch. Theol., 1966. Ordained to ministry, Presbyn. Ch., 1946. Pastor Inskip Presbyn. Ch., Knoxville, Tenn., 1954-57, First Presbyn. Ch., Winfield, Kans., 1957-61; dir. student religious life Southwestern Coll., Winfield, 1961-66; pastor Community Presbyn. Ch., Lake City, Colo., 1978—; stated clk. Presbytery of Western Colo., Gunnison, 1972—; pres. Winfield Council Chs., 1960-61. Prof. History Western State Coll., Gunnison, 1967—. Author: Studies in Southern Presbyterian History, 1979; Sermons on Minor Prophets, 1979; (with others) Oldest Church on the Western Slope, 1976. Contbr. articles on so. Presbyn. history and bibl. studies to profl. jours. Chmn. Inskip Recreation Commn., Knoxville, 1956; pres. Winfield Oratorio Soc., 1960; vice chmn. Bd. Adjustments and Appeals, Gunnison, 1972—. Recipient Thornwell award Hist. Found. of Presbyn. Ch., 1972, 1978; named Tchr. of Yr. Southwestern Coll., 1960; named Citizen of Yr. Lake City, Colo. C., 1979. Mem. Presbyn. Hist. Soc. (bd. dirs.), Soc. Bibl. Lit. (regional sec. 1977-83), Am. Soc. Ch. History, Am. Schs. Oriental Research, Phi Alpha Theta. Republican. Home: 500 E Virginia Gunnison CO 81230 Office: Western State Coll Gunnison CO 81230

PARKER, JOLORENE MILLER, minister, United Methodist Church; b. Chgo., Feb. 7, 1916; d. John Meredith and Dorothea Emeline (Hauk) Miller; B.Mus., Am. Conservatory of Music, 1933; A.A., Kendall Coll., 1952; B.A. Religion, Syracuse U., 1955; S.T.B., Boston U., 1958; m. Clarence Hanley Parker, Oct. 29, 1961. Ordained to ministry, 1958; part-time pastor Vesper (N.Y.) United Meth. Ch., summer 1955; pastor Georgetown, Sheds and Otselic United Meth. chs., N.Y., 1957, Perryville (N.Y.) United Meth. Ch., 1961-62, Otselic (N.Y.) United Meth. Ch., 1967-81, Georgetown, 1981, Georgetown-Sheds, 1982-83, Georgetown-Otselic, 1983—. Address: PO Box 40 Otselic NY 13129

PARKER, KENNETH RUSSELL, religious educator, American Baptist Churches in the U.S.A.; b. Malden, Mass., Apr. 6, 1946; s. Clarence Henry and Mildred Brown (Furbush) P.; m. Patricia Anne Waugh, July 16, 1971; children: Samuel and Danny (foster children), Ned. B.A. in Philosophy, Gordon Coll., 1969; M.Div., Am. Bapt. Sem. of West, 1974; S.T.M., N.Y. Theol.

Sem., 1977; Ph.D. in Speech Communication, Kent State U., 1984. Ordained to ministry Am. Bapt. Chs. in U.S.A., 1975. Pastor Liberty and So. Montville Bapt. Chs., Maine, 1968-70, First Congl. Ch., Bar Mills Bapt. Ch., Buxton, Maine, 1974-79; asst. prof. pastoral theology Eastern Bapt. Theol. Sem., Phila., 1982—; resource person for workshops and retreats, local, denom. and ecumenical ch. settings, 1969—. Communication cons. Pub. Sector Projects funded institutionally by Kettering, Lilly and Ford Founds., 1980—. Research fellow Acad. Contemporary Problems, summer 1981; teaching fellow Kent State U. 1979-82. Mem. Acad. for Evangelism in Theol. Edn., Assn. Theol. Field Edn., Ministers Council Am. Bapt. Chs., Nat. Assn. Preservation and Perpetuation Storytelling, Speech Communication Assn., Religious Speech Communication Assn. Democrat. Home: 14-16 Valley Rd Drexel Hill PA 19026 Office: Eastern Bapt Theol Sem City and Lancaster Aves Philadelphia PA 19151

PARKER, SIDNEY BAYNES ST. HUGH, priest, Episcopalian Church; b. Jamaica, W.I., July 13, 1922, came to U.S., 1945, naturalized, 1961; s. Luther Augustus and Rachel Elizabeth (Salmon) P.; diploma Mico Tchrs. Coll. Jamaica, 1943; B.S., Howard U., 1949, B.D., 1952, M.A., 1954, M.Div., 1960; postgrad. La. State U., 1955, Gen. Theol. Sem., 1960-61; S.T.B., St. Augustine's Coll., 1966-67; LL.B., LaSalle U., 1967; Ed.D., Columbia, 1970; postgrad. Jacksonville U., 1971; m. Bernice Eleanor Martin, Mar. 19, 1948 (dec.); children—Philip, Cynthia, Alfred; m. Carolyn Burdine, Oct. 26, 1978. Ordained priest Protestant Episcopal Ch., 1954. Vicar St. Michael's Episcopal Ch., Baton Rouge, 1954-57; chaplain So. U., instr. math. Leland Coll., Baker, La., 1954-57; vicar Trinity Episcopal Ch., Montclair, N.J., 1957-61, rector, 1961-70; rector St. Philip's, 1970-78, vicar St. Gabriel's Episcopal chs., Jacksonville, Fla., 1970—; mem. exec. com. Diocese of Fla., 1978-82, pres. standing com., 1982, mem. charter and canons com., 1984; tchr. Jacksonville Episcopal High Sch., 1970—; instr. humanities Edward Waters Coll., 1977—. Pres., Montclair Mayor's Com., 1969-70; trustee Cathedral Found., Jacksonville, Jacksonville Pub. Library, 1984—, Jacksonville council Girl Scouts U.S., 1983—. Recipient Howard U. Miller's prize in homiletics, 1951. Mem. Internat. Platform Assn., Am. Acad. Religion, Am. Acad. Social and Polit. Sci., UN Assn. U.S., Inst. Soc., Ethics and Life Scis. Home: POB 12315 Jacksonville FL 32209 Office: PO Box 9548 Jacksonville FL 32208

PARKERSON, DELAMAR EUGENE, minister, So. Baptist Conv.; b. Dodge County, Ga., Sept. 27, 1931; s. Matthew Eugene and Nancy Clyde (Lee) P.; A.B., Mercer U., 1952; M.Div., Southeastern Bapt. Theol. Sem., 1956, Th.M., 1957; m. Jessie Mae Lord, Aug. 18, 1951; 1 dau., Gail Anette. Ordained to ministry, 1950; pastor chs., Ga., 1949-53; pastor Gibson (N.C.) Bapt. Ch., 1953-58, Warsaw (N.C.) Bapt. Ch., 1958-66, Carrboro (N.C.) Bapt. Ch., 1966-69, Temple Bapt. Ch., Wilmington, N.C., 1969—. Chmn. evangelism Mercer Ministerial Assn., 1951-52; pres. pastor's conf. Pee Dee Bapt. Assn. N.C., 1955-56; moderator Eastern Bapt. Assn. N.C., 1963-65, v.p. pastor's conf., 1959-60, pres., 1960-61; pres. pastors' conf. Wilmington Bapt. Assn., 1970-71, vice moderator, 1973-74; bd. dirs. Bibl. Recorder, 1970-74, 76—, Girl's Haven, 1971-72. Mem. Orange County (N.C.) Mental Health Bd., 1966-69, Bd. Alcoholic Rehab., 1966-69; mem. Vol. Fire depts., Gibson, 1957-58, Warsaw, 1958-66, Carrboro, 1966-69. Columnist various N.C. newspapers, 1959—; writer Sunday sch. lesson commentary for Bibl. Recorder, 1967—. Home: 2222 Market St Wilmington NC 28401 Office: 1801 Market St Wilmington NC 28401

PARKHURST, LOUIS GIFFORD, JR., minister, Christian Churches; b. Broken Arrow, Okla., Aug. 13, 1946; s. Louis Gifford and Martha Gertrude (Kendall) P.; m. Patricia Ann Kirkham, June 8, 1968; children: Jonathan Edward, Kathryn Elizabeth. B.A., U. Okla., 1969; M.Div., Princeton Theol. Sem., 1973; M.A., U. Okla., 1974. Ordained to ministry Christian Ch., 1973. Assoc. minister First Christian Ch., Bartlesville, Okla., 1973-75, First Christian Ch., Mpls., 1975-77; minister First Christian Ch., Rochester, Minn., 1977—; instr. Minn. Bible Coll., Rochester, 1982—; founder, pres. Christian Life Study Ctr., Rochester, 1983—; pres. Evangelical Pastors Fellowship, Rochester, 1981-83; bd. mem. Mission of Mercy, Mpls., 1982-83. Author/editor: (with C.G. Finney) Principles of Prayer, 1980, Principles of Victory, 1981, Principles of Liberty, 1983, Answers to Prayer, 1983, Principles of Holiness, 1984; Principles of Union with Christ, 1985; author: Francis Schaeffer: The Man and His Message, 1985. Mem. Nat. Assn. Evangelicals. Lodge: Rotary. Home: 1425 22d St NW Rochester MN 55901 Office: First Christian Ch 3108 Hwy 52N Rochester MN 55901

PARKS, HENRY MILLARD, minister, Church of God (Independent); b. Roane County, Tenn., May 5, 1922; s. George Washington and Gopher Hattie (Branson) P.; m. Dora Lucille Sentell, Aug. 16, 1941; children: George Henry, Gloria Gale, Vicki Deen. B.Th., Luther Rice Sem., 1980. Ordained to ministry Church of God, 1954. Pastor, South Knoxville Ch. of God, Tenn., 1957—; chmn. Pentecostal Children's Home, Barbourville, Ky., 1958—; founder and pres. Pentecostal Youth Camp, Barbourville, 1959—. Bd. dirs. Boys Club of Am., Knoxville, 1975—, Teen Challenge, Knoxville, 1980—; trustee Oxford Grad. Sch., Dayton, Tenn., 1982—. Recipient 5 Yr. award Boys Club Am., 1981, Service award Nat. Council Christians and Jews, Knoxville, 1984, Pub. Service award City of Knoxville, 1984. Lodge: Masons (chaplain 1978-79). Home: 605 Post Oak Dr Knoxville TN 37920

PARKS, MICHAEL E., minister of music, Southern Baptist Convention. b. Columbia, S.C., Oct. 26, 1954; s. Joe E. and Wilda (Reed) P.; m. Randie Newby, Aug. 3, 1974; children: Cale, Kylie. Ed., U. Tenn.-Chattanooga, 1972-73, Belmont Coll., Nashville, 1974. Minister of music New Liberty Bapt. Ch., Ringgold, Ga., 1980, Boynton Bapt. Ch., Ringgold, 1981-84, Big Spring Bapt. Ch., Cleveland, Tenn., 1984—; clinician and guest condr. in music. Composer: (Easter cantata) The Third Day, 1981; (Christmas cantata) A King Comes, 1983; (Easter cantata) Emmanuel . . . The Sacrifice, 1984; (Christmas cantata) Love Beyond Measure, 1985; arranger: (Choral collection) Blessed Assurance, 1985. Mem. ASCAP. Home: Route 2 Box 1317 Cleveland TN 37311 Office: Big Spring Baptist Ch 1415 Hardwick St SE Cleveland TN 37311

PARMA, ROBERT WAYNE, minister, Conservative Baptist Assn. Am.; b. Oakland, Calif., Feb. 18, 1944; s. Albert Earl and Berenice (McLerran) P.; B.A., Calif. State Coll., 1966; M.Div., Western Conservative Bapt. Sem., 1969; postgrad. Eastern Bapt. Theol. Sem., 1969-70, Calif. Grad. Sch. Theol., 1973—. Ordained to ministry, 1975; pastor Central Bapt. Ch., Concord, Calif., 1970—; instr. Multnomah Sch. Bible Extension E. Bay Sch. Bible, San Leandro, Calif., 1974—, Simpson Coll. Extension, Concord, Calif., 1975—. Bd. dir. E. Bay Sch. Bible; pres. Evang. Ministerial Fellowship Central Contra Costa County, 1975-77; bd. dirs. No. Calif. Nat. Assn. Evangs.; founder, pres. Contra Costa Christian Singles; chmn. exec. com. Diablo Valley Crusade. Home: 3203 Clayton Rd Concord CA 94520 Office: 2425 Olivera Rd Concord CA 94520

PARMETER, GEORGE EDWARD, JR., priest, Episcopal Ch.; b. Deer River, Minn., Apr. 15, 1946; s. George Edward and Margaret Mary (Strickley) P.; B.A., Bemidji State Coll., 1969; M.Div., Seabury Western Theol. Sem., 1972; postgrad. Johnson Inst., 1973, Leadership Acad. New Directions, Kansas City, Mo., 1976; m. Gayle Harriet Holmberg, Oct. 26, 1974. Ordained priest, 1974; area dir. Yellowstone Nat. Park, 1972-73; also minister W. Glacier Community Ch.; intern Diocese of Minn., Mpls., 1973-74; priest-in-charge chs., White Earth, Ponsford, Park Rapids, Minn., 1974—. Diocesan dir. camp planning and programming, 1974-76, mem. diocesan council, 1976. Mem. Nat. Soc. Arts Letters (pres. 1976). Author video-tape project: Operation Northern Lights, 1976. Home and Office: Saint Columbas Episcopal Church White Earth MN 56591

PARNELL, RICKEY RAY, ch. staff mem. So. Baptist Conv.; b. Lamar, Colo., Apr. 18, 1948; s. Orville E. and Doris Virginia (Philippe) P.; B.Music Edn., Okla. Panhandle State Coll., 1970; M.R.E., Southwestern Bapt. Theol. Sem., Ft. Worth, 1972; m. Amy Lea Caddell, Aug. 10, 1968; children—Ryan Dillan, Kyle Wade. Minister music and youth First Bapt. Ch., Guymon, Okla., 1969-70; minister music and edn. Park Temple Bapt. Ch., Ft. Worth, 1971-72, Bentonville (Ark.) First Bapt. Ch., 1972-73, Pleasant Grove First Bapt. Ch., Dallas, 1973—; educator Bapt. chs., Alaska, 1976—. Mem. Religious Edn. Assn., Music Conf. Dallas Bapt. Assn. Home: 1504 Brockham Circle Dallas TX 75217 Office: 1401 S Buckner Blvd Dallas TX 75217

PARRISH, ROBERT HARWOOD, lay worker, Christian and Missionary Alliance; b. Berwyn, Ill., Jan. 16, 1937; s. Charles I. and Helen S. (Symons) P.; B.S. in Elec. Engring., U. Akron, 1962; B.Div., Wheaton Coll., 1968; m. Vida Bernice Smead, June 19, 1965; children—Tammy, Cindy, Mark. Licensed to ministry. asst. pastor Stow Alliance Fellowship, Ohio, 1973-74; pastor Clearview Christian and Missionary Alliance, Castleton, N.Y., 1975-76; elder Stow Alliance Fellowship, 1977—, bd. govs., 1985—. Sr. engring. writer Goodyear Aerospace Corp., Akron, 1982—. Mem. Stow City Council, 1970-73; charter bd. dirs. Christian Conciliation Service of Akron, 1982. Mem. IEEE (sr.), Author: The Destiny of Freedom, 1963; (with others) Transformer Maintenance Guide, 1981. Address: 2090 Marhofer Ave Stow OH 44224

PARRISH, WILBUR WILLIAM, minister, General Association of Regular Baptist Churches; b. Kalamazoo, Jan. 11, 1939; s. Ernest Chester and Areta Bell (Hotdrum) P.; m. Joyce Ann Hurne, Aug. 29, 1964; children: Tange, Timothy. B.Religious Edn., Bapt. Bible Coll., 1962; Th.B., Bapt. Bible Sem., 1964; postgrad. Morehead State U., 1970, Ohio U., 1971-72. Ordained to ministry, 1965. Youth minister Hillcrest Bapt. Ch., Elmira, N.Y., 1964-66; asst. pastor Temple Bapt. Ch., Portsmouth, Ohio, 1966-73; sr. minister First Bapt. Ch., Strongsville, Ohio, 1974—; vol. chaplain staff Southwest Hosp., Middleburg Hts., Ohio, 1975—; chmn. personnel Westside Christian Sch., Cleve., 1981—; moderator Hebron Fellowship of Regular Bapt Chs. Greater Cleve., 1982-84, vice moderator, 1978-81. Contbr. articles to profl. jours. Vis. minister City Mission, Cleve., 1982—; trustee Skyview Ranch, Millerburg, Ohio, 1978—; pres. Scioto Hills Bapt Camp, 1968-73. Commd. chaplain CAP, 1978—, advanced through ranks to capt. Mem. Narramore Christian Found. (counseling award 1979), Hebron Fellowship of Pastors. Office: First Baptist Ch 17444 Drake Rd Strongsville OH 44136

PARROTT, DOUGLAS MORRIS, educator, minister, United Presbyn. Ch. in U.S.A.; b. Utica, N.Y., July 16, 1927; s. William C. and Helen (Morris) P.; B.A., Hamilton Coll., Clinton, N.Y., 1949; M.Div., Union Theol. Sem., N.Y.C., 1952, S.T.M., 1965; Ph.D. (research fellow), Grad. Theol. Union, Berkeley, Calif., 1970; m. Anne Elder, July 13, 1957; children—Elizabeth, Kirk. Ordained minister United Presbyn. Ch. in U.S.A., 1953; pastor chs. in N.Y. and N.J., 1953-65; research asso., then research fellow Inst. Antiquity and Christianity, Claremont, Calif., 1968-71; asst. prof. religious studies U. Calif. at Riverside, 1971-77, asso. prof., 1977—, chmn. program religious studies, 1971—. Mem. Phi Beta Kappa. Home: 625 California Dr Claremont CA 91711 Office: Program Religious Studies Univ Cal Riverside CA 92502

PARRY, WALTER PHILLIP, minister, American Baptist Churches in the U.S.A.; b. Knoxville, Tenn., Dec. 9, 1939; s. William Moody and Cleo Pearl (Watson) P.; m. LeeAnn Moore, Sept. 11, 1965; children: Adrien, Jason, Jennie, Emilie, Leslie, Matthew. B.A., Berea Coll., 1961; M.Div., Berkely Bapt. Div. Sch., 1968. Ordained to ministry Am. Bapt. Ch., 1970. Ch. and community study dir. Am. Bapt. Nat. Ministries, Valley Forge, Pa., 1969-74; coordinating minister Cortland County Council Chs., N.Y., 1974-85; exec. dir. Fresno Met. Ministry, Calif., 1985—. Contbr. weekly newspaper column, Church News & Views, 1974-75; radio show host Sunday Night Dialogue WKRT radio, 1975-85. Organizer Cortland County Child Abuse Prevention Council, N.Y., 1976; bd. dirs. Cortland Access Television Council, Cortland, 1983-85. Recipient Cert. of Recognition, City of Cortland, 1985. Mem. Nat. Assn. Ecumenical Staff, N. Am. Broadcast Section-World Assn. Christian Communications, Cortland County Ministerial Assn., Assn. Regional Religious Broadcasters. Democrat. Home: 3927 E Safford Fresno CA 93704 Office: Fresno Metropolitan Ministry 4411 E Tulare Fresno CA 93702

PARSHALL, HOWARD WILSON, minister, Southern Baptist Convention; b. Houston, May 23, 1925; s. Merle Adelbert and Mary Elenor (Wilson) P.; B.A., Howard Payne U., 1949; B.D., Southwestern Bapt. Theol. Sem., 1952, M.R.E., 1953; Ed.D., New Orleans Bapt. Theol. Sem., 1969; m. Clara Louise Wiggins, Aug. 30, 1949; children—Virginia Ruth, Paul Wayne. Ordained to ministry, 1947; pastor 1st Bapt. Ch., Weimar, Tex., 1953-56; clin. pastoral intern Tex. Med. Center Inst. Religion, Houston, 1956-57; chaplain Pinecrest State Sch., Pineville, La., 1957—. Chaplain supr. Assn. Clin. Pastoral Edn., fall 1966. Fellow Am. Assn. Mental Deficiency; mem. Am. Protestant Hosp. Assn. (cert.). Home: 207 Iris Dr Pineville LA 71360 Office: PO Box 191 Pineville LA 71360

PARSONS, DONALD JAMES, bishop, Episcopal Ch.; b. Phila., Mar. 28, 1922; s. Earl and Helen (Drabble) P.; B.A., Temple U., 1943; M.Div. Phila. Div. Sch., 1946, Th.D., 1951, D.D. (hon.), 1964; postgrad. U. Nottingham (Eng.), 1968; D.C.L., Nashota (Wis.) House, 1973; m. Mary Russell, Sept. 17, 1955; children—Mary, Rebecca, Bradford. Ordained priest Episcopal Ch., 1946, consecrated bishop, 1973; curate Immanuel Ch., Wilmington, Del., 1946-49; rector St. Peter's Ch., Smyrna, Del., 1949-50; prof. N.T. Nashotah House, 1950-73, pres., dean, 1963-73; bishop Diocese of Quincy (Ill.), 1973—. Author: A Life-time Road to God, 1966; In Time with Jesus, 1973; The Holy Eucharist: Rite Two, 1976. Home: 3900 Hawthorne Pl Peoria IL 61614 Office: 3601 N North St Peoria IL 61604

PARSONS, ELMER EARL, bishop, Free Methodist Church N.Am.; b. Cloverland, Wash., Oct. 4, 1919; s. Claud Soloman and Bessie Lillian (Campbell) P.; A.B., Seattle Pacific Coll., 1942; S.T.B., Bibl. Sem. in N.Y., 1945; Th.M., Asbury Theol. Sem., Wilmore, Ky., 1955; D.D. (hon.), Greenville (Ill.) Coll., 1958; m. Marjorie E. Carlson, Aug. 29, 1942; children—Karl E., James M., H. Joy, Ann E., Lois Marie, Louise Melba. Ordained to ministry; dean Wessington Springs (S.D.) Coll., 1945-47; missionary to China, 1947-49, Japan, 1949-54; pres. Central Coll., McPherson, Kans., 1955-64, Osaka (Japan) Christian Coll., 1964-74; bishop Free Meth. Ch., Winona Lake, Ind., 1974—. Named Alumnus of Year, Seattle Pacific Coll., 1975. Author: Witness to the Resurrection, 1967. Home: 1302 W Winona Ave Warsaw IN 46580 Office: care Free Meth Ch N Am 901 College Ave Winona Lake IN 46590

PARSONS, MICHAEL LEONARD, minister, Presbyterian Church in the U.S.; b. Walsoken, Norfolk, Eng., Aug. 3, 1933; came to U.S., 1957; s. Leonard Francis and Ivy Emily (Smith) P.; m. Margaret Joy Morris, Apr. 8, 1961; children: Murray Levin, Romney

Christina. B.A., Cambridge U., 1957, M.A., 1961; M.Div., Austin Presbyn. Theol. Sem., 1960. Ordained to ministry Presbyterian Church, 1960. Asst. minister St. Philip Presbyn. Ch., Houston, 1960-62; interim supply minister Presbyn. Ch., Tenafly, N.J., 1963; minister First Presbyn. Ch., Henderson, Tex., 1963-69, St. Andrew Presbyn. Ch., Longview, Tex., 1969-70, Fain Meml. Presbyn. Ch., Wichita Falls, Tex., 1980—; asst. warden Wymondham Coll., Eng., 1952-54; tchr. St. Johns Sch., Houston, 1957-58, Earsham Hall Sch., Eng., 1970-71, Northgate High Sch., Eng., 1971-79; instr. Kilgore Jr. Coll., Tex., 1965-66; mem. Gregg County Interracial Council, Longview, Tex., 1969-70; chmn. Clergy Nuclear Awareness, Wichita Falls, Tex., 1983—. Dir. Rusk and Cherokee Counties Community Action Program, Henderson, 1966-69, Longview Community Theatre, 1967-70. Austin Presbyn. Theol. Sem. Bd. grad study fellow, 1960, Princeton Theol. Sem. teaching fellow, 1962. Mem. Palo Duro Presbytery, Interfaith Ministries Inc. Wichita Falls. Clubs: Faith City Kennel (pres. 1981-82); Labrador Retriever (Eng., Dallas, and Fort Worth). Avocations: painting; travel; acting; breeding, judging, exhibiting labrador retrievers. Home: 1721 Ridgemont Dr Wichita Falls TX 76309 Office: Fain Meml Presbyn Ch 2201 Speedway Wichita Falls TX 76308

PARTHEMORE, JOHN ALFRED, JR., minister, Churches of God General Conference; b. Harrisburg, Pa., Aug. 13, 1929; s. John Alfred and Mary Kathryn (Hoff) P.; A.B., Findlay Coll., 1951; B.D., Winebrenner Theol. Sem., 1954; B.D., Lutheran Theol. Sem., Gettysburg, Pa., 1960; m. Janet Grace Rayle, June 13, 1954; children: John, Judith, Jeffrey, Janice, Joel. Ordained to ministry Chs. of God Gen. Conf., 1954; student pastor Zion Ch. of God, Hamler, Ohio, 1951-54; pastor Bowmansdale and Mt. Pleasant Chs. of God, Dillsburg, Pa., 1954-60; editor The Church Advocate, Harrisburg, 1960-79; editor ch. publs., 1970-79; pastor First Ch. of God, Middletown, Pa., 1979—. Office: 245 W High St Middletown PA 17057

PARVEY, CONSTANCE F., pastor, Lutheran Church in America, religion educator; b. Aberdeen, S.D., Jan. 12, 1931; d. William Robert and Anna Katherine (Dunkel) P. B.A., U. Minn., 1952; B.D., Harvard U., 1963; D.D. (hon.), Redlands U., 1977. Ordained to ministry Luth. Ch. in Am., 1972. Luth. chaplain Nat. Luth. Camp Ministry, U. Wis.-Madison, 1963-66; editor Harvard Div. Bull., Cambridge, Mass., 1966-68; pastor Univ. Luth. Ch., Cambridge, 1972-77; dir. World Council Chs. Faith and Order Commn., Community of Women and Men in Ch. Study, 1978-82; Roian Fleck resident in religion Bryn Mawr Coll., Pa.; mem. Inter-Luth. Commn. on Worship, 1972-77, faith and order com. Nat. Council Chs., N.Y.C., 1975-78; bd. preachers Harvard U., 1975-77, adv. com. women's studies in religion, 1980—. Author: Come Lord Jesus, Come Quickly, 1975. Editor: Ordination of Women in Ecclesiatic Perspective, 1980; Community of Women and Men in the Church, 1983. Contbr. articles to profl. jours. Recipient DeTocqueville prize Ctr. for Vol. Soc., Washington, 1973; Danforth Found. fellow; German Nat. Com. grantee Luth. World Fedn., 1982. Mem. Am. Acad. Religion (chmn. sect. on theology and arts New Eng. region 1973-76, region program chmn. 1975-77, assoc. editor Worship mag. 1979-82, co-chmn. consultation 1985—), Phi Beta Kappa. Democrat. Home: 47 Vassal Ln Cambridge MA 02138 Office: Dept History Bryn Mawr Coll Bryn Mawr PA 19010

PASCOAL, EZEQUIEL ENES, priest, Roman Catholic Ch.; b. Petropolis, Brazil, Sept. 11, 1908; s. Manuel da Silveira Pascoal and Teresa de Jesus Enes; student sem., Macao, S.China, 1921-32. Ordained priest, 1932; missionary, Timor, Oceania, 1932-66; prof. Portugese and Portugese lit. Timor Diocesan Sem., 1938-40; prof. religion and morals Timor High Sch., 1949-56. Dir., Timor Dept. Pub. Welfare, 1952-57. Dir., editor SEARA, Diocesan Mag., 1949-57. Author: A Alma de Timor Vista na sua Fantasia. Address: 125 E Pleasant Ave Tulare CA 93274

PASKOW, SHIMON, rabbi, Conservative Jewish Congregations; b. Newark, 1932; m. Carol Bauman; 1 child, Michele. B.A., Bklyn. Coll., 1956; Amit cert., Hebrew U., 1953; M.A., Hebrew Union Coll., Jewish Instit. Religion, 1959, rabbi (hon.), 1984; D.D. (hon.), Jewish Theol. Sem. Am., 1984. Ordained rabbi, 1959. Fellow Hebrew Union Coll., Jewish Instit. Religion, Cin., 1959-60; assoc. rabbi Valley Jewish Community Center, Temple Adat Ari El, North Hollywood, Calif., 1965-69; rabbi Temple Etz Chaim, Thousand Oaks, Calif., 1969—; campaign chmn. United Jewish Welfare Fund, 1972-75, State of Israel Bonds, 1972-76. Contbr. articles to profl. jours. Mem. community relations com. San Fernando Valley Area Council; adv. com. 12th Dist. City of Los Angeles; trustee So. Calif. Council for Soviet Jews; bd. dirs. Gregor Mendel Botanic Found., Inc., 1966—. Served as chaplain U.S. Army, 1960-65; served to lt. col. USAR, 1965—. Recipient Shalom award Israel Govt. Tourist Office. Mem. Central Conf. of Am. Rabbis, Soc. Bibl. Literature, Rabbinical Assembly Am., Am. Jewish Hist. Soc., So. Calif. Bd. Rabbis, Mil. Chaplains Assn., Assn. Jewish Chaplains. Home: 42 Verde Vista Dr Thousand Oaks CA 91360 Office: Temple Etz Chaim 1080 Janss Rd Thousand Oaks CA 91360

PASS, THOMAS EMERY, minister, Presbyterian Ch. U.S.; b. Ft. Oglethorpe, Ga., Feb. 28, 1945; s. Albin George and Harriet Kerth (Hanauer) P.; B.A., La. State U., 1967; Th.M., New Orleans Bapt. Theol. Sem., 1970; postgrad. Austin Presbyn. Theol. Sem., 1970-71; D.Min., McCormick Theol. Sem., 1977; m. Suzanne Marie Sandoz, Jan. 20, 1968; 1 son, Garrick Thomas. Ordained to ministry Presbyn. Ch. U.S., 1971; asso. pastor Grace Presbyn. Ch., Houston, 1971-75; pastor First Presbyn. Ch., Post, Tex., 1975—. Author: A Love Seeking, and a Love Being Found, 1974; Gifts Worth Living, 1976. Home: 1017 Sunset Dr Post TX 79356 Office: Box 597 Post TX 79356

PASSAGE, DOUGLAS WARD, minister, American Baptist Churches in the U.S.A.; b. Mt. Vernon, N.Y., Oct. 16, 1921; s. Albert Jay and Mary Gertrude (Goodwin) P.; m. Luella Ruth Collamer, Sept. 11, 1948; children: Mary, Peter, Mark, Gail. B.A., Bucknell U., 1943; M.Div., Colgate Rochester Div. Sch., 1945; S.T.M., Boston U., 1951. Ordained to ministry Baptist Ch., 1945. Minister South Rutland Bapt. Ch., also Adams First Bapt. Ch., Adams Center, N.Y., 1945-48, Georgiaville Bapt. Ch., R.I., 1948-52, Federated Ch., West Winfield, N.Y., 1952-62, United Ch. of Christ, Elizabethtown, N.Y., also First Congregational Ch., Lewis, N.Y., 1962-72, First Bapt. Ch., Penn Yan, N.Y., 1972—; mem. dept. ministry Am. Bapt. Chs. of N.Y. State, 1981—; mem. com. on ministerial standing and ordination Finger Lakes Assn. of Am. Bapt. Chs., 1983—; chmn. com. on hosps./nursing homes Penn Yan Area Council of Chs., 1983—. Author: The Secret Place, 1979—. Bd. dirs. Yates County Assn. for Retarded Citizens, 1979—; mem. bd. edn. Penn Yan Central Sch. Dist., 1979—. Mem. Ministers Council Am. Bapt. Chs. USA. Republican. Lodge: Rotary (chmn. 1984—). Home: 104 Highland Dr Penn Yan NY 14527 Office: First Baptist Church PO Box 391 224 Main St Penn Yan NY 14527

PASSAMANECK, STEPHEN MAURICE, educator, rabbi, Reform Jewish Congregations; b. Pitts., Dec. 7, 1933; s. Herman and Dolores (Jaskol) P.; B.A., U. Pitts., 1955; M.A., Hebrew Union Coll., 1960, Ph.D., 1964; diploma in law Oxford (Eng.) U., 1963; m. Marjorie Blattner, Sept. 2, 1962; children—Daniel, Eve. Ordained rabbi, 1960; instr. rabbinics Hebrew Union Coll., Los Angeles, 1963-64, asst. prof., 1964-68, asso. prof., 1968-72, prof., 1972—. Res. chaplain Los Angeles County Sheriff's Dept. Mem. Central Conf. Am. Rabbis, Pacific Assn. Reform Rabbis, Phi Beta Kappa. Author: Insurance in Rabbinic Law, 1974; contbr. articles on Jewish law to scholarly jours. Home: 4518 Wortser Ave North Hollywood CA 91604 Office: 3077 University Mall Los Angeles CA 90007

PASTUKHIV, SERHIJ KINDZERIAVYJ See *Who's Who in America,* 43rd edition.

PASTUSZKA, THOMAS JAMES, minister, United Church of Christ; b. N.Y.C., Sept. 24, 1954; s. Stanley Thomas and Florence Theresa (Sabia) P. A.A.S., St. Francis Coll., 1975; B.S., 1976; M.Div., Princeton U., 1981; postgrad. San Francisco Theol. Sem., 1984—. Ordained to ministry United Ch. of Christ, 1981. Asst. Slackwood Presbyn. Ch., Lawrenceville, N.J., 1978-79; pastor, intern Presbyn. Ch. Mountain, Delaware Water Gap, Pa., 1979-80; asst. Madison Ave Prebyn. Ch., N.Y.C., 1980-81; minister, 1st Congl. Ch., Santa Barbara, Calif. 1981—; bd. dirs. Ecumedia So. Calif., Los Angeles, 1984—; mem. Ch. and Ministry Commn.; bd. dirs. Commn. on Nurture & Evangelism, 1982-84, Univ. Religious Center, 1981—, United Campus Ministries, U. Calif., Santa Barbara. Bd. dirs. Creekside Terr. Assn., Santa Barbara, 1984. Recipient Honor cert. Freedoms Found., Valley Forge, 1978, Outstanding Young Man, U.S. Jaycees, 1984. Mem. Sunset Assn. United Ch. Christ. Clubs: Channel City, University (Santa Barbara). Lodge: Kiwanis (dir. 1984). Office: 1st Congl Ch 2101 State St Santa Barbara CA 93105

PATAKI, ANDREW, bishop, Byzantyne Catholic Church. Titular bishop of Telmisso, aux. bishop of Byzantyne Diocese, Passaic, N.J., 1983—. Office: 101 Market St Passaic NJ 07055*

PATE, JAMES DANIEL, JR., minister, So. Bapt. Conv.; b. Birmingham, Ala., Apr. 11, 1947; s. James Daniel and Margrett (Fason) P.; B.A., Miss. Coll., 1971; m. Berlita Marie Leonard, Aug. 18, 1968. Ordained to ministry, 1967; pastor New Providence Bapt. Ch., Coy, Ala., 1965-68, McIvor Bapt. Ch., Batesville, Miss., 1967-70, Hebron Bapt. Ch., Bentonia Miss., 1970-73, Calvary Bapt. Ch., Canton, Miss., 1973, River View (Ala.) Bapt. Ch., 1973-76, East 22d Bapt. Ch., Anniston, Ala., 1976—. Mem. Blount County, Pine Barren, East Liberty, Calhoun, Madison, Yazoo, Panola ministerial assns. Home: 2821 McClellan Blvd Anniston AL 36201 Office: PO Box 2051 Anniston AL 36202

PATENAUDE, GERARD WILFRED, priest, Roman Catholic. B. Augusta, Maine, June 11, 1916; s. Wilfred and Ludie (Gilbert) P. B.A., U. Montreal, 1937, M.A., 1947; postgrad. Fordham U., 1948. Ordained priest Roman Catholic Ch., 1941. Prof. English and Music Sem. Sherbrooke (Que.), Can., 1937-80; prof. English, U. Sherbrooke, 1952-65; minister, Maine, Fla., and N.Y.; chaplain St. Joseph Home, N.Y., 1947-48; curate Winthrop, Maine and Sanibel, Fla., 1941-84. Contbr. articles to profl. publs. Bd. dirs. Sherbrooke Mus., Hist. Soc. and Geneal. Soc. Sherbrooke, Que. and Maine Arnold Trail Hist. Soc. Home: 195 Rue Marquette CP 790 Sherbrooke PQ J1H 5K8 Canada

PATHENOS, NICHOLAS GEORGE, priest, Greek Orthodox Church; b. St. Louis, Nov. 5, 1955; s. George Nicholas and Mary (Karides) P.; m. Chrysanthe Lazarides, Jan. 14, 1979; children: Andrew, Alexander. B.A. in Philosophy and Religion, Hellenic Coll., 1978; M.Div. Holy Cross Coll., 1981. Ordained priest Greek Orthodox Ch., 1981. Priest Greek Orthodox, Denver, Colo., 1981-83, Corpus Christi, Tex., 1983—; sec. Corpus Christi Ministerial Alliance, 1983—. Lodge: Lions. Home and Office: St Nicholas Greek Orthodox Ch 502 S Chaparrel Box 343 Corpus Christi TX 78401

PATT, RICHARD WILLIAM, minister, Lutheran Church-Missouri Synod; b. Madison, Wis., Sept. 13, 1935; s. Ewald Paul and Clara Gurina (Wasley) P.; m. Shirley Berniece Kolka, June 12, 1960; children: Rachel, Paul. B.A., Concordia Sem., St. Louis, 1957, M.Div., 1960. Ordained to ministry Luth. Ch., 1960. Pastor, Christ Ch.-Luth., Fort Worth, 1960-64; sr. pastor, Meml. Luth. Ch., Toledo, Ohio, 1964-73; sr. minister Sherman Park Luth. Ch., Milw., 1973—; pres. Luth. Council Met. Milw., 1975-80. Author: What's Happened to My Johnny, 1972; Out of the Depths, 1973; The Word in Sign Language, 1973; The World Declares His Glory, 1973; Wait!, 1975; The Challenge of God's Harvest, 1975; The Lord's My Shepherd, 1977; The Challenge of God's Harvest, 1975; A Time for Everything, 1977, Psallite, vol. 1, 1976, vol. 2, 1977, vol. 3, 1978; Planning A Christian Wedding Service, 1981; Partners in the Impossible, 1984. Contbr. articles to nat. mags. Mem. Am. Soc. Ch. Architecture (corp. mem., nat. v.p. 1976-77), Interfaith Forum on Religion, Arts and Architecture. Democrat. Home: 2463 N 97th St Wauwatosa WI 53226 Office: Sherman Park Luth Ch 27-3 N Sherman Blvd Milwaukee WI 53210

PATTERSON, ARTHUR LAWRENCE, minister, Southern Baptist Convention; b. Bradford, Pa., Mar. 9, 1934; s. Glenn M. and Alice Mae (Carl) P.; m. Jeanette Irene Benson, Nov. 14, 1954 (dec. Dec. 1978); children: Nancy, Alicia, Laurie. B.A., Baylor U., 1957; B.D., So. Bapt. Theol. Sem., 1961. Ordained to ministry Baptist Ch., 1955. Pastor, First Bapt. Ch., College Hill, Ohio, 1960-66, North Park Bapt. Ch., Pitts., 1966-68, First Mason Ch., Ohio, 1968—; trustee So. Bapt. Home Missions Bd., 1980—; pres. Ohio State Bapt. Conv., 1982-84, bd. dirs., 1980—. Author articles. Mem. Mason Sch. Bd., 1977—; bd. dirs. Countryside YMCA, Lebanon, Ohio, 1981-84; pres. Lebanon Citizens Adv. Council, 1974-84. Lodges: Kiwanis (pres. 1977-78), Masons, Shriners (Mason). Home: 735 Reading Rd Mason OH 45040 Office: First Baptist Ch 745 Reading Rd Mason OH 45040

PATTERSON, DONIS DEAN, priest, Episcopal Ch.; b. Holmesville, Ohio, Apr. 27, 1930; s. Raymond J. and Louella (Glasgow) P.; B.S., Ohio State U., 1952, postgrad., 1960-61; postgrad. Harvard Div. Sch., 1956, Coll. Preachers, 1959, Inst. Advanced Pastoral Studies, 1960; S.T.B., Episcopal Theol. Sch., 1957, M.Div., 1971; grad. U.S. Army Command and Gen. Staff Coll., 1975; m. JoAnne Nida, Dec. 22, 1951; children—Christopher Nida, Andrew Joseph. Ordained priest Episcopal Ch., 1957; asst. chs., South Weymouth, Mass., 1954-55, Chelmsford, Mass., 1955-57; rector St. Andrew's Ch., Washington Court House, Ohio, 1957-63, St. Mark's Episcopal Ch., Venice, Fla., 1963-70, headmaster Day Sch., 1963-70; rector All Saints Episcopal Ch., Winter Park, Fla., 1970—. Chmn. armed forces div. Episcopal Ch., 1958-63; chaplain U.S. Army, 1959—; chmn. div. evangelism Episcopal Diocese South Fla., 1964-65, div. Christian Living, 1968-69, div. Christian edn., 1969-70; mem. Orlando Deanery Council, 1970—; chmn. armed forces div. Episcopal Diocese Central Fla., 1970—, mem. commn. on ministry, 1972—; chmn. Deacon Tng. Sch., 1973—, mem. diocesan bd., 1972-74; field rep. Anglican Fellowship of Prayer. Dist. chmn. Boy Scouts Am., 1960-63, instnl. rep., 1957-72, commr., 1958-60; chmn. clergy div. United Appeal, 1970-71. Bd. dirs., commr. Venice Housing Authority; Sarasota (Fla.)-Manatee Guidance Center; trustee Fla. Episcopal Coll. Served to lt. AUS, 1952-54; PTO; lt. col. Res. Recipient, 8 George Washington medals Freedoms Found. Valley Forge, 1965-71; 1st U.S. Army Res. Component Achievement medal Chief chaplain, 1974. Mem. Soc. Colonial Wars, Mil. Order World Wars (chaplain 1964-70), Am. Legion (chaplain 1960-70), Fayette Ministerial Assn. (pres. 1967-69), Lambda Chi Alpha. Contbr. articles to various publs. Home: 210 Trisman Terr Winter Park FL 32789 Office: 338 E Lyman Ave Winter Park FL 32789

PATTERSON, EDWIN, minister, Southern Baptist Convention; b. Andalusia, Ala., Sept. 6, 1921; s. Walter Levi and Kate Edline (Aughtman) P.; degree Brennan Bus. Sch., 1940, postgrad., 1941; postgrad. Howard Coll., Samford U., 1950-57; m. Margaret Alice Hall, May 14, 1966. Ordained to ministry, 1947; pastor chs., Ala., 1947—, Hopewell, 1949-67, Harmony Bapt. Ch., Andalusia, 1967-80, Searight Bapt. Ch., Dozier, 1980—. Comptroller, Ben Williams Equipment Co., Inc., Andalusia, 1962—. Home: 407 Lakeview Dr

Andalusia AL 36420 Office: PO Box 486 Andalusia AL 36420

PATTERSON, FRANK WILLARD, minister, Southern Baptist Convention; b. Alva, Okla., July 6, 1907; s. Otis Harvey and Myrtle May (Holder) P.; B.A., Okla. Bapt. U., 1928; M.Th., Southwestern Bapt. Theol. Sem., 1932; M.A., Nat. U. Mex., 1940; D.Th., Central Bapt. Theol. Sem., 1957; m. Pauline Widner Gilliland, Sept. 7, 1933; children—Burton Harvey, Donald Ray Aldridge (foster son). Ordained to ministry, 1926; pastor Bapt. chs., Okla., Ark., 1930-38; missionary Fgn. Mission Bd., So. Bapt. Conv., Mex., 1939-40; bus. mgr. Bapt. Spanish Pub. House, El Paso, Tex., 1941-42, gen. dir., 1943-70; pastor Trinity Bapt. Ch., High Rolls-Mountain Park, N.Mex., 1974-78. Lit. promoter, cons. Latin Am., 1971-72; cons. Bapt. Pub. House, Brazil, 1973; mem. Bible Study and Membership Tng. Commn., Bapt. World Alliance, 1960-70. Recipient award for outstanding alumni achievement Okla. Bapt. U., 1968, Distinguished Alumnus award Southwestern Bapt. Theol. Sem., 1970. Author: El Plan Financiero de Dios, 1940; Manual de Finanzas para Iglesias, 1944, 52, rev. edit., 1970; J.E. Davis, Printer for God, 1956; Baptist Missionary Administration in Mexico, 1957; Evangelizando con el Espiritu Santo, 1958; Carribean Quest, 1960; Manual para la Escuela Dominical, 1962; Impresor al Servicio de Dios, 1966; A Century of Baptist Work in Mexico, 1979; editor Revista Evangelica, 1944-55, El Expositor Biblico, 1944-70. Home and Office PO Box 421 Cloudcroft NM 88317

PATTERSON, J. O., presiding bishop Church of God in Christ. Address: 1774 S Parkway E Memphis TN 38114

PATTERSON, JAMES WRIGHT, religious organization administrator, educator, Progressive National Baptist Convention; b. Monroe, La., May 10, 1909; s. George and Laura (Duncan) P.; m. Deatrice Anderson, Dec. 26, 1950. B.A., Straight Coll., 1934; M.Ed., DePaul U., 1961. Tchr., Monroe, 1935-42, Evanston, Ill., 1952-78; dir. religious edn. Monumental Bapt. Ch., Chgo., 1978—, also deacon and trustee; tchr. Progressive Bapt. Congress, St. Louis and Chgo., 1975, 80-82, Progressive Bapt. State Conv., Chgo., 1980-84; missionary, Haiti, summers 1981-83; reading and comprehension tutor DePaul U., Chgo., 1980—. Author religious dramas: A Passion Play, 1960 (Trophy award 1970); Moses and the Ten Commandments, 1970; A Prodigal Son, 1981. Mem. Assn. Retired Tchrs., Straight Coll. Alumni Assn. (corr. sec.). Democrat. Club: Church (pres. 1980—). Home: 4534 Vincennes Ave Chicago IL 60653

PATTERSON, JOHN WELLINGTON, minister, Southern Baptist Convention; b. Yuma, Ariz., Mar. 1, 1926; s. Oliver Wellington and Gail Gertrude (MacDonald) P.; m. Patricia Ann Wilson, May 31, 1950; children: Patricia Gail, John Wellington, Leighanne McGarey, Michelle McKay, Scott Wilson, Heather-Jill. B.A., Bob Jones U., 1949; postgrad. U. Richmond, 1943-44; B.D., Southwestern Bapt. Theol. Sem., 1952, Th.D., 1955; Ph.D., U. Edinburgh, Scotland, 1970. Ordained to ministry, 1949. Pastor First Bapt. Ch., Burleson, Tex., 1953-56; prof. theology Seminario Teologico Bautista, Cali, Colombia, 1956-67; pastor Hatcher Meml. Bapt. Ch., Richmond, Va., 1967-83; pastor Gambrell St. Bapt. Ch., Ft. Worth, Tex., 1983—; adj. prof. Southwestern Sem., Ft. Worth, 1984—; pres. Unified Bd. Mission, Colombia, 1960-67; mem., pres. So. Bapt. Fgn. Mission Bd., Richmond, 1972-82; moderator Richmond Bapt. Assn., 1972-74; pres. bd. dirs. Bapt. Hosp., Baranquilla, Colombia, 1956-67. Author: Look South, 1968. Chaplain, Vol. Rescue Squad, Richmond, 1967-83. Served with USN, 1944-46. Recipient Balfour award, 1943; award, Protestants & Other Ams. United, 1952. Mem. Phi Gamma Delta. Home: 4101 Alicante Ave Fort Worth TX 76133 Office: Gambrell Street Bapt Church 1616 W Gambrell St Fort Worth TX 76115

PATTERSON, RICHARD EUGENE, minister, sch. adminstr., Ch. of God (Anderson, Ind.); b. Shelbyville, Ill., Nov. 7, 1943; s. Fredric A. And Ruby Aileen (Rentfro) P.; student So. Ill. U., Carbondale, 1961-62; m. Delores Ann Stockton, Nov. 16, 1962; children—Gina Dawn, Richard Michael, MaryAnn, William Andrew. Ordained to ministry, 1974; pastor 1st Ch. of God, Farmington, Mo., 1972-76, 1st Ch. of God, Charleston, Ill., 1976—; founder, supt. Twin City Christian Acad., Charleston, 1976—. Mem. program com. Mo. Ch. of God., 1975-76; dir. So. Ill. Youth Camp, Benton, 1971, State of Mo. High Sch. and Coll. Camp, 1975. Named Outstanding Young Man, Jaycees, 1977. Author Sunday sch. curriculum materials. Home: 917 Westgate Dr Charleston IL 61920 Office: 1225 Montgomery Dr Charleston IL 61920

PATTERSON, RONALD PAUL, minister, United Methodist Church; b. Ashland, Ohio, Dec. 4, 1941; s. Donald Edward and Mildred Corrine (Niswender) P.; m. Marlene Louise Pfahler, Sept. 1, 1962; children: Paul Edward, Mark Loren. B.A., Malone Coll., 1963; M.Div., United Theol. Sem., 1967; M.A., (Ralph Stoody Journalism fellow), Syracuse U., 1969. Ordained to ministry, United Meth. Ch., 1967. Editor Youth publs., Evang. United Brethren Ch., Dayton, Ohio, 1964-68; assoc. pastor Lafayette Ave. United Meth. Ch., Syracuse, N.Y., 1968-70; editorial assoc. The Upper Room, Nashville, 1970-74; editor Alive Now, Nashville, 1970-74; editor World Books, Word, Inc., Waco, Tex., 1974-77; v.p., editorial dir. Abingdon Press, Nashville, 1977-84, v.p., dir. pub., 1984—. Author: The Kyle Rote, Jr., Story, 1975. Editor: Come On, Let's Pray, 1972; The Comming of Easter, 1973. Contbr. articles to religious pubs. Vice-pres. Y's Men Club, YMCA, Dayton, 1965. Recipient Nat. Freedom Found. award, 1960; Paul M. Hinkhouse Nat. award for Creative and Effective Religious Communication, 1973. Mem. Religious Pub. Relations Council (v.p. Nashville chpt. 1973), Asso. Ch. Press. Address: United Methodist Pub House 201 8th Ave S Nashville TN 37202

PATTERSON, WILLIAM BROWN, priest, historian, educator, Episcopal Church; b. Charlotte, N.C., Apr. 8, 1930; s. William Brown and Eleanor Selden (Miller) P.; B.A., U. South, 1952; M.A., Harvard, 1954, Ph.D., 1966; B.A., Oxford (Eng.) U., 1955, M.A., 1959; B.D., Episcopal Theol. Sch., Cambridge, Mass., 1958; m. Evelyn Byrd Hawkins, Nov. 27, 1959; children—William Brown, Evelyn Byrd, Lucy Miller, Emily Norvell. Ordained priest, 1959; grad. fellow Episcopal Theol. Sch., curate Grace Ch., N. Attleboro, Mass., 1958-61; fellow tutor Gen. Theol. Sem., N.Y.C., asst. Christ Ch., Hackensack, N.J., 1961-62; asst. prof. history Davidson (N.C.) Coll., 1963-67, asso. prof. history, 1967-76, prof., 1976-80; priest in charge St. Albans Ch., Davidson, 1969-78; dean of coll., prof. history Univ. of the South, Sewanee, Tenn., 1980—. Trustee U. of South, 1967-71; mem. internat. advisory council Univ. Coll. Buckingham (Eng.), 1975-83. Nat. Endowment for the Humanities fellow, 1967-68, 79-80; Folger Shakespeare Library fellow, 1975; fellow Inst. for Research in Humanities, U. Wis., Madison, 1976. Contbr. hist. articles to theol. jours. Home: North Carolina Ave Sewanee TN 37375 Office: Office of Dean of College Univ of the South Sewanee TN 37375

PATTISON, CARL FRANKLIN, minister, Lutheran Ch. Am.; b. Balt., July 27, 1946; s. Alfred Henry Draper Bazy and Edna May (Campbell) P.; B.A., Roanoke Coll., 1968; M.Div., Luth. Theol. So. Sem., 1972; M.Ed., Madison Coll., 1976; clin. pastoral edn. S.C. State Hosp., Brook Ln. Psychol. Inst., 1976; m. Vivian Annette Parrott, Aug. 30, 1970; 1 son, Israel Jacob Parrott, Ordained to ministry, 1972; chaplain, supt. Oliver Gospel Mission, Columbia, S.C., 1969-70; chmn. Task Force Law Enforcement, Drug Abuse and Edn., Columbia, 1970-72; chaplain Myrtle Beach (S.C.) Campground, 1972; pastor Orkney Springs (Va.) Luth. Parish, 1972-77; pastor/minister Emmanuel Luth. Ch., Roanoke, Va., 1977—. Supply pastor Bethany Am. Luth. Ch., 1977; chaplain Bryce Mt. Resort, Va., 1973—, Shenandoah Counseling Center, Woodstock, Va., 1976-77; counselor in area. Active Vol. Fire Dept., Orkney Springs; chmn. Orkney Springs Red Cross Fund, 1973. Mem. Nat. Speleol. Soc., Va. Herpetol. Soc. Contbr. article to Pastoral Psychology. Home and Office: PO Box 6164 Roanoke VA 24017

PATTON, BETHANY ANNE, minister, Disciples of Christ Church; b. Hicksville, Ohio, July 7, 1956; d. Bruce Butterick Patton and Gladys (Morrell) B.A., Hiram Coll., 1978; M.Div., Christian Theol. Sem., Indpls., 1982. Ordained to ministry Disciples of Christ Ch., 1982. Pastor, Hyndsdale Christian Ch., Martinsville, Ind., 1981-82; assoc. pastor Ch. of Christ, Williamsport, Pa., 1982—; mem. Ecumenical Concerns Commn., Ind. Region, 1980-82; steward Consultation on Ch. Union, Cin., 1979-80; chmn. Youth Task Force, Pa. region, 1983—. Intern Ind. U. Med. Ctr., Indpls., 1981-82; resident Williamsport Hosp., 1982-84. Bd. dirs. Internat. Students Coordinating Assn. of Lycoming County, Williamsport, 1984; mem. Multi-Disciplinary Team for Child Abuse, Williamsport, 1983. Grad. asst. in history Christian Theol. Sem., 1981. Mem. Assn. Clin. Pastoral Edn., Congress of Disciples Clergy, Williamsport Clergywomen Fellowship (founding). Democrat. Club: Fedn. of Music. Office: 1st Ch of Christ Disciples 1250 Almond St Williamsport PA 17701

PAUL, DAVID JEROME, university president, priest, Roman Catholic Church; b. St. Louis, Mar. 22, 1938; s. Charles A. and Cora Mae (Strebler) P. B.A., St. Mary's U., 1960; M.A., St. Louis U., 1969, M.Div., 1970; M.A. in Ednl. Adminstrn., Creighton U., 1975. Ordained priest Roman Cath. Ch., 1970. Tchr., Villa St. Jean Internat. Sch., Fribourg, Switzerland, 1965-67, Don Bosco High Sch., Milw., 1970-71; asst. prin. Daniel Gross High Sch., Omaha, 1971-74, prin., 1974-81; pres. St. Mary's U., San Antonio, 1981—, trustee, 1981—; bd. dirs. Central Cath. High Sch., San Antonio, 1983—, Incarnate Word High Sch., San Antonio, 1982—; guest chaplain U.S. Ho. of Reps., 1979. Mem. Higher Edn. Council San Antonio, 1981—, San Antonio World Affairs Council, 1982—, Univ. Round Table, 1982—. Recipient Disting. Educator award Kettering Found., 1974, 76, 79. Mem. Am. Council Edn., Ind. Colls. and Univs. Tex., Assn. Governing Bds. Colls. and Univs., Nat. Assn. Ind. Colls. and Univs., Assn. Cath. Colls. and Univs., Greater San Antoino C. of C. Office: St Mary's University One Camino Santa Maria San Antonio TX 78284

PAUL, GERALD WALTON, minister, United Church of Canada; writer; b. Sudbury, Ont., Can., June 26, 1926; s. Lloyd Walton and Clara (Thompson) P.; m. Shirley Florence Dixon, Sept. 8, 1948; children: Dennis, Catharine, Lloyd, Arnold, Gordon. B.A., Queen's U., Kingston, Ont., 1955; M.Div., Queen's Theology Coll., Kingston, 1957; Th.M., Vancouver Sch. Theology, 1974. Ordained to ministry United Ch. Can., 1957. Minister United Ch. Can., Manitouwadge, Ont., 1957-60, North Bay, Oct., 1960-64, Kincardine, Ont., 1977-83; chaplain Carleton U., Ottawa, Ont., 1964-70; chaplain, dir. Iona Coll., U. Windsor, Oct., 1970-77; ministry of writing Kingston, Ont., 1983—; chmn. Nat. Guidelines on Evangelism, United Ch. Can., Toronto, 1966-70; co-chmn. Anglican United Ch. Union, Montreal-Ottawa Conf., 1967-70; founder Coalition for Devel., Windsor, Ont., 1970-77. Author: Evangelism in the 70's, 1970; contbr. numerous articles to various publs. Recipient 1st Pl award Writer's Digest Writing Competition, 1984. Home: 1002 66 Greenview Dr Kingston ON K7M 7C5 Canada

PAUL, JOEL HENRY, religious organization administrator, educator, social worker; b. Brookline, Mass., Sept. 4, 1942; s. Samuel M. and Doris (Movchine) P.; B.S., Boston U., 1964; postgrad. in Judaic Studies and Edn., Yeshiva U., 1965-70; postgrad. Sch. Social Work, U. Pa., 1972-74; m. Lillian Amcis; children: Harold Isaac, Sheila Miriam Rena, Nathan Abraham, Elliot Mark. Founding dir. New Eng. region Nat. Conf. Synagogue Youth, 1962-64; youth dir. Baldwin Jewish Center, L.I., N.Y., 1964-65; dir. youth activities Great Neck Synagogue, L.I., 1965-68; asso. dir. youth bur. Yeshiva U., 1968-71; dir. B'nai B'rith Hillel Found., U. Pa., Phila., 1971-73; founding dir., exec. dir. Jewish Campus Activities Bd., Phila., 1973—; staff Met. N.Y. Commn. on Talmud Torah Edn., 1969-70; trustee Internat. Conf. Jewish Communal Services; mem. local services com. Phila. Fedn. Jewish Agys. and Phila. Jewish Community Relations Council, 1971—; mem. profl. adv. com. Wurzweiler Sch. Social Work, Yeshiva U.; campus and youth worker. Am. Friends of Tel Aviv U. grantee, 1974. Mem. Phila. Assn. Jewish Agy. Execs. (pres.). Home: 133 Cynwyd Rd Bala Cynwyd PA 19004 Office: 202 S 36th St Philadelphia PA 19104

PAUL, JOHN JOSEPH See *Who's Who in America*, 43rd edition.

PAUL, WILLIAM JOSEPH, priest, Roman Cath. Ch.; b. Phila., Mar. 30, 1938; s. William James and Emma (Ascolese) P.; B.A., St. Charles Sem., M.A., 1967; M.S. in Secondary Sch. Sci., Villanova (Pa.) U., 1969. Ordained priest, 1963; tchr. sci., chmn. dept. Roman Cath. High Sch., Phila., 1965—, also golf coach and basketball moderator. Mem. biology curriculum com. Roman Cath. Archdiocese Phila. Mem. steering com. Knowledgeable Action to Restore Environment; secondary sci. chmn. energy edn. adv. com. council Phila. Electric Co. Mem. Nat. Sci. Tchrs. Assn. Home: 6214 Grays Ave Philadelphia PA 19142 Office: 301 N Broad St Philadelphia PA 19107

PAULEY, EDWARD HAVEN, lay ch. worker, Baptist Ch.; b. Boston, June 17, 1939; s. Edward Lawton and Ethel (Book) P.; A.B. cum laude, Gordon Coll., 1961; A.M., Boston U., 1964, Ph.D., 1969; postgrad. Oxford (Eng.) U., 1966-67, 75; m. Shirley Stewart, May 29, 1964; children—David Stewart, Deborah Jeanne. Deacon, Rock Hill Bapt. Ch., Jamaica Plain, Mass., 1961-63; young people's leader Blaney Meml. Bapt. Ch., Dorchester, Mass., 1964-66; deacon West Kingston (R.I.) Bapt. Ch., 1970-72, moderator, 1970-76. Asso. prof. philosophy U. R.I., Kingston, 1967-76; also asst. v.p. acad. affairs, 1971-76; dean Biola Coll., La Mirada, Calif., 1976—. Edward Payson Drew scholar, 1957-58; Bordon Parker Bowne fellow, 1965; Dissertation fellow, 1966, Kent fellow Danforth Found. 1966; Mem. Am. Assn. Higher Edn., Am. Philos. Assn. Home: 12700 S Sparwood Ln La Mirada CA 90638 Office: Marshburn Hall Biola Coll La Mirada CA 90639

PAULSON, JOHN FREDERICK, minister, Lutheran Church in America; b. Portland, Oreg., Feb. 25, 1931; s. Casper Ferdinand and Anne Elizabeth (Moe) P.; m. Donna Charlotte McMullen, Aug. 8, 1954; children: Kristin Ann Paulson Landon, Timothy John. B.A., Augustana Coll., 1953; M.Div., Augustana Theol. Sem., 1957; D.Min., Pacific Luth. Theol. Sem., 1980. Ordained to ministry Lutheran Ch., 1958. Intern pastor Immanuel Luth. Ch., Jamestown, N.Y., 1957-58; pastor Bethel Luth. Ch., Firth, Idaho, 1958-61, Peace Luth. Ch., Seattle, 1961-66, Mount Cross Luth. Ch., Tacoma, Wash., 1966-76; sr. pastor Messiah Luth. Ch., Spokane, Wash., 1976-84; sr. pastor Grace Luth. Ch., Corvallis, Oreg., 1984—; bd. dirs. Riverview Retirement Home and Med. Center, Spokane, 1979—, chmn. bd., 1984; v.p. Riverview Found., Spokane, 1982—; bd. dirs. Christian Aid Network, Spokane, 1983—. Author: (with Donna C. Paulson) Kids Are Like That!, 1966; author/co-author Bible study courses. Home: 4129 NW Douglas St Corvallis OR 97330 Office: Grace Luth Ch 435 NW 21st St Corvallis OR 97330

PAULSON, WARREN LEE, minister, Lutheran Church-Missouri Synod; b. Racine, Wis., Nov. 18, 1932; s. Harvey Leonard and Gertrude Cecilia

(Anderson) P.; m. Ruth Esther Pedersen, Apr. 4, 1959; children: Joy Ruth, Katherine Esther, David Warren. A.A., Concordia Jr. Coll., Fort Wayne, Ind., 1954; B.Th., Concordia Theol. Sem., Springfield, Ill., 1958; advanced cert. in clin. pastoral tng. Inst. Pastoral Care, 1966. Ordained to ministry Luth. Ch., 1958. Pastor, Trinity Luth. Ch., Newberry, Mich., Grace Luth. Ch., Germfask, Mich., 1958-63; Faith Luth. Ch., Germantown, Wis., 1963-65; clin. tng. in univ. hosp., mental hosps. and prison, 1965-66; coordinating chaplain Mich. Corrections Camps, Grass Lake, 1966—; service to deaf Mich. Upper Peninsula, 1960-62; cir. counselor No. Wis. dist. Luth. Ch.-Mo. Synod, 1962-63; chaplains' rep. Chaplaincy Adv. Com., Mich. Dept. Corrections, 1976-80; com. mem. to various denominational convs.; chaplaincy cons. County Jail, Jackson, Mich., 1982—. Author: (Manual for Vol. Chaplains, 1983). Mem. Am. Protestant Correctional Chaplains Assn., Am. Correctional Chaplains Assn., Am. Correctional Assn. Home: 4839 Sequoia Jackson MI 49201 Office: Corrections Camps 600 Maunte Rd Grass Lake MI 49240

PAUSON, MARIAN LAGARDE, religion educator, Episcopalian Church; b. New Orleans, Mar. 8, 1923; d. William Albert and Louise Julia (Guidry) LaGarde; m. John Jerome Pauson, June 25, 1949 (div. 1973); children: John Jerome Jr., Marie-Louise, Frances Pauson Bouton, Gregory Vincent, James William; m. Paul M. Belbutowski, Jan. 27, 1984. B.A., Webster Coll., 1947; M.A., U. Montreal, Can., 1954; Ph.D., Tulane U., 1965. Assoc. prof. philosophy and religious studies Old Dominion U., Norfolk, Va., 1975—. Author: Jung the Philosopher, 1986. Contbr. articles to profl. jours. Republican. Home: 528 Warren Crescent Norfolk VA 23507 Office: Old Dominion U Norfolk VA 23508

PAVALKIS, VICTOR, priest, Roman Cath. Ch.; b. Akeciai, Lithuania, May 3, 1909; s. Joseph and Maria (Jurksaitis) P.; came to U.S., 1950, naturalized, 1962; grad. Vilkaviskis Sem., Lithuania, 1932; D. Ch. History, Pontifical Gregorian U., Rome, 1941; grad. in philosophy Angelicum U., Rome, 1944. Ordained priest, 1932; pastor chs., Lithuania, 1932-37; mem. Vatican mission, Germany, 1945-46; rep. United Lithuanian Relief Fund Am., Inc., Italy, 1946-50; asso. pastor chs., Oakland, San Francisco and San Jose, Calif., 1950-68; pastor St. John the Baptist Ch., Milpitas, Calif., 1968—. Mem. Lithuanian Community of San Francisco (founder, pres. 1951-62), Assn. Advancement Baltic Studies, Inc. Home and Office: 279 S Main St Milpitas CA 95035

PAWLOWICZ, MICHAEL WILSON, ind. gospel broadcaster; b. Balt., Oct. 25, 1938; s. Sigmund S. and Mary Elizabeth (Esterline) P.; B.D., Ravenna Sch. Ministerial Studies, 1968. Ordained to ministry, 1960; asso. dir. Youth for Christ, Balt., 1959-61, dir., Morgantown, Pa., 1965-68, bd. dirs., Huntsville, Ala., 1971—; youth dir. Meml. Presbyn. Ch., Lancaster, Pa., 1966-68; news dir. Sta. WMHR, Christian Radio, Syracuse, N.Y., 1969; mgr. gospel Sta. WGNR, Oneonta, N.Y., 1970; program mgr., news dir. Sta. WNDA, Gospel radio, Huntsville, 1970—. Student supr. Lancaster (Pa.) Bible Sch., 1964-66; bd. dirs. Madison County Child Evangelism Fellowship, 1971-76; elder Calvary Bible Ch., 1974—. Mem. Mayor's Advisory Com., Oneonta, 1970. Recipient Presdl. Commendation, 1970; Lefty Gomez Sports award, 1976; named Huntsville Gospel Music Ambassador, 1976. Mem. Huntsville Ministerial Assn., Gospel Music Assn. Contbr. articles to various religious jours. Home: 2819 Newby Rd Box 7 Huntsville AL 35805 Office: 2407 9th Ave Huntsville AL 35805

PAYNE, EDWARD CARLTON, clergyman, Ind. Cath. Ch. (Old Roman Cath.); b. Hartford, Conn., Aug. 4, 1928; s. Robert Carlton and Margaret Ilon (Bodnar-Donovan) P.; L.T., St. Francis Sem., 1966; S.T.D., St. John Chrysostom Coll., 1971; B.S., Peoples U., 1973, D.A.E.H., 1973, M.Div., 1976; D.D., Am. Coll. and Sem., 1971, D.S.M., 1971; D.D., St. Ephrem's Inst., 1974. Ordained deacon, 1947, archdeacon, 1951, elder, 1953, priest, 1966; Dean of Conn., 1968; Bishop of Conn., 1969; Archbishop of New Eng., 1972; primate, 1970; dir. and prior Order of the Cross, Hartford, 1951—, prior Holy Cross chpt., 1951—; rector Holy Cross Old Roman Cath. Ch., Hartford, 1966—; instr. Ind. Cath. Seminarium, 1970—; met. exarch of Ugro-Finnic Peoples, 1975—. Sec. Traditionalist Clergy Assn., 1974-75. Recipient God and Country awards, 1949. Editor of The Ind. Cath., 1970—, The Silver Cross, 1951-66, The Associated Traditionalist, 1974-75. Office: PO Box 261 Wethersfield CT 06109

PAYNE, LESLIE HOWARD, minister, Christian Church (Disciples of Christ); b. Emmett, Idaho, Jan. 21, 1928; s. John Henry and Nellie Jane (Swan) P.; B.Th., N.W. Christian Coll., 1954; M.Div., Christian Theol. Sem., 1959; M.A., Butler U., 1960; m. Norlene Elise Walcott, Aug. 27, 1950; children—Christina Cay, Lynn Louise. Ordained to ministry, 1954; minister Chgo. Corner Christian Ch., New Castle, Ind., 1954-60, First Christian Ch., Miles City, Mont., 1960-63; chaplain Pine Hills Sch., Miles City, Mont., 1963—, founder juvenile sexual offender treatment program, 1984. interim minister First Christian Ch., Miles City, 1971—. Grief therapist Graves Funeral Home, Miles City, Mont., 1973. Adviser, Parents Without Partners; active local mental health assn. Mem. Am. Correctional Chaplains Assn., Am. Protestant Correctional Chaplains Assn., Christian Ministers Mont., Miles City Ministerial Assn., Am. Assn. Profl. Hypnotherapists. Home: 1716 Main St Miles City MT 59301 Office: PO Box 1058 Miles City MT 59301

PAYNE, SIDNEY STEWART, bishop, Anglican Church of Canada; b. Fogo, Nfld., Can., June 6, 1932; s. Albert and Hilda Mae (Oake) P.; m. Selma Carlson Penney, Oct. 11, 1962; children: Carla Ann, Christopher, Robert, Angela. B.A., Meml. U., St. John's, Nfld., 1958; L.Th., Queen's Coll., St. John's, 1958; B.D., Gen. Synod, 1963; D.D. (hon.), King's Coll., Halifax, 1981. Ordained deacon, Anglican Ch. Can., 1957, ordained priest, 1958; consecrated bishop, 1978. Rector Anglican Ch., Happy Valley, Nfld., 1957-65, Bay Roberts, 1965-70, St. Anthony, 1970-78; bishop Western Nfld., 1978—. Address: 13 Cobb Ln Corner Brook ND A2H 2V3 Canada

PAYNE, WILLIAM LEONARD, minister, So. Baptist Conv.; b. Abilene, Tex., Dec. 17, 1940; s. William Thurman and Betty (Vaughn) P.; B.A., Hardin-Simmons U., 1964; M.Div., Southwestern Bapt. Theol. Sem., 1967; m. Carlene Wilson, Nov. 24, 1967; children—Julie Elizabeth, William Jeffrey. Ordained to ministry, 1964; minister music and youth 1st Bapt. Ch., Baird, Tex., 1962-64; minister youth and edn. Oakwood Bapt. Ch., Arlington, Tex., 1964-66; minister of music 1st Bapt. Ch., Bedford, Tex., 1967-68; pastor chs., Rotan, Tex., 1968-70, Andrews, Tex., 1970-73, 1st Bapt. Ch., Tye, Tex., 1973—. Ch. tng. dir. Abilene Bapt. Assn., 1973—; v.p. Andrews Ministerial Alliance, 1973; chaplain Hardin-Simmons U. Alumni Assn., 1974-75; program chmn. Abilene Bapt. Ministers Fellowship. Home: 209 Morgan St Tye TX 79563 Office: PO Box 235 Tye TX 79563

PEABODY, ALAN BOWE, ch. ofcl., minister, United Ch. of Christ; b. Melrose, Mass., Feb. 8, 1925; s. William Tyler and Dorothy (Atkinson) P.; B.S., Springfield Coll., 1946; B.D., Yale U., 1949; Ph.D., Syracuse U., 1964; m. Etta Mable Burghardt, Aug. 25, 1946; children: Gara, Alan Bowe, Charles, Deborah (dec.). Ordained to ministry United Ch. of Christ, 1949; pastor Riverside Salem Evang. and Ref. Ch., Buffalo, 1949-53, DeRuyter (N.Y.) Federated Ch., 1953-60, Lincklaen (N.Y.) Community Ch., 1957-60; exec. dir. Council Chs. of Mohawk Valley Area, Inc., Utica, N.Y., 1968—. Assoc. prof. Paul Quinn Coll., Waco, Tex., 1960-65, Mohawk Valley Community Coll., 1965-68; assoc. faculty Utica Coll., 1968—. Chmn., Utica Human Relations Commn., 1969-74; founder, dir. Utica Community Devel. Corp., 1968—, pres., 1970-71, 72—. Research grantee State U. N.Y., 1965. Mem. Am. Soc. Christian Ethics. Office: 1644 Genesee St Utica NY 13502

PEACE, RICHARD VERNON, theology educator, minister, writer, United Church of Christ; b. Detroit, July 6, 1938; s. Claude V. and Helen M. (Brinkman) P.; m. Judy J. Boppell, Sept. 13, 1963; children: Elizabeth, Jennifer, Stephen, Jonathan. B.E., Yale Univ., 1960; M.Div., Fuller Theol. Sem., 1964; Ph.D. candidate Univ. Natal, Pietermaritzburg, Republic of South Africa, 1985—. Ordained to ministry, United Ch. Christ, 1984. Dir. spl. projects African Enterprise, Pietermaritzburg, 1964-71; dir. publs. Clear Light Prodns., Newton, Mass., 1971-73; assoc. prof. evangelism and media Gordon-Conwell Theol. Sem., South Hamilton, Mass., 1976—; dir. Sanders Christian Found., 1978—, Still Point Films, 1976—. Author: (with others): Search The Scriptures, 1983; Where Do We Go From Here? A Program to Improve Problem Solving for Families of Impaired Elders, 1983; author: A Church's Guide to Evangelism, 1982; Giving Away Your Faith and Keeping It Too, 1979; Small Group Evangelism, 1985; Pilgrimage, 1984; many others translated into Spanish, Chinese and other langs. Contbr. articles to nat. and internat. mags. Contbr. films: Freedom '66, 1967, One In The Night, 1969, Chris Begins Again, 1974. Contbr. TV series PBS Infinity Factory, 1976-78, other projects. Mem. Acad. For Evangelism in Theol. Edn. (pres. 1981-83), Am. Soc. Missiology, Assn. for Ednl. Communication and Tech., Assn. for Multi-Image. Home: 479 Bay Rd South Hamilton MA 01982 Office: Gordon-Conwell Theol Seminary 130 Essex St South Hamilton MA 01982

PEACOCK, BEN LAMAR, minister, So. Bapt. Conv.; b. Montgomery, Ala., Oct. 1, 1930; s. Herbert and Mary Margaret (Cotton) P.; A.B., Howard Coll., 1952; postgrad. New Orleans Theol. Sem., 1953-54, Luther Rice Sem., 1976-77; m. Mary Helen Johnson, Aug. 10, 1950; children—Melody, David, Paul. Ordained to ministry So. Baptist Conv., 1950; pastor 1st Bapt. chs., Dallas, Ga., 1954-58, Chatsworth, Ga., 1958-59, Doraville, Ga., 1959-60, Southside Bapt. Ch., Miami, Fla., 1960-63, East Lake Bapt. Ch., Chattanooga; 1963-71, Arlington Bapt. Ch., Jacksonville; Fla., 1971-75, First Bapt. Ch., Panama City, Fla., 1975—. Moderator, Paulding County Assn., 1954-55; chmn. evangelism, Atlanta, Jacksonville, Fla., 1971—; chmn. State Bd. Missions, Fla. Bapt. Conv., 1974—; mem. adminstrv. com. state bd., 1973—, chmn. missions and evangelism, 1975—; mem. com. on coms. So. Bapt. Conv., 1976; chaplain Mahi Shrine, Miami; trustee, pres., chaplain Bapt. Home for Children, Jacksonville. Home: 512 S Bonita Ave Panama City FL 32401 Office: POB 1200 Panama City FL 32401

PEACOCK, EDWARD CHARLES, minister, United Presbyterian Church U.S.A.; b. Long Beach, Calif., Feb. 22, 1936; s. Darrel Vern and Beatrice Margaret (Compo) P.; B.A., Calif. State U. Long Beach, 1958; M.Div., San Francisco Theol. Sem., 1964, D.Min., 1974; m. Jacquelyn Gaye Miller, Dec. 25, 1959; children: Victoria Sue, Robert Paul, William Seward. Ordained to ministry, 1964; pastor Aztec United Presbyn. Ch., 1964-66, El Monte (Calif.) Community Presbyn. Ch., 1966-71, St. Paul's Presbyn. Ch., Anaheim, Calif., 1971—. Chmn. dept. speech and drama George Fox Coll., 1959-61; instr. Chapman Coll., 1973, Pepperdine U., 1976—; clin. mem., regional officer Am. Assn. Pastoral Counseling, 1974—; sr. staff counselor Am. Inst. Family Relations. Mem. Am. Acad. Psychotherapists, Am. Assn. Marriage and Family Counselors, Nat. Alliance Family Life, Presbyn. Ordained Profl. Counselors. Editor: Family Life. Home: 4452 Graywhaler Ln Rohnert Park CA 94928 Office: 2580 W Orange St Anaheim CA 92804

PEACOCK, HAROLD EUGENE, minister, United Methodist Church; b. Kincey, Ala., Oct. 11, 1919; s. J. P., Jr. and Mollie May (Jordan) P.; B.A., Millsaps Coll., 1941; M.Div., Emory U. Candler Sch. Theology, 1944; D.D., Birmingham-So. Coll., 1953, student Am. Sem. in Europe, 1951; m. Dorothy Heloise Burkhart, Mar. 18, 1943; children: Anne Peacock Coltrane, Eugenia Peacock Milner, Harold Eugene, Jr. Ordained to ministry United Methodist Ch., 1944. Pastor Fairlington United Meth., Arlington, Va., 1944-46, St. Francis St. United Meth. Ch., Mobile, Ala., 1946-61, Montgomery, Ala., 1961-65, First United Meth. Ch., Charlotte, N.C., 1965-72; dist. supt. United Meth. Ch., High Point, N.C., 1972-76; pastor First United Meth. Ch., Hendersonville, NC, 1976-84; pastor First United Meth. Ch., Lexington, N.C., 1984—. Chmn., Mobile Human Relations Council, 1960-61, Charlotte Community Devel. Com., 1970-72. Lodge: Rotary. Author: Hebrew Poetry and Wisdom Literature, 1974; The Trinity and the Holy Spirit. Contbr. articles to religious publs. Address: 613 Bellwood Dr Lexington NC 27292

PEALE, NORMAN VINCENT, clergyman; b. Bowersville, Ohio, May 31, 1898; s. Charles Clifford and Anna (DeLaney) P.; A.B., Ohio Wesleyan U., 1920, D.D., 1936; S.T.B., Boston U., 1924, A.M., 1924; D.D., Syracuse U., 1931, Duke, 1938, Central Coll., 1964; L.H.D., Lafayette Coll., 1952, U. Cin., 1968; LL.D., Wm. Jewell Coll., 1952, Hope Coll., 1962; Brigham Young U., 1967; S.T.D., Millikin U., 1958; Litt.D., Ia. Wesleyan U., 1958, Eastern Ky. State Coll., 1964, Jefferson Med. Coll., 1955; m. Ruth Stafford, June 20, 1930; children—Margaret (Mrs. Paul F. Everett), John, Elizabeth (Mrs. John M. Allen). Ordained to ministry M.E. Ch., 1922; pastor, Berkeley, R.I., 1922-24, Kings Hwy. Ch., Bklyn., 1924-27, Univ. Ch., Syracuse, N.Y., 1927-32, Marble Collegiate Ref. Ch., N.Y.C., 1932—; Weekly Sunday radio program WOR radio; editor Guideposts, an inspirational mag. Life trustee Ohio Wesleyan U., Central Coll. Mem. exec. com. Presbyn. Ministers Fund for Life Ins.; mem. Mid-Century White House Conf. on Children and Youth, Pres.'s Commn. for Observance 25th Anniversary UN; pres. Nat. Temperance Soc.; pres. Protestant Council City N.Y., 1965-69; pres. Ref. Church in Am., 1969-70; lectr. pub. affairs, personal effectiveness. Chaplain, Am. Legion, Kings County, N.Y., 1925-27. Recipient Freedom Found. award, 1952, 55, 59, 73, 74; Horatio Alger award, 1952; Am. Edn. award, 1955; Gov. Service award for Ohio, 1955; Nat. Salvation Army award, 1956; Distinguished Salesman's award N.Y. Sales Execs., 1957; Salvation Army award, 1957; Internat. Human Relations award Dale Carnegie Club Internat., 1958; Clergyman of Year award Religious Heritage Am., 1964; Paul Harris Fellow award Rotary Internat., 1972, Distinguished Patriot award S.A.R., 1973; Alderson-Broaddus Coll. Apollo award on Outstanding Couple in Ministry, 1982; Disting. Achievement award Ohio Wesleyan U., 1983, Ohio Sr. Citizen Hall of Fame award, 1983, Disting. award Lotos Club of N.Y., 1983, Religion in Media Gold Angel award, 1984, Presdl. Medal of Freedom, 1984, Bowery Savs. Bank 150th Ann. Disting. New Yorker award, 23rd St. Assn. of N.Y. Man of Yr., 1984, Caleb B. Smith Medal of Honor, Grand Lodge of Ind., 1984, Internat. Rotary award, 1984; Order of Aaron and Hur, Chaplains Corps U.S. Army, 1975. Mem. Am. Found. Religion and Psychiatry (pres.), Ohio Soc. N.Y. (pres. 1952-55), Episcopal Actors Guild, Am. Authors Guild, S.A.R., Alpha Delta, Phi Gamma Delta. Republican. Rotarian, Mason (33 deg., Shriner, K.T., past grand prelate). Clubs: Metropolitan, Union League, Lotos. Author: The Art of Living; You Can Win; A Guide to Confident Living, 1948; The Power of Positive Thinking, 1952; The Coming of the King, 1956; Stay Alive All Your Life, 1957; The Amazing Results of Positive Thinking, 1959; The Tough-Minded Optimist, 1962; Adventures in the Holy Land, 1963; Sin, Sex and Self-control, 1965; Jesus of Nazareth, 1966; The Healing of Sorrow, 1966;

Enthusiasm Makes the Difference, 1967; Bible Stories, 1973; You Can If You Think You Can, 1974. Co-author: Faith Is the Answer; Art of Real Happiness; chpt. in Am's. 12 Master Salesmen. TV program: What's Your Trouble; nationally syndicated weekly TV program Guideposts presents Norman Vincent Peale. Author newspaper column Positive Thinking appearing in many papers. Writer for various secular and religious periodicals. Tech. advisor representing Protestant Ch. in filming of motion picture One Foot in Heaven; motion picture One Man's Way, based on biography, 1963; (film) What It Takes To Be A Real Salesman. Office: 1025 Fifth Ave New York City NY 10028

PEALE, RUTH STAFFORD (MRS. NORMAN VINCENT PEALE), religious leader; b. Fonda, Iowa, Sept. 10, 1906; d. Frank Burton and Anna Loretta (Crosby) Stafford; A.B., Syracuse U., 1928, LL.D., 1953; Litt. D., Hope Coll., 1962; m. Norman Vincent Peale, June 20, 1930; children—Margaret Ann (Mrs. Paul F. Everett), John Stafford, Elizabeth Ruth (Mrs. John M. Allen). Tchr. math. Central High Sch., Syracuse, N.Y., 1928-31; nat. pres. women's bd. domestic missions Ref. Ch. Am., 1936-46; sec. Protestant Film Commn., 1946-51; chmn. Am. Mother's Com., 1948-49; appeared on Nat. TV program What's Your Trouble, 1952-68; appears on Nat. TV with husband, 1968—; pres., editor-in-chief, gen. sec. Found. for Christian Living, 1945—. Nat. pres. bd. domestic missions Ref. Ch. in Am., 1955-56, mem. bd. N. Am. Missions, 1963-69, pres., 1967-69; mem. gen. program council Ref. Ch. in Am., 1968—; mem. com. of 24 for merger Ref. Ch. in Am. and Presbyn. Ch. U.S., 1966-69; v.p. Protestant Council N.Y.C., 1964-66; hon. chancellor Webber Coll., 1972—. Trustee Hope Coll., Holland, Mich., Champlain Coll., Burlington, Vt., Stratford Coll., Danville, Va., Lenox Sch., N.Y.C., Interchurch Center Syracuse U., 1955-61; bd. dirs. Cook Christian Tng. Sch., Lord's Day Alliance U.S.; mem. bd. and exec. com. N.Y. Theol. Sem., N.Y.C.; sponsor Stanford Children's Convalescent Hosp., 1966—; bd. govs. Help Line Telephone Center, 1970—. Named New York State Mother of Yr., 1963; Distinguished Woman of Yr. Nat. Art Assn.; recipient Cum Laude award Syracuse U. Alumni Assn. N.Y., 1965; Honor Iowans' award Buena Vista Coll., 1966; Religious Heritage Am. Ch. Woman of Year, 1969, Am. Mother's Com. award religion, 1970, Horatio Alger award, 1977, Soc. Family of Man award, 1981. Mem. Insts. Religion and Health (bd. exec. com.), Am. Bible Soc. (bd.), Nat. Council Chs. (v.p. 1952-54, gen. bd.; treas. gen. dept. United Ch. Women, vice chmn. broadcasting and film commn., 1951-55; program chmn. gen. assembly 1966), N.Y. Fedn. of Women's Clubs (chmn. religion 1951-53, 57-58). Home Missions Council N.A. (nat. pres. 1942-44, nat. chmn. migrant com. 1948-51), P.E.O., Alpha Phi. Clubs: Sorosis (pres. 1953-56, hon. life pres. 1975—), Women's National Republican (N.Y.C.), Author: I Married A Minister, 1942; The Adventure of Being a Wife, 1971. Co-editor: Guidepost Mag., 1957—. Appears on nat. radio program with husband, 1968—; co-subject with husband film One Man's Way, 1963.

PEARL, WILLIAM ANSON, lay ch. worker, United Methodist Ch.; b. Benton, Ill., Sept. 13, 1901; s. William Alexander and Sarah Ann (Combs) P.; student Ewing (Ill.) Coll., 1917-19, Gregg Bus. Coll., Chgo., 1920; m. Opal Ona McCracken, Sept. 22, 1921; 1 dau., Peggy Jean (Mrs. John H. Hillman). Sec., Lafayette Park Meth. Ch. Sunday Sch., 1934-39, sch. supt., 1939-41, chmn. ofcl. bd., 1960-62; dist. counselor Meth. Youth Fellowship, 1941-42; writer, producer several ministrel shows, 1939-42, 51; asso. dist. lay leader St. Louis S. dist. Mo. E. Conf., 1961—; mem. adminstrv. bd., conf. rep. Shaw Ave. United Meth. Ch., St. Louis, 1969—; coordinator E. Mo. Conf. United Meth. Men for Nat. Conf. at Purdue U., 1969—; dist. dir. Meth. Men, 1969—; mem. adv. bd. Bishop's Crusade, 1974—. Sales rep. Dau Furniture Co., 1961-75; salesman Fair Mercantile Co., St. Louis, 1975—; mgr. Cokesbury Co. Book Store, Epworth Among the Hills. Mem. St. Louis Mission and Ch. Extension Soc., St. Louis Singspiration Soc. (gen. sec.). Author: History of Lafayette Park United Meth. Ch., 1964. Home: 4452 Shaw Ave St Louis MO 63110 Office: 5257 Shaw Ave St Louis MO 63110

PEARLSON, JORDAN, rabbi; b. Somerville, Mass., Sept. 2, 1924; s. Jacob and Freda (Spivak) P.; B.A. with honors in Econs., Northeastern U., 1948, J.D., 1950; B. Hebrew Letters (fellow), Hebrew Union Coll., 1954, M. Hebrew Letters, 1956; m. Geraldine S. Goldstein, Jan. 19, 1958; children—Joshua Seth, Nessa Yocheved, Abigail Sara. Ordained rabbi, 1956; mem. faculty grad. programme for Jewish religious educators Hebrew Union Coll., Cin., 1955-56. Chmn. nat. religious adv. com. Canadian Broadcasting Corp., 1974-75; nat. chmn. joint pub. relations com. Canadian Jewish Congress, 1974, mem. nat. exec., 1974—, mem. nat. bd. Can.-Israel com., 1974—; mem. exec. com. bd. govs. Hebrew Union Coll.; Canadian sr. del. Internat. Commn. on Interreligious Consultation, Geneva, 1973, London, 1975. Bd. dirs. Canadian Friends of Ben Gurion U. Mem. Hebrew Union Coll. Rabbinic Alumni Assn. (pres. 1976-77), Central Conf. Am. Rabbis (fin. sec. 1976-79). Contbr. articles to religious publs. Home: 2 Carnwath Crescent Willowdale ON Canada Office: 210 Wilson Ave Toronto ON M5M 3B1 Canada

PEARSON, CHARLES WARREN, minister of music, Southern Baptist Convention; b. Winston-Salem, N.C., June 5, 1952; s. Charles Warren Pearson and Florence Willis (Mitchell) Faulk; m. Patricia Susan Ipock, July 26, 1975; children: Aaron Benjamin, Courtney Rhea. B. Music Edn., Mars Hill Coll., 1974; Mus. M., Southwestern Bapt. Theol. Sem., 1977. Ordained to ministry Bapt. Ch., 1976. Minister music, First Bapt. Ch., Saluda, N.C., 1972-74; minister music and edn. Highland Bapt. Ch., Denton, Tex., 1974-77; minister music and youth Taylor Meml. Bapt., Hobbs, N.Mex., 1977—; trustee Southeastern Theol. Sem., Wake Forest, N.C., 1981—; bd. dirs. N.Mex. Singing Churchmen, 1985-86. Bd. dirs. Hobbs Community Concert Series, 1981. Mem. Am. Choral Dirs. Assn., Am. Guild English Handbell Ringers, Southeastern Bapt. Assn. (associational music dir. 1977—). Republican. Home: 1026 Nambe Hobbs NM 88240 Office: Taylor Meml Bapt Ch 1700 Yeso Hobbs NM 88240

PEARSON, HENNING BERNHARD, minister, Lutheran Ch. Am.; b. Bklyn., May 5, 1906; s. Bernhard Arald and Jennie (Stormbom) P.; B.A., Upsala Coll., 1932; postgrad. Moody Bible Inst./Cleve. Bible Inst., 1938, U. Nebr., U. N.D.; M.Div., Luth. Theol. Sem., Chgo., 1943; m. Blanche Irene Galloway, July 10, 1943; 1 dau., Ann Kristine. Ordained to ministry, 1943; pastor Acacia Park Luth. Ch., Chgo., 1943-44, Christ Luth. Ch., Wisner, Nebr., 1944-48; teaching chaplain Augustana Acad., Canton, S.D., 1948-52; pres., prin., teaching chaplain Dakota Luth. High Sch., Minot, N.D., 1952-54; teaching chaplain Luther Coll., Wahoo, Nebr., 1954-58; pastor Grace Luth. Ch., Ohiowa, N.B., 1954-58; chaplain Ilboru Luth. Secondary Sch., Arusha, Tanzania, 1958-71; pastor Cripple Creek Luth. Parish, Wythe County, Va., 1972—. Home and office: 140 E Ridge Rd Wytheville VA 24382

PECHILLO, JEROME ARTHUR See *Who's Who in America*, 43rd edition.

PECK, GEORGE WILLIS, educator, minister, Am. Bapt. Chs. in U.S.A.; b. Ipswich, Australia, Mar. 4, 1931; s. Albert Edward and Mildred Jackson (Ingram) P.; Dipl., Queensland Bapt. Coll., 1953; B.A. with honors U. Queensland, 1956, M.A., 1959; B.D. with honors Melbourne Coll. Div., 1961; B.D., U. London, 1959; student Harvard Div. Sch., 1963-66; m. Florence Mary Walton, Dec. 5, 1953; children—Susanne Mary, Kathryn Joy, Jennifer Ruth, Lynette Margaret. Ordained to ministry Queensland Baptist Union, 1954; pastor Albion Bapt. Ch., Brisbane, Australia, 1956-58; registrar, prof. Eastern Theol. Coll., Jorhat, Assam, India, 1958-62, prin., 1962-63; prof., dean Andover Newton Theol. Sch., Newton Centre, Mass., 1966-83, pres., 1983—. Mem. Bd. Internat. Ministries, Am. Bapt. Chs. in U.S.A., 1966-75. Bd. dirs. Fund for Theol. Edn. in S.E. Asia, Boston Theol. Inst. Mem. Mind Assn., Internat. Soc. Neoplatonic Studies, Mediaeval Acad. Am., Phi Beta Kappa. Home: 125 Herrick Circle Newton Centre MA 02159 Office: 210 Herrick Rd Newton Centre MA 02159

PECK, JAMES HAMPTON, lay church worker, United Methodist Church; b. Springfield, Tenn., Oct. 12, 1914; s. Robert Lee and Bettie (Brown) P.; B.A., Vanderbilt U., 1937, LL.B., 1939, J.D., 1969; m. Ann Knight Seay, Nov. 7, 1943; children: Ann, Mary, Robert, Nancy, Bettie. Mem. ofcl. bd. Springfield Meth. Ch., 1939-42; mem. ofcl. bd. Coral Gables (Fla.) First Meth. Ch., 1949—, chmn., 1960, lay leader, 1971-72, pres. Men's Club, 1951, trustee, 1975—, chmn. bd. trustees, 1983-85; pres. Miami Dist. Bd. Ch. Extension Meth. Ch., 1968-74; mem. legal adv. council Fla. Ann. Conf. United Meth. Ch., 1972-85. Ptnr. law firm Peck & Peck Coral Gables, 1947—. Pres., Coral Gables War Meml. Youth Center Assn., 1968-69, dir., 1957-85; mem. U. Miami Endowment Com., 1968-85. Mem. Fla., Dade County (dir. 1959-60) bar assns., Sigma Chi, Phi Delta Phi. Home: 2604 N Greenway Dr Coral Gables FL 33134 Office: 475 Biltmore Way Coral Gables FL 33134

PEDNEAULT, ROCH, évêque auxiliaire, prêtre, Clergé de Chicoutimi; b. Alam, Lac-St. Jean, Qué., Can., Apr. 10, 1927; s. Léonard Pedneault and Marie-Ange Tapin. Secondaires, Petit Séminaire, Chicoutimi, Que., Can., 1949, Collégiales, 1953; universitaires théologie Faculté de Théologie, U. Laval, Qué., Can., 1953, universitaires théologie Faculté des Sciences, 1959. Vicar, St.-Laurent de Jonqière, 1953; prof. Séminaire, Chicoutimi, 1953-60, rector Séminaire, 1967-74, évêque auxiliare, 1974—; mem. Comité du Laicat l'Assemblée des Évêques du Qué., Comité dé Diffusion des Célébrations Liturgiques, Comité Mixte Assemblée des évêques du Qué. et de la Conférence Religeuse Catholique de Qué.; secrétaire l'Inter-Québec. Address: 602 Est Rue Racine C P 278 Chicoutimi PQ G7H 5C3 Canada

PEDRONE, DINO JONATHAN, minister, Ind. Baptist Ch.; b. Binghamton, N.Y., Feb. 26, 1945; s. Fred and Bertha Olive (Lowe) P.; diploma Practical Bible Tng. Sch., Binghamton, N.Y., 1967; B.Th., Evang. Bible Coll., Denver, 1971; Th.D., Clarksville Sch. Theology, 1975; student Bob Jones U., Greenville, S.C., 1969-70; m. Roberta Dee, July 22, 1967; 1 dau., JoAnna Ruth. Ordained to ministry, 1970; dir. Christian edn. Grace Bapt. Ch., Binghamton, 1964-67; minister Open Door Ch., Chambersburg, Pa., 1970—. Pres., Cumberland Valley Christian Schs.; dir. evangelistic ministries, Chambersburg; bd. dirs. Trinity Bapt. Coll., Jacksonville, Fla. Mem. exec. bd. Citizens for Decency Through Law, Franklin County, Pa., 1974—. Recipient award Christian Life mag. for Pa.'s fastest growing Sunday Sch., 1974-75, Community Leaders and Noteworthy Americans award, 1976. Author: Why Do the Godly Suffer, 1971. Home: 435 Ohio Ave Chambersburg PA 17201 Office: 600 Miller St Chambersburg PA 17201

PEEHLMANN, WALDEMAR CARL, minister, American Lutheran Church; b. Tripoli, Iowa, Dec. 22, 1907; s. Henry Carl and Louise (Riehl) P.; m. Atemsa Rosemarie Menn, June 3, 1936; children: Waldemar Carl, Rosemarie, David John, Mark Everett, Luther Dale. Student, Tex. Luth. Coll., 1927-30, Wartburg Sem., 1930-34, Am. Sch. Law, Chgo., 1935-38. Ordained to ministry American Lutheran Church, 1934. Intern, St. John's Luth. Ch., Eau Clair, Wis., 1933, pastor, Fredericksburg, Tex., 1934-41, St. Pauls Luth. Ch., Cave Creek, Tex., 1934-41, St. Matthew Luth. Ch., Sabdy Hill, Brenham, Tex., 1941-47, Salem, Tex., 1947-53, Trinity Luth. Ch., Kingsville, Tex., 1953-62, Christ Luth. Ch., Elm Creek, La Vernia, Tex., 1962-67, Luth. Emmanuel Luth. Ch. Greenville, Burton, Tex., 1967-84 leader young people Luther League, 1942-46; mem. stewardship com. Tex. dist. Am. Luth. Ch., 1948-61; chmn. Ministerial Assn., Kingsville, 1954-56; student pastor Luth. Students Assn., Tex. Agrl. and Indsl. Coll., Kingsville, 1953-62, Naval Aux. Air Sta., Kingsville, 1953-62. Editor The Kirchenblatt, 1934-41. Chmn. membership Sam Houston council Boy Scouts Am., 1941-51; chmn. local USO, Kingsville, 1957-60. Recipient Silver Beaver award Boy Scouts Am., 1948. Home and Office: Emmanuel Luth Ch Rural Route 2 Box 40 Burton TX 77835

PEEL, MALCOLM LEE, educator, minister, United Presbyterian Church U.S.A. b. Jeffersonville, Ind., June 12, 1936; s. Frank Peyton and Ella (Ditsler) P.; m. Ruth Ann Nash, June 18, 1960; children: Noel Carol, Drew George. B.A. Ind. U., 1957; M.Div., Louisville Presbyn. Sem., 1960; M.A., Yale U., 1962, Ph.D., 1966; postgradn. Rijksuniversitaet Urecht-Netherlands, 1963, 81. Ordained to ministry, 1960. Asst. instr. Yale Div. Sch., New Haven, 1960-62; asst. prof. Lycoming Coll., Williamsport, Pa., 1965-69; asst. to full prof. religious studies Coe Coll., Cedar Rapids, Iowa, 1969-81, prof. religious studies, 1983—; exec. dir. Hoover Endowment/Presdl. Library, W. Branch, Iowa, 1981-83; task force ch. and higher edn. Presbyn. Ch., N.Y.C., 1979-81; author, tchr. 1st Synod of Lakes and Prairies Presbyn. Ch. closed circuit TV adult edn. series on N.T., Mpls., 1984—; resource leader Nat. Mariners Family Camps, N.H., 1981, N.Mex., 1985. Editor: Yale Gnosticism Seminar, 1964. Author: Epistle to Rheginos, 1969; Gnosis and Auferstehung, 1974; transl.: Teachings of Silvanus (Nag Hammadi), 1977. Contbr. over 40 articles and revs. to profl. jours. Acad. advisor Cedar Rapids community Sch. Dist., 1979-84; del. Republican State conv., 1980; advancement chmn. Hawkeye Area council Boy Scouts Am., Cedar Rapids, 1980-84; exec. dir. Religion and Pub. Schs. of Iowa study, NEH, 1978-79. Guggenheim fellow, 1971-72; Fulbright travel grantee, Netherlands, 1972; Mellon-U. House fellowship U. Iowa, 1981; Presbyn. Grad. fellow Yale U., 1962-65. Mem. Am. Acad. Religion, Soc. Bibl. Lit. (sect. chmn. 1974-78), Inst. for Antiquity and Christianity (research assoc.). Home: 3918 Wenig Rd NE Cedar Rapids IA 52402 Office: Coe Coll Dept Philosophy and Religion Cedar Rapids IA 52402

PEERS, MICHAEL GEOFFREY, archbishop, Anglican Church of Canada; b. Vancouver, B.C., Can., July 31, 1934; s. Geoffrey Hugh and Dorothy Enid (Mantle) P.; m. Dorothy Elizabeth Bradley, June 29, 1963; children: Valerie, Richard, Geoffrey. B.A. with honors, U. B.C., Vancouver, 1956; zert. dolm. U. Heidelberg, Fed. Republic of Germany, 1955; L.Th. Trinity Coll., Toronto, Ont., Can., 1959, D.D. (hon.), 1978; D.D. (hon.), St. John's Coll., Winnipeg, Man., Canada, 1980. Ordained deacon Anglican Ch. Canada, 1959, ordained priest, 1960, consecrated bishop, 1977. Parish priest Diocese Ottawa, Ont., 1959-66, Diocese of Rubert's Landing, Winnipeg, 1966-74; dean Diocese of Qu'Appelle, Regina, Sask., Can., 1974-77, bishop, 1977—, archbishop, 1982—; mem. Anglican Consultative Council, London, 1973-77; del. VI Assembly World Council Chs., Vancouver, 1983. Club: Royal United Services Inst. (chaplain 1982) (Regina). Office: Diocese of Qu-Appelle 1501 College Ave Regina SK S4P 1B8 Canada

PEERY, ED HALEY, JR., minister, So. Baptist Conv.; b. French, N. Mex., Feb. 8, 1938; s. Ed Haley and Velna (Bell) P.; B.A., Calif. Bapt. Coll., 1962; B.D., Golden Gate Bapt. Theol. Sem., 1965; Ph.D., Calif. Grad. Sch. Theology, 1972; m. Mary Alice Walker, Dec. 18, 1965; children—David Walker, Suzanne Marie. Ordained to ministry, 1962; pastor 1st Bapt. Ch., Toulumne, Calif., 1962-63, 1st. So. Bapt. Ch., Monrovia, Calif., 1964-67; asso. pastor 1st So. Bapt. Ch., Whittier, Calif., 1967-68;

pastor 1st Bapt. Ch., Santa Fe Springs, Calif., 1968-69, 1st Bapt. Ch. Walnut Valley, Walnut, Calif., 1969—. Pres., Ministerial Alliance Calif. Bapt. Coll., 1959-60; v.p. Bapt. Student Union Calif., 1960-61; chmn. Here's Life of Greater Los Angeles. Mem. So. Bapt. Conv. Calif., Alumni Assn. Calif. Bapt. Coll., Alumni Assn. Golden Gate Sem., Alumni Assn. Calif. Grad. Sch. Theology. Home: 20152 E Evening Breeze Dr Walnut CA 91789 Office: 20425 E La Puente Rd Walnut CA 91789

PEEVER, JOHNSTON BAIN, priest, Anglican Church of Canada; b. Kirkland Lake, Ont., Can., Jan. 28, 1937; s. Johnston and Olga (Parcher) P.; m. Clara Dale Clermont, Oct. 10, 1959; children: Stephen Bruce, Allan Bain. B.A., Sir. George William Coll., 1961; M.Div., McGill U., 1963; M.Div., Montreal Diocesan Coll., 1963. Ordained to deacon Anglican Ch., 1962, priest, 1963. Incumbent Parish of Mindemoya, Ont., 1963-66; asst. curate St. Luke's Cathedral, Sault St. Marie, Ont., 1966-69; dir. leadership tng. Diocese of Nfld., St. John's, Can., 1969-72; dir. program Diocese of Ont., Kingston, 1972-77; rector Trinity Ch., Cornwall, Ont., 1977—. Home: 101 2d St W Cornwall ON K6J 1G4 Canada Office: 105 2d St W Cornwall ON K6J 1G4 Canada

PEINE, LESLIE ALLEN, U.S. Air Force chaplain, United Methodist Church; b. Painesville, Ohio, May 19, 1945; s. Lester A. and Thelma Fay (Collins) P.; m. Beryl Anne Berger, Mar. 30, 1968; children: Mark Allen, Susan Elizabeth, Sarah Rebecca. B.A., Mt. Union Coll., 1967; M.Div., Meth. Theol. Sch., 1975. Ordained to ministry United Methodist Ch., 1973. Pastor Harmony and Chesterville United Meth. Ch., Ohio, 1973-75; assoc. pastor Grace United Meth. Ch., Coshocton, Ohio, 1975-77; commd. capt. U.S. Air Force, 1977, advanced through grades to maj., 1983; air force chaplain Laughlin AFB, Del Rio, Tex., 1977-79; installation staff chaplain Kalkar AF Sta., Germany, 1979-82; Protestant chaplain Seymour Johnson AFB, Goldsboro, N.C., 1982-84; asst. installation staff chaplain Brooks AFB, San Antonio, 1984—. Pres. Coshocton County Resdl. Home, Ohio, 1976-77. Am. Bible Soc. scholar 1975. Mem. Mil. Chaplains Assn., Air Force Assn. Democrat. Club: San Antonio Radio. Avocations: amateur radio; stamp collecting; music; golf; tennis. Home: 125 Vinsant St San Antonio TX 78235 Office: 6570th Air Base Group/HC Brooks Air Force Base TX 78235-5000

PEITZMAN, LLOYD JOHN, educator, lay ch. worker, United Presbyterian in U.S.A.; b. Des Moines, Feb. 18, 1937; s. Earl Lee and Laura Ann (Rittgers) P.; B.A., Macalester Coll., St. Paul, 1958; postgrad. United Theol. Sem., N.Y.C., 1963, United Theol. Sem., Mpls.-St. Paul, 1965-66; m. Carol Elizabeth Holmquist, Mar. 29, 1958; children—Linda Ruth, Robert John, James Lloyd, John Richard. Mem. edn. com. Minn. Presbyn. Synod, 1969-71; bd. dirs. Greater Mpls. Council Chs., 1967-70, chmn. dept. Christian Edn., 1967-70; chmn. div. edn. Twin Cities Met. Ch. Commn., 1970-72, bd. dirs. commn., 1970-72; chmn. TV task force Presbytery Twin Cities, 1974—; N. Central rep. nat. central com., also nat. gov. cabinet Assn. Presbyn. Ch. Educators, 1967-76, nat. pres., 1972-76; sec. spl. com. compensation Gen. Assembly United Presbyn. Ch. U.S.A., 1974-76; dir. edn., exec. dir. ministries Westminster Presbyn. Ch., Mpls., 1962—; co-founder, dir. Sunshare; nat. leader Nat. Tchr. Edn. Project. Co-chmn. Minn. Teaching Skills Blocks, Mpls., 1972—; bd. dirs. Minn. Coalition Tchr. Edn., 1972—; bd. dirs., exec. com. Center and Network for Ch. Educators, 1977—, mem. Ch. Tchrs. Nat. Advisory Bd. Mem. Protestant Com. Scouting, 1973-66; chmn. God and country rev. bd. Boy Scouts Am., 1964-67; mem. Loring-Nicollet Community Council; alumni bd. dirs. Macalester Coll. Recipient Outstanding Citizen award Iowa Bar Assn., 1954; N. Central Publishing award 1957. Mem. Assn. Presbyn. Ch. Educators (pres. 1972-76), Religious Edn. Assn., Assn. Childhood Edn. Internat., Minn. Video-Media Soc., Mpls. Ministerial Assn., Nat. Ch. Tchr. Assn., Mpls. YMCA. Club: Minn. Press (charter). Author articles. Home: 6421 Upton Ave S Minneapolis MN 55423 Office: 83 S 12th St Minneapolis MN 55403

PEKENHAM, DANIEL J., clergyman, seminary administrator, Roman Catholic. Rector St. Francis Sem., Sch. Pastoral Ministry, Milw. Office: St Francis Sem Sch Pastoral Ministry 3257 S Lake Dr Milwaukee WI 53207*

PELHAM, JAMES EARL, minister, Southern Baptist Convention; b. Slocomb, Ala., Nov. 7, 1926; s. John Edd and Bertha Irene (Griffin) P.; B.A., Stetson U., 1950; M.R.E., New Orleans Bapt. Theol. Sem., 1954; m. Mary Elanor Lavender, Dec. 25, 1948 (dec.); children—James Edward, Susan Pelham Burcham; m. Myrtice Taylor, June 27, 1980. Ordained minister So. Baptist Conv., 1951. Minister edn. First Bapt. Ch. Sweetwater, Tenn., 1954-55, Park St. Bapt. Ch., Columbia, S.C., 1955-59, Allen St. Bapt. Ch., Charlotte, N.C., 1959-60, Riverside Bapt. Ch., Tampa, Fla., 1960-62, Arlington Bapt. Ch., Jacksonville, Fla., 1963-67; minister edn., asso. pastor Byne Meml. Bapt. Ch., Albany, Ga., 1967-70; dir. associational missions Mallary Bapt. Assn., Albany, 1970—. Mem. So. Bapt. Assn. Dirs. of Missions, Dougherty Ministerial Fellowship. Home: 202 Thornton Dr Albany GA 31705 Office: 200 Thornton Dr Albany GA 31705

PELKONEN, J(OHN) PETER, minister, Lutheran Church in America. b. Boston, May 28, 1937; s. Frank Alexander and Effie Lydia (Mattson) P.; m. Nancy Lee Sprinkle, June 28, 1964. B.A., Wittenberg Univ., 1958; M.Div., Hamma Sch. Theology, 1961; Ph.D. in Religion, Duke Univ., 1972. Ordained to ministry Luth. Ch. Am., 1962. Pastor, Holy Trinity Luth. Ch., Fort Walton Beach, Fla., 1962-65; prof. church history Hamma Sch. Theology, Springfield, Ohio, 1968-70; pastor First Luth. Ch., Beach City, Ohio, 1970-74; sr. pastor Faith Luth. Ch., Akron, Ohio, 1974-81; pastor St. John's Luth. Ch., Dayton, Ohio, 1981—; dir. Trinity Luth. Sem., 1978—, Hamma Sch. Theology, 1972-78; chmn. Ohio Synod Profl. Leadership Com., 1974-78; pres. Luth. Council Greater Akron, Ohio, 1976-78. Contbr. sermons to Clergy Jour., 1979—; contbr. to other profl. jours.; translator: Practical Theology, 1962. Luth. World Fedn. Exchange Scholar (Finland), 1961-62; Duke Univ. scholar, 1965-67; G.H. Kearns fellow, 1967. Home: 3207 Allendale Dr Dayton OH 45409 Office: St John's Lutheran Ch 141 S Ludlow St Dayton OH 45402

PELLICANE, MARY M., nun, Roman Catholic Ch.; b. Bklyn., Jan. 11, 1922; d. Joseph and Cathrine Cecilia (Cuccia) P. B.A., Queens Coll., 1943; postgrad. study Rome. Joined Congregation Our Lady of Retreat in the Cenacle, Roman Cath. Ch., 1946. Spiritual dir. Cenacle Retreat House, Boston, N.Y.C., N.Z., L.I., N.Y., 1948-77, dir. Rochester, N.Y., Pitts., Charleston, W. Va., 1977—. Contbr. articles to profl. jours. Home and Office: Cenacle Retreat House 1114 Virginia St Charleston VA 25301

PELOTTE, DONALD EDMOND, clergyman, provincial superior; b. Waterville, Maine, Apr. 13, 1945; s. Norris Albert and Margaret Yvonne (LaBrie) P. A.A., Eymard Coll., Hyde Park, N.Y., 1965; B.A., John Carroll U., 1969; M.A., Fordham U., 1971, Ph.D., 1975. Ordained priest Roman Catholic Ch., 1972. Provincial superior Blessed Sacrament, Cleve., 1978-81, 81—; nat. bd. dirs. Major Superiors of Men, Silver Springs, Md., 1981—, Tekakwitha Conf., Great Falls, Mont., 1981—. Author: John Courtney Murray: Theologian in Conflict, 1976. Mem. Cath. Theol. Soc. Am., Am. Cath. Hist. Soc., Tekakwitha Nat. Conf., Conf. of Maj. Superior of Men Religious. Home and Office: Congregation of the Blessed Sacrament 5384 Wilson Mills Rd Cleveland OH 44143

PENA, RAYMOND JOSEPH, priest, Roman Cath. Ch.; b. Corpus Christi, Tex., Feb. 19, 1934; s. Cosme A. and Elisa (Ramon) P.; student St. John's Sem., San Antonio, 1950-52, Assumption Sem., San Antonio, 1952-57. Ordained priest Roman Catholic Ch., 1957; asst. pastor Tex. chs., 1957-67; diocesan youth dir. Diocese of Corpus Christi, 1967-70; pastor Our Lady of Guadalupe Ch., Corpus Christi, 1969-78; aux. bishop of San Antonio, 1976-80; bishop of El Paso, 1980—. Editor Tex. Gulf Coast Cath., 1970-75; consultor Diocese of Corpus Christi, 1968—, dir. Commn. Mexican-Am. affairs, 1971—; mem. Diocesan Liturgical Commn., 1974—; bd. dirs. Region 10 Office of Hispanic Affairs, San Antonio, 1979-81; chmn. bd. dirs. Mexican-Am. Cultural Ctr., San Antonio, 1984—. Founder, pres. Mathis Community Action Agy., 1964-66; v.p. Nueces County Child Welfare Bd., 1968-70; dir. Corpus Christi Econ. Devel. Corp., 1970-75, Goals for Corpus Christi, 1974-75; mem. nat. com. Campaign for Human Devel., 1974-77. Bd. dirs. S.W. Regional Office for Spanish Speaking, 1974—. Mem. Padres. Office: 499 St Mathew El Paso TX 79907

PENFIELD, CAROLE HARVEY, minister, American Baptist Churches in the U.S.A., instructor; b. Elmira, N.Y., Mar. 9, 1943; d. Cyril A. and Pauline (Nichols) Harvey; m. Gary M. Penfield, June 6, 1963; children: Nicole, Todd, Jason, Matthew, Ethan. B.A., SUNY-Albany, 1965; M.Ed., U. Cin., 1976; M.Div., Andover Newton Theol. Sem., 1981. Ordained to ministry American Baptist Churches in the U.S.A., 1981. Student minister Central Bapt. Ch., Providence, 1979-80; chaplain Bryant Coll., Smithfield, R.I., 1981—; assoc. pastor Central Bapt. Ch., Providence, 1981—; instr. Bryant Coll., 1981—; mem. Missions Commn., com. on ministry, bd. mgrs., Am. Bapt. Chs. R.I., 1983—; mem. exec. com. Eastern Commn. on Ministry Am. Bapt. Chs. U.S.A., 1984—; mem. Div. Ministries in Higher Edn., R.I., 1981—; senator Nat. Ministers Council, R.I., 1984—. Recipient Promise in Preaching and Pastoral Ministry award Andover Newton Theol. Sch., 1981. Mem. Am. Bapt. Ministers of R.I. (pres. 1983—). Home: 5 Juniper Ln Greenville RI 02828 Office: Central Bapt Ch 372 Wayland Ave Providence RI 02906

PENNEY, ALPHONSUS L., bishop, Roman Cath. Ch.; b. St. John's, Nfld., Can., Sept. 27, 1924. Ordained priest, 1949; bishop of Grand Falls (Nfld.), 1973—. Office: 8A Church Rd Grand Falls NF A2A 2J8 Canada*

PENROD, EDGAR ALAN, minister, marriage and family counselor; b. Zanesville, Ohio, June 5, 1947; s. Chester Carl and Lorene Clara (Ballis) P.; B.A. in Speech, Asbury Coll., Wilmore, Ky., 1969; M.Div., Meth. Theol. Sch., Delaware, Ohio, 1975, M.A. in Clin. Counseling, 1975; m. Deborah Anne Shaw, June 17, 1972. Ordained to ministry, 1975; chaplain intern Columbus (Ohio) State Hosp., 1974; asso. minister Immanuel United Meth. Ch., Logan, Ohio, 1972-74; family counselor Drug Abuse Bd., Lancaster, Ohio, 1975; minister Fairfield Community Ch., Lancaster, 1976—; counselor Pastoral Counseling Services, Columbus, 1975—; dir., founder Fairfield Community Counseling Services, Lancaster. Mem. Fairfield County Ministerial Assn., Am. Assn. Pastoral Clin. Educators. Home: 2154 Midway Blvd Lancaster OH 43130 Office: 860 E Mulberry St Lancaster OH 43130

PENT, BENJAMIN ARNOLD, minister, Evang. Free Ch. Am.; b. Pucalpa, Peru, Apr. 24, 1935; s. Philip Horter and Rose Christina (Bechtold) P.; B.A., Trinity Coll., Chgo., 1961; M.A., Denver Bapt. Theol. Sem., 1976; m. Virginia Lois Bennett, June 21, 1958; children—Mark Alan, Michael Andrew, Karen Sue, Connie Lynn, Kevin Scott, Katy Ranee. Ordained to ministry, 1957; pastor Bethel Evang. Free Ch., Washington Island, Wis., 1961-67, Itasca (Ill.) Evang. Free Ch., 1967-69, Calvary Evang. Free Ch., Broomfield, Colo., 1969-77; pastor Watertown Evang. Free Ch., Minn., 1977-84, Faith Evang. Free Ch., Redding, Calif., 1984—. Recipient Valley Forge award Freedom Found. Contbr. articles to religious jours. Home: 8884 Olney Park Dr Redding CA 96001 Office: 8790 Swasey Dr Redding CA 96001

PENTON, ROBERT DUDLEY, minister, So. Baptist Conv.; b. Bogalusa, La., Feb. 25, 1931; s. Alvin W. and Lena Mae (Townsand) P.; M.Ch.Music, New Orleans Bapt. Theol. Sem., 1967; m. Dorothy Ann Sperry, June 1, 1949; children—James, Robert, Steven, Alice. Ordained to ministry, 1975; minister music and youth Calvary Bapt. Ch., Columbus, Ga., 1967-69; minister edn. and youth Hilton Terr. Bapt. Ch., Columbus, 1969-72; asso. pastor Holloway St. Bapt. Ch., Durham, N.C., 1972-74, Merrimon Ave. Bapt. Ch., Asheville, N.C., 1974—. Home: 55 Waters Rd Asheville NC 28805 Office: 283 Merrimon Ave Asheville NC 28801

PENVOSE, LEE D., minister, Lutheran Church in America; b. Washington, Pa., Aug. 10, 1952; s. Clarence L. and Jean Marie (Weaver) P.; m. Marilyn Joyce Foringer, Aug. 19, 1972; children: Bryan, Kevan, Lisa. B.A., Washington & Jefferson Coll., 1974; M.Div., Luth. Theol. Sem., 1978. Ordained to ministry Lutheran Ch. in Am., 1978. Pastor West Sunbury Luth. Ch., Pa., 1978-80, St. Mark's Luth. Ch., New Stanton, Pa., 1980—; chmn. Com. Parish Life and Ministry Devel., W. Pa. and W.Va. Synod, 1980; sec. Com. on Congregational Support, 1981—. Contbr. articles to profl. jours. Mem. Phi Beta Kappa, Phi Sigma Tau. Democrat. Lodge: Kiwanis. Office: St Mark's Evang Luth Ch PO Box 236 New Stanton PA 15672

PEOPLES, THOMAS HOWARD, JR., minister, Progressive Nat. Bapt. Conv.; b. Lexington, Ky., June 17, 1939; s. Thomas Howard and Bettie (Davis) P.; B.Th., Simmons U., 1963; student U. Ky., 1964-66; M.Div., Lexington Theol. Sem., 1972; m. Delma Louise Bennett, June 2, 1963; children—Thomas Howard, Stewart Titus, Samuel Underwood, David Rodmann and Bettina Louise (twins). Licensed minister, Progressive Nat. Baptist Conv., Inc., 1955; ordained to ministry, 1963; pastor First Ch., Bracktown, Ky., 1963-73, First Bapt. Ch., Versailles, Ky., 1973—. Mem. Lexington Ministers and Deacons Meeting, 1955—, Sunday sch. lectr., 1973—; Bible instr. Simmons Bible Coll. Ext. Sch., 1971—; 2d v.p. Howard's Creek dist. Convention, 1970-76; 2d v.p. Bapt. Unified Christian Leadership Conf., 1972-74, 1st. v.p., 1974—. Pres. Lexington br. N.A.A.C.P., 1965-68, v.p. State br., 1966-67. Named Ky. Col., 1974. Mem. Woodford County Jr. C. of C. (chaplain 1974). Home: 115 Roan Rd Versailles KY 40383 Office: 233 S Main St Versailles KY 40383

PEREBOOM, JAN DIRK, minister, Christian Reformed Church in North America; b. Ede, Gelderland, Netherlands, Apr. 28, 1925; came to Can., 1961; s. Derk and Martha Lucia (Poppinga) P.; m. Maria Elisabeth Van Apeldoorn, Apr. 23, 1955; children: Elisabeth, Derk, Jan Pieter, Bert, Maarten, Jodie. Cand. Theol. Free U. Amsterdam, 1954. Ordained to ministry, 1955. Minister, Christian Ref. Ch., Williamsburg, Ont., 1969, Edmonton, Alta., 1969-79, Pembroke, Ont., 1979-82, Niagara Falls, Ont., 1982—. Served to maj. Netherlands Air Force, 1957-58. Home: 4880 Jepson St Niagara Falls ON L2E 1K1 Canada

PERICH, JOHN J., priest, Orthodox Church in America, Russian art consultant/lecturer; b. Yonkers, N.Y., Nov. 10, 1952; s. John T. and Sonya J. (Pishtey) P.; m. Eugenia E. Pianovich, Aug. 31, 1980; 1 child, Taisia J. B.A. in History, U. Bridgeport, 1975, M.A. in Eastern European Studies, 1975; M.Div., St. Tikhon's Theol. Sem., 1979. Ordained deacon Orthodox Church in America, 1980, priest, 1980. Prof. patristics and history St. Herman's Theol. Sem., Kodiak, Alaska,

1979-80; rector Holy Ghost Ch., Bridgeport, Conn., 1980—; adminstr. St. Nicholas Ch., Stratford, Conn., 1984—; sec.-treas. Conn. Deanery, 1984—; spiritual advisor Bridgeport Orthodox Women's Council, 1981—, Atlantic Dist. Federated Russian and Orthodox Clubs, 1981—. Appraiser-cons. Russian iconic and pre-revolutionary art, N.Y.C., 1979—. Author: From Vladimir to Autocephaly, 1979; Eklutna - A Study of a Athabascan Village, 1980. Recipient Cross of St. Herman, Diocese of Alaska, 1982, Epignation, Orthodox Ch. in Am., N.Y.C., 1982, Patriarchal award Russian Orthodox Ch., USSR, 1983. Mem. St. Vladimir's Theol. Found., St. Tikhon's Sem. Alumni Assn. (v.p. 1983—), Bridgeport Orthodox Clergy Assn. (pres. 1983—), Dobro Slovo (pres.). Home: 1520 E Main St Bridgeport CT 06608 Office: Holy Ghost Ch 1510 E Main St Bridgeport CT 06608

PERKIN, JAMES RUSSELL CONWAY, minister, educator, Baptist Church; b. Northamptonshire, Eng., Aug. 19, 1928; s. William and Lily Maude (Drage) P.; B.A., U. Oxford, 1952, M.A., 1955, D. Phil., 1955; came to Can., 1965; m. Dorothy Joan Louise Bentley, Apr. 7, 1953; children—James Russell, John Conway, Anne Louise. Ordained to ministry, 1956; minister Altrincham Bapt. Ch., Cheshire, Eng., 1956-62; lectr. N.T. Greek, U. Edinburgh (Scotland), 1963-65; asso. prof. N.T. interpretation McMaster Div. Coll., Hamilton, Ont., Can., 1965-69; prof. religious studies, also head dept., Acadia U., Wolfville, N.S., Can., 1969—, dean Faculty of Arts, 1977-80, v.p. academic, 1980-82, pres., vice chancellor, 1982—. Chmn. Wolfville Schs. Adv. Com., 1971-73. Mem. Soc. N.T. Studies, Can. Soc. Study Religion, Can. Liturgical Soc. Author: Study Notes on Romans, 1957; Handbook for Biblical Studies, 1973; Chaplain Extraordinary, 1975; Undoing of Babel, 1975; In Season, 1978; With Mind and Heart, 1979; Seedtime and Harvest, 1982; Arrows in the Mind, 1984; contbr. articles to religious publs. Home: PO Box 355 Wolfville NS B0P 1X0 Canada Office: Acadia U Wolfville NS B0P 1X0 Canada

PERKINS, DAVID WILLIAM, religious educator, Southern Baptist Convention; b. Oakdale, La., Sept. 16, 1944; s. William and Ruth Catherine (Carter) P.; m. Nancy Lee Pruett, Oct. 1, 1965; children: Benjamin David, Leigh Katherine. B.S., N.E. Louisiana U., 1967; Th.M., New Orleans Bapt. Seminary, 1972, Th.D., 1977. Ordained to ministry Bapt. Ch., 1965. Pastor Longstraw Bapt. Ch., Choudrant, La., 1965-66, Pine Grove Bapt. Ch., Monroe, La., 1966-69, Friendship Bapt. Ch., Bienville, La., 1969-70, Evans Creek Bapt. Ch., Pearl River, La., 1970-72, Knoxo Creek Bapt. Ch., Tylertown, Miss., 1973-75, First Bapt. Ch., Williamsburg, Ky., 1976-81; adj. prof. New Testament studies New Orleans Bapt. Theol. Seminary, 1973-76, asst. prof. New Testament and Greek, 1981—; trustee Bapt. Bd. Child Care, Middletown, Ky., 1977-81, S.E. Ky. Bapt. Hosp., Corbin, Ky., 1976-81; mem. Ky. Bapt. Exec. Bd., Middletown, 1979-81, Home Bible Study, Nashville, 1978-80; mem. adv. com. Southern Bapt. Conv., 1978-80. Chmn. Substance Abuse Adv. Council, Corbin, 1980-81. Mem. Soc. Bibl. Lit. Club: Optimists (Williamsburg). Office: New Orleans Bapt Theol Seminary 3939 Gentilly Blvd New Orleans LA 70126

PERKINS, FLOYD JERRY, religion educator, Church of the Nazarene; b. Bertha, Minn., May 9, 1924; s. Ray Lester and Nancy Emily (Kelley) P.; m. Elizabeth Owen, Sept. 21, 1947 (dec. June 1983); children: Douglas Jerry, David Floyd, Sheryl Pauline; m. Phyllis Hartley, July 14, 1984. B.A., B.Th., Northwestern Nazarene Coll., 1949; M.A., U. Mo., 1952; M.Div., Nazarene Theol. Sem., Kansas City, 1952; Ph.D., U. Witwatersrand, Johannesburg, Republic of South Africa, 1974. Pres. South Africa Nazarene Theol. Coll., Florida, Transvaal, 1955-67, Nazarene Sem., Lorenco Marques, Mocambique, 1967-73, Nazarene Bible Sem., Campinas, Brazil, 1973-76; prof. Nazarene Bible Coll., Colorado Springs, Colo., 1976—. Contbr. Beacon Dictionary of Theology, 1983. Served with USN, 1944-46, PTO. Mem. Am. Sch. Oriental Research. Republican. Home: 1529 Lyle Dr Colorado Springs CO 80915 Office: Nazarene Bible Coll PO Box 15749 Colorado Springs CO 80935

PERKINS, PHYLLIS HARTLEY, religious organization executive, Church of the Nazarene; b. Bluffton, Ind., Feb. 24, 1934; d. E.B. and Velda (Williams) Hartley; m. Floyd J. Perkins, July 14, 1984. A.B., Northwest Nazarene Coll., 1956; M.Ed., Oreg. State U., 1961; Ed.D., Ariz. State U., 1983. Prof. Northwest Nazarene Coll., Nampa, Idaho, 1959-62, 68-69, 74-80; missionary tchr. Ch. of the Nazarene, Japan, 1962-67; gen. dir. Nazarene World Mission Soc., Kansas City, Mo., 1980—. Mem. Nat. Assn. Evangelicals (women's fellowship commn.), Delta Pi Epsilon. Office: Ch of the Nazarene 6401 The Paseo Kansas City MO 64131

PERKINS, ROBIN DIXON, minister, American Baptist Churches in the U.S.A.; b. Madison, Ind., Feb. 4, 1953; s. Harold Ray and Dixie Dale (Hall) P.; m. Judith Lynne Harding, June 26, 1976; 1 son, Nathan Harold. B.A., Wheaton Coll., 1975; M.Div., So. Bapt. Sem., 1981. Ordained to ministry American Baptist Churches in U.S.A., 1981. Assoc. pastor First Bapt. Ch., Mattoon, Ill., 1975-78; student pastor Weston Bapt. Ch., North Vernon, Ind., 1979-81; pastor First Bapt. Ch., Olney, Ill., 1981—; chmn. area 4, Christian Edn. Com., 1982—; mem. Dept. Christian Edn., Ill. and Mo., 1982—; mem. Dept. Youth, Am. Bapt. Chs. of Great Rivers Region, 1985—. Bd. dirs. Emergency Food and Shelter, Olney, 1983-84. Named Outstanding Young Man of Am., U.S. Jaycees, 1981. Mem. Minister's Council Great Rivers Region Am. Bapt. Chs. U.S.A., Richland County Ministerial Assn. (pres. 1983-84). Office: First Baptist Ch 420 E Chestnut St Olney IL 62450

PERLMUTTER, NATHAN, community relations organization executive, Jewish; lawyer; b. N.Y.C., Mar. 2, 1923; s. Hyman and Bella (Finkelstein) P.; m. Ruth Ann Osofsky; children: Dean, Nina. Student Georgetown U., 1942-43, Villanova Coll., 1943-44; LL.B., NYU, 1949. Regional dir. Anti Defamation League, Denver, Detroit, Miami, Fla., N.Y.C., 1949-65, asst. nat. dir., 1973-78, nat. dir., 1973-78, nat. dir., N.Y.C., 1978—; assoc. dir. Am. Jewish Com., N.Y.C., 1965-69; v.p. devel. Brandeis U., Waltham, Mass., 1969-73. Author: A Bias of Reflections, 1972; (with Ruth Ann Perlmutter) The Real Anti-Semitism in America, 1982; also numerous articles on social, polit. issues. Served to 2d lt. USMC, 1943-46, CBI. Club: Harmonie (N.Y.C.). Office: Anti Defamation League of B'nai B'rith 823 UN Plaza New York NY 10017

PERMAN, JAMES H., rabbi, Reform Jewish Congregations; b. Buffalo, Nov. 6, 1940; s. Joseph C. and Ida G. (Carrel) P.; B.S., Columbia, 1972; B.H.L., Hebrew Union Coll.-Jewish Inst. Religion, 1963, M.H.L., 1967; m. Jane E. Gross, June 16, 1963; children—Deborah Elizabeth, Daniel Stephen. Ordained rabbi, 1967; chaplain capt. U.S. Air Force, 1967-69; asst. rabbi Stephen Wise Free Synagogue, N.Y.C., 1969-72; rabbi The Free Synagogue of Westchester, Mt. Vernon, N.Y., 1972—; mem. faculty dept. Theology Fordham U., N.Y.C., 1984—. Chmn. com. on bio-ethics Central Conf. Am. Rabbis, 1975—; research rev. com. Mt. Sinai Sch. Medicine, 1974—; pres. Interfaith Clery Assn. of Mt. Vernon, 1973—; bd. govs. Am. Jewish Com. (Westchester chpt.). Chmn., Commn. for Human Rights, Mt. Vernon, 1973—; active United Way Community Service. Mem. Fedn. Jewish Philanthropies, N.Y. Assn. Reform Rabbis. Home: 550 N Columbus Ave Mount Vernon NY 10552 Office: 500 N Columbus Ave Mount Vernon NY 10552

PERRITTE, LARRY EUGENE, religion educator, administrator, minister, Church of God; b. Wilmington, N.C., Nov. 2, 1938; s. Leo Robert and Geneva (Evans) P.; m. Mary Sue Brummett, Mar. 12, 1960; 1 child, Michael Eugene. Student Presbyn. Jr. Coll., 1957-59; B.A., Lee Coll., 1974; postgrad. Case Western Med. Res. U., 1974-76, Cleve. Psychiat. Inst., 1975-76; M.D., Ashland Sem., 1977. Ordained to ministry Ch. of God, 1979. Vis. lectr. European Bible Sem., Rudersburg, Federal Republic Germany, Nov. 1976, Jan. 1978; instr. Retreat for Mil., Buchtesgaden, Federal Republic Germany, Oct. 1976, Oct. 1977; vis. lectr. Leadership Conf. for Mil., Buchtesgaden, Feb. 1976; instr. Ch. of God Bible Inst., Kaiserslautern, Federal Republic Germany, spring 1978; instr. gen. and abnormal psychology and theology West Coast Christian Coll., Fresno, Calif., 1979-81, advisor, 1980-81, small group leader, 1981, internship coordinator, 1981, counselor to students, 1979-81; pastor Cumberlin Presbyn. Ch., Flint Springs, Tenn., 1974-75, Lodi Ch. of God, Ohio, 1975-76; servicemen's dir. Kaiserslautern Christian Servicemen's Ctr., 1976-78; civilian chaplain Landstul Mi. Hosp., (Fed. Republic Germany, 1977-78; chaplain advisor Women's Aglow, Kaiserslautern, 1977-78; pastor North Fresno Ch. of God, Calif., 1978-82; acad. dean N.W. Bible Coll., Minot, N.D., 1982—; mem. Dakota State Mission Com., Ch. of God, 1982; guest speaker, lectr. in field. Contbr. articles to religious jours. Recipient Chaplain's award Kaiserslautern, 1977; named Adminstr. of Yr., Northwest Bible Coll., 1984. Lodges: Rotary (Anderson, S.C.); Moose (Abbeville, S.C.). Address: 1800 1/2 8th Ave SE Minot ND 58701

PERRY, CHARLES WAYNE, minister, United Meth. Ch.; b. Montgomery, Ala., July 25, 1948; s. Collin Wade and Belle (Ray) P.; B.A., Campbell Coll., 1970; M.Div., Wesley Theol. Sem., 1974; postgrad. Emory U., 1976—; m. Joyce Marie Sumners, Apr. 12, 1968; 1 son, Christopher Warren. Ordained to ministry, 1971; pastor Morgan Circuit, United Meth. Ch., Berkeley Springs, W.Va., 1971-74, Wesley Circuit, Cumberland, Md., 1974-75, Venter's Meml. United Meth. Ch., Freeport, Fla., 1975-76, Pine Level United Meth. Ch., Prattville, Ala., 1976—. Chaplain, USAFR. Mem. Morgan County Vol. Rescue Service, 1972-74, LaVale Vol. Rescue Squad and Bedford Rd. Vol. Fire Dept., 1975. Mem. Assn. Clin. Pastoral Edn., Ala. West Fla. Conf. Council on Ministries, Inst. Soc., Ethics, and the Life Scis. (asso.). Home and Office: Rt 1 Box 368 Prattville AL 36067

PERRY, E. EUGENE, theater educator; b. Martins Ferry, Ohio, Dec. 25, 1957; s. Edwin Ray and Sally Lou (Youst) P. B.S. in Edn., Ohio U.-Athens, 1979; M.Div., U. Dubuque, 1982. Ednl. resource person Stone Presbyn. Ch., Wheeling, W.Va., 1978-79; asst. chaplain U. Dubuque, Iowa, 1981-82, sem. relations asst. Theol. Sem., 1982—; youth adv. del. United Presbyn. Ch. in the U.S.A. Gen. Assembly, 1977. Substitute tchr. Dubuque Community Schs., 1982—; instr. theater U. Dubuque, 1984—. Author play: It Works for Everybody Else, 1984. Contbr. articles to profl. jours. Mem. Dubuque County Democratic Central Com., 1984-85, office mgr. hdqrs., 1984; del. County and 2d Dist. Demo Conv., Dubuque, 1984; sec. 2d dist. Dem. Conv., Dubuque, 1984; chmn. play-selection com. Barn Community Theater, Dubuque, 1981-83. Home: 759 Bluff St Apt 3 Dubuque IA 52001

PERRY, EDWARD KERSTEN. Synodical bishop Lutheran Church in America, Syracuse, N.Y. Office: Luth Ch in Am 3049 E Genesee St Syracuse NY 13224*

PERRY, GREGORY ALEXANDER, minister, National Baptist Church of America, Inc., American Baptist Churches in the U.S.A.; b. Norwalk, Conn., July 8, 1952; s. George Henry and Helen (Thompson) P.; m. Jayne Claire Hagel, Apr. 30, 1977; children: Timothy Allen, Janine Candace, Gregory Nathaniel. B.A., Wagner coll., 1976; M.Div., Yale U., 1979. Ordained to ministry Nat. Bapt. Ch. Am., Inc., 1980, Am. Bapt. Chs. U.S.A., 1982. Asst. pastor Grace Bapt. Ch., Norwalk, 1976-80; chaplain resident Norwich Hosp., Norwich, 1980-81; protestant chaplain, 1981—; spl. ministries coordinator Conn. Missionary Bapt., 1984. Bd. dirs. Martin House Inc., Norwich, 1983—; co-chmn. Combined Health Appeal, 1983; mem. chmn. Research and Planning United Way, 1983-84; v.p. bd. dirs. Contact Telephone Ministry, 1985. Fellow Coll. Chaplains; mem. Evang. Minister's Assn. (sec., treas. 1982-84). Home: 33 Mulberry St Norwich CT 06360 Office: Norwich Hosp PO Box 508 Norwich CT 06360

PERRY, HAROLD R. See *Who's Who in America*, 43rd edition.

PERRY, JAMES MYRON, minister, United Methodist Church; b. St. Albans, Vt., Oct. 15, 1946; s. Francis William and Melba Kay (Chandler) P.; m. Kareen Ann Karr, June 15, 1968; children: Matthew Karr, William Francis. B.A., Swarthmore Coll., 1968; B.Div., Andover Newton Theol. Sch., 1971. Ordained to ministry as elder, United Meth. Ch., 1972. Pastor Danville Circuit, Vt., 1971-74; assoc. pastor Grace United Meth. Ch., St. Johnsbury, Vt., 1974-77; pastor Whitehall United Meth. Ch., N.Y., 1977-81, Queensbury Circuit, Glens Falls, N.Y., 1981—; del. Jurisdictional Conf., Selingsgrove, Pa., 1980, Annville, Pa., 1984; sec. Troy Ann. Conf., Saratoga Springs, N.Y., 1983—. Editor: (with others) Circuit Breakers Mag., 1984. Contbr. book revs. and articles to Circuit Breakers Mag. Mem. Democratic Exec. Com., Danville, Vt., 1971-74; treas. Skenesborough Emergency Squad, Whitehall, N.Y., 1980-81; bd. dirs. Geriatric Found., 1984—. Mem. Assn. for Clin. Pastoral Edn., Whitehall C. of C. (treas. 1979-81). Lodges: Masons (master 1976-77), Kiwanis (2d v.p. 1983—, bd. dirs. 1977, Kiwanian of Yr. 1977). Home: 27 Buena Vista Ave Glen Falls NY 12801 Office: United Meth Ch 74 Aviation Rd Glens Falls NY 12801

PERRY, L. TOM, church official. Mem. Quroum of the Twelve, The Church of Jesus Christ of Latter-day Saints. Office: The Church of Jesus Christ of Latter-day Saints 50 E North Temple St Salt Lake City UT 84150*

PERRY, LANNY JOSEPH, minister, Southern Baptist Convention; b. Madison, W.Va., June 19, 1944; s. Ross Perry and Lois Kathleen (Pauley) Bunch; m. Sondra Kay Morgan, June 16, 1967; children: Matthew Joseph, Meredith Leigh. B.A., Dallas Bapt. Coll., 1973; M.Div., Southwestern Bapt. Theol. Sem., 1976. Ordained to ministry So. Bapt. Conv., 1975. Pastor Ida Bapt. Ch., Sherman, Tex., 1974-76, Tabernacle Bapt. Ch., Gainesville, Tex., 1976-77, Crutchfield Bapt. Ch., Sherman, 1977-82, Emmanuel Bapt. Ch., Terrell, Tex., 1982—; assn. clk. Kaufman Bapt. Assn., Terrell, 1983—; tchr. Southwestern Bapt. Theol. Sem. Extension, Sherman, 1981-82. Contbr. articles and poems to mags. Mem. Human Relations Com., Terrell, 1984—. Served to sgt. USAF, 1965-69. Recipient Presdl. Service cert. and medal Johnson Adminstrn., 1966, White House Service cert. White House Communications Agy., 1968. Mem. Century Club of Southwestern Sem., Terrell Ministerial Alliance (pres. 1983-84), Terrell C. of C., NAACP. Avocations: writing; softball; basketball; reading. Office: Emmanuel Bapt Ch 1717 N Frances St Box 798 Terrell TX 75160

PERRY, NORMAN ROBERT, priest, religious editor; Roman Catholic Church; b. Cin., Dec. 7, 1929; s. Joseph S. and May A. (Hafertepe) P. B.A., Duns Scotus Coll., 1954. Joined Order St. Francis; ordained priest Roman Catholic Ch., 1958. Assoc. pastor St. Clement Parish, Cin., 1959-61, St. Therese Parish, Fort Wayne, Ind., 1961-62; instr. Bishop Luers High Sch., Fort Wayne, 1961-62; preaching retreats, 1962-66; assoc. editor St. Anthony Messenger, Cin., 1966-81, editor-in-chief, 1981—; vicar provincial St. John Bapt. Province, Cin., 1975-81. Recipient awards Ohio Editors, Cin. Editors. Mem. Cath. Press Assn. (1st place best analytical and interpretive reporting 1969), Cin. Editors Assn. Home: St Francis Friary 1615 Vine St Cincinnati OH 45210 Office: St Anthony Messenger 1615 Republic St Cincinnati OH 45210

PERRY, RICHARD JAMES, JR., minister, Lutheran Church in America. B. Ashland, Ky., July 31, 1948; s. Richard James Sr. and Ethyl Mae (Ross) P.; m. Theresa Marie Cosby, Dec. 21, 1974. B.A., Carthage Coll., 1973; M.Div., Luth. Sch. Theology, Chgo., 1977. Ordained to ministry Lutheran Church in America, 1977. Youth dir. Ch. of Cross, Detroit, 1968-71; camp counselor Camp Michi-Lu-Ca, Fairview, summers 1972; 73; pastor Calvary Luth. Ch., Gary, Ind., 1977-80; dir. inclusive ministry N.C. Synod, Luth. Ch. in Am., Salisbury, 1980—; sec. Luth. Human Relations, Milw., 1980-82, pres., 1982-84; mem. exec. bd. N.C. Council Chs., 1982—; del. to 7th assembly Luth. World Fedn., Budapest, Hungary, 1984; mem. mgmt. com. Div. Parish Services, Luth. Ch. in Am., Phila., 1984—; co-chairperson interfaith com., bd. dirs. NCCJ, 1984. Mem. Afro-Am. Cultural Service Ctr., Charlotte, N.C., 1983. Recipient Best Friend award Metrolina Native Am., Charlotte, 1981; named Outstanding Citizen in Religion of Northwest Ind., Gary Info. Newspaper, 1979. Mem. Charlotte Area Luth. Clergy Assn. (v.p. 1984-85), Charlotte Area Clergy Assn. Democrat. Office: NC Synod Luth Ch in Am PO Box 36186 Charlotte NC 28236

PERRY, ROBERT HAYNES, minister, Southern Baptist Convention. B. Hattiesburg, Miss., Jan. 1, 1933; s. Matthew Euodias and Edna Inez (Haynes) P.; m. Doris Helen Warnock, June 7, 1953; children: Robert Haynes, Peggy Ann, Mary Lynn, Marcia Kay. Student Clarke M. Jr. Coll., 1951-52; B.A., Miss. Coll., 1955; postgrad. New Orleans Bapt. Theol. Sem., 1958-59; Th.M., Luther Rice Theol. Sem., 1968, Th.D., 1971. Ordained, 1953. Pastor, Forkland Bapt. Ch., Winterville, Miss., 1953-56, Parkview Bapt. Ch., Leland, Miss., 1956-58, Emmanuel Bapt. Ch., Greenville, Miss., 1958-67, New Palestine Bapt. Ch., Picayune, Miss., 1967-69, Crestwood Bapt. Ch., Jackson, Miss., 1969-70, Hanging Moss Bapt. Ch., Jackson, 1970-74, 1st Bapt. Ch., Raleigh, Miss., 1975-80, 1st Bapt. Ch., Waynesboro, Miss., 1981—; dir. stewardship com. Wayne County Bapt. Assn., 1984—; assn. leader planned growth in giving Miss. Bapt. Conv. Bd., 1984—; dir. vol. chaplaincy program Wayne County Gen. Hosp., 1981—; chaplain Greenville Evening Lions Club, 1964. Author manuals: Personal Evangelism, 1971, Brief Studies I, II Peter, 1970, Brief Studies in Prophecy, 1974; contbr. articles to religious publs. Pres. Band and Athletic Booster Clubs, Raleigh, 1975-76; dir. Ann. Christmas Parade, Raleigh, 1975-78; charter mem. Smith County Hist. Soc., Raleigh, 1979. Greenville Rotary Club scholar, 1958; recipient grand prize Raleigh Art Show, 1976. Lodge: Waynesboro Lions (2d v.p. 1984—). Home: 1709 Eastwood Dr Waynesboro MS 39367 Office: First Bapt Ch 810 Azalea Dr Waynesboro MS 39367

PERRY, TROY DEROY, minister, Congregational Ch.; b. Tallahassee, July 27, 1940; s. Troy and Edith (Allen) P.; student Midwest Bible Coll., 1958-60, Moody Bible Inst., 1960-61. Ordained to ministry Congl. Ch., 1968; founder, pastor Met. Community Ch., Los Angeles, 1968-73; gen. moderator Universal Fellowship of Met. Community Chs., 1969—. Mem. Los Angeles Community Relations Com., 1973-74; chairperson Troy Perry Found., 1973—, Calif. Com. for Sexual Law Reform; mem. bd. Nat. Gay Task Force; mem. Los Angeles Commn. Human Relations. Bd. dirs. Homosexual Counseling Service, N.Y.C. Author: The Lord is my Shepherd and He Knows I'm Gay, 1972. Contbg. editor: Is Gay Good? (Overholtzer), 1970. / Office: 318 W 9th St Suite 632 Los Angeles CA 90015

PESTEL, DAVID MERLE, minister, General Association of Regular Baptist Churches; bus driver; b. River Falls, Wis., July 27, 1947; s. Merle Lambert and Beatrice Louise (Erickson) P.; m. Charlotte Ann Inabnit, June 20, 1969; children: Melissa Louise, Christie Susanne, Paul David. B.S., Faith Bapt. Bible Coll., Ankeny, Iowa, 1971. Ordained to ministry General Association of Regular Baptist Churches, 1978. Interim pastor First Bapt. Ch., Grand River, Iowa, 1969-70; assoc. pastor Saylorville Bapt. Ch., Des Moines, 1970-72; pastor Faith Bapt. Ch., New London, Wis., 1972—; dir. Camp Fairwood, Westfield, Wis., 1975—; chmn. bd. Bible Press, Weyauwega, Wis., 1976—. Bus driver New London Pub. Schs., Wis., 1974—. Home: 1512 Cardinal St New London WI 54961 Office: Faith Bapt Ch 303 W Cameron New London WI 54961

PETAIA, EMAU SIU, minister, Congregational Church of Samoa, United Church of Christ; accountant; b. Fagasa, Pago Pago, Am. Samoa, Sept. 5, 1933; came to U.S., 1963; s. Petaia Siu Malaepule and Aliimau (Iuta) Petaia; m. Sialei Vaega, Sept. 2, 1978; children: Emau S., Magdalene P. Diploma in Jr. Acctg., Honolulu Bus. Coll., 1965; A.A., Los Angeles City Coll., 1971; B.S., East Tex. State U., 1975; diploma in Theology, Malua Theol. Sem., Apia, Western Samoa, 1978. Ordained to ministry, 1979. Organist, conductor Samoan Chs., Samoa, Hawaii, Calif., Wash., 1954; minister Samoan Christian Ch., Seattle, Wash., 1979—; bd. dirs. Wash. and N. Idaho Conf., United Ch. Christ, Seattle, 1983—; mem. exec. com. Pacific Asian Am. Ministry, San Francisco, 1983—; bd. govs. Pacific Asian Ctr. Theol. Strategy, Seattle, 1985—; treas., sec. Samoan Ch. Conf., San Francisco-Seattle, 1983—. Mem. newspaper staff The Facts Newspaper, Seattle, 1984—. Cons. New Immigrants (book), 1981. Active leader Samoan Community, Los Angeles, 1974, Seattle, 1979—. Lodge: Kiwanis (Seattle officer 1979-82). Home: 416 S 132nd St Seattle WA 98168 Office: Samoan Christian Church of Seattle 437 S 126th St Seattle WA 98168

PETER, CARL JOSEPH, educator, priest, Roman Catholic Church; b. Omaha, Apr. 4, 1932; s. Carl Joseph and Anne Marie (Schinker) P.; S.T.D., Pontifical Gregorian U., Rome, 1962; Ph.D., U. Thomas Aquinas, 1964. Ordained priest Roman Cath. Ch., 1957; asst. pastor St. Patrick's Ch., Fremont, Nebr., 1958-60; asst. vice rector N.Am. Coll., Rome, 1960-64; faculty dept. theology Cath. U. Am. Sch. Religious Studies, Washington, 1964—, prof. systematics, 1972—, chmn. dept. theology, 1975-77, dean Sch. Religious Studies, 1977—. Vis. lectr. Princeton Theol. Sem., 1973, 76; vis. prof. St. Johns U., Collegeville, Minn., summers 1970—; mem. faith and order commn. Nat. Council Chs., 1971-72; peritus for 5 U.S. dels. to Synod of Bishops, Rome, 1971, 83; mem. bilateral ecumenical consultation between Luth. and Roman Cath. Chs. U.S.A., 1972—; pres. Cath. Theol. Soc. Am., 1971-72; trustee Pontifical Coll. Josephinum. Recipient John Courtney Murray award, 1975. Mem. Internat. Theol. Commn. Author: Participated Eternity in the Vision of God, 1964. Contbr. numerous articles and revs. to religious jours. Address: Curley Hall POB 49 Cath U Am Washington DC 20064

PETER, VALENTINE JOSEPH, priest, religious educator, Roman Catholic Church, child care administrator; b. Omaha, Nov. 20, 1934; s. Carl Joseph and Anne Marie (Schinker) P. Ph.B., Gregorian U., Rome, 1956, S.T.L., 1960; S.T.D., U. St. Thomas, Rome, 1965; J.C.D., Lateran U., Rome, 1967. Ordained priest, 1960. Assoc. jud. vicar Archdiocese of Omaha, 1966—; chmn. dept. theology Coll. of St. Mary, Omaha, 1969-71; prof. theology Creighton U., Omaha, 1971-84; exec. dir. Fr. Flanagan's Home, Boys Town, Nebr., 1984—; bd. dirs. Covenant Inc., Omaha, 1970—; selected del. Council of Priests, Omaha, 1983—; chmn. bd. Internat. Communio, Notre Dame, Ind., 1984—. Recipient Presdl. Citation, Creighton U., 1984, Disting. Faculty award, 1983. Mem. Cath. Theol. Soc. Am., Canon Law Soc. Am. Home and Office: Fr Flanagan's Boys Home Boys Town NE 68010

PETERS, ABE HERBERT, minister, Mennonite Church General Conference; b. nr. Henderson, Nebr., Sept. 22, 1916; s. Peter J. and Marie (Peters) P.; A.B., Bethel Coll., Kans., 1947; postgrad. Mennonite Bibl. Sem., 1967-71; m. Martha Schmidt, Aug. 1, 1940 (dec. July 1977); children: Lois (Mrs. James Loflin), Edwin, Janice (Mrs. Harold Gingerich), Galen; m. Emma Miller, Nov. 23, 1978. Ordained to ministry Mennonite Ch., Gen. Conf., 1946; pastor Geary (Okla.) Mennonite Ch., 1946-51, Burrton (Kans.) Mennonite Ch., 1951-56, Central Heights Mennonite Ch., Tampa, Kans., 1956-59, Fredonia (Kans.) Mennonite Ch., 1960-66, Topeka, (Ind.) Mennonite Ch., 1966-72, Hudson Lake Mennonite Ch., New Carlisle, Inc., 1973-76; prison minister, 1966-79. Tchr. elem. schs., Kans., 1937-67. Mem. Gen. Conf. Mennonite Ch. Am.; chaplain county jail, Wilson County, Kans., 1960-66. Active Community 4-H Clubs, 1951-64; vol. counsellor Ind. State Prison, Michigan City, 1966-79, Protestant chaplain, 1979—. Mem. Ind. State and Regional Corrections Assn., Ind. State Chaplains Assn. Home and office: Route 2 Box 330 New Carlisle IN 46552

PETERS, CLAUDE LORRAIN, minister, Am. Bapt. Conv.; b. Mayville, N.Y., Jan. 14, 1909; s. Frederick John and Sadie Wentworth (Davis) P.; grad. Mt. Hermon Sch., 1926; diploma Nat. Bible Inst., 1939; B.S., N.Y.U., 1952; M.S. in Pastoral Counseling, Iona Coll., 1974; m. Ida Boughton, Sept. 18, 1939; 1 son, Claude Lorrain. Ordained to ministry Am. Bapt. Conv., 1942; pastor First Congl. Ch. of Woodhaven, Ozone Park, N.Y., 1942-47, Meml. Bapt. Ch., Bklyn., 1947-48, Port Washington (N.Y.) Bapt. Ch., 1948-54, Stamford (Conn.) Bapt. Ch., 1954-73; hosp. chaplain Stamford-Darien Council Chs. and Synagogues, 1972—; pastor Talmadge Hill Community Ch., Darien, 1974—. Pres. Stamford-Darien Ministers League, 1959; mem. program com. YMCA. Bd. dirs. Salvation Army. Mem. radio trio The Reverend, The Priest and The Rabbi, Sta. WSTC, 1967—. Home: 96 Weed St New Canaan CT 06840 Office: 20 Forest St Stamford CT 06902

PETERS, DAVID FARR, JR., minister, United Church of Christ; b. Meriden, Conn., Aug. 18, 1958; s. David Farr and Barbara Louise (Goldstien) P. B.S., Central Conn. State Coll., 1981; M.Div., Andover Newton Theol. Sch., 1985. Minister Christian edn. 1st Congregational Ch., Waltham, Mass., 1981-84; assoc. minister 1st Congl. Ch., Danbury, Conn., 1984—; mem. staff Silver Lake Conf. Ctr., Sharon, Conn., 1975-82; del. gen. synod United Ch. of Christ, N.Y.C., 1979, 81, 85; bd. dirs. Bd. for World Ministries, N.Y.C., 1979—. Editor: Teaching for You, 1980. Home: 162 Deer Hill Ave Danbury CT 06810 Office: First Congregational Ch 164 Deer Hill Ave Danbury CT 06810

PETERS, GARY BLAINE, minister, United Methodist Church; b. Newberg, Oreg., May 31, 1943; s. Edgar F. and Lorrene P. (Markum) P.; m. Gail M. Young, Mar. 4, 1967 (div. 1984); children: Gavin Y., Genni B. B.S., Portland State U., 1970; M.Div., Iliff Sch. Theol., 1979. Ordained to ministry, United Meth. Ch., as deacon, 1977, as elder, 1980. Assoc. pastor Alameda Heights United Meth. Ch., Denver, 1975-77, First United Meth. Ch., Alliance, Nebr., 1977-79; pastor First United Meth. Ch., Pine Bluffs, Wyo., 1979-82, Palisade United Meth. Ch., Colo., 1982-85, De Beque United Meth. Ch., Colo., 1982—; readjustment counsellor for Vietnam vets. Essex Growth Ctr., Grand Junction, Colo., 1984—; chmn., rep. Rocky Mountain Town and County Network, 1982—; guest lectr. Claremont Sch. Theology, Calif., 1983. Served with U.S. Army, 1964-67, Vietnam. Recipient Merit award Boys' Club, Alliance, 1979, Cert. of Appreciation Pine Bluffs council Boy Scouts Am., 1982. Mem. Alliance C. of C. (chmn., originator Christmas parade activities 1978-79), Cosmicos, Iliff Alumni Assn., M and M Clown Troup. Republican. Lodge: Masons. Home: 702 Midland Ave Apt 14 Glenwood Springs CO 81601 Office: 826 1/2 Grand Ave Room 28 Glenwood Springs CO 81601

PETERS, JACK LAWRENCE, minister, United Pentecostal Church; b. Morton, Wash., Jan. 18, 1946; s. Kenova Imboden and Hazel Clara (Huffman) P.; m. Beverley Ann Springer, June 11, 1966; children: Ronald J., Ramon J. Student Conquerors Bible Coll., Portland, 1964-67. Ordained to ministry, 1969. Pastor, United Pentecostal Ch., Kodiak, Alaska, 1967-72; home missions dir. Alaska dist. United Pentecostal Ch., 1978-82, fgn. missions dir., 1976—; assoc. pastor First United Pentecostal Ch., Anchorage, 1975—; co-owner Alaska Haz-Mat, Anchorage, 1982—. Address: 110 Showers St Anchorage AK 99515

PETERS, LANNY LEE, minister, American Baptist Churches in the U.S.A./Southern Baptist Convention; b. Lexington, N.C., Mar. 31, 1952; s. Marcus Eugene and Gladys Mills (Neighbors) P.; m. Karen Jean Bridgman, Aug. 30, 1956. B.S. magna cum laude in Edn., Western Carolina U., 1974; M.A. in Edn., E. Carolina U., 1976; postgrad. Pacific Sch. of Religion, 1979-81; M.Div., Southeastern Bapt. Theol. Sem., 1982. Ordained to ministry, 1983. Campus minister Unitas, Berkeley, Calif., 1980-81; minister First Bapt. Ch., Washington, 1982—. Democrat. Home: 2316 N Monroe St Arlington VA 22027 Office: First Baptist Ch of Washington 1328 16th St NW Washington DC 20036

PETERSEN, JOHN LAURENS, nondenominational ch. ofcl.; b. Omaha, July 11, 1943; s. J. Allan and Evelyn Roselyn (Witt) P.; B.S. in Elec. Engring., John Brown U., 1965; m. Janet Diane Carter, July 22, 1968; 1 son, John Carter Laurens. Chmn. fin. com., deacon LaSalle St. Ch., Chgo., 1970—, coordinator Continental Congress on Family, 1974-75. Dir. Lakeview Logos Books, Chgo., 1975—, Cabrini-Green Legal Aid Clinic, Chgo., 1975—; pres. Near North Housing Corp., Chgo., 1970-75; sec., dir. Chgo.-Orleans Housing Corp., 1970—. Vice pres. Family Concern Inc., Chgo., 1974—. Home: 3507 N Bosworth Chicago IL 60657 Office: 222 W Adams St Chicago IL 60606

PETERSEN, MARLO DEAN, minister, pastoral counselor, Lutheran Church in America; b. Minot, N.D., Dec. 4, 1930; s. Chramer A. Petersen and Marie T. (Petersen) A.; m. Dorothy G. Skonnord, Aug. 22, 1953; children: Mark, Bruce, Robin, Michael. B.A., Augsburg Coll., 1952; M.Div., Northwestern Luth. Theol. Sem., 1955; S.T.M., So. Meth. U., 1968. Ordained to ministry Lutheran Ch., 1955. Asst. pastor St. Pauls Luth. Ch., Postville, Iowa, 1955-57; pastor Faith Luth. Ch., Eldridge, Iowa, 1957-62; asst. prof. Inst. of Religion, Houston, 1964-70; dir. of chaplains Harris County Hosp. Dist., Houston, 1964-70; dir. clin. pastoral edn. Decatur Mental Health Center, Ill., 1970-78; dir. Cypress Creek Center for Interface, Spring, Tex., 1978—; mem. prof. services commn. Ill. Synod, Luth. Ch. in Am., 1976-78, mem. profl. service commn. Tex.-La. Synod, 1979—. Mem. Am. Assn. for Marriage and Family Therapy (clin. mem.), Am. Assn. Pastoral Counselors (diplomate), Assn. for Clin. Pastoral Edn. (clin. supr. cert.). Office: Interface 6823 Cypresswood Dr Spring TX 77379

PETERSEN, NORMAN RICHARD, religious studies educator; b. Chgo., Aug. 25, 1933; s. Norman Richard and Mildred May (Wilson) P.; m. Antoinette Petersen, Jan. 28, 1956; children: Kristen Anne, Mark Andrew, Joanna. B.F.A., Pratt Inst., 1957; S.T.B., Harvard Div. Sch., 1961; Ph.D., Harvard U., 1967. Faculty, Williams Coll., Williamstown, Mass., 1969—, prof. dept. religion, 1978—, Washington Gladden prof. religion, 1980. Author: Literary Criticism for N.T. Critics, 1978; Rediscovering Paul, 1985. Editor Semeia 6, 1976, Semeia 16, 1979. Mem. sch. bd. Mt. Greylock Regional High Sch., Williamstown, 1980-85, chmn., 1982-85. Served with U.S. Army, 1952-54. Mem. Soc. Bibl. Lit. (mem. council 1981-83), Soc. N.T. Studies. Home: 51 Bulkley St Williamstown MA 01267 Office: Williams Coll Williamstown MA 01267

PETERSON, BARTLETT, church official, Assemblies of God; b. Boston, Oct. 29, 1908; s. Ansel Lee and Charlotte Benedicta (Anderson) P.; grad. Christie U., 1927, LL.B., 1928; postgrad. U Minn., 1943; B.Th., North Central Coll., 1946; D.D., Northwest Coll., 1973; m. Lydia Eleanor Espeseth, Sept. 24, 1930; children—Dennis Lee, Wilson Bartlett, Don Sheldon. Ordained to ministry Assemblies of God, 1928; pastor various chs., S.D., Minn., 1929-40; field sec. Minn. dist. council Assemblies of God, 1940-43, dist. supt., 1943-48; pres. Central Bible Coll., 1948-58; gen. presybter Gen. Council Assemblies of God Ch., Springfield, Mo., 1942, sec. gen., 1959—. Mem. Greene County Planning and Zoning Bd., 1967-70; chaplain Greene County Sheriff's Dept., 1968. Bd. dirs. Central Bible Coll.; bd. dirs. Assemblies of God Grad. Sch. Theology. Mem. Nat. Assn. Evangs. (dir. 1968—), Springfield C. of C. Contbr. articles to religious periodicals. Editor: Gospel Broadcast mag., 1940-48. Office: 1445 Boonville Ave Springfield MO 65802

PETERSON, CHARLES MORGAN, minister, United Methodist Church; b. Weston, W.Va., Nov. 11, 1943; s. Morgan H. and Edna Grace (Wiemer) P.; B.A., W.Va. Wesleyan Coll., 1965; B.D., Duke Div. Sch., 1969; Th.M., 1970; m. Sharon Sue Gray, Aug. 20, 1966. Ordained to ministry, 1969; asso. minister Bland St. United Meth. Ch., Bluefield, W.Va., 1971-73; pastor Mt. Pleasant/Pettyville United Meth. chs., 1973-74, Mt. Pleasant Ch., 1973-77, Winfield (W.Va.) Ch., 1977-80; dir. pastoral care Thomas Meml. Hosp., South Charleston, W.Va., 1980—. Chaplain, Pipestem (W.Va.) Resort, 1971-72; chmn. leisure and recreation com. W.Va. Council Chs., 1973-75, rec. sec., 1977—; chmn. div. pastoral care and counseling bd. higher edn. and ministry, W.Va. Ann. Conf., United Meth. Ch., 1974—. Home: 217 Autumn Dr Dunbar WV 25064 Office: 4605 MacCorkle Ave SW South Charleston WV 25309

PETERSON, CURTIS ARTHUR, minister, Wisconsin Evangelical Lutheran Synod; b. Moose Lake, Minn., Apr. 6, 1939; s. Clarence Arthur and Ferol Virginia (Boltman) P.; m. Marilynn Elizabeth McMullan, Aug. 22, 1965; children: Robert, Laurie, Kevin, Ryan. A.A. in Arts, St. John's Coll., 1959; B.A., Concordia Sr. Coll., 1962; postgrad., Moody Bible Inst., 1960-61, Wis. Luth. Sem., 1985; M.Div., Concordia Sem., 1966, M.S.T., 1984. Ordained to ministry Lutheran Ch., 1966. Pastor Redeemer Luth. Ch., Burlington, N.C., 1966-70, Good Shepherd Luth. Ch., Rock Falls, Ill., 1970-77, Peace Luth. Ch., Garland, Tex., 1977-81; sr. pastor Salem Luth. Ch., Gretna, La., 1981-85; trustee Balance, Inc., Ohio, 1975-78, 1981-85; cir. counselor No. Ill. Dist., Luth. Ch.-Mo. Synod, 1975-77, del. convention, 1971, program chmn. Tri-Cir. Pastors' Conf., 1983-84, mem. Task Force on Anglo Ministry So. Dist. Luth. Ch. - Mo. Synod, 1984. Contbr. articles to Affirm, Christian News, Church Growth: America, Lutherans Alert. Mem. Burlington Jaycees (chaplain 1967-70). Home: 3724 Inwood Dr Harvey LA 70058

PETERSON, DOROTHY MARIE, nun, Roman Catholic Church, educator; b. Providence, May 21, 1947; d. George Arthur and Anne Eileen (Pendergast) Peterson. B.A. in Edn. magna cum laude, Fitchburg State Coll., 1973; M.A., St. Michael's Coll., 1982. Joined Faithful Companions of Jesus, Roman Cath. Ch., 1969. Tchr., St. Joseph Sch., Fitchburg, Mass., 1972-79; prin. Blessed Sacrament Sch., Providence, 1980—; Del. Sisters Senate, Diocese of Worcester, Mass., 1975-79; mem. Diocesan Communication, Worcester, 1977-79, Teens Encounter Christ, Worcester, 1977-79. Mem. Nat. Cath. Edn. Assn., R.I. Cath. Elem. Prins. Assn. (sec. 1984—). Democrat. Home: 20 Atkins St Providence RI 02908 Office: Blessed Sacrament Sch 240 Regent Ave Providence RI 20908

PETERSON, DUANE S., evangelist, bible college administrator, Evangelical Free Church; b. Shenandoah, Iowa, June 14, 1934; s. George G. and Ethel J. (Almquist) P.; m. Nina Nepscha, May 7, 1960; children: Karen Lee Peterson Glastad, Steven George. A.A., North Park Coll., Chgo., 1954; B.S., Dallas Bible Coll., 1974. Ind. music ministry evangelist, 1974—; dir. pub. relations Dallas Bible Coll., 1977-80, dir. pub. affairs, 1980—; deacon Northwood Hills Bible Ch., Dallas, 1981—; dir. Christian Indian Ministries, Dallas, 1980—. Vocalist recordings God Gave the Song, 1976, Tell Them, 1978. Served with U.S. Army, 1957-59. Home: 3336 High Brook Dr Dallas TX 75234 Office: Dallas Bible Coll 8733 Prada Dr Dallas TX 75228

PETERSON, ELWYN GEORGE, lay church worker, Episcopal Church; b. Boise, Idaho, Mar. 23, 1910; s. Van Frederick and Helen (Roberts) P.; m. Alice Porter, Dec. 31, 1938; children: Helen Elizabeth, Julie Porter. B.S., U. Idaho, 1928-30. Lic. lay reader, Episcopal Ch. Exec. asst. Diocese of San Joaquin, Fresno, Calif., 1970-75, stewardship cons., 1975—; program chmn. stewardship Province of the Pacific, San Francisco, 1982—; stewardship area rep. Exec. Council, Episcopal Ch., H.Y., 1983—; del. Provincial Synod, Boise, 1967, Episcopal Ch. Nat. Conv., Houston, 1970. Trustee, pres. Visalia Bd. Edn., Calif., 1952-64; chmn. ARC, Visalia, 1960-62. Served to capt. U.S. Army, 1943-46. Decorated Army Commendation medal, Order of Chevalier, Order of Demolay, 1943. Mem. Order of San Joaquin (charter), Alpha Kappa Psi. Home: 1420 W Laurel St Visalia CA 93277 Office: Episcopal Diocese of San Joaquin 4159 E Dakota Ave Fresno CA 93726

PETERSON, GENE RICHARD, minister, American Lutheran Church; b. Columbus, Ohio, Apr. 21, 1949; s. Lauritz Irving and Genevieve Roberta (Arnold) P. B.A., Capital U., Columbus, 1971; M.Div., Luth. Theol. Sem., Columbus, 1977. Ordained to ministry Am. Lutheran Ch., 1977. Pastor Peever Luth. Ch., S.D., 1977-83, Our Saviour Luth. Ch., Highmore, S.D., 1983—; dir. evangelism S.D. dist. Am. Luth. Ch., Sioux Falls, 1983—; coordinator Glacial Lakes Leisure Ministry, NE S.D., 1978-82; bd. dirs. life and mission com. S.D. Dist., Sioux Falls, 1979-82, minority concerns com., 1981-82; dir. Luths. Outdoors in S.D., Sioux Falls, 1983—. Vol. fireman Peever Fire Dept., 1977-83; pres. Peever Community Club, 1980; v.p. Sisseton Better TV Assn., S.D., 1981. Mem. Luth. Single Clergy Assn., Highmore Booster Assn. Home: 516 Fourth St SE Highmore SD 57345 Office: Our Savior Luth Ch 515 Fourth St SE Highmore SD 57345

PETERSON, GLEN ELSTER, religious college administrator, minister, American Lutheran Church; b. Worthing, S.D., May 13, 1929; s. Alfred Emil and Christine Eline (Elster) P.; m. Irene Brandenburg, Aug. 15, 1955; children: Angela Marie, Renee Beth. B.A., Augustana Coll., 1954; B.D., Luther Theol. Sem., St. Paul, 1959; M.A., U. Minn., 1959; Ph.D., Mich. State U., 1968. Ordained to ministry American Lutheran Church, 1962. Assoc. student personnel Augustana Coll., Sioux Falls, S.D., 1963-66, exec. dir. alumni, 1968-72, exec. dir. fellows, 1972-82, asst. to pres., 1982—; mem. ch. council deacons/stewardship bd. Our Savior's Luth. Ch., Sioux Falls, 1972-84; bd. dirs. past chmn. S.D. Fellowship Christian Athletes, Sioux Falls, 1977—; del. S.D. dist. Am. Luth. Ch., Sioux Falls, 1978-83; mem. membership com. Sioux Falls YMCA, 1971—; chmn. elect bd. Howard Wood Dakota Relays Bd., Sioux Falls, 1973—; bd. dirs. Sioux Falls Sports and Recreation Com., 1976—. Recipient Faculty Growth award Am. Luth. Ch., Mpls., 1966-68, Granskou award (1st one awarded) Augustana Coll., 1984; named to Athletic Hall Fame, Augustana Coll., 1977; grad. scholar Mich. State U., 1966-68. Mem. Council for Advancement and Support Edn. (track chmn. 1977-78, conf. chmn. 1978-79, membership com. 1979-80, sec., 1980-81, treas. 1981-82, chmn.-elect, 1982-83, chmn., 1983-84). Republican. Club: Westward Ho Country. Lodge: Lions (chmn-elect 1978). Home: 1906 S Hawthorne Ave Sioux Falls SD 57105 Office: Augustana Coll Sioux Falls SD 57197

PETERSON, H. BURKE, Presiding bishop The Church of Jesus Christ of Latter-day Saints, Salt Lake City. Office: The Ch of Jesus Christ of Latter-day Saints 50 E N Temple St Salt Lake City UT 84150*

PETERSON, JOHN OTIS, minister, American Baptist Churches; b. Heathsville, Va., July 21, 1934; s. Hiram Ernest and Marie Hayne (Nutt) P.; B.S., Va. Union U., 1956; postgrad. Va. Union Sch. of Religion, 1956-57; M.A., George Washington U., 1962; Th.M., Howard U. Sch. of Religion, 1964; postgrad. Bucknell U., 1964, Wesleyan U., 1969; m. Joyce Mattie Keemer, Dec. 22, 1956; children—Jewelette Graclyn, John Otis. Ordained to ministry Am. Bapt. Ch., 1955; supply pastor New Jerusalem Bapt. Ch., Holly, Va., 1954-55; pastor First Bapt. Ch., Louisa, Va., 1955-64, Alfred St. Bapt. Ch., Alexandria, Va., 1964—. Past pres. Bapt. Gen. Conv. Va.; mem. Alexandria Sch. Bd.; trustee Va. Union U.; chmn. Alexandria Community Corrections Resources Bd. Home: 902 N Howard St Alexandria VA 22304 Office: 313 S Alfred St Alexandria VA 22314

PETERSON, KENNETH LAWRENCE, minister, Evangelical Lutheran Church in Canada; b. Chgo., Nov. 4, 1934; s. Lawrence Ludwig and Edna Marie (Olson) P.; m. Margareth Elfrieda Goos, July 9, 1959; children: Deborah, Andrew, Lois, Diana. B.A., Augustana Coll., 1956; M.Div., Augustana Theol. Sem., 1959; S.T.M., Luth. Sch. Theology, 1971, D.Min., 1985. Ordained to ministry Lutheran Ch. in Am., 1959. Pastor Holy Redeemer Luth. Ch., Cedar Rapids, Iowa, 1959-63, St. Matthew Luth. Ch., Chgo., 1964-69, Central Luth. Ch., Regina, Sask., Can., 1969-78, Augustana Luth. Ch., 1978-83; dist. sec. Can. Bible Soc., 1983—; exec. bd. Central Can. Synod, 1971-74; bd. publ. Luth. Ch. Am., Phila., 1974-78; sec. Central Can. Synod, 1978-82; mem. merger com. Saskaton Synod, 1984—. Editor (synod paper) 1971-76. Contbr. articles to profl. jours. Rep. Citizens Adv. Com., Saskatoon, 1982—, Bd. Ed., 1982-84; v.p. Saskatchewan Council Internat. Co-operation, 1974-75. Democrat. Home: 1209 Wiggins Ave Saskatoon SK S7H 2J4 Canada Office: Can Bible Soc 250 2d Ave S Saskatoon SK S7K 1K9 Canada

PETERSON, PHILIP EDWARD, educational administrator, American Lutheran Church; b. Mansan, N.D., June 22, 1952; s. Elmer P. and Lorene (Schutz) P.; m. Bonnie Raye Smokov, Aug. 25, 1973; children: Amber, Aaron, Adam. B.S., Dickinson State Coll., 1974. Dir. edn. and youth ministry First Lutheran Ch., Mandan, N.D., 1977—. Rep., Bd. for Life and Mission in the Congregation, Am. Luth. Ch., 1980-84, liaison bd. Luther League, 1980-84; mem. Western N.D. Dist. Council, 1980-84. Mem. grant rev. com. Dept. Alcoholism, N.D. Dept. Human Services, Bismarck, 1983-84; mem. lang. arts curriculum com. Mandan Public Schs., 1983-84. Mem. Bismarck-Mandan Lutheran Ministerial Assn. (sec. 1977-78), Bismarck-Mandan Assn. Christian Youth Dirs. (mentor 1982-84). Office: 1st Lutheran Ch 408 9th St NW Mandan ND 58554

PETERSON, THOMAS R., college president, Roman Catholic Church; b. Newark, June 17, 1929; s. William J. and Mathilda (Collins) P. B.A., Providence Coll., 1951; S.T.L., Coll. Immaculate Conception; M.A., St. Stephen Coll., 1961; Ph.D., Aquinas Inst., 1968; Ed.D., Mt. St. Joseph Coll., 1973; S.T.D., Our Lady of Providence Sem., 1975; D.Sc. in Bus. Adminstrn., Bryant Coll., 1977; LL.D., Johnson and Wales Coll., 1979. Ordained priest Dominican Order, Roman Catholic Ch., 1956. Assoc. prof. philosophy Providence Coll., 1957-62, asst. dean, 1962-68, dean, 1968-71, pres., 1971—. Trustee Fenwick High Sch., Oak Park, Ill.; chmn. task force on service United Way; chmn. R.I. Higher Edn. Council; vice chmn. R.I. Ind. Higher Edn. Assn.; bd. dirs. Columbus Nat. Bank, Meeting Street Sch., Narragansette council Boy Scouts Am., Roger Williams Gen. Hosp., NCCJ; mem. Gov.'s Energy Facility Commn.; mem. exec. com. Nat. Assn. Cath. Colls. and Univs.; bd. dirs., trustee R.I. Pub. Expenditure Council; mem. commn. on instns. of higher edn. New Eng. Assn. Schs. and Colls. Home and Office: Providence Coll Providence RI 02918

PETERSON, WALLACE BEDFORD, JR., hospital chaplain, pastoral education administrator, American Lutheran Church. B. Mpls., Dec. 5, 1944; s. Wallace Bedford Sr. and Carmelita Edith (Anderson) P.; m. Jill Susan Lange, Aug. 10, 1968; children: Dawn, Sara. A.A.S., Columbia Basin Coll., 1965; B.A., Gustavus Adolphus Coll., 1967; M.Div., Luther Theol. Sem., St. Paul, 1971. Ordained to ministry American Lutheran Church, 1973; cert. supr. Assn. Clin. Pastoral Edn. Chaplain, coordinator clin. pastoral edn. Fairview Hosp., Mpls., 1973—. Fellow Protestant Health and Welfare Assembly Coll. Chaplains; mem. Assn. Mental Health Clergy. Club: Arden Hills Film Soc. (pres. 1981-84) (St. Paul). Office: Fairview Hosp Dept Religion and Health 2312 S 6th St Minneapolis MN 55454

PETERSON, WALTER FRITIOF, sem. pres.; b. Idaho Falls, Idaho, July 15, 1920; s. Walter F. and Florence Leola (Danielson) P.; B.A., U. Iowa, 1942, M.A., 1948, Ph.D., 1951; m. Barbara Mae Kempe, Jan. 13, 1946; children—Walter Fritiof III, Daniel John. Pres. U. Dubuque (Iowa) Theol. Sem., 1970—; mem. exec. com. Council Theol. Sems., United Presbyn. Ch. U.S., 1970—. Dir. Home Mut. Ins. Group, Appleton, Wis., 1968—; cons. Allis-Chalmers Mfg. Co., Milw., 1959—. Bd. dirs. Dubuque Symphony Orch., 1970—, Dubuque Art Assn., 1971—; bd. dirs. Finley Hosp., 1976—, pres., 1983-84. Mem. Am. Hist. Assn., Orgn. Am. Historians, Iowa Assn. Coll. and U. Pres.'s (pres. 1975-76), Am. Studies Assn. (pres. Wis. Ill. chpt. 1970-71), Assn. Theol. Faculties Iowa (chmn. 1975-76), Phi Alpha Theta, Kappa Delta Pi. Author: The Allis-Chalmers Corporation: An Industrial History, 1977; contbr. articles to profl. jours. 52001 Office: 2050 University Dubuque IA 52001

PETERSOO, UDO, minister, Estonian Luth. Ch.; b. Tallinn, Estonia, May 8, 1934; s. Elmar and Jenny (Sild) P.; came to Can., 1951, naturalized, 1956; B.A., Waterloo Luth. U., Ont., 1963; diploma in theology Waterloo Luth. Sem., 1965; m. Reet Krabi, Dec. 17, 1966; children—Alar Toomas, Tonu Elmar, Taimi Laura. Ordained to ministry, 1975; asst. pastor Estonian Evang. Luth. Synod in Can., Toronto, Ont., 1975—; tchr. pub. schs. Toronto 1965—. Pres. Estonian Central Council in Can., 1973—; mem. exec. com. Estonian World Council, 1973—. Address: 3714 Beechollow Crescent Mississauga ON L4Y 3T2 Canada

PETOSA, JASON JOSEPH See *Who's Who in America*, 43rd edition.

PETRANEK, RICHARD JOHN, JR., priest, Episc. Ch.; b. Chgo., Dec. 5, 1947; s. Richard John and Vera (Magoc) P.; B.S., Morningside Coll., 1970; M.Th., Perkins Sch. Theology, So. Meth. U., 1973; D.Ministry, Tex. Christian U., 1976; m. Elaine Jean Sattem, June 13, 1970. Ordained priest, 1974; Cathedral Center fellow St. Matthews Episc. Cathedral, Dallas, 1973-74; curate Good Shepherd Episc. Ch., Dallas, 1975—. Adminstr. diocesan programs Diocesn Ordination Course Bishop's Sch. for Lay Leadership, 1974-75; del. Provincial Synod, 1975; dir. Bishop's Advisory Com. on Admission to Ministry, 1975—; sec. Episc. Diocese of Dallas, 1975—. Trustee Help Is Possible, drug abuse treatment center, 1976—; mem. Leadership Dallas, 1976. Home: 3546 Woodleigh Dr Dallas TX 75229 Office: 11122 Midway Rd Dallas TX 75229

PETRUSIC, ANTHONY ANDREW, priest, Roman Cath. Ch.; b. Johnstown, Pa., Dec. 10, 1930; s. Stephen C. and Sophia (Stipancic) P.; B.A., Immaculate Conception Sem., 1953; M.A., Creighton U., 1962. Ordained priest, 1957; prof. philosophy, theology Coll. St. Mary, Omaha, 1963-65; pastor Sts. Peter and Paul

Ch., Omaha, 1969—. Dir. vocations Diocese Omaha, 1962-68, asst. supt. schs., 1963-69; dean S. Urban Deanery, Omaha, 1973—; mem. Priest Senate. Bd. govs. Met. Community Coll., Omaha, chmn. bldg. and sites com.; mem. jud. nominating com. Douglas County (Nebr.) Juvenile Ct. Home and Office: 5912 S 36th St Omaha NE 68107

PETTIT, VINCENT KING, bishop, Episcopal Ch.; b. New Brunswick, N.J., Aug. 31, 1924; s. John Mervin and Marion (King) P.; B.S., Rutgers U., 1950; M.Div., Phila. Div. Sch., 1958; Th.M., Temple U., 1963; m. Virginia Elsa Sorensen, June 17, 1950; children: Joan Marie, Ann Marion, Vincent King. Ordained to ministry, 1958; pastor All Saints Ch., 1958-61, St. George's Ch., Pennsville, 1961-67, St. Mary's Ch., Keyport, 1967-72; rector Trinity Ch., Cranford, N.J., 1972-82; suffragen bishop Diocese of N.J., Trenton, 1982—; mem. exec. council Episcopal Ch., chmn. standing liturgical commn., mem. council for devel. of ministry, dep. Gen. Conv., 1979, 82. Youth dir. Diocese of N.J., 1967-75, chmn. provincial youth com., 1970-74, chmn. diocesan liturgical commn., 1974—, chmn. nat. conf. diocesan and music commn., 1975; canon Trinity Cathedral, Trenton, N.J., 1970—; asst. sec. Diocese of N.J., 1965—, mem. urban concerns com., 1969—. Office: 808 W State St Trenton NJ 08618

PETUCHOWSKI, JAKOB JOSEF, educator, rabbi; b. Berlin, Germany, July 30, 1925; s. Siegmund and Recha Lucie (Loewenthal) P.; B.A. with honors, U. London (Eng.), 1947; B. Hebrew Letters, Hebrew Union Coll., 1949, M.A., 1952, Ph.D. (teaching fellow 1952-55), 1955; m. Elizabeth Rita Mayer, Nov. 28, 1946; children: Samuel Judah, Aaron Mark, Jonathan Mayer. Came to U.S., 1948, naturalized, 1954. Rabbi, 1952; rabbi (part-time) Temple Emanuel, Welch, W.Va., 1949-55; rabbi Beth Israel Synagogue, Washington, Pa., 1955-56; asst. prof. rabbinics Hebrew Union Coll., Cin., 1956-59, asso. prof. rabbinics, 1959-63, prof. rabbinics and Jewish theology, 1965-74, research prof. Jewish theology and liturgy, 1974—. rabbi (part-time) Temple B'nai Israel, Laredo, Tex., 1956—; vis. prof. philosophy and religion Antioch Coll., Yellow Springs, Ohio, 1961; dir. Jewish studies Hebrew Union Coll., Jerusalem, Israel, 1963-64; vis. prof. Jewish philosophy Tel-Aviv (Israel) U., 1971. Fellow Am. Acad. for Jewish Research; mem. Am. Acad. Religion. Author: Ever Since Sinai, 1961; Prayerbook Reform in Europe, 1968; Heirs of the Pharisees, 1970; The Theology of Haham David Nieto, 1970; Contributions to the Scientific Study of Jewish Liturgy, 1970; Understanding Jewish Prayer, 1972; Beten im Judentum, 1976. Office: 3101 Clifton Ave Cincinnati OH 45220

PEVEC, ANTHONY EDWARD, bishop, Roman Catholic Church; b. Cleve., Apr. 16, 1925; s. Anton and Frances (Darovec) P. M.A., John Carroll U., 1956; Ph.D., Western Res. U., 1964. Ordained priest Roman Cath. Ch., 1950, consecrated bishop, 1982. Assoc. pastor St. Mary's Ch., Elyria, Ohio, 1950-52, St. Lawrence Ch., Cleve., 1952-53; rector-prin. Borromeo Sem. High Sch., Wickliffe, Ohio, 1953-75; pastor St. Vitus Ch., Cleve., 1975-79; rector-pres. Boromeo Coll. of Ohio, Wickliffe, 1979-82; aux. bishop Cleve. Diocese, 1982—. Named Man of Yr., Fedn. of Nat. Homes, 1985. Mem. Slovenian-Am. Heritage Found. (hon.), Bishop's Com. on Vocations.

PEYTON, JUSTUS BERRY, minister, Wesleyan Tabernacle Association Church; b. Turkey Knob, W.Va., Aug. 22, 1924; s. Berry Marcus and Sally Roscoe (Rupe) P.; A.B., Marshall U., Huntington, W.Va., 1949; LL.D., Fla. Research Inst., Melbourne, 1972; m. Eunice Marie Shelton, Dec. 25, 1952; 1 child, Betty Marie. Ordained to ministry Wesleyan Tabernacle Assn. Ch., 1952. Pastor Hinton Gospel Tabernacle, W.Va., 1957-58; evangelistic work, 1949-85; pastor Oak Hill Gospel Tabernacle, W.Va., 1966-71; asst. to Victor Glenn of Evangelistic Faith Missions, Bedford, Ind., 1971-74, pres., dir., 1982—. Home: 2031 27th Ave Bedford IN 47421 also Evang Faith Missions US Hwy 50E Box 609 Bedford IN 47421

PFAHLER, JOHN WHITFORD, SR., chaplain administrator, Lutheran Church in America; b. Meyersdale, Pa., Feb. 10, 1922; s. Ralph Deal and Carrie Pearl (Dannecker) P.; m. Helen MarLogan, June 25, 1945; children: John Whitford, Robert B., Thomas A., Pamela M. B.A., Gettysburg Coll., 1943; B.D., Luth. Theol. Sem., Phila., 1945; M.Ed., U. Pitts., 1952; D.D., Theil Coll., 1978. Ordained to ministry Lutheran Church in America, 1945. Pastor St. Luke's Luth. Ch., Pitts., 1947-59; dir. pastoral care Luth. Service Soc., Pitts., 1959-77, John Kane Hosp., Pitts., 1977-81, Eger Nursing Home, Staten Island, N.Y., 1981—. Served to 1st lt. USNR, 1944-47. Fellow Coll. Chaplains; mem. Assn. Clin. Pastoral Evaluation (supr. 1963—). Democrat. Home: 178 Manhattan St Staten Island NY 10307 Office: Eger Nursing Home 140 Meisner Ave Staten Island NY 10306

PFATTEICHER, PHILIP HENRY, minister, American Lutheran Church, English language educator; b. Phila., Oct. 29, 1935; s. Ernst P. and Esther T. (Linaka) P.; m. Lois Sharpless, June 24, 1961; children: Carl, Carolyn, Sarah, Linda. B.A., Amherst Coll., 1957; M.A., U. Pa., 1960, Ph.D., 1966; S.T.M., Union Theol. Sem., 1968. Ordained to ministry, 1960. Asst. pastor Trinity Ch., Phila., 1960-64; pastor Bethany Ch., Bronx, N.Y., 1964-68; campus pastor E. Stroudsburg U., Pa., 1968—; prof. English, East Stroudsburg U., Pa., 1968—; mem. Liturgical Text Com., 1968-78, Task Force on Occasional Services, 1978-82. Author: Lesser Festivals, 1975, Festivals and Commemorations, 1980, Commentary on Occasional Services, 1983. Co-author: Manual on The Liturgy, 1979. Recipient Visiting Scholar award NY U, 1985. Mem. Am. Acad. Religion, MLA, N. Am. Acad. Liturgy, Soc. Bibl. Literature, Nat. Council Tchrs. of English. Democrat. Club: Classical (Phila.). Home: Route 5 Box 362 East Stroudsburg PA 18301 Office: East Stroudsburg Univ East Stroudsburg PA 18301

PFEIFFER, WILLIAM OSWALD, ch. ofcl., minister, United Presbyterian Ch. in U.S.A.; b. Omaha, June 10, 1924; s. William Henry and Elsa Bertha (Kappelman) P.; B.A., Whitworth Coll., 1949; B.D. San Francisco Theol. Sem., 1952; D.Bus. Adminstrn., (hon.), Coll. Emporia (Kans.), 1972; m. Elizabeth Louise Henderson, Feb. 16, 1945; children—William L., Richard H. Ordained to ministry U.P. Ch. U.S.A., 1952; pastor chs., Pleasanton, Kans., 1952-54, Syracuse, Kans., 1954-57, First Presbyn. Ch., Paola, Kans., 1957-68; dir. finance Synod of Kans., Topeka, 1968-72, Synods of Mid-Am. U.P. Ch. U.S.A., Presbyn. Ch. U.S., Overland Park, Kans., 1972-73, asso. for finance, 1973—. Moderator, Jud. Commn. of Synod Kans., 1966-68; chmn. Neosho Presbytery Gen. Council, 1964-68. Treas., Mo. Council Chs., 1974—. Republican. Home: 6930 W 101 St Overland Park KS 66212 Office: 6400 Glenwood Overland Park KS 66202

PHELPS, GARY WILLIAM, chaplain, Lutheran Church, Missouri Synod, air force officer; B. Oneida, N.Y., Aug. 19, 1947; s. Lester Cleon Phelps and Eileen (Austin) Morey; m. Kristine Marie Koski, July 3, 1981; 1 child, Bernhardt Kenneth. A.A., Concordia Coll., Bronxville, N.Y., 1968; B.A., Concordia Sr. Coll., Ft. Wayne, Ind., 1969; M.Div., Concordia Sem. in Exile, St. Louis, 1974, Colloquy, 1974. Ordained, 1974. Pastor Grace Luth. Ch., Zion Luth. Ch., Grace-Zion St. Luth. Sch., Mo., 1974-76, Immanuel Luth. Ch., Trenton and Princeton, Mo., 1976; pastor Redeemer Luth. Ch. and prin. Redeemer Luth. Sch., Lancaster, Ohio, 1976-82; chaplain candidate, Scott AAFB, Ill., 1971-73, chaplain, commd. 2d lt, USAFR, 1974, served Scott AFB and MacDill AFB, Fla., 1974-75, chaplain, 1st lt., Wurthsmith AFB, Ohio, 1975, Whiteman AFB, Mo., 1976, chaplain, capt., Rickenbacker AFB, Ohio, 1976-80, Wright Patterson AFB, Ohio, 1980-82, Mountain Home AFB, Idaho, 1982-84—, chaplain Air Res. Personnel Ctr., Denver, 1971-82, 84—; chaplain VA Med. Ctr., Des Moines, 1984—; vis. chaplain CAP, Lancaster and Columbus, Ohio, and Mountain Home AFB, 1976-84; chaplain Boy Scouts Am., Washington, 1981-84, Luth. Assn. Scouters, Luth. Council USA, 1974-74, Am. Legion, Perryville, Mo., 1974-76, Lancaster, Ohio, 1976-82; mem. Mil. Chaplains Assn.; Lancaster Ministerial Assn., 1976-81, Ch. Com. on Scouting, Central Ohio Council Boy Scouts Am., 1976-81; assoc. mem. Luth. Laymen's League, St. Louis, 1974-84; founder, coordinator chaplain staff Boy Scouts Am., Concordia Sem., St. Louis, 1972; flightline chaplain, 1971-84. Contbr. articles to publs. Dist. chmn. Central Ohio Council Boy Scouts Am., Columbus, 1977; adv. mem. Peace Poll: Am. Security Council, Washington, 1978; advisor Parents Anonymous, Mountain Home, 1983. Recipient Dist. Award of Merit, Central Ohio Council Boy Scouts Am., 1979, Silver Beaver award, 1980, Air Force Commendation Medals. Mem. Air Force Assn., Am. Legion. Republican. Lodge: Order of Arrow, Boy Scouts Am., 1979-84. Home: 2415 26th St Des Moines IA 50310 Office: VA Med Ctr 30th and Euclid Des Moines IA 50310

PHERIGO, LINDSEY PRICE, theology educator, United Methodist Church; b. Miami, Fla., Dec. 29, 1920; s. Ezekiel Lindsey and Dorothy Richardson (Price) P.; m. Viola May Schmitt, Feb. 22, 1942; children: Linda J. Pherigo Burgess, Stephen A., Ruth A. Pherigo Charpie, Robert P. B.A.E., U. Fla., 1942; S.T.B., Boston U., 1945, Ph.D., 1951. Ordained elder United Meth. Ch., 1950. Instr. religion Syracuse U. (N.Y.), 1949-51; from asst. prof. to prof. Scarritt Coll., Nashville, 1951-59, acad. dean, 1957-59; prof. N.T. and early ch. history St. Paul Sch. Theology, Kansas City, Mo., 1959—; vis. lectr. Vanderbilt Div. Sch., Nashville, 1954-59. Author: The Great Physician, 1983; also articles. Ford Found. fellow, 1953-54. Mem. Am. Soc. Ch. History, Soc. Bibl. Lit. Democrat. Home: 4960 Westwood Rd Kansas City MO 64112 Office: St Paul Sch Theology 5123 Truman Rd Kansas City MO 64127

PHILARET, GEORGE VOZNESENSKY, primate, Russian Orthodox Church Outside Russia; b. Kursk, Russia, Mar. 22, 1903; came to U.S., 1964; s. Nicholas and Lydia (Vinogradova) Voznesensky. Elec. Engr., Russian-Sino Politech. Inst., Harbin, China, 1929; grad. pastoral theol. sch., Harbin, 1931. Ordained priest Russian Orthodox Ch., 1931, took vows of monkhood, 1931, named archimandrite, 1937. Consecrated Bishop of Brisbane, Australia; vicar bishop Australian Diocese Russian Orthodox Ch., 1963; elected met. primate of Russian Orthodox Ch. Outside Russia, 1964. Address: 75 E 93d St New York NY 10028*

PHILBECK, BEN F., JR., religious educator, minister, Southern Baptist Convention; b. Memphis, Jan. 4, 1931; s. Ben F. and Lida (McCoy) P.; m. Jo Sloan, June 5, 1951; children: Richard Forrest, John Walter. B.S., Wake Forest U., 1951; M.Div., Southeastern Bapt. Theol. Sem., 1956; Ph.D., So. Bapt. Theol. Sem., 1966. Ordained to ministry, 1951. Pastor, Sardinian Bapt. Ch., Westport, Ind., 1960-66, Lake Village Bapt. Ch., Ark., 1966-67; assoc. prof., then prof. religion Carson-Newman Coll., Jefferson City, Tenn., 1967-77; prof. Hebrew and O.T., Midwestern Bapt. Sem., Kansas City, Mo., 1977-79, Southeastern Bapt. Sem., Wake Forest, N.C., 1979—. Contbr. articles to profl. jours. Contbr.: Teacher's Bible Commentary, 1972; Broadman Bible Commentary 1 and 2 Samuel, 1970. Bd. dirs. C. of C., Jefferson City, 1975-76; mem. Chicot County Welfare Bd., Ark., 1966-67. Recipient Disting. Faculty award Carson Newman Coll., 1972. Mem. Am. Schs. Oriental Research, Soc. Bibl. Lit., Assn. Bapt. Profs. Religion, Alpha Chi, Phi Beta Kappa. Lodge: Lions. Office: Southeastern Bapt Theol Sem Wake Forest NC 27587

PHILIPS, J(AMES) DAVISON, seminary president, minister, Presbyterian Church U.S.A.; b. La., May 22, 1920; m. Katherine Wright; children: Jim, June, Graham. B.A., Hampden-Sydney Coll., 1940, D.D., 1963; B.D., Columbia Theol. Sem., 1943; Ph.D., U. Edinburgh, 1955; D.D., Presbyn. Coll., 1962. Ordained, 1943. Asst. pastor 1st Presbyn. Ch., Atlanta, 1947-50; pastor 1st Presbyn. Ch., Thomasville, Ga., 1950-54, Decatur Presbyn. Ch. (Ga.), 1954-75; pres. Columbia Theol. Sem., Decatur, 1976—, chmn. bd. trustees, 1966-71; moderator Presbyn. Ch. U.S.A. com. on theol. edn.; preacher coll. campuses, preaching missions, confs.; moderator Synod of Ga., 1966, Atlanta Presbytery, 1959; mem. bd. ch. extension, chmn. div. evangelism, 1961-66; mem. curriculum planning com. Bd. Christian Edn., 1960-64; mem. Atlanta Christian Council; trustee Presbyn. Coll., Clinton, S.C. Trustee Agnes Scott Coll., Decatur; vice chmn. Univ. Ctr. in Ga.; chmn. Mayor's Citizens Adv. Com., Decatur, 1966-70; chmn. operation com. Gen. Assembly, 1969-73. Served as chaplain USN, 1943-45. Mem. Atlanta Theol. Assn. Club: Rotary (Atlanta). Home: 320 Inman Dr Decatur GA 30030 Office: Columbia Theol Sem PO Box 520 Decatur GA 30031

PHILLIP, MALCOLM IRVING, minister, Church of God (Anderson, Indiana). b. Basseterre, St. Kitts, West Indies, Apr. 26, 1934; came to U.S., 1980; s. Glennis Phillip and Maislie (Walters) P.; m. Chessie Perlina Constant, Aug. 28, 1958; children: Randoline, Randolph, Alden. D.Theol., Internat. BIble Inst. and Sem., 1983; D.D. (hon.), 1985. Ordained to ministry Church of God, 1965. Cert. counselor United Assn. Christian Counselors. Pastor, Wesleyan Ch., St. Kitts, 1958-63, Ch. of God, St. Kitts, 1963-72, Ch. of God, Antiqua, West Indies, 1978-80, Ch. of God, Cin., 1980-85; evangelist, West Indies, 1972-76. Author: Reflections of Excellent Spirits, 1983, Developing and Delivering A Sermon, 1983; Bible Theology Made Simple, 1983. Mem. North Avondale Neighborhood Assn., Cin., 1984. Home: 757 Clinton Springs Ave Cincinnati OH 45229

PHILLIPS, ALFRED PATRICK, educator, priest, Roman Catholic Church; b. Mobile, Ala., Mar. 17, 1927; s. Alfred Yancey and Rosa Layet (Parker) P.; B.S., Spring Hill Coll., 1952; Licentiate in Philosophy, M.A., St. Louis U., 1958; S.T.L., St. Louis U. Div. Sch., 1963; Th.M., St. Mary's U., 1969. Joined Soc. of Jesus, 1952; ordained priest Roman Cath. Ch., 1963; prof. philosophy and theology Loyola U., New Orleans, 1963-76, dir. religious studies program, 1969, dean Campus Ministries, 1973-76; dir. Jesuit Spirituality Ctr., rector St. Charles Coll., Grand Coteau, La., 1976—. Lectr. theology and philosophy St. Patrick's Coll., Ottawa, Ont., Can., 1967-68, U. Ibero-Americana, Mexico City, Mexico, 1966; co-founder Christian Friends for Social Action in La., 1972. Mem. La. Coalition Campus Ministers, Jesuit Campus Ministry Assn., Sigma Alpha Kappa. Address: St Charles Coll Grand Coteau LA 70541

PHILLIPS, BEN HILL, minister, Church of God, Anderson, Indiana; b. Damascus, Ga., Mar. 9, 1914; s. Benjamin F. and Rhoddie Catherine (Poole) P.; m. Ruby Virginia Tipton, Oct. 30, 1938; children: Brenda Faye, Robert Leon. D.Div. (hon.), Dothan Bible Coll., 1984. Ordained to ministry, 1964. Pastor, Jakin Ch. of God, Ga., 1963-75, Bainbridge First Ch. of God, Ga., 1975-85; trustee, vice chmn., treas. Pleasantview Ch. of God, Damascus, Ga., 1949-53; trustee, vice chmn. Bainbridge Ch. of God, 1954-56. Served with USAAF, 1942-46. Democrat. Address: 509 N 1st St Colquitt GA 31737

PHILLIPS, DONALD ALLEN, minister, American Baptist Churches in the U.S.A.; b. Cin., July 30, 1937; s. Albert Allen Phillips and Stella E. (Mills) Hall; m./Sharon Sue Hatfield, Aug. 25, 1958; children: William, John, Julia. Student Ind. U., 1955-56, Anderson Coll., 1956-57, Oakland City Coll., 1957-58; Th.B., Am. Bible Coll., 1965, Th.M., 1973, Litt.D., 1974; postgrad. U. Cin., 1984—. Ordained to ministry Am. Bapt. Chs. in the U.S.A., 1958. Pastor, Peerless Bapt. Ch., Bedford, Ind., 1955-58, Bethel Bapt. Ch.,

Linton, Ind., 1958-62, New Market Bapt. Ch. (Ind.), 1962-65, First Bapt. Ch., Lawrenceburg, Ind., 1965—; evangelist 200 Revival Meetings, 1958—; chaplain Dearborn County Hosp., Lawrenceburg, 1967-75, Ind. State Police Post 73, Versaillles, 1976—; mem. mission tours Am. Bapt. Chs. in U.S.A., Haiti, Ariz., Africa, 1971, 73, 76. Author: Fading Glory, 1976. Instr., Ivy Tech. Vocat. Sch., Lawrenceburg, 1980; shelter mgr. Ind. Dept. Civil Def., Lawrenceburg, 1981; tour leader Wandering Wheels, Taylor U., Scotland and Eng., 1979; mem. assoc. faculty Greendale Middle Sch., Lawrenceburg, 1980. Named hon. dep. sheriff Marian County Sheriff Dept., 1977. Mem. Ministers' Council Am. Bapt. Chs. U.S.A., Ind. Bapt. Conv. (bd. mgrs. 1975), Ind. Ministers' Council (bd. mgrs. 1984—), Lawrenceburg Ministerial Assn. (pres. 1975). Republican. Home: 647 Ridge Ave Lawrenceburg IN 47025 Office: First Bapt Ch 45 Tebbs Lawrenceburg IN 47025

PHILLIPS, IRVING RUSSELL, minister, United Presbyterian Church; b. Warren, Ohio, July 28, 1926; s. Orlando R. and Ruth (Burlette) P.; m. Claire E. Maurer, June 26, 1927; children: I. Russell, Jill A., Mark P., Susan L., Scott M., David M. A.B., Bethany Coll., 1946; D.B., M.Th., Princeton Sem., 1949, Fellow in Adminstrn., 1976. Ordained to ministry, 1950. Pastor, E. Liberty Presbyn. Ch., Vanderbilt, Pa., 1950-55; assoc. pastor Drayton Ave. Presbyn. Ch., Ferndale, Mich., 1955-59; pastor Calvary Presbyn. Ch., Logansport, Ind., 1959-69; pastor First Presbyn. Ch., Lansing, Mich., 1969-77, First Presbyn. Ch., Las Vegas, Nev., 1977—. Author Outlook mag., 1978. Mem. Sch. Bd., Waverly Sch. Bd., Mich., 1975; chmn. Lansing Bicentennial, 1976; religious orgn. chmn. United Fund, Las Vegas, 1984. Lodge: Rotary (pres. 1968). Office: 1515 W Charleston Blvd Las Vegas NV 89102

PHILLIPS, JAMES DONALD, minister, Southern Baptist Convention; b. Mooresville, N.C., Nov. 22, 1936; s. Ulysses Truman and Lillie Margaret (Sellers) P.; B.S., Appalachian State U., 1960; M.Div., Southeastern Bapt. Sem., 1969; m. Mary Lou Brown, Aug. 6, 1961; children: Gary, Donna. Ordained to ministry, 1967; pastor Aenon Bapt. Ch., Elm City, N.C., 1967-71, Harmony Bapt. Ch., Bunnlevel, N.C., 1971-74, Warwick Bapt. Ch., Hobbsville, N.C., 1974—, Bethel Bapt. Ch., Statesville, N.C., 1979-84, Fellowship Bapt. Ch., Barium Springs, N.C., 1981—. Sec.-treas. Edenton Chowan Rescue Squad, 1976-77; bd. dirs. Troutman Fire Dept., 1984—. Address: PO Box 128 Barium Springs NC 28010

PHILLIPS, MELVIN ROMINE, ch. ofcl., minister, Am. Baptist Chs., U.S.A.; b. Parkersburg, W.Va., July 10, 1921; s. Chester Corliss and Julia Augusta (Romine) P.; B.A., Alderson-Broaddus Coll., 1944; B.D., Colgate Rochester Div. Sch., 1946; postgrad. Marshall U., 1949-50; m. Carolyn Beckner, Aug. 12, 1944; children: Ann Elizabeth (Mrs. J. Leachman), Ruth Elaine Phillips-Huyck, Ralph Beckner, Beth Carol. Ordained to ministry Am. Bapt. Ch., 1946; pastor, Mumford, N.Y., 1944-46, Kingwood-Masontown parish, Kingwood, W.Va., 1946-49; univ. pastor Marshall U., Huntington, W.Va., 1949-50; pastor Bapt. Chs., Shelbyville, Ind., 1950-57, Anderson, Ind., 1957-67, Jamestown, N.Y., 1967-73; exec. dir. Asso. Chs. of Fort Wayne and Allen County, Ind., Ft. Wayne, 1973—. Pres. bd. dirs. Mental Health Assn.; bd. dirs. Adler Inst., 1980—, Samaritan Counseling Ctr., 1982—; mem. Community Human Services Task Force, 1979—. Recipient Ecumenical citation Ind. Council Chs., 1964; named Man of Year, Jaycees, 1954. Mem. Am. Bapt. Hist. Soc., Am. Bapt. Ministerial Council, Am. Council Execs. Religion, N.Am. Acad. Ecumenists, Nat. Assn. Ecumenical Staff. Office: 227 E Washington Fort Wayne IN 46802

PHILLIPS, OSCAR GEORGE, minister, American Baptist Churches in U.S.A., educator; b. Jamaica, W.I., May 28, 1914; s. Joshua Bailey and Ida Adella (Jackson) P.; A.B., Bishop Coll., 1947, M.Ed., 1949, D.D., 1969; B.D., Andover Newton Theol Sch., 1953, D.Ministry, 1972; S.T.M., Boston U., 1955; m. Miriam Ernestine Faulcon, Dec. 19, 1954; children—Peter Joshua, Miriam Elaine. Ordained to ministry Am. Baptist Chs. of U.S.A., 1947. Organizer, pastor Macedonia Bapt. Ch., Marshall, Tex., 1946-49; asst. pastor Shiloh Bapt. Ch., Medford, Mass., 1950, pastor, 1950—, supr. clin. pastoral edn., 1960—. Dean men Bishop Coll., Marshall, 1948-49; asso. in clin. pastoral edn., adj. faculty Andover Newton Theol. Sch., 1962—, also asso. dir. pastoral clin. edn., dir. tng. in pastoral counseling; dir. tng. Middleton Counseling Ctr., Mass., Tremont Temple Counseling Ctr., Boston; past dir. tng. Melrose-Wakefield Hosp., Mass., Boston City Hosp.; dir. clin. pastoral edn. St. John's Hosp., Lowell, Mass., Tewksbury Hosp., Mass.; past pres. Medford Council Chs. Past pres. Mystic Valley Credit Union; bd. dirs. West Medford Community Center, Am. Bapt. Chs. of Mass.; mem. civic adv. com. New Eng. Meml. Hosp. Recipient Cutting award Andover Newton Theol. Sch., 1972, Community Leaders of Am. award, 1969, Walter Telfer award for Excellence in Field Edn., 1984; named Am. Bapt. Instl. Chaplain of Year, 1968. Diplomate Am. Assn. Pastoral Counselors. Mem. Am. Assn. Marriage and Family Counselors (dir. tng. Region IV), Am. Protestant Hosp. Assn. (Coll. of Chaplains). Home: 94 Monument St Medford MA 02155

PHILLIPS, PAUL LE ROY, religious educator; b. Dayton, Ohio, Sept. 12, 1933; s. Irwin William and Ruth Alberta (Singer) P.; m. Naomi Albertine Wright, Jan. 21, 1956; children: Paul L.R., Naomi Faye, Irwin W., Peggy Y. Student, Open Bible Inst., 1950-52, U. Dayton, 1950-52, Southeastern Bible Coll., 1952-53, 56-58. D.Div. (hon.), St. Peters Collegiate Acad. of Nat. Ecclesiastical U.-Eng., 1974. Ordained to interdenominational ministry, 1974. Sunday sch. tchr., sch. supt. Assemblies of God, 1960-64; pres. youth group Assemblies of God, Dayton, 1950-53, pastor, Mulberry, Fla., 1958-61; missionary/evangelist/tchr. Mission Crusades, Inc., Jamaica, W.I., 1974-82, founder, dir., pres., Columbus, Ohio, 1974—; pres., tchr. Fgn. Mission Bible Schs., 1974-82, Community Bible Colls., Columbus, Chillicothe, Peru, Ind., 1982—; founder, dir. Community Bible Colls. of Columbus, Chillicothe, Ohio and Peru, 1983—. Contbr. articles to profl. jours. Republican. Lodges: Civitan, Lions. Office: Mission Crusades Inc Columbus Community Bible Coll PO Box 14399 Columbus OH 43214

PHILOTHEOS See *Who's Who in America,* 43rd edition.

PHYLES, RAYMOND HENRY, minister, Luth. Ch. Am.; b. Balt., Dec 28, 1939; s. Thomas Edward and Anna Catherine (Butz) P.; B.A. magna cum laude, Gettysburg Coll., 1961; B.D., Luth. Sch. Theology, Chgo., 1964; postgrad. Harvard; m. Julia Ann LaRose, June 16, 1962; 1 dau., Cheryl Lynne. Ordained to ministry, 1969; pastor Luth. Ch. of the Triumphant Cross, Armonk, N.Y., 1970—. Chmn. Ednl. Design Group, mem. personnel commn. Council Met. N.Y. Synod; sec. Tappan Zee dist. N.Y. Synod; treas. No. Westchester Clergy Assn.; convenor Armonk Clergy Assn.; chaplain Armonk Rotary club; sec. treas. Timotheans Soc. Br. chmn. ARC. Luth. Brotherhood Grad. fellow, 1964-65; Luth. World Fedn. scholar, Europe, 1968-69. Mem. Arnold Air Soc., Phi Beta Kappa, Eta Sigma Phi, Phi Sigma Tau, Delta Phi Alpha. Indexer: The Marrow of Theology (W. Ames). Translator: De Conceptu Virginali et de Originali Peccato (Anselm of Canterbury). Home: 21 Thornewood Rd Armonk NY 10504 Office: 485 Bedford Rd at Banksville Rd Armonk NY 10504

PICHE, PAUL, bishop, Roman Catholic Church; b. Gravelbourg, Sask., Can., Sept. 14, 1909; s. Joseph Amedee and Eleonore (Pratte) P.; B.A. in Anthropology, Ottawa (Ont.) U., 1931; Scholasticate of Sacred Heart, Lebret, Sask., 1935. Ordained priest Roman Cath. Ch., 1934; prof. holy scripture, liturgy and history of ch. Lebret Sem., 1935-39; prof. social economy Oblates Scholasticate, Lebret, 1939-41; superior Juniorate of Holy Family, St. Boniface, Man., Can., 1941-43; superior, prin. Qu Appelle Indian Residential Sch., Lebret, 1943-51; provincial superior Oblate Fathers of Mary Immaculate, St. Boniface, Man., 1951-56; gen. dir. Oblate Indian and Eskimo Commn., Ottawa, Ont., 1956-59; bishop of MacKenzie, 1959—. Decorated Centennial medal, 1967. K.C. Author writings on Indian edn. Address: PO Box 25 Fort Smith NT X0E 0P0 Canada

PICKARD, DALE EUGENE, missions educator, Mid-America Yearly Meeting of Friends; b. Mt. Pleasant, Iowa, Mar. 21, 1947; s. Dale Owen and Louva Maude (Bailey) P.; m. Myra Lee Williamson, June 28, 1970; children: Heather Dawn, Jason David. B.A., Friends Bible Coll., 1969; M.Div., Asbury Theol. Sem., 1975. Instr. Greek, Asbury Theol. Sem., Wilmore, Ky., 1975-76; missionary Guatemala Friends Mission, Chiquimula, 1977-81; asst. prof. missions Friends Bible Coll., Haviland, Kans., 1981—. Mem. Am. Assn. Missiology. Home: Route 1 Box 7 Haviland KS 67059 Office: Friends Bible Coll Haviland KS 67059

PICKENS, ANDREW, minister, Southern Baptist Convention; b. Anderson, S.C., Feb. 28, 1928; s. Travis Richard and Emma (Stowers) P.; A.A., Anderson Coll., 1950; D.D., Neotarian Coll., 1966; C.T., Southeastern Bapt. Theol. Sem., 1972; m. Sarah Elizabeth Bailey, Nov. 26, 1952; children—Elizabeth, Andrea, Susan. Ordained to ministry, 1950; pastor Oak Bower Bapt. Ch., Hartwell, Ga., 1951-52, Triangel Bapt. Ch., Belton, S.C., 1952-54, Bethany and Old Canon Bapt. Chs., Canon, Ga., 1955-56, Fortsonia, Harmony and Bethel Bapt. Chs., Elberton, Ga., 1957-70, Ridgecrest Bapt. Ch., Wake Forest, N.C., 1970-73, 78-83, Good Hope Bapt. Ch., Carpenter, N.C., 1973-78. Chaplain Wake Hosp. System, Raleigh, N.C., 1970-83; faculty So. Bapt. Extension Sem., Morrisville, N.C., 1974-78. Pres., chmn. bd. dirs. Morrisville Rural Fire Co., 1975-78. Mem. Raleigh Bapt. Assn. Pastor's Conf., Chaplain Assos., Wake County Firemans Assn. Home: Route 1 PO Box 461 Morrisville NC 27560 Office: Route 1 Morrisville NC 27560

PICKERING, ERNEST DINWOODIE, educator, minister, Gen. Assn. Regular Bapt. Chs.; b. St. Petersburg, Fla., Dec. 14, 1928; s. Ernest Joseph and Evelyn Ida (Dinwoodie) P.; A.B., Bob Jones U., 1948; Th.M., Dallas Theol. Sem., 1952, Th.D., 1957; m. Ariel Yvonne Thomas, Aug. 16, 1952; children—Dawn Gay, Lloyd Ernest. Ordained to Baptist ministry, 1948; student pastorates, 1949-52; pastor Maranatha Bible Ch., New Kensington, Pa., 1953-56; nat. exec. sec. Ind. Fundamental Chs. of Am., Chgo., 1956-59; pastor Woodcrest Bapt. Ch., Mpls., 1959-65; prof. theology Central Bapt. Theol. Sem., 1959-65, acad. dean, 1961-65; pastor Bible Bapt. Ch., Kokomo, Ind., 1965-69; acad. dean Bapt. Bible Coll. of Pa., 1969-70, pres. Bapt. Bible Coll. of Pa. and Sch. Theology, Clarks Summit, Pa., 1970—. Pres. Minn. Bapt. Conv., 1963-65; mem. council of 18 Gen. Assn. Regular Bapt. Chs., 1965-71, 72—. Trustee Pillsbury Bapt. Coll., Owatonna, Minn. Mem. Evang. Theol. Soc., Assn. Bapts. for World Evangelism, Fellowship Bapts. Home Missions. Author various pamphlets, booklets, mag. articles. Home and office: 538 Venard Rd Clarks Summit PA 18411

PICKETT, OLIVER EUGENE See *Who's Who in America,* 43rd edition.

PIERCE, BOBBY LANE, minister Southern Baptist Convention; b. Valdosta, Ga., Mar. 20, 1944; s. Wilmont Candler and Helen Delah (Baskin) P.; m. Kay Marion Gillis, June 24, 1967; children: Kay Lynn, Kimberly Lane, Krista Lea. B.S., Valdosta State Coll., 1966; student So. Bapt. Theol. Sem., 1966-68. Lic. Baptist Ch., 1964; ordained to ministry Southern Baptist Conv., 1967. Interim pastor Hickory Head Bapt. Ch., Quitman, Ga., 1964, Beulah Bapt. Ch., 1965-66; minister of music and youth Bapt. Ch., Louisville, 1966-68; pastor Cocoli Bapt. Ch., Balboa, C.Z., Republic of Panama, 1968-71, Beallwood Bapt. Ch., Columbus, Ga., 1974-81, First Bapt. Ch., Pearson, Ga., 1981—; assoc. minister edn., youth and recreation East Hill Bapt. Ch., Tallahassee, Fla., 1971-74; chmn. Ga. Bapt. Student summer missions com., Atlanta, 1965-66; trustee Panama Bapt. Theol. Sem., Arriajan, Republic of Panama, 1969-71; assoc. ch. tng. worker Fla. Bapt. Assn., Tallahassee, 1972-74; associational Sunday Sch. improvement support team (adult div.) Columbus Bapt. Assn., 1979-81, associational clk., 1980-81, Smyrna Bapt. Assn., Douglas, Ga., 1981-83; sec., treas. Atkinson County Ministerial Assn., Pearson, Ga., 1982-83, pres., 1983-85. Author weekly articles for newspaper, 1981-83; producer weekly religious radio program, 1976-80 (recognition award 1981). Advisor coordinated vocat.-acad. edn. Atkinson County High Sch., Pearson, Ga., 1982; mem. career planning resource bd. Valdosta State Coll., 1983—. Named Outstanding Young Man in Am., Jaycees, 1975. Democrat.

PIERCE, JAMES RUSSELL, minister, Lutheran Church-Missouri Synod; b. Stamford, Conn., July 10, 1944; s. Russell Theron and Helene (Lietke) P.; m. Linda Lee Hicks, Sept. 3, 1966; children: Kevin, Anne. A.A., Concordia Jr. Coll., 1964; B.A., Concordia Sr. Coll., 1966; M.Div., Concordia Sem., 1970; M.S.T., Concordia Sem., 1971. Ordained to ministry Lutheran Ch., 1971. Pastor Trinity Luth. Ch., Farmington, Minn., 1971-76; vacancy pastor St. John & Our Savior Luth. Chs., Rosemount, Minn., 1975; pastor Our Redeemer Luth. Ch., Wilson, N.C., 1976-82; mission developer Gloria Dei Luth. Ch., Greenville, N.C., 1976-77; pastor Prince of Peace Luth. Ch., Howell, N.J., 1983—; chmn. Farmington Ministerial Assn., 1973; pres. Wilson County Ministers Assn., N.C., 1978; cir. counselor cir. 13 S.E. Dist., 1978-82, del. convention Luth. Ch. - Mo. Synod, 1979. Author (vacation Bible sch. curriculum) Christmas Comes Twice This Year, 1979. Mem. Howell & Farmingdale Team Outreach, N.J., 1983—, Wilson County Migrant Farmworkers Council, N.C., 1981-82, N.J. Dist. Commn. on Worship Luth. Ch. - Mo. Synod, 1983—, Raritan Zone Luth. Women's Missionary League (counselor, 1983—). Republican. Home: 614 Aldrich Rd Howell NJ 07731 Office: Prince of Peace Lutheran Church 400 Aldrich Rd Howell NJ 07731

PIERCE, RODERIC HALL, minister, Episcopal Church; b. Endicott, N.Y., July 23, 1928; s. Roderic and Margaret Griswold (Hall) P.; B.A., Hobart Coll., 1952; S.T.B., Berkeley Div. Sch., 1955; M.A. (Univ. fellow 1955-58), Princeton, 1957, Ph.D., 1962; m. Margaret Dorothea Partridge, June 21, 1952; children—Eric Thompson, Evan Bradford. Ordained priest Episcopal Ch., 1955; minister various chs., N.J., 1955-58; instr. O.T., Bexley Hall Div. Sch., Gambier, Ohio, 1958-60, asst. prof. ch. history, 1960-65, asso. prof., 1965-68, also registrar, 1960-65; Munds prof. ch. history Colgate Rochester Div. Sch., Rochester, N.Y., 1968-73; rector St. Andrew's Episcopal Ch., Elyria, Ohio, 1973—. Chmn. Parish Renewal Commn., Diocese of Rochester, 1971-73; mem. Diocesan Council, 1975-79, 84—, Diocesan Planning Commn., 1975-83; mem. Bd. Examining Chaplains, Ohio Diocese, 1974-78, chmn. dept. evangelism and ch. renewal, 1975-78, 83—, chmn. dept. congl. life, 1976-78. Mem. spl. task force Pub. Schs. Elyria, 1975-76. Mem. Elyria Ministerial Assn. (pres. 1974-75, 84-85). Author: George Whitefield and His Critics, 1962; Trinity Cathedral Parish Cleveland: The First 150 Years, 1969. Home: 6293 Case Rd North Ridgeville OH 44039 Office: 300 3d St Elyria OH 44035

PIERSON, ROSCOE MITCHELL, librarian, educator, minister, Christian Ch. (Disciples of Christ); b. Crenshaw, Miss., Sept. 21, 1921; s. Roscoe Peary and Esther Virginia (Mitchell) P.; A.B., Centre Coll., 1947;

M.A., U. Ky., 1950; m. Dorothy J. McCowan, July 15, 1944; 1 dau., Eugenia Pierson Attkisson. Ordained to ministry, 1953; librarian Lexington (Ky.) Theol. Sem., 1950—, dir. field placement, 1975—, prof. religious lit., 1958—. Sr. librarian fellow, 1968. Pres. Am. Theol. Library Assn., 1965; sec. Disciples Hist. Soc., 1955-75. Mem. Ky. Library Assn., Nat. Rifle Assn., Nat. Muzzle Load Rifle Assn. Contbr. articles to religious publs. Home: 624 Seattle St Lexington KY 40503 Office: 631 Limestone St Lexington KY 40508

PIES, FRANK JOHN, JR., minister, Lutheran Church-Missouri Synod. B. Detroit, Mar. 26, 1947; s. Frank John and Marie Hilma Margaret (Hirvela) P., Sr.; m. Jeanette Marie Rockfalus, June 17, 1972; children: Jonathan, Christopher, Timothy, Frank, III. B.S. in Edn., Wayne State U., 1968; B.D., Concordia Theol. Sem., Springfield, Ill., 1972, M.Div., 1972; S.T.M., Luth. Sch. Theology Chgo., 1983. Ordained to ministry Luth. Ch., 1973. Pastor Our Savior Luth. Ch., Hartland, Mich., 1973—; interim pastor Nativity Luth. Ch., Parshallville, Mich., 1978-82; tchr. Child of Christ Luth. Sch., Hartland, 1982-83; cir. counselor English dist. Detroit west cir. Luth. Ch.-Mo. Synod, 1977-78, mem. evangelism com. English dist., 1978-82. Author religious column Milford Times Newspaper, 1980—. Camp dir. Camp Fair Haven (summer camp for less fortunate children), Hartland, 1972—. Recipient Servus Ecclesiae Christi award Concordia Theol. Sem., 1984. Office: Our Savior Evangelical Luth Ch 3375 Fenton Rd Hartland MI 48029

PIETRZAK, DANIEL M., priest, religious educator, Roman Catholic Church; b. Buffalo, Mar. 12, 1939; s. Thaddeus S. and Stella G. (Cybulski) P. B.A., St. Hyacinth Coll., 1961; S.T.L., Seraphicum, Rome, 1965; M.S., South Conn. State U., 1968; Ph.D., Fordham U., 1981. Joined Order Friars Minor (Franciscans) Roman Cath. Ch., ordained priest, 1964. High sch. tchr. Kolbe High Sch., Bridgeport, Conn., 1965-67; prof. St. Hyacinth Coll.-Sem., Granby, Mass., 1967-76, registrar, 1968-76, acad. dean, 1973-76; sem. rector Seraphicum, Rome, 1977-82; minister provincial, Franciscan Order, Balt., St. Anthony Province, 1982—. Asst. gen. Order Friars Minor Conventual, Rome, 1976-82. Fordham U. fellow, 1969. Mem. Am. Psychol. Assn., Soc. Sci. Study of Religion, Nat. Cath. Edn. Assn. Home and Office: 1300 Dundalk Ave Baltimore MD 21222

PIFER, ROBERT DANIEL, minister, religious organization administrator, Seventh-day Adventists; b. York Springs, Pa., Apr. 13, 1935; s. Earl Harrison and Dorothy Virginia (Luckenbaugh) P.; m. Gerd Lind, Dec. 23, 1956; children: Linda Moyer, Randi, Lisa, Shirley, Robert L. B.A. in Theology, Columbia Union Coll., 1957; M.A. in Systematic Theology, Potomac U., 1959. Ordained to gospel ministry Seventh-day Adventists, 1963. Treas., pres. Uganda Mission, Seventh-day Adventists, 1964-70; pres. E. Mediterranean Mission, Beirut, 1971-74; adminstrv. dept. dir. Pa. Conf. Seventh-day Adventists, Reading, 1974-76; staff/bus. mgr. So. Lancaster Acad., Mass., 1976-80; Can. ops. mgr. Christian Record Braille Found., Clearbrook, B.C., 1981—; dir. various hosps. high schs. and ch. adminstrv. bds. while in Africa and Middle East. Contbr. articles to religious publs. Speaker, various service clubs, Hamburg, Pa., Mass., Oreg. and B.C. Home: PO Box 640 Sumas WA 98295 Office: Christian Record Braille Found 31897 Mercantile Way Clearbrook BC V2T 4C3 Canada

PIKE, THOMAS FREDERICK, priest, Episcopal Church; b. Dobbs Ferry, N.Y., Jan. 10, 1938; s. Frederick R. and Elizabeth M. (Smith) P.; m. Lys McLaughlin; children: Jean, Thomas F., Nicholas. B.S., SUNY-New Paltz, 1960; M.Div., Berkeley-Yale U., 1963, D.D. (hon.), 1977; D. Ministry, N.Y. Theol. Sem., 1977. Ordained to ministry Episcopal Ch. as priest, 1963. Asst. St. Marks in the Bowery, N.Y.C., 1963-65; rector St. Andrew's, Yonkers, N.Y., 1965-71, Calvary, N.Y.C., 1971-75, Calvary-St. George's, N.Y.C., 1975—; trustee Cathedral St. John Divine, N.Y.C., 1978—; pres. Episc. Peace Fellowship, 1968-71. Commr. Commn. Human Rights, Yonkers, 1966-70; pres. Preservation League N.Y. State, Albany, 1984, Beth Israel Hosp., 1983. Parish fellow Fund Theol. Edn., 1974-75. Mem. Ch. and City, Partnership for Homeless. Club: Century Assn. (N.Y.C.). Home: 61 Gramercy Pk New York NY 10010 Office: Pierce House 209 E 16th St New York NY 10003

PILARCZYK, DANIEL EDWARD, archbishop, Roman Catholic Ch.; b. Dayton, Ohio, Aug. 12, 1934; s. Daniel Joseph and Frieda S. (Hilgefort) P.; student St. Gregory Sem., Cin., 1948-53; Ph.B., Pontifical Urban U., Rome, 1955, Ph.L., 1956, S.T.B., 1958, S.T.L., 1960, S.T.D., 1961; M.A., Xavier U., 1965; Ph.D., U. Cin., 1969. Ordained priest Roman Catholic Ch., 1959, consecrated bishop, 1974, archbishop, 1982; asst. chancellor Archdiocese of Cin., 1961-63, synodal judge Archdiocesan Tribunal, 1971-82; mem. faculty Athenaeum of Ohio, St. Gregory Sem., 1963-74, v.p. Athenaeum of Ohio, also rector St. Gregory Sem., 1968-74, trustee, 1974—; archdiocesan vicar for edn., 1974-82; aux. bishop of Cin., 1974-82; vicar gen., 1974-82; archbishop Diocese of Cin., 1982—. Ohio Classical Conf. scholar to Athens, 1966. Mem. Am. Philol. Assn. Author: Praepositini Cancellarii de Sacramentis et de Novissimis, 1964-65. Office: 100 E 8th St Cincinnati OH 45202

PILCHIK, ELY EMANUEL, rabbi, Reform Jewish Congregations; b. Russia, June 12, 1913; s. Abraham and Rebecca (Lipovitch) P.; came to U.S., 1920, naturalized, 1920; A.B., U. Cin., 1935; M.H.L., Hebrew Union Coll., 1936, D.D., 1964; m. Ruth Schuchat, Nov. 20, 1941 (dec. 1977); children: Susan Pilchik Rosenbaum, Judith Pilchik Zucker; m. Harriet Perlmutter, 1981. Ordained rabbi, 1939; founder, dir. Hillel Found., U. Md., College Park, 1939-40; rabbi Har Sinai Temple, Balt., 1940-41, Temple Israel, Tulsa, 1942-47; chaplain USNR, 1944-46; rabbi Temple B'nai Jeshurum, Short Hills, N.J., 1947—; prof. Jewish thought Upsala Coll., East Orange, N.J., 1969—. Pres. N.J. Bd. Rabbis, 1974-76; v.p. Central Conf. Am. Rabbis, 1975-77, pres., 1977-79; pres. Jewish Book Council Am. Recipient Man of Year award N.J. NCCJ, 1971. Author: Hillel, 1951; From the Beginning, 1956; Judaism Outside the Holy Land, 1964; Jeshrun Essays, 1967; Toby (a Play), 1968, others; 6 cantatas. Contbr. articles to religious jours. Home: 5 Cherrywood Circle West Orange NJ 07052 Office: 1025 S Orange Ave Short Hills NJ 07078

PILKENTON, KENNETH LEO, minister, International Convention of Faith Churches and Ministries; b. Tulsa, Aug. 23, 1943; s. Leo Silvester and Wilma Hiawatha (Franklin) P.; m. Martha Marie Lamb, Sept. 14, 1968. Student, Sam Houston State Coll., 1961, U. Houston, 1963, So. Bible Coll., 1967. Ordained to ministry Full Gospel Fellowship of Churches and Ministers, 1969. Co-founder, mgr. The Timesmen Quartet, Houston, 1964-68; assoc. mgr. McDuff Bros. Ministries, Pasadena, Tex., 1968-72; v.p., adminstr., Roger McDuff Evang. Assn., Pasadena, 1982-84; founder, pres. Spiritual Life Ministries, McKinney, Tex., 1972—. Recipient Cert. Appreciation Rotary Club, 1976, Angels award, 1983. Named one of Outstanding Young Men Am. 1977. Office: Spiritual Life Ministries Inc PO Box 141 McKinney TX 75069

PILLA, ANTHONY MICHAEL, bishop, Roman Catholic Church; b. Cleve., Nov. 12, 1932; s. George and Libera (Nista) P. Student St. Gregory Coll. Sem., 1952-53, Borromeo Coll. Sem., 1955, St. Mary Sem., 1954, 56-59; B.A. in Philosophy, John Carroll U., Cleve., 1961, M.A. in History, 1967. Ordained priest Roman Cath. Ch., 1959. Assoc. St. Bartholomew Parish, Middleburg Heights, Ohio, 1959-60; prof. Borromeo Sem., Wickliffe, Ohio, 1960-72, rector-pres., 1972-75; mem. Diocese Cleve. Liturgical Commn., 1964-69, asst. dir., 1969-72; sec. for services to clergy and religious personnel Diocese Cleve., 1975-79; titular bishop of Scardona, aux. bishop of Cleve. and vicar Eastern region Diocese of Cleve., 1979, apostolic adminstr. Diocese, 1980, bishop of Cleve., 1981—; trustee Borromeo Sem., 1975-79; trustee, race relations com. Greater Cleve. Roundtable, 1981—; trustee, mem. bd. overseers St. Mary Sem., 1975-79; adv. bd. permanent diaconate program Diocese of Cleve., 1975-79, mem. hospitalization and ins. bd., 1979. Bd. dirs. Cath. Communications Found., 1981—; trustee sta. WVIZ-TV, 1982. Mem. Nat. Cath. Edn. Assn. (dir. 1972-75), U.S. Cath. Conf., Nat. Conf. Cath. Bishops, Cath. Conf. Ohio. Address: 1027 Superior Ave Cleveland OH 44114

PILLOW, NATHAN HOWELL, minister, religious organization administrator, Southern Baptist Convention; b. Poplar Bluff, Mo., Feb. 3, 1939; s. Chester and Edith (Baird) P.; m. Peggy Ruth Thefford, June 4, 1960; children: Sherry Leah Pillow Tuttle, Lisa Paige. B.S. in English, Union U., 1960; postgrad. Midwest Bapt. Theol. Sem., 1962; D.D. (hon.), Grand Canyon Coll., 1974. Ordained to ministry First Baptist Ch., 1957. Pastor, Manor Bapt. Ch., Tucson, 1961-65, First Bapt. Ch., Yuma, Ariz., 1965-75; dir. evangelism Ariz. So. Bapt. Conv., Phoenix, 1975—, bd. dirs. 1963-69; evangelist Home Bapt. Mission, 1961, 69, 72; Ariz. rep. Radio and TV Commn., 1964-73; chaplain Ariz. Senate and Ho. Reps., 1966-76; pres. ASBC Pastors' Conf., 1968; v.p. exec. bd. Ariz. So. Bapt. Conv., 1967-70, 71-74; trustee Bapt. Sunday Sch. Bd., So. Bapt. Conv., 1975—; chmn. Ariz. Bapt. Children's Services Fund, 1975; established missions Southwestern U.S.; conductor many revival campaigns. Home: 10414 Sarazen Fountain Hills AZ 85269 Office: Ariz So Bapt Conv 400 W Camel Back Phoenix AZ 85013

PINCKNEY, ROBERT BICKLEY, minister, United Meth. Ch.; b. Lincoln, Nebr., Jan. 17, 1927; s. Charles Edward and Lillian Viola (Fox) P.; B.F.A., Southwestern U., 1963; B.Th., Burton Coll. and Sem., 1966; D.D., Evang. Sem., 1970; postgrad. So. Meth. U., 1970; m. Beatrice Ann Williams, Feb. 28, 1958; children—Charles Edward, David Bruce, Melody Ann. Ordained to ministry, 1963; sr. minister 1st Meth. Ch., Round Rock, Tex., 1959-61, Florence, Tex., 1961-63, St. Andrews Meth. Ch., Killeen, Tex., 1963-66, Glendale Meth. Ch., Dallas, 1966-67, 1st Meth. chs., Avery, Tex., 1967-68, Wolf City, Tex., 1968-69, St. Jo, Tex., 1969-72, Hutchins, Tex., 1973, Oak Park United Meth. Ch., Paris, Tex., 1974-76, 1st United Meth. Ch., Cedar Hill, Tex., 1976—. Mem. bd. social concerns, bd. publs., bd. evangelism Central Tex. Conf.; dir. Meth. Info., Georgetown Dist.; div. chmn. bd. ch. and soc. N.Tex. Ann. Conf., 1968-76. Mem. adv. bd. USO, Killeen, 1965-66; chmn. heritage div. Bicentennial Commn. for Paris and Lamar County, 1975—; judge St. Jo Municipal Ct., 1973-75; justice of peace, Montague County, Tex., 1973-75; bd. dirs. Sr. Citizens Bd., St. Jo. Home: 920 Harrington St Cedar Hill TX 75104 Office: PO Box 187 Cedar Hill TX 75104

PINKSTON, MOSES SAMUEL, minister, American Baptist Churches in the U.S.A.; b. Camden, N.J., Jan. 14, 1923; s. William Lincoln and Benena (McDonald) P.; m. Esther Miller, Nov. 18, 1951; children: Moses S. Jr., Steven Alan. B.A., Gordon Coll., 1949; M.Div., Temple U. Sch. Theology, 1952; M.S.W., Rutgers U., 1968; Ph.D., Calif. Grad. Sch. Theology, 1977. Ordained to ministry American Baptist Churches in the U.S.A., 1949. Area minister American Bapt. Chs., W. Oakland, Calif., 1970-74; dir. urban ministries Am. Bapt. Chs., W. Oakland, 1970-74; pastor Antioch Bapt. Ch., San Jose, Calif., 1974—. Atuhor: Black Church Development, 1977. Commr. Human Relations Commn., Santa Clara County, Calif., 1975-77; mem. Urban Task Force, San Jose, 1980-82, San Jose Minority Comn., 1984—. Served to lt. U.S. Army, 1943-46, ETO. Recipient Disting. Citizen award San Jose City, 1981. Mem. NAACP, Nat. Assn. Social Workers, Ministerial Alliance Santa Clara (pres. 1981). Democrat. Lodge: Masons. Home: 699 N White Rd San Jose CA 95127 Office: 268 E Julian St San Jose CA 95112

PINNER, JOSEPH WALTER, JR., priest, Episcopal Church; b. Memphis, June 5, 1950; s. Joseph Walter and Dorothy (Allstadt) P.; m. Anne Lauren McMahon, Nov. 25, 1969 (div. 1980); children: Thomas Edward, Daniel Mark; m. Sharon Monica Philpott, Jan. 26, 1981; 1 child, Megan Allstadt. B.A. in History, Southwestern U., 1972; M.Div., Va. Theol. Sem., 1975. Ordained priest, 1976. Deacon, St. Peter's Ch., Columbia, Tenn., 1975-76; priest-in-charge St. Thomas' Ch., Humboldt, Tenn., 1976-81, St. Paul's Ch., Picayune, Miss., 1982—; mem. Diocesan Commn. on Family Life, Jackson, Miss., 1983—, Diocesan Commn. on Compensation Rev., 1983—, Diocesan Commn. on Evangelism/Renewal, 1985—; chaplain Civil Air Patrol, 1980—. Mem. Amnesty Internat. Republican. Lodge: Rotary. Home: 1500 Goodyear Blvd Picayune MS 39466 Office: Saint Pauls Episcopal Ch 1421 Goodyear Blvd Picayune MS 39466

PIPER, EDWARD ALAN, minister, Luth. Ch. Am.; b. Webster City, Iowa, Nov. 18, 1929; s. Edward Albert and Tena Marie (Peterson) P.; B.A., Carthage Coll., 1952; M.Div., Gettysburg Luth. Theol. Sem., 1956; m. Patricia Aileen Groom, Nov. 4, 1962; children—Brian Alan, Melissa Aileen. Ordained to ministry, 1956; intern St. John's Luth. Ch., Des Moines, 1953-54; pastor Zion Luth. Ch., Princeton, Iowa, 1956-59; chaplaincy intern Iowa Meth. Hosp., Des Moines, 1960-61; asst. pastor St. Matthew's Luth. Ch., Davenport, Iowa, 1965-66; Protestant chaplain Iowa Annie Wittenmeyer Home, Davenport, 1966-71; pastor Zion Luth. Ch., Beloit, Kans., 1971—. Mem. synodical social ministry com., 1971, worship com., 1972-73. Bd. dirs. Sunflower Mental Health Center, Concordia, Kans., 1973—. Mem. Mitchell County Mental Health Assn. (pres. 1972-74), Mitchell County Assn. for Retarded Citizens, Beloit Ministerial Assn. (v.p. 1975-76). Home: 915 N Mill St Beloit KS 67420 Office: 621 N Mill St Beloit KS 67420

PIPPENS, GLENN E., minister, So. Bapt. Conv.; b. Forest, La., Dec. 26, 1932; s. Calvin Lee and Elon (Russell) P.; B.A., La. Coll., 1957; Th.M., New Orleans Bapt. Theol. Sem., 1960; m. Martha Ann Goff, Dec. 22, 1959; children—Mark Randall, Karen Dawn. Ordained to ministry, 1957; pastor Trinity Bapt. Ch., Oak Grove, La., 1956-69, North Monroe (La.) Bapt. Ch., 1960-68, Faith Bapt. Ch., Baker, La., 1968-74, Parkview Bapt. Ch., Alexandria, La., 1974—. Moderator Quachita Parish Bapt. Assn., Judson Bapt. Assn., Central La. Bapt. Assn., 1976—; trustee Arcadia Bapt. Home for Aged; chmn. credentials com. La. Bapt. Conv., also mem. program com., 1976—; chmn. evangelism Central La. Bapt. Assn.; mem. adv. com. Bapt. Studen Union. Mem. La. Coll. Alumni Assn. Decade Club (pres.). Home: 1215 Canterbury Dr Alexandria LA 71301 Office: 2101 MacArthur Dr Alexandria LA 71301

PIRKLE, ESTUS WASHINGTON, minister, Southern Baptist Convention; b. Vienna, Ga., Mar. 12, 1930; s. Grover Washington and Bessie Nora (Jones) P.; B.A. cum laude, Mercer U., 1951; B.D., M.R.E., Southwestern Bapt. Sem., 1956, Th. M., 1958; D.D., Covington Theol. Sem., 1982; m. Annie Catherine Gregory, Aug. 18, 1955; children—Letha Dianne, Gregory Don. Ordained to ministry, 1949. Pastor Locust Grove Bapt. Ch., New Albany, Miss.; speaker Camp Zion, Myrtle, Miss. Producer religious films: The Burning Hell, 1975; If Footmen Tire You, What Will Horses Do?, 1973; Believer's Heaven, 1977. Mem. Conf. So. Bapt. Evangelists. Author: Preachers in Space; I Believe God; Sermon Outlines Book; Who Will Build Your House? Home: PO Box 721 New Albany MS 38652 Office: PO Box 80 Myrtle MS 38650

PITTELKO, ELMER HENRY, minister, educator, Lutheran Church, Missouri Synod; b. Chgo., Oct. 31, 1906; s. Paul Henry and Augusta (Grossman) P.; m. Lydia Carolina Nieman, June 3, 1930; children: Roger Dean, Elaine Faith. B.D., Concordia Sem., St. Louis, 1935, M.Div., 1971; LL.B., Blackstone Coll. Law, 1934; Th.M., Am. Div. Sch., Pineland, Fla., 1946, Th.D., 1948, D.D. (hon.), 1948; postdoctoral Chgo. Theol. Luth. Sem., 1948-53; Ph.D. (hon.), St. Andrews Ecumenical U., London, 1949. Ordained to ministry Lutheran Ch., 1930. Pastor, Prince Albert Luth. Ch., Sask., Can., 1930-31, Trinity Luth. Ch., El Reno, Okla., 1931-41, Zion Luth. Ch., Fairmont, Okla., 1941-45, Immanuel Luth. Ch., Hillside, Ill., 1945-80; prof. history and religion, Concordia Coll., River Forest, Ill., 1951-55; faculty Am. Div. Sch., Pineland, 1951—; counselor Luth. Ch., Mo. Synod, Hillside, 1977-80; bd. dirs. Okla. Luth. Ch. Mo. Synod, Fairmont, 1940-45. Author hist. supplement, 1953. Republican. Clubs: Rotary (bd. dirs. Hillside 1965-80), Country (Itasca, Ill.). Home: 64 Grand Rd Elk Grove Village IL 60007

PITTELKO, ROGER DEAN, minister, Lutheran Ch.-Mo. Synod; b. El Reno, Okla., Aug. 18, 1932; s. Elmer Herman and Lydia Emma (Nieman) P.; B.A., Concordia Sem., St. Louis, 1954, B.D., M.Div., 1957; S.T.M., Chgo. Luth. Theol. Sem., 1958; Th.D., Am. Div. Sch., Pineland, Fla., 1968; m. Beverly Ann Moellendorf, July 6, 1957; children—Dean, Susan. Ordained to ministry, 1958; pastor chs. in N.Y. and La., 1955-59; pastor Concordia Luth. Ch., Berwyn, Ill., 1959-63, Holy Spirit Luth. Ch., Elk Grove Village, Ill., 1963—; chaplain Elk Grove Village Fire Dept., 1970—. Chmn. pastoral conf., bd. dirs. English dist. Luth. Ch.-Mo. Synod. Mem. Luth. Acad. Scholarship. Author: Concordia Pulpit, 1968, 72; Augsburg Sermons, 1977. Home: 64 Grange St Elk Grove Village IL 60007 Office: 666 Elk Grove Blvd Elk Grove Village IL 60007

PITTMAN, DAVID WEST, priest, Episcopal Church; b. Greenville, S.C., June 12, 1948; s. Wayne Creekmore and Dorothy Ethel (Groves) P.; m. Alene Belle Wright, May 17, 1970; children: David Wayne, Sarah Alene. B.A. in English, Va. Mil. Inst., 1970; M.Div., Va. Theol. Sem., 1973. Ordained priest, 1973. Asst. rector Trinity Ch., Staunton, Va., 1973-74, pirest-in-charge, 1974; vis. rector St. Andrew's Ch., Kelso, Scotland, 1977; rector Trinity Ch., Staunton, 1974—; mem. standing com. Diocese of Southwestern Va., 1983—, exec. bd., 1976-82; bd. trustees Va. Theol. Sem., 1984—. Mem. United Way bd., Staunton, 1978-82, Mental Health Assn. Bd., Staunton, 1982—, Transition Industries Bd., 1982—, Gifted and Talented Adv. Bd., Staunton City Schs., 1982-84. Named Outstanding Young Man of Yr., Staunton Jaycees, 1974. Mem. Staunton Ministerial Assn. (pres.). Lodge: Kiwanis (pres. 1979). Home: 25 Church St Staunton VA 24401 Office: Trinity Episcopal Ch PO Box 208 Staunton VA 24401

PITTMAN, FLOYD ELVISE, minister, Southern Baptist Convention; b. Penescott County, Mo., Apr. 5, 1914; s. Albert Sidney and Gertrude (Jamerson) P.; student Warrensburg State Tchrs. Coll., Central Sem.; D.D. (hon.), Jackson Coll., Honolulu, 1960; m. Corrine B. Hembree, Mar. 12, 1935. Ordained to ministry, 1935; pastor, Leeton-Chilhoue, Mo., 1939-40, Eldorado Springs, Mo., 1940-41; evangelist, 1942-45; missionary So. Bapt. Home Mission Bd., Calif. 1947-49; pastor Highland Ave. Baptist Ch., National City, Calif., 1949-62, Needles, Calif., 1967-74, Balboa Park So. Bapt. Ch., San Diego, 1974—. Moderator San Diego Bapt. Assn., 1951-53, River Valley So. Bapt. Assn., 1973; mem. coll. bd. Grand Canyon Bapt. Assn., Ariz., 1970-73; sec. Modesto (Calif.) Pastors' Conf., 1963-64. Mem. Dallas Relief and Annuity Bd.; active Boy Scouts Am. Home: 1305 Harbison St National City CA 92050 Office: 1305 Harbison Ave National City CA 92050

PITTMAN, SAMUEL COLLINS, religious educator, minister, Conservative Baptist Association; b. Monett, Mo., Aug. 7, 1926; s. Pennell Samuel and Kate (Collins) P.; m. Grace Ruth Danielson, Apr. 2, 1953; children: Janet Ruth, Joann Kay. B.A., Butler U., 1949; B.D., Fuller Sem., 1953, D.Min., 1971; M.A., Hartford Sem., 1954. Ordained to ministry, 1949. Missionary, Conservative Bapt. Fgn. Mission Soc., Wheaton, Ill., 1953-73; prof. faculty religion Northwestern Coll., Roseville, Minn., 1973—. Contbr. articles to profl. jours. Served with USN, 1944-6. Mem. Evang. Theol. Soc., Assn. Evang. Profs. of Mission, Am. Soc. Missiology, Evang. Philos. Soc. Republican. Home: 2205 Haddington Rd Roseville MN 55113 Office: Northwester.ı Coll Roseville MN 55113

PITTS, BERNICE EURA, JR., minister, Southern Baptist Convention; b. Hugo, Okla., Sept. 29, 1922; s. Bernice Eura and Kate Leam (Pennington) P.; B.A., Okla. Baptist U., 1945; B.D., Southwestern Bapt. Theol. Sem., 1949; m. Rachel Anne Waggener, Aug. 5, 1949; children—Martha Jean (Mrs. Jon Wright), Jan Elizabeth, James David. Ordained to ministry So. Bapt. Conv., 1943. Pastor Parkrose First Bapt. Ch., Portland, Oreg., 1951-56, Kennewick Bapt. Ch., Wash., 1956-58; supt. missions Columbia Basin and Yakima Bapt. Assns., Grandview, Wash., 1959-62, East Bay and South Bay Assns., Oakland, Calif., 1962-67, Interstate Bapt. Assn., Portland, 1967-72; Western annuity sec. Annuity Bd., So. Bapt. Conv., Fresno, Calif., 1973—. Home: 1461 E Vartikian St Fresno CA 93710 Office: 678 E Shaw Ave Fresno CA 93755

PIZAR, MARK MICHAEL, minister, Seventh-day Adventists. B. Haverhill, Mass., June 2, 1952; s. Norman Theodore and Gladys B. (Comeau) Currier; m. Terri Leigh Tinkham, Aug. 7, 1977; 1 child, Nathaniel David Benjamin. B.A. in Theology, Atlantic Union Coll., 1980. Ordained to ministry Seventh-day Adventists. Asst. pastor Seventh-day Adventist Ch., Rochester, N.Y., 1980-81, sr. pastor, East Palmyra, N.Y., 1981-82, sem. asst., Eau Claire, Mich., 1982-83, dist. pastor, Schenectady/Amsterdam, N.Y., 1983-84, evangelist, Schenectady, 1984-85; dist. pastor, Saratoga Springs, Amsterdam and Gloversville, N.Y., 1984-85. Composer/performer gospel music records. Served to sgt. USAF, 1972-74. Home: Route 1 Box 312 Malta Gardens D79 Mechanicsville NY 12118 (518) 899-2656 Office: N Y Conf Seventh-day Adventists 4930 W Seneca Turnpike Syracuse NY 13215

PLACE, JOSEPH WILLIAM, minister, Southern Baptist Convention; b. Williams, Ariz., Nov. 17, 1940; s. Joseph Davis and Gwendoline Mary (Williams) P.; m. Rayetta Ruth Zimmer, July 6, 1960; children: Dawn Leslie, Joseph Duane. Diploma in Theology, Southwestern Bapt. Theol. Sem., Ft. Worth, 1978; B.A., Dallas Bapt. Coll., 1979. Ordained to ministry Southern Baptist Convention, 1979. House ch. missions Gambrell St. Bapt. Ch., Ft. Worth, 1978-79; pastor Calvary So. Bapt. Ch., Mesa, Ariz., 1979—; v.p. Pastors Conf., Apache Bapt. Assn., Mesa, 1981-82, ch. tng. dir. for assn., 1983-84. Served with USNR, 1958-62. Home: 3057 W Manzanita Apache Junction AZ 85220 Office: Calvary Southern Baptist Ch 10115 E University St Mesa AZ 85207

PLAISTED, EUGENE DAVID, priest, school administrator, Roman Catholic Church; b. Mpls., July 15, 1935; s. Michael Bernard and Victoria Dora (Gothman) P. Student Crosier House of Studies, 1956-62; M.A. in Psychology, Cath. U., 1975. Ordained priest Roman Catholic Ch., 1961. Prof. liturgy Crosier House, Ft. Wayne, Ind., 1966-69; prior Crosier Monastery, Onamia, Minn., 1969-72, novice master, Hastings, Nebr., 1972-76; counselor Crosier Sem., Onamia, 1976-84, rector, 1984—; photographer. Democrat. Home: Crosier Sem Onamia MN 56359

PLAMONDON, PAUL OLIVIER, priest, Roman Catholic Ch.; b. Québec, Canada, Dec. 1, 1925; s. Israel and Rachel Jeanne (Rheault) P. B.A., Ottawa U., 1949, lic. in theology, 1953, Ph.D., 1959. Ordained priest Roman Catholic Ch., 1953. Tchr. Mathieu Coll., Gravelbourg, Sask., 1953-64; chaplain Marg. Bourgeois, Québec, 1966-68, St.-Antoine Home for Aged, Québec, 1983—, St. John the Bapt. Hosp., Québec, 1983—. Home: 1080 Belvedere Sellery PQ G1S 3G3 Canada

PLATE, MARGARET ALICE (MEG), organist, director of music, Episcopal Church; b. Bay City, Tex., Dec. 22, 1938; d. William Josiah and Frances Alene (Collier) Taylor; m. George L. Johnson, 1963 (div. 1968); children: Jennifer D., Rebecca D.; m. Ronald T. Plate, Aug. 1969 (div. 1979); 1 child, Elizabeth S. A.B. in Music, Vassar Coll., 1960. Organist, choir dir. St. Matthew's Episcopal Ch., Bellaire, Tex., 1964-71; assoc. organist, choirmaster St. John the Divine Ch., Houston, 1974-79; organist, choirmaster Ch. of Epiphany, Houston, 1975-79; organist, dir. music Palmer Meml. Episcopal Ch., Houston, 1979—; vestryman St. Matthew's Episcopal Ch., Bellaire, 1973-74; mem. Tex. Diocesan Music Commn., 1978—. Contbr. articles to Tex. Churchman, 1982-84. Shepherd Sch. Music of Rice U. teaching fellow, 1983—. Mem. Am. Guild Organists (dean 1978-80), Assn. Anglican Musicians, Sigma Alpha Iota. Home: 2222 Dorrington St Houston TX 77030 Office: Palmer Meml Episcopal Ch 6221 Main St Houston TX 77030

PLATT, ALBERT THOMAS, minister, religious organization administrator, Independent Baptist Ch.; b. Atlantic City, May 17, 1927; s. Raymond and Florence Mildred (Hitchner) P.; m. Gladys Ann Hage, June 17, 1948; children: Elizabeth Gayle Platt Sandoval, Roberta Ann Platt Friesen, Brenda Joann. B.A., Wheaton Coll., 1947; Th.M., Dallas Theol. Sem., 1951, Th.D., 1962. Ordained to ministry Ind. Bapt. Ch., 1951. Adminstr. programming Sta. TGNA, Guatemala City, Guatemala, 1952-60; prof., adminstr. Central Am. Bible Inst., Guatemala City, 1960-67; founder, pres. Central Am. Theol. Sem., Guatemala City, 1967-73; pres. Central Am. Mission Internat., Dallas, Tex., 1974—. Office: CAM Internat 8625 La Prada Dr Dallas TX 75228

PLATT, CHARLES ALEXANDER, minister, United Presbyterian Ch. in U.S.A.; b. Kansas City, Mo., Feb. 22, 1908; s. Mortimer R. and Ellen T. (Peake) P.; A.B. U. Mo., 1929; Th.B., Princeton, 1932; S.T.M., Mt. Airy Sem. 1941; S.T.D., Temple U., 1943; D.D., Waynesburg Coll., 1951; m. Mary Elizabeth Tucker, Aug. 5, 1933; children—Elizabeth E., C. Tucker, Charles Alexander. Ordained to ministry United Presbyn. Ch. in the U.S.A., 1932; asst. pastor ch., Middletown, N.Y., 1932-35, East Orange, N.J., 1935-38; pastor ch., Ambler, Pa., 1938-42; pastor, Ridgewood, N.J., 1942-73, pastor emeritus, 1973—. Moderator, Presbytery of Jersey City, 1952-53, Synod of N.J., 1962-63. Trustee Beaver Coll., Blair Acad.; bd. dirs. Bloomfield Coll. Mem. Lord's Day Alliance U.S. (pres. Atlanta). Author pamphlets, articles, booklets. Address: RD 3 Box 468 Newton NJ 07860

PLATT, MARVIN EARL, minister, Christian Chs.; b. Ft. Scott, Kans., Aug. 19, 1936; s. Eldon Louie and Nora Louise (Sharpless) P.; B.S.L., Ozark Bible Coll., Joplin, Mo., 1965; D.D. (hon.), Crossroads Sch. Div., Farmland, Ind., 1976; m. Lola Emily Sproul, May 12, 1957; children—William Earl, Timothy James, Dennis Dean, Kimberly Renae. Ordained to ministry, 1962; faculty Berea Christian Coll., Wichita, Kans., 1975-76, v.p., 1976—. Dean camps Wichita, 1967; organizer, leader youth orgn. Christ Crusader, 1966-67; organizer Risen Sun Christian Camp, Louisville, Nebr., 1968-69; pres. bd. Show Me Christian Youth Home, Lamonte, Mo., 1966-73; pres. Knob Noster (Mo.) Ministerial Alliance, 1971-72. Named Tchr. of Year, Lecton, Mo., 1972. Mem. Evang. Tchrs. Assn. Home: 2419 Pattie St Wichita KS 67216 Office: 2417 Pattie St Wichita KS 67216

PLAUT, JONATHAN VICTOR, rabbi, national official, Reform Jewish Congregations; b. Chgo., Oct. 7, 1942; s. W. Gunther and Elizabeth (Strauss) P.; B.A., Macalester Coll., 1964; B.H.L., Hebrew Union Coll., Jewish Inst. Religion, Cin., 1968, M.A., 1970, D.H.L., 1977; m. Carol Ann Fainstein, July 5, 1965; children—Daniel, Deborah. Rabbi, 1970; rabbi Congregation Beth El, Windsor, Ont., Can., 1970-84; sr. rabbi Temple Emanu-El, San Jose, Calif., 1985—; mem. exec. bd. central region Can. Jewish Congress, 1970-84, mem. nat. archives com., 1974-84; mem. nat. bd. Orgn. Rehab. Tng., Can., 1973-84, chmn. Windsor chpt., 1972-84; mem. exec. com. Windsor Jewish Community Council, 1970-84, chmn. archives com., 1975-84; mem. exec. com. Can. Council Liberal Congregations, 1970-84; adj. asst. prof. religious studies U. Santa Clara, 1985—. Lectr., Coll. Jewish Studies, Southfield, Mich., 1970-72; v.p. Jewish Hist. Soc. Can., 1976-84; lectr. Assumption Coll. Sch., Windsor, 1972-84; hon. chaplain B'nai B'rith, 1970-84; mem. exec. cabinet United Jewish Appeal, Windsor, 1970-84, deputy chmn., 1980-82, chmn., 1982-84; mem. Can. nat. bd. Jewish Nat. Fund., 1974-84, pres., Windsor, 1976-80, chmn. bd. dirs., 1980-84; mem. Nat. Council Christians and Jews; host radio program Religion in the News, Windsor, 1971-84, TV program Religious Scope, 1972-84. Editor: Can. Hist. Soc. Jour., 1977—; Through the Sound of Many Voices; editorial writer and book reviewer Windsor Star, 1972; contbr. articles to Can. Jewish News, San Jose Jewish News. Home: 6216 Balderstone Dr San Jose CA 95120 Office: 1010 University Ave San Jose CA 95126

PLAUT, WOLF GUNTHER, rabbi, Reform Jewish Congregations; b. Münster, Germany, Nov. 1, 1912; s. Jonas and Selma (Gumprich) P.; came to Can., 1961; LL.B., U. Berlin, 1933; Dr.iur.utr., U. Berlin (Germany), 1934; M.H.L., Rabbi, Hebrew Union Coll., 1939, D.D. (hon.), 1964; m. Elizabeth Strauss, Nov. 10, 1938; children—Jonathan, Judith. Rabbi, Chgo., 1939-48, St. Paul, 1948-61; sr. rabbi Holy Blossom Temple, Toronto, Ont., Can., 1961—. Chaplain AUS, 1943-46; chmn. United Jewish Appeal Campaign, 1970; nat. chmn. religious affairs Canadian Jewish Congress, 1969-74, fgn. affairs, 1974—; chmn. Can. sect. Central Conf. Am. Rabbis, 1976—; mem. governing bd. World Union for Progressive Judaism, 1970—; nat. co-chmn. Can.-Israel com., 1976—. Chmn. gov.'s commn. on ethics in govt., Minn., 1958-61; pres. St. Paul Gallery and Sch. of Art, 1953-59; nat. pres. World Federalists Can., 1966-68. Editorial contbr. Globe and Mail, 1962—; author: Genesis-A Commentary, 1974; Page 2, 1971; Your Neighbour is a Jew, 1967; The Case for the Chosen People, 1965; The Growth of Reform Judaism, 1964; The Rise of Reform Judaism, 1963, others. Office: Canadian Jewish Congress 1590 Ave Docteur Penfield Montreal PQ H3B 1C5 Canada

PLEXICO, THURMOND CLAUDE, minister, Luth. Ch. Am.; b. Columbia, S.C., Oct. 10, 1928; s. Claude Good and Lida Mae (Denny) P.; A.B., Lenoir-Rhyne Coll., 1948; M.Div., Luth. Sem., Columbia, 1951, postgrad., 1956; postgrad. Princeton Theol. Sem., 1953, U. S.C., 1948-49, U. N.C., 1977; m. Mary Katherine Wilhelm, July 6, 1952; 1 son, Byron Kent. Ordained to ministry, 1951; pastor Union Ch., Salisbury, N.C., 1951-53; pastor Our Savior Ch. and dir. Luth. Servicemen's Center, Jacksonville, N.C., 1953-63; pastor St. James Ch., Concord, N.C., 1963—. Pres. Ministerial Assn. Salisbury and Jacksonville, N.C., Onslow and Cabarrus counties, N.J.; Luth. Ch. Am. rep. to Luth. Council U.S.A.; preacher numerous missions in S.W.; chaplain-preacher for ch. convs. Pres. Cabarrus and Onslow counties United Fund, ARC for Cabarrus and Onslow counties; active Boy Scouts Am.; chmn. Cabarrus Human Relations Commn.; mem. steering com. USO; instr. sociology Sch. Nursing, Concord. Mem. Luth. Soc. Rotary Found. Fellow, 1975. Author: The Church Wedding, 1963; The Christian's Funeral, 1976; contbr. articles to religious jours. Home: 97 Grove Ave NW Concord NC 28025

PLOCH, CLARENCE EARL, minister, United Meth. Ch.; b. Louisville, Feb. 3, 1914; s. George Raymond and Emma Grace (Tate) P.; B.A., U. Louisville, 1936;

M.Div., Garrett Theol. Sem., 1939; m. Helen Jane Swits, Dec. 8, 1940; children—Robert Swits, Richard Raymond, John Carl. Ordained deacon, 1940, elder, 1942; minister, Houghton-Hancock, Mich., 1939-40, Albany-Thomson, Ill., 1940-42, Warren, Ill., 1942-45, Olivet United Meth. Ch., Chgo., 1945-51, Zion (Ill.) United Meth. Ch., 1951-57, Ottawa St. Ch., Joliet, Ill., 1957-61, 1st United Meth. Ch., DeKalb, Ill., 1961-65; supt. Chgo. So. Dist., 1965-70; minister Gary Meml. United Meth. Ch., Wheaton, Ill., 1970-76, 1st United Meth. Ch., Belvidere, Ill., 1976—. Pres., Wheaton Ministerial Assn., 1975-76; chmn. higher edn. No. Ill. Conf., 1960-64, chmn. bd. edn., 1961-65, chmn. conf. program, 1972—. Recipient citation Mayor of Chgo., 1950, Scouting award of honor, 1976. Mem. Cum Laude Soc., Belvidere Ministerial Assn. Editor of Jour. No. Ill. Conf., 1954-59. Home: 532 Whitney Blvd Belvidere IL 61008 Office: 534 Whitney Blvd Belvidere IL 61008

PLONA, MARY FEBRONIA, nun, Roman Catholic Ch.; b. Gardner, Mass., Oct. 2, 1912; d. Alexander and Alexandra (Wiski) P.; diploma St. Catherine's Hosp. Sch. Nursing, Bklyn., 1944; B.S. in Nursing, St. Joseph's Coll., 1959. Joined Daus. of Mary of the Immaculate Conception, 1936; nurse New Britain (Conn.) Meml. Hosp., 1944-54; adminstr. Our Lady of Rose Hill Home, New Britain, 1954-63, St. Lucian's Home, New Britain, 1965—. Bd. dirs. Hartford Council Cath. Nurses, 1960, Sancta Maria Hosp., Cambridge, Mass., 1972-76, Monsignor Bojnowski Manor, New Britain, 1973, Conn. Assn. Non-Porfit Facilities for Aged, 1967-74, 76—. Mem. Cath. Hosp. Assn., Nat. Geriatric Soc., Conn. Soc. Gerontology, Nat. Council on Aging, New Britain Conf. Chs. Address: 532 Burritt St New Britain CT 06053

PLOURDE, J-AURELE, bishop, Roman Catholic Ch.; b. St. Francois, N.B., Can., Jan. 12, 1915; s. Antoine and Suzanne (Albert) P.; B.A., St. Joseph's U., Moncton, 1939; student Halifax Maj. Sem., 1939-44, Cath. Inst. Paris, 1947-48; Licentiate Social Scis., Ottawa U., 1948-50; L.M. in Theology, Gregorian U., Rome, 1960. Ordained priest Roman Cath. Ch., 1944; asst. St. Quentin, N.B., 1944-46; sec. to bishop Edmundston, N.B., 1946-47; prof. philosophy St. Louis Coll., Edmundston, 1950-55; pastor St. Leonard Parish, N.B., 1955-59; aux. bishop of Alexandria, 1964-67; archbishop Ottawa, 1967—. Address: 256 King Edward Ave Ottawa ON K1N 7M1 Canada

PLUMMER, ROGER ALLISON, minister, United Church of Christ, National Association Congregational-Christian Churches; b. Somerville, Mass., Dec. 18, 1937; s. Elmer Winslow and Hazel Kathleen (Allison) P.; B.A., Gordon Coll., 1960; B.D. cum laude, Eastern Seminary, 1963; D.Min., Andover Newton Theol. Sch., 1976; m. Jean Alice Cooper, May 25, 1963; children: Jonathan Mark, Victoria Leigh, Carolyn Anne. Ordained to Ministry, 1963; pastor Alton (N.H.) Federated Chs., 1963-66, pastor United Ch., Milw., 1966-71, First Congregational Ch., Wolfeboro, N.H., 1971-83, First Congregational Ch., Terre Haute, Ind., 1983—. Mem. com. on multidenoml. ministries N.H. conf. United Ch. Christ, 1962-63; sec. Wis.-Milw. Religious Broadcasting Ministry, 1967-71; chmn. Christian edn. com. Milw. Bapt. Assn., 1967-68; rep. Disciples of Christ for consultation on ch. union, Wis., 1968-70; coordinator Interdenoml. radio-TV com. Sta. WTMJ, Milw., 1968-71; Program Com. N.H. conf. United Ch. Christ, 1971-72; pres. Wolfeboro Area Ministerial Assn., 1972; chmn. program com. Geneva Point Center, Nat. Council Chs. of Christ, 1972-74; chaplaincy com. Carroll County Home, 1972, 73, 74; scribe-treas. Carroll-Stratford Assn., N.H. conf., 1974-83; clergy cons. N.H. Hosp., Concord, 1975-77; served on workshops, as lectr. for continuing edn. on death and dying Huggins Hosp., Wolfeboro, 1973, 74, 76, Ind. State U. Sch. Nursing, 1984. Mem. Boy Scouts Am. Com., Milw., 1967-68; mem. bd. Am. Cancer Soc., Carroll-South Unit, 1972-73; pres. bd. dirs. Wolfeboro area "Meals-on-Wheels" Program, 1974-80; substitute tchr. Carpenter Elementary Sch., 1974; tchr. Brewster Acad., Wolfeboro, 1974; mem. eval. com. Family Life and Sex Edn. program Gov. Wentworth Regional Sch. Dist., Wolfeboro, 1975-78; chmn. steering com. Carroll County Citizens on Alcohol, 1976—; bd. dirs. Carroll County Mental Health, 1976-83, Planned Parenthood Wabash Valley, 1984—, Alts. to Learning and Living, Terre Haute, 1984—. Parish Minister fellow, 1969. Mem. Wabash Valley Assn., Inst. of Soc. Ethics and Life Scis., Soc. for Human and Health Values. Office: 630 Ohio St Terre Haute IN 47807

PLUNK, JERE HAYNES, minister, Southern Baptist Convention. B. Jackson, Tenn., Aug. 2, 1943; s. Crolin Edgar and Annie Laurie (Haynes) P.; m. Linda Margaret West, Jan. 17, 1967; children: Jonathan Matthew, Laurie Gail, David Christopher. B.A., Samford U., 1966; M.Div., So. Bapt. Theol. Sem., 1970, D.Min., 1980. Ordained, 1967. Pastor Riverview Bapt. Ch., Berry, Ky., 1967-68; asst. pastor Jefferson St. Bapt. Ch., Louisville, 1968-70; pastor North Fork Bapt. Ch., Shelbyville, Tenn., 1972, Immanuel Bapt. Ch., Murfreesboro, Tenn., 1972-75, 1st Bapt. Ch., Carthage, Tenn., 1975—; exec. bd. Tenn. Bapt. Conv., 1980—, mem. state missions com., 1980—, rec. sec. exec. bd., 1984-85; various offices including moderator, New Salem Assn. Baptists, Carthage, 1975—; chaplain Smith County High Sch. Football and Basketball Team, 1978-84; sec. Smith County Ministerial Alliance, Carthage, 1978-83. Contbr. article to mag. Pres., Smith County Flood Relief Orgn., 1982; mem. Smith County Foster Care Rev. Bd., 1980-85; Eagle Scout, Middle Tenn. Council Boy Scouts Am., 1958, vice chmn. Explorers, Tenn., 1960. Republican. Home: 516 Carmack Ave Carthage TN 37030 Office: First Bapt Ch PO Box 191 Carthage TN 37030

POE, JACK O'BRIAN, minister, Southern Baptist Convention; b. Little Rock, Feb. 8, 1941; s. Arthur O'Brian and Velma Winifred (Owens) P.; B.A., Central State U., 1965; B.D., Southwestern Bapt. Theol. Sem., 1969; D.Min., Phillips U., 1975; m. Phyllis Ann Futrell, Aug. 18, 1961; children: David O'Brian, Robin Denise. Ordained to ministry, 1966; pastor dept. missions, First Bapt. Ch., Dallas, 1967-69; pastor Oak Ave. Bapt. Ch., Ada, Okla., 1969-71, First Bapt. Ch., Kingfisher, Okla., 1971-75, Highland Hills Bapt. Ch., Oklahoma City, 1975-84; chaplain Oklahoma city Police Dept., 1984—. Chaplain Oklahoma Nat. Guard, 1971—, Kingfisher Police Dept., 1972-75. Mem. Internat. Conf. Police Chaplains, Okla. Sheriff and Police Officers Assn., Okla. Res. Law Enforcement Assn. Contbr. articles to profl. jours. Home: 6920 Stonycreek St Oklahoma City OK 73132 Office: 7900 Devore St Oklahoma City OK 73132

POELLOT, LUTHER, minister, Lutheran Church-Missouri Synod; b. Palatine, Ill., Oct. 23, 1913; s. Sigfried Daniel and Lisette (Brueggemann) P.; student Concordia Coll., Milw., 1927-33, Concordia Sem., St. Louis, 1933-37; m. Esther Maaser, May 23, 1942; children—Sharon Ruth, Carolyn May (Mrs. Ray Gluesenkamp), Marion Kay, Celia Louise (Mrs. Terry Williams). Ordained to ministry Luth. Ch.-Mo. Synod, 1942; head clk. Concordia Sem. library, St. Louis, 1937-39; missionary, Ft. Myers, Fla., 1940; pastor chs., Dallas, 1940-50, Mercedes, Tex., 1950-52, Pitcairn, Pa., 1952-62, Waterloo, Ont., Can., 1962-64; indexer and editor Concordia Pub. House, St. Louis, 1964-78. Author: Revelation, 1962, 76; translator: Ministry, Word, and Sacraments, 1981; contbr. articles to profl. jours. Home: 753 Buckley Rd Saint Louis MO 63125

POETTCKER, HENRY, seminary pres. Mennonite Ch. Gen. Conf. Former pres. Canadian Mennonite Bible Coll., now pres. Mennonite Bibl. Sem.; pres. Gen. Conf. Mennonite Ch., 1968-74. Address: 3003 Benham Ave Elkhart IN 46517

POETZEL, RICHARD KARL, religious educator, priest, Roman Catholic Church; b. Balt., Nov. 1, 1936; s. Carl Alphonsus and Magdalen Anna (Weber) P. B.A., Mt. St. Alphonsus Sem., 1960; M.S.L.S., Cath. U. Am., 1968; M.A., U. Notre Dame, 1975. Redemptorist profession, 1958, ordained priest, 1963. Librarian, Mt. St. Alphonsus Sem., Esopus, N.Y., 1965-76, dir. liturgy, 1968-83, prof. liturgical theology, 1978—, v.p., acad. dean, 1984—. Contbr. articles to profl. jours. Editor/compiler: Manual of Community Prayers for the Baltimore and St. Louis Provinces, 1971. Mem. Nat. Assn. Pastoral Musicians, N. Am. Acad. Liturgy, Societas Liturgica, Eastern Conf. Major Sem. Deans, Am. Assn. Collegiate Registrars and Admissions Officers, Beta Phi Mu. Address: Mount Saint Alphonsus Sem Esopus NY 12429

POGANSKI, DONALD JOHN, minister, Luth. Ch.-Mo. Synod; b. Foley, Minn., Oct. 6, 1928; s. Emil Frederick and Bertha Minnie (Burski) P.; B.Th., Concordia Theol. Sem., Springfield, Ill., 1955; m. Doris Lilly Ann Mueller, June 7, 1953; children—David, Karen, Cynthia. Ordained to ministry, 1955; minister Christ Luth. Ch., Cin., 1955-63, Trinity Luth. Ch., Montclair, Calif., 1963-70, Zion Luth. Ch., San Luis Obispo, Calif., 1970—. Recipient Servus Ecclesiae Christi award Concordia Theol. Sem., 1971. Author: 50 Object Lessons, 1967; 40 Object Lessons, 1973; contbr. articles to religious jours. Home and office: 1010 Foothill Blvd San Luis Obispo CA 93401

POHL, LEIF ALAN, minister, Lutheran Church in America; b. Milw., Sept. 22, 1940; s. Neil Alan and Frieda Herma Auguste (Radtke) P.; m. Janice Jean Forsyth, May 28, 1966; children: Eric, Jennifer, Andrew, Thomas. B.A. in Botany, U. Colo.-Boulder, 1962; B.A. (M.Div.), Luth. Sch. Theology at Chgo., 1966. Ordained to ministry Lutheran Church in America, 1966. Campus pastor Ball State U., Muncie, Ind., 1966-69; assoc. pastor Holy Trinity Luth. Ch., Muncie, 1966-69; pastor Faith Luth. Ch., Owensboro, Ky., 1969-76, Our Saviour Luth. Ch., Valparaiso, Ind., 1976—; mem. exec. bd. Ind.-Ky. Synod, Luth. Ch. in Am., Indpls., 1973-76, parliamentarian, 1979—, chmn. task force on ecumenism, 1983—; dean Evansville dist. Luth. Ch. in Am., Ind., 1973-76; dir. Luth. Relief Fund, Porter County, 1984—; mem. gen. assembly, mem. nominating com., mem. dept. ecumenical concerns Ind. Council Chs. Contbr. articles to religious publs. Sec. Portage Twp. Emergency Food Pantry, 1982—. NSF research grantee, 1960, 71. Mem. Porter County Luth. Council (pres. 1980-83), Portage Ministers Fellowship. Home: 771 McCool Rd Valparaiso IN 46383 Office: Our Saviour Luth Ch 799 Capital Rd Valparaiso IN 46383

POIRÉ, MARC-VERCHÈRES, priest chaplain, Roman Catholic Church; b. Beaumont, Quebec, Can., Oct. 19, 1931; s. Edgar and Blanche (Maftel) P. B.L., Laval U., Quebec, 1952, B.A., 1954, B. Theology, 1958, M. Theology, 1964; cert. in English, Winooski U., Vt., 1960; postgrad. U. Detroit, 1961, U. Sherbrooke, 1967. Ordained priest Roman Catholic Ch., 1958. Priest Parish St. Louis-Couville, Quebec City, 1958-59, St. Agapit, Lotbiniere, Que., 1962-65; chaplain Pub. High Sch., Quebec, 1966-72, Employees and Police Dept., Quebec City, 1972—; del. Internat. Conf. Police Chaplains, Quebec, 1975-84; tchr. Seminaire du Sacré-Coeur, St. Victor, Que., 1959-62, St. Michael's Coll. High Sch., Toronto, Ont., 1965-66. Mem. Internat. Conf. Police Chaplains (recipient John A. Price Excellence in Chaplancy award 1984). Mem. Internat. Conf. Police Chaplains. Home: 490 Rue St-Jean Quèbec PQ GIR 1P4 Canada Office: Centrale De Police 475 Rue Gignac Quèbec PQ GIL 4P3 Canada

POKORNY, DANIEL HARRY, minister, Luth. Ch.-Mo. Synod; b. N.Y.C., Apr. 18, 1937; s. Harry and Anna (Kocsis) P.; M.Div., Concordia Sem., St. Louis, 1961; M.S.W., Ind. U., Indpls., 1967; m. Patricia Louise Florine, Apr. 25, 1964; children—James Duncan, Philip Daniel, David Andrew, Elizabeth Ann. Ordained to ministry, 1961; pastor in Indpls., 1961-67; chaplain Gallaudet Coll., Washington, 1967—. Dir., Center for Devel. Deaf Ministry, Southeastern Dist.; gen. sec. 2d Internat. Tng. Seminar for Pastoral Care of Deaf. Recipient Algernon Syndney Sullivan award, 1974; Spl. Service award Nat. Assn. of the Deaf, 1975. Mem. Registry of Interpreters for Deaf, Profl. Rehab. Workers Among Adult Deaf, Nat. Assn. Social Workers. Author: (with others) Lift Up Your Hands, 1976. Editor: My Eyes are My Ears, 1975; co-editor: The Word in Signs and Wonders, 1976. Originator of Rock Gospel contemporary music concerts for deaf, 1969. Home: 4703 Montgomery Pl Beltsville MD 20705 Office: Box 1024 Gallaudet Coll Washington DC 20002

POLEN, OLLY WAYNE, editor, Ch. of God; b. Clinton, Ill., Dec. 31, 1920; s. Ollie William and Allie Minerva (Mellinger) P.; student Ohio State U., 1950-52; D.D. (hon.), West Coast Bible Coll., 1973; m. Neva Grace Feucht, Aug. 27, 1942; children—Janet (Mrs. Jim Price), Connie L. Ordained to ministry Ch. of God (Cleveland, Tenn.), 1947; pastor Ch. of God, Shelby, O., 1945-46; state Sunday sch. and youth dir. of Ohio, Columbus, 1946-54; asst. nat. Sunday sch. and youth dir., 1954-56, nat. Sunday sch. and youth dir., Cleveland, Tenn., 1956-60; pastor West Flint Ch. of God, Flint, Mich., 1960-68; state overseer Ch. of God in Md., Del. and Washington, 1968-70; editor in chief Ch. of God Publs., Cleveland, Tenn., 1970—, mem. exec. council, 1966-70, 72-76. Mem. gen. editorial and publs. bd. Ch. of God, Cleveland, 1968-70. Author: The Sunday School Teachĕr, 1956; Editorially Speaking, 1975; Living By the Word, 1977. Contbr. articles to profl. jours. Home: 1140 Peoples St Cleveland TN 37311 Office: 1080 Montgomery Ave Cleveland TN 37311

POLIN, MILTON HAROLD, rabbi, Orthodox Jewish Congregations; b. Chgo., Oct. 7, 1930; s. Abraham Noah and Dorothy (Blacher) P.; m. Sainee Fagy Sachs, Aug. 15, 1954; children: Kenneth Saul, Dorothy Anne, Rena Beth, Gail Menucha, Nechama Bea. M.A., U. Chgo., 1953; B. Hebrew Lit., Hebrew Theol. Coll., Chgo., 1954, D.H.L., 1982. Ordained rabbi, 1954. Rabbi Mt. Sinai Congregation, Cheyenne, Wyo., 1954-56, Keneseth Israel Congregation, Louisville, 1956-66, Tpheris Israel Chevra Kadisha, St. Louis County, Mo., 1966-74, Kingsway Jewish Ctr., Bklyn., 1974—; adj. lectr. Touro Coll., N.Y.C., 1977; bd. govs. Union Orthodox Jewish Congregations Am., N.Y.C., 1982—; chmn. Kashruth Commn., 1979-84; rabbinical adv. council Fedn. Campaign United Jewish Appeal, N.Y.C., 1982—; bd. edn. Yeshivah of Flatbush, Bklyn., 1983—. Contbr. to RCA Sermon Manuals, 1955—. Recipient Rabbinical Communal award Yeshivat Mizrachi L'Banim, Bklyn., 1984; Disting. Service award Louisville Jr. C. of C., 1964, Citation of Honor, Jewish Nat. Fund, N.Y.C., 1984, Chief Rabbi Herzog medal Religious Zionists Am., N.Y.C., 1976. Mem. Rabbinical Council Am. (1st v.p. 1984—), Rabbinical Bd. Flatbush (pres. 1979-81), N.Y. Bd. Rabbis. Office: Kingsway Jewish Ctr 2810 Nostrand Ave Brooklyn NY 11229

POLING, DAVID, minister, United Presbyterian Church in U.S.A.; b. Spring Lake, N.J., Oct. 15, 1928; s. Paul Newton and Olive (Tomlinson) P.; B.A. in History, Coll. of Wooster (Ohio), 1950; M.Div., Yale, 1953; L.H.D., Willamette U., 1969; D.D., Hope Coll., 1970; m. Ann Reid, Sept. 5, 1950; children—John D., Lesley A. Poling Kempes, Andrew P., Charles C. Ordained to ministry, 1953; pastor Leroy (N.Y.) Presbyn. Ch., 1953-57, Lafayette Presbyn. Ch. of Buffalo, 1957-62, First Presbyn. Ch., Bartlesville, Okla., 1962-64; pres. Christian Herald, 1964-71; dir. S.W. Mission Found., Albuquerque, 1971-75; pastor First United Presbyn. Ch., Albuquerque, 1975—; nat. radio preacher The Protestant Hour, 1984. Religious editor Newspaper Enterprise Assn. Recipient Wade prize in Preaching, Yale, 1953. Author: Last Years of the Church, 1969; Schweitzer, 1971; They Walked with Christ, 1971; This Great Company, 1976; Songs of Faith/Signs of Hope, 1976; Why Billy Graham?, 1977;

The Search For America's Faith, 1980. Contbr. articles to popular mags. Home: 3735 Manchester St NW Albuquerque NM 87107 Office: 215 Locust St NE Albuquerque NM 87102

POLING, KERMIT WILLIAM, minister, United Methodist Church; b. Elkins, W.Va., Oct. 1, 1941; s. Durward Willis and Della Mae (Boyles) P.; diploma in Bible, Am. Bible Sch., 1966; B.A. in Bible, Reed Coll. Religion, 1968; A.A., W.Va. U., 1970; Th.D., Zion Theol. Sem., 1971; postgrad. Wesley Theol. Sem., 1974; LL.D., Geneva Theol. Coll., 1980; D.S.L. (hon.), Berean Christian Coll., 1981; m. Patricia Ann Groves, June 12, 1965; children—David Edward Elson, Mikael Erik. Ordained to ministry Evang. United Brethren Ch., 1967; pastor, Parkersburg-Crossroads Circuit, 1967-70; asst. sec. W.Va. Ann. Conf., 1967-69; pastor Hope-Halleck Morgantown Circuit, 1970-76, Trinity-Warren Grafton (W.Va.) Charge, 1976-83, First Trinity Pennsboro Charge, 1983—; Editor, Local Ch. News, 1968-73; instr. Bible, Bodkin Bible Inst., 1972-75; mem. staff Taylor County Coop. Parish, 1976-83; coordinator Hughes River Coop. Parish, 1983—; mem. chaplains com. Grafton City Hosp., 1976-82; mem. council Centre D'Etudes Et D'Action Oecumeniques, 1972-74. Decorated Royal Afghanistan Order of Crown of Amanullah; Order of Polonia Restituta; Mystical Order of St. Peter; recipient Good Citizenship award, Doddridge County, 1954, Silver medal Ordre Universel du Merit Humain, Geneva, 1973. Mem. Internat. Platform Assn., SAR, Sovereign Order St. John of Jerusalem, Knights of Malta, Ritchie County Ministerial Assn. (pres. 1984—), Order Sacred Cup. Author: A Crown of Thorns, 1963; A Silver Message, 1964; Eastern Rite Catholicism, 1971; History of the Halleck Church, 1970; Oriental Orthodox Churches and Church of the East, 1971; From Brahmin to Bishop, 1976; Cult and Occult: Data and Doctrine, 1978; contbr. articles and poems to religious jours. Home: 118 Ray Ave Pennsboro WV 26415 Office: Penn and Main Sts Pennsboro WV 26415

POLING, SYLVIA NETTIE, educator; b. Cripple Creek, Colo., 1902; d. William Charles and May Ernestine (Koenen) Poling; student Tempe Normal Coll., 1923; B.A., Ariz. State U., 1940, M.A., 1945. C.S. practitioner, Phoenix, 1950—; C.S. tchr., Phoenix, 1958—; lectr. C.S., U.S., Can., Eng., Europe, Australia, New Zealand, 1956-66. Republican. Contbr. articles to religious periodicals. Home: 2401 W Southern St #B65 Tempe AZ 85282 Office: 610 W Broadway Suite 120 Tempe AZ 85281

POLIZZI, SUSAN MARY PANEK, minister, American Baptist Churches in the U.S.A.; b. Plainfield, N.J., Sept. 16, 1956; d. Edward Stephen and Mary Ann (Crede) Panek; m. Emanuel Victor Polizzi, June 3, 1984. B.A., Ohio Wesleyan U., 1978; M.Div., Colgate Rochester/Bexley Hall/Crozer Theol. Sem., 1981. Ordained to ministry Am. Baptist Chs., 1981. Assoc. pastor First Bapt. Ch., Waukesha, Wis., 1981—; mem. commn. on Christian Edn., Wis. Bapt. State Conv., 1981—, chmn. commn. on Christian Edn., 1984; v.p. Roger Williams fellowship Am. Bapt. Chs. U.S.A., 1984. Bd. dirs., v.p. Kindcare, Inc., Milw., 1983—. Shelbyville Bapt. scholar Colgate Rochester/Bexley Hall/Crozer Theol. Sem., 1980, Am. Bible Soc. scholar, 1981. Mem. Wis. Bapt. Ministers Council (treas. 1982-84). Home: 426 E North Ave Apt 104 Waukesha WI 53186 Office: First Bapt Ch PO Box 244 Waukesha WI 53187

POLK, ROBERT L., minister, United Church of Christ, organization executive; b. Chgo., May 8, 1928; s. Tillman Prentice and Lilly (Bell) P.; children: George, Robert. B.A., Doane Coll., 1952, D.D. (hon.), 1972; M.Div., Hartford Theol. Sem., 1955; D.D. (hon.), Tillotson Coll., 1984. Ordained to ministry United Ch. of Christ, 1955. Pastor, First Congl. Ch., Berthold, N.D., 1955-57; youth program dir. YMCA, Minot, N.D., 1957-60; minister to youth Riverside Ch., N.Y.C., 1960-66, minister urban affairs, 1969-76; dean of chapel, acting dean student Dillard U., New Orleans, 1966-68; exec. dir. Edwin Gould Services for Children, N.Y.C., 1976-80; exec. dir. Council of Chs. in City N.Y., 1980—. Trustee CUNY Bd. Higher Edn.; chmn. CUNY Constrn. Fund; mem. Mayor's Com. Religious Leaders, Healing Community; com. mem. on religion and local humanism Nat. Council Chs., nat. assn. ecumenical staff; active Partnership for Homeless. Active, Cultural Arts Connection, N.Y.C., Assn. Black Charities, Albert Schweitzer Fellowship Bd., N.Y.C., Coaltion for Homeless, Sex Info. Edn. Council U.S., Gov.'s Wife's Com. on Child Abuse and Neglect, Gov.'s Com. on Scholastic Achievement; mem. interfaith edn. adv. council N.Y. State Dept. Edn. Club: Princeton. Home: Sheffield Apt 36-F 322 W 57th St New York NY 10019 Office: Council Chs of City NY Suite 456 475 Riverside Dr New York NY 10115

POLLARD, FRANKLIN DAWES, minister, seminary president, Southern Baptist Convention; b. Olney, Tex., Feb. 25, 1934; s. Daniel Spurgeon and Ova Roena (Boone) P.; B.B.A., Tex. A&M U., 1955; B.D., Southwestern Bapt. Theol. Sem., 1959; D.Min., New Orleans Bapt. Theol. Sem., 1983; D.D. (hon.), Miss. Coll., Clinton, 1977; L.H.D. (hon.), Calif. Bapt. Coll., Riverside, 1983; m. Jane Shepard, Sept. 1, 1955; children: Brent, Suzanne. Ordained to ministry So. Baptist Conv., 1956. Pastor chs., Seagraves, Tex., 1961-64, Dimmitt, Tex., 1964-66; pastor First Bapt. Ch., Tulia, Tex., 1966-70, Shiloh Terrace Bapt. Ch., Dallas, 1970-74, First Bapt. Ch., Jackson, Miss., 1974-80, San Antonio, 1980-83; pres. Golden Gate Bapt. Theol. Sem., Mill Valley, Calif., 1983—; preacher Bapt. Hour, 1976—. Vice pres., exec. bd. Bapt. Gen. Conv. Tex., 1973; exec. bd. Miss. Bapt. Conv., 1977-80. Trustee Howard Payne U. Author: How to Know When You're A Success, 1973 (reprinted as The Bible in Your Life, 1978); After You've Said I'm Sorry, 1982; Keeping Free, 1983. Named One of Seven Most Outstanding Prot. Preachers, Time Mag., 1979. Office: Golden Gate Bapt Theol Sem Strawberry Point Mill Valley CA 94941

POLLARD, JAMES ALFRED, minister, American Baptist Church in the U.S.A.; b. Phila., Feb. 17, 1948; s. Ernest Stien and Sophia Elanor (Morton) P.; m. Virginia Margaret Overton, May 15, 1971; children: James Alfred, Joseph, John. B.S. in Bible, Phila. Coll. Bible, 1969; M.Div., Eastern Bapt. Sem., 1972. Ordained to ministry National Baptist Convention, Inc., U.S.A., 1970. Pastor Zion Bapt. Ch., Ardmore, Pa., 1971—; bd. dirs. Phila. Bapt. Assn., 1981—; v.p. NAACP, Bryn Mawr, Pa., 1974-78. Pres. Ardmore Community Devel. Corp., 1974-78. Republican. Lodge: Masons (chaplain 1973—). Home: 221 W Spring Ave Ardmore PA 19003

POLLINGER, HAROLD WILLIAM, minister, Am. Baptist Chs. in U.S.A.; b. Hornell, N.Y., Apr. 3, 1921; s. William Joseph and Aleine Marie (Crites) P.; m. Doris G. Campbell, Aug. 12, 1942; children: Dean E., Jean D., Dan A. Student Practical Bible Tng. Sch., 1939-42; Th.B., Calif. Bapt. Sem., 1947. Ordained to ministry Am. Bapt. Ch. in U.S.A., 1942. Pastor Seaside Bapt. Ch., Long Beach, Calif., 1946-53; pastor, minister Town and Country Bapt. Ch., Bakersfield, Calif., 1953-58; assoc. pastor First Bapt. Ch., Bakersfield, 1958-61; pastor, minister Del Rosa Heights Bapt. Ch., San Bernardino, Calif., 1961-74; sr. minister Oak Knolls Bapt. Ch., Santa Maria, Calif., 1971—; mem. exec. com., bd. mgrs. Am. Bapt. Chs. Pacific Southwest, Covina, Calif., 1974—, moderator Area V, 1984—; pres. Ministerial Assn., Santa Maria, 1981-82. Pres. bd. dirs. Mental Health Assn., Santa Maria, 1982; bd. dirs. People Helping Ctr., Santa Maria, 1982—. Recipient honor award with citation for service as agt. HUD, 1983. Mem. Ministers Council Am. Bapt. Chs. U.S.A., Ministers Am. Bapt. Chs. Pacific Southwest (chmn. div. ch. devel.). Republican. Home: 4318 Edenbury Dr Santa Maria CA 93455 Office: Oak Knolls Bapt Ch 4799 S Bradley Rd Santa Maria CA 93455

POLSON, JOHN MILTON, minister, Gen. Assn. Regular Baptist Chs.; b. Millville, Minn., Feb. 20, 1925; s. William Oscar and Lela Pearl (Olin) P.; B.A., Taylor U., 1949; M.Div., Central Bapt. Theol. Sem., 1957; m. Patricia Ruth Stanford, Aug. 31, 1947; children—Karen Polson Denger, David John, John Mark. Ordained to ministry, 1951; pastor Gildead Meth. Ch., Macy, Ind., 1948-50, 1st Bapt. Ch., Morristown, Minn., 1950-53, Grace Bapt. Ch., Austin, Minn., 1953-57, Hagerman Bapt. Ch., Waterloo, Iowa, 1957-63, Ankeny (Iowa) Bapt. Ch., 1963-66, Calvary Bapt. Ch., Highland, Ind., 1969-74, Sun Coast Bapt. Ch., New Port Richey, Fla., 1974—; field rep. Faith Bapt. Bible Coll., Ankeny, 1966-69. Bd. dirs. Iowa Bapt. Camp, Council of Ten, Faith Bapt. Bible Coll., Ind. Council of Twelve, Spurgeon Bapt. Bible Coll., Fla. Council of Six, Evang. Bapt. Missions, Fellowship of Bapts. for Home Missions. Contbr. articles to Bapt. Bull. Home: 3504 Job Sail Ct New Port Richey FL 33552 Office: 19 E State Rd 54 New Port Richey FL 33552

POMEROY, WEBB DONNOLLY, religious studies educator, elder United Methodist Church; b. Fairbanks, La., Oct. 30, 1923; s. Allen Webb and Helen (Donnolly) P.; m. Juanita Newton, Oct. 8, 1928; children: Deborah Irene, Helen Leah, Allen Newton, Mark Donnolly. B.A., Centenary Coll. La., 1943; Th.M., Union Theol. Sem., 1945; Ph.D., Edinburgh U., Scotland, 1953. Ordained to ministry as elder United Meth. Ch., 1945. Dir youth La. Conf. United Meth. Ch., Shreveport, La., 1946-48; pastor Deerford Meth. Ch., La., 1951-53; prof. religion Centenary Coll., Shreveport, 1953-75, T.L. James prof. religion, 1975—. Served to lt. (j.g.) USN, 1945-46. Mem. U. Edinburgh Council, Am. Acad. Religion, Soc. Bibl. Lit. Democrat. Home: 3504 Greenway Pl Shreveport LA 71105 Office: Centenary Coll La 2911 Centenary Blvd Shreveport LA 71134

PONDER, CATHERINE, minister, Unity School Christianity; b. Hartsville, S.C., Feb. 14, 1927; d. Roy Charles and Kathleen (Parrish) Cook; m. Robert Stearns, June 19, 1970; 1 son by previous marriage: Richard. Student U. N.C. Extension, 1946, Worth Bus. Coll., 1948; B.S. in Edn., Unity Ministerial Sch., 1956; D.D. (hon.), Assn. Unity Chs., 1976. Ordained to ministry Unity Sch. Christianity, 1958. Minister Unity Ch., Birmingham, Ala., 1956-61; founder, minister Unity Ch., Austin, Tex., 1961-69, San Antonio, 1969-73, Palm Desert, Calif., 1973—. Author: The Dynamic Laws of Prosperity, 1962; The Prosperity Secret of the Ages, 1964; The Dynamic Laws of Healing, 1966; The Healing Secret of the Ages, 1967; Pray and Grow Rich, 1968; The Millionaires of Genesis, 1976; The Millionaire Moses, 1977; The Millionaire Joshua, 1978; The Millionaire from Nazareth, 1979; Secret of Unlimited Prosperity, 1980; Open Your Mind to Receive, 1983; Dare to Prosper!, 1983; The Prospering Power of Prayer, 1983; Open Your Mind to Prosperity, 1984; The Prospering Power of Love, 1984. Mem. Assn. Unity Chs., Internat. New Thought Alliance, Internat. Platform Assn. Clubs: Bermuda Dunes Country, Racquet (Palm Springs, Calif.), Los Angeles. Office: 73-669 Hwy 111 Palm Desert CA 92260

PONDER, JAMES ALTON, minister, Southern Baptist Convention; b. Ft. Worth, Jan. 20, 1933; s. Leo Alton and Mae Adele (Blair) P.; B.A., Baylor U., 1954; B.D., M.A. in Edn., Southwestern Bapt. Theol. Sem., 1965; m. Joyce Marie Hutchison, Sept. 1, 1953; children—Keli Marie, James Kenyon. Ordained to ministry So. Baptist Conv., 1953; evangelist, 1951-53, 67; pastor Tex. and Ill. chs., 1953-67; dir. evangelism Ill. Bapt. State Conv., 1967-70, Fla. Bapt. Conv., Jacksonville, 1970-81; pres. Jim Ponder Ministries, 1981—. Mem. Fellowship Christian Athletes. Author: The Devotional Life, 1970; New Church Member Training Workbook for Adults, 1973; Evangelism Men....Motivating Laymen to Witness, 1974; Evangelism Men . . . Proclaiming the Doctrines of Salvation, 1975. Contbr. articles to mags. and periodicals, Ency. So. Bapts. Office: 8420 Baymeadows Way #1 Jacksonville FL 32216

PONTIER, RALPH ANDREW, minister, Christian Reformed Church in North America; b. Passaic, N.J., Feb. 7, 1950; s. Peter L. and Grace A. (DeVries) P. m. Lois Jean Kievit, June 24, 1972; children: Grace, David, Jonathan, Sarah, Rachel. B.S., Grove City Coll., 1972; M.Div., Westminster Theol. Sem., 1976. Ordained to ministry, Christian Ref. Ch., 1977. Minister, organizing pastor Cape Coral Christian Ref. Ch., Fla., 1977—; stated clk. Classis Fla., Fla. and Ga., 1981—; del. to ann. synod Christian Ref. Ch. in N. Am., 1981, 83, 84. Mem. Cape Coral Ministerial Assn. Office: Cape Coral Christian Ref Ch 2220 Hancock Bridge Pkwy Cape Coral FL 33904

POOLE, GREGORY KELLEY, minister, United Methodist Church; b. West Point, Tenn., Sept. 13, 1921; s. George Edward and Lou Anice (Farmer) P.; B.S., Northeastern Mo. U., 1944; M.Th., Iliff Sch. Theology, 1946; D.D., Central Meth. Coll., 1968; m. June Harness, June 10, 1945; 1 child, Linda Kay (Mrs. John Klein). Ordained elder United Methodist Ch., 1946. Pastor in LaPlata, Mo., 1946-50, Liberty, Mo., 1950-60, Mexico, Mo., 1960-65; dist. supt., St. Louis, 1965-71; pastor St. Johns Ch., St. Louis, 1971-74; dist. supt. Hannibal-Kirksville Dist., 1974-77; council dir. Mo. East Conf., 1977-85; exec. dir. Mo. United Meth. Found., 1985—; adminstrv. asst. to Bishop of Mo., 1985—. Bd. dirs. Mo. Meth. Found.; bd. dirs. Ozark Meth. Manor. Address: 11705 Niehaus St Saint Louis MO 63146

POPE, DANNY WAYNE, minister, editor, Baptist Missionary Assn. Am.; b. Jacksonville, Tex., Oct. 10, 1939; s. Joe Coleman and Irene Mae (Taylor) P.; A.A., Jacksonville Coll., 1959; student Bapt. Missionary Assn. Sem., Jacksonville, 1963; m. Dian Cassity, July 1, 1960; children—Donna, Dwayne, Darla. Ordained to ministry, 1964; pastor Sanders Creek Bapt. Ch., Donie, Tex., 1964-65, Walnut Grove Bapt. Ch., Garrison, Tex., 1966-67, Temple Bapt. Ch., Port Neches, Tex., 1967-70, Friendship Bapt. Ch., Dallas, 1970-71, Myrtle Springs Bapt. Ch., Quitman, Tex., 1971-74; editor The Bapt. Progress, 1974—. Contbr. articles in field to religious jours. Home: 105 Comanche St Waxahachie TX 75165 Office: Box 4205 Dallas TX 75208

POPE, ROBERT EDWARD, accountant, Lutheran Ch. in America; b. Detroit, June 25, 1933; s. Nestor A. and Lucilia E. (Abranches) P.; m. Joan Elizabeth Brennan, June 25, 1960; children: Diana Sheryl, David George, Denise Susan. B.A., Mich. State U., 1955; postgrad., U. Hawaii, 1957, U. Detroit, 1958, Cert. ch. bus. adminstr. Fin. asst. Bd. Am. Missions, Luth. Ch. in Am., Chgo., 1966-69, asst. controller, 1969-73, chmn. synod com., 1975-81, dir. acctg. services Office Adminstrn. and Fin., Phila., 1973-78, chief acct., 1978—; treas., fin. sec., sec. Christ Luth. Ch., Phila., 1974-81; congregation rep. Northwest Luth. Parish, Phila., 1979-85; synod rep. Luth. Coalition Pub. Policy, Harrisburg, Pa., 1984-85. Treas. sch. bd. election com. Springfield Twp., Pa., 1975. Served with USN, 1955-57. Democrat. Home: 12 Glenn Circle Erdenheim Philadelphia PA 19118 Office: Dept Fiscal Mgmt Office Adminstrn and Fin 2900 Queen Ln Philadelphia PA 19129

POPP, BERNARD F., bishop, Roman Catholic Church. Titular bishop of Capsus, aux. bishop, San Antonio. Office: 114 Military Plaza San Antonio TX 78205*

POPP, KEVIN PAUL, minister, Lutheran Church-Missouri Synod; b. Cape Girardeau, Mo., Dec. 25, 1955; s. Kenneth Paul and Vera May (Lewis) P.; m. Karen Dolores Medhus, Aug. 24, 1980; children: Martin Christopher, Heidi Michelle. Student St. Paul's Coll., 1974-75; B.A. in Elem. Edn., Concordia Coll., River Forest, Ill., 1977; M.Div., Concordia Sem., St. Louis, 1981. Ordained to ministry Luth. Ch.-Mo. Synod, 1981. Vicar, Bethlehem Luth. Ch., Ridgewood, N.J., 1979-80; assoc. pastor St. Paul's Luth. Ch., Concordia, Mo., 1981-84; pastor Trinity Luth. Ch., Ottumwa, Iowa, 1984—. Home: 297 Shaul Ave Ottuma IA 52501 Office: Trinity Luth Ch 295 Shaul Ave Ottuma IA 52501

POPP, NATHANIEL, ruling bishop, Romanian Orthodox Episcopate of America; b. Aurora, Ill., June 12, 1940; s. Joseph and Vera (Boytor) P. B.A., Ill. Benedictine-St. Procopius Coll., 1962; M.Th., Pontifical Gregorian U., Vatican (Rome), 1966. Ordained priest Romanian Greek Catholic Ch., 1966; bishop consecrated Romanian Orthodox Episcopate of Am., 1980. Parish priest Holy Cross Romanian Orthodox Ch., Hermitage, Pa., 1975-80; aux. bishop Romanian Orthodox Episcopate of Am., Orthodox Ch. in Am., 1980-84, ruling bishop, 1984—; mem. Holy Synod Orthodox Ch. in Am., Syosset, N.Y., 1980—; mem. participant Monastic Consultation, Cairo, 1979, Seventh Assembly, Vancouver, Can., 1983. Author: Holy Icons, 1969. Editor newspaper Solia. Chmn. Romanian-Am. Heritage Ctr., Grass Lake, Mich. Home and Office: The Romanian Orthodox Episcopate of Am 2522 Grey Tower Rd Jackson MI 49201

POPPLEWELL, ROGER, moderator, Separate Baptists in Christ. Address: Route 5 Russell Springs KY 42642

PORT, ROBERT STANLEY, rabbi, Conservative Jewish Congregations; b. N.Y.C., Jan. 19, 1927; s. Philip and Evelyn (Schulberg) P.; B.A., N.Y. U., 1950, M.A., 1952; student Yavne Hebrew Theol. Sem., 1950-53; m. Deborah Fisch, June 23, 1953; children—Reva, Andrew, Joan, Lisa. Rabbi, Conservative Jewish Congregations, 1954; rabbi, Jeannette, Pa., 1953-56, Whitestone, N.Y., 1956-58, Farmingdale (N.Y.) Jewish Center, 1958-62, Beth Jacob Synagogue, Norwich, Conn., 1962-68, Temple Sinai, Middletown, N.Y., 1968-76, Temple Ohav Shalom, Sayreville, N.J., 1976—. Chaplain, N.Y. State Police, 1968—, Mid-Hudson Psychiat. Center, New Hampton, N.Y., 1972—. Active Marriage Encounter, Inc., 1973—. Bd. dirs. Thames Valley Council for Community Action, Norwich, 1964-68, Thames Valley Mental Health Orgn., Norwich, 1965-68, NAACP, Norwich, 1963-68, Jeannette (Pa.) Dist. Hosp., 1955-57. Mem. Interfaith Council, Mensa. Rotarian (dir. 1972—) . Home: 29 Frederick Pl Parlin NJ 08859

PORTER, BILLY GENE, minister, Ch. of God (Anderson, Ind.); b. Dexter, Mo., July 21, 1943; s. Owen Eugene and Mildred (Abney) P.; student U. Md. Extension; m. Betty Joan Sims, Aug. 29, 1961; children—Tracie Rhea, Scott Thomas. Ordained to ministry, 1975; chaplain's asst. AUS, 1962-63, chief chaplain's asst., 1964-67; asso. pastor 1st Ch. of God, East Prairie, Mo., 1973-74, pastor, 1974—. Sec.-treas. bd. evangelism S.E. Mo. dist., bd. dirs. Dist. Assembly Rest Home; sec.-treas. East Prairie Ministerial Alliance. Mem. East Prairie Parks and Recreation Bd. Home: 322 N Washington St East Prairie MO 63845 Office: PO Box 236 East Prairie MO 63845

PORTER, H(ARRY) BOONE, priest, Episcopal Church; b. Louisville, Jan. 10, 1923; s. Harry Boone and Charlotte (Wiseman) P.; m. Violet Monser, June 28, 1947; children: Charlotte M., H. Boone III, Michael T., Gabrielle R., Clarissa H., Nicholas T. B.A., Yale U., 1947; S.T.B., Berkeley Div. Sch., 1950, S.T.M., Gen. Theol. Sem., N.Y.C., 1952; D.Phil., Oxford U., Eng., 1954. Ordained priest Episcopal Ch., 1952. From asst. to assoc. prof. Nashotah House, Wis., 1954-60; prof. Gen. Theol. Sem., N.Y.C., 1960-70; dir. Roanridge Found., Kansas City, Mo., 1970-77; editor The Living Ch. Mag., Milw., 1977—; mem. Standing Liturgical Commn. of Episcopal Ch., 1961-76; mem. Gen. Bd. Examiners Episcopal Ch., 1970-82; pres. New Directions Ministries, Inc., 1980—, Episcopal Literature Fund, Inc., 1981—. Author: Ordination Prayers, 1967; Keeping the Church Year, 1977; Jeremy Taylor: Liturgist, 1979. Mem. soil stewardship com. Nat. Assn. Conservation Dists.; mem. Wis. Rural Devel. Ctr., Inc. Served as sgt. U.S. Army, 1943-46, PTO. Mem. N. Am. Acad. Liturgy, Assoc. Parishes Inc. (pres. 1973-75, council mem.), Fellowship of St. Alban and St. Sergius. Clubs: Yale (N.Y.C.); Elizabethan (New Haven, Conn.). Office: The Living Church 407 E Michigan St Milwaukee WI 53202

PORTER, JAMES LAUREN, elder, religious studies educator, Evangelical Church of North America; b. Tampa, Fla., June 20, 1947; s. Lauren D. and Phyllis Jane (Deplois) P.; m. Beverly Anne Bailey, June 8, 1968; children: Lauren James, Bethany Joy. B.S. in Edn., Oreg. Coll. Edn., 1969; M.Div., Western Evang. Sem., 1972; M.S. in Edn., Wayne State Coll., 1975; Ph.D. in Edn., U. Oreg., 1977. Ordained to ministry as elder Evang. Ch. N. Am., 1973. Pastor, Evang. Ch. N. Am., South Souix City, Nebr., 1972-74; dir. Christian Edn. Willakenzie Evang. Ch. N. Am., Eugene, Oreg., 1975-76; prof. Christian edn. Vennard Coll., University Park, Iowa, 1976-80, Wesley Bibl. Sem., Jackson, Miss., 1980—. Contbg. author: Beacon Dictionar of Theology, 1984. Pres. Right to Life of Jackson, 1983. Mem. Alpha Psi Omega, Pi Lambda Theta. Home: 702 Green Forest Rd Jackson MS 39211 Office: Wesley Bibl Sem PO Box 9938 Jackson MS 39211

PORTER, ROBERT DELANO, evangelist, So. Baptist Conv.; b. Oldhams, Va., Nov. 3, 1936; s. Thomas Jefferson and Madeline Burtha (Forrester) P.; m. Barbara Jean Nash, Dec. 1, 1955; children—Douglas Wayne, Deborah Ann, Robert Delano, Briggitt Lang. Ordained to ministry, 1972; pres., chmn. bd. dirs. Bob Porter Evangelistic Assn., Roanoke, Va., 1970—. Mem. Conf. So. Bapt. Evangelists, 1974—; mem. First Bapt. Ch., Roanoke. City councilman, Colonial Beach, Va., 1962. Mem. Roanoke Valley Bapt. Assn. Author: Witnessing Made Simple, 1973. Home 5825 Plantation Rd NE Roanoke VA 24019 Office: POB 7605 Roanoke VA 20419

PORTERFIELD, ALLEN GERALD, minister, So. Bapt. Conv.; b. Long Beach, Calif., Feb. 11, 1937; s. Ralph Gerald and Arlene (Allen) P.; student U. Alaska, 1961-62, Calif. Bapt. Coll., 1962-64, Chapman Coll., 1968-70; m. Barbara Ann Ganner, May 2, 1958; children—Allen Gerald, John Mark. Ordained to ministry, 1970; dir. music and religious edn. chs., Alaska, Calif., 1957-68; asso. pastor Melodyland Christian Center, Anaheim, Calif., 1968-72, Wescott Christian Center, Oroville, Calif., 1972; pastor Vincent Ave. Bapt. Ch. (name changed to San Gabriel Valley Christian Fellowship Center), Covina, Calif., 1972—. Mem. Nat. Assn. Dirs. Christian Edn. Office: 4315 N Vincent Ave Covina CA 91722

PORTERFIELD, RICHARD EARL, minister, Church of God (Cleveland, Tenn.); b. Greenwood, S.C., Apr. 18, 1936; s. Olin R. and Hazel M. (Suits) P.; diploma Ch. of God Bible Sch., 1970; m. Betty Jo Carroll, June 10, 1955; children: Richard Wayne, Lisa Dianne Porterfield Brownlee, Stephen Greg. Ordained to ministry, 1973; pastor Taylors Ch. of God, S.C. 1968-72, North Spartanburg Ch. of God, S.C., 1972-82; pastor Elmwood Ave. Ch. of God, Columbia, S.C., 1982—. Mem. denominational bd. youth and Christian edn., S.C., 1972—; mem. faculty and bd. Ch. of God Bible Inst., S.C., 197-76; speaker TV program Voice of Victory. Home: 7173 Caledonia Ln Columbia SC 29209 Office: 1427 Elmwood Ave Columbia SC 29201

PORTNOY, MINDY AVRA, rabbi, Hillel director, Jewish; b. New Haven, Dec. 6, 1951; d. Nathan D. and Sarah Claire (Themper) P.; m. Philip Leonard Breen, May 18, 1975; 1 child, Ceala Eloise. B.A. cum laude, Yale U., 1973; M.A. in Hebrew Lit., Hebrew Union Coll., 1978. Ordained rabbi, 1980. Prin. Brooklyn Heights Synagogue Religious Sch., N.Y.C., 1977-79; rabbi Temple Rodeph Shalom, Ellenville, N.Y., 1979-80; profl. lectr. Am. U., Washington, 1982, 85, rabbi, dir. B'nai B'rith Hillel Found., 1980—; mem. Nat. Commn. Jewish Life and Culture, adv. bd. Am. Jewish Congress, N.Y.C., 1983—; adv. bd. dept. interreligious affairs Union Am. Hebrew Congregations, N.Y.C., 1983—; co-coordinator Women's Rabbinic Network, Washington, 1984—. Mem. Central Conf. Am. Rabbis (com. on ch. and state 1982—), Washington Bd. Rabbis. Democrat. Office: B'nai B'rith Hillel Found AS Kay Spiritual Life Ctr Am U Washington DC 20016

POST, AVERY DENISON, minister, church official, United Church of Christ; b. Norwich, Conn., July 29, 1924; s. John Palmer and Dorothy (Church) P.; m. Margaret Jane Rowland, June 8, 1946; children: Susan Macalister Post Roszkowksi, Jennifer Campbell, Elizabeth Champlin, Anne Denison Post Proudman. B.A., Ohio Wesleyan U., 1945; B.D., Yale U., 1949, S.T.M., 1952; L.H.D. (hon.), Lakeland Coll., Sheboygan, Wis., 1977; D.D. (hon.), Chgo. Theol. Sem., 1978, Middlebury Coll., 1978, Defiance Coll., 1979; LL.D. (hon.), Heidelberg Coll., 1982. Ordained to ministry United Ch. of Christ, 1949. Pastor chs. in Vt., Ohio, Conn., N.Y., 1946-63; sr. minister Scarsdale Congl. Ch., N.Y., 1963-70; minister, pres. Mass. conf. United Ch. Christ, 1970-77; pres. United Ch. Christ, N.Y.C., 1977—; mem. central com. World Council Chs., 1978—; exec. com. bd. govs. Nat. Council Chs., 1977—; lectr. Bible, Adelphi Coll., Garden City, N.Y., 1958-59; Luccock lectr. Div. sch., Yale U., 1961; lectr. homiletics Union Sem., N.Y.C., 1967-69, bd. dirs., 1967-77; trustee Andover Newton Theol. Sem., 1970-80; del. numerous internat. ch. meetings. Served with USNR, 1943-45. Recipient 1st Ecumenical award Mass. Council Chs., 1976, life membership PTA, Norwich, N.Y., Disting. Achievement award Ohio Wesleyan U., 1983. Fellow Soc. Arts, Religion and Contemporary Culture; mem. Boston Athenaeum, Phi Beta Kappa, Omicron Delta Kappa. Democrat. Clubs: Yale, Appalachian Mountain; Randolph Mountain (N.Y.). Office: United Ch of Christ 105 Madison Ave New York NY 10016

POTTENGER, WILLIAM ALBERT, JR., priest, Episcopal Church; b. Chgo., June 7, 1924; s. William Albert and Martha Cobb (Livinston) P.; certificate Ch. Div. Sch. of Pacific, 1952; student Ill. Inst. Tech., 1942-44, 1946-47, U. Ariz., 1948-49; m. Beverly Ann Spies, June 11, 1949; children—Susanne Elizabeth, William A. III, Marguerite Estelle, Warren Theodore. Ordained priest, 1952; vicar St. George's Ch., Holbrook, Ariz., 1952-54; founder, vicar Ch. of Our Savior, Sholow Lake, Ariz., 1954; founding rector St. Augustine's Parish, Tempe, Ariz., 1954-76; assoc. St. Stephen's Parish, Phoenix, 1978—; Chaplain Ariz. State U., Tempe, 1954-71, St. Luke's Hosp., Phoenix, 1955-65; pres. standing com. Diocese of Ariz., mem. Ariz. Diocesan Council; pres. Ariz. Council of Chs. Bd. dirs. Tempe United Fund, 1966-72, TriCity Mental Health Clinic, Tempe, Mesa and Chandler, 1967-73, Tempe Commn. Action Agy., 1965-71, Tempe Police and Firefighters Pension, 1972-76. Appointed Canon to Ordinary by Bishop of Ariz., 1976—; recipient for Outstanding Service (United Fund) of Appreciation, Tempe Community Action Agy., 1971. Mem. Ariz. State U. Religious Conf. (past pres.), Tempe Minister Assn. (past pres.), Ariz. Central Deanery Clericus (past dean). Contbr. articles to religious jours. Home and office: 404 E Concorda Dr Tempe AZ 85282

POTTER, JOSEPH PALO, youth minister, religious organization administrator, Christian Churches; b. Roanoke, Va., Nov. 15, 1956; s. Donald Lee and Margaret (Wolfe) P.; m. Cathy Sue Pulliam, July 10, 1979; 1 child, Josiah Palo. B.S., Milligan Coll., 1979. Youth minister Lone Oak Christian Ch., Johnson City, Tenn., 1980-81, Camden Ave Christian Ch., Louisville, 1981-82, Central Holston Christian Ch., Bristol, Tenn., 1982—; dir. Fellowship Christian Athletics, Johnson City, 1985—. Program planner City Govt., Johnson City, 1985—; head resident Milligan Coll., Johnson City, 1984—; tchr. Johnson City Sch. System, 1980-81. Milligan scholar 1978. Named one of Outstanding Young Men Am., 1980. Avocations: running; tennis; hiking. Home: PO Box 745 Milligan TN 37682

POTTER, RALPH BENAJAH, JR., minister, United Presbyterian Church in the U.S.A.; educator; b. Los Angeles, May 19, 1931; s. Ralph Benajah and Vivian Irene MacNabb (Borden) P.; m. Jean Ishbel MacCormick, Aug. 15, 1953; children: Anne Elizabeth, Ralph Andrew, James David, Margaret Jean. B.A., Occidental Coll., 1952; postgrad. Pacific Sch. Religion, 1952-53; B.D., McCormick Theol. Sem., 1955; Th.D., Harvard U., 1965. Ordained to ministry Presbyn. Ch., 1955. Dir., pastor Clay County Presbyn. Larger Parish, Manchester, Ky., 1955-58; sec. social edn. Bd. Christian Edn., United Presbyn. Ch. in U.S.A., Phila., 1963-64; asst. prof. social ethics Harvard Div. Sch.; mem. Ctr. for Population Studies, Harvard U., Cambridge, Mass., 1965-69, prof., 1969—. Theologian-in-residence Am. Ch. in Paris, 1975; sr. research scholar Kennedy Inst. for Bio-ethics Georgetown U., 1974. Author: War and Moral Discourse, 1979. Contbr. chpts. to The Religious Situation, 1968; Religion and the Public Order, 1968; Toward a Discipline of Social Ethics, 1972; The Population Crisis and Moral Responsibility, 1973. Fellow Rockefeller Found., 1961-62, Kent Found., 1963-64. Fellow Inst. Soc., Ethics and Life Scis.; mem. Am. Soc. Polit. and Legal Philosophy, Soc. Christian Ethics, Soc. for Values in Higher Edn., Societe Europeene de Culture, War-Nation-Ch. Study Group. Office: 45 Francis Ave Cambridge MA 02138

POTTER, THOMAS KELLY, JR., religious organization executive, United Methodist Church; b. Sparta, Tenn., May 16, 1930; s. Thomas Kelly and Bonnie Lee (Passons) P.; m. Barbara Anne Worley, June 15, 1954 (div. Aug. 1981); children: Thomas K. III, Lee Carson, Joseph Worley; m. Renate Anna Hehn-Lass, Dec. 5, 1981. A.B. with honors in Journalism, George Washington U., 1954. Curriculum promotion dir. United Meth. Pub. House, Nashville, 1962-63, mgr. graded press, 1963-70, v.p. pub., 1970-84, v.p. planning and research, 1984—; del. Southeastern Jurisdictional Conf., 1976; pres. Coop. Publ. Assn., 1976-80. Served with USNR, 1948-49. Mem. Planning Execs. Inst., Am. Mktg. Assn. Democrat. Office: United Meth Pub House 201-8th Ave S Nashville TN 37202

POTTERTON, BRUCE ELBERT, radio broadcaster; b. Oakdale, Calif., Nov. 12, 1949; s. Ralph Elbert and Irma Mary (Andrews) P.; m. Eileen Toma, Aug. 29, 1982; children: Kristen, Danny. B.S. in Communications, Pacific Union Coll., 1976. Program dir. Sta. KLLU, Riverside, Calif., 1974-80; instr. Loma Linda U., Riverside, 1978-79; ops. mgr. Sta. KSGN, Riverside, 1980—; treas. Adventist Radio Network, Washington, 1975—. Crisis counselor Help Line, Riverside, 1982. Mem. Nat. Assn. Broadcasters, Nat. Religious Broadcasters Assn.

POTTERVELD, RIESS WILLIAM, minister, religious studies educator, United Church of Christ; b. Milw., Jan. 26, 1943; s. Burton Lee and Dorothy Audrene (Bovey) P.; children: Will, Jesse; m. Theresa Louise Tarbell, Dec. 13, 1981; stepchildren: Warren, Matthew. B.A., Trinity Coll., 1965; B.D., Yale U., Divinity Sch., 1969; M.A., Claremont Grad. Sch., 1982, Ph.D., 1982. Ordained to ministry United Ch. of Christ, 1971. Assoc. minister Congl. Ch. of Claremont, Calif., 1971-74; minister, Congl. Ch. of Northridge, United Ch. of Christ, Calif., 1974—; prof. Calif. State U.-Northridge, 1980—; dir. So. Calif. Ecumenical

Council, Los Angeles, 1982—, So. Calif. Conf., United Ch. of Christ, Pasadena, Calif., 1979-82; pres. San Fernando Valley Interfaith Council, Van Nuys, Calif., 1980-82; chmn. Stewardship Commn., So. Calif. Conf., Pasadena, 1975-77. Recipient 150th Ann. Alumni award Trinity Coll., 1973; Booth Ferris fellow, 1965-66. Mem. Am. Acad. Religion. Democrat. Office: Northridge United Ch of Christ 9659 Balboa Blvd Northridge CA 91325

POTTS, KENNETH MARVIN, priest, Roman Cath. Ch.; b. Yankton, S.D., Dec. 3, 1942; s. Alfred Ludwig and Sara Irene (Wieseler) P.; B.A., Conception Sem., 1964, M.A., 1967; B.S.T., Cath. U., 1967; M.S., U. Nebr., 1971; postgrad. Creighton U., 1974—. Ordained priest, 1968; asso. pastor St. Francis of Assisi, Omaha, 1968-69, St. Frances Carbrini, Omaha, 1969-70, St. Michael, S. Sioux City, Nebr., 1970-73, St. Peter's, Omaha, 1973—; chaplain Luth. Gen. Hosp., 1973—; dean Urban Southeast Deanery, 1974—. Mem. Omaha Priests' Senate, 1974—; chaplain K.C., 1973—. Mem. Nebr. Personnel and Guidance Assn., Augustan Soc. Home and Office: St Peter's Ch 709 S 28th St Omaha NE 68105

POVISH, KENNETH JOSEPH, bishop, Roman Catholic Church; b. Alpena, Mich., Apr. 19, 1924; s. Joseph Francis and Elizabeth (Jachcik) P.; A.B., Sacred Heart Sem., Detroit, 1946; M.A., Cath. U. Am., 1950; grad. student No. Mich. U., 1961, 63. Ordained priest Roman Cath. Ch., 1950, consecrated bishop, 1970; asst. pastorships, 1950-56; pastor in Port Sanilac, Mich., 1956-57, Munger, Mich., 1957-60, Bay City, Mich., 1966-70; dean St. Paul Sem., Saginaw, Mich., 1960-66, vice-rector, 1962-66; bishop of Crookston, Minn., 1970-76, Lansing, Mich., 1976—; bd. consulators Diocese of Saginaw, 1966-70; instr. Latin and U.S. history St. Paul Sem., 1960-66. Bd. dirs. Cath. Charities Diocese Saginaw, 1969-70. Mem. Mich., Bay County hist. socs. Kiwanian. Weekly columnist Saginaw and Lansing diocesan newspapers. Home: 1348 Cambridge St Lansing MI 48910 Office: 300 W Ottawa St Lansing MI 48933

POWELL, CATHERINE RAVENEL, priest, Episcopal Church; b. Fayetteville, N.C., Sept. 5, 1952; d. Robert Jackson and Catherine (Gant) P.; m. Charles Frederick Parthum, III, June 14, 1980; 1 child, Elizabeth. A.B., Hollins Coll., 1974; M.Div., Union Theol. Sem., 1979. Ordained priest Episcopal Ch., 1980. Assoc. chaplain Nat. Cathedral Sch., Washington, 1979-81, chaplain, 1981-84, lower sch. chaplain, 1984—; priest-in-charge St. Dunstan's Ch., Sumner, Md., 1980; clergy staff Washington Cathedral, 1980-82; mem. parish internship program com. Diocese of Washington, 1979-82, chmn., 1982-84, cons., 1984—, staff, jr. and sr. high sch. conf., 1975-76, 78-79, 81-83, mem. Christian Edn. Commn., 1985—; mem. coordinating com. Nat. Episcopal Young Adult Ministries, 1977-79. Recipient Jane Cocke Funkhauser award Hollins Coll., 1974. Mem. Washington Episcopal Clergy Assn., Phi Beta Kappa. Office: Nat Cathedral Sch Mt St Alban Washington DC 20016

POWELL, CHARLES WILLIAM, minister, Baptist General Conference; educator; b. Gilman, Colorado, May 9, 1937; s. Harold Hayes and Rosella Charlott (Collins). B.S., Colo. State U., 1970; postgrad. Western Conservative Bapt. Sem., 1982. Ordained to ministry Evangelical Ch. Alliance, 1976; cert. sch. tchr., Wash. Team leader The Navigators, Colorado Springs, 1966-72; sr. pastor Albion Community Ch., Wash., 1972-76; hon. v.p. Am. Missionary Fellowship, Portland, Oreg., 1979—; itinerant preacher, Oreg., 1976—. Contbr. articles to religious jours. Res. policeman Whitman County Sheriff's Office, Colfax, Wash., 1975-76. Served with USN, 1956-62. Mem. Am. Legion, Mensa. Republican. Avocations: reading; computer science; amateur magician. Home and Office: 2220 SE Taylor St Portland OR 97214

POWELL, CHARLES WILLIAM, minister, Southern Baptist Convention; b. Birmingham, Ala., June 18, 1928; s. Charlie Wesley and Edna Melvina (Troupe) P.; A.B., Samford U., 1953; M.R.E., Southwestern Bapt. Theol. Sem., Fort Worth, 1954; m. Betty Miles, Nov. 22, 1951; children—Charles William, Pamela Elaine. Ordained to ministry, 1951. Minister edn. chs. in Fla., Ala. and Ga., 1955-66, First Bapt. Ch., Gardendale, Ala., 1966-70, First Bapt. Ch., Jasper, Ala., 1970-83, assoc. pastor, 1983—. Trustee Cook Springs Bapt. Assn., 1966-68, Am. Bapt. Sem., 1975—; mem. faculty Ridgecrest (N.C.) Conf. Ctr., 1969; mem. joint com. Nat. and So. Bapts. Ala., 1972-75; v.p. Ala. Bapt. Religious Edn. Assn., 1971-72. Author articles. Home: 502 16th Ave Jasper AL 35501 Office: PO Box 210 Jasper AL 35501

POWELL, EUGENE MARION, minister, Lutheran Church in America; b. Springfield, Ohio, Oct. 24, 1936; s. Andrew J. and Esther Line (Hughes) P.; m. Delphine Marie Robinson, Aug. 3, 1974; children: Wendell L., Eugenia D. A.A., Highlands U., 1964, Assoc. Sci., 1964, B.A., 1976; M.Div., Hamma Luth. Sch. Theology, 1974. Ordained to ministry Luth. Ch., 1973. Campus pastor Chgo. Community Colls., 1973-79; pastor, developer N.C. Synod, Raleigh, 1979-82; coll. minister Atlanta U. Ctr., 1982—; exec. sec. Luth. Campus Ministry Council, 1982—; chmn. prison ministry task force Luth. Ministerial of Ga., 1984—. Author: Ministry to Blacks in Higher Education: A Lutheran View, 1978. Contbr. articles to profl. jours. Bd. dirs. Atlanta Fair Housing Coalition, 1984—. Mem. Am. Coll. Personnel Assn., Assn. Study of Higher Edn., Ministries to Blacks in Higher Edn. Lodge: Optimists. Home: 3136 Buford Hwy NE D-4 Atlanta GA 30329 Office: Clark Coll 240 Jame P Brawley Dr SW Atlanta GA 30314

POWELL, JOHN PAUL, minister, Presbyterian Church U.S.A.; b. Eugene, Oreg., Feb. 9, 1950; s. Robert Vincent and Marilyn Marie (Mowe) P.; m. Pamela Baker, Aug. 20, 1977; children: Stewart, Elliott, Jennifer. B.A., Northwest Christian Coll., 1972; M.Div., Fuller Theol. Sem., 1977, D.Min., 1982. Lic. to ministry Presbyn. Ch., 1972. Youth minister Dallas Christian Ch., Oreg., 1969-70; with Northwest Christian Coll., Eugene, Oreg., 1970-71; intern Peachtree Christian Ch., Atlanta, summer 1971; student pastor Elkton Christian Ch., Oreg., 1971-72; youth minister Park Ave. Christian Ch., Des Moines, 1972-74; assoc. pastor South Pasadena Christian Ch., Calif., 1974-76, Glendale Presbyn. Ch., Calif., 1977-83; co-pastor Sherman Oaks Presbyn. Ch., 1983—; panelist on Faithways, Sta. KNXT-TV, Hollywood, Calif., 1982; mem. ethics com. Children's Hosp., Hollywood, 1980-81; spiritual dir. Fuller Sem., Pasadena, 1979-84; commr. Synod of So. Calif. and Hawaii, 1984-85; faculty search com. Fuller Theol. Sem., 1978, instr. communications, 1979; faculty Coll. Brief in Forest Home Christian Conf., Forest Falls, Calif., 1980—; lectr. Fuller Theol. Sem., 1982, 84, 85. Contbr. articles to profl. jours. Developer, dir. Cross Talk Coffee House, Des Moines, 1972-74; violinist Summer Musical Assn., Eugene, 1966, 67; soloist Continental Singers World Tour, 1970; vocal solist Crystal Cathedral, Long Beach Symphony and Oragne County Choral Condrs. Guild, 1976-77; rec. soloist Gospel Light, 1977, 78; fund raiser Campbell Hall Sch., North Hollywood, 1983-84. Oreg. scholar, 1968. Mem. San Fernando Presbytery Gen. Council, Korean Congregation Organizing Adminstrv. Commn. Republican. Club: YMCA Men's. Avocations: tennis; skiing; bycycling; racquetball; travel. Home: 3620 Sepulveda Blvd Sherman Oaks CA 91403 Office: First Presbyn Ch 4445 Noble Ave Sherman Oaks CA 91403

POWELL, PETER JOHN, priest, scholar, Episcopal Ch.; b. Bryn Mawr, Pa., July 2, 1928; s. William and Helena (Teague) P.; B.A., Ripon Coll., 1950; M. Div., Nashotah House Sem., 1953, D.D., 1971; m. Virginia Lee Raisch, June 13, 1953; children—Katherine, Christine, John, Stephen. Ordained to ministry as priest Episcopal Ch., 1953; priest in charge Holy Cross-Immanuel Ch., Chgo., 1953-54, St. Timothy's Ch., 1953-61; founder and dir. St. Augustine's Center for Am. Indians, Chgo., 1962-71; scholar in residence Newberry Library, Chgo., 1972—, research asso., 1975—. Bd. dirs. Center History Am. Indian Newberry Library, Chgo.; pres. Found. Preservation Am. Indian Art and Culture, Chgo. Recipient Ann. award Chgo. Commn. Human Relations, 1961; knighted by King Peter of Yugoslavia, 1968. Fellow, Nat. Endowment for Humanities, John Simon Guggenheim Meml. Found., Bollingen Found. Mem. Phi Beta Kappa. Author: Sweet Medicine: The Continuing Role of the Sacred Arrows, the Sun Dance and the Sacred Buffalo Hat in Northern Cheyenne History, 1969; editorial adv. bd. Am. Indian Art mag., Scottsdale, Ariz. Contbr. articles to profl. jours. Home: care St Augustine's Rectory 4512 N Sheridan Rd Chicago IL 60640 Office: Newberry Library 60 W Walton St Chicago IL 60610

POWELL, PETER ROSS, JR., priest, Episcopal Church. B. Phila., Jan. 8, 1948; s. Peter Ross Powell Sr. and Rosalie Sadler Watson; m. Kathryn Elizabeth McAllister, June 13, 1970; children: Melissa, Elizabeth, Sarah. B.S. in Chem. Engring., N.C. State U., 1970; M.Div. cum laude, Va. Theol. Sem., 1976; Th.M., Princeton Theol. Sem., 1979; postgrad. U. of the South, 1984—. Ordained to ministry Episcopal Church, 1976. Curate, St. Andrew's Episc. Ch., Murray Hill, N.J., 1976-77; teaching fellow, instr. Princeton Theol. Sem., N.J., 1976-78; assoc. All Saints' Episc. Ch., Princeton, 1977-79; rector Christ Episcopal Ch., Accokeek, Md., 1979-85, Emmanuel Ch., Weston, Conn., 1985—; adj. prof. Biblical langs. Va. Theol. Sem., Alexandria, 1980-84; mem. Missionary Devel. Adv. Com., Washington, D.C., 1980-83; staff Creation Around the Chesapeake, St. Mary's City, Md., 1981; cons. ten talents program Wesley Sem., Washington, D.C., 1982-84; chmn. Commn. Healing the Abuse of Alcohol and other substances, Diocese of Washington, 1983-85; dir. youth camps, 1981-84. Reviewer Old Testaments books in numerous jours., 1976—. Bd. dirs. Henson Valley Montessori Sch., Camp Springs, Md., 1979-80, Canterbury Sch., Accokeek, Md., 1979—; trustee Accokeek Health Council, 1982-84. Proctor fellow Christ Ch., Glendale, Ohio, 1973-76, W. Crosby Bell fellow Va. Theol. Sem., 1976-79, teaching fellow Princeton Theol. Sem., 1976-79. Mem. Soc. Biblical Lit., Cath. Biblical Soc. (assoc.), Evangelical Edn. Soc. of Episcopal Ch. Republican. Home: 283 Lyons Plains Rd Weston CT 06883 Office: Emmanuel Ch 285 Lyons Plains Rd Weston CT 06883

POWELL, ROGER, minister, So. Bapt. Conv.; b. Oakdale, Tenn., Dec. 7, 1929; s. Ernest and Emma (Alley) P.; student in theology Grand Canyon Coll., 1962; diploma in theology Southwestern Bapt. Theol. Sem., 1966; m. Mary Alma Coburn, Aug. 15, 1959; children—Timothy Roger, Jeffrey Russell. Ordained to ministry, 1962; pastor chs. in Okla., Ohio, Ky., 1962-71; pastor First Bapt. Ch., Baird, Tex., 1971-75, East Patterson Rd. Bapt. Ch., Dayton, Ohio, 1975—. Associational Sunday sch. dir. Callahan County (Tex.) Assn., 1971-75; chmn. Callahan County Evangelistic Crusade, 1972-73; mem. nominating, budget and fin. coms. Greater Dayton Assn.; missionary Wings for Christ, Ariz.; broadcaster ch. services. Active Welfare Dept., parole bds. Recipient award Callahan County Assn. Contbr. editorials to mags. and newspapers. Office: 4184 E Patterson Rd Dayton OH 45430

POWELL, RONALD CLAUDE, minister, So. Baptist Conv.; b. Denver, Nov. 12, 1946; s. John A. and Emma S. (Wester) P.; B.S. in Secondary Edn. and Social Studies, Ind. U., 1971; M.Div., Southwestern Bapt. Theol. Sem., Fort Worth, 1974; m. Beverly R. Boromisa, Mar. 20, 1971; children—Ronald C., John A. II. Ordained to ministry, 1973; interim pastor North Highland Bapt. Chapel, Highland, Ind., 1969-70; pastor Gibtown (Tex.) Bapt. Ch., 1973-74; chaplain 189th Maintenance Bn. U.S. Army, Ft. Bragg, N.C., 1974—; dep. task force chaplain Operation New Arrivals for Vietnamese refugees, Ft. Indiantown Gap, Pa., 1975. Recipient Nat. Def. Service medal U.S. Army, 1974, Army Commendation medal, 1977. Home: 101 Souter Pl Fort Bragg NC 28307 Office: 189th Maintenance Bn US Army Fort Bragg NC 28307

POWER, CORNELIUS MICHAEL, archbishop, Roman Catholic Church; b. Seattle, Dec. 18, 1913; s. William and Kate (Dougherty) P.; student St. Patrick Sem., 1933-35, St. Edward Sem., 1935-39; J.C.D., Cath. U. Am., 1943. Ordained priest Roman Catholic Ch., 1939, consecrated bishop, 1969, archbishop, 1974; asst. pastor St. James Cathedral, Seattle, 1939-40; resident chaplain Holy Names Acad., Seattle, 1943-52; adminstr. Parish of Our Lady of Lake, Seattle, 1955-56, pastor, 1956-69; vice chancellor Archdiocese of Seattle, 1943-51, chancellor, 1951-69; apptd. domestic prelate, 1963; 2d bishop of Yakima, 1969; bishop of Yakima, 1969-74; archbishop, Portland, Oreg., 1974—. Office: Archdiocese Portland 2838 N Burnside St PO Box 351 Portland OR 97207

POWER, PAUL WAYNE, minister, So. Baptist Conv.; b. Liberty, Mo., Jan. 17, 1945; s. Paul Elton and Roma Pearl (Bush) P.; B.A., S.W. Bapt. Coll., 1971; M.R.E., Golden Gate Bapt. Theol. Sem., 1973; m. Judy Jennalea Johnson, Aug. 23, 1968; 1 dau., Tiffani Le Wayne. Ordained to ministry, 1975; asso. pastor Clavary Bapt. Ch., Napa, Calif., 1973-75; mgr. Bapt. Book Store, Golden Gate Bapt. Sem., Mill Valley, Calif., 1973-75; minister edn. Park Victoria Bapt. Ch., Milpitas, Calif., 1975—. Mem. Western Religious Edn. Assn., Milpitas Ministerial Alliance. Home: 2415 Fallingtree Dr San Jose CA 95131 Office: 875 S Park Victoria Milpitas CA 95035

POWER, WILLIAM EDWARD, bishop, Roman Catholic Church; b. Montreal, Que., Can., Sept. 27, 1915; s. Nicholas Walter and Bridget Elizabeth (Callaghan) P.; B.A., Montreal Coll., 1937; student Grand Sem., Montreal. Ordained priest Roman Catholic Ch., 1941; parish asst., Montreal, 1941-47; vice-chancellor Diocese Montreal, 1947-50; diocesan chaplain Young Christian Workers and Christian Family Movement, 1950-53; nat. chaplain Young Christian Workers, 1953-59; chaplain, mgr. Cath. Men's Hostel, Montreal, 1957-59; pastor St. Barbara's Ch., Lasalle, Que., 1959-60; bishop of Antigonish, N.S., 1960—; chancellor St. Francis Xavier U., 1960—. Bd. dirs. Canadian Catholic Conf. of Bishops, 1975—. Address: PO Box 1330 155 Main St Antigonish NS B2G 2L7 Canada

POWER, WILLIAM LARKIN, religious educator, United Methodist Church; b. Biloxi, Miss., Aug. 2, 1934; s. Ellis Candler and Lauraine (Barbour) P.; m. Margaret Joan Holloway, Dec. 23, 1957 (dec. 1969); children: William Keith, Richard Kevin; m. Mildred Amburn Huskins, Dec. 30, 1970. B.A., U. Miss., 1956; B.D., Emory U., 1959, Ph.D., 1965. Assoc. dir. United Christian Fellowship, Bowling Green, Ohio, 1959-62; asst. prof. philosophy Lambuth Coll., Jackson, Tenn., 1965-67; mem. faculty U. Georgia, Athens, 1967—, assoc. prof. philosophy and religion, 1976—; lectr. to numerous profl. groups; bd. dirs. Felton Williams Mission, Atlanta, 1968—. Bd. dirs. Friends of Ga. Mus. Art, 1980—, v.p., 1982-83, pres., 1983-84; bd. dirs. Hope Haven Sch., 1981—, sec., 1982-83; bd. dirs. United Fund of Athens, 1974-80, bd. dirs. Athens YMCA, 1974—; cons. for Com. Humanities Ga., 1975—; mem. scholarship bd. U. Ga. Army R.O.T.C., 1976—; trustee Athens Acad., 1982—. Named Outstanding Honors Prof. U. Ga., Athens, 1976, 84. Mem. Am. Acad. Religion (editorial bd. 1980—), Soc. Philosophy of Religion. Democrat. Club: Athens Country. Home: 165 Phimarga Ln Athens GA 30606 Office: Dept Religion U Ga Athens GA 30602

POWERS, BRUCE POSTELL, educator, minister, Southern Baptist Convention; b. Savannah, Ga., May 25, 1940; s. Bruce Postell and Lila (Goynes) P.; m. Barbara Jean Clark, July 3, 1965; children: Bruce, Jason. A.B., Mercer U., 1964; M.R.E., So. Bapt. Theol. Sem., 1967, Ed.D., 1971. Ordained to ministry So. Bapt. Conv., 1978. Staff minister Tattnall Sq. Bapt. Ch., Macon, Ga., 1959-65, Melbourne Heights Ch., Louisville, 1965-70; cons. Sunday Sch. Bd., Nashville, 1971-77; prof. Christian edn. Southeastern Bapt. Theol. Sem., Wake Forest, N.C., 1978—. Author: Growing Faith, 1982; Christian Leadership, 1979. Editor: Christian Education Handbook, 1981; Church Administration Handbook, 1985. Mem. N.C. Bapt. Religious Edn. Assn. (bd. dirs. 1982—), So. Bapt. Religious Edn. Assn. (pres., bd. dirs. 1984—), World Future Soc., N.C. Religious Edn. Assn. (bd. dirs. 1982-85), Religious Edn. Assn. Office: Southeastern Sem Box 712 Wake Forest NC 27587

POWERS, JOHN EDWARD, JR., minister; b. Willard, N.C., Jan. 3, 1917; s. John Edward and Cordelia (Glasper) P.; m. Pearl Marie McIver; children: Julie Cordelia, John Edward, III, Agnes Marie. B.A., Shaw U., 1943; M.Div., Shaw Div. Sch., 1945; M.Ed., U. Va., 1965; LL.D. (hon.), Richmond Va. Sem., 1984; D.D., 1985. Ordained to ministry Progressive Baptist Ch., 1943. Pastor St. John Bapt. Ch., Axton, Va., 1946-65, First Bapt. Ch., Rocky Mount, Va., 1949-56, East Martinsville, Va., 1959-65, Calvary Bapt. Ch., Danville, Va., 1965-69, St. Paul's High St. Bapt. Ch., Martinsville, Va., 1969—; tchr. numerous colls. throughout Va., 1945-78; instr. Richmond Va. Sem., Va., 1983—; exec. bd. mem. Va. Sem. Coll., Lynchburg, 1977—, Lott Carey Bapt. Fgn. Mission Conv., Washington, 1977—. Trustee Children's Home of Va. Bapt., Inc., 1982—. Mem. Martinsville Ministerial Alliance, (sec. 1950-51), Danville Ministerial Alliance, Martinsville Ministerial Assn. (sec. 1971-72, v.p. 1972-73, pres. 1973-74). Lodges: Masons; Knights of Pythias. Address: 517 Holbrook St Danville VA 24541

POWERS, JOSEPH DUDLEY, lay ch. worker, Ch. of the Nazarene; b. Upland, Calif., Apr. 13, 1927; s. Hardy C. and Ruby M. Powers; B.S., So. Methodist U., 1951; D.D.S., Baylor U., U. Tex., 1962; m. Mary Joan Clester, June 8, 1951; children—Bradford, Peter, Elizabeth, Stephanie. Lay mem. gen. bd. Ch. of Nazarene, 1972—, v.p., 1973—, mem.-at-large exec. com., 1976; med. missionary, hosp. adminstry Nazarene Mission Hosp., Kudjip, Papia New Guinea, 1965-69. Gen. practice medicine, Bethany, Okla., 1969—. Recipient Goldheaded Cane award U. Tex. Med. Sch., Galveston, 1962—. Diplomate Am. Bd. Family Practice, 1977. Mem. Am., Okla. med. assns., Am. Acad. Family Practice, Mu Delta. Author articles. Address: PO Box 74 Bethany OK 73008

POYTHRESS, VERN SHERIDAN, minister, religious educator Presbyterian Church in America; b. Madera, Calif., Mar. 29, 1946; s. Ransom Huron and Carola Eirene (Nasmyth) P.; m. Diane Marie Weisenborn, Aug. 6, 1983. B.S., Calif. Inst. Tech., 1966; Ph.D., Harvard U., 1970; M.Div., Th.M., Westminster Theol. Sem., 1974; M.Phil., Cambridge U., 1977; Th.D., U. Stellenbosch, 1979. Ordained to ministry Presbyn. Ch. in Am., 1981. Asst. prof. N.T., Westminster Theol. Sem., Phila., 1976-81, assoc. prof., 1981—. Author: Philosophy, Science and the Sovereignty of God, 1976. Assoc. editor Westminster Theol. Jour., 1981—. NSF fellow, 1966-70; Nat. Merit scholar, 1963-66; Ned B. Stonehouse fellow, 1974. Mem. Lingusitic Assn. Can. and U.S. Home: 510 Twickenham Rd Glenside PA 19038 Office: Westminster Theol Sem Chestnut Hill Philadelphia PA 19118

PRABHUPADA, A. C. BHAKTIVEDANTA SWAMI, leader, Hare Krishna Movement. Founder, Internat. Soc. for Krishna Consciousness, 1965. Address: care Internat Soc Krishna Consciousness 3764 Watseka Ave Los Angeles CA 90034*

PRASAD, ADAM PULIVARTI, religious organization executive, Seventh-day Adventists. B. Nuzvid, Andhra Pradesh, India, Aug. 12, 1944; came to U.S., 1975, naturalized, 1982; s. Pulivarti Adam and Avvamma (Elura), P.; m. Mary Thummalapaeli, Dec. 28, 1969; children: Salina, Norwin. B.Sc. in Religion, Spicer M. Coll., Poona, India, 1967, B.S.Ed., 1968; A.A. in Computer Sci., Montg Coll., 1978; postgrad. U. Md., 1983—. Ordained elder Seventh-day Adventists, 1974. Pastor, Seventh-day Adventists Ch., Roorkee, India, 1970-74; exec. sec., chmn. religious activities So. Asia Adventist Assn., Silver Spring, Md., 1977-80; programmer/analyst Rev. and Herald Pub. Assn., Hagerstown, Md., 1980—; vice chmn. Adventist Fellowship Internat., Takoma Park, Md., 1983—; warden Seventh-day Adventist Sem., Roorkee, India, 1970-74; dir. Christian Children's Fund, Jullundur, India, 1973-75; chmn. cultural and soc. activities Adventist Fellowship Internat., Takoma Park, 1981-83, chmn. fund raising com., 1983—. News editor Spicerian, 1965. Sec., Sligo PTA, Takoma Park, 1983—. Club: Toastmasters. Lodge: Rotary (Roorkee, India). Home: 9413 Avenel Rd Silver Spring MD 20903 Office: Rev and Herald Pub Assn 55 W Oak Ridge Dr Hagerstown MD 21740

PRATER, DANNY LEE, minister, Southern Baptist Convention; b. Pontotoc, Miss., Dec. 21, 1946; s. Harvey Lee and Pauline Imogene (Jaggers) P.; B.A., Blue Mountain Coll., 1969; M.Div., Luther Rice Sem., 1980, D.Min., 1981; m. Linda Faye Anglin, Aug. 12, 1966; 1 son, Timothy Lee. Ordained to ministry, 1966; pastor Algoma (Miss.) Bapt. Ch., 1966-68, Slayden (Miss.) Bapt. Ch., 1969-72; asso. pastor Forest Bapt. Ch., Forest, Miss., 1972-73; dir. missions Riverside Bapt. Assn., Coahoma and Tunica counties, Miss., 1973-80; pastor First Bapt. Ch., Inverness, Miss., 1980—. Vice pres. Marshall Bapt. Pastors Conf., 1969-70, pres., 1970-71, chmn. evangelism, 1971-72, co-chmn. spl. missions com., 1970-72; chmn. nominating com. Scott Bapt. Assn., 1972-73, co-chmn. evangelism, 1972-73, vacation Bible sch. dir., 1972-73; mem. Com. on Bds. of the So. Bapt. Conv., 1974-75; mem. Delta Spanish Missions Com., 1973-77; vice-moderator Sunflower Bapt. Assn., 1985; pres. Sunflower Bapt. Pastors Conf., 1984; pres. Inverness C. of C., 1985-86. Home: PO Box 4 Inverness MS 38753

PRATT, MARTIN LEE, religious organization administrator, Evangelical Covenant Church; b. Pope, Miss., Apr. 28, 1935; s. James Lee and Viola Bell (Deaton) P.; m. Sue Mihlfeld, Aug. 3, 1958; children: Kevin, Kenneth. B.A., Miss. Coll., 1957; M.Div., New Orleans Bapt. Sem., 1960; M.S.W., Washington U., St. Louis, 1968. Ordained to ministry Baptist Ch., 1960. Missionary, Home Mission Bd., So. Bapt. Conv., Washington and New Orleans, 1960-66; dir. inner city ministries St. Louis Bapt. Assn., 1970-72; coordinator campus programs Mo. Bapt. Children's Home, Bridgeton, 1976-80; exec. dir. Covenant Children's Home and Family Services, Princeton, Ill., 1980—. Mem. Nat. Assn. Social Workers, Acad. Cert. Social Workers, Ill. Child Care Assn. (bd. dirs. 1983-85). Lodge: Optimists. Avocations: coin collecting; stamp collecting; gardening. Home: Route 4 Country Oaks Princeton IL 61356 Office: 502 Elm Pl Princeton IL 61356

PREBISH, CHARLES S., religion educator; b. Chgo., Oct. 11, 1944; s. Jacob L. and Sydelle (Grossman) P.; m. Susan Lee Kodicek, Aug. 31, 1968; children: Jared Berkeley, Robinson Ashley. B.A., Western Res. U., 1966; M.A., Case-Western Res. U., 1968; Ph.D., U. Wis.-Madison, 1971. Assoc. prof. religious studies Pa. State U., University Park, 1971—. Author: Buddhist Monastic Discussion, 1975; Buddhism: A Modern Perspective, 1975; American Buddhism, 1979. Pa. State U. grantee, 1972-73, 77. Mem. Am. Oriental Soc., Assn. Asian Studies, Am. Acad. Religion (chmn. Buddhism group 1981—), Internat. Assn. Buddhist Studies (assoc. sec. 1976-81, bd. dirs. 1981—). Clubs: Nittany Valley Track (University Park), Pa. State Wrestling; State College Wrestling. Office: Religious Studies Program Pa State U University Park PA 16802

PREGNALL, WILLIAM S., clergyman, educational administrator, Episcopal. Pres., dean Ch. Div. Sch. of the Pacific, Berkeley, Calif. Office: Ch Div Sch of the Pacific 2451 Ridge Rd Berkeley CA 94709*

PREHEIM, VERN QUINCY, religious organization executive, minister, Mennonite Church; b. Hurley, S.D., June 27, 1935; s. Jacob Roy and Selma (Miller) P.; m. Marion Kathryn Keeney, Aug. 28, 1958; children: Jay, Janette, Beth, Brian, Lorie. A.A., Freeman Jr. Coll., 1956; B.A., Bethel Coll., 1957; B.D., Mennonite Bibl. Sem., 1960. Peace sec. Gen. Conf. Mennonite Ch., Newton, Kans., 1962-65; Algeria program dir. Mennonite Central Com., Algiers, 1960-62, Africa and Middle East dir., Akron, Pa., 1965-75, Asia dir., Akron, 1975-80; gen. sec. Gen. Conf. Mennonite Ch., Newton, 1980—, mission bd. sec., 1968-72, chmn., 1974-80, gen. bd. dirs., 1974-80. Home: 1112 Lorna Ln Newton KS 67114 Office: Gen Conf Mennonite Ch 722 Main Newton KS 67114

PRESTON, EARL, JR., minister, American Baptist Churches in the U.S.A. B. Cleve., Apr. 30, 1931; s. Earl Preston Sr. and Esther (Clack) Preston McAlpine; m. Marian Ella, Dec. 10, 1959; children: Cheryl, Charles, Tara, Renee. Student religious studies Cleve. State U., 1960-65, Am. Inst. Banking, 1972-77; M.A., Ashland Theol. Sem., 1980; D.Min., Trinity Theol. Sem., Newburg, Ind., 1983. Licensed evangelistic minister, 1972; ordained to ministry American Baptist Chs. in the U.S.A., 1975. Minister music Olivet Instl. Bapt. Ch., Cleve., 1957-75, assoc. minister, 1975-77; pastor Morning Star Bapt. Ch., Cleve., 1977—; chmn. bd. dirs. Nat. Conv. Gospel Choirs and Choruses, Cleve., 1959—; trustee Greater Cleve. Interchurch Council, 1979—, Inter-City Protestant Parish, 1981—; mem. Ptnr. in Ecumenism, N.Y.C., 1979; Progress Nat. Bapt. Conv., Ohio Bapt. Ministers Conf., 1980. Mem. NAACP, Cleve., 1963, Cleve. Urban League, 1975. Recipient Best Religious Program award State of Ohio, 1972, 78, Pub. Speaking award Am. Inst. Banking, 1970, Mayoral and Councilmatic citations, Cleve., 1983, Wash., 1979, 82; named Citizen Yr. Cleve. Assn. Real Estate Brokers, 1981. Mem. Cleve. Bapt. Assn. (trustee 1980—), Omega Psi Phi. Lodge: Kiwanis. Home: 17203 Talford Ave Cleveland OH 44128 Office: Morning Star Bapt Ch 650 Parkwood Dr Cleveland OH 44108

PRETTI, BRADFORD JOSEPH, lay worker, Episcopal Church; insurance agency executive; b. Glenwood Springs, Colo., Oct. 11, 1930; s. Joseph John and Ethel Elizabeth (Roe) P.; m. Nancy Ann Clayton, Mar. 30, 1951 (div. 1971); children: Kristi Pretti Micander, Terice Pretti Brownson, Bradford Joseph, Holli; m. Sarah J. Rupp, Aug. 8, 1974. B.A., U. Colo., 1952. Sr. warden St. Thomas a Beckett Ch., Roswell, N.Mex., 1978-79; mem. Program Council, Diocese of Rio Grande, Albuquerque, 1981-84, mem. Venture in Mission Commn., 1980-84, pres. Standing Commn., 1981-84, dep. to Gen. Conv., 1985. Pres. RBS Ins., Roswell, 1960—. Pres. Assurance Home Found., Roswell, 1984; v.p. United Way of Chaves County, Roswell, 1984; bd. dirs. Roswell Hospice Inc., 1984; trustee Roswell Mus. and Art Ctr., 1985—. Recipient Disting. Service award United Way of Chaves County, 1982. Mem. N.Mex. Ind. Ins. Agts. Assn. (Outstanding Service award 1964), Roswell C. of C. (treas. 1984, pres.-elect 1985, Pres.'s Club citation 1983). Republican. Home: 317 Sherrill Ln #14 Roswell NM 88201 Office: RBS Ins 1510 W Second St Roswell NM 88201

PREUS, DAVID WALTER, minister, ch. ofcl., Am. Luth. Ch.; b. Madison, Wis., May 28, 1922; s. Ove Jacob Hjort and Magdalene (Forde) P.; B.A., Luther Coll., Decorah, Iowa, 1943, D.D., 1969; B.Th., Luther Sem., St. Paul, 1950; postgrad. U. Minn., 1946-47, Union Sem., 1951, Edinburgh U., 1951-52; LL.D., Wagner Coll., 1973, Gettysburg Coll.; D.D., Luther Coll., 1969, Pacific Luth. Coll., 1974, St. Olaf Coll., 1974; L.H.D., Macalester Coll.; m. Ann Madsen, June 26, 1951; children—Martha, David, Stephen, Louise, Laura. Ordained to ministry, 1950; asst. pastor First Luth. Ch., Brookings, S.D., 1950-51; pastor Trinity Luth. Ch., Vermillion, S.D., 1952-57; campus pastor U. Minn., Mpls., 1957-58; pastor Univ. Luth. Ch. of Hope, Mpls., 1958-73; v.p. Am. Luth. Ch., 1968-73, pres., 1973—. Luccock vis. pastor Yale Div. Sch., 1969; chmn. bd. youth activity Am. Luth. Ch., 1960-68; mem. exec. com. Luth. Council U.S.A., Luth. World Fedn.; mem. central com. World Council Chs., 1973-75; Luth. del. White House Conf. on Equal Opportunity; chmn. Greater Mpls. Fair Housing Com., Mpls. Council Chs., 1960-64. Mem. Mpls. Planning Commn., 1965-67; mem. Mpls. Sch. Bd., 1965-74, chmn., 1967-69; mem. Mpls. Bd. Estimate and Taxation, 1968-73, Mpls. Urban Coalition; bd. dirs. Mpls. Inst. Art, Walker Art Center, Hennepin County United Fund, Ams. for Children's Relief, Luth. Student Fedn., Research Council of Gt. City Schs., Urban League, NAACP; bd. regents Augsburg Coll., Mpls. Decorated comdr.'s cross Royal Norwegian Order St. Olav; recipient Regents medal Augustana Coll., Sioux Falls, S.D., 1973; Torch of Liberty award Anti-Defamation League, 1973; St. Thomas Aquinas award Coll. of St. Thomas, 1983; Minn. Religious Hall of Fame award Temple Israel, Mpls., 1984. Home: 60 Seymour Ave SE Minneapolis MN 55414 Office: 422 S 5th St Minneapolis MN 55415

PREUS, ROBERT DAVID, seminary president, Lutheran Church Missouri Synod; b. St. Paul, Oct. 16, 1924; s. Jacob Aall Ottesen and Idella Louise (Haugen) P.; m. Donna Rockman, May 29, 1948; children: Daniel, Klemet, Katherine, Rolf, Peter, Solveig, Christian, Karen, Ruth, Erik. B.A., Luther Coll., Decorah, Iowa, 1944; B.D., Bethany Luth. Sem., Mankato, Minn., 1947; Ph.D., Edinburgh U., Scotland, 1952; D.Ehtol., Strasbourg U., France, 1969. Ordained to ministry Mo. Synod Luth. Ch., 1947. Luth. pastor, 1947-57; prof. Concordia Sem., St. Louis, 1957-74; pres., prof. systematic theology Concordia Theol. Sem., Springfield, Ill., 1974-76 (school moved, 1976), Ft. Wayne, Ind., 1976—; guest lectr. Luther Sem., North Adelaide, Australia, 1981. Author: The Inspiration of Scripture, 1955; The Theology of Post-Reformation Lutheranism, 2 vols., 1970, 72; Getting into the Theology of Concord, 1977. Active Ft. Wayne Hist. Soc. Mem. Am. Soc. for Reformation Research. Republican. Office: Concordia Theol Sem 6600 N Clinton St Fort Wayne IN 46825

PREUSS, WILLIAM JOHN II, minister Lutheran Church in America; b. Rockville, Conn., Sept. 13, 1946; s. William John and Dorothea H. (Escherich) P.; m. Marilyn H. Kington, June 22, 1968; children: Melissa, Kristen, William. B.A., Upsala Coll., 1968; M.Div., Luth. Sch. Theology, 1972. Ordained to ministry New Eng. Synod Luth. Ch. in Am., 1972. Pastor, St. Paul's Luth. Ch., Richmondville, N.Y., 1972-76, Zion Luth. Ch., Seward, N.Y., 1972-76, Trinity Luth. Ch., Herkimer, N.Y., 1976—; bd. dirs., treas. Luth. Home of Central N.Y., Clinton, 1981—; bd. dirs. Luth. Home Found., Clinton, 1982—; mem. cabinet Luth. Ch. in Am., 1983—; chaplain Mohawk Valley Ambulance Corps, N.Y., 1979—, Mohawk Fire Dept., N.Y., 1981—. Vice chmn. ARC, Herkimer, N.Y., 1983—. Home: 15 Catherine St Mohawk NY 13407 Office: Trinity Luth Ch 443 Henry St Herkimer NY 13350

PREWETT, THURMAN BRADFORD, minister, Southern Baptist Convention; b. Ft. Payne, Ala., Nov. 2, 1922; s. John Franklin and Beatrice (Abney) P.; B.A., Carson-Newman Coll., 1949; M.R.E., Southwestern Bapt. Theol. Sem., 1950, D.R.E., 1957; m. Catherine Jones, Dec. 28, 1940; children—James Thurman, Cathy Gail Bell. Ordained to ministry So. Bapt. Conv., 1954;

minister of edn. Frayser Bapt. Ch., 1951-58; dir. edn. and promotion Shelby Bapt. Assn., Memphis, 1959—. Mem. Tenn. Religious Edn. Assn. (pres., v.p.), Southwestern Bapt. Sem. Alumni Assn. (past pres.), Met. Edn. Dirs. (past pres.). Mason. Editor: Shelby Baptist Beacon, 1961—. Home: 6192 Moray Cove Memphis TN 38119 Office: 202 S Cooper St Memphis TN 38104

PREWITT, JAMES FRANKLIN, religion educator, General Association of Regular Baptist Churches; b. Dora, N.Mex., Nov. 25, 1914; s. William Henry and Elva Mae (Dutton) P.; m. Catherine Mildred Hannah, Nov. 28, 1935; children: Joyce, Grace, James Franklin. Student Biola Coll., 1934-35, Inst. Holy Land Studies, Jerusalem, Israel, 1960-62; B.A., Western Bapt. Coll., 1962, Th.B., 1962, D.D., 1971. Ordained to ministry Bapt. Ch., 1941. bus. v.p. Western Bapt. Coll., Salem, Oreg., 1946-60, prof. history and Bible, 1962—; resident dir. Inst. Holy Land Studies, Jerusalem, 1960-62; vis. prof. Bapt. Inst., Ilo Ilo, Philippines, 1973, Tiberias, Israel, 1981, 84; conf. lectr. Middle East. Author: A People Who Will Not Die, 1973; Prophetic Light on Arab-Israeli Conflict, 1983; contbr. articles to Internat. Bible Ency.; author Bible Land Profile Audio-Visual Series. Mem. Near East Archaell. Soc. Republican. Club: Wally Byam Caravan. Home: 10774 Mill Creek Rd Aumsville OR 97325 Office: Western Bapt Coll 5000 Deer Park Dr SE Salem OR 97302

PRIBIL, CLEMENT EUGENE, priest, Roman Catholic Ch.; b. Bison, Okla., June 30, 1932; s. Joseph A. and Rose L. (Brauner) P.; grad. Glennon Coll., St. Louis, 1952; postgrad. Inst. Philosophy U. Louvain (Belgium), 1952-54, M.A., 1967. Ordained priest, 1958; chaplain Okla. State U., 1958-66; vice rector Am. Coll. U. Louvain, 1966-70, rector, 1970-72; pastor Sacred Heart Parish, Oklahoma City, 1972—. Regional dir. Univ. Chaplains Tex., Okla., 1960-66; mem. adv. bd. Nat. Newman Chaplain's Assn., 1962-66; dir. Continuing Edn. of the Clergy, Archdiocese of Oklahoma City, 1972—, mem. Archdiocesan Pastoral Bd., archdiocesan consultor, mem. Lay Deacon Edn. Bd., Mem. Archdiocesan Rural Ministry Com. Mem. Nat. Assn. Dirs. Continuing Edn. of Roman Cath. Clergy. Home: 2706 S Shartel Oklahoma City OK 73109

PRICE, FREDERICK KENNETH CERCIE, minister, Protestant non-denominational; b. San Monica, Calif., Jan. 3, 1932; s. Fred Cercie and Winnifred Bernice (Ammons) P.; m. Betty Ruth Scott, Mar. 29, 1953; children: Angela Marie Price Evans, Cheryl Ann Price Crabbe, Stephanie Pauline, Frederick Kenneth. Diploma Rhema Bible Tng., 1976; D.D. (hon.), Oral Roberts U., 1982. Ordained to ministry Bapt. Ch., 1955, A.M.E., 1957, Kenneth Hagin Ministries, 1975. Asst. pastor Mt. Sinai Bapt. Ch., Los Angeles, 1955-57; pastor A.M.E.Ch., Val Verde, Calif., 1957-59, Christian Missionary Alliance West Washington Community Ch., Los Angeles, 1965-73, Crenshaw Christian Ctr., Inglewood, Calif., 1973—; trustee, a founder Internat. Conv. of Faith Chs. and Ministers, Tulsa, 1979—; host TV program. Author: How Faith Works, 1976, Is Healing For All, 1976, How To Obtain Strong Faith, 1977, Thank God For Everything?, 1977, The Holy Spirit, The Missing Ingredient, 1978, Now Faith Is, 1983, High Finance, God's Financial Plan, Tithes and Offerings, 1984. Democrat. Office: Crenshaw Christian Ctr PO Box 90000 Los Angeles CA 90009

PRICE, JOHN EDWARD, religious education administrator; Christian of the Roman Catholic Tradition; b. Chgo., Mar. 7, 1942; s. Edward F. Price and Carolyn Maxine Polachek; m. Luz Maria Sepulveda, Nov. 26, 1969; children: Larissa Marie, James Thomas, Elizabeth Suzanne. B.A., St. Mary of the Lake, 1964, S.T.B., 1966, S.T.L., 1968. Lic. dir. religious edn., 1984. Tchr. Mother of God Sch., Waukegan, Ill., 1968-69; tchr. chmn. religion dept. Holy Trinity High Sch., Chgo., 1969-70; coordinator of religious edn. Transfiguration Ch., Wauconda, Ill., 1970-75; dir. religious edn. Saint Athanasius, Evanston, Ill., 1975—; catechist resource person Archdiocese CCD Ctr., Chgo., 1977-80; field supr. Mundelein Coll. and Inst. Pastoral Studies, Chgo., 1979-80, 1984; team mem. North Central Evaluation, Chgo., 1984; presenter, lectr. Archdiocese of Chgo., 1979, 80, 84, 85. Author Learning Right and Wrong sound filmstrip, 1978; Religious Edn. Diagnostic Survey testing service, 1983. Contbr. articles to religious publ. Del. Ill. White House Conf. on Libraries and Info. Services, Springfield, 1978. Mem. Chgo. Assn. Religious Educators (treas. 1979-82, Care award 1983), Cath. Theol. Soc. Am., Religious Edn. Assn., Ill. Assn. Parish Dirs. and Coordinators, Nat. Assn. Parish Dirs, and Coordinators. Club: Book Discussion (North Shore). Avocations: photography, fishing, scuba diving, bicycling, poetry. Office: Saint Athanasius Religious Edn 2510 Ashland Ave Evanston IL 60201

PRICE, JOHN FRANKLIN, church official, United Methodist Church; b. Bluefield, W.Va., Aug. 3, 1939; s. Wiley Marshall and Maggie Elizabeth (Boyles) P.; A.B., Concord Coll., Athens, W.Va., 1962; B.D., Candler Sch. Theology, Emory U., Atlanta, 1965; m. June Ellen Hunt, Aug. 26, 1967; children—David Kenneth and Douglas Steven (twins), Gregory Marshall. Ordained deacon United Methodist Ch., 1963, elder, 1966, then minister; pastor Pisgah United Meth. Ch., Princeton, W.Va., 1960-61, Lovejoy-Mt. Carmel Parish, Ga., 1961-63, St. Luke Inner-City Parish, Atlanta, 1963-65; co-minister, dir. Ho. of the Carpenter, Meth. Community Center, Wheeling, W.Va., 1965-68; field rep. W.Va. Council Chs., Charleston, 1968-77, exec. sec., 1970—; mem. Council Ministries W.Va. United Meth. Ann. Conf. Bd. dirs. Kanawha-Putnam Assn. Retarded Citizens, W.Va. Welfare Conf.; chmn. Resource Moblzn. Task Force, Commn. on Religion in Appalachia. Office: 1608 Virginia St E Charleston WV 25301

PRICE, NELSON, communications executive, United Methodist Church; b. Valley City, N.D., Oct. 4, 1928; s. Nelson Allen and Charlotte (King) P.; m. Ann Freeman, Mar. 27, 1954; children: Donna Lynn, David Brent, Debra Leah, Dara Gwen. B.A., Morningside Coll., 1951; postgrad. U. Chgo., 1957-58; M.A., Goddard Coll., 1975. Dir. communication Ind. area The Meth. Ch., Indpls., 1952-57, No. Ill. Conf., Chgo., 1957-59, dir. pub. relations and field work, TV, radio and film commn., Nashville, 1959-61, dir. prodn. TV, Radio and Film Commn., 1961-64; dir. pub. media div. United Meth. Communications, N.Y.C., 1975—; pres. Media Action Research Ctr., Inc., N.Y.C., 1975—; treas., past pres. Communication Commn., Nat. Council Chs., N.Y.C., 1961—; pres. bd. dirs. Ecumedia News Service, N.Y.C., 1985—. Exec. producer Night Call, 1969 (Faith and Freedom award 1969), Begin with Goodbye, 1979 (Cine award 1979), A Fuzzy Tale, 1977 (Asifa-East award 1977), Children's Growing, 1980 (Am. Film Fest award 1980); producer Breakthru, 1966 (Ohio State award 1966); trainer TV Awareness Tng., N.Y.C., 1977—. Chmn. council on ministries New City United Meth. Ch., N.Y., 1982-85. Recipient Gabriel award Cath. Broadcasters Assn., 1969, 76, 77, Paul M. Hinkhouse award Religious Pub. Relations Assn., 1973, 74, 79, 82, 77, Brotherhood award Nat. Conf. Christians and Jews, 1969. Mem. Internat. Radio and TV Soc., Nat. Acad. TV Arts and Scis., Religious Pub. Relations Council, Inc. (past dir.), Internat. Transactional Analysis Assn., World Assn. Christian Communications. Democrat. Home: 120 N Broadway Nyack NY 10960 Office: United Methodist Communications 475 Riverside Dr Suite 1370 New York NY 10115

PRICE, ROSS EUGENE, minister, Church of the Nazarene; b. Culbertson, Mont., July 15, 1907; s. Ernest Eugene and Lydia Ann (Cuff) P.; m. Irene Elizabeth Taylor, Aug. 4, 1933; children: Dorothy Lois, Patricia Louise, Michael Kennedy. A.B., N.W. Nazarene Coll., 1932; M.A., Pasadena Coll., 1944, B.D., 1945; M.Th., McCormick Theol. Sem., 1950; Ph.D., U. So. Calif., 1966; D.D. (hon.), Pasadena Coll., 1949. Ordained to ministry Nazarene Ch., 1933. Pastor Ch. of the Nazarene, Wyo., Mont., Ill., 1932-48; prof., dean grad. studies Pasadena Coll., Calif., 1948-61; prof. theology, 1961-69; prof. theology Olivet Nazarene Coll., Kankakee, Ill., 1969-75; dist. supt. Rocky Mountain Dist. Ch. of the Nazarene, Mont., Wyo., 1970-78; prof. Bible and theology Nazarene Bible Coll., Colorado Springs, Colo., 1978-80; evangelist, 1980—; trustee, regent N.W. Nazarene Coll., Nampa, Idaho, 1942-43, 70-78; trustee Olivet Nazarene Coll., Kankakee, Ill., 1945-48; lectr. Nazarene Theol. Sem., Bethany Nazarene Coll., N.W. Nazarene Coll., Point Loma Nazarene Coll., Can. Nazarene Coll., Nazarene Bible Coll., 1962-85. Author: (with Olive M. Winchester) Crisis Experiences in the Greek New Testament, 1953; Dynamic Evangels, 1966; Some Absolutes from Jesus, 1984; others. Contbr. articles to encys. and dictionaries. Mem. Evang. Theol. Soc. (past pres. Pacific Coast sect.), Wesleyan Theol. Soc., Phi Delta Lambda, Pi Epsilon Theta. Republican. Home: 1540 Hiawatha Dr Colorado Springs CO 80915

PRICE, ROY CANTRELL, minister, Christian and Missionary Alliance Church; b. Los Angeles, May 23, 1935; s. Walter and Wilma P.; m. Sandra Lee Burns, Aug. 27, 1957; children: Steven Roy, Cynthia. B.A., Westmont Coll., 1957; Th.M., Luther Rice Sem., 1977, D.Min., 1978. Ordained to ministry Christian and Missionary Alliance Ch., 1952. Pastor Arbor Heights Alliance, Seattle, 1964-68; assoc. pastor Allegheny Ctr. Alliance, Pitts., 1968-71; sr. pastor Wadsworth Alliance, Ohio, 1971-74; pastor Internat. Protestant, Saigon, Viet Nam, 1975; sr. pastor First Alliance, Louisville, 1975-81, Paradise Alliance, Calif., 1981—; mem. dist. exec. com. Christian and Missionary Alliance, Oakland, Calif., 1982—, bd. mgrs., 1985—, exec. com. ordination council, Toledo, Ohio, 1976-81, dist. treas., Wadsworth, 1974-75. Contbr. articles to profl. jours. Republican. Lodge: Lions (1st v.p. Wadsworth 1974). Home: 585 Valley View Dr Paradise CA 95969 Office: Paradise Alliance Ch 6491 Clark Rd Paradise CA 95969

PRIDGEN, PAUL MISHUE, JR., minister, Southern Baptist Convention; b. Charleston, S.C., Oct. 4, 1927; s. Paul Mishue and Marie (Green) P.; B.A., Furman U., 1953; M.Div., Southeastern Bapt. Theol. Sem., 1958; D.D., Bapt. Coll. at Charleston, 1970; m. Millie Hawkins, Dec. 27, 1951; children—Paul Mishue III, Stephen Michael. Ordained to ministry So. Bapt. Conv., 1951; pastor chs., N.C., S.C., 1953-62; pastor First Bapt. Ch., North Charleston, S.C., 1962—. Moderator Charleston Bapt. Assn., 1969-70; mem. gen. bd. S.C. Bapt. Conv., 1971-76; co-sponsor Cath.-Bapt. Dialogue, Mepkin Abbey, Moncks Corner, S.C., 1973—. Pres. I CARE, prisoner of war program, 1971—; vice chmn. Spl. County Com. for Study of Juvenile Delinquents, 1961; mem. Bicentennial Com. Charleston County, 1972. Bd. dirs. North Charleston Choral Soc., Citizens Scholarship Found.; trustee Bapt. Coll. at Charleston. Mem. North Charleston Ministerial Assn. (pres. 1966-67). Kiwanian (pres. 1973-74). Home: 5870 N Rhett Extension Hanahan SC 29406 Office: POB 5728 North Charleston SC 29406

PRIDGEN, THOMAS J., minister, United Pentecostal Church International; silver miner; b. Kemmerer, Wyo., July 25, 1952; s. Thaddeus J. and Hazel Bernice (Ivie) P.; m. Marjorie Lolly Abeyta, Aug. 21, 1977; children: Jeffery T., Crystal D. Grad. high sch. Weiser, Idaho. Ordained to ministry United Pentecostal Ch. Internat. 1982. Sec., treas., youth dir. United Pentecostal Ch., Rawlins, Wyo., 1978-79, prison outreach minister, 1979-81, Nampa, Idaho, 1981—, retirement ctr. outreach minister, Nampa, 1981—; pastor Nampa Home Mission Ch., 1984—. Ore crusher operator Delamar Silver Mine, Jordan Valley, Oreg., 1982—. External v.p. U.S. Jaycees, Weiser, Idaho, 1973-76, internal v.p., sec., treas., 1973-76. Democrat. Home: 712 8th Ave S Nampa ID 83651 Office: Victory United Pentecostal Ch 712 8th Ave S Nampa ID 83651

PRIEBE, DENNIS EMIL, minister, educator, Seventh-day Adventists; b. Sacramento, Calif., Sept. 27, 1942; s. Emil John and Ruth (Leer) P.; m. Kay Yvonne Buzzard, Aug. 16, 1964; 1 child, Matthew. B.A., Pacific Union Coll., 1964; M.A., Andrews U., 1966, B.D., 1966. Ordained to ministry Seventh-day Adventists, 1970. Pastor, Southeastern Calif. Conf. Seventh-day Adventists, Riverside, 1966-74; instr. Pacific Union Coll., Angwin, Calif., 1974—. Author syllabus. Home: 335 McReynolds Ct Angwin CA 94508 Office: Pacific Union Coll Religion Dept Angwin CA 94508

PRIMMER, MARGARET LILLIAN (MRS. MERL E. PRIMMER), lay church worker, Am. Lutheran Ch.; b. Logan, Ohio, Aug. 19, 1917; d. Charles Ebert and Margaret Catherine (Beery) McBroom; grad. high sch.; m. Merl E. Primmer, July 3, 1943. Pres., Women of the Ch., St. Matthew, 1956; pres. S.E. Group, Womens Missionary Fedn., 1958-59; del. Constituting Constn., Am. Luth. Ch. Women, 1960, v.p. Columbus Conf., 1961, pres. Ohio Dist., 1962-68, mem. nat. bd., 1962-68, pres. St. Matthew, 1960-62; mem. dist. research and social action com. Am. Luth. Ch., 1971-72; fin. sec. St. Matthew Am. Luth. Ch., 1970-72; first woman dist. sec. Am. Luth. Ch., 1972; mem. planning com. and gen. bd. Ohio Council Chs., 1972—; Tri-State Conf. rep. Dist. Council Am. Luth. Ch., 1977-78, 82-83, pres., 1984-85. Active Bloodmobile, ARC, 1948—, pres. chpt., 1980-81. Recipient Clara Barton Vol. award ARC, 1984. Mem. D.A.R. (regent Gov. Worthington chpt. 1969-72, State Officers Club), Hocking County Agrl. Soc. (life), Hocking Grange. Home: 31243 Primmer Rd Logan OH 43138

PRIMO, QUINTIN EBENEZER, JR., bishop, Episcopal Church; b. Liberty County, Ga., July 1, 1913; s. Quintin Ebenezer and Alvira Wilhemenia (Wellington) P.; B.A., Lincoln U. (Pa.), 1934, S.T.B., 1937; M.Div., Va. Theol. Sem., 1941, D.D., 1973; D.D., Seabury-Western Sem., 1972, Gen. Theol. Sem., 1973; L.H.D., St. Augustine's Coll., 1972; m. Winifred Priscilla Thompson, July 5, 1942; children—Cynthia Priscilla, Quintin Ebenezer, Susan Alvira. Ordained priest, 1942; curate St. Agnes' Ch., Miami, Fla., 1941-42; Vicar ch., Rutherfordton, N.C., 1942-44, Bklyn., 1945-47; priest-in-charge St. Stephen's Ch., Winston-Salem, N.C., 1944-45, St. Simon's Ch., Rochester, N.Y., 1947-61, St. Matthew's Ch., Wilmington, Del., 1963-66; rector ch., Wilmington, 1966-69, Detroit, 1969-71, St. Matthew's and St. Joseph's Ch., Detroit, 1971-72; suffragan bishop Diocese of Chgo., 1972-84. Chmn. Diocese of Chgo. Commn. on Met. Affairs; co-founder Union Black Episcopalian. Life trustee Rush-Presbyn.-St. Luke's Med. Center, Chgo.; Mem. Clergy Assn. of Diocese of Chgo. Home: 2140 Evans Rd Flossmoor IL 60422

PRINCE, BERNARD AMBROSE, priest, Roman Catholic Church, educator; b. Wilno, Ont., Can., Apr. 26, 1934; s. Ambrose V. and Mary C. (O'Malley) P.; S.T.L., U. Montreal, 1963; J.C.D., St. Thomas (Angelicum), Rome, 1966; M.A. in Slavic Studies, U. Ottawa, 1974; M.A. in History of Religion, U. Notre Dame. Ordained priest Roman Catholic Ch., 1963; vice chancellor Pembroke Diocese, 1966-67; English sec. Apostolic Delegation, Ottawa, Ont., 1967-69; asst. gen. sec. Canadian Cath. Conf., Ottawa, 1969-75; lectr. U. Notre Dame, South Bend, Ind., 1975-76, rector Morrissey Hall, 1975-76; faculty Nat. Def. Coll. of Can., Fort Frontenac, Kingston, Ont., 1976—; dir. Pax Vobis Found., Ottawa, 1976-80; lectr. canon law St. Paul U., Ottawa, 1980-82; asst. gen. sec. Can. Cath. Conf., Ottawa, 1981-84; chaplain Knight of Lazarus of Jerusalem. Mem. Canadian Assn. Ethnic Studies, Can. Canon Law Soc., Polish Pioneer Assn. K.C. (3D).

Contbr. articles to publs.; translator from French and Italian. Home: Wilno ON K0J ZN0 Canada

PRINCE, DEREK, minister, educator, Free Church; b. Bangalore, India, Aug. 14, 1915; came to U.S., 1963; s. Paul Ernest and Gwendolyn (Vaughan) P.; m. Lydia Christensen, Feb. 16, 1946 (dec. Oct. 1975); children: Tikva, Peninah, Magdal, Johanne, Ruth, Kirsten, Anna, Elisabeth, Jesika; m. Ruth Hemmingson Baker, Oct. 17, 1978; children: Pamela Baker, Paul Baker, Erika Baker. Grad. with distinction, Eton Coll., Eng., 1934; B.A. in Classics, Kings Coll., Cambridge U., Eng., 1938. M.A. in Classics, 1941. Ordained to ministry Free Ch., 1946. Prof. philosophy, 1940-49; head, Swedish Children's Home, Jerusalem, Israel. 1946-48; pastor Free Ch., London, 1948-56; prin. Nyan&g)oriTchr. Tng. Coll., Kisumu, Kenya, 1957-61; itinerant missionary Pentecostal Assemblies of Can., 1962; pastor, assoc. pastor, Mpls., Seattle, Chgo., 1963-67; tchr. Bible, author, founder Derek Prince Mininstries, Fort Lauderdale, Fla., 1968—; elder Good News Ch., Fort Lauderdale, 1975—; tchr. Bible Daily radio braodcast: Today with Derek Prince, 1978—. Chmn. bd. Fellowship Travel, Fort Lauderdale, 1978—; pres. Audio Duplicating Service, Fort Lauderdale, 1978—. Author: Self Study Bible Course, 1964; Eternal Judgment, 1964; Resurrection of the Dead, 1964; Laying on of Hands, 1964; Purposes of Pentecost, 1964; From Jordan to Pentecost, 1964; Repent and Believe, 1964; Foundation for Faith, 1964; The Baptism in the Holy Spirit, 1964; Three Messages for Israel, 1969; Praying for the Government, 1970; Restoration Through Fasting, 1970; How To Judge Prophecy, 1971; Shaping History Through Prayer and Fasting, 1973; Appointment in Jerusalem, 1975; (pamphlet) Our Debt to Israel, 1976; How to Fast Successfully, 1977; The Grace of Yielding, 1977; Faith to Live By, 1977; The Marriage Covenant, 1978; The Last Word on the Middle East, 1982; Chords From David's Harp, 1983; God is A Matchmaker, 1985 (all works transl. into numerous langs). Contbr. articles to profl. jours. Served with Brit. Army, 1941-46. Kings scholar, 1929-34, 34-38, Craven Research Student Kings Coll., 1939-40. Office: Derek Prince Ministeries PO Box 300 Fort Lauderdale FL 33302

PRINCE, JAMES HENDERSON, minister, So. Bapt. Conv.; b. Fort Worth, May 30, 1947; s. Wade Worth and Lucille (Harris) P.; Mus.B., U. Ariz., 1972, postgrad., 1975—; postgrad. Grand Canyon Coll. Sem., 1972—; m. Mary Christine Knost, June 1, 1969; 1 dau., Christine Michelle. Ordained to ministry, 19—; asso. pastor Pima St. Bapt. Ch., Tucson, 1975—. Youth dir. Cataline Bapt. Assn., 1973-75. Home: 6652 E Calle Dened Tucson AZ 85710 Office: 5056 E Pima St Tucson AZ 85712

PRINCE, JOHN FREDERICK LEWIS, priest, Anglican Ch. Can.; b. Truro, N.S., Can., June 5, 1937; s. Arthur Reginald and Honor Jessie (White) P.; B.A., Bishop's U., Lennoxville, Que., 1962, M.A., 1974; S.T.B., Trinity Coll., U. Toronto, 1965. Ordained to ministry Anglican Ch. Can., as deacon, 1965, priest, 1966, mem. Oblates of Mt. Calvary, Order Holy Cross, 1967—; pastor chs. in B.C., 1965-67; precentor Cathedral Ch. of Redeemer, Calgary, Alta., Can., 1967-68; incumbent mission to Blackfoot Res., Gleichen, Atla., 1968-70; rector Claresholm and Nanton (Alta.) Ch., 1971-76, Ch. of Holy Trinity, White Rock, B.C., 1976—. Chaplain, Claresholm chpt. Royal Canadian Legion, 1974-76; regional dean High River, Diocese of Calgary, 1974-76; pres. Claresholm Ministerial Assn., 1974-76. dir. Claresholm Housing Authority, 1974-76, chmn., 1976. Recipient Mission Study prize Trinity Coll., 1965; S.C. Kennedy Indian Mission scholar, 1970-71. Contbr. articles to profl. publs. Address: Holy Trinity Ch 1320 Foster St White Rock BC V4B 3X4 Canada

PRINSEN, MARTHA LOCKE, lay ch. worker, Unitarian Universalist Assn.; b. Lexington, Mass., May 9, 1922; d. Errol Hastings and Elinor (Whitney) Locke; student Colby Jr. Coll., 1940, Perry Kindergarten Normal, 1940-41; grad. Cushing Acad., 1940; m. Aug. 20, 1941; (now div.); children—Karl Errol, Edward Locke, Clayton George, Sheila K. (Mrs. Wayne Robert Cassidy). Tchr. Sunday sch. First Parish Ch., Lexington, Mass., 1938-39; trustee Unitarian Universalist Soc., Springfield, Vt., 1972—, pres. trustees, 1974-77; pres. N.H.-Vt. dist. Unitarian Universalist Assn., 1976—, mem. adult program com., 1972-76, v.p., 1976-77; editor news N.H.-Vt. dist. N.H.-Vt. dist. Unitarian Universalist Women's Fedn., 1972—; trustee Vt.-Que. Conv., 1973—. Chmn., Reading (Vt.) Charter BiCentennial Celebration, 1972, mem. Bicentennial Com., 1975—; sch. dir., 1974-77, chmn., 1975-77; mem. Vt. Ednl. Adv. Council, 1975—; active Boy Scouts Am., 1952-58, 4-H Clubs Am., 1957-64. Mem. Nat. (v.p. 1969-71, hon life mem. 1967), Vt. (pres. 1966-68, hon. life mem.) PTA's, Lexington Hist. Soc. (life mem. 1974), Vt. State Sch. Dirs. Assn. (2d v.p. 1976-77). Home: Star Route Reading VT 05062

PRINZ, JOACHIM, rabbi; b. Burkhardsdorf, Germany, May 10, 1902; s. Joseph and Nani (Berg) P.; grad. Jewish Theol. Sem., Breslau, Germany, 1925; postgrad. U. Berlin, 1922-23; Ph.D., U. Giessen, Germany, 1924; D.D. (hon.), Hebrew Union Coll., 1959; D.H.L., Hofstra U., 1975; m. Hilde Goldschmidt, May 24, 1932; children: Ludie P., Jo (Mrs. Harold Jaffe), Michael, Jonathan J., Deborah. Came to U.S., 1937; naturalized, 1943. Rabbi, 1925; pres. Am. Jewish Congress, N.Y.C., 1958-66; chmn. governing council World Jewish Congress, N.Y.C., 1968—, v.p., 1975—; chmn. Conf. Presidents Major Am. Jewish Orgns., 1965-67; chmn. World Conf. Jewish Orgns., 1975—. Author: Dilemma of the Modern Jew, 1962; Popes from the Ghetto, 1966; the Secret Jews, 1973. Office: 300 E Northfield Rd Livingston NJ 07039

PRIVETT, GERALD HERMAN, minister, Independent Baptists; b. Muncie, Ind., Aug. 16, 1943; s. Louis Homer and Helen Rosemary (Rogers) P.; m. Phyllis Ann Upchurch, Mar. 13, 1964; children: Ruth Ellen, Rebecca Eileen, Richard Earon. Grad. of theology Bapt. Bible Coll., Springfield, Mo., 1971; B. Ministry, Gt. Plains Bapt. Coll., Sioux Falls, S.D., 1981, D.D. (hon.), 1981, M. Ministry, 1985. Ordained to ministry Baptist Ch., 1971. Asst. pastor Temple Bapt. Ch., Muncie, Ind., 1971-72; pastor First Guyandotte Bapt. Ch., Huntington, W.Va., 1972; founder, pastor Bible Bapt. Ch., Rapid City, S.C., 1973-74; pastor Lickspring Bapt. Ch., Trafalgar, Ind., 1975-81, Broadway Bapt. Ch., Indpls., 1981—; pres. Broadway Christian Sch., Indpls., 1981—; mem. bd. reference Gt. Plains Bapt. Coll., Sioux Falls, 1982—. Republican. Avocations: computer programming; canoeing. Home: 8037 Murphy Ct Indianapolis IN 46256 Office: Broadway Bapt Ch 7676 E 38th St Indianapolis IN 46226

PRO, JOHN PAUL, minister, pastoral psychotherapist, American Baptist Churches in the U.S.A.; b. Pitts., Apr. 7, 1925; s. John Baptista and Mary (DiBartolo) P.; m. Katherine Mary Vazzano, June 2, 1945; children: Patricia, Paul, Carol Ann, Anita, Robert. B.Edn., Duquesne U., 1949; M.Div., Pitts.-Xenia Sem., 1957; Th.M., Pitts. Sem., 1969; D.Min., Luther Rice Sem., 1977; D.D. (hon.), Alderson-Broaddus Coll., 1976. Ordained to ministry Am. Bapt. Chs. in U.S.A., 1954; diplomate Am. Assn. Pastoral Counselors. Pastor Knoxville Bapt. Ch., Pitts., 1953-57; sr. pastor First Bapt. Ch., Jeannette, Pa., 1957—; sr. pastoral counselor Pitts. Pastoral Inst., 1970—; bd. dirs. Am. Bapt. Chs. of Pa., Valley Forge, 1976—, Am. Bapt. Chs., Valley Forge, 1980—. Author: From Parochial Schools to the Protestant Pulpit, 1957; Evangelism in Pastoral Counseling, 1980. Bd. dirs. United Fund, Jeannette, 1970-75. Served to petty officer 1st class U.S. Navy, 1943-45, 50-52, PTO, Korea. Mem. Am. Assn. Marriage and Family Therapists (clin.), Alpha Phi Delta. Republican. Home: 436 Sloan Ave Jeannette PA 15644 Office: First Bapt Ch 131 N 2d St Jeannette PA 15644

PROBASCO, CALVIN HENRY CHARLES, minister, college president, Independent Fundamental Churches of America; b. Petaluma, Calif., Apr. 5, 1926; s. Calvin Warren and Ruth Charlene (Winans) P.; m. Nixie June Farnsworth, Feb. 14, 1947; children: Calvin, Carol, David, Ruth. B.A. cum laude, Biola Bible Coll., 1953; D.D. (hon.), Talbot Theol. Sem., 1983. Ordained to ministry Independent Fundamental Chs. of America, 1950. Pastor, Sharon Baptist Ch., El Monte, Calif., 1951-58, Carmichael Bible Ch., Calif., 1958—; pres. Sacramento Bible Inst., Carmichael, 1968—; bd. dirs. United Missionary Fellowship, Sacramento, Calif., 1958—; rec. sec. Ind. Fundamental Chs. of Am., 1978-81, pres., 1981-84. Mem. Delta Epsilon Chi.

PROBST, WALTER CARL, JR., minister, American Lutheran Church; b. Kerrville, Tex., Apr. 4, 1937; s. Walter Carl Sr. and Selma Adela (Pfluger) P.; m. Marilyn Faye Jorgensen, Dec. 7, 1963; children: Christie Ann, Michelle Renee. B.S., Tex. Luth. Coll., 1960; B.D., Wartburg Theol. Sem., 1963. Ordained to ministry Am. Luth. Ch., 1963. Pastor, Salem Luth. Ch., Roscoe, Tex., 1964-67, St. John Luth. Ch., Rutersville, Tex., 1967-75, St. John Luth. Ch., Cat Spring, Tex., 1975—; bd. dirs. Luther League, Brenham Conf., 1972-75; dean Cat Spring Deanery, 1983—; chaplain Cat Spring Vol. Fire Dept., 1976—. Mem. Brenham Conf. Mission Soc. (sec. 1981—). Home and Office: St John Luth Ch Route 1 Box 57-A Cat Spring TX 79933

PROSSER, PETER EDWARD, priest, educator, Anglican Church of Canada; b. Birmingham, Eng., Dec. 16, 1946; s. Norman Albert and Lily May (Taylor) P.; m. Elfriede Biermayer, May 2, 1970; children: Nathalie Lorraine, Andrea Gwynneth. Diploma in Theology, Eastern Coll., 1970; B.A., Bethel Coll.; M.Div., U. Montreal, Que., Can., 1975, M.A., 1978, Ph.D., 1985. Ordained to ministry Assemblies of God, 1973; ordained priest Anglican Ch., 1975. Pastor Assemblies of God, Montreal, 1970-75; asst. parish priest Anglican Ch., Montreal, 1975-77; parish priest Episcopal Ch., Springfield, Mo., 1977-78, Anglican Ch., Montreal, 1978-83; prof. CBN U. Grad. Sch., Virginia Beach, Va., 1983—, extended univ. coordinator, 1983—; interim rector Episcopal Ch., Chesapeake, 1984; asst. rector Galilee Ch., Virginia Beach, 1984—; organizing mem. Ministry to Prisons, Montreal, 1972. Co-author: Death and Dying, 1981. Contbr. articles to profl. jours. Served with cadets RAF, 1962-67. U. Montreal fellow, 1980, 81. Mem. Soc. Pentecostal Studies, Am. Acad. Religion, Soc. Bibl. Lit., Ch. History Soc., Scandinavian Christian U. Club: Rotary. Home: 3341 King Richard Ct Virginia Beach VA 23452 Office: CBN U CBN Ctr Virginia Beach VA 23452

PROUDFOOT, WAYNE LEE, educator; b. Peterborough, N.H., Nov. 17, 1939; s. Raymond Stanley and Sarah Alice (King) P.; B.S., Yale U., 1961; B.D., Harvard U., 1964, Th.M., 1966, Ph.D., 1972. Asst. prof. philosophy of religion Andover-Newton Theol. Sch., 1969-70; asst. prof. religion Fordham U., N.Y.C., 1970-72; prof. religion Columbia, N.Y.C., 1972—. Bd. dirs. Fund for Theol. Edn. Kent fellow, 1965-68. Mem. Am. Acad. Religion, Soc. Values in Higher Edn. Home: 315 W 106th St New York NY 10025

PROULX, ADOLPHE, clergyman, Roman Catholic Ch.; b. Hanmer, Ont., Can., Dec. 12, 1927; s. Augustin and Marie-Louise (Tremblay) P.; B.A., St. Augustine's Sem., Toronto, Ont.; postgrad. in canon law, Rome, Italy, 1958-60. Ordained priest Roman Catholic Ch., 1954; parish priest, North Bay and Sudbury, Ont., Can., 1954-57; chancellor Sault Ste. Marie (Ont.) Diocese, 1960-64, aux. bishop, 1965-67; bishop Alexandria (Ont.) Diocese, 1967-74; bishop Hull, Que., Canada, 1974—. Address: 119 Rue Carillon Hull PQ J8X 2P8 Canada

PROULX, AMEDEE WILFRID, auxiliary bishop, Roman Catholic Church; b. Sanford, Maine, Aug. 31, 1932; s. Francis A. and Rose Anna (Seviegny) P. B.A., St. Hyacinth Coll., 1954; S.T.L., St. Pauls U. Sem., 1958; J.C.L., Cath. U. Am., 1968; D.H.L., St. Joseph's Coll., 1977, Assumption Coll., 1978. Ordained priest Roman Catholic Ch., 1958. Assoc. pastor various parishes, Portland, Maine, 1958-66; vice officialis Portland Tribunal, 1968—; vicar for religious Diocese of Portland, 1970-76, aux. bishop, 1975—; mem. women's com. Nat. Conf. Cath. Bishops, Washington, 1976—, chmn. liaison com. Leadership Conf. Women Religious, 1982—. Trustee Nat. Council on Alcoholism/Maine, Augusta, 1979—. Mem. Canon Law Soc. Am.

PROVOST, JAMES HARRISON, priest, Roman Catholic Church. b. Washington, Oct. 15, 1939; s. Oscar A. and Mary (Howe) Ryan P. B.A., Carroll Coll., 1959; S.T.B., U. Louvain, Belgium, 1963, M.A., 1963; J.C.D., Lateran U., Rome, 1967. Ordained priest Roman Catholic Ch., 1963. Asst. pastor St. John the Evangelist, Butte, Mont., 1963-64; chancellor Diocese of Helena, Mont., 1967-79, officialis, 1967-79; assoc. prof. dept. canon law Cath. U., Washington, 1979—. Editor: Code, Community, Ministry, 1983; Ministry in a New Age, 1983; mng. editor The Jurist, 1979—. Mem. Canon Law Soc. Am. (pres. 1977-78), Cath. Theol. Soc. Am., Can. Canon Law Soc., Canon Law Soc. Gt. Britain and Ireland, Consociatio Internationalis Studio Iuris Canonici Promovendo. Office: Dept Canon Law Cath U Washington DC 20064

PRUETT, WALTER BURWELL, retired minister, United Methodist Church; b. Kinmundy, Ill., Oct. 5, 1917; s. Walter Simpson and Bertha Wilhelmina (Steuber) P.; A.B., McKendree Coll., 1938; M.Div., Drew U., 1941; postgrad Garrett Theol. Sem., 1949, 50, Western Ill. U., 1948; m. Beulah Mae Jones, Jan. 22, 1938; children: Patricia Louise, Peggy Lou. Ordained to ministry, 1941; pastor chs., Ill., 1936-38, N.J., 1939-40, W.Va., 1941-42, Armstrong, Ill., 1943-44; chaplain U.S. Army, 1944-47; pastor Golden Ill., 1947-49, Carrollton, Ill., 1950-54, Auburn, Ill., 1955-59, Centenary Ch., Jacksonville, Ill., 1960-62, Pana, Ill., 1963-68, Monticello, Ill., 1969-73, Aledo, Ill., 1974-79, Lewistown, Ill., 1980-82. Trustee, Baby Fold, Normal, Ill., 1966-76; mem. Dist. Com. on Ministry, 1967-80; v.p. Aledo Minsterial Assn., 1976; treas. Mercer County Hosp. Chaplaincy Service, 1976. Trustee, Pana Community Hosp., 1967-69. Home: 633 N Riverview Dr Vandalia IL 62471

PRUITT, TIMOTHY CAROL, minister, United Pentecostal Church International; engineer; b. Beech Grove, Ind., June 12, 1956; s. Carol Merrill Roger and Martha Jean (French) P.; m. Rita Jo Helms, June 14, 1980. B.S. in Physics, Rose-Hulman Inst. Tech., 1978; Degree in Missions, Jackson Coll. Ministries, 1981. Lic. to ministry United Pentecostal Ch., 1983. Assoc. missionary United Pentecostal Ch. Internat., Leeward Islands, 1982-83; tchr. coll., career Calvary Tabernacle, Indpls., 1983—, mem. youth com., 1983-84, team minister, 1984—, chmn. home Bible study advertising, 1984—. Electronics engr. Naval Avionics Ctr., Indpls., 1983—. Mem. Pi Mu Epsilon. Republican. Home: 3354 Sherburne Circle Apt A Indianapolis IN 46222 Office: Naval Avionics Ctr B 432 6000 E 21st St Indianapolis IN 46218

PRUITT, WILLIAM CHARLES, JR., pastor, educator, Baptist Missionary Assn. Am.; b. Reed, Okla., May 31, 1926; s. William Charles and Helen Irene (Sanders) P.; B.S., Stephen F. Austin State U., 1956, M.Ed., 1958; B.D., M.R.E., Bapt. Missionary Assn. Theol. Sem., 1959, D.R.E., 1963; M.S. in L.S., East Tex. State U., 1963; m. Ellen Ruth Palmer, Aug. 25, 1953; children-Philip, Suzanne, John. Ordained to ministry Bapt. Missionary Assn. Am., 1955; pastor Mt. Pleasant Bapt. Ch., Bedias, Tex., 1955-60, Calvary Bapt. Ch., Commerce, Tex., 1960-63, Glenfawn Bapt. Ch.,

Laneville, Tex., 1963-66, New Hope Bapt. Ch., Winkler, Tex., 1966-70, Pleasant Ridge Bapt. Chs., Centerville, Tex., 1970-74, and Redland Bapt. Ch., Centerville, 1970-79, Concord Bapt. Ch., Concord Tex., 1983—. Tex. wing chaplain Civil Air Patrol, 1971-77; exec. dir. Armed Forces Chaplaincy Com., Bapt. Missionary Assn. Am., Jacksonville, Tex., 1965—; dir. library service, instr. Bapt. Missionary Assn. Theol. Sem., 1958-67, prof. missions and religious edn. 1967-72; instr. psychology Jacksonville Coll., 1971-76. Asst. dir. East Tex. Adult Edn. Coop., 1973—. Mem. Mil. Chaplains Assn. U.S., Tex. Assn. for Continuing Adult Edn. Lion. Home: Route 8 Box 327 Jacksonville TX 75766 Office: PO Box 912 Jacksonville TX 75766

PRUTER, KARL, bishop, Christ Catholic Church (Diocese of Boston); b. Poughkeepsie, N.Y., July 3, 1920; s. William Karl and Katherine (Rehling) P.; A.B., Northeastern U., 1943; M.Div., Lutheran Theol. Sem., Phila., 1954; M.A., Roosevelt U., 1963; M.A., Boston U., 1968. Ordained to ministry Congl. Ch., 1946, priest Christ Catholic Ch., 1965; consecrated bishop, 1967; leader Free Cath. Movement, 1946-64; pastor Ch. of the Transfiguration, Boston, 1965-70; presiding bishop Christ Cath. Ch. (Diocese of Boston), 1967—. Author: The Teachings of the Great Mystics, 1969; A History of the Old Catholic Church, 1973. Address: PO Box 98 Highlandville MO 65669*

PRZYGODA, JACEK STANISLAW, priest, Roman Cath. Ch.; b. Brzescie, Poland, Oct. 31, 1910; s. Jan and Zofia (Sobocha) P.; M.A., Cath. U. (Belgium), 1947; Ph.D., U. Ottawa (Can.), 1952. Ordained priest, 1933; tchr. religion Jedlinsk Sch., Ilza, Poland, 1933-36; editor Diocesan Weekly, Sandomierz, Poland, 1937-38; chaplain Polish Cath. Mission, Charleroi, Belgium. 1938-41, rector, 1941-48; instr. religion St. Mary's Coll. Prep. Sch., Orchard Lake, Mich., 1954-55; instr. econs. St. Mary's Coll., Orchard Lake, 1949-50; instr. Loyola U. of Los Angeles, 1955-56, asst. prof., 1956-58, asso. prof., 1958-60. prof., chmn. dept. econs., 1960-76; faculty social scis. Queen of Angels Sem., San Fernando, Calif., 1976—. Recipient Gold Apple, Tchr. Remembrance Day Found., Los Angeles, 1976; Tchr. Remembrance Scroll, City of Los Angeles, 1976. Mem. Am. Cath. Hist. Assn., Polish Am. Hist. Assn. (pres. 1972), Assn. for Social Economy. Author: Dla Ciebie Dziecko, cathechism in Polish, 1941; Life with Poles in Belgium, 1942; Jezu, Ufam Tobie, Prayer book, 1945; Texas Pioneers from Poland, 1971; Polish Catholic Homiletic Literature in U.S., 1955. Address: 15101 San Fernando Mission Blvd San Fernando CA 91341

PSALMONDS, (WALTER) GORDON, minister, Southern Baptist Convention; b. Cotton Plant, Ark., Sept. 24, 1916; s. Walter Lowrie and Ionia (Anderson) P.; A.A., S.W. Bapt. Coll., 1941; B.A., William Jewell Coll., 1943; M.R.E., Southwestern Bapt. Sem., 1947, D.R.E., 1958; m. Marjorie Varner, Mar. 23, 1940; 1 son, Jonathan Lowrie, Ordained to ministry, 1940; minister edn. 1st Bapt. Ch., Bartlesville, Okla., 1947-49, Park Cities Bapt. Ch., Dallas, 1950, 1st Bapt. Ch., McAlester, Okla., 1951, Duncan, Okla., 1952-54; prof. religion Grand Canyon Coll., 1954-71, editor coll. catalog, 1965-71; prof. religion Mo. Bapt. Coll., 1971-83, prof. emeritus, 1983—, also chmn. div. humanities and acad. com. Trustee Southeastern Bapt. Sem., Wake Forest, N.C., 1961-71. Mem. Mayor's Planning Com., Bartlesville, 1948; mem. exec. com. PTA, Phoenix, 1966-68. Mem. Am. Acad. Religion, Ariz. Coll. Assn. (pres. 1971), Ariz. Higher Edn. Coordination Council, So., Southwestern Bapt. religious edn. assns., So. Bapt. Hist. Soc. Contbr. to ch. periodicals and study materials. Home: 12340 Oak Hollow Dr Saint Louis MO 63141

PUCKETT, JOSEPH DONALD, minister, American Baptist Churches in the U.S.A.; realtor associate; b. McKeesport, Pa., Jan. 1, 1957; s. Joseph Earl and Lorine Glenna (Pryor) P.; m. Joanne Elizabeth Dempsey, Dec. 17, 1977; 1 child, Jennifer Danielle. B.A., Eastern Coll., 1978; M.Div., Eastern Bapt. Theol. Sem., 1981. Ordained to ministry Am. Bapt. Chs. in U.S.A., 1981. Pastoral intern First Bapt. Ch., Dover, Del., 1979-81; pastor First Bapt. Ch., Greenville, Mich., 1981—; realtor assoc. Brandywine Realty, Greenville, Mich., 1983-85; cluster chmn. Am. Bapt. Chs. in the U.S.A. of Mich., 1981—; treas. Greenville Ministerial Fellowship, 1981-82. Republican. Club: Flat River Players (Greenville). Home: 407 S Franklin St Greenville MI 48838 Office: First Bapt Ch 401 S Franklin St Greenville MI 48838

PUCKETT, OLAF MARVIS, minister, Southern Baptist Convention; b. Cave City, Ark., May 9, 1920; s. Earl Ditzler and Dora Minnie (Voyles) P.; student Sem. Extension dept., Nashville, 1956-60, also Moody Bible Inst.; m. Dorothy Louise Strickland, Oct. 1, 1949; children—Donna Sue, Victoria Lynn. Ordained to ministry, 1963; pastor chs., Okla., 1958—; pastor Crescent Valley Bapt. Ch., Tahlequah, Okla., 1965-72, Boudinot Bapt. Ch., Tahlequah, 1972—. Vice moderator local assn. Bd. dirs. B.S.U. Northeastern Okla. State U., Tahlequah, 1971-77. Contbr. sermons to denoml. jours. Home and Office: Rt 2 Box 171 Tahlequah OK 74464

PUDAITE, ROCHUNGA, church official, minister, Evangelical Free Church; b. Senvon, Manipur, India, Dec. 4, 1927; s. Chawnga and Daii (Zote) P.; student St. Paul's Coll., Calcutta U., 1949-52; B.A., Allahabad U., India, 1954; postgrad. Wheaton Coll., 1955-58; M.A., No. Ill. U., 1961; LL.D., Malone Coll., Canton, Ohio, 1977; m. Lalrimawi Pakhuongte, Jan. 1, 1959; children—Paul Rozarlien, John Lalnunsang, Mary Lalsangpui. Ordained to ministry Evang. Free Ch., 1959; exec. dir. Indo-Burma Pioneer Mission, 1958-67; pres. Partnership Mission, Inc., Wheaton, Ill., 1968-72; founder, pres. Bibles for the World, Inc., Wheaton, 1973—. Pres., Evang. Free Ch. of India, 1963-73; translator Bible into Hmar tribal lang. of India; moderator Evang. Free Ch. of India, 1972—. Mem. Evang. Press Assn., Internat. Platform Assn. Club: Rotary (Wheaton). Author: Hmar-English Grammar, 1958; The Education of the Hmar People, 1961; My Billion Bible Dream, 1983; The Dime Lasted Forever, 1985. Editor Kristien, 1957-63, Khawnvar, 1970-72, Bibles for the World News, 1973. Home: 1555 E Forest Ave Wheaton IL 60187 Office: POB 805 Wheaton IL 60187

PUGH, JESSIE TRUMAN, minister, United Pentecostal Church, International; b. Noble, La., Oct. 28, 1923; s. Jessie Trulonzer and Lucy (Sanderson) P.; B.Th., Tex. Bible Coll., 1971; D.D., Berean Christian Coll., 1973; m. Bessie Byrl Halbrooks, Aug. 20, 1944; children: James Terry, Datha Jo, Nathanael Brent. Ordained to ministry; youth sec. Tex. Dist., 1940, pres. youth camps, 1954; instr. Tex. Bible Coll., Houston, 1962-67; pastor chs., 1944-67; gen. dir. home missions, U.S. and Can., 1967-74; pastor 1st Pentecostal Ch., Odessa, Tex., 1974—; dist. supt. Texico Dist. United Pentecostal Ch., 1983—. Speaker camp meetings and convs.; overseas lectr. Contbr. articles to religious jours. Home: 1500 Tangelwood St Odessa TX 79760

PULIDO, RODOLFO ANTONIO, minister, So. Baptist Conv.; b. Laredo, Tex., Sept. 22, 1945; s. Peter and Jessie (Mata) P.; B.A., Miss. Coll., Clinton, 1968; M.Div., Southwestern Bapt. Theol. Sem., Ft. Worth, 1973; m. Doris Jean Ewens, Sept. 3, 1966; children—Preston Scott, Jennifer Lynn. Ordained to ministry, 1967; pastor Anding (Miss.) Bapt. Ch., 1967-69; minister youth and recreation Lake Highlands Bapt. Ch., Dallas, 1971-73; pastor Calvary Bapt. Ch., Jefferson City, Mo., 1974—; instr. ch. history and O.T., Lincoln U., Jefferson City, Mo., 1975—. Curator, Redford, Sch. Theology, SW Bapt. Coll., Bolivar, Mo.; cons. youth edn. Mo. Bapt. Conv., also mem. exec. bd. Home: 207 Johnson St Jefferson City MO 65101 Office: 1436 Hough St Jefferson City MO 65101

PULLEN, LOWELL LARRY, religious organization executive, American Baptist Churches in the U.S.A. b. Charleston, W.Va., Mar. 12, 1947; s. Lowell Leon and Nora Mabel (McCue) P.; m. Terry Ellen Sparkers, May 4, 1980 (div. 19—). Student, Marshall U., 1965-67; B.A., W.Va. U., 1969; M. in Internat. Service, Am. U., 1972; M.Div., Colgate Rochester-Bexley Hall-Crozer Theol. Sem., 1980. Ordained to ministry Baptist Church, 1980. Dir. peace concern program Nat. Ministries Am. Bapt. Ch. of the U.S.A., Valley Forge, Pa., 1980—; rep. to world council of chs. Disarmament Conf., Amsterdam, 1981; rep. interunit com. on internat. concerns Nat. Council of Chs. of Christ, N.Y., 1981—. Author: Swords into Plowshares, 1984. Recipient Outstanding Young Man of Year award 1981, 82. Mem. Am. Soc. of Internat. Law, Bapt. Peace Fellowship N. Am. (mem. exec. com.). Democrat. Club: World Affairs Council (Phila.). Home: 1170 Kingsway Rd Apt 6 West Chester PA 19380 Office: Nat Ministries Am Bapt Chs Box 851 Valley Forge PA 19482-0851

PULLIAM, RUSSELL B., deacon, Reformed Presbyterian Church of N.A.; editorial writer, columnist; b. Indpls., Sept. 20, 1949; s. Eugene S. and Jane B. Pulliam; m. Ruth Eichling, Nov. 26, 1977; children: Christine, Daniel, John. B.A. cum laude, Williams Coll., 1971. Deacon Second Reformed Presbyn. Ch., Indpls., 1983—. Editorial writer, columnist AP Indpls. News, 1978—. Contbr. articles to religious jours. Bd. dirs. Community Outreach Ctr., Noble Ctrs. Marion County Assn. for the Mentally Retarded, Indpls., 1984—; commentator Sta. WIAN-FM All Things Considered. Recipient Casper award Community Service Council, 1980, 81, Hoosier State Press Assn. award, 1979, 80, UPI Editorial Writing award, 1984. Mem. Bread for the World, NAACP, Prison Fellowship, Ind. Assn. for Home Educators, Indpls. C. of C., Sigma Delta Chi (treas. Ind. chpt. 1982-85). Home: 1241 N New Jersey Indianapolis IN 46202 Office: The Indianapolis News 307 N Penn Indianapolis IN 46204

PUMPHREY, CHARLES MICHAEL, priest, Episcopal Church; b. Balt., July 22, 1956; s. Charles Merritt and Dorothy May (Iglehart) P.; m. Donna Jean Gambill, Aug. 12, 1978; children: Abigail Jean, Gregory Michael, James Norman. B.A. in Religious Studies, Randolph-Macon Coll., 1978; M.Div., Episcopal Theol. Sem. Va., 1981. Ordained priest Episcopal Ch., 1982. Curate, St. Peter's Ch., Salisbury, Md., 1981—; priest-in-charge St. Mary's Ch., Tyaskin, Md., 1982—; mem. Commn. on Ministry, Diocese of Easton, Md., 1983—, hunger coordinator dept. Christian social relations, 1982—, pres. Clericus, 1984—. Democrat. Home: 316 Cedar Dr Salisbury MD 21801 Office: St Peters Ch Church and St Peters Sts Salisbury MD 21801

PURCELL, GEORGE RICHARD, lay church worker, Roman Catholic Church; b. Clayton, N.Y., May 4, 1921; s. George Thomas and Katherine Eileen (Eagan) P.; B.S., Niagara U., 1947; m. Mary Sutter, Apr. 3, 1961. Founder, Syracuse (N.Y.) chpt. Catholic Med. Mission Bd., Roman Cath. Ch., 1973, pres., 1973-76; rep., 1976—. Fed. employee, Syracuse, 1957—. N.Y. State War Service scholar, 1955. Fellow Internat. Biog. Assn.; mem. Am. Cath. Philos. Assn., Internat. Soc. Neoplatonic Studies, Soc. Christian Philosophers, Am. Biog. Inst. (research bd. advisors nat. div.). Address: 1 Gregory Pkwy Syracuse NY 13214

PURSELL, CLEO WILBURN, church official, National Association Free Will Baptists; b. Ft. Worth, Feb. 16, 1918; d. Charles P. and Eltrie Lee (Tice) Dalton; grad. high sch.; m. Paul Edgar Pursell, Feb. 16, 1939 (dec. 1973). Ordained to ministry Nat. Assn. Free Will Baptists, 1939; asst. pastor various chs. in Okla., 1939-57; pres. Okla. State Aux.; pres. First Okla. and First Mission Dists.; West Coast officer Cal. Dist., 1958-63; officer Cal. State Aux., 1960; 2d v.p., youth chmn. Woman's Nat. Aux. Conv., 1946-48, 52-55, nat. study chmn., 1955-57, exec. sec.-tres., Nashville, 1963-85. Prominent in youth work Okla., 1939-57; tchr. dist., state Sunday Sch. Workshops. Mem. Women's Fellowship, Federated Womens Missionary Socs. (treas. Bristow, Okla. 1955). Author: Missionary Education of Our Youth, 1955; Woman's Auxiliary Manual, 1965; Triumph Over Suffering, 1982; Death and Dying, 1982; column Words for Women, Contact mag., 1966-70. Editor: Co-Laborer, 1963-85. Contbr. articles to profl. jours. Home: 1148 Vultee Blvd Apt 12 Nashville TN 37217 Office: POB 1088 Nashville TN 37202

PURSLEY, GEORGE WILLIAM, religion educator, Churches of Christ in Christian Union; b. Parker City, Ind., Jan. 9, 1954; s. George Oscar and Billie Faye (Baker) P.; m. Rebecca Lynn Mathias, June 10, 1978; 1 child, Ashley Danielle. Student U.S. Mil Acad., 1972-73; A.B., Asbury Coll., 1976; M.Div., Asbury Theol. Sch., 1979; postgrad. Ohio State U., 1982—. Ordained to ministry Chs. of Christ in Christian Union, 1983. Intern, The Christ Hosp., Con., 1977, United Meth. Chs., Monticello, Ind., Terre Haute, Ohio and Lexington, Ky., 1974-78; pastor Ch. of Christ in Christian Union, Richland Center, Wis., 1979-80; asst. prof. history Circleville Bible Coll. (Ohio), 1981—, dir. fin. aid, 1980—; tchr. Faith Meml. Ch., Lancaster, Ohio, 1982—; chaplain Ohio Nat. Guard 383d Med. Oo., Cin., 1984—; speaker Hitler-Ludwig Cemetery Assn., Circleville, 1982—, Circleville Monument Assn., 1982—, Vietnam Vets Am., Circleville, 1983—, VFW, Williamsport, Ohio, 1984. Contbr. articles to profl. publs. Mem. Fairfield County Republican Central Com., 1984—. Mem. Ohio Assn. Student Fin. Aid Adminstrs. (cert. appreciation 1984), Nat. Assn. Student Fin. Aid Adminstrs. Home: 538 Westview Dr Lancaster OH 43130 Office: Circleville Bible Coll 1476 Lancaster Pike Circleville OH 43113

PUSCAS, LOUIS, clergyman. Apostolic exarch for the Romanian Byzantine Faithful of the U.S., 1983—. Office: 1121 44th St NE Canton OH 44714*

PUTNAM, ROBERT GENE, minister, Assemblies of God; b. Alton, Mo., Sept. 8, 1927; s. Stacy Robert and Mary Pearl P.; A.A., Mineral Area Jr. Coll., 1947; B.D., Central Bible Coll., 1951; postgrad. Southwestern Mo. State U., 1951; m. Mary Catherine Hodge, Sept. 1, 1951; 1 son, Robert David. Ordained to ministry, 1952; pastor chs., St. Louis, 1951-52, El Paso, Tex., 1952-53, Rolla, Mo., 1953-54; founder, pastor Lindbergh Assembly of God, St. Louis, 1962; now sr. pastor South County Christian Fellowship. Past mem. Nat. Christ Ambassador Com., Nat. Sunday Sch. Com.; past coordinator Regional Sunday Sch. Conv., Nat. Council Evangelism; tchr. Advanced Christian Tng. Sch.; pres. So. Mo. dist. Christ Ambassador; dir. So. Mo. dist. Sunday sch.; producer, speaker Words of Spirit and Life radio series; bd. dirs., exec. prebyter So. Mo. Dist., Assemblies of God; regional bd. dirs. Women's Aglow; mem. Highlands Child Placement Service, Assemblies of God; speaker youth camps; counselor to ministers; bd. dirs. Christian Civic Found.; founder, dir. Christian Cadets. Mem. Nat. Assn. Religious Broadcasters. Author Christian Cadet publs.; contbr. articles to Pentecostal Evangel, Internat. Correspondence Inst. Home and Office: 4646 S Lindberg Blvd Saint Louis MO 63127

PYNE, DONALD EUGENE, priest, Roman Catholic Church; b. San Francisco, Dec. 24, 1929; s. Thomas Francis and Marcia Aileen (Worth) P. B.A., St. Patrick's Coll., 1952, M.Div., 1977; D. Min. candidate San Francisco Theol. Sem., 1979; M.A. candidate Calif. State U.-Dominquez Hills, 1980. Ordained priest Roman Cath. Ch., 1956. Tchr. Marin Cath. High Sch., Kentfield, Calif., 1957-66; faculty Coll. of Notre Dame, Belmont, Calif., 1981-83; parish priest Archdiocese of San Francisco Bay Area, 1966—; pastor St. Charles Ch.,

San Carlos, Calif., 1982—; dean Deanery G, So. San Mateo County, 1983—; cons. Archdiocese San Francisco, 1983--; vice chmn. San Francisco Council Priests, 1984-85; mem. Com. On-Going Edn. of Priests. Address: 880 Tamarack Ave San Carlos CA 94070

QUAM, JOHN ELLIOTT, minister, American Lutheran Church; b. Randall, Iowa, Jan. 31, 1931; S. Nels Eliassen and Thora Elizabeth (Larsen) Q.; m. Louise Estelle Hammer, June 16, 1956; children: Joel Eric, Lois Elaine, Mary Elizabeth, David Eugene. Student Oslo U., Norway, summer 1951; B.A., St. Olaf Coll., 1953; B.Th., Luth. Theol. Sem., St. Paul, 1957; M.A., Yale U., 1963, Ph.D., 1968. Ordained to ministry Am. Luth. Ch., 1957. Pastor United Luth. Ch., Henning, Minn., 1957-60, various locations in Conn., 1960-63, St. Stephen Luth. Ch., Marshall, Minn., 1963—; bd. dirs. Luth. Student Found. Minn., 1968-74; mem. Bd. Parish Edn., Am. Luth. Ch., 1970-74, Bd. Life and Mission, 1973-78, mem. Ch. Council, 1982—. Mem. Phi Beta Kappa. Democrat. Home: 306 N Whitney St Marshall MN 56258 Office: St Stephen Luth Ch Box 198 Marshall MN 56258

QUASTEN, JOHANNES, priest, Roman Catholic Ch.; b. Homberg, Germany, May 3, 1900; s. Wilhelm and Sibilla (Schmitz) Q.; D.Theology, U. Muenster (Germany), 1927; postgrad. Pontifical Inst. Archeology, Rome, Italy, 1926-29; L.H.D., Cath. U. Am., 1976. Ordained priest Roman Cath. Ch., 1926, named monsignor, 1976; pvt. docent ancient ch. history and Christian liturgy U. Muenster, 1931-37; prof. patristic theology and Christian archeology Cath. U. Am., Washington, 1938—. Hon. prof. U. Freiburg (Germany), 1970—; named Papal Prelate of Honor, 1976. Mem. Henry Bradshaw Soc. London (v.p. 1951—) , Oxford Hist. Soc., Cath. Com. for Cultural Affairs, Am. Cath. Theol. Assn., Patristic Soc. N.Am. (hon.). Author: Monumenta Eucharistica et Liturgica Vetustissima, 7 vols., 1935-37; Patrology, 3 vols., 1950-60; Music und Gesang in den Kulten der heidnischen Antike und christlichen Fruehzeit, 1974. Subject of Kyriakon, Festschrift J. Quasten. (P. Granfield, J.A. Jungmann), 2 vols., 1970. Home and office: Catholic U America Washington DC 20064

QUIGLEY, MARTIN SCHOFIELD, lay church worker, Roman Catholic Church; b. Chgo., Nov. 24, 1917; s. Martin Joseph and Gertrude (Schofield) Q.; A.B. magna cum laude, Georgetown U., 1939; M.A., Columbia, 1973, Ed.D., 1975; m. Katherine J. Dunphy, July 2, 1946; children—Martin Mark, Elin, William, Kevin, Karen, Patricia, John, Mary Katherine, Peter. Pres. N.Y. Christian Family Movement, Roman Catholic Ch., 1960-62, mem. nat. exec. com., 1960-65; pres. Found. Internat. Coop., 1960-65, bd. dirs., 1965—; adv. bd. Religious Heritage Am., 1972. Pres. Quigley Pub. Co. Inc., N.Y.C., 1964—, QWS, Inc., N.Y.C., 1975—; adj. prof. dept. edn. Baruch Coll., CUNY, 1977—. Bd. dirs. Found. Motion Picture Pioneers. Mem. Religious Edn. Assn. (dir. 1975—, treas. 1975-81, chmn. 1981-84), Am. Assn. Higher Edn., Adult Edn. Assn. Author: Great Gaels, 1944; Roman Notes, 1946; Magic Shadows-The Story of the Origin of Motion Pictures, 1948; co-author: Catholic Action in Practice, 1968; Films in America, 1970. Home: 1 Locust Av Larchmont NY 10538 Office: 159 W 53d St New York NY 10019

QUIGLEY, THOMAS HARRY, JR., minister, Christian Church (Disciples of Christ); b. Cin., Aug. 4, 1942; s. Thomas Harry and Ruth (Raleigh) Q.; m. Helen Jane Wertz, July 9, 1966; children: Christine Amy, Thomas Charles. B.A., Ohio State U., 1964; D.B., Div. Sch., U. Chgo., 1967. Ordained to ministry, 1967. Assoc. minister First Christian Ch., Louisville, 1967-72; exec. dir. Louisville Area Interch. Orgn., 1972-78; exec. dir. Ind. Interreligious Commn. on Human Equality, Indpls., 1978-80, Greater Mpls. Council of Chs., 1980—. Mem. Nat. Assn. Ecumenical Staff (v.p.), Beta Theta Pi. Democrat. Home: 5101 Valley View Rd Edina MN 55436 Office: Greater Mpls Council Chs 122 W Franklin Minneapolis MN 55404

QUILLEN, MARK LAVERN, educational administrator, Roman Catholic Church; b. Greeley, Colo., May 10, 1951; s. Perry L. and Shirley J. (Cummins) Q. A.A., Ulster County Community Coll., 1972; B.S. in Elem. Edn., SUNY-New Paltz, 1974; M.A. in Theology, St. Michael's Coll., 1983. Cert. tchr., Vt. Mem. High Sch. Retreat Team, Diocese of Davenport, Iowa, 1976-77, Confraternity of Christian Doctrine tchr., 1976-78; chmn. spiritual life com. Mater Christi Sch., Burlington, Vt., 1982—, dir. religious edn., 1983—, also drama dir., 1983—; lay minister of eucharist Cathedral of Immaculate Conception, Burlington, 1979—. Recreation coordinator migrant program Campus Learning Ctr., SUNY-New Paltz, 1973-74; treas. Green Mountain Skating Club, Burlington, 1981—. Mem. Nat. Cath. Edn. Assn. Avocations: competitive figure skating; reading; writing poetry. Home: 102 Mansfield Ave Burlington VT 05401 Office: Mater Christi Sch 50 Mansfield Ave Burlington VT 05401

QUINN, ALEXANDER JAMES, bishop, Roman Catholic Church. Titular bishop of Socia, aux. bishop, Cleve., 1983—. Office: 2500 Euclid Ave Lorain OH 44055*

QUINN, FRANCIS A. See *Who's Who in America*, 43rd edition.

QUINN, JEROME DONALD, educator, Roman Catholic Church; b. Litchfield, Minn., Feb. 24, 1927; s. Donald Louis and Irene Barbara (Lenz) Q.; B.A., St. Paul Sem., 1947, M.A., 1951; postgrad. U. Minn., 1947-61, U. Notre Dame, 1949, 55; S.T.L., Gregorian U. (Italy), 1959; Sacrae Scripturae Baccalaureatus, Pontifical Bibl. Inst., 1960, Sacrae Scripturae Licentiatus, 1961. Ordained priest Roman Catholic Ch., 1951; asst. pastor Ch. of Incarnation, Mpls., 1951-53; tchr. Nazareth Hall, St. Paul, 1953-58; prof. scripture and Hebrew St. Paul Sem., St. Paul, 1961—, dean grad. dept., 1967-72. Guest prof. Pontifical Bibl. Inst., Rome, Italy, 1971-72, 79-80; chmn. commn. for ecumenism Archdiocese of St. Paul, 1966-77; mem. Luth.-Cath. Dialog U.S. Bishops Com. for Ecumenical Affairs, 1966-84; mem. Pontifical Bibl. Commn., Rome, 1978-84. Fulbright scholar Am. Acad., Rome, 1957; named monsignor, 1973. Mem. Cath. Bibl. Assn. (pres. 1970-71, exec. bd. 1972-74), Archaeol. Inst. Am. (chpt. pres. 1970-71), Soc. Bibl. Lit. Asso. editor Cath. Bibl. Quarterly, 1966-74. Contbr. articles to archaeol. and religious jours., books. Translator: The New American Bible, 1970; Roman Missal, 1964. Address: 2260 Summit Ave St Paul MN 55105

QUINN, JOHN R., archbishop, Roman Catholic Church; b. Riverside, Calif., Mar. 28, 1929; s. Ralph J. and Elizabeth (Carroll) Q.; Ph.B., Gregorian U., Rome, 1950, S.T.B., 1952, S.T.L., 1954. Ordained priest Roman Cath. Ch., 1953, consecrated bishop, 1967, archbishop, 1973. Asst. priest St. George Ch., Ontario, Calif., 1954-55; prof. theology Immaculate Heart Sem., San Diego, 1955-62, vice rector, 1960-62; rector St. Francis Coll. Sem., El Cajon, Calif., 1962-64, Immaculate Heart Sem., 1964-68; aux. bishop, vicar gen., San Diego, 1967-72; bishop of Oklahoma City, 1972-73, archbishop, 1973-77; archbishop of San Francisco, 1977—; apptd. Pontifical Del. for Religious in U.S., 1983; provost U. San Diego, 1968-72. Mem. Cath. Theol. Soc. Am., Canon Law Soc. Am., Am. Cath. Hist. Soc. Address: 1521 N Hudson Oklahoma OK 73103

QUINTERO, CARLOS ARCE, archbishop, Roman Catholic Church; b. Etzatlan, Jalisco, Mex., Feb. 13, 1920; s. Silverio Real Quintero and Lucrecia (Meza) Arce. Licenciad Philos, P.U.G., Roma-Italia, 1940, D.O., 1946. Ordained priest Roman Catholic Ch., 1944, bishop, 1961. Prof. theology Sem., Guadalajara, Mex., 1947-61; first bishop Catedral, Cuidad Valle, S.L.P., 1961-66, archbishop coaddj., Herosillo, Sonora, 1966-68, archbishop, 1968—; pres. Edn., Mex., 1968-72, CELAM-Edn., Latin Am., 1974-79. Home and Office: Dr Paliza #81 Hermosillo Sonora

QUIRANTE, LU LAFUENTE, minister, Seventh-day Adventist Church; former education educator; b. Tayabas, Quezon, Philippines, Apr. 2, 1913; came to U.S., 1966; s. Ponciano Valde and Felipa (Lafuente) Q.; m. Melba Andal, May 1, 1938; children: Melu Jean, Delma Eden, Lou and Ednardo. A.B., B.S. in Edn., Philippine Union Coll., 1936; M.A., Far Eastern U., Manila, 1947; Ed.D., U. Md., 1953. Ordained to ministry Seventh-day Adventist Ch., 1956. Bible instr. Philippine Union Coll. Acad., Manila, 1936-40; missionary Philippine Union Mission, Manila, 1937-52, minister, 1953-55; minister North Philippine Union Mission, Manila, 1956—; elder Oakwood Coll. Ch., Huntsville, Ala., 1970—. Prof. edn. Oakwood Coll., Huntsville, 1966-78, prof. edn. emeritus, 1978—. Dir. Philippine Inst. Sci. Studies for Prevention of Alcoholism, 1960-66; del. Third World Congress for Prevention of Alcoholism, 1979. Fulbright-Smith-Mundt scholar, 1951-53; recipient Philippine Union Coll. Outstanding Alumnus award, 1967; named Educator of Yr., Oakwood Coll., 1979. Mem. Philippine Fulbright Scholars Assn. (life), AAUP, Internat. Edn. Assn. (sec.-treas. div. Ala. Edn. Assn. 1970-72), Am. Assn. Colls. of Tchr. Edn., Phi Delta Kappa. Lodge: Lions. Home: 7822 Horseshoe Trail SE Huntsville AL 35802 Office: Oakwood Coll Oakwood Rd Huntsville AL 35806

RABB, JOHN LESLIE, priest, Episcopal Church; b. Des Moines, Iowa, Oct. 11, 1944; s. Carleton Alexander and Jo Ann (Robinson) R.; m. Sharon Elaine Rafter, Apr. 17, 1976; children: Alison, Jennifer. B.A., DePauw U., 1966; M.A., U. Iowa, 1969; M.Div., Episcopal Div. Sch., Cambridge, Mass., 1976. Ordained to ministry Episcopal Ch. as deacon, 1976, as priest, 1977. Curate, Ascension Chapel, Gaithersburg, Md., 1976-78, asst. rector, 1978-79, priest-in-charge, 1979; rector Holy Apostles Episcopal Ch., Arbutus, Md., 1979—; chmn. bd. Province III Conf., Frederick, Md., 1979-81; mem. seminarians com. Diocese of Md., Balt., 1981—, mem. commn. on ministry, 1982—, mem. cathedral chpt., 1984—. Named Tchr. of Yr., Palmer Jr. Coll., 1969. Mem. Assn. Clin. Pastoral Edn., Greater Arbutus Ministerial Assn. (pres. 1980-81), ACLU. Home and Office: Holy Apostles 4922 Leeds Ave Arbutus MD 21227

RABB, MUHAMMAD ABDUR, educator; b. Bangladesh, Dec. 25, 1935; s. Muhammad Sonamaddin and Rahila (Khatun) Munsi; B.A. (Pakistan Govt. scholar), Dacca U., 1955, M.A., 1958; M.A. (Ford Found. scholar), McGill U., 1967, Ph.D. (Ford Found. scholar), 1970; m. Aishah Forhat, Nov. 17, 1959; children—Hamid Abdur, Shinin Abdur. Asst. prof. Western philosophy Dacca U., 1958-63, asso. prof. Muslim philosophy, 1970-71; prof., dir. Iqbal Acad., Pakistan, 1971-72; prof. dept. religion Dawson Coll., Montreal, Que., Can., 1973—, founder Centre for Intercultural Studies. Part-time lectr. Sir George Williams U., 1967-70; sessional lectr. Carleton U., 1972-73; delivered sermons in Mosque; Author: Persian Mysticism: Abu Yazid al-Bistami, 2d edit., 1976. Contbr. articles to profl. jours. Home: 532 Prince Arthur St W Montreal PQ H2X 1T7 Canada Office: 1001 Sherbrooke St E Montreal PQ Canada

RABBITT, GERALD LEE, religion educator, Inter Varsity Christian Fellowship; b. Toledo, July 31, 1946; s. James Edward and Clara (Metzger) R.; m. Emily G. Thiessen, June 30, 1970; children: Trudy Joy, Jeremy, Christa, Bobby, Emily Ruth. B.Ed., U. Toledo, 1971, M.Ed., 1972, Ed.S., 1981. Instr. math dept., also internat. student adviser Rio Grande Coll., Ohio, 1980—, instr. history and lit. of N.T., 1984—, adviser Inter Varsity Christian Fellowship, 1981—; dir. internat. student houseparties Cedar Campus, Cedarville, Mich., 1982-83, 83-84, 84-85; Served with USAR, 1971—. Named Outstanding Young Man of Am., Jaycees, 1983. Mem. Assn. of Christian Ministries to Internats. Republican. Home: 700 Pine St Box 13 Rio Grande OH 45674 Office: Rio Grande Coll Rio Grande OH 45674

RABE, VIRGIL WILLIAM, minister, religious educator, United Presbyterian Church in U.S.A.; b. Monroe, Wis., Nov. 3, 1930; s. Albert and Beulah (Davidson) R.; m. Nancy Ann Fay, July 9, 1955; children: Johathan Paul, Laurie Fay. B.A., U. Wis., 1954; B.S., McCormick Theol. Sem., 1957; Th.D., Harvard U., 1963. Ordained to ministry United Presbyn. Ch. in U.S.A., 1957. Pastor, First Presbyn. Ch., Waltham, Mass., 1957-59; prof. religion and philosophy Mo. Valley Coll., Marshall, 1961—. Contbr. articles to profl. jours. Rockefeller doctoral fellow, 1959-61. Mem. Am. Schs. of Oriental Research, Soc. Bibl. Lit., Mo. Union Presbytery, Alpha Sigma Phi. Home: 316 E Black St Marshall MO 65340 Office: Mo Valley Coll Marshall MO 65340

RABUN, GENE TERRY, minister of music, So. Bapt. Conv.; b. Sanford, Fla., Apr. 27, 1947; s. Charles Tolar and Voncile (Yates) R.; A.A., Orlando Jr. Coll., 1967; B.A., Stetson U., 1970; M.A., Rollins Coll., 1975. Minister of music First Bapt. Ch., Altoona, Fla., 1967-68, First Bapt. Ch., Oviedo, Fla., 1968—, dir. single adults Sunday Sch. dept., 1976—. Tchr., Eastbrook Elementary Sch., Winter Park, Fla., 1970—. Mem. NEA, Fla., Seminole edn. assns., Phi Mu Alpha. Home: 1609 Terrace Dr Sanford FL 32771 Office: PO Box 487 Oviedo FL 32765

RACHUY, VIOLA HELEN, lay church worker, United Methodist Church; b. German Valley, Ill., Apr. 15, 1919; d. John Frederick and Jennie (Harma) Stratmann; m. Lyle A. Rachuy, Jan. 24, 1938; children: Judith Ann Rachuy Decker, James Lyle. Student, Central Coll., 1936-38. Sunday sch. tchr. United Meth. Ch., Iowa, S.D. and Ill., 1938-70, youth dir., 1938-74; pres. Women's Soc. Christian Service, United Meth. Ch., Stockton, Ill., 1974-75, 80-84, dist. pres., Rockford, 1968-73, chmn. for publicity No. Ill. conf., 1970-73; mem. Conf. Bd. World Service and Fin., 1971-72. Bd. dirs. Martha Hall Home for Girls, 1967-72, Rosecrance Homes for Children, 1968-74, Rainbow Ridge, 1983—. Home: 512 Stockton St Stockton IL 61085

RADA, HEATH K., educational adminstrator. Pres. Presbyterian Sch. of Christian Edn., Richmond, Va. Office: Presbyn Sch of Christian Edn 1205 Palmyra Ave Richmond VA 23227*

RADDE, LEONARD CARL, minister, United Methodist Church; b. Big Spring, Tex., Sept. 27, 1935; s. Samuel Carla and Rebecca Doris (Dickerson) R.; m. Elizabeth Ann Poteet, May 31, 1969; children: Timothy Lynn, James Allen, John Wesley. Assoc. in Agr., Tarleton State U., 1955; B.S., Tex. Wesleyan Coll., 1958; B.D., So. Meth. U., 1964; postgrad. Baylor U., 1968, Drew U., 1983—. Ordained to ministry United Meth. Ch., as deacon, 1960, as elder, 1964. Pastor Itasca Meth. Parish, Tex., 1970-74, First Meth. Ch., Coleman, Tex., 1974-78; sr. pastor First Meth. Ch., Ennis, Tex., 1978-83, First Meth. Ch., Killeen, Tex., 1983—; statistician Central Tex. Conf. United Meth. Ch., 1982—, mem. Bd. Global Ministry, 1976-80, 84—, trustee, 1984—, mem. exec. com. Council on Fin., 1980—; chmn. bd. dirs. Wesley Voice Ministries, Floyd Knob, Ind. Author: Pre-Employment Training, 1968; Bible Study in Moral Decision, 1977; (book and study guide) Camping Together as Christians, 1976; (training curriculum) Re-Training for Hard-Core Unemployed, 1969. Chmn. bd. dirs. Ennis Airport, 1980-82; mem. dist. com. Circle 10 council Boy Scouts Am., 1981-82. Named Rural Pastor of Yr., Central Tex. Conf. United Meth. Ch., 1963. Mem. Killeen/Fort Hood Christian

Ministers Assn., Killeen C. of C., Ennis C. of C. (bd. dirs. 1980-82). Lodge: Lions (pres. Meridian, Tex., 1968-69, Lion of Yr. 1969). Home: 1902 Halbert Killeen TX 76541 Office: First United Meth Ch 508 N Gray Killeen TX 76541

RADDIN, ROY DAVID, minister, Southern Baptist Convention; b. Hattiesburg, Miss., Apr. 18, 1930; s. James Thomas and Pellie (Tisdale) R.; m. Myra Ray Corley, June 2, 1953; children: Roy David, Donna Jo Raddin Babb. B.A., Miss. Coll., 1952; M.Div., New Orleans Bapt. Theol. Sem., 1955; D.Ministry, Miss. Bapt. Sem., 1982. Ordained to ministry So. Bapt. Conv., 1950. Pastor Anguilla Bapt. Ch., Miss., 1955-58, Tchula Bapt. Ch., Miss., 1958-63, Second Bapt. Ch., Greenville, Miss., 1963-79; dir. missions Washington County Bapt. Assn., 1979—. Trustee Am. Bapt. Sem., Nashville, 1981—. Democrat. Lodge: Rotary. Home: 825 Adams Dr Greenville MS 38701 Office: Washington County Bapt Assn PO Box 4511 Greenville MS 34704

RADECKE, MARK WILLIAM, minister, Lutheran Church in America; b. Balt., June 16, 1952; s. William Herman and Gloria Louise (Edwards) R.; m. Lee Benney, June 7, 1974; children: Jessica Brooke, Christopher Mark, Jaime Elizabeth. B.A., U. Md., 1974; M.Div., Luth. Theol. Sem., Gettysburg, Pa., 1978. Ordained to ministry Luth. Ch., 1978. Pastor Christ Luth. Ch., Roanoke, Va., 1978—; pres. Luth. Coop. Ministry, Roanoke, 1979-81; bd. dirs. Roanoke Area Ministries, 1982—; adj. prof. religion Roanoke Coll., Salem, Va., 1984—. Author: In Many and Various Ways, 1985. Contbr. sermons and book revs. to religious jour. Office: Christ Luth Ch 2011 Brandon Ave SW Roanoke VA 24015

RADEMACHER, ROBERT PAUL, minister, Evangelical Lutheran Church of Canada; b. Omaha, Sept. 21, 1942; s. Heye J. and Johanna (Stoehr) R.; m. Darlene Edna Haecker, June 9, 1968; children: Jonathan, Jeffrey, Jeremy, Jennifer. B.A., Dana Coll., 1964; M.Div., Wartburg Sem., 1968; D.Min., McCormick Sem., Chgo., 1985—. Ordained to ministry, Evang. Luth. Ch. of Can., 1968. Pastor, Kyle Luth. Parish, Sask., Can., 1968-70, Midale Luth. Parish, Sask., 1970-81, Christ Luth. Ch., Neudorf, Sask., 1981—; mgr., treas. Luth. Bible Camp, Midale, Sask., 1970-81; sec. St. Paul Luth. Home Bd., Melville, Sask., 1981—. Sec. supervisory com. Midale Credit Union. Mem. Acad. Parish Clergy. Democrat. Home and Office: Christ Luth Ch Box 10 Neudorf SK S0A 2T0 Canada

RADEN, LOUIS, lay church worker, Episcopal Church; tape and label company executive; b. Detroit, June 17, 1929; s. Harry M. Raden and Joan (Morris) Raden Shumway; m. Mary K. Knowlton, June 18, 1949; children: Louis III, Pamela, Jacqueline. B.A., Trinity Coll., 1951; student NY U, 1952. Mem. Diocesan Urban Evaluation Com., Detroit, 1975-78, chmn., 1978; mem. Diocesan Urban Affairs Com., Detroit, 1978-80, chmn. 1979-80; mem. Diocesan Bd. Trustees, Detroit, 1980-82, v.p., 1981-82; vice chmn. bd. dirs. Robert H. Whitaker Sch. Theology, Mich. Diocese, Detroit, 1983-85; mem. Christ Ch. Cranbrook, Bloomfield Hills, Mich. Pres., chmn. bd. dirs. Gen. Tape and Supply, Inc., Detroit, 1963—. Recipient Key Man award Greater Hartford Jaycees, 1957. Mem. Nat. Cathedral Assn., Theta Xi (Disting. Service award 1957). Republican. Clubs: Detroit Golf, Detroit Gun. Home: 1133 Ivyglen Circle Bloomfield Hills MI 48013 Office: Gen Tape and Supply Inc 7451 W 8 Mile Rd Detroit MI 48221

RADFORD, DENNIS WAYNE, minister, religion and literature educator Seventh-day Adventists; b. Pueblo, Colo., Mar. 10, 1947; s. John Rice and Bilie Vaughn (Nichols) R.; m. Kari Anne Vetne, Sept. 5, 1971; children: Rachel, Danielle, Nathan. B.A., Atlantic Union Coll., 1975; M.A., Andrews U., 1977; M.Div., Seventh Day Adventist Sem., 1980. Asst. pastor Hudson/Framingham Seventh-day Adventist Chs., Mass., 1974-75; pastor Upper Columbia Conf., Spokane, Wash., 1979-81; asst. prof. English, Atlantic Union Coll., South Lancaster, Mass., 1981—; instr. religion South Lancaster Acad., 1974-75, Tri Cities Jr. Acad., Pasco, Wash., 1980. Served with USN, 1966-70, Vietnam. Decorated Purple Heart, Bronze Star. Mem. Am. Acad. Religion, Soc. Bibl. Lit., Nat. Council Tchrs. English, Medieval Acad. Am., Vietnam Vets. Am. (sec. 1983-84), DAV. Office: Atlantic Union Coll Main St South Lancaster MA 01561

RADHA, SIVANANDA (SYLVIA HELLMANN), swami, Saraswati Order of Sannyas; b. Berlin, 1911; came to Can., 1951, naturalized, 1959. Initiated as swami, 1956; spiritual dir. Yasodhara Ashram, Kootenay Bay, B.C., Can., 1963—; founder 6 Shambala Houses in N. Am.; workshop leader; lectr. in field. Author: Kundalini Yoga for the West, 1978; Mantras Words of Power, 1980; Aphorisms of Swami Sivanda Radha, 1980; Radha: Diary of a Woman's Search, 1981; Gods Who Walk the Rainbow, 1981. Address: Box 9 Kootenay Bay BC V0B 1X0 Canada

RAFTER, FRANK FURZE, minister, American Baptist Churches in the U.S.A.; b. Bronx, N.Y., Apr. 22, 1935; s. Francis Donald Furze and Lena (Relph) Berwin; m. Deborah Ann Trockel, Sept. 4, 1982. B.S., Am. Coll., 1974; B. Religious Edn., Am. Sem., 1975; M. Profl. Studies, N.Y. Theol. Sem., 1977; D. Humanities (hon.), Far East Grad. Theol. Sem., Macau, China, 1967. Ordained to ministry Am. Bapt. Chs. U.S.A., 1977. Pastor, Richmond Hill Bapt. Ch., N.Y.C., 1973—; Chaplain N.Y. Bible Soc., N.Y.C., 1963-73, Jamaica Hosp., N.Y.C., 1973—, Emergency Med. Service, N.Y.C., 1975—; counselor Plaza Bus. Inst., N.Y.C., 1980—. Author: Street Preacher, 1984. Chaplain, Civil Air Patrol, N.Y.C., 1969, Queens Council Girl Scouts Am., 1968—, Aux. Police, N.Y.C., 1975-77, Nat. Boy Scouts Am. Jamboree, Va., 1981; counselor Family Ct. Queens, N.Y., 1973-77. Served with USN, 1954-58, Korea. Recipient Shofar award Jewish Com. Scouting, 1972, St. George Emblem award Catholic Com. Scouting, 1977, Silver Beaver award Boy Scouts Am., 1977, Good Shepherd award Bapt. Com. Scouting, 1982. Mem. Interfaith Council Queens (merit award 1977), AMVETS (chaplain 1975—, merit award 1978), Protestant Com. (chaplain 1974-84, Interfaith award 1981), Yankee Tunesmiths (chaplain 1976-84). Republican. Lodge: Kiwanis (pres. 1976-77).

RAFTERY, WILLIAM JOHN, priest, Roman Catholic Church; b. Somerville, Mass., July 16, 1916; s. William Francis and Beatrice Mary (Cody) R.; B.A., Cath. U., 1945; M.A., Villanova U., 1953. Ordained priest, 1945; tchr. St. Mary's Prep. Sch., Penndel, Pa., 1945-58; rector, prin. Immaculata Sem., Lafayette, La., 1958-64; rector, pres. Notre Dame Sem. Coll. Grad. Sch., New Orleans, 1964-67; parish priest Diocese Worcester (Mass.), 1968—. Chaplain Lafayette Serra Club. Mem. Sch. Prins. Assn., Coll. Pres's. Assn. Home and office: Box 307 Manomet MA 02345

RAGANAS, ROLANDO ALIA, minister, Southern Baptist Convention; b. Davao City, Philippines, June 21, 1937; s. Leoncio N. and Celerina (Alia) R.; came to U.S., 1969; B.A., Mindanao U., 1961; B.D., Philippine Bapt. Sem., 1962; M.Ch. Music, Southwestern Bapt. Theol. Sem., 1974; m. Nelly Baja, Apr. 17, 1961; children—Ronnell, Johnferdi, Rolando. Ordained to ministry, 1964; pastor Immanuel Bapt. Ch., Davao City, 1964-68; tchr. Mindanao Bapt. Bible Sch., Davao City, 1964-68; minister of music West Athens (Tex.) Bapt. Ch., 1970-72, Campbellsville (Ky.) Bapt. Ch., 1972-84, Sta. WGRB-TV, Columbia, Ky., 1984—. Pres. Mindanao Conv. So. Bapt. Chs., 1967-68. Home: Rt 5 Box 89 Campbellsville KY 42718 Office: 420 N Central St Campbellsville KY 42718

RAINES, ELESTER EVANS, minister, Am. Bapt. Assn.; b. Folsom, La., Feb. 28, 1926; s. Elester Scales and Alice (Reid) R.; student Jacksonville Bapt. Coll., 1947-48; B.A., Tulane U., 1951; postgrad. La. Bapt. Sem., 1957-58; m. Verbia Marie Parent, Aug. 8, 1947; children—Sheilah C., Kerry B. Ordained to ministry, 1948; pastor Bethel Missionary Bapt. Ch., New Orleans, 1949-50, Crescent City Missionary Bapt. Ch., New Orleans, 1951-58, Glendale Missionary Bapt. Ch., Kenner, La., 1959—. Missionary committeeman Am. Bapt. Assn., 1954-67; instr. English and Koine Greek, acting dean La. Missionary Bapt. Inst. and Sem., Minden, 1957-58; dean, instr. Missionary Bapt. Inst. Theology, New Orleans, 1959-60; moderator Trinity Missionary Bapt. Assn., 1956, 57, 72, 73, La. State Missionary Bapt. Assn., 1965, 66; Sunday Sch. committeeman Am. Bapt. Assn., 1967-77; founder Glenwood Bapt. Youth Camp, Folsom, La., 1969; organizer/dir. S.E. La. Youth Encampments, 1970-73. Author: Let There Be Light, 1957; pub., editor The Gospel Trumpet, 1961-65. Home: 2727 Gadsen Ave Kenner LA 70062 Office: 2715 Gadsen St Kenner LA 70062

RAINES, JERRY RICHARD, minister, Southern Baptist Convention; b. Lamesa, Tex., Sept. 29, 1946; s. Hershel Edwin and Dorothy Louise (Painter) R.; m. Sue Ann Davis, Aug. 17, 1968; children: Jay Richard, Rebecca SuAnn, Hannah Maryelle. B.A., Howard Payne Coll., 1969; M.Div., Southwestern Bapt. Theol. Sem., 1972. Ordained to ministry So. Bapt. Conv., 1968. Pastor, Ireland Bapt. Ch., Gatesville, Tex., 1968-69; youth minister Calvary Bapt. Ch., Harlingen, Tex., 1969-70; pastor Live Oak Bapt. Ch., Gatesville, 1973-78, Canyon Creek Bapt. Ch., Temple, Tex., 1978—; trustee Faith Rescue Mission, Temple, 1983—; mem. missions com. Bell Bapt. Assn., Belton, Tex., 1981—. Office: Canyon Creek Bapt Ch 4306 S 31st St Temple TX 76502

RAINEY, TERRY JOE, minister, Southern Baptist Convention; b. Greenville, S.C., Aug. 13, 1949; s. Harold D. and Frances R. (Hiott) R.; m. Harriette G. Smith, Nov. 7, 1969; 1 child, Shannon. A.A., Anderson Jr. Coll., 1974; student Gardner Webb Coll., 1972-73, Central Wesleyan Coll., 1973-75, Columbia Bible Coll., 1977-79. Ordained to ministry Bapt. Ch., 1974. Pastor Unity Bapt. Ch., Woodruff, S.C., 1974-77, Airport Bapt. Ch., Columbia, S.C., 1977-80, Centerville Bapt. Ch., Anderson, S.C., 1980—; TV minister stas. WGGS, WAXA, WGSE; organizer, dir., host television broadcast Lift Him Up, 1985—. Home: Route 12 Box 419 Dunhill Dr Anderson SC 29621 Office: Route 12 Box 317 Gerrard Rd Anderson SC 29621

RAKESTRAW, ROBERT VINCENT, minister Southern Baptist Convention, educator; b. Phila., Nov. 16, 1943; s. Arthur Jesse and Mary Anne (Stenella) R.; m. Judy Kay Engevik, July 22, 1967; children: Joan Marie, Laureen Dawn. Student St. Joseph's Coll., Phila., 1961-63; diploma in Bible, Prairie Bible Inst., Three Hills, Alta., Can., 1967; B.S. in Missions, Calvary Bible Coll., 1968, M.A. in Bibl. Lit., 1970; M.Phil. in Theology, Drew U., 1982, Ph.D. in Theology, 1985. Ordained to ministry, 1967. Asst. pastor, Harmony Bapt. Bible Ch., Kansas City, Mo., 1968, pastor, 1968-69; grad. instr. in Bible, Calvary Bible Coll., Kansas City, Mo., 1970; instr. in Bible and practical theology Prairie Bible Inst., Three Hills, 1970-75; pastor Calvary Bapt. Ch., Flemington, N.J., 1976-80; vis. instr. religion King's Coll., Briarcliff Manor, N.Y., 1981; teaching fellow Christian ethics Drew Theol. Sem., Madison, N.J., 1982-83; prof. theology and Christian ethics Criswell Bible Coll. and Grad. Sch., Dallas, 1985—; assoc. pastor First Bapt. Ch., Dallas, 1985—; treas. Heart of Am. region Independent Fundamental Chs. of Am., Kansas City, Mo., 1969; leader of tours to Bible lands, 1973, 75. Author: Spiritual Gifts Today, 1979, 85. Contbr. column to newspaper, 1973-74, articles to Lockyer's Bible Dictionary, articles and book revs. to religious periodicals and jours. Chmn. parents adv. council Prairie Kindergarten, Alta., 1973-74; mem. parents adv. council Flemington-Raritan Sch. Dist., N.J., 1978-79. Recipient scholarship St. Joseph's Coll., 1961-63, Drew U., 1980-82; teaching fellow Drew U., 1982-83. Mem. Evangelical Theol. Soc. (sec.-treas. Eastern region 1978-80), Evangelical Philos. Soc., Am. Acad. Religion, Soc. Christian Ethics, Wesleyan Theol. Soc. Lodge: Rotary. Office: Criswell Bible Coll and Grad Sch 525 N Ervay Dallas TX 75201

RAMAGE, DAVID, JR., seminary administrator, Presbyterian. Pres. McCormick Theol. Sem., Chgo., 1985—. Office: 5555 S Woodlawn Ave Chicago IL 60637*

RAMBO, DAVID LLOYD, religion educator, Christian and Missionary Alliance; b. Williamsport, Pa., June 8, 1934; s. Harold Merle and Mazie Dorothea (Cupples) R.; m. Ruth Claudette Retallack, July 9, 1960; children: Elizabeth, Jody, Shelly. Student St. Paul Bible Coll., 1952-55; B.S., Nyack Coll., 1957; M.Div., Gordon-Conwell Theol. Sem., 1960; M.A., Fuller Theol. Sem., 1968; Ph.D., NYU, 1973. Ordained to ministry Christian and Missionary Alliance, Casco, Maine, 1960-62. Missionary, Philippines, 1962-67, v.p. overseas ministries, Nyack, N.Y., 1978-82; prof. Can. Bible Coll. and Theol. Sem., Regina, Sask., Can., 1970-72, pres., 1972-78; pres. Nyack Coll., and Alliance Theol. Sem., N.Y., 1982—. Lodge: Rotary (Nyack). Office: Nyack Coll Nyack NY 10960

RAMEY, GORDON FRANKLIN, minister, Ch. of God-Anderson, Ind.; b. Longacre, W.Va., Sept. 14, 1940; s. John and Thelma Oreal (Bess) R.; B.S. cum laude, Gulf Coast Bible Coll., 1976; m. Lillian Mae Matney, Aug. 31, 1962; 1 son, Allen Franklin. Ordained to ministry Ch. of God-Anderson, Ind., 1971; asst. dir. Missions Through Faith Program, Andros Island, Bahamas, 1959-61, P.R., 1961; pastor Ch. of God, Rittman, Ohio, 1964, Cookville, Tenn., 1968-69, Willshire, Ohio, 1970-72; pastor Baytown (Tex.) Ch. of God, 1974—. Mem. Delta Epsilon Chi. Home: 110 Bob Smith Rd Baytown TX 77520

RAMIREZ, RICARDO, bishop, Roman Catholic Church; b. Bay City, Tex., Sept. 12, 1934; s. Natividad Espitia and Maria (Espinosa) R. B.A., U. St. Thomas, 1959; M.A., U. Detroit, 1968; postgrad., St. Basils Sem., Toronto, Can., 1963-65, Seminario Conciliar, Mex. City, 1965-66, East Asian Pastoral Inst., Manilia, 1973-74. Ordained priest Roman Cath. Ch., 1966, bishop, 1981. Chaplain, U. Centro Cultural, Aragon, Mex. City, 1968-70, Family Religious Edn. Project, Tehuacan, Mex., 1970-76; exec. v.p. Mexican Am. Cultural Ctr., San Antonio, 1976-81; first bishop Diocese of Las Cruces, N.Mex., 1982—; mem. U.S. Bishops Com. on Latin Am., Washington, Am. Bd. of Cath. Missions, Litury; chmn. Hispanic Litury Subcom. Mem. N. Am. Acad. Liturgy (chmn.), Inst. Hispanic Liturgy, N.Mex. Humanities Council. Home: 455 W Palmer St Las Cruces NM 88004 Office: Cath Diocese of Las Cruces 1280 Med Park Las Cruces NM 88001

RAMIREZ, RUBÉN RODRÍGUEZ, minister, Seventh-day Adventist Church; b. Jaltipán, Veracruz, México, Oct. 18, 1953; s. Santos Rodríguez Martínez and Estéfana (Ramírez) Soto; m. Lily Ramos Escobedo, May 7, 1977; children: Rubén Rodríguez Ramos, Rogel Rodríguez Ramos, Lily E. Rodríguez Ramos. B.Theology, Universidad de Montemorelos, Mex., 1978; M.A. in Religion, Andrews U., 1981. Ordained to ministry Seventh-day Adventist Ch., 1981. Dist. pastor South Conf. of Seventh-day Adventist Ch., Tuxtla Gutierrez, Chiapas, 1978-81; dept. dir. Isthmus Conf., Oaxaca, Oaxaca, 1982—; newspaper corr. Asociación Nacional de Periodistas, México, D.F., 1982-84. Home: Apartado 1 C Col Reforma Oaxaca Oaxaca 68050 Mexico Office: Isthmus Conf H Colegio M 523 Oaxaca Oaxaca 68050 Mexico

RAMON, INEZ SALINAS, JR., minister, So. Baptist Conv.; b. Robstown, Tex., Apr. 30, 1944; s. Inez Chavez and Velia (Barrera) S.; B.A., Howard Payne U., 1968; B.S., Okla. Bapt. U., 1971; postgrad. Pan Am. U., 1976; m. Gamaila Ann Davis, June 10, 1972; children—Stephanie Kristen, David Brian. Ordained to ministry, 1969; pastor Bapt. Spanish Mission of 1st Bapt. Ch., Altus, Okla., 1968-71, Los Encinos Bapt. Ch., Corpus Christi, Tex., 1975, 1st Bapt. Ch., Hargill, Tex., 1976—, Primavera Bapt. Ch., Fort Worth, 1977—. Address: 2205 Clinton Ave Fort Worth TX 76106

RAMOS, JOVELINO P., administrator, Presbyterian Church (U.S.A.); b. Tarumirim, Minas, Brazil, Aug. 27, 1934; naturalized U.S. citizen, 1968; s. Jovelino and Antonia (Ramos) Pereira; m. Myra Bergman, Dec. 17, 1960 (div. 1972); children: Lyria, Barton, Tarso; m. Joan Howard, Jan. 20, 1973; children: Helena, Carlos. M.A. in Social Ethics and N.T., Yale Div. Sch., 1962; M.A. in Latin Am. History, Columbia U., 1970. Ordained to ministry Presbyterian Ch. (U.S.A.). Pastor, Ipanema Presbyn. Ch., Rio de Janeiro, Brazil, 1962-68; dir. racial justice NCCC, N.Y.C., 1973-82; dir. ch. and race Presbyn. Ch. (USA), N.Y.C., 1982—; dir. Council on Ch. and Race, N.Y.C., 1982—; mem. Bi-Nat. Service, N.Y.C., 1978—; co-commr. Program to Combat Racism, Geneva, Switzerland, 1984—; mem. Racial Justice Working Group, NCCC, N.Y.C., 1982—. Co-editor jours. Paz e Terra 1967, The Fifth Commn., 1974-82, Cocar News, 1982—. Co-editor book Memoirs of Exiles, 1976. Columbia U. fellow, 1971; recipient Gold Plate, Nat. Council Chs., 1982. Home: 80 LaSalle St #14G New York NY 10115 Office: Council on Church and Race 475 Riverside Dr #1260 New York NY 10115

RAMSTAD, PHILIP JULIAN, minister, United Church of Christ; b. St. Paul, Aug. 16, 1929; s. Otto and Otilia (Ellertson) R.; B.A., U. Minn., 1950; M.Div., Union Theol. Sem., 1953; m. Lucille Mortvedt Baker, June 15, 1962; children—Robert Evan, Kari Anne. Ordained to ministry, 1953; chaplain, tchr. Kiski Sch., Saltsburg, Pa., 1953-54; pastor West End United Ch. of Christ, Pitts., 1954-63, Horace Bushnell Congl. Ch., Hartford, Conn., 1963-67, West United Ch. of Christ, Akron, Ohio, 1967-73; interim pastor Bath (Ohio) Ch., 1974; pastor United Ch. of Christ-Congl., Grinnell, Iowa, 1974—. Chaplain, Congl. Homes, Pitts., 1956-63; moderator Western Pa. Assn. Congl. Christian Chs. and Ministers, 1958-60, 62-63; bd. dirs. Pa. Conf. Congl. Christian Chs., 1958-63, Pa. West Conf. United Ch. Christ, 1962-63, Congl. Homes Pitts., 1954-63; pres. Greater Hartford Ministers Fellowship, 1965, Greater Akron Ministerial Assn., 1970; v.p.-communication Council Chs. Akron, 1970-73; founding chmn. Akron Area Mission Priority Bd. United Ch. of Christ, 1972-74; regional bd. dirs. NCCJ, 1960-63; chmn. Grinnell Gen. Hosp. Chaplaincy, 1976-78; chmn. ch. and ministry Central Iowa United Ch. of Christ Assn., 1976-78; broadcaster WPIT, 1958-63, WRCH, Hartford, and New Britain, 1965-67, WAKR, Akron, 1969-74, KGRN, Grinnell, 1975—. Mem. Citizens Adv. Council Hartford, 1964-67; bd. dirs. Florence Crittenton Services Akron, 1970-73, United Fund, 1975-80, Poweshiek County Mental Health Center, Grinnell, 1975-77, pres., 1977-78; moderator Central Assn. Iowa Conf., 1985—; pres. Grinnell Ministerial Assn., 1982-84; mem. long range planning com. Grinnell Hosp., 1981—; Mem. Insts. Religion and Health. Home: 1810 Manor Dr Grinnell IA 50112 Office: PO Box 322 Grinnell IA 50112

RAND, HOWARD BENJAMIN, religious organization administrator, educator, editor, lawyer; b. Haverhill, Mass., June 13, 1889; s. Frank Nathenial and Letty May (Lepper) R.; m. Hazel Gertrude Smith, July 23, 1913 (dec. 1982). B.Law U. Maine, 1912. Instr., lectr. on bibl. truths Anglo Saxon Fedn. Am., Haverhill, 1928-46, nat. commr., 1946—; treas., editor Destiny Pubs. Fedn., Haverhill, and Merrimac, Mass., 1928—. Author: The Story the Bible Tells, 1953; Study in Revelation, 1951; Digest of the Divine Law, 1943; Study in Hosea, 1955; The Challenge of the Great Pyramid, 1943; others; also editor. Served with USNG, 1909-12. Mem. Phi Alpha Delta. Home and Office: Destiny Pubs 43 Grove St Merrimac MA 01860

RANDALL, MAX WARD, minister, Christian Church (Disciples of Christ); b. Readstown, Wis., Oct. 17, 1917; s. Milton Roy and Melissa Pearl (Ward) R.; B.A., Minn. Bible Coll., 1939, D.D., 1966; M.A., Cin. Bible Sem., 1942, B.D., 1943; M.A., Fuller Theol. Sem., 1968, D.Missiology, 1979; m. Gladys Waller, Sept. 3, 1938; children—Leroy, Ramona (Mrs. Kenneth Goble), Jeannette (Mrs. Terry Crane), Karen (Mrs. David Roadcup), Morris, Dwight. Ordained minister Christian Ch., 1944; pastor Ohio and Minn., 1938-50; missionary, So. Africa, 1950-66; prof. world mission and church growth Lincoln (Ill.) Christian Coll. and Sem., 1967—. Co-founder, Coll. Scriptures, Louisville, 1945; founder South Africa Ch. of Christ Mission, Kimberley, 1948, Zambia Christian Mission, Lusaka, 1968. Trustee Zambia Christian Mission, 1968, Isles of Pacific Christian Mission, 1970, S. Pacific Evang. Fellowship, 1972, Mission Services, 1973, Pioneer Bible Translators, 1976. Author: We Would Do It Again, 1956; Light for the Dark Country, 1960; Profile for Victory, 1971; The Great Awakenings and the Restoration Movement, 1983. Contbr. articles to religious jours. Home: 220 Campus View Dr Lincoln IL 62656 Office: Box 178 Lincoln IL 62656

RANDOLPH, WILLIAM MARVIN, minister, Presbyn. Ch. U.S./United Presbyn. Ch. U.S.A.; b. S. Norfolk, Va., Oct. 9, 1934; s. James Edward and Beulah Adelia (Trevathan) R.; B.A. cum laude, King Coll., Bristol, Tenn., 1958; B.D. magna cum laude, Columbia Theol. Sem., Decatur, Ga., 1961, M.Div., 1971; D.Min., Vanderbilt U., 1976; m. Anna Lou Roberts, May 27, 1958; children—Donna Anne, William Marvin. Ordained to ministry, 1961; pastor chs. in Ga., 1961-64; pastor First Presbyn. Ch., Warner Robins, Ga., 1964-73; sr. pastor Presbyn. Ch., Henderson, Ky., 1973—; vol. chaplain Houston County Hosp., 1966-73. Chmn. com. nat. ministries Presbytery Augusta-Macon (Ga.), 1967-73, moderator, 1970; commr. gen. assembly Presbyn. Ch. U.S., 1969, 82, mem. spl. adv. council evangelism, gen. exec. bd., 1976; pres. Houston County Ministerial Assn., 1966; gen. chmn. Greater Warner Robins, Billy Graham Evangelist Crusade, 1966; chmn. congl. support com. Presbytery Western Ky.-Union, 1974—, chmn., judicatory Support com., 1978-82; coordinating chmn. spl. events Key 73 Celebration, Ga. Council Chs., 1973; commr. Synod of Covenant, United Presbyn. Ch. in U.S.A., 1976-77, design team, 1981-84, adminstrv. cabinet, 1982-83, Tri-court negotiations chmn., 1983; v.p. Henderson County Ministeral Assn., 1976, pres., 1977 Staff counselor Houston County Alcoholic Problems Treatment Center, 1971-73; bd. dirs. Houston County chpt. ARC, 1971-73, Henderson County chpt. ARC, 1976—, chmn., 1980-83; bd. dirs.; chmn. ARC Tri-State Blood Adv. Council, 1980-81; adminstrv. cons. ARC Region 9, 1984—. chmn., adv. council, 1985; Houston County USO, 1969-73, Houston County Recreation Dept., 1968-73. Alumni fellow Columbia Theol. Sem., 1961. Mem. Am. Mgmt. Assn. Home: 2775 Heather Ln Henderson KY 42420 Office: PO Box 1016 Henderson KY 42420

RANEY, OWEN FRANKLIN, minister, Church of God, Anderson, Indiana; b. Wolf Bayou, Ark., Sept. 29, 1917; s. William Franklin and Bonnie (Davis) R.; m. Mildred Lavonia Anderson, Mar. 8, 1939; children: Paul, Lavonia, Michael, Pamela. Student, Anderson Coll., 1945, Ind. State Tchrs. Coll., 1949, S.W. Mo. State Coll., 1950, U. Mo.-Columbia, 1958. Ordained to ministry, Ch. of God, 1936. Evangelist, Ch. of God, 1932-39; pastor Ch. of God, Ill., 1939, 46, Mo., 1941-43, 51-81, Ind., 1947-49; supply pastor United Meth. Ch., Stoutland and Hazelgreen, Mo., 1983—. Author: How to Be Saved, 1953; Always in Grace, 1972; The New Testament Church, 1973. Editor: Christian Baptism, 1972. Chmn. Cancer Found., 1952. Mem. Mid-States Translators. Republican.

RANGE, WILLIAM HERMAN, minister, Am. Luth. Ch.; b. Detroit, Sept. 5, 1926; s. William Carl and Mamie (Young) R.; B.A., Capital U., 1947; B.D., Evang. Luth. Theol. Sem., 1952, M.Div., 1974; m. Jacqueline Ann Schroeder, June 21, 1952; children—William Carl, Jill Suzanne, Stephen David. Ordained to ministry, 1952; pastor Bethel Luth. Ch., St. Clair Shores, Mich., 1952—. Chmn. Detroit Met. Ministries Com., 1971-73; mem. dist. directing com. United Mission Appeal, 1974—; pres. Detroit Conf. Am. Luth. Ch., 1967-68; del. Am. Luth. Ch. Convs., 1962, 66, 70; pres. Wayne State U. Luth. Found., 1960-64; chmn. Mich. dist. Am. Missions Com., 1960-64. Regent, Capital U., Columbus, Ohio, 1960—; bd. dirs. Inter-Faith Center Racial Justice NE Detroit, 1970—; trustee St. Clair Shores Youth and Community Center, 1962-65; pres. Macomb County Mental Health Soc., 1968; dir. St. Clair Shores Adv. Bd. for Urban Renewal, 1963-65; mem. St. Clair Shores Community Edn. Adv. Bd., 1974—. Home: 26400 Little Mack St Clair Shores MI 48081

RANSOM, ROBERT LOUIS, minister, Missionary Church, Inc.; b. Jeffersonville, Ind., June 22, 1950; s. William Robert Ransom and Ruthanna (Moore) Ransom Dodd; m. Donna Evelyn Pottschmidt, Aug. 12, 1972; children: Matthew Robert, Sarah Elizabeth. B.A., Fort Wayne Bible Coll., 1972; M.Div., Asbury Theol. Sem., 1975. Ordained to ministry, Missionary Ch., 1977. Pastor First Missionary Ch., Bluffton, Ohio, 1975-79, Newson Missionary Ch., Saint Paris, Ohio, 1979-84; dir. Christian edn. ministries Mich. Dist. of Missionary Ch., Burton (Flint), Mich., 1984—, also mem. children's bd., youth bd., Christian edn. bd., bd. dirs. Missionary Men Internat.; rep. constl. commn. Missionary Ch., Fort Wayne, Ind., 1981—, dist. rep. ednl. ministries com., 1978—; dist. youth dir. East Central dist. Missionary Ch., Troy, Ohio, 1978-84; pres. Lima chpt. Nat. Assn. Evangs., Ohio, 1978-79; chmn., fundraiser Christian Rural Overseas Program, Bluffton, Ohio, 1977. Contbr. articles to profl. jours. Bd. dirs. Cystic-Fibrosis, Northwest Clark County, Ohio, 1981. State of Ind. scholar, 1968; Fort Wayne Bible Coll. Women's Aux. grantee, 1971. Mem. Kappa Kappa Kappa. Republican. Home and Office: 2183 Covert Rd Burton MI 48509

RANUM, PAUL ARTHUR, minister, religious organization executive; American Lutheran Church; b. Starbuck, Minn., Feb. 22, 1929; s. Arthur R. and Agnes C. (Kirkwold) R.; m. Sylvia H. Almlie, Sept. 7, 1956; children: Eric, Heidi, Gretchen, Ingrid. B.A., Luther Coll., 1952; C.Th., Luther Theol. Sem., 1956. Ordained to ministry, Am. Luth. Ch., 1956. Pastor Am. Luth. Ch., Newport, Wash., 1956-62, Our Saviour's Luth. Ch., Spirit Lake, Idaho, 1956-62, Our Savior Luth. Ch., Laurel, Mont., 1962-69, Bethesda-Our Savior's Parish, Alexandria and Nelson, Minn., 1969-79; dist. minister, asst. to bishop Southwest Minn. Dist. Am. Luth. Ch., Willmar, 1979—. Home: 2800 NW 12th Ave Willmar MN 56201 Office: Southwestern Minn Dist Am Luth Ch Box 773 Willmar MN 56201

RAO, KOLAR LAKSHMINARAYA SESHAGIRI, religious studies educator, Hinduism; b. Mulbagal, Mysore, Karnataka, India, Oct. 14, 1929; came to U.S., 1962; s. K. Lakshminarayana and Kamakshamma Rao; m. Saraswati S. Malati, May 20, 1954; children: Niranjan, Nandakumar, Santosh, Sudhir. B.A. with honors, U. Mysore, 1950, M.A., 1951; Ph.D., Harvard U., 1967. Lectr. philosophy Chhattisgarh Coll., Raipur, India, 1951-60; fellow Grand Peace Found., Delhi, India, 1960-62; Center for Study of World Religions Assoc. Harvard U., 1962-66; vis. lectr. U. Calif.-Santa Barbara, 1966-67; prof. comp. religion Punjahi U., Patiala, India, 1966-71; prof. religious studies U. Va., Charlottesville, 1971—; editor World Faiths Insight, Washington and London, 1966—; internat. cons. Gandhi Marg, Delhi, 1978—. Author: Gandhi and Andrews, 1969; The Concept of Sraddha, 1971; Mahatma Gandhi and Comparative Religion, 1978. Chmn. Internat. Students Com. U. Va., 1982—; mem. Indian Council of Cultural Relations, Delhi, 1968-71, Soc. of Asian and Camparative Philosophy Honolulu, Hawaii, 1971—; treas. Global Congress Worlds' Relegions, Washington, 1982—. Recipient Hall of Fame Anim award Internat. Parapsychology Assn., 1983, Nat. award for devel. of consciousness Coll. of Natural Laws, 1983. Mem. Internat. Soc. for Metaphysics, 4th World Council, World Union Internat. Ctr., World Religions Series (bd. editors New Delhi). Office: Univ Va Cocke Hall 103 Charlottesville VA 22903

RAPPS, DENNIS, Jewish organization executive. Exec. dir. Nat. Jewish Commn. on Law and Pub. Affairs. Office: Nat Jewish Commn on Law and Pub Affairs 71 Broadway 6th Fl New York NY 10006*

RASMUSSEN, A. W., secretary, Independent Assemblies of God, Internat. Address: 3840 5th Ave San Diego CA 92103

RASMUSSEN, CARL LAWRENCE MARLOE, minister, Evangelical Lutheran Church of Canada; b. Mpls., June 14, 1953; s. Bjarne Bent and Margaret Gotsche (Jensen) R.; m. Nancy Jeanette Feiertag, Aug. 5, 1978; 1 child, Andrew. B.A., Dana Coll., 1975; M.Div., Luther Theol. Sem., St. Paul, 1979. Ordained to ministry Luth. Ch., 1979. Pastor Hodgeville Luth. Parish, Sask., Can., 1979-82, Highwood Luth. Ch., Calgary, Alta., Can., 1982—; pres. Swift Current Conf., Evang. Luth. Ch. of Can., 1980-82; mem. planning com. Praise Throughout the Land, Winnepeg, Man., Can., 1981-82; sec.-treas. Hodgeville Inter-Ch. Refugee Com., 1980-82; mem. Nat. Worship Com., Saskatoon, Sask., 1982—; mem. planning com. all city worship and hymn festival, Luther's 500th Birthday, Calgary, 1983. Office: Highwood Luth Ch 419 Northmount Dr NW Calgary AB T2K 3H7 Canada

RASMUSSEN, KEITH MARTIN, music educator; minister of music, Seventh-day Adventist; b. Janesville, Wis., Oct. 15, 1953; s. Sherrill Keer and Alice May (Herwick) R.; m. Kathy Fay Pound, June 18, 1978; children: Joanne Marie, Janelle Aileen. B.Mus., Andrews U., 1977, M.Mus., 1978; student Eastman Sch. Music, 1984—. Tchr. piano, organ, harpsichord Kingsway Coll., Oshawa, Ont., 1978—; organist, Keyboard coordinator College Park Seventh-day Adventist Ch., Oshawa, 1978—; minister of music Simcoe St. United Ch., Oshawa, 1984—; organ recitalist Ont., U.S.A.; dir. organ workshops, Ont.; organ cons., Ont. Mem. Royal Canadian Coll. Organists (sec. of center 1982—). Progressive Conservative. Home: 1156 King St E Unit 71 Oshawa ON L1H 7M6 Canada

RATCHFORD, WILLIAM CLIFTON, SR., minister, Church of God. B. Big Springs, Tex., Aug. 23, 1934; s. Benjamin Arthur and Myrtle Lena (Ruff) R.; m. Monte Laverne Gray, July 20, 1952; children: William Clifton, David Arthur. Student Southwestern Coll., Oklahoma City, 1974-77. Ordained in ministry Church of God, 1964. Pastor, Ch. of God, Petrolia, Tex., 1958-59, Olney, Tex., 1959-62, Amarillo, Tex., 1962-67, Mesquite, Tex., 1967-68, Hurst, Tex., 1968-70, state supt., State of Nebr., 1970-76, State of Miss., 1978-80, State of Va., 1980-82, asst. gen. dir. evangelism and home missions, Cleveland, Tenn., 1980—; bd. dirs. Northwest Bible Coll., Minot, N.D., 1972-74; prin. speaker 48 state convs. and confs. Home: PO Box 4435 Cleveland TN 37311 Office: Church of God Gen Offices Keith at 25th St NW Cleveland TN 37311

RATCLIFF, DONALD EARL, minister, religious educator, Christian Nation Ch.; b. Pomeroy, Ohio, Apr. 6, 1951; s. Clarence Earl and Lois Anna (Harris) R.; m. Brenda Sue Campbell, Dec. 16, 1978; children: John Wesley, Stephen Earl. B.A., Spring Arbor Coll., 1973; M.A., Mich. State U., 1975; postgrad., U. Ga., 1984—. Ordained to ministry Christian Nation Ch., 1978; Asst.

prof. Circleville Bible Coll., 1975-78; tchr., adminstr., dean of men Christian Union Bible Sch., Roseau, Dominica, W.I., 1978-79; dir. Christian edn. Vinton Bapt. Ch., Ohio, 1981-82; interim pastor Mt. Pleasant Bapt. Ch., Toccoa, Ga., 1983-84; asst. prof. Toccoa Falls Coll., Ga., 1982—. Contbr. articles to profl. jours. Mem. Right to Life Orgn. Mem. Christian Assn. Psychol. Studies (com. to rev. manuscripts 1977), Am. Sci. Affiliation. Republican. Office: Toccoa Falls Coll PO Box 800207 Toccoa Falls GA 30598

RATCLIFF, JOE HUGH, minister, Southern Baptist Convention; b. Baton Rouge, La., Dec. 7, 1940; s. Elious Virgil and Annabel Cairie (Tanner) R.; m. Carol Ann Brock, June 22, 1962; children: Pamela, Bryan, Rebecca, Brock. B.A., Miss. Coll., 1962; B.Div., New Orleans Bapt. Theol. Sem., 1965, M.R.E., 1966, Th.M., 1969. Ordained to ministry Bapt. Ch., 1960. Pastor Pine Bapt. Ch., Carthage, Miss., 1959-65, Salem Bapt. Ch., Raymond, Miss., 1965-70, Foster Rd. Bapt. Ch., Baton Rouge, 1970-72, North McComb Bapt. Ch., Miss., 1972-80, First Bapt. Ch., Many, La., 1980—; trustee La. Bapt. Conv., Alexandria, 1982—; trustee Miss. Bapt. Found., Jackson, 1978-80; clk. Pike County Bapt. Assn., McComb, 1974-80. Pres. Pike County Council on Disabled Adults, McComb, 1978-79; mem. Sabine Parish Mental Health, Many, 1982-84. Mem. Sabine Parish C. of C. Lodge: Lions. Office: First Bapt Ch PO Box 239 Many LA 71449

RATINI, MARGARET, religion educator, Roman Catholic Church; b. Newton Falls, Ohio, June 29, 1931; d. Rudolph and Julia (Trenka) Wiczen; m. Joseph Ratini, Mar. 17, 1962 (div. 1971); children: Brenda Susan, Jeffrey Joel. Student pub. schs., Newton Falls. Confraternity Christian Doctrine tchr. St. Robert's Ch., Cortland, Ohio, 1977—. Home: 5695 St Route 45 Bristolville OH 44402

RATLEDGE, WILBERT HAROLD, JR., Bible college dean; b. Atlanta, May 2, 1940; s. Wilbert Harold and Nora Mae (Coleman) R.; m. Helen Marie Siemens, Aug. 1965; children: Philip, Rebekah. B.A., Tenn. Temple Coll., 1962; Th.M., Dallas Theol. Sem., 1966; M.A., North Tex. State U., 1970, Ph.D., 1982. Ordained to ministry, 1964. Pastor, Cunningham Bapt. Ch., Tex., 1964-67; instr. Dallas Bible Coll., 1966-67; tchr. Bamboo River Acad., West Borneo, Indonesia, 1967-68; athletic dir., dir. admissions, registrar Dallas Bible Coll., 1968-78, dean acad. affairs, 1978—; dir. children's worship First Bapt. Ch. Urbandale, Dallas, 1975-78; lectr. in field. Editor Tenn. Temple Times, 1960-61. Mem. Evang. Theol. Soc., Soc. Christian Philosophers, Am. Assn. Bible Colls. (presiding dean acad. conf. western region 1984), Phi Alpha Theta. Clubs: DBC Chess (sponsor). Office: Dallas Bible Coll 8733 La Prada Dallas TX 72228

RATZLAFF, RUBEN MENNO, educator, minister, Christian Church/Churches of Christ; b. Burrton, Kans., Jan. 8, 1917; s. Henry and Julia (Foth) R.; m. Frances Irene King, Sept. 7, 1941; children: Keith Lowell, Paul Dennis, Mark Henry, Loren Lee. B.A., Johnson Bible Coll., 1940; B.D., Butler U., 1955, M.A., 1959. Ordained to ministry, 1938. Minister, Pleasant Hill Christian Ch., Hall, Ind., 1948-50, Christian Ch., Clermont, Ind., 1950-55, Kennard, Ind., 1955-59; prof. San Jose Bible Coll., Calif., 1959—; vis. prof. Springdale Coll., Birmingham, Eng., 1985. Author: Ezra Nehemiah, 1982. Contbr. articles to profl. jours. Recipient Hebrew award, Hebrew Synagogue, Indpls., 1950. Mem. Theta Phi. Republican. Home: 1567 Willowdale Dr San Jose CA 95118 Office: San Jose Bible Coll 790 S 12th St San Jose CA 95112

RAUDSEPP, KARL, bishop, Estonian Evangelical Lutheran Church; b. Puurmanni, Estonia, Mar. 26, 1908; s. Jaan and Liisa (Gruner) R.; came to Canada, 1948, naturalized, 1950; cand. theol. U.Tartu (Estonia), 1933; m. Ellen Feldmann, July 20, 1935; 4 children. Ordained to ministry, 1933, became dean, 1958, bishop, 1976; pastor St. Michael Ch., Vändra, Estonia, refugee camps, W. Ger.; pastor Luth. World Fedn. Service to Refugees, St. John's Estonian Ch., Montreal, Que., Can. Author: Marked by Cross, 1982; author 3 edits. of sermons in Estonian. Office: PO Box 291 Jordan Station ON L0R 1S0 Canada

RAUFF, EDWARD ALLEN, minister, Lutheran Church - Missouri Synod; b. N.Y.C., July 19, 1929; s. Edward and Olga (Keene) R.; m. Elaine Carol Schacht, June 16, 1956 (div. Sept. 1982); children: Pauline, David, Dawn, Kathryn, Mark, Caitlin; m. Naomi Kathryn Gutheil, Apr. 9, 1983. B.A., Concordia Sem., St. Louis, 1956, M.Div., 1956; M.A., Columbia U., 1958. Ordained to ministry Luth. Ch., 1956. Pastor Gethsemane Luth. Ch., Columbus, Ohio, 1956-62, St. John Luth. Ch., Detroit, 1962-67, Emanuel Luth. Ch., Patchogue, N.Y., 1967-70; adminstr. Luth. Council U.S.A., N.Y.C., 1970-80; exec. dir. Southeast Luth. High Sch., Los Angeles, 1981-84; pastor Christ Luth. Ch., Burbank, Calif., 1984—; pres. Census Access for Planning in the Ch., 1975-77. Co-author: Lutheran Church Statistics, 1975; author: Why People Join the Church, 1979. Mem. Religious Research Assn. (treas. 1977-79). Home: 7962 5th St Downey CA 90241 Office: Christ Luth Church 2400 W Burbank CA 91506

RAUSCH, THOMAS PETER, priest, theology educator, administrator, Roman Catholic Church; b. Chgo., Feb. 12, 1941; s. Charles Joseph and Imelda Clair (Claffy) R. M.A. in Philosophy, Gonzaga U., 1967; S.T.M., Jesuit Sch. Theology, 1972; Ph.D. in Religion, Duke U., 1976. Ordained priest Roman Cath. Ch., 1972. Assoc. prof. theology Loyola Marymount U., Los Angeles, 1976—, dir. campus ministry, 1981—. Contbr. articles to religious jours. Trustee U. San Francisco, 1980-83. Mem. Cath. Theol. Soc. Am. Democrat. Address: Loyola Marymount U Los Angeles CA 90045

RAWLS, HENRY CLAY MICHAEL JOHN, priest, Roman Catholic Church; b. Newark, Dec. 3, 1949; s. Ruth Elaine Mills; B.A. in Classical Langs., Seton Hall U., 1971; M.A. candidate for Dogmatic Theology, Darlington Sch. Theology; M.F.A. candidate for Music, Julliard Sch. Music. Ordained deacon, 1974, priest, 1975; sec. student council, choir dir. Darlington Sem., 1969-74; deacon St. Vincent de Paul Ch., Bayonne, N.J., 1974-75; curate Our Lady Star of the Sea, Bayonne, 1975-83; pastor Holy Spirit and Our Lady Help of Christians' Ch., East Orange, N.J., 1983—. Team mem. N.J. Marriage Encounter. Mem. N.J. Schola Cantorum, 1964—, N.J. Allstate Chorus, 1966. Mem. adv. editorial bd. Diocesan Newspaper of Newark. Home: 1380 Bellview Ct Plainfield NJ 07060 Office: 326 Ave C Bayonne NJ 07002

RAY, LEXIE B., minister, Church of Christ; b. Lynnville, Ky., Sept. 19, 1932; s. Onyx B. and Ola Jane (Seay) R.; m. Zann Patton, July 19, 1953; children: Karyn, Latetia. A.A., Freed-Hardeman Coll., 1951; B.S., Murray State U., 1953. Named to ministry Church of Christ, 1950. Minister Ch. of Christ, Apopka, Fla., 1954-56, Arlington Ch. of Christ, Jacksonville, Fla., 1956-59, Exchange St. Ch. of Christ, Union City, Tenn., 1961-69, Ch. of Christ, Poole, Ky., 1959-61, Ch. of Christ, Kingston, Ky., 1969-84; Franklin Ch. of Christ, Ky., 1984—. chaplain Roane County High Sch. Band, Kingston, 1971-78. Named Outstanding Young Man of Yr., Union City Kiwanis, 1967, 68, 69, hon. life mem. Tenn. Congress of PTAs, 1967. Republican. Home: 615 S College St Franklin KY 42134 Office: Franklin Ch of Christ 700 S Main St Franklin KY 42134

RAYBORN, TALMADGE MADISON, minister, So. Baptist Conv.; b. Sumrall, Miss., Aug. 22, 1921; s. Billey Gray and Ora Mae (Barr) R.; B.S., Miss. State U., 1949; m. Rena Jean Templeton, Oct. 10, 1946; children—Brenda Gail, Kenneth Wayne, Sandra Kay. Vice pres. Miss. Bapt. Layman, 1964-65; lay pastor 6 chs., 1965-66; trustee Miss. Bapt. Children's Village, 1964—; Sunday sch. tchr., tng. union leader, Geidion, deacon various chs., 1949-76; ordained to ministry, 1976; pastor 1st Bapt. Ch., Pass Christian, Miss., 1973—. Instr., Miss. State U., 1947-49. Mem. Miss. Econ. Council, Miss. C. of C. (dir.), So., Miss. indsl. devel. councils, Regional Export Expansion Council. Home: 102 Whispering Pines Waveland MS 39576 Office: 322 2d St Pass Christian MS 39571

RAYBURN, STEPHEN EARL, minister, So. Bapt. Conv.; b. Panama City, Fla., Nov. 27, 1947; s. Henry Louis and Doris June (Rogers) R.; A.A., Gulf Coast Community Coll., 1967; M.A., Miss. Coll., 1969; M.Div., So. Bapt. Theol. Sem., 1974, D.Min., 1977; m. Patsy Ruth Harrell, Aug. 1, 1970; children—Christopher Louis, Jennifer June. Ordained to ministry, 1971; minister of edn. Parkway Bapt. Ch., Jackson, Miss., 1968-69; pastor Walnut St. Bapt. Ch., Louisville, 1970-71; minister of edn. and youth East Hill Bapt. Ch., Tallahassee, Fla., 1971; asso. pastor Hazelwood Bapt. Ch., Louisville, 1972-73, pastor, 1973-76; chaplain Norton Children's Hosp., Louisville, 1974; asso. pastor East Hill Bapt. Ch., Tallahassee, 1974—. Mem. student ministry com. Fla. State U., Tallahassee, 1974-77; mem. religious edn. com. Fla. Bapt. Assn., 1974-76. Mem. Assn. for Clin. Pastoral Edn., Am. Assn. Pastoral Counselors. Home: 1933 Lawson St Tallahassee FL 32303 Office: 912 Miccosukee Rd Tallahassee FL 32303

RAYNOR, JOHN PATRICK, priest, univ. pres., Roman Catholic Ch.; b. Omaha, Oct. 1, 1923; s. Walter V. and Mary Clare (May) R.; A.B., St. Louis U., 1947, M.A., 1948; Ph.D., U. Chgo., 1959; LL.D., Cardinal Stritch Coll., 1973. Ordained priest Roman Catholic Ch., 1954; instr. St. Louis U. High Sch., 1948-51, asst. to prin., 1951; asst. to dean Coll. Liberal Arts, Marquette U., 1951-61, asst. to v.p. for acad. affairs, 1961-62, v.p. acad. affairs, 1962-65, pres., 1965—. Dir. Kimberly-Clark Corp. Treas. steering, exec. coms. Edn. Commn. of the States, 1972—; state chmn. NCCJ, 1972-74; mem. Greater Milw. Com., 1967—; corp. mem. Wis. Regional Med. Program, 1967—; mem. Citizens Govtl. Research Bur., Wis. Higher Ednl. Aids Bd.; corporate mem., chmn. edn. div. United Way Greater Milw.; sponsor United Negro Coll. Fund. Hon. bd. dirs. Goethe House. Recipient Distinguished Community Service award Allied Constrn. Employers Assn., 1973; Headliner of Year award Milw. Press Club, 1974; Human Relations award NCCJ, 1975. Mem. Assn. Jesuit Colls. and Univs. (chmn. bd. dirs.), Wis. Assn. Ind. Colls. and Univs. (past pres., exec. com.), Wis. Found. Ind. Colls. (pres. 1970-72), Nat. Catholic Edn. Assn. (bishops and presidents com.), Am. Council Edn. (dir. Greater Milw. com.), North Central Assn. Colls. and Secondary Schs. (cons., examiner), Newcomen Soc. N. Am., Internat. Fedn. Catholic Univs., Phi Beta Kappa, Phi Delta Kappa, Alpha Sigma Nu. Address: 615 N 11th St Milwaukee WI 53233

READ, ALLAN ALEXANDER, bishop, Anglican Church; b. Toronto, Ont., Canada, Sept. 19, 1923; s. Alex P. and Lillice Marie (Matthews) R.; m. Mary Beverly Sophia Roberts, Sept. 28, 1949; children: John, Elizabeth, Michael, Martha. B.A., U. Toronto, 1945; L.Th., Trinity Coll., 1948, D.D. (hon.), 1972; D.D., Wycliffe Coll., 1972; S.T.D., Thornloe Coll., 1982. Ordained deacon Anglican Ch., 1948, priest, 1949, bishop, 1972. Incumbent Mono, Toronto, 1947-54; priest Barrie Ch., Toronto, 1954-71; archdeacon of Simcoe, Diocese of Toronto, 1961-72; suffragan bishop of Toronto, 1972-81, bishop, 1981—; bd. dirs. Anglican Found. Author: Shepherds in Green Pastures, 1952. Mem. Simcoe County Sch. Bd., 1958-66. Recipient Rural Worker's Fellowship award N. Am., 1952; named Citizen of Yr., City of Barrie, 1957. Mem. Can. Churchman (bd. dirs.), Rural Workers' Fellowship (hon. pres.). Home: Rural Route 1 Kingston ON K7L 4V1 Canada Office: Diocese of Ontario 90 Johnson St Kingston ON K7L 1X7 Canada

READ, DAVID HAXTON CARSWELL See *Who's Who in America*, 43rd edition.

READ, HERBERT GARFIELD, minister, Christian Churches and Churches of Christ; b. Troy, N.Y., Oct. 3, 1918; s. Herbert Garfield and Agnes (Fileau) R.; student Pacific Christian Coll., 1957-60; m. Thelma Mildred Candee, Oct. 29, 1938; children—Miriam Edna Read, Cheryl Lee Read Colombero, H. Richard. Ordained to ministry, 1962; rep. Keister Ad Church Service, N.Y. and Calif., 1954-59; minister Westminster Ch. of Christ, 1961-62, Milwaukie Ch. of Christ, Oreg., 1963-67; coll. career minister, minister of evangelism 1st Christian Ch., Long Beach, Calif., 1967-68; mng. dir. Boys Clubs of Long Beach, 1968-70; minister Lawndale Ch. of Christ, Lawndale, Calif., 1970—. Bd. dirs. Assn. Coll. Advisors for Project Challenge; group leader Continental Congress on the Family, St. Louis, 1975; dir. coll.-career camp Angeles Crest Christian Camp; pres. Milwaukie Ministerial Assn., 1965; internship supr. students Pacific Christian Coll., 1975-76; v.p. Los Angeles County Protestant Com. on Scouting, 1976; chaplain Bus. and Profl. Women, 1961; police chaplain City of Hawthorne, Calif., 1981—; Los Angeles county rep. Centenela Valley Juvenile Delinquency Project. Mem. Hawthorne-Lawndale Ministerial Assn. (pres. 1980—). Home: 4106 W 177th St Torrance CA 90504 Office: 4234 W 147th St Lawndale CA 90260

READY, GLENNA ELTHA, practitioner, Ch. of Christ Scientist; b. Umpire, Ark., July 23, 1899; d. Ruben Franklin and Amanda Lucinda (Gober) Jackson; student U. Okla., 1938-39, S.W. Jr. Coll., 1976; m. Ewing Howard Ready, June 28, 1918; 1 dau., Wilma Jean Ready Ward. Became practitioner, 1952; charter mem. Christian Sci. Soc., Dalhart, Tex., 1935-36; services in home, Hollis, Okla., 1937-38, also Keeper reading room, asst. reader; usher, Keeper reading room 2d Ch., San Antonio, 1969-70. Recipient letter of recognition 1st Ch. of Christ Scientist, Boston, 1971. Home: 206 East Eula St Hollis OK 73550

REBOL, ANTHONY, priest, Roman Catholic Church; b. Smartno, Yugoslavia, Feb. 28, 1928; came to U.S., 1939, naturalized, 1948; s. Frank and Frances (Sustar) R. B.A., John Carroll U., 1962, M.A. in Counseling, 1964; M.A. in Sociology, Cath. U., 1969. Ordained priest Roman Cath. Ch., 1956. Assoc. pastor various chs., Ohio, 1956-67; pastor St. Lawrence Ch., Cleve., 1979—; dir. family life Diocese of Cleve., 1979—, marriage and family counselor, 1969—; bd. dirs. Fedn. Cath. Community Service, 1974. Co-author: Cleveland Diocese Evaluation for Marriage, 1979. Recipient Recognition award Fedn. Cath. Community Service, 1979. Address: St Lawrence's Ch 3547 E 80th St Cleveland OH 44105

RECACHINAS, DEMETRIOS ANASTASIOS, Greek Orthodox Archdiocese of North and South America; b. Kafkada, Greece, Jan. 11, 1949; s. Anastasios and Katerina (Arvanitis) R.; came to U.S., 1966, naturalized, 1977; m. Eleftheria Bakiris, Jan. 2, 1977; children: Anastasios, Katerina-Despina. B.A., Hellenic Coll., 1972; M.Div., Holy Cross Coll., 1975; Th.M., Princeton U., 1976; Ph.D. candidate Catholic U., 1977. Ordained priest Greek Orthodox Ch., 1977. Lay asst. Sts. Constantine and Helen Ch., Washington, 1975-77, asst. pastor, 1977-83; pastor Holy Trinity Greek Orthodox Ch., Bridgeport, Conn., 1983—. Research bd. White House Conf. Ethnic Groups, Washington, 1977-83. Mem. NCCJ (exec. bd. dirs. 1977-83). Home: 130 Brookfield Ave Fairfield CT 06430 Office: Holy Trinity Greek Orthodox Ch 4070 Park Ave Bridgeport CT 06604

REDAL, RUEBEN HERBERT, minister, World Confessional Lutheran Association; b. Souris, N.D., Nov. 7, 1920; s. Jacob Lars and Caroline (Aasen) R.; B.A., St. Olaf Coll., 1942; B.Th. (M.Div.), Luther Theol. Sem., 1945; D.D., Linda Vista Bible Coll. and Sem., 1974; H.H.D., Pierson Meml. Bibl. Sem., Seoul, Korea; m. Violet Eleanor Sillerud, Sept. 12, 1943;

children—Karen, Mark, Paul, John. Ordained to ministry, 1945; pastor chs. Iowa, 1945-52, Central Luth. Ch., Tacoma, 1952—. Pres., Luths. Alert Nat.; bd. dirs. Teen Life Internat.; pres. Faith Evang. Luth. Sem., Tacoma. Home: 425 Tacoma Ave N Tacoma WA 98403 Office: 409 Tacoma Ave N Tacoma WA 98403

REDARD, RODMAN DORIAN, minister, Southern Baptist Convention; b. Chambersburg, Pa., May 28, 1941; s. Dorian Ruben and Margaret Louise (Overcash) R.; B.A., Wayland Bapt. Coll., 1973; m. Dorothy Lynn Caldwell, June 25, 1962; children—Robert Daniel, Christopher Jon, Laura Joelle, Andrew Caleb. Ordained to ministry, 1973; pastor Dickens (Tex.) Bapt. Ch., 1973-75, Oak Grove Bapt. Ch., Nacogdoches, Tex., 1976-77; pastor Rayburn Drive Bapt. Ch., Nacogdoches, 1978-79, New Faith Bapt. Ch., Nacogdoches, 1979-80. Tchr. English, Patton Springs Sch., Afton, Tex., 1974-75; tchr. govt. and history Broaddus (Tex.) High Sch., 1975-78; tchr. Central Heights High Sch., Nacogdoches, 1978-80. Mem. Nacogdoches Ministerial Alliance, Tex. State Tchrs. Assn. (v.p. Broaddus High Sch. chpt. 1976—), NEA. Home: 604 Burk St Rd Nacogdoches TX 75961

REDDINGTON, FRED JAMES, minister, Evangelical Church Alliance; b. Honolulu, Feb. 26, 1928; s. Herbert Benjamin and Barbara Caroline (Bailey) R.; m. Joanne Marilyn Reddington, June 22, 1951; children: Ruth, Tim, Mark, Joh. Ordained to ministry Evang. Ch. Alliance, 1952; registered healthologist. Missionary, United World Missions, 1956-64; missionary Assn. for World Evangelism, 1964-70, dir., Portland, Oreg., 1970—; chaplain CAP, Portland, 1967—. Pres. Trans-World Distbrs., Portland, 1969—. Area chmn. Neighborhood Assn. Portland, 1984—; precinct committeeman, Portland, 1974—. Served to lt. col. USAF Aux., 1968—. Mem. Oreg. Assn. Family Counselors, Cert. Bus. Counselors, Washington County Sheriff's Res. Lodge: Kiwanis. Office: 4521 SE 52d Ave Portland OR 97206

REDEKOP, DAVID EDWARD, minister, Mennonite Brethren Churches, General Conference of Mennonite Church; electric company executive; b. Kronstal, Ukraine, Russia, Nov. 5, 1917; came to Can., 1923, naturalized, 1930; s. Henry and Susanna (Froese) R.; m. Katie Hiebert, Feb. 28, 1942 (dec. July 1971); children: David, Kathy, Charlotte, Marlene, Edward; m. Anne Hiebert Pauls, Dec. 31, 1972. Student, Winkler Bible Inst., Man., Can., 1937-41. Elected minister Mennonite Brethren Ch., 1970. Sunday sch. supt. Portage Ave. Mennonite Brethren Ch., 1948-72, moderator, 1972-84. Pres. Redekop Electric Co., Ltd., Winnipeg, Man., 1945—; chmn. Belnor Electric, 1980—; pres. Redekop Enterprises, Ltd., 1984—. Chmn. Christian Bus. Men (editor manual, newsgram, pamphlets 1976-81), Winnipeg, 1973-76; exec. dir. Christian Bus. Men of Can., 1976-81; chmn. Christian Bus. Men Internat., 1977-81. Moderator Can. Mennonite Brethren Conf., 1980-83; pres. Camp Arnes, Manitoba, 1950-53. Mem. Elec. Contractors Assn., Winnipeg C. of C. (chmn. employer-employee relations), Mennonite Central Com. (bd. dirs. 1980), Winnipeg Constrn. Assn. Office: Redekop Electric Co Ltd 966 Portage Ave Winnipeg MB R3G 0R3 Canada

REDENBACH, SIEGMUND HENRY, minister, Lutheran Church-Missouri Synod; b. Oakshella, Sask., Can., Mar. 13, 1936; s. Philip and Sophia (Sander) R.; B.A., U.B.C., 1969; B.D., Concordia Theol. Sem., 1970; m. Shireen Stella Saggau, June 8, 1966; children—Ann Marie, Nancy Kay, John Michael. Ordained to ministry, 1970; pastor Our Saviour Luth. Ch., Chatham, Ont., Can., 1970-72, Mt. Calvary Luth. Ch., New Westminster, B.C., 1972—. Sec. pastoral conf. Synod of Evang. Luth. Chs., 1971; pastoral counselor Fraser Valley Zone, Luth. Laymen's League, 1973-75; sec. Alta.-B.C. Dist. Evangelism Dept., 1974-78; pastoral counselor Vancouver Zone, Luth. Women's Missionary League, 1974-75; circuit pastoral counselor Vancouver Circuit, Luth. Ch.-Mo. Synod, 1975—; del., mem. floor com. on constl. matters Luth. Ch.-Mo. Synod Conv., Anaheim, Calif., 1975; organizer Luth. Camp Concordia Soc., 1974. Trustee New Westminster Sch. Bd., 1978-83, chmn., 1979; chmn. steering com. for Luth. Schs., 1984. Mem. Luth. Camp Concordia Soc. Contbr. articles in field to profl. jours. Home: 701 6th St New Westminster BC V3L 3C6 Canada

REDFORD, FRANCIS JACKSON, minister, Southern Baptist Convention; b. Memphis, Oct. 22, 1922; s. Addison Franklin and Addie Myrtle (Lang) R.; m. Mildred Gertrude Evans, Dec. 18, 1946; children—Kenneth, Charlotte, William, Rita. A.A., Decatur Bapt. Coll., 1942; B.A., Howard Payne U., 1947; postgrad., Hardin-Simmons U., 1947,49,50; D.D. (hon.), Linda Vista Coll., 1974. Ordained to ministry Southern Baptist Conv., 1946. Pastor various chs., Ark., Tex., La., Colo., Ind., 1948-60; dir. missions Bapts. in Ind. Indpls., 1960-67; assoc. dir. Pioneer Missions, Bapt. Home Mission Bd., Atlanta, 1967-70, dir. ch. extension div., 1971—; adj. prof. Southeastern Bapt. Sem., Wake Forest, N.C., 1972, Southwestern Bapt. Sem., Fort Worth, summers 1973,77, 80, 82, 84, Midwestern Bapt. Sem., Kansas City, Mo., fall 1975, Golden Gate Bapt. Sem., Mill Valley, Calif., 1979, 83, 85. Author: Planting New Churches, 1979. Served to maj. U.S. Army,

1943-45,53-57,58-60. Recipient Disting. Alumni award Howard Payne U. 1977. Avocation: reading. Office: Bapt Home Mission Bd 1350 Spring St NW Atlanta GA 30367

REDHEFFER, KENNETH WILLIAM, SR., church musician, Lutheran Church in America; postal agency administrator; b. Woodbury, N.J., Nov. 19, 1935; s. Samuel Fredly and Myrtle Reece (Ellis) Simkins; m. Beatrice Foster, Mar. 9, 1956 (dec. 1969); children: Kenneth, Jr., Barbara Anne, Kevin Thomas, Bruce David; m. Esther Tann, Feb. 14, 1970; 1 stepdau.: Joyce Esther Redheffer Walters. B.A., Glassboro Coll., 1975. Cert. lay profl. musician Lutheran Church in America. Dir. music St. Stephen's Luth Ch., Woodbury, N.J., 1961-70, sec. ch. council, 1961-67; dir. music Luther Meml. Ch., Blackwood, N.J., 1970-80, Trinity Luth. Ch., Roanoke, Va., 1980-83; minister music St. Paul's Luth Ch., Roanoke, 1983—; music coordinator Lutherans Combined, Roanoke, 1982—; mem. local com. Luth. Music Inst., Phila., 1982; del. Worship-Witness program, Mpls., 1983. Various positions United States Postal Service, Roanoke, 1959—, mgr. Postal Employee Devel. Ctr., 1982—. Pres. PTA Westville, N.J., 1963-64. Recipient Cert. of Appreciation, U.S. Postal Service, 1984. Mem. Luth. Liturgical Renewal, Nat. Assn. Pastoral Musicians, NAPS Postal Suprs. Assn. (v.p. 1983). Republican. Home: 933 Anchor Dr NW Roanoke VA 24012-1101 Office: PEDC Postal Service 419 Rutherford Ave Roanoke VA 24022-9402

REDINGTON, PATRICK EDWARD, educator, Roman Catholic Church; b. Galesburg, Ill., Sept. 30, 1946; s. Edward Patrick and Aileen (Lee) R.; m. Deirdre Eileen Aukward, Aug. 19, 1972; children: Maura Eileen, Edward Patrick. B.A. in History cum laude, Loras Coll., 1969; M.A. in Religious Edn., Cath. U. Am., 1972. Grad. teaching asst. Cath. U. Am., Washington, 1971; dir. religious edn. St. Clement Parish, Balt., 1972-74; tchr. Good Counsel High Sch., Wheaton, Md., 1974-81; dir. religious edn. St. Malachy Parish, Geneseo, Ill., 1981—; mem. religion curriculum com. Peoria Diocese, 1982-83; coordinator Geneseo Christian Rural Overseas Program. Author: Catholics in America, 1979; Our Church History, 1980; also articles. Mem. congl. intern selection com. Md. 8th Congl. Dist., 1978. Mem. Religious Edn. Assn., Nat. Cath. Edn. Assn., Ill. Parish Coordinators and Dirs. Religious Edn., Christian Peace Fellowship. Democrat. Home: 412 S State St Geneseo IL 61254 Office: St Malachy Ch 217 N Russell Ave Geneseo IL 61254

REDMAN, DAVID, minister, American Lutheran Church; b. Waupun, Wis., Feb. 26, 1933; s. Albert and Laura (Wruck) R.; B.A., Wartburg Coll., 1955; B.D., Wartburg Sem., 1959; student clin. pastoral edn. Luth. Social Services, Milw., 1973; m. Lucille Hoge, June 5, 1954; children—Susan, Barbara, William. Ordained to ministry, 1959; minister chs. Iowa, 1959-61, South Wayne, Wis., 1961-63, Trinity Luth. Ch., Cedarburg, Wis., 1963-84, St. Paul Luth. Ch., Mayville, Wis., 1984—. Dir. Lutherdale Bible Camp, 1962-63; So. Wis. Dist. del. Am. Luth. Ch. Conv., 1962, 64; mem. council So. Wis. Dist., 1972-73, 79-84, chmn. Fond du Lac Conf. stewardship com., 1967-72, pres. Conf., 1972-73; chmn. Lakeshore Conf., 1980-84. pres. Wis. Dist. Luther League, 1952-56; mem. Nat. Stewardship Conf., Chgo., 1968; chaplain Cedarburg Common Council, 1964-73; chmn. Cedarburg Clergy Assn., 1974-83, Fond du Lac Conf. Pastoral Assn., 1973; coordinator Lasata Home Pastoral Assn., 1974-84. Contbr. articles to Luth. Standard. Address: 4 S Walnut St Mayville WI 53050

REDMOND, DONALD EDWARD, minister, Ch. of the Nazarene; b. Delta, Colo., Aug. 10, 1933; s. George Miller and Cleta Mignon (Shannon) R.; A.B., Pasadena Coll., 1955, M.A., 1957; postgrad. So. Calif. Sch. Religion, 1962-64; m. Jimmie Lee Blanchette, Apr. 15, 1956; children—Sherry, Steven, Scott, Shawn. Ordained to ministry, 1958; pastor Ch. of the Nazarene, Lake Elsinore, Calif., 1958-60, Indio, Calif., 1960-68, Anaheim, Calif., 1968-70, LaHabra, Calif., 1970-76, El Cajon, Calif., 1976—; chaplain El Cajon Valley Hosp., 1976—. Chmn. Council of Chs., Desert Zone, Indio, 1961-63; pres. Indio Ministerial Assn., 1963-65; bd. dirs. Indio Community Hosp., 1962-64, chaplain, 1962-68; mem. bd. orders and relations So. Calif. Dist., Ch. of the Nazarene, 1975—, mem. bd. ministerial studies, 1975. Mem. adv. bd. W.D. Hall Elementary Sch., El Cajon, 1976—, Pop Warner and Little League Softball, El Cajon, 1976—. Mem. E. County Mental Health Assn., San Diego Evang. Assn., Pasadena Coll. Alumni Assn. Editor So. Californian, 1960—; contbr. articles to religious jours. Home: 1804 Jasmine St El Cajon CA 92021 Office: 1123 N Mollison Ave El Cajon CA 92021

REECE, ROBERT DENTON, religion educator, Presbyterian Church in the U.S.A.; b. Bonham, Tex., Oct. 25, 1939; s. Clovis D. and Bonnie (Hyatt) R.; m. Donna Jayne Walters, June 5, 1965; children: Gwendolyn, Gregory, David, Emily. B.A., Baylor U., 1961; B.D., So. Bapt. Theol. Sem., 1964; Ph.D., Yale U., 1969. Asst. to assoc. prof. dept. religion Wright State U., Dayton, Ohio, 1969—, assoc. prof., chmn. dept. medicine in soc., 1975—. Contbr. articles to profl. jours.

Mem. Am. Acad. Religion (convener of med. ethics cons.), Soc. Health and Human Values (chmn. program dirs. group), Soc. for Values in Higher Edn., Soc. Christian Ethics. Home: 333 Volusia Ave Dayton OH 45409 Office: Wright State U Sch Medicine PO Box 927 Dayton OH 45401

REED, CARLYNN LEAH, family life minister, Episcopal Church; b. Montreal, Que., Can., Nov. 28, 1944; came to U.S., 1965; d. Arthur Joseph and Leah Eleanor (Lyons) Roy; m. David Arthur Reed, July 10, 1965; children: Kirkland Dow, Christopher Clark. B.A., Barrington Coll., 1968; M.A., Brown U., 1969. Program coordinator Episcopal Social Service, Bridgeport, Conn., 1980—; dir. Timbrel & Dance, Shelton, Conn., 1974-78; dir. Ch. St. Players, Shelton, 1980-84, playwright, 1978—; playwright Episcopal Social Services, Bridgeport. Author: And We Have Danced, 1978; (play) The Family, 1980. Recipient ann. award Bible and theology dept. Barrington Coll., 1967. Mem. Sacred Dance Guild (pres. 1979-82). Home: 25 Church St Shelton CT 06484 Office: Episcopal Social Service 1067 Park Ave Bridgeport CT 06604

REED, DAVID ARTHUR, priest, Episcopal Church; b. Springfield, N.B., Can., Jan. 1, 1941; s. Harry Dow and Bessie Florence (Clark) R.; came to U.S., 1965; diploma New Brunswick Inst. Tech., 1961; B.A., Barrington Coll., 1968; M.A., Andover Newton Theol. Sch., 1969; Ph.D., Boston U., 1978; m. Carlynn Leah Roy, July 10, 1965; children—Kirkland, Christopher. Ordained priest, 1970; instr. math., physics New Brunswick Inst. Tech., 1961-65; registrar Atlantic Provinces Vocat. Tchr. Tng. Summer Sch., Moncton, N.B., summers 1965-67; migrant chaplain R.I. Council Chs., Providence, summers 1968-69; asso. pastor All Saints' Episcopal Ch., Attleboro, Mass., 1969-74; rector St. Paul's Episcopal Ch., Shelton, Conn., 1974—; chmn. diocesan com. on evangelism, 1981—; diocesan rep. Episc. Charismatic Fellowship; mem. Anglican-Roman Catholic Dialogue Team, Fairfield County, Conn. Mem. N. Am. Acad. Ecumenists, Soc. for Pentecostal Studies. Contbg. author: Aspects of Pentecostal-Charismatic Origins, 1976. Address: 31 Church St Shelton CT 06484

REED, DAVID BENSON, bishop, Episcopal Church; b. Tulsa, Feb. 16, 1927; s. Paul Spencer and Bonnie Frances (Taylor) R.; A.B., Harvard, 1948; M.Div., Va. Theol. Sem., 1951, D.D., 1964; D.D., U. of South, 1972; m. Susan Henry Riggs, Oct. 30, 1954; children—Mary, Jennifer, David, Sarah, Catherine. Ordained priest Episcopal Ch., 1952; missionary priest in Panama and Colombia, 1951-58; with Nat. Ch. Exec. Office, 1958-61; mission priest, S.D., 1961-63; missionary bishop of Colombia, 1964-72; bishop coadjutor Diocese of Ky., Louisville, 1972-74, bishop of Ky., 1974—; 1st pres. Anglican Council Latin Am., 1969-72. Bd. dirs. Norton Childrens Hosp., Louisville, 1972—; trustee U. of South, 1972—, regent, 1979-82. Democrat. Home: 1823 Ballard Mill Ln Louisville KY 40207 Office: 421 S 2d St Louisville KY 40202

REED, JOHN W., educator. Pres. The Ministers and Missionaries Benefit Bd., American Baptist Churches in the U.S.A., N.Y.C. Office: 475 Riverside Dr New York NY 10115*

REED, LOY WAYNE, pastor, Southern Baptist Convention; b. Springfield, Mo., June 19, 1948; s. George Wayne and Stella Gertrude (Miller) R.; m. Glenda Ann Shores, Aug. 24, 1968; children: Danna Ann, Dania Annette, Dawn Angela, Diedra Alisha. B.A., William Jewell Coll., 1970; M.Div., Midwestern Bapt., 1978; D.Ministry, Midwestern Bapt. Theol. Sem., 1984. Ordained to gospel ministry Southern Baptist Conv., 1970. Minister music, youth Liberty Manor Bapt. Ch., Mo., 1968-71, First Bapt. Ch., Warrensburg, Mo., 1971-74, N. Kansas City, Mo., 1974-76; campus minister, adminstr. U. Mo., Columbia, 1976-81; pastor Harmony Bapt. Ch., Rogersville, Mo., 1981—; conf. speaker Mo. Bapt. Evangelism Dept., Jefferson City, 1975-78, 1983-84; evangelism cons. Dept. Student Ministry, Jefferson City, 1978-81; keynote speaker Youth Music Week, Windermere Bapt. Assembly, 1984; chmn. evangelism Greene County Bapt. Assn., Springfield, 1984, 1985. Contbr. numerous articles to mags. Pres. Assn. of Campus Religious Advs., Columbia, 1980; mem. exec. com. Leighton Ford Crusade, Springfield, 1984. Named to Outstanding Young Men of Am. Jaycees, 1976, 1979, 1980. Mem. Assn. for Clin. Pastoral Edn., Charles Haddon Spurgeon Soc. William Jewell Coll. Democrat. Lodge: Lions (chaplain). Home: Route 4 Box 256 Rogersville MO 65742

REED, MELVIN, lay church worker, Methodist Church; b. Atlanta, May 15, 1933; s. Wallace and Emma G. Reed; m. Vera L. Cross, Aug. 6, 1958; children: Pat Marian, Kelvin, Wallace, Alan, Trina. Hon. degree Rose Croix Univers San Jose, Calif., 1975. Lay worker Bread of World Covenant Chs., Washington, 1982—. Mem. assembly GM Div., Atlanta, 1965—. Notary, Am. Council of Notaries, Atlanta, 1967; mem. Rep. Presdl. Task Force. Served to sgt. U.S. Army, 1951-54. Mem. Bibl. Archaeology Soc., Am. Arab Com. Republican. Lodge: Masons. Home: 1899 Goddard St SE Atlnata GA 30315

REED, MILLARD CLIFTON, minister, Church of the Nazarene; b. Hannibal, Mo., Nov. 19, 1933; s. Harlow and Mary Agnes R.; m. Barbara Jean Cunningham, Nov. 26, 1953; children: Stephen, Deborah, Paul, John. A.B., Olivet Nazrene Coll., 1955; M.Div., Eden Theol. Sem., 1961; D.Min., Vanderbilt U., 1979; Ph.D. (hon.), Revecca Nazarene Coll., 1978. Ordained to ministry, 1958. Pastor, Page-Warson Nazarene Ch., St. Louis, 1957-61, First Ch. of Nazarene, Kenosha, Wis., 1961-66, Overland Park Nazarene Ch., Kans., 1966-74, First Ch. of Nazarene, Nashville, 1974—. Author: Let Your Church Grow; Take Care Man; (with Harold Bonner) Proclaiming the Spirit, 1975; (with John B. Nielson) Family Love in All Dimensions, 1976. Club: Palaver. Home: 2425 Eastland St Nashville TN 37206 Office: First Church of the Nazarene 510 Woodland St Nashville TN 37206

REED, RICHARD GLENN, minister, American Baptist Churches in U.S.A.; b. Sayre, Pa., Aug. 22, 1956; s. Clifford Ernest and Doris Jean (Smith) R.; m. Sharon-Lynn Roberts, June 6, 1981; 1 child, Andrew Cliftin. B.A., Eastern Coll., St. Davids, Pa., 1978; M.Div., Eastern Bapt. Sem., Phila., 1981. Ordained to ministry Bapt. Ch., 1981. Pastoral intern Drexel Hill Bapt. Ch., Pa., 1980-81; pastor First Bapt. Ch., Deposit, N.Y., 1981—; mem. area lay-edn. bd. Am. Bapt. Chs. of N.Y. State, 1983—, bd. mgrs., 1984—; chair Christian edn. com. Deposit Council of Chs., N.Y., 1984—. Bd. dirs. Deposit Found., 1984—. Democrat. Lodge: Rotary (chaplain Deposit 1982—, chair youth exchange 1984, bd. dirs. 1985—). Home: 141 2d St Deposit NY 13754 Office: First Baptist Church 139 2d St Deposit NY 13754

REED, ROBERT JAMES, bishop, religious organization administrator, Independent Christian Churches International; b. Portis, Kans., Aug. 4, 1947; s. James Cecil and Melba (Coop) R.; m. Brenda Gayle Whitmore, June 23, 1973. B.S. in Edn., Bob Jones U., 1969; B.A. in Bible, Oklahoma City Southwestern Coll., 1973; LL.D. (hon.) Burton Coll., 1980; D.Theology (hon.), Am. Sch. of Bible, 1982. Ordained to ministry, 1968. Assoc. pastor Ch. of Christian Crusade, Tulsa, 1969-74; pastor First Ind. Methodist Ch., Dallas, 1974-84; bishop Ind. Christian Chs. Internat., 1979—; dir. admissions Am. Christian Coll., 1969-74; bd. dirs. World Wide Compassion Missions, 1979—; dir. pub. relations Okla. Coll., Tulsa, 1985—; pres., dir. Am. Prison Ministry, Tulsa, 1983—; book reviewer; radio speaker, 1974-84; tchr. Boston Ave. Ch. (United Meth.), Tulsa. Editor, Across the Fence. Assoc. editor Christian Crusade newspaper, 1969-74. Mem. Civitan Internat. (lt. gov. 1985—). Republican. Avocations: motivational speaker to secular groups; world traveler. Office: Box 1765 Tulsa OK 74101

REED, SHERMAN RAY, minister, Army Reserve chaplain, Church of the Nazarene; b. Jasonville, Ind., June 24, 1941; s. John Dennis and Levina Ruth (Mattox) R.; m. Janet Joyce Hayman, June 19, 1965; children: Angela Dawn, John Robert. B.S., Purdue U., 1963; M.Div., Nazarene Theol. Sem., 1967-71, postgrad., 1985—. Ordained to ministry Ch. of the Nazarene, 1973. Pastor, First Ch. of the Nazarene, Astoria, Oreg., 1970-75, Ch. of the Nazarene, Osawatomie, Kans., 1975-80, Trinity Ch. of the Nazarene, Naperville, Ill., 1980—; chaplain 138th Mil. Intelligence BN, Rosemont, Ill., 1982—; mem. Bd. of Orders and Relations, Kansas City, Mo., 1978-79; chaplain Police-Sheriff Dept., Osawatomie, 1977-80, Police Dept., Naperville, 1980—; Pres. Greater Chgo. Nazarene Assn. Mem. Fin. Com., Central Dist., Chgo., 1982—; sec. Bd. of Ch. Properties, 1982—. Decorated Nat. Def. Service medal Army Res. Achievement medal, Meritorious Service medal, Overseas ribbon; recipient Cert. of Commendation, Kans. Dept. of Aging, 1978; named Chapel Man of Yr. U.S. Air Force, 1967. Mem. Nazarene Chaplains Assn., Mil. Chaplains Assn., Nat. Assn. Police Chaplains, Wesley Theol. Soc., Christian Holiness Assn., Res. Officers Assn. (state chaplain Kans. 1978-79), Osawatomie C. of C. (bd. dirs. 1976-79). Lodges: Kiwanis, Rotary (pres., v.p. 1976-80).

REED, THOMAS RICHARD, minister, United Pentecostal Ch.; b. Success, Ark., May 26, 1911; s. Thomas S. and Beulah Z. (Lewis) R.; student U. Ark., 1929, Moody Bible Inst., 1930-31, Winona Lake Sch. Theology, 1952; m. Vernita Chloe Craine, Aug. 29, 1944; children—Thomas Richard, Robert Michael, Samuel Timothy, Cynthia Denice. Ordained to ministry United Pentecostal Ch., 1934; pastor Pentecostal Ch., Corning, Ark., 1929, 37, Pentecostal Ch., Trumann, Ark., 1937-42, Bible Hour Tabernacle, Jonesboro, Ark., 1942-58, First Pentecostal Ch., Laurel, Miss., 1958-62, First United Pentecostal Ch., Memphis, 1963—. Preacher various radio stas., 1934—; mem. radio commn. United Pentecostal Ch., 1960-77. Author: Bird's Eye View of Holy Land, 1953. Editor Pentecostal Voice of Tenn., 1963-76. Home: 1835 Oliver Ave Memphis TN 38114 Office: 1915 Young Ave Memphis TN 38104

REES, PAUL STROMBERG, minister, Evangelical Covenant Church; b. Providence, R.I., Sept. 4, 1900; s. Seth Cook and Frida Marie (Stromberg) R.; m. Edith Alice Brown, June 3, 1926; children: Evelyn Joy Rees Moore (dec.), Daniel Seth, Julianna Rees Robertson. A.B., U. So. Calif., 1923; D.D. (hon.), Asbury Coll., 1939, U. Co. Calif., 1944, North Park Coll., 1965, Warner Pacific Coll., 1982; D.Litt. (hon.), Houghton Coll., 1953; D. Humanities (hon.), Seattle Pacific U., 1959. Interdenominational evangelist, 1922-38; pastor First Covenant Ch., Mpls., 1938-58; assoc. World Vision Internat., Monrovia, Calif., 1958—, v.p. at large, 1958-75. Moderator, Evang. Covenant Ch. Am., 1948, v.p., 1950-55; v.p. World Evang. Fellowship, Minister to Ministers, Billy Graham Crusades, London, 1954, Glasgow, Scotland, 1955, N.Y.C., 1957, Sydney, Australia, 1959; adviser World Council Chs. Assembly, New Delhi, India, 1961, Uppsala, Sweden, 1968; lectr. Staley Found. Disting. Lectures series; bd. dirs. Christianity Today, 1958-80, contbg. editor, 1958-75, hon. life mem. Bd. dirs. Bread for the World, 1974-81. Columnist Covenant Companion, 1958-75, columnist, 1975-79. Assoc. editor, The Herald, 1955-57, contbg. editor, 1975-79. Cons. editor Eternity, 1960-77. Editor Nairobi to Berkeley, 1967. Editor World Vision mag., 1964-72, contbg. editor, 1972-74, editor at large, 1974—. Author: Stand Up in Praise to God, 1960; Triumphant in Trouble, 1962; Proclaiming the New Testament-Philippians, Colossians, Philemon, 1964; Men. of Action in the Book of Acts, 1966; Don't Sleep Through the Revolution, 1969. Trustee Asbury Coll., 1935-65, Asbury Theol. Sem., 1967-82, hon. life mem.; bd. dirs. William Penn Coll., 1950-58, Paul Carlson Med. Found., 1965-72. Mem. Nat. Assn. Evangelicals (pres. 1952-54, hon. life mem.), Phi Beta Kappa. Home: Boca Towers Apt 1109 E 2121 North Ocean Blvd Boca Raton FL 33431 and 2527 Mayapple Ct Northbrook IL 60062

REESE, JAMES FINLEY, minister, So. Baptist Conv.; b. Gainesville, Tex., Sept. 26, 1935; s. Carroll Lee and Martha Adeline (Proffer) R.; B.A., Okla. Bapt. U., 1958; B.S., Panhandle State U., Goodwell, Okla., 1964; B.D., Southwestern Bapt. Theol. Sem., 1963; m. Frances Elaine Allen, May 27, 1967; 1 son, Shane Allen. Ordained to ministry, 1956; leader Jimmy Reese Evang. Assn., 1957—; pastor Natura Bapt. Mission, 1956; pastor chs. in Kans., Okla. and Tex., 1965-72; asso. pastor Dauphin Way Bapt. Ch., Mobile, 1972-73; pastor Gracemont Bapt. Ch., Tulsa, 1973—; chaplain local Boy Scouts Am., also Tulsa Police and Fire depts. Mem. Tex. Bapt. Men (past v.p.), Bass Masters, Okla. Forensic League, Okla. Tchrs. Assn., Okla. Football Coaches Assn., Four Cities C. of C. Contbr. to ch. publs. Home: 8038 S Peach Circle Broken Arrow OK 74012 Office: 3160 S 129th E Ave Tulsa OK 74134

REESE, KERRY DAVID, minister, Lutheran Church-Missouri Synod; b. Kennewick, Wash., Dec. 17, 1953; s. Walter Theodore and Arline Winefred (Botz) R.; m. Robin Marie Harm, Aug. 18, 1978; 1 child, Michelle Lynn. A.A., Concordia Coll., Portland Oreg., 1974; B.A., Concordia Sr. Coll., Ft. Wayne, Ind., 1976; M.Div., Concordia Sem., St. Louis, 1980. Ordained to ministry Luth. Ch.-Mo. Synod, 1981. Asst. pastor St. Peter-Immanuel Ch., Milw., 1982-83; pastor Messiah Luth. Ch., Highland, Calif., 1983—. Republican.

REESE, PERCY NOCK, priest, Episcopal Church; b. Crisfield, Md., Jan. 11, 1911; s. Chauncy Clifford and Agnes (Nock) R.; m. Frances Walton Unglaub, Apr. 11, 1936. Student, Washington Coll., Cherstertown, Md., 1927-28. Ordained priest Episcopal ch., 1974. Lay reader Episcopal Ch., Crisfield, 1953-73, deacon, 1973-74, priest, 1974—. Mem. Lower Somerset Ministerium (pres. 1975-76). Lodges: Rotary (sec.-treas.), Masons (past master), Order Eastern Star (past pres., treas.).

REEVES, GENE, educator, minister, Unitarian Universalist Association; b. Franklin, N.H., Apr. 2, 1933; s. Eugene V. and Parmelie (Twombly) R.; B.A., U. N.H., 1956; S.T.B., Boston U., 1959; Ph.D., Emory U., 1963; m. Joan D. Shaw, Sept. 11, 1957; children—Eva Shaw, Anna Marie. Ordained to ministry Unitarian Universalist Assn., 1961; asst. prof. philosophy and theology Tufts U., 1962-67; prof. philosophy Wilberforce U., 1967—, chmn. humanities div., 1971-72, asso. acad. dean, 1972—, also minister 1st Unitarian Ch., Dayton, Ohio, 1968—. Mem. ACLU, NAACP, SANE, United World Federalists, Ams. Dem. Action (chpt. vice chmn. 1972-73), UN Assn., Zero Population Growth (nat. bd., chpt. chmn.). Cogswell scholar, 1951-52; Robinson fellow, 1959-60; Emory fellow, 1960-62. Mem. Am. Philos. Assn., Metaphys. Soc. Am., Am. Acad. Religion, Soc. Sci. Study of Religion, Soc. Philosophy and Pub. Policy, Center Process Studies, AAUP (chpt. pres. 1968), Am. Assn. Higher Edn. Author: (with D. Brown and R. James) Process Philosophy and Christian Thought, 1971. Editor of The Crane Review, 1965-67. Office: Wilberforce University Wilberforce OH 45384

REEVES, GEORGE PAUL, bishop, Episcopal Church; b. Roanoke, Va., Oct. 14, 1918; s. George Floyd and Harriett Faye (Foster) R.; B.A., Randolph-Macon Coll., 1940; B.D., Yale, 1943; D.D., U. of South, 1970, Nashotah House, 1970; m. Adele Beer, Dec. 18, 1943; children—Cynthia (Mrs. Karl Pond), George Floyd II. Ordained priest Episcopal Ch.; consecrated bishop, 1969; chaplain USN, 1943-47, Fla. State U., 1947-50; rector All Saints Ch., Winter Park, Fla., 1950-59, Ch. of Redeemer, Sarasota, Fla., 1959-65, St. Stephens Ch., Miami, Fla., 1965-69; bishop of Ga., Savannah, 1969—. Mem. Phi Beta Kappa. Home: 112 E 52d St Savannah GA 31405 Office: 611 E Bay St Savannah GA 31401

REGAN, DENNIS MARTIN, priest, seminary president; b. Rockville Centre, N.Y., July 11, 1937; s. W. Kenneth and Isabella (Martin) R. B.A., St. Bernard Sem., Rochester, N.Y., 1964; S.T.L., Pontifical Lateran U., Rome, Italy, 1968, S.T.D., 1970. Ordained priest Roman Catholic Ch., 1964; assoc. pastor Sacred Heart Ch., North Merrick, N.Y., 1964-67; professorial asst. N. Am. Coll., Rome, 1968-70; acad. dean Sem. of Immaculate Conception, Huntington, N.Y., 1971-78, rector, pres., 1979—, prof. moral theology, 1970—. Author: Violent Revolution, 1970; also articles and papers. Chmn., Central Am. Refugee Ctr., Westbury, N.Y., 1983—; mem. com. for revision of standards Assn. Theol. Schs., 1982—; mem. Commn. on Justice and Peace, Diocese of Rockville Ctr., 1982—; trustee Cathedral Coll., Douglaston, N.Y., 1979—, St. John Sem., Boston, 1982—. Named Prelate of Honor by Pope John Paul II, 1980. Mem. Cath. Theol. Soc. Am., Am. Acad. Religion, Am. Soc. Christian Ethics. Home and Office: Sem of Immaculate Conception West Neck Rd Huntington NY 11743

REGAN, JAMES ROBERT, JR., minister, United Methodist Church; b. Manteo, N.C., June 25, 1930; s. James Robert and Selma Adelaide (Cain) R.; m. S. Jeanette Leonard, Dec. 22, 1956; children: Curtis Randall, Robert Steven, David Leonard, Jennifer Leigh. A.B., Duke U., 1949, M.Div., 1952; D.Min., Howard U., 1975. Ordained elder United Methodist Ch., 1953, ordained to ministry, 1952. Assoc. pastor Hay St. United Meth. Ch., Fayetteville, N.C., 1952-54; state dir. Meth. Student Movement of N.C., Durham, 1954-57; assoc. gen. sec. Gen. Bd. Ch. and Soc., Washington, 1957-64; co-pastor United Christian Parish, Reston, Va., 1964-79; pastor Trinity United Meth. Ch., McLean, Va., 1979-83, Peakland United Meth. Ch., Lynchburg, 1983—; pres. Va. Conf. Bd. of Ch. and Soc., 1964-72, Va. United Meth. Family Service, Richmond, 1978-80, Va. United Meth. Housing Corp., Richmond, 1978—, bd. trustees Charterhouse Sch., Richmond, 1982-84. Author: What About Alcohol, 1962. Pres. Fairfax Community Action Program, Fairfax County, Va., 1970-74. Mem. Am. Assn. Homes for Aging, Va. Conf. United Meth. Ch., Democrat. Home: 1501 Lexington Dr Lynchburg VA 24503 Office: Peakland United Meth Ch 4434 Boonsboro Rd Lynchburg VA 24503

REGIER, JON LOUIS, minister, United Presbyterian Church in U.S.A.; b. Dinuba, Calif., May 24, 1922; s. John and Adeline (Roth) R.; A.B., Huntington (Ind.) Coll., 1944; B.D., McCormick Theol. Sem., 1947; student U. Mich. Sch. Social Work; D.D., Payne Theol. Sem., Wilberforce, Ohio, 1959; m. Joyce Palmer, June 12, 1948; children—Jon Denniston, Marjorie Grace, Susan Marie, Luke Roth. Ordained to ministry, 1947; asso. dir. Dodge Christian Community House, Detroit House, Detroit, 1947-49; head resident Howell Neighborhood House, pastor Howell Meml. Ch., Chgo., 1949-58; lectr. social group work McCormick Theol. Sem., Chgo., 1952-58; exec. sec. div. home missions Nat. Council Chs., 1958-64, asso. gen. sec., chief exec. officer div. Christian life and mission, 1965-73; exec. dir. N.Y. State Council Chs., Syracuse, 1973—. Del. to Assembly of Div. World Mission and Evangelism, World Council Chs., mem. exec. com. world mission and evangelism, del. World Conf. Ch. and Soc., Geneva, 1966; founding mem. IDOC Internat., Rome, pres., 1972. Exec. council div. edn. and recreation Welfare Council Met. Chgo., 1953; mem. hard-to-reach youth research com., 1953-58; mem. Chgo. Youth Commn., 1954-58; chmn. spl. study on delinquency, 1956-58; exec. com. Citizens Crusade Against Poverty, 1964—; exec. com. Citizens Adv. Center, 1967—; trustee North Conway Inst. Mem. Nat. Fedn. Settlements and Neighborhood Centers (dir. 1954-58), Nat. Assn. Social Workers (exec. council Chgo. chpt. 1955-58), Soc. Propagation of Gospel Among Indians and Others of N.Am., Nat. Assembly for Social Policy and Devel. (founding mem.). Office: 3049 E Genesee St Syracuse NY 13224

REHKOPF, CHARLES FREDERICK, priest, Episcopal Church; b. Topeka, Dec. 24, 1908; s. Frederick Adams and Mary Gertrude (Jennings) R.; m. Dorothy Arnold Getchell, July 30, 1936; children: Frederick Arthur, Jeane Elizabeth Rehkopf Cessna, Susan Gail. B.S., Washburn U., 1932; diploma Episcopal Theol. Sch., 1935. Ordained to ministry Episcopal Ch. as deacon, 1935, as priest, 1936. Rector Trinity Episcopal Ch., El Dorado, Kans., 1935-44, St. John's Episcopal Ch., St. Louis, 1944-52; archdeacon, exec. sec. Diocese of Mo., St. Louis, 1953-76, registrar, historiographer, 1948—; staff priest Emmanuel Episcopal Ch., Webster Groves, Mo., 1977—; bd. dirs. Hist. Soc. of Episcopal Ch., Austin, Tex., 1973—; Episcopal-Presbyterian Found. for Aging, St. Louis, 1964—, Met. Ch. Fedn., St. Louis, 1945-69; sec., bd. dirs. Thompson Retreat and Conf. Ctr., St. Louis, 1952-76; treas. Episcopal Home for Children, St. Louis, 1970—. Author: Missouri's Episcopal Church, 1976. Editor Historiographers Newsletter, 1970-82. Bd. dirs., editor Webster Groves Hist. Soc., 1975. Recipient Citation, Mo. Senate, 1976; Citation, Bd. of Aldermen, St. Louis, 1983; named Diocesan Exec. of Yr., Conf. of Diocesan Execs., 1966. Mem. Soc. Am. Archivists (sect. sec. 1982—), Nat. Episcopal Historians Assn. Lodge: Masons. Home: 642 Clark Ave Webster Groves MO 63119 Office: Diocese of Mo 1210 Locust St Saint Louis MO 63119

REHRER, LEROY RIDLEY, III, minister, Lutheran Church In America; b. Riverside, Calif., Jan. 9, 1950; s. Leroy Ridley and Virginia Evelyn (O'Neil) R.; m. Valerie June Fulks, Apr. 16, 1972. B.A., Calif. Luth. Coll., 1972; M.Div., Christ Sem., 1976. Ordained to ministry Luth. Ch. in Am., 1977. Youth minister Woodland Hills Christian Ch., Calif., 1971-72; asst. pastor Our Saviour's Luth. Ch., Phoenix, 1976-78; pastor Holy Trinity Luth. Ch., Chandler, Ariz., 1978—; bd. dirs. pastor's adv. com. ARCA Agy. on Alcoholism, Phoenix, 1979-81; pres., v.p., sec., treas. Chandler Ministerial Fellowship, 1978-84. Bd. dirs. Salvation Army, Chandler, 1978-81; mem. Chandler Area Council, 1984-85. Named Outstanding Young Religious Leader of Chandler, Jaycees, 1980, Outstanding Young Religious Leader of Ariz., Jaycees, 1980. Democrat. Office: Holy Trinity Luth Ch 739 W Erie St Chandler AZ 85224

REICHARDT, LOWELL KEITH, minister, Southern Baptist Convention; b. Des Moines, Mar. 8, 1932; s. Author August Reichardt and Iva Leona (Huey) Treaster; m. Donnis Belle Harmon, Mar. 4, 1933; children: Rebecca Paige, Lowell Keith, Jr., Ingrid Leah, Donn-Evans. Student Mo. Sch. of Mines, 1950-51, U. Md., extension, Italy, 1953; B.A., Bob Jones U., 1961; M.Theology, Am. Div. Sch., 1969, D.Theology, 1972. Ordained to ministry Bapt. Ch., 1960. Assoc. pastor Jonesboro First Bapt. Ch., La., 1968-73; pastor Quitman First Bapt. Ch., 1974-78, Pollock First Bapt. Ch., La., 1978—; shaping 70's dir. Jackson Bapt. Assn., Jonesboro, 1969-70, bd. dirs., 1970-71, sem. tchr., 1972; mem. nominating com. exec. bd. La. Bapt. Assn., Jonesboro, 1970-72; missionary tchr. So. Bapt. Conv., Union of South Africa, 1980, State of Karnataka, India, 1982; mem. exec. bd. La. Bapt. Conv., 1982-83, 84—; sem. extension dir., tchr. Bapt. Joint Assn., Pineville, 1984. Mem. library bd. Grant Parish Library, Colfax, La., 1984. Served as sgt. U.S. Army, 1952-56. Mem. La. Library Assn., Nat. Rifle Assn., Grant Parish Artist Guild. Democrat. Lodge: Lions. Home: Box 308 Pollock LA 71467 Office: Box 308 Hickory St and Hwy 165 Pollock LA 71467-0308

REICHEL, CHARLES EDWARD, minister, educator, consultant Lutheran Church-Missouri Synod; b. Shawano, Wis., Oct. 16, 1943; s. Edward Charles and Eleanor Anne (Koenig) R.; B.A., Concordia Sr. Coll., 1965; M.A. in Urban Affairs, St. Louis U., 1969; B.Div., Concordia Sem., 1969, M.Div., 1971; Ph.D. in Counseling and Ednl. Psychology, U. Miss., 1977; m. Sharon Anne Werfelmann, June 14, 1970; children: Cara Loelle; Carsten Martin, Carlyn Anne. Ordained to ministry, 1969; pastor Peace Luth. Ch., Oxford Miss., 1969-84, Zion Luth. Ch., Holly Springs, Miss., 1969-74; minister, instr. adolescent psychology, philosophy and religion U. Miss., 1969-84; dir. career devel. Shorter Coll., Rome, Ga., 1984—; prin. New Perspective Cons., 1985—. Parent Effectiveness trainer, 1976—; cons. so. dist. Urban Affairs com. Luth. Ch.; dir. to S.E. area Luth. immigration and refugee service Luth. Council U.S.A.; past pres. Oxford Ministerial Alliance. Bd. dirs. Lafayette County Assn. for Retarded Citizens, 1971-84, Lafayette County Laubach Literacy Adv. Bd., 1982-84; chmn. Oxford Concerned Citizens for Refugee Resettlement, 1975-76; designer, coordinator Holly Springs program of tng. for community tutors, 1973-74; coordinator Oxford Afterschool Childcare Program, 1983-84. Mem. Am. Assn. for Counseling and Devel., Nat. Vocat. Guidance Assn., So. Coll. Placement Assn., Ga. Coll. Placement Assn., Phi Kappa Phi, Phi Delta Kappa. Home: 1505 Mt Alto Rd Rome GA 30161 Office: Box 305 Shorter Coll Rome GA 30161

REICHTER, ARLO RAY, minister, American Baptist Churches in U.S.A.; b. Eagle Grove, Iowa, May 22, 1947; s. Verven Leonard and Marvyl Nellie (Harvey) R.; m. Dianne Kristine Stueland, June 22, 1968; children: Kristi, Kari. B.A., Sioux Falls Coll., 1969; M.Div., Am. Bapt. Sem., 1971; M.A., U. So. Calif., 1976; D.Min., Jesuit Sch. Theol., 1980. Ordained to ministry Am. Bapt. Chs. in U.S.A., 1971. Co-pastor First Bapt. Ch., Los Angeles, 1971-83; program dir. Am. Bapt. Assembly, Green Lake, Wis., 1983—; mem. Central Sectional Christian Edn. Team, Am. Bapt. Chs., 1983—. Author: The Group Retreat Book, 1983, also devotionals. Contbr. articles to profl. jours. Vice chmn. study com. Los Angeles Unified Sch. Dist., 1981-83; chmn. Com. on Protestant Scouting, Los Angeles, 1981-83. Home: Nordane Ave Ripon WI 54971

REID, ANDREW DAVIS, ecumenical religious organization executive; b. York, Maine, Aug. 26, 1947; s. Ralph Linn and Vivien L. (Davis) R. B.S., Baldwin-Wallace Coll., 1969. Dir. Pike County Outreach Council, Waverly, Ohio, 1978—; dir., past pres. HEAD Corp., Berea, Ky., 1981-82. Office: Pike County Outreach Council 122 E 2d St Waverly OH 45690

REID, BENJAMIN FRANKLIN, minister, Church of God-Anderson, Indiana; b. N.Y.C., Oct. 5, 1937; s. Noah W. and Viola M. (Samuels) R.; student U. Pitts., 1955-57, No. Baptist Theol. Sem., 1957-58; D.D., Am. Bible Inst., Kansas City, Mo., 1971; Ph.D., Calif. Western U., 1974; Litt.D., Calif. Grad. Sch. Theology, 1981; D.D., Anderson Coll., 1982; m. Anna Pearl Batie, June 28, 1958; children—Benjamin Franklin, Sylvia, Angela. Ordained to ministry, 1960; pastor Adams Street Ch. of God, Springfield, Ill., 1958-59, 1st Ch. of God, Junction City, Kans., 1959-63, Southwestern Ch. of God, Detroit, 1963-71, 1st Ch. of God, Los Angeles, 1971—. Chaplain, Inglewood (Calif.) Police Dept., 1973—; vice chmn. Nat. Gen. Assembly of the Ch. of God, 1978-79; mem. nat. bd. ch. extension Ch. of God, 1968-82; pres. bishop 1st Ch. of God, Nigeria, 1981—; chmn. Interstate Assn. Ch. of God—Alaska, Ariz., Calif., Nev., Oreg., Wash., 1982—; chaplain Los Angeles Police Dept., 1974-76; pres. SW Los Angeles Police-Clergy Council, 1974-75; mem. Urban Coalition of Ch. of God, 1981-82; cons. Nat. Higher Edn. Commn. Ch. of God, 1976-80, Long Range Planning Commn., Ch. of God, 1981-82. Dir. minority affairs Azusa (Calif.) Pacific U., 1972-80; mem. community adv. bd. U. So. Calif., Los Angeles, 1975—; bd. dirs. Los Angeles Council of Chs., pres., 1980; bd. dirs. Los Angeles Met. Learning Center, Los Angeles Urban League, Ecumenical Center Black Ch. Studies, Los Angeles, So. Christian Leadership Conf. West, Black Am. Response to African Crisis; trustee Anderson Coll. and Sch. Theology, 1982—; mem. adv. bd. Azusa Pacific U. Sch. Theology, 1983—; founding pres. So. Calif. Sch. Ministry, 1980—; dir. Interstate Effective Ministries Inst., 1971—. Mem. Los Angeles Interdenominational Ministers Alliance (pres. 1972-74, v.p. 1977—). Author: Confessions of a Happy Preacher, 1972; Black Preacher-Black Church, 1974; Another Look at "Other Tongues", 1977, 2d edit., 1983; Church Growth Workbook, 1980; Discipleship Manual, 1984; Fire in My Bones—Sermons from a Burning Heart, 1984. Office: 2941 W 70th St Los Angeles CA 90043

REID, CLYDE HENDERSON, minister, pastoral psychotherapist, United Church of Christ; educator; b. Peoria, Ill., Dec. 13, 1928; s. Clyde Henderson and Marguerite (Barham) R.; children: Laurie Beth, Eric James, Robin Joye, Kelton Jud. B.S., Bradley U., 1949; M.Th., Pacific Sch. Religion, 1953; M.A., 1952; Th.D., Boston U., 1960. Ordained to ministry United Ch. of Christ, 1954; diplomate Am. Assn. Pastoral Counselors. Asst. prof. Union Theol. Sem., N.Y.C., 1960-64; evangelism sec. bd. homeland ministries United Ch. of Christ, 1965-67; assoc. dir. Inst. Advanced Pastoral Studies, Bloomfield Hills, Mich., 1967-70; assoc. prof. Iliff Sch. Theology, Denver, 1971-74; exec. dir. Ctr. for New Beginnings, Denver, 1974-80; pastoral psychotherapist in pvt. practice, Denver, 1980—; mem. faculty Colo. Inst. Transpersonal Psychology, Boulder, 1982-84. Author 12 books including: Celebrate the Temporary, 1972; The Return to Faith, 1974; You Can Choose Christmas, 1975; Dreams: Discovering Your Inner Teacher, 1983. Contbr. numerous articles to various publs. Fellow Assn. Past-Life Research and Therapy (bd. dirs.). Democrat. Home: 1035 Tantra Park Circle Boulder CO 80303

REID, FRANK M., JR. Bishop, African Methodist Episcopal Church, 9th dist., also sec. Council of Bishops. Office: African Meth Episcopal Ch 1738 3d Ave N Birmingham AL 35203*

REID, JAMES JOHN, minister, Ref. Ch. in Am.; b. Teaneck, N.J., July 28, 1942; s. John James and Lillian May (Dale) R.; B.A., Hope Coll., 1964; M.Div., New Brunswick Theol. Sem., 1968; M.S., State U. N.Y. at Albany, 1973; m. Janet Anne Lewis, Aug. 22, 1964; children—William, Michael. Ordained to ministry, 1968; minister Altamont (N.Y.) Ref. Ch., 1968-75; chaplain Albany County (N.Y.) Jail, 1973—; exec. dir. Christians United in Mission Inc., Albany; dir. Family Life Center, Ref. Ch. Am., 1976—. Co-therapist Ellis Hosp. Psychiat. Day Center, Schenectady, 1973—; convenor Albany County Coalition for Criminal Justice, 1974. Mem. community adv. bd. Eleanor Roosevelt Developmental Services, Delmar, N.Y., 1973-75; bd. dirs. Helderberg House Hostel for Adult Retarded, Altamont, 1974-75. Mem. Phi Alpha Theta, Pi Kappa Delta. Home and Office: Bozenkill Rd Altamont NY 12009

REID, RICHARD, seminary adminstrator. Pres., dean Protestant Episcopal Theol. Sem. in Va., Alexandria. Office: Protestant Episcopal Theol Sem in Va 3737 Seminary Rd Alexandria VA 22304*

REID, ROBERT ORLO, educator, United Church of Canada; b. Stirling, Ont., Sept. 29, 1932; s. Bryson Caldwell and Emily Emmanda (Smith) R.; B.A., U. Toronto, 1955; B.D., Victoria U., 1959; M.Ed., Syracuse U., 1967, Ph.D., 1970; m. June Helen Reid, May 14, 1955; children—Deborah, Donald, Darren. Ordained to ministry United Church of Canada, 1959; pastor chs. Cold Lake, Alta., 1959-62; pastor, Foxboro, Ont., 1962-65; supr. communication edn. United Ch. Can., 1965-73; minister Riverdale United Ch., Toronto; dir. curriculum devel. Davar Media Devel. Assn., Thornhill, Ont., Can., 1973—; chmn. dept. communication Toronto Sch. Theology, 1970—. Pres. bd. govs. John Neil Hosp., Cold Lake, 1959-62. Mem. Soc. for Study Bibl. Lit., Assn. Ednl. Communications Tech., Ednl. Media Assn. Can., Ednl. TV and Radio Assn. Can. Author: The Mindbenders, 1967; Introductory Concepts in Communication Education, 1973. Research Multi image film and its effect on religious attitudes, 1970; radio and TV effects, 1974. Home: 78 Meldazy Dr Scarborough ON M1P 4G1 Canada Office: 1117 Gerrard St East Toronto ON M4M 1Z9 Canada

REID, THOMAS FENTON, minister, Assemblies of God; b. Buffalo, Sept. 9, 1932; s. Albert E. and Helen Gertrude (Rice) R.; m. Wanda Darlene Bousum, July 7, 1968; 1 child, Aimee Linette. Diploma Central Bible Coll., Springfield, Mo., 1953; D.D. (hon.), Calif. Grad. Sch. Theology, 1981. Ordained to ministry Assemblies of God, 1956. Missionary, evangelist Assemblies of God, Springfield, Mo., 1953-63; pastor Bethel Temple, Manila, Philippines, 1959-60; sr. pastor Full Gospel Tabernacle, Orchard Park, N.Y., 1963—; pres. Buffalo Sch. of Bible, 1976—, Gibraltar Network, Buffalo, 1983—, Nat. Ch. Growth Conf., Washington, 1984; sec., bd. dirs. Ch. Growth Inc., Seoul, Korea, 1979—; mem. Christians for Friends in Middle East, Buffalo. Author: The Exploding Church, 1979. Contbr. articles to religious publs. Mem. Friends of Anwar Sadat, Nat. Religious Broadcasters, Nat. Assn. Evangelicals (bd. dirs. 1979—). Republican. Home: 65 Hawthorne Dr Orchard Park NY 14127 Office: Full Gospel Tabernacle 3210 Southwestern Blvd Orchard Park NY 14127

REIF, JOEL ALLEN, minister, United Church of Christ; b. Stanley, N.D., May 4, 1952; s. Jack Wessles and Martha Nell (Wallace) R.; m. Barbara Ellen Zeissler, Sept. 6, 1975; children: Karlie Lynn, Clinton Joel. B.A., Ottawa U., 1973; M.Div., No. Bapt. Theol. Sem., 1976. Ordained to ministry United Ch. of Christ, 1976. Youth minister Christ Ch., DesPlaines, Ill., 1974-76; pastor St. John's United Ch. Christ, Brighton, Ill., 1976-79, Lyons, Ill., 1979—; mng. com. mem. Hitz Home Aged, Alhambra, Ill., 1977-79; camp dir. Mission Council #5 Camp Chgo. Met. Assn. United Ch. Christ, 1982; del. Gen. Synod Meeting United Ch. Christ, Pitts., 1983; sec. Ill. Conf. United Ch. Christ, 1982-84; mem. Task Force Ministry with and to Disabled, Conf. United Ch. Christ, 1984—, personnel com. Ill. Conf. United Ch. Christ, 1984—. Active Handicapped Evaluation Com., Lyons, 1984—, Citizens Liquor Commn., Lyons, 1985—. Home: 4446 Center Ave Lyons IL 60534 Office: St Johns United Ch Christ 4500 S Prescott Ave Lyons IL 60534

REIFF, JAMES ELLING, minister, American Lutheran Church; b. Marshfield, Wis., Apr. 13, 1944; s. Gerhardt Paul and Francis Threne (Tweito) R.; m. Kristine Marie Olsen, May 24, 1974 (div. Nov. 1976); 1 child, Jacob M.; m. Linda Jean Lexau, Nov. 10, 1979; children: Mark A., Timothy J. B.A., Augsburg Coll., 1967; M.Div., Wartburg Sem., 1971; postgrad. Wausau Hosp., 1976; M.A.R., U. Dubuque, 1984. Ordained to ministry Am. Luth. Ch., 1974. Assoc. pastor Grace Luth. Ch., Tomahawk, Wis., 1973-74; pastor St. John Luth. Ch., Edgar, Wis., 1974-79, Trinity Luth. Ch., Washington Island, Wis., 1979—; gen. mem. Spiritual Frontiers Fellowship, Chgo., 1968-70; mem. Fellowship St. Augustine, Oxford, Mich., 1978-84. Contbr. articles to religious publs. Served with U.S. Mcht. Marine, 1968-71. Mem. Nat. Rifle Assn. (life). Home: Town Line Rd Washington Island WI 54246

REIGHARD, DWIGHT ARTHUR, minister, Bapt. Ch.; b. Andrews, N.C., Dec. 12, 1950; s. Ernest Woodrow and Ruth Ida (Matheson) R.; student Kennesaw Jr. Coll., 1968-69, Mercer U., 1974-77; m. Cindy Sue Mitchell, June 11, 1971. Ordained to ministry, 1975; youth minister (part-time) First Bapt. Ch. of Chattahoochee, Atlanta, 1972-73, asso. pastor, 1973-75; asso. pastor, youth minister, New Hope Bapt. Ch., Fayetteville, Ga., 1976—; appeared on Midnight Minister radio program sta. WSB, Atlanta; speaker youth rallies and revivals; outreach dir. Bapt. Student Union, 1976-77; producer, moderator Young Generation radio program Sta. WZGC, Atlanta; vol. staff Atlanta Interfaith Broadcasting; announcer weekly TV program Miracle Hour, Channel 46, Atlanta. Mem. assembly com. Atlanta Bapt. Assn., 1975—; coordinator for ch. ministerial relations Ministerial Assn., Mercer, 1975—, pres., 1976-77; mem. Atlanta Bapt. Pastor's Conf., 1973-76. Mem. ARC blood drive com., Mercer, Atlanta, 1975-76; vol. in Drug Rehab. Programs, Atlanta. Mem. Ministerial Assn. of Mercer, Fairburn Bapt. Assn., Religious Edn. Assn. Home: 1097 Longley Ave NW Atlanta GA 30318 Office: New Hope Baptist Church New Hope Rd Fayetteville GA

REILE, LLOYD LEON, minister, ch. adminstr., Seventh-day Adventists; b. Harvey, N.D., June 12, 1915; s. Samuel A. and Lydia (Lang) R.; B.Th., Walla Walla Coll., 1937; m. Elsie Viola Ruth, June 6, 1937; children—Carol Joy Reile Powers, Loella Jean Reile Johnson. Ordained to ministry; pastor chs.; evangelist; departmental dir.; missionary; adminstr. Seventh-day Adventist Ch., Oshawa, Ont., Can. Mem. Gen. Conf. Com. of Seventh-day Adventists; chmn. Canadian Union Conf. Com.; bd. dirs. Walla Walla Coll., Atlantic Union Coll., Christian Record Braille Found., Kingsway Coll., Canadian Union Coll. Home: 65 Townline Rd N

Oshawa ON L1H 7K5 Canada Office: 1148 King St E Oshawa ON L1H 1H8 Canada

REILEY, KEITH, minister, Church of God, Anderson, Indiana; b. Stillwater, Okla., Nov. 25, 1947; s. Robert Nelson and Laura May (Delap) R.; m. Karen Elaine Graves, May 1, 1970; children: Patricia Lynn, Kaherine Sue. B.A., Warner So. Coll., 1983. Ordained to ministry, 1982. Pastor assoc. First Ch. of God, Plant City, Fla., 1975-77; pastor First Ch. of God, Avon Park, Fla., 1977-82, Community Chapel, Zephyrhills, Fla., 1983—. Served with USAF, 1967-71. Mem. Zephyrhills Ministerial Assn. (pres. 1985), Soc. for Preservation and Encouragement of Barber-shop Quartet Singing in Am. (treas.). Republican. Home: 2158th Ave Zephryhills FL 34248 Office: Community Chapel Church of God PO Box 1086 Zephyrhills FL 34248

REILLY, DANIEL PATRICK, bishop, Roman Catholic Church; b. Providence, May 12, 1928; s. Francis E. and Mary (Burns) R.; student Our Lady of Providence Sem., 1943-48, Grand Seminarire, St. Brieuc, France, 1948-53, Harvard Grad. Sch. Bus. Adminstrn., 1954-55, Boston Coll. Sch. Bus. Adminstrn., 1955-56. Ordained priest, 1953, became monsignor, 1965; asst. pastor Cathedral Saints Peter and Paul, Providence, 1953-54; asst. chancellor Diocese of Providence, 1954-56, sec. to bishop, 1956-64, chancellor diocese, 1964-72, adminstr. diocese, 1971-72, vicar gen., 1972-75; bishop Diocese of Norwich (Conn.), 1975—. State chaplain K.C., 1964—. Trustee St. Joseph's Hosp., Providence, 1964—, Providence Coll., 1969—, Our Lady of Providence Sem. Coll., Warwick, R.I., 1969—; chmn. bd. dirs. Cath. Relief Services, N.Y.C., 1978—; bd. dirs. Cath. Conf., Hartford, Conn., 1976—. Recipient Ann. award NCCJ, 1972. Office: 201 Broadway Norwich CT 06360

REIMER, DONALD ARTHUR, minister, Evangelical Lutheran Church of Canada; b. Winnipeg, Man., Can., Dec. 22, 1948; s. Erdman and Elsie (Wonneck) R.; m. A. Dolores Josephine Reimer, May 17, 1971; children: Holly, Richard. B.A., U. Winnipeg, 1969; M.Div., Luth. Theol. Sem., 1974. Ordained to ministry, 1974. Pastor, Francis-Stoughton Luth. Ch., Francis, Sask., 1974-80, Trinity Luth. Ch., Lemberg, Sask., 1980—; sec. Regina conf. Bible Camp, Midale, Sask., 1976-80, Evang. Luth. Ch. Can., Saskatoon, 1981—. Pres., Lemberg Housing Authority, Sask., 1983—. Home: PO Box 63 Lemberg SK S0A 2B0 Canada Office: Trinity Luth Ch PO Box 63 Lemberg SK S0A 2B0 Canada

REIMER, ELMER ISAAC, minister, Evangelical Mennonite Brethren Conf.; B. Drake, Sask., Can., May 18, 1922; s. Frank E. and Gertrude (Boese) R.; m. Catharina Peters, Sept. 26, 1943; 1 child: David Elmer. Pastor, Jansen Evang. Mennonite Brethren Ch., Nebr., 1948-53; pulpit supply, 1954-57; pastor, Springfield, S.D., 1957-62; pastor, evangelist, Carter, S.D., 1963—; pres., evangelist Assoc. Gospel Ministries, Winner, S.D., 1973—. Home: 401 W 8th St Box 209 Winner SD 57580 Office: Associated Gospel Ministries 401 W 8th St Winner SD 57580

REIMNITZ, ELROI, minister, Lutheran Church-Missouri Synod; b. Porto Alegre, Brazil, June 20, 1948; came to U.S., 1969, naturalized, 1974; s. Elmer and Kordula Luise (Schelp) R.; m. Ruth Sonaide Weimer, June 16, 1973; children: Patrick Jonathan, Kristeen Nicole, Nicholas Alexander. Diploma, Seminario Concordia, Brazil, 1966; M.Div., Concordia Sem., St. Louis, 1971, Th.D., 1975. Ordained to ministry Lutheran Ch., 1975. Asst. to pastor Our Savior's First Luth. Ch., Granada Hills, Calif., 1974-75; prof. Faculdade Canoense, Canoas, Brazel, 1976-77; adminstrv. pastor Trinity Luth. Ch., Grand Island, Neb., 1978—. Lodge: Rotary. Home: 1320 N Wheeler Grand Island NE 68801 Office: Trinity Lutheran Church 212 W 12th St Grand Island NE 68801

REINECKE, RODERICK LAURY, minister, Episcopal Church; b. Washington, Oct. 8, 1933; s. Paul Sorg and Esther Jean (Runyan) R.; m. Carolyn Lee Miser, Feb. 1, 1955 (div. 1974); children: Michael, David, Bruce, John; m. Ruthmary Ragsdale Wright, July 9, 1976; stepchildren: Paul, Christopher, Leslie, Laura Wright. M.Div., Va. Theol. Sem., 1958; B.A., U. N.C., 1955. Ordained priest, 1958. Minister, St. Paul's Ch., Cary, N.C., 1958-59; chaplain N.C. State U., Raleigh, 1958-63; rector St. Timothy's Ch., Winston-Salem, 1963-68, Holy Comforter Ch., Burlington, N.C., 1968-83; cons., therapist Piedmont Counseling Assocs., Controd Assocs., Burlington, 1984—; dir. tng. Episcopal Diocese of N.C., 1974—. Mem., program chmn. Community Council, Alamance, County, N.C., 1980—. Named Clergyman of the Yr., Civitan Club, 1973. Mem. Am. Assn. Marriage and Family Therapy, N.C. Episcopal Clergy Assn. (pres. 1974), N.C. Group Behavior Assn., Mid-Atlantic Assn. for Tng. and Cons. (bd. dirs.), Assn. Creative Change. Home: 1117 Briarcliff Rd Burlington NC 27215

REINELT, HERBERT R., educator, United Church of Christ; b. Seattle, Apr. 17, 1929; s. Herbert and Lillian (Goff) R.; m. Janelle J. Gobby, Aug. 18, 1968; children by previous marriage: Claire Louise, Douglas Alan, Lorin Edward, Peter Scott. B.A., U. Wash., 1951; B.D., Yale U., 1954, M.A., 1958, Ph.D., 1962. Ordained to ministry, 1954. Minister, Congl. Ch., Centerbrook, Conn., 1954-57; asst. prof. Hamline U., St. Paul, 1959-62; asst. prof. U. of Pacific, Stockton, Calif., 1962-65, assoc. prof., 1965-68, prof. philosophy, 1968—. Contbr. articles to profl. jours. Mem. Am. Acad. Religion, Am. Philos. Assn., Pacific Coast Theol. Soc., Soc. for Process Philosophy, AAUP. Democrat. Home: 7640 Greenhaven Dr Sacramento CA 95831 Office: Dept Philosophy Univ of Pacific 3600 Pacific Ave Stockton CA 95211

REINKE, RALPH LOUIS, religious publisher, Lutheran Ch.-Mo. Synod; b. Elmhurst, Ill., June 22, 1927; s. Louis Fred and Malinda Marie (Beckmann) R.; B.S., Concordia Tchrs. Coll., River Forest, Ill., 1949; M.A., Northwestern U., 1952; postgrad. U. Chgo., 1956-65; Litt.D., Concordia Sem., Springfield, Ill., 1971; m. Lois H. Borneman, Aug. 28, 1948 (dec. 1984); children: Janice Reinke Eisenloeffel, Stephan, Sharon Reinke Holaway. Prin., St. John Christian Day Sch., Houston, 1950-56; asso. prof. edn./psychology Concordia Tchrs. Coll., 1956-68; pres. Concordia Pub. House, St. Louis, 1971-85. Mem. Lutheran Edn. Assn. (pres. 1968-70), Protestant Ch. Pubs. (pres. 1982-84), Phi Delta Kappa. Lodge: Rotary. Office: 3558 S Jefferson St Saint Louis MO 63118

REINKE, ROBERT JOHN, brother, Roman Catholic Church; b. Chgo., Jan. 6, 1941; s. Joseph and Helen Claire (Woznicki) R.; B.S. in English, Xavier U., 1965, M.Ed., 1972, postgrad., 1969-70. Joined Bros. of the Poor of St. Francis, 1959, mem. provincial council of brotherhood, Cin., 1968-71, 73-74; regional chpt. del. for Brotherhood of St. Francis, 1969-81, gen. chpt. del. for U.S. region at Brotherhood's hdqrs. in Germany, 1969-82; mem. Diocese of Davenport (Iowa) Synod Preparatory Commn., 1973-75; bd. dirs. Christian Action, Burlington, Iowa, 1972-73, St. Vincent's Home, 1972-73; bd. dirs. Burlington Charismatic Prayer Group, Inc., pres., 1976-80. Founder, adminstr. The Young House, Inc., Burlington, 1971—. Mem. Conf. of Major Superiors of Men. Mem. Nat. Assn. of Religious Bros., Iowa Welfare Assn. (sec. southeast chpt. 1973-74), Iowa Group Home Personnel Assn. (pres. 1975-81, 83—). Home: 417 Franklin St Burlington IA 52601 Office: 105 Valley St Burlington IA 52601

REINSEL, THOMAS HERBERT, minister, Lutheran Church in America; b. Reading, Pa., Mar. 10, 1939; s. Herbert M. and Elizabeth C. (Flickinger) R.; m. Amy Lou Hawman, Aug. 24, 1963; children: Kathleen A., Karin L. B.S., Muhlenberg Coll., 1961; M.Div., Luth. Theol. Sem., Phila., 1964. Ordained to ministry Lutheran Ch. Am., 1964. Asst. pastor Trinity Luth. Ch., Pottsville, Pa., 1964-66; pastor St. Timothy's Ch., Aston, Pa., 1966-69, Hope Luth. Ch., Bowers, Pa., 1969-76, Luth. Ch. of the Holy Spirit, Emmaus, Pa., 1976—. Trustee Gt. Valley council Girl Scouts U.S.A., Allentown, 1984, Swain Sch., Allentown, 1984. Office: Lutheran Church of the Holy Spirit PO Box 414 Emmaus PA 18049

REIS, MICHAEL JAMES, priest, Roman Cath. Ch.; b. Columbus, Ohio, June 29, 1941; s. Leo James and Margaret (George) R.; B.S. in Philosophy, St. Charles Coll. Sem., 1963; student Mt. St. Mary's of the West, Norwood, Ohio, 1967; M.A.R.E., Fordham U., N.Y.C., 1971. Ordained priest, 1967; asst. pastor St. Michael's Ch., Worthington, Ohio, 1969-71; religion tchr. Watterson High Sch., 1969-71; dir. religious edn. Notre Dame High Sch., Portsmouth, Ohio, also Scioto County, 1971-73, Wehrle High Sch., 1973-75; dir. TV and radio services Diocese of Columbus, 1975—; chairperson dept. communications Cath. Conf. of Ohio, 1976—, also spiritual dir. Cursillo, Diocese of Columbus, 1976—. Mem. Columbus Area Cable TV Commn. Mem. UNDA-U.S.A., N.Am. Broadcast sect. World Assn. Christian Communicators, Ohio Assn. Broadcasters (asso.), Ohio Cable TV assn. Home: 648 S Ohio Ave Columbus OH 43205 Office: 197 E Gay St Columbus OH 43215

REISCH, PAUL CONRAD, minister, Lutheran Church in America; b. Southington Conn., Apr. 24, 1923; s. William C. and Bertha (Ensle) R.; m. Catherine Dubs. Aug. 24, 1946; children: Paul C. Jr., David, Susan, Jonathan. B.A., Wagner Coll., 1944; B.D. Luth. Sem., 1946. Ordained to ministry Lutheran Church in America 1946. Pastor St. Mark Luth. Ch., Canajoharie, N.Y., 1946-52, Grace Luth. Ch., Startford, Conn., 1952-60, St. John's Luth. Ch., Richmond Hill, N.Y., 1960-71, Christ Luth. Ch., Wantagh, N.Y., 1971—; chmn. Am. Missions Com., Metro N.Y. synod, N.Y.C. Home: 1587 Church Rd Wantagh NY 11793 Office: Christ Luth Ch 3384 Island Rd Wantagh NY 11793

REISMAN, BERNARD, theology educator, Jewish religion; b. N.Y.C., July 15, 1926; s. Herman and Esther Sarah (Kavesh) R.; m. Elaine Betty Sokol, Aug. 26, 1951; children: Joel Ira, Sharon Fay, Eric K., Robin Sue. B.Social Sci., CCNY, 1949; M.Social Sci. Adminstrn., Western Reserve U., 1951; Ph.D., Brandeis U., 1970. Agy. dir. Jewish Community Ctr., Chgo., 1951-67; assoc. prof. Am. Jewish communal studies Brandeis U., Waltham, Mass., 1969—; dir. Hornstein Program in Jewish Communal Service, 1971—; lectr. in field; vis. prof. Baerwald Sch. Social Work, Hebrew U., Jerusalem, 1978, Ctr. Jewish Edn. in Diaspora, 1978; sr. cons. Josephtal Found., Jerusalem, 1978, cons. Am. Joint Distribution Com., European Council, 1978, Inst. for Jewish Life, N.Y.C., 1972-76, Organizational Theory, Boston U. Med. Sch., 1969-70; research assoc. on Future of Religion, Nat. Council Chs., 1972-73. Author: Reform is a Verb, 1972; The Jewish Experiential Book: Quest for Jewish Identity, 1978; The Chavurah: A Contemporary Jewish Experience, 1977. Contbr. articles to profl. jours. Served with U.S. Army, 1944-46, ETO. Recipient 75th Anniversary award Am. Jewish Com., Boston, 1981; Arnulf Pins Meml. Lectr. award Hebrew U., Jerusalem, 1983, 84; Farfel Jewish Family Service award for exemplary support to the Jewish family, Houston, 1984; Whiting Found. grantee, 1977. Mem. Conf. Jewish Communal Service (chmn. publs. com. 1980—), Nat. Jewish Family Ctr., Am. Jewish Com. (1st chmn. acad. adv. com. 1979-82), Am. Jewish Hist. Soc. (acad. council 1979—), Radius Inst. (bd. dirs. 1980—), Assn. for Jewish Studies. Home: 28 Fairway Dr West Newton MA 02165 Office: Hornstein Program in Jewish Communal Service Brandeis U Waltham MA 02254

REISMAN, WILLIAM SEGERS, minister, Episcopal Church; b. St. Paul, Nov. 12, 1916; s. Philip Harry and Irene (Segers) R.; m. Janice McKinley, June 28, 1946; children: William, Thomas, Mark. A.B., Brown U., 1940; M.Div., Va. Theol. Sem., 1958. Ordained priest, Episcopal Ch., 1958. Vicar, St. David's Ch., Highland Falls, N.Y., 1958-60; rector St. Philips in the Highlands Ch., Garrison, N.Y., 1960—. Author: Short History of St. Philip's Church, 1970. Served to capt. U.S. Army, 1940-46; ETO. Decorated Bronze Star with "V". Republican. Address: Rt 9D Garrison NY 10524

REISS, ELLEN DIANE MISHEY, music educator, Lutheran Church in America; b. Mt. Vernon, Ohio, Jan. 30, 1950; d. Lawrence Russell and Juanita Althea (Hillman) Mishey; m. Garry Keith Reiss, June 5, 1976; 1 dau., Lauren Marie. B.Music in Edn., Capital U., 1972; M. Vocal Pedagogy, Ohio State U., Columbus, 1974-76. Dir. choirs Grace Luth. Ch., Columbus, Ohio, 1972-74; mem. faculty Mt. Vernon Nazarene Coll., Ohio, 1974—, asst. prof. music, 1983—; dir. children's music Faith Luth. Ch., Mt. Vernon, 1983. Composer Sacred Songs for Children, 1983, 84, 85. Home: 807 Southridge Dr Mount Vernon OH 43050 Office: Mt Vernon Nazarene Coll 800 Martinsburg Rd Mount Vernon OH 43050

REISS, JOHN C. See *Who's Who in America,* 43rd edition.

REITER, EDWARD BERNARD, priest, Roman Catholic Church; b. Flushing, N.Y., Sept. 12, 1942; s. Edward John and Elizabeth Madlin (Feitz) R.; B.A. in Philosophy, Holy Apostles Sem., Cromwell, Conn., 1969; B.A. in Religious Studies, Calif. State U.-Northridge, 1974; M.Div., Holy Apostles Sem., 1978; M.S. in Social Scis., L.I. U., 1983; Ph.D. candidate, 1983—. Ordained priest Roman Cath. Ch. Prof. theology Holy Apostles Sem., Cromwell, Conn., 1978-84, vocation dir., 1978-83; chaplain St. Francis Hosp., Hartford, Conn., 1979-82; adj. assoc. pastor Sacred Heart Ch., Dobbs Ferry, N.Y., 1982—; adj. assoc. clergy St. Paul's the Apostles Ch., Yonkers, N.Y., 1983—; dir. religious edn. Sacred Heart Parish, Dobbs Ferry, 1983—; chaplain Sisters of Mercy, Dobbs Ferry, 1984—; mem. Confraternity of Christian Doctrine, Washington, 1980—. Author: The Natural Right of Self-Determination, 1983; Global Communications and Information, 1984; Oil and Gas, 1985. Editor: The Dean's List of Recommended Readings, 1984; Practice and Methods of Internat-national Law, 1984. Recipient Dragos D. Kostich award L.I. U. Alumni Assn., 1982, Award for Leadership in Catechical Ministry, Cathechical Office Archdiocese of N.Y., 1985. Mem. Nat. Conf. Diocesean Dirs. of Religious Edn., Canon Law Soc. Am., Nat. Cath. Edn. Assn., Club: KC (Meriden Conn.) (chaplain 1981-82). Avocations: tennis; horseback riding. Home: PO Box 132 Hastings-On-Hudson NY 10706 Office: Mount Mercy Broadway St Dobbs Ferry NY 10522

REKLAU, FREDERICK WALTER, minister, English Synod Evangelical Lutheran Church; b. Marshfield, Wis., July 16, 1937; s. Walter Albert and Hildegarde Clara (Seefeldt) R.; B.A., Concordia Sr. Coll., Ft. Wayne, Ind., 1959; M.Div., Concordia Sem., St. Louis, 1963; m. Tecla Marie Sund, July 19, 1969; children—Angela, Rachel. Ordained to ministry Luth. Ch.-Mo. Synod, 1963, trans. to English Synod Assn. of Evang. Luth. Ch., 1976; pastor chs. in Nebr. and Ill., 1963-68; pastor Windsor Park Luth. Ch., Chgo., 1968-75, Grace Luth. Ch., Evanston, Ill., 1975—; dir. A Joyful Noise, religious folksinging group, 1968-74. Circuit counselor Luth. Ch.-Mo. Synod, 1972-75; pres. South Shore Ministerial Assn., 1971-73, Luth. Campus Ministry Commn. Ill., 1973-75; conf. counselor English synod, Assn. Evang. Luth. Chs., 1979-83; co-chmn. Police-Clergy Liaison Team, Evanston, 1982—; co-chmn. Social Ministry Task Force, Evanston Ecumenical Action Council, 1983-85; bd. govs. Augustana Ctr. Devel. Disabled, 1983—. Trustee Luth. Student Found. Met. Chgo., 1969-76, pres., 1976. bd. dirs. South Shore Commn., 1972-75, Rainbow Neighbors, 1972-75, South Shore Community Center,

1970-72. Home: 1409 Dobson Evanston IL 60202 Office: 1430 South Blvd Evanston IL 60202

REMSON, MICHAEL M., rabbi, Reform-Reconstructionist Jew; b. Buffalo, Feb. 14, 1944; s. Louis H. and Yetta Rae (Davidoff) R.; m. Susan Tee Kotick, June 22, 1969; children: Aviva Miriam, Benjamin Dan. Student Hebrew U., Jerusalem, 1969-70; B.S., Canisius Coll., 1966; B.A., in Hebrew Lit., Hebrew Union Coll., Jewish Inst. of Religion, N.Y.C., 1971, M.A. in Hebrew Lit., 1973. Ordained rabbi, 1973. Rabbi Beth Hillel Temple, Kenosha, Wis., 1973-83, Congregation Beth Shalom, Naperville, Ill., 1983—; chmn. com. on family life Central Conf. of Am. Rabbis, 1983—; v.p. Mid-west Assn. of Reform Rabbis, 1981-83; mem. Chgo. Bd. Jewish Edn.; pres. Kenosha County Clergy Assn., 1981-83. Editor booklet A Rabbi's Guide to Adoopion, 1981. Contbr. articles to profl. jours. Vol. VISTA, Wilmington, Del., 1966-67; sec. Women's Horizons, Kenosha, 1979-81; bd. dirs. Devel. Disabilities Service Ctr., Kenosha, 1981-83; mem. adv. bd. Children's Service Soc., Kenosha, 1981-83; bd. dirs. Clergy and Laity Concerned. Mem. Chgo. Assn. Reform Rabbis, Central Conf. of Am. Rabbis, Reconstructionist Rabbinical Assn., Naperville Ministerium. Home: 426 E Hillside Rd Naperville IL 60540 Office: Congregation Beth Shalom 21 E Franklin St Naperville IL 60540

RENDSBURG, GARY ALAN, Biblical studies educator, conservative Jewish Congregations; b. Balt., Feb. 13, 1954; s. Julius and Irene (Schneemann) R.; m. Susan Ladenheim, Nov. 23, 1977; children: David, Rachel. B.A., U. N.C., 1975; M.A., NY U, 1977, Ph.D., 1980. Asst. prof. Biblical studies Canisius Coll., Buffalo, 1980—. Author: The Redaction of Genesis, 1985. Editor: The Bible World, 1980. Contbr. articles to religious jours. Mem. Soc. Biblical Lit., Assn. Jewish Studies, Am. Oriental Soc. Home: 159 Brooklane Dr Williamsville NY 14221 Office: Canisius Coll 2001 Main St Buffalo NY 14221

RENKEN, JOHN ANTHONY, priest, religious organization executive, Roman Catholic Church; b. Staunton, Ill., Jan. 18, 1953; s. William Fredrick and Gertrude Ann (Klotz) R. B.A., Cardinal Glennon Coll., 1975; S.T.D., Angelicum U., Rome, 1981, J.C.D., 1981. Ordained priest Roman Cath. Ch., 1979. Assoc. pastor Cathedral, Springfield, Ill., 1981—; coordinator, vice officialis Tribunal Office, Springfield, 1981—, vice chancellor of Diocese Chancery, Springfield, 1981-84, chancellor of Diocese, 1984—, Diocesan consultor, 1984—, Episcopal Vicar, 1984—. Mem. Canon Law Soc. Am. Office: Chancery Office 524 E Lawrence Ave Springfield IL 62703

RENSHAW, DONALD FRANK, JR., minister, religious organization executive, The United Methodist Church; b. Dec. 4, 1934; s. Donald F. Renshaw Sr. and Marie Teresa (Hester) Gilbert; m. Barbara J. Howie, July 3, 1953; children: Mark David, Scott Andrew, Todd Vincent. B.S., Tex. Wesleyan Coll., 1957, M. Edn., 1958; B.D., S. Meth. U., 1960, D.Ministry, 1976. Ordained to ministry United Meth. Ch. Pastor Joshua Meth. Ch., Tex., 1960-62, Grace Ch., Ft. Worth, 1962-65, Wedgewood Meth. Ch., Ft. Worth, 1965-72, Ridgewood Park Meth. Ch., Dallas, 1972-73, First Sulpur Springs Meth. Ch., Tex., 1973-76, First Plano Meth. Ch., Tex., 1976-82; dist. supt. Paris-Sulphur, Dist., Paris, Tex., 1982—; del. gen. conf. United Meth. Ch., Balt., 1984, Jurisdictional Conf. United Meth. Ch., Lubbock, Tex., 1984; trustee Lydia Patterson Inst., El Paso, 1984—, commr. Meth. Home, 1984—. Served to 1st lt. U.S. Army, 1952-55. Recipient Citation award Tex. Meth. Coll. Assn., 1976. Mem. Gerontol. Soc. Democrat. Lodges: Rotary, Masons. Home: 660 Twin Oaks Paris TX 75460 Office: United Meth Dist Office PO Box 842 Paris TX 75460

RENSHAW, GEORGIE GORDON, minister, Baptist Missionary Association of America; b. Chickasha, Okla., Apr. 22, 1927; s. James Otis and Bessie Telah (Moody) R.; m. LaJuana Jo Dean, Aug. 18, 1950; children: Richard Curtis, Rhonda Gail Renshaw Irvin, Regina Sue Renshaw Hodnett. A.A., Jacksonville Bapt. Coll., 1953, B.A., 1954; Th.B. and B.D., Bapt. Missionary Assn. Theol. Sem., 1958, Th.M., 1965. Ordained to ministry Oaklawn Bapt. Ch., Hot Springs, Ark., 1950. Pastor several chs., Tex., 1950-60, Unity Bapt. Ch., Hope, Ark., 1960-80, Farmington Bapt. Ch., Corinth, Miss., 1980-82, Coll. Ave. Bapt. Ch., Levelland, Tex., 1982—; trustee Central Bapt. Coll., Conway, Ark., 1961-63, Bapt. Missionary Assn. Theol. Sem., Jacksonville, Tex., 1962-64, Ark. Children's Home, Magnolia, 1978-80; personnel committeeman Bapt. Missionary Assn. of Am., 1976-78, pres., 1981-82. Writer adult dept. Golden Words Publ., 1966. Chmn. Southwest Ark. Devel. Council, Hope, 1974-75; chmn. Hempstead county chpt. Ark. Regional Blood Services, 1977-80; pres. Hope Concerned Citizens, 1968. Served with USN, 1948-49. Republican. Lodge: Kiwanis (pres. 1970-71). Office: Coll Ave Baptist Church 213 N College St Levelland TX 79336

RENTEL, DANIEL WILLIAM, priest, Orthodox Church in America; educator. B. Altoona, Pa., July 16, 1939; s. Victor Albert and Mary (Twardon) R.; m. Elaine Holovach, Sept. 2, 1962; children: Victoria, Judith, Alexander. Diploma in Sacred Theology, St. Tikhon's Sem., 1961; B.A., Indiana U. of Pa., 1970; M.A., Pa. State U., 1972; postgrad. Ohio State U., 1977. Ordained priest Orthodox Church in America, 1962; cert. tchr. soc. studies and Russian, Ohio. Rector St. John's Orthodox Ch., Phillipsburg, Pa., 1962-64, Holy Annunciation Orthodox Ch., Berwick, Pa., 1964-65, All Saints Orthodox Ch., Indiana, Pa., 1965-71, Christ the Savior Orthodox Ch., Cin., 1975-82; chaplain St. Gregory's Campus Ctr., Columbus, Ohio, 1983—; chaplain Orthodox Christian Fellowship, Indiana, Pa., 1965-71; council mem. Pitts. Archdiocese, 1971-72. Tchr. Columbus Pub. Sch., Ohio, 1978—. Author: (with others) Global Issues - Geography, 1983. Contbr. articles on mission work to ch. newspapers. Named archpriest Diocese of the Midwest, Chgo., 1984; recipient fellowship Ohio State U., 1973-77. Mem. Phi Alpha Theta. Home and Office: 345 Tibet Rd Columbus OH 43202

RENTZ, WILLIE DERRELL, minister, Southern Baptist Convention; b. Jacksonville, Fla., July 5, 1942; s. Willie George Rentz and Mattie May Louise (Cannady) Felberg; m. Virginia Inez Baxley, Dec. 7, 1963; children: Sheryl Lynn, Kelley Michelle, Karen Renee, Julie Ann. B.A. in Bibl. Studies, Luther Rice Sem., 1971, S.T.M., 1974, D.Edn. in Religion, 1977, postgrad., 1984—. Ordained to ministry Baptist Ch., 1967. Pastor, Beaumont, Pa., 1967-68, Faith Bapt. Ch., Boston, Ga., 1968-69, Fellowship Bapt. Ch., Jacksonville, 1970-77, Hickox Bapt. Ch., Nahunta, Ga., 1977—; sec. Fla. Regional of Ind. Fundamental Chs. of Am., 1972-74. Pres. PTA, Nahunta, 1981-82. Mem. Piedmont-Okefenokee Bapt. Assn. (chmn. exec. com. 1978-81, chmn. missions com. 1978—, vice moderator 1983-85). Democrat. Avocations: tennis; reading. Home: Route 1 Box 84A Nahunta GA 31553 Office: Hickox Bapt Ch PO Box 656 Nahunta GA 31553

RESCH, DAPHNE, minister, National Association of Congregational Christian Churches; b. Yokosuka, Japan, Sept. 12, 1953; d. David John and Virginia Emma (Madden) R. B.S., Bowling Green State U., 1975; M.Div., Princeton Theol. Sem., 1978. Ordained to ministry Nat. Assn. Congregational Christian Churches, 1978. Pastor, Little Kyger Congl. Christian Ch., Cheshire, Ohio, 1978-81, 1st Congl. Ch., Ashland, Nebr., 1981—. Mem. Commn. on Ministry, Nat. Assn. Congl. Christian Chs., 1979-82, chmn. com., 1982-83. Emergency med technician Ashland Rescue Squad, 1982—. Mem. Nebr. Assn. Congl. Christian Chs. (exec. com. 1982-84, chmn. budget com. 1984—), Alpha Lambda Delta, Kappa Delta Pi. Office: 1st Congregational Ch 1542 Boyd St Ashland NE 68003

RESSMEYER, RUDOLPH PAUL FREDERICK, bishop, East Coast Synod, Association of Evangelical Lutheran Churches; b. Balt., Feb. 22, 1924; s. Rudolph Stang and Clara (Pieper) R.; m. Virginia Christiana Werberig, Jan. 1, 1949; children: Faith, Judith, Marcia, Paul, Timothy. A.A., Concordia Jr. Coll., 1943; B.A., Concordia Sem., 1945, M.Div., 1947; D.D. (hon.), Wagner Coll., 1976. Ordained to ministry Lutheran Ch.-Mo. Synod. Asst. prof. Concordia Acad., Portland, Oreg., 1947-48; pastor Holy Cross Luth. Ch., Spokane, Wash., 1948-50; asst. pastor Emmanuel Luth. Ch., Balt., 1950-54; pastor Our Redeemer Lutheran Ch., Seaford, N.Y., 1954-66; exec. dir. L.I. Luth. High Sch., Brookville, N.Y., 1966-68; pres. Atlantic Dist. Luth. Ch. Mo. Synod, N.Y.C., 1967-76; bishop East Coast Synod, Assn. Evang. Luth. Ch., N.Y.C., 1977—; chmn. div. Pub. Relations Luth. Council U.S.A., N.Y.C., 1965-68; pres. Am. Luth. Publicity Bur., N.Y.C., 1961-66; chmn. bd. trustees Concordia Coll., Bronxville, N.Y., 1967-75; chmn. Council of Bishops, Assn. Evang. Luth. Ch., St. Louis, 1978—. Office: East Coast Synod Assn Evang Luth Ch 132 Jefferson Ave Mineola NY 11501

REST, FRIEDRICH OTTO, minister, United Church of Christ; b. Marshalltown, Iowa, Aug. 28, 1913; s. Karl and Bertha (Leisy) R.; m. Dorothy Evelyn Schumacher, Aug. 20, 1940; children: Paul Frederick, Elizabeth Rest Bean, John Marvin. A.B., Elmhurst Coll., 1935; B.D., Eden Theol. Sem., 1937; D.D., Mission House Theol. Sem., 1962. Ordained minister to United Ch. of Christ, 1937. Pastor St. Paul United Ch. of Christ, Hermann, Mo., 1948-55; sr. pastor St. Paul United Ch. of Christ, Evansville, Ind., 1955-64; sr. pastor Salem United Ch. of Christ, Rochester, N.Y., 1964-70; pastor St. Peter United Ch. of Christ, Houston, 1970-75; assoc. pastor First Protestant Ch., New Braunfels, Tex., 1975-85. Author: Our Christian Symbols, 1954, 9th edition, 1985; Funeral Handbook, 1982; The Cross in Hymns, 1961; Fourteen Messages of Hope: Thoughts for Funerals and Other Occasions, 1985; others. Contbr. articles to profl. jours. Lodges: Lions (bd. dirs.); Rotary (1st v.p. 1974). Home: 827 W Merriweather St New Braunfels TX 78130

RESZKOWSKI, JOSEPH VALENTINE, priest, Roman Catholic Church; b. Erie, Pa., June 20, 1928; s. Joseph Valentine and Josephine Mary (Szymanowski) R. B.A., St. Mary's Coll., 1950, S.T.B., 1952, S.T.L., 1954. Ordained priest Roman Catholic Ch., 1954. Assoc. pastor St. Stanislaus Ch., Erie, Pa., 1954-67; tchr. Cathedral Prep. Sch., Erie, 1962-67; pastor various chs., Pa., 1967-79; pastor St. Bernard's Ch., Bradford, Pa., 1979—; personnel bd. Diocese of Erie, 1983—, vicar forain, 1983—; chaplain to His Holiness Pope John Paul II. Democrat. Club: Exchange. Lodge: Lnights of Columbus. Address: Bernard's Ch 98 E Corydon St Bradford PA 16701

REUSS, CARL FREDERICK, church official, American Lutheran Church; b. Phila., June 7, 1915; s. Charles F. and Marie A. (Kick) R.; B.S., U. Va., 1934, M.S., 1935, Ph.D., 1937; m. Thelma L. Steinmann, June 24, 1938; children—Paula L. (Mrs. Robert Schanz), Ellen M. (Mrs. Thomas Jeppesen), Betty J. Shovelin. Exec. sec. Bd. Christian Social Action, Am. Luth. Ch., 1947-60, exec. dir. Commn. on Research and Social Action, 1960-74, dir. Office Research and Analysis, 1974-81, asst. for research coordination Office of Pres. Bishop, 1982—; mem. com. on ch. and soc. World Council Chs., 1954-60; sec. commn. on inner missions Luth. World Fedn., 1955-63; del. Assemblies of Luth. World Fedn., 1957, 63, 70, Assembly of World Council Chs., 1968—; mem. various coms. and task forces Luth. Council in U.S.A., 1966—. Bd. dirs. Nat. Safety Council, 1972-78; v.p. for religious leaders, mem. exec. com., 1973-78. Fellow Am. Sociol. Assn.; mem. Nat. Council on Family Relations, Rural Sociol. Soc., Soc. for Sci. Study Religion, Religious Research Assn. Author: Profiles of Lutherans in the U.S.A., 1982. Editor: Conscience and Action, 1971. Contbr. to Ency. of the Luth. Ch., 1965. Home: 5311 Vincent Ave S Minneapolis MN 55410 Office: 422 S 5th St Minneapolis MN 55415

REVEL, ANNA CARTER, deacon, Episcopal Church; school psychologist; b. Marion, Ky., June 26, 1924; d. Thomas Homer and Ruth (Cook) Carter; m. John Clarence Revel, Jr., Nov. 26, 1948 (div. 1967); 1 dau., Mary Linda Revel Shaw. B.S. in Home Econs., U. Ky., 1948; M.Ed. in Sch. Psychology, U. Wis.-Whitewater, 1973; Grad., Inst. Christian Studies, Nashotah Theol. Sem., Wis., 1980; postgrad. U. Wis.-Madison, 1976-77, U. Minn., 1983. Ordained deacon Episcopal Ch., 1981; cert. sch. psychologist level II, Wis. Dept. Pub. Instrn. Pres. Episc. Ch. Women, St. Edward's Episc. Ch., Columbus, Ohio, 1965-66; workshop leader Episc. Ch. Women, Diocese of Milw., 1984; spiritual dir. Cursillo, Diocese of Milw., 1984; workshop leader Diocese of Milw., 1981, 82; del. for bishop selection Trinity Episc. Ch., Janesville, Wis., 1983-84, lay reader, mem. vestry, liturgical commn., altar guild, 1973—, deacon, 1981—. Sch. psychologist Sch. Dist. of Janesville, 1973—. Bd. dirs. Beginnings Group Home for Delinquent Boys, Janesville Community Day Care Ctr., 1974-76; mem. Rock County Mental Health Assn., Friends of Janesville Pub. Library; vol. chaplain Anderson Rehab. Hosp., Rock County Hosp., Rock Haven Nursing Home, Janesville. Grantee Wis. Dept. Pub. Instrn., 1983. Mem. Nat. Assn. Sch. Psychologists (presenter at nat. conv. 1980), Wis. Sch. Psychologist Assn. (presenter at 3 state convs. 1981), Janesville Sch. Psychologists (chmn. 1979-80, 84—), NEA, Wis. Edn. Assn., Mensa, Pi Lambda Theta. Democrat. Home: 59 Lapidary Ln Janesville WI 53545 Office: Ednl Services Ctr 527 S Franklin St Janesville WI 53545

REVELS, PERCY BURTON, lay ch. worker, United Methodist Ch.; b. McRae, Fla., Dec. 16, 1901; s. William R. and Alice (Tyre) R.; student U. Fla., 1924-27; LL.B., Southeastern U., Washington, 1943; LL.D., Bethune-Cookman Coll., 1966; m. Bernice Hardy, June 20, 1929; children—Joan Dell (Mrs. John F. Gaines), Percy Burton. Mem., rec. sec. ofcl. bd., mem. adminstrv. bd., trustee, ch. sch. supt. St. James United Meth. Ch., Palatka, Fla., 1930—; vice chmn. conf. merging com. Fla. Conf., Southeastern and Central Juridictions, 1964; chmn. Conf. Bd. Christian Social Concern, 1968-73; vice chmn. Fla. Ann. Conf. Com. on Program Coordinating, 1970-72; dean Fla. United Meth. Conf. Sch. Christian Mission, 1970-72; del. Fla. to Gen. Conf., United Meth. Ch., 1971, mem. legislative com. on Christian social concerns, 1971, mem. Gen. Bd. on Ch. and Soc., 1972; vice chmn. div. gen. welfare Gen. Bd. Ch. and Soc., 1972; chmn. bd. trustees endowment fund and property div. gen. welfare United Meth. Ch., 1972; mem. United Meth. Women, 1972—; lectr. on community and ch. responsibility to humanity, 1971-72; del. Fla. Council Chs., 1972—; mem. World Meth. Council, 1976, del. Conf., Dublin, Ireland, 1976. Circuit judge Fla., 1951—. Exec. sec., pres. Young Democratic Clubs Fla., 1930-42; mem. State Dem. Exec. Com., 1942-48. Trustee Bethune-Cookman Coll. Recipient Good Govt. award Jr. C. of C., 1960. Mem. Am., Fla., Putnam County bar assns., Nat. Assn. State Trial Judges. Author: Florida Civil Law, 1967. Vice chmn. editorial com. Nat. Trial Judges Jour., 1958-64. Contbr. articles to profl. jours. Home: 1800 Laurel St Palatka FL 32077 Office: PO Drawer 250 Palatka FL 32077

REWAK, WILLIAM JOHN, priest, Roman Catholic Church, university president; b. Syracuse, N.Y., Dec. 22, 1933; s. William Alexander and Eldora Venetia (Carroll) R. B.A., M.A., Gonzaga U., 1958; M.A. in Theology, Regis Coll., Toronto, Ont., Can., 1964; Ph.D. in English, U. Minn., 1970. Ordained priest Roman Catholic Church, 1964. Asst. prof. religion U. Santa Clara, Calif., 1970-71, religious superior Jesuit community, 1971-76, pres., 1976—; bd. govs. NCCJ, San Jose, Calif., 1977—. Contbr. articles on theology, lit. criticism and edn. to profl. publs. Mem. nat. bd. dirs. Boys Clubs Am., 1981—; mem. adv. bd. Triton Mus. Art, Santa Clara, 1981—; pres. Western Football Conf., 1983—; mem. bd. govs. Inst. European Studies, Chgo., 1984—. Recipient Brotherhood award NCCJ, 1982. Mem. Assn. Jesuit Colls. and Univs. (bd. dirs. 1976—), Assn. Cath. Colls. and Univs. Democrat. Home and Office: U Santa Clara Santa Clara CA 95053

REYES, LONNIE C., priest, Roman Catholic Church; b. Lockhart, Tex., June 1, 1942; s. Jose M. and Angela (Contreras) R. M.Th., U. St. Thomas, Houston, 1969. Ordained priest, Roman Cath. Ch., 1969. Parochia vicar St. Louis Ch., Waco, Tex., 1969-70; exec. sec. Hispanic Ministry, Diocese of Austin, Tex., 1970-73, vice chancellor Diocese of Austin, 1973-75, chancellor, 1975—; pastor Cristo Rey Parish, Austin, 1978-82. Trustee Laguna Gloria Art Mus., Austin, 1984—; mem. integrity task force Travis County Democratic Party, 1984—; chmn. Police and Fire Commn., Austin, 1976—; chmn. Father Joe Znotas Community Scholarship, Austin, 1984—; mem. blue ribbon ethics rev. com. City of Austin, 1985. Mem. Nat. Assn. Ch. Personnel Adminstrs., Diocesan Fiscal Mgmt. Conf., Canon Law Soc. Am. Home: 3010 Lyons Rd Austin TX 78702 Office: Chancery Office 1600 N Congress PO Box 13327 Austin TX 78711

REYNOLDS, BEATRICE, evangelist, Church of God in Christ; b. Sherrells, Ark., Nov. 19, 1932; d. Bonnie and Burnesteen (Davis) Daniels; Asso. degree in social service Milw. Area Tech. Coll., 1972; B.Ed., U. Wis.-Milw., 1976; m. Vernon Reynolds, Sept. 18, 1950; children—Carolyn (Mrs. Nathanal Stampley), Catherine (Mrs. Williams Fowlkes, Jr.), Jeffery, Tina. Missionary, Ch. of God in Christ, 1959—, evangelist 1962—; Sunday sch. tchr., 1955-71; pres. missionaries bd. West Side Ch. of God in Christ, Milw., 1963-76, pres. home and fgn. mission, 1964-77, Bible tchr., 1960—, pres. ch. choir, 1961-64, dir., 1964-67; dean Charles Harrison Mason Bible Coll., Milw., 1974—; dist. missionary New Hope Dist., 1974—; regional evangelist, 1976-80. Case worker Milw. County Welfare Dept., Milw. Home: 6112 N River Trail Dr Milwaukee WI 53225

REYNOLDS, DANIEL HARRISON, priest, Roman Catholic Church; b. Rainier, Oreg., Oct. 11, 1926; s. Frank Harrison and Alisha Teresa (Meehan) R. B.A., Mt. Angel Sem., 1949; B.Div., St. Edward Sem., 1953. Ordained priest, 1953. Assoc. pastor Archdiocese of Portland, Oreg., 1953-67; pastor St. Peter Ch., Newberg, Oreg., 1967-70, Queen of Peace Ch., Salem, Oreg., 1970-78, St. Anne Ch., Grants Pass, 1978—, fedn. chaplain Christian Family Movement, 1953-62, dir. vocations, 1967-69; mem. Priests' Senate, Archdiocese of Portland, 1980—. Democrat. Lodges: Elks, Rotary. Home: 1131 NE 10th St Grants Pass OR 97526

REYNOLDS, JAMES CURTIS, minister, United Pentecostal Church International. B. Athens, Ga., June 30, 1949; s. Enoch James and Emmie Lorene (Bellow) R.; m. Jennifer Carol Colquitt, Oct. 9, 1970; children: Joy Christina, Jennifer Caryn. Assoc. in Christian Edn., Pentecostal Bible Inst., 1968; Assoc. in Acctg., Athens Tech., 1970, postgrad., U. Ga., 1970-72. Ordained to ministry, United Pentecostal Ch. Internat. 1983. Sunday sch. supt. First Pentecostal Ch., Athens, 1972-76, youth minister, 1976-81, ch. adminstr., 1981-82; pastor First United Pentecostal Ch., Waynesboro, Ga., 1982-83; assoc. pastor Faith Tabernacle United Pentecostal Ch., Conyers, Ga., 1983—; mgr. Dove Christian Bookstore, Conyers, 1984—; radio announcer Gospel Music Caravan Sta. WDOL-AM, Athens, 1974-76; Southeast regional rep. Boy Scouts Am., United Pentecostal Ch., Atlanta, 1983—, Ga. dist. dir. Sunday Sch. Promotional, Conyers, 1983—, Ga. dist. sect. sec., Athens, 1980-83, Ga. dist. youth commn. rep., 1977-80; mem. Burke County Ministerial Assn., Waynesboro, Ga., 1983, Conyers-Rockdale Community Ministries, 1984. Author weekly newspaper column Notes From A Pastor's Desk, True Citizen, Waynesboro, Ga., 1982-83; (plays) Jonah: A Whale of a Man, Judas Now. Contbr. articles to profl. jours. Mem. Mayor's P.O. Search Com., Waynesboro, 1983; Social Services-Ch. Liaison Com., Conyers, 1984. Mem. Modern Music Masters Soc. Democrat. Lodge: Sertoma (sgt. at arms 1974-75). Home: 1368 Classic Dr NE Conyers GA 30208 Office: Faith Tabernacle United Pentecostal Ch 2143 Gees Mill Rd Conyers GA 30208

REYNOLDS, JOHN PETER, priest, Roman Catholic Ch.; b. New Orleans, Apr. 23, 1925; s. John P. and Elma (Coburn) R.; student St. Joseph's Sem., 1944, Notre Dame Sem., New Orleans, 1949; M. Ed., Loyola U., New Orleans, 1952. Ordained priest, 1949; pastor St. Patrick Ch., New Orleans, 1965—, dir. St. Patrick's cemeteries, 1965-68. Asso. dir. St. Ann's Nat. Shrine, New Orleans, 1949-65, Sodalities, Archdiocese New Orleans, 1950-55; asst. editor-in-chief Catholic Action of the South, 1955-62; adminstrv. dir. and treas. Clarion Herald Pub. Co., New Orleans, 1962-74; supr. sch. food services Archdiocese New Orleans, 1967—; dir. Ozanam Inn, New Orleans, 1966—. Mem. Am. Sch. Food Service Assn., Kappa Delta Pi. Home: 724 Camp St New Orleans LA 70130 Office: 3003 S Carrollton Ave New Orleans LA 70118

REYNOLDS, LOUIS BERNARD, minister, Seventh-day Adventists; b. Verdery, S.C., Feb. 23, 1917; s. Albert and Josephine (Harris) R.; B.A., Fisk U., 1958; M.A., Howard U., 1968; LL.D., Union Bapt. Sem., 1970; m. Ann Bernice Johnson, May 28, 1938; children—Dawn Reynolds, Joan Reynolds Cruz. Pastor, Kansas City, Mo., 1938-41; dist. supt. State Kans., 1941-44; editor So. Pub. House, 1944-59; pastor, New Rochelle, N.Y., 1960-62; asso. dir., editor World Sabbath Sch. Dept. Publs., Washington, 1962-75; field sec. Gen. Conf. Seventh-day Adventists, Washington, 1975—. Columnist, Kansas City Call, 1938-44; mem. bd. Asso. Ch. Press, 1952-59, Oakwood Coll., 1949-59, Riverside Hosp., 1944-59; mem. Gen. Conf. Com., 1962—. Recipient First prize Elks Oratorical Contest for No. Ala., 1931, award of merit Daniel Payne Coll., Birmingham, Ala., 1970. Author: Dawn of Tomorrow, 1945; Look to the Hills, 1960; Journeys to Storyland, 1945; Great Texts from Romans, 1972; (with Robert L. Peerson) Bible Answers, 1974. Home: 7510 Dundalk Rd Takoma Park MD 20012 Office: 6840 Eastern Ave NW Washington DC 20012

REYNOLDS, MARTI DAVID, minister, Lutheran Church in America; b. Beloit, Wis., May 2, 1953; s. David Derwin and Carol Joann (Pilz) R. B.A., U. S.C., 1977; M.Div., Luth. Theol. So. Sem., 1981. Ordained to ministry Lutheran Ch., 1982. Vol. chaplain Children's Hosp., Birmingham, Ala., 1979-80; resident chaplain S.C. State Hosp., Columbia, 1981-82; chaplain fellow U. Tex.-M.D. Anderson Hosp., Houston, 1983-84; pastor Trinity Luth. Ch., LaMarque, Tex., 1984—. Served with U.S. Army, 1972-75. S.C. Synod scholar, 1976. Republican. Lodge: Lions. Home: 2104 12th Ave LaMarque TX 77568 Office: Trinity Lutheran Ch 2024 12th Ave LaMarque TX 77568

REYNOLDS, MICHAEL EUGENE, minister, army chaplain, marriage and family therapist, Christian Church (Disciples of Christ); b. Vincennes, Ind., July 3, 1945; s. Clyde Eugene and Rachel Pauline (Gilmore) R.; m. Annette Baugh, Feb. 8, 1974; children: Michael Eugene, Aaron Bradley Dyke. B.A., Asbury Coll., 1969; D.Min., Lexington Theol. Sem., 1973; M.S. in Edn., U. Ky., 1983. Ordained to ministry Christian Ch. (Disciples of Christ), 1973. Minister, Mt. Carmel United Meth. Ch., Bedford, Ky., 1967-69, Mt. Beulah United Meth. Ch., Nicholasville, Ky., 1969-71; assoc. minister Epworth United Meth. Ch., Lexington, Ky., 1971-73; chaplain Blackburn Correctional Complex, Lexington, 1973-74; commd. 2d lt. U.S. Army, 1974, advanced through grades to maj., 1982; chaplain, 1974—; dir. family life ctr., Schofield Barracks, Hawaii, 1979-80; plans, program and tng. chaplain Ft. Carson, Colo., 1983, dir. clin. pastoral edn. ctr., 1983—; staff chaplain, Honduras, 1984—. Pvt. practice hypnotherapy, marriage and family therapy, Colorado Springs, Colo., 1983—. Bd. dirs. Colo. Interfaith Counseling Ctr., Colorado Springs, 1983—; v.p., bd. dirs. Shannon Green Condominium Assn., Colorado Springs, 1983—; pastoral adviser Child Protection Case Mgmt. Team, Ft. Carson, 1983—; vol. trainer El Paso County Dept. Social Services, Colorado Springs, 1983—. Mem. Assn. for Clin. Pastoral Edn. (acting supr. 1982—), Am. Assn. Profl. Hypnotherapists (profl.), Inst. for Advanced Study in Rational Psychotherapy, Assn. for Rational Thinkers. Democrat. Home: 2953 E Fountain Blvd Colorado Springs CO 80910 Office: Office of Staff Chaplain Fort Carson CO 80913

RHEIN, DON WILLIAM, minister, Ch. of God (Cleveland, Tenn.); b. Grayville, Ill., Dec. 12, 1930; s. Benjamin F. and Mary E. (Sigler) R.; hon. grad. Lee Coll., Cleveland, 1963; m. Viola Mae Carter, Jan. 24, 1953; 1 dau., Sheri Renea. Ordained to ministry, 1957; evangelist, Ill., Ind., Ky., N.C., S.C., Fla. and Mo.; pastor Bradley (Ill.) Ch. of God, 1960-62, So. Boston (Va.) Ch. of God, 1962-64, Meadowood Ch. of God, Richmond, Va., 1964-74, Carmi (Ill.) Ch. of God, 1974—. Mem. Va. youth bd. Ch. of God, 1962-66, mem. Va. bd. evangelism, 1966-72, Va. state council, 1966-74; mem. nat. radio and TV bd., 1966-72, chmn., 1968-72; dir. evangelism Ill., 1974-76; mem. Ill. state council, 1976—; founder Meadowood Christian Sch., Richmond, 1969-74, bd. dirs., 1969-74; pres. Carmi Ministerial Assn., 1976—. Mem. Carmi C. of C. (dir. 1976—). Address: 400 W Fackney St Carmi IL 62821

RHOADS, JAMES LAWRENCE, minister, Christian Union; b. Bainbridge, Ohio, May 12, 1922; s. James McKibben and Della Elizabeth (Zickafoose) R.; student Christian Union Extension Sch., Mo., 1955; m. Marjorie Lorene Rhoads, July 18, 1940. Ordained to ministry Christian Union, 1958; pres. Ohio Council, Christian Union, 1966-73, Gen. Council Christian Union, 1973—. Chaplain, Otway (Ohio) Fire Dept. Active Boy Scouts Am. Address: 106 W Broadway Excelsior Springs MO 64024

RHODES, DENNIS ROBERT, church archivist, Orthodox Church in America; b. Hamilton AFB, Calif., June 15, 1948; s. Robert Aaron Rhodes and Marion Margery (Levisee) Rhodes Cotter; m. Valentina Tichy, Sept. 11, 1977; children: Sarah, Jonathan. Ordained deacon Orthodox Church in America, 1978, priest, 1979; cert. in archives administrn. Nat. Archives. Assn. archivist Orthodox Ch. in Am., Syosset, N.Y., 1978-79, 81-82, archival cons., 1980-81, archivist, 1982—; sec. dept. history and archives Orthodox Ch. in Am., Syosset, 1978—. Editor: Orthodoxy and Native Americans, 1980. Mem. Soc. Am. Archivists, Archivists of Religious Instns., Orthodox Theol. Soc. Am. Home: 11 Lee Ave Bethpage NY 11714 Office: Orthodox Ch in Am PO Box 675 Syosset NY 11791

RHODES, NORMAN K(AY), religious broadcasting executive, Church of Christ; b. Mulvane, Kans., Feb. 12, 1930; s. Andrew Harold and Margaret Alice (Higginson) R.; m. Mary Joyce Darling, Dec. 27, 1951; children: Mark Andrew, Linda Kay, Sara Lynn, Leonard Dean, Martha Jean. B.A., Friends U., Wichita, Kans., 1953. Deacon Webb Chapel Ch. of Christ, Dallas, 1962-67, elder, 1967-68; elder White's Ferry Rd. Ch. of Christ, West Monroe, La., 1970—; dir. World Radio, West Monroe, 1977—; mem. adv. bd. World Christian Broadcasting Corp., Abilene, Tex., 1982—. Office: White's Ferry Rd Ch of Christ 3201 N 7th St West Monroe LA 71291

RIANI, PETER ROBARGE, priest, Roman Catholic Church; b. Plattsburgh, N.Y., Aug. 16, 1929; s. Peter L. and Mary Elizabeth (Robarge) R. B.A., Wadhams Hall, 1951; S.T.L., St. Mary's Sem., 1955; S.T.D., Angelicum U., Rome, 1960, M.Ed., U. Ottawa, Ont., Can., 1963. Ordained priest, Roman Cath. Ch. Asst. pastor St. Paul's Ch., Black River, N.Y., 1955-57, St. Bernard's Ch., Saranac Lake, N.Y., 1957-59; prof. Wadhams Hall, Ogdensburg, N.Y., 1960-74; pres., 1974-82; pastor St. Agnes Ch., Lake Placid, N.Y., 1982—. Lodge: Kiwanis. Home and Office: 6 Hillcrest Ave Lake Placid NY 12946

RICARD, JOHN, priest, Roman Catholic Church; b. Baton Rouge, Feb. 29, 1940; s. Maceo and Albanie (St. Amant) R.; B.A., St. Joseph Sem., 1962, M.A., 1968; M.S., Tulane U., 1970. Ordained priest, 1968; pastor Holy Redeemer Ch., Washington, 1972-75, Holy Comforter Ch., Washington, 1975-84; ordained titular bishop of Rucuma and aux. bishop of Balt., 1984; asso. prof. Cath. U. Am., Washington, 1973—. Mem. sch. bd. Archdiocese of Washington, 1976—, mem. priests senate, 1974—. Mem. Secretariat of Black Catholics. Address: 320 Cathedral St Baltimore MD 21201*

RICCIARDELLI, ANGELA ROSE, lay worker, Roman Catholic Church; b. Jersey City, Feb. 18, 1935; d. Quirinus Armand and Lena Mary (Campanella) R. B.A., Georgian Ct., 1956; M.A., Cath. U. Am., 1974; Ph.D., Georgetown U., 1984. Editor, Cath. U. Am., Washington, 1972-76; cons. Theol. Coll., Washington, 1976-79; dir. publs. office U.S. Cath. Conf., Washington, 1979-81; dir. orgn. services Nat. Council Cath. Women, Washington, 1981—. Author: Relation of Faith and Reason in Philosophy of Kierkegaard, 1974; Philosophical Basis of Survival in a United World, 1984. Recipient Human Rights award Capital Area chpt. UN Assn., 1982; Trustees scholar Cath. U. Am., 1971. Republican. Lodge: Zonta (pres. Washington chpt. 1982-84, Leadership award 1984). Office: Nat Council Cath Women 1312 Massachusetts Ave NW Washington DC 20005

RICE, ARTHUR HOPKINS, lay church worker, Episcopal Church; b. Portsmouth, N.H., May 22, 1914; s. Arthur Hopkins and Ellnora (Richter) R.; A.B., Harvard U., 1937; M.A., U. Miss., 1948. Pres., Potomac Assembly, Episc. Diocese of Washington, 1959-60, 67-85, Nat. Council, Brotherhood of St. Andrew, Washington, 1960-85. Mem. Res. Officers Assn., YMCA, Newcomen Soc. Home: 180 Middle St Portsmouth NH 03801 Office: 2231 California St NW Washington DC 20008

RICE, GEORGE EDWARD, theology educator; Seventh-day Adventists; b. Waterbury, Conn., Apr. 23, 1933; George Harry and Dorothy Louise (Book) R.; m. Janet Mildred Bowen, June 7, 1953; 1 dau., Shereen Beverly. B.A., Atlantic Union Coll., 1955; M.A., Andrews U., 1957, B.D., 1968; Ph.D., Case Western Res. U., 1974. Ordained to ministry Seventh-day Adventists, 1960. Pastor, So. New Eng. Conf., Mass. and R.I., 1955-62, No. New Eng. Conf., N.H., 1962-64, Nev. Utah Conf., Ogden, Utah, 1964-67; religion educator So. Missionary Coll., Collegdale, Tenn., 1970-72, Atlantic Union Coll., South Lancaster, Mass., 1972-78, Andrews U., Berrien Springs, Mich., 1978—. Author: Christ in Collision, 1982; Luke, a Plagiarist?, 1983; contbr. articles to profl. jours. Mem. Soc. Bibl. Lit., Chgo. Soc. Bibl. Research. Home: 1410 Ridgewood Trail Berrien Springs MI 49103 Office: Andrews Univ Sem Berrien Springs MI 49104

RICE, HAROLD ALBERT, chaplain, American Lutheran Church; b. Boston, Feb. 4, 1940; s. Harold Ellsworth and Mathilda Marie (Salvesen) R.; m. Caroline Elizabeth Zirkman, Mar. 1, 1963; children: Eric Charles, Bryan Jon, Alyssa Elizabeth. B.A., St. Olaf Coll., 1961; M.Div., Luther Theol. Sem., 1965; postgrad. Iliff, 1972-73, Menninger Inst., 1982. Ordained to ministry. Vicar, Trinity Luth. Ch.,

Owatonna, Minn., 1963-64; pastor Gilbert Luth. Ch., Iowa, 1965-68; chaplain U.S. Air Force, 1968—, Air Base Wing/Hdqrs., Offutt AFB. Author curriculum: The Last Book of Bible, 1971; What Happened Between the Testaments, 1981. Active Girl Scouts U.S.A. Republican. Home: 3206 Daniell St Omaha NE 68123 Office: 3902 Air Base Wing Hdqrs Offutt AFB NE 68123

RICE, HAROLD LILBORN, minister, Christian Church (Disciples of Christ); b. Raceland, Ky., June 3, 1921; s. John Basil and Willa Ann (Heaberlin) R.; student in Bible, Ky. Christian Coll., 1958-59; m. Majel Mitchell, May 21, 1941; children: Gary Joe, Thomas Mitchell. Ordained to ministry, 1953; pastor chs., South Shore, Ky., 1953-54, Leaksville, N.C., 1954-56, New Boston, Ohio, 1957-65, Charleston, W.Va., 1965-67, Carlisle (Ky.) Christian Ch., 1967-74, 1st Christian Ch., Wrightsville, Ga., 1974—; evangelist states including Miss., W.Va., Fla. and Ill. Pres. Kyowva Evang. Assn., 1961-62, Middle Ky. Evang. Assn., 1968-69, Kyowva Christian Camp Assn., 1957-62. Mem. Johnson County (Ga.) Bicentennial Com., 1976. Recipient Ky. Col. awards State of Ky., 1973, 1974. Mem. 1976 Council for Nat. Righteousness. Author: For Such A Time As This, 1976. Home and Office: 302 N Marcus St Wrightsville GA 31096

RICE, JONATHAN CLEVELAND, JR., minister, Southern Baptist Convention; b. Westminster, S.C., May 6, 1922; s. Jonathan Cleveland and Mary Lillie (Marett) R.; B.A., Furman U., 1949; D.Div., Bapt. Coll., Charleston, S.C., 1982; m. Lydia Margaret Campbell, Feb. 12, 1944; children: Frankie (Mrs. James Abrams), Jonathan Cleveland III, Ernest, Lydia (Mrs. George Tolleson). Ordained to ministry, 1948; pastor chs. in S.C., 1948-54; pastor Poplar Springs Ch., Ware Shoals, S.C., 1954-71; dir. missions Saluda Bapt. Assn., Anderson, S.C., 1971—; columnist Daily Mail, Anderson, 1973—; devotional writer Bapt. Courier, 1973-74. Pres. S.C. Bapt. Conv., 1970; mem. Christian Life and Pub. Affairs Com., S.C. Bapt. Conv., 1982—. Chmn. Edgefield County chpt. Nat. Found. Infantile Paralysis, 1951-54; active N.C. Tb and Respiratory Diseases Assn. Trustee Bethea Home for Aging, Darlington, S.C., Bapt. Courier; advisory bd. Baptist Coll. at Charleston (S.C.); trustee Furman U. Mem. Anderson Area C. of C. Home: 100 Pine Bark Rd Anderson SC 29621 Office: POB 3004 Anderson SC 29621

RICE, PHYLLIS MATHER See *Who's Who in America*, 43rd edition.

RICE, RICHARD, minister, educator, Seventh-day Adventist; b. Loma Linda, Calif., Nov. 14, 1944; s. Bruce H. and Alyse (Klose) R.; m. Gail Louise Taylor, Aug. 14, 1966; children: Alison Heather, Jonathan Taylor. B.A., Loma Linda U., 1966; M.Div., Andrews U., 1969; M.A., U. Chgo., 1972, Ph.D., 1974. Ordained to ministry Seventh-day Adventist Ch., 1977, Pastor, Seventh-day Adventist Ch., Southeastern Calif. Conf., 1967-70; prof. Loma Linda U., Riverside, Calif., 1974—. Author: The Openness of God, 1980. Fellow U. Chgo., 1972-73, 73-74. Home: 5241 Sierra Vista Riverside CA 92505 Office: Loma Linda U Riverside CA 92515

RICE, RONALD ALASTER, JR., minister, United Methodist Church; b. Asheville, N.C., July 20, 1950; s. Ronald Alaster and Kathryn Virginia (Pitman) R.; m. Peggy Lynn Burley, June 5, 1971; 1 child, Sean Elijah. B.C.E., N.C. State U., 1972; M.Div. Asbury Theol. Sem., 1982, postgrad., 1985. Ordained to ministry Methodist Ch. as elder, 1984. Chmn. of evangelism Weaverville United Meth. Ch., N.C., chmn. adv. bd., 1977-78; constrn. supr. Christ United Meth. Ch., Lexington, Ky., 1980-81, asst. pastor, 1980-82; pastor Sardis and Reeves Chapel, Asheville, 1982—; mem. bd. discipleship, edn. com. Conf. of N.C.-United Meth. Ch., Charlotte, 1984—, mem. confirmation design group, 1984-85, mem. archtl. bd., 1984-85. Contbr. articles to profl. jours. Scoutmaster Daniel Boone council Boy Scouts Am., Weaverville, 1973-74. Named Ky. Col., State of Ky., 1982, Mem. Jaycees (Jaycee of Yr. 1979, Keith Hawkins Faith in God award N.C. sect. 1979, chaplain, sec., treas., Weaverville sect. 1977-79), West N.C. Profl. Engrs. (sec., treas. 1975), Blue Ridge Contractors Assn. (pres. 1977-78). Avocations: motorcross; motorcycle trail riding; construction. Home: 142 Stradley Mountain Rd Asheville NC 28806 Office: Sardis and Reeves Chapel United Meth Ch 897 Brevard Rd Asheville NC 28806

RICHARD, THOMAS MATTHEW, minister, National Association of Congregational Christian Churches; b. Rumford, Maine, Oct. 20, 1947; s. Clayton E. and Lois Rosemond (Smith) R.; m. Sherry Lynn, May 30, 1969; children: Todd Matthew, Travis Matthew. Student Norwich Free Acad., Norwich, Conn., 1966; B.A., Piedmont Coll., 1970; M.Divinity, Bangor Theol. Seminary, 1974; D.Ministry, U. Dubuque Theol. Sch., 1985. Minister Newbury Congl. Ch., Brookfield Center, Conn., 1973-76, First Cong. Ch., South Paris, Maine, 1976-80; sr. minister First Congl. Ch., Marshalltown, Iowa, 1980—; fellow Congl. Found. for Theol. Studies, Oak Creek, Wis., 1970—; chmn. Nat. Assn. Congl., Chs. Youth Commn., Oak Creek, Wis., 1978-85; v.p. Vis. Nurses Assn., Marshalltown, Iowa, 1980-84; v.p. Hospice, Marshalltown, 1981-84, Friendship Center West, Marshalltown, 1984; mem. Marshalltown County Peace Fellowship, 1983; adj. chaplain Iowa Veterans Home, Marshalltown, 1982; adj. faculty mem. Marshalltown Community Coll., 1983; co-founder tchr. Nat. Youth Worker's Inst., Oak Creek, Wis., 1983. Editor, author Curriculum, Confirmation, 1978, 85, Resources for Youth, 1982; author handbook project Leadership Handbook, 1983. Chmn. Polit. Action Com. Chs. United in Compassion and Concern, Marshalltown, 1982; mem. Congl. Sensitizing Task Force, Marshalltown, 1983-84. Mem. Marshalltown Clergy Assn. (v.p. 1983; treas. 1984). Democrat. Club: Rotary. Home: 506 N 4th St Marshalltown IA 50158 Office: First Congl Ch 312 W Main St Marshalltown IA 50158

RICHARDS, HERBERT EAST, minister, United Methodist Church; b. Hazleton, Pa., Dec. 30, 1919; s. Herbert E. and Mable (Vannaucker) R.; m. Lois Marcey, Jan. 1, 1942; children: Herbert, Marcey, Fredrick, Robyn, Mark Allen. A.B. cum laude, Dickinson Coll., 1941; B.Div. magna cum laude, Drew U., 1944; M.A., Columbia U., 1944; D.Div., Coll. Idaho, 1953. Ordained to ministry United Meth. Ch. Assoc. prof. preaching Drew U., Madison, N.J., 1944-51; minister United Meth. Ch., Boise, 1951-68, 1st United Meth. Ch., Eugene, Oreg., 1968-78, Tabor Heights United Meth. Ch., Portland, Oreg., 1978—; assoc. prof., asst. dean Drew U., Madison, 1944-51; pres. Inspiration, Inc. Religious Radio and TV, 1954—; chaplain Idaho State Senate, Boise, 1952-65, Idaho Supreme Ct., Boise, 1958-66. Composer: Prophet Unwilling, 1954. Contbr. articles to profl. jours. Contbr. articles to profl. jours. Bd. dirs. ARC, Eugene, 1968-78, Boy Scouts Am., Eugene, 1968-78; trustee Willamette U., Salem, Oreg., 1982—, Cascade Manor Home, Eugene, 1968-78. Recipient Clergyman of Yr., Religious Heritage Am., 1965. Mem. Am. Found. Religion and Psychiatry (bd. govs.), Am. Acad. Achievement (v.p. 1976). Club: Eugene Country. Lodges: Rotary, Masons, Elks (state chaplain), Shriners. Home: 10172 SE 99th St Portland OR 97266 Office: Inspiration IAIC TV 6161 SW Stark Portland OR 97215

RICHARDS, LORETTA THERESA, nun, religion educator, Roman Catholic Church; b. N.Y.C., Apr. 8, 1929; d. David Alexander and Mary Elizabeth (Cornelius) Richards. B.A., Mt. St. Vincent, Riverdale, N.Y., 1954; M.A., Cath. U., 1960; M.A., Catechetical Inst., Yonkers, N.Y., 1984; D.Pedagogy (hon.), N.Y. Coll. Podiatric Medicine, 1981. Joined Franciscan Handmaids of Mary, Roman Cath. Ch., 1948. Tchr. Archdiocesan Schs., N.Y.C., 1954-64; community supr. Franciscan Handmaids of Mary, N.Y.C., 1964-68, vicar gen., 1968-74, supr. gen., 1974-82; religious edn. coordinator St. Aloysius Parish, N.Y.C., 1982—; sec. gen. Franciscan Handmaids of Mary, N.Y.C., 1982; co-moderator Guild of Praying Hands, N.Y.C., 1982; mem. pastoral team Manhattan Leaders Cath. Charismatics, N.Y.C., 1983. Trustee N.Y. Coll. Podiatric Medicine, N.Y.C., 1974—. Recipient Plaque, N.E. regional chpt. Black Lay Caucus, L.I., N.Y., 1981. Mem. Religious Educators Harlem Area (coordinator 1984). Home: 15 W 124th St New York NY 10027 Office: Saint Aloysius Parish 219 W 132d St New York NY 10027

RICHARDS, RILEY H., lay church worker. Chmn. bd. United Presbyterian Found. Office: Presbyterian Ch (USA) 475 Riverside Dr New York NY 10115*

RICHARDS, RUSSELL DUBOIS, social ministry exec., Lutheran Ch. Am.; b. Frederiksted, V.I., Sept. 7, 1930; s. Claude Jacobsen and Evelyn Marie (DuBois) R.; B.A., Lincoln U., 1960; M.S.W., U. Denver, 1965; m. Elena Luzunaris, Mar. 4, 1961; children—Russell DuBois, Wesley, Gregory. Ch. vocations com. Caribbean Synod, Luth. Ch. Am., 1971, mem. budget com., 1973, continuing edn. com., 1972; del. Caribbean Conf. Chs., 1972; mem. ch. council Holy Trinity Luth. Ch., Frederiksted, 1971-72; exec. dir. Luth. Social Services, V.I., St. Croix, 1970—. Instr. sociology Coll. V.I., part-time 1969—. Mem. Gov.'s Citizens Adv. Council, 1974; active Community Chest; chmn. V.I. Bd. Social Welfare, 1972—. Mem. Nat. Assn. Social Workers, Am. Pub. Welfare Assn., Clan of St. Croix. Home: POB 204 Frederiksted St Croix VI 00840 Office: POB 866 Frederiksted St Croix VI 00840

RICHARDSON, CHARLES RAYMOND, pastor, Southern Baptist Convention; b. Pittsburg, Tex., Sept. 12, 1934; s. Earl Roscoe and Dora Mae (Keeling) R.; m. Betty Ruth Birdsong, Aug. 14, 1959; children: Christi, David, Mark. B.A., Baylor U., 1957; B.D., Southwestern Bapt. Theol. Sem., 1961. Ordained, 1954. Moderator Van Zandt Bapt. Assn., Van Zandt County, Tex., 1978-80; pastor 1st Bapt. Ch., Canton, Tex., 1981—; mem. exec. bd. Bapt. Gen. Conv. Tex., Dallas, 1968-77. Mem. Salvation Army Service Unit, Pittsburg, 1960-65, Canton, 1966-70. Lodge: Lions (Canton). Home: PO Box 336 Canton TX 75103 Office: First Bapt Ch 303 S Athens St Canton TX 75103

RICHARDSON, GEORGE MCLEAN, minister, United Church of Canada; b. Renfrew, Ont., Can., Jan. 5, 1924; s. Garfield Newton and Mary Grace (McLean) R.; m. Eunice Marjorie Buchan, Sept. 15, 1950; children: Gwendolyn, Joyce, Gloria, Ruth, Susan. B.A., Queen's U., 1958, B.Div., 1961, D.Div. (hon.), 1983. Ordained to ministry United Ch. Can., 1960. Student Pastor Westport Pastoral Charge, Ont., 1955-58, Inverary Pastoral Ch., Ont., 1958-60; minister Manvers Pastoral Charge, Ont., 1960-62, Athens Pastoral Charge, Ont., 1962-66; sr. minister St. Paul's Ch., Perth, Ont., 1966—; pres. Bay of Quinte Conf., Ont., 1974-75; chmn. Renfrew Presbytery, Ont., 1968-69; conf. rep. Gen. Council Exec., 1982-86. Lodge: Masons (chaplain 1967-69). Address: 20 Gore St W Perth ON K7H 2L8 Canada

RICHARDSON, HARVEY LEE, minister, Southern Baptist Convention; b. Louisville, June 3, 1930; s. Ezra Hasely and Elizabeth Earmon (Gault) R.; m. Patricia Ann Wells, June 2, 1956; children: Craig, Mark, Jeffrey. B.A., U. Louisville, 1969; M.Div., So. Sem., Louisville, 1972, D.Min., 1980. Ordained to ministry, 1969. Pastor, Rowletts Bapt. Ch., Ky., 1966-68, First Bapt. Ch., Austin, Ind., 1968-70, Parkway Bapt. Ch., New Albany, Ind., 1970-72, Plum Creek Bapt. Ch., Taylorsville, Ky., 1972-76, Kenwood Bapt. Ch., Louisville, 1976—; mem. ch. relations com. Cumberland Coll., Williamsburg, Ky., 1982—; Sunday sch. dir. Long Run Assn., Louisville, 1982—; pres. Pastor's Conf., Louisville, 1983; exec. bd. Ky. Bapt., Middletown, 1980-83. Pres. Concerned Citizens, Taylorsville, Ky., 1973, S. Louisville Community Ministries, 1983; treas. Star-Lite Crusade, Louisville, 1980. Served with USAF, 1950-54. Republican. Home: 5356 Southdale Rd Louisville KY 40214 Office: Kenwood Bapt Ch 6603 S 3d St Louisville KY 40214

RICHARDSON, JAMES BRINSON, minister, So. Bapt. Conv.; b. Charlotte, N.C., May 12, 1945; s. James Preston and Margaret Elizabeth (Granberry) R.; B.A., Mars Hill Coll., 1968; M.Div., So. Bapt. Theol. Sem., 1971; m. Carol Ann Hayes, June 9, 1972; children—Michael Brinson Richardson. Ordained to ministry, 1970; youth worker Shawnee Bapt. Ch., Louisville, Ky., 1968-71; pastor English (Ky.) Bapt. Ch., 1972-74, 1st Bapt. Ch., Tryon, N.C., 1974—. Named Outstanding Young Minister, Polk County Jaycees, 1973. Home: Glenwalden Circle Tryon NC 28782 Office: Box 1287 Tryon NC 28782

RICHARDSON, JOHN THOMAS See *Who's Who in America*, 43rd edition.

RICHARDSON, LINCOLN, minister, Presbyterian Church in the U.S.A.; b. Turtle Creek, Pa., July 25, 1938; s. Ralph Holmes and Margaret Rebecca (Chew) R.; m. Gloria Edith Munkberg, Aug. 30, 1980; children: Hilary, Matthew Lincoln, Eli Jeremy. B.A. with honors, Northwestern U., 1960; M.Div., Yale U., 1963. Ordained to ministry, 1963. Pastor Ecumenical Fellowship, Madison, N.J., 1963-66; assoc. editor Presbyterian Life mag., Phila., 1966-73; dir. communications Synod of Lakes and Prairies, Bloomington, Minn., 1973-79; pastor First Presbyn. Ch., Pine City, Minn., 1980-82, Dixon, Ill., 1982—; bd. dirs. People, Inc., St. Paul, 1975-80; chmn. Christian edn. com. Twin City Area Presbytery, Mpls., 1980-82. Author: Contemporary Faiths in Familiar Forms, 1967. Contbr. numerous articles to profl. jours. Recipient Mersick prize Yale U., 1963. Home: 122 E 3d St Dixon IL 61021 Office: First Presbyn Ch 110 E 3d St Dixon IL 61021

RICHARDSON, TERRANCE KEITH, minister, Lutheran Church-Missouri Synod; b. Edmonton, Alta., Can., Jan. 14, 1955; s. Keith Wesley and Bertha Louise (Jacobson) R.; m. Mona Helga Lippert, Aug. 15, 1976; 1 child, Colleen. B.A. (gen.), U. Alta., Edmonton, 1974, B.A. (spl.), 1976; M.Div., Luth. Theol. Sem., Saskatoon, Sask., Can., 1981. Ordained to ministry Luth. Ch., 1981. Intern, St. Matthew's Luth. Ch., Stony Plain, Alta., 1979-80; pastor, mission developer St. Paul's Luth. Ch., Mannville, Alta., 1981—, Faith Luth. Ch., Verminion, Alta., 1981—. Contbr. to book: The Road To Jasper, 1978. Mem. Vermilion Ministerial Assn. (chmn. 1983-85). Home: PO Box 395 Vermilion AB T0B 4M0 Canada Office: Vermilion Mannville Luth Ch PO Box 395 Vermilion AB T0B 4M0 Canada

RICHARDSON, WILBUR JEAN, minister, Cumberland Presbyterian Church; b. Elizabethtown, Ky., Apr. 11, 1930; s. Wilbur Brandon and Bertha Edna (Powell) R.; m. Regena Laycock, Sept. 18, 1953; children: Sheena Lynn Richardson Beal, Jeana Ray Richardson Daniel. B.A., Bethel Coll., 1951; B.D., Cumberland Presbyn. Theol. Sem., 1955. Ordained minister, 1951. Pastor Beaver Creek Ch., Knoxville, Tenn., 1956-61, Red Bank Ch., Chattenooga, 1961-64; assoc. pastor First Ch., Chattanooga, 1964-66; pastor First Ch., Evansville, Ind., 1966-71, Beaver Creek Ch., Knoxville, 1971—; gen. assembly exec. com. Cumberland Presbyn. Ch., Memphis, 1981-83, bd. missions pres., 1976-84, moderator, 1981-82. Contbr. articles to religious jours. Active TVA. Lodges: Masons, Kiwanis, Scottish Rite, Shriners. Home: 7533 Lancashire Blvd Powell TN 37849 Office: Beaver Creek

Cumberland Presbyn Ch 7225 Old Clinton Pike Knoxville TN 37921

RICHARDSON, WILLIAM RAMSEY, priest, Episcopal Ch.; b. Charleston, W.Va., Jan. 24, 1931; s. Jewel Burgess and Zelema Miriam (Atkinson) R.; B.A., Hampden-Sydney Coll., 1952; M.Ed., U. Va., 1960; M.Div., Protestant Episc. Theol. Sem., Alexandria, Va., 1963; m. Emily Howard Tongue, May 27, 1967; children—Thomas Ramsey, David Kirk, James Smiley. Ordained priest, 1964; asst. rector St. Paul's Ch., Lynchburg, Va., 1963-66; vicar-in-charge Emmanuel Ch., Madison Heights, Va., 1964-66; rector Episc. Ch. of the Redeemer, Richmond, Va., 1966—. Chaplain Protestant Episc. Ch. Home for Ladies, Richmond, 1973-75; diocesan chmn. Presiding Bishop's Fund for World Relief, 1972—; mem. Va. Council Chs., 1973-75, exec. bd., 1974-75; examining chaplain Diocese of So. Va., 1974—, mem. exec. bd., 1975—, mem. commn. on ministry, 1974—, chmn. dept. spl. ministries, 1976—; bd. dirs. Norfolk Urban Outreach, 1976—. Bd. dirs. Traveler's Aid Soc., Richmond, 1967—; trustee Fishburne-Hudgins Ednl. Found., Waynesboro, Va., 1972-75. Mem. SAR. Contbr. articles to religious publs., Sermon Subscription Service. Home: 8330 W Weyburn Rd Richmond VA 23235 Office: 8401 Chippenham Pkwy Richmond VA 23235

RICHARDSON, WILLIAM WOOLEY, lay worker, United Church of Christ; b. Victory Mills, N.Y., Sept. 9, 1908; s. Harry and Catherine (Wooley) R.; m. Ruth Henrich; children: Carol Richardson Ray, Gail Richardson Mason. Student indsl. engring. Worcester Poly. Inst., 1928-32, Northeastern U., 1929-34. Pres., R.I. Bible Soc., Barrington, 1957-84, distbn. sec., 1983-85; chmn. Pine Mountain Lay Sch. Theology, 1960-61; pres. R.I. Council United Ch. Men, 1961-62; gen. sec. United Christian Ashrams, 1961-76; bd. dirs. United Ch. Bd. for World Ministries, 1965-81, chmn. S. Am. projects. European projects service div., 1962-78; trustee Barrington Coll.; corr. Christian Century radio programs; lectr. mission work to local chs. and groups on behalf of World Missions and Ch. World Services. Former pres., treas. W.W. Richardson Ins. Agy., Inc. Mem. Bristol County Assn. Ins. Agts. (pres., treas. 1975-84). Republican. Lodge: Rotary. Avocations: photography; travel. Home and Office: Bible Distbn Ctr 91 Prospect St Barrington RI 02806

RICHEY, MCMURRY SMITH, theology educator, United Methodist Church; b. Marlin, Tex., Oct. 10, 1914; s. McMurry and Ruby Elna (Smith) R.; m. Erika Marx, Aug. 12, 1938; children: Russell Earle, Thomas Samuel, Douglas Grady. A.A., Brownsville Jr. Coll. (named changed to Tex. Southmost Coll.), 1933; A.B., Duke U., 1936, B.D., 1939, Ph.D., 1954. Ordained elder United Methodist Ch., 1943. Assoc. pastor, dir. Christian edn. Central Meth. Ch., Asheville, N.C., 1939-41; pastor Cullowhee Meth. Ch., N.C., 1941-45; asst. prof. math. Western Caolina Coll., 1943-45; pastor Kerr St. Meth. Ch., Concord, N.C., 1945-46, Brevard St. Meth. Ch., Charlotte, N.C., 1946-47; dir. Meth. student work, asst. prof. philosophy and religion U. Houston, 1947-51; from asst. prof. to prof. theology and christian nurture The Div. Sch. Duke U., Durham, N.C., 1954-84, ret., 1984; dir. continuing edn., 1972-80; chmn., exec. com. profs. of religion sect. Nat. Meth. Conf. on Christian Edn., 1963-65; exec. com. profs. and research sect. div. Christian edn. Nat. Council of Chs., 1968-70. Co-author: The Ministry in the Methodist Heritage, 1960; A Miscellany of American Christianity, 1963. Contbr. articles to profl. jours. Fellow Kearns, 1952-54, Kent, 1953—; faculty fellow Assn. Theol. Schs., 1969-70. Mem. Religious Edn. Assn., Soc. Advancement of Continuing Edn. for Ministry, Assn. United Meth. Christian Edn., Profs. and Research sect. div. Christian Edn. Nat. Council of Chs., Soc. for Religion in Higher Edn., Phi Beta Kappa, Pi Gamma Mu, Phi Theta Kappa. Democrat.

RICHTER, ROBERT LAWRENCE, minister, Lutheran Church-Missouri Synod; b. Memphis, Oct. 20, 1934; s. Edwin Michael and Hettie Elizabeth (Meek) R.; m. Suzanne Doretha Landry, July 14, 1960; children: Rachael, Christian, Ingrid. A.A., St. John's U., 1953-55; B.A., Concordia Sem., St. Louis, 1958, M.Div., 1960; D.Min., Wartburg Sem., 1981. Ordained to ministry, 1960. Pastor, Gethsemane Luth. Ch., St. Paul, 1960-62, University Luth. Ch., Tuscaloosa, Ala., 1962-64; chaplain U.S. Navy, Charleston, S.C., 1964-66, Jacksonville, Fla., 1966-67; pastor Grace Luth. Ch., Pensacola, Fla., 1967-75; chief, chaplain VA Hosp., Madison, Wis., 1975—; pres. Madison Area Luth. Council Chs., 1981-82; chmn. Pensacola Area Luth. Council Chs., 1970-72. Author: The Last Enemy, 1983; Concordia Pulpit, 1974. Contbr. articles to profl. jours. Recipient St. Martin of Tours medal Luth. Ch.-Mo. Synod, 1983, Republican. Home: 1602 Prairie Rd Madison WI 53711 Office: Wm S Middleton Meml VA Hosp 2500 Overlook Terr Madison WI 53705

RICK, JOHN WILLIAM, II, priest, Episcopal Ch.; b. St. Louis, June 15, 1941; s. John William and Mildred Arline (Robben) R.; A.B., Washington U., St. Louis, 1965; M.B.A., U. Va., Charlottesville, 1967; M.Div., Yale, 1974, postgrad., 1974-75. Mktg. mgr. Gen. Foods Corp., N.Y.C., 1967-71; ordained priest, 1975; asst. master Jonathan Edwards Coll., Yale, 1972-75; asst. minister Christ Episc. Ch., Greenwich, Conn., 1974-75; dir. devel. and alumni affairs, mem. faculty, master Brooks Sch., North Andover, Mass., 1975—. Vis. instr. U. Va. Bus. Sch., 1969-74, U. Va. Nursing Sch., 1975-76. Dir., treas. Episc. Ch. at Yale; summer supply priest St. Saviour's Ch., Bar Harbor, Maine. Bd. dirs. Yale Coop Corp., DBL & Assos. North Andover; chmn. bd. Gray Meml. Found. at U. Va. Mem. Mass. Soc. Fund Raisers, Assn. Yale Alumni, Council for Advancement, Support Edn. Editor, chmn. editorial bd. Brooks Bull., 1975—. Home and Office: Brooks Sch North Andover MA 01845

RICKENBAKER, GLEATON FOREMAN, JR., minister, Southern Baptist Convention; b. Charleston, S.C., Dec. 14, 1933; s. Gleaton Foreman and Pauline Lois (Fender) R.; m. Charlotte Ann Wyatt, Aug. 27, 1959; children: Gleaton Paul, Janet Kay, David Foreman. A.B., U. Corpus Christi, 1960; D.Min., Southeastern Bapt. Theol. Sem., 1965. Ordained to ministry, 1959. Music edn. dir. Parkway Bapt. Ch., Corpus Christi, Tex., 1958-59; pastor Collegeport Bapt. Ch., Tex., 1959-61, Bullock Bapt. Ch., N.C., 1963-66; assoc. pastor Melbourne Bapt. Ch., Fla., 1966-69; pastor First Bapt. Ch. St. Charles, Waldorf, Md., 1960—; moderator Potomac Bapt. Assn., Waldorf, 1974, 75, 81, 82, vice moderator, 1973, mem. exec. com., Sun. sch. dir., 1973, chmn. mission com., 1974-79, 82-84, sem. extension com., 1975-77, dir. vacation Bible sch., 1969, Sunday sch. youth resource person, 1975-79, pres. pastor's conf., 1975; chmn. exec. com. Bapt. Conv. Md., 1977, mem. exec. com., 1977-81, mem. state mission bd., 1972-81, 83—, vice chmn. Md. Bapt. Com., 1976, 84, mem. Christian life and pub. affairs com., 1972-75; D.C. Md. Cooperation mem. com. on bds. and agys. So. Bapt. Conv., 1980. Author: Youth in Discovery, Sunday Sch. Lessons, 1974. Mem. Citizens Adv. Bd. of Crownsville State Hosp., Md., 1984—; bd. dirs. Waldorf Pastoral Counseling Service, 1979-84. Served with U.S. Army, 1955-66. Home: 2210 Elgin Ct Waldorf MD 20601 Office: First Baptist Ch of Saint Charles 136 Stoddert Ave Waldorf MD 20601

RICKETT, GENE, lay worker, Southern Baptist Convention; b. Tinsley, Ky., Dec. 6, 1931; s. Elmer Oscar and Mary Ellen (Slusher) R.; m. Virginia May Johnson, Jan. 27, 1971. Student pub. schs., Washington. Pres., Poets for Christ, Seymour, Tenn., 1965—. Author: Poems of Inspiration, 1964; Poetic Post Cards, 1972. Served with USAF, 1950-70. Lodge: Masons. Address: Route 6 Box 266 Tennessee Dr Seymour TN 37865

RICKETT, KENNETH LEE, minister, Christian Church (Disciples of Christ). B. Andrews, N.C., Feb. 27, 1949; s. Paul Kenneth and Lenna Susan (Calhoun) R.; m. Della Lorraine Mull, Nov. 24, 1972; 1 child: Kevin Scott. B.A., Mars Hill Coll., N.C., 1971; M.Div., Southeastern Bapt. Theol., Wakes Forest, N.C., 1974. Ordained to ministry Baptist Ch., 1974; recognition and standing in Christian Ch. (Disciples of Christ), 1979. Minister, Cartledge Creek Bapt. Ch., Rockingham, N.C., 1975-77, Salem Fork Christian Ch., Dobson, N.C., 1977-82, First Christian Ch., Richlands, N.C., 1982—; mem. camp and conf. com. N.C. Disciples of Christ, Wilson, 1982-84, chmn. N.C. Educare, 1982-84, chmn. commn. on leadership devel., 1984—; mem. long range and coordinating council N.C. Regional Ch., 1984-86, mem. fin. com., 1984-86. Co-author: Under the Beechnut Trees, 1983. Asst. coach Little League Baseball, Richlands, 1984; mem. adv. com. Christian treatment program Brynn Marr Psychiat. Hosp., Jacksonville, N.C., 1984—. Mem. Disciples of Christ Hist. Soc. (life), N.C. Chaplain's Assn. (assoc.), Richlands Ministerial Assn. (pres. 1984—). Democrat. Home: PO Box 425 Richlands NC 28574

RICKMAN, CLAUDE ROGER, minister, educational administrator Wesleyan Church; b. Brevard, N.C., Nov. 10, 1917; s. Andrew Cornelius and Flora Pearl (Powell) R.; m. Evelyn Thornton Tucker, Jan. 1, 1942; children: Claude Merideth, Sharon Carol Rickman Wallace, Bryan Cary. A.B., B.S., Marion Coll., 1941; M.A., U. N.C., 1952, Ph.D., 1956; LL.D. (hon.), Central Wesleyan Coll., 1982. Ordained elder, Wesleyan Methodist Ch., 1947. Pastor Ragan Wesleyan Ch. Gastonia, N.C., 1946, 1948-50; dean Central Wesleyan Coll., Central, S.C., 1946-68, pres., 1968-79, asst. to pres., 1980—; pres. N.C. dist. Wesleyan Youth, Colfax, 1951-56; del. Gen. Conf. Wesleyan Ch. (every 4 yrs.) 1956-80; mem. Wesleyan Council of Edn., 1968-79. Mem. Pickens County Sch. Bd., S.C., 1983—. Served with USN, 1942-45, lt. comdr. Res. ret. Mem. Central C. of C. (past pres.). Republican. Lodge: Lions. Home: Box 458 Central Wesleyan Coll Central SC 29630 Office: Central Wesleyan Coll Central SC 29630

RIDDLE, EARL WALDO, ch. ofcl., United Meth. Ch.; b. St. Joseph, Mo., Jan. 29, 1920; s. Roderick Edwin and Nannie Myrtle (Albertson) R.; Asso. Sci., Mo. Western Coll., 1940; A.B., U. Kans., 1942; M.Div., Boston U., 1945, postgrad., 1946-50; D.Ministry, San Francisco Theol. Sem., 1976; m. Etta Kathryn McGauhey, Aug. 23, 1942; children—Martha Anne (Mrs. Donald Moretty), Mary Janet (Mrs. John Switzer), David Earl. Dir. youth work Morgan Meml. Ch. All Nations, Boston, 1942-45; ordained to ministry as elder, 1945; chaplain USNR, 1945-46; asso. pastor College Ave. Meth. Ch., West Somerville, Mass., 1946-50; dir. Wesley Found., Oreg. State U., Corvallis, 1950-54; pastor Forest Grove (Oreg.) Meth. Ch., 1954-60; sr. pastor First Meth. Ch., Twin Falls, Idaho, 1960-65; sr. pastor First Meth. Ch., Caldwell, Idaho, 1965-68; conf. council dir. Oreg.-Idaho Conf. United Meth. Ch., Portland, Oreg., 1968—. Exec. dir. local com. Gen. Conf. United Meth. Ch., Portland, 1976, mem. gen. conf., 1964, 66, 68, 70, mem. jurisdictional conf., 1964, 68, mem. gen. bd. edn., 1966-72, mem. interbd. com. on missionary edn., 1968-72, mem. exec. com. Conf. Program Dirs. Assn., 1968-72, mem. exec. com. Conf. Officers Assn., 1973—. Founder, owner Riddle Photos, Portland, 1968—. Scoutmaster Columbia Pacific council Boy Scouts Am., 1972-76, chmn. scout com., 1976—; exec. sec. Oreg. Meth. Found., Inc., 1970—. Bd. dirs., chmn. Forest Grove Union High Sch. Dist., 1955-60; mem. Gov.'s Com. on Sexual Preference, 1976; mem. human research com. U. Oreg. Med. Sch., 1975—; bd. dirs. Portland State Wesley Found., U. Oreg. Wesley Found. Recipient plaques and awards Boy Scouts Am. Author: Evaluative Study of Conference Council Director, 1976; also articles in profl. jours. Home: 465 NW 95th Ave Portland OR 97229 Office: 1505 SW 18th Ave Portland OR 97201

RIDER, ALAN JAMES, minister, Lutheran Church in America. b. Unionville, Mich., Mar. 8, 1948; s. Kenneth W. and Hannah (Beck) R.; m. Karen Letke, Sept. 26, 1981; 1 child, Mark. B.A., Valparaiso U., 1970; M.Div., Gettysburg Sem., 1977. Ordained to ministry Lutheran Church in America, 1977. Assoc. pastor St. Marks Luth. Ch., Springfield, Va., 1977-80; pastor Christ the Servant Luth. Ch., Reston, Va., 1980—; bd. dirs. Vesper Exchange mag., San Leandro, Calif., 1976-82, Council for Parish Life, 1984—, Reston Interfaith Inc., 1982—, Inter-Luth. Commn., D.C., 1983—; chmn. Youth Ministry, Va. Synod, 1978-81, Ednl. Ministry, Va. Synod, 1984—. Danforth fellow U. Va., 1970-71. Office: Christ the Servant Lutheran Church 2300 Hunters Woods Center Reston VA 22091

RIDLEY, ROBERT HENDERSON, minister, United Methodist Church; b. Campbell, Tex., Jan. 27, 1911; s. Fred Reginald and Chloe Wan (Henderson) R.; student Wesley Coll., 1930, Dallas Theol. Sem., 1930-33; B.A., E. Tex. State U., 1935; m. Margaret Elizabeth Low, June 9, 1939; 1 son, Robert Low. Ordained to ministry, 1938; pastor South Wilcox Ch., McKinney, Tex., 1940-44, First Meth. Ch., Carrollton, Tex., 1944-50, Trinity Ch., Dallas, 1950-74; interim pastor Brashear Charge, Hopkins County, Tex., 1975—. Mem. reference com. Am. Bd. Missions to the Jews, Dallas, 1970-74; trustee N. Tex. Conf. United Meth. Ch., 1959-70, chmn. bd., 1962-63. Recipient Certificate of Achievement, E. Tex. State U. Alumni Assn., 1974. Author: (with Margaret Low Ridley) Candles at Dusk, 1954; (with Margaret Low Ridley) Another Dawn, 1967. Home: Box 118 Campbell TX 75422

RIDLEY, ROBERT KEITH, minister of music, Southern Baptist Convention; b. Mt. Morris, Mich., Feb. 15, 1924; s. Charles Albert and Rosetta Margaret (Schofield) R.; grad. Baker Bus. U., 1947; certificate So. Bapt. Theol. Sem., 1958; m. Lois Mamie Montague, Oct. 8, 1943; children: Vivian Marie Ridley Wymer, Dell Robert, Ann Louise Ridley Cascarelle, Daniel Carlyle, Jeanette Ilene Ridley Swords, Stephen Glenn. Mem. choir 1st Bapt. Ch. of Mt. Morris, 1947-57, 1st violin of orch., 1947-57, mem. Victorious Christian Youth Choral, 1949-50, mem. male quarter, 1950-54; minister of music 1st Bapt. Ch. of Clio (Mich.), 1957-75, 78—, Harvest Bapt. Ch. of Clio, 1976-78. Cabinet maker Woodcraft Kitchens, Inc., Flint, Mich., 1970—. Vol. juvenile div. Probate Ct. Genesee County (Mich.), 1966—. Home: 1364 W Dodge Rd Clio MI 48420 Office: 3573 Flushing Rd Flint MI 48502

RIECKE, CONRAD CHARLES, minister, So. Baptist Conv.; b. N.Y.C., Aug. 24, 1933; s. Carl Hugo and Bertha (Koster) R.; student Community Coll., 1973—; m. Joan Yvonne Cox (dec. 1967); children—Susan Carol, Timothy Carl, Teresa Lynn; m. 2d, Carolyn Susan Blackburn, Nov. 23, 1974; 1 dau., Sara Jean. Ordained to ministry, 1960; pastor Japan Kasugabaru Bapt. Mission, 1960-63, Brentwood Bapt. Ch., Portland, 1963-65; chaplain Edgemeade Boys Sch., Malborough, Md., 1965-67; pastor Pecan Way Bapt. Mission, Wichita Falls, Tex., 1973-76. With USAF, 1954—. First aid instr. ARC, 1960—. Recipient 13th Ann. Brotherhood award NCCJ, 1973. Address: PSC Box 409 APO New York NY 09692

RIEDEL, ERNEST GOTTFRIED, minister, Lutheran Church-Missouri Synod; b. Dover, Ark., Jan. 16, 1915; s. Paul J. and Clara E. (Knoernschild) R.; m. Hildegarde Charlotte Bojarzin, June 26, 1943; children: Dorothy, Debra, Cheryl. B.Theology, Concordia Theol. Sem., Springfield, Ill., 1943; postgrad. Concordia Theol. Sem., St. Louis, 1953-54; student clin. pastoral edn. U. Minn. Hosps., 1973-74. Ordained to ministry Lutheran Church-Missouri Synod, 1943. Pastor, Trinity and St. James Luth. Ch., Hazen, N.D., 1943-47, Trinity Luth. Ch., Spencer, S.D., 1947-50, Bethlehem Luth. Ch., Altamont, Ill., 1950-55, Immanuel Luth. Ch., Crystal City, Mo., 1955-57, St. John's Luth. Ch., Idaho Falls, 1957-59, Concordia Luth. Ch., Springfield, Ill., 1960-71, Olive Branch Luth. Ch., Coon Rapids, Minn.,

1976-79; Faith Luth. Ch., Fairfield Bay, Ark., 1981—; cir. counselor Altamont Cir., 1953-55, Yellowstone Cir., Idaho Falls, Idaho, 1957-59; pastoral advisor Utah/Idaho Dist. Luth. Layman's League, Idaho Falls, 1957-58; chaplain Crest View Luth. Home, Mpls., 1974-76; counselor, group therapist Mercy Hosp. De-Tox Ctr., Coon Rapids, 1976-78. Mem. Coll. of Chaplains, Am. Protestant Hosp. Assn., Assn. Mental Health Clergy. Republican. Home: Route 2 Box 381 Fairfield Bay AR 72088 Office: Faith Luth Ch Route 3 Box 207 Fairfield Bay AR 72088

RIEGEL, ARTHUR WILLIAM, church official, college official, Evangelical Church in Canada; b. Lipton, Sask., Can., Sept. 13, 1921; s. William and Dorothea (Zahn) R.; student Luther Coll., Regina, Sask., 1939-40, Regina Bible Inst., 1941-43; B.R.E., Hillcrest Christian Coll., 1974; m. Lydia Bertha Heinrich; children—Beverley Lynn (Mrs. Montgomery Chabun), Cheryl Ann (Mrs. Richard Schatz), Gloria Fay (Mrs. Brian Stevenson). Ordained to ministry, 1944; treas. Hillcrest Christian Coll., Medicine Hat, Alta., 1957-65, v.p., 1959—, registrar, 1973—; conf. chmn. Evang. Ch. in Can., 1970—; chmn. Evang. Inter-Church Fellowship, 1976—. Office: 264 Broadway W Yorkton SK S3N 0N3 Canada

RIEGNER, GERHART MORITZ, religious organization executive, Judaism; b. Berlin, Germany, Sept. 12, 1911; came to Switzerland, 1934; s. Henrich and Agnes (Arnheim) R. Law Degrees in Germany and France, 1932-34; L.H.D. (hon.), Jewish Theol. Sem. of Am., 1982. With World Jewish Congress, Geneva, 1936—, sec. gen., 1965-83, co-chmn. governing bd., 1983—; chmn. Internat. Jewish Com. on interreligious consultations, 1982-84. Contbr. articles to profl. jours. Chmn. Conf. on Non Governmental Orgns. in consultative status with UN, 1953-55, in consultative status with UNESCO, 1956-58; chmn. World Univ. Service, Geneva, 1949-55. Recipient Nahum Golmann medal, World Jewish Congress, 1981; Humanitarian award Internat. Council of Christians and Jews, 1981; Roger Joseph prize Hebrew Union Coll., 1984. Mem. Meml. Found. for Jewish Culture (bd. dirs.), Beth Hatefutsdth-Mus. of the Jewish Diaspora (Telaviu), Internat. Council, Yad Vashem (Jerusalem). Office: World Jewish Congress 1 Rue Varembe Geneva Switzerland 1211

RIEK, FOREST O., JR., priest, Episcopal Ch.; b. Rhinelander, Wis., Sept. 1, 1928; s. Forest O. and Dorothea (Maier) R.; B.S. in Mech. Engring., U. So. Calif., 1951; certificate in theol. studies Bloy Episcopal Sch. Theology, 1972; m. Elizabeth Ann Paterson, June 4, 1955; children—Elizabeth Ann, Forest O., III, Karl Christian. Ordained priest, 1973; resident priest, liturgical authority St. Stephen's Episcopal Ch., Hollywood, Calif., 1973—. Mem. Diocesan Commn. on Ministry, Diocesan Commn. on Scouting. Home: 3722 Effingham Pl Los Angeles CA 90027

RIEMER, CARLTON LESTER, minister, Lutheran Church-Missouri Synod. B. Mequon, Wis. Sept. 15, 1941; s. Erwin John and Gertrude Augusta (Radue) R.; m. Arlene Lydia Haefker, Aug. 23, 1967; children: Sushela, Elizabeth, Melanie. B.A., Concordia Sr. Coll., Fort Wayne, Ind., 1963; M.Div., Concordia Sem., St. Louis, 1967; M.A. in History of Religions, Hartford Sem. Found., 1970. Ordained to ministry Luth. Ch., 1967. Muslim missionary India Evangelical Luth. Ch., Nagercoil Dist. Synod, 1969-70, Luth. Ch. in the Philippines, Mindanao Dist., 1970-78; clin. pastoral edn. Trinity Luth. Hosp., Kansas City, Mo., 1978; pastor St. Paul Luth. Ch., Ruston, La., 1979—; pres., sec. La. Tech. Uniting Campus Ministries, Ruston, 1980—; pastoral conf. chmn. circle V, So. dist. Luth. Ch.-Mo. Synod, 1981-84, campus ministry coordinator So. dist., 1982—. Chmn. bd. dirs. Lincoln Gen. Hosp. Chaplaincy Service, Ruston, 1984; chmn., convenor Ruston Bread for World Group, 1981—; mem. Lincoln Energy Trust, Ruston, 1983—. Mem. Ruston Area Alliance for Ministry. Republican. Home: 1500 Caddo St Ruston LA 71270 Office: St Paul Luth Ch 500 W Texas Ave Ruston LA 71270

RIGHTER, WALTER CAMERON, bishop, Episcopal Church; b. Phila., Oct. 23, 1923; s. Richard and Dorothy Mae (Bottomley) R.; B.A., U. Pitts., 1948; M.Div., Berkeley Div. Sch., New Haven, 1951, D.D., 1972; m. Marguerite Jeanne Burroughs, Jan. 26, 1946; children—Richard, Rebecca. Ordained priest Episcopal Ch., 1951; consecrated bishop, 1972; lay missioner St. Michael's Ch., Rector, Pa., 1947-48; priest-in-charge All Saints Ch., Aliquippa, Pa., 1951-54; rector Ch. of Good Shepherd, Nashua, N.H., 1954-71; bishop Diocese of Iowa, Des Moines, 1972—. Del. from N.H., Nat. Council Chs., 1963; exec. council Protestant Episcopal Ch. U.S.A., 1979—. Mem. N.H. com. White House Conf. on Youth, 1962, Regional Crime Commn., Hillsboro County, N.H., 1969-71. Trustee Nashua Library, 1968-71. Fellow Coll. of Preachers, Washington Cathedral, 1964. Office: 225 37th St Des Moines IA 50312

RIHERD, LESLIE MARTIN, minister, Southern Baptist Convention; b. Park City, Ky., May 1, 1916; s. Clitus and Sarah Anne (Martin) R.; A.B., Georgetown (Ky.) Coll., 1937; postgrad. Southwestern Bapt. Theol. Sem., Ft. Worth, 1937-39; m. Cleopatra Bernice Krapf, May 12, 1940; children—Leslie Martin, Hazel Anne, Robert Lee. Ordained to ministry, 1935; pastor Kidville (Ky.) Bapt. Ch., 1936-37, First Bapt. Ch., Lepanto, Ark., 1938-53, West Bapt. Ch., Batesville, Ark., 1953-64, First Bapt. Ch., Newport, Ark., 1964-81. Moderator, Trinity Bapt. Assn., 1952-53, Independence Assn., 1957-58, Black River Bapt. Assn., 1967-69; mem. fin. com., chmn. operating com. Ark. Bapt. Conv.; pres. Batesville and Newport Ministerial Alliance; past pres. Ark. Bapt. Pastors Conf.; bd. dirs. So. Bapt. Coll., Bapt. Meml. Hosp., Ark. Bapt. Hosp. Mem. Newport C. of C. Home: 402 Laurel St Newport AR 72112

RIKLI, CARROLL K., ecumenical agency executive, United Methodist Church; b. Enid, Okla., Oct. 21, 1921; s. Oscar and Hazel (Glenn) R.; m. Clarice Ellen; children: Steven, Linda. A.B., Phillips U., 1943, M.A., 1948. Exec. dir. Christian Youth Council, Kenosha, Wis., 1955—; sec. Ecumenical Ch. Housing, Inc., 1978-84; bd. dirs. Midwest Ecumenical Ctr., Williams Bay, Wis., 1979-83; pres. Wis. Bus. and Indsl. Chaplaincy, Inc., Kenosha, 1980—. Pres. Human Relations Commn., Kenosha, 1970-78; pres. Unified Sch. Bd., Kenosha, 1980. Served to 1st sgt. USAAF, 1943-46. Honored in naming of Rikli Park, Christian Youth Council, Kenosha, 1970; recipient Recreation Disting. Service award Christian Youth Council, 1980. Mem. Nat. Assn. Ecumenical Staff (bd. dirs. 1984—, Disting. Service award 1984). Democrat. Lodges: Rotary (v.p. 1975), Toastmasters (pres. 1954-55), Elks. Office: Christian Youth Council 1715 52d St Kenosha WI 53140

RILEY, EUGENE SCOTT, minister, Disciples of Christ Church; b. Lynchburg, Va., Aug. 27, 1942; s. James Donald Sr. and Mary Loveonia (Creasy) R.; m. Janet Lockhart, June 27, 1964; children: Eugene Scott, Jeannette Ann, Audrey Denise. A.A., Ferrum Coll., 1976, B.S., 1978; M.Div., Lexington Theol. Sem., 1983. Ordained to ministry Disciples of Christ Ch., 1978. Interim pastor 1st Christian Ch., Berea Christian Ch., Galilee Christian Ch., Wytheville, Va., 1969-70, Cool Springs Christian Ch., Va., 1970, Perkins Park Christian Ch., Lynchburg, 1970-71; minister Wintergreen Christian Ch., Faber, Va., 1971-74, Liberty Christian Ch., Sandy Level, Va., 1974-79, Bethel Christian Ch., Ky., 1979-82, Zion Christian Ch., Beaverdam, Va., 1982—; chaplain Beaverdam Vol. Fire Dept., 1984. Democrat. Home: PO Box 55 Beaverdam VA 23015

RILEY, LAWRENCE JOSEPH See *Who's Who in America*, 43rd edition.

RILEY, LONNIE, minister, religious organization administrator, Southern Baptist Convention; b. Gays Creek, Ky., Sept. 12, 1949; s. Fred and Pearlie (Smith) R.; m. Belinda Brummitt, Apr. 17, 1970; children: Lisa, Brian, Amy. A.A. in Engring., U. Ky., 1970; B.A. in Religion, Cumberland Coll., 1980; postgrad. So. Bapt. Theol. Sem., 1981. Ordained to ministry So. Bapt. Conv., 1971. Pastor, Townview Bapt. Ch., Dayton, Ohio, 1976-78, Saxton Bapt. Ch., Williamsburg, Ky., 1978-80; mem. exec. bd. Ky. Bapt. Conv., Middletown, 1978-81; asst. to pres. Cumberland Coll., Williamsburg, 1979-81; assoc. dir. evangelism State Conv. Bapts. Ohio, Columbus, 1981—; com. mem. The Ten Commandments, Ky. Region, 1979; com. chmn. Ch. Relations Adv. Bd., 1981—; mem. Nat. Youth Com., 1981—. Compiler book studies on James and Colossians. Named one of Outstanding Young Men of Am., 1983. Republican. Avocations: basketball; swimming; writing. Home: 8945 Canoe Dr Galloway OH 43119 Office: State Conv Bapts Ohio 1680 E Broad St Columbus OH 43203

RILEY, RALPH WILLIAM, minister, So. Baptist Conv.; b. Lowell, N.C., Sept. 30, 1932; s. James Robert and Mary Ida (Whitman) R.; student Mars Hill Jr. Coll., 1950-52; B.R.E., New Orleans Bapt. Theol. Sem., 1955; m. Jessie Mae Thompson, June 26, 1954; children—Michael Glenn, Melody Lynn, Martin Lee. Ordained to ministry, 1969; minister music and edn. First Bapt. Ch., Cuthbert, Ga., 1954-55, East Bapt. Ch., Belmont, N.C., 1956-58, Remount Bapt. Ch., North Charleston, S.C., 1959-65; minister adminstrn., music and edn. Mt. Vernon Bapt. Ch., Richmond, Va., 1965—. Mem. Va. Bapt., So. Bapt. ednl. assns., Va. Bapt. Ch. Library Assn. Home: 2400 Gurley Rd Richmond VA 23229 Office: 8100 W Broad St Richmond VA 23229

RILEY, WALTER KEITH, practitioner, Ch. of Christ Scientist; b. Portland, Oreg., Sept. 2, 1915; s. John and Ida (Knapp) R.; student U. Oreg., 1940, Cuesta Coll., 1964-66. Became practitioner, 1967; jour. listed, 1971; 1st reader Christian Sci. Ch., Atascadero, Calif., 1965-68, San Luis Obispo, Calif., 1969-74, pres. ch., 1975-76, chmn. exec. bd., 1975-76. Mem. Students' Assn. of Miss Anna Friendlich, Ams. United for State-Ch. Separation, Calif. Anti-Vivisection League, Nat. Cat Protection Soc. Address: 288 Hermosa Way San Luis Obispo CA 93401

RING, NANCY C., religion educator; b. Memphis, Aug. 26, 1937; d. Louis Cappall and Lyda (Greer) R. B.A., Siena Coll., 1963; M.A. in Theology, Marquette U., 1972, Ph.D., 1980; M.A. in French, Middlebury Coll., 1972. Prof. theology LeMoyne Coll., Syracuse, N.Y., 1979-83, 85—. Contbr. articles to profl. jours. Mem. Am. Acad. Religion, Cath. Theol. Soc. Am. Roman Catholic. Home: Apt F 143 Croyden Ln Syracuse NY 13224 Office: Dept Theology LeMoyne Coll Le Moyne Heights Syracuse NY

RINGENBERG, WILLIAM CAREY, minister, Evangelical Mennonite Ch., history educator; b. Fort Wayne, Ind., Aug. 18, 1939; s. Loyal Robert and Rhoda (Roth) R.; m. Rebecca Helen Lehman, Aug. 18, 1962; children: Matthew, Mark, Peter, Melodie. B.S., Taylor U., 1961; M.A. in Social Sci., Ind. U., 1964; Ph.D., Mich. State U., 1970. Ordained to ministry Evangelical Mennonite Church., 1979. Minister, Bailey Chapel United Meth. Ch., Anderson, Ind., 1979-80, Mount Carmel United Meth. Ch., Hartford City, Ind., 1980—. Prof. history, dir. Honors program Taylor U., Upland, Ind., 1968—. Author: Taylor University: The First 125 Years, 1973; The Christian College: A History of Protestant Higher Education in America, 1984. Mem. editorial bd. Christian Scholar's Review, 1970-74. Contbr. articles, reviews to religious publs. Lilly fellow in Am. history Ind. U., 1962-63; fellow Inst. for Advanced Christian Studies, 1981. Mem. Am. Hist. Assn., Am. Soc. Ch. History, Conf. on Faith and History, Orgn. Am. Historians, Chi Alpha Omega. Office: Taylor U Reade Ave Upland IN 46989

RINK, SUSAN, college president, Roman Catholic Church; b. Tulsa, Aug. 8, 1927; d. Raymond B. and Helen (McEvoy) R. B.A. in Biology, Clarke Coll., 1948; M.A. in Biology, Purdue U., 1963; M.A. in Counseling Psychology, Northwestern U., 1971, Ph.D., 1973. Joined Sisters of Blessed Virgin Mary, Roman Catholic Ch., 1948. Instr. Sci. Holy Angels Acad., Milw., 1951-53; chmn. dept. sci. Xavier High Sch., St. Louis, 1953-66; chmn. dept. biology Clarke Coll., Dubuque, Iowa, 1966-69, asst. prof., 1969; lectr. edn. Mundelein Coll., Chgo., 1969-71, dir. div. continuing edn., 1971-73, assoc. prof. edn., 1973—, acad. dean, 1973-75, pres., 1975—; mem. staff counseling lab. Northwestern U., 1970-71. Mem. higher edn. com. Blessed Virgin Mary Commn.; v.p. Assoc. Colls. Ill.; corp. mem. Health Care Service Corp. Northwestern U. scholar, 1971; recipient Disting. Service award Northwestern U. Sch. Edn., 1975. Mem. Am. Assn. Higher Edn., Pi Lambda Theta, Kappa Gamma Pi. Club: Econ. (Chgo.). Office: Mindelein Coll 6363 N Sheridan Rd Chicago IL 60660

RIPPIN, ANDREW LAWRENCE, religion educator; b. London, May 16, 1950; came to Can., 1959; B.A., U. Toronto, 1974; M.A., McGill U., 1977, Ph.D., 1981. Lectr. Mich. State U., East Lansing, 1979-80; asst. prof. religious studies U. Calgary, Alta., Can., 1980-84, assoc. prof. religious studies, 1984—. Contbr. articles to theol. and sociol. jours. Mem. Am. Oriental Soc., Am. Acad. Religion, Brit. Soc. Middle Eastern Studies, Can. Soc. Study of Religion, Can. Mediterranean Inst. Office: U Calgary Dept Religious Studies Calgary AB T2N 1N4 Canada

RIQUIER, WILLIE DEAN, religious organization administrator, Roman Catholic Church; b. Maude, Okla., Dec. 5, 1929; d. William J. and Beatrice (Henson) Robinson; m. Leo J. Riquier, Sept. 1, 1946; 1 child, James Joseph. B.S. in Elem. Edn., U. Hartford, 1969; M.S. in Gen. Edn., Central Conn. U., 1983; M.A. in Religious Studies, St. Joseph Coll., 1984. Dir. religious edn. St. Ann Ch., Bristol, Conn., 1955—; with speaker's bur. Schs. of Contemporary Christianity, Archdiocese of Hartford, Conn., 1968—, lectr. adult edn., 1968—; tchr. St. Joseph Sch., Bristol, 1977—; pres. Conf. of Congregations, Bristol, 1984—; chmn. religion curriculum Archdiocese of Hartford, 1984—. Contbr. articles to profl. jours. Active Task Force on Housing, Bristol, 1984—. Recipient God and Youth award Archdiocesan Cath. Youth Orgn., 1967. Democrat. Avocations: creative writing; cooking; needlework; outdoor life. Home: 209 Wolcott St Bristol CT 06010

RISING, RICHARD LINN, priest, Episcopal Church; b. Columbus, Ohio, May 7, 1920; s. Francis Russell and Cicely Fay (Rodgers) R.; B.A., Williams Coll., 1942; M.A., Harvard U., 1949; M.Div., Episc. Theol. Sch., Cambridge, Mass., 1952; m. Charlotte Elizabeth Drea, Sept. 20, 1969; children: John Reed, Cynthia Anne, Caroline Fay, Stephen Reed, Catherine Reed, William Reed. Ordained priest, 1952; pastor chs. in Ohio, Philippines, Mass. and Caribbean, 1952-68; staff asso. Am. Assn. Theol. Schs., Dayton, Ohio, 1968-70; asso. dir. Episc. Bd. Theol. Edn., 1970-76; coordinator, editor Episc. Study Com. Preparation Ordained Ministry, 1974-76; rector St. Barnabas Parish, Cortez, Colo., 1976-80, ret. Adv. bd. St. Andrew's Theol. Sem., Manila, 1959-60; editorial bd. Overseas Mission Rev., 1958-68; mem. Episc. Joint Commn. Edn. for Holy Orders, 1965-68. Mem. Phi Beta Kappa. Contbr. articles to religious jours. Address: 1391 Avenida Sebastiani Sonoma CA 95476

RITCHIE, ROBERT. Bishop The Old Catholic Church of Canada, Hamilton, Ont. Office: The Old Cath Ch of Can 216 Tragina Ave N Hamilton ON L8H 5E1 Canada*

RITCHIE, ROBERT THOMAS, priest, Roman Catholic Church; b. N.Y.C., Mar. 26, 1945; s. David John and Eugenia Marie (Wood) R.; B.A., St. Joseph's

Sem., 1967, M. Div., 1970. Ordained priest, 1971; asso. pastor St. Catherine of Genoa Ch., N.Y.C., 1971-75; dir. youth ministry Cath. Youth Orgn., Archdiocese of N.Y., N.Y.C., 1975—; pastor St. Catherines of Benda Ch., N.Y.C. Exec. com. Senate of Priests, Archdiocese of N.Y., 1972—; asso. 15 chs. United for a Better Manhattan, 1972-75. Mem. N.Y.C. Community Sch. Bd. #6, 1975-77; chmn. community planning bd. #9, N.Y.C., 1974-75; mem. adv. bd. for west side hwy., 1974-75. Home: 506 W 153rd St New York City NY 10031 Office: 506 W 153d St New York NY 10031

RITTENHOUSE, WILLIAM HENRY, minister, religious found. exec., So. Bapt. Conv.; b. Macon, Ga., Apr. 6, 1922; s. William Henry and Florence (Perry) R.; B.S., Stetson U., 1941; Ph.D., U. N.C., 1949; m. Nell Crider, Dec. 20, 1944; children—Sherrie Rittenhouse Forshey, JoAnn Rittenhouse Crye, Nancy Rittenhouse Tulley. Ordained to ministry, 1945; pastor Southside Bapt. Ch., Miami, Fla., 1949-55, Sylvan Hills Bapt. Ch., Atlanta, 1955-62, Roswell St. Bapt. Ch., Marietta, Ga., 1962-64, Nassau Bay Bapt. Ch., Houston, 1965-72; pres. High Flight Found., 1972—. Citizen adviser Atlanta Sch. Bd., 1960-62. Home: 5702 Red Onion Way Colorado Springs CO 80918 Office: 5010 Edison Ave Colorado Springs CO 80915

RITTER, BRUCE, priest Roman Catholic Church; founder Covenant House (for runaway youths), N.Y.C. Office: Covenant House 460 W 41st St New York NY 10036*

RITTER, GEORGE EDWARD, minister, Nat. Assn. Free Will Baptists; b. Johnston City, Ill., July 21, 1923; s. George Edward and Alice Arada (Shelton) R.; student Southeastern Ill. Coll., 1966-67, Free Will Bapt. Coll., Nashville, 1972; m. Reba Horton, June 23, 1946. Ordained to ministry, 1952; pastor Freedom Free Will Bapt. Ch., Marion, Ill., 1950-55, Pittsburgh (Ill.) Free Will Bapt. Ch., 1955-60, Arnold View Free Will Bapt. Ch., Creal Springs, Ill., 1960-68, 71-74, First Free Will Bapt. Ch., Elgin, Ill., 1968-71, First Free Will Bapt. Ch., Pocahontas, Ark., 1974—. Dir. Ill. Free Will Bapt. Home Missions, 1952-53, treas. 1964-67; moderator Ill. State Assn. Free Will Bapt., 1964-65, clk., 1972-73; mem. Greater Elgin (Ill.) Evang. Ministerial Fellowship, pres. 1970-71; pres. Pocahontas Ministerial Alliance, 1975-76; chmn. exec. bd., presbytery bd. Social Band Dist. Assn. Free Will Bapts., Ark. Contbr. articles to religious jours. Home and Office: PO Box 86 Pocahontas AR 72455

RITTER, WALTER ADOLF, minister, educator, Luth. Ch.—Mo. Synod; b. Edmonton, Alta., Can., June 24, 1932; s. Carl and Natalie (Gliege) R.; B.A., Concordia Sem., 1954, B.D., 1957; m. Doris Paulin Elizabeth Andres, June 11, 1957; 1 dau., Libby. Ordained to ministry, 1957; pastor Christ Luth. Ch., MacNutt, Sask., Can., 1957-60, Faith Luth. Ch., Winnipeg, Can., 1960-67, Bethel Luth. Ch., Edmonton, Alta., 1967-76; instr. Camrose Luth. Coll., Alta., 1976—. Nat. coordinator coll. and univ. work for Luth. Ch. Can., 1966-70; mem. joint commn. Inter-Luth. Relations, 1961-67; chmn. Concordia Coll., Edmonton Bd. Control, 1973-75, chmn. master plan com., 1975-76; participant First Nat. Luth.-Roman Cath. Ch. Dialogue, 1969. Contbr. articles to religious jours. Home: 6109 Marler Dr Camrose AB T4V 2Y4 Canada Office: Camrose Luth Coll Camrose AB T4V 2R3 Canada

RIVERA, VICTOR MANUEL, bishop, Episcopal Church; b. Penuelas, P.R., Oct. 16, 1929; s. Victor and Filomena (Toro) R.; student Modern Bus. Coll. P.R., 1937, DuBose Meml. Ch. Tng. Sch., 1938; B.D., Ch. Div. Sch. Pacific, 1944, D.D., 1965; postgrad. St. Augustine Coll., Eng., 1957; m. Barbara Ross Lamb, Dec. 1944; 3 children. Ordained deacon Episcopal Ch., 1943, priest, 1944; curate St. John's Cathedral, Santurce, P.R., 1944-45; rector St. Paul's Ch., Visalia, Cal., 1945-68; consecrated bishop San Joaquin, Stockton, Cal., 1968. Address: 4159 E Dakota Fresno CA 93726*

RIVERS, RALPH WILLIAM, minister, United Methodist Church; b. Bronson, Fla., May 15, 1917; s. William Eugene and Vida Mae (Outland) R.; student Fla. So. Coll., 1934-36; A.B., U. Fla., 1945; postgrad. U. Fla., 1945-47, Emory U., 1948-49, U. Edinburgh (Scotland), 1974; m. Martha L. Hogan, May 30; children—Martha Jane, Robin Dale, Teresa Mae; children by previous marriage—Ralph Eugene, Charles David, Prudence Mae. Ordained deacon, 1941, elder, 1943; pastor, Melrose, Fla., 1941-48, Fruitland Park Community Ch., Leesburg, Fla., 1948-50, Ellenton (Fla.) Community Ch., 1950-54, Christ Meth. Ch., Miami, Fla., 1954-59, First Meth. Ch., OpaLocka, Fla., 1959-61, Concord Park Meth. Ch., Orlando, Fla., 1961-64, Epperson Meml. Meth. Ch., Jacksonville, Fla., 1964-68, Calvary United Meth. Ch., Tampa, Fla., 1968—; exec. sec., treas. Tampa Ministers Assn., 1985—; mem. bd. edn. Fla. Conf., United Meth. Ch., 1964-72, mem. bd. of missions Fla. Conf., 1945-50, Commn. of Town and Country, Fla. Conf., 1947-50; sec. Family Life Commn., Fla. Conf. Com. on Family Life, 1958-62, chmn., 1962-64; chmn. Family Ministry Fla. Conf. 1964-66; mem. Health and Welfare Ministries Bd., United Meth. Ch., 1975—. Chmn. Alachua County (Fla.) Citizens Com. on Pub. Edn., 1945-48. Recipient award U.S. Treasury, 1945, Merit award Nat. Red Cross, 1946, Spl. Service award Dade County, Fla., 1958. Mem. Fla. Peace Officers Assn. Author: Roads to God's World, 1950; contbr. articles to religious publs. Address: 9520 N Tampa St Tampa FL 33612

ROACH, CHANWICK ALTON, minister, Church of God, Anderson, Indiana; b. Anderson, Ind., June 24, 1947; s. Carl Fay and Gwendlyn Mae (Stickney) R.; m. Louella Kay McPherson, July 7, 1973; children: Jonathan, Alicia, Derek. A.B., Anderson Coll., 1969; M.Div., Anderson Sch. Theology, 1972. Ordained to ministry, 1973. Pastor, Fellowship Ch., Terre Haute, Ind., 1970-77, First Ch. of God, Danville, Ind., 1977-80, Dennison, Ohio, 1980—; pres., treas. Youth Camp program com., Bedford, Ind., 1971-77; dir. Twin City Hosp. Chaplains, Dennison, Ohio, 1981—; bd. dirs. E. Ohio Bd. Christian Edn., Ravenna, 1983—; pres. Hendricks County Chaplains, 1979-80. Columnist Chronicle, 1983-84. Bd. dirs. Hendricks County Spl. Services, Danville, Ind., 1979-80. Recipient Ellis Preaching award Sch. Theology, Anderson, Ind., 1972. Mem. Nat. Assn. Evangelicals, Twin City Ministerial Assn. (pres.). Club: Wilderness Ctr. Home: 481B Rt 2 Uhrichsville OH 44683 (614) 922-2283 Office: First Ch of God 403 N 3d St Dennison OH 44621

ROACH, JEWELL SMITH, lay ch. worker, Baptist Ch.; b. Childress, Tex., Dec. 21, 1913; d. Marion and Annie (Dempsey) Smith; grad. high sch.; m. Sears Price, July 26, 1936; children—Alice Roach Atkinson, Anita Roach Lichtenwalner. Mem. state bd. Am. Bapt. Women Utah, 1955-65, v.p. missions, 1970-71, state pres., 1972-75; sec./treas. Utah Am. Bapts., 1969-70. Address: 2856 Malan Ave Ogden UT 84403

ROACH, JOHN ROBERT, archbishop, Roman Catholic Church; b. Prior Lake, Minn., July 31, 1921; s. Simon J. and Mary V. Roach; B.A., St. Paul Sem.; M.A., U. Minn. Ordained priest Roman Catholic Ch., 1946; named domestic prelate, 1966; instr. St. Thomas Acad., 1946-50, headmaster, 1951-68; rector St. John Vianney Sem., 1968-71; aux. bishop St. Paul and Mpls., 1971; pastor St. Charles Borromeo Ch., Mpls., 1971, St. Cecilia Ch., St. Paul, 1973-75; archbishop of St. Paul and Mpls., 1975—. Apptd. vicar for parishes, 1971-75; vicar for clergy, 1972-75; mem. Priests Senate, 1968-72; pres. Priests Senate and Presbytery, 1970; Episcopal moderator Nat. Apostolate for Mentally Retarded, 1974; v.p. Nat. Conf. Cath. Bishops, 1977-80, pres., 1980-83. Chmn., Com. on Accreditation Pvt. Schs. in Minn., 1952-57; mem. adv. com. Coll. Entrance Exam. Bd., 1964. Trustee St. Paul Sem., 1971—, Coll. of St. Thomas, Cath. U. Am., 1978-81, St. Thomas Acad., Coll. of St. Catherine, Visitation Convent and Sch. Mem. Minn. Cath. Edn. Assn. (pres. 1959-61), Assn. Mil. Colls. and Schs. U.S. (pres. 1961-62), N.Central Assn. Colls and Secondary Schs. (adv. com. 1963-66), Am. Council Edn. (del. 1963-65), Am. Assn. Theol. Schs. (dir.), Nat. Conf. Cath. Bishops. Office: 226 Summit Ave St Paul MN 55102*

ROACH, KENNETH MAYES, minister, Southern Baptist Church; b. Marietta, Ga., July 22, 1951; s. Artis Steve and Dorothy Louise (Hunnicutt) R.; m. Susan Elaine Bridges, Dec. 3, 1977; 1 dau., Wendy Rebekah. A.A., Reinhardt COll., Waleska, Ga., 1971; B.A. in Bible, Antioch Bapt. Coll. and Sem., Marietta, 1973. Ordained to ministry Bapt. Ch., 1978; prof. Shiloh Bible Coll., Kennesaw, Ga., 1974-78; assoc. pastor Toonigh Bapt. Ch., Lebanon, Ga., 1976-77, Legend Heights Bapt. Ch., Smyrna, Ga., 1978-80; pastor Dalton 2d Bapt. Ch., (Ga.), 1980—. Mem. N. Ga. Bapt. Assn., Ga. Bapt. Conv., So. Bapt. Conv. Home: 2125 Dug Gap Rd Dalton GA 30720

ROACH, WILFRED EVERARD, II, minister Episcopal Church; b. Marshall, Va., June 2, 1917; s. Wilfred Everard and Carolyn Awilda (Mosher) R.; m. Dorothy Stickley Bear, June 30, 1943; children: David Michael, Kenneth Slater, Ann Fellows Roach Crawford. B.A., U. Va., 1939; M.Div. cum laude, Va. Theol. Sem., 1942. Ordained deacon Episcopal Ch., 1942, priest, 1943. Minister in charge Grace Episc. Ch., Radford, Va., 1942-45, St. Thomas Episc. Ch., Christiansburg, Va., 1942-45; rector Grace Episc. Ch., Radford, 1945-64; vicar, rector Nelson Parish, Christ Ch., Norwood, Va., Grace Ch., Massies Mill, Va., Trinity Ch., Oak Ridge, Va., 1964-82; pastor neighborhood Episc. chs., 1964-82; clerical dep. gen. convs. Episc. Ch., 1954, 60, 64; bd. dirs. Va. Episc. Sch., Lynchburg, 1947-60, Boys Home, Covington, Va., 1952-60; examining chaplain Diocese of Southwestern Va., Roanoke, 1954-68. Contbr. articles to profl. jours. Founder, pres. Mountain Empire Guidance Ctr., 1945; mem. adv. bd. Juvenile and Domestic Ct., 1950-60; bd. dirs. Redford Community Hosp. Recipient awards Episcopal Ch. Mem. Associates for Religion and Intellectual Life (assoc.). Democrat. Clubs: Winton Country (Clifford, Va.); Nelson County Men's. Lodges (Masons, Rotary. Home: Route 5 Box 86 Amherst VA 24521

ROBB, DALE WILLARD, minister, Presbyterian Church (U.S.A.); b. Swanwick, Ill., Aug. 13, 1921; s. George Willard and Caroline Asenath (Cunningham) R.; B.A., U. Ill., Urbana, 1943; M.Div., McCormick Theol. Sem., Chgo., 1946; M.A., Miami U., Oxford, Ohio, 1954; D.D., Ill. Coll., Jacksonville, 1974; m. Arlene Jay, May 19, 1945; children—Darel Jay, Ronda Ardelle. Ordained to ministry, 1946; pastor chs. in Ill., 1946-49; dir. Westminster Found., Oxford, 1949-59; acting dir. Student Christian Center, Bangkok, Thailand, 1954-55; asso. gen. sec. Korean Student Christian Movement, Seoul, 1959-62; pastor First Presbyn. Ch., Jacksonville, 1963—. Del. World Christian Youth Conf., Oslo, 1947; moderator Miami Presbytery, Dayton, Ohio, 1958, Gt. Rivers Presbytery, Peoria, Ill., 1972, Synod of Lincoln Trails, Indpls., 1977; mem. Presbyn. Support Agy. Bd., N.Y.C., 1980—. Chmn. Jacksonville Human Relations Commn., 1964-72; mem. Fulbright scholarship com. Am. embassy, Seoul, 1961-62; mem. Nat. Com. on Self-Devel. of People, 1983—. Recipient honor medal preaching Freedoms Found., 1952; plaque outstanding leadership in human relations, Jacksonville, 1970. Mem. Jacksonville Lit. Union. Republican. Author: Love and Living Together, 1978; author articles. Home: 823 W State St Jacksonville IL 62650 Office: 870 W College St Jacksonville IL 62650

ROBBINS, ANDREW JOSEPH, minister, Seventh-day Adventists; b. Morgantown, W.Va., Nov. 19, 1910; s. Strawn Murphy and Oakie Urbana (Christner) R.; B.Th., Columbia Union Coll., 1931; M.A., U. Chgo., 1942; m. Ollie Mae Robertson, July 28, 1931; children—David Bruce, Linda Jean. Ordained to ministry, 1935; pastor, Johnstown, Pa., 1931-35; overseas missionary in China, 1935-41; tchr. Columbia Union Coll., 1942-50; pres. W. Pa. Conf. Seventh-day Adventists, 1950-58; pres. N. Phillipine Union Mission Seventh-day Adventists, 1958-63, Hong Kong-Macao Mission Seventh-day Adventists, 1964-69; dept. sec. Ariz. Conf. Seventh-day Adventists, 1969-71; chaplain Tempe Community Hosp. (Ariz.), 1971-77. Pres., Tempe Ministerial Assn., 1975-76, Ariz. Assn. Hosp. Chaplains, 1976-77; sec.-treas. Tri-City Evangelicals, 1975-76. Address: 22724 De Soto St Grand Terrace CA 92324

ROBBINS, ARTHUR FREEMAN, JR., minister; b. Leominster, Mass., Sept. 25, 1919; s. Arthur Freeman and Bertha Jeanette (Merrill) R.; grad. Bible Inst. Los Angeles, 1949; D.D. (hon.), Linda Vista Baptist Bible Coll. and Sem., San Diego, 1965; D.H. (hon.), San Diego Bible Coll. and Sem., 1979; m. Esther Violet Spath, Jan. 20, 1946; children—Kathleen, William, Shirley. Ordained to ministry Am. Baptist Conv., 1949, now independent; pastor Otay Bapt. Ch., Chula Vista, Calif., 1949—; pres. San Diego Bible Coll. and Sem., Chula Vista, 1970—; founder Southland Christian Schs., 1971—. Vice-pres. Evangelize China Fellowship, Los Angeles, 1961—. Home: 718 J Pl Chula Vista CA 92010

ROBBINS, JAMES WILLIAM, minister, United Church of Christ; b. Des Moines, Iowa, Feb. 13, 1929; s. Brian Laney and Mabel Iowa (Jones) R.; m. Rosemary Hargesheimer, July 1, 1953 (dec. 1976); m. Alice Lenore Creger, June 4, 1982; children: David, Virginia Ann. B.A., Drake U., 1950, M.S., 1950, M.R.E., 1952; A.M., U. N.D., 1959. Ordained to ministry, United Ch. Christ, 1952. Pastor Eastgate Ch., Independence, Mo., 1969-74, Ch. Good Shepherd, Kansas City, Kans., 1975-82, St. Matthew's Ch., Kansas City, 1977-82; sr. pastor St. James Ch., Dearborn, Mich., 1982; alt. del. Gen. Synod, United Ch. Christ, 1984—; mem. Ch. and Ministry Com., Detroit Assn. United Ch. Christ, 1983—; mem. Affirmative Action Com., Mich. Conf. United Ch. Christ, 1983—. Contbr. articles to profl. jours. Active Adv. Com. Supt. Schs., Dearborn, Mich., 1983—. Mem. East Dearborn Ministerial Assn. Republican. Lodges: Rotary (pres. Kansas City 1973-74, 1979-80), Masons (Grand Master, Kans. 1979-80, many other offices, honors). Home: 1866 Linden Dearborn MI 48124 Office: St James United Ch Christ 4920 Greenfield Rd Dearborn MI 48126

ROBBINS, LARRY JACK, religious educator, administrator, minister, Independent Baptist Churches; b. Chesapeake, Ohio, Aug. 8, 1935; s. Lawrence Loring and Blanche Margaret (Earls) R.; m. Wanda Lee True, Aug. 20, 1961; 1 child, Katherine Loring Robbins, Herald. B.A., Lexington Bapt. Coll., Ky., 1964, Th.B., 1969, B.R.E., 1973, M.R.E., 1977, D.D., 1981. B.S., Cumberland Coll., 1976; M. of Higher Edn., Morehead State U., Ky., 1978. Ordained to ministry Bapt. Ch., 1964. Pastor, Stewartsville Bapt. Ch., Williamstown, Ky., 1964-68, Lusby's Mill Bapt. Ch., Owenton, Ky., 1968-72; asst. pastor Devondale Bapt. Ch., Lexington, 1972-79; from registrar to exec. v.p. Lexington Bapt. Coll., 1968—. Served with U.S. Army, 1958-60; ETO. Home: 188 N Ashland Ave Lexington KY 40502 Office: Lexington Bapt Coll 163 N Ashland Ave Lexington KY 40502

ROBBINS, VERNON KAY, minister, religion educator, United Methodist Church; b. Wahoo, Nebr., Mar. 13, 1939; s. Earl Willard and Mildred Irene (Hanson) R.; m. Deanna Shirley Moritz, Aug. 6, 1960; children: Rick Anthony, Chimene Alise. B.A. cum laude, Westmar Coll., 1960; B.D. cum laude, United Theol. Sem., 1963; M.A., U. Chgo., 1966, Ph.D., 1969. Ordained to ministry, United Meth. Ch., 1963. Asst. prof. U. Ill., Urbana, 1968-74, assoc. prof., 1974-84, dir. Religious Studies, 1978-80; assoc. prof. Emory U., Atlanta, 1984—; mem. editorial bd. Jour. Bibl. Lit.,

1981—. Author: Jesus the Teacher, 1984. Contbr. articles to profl. jours. Research fellow Inst. for Ecumenical and Cultural Research, 1975, U. Ill., 1982, Soc. Bibl. Lit., 1982, Fulbright-Hayes, 1983-84. Mem. Studiorum Novi Testamenti Societas, Soc. Bibl. Lit. (dir. pronouncement story research group 1981—), Chgo. Soc. Bibl. Research, Internat. Soc. for History of Rhetoric. Home: 1634 Stonecliff Dr Decatur GA 30033 Office: Dept Religion Emory U Atlanta GA 30322

ROBERTS, BILLY JACK, minister, Assemblies of God; b. Custer City, Okla., Dec. 2, 1943; s. Chester Lois and Beatrice N. (Hammer) R.; diploma Brean Sch. Bible, Springfield, Mo., 1971, 73; postgrad. psychology Friends Bible Coll., Haniland, Kans.; m. Nancy Ann May, Sept. 2, 1961; children—Benjamin Stephen, Jeanna Lynn. Ordained to ministry, 1971; pastor chs. in Kans., 1968-77; pastor Coll. Dr. Assembly of God, Colby, Kans., 1974—; mem. faculty N.W. Kans. Sch. Bible, 1976-77. Sec., Christ Ambassadors, Kans.; sec. Kans. Sunday sch. dept. Assemblies of God. Bd. dirs. New Life for Girls, Gem, Kans.; founder, chmn. bd. New Wine Care and Counseling Center, Colby, Kans., 1977—. Address: 910 Court Terr Colby KS 67701

ROBERTS, CHARLES BANKSTON, priest, Episcopal Church; b. Atlanta, Nov. 5, 1939; s. Charles Speer and Mary Helen (Walton) R.; m. Mary Gaston Sparrow, Aug. 10, 1962; children: Laura Melissa Roberts Luckie, Charles Walton Roberts, Mary Rebecca. B.S., Auburn U., 1962, M.S., 1969; M.Div., U. South, 1980. Ordained priest, 1980. Asst. chaplain U. South, Sewanee, Tenn., 1980-81; rector St. Jame's Ch., Alexander City, Ala., 1981—. Founder, pres. Tallapoosa Aid to People, Alexander City, Ala., 1983—; dir. E. Ala. Mental Health, Opelika, Ala., 1982—; treas. E. Ala. Alcohol Council, 1983—. Served to 1st lt. U.S. Army, 1963-65. Rotary fellow to Brazil, 1960; Humanitarian Service award, Delta Sigma Theta, 1975; Leadership award. ODK, 1976. Club: Quarterback (dir. 1983). Lodge: Kiwanis. Home: 305 University Circle Alexander City AL 35010 Office Saint James Episcopal Church 122 S Central Ave Alexander City AL 35101

ROBERTS, CHARLES MERWYN, minister, So. Baptist Conv.; b. Alexandria, La., July 26, 1945; s. Hugh Dorsey and Angieline (Crooks) R.; B.A., La. Coll., 1970; M.Div., New Orleans Bapt. Theol. Sem., 1974; m. Doris Lane Hooper, June 3, 1965; children—Chris, Chad. Ordained to ministry, 1966; asso. pastor Fairfield Bapt. Ch., Colfax, La., 1963-64, Donahue Bapt. Ch., Pineville, La., 1964-67, Big Island Bapt. Ch., Deville, La., 1967-70, Oak Grove Bapt. Ch., Bentley, La., 1970-74, Rio Vista Bapt. Ch., New Orleans, 1974—. Vice-pres. Pastor's Conf., 1967-68, sec., 1968-70 76—; mem. evangelism com. New Orleans Bapt. Assn. Home: 429 Riverdale Dr Jefferson LA 70121 Office: 3800 Jefferson Hwy Jefferson LA 70121

ROBERTS, HEYWARD DELAIN, minister, Southern Baptist Convention; b. Paducah, Ky., Nov. 12, 1933; s. Eucle Smith and Thelma (Miller) R.; student Mid-Continent Bapt. Coll., 1960, Bethel Coll., Hopkinsville, Ky., 1962, So. Sem., Louisville, 1963-64; m. Wanda Taylor, Jan. 23, 1960; 1 child, John Mark. Ordained to ministry; pastor Union Ridge Bapt. Ch., Benton, Ky., 1960-64, Hardin (Ky.) Bapt. Ch., 1964, West Fork Bapt. Ch., Murray, Ky., 1965-73, Flint Bapt. Ch., Murray, 1974-84, Scotts Grove Bapt. Ch., 1984—. Mem. Blood River Bapt. Assn. Home and Office: Route 2 PO Box 74 Murray KY 42071

ROBERTS, HOWARD WALLACE, minister, Southern Baptist Convention; b. Monticello, Ky., June 16, 1947; s. Milton and Doris (Cooper) R.; m. Peggy Joan Griesser, May 24, 1969; children: Melanie Kaye, Danita Carelle, Brandton Thomas. B.A., Georgetown Coll., 1969; M.Div., So. Bapt. Theol. Sem., 1973, Th.M., 1973; D.Min., Southeastern Bapt. Theol. Sem., 1978. Ordained to ministry Baptist Ch., 1966. Minister Stonelick Bapt. Ch., Maysville, Ky., 1966-68; missionary Guyana Bapt. Mission, South Am., summer 1968; minister Belleview Bapt. Ch., Grant, Ky., 1968-74, Meml. Bapt. Ch., Savannah, Ga., 1974-77, Broadview Bapt. Ch., Temple Hills, Md., 1977—; mem. Christian life and public affairs com. Bapt. Conv. of Md., 1981-83; mem. Bapt. Peace tour to USSR, 1983; guest chaplain U.S. Ho. of Reps., 1981. Author: Learning to Pray, 1984. First v.p. Allenwood Elem. PTA, Temple Hills, 1983. Merrill fellow Harvard Divinity Sch., 1985. Democrat. Club: Interchurch (pres. 1981-82) (Washington). Home: 4107 Canterbury Way Temple Hills MD 20748 Office: Broadview Baptist Church 5757 Temple Hills Rd Temple Hills MD 20748

ROBERTS, JANET SEDAM, minister, American Baptist Churches in the U.S.A.; b. N.Y.C., May 30, 1936; d. Oscar Whitson and Margaret Isabel (Soars) Sedam; m. Leffie Lamar Roberts, Dec. 28, 1968. B.R.E., Bapt. Missionary Tng. Sch., 1958; B.D., Berkeley Bapt. Div. Sch., 1964. Ordained to ministry American Baptist Churches in the U.S.A., 1975. Dir. Girls' Work Milw. Christian Center, 1958-59; program asst. No. Ariz. Bapt. Missions, Keams Canyon, Ariz., 1959-61; staff Good Neighbor Center, Los Angeles, 1968-74; chaplaincy cons. Los Angeles Council Chs., 1978-83; chaplain Visiting Nurse Assn. Los Angeles, 1983—; sec. Southern Calif. Interfaith Coalition Aging, Los Angeles, 1976-78; v.p. Ministers Council Bapt. Chs., Pacific S.W., 1976-79. Bd. dirs. Los Angeles Funeral Soc., 1980—. Fellow Coll. Chaplains, Am. Protestant Hosp. Assn.; mem. Hospice Orgn. Southern Calif. Home: 840 S Ardmore Ave Apt 306 Los Angeles CA 90005 Office: Visiting Nurses Assn 3755 Beverly Blvd PO Box 74912 Los Angeles CA 90004-0912

ROBERTS, JOHN ELGIN, editor, minister, Southern Baptist Convention; b. Shelby, N.C., Sept. 14, 1926; s. John Ellis and Annie Elizabeth (Spake) R.; B.A., Furman U., 1951, LL.D., 1972; M.A., George Peabody Coll., 1952; D.Litt., Bapt. Coll. at Charleston, 1971; m. Helen Elizabeth Goodwin, Sept. 8, 1950; children—Wayne, Mark, Glenn, Jonna, Jill, Julie. Dir. pub. relations Gardner-Webb Coll., Boiling Springs, N.C., 1954-60; editor Charity and Children, dir. pub. relations Bapt. Children's Homes of N.C., 1960-65; editor, bus. mgr. The Bapt. Courier publ. S.C. Baptists, Greenville, 1966—; chmn. bd. deacons, Sunday sch. tchr. First Bapt. Ch., Greenville, 1976-77. Pres., Bapt. Pub. Relations Assn., 1963; trustee So. Bapt. Radio and TV Commn., 1978-85, chmn. bd., 1984-85; mem. Bapt. World Alliance Exec. Com., 1970-85; pres. S.C. Bapt. Conv., 1979-80. Mem. Thomasville (N.C.) Bd. Edn., 1963-65; mem. City Recreation Commn., 1963-65. Named Faculty Mem. of Year, Gardner-Webb Coll., 1958, Alumnus of Year, 1968. Mem. So. Bapt. Press Assn. (pres. 1979), Asso. Ch. Press, S.C. Press Assn. Home: 106 Trinity Way Greenville SC 29609 Office: 100 Manly St Greenville SC 29602

ROBERTS, KENNETH HOWARD, minister, Lutheran Church-Mo. Synod; b. Shreveport, La., Apr. 19, 1955; s. Roy Gerald and Barbara Agnes (Harman) R.; m. Kathy Lynn Kaminska, Aug. 20, 1978; 1 child, Kelly. A.A., Concordia Coll., Bronxville, N.Y., 1975, B.A., 1977, M.Div., Concordia Sem., St. Louis, 1981. Ordained to ministry Luth. Ch., 1981. Radio prodn. asst. Internat. Luth. Laymen's League, St. Louis, 1978-81, mgr. radio programs, 1981—; producer Lutheran Hour, writer syndicated Christmas spl. radio programs, 1983. Mem. Sons of Republic Tex., Nat. Assn. Religious Broadcasters. Home: 2109A McKelvey Hill Saint Louis MO 63043

ROBERTS, MARION EDWARD, minister, So. Bapt. Conv.; b. Fairland, Okla., Sept. 1, 1908; s. Marion Presley and Jessie Lee (Clark) R.; student Okla. Bapt. U.; m. Opal Mae Dillinger, Oct. 25, 1930; children—Marion Edward, R.D. Ordained to ministry, 1948; pastor chs. in Okla.; pastor First Bapt. Ch., Chouteau, Okla., 1949; chaplain Grand Valley Hosp., Pryor, Okla., 1974—. Bd. dirs. Bapt. Gen. Conv. Okla. Mem. Am. Protestant Hosp. Chaplains Assn., Chouteau C. of C. Home: 314 W Olney St Chouteau OK 74337 Office: Grand Valley Hosp Pryor OK 74361

ROBERTS, (GRANVILLE) ORAL, university president, evangelist; b. Ada, Okla., Jan. 24, 1918; s. Ellis Melvin and Claudius Priscilla (Irwin) R.; student Okla. Bapt. U., 1942-44, Phillips U., 1947; m. Evelyn Lutman, Dec. 25, 1938; children—Rebecca (Mrs. Marshall Nash) (dec.), Roberta (Mrs. Ronald Potts), Richard, Ronald. Ordained to ministry Pentecostal Holiness Ch., 1936, United Meth. Ch., 1968; evangelist, 1936-41; pastor various chs., N.C., Okla., and Ga., 1941-47; worldwide evangelist in crusades, radio, television, 1947—; founder, pres. Oral Roberts Assn., Inc., 1947-70; pres., founder Oral Roberts U., Tulsa, 1963—. Dir. Okla. Natural Gas Co., Bank of Okla. Named Indian of Yr., Am. Indian Expn., Anadarko, Okla., 1963, Oklahoman of year, Okla. Broadcasters Assn., 1974; named to Okla. Hall of Fame, 1973. Mem. Tulsa C. of C. (dir.). Author: Miracle of Seed Faith, 1970; Daily Guide of Miracles, 1972; 3 Steps to Better Health and Miracle Healing, 1976; Better Health and Miracle Living, 1976; How to Get Through Your Struggles, 1977; Receiving Your Miracle, 1978; Don't Give Up, 1980. Office: Oral Roberts University 7777 S Lewis Ave Tulsa OK 74171

ROBERTS, RONALD ELDRIDGE, minister, Baptist General Conference; b. Mt. Holly, N.J., Jan. 30, 1942; s. Benjamin Charles and Juanita Odessa (Jacobs) R.; m. Gertrude Inez Timpson Carney, Jan. 30, 1965; children: Ronald E. Jr., Reginald E. B.S., Phila. Coll. of Bible, 1970; Th.M., Dallas Theol. Sem., 1975, D.Min., 1985. Ordained to ministry Bapt. Ch., 1969. Assoc. minister Mt. Calvary Bapt. Ch., Camden, N.J., 1965-70, 1975-77, Golden Gate Bapt. Ch., Dallas, 1970-71; minister of Christian edn. St. John Bapt. Ch., Dallas, 1972-75; dean of students and mem. faculty Manna Bible Inst., Phila., 1975-77; sr. pastor Baldwin Hills Bapt. Ch., Los Angeles, 1977—; mem. adj. faculty Talbot Theol. Sem., Los Angeles, 1982—; dir. Christian edn. dept. Nat. Black Evang. Assn., N.Y.C., 1973-75. Author: A Historical Study of the Baldwin Hills Baptist Church, 1983 (award 1983); (doctoral dissertation) Leadership Styles in Black Evangelism, 1985. Served with USAF, 1960-64. Mem. Southwest Bapt. Conf. Missions Bd. (bd. dirs. 1980-82, 84—), Black Evangelistic Enterprise (co-founder, bd. dirs. 1972—), Evang. Tchr. Tng. Assn. Club: Baldwin Hill Bapt. Ch. Camera. Avocations: photography; swimming; personal computering. Office: Baldwin Hills Bapt Ch 4700 W King Blvd Los Angeles CA 90016

ROBERTSEN, ANNA RUTH, practitioner, Ch. of Christ Scientist; b. Oakland, Calif., Apr. 13; s. William Francis and Elizabeth H. (Stuart) Lewis; student U. So. Calif., 1934-35, U. Calif., Berkeley, 1936-37; m. Robert Kaare Robertsen, Sept. 13, 1939; children—Anthony Lewis, Eric Hal. Licensed as practitioner, 1959; 2d reader 1st Ch. of Christ Scientist, Monrovia, Calif., 1963-66. Bd. dirs. Plaza Park Playhouse, 1976. Contbr. articles to religious jours. Home and Office: 721 E Foothill Blvd Monrovia CA 91016

ROBERTSON, ALICE SMITH, religious organization administrator, Seventh-day Adventist Church; b. N.Y.C., Sept. 11, 1926; d. Henry Philip and Nancy Dagmar (Benson) Smith; m. Oscar Leroy Robertson, May 12, 1946 (dec. 1970); children: Willis Roy, Philip Gene, Janita Rae; m. Arl Vandevere Voorheis, Dec. 23, 1984. B.S. in Elem. Edn., So. Coll., 1975; M.A., Andrews U., 1979. Commd. minister. Sch. bd. chmn. Winter Haven Seventh-day Adventist Sch., Freeland, N.C., 1953-55; elem. tchr. Carolina Conf. of Seventh-day Adventists, Raleigh, N.C., Elizabethtown, N.C., Charleston, S.C., 1962-71; dean of girls Mt. Pisgah Acad., Candler, N.C., 1971-77; assoc. supt. edn. Carolina Conf. of Seventh-day Adventists, Charlotte, N.C., 1977-83; supt. edn. Gulf States Conf. of Seventh-day Adventists, Montgomery, Ala., 1983—. Contbr. articles to profl. jours. Civil def. worker White Lake, N.C., Elizabethtown, N.C., Civil Def. Squad, 1966. Club: Community Services (Charleston) (pres. 1970-71). Office: PO Box 17100 Montgomery AL 36193

ROBERTSON, BYRON K., minister, Internat. Ch. of Foursquare Gospel; b. Newport, Ind., Nov. 22, 1936; s. Allen Neil and Myrtel (Foos) R.; student Life Bibl. Coll., Los Angeles, 1957-61; m. Donna L. Edwards, June 21, 1958; children—Donald N., Lorraine S., Dawn M. Ordained to ministry, 1964; pastor Fort Morgan (Colo.) Foursquare Ch., 1961-63; layman, S.W. Denver, 1963-64; youth pastor, Terre Haute, Ind., 1964-65; pastor Galva (Ill.) Foursquare Ch., 1965—. Mgr. Galva Super Valu, 1976—. Mem. Galva Ministerial Assn. Home: 210 SE 1st St Galva IL 61434 Office: 117 E Division St PO Box U Galva IL 61434

ROBERTSON, DONALD ERID, minister, Atlantic United Baptist Convention; b. North Sydney, N.S., Can., Sept. 30, 1934; s. Alvin Gordon and Marjorie Helen (Mason) R.; m. Cairine Anne Fraser, Aug. 15, 1964; children: Iain, Leslie. B.A., Acadia U., N.S., 1955, M.Div., 1957. Ordained to ministry Atlantic United Baptist Convention, 1956. Pastor Caledonia Bapt. Ch., N.S., 1957-62, New Germany Bapt. Pastorate, Barss Corner, N.S., 1962-68, Digby Bapt. Ch., N.S., 1968-74, Grace Meml. Bapt. Ch., Fredericton, N.S., 1974-80, Middleton Bapt. Ch., N.S., 1980—; trustee Acadia Div. Coll., Wolfville, N.S., 1981—; dir. Standards United Bapt. Conv., 1981—. Home: 32 Church St Middleton NS B0S 1P0 Canada

ROBERTSON, LAVOID OTHA, minister, Southern Baptist Convention; b. Weinert, Tex., May 31, 1926; s. Arthur Chester and Mollie Viola (Harris) R.; B.S., Howard Payne U., 1955; m. Margie Geneva Drinnon, June 4, 1950; children—Kyle, Ron. Ordained to ministry, 1952; pastor chs. in Tex., 1952-62; pastor First So. Bapt. Ch., Twin Falls, Idaho, 1962-69, First So. Bapt. Ch., Clearfield, Utah, 1969, now dir. evangelism and stewardship Utah-Idaho So. Bapt. Conv., Salt Lake City. Pres. Utah-Idaho So. Bapt. Conv., 1968-69, gen. chmn. Crusade of the Americas, 1969; vice moderator Brown County Bapt. Assn., 1958-59, moderator, 1963-64; moderator Golden Spike Bapt. Assn., 1970-71. Home: 3223 W 4960 S Salt Lake City UT 84118

ROBERTSON, MARION GORDON, broadcaster Southern Baptist Convention; b. Lexington, Va., Mar. 22, 1930; s. A. Willis and Gladys (Churchill) R.; m. Adelia Elmer; children: Timothy, Elizabeth, Gordon, Ann. B.A., Washington and Lee U., 1950; J.D., Yale U., 1955; M.Div., N.Y. Theol. Sem., 1959; D.T. (hon.), Oral Roberts U., 1983. Ordained minister Southern Baptist Convention, 1961. Founder, pres. Christian Broadcast Network, Virginia Beach, Va., 1960—, CBN Univ., 1977—, CBN Continental Broadcasting Network, 1978—; host The 700 Club, 1968—; bd. dirs. Nat. Religious Broadcasters, Morristown, N.J., 1973—. Author: My Prayer for You, 1977; Answers to 200 of Life's Most Probing Questions, 1984; Beyond Reason, 1984; The Secret Kingdom, 1982. Dir. United Va. Bank, Norfolk, 1977—. Mem. Pres.'s Task Force on Victims of Crime, Washington, 1982. Recipient Disting. Merit citation NCCJ; Knesset medallion Israel Pilgrimage Com. (Jerusalem); Faith and Freedom award Religious Heritage of Am.; Internat. Clergyman of Yr., Religion in Media, 1981; Man of Yr., Internat. Com. for Goodwill, 1981; Bronze halo Southern Calif. Motion Picture Council; Humanitarian award Food for the Hungry, 1982; George Washington Honor medal for individual achievement Freedoms Found. at Valley Forge, 1983. Office: The Christian Broadcasting Network Inc CBN Ctr Virginia Beach VA 23463

ROBERTSON, TERRY MICHAEL, minister, church official, Southern Baptist Convention; b. Dutton, Ala., Sept. 29, 1954; s. Winford Ellis and Wanda Faye

(Leverrett) R.; m. Elizabeth Ann Bell, Jan. 8, 1977; 1 son, Nathan Terry. B.A., Samford U., 1977; M.R.E., New Orleans Bapt. Theol. Sem., 1979. Ordained, 1973. Assoc. pastor Broadway Bapt. Ch., Rainsville, Ala., 1973-74; pastor Nicholsville Bapt. Ch., Thomasville, Ala., 1974-80, 1st Bapt. Ch., Grand Island, N.Y., 1980-85; moderator Frontier Bapt. Assn., Buffalo, 1983-85, dir. missions, Depew, NY, 1985—. Mem. New Orleans Bapt. Theol. Sem. Alumni Assn. (pres. N.Y.-N.J. chpt. 1983-84). Home: 3402 Sandy Beach Rd Grand Island NY 14072 Office: Frontier Bapt Assn 96 Meridian St PO Box 431 Depew NY 14043

ROBIDOUX, OMER, bishop, Roman Catholic Church; b. Saint-Pierre-Jolys, Man., Can., Dec. 19, 1913. Ordained priest, 1939, consecrated bishop, 1970; bishop Churchill-Hudson Bay, Man., 1970—. Address: CP 10 Churchill MB R0B 0E0 Canada*

ROBILLARD, EDMOND, member Dominican Order, Roman Catholic Church; b. St.-Paul-l'Ermite, Que., Dec. 20, 1917; s. William and Marie (Lachapelle) R. B.Arts and Scis., Coll. de l'Assomption, 1936; postgrad. in philosophy and theology, Couvent Dominicain d'Ottawa, 1938-41; Lic. in Theology, Cath. U. Am., 1943; Doctorate, U. Montreal, 1944-45. Joined Dominican Order, Roman Cath. Ch., ordained priest, 1941. Prof. theology College Dominicain, Ottawa, Ont., 1943-50; prof. theology U. Montreal, 1955-83, prof. titulaire, 1970—; dir. jour. Carrefour Chretien, 1984—; sec. de l'Academie canadienne francaise, 1977-83; pres. Societe des Ecrivains canadiens, 1973-77. Author: De l'analogie et du concept d'etre, 1963; John Henry Newman: L'idee d'universite, 1968; John Henry Newman: Conferences sur la Doctrine de la justification, 1980; Reincarnation Illusion or Reality, 1982; Quebec Blues, 1983; Sous presse: Nos racines chrétiennes, 1985. Contbr. articles to profl. jours. Mem. Société canadienne de theologie, Assn. canadienne francaise pour l'avancement des sciences. Address: Monastere Saint-Albert-le-Grand 2715 Côte du Chemin Ste-Catherine Montreal PQ H3T 1B6 Canada

ROBINS, MILTON FRANKLIN, minister, Pentecostal Ch. of God of Am., Inc.; b. Mount Ida, Ark., Aug. 5, 1922; s. Claud and Cora Bethel (Ragan) R.; student pub. schs., Tex.; m. Betty Lee Ayres, Mar. 11, 1950; children—Norbert, Lynda, Jamie, Eugene, Betty, Philip, Marilyn, Roger. Ordained to ministry, 1953; founder, pastor Pentecostal Ch. of God, Jacksonville, Tex., 1953-55; pastor First Pentecostal Ch. of God, Irving, Tex., 1955—; evangelist Irving, 1955—. Organizer, bd. dirs. So. Bible Coll., Houston, 1957—; sect. presbyter Dallas, Pentecostal Ch. of God of Am., 1955-67, 74—, mem. gen. bd., 1967-73, chmn. dist. home missions com., dist. presbyter, 1967-73, chmn. resolutions com., 1957—. Contbr. articles to newspapers and religious jours. Home: 1201 Maryland St Irving TX 75061 Office: 2437 Hinton St Irving TX 75061

ROBINSON, CHARLES JAY, minister, So. Bapt. Conv.; b. Memphis, Aug. 29, 1954; s. Richard Shelton and Nettie (Hanson) R.; B.S., Union U., 1976. Ordained to ministry, 1974; vol. music dir. Union Grove Bapt. Ch., Henderson County, Tenn., 1973-74; mem. staff Tenn. Royal Ambassador Camp, summers 1971-73; asst. pastor Blue Ridge Park Bapt. Ch., Memphis, 1974—. Mem. Memphis Religious Edn. and Music Assn., Phi Mu Alpa. Home: 498 Swan Ridge Circle Memphis TN 38122 Office: 2018 Bartlett Rd Memphis TN 38134

ROBINSON, CLARENCE ANDREW, minister, Southern Baptist Convention; b. Falls Church, Va., Mar. 16, 1927; s. Clarence Lee and Lorraine Naomi (Hampton) R.; diploma Washington Bapt. Sem., 1957; B.Th., Nat. Bible Coll., 1960; D.D., Bapt. Coll. of Bible, 1970; m. Winnie Verdell Aiken, Dec. 11, 1950; children—A. Delores Robinson Bailey, Delano L., Rita C. Robinson Montague, Clarence Andrew, Charles E., Robin E. Ordained to ministry, 1957; pastor Mt. Calvary Bapt. Ch., Fairfax, Va., 1959-69, Macedonia Bapt. Ch., Arlington, Va., 1969—. Mem. exec. bd. of Lott Carey Fgn. Mission, No. Va. Bapt. Assn.; mem. No. Va. Bapt. Ministers Conf. Mem. Alcohol Control Advisory Com., Arlington, Va.; mem. Community Mental Health and Mental Retardation Services Bd., Arlington, bd. dirs. Am. Cancer Soc., Social Center, Falls Church, Vis. Nurse Assn. No. Va., 1984-87. Recipient Distinguished Service Merit award. Mem. Mt. Vernon Bapt. Assn., NAACP (pres. Fairfax county br.), McLean Citizens Assn., Nat. Assn., Christian Marriage Counselors. Clubs: Mason (33 deg.), Shriner. Home: 1345 Gordon Ln McLean VA 22102 Office: 3412 S 22nd St Arlington VA 22206

ROBINSON, DONALD FAY, minister, Unitarian Universalist Association; b. Boston, Feb. 6, 1905; s. Thomas Pendleton and Ethel Lincoln (Fay) R.; A.B., Harvard, 1926; postgrad. Crozer Theol. Sem., 1937-38; m. Carol Howard, May 9, 1942; children—Mary Howard Robinson Rizzotto, Thomas Howard. Ordained to ministry Unitarian Universalist Assn., 1957; minister Second Parish, Hingham, Mass., 1957-77, emeritus, 1977—; dir. Unitarian Universalist Christian Fellowship, Boston, 1970-71, v.p., 1971-73, pres., 1973-75. Pres., Hingham Hist. Soc., 1960-63. Trustee, Wilder Charitable and Ednl. Fund, Hingham, 1966—. Recipient Christian Research Found. award, 1961. Mem. Soc. Bibl. Lit., Unitarian Universalist Ministers Assn., Internat. Platform Assn. Author: Out of the East (poems), 1927; Harvard Dramatic Club Miracle Plays, 1928; In Search of a Religion, 1938; Jesus Son of Joseph, 1964; Two Hundred Years in South Hingham, 1746-1946, 1980; Poems for People, 1982; contbr. articles to religious jours. Home: 46 S Pleasant St Hingham MA 02043 Office: 685 Main St Hingham MA 02043

ROBINSON, EDWARD MERRITT, minister, United Church of Christ; b. Norwood, Mass., Dec. 12, 1939; s. Edward E. and Hester E. (Merritt) R.; m. Barbara Julia Brown June 26, 1965; children: Sarah E., Jonathan E. B.A., Yankton Coll., 1961; Th.B., 1962; M.Div., United Theol. Sem., 1964; S.T.M., Iliff Sch. Theology, 1975. Ordained to ministry United Ch. of Christ, 1964. Asst. minister Hazel Park Congl. Ch., St. Paul, 1962-65; minister United Ch., Mapleton, Minn., 1966-70, Parkview Congl. Ch., Aurora, Colo., 1970-75; sr. minister Hillcrest Congl. Ch., LaHabra Heights, Calif., 1975-85; sr. minister Central Union Ch., Honolulu, 1985—; lectr. in religion Whittier Coll., Calif., 1977-80; moderator So. Calif. Conf. United Ch. Christ, 1983—, bd. dirs., 1982—; bd. dirs. Pilgrim Pines Camp, Yucaipa, Calif., 1983—; deans adv. bd. Pacific Sch. Religion, San Francisco, 1982—. Bd. dirs. Whittier YMCA, 1982—; mem. adv. bd. Summit Place Drug Ctr., Whittier, 1983. Mem. Whittier Clergy Assn. (pres. 1982), Whittier Ecumenical Council (pres. 1981). Republican. Lodge: Lions. Office: Hillcrest Congl Ch 2000 West Rd La Habra Heights CA 90631

ROBINSON, GARY GARTH, minister, Internat. Ch. of Foursquare Gospel; b. Grand Junction, Colo., Sept. 9, 1932; s. Clayton and Iola (Griffith) R.; B.Th., L.I.F.E. Bible Coll., 1954; A.A., Orange Coast Coll., 1966; B.A., Long Beach State U., 1968, M.A., 1970; m. Gay Elizabeth Clara Guilmette, Feb. 3, 1952; children—Joy Leah, Clayton David. Ordained to ministry, 1954; pastor, Peris, Calif., 1955-58; Southwestern dist. evangelist, 1958-60; pastor, Huntington Beach, Calif., 1960-84, also missionary-evangelist, 1965—. Conv., conf. and youth camp speaker Internat. Ch. of the Foursquare Gospel, 1968—, TV and radio broadcaster, 1958-60, mem. internat. bldg. com., 1967-73, mem. internat. com. higher edn., 1968-70; del. Ofcl. World Pentecostal Conf., 1976; mem. Internat. Sunday Sch. com., 1975-84, dist. coordinator, 1972-75, Sunday Sch. coordinator, 1975-84, mem. coms. ins., ordination, bldg. and planning, 1974-84; sec. Huntington Beach Ministerial Assn., 1961. Mem. Phi Kappa Phi, Western Psychol. Assn. Author; Cross-Cultural Study of Siriono Indians in Bolivia, 1969, 70. Home and Office: 20421 Ravenwood Ln Huntington Beach CA 92646

ROBINSON, HADDON WILLIAM, seminary president, minister, Conservative Baptist Association of America; b. N.Y.C., Mar. 21, 1931; s. William Andrew and Anna (Clements) R.; m. Bonita Beverly Vick, Aug. 11, 1951; children: Vicki Ann, Talley William. A.B., Bob Jones U., 1951; Th.M., Dallas Theol. Sem., 1955; M.S., So. Meth. U., 1960; Ph.D., U. Ill., 1964. Ordained to ministry Conservative Bapt. Assn. of Am. Dir. Dallas Youth for Christ, 1952-54; assoc. pastor First Bapt. Ch., Medford, Oreg., 1956-58; gen. dir. Christian Med. Soc., Richardson, Tex., 1968-78; mem. faculty Dallas Theol. Sem., 1958-78; pres. Denver Sem., 1978—; trustee Black Evangelistic Enterprise, Dallas, 1975—. Author: Psalm 23, 1968; Grief, 1976; Biblical Preaching, 1982. Mem. Religious Communications Assn., Evang. Theol. Soc. (pres. 1983-84). Office: Denver Sem PO Box 10000 Denver CO 80210

ROBINSON, HAROLD BARRETT, bishop, Episcopal Church; b. Nelson, Eng., June 14, 1922; s. Harold and Mary (Barrett) R.; m. Marie Allison Little, May 17, 1952; children: Mary Elizabeth Robinson Jewett, Martha Marie Robinson Higgins, Anne Victoria Robinson Wadsworth, Jane Barrett. B.A., UCLA, 1943; S.T.B., Gen. Theol. Sem., 1946, S.T.D. (hon.), 1967; L.H.D. (hon.), Niagara U., 1979. Ordained deacon Episcopal Ch., 1946, priest, 1946, consecrated bishop, 1968. Chaplain, Harvey Sch., Hawthorne, N.Y., 1944-46; curate St. Paul's Ch., San Diego, 1946-47, rector, 1947-62; dean St. Paul's Cathedral, Buffalo, 1962-68; bishop coadjutor Diocese of Western N.Y., Buffalo, 1968-70, bishop, 1970—; chmn. bd. Episc. Radio/TV Found., Atlanta, 1976—; pres. Province II, Episcopal Ch., 1981—, mem. presiding bishop's council of advice, N.Y.C., 1981—, mem. standing com. ecumenical relations, 1980—; trustee Gen. Theol. Sem., 1982—; former chaplain San Diego Fire Dept., Buffalo Fire Dept. Mem. Buffalo C. of C. Republican. Clubs: Saturn, Thursday (Buffalo). Lodge: Rotary. Home: 1112 Delaware Ave Buffalo NY 14209 Office: 1114 Delaware Ave Buffalo NY 14209

ROBINSON, HOWARD ARTHUR, JR., minister, American Baptist Churches U.S.A., National Nat. Baptist Convention of America; b. Columbus, Ohio, May 31, 1948; s. Howard Arthur and Mary Belle (Hairston) R.; m. Sandra Marie Sims, July 17, 1970 (div. Nov. 1979); children: Dionne Carol, Angela Marie, Howard Arthur; m. Etta Louise Gilstrap, Apr. 2, 1984; children: Teri Lynn, A. Byron. B.A., Northwest Coll., 1976; M.Div., Interdenominational Theol. Ctr., Morehouse Sch. Religion, 1979. Ordained to ministry Baptist Ch., 1976. Chaplain, Fulton County Juvenile Ct., Atlanta, 1976-79; asst. pastor First Congregational Bapt. Ch., Atlanta, 1978-79; pastor Algona Community Bapt. Ch., Wash., 1982-85, Greater Mt. Baker Bapt. Ch., 1985—. chaplain U.S. Air Force Res., MCCHORD AFB, 1982—; dir. Youth Chaplaincy Program, Seattle, 1982—; pres. Inst. for Ch. Devel., Wash. state, 1981-83; mem. task force revising religious policy Dept. of Corrections, Wash. state, 1982-83, adv. council on religious issues, 1984—; mem. task force on teen pregnancy and birth defects Wash. Assn. Chs., Seattle, 1982-83, task force on criminal justice, 1982—; chmn. pastoral care task force Ch. Council Greater Seattle. Coordinator, founder Nat. Conference for Black Seminarians, Atlanta, 1978-79; del. Wash. State Democratic Convention, 1980; pres., dir. Mt. Baker/Central Seattle Youth Service Bur., Seattle, 1980-81; mem. steering com. Coalition on Youth in Crisis, Seattle, 1981-83. Served as sgt. U.S. Army, 1967-70. Recipient Martin Luther King Jr. award Seattle Council of Chs. for Social Action, 1984, cert. appreciation Dept. of Corrections Wash. State, 1983, D.E. King award Interdenominational Theol. Ctr., Atlanta, 1979, dedicated service award, 1979. Mem. Nat. Assn. Ecumenical Staff (mem. nominating com. 1984—), Bapt. Pastors Conference (fin. sec. 1983-84), Am. Protestant Correctional Chaplains Assn., U.S. Military Chaplains Assn., Black United Clergy for Action. Democrat. Lodges: Rotary (Seattle), Masons. Home: PO Box 1572 Kent WA 98032 Office Youth Chaplaincy Program 1211 E Alder St Seattle WA 98122

ROBINSON, IRA MEREDITH, minister, United Methodist Church. B. Brandon, Miss., Aug. 15, 1930; s. Ira Robartus and Eula Lee (Sheely) R.; m. Mary Carolyn Moore, Nov. 23, 1956; children: Douglas Ray, Jill Eileen, Tony Lewis. B.A., Milsaps Coll., 1952; B.D., Emory U., 1955, M.Div., 1972. Ordained to ministry United Meth. Ch. Pastor United Meth. Ch., Elizabeth, La., 1961-64, Colfax, La., 1964-67, Golden Meadow, La., 1967-72, Welsh, La., 1972-76, Bastrop, La., 1976-80, Franklin, La., 1980—; pres. West St. Mary Parish Ministerial Assn., 1982; sec. equitable salaries commn. La. Conf. United Meth. Ch., 1976-80, chmn. 1980—; chmn. Monroe dist. council on ministries United Meth. Ch., 1975-76. Pres. PTO, Welsh, La., 1976; active band booster Welsh, 1972-76, Bastrop, 1976-80, football booster, Franklin, 1982—. Home and Office: 922 Main St Franklin LA 70538

ROBINSON, JACK FAY, minister, United Church Christ; b. Wilmington, Mass., Mar. 7, 1914; s. Thomas Pendleton and Ethel Lincoln (Fay) R.; B.A., U. Mont., 1936; B.D., Crozer Theol. Sem., 1939; A.M., U. Chgo., 1949; m. Eleanor Smith, Sept. 1, 1937 (dec. 1966); 1 child, Alice Robinson Dungey; m. Lois Henze, July 16, 1968. Ordained to ministry, 1939; pastor chs., American Falls, Idaho, 1939-41, Council Grove, Kans., 1944-49, Chebanse, Ill., 1949-52, Argo, Ill, 1954-58, St. Charles, Ill., 1958-64, Lansing, Mich., 1964-66, Waveland Ave. Congl. Ch., Chgo., 1967-79; interim pastor Chgo. Met. Assn., United Ch. of Christ, 1979—, First Congl. Ch., Des Plaines, Ill., 1979, Bethany Ch., Chgo., 1980, Eden Ch., Chgo., 1983-84, St. Nicolai Ch., Chgo., 1984. Mem. gen. bd. Ch. Fedn. Greater Chgo., 1971-73; dean Northside Mission Council, 1975-77; sec. Chgo. Met. Assn. Ch. and Ministry Com., 1982—, chmn. nominating com., 1982-85; tchr. Chgo. Bd. Edn., 1966-68. Mem. Internat. Platform Assn., Am. Soc. Ch. History. Author: Growth of the Bible, 1967; From a Mission to a Church, 1976; Bell and Howell: a 75 Year History, 1982; editor Pastor's Newsletter, Ill. Conf., 1972-74. Home: 2614 Lincolnwood Dr Evanston IL 60201 Office: PO Box 4578 Chicago IL 60680

ROBINSON, JAMES, evangelist, Southern Baptist Convention; b. Houston, Oct. 9, 1943; m. Betty, Feb. 23; children: Rhonda, Randy, Robin. Evangelist, pres. James Robison Evangelistic Assn., Ft. Worth; host daily and weekly TV programs. Author several books. Publisher monthly mag. Days of Restoration. Address: Evangelistic Association Box 18489 Fort Worth TX 76118

ROBINSON, LARRY ERNEST, minister, Southern Baptist Convention; b. Wrightsville, Ga., Dec. 13, 1945; s. Ernest David and Dorothy (Alexandra) R.; B.A., Campbellsville Coll., 1970; M.Div., Southeastern Bapt. Theol. Sem., 1973; D.Min., New Orleans Bapt. Theol. Sem., 1982; m. Nancy Ellen Hansen, Mar. 27, 1966; children—David Emanual, Esther Michelle, James Douglas. Ordained to ministry, 1967; pastor Smyrna Bapt. Ch., Deepstep, Ga., 1967-68, Hardyville (Ky.) Bapt. Ch., 1969; Welfare Bapt. Ch., Russell Springs, Ky., 1969, Moycock (N.C.) Bapt. Ch., 1970-73; minister of edn. and youth 1st Bapt. Ch., Hawkinsville, Ga., 1973-74; campus minister Ga. Bapt. State Missions, Milledgeville, Ga., 1974-76; campus ministry Mercer U., Macon, Ga., 1976-83, adminstrv. officer, dir. univ. religious life, Macon and Atlanta, 1984—. Ch. tng. dir. Pulaski-Bleakley Assn., 1973-74; clk., dir. campus ministry Washington Assn., 1974-76; writer Bapt. Sunday Sch. Bd., So. Bapt. Conv., 1975-84. Mem. Phi Tau Chi. Home: 1303 Forest Hill Rd Macon GA 31210 Office: Mercer U Macon GA 31207

ROBINSON, ROBERT ARMSTRONG, financial executive, Episcopal Church; b. Waterbury, Conn., Sept. 11, 1925; s. Robert and Ethel Marie (Armstrong) R.; m. Ann Harding, June 7, 1947; 1 child, Gayllis Harding. B.A., Brown U., 1950, M.A., 1952; postgrad. U. Ill., 1952-54; D.Lit.(hon.), Episcopal Theol. Sem., 1971; D.C.L. (hon.), U. South, 1972; LL.D. (hon.), Nashotah Theol. Sem., 1980. Instr. English, U. Ill., Urbana, 1952-54; trainee Thomaston Mfg. Co., Conn., 1954-56; sr. v.p., sr. trust officer Colonial Bank & Trust Co., 1956-66; officer Conn. Life Ins. & Trust Council, 1965-66; pres., dir. Ch. Pension Fund, Episcopal Ch., N.Y.C., 1966—; cons. Pension Ben. Guaranty Corp., Washington, 1984—. Author: The Church Pension Fund, a Great Venture of Vision and Faith, 1980. Trustee, Washington Nat. Cathedral, 1974-82; trustee Nashotah Theol. Sem., Canterbury Cath. Trust in Am., N.Y. Council Boyscouts Am., 1974—; vestryman Trinity Parish, N.Y.C., 1969-77. Served with U.S. Army, 1943-46. Named Man of the Year, Episcopal Churchwomen, Diocese of Conn., 1977. Mem. Ch. Pension Conf., Am. Numismatic Soc., Dickens Fellowship, London, Phi Beta Kappa. Republican. Clubs: Union, Union League, Church, Met. Athenaeum (London). Lodge: Masons. Home: 251 Laurel Rd New Canaan CT 06840 Office: Church Pension Fund 800 Second Ave New York NY 10017

ROBINSON, ROBERT J., clergyman. Moderator, Associate Reformed Presbyterian Church (General Synod), 1985-86. Office: Assoc Reformed Presbyn Ch Box 3114 CRS Rock Hill SC 29730*

ROBINSON, SANDY CORNELIUS, JR., minister, Seventh-day Adventists; b. Thomasville, Ala., Oct. 9, 1927; s. Sandy Cornelius and Birtha Lue (Foreman) R.; m. Savannah Patricia Atwood, Mar. 18, 1950; children: Wilatra Robinson Awoniyi, Harrell E., Sandy Cornelius III, Theodore Odell, Walesia, Jonathan T., Princess N. Maria. B.A. in Religion, Oakwood Coll., 1979; student Andrew U. Extension, Huntsville, Ala., 1980. Ordained to ministry Seventh-day Adventists, 1966. Sunday sch. tchr., deacon, Bible instr. for youth Bapt. Ch., 1951-52; lit. evangelist South Central Conf. Seventh-day Adventists, Mobile, Ala., 1953-55; field dir. pub. South Atlantic Conf. Seventh-day Adventists, Orlando, Fla., 1955-66, State of Fla., 1955-66, exec. pub. dept. dir., Atlanta, 1967-73; lectr., dir. coordinator Oakwood Coll., Huntsville, Ala., 1973-84; mem. council/sales devel. Seventh-day Adventist Ch., Washington, 1967-84, revivalist/youth services condr. nationally and internationally, 1969—, drug abuse prevention/character educator, Huntsville, 1973-84; recruiter/trainer Christian salesmen South Atlantic Conf./Oakwood Coll., 1973-84. Writer, editor bi-weekly newsletter South Atlantic Echo (excellence award 1967), 1973—; developer coll. course Christian Lit. Salesmanship, 1973. Mem. Madison County Drug Abuse Bd., 1975-80; active United Negro Coll. Fund, 1978-85, NAACP; voter registration drive promotor Ala. Democratic Conv., 1983, 84. Recipient citation of excellence Daniel Payne Coll., 1970. Mem. Nat. Acad. Adventists Workers, J.L. Moran Chapel Alumni Assn., Regional Evangelistic Assn., N. Am. Pubs. (bd. dirs., coordinator). Office: Oakwood Coll PO Box 109 Oakville AL 35896 also 55 Oak Ridge Dr W Hagerstown MD 21740

ROBINSON, STEPHEN EDWARD, religion educator, Church Jesus Christ of Latter-Day Saints; b. Los Angeles, May 23, 1947; s. Edward Brown and Myrtle Anna (Egan) R.; m. Janet Lynn Bowen, June 2, 1972; children: Sarah Joy, Rebekah Lynn, Emily Anna, Michael Edward. B.A., Brigham Young U., 1974; Ph.D., Duke U., 1978. Bishop, Ch. of Jesus Christ of Latter Day Saints, 1983—; asst. prof. religion Lycoming Coll., Williamsport, Pa., 1979-85, assoc. prof., 1985— chmn. dept. religion, 1984—. Author: The Testament of Adam, 1982; asst. to editor The Old Testament Pseudepigrapha, 1983. Mem. Soc. Bibl. Lit., Phi Kappa Phi. Republican. Office: Box 37 Lycoming Coll Williamsport PA 17701

ROBINSON, STEWART HAROLD, minister, Assemblies of God; b. Hot Springs, S.D., Jan. 17, 1921; s. Martin Guy and Amy Leota (Robinson) Orr; student Ariz. State U., Tempe; grad. Central Bible Coll., 1951, B.A., 1952, B.Th., 1953; m. Roslouise Kitty Yancey, Nov. 21, 1941; children—Stewart Harold II, Joel Martin, Russell Lowell. Ordained to ministry, 1952; pastor Rimby Assembly of God, Louisburg, Mo., 1948-49, Cave Springs Assembly of God, Willard, Mo., 1950-52, Faith City Assembly of God, Michigan City, Ind., 1952-65, Calvary Temple, Springfield, Mo., 1965-78, Central Bible Ch., Miami, Fla., 1978-81, First Assembly of God, Pensacola, Fla., 1981; evangelist, seminar speaker, 1981—; also TV-radio broadcaster; gospel minister, U.S. and abroad. Exec. officer Ind. dist. Assemblies of God, Michigan City, 1954-65; gen. presbyter Gen. Council Assemblies of God, Springfield, Mo., 1959-65, exec. officer So. Mo. dist., 1966—. Hon. mem. Ind. State Prison Parole Bd., 1960-65. Home: Route 1 Box 151B Willard MO 65781 Office: 444 W Grand St Springfield MO 65807

ROBINSON, VALENTINE KEENE, minister, So. Baptist Conv.; b. Washington, Feb. 14, 1949; s. Wade Addison and Mildred B. (Bradshaw) R.; B.A., William Carey Coll., Hattiesburg, Miss., 1971; M.Div., New Orleans Bapt. Theol. Sem., 1974; m. Janette Howell Robinson, Aug. 1, 1969; children—M. Sean, Candice Rene, Tracy Nanett. Ordained to ministry, 1969; asso. pastor First Bapt. Ch., Quitman, Miss., 1969, Riverside Bapt. Ch., New Orleans, 1971-74; pastor Oak Grove Bapt. Ch., Shubuta, Miss., 1969-71; asso. youth pastor Leesburg (Fla.) First Bapt. Ch., 1974-75; youth pastor First Bapt. Ch., Lake Charles, La., 1975—. Dir. vacation Bible Sch. New Orleans Bapt. Assn., 1974; youth dir. Carey Bapt. Assn., 1976; vol. dir. Bapt. Student Union, Lake Sumter Community Coll., 1975. Address: 4722 DeSoto Ct Lake Charles LA 70601

ROBISON, KLANE ERVING, minister, Religious Society of Friends; b. Pueblo, Colo., June 13, 1931; s. Kenneth Erving and Flossie Leona (Johnson) R.; m. Sandra May Nordke, Aug. 17, 1954; children: Kara, Kurt, Amy; m. Kathleen Margaret Hall, July 15, 1982; children: Bryan, Darin. B.A., George Fox Coll., 1953; Mus.M., Lewis and Clark Coll., 1954; M.R.E., Sch. Theology, Claremont, Calif., 1961. Recorded minister Society of Friends, 1961. Minister of music and Christian edn. Multomah United Presbyn. Ch., Portland, Oreg., 1954-55, Alamitos Friends Ch., Garden Grove, Calif., 1955-57; assoc. minister First Friends Ch., Whittier, Calif., 1955-69, sr. minister, 1969—; mem. alumni bd. Sch. Theology, Claremont, Calif., 1969-72, 1980—; bd. trustees Calif. Friends Home, Stanton, Calif., 1968-71, 1984—, Earlham Sch. Religion, Richmond, Ind., 1980—; dir. music Friends United Meeting Triennial, Richmond, Ind., 1972, 75, 84; co-founder Interchurch Samaritan Counseling Center, Whittier, 1975. Contbr. articles to various publs. Bd. trustees Boys and Girls Club Whittier, 1971—, pres., 1977-79; bd. dirs. Whittier Mus. Found., 1979-82; mem. centennial com. Whittier Coll., 1984—. Recipient Bronze medallion award Boys Clubs Am., N.Y., 1981; various awards Kiwanis Internat., 1963—. Mem. Friends Assn. Higher Edn. Republican. Lodge: Kiwanis (pres. 1966). Office: First Friends Ch 13205 Philadelphia St Whittier CA 90601

ROBLES-COTA, ALFONSO HUMBERTO, bishop, Roman Catholic Church; b. Los Mochis, Sinaloa, Mex., Oct. 30, 1931; s. Gumersindo E. Robles-Cota and Refugio Cota-Ruiz. Seminary student, Culiacan, Mex., Montezuma Sem., N.J.; Sacred Theology Licence, Gregoriana U., Rome, 1956. Prefect of studies, prefect of discipline, spiritual dir., prof. canon law, liturgy, and holy scripture Minor and Mayor Sem., Culiacan, Mex., 1956-78, vice-rector, 1968-69, rector, 1969-78; vicar gen. of Diocese Tepic, Mex., 1978-81, bishop, 1981—. Office: Curia Diocesana Apartado P 15 Tepic Nayarit Mexico 63000

ROBY, JASPER, bishop, Apostolic Overcoming Holy Church of God; b. Brookville, Miss., Apr. 19, 1912; s. Jasper and Allie F. (Horton) R.; B.Th., Am. Div. Sch., 1957, Th.M., 1964; D.D., Universal Bible Inst., 1972, Miles Coll., 1984; LL.D., Faith Coll., 1976; m. Malinda Sanders, Oct. 17, 1931; children—Dorothy, Robert, Juanita (Mrs. J. Arrington), Aretha, Linda, Vanessa. Ordained to ministry, 1942; pastor Greater 17th St Apostolic Overcoming Holy Ch. of God, Birmingham, 1942—. Presiding elder Apostolic Overcoming Holy Ch. of God Central Ala., 1945-53, Fla., 1945-53; bishop in states of N.Y., also Ohio, Conn., 1953-70, Mich., North Ala., 1953-70, Pa., 1953-69, Tenn., 1956-70; sr. bishop Nat. Body of Apostolic Overcoming Holy Ch. of God, 1973—; Conductor of program His Word sta. WVTM-TV, 1983—. Mem. Downtown Action Com., Birmingham, 1970—. Bd. dirs. Gaston Boys Club. Recipient awards Lawson State Community Coll., Booker T. Washington Bus. Coll. Mem. NAACP (life), Birmingham Urban League (dir. 1969—), Omega Psi Phi, Pi Lambda Sigma. Home: 514 10th Ave West Birmingham AL 35204 Office: 1120 24th St N Birmingham AL 35234

ROCHELLE, JAY COOPER, minister, theology educator Lutheran Church in America; b. Southampton, Pa., Dec. 28, 1938; s. Norman Harold and Marion Emma (Sommer) R.; m. Cynthia Ann Hull, June 16, 1962 (div. 1983); m. Susan Etta Steinhaus, Nov. 26, 1983; children: Leah, Peter, Glynis, Micah. A.A., St. John's Coll., Winfield, Kans., 1959; B.A., Concordia Sr. Coll., Ft. Wayne, Ind., 1961; student Luth. Sch. Theol., 1961-63; M.Div., Concordia Sem., St. Louis, 1965; Th.M., Phila. Luth. Theol. Sem., 1968. Ordained to ministry Lutheran Ch. in Am., 1965. Pastor Ascension Luth. Ch., Pitts., 1965-68, St. John's Ch., Allentown, Pa., 1968-70; campus pastor Bloomsburg U. Pa., 1970-77, Yale U., New Haven 1977-81; professor Luth. Sch. Theol., Chgo., 1982—. Author: Create and Celebrate, 1971; The Revolutionary Year, 1973; I'm Not the Same Person I Was Yesterday, 1974; Spiritual Care, 1985. Contbr. articles to profl. jours. Adv. bd. New Haven Center for Peace Edn. and Action, 1978-81; pres. New Haven Calligraphers' Guild, 1978-81; bd. dirs. Society of Scribes, N.Y.C., 1981. Named First Visiting Faculty, Gruenwald Guild, Leavenworth Wash., 1982, invited mem. first conf. on Thomas Merton, Pendle Hill, Wallingford, Pa., 1975. Fellow Fellowship of St. Augustine, Fellowship of Saints Alban and Sergius; mem. Am. Acad. Religion, Assn. for Religion in Intellectual Life, N. Am. Acad. Liturgy, Soc. for Art, Religion and Culture. Democrat. Home: 5400 S Woodlawn Ave Apt 3 Chicago IL 60615 Office: Luth Sch of Theology 1100 E 55th St Chicago IL 60615

ROCKETT, BILLY CLYDE, minister, So. Baptist Conv.; b. Spearsville, La., Oct. 10, 1933; s. Lowell B. and Bera I. (Black) R.; B.A., La. Coll., 1956; M.Div., New Orleans Bapt. Theol. Sem., 1960; m. Dorothy Lou Bruner, Sept. 2, 1961; children—Katherine Ann, Clyde Mark, Lowell Matthew. Ordained to ministry, 1956; pastor Whitehouse Forks Bapt. Ch., Bay Minette, Ala., 1956-59, Campti (La.) Bapt. Ch., 1960-65, Calvary Bapt. Ch., San Juan, P.R., 1965-71, Mystic Islands Bapt. Ch., Tuckerton, N.J., 1971-73, Emmanuel Bapt. Ch., Springfield, Mass., 1973-76, Laytonsville (Md.) Bapt. Ch., 1976—; missionary Home Mission Bd., So. Bapt. Conv., Atlanta, 1965—. Pres. Evang. Ministers Assn. of Greater Springfield, 1974-76; v.p. Western New Eng. Crusade for Christ, 1974-75; chmn. of evangelism Mass. Bapt. Assn., 1974-76; condr. revivals, Ala., La., Tex., P.R., Jamaica. Pres. Springfield PTA, 1974-75. Home: 7009 Dorsey Rd Laytonsville MD 20760 Office: Route 108 at Warfield Rd Laytonsville MD 20760

RODE, ARTHUR EMIL, minister, American Lutheran Church. B. Hallettsville, Tex., Oct. 14, 1923; s. Arthur Daniel and Lydia Marie (Hannemann) R.; m. Dorothy Mae Arning, Apr. 26, 1948; children: Arthur Stephen, Christine Rebecca Rode Borchardt. B.A., U. Tex., 1944; B.Div., Wartburg Theol. Sem., 1946, M.Div., 1976, D.D. (hon.), 1983. Ordained to ministry, Am. Luth. Ch., 1946. Pastor. Grace Luth. Ch., Sinton, Tex., 1946-48, Govt. Hill Luth. Ch., San Antonio, 1948-50, Our Savior Luth. Ch., Fort Worth, 1950-57, First English Luth. Ch., Victoria, Tex., 1958-63, Faith Luth. Ch., Austin, Tex., 1963-74; sr. pastor Christ Luth. Ch., San Antonio, 1974—; v.p. bd. regents Tex. Luth. Coll., Seguin, 1970—; v.p. bd. dirs. St. Luke Luth. Hosp., San Antonio, 1975—; bd. dirs. San Antonio Community of Chs., 1984—; sec. div. Service to Mil. Luth. Council, Washington, 1981—. Author Augsburg Sermons 2, 1983. Contbr. articles to Luth. Standard Mag. Active Exchange Club, Austin and San Antonio, 1963-83. Served with USAR, 1948-76, col. Res. ret. Recipient Disting. Churchman's award Tex. Luth. Coll., 1981. Democrat. Home: 518 Oakleaf San Antonio TX 78209 Office: Christ Luth Ch 6720 Broadway San Antonio TX 78209

RODERICK, RICHARD HUGH, minister, Seventh-day Adventist Church; b. Mason City, Iowa, Oct. 27, 1932; s. Mark Hugh and Anna Viola (Thake) R.; m. Althea Elizabeth Rea, Nov. 27, 1955; children: Alline, Ronald, Shana. B.S. in B.A., Union Coll., 1958. Ordained to ministry, Seventh-day Adventist ch., 1973. Asst. auditor Ohio Conf. Seventh-day Adventists, Mt. Vernon, Ohio, 1958-59; asst. treas. Wis. Conf., Madison, 1960; cashier Far Eastern div. Seventh-day Adventists, Singapore, 1961-62, asst. treas., 1962-65; treas. Korean Union Mission, 1965-71, Trans Africa Div., Salisbury, Rhodesia, 1971-76; treas. No. Calif. Conf. Seventh-day Adventists, Pleasant Hill, Calif., 1976—; trustee Paradise Adventist Hosp., Calif., 1981—. Served with U.S. Army, 1954-56. Home: 330 Heavenly Pl Martinez CA 94553 Office: No Calif Conf Seventh-day Adventist 401 Taylor Blvd Pleasant Hill CA 94523

RODGERS, BRUCE, minister, Christians Inc.; b. Waco, Tex., Oct. 23, 1921; s. Solas O. Rodgers and Dora Mae (Moore) Rodgers Hale; m. Jimmie Lee, June 3, 1939; children: Gary Don, Mickey Joe. Ordained to ministry Christians Ch., 1960. Pastor, Bruceville Community Ch., Tex., 1959—; bd. dirs. Christians, Inc., Bruceville, 1960—. Served with USN, 1943-45, PTO. Named to Legion of Leaders, Cheverolet, 1968. Avocations: golf; hunting. Home: Rural Route 1 Bruceville TX 76630

RODGERS, CHRISTOPHER RAYMOND PERRY, lay worker, Episcopal Church; former banker; b. Washington, Nov. 29, 1920; s. C. Raymong P. Rodgers and Alice Appleton (Meyer) Coffin; m. Mary Pardee, May 5, 1951 (dec. 1983); 11 children: m. Katharine Sage Bolton, Aug. 11, 1984. A.B., Princeton U., 1942. Vestryman, Trinity Ch., Princeton, N.J., 1958-61, 69-70, jr. warden, 1970-71, sr. warden, 1971-75; vestryman Trinity Ch., N.Y.C., 1975-82; trustee Diocesan Found., Diocese of N.J., Trenton, 1980-83, mem. investment adv. com., 1982—. With CitiBank N.A., N.Y.C., 1946-80, v.p., ret., 1980. Served to lt. USNR, 1942-46, PTO. Republican. Clubs: Bedens Brook (treas. 1963-68, pres. 1969-71), Pine Valley Golf. Home: 270 Cherry Hill Rd Princeton NJ 08540

RODGERS, LAWRENCE EVERETT, minister, Ch. of Christ (Christian); b. Oregon City, Oreg., Nov. 4, 1941; s. Everet Kelsey and Grace Lydia (Rowlett) R.; B.A., Puget Sound Coll. of Bible, 1965; M.R.E., Emmanuel Sch. Religion, 1971; postgrad. Seattle Pacific Coll., 1965-66, U. Wash., 1960-61; m. Charlene Mae Bates, Aug. 25, 1962; children—Charles Lawrence, Saundra Laree. Ordained to ministry, 1967; minister Ch. of Christ (Christian), Sedro Woolley, Wash., 1972—. Pres. Ministerial Assn., Monroe County, W.Va., 1969-71; pres. Area C Christian Men's Fellowship Christian Chs. Lower W.Va., 1971; trustee Christian Acres Camp, Bluefield, W. Va., 1971; pres. Christian Evang. Assn.,

Puget Sound Area Christian Chs., 1972; Sedro Woolley Ministerial Assn., 1973; trustee Christian Evang. Assn., 1972-75; advisor Puget Sound Coll. Bible, 1972-74, trustee, 1975—; mem. chaplain com. United Gen. Hosp., Sedro Woolley; coordinator sr. citizen Bible Study Program, Sedro Woolley, 1972-76; trustee Skagit County (Wash.) Sr. Citizen Program, 1974—. Pres. Ruritan Club, Lindside, W.Va., 1972; sec. Kiwanis, Sedro Woolley, 1974, 2d v.p., 1977; mem. Com. for Better Schs., Monroe County, W.Va., 1971. Home: 532 Township St Sedro Woolley WA 98284 Office: 534 Township St Sedro Woolley WA 98284

RODIMER, FRANK JOSEPH See *Who's Who in America*, 43rd edition.

RODNEY, HARRY SCOTT, minister, Presbyterian Church in Canada; b. Calgary, Alta., Can., Feb. 22, 1915; s. William John and Sarah Frances (Scott) R.; student U. Ottawa (Can.), 1935-36; B.A., Queen's U., Can., 1938, B.D., 1952; D.D., Presbyn. Coll. Can., 1963; m. Mary Margaret Hughston, Aug. 23, 1941. Ordained to ministry, 1941; pastor Ephraim Scott Meml. Ch., Montreal., Que., Can., 1941-44, Knox Ch., St. Thomas, Ont., Can., 1944—. Moderator Presbytery London, Ont., 1948-49, 53, 57, 62, 71; Synod Hamilton and London, 1963; bd. gen. assembly Presbyn. Ch. Can.; bd. dirs. senate Presbyn. Coll., Montreal; chaplain Elgin Regiment, Canadian Armored Regiment, 1961-63; pres. St. Thomas Dist. Ministerial Assn., 1950. Bd. dirs. Maple Leaf Found., Timken Co., St. Thomas, 1976; bd. mgmt. Alma Coll., St. Thomas, 1948—. Decorated Queen Elizabeth Jubilee medal, 1978. Mem. St. Thomas Ministerial Assn. Contbr. articles to religious jours. Home: 100 Hincks St Saint Thomas ON N5R 3P2 Canada Office: 55 Hincks St Saint Thomas ON N5R 3N9 Canada

RODRIGUEZ, PLACIDO, bishop, Roman Catholic Church; b. Celaya, Mex., Oct. 11, 1940; came to U.S., 1953, naturalized, 1964; s. Eutimio and Maria Concepcion (Rosiles) R. S.T.B., Catholic U., Washington, 1968, S.T.L., 1968; M.A., Loyola U., 1971. Ordained priest Roman Cath. Ch., 1968, ordained to bishop, 1983. Pastor, Our Lady Guadalupe Ch., Chgo., 1972-75, Our Lady of Fatima Ch., Perth Amboy, N.J., 1981-83; vocation dir. Claretians, Chgo., 1975-81; bishop aux. Archdiocese of Chgo., 1983—.

RODRIGUEZ, ROBERT JOSEPH, minister, Lutheran Church America; b. N.Y.C., Jan. 1, 1946; s. Joseph and Anna Katherine (Heizmann) R.; B.A., Concordia Coll., 1967; M.Div., Luth. Theol. Sem., 1972; postgrad. Cath. U., Ponce, P.R., summer 1974. Ordained to ministry, 1972; pastor St. Paul's Luth. Ch. of Coney Island, Bklyn., 1972-76, Christ Luth. Ch., Floral Park, N.Y., 1976-83; chaplain U.S. Navy, 1983—. Sr. mem. Clergy Vol. Program, Bklyn. House of Detention for Men, 1972—; chmn. adv. council Flatbush office Luth. Community Services; chaplain Floral Park Fire Dept. Home: 319 Gambrill Ct Virginia Beach VA 23462

RODRIGUEZ RODRIGUEZ, MIGUEL See *Who's Who in America*, 43rd edition.

RODY, CHRISTINE MARIE, nun, general superior, Roman Catholic Church; b. Bedford, Ohio, Sept. 12, 1942; d. Joseph Albert and Ruth (Sisler) R. B.S.E., St. John Coll., Cleve., 1969; M.A., St. John's U., Collegeville, Minn., 1976. Elementary tchr. Diocese of Cleve., 1962-69, secondary tchr., 1969-75; mission team mem. Diocesan Team-El Salvador, 1975-80; gen. superior Vincentian Sisters of Charity, Bedford, Ohio, 1983—; pres. Major Superiors Assn., Cleve., 1984—.

ROEGER, SANDRA, music director, Presbyterian Church U.S.A.; musician; b. Akron, Ohio, June 30, 1938; d. Thomas Wilbur and Martha Pheobe (Fliger) Grubaugh; m. Robert Vernon Roeger, June 29, 1963; children: Jeffrey, Jennifer, Melissa. B.S. in Music Edn., Muskingum Coll., 1960; M.Mus., U. Akron, 1978. Choir dir. Meth. Ch., Dubois, Pa., 1968-69; organist Firestone Park Meth. Ch., Akron, 1970-72, Fireston Park United Presbyn. Ch., Akron, 1972-77; organist, music dir. Monroe United Presbyn. Ch., Akron, 1977-78; organist, choir dir. North Springfield United Presbyn. Ch., Akron, 1979—, dir. youth choir, 1980—; organist Ch. Women United, Summit County, Ohio, 1984. Music tchr. Firestone Park Coop. Nursery Sch., Akron, 1975—. Pres. PTA, Roosevelt High Sch., Kent, Ohio, 1981; dir. Celebration Bells, Akron, 1984—; North Springfield Ringers, Akron, 1982—; vol. entertainer hosps., sr. citizen homes. Mem. Ohio Music Tchrs. Assn., Am. Guild English Handbell Ringers. Republican. Avocation: music, golf. Home: 813 Gemberling Dr Kent OH 44240 Office: North Springfield United Presbyn Ch 6 Canton Rd Akron OH 44240

ROESEL, CHARLES LOUIS, minister, Southern Baptist Convention; b. Ocala, Fla., Sept. 22, 1926; s. John Frank and Melissa Ann (Lovett) R.; m. Edna Sue Pate, June 19, 1960; children: Charles Louis Jr., Cathy Lynn, Carey Lance. B.A., Stetson Coll., 1958; B.D., Southern Bapt. Theol. Sem., Louisville, 1961. Ordained to ministry So. Bapt. Conv., 1956. Minister Coronado Bapt. Ch., New Smyrna, Fla., 1961-66, First Bapt. Ch.,

Zephyrhills, Fla., 1966-76, First Bapt. Ch., Leesburg, Fla., 1976—; mem. Fla. State Bd. Missions, 1971-76; mem. exec. bd. Fla. Bapt. Conv., 1975-76; pres. Fla. Bapt. Pastor's Conf., Leesburg, 1982-83; establisher Christian Youth Care, Zepherhills. Named Urban Pastor Yr., State of Fla., 1973; 13th in Nation in Evangelism among So. Baptists, 1976; minister one of Top Twenty Chs. in Fla. Bapt. Conv. in Evangelism, 1977-84; named to Wildwood Hall Fame, Fla., 1984. Republican. Home: 1205 Bonaire Dr Leesburg FL 32748 Office: First Bapt Ch PO Box 957 Leesburg FL 32749

ROG, FRANCIS S., priest, Roman Catholic Church; b. Chgo., Jan. 12, 1930; s. Frank and Stella (Madej) R. B.S. in Commerce, St. Louis U., 1951, M.S. in Commerce, 1953; Ph.D., Northwestern U., 1973. Ordained priest Roman Catholic Ch., 1955. Assoc. pastor Our Lady of Loretto, St. Louis, 1963-65; dir. retreats Gordon Tech. High Sch., Chgo., 1967-73, asst. prin., 1973-74; pastor St. Stanislaus Kostka, Chgo., 1974-75; provincial superior Congregation of Resurrection U.S.A., Chgo. 1976—; archdiocesan consultor Chgo., 1984, senator, 1984, exec. mem. for religious ministry, 1983, ecclesiastical notary, 1979. Home and Office: 2250 N Latrobe Ave Chicago IL 60639

ROGERS, CLEETA JOHN, deacon, Southern Baptist Convention; b. Perryville, Ark., July 24, 1930; s. Cyril and Lucy (Shelton) R.; B.A., Central State U., 1951; J.D., Oklahoma City U., 1955; m. Mary Myles Smith, May 20, 1956; children: Rosemary Myles, Randel Cleeta-John, Rodman Shelton. Ordained deacon, 1954; soloist religious radio programs, 1950-59; religious rec. artist, 1964—; v.p. So. Bapt. Radio and TV Commn., 1962-68; music dir. Agnew Ave. Bapt. Ch., Oklahoma City, 1967-69, Shields Blvd. Bapt. Ch., Oklahoma City, 1969—. Individual practice law, Oklahoma City, 1955—. Mem. Okla. Ho. of Reps., 1952-60, Okla. Senate, 1960-74, Oklahoma City Community Council, 1959-60. Knight Order St. John of Jerusalem. Named Man of Year Oklahoma City Jr. C. of C., 1957. Mem. Okla. Civic Music Assn. (pres. 1958-63), Okla. Bar Assn., Am. Trial Lawyers Assn., Christian Legal Soc. Home: 415 NW 18th St Oklahoma City OK 73101

ROGERS, CLYDE CARITHERS, JR., retired minister, Southern Baptist Convention; b. Majestic, Ala., May 5, 1921; s. Clyde C. and Lena Helen (Hinton) R.; B.A., Howard Coll., 1945; B.D., New Orleans Bapt. Theol. Sem., 1953; D.D., Universal Bible Coll., 1974; m. Doris Louise Mitchell, Feb. 27, 1942; children: Clyde Mitchell, Marcia Lynn. Ordained to ministry, 1941; pastor First Bapt. Ch., Townley, Ala., 1941-45, South Park Bapt. Ch., Birmingham, Ala., 1945-50, Riverside Bapt. Ch., New Orleans, 1950-53, Osyka (Miss.) Bapt. Ch., 1953-58, First Bapt. Ch., Bruce, Miss., 1958-61, First Bapt. Ch., Olive Branch, Miss., 1961-67, Southside Bapt. Ch., Talladega, Ala., 1967-71, Como (Miss.) Bapt. Ch., 1971-76, Lucy Rd. Bapt. Ch., Millington, Tenn., 1976-84. Chmn. missions com., Calhoun, DeSoto and Panola Assns., Miss., 1958-65, 72, pres. Pastor's Confs., 1959, 62, 68, 73; mem. state conv. bd. Miss. Bapt. Conv., 1963-65; moderator De Soto Bapt. Assn., 1962, Panola Bapt. Assn., 1972. Pres. PTA, Olive Branch, 1965-66. Contbr. articles to religious publs. Lodge: Rotary (pres. local club 1973-74, 81-82). Home: 3011 Oakland Hills Cove Memphis TN 38115

ROGERS, EDWARD BARRETT, minister, Lutheran Church-Missouri Synod, real estate sales representative; b. Danielsville, Ga., Nov. 14, 1929; s. James Murray and Elizabeth Jackson (Barrett) R.; m. Wilma Ruth Hogrefe, Dec. 3, 1948; children: Deanna Ruth Rogers Casango, Angela Elizabeth Rogers Reeves, Mark Edward, Pamela Ann. B.A., Phillips U., 1959; M.Th., Concordia Theol. Sem., 1963, postgrad., 1959-63, postgrad. Troy State U., 1977. Ordained to ministry Lutheran Ch., 1963. Pastor, St. Matthew Luth. Ch., Marion, N.C., 1963-67; chaplain U.S. Army, U.S., Vietnam, Germany, 1967-76; pastor Trinity Luth. Ch., Dothan, Ala., 1978-84; pres. Redeemer Luth. Ch., Enid, Okla., 1957-59; panelist Pastors Forum local TV, Dothan, 1978-85; speaker Portals of Prayer local radio show, Dothan, 1978—. Sales rep. Reyes Real Estate Co., Ozark, Ala., 1978—. Author (annotated catechism) Confirmation Manual, 1977. Served to major U.S. Army, 1947-56, 1967-76. Decorated 5 Army Commendation Medals, 3 Bronze Star; recipient St. Martin of Tours Medal Luth. Ch. - Mo. Synod, 1981. Mem. Nat. Assn. Realtors, Ozark C. of C. Lodge: Rotary. Home: 100 Heather Dr Ozark AL 36360

ROGERS, HARRY DOUGLAS, educator, Seventh-day Adventists; b. Peoria, Ill., Mar. 16, 1942; s. Irving Holt and Vivan (Burroughs) R.; m. Ingrid Reimann, June 30, 1963; children: Douglas, Gail, Debbie. B.A. in Edn., Andrews U., 1966, M.A., 1971. Tchr./prin. Seventh-day Adventist Sch., Lake Orion, Mich., 1966-67; tchr. Seventh-day Adventist Sch., Berrien Springs, Mich., 1967—, vice prin., 1974—; prin., arts coordinator, tchr. Bible and sci. Seventh-day Adventist Ch., Berrien Springs, 1979—, gen. Sabbath sch. supt., 1978-80; sponsor Teens for Christ Singers, 1981-84. Owner, adminstr. Rogers Constrn., Baroda, Mich., 1979—. Author: Step Ahead with Practical Arts, 1980. Probation officer Vols. in Probation, 5th dist. Ct., St. Joseph, Mich., 1977-80. Republican. Home: Route 1

Box 14-B Berrien Center MI 49102 Office: Seventh-day Adventist Sch 409 W Mars PO Box 230 Berrien Springs MI 49103

ROGERS, IVAN ARTHUR, minister, Open Bible Standard Churches; b. Des Moines, July 2, 1929; s. Ivan Jesse and Gretchen Fayree (Byars) R.; B.A., Open Bible Coll., 1952; degree in nursing home adminstrn. U. Iowa, 1970; m. Elsie Marguerita Jones, Dec. 17, 1949; children—Steven, David, Gregg, Donna. Ordained to ministry, 1954; pastor Clive, Iowa, 1953-56, Des Moines, 1956-59, Clarinda, Iowa, 1959-62, Waterloo, Iowa, 1962-68; dir. devel. Open Bible Standard Chs., Inc., Des Moines, 1968-69; adminstr. Valley View Village Nursing and Retirement Home, Des Moines, 1969-73; pres. Open Bible Coll., Des Moines, 1973-78. Supt. Central div. Open Bible Standard Chs., 1973—. Named Outstanding Citizen, Boy Scouts Am., 1974. Mem. Nat. Assn. Evangs., Pentecostal Fellowship N. Am., Evang. Ministerial Assn. Des Moines. Contbr. articles to religious jours. Home: 5002 SW 17 St Des Moines IA 50315 Office: 2633 Fleur Dr Des Moines IA 50321

ROGERS, JAMES H., archbishop. Primate Metropolitan-N. Am. Old Roman Catholic Church. Address: 118-09 Farmer Blvd Saint Albans NY 11412*

ROGERS, PETER VINCENT, priest, Roman Cath. Ch.; b. Bklyn., Nov. 19, 1924; s. Peter Vincent and Agnes (White) R.; student Oblate Coll. of S.W.; M.A., Fordham U., N.Y.C.; postgrad. Cath. U., Washington. Ordained priest, 1950; editor Nat. Oblate Mag., Mary Immaculate; missionary, Prince George No. B.C., Can.; now pastor Our Lady of Guadalupe Ch., New Orleans. Bd. dirs., Cath. Press Assn. Am., Internat. Shrie St. Jude; chaplain New Orleans Police and Fire depts.; dir. League St. Jude. Bd. dirs. Goodwill Industries, Inc. New Orleans. Recipient Valor award Am. Fedn. Police Officers, Good Samaritan award Fedn. Police, 1970, Bergeron award True Detective mag., Spl. award Sales Marketing Execs., medal of Merit, Police Dept. New Orleans. Home and Office: 411 N Rampart St New Orleans LA 70112

ROGERS, REX MARTIN, lay worker General Association of Regular Baptist Churches, political science education; b. Pasadena, Tex., Oct. 25, 1952; s. Ernest Bartholow and Yvonne Lee (Davis) R.; m. Sarah Lee Stone, Aug. 10, 1974; children: Elizabeth Ann, Eric Thomas, Andrew Lewis, Adam Lee. B.A., Cedarville Coll., 1974; M.A., U. Akron, 1978; postgrad. Marshall U., 1978; Ph.D., U. Cin., 1982. Tchr. Heritage Christian Sch., Cleve., 1974-77, vice prin., 1976-77; secondary tchr. Cross Lanes Christian Sch., Charleston, W. Va., 1977-79; prof. polit. sci. Cedarville Coll., Ohio, 1982—, dir. computer Services, 1983—; area liaison rep. Campus Bible Fellowship, Dayton, Ohio, 1983-84, Contbr. articles to profl. jours. Dist. survey supr. DeWine for Congress Campaign, Greene County, Ohio, 1982—; co-sponsor Cedarville Coll., Young Republicans, 1983—. Named Outstanding Young Men in Am., Jaycees, 1984. Mem. Right-to-Life Soc., Am. Polit. Sci. Assn., So. Polit. Sci. Assn., Am. Soc. Pub. Adminstrn., Am. Acad. Polit. Sci., Christian Computer Users Assn., Nat. Woodcarvers Assn., Nat. Honor Soc., Alpha Chi (Cedarville chpt. v.p. 1972-73, 1973-74). Home: 3332 Route 42 E Cedarville OH 45314 Office: Cedarville Coll PO Box 601 Cedarville OH 45314

ROGERS, RIX GORDON, social service association executive, Presbyterian Church in Canada; b. Fort William, Ont., Can., June 5, 1931; s. Albert Henry and Evelyn Sadie (Heard) R.; m. Barbara Ann Dawes, Dec. 22, 1956; children: Mark, Scott, Susan, Deborah, Karen. B.A., U. Toronto, Ont., 1954; M.S., Springfield Coll., 1956. Cert. profl. YMCA sec. Exec. sec. Lakeshore br. Montreal YMCA, Que., Can., 1956-63; program and staff devel. sec. Met. office YMCA 1963-65; asst. gen. sec. Montreal YMCA, 1965-68, gen. sec., 1968-71; gen. sec., chief exec. officer Nat. Council YMCAs of Can., Toronto, 1971—; nat. chmn. Coalition Nat. Vol. Orgns.; mem. adv. com. Nat. Health and Welfare Grants Com., Govt. Can.; trustee YMCA Retirement Fund, 1976-84, Can. adminstr., 1976-82; trustee Can. YMCA Retirement Fund, 1982—; participant prayer breakfast groups, 1966—; participant various seminars, workshops, 1971—. Mem. planning com. Can.'s Econ. Conf., 1985. Decorated Queen's Commemorative medal. Mem. Nat. Voluntary Health Agys. Can. (chmn. 1982-83), YMCA N. Am. Urban Group (founding), Assn. Profl. Dirs. (assoc.), Inst. Assn. Execs. Can. Clubs: Can. of Toronto, Toronto Bd. of Trade. Office: Nat Council YMCAs of Can 2160 Yonge St Toronto ON M4S 2A9 Canada

ROGERS, SCOTT BAILEY, minister, Christian Church; b. Jacksonville, Ill., July 16, 1955; s. Turner Alfred and Audrey (Bailey) R.; m. Shirley Moody, Dec. 20, 1975; children: Audrey, Adam, Nathan. B.A., Lincoln Christian Coll., 1977; M.A., Sangamon State U., 1980. Assoc. pastor Deland Christian Ch., Ill., 1974-77; minister Cornland Christian Ch., Ill., 1978-81; exec. dir. Asheville Buncombe Community Christian Ministry, Asheville, N.C., 1981—. Participant Leadership Asheville, bd. dirs. Vis. Health Profls., Asheville, 1983-84, Mental Assn. Buncombe County, 1983-84, Consumer Credit Counseling Service,

Asheville, 1984, Buncombe County Health Dept., 1984—; pres. Mountain Area Needs Alliance Food Bank, 1982-83. Recipient Leadership award City of Lincoln, Ill., 1977; Gov.'s Vol. award Gov. N.C., 1982. Republican. Club: Kiwanis Internat. Office: ABCCM 201 Broadway Asheville NC 28801

ROGERS, WILLIAM JOHN, priest, Roman Cath. Ch.; b. Tarrytown, N.Y., July 4, 1929; s. John Jerome and Catherine Margaret (Murphy) R.; B.A., St. Bonaventure U., N.Y., 1952; M.S., Iona Coll., N.Y., 1969. Ordained priest, 1954; tchr. Nativity High Sch., Pottsville, Pa., 1955-56; chaplain Bellevue Hosp., N.Y.C., 1957; asst. pastor Mt. Carmel Ch., Middletown, N.Y., 1957-61; moderator Cath. Young Orgn., chaplain Otisville Tng., chaplain K.C. and Columbietres, also chaplain Newman Club, Middletown, 1957-61; rector students St. Albert's Sem., Middletown, 1961-64; asst. pastor Transfiguration Ch., Tarrytown, also Cath. Youth Orgn. moderator and chaplain K.C., 1964-68; chaplain VA Hosp., Montrose, N.Y., 1968—; chief chaplains VA, 1975—. Named Outstanding Youth Worker, Cath. Youth Orgn., 1967. Mem. Nat. Assn. Cath. Chaplains), Assn. Pastoral Counselors (pres. 1973), Assn. Mental Health Clergy (bd. examiners 1975), NAACP, Assn. Religion and Mental Health, Assn. Sci. Study Religion, Iona Coll. Alumni Assn. (pres. 1974). Contbr. articles to religious jours. Home: 268 S Broadway Tarrytown NY 10591 Office: VA Hosp Montrose NY 10548

ROGGENKAMP, GERHARD HEINRICH WILHELM, minister, Lutheran Church in America; b. N.Y.C., Mar. 25, 1936; s. Johannes Friederich and Hanna Maria (Flicker) R.; m. Suzanne Morrow Joynt, Sept. 5, 1970; children: Christoph Johannes, John Paul, Hannah Carolyn. A.A., Concordia Coll., 1956; postgrad. Concordia Sem., 1956-57; B.A., Valparaiso U., 1959; postgrad. Westfaelische U., W. Ger., 1972-74; Ph.D., Syracuse U., 1982; M.Div., Luth. Theol. Sem., 1978. Ordained to ministry, 1978. Pastor, St. Paul/St. Bartholomew Ch., Hanover, Pa., 1978—, Latimore Parish, York Springs, Pa., 1977-78; exec. com. Luth. Social Service, S. Region, York, Pa., 1979—; chmn. Central Pa. Commn. on Ch. in Soc., 1980—; pres. Hanover Council Chs., Pa., 1978—; bd. dirs. Life Skills Unltd., Gettysburg, Pa., 1984—. Contbr. articles to profl. jours. Served to lt. comdr., USN, 1959-67. Fulbright-Hayes Grad. scholar, 1972-74. Office: West Manheim Luth Parish RD 3 Box 173 Hanover PA 17331

ROGNESS, PETER, minister, American Lutheran Church; b. Mason City, Iowa, June 9, 1945; s. Alvin Nathaniel and Nora Margaret (Preus) R.; m. Geraldine Rae Sheridan, Sept. 14, 1968; children: Rebecca, Sarah, David, Rachel. B.A., Augustana Coll., 1967; M.Div., Luther Theol. Sem., St. Paul, 1972. Ordained to ministry American Lutheran Church, 1973. Dir., Camp Amnicon, Mpls., 1968-70; assoc. pastor Wellington park Luth. Ch., Milw., 1973-75; pastor, Hephatha Luth. Ch., Milw., 1975—; bd. dirs., chmn. CHURCH (Chs. Helping Uniting Reviving Community Here) Inc., Milw., 1976—; chmn. Urban Parish Bd., Milw., 1979-82; vice chmn. Greater Milw. Conf. on Religion and Urban Affairs, Milw., 1981—; v.p. So. Wis. dist. Am. Luth. Ch., 1982—. Adv. bd. mem. United Way of Greater Milw., 1979. Home: 2876 N Grant Blvd Milwaukee WI 53210 Office: Hephatha Luth Ch 1720 W Locust St Box 06437 Milwaukee WI 53206

ROH, ROBERT LAWRENCE, minister, Bethany Tabernacle; b. Madison, Wis., Jan. 16, 1931; s. Lawrence Edward and Lucille Helen (Gardner) R.; student U. Wis., 1948-49; Th.B., Apostolic Bible Inst., 1952; M., U. Copenhagen, 1963-67; m. Mary Elizabeth Snyder, Sept. 8, 1951; children—Timothy, Thomas, Terry. Ordained to ministry, 1954; pastor, Morris, Ill., 1952-53, Janesville, Wis., 1953-54, Oshkosh, Wis., 1954-61; pres. Wis. Youth, 1956-61; founder, 1st supt. United Pentecostal Ch. of Europe and the Brit. Isles, 1961-69, European sec.-treas., 1970-73; Presbyter, mem. bd. Pa. dist. United Pentecostal Ch., Internat., 1976—. Established United Pentecostal chs. in Amsterdam and The Hague, Holland, 1969; Pa. rep. Harvestime Internat. Radio Broadcast, 1974-76; editor European Pentecostal Herald, 1962-68; profl. nursing home adminstr. for United Pentecostal Ch., 1973-76, for CHC Corp., 1976—; dir. missions bd. Bethany Tabernacle; chaplain Oshkosh City Council, 1959-61. Mem. adv. council Blue Cross, Harrisburg, Pa., 1975—. Mem. Health Care Facilities of Pa., Am. Nursing Home Assn., Pa. Assn. Non-Profit Homes for Aging, Internat. Platform Assn. Home: 202 N Arch St Mechanicsburg PA 17055 Office: PO Box 3280 Hwy 15 and Slate Hill Rd Camp Hill PA 17011

ROHRBAUGH, MARK LEROY, religious organization executive, minister, United Church of Christ; b. Spring Grove, Pa., May 21, 1936; s. Edward L. and Viola M. (Walker) R.; m. Winigred Alyse Hoffman, June 11, 1960; children: Beth, Mark, Susan. B.S., Nyack Coll., 1957; M.Div., Gordon-Conwell Theol. Sem., 1961. Ordained to ministry United Ch. of Christ, 1964. Assoc. minister Mt. Bellingham Meth. Ch., Chelsea, Mass., 1957-61; sr. minister Stevens Mills Ch., Auburn, Maine, 1961-64, Bethel Ch., New Britain, Conn., 1964-70; exec. dir. New Britain Area Conf. of Chs. (NEWBRACC), 1970-77; gen. sec. Christian Conf. of Conn. (CHRISCON), Hartford, 1977—; trustee Hartford Sem., 1979—; dir. Conn. Interfaith Housing and Human Services Corp., Hartford, 1983—, Tri-state Media Ministry, N.Y.C.; pres., dir. Conn. Energy Found. subs. Conn. Natural Gas Corp., Hartford, 1984—; bd. dir. Burrit Interfin. New Britain. Bd. dirs. St. Francis Hosp., Hartford, YMCA, New Britain, 1984—, Central Assn. Police Community Relations Officers, Hartford, United Way of New Britain-Berlin, Conn., Am. Cancer Soc., New Britain, New Britain Symphony Soc., Klingberg Family Ctrs., New Britain, Conn. Joint Council on Econ. Edn., Storrs; corporator New Britain Gen. Hosp., YMCA. Mem. Conn. Bible Soc. (bd. dirs. 1976—), Conn. Council on Alcohol Problems (bd. dirs. 1976—). Office: Christian Conf of Conn 60 Lorraine St Hartford CT 06105

ROHRBAUGH, RICHARD LEANDER, minister, educator, Presbyterian Church in the U.S.A.; b. Addis Ababa, Ethiopia, Dec. 12, 1936 (parents Am. citizens); s. James Leander and Marion (Walker) R.; m. Miriam Ruth Gathman, Apr. 11, 1960; children: Douglas Brian, Janet Marie. B.A. in Chemistry, Sterling Coll., 1958; M.Div., Pitts. Theol. Sem., 1961; S.T.D., San Francisco Theol. Sem., 1977. Ordained to ministry Presbyn. Ch., 1961. Pastor, Tri-City Presbyn. Ch., Myrtle Creek, Oreg., 1961-68, St. Mark Presbyn. Ch., Portland, Oreg., 1968-77; assoc. prof. religious studies Lewis and Clark Coll., Portland, 1977—. Author: Into All the World, 1976, 80; The Biblical Interpreter, 1978; Une Bible Agraire Pour un Monde Industriel, 1981; Interpretation, 1985. Contbr. articles to religious jours. Bd. dirs. Oreg. Mountain Rescue, Portland, 1980—; chmn. Mazama Climbing Program, Portland, 1982—; council mem. Friends of Seasonal Service Workers, Portland, 1983—. James Purdy scholar Pitts. Theol. Sem., 1971; fellow Fund for Theol. Edn., 1972. Mem. Am. Acad. Religion, Soc. Biblical Lit. (chmn. regional sect. 1983—), Pacific Theol. Soc., Am. Schs. Oriental Research. Democrat. Home: 7010 SW 4th St Portland OR 97219 Office: Lewis and Clark Coll 0615 SW Palatine Hill Rd Portland OR 97219

ROLAND, EMMERETT WILBUR, minister, American Baptist Convention; b. Red Bird, Okla., Oct. 24, 1931; s. Melvin Fred and Maggie Elizabeth (Wright) R.; B.D., St. Matthew U., 1956; D.D., Mt. Sinai Theol. Sem., 1970; m. Virginia Mae Bishop, Aug. 5, 1965. Ordained to ministry Am. Bapt. Conv., 1956; pastor, North Oakland, Calif., 1961-66, Oakland, Calif., 1966-69, 2d Bapt. Ch., Merced, Calif., 1969, now pastor 1st St. Paul Bapt. Ch., North Oakland. Mem. adv. bd., extended opportunities program Merced Coll. 1972-74; mem. Koininia Scholarship Found., Oakland, 1964—. Mem. Shiloh Dist. Bapt. Assn. (moderator 1973), Gamma Chi Epsilon. Editorial staff writer Nat. Bapt. Publ. Bd., 1965-75; editor Intermediate Quar., 1967-75. Home: 396 E Brookdale Dr Merced CA 95340 Office: 501 Q St Merced CA 95340

ROLLEFSON, JOHN, minister, American Lutheran Church; b. Oconomowoc, Wis., Oct. 13, 1946; s. Irving G. and Mary (Griffith) R.; m. Ruthanne Gordon, June 17, 1972; children: J. Griffith, N. Jakob. B.A., Luther Coll., 1968; student New Coll., U. Edinburgh, Scotland, 1969-70; M.Div. Yale U., 1971; M.A., U. London, 1973; M.A., Grad. Theol. Union, Berkeley, Calif., 1983. Ordained to ministry American Lutheran Church, 1975. Pastor St. Francis Luth. Ch., San Francisco, 1974-79; fellow Inst. Ecumenical and Cultural Research, St. John's U., Collegeville, Minn., 1979-80; co-pastor Our Savior's Luth. Ch., Milw., 1980—; chairperson task force on criminal justice Greater Milw. Conf. Religion and Urban Affairs, 1982—; dir. Milw. Theol. Inst., 1980-83. Chmn. editorial bd. Westside News, 1982—. Bd. dirs. Friends Outside in San Francisco, 1976-79; mem. citizens com. Menomonee Valley Prison, Milw., 1983—. Mem. Milw. Assn. Interfaith Relations (bd. dirs. 1984—). Democrat. Home: 517 N 32d St Milwaukee WI 53208 Office: Our Savior's Luth Ch 3022 W Wisconsin Ave Milwaukee WI 53208

ROLLINS, V. JOHN, minister, United Meth. Ch.; b. Louisville, Dec. 18, 1936; s. Virgil Lewis and Lucille Rachel (Byrd) R.; B.S., Morehead State U., 1965; M.S.T., Middle Tenn. State U., 1970; M.Div., Luth. Theol. Sem., 1973; postgrad. McCormick Theol. Sem.; 1977; m. Barbara Jean Bowen, Aug. 14, 1960; children—Jean Laurie, Deborah Lynn, David Jonathan. Ordained to ministry, 1968; sec. Dist. Pastors, Hartsville dist. S.C. Conf., 1970; dist. dir. Ch. and Soc., Hartsville and Walterboro dists., 1972—. Chairperson Dist. Crusade, 1972; clusterleader ann. conf., 1973; chairperson com. subdist. clusters, 1974; chairperson com. on needs, 1975; exec. Lake Junaluska SE Jurisdiction Assembly; chmn. dept. sci. Mather Acad. Mission Sch. Active Drug Encounter Group. Recipient Commendations for drug program, 1975. Author; Mandate to Methodism, 1970; Drugs, Not My Child, 1971. Home: 135 Riley St Anderson SC 29621 Office: Marshall Meml United Meth Ch Anderson SC 29621

ROLLINS, WAYNE GILBERT, minister, United Church of Christ, religion educator; b. Detroit, Aug. 24, 1929; s. Arthur Gilchrist and Ethel (Kamin) R.; m. Donnalou Myerholtz, Aug. 30, 1953; children: Michael W., Thomas L., David M. B.A., Capital U., 1951; B.D., Yale U., 1954, M.A., 1958, Ph.D., 1960. Ordained to ministry United Ch. of Christ. Instr. religion Princeton U., 1958-59; asst. prof. bibl. history Wellesley Coll., 1959-66; prof. bibl. studies Hartford Sem. Found., Conn., 1966-74; prof. religious studies Assumption Coll., Worcester, Mass., 1974—; interim minister Broadview Ch., Hartford, 1973-74; vice chmn. bd. trustees Notre Dame Acad., Worcester, 1977-79. Author: The Gospels - Portraits of Christ, 1964; Jung and the Bible, 1983. Contbr. articles, book revs. to profl. jours. Mem. Worcester County Ecumenical Council, 1981—. Am. Assn. Theol. Schs. fellow, 1970. Mem. Am. Acad. Religion (pres. New Eng. 1984-85), Soc. Bibl. Lit., Studiorum Novi Testamenti Societas. Democrat. Home: 75 Craigmoor Rd West Hartford CT 06107 Office: Dept Religion Assumption Coll 500 Salisbury St Worcester MA 01609

ROLSTON, HOLMES, III, religion educator, Presbyterian Church in the U.S.A.; b. Staunton, Va., Nov. 19, 1932; s. Holmes Jr. and Mary Winifred (Long) R.; m. Jane Irving Wilson, June 1, 1956; children: Shonny Hunter, Giles Campbell. B.S., Davidson Coll., 1953; B.D., Union Theol. Sem., 1956; Ph.D. in Theology, U. Edinburgh, 1958; M.A. in Philosophy of Sci., U. Pitts., 1968. Ordained to ministry Presbyterian Church in the U.S.A., 1956. Pastor, Walnut Grove Presbyn. Ch., Bristol, Va., 1959-67; asst. prof. dept. philosophy Colo. State U., 1968-71, assoc. prof., 1971-76, prof., 1976—; chmn. religious studies program, 1968-81; vis. scholar Ctr. Study World Religions, Harvard U. Divinity Sch., Cambridge, Mass., 1974-75. Author: The Cosmic Christ, 1966; John Calvin versus the Westminster Confession, 1972; Religious Inquiry - Participation and Detachment, 1985; Science and Religion: An Introduction, (in press). Assoc. editor Environmental Ethics, 1979—. Contbr. articles, revs., curriculum materials in religious and philos. jours. and publs. Recipient Oliver P. Penock award Colo. State U., 1983. Mem. Am. Acad. Religion, Phi Beta Kappa. Home: 1712 Concord Dr Fort Collins CO 80523 Office: Colo State U Dept Philosophy Fort Collins CO 80526

ROMAN, AGUSTIN A., auxiliary bishop Roman Catholic Church; b. San Antonio de los Baños, Cuba, May 5, 1928; came to U.S., 1966; s. Rosendo and Juana (Rodriguez) R. B.A., Sem. for Fgn. Missions, Montreal; M.A. in Religious Studies, Barry U., Miami, Biscayne Coll., Opa Locka, Fla., Ordained priest Roman Catholic Ch., 1959. Pastor parishes Diocese of Matanzas, Cuba, 1959-61, spiritual dir. youth; expelled by Cuban Govt., 1961; pastor Holy Spirit Parish, Temuco, Chile, 1962-66; spiritual dir., prof. Inst. Humanities, 1962-66; spiritual dir. Cursillo Movement, Diocese of Temuco, 1962-66; asst. pastor St. Mary's Cathedral, Miami, 1966-67, St. Kieran's Parish, 1967-68; chaplain Mercy Hosp., Miami, 1967-73, Shrine of Our Lady of Charity, 1967; named monsignor Archdiocese of Miami, 1974, named vicar for hispanics, 1976, elected aux. bishop, 1979—; Episcopal ordination, 1979. Mem. Nat. Conf. Cath. Bishops (mem. ad hoc com. on migration and tourism 1980—, mem. ad hoc com. for hispanic affairs 1980—). Home: 3609 S Miami Ave Miami FL 33133 Office: Archdiocese of Miami 9401 Biscayne Blvd Miami Shores FL 33138

ROMANO, GERARD JOHN, priest, Roman Catholic Church; b. Bklyn., Jan. 9, 1955; s. John Burleigh and Mary (Tramontana) R. B.A. in Sociology, Cathedral Coll., 1977; M.Div., Sem. of Immaculate Conception, 1981. Ordained priest Roman Catholic Ch., 1981. Parochial vicar St. Frances de Chantal, Bklyn., 1981-84, St. Aloysius Ch., Ridgewood, N.Y., 1984—; chaplain Bishop Kearney High Sch., Bklyn., 1984—; moderator of youth St. Aloysius Ch., Queens, N.Y., 1984, dir. liturgy, Ridgewood, 1984—; lectr. Diocesan Pre-Cana, Bklyn., 1982—; counselor Diocesan Pre and Post Abortion, Bklyn., 1983—. Active community bd. 12 Youth Planning Services, Bklyn., 1984, 5 Youth Planning Services, Queens, N.Y., 1985—. Lodge: KC. Office: St Aloysius Rectory 382 Onderdonk Ave Ridgewood NY 11385

ROMANO, JOSEPH RALPH, priest, Roman Cath. Ch.; b. Amsterdam, N.Y., Oct. 27, 1939; s. Joseph Anthony and Carmella Grace (De Matteo) R.; B.A., St. Mary's Sem. Coll., 1962, S.T.L., 1966; M.A. in Am. History, Johns Hopkins, 1965. Ordained priest, 1966; mem. faculty St. Joseph's High Sch., Albany, N.Y., 1970, Cardinal McCloskey High Sch., Albany, 1970-74; Pastor St. Ann's Parish, Albany, 1974—. Chmn. Diocesan Parish Realignment Com.; chaplain Albany Fire Dept., Albany Sons of Italy, Elks. Mem. N.Y. State Fire Chaplains Assn., N.Y. Cath. High Sch. Athletic Assn., Italian-Am. Community Assn. of Albany. Office: Saint Ann's Ch 95 4th Ave Albany NY 12202

ROMERO, JOSE TOBIAS, priest, Roman Catholic Church; b. Taos, N.Mex., Oct. 23, 1913; s. Juan Bautista and Margarita (Vigil) R.; B.A., U. San Francisco, 1974; m. Maria Claudia Garcia, Apr. 16, 1934 (dec. 1969); children—Jose Tobias, Claudio Gilberto, Juan Ricardo. Treas., fin. sec. Council 2550, K.C., Los Angeles, 1947-71; mem. Archdiocesan com. on Cath. scouting, Los Angeles, 1948-60; v.p. Perpetual Adoration Soc., Old Plaza Ch., Los Angeles, 1962-71; parish capt., v.p. Mater Dolorosa Retreat League, Sierra Madre, Calif.,

1963-71; archdiocesan pres. Holy Name Union, Los Angeles, 1964-66, asso. moderator, 1976—; ordained priest, Claretian Missionaries, 1975; asso. pastor Our Lady Queen of Angels, Los Angeles, 1975—. Decorated Kt. Comdr. of St. Gregory, 1967. Address: 100 Sunset Blvd Los Angeles CA 90012

ROMERO, JOSEPH ROBERT, priest, Roman Cath. Ch.; b. Abbeville, La., Sept. 27, 1948; s. Joseph Robert and Ruby (Gaspard) R.; B.A. in History, St. Joseph Sem. Coll., St. Benedict, La., 1971; S.T.B., M.A. in Sacred Theology, Cath. U. Louvain (Belgium), 1974. Ordained priest, 1975; asso. pastor Our Lady of Sacred Heart Ch., Church Point, La., 1975—. Chaplain local K.C., Jr. Cath. Daus. Am., Jaycees, 1975—; youth coordinator S.W. Acadiana Deanery, 1976—. Contbr. articles to local newspapers. Address: 114 N Bienvenu St Church Point LA 70525

ROMERO, MARY ROSELLA, nun, religious organization administrator, Roman Catholic Church; b. Aragon, N.Mex., Feb. 28, 1929; d. Jose N. and Tomasita (Aragon) R. B.S. in Edn., Mt. Mary Coll., 1960; M.Ed., Marquette U., 1969; M.A. in Religion Edn., U. San Francisco, 1973. Joined Franciscan Sisters of the Sorrowful Mother, Roman Catholic Ch., 1949. Tchr. Cath. Schs., Wis., Iowa, prin., Wis., N.Mex., Kans.; assoc. dir. edn. Diocesan Religious Edn., Tulsa; coordinator Parish Religious Edn., Albuquerque, Dexter, N.Mex., San Antonio, 1981—; del. Provincial Assemblies Franciscan Sisters Sorrowful Mother, Broken Arrow, Okla., 1978—. Recipient Cert. of Recognition, Archdiocesan Catechetical Ctr., 1985. Fellow Parish Coordinators Religious Edn. (facilitator archdiocesan workshops). Club: Sisters, Senate. Avocations: piano; organ; singing; guitar; arts and crafts. Home and Office: Saint Ann Parish 210 Saint Ann St San Antonio TX 78201

ROMNEY, MARION GEORGE, Church official, Church of Jesus Christ of Latter-day Saints; b. Colonia Juarez, Mex., Sept. 19, 1897; s. George Samuel and Artemesia (Redd) R. (parents U.S. citizens); student Brigham Young U., 1924; B.S., U. Utah, 1926, LL.B., 1932, J.D., 1968; m. Ida Olivia Jensen, Sept. 12, 1924; children—Richard J., Janet Ida (dec.), George J. Ordained apostle, 1951; served ch. mission in Australia, 1920-23; bishop Salt Lake 33d Ward, 1935-38; pres. Bonneville (Utah) Stake, 1938-41; asst. to Council of the Twelve, 1941-51; mem. Council of Twelve Apostles, 1951-72; 2d counselor in the First Presidency, 1972-82, 1st counselor to 1st Presidency, 1982—; 2d v.p. Ch. Bd. Edn. Chmn. bd., dir. Beneficial Life Ins. Co., Utah Hotel Corp., Zions Securities Corp.; dir. Bonneville Internat. Corp., KSL Radio-TV, Deseret Mgmt., Peoples 1st Thrift. Mem. Utah Legislature, 1935-36. Second v.p. bd. trustees Brigham Young U. Recipient distinguished alumni award U. Utah, 1972, alumni distinguished service award Brigham Young U., 1962. Author: Look to God and Live, 1971. Home: 1909 Yalecrest Ave Salt Lake City UT 84108 Office: 47 E S Temple St Salt Lake City UT 84111

ROMO, OSCAR ISHMAEL, minister, So. Baptist Conv.; b. Lockhart, Tex., Jan. 29, 1929; s. Jose Ishmael and Concepcion (Ortega) R.; B.A., Howard Payne Coll., 1951; B.D., Southwestern Bapt. Theol. Sem., 1956; D.H.L., Linda Vista Bapt. Coll., 1975; D.D. (hon.), Calif. Bapt. Coll., 1976; m. Zoe Harmon, June 21, 1956; children—Nelson Oscar, Miriam Lois. Ordained to ministry, 1949; pastor chs., Tex., 1948-56; asso. lang. missions dept. Bapt. Gen. Conv. Tex., Dallas, 1956-65, asst. sec. lang. missions dept. Home Mission Bd., Atlanta, 1965-70, dir., 1971—. Adj. prof. Midwestern Bapt. Theol. Sem., Golden Gate Bapt. Theol. Sem.; editor Spanish edit. The Bapt. Standard, 1957-60. Mem. Missiology, Bapt. Religious Press Assn. Home: 2895 Delcourt Dr Decatur GA 30033 Office: 1350 Spring St NW Atlanta GA 30309

RONDEAU, THOMAS ONIL, priest, Roman Catholic Church; b. Kingsey Falls, Que., Can., Mar. 22, 1904; s. Edouard and Celestine (Martineau) R. B.A., Séminaire St. Charles, Sherbrooke, Que., 1925; lic. theologie, Collège Dominicain, 1932; lic. pastorale, 1968. Joined Dominican Order, Roman Catholic Ch., ordained priest, 1930. Curate St. Jean Baptiste Parish, Ottawa, Ont., 1932-35; prior of Dominicans, St. Hyacinthe, Que., 1939-42; master of Dominican students, Ottawa, 1942-54; provincial of Dominicans in Can., Montreal, Que., 1955-67; missionary St. Jude Shrine, Montreal, 1968—; chmn. Can. Religious Conf., 1961-67. Home: 3980 St Denis Montreal PQ H2W 2M3 Canada

RONKOS, CHARLES GEORGE, theology educator, Lutheran Church in America; b. Buffalo, Feb. 14, 1924; s. Charles and Mary (Keresztes) R.; m. A. Louise Finta, Oct. 4, 1952; children: Carolynne, Charles, Peter. B.A., U. Pitts., 1955; B.D., Hamma Sch. Theology, 1957, M.Div., 1972; M.Div. Ashland Theol. Sem., 1970; D.Ministry, Consortium for Higher Edn. Religion Studies, 1973. Ordained to ministry Lutheran Ch., 1957. Pastor, St. Paul Luth. Ch., Springfield, Ohio, 1957-59; missionary pastor Missions Bd., Luth. Ch. Am., Rivera, Uruguay, 1962-65; hosp. chaplain Cleve. Psychiat. Inst., 1967-77; prof. pastoral counseling Ashland Theol. Sem., Ohio, 1970—; bd. dirs. Luth. Chaplaincy Service, Cleve., 1983—. Served with USAF, 1943-46. Recipient Appreciation award Inner City Renewal Soc., 1984. Fellow Coll. of Chaplains Am. Protestant Hosp. Assn.; mem. Am. Assn. Pastoral Counselors (diplomate), Assn. Clin. Pastoral Edn. Lodge: Kiwanis (Solon). Home: 30450 Cannon Rd Solon OH 44139 Office: Ashland Theol Sem 910 Center St Ashland OH 44805

RONSISVALLE, DANIEL, minister, Assemblies of God; b. Washington, May 3, 1936; s. Benjamin Sebastian and Josephine (Castro) R.; B.S., Southwestern Coll., Waxahachie, Tex., 1959; m. Violet Fern Tidwell, June 8, 1956; children: Sheree Fern, Kenneth Daniel. Ordained to ministry, 1959; pastor Lakeview Ch. Assemblies God, New Orleans, 1961-70, Huffman Assembly God, Birmingham, Ala., 1970—; radio minister Decision Time Broadcast, 1962-70, revival hour broadcast, 1970-76; producer Ronsisvalle Family TV Series, 1965-75, Guideline TV Program, 1975-76, Huffman Assembly Presents, 1981—, also TV spls. Recipient Ann. Christian Life award, 1974-76, Ann. Brother Bryan humanitarian award. Home: 1847 6th St NW Birmingham AL 35215 Office: 9553 Parkway E Birmingham AL 35215

ROOKS, CHARLES SHELBY, minister, religious organization administrator, United Church of Christ; b. Beaufort, N.C., Oct. 19, 1924; s. Shelby A. and Maggie (Hawkins) R.; m. Adrienne Rita Martinez, Aug. 7, 1946; children: Laurence Gaylord, Carol Ann. A.B., Va. State U., 1949; M.Div., Union Theol. Sem., 1953; D.D. (hon.), Coll. Wooster, 1968, Interdenominational Theol. Ctr., 1980, Va. Union U., 1981; L.H.D. (hon.) Howard U., 1982, Va. State U., 1984. Ordained to ministry United Ch. of Christ. Pastor, Lincoln Meml. Temple, Washington, 1953-60; assoc. dir. Fund for Theol. Edn., Princeton, N.J., 1960-67, exec. dir., 1967-74; pres. Chgo. Theol. Sem., 1974-84; exec. v.p., United Ch. Bd. for Homeland Ministries, N.Y.C., 1984—. Contbr. articles to religious jours. Bd. dirs. Washington Urban League, 1956-60, Chgo. Urban League, 1975-79, Princeton School Bd., 1968. Served with AUS, 1943-46. Mem. Soc. Study of Black Religions. Home: 83 Riverbend Dr N Brunswick NJ 08902 Office: United Ch Bd for Homeland Ministries 132 W 31st St New York NY 10001

ROOT, DAVID EUGENE, minister, Church of God (Anderson, Ind.), educator; b. Houston, Sept. 5, 1949; s. William Dewitt Root and Mary Josephine (Davis) Neilsen; m. Christine Victoria Ortiz, Sept. 11, 1970 (div. 1978); 1 child, Laura Elizabeth; m. Jeanine Rene Bostwick, Feb. 14, 1981; 1 child, Heather Lynnea. A.A., Monterey Peninsula Jr. Coll., 1973; B.S., U. Houston, 1975, M.A., 1978; M.Div., Anderson Sch. Theology, 1980. Ordained to ministry Ch. of God, 1983; cert. tchr. Tex., 1975. Minister of Christian edn. South Bay Ch. of God, Torrance, Calif., 1980-81; pastor First Ch. of God, Merced, Calif., 1981—; mem. bd. Christian edn. Ch. of God, No. Calif., 1984—; dir. Ch. of God Jr. Camp, No. Calif., 1984; presenter seminar, 1984. Phys. edn. tchr. Rivera Jr. High Sch., Merced, 1983—. Served with U.S. Army, 1971-73. Mem. Ch. of God Ministerial Assn. (sec. 1983—), Merced Ministerial Assn. (pres. 1983-84), Toastmasters Internat. (1st place award 1984). Home: 3025 N Parsons Ave Merced CA 95340 Office: First Ch of God 3022 N Parsons Merced CA 93540

ROOT, MICHAEL JOHN, theology educator, Lutheran Church in America; b. Norfolk, Va., Apr. 27, 1951; s. Joseph Ernest and Inez Mildred (McGuire) R.; m. Sarah Elizabeth Duncan, May 24, 1975. B.A., Dartmouth Coll., 1973; M.A., Yale U., 1975, Ph.D., 1979. Cert. lay professional S.C. Synod, Lutheran Ch. in America. Instr. religion Davidson Coll., N.C., 1978-80; asst. prof. systematic theology Luth. Theol. So. Sem., Columbia, S.C., 1980-84, assoc. prof., 1984—; mem. exec. council Luth. Ch. in Am., N.Y.C., 1984—, Luth./Methodist Dialogue, 1984—. Contbr. articles on soteriology and creation to jours. Mem. steering com. Columbia Nuclear Weapons Freeze campaign, 1983-84. D.C. Mackintosh fellow Yale U., 1977-78. Mem. Am. Acad. Religion. Home: 1101 Duke Ave Columbia SC 29203 Office: Luth Theol So Sem 4201 N Main St Columbia SC 29203

ROPER, BILL LEE, minister of music, Southern Baptist Convention; b. Christian County, Ky., Apr. 16, 1937; s. Willie Marian and Katherine (Fleming) R.; B.S., Austin Peay State U., 1959; M.Ch. Music, So. Sem., Louisville, 1966; m. Patricia Ann Phillips, Aug. 25, 1961; children—Elizabeth Ann, Katherine Ann. Minister of music, Guthrie (Ky.) Bapt. Ch., 1957-59, 1st Bapt. Ch., Hopkinsville, Ky., 1959-62, Lyndon Bapt. Ch., Louisville, 1963-72, First Bapt. Ch., Montgomery, Ala., 1972—; music fieldwork adviser So. Sem., Louisville, 1968-72, guest lectr., 1967, 68, 69, 76. Pres. Bapt. Student Union, Austin Peay State U., Clarksville, Tenn., 1958-59; mem. exec. com. Tenn. State Bapt. Student Union, 1958-59; mem. faculty Ridgecrest Bapt. Assembly, 1968, Glorieta Bapt. Assembly, 1974. Mem. Am. Guild Organists, Choristers Guild (pres. 1974-75), So. Bapt. Ch. Music Conf. Author, composer for Broadman Press, 1973—. Home: 2444 Winchester Rd Montgomery AL 36106 Office: First Baptist Church 305 S Perry St Montgomery AL 36106

ROPER, MELINDA, religious organization executive, Roman Catholic Church; b. Chgo., Nov. 18, 1937; d. Edwin C. and Marie (Voelker) R. Student Mich. State U., 1955-57; B.A. in Theology, Loyola U., 1971, L.H.D. (hon.), 1981; L.H.D. (hon.), Emmanuel Coll., 1982, Fordham U., 1982, Cath. U. Am., 1983, New Sch. for Social Research, 1984, Albertus Magnus Coll., 1984; Litt.D. (hon.), Regis Coll., 1983. Pastoral-catechetical tchr. Roman Cath. Diocese, Mérida, Yucatán, Mex., 1965-71; regional coordinator Maryknoll Sisters in Central Am., Guatemala City, Guatemala, 1972-74; staff mem. Pastoral Inst., Roman Catholic Diocese, Huehuetenango, Guatemala, 1974-78, exec. sec. Diocese or Huehuetenango, 1978, dir. diocesan Caritas services, 1978; pres. Maryknoll Sisters, Ossining, N.Y., 1978—; mem. Leadership Conf. of Women in Religion, Washington, 1979—, Comisión de Derechos Humanos de Guatemala-USA, 1983—, Commn. of Human Rights for El Salvador-Mex., 1981—; bd. dirs. U.S. Catholic Mission Assn., 1979—; mem. adv. bd. Witness for Peace-U.S.-Nicaragua, 1983—. Contbr. articles to mags. and prof. jours. Recipient Kenneth David Kaunda award for humanism Pan African Assn. at the UN, 1981, Letelier-Moffet award for human rights Justice and Peace in Latin Am., 1981, Pope John XXIII Peace award Coll. of New Rochelle, 1983. Office: Maryknoll Sisters Maryknoll NY 10545

ROQUE, FRANCIS XAVIER, auxiliary bishop, Roman Catholic Church; b. Providence, Oct. 9, 1928; s. Warren Edward and Mary Loretta (Gallagher) R. B.A., St. John's Sem., 1950. Ordained priest Roman Cath. Ch., 1953. Priest Diocese of Providence, 1953-61; chaplain U.S. Army, 1961-83; aux. bishop Mil. Vicariate Hdqrs., N.Y.C., 1983—, also regional vicar Europe. Served to col. U.S. Army, 1961-83, Vietnam, other. Decorated Bronze Star, Meritorious Service medal, Disting. Service medal. Home: Mil Vicariate U S 1011 First Ave New York NY 10022

ROSAZZA, PETER ANTHONY See *Who's Who in America*, 43rd edition.

ROSCHKE, DAVID ARTHUR, minister, Lutheran Church in America; b. St. Louis, Apr. 23, 1948; s. Francis Earl and Anna Charlotte (Gross) R.; m. Jennifer Ruth Hanske, Dec. 27, 1974; children: Daniel, Timothy, Jonathan. B.A., Concordia Sr. Coll., 1970; M.Div., Christ Sem., 1974. Ordained to ministry Lutheran Ch. in Am., 1974. Nat. staff mem. Youth Ministry Dept., St. Louis, 1971; assoc. pastor Luth. Memorial Ch., Richmond Heights, Mo., 1974-77; managing editor Missouri in Perspective, St. Louis, 1973-77; sr. pastor Madla Interdenominational Ch., Stavanger, Norway, 1977-82, Salem Luth. Ch., Houston, 1982—; v.p. Assn. English Speaking Chs. in Europe and Middle East, 1980-81; dean Houston Synodical area Luth. Ch. Am., 1984—. Contbr. articles to profl. jours. Recipient Disting. Service award Evang. Luths. in Missions, 1978; named to Outstanding Young Men of Am., 1970. Home: 6110 Dumfries Dr Houston TX 77096 Office: Salem Luth Ch 4930 W Bellfort Ave Houston TX 77035

ROSCHKE, FRANCIS EARL, minister, Lutheran Church-Missouri Synod; b. Collinsville, Ill., Dec. 22, 1923; s. Theodore Henry and Hilda Amalia (Pennekamp) R.; m. Anna Charlotte Gross, July 3, 1947; children: David, Charleen, Richard, Deborah. B.A., Concordia Sem., 1945; D.Min., Christ Sem., 1984. Ordained to ministry, 1947. Intern pastor Christ Luth. Ch., Detroit, 1945-46; asst. pastor Holy Cross Luth. Ch., Collinsville, Ill., 1947-50; pastor Peace Luth. Ch., St. Louis, 1950-57, St. Andrew Luth. Ch., Cape Girardeau, Mo., 1957-63, Holy Cross Luth. Ch., Kansas City, Mo., 1963—; cabinet mem. Met. Inter-ch. Agy. Greater Kansas City, 1970-72; zone counselor Luth. Women's Missionary League, 1979-82. Contbr. The New Days Worship, 1966; Forty Chapel Talks for Lutheran Elementary Schools, 1969. Mem. St. Paul's Coll. Alumni Assn. (bd. dirs.).

ROSE, ALAN, religious organization executive, Jewish. Exec. v.p. Canadian Jewish Congress, Montreal, Que. Office: Can Jewish Conf 1590 Ave Docteur Penfield Montreal PQ H3G 1C5 Canada*

ROSE, BOBBY ALLEN, minister, Church of God (Cleveland, Tennessee); b. Crystal, Mich., Aug. 25, 1936; s. Denton L. and Gladys C. (Stamper) R.; student Southwestern Coll., Oklahoma City, 1955-56, Lee Coll., 1958-59, Covanant Theol. Sem., St. Louis, 1964; m. Rose Marie Anselmo, May 13, 1962; 1 dau., Maria Raquel Elizabeth. Ordained to ministry, 1965; evangelist, Okla., Ky., Tenn., Calif., Tex., Ohio, Kans., 1956-60, state evangelist, Mich., 1968-69; dir. Christian Edn., Mo., Ch. of God (Cleveland, Tenn.), 1960-62, Tex., 1964-67, Eastern Can., 1967-68; pastor Northside Ch. of God, St. Louis, 1962-64, Ch. of God, Windsor, Ont., 1967-68, Mount Clemens, Mich., 1969-74, Riverview, Mich., 1974—. Mem. Mich. evangelism bd. Ch. of God (Cleveland, Tenn.), 1969-70, 71-74, mem. youth and Christian edn. bd., 1970-71, mem. state council, 1974—, dist. overseer Riverview, 1974—; pres. Greater Detroit Ch. of God Ministers' Fellowship, 1974-75, 78-79; bd. dirs. N.W. Bible Coll., Minot, N.D., 1982—; mem. Ch. of God Spl. Study Commn., 1979-84. Named Pastor of Year, Mid Am. Sunday Sch. Assn.,

1977. Home: 17065 Grange St Riverview MI 48192 Office: 15633 Pennsylvania Rd Riverview MI 48192

ROSE, DELBERT WAYNE, minister, Ch. of the Nazarene; b. Hoburg, Mo., Aug. 14, 1939; s. Loren V. and Nelda L. (Devers) R.; A.B., Nazarene Bible Coll., Colorado Springs, Colo., 1970; m. Pauline Marie Haley, Nov. 23, 1973; children—Hally Christine, Heath Tyson. Ordained to ministry, 1973; minister Ch. of the Nazarene, Monett, Mo. Home: 416 W County St Monett MO 65708 Office: 8th and Bond Sts Monett MO 65708

ROSE, JOSEPH HUGH, minister, United Pentecostal Church; b. Jewett, Ohio, Nov. 21, 1934; s. J. Harper and Lottie Louella (Van Allen) R.; m. Nila Jayne Habig, Feb. 14, 1958; children: J. Hugh II, Stephanie, David, Dawnella. Student Macphail Coll. Music, Mpls. Th.B., Apostolic Bible Inst., 1955. Ordained to ministry, 1958. Assoc. minister Calvary Tabernacle, Indpls., 1956-73; state youth sec,-treas. Ind. Dist., United Pentecostal Ch. Internat., Fortville, 1959-61, pres., 1961-72; narrator, choir dir., music dir. Harvestime, St. Louis, 1960—; pastor Harrison Hills Ch., Jewett, 1973—; presbyter Ohio Dist., 1975—; coordinator Harvestime, St. Louis, 1982—. Editor Ind. Dist. News, 1958-68 (named outstanding editor 1968). Republican. Home: 698 Kerr Ave Cadiz OH 43907 Office: World Evangelism Ctr 8855 Dunn Rd Hazelwood MO 63042

ROSE, MARVIN STEPHEN, rabbi; b. N.Y.C., Feb. 20, 1944; s. Walter and Irene R.; B.A., Queens Coll., 1965; M.S., Yeshiva U., 1969; m. Sandra Markowitz, Mar. 19, 1972; children: Shira Malka, Jonathan David. Ordained rabbi, 1970. Rabbi Morris Park Hebrew Ctr., Bronx, N.Y., 1970-72, Congregation Agudas Israel, Newburgh, N.Y., 1972-74; lectr. in Bible, Mt. St. Mary Coll., Newburgh, 1973-74; ednl. dir., assoc. rabbi Beth David Congregation, Miami, Fla., 1974-76; rabbi Temple Beth El of North Bay Village (name formerly North Bay Village Jewish Ctr.), Fla., 1976—; chmn. adult Jewish edn. South Fla. council B'nai B'rith, 1980—; founder, pres. You're Not Alone; host TV spls. You're Not Alone. Author: Five Easy Steps to a Happier Life. Mem. Dade County Youth Adv. Bd., Miami, 1976-78. Mem. Assn. for Jewish Spl. Edn. (charter mem.; profl. standards com.), Rabbinical Council Am., Greater Miami Rabbinical Assn. Office: 7800 Hispanola Ave North Bay Village FL 33141

ROSE, ROBERT JOHN, bishop, Roman Catholic Church; b. Grand Rapids, Mich., Feb. 28, 1930; s. Urban Henry and Maida Ann (Glerum) R. Student St. Joseph Sem., 1944-50; B.A. Sem. of Philosophy, Montreal, 1952; S.T.B., Pontifical Urban U., Rome, 1954, S.T.L., 1956; M.A., U. Mich., 1962. Ordained priest Roman Cath. Ch., 1955, consecrated bishop, 1981. High sch. tchr. and counselor St. Joseph Sem., Grand Rapids, Mich., 1956-66, dean of coll. dept., 1966-69; dir. Christopher House, Grand Rapids, 1969-71; rector St. John's Provincial Sem., Plymouth, Mich., 1971-77; pastor Sacred Heart Parish, Muskegon Heights, Mich., 1977-81; bishop Diocese of Gaylord, Mich., 1981—; sec.-treas. Mich. Cath. Conf., Lansing, 1983. Mem. Nat. Conf. Cath. Bishops. Address: Diocese of Gaylord PO Box 1020 Gaylord MI 49735

ROSEDALE, ROY STANLEY, missions educator, Mennonite Brethren Church; b. Whittier, Calif., Apr. 6, 1933; s. Selmer M. and Margaret (White) R.; m. Eleanor Hilda Boehringer, Aug. 15, 1959; children: Karen, Michael, Robin. B.Sc., U. Calif.-Davis, 1955; B.D., Bibl. Sem., 1966; Ph.D., Calif. Grad. Sch. Theology, 1981. Ordained to ministry, 1981. Missionary to India, Soc. Friends, Orissa, India, 1955-58; lay minister Campus Crusade for Christ, San Bernardino, Calif., 1967-85, missionary to Indonesia, 1968-73, dir. Agape missionary tng., 1973-79; prof., missions dept. chmn. and dir. internat. programs Internat. Sch. Theology, San Bernardino, 1979-85; del. Evang. Fgn. Missions Assn., 1967-85; elder Calvary Chapel, Lake Arrowhead, Calif., 1975-85. Mem. Evang. Fgn. Missions Assn., Missiology Assn., Missions Profs. Assn., Christian Businessmen's Com. Republican. Home: Box 36 Blue Jay CA 92317 Office: Internat Sch Theology Arrowhead Springs San Bernardino CA 92414

ROSEN, MOISHE MARTIN, clergyman, religious organization leader; b. Kansas City, Mo., Apr. 12, 1932; s. Ben and Rose (Baker) R.; m. Ceil Starr, Aug. 18, 1950; children: Lyn Rosen Bond, Ruth. Grad. Northeastern Collegiate Bible Inst., 1957. Ordained to ministry Baptist Ch., 1957. Missionary, Am. Bd. Missions to the Jews, N.Y.C., 1956, dir. recruiting and tng., 1967-70; minister Beth Sar Shalom Congregation, Los Angeles, 1957-67; founder, leader Jews for Jesus Movement, San Francisco, 1970-73, chmn., 1973—; speaker in field. Author: Jews for Jesus Book, 1974; Share the New Life with a Jew, 1976; Christ in the Passover, 1977; Y'shua, The Jewish Way to Say Jesus, 1982. Composer songs. Contbr. articles to profl. jours. Bd. trustees Christian Witness to Israel, Kent, Eng., Western Conservative Bapt. Sem., Portland, Internat. Council on Biblical Inerrancy, Oakland, Calif. Office: 60 Haight St San Francisco CA 94102

ROSEN, PETER, film-TV producer; b. N.Y.C., Sept. 1, 1943; s. Herman H. and Tamara T. (Tamarkina) R.; B.Arch., Cornell U., 1966; B.F.A., Yale, 1968, M.F.A., 1968; m. Anne Marie Johnson, Sept. 7, 1971; children—Tanya, Sasha. Pres. Peter Rosen Prodns., Inc., producer religious films and TV programming, N.Y.C., 1970—. Recipient Faith and Freedom award Religious Heritage of Am., 1973, 75, George Washington honor medal Freedoms Found. at Valley Forge, 1974; fellow Trumbull Coll., Yale, 1968-74. Mem. Religious Heritage Am. (mem. exec. com. 1974—), Religious Pub. Relations Council. Club: Yale (N.Y.C.). Home: 114 E 71st St New York NY 10021 Office: 34 E 68th St New York NY 10021

ROSENBAUM, STANLEY NED, Jewish theology educator; b. Highland Park, Ill., Dec. 8, 1939; s. Stanley Menz and Wilma (Nussbaum) R.; m. Mary Helene Pottker, Sept. 2, 1963; children: Sarah Catherine, William David, Ephraim Samuel. B.A., Tulane U., 1961; postgrad. U. Chgo., 1961-64; M.A., Brandeis U., 1967, Ph.D., 1974. Assoc. prof. Dickinson Coll., Carlisle, Pa., 1970—, counselor Dickinson Coll. Hillel, 1971—. Contbr. articles to religious publs. Woodrow Wilson fellow, 1961. Mem. Assn. Jewish Studies, Nat. Assn. Profs. Hebrew. Lodge: B'nai B'rith. Home: 431 S College St Carlisle PA 17013 Office: Box 162 Dickinson Coll Carlisle PA 17013

ROSENBERRY, EDWARD LESTER, minister, Churches of God, General Conference; b. Chambersburg, Pa., Feb. 7, 1951; s. Clarence Lester and Dorothy May (Miller) R.; m. Linda Kay Long, May 25, 1974; children: J. Daniel, Elizabeth, Caroline, Christina, Emily. B.A., Shippensburg U., 1973; M.Div., Evang. Sch. Theology, 1976. Ordained to ministry, Ch. of God, 1976. Pastor, Maytown Ch. of God, Pa., 1973-79, Plainfield Ch. of God, Pa., 1979—; pres. E. Pa. Conf. Chs. of God, 1985—, mem. adminstrv. council, 1977-82, v.p., 1984-85; mem. Gen. Conf. Adminstrv. Council, 1983—. Author: (with Myra Fields) Three Centuries with the Rosenberry Family, 1983. Editor: The Valley Jour., 1983-84. Club: Palam (v.p. 1984).

ROSENHAMER, JOHN HENRY, priest, Roman Catholic Church. b. Altoona, Pa., Aug. 26, 1938; s. J. Harry and Mary Elizabeth (McCrossin) R. A.B., St. Mary's U., 1960, S.T.B., 1963; M.S. in Library Sci., Western Res. U., 1965. Ordained priest Roman Catholic Ch., 1964. Tchr. Bradford Central Christian High Sch., Pa., 1964-66; tchr., adminstr. Venango Christian High Sch., Oil City, Pa., 1966-82; pastor St. Venantius Ch., Rouseville, Pa., 1979-82, St. Joseph Ch., Erie, Pa., 1982—; judge Tribunal Diocese of Erie, 1980—, personal bd., 1983—; bd. dirs. Inter-Ch. Ministries, Erie, 1982—; clergy reference Hospice, Erie, 1983—. Democrat. Clubs: Mashneechor, Siebenbuerger, East Erie Turners. Lodges: K.C., Elks. Address: 147 W 24th St Erie PA 16502

ROSENSTOCK, ELLIOT DAVID, rabbi, Reform Judaism; b. Kansas City, Dec. 18, 1932; s. Gustav and Edna Viola (Straus) R.; m. Nancy Scharff, July 10, 1958; children: Emily, David Gustav. B.A., Cornell U., 1953; B.H.L., Hebrew Union Coll./Jewish Inst. Religion, 1958, M.A.H.L., 1961, D.H.L., 1976. Ordained rabbi, 1958. Asst. and assoc. rabbi Collingwood Ave. Temple, Toledo, Ohio, 1961-67; rabbi Temple Beth-El, South Bend, Ind., 1967—; resident lectr. dept. religion Defiance Coll., 1960-64; faculty O.T., U. Toledo, 1963-67; vis. asst. prof. dept. theology U. Notre Dame, 1967-76; mem. Central Conf. Rabbis, 1958—, mem. Commn. on Jewish Edn.; pres. Great Lakes-Ohio Valley Region, and exec. bd. Central Conf., 1981-83, mem. long range planning com., 1981—; mem. exec. com. Clergy Assn. St. Joseph County, pres., 1974-76. Contbr. articles to profl. jours. Bd. dirs. Big Bros., 1969-75, United Community Services, 1972-76, Hospice, 1980-83; mem. Commn. on Human Relations and Fair Employment Practices, City of South Bend, 1973-77; bd. dirs. Phoenix House, 1979-84; pres. Resources for Enriching Adult Living, 1984-85, chmn. bd., 1985—. Home: 5914 S Gotham Dr South Bend IN 46614 Office: Temple Beth-El 305 W Madison St South Bend IN 46601

ROSET, WILFRED LAURIER, minister, Assemblies of God; b. Herbert, Sask., Can., Jan. 10, 1927; s. Bent Christian and Eline Margaret (Rorstrand) R.; came to U.S., 1952, naturalized, 1967; B.Th., Western Bible Coll., Winnipeg, Man., Can., 1949; cert. alcoholism and counseling, U. Utah, 1967, 69; m. Leila Margaret MacIntosh, Oct. 2, 1948; children: Grant, Gayle, Gregory. Ordained to ministry, 1950; pastor chs. in Man., N.D. and Mont., 1949-68; chaplain Mont. State Hosp., Warm Springs, 1968—; mem. Assemblies of God Commn. on Chaplains, 1980-83. Vice pres. youth dept. Man. dist. province Assemblies of God, 1950-52; youth pres. N.D. dist., 1953-58; sec. N.D. Evang. Sunday Sch. Assn., 1956-57; host pastor 1st Pentecostal Ecumenical Fellowship Week, New England, N.D., 1961; pres. Anaconda (Mont.) Ministerial Assn., 1968, 73; bd. adminstrn. High Acres Manor, Jamestown, N.D., 1958-59; bd. dirs. Lakewood Park Bible Sch., 1953-58; dir. N.D. Youth Camps, 1953-59. Recipient award contbn. youth programs Assemblies of God, 1957. Mem. Assn. Mental Health Chaplains. Home: 103 Madison St Anaconda MT 59711 Office: Box 103 Warm Springs MT 59756

ROSHAK, MICHAEL GREGORY, educational administrator, religious organization executive, Orthodox Church in America; b. Carbondale, Pa., Aug. 9, 1946; s. Frederick Vincent and Helen (Kutch) R.; m. Olga Ptach, Oct. 19, 1975; children: Michael John, Peter Alexis, Julianna. B.S. in Edn., Millersville State U., 1967; M.A., Ohio State U., 1972; student Inst. Theologie Orthodoxe, Paris, 1970-71, Leningrad Theol. Acad., USSR, 1973-74; M.Div., St. Vladimir's Sem., 1979. Ordained to ministry Orthodox Church in America as deacon, 1976. Choir dir., youth dir. Foyer des Engants, Montgeron, France, 1970-71; exec. dir. St. Vladimir's Theol. Found., Crestwood, N.Y., 1974—; dir. devel. and pub. relations St. Vladimir's Sem., 1974—; chmn. Orthodox christian communications commn. Standing Conf. Canonical Orthodox Bishops in Ams., 1982—; mem. dept. info. and pub. relations Orthodox Ch. in Am., 1982—, mem. task force on ecumenism, 1983—; clergy rep. Council on Alcoholism, Westchester County, N.Y., 1983-84; lectr. Russian St. Vladimir's Sem., 1974—. Recipient nat. def. fellowship Ind. U., 1967, teaching assistantship Ohio State U., 1968-69. Mem. Phi Sigma Pi. Home and Office: St Vladimir's Sem 575 Scarsdale Rd Crestwood NY 10707

ROSS, CHESTER WHEELER, minister, United Methodist Church; b. Evansville, Ind., Nov. 3, 1922; s. Mylo Wheeler and Irma Katherine Julia (Berning) R.; m. Ruth Eulaine Briney, Aug. 30, 1949; children: James W., Deborah R., Judith R., Martha S., John W. A.B. cum laude, Kans. Wesleyan U., 1952; M.Div. with distinction, Garrett Evang. Theol. Sem., 1954; D.Ministry, St. Paul Sch. Theology, 1979; postgrad. U. Tex., 1959, Oxford U., Eng., 1963. Ordained elder Meth. Ch., 1954. Pastor United Meth. Ch., Mentor, Kans., 1949-52, Bogue, Kans., 1954-55; enlisted U.S. Air Force, 1942, advanced through grades to lt. col., 1975; chaplain, 1955-75; pastor United Meth. Ch., Iuka, Kans., 1975-80, Ness City, Kans., 1980—; vice chmn. parish devel. council United Meth. Ch. Kans. West Conf., 1979-82, mem. global ministry council, 1975-82, mem. conf. council on fin. and adminstrn., 1983—; mem. Hays Dist. Council on Ministry, 1980-81. Contbr. articles to profl. jours. Scoutmaster Santa Fe Trails Boy Scouts Am., 1981-84; rehab. counselor, Ness County, 1982-84. Decorated Air medal (2). Recipient Silver Beaver award Pushmataha council Boy Scouts Am., 1975. Mem. Acad. Parish Clergy, Internat. Platform Assn., VFW, Am. Legion, Mil. Chaplains Assn., Ret. Officers Assn., Ness City Ministers Assn. (pres. 1982-84). Lodge: Rotary. Home: 417 N School St Ness City KS 67560 Office: United Meth Ch 316 N Pennsylvania St Ness City KS 67560

ROSS, GEORGE EVERETT, minister, Episcopal Church; b. Kansas City, Mo., Nov. 20, 1933 ; s. Walter W. and Eugenia C. (Moeckel) R.; m. Joan M. Ruda, June 4, 1960 (div. 1983); children: Mary, Ann. B.A., Ohio Wesleyan U., 1955; M.Div., Episcopal Theol. Sem., 1958. Ordained to ministry Episcopal Ch., 1958. Asst. St. Stephen's Ch., Columbus, Ohio, 1958-61; rector St. Peter's Ch., Delaware, Ohio, 1963-63; archdeacon Diocese of Idaho, Boise, 1963-69; dean St. Michael's Cathedral, Boise, 1969-72; rector St. Paul's Ch., Akron, Ohio, 1972—; trustee Ohio Wesleyan U., Delaware, 1974-77, Trinity Episcopal Sch. for Ministry, Ambridge, Pa., 1979—. Home: 2547 Falmouth Rd Akron OH 44313 Office: St Paul's Ch 1361 W Market St Akron OH 44313

ROSS, GERMAN REED, bishop, Church of God in Christ; b. Mart, Tex.; s. Ira and Mary (Lewis) R.; m. Grace Y. Searcy, July 4, 1942 (dec. Jan. 1971); children: Merria A., Winston R., Ira G. B.B.A., Golden Gate U., 1950; M.Div., Pacific Luth. Sem., 1966; student Philander Smith Coll., 1940-42, U. Calif.-Berkeley, 1947-48. Ordained to ministry Ch. of God in Christ, 1955. C.P.A. Gen. sec. Ch. of God in Christ, Memphis, 1976—, jurisdictional bishop, No. Calif., 1973—, nat. auditor, 1973—; pastor Good Samaritan Cathedral, Oakland, Calif., 1979—, Mt. Sinai and Good Samaritan Ch., Oakland, 1955-79; sec. Congress Nat. Black Chs., 1978—; mem. Nat. Bd. Bishops, 1973—. Author: History and Formative Years of Church of God In Christ, 1968; (with others) Here Am I, 1969. Co-chmn. Assault on Illiteracy Program, Washington, 1981—. Served with USNR, 1942-45. Recipient Disting. Service award Religious Workers Guild, 1975, 81; others. Democrat. Home: PO Box 10013 Oakland CA 94610 Office: 625 W MacArthur St Oakland CA 94608

ROSS, HENRY, bishop, Church of Our Lord Jesus Christ of the Apostolic Faith, Inc. Office: 2081 Adam Clayton Powell Jr Blvd New York NY 10027*

ROSS, JAMES ROBERT, minister, Christian Churches. B. Clarksville, Tenn., Aug. 11, 1934; s. Clyde D. and Claudine Evelyn (Singleton) R.; m. Doris Naugle, Sept. 3, 1950; children: Joy, Thomas, Lisa. B.S., Southeastern La. U., 1962; B.D., Columbia Theol. Sem., 1962; Ph.D., Emory U., 1969. Ordained to ministry Christian Churches, 1962. Prof. Bible, Southeastern

Christian Coll., Winchester, Ky., 1960-64; prof. philosophy Ala. A&M U., Huntsville, 1968-70; campus minister Christian Campus House, Charleston, Ill., 1970-80, Purdue Christian Campus House, West Lafayette, Inc., 1984—; dir. Christian Counseling Service, Mount Vernon, Ill., 1980-84. Author: The War Within, 1970. contbr. articles to scholarly jours. Dist. coordinator Bread for the World, Washington, 1976-79. Mem. Am. Assn. Pastoral Counselors, Am. Assn. Marriage and Family Therapy. Lodge: Rotary. Home: 602 Dodge St West Lafayette IN 47906 Office: Purdue Christian Campus House 1000 State St West Lafayette IN 47906

ROSS, JAMES RUSSELL, minister, Salvation Army; b. Sheridan, Wyo., Dec. 30, 1942; s. Russell B. and Vivian Estella (Moore) R.; B.A., Seattle Pacific Coll., 1965; M.Div., Nazarene Theol. Sem., 1972; m. Peggy Gene Barringer, Aug. 1, 1970; children—Stephen James, Renee Christine, Elizabeth Estelle. Ordained to ministry; cadet in tng. Salvation Army Sch. Officers Tng., San Francisco, 1968-69; assisting officer Bellingham (Wash.) Corps, 1969-70; officer in command Anacortes, (Wash.) Corps, 1970, Englewood (Colo.) Corps, 1970-71, Butte (Mont.) Corps, 1971-72, Casper (Wyo.) Corps, 1972-75, Van Nuys (Calif.) Corps, 1975-76; spl. services officer San Diego Citadel, 1976—. Mem. Wyo. Human Resources Council, 1972-75; bd. dirs. Meals on Wheels of Natrona County, Wyo., 1972-74. Named Kiwanis Minister of the Month, 1975. Mem. San Fernando Valley Nat. Assn. Evangelicals. Home: 3435 Quince St San Diego CA 92104 Office: 825 7th Ave San Diego CA 92101

ROSS, LOUIS PHILIP, lay church worker, Southern Baptist Convention; b. Sumter, S.C., Jan. 4, 1944; s. John Quincy and Dorothy Irene (Jackson) R.; B.S., U. S.C., 1967; M.A. in Religious Edn., Southwestern Bapt. Theol. Sem., 1969; m. Judith Lucille Starr, Dec. 16, 1966; 1 son, Christopher Philip. Minister music Bayview Bapt. Ch., Columbia, S.C., 1971-74, Trinity Bapt. Ch., West Columbia, S.C., 1975-77, Northgate Bapt. Ch., Orangeburg, S.C., 1979-81; interim minister music First Presbyn. Ch., Orangeburg, 1983-84. Dir. social services Carolina Children's Home, Columbia, 1970-77; exec. dir. Brookland Plantation Home for Boys, Orangeburg, 1979—. Mem. Southeastern Child Care Assn., Southwestern Religious Edn. Assn., U. S.C. Alumni Assn., S.C. Assn. for Vol. Adminstrn. Office: PO Box 4465 Columbia SC 29240

ROSS, ROBERT DUANE, minister, Assemblies of God; b. Kalispell, Mont., Jan. 7, 1935; s. Ted Isaac and Ester (Rasmussen) R.; B.A., N. Central Bible Coll., 1957; m. Roberta Jean Cutsforth, Aug. 4, 1956; children—Ronald Duane, Rachel Lynn. Ordained to ministry, 1959; minister Gospel Tabernacle, Dallas, Wis., 1957-59, Hwy. Tabernacle, Hungry-Horse, Mont., 1959-64, Parkhill Assembly, Billings, Mont., 1964-71, Rapids Assembly of God, Wisconsin Rapids, 1971—. Youth rep. Wis. sect. Assemblies of God, 1957-59, presbyter Mont. dist., 1967-68, exec. sec., 1968-71, asst. supt. Wis. dist., 1973—; bd. regents Northwest Coll., Seattle, 1968-71, N. Central Bible Coll., Mpls., 1973—. Editor Full Gospel Tidings, 1976—. Contbr. articles to religious jours. Home: 408 Woodland Dr Wisconsin Rapids WI 54494 Office: Box 128 Wisconsin Rapids WI 54494

ROSS, ZANE GREY, minister, Southern Baptist Convention; b. Troutdale, Va., Sept. 2, 1920; s. Lester C. and Lola (Pennington) R.; student Bluefield Coll., 1938-40; B.A., U. Richmond, 1946; postgrad Union Theol. Sem., 1947-48; m. Eva Courtney Burton, Dec. 21, 1943; children—Burton Blakeley, David Courtney. Ordained to ministry, 1944; pastor Skinquarter and Chesterfield Bapt. Chs., Va., 1946-50, Indian Head Bapt. Ch., Md., 1950-57, First Bapt. Ch., Dundalk, Md., 1957-60, Wayne Hills Bapt. Ch., Waynesboro, Va., 1960-62, Cool Spring Bapt. Ch., Mechanicsville, Va., 1963—, Berea Bapt. Ch., Louisa, Va., 1983, Hebron Bapt. Ch., Hanover, Va., 1984—. Pres., Augusta (1961), Dover (1974), Richmond Area (1972) Bapt. pastors confs.; sec.-treas. Md. Bapt. Pastors Conf., 1951; v.p. Va. Bapt. Pastors Conf., 1962; active Va. Bapt. Men's Mission Team, S.D., 1963, 1965; moderator So. Dist. (1954-56), Dover (1973) Bapt. assns.; former mem. Md. State Mission Bd. Trustee Bluefield (Va.) Coll., 1972—, named Best Declaimer, 1940; charter mem. Univ. Richmond (Va.) Lake Soc., 1976; chaplain Humana Saint Luke's Hosp., Richmond, 1983—. Mem. Richmond Area Interdenominational, Richmond Area, Dover Bapt. pastor's confs., Hanover County Ministerial Assn. Home: 8200 Penobscot Rd Richmond VA 23227

ROSSING, LYLE ERLING, minister, American Lutheran Church; b. Duluth, Minn., Jan. 23, 1938; s. Erling William and Irene Clara (Norby) R.; m. Betty Elaine Hanson, June 13, 1964; children: Christopher, Theodore. B.A., Augustana Coll., 1960; B.D., Luther Theol. Sem., 1964; M.Th., Princeton U., 1966; D.Min., Luther Theol. Sem., 1981. Ordained to ministry, 1966. Pastor, Bergen Calvary Luth. Chs., Rural Lidgerwood and Hankinson, N.D., 1966-71; pastor Ezekiel Luth. Ch., River Falls, Wis., 1971-82, Emmaus Luth. Ch., Racine, Wis., 1982—; chmn. Am. Luth. Ch. wills awareness com., Racine conf., 1983—; trustee Carthage Coll., Kenosha, Wis., 1984—. Contbr. articles to profl. jours. Chmn., Crop Walk for Hunger Relief, River Falls, Wis., 1980, 81; bd. dirs. Recycling Ctr., River Falls, 1981-82. Am. Luth. Ch. scholar, 1964; Luth. World Fedn. scholar, 1965-66. Fellow Augustana Coll. Fellows; mem. Racine Clergy Assn.

ROSTE, DARRYL MELVIN, religious educator, Evangelical Lutheran Church of Canada. B. Preeceville, Sask., Can., Oct. 17, 1946; s. Rudolph Melvin and Anna (Mosell) R.; m. Rita Elaine Salte, Oct. 12, 1968; children: Vaughn, Erica. B.A., U. Sask., Saskatoon, Can., 1969; M.Div., Luth. Theol. Sem., Saskatoon, 1972. Ordained to ministry Evangel. Luth. Ch. Can., 1972. Pastor, Bethany Luth. Ch., Tillery, Alta., Can., 1972-77, Peace Luth. Ch., Fort St. John, B.C., Can., 1977-82; faculty mem. Can. Luth. Bible Inst., Camrose, Alta., 1982—. Office: Can Luth Bible Inst 4837 52A St Camrose AB T4V 1W5 Canada

ROTERT, NORMAN FRANCIS, priest, Roman Catholic Church. B. Montrose, Mo., June 22, 1931; s. Clement William and Freda Marie (Cook) R. M.A. Kenrick Sem., 1957. Ordained priest, Roman Cath. Ch., 1957. Assoc. pastor Diocese of Springfield-Cape Girardeau, Mo., 1957-59; assoc. pastor Diocese of Kansas City-St. Joseph, Mo., 1959-68; vicar for social concerns, 1970—, vicar gen., 1984—; pastor St. Peter's ch., Kansas City, 1979—; sec. Cath. Charities, Kansas City, 1970—; Kansas City Diocesan dir. Campaign for Human Devel., 1979—; founder, adminstr. Bishop Helmsing Early Childhood Ctr., Kansas City, 1974—. Pres. Blue Hills Homes Corp., Kansas City, 1974—; sec. Kansas City Orgn. Project, 1976—; dir. Kansas City Consensus, 1984—. Democrat. Home and Office: 6415 Holmes St Kansas City MO 64131

ROTH, DON ANDREW, administrator, Seventh-day Adventist; b. Cin., Apr. 14, 1927; s. Daniel F. and Matilda (Gatz) R.; m. Doris Ann Behringer, Aug. 28, 1948; children: David Alan, Diane Arlene, Dan Andrew. B.A., Columbia Union Coll., 1950. Ordained to ministry, 1959. Dir. pub. relations East Pa. Conf., Reading, Pa., 1950-54; pub. relations sec. Columbia Union Conf., Takoma Park, Md., 1954-65; asst. sec. Far Eastern Div., Singapore, 1965-75; assoc. sec. Gen. Conf. Seventh-day Adventists, Takoma, Park, Md., 1975—; pres. Vellore Christian Med. Coll. Bd., N.Y.C., 1982—. Author: The Individualist, 1964; Mundahoi, 1970. Home: 3004 Shanandale Dr Silver Spring MD 20904 Office: 6840 Eastern Ave Washington DC 20012

ROTH, WILLARD EDWARD, mission administrator, Mennonite Church; b. Wayland, Iowa, Mar. 10, 1933; s. Elmer G. and Minnie Fannie (Wenger) R.; m. Alice Metzler, Aug. 25, 1956; children: Carla Joy, Kevin Roy. A.A., Hesston Coll., 1953; B.A., U. Iowa, 1955, cert. in Journalism, 1955; M.Div., Goshen Bibl. Sem., 1971. Ordained to ministry Mennonite Ch., 1961. Organizing pastor Mennonite Ch., Des Moines, 1956-58; info. dir. Mennonite Central Com., Akron, Pa., 1959-60; youth editor Mennonite Pub. House, Scottdale, Pa., 1961-68; West Africa coordinator Mennonite Bd. of Missions, Accra, Ghana, 1968-73, ch. relations dir., Elkhart, Ind., 1973—. Author: (with others) Becoming God's People Today, 1966; No More The Round Mud Hut, 1971. Editor: Hunger Hurts, 1968; mag. Sent. Mem. Religious Pub. Relations Council, Internat. Assn. Mission Studies, World Assn. Christian Communication, Am. Soc. Missiology (pub. 1978—), Sigma Delta Chi. Home: 2313 Morehouse Ave Elkhart IN 46517 Office: Mennonite Bd of Missions Box 370 Elkhart IN 46515

ROTH, WILLIAM GLENN, Bible educator, Evangelical Free Church; psychological assistant; b. Buffalo, May 21, 1947; s. Clarence A. and Betty K. (Mitchell) R.; m. Patricia Jean Davis, June 8, 1969; children: Michele, Kristopher. B.S., Indiana U., 1969; Th.M. with honors, Dallas Theol. Sem., 1979; M.A. in Psychology, Rosemead Sch. Psychology, 1981, postgrad., 1981—. Registered psychol. asst., Calif. Staff mem. Campus Crusade for Christ, San Bernardino, Calif., 1969-79, internat. rep., 1972-75; faculty member Internat. Sch. Theology, San Bernardino, 1979—; psychol. cons. Mission Avaiation Fellowship, Redlands, Calif., 1984—, Air Serv Internat., Redlands, Calif., 1985—; psychol. asst. Christian Psychol. Services, Riverside, Calif., 1983—. Bd. dirs. YMCA, San Bernardino, 1980-81. Recipient academic scholarship Scalp and Blade Soc., 1965-69. Republican. Lodge: Rotary. Office: Internat Sch Theology Arrowhead Springs San Bernardino CA 92414

ROTHAAR, MICHAEL ROBERT, pastor, American Lutheran Church. B. Bayreuth, Federal Republic Germany, May 2, 1946; came to U.S., 1946, naturalized, 1947; s. Ernest William and Uleva Catherine (Cecil) R.; m. Linda Lee Athey, Aug. 15, 1970; children: Sarah Catherine, Marcus James, Lucas Michael. B.A., Capital U., 1967; M.Div., Trinity Sem., Columbus, Ohio, 1971; M.S., St. Francis Coll., Fort Wayne, Ind., 1974; D.Min., Drew U., 1980. Ordained to ministry American Lutheran Ch., 1971. Pastor St. Peter's Luth. Ch., Edon, Ohio, 1971-74, Christus Victor Luth. Ch., Dearborn Heights, Mich., 1974—; clergy dir. for Mich. Luth. Book of Worship Introduction Project, Mpls., 1977-79; dir. So. Mich., Sem. Appeal, Mpls., 1980-81; mem. urban issues com. Sch. for Min., Ann Arbor, Mich., 1983—; rep. Mich. dist. council Am. Luth. Ch., Detroit, 1984—. Author: (with others) Worship Blueprints, Series A, 1980; also articles. Mem. cable TV commn., Garden City, Mich., 1982-83; pres. Garden City Civic Theatre, 1983—. Home: 137 Central Garden City MI 48135 Office: Christus Victor Luth Ch 25535 Ford Rd Dearborn Heights MI 48127

ROTHENBERGER, JACK RENNINGER, clergyman, Schwenkfelder Church; b. Boyertown, Pa., Oct. 4, 1930; s. Stuart Henry and Beulah (Renninger) R.; m. Jean Delores Schultz, Sept. 8, 1951; children: Susan Marie, Bruce Wayne. B.S., Juniata Coll., 1952; M.Div., Hartford Theol. Sem., 1955; S.T.M., Temple U., 1962; D.Min., Lancaster Theol. Sem., 1977. Ordained to ministry, Schwenkfelder Ch., 1955. Pastor, Palm and Landsale Schwenkfelder Ch., 1955-63, 65-66; stated supply, interim pastor Pa. United Ch. of Christ, 1963-69; chaplain, tchr., coordinator, dir. admissions Perkiomen Sch., Pennsburg, Pa., 1955-56, 62-67; asst. headmaster, headmaster Perkiomen Sch., 1967-69; minister Christian edn. Central Schwenkfelder Ch., Worcester, Pa., 1969-74, sr. minister, 1974—; pres. Internat. Christian Endeavor, Columbus, Ohio, 1983—; mem. cabinet and bd. Pa. Council Chs., 1957—; mem. Pa. Conf. Interch. Cooperation. Editor: The Schwenkfeldion mag., 1964—. Author: Casper Schwenkfeld and the Ecumenical Ideal, 1962. Contbr. articles to profl. jours. First v.p. Schwenckfeld Manor, Lansdale, Pa., 1973—; v.p. Meadowood Total Care Retirement Community, Worcester, Pa., 1983—; mem. Schwenkfeld Mission Bd., 1957, Schwenkfelder Bd. Pubs., 1957—, Schwenkfelder Library Bd., 1957—, Schwenkfeldian in Exile Soc., 1955—, others. Mem. N. Pa. Assn. United Ch. Christ Ministerium, N. Pa. Ministerium, Methacton Area Ministerium, United Schwenkfelder Youth Fellowship, Montgomery County Sunday Sch. Assn., others. Republican. Home: 3914 Gate House Ln Skippack PA 19474 Office: Central Schwenkfelder Ch Valley Forge Rd Worcester PA 19490

ROTHENBERGER, VICTOR CONRAD, minister, Evangelical Lutheran Church of Canada; b. Rhein, Sask., Can., Feb. 14, 1923; s. Conrad and Amalia (Propp) R.; m. Martha Ida Redlich, July 9, 1947; children: Sharon Thomson, Wayne, Deborah Hick, Richard. A.A., Luther Coll., 1942; B.A., U. Sask., 1947; ministerial diploma, Capital U. and Sem., Columbus, Ohio, 1947; B.D., Knox Coll., Toronto, Ont., Can., 1965; M.A., M.Edn., Wright State U., 1975. Ordained to ministry Am. Luth. Ch., 1947. Pastor various chs. in Sask., B.C. and Alta., Can., 1947-56, Sharon Luth. Ch., Pasadena, Tex., 195659, Peace Luth. Ch., Linton, N.D., 1959-62, Peace Luth. Ch., Pickering, Ont., 1962-65, Christ Luth. Ch., Dayton, Ohio, 1965-74, Martin Luther Ch., Vancouver, B.C., 1974—; chmn. B.C. conf. Am. Luth. Ch., Vancouver, 1952-53; mem. stewardship com. Can. dist. Am. Luth. Ch., Vancouver, 1951-53; mem. campus ministry bd. Evang. Luth. Ch. Can., Vancouver, 1981-84; bd. dirs. Luth. Bible Sch. of B.C., Evang. Luth. Ch. Can., 1981—. Served with Canadian Armed Forces, 1940-43. Home: 535 E 46th Ave Vancouver BC V5W 2A2 Canada Office: Martin Luther Evang Luth Ch 505 E 46th Ave Vancouver BC V5W 2A2 Canada

ROTHERMEL, DAVID EDWIN, minister, Lutheran Church in America; b. Minersville, Pa., Aug. 13, 1935; s. Edwin F. and Violet (Komorosky) R.; m. Lois Joan Redinger, Mar. 4, 1961; children: Mark D., Deborah A. A.B., Muhlenburg, Coll., 1957; B.D., Phila. Theol. Sem., 1960, M.Div., 1960; M.A., Lehigh U., 1972; Ph.D., Pa. State U., 1984. Ordained to ministry Lutheran Ch., 1960. Asst. pastor St. John Luth. Ch., Phila., 1960-61; pastor First Luth. Ch., Collingdale, Pa., 1961-65, Trinity Meml. Luth. Ch., Catasauqua, Pa., 1965-75, Rife-Killinger Luth. Parish, Millersburg, Pa., 1975—; chmn. social ministry Lykens Dist., Millersburg, 1979-82. Mem. Lykens Pastoral Assn. Republican. Club: Sportsmen. Home and Office: 545 Ruby Rd Millersburg PA 17061

ROTHMAN, MURRAY ISRAEL, rabbi Jewish; educator; b. N.Y.C., Mar. 16, 1921; s. Hyman and Eva (Esrig) R.; B.A., Yeshiva Coll., 1944; M. Hebrew Lit., Hebrew Union Coll., 1949, D.D. (hon.), 1974; m. Charlotte Hamburg, May 28, 1950; children—Jo Amy, Lily Ann. Rabbi, 1949; asst. rabbi Rodef Shalom Temple, Pitts., 1949-51; chaplain USNR, 1951-53; rabbi Temple Shalom, Newton, Mass., 1954—. Vis. lectr. Judaism, Andover Newton (Mass.) Theol. Sem., 1969—; mem. Archdiocesan Com. on Catholics and Jews, 1969—; pres. Mass. Bd. Rabbis, 1967-70. Past pres. Newton Clergy Assn.; mem. nat. commn. on interfaith activities Union Am. Hebrew Congregations, 1967—, mem. nat. bd., 1968—. Mem. Joint Com. on Mid-East Policy, 1974—; mem. Mayor's Human Relations Adv. Commn., Newton, 1970—. Bd. dirs. Am. Friends of Hebrew U., Newton chpt. ARC. Recipient citation NCCJ, 1974. Mem. Central Conf. Am. Rabbis (nat. treas. 1983—). Home: 35 Kingston Rd Newton MA 02161 Office: 175 Temple St Newton MA 02165

ROTHSCHILD, KURT, religious organization executive, Jewish. Nat. pres. Mizrachi-Hapoel Hamizrachi Orgn., Can., Montreal, Que. Office:

Mizrachi-Hapoel Hamizrachi Orgn Can 5497A Victoria Ave Suite 101 Montreal PQ H3W 2R1 Canada*

ROUELLE, FORREST WILLIAM, priest, Roman Catholic Church; b. Montpelier, Vt., Dec. 5, 1927; s. Leon George and Alma Genevive (Mathieu) R.; student St. Michael's Coll., Winooski, Vt., 1950-52, Grand Sem. Philosophy, Montreal, 1952-56. Ordained priest, 1956; dir. Don Bosco Home Boys, Burlington, Vt., 1956-59; asst. pastor chs. in Vt., 1959-67; chaplain Vt. State Prison, Windsor, 1963-65; pastor chs. in Vt., 1967—; pastor St. Francis of Assisi Ch., Windsor, 1975—. Past chaplain Vt. Elk's youth program; past father prior Vt. Columbian Squires. Founder People Helping People, Grand Isle, Vt., 1967-68, Interfaith Community Recreation Program. Barton, Vt., 1958-59, Jefferson's Market, Inc., low income food, Royalton, Vt., 1975, Faith, Hope and Charity, Bethel, Vt., 1970, Interfaith Sharing of Ch. Properties, Pittsfield, Vt., 1971, Home Health Agy., Randolph, Vt., 1974, Northeast Family Counseling Service, Newport, Vt., 1960; chmn. bd. Champlain Valley Office Econ. Opportunity, Burlington, 1964; Episcopal liaison to Vt. Cath. Charismatic Renewal, 1981—; chaplain Vt. State Prison, 1982—; mem. Vt. Cath. Charities Bd., 1983—. Recipient citations and certificates of appreciation. Mem. Vt. Ecumenical Assn., Windsor Ministerial Assn. Address: 30 Union St Windsor VT 05089

ROUNTREE, H. G. (JIM), lay church worker, Roman Catholic Ch.; b. Pelican, La., Oct. 19, 1931; s. Perry and Ada Marguerite (DeSoto) R.; B.S., S.W. Mo. State U., 1959; M.Ed., U. Okla.; postgrad. Washington U., St. Louis, 1965, U. Ark., 1971-72; m. Carol Jean Thompson, June 23, 1962; children—William Hunter, Clare Marguerite. Charter pres. Nat. Council Cath. Laity, 1971-73, bd. dirs., 1973—; bd. dirs. Nat. Council Cath. Men, 1968-70; pres. Diocesan Council Cath. Men, Little Rock, 1967-70. Vice pres. pub. relations Wal-Mart Stores, Inc., Bentonville, Ark., 1972-76; to 1983; pub. relations cons., Author: Thy Will Be Done In All Things, 1965. Editor: Eight Hundred Colleges Face the Future, 1966 (Manning Patillo). Contbr. articles to edn. and religious jours. Chmn. bd., pres. Ozark Guidance Center, 1973-75; trustee Ark. Found. Assoc. Colls., 1975—; bd. dirs. Beaver Lake Waler Comm. Recipient Distinguished Service award Westark Area council Boy Scouts Am., 1971; Disting. Service award Jr. C. of C., Rogers, Ark., 1968; American Citizenship award Rogers Rotary Club, 1971. Mem. Rogers C. of C. (dir. 1967-69), Am. Personnel and Guidance Assn., Am. Soc. Personnel Adminstrs., Phi Delta Kappa, Sigma Phi Epsilon. Lodge: Rotary (pub. relations com. 1981-84). Home: 126 Dutchman Dr Rogers AR 72756

ROUSE, MILFORD OWEN, lay ch. worker, So. Baptist Conv.; b. Jacksonville, Tex., Aug. 10, 1902; s. William Thomas and Sallie Lee (Milford) R.; A.B., Baylor U., 1922, M.A., 1923, M.D., 1927, LL.D., 1967; m. Leaureame McDavid, July 26, 1927; 1 dau., Leaureame Anne (Mrs. Curtis L. Sawyer). Deacon 1st Bapt. Ch., Dallas, 1932-46, Lakeside Bapt. Ch., 1946-76, Wilshire Bapt. Ch., 1976—; 1st sec. Tex. Bapt. Student Union, 1918; developer missions library Lakeside Bapt. Ch., 1971, tchr. adult men's Bible class, 1946-70; bd. dirs. Bapt. Standard, 1959-68; trustee Sunday sch. bd. of So. Bapt. Conv., 1972-75; chmn. com. on medicine and religion AMA, 1962-64; speaker medicine and religion. Practicing physician, Dallas, 1928-74; clin. prof. medicine Southwestern Med. Sch., 1942—. Founder, pres. Dallas Health and Sci. Mus., 1947; pres. Greater Dallas Community Nutrition Council, 1971. Recipient Distinguished Service award Tex. Med. Assn., 1964, So. Med. Assn., 1965, citation Tex. Council Chs., 1967. Diplomate Am. Bd. Internal Medicine, Am. Bd. Gastroenterology. Life fellow A.C.P.; mem. Tex. (pres. 1956-57), So. (pres. 1958-59) med. assns., AMA (speaker ho. of dels. 1960-66, pres. 1967-68), Ex-Students Assn. Baylor U. (pres. 1942-43). Contbr. articles to profl. jours. Home: 4427 Abrams Rd Dallas TX 75214

ROWE, ALBERT PRINCE, minister, American Baptist Churches, U.S.A.; b. Columbia, S.C., Sept. 22, 1934; s. John Henry and Esther (Bowman) R.; B.A., Morgan State Coll., Balt., 1958; B.D., Crozer Theol. Sem., Chester, Pa., 1962; Th.M., Princeton Theol. Sem., 1969; D.Min., Eastern Theol. Sem., Phila., 1982; m. Dorothy Lee Collins, Aug. 1, 1964. Ordained to ministry, 1968; pastor chs. in Del. and N.J., 1960-68; pastor Calvary Bapt. Ch., Paterson, N.J., 1968—; chmn. home mission bd., 1977-80; Lectr. urban ministries N.Y. Theol. Sem., 1971. Mem. Paterson City Council, 1982—; commr. Paterson Bd. Edn., 1977-82; trustee Barnert Meml. Ctr., 1978—; active United Way of Passaic Valley, 1979—; pres. Paterson United Against Drug Abuse, 1973—; mem. Mayor's Commn. Prevention Drug Abuse, 1971—, Mayor's Council on Youth Service, 1974—; chmn. Paterson Leadership Reinforcement Com., 1974—; v.p. Paterson Sponsors for Better Housing Assns. Bd. dirs. Paterson Boys Club, Paterson YMCA, H.E.L.P. Served to 1st lt. U.S. Army, 1958. Mem. Willowbrook Ministries, The Remnant, NCAAP (life), Alpha Phi Alpha. Home: 415 19th Ave Paterson NJ 07514 Office: 575 E 18th St Paterson NJ 07514

ROWINSKI, FRANCIS C., Prime bishop Polish National Catholic Church of America, Scranton, Pa. Office: Polish Nat Cath Ch of Am 115 Lake Scranton Scranton PA 18505*

ROWLAND, DAVID RAY, minister, So. Baptist Conv.; b. Baton Rouge, Dec. 21, 1933; s. Louis Alexander and Winnie David (May) R.; B.A., Baylor U., 1956; B.D., Southwestern Bapt. Theol. Sem., 1960; m. Norma Lucille Shepard, Dec. 19, 1953; children—Brenda Lucille, Melissa Dianne. Ordained to ministry, 1957; pastor chs., Rosston, Tex., 1957-60, Bryan, Tex., 1960-63, Los Alamos, N.Mex., 1963-65, College Station, Tex., 1965—. Dist. Sunday sch. dir. Creath-Brazos Bapt. Assn.; mem. Tex. Bapt. Annuity Com. Asso. dir. United Chest College Station. Mem. Southwestern Bapt. Theol. Sem. Religious Educators Assn., Tex. Bapt. Pub. Relations Assn., Tex. A. and M. Campus Religious Workers Assn. Home: 1002 Holik College Station TX Office: 200 College Main College Station TX

ROWNEY, MARY LOUISE, nun, Roman Catholic Church; b. Kokomo, Ind., Apr. 6, 1934; d. Roy Thomas and Bertha M. (Chamberlin) R. B.A. in Theology, Marquette U., 1968; M.R.E., U. St. Thomas, Houston, 1973. Joined Our Lady of Victory Missionary Sisters, Roman Cath. Ch., 1952. Councilor/coordinator mountain area Our Lady of Victory Missionary Sisters, 1974-80, pres., Huntington, Ind., 1984—. Mem. Leadership Conf. of Women Religious.

ROY, ELMON HAROLD, minister, Seventh-day Adventist Ch.; b. Russell Springs, Ky., Dec. 17, 1924; s. Leslie Combs and Olza Myrtle (Gosser) R.; B.A., So. Missionary Coll., 1953; M.A., Belin U., 1958; Ph.D., Colo. Coll. and Sem., 1966; postgrad. Spalding Coll., Andrews U.; m. Retha Adkins, Mar. 16, 1946; children—Joel, Michael. Ordained to ministry, 1959; pastor Barberton (Ohio) Seventh-day Adventist Ch., 1956-57, East Liverpool (Ohio) Seventh-day Adventist Ch., 1957-60, Coudersport, Pa., 1960-64, St. Matthew's Seventh-day Adventist . Ch., Louisville, 1965-71; chaplain Seventh-day Adventist Hosp., Louisville, 1971-75; pastor Springfield (Ohio) Seventh-day Adventist Ch., 1975—. Pres. S. Oldham Inter-ch. Council, Louisville, 1971-72; chaplain Jefferson County Ct., Louisville, 1975, S.A.R., Louisville, 1974, 75. Named hon. citizen Tenn., 1975; Ky. col. Fellow Royal Soc. Arts; mem. Acad. Parish Clergy, Am. Acad. Religion, Acad. Adventist Ministers, Knights of Malta, Sovereign Order St. John (knight 1975). Author: Earth's Coming Events, 1968; Bible Promises, 1971; Courage for the Hospital Days, 1973; Moments of Meditation, 1975; also articles. Home: 1541 Villa Rd Springfield OH 45503 Office: PO Box 1563 Springfield OH 45501

ROY, LUCIEN, priest, Roman Catholic Church; b. St. Michel, Quebec, Can., Jan. 17, 1913; s. Louis Arthur and Eugenie Dumas. B.A., St. Marie Coll., Montreal, Can., 1925, M. Theology, 1938; D. Theology, Immaculate Conception U., Montreal, 1947. Ordained priest Roman Cath. Ch., 1948. Prof. Theology, Immaculate Conception, U., 1948-50; spiritual counselor, master retreats, tchr. Charismatic Renewal, various parishes, Montreal and Quebec, 1950-84; superior cooperator Vila Manrese Spirituality Ctr., Quebec, 1984—; asst. Renewal Charismatic Diocese of Quebec; mem. com. pastors Renewal Charismatic Can. Author books, 1948, 57, 80. Contbr. articles to profl. jours. Mem. Am. Soc. Theology. Home and Office: 2370 rue Nicolas Pinel St Foy PQ G1V 4L6 Canada

ROY, MOISE, priest, Roman Catholic Church; b. Saint-Vital de Lambton, Que., Can., Sept. 4, 1899; s. George R. D.Cn.L., Laval U., 1940. Joined Fathers of the Blessed Sacrament, 1918, ordained priest Roman Catholic Ch., 1928. Asst., Saint Jean-Baptiste Ch., N.Y., 1928-29, Notre Dame Parish, Chgo., 1929-31; prof. moral theology and canon law St. Joseph Sem., Cleve., 1931-36, Blessed Sacrament Sem., Montreal, Que., Can., 1936-51; dir. Revue Eucharistique du Clerge, Montreal, 1942-52; judge Provincial Ecclesiastical Tribunal of Montreal for Marriage Causes, 1945-52; procurator gen. to the Holy See for Cong. Blessed Sacrament, Rome, 1952-70; defender of marriage bond Ecclesiastical Tribunal, Montreal, 1970—; mem. Pontifical Com. Sacred Cong. of Sacraments for non-consummated marriages, Rome, 1954-70; mem. Pontifical Com. on Vigilance over Ecclesiastical Tribunals, 1959—; postulator for cause of beatification of Ven. Marie de l'Incarnation and Zephirin Moreau, bishop of St. Hyacinthe, Que., 1956-70. Recipient Bronze medal Lt. Gov. Que., 1940. Address: 4450 St Hubert St Montreal PQ H2J 2W9 Canada

ROY, RAYMOND, bishop, Roman Catholic Church; b. St. Boniface, Man., Can., May 3, 1919. Ordained priest, 1947, consecrated bishop, 1972; bishop of St. Paul (Alta., Can.), 1972—. Office: 4410 51st Ave Box 339 Saint Paul AB T0A 3A0 Canada*

ROYNESDAL, OLAF, minister, American Lutheran Church; b. Bklyn., Aug. 14, 1952; s. Torvald and Anne Marie (Traeland) R.; m. Marcia Ann Houck, Sept. 1, 1973; children: Emily Susan, Elizabeth Ann. B.A., Augustana Coll., 1974; M.Div., Luther Theol. Sem., 1978; postgrad. Marquette U., 1978-81. Ordained to ministry, 1981. Instr. religion Augustana Coll., Sioux Falls, S.D., 1984; pastor Bethany Luth. Ch., Viborg, S.D., 1981—. Smith fellow, Marquette U., 1981; Diet Theologican Award, Luther Theol. Sem., 1978. Mem. Am. Acad. Religion, Am. Soc. for Church History, Luther-Gesellschaft, Am. Soc. for Reformation Research. Democrat. Address: PO Box 195 Viborg SD 57070

RUBENSTEIN, RICHARD LOWELL, theologian, educator; b. N.Y.C., Jan. 8, 1924; s. Jesse George and Sara (Fine) R.; m. Betty Rogers, Aug. 21, 1966; children by previous marriage: Aaron, Nathaniel (dec.), Hannah Rachel, Jeremy. Student Hebrew Union Coll., 1942-45; A.B., U. Cin., 1946; M.H.L., Rabbi, Jewish Theol. Sem., 1952; S.T.M., Harvard Div. Sch., 1955; Ph.D., Harvard U., 1960. Rabbi, Temple Beth Emunah, Brockton, Mass. 1952-54, Temple Israel, Natick, Mass., 1954-56; chaplain Jewish students Harvard U., 1956-58, U. Pitts., 1958-70; prof. religion Fla. State U., Tallahassee, 1970-77, Robert O. Lawton disting. prof. religion, 1977—; pres. Washington Inst. for Values in Pub. Policy, 1982—; mem. editorial adv. bd. Washington Times, 1982—; sr. cons. Internat. Cultural Fedn., N.Y.C., 1982—; editorial bd. Paragon House Pubrs., 1982—; pres. Profs. World Peace Acad. Am., 1981-82. Author: After Auschwitz, 1966; The Religious Imagination, 1968 (Portico d'Ottavia Literary prize, Rome, Italy); My Brother Paul, 1972; Morality and Eros, 1970; Power Struggle, 1974; The Cunning of History, 1975; The Age of Triage, 1983. Editor: Modernization: The Humanist Response, 1982. NEH grantee, 1978; NEH fellow, 1976. Mem. Am. Acad. Religion, Soc. Bibl. Lit., Soc. for Sci. Study of Religion, Rabbinical Assembly of Am. Clubs: Governors (Tallahassee); Cosmos (Washington). Home: 751 Lake Shore Dr Tallahassee FL 32312 Office: Dept Religion Fla State Univ Tallahassee FL 32306 also Washington Inst Suite 910 1333 New Hampshire Ave NW Washington DC 20036

RUBIN, ALVAN DANIEL, rabbi; b. Roxbury, Mass., Dec. 1, 1920; s. Morris and Edith (Crockett) R.; B.S., Northeastern U., 1942; M.A., N.Y. U., 1952; M.Hebrew Lit., Hebrew Union Coll.-Jewish Inst. Religion, 1950, D.D. (hon.), 1975; m. Ruth Ann Silverman, June 19, 1949; children—David H., Amy Phyllis, Carol. Rabbi, 1950; rabbi Temple Sinai, Roslyn Heights, N.Y., 1950-67, Temple Israel, St. Louis, 1967—. Chaplain, Travelers Protective Assn., 1973; nat. chaplain AMVETS, 1972; grand chaplain Grand Lodge Mo. Masons, 1974—; cons. Jewish chaplain VA Hosp., Jefferson Barracks, Mo.; bd. govs. Hebrew Union Coll.; bd. overseers Hebrew Union Coll.; mem. Jewish Fedn. St. Louis (dir.), Jewish Welfare Bd., Nat. Commn. of Chaplaincy, 1969—. Asso. prof. St. Louis U., 1967—. Mem. Alumni Assn. Hebrew Union Coll. (past pres.). Author: Picture Dictionary of Jewish Life, 1964; Your Bar/Bat Mitzvah, 1977. Home: 512 S Meramec St Louis MO 63105 Office: Temple Israel 10675 Ladue Rd St Louis MO 63141

RUBIN, SAUL JACOB, rabbi, Reform Jewish; b. Newark, May 23, 1930; s. Hyman and Pearl R.; B.A. magna cum laude, Drew U., 1952; B.Hebrew Lit., Hebrew Union Coll., 1958, M. Hebrew Lit., 1970, D.D., 1982; m. Elsie Parsons, Dec. 20, 1959; children—Lance Hays, Stephanie Lynn. Ordained rabbi, 1958; rabbi Temple Beth Israel, Gadseden, Ala., 1958-60, Temple Beth Ahabah, Richmond, Va., 1960-72, Temple Mickve Israel, Savannah, Ga., 1972—. Bd. dirs. Savannah chpt. Nat. Conf. Christians and Jews; co-organizer Downtown Hist. Chs. Assn., Savannah, 1973; mem. nat. bicentennial commn. Union Am. Hebrew Congregations; chmn., mem. exec. bd. Havurah com. Central Conf. Am. Rabbis; officer Chatham County (Ga.) Clergy Conf.; Jewish chaplain Ft. Stewart, Ga.; state chmn. religious activities commn. Ga. Semiquincentary Com. Chmn. Minute Men, Savannah Rotary, 1975. Pres. Savannah Conf. Rabbis and Profl. Workers. Author: Third to None: The Saga of Savannah Jewry 1733-1983, 1983. Co-editor: The Religious Heritage of Savannah. Head del. of rabbis of colonial Jewish congregations that prepared bicentennial letter to Pres. Ford, delivered summer 1976. Office: 20 E Gordon St Savannah GA 31401

RUBINSTEIN, KAREN, religious organization executive, Jewish. Exec. dir. American Zionist Fedn., N.Y.C. Office: Am Zionist Fedn 515 Park Ave New York NY 10022*

RUBINSTEIN, LAURENCE HENRY, rabbi, Reform Jewish; b. N.Y.C., Mar. 1, 1940; s. Benjamin and Irene (Schwartz) R.; B.A., Columbia, 1960; B. Hebrew Lit., Hebrew Union Coll.-Jewish Inst. Religion, 1963, M.Hebrew Lit., 1965; m. Robin Spero, June 16, 1963; children—Mara, Eve. Rabbi, 1965; asst. rabbi Temple Israel, Omaha, 1965-68; asso. rabbi Reform Congregation Keneseth Israel, Elkins Park, Pa., 1968-72; rabbi Temple Shalom Lower Bucks County, Levittown, Pa., 1972-78; exec. dir. nat. young leadership cabinet United Jewish Appeal, 1978-82; dir. Fedn. Jewish Agys. of Greater Phila., 1982—; asst. prof. religion Rosemont (Pa.) Coll., 1968-78. Campaign chmn. Bucks County United Jewish Appeal, 1974-76; v.p. Jewish Fedn. Lower Bucks County, 1974-78; mem.

Phila. Bd. Rabbis, 1968—; mem. exec. com., rabbinic cabinet United Jewish Appeal. Recipient award Jewish Fedn. Lower Bucks County, 1976; Ben Gurion award Israel Bond Assn., 1976; citation United Jewish Appeal, 1982, Jewish Chautauqua Soc., 1980. Mem. Central Conf. Reform Rabbis, Phila. Assn. Reform Rabbis., Israel Exploration Soc., Am. Jewish Hist. Soc. Home: 53 Rust Hill Rd Levittown PA 19056 Office: Fedn of Jewish Agencies 226 S 16th St Philadelphia PA 19002

RUDD, JOHN WILLIAM, minister, Southern Baptist Convention; b. Winnie, Tex., May 11, 1941; s. Eddie and Veta Mae (Bales) R.; m. Sharon Lucille Bunzedahl, Jan. 25, 1964; children: John William, Jr., Robert Wayne. B.A., Baylor U., 1963; M.Div., Southwestern Bapt. Theol. Sem., 1968; D. Ministry, New Orleans Bapt. Theol. Sem., 1981. Ordained to ministry So. Bapt. Conv., 1963. Pastor, First Bapt. Ch., Midkiff, Tex., 1966-67, Buckner Boys Ranch Bapt. Ch., Burnet, Tex., 1967-69, Pond Springs Bapt. Ch., Round Rock, Tex., 1969-78, Southside Bapt. Ch., Greenville, Miss., 1978-81, Connell Bapt. Ch., Ft. Worth, Tex., 1981—. Author: God Calls Outreach Leaders, 1980. Mem. Tarrant Bapt. Pastor's Conf. (v.p. 1983—), Westside Ministerial Alliance (v.p. 1983—), Tarrant Bapt. Assn. (mem. fin. com. 1982—, chmn. BSU com. 1984—). Home: 3209 Reno Fort Worth TX 76116 Office: Connell Bapt Ch 4736 Bryce Fort Worth TX 76107

RUDISILL, ALVIN STEWART, university chaplain, religious educator, Lutheran Church in America; b. Elizabeth, N.J., Jan. 10, 1929; s. Stewart Hartman and Ethel Alice (Whitaker) R.; m. Shirley Louise Erickson, Jan. 22, 1955; children: Suzanne, Alan S.; m. Nancy Jane Westen, Dec. 30, 1977. B.A., Gettysburg Coll., 1950; M.A., U. Pa., 1953; M. Divinity, Luth. Sch. Theology, 1953; Ph.D., Drew U., 1967; postgrad. U. So. Calif., 1977-78. Ordained to ministry Luth. Ch. Am., 1954. Intern, St. Mark's Ch., Phila., 1950-51, St. Paul's Luth. Ch., Collingswood, N.J., 1951-53; guest lectr. U. So. Calif., Los Angeles, 1967-69, mem. faculty, 1969—, chaplain, 1969—, assoc. prof. religion and medicine, 1969—; campus pastor Calif. State U., Los Angeles, 1962-69; guest lectr. Sch. Religion, U. So. Calif., 1967-69; faculty advisor Campus Religious Orgns. Coordinating Council, 1979—; ch. councilman Trinity Luth. Ch., Pasadena, 1970-72, chmn. stewardship com., 1970-72, advisor, tchr. Trinity Teen Forum, 1970-72; theological cons. Sabini Small Group Project, All Sts. Episcopal Ch., Pasadena, 1972; chmn. urban ed. and intern program Luth. Ch. in Am., 1980-82, cons., 1982—; faculty advisor Campus Religious Orgns. Coordinating Council, 1979—. Author: Peace Is the Way, 1983; contbr. articles to various publs. Bd. dirs. Community Counseling Center, 1981—; mem. joint planning com. Vesper Soc. and Leiterkries of Evangelical Academies of Fed. Republic of Germany, 1981—, co-chmn., 1983-84; mem. com. for protection of human subjects, State of Calif. Dept. Health Services, 1982—; mem. infant care review com. Los Angeles County-U. So. Calif. Med. Center, 1984—; mem. bd., treas. COMMIT, the West Coast Urban Tng. Center, 1965-74; supr. Intern Project, Luth. Ch. Am. Bd. Social Missions, 1968; active Boy Scouts Am., 1970-71; bd. dirs., mem. exec. com. Los Angeles Met. Project, 1975-77; mem. Los Angeles County Health Services Task Force on Hospice, 1979-80; mem. steering com. Luth. Ch. Am. Consultation on Biothetics, 1979-80; bd. dirs. Vesper Meml. Hosp., San Leandro, Calif., 1979-84, mem. joint conf. com., 1981-84, chmn. med. care com., 1980-82, chmn. bd., 1983-84. Fulbright scholar Heidelberg Universitat, Germany, 1953-54. Mem. Am. Acad. Pediatrics (mem. chpt. com. 1983—), Vesper Soc. San Leandro (cons. health and bioethics). Democrat. Office: Office of Univ Chaplain 835 W 34th St Los Angeles CA 90089

RUDOLF, RUSSELL, minister, American Lutheran Church. B. Zeeland, N.D., July 4, 1933; s. Leopold and Frieda (Ketterling) R.; m. Jane Jeanette Buenzow, June 3, 1955; children: Thomas, Peter. B.A., Wartburg Coll.,1955; student in speech, Northwestern U., 1957; B.D., Wartburg Theol. Sem., 1960, M.Div., 1976. Intern Good Shepherd Luth. Ch., San Diego, 1958-59; pastor St. John Luth. Ch., Raymond, Minn., 1960-63; asst. pastor Bethlehem Luth. Ch., Mankato, Minn., 1963-67; sr. pastor St. John Luth. Ch., Owatonna, Minn., 1967—; leader worship services Owatonna Kampground of Am.; chaplain on call Owatonna Holiday Inn; chmn. pub. relations commn., chmn. town and country commn. sec. Am. missions com. bus. mgr. tri-dist. Lutheran standard insert com. Am. Luth. Ch. (Southwestern Minn. dist.); mem. tri-dist. Luth. standard insert com., mem. parish edn. com. mem. Mankato State Coll. Luth. students directing com., bd. dirs. Logos/Onamia (Am. Meml.) Bible Camp, mem. council, mem. task force on conflict of staff/ch. council at Grace Luth. Ch., mem. task force on staff ministries Am. Luth. Ch. (Southwestern Minn. dist.), chmn. Albert Lea Pastoral Seminar, 1970-71, chmn. Albert Lea Conf., 1976, 77. Contbr. articles to religious publs. Mem. Owatonna Exchange Club, chmn. Book Golden Deeds, 1971-72, Minnesota Jr. Miss state pagent, 1972-83, v.p., 1978-79, pres., 1979-80, past-pres., bd. dirs., 1980-81, past publicity chmn, travelogue; past bd. dirs. Owatonna Concert Assn.; baseball coach, basketball coach Owatonna City Recreation Program; mem. budget com. Steele County United Way, 1972-79; mem. safety commn. City of Owatonna, 1974-77; mem. state bd. dirs. Minnesota Jr. Miss pagent, 1980—. Mem. Owatonna C. of C. (formerly active). Home and Office: St John Luth Ch 1301 Lincoln Ave Owatonna MN 55060

RUEF, JOHN SAMUEL, religion educator; Episcopal Church; b. Chgo., Jan. 24, 1927; s. John E. and Leota Alice (Rice) R.; m. Jane Margraves Hort; children: Marcus, Adam, Seth, Sarah. A.B., U. Chgo., 1947; B.D., Seabury-Western Sem., 1950, S.T.M., 1956, S.T.D., 1976; Th.D., Harvard U., 1960. Ordained to ministry Episcopal Ch., 1950. Prof., Berkeley Divinity, New Haven, 1960-71; dean Nashotah House, Wis., 1974-84, prof., 1984-85; chaplain, tchr. religion Chatham Hall, Va., 1985—. Author: Understanding the Gospels, 1967; The Gospels and the Teaching of Jesus, 1967; First Letter of Paul to Corinth, 1971. Fellow Ch. Soc. for Coll. Work, 1958, St. John's Parish, Washington, 1968. Mem. Soc. Bibl. Lit. Office: Chatham Hall Chatham VA 24531

RUETHER, ROSEMARY RADFORD, educator; b. St. Paul, Nov. 2, 1936; d. Robert Armstrong and Rebecca Cresap (Ord) Radford; B.A., Scripps Coll., 1958; M.A., Claremont Grad. Sch., 1960, Ph.D., 1965; m. Herman J. Ruether, Aug. 31, 1957; children—Rebecca, David, Mary Elizabeth. Prof. theology and ch. history Howard U., 1966—; lectr. Roman Cath. studies Harvard Div. Sch., 1972-73, Princeton Theol. Sem., Yale Div. Sch., 1973-74; Georgia Harkness prof. Garrett-Evang. Theol. Sem., Evanston, Ill., 1976—; editorial bd. Christianity and Crisis, Ecumenist. Fellow Soc. Religion in Higher Edn., Soc. Arts, Religion and Culture; mem. Am. Theol. Soc. Author: Faith and Fratricide, 1974; The Radical Kingdom, 1970; The Liberating Bond, 1978; Women of Spirit, 1979; On Being a Christian, 1982; Sexism and God Talk, 1983; many others. Contbr. articles to religious jours. Office: Garrett-Evang Theol Sem Evanston IL 60202

RUFFCORN, KEVIN EDWARD, minister, American Lutheran Ch. B. Mpls., Aug. 19, 1951; s. William Edward and Evelyn (Baldwyn) R.; m. Faye Ann Iverson, Apr. 28, 1972; children: Shane Edward, Ryan Edward. B.A. in Speech and History, Concordia Coll., 1973; M.Div., Luther/Northwestern Sem., 1979. Ordained to ministry Lutheran Ch., 1979. Pastoral asst. Hope Luth. Ch., Mpls., 1974-76; chaplain High Plains Baptist Hosp., Amarillo, Tex., 1977-78; pastor Peace Luth. Ch., Dunseith, N.D., 1979-82, Grace Luth. Ch., East Dubuque, Ill., 1982—; parish evangelist Am. Luth. Ch., Mpls., 1980—; mem. com. Dist. Div. for Service Mission in Am., Hoffman Estates, Ill., 1981—; chpt. pres. N.D., Acad. Parish Clergy, Minot, 1981-82. Author: Share the Word, 1982, Bible Readings for Growing Christians, 1984. Contbr. articles to religious publs. Luth. Brotherhood scholar, 1972. Lodges: Lions, Optimist. Home: 214 Park Lane Dr East Dubuque IL 61025 Office: Grace Luth Ch 1775 Route 35 N East Dubuque IL 61025

RUFFIN, CAULBERT BERNARD, III, minister, Lutheran Church America; b. Washington, Nov. 22, 1947; s. Caulbert Bernard and Lillian Rebecca (Jones) R.; A.B., Bowdoin Coll., 1969; M.Div., Yale, 1972. Ordained to ministry, 1974; parish assoc. Trinity Luth. Ch., New Haven, 1969-70; deacon Zion Evang. Luth. Ch., Luth. Ch.—Mo. Synod, New Haven, 1970-72; intern pastor Sugar Valley Luth. Parish, Longanton, Booneville, Salona (all Pa.), 1972-73; pastor Gloria Dei Evang. Luth. Ch., Alexandria, Va., 1974-76; asst. pastor Luth. Ch. of Holy Comforter, Washington, 1976—; tchr. social studies South Lakes High Sch., Reston, Va., 1982—. Bd. dirs. Capital Lutheran High Sch., 1979-82; mem. exec. bd. Hymn Soc. of Am., 1980-82. Mem. Alexandria Clergy Assn., Phi Beta Kappa. Author: Fanny Crosby, 1976; Padra Pio: The True Story, 1982; The Twelve: The Apostles after Calvary, 1984; The Days of the Martyrs, 1985. Home: 767 N Van Dorn St Alexandria VA 22304

RUHL, WILLIAM JOSEPH, priest, religious educator, Roman Catholic Church; b. Phila., Apr. 19, 1935; s. William Joseph and Helen Rita (Weber) R. B.S., Niagara U., 1959; S.T.L., Cath. U. Am., 1968, S.T.D., 1971. Ordained priest Roman Catholic Ch. Vice pres. Cluster Ind. Theol. Schs., Washington, 1984—; pres. DeSales Sch. Theology, Washington, 1976—. Mem. Am. Acad. Religion, Nat. Cath. Ednl. Assn., Cath. Theol. Soc. Am. Democrat. Office: Desales Hall Sch Theology 721 Lawrence St NE Washington DC 20017

RUMSCHEIDT, MARTIN, educator, minister, United Church Canada; b. Leuna, Germany, July 24, 1935; s. Carl Friedrich and Edith Marie (Oeckinghaus) R.; came to Can., 1952, naturalized, 1957; B.A., McGill U., 1958, B.D., 1961, S.T.M., 1963, Ph.D., 1967; m. Barbara Lawrence Guild, Dec. 28, 1962; children—Peter, Robert, Heidi. Ordained to ministry United Ch. of Can., 1961; minister chs., Montreal, Que., Can., 1962-65, Enterprise, Ont., Can., 1965-67; asst. minister Deer Park United Ch., Toronto, Ont., 1967-70; prof. hist. theology U. Windsor (Ont.), 1970-75; prof. systematic theology Atlantic Sch. Theology, Halifax, N.S., 1975—. Sec., Canadian Theol. Soc., 1968-70, pres., 1972-73. Mem. Am. Acad. Religion, Canadian Soc. for Study Religion, Karl Barth Soc. N.Am. Author: Revelation and Theology-An Analysis of the Barth Harnack Correspondence of 1923, 1972. Editor: Fragments Grave and Gay (Karl Barth), 1971; Footnotes to a Theology-The Karl Barth Colloquium of 1972, 1974; Karl Barth in Re-View: Posthumous Works Reviewed and Assessed, 1981; The Way of Theology in Karl Barth-Essays and Comments, 1985; translator: The Theology of Dietrich Bonhoeffer, 1985. Home: 600 Francklyn St Halifax NS B3H 3B4 Canada

RUNION, CLYDE LESLIE, minister, So. Baptist Conv.,; b. Great Falls, S.C., Aug. 11, 1930; s. Thomas William and Emma Lillian (Lineberger) R.; B.A., Furman U., 1957; B.D., Southeastern Bapt. Theol. Sem., 1960; m. Peggy Lee Killian, July 16, 1950; children—Thomas Martin, Michael Munn. Ordained to ministry, 1957; pastor Wampee Bapt. Ch., N. Myrtle Beach, S.C., 1957-59, Pleasant Dale Bapt. Ch., Lancaster, S.C., 1959-62, Wateree Bapt. Ch., Camden, S.C., 1962-67, 2d Bapt. Ch., Lancaster, 1967—. Moderator Kershaw Bapt. Assn., 1963-64, vice moderator, 1965-66, chmn. evangelism, 1967; mem. Camden (S.C.) Youth Baseball Commn., 1964-67; chmn. evangelism Morah Bapt. Assn., 1972-76, vice-moderator, 1975-76; pres. Morah Bapt. Pastors Conf., 1975-76; pres. Elliott White Springs Meml. Hosp. Clergy Staff, 1975-76. Pres. Lancaster United Way, 1976; bd. dirs. ARC; dir. Lancaster County Council on Aging, 1975-76; dir. Catawba Health Dist., 1974-76. Mem. Greater Lancaster Ministerial Assn. Contbr. articles to religious jours. Home: 122 Springdale Rd Lancaster SC 29720 Office: 29 Brooklyn Ave Lancaster SC 29720

RUNNELS, ALVIN EUGENE, minister, Southern Baptist Convention; b. Kirksville, Mo., Jan. 20, 1939; s. Alvin Lester and Florence (Hays) Runnels Mock; m. Donna Jeanette Doner, May 25, 1957; children: Mark, Jeffrey. A.A., Hannibal LaGrange Coll., 1960; B.A., S.E. Mo. State U., 1965; M.Div., Midwestern Bapt. Theol. Sem., 1970. Ordained to ministry Southern Baptist Conv., 1961. Pastor, Mt. Zion Bapt. Ch., Edgerton, Mo., 1968-71, Necker Valley Bapt. Ch., Sindelfingen, W. Ger., 1971-74, Southside Bapt. Ch., Charlston, Mo., 1965-67, 74-75, Anne Heights Bapt. Ch., Anne, Ill., 1976-78, Linden Bapt. Ch., Kansas City, Mo., 1978-85, Mountain View Bapt. Ch., Phoenix, 1985—. Vice pres. European Bapt. Conv., W. Ger., 1972-73. Home: 13833 N 22d St Phoenix AZ 85022 Office: Mountain View Bapt Ch 4233 N 40th St Phoenix AZ 85018

RUNNELS, ROBERT, JR., religious organization executive, Roman Catholic Church; b. Houston, Aug. 26, 1925; s. Robert and Mellie Bridget (Nonus) R.; m. Billie Van Houten, Mar. 1, 1947; children: Robert III, Lucia Lee, Rebecca, Deborah Ann, Elizabeth Angelica, Janice Mary, Martha Susan. B.B.A., U. Houston, 1949. Exec. dir. Kans. Cath. Conf., Kansas City, 1982—. Pres. Heart of Am. Scout Council, Boy Scouts Am., East Kans., West Mo., 1973, Johnson County United Way, Kans., 1973, Serra Club, Kansas City, 1974; dist. gov. Serra Found., 1980. Served as cadet USAAF, 1943-45. Recipient Silver Beaver award Boy Scouts Am., 1972; Vigil Honors Order of the Arrow, 1971; Silver Bow award Kaw Council, 1969; decorated Order of Holy Sepulcher, 1984—, St. George Cath. Com. on Scouting Nat., 1972-84. Republican. Clubs: Leawood Country (Kans.); Learned (Lawrence, Kans.); Advt. (v.p., treas. 1960-72). Lodge: K.C. Home: 8900 Mohawk Rd Leawood KS 66206

RUPP, GEORGE ERIK, educator, minister, Presbyn. Ch. in the U.S.; b. Summit, N.J., Sept. 22, 1942; s. Gustav Wilhelm and Erika (Braunoehler) R.; A.B., Princeton U., 1964; student Ludwig Maximilians U., Munich, Germany, 1962-63; B.D., Yale U., 1967; postgrad. U. Ceylon, Peradeniya, 1969-70; Ph.D., Harvard U., 1972; m. Nancy Katherine Farrar, Aug. 22, 1964; children—Katherine Heather, Stephanie Karin. Ordained to ministry Presbyn. Ch. in U.S., 1971; faculty fellow religion, vice chancellor Johnston Coll., U. Redlands, Calif., 1971-74; asst. prof. Harvard Div. Sch., Cambridge, Mass., 1974-76, assoc. prof., 1976-77; dean for acad. affairs and prof. humanistic studies U. Wis., Green Bay, 1977-79; dean, John Lord O'Brian prof. divinity Harvard Divinity Sch., 1979-85; pres., prof. religious studies Rich U., Houston, 1985—. Danforth Grad. fellow, 1964-71. Mem. Soc. for Religion in Higher Edn., Am. Acad. Religion. Author: Christologies and Cultures: Toward a Typology of Religious Worldviews, 1974; Culture-Protestantism: German Liberal Theology at the Turn of the 20th Century, 1977; Beyond Existentialism and Zen: Religion in a Pluralistic World, 1979. Contbr. articles to profl. jours. Home: President's Home Rice Univ Houston TX 77251

RUSACK, ROBERT CLAFLIN, bishop, Episcopal Ch.; b. Worcester, Mass., June 16, 1926; s. Roy Leonard and Dorothy Rathbun (Claflin) R.; B.A., Hobart Coll., 1946, D.D., 1967; postgrad. Gen. Theol. Sem., 1951, S.T.D., 1965; m. Janice Morrison Overfield, June 26, 1951; children: Rebecca Morrison, Geoffrey Claflin. Ordained deacon, 1951, priest, 1951, consecrated bishop, 1964; rector St. James Ch., Deer Lodge, Mont., 1951-57; priest-fellow St. Augustine's Coll., Canterbury, Eng., 1957-58; rector St.

Augustine-by-the-Sea Parish, Santa Monica, Calif., 1958-64; suffragan bishop of Los Angeles, 1964-72, bishop coadjutor, 1972-73, bishop, 1974—. Chmn. bd. Good Samaritan Hosp.; chmn. bd. trustees Gen. Theol. Sem., N.Y.C. Office: 1220 W 4th St Los Angeles CA 90051

RUSH, JAMES EDWARD, minister, religion educator, United Methodist Church; b. Oskaloosa, Iowa, Jan. 2, 1941; s. Harold Madison and Thelma Irene (Lewers). B.S. in Biology and Chemistry, Geneva Coll., 1963; M.Div., Crozer Theol. Sem., 1968; Ph.D., Hartford Sem. Found., 1975. Ordained elder United Methodist Ch., 1971. Chaplain, Meth. Home for Children, Phila., 1967-68; assoc. pastor Grace United Meth. Ch., Newburgh, N.Y., 1968-70; pastor United Meth. Ch., East Berlin, Conn., 1970-72, Morrilton Parish, United Meth. Ch. (Ark.), 1982—; chmn. div. humanities Philander Smith Coll., 1984, chmn. dept. philosophy and religion, 1976—; asst. prof. div. med. humanities Ark. Sch. Medicine, Little Rock, 1983—; mem. com. on religion and race United Meth. Ch., Little Rock, 1984. Author: Toward a General Theory of Healing, 1981. Contbr. articles to religious jours. Mem. biomed. ethics com. Ark. Children's Hosp., Little Rock, 1984; trustee Raphealite I Inst., Laicester, N.C., 1984. Grantee Phelps-Stokes Found., 1978. Mem. Soc. Health and Human Values, Assn. Faculty in Med. Humanities, Am. Soc. Law and Medicine. Democrat. Office: Philander Smith Coll 813 W 13th St Little Rock AR 72203

RUSSEL, R. ALAN, minister, theology educator; Church of God (Anderson, Ind.); b. McKeesport, Pa., Sept. 3, 1926; s. Richard Alan and Sarah Mary (Saunders) R.; m. Lottie Klinger, June 27, 1961; 1 child, Lottie Jane. B.Th., Hamilton State U., 1958; M.Bible, Kingdom Bible Inst., Dallas, 1960; D.D. (hon.), Bethany Bible Sem., Dothan, Ala., 1982. Ordained to ministry Ch. of God (Anderson, Ind.), 1959. Asst. to rescue missions in ghetto, Phila., 1958-76; tchr., leader various Christian edn. confs., 1976—; chmn. bd. of evangelism Gen. Assembly of Ch. of God in East, 1977—, bd. of ch. extension, 1977—; budget dir. Kingdom Builders, Boyertown, Pa., 1977—; bd. dirs. Montgomery County Sunday Sch. Assn., Worcester, Pa., 1975—. Served to maj. AUS, 1943-52, PTO. Recipient Service Recognition award Internat. Bible Inst. and Sem., 1984. Mem. United Assn. of Christian Counselors, Assocs. for Bibl. Research. Republican. Home and Office: Christian Growth Ministries 869 Andover Rd Lansdale PA 19446

RUSSELL, CHARLES EDWARD, minister of edn., So. Bapt. Conv.; b. Wilmington, Ohio, Sept. 30, 1949; s. Edward E. and Anna Lee (Vance) R.; B.A. in Christian Edn., Bryan Coll., 1972; m. Darlene Lynn Cook, Aug. 22, 1971; children—Bronlyn Kaye, Corryn Ann. Ordained to ministry, 1976; supr. Grace Christian Acad., Bible Bapt. Ch., Fort Pierce, Fla., 1972-74; minister of edn. and music Northside Bapt. Ch., Fort Pierce, Fla., 1974—. Mem. Fla. Bapt. Religious Edn. Assn., Fla. Bapt. Ch. Music Conf., Evang. Tchr. Tng. Assn. Home and Office: Route 5 Box 107 Fort Pierce FL 33450

RUSSELL, GARY EUGENE, minister, Seventh-day Adventists; b. Detroit, Feb. 10, 1950; s. Billy Eugene Russell and Betty Mae (Harden) Russell Berzley; m. Diane L. Rendel, Aug. 9, 1970; children: Chad M., Kurt L., Tara N. B.A. in theology, Andrews U., 1972, M.Div., 1974; M.P.H., Loma Linda U., 1981. Ordained to ministry, Seventh-day Adventists, 1979. Assoc. pastor Fla. Conf. Seventh-day Adventists, Winter Park, 1975-77, pastor, Okeechobee,1977-79, Vero Beach, 1977-81; pastor Mich. Conf. Seventh-day Adventists, Boyne City, 1981-; Sec.-treas. Okeechobee Ministerial Assn., 1979; dir. Adventist Health Edn. Services, Boyne City, 1981-84; Traverse City; Mich., 1985—. Participant, Charlevoix Area Hosp. Health Fair, Mich., 1982-83. Recipient Service award Mich. Conf. Seventh-day Adventists Community Services, 1984. Mem. Boyne City Ministerial Assn. (sec.-treas. 1983, pres. 1984), Charlevoix County Ministerial Assn. (treas. 1984). Home: 1496 Healey Rd Boyne City MI 49712 Office: Traverse City Seventh-day Adventist 442 W 7th St Traverse City MI 49684

RUSSELL, JAMES SHEPHERD, JR., minister, Presbyterian Ch. in U.S.; b. Petersburg, Va., July 26, 1930; s. James Shepherd and Elizabeth Patterson (Bragg) R.; B.A., Hampden-Sydney Coll., 1951; M.Div., Union Theol. Sem., Richmond, Va., 1954; m. Jean Bernard Feild, June 12, 1952; children—James Shepherd, III, Margaret Bolling, Daniel Lindsay, Theophilus Feild. Ordained to ministry, 1954; pastor Lake Waccamaw and White Plains Presbyn. chs., Lake Waccamaw, N.C., 1954-59; Kingston Presbyn. Ch., Conway, S.C., 1959-64, 1st Presbyn. Ch., Albemarle, N.C., 1964-71, Ft. Smith, Ark., 1971—. Moderator Wilmington Presbytery, 1956, Pee Dee Presbytery, 1963, Mecklenburg Presbytery, 1970; pres. Stanly County Ministerial Assn., Albemarle, N.C., 1967, Ft. Smith Ministerial Assn., 1972-73; pres. Union Theol. Sem. Alumni Assn., 1972-73. Named Sr. Man of Year of Stanly County Albemarle Jaycees, 1966. Home: 3400 S Cliff Dr Fort Smith AR 72901 Office: 116 N 12th St Fort Smith AR 72901

RUSSELL, JOHN See *Who's Who in America*, 43rd edition.

RUSSELL, JOHN DOUGLAS, minister, Luth. Ch. Am.; b. Glendale, Calif., Dec. 21, 1937; s. Harry Edward and Hazel Alvina (Hilligoss) R.; B.A. Midland Luth. Theol. Sem., 1959; B.D., Pacific Luth. Theol. Sem., 1963, M.Div., 1963; m. Colleen Faye Bonderson, June 3, 1959; children—Martin, Matthew, Kathleen. Ordained to ministry, 1963; pastor, developer Faith Luth. Ch., San Jose, Calif., 1963-68; pastor Calvary Luth. Ch., San Diego, 1968-72, Grace Luth. Ch., Culver City, Calif., 1972—; dean San Diego dist., 1971-72; dir. Luth. Assn. for Retarded Children, 1969-73, v.p. 1973; dean central dist. Pacific S.W. Synod, 1973-75; dir. Luth. Social Services So. Calif., 1970—, pres. 1973—; coordinator evangelism outreach emphasis Luth. Ch. Am., 1976—; Luth. Ch. Am. rep on Luth. Council U.S. Region 16, 1971—, chmn. 1974—. Mem. supts. clergy adv. com. Los Angeles City Schs., 1973-76. Home: 4279 LeBoorget Culver City CA 90230 Office: 4427 Overland Ave Culver City CA 90230

RUSSELL, JOHN JOSEPH, JR., lay worker, book store employee, Baptist General Conference; b. Wilmington, Del., Mar. 27, 1957; s. John Joseph and Mary Jane (Schofield) R. Lay vol. staff Campus Crusade for Christ, Wilmington, Del., 1983—; shipping clk. Puritan Reformed Discount Book Service, Wilmington, Del., 1981—. Home: 2350 Overlook Dr Naamans Manor Wilmington DE 19810

RUSSELL, RONALD LEE, minister, Southern Baptist Convention; b. Mt. Gilead, N.C., June 11, 1947; s. Leroy and Mary Anna (Hines) R.; m. Judy Carol Hudson, Aug. 17, 1968; children: Jennifer Leigh, David Alexander. A.A., Wingate Coll., 1967; B.S., U. N.C., 1969; M.Div., Southeastern Bapt. Sem., 1975; D.Min., So. Bapt. Sem., 1985. Ordained to ministry Bapt. Ch., 1974. Pastor, Mission Bapt. Ch., Stanfield, N.C., 1974—; trustee Christian Action League, N.C., 1983—; revival and conf. speaker N.C. chs.; leader Smith/Russell Holy land Tours, 1980-84, study team mem. So. Bapt./Anti-Defamation League Holy Land Tour, 1982. Mem. adv. council Health Screening Clinic, Albemarle, N.C., 1978-80, Ridgecrest Sch., Stanfield, N.C., 1979-82. Mem. Bapt. Minister's Conf. (pres. 1981), Stanly Bapt. Assn., Stanly County Ministerial Assn. (pres. 1978). Home: 12729 Barrier Store Rd Stanfield NC 28163 Office: Mission Bapt Ch Rt 1 Stanfield NC 28163

RUSSELL, ROY GLEN, minister, Advent Christian Ch.; b. Charleston, W.Va., Nov. 14, 1938; s. Kenneth Bartley and Hettie Frances (Price) R.; student Mason Coll. Sch. Music, 1950, W.Va. State Coll., 1956, W.Va. Inst. Tech., 1976—; m. Sandra Sue Farrell, Dec. 17, 1960; children—Wayne Roy, Glenna Sue. Ordained to ministry, 1969 pastor Otto Advent Christian Ch., 1966-68, Mt. Welcome Union Ch., 1968-70, Coopers Creek Advent Christian Ch., Charleston, 1970—. Pianist, Blue Creek Advent Christian Ch., 1954-57, Sunday Sch. tchr., 1954—; bd. mem. Advent Christian Regional Youth Fellowship, 1955-62; pres. State Youth Fellowship, 1955-62; mem. bd. State Advent Christian Conf., 1959-68; sr. worker, mem. bd. Local Contact Teleministries, U.S.A., 1973—. Instr. automotive counter parts in vocat. edn. Kanawha County Bd. Edn., 1975. Named Conservation Minister of Capitol Soil Conservation Dist. of Kanawha County, 1972, 73. Home: PO Box 163 Church Rd Pinch WV 25156

RUSSELL, STANLEY GORDON, minister, United Ch. Christ; b. Medford, Mass., Feb. 5, 1932; s. Stanley Gordon and Anna Elizabeth (Glynn) R.; Mus.B., Boston U., 1956; M.Div., Andover Newton Theol. Sem., 1965; m. Sally Ann Cobb, Nov. 23, 1958; children—Judith, Ann. Ordained to ministry, 1965; minister music, asst. minister United Ch. Christ, Walpole, Mass., 1957-66; pres. New Eng. Choir Dirs. Guild, Boston, 1958-60; pastor Central Congl. Ch., Orange, Mass., 1966-70; pastor Tabernacle Ch., Salem, Mass., 1970-73, Meml. Congl. Ch., Sudbury, Mass., 1973—. Pres., Orange Ministerial Assn., 1967-70; chmn. Western Area Study Com., 1970; mem. program devel. com. Mass. Conf., 1974, chmn. ch. and leadership com., 1976; convenor Sudbury Clergy Group, 1975-76; bd. dirs. Mass. Conv. Congl. Ministers, 1975—; guest lectr. theology and social issues Claflin Coll., Orangeburg, S.C., 1968, Defiance (Ohio) Coll., 1970. Mem. Gardner Area (Mass.) Bd. Mental Health, 1968; bd. dirs. Essex County (Mass.) Community Concert Assn., 1971-73, Framingham (Mass.) Community Concert Assn., 1973-76; mem. youth study com. Town of Sudbury, 1974. Recipient Bell Ringer award Outstanding Citizenship, Orange, 1967; Service to Elderly award Salem Council Aging, 1973. Founder, United Youth Ministry, Orange, 1967. Office: Memorial Congl Ch Church St Sudbury MA 01776

RUSSELL, WILLIAM JAMES, minister, Southern Baptist Convention; b. Tulsa, May 8, 1945; s. Wilson Arthur and Vesta Beula (Smith) R.; m. Betty Sue Gandy, Nov. 22, 1963; children: Jamie Suzanne, Rebecca Michelle, David William. B.A., Dallas Bapt. Coll., 1974; postgrad. Southwestern Bapt. Theol. Sem., Ft. Worth, 1974, 75, 82. Ordained to ministry So. Bapt. Conv., 1968. Pastor, Limestone Bapt. Ch., Sand Springs, Okla., 1969-71, Hillburn Dr. Bapt. Ch., Dallas, 1973-74, Ardis Heights Bapt. Ch., Greenville, Tex., 1974-76, Liberty So. Bapt. Ch., Enid, Okla., 1976—. Pres., Cleveland Sch. PTA, Enid, 1978-80; chmn. Republican Precinct Com., Greenville, 1974. Recipient Youth Service award YMCA, Enid, 1978. Mem. Perry Bapt. Assn. (chmn. evangelism com.). Home: 1628 S Jackson St Enid OK 73701 Office: Liberty So Bapt Ch 1616 S Jackson St PO Box 725 Enid OK 72702

RUSSELL, WILLIAM R., clergyman, gen. sec. Can. Bible Soc., Toronto, Ont. Office: 10 Carnforth Rd Toronto ON M4A 2S4 Canada*

RUSSO, ROBERT JOSEPH, minister, Baptist Bible Fellowship; b. Bainbridge, Md., Sept. 4, 1955; s. Anthony Henry and Frances (Haithcock) R.; m. Lesa Lynn Starkes, Nov. 21, 1980. B.A., Baptist Bible Coll., Springfield, Mo., 1978. Ordained to ministry Bapt. Ch. Interim pastor Brean Bapt. Ch., St. Augustine, Fla., 1978; assoc. pastor St. Augustine Bapt. Ch., Fla., 1979-80, Bethel Bapt. Ch., Melbourne, Fla., 1980; minister edn. Jupiter Rd. Bapt. Ch., Garland, Tex., 1981-84, assoc. pastor, 1984—; with contacted mgmt. Verandah Club, Dallas, 1985—; dir. Youth Camp, Lone Star, Tex., 1984; vol. in numerous activities. Editor: (yr. book) Sojourner, 1978. Bapt. Bible Coll. Journalism scholar, 1978. Avocations: reading; music; racquet sports; golf; photography; fine arts. Home: 3305 S Glenbrook Garland TX 75041 Office: Jupiter Rd Bapt Ch 2422 N Jupiter Garland TX 75042

RUSSO, STEPHEN RICHARD, evangelist, Baptist General Conference; b. San Jose, Calif., Mar. 27, 1953; s. Paul Richard Russo and Pauline Mae (Rodoni) Russo Zolnak; m. Tamera Ann McKee, June 10, 1978. B.A., Biola U., 1979; M.A., Talbot Sem., 1980. Ordained to ministry Baptist Ch., 1979. Mem. program staff Hume Lake Christian Camps, Hume, Calif., 1977—, conf. speaker, 1980—; youth pastor Eagle Rock Bapt. Ch., Los Angeles, 1977-80; campus life area dir. Youth for Christ, Covina, Calif., 1980-82, Anaheim, Calif., 1982-84; founder, pres. Steve Russo Evangelistic Team, Ontario, Calif., 1984—; mem. youth task force Southwest Bapt. Conf., West Covina, Calif., 1980—, mem. Christian edn. bd., 1983-86; mem. nat. youth task force Bapt. Gen. Conf., 1983-84; del., participant Amsterdam '83, The Netherlands, 1983; nat. youth cons.; gospel musician. Author gospel tract: Fear, 1985. Named one of Outstanding Young Men Am., U.S. Jaycees, 1981. Mem. Nat. Assn. Evang. Tchrs. (diploma 1979). Home: 2057 Evergreen St La Verne CA 91750 Office: Steve Russo Evangelistic Team PO Box 1549 Ontario CA 91762

RUST, MALCOLM CYRIL, minister, Baptist Conv. Ont. and Que.; b. Felixstowe, Suffolk, Eng., Apr. 13, 1938; s. Cyril Frank and Margaret Aileen (Jacobs) R.; came to Can., 1968; diploma theology U. London (Eng.), 1960; m. Marjorie Fillingham, July 16, 1960; children—Andrew Thomas, Martin David. Ordained to ministry, 1961; minister Broadway Bapt. Ch., Douglas, Isle of Man, U.K., 1961-64, Thame Bapt. Ch., Oxfordshire, Eng., 1964-68, Clyde Ave. Bapt. Ch., Sydney Mines, N.S., Can., 1968-70, Woodbine Heights Bapt. Ch., Toronto, Ont., Can., 1970—. Vice moderator Toronto Assn. Bapt. Chs., 1976—; sessional lectr. Ont. Bible Coll., Toronto, 1975-76. Home: 55 Southwood Dr Toronto ON M4E 2T8 Canada Office: 1171 Woodbine Ave Toronto ON M4C 4E1 Canada

RUSTED, EDWARD CHARLES WILLIAM, priest, Anglican Church of Canada; b. Upper Island Cove, Nfld., Can., Jan. 20, 1919; s. Ernest Edward and Faith Amy Margaret (Hollands) R.; m. Marjorie Shuk-Fun Chan, Apr. 6, 1961; 1 child, Anthea Patricia. B.A., U. Durham, Eng., 1941, M.A., 1944; L.Th., Warminster Missionary Coll., Eng., 1940; postgrad. cert. edn. U. London, 1955. Ordained deacon, 1942, priest, 1943. Curate St. Gabrield's, Bounds Green, London, 1942-44, St. Mark's, London, 1947-50; prin. All Saints Mission Sch., Sabah, Malaysia, 1950-68; vicar St. Oswald's, Norbury, London, 1968-77; dean, rector Cathedral of St. John Bapt., St. John's, Nfld., 1977—; hon. chaplain Royal Can. Legion I, Booth Meml. High Sch., Boy Scouts Assn., St. John's, Nfld., 1979—; chmn. pastoral care com. Gen. Hosp., St. John's, 1982—. Editor: The Fulfillment of the Law, 1949; the Sabah Story, 1956. Served as chaplain Royal Navy, 1944-47. Chmn. trustees English campus Meml. U. Nfld., Harlow, Eng., 1974-77. Decorated comdr. Order Brit. Empire, 1960; named canon emeritus and Episcopal commissary Diocese of Sabah, Malaysia, 1968. Mem. Sergeants' Mess of Nfld. (life), Royal Naval Assn. Nfld. (life). Home: 22 Church Hill St John's NF A1C 3Z9 Canada

RUSU, GEORGE NICHOLAS, priest, Romanian Byzantine Rite Catholic Ch.; b. Vilcan, Romania, May 17, 1917; s. Nicholas and Maria (Bogdan) R.; came to U.S., 1954, naturalized, 1972; S.T.D., Propaganda Fide, Rome, 1943; Ph.D., Angelicum, Rome, 1949. Ordained priest, 1941; speaker for Romania, Vatican Radio, 1949-50; chaplain Romanian community in Buenos Aires, 1950-54; pastor St. Mary Ch., McKeesport, Pa., 1954—; mem. faculty Cath. U. Buenos Aires, 1950-54, Maj. Sem. Buenos Aires, 1950-54, Byzantine Rite Cath. Sem., Pitts., 1955-65, La Roche Coll., Pitts., 1965, Canevin Cath. High Sch., Pitts., 1971-74. Author numerous articles. Editor, pub. Curierul Crestin, Buenos Aires, 1951-54; editor Unirea, U.S.A., 1955-59. Home: 2900 Noblestown Rd Pittsburg PA 15205 Office: 318 26th St McKeesport PA 15132

RUTH, DONALD WILLIAM, minister, Presbyterian Church (U.S.A.); b. Solsberry, Ind., Sept. 12, 1918; s. Harry William and Leona (Bridges) R.; A.B., Ind. U., 1941; B.D., Princeton, 1944; D.D., Waynesburg Coll., 1949; m. Mary Elizabeth Braden, May 24, 1942; children—William, Susan, Catharine. Ordained to ministry, 1944; minister 1st Presbyn. Ch., Jamaica, N.Y., 1944-55, Muskogee, Okla., 1955-69, Yale Ave. Presbyn. Ch., Tulsa, 1969—; moderator Bklyn.-Nassau Presbytery, 1955, East Ark. Valley Presbytery, 1965. Co-founder, Muskogee Guidance Clinic, 1960. Mem. Acad. Parish Clergy, Assn. Mental Health Clergy, Presbyn. Hist. Soc., Okla. Hist. Soc., Am. Schs. Oriental Research (assoc.), Cath. Bibl. Assn., Soc. Bibl. Lit., Israel Exploration Soc. Author: The First Presbyterian Sunday School in America, 1944; Ten Years on Broadway, 1965; The Story of Sally Brown, 1966; Living in a Supermarket World, 1967; People of the Way, 1976; also articles. Home: 520 S Allegheny Rd Tulsa OK 74112 Office: 510 S Yale St Tulsa OK 74112

RUTH, HOWARD HUNTER, minister, American Baptist Churches in the U.S.A.; b. Phila., Oct. 13, 1919; s. Charles Louis and Isabel (Hunter) R.; m. Mildred June Gerbron, May 19, 1945; children: Janice Ruth Fullerton, Paul Howard. B.A., Eastern Bapt. Theol. Sem., 1952, Th.B., 1952, M.Div., 1979. Ordained to ministry Am. Bapt. Chs. U.S.A., 1952. Pastor, Calvary Bapt. Ch., Franklin, Pa., 1952-56; dir. Seneca Hills Bible Conf., Franklin, Pa., 1953-56; pastor First Bapt. Ch., Berwick, Pa., 1956-63; sr. pastor Goshen Bapt. Ch., West Chester, Pa., 1963-85; pres. Pa. Bapt. Ministers, 1970-72. Served with U.S. Army, 1942-46. Mem. Eastern Bapt. Sem. Alumni Assn. (pres. 1976-78). Lodge: Lions. (asst. sec. 1971—). Home and Office: 523 Merioneth Dr Exton PA 19341

RUTH, RONALD ANDREW, priest, Roman Catholic Church. B. Newark, Nov. 22, 1942; s. Franklin Andrew and Stella Rose (Hanas) R. B.A. in Philosophy, Mount St. Mary's Coll,, 1966; M.A. in Theol., Mount St. Mary's Sem., 1970. Ordained priest, Roman Cath. Ch., 1970. Assoc. pastor Queen of Apostles Ch., Alexander, Va., 1970-72; vocations dir. Cath. Diocese of Richmond, Va., 1972-77; pastor Sacred Heart Ch., South Richmond, Va., 1977-82; Saint Pius X, Norfolk, Va., 1982—. Democrat. Lodge: K.C. (chaplain 1972-73, statewide asst. chaplain 1974-75). Home and Office: St Pius X Ch 7800 Halprin Dr Norfolk VA 23518

RUTTER, CHARLES ALBERT, minister, United Pentecostal Church International; b. Beecher, Ont., Can., Nov. 20, 1945; s. Charles Joseph and Emma Grace (Rabbie) R.; m. Janice Louise Cooling, May 13, 1967; children: Vicki Lynne, Charlene Grace. Student Prince Edward Coll., 1960-64. Ordained to ministry United Pentecostal Ch., 1981. Asst. pastor United Pentecostal Ch,, Windsor, Ont., 1977-79; pastor, Picton, Ont., 1979—; instr. Apostolic Missionary Inst., Oshawa, Ont., 1980—, bd. dirs., 1984—. Home: Box 90 Picton ON K0K 2T0 Canada

RUTZ, KARL WILLIAM, minister, religion educator, Lutheran Church-Missouri Synod; b. Chgo., Feb. 25, 1930; s. Emil William Ferdinand and Bertha Louise (Irsch) R.; m. Killie Ann Luecker, June 8, 1957; children: Karen Marie, John Michael, Pamela Ann. A.A., St. John's Coll., 1950; B.A., Concordia Sem., 1952, M.Div., 1956, D.S.T., 1963; M.A., Washington U., St. Louis, 1958. Ordained to ministry Luth. Ch.-Mo. Synod, 1958. Asst. prof. religion Concordia Coll., St. Paul, 1961-68, assoc. prof., 1969—; seminary instr. Luth. Sem., Saguio City, Philippines, 1964-66, Concordia Sem., St. Louis, 1967, summer 1968; chmn. religion div. Concordia Coll., St. Paul, 1968-82; mem. Oberseminar Westfälische Wilhelms U., Münster, W.Ger. 1973; membership chmn. Luth. Layman's League, King of Kings Luth. Ch., Roseville, Minn., 1981—. Author publs. in field. Mem. Ramsey County IndoChinese Refugee Adv. Com., Minn., 1982—. Scheele fellow, 1959, NEH fellow, 1976; Committee for Scholarly Research Luth. Ch.-Mo. Synod fellow, 1958. Mem. Soc. Bibl. Lit. Home: 1269 W Shryer St Roseville Saint Paul MN 55113 Office: Concordia Coll 275 N Syndicate Saint Paul MN 55104

RYAN, DANIEL LEO, bishop, Roman Catholic Church; b. Mankato, Minn., Sept. 28, 1930; s. Leonard Bennett and Irene Ruth (Larson) R. B.A., Ill. Benedictine Coll., 1952; J.C.L., Pontificia Universita Lateranense, Rome, Italy, 1960. Ordained priest Roman Cath. Ch., 1956, consecrated bishop, 1981. Priest, Diocese of Joliet, Ill., 1956-81, aux. bishop, 1981-84; bishop Diocese of Springfield, Ill., 1984—. Home and Office: PO Box 1667 Springfield IL 62705

RYAN, GERALD J., bishop, Roman Catholic Church. Titular bishop of Munatiana, aux. bishop, Rockville Centr, 1977—. Office: St Joseph's Convent Box 33 Brentwood NY 11717*

RYAN, HERBERT JOSEPH, historical theology educator, Roman Catholic Church; b. Scarsdale, N.Y., Feb. 19, 1931; s. Herbert Joseph and Elizabeth Angela (Gallagher) R. A.B. in Classical Langs., Loyola U., Chgo., 1954, Ph.L., 1955, M.A. in History, 1960; S.T.L., Woodstock Coll., 1963; S.T.D,, Gregorian U., Rome, 1967; S.T.D. (hon.), Gen. Theol. Sem., N.Y.C., 1973. Joined S.J., 1949, ordained priest Roman Catholic Church, 1962, professed in S.J., 1966. Assoc. prof. theology Woodstock and Union Theol. Sem., N.Y.C., 1967-74; prof. hist. theology Loyola Marymount U., Los Angeles, 1974—; cons. on ecumenical and interreligious affairs to Vatican and Nat. Conf. Cath. Bishops, 1966—; mem. Anglical Roman Cath. Consultation U.S.A., N.Y., Washington, 1969-84, Anglican Roman Cath. Internat. Commn., London, Vatican City, 1969-83; N.Y. Archdiocesan Ecumenical Commn., 1969-74, Los Angeles Archdiocesan Ecumenical Commn., 1974—. Author: De Praedestinatione of J.S. Eriugena, 1967; Anglicans and Roman Catholics, 1973. Editor: (series) Documents on Anglical-Roman Catholic Relations, 1970-84. Contbr. articles on ecumenism to profl. jours. Mem. editorial bd. Thought, 1982—. Recipient Christian Unity award Graymoor Ecumenical Inst., London, 1973; medal St. Augustine, Archbishop Canterbury, London, 1981; named DeBose Lectr. U. South, Sewanee, Tenn., 1974. Mem. Cath. Hist. Soc., Ch. Hist. Soc., Cath. Theol. Soc. Am., Am. Acad. Religion, N.Am. Acad. Ecumenists, Council on Study Religion (charter), Mediaeval Acad. Am., Fellowship Cath. Scholars, Mariological Soc. Home: 7101 W 80th St Los Angeles CA 90045 Office: Loyola Marymount U Xavier Hall Los Angeles CA 90045

RYAN, JOHN BARRY, religious educator, Roman Catholic Ch.; b. N.Y.C., Apr. 7, 1933; s. John Michael and Winifred Mary (Barry) R.; m. Jeanette Calvo, June 12, 1976; 1 child, John Barry. B.A. in English Lit., Catholic U. Am., 1955; M.A., Manhattan Coll., 1961; lic. in theology U. Strasbourg, 1969; Th.D., Institut Catholique, Paris, 1973. Mem. Bros. Christian Schs., N.Y.C., 1950-75; assoc. prof. Manhattan Coll., N.Y.C., 1972—; mem. Archdiocesan Liturgical Commn., N.Y., 1974—; cons. Internat. Com. on English in Liturgy, 1979—; del. Council on Study Religion, Ont., Can., 1980-84. Author: The Eucharistic Prayer, 1974; (with Robert Crotty) Commentaries on the Readings of the Rites, 1982. Editor: (with Anthony Sherman et al), Symbol the Language of Liturgy, 1982. Mem. N. Am. Acad. Liturgy (sec. 1975-82, v.p. 1985), Cath. Theol. Soc. Am., Societas Liturgica, AAUP. Club: Alcuin. Home: 4214 Van Cortlandt Park E Bronx NY 10470 Office: Manhattan Coll Bronx NY 10471

RYAN, MARY HOFFMANN, minister, Christian Church (Disciples of Christ) and United Church Christ; b. Mansfield, Ohio, Aug. 17, 1903; d. Irving Singleton and Ethleen May (Carter) Hoffmann; B.S. in Edn., Ohio State U., 1924; M.A. in Edn., Case-Western Res. U., 1960; M.R.E., Oberlin Grad. Sch. Theology, 1966; m. Norman Arden Ryan, Aug. 17, 1925; children—Frances Millward, Katherine McWilliams, Irving, John. Ordained to ministry, 1966; asst. pastor Dunham Christian Ch., Cleve., 1951-56; dir. Christian edn. Olmsted Community Ch., Olmsted Falls, Ohio, 1960-66; asst. to pastor Euclid Ave. Congl. Ch., United Ch. Christ, Cleve., 1966-68; minister Christian edn. Trinity Congl. Ch., United Ch. Christ, Pepper Pike, Ohio, 1968-70, Calvary Presbyn. Ch., Cleve., 1970-74; ret., 1974. Dir. childrens programs various Camps Farthest Out, 1947-82; leader retreats and spiritual growth, past trustee Shadybrook House, Mentor, Ohio; past chaplain Cleve. Pilot Club, mem. task force on Christian edn. United Ch. Christ-Western Res. Assn., 1966-70; treas., trustee Internat. Assn. Women Ministers, 1970-84. Tchr. Laubach Literacy adult classes Cleve. Bd. Edn., 1954-59; tutor Project Learn, Cleve., 1974—; dir. edn. and recreation House of Correction for Women, Cleve., 1951-59. Mem. Ch. Employed Women, United Presbyn. Ch. in U.S.A. Home: 414 Beeler Dr Berea OH 44017

RYAN, MICHAEL RUSSELL, minister, Evangelical Covenant Church of America; b. San Francisco, Dec. 25, 1950; s. Charles Franklin and Sue Arlene (Goade) R.; m. Donna Sue Carter, June 17, 1972; children: Kasey Rene, Kelly Colleen. B.S., U. So. Calif., 1973; M.A., Grace Grad. Sch. Theology, 1979; M.Div., Talbot Theol. Sem., 1984. Field assoc. Fellowship Christian Athletes, Los Angeles, 1973-74; assoc. pastor Grace Brethren Ch., Seal Beach, Calif., 1973-79; sr. pastor Grace Brethren Ch., Seal Beach, 1979-83, First Covenant Ch., San Francisco, 1983—; bd. advisors Fellowship Christian Athletes, Kansas City, 1976—; v.p., bd. dirs. Horizon Ministries, Fullerton, Calif., 1981—; co-chmn. Internat. Christian Sports Conf., Hong Kong, 1982; co-chmn. N. Am. Conf. Evangelism Thru Sports, Dallas, 1984. Bd. dirs. Calif. Restitution Bd., 1977-83. Mem. So. Calif./Ariz. Dist. Ministerium. Republican. Home: 52 Chenery St San Francisco CA 94131 Office: First Covenant Ch 455 Dolores St San Francisco CA 94110

RYAN, THOMAS FRANCIS, JR., priest, Episcopal Church; b. West Palm Beach, Fla., Oct. 9, 1936; s. Thomas Francis and Anice (Hart) R.; B.Ed., U. Miami (Fla.), 1960; postgrad., 1962-67; M.Div., Yale Div. Sch., 1972; postgrad. U. Ga., 1963, Peabody Coll., 1965, Butler U., 1966; M.A. in Psychology, Eastern Ill. U., 1977; m. Courtenay Claire DeSaussure, Apr. 15; children—Courtenay Lane, Lori Allison. Ordained to ministry, 1971; chaplain-in-residence Hartford Hosp., Conn., 1971-72; rector Episcopal Ch. of St. Mary Magdalene, Margate, Fla., 1972-74, Trinity Episcopal Ch., Mattoon, Ill., 1975—. Chaplain Eastern Ill. U., Charleston, 1975—; mem. dept. litury and life Diocese of Springfield, Ill., 1975—, mem. com. on ministry, 1976—; developer program for lay visitation Imperial Point Hosp., Fort Lauderdale, Fla., 1973. Bd. dirs. Broward Counseling Center, Fort Lauderdale, 1973-74. Home: Mattoon IL 61938 Office: 3747 34th St S Saint Petersburg FL 33711

RYBOLT, JOHN EARL, seminary president, Roman Catholic Church; b. Los Angeles, Aug. 13, 1939; s. John Wilms and Eunice Margaret (McLarney) R.; B.A., St. Mary's Sem., Perryville, Mo., 1963; M.A., De Paul U., 1967, Harvard, 1968; S.T.L., Cath. U., 1969; Sacred Scripture License, Pontifical Bibl. Inst., Rome, Italy, 1972; postgrad. St. Louis U., 1973—. Joined Vincentian Fathers, 1959; ordained priest Roman Cath. Ch., 1967; prof. O.T., St. Thomas Sem., Denver, 1969-70; prof. O.T., Kenrick Sem., St. Louis, 1970—, acad. dean, 1970—, vice rector, 1977-84; pres., rector St. Thomas Sem., Denver, 1984—. Mem. bd. St. Louis Theol. Consortium, Inc., 1970—, chmn. bd., 1974-76. Mem. Cath. Bible. Assn., Soc. Bibl. Lit., St. Louis Bibl. Studies Soc. Asso. editor: Old Testament Abstracts, 1977—. Address: St Thomas Sem Pres Office 1300 S Steele St Denver CO 80210*

RYDEN, ERNEST EDWIN, JR., minister, Lutheran Ch. Am.; b. St. Paul, Mar. 9, 1931; s. Ernest Edwin and Agnes Elizabeth (Johnson) R.; B.A., Augustana Coll., 1953; M.Div., Luth. Sch. Theology, 1959; postgrad. R.I. Coll., 1971; m. Lois Elizabeth Beck, Aug. 19, 1956; children—Paul Howard, Janice Beth, David Beck. Ordained to ministry, 1959; pastor ch., Orange, Mass., 1959-66, Barrington, R.I., 1966—. Asso. dir. communications R.I. State Council Chs., 1971—; producer, host Face the News, WPRI-TV, 1971-72; producer Worship, WTEV-TV, 1971—; producer, host The Week Starts Here, WJAR-TV, 1971—; dean R.I. dist. Luth. Ch. Am., 1971-75; mem. gov. bd. R.I. State Council Chs., 1971—, mem. presidium, 1971—, chmn. communications dept., 1972-74; mem. press, radio and TV com. New Eng. Synod, 1966—; bd. dirs., mem. policy com. R.I. Bible Soc., 1977—. Mem. Toastmasters Internat., Aircraft Owners and Pilots Assn., Nat. Assn. Council Broadcast Execs., World Assn. Christian Communications. Home: 224 New Meadow Rd Barrington RI 02806 Office: Middle Hwy and County Rd Barrington RI 02806

RYKEN, LELAND, Christian educator, Orthodox Presbyterian Church; b. Pella, Iowa, May 17, 1942; s. Frank and Eva (Bos) R.; m. Mary Alice Graham, Aug. 22, 1964; children: Philip Graham, Margaret Lynn, Nancy Elizabeth. B.A., Central Coll., 1964; Ph.D., U. Oreg., 1968. Faculty, Wheaton Coll., Ill., 1968—, now prof. English; bd. dirs. Conf. on Christianity and Lit., Grand Rapids, Mich., 1977-80. Assoc. editor Christian Scholar's Rev., 1972-76. Author: The Literature of the Bible, 1974; Triumphs of the Imagination, 1979; The Christian Imagination, 1981; How to Read the Bible as Literature, 1984. Editor: The New Testament in Literary Criticism, 1985. Mem. MLA, Conf. on Christianity and Lit. Republican. Home: 1118 N Howard Wheaton IL 60187 Office: Wheaton Coll Wheaton IL 60187

RYSZ, ANTHONY M., bishop, Polish National Catholic Church of America, Central Diocese. Office: 529 E Locust St Scranton PA 18505*

RYU, JOSEPH HYO-KEUN, minister, United Presbyn. Ch. in U.S.A.; b. Pyung-yang, Korea, Feb. 6, 1934; s. Dong-hi and Wi-soon (Lee) R.; came to U.S., 1956, naturalized, 1968; B.A., Yonsei U., Seoul, Korea, 1956; B.D., U. Dubuque, 1960; Th.M., Princeton, 1961; M.S.W., U. Mich., 1970; m. Hannah Shyn, Sept. 3, 1960; children—Frances, Florence, Joyce, Julie. Ordained to ministry, 1962; pastor Post Oak and Union Grove Presbyn. chs., Cookeville, Tenn., 1961-62; asst. pastor Throop Meml. Presbyn. Ch., Rosedale, N.Y., 1963-65; research asst. Council of Chs. City of N.Y., 1963-66. Caseworker, N.Y.C. Dept. Social Services, 1967-68. Founding mem. Nat. Asian Presbyn. Council United Presbyn. Ch. in U.S.A., 1972, mem. steering bd., 1973-76, 77—, chmn. Eastern region, 1973-75, mem. steering council Eastern Region, 1973—; mem. racial and ethnic concerns team N.E. synod United Presbyn. Ch. in U.S.A., 1974—, mem. synod mission council, 1975-76; mem. spl. com. on Korean Am. ministries Gen. Assembly United Presbyn. Ch. in U.S.A., 1975—, mem. Gen. Assembly Mission Council, 1976—; mem. Chinese Am. congregation com. Presbytery of Albany United Presbyn. Ch. in U.S.A., 1976—, chmn. Nat. Korean Presbyn. Council, 1977—. Mem. Assn. Korean Christian Scholars in N.Am., Nat. Coalition Asian-Ams. and Pacific Island Peoples for Human Services and Action (organizer mid-Atlantic region chpt., mem. nat. bd., 1973-75). Home: 3010 Williamsburg Dr Schenectady NY 12303 Office: 40 N Pearl St Albany NY 12243

SABATINI, LAWRENCE See *Who's Who in America,* 43rd edition.

SABOM, WILLIAM STEPHEN, religious editor, psychotherapist; b. Houston, July 10, 1942; s. William

Oscar and Felicia (Slataper) S.; m. Gay Morrison, Apr. 7, 1973; 1 child, Clinton Stephen. M.Div., Va. Theol. Sem., 1970; Th.M., Duke U., 1974; S.T.D., San Francisco Theol. Sem. 1980. Counselor, Meml. Dr. Presbyn. Ch., Houston, 1974-81; vicar St. James/St. Vincent Ch., Beaumont, Tex., 1970. Psychotherapist pvt. practice, Houston, 1981—; contbg. editor Jour. Psychology and Theology, 1983—. Contbr. articles to profl. jours. Served to 1st lt. U.S. Army, 1965-66. Fellow Am. Assn. Pastoral Counselors, Am. Orthospychiat. Assn.; mem. Am. Assn. Marriage and Family Therapists, Am. Acad. Psychotherapists, Am. Assn. Sex Educators, Counselors and Therapists. Office: 1200 Blalock #116 Houston TX 77055

SACHS, WILLIAM LEWIS, priest, Episcopal Church; b. Richmond, Va., Aug. 22, 1947; s. Lewis S. and Dorothy (Creasy) S. B.A., Baylor U., 1969; M.Div., Vanderbilt U., 1972; S.T.M., Yale U., 1973; Ph.D., U. Chgo., 1981. Ordained Episcopal Ch., 1974. Curate, Emmanuel Ch., Richmond, Va., 1973-75; asst. rector St. Chrysostom's Ch., Chgo., 1975-80, St. Stephen's Ch., Richmond, 1980—; co-producer religious TV programs, Richmond, Va., 1981—; pres. Richmond Clericus, 1984—; bd. dirs. Communications Commn., Richmond, 1983—, reader gen. ordination exams, 1982—. Author: Of One Body. Contbr. articles to profl. jours. Pres., Chgo. Vanderbilt Club, 1978; bd. dirs. Va. Planned Parenthood, Richmond, 1983. Stevenson fellow, 1972; Episcopal Ch. Found. fellow, 1976. Mem. Am. Hist. Assn., Am. Soc. Ch. History, Am. Acad. Religion. Club: The Arts. Home: 6003 York Rd Richmond VA 23226 Office: Saint Stephens Church 3 Chopt Rd Richmond VA 23226

SACKSCHEWSKY, MARVIN LOWELL, minister, Am. Luth. Ch.; b. Thayer, Nebr., Feb. 27, 1932; s. William Alfred and Gertrude Emma Marie (Ehlers) S.; B.S., Colo. State U., 1954; B.D., Concordia Theol. Sem., 1962, M.Div., 1972; S.T.M., Iliff Sch. Theology, Denver, 1975; m. Christa Maria Gerlinde Goy, Aug. 12, 1962; 1 son, Paul Jonathan; stepchildren—Kayrene Pohlmeyer Schultz, Bradley Pohlmeyer. Ordained to ministry, 1962; instr., counselor St. Paul's Coll., Concordia, Mo., 1963-64; pastor Our Savior Luth. Ch., Sedalia, Mo., 1964-66; missionary, New Guinea, 1966-71; pastor chs., Wyo., 1972-75; pastor Covenant Luth. Ch., Wheatland, Wyo., 1975—. Adv. mem. Center of Indian Ministries and Studies, Seward, Nebr.; adv. bd. Platte County Human Services Project; dist. rep. Wheat Ridge Found., Chgo.; chaplain coordinator Platte County Hosp., Wyo., 1974—; chaplain USAF Res., 1972—, Civil Air Patrol Squadron, Wheatland, 1975—. Mem. Soc. Bibl. Lit., Platte County Ministerial Assn. (chmn. 1977—), Luth. Soc. Worship, Music and Arts. Co-author Values for Living, Part V. Home and office: 1852 South Rd Box 1085 Wheatland WY 82201

SAGER, STEVEN. rabbi; pres. Reconstructionist Rabbinical Assn. Office: Reconstructionist Rabbinical Assn Wyncote PA 19095*

ST. ANDRE, GLYNN DWIGHT, minister, Southern Baptist Church; b. Montgomery, La., Apr. 19, 1933; s. Gilbert Harrison and Altha Iliene (Drewett) St. A.; m. Dortha Jeanne Gregg, Apr. 22, 1951; children: Danny, David, Dianne. B.A., U. Nebr.-Omaha, 1970; M.Div., Luther Rice Sem., 1980; D.Min., Covington Sem., 1983, D.Div. (hon.), 1980. Lic., 1971; ordained, 1972. Enlisted U.S. Air Force, 1951, advanced through grades to E-8, 1967, ret., 1970; minister edn. Alameda Hills Ch., Denver, 1970-72; assoc. pastor 1st Bapt. Ch., Bellevue, Nebr., 1972-74; pastor Westside Bapt. Ch., Natchitoches, La., 1974-79; pastor 1st Bapt. Ch., Loxley, Ala., 1980—; mem. exec. bd. La. Bapt. Conv., 1976-79; chmn. evangelism Natchitoches Assn., 1976-78; pres. dist. 5 Assn. of Baptists, Natchitoches, 1977-79; chmn. missions Baldwin Bapt. Assn., Loxley, 1982-84; chaplain Holiday Inn, Natchitoches, 1975. Active State Drug Rehab. Program, Shreveport, La., 1978, Personnel Bd., Natchitoches, 1977, State Sr. Citizens Program, Natchitoches, 1978. Named Outstanding non-commd. officer European Command, USAF, 1967. Club: Optomist (v.p. 1981-82). Home: PO Box 114 Loxley AL 36551

ST. CLAIRE, ELBERT KYLE, priest, Episcopal Ch.; b. Trenton, N.J., Nov. 29, 1917; s. George E. and Caroline I. (Green) St.C.; A.B. cum laude, Princeton, 1941; S.T.M., Episcopal Theol. Sch., 1943; m. Barbara Walton, Jan. 8, 1944; children—Elbert Kyle, Alice (Mrs. D.A. Long). Ordained priest Episcopal Ch., 1944; asst. Christ Ch., Fitchburg, Mass., 1943-45; chaplain Episcopal Acad., Phila., 1945-52; rector Ch. of the Advent, Kennett Square, Pa., 1952—. Mem. dept. Christian edn., Diocese of Pa., 1950-64, chmn., 1958-64; sec. Pa. chpt., Episcopal Evang. Fellowship, 1958-63, v.p., 1963-67; mem. Diocesan Council, Diocese of Pa., 1958-64, Christian Social Relations dept., 1959-65, mem. com. abolition of death penalty, 1959-65, mem. Cathedral chpt., 1966-70, chmn. nominating com., 1968-72, diocesan world relief com., 1969-72, dean Brandywine Deanery, 1970-73. Bd. dirs. Chester County (Pa.) Children's Services, 1959-72, chmn., 1968-72. Mem. Kennett Council Chs. (pres. 1963-68). Mem. Pa. Soc. Clubs: Greenville Country (Del.), Merion Cricket (Haverford, Pa.). Home: Crestline Rd Kennett Square PA 19348 Office: North Union St Kennett Square PA 19348

ST. JOHN, SHAY, minister, Association of Unity Churches; b. Roanoke, Va., June 17, 1944; d. Stuart Dexter and Reba Claudine (Summers) Bancroft; m. Glenn Philip Robinson, Aug. 17, 1963 (div. 1972); children: Sandra Lynn, Deborah Shay; m. Al Sears, Aug. 30, 1985. B.A., Va. Poly. Tech., 1969. Ordained to ministry Association of Unity Chs., 1982. Founding minister Unity of Savannah, Ga., 1978-84; pioneer minister Unity of St. Simons, Ga., 1981; supporting minister Unity of Charleston, S.C., 1983; minister Unity Christ Ch., San Francisco, 1984—; sec., treas. Southeast Unity Ministries, 1981-84; chaplain Women Police Officers, San Francisco, 1984—; bd. dirs. Western Central Region Unity Chs., 1985. Founding editor New Age newsletter Adventure in Truth, 1978; editor New Age newsletter Gateway to Truth, 1984. Contbr. articles to Unity Mag. Filmmaker, New Age film Living Together, Growing Together, 1983. Mem. Nat. Assn. Female Execs., Assn. Unity Chs. (program com. 1981—), Internat. New Thought Assn., Phi Kappa Phi. Avocations: needlepoint; creating slide shows; writing. Office: Unity Christ Ch 2690 Ocean Ave San Francisco CA 94132

ST MERAN, DELINCE L. G., minister, Haitian Baptist; b. Cap-Haitien, Haiti, Jan. 10, 1929; s. Dantes Baptiste and Almaide (Henri) St. M.; came to U.S., 1965; student N.Y.C. Community Coll., 1972-76; m. Edith Charles, Mar. 7, 1964; children—Joshuah, Deline, Jessy, Ronyx. Ordained to ministry, 1972; pastor Haitian Baptist Ch., Bklyn., 1965—. Home: 86 E 43d St Brooklyn NY 11203 Office: 241 Prospect Pl Brooklyn NY 11238

SAKENFELD, KATHARINE DOOB, religion educator, Presbyterian Church in U.S.A. b. Ithaca, N.Y., Aug. 24, 1940; d. Hugo Jr. and Hilda Agnes (Smith) Doob; m, Helmar Peter Sakenfeld, June 17, 1967. B.A., Coll. Wooster, 1961; M.A., Univ. R.I., 1962; B.D., Harvard Div. Sch., 1965, Ph.D., Harvard Univ., 1971. Ordained to ministry Presbyn. Ch. (U.S.A.), 1970. Instr. Old Testament Princeton Theol. Sem., N.J., 1970-71, asst. prof., 1971-76, assoc. prof,, 1976—, dir. Ph.D. Studies, 1984—; mem. commn. faith and order Nat. Council Chs., N.Y.C., 1979—, rep. Presbyn. Ch. (U.S.A.), N.Y.C.; cons. on ch. union, 1976-84, alt. del., 1976-84. Author: The Meaning of Hesed in the Hebrew Bible, 1978; Faithfulness in Action, 1985; contbr. articles, book revs. to profl. jours. Mem. editorial bd. Jour. Bibl. Lit., 1974-77. Assn. Theol. Schs. grantee 1978. Mem. Soc. Sch. Bibl. Lit. (assoc. in council 1977-80), Am. Schs. Oriental Research, Columbia Univ. Seminar on Hebrew Bible, Bibl. Colloquium, Bibl. Theologians, Rev. Standard Version Trans. Com., Phi Beta Kappa. Office: Princeton Theol Seminary CN 821 Princeton NJ 08542

SALA, HAROLD JAMES, minister, Gospel Fellowship Assn.; b. Denver, July 15, 1937; s. Delmar Harold and Ruby Edith (Irby) S.; m. Darlene Starr Duffield, Dec. 23, 1959; children: Bonnie, Steven, Nancy. B.A. magna cum laude, Bob Jones U., 1958, M.A., 1959, Ph.D., 1963. Ordained to ministry, 1958. Assoc. pastor Calvary Temple, Denver, 1960-63; grad. asst. Bob Jones U., Greenville, S.C., 1963-66; pastor So. Bay Bible Ch., Redondo Beach, Calif., 1966-74; founder, pres. Guidelines, Inc., Laguna Niguel, Calif., 1963—; bd. dirs. Orinoco River Mission, Los Angeles, 1972-74, Revival Prayer Fellowship, Laguna Niguel, Calif., 1984—, G.L.A.S.S., Los Angeles, 1970-74, Hosp. Chaplin Ministers Am., Los Angeles, 1970-74; adv. bd. Harvesting in Spanish, Denver, 1982—. Author: Guidelines for Living, 1967; Guidelines for Successful Living, 1972; They Shall be One Flesh, 1978; Train up a Child, 1978; A Love to Live By, 1973; Science and God in the 80's, 1980; The Power of Positive Parenting, 1982; You Can Live Successfully, 1982; Something More Than Love, 1983; How to Enjoy Raising Your Children, 1984. Contbr. articles to profl. jours. Columnist, Sidestreets, 1976—. Recipient Civic award, Los Angeles County, 1973; named Outstanding Citizen, City of Redondo Beach, 1974. Mem. Western Religious Broadcasters, Nat. Religious Broadcasters. Republican. Office: Guidelines Inc 26076 Getty Dr Laguna Niguel CA 92677

SALATKA, CHARLES ALEXANDER, bishop, Roman Cath. Ch.; b. Grand Rapids, Mich., Feb. 26, 1918; s. Charles and Mary (Balun) S.; M.A., Catholic U. Am., 1941; J.C.L., Inst. Civil and Canon Law, Rome, Italy, 1948. Ordained priest Roman Catholic Ch., 1945; assigned to Chancery Office, Diocese of Grand Rapids, 1948-54, vice chancellor, 1954-61, aux. bishop, 1961, vicar gen., 1961, consecrated bishop, 1962; pastor St. James Parish, Grand Rapids, 1962-68; bishop Diocese of Marquette (Mich.), 1968-77; archbishop of Oklahoma City, 1977—. Pres., Mich. Cath. Conf. Mem. Canon Law Soc. Office: PO Box 32180 Oklahoma City OK 73123

SALAZAR LOPEZ, JOSE CARDINAL, archbishop, Roman Catholic Church; b. Ameca, Mex., Jan. 12, 1910. Ordained priest Roman Cath. Ch., 1934. Named titular bishop of Prusiade, 1961, named bishop of Zamora, 1967, named archbishop of Guadalajara, 1970—. Office: Arzobispado Apartado Postal 1-331 Guadalajara Jalisco Mexico 44100*

SALDARINI, ANTHONY JOSEPH, theology educator, Roman Catholic Church. b. Boston, Sept. 18, 1941; s. Roger Louis and Harriet Carroll (Byrne) S.; m. Maureen Barbara Cusack, July 15, 1978; children: Daniel, Bryan. A.B., Boston Coll., 1965, M.A., 1966; Ph.L., Weston Coll., 1966; M.Phil., Yale U., 1970, Ph.D., 1971. Assoc. prof. dept. theology Boston Coll., 1975—; trustee Am. Acad. Religion, 1983—. Author: The Fathers According to Rabbi Nathan, 1975; Scholastic Rabbinism, 1982; Jesus and Passover, 1984; contbr. articles to religious jours. Mem. Soc. Biblical Lit., Cath. Biblical Assn. Democrat. Home: 46 Walker St Newtonville MA 02160 Office: Boston Coll Dept Theology Chestnut Hill MA 02167

SALIBA, PHILIP E., archbishop, Antiochian Orthodox Christian Ch.; b. Abou-Mizan, Lebanon, June 10, 1931; s. Abdallah Elias and Salema (Saliba) S.; B.A., Wayne State U., 1959; M.Sacred Theology, St. Vladimir's Sem., N.Y., 1964. Sub-deacon Antiochian Orthodox Christian Ch., 1945-49, deacon, 1949-59, ordained priest, 1959, consecrated archbishop, 1966, now met. archbishop. Trustee St. Valdimir's Orthodox Theol. Sem. Address: 358 Mountain Rd Englewood NJ 07631

SALICO, DALE VINCENT; minister, American Baptist Churches in the U.S.A.; b. Johnson City, N.Y., Dec. 17, 1946; s. Charles Gerrard and Joy Bondelyn (Crispel) S.; m. Elaine Claudia Vining, June 21, 1969; children: Angela Joy, Claudia Rose. B.A., Houghton Coll., 1969; M.Div., Gordon-Conwell Theol. Sem., 1972, postgrad., 1983-86. Ordained to ministry Baptist Ch., 1973, Asst. pastor Little White Ch., Conklin, N.Y., 1967-69; pastor Forestdalle Community Ch., Malden, Mass., 1969-71; minister with youth First Bapt. Ch., Wakefield, Mass., 1971-72; pastor First Bapt. Ch., Sharpsville, Pa., 1973-78, First Bapt. Ch., Clarion, Pa., 1978—; bd. dirs. Koinonia Christian Fellowship at Clarion U. of Pa., 1979—; mem. evangelism community task force Am. Bapt. Chs. of Pa. and Del., 1981—. Mem. Mental Health and Retardation Adv. Bd., Clarion County, 1981-83; mem. interim bd. dirs. Clarion Community Counseling Ctr., 1982-83. Author: New Birth - New Life, 1980. Mem. Sharpsville-Clark Ministerium (pres. 1975-78), Clarion Ministerial Assn. (pres. 1984—). Democrat. Home: RD 2 Box 547 Shippenville PA 16254 Office: First Baptist Ch Main St at 7th Ave Clarion PA 16214

SALT, ALFRED LEWIS, priest, Episcopal Church; b. Hackensack, N.J., Apr. 30, 1927; s. Alfred John and Lily (Tittle) S.; m. Elizabeth May Loveland, June 18, 1949; children: Richard John, Michael Rob, Christopher William, Katharine Anne. B.A. with 1st class honors, Bishop's U., Lennoxville, P.Q., Can., 1949, M.A. in History, 1951, B.D., 1960; grad. Advanced Mgmt. Program, Harvard U., 1970. Ordained to ministry Anglican Ch. as deacon, 1951, priest, 1952. Incumbent, St. Philip's, Sawyerville, P.Q., 1951-52, St. John the Evangelist, Portneuf, P.Q., 1952-54; rector Christ Ch., Stanstead, P.Q., 1954-62, St. Michael's Ch., Sillery, P.Q., 1962-72, All Saints' Ch., Millington, N.J., 1972—; trustee Heath Village, Hackettstown, N.J., 1974-76; pres. Morris Convocation, Morris County, N.J., 1974-78; retreat condr. various chs., 1979—; coordinator prayer sch. Victorious Ministry through Christ, 1984—. Contbr. to Sharing mag. Mem. Superior Council of Edn., Quebec, P.Q., 1964-70, Twp. Welfare Bd., Millington, 1977-78, 82; commr. Quebec Protestant Sch. Bd., 1970-72. Served with U.S. Navy, 1945-46. Named Bishop's Chaplain, Diocese of Que., 1962, hon. canon, 1970. Mem. Somerset Hills Ministerial Assn., Order of St. Luke (chaplain 1980—). Avocations: golf; sailing. Home: 15 Cross Hill Rd Millington NJ 07946 Office: All Saints' Ch 15 Basking Ridge Rd Millington NJ 07946

SALTER, J(AMES) EDWARD, minister, Southern Baptist Convention. B. Savannah, Ga., Aug. 15, 1944; s. George C. and Louise (Bagwell) S.; m. Christine Varnadore, June 14, 1964; children: Angela, Pamela, Brian. A.A., Brenton-Parker Coll., 1964; B.S. in Edn., Ga. So. Coll., 1968; M.Div., Southwestern Theol. Sem., 1972; D.Min., New Orleans Bapt. Sem., 1983. Ordained, 1962. Minister, Unity Bapt. Ch., Alma, Ga., 1962-64, Double Heads Bapt. Ch., Sylvania, Ga., 1964-66, Turkey Br. Bapt. Ch., Springfield, Ga., 1966-69, Antelope Bapt. Ch. (Tex.), 1969-72, Franklin Rd. Bapt. Ch., LaGrange, Ga., 1972-73, Zion Hill Bapt. Ch., Buford, Ga., 1973-75, Redan 1st Bapt. Ch. (Ga.), 1975—; chmn. Metro Reach Growth Campaign, Atlanta, 1975; moderator Stone Mountain Bapt. Assn., 1977-79; mem. exec. com. Ga. Bapt. Conv., 1978-81; pres. Stone Mountain Pastors Conf., 1980; chaplain Gwinnett County Police Dept., Lawrenceville, Ga., 1974-75. Author project report, 1983. Leader, advisor Coastal Empire council and Atlanta council Boy Scouts Am., 1962-84. Eagle Scout, Vigil Honor award, God and Country award, Boy Scouts Am.; named Star Tchr., Effingham County, Ga., 1969. Home: Box 216 Redan GA 30074 Office: Redan First Bapt Ch Box 216 Redan GA 30074

SALTZMAN, RUSSELL EDWARD, minister, AMerican Lutheran Church; b. Kansas City, Kans., Apr. 26, 1947; s. Harry Albert and Lola (Lacy) S.; m. Kate Baker, May 30, 1970; children: Karl Fredrick (adopted), Paul William, Elizabeth Lacy, Richard John. B.S., Missouri Valley Coll., 1970; postgrad. in Am. history U. Kans., 1976; M.Div., Trinity Luth. Sem.,

1980. Ordained to ministry Am. Luth. Ch., 1980. Pastor Luth. Parish of Emmaus and Immanuel Congregations, Kennard, Nebr., 1980—; bishop's staff Central Dist., Am. Luth. Ch., Denver, 1981—; bd. dirs. Luth. Forum, N.Y.C., 1984—, editorial advisor, 1984—. Editor: The Heartbeat, 1981—. Contbr. articles to religious publs. Press sec. Congressman Larry Winn, Jr., Washington, 1972-73; dep. sec. state State of Kans., Topeka, 1973-76; pres. Shawnee County Young Republicans, Kans., 1974-76; v.p. Village of Kennard Planning Commn., 1980-83; coordinator CROP Community Hunger Appeal, Washington County, Nebr., 1981-83; bd. dirs. Washington County unit Am. Cancer Soc., 1983—; mem. adv. bd. Region IV, Eastern Nebr. Mental Health, 1983-84. Mem. Washington County Ministerial Assn. (pres. 1981-82), Acad. for Luth. Scholarship (editorial assoc. 1981-84). Home: Lutheran Parish House Kennard NE 68034 Office: PO Box 216 Kennard NE 68034

SALVERSON, CAROL ANN, theological library administrator, clergyman; b. Buffalo, N.Y., June 30, 1944; d. Howard F. and Estella G. (Zelie) Heavener. B.A. in Philosophy, SUNY-Buffalo, 1966; M.S. in L.S., Syracuse U., 1968; grad. Sacred Coll. of Jamilian Theology and Divinity Sch., Reno, Nev., 1976. Ordained to ministry Internat. Community of Christ, 1974. Dir., Jamilian Theol. Research Library, Reno, 1975—, also Gene Savoy Heritage Mus. & Library, 1984—; mem. faculty Jamilian Parochial Sch., Reno, 1979—; librarian Sacred Coll. Jamilian Univ. of Ordained, Reno, 1979—; sexton Jamilian Handbell Choir, Reno, 1981—; research librarian Advocates for Religious Rights and Freedoms, Reno, 1982—; violist Symphonietta, Reno, 1983—. Contbr. articles to profl. jours. Mem. Nat. League Concerned Clergywomen, Am. Library Assn., Nev. Library Assn. Home: 2025 LaFond Dr Reno NV 89509 Office: Internat Community Christ Chancellery Complex 643 Ralston St Reno NV 89503

SALZMAN, JOHN WARREN, minister, So. Bapt. Conv.; b. Burlington, Ia., Sept. 23, 1921; s. Elmer Alan and Florence Emma (Sloneker) S.; B.A., Wheaton Coll., 1943; Th.M., Southwestern Bapt. Theol. Sem., 1946; D.D., Howard Payne U., 1960; m. Pauline Lytle, June 14, 1947; children—John Warren, David Lee, Stephanie Ann. Ordained to ministry So. Baptist Conv., 1944; pastor Mo., Ill., Tex., Ind., 1943-72; pastor First Bapt. Ch., Bonham, Tex., 1946-50, First Bapt. Ch., Muskogee, Okla., 1950-55, First Bapt. Ch., Galveston, Tex., 1955-62, First So. Bapt. Ch., Tucson, 1962-64, Hillcrest Bapt. Ch., Dallas, 1964-70, First Bapt. Ch., Orleans, Ind., 1971-72, Immanuel Bapt. Ch., Grand Rapids, Mich., 1972—. Bible tchr. Nat. Summer Confs.; preacher Nat. Religious Convocations; mem. state exec. bd. Mich. Bapt. Conv., 1974—. Mem. Muskogee Inter-racial Bd., 1952-54; mem. Dallas Inter-racial Com., 1966-70. Trustee Okla. Bapt. U., 1952-54, Bapt. Sunday Sch. Bd., So. Bapt. Conv.; mem. State Hosp. Bd. Okla. and Ariz., 1950-54, 62-64. Contbr. articles to religious jours. Home: 1616 Millbrook St SE Grand Rapids MI 49508 Office: 1935 44th St SE Grand Rapids MI 49508

SAMANO, BERNARDO, church official, Seventh-day Adventist Church; b. Cd. Mante, Tamaulipas, Mexico, Oct. 20, 1956; s. Jose and Felicitas (Ruiz) S.; m. Silvia Lazaro, Aug. 24, 1980; 1 child, Elias Obed. Licenciado en Teologia, Montemorelos U., 1980. Pres. Ministerial Club, Montemorelos, Nuevo Leon, 1979-80; pastor Seventh-day Adventist Ch., Los Mochis, Sinaloa, 1980-82, Oaxaca, Mex., 1982—; edn. dir. Association Civil Filantropica y Educativa, Oaxaca, 1982—. Contbr. articles to profl. jours. Served with Mexican Army, 1976. Office: Seventh Day Adventists Ch Colegio Militar #523 Oaxaca Oaxaca Mexico 68050

SAMARTHA, MICHAEL PRAKASH, priest, Episcopal Church. b. Mangalore, Karnaraka, India, Mar. 10, 1941; came to U.S., 1967; s. Lucas J. and Sahadevi (Soans) S.; m. Eunice Evelyn Reynolds, June 9, 1979; children: Rebekah Shanthi and Mark Sanjay (twins), Ruth Asha and Anne Jyothi (twins). B.A., St. Aloysius Coll., Mangalore, 1962; B.D., United Theol. Coll., Bangalore, 1965; Th.M., Princeton Theol. Sem., 1968; Ph.D., Hartford Sem., 1972. Ordained to ministry Episcopal Ch., 1967. Deacon Ch. of South India, Mangalore, 1965-67; asst. prof. Calif. State U., Northridge, 1972-75; asst. presbyter St. Mark's Cathedral, Bangalore, India, 1975-77; assoc. rector St. Martins Episcopal Ch., Canoga Park, Calif., 1977-83; rector St. John's Episcopal Ch., San Bernardino, Calif., 1983—; prof. Calif. State U., San Bernardino, 1979—, Whittier Coll., Calif., 1982—. Contbr. articles and book reviews to profl. jours. Judge Bank of Am. Achievement Awards, San Bernardino, 1984; com. mem. Arrowhead United Way, San Bernardino, 1984. Mem. Am. Acad. Religion, Soc. Asian Studies, Soc. Bibl. Lit. Home: 264 W 14th St San Bernardino CA 92405 Office: St John's Episcopal Ch 1407 Arrowhead Ave San Bernardino CA 92405

SAMMONS, DAVID G., minister, Unitarian Universalist Church; b. Chgo., Feb. 11, 1938; s. Joseph Albert and Helen Louise (Leonard) S.; m. Rosemary Louise Sturtz, Aug. 30, 1959 (div. 1973); children: Donna, David, Michal Ann, Benjamin; m. Janis Miller, Jan. 24, 1974; 1 son, Matthew. A.B., Dartmouth Coll., 1960; postgrad. Meadville/Lombard Coll., 1961-62; M.Div., Starr King Sch. Ministry, 1965; D.Min., Pacific Sch. Religion, 1978. Ordained to ministry, 1965. Assoc. minister First Unitarian Ch., Rochester, N.Y., 1965-67; minister St. John's Unitarian Ch., Cin., 1967-78; sr. minister Unitarian Ch. of Evanston, Ill., 1978-84, Mt. Diablo Unitarian Universalist Ch., Walnut Creek, Calif., 1984—; bd. dirs. Beacon Press, Boston, 1969-75, Urban Ch. Coalition, N.Y.C., 1983, Unitarian Universalist Service Com., Boston, 1983; mem. Extension Task Force, PCD, Berkeley, Calif., 1984—. Author: The Marriage Option, 1977. Contbr. articles to profl. jours. Pres. Cin. Action for Peace, 1968, Lake Geneva Summer Assembly, 1971, N. Shore Peach Initiative, Evanston, Ill., 1981-83; coordinator Clergy Cons. Service, Cin., 1969; scribe Downtown Clergy Group, Evanston, 1982; chmn. Ill. Nuclear Freeze Adv. Com., Chgo., 1983; bd. dirs. Mt. Diablo Peace Ctr., 1984—. Recipient Award of Honor, N. Shore Peach Initiative, 1983. Mem. Unitarian Universalist Ministers Assn. (sec.), Phi Beta Kappa. Democrat. Home: 829 Hutchinson Walnut Creek CA 94598 Office: Mount Diablo Unitarian Univeralist Church 55 Eckley Ln Walnut Creek CA 94596

SAMORAJCZYK, MARY ANN THERESE, lay volunteer, nurse, Roman Catholic Church; b. Bridgeport, Conn., Apr. 29, 1934; d. John Francis and Sophia Ladislaus (Zysk) S. Diploma in Nursing, St. Vincent Hosp., Bridgeport, Conn., 1954; B.S., Cath. U., 1964; M.A., Fairfield U., 1974; postgrad. Trinity Coll., Washington. R.N., Conn., Md., D.C. Secular Franciscan, Assumption Fraternity, Bethesda, Md., 1966—, parish council, sec., 1980—; liturgy com., 1983—; sec. St. John Cath. Community, 1981—, coordinator, tchr. religious edn. presch. program St. John Neumann Cath. Community, Gaithersburg, Md., 1979—, lay minister, 1980—; instr. in nursing Alexandria Hosp., Va., 1977-84; pastoral counseling Samorajczyk Psychol. Services, Gaithersburg, 1983-84; cons. and lectr. in religious needs of children and families. Co-author: (bibliography) Hospitalized Child, 1979. Co-editor: St. John Neumann Parish Sunday Bull., 1981-84. Designer, coordinator seminars and workshops. Instr. resuscitation Am. Heart Assn., Md., 1984-85. Served to capt. Nurses Corps, U.S. Army, 1966-67. Mem. Am. Nurses Assn., Assn. Care Children's Health (bd. dirs. Met. Washington chpt. 1978-80), Nat. Capital Area Hosp. Council (Edn. and tng. div.), Staff Devel. Council Greater Washington Area, Md. Nurses Assn. Club: Women's (St. John Neumann Parish). Office: Hosp Sick Children 1731 Bunker Hill Rd NE Washington DC 20017

SAMPLES, MAX JEROME, minister, So. Baptist Conv.; b. W. Frankfort, Ill., Oct. 26, 1934; s. Luther Martin and Oarlee (Edwards) S.; B.A., So. Ill. U., Carbondale, 1968; m. Elizabeth Peek, Apr. 30, 1955; 1 dau., Carol. Ordained to ministry, 1960; pastor New Hope Bapt. Ch., Benton, Ill., 1959-61, Third Bapt. Ch., W. Frankfort, 1961—; dir. religious radio program, 1971—; chaplain CAP, 1974—. Youth dir. Franklin Bapt. Assn., 1959-62, stewardship chmn., 1966, moderator, 1965, 72, 73; bd. dirs. Ill. Bapt. Assn., 1968-74, mem. order of bus. com., 1973-76. Home: 614 Franklin Ave West Frankfort IL 62896 Office: Third Baptist Ch Washington Blvd and 6th St West Frankfort IL 62896

SAMRA, NICHOLAS JAMES, priest, Byzantine Melkite Catholic Church. B. Paterson, N.J., Aug. 15, 1944; s. George Harold and Elizabeth L. (Balady) S. B.A. in Philosophy, St. Anselm Coll., 1966; B.D. in Theology, St. John Sem., 1970. Ordained priest Byzantine Melkite Cath. Ch., 1970. Assoc. pastor St. Anne Ch., North Hollywood, Calif., 1970-78; adminstr. Holy Cross Mission, Anaheim, Calif., 1973-78; pastor St. John Ch., Northlake, Ill. and St. Michael Ch. Southeast, Chgo., 1978-81, St. Ann Ch., West Paterson, N.J., 1981—; bd. dirs. Adult Religious Edn. of Los Angeles 1975-78; chaplain Police Athletic League Supporters, North Hollywood, 1974-77; v.p. Eastern Clergy Assn., Chgo., 1979-80; mem. Ecumenical Commn., Los Angeles, 1977-78. Contbr. articles to Byzantine Anthology, 1978. Home and Office: St Ann Melkite Cath Ch 802 Rifle Camp Rd West Paterson NJ 07424

SAMS, RONALD WAYNE, minister, non-denominational Christian Church; b. Kingsport, Tenn., Sept. 7, 1940; s. Elijah Marcelle and Lillian Mae (Stata) S.; A.B., Johnson Bible Coll., 1962; postgrad. Lincoln (Ill.) Christian Sem., 1971, Christian Heritage Coll., 1976, Huntington Coll. (Ind.), 1979-80, Anderson Coll. (Ind.), 1980-84; m. Dee Ann Lowe, June 23, 1963; children—Patricia Yolanda, David Marcelle. Ordained to ministry, 1961; minister Artemus (Ky.) Christian Ch., 1961, Southgate Christian Ch., Greenville, S.C., 1961-66, Dive Christian Ch., Bedford, Ind., 1966-72, First Christian Ch., Mt. Vernon, Ky., 1972-74, Center Christian Ch., Mays, Ind., 1974—. Co-founder, mgr. Christian Service Camps, Piedmont-Greenville, S.C., 1964-66; mgr. Wonder Valley Christian Assn., Salem, Ind., 1969-72; mgr. Ky. Christian Assn., Brodhead, 1973; chmn. deans Mahoning Valley Christian Assn., 1975; sec.-treas. So. Ind. Christian Minister's Assn., 1967-70; asso. evangelist Christian Evangelizers Assn., 1973. Founding mem. Americans Against Union Control of Govt., 1974; founding mem. Conservative Caucus, 1974, Concerned Alliance of Parents of Rush County, 1984. sec.-treas. United Cerebral Palsy of Rush County, Ind., 1975-78, 81-84, pres., 1979-80, mem. state bd., 1975-76; exec. sec. United Cerebral Palsy Ind., 1980-84, bd. dirs., 1975—, legis. chmn., 1972-82. Mem. Alumni Assn. Johnson Bible Coll.; mem. council of seventy adv. bd. Johnson Bible Coll., 1979-81, 83-84; trustee Ctr. Civil Twp. of Rush County, 1983-84. Home: PO Box 125 Mays IN 46155 Office: Route 1 Knightstown IN 46148

SAMUEL, ATHANASIUS YESHUE, archbishop, Syrian Orthodox Ch. of Antioch; b. Hilwah, Syria, Dec. 25, 1907; s. Sowmey Malkey and Khatoun Malkey (Hido) S, Student, St. Mark's Sem., 1923-27, 29-31, Cairo Theol. Coll., 1927-29. Ordained priest, 1932. Sec. to Syrian orthodox patriarch of Antioch, 1931-32; father superior St. Mark's Monastery, Jerusalem, 1933-43; patriarchal vicar of Jerusalem, 1943-46, archbishop, 1946-52, patriarchal del. to U.S. and Can., 1949-57; archbishop, Hackensack, N.J., 1957—. Author: Treasure of Qumran, 1966; Liturgy of St. James, 1967; Rites of Baptism, Holy Matrimony and Burial, 1974, Decorated, Emperor Haile Selassie I Gold Cross and papal medallion Pope Paul VI, Cross Knights of St. John of Jerusalem, Grand Cross of St. Ignatius Theophoros. Mem. World Council Chs., Nat. Council Chs. Christ in U.S. Address: 49 Kipp Ave Lodi NJ 07644

SAMUELS, WESLEY EDDIE, lay ch. worker, Pentecostal Ch. of God of Am., Inc.; b. Columbia, S.C., Apr. 6, 1931; s. Willie and Eva Sue (Etheridge) S.; student pub. schs., Columbia, Boys High Sch., Bklyn.; m. Geneva Carter, June 23, 1951; children—Darryl, Meldrena. Nat. asst. Sunday Sch. supt. St. John Pentecostal Ch., N.Y.C., 1974—, broadcast narrator, 1967—, ch. treas., 1965—, Sunday sch. tchr., 1966-74, chmn. program com., 1969—, youth leader, 1966—; asst. nat. Sunday sch. supt. Mt. Pisgah Pentecostal Chs. Am., 1974—. Sr. clk. Harlem Hosp., N.Y.C., 1966—. Home: 496 W 133d St New York City NY 10027 Office: 506 Lenox Ave New York City NY 10037

SANBORN, HUGH WIEDMAN, religion educator, administrator, pastoral therapist, United Church of Christ. B. Albany, N.Y., Nov. 29, 1939; s. Hugh Wallace and Elizabeth (Wiedman) S.; m. Barbara Ann Mortensen, June 16, 1962; children: Elisabeth, Daniel, B.A. in Psychology, Muhlenberg Coll., 1962; B.D., Andover Newton Theol. Sch., 1966, S.T.M., 1967; Ph.D. in Religion and Personality, U. Iowa, 1975. Ordained to minister United Ch. of Christ, 1965; licensed profl. counselor Tex. Chaplain, Iowa Security Med. Facility, Coralville, 1969-71; adj. asst. prof. Rice U., Houston, 1973—; pastoral therapist St. Peter United Ch., Houston, 1978—; dir. campus ministries Houston United Campus Christian Life Com., Houston, 1980—; dir., v.p. Meeting House West Counseling Ctr., Houston, 1980—; vis. lectr. San Francisco Theol. Sem., 1982; Houston liaison World Council Chs., 1982-83; sec. ch. and ministry com. Houston Assn. United Ch. Christ, 1983-84, pastoral relator to clergy So. Centra. Conf., Austin, Tex., 1984—; mem. Spl. Commn. Ministry in Higher Edn., Auston, 1984—. Trustee Houston Rape Crisis Coalition, 1977-80; mem. Interfaith Peaceforce Houston, 1981—; Houston coordinator Union Concerned Scientists Peace Conv., 1981—; organizer Peace Studies Ctr., U. Houston, 1982—. Page fellow Andover-Newton Theol. Sch., 1966-67. Mem. Assn. Clin. Pastoral Edn. (clin. mem.), Acad. Religion. Democrat. Home: 3739 Tartan Ln Houston TX 77025 Office: Houston United Campus Christian Life Com 208 A D Bruce Religion Ctr U Houston Houston TX 77004

SANCHEZ, ROBERT FORTUNE, archbishop, Roman Catholic Church; b. Socorro, N.Mex., Mar. 20, 1934; s. Julius C. and Priscilla (Fortune) S.; grad. Immaculate Heart Sem., Santa Fe, N.Mex., 1954, Gregorian U., Rome, 1960. Ordained priest, 1959; tchr., asst. prin. St. Pius X High Sch., Albuquerque, 1960-68; pastor St. Joseph Parish, Masquero, N.Mex., 1968-71, San Felipe Parish, Albuquerque, 1971-74; vicar gen. Archdiocese of Santa Fe, 1974; ordained archbishop of Santa Fe, 1974—. Dir., Extension Lay Vols., 1965; rep. N.Mex. Council Chs., 1968; Santa Fe rep. Nat. Fedn. Priests Council, 1972-73; pres. Archdiocesan Priests Senate, 1973. Mem. Nat. Conf. Bishops. Office: Archdiocese of Santa Fe 202 Morningside Dr SE Albuquerque NM 87108*

SANCHEZ, RUBEN DARIO, minister, educator, author, Seventh-day Adventist Church; b. Buenos Aires, Argentina, Feb. 13, 1943; came to U.S., 1970. s. Ramon Jose and Maria Concepcion (Pardino) S.; m. Lina Alcira Tabuenca, Feb. 7, 1966; children: Adrian Nelson, Vivian Ethel. B.A., River Plate Coll., Puiggari, Argentina, 1968; postgrad. Andrews U., 1971-72, M.A., 1975; Ph.D. Calif. Grad. Sch. Theology, 1979.

Ordained, 1976. Pastor, tchr. River Plate Coll., Puiggari, Argentina, 1969; minister Lit., So. Calif. Conf., Glendale, 1970-71; minister Ill. Conf., Brookfield, 1972-77, Oreg. Conf., Portland, 1977-80; Bible Sch. dir., assoc. speaker Spanish Voice of Prophecy, Thousand Oaks, Calif., 1980-84; assoc. dir. devel. His Written Telecast, 1985—; founder Pacific Northwest Christian Sch., Woodburn, Oreg., 1979; founder, dir. Instituto Biblico Christiano, 1979-80; dir. Escuala Radiopostal (Corr. Bible Sch.), 1980-84; mem. Hispanic Nat. Religious Broadcasters. Editor Antologia Poetica, 1976; author textbook: Apasionante Exploracion de la Biblia, 1977; Introduction to the Old Testament, 1979, doctrinal, devotional; Hungary Heart, 1984; contbr. religious edn. articles to publs. Recipient Master Guide award, River Plate Coll., 1968, Outstanding Service to Spanish Community in Oreg. award, sta. KROW, Woodburn, 1980; Andrews U. scholarship to study in Eng., 1972. Club: Unidos Para Crecer (pres. Newbury Park 1981-84). Home: 3780 San Felipe Ave Newbury Park CA 91320 Office: Adventist Media Ctr 1100 Rancho Conejo Blvd Newbury Park CA 91320

SANCHEZ, RUDY, minister, Southern Baptist Convention; religious organization executive; b. San Antonio, July 15, 1936; s. Ignacio Ingle and Angelita (Garcia) S.; B.A., Howard Payne U., Brownwood, Tex., 1958, D.D., 1974; m. Ruth Menchaca, Sept. 10, 1960; children—Rhoda Sue, Rebekah Selene, Reuel Scott, Regem Saul. Ordained to ministry, 1955; mem. State Missions Commn. Bapt. Gen. Conv. Tex.; v.p. Bapt. Gen. Conv. Tex., 1969; pres. Mex. Bapt. Conv. Tex., 1973-75. Participant White House Conf. on Aging, 1972; bd. dirs. Nueces County (Tex.) Center for Mentally Handicapped, Mentally Retarded. Home and office: 848 Joanna Dr Hurst TX 76053

SANDBERG, NEIL C., lay worker, Reform Jewish; b. N.Y.C., Apr. 25, 1925; s. Jacob and Lena (Schnitzer) S.; B.A., Columbia, 1949; M.Pl., U. So. Calif., 1971, Ph.D., 1972; m. Mary Keiser, Dec. 26, 1954; 1 son, Curtis N. Prof. sociology Loyola-Marymount U., Los Angeles, 1964—, dir. Inst. Intergroup Relations Tng., 1974—; prof. contemporary Jewish studies Hebrew Union Coll.-Jewish Inst. Religion, Los Angeles, 1975—; 1st fellow Center Contemporary Jewish Life, U. Judaism, Los Angeles, 1975—; research dir. study Jewish identity, 1976; bd. dirs. Interreligious Council So. Calif., 1973—; Western regional dir. Am. Jewish Com., Los Angeles, 1962—. Mem. Atty. Gen. Calif. Commn. Police-Community Relations, 1972, Higher Edn. for Los Angeles Minorities, 1966-67. Recipient award Urban League, 1976; award merit Los Angeles city schs., 1970; award Kosciuszko Found., 1972. Author: New Towns: Why-And For Whom?, 1973; Ethnic Identity and Assimilation: The Polish-American Community, 1974; Stairwell 7, 1977; Ethnic Identity and Assimilation: The Welsh-English Dichotomy, 1981. Home: 2001 Sunset Plaza Dr Los Angeles CA Office: 6505 Wilshire Blvd Los Angeles CA 90069

SANDERFORD, MATTHEW ANDERSON, minister, Southern Baptist Convention; b. Waco, Tex., Jan. 8, 1920; s. Roger Monroe and Willie (Anderson) S.; B.A., Baylor U.; B.D., Southwestern Bapt. Theol. Sem.; m. Dora Jean Mc Donald, Aug. 23, 1943; children—Matthew Anderson, Sharon Jean, Lee Bell, John Mark. Ordained to ministry, 1941; chaplain U.S. Army, 1945-47; pastor chs., Tex., 1941-52; fgn. missionary to Uruguay So. Bapt. Conv. Fgn. Mission Bd., Richmond, Va., 1952—; fgn. missionary, dir. dept. info. process Bapt. Spanish Pub. House, El Paso, Tex., 1961—; interim pastor chs., El Paso area, 1970—; founder El Paso Hot Line, bd. dirs., 1969-70; vol. chaplain Police, Sheriff Dept. Pres. Irvin High Sch. PTA, 1971-72. Mem. Pastors Assn. Home: 3631 Titanic St El Paso TX 79904 Office: PO Box 4255 El Paso TX 79914

SANDERS, GERALD JOSEPH, JR., minister, Lutheran Church in America; b. Oakland, Md., Dec. 2, 1953; s. Gerald Joseph and Wilda Juanita (Durst) S.; B.S., Frostburg State Coll., 1975; M.Div., Luth. Theol. Sem., 1981. Ordained to ministry Lutheran Church in America, 1981. Pastor Spring Ch. Luth. Ch., Apollo, Pa., 1981—; sec. Armstrong dist. Western Pa./W.Va. Synod, 1983, dean, 1984—; bd. dirs. Passavant Health Ctr., Zelienople, Pa., 1983—; coordinator ann. pastor's conv. Western Pa./W.Va. Synod, 1984—, coordinator bishop shepherding cluster, 1982—; chaplain Kiski Twp. Sr. Citizens, Apollo, 1983, 84, 85. Mem. Apollo Area Ministerium. Republican. Home and Office: Spring Ch Luth Ch 3623 Lutheran Church Rd Apollo PA 15613-8954

SANDERS, JACK THOMAS, educator; b. Grand Prairie, Tex., Feb. 28, 1935; s. Eula Thomas and Mildred Madge (Parish) S.; B.A., Tex. Wesleyan Coll., 1956; M.Div., Emory U., 1960; Ph.D., Claremont Grad. Sch., 1963; postdoctoral U. Tuebingen, Germany, 1963-64; m. M. Patricia Chism, Aug. 9, 1959 (dec. Oct. 1973); 1 son, Collin Thomas; m. Susan E. Plass, Mar. 3, 1979. Ordained elder United Methodist Ch., 1960; student pastor, 1955-60; asst. prof. N.T., Emory 1964-67; vis. asst. prof. N.T., Garrett Theol. Sem., 1967-68, McCormick Theol. Sem., 1968-69; asso. prof. religious studies U. Oreg., 1969-75, prof., 1975—, head dept., 1973—; vis. scholar Harvard Div. Sch., 1983-84; fellow Center for Bibl. Research and Archives, Claremont, Calif., 1976-77; NEH sr. fellow for ind. study and research, 1983-84. Mem. policy bd. dept. higher edn. Nat. Council Chs. 1971-73. Mem. Am. Civil Liberties Union. Mem. exec com. Lane County McGovern for Pres. Com., 1972. Mem. Soc. Bibl. Lit. (regional sec. 1970-76) Am. Acad. Religion, Studiorum Novi Testamenti Societas, AAUP. Author: The New Testament Christological Hymns, Their Historical Religious Background, 1971; Ethics in the New Testament, Change and Development, 1975; Ben Sira and Demotic Wisdom, 1983; editorial bd.: Jour. Bibl. Lit., 1977-80. Home: 390 E 50th Ave Eugene OR 97405

SANDERS, JOHN CLARKE, priest, Episcopal Church; m. Frances Jameson, 1955; children: Clarke, Scott, David. B.B.A. in Personnel Mgmt., U. Tex., 1955; B.D., Sem. of SW, Austin, Tex., 1955; S.T.M. cum laude, Va. Theol. Sem., 1969. Ordained to ministry Episcopal Church, 1958. Victor, Holy Trinity Ch., Port Neches, Tex., 1958-61, rector, 1961-63; rector St. James Ch., Houston, 1963-70, Christ Episcopal Ch., Shaker Heights, Ohio, 1975—; dean St. John Cathedral, Wilmington, Del., 1970-75; dean SE conv. Diocese of Tex., 1963, mem. exec. bd., 1965-67, chmn. dept. soc. relations, 1965; chmn. Episcopal Loyalty Fund, East Harris County, Tex.; alumni trustee Sem. of Southwest, 1967-68; chairperson Episcopal Soc. Cultural and Racial Unity, 1964-65; area clergy chmn. Resources for Leadership in the '70s Diocesan Fund Campaign; mem. exec. bd. Diocese of Del., 1970-75, co-chmn. dept. ministries, 1970, chmn. clergy support div., 1971-75; Protestant chmn. clergy dialog group NCCJ, Wilmington; dep. to Gen. Conv. Episcopal Ch., 1973; commencement speaker Sem. of SW, 1974; chairperson Placement Com. for Women and Minority Clergy; mem. task force on role and status of women Diocese of Ohio, companion workshop, province V, mem. personnel com., mem. fin. com., mem. dept. evangelism and renewal, mem. council, 1977-81, v.p., 1981, mem. dept. nat. and world mission, mem. liturgical commn.; dep. to Gen. Conv. Episcopal Ch., 1982, 85; bd. dirs. Greater Cleveland Inter-Ch. Council, 1976-82; field work supr. St. Mary's Roman Cath. Sem., 1981-83; clergy chairperson Greater Cleve. United Way, 1983; mem. Cleve. Covenant Design Team; mem. L.E.A.D. Consultants Calling Ministry Labs I and II; chairperson Commn. on Ministry. Chmn., Port Neches Community Chest, Tex., 1959-63; vice-chmn. Mid County Am. Cancer Soc., 1960-63, Houston Housing Corp.; mem. governing bd. Negro Child Ctr. Houston, 1964-68; mem. steering com. Wilmington Housing Alliance; bd. dirs. Early Childhood Enrichment Ctr., Ohio, Shaker Heights Youth Ctr. Recipient Distinguished Congregation award Living Ch.'s, 1965; Rossiter scholar Bexley Hall, 1982. Mem. Cleve. Alathean Soc. (chairperson). Home: 20889 Colby Rd Shaker Heights OH 44122 Office: Christ Episcopal Ch 3445 Warrensville Center Rd Shaker Heights OH 44122

SANDERS, JOHNNY LEE, minister, Southern Baptist Convention; b. Calhoun City, Miss., May 12, 1937; s. Joe B. and Claudine (Cofer) S.; m. Rebecca Turner, July 17, 1962; children: Johnny L. II, Mark K. B.A., Miss. Coll., 1959; M.Div., New Orleans Bapt. Theol. Sem., 1963; D. Ministry, Luther Rice Sem., 1978. Ordained to ministry, Bapt. Ch., 1957. Pastor, Glendale Bapt. Ch., Greenville, Miss., 1963-65, West Side Bapt. Ch., Bastrop, La., 1965-73, Hillcrest Bapt. Ch., Nederland, Tex., 1973-74, West Side Bapt. Ch., Bastrop, La., 1974-78, Forest Bapt. Ch., La., 1978—; revival preacher, Bible tchr. So. Bapt. chs.; moderator Morehouse Bapt. Assn., Bastrop, 1972-73; La. coordinator Luther Rice Sem., Jacksonville, Fl., 1980—. Contbr. articles to religious jours. Recipient placque for contbns. New Orleans Bapt. Sem., 1976. Mem. Bayou Macon Bapt. Assn. (mem. exec. bd., moderator 1979-80), La. Bapt. Conv., So. Bapt. Conv. Democrat. Club: PJA (Forest). Home and Office: PO Box 339 Forest LA 71242

SANDERS, MARSHALL JAMES, religious publisher, construction consultant, Church of God (Anderson, Indiana); b. Wichita, Kans., Mar. 23, 1952; s. James Thomas and Twila Maxine (Brown) S.; m. Cynthia Sue Andrist, Aug. 26, 1972; 1 child, Benjamin James. Student, Anderson Coll., 1970-74. Assoc. ministry of music Crystal Cathedral, Garden Grove, Calif., 1979-81; minister of music Central Com. Ch., Wichita, Kans., 1983-84; pub. and pres. Creator Magazine, Inc., Wichita, 1977—; cons. lighting and constrn. projects, 1983—. Contbr. articles to prof. jours. Mem. Evangel. Press Assn. Democrat. Home and Office: 25 Rolling Hills Wichita KS 67212

SANDERS, RAY H., minister, church official, Ch. of God; b. Bath, S.C., Oct. 5, 1936; s. Darlin A. and Lillian Elizabeth (Hutto) S.; B.A. in Bibl. Edn., Lee Coll., 1965; m. Kathy Virginai Hucklebridge, Aug. 14, 1964; children—Delta, Virginia, Tonya. Ordained to ministry, 1968; v.p. Pioneers for Christ, 1963, 64, Met. evang. dir., Ind., La., Colo., Calif., 1965-74; mem. Evangelism and Home Mission bd., Cleveland, Tenn., 1972—, chmn., 1978-82; state overseer, Mpls., 1974—; mem. gen. exec. council Ch. of God, 1982—; state overseer of Ill., 1982—. guest speaker youth camps. Contbr. articles to religious jours. Home and Office: 1411 Post Ct Decatur IL 62521

SANDERS, TERRELL C., JR., seminary adminstrator. Pres. Nazarene Theol. Sem. (Church of Nazarene), Kansas City, Mo. Office: Nazarene Theol Sem 1700 E Meyer Blvd Kansas City MO 64131*

SANDERSON, JAMES LAVERN, minister, So. Bapt. Conv.; b. Plum City, Wis., Aug. 24, 1946; s. Arthur James and Bernice Hazel (Merriman) S.; B.A., Okla. State U., 1968; M.Div., Southwestern Bapt. Theol. Sem., 1972; m. Barbara Sue Goins, Nov. 29, 1968; children—Christopher James, Matthew Todd. Ordained to ministry, 1968; pastor First Bapt. Ch., Morrison, Okla., 1966, Trinity Bapt. Ch., Duncan, Okla., 1968-72, First Bapt. Ch., Lazbuddie, Tex., 1972-74, Eastern Hts. Bapt. Ch., Bartlesville, Okla., 1974—. Moderator, Mullins Bapt. Assn., 1972; chmn. City-side Crusade, Bartlesville, Okla., 1976; bd. dirs. Bapt. Gen. Conv. Okla., 1976. Mem. Okla. State U., Southwestern Bapt. Theol. Sem. alumni assns. Home: 1536 S Johnstone St Bartlesville OK 74003 Office: 1331 SE Swan Dr Bartlesville OK 74003

SANDFORD, JOHN LOREN, minister, United Church of Christ; b. Joplin, Mo., July 23, 1929; s. George Oliver and Zelma Edith (Potter) S.; Paula Ann Bowman, Jan. 12, 1951; children: Loren, Amilee, Mark, John, Timothy, Andrea. B.A., Drury Coll., 1951; M.Div., Chgo. Theol. Sem., 1958. Ordained to ministry United Ch. of Christ, 1958. Pastor, First Congl. United Ch. of Christ, Streator, Ill., 1956-61, Council Grove, Kans., 1961-65, Wallace, Idaho, 1965-73; writer, tchr., counselor Elijah House, Inc., Coeur D'Alene, Idaho, 1973—; tchr. Sch. of Pastoral Care, Whitinsville, Mass., 1961-70, Camps Farthest Out, Mpls., 1961—. Author: (with Paula Sandford) The Elijah Task, 1977, Restoring the Christian Family, 1979, The Transformation of the Inner Man, 1982, Healing the Wounded Spirit, 1985. Home: 3657 Highland Dr Coeur D'Alene ID 83814 Office: Elijah House Inc 3657 Highland Dr Coeur D'Alene ID 83814

SANDIN, PAUL LEONARD, minister, International Council of Community Churches; b. Chgo., Feb. 5, 1939; s. Ernest Clifford and Hazel Sophia (Johnson) S.; m. Irene Lois VanDyke, May 30, 1957; children: Debra Lynn Sandin Dockendorf, Peter Clifford. B.A., Shurtleff Coll., 1957; M.Div., Colgate Rochester Coll., 1960; D. Ministry, Drew U., 1981. Ordained to ministry American Baptist Churches in the U.S.A., 1960. Capital funds dir. Central Bapt. Theol. Sem., Kansas City, Kans., 1963-64; minister Countryside Bapt. Ch., Hutchinson, Kans., 1964-67; assoc. minister The S. Ch., Mt. Prospect, Ill., 1967-73; minister First Bapt. Ch., Iowa City, Iowa, 1973-79; Sr. minister Community Ch., East Williston, N.Y.; 1979—; trustee Internat. Council Community Chs., Homewood, Ill., 1982—; v.p. Long Island Council of Chs., 1982—; nat. program chmn. Internat. Council Community Chs., 1984—. Home: 202 Ward St East Williston NY 11596 Office: Community Ch East Williston East Williston Ave & High St East Williston NY 11596

SANDLIN, S.Z., minister, Southern Baptist Convention. B. Lubbock, Tex., Aug. 10, 1949; s. Horace E. and Helen B. (Zeh) Sandlin; m. Cheryl Anne Colclazer, July 17, 1971; children: Summer, Suzanna. B.B.A., Tex. Tech. U., 1971; M. Divinity, Southwestern Bapt. Theol. Sem., Ft. Worth, 1975, D.Min., 1980. Ordained to ministry So. Bapt. Conv., 1975; dir. Bapt. Student Union, Kilgore (Tex.) Coll. and Panola (Tex.) Coll., 1974-76; pastor Midway Bapt. Ch., Big Spring, Tex., 1976-78, S. Plains Bapt. Ch., Levelland, Tex., 1978-80, Faith Bapt. Ch., Wichita Falls, Tex., 1980—. Bd. dirs. Wichita Falls YMCA, 1982-84. Mem. So. Bapt. Conv., Wichita-Archer-Clay Bapt. Assn. (chmn. student work com. 1980-82, personnel com., 1983—). Recipient Order of Arrow, Boy Scouts Am., 1967. Home: 4507 Wynnwood St Wichita Falls TX 76308 Office: Faith Bapt Ch 3001 Southwest Pkwy Wichita Falls TX 76308

SANDMAN, J(OHN) ROBERT, minister, United Ch. of Christ; b. Newport, Ky., July 14, 1927; s. Albert and Erma E. (Wald) S.; A.B., Oberlin (Ohio) Coll., 1949; M.Div., Union Theol. Sem., N.Y.C., 1952; D.Min., United Theol. Sem., Dayton, Ohio, 1975; m. Olgha Sierra-Ramos, Feb. 26, 1955; children—Robert, Linda, Richard, Rodney. Ordained to ministry 1952; migrant ministry field staff Nat. Council Chs., Midwest, 1952-54, migrant ministry, Tex. dir., Austin, 1955-57; pastor North Congl. Ch., Columbus, Ohio, 1957-62; minister parish program/mission priorities S.W. Ohio Assn., Ohio Conf. United Ch. of Christ, Dayton, 1963-73; assn. minister Central Assn., Ill. Conf., Peoria, 1974—; bd. dirs., chmn. dept. pub. affairs Ohio Council Chs., 1966-67. Mem. Ohio Gov.'s Com. on Migrant Labor, 1964-71; mem. dist. and troop com. Kettering council Boy Scouts Am., 1968-70; chmn. FORCE Assos., Dayton, 1968. Bd. dirs. Friendship House, Peoria, 1974—. Home: 225 Coventry St East Peoria IL 61611 Office: 2508 N Sheridan St Peoria IL 61604

SANDOVAL, MOISES, lay church worker, Roman Catholic Church; b. Sapello, N.Mex., Mar. 29, 1930; s. Eusebio and Amada (Perea) S.; m. Penelope Ann

Gartman, Nov. 5, 1955; children: Margaret, Michael, Rose, Jim, Mary. B.S. in Journalism, Marquette U., 1955; cert. internat. reporting Columbia U., 1964. Sr. editor Pflaum Publishers, Dayton, Ohio, 1964-70; mng. editor Cath. Fgn. Mission Soc., Maryknoll, N.Y., 1970-79, editor, 1980—; bd. dirs. Cath. Press Assn. of U.A. and Can., Rockville Center, N.Y., 1977—, Assn. for the Rights of Caths., 1980—. Editor: Fronteras: The History of Hispanic Churches in U.S., 1983. Contbr. articles to profl. jours. and chpts. to books. Served to 1st lt. USAR, 1955-63. Ford Found. fellow, 1963; Alicia Patterson fellow, 1977. Democrat. Office: Maryknoll Fathers Maryknoll NY 10545

SANDY, D. BRENT, minister, religion educator, Fellowship of Grace Brethen Churches; b. Lebanon, Pa., Mar. 19, 1947; s. A. Rollin and Omega V. (Hartman) S.; m. Cheryl J. Ackerly, June 26, 1971; children: Jason Brent, Jaron Chad. B.A., Grace Coll., Winona Lake, Ind., 1969; postgrad. SUNY-Binghamton, 1969-70; M.Div. with honors, Grace Sem., 1970-73; Ph.D. (grad. fellow) Duke Univ., 1977. Licensed to ministry, Fellowship Grace Brethen Chs., 1984. Minister of music Calvary Bapt. Tabernacle, Vestal, N.Y., 1969-70, Edgemont Bapt. Ch., Durham, N.C., 1973-77; asst. prof. Grace Coll. and Sem., Winona Lake, Ind., 1977-82, assoc. prof., 1982—; vis. scholar Univ. Mich., Ann Arbor, 1984; participant Conf. on Teaching in Ancient World, NEH, Nashville, 1982, Judaism and Early Christianity Seminar, Nat. Endowment Humanities, Duke U., 1982. Author: Ptolemaic Oils, 1985. Contbr. articles to profl. jours., chpts. in books. Recipient award in New Testament, Grace Theol. Sem., 1973. Mem. Soc. Bibl. Lit., Evang. Theol. Soc., Am. Philol. Assn., Am. Soc. Papyrology, Am. Classical League, Assn. Ancient Historians, Association Internationale de Papyrologues. Republican. Home: Route 3 Box 36 Warsaw IN 46580 Office: Grace Coll & Theol Sem 200 Seminary Dr Winona Lake IN 46590

SANFILIPPO, RONALD JOSEPH, educational administrator, Roman Catholic Church; swimming coach; b. San Jose, Calif., Apr. 7, 1947; s. Joseph Ignatius and Catherine (Hilje) S. B.A. in Philosophy, Gonzagu U., 1971; M.Div. in Theology, Grad. Theol. Union, Berkeley, Calif., 1976. Ordained priest Roman Catholic Ch., 1976. Assoc. pastor St. Ignatius Parish, Sacramento, 1976-83; chaplain Sacramento Juvenile Hall, 1976-79; dir. campus ministry Brophy Coll. Prep., Phoenix, 1984—, also asst. swim coach. Vol., Children of the Night, Hollywood, Calif., 1984. Democrat. Club: Universal Autograph Collector's. Avocations: autograph collecting; swimming; entertainment field and arts. Home and Office: 4701 N Central Ave Phoenix AZ 85012

SAPP, CARL ROBERT, church consultant, Southern Baptist Convention; b. McLeansboro, Ill., June 27, 1914; s. John Edla and Carrie Ethel (Marshall) S.; m. Dorothy Pearl Angle, Dec. 22, 1937; children: David Gordon, Jean Carolyn Sapp Ingram. A.B., George Washington U., 1941; M.A., Am. U., 1962; postgrad. So. Bapt. Theol. Sem., 1971. Ch. cons., Arlington, Va., 1966-71, 76-77, 83—; minister Edn. Providence Bapt. Ch., Vienna, Va., 1971-75; dir. dept. Christian edn. D.C. Bapt. Conv., Washington, 1978-83; chmn. edn. com. Va. Bapt. Gen. Bd., Richmond, 1967-68; 2d v.p. Bapt. Gen. Assn. Va., Richmond, 1967-68; trustee So. Bapt. Sunday Sch. Bd., Nashville, 1970-78. Contbr. articles to religious publs. Recipient Superior Service award Sec. Agr., 1968. Fellow Soc. Religious Orgn. Mgmt. (bd. dirs. 1984); mem. Pi Sigma Alpha. Home: 5534 N 18th Rd Arlington VA 22205 Office: Westover Bapt Ch 1125 N Patrick Henry Dr Arlington VA 22205

SAPP, WARREN HENRY, priest, Episcopal Church; b. Chgo., Sept. 24, 1919; s. Warren Henry and Hattie Sophia (Hann) S.; m. Eleanor Ruth Gustafson, Mar. 24, 1939; children: Warren Henry III, Kathleen Eleanor, Andrew Paul. Student U. Kans., 1937-38, North Park Coll., Chgo., 1938-39. Ordained priest Episcopal Ch., 1957. Vicar, various chs., Kans., Mo., 1957-67; vol. priest, various chs., Mo., Oreg., 1967-77; vicar St. Mark's Ch., Madras, Oreg., 1977-84; mem. Commn. on Ministry, Diocese of Eastern Oreg., 1976-82. Cost acct., various other positions Armour & Co., meat packers, 1939-55; claims examiner, claims rep. Social Adminstrn., 1967-76. Served to 1st lt. AUS, 1944-46, 50-53. Home: 788 NW 1st St Madras OR 97741

SAPPINGTON, ROGER EDWIN, religious history educator, minister, Church of the Brethren; b. Avon Park, Fla., Mar. 6, 1929; s. Ross Frazier and Beulah Elizabeth (Snader) S.; m. LeVerle Hochstetler, June 5, 1949; children: Charlotte, David, Paul, Mark. B.A., Manchester Coll., 1951; B.D., Bethany Theol. Sem., 1954; M.A., Duke U., 1954, Ph.D., 1959. Ordained to ministry Ch. of the Brethren, 19—. Pastor, Pleasant View Ch. of Brethren, Lima, Ohio, 1955-58; prof. history Bridgewater Coll., Va., 1958—. Contbr. articles to religious jours. Author: The Brethren in the New Nation: 1785-1865, 1976, others. Ford Found. humanities fellow, 1966-67. Mem. Am. History Assn., Orgn. Am. Historians, Pa. German Soc., Am. Assn. State and Local History. Home: Route 1 PO Box 3 Bridgewater VA 22812 Office: Bridgewater Coll Bridgewater VA 22812

SARDINA, JOHN JOSEPH, priest, Roman Catholic Church. B. Buffalo, May 3, 1932; s. Pasquale Jerome and Maria Lucy (Provenzano) S. Ordained priest, Roman Cath. Ch., 1960. Asst. pastor Nativity of Blessed Virgin Mary, Buffalo, 1960-63, Our lady of Pompeii, Lancaster, N.Y., 1963-65, Holy Cross, Buffalo, 1965-67, 77-79, Cornonation of Blessed Virgin Mary, Buffalo, 1967-77; pastor St. Anthony's Ch., Fredonia, N.Y., 1980—. Home and Office: St Anthony's Ch 42 Orchard St Fredonia NY 14063

SARGEANT, DOUGLAS JACK, minister, United Pentecostal Church International; b. Aberdeen, Wash., May 3, 1937; s. Donald J. and Wretha Lora (Bailey) S.; m. Donna Mae Austin, June 22, 1957; children: Renae L. (dec.), Kendall Douglas, Brian Lynn. Grad. Conquerors Bible Coll., 1958. Ordained to ministry United Pentecostal Ch., 1961. Evangelist, United Pentecostal Ch., Pacific Northwest, 1959-60, pastor, Great Falls, Mont., 1960-65, Sandoval, Ill., 1970-73, Sparta, Ill., 1973-81; Creston Apostolic Lighthouse United Pentecostal Ch., Creston, Iowa, 1984—; Sunday sch. dir. United Pentecostal Ch., sect. one, 1973-75, sec. two, 1975-77, sec. Ill. dist., 1974-81, bd. govs. Ill. dist. youth camps, 1974-81, Ill. dist. federal credit union, 1974-81, Tupelo Children's Mansion, Miss., 1981-82. Mem. Smithsonian Instution. Republican. Home: 605 S Maple Creston IA 50801 Office: United Pentecostal Ch PO Box 576 Creston IA 50801

SARUBBI, DOMINIC WILLIAM, priest, Episcopal Church; b. San Francisco, July 18, 1934; s. Francis Samuel and Rose (Cirimeli) S.; m. Margaret Mary Smith, Oct. 28, 1972; children: Christine Mary. A.B., St. Patrick's Coll., 1956; B.D., St. Patrick's Sem., 1960; M.A., Dominican Coll., 1968; D.R.Ed., Internat. Bible Inst. and Sem., 1983. Ordained priest, Roman Cath. Ch., 1960. Asst. pastor, Holy Name Roman Cath. Ch., San Francisco, 1960-61; tchr. Marian Cath. Sch., Kentfield, Calif., 1961-72; adminstr., 1963-65; vice prin. St. John's Sch., Healdsburg, Calif., 1973-74; headmaster St. Michael Episcopal Sch., Carmichael, Calif., 1974-76; rector St. Stephen's Episcopal Ch., Sebastopol, Calif., 1976—. Democrat. Home: PO Box 186 Sebastopol CA 95472 Office: Saint Stephens Ch PO Box 98 500 Robinson Rd Sebastopol CA 95472

SARVELLO, MARY NICOLA, nun, Roman Cath. Ch.; b. Spokane, Wash.; d. Francis Anthony and Frances Marie (Servello) S.; B.A., Holy Names Coll., 1961; M.A., Gonzaga U., 1968. Joined Sisters of St. Francis, 1930; prin. St. Andrew's Sch., Pendleton, Oreg., 1950-55; asst. Confraternity Christian Doctrine coordinatory Diocesan Office, Baker, Oreg., 1960-62; parish Confraternity Christian Doctrine coordinator, Pendleton, Oreg., 1962-64; adminstr. St. Joseph's Children's Home, Spokane, Wash., 1969—. Mem. Nat. Cath. Charities Conf., Nat. Assn. Homes for Children, Wash. Assn. Social Welfare, Wash. Child Caring Inst. Home and Office: N 1016 Superior St Spokane WA 99202

SATCHIDANANDA, SWAMI, monk, Santana Dharmi; b. Chettipalayam, Coimbatore, India, Dec. 22, 1914; came to U.S., 1966, naturalized, 1976; ed. in sci. and tech., S. India; student religion Swami Chidbavanandaji, Swami Rajeswaranandaji, Ramana Maharshi, Swami Sivanandaji. Co-dir. Center for Spiritual Studies, N.Y.C.; pres. Integral Yoga Inst., Coimbatore; trustee Satchidananda Thapovanam monastery, Kandy, Sri Lanka; prof. Hatha and Raja Yoga, Yoga Vedanta Forest Acad., Himalayas; spiritual head Satchidananda Ashram, Pomfret Center, Conn.; organizer Ann. All-Prophets Days, Sri Lanka, also brs. Divine Life Soc., Sri Lanka; lectr. U.S., Europe, S. Pacific, Australia, S.Am. Recipient Martin Buber award for Outstanding Service to Humanity. Author: Integral Yoga Hatha; also pamphlets on meditation and Yoga-related subjects. Home and Office: Satchidananda Ashram Yogaville East PO Box 108 Pomfret Center CT 06259

SATO, EUNICE NODA, ch. ofcl., United Methodist Ch.; b. Livingston, Calif., June 8, 1921; d. Bunsaku and Sawa (Maeda) Noda; A.A., Modesto Jr. Coll., 1941; B.A., U. No. Colo., 1944; M.A., Columbia Tchrs. Coll., 1948; m. Thomas T. Sato, Dec. 9, 1950; children—Charlotte Patricia, Daniel Ryuichi and Douglas Ryuji (twins). Ednl. missionary, Japan, 1948-51; childrens supt. Silverado United Methodist Ch., 1961-63, ch. sch. supt., 1966-67; chmn. Commn. on Missions, 1968; supt. Vacation Ch. Sch., 1965; lay del. to Council Chs., lay del. So. Calif./Ariz. Conf., 1967-71; chmn. Adminstrn. Bd., 1969-72; mem. Bd. Edn. So. Calif./Ariz. Conf., 1972-74, adult ministries rep. Global Ministries Bd.; chmn. Council on Ministries, 1973—; pres. Long Beach Area Council Chs., 1972-74. Mem. Long Beach City Council, 1975—. Pres., Long Beach Council PTA, 1972-74, mem. exec. bd., 1961—; mem. Long Beach Human Relations Commn., 1972-74; pres. Long Beach Area Community Planning Council, 1970; mem. UN Assn.; mem. edn. com. Cancer Soc.; mem. steering com. Long Beach Am. Revolution Bicentennial, Long Beach Safety Council. Bd. dirs., sec. Girl Scouts U.S.A.,; bd. dirs. Long Beach chpt. ARC, Long Beach Day Nursery, United Way-United Crusade, Long Beach Meml. Hosp. Med. Center, Psychiat. Clinic for Children. Recipient Outstanding Service award Long Beach Coordinating Council, 1969; Hon. Service award PTA, 1963; Continuing Service award, 1974; named Mother of Year, Silverado United Meth. Ch., 1973. Contbr. monthly page Long Beach Council PTA Newsetter. Home: 2895 Easy Ave Long Beach CA 90810

SATRE, CARL HERSCH, minister, Lutheran Church in America; b. Lena, Ill., May 6, 1934; s. W. Carl and Elizabeth (Hersch) S.; m. Esther Joyce, June 5, 1956; children: Caroline, Mary. A.B., Carthage Coll., 1956; M.Div., Hamma Sch. Theology, 1959; M.A., U. Notre Dame, 1964. Ordained to ministry Luth. Ch. in Am., 1959. Pastor, Grace Luth. Ch., Syracuse, Ind., 1959-65; sr. pastor Messiah Luth. Ch., Fort Wayne, Ind., 1965—; dir. Wittenberg U., Springfield, Ohio, 1965-72, 78-82; Ind.-Ky. Synod, Indpls., 1972-78, 82—; dean Ind.-Ky. Synod Fort Wayne Dist., 1968-78, 82—. Served to 1st lt. chaplain U.S. Army, 1960-65. Republican. Home: 6115 Groveland Dr Fort Wayne IN 46815 Office: Messiah Lutheran Church 6201 Stellhorn Rd Fort Wayne IN 46815

SATTERWHITE, DAVID EARL, minister, So. Bapt. Ch.; b. Amory, Miss., Mar. 15, 1936; s. James Doyle and Hazel (Francis) S.; diploma theology Southwestern Bapt. Theol. Sem., 1975, postgrad., 1975—; m. Mavis Wade, July 16, 1960; 1 dau., Sophia Dawn. Ordained to ministry, 1974; pastor Hulen St. Bapt. Ch., Fort Worth, 1974-75, Unity Bapt. Ch., Tuscaloosa, Ala., 1976—. Mem. Alcohol Abuse Com.; active as speaker and writer for Gideons. Mem. Tuscaloosa Bapt. Assn. Home: 3821 65th Ave Tuscaloosa AL 35401 Office: Route 3 Unity Rd Tuscaloosa AL 35401

SATTERWHITE, GRADY CHARLES, minister, Church of God (Cleveland, Tenn.); b. Lufkin, Tex., Jan. 28, 1947; s. Bradly Boswell Satterwhite and Mary Louise (Jackson) Satterwhite Fulcher; b. Ramona Duhon, Dec. 30, 1971; children: Charity Leone, Elizabeth Hope. B.S., Southwestern Coll. Assemblies of God, Waxahachie, Tex., 1972; Th.M., Southwestern Sem., Ft. Worth, 1975. Ordained to ministry Assemblies of God, 1970. Evangelist, pastor Assemblies of God, Tex., 1961-72; pastor, Arp, Tex., 1973-75; missionary to mil. Ch. of God, Spain and Germany, 1977-82; pastor Ch. of God, Baumholdar, Fed. Republic Germany, 1981-82, Copeland Ch. of God, Millry, Ala., 1982—; prof. Ch. of God, Rudersberg, Fed. Republic Germany, 1980-81; dist. dir. Christian edn. Ch. of God, Choctaw County, Ala., 1982—. Coordinator Young Republicans, Tyler, Tex., 1963-65; coordinator Nat. Fedn. for Decency, Millry, 1984. Home and Office: Route 2 Box 131 Millry AL 36558

SAUDER, ELIZABETH WEAVER, lay ch. worker, Mennonite Ch.; b. nr. Lancaster, Pa., Sept. 20, 1916; d. Samuel Reiff and Elizabeth Zimmerman (Good) Weaver; grad. high sch.; m. Paul Noah Sauder, Feb. 5, 1938. Tchr. Sunday sch. Lancaster Conf. Mennonite Ch., 1939—; v.p. Sr. Sewing Circle, 1954-55, treas., 1960, pres., 1967; area v.p. Asso. Sewing Circles of Lancaster Conf., 1967, pres., 1968-76; sec. Women's Work Coordinating Com., 1967-71; mem. Women's Missionary Service Commn., Mennonite Ch. Mem. Landis Homes Retirement Community Aux., Conestoga View Aux., Lancaster Mental Health Assn., Black Rock Camp Aux. Home: 343 W Main St New Holland PA 17557

SAUDER, RAY E. Elder, Apostolic Christian Church of America. Office: 1100 E St Luke Ct Peoria IL 61614*

SAUER, KENNETH H. Synodical bishop Lutheran Church in America, Columbus, Ohio. Office: Luth Ch in Am 1233 Dublin Rd Columbus OH 43215*

SAUER, VAL JOHN, JR., minister, American Baptist Churches in the U.S.A.; b. Herried, S.D., June 12, 1938; s. Valentine John and Freda (Reidlinger) S.; m. Connie Jean Olmsted, Feb. 5, 1966; children: Colleen June, Crystal Joy. B.S. in Elec. Engring., S.D. State U., 1965; M.Div., Am. Bapt. Sem., 1969, D. Ministry, 1974. Ordained to ministry Baptist Ch., 1969. Sr. pastor First Bapt. Ch., Mitchell, S.D., 1969-73, Meml. Bapt. Ch., Fond du Lac, Wis., 1974-78, First Bapt. Ch., Watertown, S.D., 1978—; v.p. S.D. Bapt. Conv., 1970-72, mem. bd. dirs., 1979—. Author: The Eschatology Handbook, 1981; contbr. articles to religious publs. Bd. dirs. St. Ann's Hosp., Watertown, 1983—; pres. Davison County Mental Health Assn., Mitchell, 1972. Served with USMC, 1956-61. Named Minister of Yr., S.D. Bapt. Conv., 1983. Mem. Am. Bapt. Ministers Council, Acad. of Parish Clergy. Democrat. Home: 1334 Harmony Ln Watertown SD 57201 Office: First Baptist Ch 111 14th Ave NE Watertown SD 57201

SAULS, DONALD GERALD, minister, Pentecostal Free Will Baptist Church, Inc.; b. Wayne County, N.C., Sept. 22, 1946; s. Sidney Russell and Clara Lee (Sorrell) S.; m. Alta Marie Brown, July 15, 1966; children: Donna Marie, Dale Michael. B.S.L., Holmes Sch. of Bible, 1967; postgrad. N.C. Wesleyan, 1974-75, N.C. State U.-Raliegh, 1983—. Ordained to ministry, 1966. Dir. ministerial dept. Pentecostal Free Will Bapt. Ch., Inc., Dunn, N.C., 1970-74, mem. gen. bd., 1970—, dir. Christian edn., 1971-84, exec. sec., 1971-84, dir.

Crusader Youth Camp, 1974-84, gen. supt., 1984—, dir. Laity dept., 1974-82; chmn. youth commn. Pentecostal Fellowship of N. Am., 1975-77, bd. adminstrn., 1984—; exec. mgr. to mgr. Blessings Bookstore, 1971-84; prof. Hentiga Bible Coll., Dunn, 1971-83. Home: Route 1 Box 40 Dunn NC 28334 Office: Pentecostal Free Will Bapt Ch Inc Route 1 PO Box 1568 Dunn NC 28334

SAUNDERS, GEORGE MICHAEL, SR., minister, Presbyterian Church in America; b. Wolfboro, N.H., June 27, 1955; s. George William and Theresa Alice (Waterman) S.; m. Deborah Anne Baucom, Jan. 1, 1976; children: George Michael, Deborah JoAnne, Joseph Adam. Student Berkshire Christian Coll., 1973-75; B.A. in Bible, Belhaven Coll., 1978; M.Div., Reformed Theol. Sem., Jackson, Miss., 1983. Ordained to ministry Presbyterian Ch., 1983. Asst. pastor Portsmouth Advent Christian Ch., N.H., 1979, Back Creek Assoc. Reformed Presbyn. Ch., Charlotte, N.C., 1979-80; pastor First Presbyn. Ch., Enterprise, Ala., 1983—; founder, dir. chaplaincy Humana Hosp., Enterprise, 1984—, Enterprise Hosp., 1985—. Mem. Evang. Theol. Soc., Enterprise Christian Minister's Fellowship (treas. 1983-84, sec. 1984-85), Enterprise C. of C., Pea River Hist. and Geneal. Soc. Republican. Home: 103 Rosewood Dr Enterprise AL 36330 Office: First Presbyn Ch 100 Daleville Ave Enterprise AL 36330

SAUNDERS, HERBERT EUGENE, minister, Seventh Day Baptist General Conference; b. Nortonville, Kans., May 31, 1940; s. Francis Davis and Lila Margaret (Stephan) S.; m. Barbara Louise Crandall, June 24, 1962; children: Brian Eugene, Peggy Susan, Michael David. B.A., Salem Coll., 1962; M.Div., Colgate Rochester Div. Sch., 1966. Ordained to ministry, Seventh-Day Baptist Gen. Conf., 1966. Pastor Seventh Day Bapt. Ch., Little Genesee, N.Y., 1962-67, Hebron, Pa., 1964-67, Plainfield, N.J., 1967-75; dean Seventh Day Bapt. Ctr. on Ministry, Plainfield, N.J., 1975-82; pastor Seventh Day Bapt. Ch., Milton, Wis., 1982—; chmn. Seventh Day Bapt. com. on faith and order, Janesville, Wis., 1983—. Author: Sabbath: Symbol of Creation and Re-Creation, 1971. Editor: (ch. sch. helps) The Helping Hand, 1984. Lodge: Kiwanis. Home: 712 E Madison Ave Milton WI 53563 Office: Seventh Day Bapt Ch 720 E Madison Ave Milton WI 53563

SAUNDERS, JAMES DALE, chaplain, Lutheran Church-Missouri Synod; b. Milw., Aug. 21, 1950; s. Jack Louis and Betty Jane (Werner) S.; m. Barbara Jean Gariepy, July 13, 1974; children: Daniel Paul-Louis, Timothy Michael-John. B.A., Carthage Coll., 1973; M.Div., Concordia Sem., 1977. Ordained to ministry, 1977. Pastor, Trinity Luth. Ch., Casey, Ill., 1977-79; chaplain U.S. Air Force, Sheppard AFB, Wichita Falls, Tex., 1979-82, Hickam AFB, Honolulu, 1982—. Decorated Air Force Commendation medal. Address: 204B Signer Blvd Honolulu HI 96818

SAUPE, WALTER ROBERT, minister, Lutheran Church in America; b. Dayton, OH, Nov. 9, 1934; s. Waldemar Max and Emilie (Knodel) S.; m. Margaret Ann Gordon, Sept. 7, 1957; children: Karen Emili, Eric Gordon. B.M.E. in Mechanical Engring., Gen. Motors Inst., 1957; M.Div., Hamma Sch. Theology, 1964. Ordained to ministry Lutheran Ch. in Am., 1964. Asst. pastor First Luth. Ch., Dayton, Ohio, 1964-67; sr. pastor, 1967-77; pastor St. John's Luth. Ch., London, Ohio, 1977—; del. Biennial Conv. Luth. Ch. Am., 1974-84; dir. Wittenberg U., Springfield, Ohio, 1977—, Trinity Luth. Sem., Columbus, Ohio, 1984—. Mem. Madison County Substance Abuse Council, London, 1982—, Central Ohio Regional Council on Alcoholism, Columbus, 1984—. Republican. Lodge: Rotary (dir. 1983—, v.p. 1984—). Home: 176 East High St London OH 43140 Office: St John's Luth Ch 62 E 2d St London OH 43140

SAVAGE, JAMES HENRY, minister, United Methodist Church; b. Gadsden, Ala. Sept. 30, 1957; s. Joseph Luther and Mattie Sue (Arnold) S.; m. Sherri Lynn Stepps, Apr. 27, 1979; children: James Wesley, Cassi Lynn. B.A. with honors in English and Sociology, Jacksonville U., 1978, B.S. with honors, in Secondary Edn., 1979; M.Div., with honors, Emory U., 1980. Ordained to ministry, United Meth. Ch., as deacon, 1979, as elder, 1982. Asst. pastor, youth dir. Centre First United Meth. Ch., Ala., 1974-77, Saks First United Meth. Ch., Ala., 1977-78; student pastor sem. Lookout Valley United Meth. Circuit, Blanche, Ala., 1978-80; sr. pastor New Oregon United Meth. Ch., Fort Payne, Ala., 1980—; dist. scout coordinator Gadsden dist. United Meth. Ch., 1982—, dist. rep. for Bd. of Ch. and Soc., Birmingham, Ala., 1982—, mem. Commn. on Edn., North Ala. Conf., 1984—; chaplain Fischer Rescue Squad, Fort Payne, 1980—, Choccolocco Council Boy Scouts Am., 1980—; coordinator chs. DeKalb County United Givers Fund, Fort Payne, 1983—; Rep., counselor Bridge Drug and Alcohol Ctr., Gadsden, and Fort Payne, 1980—; pres. DeKalb County Human Resources Council, 1984—. Emory U. scholar, 1978. Mem. Fort Payne Ministerial Assn. (pres. 1983—), North Ala. Study Club, DeSoto Laity Club (pres. 1983), Alpha Nu Gamma. Club: New Oregon Men's (organizer, 1980—) (Fort Payne). Home and Office: New Oregon United Meth Ch Route 1 Box 52 Fort Payne AL 35967

SAVAGE, JOHN EDMUND, minister, So. Bapt. Conv.; b. Shreveport, La., June 1, 1947; s. Edmund Fredrick and Nellie May (Inzer) S.; A.A., So. Bapt. Coll., 1967; B.S.E., Ouachita Bapt. U., 1970, B.A. in Pastoral Ministry, 1979; children—Deborah Lynette, Jonathan Eli. Ordained to ministry, 1966; pastor Big Creek Bapt. Ch., Hooker, Ark., 1965-67, Northside Bapt. Chapel, Arkadelphia, Ark., 1967-69, Shiloh Bapt. Ch., Arkadelphia, Ark., 1969-70, Parks (Ark.) Bapt. Ch., 1970-73, New Hope Bapt. Ch., Pollard, Ark., 1973-75; youth dir. Gainesville Bapt. Assn., 1973-75, vice-moderator, 1974-75; pastor Anchor Bapt. Ch., Donaldson, Ark., 1975-83, Mt. Bethel Bapt. Ch., Arkadelphia, Ark., 1984—. Dir. printing dept. Ouachita Bapt. U., 1975—; clk. Red River Bapt. Assn., 1977-84. Named Outstanding Rural Minister, So. Bapt. Coll., 1967. Home: 218 Main St Arkadelphia AR 71923 Office: OBU Box 3782 Arkadelphia AR 71923

SAVAGE, KENZY KULMAN, minister, Assemblies of God; b. Alvord, Tex., Mar. 17, 1912; s. Hulet Melton and Annie Mae (Gregg) S.; grad. Latin Am. Bible Inst., San Antonio, 1935; m. Esther Winona Dodson, May 8, 1930; children—Bobbie Jean, Patsy Joyce. Ordained to ministry, 1931; truck evangelist Latin Am. dist. Assemblies of God, 1932, presbyter conf., 1932; supt. Latin Am. Bible Inst., 1943-50, 52-60, 76; supt. central conf. Latin Am. dist., 1960-66, exec. treas., 1966-70; sec.-treas. Central Latin Am. dist., 1970-73, exec. presbyter, 1973—. Recipient service plaques. Author: Las Siete Palabras, 1951: La Palabra Sanadora, 1951. Address: Hereford AZ 85615

SAVARYN, NEIL NICHOLAS, bishop, Ukrainian Byzantine Rite; b. Stary Sambir, Ukraine, May 19, 1905; s. Wasyl and Anna (Sygerych) S.; classical and rhetorical studies, Lavriv, Ukraine, 1924; philos. studies, Dobromyl, 1927; theol. studies, Krystynopil, Ukraine, 1928; Canadian citizen, 1939. Entered Order of St. Basil the Great, 1922; ordained priest, 1931; aux. Bishop Ukrainian Cath. Diocese Toronto, 1943-48; bishop of Edmonton, Alta, Can., 1948—; missionary priest in Mundare, Chipman, St. Michael, Krakiv and Wostok, Alta., 1932—; prof. rhetoric and philosophy Basilian Fathers Monastery, Mundare, 1932—; superior Brasilian Fathers Monastery, 1938—. Address: 6240 Ada Blvd Edmonton AB T5W 4P1 Canada

SAVERANCE, EDDIE GRANT, minister, Nat. Assn. Free Will Bapts.; b. Timmonsville, S.C., Mar. 4, 1942; s. Eddie Rudolph and Mary Louise (Fraley) S.; student Free Will Bapt. Coll., 1960-64; m. Carolyn Ann Siler, Aug. 2, 1963; children—Deborah Lee, Eddie Grant. Ordained to ministry, 1962; clk. S. Ga. Assn., 1966-68; mem. Bd. Christian Edn., Ga., 1967-68; mem. ordaining council N.C. Gen. Conf., 1969-70; chmn. ordaining council S. Ga. Assn., 1975-76; mem. S. Ga. Mission Bd., 1976—. Mem. bd. edn. Harriet County Christian Acad., Dunn, N.C., 1968-70. Home: 337 Davis Ct Flat River MO 63601

SAWHILL, LAWRENCE WILLIAM, minister, Lutheran Church-Missouri Synod. B. Truro, Iowa, Mar. 19, 1920; s. William Lincoln and Rosa Angeline (Foreman) S.; m. Violet Evelyn Villwock, Aug. 1, 1943; children: Sheila Ann Sawhill Kimle, Philip William, David Lynn. Student, Knox Coll., 1938-39; B.Th., Concordia Coll. and Sem., Springfield, Ill., 1951. Ordained to ministry, 1951. Pastor, First English Luth. Ch., Spring Valley, Minn., 1951-53, Christ Luth. Ch., Wolverton, Minn., 1953-56, Immanuel Luth. Ch., Prior Lake, Minn., 1956-60, Luth. Ch. of Redeemer, Winnipeg, Man. Can., 1960-65, St. Paul's Luth. Ch., Kenesaw, Nebr., 1965-70, Zion Luth. Ch., Arcadia, Iowa, 1970—; sec. Park Region Pastoral Conf., Minn. dist. Luth. Ch.-Mo. Synod, 1954-56, mem. dist. bd. edn. Man.-Sask. Dist., 1961-65. Served to sr. sgt. USAF, 1941-45. Republican. Home: 200 W Tracy St Box 59 Arcadia IA 51430 Office: Zion Luth Ch 108 W Tracy St Box 59 Arcadia IA 51430

SAYLOR, JOSEPH RICE, JR., minister, United Methodist Church; b. Weatherford, Tex., Dec. 11, 1936; s. Joseph Rice and Fern Lucille (Yost) S.; m. Peggy Leverne Duckworth, Aug. 19, 1965; children: Joseph Rice S. III, Lawrence Emory S. B.A., East Tex. State Coll., 1959; M.Div., Perkins Sch. of Theology, So. Meth. U., 1962. Ordained to ministry United Meth. Ch., 1962. Pastor various chs. throughout Tex., 1959-80, First United Metho- Ch., Waxahachie, Tex., 1980-83, Richland Hills United Meth. Ch., Fort Worth, 1983—. Sec. North Tex. Conf. Bd. of Ordained Ministry, 1968-72, sec. central Tex. conf., 1973-80. Named Outstanding Young Men of Am., 1965. Democrat. Lodge: Rotary (bd. dirs. 1981-83).

SAYLOR, PHILIP P., priest, editor, Roman Catholic Church; b. Bellefonte, Pa., Oct. 1, 1929; s. Philip P. and Kathryn M. (Hoy) S. B.A., Mt. St. Mary's Coll., 1951; M.Div., St. Francis Sem., Loretto, Pa., 1972. Ordained priest, Roman Cath. Ch., 1955. Asst. pastor Our Mother of Sorrows Ch., Johnstown, Pa., 1955-63; pastor St. John's Ch., Altoona, Pa., 1963—; instr. theology St. Francis Coll., Loretto, Pa., 1968-77; dir. ecumenism Diocese of Altoona, 1965—, editor Diocesan newspaper, 1977—; mem. exec. com. Pa. Cath. Conf., Harrisburg, 1964—; papal chaplain, 1974; prelate of honor, 1983. Chmn., Pub. Ambulance Authority, Altoona, 1974—; trustee Mt. St. Mary's Coll., Emmitsburg, Md., 1974—; bd. dirs. Mercy Hosp., Altoona, 1974—. Mem. Canon Law Soc. Lodge: Lions. Home: 309 Lotz Ave Altoona PA 16602 Office: PO Box 413 126 C Logan Blvd Hollidaysburg PA 16648

SAYRE, JOHN LESLIE, minister, Christian Ch. (Disciples of Christ); b. Hannibal, Mo., Mar. 28, 1924; s. John Leslie and Clara Lucile (Haden) S.; B.A., Phillips U., 1947; M.Div., Yale, 1950; M.L.S., U. Tex., Austin, 1963, Ph.D., 1973; m. Herwanna Lee Harrouff, June 18, 1948; children—Barbara Ann, John Richard, Alan Douglas, Melody Lyn. Ordained to ministry, 1946; campus minister Okla. State U., 1950-57, U. Tex., Austin, 1957-62; librarian Grad. Sem., Phillips U., Enid, Okla., 1962—. Pres. Fellowship of Campus Ministry, 1953; bd. dirs. Am. Theol. Library Assn., 1974—. Mem. Disciples of Christ Hist. Soc., Theta Phi. Author: History of Disciples Student Work, United Christian Missionary Society, 1950; Basic Books for the Minister's Library, 1966; An Index of Festschriften in Religion, 1970; Tools for Theological Research, 1975. Home: 2416 E Elm St Enid OK 73701 Office: Box 2212 University Sta Enid OK 73701

SCAER, DAVID PAUL, religion educator, minister, Lutheran Church-Missouri Synod; b. Bklyn., Mar. 13, 1936; s. Paul Henry and Victoria Ann (Zimmermann) S.; m. Dorothy Marie Hronetz, June 18, 1960; children: David Paul, Stephen Charles, Peter James. A.A., Concordia Coll., 1955; B.A., Concordia Sem.-St. Louis, 1957, M.Div., 1960, Th.D., 1963. Ordained to ministry, 1962. Pastor, Redeemer Luth. Ch., Gillespie, Ill., 1962-64, Trinity Luth. Ch., Rockville, Conn., 1964-66; instr. religion U. Ill., Champaign, 1966-76; prof. systematics and N.T., Concordia Sem., Ft. Wayne, Ind., 1966—, acad. dean, 1984—, editor Concordia Theol. Quar., 1969—. Author: James the Apostle of Faith, 1984; Getting in the Story of Concord, 1978; What do You Think of Jesus, 1972; Apostolic Scriptures, 1971. Republican. Home: 1912 Brandywine Trail Fort Wayne IN 46825-4996 Office: Concordia Theol Sem 6600 N Clinton St Fort Wayne IN 46825-4996

SCANLON, MICHAEL JOSEPH, educator, Roman Catholic Church; b. N.Y.C., Aug. 1, 1937; s. Michael Joseph and Christine Mary (Costello) S.; B.A., Villanova U., 1960; S.T.L., Cath. U. Am., 1964, S.T.D., 1969. Entered Augustinian Order, Roman Cath. Ch., 1956, ordained priest, 1964; tchr. Archbishop Carroll High Sch., Washington, 1964-65; prof. systematic theology Augustinian Coll., Washington, 1965-68; asso. prof. systematic theology, dept. chmn. Washington Theol. Coalition, Silver Spring, Md., 1968—. Co-founder, 2d pres. Washington Theol. Consortium, 1969-71. Mem. Am. Acad. Religion, Cath. Theol. Soc. Am. Home: 3900 Harewood Rd NE Washington DC 20017 Office: 9001 New Hampshire Ave Silver Spring MD 20910

SCANLON, PETER JOSEPH, priest, Roman Catholic Church; b. Worcester, Mass., Sept. 2, 1931; s. Peter and Julia (O'Sullivan) S.; student Holy Cross Coll., 1949-51; A.B., St. Mary's U. and Sem., 1953, S.T.B., 1955, S.T.L. with honors, 1957. Ordained priest Roman Catholic Ch., 1957; asst. pastor St. Mary's Parish, Southbridge, Mass., 1957-58, Ascension Parish, Worcester, 1958, St. Patrick's Parish, Rutland, Mass., 1958—, Cath. chaplain Worcester Poly. Inst., 1961—; pastor Our Lady of Fatima, Worcester, 1976-83; diocesan dir. Newman Apostolate, Diocese of Worcester, 1969-71, episcopal vicar for coll. communities and adminstrn. Newman Div., 1971—. Mem. edn. revision study com. Diocese of Worcester, 1969; New Eng. rep. to nat. com. Diocesan Dirs. Campus Ministry of U.S. Cath. Conf., 1974-77; fire chaplain City of Worcester, 1961—. Trustee Worcester Area Campus Ministry, 1969—; trustee Becker Jr. Coll., 1970—, trustee faculty com., 1974—. Recipient For God and For Youth award Cath. Youth Council Worcester, 1969, Worcester Poly. Inst. award for Disting. Service to Coll., 1984. Mem. Cath. Campus Ministry Assn., Phi Kappa Theta. Contbr. articles to religious jours. Home: 19 Schussler Rd Worcester MA 01609 Office: Religious Center Worcester Poly Inst 19 Schussler Rd Worcester MA 01609

SCARBEARY, EARL WILLIAM, religious agency executive, Christian Church (Disciples of Christ); b. Hudson, Ill., Oct. 25, 1921; s. George H. and Erma Lois (Anderson) S.; m. Frances L. Lockhart, June 2, 1949 (dec. 1966); m. Mary Ellen Pearman, July 29, 1967; children: Stephen Earl, Timothy Robert, Mark Edwin. Student Ill. State U., 1940-43, U. Ill.-Urbana, 1946; B.A., Phillips U., 1948; B.D., Graduate Sem., 1951; D.D. (hon.), Eureka Coll., 1968. Ordained to ministry Christian Ch. (Disciples of Christ), 1948. Minister Canton Christian Ch., Okla., 1949-51, Bethany Park Christian Ch., Rantoul, Ill., 1951-58, First Christian Ch., Paris, Ill., 1958-63; sr. minister Central Christian Ch., Orlando, Fla., 1963-78; exec. dir. Christian Service Ctr., Orlando, 1978—; chmn. Ill. Disciples Found., Urbana, Ill., 1952-59; trustee Eureka Coll., Ill., 1954-60, 61-63; pres. Fla. Council Chs., Orlando, 1974-76, Fla. Christian Assembly, St. Petersburg, Fla., 1970-71;

chmn. New Congregation Establishment Com., Fla. Christian Ch., 1983—. Moderator TV program Moral Issues, 1977—, Community Tapestry radio program, 1983—. Bd. dirs. Citizens Com. for Better Schs., Orlando, 1977; trustee Pub. TV and radio, Orlando, 1981-84. Served with USAF, 1943-46. Recipient Ky. Col. award, 1980. Mem. Council on Christian Unity (bd. dirs.), Nat. Evang. Assn., (bd. dirs.), Mental Health Assn. Orange County, Inter-Faith Group, Pi Kappa Delta, Kappa Mu Epsilon. Clubs: Kiwanis (program chmn. 1981-82, bd. dirs. 1980-83). Home: 441 E Purdue St Orlando FL 32806 Office: Christian Service Ctr Central Fla Inc PO Box 232 Orlando FL 32802

SCARBOROUGH, CURTISS CLINTON, FOUNDATION EXECUTIVE, minister, So. Baptist Conv.; b. West Frankfort, Ill., Dec. 10, 1935; s. Curtis Clinton and Olive Evanelle (Keith) S.; B.A., So. Ill. U., 1956; B.C.M., M.R.E., Southwestern Bapt. Sem., Ft. Worth, 1959; M.A., Evang. Coll., Chgo., 1961; Litt.D. (hon.) Stanton U. , 1976; Ph.D., Columbia Pacific U., 1980; m. Ruth Ann Jent, Nov. 22, 1955; children—Karol Ruth, Keith Curtiss. Ordained to ministry, Baptist Ch., 1964; pastor chs. in Ill. and Mo., 1959-67; pastor North Side Bapt. Ch., Florissant, Mo., 1967-75; dir. communications Christian Civic Found., St. Louis, 1975-83, pres., 1983—; pres., chmn. bd. Drug Alcohol Tobacco Edn., Inc., 1983—; pres. Paradox Enterprises, Inc. Mem. Youth Adv. Commn., St. Louis County, Mo., 1981—; bd. dirs. Mo. Chpt. Fedn. parents for Drug Free Youth, Am. Council Alcohol Problems, Am. Council Against Gambling; Mem. Eastern regional adv. commn. Mo. Dept. Mental Health. Mem. Internat. Platform Assn., Nat. writers' club, Religions Pub. Relations Council, Mo. Prevention Network. Author: (with Cleveland R. Horne) Citizens, Under God, 1979; (with JOhn D. King) An Ounce of Prevention, 1980. Basics on Abused Drugs, 1981, Take the Freeway, 1983; author, complies (with Gerald Young) Choice Sermons from Missouri Pulpits, 1981; newspaper editor, The Christian Citizen, 1975-83, Dateline, 1975-83; syndicated columnist Drug Quiz, 1979—. Home: 2476 Buttonwood Ct Florissant MO 63031 Office: 3426 Bridgeland Dr Bridgeton MO 63044

SCARBOROUGH, RUTHANN, minister, Southern and American Baptist Convention; b. Marion, Ill., July 30, 1936; d. Floyd and Aretha (Stilley) Jent; m. Curtiss Clinton Scarborough, Nov. 23, 1955; children: Karol Ruth Scarborough Haskins, Keith Curtiss. B.S., So. Ill. U., 1956; M.R.E., Southwestern Bapt. Theol. Sem., 1958. Presch. tchr. St. Mark's Methodist Ch., Florissant, Mo., 1966-72; dir. daycare ctr. North Side Bapt. Ch., Florissant, 1972-82; pastoral staff Third Bapt. Ch., St. Louis, 1982—; spl. presch. leader Mo Bapt. Conv., Jefferson City, 1965—; conf. leader Southern Synod Bd., Nashville, 1984, Mo. Bapt. Conv., Jefferson City, Mo., 1982. Contbr. articles to profl. jours. Mem. Nat. Assn. Edn. Young Children, St. Louis Bapt. Assn. (pres. 1977-82). Home: 2476 Buttonwood Ct Florissant MO 63031 Office: Third Bapt Ch 620 N Grand Saint Louis MO 63103

SCARVIE, WALTER BERNARD, minister, Am. Luth. Ch.; b. Story City, Iowa, July 23, 1934; s. Walter Bernard and Florence Emily (Thompson) S.; B.A., Luther Coll., Decorah, Iowa, 1956; B.D., Luther Theol. Sem., St. Paul, 1963; M.A., Cath. U. Am., 1973, postgrad. (Eastern Dist. Am. Luth. Ch. Osterman fellow), 1975—; m. Korinne Mary Thompson, June 1, 1975. Ordained to ministry, 1964; pastor St. Peter Luth. Ch., St. Clair, Mich., 1964-67; campus pastor to univs. in Washington, Luth. Campus Ministry of Washington, 1967—. Leader ritual, liturgy and communication arts workshops. Mem. St. Clair Housing Commn., 1965-67. Mem. Liturgical Conf., Luth. Soc. Worship, Music and Arts, Luth., Nat. campus ministry assns., Nat. Acad. Rec. Arts, Scis., Choral Arts Soc. Washington, Friends of Kennedy Center for Performing Arts (founding), ACLU. Contbr. articles to religious jours.; editor worship supplement Circle mag., 1972-73, Jour. Religious Concern, 1976. Home: 1806 Irving St NW Washington DC 20010 Office: Kay Spiritual Life Center Am U Washington DC 20016

SCHACHTE, HERSHEL, rabbi; dir. Inst. for Advanced Research in Rabbinics, Rabbi Isaac Elchaman Theol. Sem. Office: 2540 Amsterdan Ave New York NY 10033*

SCHACTER, JACOB JOSEPH, rabbi, orthodox Judaism; b. N.Y.C., Dec. 11, 1950; s. Herschel and Pnina (Gewirtz) S.; m. Yocheved Weisbord, Sept. 4, 1972; children: Leah Tehilla, Sarah Ahuva. A.B., Bklyn. Coll., 1973; M.A., Harvard U., 1978, Ph.D., 1986. Ordained rabbi, 1973. Rabbi, Young Israel of Sharon, Sharon, Mass., 1977-81, The Jewish Ctr., N.Y.C., 1981—; inster. Stern Coll., N.Y.C., 1983-84; chmn. Midtown Bd. Kashruth, N.Y.C., 1983—. Author/translator: Autobiography of Rabbi Jacob Emden, 1986. Contbr. articles to profl. jours. Recipient Goodhartz award of excellence, Judaic Studies, Bklyn. Coll., 1973; Meml. Found. Jewish Culture grantee, 1973-75; Harvard U. grad. fellow, 1973-75. Mem. N.Y. Bd. Rabbis (bd. govs. 1983—), Union Orthodox Jewish Congregations of Am. (bd. govs.), Jewish Nat. Fund (dir.), Commn. on Synagogue Relations (exec. council), Phi Beta Kappa. Office: Jewish Center 131 W 86th St New York NY 10024

SCHAD, JAMES L., bishop, Roman Catholic Church. Titular bishop of Panatoria, aux. bishop, Camden, N.J., 1966—. Office: Maris Stella Rectory 4912 Dune St Avalon NJ 08202*

SCHADE, EDWARD JOSEPH, minister, Wesleyan Ch.; b. Nashville, Apr. 2, 1917; s. John Henry and Anna Louise (Carruthers) S.; Th.B., Lighthouse Bible Coll., 1942, B.D., 1944, Ph.B.D., 1948; Th.D., Pioneer Sem., 1960, D.D., 1962; Litt.D., Emmanuel Bible Coll., 1965; m. Eunice Kathrine Dutton, June 1, 1940; children—Edward Joseph, Eunice Karen, Tommye Molita, James Patrick, Debby Ann. Ordained to ministry, 1948; founder, pastor First Wesleyan Ch., Nashville, 1942-75; founder, tchr. preaching, pres. Emmanuel Bible Coll., Nashville, 1962—; chaplain Tenn. Dept. Corrections, Spencer Youth Center, 1962-73; v.p. Tenn. Conf. Wesleyan Ch., 1967, pres., 1967-68; sr. chaplain Sheriff's Dept. Corrections, Nashville Metro Govt., 1975—. Maj., CAP, 1970—; counselor Sci. Marriage Found. Named Outstanding Pastor of Year, Wesleyan Ch., 1965. Mem. Mil. Chaplains Assn. U.S.A., Am. Protestant Chaplains Assn., Am. Correctional Chaplains Assn. Home: 617 Shelby Ave Nashville TN 37206 Office: PO Box 60508 Emmanuel Coll 610 Boscobel St Nashville TN 37206

SCHAEFER, EMIL FREDERICK, lay ch. worker, Lutheran Ch.-Mo. Synod; b. Delmont, S.D., Feb. 20, 1898; s. John and Christina (Baumann) S.; student Luth. Normal Coll., Seward, Nebr., 1913-16; m. Agnes Hannah Oberheu, June 8, 1920; children—Robert Arno, Maxine Marie Schwerin. Dist. organizer Luth. Laymen's League, S.D. dist., 1941-46, 1st pres., 1956-57; archivist, S.D. dist., 1966—; dist. editor Luth. Witness, 1970-76. Ret. asst. postmaster, Sioux Falls, S.D. Recipient Certificate of Appreciation Luth. Laymen's League, 1974. Mem. Concordia Hist. Inst. (life), Am. Automobile Assn., DAV, VFW. Home: 3505 S Willow Ave Sioux Falls SD 57105 Office: 101 E 38th St Sioux Falls SD 57105

SCHAEFER, JAMES PALMER, minister, Wisconsin Evangelical Lutheran Synod, editor; b. Colome, S.D., Dec. 24, 1922; s. William John and Pency (Palmer) S.; m. Ruth Marie Eggert, Nov. 2, 1947; children: Paul, Ruth William, Grace, James Palmer, Pency. B.A., Northwestern Coll., Watertown, Wis., 1944; M.Div., Wis. Lutheran Sem., 1947; M.A., Marquette U., 1951. Ordained to ministry Wis. Evangel. Luth. Synod, 1947. Pastor, Atonement Ch., Milw., 1947-67; dir. stewardship Wis. Evang. Luth. Synod, Milw., 1967-80; editor The Northwestern Lutheran, Milw., 1981—. Dir. Protestant Legis. Council, Madison, 1971—, Wis. Evang. Luth. Synod Found., Milw., 1983—, dir. pub. relations, 1962—. Bd. dirs. Aid Asn. Lutherans Appleton, Wis., 1984—; editor WELS Hist. Jour., Milw., 1982—. Mem. Assoc. Ch. Press. Club: Milw. Press Office: Wis Evangel Lutheran Synod 2929 Mayfair Rd Milwaukee WI 53222

SCHAEFER, JAMES RICHARD, priest, Roman Catholic Church; b. Balt., Oct. 17, 1931; s. John Herman and Caroline Ellen (Doran) S. Ph.B. Gregorian U.-Rome, 1953, S.T.L., 1957; Ph.D., Cath. U. Am., 1971. Ordained priest, 1956. Asst. pastor St. Joseph Ch., Cockeysville, Md., 1957-66; dir. adult edn. Archdiocese of Balt., 1969-77; pastor St. Ann Ch., Hagerstown, Md., 1978—; chmn. Archdiocesan Task Force for Sch. Financing, Balt., 1983—. Author: Program Planning for Adult Christian Education, 1972. Editor: Gift—Growth in Faith Together, 1973. Mem. Cath. Bible. Assn., Religious Edn. Assn. Democrat. Lodge: Rotary. Home: 1010 Oak Hill Ave Hagerstown MD 21740 Office: Saint Ann Ch 1525 Oak Hill Ave Hagerstown MD 21740

SCHAFER, JERRY LYNN, pastor, American Lutheran Church; b. Sandusky, Ohio, Apr. 20, 1953; s. Wayne Cletus and Leola Marie (Niemann) S.; m. Catherine Ann Miller, Sept. 9, 1978. B.A. in Govt., Politics, Muskingum Coll., 1975; M.Div. in Parish Ministry, Trinity Luth. Sem., Columbus, Ohio, 1979, M.Div. in Christian Min. (hon.), 1979. Ordained to ministry American Lutheran Church, 1979. Pastor St. Paul Luth. Ch., Oak Harbor, Ohio, 1979-81, Salem Luth. Ch., Woodhaven, Mich., 1981-83; assoc. pastor Prince of Peace Luth. Ch., Kalamazoo, Mich., 1983—; chmn. Dist. Personnel, Detroit, 1981-82; advisor Dist. Luther League Bd., Detroit, 1983—. Author: (with others) (theol. statement) Theology of Compensation, 1981. Chmn. Concerned Citizens Oak harbor, Ohio, 1980-81; bd. dirs. Kalamazoo Youth Ministry, 1984—. Named Outstanding Contbr. to Spiritual Welfare, Kiwanis, 1982. Mem. Phi Kappa Tau (Delta Lambda chpt., pres. 1973-75). Office: Prince Peace Luth Ch 1747 W Milham Rd Kalamazoo MI 49002

SCHAGRIN, ELIHU, rabbi, Reform Jew; b. Wilmington, Del., June 20, 1918; s. Charles Wolfe and Frances (Schwartz) S.; children: Gail Isaacs, Charles W., Judith M. B.A., U. Pa., 1940; M.H.L., Jewish Inst. Religion, 1946; D.Div. (hon.), Hebrew Union Coll.-Jewish Inst. Religion, 1971. Ordained rabbi, 1946. Rabbi Beth Israel Congregation, Coatesville, Pa., 1945-35, Temple Concord, Binghamton, N.Y., 1953—; mem. exec. bd. Central Conf. Am. Rabbis, N.Y.C., 1968-70, 80-82, rabbinic placement commn., 1978-83; pres. Metro Interfaith Services, Inc., Binghamton, 1976-78; dir. ministerial bd. Planned Parenthood Assn., 1953-83; bd. dirs. Metro Interfaith Services, Inc., 1968—, Jewish Fedn. Broome County, 1957—. Bd. dirs. Am. Heart Assn., Broome County chpt., 1979—, Roberson Ctr. for Arts and Scis., 1982-84. Recipient Service award Broome County Med. Soc., Binghamton, 1967; named Man of Yr., Beth David Orthodox Congregation, Binghamton, 1981. Lodge: Rotary, Masons. Home: 5 Chapin St Binghamton NY 13905 Office: Temple Concord 9 Riverside Dr Binghamton NY 13905

SCHAMBER, KENNETH GEORGE, minister, Lutheran Church-Missouri Synod; b. Scotland, S.D., Jan. 17, 1948; s. Edgar George and Ruth Karolina (Buchmann) S.; m. Diane Naomi Russell, May 28, 1972; children: Naomi, Jeremy, Lynnae. A.A., Concordia Coll., St. Paul, 1968; B.A., Concordia St. Coll., Fort Wayne, Ind., 1970, M.Div., Concordia Sem., St. Louis, 1974. Ordained to ministry Luth. Ch., 19—. Pastor, Mount Hulda Luth. Ch., Cole Camp, Mo., 1974-76, Immanuel Luth. Ch., Hannibal and Our Savior Ch., Monroe City, Mo., 1978—; cir. counselor Luth. Ch.-Mo. Synod, 1981—; sec.-treas. Monroe City Alliance (Mo.), 1981—. Republican. Home: Route 2 Box 169 Hannibal MO 63401

SCHANDER, HARLEY LESTER, minister, Seventh-day Adventist Church; b. Heaton, N.D., Apr. 26, 1918; s. Frederick and Katherina (Pfaffenroth) S.; m. Susan Mae Lehmann, Sept. 5, 1943; children: Quentin Roger, Kenneth Lee, Mary Kaye, Alice Renee. B.S., Union Coll., 1945; postgrad. Andrews U., 1958-59. Ordained to ministry Seventh-day Adventist Ch. Dist. pastor No. Union Ch., Minn., S.D., 1945-54; pastor Kenhorst Ch., Reading, Pa., 1960-64, Willowdale Ch., Toronto, Ont., Can., 1968-74, Campus Ch., Nashville, 1974-78; pastoral cons. Maritime Conf., Dartmouth, N.S., Can. 1983—; exec. com. South New Eng. Conf., Stoneham, Mass., 1964-68, Kingsway Coll., Oshawa, Ont., Can., 1968-74, Ky.-Tenn. Conf., Nashville, 1974-78, B.C. Conf., Kelowna, 1978-83. Home: 45 Hannebury Dr Dartmouth NS B2V 1P7 Canada Office: Maritime Conf Seventh-day Adventist Ch 121 Salisbury Rd Moncton E1E 1A6 Canada

SCHARLEMANN, HERBERT KARL, minister, Luth. Ch.-Mo. Synod; b. Lake City, Minn., Aug. 5, 1927; s. Ernst Karl and Johanna (Harre) S.; B.A., Northwestern Coll., 1949; B.D., Evang. Luth. Theol. Sem., 1953; C.R.M., Concordia Sem., 1954, Dr. Min., 1960; m. Elizabeth Mae Fahrmann, July 1, 1956; children—Lizbeth, Timothy, Nancy, Daniel, James Mary, Benjamin. Ordained to ministry, 1956; pastor Grace Luth. Ch., Dodge Center, Minn., 1956-58, Trinity Luth. Ch., Hoffman, Ill., 1958—. Staff mem. Kaskaskia Coll., Centralia, Ill., 1965—; chmn. South Ill. Dist. Worship Com., 1965—; pres. Centralia Area Ministerial Alliance, 1962-64; chaplain Kaskaskia Coll., 1965—. Precinctman Dem. Party. Mem. Luth. Acad. for Scholarship (award 1963), Luth. Edn. Assn., Soc. Bibl. Lit., Luth. Soc. for Worship and Arts, Luth. Human Relations Soc., Century Club (Valparaiso U.). Contbr. articles to religious jours. Home: Box 56 Hoffman IL 62250 Office: Trinity Church Hoffman IL 62250

SCHARLEMANN, ROBERT PAUL, educator, minister, Lutheran Church in America; b. Lake City, Minn., Apr. 4, 1929; s. Ernst Karl and Johanna Meta (Harre) S. B.A., Concordia Coll., 1952; B.D., Concordia Sem., 1955; Dr.Theol. U. Heidelberg-Ger., 1957. Ordained to ministry, 1960. Pastor, Bethlehem Luth. Ch., Carlyle Ferrin, Ill., 1960-62, Grace Luth. Ch., Durham, N.C., 1962-63; faculty, U. Va., Charlottesville, Commonwealth prof. religious studies, 1981—. Author: Thomas Aquinas and John Gerhard, 1964; Reflection and Doubt in the Thought of Paul Tillich, 1969; The Being of God, 1981. Editor Jour. Am. Acad. Religion, 1979-84. Fulbright grantee, 1955-56, 56-57; Fulbright-Hays Commn. sr. research grantee, 1975-76. Home: 1529 Rutledge Ave Charlottesville VA 22903 Office: Univ Va Dept Religious Studies Cocke Hall Charlottesville VA 22901

SCHATKIN, MARGARET AMY, theology educator, Lutheran Church-Missouri Synod; B. N.Y.C., Apr. 29, 1944; d. Sidney Bernhard and Amy Wheeler (White) S. B.A., City U. N.Y., 1964; M.A., Fordham U., 1966, Ph.D., 1967; Th.D., Princeton U., 1982. Assoc. prof. Boston Coll., Chestnut Hill, Mass., 1969—. Author: St. John Chrysostom: Apologist, 1985. Editor: Heritage of the Early Church, 1973. Contbr. articles to religious publs. Woodrow Wilson fellow, 1964, 66, Nat. Endowment for Humanities fellow, 1976; Mellon grantee, 1981. Mem. Am. Philol. Assn., N. Am. Patristic Soc., Assn. Internationale d'Etudes Patristique. Home: 215-05 39th Ave Bayside NY 11361 Office: Boston Coll Dept Theology Chestnut Hill MA 02167

SCHATZMANN, SIEGFRIED SAMUEL, minister, religion educator, Southern Baptist Convention; b. Uster, Zurich, Switzerland, Aug. 8, 1941; came to U.S.,

1972; s. Karl Johann and Ida Maria (Gatzi) S.; m. Madi Hirzel, Apr. 21, 1962; children: Myriam, David Alan, Marcel Mark. B.S., Bethany Bible Coll., 1974; M.Div., S.W. Bapt. Theol. Sem., 1976, Ph.D., 1981. Ordained to ministry Swiss Pentecostal Mission, 1965, Southern Baptist Conv., 1984. Minister, Swiss Pentecostal Mission. Glarus, Switzerland, 1963-66, missionary, Lesotho, 1966-72; assoc. minister Rockland Park Assembly of God, Fort Worth, 1978-81; asst. prof. Oral Roberts U., Tulsa, 1981—. Recipient Systems Approach to Instructional Devel. award Oral Roberts U., 1983. Mem. Soc. Bibl. Lit. Home: 2316 W Broadway Ct Broken Arrow OK 74012 Office: Oral Roberts U Dept Undergrad Theology 7777 S Lewis Tulsa OK 74171

SCHEBERA, RICHARD LOUIS, priest, Roman Catholic Church; b. N.Y.C., Aug. 6, 1937; s. Richard John and Mary Ann (Boylan) S. B.D., Montfort Theol. Sem., 1964; S.T.L., Institut Catholique-Paris, 1967; Ph.D., Fordham U., 1974. Ordained priest, 1964. Dir. edn. Montfort Sem., St. Louis, 1967-70; asst. prof. St. Louis U., 1974-77, assoc. prof. religion, 1978—; assoc. prof. MaryKnoll Theolgate, N.Y., 1977-78; adj. prof. Paul VI Inst., St. Louis, 1978-84. Fordham U. scholar, 1970-72; Am.-Israel Cultural Found. grantee, 1970. Mem. Coll. Theology Soc. (nat. sec. 1975-77). Home: 2123 N Geyer Rd Saint Louis MO 63131 Office: Dept Theol Studies 3634 Lindell Blvd Saint Louis U Saint Louis MO 63108

SCHEETZ, MARY JOELLEN See *Who's Who in America*, 43rd edition.

SCHENEMAN, MARK ALLAN, clergyman, Episcopal Church; b. Washington, Oct. 13, 1948; s. William A. and Jeanne K. (Lorah) S.; m. Dorothy M. Hoshauer, Aug. 15, 1970; children: Katherine Elaine, Elisabeth Clair. B.A., Moravian Coll., 1970; M.Div., Gen. Theol. Sem., 1973; M.A., Temple U., 1976; D.Min., Eastern Bapt. Theol. Sem., 1983. Ordained priest, 1975. Asst. St. Mary's Ch., Ardmore, Pa., 1973-75, St. Anne's Ch., Abington, Pa., 1975-77; rector St. Peter's Ch., Broomall, Pa., 1977—; chmn. program and budget com. Diocese of Pa., Phila., 1984—, convenor com. on cult abuse, 1981—. Editor: Way of the Cross, pamphlet, 1981. Com. mem. Marple Twp. Tricentennial, Broomall, 1984. Mem. Profl. Soc. Eastern Bapt. Sem., Citizens Freedom Found., Am. Family Found. Club: United Bowmen of Phila. Office: Saint Peters Episcopal Ch West Chester Park Broomall PA 19008

SCHENIDER, DELWIN BYRON, religious educator; b. Oshkosh, Wis., May 14, 1926; m. Katherine Schneider; children: Kathi Del, Mark, Michael, Lisa. B.A., Concordia Coll., 1948; B.D., Concordia Sem.-St. Louis, 1951; M.A., Pepperdine U., 1950; postgrad. U. Chgo., 1954-56, Japanese Lang. Ctr., 1956-58, Rikkyo U.-Tokyo, 1958-61, Ph.D., 1961; postgrad. Harvard U. (vis. scholar), 1961-62. Ordained to ministry, Bethlehem Luth. Ch., 1951. Pastor, St. Paul Luth. Ch., Oak Lawn, Ill., 1951-56; dir. Japan Luth. Hour, Tokyo, 1956-61; chaplain, lectr. Boston U., 1962-65; assoc. prof. history of religions Gustavus Adolphus Coll., St. Peter, Minn., 1965-70; edn. TV lectr. World Religions, KTCA-Tv, Channel 2, St. Paul, 1967; dir. Inst. East Asian Studies, 1967-70; SPAN prof. U. Minn., Mpls., 1968-69; asst. dean acad. affairs and coordinator Internat. programs Gustavus Adolphus Coll., 1968-70; coordinator Ecumenical Ctr. for World Religions, U. San Diego, 1972—; lectr. Ctr. for Theol. Study, 1983. Author: Konkokyo: A Japanese Religion, 1962; The Life of the Founder, 1962; contbr.: 89 Modern Mission Stories, 1962, God and Our Parish, 1963, Systems of Human Guidance, 1972, Religion in Human Culture: The Buddhist Tradition, 1978, Christian Prescence in Japan, 1981, others. Address: Univ San Diego Alcala Park San Diego CA 92110

SCHENKELBERG, JEANNE MARIE, educational administrator, Roman Catholic Church. B. Cleve., Sept. 2, 1942; d. George John and Helen Marie (Fredrich) S. B. Sci. Edn., St. John Coll., 1965, M.S. in Edn., 1971. Joined Sisters of St. Joseph, Roman Catholic, 1960. Tchr., Diocese Cleve., 1965-79; dir. religious edn. St. Richard Parish, North Olmsted, Ohio, 1972-74; prin. St. Mel Sch., Cleve., 1979—. Contbg. author text: Our Country, 1974, The Making of Our America, 1974. Mem. Nat. Cath. Edn. Assn., Ohio Cath. Edn. Assn. Assn. Supervision and Curriculum Devel., Diocesan Prin.'s Exec. Bd. (v.p. 1983, pres. 1984). Republican. Office: St Mel Sch 14440 Triskett Rd Cleveland OH 44111

SCHEPER, GEORGE LOUIS, lay minister, Roman Catholic Church, English educator; b. N.Y.C., Oct. 1, 1939; s. George Louis and Anne Maria (Znojemsha) S.; m. Nancy K. Lawler, June 18, 1966 (div. 1981); children: Jeanne Anne, David John. B.A., Duke U., 1960; Ph.D., Princeton U., 1971. Lay minister Corpus Christi Ch., Balt., 1978—. Prof. English and humanities Essex Community Coll., Baltimore County, Md., 1970—. Author: Michael Innes, 1985. Recipient NEH Summer Stipend, Oxford, 1972; Woodrow Wilson fellow Princeton U., 1960, NEH grantee, 1978, 79, 80. Mem. MLA, Conf. Christianity and Lit., Community Coll. Humanities Assn., Phi Beta Kappa. Democrat. Home: 240 W Lanvale St Baltimore MD 21217 Office: Essex Community Coll Rossville Blvd Baltimore County MD 21237

SCHERER, ROSS PAUL, minister, Assn. Evang. Lutheran Chs., Lutheran Church-Missouri Synod, sociology educator; b. Fort Wayne, Ind., Mar. 30, 1922; s. Arnold Frederick and Eleanor Margaret (Vonderau) S.; m. Doris Emelie Hoffmeier, July 6, 1946; children: Rebecca, Thomas, Mary. Diploma, Concordia Jr. Coll., 1941; A.B., Concordia Sem., 1943, Diploma in Theol., 1946; A.M., U. Chgo., 1947, Ph.D., 1963. Ordained to ministry Lutheran Ch., 1950. Caseworker Luth. Child Welfare Assn., Addison, Ill., 1948-50; asst. to pastor Windsor Park Luth. Ch., Chgo., 1949-50; dir. ministry studies Nat. Council Chs. N.Y., N.Y.C., 1963-66; mng. editor Review of Religious Research, 1966-72; instr., asst. prof. Valparaiso U., Ind., 1950-63; assoc. prof. sociology Loyola U., Chgo., 1966—. Editor, author: The Church & Its Manpower Management, 1966, American Denominational Organization, A Sociological View, 1980. Mem. Ch. Fed. Chgo. (mem. pub. issues com., 1974-75), Religious Research Assn. (v.p., pres., 1974-77), Soc. for Sci. Study of Religion, Assn. for Sociol. of Religion, Am. Sociol. Assn., Ill. Sociol. Assn. (bd. dirs. 1983-85). Democrat. Home: 202 S Gibbons Ave Arlington Heights IL 60004 Office: Dept Sociology/Anthropology Loyola U 6525 N Sheridan Rd Chicago IL 60626

SCHEVE, MARK RUSSELL, minister, Lutheran Ch. - Missouri Synod; b. Painesville, Ohio, July 25, 1948; s. Jack Wallace and Lucille Jessie (Whitmore) Ballard. A.A., Concordia Luth. Coll., 1968; B.A., Concordia Sr. Coll., 1970; student, Concordia Theol. Sem., 1970-72; M.Div., Concordia Sem., 1976. Ordained to ministry Lutheran Ch., 1976. Vicar Gethsemane Luth. Ch., Lakewood, Ohio, 1972, St. John's Luth. Ch., Red Bud, Ill., 1975; pastor Holy Cross Luth. Ch., Wartburg, Ill., 1976-81; substitute preacher Luth. Ch. - Mo. Synod, Ohio, 1981-85; Bible class tchr. state sch. for mentally handicapped, Ft. Wayne, Ind., 1966-68; asst. playground dir. Community Action Program, Painesville, 1970. Mem. Luth. Ch. - Mo. Synod, Coll. Young Republicans (bd. dirs. Concordia Sr. Coll. campus chapt. 1969-70). Home: 135 Overlook Rd Painesville OH 44077

SCHIESS, BETTY BONE, priest, Episcopal Ch.; b. Cin., Apr. 2, 1923; d. Evan Paul and Leah (Mitchell) B.; B.A., U. Cin., 1945; M.A. Ed., Syracuse U., 1947; M.Div., Colgate Rochester/Bexley Hall/Crozer, 1972; m. William Arnold Scheiss, Aug. 28, 1947; children—William, Richard Corwine, Sarah. Ordained priest, 1974; curate Grace Ch., Baldwinsville, N.Y., 1972-73; exec. dir. Ednl. Center for Aging, Syracuse, 1973-75; priest asso. Grace Ch., Syracuse, 1975—; chaplain-at-large Syracuse U., 1977—. Founder, Episcopal Soc. for Examination of Feminist Issues; mem. com. legis. concerns N.Y. State Council Chs.; past mem. draft bd. Ch. state com. ACLU; mem. nat. adv. bd. Jr. League Syracuse; mem. adv. bd. Colgate Rochester/Bexley Hall/Crozer; mem. com. religious liberty Nat. Council Chs. Bd. dirs. YWCA; mem. bd. County-City Human Rights Commn. Named Post Standard Woman of Year in Religion, 1972. Mem. NOW (founder Syracuse), Religious Coalition for Abortion Rights, Theta Chi Beta, Pi Lambda Theta. One of 1st eleven women in U.S. ordained to priesthood. Home: 107 Bradford Ln Syracuse NY 13224 Office: 601 Allen St Syracuse NY 13224

SCHINDLER, ALEXANDER MOSHE, religious organization executive, Reform Jewish Congregations; b. Munich, Germany, Oct. 4, 1925; s. Eliezer and Sali (Hoyda) S.; came to U.S., 1938, naturalized, 1943; B.S.S., Coll. City N.Y., 1950; Rabbi, Hebrew Union Coll.-Jewish Inst. Religion, Cin., 1953, B.H.L., 1953, M.H.L., 1953; m. Rhea Rosenblum, Sept. 29, 1956; children—Elisa Ruth, Debra Lee, Joshua Michael, Judith Rachel, Jonathan David. Rabbi Reform Jewish Congregations, 1953; asst., then asso. rabbi Temple Emanuel, Worcester, Mass., 1953-59; dir. New Eng. council Union Am. Hebrew Congregations, Boston, 1959-63, dir. edn., N.Y.C., 1963-67, v.p., 1967-73, pres., 1973—; mem. governing bd. World Union Progressive Judaism, 1973, v.p., 1974; mem. governing bd. World Jewish Congress, 1971, v.p., 1985; mem. Nat. Jewish Community Relations Adv. Com., 1973, Meml. Found. Jewish Culture, 1967, Central Conf. Am. Rabbis, 1967; mem. praesidium World Council Jewish Edn., 1967-70; chmn. Conf. Pres.'s Maj. Jewish Orgns., 1976—. Mem. governing bd. United Jewish Appeal, 1974—. Mem. governing bd. Hebrew Union Coll.-Jewish Inst. Religion, 1973—, Jewish Agy. for Israel, 1981. Author: From Discrimination to Extermination, 1950. Lit. editor of CCAR Jour., 1953-59; founding editor Dimensions, 1965. Contbr. articles to profl. jours. Home: 6 River Ln Westport CT 06880 Office: 838 Fifth Ave New York City NY 10021

SCHIPANI, DANIEL S., religious educator, psychologist, minister, Mennonite Church. B. Pehuaó, Buenos Aires, Apr. 16, 1943; came to Puerto Rico, 1976; s. Serafin Pascual and Carmen Antonia (Fatone) S.; m. Margaret Anne Snyder, June 17, 1967; children: David, Marisa. Licenciate in Psychology, U. Buenos Aires, 1965, Prof. in Psychology, 1965; D. Psychology, Catholic U., Buenos Aires, 1968; M. Religion, Goshen Biblical Sen., 1974; Ph.D., Princeton Theol. Sem., 1981. Dir. orientation dept. Escuela Cristiana Evangelica Argentina, Buenos Aires, 1968-72; assoc. prof. pastoral psychology and Christian edn. Seminario Evangelico de Puerto Rico, San Juan, 1976-85; prof. Christian edn. and personality Assoc. Mennonite Bibl. Sems., Elkhart, Ind., 1985—. Author: La Angustia, 1969; Orientacion Existencial del Adolescente, 1971 (1st prize, 1971); El Arte de ser Familia, 1982; El Reino de Dios y ed Ministeria Educativo de la Iglesia, 1983; Conscientazation and Creativity, 1984; (with others) Educacion y Comunidad, 1973; (with others) Y Fueron Felices, 1974. Sec. Com. on Quality of Life, San Juan C. of C., 1981-83. Mem. Latin Am. Theol. Fraternity, Assn. Researchers and Profs. Religious Edn., Christian Assn. Psychol. Studies, Soc. Sci. Study of Religion, Am. Psychol. Assn., Am. Assn. Pastoral Counselors. Office: Assoc Mennonite Biblical Sem 3003 Benham Ave Elkhart IN 46517

SCHKADE, RAY CHARLES, religious organization administrator, minister, Lutheran Church-Missouri Synod; b. Giddings, Tex., Aug. 14, 1928; s. Edmund E. and Meta (Jatzlau) S.; m. Kathryn Martha Kirshberger, Aug. 13, 1950; children: Craig, Kevin, Tammy, Dean. A.A., St. John's Coll., Winfield, Kans., 1948; B.A., Concordia Sem., St. Louis, 1950; Th.M., Concordia Sem., Springfield, Ill., 1954. Ordained to ministry Lutheran Ch.-Mo. Synod, 1954. Founder, pastor Redeemer Luth. Ch., Austin, Tex., 1954-67; exec. dir. Parish Services, Tex. Dist. Lutheran Ch.-Mo. Synod, Austin, 1967—; div. chaplain Nat. Guard, 1980—. Author: God's Ownership-My Stewardship, 1970. Organizer: (total stewardship process) In His Service, 1983. Decorated Army Commendation medal, Meritorious Service medal. Home: 7101 Creighton Ln Austin TX 78723 Office: Tex Dist Luth Ch-Mo Synod 7900 U S 290 E Austin TX 78724

SCHLARMAN, STANLEY GERARD, bishop, Roman Catholic Church; bishop of Dodge City, Kans., 1983—. Office: 1608 Ave C Dodge City KS 67801*

SCHLEIF, PAUL EDWARD, minister, American Lutheran Church. B. Detroit, Sept. 22, 1946; s. Norman W. and Dollie B. (Still) S.; m. Jill M. Kramer, Aug. 17, 1968; children: Karin, Katherine, Kurt, Kristin. B.A. in Religion, Mich. State U., 1969; M.Div., Luth. Theol. Sem., Columbus, Ohio, 1972. Ordained to ministry American Lutheran Church, 1972. Pastor, St. Paul Luth. Ch., Oak Harbor, Ohio, 1972-78, St. James Luth. Ch., Toledo, 1979—; pres. Portage Conf. Am. Luth. Ch., Ottawa County, Ohio, 1972-76; dist. rep. div. life and mission in the congregation Am. Luth. Ch., Mpls., 1979-80; pres. Ecumenical Communications, Toledo, 1982-83; nominated bishop Mich. dist. Am. Luth. Ch., Detroit, 1984. Named Outstanding Young Man. Internat. Jaycees, 1975. Office: St James Luth Ch 3948 Brockton Dr Toledo OH 43623

SCHLIEP, DUANE WILLIAM, minister, Southern Baptist Convention; b. Red Wing, Minn., Jan. 13, 1945; s. Frederick F. and Annabelle (Chamberlain) S.; m. Helen Annette Grimes, July 29, 1968; children: Lisa Marie, Lori Anne. B.Min., Bapt. Bible Inst., Fla., 1977; M.Min., Luther Rice Sem., 1980. Ordained to ministry Baptist Ch., 1975. Pastor Enon Bapt. Ch., Camden, Ala., 1981—, River Falls Bapt. Ch., Ala., 1978-80; dir. edn. Kathleen Bapt. Ch., Fla., 1977-78. Served with USN, 1963-73. Democrat. Home: Rt 2 Box 320 Camden AL 36726

SCHLUTOW, BRYANT K., minister, So. Baptist Conv.; b. Cleve., May 25, 1924; s. Charles John and Elsa Irene (Bryant) S.; B.A., Bob Jones U., Greenville, S.C., 1950. Ordained to ministry, 1950; asst. exec. sec. Evang. Fgn. Missions Assn., Washington, 1951-58; pastor Crater View Bapt. Mission, Petersburg, Va., 1962-63; Sunday sch. tchr., deacon Immanuel Bapt. Ch., Colonial Heights, Va., 1968—, also chmn. youth adv. com., leader Royal Ambassadors; leader Royal Ambassadors, Petersburg Bapt. Assn., 1976—. Dir. fin. Petersburg Pub. Schs., 1972—; mem. Republican Nat. Com., 1976—. Mem. S.E., Va. assns. bus. sch. ofcls. Home: 1112 Briarcliffe Dr Colonial Heights VA 23834 Office: Petersburg Sch Bd Wythe and Jefferson Sts Petersburg VA 23803

SCHMALENBERGER, JERRY L., minister, Lutheran Church in America; b. Greenville Ohio, Jan. 23, 1934; s. Harry Henry and Lima Marie (Hormell) S.; m. Carol Ann Walthall, June 8, 1956; children: Stephen L., Beth L., Sarah L., A.B., Wittenberg U., 1956; M.S.T., Hamma Sch. Theology, 1959; D.Min., Consortium Higher Edn. Religious Studies, 1976; D.D. (hon.), Wittenberg U., 1984. Ordained to ministry Luth. Ch. in Am., 1959. Pastor Third Luth. Ch., Springfield, Ohio, 1959-61; sr. pastor First Luth. Ch., Bellefontaine, Ohio, 1961-65, First Luth. Ch., Tiffin, Ohio, 1965-70, First Luth. Ch., Mansfield, Ohio, 1970-79, St. John's Luth. Ch., Des Moines, Iowa, 1979—; dir. Wittenberg U., Springfield, 1974—; mem. Consulting Com. Minorities, 1978—; pastor, evangelist, Luth. Ch. Am., 1976-84; chmn. Minority Ministry Com., Iowa Synod, 1980-81; pastor, dir. Evang. Outreach, 1983-84. Author: Letters from the Pulpit, 1983; We Have Good News, 1978; Iowa Parables, 1984; Lutheran Christians, 1984; pub. Iowa Psalms, 1985. Pres., Seneca County Regional

Planning Commn., Tiffin, 1972; mem. Criminal Justice Commn., Columbus, Ohia, 1977; pres. Downtown Revitalization Com., Mansfield, Ohio, 1978; bd. dirs. Luth. Social Service, Iowa, 1980—, Grand View Coll. Named Young Man of Year in Ohio Jr. C. of C., 1965, Young Man of the Year Jr. C. of C., 1968, Exemplary Citizen Ohio Senate, 1970. Mem. Sr. Pastors of Large Chs., Assn. Governing Bds. Lodge: Rotary.

SCHMELING, JOHN PETER, minister, educator, American Lutheran Church; b. Beach, N.D., Oct. 31, 1938; s. John Freidrich William and Violet Marie (Weinreis) S.; A.A., Concordia Coll., St. Paul, 1959; B.S., Dickinson (N.D.) State Coll., 1961; B.D., Wartburg Theol. Sem., Dubuque, Iowa, 1968; M.S., Ind. State U., 1970, Ph.D., 1977; m. Susan Ellen Reinhart, Mar. 9, 1976; children—Linda Sue, Erich Stefan, Kimberly Jane, John Reinhart, Heather Celeste, Kirsten Ellen. Ordained to ministry, 1968; pastor Trinity Luth. Ch., Linton, Ind., 1968-74; asst. prof. religion Vincennes U., 1974—, v.p., dean of faculty, 1981—. Weekend pastor St. John Luth Ch., Shelbyville, Ill. Home: Rural Route 1 Vincennes IN 47591 Office: N 2d St Vincennes U Vincennes IN 47591

SCHMELZER, DELBERT LEROY, priest, Roman Catholic Church. b. Avoca, Wis., Jan. 4, 1930; s. Roy Alvin and Baptista Anna (Dolan) S. M.Div., St. Francis Sem., 1956. Ordained priest Roman Catholic Ch., 1956. Assoc. pastor various chs., Wis., 1956-65; pastor Our Lady of Hope, Shullsburg, Wis., 1965-67, St. John Ch., Montello, Wis., 1967-69, St. John Ch., Janesville, Wis., 1969-81, St. Andrew Ch., Verona, Wis., 1981—; assoc. dir. Propagation of Faith, Madison, Wis., 1968-81, dir., 1981—; chaplain Janesville Senna Club, 1972-81. Address: St Andrew Ch 301 N Main St Verona WI 53593

SCHMELZLE, MARIE CLARE, nun, ednl. adminstr., Roman Catholic Ch.; b. Manitowoc, Wis., Mar. 29, 1943; d. Marvin Frank and Eleanor Katherine (Lallensack) Schmelzle; B.A., Silver Lake Coll., 1971; postgrad. Marquette U., Milw., 1973—. Elementary sch. tchr., 1964—, prin., 1970—; mem. Vicariate Area XII Council, 1970—, Green Bay Diocesan Sisters Council, 1973—; mem. worship com. St. Anne Parish, Francis Creek, Wis., 1975—, mem. Bd. Edn. and Parish Council, 1970—, organist, song leader St. Anne Parish, 1970—, grade sch. CCD coordinator, 1970—, faculty mem. St. Anne High Sch. CCD program, 1975—, coordinator, 1976—, sec. parish council, 1976—; mem. adv. bd. Mishicot Pub. Sch. Dist., 1970—. Mem. Nat. Council Ednl. Adminstrs., Diocesan Elementary Sch. Prins. Assn. Home: St Anne Convent 202 Packer Dr Francis Creek WI 54214 Office: St Anne Sch 202 Packer Dr Francis Creek WI 54214

SCHMENK, MARY JANE, nun, religious organization executive, Roman Catholic Church; b. New Cleveland, Ohio, Jan. 13, 1918; d. Casper Lewis and Theresa Elizabeth (Meyer) S. B.A., Coll. of St. Francis, 1948; M.A., Marquette U., 1956; postgrad. Notre Dame U., 1958, Cath. U., 1961, U. Saltillo, Mexico, 1970. Joined Sisters of St. Francis, Tiffin, Ohio, 1932. Tchr., Calvert High Sch., Tiffin, Ohio, 1948-56, Central High Sch., Toledo, 1957-61; mem. adminstrn. Sisters of St. Francis, Tiffin, 1961-70; adminstr. Living Waters Reflection Ctr., Maggie Valley, N.C., 1976—, bd. dirs. Retreats Internat. Southeast Region, 1983—; tchr. of catechists Diocese of Toledo, 1960-70; part-time tchr. Mary Manse Coll., Toledo, 1960-70; sec. Sisters' Senate, Diocese of Charlotte, 1982—. Mem. Nat. Assn. Religious Women, Profl. and Bus. Women's Club (pres. 1984—). Democrat. Home and Office: Living Waters Cath Reflection Ctr Route 1 Box 476 Maggie Valley NC 28751

SCHMID, THOMAS HENDERSON, minister, Presbyterian Church (U.S.A.); b. Houston, Aug. 6, 1943; s. Albert Darwin and Nancy Bell (Hunter) S.; m. Elizabeth Anne Wheatcroft, Sept. 6, 1966; children: Albert, Gretchen, Rachel, Bennett. B.A., Austin Coll., 1965; M.Div., Austin Presbyn. Theol. Sem., 1971; D.Min., McCormick Theol. Sem., 1979. Ordained to ministry Presbyterian Church (U.S.A.), 1971. Assoc. pastor Grace Presbyn. Ch., Lafayette, La., 1971-73; pastor Eastminster Presbyn. Ch., New Orleans, 1973-77, San Pedro Presbyn. Ch., San Antonio, 1977—; trustee Austin Presbyn. Theol. Sem., 1974-83, 84—; chmn. com. justice and human devel. Presbyn. Ch., Gen. Assembly, 1980. Mem. Met. Congl. Alliance, San Antonio, 1980—; foster parent Meth. Mission Home of Tex., 1980—; dir. San Antonio Urban Council, 1978-82, pres., 1980-81. Served with USCGR, 1966-68. Democrat. Office: San Pedro Presbyn Ch 1605 Timber Oak San Antonio TX 78232

SCHMIDT, GALE DWIGHT, minister, Lutheran Ch. - Missouri Synod; b. Daykin, Neb., Nov. 25, 1936; s. Lawrence Frederick and Hazel Caroline (Jarchow) S.; m. Lois Elizabeth Mayer, July 10, 1960; children: Beth, Daniel, Jennifer, Julie. B.A., Concordia Sem., 1958, M.Div., 1967. Ordained to ministry Lutheran Ch., 1962. Pastor First Immanuel Luth. Ch., Chgo., 1962-66, St. Matthew Luth. Ch., Chgo., 1967-79, El Buen Pastor, Chgo., 1979—; pres. Luth. Council Greater Chgo., 1972-73; bd. dirs. Luth. Child & Family Services, River Forest, Ill., 1982—; sec. Luth. Hispanic Com., Chgo., 1982—. Democrat. Home: 6145 W Barry Chicago IL 60634 Office: El Buen Pastor Lutheran Ch 3740 W Belden Chicago IL 60647

SCHMIDT, HENRY JAKE, educator, minister, Mennonite Brethren Church; b. Grande Prairie, Alta., Can., July 2, 1940; came to U,S., 1964; s. Peter and Margaret (Unger) S.; m. Elvera Agnes Schmidt, Aug. 27, 1960; children: Debra Elaine, Laura Jean. B.Th., Mennonite Brethren Bible Coll., 1964, M.Div., 1972; B.A., Fresno Pacific Coll., 1970; Ph.D., U. So. Calif., 1981. Ordained to ministry, 1966. Pastor, Emmanuel Mennonite Brethren Ch., Onida, S.D., 1964-69; insterim pastor Neighborhood Ch., Visalia, Calif., 1970-71; exec. dir. evangelism U.S. Conf., Fresno, 1971-77; ch. planterFig Garden Bible Ch., Fresno, 1980-84; assoc. prof. world mission Mennonite Brethren Bibl. Sem., Fresno, 1979—, dir. Ctr. Tng. in Mission, 1984—; ch. growth cons. Mennonite Brethren Ch., 1972—; chmn. Pacific Dist. Bd. Home Missions, 1978-80; chmn. U.S. Conf. Bd. Evangelism, Fresno, 1980-83, U.S. Mennonite Brethren Conf., 1983—; chmn. Dept. World Mission, Bibl. Sem., Fresno, 1982—. Editor: Conversion: Doorway to Discipleship, 1980. Contbr. articles to profl. jours. Recipient Acad. award, Mennonite Brethren Bibl. Sem., 1972; Sermon award, Decision Mag., 1972; U. So. Calif. scholar, 1977-78. Mem. Acad. Evangelism in Theol. Edn., Nat. Assn. Evangelicals (dir.). Club: Cabana. Home: 4411 North Winery Fresno CA 93727 Office: Mennonite Brethren Bibl Sem 4824 E Butler Ave Fresno CA 93727

SCHMIDT, ROBERTA JEANNE, nun, Roman Catholic Church; b. Kansas City, Mo., May 9, 1928; d. Ernest Louis and Florence Marie (Noonan) S. B.A., Avila Coll., 1949; M.A., St. Louis U., 1958, Ph.D., 1964; LL.D., Lindenwood Coll., 1968. Tchr. Archdiocese of St. Louis, 1952-61; faculty Fontbonne Coll., St. Louis, 1961-66, pres., 1966-72; consortium dir. United Colls. San Antonio, 1973-75; v.p. acad. affairs So. Benedictine Coll., Cullman, Ala., 1975-79; supt. schs. Archdiocese of Atlanta, 1980-82, sec. for edn., supt., 1982—. Democrat. Office: Dept Cath Edn 680 W Peachtree St NW Atlanta GA 30308

SCHMIDT, STEVEN JAMES, minister, American Baptist Association; b. Grand Rapids, Mich., June 6, 1947; s. Clayton Joseph and Ruth Gladuce (Schlief) S.; m. Mary Jule Veldman, Dec. 11, 1970; children: Matthew, Nicholas, Kathleen, Laura. Student No. Mich. U., 1965-67, Grand Rapids Jr. Coll., 1967-68, So. Theol. Sem., 1980-82, U. Bibl. Studies, 1980—. Ordained to ministry Baptist Ch., 1982. Assoc. minister and minister of evangelism North Parkersburg Bapt. Ch., Parkersburg, W.Va., 1980-82; sr. minister Porterfield Bapt. Ch., Little Hocking, Ohio, 1983—; assoc. chaplain Camden-Clark Hosp., Parkersburg, 1981—; pres. Ministers Fellowship Parkersburg Assn., 1982—; advisor Ministers Adv. Council Alderson Broaddus Coll., Philippi, W.Va., 1984—. Author (tape and manual seminars) Heart To Heart Evangelism, 1981; (study guide) The Enquirers, 1982. Contbr. articles to local papers, hosp. publication. Served to 1st lt. U.S. Army, 1968-71, Vietnam. Decorated Silver Star, 3 Distinguished Flying Cross, 5 Bronze Stars, 45 Air Medals, Purple Heart, Vietnamese Cross of Gallantry. Mem. Belpre Ministerial Alliance, Ohio Bapt. Convention, Parkersburg Ministerial Alliance (assoc.). Republican. Home: Route 2 Box 129 Little Hocking OH 45742 Office: Portersfield Baptist Ch Route 2 Box 129-A Little Hocking OH 45742

SCHMIDTKE, RICHARD L., minister, Lutheran Church-Missouri Synod, effectiveness training instructor; b. Minot, N.D., June 16, 1945; s. Albert Arthur John and Ilo Maurine (Nelson) S.; m. Shelah Jane Stender, Dec. 16, 1967; children: Shawn Albert, Shannon Lee. A.A., Concordia Jr. Coll., Portland, Oreg., 1965; B.A., Concordia St. Coll., Fort Wayne, Ind., 1967; M.Div., Concordia Sem., St. Louis, 1971. Ordained to ministry Luth, Ch., 1977. Minister, Pincher Creek Parish, (Alta., Can.), 1971-78, Our Savior's Luth. Ch., Bottineau, N.D., 1979—; cir. counselor Luth. Ch.-Mo. Synod, Bottineau, 1979—, marriage enrichment instr., St. Louis, 1982—; family life coordinator Bd. Parish Services, St. Louis, 1982—; spl. ministry coordinator Bd. Missions, Fargo, N.D., 1982—; workshop leader, lectr. in field. Instr. Effectiveness Tng., Inc., Solana Beach, Calif., 1977—. Mem. Psychol. Publs, Inc. Home: 1310 S Thompson Bottineau ND 58318 Office: Our Savior's Luth Ch RR #3 Bottineau ND 58318

SCHMITKE, KATHLEEN ANN, minister, Lutheran Church in America; b. Edmont, Alta., Can., Feb, 20, 1952; d. Milton Raymond and Dorothy Joanne (Baron) S. B.Ed., U. Alta., 1974; M.Div., Luth. Theol. Sem., Saskatoon, Sask., Can., 1980. Ordained to ministry Lutheran Ch., 1980. Pastor, Trinity Luth. Ch., Falun, Alta., 1980—, St. John's Luth. Ch., Wetaskiwin, Alta., 1980—; mem. task force for justice for men and women Western Can. Synod, Luth. Ch. Am., 1981-85; mem. profl. preparations com., 1981—, mem. examining com., 1983—. Mem. Can. Assn. for Pastoral Edn. (sec. Alta. region 1983-85), Liturgical Conf., Wetaskiwin Ministerial Assn. (v.p. 1982-83). Home and Office: Rural Route 1 Wetaskiwin AB T9A 1W8 Canada

SCHMITT, CONRAD, priest, Roman Cath. Ch.; b. Balt., Nov. 8, 1928; s. Louis Raymond and Mary Angela (Neser) S.; student St. Joseph's Sem., Holy Trinity, Ala., 1944-49; Holy Trinity Mission Sem., Silver Spring, Md., 1949-55; M.B.A., Wharton Sch., U. Pa., 1967. Joined Missionary Servants of Most Holy Trinity, 1949; ordained priest Roman Catholic Ch., 1955; asst. mission procurator, Silver Spring, Md., 1955-63; asst. pastor St. Agnes, Cleve., 1963-65; treas. gen. Missionary Servants Order, Silver Spring, 1967-73, asst. superior gen., 1973—; mem. Union Superiors Gen., Rome. Bd. dirs. Trinity Cons. Center, 1972-76; chmn. bd. trustees Washington Theol. Union, Silver Spring, Md.; mem. finance com. Conf. Major Superiors of Men, 1972-76. Office: 1215 N Scott St Arlington VA 22209

SCHMITT, JOHN JACOB, religion educator, Roman Catholic Church. b. Milw., May 6, 1938; s. Silvester Joseph and Frances Josephine (Knar) S.; m. Roberta Ann O'Hara, July 8, 1967; children: Maria-Kristina, Tara Elizabeth. B.A., Marquette U., 1966; A.M., U. Chgo., 1970, Ph.D., 1977. Asst. prof. St. Bonaventure U., N.Y., 1972-80, Marquette U., Milw., 1980—. Contbr. articles to religious jours. Fulbright fellow, 1968-69; recipient Nat. Endowment for Humanities award, 1978. Mem. Cath. Bibl. Assn., Soc. Bibl. Lit., Nat. Assn. Profs. Hebrew, Am. Acad. Religion. Home: 1843 N 84th St Wauwatosa WI 53226 Office: Marquette U Theology Dept Milwaukee WI 53233

SCHMITT, MARK F. See *Who's Who in America*, 43rd edition.

SCHMITZ, CHARLES EDISON, minister, educational administrator, American Lutheran Church; b. Mendota, Ill., July 18, 1919; s. Charles Francis Schmitz and Lucetta Margaret (Foulk) Schmitz Kaufmann; m. Eunice Magdalene Ewy, June 1, 1942; children: Charles Elwood, Jon Lee. Student, Wheaton Coll., 1936-39; B.A., Wartburg Coll., 1940; B.D., Wartburg Theol. Sem., 1942, M.Div., 1977. Ordained to ministry American Lutheran Church, 1942. Pastor, Ascension Luth. Ch., Los Angeles, 1942-48, prin. day sch., 1946-48; pastor Am. Evangelical Luth. Ch., Phoenix, 1948-65, prin. day sch., 1950-65; dir. Intermountain Missions, Am. Luth. Ch., Phoenix, 1948-65, evangelist, Mpls., 1965-73; sr. pastor Peace Luth. Ch., Palm Bay, Fla., 1973—, prin. day sch., 1983—; v.p. Calif. dist. Am. Luth. Ch., Phoenix, 1949-55, vice chmn. synodical worship and ch. music, Mpls., 1960-66, chmn. space coast conf., 1980—; cassette study lectr. Paul's Messianic Ministry, 1970-73; mem. exec. com. Fla. Council Chs., Orlando, 1982—. Author: Evangelism for the Seventies, 1969; (with others) ABC's of Life, Evangelism System, 1969. Assoc. editor Good News mag. Contbr. articles to religious publs. Chmn. Ariz. Christian Conf. on Adult and Youth Problems, Phoenix, 1955-65; mem. Ariz. Gov.'s Com. on Marriage and Divorce Problems, Phoenix, 1962-64, Palm Bay City Planning Commn., 1975-83; mem., Mayor's Assistance Com., Palm Bay, 1975—, chmn., 1984-85; mem. hosp. commn. City of Palm Bay, 1980-83. Recipient Civil Def. Chaplain award Los Angeles, 1945, Phoenix, 1960-65, Disting. Alumni award Wartburg Coll., 1959; named Citizen of Yr., Palm Bar Area C. of C., 1979. Mem. Div. World Missions and Interchurch Coop. (chmn. 1980—). Republican. Lodges: Lions (chaplain, first v.p., editor), Kiwanis (editor 1943-48). Home and Office: Peace Luth Ch 1801 Port Malabar Blvd NE Palm Bay FL 32905

SCHNABEL, ROBERT VICTOR See *Who's Who in America*, 43rd edition.

SCHNEERSON, MENACHEM MENDEL, rabbi, Jewish Congretaion; b. Nikolaev, Russia, 1902; came to U.S., 1941; s. Levi Yitzchak and Rebbetzin (Chana) S.; m. Rebbetzin Chayo Moussia, 1929. Student, U. Berlin, Sorbonne, Paris. Head, Machne Israel, 1941—, Lubavitcher Pub. House, Bklyn., N.Y., 1941—; established communities and instns. throughout the world; established Tzivos Hashem for pre-Bar; established Tifereth Zekeinim Colel Leby Yitzchak for elderly; speaker on Jewish movement throughout world; established schs., youth ctrs., various instns. agys. and activities; various Cable TV appearances.

SCHNEIDER, DAVID JOHN, minister, Lutheran Church-Missouri Synod; b. Royal Oak, Mich., June 2, 1935; s. Carl William and Marie (Kionka) S.; m. Darlene Mae Laseman, June 11, 1960; children: Carolyn, Susan, Stephen. A.A., Concordia Coll., Ft. Wayne, Ind., 1955; B.A., Concordia Sem., St. Louis, 1957, B.D., M.Div., 1960, M.S.T., 1971. Ordained to ministry, Luth. Ch., 1960. Missionary, Luth. Ch., Philippines, 1960-78; pastor Holy Trinity Luth. Ch., Gulfport, Miss., 1978—; chmn. Commn. for Ecumenical Affairs, Luth. Ch. in Philippines, 1967-72; prof. Luth. Sem., Baguio City, Philippines, 1971-78; pres. Luth. Ch. in Philippines, 1972-74; chmn. steering com. Great Commn. Convocation, So. Dist., Luth. Ch.-Mo. Synod., 1984. Author: (text) Introduction to Theology, 1977. Contbr. articles to religious jours. Lodges: Lions, Rotary. Home: 606 Rosemary Dr Gulfport MS 39501 Office: Holy Trinity Cath Ch 505 Cowan Rd Gulfport MS 39501

SCHNEIDER, EDWARD D., assistant to presiding bishop, American Lutheran Church; b. Oconomowoc, Wis., Jan. 8, 1936; s. ALexander and Wilhelmine Elsie (Kroll) S.; m. Nancy Kay Crosman, July 3, 1965; children: Ann, Mary. B.A., Wartburg Coll., 1957; B.D., Wartburg Theol. Sem., 1961; Th.M., Princeton Theol. Sem., 1962; Ph.D., U. Iowa, 1978. Ordained to ministry American Lutheran Church, 1962. Pastor, Moreland Luth. Ch., Chgo., 1962-67, St. James Luth. Ch., Western Springs, Ill., 1967-71; teaching asst., coordinator religion core courses Sch. Religion, U. Iowa, Iowa City, 1972-76; various pastorates, 1971-76; asst. dir. Office of Research and Analysis, Am. Luth. Ch., Mpls., 1976-81; part-time instr. Christian ethics Luther Northwestern Theol. Sem., St. Paul, 1979, 81; assoc. dir. for studies Office of Ch. in Soc., Am. Luth. Ch., Mpls., 1981-83; asst. to presiding bishop Am. Luth. Ch., Mpls., 1983—; pres. North Chgo. Conf., Am. Luth. Ch., 1967-69, Western Springs Clergy Assn., Ill., 1970-71; sec., cons. ch. and its relationship to govt. Luth. Council in U.S.A., 1979; accredited visitor World Council of Chs. Conf. on Faith, Sci. and Future, 1979; mem. standing com. on studies Luth. World Ministries, 1981—, mem. task force on The Eucharist, 1981; mem. standing com. on theol. studies Luth. Council in U.S.A., 1983—, mem. study group on historic Episcopate, 1984; mem. Luth.-Episcopal Dialogue III, 1983—; mem. Luth. World Fedn. Consultation on Christian Ethics - Property and Poverty, 1984. Author and editor, Questions about the Beginning of Life (Augsburg: 1985). Contrib. articles to religious publs. Bd. dirs. Austin YMCA, Chgo. Mem. Soc. Christian Ethics. Home: 3500 Canterbury Dr Bloomington MN 55431 Office: Am Luth Ch 422 S 5th St Minneapolis MN 55415

SCHNEIDER, KENT EDWARD, minister, United Ch. of Christ; b. Chgo., Apr. 6, 1945; s. Edward George and Alice Jane (Montgomery) S.; B.A., N. Central Coll., 1966; M.Div. cum laude, Chgo. Theol. Sem., 1969; m. Patricia Rae Wheeler, June 2, 1973. Ordained to ministry United Ch. of Christ, 1970; dir. Center for Contemporary Celebration, West Lafayette, Ind., 1968—; Developer of jazz worship Bread Sessions, Detroit, Chgo., Indpls., 1972; cons. to Armed Forces chaplains, Pentagon, Washington, 1971; mem. Nat. Commn. Worship, United Ch. of Christ, 1973—. Recipient grant Lilly Endowment Inc., 1974-76; first place award Nat. Hymn Contest United Ch. of Christ, 1963. Mem. Broadcast Music, Inc., Musicians Union. Author: (with Adelaide Ortegel) Light: A Language of Celebration, 1973; The Creative Musician in the Church, 1976. Producer, creator, pub. music albums: Celebration for Modern Man 1968, Voice in the Wilderness, 1977; editor, pub. Directory of Artists and Religious Communities, 1974. Author, pub. (hymnals) Songs for Celebration, 1968; Come Share the Spirit, 1976; (vocal solos) Songs of Love, 1976. Composer Sonrise of Imagination (religious jazz concert, recording), 1973. Home: 2354 N 20th St West Lafayette IN 47904 Office: 435 W State St West Lafayette IN 47906

SCHNEIER, ARTHUR, rabbi, Orthodox Jewish; b. Vienna, Austria, Mar. 20, 1930; came to U.S., 1947, naturalized, 1952; s. Chiam and Gisela (Bergman) S.; m. Donna F. Makovsky, Jan. 12, 1958; children: Marc, Karen. B.A., Yeshiva U., 1951; M.A., NY U, 1953; D.H.L. (hon.), Fordham U., 1977, L.I. U., 1981; Ph.D. (hon.), U. Budapest, Hungary, 1984. Ordained rabbi, 1955. Rabbi, Congregation B'Nai Jacob, Bklyn., 1956-62, Park East Synagogue, 1962—; founder, pres. Appeal of Conscience Found., 1965—; founder, chancellor Park East Day Sch. and Minskoff Cultural Ctr., 1967—; chmn. Am. sect. World Jewish Congress, 1979-84, hon. chmn., 1984; vice chmn. N. Am. Bd. World Jewish Congress, 1981, chmn. third world commn., 1981; chmn. adminstrv. com., former v.p. Religious Zionists Am.; spiritual leader World Fedn. Hungarian Jews; mem. Council Fgn. Relations, 1978—; mem. inter-religious group concerned with religious freedom throughout the world, headed Appeal Conscience missions to USSR, Eastern Europe, China, Morocco, Spain, Argentina, No. Ireland. Mem. U.S. Presdl. Del. for Return of the Crown to Hungary; chmn. Am. Romanian Flood and Earthquake Relief, 1977—; founding trustee U.S. Japan Found.; former dir. UN Devel. Corp.; mem. Holocaust Commn., N.Y.C. Named Clergyman of Yr., Protestant Council Chs., 1982. Home: 251 E 71st St New York NY 10021 Office: 164 E 68th St New York NY 10021

SCHNEIER, ARTHUR, rabbi, Orthodox Jewish Congregations; b. Vienna, Austria, Mar. 20, 1930; s. Chaim and Gisela (Bergman) S.; came to U.S., 1947, naturalized, 1952; B.A., Yeshiva U., 1951; M.A., N.Y. U., 1953; D.H.L., Fordham U., 1977; m. Donna F. Makovsky, Jan. 12, 1958; children: Marc, Karen. Ordained rabbi, 1955; rabbi Congregation B'nai Jacob, Bklyn., 1956-62, Park East Synagogue, N.Y.C., 1962—. Co-chmn. Internat. Affairs Com. Rabbinical Council Am., 1976—; bd. govs. N.Y. Bd. Rabbis, 1966—; v.p. Fedn. Jewish Philanthropies, 1965-70; bd. dirs. Jewish Nat. Fund. Founder, pres. Appeal of Conscience Found., 1965—, head interfaith missions to USSR, 1966—; founder, chancellor Park East Day Sch. and Minskoff Cultural Center, 1967—; chmn. bd. dirs. Am.-Romanian Flood Relief, 1970, 75; chmn. Am.-Romanian Earthquake Relief, 1977; dir. UN Devel. Corp., 1973—; v.p., bd. govs. World Jewish Congress Am. sect., 1976—; mem. N.Y.C. Community Planning Bd. 8, 1963-66; v.p. Religious Zionists of Am., 1966-75; del. World Conf. on Soviet Jewry, Brussels, 1971, 76; chmn. Met. Region Gov.'s Conf. on Human Rights, 1966. Recipient citation for distinguished and exceptional service, Mayor Lindsay, N.Y.C., 1973. Contbr. articles to periodicals. Office: 164 E 68th St New York City NY 10021

SCHNELL, MICHAEL LEROY, minister, Lutheran Church in America; b. Moline, Ill., Oct. 29, 1941; s. William and Ruby D. (Gilligan) S.; m. Rita Kay Mentzer, July 18, 1965; children: Kristin, Kara. A.B., Augustana Coll., Rock Island, Ill., 1963; M.Div., Luth. Sch. Theology at Chgo., Rock Island, 1967; D.Min., McCormick Theol. Sem., 1975. Ordained to ministry Luth. Ch. Am., 1968. Asst. pastor Edgebrook Luth. Ch., Chgo., 1968; pastor St. John's Luth. Ch., Bluff Springs, Ill., also Grace Luth. Ch., Virginia, Ill., 1969-72; pastor Gethsemane Luth. Ch., Cicero, Ill., 1972-76; synod cons. Div. for Mission in N. Am., Luth. Ch. in Am., N.Y.C., 1976-82; dir. planning Luth. Social Services of Ill., Des Plaines, 1982—. Author: Manual for Synodical Fiscal Proposal, 1981. Office: Lutheran Social Services of Illinois 880 Lee St Des Plaines IL 60016

SCHNITZER, JONATHAN AARON, rabbi, Conservative Judaism; b. N.Y.C., Aug. 6, 1948; s. Jeshaia and Hilde (Maier) S.; m. Beverly Gottlieb, June 25, 1972; children: Shira Danielle, David Ari. B.A., Columbia Coll., 1969; M.A., Jewish Theol. Sem. Am., 1972. Ordained rabbi 1974. Rabbi, Bnai Abraham Synagogue, Easton, Pa., 1974—; lectr. dept. religion Lafayette Coll., Easton, 1984—; co-chmn. Easton United Jewish Appeal, 1976; mem. Easton Hosp. Chaplaincy Bd., 1980—. Contbr. articles to profl. jours. Pres., ProJeCt Easton, 1981-82, Family Counseling Service Northampton County, Bethlehem, Pa., 1979-81, dir., 1975—. Recipient Disting. Service award United Jewish Appeal Rabbinic Cabinet, 1981. Mem. Rabbinical Assembly (pres. eastern Pa. region 1978-79), Rabbinic Cabinet United Jewish Appeal (chmn. new Rabbinic leadership com. 1979-81, chmn. small communities com. 1982-84). Home: 1458 Spring Garden St Easton PA 18042 Office: Bnai Abraham Synagogue 16th and Bushkill Sts Easton PA 18042

SCHNUCKER, ROBERT VICTOR, minister, Presbyterian Church U.S.A.; educator; b. Waterloo, Iowa, Sept. 30, 1932; s. Felix Victor and Josephine Fear (Maasdam) S.; A.B., N.E. Mo. State U., 1953; B.D. Theol. Sem. U. Dubuque, 1956; M.A., U. Iowa, 1960, Ph.D., 1969; m. Anna Mae Engelkes, Sept. 18, 1955; children: Sarai Ann, Sar Victor, Christjahn Dietrich. Ordained to ministry United Presbyn. Ch. U.S.A., 1956; pastor United Presbyn. Ch., Springville, Iowa, 1956-63; prof. history and religion Northeastern Mo. State U., Kirksville, 1963—, chmn. dept. philosophy and religion, 1972—. Mem. Mo. Com. for Humanities; chmn. Mo. Com. for Religion in Pub. Edn. Postdoctoral fellow Soc. Religion in Higher Edn., 1971; named Pastor of Distinction Iowa Synod, 1958, 1960, Mo. Synod, 1965. Mem. Am. Assn. Univ. Profs., Am. Acad. Religion, Am. Soc. Ch. History, Soc. Bibl. Lit., Am. Soc. for Reformation Research, Am. Hist. Assn., Soc. for Sci. Study Religion, Central Renaissance Conf., Conf. Faith and History, Sixteenth Century Studies Conf. (pres. 1973, sec. 1974, exec. sec. 1975—), Ctr. for Reformation Research (dir.), Soc. History Edn., 16th Century Jour. Pubs. (pres.), Blue Key, Phi Mu Alpha Sinfonia, Phi Alpha Theta, Alpha Phi Sigma, Pi Kappa Delta. Author: Modular Learning Program for Western Civilization, 1973; Helping the Humanities Journal Survive, 1983. Editor: Editing History; mng. editor, book rev. editor The Sixteenth Century Jour., 1971; editor Network News Exchange, Newsletter Historians of Early Modern Europe. Contbr. articles to profl. jours. Home: 40 Overbrook Kirksville MO 63501

SCHOCHET, ELIJAH JUDAH, rabbi, Conservative Jewish Congregations; b. Chgo., May 27, 1934; s. Jacob A. and Rachel (Rubinstein) S.; B.A., U. Calif. at Los Angeles, 1955; M.H.L., Jewish Theol. Sem. Am., 1960, D.H.L., 1967; m. Penina Fohrman, July 4, 1965; children—Daniel Chaim, Joel Michael, Lisa Deborah. Rabbi, 1960; rabbi Congregation Beth Kodesh, Canoga Park, Calif., 1960—; prof. rabbinic lit. U. Judaism, Los Angeles, 1968—. Pres., Western States region Rabbinical Assembly of Am., 1976; mem. com. on Jewish law and standards Rabbinical Assembly, 1976; mem. exec. com. So. Calif. Bd. Rabbis, 1976. Licensed marriage family and child counselor, Calif. Author: Bach, Rabbi Joel Sirkes, His Life, Works and Times; A Responsum of Surrender, Translation and Analysis. Home: 7454 Sausalito Ave Canoga Park CA 91307 Office: 7401 Shoup Ave Canoga Park CA 91307

SCHOELLERMAN, ESTHER JEAN, educator, non-denominational Christian school; b. Pinedale, Wyo., Aug. 28, 1934; d. William and Mary Edith Webber; B.A., Coll. of Pacific, 1957; m. Willard D. Schoellerman, Aug. 4, 1957; children—Lori, Julie, Curt. Founder, dir. Forest Lake Christian Sch., Auburn, Calif., 1967—. Home and Office: 12504 Combie Rd Auburn CA 95603

SCHOENHERR, WALTER JOSEPH See *Who's Who in America*, 43rd edition.

SCHOLL, FENTON THOMAS, JR., minister, American Baptist Churches in the U.S.A.; b. Louisville, June 25, 1950; s. Fenton Thomas and Grace (Adair) S.; m. Darba Sue Bowers, Apr. 14, 1979. A.A.S., Lexington Tech. Inst., 1972; B.A., Georgetown Coll., 1975; M.Div. Princeton Theol. Sem., 1978; postgrad., So. Bapt. Theol. Sem., 1979, Ordained to ministry So. Bapt. Conv., 1975, Am. Bapt. Chs. U.S.A., 1980. Minister, Calvary Bapt. Ch., Dayton, Ohio, 1980-82, Madison Ave Bapt. Ch., Albany, N.Y., 1982—; del. observer 5th assembly World Council Chs. So. Bapt. Conv., Nairobi, Kenya, 1975. Vol. chaplain Miami Valley Hosp., Dayton, Ohio, 1980-82; founder, bd. dirs. Ethiopian Refugee Relief Program., Albany, 1983—; bd. dirs. East African Relief Fund of Albany, 1985—. Scholar-in-residence Andover Newton Theol. Sem., 1982. Mem., Capital Area Council Chs. (bd. dirs.). Home: 26 Penn Ln Glenmont NY 12077 Office: Madison Ave Bapt Ch 901 Madison Ave Albany NY 12208

SCHOLSKY, MARTIN JOSEPH, priest, Roman Cath. Ch.; b. Stafford Springs, Conn., Jan. 16, 1930; s. Sigmund Felix and Mary Magdalen (Wysocki) S.; B.A., St. John's Sem., Mass., 1952, M.A. in History, 1956; M.A. in Classical Greek, Cath. U. Am., 1966. Ordained priest Roman Catholic Ch., 1956; asst. pastor ch., Hartford, 1956-61; prin. St. Peter's Grammar Sch., Hartford, 1956-58; instr. St. Thomas Sem., Bloomfield, Conn., 1961-67, dir. admissions, 1965-67; dir. vocations Archdiocese of Hartford, 1967—, mem. adv. bd. for permanent diaconate, 1969—; Cath. chaplain Newington (Conn.) Children's Hosp., 1961—; asst. St. Mary's Ch., Newington, 1961—. Contbr. to New Cath. Ency., Cath. Ency. for Sch. and Home, newspapers. Address: St Thomas Sem Bloomfield CT 06002

SCHOOLER, MARVIN EDWARD, minister, Church of God Reformation Movement (Anderson, Ind.); b. Beattyville, Ky., Aug. 20, 1958; s. Albert F. and Pauline (Pasley) S.; m. Lucinda Jane Ferguson, Aug. 28, 1976; 1 child, Joshua Aron. B.A., Warner So. Coll., 1980. Ordained to ministry, 1981. Pastor, First Ch. of God, Summerville, S.C., 1980-83, Bowen, Ky., 1983—; chmn. bd. Christian edn. Ch. of God, Bishopville, S.C., 1982-83; del. Gen. Assembly, Anderson, 1980—; chmn. Bd. Christian Edn., 1982-83. Coordinator Boy Scouts Am., 1983. Home: Route 1 Box 361 Stanton KY 40380 Office: Bowen First Ch of God Route 1 Box 361 Stanton KY 40380

SCHORSCH, ISMAR. Rabbi; provost The Jewish Theol. Sem. Am., also Rabbi Herman Abramovitz prof. in Jewish hist. Office: 3080 Broadway New York NY 10027*

SCHOWENGERDT, L. W. Bishop The United Methodist Church, N.Mex. Conf. and N.W. Tex. Conf. Office: The United Methodist Ch 1415 Ave M Lubbock TX 79401 also 209 San Pedro NE Albuquerque NM 87108*

SCHRAMM, DAVID CARL, minister, religion educator, United Methodist Church; b. Muncie, Ind., May 2, 1939; s. Donald Albert and Catherine Amanda (Mitchell) S.; m. Joyce Elaine Arnold, June 21, 1961; children: Jeanne Carolyn, John Mark, Mary Jane, Julia Lynne. B.A., DePauw U., 1961; B.D., Garrett Evangel. Sem., 1964; postgrad. Harvard U., 1964-65. Ordained to ministry as elder United Meth. Ch., 1964. Pastor, Wesley Parish, Lynn, Ind., 1965-69, East United Meth. Ch., Mishawaka, Ind., 1980—; campus minister Ball State U., Muncie, Ind., 1969-76; assoc. pastor Merrillville U. Meth. Ch. (Ind.), 1976-80; instr. World Harvest Bible Coll., South Bend, Inc., 1982—; chmn. emerging social issues div. bd. ch. and soc. N. Ind. Conf. United Meth. Ch., 1972-75; mem. Wesley Found. Bd. Purdue U., Lafayette, Ind., 1980—. Republican.

SCHRECK, ALAN EDWARD, theology educator, Roman Catholic Church; b. Rochester, N.Y., Dec. 7, 1951; s. Karl Joseph and Irene Elizabeth (Varga) S.; m. Nancy Elizabeth Pflug, May 15, 1982; 1 child, Paul Alan. B.A. in English/Theology, U. Notre Dame, 1973; M.A. in Theology, U. St. Michael's Coll., 1975, Ph.D. in Theology, 1979. Asst. prof. theology U. Steubenville, Ohio, 1978-82, assoc. prof., 1982—. Author: Catholic and Christian: An Explanation of Commonly Misunderstood Catholic Beliefs, 1984. Office: The Franciscan U Steubenville Franciscan Way Steubenville OH 43952

SCHROCK, PAUL MELVIN, editor; b. Tangent, Oreg., Aug. 4, 1935; s. Melvin and Anna Magdalena (Roth) S.; B.A., Eastern Mennonite Coll., 1958; M.A., in Journalism, Syracuse U., 1963; m. June Darlene Bontrager, Sept. 7, 1957; children: Carmen Joy Schrock-Hurst, Brent Lamar, Andrea Denise Wenger. With Mennonite Pub. House, Scottdale, Pa., 1959—, asst. editor Gospel Herald, 1959-61, asst. to Herald Press book editor, 1959-61, editor Words of Cheer, 1961-70, Herald Graded Sunday Sch. Series, 1967-68, founding editor Purpose mag., 1968-71, editor The Way, 1970-75, book editor Herald Press, 1972—; instr. linguistics and rhetoric, creative writing and photojournalism Eastern Mennonite Coll., 1970-72; with Mennonite Bd. Missions Media Ministries, Harrisonburg, Va., 1970-72, producer Mennonite Hour and Way to Life programs, 1971-72; editor of Alive Mag., 1970-75; free lance photographer. Home: 14 Park Ave Scottdale PA 15683 Office: 616 Walnut Ave Scottdale PA 15683

SCHROEDER, CARL EDWARD, church musician, Lutheran Church in America. B. Narrowsburg, N.Y., June 1, 1934; s. Hugo William and Florence May (Smith) S.; m. Elsie Emilie Hansen, Dec. 24, 1956 (div. Jan. 1974); children: Stephanie, Charles; m. Jane Elizabeth Hymes, Aug. 3, 1974. Tchr.'s cert. in Organ, Peabody Conservatory, Balt., 1956, B.M. Mus.B, 1960, Mus.M., 1969. Cert. lay profl. leader Lutheran Church in America, 1972. Organist, choirmaster, various chs., Balt., 1949-72, Trinity Luth. Ch., Lancaster, Pa., 1964-72, Zion Luth. Ch., Lancaster, 1972-82, St. Andrew United Ch. of Christ, Lancaster, 1983-84, St. John's Luth. Ch., Columbia, Pa., 1984—; organist All Saints Anglican Ch., Lancaster, 1980-84; organist, choir master Trinity United Ch. of Christ, Mountville, Pa., 1984—. Cons. Gundling Organ Co., Lancaster, 1972—; self-employed music tchr. Author: Buying an Organ for your Church, 1979, 2d edit., 1981. Contbr. revs. music, books and records to music publs. Composer anthems, song; editor motet, organist record. Mem. Am. Guild Organists (Lancaster chpt., exec. bd. 1964—, sub.-dean 1981, dean 1982, 83). Republican. Home: RD #1 Box 39 Jane Ave Donegal Heights Mt Joy PA 17552 Office: St John's Luth Ch 6th and Locust Sts Columbia PA 17512

SCHROEDER, ROY PHILIP, minister, Lutheran Church-Missouri Synod; b. Caro, Mich., Sept. 8, 1929; s. Philip and Esther (Ude) S.; m. Phyllis Joy Helge, June 4, 1955; children: Paul, Stephanie, Deborah, Suzanne, John. B.A., Concordia Sem.-St. Louis, 1950, B.D., 1954, M.S.T., 1955, Th.D., 1968. Ordained to ministry, 1955. Vicar, Japan Luth. Ch., Sapporo, Hokkaido, Japan, 1951-53; pastor St. Peter's Luth. Ch., Vincennes, Ind., 1955-57, St. John Luth. Ch., Monroeville, Ind., 1957-59, Peace Luth. Ch., Sparta, Mich., 1959-71, Ascension Luth. Ch., East Lansing, Mich., 1971—; mem. Dist. Bd. Edn., Ann Arbor, 1968-70, dist. bd. dirs., 1970-74; chmn. Grand Rapids Area Pastor's Conf., 1969-72, Western Mich. Pastors Conf., 1971-73; mem. Bd. mgrs. YMCA, East Lansing, 1979—. Contbr. articles to profl. jours. Home: 5190 Park Lake Rd East Lansing MI 48823 Office: Ascension Luth Ch 2780 Haslett Rd East Lansing MI 48823

SCHROM, H. DERAL, minister, Disciples of Christ; b. Grangeville, Idaho, Sept. 25, 1951; s. John H. and Georgia M. (Lance) S.; m. Garren Sue Rollins, Sept. 3, 1972; children: Andrew John, Mandy Kay. B.A., Northwest Christian Coll., 1973; M.Div., Tex. Christian U., 1978. Ordained to ministry Christian Ch., 1978. Youth pastor First Christian Ch., Springfield, Oreg., 1971-73; pastor Polson Christian Ch., Mont., 1973-75, First Christian Ch., Anna, Tex., 1975-78, South Suburban Christian Ch., Littleton, Colo., 1978—; chmn. Central Rocky Mountain Regional Evangelism Com., Denver, 1980-82. Author advertising media Life Stream Evangelism, 1981—. Mem. outreach bd. Anna Christian Community Outreach, Tex., 1976-77. Recipient Worthy Grand Matron award Order of Eastern Star, 1976, Brite Div. Sch. Field Edn. award Tex. Christian U., 1978, Professor's Book award Tex. Christian U., 1978; named Outstanding Young Man, of Am., U.S. Jaycees, 1983; Tex. Christian U. scholar, 1976. Mem. Theta Phi. Lodge: Kiwanis. Office South Suburban Christian Ch 7275 S Broadway Littleton CO 80122

SCHUBERT, JOE DAVID, minister, Churches of Christ; b. Fairfax, Okla., Oct. 27, 1935; s. Floyd Milton and Nancy (Sexson) S.; B.A., Abilene Christian Coll., 1957, M.A., 1959; postgrad. Vanderbilt Sch. Religion, 1959-60; Ed. D., U. So. Cal., 1967; m. Kathleen Kelley, Aug. 25, 1959; children—David, Kelley, Philip. Entered ministry Chs. of Christ, 1960; minister San Fernando (Calif.) Ch. of Christ, 1960-64, Stillwater (Okla.) Ch. of Christ, 1964-67; dean of students Okla. Christian Coll., Oklahoma City, 1967-70; minister San Jose Ch. of Christ, Jacksonville, Fla., 1970-73, Bammel Rd. Ch. of Christ, Houston, 1973-83; pres. Ctr. for Ch. Growth, Houston, 1983—. Asso. bd. mem. Abilene Christian Coll. Rockefeller Theol. fellow, 1959. Author: Marriage, Divorce and Purity, 1966; (with others) The Devil, You Say?, 1974. Home: 1010 Abana Houston TX 77090 Office: PO Box 73362 Houston TX 77273

SCHUBKEGEL, THEODORE VINCENT, minister, Lutheran Church Missouri Synod; b. Austin, Tex., June 6, 1948; s. Theodore Walter and Quinta Lily (Schlecht) S.; m. Ruth Ethyl Manns, July 20, 1975; children: Sarah Beth, Rebecca Joy. A.A., Blinn Jr. Coll., 1968; B.A., U. Tex., 1970; M.Div., Concordia Luth. Sem., Ft. Wayne, 1976. Ordained to ministry Luth. Ch. Mo. Synod, 1976. Assoc. minister Calvary Luth. Ch., Kansas City, Mo., 1976-82; head minister Bethel Luth. Ch., Kansas City, Kans., 1982—; sec. Circuit #2 Pastoral Conf., Kansas City, Kans., 1983—; pastoral advisor Lutherans for Life, Kansas City, Kans. area, 1984—. Club: Kiwanis. Home: 7906 Yecker Kansas City KS 66109 Office: Bethel Lutheran Ch 2801 N 83rd St Kansas City KS 66109

SCHUK, ERIC JOSEPH, minister, Lutheran Ch.-Mo. Synod; b. Niagara Falls, N.Y., Dec. 15, 1933; s. Joseph P. and Violet (Jordan) S.; A.A., Concordia Jr. Coll., Fort Wayne, 1953; B.A., Concordia Theol. Sem., St. Louis, 1955, theol. diploma, 1958; m. (Rose) Marian Epperson, June 22, 1958. Ordained to ministry Lutheran Ch.-Mo. Synod, 1958; pastor, Newkirk, Okla., 1958-60, Lawrenceburg, Ind., 1960-68, Peace Luth. Ch., Cin., 1968—. Mem. Okla. Dist. Bd. Parish Edn., 1959-60; sec. So. Ind. Pastors Conf., 1961-66; circuit counselor Ind. Dist., 1963-68; sec. So. Ohio Pastors Conf., 1969-71; regional pub. relations rep. Synod, 1969—; pres. Ohio Dist. Missionary Pastors, 1970; mem. Ohio Dist. Bd. Stewardship, 1973-76. Editor: Ohio Concerns. Home: 6492 Timberhill Ct Cincinnati OH 45238 Office: 1451 Ebenezer Rd Cincinnati OH 45238

SCHULER, RICHARD JOSEPH, priest, Roman Catholic Church; b. Mpls., Dec. 30, 1920; s. Otto Henry and Wilhelmine Mary (Hauk) S. B.A., Coll. St. Thomas, 1942; M.A., U. Rochester, N.Y., 1950; Ph.D., U. Minn., 1963. Ordained priest, 1945. Prof. music Nazareth Hall Sem., St. Paul, 1954; assoc. prof. music Coll. St. Thomas, St. Paul, 1955-69; pastor Ch. of St. Agnes, St. Paul, 1969—. Named hon. papal prelate (monsignor), 1970. Recipient Gold Lassus medal Caecilia Soc., Germany, 1973. Fulbright scholar, 1954-55. Mem. Ch. Music Assn. Am. (gen. sec. 1972—), Consociatio Internat. Musicae Sacrae (v.p. 1967-80). Editor: Fourteen Liturgical Works of Giovanni Maria Nanino, 1969. Editor Sacred Music quar., 1975—. Address: 548 Lafond Ave Saint Paul MN 55103

SCHULLER, ROBERT HAROLD, minister, Reformed Church in America; b. Alton, Iowa, Sept. 16, 1926; s. Anthony and Jennie (Beltman) S.; B.A., Hope Coll., 1947, D.D., (hon.), 1973; B.D., Western Theol. Sem., 1950; LL.D., Azusa Pacific Coll., 1970, Pepperdine U., 1976; m. Arvella DeHaan, June 15, 1950; children—Sheila, Robert, Jeanne, Carol, Gretchen. Ordained to ministry, Reformed Ch. Am., 1950; pastor Ivanhoe Ref. Ch., Chgo., 1950-55; founder, pastor Garden Grove Community Ch., Garden Grove, Calif., 1955—. Founder, pres. Hour of Power, TV ministry, Garden Grove, 1970—; founder, dir. Robert H. Schuller Inst. for Success Ch. Leadership, Garden Grove, 1970—; founder Robert H. Schuller Correspondence Center for Possibility Thinkers, 1976; pres. bd. Christian Counseling Service; bd. dirs. Religion in Am. Life; chmn. program Religion in Am. Life, N.Y.C., 1975—. Recipient Distinguished Alumnus award, Hope Coll., 1970; Freedoms Found. prin. award, 1974, 75, 76. Mem. Religious Guild Architects (hon.). Rotarian. Author: God's Way to the Good Life, 1963; Your Future is Your Friend, 1964; Move Ahead with Possibility Thinking, 1967; Self Love, the Dynamic Force of Success, 1969; Power Ideas for a Happy Family, 1972; The Greatest Possibility Thinker That Ever Lived, 1973; Turn Your Scars into Stars, 1973; You can Become the Person You Want to Be, 1973; Your Church Has Real Possibilities, 1974; Love or Loneliness—You Decide, 1974; Positive Prayers for Power Filled Living, 1976; Keep On Believing, 1976; Peace of Mind Through Positive Thinking, 1977; Turn Your Stress Into Strength, 1978; One Day at a Time, 1981; Tough Times Never Last But Tough People Do!, 1984; Tough Minded Faith for Tenderhearted People, 1984; (with Paul David Dunn) The Power of Being Debt Free, 1985. Address: 12141 Lewis St Garden Grove CA 92640

SCHULTE, FRANCIS B., bishop, Roman Catholic Church. Titular bishop of Efufenia, aux. bishop, Phila., 1981—. Office: St Margaret Ch 208 N Narberth Ave Narberth PA 19072*

SCHULTZ, EDWARD LLOYD, JR., priest, Episcopal Church; b. Quincy, Mass., July 13, 1948; s. Edward Lloyd and Lena Antoinette (Ruggiano) S.; m. Ruth Elizabeth Annis, Aug. 30, 1969; children: Christopher, Jennifer. A.B., Gordon Coll., 1969; Th.M., Boston U., 1973. Ordained priest, 1973. Pastoral asst. St. Andrews Ch., Hanover, Mass., 1972-73; rector Christ Ch., Medway, Mass., 1973-76; asst. to rector St. Stephens Ch., Ridgefield, Conn., 1976-80; rector Holy Nativity Ch., Rockledge, Pa., 1980—; mem. Diocesan Spiritual Growth Com., Phila., 1980—; del. Anglican Fellowship of Prayer, Phila., 1981—. Editor Soul Searcher, 1978-80. Contbr. articles to profl. jours. Bd. dirs. Rockledge Community Services, 1981—; chaplain Rockledge Fire Co., 1981—; mem. Rockledge Civil Service Bd., 1982—. Mem. Fox Chase/Rockledge Ministerium (v.p. 1982-84). Home: 205 Huntingdon Pike Rockledge PA 19111 Office: Holy Nativity Ch 205 Huntington Pike Rockledge PA 19111

SCHULTZ, ERICH RICHARD WILLIAM, minister, librarian, archivist, Lutheran Church of America; b. Rankin, Ont., Can., June 1, 1930; s. William Henry and Martha Frieda (Geelhaar) S. B.A., U. Western Ont., 1951; B.D., Waterloo Luth. Sem., 1954; M.Th., U. Toronto, 1958, B.L.S., 1959. Ordained to ministry Luth. Ch. Am., 1954. Pastor St. Paul's Luth. Ch., Ellice Twp., Ont., 1954-56; librarian Waterloo Luth. Sem., Ont., 1959-60, lectr., 1959-70; librarian, archivist Waterloo Luth. U. (name changed to Wilfrid Laurier U. 1973), 1960—; archivist Eastern Can. Synod, Luth. Ch. Am., 1961—. Editor, bibliographer: Ambulatio Fidei: Essays in Honor of Otto W. Heick, 1965; Vita Laudanda: essays in memory of Ulrich S. Leopold, 1975. Translator: Getting Along with Difficult People (Friederich Schmitt) 1970. Bd. dirs. Kitchener-Waterloo Community Concert Assn. Mem. Can. Library Assn. (convenor outstanding service award com. 1978-80, Assn. Can. Archivists, Can. Luth. Hist. Assn., Luth. Hist. Conf., Toronto Area Archivist Group, Waterloo Hist. Soc. (v.p. 1980-82, pres. 1982-84), Ont Library Assn. (v.p. 1967-68, pres. 1968-69), Inst. Profl. Librarians Ont. (v.p., pres. 1969-70), Am. Theol. Library Assn. (v.p., pres. 1975-77, chmn. program com. 1982—). Home: 235 Erb St E Waterloo ON N2J 1M9 Canada Office: 75 University Ave W Waterloo ON N2L 3C5 Canada

SCHULTZ, KURTIS DEAN, minister, Lutheran Ch.-Missouri Synod; b. Melrose Park, Ill., Nov. 2, 1953; s. Darrell Lee and Barbara K. (Schuppe) S.; m. Becky Lynn Schmidt, June 27, 1975. B.A., Concordia Tchrs. Coll., 1975; M.Div., Concordia Theol. Sem., 1979. Ordained to ministry Lutheran Ch., 1979. Pastor Christ the King Luth. Ch., Enterprise, Ala., 1979—; vacancy pastor Prince of Peace Luth. Ch., Ozark, Ala., 1979—; cir. youth counselor so. dist. Luth. Ch. - Mo. Synod, 1980; introduction team mem. Lutheran Worship hymnal, Ala., Miss., Fla., 1981; worship and music chmn. 84 Great Comission Convocation, Ala., Miss., Fla., La., 1984; program chmn. Promises 84 youth gathering, Ala., Miss., Fla., La., 1984; pastoral counselor Luth. Women's Missionary League, Gulf States, 1984—; hosp. chaplain Humana Hosp., Enterprise, 1983—. Mem. Luth. Council in the U.S.A. (southeast Ala. rep. 1980), Enterprise Christian Ministers Fellowship (pres. 1982—, transient benevolence chmn., 1979—), Aid Assn. for Luths. (southeast Ala. branch pres. 1983—). Clubs: Wiregrass Micro-Computer (Enterprise), Enterprise Volksmarchers. Office: 208 E Watts Ave Enterprise AL 36330

SCHULTZ, MARVYN ROSCOE, minister, Presbyn. Ch. in U.S.; b. DeSmet S.D., Apr. 11, 1927; s. Charley Fredrick and Hulda Wilhelmina (Krueger) S.; B.S., Morningside Coll., 1949; grad. Moody Bible Inst., 1953; M.Div., N.Am. Bapt. Sem., 1976; m. Martha Kingma, Aug. 25, 1949; children—James, Alice, Cynthia, Philip. Ordained to ministry, 1953; pastor Alton, Ill., 1953-59, First Presbyn. Ch. Little Rock, Iowa, 1959—. Vice pres. Sr. Citizens Housing Little Rock; active Little Rock Playhouse and Choir. Contbr. youth sect. The Messenger. Home and Office: Little Rock IA 51243

SCHULTZ, THOMAS, pastor, educator, Reformed Church in America; b. Phila., Jan. 31, 1931; s. Thomas Samuel and Mary Margaret (Smith) S.; m. Elizabeth Braun; children: Thomas Allen, Tamra Mae. B.Sc., U. Del., 1953; Th.M., Dallae Theol. Sem., 1959, Th.D., 1962. Ordained to ministry, 1962, Reformed Ch. in Am., 1983. Pastor Calvary Presbyn. Ch., Ft. Lauderdale, Fla., 1962-66, Elim Chapel, Winnipeg, Man., Can., 1966-75, Ch. of Cross, Sarasota, Fla., 1983—; prof. Winnipeg Theol. Sem., 1967-75; mem. adv. council B'nai B'rith, Winnipeg, 1970-75; pres. Man. Evang. Fellowship, 1971; cons. Scripture Press of Can., 1968-74. Exec. dir. Big Bros. of Winnipeg, 1975-81, Big Bros./Big Sisters of Sarasota, 1981-83. Recipient Communication and Leadership award Toastmasters of Winnipeg, 1979; named Hon. Citizen of Winnipeg, 1980. Home: 330 Gershwin Dr Sarasota FL 33577 Office: Ch of Cross 3005 S Tuttle Ave Sarasota FL 33579

SCHULTZ, WALTER ARTHUR, lay ch. worker, Luth. Ch. Am.; b. Winnipeg, Man., Can., Jan. 16, 1928; s. Ludwig and Matilda (Hoffman) S.; chartered accountant, U. Man., 1954; m. Dorothea Marie Brethauer, Aug. 8, 1952; children: Laurie Ann, Walter David, Brenda Marie, Mark Douglas. Youth group ch. activities, 1947-57; active ch. council, 1953-65; treas. Canadian Luth. Council, 1955-62, exec. sec. div. information services, 1963-67; exec. sec. div. info. services, asst. treas. Luth. Council in Can., 1967-76, exec. dir., 1976—; treas. Can. sect. Luth. Ch. in Am., 1963-85, mem. Love Compels Action com., 1972-82; mem. finance com. Can. Council Chs., 1971-85; mem. commn. on world service Luth. World Fedn., Geneva, 1977—. Dir., mem. fraternal activity com. Luth. Life Ins. Soc. Can., Waterloo, Ont. Mem. allocation com. United Way of Winnipeg. Chmn. bd. Sr. Citizen Day Centres, 1963-69. Recipient Disting. Service award Luth. Brotherhood Fraternal Ins. Soc., Mpls., 1967. Mem. Inst. Chartered Accountants of Man. Office: 500-365 Hargrave St Winnipeg MB R3B 2K3 Canada

SCHULZ, VICTOR ARTHUR, evangelist, Seventh-day Adventists; b. Hohenau, Paraguay, Feb. 5, 1943; s. Lucas Juan and Mary (Hein) S.; came to U.S., 1973; B.A.Th., River Platte Coll., 1964; postgrad Ohio U., 1975; M.Div., Andrews U., 1978, D.Min., 1979; m. Elsa Ruth Esparcia, Jan. 25, 1967; children: Ronald Arthur, Leroy Edgard. Ordained to ministry Seventh-day Adventists, 1969; pastor chs. in Argentina, 1965-70; tchr. theology, chaplain Uruguay Seventh-day Adventist Coll., Canelones, 1971-72; evangelist, Uruguay, 1972-73; minister chs., Youngstown, Ohio and Cleve., 1973-76, East Chicago, Ind., 1976; leader profl. tours to Holy Land and Europe, 1973-82; major evangelistic crusades include Salta, Argentina, 1966, Corrientes, Argentina, 1968, Canelones, Uruguay, 1972, Youngstown, 1974, East Chicago, 1976, New Orleans, 1978, Houston, 1980, Washington, 1982, Cleve., Kansas City, Mo., Denver, 1983, Toronto, Ont., Can., Trenton, Wilmington, Del., Melbourne and Sydney, Australia, 1984. Bd. dirs. Spanish Am. Assn., 1974-76, pres., 1975. Bur. Econ. Opportunity grantee, 1975; postgrad. scholar, 1976-79. Author: Secrets for a Happy Home, 1968; Flight 657 to Jerusalem, 1976. Contbr. numerous articles to religious mags. Named hon. citizen of Houston, 1980, Washington, 1982, Toronto, 1984; recipient proclamation City of Sydney, 1984, numerous other awards. Home: 3296 W 74th Pl Merrillville IN 46410

SCHULZ, WILLIAM FREDERICK, minister, executive, Unitarian Universalist Association; b. Pitts., Nov. 14, 1949; s. William Frederick and Jean Holman (Smith) S.; m. Linda Lu Cotney, Nov. 17, 1978; children: Jeneanne, Jason. A.B., Oberlin Coll., 1971; M.A. in Theology, Meadville/Lombard Theol. Sch., Chgo., 1973, D.Min., 1975; M.A. in Philosophy, U. Chgo., 1974. Ordained to ministry Unitarian Universalist Assn., 1975. Minister, First Parish, Bedford, Mass., 1975-78; dir. social responsibility Unitarian Universalist Assn., Boston, 1978-79, acting dir. ministerial and congregational services dept., 1979, exec. v.p., 1979—. Contbg. editor: Transforming Words: Six Essays on Preaching, 1984. Recipient Francis Albert Christie prize Meadville/Lombard Theol. Sch., 1972, 75. Mem. Unitarian Universalist Ministers Assn., Soc. for Theol. Edn. (bd. dirs. 1982—), Mass. Civil Liberties Union, Phi Beta Kappa. Democrat. Club: Fortnightly (Newburyport, Mass.). Office: Unitarian Universalist Assn 25 Beacon St Boston MA 02108

SCHUMACHER, A(LBERT) C(HARLES), bishop and district president, American Lutheran Church; b. Eureka, S.D., July 2, 1918; s. Christian and Christine (Klooz) S.; m. Olivia Denef, Aug. 23, 1944 (dec. May 1978); children: Timothy Albert, Anthony Alan, Jonathan James. B.A., Wartburg Coll., 1940; M.S.T., Wartburg Sem., 1943, D.Div. (hon.), 1973; postgrad. Drake U., 1944-46; D.Div. (hon.), Luther Coll., 1979. Ordained to ministry American Luth. Ch., 1943. Pastor, Windsor Heights Luth. Ch., Des Moines, 1943-54, St. John's Luth. Ch., Madison, 1954-64, 66-75; cons. Luth. World Fedn., Alsace-Lorraine, France, 1964-65; bishop, pres. So. Wis. Dist. Am. Luth. Ch., Madison, 1976—; mem. ch. council Am. Luth. Ch., Mpls., 1968—, mem. council pres., 1976—; trustee Carthage Coll., Kenosha, Wis., 1970—; bd. dirs. Luth. Social Services, Wis. and Upper Mich., 1976—, Luth. Campus Ministry, Wis. and Upper Mich., 1976—; pres. Wis. Conf. chs., Madison, 1982-84. Pres. bd. dirs. Briarpatch, Inc., Madison, 1982-84; bd. dirs. Oakwood Luth. Found., Madison, 1982—; trustee Suomi Coll., Hancock, Mich., 1985—. Recipient Outstanding Civic Contbn. award Windsor Heights Community, Iowa, 1952, citation of appreciation Luth. Social Services, Milw., 1963, Community Service award Wartburg Coll. Alumni Assn., 1973, Suomi award Suomi Coll., 1984. Republican. Club: Maple Bluff Country (Madison). Lodge: Rotary. Office: Am Luth Ch So Wis Dist 2705 Packers Ave Madison WI 53704

SCHUMACHER, FREDERICK JOHN, minister, Lutheran Church America; b. Bklyn., Mar. 8, 1939; s. Friedrich and Elizabeth Marie (Perley) S.; B.S., U. Okla., 1961; B.D., Central Luth. Theol. Sem., 1964; M.Div., Luth. Sch. Theology, 1972; S.T.M., N.Y. Theol. Sem., 1972; D.Min., Princeton Theol. Sem., 1978; m. Joyce Elaine Morris, June 9, 1961; children—Frederick Eugene, John Frederick, Joy Elaine. Ordained to ministry, 1964; asst. pastor, dir. religious edn. and evangelism St. Matthew's Luth. Ch., White Plains, N.Y., 1964-66, pastor, 1966—. Pres., White Plains Clergy Assn., 1968-70; vice-chmn. cons. com. on aging Luth. Ch. in Am., 1974-78, mem. exec. bd. Metropolitan N.Y. Synod, 1974-77; trustee St. Agnes Hosp., White Plains, 1983—; dean Tappan Zee dist. Luth. Ch. in Am., 1983—; chaplain, White Plains Police and Fire Depts., 1966—; Protestant chaplain White Plains Extended Care and Nursing Facility, Inc., 1972—. Bd. dirs. White Plains YMCA, 1972-74. Recipient Pioneer Friendship award United Cerebral Palsy of Westchester, 1970; parish minister's fellow Fund for Theol. Edn., Inc., 1971, Samuel Trexler scholar, 1973. Contbr. articles to religious jours. Home: 79 Greenridge Ave White Plains NY 10605 Office: 3 Carhart Ave White Plains NY 10605

SCHUMAKER, MILLARD KENT, educator, minister, United Presbyterian Church U.S.A.; b. Genoa, Nebr., July 26, 1936; s. Lester Melvin and Viola Sophia (Anderson) S.; m. Elizabeth Ann McKnight, Nov. 7, 1976; children: Alexandra, Katherine; children by previous marriage: Robin, Albert. A.B., Colgate U., 1958, M.A., 1967; S.T.B., Harvard U., 1961; Ph.D., Queen's U., Kingston, Ont., 1970. Ordained to ministry, 1961. Pastor, Babcock Meml. Chapel, Ashaway, R.I., 1958-65; instr. Colgate U., Hamilton, N.Y., 1965-67; prof. Christian ethics Queens Theol. Coll., Kingston, Ont., 1969—; Chautauqua lectr., 1983. Contbr. articles to profl. jours. Author monographs: Supererogation, 1977; Moral Poise, 1977; Appreciating our Good Earth, 1980. Guggenheim fellow, 1978. Home: 19 Sydenham St Kingston ON K7L 3G8 Canada Office: Queens Theol Coll Kingston ON K7L 3N6 Canada

SCHUMAN MARY ANNE, contemplative nun, Roman Catholic Church; b. Milw., Mar. 10, 1922; d. Raymond Alexander and Anita Sophia Matilda (Efflandt) S. B.A., St. Mary of the Woods, 1977. Joined Discalced Carmelite Nuns, Roman Cath. Ch., 1943. Dir., composer liturgical music Discalced Carmelites, Eldridge, Iowa, 1950—, prioress, 1980—, novice mistress formation dir., editor newsletter, archivist. Editor music collection Songs from Carmel, 1970. Contbr. book revs. to religious publs. Mem. Assn. Contemplative Sisters (regional del. 1983—). Home and Office: Carmelite Monastery Monastery Rd Eldridge IA 52748

SCHURTER, DENNIS DEAN, minister, Lutheran Church-Missouri Synod; b. Great Falls, Mont., Sept. 19, 1942; s. Orie Olin and Martha Mary (Priboth) S.; m. Sandra Carol Boehme, Aug. 21, 1965; children: Stephanie Ann, Kyle Christopher. A.A., Concordia Jr. Coll., Austin, Tex., 1962; B.A., Concordia Sr. Coll., Fort Wayne, Ind., 1964; M.Div., Concordia Theol. Sem., St. Louis, 1968. Ordained to ministry Luth. Ch., 1968. Pastor, Christ The King Luth. Ch., Waxahachie, Tex., 1968-72, Our Redeemer Luth. Ch., Greenville, Tex., 1972-74; chaplain-in-tng. Terrell State Hosp., Terrell, Tex., 1973-74; chaplain Denton State Sch., Tex. Dept. Mental Health and Mental Retardation, Denton, 1975—; chmn., treas. Denton Area Hosp. Chaplaincy Bd., 1980—. Adult leader Longhorn council Boy Scouts Am., 1980—. Fellow Am. Protestant Hosp. Assn. (Coll. Chaplains); mem. Am. Assn. Mental Deficiency (religion div., sec. 1977-79). Office: Denton State Sch PO Box 368 Denton TX 76202

SCHUSTER, JEAN DOROTHY, nun, religious organization administrator, Roman Catholic Church; encyclopedia saleswoman; b. Madison, Wis., June 17, 1945; d. Bernard William and Dorothy Gertrude (Conrad) S. B.A. in Religious Studies, Cardinal Stritch Coll., Milw., 1975; M.A. in Social Ministry, St. Mary's Coll., Winona, Minn., 1979. Joined Sisters for Christian Community, Roman Catholic Ch., 1972. Cert. secondary tchr. Tchr. St. Francis Xavier Sch., Spalding, Mich., 1965-70; dir. religious edn. Sts. Peter and Paul Sch., Milw., 1970-72, St. Aloysius Sch., Sauk City, Wis., 1975—; supr. St. Boniface Sch., Milw., summer 1968; mem. choir, lector and Eucharist minister St. Aloysius Ch., 1975—; Wis. contact person Sisters for Christian Community, Wis., 1975—. Saleswoman, World Book Encyc., Sauk City, 1980-85. Author: ednl. lesson plans, parish needs assessment. Sec. Alcohol and Other Drug Abuse, Sauk City, 1979-85; donor ARC Blood Bank, Sauk City, Madison chpt., 1975-85; speech judge Sauk-Prairie and Wisconsin Heights High Sch., Wis., 1983, 84. Scholar Cardinal Stritch Coll., 1972-75, K.C., 1984. Mem. Madison Dirs. Religious Edn. Orgn. (treas. 1983-84), Wis. Dirs. Religious Edn. Fedn. (bd. dirs. 1981-83), Nat. Apostle Wis. Retarded Persons, Nat. Cath. Edn. Assn., Cath. Daughters Am. (hon.), Delta Epsilon Sigma. Democrat. Avocations: Gardening; horseback riding; sewing; reading. Home: 608 Oak St Sauk City WI 53583 Office: St Aloysius Religious Edn Office 608 Oak St Sauk City WI 53583

SCHUSTER, RICHARD LOUIS, priest, Episcopal Church; b. Waterbury, Conn., Apr. 5, 1945; s. Robert Bryan and Mabel Margaret (Bristol) S.; children: Wendi, Alyson. B.A. in Bus. and Econs., Nasson Coll., 1968; M.Div., Berkeley Div. Sch., 1971. Ordained priest, Episcopal Ch., 1972. Curate, Ch. of Holy Trinity, Middletown, Conn., 1971-75; rector Joint Ministry of Immanuel and St. James Episcopal Chs., Ansonia and Derby, Conn., 1975-84; asst. dir. Episcopal Social Service, Inc., 1984—; trustee Berkeley Div. Sch., New Haven, 1968-71; chmn. mission com. Diocese of Conn., 1981-83, mem. standing com., 1983—, mem. exec. council, 1980-83. Founder, Lower Naugatuck Valley Community Mental Health Ctr., 1979; pres. Conn. Coalition for Homeless, 1984—, Pub. Health Nursing and Homemaker Services, Derby, Conn., 1980-82, Regional Mental Health Bd., Region II, New Haven, 1978-79; chmn. InterFaith Emergency Housing Project, Derby, 1981-84. Recipient Charles H. Flynn Humanitarian award Valley United Way, 1983; Gold Seal award Lower Naugatuck Valley C. of C., 1981; Good Neighbor award Lower Naugatuck Valley Community Mental Health, 1984. Lodge: Rotary (v.p.). Home: 341 Alden Ave New Haven CT 06151 Office: Episcopal Social Service 1067 Park Ave Bridgeport CT 06604

SCHUTT, RONALD PAUL, minister, Luth. Ch.-Mo. Synod; b. Frankenmuth, Mich., Mar. 12, 1937; s. Paul Emmanuel and Meta Martha Naphteli (Heine) S.; B.A., Concordia Sr. Coll., 1960; M.Div., Concordia Sem., 1964; m. Karen Ann Maxwell, Sept. 19, 1964; children—Paul Robert, David Mark, Andrew Jon. Ordained to ministry, 1964; pastor St. Paul Luth. Ch., Kemmerer, Wyo., 1964-72, Emmanuel Luth. Ch., Green River, Wyo., 1965-72, Evergreen Luth. Ch., Evergreen, Colo., 1973—. Sec. Wyo. dist. Luth. Ch.-Mo. Synod, 1970-72. Named Outstanding Young Man, Green River Jr. C. of C., 1972. Mem. Am. Assn. Pastoral Counselors. Home: 6398 S Far View Ln Evergreen CO 80439 Office: 5980 Hwy 73 Evergreen CO 80439

SCHUTZ, JOHN HOWARD, history of religion educator; b. Orange, N.J., Mar. 11, 1933; s. John Paul and Frances Virginia (Wolfe) S.; m. Barbara Jane Foster, June 20, 1953; children: Martha Anne, Amy Thorndike. B.S., Northwestern U., 1954; B.D., Yale U., 1958, M.A., 1960, Ph.D., 1964. Instr., Yale U., New Haven, 1961-65, asst. prof., 1965-68; assoc. prof. U. N.C., Chapel Hill, 1968-73, prof., 1973-83, Bowman and Gordon Gray prof. history of religion, 1983—. Author: Paul and the Anatomy of Apostolic Authority, 1975. Editor/translator: The Social Setting of Pauline Christianity, 1982. Mem. Studiorum Novi Testamenti Societas, Soc. Bibl. Lit., N. Am. Patristics Soc., Cath. Bibl. Assn. Home: 311 Birch Circle Chapel Hill NC 27514 Office: Dept Religious Studies U NC Chapel Hill NC 27514

SCHWAB, J. MILTON, minister, American Baptist Churches in the U.S.A.; b. Fulton, Mo., July 10, 1928; s. Orval L. and Thelma (Sims) S.; m. Pauline Hauser, May 23, 1953; children: David, Linda, James (dec.), Jennifer. Student Moody Bible Inst., 1948-49. B.A., Roosevelt U., 1952-53; student Northern Bapt. Coll., 1949-53; M.Div., Northern Bapt. Sem., 1952-55. Ordained to ministry American Baptist Chs. in U.S.A., 1955. Pastor, North Scott Bapt. Ch., Pardeeville, Wisc., 1954-60, First Bapt. Ch., Sunbury, Ohio, 1960-63, Pleasant Run Bapt. Ch., Cin., 1963-76, First Bapt. Ch., Lancaster, Pa., 1976-81, Central Bapt. Ch., Indpls., 1981—. Served to ETM 2 U.S.Navy, 1946-48. Home: 8706 Holliday Indpls IN 46260 Office: Central Bapt Ch 6151 Central Indpls IN 46220

SCHWARTZ, CORMI, organization executive, Jewish. Exec. v.p. Council of Jerish Fedn., Inc. Office: 575 Lexington Ave New York NY 10022*

SCHWARTZ, ELEANOR R., lay federation executive, Reform Jewish Congregation; b. Chgo., Dec. 5, 1923; d. Michael and Gertrude (Fagen) S. B.A. in Polit. Sci. and Psychology, U. Chgo., 1941. Dir. youth N.Y. Fedn. Reform Synagogues; dir. young people's div. Jewish Fedn. and Welfare Fund Chgo.; assoc. dir. Nat. Fedn. Temple Youth, youth affiliate Union Am. Hebrew Congregations; assoc. dir. Nat. Fedn. Temple Sisterhoods, N.Y.C., 1959-76, exec. dir., 1976—; also past rep. to UNICEF and rep. to Joint Commns. Social Action and Israel, N. Am. bd. and governing body World Union for Progressive Judaism; past rep. Union Am. Hebrew Congregations on Rabbinical Placement Commn., also past mem. exec. com.; past coordinator Joint Steering Com. of Reform Judaism on Jewish Family; past observer UN; past mem. bd. dirs. and speakers bur. Joint Distbn. Com., Chgo. Conf. Christians and Jews, Combined Jewish Appeal, USO; past rep. Nat. Fedn. of Temple Sisterhoods and UNICEF at internat. gatherings in Europe, Mid-East, Africa; past organizing mem. Religious Coalition for Abortion Rights (now Religious Network for Equality for Women); bd. dirs. Nat. Interfaith Coalition on Aging. Past mem. policy council Nat. Orgn.'s Adv. Council, a sustaining orgn. Internat. Yr. of the Child. Office: Nat Fedn Temple Sisterhoods 838 Fifth Ave New York NY 10021

SCHWARTZ, JUDE, nun, Roman Catholic, educator; b. St. Louis, Feb. 9, 1940; d. John Joseph and Angela (Gardner) S. B.A., Webster Coll., 1963; M.A., St. Louis U., 1975. Joined Sisters of Loretto, Roman Cath. Ch., 1959; cert. sch. adminstr. U. Tex. Tchr., Loretto Acad., El Paso, Tex., 1963-66, Loretto Acad. Kansas City, Mo., 1966-70, Loretto Acad. El Paso, 1970-75, prin., 1976—. Mem. reviewing com. El Paso Cath. Bd. Edn., 1978-83. Recipient Women's Equality Day award El Paso Women's Polit. Caucus, 1984. Mem. Nat. Assn. Secondary Sch. Prins., Assn. Supervision and Curriculum Devel., So. Assn. Colls. and Sch. (chmn. 1977—), So. Assn. Colls. and Schs. Secondary Commn. Office: Loretto Acad High Sch 1300 Hardaway El Paso TX 79903

SCHWARTZ, SUSAN CHRISTINE, minister, American Lutheran Church; b. Columbus, Ohio, Dec. 4, 1949; s. Francis Edward and Sara Alice (Montgomery) S. B.A., Capital U., 1975; M.Div., Trinity Luth. Sem., Columbus, Ohio, 1980. Ordained to ministry American Lutheran Church, 1980. Asst. pastor Our Savior's Luth. Ch., Burbank, Ill., 1980—; mem. exec. bd. S. Chgo. cong. Am. Luth. Ch., 1982-85, mem. dist. faculty Ill. SEARCH Bible Studies, 1983-85; mem. dist. bd. Ill. div. World Mission and Interchurch Cooperation, 1982-85; mem. standing com. Ill. dist. Office Communication and Mission Support, 1982-85. Mem. Burbank Police and Fire Chaplains (v.p. 1981-83), Chgo. Zool. Soc., Mus. Sci. and Industry, Luths. for Life, Evangels. for Social Action. Home: 8101 Willow Dr Palos Hills IL 60465 Office: Our Savior's Luth Ch 8607 S Narragansett Burbank IL 60465

SCHWEIGARDT, ERWIN HERMAN, priest, Roman Catholic Church; b. Albany, N.Y., June 29, 1939; s. Hermann R. and Elsie Rose (Teufer) S.; B.A., Manhattan Coll., 1961; M.S., Fordham U., 1963; Ph.D., Cath. U. Am., 1972. Ordained priest, 1967; tchr., guidance counselor high schs. in N.Y., 1961-70; dir.

ednl. research Roman Cath. Diocese Albany, 1972-75, dist. supt. schs., 1975-78; chaplain Union Coll., Schenectady, 1973-80; pastor Ch. of St. Patrick, Watervliet, N.Y., 1980—. Mem. campus bd. Holy Names Acad., Albany, 1972-80; bd. dirs. Schenectady Cath. Family Services, 1973-76. Pres. Rensselaer (N.Y.) Community Council, 1967-70; mem. nat. devel. council Manhattan Coll., 1972—; bd. dirs. Hospice of Schenectady, 1979-84, Hospice Found., 1984—; cons. Nat. Assn. Bds. Edn., 1972-80. Recipient Cardinal Spellman award Manhattan Coll., 1961; Frank Gannett Newsboys scholar, 1957-61. Mem. Nat. Cath. Ednl. Assn., Cath. U. Am. (govs. 1972-75), Manhattan Coll. (treas. 1976-80) alumni socs., Phi Alpha Theta, Delta Phi Alpha, Phi Kappa Theta. Home: 515 19th St Watervliet NY 12189

SCHWEIKERT, JOHN E., bishop, North American Old Roman Catholic Church Ordained priest N.Am. Old Roman Catholic Ch., 1955, consecrated bishop, 1958; chaplain Chgo. Tech. Coll., 1959-71; now presiding bishop of the Americas and Can., N.Am. Old Roman Catholic Ch. Founder, dir. Little Sisters Sch. for Retarded Children, 1971—. Mem. Nat. Assn. Coll. Chaplains. Address: 4200 N Kedvale Ave Chicago IL 60641

SCHWEITZER, ALVIN AUSTIN, minister, Luth. Ch. in Am.; b. Newton, Ont., Can., Nov. 3, 1917; s. George Henry and Annie (Doerr); B.A., U. Western Ont., 1937; B.Div., 1944; m. Nora Catharine Dorland, Nov. 4, 1944; children—Paul Alvin, Mary Ann, Julia Margery. Ordained to ministry, 1941; asst. pastor St. John's Luth. Ch., Waterloo, Ont., 1941; pastor Linwood Parish, Waterloo, County, 1942-45, Brantford-Woodstock (Ont.) Parish, 1945-54, Redeemer Luth. Ch., Vancouver, B.C., 1954-59, 69—, Our Savior's Luth. Ch., Lachine, Que., 1959-62, St. Mark's Luth. Ch., Kitchener, Ont., 1963-69, Dean B.C. dist., Western Can. Synod, Luth. Ch. Am., 1970-74. Home: 1041 W 49th Ave Vancouver BC V6M 2P7 Canada Office: 1499 Laurier Ave Vancouver BC V6H 1Z2 Canada

SCHWERTZ, FREDERICK JOSEPH, church official, Roman Catholic Church; b. Millersville, Pa., May 7, 1896; s. Celestin and Anna B. (Rees) S.; B.A., Pontifical Coll. Josephinum, Columbus, O., 1916, M.A., 1920; Litt.D., Sch. Journalism, Denver, 1956. Ordained priest Roman Catholic Ch., 1922; prof. St. Edward Coll., Huntington, W. Va., 1922-23; asst. chancellor Diocese of Wheeling (W. Va.), 1923-41, chancellor, 1941-76, also diocesan consultor, 1926-76, dir. bur. publicity, 1941-72, mem. council of adminstrn., 1941-76, supt. orphan homes, 1942-56, dir. Catholic relief services, 1943-75, dir. cemeteries, 1949—. Chmn. UN Refugee Relief Assn. Clothing Drive, City of Wheeling, 1943. Sec. bd. dirs. Wheeling Hosp., 1941-76; sec. bd. dirs., Welty Home for Aged, Wheeling, 1950-84, v.p., 1984—; sec.-treas. Infirm Priests' Assn., 1941-76. Named Domestic Prelate, Roman Catholic Ch., 1949, Protonotary Apostolic, 1968. K.C. Editor Diocesan Weekly, 1923-63. Home: Mt de Chantel Acad 410 Washington Ave Wheeling WV 26003 Office: 1300 Byron St Wheeling WV 26003

SCHWICHTENBERG, WILLIS ROBERT, minister, Lutheran Church-Missouri Synod; b. Morristown, Minn., Nov. 21, 1946; s. Harold Arthur and Mabel Elizabeth (Fratzke) S.; m. Alice Marie Fischer, Sept. 2, 1967; children: Jonathan, Jennifer, Jason, Jodee. B.S., Mankato State Coll., 1968; B.D., Concordia Theol. Sem., Springfield, Ill., 1972, M.Div., 1973. Ordained to ministry Luth. Ch., 1972. Pastor, Trinity Luth. Ch., Sheldon, Wis., Zion Luth. Ch., Gilman, Wis., 1972-76, Our Savior Luth. Ch., Milford, Ill., 1977-82, Immanuel Luth. Ch., Freeport, Ill., 1982—; vacancy pastor Good Shepherd Luth. Ch., Hoopeston, Ill., 1978-79, 81-82; sub.dist. dir. Foreward In Remembrance Synodical Appeal, 1980-81; dean Iroquois Bible Inst., Iroquois County, Ill., 1981-82; speaker Instrospect radio program, Freeport, 1983—. Contbr. editor Adventures With Youth, 1977-81. Contbr. articles to religious publs. Home: 617 S Chicago Freeport IL 61032 Office: Immanuel Luth Ch 615 S Chicago Freeport IL 61032

SCHWIER, STEVEN LAYNE, minister, Lutheran Ch. in America; b. Batesville, Ind., Oct. 6, 1949; s. Henry Layne and Cleona Ilene (Miller) S.; m. Kathy Ann Doenges, July 24, 1971; children: Henry Layne II, Julie Ann. B.S., Ball St. U., 1973; M.Div., Luth. Theol. Southern Sem., 1977. Ordained to ministry Luth. Ch. in Am., 1977. Pastor Our Saviour Luth. Ch., Princeton, Ind., 1977—; exec. bd. Ind.-Ky. Synod, 1980—; dean Evansville Dist., Ind.-Ky. Synod, 1980—; del. Luth. Ch. in Am. Conv., Louisville, 1982; chaplain Ind.-Ky. Synod Conv., Bloomington, Ind., 1982. Pres. Boys' Club Princeton, 1982—; bd. dirs. United Way of Gibson County, 1978-84; Princeton Soccer League, 1979-84, Princeton Little League, 1983-84. Served to spec. 4 U.S. Army, 1969-71, Ger. Cum Laude Luth. Theol. Southern Sem., 1977. Lodge: Rotary. Home: S Hart St Princeton IN 47670

SCHWOCHOW, ALAN ARTHUR, minister, American Lutheran Church. B. Castalia, Ohio, June 7, 1953; s. Eric Ernest and Lucille Mae (Norman) S.; m. Elizabeth Ann Tonn, Feb. 15, 1981. B.A., Capital U.,

1975; M.Div., Trinity Luth. Sem., Columbus, Ohio, 1979. Ordained to ministry American Lutheran Church, 1979. Pastor, Martin Luther Luth. Ch., Bucyrus, Ohio, 1979; v.p. N. Central Conf., Ohio dist. Am. Luth. Ch., 1983—. Chairperson Bucyrus Area CROP Walk for Hunger, Ohio, 1982, 83. Mem. Bucyrus Area Ministerial Assn. (sec. 1980-81, pres. 1981-83), Liturgical Conf. Home and Office: Martin Luther Luth Ch 2984 Knauss Rd Bucyrus OH 44820

SCICERE, LEO EARL, minister, Baptist Church of God and Christ; psychotherapist; b. Toledo, Ohio, May 13, 1933; s. James and Anna (Bunkly) S. B.A. summa cum laude, CCNY, 1958; M.A., Harvard U., 1960, Ph.D., 1963; D.Min., N.Y. Theol. Sem., 1979. Ordained to ministry Bapt. Ch., 1979. Pastor, Little Zion Bapt. Ch., Bklyn., 1970—. Pvt. practice psychotherapy, Queens, N.Y., 1970—. Mem. legis. adv. com. Sen. Andrew Jenkins 10th Dist., Queens., 1984-85. NSF fellow, 1958-62; Fulbright scholar, 1975-76. Mem. N.Y. Acad. Sci., Nat. Psychiat. Assn., AAAS, Assn. Mental Health Clergy, Assn. for Alcoholism Communication. Home: 13507 219th St Springfield Gardens NY 11413

SCOATES, HARRY WILLIAM, JR., minister, United Methodist Ch.; b. Palatka, Fla., Sept. 13, 1920; s. Harry William and Orlene (Buffkin) S.; A.B., Emory U., 1949; M.Div., Candler Sch. Theology, 1952; postgrad. Valdosta State U., 1970-72; m. Mary Grace Patten, Nov. 8, 1942; children—Luellen (Mrs. T. Ed Hart), Gaylon, Dana (Mrs. Don Wildsmith). Ordained to ministry United Methodist Ch., 1952; pastor, Jeffersonville, Ga., 1950-55, Crosskeys United Meth. Ch., Macon, Ga., 1955-60, Vidalia, Ga., 1960-65, Trinity United Meth. Ch., Savannah, Ga., 1965-70; dist. supt. Americus Dist. United Meth. Ch., Cordele, Ga., 1970-72; council dir., dir. missions and ch. extension, dir. So. Ga. Investment Fund, Inc. (all S. Ga. Conf. United Meth. Ch.), St. Simons Island, Ga., 1972-76; field rep. Bd. Global Ministries United Meth. Ch., N.Y.C., 1976—. Mem. Internat. Congress on World Evangelization, 1974; dir. research projects So. Ga. Conf., 1956, 60, Savannah-Statesboro dists., 1974; mem. World Meth. Council, 1972-76, 76—. Active Boy Scouts Am., Macon, also Vidalia, Savannah, Albany, Ga., 1955-72; mem. Ga. Gov.'s Com. State Reorgn., 1971. Bd. dirs. March of Dimes, Jeffersonville, Macon, Vidalia, 1952-65, ARC, Jeffersonville, Macon, Vidalia, Savannah, 1953-70; trustee Dooly Camp Ground, Vienna, Ga., 1970-72, So. Ga. Home for Aging, Americus, 1970-72, Vashti Sch., Thomasville, Ga., 1972—, Paul Anderson Home, Vidalia, 1961-65. Named Rural Pastor of Year, Emory U.-Progress Farmer mag., 1955. Mem. Nat. Trust Historic Preservation, United Meth. Rural Ch. Fellowship, Nat. Assn. Council Dirs. United Meth. Ch. (sec.-treas. 1975-76), Am. Mgmt. Assn., Nat. Eagle Scout Assn. Author: Vidalia Moments, 1962; Riding the Wire, 1964. Contbr. articles to religious jours. Home: Route 1 Box 149 Bethlehem GA 30620 Office: 475 Riverside Dr New York City NY 10027

SCOTT, CLIFFORD RAY, religious broadcasting executive, Baptist General Conference; b. Wilmington, N.C., June 15, 1930; s. DeWitt Talmadge and Ruth Elvera (Hufham) S.; student Reedley (Calif.) Coll., 1963-64, Internat. Coll., Honolulu, 1977-80; m. Billie Jean Gibson, Jan. 3, 1956; children—Clifford, Lisa, David, Rebecca. Deacon, tchr. Calvary Bapt. Ch., Dinuba, Calif., 1962-67; gen. mgr. KAIM Radio, Christian Broadcasting Assn., Honolulu, 1971—. Home: Apt 10B 38 S Judd St Honolulu HI 96817 Office: PO Box 375 Honolulu HI 96809

SCOTT, DAMON SMITH, minister, United Meth. Ch.; b. DeLeon, Tex., Nov. 22, 1914; s. Willie James and Annie Arnold (Smith) S.; ed. Moody Bible Inst., 1939, U. Miami (Fla.), 1959, Candler Sch. Theology, 1961; m. Verbie Price, Nov. 6, 1944; children—Edgar Allen, Vicki Ann. Ordained to ministry, 1962; dir. Gospel Broadcasting Co., Jackson, Miss., 1939-40; dir. music, youth Comer Meml. Ch., Alexander City, Ala., 1952-54; pastor Tavernier, Fla., 1954-56, Florida City, Fla., 1956-59, Miami, Fla., 1959-61, DeBary, Fla., 1961-63, Palatka, Fla., 1963-67, Monticello, Fla., 1967-69, Wesley United Meth. Ch., Jacksonville, Fla., 1969—. Youth dir. Deland Dist., 1964-67, Tallahassee Dist., 1967-69; chief of chaplains Putnam County Civil Def., 1965-67; pres. Putnam County Ministerial Assn., 1964-66. Mem. Putnam County Bi-Racial Com., 1965-67; bd. dirs. Monroe County Hosp. Authority, 1954-56; bd. dirs. Putnam County Bd. Mental Health, 1963-67. Named Minister of Yr., DeLand Dist., 1962-64, Minister of Yr., Fla. Conf., 1962. Mem. Jacksonville Gospel Singers Assn. (pres. 1974-75). Author: Praying Effectively, 1966; weekly contbr. Monticello News, 1967-69. Home: 2014 Woodmere Circle Jacksonville FL 32210 Office: 1140 S McDuff Ave Jacksonville FL 32205

SCOTT, DOUGLAS GORDON, priest, Episcopal Church; b. Phila., Jan. 14, 1949; s. Robert Allen and Jean Hamilton (Torrey) S.; m. Jane Elizabeth Kirkby, Aug. 13, 1977; children: Claire Aileen, Mhari Gordon, Joy Francis. B.A., Muskingum Coll., 1970; M.Div., Phila. Div. Sch., 1974; M.S.T., Gen. Theol. Sem., 1979. Ordained priest, 1974. Asst. St. Mary's Ch., Wayne, Pa., 1974-75; staff assoc. Diocese of Pa., Phila.,

1974-75; curate Ch. of the Atonement, Tenafly, N.J., 1975-77; rector St. John the Divine, Hasbrouck Heights, N.J., 1977-80, Ch. of St. Thomas of Canterbury, Smithtown, N.Y., 1980-84, St. Martin's Ch., Radnor, Pa., 1985—; bd. dirs. H.E.A.L., Smithtown, 1983-84; supr. Lay Chaplains Program, St. John Hosp., 1982-84; episcopal chaplain St. Johnland Nursing Home, Kings Park, N.Y., 1980-84; mem. community bd. St. John's Hosp., 1980-81. Author: The Piobaireachd Index, 1978; co-author: The Fast I Choose, 1976. Author Christian edn. curriculum: Sharing the Faith, 1985. Contbr. articles to profl. jours. Chmn., Com. on Nutritional Alternatives, Phila., 1975; lectr. Alfred Noyes Med. Conf., Norristown, Pa., 1975; bd. dirs. R.E.A.C.H., Hasbrouck Heights, 1979. Club: Mensa. Home: PO Box 56 Radnor PA 19087 Office: St Martin's Ch Radnor PA 19087

SCOTT, DURWARD LEROY, minister, So. Bapt. Conv.; b. Benton County, Mo., June 27, 1925; s. Erban E. and Mary C. (Smith) S.; student S.W. Bapt. Coll., 1962-63; diploma in theology Midwestern Bapt. Theol. Sem., 1967; m. Lena Loraine Bunch, Dec. 8, 1945; 1 dau., Winnie Lou. Ordained to ministry, 1961; pastor Parks Chapel Bapt. Ch., Clinton, Mo., 1961-67, 1st Bapt. Ch., Huntsville, Mo., 1967-73, Elm St. Bapt. Ch., Murphysboro, Ill., 1973—. Chmn. mission com. Nine Mile Bapt. Assn., 1974—; moderator Mt. Pleasant Assn., 1973. Address: PO Box 586 1240 Crescent Dr Murphysboro IL 62966

SCOTT, EDWARD WALTER, primate, Anglican Ch. of Can.; b. Edmonton, Alta., Can., Apr. 30, 1919; s. Thomas and Kathleen S.; B.A., U. B.C., 1940; L.Th., Anglican Theol. Coll., 1942; D.D. (hon.), Anglican Theol. Coll. of B.C., Trinity Coll., U. Toronto, Wycliffe Coll., Toronto, Huron Coll., U. Western Ont.; D.C.L. (hon.), St. Johns Coll., U. Man., also S.T.D.; m. Isabel Florence Brannan, Aug. 5, 1942; children—Douglas, Maureen Scott Harris, Patricia Ann Scott Robinson, Elizabeth Jean. Ordained priest; priest St. Peters Ch., Seal Cove, Prince Rupert, B.C., 1942-45; gen. sec. Student Christian Movement, U. Man., Winnipeg, 1945-49; tchr. St. Johns Coll., Winnipeg, 1949-55; parish priest St. Jude's Ch., Winnipeg, 1955-60; dir. social service, priest dir. Indian work Diocese of Rupert's Land, Man., 1960-64; asso. sec. Council for Social Service, Nat. Hdqrs. Anglican Ch. of Can., Toronto, 1964-66; consecrated bishop of Kootenay, 1966; elected primate Anglican Ch. of Can., Toronto, Ont., 1971—. Moderator central com. World Council Chs., 1975—. Home: 29 Hawthorn Ave Toronto ON M4W 2Z1 Canada Office: 600 Jarvis St Toronto ON M4Y 2J6 Canada

SCOTT, GEORGE WILLIAM, minister, United Methodist Church; b. Greenfield, Mo., Oct. 10, 1922; s. Homer Ethel and Harriett Pauline (Odell) S.; B.A. in Sociology, So. Mo. State U., Springfield, 1967; M.Div., St. Paul Sch. Theology, Kansas City, Mo., 1970; m. Wealtha Belle Chaplin, Oct. 31, 1943; children—Alice, Elizabeth, James, Donald. Ordained deacon, 1968, elder, 1970; minister Versailles (Mo.) United Meth. Ch., 1976-84, Broadway United Meth. Ch., Springfield, Mo., 1984—. Mem. conf. bd. minimum salaries United Meth. Ch., 1971-72, mem. dist. council on ministries, 1972-84; sec.-treas. Webb City (Mo.) Ministerial Alliance, 1972-74; trustee Mo. West Conf., United Meth. Ch., 1980-84; mem. Lakes Dist. Bldg. Com., 1982-84, Lakes Dist. Superintendency Com., 1982-84. Bd. dirs. Morgan County (Mo.) Sheltered Workshop, 1983—; v.p. Morgan County Mental Health Bd., 1982—; pres. Morgan County Ministerial Alliance, 1978-79. Home: 3226 S Benton Springfield MO 65807 Office: 545 S Broadway Springfield MO 65806

SCOTT, JAMES FRANCIS, theology educator, Evangelical Free Church America, librarian; b. Wheatland, Wyo., Feb. 20, 1932; s. William F. and E. Violet (Hampton) S.; m. Ethel Lewis, June 10, 1951. Th.B., Midwest Bible Coll., 1958; A.B., Greenville Coll., 1960; M.A. in Library Sci., East Tex. State U., 1971; M.A. in Bibl. Studies, Dallas Theol. Sem., 1977. Ordained to ministry Evangel. Free Ch. of Am., 1978. Asst. librarian Dallas Theol. Sem., 1969-78; dir. library Multnomah Sch. Bible, Portland, Oreg., 1979—, also asst. prof. of Bible. Author: Analytical Index to Bibliotheca Sacra, 1971; book rev. editor The Christian librarian, 1983—. Mem. Pacific Northwest Christian Library Media Assn. (pres. 1983—), Am. Theol. Library Assn., Assn. Christian Librarians. Home: 11303 NE Siskiyou St Portland OR 92220 Office: Multnomah Sch Bible 8435 NE Glisan St Portland OR 97220

SCOTT, JAMES JULIUS, JR., religious educator, minister, Presbyterian Church U.S.A.; b. Decatur, Ga., Feb. 2, 1935; s. J. Julius and Tena Laverne (Schonert) S.; m. Florence Richardson, Sept. 2, 1958; children: Mary Eleanor, Julia Wymond, James Julius. B.A., Wheaton Coll., 1956; B.D., Columbia Theol. Sem., 1959; Ph.D., U. Manchester-Eng., 1969. Ordained to ministry, 1959. Asst. to pastor Westminster Presbyn. Ch., Atlanta, 1955-58; pastor Brandon Presbyn. Ch., Miss., 1959-61; prof., dept. chmn. Belhaven Coll., Jackson, Miss., 1963-70; prof. Western Ky. U., Bowling Green, 1970-77; prof. religion, chmn. dept. Wheaton Coll., Ill., 1977—. Contbr. articles to profl. jours. Named Tchr. of Year, Belhaven Coll., 1969; Distinctive

Tchr., Western Ky. U., 1976. Fellow Inst. Bibl. Research; mem. Chgo. Soc. Bibl. Research, Evang. Theol. Soc., Soc. Bible. Lit. Home: 924 Eddy Ct Wheaton IL 60187 Office: Dept Theol Studies Wheaton Coll Grad Sch Wheaton IL 60187

SCOTT, JOHN ATWOOD, educator, minister, Chs. of Christ; b. Muskogee, Okla., Feb. 6, 1925; s. Clarence E. and Ruby (Register) S.; B.A., Abilene (Tex.) Christian Coll., 1945, B.S., 1946; M.A., U. Pa., 1952, Ph.D., 1965; m. Mary Joyce Forrester, Aug. 30, 1945; children—John Atwood, David Ray, Emily Joyce. Ordained minister Chs. of Christ, 1942; minister chs. in Pa. and Tenn., 1945-58, 61-72; dir. Bible camps in N.Y., 1950-61; prof. O.T. and counseling Harding Grad. Sch. Religion, Memphis, 1959—; pvt. practice marriage and family counseling, Memphis, 1971—. Bd. dirs. Northeastern Christian Coll., Villanova, Pa., 1954-58. Mem. Soc. Bibl. Lit., Nat. Alliance Family Life, Nat. Assn. Christian Marriage Counselors, Am. Inst. Hypnosis (v.p.), Insts. Religion and Health, Am. Assn. U. Profs. Home: 3454 Forest Hill Rd Germantown TN 38138 Office: 5100 Poplar Ave Memphis TN 38137

SCOTT, JOHN DANIEL, minister, Southern Baptist Convention; b. Portland, Ark., Sept. 8, 1904; s. Thomas Anguris and Mettie Earl (Worthy) S.; diploma Christian tng. New Orleans Bapt. Theol. Sem., 1939; D.D., Union Bapt. Sem., New Orleans, 1954; m. Mamie Ophelia Sutton, Feb. 18, 1923; children—John Daniel, Harvey Edward, Louis Ray. Ordained to ministry, 1935; pastor chs. in Ala. and La., 1935-42; rural field worker La. Bapt. Conv., 1942-54, field sec., 1954-64, dir. rural ch. devel. and planning processes, 1964-71, organizer and chaplain resort ministry, 1971-74; pastor First Bapt. Ch., Georgetown, La., 1974—; active Bible confs., revivals, denominational confs. Chmn. ch. achievement program Big Creek Bapt. Assn., 1975—; chaplain La. Campers on Missions, 1974—. Named Rural Pastor of Year, Progressive Farmer Rural Ch. Mag. and Sears Roebuck & Co., 1942. Author guidebooks, manuals on rural ch. life. Address: 5627 North Dr Alexandria LA 71301

SCOTT, NATHAN ALEXANDER, JR., educator, Episcopal Church; b. Cleve., Apr. 24, 1925; s. Nathan Alexander and Maggie (Martin) S.; A.B., U. Mich., 1944; B.D., Union Theol. Sem., 1946; Ph.D., Columbia, 1949; Litt.D., Ripon Coll., 1965; L.H.D., Wittenberg U., 1965, Fed. City Coll., 1976; D.D., Phila. Div. Sch., 1967; S.T.D., Gen. Theol. Sem., 1968; Litt.D., St. Mary's Coll., Notre Dame, 1969, Denison U., 1976; m. Charlotte Hanley, Dec. 21, 1946; children—Nathan Alexander III, Leslie K. Ordained priest Episcopal Ch., 1960; canon theologian Cathedral of St. James, Chgo., 1966-76; Commonwealth prof. religious studies U. Va., 1976—. Shailer Mathews prof. theology and lit. U. Chgo., 1955-76. Trustee, Soc. for Arts, Religion and Contemporary Culture, Episcopal Radio-TV Found.; trustee Seaburg-Western Theol. Sem., 1970-75. Kent fellow Soc. for Values in Higher Edn. Fellow Am. Acad. Arts and Scis.; mem. Am. Philos. Assn., Modern Lang. Assn., Ch. Hist. Soc., Am. Acad. Religion. Author: The Broken Center, 1966; Negative Capability, 1969; The Wild Prayer of Longing, 1971; Three American Moralists, 1973; The Poetry of Civic Virtue, 1976; The Modern Vision of Death, 1967; Mirrors of Man in Existentialism, 1978; others. Co-editor Jour. Religion, 1963—. Home: 1419 Hilltop Rd Charlottesville VA 22903 Office: Dept Religious Studies U Va Charlottesville VA 22903

SCOTT, OLOF HENDERSON, JR., priest, dean of clergy, Antiochian Orthodox Christian Church. b. Phila., May 13, 1942; s. Olof Henderson and Julia Irene (Rutroff) S.; m. Eva Jakowenko, Sept. 13, 1969; children: Lisa Ann, Christopher Olof, Timothy Nicholas. B.A. in Physics, Franklin and Marshall Coll., 1964; M.S. in Nuclear Engring., Pa. State U., 1966; postgrad. St. Vladimir's Orthodox Theol. Sem., 1975-76. Ordained deacon Antiochian Orthodox Christian Ch., 1975, priest, 1976. Pastor, St. George Orthodox Ch., Charleston, W.Va., 1976—; dean of clergy Appalachian-Ohio Valley Deanery, 1976—; spiritual advisor NAC-SOYO of Archdiocese, 1977-82; mem. exec. bd. W.Va. Council of Chs., 1977—; bd. govs. Nat. Council of Chs., 1977—, mem. nominating com., 1979-81, exec. com., 1985—. Contbr. articles to religious jours. Mem. long-range planning com. W.Va. State Republican Exec. Com., 1985—. Mem. Acad. Parish Clergy (pres. W.Va. chpt. 1983-85), Am. Nuclear Soc., St. Vladimir's Theol. Found., Charleston Ministerial Assn., Order of St. John of Jerusalem-Knights Hospitellers (chaplain 1985—), Sigma Pi Sigma. Club: SPEBSQSA Inc (Charleston)(v.p. 1984-85), Penn State of W.Va. (pres. 1984—). Avocations: camping; barbershop quartet. Home: 4409 Staunton Ave SE Charleston WV 25304 Office: St George Orthodox Ch PO Box 2044 Charleston WV 25327

SCOTT, RANDALL REED, minister, Lutheran Church in America. b. St. Louis, Mar. 16, 1953; s. Harry Sylvester and Virginia Lee (Reed) S.; m. Therese M. Labriola, May 25, 1974 (div. Feb. 1984); 1 child, Sarah Labriola. B.B.A., U. Mo.-Columbia, 1975; M.Div., Luth. Sch. Theology, Chgo., 1979. Ordained to ministry Lutheran Church in America, 1979. Pastor, Immanuel Luth. Ch., Cairo, Ill., 1979—; mem. World Hunger task force, Chgo., 1981—, mem. com. social ministry, 1982—; mem. com. Parish Life, Chgo., 1982—. Contbr. articles to profl. jours. (pres. bd. dirs. Love God Over Self (LOGOS), Inc., Cairo, 1981-83, So. Med. Bldg. Home Assn., Cairo, 1980—. Recipient Gen. Harry L. Bolen award City of Cairo, 1984. Mem. NAACP. Democrat. Home: 626 26th St Cairo IL 62914 Office: 413 Douglas St Cairo IL 62914

SCOTT, ROBERT JOSEPH, minister, counselor, Christian Methodist Episcopal Church; b. Atlanta, Sept. 24, 1938; s. John Scott and Lovie Ruth S. (Brown) Dozier; m. Patricia Watson, June, 1966 (div. 1975); 1 child, Christopher Adrian; m. Imogene Bush, Nov. 16, 1979. B.A., Clark Coll., 1976; M.Div., Interdenominational Theol. Ctr., 1979. Ordained to ministry Christian Methodist Episcopal Ch., 1975; eccles. endorsed chaplain U.S. Navy, 1979. Pastor, St. Mary's Christian Meth. Episcopal Ch., Elberton, Ga., 1981—; counselor, chaplain Atlanta Job Corp, 1978-79; pres. Christian Meth. Episcopal Ch. Fellowship, Atlanta, 1978-79; counselor Hall County Correctional Inst., Gainesville, Ga., 1982—; sponsor Hall County Jaycees, Gainesville, 1982—. Founder, Linden Inst. Boys Club, Atlanta, 1976-79. Served with USN, 1957-61. Grantee Interdenominational Theol. Ctr., 1976, Garrett Theol. Sem. 1976; Clark Coll. scholar, 1956. Mem. NAACP, United Negro Coll. Fund. Avocations: public speaking; writing; word games; swimming; softball. Home: 1845 Calvary Dr Gainesville GA 30501 Office: Hall County Correctional Inst Route 3 PO Box 118-A Gainesville GA 30501

SCRAPER, RANDY LEE, minister, United Methodist Church; b. Beloit, Kans., July 5, 1950; s. Robert Dale and Vida Lee (Davis) S.; m. Wanda Joy Jones, Aug. 16, 1970; children: Heather, Matthew, Stephanie. B.M.E., Baker U., 1971; postgrad. Berean Coll., 1975-76, Asbury Theol. Sch., 1973-74; M.A. in Theology, Oral Roberts U., 1978, D.Min., 1984; M.Div., St. Paul's Sch. Theology, Kansas City, Mo., 1980. Ordained to ministry United Methodist Ch., 1974. Dir. music and youth First United Meth. Ch., Pecos, Tex., 1972-73; student pastor Edenton-2d Creek United Meth. Ch., Edenton, Ohio, 1973-74; pastor Ch. of Pecos, Tex., 1974-76; student pastor Robinson United Meth. Ch., Kans., 1978-80; founding pastor St. Peter's United Meth. Ch., Topeka, Kans., 1980-85; pastor Leawood United Meth. Ch., Kans., 1985—; trustee ex-officio Baker U., Baldwin, Kans., 1981—; adviser Granite Publs., Topeka, 1981—; evangelism chmn. Topeka dist. United Meth. Ch., 1980—, chmn. Bd. Higher Edn. and Campus Ministry, Kans. East Conf., 1981—; bd. dirs. Ecumenical Christian Ministries, State of Kans., 1981—. Author: On Golden Wings, 1985; The Pregnant Father, 1985. Contbr. poetry to ch. mags. Club: Sunflower Shutterbugs (Topeka). Avocations: writing; golf; photography; music.

SCROGGS, ROBERT LEE, minister, So. Baptist Conv.; b. Greenville, S.C., Apr. 24, 1929; s. Egar Hubert and Ida (Bennett) S.; A.A., N. Greenville Jr. Coll., 1957; B.A., Furman U., 1959; m. Earnestine Blackwell, Dec. 3, 1949; children—Diane Moon, Robert Lee. Ordained to ministry, 1957; pastor Fork Shoals Mills (S.C.) Bapt. Ch., 1957-59, Welcome Bapt. Ch., Laurens, S.C., 1959-61, Pelham (S.C.) Bapt. Ch., 1961—. Moderator Greer Assn., chmn. mission com., co-chmn. fin. com., mem. recreation com., exec. com.; marriage counselor, 1965—; referee Family Ct. (juvenile div.), youth counselor, Greenville, S.C., 1976; chaplain local fire dept., 1968—; mem. evangelistic com. Pastors Conf. Recipient Recreational Award for Youth Activities, 1972. Home: Route 5 Greer SC 29651 Office: PO Box 757 Greenville SC 29602

SCRUGGS, JULIUS RICHARD, minister, Missionary Bapt. Ch.; b. Elkton, Tenn., Feb. 1, 1942; s. Earl and Georgia Anna (Seay) S.; B.A., Am. Bapt. Coll., 1965; M.Div., Vanderbilt U., 1968, D.Min., 1975; m. Francina Bannister, June 3, 1963; 1 dau., Jennifer Juliette. Ordained to ministry, 1960; pastor Antioch Bapt. Ch., East Chgo., Ind., 1972-76, 1st Bapt. Ch., Huntsville, Ala., 1977—. Editor, tchr. quar. Nat. Bapt. Pub. Bd., Nashville, 1969—; pres. Pastor's Conf., Nat. Bapt. Conv. Am., 1973-74; dean Nat. Bapt. Pastors Conf., 1974-75. Recipient Theta Epsilon honor award. Mem. NAACP, People United to Save Humanity, Com. on Uniform Series. Author: Meditations on the Church, 1976. Home: 3923 Melville St East Chicago IN 46312 Office: 236 Church St Huntsville AL 35801

SCUDDER, ROBERT, minister, Southern Baptist Convention; youth home administrator; b. Monroe, La., May 1, 1926; s. Lee and Aldyth (Flenniken) S.; m. Mary Nichols, Oct. 28, 1967; children: Lee, Doug, Vicki, Dana. B.A. in Human Behavior, Newport U., Newport Beach, Calif., 1983. Ordained to ministry So. Bapt. Conv., 1979. Minister, tchr. Books 'n' Tapes, Shreveport, La., 1974—; counselor Shreveport Counsel Ctr., 1975-80; asst. pastor Woodlawn Bapt. Ch., Shreveport, 1976; exec. dir., adminstr. Joy Home for Boys, Greenwood, La., 1979—; bd. dirs. Johnny Robinson Youth Shelter, Monroe, La., 1980—. Author: Genesis, 1976; Cults Exposed, 1981; Customs & Prayer, 1983. Author child care pamphlet. Served with USN, 1941-43, PTO. Recipient Child Care award Kiwanis, 1984. Mem. Am. Assn. on Mental Deficiency (religious v.p. 1984-86). Lodge: Kiwanis (pres. 1971-72). Home: Box 550 Greenwood LA 71033 Office: Joy Home for Boys Box 550 Greenwood LA 71033

SEABORG, GLEN E., clergyman. Exec. sec. The Evangelical Church Alliance, Bradley, Ill. Office: The Evang Ch Alliance 1273 Cardinal Dr PO Box 9 Bradley IL 60915*

SEAL, WILLIAM OTIS, minister, So. Bapt. Conv.; b. Cybur, Miss., Oct. 8, 1919; s. Melvin and Mamie (Woodard) S.; B.S., Miss. State U., 1943; postgrad. Southwestern Theol. Sem., Ft. Worth, Tex., 1948-49, New Orleans Theol. Sem., 1950; D.D., William Carey Coll., 1977; m. Jacque Edwards, Nov. 28, 1941; children—Ann Seal, McMullen, Alton Otis. Ordained to ministry, 1948; minister edn. 1st Bapt. Ch., Picayune, Miss., 1946-47, 1st Bapt. Ch., Columbus, Miss., 1948-50; pastor 1st Bapt. Ch., Ita Bena, Miss., 1951-56; Calvary Bapt. Ch., Meridian, Miss., 1957—. Owner, operator Seal's Registered Quarter Horse Ranches. Pres., Miss. Religious Edn. Assn., Miss. Tng. Union; bd. dirs. Universal Concern Found.; conductor revivals U.S. and India; touring preacher, Israel, Africa, Europe. Author: 103 Years of Trials and Triumphs, 1968; This Is the Work of God, 1971; contbr. articles to religious jours. Home: Rt 9 Box 121 Meridian MS 39301

SEALS, ROBERT JOSEPH, minister, Southern Baptist/Transdenominational; b. Paintsville, Ky., May 18, 1938; s. Charles and Mayselle (Taylor) S.; B.A., Southwest Bapt. Coll., Bolivar, Mo., 1972; m. Clarlaine Sue Grimmett, Mar. 21, 1959; children—Kimberly M., Sharon K., Robert J., Nathan C. Ordained to ministry, 1962; pastor chs. in W.Va., Alaska, Mo. and Ariz., 1962—; youth dir., Tenn., 1961; camp dir., Alaska and Ariz., 1968, 73-74; pastor Valley of Son Christian Center, Chandler, Ariz., 1975-84; pres. Mara-Natha Ministries Internat., Inc., 1973—; pastor Mara-Natha Covenant Assembly, 1984—; adminstr. Mara-Natha Christian Acad., 1977—; pres. Ariz. Christian Tng. Sch., 1979—; realtor-assoc. ERA SAVE-COM Realty, 1984—. Officer, Tanana (Alaska) Bapt. Assn., 1968; mem. adv. bd. Chandler Salvation Army. Mem. Chandler Ministerial Fellowship (v.p. 1976—), Nat. Assn. Christian Marriage Counselors, Full Gospel Bus. Men's Fellowship Internat. Lodge: Kiwanis. Author religious tracts. Home: 1803 N Arrowhead Circle Chandler AZ 85224 Office: PO Box 699 Chandler AZ 85224

SECOR, GARY LEE, priest, Roman Catholic Church; b. Berkeley, Calif., Apr. 16, 1951; s. Donald E. and Alice E. (Baptiste) S. B.A. in Philosophy, Chaminade Coll., 1973; postgrad. St. Patrick's Sem., 1973-76. Ordained priest Roman Cath. Ch., 1977. Assoc. pastor St. Anthony's Ch., Kailua, Hawaii, 1977-81; dir. vocations Diocese of Honolulu, Hawaii, 1981—; active various diocesan coms. and orgns. Home: 6301 Pali Hwy Kaneohe HI 96744 Office: Diocese of Honolulu 1184 Bishop St Honolulu HI 96813

SEDGEWICK, TIMOTHY FOSTER, religion educator, Episcopalian Church. B. Melrose Park, Ill., Dec. 6, 1946; s. Roger Stanley and Virginia May (Karau) S.; m. Martha Wallace Wilkinson, Aug. 24, 1968; children: Sarah Wallace, Ellen Foster. A.B., Albion Coll., 1969; Ph.D., Vanderbilt U., 1975. Asst. prof. Denison U., Granville, Ohio, 1975-76, Marshall U., Huntington, W.Va., 1976-77, Blackburn Coll., Carlinville, Ill., 1977-78; assoc. prof. Christian ethics and moral theology, Seabury-Western Theol. Sem., Evanston, Ill., 1978—; vice chmn. Council Devel. Ministry (Episcopal), 1979-84. Book rev. editor Anglican Theol. Rev., 1980—. Mem. Soc. Christian Ethics, Conf. Anglican Theologians. Home: 2135 Orrington Evanston IL 60201 Office: Seabury-Western Theol Sem 2122 Sheridan Rd Evanston IL 60201

SEDGWICK, HAROLD BEND, minister, Episcopal Ch.; b. St. Paul, Feb. 13, 1908; s. Theodore and Mary Aspinwall (Bend) S.; B.A., Harvard, 1930; B.D., Episc. Theol. Sch., 1935. Ordained to ministry, 1935; asst. Christ Ch., Cambridge, Mass., 1935-38; rector All Saints' Ch., Brookline, Mass., 1938-48, St. Thomas Ch., Washington, 1948-57, Emmanuel Ch., Boston, 1957-62; canon St. Paul's Cathedral, Boston, 1962-75; lectr., preacher, 1975—. Trustee, pres., 1976—. Mem. Soc. of Men for Ministry, 1962—, Bostonian Soc., Friends of Boston Common, Soc. Colonial Wars, Order of Founders and Patriots Am., Descendants of Signers of Declaration of Independence (nat. chaplain gen. 1973—), New Eng. Hist. Geneal. Soc. Contbr. articles in field to religious jours. Address: Blueberry Ln PO Box 23 Lincoln Centre MA 01773

SEEKER, MARY ANN, nun, educational administrator, Roman Catholic Church; b. Jefferson City, Mo., May 20, 1929; d. William Francis and Helen Frances (Finnegan) S. B.A., Incarnate Word Coll., 1965; M.A., St. Mary's Coll., Notre Dame, Ind., 1966. Joined Sisters of Charity of the Incarnate Word, Roman Catholic Ch., San Antonio, 1955. Prin. St. Francis Xavier Sch., Taos, Mo., 1961-64; instr. Incarnate Word Coll., San Antonio, 1969-70; prin. St. Mary's Sch., Amarillo, Tex., 1970-72, Immaculate Conception Sch., Jefferson City, 1972-83, Mary Immaculate Sch.,

Kirksville, Mo., 1984—; del. Diocesan Pastoral Council, Jefferson City, 1984—; mem. Diocesan Sisters Orgn., Jefferson City, 1984—. Co-author: Diocesan School Handbook, 1978. Bd. dirs. Zonta Internat., Jefferson City, 1981; active Girl Scouts U.S.A., Jefferson City, 1985. Recipient Mother Seton award Girl Scouts U.S.A., 1982. Mem. Nat. Cath. Edn. Assn., Internat. Reading Assn. (pres. local chpt. 1975-76). Avocations: sewing; reading; music; walking; travel. Home: 902 E Washington Kirksville MO 63501 Office: Mary Immaculate Sch 712 E Washington Kirksville MO 63501

SEEKS, DONALD AUSTIN, priest, Episcopal Church; b. Cedar Rapids, Iowa, June 9, 1929; s. James Donald and Helen Elizabeth (Neff) S.; m. Carol Ritchie, Aug. 18, 1951; children: James Frederic, Ann Elizabeth, Barbara Helen. A.A., E. Los Angeles Coll., 1963; B.A., Calif. State U., 1967. Ordained priest, 1972. Curate, St. Mark's, Downey, Calif., 1971-75; asst. to rector Blessed Sacrament Ch., Placentia, Calif., 1975-77; vicar St. Clement's Ch., Woodlake, Calif., 1977-84; rector St. Stephen's Ch., Stockton, Calif., 1985—; sec. Registrar Diocese of San Joaquin, 1979—, mem. council, 1981—, chmn. communications commn., 1978—; dep. to Gen. Conv. Episcopal Ch., 1982-85. Contbr. articles to profl. jours. Mem. Los Angeles County Republican Central Com., 1963. Mem. Sisterhood of Holy Nativity (assoc.), Evang. Cath. Mission, Woodlake-Three Rivers Ministerial Assn. (sec.-treas.). Lodge: Rotary (exec. bd. 1982-83). Office: Saint Stephen's Episcopal Ch 3832 N Plymouth Rd Stockton CA 95204

SEERVELD, CALVIN GEORGE, educator, Christian Reformed Church of North America; b. Bayshore, N.Y., Aug. 18, 1930; s. Lester Benjamin and Letitia (Van Tielen) S.; m. Ines Cecile Naudin ten Cate, Sept. 8, 1956; children: Anya, Gioia, Lucas. B.A., Calvin Coll., 1952; M.A., U. Mich., 1953; Ph.D,, Free U. Amsterdam, 1958. Faculty, Inst. for Christian Studies, Toronto, Ont., 1972—; prof. aesthetics, 1972—. Editor: Opuscula Aesthetica Nostra, 1984; author translation from Hebrew and prepred for oratorio performance: Song of Songs, 1967. Mem. Societe Candienne d'Esthetique (copres.). Address: Inst Christian Studies 229 College St W Toronto ON M5T 1R4 Canada

SEGAL, JACK, rabbi; b. Bklyn., Apr. 18, 1929; s. Henry and Bertha (Bienstock) S.; B.A., NYU, 1951; grad. Chaim Berlin Sem., 1954; B.S., U. Pitts., 1957; M.Ed., Oreg. State U., 1960, M.A., 1965; D.H.L., Hebrew Union Coll., 1962; Ed.D., Houston U., 1973; m. Toby Faye Chotiner, Nov. 24, 1957; children—Jeffrey, Michael, Lisa, Scott. Rabbi, 1954; rabbi congregations, Pa., 1954-57, Ore., 1957-61; asso. rabbi Beth Yeshurun Congregation, Houston, 1965-73, sr. rabbi, 1973—. Mem. Nat. Assn. Marriage and Family, Am. Psychol. Assn., Sigma Pi Sigma, Beta Beta Beta, Phi Delta Kappa. Home: 4039 Falkirk Ln Houston TX 77025 Office: 4525 Beechnut St Houston TX 77096

SEIBERT, MARY ANGELICE, nun, religious order executive, Roman Catholic Church; b. Louisville, Jan. 16, 1922; d. William Karl and Catherine A. (Schmidt) S. B.S. in Chemistry, Ursuline Coll., Louisville, 1947; M.S. in Biochemistry, Institutum Divi Thomae, Cin., 1950, Ph.D. in Biochemistry, 1952. Joined Ursuline Sisters, Roman Cath. Ch., 1940. Pres., Ursuline Coll., Louisville, 1963-68, Ursuline Sisters, Louisville, 1980—; dir. Monseignor Pitt Learning Ctr., Louisville, 1974; trustee St. Mary Coll., Ky., 1975-77, Bellarmine Coll., Louisville, 1982—, Coll. New Rochelle, Ky., 1983—. Damon Runyon postdoctoral fellow St. Louis U. Med. Sch., 1953-54; Fulbright-Hays lectr. Univ. Coll., Galway, Ireland, 1968-69; prof., chmn. div. allied health Jefferson Community Coll., Louisville, 1970-79; vis. prof. Smith Coll., Northampton, Mass., 1969-70. Recipient Woman of Yr. in Edn. award YWCA, Louisville, 1976, Cert. for Outstanding Service to Higher Edn., Louisville chpt. Phi Delta Kappa, 1977, Cert. Meritorious Service Jefferson Community Coll., 1978, Alumna of Yr. award Bellarmine Coll., 1980. Mem. AAAS, Leadership Conf. Women Religious, Inst. for Theol. Encounter with Sci. and Tech., World Future Soc. Democrat. Home and Office: Ursuline Sisters 3105 Lexington Rd Louisville KY 40206

SEIDEL, WILLIAM RONALD, minister, Missionary Church; b. Hollywood, Calif., May 27, 1945; s. Bill Seidel and Mitty (Lillian) Seidel Hooks; m. Kathryn Louise Nelson, Sept. 20, 1969; children: Mindy, Julie, Ron Jr. A.A., Los Angeles Pierce Coll., 1971; B.A., Calif. State U., Northridge, 1972; M.P.A., Pepperdine U., 1976; M.Div., Talbot Theol. Sem. 1984. Lic., Missionary Ch. Student evangelist Campus Crusade for Christ, Los Angeles, 1967-69; deacon, shepherd leader Grace Community Ch., Sun Valley, Calif., 1978-83; intern student pastor Granada Hills Community Ch., Calif., 1983-84, assoc. pastor, 1984—, elder, 1983—; tchr. Evangel. Tchr. Tng. Assn., 1983. Police officer Manhattan Beach Police Dept., Calif., 1974-76, Santa Monica Police Dept., Calif., 1976-80. Served with USAF, 1963-67. Mem. Calif. Community Coll. Assn., Alpha Gamma Sigma, Sigma Tau Sigma. Republican. Avocations: swimming; weight lifting; reading; gardening; target shooting. Home: 20132 Elkwood St Canoga Park CA 91306 Office: Granada Hills

Community Ch 11263 Balboa Blvd Granada Hills CA 91344

SEIPLE, ROBERT ALLEN, seminary administrator, American Baptist Association; b. Easton, Pa., Dec. 6, 1942; s. Chris and Gertrude Helen (Crozier) S.; m. Margaret Ann Goebel, May 14, 1966; children: Chris, Amy, Jesse. A.B. in Am. Lit., Brown U., 1965. Field sales rep. Boise Cascade Corp., 1971-72; admissions officer Brown U., 1973-75, asst. athletic dir., 1975-78, athletic dir., 1978-83; pres. Eastern Coll., East Bapt. Theol. Sem., St. David's, Pa., 1983—. Trustee Barrington Coll., R.I., 1981-83, Brit. Am. Ednl. Found., N.Y.C., 1982—; chmn. ch. council Barrington Bapt. Ch., 1977-80. Served to capt. USMC, 1966-69; Vietnam. Decorated 28 Air medals, D.F.C. Mem. Sunday Morning Breakfast Club. Home: 1300 Eagle Rd St David's PA 19087 Office: Eastern Coll St David's PA 19087

SEITZ, LANE RICHARD, minister, Lutheran Ch.-Missouri Synod; b. Painesville, Ohio, Dec. 6, 1946; s. Tony Frank and Ruth Marie (Schaefer) S.; m. Donna Kae Lehrbass, Dec. 21, 1968; children: Jodi Lynn, Timothy John. A.A., Concordia Coll., 1966; B.A., Concordia Tchr.'s Coll., 1970; M.Div., Concordia Sem., 1974. Ordained to ministry Lutheran Ch., 1974. Minister St. Timothy Luth. Ch., Bedford, Iowa, 1974-76, Faith Luth. Ch., Spooner, Wis., Christ Luth. Ch., Lampson, Wis., 1976-80, Faith Luth. Ch., Spooner, 1980—; subdist. dir. Forward in Remembrance Luth. Ch. - Mo. Synod, St. Louis, 1980-82; chmn. No. Wis. Dist. Bd. of Evangelism, Wausau, 1982—, mem. Dist. Planning Council, 1982—, chmn. 1985 Great Commn. Convocation, 1984—; dir. Spooner Ambulance Service, 1980—. Mem. Spooner Volunteer Fire Dept., 1980-82; Recipient 1983 EMT of Yr. award Spooner Ambulance Service. Mem. Nat. Assn. Emergency Med. Technicians (instr., coordinator), Wis. Emergency Med. Technician Assn. Republican. Home and Office: Faith Luth Ch Route 1 Box 1507 Spooner WI 54801

SEITZ, SUSAN, nun, order official, Roman Catholic Church; b. Dubuque, Iowa, Feb. 9, 1935; d. Raymond Francis and Aileen Margaret (Takes) S. B.A. in Elem. Edn., Briar Cliff Coll., 1965; M.A. in Religious Studies, U. Detroit, 1973. Joined Order Sisters of St. Francis, Roman Cath. Ch., 1953. Primary tchr. schs., Ill., Iowa, 1956-68; dir. religious edn. Archdiocese of Dubuque, 1968-78; regional coordinator Sisters of St. Francis of Dubuque, 1978-80, pres. 1980—; pres. bd. dirs. Stonehill Care Ctr., Dubuque, 1980—; chairperson bd. trustees Briar Cliff Coll., Sioux City, Iowa, 1980—; chairperson divisional bd. Mercy Health Ctr., Dubuque, 1984—; co-chairperson social justice com. Archdiocese of Dubuque, 1982—; mem. Intercongregational Com. on Call to Justice, 1976-80. Author: Becoming Fully Alive, 1976. Home, 1978. Mem. Leadership Conf. of Women Religious. Democrat. Office: Sisters of St Francis of Dubuque 3390 Windsor Dubuque IA 52001

SELEMAN, STEPHEN JOSEPH, lay ch. worker, Roman Cath. Ch.; b. New Britain, Conn., June 30, 1950; s. Paul and Ann Dolores (Miynarski) S.; B.A. in Philosophy, U. Hartford (Conn.), 1972; M.A., St. Joseph Coll., West Hartford; 1973, certificate Medieval Research, 1974; postgrad. in philosophy (Loyola fellow) Fordham U., 1975—. Mem. St. Gregory the Gt. Parish, Roman Catholic Ch., Bristol, Conn., 1957—, lector 1971—; mem. liturgy, social action coms., 1973—; extraordinary minister of the eucharist, 1977—; pres. Bristol-1 chpt. Christians Against Abortion, 1974, Greater Bristol chpt. Conn. Right to Life Corp., 1974. Adj. lectr. philosophy, religious studies Holy Apostles Coll., Cromwell, Conn., 1972-74. Mem. Am. Cath. Philos. Assn., AAUP. Address: 15 Roberge Rd Bristol CT 06010

SELF, CHARLES DELOYD, minister, So. Baptist Conv.; b. Tuscumiba, Mo., July 14, 1919; s. William Chanoch and Elda (McCubbin) S.; A.A., Hannibal LaGrange Coll., 1942; B.A., William Jewell Coll., 1944; B.Div., So. Bapt. Theol. Sem., 1947; postgrad. Central Sem., Kansas City, 1949-51; m. Dorothy Lucille Vermillion, Dec. 25, 1939; children—Larry, Barbara Self Edwards, Beverly Self Smart. Ordained to ministry, 1941; pastor chs., Mo., 1940-44, Ky., 1944-47, Mo., 1947-50, Kans., 1950-57, Augusta Heights Bapt. Ch., Greenville, S.C., 1957—. Mem. exec. bd. Kans. Bapt. Conv.; missionary to Brazil, 1968; mem. gen. bd. S.C. Bapts., 1971-76; TV Sunday sch. lesson, WFBC, 1965-75; trustee Furman U., Greenville, 1962-67. Home: 3100 Augusta St Greenville SC 29605 Office: 3118 Augusta St Greenville SC 29605

SELF, WILLIAM LEE, minister, Southern Baptist Convention; b. Winston-Salem, N.C., Jan. 10, 1932; s. Edgar Greenleaf and Della Mae (Curry) S.; B.A., Stetson U., 1954; D.D., 1969; B.D., Southeastern Bapt. Theol. Sem., 1957; D.D., Mercer U., 1970; S.T.D., Emory U., 1971; Litt.D., Hanyang U. (Korea), 1975; m. Carolyn Shealy, Aug. 2, 1953; children—Lee, Bryan. Ordained to ministry, 1952; pastor N.C. and Fla. chs., 1957-64, Wieuca Rd. Bapt. Ch., Atlanta, 1964—. Mem. fgn. mission bd. So. Bapt. Conv., 1973-81, mem. Ga. exec. com., 1966-71, 74—, chmn. exec. com. 1975-76, v.p., 1979; pres. Ga. Bapt. Conv., 1976-77; regular appearances WSB-TV, Today in Ga., 1966-79; pres. Ga.

Bapt. Pastors Conf., 1971-72. Trustee Shorter Coll., Rome, Ga., 1970-75, Ga. Bapt. Hosp., 1970-72, Westminster Schs., Atlanta, 1984-85, Stetson U., DeLand, Fla., 1984-85. Named an outstanding young man of Atlanta, Jaycees, 1967. Author: Bridging the Generation Gap, 1970; (with Carolyn Self) Survival Kit for the Stranded, 1975, Learning to Pray, 1978, A Survival Kit for Marriage, 1981, Confessions of a Nomad, 1983. Home: 609 Old Ivy Rd Atlanta GA 30342 Office: 3626 Peachtree Rd NE Atlanta GA 30326

SELIG, ALAN DEE, minister, Am. Baptist Chs. U.S.A.; b. Wichita, Kans., Mar. 23, 1952; s. Leonard W, and Frances M. (Shirley) S.; m. Karen Ann Kruskop, May 18, 1974; children: Jennette, Caroline. B.Gen. Studies, Kans. U., 1974; M.Div., Central Bapt. Theol. Sem., 1978. Ordained to ministry Baptist Ch., 1978. Pastor First Bapt. Ch., Larned, Kans., 1978-82, First Bapt. Ch., Dubuque, Iowa, 1982—; mem. Hunger Task Force Am. Bapt. Chs. of Central Region, Kans., 1980-81. Walk coordinator CROP-Church World Service, Larned, 1979-81. Mem. Am. Bapt. Chs. Ministers Council, Dubuque Area Christians United (bd. dirs. 1938—), Mid-Am. Bapt. Peace Fellowship (pres. 1982—). Office: First Baptist Church 2143 Judson Dr Dubuque IA 52001

SELLERS, J. W., minister, United Methodist Ch.; b. Hamilton County, Tex., Nov. 26, 1931; s. Wert Allen and Ruby E. (Blum) S.; m. Gayla Jean Melver, Oct. 15, 1971; children: Lori Hornell, Allen Hornell, Jorge-Wert, Ruby. B.S., Tex. Wesleyan Coll., 1956; B.D., So. Meth. U.-Perkins, 1961. Ordained to ministry United Methodist Ch. as deacon, 1958, as elder, 1961. Pastor, St. John's United Meth. Ch., Ft. Worth, 1965-68, Robinson Dr. United Meth. Ch., Waco, Tex., 1968-75, First United Meth. Ch., Comanche, Tex., 1975-77, Mexia, Tex., 1977-81, St. Mark's United Meth. Ch., Cleburne, Tex., 1981—. Mem. Cleburne Ministerial Alliance (pres. 1984-85). Home: 807 Berkley Cleburne TX 76031

SELLINGER, JOSEPH ANTHONY, college president, Roman Catholic Church; b. Phila., Jan. 17, 1921; s. Frank and L. Caroline (Wiseman) S. Ph.L., Spring Hill Coll., 1945; B.S. in Chemistry, 1945; student theology Weston Coll., 1948-49, Woodstock Coll., 1949-50; S.T.L., Facultes St. Albert, Louvain, Belgium, 1952. Joined Soc. of Jesus, Roman Catholic Ch., 1938, ordained priest, 1951. Assoc. dean Coll. Arts and Scis., Georgetown U., 1955-57, dean, 1957-64, sec. corp., dir., 1957-64; pres., rector Loyola Coll., Balt., 1964—. Mem. Am. Council on Edn. (vice chmn.), Assn. for Higher Edn., Middle States Assn., Nat. Cath. Ednl. Assn., Cath. Theol. Soc., Assn. Am. Colls., Phi Beta Kappa (hon.). Address: Loyola Coll 4501 N Charles St Baltimore MD 21210

SELZER, CHARLES LOUIS, religious organization official, Amana Church Society; b. Homestead, Iowa, Dec. 21, 1914; s. Louis C. and Caroline (Shoup) S.; B.A., Coe Coll., 1935; M.A., magna cum laude, State U. of Iowa, 1950; m. Louise Kippenhan, Mar. 9, 1935; 1 dau., Patricia (Mrs. Robert Carstensen). Elder, trustee Amana (Iowa) Ch. Soc., 1950—, pres., 1971—; writer Ch. News, Amana News Bull., 1968—. Supt. Amana Community Schs., Middle, Iowa, 1950—. Dir. Amana Soc., Inc., Amana Soc. Service Co., 1970—, Amana Telephone Co., 1970—, Amana Woolens, Inc., 1970—, Amana Soc. Farms, Inc. Mem. Iowa Schoolmen's legislative com., 1948—; ex-officio mem. Amana Community Sch. Bd., 1950—. Mem. Benton-Iowa Conf. Bd., 1948, Homestead Fire dept., 1932; mem. Iowa County Bd. on Narcotics and Drug Edn., 1970—; chmn. Amana Bicentennial Commn. Mem. Adv. Bd. Kirkwood Cedar Rapids (Iowa) Coll., 1970; bd. dirs. Amana Travel Council, 1970—, v.p., 1972—; bd. dirs. Iowa County Crime Commn., 1970—. Mem. Nat., Iowa, Amana edn. assns., Nat., Iowa assns. sch. adminstrs., Iowa-Poweshiek Supt.'s Assn., Iowa Peace Officer's Assn., Iowa Justices and Constables Assn., Iowa State, Iowa County hist. socs., Amana Heritage Soc., Nat. Assn. Notary Pubs., The Amana Cooperative Education Plan, 1950. Office: Amana Church Society Amana IA 52203

SEMPLE, JAMES HENRY, pastor, Southern Baptist Convention. B. Tifton, Ga., Aug. 23, 1931; s. Henry, Jr., and Mary Frances (Poole) S.; m. Betty Jane Bennett; children: Jim, John, Jan, Jill, Jenene, Jonel. A.B., Stetson U., 1953, B.D., Southwestern Bapt. Theol. Sem., 1957, Th.D., 1962. Ordained So. Bapt. Conv., 1952. Pastor, Northside Bapt. Ch., Mineral Wells, Tex., 1955-56, Oakview Bapt. Ch., Ft. Worth, 1958-61, 1st Bapt. Ch., Plano, Tex., 1961-63, 1st Bapt. Ch., Paris, Tex., 1963—; parliamentarian So. Bapt. Conv., 1983-84; dir. Bapt. Standard of Tex., Dallas, 1984—; chmn. adminstrv. com. Bapt. Gen. Conv. Tex., Dallas, 1978-84, exec. bd., 1977-83; exec. com. So. Bapt. Conv., 1967-75. Author: On Wings of Eagles, 1968; contbr. articles to religious jours. Mem. Tex. Bapt. Hist. Soc. Home: 3150 Dogwood Ln Paris TX 75460 Office: First Bapt Ch 207 S Church St Paris TX 75460

SENFT, KENNETH CHARLES, minister, religious organization executive, Lutheran Church in America; b. York County, Pa., Aug. 20, 1925; s. Harry and Effie

(Krebs) S.; m. Josephine Haugen, Oct. 21, 1949; children: Elizabeth, Catharine. A.B., Gettysburg Coll., 1946, M.Div., 1952, D.D. (hon.), 1973. Ordained to ministry, Luth. Ch. in Am., 1952. Mem. staff Luth. World Fedn., Germany, 1947-50; pastor Messiah Ch., Redwood City, Calif., 1952-63, Berkeley Luth. Ch., Calif., 1964-67, Holy Divinity Ch., Pasadena, Calif., 1967-70; exec. dir. for Mission in N. Am., Luth. Ch. Am., N.Y.C., 1972—; mem. bd. govs. Nat. Council Chs. of Christ U.S.A., N.Y.C., 1973—; v.p. Pacific Southwest Synod, Luth. Ch., Am., Los Angeles, 1954-64; mem. bd. Am. Missions, Luth. Ch. Am., N.Y.C., 1966-70; commn. on stewardship, Luth. Ch., Am., N.Y.C., 1958-66. Author: God Lives in Word and World, 1964; New Life in the Parish, 1967. Recipient Suomi Coll. award, Hancock, Mich., 1975. Democrat. Home: 370 A Claremont Ave Montclair NJ 07042 Office: DMNA Luth Ch Am 231 Madison Ave New York NY 10016

SENTER, MARK HOUSTON, III, educator, Evangelical Free Church of America; b. Warsaw, Ind., Dec. 8, 1943; s. Mark Houston and Alice Ann (Watkins) S.; m. Ruth Ann Hollinger, Sept. 4, 1965; children: Jori Lynn, Nicholas Martin, Diploma Moody Bible Inst., 1964; B.A., U. Ill.-Chgo. Cir., 1968; M.A., Trinity Evang. Div. Sch., 1971; postgrad. Loyola U.-Chgo., 1981—. Ordained to ministry, 1976. Youth dir. Cicero Bible Ch., Ill., 1964-68; youth pastor Arlington Hts. Evang. Free Ch., Ill., 1968-75; pastor Christian Edn., Wheaton Bible Ch., Ill., 1975-82; asst. prof. Christian edn. Trinity Evang. Div. Sch., Deerfield, Ill., 1982—; mem. youth commn. Evang. Free Ch. Am., 1970-72, 73-75; mem. West Suburban Evang. Fellowship, Wheaton, 1975—, chmn., 1980-81; adv. bd. Pioneer Ministries, Wheaton, 1984—. Author: The Art of Recruiting Volunteers, 1983; Free to Dream, 1984. Contbr. articles to profl. jours. Named Christian Edn. dir. of the Year, Greater Chgo. Sun. Sch. Assn., 1972. Creator, host TV series, 1979. Mem. Ministerial Assn. Evang. Free Ch. Am., Nat. Assn. Dirs. Christian Edn., Nat. Assn. Profs. Christian Edn., Phi Delta Kappa. Home: 295 Arapahoe Trail Carol Stream IL 60188 Office: Trinity Evang Div Sch 2065 Half Day Rd Deerfield IL 60015

SENTER, WILLIAM ROBERT, III, priest, Episcopal Church; b. Chattanooga, Sept. 18, 1935; s. William R. and Virginia (Mack) S.; B.S., U. South (Tenn.), 1957; postgrad. U. Chattanooga, 1955, U. Tenn., 1958; B.D., Bexley Hall, Div. Sch. Kenyon Coll., 1961; M.Div., Bexley Hall/Colgate Rochester/Crozer Theol. Sem., 1973; postgrad. Vanderbilt Div. Sch., 1969-71, Southeastern Sch. Alcohol and Drug Studies, Athens, Ga., 1976; m. Linda Anne Howard, Feb. 9, 1963; children: Lydia Elizabeth, Matthew Mack. Ordained deacon, 1961, priest, 1962; cert. substance abuse counselor, Tenn. Asst., St. James Ch., Knoxville, Tenn., 1961-63; priest-in-charge St. Columba's Ch., Bristol, Tenn., 1963-68, Epiphany Episc. Ch., Lebanon, Tenn., 1968-84; rector Grace Episc. Ch., Canton, Miss., 1984—. Chaplain Camp Allegheny for Girls, Lewisburg, W.Va., 1976; hon. chaplain for a day U.S. Senate, 1976; pres., treas. Senter Sch., Chattanooga, 1973-78. Founder "Hangout", Lebanon, 1968-71; originator, first chmn. Project Help (free clothing distbn. project), Lebanon, 1970-73; originator, mem. Lebanon-Wilson County Drug Abuse Commn., 1969-71, chmn., 1974-84; incorporater Lebanon-Wilson County Mental Health Center, 1972; mem. Wilson County Welfare adv. bd., 1974-84; chmn. Horizons com., mem. exec. com. Wilson County Bicentennial Commn., 1974-76; personnel and mgmt. tng. cons. Cracker Barrel Old Country Stores, Lebanon, 1974-76; mem. Gov.'s Commn. on Alcohol and Drug Abuse, 1972-77, vice chmn., 1975-77; bd. dirs. Lebanon YMCA, 1973-78. Mem. Tenn. Ornithol. Soc. (v.p. 1973-75), Alumni Council U. of South, SAR, Nat. Model R.R. Assn., Am. Assn. Arts and Scis., Profl. Alcohol and Drug Counselors Tenn., Delta Tau Delta. Address: Grace Episcopal Ch PO Box 252 Canton MS 39046

SERAPHIM (SERAPHIM IVANOV), Archbishop of Detroit and Chgo., Russian Orthodox Church Outside of Russia, also mem. Council of Bishops. Office: 75 E 93d St New York NY 10028*

SERIO, HARRY LOUIS, minister, United Church of Christ. b. Newark, Sept. 16, 1941; s. Harry F. and Matilda (Wertz) S.; m. Mary Ann Kocsi, Sept. 7, 1963; children: Stuart, Tasha, Matthew. B.A., Ursinus Coll., 1963; B.D., Lancaster Theo. Sem., 1966, M.Div., 1975. Ordained to ministry United Ch. of Christ, 1966. Pastor, Mt. Zion United Ch. Christ, Martins Creek, Pa., 1966-70, Zion United Ch., Womelsdorf, Pa., 1970-76, St. John's United Ch., Kutztown, Pa., 1976—; doctoral fellow Lancaster Theol. Sem., Lancaster, 1982—; dir. Saucony Cross, Kutztown, 1983—; sec. East Penn Camps, Collegeville, Pa., 1974—. Author: Voyage of Faith Resources, 1980. Mem. Berks Ministerial Assn United Ch. Christ (pres. 1983-84); acad. mem. Acad. Religion and Psychical Research. Democrat. Lodge: Rotary (pres. Kutztown, Pa.). Home: 550 W Spring St Fleetwood PA 19522

SESSUM, ROBERT LEE, minister, Episcopal Church; b. Memphis, Feb. 17, 1943; s. William Calvin and Elaine Melba (Holt) S.; m. Donna Ann Snyder, July 8, 1967; 1 child, William Paul. B.A., Rhodes Coll., 1965; M.Div., Va. Theol. Sem., 1970. Ordained priest, 1971. Asst. to rector St. Paul's Ch., Chattanooga, 1970-72; vicar Ch. of the Nativity, Ft. Oglethorpe, Ga., 1972-74; assoc. rector Christ Ch., Raleigh, 1974-79; rector All Saints' Parish, Concord, N.C., 1979—; mem. standing com. Diocese of N.C., Raleigh, 1984—, del. to gen. conv., 1984—, bd. dirs. Conf. Ctr., 1982-85, chmn. Communication Commn., 1983—; mem. Cursillo Secretariat for Diocese of N.C., 1985—. Founding pres. Hosp. Pastoral Care, Inc., Concord, N.C., 1979; chmn. bd. Piedmont Area Mental Health Authority, 1984—; bd. dirs. Cabarrus Coop. Ministries, 1984-85, Penick Home, 1984-86. founding father Cabarrus County Winter Night Shelter, 1984. Recipient Community Vol. Service award, Cabarrus County United Way, 1984; Sr. Man of the Year, Concord Jaycees, 1984; Outstanding Young Man of Year, Ft. Oglethorpe C. of C., 1974. Mem. Concord Ministerial Assn. (chmn. hosp. com.), Kannapolis Ministerial Assn. (mem. hosp. com.), N.C. Clergy Assn. Democrat. Home: 271 Palaside Dr NE Concord NC 28025 Office: All Saints Episcopal Church 525 Lake Concord Rd NE Concord NC 28025

SETCHKO, EDWARD STEPHEN, minister, educator, United Ch. Christ; b. Yonkers, N.Y., Apr. 27, 1926; s. Stephen John and Mary Elizabeth (Dulak) S.; B.S., Union Coll., 1948; B.D. cum laude, Andover-Newton Theol. Sch., 1953, S.T.M., 1954; Th.D. (Danforth grantee), Pacific Sch. Religion, 1961; m. Penelope Sayre, Nov. 18, 1950; children—Marc Edward, Kip Sherman, Robin Elizabeth, Jan Sayre, Dirk Stephen. Psychometrician, Union Coll. Character Research Project, 1947-50; clin. tng. supr. Boston City Hosp., 1951-54; ordained to ministry, 1954; asst. minister Eliot Ch. of Newton, 1950-54; univ. campus minister U. Wash., 1954-58; instr. dept. pastoral psychology Pacific Sch. Religion, Berkeley, Calif., 1960-61; asst. prof., 1962-63; field research sec. nat. staff United Ch. of Christ, Berkeley, 1963-68; prof. religion and society Starr King Sch. for Ministry and Grad. Theol. Union, Berkeley, 1969—. Mem. Com. for the Protection of Human Subjects, U. Calif., Berkeley. Active ACLU, Council for Civic Unity of San Francisco Bay Area, Berkeley Council for Social Planning, Assos. of Berkeley Center for Human Interaction. Certified profl. hosp. chaplain. Mem. Am. Psychol. Assn., Religious Research Assn., Am. Assn. for Humanistic Psychology, AAAS, Assn. for Clin. Pastoral Edn., Assn. of World Colls. and Univs., Am. Protestant Hosp. Assn., Soc. for Sci. Study of Religion, World Future Soc. Contbr. articles to ednl. and religious jours.

SETLIFFE, ANDREW BENTON, JR., minister of education, Southern Baptist Convention; b. Reidsville, N.C., June 24, 1922; s. Andrew Benton and Nannie Belle (Dockery) S.; B.A., Baylor U., 1950; M.R.E., Southwestern Bapt. Theol. Sem., Ft. Worth, 1952, D.R.E., 1959; m. Dorothy Mae Cardwell, Mar. 2, 1946; children—Dorothy Jean, Marianne, Andrea Leigh. Ordained to ministry, 1956; minister edn. Parkside Bapt. Ch., Denison, Tex., 1952-55, First Bapt. Ch., Cleburne, Tex., 1955-58; minister edn. and adminstrn. Central Bapt. Ch., Waycross, Ga., 1958-60, Grand Ave. Bapt. Ch., Ft. Smith, Ark., 1960-70; minister edn. Pulaski Heights Bapt. Ch., Little Rock, 1970-76. Mem. Ridgecrest faculty So. Bapt. Youth Week, 1964, Tng. Union Week, 1966, 67; mem. Glorieta faculty Tng. Union Week, 1968; chmn. nominating com. Ark. Bapt. State Conv., 1973, pres., mem. exec. bd., 1976—; adult conf. leader Ark. Bapt. Sunday Sch. Conv.; pres. Ark. Bapt. Religious Edn. Assn., 1974; 1st non-pastor to serve as pres. exec. bd. Ark. Bapt. Conv. Mem. So., Southwestern Bapt. religious edn. assns. Contbr. articles to religious publs. Home: 6700 Granada Dr Little Rock AR 72205 Office: 2200 Kavanaugh Blvd Little Rock AR 72205

SETLOCK, WILLIAM, priest, Roman Catholic Church; b. Buffalo, Apr. 12, 1920; s. Stephen and Mary (Faltisko) S. B.S., Tri-State U., 1949; M.Div., Pope John XXIII Nat. Sem., 1968. Ordained priest Roman Catholic Ch., 1968. Aerospace engr. Bell Aircraft Corp., Buffalo, 1949-64; assoc. pastor All Saints Ch., Buffalo, 1968-70, St. John Evangelist Ch., Buffalo, 1970-71; chaplain St. Mary's Deaf Sch., Buffalo, 1971-74; assoc. pastor Our Lady Help/Christians Ch., Cheektowaga, N.Y., 1974-81; pastor St. Monica's Ch., Buffalo, 1981—. Served as cpl. USAAF, 1942-46. Avocations: astronomy; photography. Home: 206 Orlando St Buffalo NY 14210 Office: St Monica's Ch 206 Orlando St Buffalo NY 14210

SETTGAST, LELAND G., chaplain, Lutheran Church-Missouri Synod; b. Columbus, Nebr., June 6, 1939; s. George E. and Dena (Henke) S.; m. Eunice Wurdeman, Apr. 29, 1964; children: Bradford Lee, Christine Renee. Student U. Nebr.-Lincoln, 1956-57, St. Paul's Coll., 1958-59; B.Th., Concordia Sem., Ft. Wayne, 1964; M.A. in Psychology, Calif. Coast U., 1977. Ordained to ministry Luth. Ch.-Mo. Synod, 1964. Pastor, Immanuel Luth. Ch., Osceola, Iowa, 1964-66, Highland Park Luth. Ch., Los Angeles, 1966-68; sr. pastor Christ Luth. Ch., Norfolk, Nebr., 1968-73; asst. exec. dir. Luth. Bible Translators, Orange, Calif., 1974-75; dir. chaplains, Christian Jail Workers, Inc., and Los Angeles County Sheriff and Probation Depts., Los Angeles, 1976—; dir. pub. relations English Dist., Luth. Ch. Mo. Synod, Detroit, 1978—; bd. dirs. Friends Christ Coll., Irvine, Calif., 1980-81; panelist radio talk show Religion on the Line, Los Angeles, 1983—; mem. TV talk shows, Los Angeles, 1980—; editor newspaper Religion in Media. Producer, dir. filmstrip: Victory is Sobriety, 1983 (award of merit 1984); (radio broadcast) Beyond Prison Walls, 1977-79; editor newspaper Broken Shackles, 1976-83. Bd. dirs. Highland Park Symphony, Los Angeles, 1967-68, Big Bros. Am., Norfolk, 1972-73. Mem. Am. Protestant Correctional Assn., Am. Film Inst., So. Calif. Broadcasters Assn. Republican. Club: Kiwanis (Norfolk and Anaheim). Home: 2875 E Virginia Anaheim CA 92806 Office: Chaplains Office Los Angeles County Sheriff's Dept PO Box 4009 Los Angeles CA 90051

SEVIER, FREDERICK MERLE, minister, National Association Congregational Christian Chs.; b. Gardena, Calif., Nov. 19, 1919; s. Frederick Charles and Emma Adelaide (Case) S.; m. Ruth Miriam Thomas, Feb. 16, 1945 (dec. Apr. 1982); children: David, Jane. B.A., UCLA, 1942; B.A., Princeton Sem., 1949; S.T.M., Boston U., 1957; M.A., Pepperdine Coll., 1965. Ordained to ministry Congregational Ch., 1949. Minister Harundale Presbytery Ch., Glen Burnie, Md., 1949-53, Congregational Ch., Harvard, Mass., 1955-58; minister counseling Mt. Lebanon Presbyn. Ch., Pitts., 1958-61; minister Bethany Presbyn. Ch., Phoenix, 1961-64, Congregational Ch., Huntington Pk., Calif., 1971—; moderator Calif. Assn. Congl. Christian Chs., 1977; mem. commn. on world Christian religions Nat. Assn. Congl. Christian Chs., 1978-82. Mem. adv. bd. Family Service, Inglewood, Calif., 1967-70; bd. dirs. Southwest Child Guidance Clinic, Inglewood, 1967-71. Served to lt. col. U.S. Air Force, 1942-46, 1953-55. Recipient sermon award Freedoms Found., 1975. Mem. Military Chaplains Assn., Huntington Park Ministerial Assn. (pres. 1977). Republican. Home: 7628 De Palma St Downey CA 90241 Office: Congregational Christian Ch 2965 E Gage Ave Huntington Park CA 90255

SEWELL, DONALD EUGENE, religion educator, Southern Baptist Convention. B. Borger, Tex., July 17, 1952; s. Julius Eugene and Lois Marie (Harris) S.; m. Rebecca Elaine Graves, Aug. 8, 1975; children: Benjamin Brent, Donald Keith. B.A., Baylor U., 1973; M.A. in Religious Edn., Southwestern Sem., 1975, Ed.D., 1982. Ordained to ministry Bapt. Ch., 1976. Minister to youth Immanuel Bapt. Ch., Temple, Tex., 1973-75, First Bapt. Ch., Plano, Tex., 1976-78; assoc. pastor Lakewood Bapt. Ch., Dallas, 1975-76; prof. Mex. Bapt. Sem., Mexico City, 1978-82; asst. prof. Golden Gate Bapt. Sem., Mill Valley, Calif., 1983—, interim dir. continuing edn. program, 1984—. Author: Effective Teaching in the Church (in Spanish-Mexico), 1980. Campaign coordinator Plano City Council, 1978; bd. dirs. GG-BTS Festival of the Arts for Marin County, Mill Valley, 1984—. Named to Disting. Men of Yr. Oxford U. Library, London, 1979. Mem. So. Bapt. Religious Edn. Assn., Western Bapt. Religious Edn. Assn. Home: 1021 Catalpa Way Petaluma CA 94952 Office: Golden Gate Bapt Theol Sem Strawberry Point Mill Valley CA 94941

SEWELL, LEON OTIS, minister, So. Bapt. Conv.; b. Hobart, Okla., May 5, 1930; s. Bailey Otis and Ruby Elizabeth (Cagle) S.; B.A., Okla. Bapt. U., 1953; postgrad. Southwestern Bapt. Theol. Sem., 1953-56; m. Delores Charlene Reid, Jan. 31, 1953; children—Redina Darlene, Lenora Jean, Charles Bailey. Ordained to ministry, 1948; minister, Pleasant Hill Bapt. Ch., 1949-50, 51-53, Hulen Bapt. Ch., 1950-51; mission pastor 1st Bapt. Ch., Chickasha, Okla., 1953-55; asso. pastor Nichols Hills Bapt. Ch., Oklahoma City, 1955-56; pastor chs. Okla., 1956—, 1st Bapt. Ch., Weatherford, 1965-74, Weslaco, 1974—. Chaplain Okla. Senate, 1968, 70, 73; pres. Weatherford Ministerial Alliance, 1969-71, Weslaco Ministerial Alliance, 1975-76. Recipient Key to City of Weatherford, 1972. Mem. Okla. Poetry Soc., Magic Valley Bapt. Assn. Contbr. articles to Bapt. Messenger of Okla., including You Can't Earn The Right to be Rude, 1972 (reprinted in Bapt. newspapers in 5 other states). Home: 706 S Ohio Ave Weslaco TX 78596 Office: 6th and Kansas Sts Weslaco TX 78596

SEWELL, OTTO LEROY, minister, United Methodist Church. b. Skadee, Okla., Oct. 12, 1916; s. Otto Haman and Lillie Mae (Harris) S.; m. Fay Del Black, May 28, 1944; children: Stanford LeRoy, Carol Collier, Mark LeRoy. B.A., Oklahoma City U., 1943; M.Div., Boston U., 1946; postgrad. Perkins Sch. Theology; D.D. (hon.), Oklahoma City U., 1969. Ordained to ministry Methodist Ch., 1946. Pastor, Goodrich Meml. Ch., Norman, Okla., 1946-48, Trinity Ch., Tulsa, 1948-51, First St. Ch., Alpine, Tex., 1951-53, Hobbs, N.Mex., 1953-57, Epworth Ch., Chickasha, N.Mex., 1957-59, May Ave. Meth. Ch., Oklahoma City, 1959-63, St. Paul's Ch., Shawnee, Okla., 1963-66, First Ch., Alva, Okla., 1966-70, First Ch., Oklahoma City, 1970-77, First Ch., Muskogee, Okla., 1977-78, Grand Ave. Ch., McAlester, Okla., 1978-82; dist. supt. Bartlesville Dist., Okla., 1982—; mem. exec. com. Nat. Assn. Equitable Salary United Meth. Ch., 1980—; chmn. Commn. on Equitable Salary Okla. Ann. Conf., 1976-82; mem. Bd. Evangelism United Methodist Ch., Nashville, 1964-72; mem. Bd. Social Concerns, South Central Jurisdiction, 1956-64; del, South Central Jurisdiction Conf., 1984;

chmn. Bd. Evangelism Okla. Ann. Conf., 1960-76. Contbr. articles on practical evangelism and pastors' fin. support to profl. jours. Trustee Oklahoma City U., 1982—. Democrat. Lodges: Rotary, Lions, Masons, Shriners. Home: 4702 SE Harned Ct Bartlesville OK 74006 Office: The United Meth Ch Box 2524 Bartlesville OK 74005

SEWELL, WILLIAM LAMAR, minister, So. Baptist Conv.; b. Birmingham, Ala., Sept. 9, 1912; s. William Lunsford and Elizabeth Victoria (Watkins) S.; B.A., Miss. Coll., Clinton, 1937; Th.M., New Orleans Bapt. Theol. Sem., 1941, Th.D., 1944; m. Willie Maude Reeves, Oct. 11, 1931; children—Evelyn Joyce Sewell Muller, Carol Ann Sewell Beason. Ordained to ministry, 1934; pastor chs. in Miss. and La., 1934-48; pastor First Bapt. Ch., Bossier City, La., 1948-59; asso. exec. sec. La. Bapt. Conv., Alexandria, 1959—, pres., 1952-53, exec. com., exec. bd., 1948-58. Trustee Clarke Meml. Coll., Newton, Miss., 1944-48, Acadia Bapt. Acad., Eunice, La., 1949-58, So. Bapt. Theol. Sem., Louisville. Home: 103 Hill Top Dr Pineville LA 71360 Office: Box 311 Alexandria LA 71301

SEXTON, JAMES REUBEN, JR., minister, Southern Baptist Convention. B. Tuscaloosa, Ala., July 8, 1953; s. James Reuben and Betty Sue (Keene) S.; m. Evelyn Elizabeth Davis, Aug. 3, 1974; children: Eric, Justin, Amy. B.A., U. Ala., 1975; M.Div., So. Bapt. Theol. Sem., 1978. Ordained to ministry So. Bapt. Conv., 1977. Assoc. pastor Poplar Level Bapt. Ch., Louisville, 1976-78; pastor Bethel Bapt. Ch., Ft. Deposit, Ala., 1978-81, 1st Bapt. Ch., Wetumpka, Ala., 1982—; sec., treas. Montgomery Bapt. Ministers Conf., 1981; sec. Wetumpka Area Ministerial Fellowship, 1984; v.p. Elmore Bapt. Pastors Conf., Wetumpka, 1982-83. Pres. Wetumpka Elem. Sch. PTO, 1984-85. Named Man of Yr. Ft. Deposit C. of C., 1981. Democrat. Club: Lions. Office: First Bapt Ch 205 W Bridge St Wetumpka AL 36092

SEYDA, ROBERT RUDOLPH, minister, Church of God, Cleveland, Tennessee; b. Crisfield, Md., May 19, 1938; s. Robert Rudolph and Hilda Rae (Lane) S.; B.A. in Philosophy and Religion, U. N.D., 1975; postgrad. Christian edn. Winnipeg Theol. Sem.; Th.M., Trinity Theol. Sem., 1980, Th.D., 1982; m. Kay Louise Bolle, June 5, 1959; children—Cynthia Kay Seyda Roso, Suzanne Ruth, Robert Rudolph III, Michelle Dawn. Ordained to ministry, 1969; mem. faculty Internat. Bible Sem., Wienacht, Switzerland, 1966-68; European evangelism, youth dir. Ch. of God, 1968-72; pastor Ch. of God, Grand Forks, N.D., 1972-77, Lemmon, S.D., 1979—; dean students N.W. Bible Coll., Minot, N.D., 1977-79; pres. Evang. Ministers Fellowship, Grand Forks, 1975, Greater Grand Forks Ministerium, 1976-77; pres., chmn. bd. dirs. Profl. Consultation Services, Lemmon, 1982-84, LIVE Ctr., Inc., Lemmon, 1984—. Bd. dirs. Grand Forks County Big Bros., 1973-77. Mem. Nat. Assn. Evangelicals, Am. Assn. Christian Counselors. Author: Transforming Love, An In-Depth Study of the Fruit of the Spirit, 1984; contbr. articles to religious jours. Home: 612 Gem Dr Lemmon SD 57638 Office: 212 2d Ave W Lemmon SD 57638

SEYFERT, FREDERICK CHARLES, JR., minister, United Methodist Church; b. Brockton, Mass., Feb. 15, 1927; s. Frederick Charles and Ruth Alice (Tidmarsh) S.; m. JoAnn Springstead, Dec. 30, 1949; children: Robert, William. B.A., Houghton Coll., 1951; M.A. in Edn., Allegheny Coll., 1957; B.D., Moravian Thoel. Sem., 1962; S.T.M., Luth. Theol. Sem., 1970; D.Min., Drew U., 1978. Ordained to ministry, 1962. Assoc. and minister of edn. Wesley United Meth. Ch., Dover, Del., 1968-71; minister Calvary United Meth. Ch., Milford, Del., 1971-73, Holly Oak United Meth. Ch., Wilmington, Del., 1974-79, Christiana United Meth. Ch., Del., 1980-84, Sudlersville Charge, Md., 1984—; pres. Northwest Parish, Wilmington, 1979-80, Newark Clergy Group, 1983-84. Editor book rev. column The Worlds Crisis, 1951-53. Contbr. articles to profl. jours. Mem. Religious Edn. Assn., Christian Educators Fellowship (pres. Peninsula Conf. chpt. 1970, 74). Republican. Home: PO Box 202 Sudlersville MD 21668 Office: PO Box 202 Sudlersville MD 21668

SHAFER, ERIC CHRISTOPHER, minister, Lutheran Church in America. b. Hanover, Pa., Apr. 10, 1950; s. B. Henry and Doris M. (Von Bergen) S.; m. Kristi L. Owens, Nov. 24, 1973. B.A., Muhlenberg Coll., 1972; M.Div., Hamma Sch. Theology, 1976. Ordained to ministry Lutheran Church in America, 1976. Pastor, Holy Trinity Meml. Luth. Ch., Catasauqua, Pa., 1976-83; asst. to Bishop Northeastern Pa. Synod, Wescosville, 1983—; Del., 5th Assembly Luth. World Fedn., Evian, France, 1970; trustee Muhlenberg Coll., Allentown, Pa., 1972-83; editor: The Northeaster newsletter, 1984. Corr. to The Lutheran mag., 1978--. Bd. dirs. Catasauqua Fellowship in Serving Humanity, 1976-79, Catasauqua Community Thrift Shop, 1976-82, Planned Parenthood of Lehigh Valley, Allentown, Pa., 1982-83; founder, chmn. Catasauqua Emergency Fund, 1979-83. Democrat. Home: 62 Wall St Bethlehem PA 18018 Office: Northeastern Pennsylvania Synod 4865 Hamilton Blvd Wescosville PA 18106

SHAFER, RAYMOND DONALD, church official, Brethren in Christ Church; b. Waynesboro, Pa., May 22, 1936; s. Raymond N. and Hannah O. (Paxton) S.; m. C. Marlene Engle, Aug. 30, 1956; children: Bernice Elaine Worley, Bruce Eric. A.B., Messiah Coll.; postgrad. Lancaster Theol. Sem.; B.D., Eastern Bapt. Theol. Sem.; D.Min., Fuller Theol. Sem. Ordained to ministry Brethren in Christ Ch., 1959. Pastor Brethren in Christ Ch., Elizabethtown, Pa., 1959-65; exec. dir. Christian edn. Brethren in Christ Ch., Upland, Calif., 1968-72, dir. ch. planning and evangelism, 1978-84, bishop, 1972-84, gen. sec., 1984—; moderator gen. conf., 1976-78, 82-84. Bd. dirs. Azusa Pacific U., Calif., 1972-84; trustee Western Evang. Sem., Portland, Oreg., 1972-84, Messiah Coll., Grantham, Pa., 1972—. Office: Gen Conf Brethren in Christ Ch 377 N 2d Ave Upland CA 91786

SHAH, IDRIES ABUTAHIR, church official, Islamic and Sufi authority; b. Simla, India, June 16, 1924; s. Ikbal Ali and Sharifa Saira (Khanum) S.; student Traditional Sufi schs. in Near and Middle East. Teaching and writing on Sufi way and history of human thought, 1943—; dir. Inst. for Cultural Research, 1966—; prof. ad honorem Nat. U., La Plata, Argentina, 1974—; vis. prof. U. Calif., San Francisco, 1976; prof. U. Geneva, 1972-73. Bd. govs. Royal Hosp. and Home for Incurables (London), Royal Humane Soc. Recipient 1st prizes (6) UNESCO Book Year, 1972, Cambridge Poetry Gold medal, 1973, Distinguished Service to Internat. Understanding award, 1974, Gold medal Internat. Community Service, 1975. Fellow Royal Soc. Arts (London); mem. Brit. Assn. for Advancement Sci. (London) (life). Author 30 books and numerous articles on human thought, Sufi thought and teaching; contbr. to Oxford Companion to the Mind, 1977; work assessed in Sufi Studies East and West, 1973, Journeys with a Sufi Master (Dervish), 1982. Office: Inst for Cultural Research PO Box 13 Tunbridge Wells England also PO Box 176 Los Altos CA 94022 also care Collins-Knowlton Wing Inc 60 E 56th St New York NY 10022

SHALOWITZ, MORTON, rabbi, Orthodox Judaism; b. Chgo., Dec. 27, 1923; s. Milton and Mary (Halpert) S. B.A., Central YMCA Coll., Chgo., 1945. Ordained rabbi, 1949. Rabbi Minot Hebrew Congregation, N.D., 1950-52, Kehilath Israel, Kansas City, Mo., 1954-57, Heska Amuna Congregation, Knoxville, Tenn., 1957-62, Congregation Yehuda Moshe, N. Miami, Fla., 1962-63, Temple Beth Israel, Fond du Lac, Wis., 1963—. Served to col. U.S. Army, 1952-83, Korean War. Mem. Jewish War Vets., Am. Legion, VFW, Mil. Chaplains Assn. Armed Forces, Res. Officers Assn. Lodge: Bnai Brith. Home and Office: 6 Woods Pl Fond du Lac WI 54935

SHANBLATT, SANFORD DAVID, rabbi; b. Pitts., July 20, 1931; s. Benjamin and Edith (Shelkrot) S.; A.B., U. Mich., 1953; postgrad. Columbia U., 1958-59; M.Hebrew Lit., Jewish Theol. Sem. Am., 1958, D.D. (hon.), 1984; m. Charlotte Shapiro, Aug. 7, 1960; children: Jonathan, Brian, Neal. Rabbi, 1958; chaplain U.S. Army, 1958-60; rabbi Congregation Knesses Israel, Pittsfield, Mass., 1960-74, Temple Shaarey Zedek, Buffalo, 1974-77, Temple Israel of Swampscott and Marblehead, Swampscott, Mass., 1977—; mem. faculty Acad. Jewish Studies, Pittsfield, Mass., 1965-74, Coll. Jewish Studies, Buffalo, 1974—; mem. Berkshire (Mass.) Bd. of Rabbis, Capital Dist. Bd. of Rabbis, Buffalo Bd. of Rabbis. Mem. Rabbinical Assembly Am., North Shore Rabbinical Assn. (pres. 1981-85). Author: The Rabbi's Corner: Personal Insights on Jewish and World Problems, 1973. Contbr. articles to religious and secular publs. Shanblatt scholarship named and endowed in his honor by Temple Israel at Jewish Theol. Sem. Am., 1984. Home: 44 Atlantic Ave Swampscott MA 01907 Office: 837 Humphrey St Swampscott MA 01907

SHANKEL, JACK EUGENE, minister, Church of the Nazarene; b. Mayport, Pa., Aug. 20, 1932; s. Fred Cameron and Chloie Irene (Huffman) S.; m. Joyce Joan Bish, June 15, 1957; 1 child, Christi-Le. A.B. in Religion, Eastern Nazarene Coll., 1961, Th.B., 1963, D.D. (hon.), 1980; postgrad. Andover Newton Theol. Sem., 1964-66. Ordained to ministry Ch. of Nazarene, 1964. Pastor, Ch. of Nazarene, Duxbury, Mass., 1962-65, Augusta, Maine, 1965-71; dist. supt. Maine dist. Ch. of Nazarene, Augusta, 1971—; trustee Eastern Nazarene Coll., Quincy, Mass., 1969—, Nazarene Bible Coll., Colorado Springs, Colo., 1980—. Contbr. articles to religious and civic publs. Served with USN, 1952-56, N. Africa. Mem. Bible Soc. Maine (bd. dirs. 1974-82), Christian Civic League Maine (v.p. 1975-80, bd. dirs. 1975—), Assn. for Pastoral Care. Home: 1040 Riverside Dr Augusta ME 04330 Office: Maine Dist Ch of Nazarene RFD 1 PO Box 300 Augusta ME 04330

SHANKWEILER, CARL DAVID, minister, Lutheran Church in America; b. Ashland, Pa., Nov. 23, 1946; s. Carl Benfield and Grace Amanda (Starr) S.; m. Cynthia Louise Rebecca Herb, June 23, 1963. B.A., Pa. State U.-Univ. Park, Pa., 1967, M.A., 1971; M.Div., Luth. Theol. Sem., Phila., 1972; Th.M., Princeton Theol. Sem., 1973. Ordained to ministry Lutheran Church in America, 1973. Tchr., J.L. Schneller Sch., Khirbet Kanafar, Lebanon, 1970-71; pastor St. James Luth. Ch., Geigertown, Pa., 1973-78; asst. pastor St. Mark's Luth. Ch., Birdsboro, Pa., 1973-78; pastor Trinity Luth. Ch., Wernersville, Pa., 1978-83; editor Adult Resources Div. for Parish, Phila., 1983—; sec. Long Range Planning Com., Luth Synod Northeast Pa., 1977-79; treas. Am. Bd. Syrian Orphanage at Jerusalem, Inc., Gettysburg, Pa., 1978—; dean West Berks Luth. Destrict, Reading, Pa., 1981-83. Author various edn. curriculums and study guides. Dir., v.p. Daniel Boone Area Sch. District, Birdsboro, 1975-78, sec. Luth. Hist. Soc. Eastern Pa., 1976-80. Recipient Schuykill award, Pa. State U., 1966; Hoh scholarship award Luth. Theol. Sem. at Pa., 1978,70, Sem. grad. scholarship Luth. Brotherhood Ins., 1972. Mem. Religious Edn. Assn., Am. Philatelic Soc., Luth. Hist. Soc. Eastern Pa. (sec. 1976-80). Home: 2809 W Queen Ln Phila PA 19129 Office: Div Parish Services 2900 Queen Ln Phila PA 19129

SHANLEY, LEONIE, nun, diocesan administrator, Roman Catholic Church; b. Pawtucket, R.I., Oct. 24, 1927; d. Leo Bernard and Grace Margaret (Quinn) S. B.A. in French, Villa Maria Coll., Erie, Pa., 1959; M.A. in French, Case Western Res. U., 1964; postgrad. Cath. U. Am., Fairfield U. Joined Sisters of St. Joseph, Roman Catholic Ch. Tchr. elem. and secondary schs. Diocese of Erie, Pa., 1945-68, sec. for Christian edn. and formation, 1982—; dean of students Villa Maria Coll., 1968-73; gen. superior Sisters of St. Joseph of Northwestern Pa., 1973-81; trustee St. Vincent Health Ctr., Erie, 1974—; incorporator Spencer Hosp., Meadville, Pa., 1975—. Mem. Nat. Cath. Edn. Assn., Chief Adminstrs. Cath. Educators, Nat. Conf. Diocesan Dirs. Home: 910 Cherry St Erie PA 16504 Office: Diocese of Erie 517 E 26th St Erie PA 16504

SHANNON, DAVID THOMAS, seminary official, minister, educator, American Baptist Church; b. Richmond, Va., Sept. 26, 1933; s. Charlie Lee and Phyllis (Gary) S.; B.A., Va. Union U., Richmond, 1954, B.D., 1957; S.T.M., Oberlin (Ohio) Grad. Sch. Theology, 1959; D. Ministry, Vanderbilt U., 1974; Ph.D., U. Pitts. 1975; m. Averett Powell, June 15, 1957; children—Vernitia Averett, Davine Belinda, David T. Ordained to ministry, 1954; pastor Fair Oaks (Va.) Bapt. Ch., 1954-57; student asst. Antioch Bapt. Ch., Cleve., 1957-59; grad. asst. Oberlin Grad. Sch. of Theology, 1958-59; univ. pastor Va. Union U., 1960-61; pastor Ebenezer Bapt. Ch., Richmond, 1960-69; vis. lectr. O. T. studies Howard U. Div. Sch., Washington, 1968; Eastern dir. Christian Higher Edn. Services, Am. Bapt. Bd. Edn. and Publ., Valley Forge, Pa., 1969-71; vis. prof. St. Mary's Sem., Cleve., 1969-72; assoc. prof. religion Bucknell U., Lewisburg, Pa., 1971-72, also dir. minority studies, 1971-72; dean faculty Pitts. Theol. Sem., 1972—. Mem. commn. on theol. concerns Am. Bapt. Conv., 1972—; mem. council on theol. edn. United Presbyn. Ch., 1972-76. Mem. exec. bd. Pitts. chpt. Ames. for Democratic Action, 1975—. Mem. Soc. Bibl. Lit., Am. Assn. Higher Edn., Soc. Study Black Religion. Author: Studies in the Life and Works of Paul, 1961; The Old Testament Experience of Faith, 1977; contbr. articles to religious publs. Office: 616 N Highland Ave Pittsburgh PA 15206

SHANNON, DON MICHAEL, minister, Southern Baptist Convention; b. Beaumont, Tex., May 18, 1945; s. Carl Lynn and Margaret Evangeline (Miller) S.; B.A. in Theology, Speech and Philosophy, Houston Bapt. U., 1969; M.Div., Southwestern Bapt. Theol. Sem., 1979; m. Beverly Ann Richardson, July 16, 1967; children—Michael, Kelly, Melissa. Ordained to ministry, 1965; missions pastor 1st Bapt. Ch., Liberty, Tex., 1964-68; associational youth leader Trinity River Bapt. Assn., Tex., 1965; pastor 1st Bapt. Ch., Coldspring, Tex., 1969—. Mem. missions com., stewardship budget com., hist. com., Christian life com. Tryon-Evergreen Bapt. Assn. Tex.; mem. staff Glorieta (N. Mex.) Bapt. Assembly, 1963. Mem. San Jacinto County (Tex.) Child Welfare Bd., 1971-73, San Jacinto County Program Bldg. Com., 1975—, San Jacinto County Aging Com. Winner 1st place Persuasive Speaking Tex. Interscholastic League Competition, 1964; author: Joining Jesus, 1975. Home and Office: PO Box 26 Coldsspring TX 77331

SHANOR, CLARENCE RICHARD, minister educator, United Methodist Church. b. Butler, Pa., Dec. 26, 1924; s. Paul L. and Marion (McCandless) S.; m. Anna Lou Watts, June 23, 1948; 1 son, Richard Watts. B.A., Allegheny Coll., 1948; S.T.B., Boston Univ., 1951; Ph.D., 1958. Ordained to ministry Meth. Ch., 1950. Pastor Meth. Ch., South Hamilton, Mass., 1951-54; research assoc. Union Coll., Schenectady, 1954-55; prof. Christian edn. Nat. Coll., Kansas City, Mo., 1956-58; assoc. minister First United Meth. Ch., St. Petersburg, Fla., 1958-61, First United Ch., Fullerton, Calif., 1961-66; coordinator Met. dept. San Diego dist. United Meth. Union, San Diego, 1966—; pres. Human Services Corp., 1972-77. Treas. San Diego County Ecumenical Conf., 1970-71, pres., 1975-77; chmn. Coalition Urban Ministries, 1970-71, Cultural and Religious Task Force Rancho San Diego, 1970-74; chmn. western jurisdiction Urban Network United Meth. Ch., 1978. Author: (with Anna Lou Shanor) Kindergartner Meet Your World, 1966. Chmn. San Diego Citizens Com. Against Hunger, 1969-72; bd. dirs. Interfaith Housing Found., chmn. 1979; mem. Gaslamp Quarter Project Area Com., San Diego, 1978; chmn. bd.

Horton House Corp., 1978; chmn. San Diego Downtown Coordinating Council, 1981—. Recipient San Diego Inst. for Creativity award, 1969, Boss of Yr. award Am. Bus. Women's Assn., 1972. Home: 6919 Maury Dr San Diego CA 92119 Office: 861 6th Ave Suite 810 San Diego CA 92101

SHAPIRO, MAX ANDREW, rabbi, Reform Jewish Congregations; b. Worcester, Mass., Jan. 31, 1917; s. Samuel and Clara (Wolfgang) S.; A.B., Clark U., 1939; M.Ed., Boston Tchrs. Coll., 1940; B.H.L., Hebrew Union Coll., 1953, M.H.L., 1955, D.D. (hon.), 1980; D.Ed., U. Cin., 1960; m. Bernice Clein, Dec. 31, 1944; children: Susan, Steven. Rabbi, 1955; sr. rabbi Temple Israel, Mpls., 1963-85, rabbi emeritus, 1985—; lectr. dept. religion and philosophy Hamline U., 1958—; adj. prof. United Theol. Sem., 1975—; bd. govs. Hebrew Union Coll., Jewish Inst. Religion; co-chmn. task force on reform outreach Union Am. Hebrew Congregations, Central Conf. Am. Rabbis, 1979-83; dirs. Ctr. for Christian-Jewish Learning, Coll. St. Thomas, St. Paul, 1985—. State commr. against discrimination, 1961-65; bd. dirs. Mt. Sinai Hosp., Mpls., Mpls. United Way, Minn. Council on Religion and Race. Rabbi Max A. Shapiro Forest in Israel established in his honor Jewish Nat. Fund, 1976; recipient Humanitarian award Nat. Jewish Hosp., Denver, 1978; named Outstanding Citizen, United Way, 1970, City of Mpls., 1966; recipient State of Israel Bonds award, 1972. Mem. Midwest Assn. Reform Rabbis (pres. 1970-71), Rabbinic Alumni Assn. (pres. 1973—), Central Conf. Am. Rabbis (sec.), Central Conf. Am. Rabbis, Minn. Rabbinical Assn. (pres. 1962-64). Home: 2830 Inglewood Ave Minneapolis MN 55416 Office: Temple Israel 2324 Emerson Ave S Minneapolis MN 55405

SHAPIRO, SOLOMON BERNARD, rabbi, Jewish; b. Rumania, Mar. 29, 1922; s. Mordecai and Molly (Rabinowitz) S.; m. Mildred Sodden, June 11, 1946; children: Mordecai, Brocha, Miriam, Mala. Grad. Mesvta Talmudaical Sem., 1943; B.A., Bklyn. Coll., 1943; D.D., Phila. Coll., 1962. Ordained rabbi, 1943. Prin., Bath Rivkah Sch. for Girls, 1943-45; exec. dir. Mesifta Rabbi Chaim Berlin, 1946-48; rabbi Congl. Anshei Ozaritz, Bklyn., 1945-47, B'nai Abraham of East Flatbush, N.Y., 1974—, Degal Mordecai of Bklyn., 1974—; rabbi and chaplain Kingsbrook Jewish Med. Ctr., 1944—; chaplain Kings County Hosp. Ctr., 1950—, chmn. chaplaincy dept., 1982—; religious adviser Downstate Med. U., 1957-59; mem. exec. bd. Rabbinical Council Am., chmn. membership commn., 1972—; mem. Rabbinical Bd. Greater N.Y.; pres. rabbinical Alumni Mesivta Torah Vodath; pres. Rugby-East Flatbush United Jewish Community Council, 1972-75; trustee Union of Orthodox Rabbis, U.S. and Can., Vaad Haraboniem of Queens. Contbr. articles to religious publs. Bd. dirs. Bklyn. Assn. Mental Health. Named one of Religious Zionists of Am., 1984. Mem. Free Sons Israel, Mizrachi Orgn. Am., Nonparil Soc. Club, Am. Correctional Assn., Am. Sociol. Assn., Acad. Religion and Mental Health. Home: 73-09 136th St Flushing NY 11367 Office: 75-03 Main St Flushing NY 11367

SHAPIRO, SOLOMON KEHANE, rabbi, seminary administrator, educator; social worker. b. Jerusalem, Apr. 23, 1914; s. Jacob M. and Gittle (Kehane) S.; came to U.S., 1929; m. Rebecca E. Mandel, 1946; children: Eli, Vivian, Harold, Stanley, Abraham, Mitchell. B.A., Bklyn. Coll., 1942; M.A., Hunter Coll., 1971. Ordained rabbi, 1938. Rabbi, Hebrew Inst., Bklyn., 1938-41, Stevens Point, Wis., 1947-49, Beth Israel, Salisbury, Md., 1949-51; exec. dir. Yavne Hebrew Theol. Sem., Bklyn., 1953—; supporter Jewish research Resposa Index, 1972—. Co-founder, bd. dirs. Machon Maharshal Inst., Jerusalem, 1951—. Home: 718 East 7th St Brooklyn NY 11218

SHARKEY, MARIETTA, nun, religion educator, Roman Catholic Church; b. Indpls., Aug. 18, 1934; d. William Joseph and Mary Elizabeth (Duffey) S. B.S., Marian Coll., 1960; Ed.M. in Theology, Xavier U., 1974. Joined Sisters of St. Francis, 1952. Classroom tchr. various parishes, Ind., Ohio, 1954-71; first dir. religious edn. St. Monica Parish, Indpls., 1971-76, St. Bartholomew Parish, Cin., 1976-79, St. Ignatius Parish, Cin., 1979—; elected religious edn. rep. Archdiocese of Indpls., 1976, instr., religious studies program, 1975-76, mem. speaker bur., 1973-76; instr. adult religious edn. Archdiocese of Cin., 1981, St. Richard's Ctr., Cin., 1983—; catalyst First Ecumenical Adult Faith and Life Experience, Cin., 1977-79. Contbr. articles to profl. jours. Mem. Cin. Religious Edn. Assn. (chmn. 1982-83, agenda com. 1979-80, statewide task force 1983—), Dirs. Religious Edn. Ministry (effectiveness of study com. 1983—), Nat. Assn. Parish Coordinators and Dirs. Avocation: Irish culture and festivities. Office: Saint Ignatius Parish 5222 N Bend Rd Cincinnati OH 45247

SHARKEY, PAUL WILLIAM philosopher, religious educator, Roman Catholic Church; psychiatry educator; b. Oakland, Calif., Mar. 22, 1945; s. Paul Raymond and Alma Shirley (Bach) S.; m. Karen Kristine Efker, Mar. 31, 1967; 1 child, Erin Kathleen. A.A., Pasadena City Coll., 1963; B.A. with high honors, Calif. State U.-Los Angeles, 1969; Ph.D., U. Notre Dame, 1973. Assoc. prof. philosophy and religion U. So. Miss., Hattiesburg, 1975—; faculty adviser St. Thomas Newman Ctr., Hattiesburg, 1980—. Clin. asst. prof. psychiatry U. Miss. Sch. Medicine, Jackson, 1983—; acad. adviser Inst. on Comparative Polit. and Econ. Systems, Georgetown U., 1981—. Editor: Philosophy, Religion and Psychotherapy, 1982. Contbr. articles to religious publs. Served with USN, 1964-69. Recipient Excellence in Teaching award U. So. Miss., 1979. Mem. Soc. Christian Philosophers, New Ecumenical Research Assn. (So. regional dir. 1981—), Inst. for Advanced Philosophic Research (sr. adviser 1980—), Soc. Advancement Am. Philosophy, Soc. Philosophy Religion, Miss. Philos. Assn. (pres. 1980-81). Home: 128 E Lakeside Dr Hattiesburg MS 39401 Office: Box 5015 U So Miss Hattiesburg MS 39406

SHARP, JOHN, minister, Seventh-day Adventist; trust officer; b. Beemer, Neb., Sept. 20, 1933; s. Grover Cleveland and Esther Matilda (English) S.; m. Muriel Dolores Lehto, Feb. 21, 1954; children: Janet Louise, Jeanine Karen. B.A., Union Coll., 1963; M.A. in Religion, Andrews U., 1964. Ordained to ministry Seventh-day Adventist Ch., 1968. Pastor, Seventh-day Adventist Ch., South Sioux City, Neb., 1964-67, Holdredge, Neb., 1967-68, Carmichael, Calif., 1968-71, Red Bluff, Placerville, Calif., 1971-78; trust officer No. Calif. Conf., Pleasant Hill, 1978-80; pastor, evangelist, Aiea, Hawaii, 1980—; pastor, evangelist Hawaii Conf., Honolulu, 1982—, ministerial dir., 1984. Author lecture series Archeology Speaks, 1971. Served to cpl. U.S. Army, 1955-57. Home: 1644 Puananala St Pearl City HI 96782 Office: Aiea Seventh-day Adventist Ch 99-005 Moanalua Rd Aiea HI 96701

SHARP, URIE JONATHAN, minister, Mennonite Ch.; b. Belleville, Pa., June 19, 1936; s. Jesse D. and Amelia (Peachey) S.; B.A., Eastern Mennonite Coll., 1958; m. Delilah A. Miller, June 20, 1959; children—Dorcas Yvonne, Julia Lucille, Marcus Allen, Jana Lois, Jonathan Roger. Ordained to ministry, 1963; tchr. Hartville (Ohio) Christian Sch., 1962—, also prin.; missionary to Guatemala, 1968, 76—. Mem. mission bd. Conservative Mennonite Ch., 1965-70; sec. Mennonite Air Missions in Guatemala, 1972. Editor Harvest Call, 1969-70, Fellowship Messenger, 1969-70; contbr. articles in field to religious jours. Home: 12500 N Market Ave Hartville OH 44632 Office: 10515 N Market Ave Hartville OH 44632

SHATZ, EDWARD SIMPSON, lay synagogue worker, Conservative Jewish Congregations; b. Boston, Dec. 11, 1918; s. David Meyer and Rose (Grossman) S.; student Boston U. Coll. Commerce, eves., 1938-41; m. Beatrice Fellman, May 14, 1941 (dec. 1972); children—Karen (Mrs. Alan Ross), Ruth (Mrs. Kenneth Weiner); m. 2d, Edith Dorfman, 1973; children—Cheryl Dorfman (Mrs. Jerry Sher), Sandra Dorfman (Mrs. Sheldon Katz). Bd. dirs. Temple Shalom, Milton, Mass., 1950—, sec., 1966-70, v.p., 1970-72, pres., 1972-74; mem. adminstrv. bd. Asso. Synagogues Greater Boston, 1976—. Salesman, Joyva Corp., N.Y. Mem. Milton Hist. Commn., 1973—. Recipient scroll of honor State of Israel Bonds, 1962, Gates of Jerusalem award, 1973. Mem. Jewish War Vets. (past post comdr., nat. aide; comdr. Milton post 1975—), Phi Pi Chi. Address: 353 Blue Hills Pkwy Milton MA 02187

SHAW, MICHAEL EDWARD, minister, Southern Baptist Convention; b. Birmingham, Ala., May 7, 1948; s. Walter Edward and Frances Laura (Glidewell) S.; m. Mary Johnston, June 25, 1971; children: John Scott, Jacob Johnston. B.A., Samford U., Birmingham, 1970; Th.M., New Orleans Bapt. Sem., 1973, D. Ministry, 1976. Ordained to ministry So. Bapt. Conv., 1976; pastor Carrollton Ave. Bapt. Ch., New Orleans, 1971-73, Munford Bapt. Ch. (Ala.), 1973-75, Millry Bapt. Ch. (Ala.), 1976-79, 1st Bapt. Ch., Pelham, Ala., 1979—; evangelist Christ for the World, Jeon Ju, S. Korea, 1978. Author: One Hundred Years of Service for Christ, 1975. Bd. dirs. Developing Ala. Youth Found., Columbiana, 1984. Named Outstanding Young Religious Leader, Jaycees, Alabaster, Ala., 1982. Mem. Shelby Pastors' Conf. (pres. 1981-82), Ala. Bapt. Pastors' Conf. (v.p. 1977-78, sec.-treas., 1982-83). Office: 1st Bapt Ch 3174 Church St Pelham AL 35124

SHEA, FRANCIS R., bishop, Roman Catholic Church; b. Knoxville, Tenn., Dec. 4, 1913. S.A.B., St. Mary's Sem., Balt., 1935. priest Roman Catholic Ch., 1939. Tchr. Christian Bros. Coll. and Siena Coll., Memphis, 1940-45; prin. Father Ryan High Sch., Nashville, 1945-46; pastor Immaculate Conception Ch., Knoxville, 1956-69; apptd. 3d bishop, Evansville, Ind., 1969, ordained, installed, 1970. Address: 4200 N Kennedy Ave Evansville IN 47710

SHEA, LOUIS CHARLES, priest, Roman Cath. Ch.; b. Springfield, Ill., May 2, 1929; s. George Edward and Agnes (Mueller) S.; student Pontifical Coll. Josephinum, Worthington, Ohio, 1943-55. Ordained priest, 1955; asst. pastor St. James Ch., Decatur, Ill., 1955-59, St. Marys Ch., Taylorville, Ill., 1959-63, St. Rose Ch., Quincy, Ill., 1963-67; asst. dir. Cath. Charities of Quincy, 1963-67, 71—; asst. chaplain St. John Hosp., Springfield, Ill., 1967-69; pastor St. Stanislaus Chs., Macon and Moweaqua, Ill., 1969-70, St. Marys Ch., Mt. Sterling, Ill., 1970-77, St. Dominic Parish, Quincy, 1977—. Supt., St. Mary Acad., Mt. Sterling, 1970-77; deanery rep. Springfield Diocesan Secular Priests Trust Fund; past v.p. Brown County Ministerial Assn. Mem. Brown County Welfare Adv. Bd. Mem. Josephinum Coll. Alumni Assn. Home: 401 W North St Mount Sterling IL 62353 Office: PO Box 3364 Quincy IL 62301

SHEAN, JEANNETTE MARY, educator, nun, Roman Catholic Church; b. Chgo., Dec. 13, 1923; d. John Sylvester and Mary Cecilia (White) S. B.A., DePaul U., 1953, M.A., 1958; Ed.D., No. Ariz. U., 1977. Entered Inst. Blessed Virgin Mary, 1942. Tchr., Archdiocese Chgo., 1945-58, Diocese of Joliet, Ill., 1958-62; instr. Ill. Benedictine Coll., Lisle, Ill., 1958-70; tchr. Diocese Phoenix, 1970-75; grad. asst. No. Ariz. U., Flagstaff, 1975-77; asst. prof. U. Seattle, 1977-79; prin. St. Mark/St. Gregory Sch., Phoenix, 1979—; cons. Creative Problem Solving Inst., 1975, cons. in field. Contbr. articles to profl. jours. St. Xavier Coll. scholar, 1941-44. Mem. Am. Assn. Supervision and Curriculum Devel., Principals Phoenix, Kappa Delta Pi, Phi Delta Kappa. Address: 3437 N 18th Ave Phoenix AZ 85015 Office: Saint Gregory Sch 3437 N 18th Ave Phoenix AZ 85015

SHEARER, RODNEY HAIN, minister, United Methodist Church; b. Reading, Pa., Sept. 21, 1944; s. James Warren and Helen Rettew (Hain) S.; m. Mary Ellen Olmsted, July 2, 1966; children: Laura Beth, Angela Gail, Sara Helene. B.A., Lebanon Valley Coll., 1966; student Luth. Theol. Sem., 1966-68; M.Div., United Theol. Sem., 1969; postgrad. Drew U., 1970—. Ordained to ministry United Meth. Ch., as elder, 1969. Assoc. pastor St. Paul's United Meth. Ch., Elizabethtown, Pa., 1969-72; pastor Green Village United Meth. Ch., N.J., 1972-76; chaplain, adj. asst. prof. Religion Lebanon Valley Coll., Annville, Pa., 1976-80; instr. Old Testament Moravian theol. Sem., Bethlehem, Pa., 1984; pastor Fritz Meml. United Meth. Ch., Bethlehem, 1980—; sec. Eastern Pa. Conf. Commn. on Religion and Race, 1978-82, mem. Commn. on Higher Edn., 1984—; pres., v.p. United Ch. Elizabethtown, 1970-72. Bd. dirs. Lancaster County Family and Children's Services, 1970-71; active Green Village Vol. Fire Dept., N.J., 1972-76. Recipient Eagle Scout award Boy Scouts Am., 1962. Mem. Soc. Bibl. Lit. Home: 468 Montclair Ave Bethlehem PA 18015 Office: Fritz Meml United Meth Ch W Packer and Montclair Bethlehem PA 18015

SHEEHAN, DANIEL EUGENE, archbishop, Roman Cath. Ch.; b. Emerson, Nebr., May 14, 1917; s. Daniel F. and Mary Helen (Crahan) S.; student Creighton U., 1934-36, LL.D. (hon.), 1964; student Kenrick Sem., St. Louis, 1936-42; J.C.D., Cath. U. Am., 1949. Ordained priest Roman Cath. Ch., 1942, consecrated bishop, 1964; asst. pastor, Omaha, 1942-46; chancellor Archdiocese Omaha, 1949—, auxiliary bishop Omaha, 1964-69; archbishop of Omaha, 1969—. Pres. the Canan Law Soc. of America, 1953; del. 3d session Ecumenical Council, Rome, Italy, 1964; chaplain Omaha club Serra Internat., 1950—. Address: 100 N 62d St Omaha NE 68132

SHEEHAN, MICHAEL J., bishop, Roman Catholic Church. Bishop of Lubbock, Tex., 1983—. Office: 4011 54th St Lubbock TX 79413*

SHEEHY, HOWARD S., church official. Mem. first presidency Reorganized Ch. of Jesus Christ of Latter Day Saints. Office: The Auditorium PO Box 1059 Independence MO 64051*

SHELDON, GILBERT IGNATIUS See *Who's Who in America*, 43rd edition.

SHELDON, STEVEN RAY, minister, Southern Baptist Convention; b. Waynesboro, Pa., Nov. 21, 1952; s. Eldon K. and Doris B. (Barnhart) S.; m. Kathy Sue Johnson, Feb. 18, 1973; 1 child, Samuel David. B.A. cum laude, Campbellsville Coll., 1980; M.Div., So. Bapt. Theol. Sem., 1984. Ordained to ministry Baptist Ch., 1977. Deacon First So. Bapt. Ch., San Diego, 1975-76; pastor Arbuckle Bapt. Ch., Lebanon, Ky., 1977-80, Ovesen Heights Bapt. Ch., Hodgenville, Ky., 1980-84, Box-Mont Bapt. Ch., Hatboro, Pa., 1984—; pres. LaRue County Ministerial Assn., 1981-82; chairmissions com. Ky. Bapt. Conv., 1982—. Mem. Sunrise Vols., 1983—; mem. ch. relations com. Campbellsville Coll., 1983—. Served with USN, 1972-76. Recipient Christian Studies award Campbellsville Coll., 1980. Democrat. Home: 550 Lowell Rd Warminster PA 18974 Office: Box-Mont Baptist Ch 309 W County Line Rd Hatboro PA 18974

SHELEY, VERNITA LOREE, ednl. adminstr., undenominational; b. Modesto, Calif., Jan. 19, 1930; d. C. Ely and Zelna B. (Stokes) Persing; student Bethany Bible Coll., 1951; San Francisco State U., U. Calif. at Berkeley; Donald B. Sheley, Feb. 5, 1955; children—Leighton Grant, Cabot Layne, Karlton Blair. Dir., Highlands Presch. and Acad., San Bruno, Calif., 1966—; organist, pianist Ch. of the Highlands, San Bruno, Calif., 1960—. Mem. Am., Western assns. Christian schs. Home: PO Box B Daly City CA 94017 Office: PO Box 127 1900 Monterey Dr San Bruno CA 94066

SHELL, JOHN ROBERT, minister, Presbyterian Church (U.S.A.); b. Pine Bluff, Ark., Aug. 16, 1925; s. Claude Irving and Ela Evelyn (Hartsell) S.; B.A., Maryville (Tenn.) Coll., 1947; B.D., Austin Presbyn. Theol. Sem., 1954, Th.M., 1961, D.Min., 1980; accredited Assn. Couples for Marriage Enrichment, 1980; m. Gwendolen Rees-Jones, June 6, 1948; children—John Robert, Elizabeth Jane, Martin William, Paul Calvin, Philip Andrew. Ordained to ministry, 1954; pastor chs., Dermott and Tillar, Ark., 1954-58; pastor 1st Presbyn. Ch., Conway, Ark., 1958—; supply pastor Cove Chapel Presbyn. Ch., Damascus, Ark., 1959—. Home: 1971 Hillman St Conway AR 72032 Office: Caldwell and Faulkner Sts Conway AR 72032

SHELLEM, JOHN JOSEPH, priest, religion educator, librarian, Roman Catholic Church; b. Phila., Apr. 11, 1926; s. Eugene Joseph and Barbara Dena (Johnson) S. B.A., St. Charles Sem., 1948, M.A., 1959, M.Div., 1971; B.L.S., Villanova U., 1950, M.L.S., 1963. Asst. pastor various parishes, Pottsville, Bethlehem, Phila., Pa., 1952-58; tchr., librarian Cardinal Dougherty High Sch., Phila., 1958-63; librarian Cardinal O'Hara High Sch., Springfield, Pa., 1963-67; instr. Villanova U., 1962-70; librarian St. Charles Sem., Phila., 1967-78; pastor St. Madeleine Sophie Parish, Phila., 1978—; del. Archdiocesan Priests Council, Phila., 1979-84; bd. dirs. Am. Cath. Hist. Soc., 1977—, past pres.; mem. com. Free Library Religious Books, 1964-66. Asst. editor jour. pastoral concern, 1969-78. Contbr. articles to profl. jours. Mem. Cath. Library Assn. (chmn. Eastern Pa. unit, 1964, 1966-71), Library Pub. Relations Assn. (v.p. 1974—). Lodge: K.C. (chaplain 1955—). Home and Office: St Madeleine Sophie Ch 6440 Greene St Philadelphia PA 19119

SHELTON, GEORGE, university dean, minister, National Baptist Convention U.S.A., Inc.; b. Selma, Ala., July 2, 1943; s. Bill and Will Ella (Lawson) S.; A.A., Selma U., 1963, B.Th., 1965; M.Div., Va. Union U., 1969; M.A., Presbyn. Sch. Christian Edn., 1970; m. Haddie Askew, June 24, 1972. Ordained to ministry, 1967; asst., pastor chs., Ala., Va., 1963-70; dean Sch. Religion, Selma U., 1971-84; pastor Mt. Zion Bapt. Ch., Selma, Ala., 1981—; dean religious activities Selma U., 1984—, dir. student union, 1976—. Student asst., univ. pastor Va. Union U., 1967-68; project dir. Am. Bible Soc., 1969; pastor asst. Green St. Bapt. Ch., 1971—; pastor Vilula Bapt. Ch., Marion, Ala., 1972—; dean of congress New Cahaba Dist. Sunday Sch. and Bapt. Tng. Union, 1972—; corr. sec. New Cahabra Dist. Assn., 1982—. Mem. membership com. Carver br. YMCA, 1972; coll. dir. Dallas County Crusade, 1973; active Dallas County Voters League, 1965-67, Friends of Carnegie Library, Inc., 1972-73. Recipient Alumni award Selma U. Alumni Assn., 1964. Mem. Assn. Bapt. Profs. Religion, Am. Assn. Higher Edn., N.A.A.C.P., Am. Security Council. Mason; mem. Order Eastern Star. Contbr. articles to religious jours. Home: 525 3d Ave Selma AL 36701 Office: 1501 Lapsley St Selma AL 36701

SHELTON, JANICE PAULINE, minister, American Baptist Association; b. Eldorado, Kans., Nov. 19, 1950; d. Roy E. Osborne and V. Pauline (Church) O.; m. Larry A. Shelton, July 26, 1980; children: James, Debra, L. Lance. B.A., Ottawa U., 1972; M.Div., Central Bapt. Theol. Sem., 1975. Ordained to ministry Am. Bapt. Assn., 1978. Minister Christian Edn. First Bapt. Ch., Mt. Pleasant Iowa, 1975-77; chaplain recreation Stockton Lake Ministries, Mo., 1977; chaplain intern Prairie View Mental Health Ctr., Newton, Kans., 1977-78; minister First Bapt. Ch., Dexter, Kans., 1979—; dir. adv. com. Grouse Valley Manor, Dexter, 1982—. Mem., Women in Ministry (Kans.). Home: PO Box 167 Dexter KS 67038

SHELTON, RAYMOND LARRY, educator, Free Methodist Church; b. Hooper's Creek, N.C., Jan. 10, 1942; s. Raymond Samuel and Viola Gladys (Hoots) S.; m. Evangeline Deal, Aug. 25, 1967; children: Annalisa Tung-Yo, Alison Leigh. B.A., Pfeiffer Coll., 1964; M.Div., Asbury Theol. Sem., 1967, Th.M., 1968; Th.D., Fuller Theol. Sem., 1974. Ordained elder, 1966. Asst./assoc. prof. Azusa Pacific U., Calif., 1968-74; asst. pastor Pasadena Wesleyan Ch., 1968-70, First Wesleyan Ch., High Point, N.C., 1974-77; prof. theology John Wesley Coll., Greensboro, N.C., 1974-77, acad. dean., 1975-77; dean Sch. Religion, Seattle Pacific U., 1977—; exec. com. Bd. Ministerial Edn., Free Meth. Ch., Pacific Northwest Conf., Seattle, 1980—; bd. dirs. Fuller Theol. Sem., Seattle, 1979—. Editor 5 vol. theol. series, Wesleyan Theological Perspectives, 1980—. Contbr. articles to profl. jours. Recipient Disting. Faculty award, Azusa Pacific U., 1969. Mem. Wesleyan Theol. Soc. (pres. 1984—), Am. Soc. Ch. History, Soc. Bibl. Lit., Am. Acad. Religion, Internat. Soc. Theta Phi. Republican. Home: 13326 52d Pl W Edmonds WA 98020 Office: Seattle Pacific U Seattle WA 98119

SHELTON, TOM WILLIAM, minister, General Association Regular Baptist Churches; b. Cin., Feb. 5, 1935; s. William and Martha (Jones) S.; m. Peggy Jean Lowe, June 5, 1957; children: Tom W., Richard A. A.A., Bapt. Coll. Bible of Pa., 1976, B.R.E., 1978, Th.B., 1979. Ordained to ministry Gen. Assn. Regular Bapt. Chs., 1979. Pastor New Boston Bapt. Ch., N.H., 1979—; sec. Pastoral Internat. Fellowship, Clarks Summit, Pa., 1977; sec.-treas. Heritage Pastoral Fellowship, 1979-80. Author booklets: Revelation, 1983, Atributes of God, 1984. Served with USCG, 1954-74. Recipient Nat. Youth award Soc. Dist. High Schs., 1984. Mem. Bapt. Bible Coll. Northeastern Alumni Assn. (pres. 1981-83). Address: 2 Lyndeboro Rd New Boston NH 03070

SHEPARD, WILLIAM DAVID, brother, ednl. adminstr., Roman Cath. Ch.; b. Somerville, Mass., Oct. 2, 1929; s. George Edward and Anna Veronica (Sheehan) S.; B.A. in Chemistry, Cath. U. Am., 1954; M.A., N.Y. U., 1968, Ed.D. in Ednl. Adminstrn. (Edn. Professions Devel. Act fellow), 1975. Joined Congregation of Bros. of St. Francis Xavier, 1948; tchr. math., chemistry and physics in high schs., Mass., Md., Ky., N.Y., 1954-64; asst. prin. St. Joseph Regional High Sch., Montvale, N.J., 1964-68, prin., 1968-77; dir. fin. affairs, asst. prof. mathematics St. Thomas Aquinas Coll., Sparkill, N.Y., 1977—; adj. asst. prof. Grad. Sch. Edn., Fordham U., Lincoln Center, N.Y.C. Pres. Regional Secondary Sch. Prins. of Archdiocese of Newark, 1969-77; instr. mathematics Dominican Coll., Blauvelt, N.Y. NSF grantee, 1958-59, 61-62, 64-65. Mem. Am. Assn. Sch. Adminstrs., Am. Assn. Supervision, Curriculum Devel., Nat. Assn. Secondary Sch. Prins., Nat. Cath. Ednl. Assn., AAUP, Phi Delta Kappa. Home: 40 Chestnut Ridge Rd Montvale NJ 07645 Office: Saint Thomas Aquinas Coll Sparkill NY 10976

SHEPPARD, WILLIAM RAYMOND, minister, counselor, Christian Church (Disciples of Christ); b. Harvey, Ill., Nov. 1, 1930; s. Walter VanBuren and Flossie Nina (Davis) S.; A.A.S., Carl Sandburg Jr. Coll., 1973; B.A., Colonial Acad., Rockford, Ill., 1959; gen. certificate religious knowledge (advanced level) U. London, 1965; m. Betty Ruth Seidel, June 27, 1952; children—David Raymond, Jonathan William. Ordained to ministry, 1953; minister God's House, Cameron, Ill., 1982—; tutorial counselor, alcohol treatment center Galesburg Cottage Hosp., Ill., 1974-77. Mem. Internat. Brotherhood of Magicians. Author: I Never Thought I Would Sink So Low. Home: 13 Gerlaw St Gerlaw IL 61435

SHERARD, ROBERT DOUGLAS, minister, United Church of Christ; b. Memphis, June 10, 1922; s. Major James and Elizabeth Perkins S.; m. Lois Johnson Sept. 8, 1956; children: Robert, Jr., Lynn Case, Dawna Jean. A.B., Morehouse Coll., 1949; M.Div., Gammon Theol. Sem., 1952; S.T.M., N.Y. Theol. Sem., 1974, D.Min., 1976. Ordained to ministry United Ch. Christ, 1953. Minister Beecher United Ch., New Orleans, La., 1953-58, Corona United Ch., Corona, Queens, N.Y., 1958—; bd. dirs. World Ministries United Ch. Christ, N.Y.C., 1966-70, Homeland Ministries, 1979—; moderator Met. Assn. Chs., United Ch. Christ, 1978-80. Pres. NAACP, 1958-64; regional convenor Commn. Racial Justice, 1974, Mayor's Task Force on Poverty, 1968; mem. adv. com. Queens Urban League, 1962, Vis. Nurses Assn., 1980, Ptnrs. for the Homeless, 1984—. Served with USN, 1942-45, ETO. Named Man of Yr., Morehouse Coll. Alumni Assn., 1970; recipient Humanitarian award Abu Beka, Shriners, 1968. Democrat. Home: 27-21 99th St East Elmhurst NY 11369 Office: Corona United Ch Christ 102-18 34th Ave Corona NY 11368

SHERER, MORRIS, rabbi, Jewish religion; b. Bklyn., June 18, 1921; s. Hyman and Bessie (Morochnik) S.; student Mesivta Torah Vodaath Rabbinical Sem., 1934-39; rabbi Ner Israel Rabbinical Coll., Balt., 1942; m. Deborah Fortman, Nov., 1943; children—Rochelle (Mrs. Ira Langer), Elky (Mrs. Robert Goldschmidt), Shimshon. Rabbi, 1942; exec. dir. Agudath Israel Youth Council Am., 1943-50; exec. v.p. Agudath Israel of Am., 1951-62, exec. pres., 1963-78, pres., 1978—; prof. homiletics Mesivta Torah Vodaath Rabbinical Sem., 1949—; founder, dir. Nat. Jewish Commn. Law and Pub. Affairs, 1965—; dir. N.Y. Met. Coordinating Council on Jewish Poverty, 1973-78; co-chmn. Am. sect. Agudath Israel World Orgn., 1964-80, chmn., 1980—; Jewish community rep. N.Y. State Edn. Commr.'s Adv. Council Sch. Dist. Adminstrs., 1973-80; founder, pres. commn. sr. citizens Agudath Israel of Am., 1973—, commn. legislation and civic action, 1965—; dir. Nat. Assn. Rabbinic and Talmudic Schs., 1973—; cons., rep. Jewish day sch. movement, 1954—; dir. Welfare Research, Inc., 1975—. Mem. exec. com. Citizens' Com. N.Y.C.; bd. visitors Grad. Center City U. N.Y., 1975—. Office: 5 Beekman St New York City NY 10038

SHERIDAN, WILLIAM COCKBURN RUSSELL, bishop, Episcopal Church; b. N.Y.C., Mar. 25, 1917; s. John Russell Fortesque and Gertrude Magdalene (Hurley) S.; B.A., Carroll Coll., 1939; M.Div., Nashotah House Sem., 1946, S.T.M., 1968, D.D., 1966, D.C.L., 1984; m. Rudith Treder, Nov. 13, 1943; children—Elizabeth (Mrs. Allen Wilson Beeler), Margaret (Mrs. Gerald Wilson), Mary (Mrs. James Janda), Peter, Stephen. Ordained priest, 1943, bishop, 1972; asst. priest St. Pauls Ch., Chgo., 1943-44; rector Gethsemane Ch., Marion, Ind., 1944-47, St. Thomas Ch., 1947-72; Episc. chaplain Culver (Ind.) Mil. Acad., 1953-58, 70-72; bishop Diocese of No. Ind., South Bend, 1972—. Clerical dep. to Gen. Conv., Nat. Synod, 1952-70. Pres. bd. trustees Howe (Ind.) Mil. Sch., 1972; pres. bd. trustees Nashotah House Sem., 1985. Recipient Disting. Service award Ancilla Coll. Mem. Alumni Assn. Nashotah House Sem. (pres. 1953-55). Author: Journey to Priesthood, 1950; For High School Boys Only, 1955; Between Catholics, 1968. Home: 2502 S Twyckenham Dr South Bend IN 46614 Office: 117 N LaFayette Blvd South Bend IN 46601

SHERLOCK, JOHN MICHAEL See *Who's Who in America*, 43rd edition.

SHERMAN, CHARLES PHILLIP, rabbi, Reform Jewish; b. Warren, Pa., Dec. 14, 1943; s. Samuel Louis and Ruth (Kovacs) S.; m. Nancy Rae Slone, Feb. 7, 1965; children; Aaron Reuben, Daniel Micah, Ruth Miriam. B.A., U. Pitts., 1963; B. Hebrew Letters, Hebrew Union Coll., 1966, M.A. Hebrew Letters, 1969. Ordained rabbi Reform Jewish, 1969. Assoc. rabbi Temple Beth Israel, West Hartford, Conn., 1969-76; sr. rabbi Temple Israel, Tulsa, 1976—; v.p. Tulsa Met. Ministry, 1982—. Contbg. editor Tulsa Jewish Rev. Contbr. articles to profl. jours. Bd. dirs. Instl. Review Hillcrest Med. Ctr., Tulsa, 1980, Planned Parenthood, 1977-83, Okla. Religious Coalition for Abortion Rights; mem. Task Force to Study Religious Programs Pub. Schs., Tulsa, 1979-80. Mem. Central Conf. Am. Rabbis (exec. bd. 1982—), Tulsa Ministerial Alliance (pres. 1980-81), S.W. Assn. Reform Rabbis. Democrat. Office: Temple Israel 2004 E 22nd Pl Tulsa OK 74114

SHERMAN, JOSEPH HOWARD, bishop, Church of God in Christ; b. Marion, S.C., June 14, 1923; s. Sam and Alma (Cannon) S.; m. Daisy Lee Littles; children: Joseph Howard, Beatrice Sherman Boone. D.D. (hon.), Trinity Hall Coll., 1968; LL.D. (hon.), New Haven Theol. Sem., 1981. Ordained to ministry Ch. of God in Christ, 1943, consecrated bishop, 1963. Founder, organizer more than 10 missions and chs. Ch. of God in Christ, chmn. Council of Bishops, Memphis, 1976—; pres. C.H. Mason System of Bible Colls., Charlotte, 1975; bd. dirs. C.H. Mason Scholarship Found., Memphis, 1969—; pres., founder, J. Howard Sherman Scholarship Fund, 1974—; founder Mighty Voice that Crieth TV ministry, 1984—. Author: Weapons of the Righteous, 1975. Editor The Mighty Voice That Crieth, 1984—. Recorder album: Peace That Only Christ Can Give, 1973. Mem. steering com. Democratic Governorship of N.C., 1984; mem. grievance com. Housing Authority, Charlotte, 1983-84; mem. Hiring of the Handicapped, Charlotte, 1984. J.H. Sherman Day proclaimed in his honor City of Charlotte, annually, 1974-84; named Hon. Citizen, State of Tex., 1973, Knight of Queen City 1976, Hon. Citizen, Commonwealth of Va., 1980, Hon. Citizen, City of Balt., 1981, Hon. Atty. Gen., State of N.C., 1983. Mem. NAACP (cert. of appreciation 1976). Office: Pentecostal Temple Ch of God in Christ 1401 Parkwood Ave Charlotte NC 28205

SHERMAN, RAYMOND LAMAR, minister, So. Bapt. Conv.; b. Lee County, Tex., Feb. 28, 1940; s. Vernon T. and Mary Nell (Turnipseed) S.; student Howard Payne Coll., 1958-59; B.A. in religion, E. Tex. Bapt. Coll., 1970; postgrad. Kansas State Coll., 1973-75, U. Nebr., summer 1975; m. Doris Ann Haydon, June 6, 1959; children—Raymond Terrell, Pamela Gail. Ordained to ministry, 1962; pastor various Bapt. chs. in Tex., 1964-72, Ravanna (Ark.) Bapt. Mission, 1971-72, First Bapt. Ch., Chetopa, Kans., 1972-76, First So. Bapt. Ch., Emporia, Kans., 1976—. Chmn. missions com. Twin Valley Bapt. Assn. of So. Bapt. Conv., 1972-76; chmn. sem. extension com. Twin Valley Sem. Extension Center, Independence, Kans., 1972-76; mem. bd. Virgil Bapt. Assembly, 1972-76, pres., 1975. Home: 67 Apache Rd Emporia KS 66801 Office: 1028 Whittier Emporia KS 66801

SHERTZER, LEONARD EUGENE, minister, Lutheran Church; b. Harrisburg, Pa., May 1, 1929; s. Charles Stephen Shertzer and Charlotte (Fitzweiler) S.; m. Brenda Warin, Sept. 21, 1957 (div. 1983); children: Denise, David, Diane. A.B., Elizabethtown, Pa., 1953; B.D., Gettysburg Sem., 1957, S.T.M., 1975. Ordained to ministry Lutheran Ch., 1957. Pres. Johnstown Pastoral Assn., 1959-60; dean of Harrisburg Dist., 1972-74; pastor Union Lutheran Ch., York, Pa. 1979—. Mem. Commn. of Mission and Ecumenicity. Republican. Club: Optimist. Home: 321 N Penn St York PA 17404

SHIBATA, GEORGE EISHIN, minister, Jodo Shinshu Honganji Sect Buddhist Churches America; b. Fukuoka-ken, Japan, Apr. 13, 1938; s. Tesshin and Haruko (Fukuyoshi) S.; came to U.S., 1939, naturalized, 1963; student U. Wash., 1957-62; B.A., Ryukoku U. (Japan), 1966, M.A., 1969; m. Yasuko Kawasaki, Oct. 27, 1973. Ordained to ministry, 1964; asst. minister Gardena (Calif.) Buddhist Ch., 1970-73; asst. dir. Bur. Buddhist Edn., Buddhist Chs. Am. Hdqrs., San Francisco, 1974; resident minister Reedley (Calif.) Buddhist Ch., 1975—. Mem. literary propagation com. Buddhist Chs. Am., 1975-81, Sunday sch. dept. exec. com., 1976-78, 81—, chmn., 1982—, mem. ministerial affairs com., 1980—; trustee Inst. Buddhist Studies, 1982-83; chmn. Central Calif. Buddhist Ministerial

Assn., 1978-80, vice chmn., 1981-82, treas., 1975-77, 83—. Author: Buddhist Holidays, 1974. Home: PO Box 24 1459 J St Reedley CA 93654 Office: 2035 15th St Reedley CA 93654

SHIELDS, JERRY KERMIT, minister, naval chaplain, United Methodist Church; b. Charleston, W.Va., Apr. 19, 1944; s. Kermit and Gennie Faye (Keaton) S.; m. Margaret Ann Stewart, Nov. 20, 1966; children: Christie Ann, Thomas Scott. B.A., Marshall U., 1967; M.Div., Drew U., 1971; S.T.M., Yale U. Div. Sch., 1984. Ordained to ministry United Meth. Ch., as elder, 1972. Pastor, W.Va. Conf. United Meth. Ch., Charleston, W.Va., 1971-78; commd. lt. U.S. Navy, 1978 advanced through grades to lt. comdr., 1983; circuit riding chaplain Fleet Religious Support Activity, Norfolk, Va., 1978-79; ship's chaplain USS Puget Sound, Norfolk and Gaeta, Italy, 1979-81; asst. dir. Credo Pier Ministry, Naples, Italy, 1981-83; gen. chaplain Naval Tng. Ctr., San Diego, 1984—. Recorder, mayor Town of Matoaka, W.Va., 1972-73; chmn. Mercer County Commn. on Aging, Bluefield, W.Va., 1975-76. Recipient John Heston Willey award Drew U. Theol. Sch., 1971, George C. Crooks award, 1971. Democrat. Lodge: Masons (master mason 1978). Home: 3355 Corporal Dr San Diego CA 92124 Office: Naval Tng Ctr Adminstrv Command San Diego CA 92133

SHIELDS, ROBERT WILLIAM, church official, minister, editorial consultant, United Church of Christ; b. Seymour, Ind., May 17, 1918; s. John Arthen and Ada Beatrice (Vincent) S.; m. Billie D. Bichacoff, May 17, 1956 (div. May 1960); m. Grace Hotson, Aug. 20, 1960; children: Cornelia M., Heidi E., Klara K. A.B. magna cum laude, Franklin Coll., 1944; postgrad. U. Ky., Andover-Newton Theol. Sch., Drake U. Coll. of Bible, Garrett Bibl. Inst., Harvard U. Div. Sch., U. Colo., Mont. State U. Ordained to ministry United Ch. of Christ, 1953. Pastor, Bapt. Chs., so. Ind., 1941-44, Congregational-Christian Pastorates, Deerfield, N.H., 1945-49, Congregational-United Ch. of Christ Pastorates, Iowa, 1949-50, United Meth. Pastorates, Iowa, 1950-51, Congregational/United Ch. of Christ, S.D., 1951-54; asst. minister 1st Congregational/United Ch. of Christ, Dayton, Wash., 1973—; nat. pres. Ch. of the Servant, Inc., Dayton, 1963—; pres. Am. Div. Acad., Ind., 1943-54, Ch. of the Servant Inc., Dayton, 1963-84. Editorial dir. MANUSCRIPTS, Dayton, 1959—. Author: Day I Was Proudest to Be An American, 1958; author story base for screenplay movie Love Me Tender, 1955, World's Worst Sentence award for Gothic Novel, 1983. Republican. Mason (chaplain/sr deacon 1980-84). Home: 217 E Oak St Dayton WA 99328

SHIN, SUNG KOOK, minister, Presbyterian Church (U.S.A.); b. Seoul, Korea, Sept. 19, 1926; s. Chang Bok and Soon Bok (Cha) S.; B.D., Han-Kuk Theol. Sem., (Korea), 1961; M.Th., Emmanuel Coll. Victoria U. (Can.), 1963; postgrad. Boston U., 1964-65; m. Chung Hee Kim, Nov. 20, 1945; children: Cho-Um, Cho-Hyun, Dai-Bong. Came to U.S., 1964, naturalized, 1974. Ordained to ministry Presbyn. Ch. in Korea, 1951; chaplain Korean Navy, 1951-56; gen. sec. Korean Student Christian Fed., 1951-58; asso. gen. sec. Korean Presbyn. Ch., 1958-60; assoc. pastor Lafayette Ave. Presbyn. Ch., Bklyn., 1965-69; pastor Korean Central Ch. N.Y., N.Y.C., 1970-80; cons. Korean-Am. ministry Presbyn. Ch. (U.S.A.), 1981—; chmn. ecumenical relations com. Presbytery N.Y.C., United Presbyn. Ch. U.S.A., 1972—, vice moderator presbytery, 1976—, chmn. Korean Presbyn. Caucus, 1974-75; chmn. Korean Ministers Assn. Greater N.Y., 1975-76; mem. governing bd. Nat. Council Ch. of Christ in U.S.A., 1976-82. Recipient certificates Order of Merit, Korean Christian Press, 1957, Pres. Republic Korea, 1970. Editor, pub. Church and World mag., 1964—. Home: 88-23 218th St Queens Village NY 11427 Office: 7 W 11th St New York NY 10011

SHIVELY, STEVEN GLEN, youth minister, Presbyterian Church in U.S.A.; b. Encino Calif., Aug. 30, 1961; s. Richard Paul and Barbara (Saunders) S. B.B.A., Calif. State U.-Northridge, 1985, B.A. in Speech Communication, 1985, postgrad., 1985—. Campus dir. Inter Varsity Christian Fellowship, Woodland Hills, Calif., 1981-83; mgr., founder ALIVE! concerts, Canoga Park, Calif., 1981-83; assoc. dir. Youth for Christ, Canoga Park, 1982-83; youth dir. St. Stephen Presbyn. Ch., Chatsworth, Calif., 1983—. Mem., del. UPCUSA Triennium, Ind., 1980; dean sr. high camps Synod Co. Calif. and Hawaii, Los Angeles, 1984—; mem. U.S.-USSR Global Ministries Peacemaking Seminar in Soviet Union, 1985. Dir. Rec-Specs and Message Communications Ministries, Inc., 1979—. Republican. Avocations: photography; alpine-nordic skiing; mountaineering; rafting; audio productions. Home: 21115 Devonshire Apt 249 Chatsworth CA 91311 Office: St Stephen Presbyn Ch 20121 Devonshire Chatsworth CA 91311

SHIZGAL, SENDER, rabbi, religious organization executive. Nat. exec. dir. Mizrachi-Hapoel Hamizrachi Orgn., Montreal, Que. Office: 5497A Victoria Ave Suite 101 Montreal PQ H3W 2R1 Canada*

SHOEMAKE, BURL PALMER, minister, counseling dir., Christian Chs., Chs. Christ; b. Vader, Wash., May 1, 1921; s. William Perry and Leah Fay (Armstrong) S.; B. Sacred Lit., San Jose (Calif.) Bible Coll., 1949; M.S., Ft. Hays (Kans.) State Coll., 1973; postgrad. Freedom U., Orlando, Fla., 1976—; m. Bernita June Chambers, June 2, 1947; children—Donita Rae, Burl Palmer, II, Perry Bob, Doylanne, Monte, Lynn. Ordained to ministry, 1949; establisher pastor chs., Calif., Bahamas, Colo., Oreg., 1949-66; Sebastopol, Sonoma, Calif., 1966-68, Siletz, Oreg., 1969-74; dir., counselor Lincoln County Family Counseling Clinic, Toledo, Oreg., 1969-72; dir., cons. Civic Center Counseling Clinic, Topeka, Kans., 1973—; dir., counselor Community Counseling Center, Sweet Home, Oreg., 1974—, New Direction Counseling Center, Eugene, Oreg., 1975—; tchr. Bible and human relations, community edn. dept. Linn Benton Community Coll., Albany, Oreg., 1973—. Pres. Toledo Ministerial Assn. City councilman City of Toledo, 1968-71. Mem. Phi Delta Kappa. Editor publisher Beachcomber, 1965-66. Home: 660 Oak Terr Sweet Home OR 97386

SHOEMAKER, CHARLES CLINTON, JR., minister, Bapt. Gen. Conf.; b. Distant, Pa., Sept. 28, 1915; s. Charles Clinton and Annie Lavera (Chapman) S.; Th.G., Practical Bible Tng. Sch., 1938; B.A., Burton Coll., 1942; Th.M., Bible Bapt. Sem., 1946; Th.D., Burton Sem., 1957; D.D. (hon.), John Brown U., 1960; postgrad. Bethany Coll., 1947-48. U. Wash., 1949-50; m. Dorothy Evelyn Weyhe, Feb. 28, 1939; children—Ruth G., Naomi A. (Mrs. Keith M. Austin), James L. Ordained to ministry, 1938; minister N.Y., Ohio, Wash., Calif.; founder Evang. Mission, Martinique, French West Indies, 1946; dir. Christian Missions, Antilles, 1946-48; founder First Bapt. Ch., Kirkland, Wash., 1949-65; sr. minister Fountain Ave. Bapt. Ch., Hollywood, Calif., 1965-69, Trinity Bapt. Ch., Indio, Calif., 1969-74, Lincoln Ave. Bapt. Ch., Escondido, Calif., 1974—. Guest minister Abbey Rd. Bapt. Ch., London, Eng., 1967; condr. Sunday worship broadcast, Kirkland, Wash., 1949-65; pres. Coachella Valley Ch. Alliance, 1972-73; West area moderator, bd. dirs. Conservative Bapt. Assn. So. Calif., 1967-69; trustee S.W. Bapt. Conf., 1976—. Vice pres. Alcohol Problems Assn. Wash., 1964. Bd. promotion Denver Conservative Bapt. Sem., 1962; bd. reference Western Conservative Bapt. Sem., 1968. Mem. Escondido Ministerial Assn. (pres. 1976—). Home: 2170 Jefferson Ave Escondido CA 92027 Office: 1717 E Lincoln Ave Escondido CA 92025

SHOEMAKER, MARK THOMAS, minister, religious organization administrator, National Baptist Convention USA; b. Kokomo, Ind., Aug. 29, 1947; s. Ithel Devon and Delsie Lee (McQueary) S.; m. Ruth Ann Lennington, Oct. 15, 1977; 1 child, Melissa Marie. B.S., Ill. Inst. Tech., 1969; M.Div., So. Bapt. Theol. Sem., 1982. Ordained to ministry Bapt. Ch., 1979. Assoc. minister Mount Lebanon Bapt. Ch., Louisville, Ky., 1978—, interim minister, 1980; assoc. minister Shiloh Bapt. Ch., Newark, Ohio, 1979—; exec. dir. EUMBA Assembly Ground, Newark, 1983—; chaplain Madison Twp. Fire Dept., Marne, Ohio, 1984—, Jewish Hosp., Louisville, 1982. Artist-photographer visual images exhibited primarily at Licking County Art Mus., Chgo. Artists Guild, Ind. State Fair. Sec. IIT Concerned Students, Chgo., 1967-69; pres. bd. dirs. Leads Community Action Agy., Newark, 1974-76; dist. exec. Licking County council Boy Scouts Am., 1973-76; edn. exec. Old Ky. Home council Boy Scouts Am., 1976-79. Named Ky. Col., Commonwealth of Ky., 1977. Lodges: Kiwanis (bd. dirs. 1975-76), Rotary (bd. dirs. 1978-79). Office: EUMBA Assembly Ground 3302 Hickman Rd NE Newark OH 43055-9157

SHOEMAKER, MELVIN HUGH, minister, Free Meth. Ch.; b. Bryant, Ind., Feb. 11, 1940; s. H. Vaughn and Thelora M. S.; A.B., Marion Coll., 1962; M. Div. with honors, Asbury Theol. Sem., 1967; postgrad. U. Wis. Hebrew Seminar in Israel, 1966, (fellow) Spring Arbor Coll., 1977; m. Glenna Joan Cockrell, Dec. 29, 1961; children—David Wesley, Diana Marie, Daniel Luther. Ordained to ministry, 1964; pastor Leith St. Wesleyan Ch., Ft. Wayne, Ind., 1962-64, Hillside Wesleyan Ch., Marion, Ind., 1967-70; sr. minister Houghton (N.Y.) Coll. Wesleyan Ch., 1970-73, Dearborn (Mich.) Free Meth. Ch., 1973—. Instr. Marion Coll., 1967; v.p. Marion Area Ministerial Assn., 1968-69, pres., 1969-70; v.p. Allegheny County (N.Y.) Ministerial Assn., 1972-73; pres. Dearborn Area Clergy, 1975-76. Vol. fireman, Houghton, 1970-73; mem. Dearborn Youth Affairs Commn., 1976—. Mem. Nat. Assn. Evangs. Contbr. articles to denominational publs. Home: 18307 Oakwood Blvd Dearborn MI 48124 Office: 21360 W Outer Dr Dearborn MI 48124

SHOEMAKER, WARREN ALCOTT, minister, American Baptist Churches in the U.S.A.; b. Chgo., July 15, 1903; s. George A. and Gertrude Elizabeth (Alcott) S.; B.A., M.A., U. Wash., Ph.D., 1927; D.D., Eastern Bapt. Sem., 1930; m. Louise Ernestine Ladner, June 15, 1950; children: Vicky Louise, Louis Allan. Ordained to ministry, 1930; pastor chs., Wash., Calif., Wis., 1930-53; organizer Maracay (Venezuela) Community Ch., 1953-58; pastor chs. in Europe, 1958-61; pastor chs. in Calif., 1961—; pastor First Bapt. Ch., Milpitas, Calif., 1972-80, First Bapt. Ch., Chowchilla, Calif., 1980—. Bd. mgrs. Am. Bapt. Conv.; pres. Milpitas Ministers Fellowship, 1972-75. Active local Boy Scouts Am. Home: PO Box 565 Chowchilla CA 93610 Office: 717 Robertson Blvd Chowchilla CA 93610

SHOFF, DONALD GENE, minister, Independent Bible Church and Southern Baptist Convention; b. Ponca City, Okla., Aug. 19, 1934; s. George Arthur and Mary Dema (Pickett) S.; B.A., Bob Jones U., Greenville, S.C., 1956; M.Div., Southwestern Bapt. Theol. Sem., Ft. Worth, 1963; Ph.D., Calif. Grad. Sch. Theology, Glendale, 1975; m. Judy Hellen Sivulka, Aug. 18, 1956; children—Christine Annette, Ellen Michelle. Ordained to ministry, 1956; pastor chs. in Ill. and Tex., 1957-63; pastor Trinity Bapt. Ch., Westminster, Calif., 1963—, Bethany Bible Fellowship, Westminster, 1975—; mem. Los Angeles com. Africa Inland Mission, chmn., 1983-85. Mem. Nat. Assn. Evangelicals (v.p. Orange County 1975—, pres. 1979-81), Am. Bd. Hindustan Bible Inst. (pres. 1983-84). Home: 10082 Banbury Ave Westminster CA 92683 Office: 15751 Brookhurst St Suite 208 Westminster CA 92683

SHOOP, PAUL EDWARD, minister, Lutheran Church in America; b. Buffalo, Nov. 16, 1952; s. John Robert and Mary Ellen (Barth) S.; m. Joan Lee Kaufman, Aug. 17, 1974; children: Joel Stephen, Jeremy Paul. B.A., Thiel Coll., 1974; M.Div., Luth. Theol. Sem. at Phila., 1978. Ordained to ministry Luth. Ch. in Am., 1978. Pastor, St. John's Luth. Ch., Victor, N.Y., 1978—; mem. Upper N.Y. Synod Mission Devel. Team, 1978—, chmn., 1980-83; mem. dist. cabinet Genesee Valley Dist., Upper N.Y. Synod, Luth. Ch. Am., 1979-83, sec. dist., 1983—; founding mem. Genesee Valley Luth. Consortium, Rochester, 1982—. Mem. Spl. Com. on Aging, Victor, 1983. Home: 31 Hillcrest Dr Victor NY 14564 Office: St John's Luth Ch 888 Victor Egypt Rd Victor NY 14564

SHORROCK, FRANCES FLORENCE, minister, Christian Church (Disciples of Christ); b. Seattle, July 30, 1930; d. Hallam Carey Sr. and Alice Emily (Maxfield) S. B.A., U. Wash., 1954; M.A., Pacific Sch. Religion, 1956. Ordained to ministry Disciples of Christ Ch., 1962. Minister of edn. Univ. Christian Ch., San Diego, 1956-62; assoc. pastor 1st Christian Ch., Orange, Calif., 1962-66, 69-76, Central Christian Ch., Phoenix, 1966-69, 1st Christian Ch., Corvalis, Oreg., 1976-79; pastor 1st Christian Ch., Stockton, Calif., 1979—; del. UN seminar Christian Ch., 1962, 70; co-chmn. Regional Assembly No. Calif., 1984-85; mem. regional bd. dirs. No. Calif. Christian Chs., 1984—; vice-moderator No. Calif. Region, 1985—; clergy mem. St. Joseph's Hosp. staff, 1980—. Author pamphlet; contbr. articles to profl. jours. Organizer, mem. Corvallis Pastoral Counseling Ctr., 1978; mem. Friends of Library, Orange and Stockton, 1983—, Peninsula Chorale, Los Angeles, 1967, Commn. on Aging in Oreg., Corvallis, 1978. Mem. Western Assn. for Theol. Discussion, San Joaquin Peace Com., Western Assn. Theologians (pres. Western Region 1984-85), Disciples Peace Orgn. Democrat. Office: 1st Christian Ch 405 E Lindsay Stockton CA 95202

SHORROSH, ANIS AUGUSTINE, evangelist, Southern Baptist Convention; b. Nazareth, Palestine, Jan. 6, 1933; s. Augustine Assad and Olga Saleem (Khbais) S.; came to U.S., 1953, naturalized, 1972; diploma Clark Jr. Meml. Coll. 1955; B.A., Miss. Coll., 1956; M.Div., New Orleans Bapt. Theol. Sem., 1959; D.Min., Luther Rice Bapt. and Internat. Sem., 1978; m. Nellie Pearl Martz, Aug. 31, 1957; children—Salam, Paul, Steven, Victoria. Ordained to ministry, 1959; pastor, evangelist, Jordan, 1959-63; pastor Jerusalem (Jordan) Bapt. Ch., 1964-66; world evangelist, 1966—. Author: The Glory of Christ in the Church, 1965; An Ambassador for Jesus, 1969; The Ultimate Reality, 1971; The Fig Tree, 1974; The Liberated Palestinian, 1975; Jesus, Prophecy, and the Middle East, 1979; Where Jesus Walked, 1979; The Ark of the Covenant, 1984. Home: Daphne AL 36526 Office: PO Box 577 Spanish Fort AL 36527

SHORT, HEDLEY VICARS ROYCRAFT, bishop, Anglican Church Canada; b. Toronto, Jan. 24, 1914; s. Hedley Vicars and Martha Hallam (Parke) S.; B.A., U. Toronto, 1941; L.Th., Trinity Coll., Toronto, 1943, B.D., 1945, D.D., 1964; m. Elizabeth Frances Louise Shirley, Apr. 14, 1953; children—Martha, Elizabeth, Janet, Margaret, Desmond. Ordained deacon, 1943, priest, 1944, consecrated bishop, 1970; asst. curate, Toronto, 1943-46; jr. chaplain, Coventry, Eng., 1946-47; lectr., sr. tutor, dean of residence Trinity Coll., Toronto, 1947-51; rector, Cochrane, Ont., 1951-56, St. Catharines, Ont., 1956-63; canon Diocese of Niagara, 1963-70; dean, rector St. Alban's Cathedral, Prince Albert, Sask., 1963-70; archdeacon, Prince Albert, 1966-70; bishop of Sask., 1970—. Chmn. high sch. bd., Cochrane, Ont., 1953-56, Prince Albert, 1970. Chmn. bd. dirs. Prince Albert Community Coll.; pres. council Coll. Emmanual and St. Chard; chancellor U. of Emmanuel Coll., Saskatoon, 1975. Office: PO Box 1088 Prince Albert SK Canada

SHOTWELL, JOHN RALPH, minister, American Baptist Churches U.S.A.; b. Brookneal, Va., Sept. 30, 1926; s. John Henry and Ada Mildred (Puckett) S.;

B.A., U. Richmond, 1946; B.D. (M.Div.), Colgate Rochester Div. Sch., 1949; m. Virginia Lambeth, June 22, 1947; children—Donna Lynn, Jo Ann. Ordained to ministry, 1949; pastor Union Av. Bapt. Ch., Paterson, N.J., 1949-52; dir. religious activities, asst. prof. religious edn. U. Richmond, 1952-56; sr. pastor Greece Bapt. Ch., Rochester, N.Y., 1956-65; pastor sr. minister Central Bapt. Ch., Hartford, Conn., 1965-75; sr. pastor Flossmoor (Ill.) Community Ch., 1975—. Guest lectr. Colgate Rochester Div. Sch. and Hartford Sem.; founder Center City Chs. of Hartford, 1966; pres. Greater Hartford Council Chs., 1971; dir. Paterson, Rochester, Hartford councils of chs. Founder, Greater Paterson Interfaith Youth Council, 1950, Greater Paterson Anti-Crime Commn., 1951; pres. Family Service, Rochester, 1962-64. Bd. dirs. Paterson chpt. ARC, Vols. of Am., Vocat. Guidance, Hartford Community Renewal Team, Planned Parenthood, Family Service; trustee Hartford Sem. Found. Mem. Sigma Alpha Epsilon, Omicron Delta Kappa, Tau Kappa Alpha, Pi Delta Epsilon. Contbr. articles to profl. publs. Office: Carroll Pkwy and Hutchison Rd Flossmoor IL 60422

SHOUSE, KENNETH LEE, minister, Independent Christian Church; b. Louisville, Mar. 5, 1934; s. Earldon Lee and Ruth (Morris) S.; A.B., Ky. Christian Coll., 1958; m. Verlie Evelyn Maddox, June 5, 1953; children—Bruce, Blake. Ordained to ministry, 1958; minister Ninevah Christian Ch., Lawrenceburg, Ky., 1955-60, Antioch Christian Ch., Mt. Sterling, Ky., 1960-68, Shelby Christian Ch., Shelbyville, Ky., 1968—; dean Calvary Assembly, 1976; chmn. Statewide Ky. Minister's Retreat, 1976-77; chmn. Salt River Christian Men's Fellowship Com. of Evangelism for New Locations, 1976. Chmn. fund drive ARC, Shelby County, Ky., 1971. Recipient Honor award Soil Conservation Dist., 1967, Christian Hour TV award, 1968, award Nat. Red Cross, 1971. Mem. Ky. Christian Minister's Assn., Ky. Christian Coll. Alumni Assn. Home: Rt 5 Shelbyville KY 40065 Office: Box 13 Shelbyville KY 40065

SHOWALTER, MONTE DEAN, minister, United Pentecostal Church International. B. Omaha, Aug. 12, 1951; s. Henry Martin and Thelma May (Myers) S.; m. Kathy Dianne Freeman, July 15, 1972; children: Layna Lachelle, Monte Matthew, Keirstin Deanne. Grad. diploma Gateway Coll. Evangelism, 1972. Ordained to ministry, United Pentecostal Ch. Internat., 1980. Evangelist Pentecostal Students Fellowship Internat., Hazelwood, Mo., 1972-74; evangelist United Pentecostal Ch. Internat., Hazelwood, 1974-75, 77-78; asst. to pastor, youth pastor First pentecostal ch., Odessa, Tex., 1976; dir. Carpenter's Shop Youth Ministry, Odessa, 1976; pastor New Life Christian Ctr., Marshfield, Wis., 1978-84; evangelist United Pentecostal Ch. Internat., home and overseas, 1984—; leadership Servants of the Word, Prayer Group, Marshfield, 1979-81; dir. Ark Youth Outreach Ministry, Marshfield, 1979-81; Northeast region Youth Leader Wis. Youth Ministries, 1980-83. Contbr. articles to profl. jours. Bd. dirs. We Care, Marshfield, 1982-84. Mem. Marshfield Ministerial Assn. Home: 5745 Clinto Blvd Jackson MS 39209

SHOWERS, RUTH IRETA, minister, Churches of God General Conference; retired educator, school counselor; b. Sumner, Mich., July 24, 1913; d. George Eugene and Florence Josephine (Gager) Manning; m. Lawrence Showers, June 24, 1934; children: George, James. B.S., Central Mich. U., 1958, M.A., 1967. Ordained to ministry Chs. of God Gen. Conf., 1959. Mich. Conf. camp registrar, 1954—; sec. commn. on edn. Mich. Conf. Chs. of God, 1974—, Mich. Conf. sec., 1974-84; sec., spiritual life chmn. Gen. Conf. Women's Christian Service Council, 1964-83, state pres., v.p., 1968—, treas., 1974—; parliamentarian Mich. Conf. Chs. of God, 1974—; trustee Findlay Coll., Ohio, 1983—. Contbr. articles to profl. jours. Sec. Vestaburg Women's Club, Mich., 1970-73; active Federated Women's Club, Vestaburg, 1959—; leader Gratiot County 4H Clubs, 1948-55. Recipient Merit Mother of Yr. award Am. Mothers, Inc., Mich., 1968. Mem. Am. Assn. Ret. Persons, Mich. Assn. Ret. Sch. Personnel. Home: Vestaburg MI

SHRIVER, DONALD WOODS, JR., theology educator, clergyman, Presbyterian Church; b. Norfolk, Va., Dec. 20, 1927; s. Donald Woods and Gladys (Roberts) S.; m. Peggy Ann Leu, Aug. 9, 1953; children: Gregory Bruce, Margaret Ann, Timothy Donald. B.A., Davidson Coll., 1951; B.D., Union Theol. Sem. Va., 1955; S.T.M., Yale U., 1957; Ph.D., Harvard U., 1973; LL.D. (hon.), Central Coll., 1970; D.D. (hon.), Wagner Col., 1978, Southwestern Coll., 1983. Ordained to ministry Presbyterian Ch., 1955. Pastor Linwood Presbyn. Ch., Gastonia, N.C., 1956-59; univ. minister, prof. religion N.C. State U., Raleigh, 1963-72, dir. univ. program on sci. and soc., 1968-72; prof. ethics and soc. Emory U., Atlanta, 1972-75; pres. faculty, William E. Dodge prof. applied Christianity, Union Theol. Sem., N.Y.C., 1975—; lectr. Duke U., Va. State U., GA. State U., numerous colls., univs. in Can., Kenya, India, Japan, Korea. Author: How Do You Do and Why: An Introduction of Christian Ethics for Young People, 1966; Rich Man Poor Man; Christian Ethics for Modern Man Series, 1972; (with Dean D. Knudsen and John R. Earle) Spindles and Spires: A Restudy of Religion and Social Change in Gastonia, 1976; (with Karl A. Ostrom) Is There Hope for the City?, 1977; The Social Ethics of the Lord's Prayer, 1980; The Gospel, The Church, and Social Change, 1980; The Lord's Prayer: A Way of Life, 1983; co-author: Redeeming the City, 1982. Editor: The Unsilent South, 1965; Medicine and Religion: Strategies of Care, 1979. Dir. urban policy study N.C. State U., 1971-73; mem. Mayor's Com. on Human Relations, Raleigh, 1967-71; chmn. Urban Policy Seminar, Ctr. for Theology and Pub. Policy, 1978-82; Raleigh Democratic precinct chmn.; del. Nat. Dem. Conv., 1968. Served with Signal Corps, U.S. Army, 1946-47. Kent fellow in religion, 1959; Rockefeller doctoral fellow Harvard U. Mem. Am. Soc. Christian Ethics (pres. 1979-80), Soc. for Values in Higher Edn., Soc. for Health and Human Values, Soc. for Sci. Study Religion, AAAS, Am. Sociol. Assn., Am. Soc. Engring. Edn. (chmn. liberal arts div. 1972-73), United Christian Youth Movement of Nat. Council of Chs. (nat. chmn. 1951-53). Office: Union Theol Sem 3041 Broadway New York NY 10027

SHRIVER, PEGGY ANN LEU, lay administrator, Presbyterian Church USA; b. Muscatine, Iowa, July 23, 1931; d. George Chester and Zelda Marguerita (Wunder) Leu; m. Donald Woods Shriver, Aug. 9, 1953; children: Gregory, Margaret Ann, Timothy. B.A., Central Coll., 1953, H.H.D. (hon.), 1979. Staff exec. office of rev. and evaluation Gen. Assembly Presbyn. Ch. U.S.A., Atlanta, 1973-75; asst. gen. sec. office of research evaluation and planning, Nat. Council Chs. of Christ, U.S.A., N.Y.C., 1976—, del. to World Council Chs. Faith, Sci. and Future Consultation, 1979; nat. sec. United Christian Youth Movement, 1951-53; mem. interreligious delegation to Romania, Appeal to Conscience Found., 1980; bd. dirs. Christianity and Crisis mag., 1977—, Ctr. for Theology and Pub. Policy, Washington, 1978—. Author: The Bible Vote: Religion and the New Right, 1981. Contbr. articles to profl. jours. Organizer, bd. chmn. New Bern Ave. Day Care Ctr., 1968-72; state pres. N.C. Consumers Council, 1969-72; bd. dirs. So. Regional Council, Atlanta, 1974-75, League of Women Voters, Raleigh, 1963-72, Wake Opportunities, 1966-68. Mem. Religious Research Assn., Nat. Assn. Ecumenical Staff. Democrat. Home: 606 W 122nd St 4E New York NY 10027 Office: Nat Council of Chs of Christ USA 475 Riverside Dr New York NY 10115

SHUBSDA, THADDEUS A. See *Who's Who in America*, 43rd edition.

SHUGRUE, TIMOTHY JOSEPH, priest, Roman Catholic Church; b. Elizabeth, N.J., Feb. 4, 1948; s. Timothy Daniel and Rita Catherine (Murphy) S. B.A. in Classical Langs., Seton Hall U., 1969; M.A. in Systematic Theol., Immaculate Conception Sem., 1976. Ordained priest Roman Cath. Ch., 1973. Assoc. pastor St. Aedan's Ch., Jersey City, 1973-78; chaplain Essex Cath. Boys High Sch., East Orange, N.J., 1978-84; dir. Permanent Diaconate, Archdiocese of Newark, 1979—; chaplain N.J. Boystown, Kearny, 1984—; pres. Senate of Priests, Archdiocese of Newark, 1982-84; coordinator Office of Pro-Life Activities, Archdiocese of Newark, 1976-82. Author-editor booklet Revised Diocesan Diaconate Formation Guidelines, Renewing the Vision, 1982. Mem. Nat. Assn. of Permanent Diaconate Dirs. (pres. 1984-85). Office: Office of Personnel in Ministry 97 Ridge St Newark NJ 07104

SHULTZ, JOSEPH RANDOLPH See *Who's Who in America*, 43rd edition.

SHUSTER, CARROLL LLOYD, minister, Presbyterian Church (U.S.A.); b. Eureka, Calif., Jan. 16, 1917; s. William Colwell and Serena (Nilson) S.; B.A. cum laude, Pasadena Coll., 1938; S.T.B., Harvard, 1942; D.D., Occidental Coll., 1953; m. Grace Margaret Hornbeck, Jan. 14, 1939; children: Marguerite, Lorraine. Ordained to ministry, 1940; pastor First Presbyn. Ch., Santa Paula, Calif., 1946-50; chief exec. So. area Synod of Calif., Presbyn. Ch. (U.S.A.), Los Angeles, 1952-69; chief exec. officer Synod of Fla., Lauderdale by the Sea, 1970-73; pastor First Presbyn. Ch., Coral Gables, Fla., 1973—; v.p. Greater Miami Fellowship of Chs., 1976-77; bd. dirs. Christian Community Service Agency, Miami, 1971—, v.p., 1977; bd. dirs. Wasatch Acad., Utah, 1974-77. Mem. com. on Rumford Act, State of Calif., 1967; mem. spl. com. Los Angeles Sch. Bd., 1968. Named Ecumenical Churchman of Year, Ch. Fedn. Los Angeles, 1964; recipient spl. citations for work with minorities Los Angeles City Council 1967, Los Angeles County Bd. Suprs., 1969. Home: 17221 SW 86th Ave Miami FL 33157 Office: 121 Alhambra Plaza Coral Gables FL 33134

SHYNE, JOHN ALBERT, SR., minister, non-denominational; b. Athens, La., Apr. 1, 1925; s. Albert and Mary Jessie (Ferrell) Shine; children: Lizzie, John, Isaac, Essie, Jessie, Lillie, Lenord, Thelma. Ordained to minister Berean Grace Ch., 1957. Supt. West Side Grace Mission, Muskegon Heights, Mich., 1949-53, youth minister, 1953-56; pastor, founder Berean Grace Ch., Muskegon Heights, 1956-84; state chaplain NAACP, Mich., 1983—; bd. mem. Grace Bible Coll., Grand Rapids, Mich., 1962—. Chmn. Dist. Council, Muskegon Heights, 1973. Democrat. Lodge: King David Prince Hall Grand.

SIBLEY, WALLACE JEROME, minister, church official, Pentecostal Church of God; b. St. Mary's, Ga., June 30, 1938; s. Peter James and Ernestine (Campbell) S.; m. Dorothy Mae Herring, Aug. 23, 1964; children: Wallace, Jr., Kevin E., Anita A. B.S., Edward Waters Coll., 1969; M.Ed., Fla. A&M U., 1972; Litt.D. (hon.), Ind. Central U., 1980. Pastor Ch. of God, Valdosta, Ga., 1964-68, Ch. of God, Jacksonville, Fla., 1969-71, Ch. of God, St. Marys, 1974-78; state edn. dir. Fla. Chs. of God, Jacksonville, 1971-74, state overseer, Cocoa, 1982—; southeast dir. of evangelism Ch. of God gen. hdqrs., Cleveland, Tenn., 1978-82; dist. youth edn. dir. Ch. of God, St. Marys, 1964-65; dist. overseer, 1974-78; state youth edn. dir. Ga. Chs. of God, St. Marys, 1965-68, state liaison for Black affairs, 1976-78. Contbr. articles to profl. jours., books. Served with USAF, 1956-59. Democrat. Home: 2208 Salem Dr Cocoa FL 32922 Office: Choof God State Hdqrs PO Box 1966 Cocoa FL 32922

SIDER, HARVEY RAY, bishop, Brethren in Christ Church; b. Hagersville, Ont., Can., June 20, 1930; s. Earl Morris and Elsie (Sheffer) S.; m. Erma Jean Heise, July 20, 1957; children: Cheryl, Steven. B.A., Western U., 1956; B.D., Winona Lake Sch. Theology, 1962. Ordained to ministry Brethren in Christ Ch., 1953. Pastor Brethren in Christ Ch., Toronto, Ont., 1957-62; adminstr. Brethren in Christ missions, Bihar, India, 1962-74; pastor, Stayner, Ont., 1974-76; pres. Niagara Christian Coll., Fort Erie, Ont., 1976-78; bishop, Fort Erie, 1978—; del. Mennonite World Fellowship, Strasbourg, France, 1984. Author: The Church in Mission, 1975. Mem. Brethren in Christ Hist. Soc. Office: 2519 Stevensville Rd Stevensville ON L0S 1S0 Canada

SIDORAK, STEPHEN JAMES, JR., clergyman; United Methodist Church; b. Cleve., Dec. 5, 1949; s. Stephen James and Anne (Hirus) S.; m. Alexis Carol Rascati, Dec. 18, 1976; children: Alissa Anne, Stephen Alexander, Kristin Carol. B.A., Baldwin Wallace Coll., 1971; M.Div., Div. Sch., Yale U., 1975, S.T.M., 1976; postgrad. San Francisco Theol. Sem., San Anselmo, Calif., 1982-84. Ordained to ministry United Meth. Ch., 1975, elder Rocky Mountain Conf., 1978; accredited visitor World Council Chs. Sixth Assembly. Intern minister United Meth. Ch. Palm Springs, Ca., 1976-77; assoc. minister First United Meth. Ch., Fort Collins, Colo., 1977-78; pastor Centenary United Meth. Ch., Salt Lake City, 1978-80, First United Meth. Ch., Aurora, Colo., 1980-82; exec. dir. Colo. Council Chs., Denver, 1982—; speaker on Christian ethics and nuclear arms race. Charter mem. nat. com. Nuclear Weapons Freeze Campaign, St. Louis, 1981; co-convenor No Casino Gambling, Inc., Denver, 1982; co-host An Evening For Peace, Denver, 1982; mem. adv. bd. Colo. chpt. World Federalist Assn., UN Assn. Mem. Nat. Assn. Ecumenical Staff, Colo. Yale Assn. Office: Colo Council Chs 5209 Montview Blvd Denver CO 80207

SIEBENMORGEN, PAUL, lay church worker, Christian Church (Disciples of Christ); b. Terre Haute, Ind., Sept. 16, 1920; s. Louis and Ruby E. (Curtis) S.; B.S. in Edn., Ind. State U., 1941; M.D., Ind. U., 1944; m. Jane Maxine Waggoner, June 20, 1948; children: Paul Stephen, Elizabeth Ann (Mrs. Thomas K. Brentlinger), Susan Lynn (Mrs. Kenneth A. Amos). Deacon, Central Christian Ch., Terre Haute, 1947, elder, 1948—, trustee, 1966—, chmn. bd., 1957-59; mem. bd. Ind. Region Christian Ch. (Disciples of Christ), 1966-76, pres.-elect, 1972-74, moderator, 1974-76, mem. program audit com., 1981-84, chmn., 1983; del. Internat. Conv. and Gen. Assembly, 1966-69, 71, 73, 75, 77, 79, 81; mem. gen. bd. Christian Ch. U.S.A. and Can., 1969-75, 77-80; mem. exec. com. Conf. Regional Ministers and Bd. Chmn., 1974-76. Pvt. practice medicine, Terre Haute, 1947—; pres. med. and dental staff Terre Haute Regional Hosp., 1974-75, trustee hosp., 1975-81; assoc. clin. faculty Ind. U. Sch. Medicine, 1975—. Pres. Vigo County Bd. Health, 1967-68, 71-75, 80-81, v.p., 1976-79; trustee Ind. State U., 1975-83. Recipient Sustained Outstanding Service award Scottish Rite Valley of Terre Haute, 1972, Meritorious Service award Ind. State U. Alumni Assn., 1972. Fellow Am. Acad. Family Physicians; mem. AMA, Ind. State Med. Assn. (chmn. bd. trustees 1981-84, pres.-elect 1984), Vigo County Med. Soc. (pres. 1970), Ind. Acad. Family Physicians (dir. 1973—, dist. pres. 1961, 71, pres. 1981), Aesculapian Soc. Wabash Valley, Vigo County Comprehensive Health Planning Council (sec.), So. Ind. Health Systems Agy. (bd. 1975-78), Ind. Statewide Health Coordinating Council (exec. com. 1982-84), Vigo County Heart Assn. (pres. 1965-66), Terre Haute C. of C., Blue Key, Sigma Alpha Epsilon, Alpha Phi Omega, Kappa Delta Pi, Phi Rho Sigma. Home: 2515 N 7th St Terre Haute IN 47804 Office: 501 Hospital Ln Terre Haute IN 47802

SIEGEL, MORTON, religious organization administrator, educational administrator; b. N.Y.C., Dec. 5, 1924; s. Samuel William and Esther (Sackin) S.; B.A. summa cum laude, Yeshiva U., 1945; M.A. in Philosophy and History, Columbia U., 1946, Ph.D., 1952; m. Pearl Fox, June 28, 1949; children: Deborah

(Mrs. Howard Eisenstadt), Daniel, Deenah (Mrs. Mark Speiser). Ednl. dir. Laurelton Jewish Center, Queens, N.Y., 1945-49; ednl. dir., dir. educator placement United Synagogue Am., N.Y.C., 1949-51, dir. youth activities, 1953-64, exec. dir., 1970-75, ednl. dir., 1964—; adj. asst. prof. Sch. Edn., NYU, 1971—. Bd. dirs. Educators Assembly. Mem. Nat. Council Jewish Edn. Contbr. numerous articles on pedagogy to profl. publs. Home: 43 Cross Bow Ln Commack NY 11725 Office: 155 Fifth Ave New York NY 10010

SIEGEL, SEYMOUR See *Who's Who in America,* 43rd edition.

SIEGENTHALER, CARL EDWARD, minister, church agency executive, lecturer, Presbyterian Church U.S.A.; b. Buffalo, Dec. 11, 1923; s. Gottlieb and Agatha (LeBlanc) S.; m. Eva Louise Beck, Dec. 26, 1950; children: Kathryn, Margaret, David, Susan, Theresa, Heidi. A.B., Franklin-Marshall Coll., 1944; B.D., Yale U., 1946; M.S.W., Washington U.-St. Louis, 1957. Ordained to ministry Evangel. and Ref. Ch., 1948. Pastor, supt. Caroline Mission, St. Louis, 1948-59; assoc. dir. Dept. Social Work So. Area, Synod of Calif., 1959-64; dir. of project devel. Nat. Urban Tng. Ctr. Christian Mission, Chgo., 1964-74; faculty Austin Presbyn. Sem., Tex., 1974—; dir. Metro-Ministries of Austin, 1974—; co-chmn. Austin Interfaith Com., 1983—; mem. exec. com. Austin Confs. of Chs., 1982—; bd. dirs. Texas IMPACT, 1977—; div. mem. Soc., Tex. Conf. of Chs., 1979—. Contbr. articles to profl. jours. Treas. Capital Area Food Bank, Austin, 1981—; chmn. Austin Tomorrow Ongoing Commn., Austin, 1984—; vice chmn. Community Edn. Consortium, Austin, 1980—. Fellow Case Study Inst.; mem. Presbyn. Health Welfare Assn., Tex. Econ. Demographic Assn., Witherspoon Soc., Nat. Assn. Social Workers (cert.; Social Worker of Yr. Austin Chpt. 1983). Home: 1905 Greenbrook Pwky Austin TX 78723 Office: Metro-Ministries of Austin 100 E 27th St Austin TX 78705

SIEGMAN, HENRY, rabbi, administrator, Orthodox Jewish Congregation; b. Germany, Dec. 12, 1930; came to U.S., 1942, naturalized, 1948; s. Mendel and Sara (Scharf) S.; m. Selma Goldberger, Nov. 8, 1953; children: Bonnie, Debra, Alan. Rabbi, Torah Vodaath Sem., N.Y.C., 1951; B.A., New Sch. Social Research, 1961, postgrad., 1961-64. Nat. dir. community activities div. Union Orthodox Jewish Congregations Am., 1953-59; exec. sec. Am. Assn. Middle East Studies, 1959-64; dir. internat. affairs Nat. Community Relations Adv. Council, N.Y.C., 1964-65; exec. v.p. Synagogue Council Am., N.Y.C., 1965-78; exec. dir. Am. Jewish Congress, N.Y.C., 1978—; guest lectr. U. Ill., Columbia, Williams Coll.; nat. vice chmn. Religion in Am. Life, 1966—; exec. com. Interreligious Com. on Peace, 1966—; chmn. Interreligious Com. Gen. Secs. (Nat. Council Chs.-U.S. Cath. Conf.-Synagogue Council Am.), 1973; served to 1st lt., chaplain U.S. Army, 1952-54. An organizer White House Conf. Civil Rights, 1967. Editor: Middle East Studies, 1959-64; contbr. articles to profl. jours. Bd. dirs. Nat. Com. Against Discrimination in Housing, 1966—; sterring com., exec. com. Nat. Urban Coalition. Decorated Bronze Star; designated Disting. American, Pres. U.S., 1970. Mem. AAUP, Nat. Conf. Jewish Communal Service, Assn. Jewish Community Relations Workers.

SIEMENS, STEPHEN KENNETH, college president, minister; Church of Christ; b. Fort Dodge, Iowa, Apr. 21, 1952; s. Kenneth Marinus and Harriett Lucille (Ruberg) S.; m. Barbara Jean Price, Dec. 22, 1972; children: Staci Jean, Leisl Suzanne, Christopher Stephen. B.A. in Christian Edn., Ozark Bible Coll., 1974, A.A. in Music, 1974; postgrad. Drake U. Minister, First Christian Ch., Grove, Okla., 1971-75; part time instr. Ozark Bible Coll., Joplin, Mo., 1973-75; prof. Platte Valley Bible Coll., Scottsbluff, Nebr., 1975-77; prof. Iowa Christian Coll., Des Moines, 1977-82, pres., 1982—; pres. Iowa Sunday Sch. Assn., Des Moines, 1983—; bd. dirs. 1980-83; bd. dirs. Rising Sun Ch. of Christ, Des Moines, 1979-82, chmn., 1982—. Author: What the Bible Says About Positive Living, 1984. Contbr. articles to profl. jours. Recipient Disting. Service award Iowa Christian Coll., 1984; named Outstanding Young Man in Am., Iowa Christian Coll., 1982. Mem. Evang. Ministers Assn. Republican. Lodge: Kiwanis (Scottsbluff, Nebr. exec. com. 1975-77). Home: 6478 NE 5th Ave Runnells IA 50237 Office: Iowa Christian Coll and Equipping Ctr 2847 Indianola Rd Des Moines IA 50315

SIGHTLER, HAROLD BENNETT, minister, Independent Baptist; b. St. George, S.C., May 15, 1914; s. Horace C. and Pauline (Bennett) S.; m. Helene Grace Vaugh, Dec. 11, 1935; children: James Harold, Elizabeth Ann Carper. B.A., Furman U., 1946; D.D., Tenn. Tenple U., 1960; LLT.D., Emmanuel Coll., 1971. Ordained to ministry Bapt. Ch., 1942. Pastor 1st Bapt. Ch., Mauldin, S.C., 1943-48, 1st Bapt. Ch., Pelham, S.C., 1943-52, Tabernacle Bapt. Ch., Greenville, S.C., 1952—. Mem. bd. Bapt. Internat. Missions, Chattanooga, 1954—; pres. Tabernacle Bapt. Coll., Greenville, 1963—. Author books including: Revelation Commentary, 1983, Romans Commentary, 1984, Hebrews and James Commentary, 1984. Office: Tabernacle Bapt Bible Coll 3931 White Horse Rd Greenville SC 29611

SIGLER, RICHARD EYSTER, minister, Presbyterian Church (U.S.A.); b. Harrisburg, Pa., Sept. 24, 1926; s. Howard Forney and Alice Bowman (Myers) S.; A.B., Lafayette Coll., 1949; M.Div., Pitts. Theol. Sem., 1952; postgrad. Gettysburg Theol. Sem., 1953-56; D.Min., McCormick Theol. Sem., 1981; m. Judith Kirkpatrick, June 27, 1953; children—Judith Louise, Alice Myers, Sarah Kirkpatrick. Ordained to ministry, 1952; pastor Centre Presbyn. Ch., Loysville, Pa., 1952-58; dir. admissions and registrar Western Theol. Sem., Pitts., 1958-60, dir. devel., 1960-63; pastor Trinity Presbyn. Ch., Pitts., 1963-67; minister evangelism Wayne (Pa.) Presbyn. Ch., 1967-70; pastor Presbyn. Ch. of Falling Spring, Chambersburg, Pa., 1970-76; exec. presbyter Presbytery of Kiskiminetas, 1976—; mem. council Synod of Trinity, 1976—; v.p. alumni council Pitts. Theol. Sem., 1984—; Radio broadcaster WHP, Harrisburg, Pa., 1952-57, WCHA, Chambersburg, Pa., 1970-76. Active United Way of Chambersburg, Pa., 1976—; chmn. citizens adv. com. Franklin County Child Care Agy., 1971-76; bd. dirs. Children's Aid Soc., Franklin County, 1972-76. Mem. Presbytery of Kiskiminetas, Carlisle Presbytery Cleric. Contbr. articles in field to religious jours. Home: 2674 Elaine Dr Lower Burrell PA 15068 Office: Presbyterian Center 150 Arch St Kittanning PA 16201

SIGMAN, WALTER AUGUSTUS, minister, Lutheran Ch. Am.; b. Newton, N.C., Oct. 3, 1905; s. William Vernon and Lula Mertie S.; A.B., Lenoir Rhyne Coll., 1928; B.D., Luth. Theol. Sem., Columbia, S.C., 1931, postgrad., 1955-56; m. Emma Lee Cathey, May 24, 1931; children—Mertie Lee, Walter Augustus, Vernon Reeves, Stephen Douglas. Ordained to ministry, 1931; pastor rural and suburban chs., N.C., S.C., Va., 1931-72, including Bethlehem Ch., Waynesboro, Va., 1965-68, Orkney Springs (Va.) Luth. Parish, 1968-72; ret., 1972; chaplain U.S. Army, 1942-46. Active Boy Scouts Am., 1940-69; committeeman, instl. rep., treas. S.C. chpt. Am. Assn. Ret. Persons. Mem. Waynesboro (Va.), Clinton (S.C.), Shenandoah County (Va.) ministerial assns. Home: Route 2 PO Box 127 Clinton SC 29325

SILAS (KOSKINAS SILAS), bishop, Greek Orthodox Church; b. Corfu, Greece, Dec. 27, 1919; came to U.S., 1946. Grad. U. Athens Theol. Sch., 1943; M.S.T., Boston U., 1957. Ordained deacon Greek Orthodox Ch., 1941, ordained priest, 1943. Pastor, Albuquerque, 1946, parishes in New London, Conn., Boston, Pitts.; dean St. Nicholas Cathedral, Pitts.; elevated to bishop, 1960, bishop of 8th archdiocesan dist., New Orleans, 1960-65, 1st archdiocesan dist., N.Y.C., 1965—; bishop new diocese N.J., 1979, mem. spl. del. to Rumania, 1970; vice pres. Religion in Am. Life, 1972—; mem. Archdiocesan Council of Greek Orthodox Archdiocese, 1972—; chmn. Office of Fgn. Missions, Greek Orthodox Ch. Contbr. articles on Greek Orthodox faith to religious publs. Mem. bd. Appeal of Conscience Found. Recipient Gold Medallion award NCCJ. Address: 8 E 79th St New York NY 10021*

SILL, STERLING WELLING, church official, Church of Jesus Christ of Latter-day Saints; b. Layton, Utah, Mar. 31, 1903; s. Joseph A. and Marietta (Welling) S.; student Utah State U., 1921-22; student U. Utah, 1926-27, LL.D., 1953; m. Doris Mary Thornley, Sept. 4, 1929; children: John Michael, David S., Carolyn (Mrs. Donald Knepper). Sunday sch. tchr. Ch. of Jesus Christ of Latter-day Saints, 1918-21; preaching missionary So. States, 1924-26; Sunday Sch. supt., 1926-31; mem. North Davis Stake High Council, 1931-33; leader young peoples orgn. Yale Ward, 1935-36; bishop Garden Park Ward, Salt Lake City, 1936-46; mem. Bonneville Stake High Council, Salt Lake City, 1946-51; mem. Latter-day Saints Ch. Sunday Sch. Gen. Bd., 1951-54; asst. to Quorum of Twelve Apostles of Latter-day Saints Ch., Salt Lake City, 1954-76; First Quorum of Seventy, 1976—. Insp. agys. N.Y. Life Ins. Co., 1940-68. Scoutmaster, Ogden Gateway council Boy Scouts Am., 1922-23, 26-31. Mem. City Council, Layton, 1928-32. Chmn. bd. regents U. Utah, 1947-51. Recipient Carnegie Hero medal, 1959, Distinguished Service award in arts and humanities Ricks Coll., Rexburg, Idaho, 1974. Mem. Am. Coll. Life Underwriters. Author: Leadership 1, 1958; Leadership II, 1960; Leadership III, 1978; The Glory of the Sun, 1961; The Upward Reach, 1962; The Law of the Harvest, 1963; The Way of Success, 1964; What Doth It Profit, 1965; The Miracle of Personality, 1966; The Quest for Excellence, 1967; The Power of Believing, 1968; The Three Infinities, 1969; The Strength of Great Possessions, 1970; Making the Most of Yourself, 1971; The Keys of the Kingdom, 1972; Principles, Promises and Powers, 1973; Christmas Sermons, 1973; The Majesty of Books, 1974; That Ye Might Have Life, 1974; The Laws of Success, 1975; Thy Kingdom Come, 1975; This Nation Under God, 1976; The Wealth of Wisdom, 1977; The International Journal of Success, 1974; This We Believe, 1980; Lessons from Great Lives, 1981; Meditations on Death and Life, 1982; The Power of Poetry, 1983, others. Speaker, Sta. KSL program Sunday Evening on Temple Square, 1960-77. Home: 1264 Yale Ave Salt Lake City UT 84105 Office: 50 E North Temple St Salt Lake City UT 84150

SILLS, HORACE STEVENSON, minister, church official, United Church of Christ; b. Gaston County, N.C., Nov. 16, 1922; s. John Hartsell and Martha Rosella (Perry) S.; student Catawba Coll., 1950, D.D., 1976; B.P.S., Elizabethtown Coll., 1973; M.Div., Lancaster Theol. Sem., 1953; m. Anne Louise Cloninger, Oct. 13, 1940; children—Rebecca (Mrs. John F. Harrison), Horace Stevenson, Robert A., Timothy P. Ordained to ministry, 1953; pastor, Lexington, N.C., 1953-59, Orlando, Fla., 1959-61; field sec. United Ch. Bd. for Homeland Ministries, Lancaster, Pa., 1961-68; pres. Pa. W. Conf., Greensburg, 1968-71, Pa. Central Conf., 1973—; v.p. Lancaster Theol. Sem., 1971-73. Pres., Pa. Council Chs., 1971—; mem. Commn. Religion in Appalachia. Mem. bd. ethics State of Pa., 1974—. Bd. dirs. Lancaster Theol. Sem. Author: Grassroots Ecumenicity, 1967; also articles and booklets. Office: 900 S Arlington Ave Harrisburg PA 17109

SILVER, DAN WILLIAM, minister, Southern Baptist Convention; b. Avondale, N.C., June 25, 1927; s. George Alfred and Mary Alice Elizbeth (Mashburn) S.; A.A., Gardner-Webb Coll., 1952; student Wake Forest Coll., 1955-56; B.S., Atlantic Christian Coll., 1959; B.D., Southeastern Bapt. Sem., 1961; m. Colleen V. Lane, June 1, 1946; children: Patricia Elizabeth Silver Melton, Michael Dan. Ordained to ministry, 1956; pastor Shady Grove Bapt. Ch., Cherryville, N.C., 1976—. Mem. faculty Bapt. Assembly, 1965-67; pres. Assoc. Coll. Com., 1973-77. Mem. Greater Cherryville Ministers Assn., Gaston Bapt. Assn. (moderator 1982-83). Contbr. articles to religious jours. Lodge: Masons (chaplain). Home: Box 186 Cherryville NC 28021 Office: Route 2 Box 462 Cherryville NC 28021

SILVER, DANIEL JEREMY, rabbi, Reform Jewish Congregations; b. Cleve., Mar. 26, 1928; s. Abba Hillel and Virginia (Horkheimer) S.; A.B., Harvard, 1948; M.H.L., Hebrew Union Coll., 1952; Ph.D., U. Chgo., 1962; m. Adele F. Zeidman, July 19, 1956; children—Jonathan Moses, Michael Louis, Sarah Jean. Ordained rabbi, 1952; chaplain USNR, 1952-54; rabbi Beth Torah Congregation, Chgo., 1954-56, The Temple, Cleve., 1956—. Adj. prof. religion Case Western Res. U., 1966—, Cleve. State U., 1970—; pres. Nat. Found. Jewish Culture, 1966-75; pres. Cleve. Bd. Rabbis, 1975—; chmn. Israel task force Cleve. Jewish Fedn., 1966—; chmn. task force on Jewish identity Central Conf. Am. Rabbis, 1974—; chmn. acad. adv. council Nat. Found. Jewish Culture, 1970—; mem. bd. Synagogue Council Am., 1972—. Vice-pres. Cleve. Mus. Art, 1972—. Mem. Synagogue Council Am., Am. Acad. Religion, Assn. Jewish Studies. Author: Maimonidean Criticism and the Maimonidean Controversy (1160-1240), 1965; (with B. Martin) A History of Judaism, 1974; Images of Moses, 1982; editor: Judaism and Ethics, 1970; sr. editor Jour. Central Conf. Am. Rabbis, 1964-72. Home: 2841 Weybridge Rd Cleveland OH 44120 Office: 26000 Shaker Blvd Cleveland OH 44122

SILVER, MARC S., religious organization editor, Jewish; b. Balt., Dec. 26, 1951; s. Donald Leon and Shirley Elginor (Freeman) S.; m. Marsha Dale, June 8, 1980. B.A., U. Md., 1973. Editor, B'nai B'rith Jewish Monthly, Washington, 1981—. Council of Jewish Fedns. Smolar award for excellence in N. Am. Jewish Journalism, 1984. Office: B'nai B'rith Jewish Monthly 1640 Rhode Island Ave NW Washington DC 20036

SILVERMAN, DAVID WOLF, rabbi, Conservative Jewish; b. Chgo., Sept. 22, 1926; s. Samuel Jacob and Esther Chana (Steinberg) S.; m. Sylvia Zion, Dec. 23, 1951; children: Shira Ahuva, Deborah Lea, Eve Hinda, Ethan Elijah. B.A., U. Chgo., 1946, M.A., 1948; M.H.L., Jewish Theol. Sem., N.Y.C., 1952, D.D. (hon.), 1977; M.Phil., Columbia U., 1973, Ph.D., 1974. Rabbi, 1952. Rabbi, Conservative Synagogue, Riverdale, N.Y., 1958-63; prof. Jewish Theol. Sem., N.Y.C., 19639-79; pres. Spertus Coll. of Judaica, Chgo., 1979-81, disting. service prof., 1981-83; rabbi Temple Beth Zion, Phila., 1983—. Translator: Philosophies of Judaism, 1963. Author: (with Deede) Religious Press in America, 1963; Foundations of Judaism, 1974. Mng. editor Judaism: A Quar., 1970-71; editor Conservative Judaism, 1984—. Served to capt. as chaplain U.S. Army, 1952-54. Fellow Acad. for Jewish Philosophy (co-founder 1980); mem. AAUP, Religious Edn. Assn. (pres. 1975-77, chmn. bd. 1977-79). Home: 209 S Bonsall Philadelphia PA 19103

SILVERMAN, IRA, college administrator, Jewish. Pres., Reconstructionist Rabbinical Coll., Wyncote, Pa. Office: Reconstructionist Rabbinical Coll Church Rd and Greenwood Ave Wyncote PA 19095*

SIMBOLI, RONALD LEWIS, priest, Roman Cath. Ch.; b. Charleroi, Pa., Oct. 3, 1944; s. Guido Louis and Irene Elizabeth (DeFazio) S.; student Point Park Coll., Pitts., 1964; diploma Pitts. Inst. Mortuary Sci., 1965; student Pope John XXIII Nat. Sem., Weston, Mass., 1971-75. Ordained priest, 1975; asso. pastor Holy Family Ch., Latrobe, Pa., 1975-76; dir. hosp. ministry Diocese of Greensburg (Pa.), chaplain Westmoreland Hosp. and Westmoreland Manor, Greensburg, 1976—.

Recipient Meml. award Pitts. Inst. Mortuary Sci., 1965; licensed funeral dir., Pa. Mem. Christians of Greater Greensburg, Nat. Assn. Cath. Chaplains, Greensburg Diocese Assn. Priests. Office: Westmoreland Hosp 532 W Pittsburgh St Greensburg PA 15601

SIMCOSKY, PHILIP DEAN, minister, Southern Baptist Convention; b. Independence, Mo., Sept. 29, 1952; s. Roy Allen and Norma Lee (Lowe) S.; m. Julia May Hinton, July 23, 1977; 1 son, Jonathan Hinton. B.S. in Music Edn., William Jewell Coll., 1975; M.Div., Southwestern Bapt. Theol. Sem., 1978. Ordained to ministry Bapt. Ch., 1979. Music minister 1st Bapt. Ch., Grain Valley, Mo., 1971-72; youth minister Waldo Ave. Bapt. Ch., Independence, Mo., 1972-73; music and youth minister Posey Bapt. Ch., Sulphur Springs, Tex., 1975-76; pastor Waverly Bapt. Ch., Mo., 1979-83, Suburban Bapt. Ch., Granite City, Ill., 1983—; chmn. program com. Madison County Bapt. Assn., Granite City, 1983—. Republican. Club: Rotary (sr. citizen com.). Home: 3248 Erin Dr Granite City IL 62040 Office: Suburban Bapt Ch 2500 St Clair Ave Granite City IL 62040

SIMMONS, CHARLES BRYANT, minister, United Methodist Church; b. DeQuincy, La., Sept. 23, 1949; s. Cubic Stuart and Jen (Knight) S.; m. Linda Lee Garrett, Nov. 20, 1970; children: Jeffrey Stuart, Christopher Bryant. B.A., Centenary Coll. of La., 1971; M.Div. magna cum laude, Emory U., 1974; D.Ministry, 1978; postdoctoral, Institut Ecumenique U., Geneva, 1978. Ordained as elder United Meth. Ch., 1975. Assoc. minister Avondale-Patillo United Meth. Ch., Decatur, Ga., 1973-75, Univ. United Meth. Ch., Baton Rouge, 1975-78; dir. ch. relations Centenary Coll., Shreveport, La., 1978-80; minister St. Luke United Meth. Ch., Lake Charles, La., 1980-82, St. Luke Simpson United Meth. Ch., 1982-85; sr. minister Noel United Meth. Ch., Shreveport, 1985—. Founder, Centenary Ch. Council, chmn. 1980-82; sec. faith and order div. La. Interch. Conf., 1982—; del. to La. Interch. Assembly, 1980—; bd. dirs. Meth. Children's Home, Rushton, La., 1984; dean La. Conf. Pastors Sch., 1983—; chmn. La. Ann. Conf. Council on Ministries, 1984—. Contbg. author: World Council Div. Laity, 1973; World Council, Church and Society, 1973. Bd. dirs. Campfire Girls, Baton Rouge, 1976-78, Family Youth Counseling, Lake Charles, 1981-84, New Directions Drug Abuse Program, Calcasieu Parish, La., 1983—. Meth. fellow Global Ministries, United Meth. Ch., 1973. Mem. Christian Educators fellowship Ch. Resource Assocs., Omicron Delta Kappa, Theta Phi. Democrat. Lodge: Rotary (bd. dirs. 1982-84). Avocations: bass fishing; music. Home: 3522 Madison Park Blvd Shreveport LA 71104 Office: Noel United Meth Ch 520 Herdon Shreveport LA 71101

SIMMONS, CHARLES LEE, SR., minister, Southern Baptist Convention; b. Winchester, Va., Nov. 5, 1932; s. Clyde William and Effie Mae (Rotruck) S.; A.A., Anchorage Community Coll., 1974; B.A., U. Alaska, 1976; M.R.E., Southeastern Bapt. Theol. Sem.; m. Janet Virginia Kerns, Mar. 7, 1953; children: Charles Lee, Connie, Bryan, Tracy. Ordained to ministry, 1973; assoc. and interim pastor Sunset Hills Bapt. Ch., Anchorage, 1973-74, Palmer Bapt. Mission, 1974-75, Big Lake Bapt. Mission, Wasilla, Alaska, 1975; interim pastor Immanuel Bapt. Ch., Anchorage, 1976; vol. chaplain Alaska Prison System. Owner, Alaska Mud Puddle. Counselor, Juvenile Boys' Home, Anchorage, 1976-82. Home: 128 W 23d Ave Anchorage AK 99503

SIMMONS, DUDLEY GLENN, minister, Southern Baptist Convention; b. Franklinton, La., Aug. 8, 1949; s. Dudley W. and Essie Jean (Foil) S.; m. Sherry Marguerite Smith, Apr. 20, 1973; children: Jennifer, Glenna, Jason, Sandra. B.S., William Carey Coll., Miss., 1972; M.Div., New Orleans Bapt. Theol. Sem., 1976; Th.D., 1980. Ordained to ministry Baptist Ch. Pastor, Ebenezer Bapt. Ch., Bassfield, Miss., 1973-76, Morgan City Bapt. Ch., Miss., 1976-80, First Bapt. Ch., Homer, La., 1980—; moderator Holmes-LeFlore Bapt. Assn., Greenwood, Miss., 1979-80; Webster-Claiborne Bapt. Assn., Homer, 1983—; bd. dirs. La. Bapt. Assn., 1983—. Author: Young Adult Pupil Book. Contbr. articles to ch. jours.; Bd. dirs. Minden Mental Health Ctr., La., 1984—, Claiborne Rural Ind. Living Network, Homer, 1984. Mem. Homer C. of C., Am. Acad. Religion, Soc. Bibl. Lit. Lodge: Lions (sec. 1984-85) (Homer). Home: 1105 N Main St Homer LA 71040 Office: PO Box 30 Homer LA 71040

SIMMONS, ERNEST LEE, JR., religion educator, minister, American Lutheran Church; b. Ennis, Tex., Sept. 19, 1947; s. Ernest Lee Sr. and Anna Louise (Moseley) S.; m. Martha Jean Johnson, June 14, 1970; 1 child, Scott Ernest. B.A., Colo. State U., 1970; M.Div., Luther Theol. Sem., St. Paul, 1973; Ph.D., Claremont Grad. Sch., 1981. Ordained to ministry Am. Luth. Ch., 1978. Intern pastor St. Paul's Luth. Parish, Butte, N.D., 1977-78; pastor Carpio Luth. Ch., N.D., 1978-79; instr. Great Plains Inst. Theology, Bismark, N.D., 1977-79, Charis Ecumenical Ctr., Moorhead, Minn., 1979—; asst. prof. dept. religion Concordia Coll., Moorhead, 1979—; asst. dir. Ctr. for Process Studies, Claremont, Calif., 1973-77; supporter Minn. Congl. Senatorial Democratic Campaigns, 1982-84; participant Hunger Task Force, Good Shepard Luth. Ch., Moorhead, 1983-84. Contbr. articles and book revs. to religious publs. Recipient scholarship Aid Assn. for Luths., 1970-73; fellow Luth. Brotherhood, 1973-74, Am. Luth. Ch., 1973-77, Claremont Grad. Sch., 1973-76. Fellow Ctr. for Process Studies; mem. Am. Acad. Religion (sec. Upper Midwest region 1981—, nat. bd. dirs. 1983—), Luth. Human Relations. Home: 1109 S 5th St Moorhead MN 56560 Office: Concordia Coll 901 8th St Moorhead MN 56560

SIMMONS, KENNETH WILLIAM, priest, Episcopal Church; b. Ponca City, Okla., Aug. 7, 1935; s. Lyle Cole and Karolyn Frances (Stiles) S.; B.A., U. Tulsa, 1958; M.Div., Episcopal Theol. Sem., Austin, Tex., 1963; certificate in group counseling Met. Mental Health Center, Mpls., 1973; m. Barbara Ann Langer, June 29, 1975; children: Jennifer, Stephanie. Ordained priest, 1964; rector Grace Ch. Parish, Pine Island, Minn., 1963-66, Ch. of the Good Shepherd, St. Paul, 1966-83; dean St. Paul region, 1980—; examining chaplain Episcopal Ch., 1969—, chmn. dept. higher edn. Diocese of Minn., 1970-74, mem. council, 1966-69, 71-74, grand marshall gen. conv., 1976; del. Coll. of Preachers, Washington, 1967, 70, 74; trustee Episcopal Center, U. Minn., Mpls., 1972—; mem. Liturtical Commn., 1973-83, Anglican/Roman Catholic Commn., 1978-83, Diocesan Council, 1980-83. Bd. dirs. St. Paul Planned Parenthood Assn., 1967-73, Minn. Planned Parenthood Assn., 1973-75. Mem. Episcopal Soc. to Ministry in Higher Edn., Minn. Clergy and Laity Assn., Cursillo. Home and Office: 2050 Delaware Saint Paul MN 55118

SIMMONS, LOLARD ALAN, minister, So. Baptist Conv.; b. Fredericktown, Mo., Jan. 25, 1926; s. Fred William and Emma Virena (Pogue) S.; B.S., So. Ill. U., Edwardsville, 1971; Th.M., Luther Rice Sem., Jacksonville, Fla., 1973, D.Min., 1976; m. Dorothy Blanche McPherson, June 4, 1944; children—Lolard Alan, Doris Jean, Mark Lee, Twyla Sue. Ordained to ministry, 1953; pastor Curdie Heights Bapt. Ch., Alton, Ill., 1952-74, Calvary Bapt. Ch., Casa Grande, Ariz., 1974-76; dir. associational missions River Valley Bapt. Assn., Ariz., 1976—; home missionary So. Bapt. Conv. Author: The Eternal Abode of Man, 1973; The Precious Blood, 1976. Address: 940 Hillside Dr Kingman AZ 86401

SIMMONS, THOMAS SAMUAL, minister, American Baptist Churches in the U.S.A.; b. Arcadia, Fla., May 7, 1939; s. Paul James and Rubye Mae (Martin) Simmons Meeks; m. Norma (Bunny) Bernice Thomas, June 12, 1959; children: Lisa Michelle, Deborah Lynn, David Thomas, Jonathan Thomas. B.A., U. Tampa, 1961; Th.M., Dallas Sem., 1968; D. of Ministries, Luther Rice Sem., 1977. Ordained to ministry Bapt. Ch., 1961; chaplain cert. Ga. Bapt. Hosp., 1964. Chaplain, Baylor Hosp., Dallas, 1966-68; prof. Southeastern Bible Coll., Birmingham, Ala., 1971-74; pastor Valley View Bapt. Ch., Council Bluffs, Ia., 1974-79, Bethel Bapt. Ch., Sioux City, Ia., 1979-81, First Bapt. Ch., Muscatine, Ia., 1981—; bd. advisors Grace Coll. of Bible, Omaha, 1978—; mem. regional policy bd. Mid-Am. Bapt. Chs., Des Moines, 1983—; mem. hosp. crisis team Jennie Edmundson Hosp., Council Bluffs, 1976-79; mem. bd. reference Western Bapt. Sem., Portland, 1973—; part-time tax preparer H.R. Block, 1979—. Author: Sunday School Superintendent, 1974; Sunday School Adult Lessons, 1973; contbr. articles to profl. jours. Del. Republican County Conv., Muscatine, Ia., 1984; worker United Way Muscatine, 1982; chaplain vol. Muscatine Gen. Hosp., 1981—; police chaplain Sioux City and Council Bluffs Police Dept., 1975-81. Served with Air N.G., 1955-59. Mem. Muscatine Area Assn. Evangelicals (pres. 1983), Muscatine Area Ministers Assn. (jail chaplain 1984), Met. Assn. Evangelicals (pres. Omaha chpt. 1978-79), Ministers Council Am. Bapt. Clergy. Republican. Lodge: Kiwanis. Home: 902 W Eighth St Muscatine IA 52761 Office: First Bapt Ch 224 E Third St Muscatine IA 52761

SIMMONS, WILLIAM KYLE, minister, So. Bapt. Conv.; b. Atlanta, Apr. 1, 1926; s. William Guy and Nelle (Walker) S.; B.B.A., Emory U., 1949; M.R.E., Southwestern Bapt. Sem., 1952; m. Barbara Landrum, Feb. 24, 1950; children—Anne, Debra, Robert, Kyle. Ordained to ministry, 1958; minister of edn. 1st Bapt. Ch., St. Petersburg, Fla., 1952-62, 1st Bapt. Ch., Birmingham, Ala., 1962-65, Calvary Bapt. Ch., Lexington, Ky., 1965—. Pres., Ky. Bapt. Religious Edn. Assn., 1970-71; pres. Southwestern Bapt. Sem. Alumni of Ky., 1970-71; 1st v.p. Fla. Bapt. Conv., So. Bapt. Conv., 1960-61. Mem. Eastern, Southwestern, So. Bapt. religious edn. assns. Home: 1043 Elmendorf Dr Lexington KY 40502 Office: 150 E High St Lexington KY 40507

SIMMS, ALBERT EGERTON, minister, Southern Baptist Convention; b. Raleigh, N.C., Jan. 24, 1918; s. Robert Nirwana and Virginia Adelaide (Egerton) S.; B.A. (A.D. Ward Orator's medal 1938), Wake Forest U., 1938; postgrad. So. Bapt. Theol. Sem., Louisville, 1939-40, Va. Bapt. Hosp. Sch. Pastoral Care, 1967; m. Helen Canaday, Jan. 1, 1941; children: Albert Egerton, Mary Helen Simms Patterson, David E. Ordained to ministry, 1938; pastor chs. in N.C. and Va., 1941-60; pastor Rivermont Ave. Bapt. Ch., Lynchburg, Va., 1960-74; founding adminstr. Lakewood Manor Retirement Community of Va. Bapt. Homes, Richmond, 1974-83; dir. So. Bapt. Conv. Home Mission Bd., 1984—; pres. Bapt. Gen. Assn. Va., 1960, bd. dirs. 1953-60, chmn. long-range planning com., 1972-74; exec. com. So. Bapt. Conv., 1964-70; moderator Lynchburg Bapt. Assn., 1965-66, Peninsula Bapt. Assn., 1948-49, Strawberry Bapt. Assn., 1963-64; pres. Va. Peninsula Christian Ministers Assn., 1951. Bd. dirs. Peninsula div. U. Richmond extension sch., 1952-54, Peninsula YMCA, 1948-54; bd. dirs. Va. Assn. Non-Profit Homes for Aging, 1976-81, sec. bd., 1979-81. Mem. Omicron Delta Kappa. Author tracts, articles. Home: 1514 Chauncey Ln Richmond VA 23233

SIMON, HUGH VERNON, minister, Presbyterian Church (U.S.A.); b. Overbrook, Kans., Oct. 22, 1919; s. August Joseph and Rebecca (Heberling) S.; B.A., Washburn U., Topeka, 1947; B.Div., Louisville Presbyn. Theol. Sem., 1950; D.D. (hon.), Tusculum Coll., Greeneville, Tenn., 1961; m. Sophie Fontaine Vass, Nov. 14, 1943; children: Hugh Vernon, Celia Simon Barrett. Ordained to ministry, 1950; pastor chs. in Tenn. and Kans., 1950-60; pastor First Presbyn. Ch., Greeneville, Tenn., 1960-84. Moderator Synod Mid-South, 1966; chmn. organizing commn. Synod of South, 1972, chmn. ministerials relations com., 1974—; mem. com. regional synods Gen. Assembly Presbyn. Ch. (U.S.A.), 1972; organizer Holston Acad. Parish Clergy, 1964. Sec. bd. trustees Tusculum Coll.; chmn. bd. govs. adv. com. Greene County Welfare Dept.; chmn. Greeneville Day Care Center, 1968-72; active Greenville Salvation Army. Mem. Holston Acad. Parish Clergy, Greene County Ministerial Assn. Club: Greeneville Exchange (past pres.). Home: Route 8 Box 186D Greenville TN 37743

SIMON, KUNNUMPURATH MATHEW, priest, educator, Syrian Orthodox Church of Antioch; b. Kerala, India, Jan. 5, 1917; s. Kunnumpurath Chummar and Sarah (Poonoose) Mathew; came to U.S., 1947, naturalized, 1973; M.A., Columbia, 1948; B.D., Union Theol. Sem., 1949; D.D., Lincoln U., 1951; m. Thankamma Abraham, Apr. 20, 1953; children—John Mathew, Abraham Ronald. Ordained priest, 1954; gen. sec. Knanaya Diocese Syrian Ch. of India, prof. ch. history Syrian Theol. Sem., Kottayam, S. India, 1943-45; gen. sec. World Conf. Christian Youth, 1950-53; dean Theol. Coll. Addis Ababa, Ethiopia, 1953-59; core-episcopos Syrian Ch.; pres., adminstr. Knamaya Community N. Am.; prof. history Fairleigh Dickinson U., Teaneck, N.J., 1961—. Mem. gen. bd. Nat. Council Chs. U.S.A.; mem. central com. World Council Chs., 1961—; sec. Am. Friends of Ethiopian Orthodox Ch. Recipient medal of honor Emperor of Ethiopia, 1951; Doctorial Cross, Patriarch of Moscow and All Russia. Mem. AAUP, Knanaya Service Assn. U.S.A. (pres., dir.), Fedn. Indians Overseas Internat. Home: 12 Dogwood Ln Ho Ho Kus NJ 07423 Office: 1000 River Rd Teaneck NJ 07666

SIMON, MORDECAI, rabbi; b. St. Louis, July 19, 1925; s. Abraham M. and Rose (Solomon) S.; m. Maxine Ruth Abrams, July 4, 1954; children: Ora, Eve, Avrom. B.A., St. Louis U., 1947; M.A., Washington U., 1952; M.H.L., Jewish Theol. Sem., N.Y.C., 1952; D.D., Jewish Theol. Sem. of Am., 1977. Ordained rabbi, 1952. Rabbi, Beth El Synagogue, Mpls., 1952-56, Sons of Jacob Synagogue, Waterloo, Iowa, 1956-63; exec. v.p. Chgo. Bd. Rabbis, 1963—. Host: (weekly TV program) What's Nu?, Chgo., 1971—. Mem. exec. com. Chgo. unit Am. Cancer Soc., 1983; bd. dirs. Pub. Affairs Com. Jewish United Fund, 1970—, Chgo. USO Bd., 1974—. Served as staff sgt. U.S. Army, 1943-46; PTO. Recipient citation Jewish War Veterans, 1965; Shofar award Jewish Com. on Scouting, Chgo., 1974; Rabbinical Honor award Council of Jewish Fedns., 1982, 83; Honor plaque Jewish United Fund, Chgo., 1984. Mem. Rabbinical Assembly N.Y. Office: Chicago Bd Rabbis 1 S Franklin St Chicago IL 60606

SIMONIS, RAPHAELA ELENA, nun, Roman Catholic Ch.; b. Kaunas, Lithuania, Jan. 4, 1908; d. Stanislaus and Anastasia (Piliponis) Simonis; grad. Tchrs. Sem., Kaunas, 1926, Art Acad., Kaunas, 1936; came to U.S., 1950, naturalized, 1956. Joined Benedictine Sisters, 1928; vicar of the Mother Priores, Kaunas, 1937-40; superior and supr. Orphanage of Cioliskig, Lithuania, 1940-43; supr. Regina Pacis Found., Bedford, N.H. Author: Deo Gratias et Mariae, 1973. Address: 75 Wallace Rd Bedford NH 03102

SIMONS, WENDELL WAYNE, educator, librarian, Conservative Baptist Assn. Am.; b. Independence, Mo., Nov. 10, 1928; s. William Francis and Mabel Granville (Loren) S.; m. Judith Rae Shaw, Mar. 13, 1953; children: Gary, Teresa. A.B., U. Calif.-Berkeley, 1949, B.L.S., 1954; postgrad. Mexico City Coll., 1960; M.A. in Theology, Fuller Theol. Sem., 1980. Librarian, U. Calif., Santa Barbara, 1954-63; librarian U. Calif., Santa Cruz, 1963-80, assoc. univ. librarian emeritus, 1980—; librarian Inst. Linguistics, Ukarumpa, Papua, New Guinea, 1972; librarian, assoc. prof. Bibl. studies Judson Bapt. Coll., The Dalles, Oreg., 1980—. Contbr. articles to Christianity Today, Christian Librarian Mag. Served with USN, 1950-52. Mem. Oreg. Library Assn., Christian Librarians Assn., Pacific NW Christian

Library/Media Assn. (treas. 1983—). Home: 610 E 20th St The Dalles OR 97058 Office: Judson Baptist College 400 E Scenic Dr The Dalles OR 97058

SIMPSON, CHARLES EDWARD, minister, Southern Baptist Convention; b. Little Rock, Feb. 11, 1948; s. Charles L. and Ruth M. (Greenwood) S.; m. Helen L. Jackson, Aug. 2, 1969; children: Kelli Joe, Amanda Michel. B.A., Ouachita U., 1970; M.Div., Southwestern Bapt. Theol. Sem., 1973; postgrad. Midwestern Theol. Sem., Mo., 1982—. Ordained to ministry Bapt. Ch., 1966. Pastor chs. in La., 1969-70, Tex., 1972-73, Ark., 1973—, Lonoke Bapt. Ch., 1978—; mem. exec. bd. Ark. State Bapt. Conv., 1975-77, mem. nominating com., 1982—; bd. dirs. Christian Civic Found., Little Rock, 1976-79. Author: History of the Baptists in Israel, 1973; From My Life to His, 1984. Served to capt. USAR, 1982-84. Mem. Lonoke C. of C. (exec. bd. 1984). Lodges: Kiwanis (pres. 1980), Optimists (pres. 1974-75). Home: 120 Church St Lonoke AR 72086

SIMPSON, DOUGLAS FORSYTH, minister, So. Bapt. Conv.; b. Louisville, Aug. 25, 1939; s. William Martin and Virginia (Forsyth) S.; B.A., Wayland Bapt. Coll., 1962; M.Div., Golden Gate Bapt. Theol. Sem., 1969; m. Margaret DeLoy Taylor, June 20, 1961; children—Douglas Forsyth II, Margaret Denise. Ordained to ministry, 1964; asso. pastor Angle Lake Bapt. Ch., Seattle, 1962; asso. pastor Shellville (Calif.) Bapt. Mission, 1963-64, Trinity Bapt. Ch., Modesto, Calif., 1964; pastor First Bapt. Ch., Toul, France, 1964-66, First So. Bapt. Ch., Darmstadt, Germany, 1966-68, First Bapt. Ch., Biggs, Calif., 1968-73, First So. Bapt. Ch., Apple Valley, Calif., 1973—. Vice pres. European Bapt. Conv., 1966-67; vice moderator Sierra Butte So. Bapt. Assn., 1969, moderator, 1970-72; moderator High Desert So. Bapt. Assn., 1974-76. Call fireman, Apple Valley, 1973—; baseball mgr. Little League, 1971—. Mem. Pastors Fellowship Sierra Butte So. Bapt. Assn. Home: 22190 Sioux St Apple Valley CA 92307 Office: 21880 Cherokee Rd Apple Valley CA 92307

SIMPSON, MARSHALL RANDOLPH, minister, Southern Baptist Convention; b. Anderson County, S.C., May 23, 1914; s. Willie McDuffie and Carrie (Sanders) S.; A.B., Furman U., 1945; B.D., Luther Rice Sem., 1965, Th.M., 1968; m. Inez Meredith, Apr. 7, 1935 (dec.); m. 2d, Mildred Pace, Nov. 22, 1968; 1 son, William M. Ordained to the ministry, 1943; pastor chs. in S.C., Ga., 1973—, Mt. Hebron Baptist Ch., Hartwell, Ga., 1973-77, Saluda, N.C., 1977—. Chmn. chaplaincy services Hart County Hosp. and Nursing Home; pres. Pastors Conf., Greer, S.C.; dir. missions Polk Bapt. Assn., 1978—; gen. bd. S.C. Bapt. Conv.; moderator Aiken-Colleton Bapt. Assn. Mem. Ga. Bapt. Conv., Hart County Ministers-Pastors Conf., Hebron Assn. N.E. Bapt. Pastors Conf. Home: PO Box 265 Saluda NC 28773

SIMPSON, MARSHALL WAYNE, minister, Presbyterian Church (U.S.A.); b. Alexis, Ill., Feb. 7, 1918; s. Clifford Hill and Edna Grace (Josephson) S.; B.S., Monmouth Coll., 1940; diploma McCormick Sem., 1943; D.D., Millikin U., 1975; m. Edith Berniece Smith, Sept. 6, 1941; children: William M., Barbara Marti, Margaret Selburg, Mary Anne Logan, Deborah Carlson, Timothy W. Ordained to ministry, 1943; pastor, Garden Plain, Ill., 1941-44, Kinde, Mich., 1944-46, Mason, Mich., 1946-50, Peru, Ind., 1951-55, First Ch., Peoria, Ill., 1955-57, Arcadia Ave. Ch., Peoria, Ill., 1957-64, Henry and LaPrairie Chs., Henry, Ill., 1964-83, pastor emeritus, 1983; supply pastor Wenona Presbyn. Ch., Ill., 1984-86; moderator, Muncie Presbytery, 1954, Synod Ill., 1965, Peoria Presbytery, 1969, Synod Lincoln Trails, 1973; stated clk. Peoria Presbytery, 1961-67; chmn. gen. council Blackhawk Presbytery, 1972-78. Pres., Lake Thunderbird Assn., 1974-76. Recipient Gold medals Freedoms Found., 1956-85. Author: The Flowering Tree of Gethsemane, 1968; From Tea to a Righteous Cause, 1976; This Is My Own, 1977; Simpsonisms, 1982; Wanted: A Faith that Works, 1983. Home: 239 Lake Thunderbird Dr Putnam IL 61560

SIMPSON, MICHAEL DAVID, minister, Christian Church (Disciples of Christ); b. San Diego, June 1, 1953; s. David Keith and Kathryn Dorothy (Collett) S.; m. Nancy Lee Christianson, May 23, 1975; children: Brian Patrick, Benjamin David, Sara Katherine. B.A., North Tex. State U., 1975; M.Div., Vanderbilt U., 1978. Ordained to ministry Christian Ch., 1978. Assoc. minister First Christian Ch., Plano, Tex., 1978-81; minister Bethany Christian Ch., Dallas, 1981—. Author: Song to the Father's, 1974. Editor Christian Courier, Dist. 17, Tex., 1979-81. Course instr. Emeritus Inst., Dallas County Community Coll., 1984; facilitator Routh St. Adolescent Seminar, Dallas, 1980, 81; bd. dirs. Plano Coop. Presch., Tex., 1978-80. Mem. Ministerial Alliance (pres. 1979-80), Phi Eta Sigma, Phi Alpha Theta. Home: 5848 Sunny Wood Dallas TX 75228 Office: Bethany Christian Ch 6282 Oram Dallas TX 75214

SIMS, BOBBY EUGENE, minister, Southern Baptist Convention; b. Rome, Ga., Apr. 28, 1939; s. James Buford S.; B.S. in Music Edn., Berry Coll., Rome, 1965; M.Mus. in Ch. Music, So. Bapt. Theol. Sem., Louisville, 1969; postgrad. clin. pastoral edn. Ga. Bapt. Hosp., Atlanta, 1972-73; m. Katie Marlene Hawkins, June 12, 1960; children: Melanie Dawn, Anne Alison. Ordained to ministry, 1969; minister music, assoc. pastor Riverside Bapt. Ch., Celanese, 1958, First Bapt. Chs., Lindale, Ga., 1958-61, Pisgah Bapt. Ch., Coosa, Ga., 1961-62, Garden Lakes Bapt. Ch., Rome, 1962-65, Midlane Park Bapt. Ch., Louisville, 1965-69, Columbia Dr. Bapt. Ch., Decatur, Ga., 1969-74, Peachtree Bapt. Ch., Atlanta, 1974-80, Rehoboth Bapt. Ch., Ga., 1980-83, Alpharetta Frist Bapt. Ch., Ga., 1983—; music dir. Atlanta Bapt. Assn., 1975-79. Mem. Atlanta Symphony Orch. Chorus, 1973-83; bd. dirs. Dekalb County Council on Aging. Mem. Ga. Bapt. Conv. Sons of Jubal, Ga. Bapt. Music Conf., Am. Guild Organists, Roswell Bapt. Assn. (exec. com. 1983—). Composer: Alma Mater, Atlanta Bapt. Coll., 1972. Home: 4825 Candacraig Dr Alpharetta GA 30201 Office: 44 Academy St Alpharetta GA 30201

SIMS, HORACE BRYANT, JR., minister, Southern Baptist Convention; b. Greenville, S.C., Jan. 2, 1940; s. Horace Bryant and Mary (Davis) S.; certificate Furman U., 1962; m. Mary Jane, Bridwell, Jan. 27, 1968; children—Stacy Lee, Horace Bryant. Ordained to ministry, 1969; pastor Middleton St. Bapt. Ch., Cayce, S.C., 1969-70, Abney Meml. Bapt. Ch., Greenwood, S.C., 1971—. Vice-moderator Abbeville Bapt. Assn., 1971, moderator, 1976—; pres. Lexington Pastor's Assn., 1970; pres. Abbeville Bapt. Pastors Conf., 1973-75; v.p. clergy staff Self Meml. Hosp., Greenwood, 1975-76, pres. clergy staff, 1976-77; mem. clergy staff Greenville Hosp. System, 1971—; tchr. Greenwood Sem. Extension Center, 1976—; mem. staff Faith Home for Alcoholics, Greenwood, 1975—; mem. gen. bd. S.C. Bapt. Conv., 1979-83, chmn. budget com., 1983, chmn. order of bus. com., 1983-86, 1st v.p., 1981, pres., 1982; mem. com. on coms. So. Bapt. Conv., 1983. Chmn. ch. sect. United Fund, Greenwood, 1971; fund raiser Radio Free Europe, 1967—. Recipient plaque Abney Meml. Bapt. Ch., 1976. Mem. Greenwood Ministerial Assn., S.C. State Bapt. Pastor's Conf. Home: 307 Ellenberg Ave Greenwood SC 29646 Office: Panola Ave Greenwood SC 29646

SIMS, JOHN STEPHEN, minister, Luth. Ch. Am.; b. Atlanta, Aug. 12, 1946; s. Samuel Edgar and Mabel Grace (Howard) S.; B.A., Oglethorpe U., 1968; M.R.E., Luth. Theol. So. Sem., 1972; m. Phyllis Ann Smith, Sept. 5, 1970. Ordained to ministry, 1972; chaplain intern Bapt. Hosp., Nashville, 1970-71; asso. pastor, minister of youth, dir. Christian edn., Luth. Ch. of Good Shepherd, College Park, Ga., 1972-76; interim pastor Emmanuel Luth. Ch., Atlanta, 1975-76; congregation/synod consultation coordinator Southeastern Synod of Luth. Ch. Am., Atlanta, 1976—. Sec. Luth. Council Metro-Atlanta, 1973-75; S.E. Synod youth staffer contact person, 1975—; co-dir. Youth Awareness Seminar, 1975; mem. S.E. Synod youth ministry com., 1974-76. Mem. S. Fulton Hosp. Chaplaincy Assn. (pres. 1974-75), Am. Clin. Pastoral Edn. Assn., Fellowship of St. Augustine, Atlanta Christian Council, Chi Phi. Home: 1891 W Rugby Ave College Park GA 30337 Office: 1644 Tully Circle NE Suite 124 Atlanta GA 30329

SINCLAIR, DAVID WILLIAM, rector, Anglican Church; b. Rochester, N.Y., Sept. 14, 1936; s. Robert Gordon and Elizabeth (Broadbridge) S.; m. Mary Frances Evelyn Colbeck, May 19, 1962; children: Heather M., Laurel E. B.A. with honors, Queen's U., Kingston, Ont., Can., 1959; B.Th. with honors, Wycliffe Coll., Toronto, Ont., 1962. Ordained deacon Anglican Ch., 1961, priest, 1962. Served various parishes, Ont. Diocese, 1961-74; exec. dir. Aberdeen House, Kingston, 1974-76; assoc. rector St. George's Cathedral, Kingston, 1976-78; rector St. Stephen's and St. John's, Hornby, Ont., 1978-83, Holy Trinity, Fonthill, Ont., 1983—; mem. bd. Interval House, Kingston, 1976-78, Canterbury Hills, Ancaster, Ont., 1978-83; pastoral coordinator Sunset Haven, Welland, Ont., 1983—. Town councillor Village of Tweed, Ont., 1965-67. Served to capt. Can. Army Res., 1962-71. Mem. Can. Soc. Religion and Gerontology. Office: Holy Trinity Ch 1557 Pelham St Fonthill ON L0S IE0 Canada

SINCLAIR, WILLIAM DONALD, church official Presbyterian Church in America; b. Los Angeles, Dec. 27, 1924; s. Arthur Livingston and Lillian Mae (Holt) S.; m. Barbara Jean Hughes, Aug. 9, 1952; children: Paul Scott, Victoria Sharon. B.A. summa cum laude, St. Martin's Coll., 1975; postgrad. Emory U., 1978-79. Cert. ch. bus. adminstr. Commd. 2d lt. U.S. Air Force, 1947, advanced through grades to col., 1970, ret., 1975; ch. bus. adminstr. First United Meth. Ch., Colorado Springs, Colo., 1976-85, Village Seven Presbyn. Ch., Colorado Springs, 1985—; vice chmn. council on fin. and adminstrn. Rocky Mountain Conf. of United Meth. Ch., Denver, 1980-84. Contbr. articles to religious publs. Mem. Citizens Goals for Colorado Springs, 1982; del. Colo. State Republican Assembly, Denver, 1984; bd. dirs. Chins-UP of Colorado Springs, 1982—. Fellow Nat. Assn. Ch. Bus. Adminstrs. (pres. 1985; Ch. Bus. Adminstr. of Yr. 1984); mem. United Meth. Assn. Ch. Bus. Adminstrs. (nat. sec. 1979-81), Christian Ministries Mgmt. Assn. (bd. dirs. 1982—). Club: Colorado Springs Country. Lodge: Rotary (pres. 1985). Home: 3007 Chelton Dr Colorado Springs CO 80909 Office: Village of Seven Presbyn Ch 4050 S Nonchalant Circle Colorado Springs CO 80917

SINGER, ISRAEL. Exec. dir. World Jewish Congress. Office: 1 Park Ave Suite 418 New York NY 10016*

SINGER, MERLE ELLIOT, rabbi, Reform Jewish Congregations; b. Duluth, Minn., May 11, 1939; s. Samuel and Bertha (Naymark) S.; A.B., U. Cin., 1961; B.H.L., Hebrew Union Coll., Cin., 1963, M.H.L., 1966; m. Myra Golden, Aug. 29, 1965; children—Jonathan, Jeremy, Michael, Mark. Rabbi, 1966; rabbi Temple Sinai, Washington, 1966-71, Reform Congregation Beth Or, Spring House, Pa., 1971—. Program dir. summer camp Union Am. Hebrew Congregations Camp Inst., Cleveland, Ga., 1964-65; asso. mem. bd. dirs. Phila. Jewish Campus Activities Bd.; rabbinic adviser Mid-Atlantic council Union Am. Hebrew Congregations Fedn. Temple Youth, 1969-71; mem. faculty Nat. Leadership Tng. Inst. Nat. Fedn. Temple Youth, 1964; mem. faculty Camp Harlam, 1972—, Gwynedd Mercy Coll. (Pa.), 1974—, Gratz Coll., Phila., 1971—; Hillel adviser Phila. Coll. Textiles and Scis., 1976—. Recipient Beth Or Man of Year award, 1976. Home: 2912 Arch Rd Norristown PA 19403 Office: Penllyn Pike and Dager Rd Spring House PA 19477

SINGER, SHIRLEY, religious organization executive, Jewish. Exec. dir. Emunah Women of Am., N.Y.C. Office: Emunah Women of Am 370 7th Ave New York NY 10001*

SIRILLA, FLORANNE, director of religious education, Roman Catholic Church; b. Shamokin, Pa., Jan. 16, 1943; d. Joseph Edward and Florence Angela (Choplick) Zalewski; m. George Michael Sirilla, Nov. 23, 1968; children: Michael, Joseph. Student George Washington U., Georgetown U., 1984—. Tchr. religion St. Jane Francis De Chantal, Bethesda, Md., 1974-77, dir. religious edn., 1977-79; dir. assocs. Paul VI Inst. for Arts, Washington, 1980-81; dir. religious edn. Our Lady of Lourdes, Bethesda, 1982—; chmn. publicity Community of Catechetical Leaders of Washington, 1984—. Contbg. author: Liturgy Guide, 1985. Mem. Nat. Assn. Parish Dirs. and Coordinators of Religious Edn., Mid-East Religious Educators Fedn. Avocations: Writing; reading; dancing; music. Home: 6524 Windermere Cir Rockville MD 20852

SIRON, TERRY WAYNE, minister, So. Bapt. Conv.; b. Sedalia, Mo., Mar. 28, 1951; s. Charles Rosser and Alice Mae (Carver) S.; B.A., William-Jewell Coll., 1973; postgrad. Midwestern Bapt. Theol. Sem.; m. Judith Ann Eshelman, Oct. 25, 1974. Ordained to ministry, 1971; pastor Lamonte (Mo.) Bapt. Ch., 1974—. Dir. camp program; mem. brotherhood com., Harmony Bapt. Assn., Lamonte Ministerial Alliance. Mem. Lamonte Community Bicentennial Planning Com. Mem. Kappa Alpha, Pi Kappa Delta. Home: 1004 Midland Box 370 Lamonte MO 65337 Office: 1005 Midland Box 370 Lamonte MO 65337

SISCO, L. VERNON, minister, So. Bapt. Conv.; b. Whiteville, Tenn., July 22, 1915; s. Rosco C. and Monnie (Russell) S.; B.A., Union U., 1948; B.Div., M.Th., So. Bapt. Theol. Sem., 1956; m. Mildred Edith Marlowe, Dec. 20, 1936; children—Dorothy Nell, Mary Margaret, Bettye Carol, Charles Kimberly. Ordained to ministry, 1936; pastor First Bapt. Ch., Halls, Tenn., 1944-47, First Bapt. Ch., Caruthersville, Mo., 1948-53, Maplewood Bapt. Ch., St. Louis, 1955-57, Lincoln Park Bapt. Ch., 1958-62, First Bapt. Ch., Miami Beach, Fla., 1963-65, East Corinth Bapt. Ch., Corinth, Miss., 1965-68, First Bapt. Ch., Ewa Beach, Hawaii, 1968-72, First Bapt. Ch., Campbell, Calif., 1972-75, Anderson Meml. Bapt. Ch., Schweinfurt, Germany, 1975—. Founder, dir. Worldwide Evangelistic Service, 1964, Filmorama Evangelistic Assn., 1970; exec. bd. Hawaii Bapt. Conv., 1968-72; mem. exec. bd., dir. tng. evangelism and edn. European Bapt. Conv., 1976—; dir. Action Crusades for Europe, 1975—. Trustee So. Bapt. Coll., Walnut Ridge, Ark., 1949-50. Named Hon. Citizen, Jenola-Bukdo Province, S. Hwang, Chun-ju, Korea, 1974. Mem. So. Bapt. Theol. Sem. Alumni Assn. (pres. 1947-48). Author: Church Member's Handbook, 1962; Evangelism Evangelized, 1963. Home: 16 Rhonstrasse Schweinfurt West Germany 872 Office: Benno-Merkle and Georg Schwarz Schweinfurt West Germany

SISEL, ERIC DESBIENS, non-denominational minister; b. Paris, France, July 12, 1932; s. Antoine Jean and Térèse Sophie (Desbiens) S.; Ph.D., Sorbonne (France), 1953, U. Vienna (Austria), 1956; B.D., U. Toronto, 1969; m. Mary Louise Pomeroy, Apr. 11, 1958; children—Kevin, Jennifer, Jeffrey, Cindy Lou, Andrew. Ordained to ministry, United Ch. Can., 1969; pastor Lake of Bays Pastoral Charge, Huntsville, Ont., Can., 1969-78; pastor Lake of Bays Mission Ch., 1978—. Host An Hour with Eric Sisel, weekly radio show, CFKI, Huntsville, 1969-77. Pres. Big Bros. Muskoka, Huntsville, 1972-73, Franklin Home and Sch. Assn., Dwight, Ont., 1974-76. Trustee Muskoka Bd. Edn., Bracebridge, Ont., 1975-78; bd. dirs. Huntsville Fair Bd., 1972-76; pres. Huntsville and Dist. Assn. for Mentally Retarded, 1980—. Mem. Huntsville Agrl. Soc. (dir. 1971-75), Evang. Fellowship Can. Rotarian (dist.

gov. 1973-74), Mason (Shriner, chaplain 1973—). Editor Encounter, 1972-76. Address: Box 2461 Huntsville ON P0A 1K0 Canada

SISEMORE, JOHN THEOPHILUS, ch. ofcl., So. Bapt. Conv.; b. Hulen, Okla., Apr. 9, 1913; s. Jesse Carl and Janie Melissa (Dayton) S.; student Moody Bible Inst., 1932-34, Chgo. Music Coll., 1933; So. Bapt. Sem., 1934, Multnomah Coll., 1952; LL.D., Am. Bible Coll., 1960; m. Margaret Lois Dornhoefer, Aug. 7, 1934. Ordained to ministry, 1972; minister edn. and music Buchanan St. Bapt. Ch., Amarillo, Tex., 1934-44, Hillcrest Bapt. Ch., Dallas, 1944-50; dir. dept. religious edn. N.W. Bapt. Conv., 1950-57; adult cons. Bapt. Sunday Sch. Bd. of So. Bapt. Conv., 1957-72; dir. Sunday sch. div. Bapt. Gen. Conv. Tex., Dallas, 1972—; mem. So. Bapt. Conv. Religious Edn. Assn. Mem. Eastern (pres. 1966), Southwestern (pres. 1976-77) Bapt. religious edn. assns., Adult Edn. Assn. Am. Author: Program Planning and Presentation, 1947; Building Better Programs, 1947; Ministry of Visitation, 1954; Sunday School Ministry to Adults, 1959; Rozell's Lesson Commentary, 1960; Blueprint for Teaching, 1964; Vital Principles in Religious Education, 1966; Rejoice, You Are a Sunday School Teacher, 1976. Contbr. articles periodicals, chpts. in books. Compiler: The Ministry of Religious Education, 1976. Home: 6721 Inverness St Dallas TX 75214 Office: Baptist Bldg Dallas TX 75201

SISK, MARK SEAN, religion educator, seminary dean, priest, Episcopal Church; b. Takoma Park, Md., Aug. 18, 1942; s. Robert James and Alma Irene (Davis) S.; m. Karen Lynn Womack, Aug. 31, 1963; children: Michael A., Heather K., Bronwyn E. B.S., U. Md., 1964; M.Div., Gen. Theol. Sem., 1967. Ordained priest Episcopal Ch., 1967. Asst. Christ Ch., New Brunswick, N.J., 1967-70; assoc. Christ Ch., Bronxville, N.Y., 1970-73; rector St. John's Episcopal Ch., Kingston, N.Y., 1973-77; archdeacon Diocese of N.Y., N.Y.C., 1977-84; pres., dean Seabury-Western Theol. Sem., Evanston, Ill., 1984—. Mem. Soc. Bibl. Lit., Chgo. Area Theol. Schs. Office: Seabury-Western Theol Sem 2122 Sheridan Evanston IL 60201

SISLER, DANNY FAIRFAX, minister, So. Bapt. Conv.; b. Greer, W.Va., Nov. 22, 1936; s. Fred Chester and Sarah Priscilla (Snyder) S.; B.Th., S.W. Bapt. Theol. Sem., 1974; m. Dorothy V. Evans, Dec. 22, 1956; children—Susan Catherine, Joyce Ann, Melinda Kay. Ordained to ministry, 1974; pastor Oak Street Bapt. Ch., Kingfisher, Okla., 1974—. Chaplain Kingfisher Police Force; devel. sem. extension program. Home: 314 W Locust Ave Kingfisher OK 73750 Office: 1509 S Oak St Kingfisher OK 73750

SITES, WILBER LAWRENCE, JR., minister, United Brethren in Christ Ch.; b. Chambersburg, Pa., Oct. 1, 1926; s. Wilber Lawrence and Della Lee (Stewart) S.; B.A. summa cum laude, Huntington (Ind.) Coll., 1958, D.D., 1978; B.D., Huntington Sem., 1961, M.Div., 1973; m. Mossie Baker, Nov. 29, 1946; children—Judy (Mrs. Gary A. Baker), Linda (Mrs. Donald Etter), Dennis Allen. Ordained elder United Brethren in Christ Ch., 1961, bishop, 1977; pastor chs. in Pa., Ind. and Ohio, 1953-69, Otterbein Ch., Waynesboro, Pa., 1969—. Mem. gen. bd. United Brethren in Christ, 1964—, mem. pub. bd., 1961—, mem. bd. adminstrn., 1965—, mem. bd. edn., 1981, sec. gen. conf., 1965, del., 1965, 69, 73; supt. Pa. conf., 1965, sec., 1962-65, chmn. Cabinet Supts. Bd. dirs. Milton Wright Home Children and Aged, Fayetteville, Pa., Franklin County Sunday Sch. Assn., Franklin County Welfare Assn., Waynesboro Area United Way Fund (gen. chmn. 1974); trustee Huntington Coll., 1982—. Author articles. Office: United Brethren Ch 302 Lake St Huntington IN 46750

SITTON, PHILLIP EARL, minister, Southern Baptist Convention; b. Stamford, Tex., Mar. 12, 1945; s. Allie Buron and Lillian Carol (Bushell) S.; B.Mus., Baylor U., 1967; M.R.E., Southwestern Bapt. Theol. Sem., 1971; m. Patricia Ann Harvey, Apr. 27, 1967; children: Darren Christopher, Jennifer Leigh. Ordained to ministry, 1973; organist 1st Bapt. Ch., Stamford, 1961-63; minister of music and youth Leroy (Tex.) Ch., 1964-66; asst. minister of music, dir. jr. high activities Highland Bapt. Ch., Waco, Tex., 1966-67; missionary Home Mission Bd., So. Bapt. Conv., Grand Junction, Colo., 1967-69; minister of music 1st Bapt. Ch., Watauga, Tex., 1969-71; mem. staff Mexican Bapt. Home, San Antonio, 1971; assoc. pastor fine arts Shearer Hills Bapt. Ch., San Antonio, 1971—; pvt. tchr. voice, piano, organ, 1962—. Organist Bapt. Gen. Conv. Colo., 1968; dir. music San Antonio Bapt. Assn., 1975—; composer, arranger and accompanist. Home: 1738 Brogan St San Antonio TX 78232 Office: 802 Oblate St San Antonio TX 78216

SJOBERG, DONALD W., bishop Evangelical Lutheran Church in Canada, also president, 1985—. Office: 9901 107th St Edmonton AB T5K 1G4 Canada*

SKAGGS, FRED RANDALL, minister, Southern Baptist Convention; b. Jonesville, Va., Nov. 16, 1933; s. Jesse Milton and Osalene (Spurrier) S.; B.A., U. Richmond (Va.), 1955; M.Div., Southwestern Bapt. Theol. Sem., Ft. Worth, 1963, M.A., 1965; D.Ministry, Union Theol. Sem., Richmond, 1974; lic. marriage and family therapist; m. Jane Brugos, Sept. 12, 1953; children: Debra Jane, Fred Randall, Angela Ruth, Cynthia Lou, John Milton. Ordained minister, 1962; pastor chs. in Va. and Okla., 1952—; pastor Skipwith Bapt. Ch., Richmond, 1966-73, Walnut Grove Bapt. Ch., Mechanicsville, Va., 1974—; instr. Sch. Christian Studies, U. Richmond. Pres. Laurel (Va.) Athletic Assn., 1969; founder, pres. Skipwith Football Assn., 1971; chmn. bd. Met. Youth Football League, 1973. Named Orator of Yr., U. Richmond, 1951. Fellow Acad. Parish Clergy; assoc. mem. Am. Sci. Affiliation, Am. Assn. Marriage and Family Counselors; mem. Am. Assn. Pastoral Counselors (pastoral affiliate). Co-author: The Sound of Falling Chains, Colors of the Mind; author: A Bridge Over Troubled Waters, The Symphony of Marriage; asso. editor Bapt. Rev.; contbg. editor Jour. Acad. Parish Clergy. Home: 6308 Walnut Grove Ct Mechanicsville VA 23111 Office: POB 428 Mechanicsville VA 23111

SKAGGS, HAROLD FRANKLIN, minister, Southern Baptist Convention; b. Martin, Tenn., May 4, 1932; s. Don S. and Vida L. (Hutchens) S.; m. Mary Glynn Braswell, Dec. 19, 1959; children: Donald R., James E. A.A., Paducah Jr. Coll., 1952; B.A., Murray State U., 1954; B.D., So. Bapt. Theol. Sem., 1962, M.Div., 1969, D.Min., 1984. Ordained to ministry So. Bapt. Conv., 1952. Bible tchr., Paducah, Ky., 1956-59; pastor First Bapt. Ch., Fisherville, Ky., 1959-62, Oak Grove, Ky., 1962-69, Calhoun Bapt. Ch., Ky., 1969-79, Cadiz Bapt. Ch., Ky., 1979—; mem. exec. bd. Ky. Bapt. Conv., 1973-78, 80—, chmn. nominating com., 1977; trustee Ky. Bapt. Homes for Children, 1981—. Trustee, Trigg County Hosp., Cadiz, 1984, Green River Comprehensive Mental Health Care, Owensboro, Ky., 1975-79; mem. adv. com. Trigg County Fiscal Ct., 1982—. Named hon. Ky. Col., 1979. Democrat. Lodge: Rotary (Cadiz). Home: Hospital St Cadiz KY 42211 Office: Cadiz Baptist Ch PO Box 606 Cadiz KY 42211

SKAGGS, STEPHEN RAY, minister, American Baptist Churches in the U.S.A.; b. Princeton, Ky., Mar. 14, 1947; s. Regnal Ray and Ruth Camilla (Cash) S.; m. Mary Louise Wright, Nov. 24, 1966 (div. June 1976); 1 child, Darrell Gregory; m. Peggi Kephart Boyce, June 30, 1979. B.A. cum laude, Union U., 1969; M.Div., So. Bapt. Theol. Sem., 1973. Ordained to ministry Am. Bapt. Chs. U.S.A., 1973, endorsed to chaplaincy, 1978. Pastor, First Bapt. Ch., Middleport, Ohio, 1973-75; chaplain intern Central State Hosp., Milledgeville, Ga., 1975-76; chaplain resident Morris Village Alcohol and Drug Treatment Ctr., Columbia, S.C., 1976-77; sr. chaplain Eastern State Hosp., Lexington, Ky., 1977-81, prin. chaplain, 1982-83; staff chaplain, Protestant supr. pastoral care VA Med. Ctr., Lexington, 1983—; adj. prof., field supr. Asbury Theol. Sem., Wilmore, Ky., 1978—. Contbr. articles to profl. jours. Mem. Assn. Clin. Pastoral Edn. (clin. mem.). Democrat. Home: PO Box 11593 Lexington KY 40576 Office: VA Med Ctr 008-LD Leestown Rd Lexington KY 40511

SKEETE, F. HERBERT, minister, United Methodist Church; b. N.Y.C., Mar. 22, 1930; s. Ernest A. and Elma I. (Ramsey) S.; B.A., Bklyn. Coll., 1959; M.Div., Drew U., 1962; S.T.M., N.Y. Theol. Sem., 1970; D.Ministry, Drew U., 1975; m. Shirley C. Hunte, Oct. 4, 1952; children—Michael H., Mark C. Ordained to ministry, 1961; pastor Union United Meth. Ch., South Ozone Park, N.Y.C., 1960-67, N.Y.C. Mission Soc., 1967-68, Salem United Meth. Ch., Harlem, N.Y.C., 1968—. Religious commentator WINS Radio, 1969; bd. mem. Bd. Global Ministries, United Meth. Ch., 1972—, v.p. nat. div., 1972—; treas. Haryou-Act Bd., 1974-76; v.p. Ministerial Interfaith Assn. Harlem, 1968; mem. bd. Fedn. Protestant Welfare Agys., 1975—, Am. Bible Soc., 1975—. Mem. bd. Meth. Hosp., Bklyn., 1972—, Drew U., 1976—. Mem. NAACP. Office: 2190 Adam Powell Blvd New York NY 10027

SKERIS, ROBERT EDWARD, priest, Roman Catholic Church; b. Sheboygan, Wis., Nov. 17, 1942; s. Anthony Joseph and Vivian Elizabeth (Krick) S.; B.A., St. Joseph's Coll., 1965; postgrad. St. Anthony Sem., 1965-69, Marquette U., 1970-71; B.S. in Psychology/Alcohol and Drug Abuse Counseling, 1984; candidate M.S.W., Wayne State U., 1984. Ordained to ministry, 1968; bd. dirs., staff mem. House of Peace Community Center, Milw., 1969; mem. Priest Worker Movement, Milw., 1969; co-pastor St. Francis Ch., Milw., 1970-74, pastor, 1974-75; mem. governing bd. St. Bonaventure Monastery, Detroit, 1975-77; mem. pastoral team St. Aloysius Parish, Detroit, 1975-79. Bd. dirs. Capuchin Community Center, Detroit, 1975-83; founding dir. Jefferson House, Detroit, 1975-83. Bd. dirs. Operation Breadbasket, Milw., 1971-72, Braggs-Brooks Phys. Fitness Center, Milw., 1973-75; pres. DePorres Community Sch. Bd., Milw., 1972-74; chmn. health and welfare com. Community Relations-Social Devel. Commn., Milw., 1973-75, v.p. coordinating council, 1973-75, vice chmn. area council, 1973-75; bd. dirs. Minorities Permanent Deaconate Com., Milw., 1973-75; advisor Inner City Council on Alcoholism, Milw., 1972-75; bd. dirs. Upward Bound program, U. Wis., Milw., 1972-73. Recipient Community Service award, Milw. Commn. on Community Relations, 1973. Mem. NAACP, Wis. Council Chs., Council on Urban Life, Milw. Assn. Concerned Citizens. Home: 1740 Mt Elliott Ave Detroit MI 48207

SKERRITT, WALTER EARDLEY WYKEHAM, minister, Progressive National Baptist Convention, Inc.; b. Sandy Point, B.W.I., June 3, 1931; came to U.S., 1961, naturalized, 1966; s. James Adolphus Skerritt and Ruth Anne Eliza (Nicholls) Joseph; m. Vira Gwendolyn Lawrence, Dec. 30, 1954; children: Shirley, Eardley, Corinne, Dwight, Zachary, Janine, Cornel. Diplomate in Theology, Caribbean Pilgrim Bible Coll., B.W.I., 1954; Th.B., Clarksville Sch. Theology, 1966; Th.M., Internat. Bible Inst. and Sem., 1983, D.D. (hon.), 1985. Ordained to ministry Bapt. Ch., 1959. Pastor, evangelist Pilgrim Holiness Ch., St. Kitts, B.W.I., 1954-61, sec. dist. adv. bd., 1959-61; pastor, founder Calvary Ch. Nazarene, Hartford, Conn., 1963-73; pastor 1st Ch. Nazarene, Wakefield, R.I. 1973-76; assoc. minister Congdon St. Bapt. Ch., Providence, 1976-79, New Light Bapt. Ch., Detroit, 1979-82; pastor King Solomon Bapt. Ch., Detroit, 1982—; dir. Christian edn. div. Mich. Progressive Bapt. Conv., 1981-84; chmn. resolution com. Progressive Nat. Bapt. Conv., 1982—, asst. dean Christian edn. Midwest region, 1984—. Mem. econ. and devel. com. Hartford Urban League, 1966-73; v.p. Hartford chpt. NAACP, 1970-72; pres. Detroit Inner-City Council for Ch. and Community Change, 1984—; bd. dirs. New Ctr. Community Mental Health Services, 1985. Recipient Spirit of Detroit award Detroit City Council, 1982, Spl. Tribute by Mich. State Senate, 1982, Cert. of Merit, Mich. State Senate, 1982, Outstanding Service award Detroit City Council, 1984; honored by Testimonial Resolution, Detroit City Council, 1982, Mich. House and Senate Resolution #159, 1983, Spl. Proclamation, Wayne County, Mich., 1984, Spl. Recognition award Wayne County Coop. Extension Service, Mich. State U., 1985, presentation Great Seal of State of Mich. in recognition of achievement, 1985. Mem. Council Bapt. Ministers, Thursday Luncheon Group. Democrat. Avocations: ping-pong; soccer; swimming; boating. Home: 14000 Asbury Park Detroit MI 48227 Office: King Solomon Bapt Ch 6125 Fourteenth St Detroit MI 48208

SKILES, CLEMENT SAMUEL, ch. ofcl., Old German Bapt. Brethren; b. Rossville, Ind., Feb. 26, 1917; s. David A. and Hettie V. (Milyard) S.; student Rossville pub. schs.; m. Esther Flora Aug. 30, 1940; children: Leann (Mrs. Dale Garber), Richard. Ordained to ministry, 1948, elder, 1958, mem. standing com., 1967—, foreman, 1975—. Farmer, Bringhurst, Ind., 1941—. Home: Box 140 Route 1 Bringhurst IN 46913

SKILLIN, EDWARD SIMEON See *Who's Who in America*, 43rd edition.

SKILLRUD, HAROLD CLAYTON, minister, Lutheran Church in America; b. St. Cloud, Minn., June 29, 1928; s. Harold B. and Amanda T. (Haugen) S.; m. Lois Dickhart, June 8, 1951; children: David, Janet, John. B.A., Gustavus Adolphus Coll., 1950; M.Div., Augustana Theol. Sem., Rock Island, Ill., 1954; S.T.M., Luth. Sch. Theology at Chgo., 1969; D.D. (hon.), Augustana Coll., Rock Island, 1978. Ordained to ministry Luth. Ch., 1954. Sr. pastor St. John's Luth. Ch., Bloomington, Ill., 1954-79, Ch. of Redeemer, Atlanta, 1979—; mem. exec. council Luth. Ch. in Am., 1984—, mem. exec. bd. S.E. Synod, Atlanta, 1984—. Author: LSTC: Decade of Decision, 1969. Contbr. articles to religious publs. Recipient Ann. Alumni award Luth. Sch. Theology at Chgo., 1976. Club: Kiwanis (pres. 1983-84). Home: 368 E Wesley Rd NE Atlanta GA 30305 Office: Lutheran Church of the Redeemer 731 Peachtree St NE Atlanta GA 30308

SKINNER, BILLY WAYNE, minister, Southern Baptist Convention; b. Houston, Oct. 11, 1933; s. George P. and Virgie (Griffin) S.; m. Eva Louise Inman, Sept. 6, 1958; children: Cynthia Sue, Charles Randal, Larry Michael Wayne. B.A., E. Tex. Bapt. Coll., 1965; M.Div., Southwestern Bapt. Theol. Sem., 1969. Ordained to ministry Baptist Ch., 1962. Pastor chs. in Tex., 1962-66, Market St. Bapt. Ch., Youngstown, Ohio, 1971—; pres. P.T.L. Youngstown Christian Sch., 1984. Served with U.S. Army, 1956-58, Europe. Home: 715 Cheriwood Ct Youngstown OH 44512 Office: PO Box 3537 Youngstown OH 44512

SKINNER, RICHARD DAVID, religion educator, minister, Southern Baptist Convention; b. Lexington, Miss., Jan. 26, 1933; s. Emmett Henry and Callie (Vinson) S.; m. Maudie Louise Gregory, Aug. 7, 1960; children: Tammy, David Jr., Ray, Steven, Robert. B.A., Miss. Coll., 1959; B.D., New Orleans Bapt. Theol. Sem., 1962; Th.D., Mid-Am. Bapt. Sem., 1975. Ordained to ministry So. Bapt. Conv., 1957. Pastor, Beulah Bapt. Ch., Lexington, Miss., 1957-62, Roseland Bapt. Ch., La., 1962-65, DeKalb Bapt. Ch., Miss., 1965-67, Mt. Zion Bapt. Ch., Columbus, Miss., 1967-74; prof. Mid-Am. Bapt. Theol. Sem., Memphis, 1974—. Assoc. editor Mid-Am. Theol. Jour., 1977. Contbr. articles to religious jours. Served with USAF, 1952-56, ETO. Mem. Am. Schs. Oriental Research. Office: Mid-Am Bapt Theol Sem 1255 Poplar Memphis TN 38104

SKRYPNYK, MSTYSLAV STEPAN, archbishop, metropolitan, prelate Ukrainian Orthodox Ch. in U.S.A.; b. Poltava, Ukraine, Apr. 10, 1898; s. Ivan and

Mariamna (Petlura) S.; postgrad. Warsaw U., Sch. Polit. Sci. Warsaw, 1930; Ph.D. (hon.), Ukrainian Free U., 1950; m. Ivanna Witkovytsky, Jan. 8, 1921; children: Yaroslav, Tamara Yarovenko, Mariamna Suchoversky. Came to U.S., 1950. Mem. Orthodox Diocesan Council, Volyn, 1932-39; ordained priest Ukrainian Orthodox Ch., 1942; bishop of Pereyaslav, 1942-44; sec. Council of Bishops in Exile, 1945-46; bishop Ukrainian Orthodox Ch. in Western Europe, 1946-47; archbishop Ukrainian Orthodox Ch. in Can., 1947-50; archbishop, pres. consistory Ukrainian Orthodox Ch. U.S.A., 1950-71; archbishop of Phila., metropolitan Ukrainian Orthodox Ch. U.S.A., 1971—; South Ukrainian Orthodox Ch. in Free World (except U.S. and Can.), 1960—. Dir. Coop. Union, Halychyna, 1923-26; mem. Fgn. Affairs Commn. and Budget Com., 1931-39. Dep. to Mayor Rivne, Volyn, 1930-31; mem. Polish Parliament, Warsaw, sec. Seym Presidium, 1931-39; pres. Ukrainian Sch. Assn. in Poland, Volyn, 1932-39. Address: PO Box 445 South Bound Brook NJ 08880

SKUDLAREK, WILLIAM, clergyman, educational administrator, Roman Catholic. Rector, dean St. John's U. Sch. Theology, Collegeville, Minn. Office: St John's U Sch Theology Collegeville MN 56321*

SKUTT, CHARLES HENRY, minister, So. Bapt. Conv.; b. Portsmouth, Va., Aug. 20, 1916; s. George Henry and Helen Louise (Wright) S.; B.A., Miss. Coll., 1945; D.D., Am. Div. Sch., Pineland, Fla., 1957, Litt.D., 1969; m. Wilma Louise Kenney, May 15, 1943; children—Barbara, Charles Robert. Ordained to ministry, 1942; pastor chs. in Miss., 1942-60; pastor LaBelle Pl. Bapt. Ch., Memphis, 1960-66, Spradling Bapt. Ch., Ft. Smith, Ark., 1966—; mem. extension faculty Am. Div. Sch., So. Bapt. seminaries; chaplain-on-call Holiday Inns. Moderator Prentiss County (Miss.) Bapt. Assn., 1951-52, Desoto County (Miss.) Bapt. Assn., 1955-56, Concord (Ark.) Bapt. Assn., 1970-72; pres. Ft. Smith Bapt. Pastors Conf., 1970-71. Mem. Ft. Smith Housing Assistance Bd., Ft. Smith Citizens Com. Urban Improvement. Recipient award of merit Holiday Inns. Author textbook materials. Home: 4100 Marshall Dr Fort Smith AR 72904 Office: Spradling Baptist Ch 3515 Waldron Rd Fort Smith AR 72904

SKWOR, DONALD P., clergyman, Roman Catholic. Exec. dir. Conf. of Major Superiors of Men, Silver Spring, Md. Office: Conf of Major Superiors of Men 8808 Cameron St Silver Spring MD 20910*

SKY, HARRY Z., rabbi, Conservative Judaism; b. Newark, Apr. 17, 1924; s. Louis and Ida (Furman) S.; B.A., Yeshiva U., 1945; M.Hebrew Lit., Jewish Theol. Sem., 1951, D.D., 1977; D.D., Nasson Coll., 1976; m. Ruth Helen Levinson, Dec. 24, 1950; children—Rina, Uri, Ari. Ordained rabbi, 1951; rabbi, Mass., N.Y., Va., Tex., Indpls., to 1961; rabbi Temple Beth El, Portland, Maine, 1961—; former mem. faculty U. Maine, Portland-Gorham, Nasson Coll., St. Francis Coll. Mem. Maine Human Services Council; trustee Portland Stage Co., Maine Hist. Soc., Portland Symphony Orch. Mem. Rabbinical Assembly. Home: 400 Deering Ave Portland ME 04103

SKYLSTAD, WILLIAM S. See *Who's Who in America*, 43rd edition.

SLANEY, WILLIAM THOMAS, priest, Roman Catholic Church; b. Dartmouth, N.S., Can., July 19, 1929; s. Michael and Theresa Mary (Gray) S. B.A., St. Joseph's U., 1951; B.Theol., Holy Heart Sem., 1956; M.Theol. Studies, Atlantic Sch. Theology, 1974. Ordained priest Roman Cath. Ch., 1956; cert. chaplain. Asst. or curate St. Joseph's Ch., Halifax, N.S., 1956-62, Immaculate Conception Ch., Truro, N.S., 1962-64, St. Patrick's Ch., Halifax, 1964-66; parish priest St. Denis Ch., East Ship Harbour, N.S., 1966-69, St. Peter's Ch., Sheet Harbour, N.S., 1969-72; chaplain V.G. Hosp., Halifax, 1972-76; parish priest St. Thomas Aquinas Ch., Joggins, N.S., 1976-83, Star of Sea Ch., Terence Bay, N.S., 1983—; senator Senate of Priests, Halifax, 1984-86; dean-elect Coll. of Fellows APC, 1984-85; dir. Acad. of parish Clergy, 1982-85; sec. Atlantic Seminar in Theol. Edn., Truro, Author: Viewpoint, 1979. Chmn. Eastern Shore Meml. Hosp., Sheet Harbour, 1970-72. Recipient People Helping People award Sta. CKDH, Amherst, N.S., 1983. Fellow Acad. parish Clergy; mem. Diocesan Ecumenical Commn., Atlantic Sch. Theology Assn., Can. Assn. for Pastoral Edn. Lodge: K.C.

SLATER, OLIVER EUGENE, bishop, United Methodist Church; b. Sibley, La., Sept. 10, 1906; s. Oliver Thornwell and Mattie (Kennon) S.; B.A., So. Meth. U., 1930, LL.D., 1964; B.D., Perkins Sch. Theology, 1932; D.D., McMur Coll., Abilene, Tex., 1951; H.H.D., Southwestern Coll., Winfield, Kans., 1961; LL.D., Baker U., Baldwin, Kans., 1962; m. Eva B Richardson, Nov. 25, 1931; children: Susan (Mrs. H. Kipling Edenborough), Stewart Eugene. Ordained to ministry as deacon, 1932, elder, 1936; elected bishop, 1960; pastor chs., Tex., 1932-60; assigned to Kans. Area, Topeka, 1960-64, N.W. Tex.-S.W. Tex. Area, 1964-68, San Antonio, 1968-76; bishop-in-residence Perkins Sch. Theology, Dallas, 1976-80; mem. Gen. Bd. Edn. United Meth. Ch., 1960-72, pres., 1964-72; mem. Gen. Bd. Lay Activities, 1960-68; chmn. Com. to Study Employed Lay Career Work in Meth. Ch., 1964-68; vice chmn. Interbd. Com. on Enlistment for Ch. Occupations, 1968-72; rep. United Meth. Council Bishops to Brit. Meth. Conf., 1972; visitor Meth. missions, S.Am., 1956; visitor World Council Chs., Evanston, Ill., 1954; attended World Meth. Conf., Oslo, Norway, 1961; pres. Commn. Archives and History, 1972-76; mem. bd. Global Missions, 1972-76. Trustee So. Meth. U., Southwestern U., Georgetown, S.W. Tex. Meth. Hosp., San Antonio, Ecumenical Center for Religion and Health, San Antonio, Morningside Manor, San Antonio. Mem. Council Bishops (pres. 1972-73). Recipient Distinguished Alumnus award So. Meth. U., 1975. Home: 7424-9 W Northwest Hwy Dallas TX 75225 Office: Selecman Hall Perkins School of Theology Dallas TX 75275

SLAUBAUGH, VICTOR HARRY, minister, Independent Baptist Church; truck driver; b. Horse Shoe Run, W.Va., Nov. 5, 1949; s. Webster Wade and Fayetta Williams (Griffith) S.; m. Ruby Loraine Bray, Nov. 4, 1972; children: Denise Dawn, Dana Loraine, Deanna Marie. Grad. Aurora High Schs. Minister ch. services Hope Mont State Hosp., W.Va., 1976—, Cuppet & Weeks Nursing Home, Oakland, Md., 1974—, Garrett County Jail, Oakland, 1983—; supt. Lighthouse Independent Bapt. Ch., Red House, Md., 1979—. Truck driver Hill Top Constrn. Co., Clarksburg, W.Va., 1984—. Served with U.S. Army, 1969-72; Germany. Democrat. Avocation: bible study.

SLAUGHT, MARTIN E., priest, Roman Catholic Church; b. Los Angeles, Aug. 16, 1926; s. Francis Ellsworth and Ann (Martin) S. B.A., St. John's Coll., 1947; postgrad. in social work U. So. Calif., 1956-57, in sociology U. Calif.-Santa Barbara, 1961-66, Calif. State U.-Northridge, 1970-73. Ordained priest Roman Catholic Ch., 1951. Asst. pastor St. Charles of Assumption, Los Angeles, 1951-56; asst. dir. Cath. Welfare Bur., Santa Barbara, 1956-69; dir. campus ministry Archdiocese Los Angeles, 1970-73; pastor St. Elizabeth's Ch., Altadena, Calif., 1973—. Democrat. Address: St Elizabeth's Ch 1849 N Lake Ave Altadena CA 91001

SLIMAK, BASIL WILLIAM W, priest, psychiatric chaplain, Orthodox Church in America; b. Detroit, Feb. 27, 1935; s. Michael and Nettie (Shishko) S.; m. Patricia Stop, June 23, 1962; children: Samuel, Juliane, Nadine. B.B.A., Detroit Inst. Tech., 1961; M.Div., St. Vladimir's Sem., 1964; M.Div., Ashland Theol. Sem., 1973. Ordained priest Orthodox Ch. in Am., 1964. Pastor, Christ the Savior Ch., Byesville, Ohio, 1964-68; Eastern Orthodox chaplain Cambridge State Hosp., Ohio, 1964-68; chaplain Massillon State Hosp., Ohio, 1970—; mem. exec. bd. Stark County Council Chs., Canton, Ohio, 1969—. Editor: Sacraments for Orthodox, 1974. Mem. Ohio State Chaplains Assn., Assn. Fedn. State and Mcpl. Employees. Home: 5125 12th St NW Canton OH 44708 Office: Box 540 Massillon OH 44648

SLOAN, JOHN OWEN, minister, General Association of General Baptists; b. Newburgh, Ind., Oct. 27, 1941; s. Benjamin Harrison and Mary Margaret (Owens) S.; m. Gladys Marie Phillips, Nov. 26, 1966; children: Angela Marie, Renee Lynn, Rodney Aaron. B.A., Oakland City Coll., 1966. Ordained to ministry Liberty Assn. Gen. Baptists. Pastor various chs., Ind., Ill., Ky., 1963-77, Twelfth Ave. Gen. Bapt. Ch., Evansville, Ind., 1977—; moderator Liberty Assn. Gen. Bapts., Ind., 1970, 79; mem. home mission bd., 1966-72, 1976-83, pres., 1979, 81, 83. Clubs: Men's (Dixon, Ky.), Lions (Outstanding Citizen award 1976), Kiwanis (dir. 1977). Home: 2300 W Indiana St Evansville IN 47712 Office: Twelfth Ave Gen Bapt Ch 2225 W Indiana St Evansville IN 47712

SLOCUMB, DOUGLAS WAYNE, minister, Church of God; b. Carmi, Ill., June 30, 1942; s. William Paul and Fern Elosie (Given) S.; m. Esther Joyce Lilly, Oct. 5, 1963; children: Douglas Wayne II, Robert Paul. A.A., Lee Coll., 1965, B.A., 1967; M.Ed., U. N.C., 1979; A.A.S., Cleveland State Community Coll., 1983. Ordained to ministry Ch. of God. Assoc. pastor, dir. Christian edn. Ch. of God, Dayton, Ohio, 1967-69, pastor, 1969-72; pastor Ch. of God, Lowell, N.C., 1972-77, Thomasville, N.C., 1977-78; coordinator of communication Ch. of God, Cleveland, Tenn., 1978—; liaison internat. students Ch. of God, 4 campuses in U.S., 1979—; mem. scholarship and internship coms. Ch. of God Sch. of Theology, Cleveland, 1980—; sec. Pentecostal Fellowship of North Am., Dayton, 1968-72; sec., v.p., pres. Ministerial Assn., Gastonia, N.C., 1972-79. Author: Church of God in North Carolina, 1978; Lowell Zoning and Planning, 1977; (with others) Photo Tips, 1984. Contbr. articles to religious publs. Chmn. United Fund, Lowell, N.C., 1974, Zoning and Planning Commn., Lowell, 1976-77; trustee Gaston County Mental Health Assn., N.C., 1975-77. Recipient Photography award Mchts. Assn. Mem. Profl. Photography Assn., Internat. Communications Assn., Assn. Multi-Image Internat., Internat. Council of Accrediting Assns., Soc. Pentecostal Studies, Evang. Fgn. Mission Assn. Home: 4009 Laurel Dr Cleveland TN 37311 Office: Church of God World Missions Keith at 25th Sts Cleveland TN 37311

SLOSARCIK, EDWARD AUGUSTINE, priest, Roman Cath. Ch.; b. Chgo., Mar. 4, 1924; s. Karol and Annastasia (Matonog) S.; M.A., St. Mary of Lake Seminary, 1949; M.Ed., DePaul U., 1970; M.A. in Sociology, U. Ill., 1972. Ordained priest, 1950; asso. pastor Chgo. parishes, 1950—; religion tchr. Maria High Sch., Chgo., 1966—; prof. med. ethics De Lourdes Coll., St. Mary of Nazareth Nursing Sch., 1973—. Mem. Religious Edn. Assn., Ill. Guidance Personnel Assn., Nat. Cath. Edn. Assn., Inst. of Society, Ethics and Life Scis. Home and Office: 3111 S Aberdeen St Chicago IL 60608

SLOTNICK, MICHAEL COTLER, lay church worker, Conservative Jewish Congregations; b. Utica, N.Y., Apr. 30, 1935; s. Morris and Sylvia (Cotler) S.; B.A., U. Miami, 1957, J.D., 1960; m. Susan Jean Zeientz, Nov. 25, 1964; children: Marc Jeffrey, Deborah Lynn. Rec. sec. Temple Zion, Miami, Fla., 1962-69, 2d v.p., 1969-71, 1st v.p., 1971-72, pres., 1972-74, mem. exec. bd., 1974-76, chmn. bd. trustees, 1976-77; rec. sec. Temple Samu-El, Miami, 1978-82, edn. v.p., 1982-84. Partner firm Pallot, Poppell, Goodman & Slotnick, Miami, 1973-83, Pestcoe, Slotnick & Garcia, Miami, 1983—. Pres., Kendale Home Owners Assn., Miami, 1970-72; chmn. citizens adv. com. Kendale Elementary Sch., 1975-76. Mem. Am., Dade County bar assns., Fla. Bar. Home: 10340 SW 96th Terr Miami FL 33176 Office: 2655 Le Jeune Rd Suite 201 Coral Gables FL 33134

SLOYAN, GERARD STEPHEN, priest, educator, Roman Catholic Church; b. N.Y.C., Dec. 13, 1919; s. Jerome James and Marie Virginia (Kelley) S. A.B., Seton Hall U., 1940; LL.D. (hon.), 1983; S.T.L., Cath. U. Am., 1944, Ph.D., 1948. Ordained priest Roman Catholic Church, 1944. Asst. pastor Diocese of Trenton, N.J., 1947-50; instr. to prof. religion Cath. U. Am., Washington, 1950-67, chmn. dept., 1957-67; prof. religion Temple U., Phila., 1967—, chmn. dept., 1970-74, 84—; mem. Roman Cath.-United Meth. Ch. Bilateral Dialogue, U.S.A., 1974-80, mem. Roman Cath.-Reformed Chs., 1981-84; observer Ch. Order Commn., Consultation on Ch. Union, 1980—; chmn. bd. dirs. Liturgical Conf., Washington, D.C., 1980—. Author: Jesus on Trial, 1974; A Commentary on the New Lectionary, 1975; Jesus in Focus: The Story of a Life in Its Setting, (second pl. award best adult book Cath. Press Assn. 1984), 1984. Mem. Coll. Theology Soc. (pres. 1966-68, best book by mem. 1980, best article by mem. 1981), Cath. Biblical Assn., Soc. Biblical Lit., Cath. Theol. Soc. Am. (John Courtney Murray award 1981). Democrat. Home: 2313 Sansom St Philadelphia PA 19103 Office: Temple U Dept Religion Broad and Montgomery Sts Philadelphia PA 19122

SLUBERSKI, THOMAS RICHARD, theologian, educator, minister, Lutheran Church-Mo. Synod; b. Jersey City, Dec. 7, 1939; s. Walter and Anna Louise (Gall) S. B.A. with honors, Concordia Coll., 1962; M.Div. with high honors, Concordia Sem., 1966; postgrad. U. Vienna (Austria), summer 1966, U. Erlangen-Nuremberg (W. Ger.), 1966-68; M.A. in English Lit., Washington U., 1970; Th.D. with honors, U. Heidelberg (W. Ger.), 1973. Ordained to ministry, 1969; vicar Zion Luth. Ch., Wausau, Wis., 1964-65; asst. to dean chapel, lectr. dept. theology Valparaiso (Ind.) U., 1969-70; assoc. prof. English, humanities ch. history, Old and New Testament, Concordia Coll., Bronxville, N.Y., 1972—, chmn. depts. English and philosophy, 1974—; pastor St. Matthew's Luth. Ch., Hastings-on-Hudson, N.Y.; fellow Center for Creative Persons, Montauk, L.I., N.Y., 1975. Asst. dir. pub. relations Atlantic Dist. Conv., Luth. Ch.-Mo. Synod, 1976; bd. dirs. Luth. Soc. Worship, Music and Arts, 1971-73. Juror Am. Film Festival, N.Y.C., 1976-85. Austrian State scholar, 1966; Bavarian State scholar, 1966-67; World Council Chs. fellow, 1967; Deutscher Akademischer Austauschdienst fellow, 1970-72; Aid Assn. for Lutherans Faculty Study grantee, 1972. Fellow Christian Writers Inst. Contbr. articles to religious publs.; asst. editor Seminarian jour., 1965-66; lit. survey editor Luth. World, 1968-69. Home: 15 Farragut Ave Hastings-on-Hudson NY 10706 Office: Concordia College Bronxville NY 10708

SLY, JAMES EDWARD, JR., lay worker, Independent Fundamental Churches of America; Air force policeman; b. Dowagiac, Mich., May 19, 1958; s. James Edward and Margaret Ellen (Hutson) S. B.R.E., Grand Rapids Bapt. Coll., 1981; M.R.E., Covington Theol. Sem., 1985; Assoc. Applied Sci., Community Coll. of Air Force, 1985. Dir. juvenile home ministry Grand Rapids Bapt. Coll., Mich., 1978-81, evangelism dir., 1980-81; youth pastor Bethany Chapel, Three Rivers, Mich., 1979-81; asst. dir. Christy Lake Bible Camp, Lawrence, Mich., 1981; youth dir. Las Vegas Bible Ch,, Nev., 1983-84, youth pastor, 1985—. Security policeman U.S. Air Force, Nellis AFB, Nev., 1982—. Court appointed spl. advocate Clark County Juvenile Court System, Las Vegas, 1983—; cubmaster Boulder Dam area council Boy Scouts Am., 1985—. Mich. State Bd. Edn. scholar, 1977. Avocations: hiking; camping; canoeing; photography; stamp collecting. Home: 29 N 28th St #3A Las Vegas NV 89101 Office: 4461st SG/SP Nellis AFB NV 89191

SMALL, RALPH MILTON, publisher, minister, Churches of Christ; b. Richland Center, Wis., Oct. 26, 1917; s. John Marion and Jessie Angeline (Rowe) S.; B.A. cum laude, Cin. Bible Sem., 1939, postgrad., 1939-41; postgrad. U. Cin., 1941, Lincoln Christian Sem., 1947; D.D., Pacific Christian Coll., 1971. Ordained to ministry, 1939; minister Antioch Ch. of Christ, Rossville, Ill., 1939-63; chaplain AUS, 1945; cons. Bible sch. Standard Pub., Cin., 1963-66, editor Seek Mag., 1967, dir. ch. growth dept., 1968-71, exec. editor, 1970, v.p. and publisher, 1971—. Chmn. Chaplaincy Endorsement Commn., 1968-72; dir. Nat. Christian Edn. Conv., 1963—; tchr. White Oak Christian Ch., 1963—; bd. dirs. Directory of the Ministry, Springfield, Ill., 1971—, Ch. Found. for the Handicapped, Knoxville, Tenn., 1984—. Trustee Milligan Coll. (Tenn.), 1972—; bd. dirs. Muscular Dystrophy Assn., Danville, Ill., 1958-61; sec. bd. advisers Directory Ministry, Christian Chs. and Chs. of Christ, 1972—. Mem. Nat. Assn. Evangs., Internat. Platform Assn., Delta Aleph Tau. Home: 1010 Newcastle Dr Cincinnati OH 45231 Office: 8121 Hamilton Ave Cincinnati OH 45231

SMALLEY, WILLIAM RICHARD, priest, Roman Catholic Church; b. Bayonne, N.J., Mar. 26, 1928; s. Denis William and Margaret (Brown) S. A.B., Seton Hall U., 1951; Grad. classical langs., philosophy, Immaculate Conception Sem., 1953, M.Div., 1978; grad. Nat. Staff Coll. USAF, 1974. Ordained priest Roman Catholic Ch., 1955. First asst. pastor Immaculate Conception, Secaucus, N.J., 1955-62, Christ the King Ch., Hillside, N.J., 1962-79; pastor St. Paul the Apostle, Irvington, N.J., 1979—; police and fire chaplain, Irvington, N.J., 1982—; Essex County Sheriff's chaplain, 1984; pastor, sec.-treas. St. Paul the Apostle, Irvington, 1979; lt. col., chaplain N.Y. Guard, Albany, 1983. Com. mem. nat. legis. com. USAF Aux. CAP, Maxwell AFB, Ala., 1976—, legis. liaison N.J. Wing, McGuire AFB, 1976—. Served to lt. col. USAF, 1974—, chief chaplains N.J. wing, 1980—. Mem. Mil. Chaplains U.S. (chaplain). Clubs: Blizzard (Bayonne, N.J.) (chaplain 1955); Panther Valley Golf and Country (Allamuchy, N.J.); U.S. Golf Assn. Lodge: KC (chaplain 1980). Home and Office: 954 Stuyvesant Ave Irvington NJ 07111

SMATT, EDDIE GEORGE, minister, Southern Baptist Convention; b. Bklyn., Apr. 5, 1951; s. William and Hypha (Bardowell) Smatt; m. Donna Lynn Throckmorton, May 14, 1977; children: Brian, Justin, Angela. A.A., Coll. Orlando (Fla.), 1971; B.A., Union U., Jackson, Tenn., 1973; M.Div., Southwestern Bapt. Theol. Sem., Ft. Worth, 1977. Ordained minister So. Bapt. Conv., 1973, evangelist, Miami, Fla., 1975-79; pastor St. Helen Bapt. Ch., (Mich.), 1977-78, 1st Bapt. Ch., Center Hill, Fla., 1979-81, Eagle Lake, Fla., 1981—. Mem. Republican Nat. Com., Washington, 1984. Mem. Ridge Bapt. Assn. (budget com. 1982-85, resolutions com. 1982, Christian life commn. com., 1984—). Home: PO Box 1103 Eagle Lake FL 33839 Office: 1st Bapt Ch PO Box 155 Eagle Lake FL 33839

SMICK, ELMER BERNARD, minister, educator Presbyterian Church in America; b. Balt., July 10, 1921; s. Frank and Marie (Hagert) S.; m. Jane Harrison, Aug. 19, 1944; children: Peter, Karen, Theodore, Rebecca. B.A., King's Coll., 1944; Th.B., S.T.M., Faith Theol. Sem., 1948; Ph.D., Dropsie Coll., 1951. Ordained to ministry Presbyn. Ch. in Am., 1947. Pastor, Evang. Presbyn. Ch., Trenton, N.J., 1947-56; prof. Old Testament langs. Covenant Theol. Sem., St. Louis, 1956-71; prof. Old Testament, Gordon Conwell Theol. Sem., South Hamilton, Mass., 1971—; moderator N.J. Presbytery, Ref. Presbyn. Ch., 1953-54, asst. clk. of synod, 1965; trustee Nat. Presbyn. Missions, 1948-68, World Presbyn. Missions, 1979-81. Author: Archaeology of the Jordan Valley, 1973. Editor: The New International Version of the Bible, 1968-78. Named Alumnus of Yr., King's Coll., 1984. Fellow Inst. Bibl. Research (exec. com.); mem. Nat. Assn. Profs. Hebrew (exec. com.), Evang. Theol. Soc., Am. Oriental Soc., Soc. Bibl. Lit. Home: 84 Old Cart Rd South Hamilton MA 01982 Office: Gordon Conwell Theol Sem South Hamilton MA 01982

SMILEY, ALBERT KEITH, lay church worker, Society of Friends; b. Mohonk Lake, N.Y., May 13, 1910; s. Albert K. and Mable (Craven) S.; A.B., Haverford Coll., 1932; m. Ruth Happel, Apr. 30, 1939; children: Sandra, Albert K. Clk. of ministry and counsel N.Y. Yearly Meeting, Religious Soc. Friends, 1960-62, chmn. com. for study of faith and beliefs, 1959-63; mem. exec. com. Friends World Com., Sect. of Americas, 1962-82; clk. com. on right sharing of world's resources, 1973-82; mem. Task Force on Christian Peacemaking as Lifestyle, New Call to Peacemaking, 1977-79; bd. advisers Earlham Sch. Religion, Richmond, Ind., 1972—. Pres. Smiley Bros., Inc., Mohonk Mountain House, 1969-80, chmn., 1980—; clk. bd. mgrs. Mohonk Cons., Inc., Mohonk Lake, New Paltz, N.Y., 1980—. Coordinator New Paltz Area Common Cause, 1973-75; mem. bd. mgrs. Oakwood Sch., Poughkeepsie, N.Y., 1958-67. Home and Office: Mohonk Lake New Paltz NY 12561

SMITH, BAILEY EUGENE, minister, Southern Baptist Church; b. Jan. 30, 1939; s. Bailey Ezell and Amber Frances (Lucky) S.; m. Sandra Lee Elliff, June 8, 1963; children: Scott, Steven, Josh. B.A., Ouachita Bapt. U., 1962, D. Div. (hon.), 1978; B.D., Southwestern Bapt. Theol. Sem., 1966; D.Bibl. Studies (hon.), Dallas Bapt. Coll., 1981. Pastor Meml. Bapt. Ch., Waldo, Ark., First Bapt. Ch., Hobbs, N.Mex., First So. Bapt. Ch., Del City, Okla., 1973—; pres. Pastor's Conf. of So. Bapt. Conv., 1978, Okla. Bapt. Gen. Conv., Oklahoma City, 1980, So. Bapt. Conv., St. Louis, 1980, Los Angeles, 1981. Author: Real Evangelism, 1978; Real Christianity, 1979; Real Evangelistic Preaching, 1981; Real Revival Preaching, 1982. Mem. Del City C. of C. Lodges: Rotary, Lions. Office: First So Bapt Ch SE 28th and S Sunnylane PO Box 15039 Del City OK 73155

SMITH, BARDWELL LEITH, religious educator, priest, Episcopal Church; b. Springfield, Mass., July 28, 1925; s. Winthrop Hiram and Gertrude (Ingram) S.; m. Charlotte McCorkindale, Aug. 19, 1961; children: Peter, Susan, Laura, Brooks, Samuel. B.A., Yale U., 1950, B.D., 1953, M.A., 1957, Ph.D., 1964. Ordained priest Episcopal Ch., 1954. Curate, Trinity Episcopal Ch., Highland Park, Ill., 1954-56; asst. instr. Yale U., New Haven, 1958, Yale Div. Sch., 1958-60; asst. prof. religion Carleton Coll., Northfield, Minn., 1960-65, assoc. prof., 1965-69, prof., 1969—; cons. in field; co-editor Contributions to Asian Studies, 1973—; bd. internat. advisors Internat. Asian Studies Programme, Chinese U. Hong Kong, 1976—; bd. dirs. Gen. Service Found., 1971-77; trustee The Blake Schs., Mpls., 1980-83. Editor and contbr: Essays on Gupta Culture, 1983; co-editor and contbr.: Warlords, Artists and Commoners: Japan in the Sixteenth Century, 1981; editor, contbr.: Religion and Legitimazation of Power in Sri Lanka, 1978, others. Contbr. articles to profl. jours. State del. Dem. Farm Labor Party, Minn., 1968. Served with USMC, 1944-46; PTO. Mem. Am. Acad. Religion (dir. 1969-72), Internat. Assn. Buddhist Studies (dir. 1976—), Can. Assn. S. Asian Studies (v.p. 1972-73), Am. Soc. Study of Religion, Phi Beta Kappa. Democrat. Home: 104 Maple St Northfield MN 55057 Office: Dept Religion Carleton Coll Northfield MN 55057

SMITH, BENNETT WALKER, minister, Progressive National Baptist Convention, Inc.; b. Florence, Ala., Apr. 7, 1933; s. Pearline Smith; m. Trixie C Clement, Sept. 19, 1955 (div. May 1982); children: Debra T., Bennett Jr., Lydia R., Matthew T. B.S., Tenn. State U., 1958; D.D. (hon.) Cin. Bapt. Theol. Sem., 1967; L.H.D. (hon.), Medialle Coll., 1979. Ordained to ministry Progressive Nat. Bapt. Conv., Inc., 1962. Pastor, First Bapt. Ch., Cin., 1963-65, Lincoln Hgts., Bapt. Ch., Cin., 1965-72; instr. Congress Christian Edn., 1968-80; v.p. Progressive Baptists, 1980-82; pastor St. John Baptist Ch., Buffalo, N.Y., 1972—. Author: Tithing Handbook, 1980. Contbg. editor missionary handbook. Bd. dirs. People United to Serve Humanity, Buffalo, 1974—; nat. chmn. arrangement com. Progressive Nat. Bapt. Conv., Washington D.C., 1980—; pres. Va./Mich. Housing Co., 1982—. Recipient Outstanding Leadership award 1490 Entreprise, Inc., 1982, Medgar Evers award NAACP, 1982, Community Leadership award Black Elected Officials, 1982, Outstanding Clergy award Black Religious Broadcasters, 1983. Mem. NAACP (life), Ptnrs. in Ecuminism, Operation PUSH (nat. bd. dirs., chaplain), Kappa Alpha Psi. Democrat. Home: 105 Humboldt Pkwy Buffalo NY 14214 Office: St John Bapt Ch 184 Goodell St Buffalo NY 14204

SMITH, BILL NEWTON, minister, Southern Baptist Convention; b. Petersburg, Tex., Aug. 28, 1929; s. Cager M. and Carrie A. (Admire) S.; m. Eva Pearl White, Aug. 27, 1949; children: Rita Anette, Edward Monroe, Fred Dewayne, Elizabeth Ann. B.A., U. Corpus Christi, 1960; B.D., Southwestern Bapt. Theol. Sem., 1966. Ordained to ministry Bapt. Ch., 1960. Pastor chs. in Tex., 1960-66, Ind., 1966-84, Okla., 1985—; 2d v.p. Ind. State Bapt. Conv., 1980-83, chmn. missions com., 1977-79. Mem. Evang. Ministers Assn. Republican. Home: 1721 Custer Ave Clinton OK 73601 Office: 17th and Custer Ave Clinton OK 73601

SMITH, CHARLES BROWN, minister of education, Churches of Christ; b. Dallas, May 7, 1950; s. Lawrence Lester and Norma Fern (Locke) S.; m. M. Deanne Monk, Oct. 21, 1978; children: Jessica Erin, Jonathan Vincent. B.Arch., Tex. Tech. U., 1973; M.R.E., Abilene Christian U., 1976. Minister edn. Ch. of Christ, Duncanville, Tex., 1976-80, Mesquite, Tex., 1980—; Contbr. articles to mags. Named one of Outstanding Young Men Am., 1977. Mem. Assn. Leaders Christian Ministry. Avocations: softball; gardening. Home: 705 Melinda Mesquite TX 75149 Office: College and Locust Ch of Christ 400 W Davis Mesquite TX 75149

SMITH, CLYDE CURRY, minister, religion educator, Christian Church (Disciples of Christ); b. Hamilton, Ohio, Dec. 16, 1929; s. Charles Clyde and Mabel Ethel (Curry) S.; m. Ellen Marie Gormsen, June 13, 1953; children: Harald Clyde, Karen Margaret. B.A. cum laude, Miami U., Oxford, Ohio, 1951, M.S., 1951; B.Div., U. Chgo., 1954, M.A., 1961, Ph.D., 1968. Ordained to ministry Christian Ch., 1954. Asst. to dean Disciples Div. House, Chgo., 1956-57; prof. St. John's Coll., Winnipeg, Man., Can., 1958-63; instr. Brandeis U., Waltham, Mass., 1963-65; prof. ancient history and religion U. Wis.-River Falls, 1965—; vis. lectr. div. Edge Hill Coll., Ormskirk, Eng., 1970-71; vis. fellow U. Aberdeen, Scotland, 1980, 85-86; NEH fellow in residence U. Calif.-Santa Barbara, 1978-79. Research grantee Can. Council, 1961, 63, bd. regents U. Wis., 1968, 72, 76, NEH, 1974, 77, 78-79, 81, Univ. Found., River Falls, Wis., 1983, 84. Mem. Can. Soc. Ch. History (treas. 1960-63), Assn. Ancient Historians, N. Am. Patristic Soc., Hellenic Soc. (London), Soc. for Promotion of Roman Studies (London), Brit. Sch. Archaeology in Iraq (London), Soc. Mesopotamian Studies (Toronto), Pierce County Hist. Assn., Minn. Hist. Soc. Democrat. Home: 939 W Maple St River Falls WI 54022 Office: U Wis River Falls WI 54022

SMITH, DANA PROM, minister, United Presbyn. Ch. in U.S.A.; b. Glendale, Calif., Apr. 7, 1927; s. Tom Nelson Miles and Hazel Marguerite (Prom) S.; A.B., Princeton, 1951; B.D., Louisville Presbyn. Sem., 1954, Th.M., 1955; M.A., U. Ariz., 1958; m. Grace Marie Rinck, Aug. 11, 1951; children—Paul Prom, Timothy Rinck, Elizabeth Marie. Ordained to ministry, 1954; pastor chs., Manchester, Ohio, 1953-55, Tucson, 1955-58, Fulton, Ill., 1958-60, Fox Valley Presbyn. Ch., Geneva, Ill., 1960-68, St. Luke's Presbyn. Ch., Rolling Hills, Calif., 1968—. Author: The Educated Servant, 1967; The Debonair Disciple, 1973; Old Creed for a New Day, 1975; Reflections on the Light of God, 1976; contbr. to Opinion page Los Angeles Times. Home: 6425 Parklynn Dr Rancho Palos Verdes CA 90274 Office: 26825 Rolling Hills Rd Rolling Hills Estates CA 90274

SMITH, DAVID TERRENCE, minister, Independent Baptist Church; b. Norwood, Ohio, Jan. 4, 1947; s. Carlie Earthel and Marcella (Johnson) S.; B.A., Pillsbury Bapt. Bible Coll., 1969; postgrad. Grand Rapids Bapt. Theol. Sem., 1969-71; m. Marilyn Mardel Sutter, June 8, 1968; children: Jason, Jeremy. Ordained to ministry, 1971; asst. pastor Central Bapt. Ch., Panama City, Fla., 1971-73; pastor Langston Meml. Bapt. Ch., Conway, S.C., 1973-76, Good News Bapt. Ch., Cedar Rapids, Iowa, 1976—; youth chmn. Van Impe (Mich.) Crusade, 1971, Southwide Bapt. Fellowship, Panama City, Fla., 1973; mem. Sword of the Lord Evangelism Council. Recipient Sermon Contest award Pillsbury Coll., 1969. Mem. Southwide Bapt. Fellowship. Author: You're a Beautiful Person, 1971. Home and Office: 1130 10th St NW Cedar Rapids IA 52405

SMITH, DONALD ALBERT, religious educator, American Baptist Churches in the U.S.A.; b. Yonkers, N.Y., Nov. 19, 1931; s. Albert Henry and Ruth Isabelle (Joudrey) S.; m. Barbara Eleanor Atkeson, Dec. 28, 1957; children: Jean Marie, David Andrew, Carolyn René. B.A., Columbia Coll., 1953; M.Div., Union Theol. Sem., 1956; M.A., Tchrs. Coll., Columbia U., 1959, Ed.D., 1965. Ordained to ministry Am. Bapt. Chs. U.S.A., 1956. Assoc. dean students Alderson-Broaddus Coll., Philippi, W. Va., assoc. dean for experimental edn., 1964-77, v.p., 1977—; chmn. bd. fin. Philippi Bapt. Ch., 1983—. Mem. editorial bd. Jour. Regional Council for Internat. Edn., 1964-65. Contbr. articles on coop., experimental edn. and glacial expdn. to mags. and jours. Bd. dirs. Barbour County Devel. Corp., W. Va. 1963-65, Mountaineer Country Travel Council, W. Va., 1976-81, W. Va. Assn. Colls., 1966-67; chmn. exec. com. Barbour County Republican Party, 1960-68; chmn. Community Arts Assn., 1960-68; pres. Student Personnel Adminstrs. W. Va., 1964-65; mem. W. Va. council Boy Scouts Am., 1968-70; sec.-treas. Barbour County Parks and Recreation Commn., 1970—; chmn. lit. exchange Middle Atlantic dist. Council for Advancement and Support Edn., 1976-78; mem. exec. com. W. Va. Council on Econ. Edn., 1982—. Danforth assoc., 1961-63; named Ky. col., 1975. Mem. Coop. Edn. Assn. (v.p., newsletter editor 1968-76), Middle Atlantic Placement Assn. (v.p., treas. 1971-75), W. Va. C. of C. (vice chmn. edn. com. 1980—), Phi Delta Kappa, Kappa Delta Pi. Lodge: Lions (local pres. 1967-68, dist. sec. 1967-68). Home: 277 Broaddus Sta Philippi WV 26416 Office: Alderson-Broaddus Coll Philippi WV 26416

SMITH, DONNIE WILBURN, minister, Church of God; b. Sylacauga, Ala., Nov. 4, 1950; s. Dewey Wilburn and Jewel Christine (Hudgins) S.; m. Barbara June Masters, Dec. 30, 1967; children: Timothy Shane, Casey Braden. B.A., Lee Coll., 1973; postgrad. U. Okla., 1978-80, Ch. of God Sch. Theology, Cleveland, Tenn., 1982-85. Ordained to ministry Ch. of God, 1978. State evangelist Ch. of God, Ala., 1973; pastor Ch. of God, Leeds, Ala., 1974; state youth and Christian edn. dir. Ch. of God, State of Kans., 1974-78, State of Okla., 1978-80, State of Miss., 1980-81; sr. pastor Mountain West Ch. of God, Stone Mountain, Ga., 1981—; mem. state bd. edn. North Ga. Conf., Ch. of God, 1984—; chmn. evangelism bd. Ch. of God, State of Kans., 1974-78, State of Okla., 1978-80. Contbr. articles to Evangel mag. Author curriculum materials. Group leader Am. Cancer Soc., Wichita, Kans., 1974-78. Recipient Citation of Achievement, Ch. of God, 1974, 78, Christian Edn. Leadership award Ch. of God, 1976, Youth World Evangelism award Ch. of God, 1978, 81; named one of Outstanding Young Men Am., Jaycees, 1978. Mem. Christian Assn. for Retarded. Republican.

Home: 2857 Highland Park Dr Stone Mountain GA 30087 Office: Mountain West Ch of God 4818 Hugh Howell Rd Stone Mountain GA 30087

SMITH, DWIGHT MOODY, JR., educator, United Methodist Church; b. Murfreesboro, Tenn., Nov. 20, 1931; s. Dwight Moody and Nellie (Beckwith) S.; A.B., Davidson Coll., 1954; B.D., Duke U., 1957; Ph.D., Yale U., 1961, M.A., 1958; postdoctoral U. Zurich (Switzerland), 1963-64, U. Cambridge (England), 1970-71; m. Cynthia Jane Allen, Nov. 26, 1954; children: Cynthia Beckwith, Catherine Mitchell, David Burton, John Allen. Ordained elder, 1959; instr. New Testament, Methodist Theol. Sch. in Ohio, 1960-61, asst. prof., 1962-65; assoc. prof. N.T. interpretation Duke U., 1965-70, prof., 1970—, asso. dean divinity sch., 1973-74, dir. grad. studies in religion, 1974-80. Guggenheim fellow, 1970-71, Lilly fellow, 1963-64; Assn. Theol. Schs. research fellow, 1977-78. Mem. Soc. Bibl. Lit., Am. Theol. Soc., Studiorum Novi Testamenti Societas, Soc. Religion in Higher Edn., Phi Beta Kappa. Author: The Composition and Order of the Fourth Gospel, 1965; (with Robert A. Spivey) Anatomy of the New Testament, 3d edit., 1982; Proclamation Commentaries: John, 1976; Interpreting the Gospels for Preaching, 1980; Johannine Christianity, 1985. Office: Box 35 Divinity Duke U Durham NC 27706

SMITH, EDWARD GEORGE, minister, Presbyterian Church in Canada; b. Albany, N.Y., Feb. 21, 1924; s. Edward William and Anna Margaret (Hermann) S.; m. Lois Margaret Whyte, July 8, 1961; children: Peter Edward, Colleen Ruth. B.A., Gordon Coll., 1954; M.Div., Westminster Theol. Sem., 1957; M.Th., Knox Coll., 1976. Ordained to ministry Presbyn. Ch. in Can., 1957. Minister, Bobcaygeon, Ont., Can., 1960-64, South Nissouri, Ont., 1964-69, King City, Ont., 1969-76, Almonte, Ont., 1976—; exec. officer and contbr. Faith in Action Publs., Almonte, 1965—; main speaker to children Christian Festivals, 1980—; tchr. Old Testament, Ottawa Extension Sch. of Ont. Bible Coll., 1985—. Mem. Evang. Fellowship Can., Renewal Fellowship Presbyn. Ch. Can., Evang. Theol. Soc., Fellowship Christian Magicians, Internat. Brotherhood Magicians, N. Am. Assn. Ventriloquists. Address: Box 942 Almonte ON K0A 1AO Canada

SMITH, EDWARD THOMAS, philosophy educator, Roman Catholic Church; b. Denver, Dec. 6, 1920; s. Thomas Matthew and Florence Alice (Healy) S.; m. Betty Ann Dwyer, Jan. 3, 1950; children: Sharon Elizabeth, Daniel Sean. B.A., Cath. U. Am., 1942, M.A., 1943; Ph.D., U. Ottawa, 1954. City editor Denver Cath. Register, 1962-65; asst. prof. religion U. Denver, 1966-71, assoc. prof. philosophy, 1966—; dir. Catholic Campus Ministry, Denver, 1973-74. Contbr. articles to profl. jours. Democrat. Home: 959 S York St Denver CO 80209 Office: Dept Philosophy Univ Denver Denver CO 80208

SMITH, FRANCIS SAMUEL, minister, United Meth. Ch.; b. Cleve., Jan. 4, 1905; s. Philotus M. and Della Maria (Mehollin) S.; B.A., Muskingum Coll., 1950; postgrad. Boston U., summers 1954-59; m. Mary Alice Major, Jan. 17, 1928; children—Ruth Lucile, Samuel Emerson, Paul Edwin, Donald Francis. Ordained to ministry, 1959; minister Cumberland Meth. Ch., 1945-48, Bethesda (Ohio) Meth. Ch., 1948-68; supt. Epworth Park Learning Center, Bethesda, 1948-68; now project dir. Nat. Ret. Tchrs. Assn.-Am. Assn. Ret. Persons Community Service Employment Program. Founder, Barnesville Sr. Citizens Center, 1974—; mem. steering com. Belmont Tech. Coll., St. Clairsville, Ohio, 1973-76. Mem. Nat., Ohio hist. socs. Editor: (with H. H. Ault) Belmont County History, Facts and Traditions; The History of Epworth Park. Home: Route 1 Bethesda OH 43719 Office: 134 W Main St Barnesville OH 43713

SMITH, FREDA MARY, minister, vice moderator Universal Fellowship of Metropolitan Community Churches; b. Pocatello, Idaho, Nov. 22, 1935; d. Alfred Avery and Mary Violet (Clark) Smith; B.A. with honors, Calif. State U., 1974. Ordained to ministry, 1972; pastor Metropolitan Community Ch., Sacramento, 1973—. Mem. UFMCC Bd. of Evangelism, 1972—, elder, governing body of fellowship, 1973—; liaison elder to Commns. on Campus Ministry, Religious Orders, 1973; exec. sec. UFMCC World Ch. Extension, 1977—. Mem. Phi Kappa Phi. Home: 6411 Capital Circle Sacramento CA 95828 Office: PO Box 20125 Sacramento CA 95820

SMITH, GARY DEAN, minister, American Baptist Churches in the U.S.A.; b. Greenville, S.C., Feb. 9, 1951; s. Kyle Thornton and Elma Precess (Thornton) S.; m. Carol Adair Roberts, Nov. 17, 1972; children: Amy, Aaron, Abbey. B.A., Stanford U., 1973; M.Div., No. Bapt. Sem., 1976; Ph.D., So. Bapt. Sem., 1981; postgrad. Hebrew Union Coll.-Jewish Inst. Religion, Stanford Cath. Theol. Union, Grad. Theol. Union, 1984, Fuller Theol. Sem., 1984—. Ordained to ministry Baptist Ch., 1976. Youth minister First Bapt. Ch., Menlo Park, Calif., 1972-73; sr. minister First Bapt. Ch., Shabbona, Ill., 1973-76, First Bapt. Ch., Madison, Ind., 1976-80, First Bapt. Ch., Carmichael, Calif., 1980—; chmn. Campaign New Churches, Oakland. Calif., 1984—. Founder, bd. dirs., interim dir. New Horizons Counseling Ctr., Carmichael, Calif., 1982-85; mem. exec. com. Statements of Concern Am. Bapt. Chs. 1983-87; ex-officio Wonder-land Sch., Carmichael, 1980—. Mem. Ministers Council Am. Bapt. Chs., Soc. Bibl. Lit., Order of St. Lukes. Lodge: Rotary (Foothill-Highlands). Home: 4731 Oakbough Way Carmichael CA 95608 Office: First Baptist Ch 3300 Walnut Ave Carmichael CA 95608

SMITH, GARY ROBERT, minister, So. Bapt. Conv.; b. Houston, Dec. 12, 1946; s. John Howell and Gladys Marie (Williamson) S.; student Lee Jr. Coll, 1965-66, Tex. Coll. Theology, 1971-72; m. Mary Katherine Schlink, Oct. 18, 1965; children—Dawn Lorraine, Shan Marie, Mark Robert, Ordained to ministry, 1976; minister music and youth First Bapt. Ch., Lomax, Tex., 1971; asso. pastor Westview Bapt. Ch., Houston, 1972-73; minister youth and music Spring (Tex.) Bapt. Ch., 1973-74; vocat. evangelist, pres. Gospel Senders, Inc., 1974—; staff evangelist Sunnyland Bapt. Ch., 1976—. Founder, coordinator Houston Northside Bible Conf., 1974; rec. artist, writer Internat. Artist Rec. Co., 1969-70; rec. artist, owner Redeemer Record Co., 1974—; writer Redeemer Pub. Co., 1975—; co-dir. The King is Coming, radio program; editor-in-chief Messenger News. Home: 6606 Maybank Dr Houston TX 77055 Office: PO Box 55943 Houston TX 77055

SMITH, GARY SCOTT, religious educator, Presbyterian Church (U.S.A.); b. Franklin, Pa., Oct. 12, 1950; s. Roger Gary and Cary Arlene (Boardman) S.; m. Patricia Marie Jamison, May 27, 1972; children: Gregory Scott, Joel Andrew. B.A., Grove City Coll., 1972; M.Div., Gordon-Conwell Theol. Sem., 1977; M.A. in History, Johns Hopkins, 1979, Ph.D. in History, 1981. Ordained to ministry Presbyn. Ch. (U.S.A.), 1982. Campus missioner Coalition for Christian Outreach, Edinboro State Coll., Pa., 1972-74; guest lectr. religion and philosophy Grove City Coll., Pa., 1978-80, instr. sociology, 1980-81, asst. prof. sociology, co-dir. Christian Ministries program, 1981—; interim pastor Clen-Moore United Presbyn. Ch., New Castle, Pa., 1983. Author: The Seeds of Secularization: Calvinism, Culture and Pluralism in America, 1870-1915, 1985; also articles in profl. jours. Mem. Christian Sociol. Soc. Republican. Home: 526 Superior St Grove City PA 16127 Office: Grove City Coll Grove City PA 16127

SMITH, GREGORY MICHAEL, priest, chancellor, Roman Catholic Church; b. Danbury, Conn., May 25, 1941; s. Michael Paul and Helen Marie (McFarland) S.; A.B. in Philosophy, St. Mary Coll., Balt., 1963, M.Div., 1967; M.A. in Psychology, Fairfield U., 1973; M.S. in Religious Edn., Fordham U., 1976; Ed.D. in Adult Edn., NYU, 1982. Ordained priest, 1967; assoc. pastor chs., Trumbull and Danbury, Conn., 1967-72; dir. religious edn. Diocese of Bridgeport, Conn., 1972-82; bd. dirs. Nat. Conf. Diocesan Dirs., Washington, 1974-77; pres. New Eng. Conf. Diocesan Dirs., 1975-77; chmn. New Eng. Adult Religious Edn. Dirs., 1975-79; adj. faculty Fairfield U., 1982—. Chmn. Trumbull Human Relations Council, Conn., 1968-69; commr. youth City of Danbury, 1971-72; bd. dirs. Fairfield Found., Inc., 1983—. Contbr. articles to religious jours. Home: 163 Ortega Ave Bridgeport CT 06606 Office: Catholic Ctr 238 Jewett Ave Bridgeport CT 06606-2892

SMITH, HAROLD PHILIP See *Who's Who in America*, 43rd edition.

SMITH, HARRY CLARENCE, II, minister, Southern Baptist Convention; b. Washington, May 13, 1942; s. Norman S. and Lena G. (Estes) S.; m. Joy Watkins, May 30, 1964; children: James Stanley, David Scott. B.A., High Point Coll., 1964; M.Div., Southeastern Bapt. Theol. Sem., 1977. Ordained to ministry Bapt. Ch., 1975. Pastor North Fork Bapt. Ch., Virgilina, Va., 1974-79, 1st Bapt. Ch., Eden, N.C., 1979—; pres. Dan Valley Pastors Conf., 1981-82, Morehead Hosp. Chaplains Assn., 1982-83; moderator Dan Valley Bapt. Assn., 1983-84. Mem. adv. bd. Salvation Army, Eden, 1980-83; bd. dirs. United Way, 1981; chaplain YMCA Men's Club, Eden, 1980, bd. dirs. YMCA, 1983-85. Recipient Recognition award Morehead Hosp., 1981; cert. of appreciation Clide Dupin Ministries, N.C., 1981, Bethel Bapt. Ch., Frankfurt, Fed. Republic Germany, 1981. Lodge: Rotary (v.p. 1983-84, pres. 1984-85) (Eden). Office: 533 Greenwood St Eden NC 27288

SMITH, HENRY JORDAN, minister, Ch. of God, Cleveland, Tenn.; b. Goldsboro, N.C., Oct. 26, 1931; s. Herman and Little Gertrude (Best) S.; A.A., Lee Coll., 1957; B.A., Atlantic Christian Coll., 1960; M.A., Calif. State U., Fresno, 1971; postgrad Calif. Grad. Sch. Theology, 1976-77; m. Betty Lou Smith, Dec. 30, 1950; children—Michael H., Patricia Lynn. Ordained to ministry, 1956; pastor Ch. of God, Farner, Tenn., 1956-57, Pinetops, N.C., 1957-58; evangelist in N.C., 1958-59; pastor Ch. of God, Hudson, N.C., 1959-63, Norwood, N.C., 1963-67, Mooresville, N.C., 1968, Fresno, Calif., 1968-69; dean W. Coast Bible Coll., Fresno, 1969—. Mem. Nat. Assn. Evang., Soc. Pentecostal Studies, Ministerial Assn. (pres. 1965-67), Fresno Assn. Evang. (pres. 1972-74). Contbr. articles in field to profl. jours. Home: 424 W Pico Ave Clovis CA 93612 Office: 6901 N Maple Ave Fresno CA 93710

SMITH, J. ANDY, III, national denominational executive, American Baptist Churches USA; m. Atlanta Apr. 13, 1943; s. John Andy and Dorothy Grace (Smith) S.; m. Nancy Daniel, Oct. 18, 1980. A.B., Duke U., 1965; postgrad. Heidelberg U., 1963-64; S.T.B., Harvard Div. Sch., 1968; Ph.D., Drew U., 1983. Ordained to ministry, 1968. Baptist chaplain MIT, Cambridge, 1965-68; dir. Internat. Ministry in Cambridge, 1968-69; protestant chaplain Rensselaer Poly. Inst., Troy, N.Y., 1969-72; minister higher edn. Capital Area Ministries in Higher Edn., Albany, N.Y., 1972-80; dir. social and ethical responsibility in investments Nat. Ministries, Am. Bapt. Chs. USA, Valley Forge, Pa., 1980—; bd. dirs., exec. com. Interfaith Ctr. on Corp. Responsibility, 1980—, Christians United in Mission, Albany, N.Y., 1972-75, Religious Broadcasting Commn., Albany, 1970-72; coordinator Capital Area Clergy Consultation Service, 1970-72. Contbr. articles to profl. jours. Editor Corporate Responsibility in Investment, 1980—. Mem. Soc. Christian Ethics, Am. Acad. Religion. Office: Nat Ministries Am Bapt Chs USA Box 851 Valley Forge PA 19482-0851

SMITH, JAMES ALFRED, minister, American Baptist Churches, U.S.A. and Progressive National Baptist Convention, Inc.; b. Kansas City, Mo., May 19, 1931; s. Clyde Anderson and Amy Elnora S.; m. Jo Anna Goodwin, Sept. 9, 1950; children: Amy, James Alfred, Jori Lynn, Ronald Craig, Anthony Gerard. Ordained to ministry, 1951; prin. Lincoln Sch., Keytesville, Mo., 1952; v.p. Bishop Coll., Dallas, 1960-63; mem. nat. staff Am. Bapt. Chs., U.S.A., Valley Forge, Pa., 1965-70; pastor Allen Temple Bapt. Ch., Oakland, Calif., 1970—; prof. preaching Golden Gate Bapt. Theol. Sem., Oakland, 1976—; instr. Merritt Coll., Oakland, 1971. Bd. dirs. Oakland Spanish Speaking Unity Council, New Oakland Com. Mem. Am. Bapt. Hist. Soc., Oakland NAACP, Nat. Black Police Officers Assn., Nat. Alliance Black Sch. Educators, Nat. Com. Black Churchmen. Author: Thus Far by Faith, 1973; Don't Be Squeezed into the World's Mold, 1973; In the Name of Our Elder Brother, 1976; Baptist and the Story of Our Nation, 1976; Outstanding Black Sermons, 1977. Home: 8453 Aster St Oakland CA 94605 Office: 8500 A St Oakland CA 95621

SMITH, JAMES EDWARD, II, minister, General Association Regular Baptist Churches; b. Teaneck, N.J., Nov. 15, 1942; s. James E. and Mary E. (Barnes) S.; A.B., Muhlenberg Coll., 1964; M.Div., Faith Theol. Sem., 1967; m. Carol Ann Miller, July 11, 1964; children—Lori Carol, Heather Ruth, Cynthia Mary. Ordained to ministry, 1967; pastor Faith Bapt. Ch., Erial, N.J., 1967-77, Grace Bapt. Ch., Tonawanda, N.Y., 1977—. Missionary Fellowship of Bapts. for Home Missions, 1967-75; chmn. bd. dirs. New Life Island Regular Bapt. Youth Camp, 1972-73; chmn. Council of Six, Garden State Fellowship Regular Bapt. Chs., 1976-77; trustee Buffalo Hebrew Christian Mission, 1977-78; Campground Ministries, 1979-84, TELL Ministries, 1979—. Mem. council of ten Empire State Fellowship of Regular Bapt. Chs., 1978-83, vice chmn., 1979-83. Mem. Sigma Tau Delta. Contbr. articles to profl. jours. Home: 316 Grayton Rd Tonawanda NY 14150 Office: 2525 Eggert Rd Tonawanda NY 14150

SMITH, JAMES EDWIN, minister, Ch. of Christ (Christian); b. Flora, Ill., Sept. 8, 1921; s. Floyd and Hazel (Hadden) S.; student U. Cin., summer 1944; A.B. in Ministry, Cin. Bible Sem., 1945; postgrad. Lincoln Christian Sem., 1959-60; m. Bonnie May Tucker, July 13, 1942; children—Carol Smith Schlueter, Thomas, Beth Smith Henwodd, Timothy. Ordained to ministry; pastor Covington, Ind., 1945-46, Catlin, Ill., 1946-49, Salem, Ill., 1949-58, Medaryville, Ind., 1959-61; evangelist for Northeastern Ohio Assn. Helpers, 1961—. Trustee Lincoln Christian Coll., 1956-61; mgr. Youth Camp, Flora, Ill., 1955, 56; dean jr. high week Christian Service Camps, 1953-57; co-founder So. Ill. Christian Conv., pres. 1959, chmn. program com. 1958; mem. adv. com. for New Ch. Evangelism in Ill., 1957-58. Clubs: Masons, Rotary, Washington Twp. Ruritan Club. Author: The Church of Christ (Christian), 1965. Home and office: 13911 Bayton Alliance OH 44601

SMITH, JAMES EVERETT, minister, Christian Church (Disciples of Christ); b. Winnipeg, Mo., May 6, 1927; s. Clarence Everett and Myrtle Frances (Woody) S.; m. Virginia Juanita Jones, June 14, 1953; children: Karen, Melinda. B.A., Tex. Christian U., 1962, M.Div., Brite Sch. Divinity, 1962, D.Min., 1980. Ordained to ministry Christian Ch. (Disciples of Christ), 1961. Minister 1st Christian Ch., Howe, Tex., 1953-54, Central Christian Ch., Stamford, Tex., 1954-61, Urbandale Christian Ch., Dallas, 1962-71; sr. minister 1st Christian Ch., Duncan, Okla., 1972—; mem. com. on ministry Christian Ch. (Disciples of Christ) Okla., 1982-84; mem. nat. gen. bd. Christian Ch. (Disciples of Christ), 1980-84; bd. dirs. Okla. Christian Home, Edmond, 1976-82; tour condr. Faith Roots Tour of Middle East, 1972, 75, 78, 84, tour Far East, 1973; moderator dist. 9 Okla. Disciples of Christ, 1982-84.

Author: Standing on Holy Ground: An Ecumenical Study of Significant Biblical Sites, 1980. Pres. Duncan Community Residence, 1975-77, Duncan Sr. Citizens, 1976, Stephens County Mental Health Assn., 1976; v.p. Duncan United Way, 1979. Recipient Liberty Bell award Stephens County Bar Assn., 1980. Mem. Duncan Ministerial Alliance (pres. 1976). Lodge: Rotary (sec. Duncan). Home: 1201 Harville Rd Duncan OK 73533 Office: 1st Christian Ch 916 Walnut Duncan OK 73533

SMITH, JAMES GARLAND, minister, So. Bapt. conv.; b. Village, Ark., May 16, 1930; s. Dee Witt and Alza Mae (Nall) S.; B.S., Miss. Coll., 1974; M.R.E., New Orleans Bapt. Theol. Sem., 1976; m. Bettie Jean Godbee, Dec. 30, 1950; children—James L., Joyce A., Eugene B. Ordained to ministry, 1974; enlisted U.S. Air Force, 1948, assigned Alaskan Air Command, 1955-57, Amarillo AFB, Tex., 1957-59, Keesler AFB, Miss., 1959-61, Pacific Air Command, 1961-62, 67-70, Air Force Logistics Command, 1961-67, ret. 1971; children's worship leader Morrison Heights Bapt. Ch., 1973-74; minister of edn. Carol Estates Bapt. Ch., Gainesville, Fla., 1974-75, 1st Bapt. Ch., Luling, La., 1975-76, 1st Bapt. Ch., Canton, Miss., 1977—. Planner, coordinator, condr. religious edn. workshops Nat. Bapt. Chs., New Orleans area, 1975, 76; initiated puppet ministry, New Orleans, 1975-76. Recipient Good Citizenship award City of Tachikawa, Japan, 1970. Mem. So., Southeastern, Miss., Fla., Hinds-Madison Bapt. religious edn. assns. Home: 125 E Fulton St Canton MS 39046 Office: Box 377 Canton MS 39046

SMITH, JERRY ALLAN, minister, Southern Baptist Convention; b. Wichita, Kans., Feb. 17, 1954; s. Larnard Elvin and Eva Ilean (Miller) S.; m. Vicky Lynn Beery, May 17, 1980. B.B.A., Wichita State U., 1976; M.R.E., So. Bapt. Theol. Sem., 1980; postgrad. Dallas Theol. Sem., 1979, Liberty Bapt. Coll., 1978, Midwestern Sem., 1978. Ordained to ministry So. Bapt. Conv., 1978. Dir. Mid-West Ministries, Wichita, Kans., 1975-79; minister edn. Midway Bapt. Ch., Wichita, 1978-80; minister edn./adminstrn. First Bapt. Ch., Gonzales, Tex., 1980-82; pastor Sublette So. Bapt. Ch., Kans., 1982—; team leader Project Ptnr. Evangelism Assn., Seoul, Korea, 1982; sec. Haskell County Ministers Alliance, Sublette, Kans., 1983—; sec.-treas. Kans.-Nebr. Pastor's Conf., Topeka, 1983—; cons. Assist Team Ministries, Topeka, 1978-80. Sta. mgr. ACTS-TV 11, Sublette, Kans., 1984—. Recipient Fastest Growing Ch. award Moody Monthly mag. and Internat. Christian Edn. Assn., 1979. Mem. Nat. Assn. Ch. Bus. Adminstrs., Am. Assn. Christian Counselors. Home: 309 Cox St Sublette KS 67877 Office: Sublette So Bapt Ch Hwy 56 Sublette KS 67877

SMITH, JERRY RAY, minister, Lutheran Church in America; college dean; b. Dallastown, Pa., Oct. 18, 1934; s. George William and Lurlene Lillian (Geesey) S.; m. Geraldine Ann Fehr, Mar. 7, 1959 (div. Nov. 1983). B.F.A., Phila. Coll. Art, 1958; B.D., Luth. Theol. Sem., Gettysburg, Pa., 1961; M.Ed., Temple U., 1968, Ed.D., 1973. Ordained to ministry Lutheran Ch., 1961. Pastor, St. John Evang. Luth. Ch., Maytown, Pa., 1961-62, Trinity Evang. Luth. Ch., Darby, Pa., 1962—; pres. Central Pa. Luther League, 1957-59; mem. exec. com. Luther League Am., 1959-61; mem. worship and music com. Southeastern Pa. Synod, Luth. Ch. in Am., 1968-74, chmn., 1972-74. Asst. prof. West Chester State U., Pa., 1969-70; adj. faculty Temple U., Phila., 1972, Montgomery County Community Coll., Blue Bell, Pa., 1976; adj. faculty Del. County Community Coll., Media, Pa., 1975, assoc. dean of instrn., 1976-83. Mem. Darby Human Relations Council, 1967-71, chmn., 1967-69; pres. Darby-Colwyn Joint Bd. Sch. Dirs., 1971-72; mem. William Penn Bd. of Sch. Dirs., 1972-75, pres., 1973-75; mem. Del. County Intermediate Unit Bd. of Sch. Dirs., 1974-75. Luth. Ch. in Am. grantee, 1971; recipient Outstanding Service to Edn. award Pa. Sch. Bds. Assn., 1973, 75, Legion of Honor award Chapel of Four Chaplains, Phila., 1981. Mem. Luth. Soc. for Worship, Music and the Arts (chpt. chmn. 1968-69), Darby-Colwyn Ministerial Assn. (pres. 1968-78), Artists Guild of Del. County (pres. 1982-84). Republican. Club: Players (Swarthmore, Pa.). Home: 206 S 5th St Darby PA 19023 Office: Trinity Evang Luth Ch S 5th and Walnut Sts Darby PA 19023

SMITH, JOHN ABERNATHY, college chaplain; b. Pulaski, Tenn., Apr. 25, 1939; s. John Floyd and Julia Jackson (Abernathy) S.; m. Helen Louise Bryan, Aug. 18, 1962; children: Julia Elizabeth, John Abernathy II. B.A. cum laude, Vanderbilt U., 1961; M.Div. magna cum laude, Drew U., 1965; M.A., Johns Hopkins U., 1967, Ph.D. in History, 1971. Ordained elder Tenn. Conf. United Methodist Ch., 1969. Asst. prof. Am. U., 1968-74; pastor Walnut Grove United Meth. Ch., Cottontown, Tenn., 1974-76, Wesley Heights United Meth. Ch., Tullahoma, Tenn., 1976-77, Nolensville United Meth. Ch., Tenn., 1977-79; prof. history Martin Coll., Pulaski, Tenn., 1979-80; chaplain Lebanon Valley Coll., Annville, Pa., 1980—; pres. Tenn. Conf. United Meth. Ch. Commn. on Archives and History, 1977-80. Author: Cross and Flame, 1984. Woodrow Wilson fellow, 1961-62, Eisenhower fellow, 1966-68. Mem. Am. Hist. Assn., Orgn. Am. Historians, Am. Soc. Church History, Nat. Assn. Coll. and Univ. Chaplains, Assocs. for Religion and Intellectual Life. Democrat. Home: 121 N Garfield St Cleona PA 17042 Office: Lebanon Valley Coll Annville PA 17003

SMITH, JOHN GEORGE, III, minister, Southern Baptist Convention; b. Jacksonville, N.C., May 27, 1950; s. John George, Jr., and Margaret Grace (Dodd) S.; m. Melanie Ann Whittle, Aug. 12, 1972; children: Robert Brian, William Leonard. B.S. in Edn., U. Ga., 1972; M.Ed., Ga. Southwestern U., 1975; M.Div., Southwestern Bapt. Theol. Sem., 1984, postgrad., 1984—. Ordained to ministry Bapt. Ch., 1978. Minister of youth 1st Bapt. Ch., Albany, Ga., 1977-79; pastor Pleasant Glade Bapt. Ch., Colleyville, Tex., 1980—. Named to Jaycees Outstanding Young Men in Am., 1980, 82. Mem. Tarrant Assn. (coms.). Republican. Home: 3708 Glade Rd Colleyville TX 76034

SMITH, JOHN LEE, JR., minister, Southern Baptist Convention; b. Fairfax, Ala., Dec. 11, 1920; s. John Lee and Mae Celia (Smith) S.; A.B., Samford U., Birmingham, Ala., 1949; student New Orleans Bapt. Theol. Sem., 1950-51, 53, Auburn (Ala.) U., 1956; D.D., Ohio Christian Coll., Columbus, 1967; LL.D., Nat. Christian U., Dallas, Tex., 1974; D.D., Birmingham Bapt. Bible Coll., 1979; m. Vivian Herrington, Aug. 15, 1942; children—Vicky (Mrs. Joseph E. Hawkins), Joan (Mrs. Larry T. Wimberly), Jennifer. Ordained to ministry, 1947; pastor chs. in Ala. and Ga., 1948—; pastor Dalraida Bapt. Ch., Montgomery, Ala., 1959-66, 84—; evangelist, 1969-71; exec. dir. Ala. Council Alcohol Problems, 1969-78, Am. Council Alcohol Problems, Washington, 1972-74; dir. missions Bessemer Bapt. Assn., Ala., 1978-84; lectr., cons. on alcohol, drugs and driving to schs., clubs and civic groups. Mem. exec. bd., mem. adminstrn. com., Ala. Bapt. Conv., 1963-66, moderator, 1951-52; exec. com. Ga. Bapt. Conv., 1951-52; mem. Ala. Bd. Ministerial Edn., 1958-60. Mem. Gov. Ala. Com. Pornography, 1970—; bd. dirs. Nat. Com. Prevention Alcoholism, Temperance Edn. Mem. Alcohol-Drug Problems Assn., Nat. Temperance and Prohibition Council, Phi Kappa Phi. Mason. Contbr. papers in field. Home and office: 3783 Wares Ferry Rd Montgomery AL 36109

SMITH, JONATHAN WAYNE, minister, United Methodist Church; b. Findlay, Ohio, Apr. 23, 1950; s. Carl Herbert and Ura Amy (Davis) S.; m. Diane Lee Smith, June 23, 1973; children: Melissa Amy, Christopher Jon, Amanda Lee. B.A., Cedarville Coll., 1972; M.Div., Meth. Theol. Sch. in Ohio, 1977. Ordained deacon United Meth. Ch., 1975, elder, 1978. Student assoc. Logan United Meth. Ch., Ohio, 1975-76; resort minister Shelbyville United Meth. Ch., Mich., summers 1975, 76; campus minister Ohio State U.-Newark, 1976-77; pastor Le Roy United Meth. Ch., N.Y., 1977-82, Cattaraugus United Meth. Ch., N.Y., 1982—; chmn. Standing Com. on Higher Edn. and Campus Ministry, Buffalo, 1981—; adv. bd. Protestant Chaplaincy, Syracuse U., N.Y., 1983—. Troop chmn. Geniusha council Boy Scouts Am., 1978-82; chmn. Genesee Jud. Process Commn., Batavia, N.Y., 1981-82; chaplain Le Roy Fire Dept., 1980-82, Cattaraugus Fire Dept., 1982—. Named to Jaycees Outstanding Young Men in Am., 1975. Mem. Albin Inst. Democrat. Home: 28 N Franklin St Cattaraugus NY 14719 Office: Cattaraugus United Meth Ch 53 Washington St Cattaraugus NY 14719

SMITH, JOSEPH DANIEL, JR., minister, religious educator, United Methodist Church. B. Tallahassee, Mar. 27, 1940; s. Joseph Daniel and Marjorie (Boland) S. B.A., Fla. State U., 1962; B.D., Yale U., 1965, S.T.M., 1967, M.A., 1969, M.Phil., 1972, Ph.D., 1979; student Princeton Theol. Sem., summers 1963, 65, Sorbonne, U. Paris, 1969-71, l'Institut catholique Paris, 1969-71. Ordained, elder, 1969. Part time assoc. minister Am. Ch. in Paris, 1969-71, interim minister, 1970; pastor Wakulla United Meth. Ch. (Fla.), 1974; univ. chaplain Baker U., Baldwin City, Kans., 1975-77; assoc. minister Christ United Meth. Ch., Bradenton, Fla., 1978-79. Instr. Fla. State U., Tallahassee, 1973-74; asst. prof. Baker U., 1975-77, Willamette U., Salem, Oreg., 1979-82, Wagner Coll., Staten Island, N.Y., 1982—. Contbr. book rev. to publ. Yale Divinity Sch. Research fellow, Yale U., 1978-79; recipient Two Brothers award, Yale Divinity Sch., Paris, 1969-70, 70-71. Fellow Am. Acad. Religion, Soc. Bibl. Lit., Council for Study of Religion, NCCJ, Omicron Delta Kappa. Office: Dept Religious Studies Wagner Coll 631 Howard Ave Staten Island NY 10301

SMITH, KENNETH ARNINK, minister, Presbyterian Church America; b. Yonkers, N.Y., Nov. 12, 1947; s. Thomas Roy and Lucy (Kalata) S.; m. Carol Springer, Sept. 8, 1973; children: Nathan, Benjamin, Thomas, Mary. B.A., The King's Coll., Briarcliff Manor, N.Y., 1969; M.A., U. No. Colo., 1973; M.Div., Princeton U., 1978. Ordained to ministry Presbyn. Ch. Am., 1978; family counselor First Christian Ch., Lubbock, Tex., 1973-75; minister Princeton Presby. Ch., N.J., 1978—. Author: (mag.) Liberty, 1985. Host radio show From the Word of God, 1979—, regional TV show, A New Day, 1985. Bd. dirs. Alpha Pregnancy Ctr., Princeton, 1979—. Served to capt. USAF, 1970-73. Republican. Home: 28 Pierson Ave Princeton NJ 08540 Office: Princeton Presbyn Ch PO Box 3003 Princeton NJ 08540

SMITH, KENNETH B., seminary adminstrator. Pres. Chgo. Theol. Sem. (United Church of Christ), 1984—. Office: Chgo Theol Sem 5757 S University Ave Chicago IL 60637*

SMITH, KENNETH LELAND, church official; b. Hong Kong, Apr. 21, 1924 (parents Am. citizens); s. Albert Ray and Verona Martha (Kreider) S.; B.A., Denison U., 1949; M.Div., Colgate Rochester Div. Sch., 1956; M.S.W., U. Wis., 1965; m. Phyllis Grace Vander Plaats, Aug. 16, 1952; children: Cheri Lynette, Grantley H., Andrew R., Kermit M. Ordained minister Am. Baptist Chs., 1956; pastor chs. in N.Y., Wis., Ill., 1953-60; exec. dir. Milw. Christian Center, 1956—. Sec., Greater Milw. Ministerial Assn., 1973-74. Founder, chpt. Southside Inter Agy. Inter Ch. Com., 1965-66, Inner City Youth Serving Agencies, 1970-72. Bd. dirs. Planned Parenthood Milw., 1968-73, Pathfinders for Run-aways, 1972-76, Am. Bapt. Mgmt. Corp., 1968—; mem. community adv. bd. Walker Jr. High, Ethnic Heritage Com., Neighborhood Centers Council, Neighborhood Improvement Project, South East Community Center. Mem. Nat. Assn. Social Workers (chmn. group workers 1968-69), Inter-Faith Clergy, ACLU, Common Cause, YMCA, Am. Commons Club, Alpha Delta Phi. Home: 6930 W Mill Rd Milwaukee WI 53218 Office: 2137 W Greenfield Ave Milwaukee WI 53204

SMITH, LANNIE WILSON, minister, Southern Baptist Convention; b. Star City, Ark., Nov. 7, 1950; s. Jack Wilson and Alice Lemoine (Jones) S.; B.A., U. Ark., 1972; M.Div., New Orleans Bapt. Theol. Sem., 1976; m. LaDonna Frances Byrd, May 25, 1973. Ordained to ministry, 1970; pastor Rankin's Chapel Bapt. Ch., Dumas, Ark., 1970-73, New Hope Bapt. Ch., Folsom, La., 1973-74, Piave Bapt. Ch., 1974-76, Towaliga Bapt. Ch., Jackson, Ga., 1976-78, Providence Bapt. Ch., Williamson, Ga., 1979-80, Northside Bapt. Ch., Manchester, Ga., 1980-81, Humphrey Bapt. Ch., Ark., 1981-83, Sulphur Springs Bapt. Ch., Pine Bluff, Ark., 1983-84, 2d Bapt. Ch., Jackson, Ga., 1984—. Recipient Danforth I Dare You award. Home and office: PO Box 3752 Jackson GA 30233

SMITH, LEO WILLIAM, minister So. Bapt. Conv.; b. Ysleta, El Paso, Tex., July 14, 1937; s. Arthur Edward and Verna Belle (Wilcox) S.; B.A., U. Corpus Christi, 1965; m. Cordelia Dean, Feb. 14, 1959; children—Vernon Lee, Terry Lynn, Timothy Lane, Tammy Leigh, Vikki L'Dawn. Ordained to ministry, 1960; pastor Marcelina Bapt. Ch., Florisville, Tex., 1960-61, Choate Bapt. Ch., Kennedy, Tex., 1961-66, Crescent Valley Bapt. Ch., Victoria, Tex., 1966-70, 1st Bapt. Ch., Richmond, Tex., 1970-73, Highlands Bapt. Ch., La Marque, Tex., 1973—. Vice pres. Tex. Bapt. Men; camp dir. Royal Ambassador; Am. Campcraft instr., 1972-76. Recipient Legion of Honor award, 1975. Mem. Bapt. Gen. Conv. Tex., Galveston Bapt. Assn., Am. Camping Assn. Contbr. articles to state Bapt. papers. Home: 2913 Verkin St La Marque TX 77568 Office: Box 68 La Marque TX 77568

SMITH, MICHAEL ODELL, minister, American Lutheran Church; b. Wichita Falls, Tex., Dec. 12, 1947; s. Clyde Odell and Frances Raylene (England) S.; m. Judith Evelyn Johnson, June 6, 1970; children: Rebecca Rae, Matthew Neal. B.A., Tex. Luth. Coll., 1969; student U. Bonn, Fed. Republic Germany, 1967-68; M.T.S., Harvard U., 1971; Th.D., Trinity Theol. Sem., 1981. Ordained to ministry Luth. Ch., 1974. Pastor, Bisbee Luth. Ch., N.D. and Lakeview Luth. Ch., Egeland, N.D., 1974-77; Zion Luth. Ch., Towner, N.D., 1978—; del. nat. conv. Am. Luth. Ch., Mpls., 1980, parish evangelist, 1982—; bd. dirs. Metigoshe Ministries (camp), Bottineau, N.D., 1982—; mem. bd. theol. edn. Western N.D. dist. Am. Luth. Ch., Bismarck, 1983—. Mem. McHenry County Juvenile Adv. Bd., Towner, 1979—, Nat. Right to Life Com., Washington, 1982—. Served to capt. U.S. Army, 1977-78. Home: PO Box 569 Towner ND 58788 Office: Zion Lutheran Ch 107 4th Ave SW Towner ND 58788

SMITH, MORTON H. Clergyman, stated clk. Presbyterian Church of America. Office: PO Box 1428 Decatur GA 30031*

SMITH, MYRL ELDEN, minister, Episcopal Church; b. Circleville, Ohio, Oct. 21, 1938; s. Myrl Elden and Helen Goldie (Valentine) S.; m. Patricia Evelyn McBride, June 16, 1962; children: Gregory, Gretchen, Amy, David. B.S. in Edn., Wittenberg U., 1960; M.Div., Episcopal Div. Sch., 1964. Ordained deacon Episcopal Ch., 1964, priest, 1964. Asst. St. Philip's Ch., Columbus, Ohio, 1964-66; vicar St. Matthew's Mission, Ashland, Ohio, 1966-72; rector St. Paul's Ch., Norwalk, Ohio, 1972-79, Trinity Ch., Findlay, Ohio, 1979—; instr. philosophy Ashland Coll., Ohio, 1967-71; examining chaplain Diocese of Ohio, Cleve., 1967-72, mem. diocesan council, 1976-80, mem. planning commn., 1982-84, mem. liturgical commn., 1984—. Pres. Services for Aging, Huron County, Norwalk, Ohio, 1975-79, Alcohol Ctr. for Huron County, Norwalk, 1978-79; pres., trustee Hancock County unit Am. Cancer Soc., Findlay, Ohio, 1982-84. Recipient Red Apple award Findlay Bd. Edn., Ohio, 1983; named Clergyman of Yr., Findlay Civitan Club, 1983. Democrat. Home: 208 Howard St Findlay OH 45840

Office: Trinity Episcopal Ch 128 W Hardin St Findlay OH 45840

SMITH, NELSON HENRY, JR., minister, Prog. Nat. Baptist Conv., Inc.; b. Brewton, Ala., Aug. 23, 1930; s. Nelson Henry and Lillie Alemta S.; A.B., Selma U., 1952, D.D., 1971; D.D., Birmingham Bapt. Coll., 1969; m. Lessie M. Edwards, 1951; children—Beverly, Constance, Nelson Bernard, Monica. Ordained to ministry, 1948; pastor New Pilgrim Bapt. Ch., Birmingham, Ala., 1953—; 2d v.p. Prog. Nat. Bapt. Conv., Inc., Birmingham, 1970-72, 1st v.p., 1972-74, pres., 1974—; mem. dept. internat. affairs Nat. Council Chs. Bd. dirs. Morehouse Sch. Religion, Internat. Fellowship Reconciliation, Crisis Center of Jefferson County; mem. bd. govs. Nat. Council Chs. Democratic committeeman, 1962; sec. Ala. Christian Movement for Human Rights; bd. dirs. SCLC, Birmingham Urban League. Recipient award of merit Pi Lambda Sigma, 1960, Distinguished Service award Alpha Eta chpt. Iota Phi Lambda, 1976. Author: What Jesus Means to Me, 1971. Home: 917 Goldwire Pl SW Birmingham AL 35211 Office: 903 6th Ave S Birmingham AL 35233

SMITH, NOLAN WAYNE, minister, Southern Baptist Convention; b. Paducah, Ky., Oct. 16, 1936; s. Richard Fowler and Daisy Opal (Edwards) S.; B.A., Union U., Jackson, Tenn., 1972; m. Janice Tolar, Oct. 14, 1955; children—Mona Rae, Keith Wayne. Ordained to ministry, 1959; pastor Cave Springs Bapt. Ch., Carrsville, Ky., 1959-60, First Bapt. Ch., Golconda, Ill., 1961-64, College Heights Bapt. Ch., 1964-68, Pleasant Hill Bapt. Ch., Jackson, Tenn., 1968-70, Calvary Bapt. Ch., Humboldt, Tenn., 1970-73, First Bapt. Ch., Raleigh, Ill., 1973—; chaplain Civitan Club, Humboldt, 1970-73, CAP, 1979—; moderator, Saline Bapt. Assn., 1974-76; pres. Bapt. Hour Assn., 1974—; mem. exec. bd. Ill. council Ch. for Alcohol Problems, 1981—. Home: PO Box 154 Raleigh IL 62977 Office: PO Box 27 Raleigh IL 62977

SMITH, NORMAN DOUGLAS, priest, Ch. of Eng., educator; b. Banstead, Surrey, Eng., July 26, 1923; s. Douglas George and Florence Mary (Sillence) S.; B.A., Balliol Coll., Oxford (Eng.) U., 1945, M.A., 1948, Dip. Theol., Wycliffe Hall, 1946; honor postgrad. Naganuma Sch. Japanese Lang., Tokyo, 1951-52, London U., 1956-57, U. Calif. at Berkeley Extension, 1958-67, San Francisco State Coll., 1961-62, 69, Dominican Coll., San Rafael, Calif., 1969, Stanford, summers 1959-60. Came to U.S., 1958, naturalized, 1963. Ordained deacon Ch. of Eng., 1948, priest, 1949; transfer Episcopal Ch., 1958; pastor chs., Eng., Calif., 1948-50, 58-60; missionary in Japan, 1950-58; chaplain Cathedral Sch. for Boys, 1960-70, minor canon Grace Cathedral, San Francisco, 1966-70; tchr. fgn. langs., religion St. Mathew's Episcopal Day Sch., San Mateo, Calif., 1970—, also asst. minister St. Matthew's Ch., San Mateo. Bd. dirs. Sister Cities Assn. San Mateo, v.p., 1976-77. Council, Golden Hours Fellowship, Surbiton, Surrey, 1957—. Mem. Japan Soc. San Francisco, Am. Assn. Tchrs. French, Fgn. Lang. Assn. No. Calif., Brit.-Am. Club No. Calif., Friends of Lee Abbey (Eng.), San Francisco Gem and Mineral Soc., Mensa, Calif. Arts Soc., U. Calif. Alumni Assn. (life), Nat. Audubon Soc. Home: 967 Flying Fish St Foster City CA 94404 Office: St Matthew's Episcopal Day Sch Baldwin and El Camino Real San Mateo CA 94401

SMITH, PAUL EDMUND, JR., minister, religion educator, Presbyterian Church in the U.S.A.; b. Northampton, Mass., Feb. 6, 1927; s. Paul Edmund Sr. and Mary Jane (Murphy) S. B.A., U. Mass., 1948; postgrad. Harvard U., 1948-49; M.A., Boston U., 1953; M.Div., Columbia Theol. Sem., Decatur, Ga., 1957; postgrad. U. N.C., 1967-68. Ordained to ministry Presbyterian Ch., 1957. Minister, Henderson Presbyn Ch., Albany, Ga., 1956-59, Rocky Mountain Presbyn. Ch., Va., 1959-64; asst. prof. religion Ferrum Coll., Va., 1964-68; assoc. prof. religion Richard Bland Coll., Petersburg, Va., 1968—; vis. lectr. in history Roanoke Ctr., U. Va., 1964-68. Mem. Presbytery of Fincastle. Democrat. Home: 3774 Westwood Dr Petersburg VA 23805 Office: Commerce Hall Richard Bland Coll Petersburg VA 23805

SMITH, PAUL RICHARD, pastor, Southern Baptist Convention; b. St. Louis, June 22, 1937; s. Paul Weston and Mildren Catherine (Utterback) S.; m. Karen Sue Hiserote, May 7, 1966; children: Elizabeth Ann, Montgomery Weston. B.A., Washington U., St. Louis, 1959; M.Div., Midwestern Bapt. Theol. Sem., 1964. Ordained to ministry, 1962. Sr. pastor Broadway Bapt. Ch., Kansas City, Mo., 1964—. Writer articles, creator workshops and seminars on ch. renewal. Home: 11005 E 71st Terr Raytown MO 64133 Office: Broadway Baptist Ch 3931 Washington Kansas City MO 64111

SMITH, PERRY MICHAEL, priest, Episcopal Church; b. Springfield, Mo., Sept. 1, 1937; s. Perry Edmunds and Marian Beverley (Hagan) S.; B.A., Harvard U., 1959; S.T.M., Berkeley Div. Sch., 1962. Curate, St. Luke's Parish, Evanston, Ill., 1963-66; dir. coll. work Diocese of W. N.Y., Buffalo, 1966-73; chaplain Community of the Holy Spirit, Brewster, N.Y., 1974-77; vicar Ch. of the Holy Name, Dolton, Ill., 1978—. Author: Last Rites, 1972. Contbr. articles to profl. jours. Recipient Dana Reed prize Harvard U., 1958. Mem. Liturgical Commn., Commn. on Ministry, Ecumenical Commn. Home: 14645 Kenwood Ave Dolton IL 60419 Office: Ch of the Holy Name 1630 E 154th St Dolton IL 60419

SMITH, PHILIP ALAN, bishop, Episcopal Church; b. Belmont, Mass., Apr. 2, 1920; s. Herbert Leonard and Elizabeth (MacDonald) S.; B.A., Harvard, 1942; B.D., Va. Theol. Sem., 1949; m. Barbara Ann Taylor, June 12, 1949; children—Sarah, Ann, Jeremy. Ordained priest Episcopal Ch., 1949; rector Christ Ch., Exeter, N.H., 1952-59; asst. prof. pastoral theology Va. Theol. Sem., 1959-62, chaplain, assoc. dean student affairs, 1962-70; suffragan bishop of Va., 1970-73; bishop of N.H., Concord, 1973—. Trustee, Holderness Sch., Plymouth, N.H., White Mountain Sch., Littleton, N.H. Office: 63 Green St Concord NH 03301

SMITH, RAYMOND EVERETT, minister, church official, Open Bible Standard Chs.; b. Kanawha, Iowa, Mar. 29, 1932; s. Earl M. and Anna (Lehman) S.; diploma Open Bible Coll., Des Moines, 1953; student Eastern Mont. Coll., 1958-59; m. Helen Alice Norris; children: Danene Rae, Stephen Alan. Ordained to ministry, 1954. Pastor Chs. of the Open Bible, Billings, 1953-59, Rapid City, S.D., 1959-67; S.D. dist. supt. Open Bible Standard Chs., Inc., 1959-63, Midwest div. supt., 1963-67, gen. supt., Des Moines, 1967-76, 79—; pastor Lighthouse Temple, Eugene, Oreg., 1976-79. Chmn., Iowa Key 73, 1972-73; convener, chmn. steering com. Iowans Concerned About Pornography, 1984—. Mem. Des Moines C. of C., Nat. Assn. Evangs. (bd. adminstrn.), Pentecostal Fellowship of N.Am. (bd. adminstrn.). Address: 2020 Bell Ave Des Moines IA 50315

SMITH, RICHARD ANTHONY, church music director, Presbyterian Church in the U.S.A.; b. Birmingham, Ala., Aug. 3, 1958; s. Alton Leo and Wilma Jean (McGriff) S.; m. Cynthia Lee Burbage, June 14, 1980. B.Music, Birmingham-So. Coll., 1980; M.Music, U. Miami, 1982. Dir. music Fultondale United Meth. Ch., Ala., 1978-80; dir. music and spl. ministries Coral Gables First Presbyn. Ch., Fla., 1980-84; dir. music ministries Meml. Presbyn. Ch., Montgomery, Ala., 1984—; mem. Fla. Synod Com. on Higher Edn., 1983-84; clinician Tex. Choral Dirs. Assn., 1984; bd. dirs. Coral Gables Chamber Players, 1984. Mem. Presbyn. Assn. Musicians, Am. Choral Dirs. Assn., Hymn Soc. Am. Home: 601 1/2 E Fairview Ave Montgomery AL 36106 Office: Meml Presbyn Ch 3424 S Court St Montgomery AL 36105

SMITH, RICHARD BROOKS, minister, So. Bapt. Conv.; b. Meridian, Miss., July 1, 1932; s. Louie Brooks and Gladys Elizabeth (Williams) S.; A.A., Meridian Jr. Coll., 1952; B.A., Miss. Coll., 1954; B.D., So. Bapt. Theol. Sem., 1957, M.Th., 1959; m. Margaret Joy Hulette, June 16, 1961; children—Richard Scott, Joy Suzanne. Ordained to ministry, 1954; pastor Buena Vista (Ky.) Bapt. Ch., 1959-62, Marion (Miss.) Bapt. Ch., 1962-66, Pinecroft Bapt. Ch., Greensboro, N.C., 1966-70, Glendale Bapt. Ch., Nashville, 1970—; instr. O.T. history Belmont Coll., Nashville, 1972; supr. field work Vanderbilt U. Div. Sch., Nashville, 1975-76. Mem. exec. com. Nashville Bapt. Assn., 1970—. Bd. dirs. Project Foresight, Nashville, 1973-75, Rap House Crisis Center, Nashville, 1971-72. Fellow, Interpreter's House, Juna Luska, N.C., 1974. Mem. Nashville Bapt. Pastors Conf. Home: 1012 Draughon Ave Nashville TN 37204 Office: Glendale Baptist Ch Glendale Ln at Scenic Dr Nashville TN 37204

SMITH, RICHARD KNOX, church official United Presbyterian Church U.S.A.; b. Eugene, Oreg., Aug. 7, 1923; s. Joseph Thomas and Mabel Preston (Veatch) S.; B.S., Oreg. State U., 1947; M.Div., Yale, 1950; D.D., Whitworth Coll., 1969; m. Harriet Griffith Van Riper, June 11, 1949; children—Kirk Stevan, Paul Andrew. Ordained to ministry, 1950; pastor 1st Ch., Ephrata, Wash., 1950-54; nat. mission adminstr. Synod of Wash., 1954-57; asso. dir. to dir. dept. town and country ch. Indian work Bd. Nat. Missions, 1957-63; exec. Synod of Ariz., 1963-72; exec. Synod of S.W., Phoenix, 1973—. Pres., Ariz. Council Chs., 1968; pres. Ariz. Ecumenical Council, 1972; mem. Gen. Assembly Mission Council, 1972-74. Mem. adv. com. Save-a-Child League; mem. adv. com. Coll. Granado. Trustee Cook Christian Tng. Sch., 1957-66, Nat. Found. Asthmatic Children, 1965-67. Named prin. architect of Ariz. Ecumenical Council, 1969; recipient Civitan Internat. Clergy Week award, 1973. Author: Datelines and By-Lines, 1969; 49 and Holding, 1975. Home: 4602 E Pinchot St Phoenix AZ 85018 Office: 10 E Roanoke St Phoenix AZ 85004

SMITH, RICHARD LEE, minister, Southern Baptist Convention. B. Denville, Ill., Oct. 30, 1936; s. Ernest Lee and Nora Edna (Blue) S.; m. Suzanne Elizabeth Gass, Oct. 6, 1955; children: Richard Lee, Michael Lynn, Vickie Lou. B.S., Calif. Bapt. Coll., 1978. Ordained, 1972. Pastor, Ramona Bapt. Ch. (Calif.), 1972-73, Broadway Bapt. Ch., Escondido, Calif., 1974-75, Vineyard Bapt. Ch., Ontatio, Calif., 1975-78, Trinity Bapt. Ch., Roswell, N.Mex., 1978-81, Highland Bapt. Ch., Roswell, 1981—; cir. Associational Sunday Sch., Roswell, 1979-83; chaplain St. Mary's Hosp., Roswell, 1983-84. Treas. Starlight Ctr., Chula Vista, Calif., 1964-66; chmn. Obscenity Rev. Bd., Roswell, 1983. Served with USN, 1954-74. Recipient Bill McGregor award, Calif. Bapt. Coll., 1978; named Outstanding Enlisted Man of Yr., USN, 1965. Mem. Ministerial Alliance. Republican. Clubs: Kiwanis (pres. elect Roswell 1984), United Ostomy (pres. Roswell 1981-83). Home: 908 W Deming Roswell NM 88201 Office: Highland Bapt Ch 2001 S Lea Roswell NM 88201

SMITH, ROBERT JOHNSON, minister, Am. Bapt. Conv.; b. Chgo., Sept. 26, 1920; s. James Howard Lorenzo and Anne Eugenia (Johnson) S.; A.B., Morehouse Coll., 1937, D.D. (hon.), 1966; M.Div., Andover Newton Theol. Sch., 1940, M.S.T., 1946, D. Ministry, 1974; M.S.W., Bryn Mawr Coll., 1961; D.D. (hon.), Va. Sem., 1958; m. Jennie Mae Smith, June 29, 1940; children—Estelle Anne (dec.), Everett Newton, Renee Denise, Robert. Ordained to ministry, 1940; chaplain U.S. Army, 1941-45; pastor High St. Bapt. Ch., Roanoke, Va., 1946-52, Hill St. Bapt. Ch., Roanoke, 1954-56, Salem Bapt. Ch., Jenkintown, Pa., 1956—. Chaplain VA Hosp., Roanoke, 1946-55; counselor Phila. Bd. Edn., 1960—; moderator Suburban Baptist Assn., 1960-74. Trustee Abington (Pa.) Meml. Hosp.; chmn. bd. trustee Berean Inst., Phila.; mem. Pa. Human Relations Commn., 1965—. Mem. Nat. Assn. Social Workers, Acad. Certified Social Workers, Phila. Fedn. Tchrs., Jenkintown Ministerium. Home: 191 Serrill Rd Elkins Park PA 19117 Office: 610 Summit Ave Jenkintown PA 19046

SMITH, ROLAND COLBURN, minister, Southern Baptist Convention; b. Muskegon, Mich., June 21, 1928; s. Gerald and Viola Henrietta May (Wood) S.; m. Elizabeth May Reid, Aug. 5, 1950; 1 son, Patrick William. Student Moody Bible Inst., 1948-50, U. Louisville, 1952-53; B.A., Northwestern Coll., Mpls., 1952; B.D., So. Bapt. Theol. Sem., 1955, Th.M., 1956; postgrad. Johns Hopkins U., 1956-61; Th.D., Am. Div. Sch., Pineland, Fla., 1967; M.S., Loyola Coll., Balt., 1980. Ordained to ministry Bapt. Ch., 1956. Student evangelist Youth for Christ, Mpls., 1950-52; asst. pastor, music dir. Church of Open Door, Louisville, 1952-56; pastor Weems Creek Bapt. Ch., Annapolis, Md., 1956—; moderator So. Dist. Bapt. Assn., 1962-63, Severn Bapt. Assn., 1964-65; moderator Arundel Bapt. Assn., 1968-71, preacher ann. sermon, chmn. fin. com., 1977, 80-82; mem. state mission bd. Bapt. Conv. Md., Balt., 1964-69, chmn. nominating com. State Bds., 1971-72, alt. preacher for ann. conv. sermon, 1971. Mem. Soc. Bibl. Lit., Am. Schs. Oriental Research, Md./Del. Alumni Assn. So. Bapt. Theol. Sem. (pres. 1963-64). Democrat. Home: 661 Ridgely Ave Annapolis MD 21401 Office: Weems Creek Bapt Ch Bestgate Rd and Ridgely Ave Annapolis MD 21401

SMITH, THERESE MARIE, religion educator, nun, Roman Catholic Church; b. Hanover, Pa., Aug. 18, 1929; d. Maurice Joseph and Evelyn Mary (Adams) Smith. B.A., Carlow Coll., 1962; postgrad. Cath. U., 1962-63. Tchr. parochial schs., Pa., Ind., N.C., 1950-62, Columbia, Pa., 1964-68; formation dir. Adorers of the Blood of Christ, Columbia, 1968-77, provincial coordinator, 1977-83; religion tchr./youth moderator St. Joseph Acad., Columbia, 1984—; mem. provincial assembly Adorers of the Blood of Christ, 1968-83, del. to gen. assembly, Rome, 1975, 79, 83. Democrat. Home: Saint Joseph Convent Columbia PA 17512 Office: Saint Joseph Acad RD 2 Columbia PA 17512

SMITH, VINCENT BRYANT, III, minister, Southern Baptist Convention; b. Moulton, Ala., May 29, 1950; s. Vincent Bryant and Billie Anita (Foutch) S.; m. Carolyn June Day, Jan. 14, 1972; children: Keith, Mark, Sean Adam. B.A., Dallas Bapt. U., 1971; M.Div., Southwestern Bapt. Theol. Sem., 1974; D.Min., New Orleans Bapt. Theol. Sem., 1982. Ordained to ministry So. Bapt. Conv., 1974. Minister to youth Edgemont Park Bapt. Ch., Mesquite, Tex., 1969-70, North Euless Bapt. Ch., Tex., 1971; asst. pastor First Bapt. Ch., Dallas, 1971-75; cons. Sunday sch. div. Bapt. Gen. Conv. of Tex., 1975-79; pastor South Garland Bapt. Ch., Tex., 1979-83, Fifteenth Ave. Bapt. Ch., Meridian, Miss., 1983—; instr. in religion Meridian Jr. Coll., 1984—, Dallas Bapt. U., 1982; chmn. Meridian/Lauderdale County Am. Christian TV System, 1983—; mem. adv. com. Salvation Army, Meridian, 1985—, Author resource packet: Youth Are Witnesses Too!, 1980; also chpt., articles. Active Leadership Garland, 1981. Named to Outstanding Young Men Am., U.S. Jaycees, 1980; Judge Frank Ryburn Theol. scholar First Bapt. Ch., Dallas, 1971-73. Mem. Dallas Bapt. U. Alumni Assn. (pres. 1971-72), Minister' Conf. of Lauderdale Bapt. Assn., Lauderdale County Bapt. Assn. (exec. bd. 1983—), Meridian C. of C. Home: 1125 S Hillview Dr Meridian MS 39305 Office: Fifteenth Ave Bapt Ch 1318 15th Ave Meridian MS 39301

SMITH, WALLACE BUNNELL See *Who's Who in America*, 43rd edition.

SMITH, WILBON, minister, Am. Baptist Chs., U.S.A.; b. Macon, Ga., Oct. 6, 1919; s. David and Hattie (White) S.; student Harrisburg (Pa.) Community Coll., 1962-63, Thompson Bus. Coll., Harrisburg, 1946-48, Lancaster (Pa.) Theol. Sem., 1967-68; m. Mildred Hill Gaines, Sept. 29, 1975; children by previous marriage—Michael, Cynthia, Timothy. Ordained to ministry, 1968; pastor chs. in Pa., 1969—; pastor Pine St. Bapt. Ch., Scranton, Pa., 1969—; Protestant chaplain Adams Manor Convalescense Residence, Scranton, CMC Hosp., Scranton. Past v.p.-at-large Pa. Bapt. Congress of Christian Edn.; mem. ministerium RCA Tng. Center, Drums, Pa., 1973; mem. exec. bd. Northeastern Pa. Congregations in Christian Missions, 1973. Mem. Central City Clergy Assn., Abington Bapt. Assn. Address: 915 N Washington Ave Scranton PA 18509

SMITH, WILFRED CANTWELL, educator, United Church of Canada; b. Toronto, Ont., Can., July 21, 1916; s. Victor Arnold and Sarah Cory (Cantwell) S.; B.A., U. Toronto, 1938; postgrad. Westminister Coll., Cambridge, Eng., 1938-40, St. John's Coll., Cambridge U., 1938-40; M.A., Princeton, 1947, Ph.D., 1948; D.D., United Theol. Coll., Montreal, 1966, McGill U., 1973; m. Muriel McKenzie Struthers, Sept. 23, 1939; children—Arnold Gordon, Julian Struthers, Heather Patricia (Mrs. William Hines), Brian Cantwell, Rosemary Muriel. Ordained to ministry United Ch. of North India, 1944, Presbyn. Ch. in Can., 1945, United Ch. of Can., 1961; lectr. Indian and Islamic history Forman Christian Coll., India, 1941-45; research asso. Henry Martyn Sch. Islamic Studies, India, 1941-46; prof. comparative religion McGill U., 1949-63, dir. Inst. Islamic Studies, 1951-63; prof. world religions, dir. Center Study of World Religions of Harvard, 1964-73; McCulloch prof. religion, chmn. dept. Religion Dalhousie U., Halifax, N.S., 1973-80; prof. Harvard Div. Sch., 1980—. Recipient Chauveau medal, Royal Soc. Can., 1974. Fellow Am. Acad. Arts and Scis., Royal Soc. Can. (pres. Humanities and social scis. 1973); mem. Am. Acad. Religion (pres. 1966-69). Author: Modern Islam in India, 1943; Islam in Modern History, 1957; Faith of Other Men, 1963; Meaning and End of Religion, 1963; Questions of Religious Truth, 1967; Religious Diversity, 1976; Belief and History, 1977. Adv. editor The Middle East Jour., 1950-77, The Muslim World, 1956—, Religious Studies, 1964—, Studies in Religion, 1970—. Office: Harvard Div Sch 48 Quincy St Cambridge MA 02138

SMITH, WILLIAM CLARKE, minister, Southern Baptist Convention; b. Bend, Oreg., Jan. 22, 1926; s. Jay Harvey Smith and Amelia Grace (Starr) Poor; A.B. cum laude, Ouachita Bapt. U., 1949; postgrad. Golden Gate Bapt. Theol. Sem., 1951-53; m. Veta Maxine Davidson, Mar. 11, 1945; children: Carolyn Jean Aldama, Virginia Ann, Barbara Lynn Farstad, Rebecca Ruth Sickler, Donald Allen, Patricia Bea Weinbrenner, Dwight David. Ordained to ministry, 1948; pastor Owensville (Ark.) Bapt. Ch., 1949-50, Grace Bapt. Ch., Corning, Calif., 1951; assoc. pastor 1st So. Bapt. Ch., Richmond, Calif., 1951-53; pastor Montalvin Bapt. Ch., San Pablo, Calif., 1953-60, 1st So. Bapt. Ch., Clovis, Calif., 1961-85, Hillside Bapt. Ch., Industry, Calif., 1985—; moderator Fresno Bapt. Assn., 1962-64; moderator Mid-Valley So. Bapt. Assn., 1965-66, clk., 1969-78; pres. Clovis Ministerial Fellowship, 1963-65, 67-70, 75-77; mem. Calif. So. Bapt. Bd. Child Care, 1964-67, pres., 1966-67; parliamentarian So. Bapt. Gen. Conv. Calif., 1964, 69, 74, 78, cons. stewardship dept., 1976—, mem. exec. bd., 1981-85, vice chmn. program com., 1984, 85. Mem. Clovis Bicentennial Com., 1975-77, Clovis Civic Improvement Com., 1976. Mem. Nat. Hist. Soc., Nat. Geog. Soc. Home and Office: 123 N Azusa Ave La Puente CA 91744

SMITH, WILLIAM LAWRENCE, minister, Southern Baptist Convention; b. Pensacola, Fla., July 25, 1946; s. Clemen Turner and Enid Harrison (Rich) S.; B.A., La. Bapt. Coll., 1968; Th.M., New Orleans Bapt. Theol. Sem., 1970; m. Luna Annette Livingston, June 9, 1967; children: Christy Annette, Matthew Lawrence. Ordained to ministry, 1967; asso. pastor, dir. music and youth Lee Heights Bapt. Ch., Pineville, La., 1964-65, 1st Bapt. Ch., Georgetown, La., 1965-66; pastor Zion Bapt. Ch., Georgetown, 1966-77, Lakeshore Bapt. Ch., Monroe, La., 1977—. Mem. exec. bd. La. Bapt. Conv., 1976—; moderator Shady Grove Bapt. Assn., 1970—, Northeast Bapt. Assn., 1981, 82; trustee La. Bapt. Coll., 1982—. Named Outstanding Rural Pastor State of La., La. Bapt. Conv., 1974. Address: 104 McCoy St Monroe LA 71203

SMITH, WILLIAM MILTON, bishop, African Methodist Episcopal Zion Church; b. Stockton, Ala. Dec. 18, 1918; s. George and Elizabeth S.; m. Ida M. Anderson, Jan. 19, 1935; 1 dau., Eula C. Smith Goole. Ed. Ala. State U., Tuskegee Inst., Livinstone Coll., Hool Sem., So. Meth. U., Perkins Sch. Theology. Ordained to ministry African Methodist Episcopal Zion Ch. Pastor various chs.; bishop A.M.E. Zion Ch., Bufalo, from 1960; now sr. bishop, Mobile, Ala. Trustee Ala. State U., 1980. Recipient award Ebony mag., 1980. Republican. Office: AME Zion Ch 3753 Springhill Ave Mobile AL 36608*

SMITH, WILLIAM ROBERT, minister, religion educator, Church of Christ; b. Woodbury, Tenn., Nov. 5, 1950; s. Cecil and Opal (Mears) S.; m. Joan Marilyn Vernon, June 18, 1971; children: Scotty, Monica. A.A., Freed-Hardeman Coll., 1971; B.A., David Lipscomb Coll., 1972; M.A., Harding Grad. Sch. Religion, 1976. Ordained to ministry Ch. of Christ, 1967. Asst. minister Ch. of Christ, Henderson, Tenn., 1973-74; adminstr. Freed-Hardeman Coll., Henderson, 1974-83, Bible tchr., 1978—; minister Ch. of Christ, Humboldt, Tenn., 1975—; dir. Future Ch. Leaders Workshop, Henderson, 1983—; mem. athletic bd. Jackson Christian Sch., Tenn., 1984—; Freed-Hardeman Coll. lectr., 1977—, Spiritual Sword lectr., 1979—. City chmn. Heart Fund, Henderson, 1974. Republican. Home: 804 Mifflin Ave Henderson TN 38340 Office: Freed-Hardeman Coll Faculty Box 80 158 E Main St Henderson TN 38340

SMURL, JAMES FREDERICK, religious educator; b. Wilkes-Barre, Pa., Aug. 20, 1934; m. Mary A. Hennigan; children: Peter, Linda, Beth, Paul. B.A. cum laude, St. Mary's U., Balt., 1955; S.T.B., Gregorian U., Rome, 1957, S.T.L. magna cum laude, 1959; S.T.D. magna cum laude, Cath. U. Am., 1963. Ordained priest Roman Catholic Ch., 1959. Pastoral appointments, 1959-67; instr. Marywood Coll., Scranton, Pa., 1959-61, 63-64; asst. prof. Christian ethics Pius X Sem., Dalton, Pa., 1964-67; asst. prof. humanities and religion Okla. State U., Stillwater, 1968-70, assoc. prof., chmn. faculty humanities, 1970-73; assoc. prof., chmn. dept. religious studies Ind. U., Indpls., 1973-80, vis. assoc. prof., 1979, prof. social and comparative ethics, adj. prof. dept. med. genetics, adj. prof. health and soc., 1980—; vis. prof. med. ethics Christian Theol. Sem., Indpls., 1981, 84; mem. com. on protection of human subjects Ind. U. Med. Ctr., 1981—; mem., vice chmn. genetics adv. com. Ind. State Bd. Health, 1983—; vis. scholar Kennedy Inst. Bioethics, 1978; scholar-in-residence Am. Bar Ctr., 1978; Lilly Open Faculty fellow, 1981; cons. in field; ethics lectr. Nat. Assn. Biology Tchrs, 1975-77; reviewer proposals to pub. programs div. NEH, 1973-74. Author: Religious Ethics, 1972. Contbr. numerous articles to profl. jours. Thomas Lee scholar, 1961-63; named Outstanding Tchr., Okla. State U., 1970-71. Mem. Am. Acad. Religion, Soc. Christian Ethics, Hastings Inst. for Soc., Ethics and Life Scis. (assoc.), Com. on Religion and Law, Soc. for Values in Higher Edn., Omicron Delta Kappa. Office: Indiana U 425 Agnes St Indianapolis IN 46202

SNEED, DAN CALVIN, minister, International Church of the Foursquare Gospel; b. Los Angeles, Dec. 13, 1944; s. George Calvin and Celia May (Lewis) S.; m. Beverly Ruth Carlson, June 24, 1967; children: Robert, Russell, Beckey, Debbie. B.A., Light-house of Internat. Foursquare Evangelism, Los Angeles, 1966. Ordained to ministry International Ch. of the Foursquare Gospel, 1967. Pastor, Christ Faith Mission, Los Angeles, 1966-68, Foursquare Ch., Altadena, Calif., 1968-70; youth pastor Central Luth. Ch., Van Nuys, Calif., 1970-73; dir. Teen Challenge, Los Angeles, 1973-75; pastor Northridge Foursquare Ch., Calif., 1974—; chmn. Found. for His Ministry, 1977—; dir. Jesus West Coast, Los Angeles, 1980—; co-chmn. 1984 Olympic Outreach, Los Angeles, 1984; chmn. Internat. Praise Rally, Los Angeles, 1984; mem. southwest council Youth With A Mission, 1985; co-chmn. S.O.S. Hollywood Youth Outreach, 1985. Bd. dirs. Centrum of Hollywood, 1984—. Home: 9950 Balboa Blvd Northridge CA 91324 Office: Northridge Foursquare Ch 9950 Balboa Blvd Northridge CA 91324

SNELL, JACK ALTON, minister, Southern Baptist Convention; b. Graceville, Fla., Jan. 21, 1941; s. James C. and Ruby J. (Whiddon) S.; m. Anita Ruth Funderburk, June 1, 1963; children: Stephanie Lynn, Charles Jackson. B.A., Samford U., 1963; M.Div., So. Bapt. Theol. Sem., 1966, M.Th., 1968; D.Min., Southeastern Bapt. Theol. Sem., 1975. Ordained to ministry, So. Bapt. Conv., 1961. Pastor, Points Five Points Bapt. Ch., Ala., 1961-63, Union Grove Bapt. Ch., Milton, Ky., 1963-66, Long Run Bapt. Ch., Anchorage, Ky., 1966-68; assoc. pastor First Bapt. Ch., Avondale Estates, Ga., 1968-71; pastor Central Bapt. Ch., Newnan, Ga., 1971-80; pastor Hendricks Ave. Bapt. Ch., Jacksonville, Fla., 1980—; trustee Shorter Coll., Rome, Ga., 1976-80; pres. Ga. Bapt. Pastor's Conf., Atlanta, 1977-78; 1st v.p. Ga. Bapt. Conv., 1978-79. Author: The Christian Index, 1979. Writer newspaper column Fla. Times Union, 1981. Trustee, The Heritage Sch., 1975-80; bd. dirs., exec. com. United Way, Newnan, Ga., 1972-77. Mem. NCCJ, Clergy Roundtable (rep., co-convenor), Jacksonville Ministerial Assn. (exec. sec.), Jacksonville Bapt. Assn. (chmn. exec. com., moderator). Lodge: Rotary (pres. 1978-79, bd. dirs. 1984—). Home: 4308 Heaven Trees Rd Jacksonville FL 32207 Office: Hendricks Ave Bapt Ch 4001 Hendricks Ave Jacksonville FL 32207

SNIDER, DOROTHY ELIZABETH, minister, United Pentecostal Church; b. Deming, N.Mex., May 21, 1923; d. George Ernest and Rebecca (Usrey) Still; m. Hubert Wesley Parks, Jan. 1, 1943 (div. 1977); children: Sharon, Dorothy, Rebecca, Faith, Jonathan; m. Donald Ward Snider, Nov. 6, 1978. Student Apostolic Bible Coll., 1955. Ordained to ministry United Pentecostal Ch., 1945. Dir. child evangelism Christian Life Ctr., Stockton, Calif., 1977-78; dir. youth Life Tabernacle, Kansas City, Mo., 1979-82; evangelist United Pentecostal Ch., various locations, 1983-84; pvt. instr. ch. music Life Tabernacle First United Pentecostal Ch., Kansas City, and Lakeview United Pentecostal Ch., Blue Springs, 1980-84; asst. pastor various schs. Stockton, Calif., 1947-50, Morris, Okla., 1951-52; co-pastor chs., Monahans, Tex., 1955-56, Alamogordo, N.Mex., 1963-64, Tucson, 1964-69, Santa Paula, Calif., 1972-75; missionary Liberia, W. Africa, 1953-54, Japan, 1956-62; pres. Western Dist. Ladies Aux., 1973-77; tchr. Loomis Christian Sch., Calif., 1971-72, Christian Life Coll., Stockton, 1977-78. Republican. Home: 2900 Milford Pl Blue Springs MO 64015 Office: United Pentecostal Church Hazlewood MO 63042

SNIDER, MICHAEL LEE, SR., minister, United Methodist Church; b. Rockbridge Baths, Va., Nov. 20, 1946; s. Harry McDonald and Rebecca Isabelle (Tyree) S.; m. Linda Jane Humphries, July 14, 1973; children: Stacey, Kristen, Michael. A.A., Ferrum Coll., 1967; B.A., Randolph-Macon Coll., 1969; M.Div., Wesley Sem., Washington, 1978. Ordained to ministry Methodist Ch., 1978; cert. instr. Conf. Christian Workers Sch. Student asst. St. Matthew's United Meth. Ch., Annandale, Va., 1970-72; pastor Potomac Charge, Brooke, Va., 1972-73; assoc. pastor Fairfax United Meth. Ch., Va., 1973; lay asst. Arlington Temple, Va., 1974-76; pastor Cedar Run Charge, Catlett, Va., 1976-82, Epworth United Meth. Ch., Falls Church, Va., 1982-85, Mt. Clinton United Meth. Ch., 1985—; worship chmn. Arlington Dist. Council of Ministries, 1982—, mem. dist. evangelism team, 1984—. Republican. Lodge: Kiwanis (v.p. Annandale 1984-85). Home: Route 5 Box 267 Harrisonburg VA 22801 Office: Mt Clinton United Meth Ch Harrisonburg VA 22801

SNIDER, NEAL EDWARD, pastor, American Lutheran Church; career counselor; b. Grand Forks, N.D., June 19, 1935; s. Frank Paul and Mabel Henrietta (Ottem) S.; m. Judy Louise Fosse, Dec. 27, 1958; children: Debra, Nancy, Paul. B.A., Augsburg Coll., 1957; B.Th., Augsburg Sem., 1960; M.Th., Luther Northwestern Sem., St. Paul, 1984. Ordained to ministry Luth. Free Ch., 1960. Pastor, Westby Luth. Parish, Mont., 1960-62, 1st Luth. Ch., Port Orchard, Wash., 1963-69, St. John's Luth. Ch., Bellingham, Wash., 1973-84, Bethesda Luth. Ch., Eugene, Oreg., 1985—; dean North Puget Sound conf. Am. Luth. Ch., 1976-78, 81-83; dir. Luther Child Ctr., Everett, Wash., 1977-83; chmn. chaplaincy adv. com. St. Luke's Hosp., Bellingham, 1977-84; Instr. career assessment and devel., Bellingham, 1983—; owner, pres. Heritage Tours, Inc. Republican candidate for U.S. Ho. of Reps., 1980. Served to lt. col. USN, USAF, U.S. Army (only chaplain in U.S. history to have held commn. in Army, Navy and Air Force). Mem. DAV. Home: 2409 Crestline Dr Bellingham WA 98226 Office: Bethesda Luth Ch 4445 Royal Ave Eugene OR 97402

SNIDER, RONALD LYNN, minister, Southern Baptist Convention. b. Amarillo, Tex., Oct. 13, 1950; s. Weldon Leo and Melba Janette (Isaacs) S.; m. Brenda Dee Barrier, Jan. 11, 1975; 1 son, Luke. B.S. in Natural Sci., Southwestern Okla. State U., Weatherford, 1974; M.Divinity, Southwestern Bapt. Theol. Sem., Ft. Worth, 1981. Ordained to ministry, So. Bapt. Conv., 1975. Dormitory supr. Glorieta Bapt. Conf. Ctr., N.Mex., 1973, 74; pastor 1st Bapt. Ch., Cleo Springs, Okla., 1975-76; assoc. pastor, singles minister 1st Bapt. Ch., Carrollton, Tex., 1977-81; pastor Fairway Bapt. Ch., Wichita Falls, Tex., 1981—; team leader, speaker Internat. Crusades, Guyaquil, Ecuador, 1980, group leader, speaker, Cartegen, Colombia, 1983. Mem. Bapt. Student Union Com. (service award 1984), Right to Life Orgn. (service award 1984), Wichita Archer Clay Pastors Conf. (pres. 1984—), Wichita Archer Clay Evang. Conf. (speaker 1983), Dallas Bapt. Assn. (single adult conf. pres. 1979-80), Phi Delta Theta. Home: Route 3 Box 565 Wichita Falls TX 76308 Office: Fairway Bapt Ch 4408 Fairway Wichita Falls TX 76308

SNIEZAK, RITA MARIE, religion educator, Roman Catholic Church; b. Lackawanna, N.Y., June 30, 1938; d. Louis Joseph and Rose Mary (Pacillo) Mauro; m. Richary Roy Sniezak, Aug. 4, 1962; children: Andrew, Rosemary, Elaine, Nancy. B.S. in Elem. Edn., SUNY-Buffalo, 1960; M.S. in Elem. Edn., 1971. Team leader spl. edn. St. Amelia's Ch., Tonawanda, N.Y., 1976—; elem. tchr. St. Andrew's Country Day Sch., Kenmore, N.Y., 1978—; instr. infusion technique for peace and justice Diocese of Buffalo, 1984—, dept. chmn. elem. social studies, 1984-85. Reviewer chpts. jr. high sch. social studies text, Laidlaw Pub. Co., 1985. Merit badge counselor Greater Niagara Frontier Council, Boy Scouts Am., 1980-84; neighborhood capt. Am. Cancer Soc., Buffalo; mem. edn. com. Buffalo Hist. Soc., 1984—. Named Religious Educator of Yr., Buffalo Diocese Dept. Cath. Edn., 1984. Mem. Niagara Frontier Social Studies League, Nat. Cath. Edn. Assn. Democrat. Club: Green Acres Village (past pres. Tonawanda, N.Y.). Avocations: reading; piano; cooking. Home: 5 Avon Rd Tonawanda NY 14150

SNOW, IRA NOEL, minister, Southern Baptist Convention; b. nr. Dublin, Tex., Sept. 9, 1907; s. Isaac Newton and Beatrice Araminta (Hood) S.; B.A., Tex. Christian U., 1932; M.S., U. Houston, 1952; Th.M., Southwestern Bapt. Theol. Sem., 1939; m. Anna Belle Ellis, July 1, 1939; children: Billy John, George Edward, James Arthur (dec.). Ordained to ministry, 1927; pastor chs., Tex., 1927-58; chaplain USAAF, 1942-46; dir. missions Gulf Coast Bapt. Assn., Brazoria County, Angleton, Tex., 1958—. Pres., Beaumont-Port Arthur

Bapt. Pastors Conf., 1957; chaplain Am. Legion, West Columbia, Tex., 1946-52, 58—. Pres., PTA, West Columbia, 1965, 66; chmn. Community Chest, Port Neches, 1956-57, mem. Brazoria County Welfare Planning Council, 1971—, City Planning Commn. West Columbia, 1951. Mem. Ministerial Alliance West Columbia (pres. 1972), Supts. of Missions So. Bapt. Conv., Am. Legion. Author: (booklets) What is Faith, 1943; Where Is God?, 1944; Forty-Five Questions, and Answers on Marriage, 1944. Editor: Gulf Coast Baptist Breezes, 1958-76. Home: PO Box 535 West Columbia TX 77486 Office: PO Box 598 Angleton TX 77515

SNOW, VERNE, minister, Seventh-Day Adventists; b. Port Arthur, Ont., Can., May 29, 1942; s. Harold Eldon and Nellie (Korchenski) S.; m. Mildred Ruth Jameison, Aug. 1, 1964; children: Mark, John, Paul. B.Th., Can. Union Coll., 1968; postgrad. Andrews U., 1970-71. Ordained to ministry Seventh-day Adventists. Pastor, 7th Day Adventist Ch., B.C., Can., 1968-69, evangelist, 1969-70, 71-72; evangelist throughout Can., 1972-74, Alta., also U.S., Scotland, 1974—. Home: 11 Westview Dr Lacombe AB TOC 1SO Canada Office: Conf Seventh Day Adventists Box 5007 Red Deer AB T4N 6A1 Canada

SNOWDEN, J.S.P., bishop Lutheran Church of Canada. Office: 360 Nicola St Kamloops BC V2C 2P5 Canada*

SNUSTEAD, MERLE ELLSWORTH, chaplain, Lutheran Church in America; b. Strongfield, Sask., Can., Oct. 3, 1935; s. William and Alice Dorothy (Grunerud) S.; m. Lucille Rose Staflund, Aug. 28, 1965; children: Myrl Alyson, Kevin Anthony. B.Ed., U. Sask., 1966; M.Div., Luth. Theol. Sem., Saskatoon, Sask., 1973, also postgrad. Ordained to ministry Lutheran Ch., 1972. Pastor, Christ Luth. Ch., Tisdale, Sask., 1972-80; chaplain Lions Gate Hosp., North Vancouver, B.C., 1980-83, Bethany Care Centre, Calgary, Alta., 1984—; instr. Luth. Theol. Sem., Saskatoon, Sask., 1983-84; counsellor North East Family Life Assn., Tisdale, 1975-80. Pres. Tisdale Home and Sch. Assn., 1975-80; v.p. Boundary Community Schs. Assn., North Vancouver, 1981-83. Schneider fellow Luth. Theol. Sem., 1973, fellow/scholar Luth. Theol. Sem., 1983. Mem. Can. Assn. Pastoral Care, Luth. Theol. Sem. Alumni Assn., Western Can. Synod Ministerial Assn., Alta. Pastoral Care Assn., Luth. Ministerial Assn. (v.p. 1981-82, treas. 1982-83). Mem. New Democratic Party. Home: 3653 Diefenbaker Dr Saskatoon SK S7L 4W1 Canada

SNYDER, DEAN EDWIN, minister, Assemblies of God; b. Findlay, Ohio, Oct. 23, 1946; s. Dwight J. and Violet Monte (Schell) S.; certificate N.E. Bible Coll., 1969; m. Donna Lee Chapman, Jan. 1, 1970; children—Holly Lyn, Heather Lee. Ordained to ministry, 1974; children's evangelist, 1967-70; founding pastor Cross Lanes Assembly of God (W.Va.), 1970-71; asst. pastor, dir. Christian edn., dir. Neighborhood Bible Clubs, First Assembly of God, Findlay, 1971-73; children's pastor, dir. Neighborhood Bible Clubs, dir. elementary and pre-sch. edn. Tri-County Assembly of God, Fairfield, Ohio, 1973—; coordinator Bible curriculum, Bible tchr. Tri-County Christian Elementary Sch., Fairfield, 1973-80. Mem. N.E. Bible Coll. Alumni Assn. (v.p. Ohio chpt.). Author: Facts for Faith in Fun, 2 vols., 1974; The Treasure Chest, 4 vols., 1984-85; editor Tri-County Assembly Trumpet, 1974-83. Home: 10334 Pippin Ln Cincinnati OH 45231 Office: 7350 Dixie Hwy Fairfield OH 45014

SNYDER, DOROTHEA JONES, lay ch. worker, United Presbyn. Ch. U.S.A.; b. Sterling City, Tex., July 1, 1926; d. Evan and Marguerite (Green) Jones; B.A., N. Tex. State U., 1945; m. Alan Howard Snyder, Jr., Feb. 16, 1946; children—Mark Evan, Cathleen. Ordained elder, 1971; pres. Trinity Presbyterial, 1967-70; moderator Presbytery of Trinity, 1972, chmn. coordinating council, 1973; v.p., mem. exec. com. bd. Program Agy., United Presbyn. Ch. U.S.A., 1973—; del. World Council Chs., Nairobi, 1975. Active Boy Scouts U.S.A., hosp. vol. services. Vice pres. bd. trustees Memphis Theol. Sem., 1974-75. Mem. Dallas Council World Affairs, P.E.O. (chpt. pres. 1962-64, pres. Dallas council 1964-65). Home: 4526 Harvest Hill Dallas TX 75234

SNYDER, JOHN JOSEPH See *Who's Who in America*, 43rd edition.

SNYDER, LAVERN HENRY, minister, Assemblies of God; b. Paynesville, Minn., Dec. 15, 1930; s. Alvin Duane and Minnie (Kohler) S.; diploma theology N. Central Bible Coll., Mpls., 1953; m. Peggy Edith Booker, Aug. 16, 1953; children—Janice LaVerne, Timothy Wayne. Ordained to ministry, 1955; pastor chs. in Ky., 1953—; founder Bethel Temple Assembly of God, Lexington, Ky., 1959-68; founder, pastor Salem Assembly of God, Anchorage, Ky., 1972-76; traveling evangelist, 1968-69. Pres. Christ's Ambassadors, Ky. dist. Assemblies of God, 1954-58, presbyter Bluegrass sect., 1959-68, sec.-treas., Sunday sch. dir. Ky. dist. council, 1969-76, exec. presbyter Ky. dist., also gen. Presbyter Gen. Council, 1969-76. Mem. Oldham County Farm Bur. Recipient Goal Achievement award Assemblies of God, 1976. Author articles in field. Home: Route 3 Box 317 Lark Rd Crestwood KY 40014 Office: PO Box 98 Crestwood KY 40014

SNYDER, LYNN EDWARD, minister, United Brethren in Christ; b. Kitchener, Ont., Can., Feb. 21, 1944; s. Walter Sheldon and Adeline Velma (Kreuger) S.; m. Donna Marie Barnell, May 17, 1969; children: Cynthia, Deborah, Brenda. B.Th., Emmanuel Bible Coll., Kitchener, 1967; M.Div., Christian Internat. Grad. Sch. Theology, 1983. Ordained to ministry United Brethren in Christ, 1982. Tchr. Calvary Holiness Coll., Wellesley, Ont., 1970-76; editor Gospel Tidings, Wellesley, 1971-75; minister Free Meth. Ch., Kakabeka Falls, Ont., 1977-79, United Brethren Ch., Stevensville, Ont., 1979—; bd. dirs. Koinonia Bible Sch., Kitchener, 1976—. Author: Destiny of Hope, 1982; Making Sense of Suffering, 1984. Home: 2542 Stevensville Rd Stevensville ON LOS 1SO Canada Office: United Brethren Ch 2536 Stevensville Rd Stevensville ON LOS 1SO Canada

SNYDER, STEPHEN HARLEY, religion educator, American Baptist Churches U.S.A.; b. Los Angeles, Aug. 17, 1944; s. Harley and Helen Winifred (White) S.; A.B., Stanford U., 1967; M.Div., Am. Bapt. Sem. West, 1971; A.M., U. Chgo., 1973, Ph.D., 1975. Ordained to ministry Bapt. Ch., 1971. Asst. prof. Wright State U., Dayton, Ohio, 1976-77; lectr. U. Wis., Oshkosh, 1977-78; asst. prof. Linfield Coll., McMinnville, Oreg., 1978-82, assoc. prof., 1982—. Contbr. articles to Linfield Casements, Willamette Jour., religious periodicals, book revs. to Church History, Choice, Christian Century. NEH grantee, summers 1981, 84. Mem. Am. Acad. Religion, Am. Soc. Ch. History, Sierra Club, World Wildlife Fedn., NOW. Democrat. Home: 1107 Summerwood Dr McMinnville OR 97128 Office: Dept Religious Studies Linfield College McMinnville OR 97128

SOENS, LAWRENCE D., bishop, Roman Catholic Church. Bishop of Sioux City, Iowa, 1983—. Office: Chancery Offite 1812 Jackson St PO Box 1530 Sioux City IA 51102*

SOLAND, EUGENE FREDERICK, minister, American Lutheran Church; b. Decorah, Iowa, Jan. 8, 1936; s. Embret G. and Louise (Arness) S.; B.A., Luther Coll., Decorah, 1959; B.D., Luther Theol. Sem., St. Paul, 1967, postgrad., 1967-69; m. Wanda Gish, Nov. 4, 1961; children: Robert, Ronald, Brenda. Ordained to ministry, 1967; pastor Immanuel Luth. Ch., Glenwood City, Wis., 1956-59, Peace Ch., Sioux Center, Iowa and Our Savior's Ch., Rock Valley, 1969-76, Elk Horn (Iowa) Luth. Ch., 1976—. Active Cub Scouts Boy Scouts Am., Rock Valley Betterment Council, bd. dirs. Salem Homes, Elk Horn, Okoboji Bible Camp, Milford, Iowa. Home: Bjorholm St Elk Horn IA 51531 Office: Elk Horn Luth Ch Elk Horn IA 51531

SOLIE, ROLAND O., lay church worker. Gen. sec. Evangelical Free Church, Mpls. Office: Evang Free Ch 4201 13th Ave S Minneapolis MN 55407*

SOLON, ROLANDO LOREGA, minister, Lutheran Church in America; b. Cebu City, Phillipines, July 29, 1944; came to U.S., 1976, naturalized 1982; s. Victoriano Genson and Felina Taparra (Lorega) S.; m. Suzanne Lois Newman, Dec. 9, 1973. B.S. in Bus. Adminstrn., U. Visayas, Cebu City, 1968; M.Div., Gettysburg Sem., 1981. Ordained to ministry Luth. Ch. in Am., 1981. Pastor Holy Trinity Ch., Elkins, W.Va., 1981—; v.p. Luth. Campus Ministry, W.Va. U., Morgantown, 1981—. Democrat. Home: 201 Ferndale Dr Elkins WV 26241 (304) 636-4326 Office: Holy Trinity Luth Ch 302 1st St Elkins WV 26241

SOLOVEITCHIK, JOSEPH B. Rabbi; prof. philosophy Rabbi Isaac Elchaman Theol. Sem. Office: 2504 Amsterdam Ave New York NY 10033*

SOMERS, CARMEL THERESE, nun, Roman Catholic Church; b. Dublin, Ireland, June 12, 1939; came to U.S., 1965; d. Kevin Lawrence and Mary Eleanor (Malone) S. B.A., U. San Diego, 1970; M.Ed. in Guidance and Counseling, Loyola U., Los Angeles, 1974; diploma in Applied Theology, Jesuit Sch. Applied Theology, 1977. Joined Religious Sisters of Charity, 1957. Tchr. Cath. elem. schs., Long Beach, Calif., 1965-66, Garden Grove, Calif., 1966-68, Los Alamitos, Calif., 1968-71, Los Angeles, 1971-72, Van Nuys, Calif., 1972-74; dir. religious edn. St. Bridget of Sweden Parish, Van Nuys, 1974-77; assoc. dir. field edn. St. John's Sem., Camarillo, Calif., 1977-83, prof. pastoral theology, 1977-82; vocation/formation dir. Religious Sisters of Charity, Culver City, Calif., 1982—; mem. parents adv. bd. Office Religious Edn., Los Angeles, 1974-77, master catechist steering com., 1974-76, mem. Los Angeles Met. Interreligious Steering Com., 1984—; sec. Western Assn. Spiritual Dirs., Los Angeles, 1979-82. Recipient Pius X award for religious edn. Archdiocese Los Angeles, 1977. Mem. Western Vocation Dirs. Assn., Nat. Vocation Dirs. Assn. Address: 10664 St James Dr Culver City CA 90230

SOMMER, DANIEL GORDON, minister, American Baptist Churches in the U.S.A.; b. Altoona, Pa., Aug. 25, 1932; s. Carl Theodore and Dorothea Rebecca (Graham) S.; m. Helen Rebecca Carnes, July 31, 1955; children: Daniel Jonathan, Matthew David, Rebecca Ann, Mary Priscilla. B.A., U. Pitts., 1954, M.Ed., 1955; M.Div., Pitts. Theol. Sem., 1958. Ordained to ministry Am. Bapt. Chs. U.S.A., 1958. Pastor, Emmanuel Bapt. Ch., Pitts., 1955-64, First Bapt. Ch., Monongahela, Pa., 1964-72, Lincoln Bapt. Ch., Columbus, Ohio, 1972—; nat. clinic dir. Evangelism Explosion Internat., Fort Lauderdale, Fla., 1972—; trustee Ohio Bapt. Conv., Granville, Ohio, 1972—; pres. Ohio div. Race Track Chaplaincy Am., Columbus, 1978—, nat. pres., Dallas, 1981—. Co-founder Lincoln Edn. Assn., 1979, Apple Child Care - Mgmt. Firm, 1984; cons. Performax Systems Internat., Inc. Named Citizen of Week, WHYT, Pitts., 1960. Mem. Christian Harness Horsemen's Assn. Home: PO Box 110 Galloway OH 43119 Office: Lincoln Bapt Ch 5755 Feder Rd Columbus OH 43228

SOMMERKAMP, THEO ENOCH, editor, Southern Baptist Convention; b. Tampa, Fla., Feb. 11, 1929; s. Theo E. and Mozelle (King) S.; B.S., Okla. Bapt. U., 1951; M.S., Fla. State U., 1954; m. Jean Childers, July 28, 1951; children: Bradley, Julia, Karl. Asst. dir. Bapt. Press, So. Bapt. Conv., 1955-65; dir. European Bapt. Press Service, Ruschlikon, Switzerland, 1965-71; assoc. dir. pub. relations Bapt. Annuity Bd., Dallas, 1971-76; editor Ohio Bapt. Messenger, Columbus, 1976—. Mem. Pub. Relations Soc. Am., Bapt. Pub. Relations Assn., Religious Pub. Relations Council. Home: 3000 Easthaven Ct S Columbus OH 43227 Office: 1680 E Broad St Columbus OH 43203

SONGER, JERRY ALAN, minister, So. Baptist Conv.; b. Olney, Ill., Jan. 27, 1936; s. W.A. and Mary Kathryn (Robinson) S.; B.A. (Outstanding Ministerial Student award 1958), Belmont Coll., Nashville, 1958; B.D. (Centennial scholar 1958), So. Bapt. Theol. Sem., Louisville, 1961; D.Min., Southeastern Bapt. Theol. Sem., Wake Forest, N.C., 1975; m. Jane Elizabeth Jones, June 11, 1957; children—Sheree, Mark, Brent, Shane. Ordained to ministry, 1957; pastor chs. in Tenn., 1961-70; pastor Central Bapt. Ch., Waycross, Ga., 1970-75, Central Bapt. Ch., Chattanooga, 1976—. Trustee Belmont Coll., also Tenn. Bapt. Children's Home; mem. exec. bd. Tenn. Bapt. Conv.; past pres. Piedmont Okefenokee Bapt. Pastors Conf., Waycross Area Ministerial Assn.; v.p. Ga. Bapt. Pastor's Conf., 1975. Mem. Belmont Coll. Alumni Assn. (past pres.). Contbr. ch. publs. Home: 7021 Pauline Circle Chattanooga TN 37421 Office: 901 Woodmore Ln Chattanooga TN 37411

SONNEN, JON ANTON, priest, Episcopal Ch.; b. Houston, Nov. 19, 1936; s. Louis Carl and Waldene (Burdett) S.; B.A. in Psychology, So. Meth. U., 1959, M.A. in Philosophy, 1965; M.Div., Episc. Theol. Sem. SW, 1974; m. Marilyn Braly Sonnen, Dec. 28, 1957; children—Elizabeth Dawn, Janet Marie, Stephen Louis, Eric Joseph. Ordained deacon, 1974, priest, 1975; vicar Episc. Ch. Advent, Stafford, Tex., 1974—. Chmn., Tri-Cities Ministerial Fellowship, Tex. Home: 12119 Brighton Ln Stafford TX 77477

SONNENBURG, EMIL, lay worker, Church of God (Anderson, Ind.), industrial manager; b. Gruenthal, Russia, Jan. 22, 1928; came to Can., 1949; s. Adolf and Leontine (Ulmer) S.; m. Ida Herta Berg, Dec. 5, 1953; children: Siegbert, Arthur, George. Chmn. bd. Ch. of God, Edmonton, Alta., Can., 1949-50; lay minister Ch. of God, Kitchener, Ont., Can., 1953-63; mem. provincial bd. trustees Ch. of God, Ont., 1965-78; chmn. gen. assembly Ch. of God, Ont., 1978—, chmn. coordinating com., 1978—. Prodn. mgr. Electrohome Industries, Cambridge, Ont., 1973—. Served with German Armed Forces, 1944-45. Conservative. Home: 319 Winston Blvd Cambridge ON N3C 3C4 Canada Office: Electrohome Industries 505 Conestoga Blvd Cambridge ON N3C 3C4 Canada

SONO, ROY I., bishop, United Methodist Church, Rocky Mountain and Yellowstone Conf. Office: 2200 S University Blvd Denver CO 80210*

SORENSEN, DAVID ALLEN, minister, author, American Lutheran Church; b. Grand Forks, N.D., June 18, 1953; s. Donald Albin and Beverly Jean (Medchill) S.; m. Barbara Ann DeGrote, June 26, 1976; children: Katherine, Jillian. B.S. in Sociology, Mankato State U., 1978; M.Div., Luther Theol. Sem., 1982. Ordained to ministry Am. Luth. Ch., 1982. Chaplain Fairview Hosp., Mpls., 1980; intern pastor Faith Luth. Ch., Duluth, Minn., 1980-81; pastor Blair Luth. Chs., Wis., 1982-85, Grace Luth. Ch., Eau Claire, Wis., 1985—; chmn. No. Wis. Dist. Youth Com., N. Wis. Dist. Am. Luth. Ch., 1983—, Mondovi Conf. Youth Com., 1982—, sec., 1984; dist. coordinator Am. Luth. Ch. Nat. Youth Gathering, Denver, 1984-85. Author: It's A Mystery To Me, Lord, 1985. Contbg. editor The Clergy Jour., 1984—; syndicated columnist Pause for a Promise, 1982—; contbr. articles to religious jours. Founding chmn. Emergency Food Pantry, Blair, Wis., 1982—; bd. dirs. fin. Western Dairyland Econ. Opportunity Council, Whitehall, Wis., 1983, 85—; chem. abuse presenter Miss. Valley Human Services Ctr., Independence, Wis., 1983. Served with USAF, 1973-75, Vietnam. Rockefeller Found. grantee, 1982; recipient Disting. Service award Blair Jaycees, 1983. Mem. Clergy Roster, U.S. Jaycees (Disting. Service award, 1983, pres. 1982-83; v.p. 1983-84). Home: 2223 Trenton Ct Eau Claire WI 54703

SORENSON, MORRIS ALVIN, JR., minister, American Lutheran Church; b. Bismarck, N.D., Sept. 7, 1927; s. Morris Alvin and Bertha (Megorden) S.; m. Dorothy Austin, Aug. 31, 1952; children: Robert A., Mary Sorenson Ranum, Arne M., Michael D. B.A., Luther Coll., 1949; C.T., Luther Theol. Sem., St. Paul, 1953, B.Th., 1966, M.Th., 1967; D.D., Trinity Sem., Columbus, Ohio, 1977. Ordained to ministry Am. Luth. Ch., 1953. Missionary to Japan, 1953-66; area sec. World Mission, Am. Luth. Ch., Mpls., 1966-70, dir. World Mission, 1970-81, exec. asst. to presiding bishop, 1981—; mem. coms. and assembly World Council Chs. and Luth. World Fedn., Geneva, Switzerland, 1967-81; dir. Luth. World Relief, N.Y.C., 1971-82; mem. coms. annual meeting Luth. Council U.S.A., N.Y.C., 1967—. Contbr. revs. and articles to religious jours. Served with U.S. Army, 1946-47. Recipient Disting. Alumni award Luther Coll., 1971. Office: Am Luth Ch 422 S 5th St Minneapolis MN 55415

SORSCHER, MARVIN, educator, rabbi, Orthodox Jewish Congregations; b. Bklyn., Apr. 29, 1924; s. Abraham and Miriam (Cohen) S.; B.A., Yeshiva Coll., 1946; M.A., Hunter Coll., 1950; M.H.L., Yeshiva U., 1950, M.S., 1958; D.H.L., 1968; m. Sylvia London, Feb. 7, 1954; children—Esther Shulamis (Mrs. Tuvia Rister), Abraham Mordecai, Sroya Shalom Yoseph. Rabbi, 1952; pres. Yeshiva Haichel Hatorah, N.Y.C., 1969—; pres. Am. Assn. Tchrs. Hebrew, 1970—; guidance counselor John D. Wells Jr. High Sch., Bklyn., 1970-74, Franklin D. Roosevelt High Sch., Bklyn., 1975—; chmn. fgn. lang. dept. Washington Irving Evening High Sch., N.Y.C., 1973—. Mem. Assn. Orthodox Jewish Tchrs. (v.p., exec. bd.). Author: Havah Nesocheach, 1972, part 2, 1977; Manual of Tape Scripts, 1970; Lashon V Dibbur, 1971; The Laws of Shabbos Erev Pesach, 1974; Blessings and Prayers for the Sabbath, Holidays and Special Occasions, 1974; Hakshaiv Va'Anai, 1976. Home: 1375 57th St Brooklyn NY 11219 Office: 5800-20th Ave Brooklyn NY 11204

SORTEBERG, WARREN ANDREW, pastor, church executive, American Lutheran Church; b. Canton, S.D., Nov. 15, 1932; s. Andrew E. and Rose H. (Ring) S.; m. Phyllis M. Nielsen, June 21, 1958; children: Kristi, David, Karin, Mary. B.A., Augustana Coll., 1954; B.Th., Luther Theol. Sem., St. Paul, 1958; student Freidrich William U., Erlangen, Fed. Republic Germany, 1958-59, Harvard Div. Sch., 1970; D.D. (hon.), NW Theol. Sem., St. Paul, 1977. Ordained to ministry Am. Luth. Ch., 1959. Pastor asst. Our Savior's Luth. Ch., Mpls., 1959-61, sr. pastor, 1961-78; sr. pastor Christ the King Luth. Ch., Denver, 1978-82; service mission dir. Am. Luth. Ch., Mpls., 1982-84, dir. urban and ethnic ministries, 1984—; chmn. bd. regents Luther Theol. Sem., St. Paul, 1972-76; mem. bd. theol. edn. and ministry Am. Luth. Ch., Mpls., 1976-82. Chmn. Phillips Neighborhood Improvement Assn., Mpls., 1964-70, Mpls. Model City Program, 1969-70. Recipient Good Neighbor award Phillips Neighborhood Improvement Assn., 1978; Merrill fellow Harvard Div. Sch., 1970. Office: Am Luth Ch 422 S 5th St Minneapolis MN 55415

SOTEROPOULOS, NICHOLAS, priest, Greek Orthodox Archdiocese of North and South America; b. N.Y.C., Dec. 19, 1933; s. Costas and Maria (Trihas) S.; m. Mary Cotzias, Nov. 27, 1960; children: Nikki-Marie Margarites, Michele, Dean, Lisa. B.A. in Theology, Holy Cross Seminary, 1959; student U. Chgo., 1975, 1976. Ordained to diaconate Greek Orthodox Archdiocese of N. and S. Am., 1961, priest, 1961. Pastor St. Demetrios Greek Orthodox Ch., Waterloo, Iowa, 1961-64; assoc. pastor St. Demetrios Greek Orthodox Ch., Astoria, N.Y., 1964-67; pastor Assumption Greek Orthodox Ch., Poughkeepsie, N.Y., 1967-70; dir. youth ministry Greek Orthodox Archdiocese, N.Y.C., 1970-74; bd. dirs. St. Basil's Acad., Garrison, N.Y., 1975-77; pastor Ch. of Saint Paraskevi, Greenlawn, N.Y., 1977—; sec. L.I. Clergy Assn., 1982-84. Author youth program. Named Protopresbyter, Patriarchate of Constantanople, 1984. Office: Ch of St Paraskevi Shrine Pl Greenlawn NY 11740

SOTO, JUAN SIGIFREDO, minister, United Methodist Church. b. Majagua, Cuba, Mar. 30, 1928; came to U.S., 1967, naturalized, 1973; s. Bereno Rodriguez Soto and Maria Borges; m. Felicita Oldy Brocard, Mar. 16, 1957; children: Laudeline, Ruben, Ricard. A.B., Matanzas Coll. (Cuba), 1965; B.D., Seminario De Teologia (Cuba), 1966. Ordained to ministry United Meth. Ch., 1968. Statistician, Rio Grande Conf., San Antonio, 1972-76; chmn. Alianza Ministerial, Laredo, Tex., 1977-78; mem. Ordained Ministry, Austin, Tex., 1978—; staffwriter Reportero Metodista, Austin, 1982—. Contbr. articles to profl. jours. Author numerous poems. Trustee No. Dist., San Antonio, 1983—. Recipient Arte de Escribir, 1979. Republican. Home: 4606 Milburn Ln Austin TX 78702

SOTO, ONELL ASISELO, minister, Episcopal Ch.; b. Cuba, Nov. 17, 1932; s. Juan Aurelio and Aurelia de los Angeles (Almaguer) S.; B.A., Irene Toland Coll., Cuba, 1952; B.S., U. Havana (Cuba), 1956; B.D., U. of the South, 1964; m. Nina Ulloa, July 4, 1960; children—Ana, Lidia, Onell, Elena. Ordained priest, 1965; vicar St. Nicholas Ch., Quito, Ecuador, 1965-71; exec. provincial sec. Episc. Ch., San Salvador, El Salvador, 1971—; editor Rapidas News Service, San Salvador, 1971. Editor La Santa Eucaristía, 1972, El Libro de Oficios, 1974; contbg. editor WACC Jour., London, The Asian Messenger, Hong Kong, The Episcopalian, Phila., 1976—. Home: 4316 15 CP San Salvador El Salvador Office: Apartado (01) 142 San Salvador El Salvador Central America

SOUGSTAD, ORRIS WESTON, minister, Am. Luth. Ch.; b. Fulton, S.D., June 20, 1924; s. Edward Evan and Ora Mae (Wicks) S.; B.A., Augustana Coll., 1947; C.Th., Luther Theol. Sem., St. Paul, 1950, M.Div., 1975; m. Mildred Ruth Hanson, Sept. 14, 1947; children—Ruth, David, Timothy. Ordained to ministry, 1950; pastor Parker (S.D.) Luth. Parish, 1950-52, Faith Luth. Ch., Calamus, Ia., 1952-55; pastor-organizer Calvary Luth. Ch., Fort Worth, 1955-63; pastor Beautiful Savior Luth. Ch., Amarillo, Tex., 1963-70, First Luth. Ch., Waco, Tex., 1970—. Designer, owner ch. data processing program, 1972—; area resource pastor Evang. Outreach, Am. Luth. Ch., 1976-77. Mem. bd. programming policy adv. council, Waco-McLennan County Community Action Program, 1972—, pres., 1974-75, mem. exec. com., 1974-76, chmn., 1976—. Mem. Waco Ministers Assn. (pres. 1974), Clergy Am. Luth. Ch. Home: 1209 Westwood Dr Waco TX 76710 Office: 1008 Jefferson St Waco TX 76702

SOUKUP, ERWIN MYRON, priest, Episcopal Church; b. Oak Park, Ill., Mar. 1, 1921; s. Erwin R. and Libby V. (Hofreiter) S.; m. Janet McKay, June 3, 1944; children: Stephen M. and Sarah. B.A., North Central, 1947; M.Div. cum laude, Seabury-Western, 1961, D.D. (hon.), 1980. Postulant, candidate diocese of Chgo., Evanston Ill., 1958-61; vicar St. Helena's, Burr Ridge, Ill., 1961-67; rector Grace Ch., Freeport, Ill., 1967-70; priest-in-charge Grace Ch., Galena, Ill., 1967-70; canon to ordinary Diocese of Chgo., 1970—, archdeacon, 1978—; trustee Episcopal Charities, 1975—; pres. Episc. Found. of Chgo., 1967—; sec. SWTS Trustees, Evanston, 1975—; editor Advance mag, Chgo., 1971—; convenor Episc Communicators, Chgo., 1972-77. Trustee Radio and TV Found., 1962—. Served to maj., AUS, 1943-54. Home: 5 E 51st St LaGrange IL 60525 Office: Diocese of Chgo 65 E Huron St Chicago IL 60611

SOUTH, CHARLES EDWARD, priest Episcopal Church; b. Glen Ridge, N.J., Nov. 8, 1933; s. Edward McLeod and Evelyn (Allison) S.; student Wabash Coll., 1951-52; B.A., U. of South, 1969, M.Div., 1970; m. Lee Smith Greenwood; children: Christopher, David, Melanie, Megan, Kathryn, Joshua. Ordained to ministry as priest, 1971; deacon intern Cathedral Ch. of Nativity, Bethlehem, Pa., 1970-71; asso. rector St. Mary's on the Highlands, Birmingham, Ala., 1971-72; rector Grace Episc. Ch., Birmingham, 1972-76, St. Stephen's Episc. Ch., Huntsville, Ala., 1976—; adj. faculty Sch. Theology, U. of South. Mem. dept. Christian edn. Diocese Ala. Episc. Ch., 1971-74, dept. fin., Diocese of Ala., 1978-81. Mem. Drug Commn., Bethlehem, 1970-71; mem. youth, vols. coms. ARC, Birmingham, 1974-75; bd. dirs. St. Martins in the Pines, Birmingham, 1970-76. Home: 116 Noble Dr SE Huntsville AL 35802 Office: 8020 Whitesburg Dr SE Huntsville AL 35802

SOUTHERN, LONNIE STEVEN, minister, Christian Church (Disciples of Christ); b. San Diego, Sept. 6, 1947; s. Henry Benjamin and Juanita Hilda (Bandy-Fishburn) S.; m. Vicki Leona Musgrave, Aug. 18, 1968; children: Katherine Michelle, Jesse Ryan. B.Th., Northwest Christian Coll., 1970; D.Ministry, Sch. Theology at Claremont, 1977. Ordained to ministry Christian Ch. (Disciples of Christ), 1974. Youth minister Hillsboro Christian Ch., Oreg., 1968-69; assoc. minister Lebanon Christian Ch., Oreg., 1969-70; minister in tng. Pomona Christian Ch., Calif., 1970-74; intern Windward Christian Ch., Kailua, Hawaii, 19[illegible]; minister (joint ministry) Allenville and Sullivan Christian Chs., Sullivan, Ill., 1974-76; sr. minister South Bay Christian Ch., Redondo Beach, Calif., 1976-80; minister Allenville Christian Ch., Ill., 1980—; chaplain Ill. N.G., Decatur, Ill., 1983—; v.p. South Bay Interfaith Council, Redondo Beach, 1976-78, pres., 1978-80; bd. dirs. So. Calif. Council of Chs., Los Angeles, 1977-80, exec. com., 1979-80; v.p., bd. dirs. All Peoples Community Ctr., Los Angeles, 1977-80; mem. Shalom: Peace With Justice Congregational Project, Indpls., 1982—; mem. Regional Pastor-Parish Mgmt. Team, Bloomington, Ill., 1982—; pres. Lakeland Cluster Christian Chs., East Central Ill., 1983—; bd. dirs. Christian Chs. in Ill. and Wis., Bloomington, 1983—. Mem. Redondo Beach Co-ordinating Council, 1976-80, Disabled Services, Redondo Beach, 1977-80, Redondo Beach Mayor's Round Table, 1978-80, Moultrie County Youth Awareness Council, Sullivan, 1982—. Mem. Sullivan Ministerial Assn. (pres. 1981-83), Sch. of Theology at Claremont Alumni Assn. (sec. 1978-80). Home: 713 S Hamilton Sullivan IL 61951 Office: Allenville Christian Ch Rural Route 1 Box 72 Allenville IL 61951

SOVIC, RUTH, religious organization executive. Sec. gen. World Young Women's Christian Assn. Office: 37 Quai Wilson 1201 Geneva Switzerland*

SOWERS, BETSY JILL, minister, American Baptist Churches in the U.S.A.; flight attendant; b. Memphis, June 19, 1948; d. Paul Williams and Betty Ann (Speight) S.; m. Paul Elwyn Thomas, Sept. 3, 1979. Student Agnes Scott Coll., 1966-68; B.A. in Psychology, Fla. State U., 1970; M.S.W., Boston Coll., 1977; M.Div. magna cum laude, Harvard U., 1981. Ordained to ministry Am. Bapt. Chs. in U.S.A., 1982. Field assoc. Am. Bapt. Chs. of Mass., Boston, 1981—, mem. bd. dirs., 1981—, mem. commn. on ministry, 1982—, mem. pastoral settlement com., 1982—, mem. staff, dept. church and society, 1981—, mem. task force on women and ministry, 1981—; bd. dirs. Am. Bapt. Women Mass., 1982—; moderator Old Cambridge Bapt. Ch., Mass., 1984-85, Boston Theol. Circle, 1983—. Flight attendant Pan Am. World Airways, N.Y.C., 1970—. Contbg. editor periodic publs. Am. Bapt. Ch. Mass., 1981—; contbr. articles and revs. to ch. mag. Mem. New Eng. Women Ministers Assn. (bd. dirs.), Conf. Bapt. Ministers Mass., Phi Beta Kappa. Democrat. Office: Am Baptist Churches of Mass 88 Tremont St Room 500 Boston MA 02108

SPALDING, JAMES COLWELL, educator, minister, U.P. Ch. in U.S.A.; b. Kansas City, Mo., Nov. 6, 1921; s. John W. and Helen Muriel (Kerr) S.; student Kansas City Jr. Coll., 1938-40; B.A., U. Ill., 1942; B.D., Hartford Theol. Sem., 1945; Ph.D., Columbia, 1950; postgrad. Union Theol. Sem., U. Zurich, U. Basel, U. Tubingen: m. Virginia Esther Burford, Oct. 21, 1945; children—Paul, Helen, Peter, Mary, Ann. Ordained to ministry, 1945; pastor chs., Poplar, Mont., 1945-46, Slater, Mo., 1950-53; prof., chaplain Missouri Valley Coll., 1949-53; asso. prof. Trinity U., San Antonio, 1953-56; asst. prof. U. Iowa, 1956-59, asso. prof., 1959-68, prof., 1968—, dir. sch. religion, 1971-79. Mem. Am. Soc. Ch. History, Am. Soc. Reformation Research, Sixteenth Century Studies Conf., Am. Acad. Religion. Democrat. Contbr. to Ency. Brit. 1974, Church History, 1959, 61, 67, 70, 76. Home: 315 Ridgeview Iowa City IA 52240

SPANN, HAROLD ELLIOTT, minister, United Church of Christ; B. Washington, Ind., June 4, 1948; s. Roy Elliott and Wynemia (Blakey) S.; m. Sandra Ellen Hayden, Aug. 16, 1969; children: Jill Dian, Nathaniel Elliott, Blake Hayden. B.S., Purdue U., 1971, M.Div., Christian Theol. Sem., 1977. Ordained to ministry United Ch. Christ, 1977. Pastor, Sulphur Springs United Ch. Christ, Ind., 1973-78, St. John's United Ch. Christ, Crown Point, Ind., 1978—; del. Gen. Synod United Ch. Christ, 1984—. Bd. dirs. Southlake YMCA, 1984—. Mem. Soc. Bibl. Lit., Christian Theol. Sem. Alumni Assn. (pres. 1984—), Theta Phi. Lodge: Kiwanis. Address: St John's United Ch Christ 12213 Grant St Crown Point IN 46307

SPARKMAN, DANIEL RICHARD, minister, American Baptist Churches U.S.A.; b. Yamagata, Japan, Jan. 19, 1950; came to U.S. 1958, naturalized, 1976; adopted s. Lois Sparkman; m. Sharlean Jan Harris, Mar. 27, 1976; children: James Riley, Rachel Serah. B.A., Northwest Christian Coll., 1973; M.Div., Southeastern Bapt. Theol. Sem., 1978. Ordained to ministry Bapt. Ch., 1979. Interim pastor First Bapt. Ch., Florence, Oreg., 1975-76; social ministries intern D.C. Bapt. Conv., Washington, 1977; parish minister First Bapt. Ch., Reedsport, Oreg., 1978-82; Berkeley Bapt. Ch., Denver, 1982—; dir. Denver Inner City Parish, 1983—, Cooperative Lay Ministry, Denver, 1982—. Mem. ABC Players (religious drama group based in Denver). Democrat. Office: Berkeley Baptist Church 4050 W 44th Ave Denver CO 80212

SPARKS, DANNY VINSON, minister, Southern Baptist Convention; b. Belmont, Miss., June 5, 1952; s. Dalton V. Sparks and Maxine (Pendegraph) Sanders; m. Marilyn Dean West, Dec. 23, 1971; children: Joshua Vinson, Rebecca Shea. B.S., Blue Mountain Coll., Miss., 1976. Ordained to ministry Baptist Ch., 1971. Asst. pastor Hickory Flat Bapt. Ch., Miss., 1970-71, Wheeler Grove Bapt. Ch., Kossuth, Miss., 1971-72; pastor Pleasant Hill Bapt. Ch., Falkner, Miss., 1972-79, Shady Grove Bapt. Ch., New Albany, Miss., 1979—; del. So. Bapt. Conv., Nashville, 1972—. Hon. col. Miss. Gov.'s staff, 1976-80; officer Pontotoc County Electoral Commn., 1982. Republican. Lodge: Masons. Home: Route 4 New Albany MS 38652 Office: Route 2 Pontotoc MS 38652

SPARKS, JAMES A., minister, United Presbyterian Church (U.S.A.), educator; b. Mays Lick, Ky., May 31, 1933; s. Sherley Lee and Lillie Mae (Snyder) S.; m. Pauline Lenore Zahrte, Aug. 13, 1955; 1 child, Elizabeth Carole. B.A., Transylvania Col., 1955; M.Div., Pitts. Theol. Sem., 1958; M.S., U. Wis., 1972. Ordained to ministry United Prebytn. Ch. (U.S.A.), 1958. Pastor, Lisbon United Presbyn. Ch., Sussex, Wis., 1958-64; pastor Dale Heights United Presbyn. Ch., Madison, 1964-73; assoc. prof. clergy continuing edn. U. Wis. Extension, Madison, 1973—. Author: Potshots at the Preacher, 1977; Friendship After Forty, 1980; Living the Bad Days, 1982; If This Pew Could Talk, 1985; columnist Clergy Jour. monthly, 1983—.

Recipient Creativity award Nat. Univ. Extension Assn., 1979, Nonfiction Merit award Council Wis. Writers, 1980. Mem. Soc. Advancement Continuing Edn. for Ministry (bd. dirs. 1970-73, 79-81), Council Wis. Writers, Nat Com. Extension Continuing Edn. for Clergy and Laity. Office: U Wis Extension 610 Langdon St Madison WI 53703

SPARKS, JAMES LESLIE, minister, Church of God (Anderson, Ind.); b. New Albany, Ind., June 19, 1946; s. Howard Homer and Fern Ellen (Werts) S.; m. Susan Meeks, Aug. 23, 1969; 1 child, Dawna Diann. B.A., Anderson Coll., Ind., 1969. Ordained to ministry Ch. of God (Anderson, Ind.), 1972. Youth pastor 1st Ch. of God, Elwood, Ind., 1970-72, pastor, 1972-74; pastor Morgantown Ch. of God, W.Va., 1974-75, 1st Ch. of God, Cassopolis, Mich., 1975-77; minister Christian edn. and youth, 1st Congl. Ch., Muskegon, Mich., 1977-80; sr. pastor 1st Ch. of God, Munster, Ind., 1980—; sec. Ind. Ministries of Ch. of God, Indpls., 1981-83. Contbr. to religious publs. Chmn. bd. dirs. Samaritan Ctr. on the Ridge, Munster, 1981. Avocation: breeding and training horses. Office: 1st Ch of God 900 Ridgeway Ave Munster IN 46321

SPARKS, JOHN WAYNE, minister, Baptist Bible Fellowship Internat.; b. Boone, Iowa, June 1, 1934; s. John F. and Ella Myrtle (Daily) S.; B.A., U.S. Air Force, 1954; M.Th., Bapt. Bible Coll., Springfield, Mo., 1964; postgrad., child evangelism fellow, Los Angeles, 1961-62; now postgrad. U. Calif. at Los Angeles extension Pacific Coast Bapt. Bible Coll.; m. Marlena Belle Miller, June 30, 1955; children—Rachelle Renee, John David. Ordained to ministry, 1963; youth pastor N.T. Bapt. Ch., Miami, Fla., 1964-66; pastor Lumpkin Rd. Bapt. Ch., Augusta, Ga., 1966-68, Calvary Bapt. Ch., Balt., 1968-71; co-pastor Berean Bapt. Ch., Orange, Calif., 1971-73; pastor Bible Bapt. Ch., Gardena, Calif., 1973-76, Berean Bapt. Ch., Orange, 1976—. Vice chmn. Calif. Bapt. Bible Fellowship, 1975-76; missions committeeman Bapt. Bible Fellowship Internat., 1973-76; prof. Pacific Coast Bible Coll., 1973-76; adminstr. KBSA-TV, Los Angeles, 1976—; founder South Bay Bapt. Schs., Gardena, 1973; prin. Berean Christian Schs., 1972-73. Mem. Boone Soc. Calif. (pres.), Sparks Family Assn. Am. Home: 1130 Palmyra St Orange CA 92667 Office: 710 S Cambridge St Orange CA 92666

SPARKS, ROBERT GLENN, minister, So. Baptist Conv.; b. Shelby, N.C., Jan. 29, 1947; s. Robert Bruce and Louise (Barnes) B.; B.Mus. in Edn., Mars Hill (N.C.) Coll., 1970; m. Virginia Brooks, Nov. 15, 1969; 1 dau., Virginia Louise. Minister ch., music and youth, Spindale, N.C., 1969-72, 1st Bapt. Ch., Burlington, N.C., 1972—. Recipient Fine Arts Vocal award Governor's Sch. N.C., 1964; Sarah Hollands Edwards Vocal award Gardner-Webb Coll., 1967. Mem. Phi Mu Alpha Sinfonia. Home: 531 Hillcrest St Burlington NC 27215 Office: PO Box 2686 Burlington NC 27215

SPARLING, PAUL WILLIAM, minister, Lutheran Church - Missouri Synod; b. Adair, Iowa, June 25, 1929; s. Leon O. and Anna A. (Mueller) S.; m. Sally Sue Benson, June 11, 1961; children: Joel, Daniel, Elizabeth. M.Th., Princeton Theol. Sem., 1968. Ordained to ministry Luth. Ch., 1954. Pastor Trinity Luth. Ch., Glenwood, Iowa, 1954-62; chaplain Atlantic Dist., N.Y.C., 1962-75, Greystone Park Hosp., N.J., 1964-75; pastor Trinity Luth. Ch., Morris Plains, NJ, 1975—. Home: 145 Mt Way Morris Plains NJ 07950 Office: Trinity Lutheran Church 131 Mt Way Morris Plains NJ 07950

SPARROWK, CORA CATHERINE, lay church worker, American Baptist Churches U.S.A.; b. Martin, Tenn., Aug. 23, 1917; s. Ernest Clark and Edna (Harris) Carter; b. John Sparrowk, Jan. 19, 1937; children: Jack Ernest, Jill Ann. D.Div. (Hon.), Am. Bapt. Sem. of West, 1978. Mem. Commn. on Christian Ethics, Gen. Council Bapt. World Alliance, Washington, 1980—; mem. Internat. Com. World Day of Prayer, 1982—; dep. v.p. Ch. Women United U.S.A., N.Y.C., 1980-84; bd. dirs. Eastern Bapt. Sem. and Eastern Coll., 1981—; pres. Am. Bapt. Chs. U.S.A., Valley Forge, 1978-79, Am. Bapt. Bd. Internat. Ministries, 1976-78. Contbr. articles to profl. jours. Active ARC. Named Layman of the Yr., Berkeley Bapt. Div. Sch., 1959; citation, Central Bapt. Theol. Sem., m1978; Valiant Woman award, Ch. Women United U.S.A., 1984. Democrat. Club: Round Hill Country. Address: 3370 Camanche Pkwy N Ione CA 95640

SPATTI, RAYMOND JOHN, priest, Roman Cath. Ch.; b. Brescia, Italy, Feb. 7, 1939; s. Luigi and Pasqua (Castelanelli) S.; B.A., Pontifical Coll. Josephinum, 1961, M.Div., 1975; M.S.W., U. Pitts., 1970, postgrad., 1976—. Ordained priest, 1965; asso. pastor, Latrobe and Monessen, Pa., 1965-67; asst. dir. Cath. Charities Diocese of Greensburg, Pa., 1967-71, dir. human life activities, 1970-71, diocesan dir. campus ministries, 1971-74; dir., pastor Newman Center, Univ. Parish of St. Thomas More, Indiana U. of Pa., 1971—. Bd. dirs. Indiana County (Pa.) Guidance Center, 1971—, pres., 1974-75; pres. Indiana County Coordinated Community Child Care Program, 1973-74. Mem. Greensburg Diocese Assn. Priests (past pres.), Priests Council of Greensburg Diocese (pres. 1976—), Indiana Deanery of Priests (social action chmn.), Nat. Assn. Social Workers, Nat. Cath. Campus Ministers Assn., Acad. Certified Social Workers. Home and Office: 1200 Oakland Ave Indiana PA 15701

SPEAKS, RUBEN LEE See *Who's Who in America*, 43rd edition.

SPEARS, WILLIAM EUGENE, JR., minister, Southern Baptist Convention; b. Union S.C., June 7, 1927; s. William Eugene and Edna (Moore) Spears; A.B., U. S.C., 1948; B.D., So. Bapt. Theol. Sem., 1951, M.Div., 1975; Ph.D. in Theology, U. Edinburgh (Scotland), 1953; postgrad. Oxford (Eng.) U., 1952, Cambridge (Eng.) U., 1952, Bapt. Sem., Zurich, Switzerland, 1952; m. Lillian Wilson Adams, Sept. 9, 1952; children—Sally Adams, William Eugene III. Ordained to ministry, 1950; pastor 1st Bapt. Ch., Mooresville, N.C., 1953-58, North Augusta, S.C., 1958-64, Emerywood Bapt. Ch., High Point, N.C., 1964-69, 1st Bapt. Ch., Chattanooga, 1969-72, Bapt. Ch. Beaufort (S.C.), 1972—; mem. gen. bd. N.C. Bapt. Conv., 1958-64; mem. gen. bd. S.C. Bapt. Conv., 1963, preacher conv. sermon, 1981, chmn. exec. com. of gen. bd., 1983, 84; preacher Tenn. Bapt. Conv. Evangelism Conf., 1971; trustee Bapt. Hosps. S.C., 1973—. Author: Seventy Feet Nearer the Stars, 1964; Faith of our Families, 1982; The Church on Assignment, 1985. contbr. articles to religious jours. Home: 2208 Bay St Beaufort SC 29902 Office: PO Box 869 Beaufort SC 29902

SPEERSTRA, JOHN ANDERS, minister, American Lutheran Church; b. Whitehall, Wis., June 30, 1933; s. Peter John and Josephine Marie (Foss) S.; m. Karen Marie Anderson, June 24, 1964; children: Joel Peter, Nathan John. B.A., U. Wis., 1957; B.D. Luther Theol. Sem., 1961; postgrad. Wartburg Theol. Sem., 1980—. Ordained to ministry Luth. Ch., 1961. Asst. pastor Chetek Luth. Ch., Wis., 1961-64; pastor Our Saviour Luth. Ch., Cornell, Wis., 1964-68, St. John Luth. Ch., Mosinee, Wis., 1968-72, St. Peter Luth. Ch., Prairie du Chien, Wis., 1972-81; co-pastor Holy Trinity Luth. Ch., Dubuque, Iowa 1981—; chmn. Dubuque Luth. Cluster, 1983-84; mem. news/info. com. Iowa dist. Am. Luth. Ch., Des Moines, 1984. Contbr. articles to Luth. Standard, devotions to Christ in Our Home. Chmn., Chippewa County Unit Am. Cancer Soc., 1966; mem. adv. bd. Project Concern, 1981-84. Served with U.S. Army, 1954-56. Democrat. Club: Dubuque Golf and Country. Home: 1548 Pego Ct Dubuque IA 52001 Office: Holy Trinity Luth Ch 1755 Delhi St Dubuque IA 52001

SPEICHER, RICHARD DWAYNE, association executive, minister, Ch. of The Brethren; b. Holsopple, Pa., May 19, 1924; s. John Wesley and Annie Edith (Thomas) S.; A.B., Manchester Coll., 1949; M.Div., Bethany Theol. Sem., 1952; postgrad. Garrett Theol. Sem., 1960; m. Marianne Miller, Mar. 15, 1952; children—Timothy, Anna, Ellen, Sara. Ordained to ministry Ch. of the Brethren, 1946; pastor Kokomo (Ind.) Ch. of the Brethren, 1952-60; pastor Woodworth Ch. of the Brethren, Youngstown, Ohio, 1960-70; Protestant chaplain Youngstown State U., 1970-76; exec. dir. Mahoning Valley Assn. Chs., Youngstown, 1975—. Pres. Howard County Council Chs., Kokomo, 1956; chmn. So. Ind. Dist. Bd., 1957-60; pres. Boardman Ministerial Assn., 1962, 67; chmn. N.Ohio Camp Devel. Com., 1967-70; chmn., Mahoning County (O.) Ch. World Service-CROP, 1966, 68. Trustee Woodworth Community Area. Office: 631 Wick Ave Youngstown OH 44502

SPEICHINGER, STEVEN ROBERT, minister, American Baptist Churches in the U.S.A.; b. Sioux City, Iowa, Aug. 4, 1949; s. Robert Jerome and Luella Josephine (Taute) S.; m. Rhonda Kay Holm, June 6, 1981. B.A., Morningside Coll., 1971; M.Div., Denver Theol. Sem., 1982. Ordained to ministry Gen. Conf. Baptist, 1982, Am. Baptist, 1983. Missionary trainee Navigators, Philippines and Colorado Springs, 1974-77; youth worker Lake Sarah Bapt. Ch., Slayton, Minn., 1977-79, Foothills Bible Ch., Morrison, Colo., 1979-82; pastor First Baptist Ch., Goodland, Kans., 1982—; treas. Ministerial Alliance, Goodland, 1984—. Mem. Main St. Redevel. Com., Inc., Goodland, 1984—; bd. dirs. Good Samaritan Ctr., Goodland, 1983—, Drug & Alcohol Abuse Hosp., Goodland, 1983-84. Served to sgt. USAF, 1971-75. Mem. Great Plains Assn. (moderator 1986—). Avocations: stamp collecting; racquetball; backpacking. Home: 418 Main St Goodland KS 67735 Office: First Baptist Ch 5th St and Center St Goodland KS 67735

SPELTZ, GEORGE HENRY, bishop, Roman Cath. Ch.; b. Altura, Minn., May 29, 1912; s. Henry and Josephine (Jung) S.; B.S., St. Mary's Coll., Winona, Minn., 1932, LL.D., 1963; student theology St. Paul Sem., 1936-40; M.A., Cath. U. Am., 1942, Ph.D., 1944; D.D., Holy See, Rome, Italy, 1963. Ordained priest Roman Cath. Ch., 1940, consecrated bishop, 1963; vice chancellor Diocese of Winona, 1944-47, supt. schs., 1946-49, aux. bishop, 1963-66; pastor St. Mary's Ch., Minneiska, Minn., 1946-47; tchr. St. Mary's Coll., 1947-63; rector Immaculate Heart of Mary Sem., Winona, 1948-63; co-adjutor bishop, St. Cloud, Minn., 1966-68, bishop, 1968—. Pres., Nat. Cath. Rural Life Conf., 1970-72; mem. Bishops Com. for Pastoral on Cath. Social Thought and U.S. Economy, 1981—. Address: PO Box 1248 Saint Cloud MN 56301

SPENCE, FRANCIS J., archbishop, Roman Catholic Church; b. Perth, Ont., Can., June 16, 1927. Ordained priest, 1950; ordained titular bishop of N.S., aux. bishop Mil. Vicariate, 1967; bishop of Charlottetown (P.E.I., Can.), 1970-82; archbishop of Kingston, Ont., 1982—. Office: Archdiocese of Kingston PO Box 997 390 Place Rd Kingston ON K7L 4X8 Canada*

SPENCE, GLEN O., organization executive. Exec. sec. Gen. Baptists (Gen. Assn.). Office: 100 Stinson Dr Poplar Bluff MO 63901*

SPENCE, HUBERT TALMADGE, pastor, religion educator, Foundations Bible Church; b. Greenville, S.C., Oct. 18, 1948; s. Othniel Talmadge and Joye McGee (Spinney) S.; m. Joy Kathryn Klepper, July 11, 1970; children: Othniel Talmadge II, Carrie Elizabeth, Jessica Kathryn. B.Th., Holmes Theol. Sem., 1970; B.A., B.D., Trinity Coll., 1971; Th.M., Heritage Bible Coll., 1974; M.Div., Th.D., Foundations Bible Coll., 1984. Ordained to ministry Founds. Bible Ch., 1970. Pastor, Plainview Ch., Clinton, N.C., 1971-73; tchr. theology Heritage Bible Coll., Dunn, N.C., 1971-74; head. theology dept. Founds. Bible Coll., Dunn, 1974-79; assoc. pastor Foundations Bible Ch., Dunn, 1979—; v.p. Founds. Ministries, Dunn, 1979—; prin. Foundations Christian Acad., Dunn, 1983—; mem. Men's Prayer Conf., co-host, 1983-84; evangelist, tchr., nat. lectr. on contemporary rock and gospel music. Author: A Preacher Am I, 1984. Editor: Sunday Bible Pointer, 1976-84; founding editor (monthly newsletter) The Timotheus Commitment, 1980-84. Composer/author: 70 hymns, musical dramas, 5 religious dramas; author/dir.: Militant, Yet Magnificant, two additional multi-media prodns. Mem. Christian Purities Fellowship (v.p. 1980-84), Dunn C. of C. Home: Route 1 Box 422-Al Benson NC 27504 Office: Foundations Ministries PO Box 1166 Dunn NC 28334

SPENCE, JEFFREY BENNETT, minister, United Church of Christ; b. White Plains, N.Y., July 16, 1949; s. Edwin Bartlett and Jean (Fowler) S.; m. Laura Mary Walkiewicz, Jan. 19, 1974. B.A., Washington-Lee U., 1971; M.Div., Drew U., 1974; D.D., 1980. Ordained to ministry United Ch. of Christ, 1974. Pastor Bethlehem United Ch. of Christ, Tenth Legion, Va., 1974-77, Schroon Lake Community Ch., N.Y., 1977-78; exec. dir. NCCJ, Richmond, Va., 1978—; pres. Shenandoah Assn. Ministerium, Harrisburg, Va., 1976-77. Bd. dirs. Leadership Met. Richmond, 1981-82; bd. dirs. Richmond Urban League, 1984—; mem. Nat. Abortion Rights Action League, Washington, 1984—. Named Outstanding Young Man of Yr. Jaycees, 1982. Mem. Eastern Va. Assn. United Ch. of Christ, Am. Soc. Tng. Devel. Democrat. Club: Bullard Bear (Richmond). Lodges: Masons, Elks (chaplain 1979-80). Office: NCCJ 2317 Westwood Ave Richmond VA 23230

SPENCER, AIDA DINA BESANCON, minister, educator, United Presbyn. Ch. U.S.A.; b. Santo Domingo, Dominican Republic, Jan. 2, 1947; d. Frederick Heinrich Julius and Adelaida (Guzman) Besancon; B.A., Douglass Coll., 1968; M.Div., Princeton Theol. Sem., 1973, Th.M., 1975; postgrad. Australian Coll. Theology: m. William David Spencer, Aug. 12, 1972. Community organizer Community Action-Plainfield, Inc. (N.J.), 1969-70; intern, N.J. Dept. Community Affairs, Newark, summer 1970; ordained to ministry, 1973; campus minister Trenton (N.J.) State Coll., 1973-74; prof. N.Y. Theol. Sem., master-in-residence Salvation Army, Newark, 1974—; organizer, prof. Alpha-Omega Community Theol. Sch., Newark, 1976—. Instr., researcher Hispanic community services YWCA, Plainfield, summer 1970; student asst. minister First Presbyn. Ch., Hightstown, N.J., 1971-72; instr. English, Trenton State Coll., fall 1973, Trenton State Prison, 1973; vol. religious coordinator United Latins for Progress, Trenton State Prison, 1973-74. Mem. adv. bd. N.J. Correctional Master Plan for Hispanic Inmates, 1975—; bd. dirs. Plainfield Model Cities, 1969-70; organizer, personnel com. Day Care 100, Plainfield, 1969-70. Recipient Samuel Robinson Found. prize Princeton Theol. Sem., 1971. Mem. Evang. Theol. Soc., Evangelicals for Social Action, Evang. Women's Caucus. Contbr. articles in field to religious jours. Home: 86 Washington St Newark NJ 07102

SPENCER, HARRY CHADWICK, minister, retired religious organization administrator, United Methodist Church; b. Chgo., Apr. 10, 1905; s. John Carroll and Jessie Grace (Chadwick) S.; m. Mary Louise Wakefield, May 26, 1935; children: Mary Grace Spencer Lyman, Ralph Wakefield. B.A., Willamette U., 1925, D.D. (hon.), 1953; postgrad. U. Chgo., 1926-28; M.Div., Garrett Theol. Sem., 1929; M.A., Harvard U., 1932. Ordained elder Methodist Ch., 1933. Pastor Meth. Episcopal Ch., Washington Heights, Chgo., 1931-33, Portage Park, Chgo., 1933-35; recording sec. Bd. Fgn. Missions, N.Y.C., 1935-40; asst. exec. sec. div. edn. and cultivation bd. missions and ch. extension The Meth. Ch., N.Y.C., 1940-45, recording sec., 1940-43, sec. dept. audio-visual edn., 1944-52; exec. sec. Radio and

Film Commn., Nashville, 1952-56; gen. sec. TV, Radio and Film Commn., Nashville, 1956-58; assoc. gen. sec. program council, head div. TV, Radio and Film Communication, United Meth. Ch., Nashville, 1968-73; dir. mass communication publicity com. World Council Chs. Assembly, Evanston, Ill., 1955, New Delhi, 1961; chmn. Constituting Assembly of World Assn. for Christian Communication, Nairobi, 1963, Stockholm, 1968; chmn. Radio Visual Edn. Mass Communications Com., N.Y.C., 1948-51; mem. exec. com. Nat. Council Chs., N.Y.C., 1960-63; chmn. Nat. Council Chs. Broadcasting and Film Commn., N.Y.C., 1960-63, mem. exec. com., 1950-73; vis. prof. Garrett-Evang. Theol. Sem., 1975; trustee Scarritt Coll., Nashville, 1967-74, hon., 1974—; bd. dirs. Out Look Nashville, 1977-83, bd. dirs. chpt. UN Assn., Nashville, 1976-83. Producer movies including John Wesley, radio series, TV series. Recipient Excellence in Art of Communications award Claremont Sch. Theology, Calif., 1973. Mem. United Meth. Assn. Communicators (Hall of Fame 1983). Club: Soc. Preservation Barber Shop Quartet Singing in Am. Lodge: Kiwanis. Home: PO Box 150063 Nashville TN 37215

SPENCER, IVAN CARLTON, minister, institute executive, religious organization administrator, Elim Fellowship; b. Bradford County, Pa., July 8, 1914; s. Ivan Quay and Annie Minnie (Back) S.; m. Elizabeth Garate, Apr. 14, 1935; children: David Carlton, Esther Elizabeth (Mrs. Saied Adour), John Wesley. Diploma, Elim Bible Inst., 1933; D.D., Am. Bible Coll., 1966. Ordained to ministry Elim Missionary Assemblies (now Elim Fellowship), 1935. Instr. Elim Bible Inst., Lima, N.Y., 1938-49, pres., 1949-82, chmn. bd., 1982—; gen. chmn. Elim Fellowship, Lima, 1954—; mem. adminstrv. bd. Nat. Assn. Evangelicals, Wheaton, Ill., 1958—, Pentecostal Fellowship of N. Am., 1961—. Lodge: Rotary. Home: 7245 College St Lima NY 14485 Office: Elim Fellowship 7245 College St Lima NY 14485

SPENCER, JOHN RICHARD, religion educator, United Methodist Church; b. Long Beach, Calif., Jan. 19, 1945; s. Frank Richard and Betty Louise (Bean) S.; m. Claudia Jean Avitabile, June 15, 1968; children: Beth N., Sandra P. B.S., U. Calif.-Berkeley, 1966; B.D., M.A., Pacific Sch. Religion, 1970; M.A., U. Chgo., 1973, Ph.D., 1980. Assoc. prof. dept. religious studies John Carroll U., University Heights, Ohio, 1977—; bd. dirs. Tell el-Hesi Archeol. Expdn., Midland, Mich., 1980—, vice chmn., 1984—, dir. vol. program, 1982—. Editor: In the Shelter of Elyon, 1984. Contbr. articles to profl. jours. Frank scholar, 1973-74; fellow U. Chgo., 1970-75, John Carroll U., 1983; Ann. prof. Am. Sch. Oriental Research, Jerusalem, 1984-85. Mem. AAUP, Am. Schs. Oriental Research, Cath. Bibl. Assn., Soc. Bibl. Lit., Israel Exploration Soc. Office: Dept Religion Studies John Carroll U University Heights OH 44118

SPENCER, LLOYD KIRTLAND, minister, Southern Baptist Convention. b. Roodhouse, Ill., Oct. 9, 1910; s. Earl Grover and Fannie Delores (Little) S.; m. Ruby Mae Smith, Dec. 23, 1939; children: Marilyn Spencer Roberson, Wilma Spencer Crawford. Student So. Ill. U., 1946-49; diploma English Bible, So. Ill. Coll. Bible, 1949. Ordained to ministry Southern Baptist Convention, 1937. Pastor chs. So. Bapt. Conv., Roodhouse, Ill., 1934-49; supt. assn. missions Sandy Creek Assn., Roodhouse, Ill., 1949-53, Madison County Assn., Wood River, Ill., 1953-60; pioneer missions Western Ill., Macomb, Ill., 1960-64; supt. missions Sinnissippi-Blackhawk, Rochelle, Ill., 1964-68; supt. missions Blackhawk Assocs., Rockford, Ill., 1968-76; chaplain Americana/Amberwood/Brian Glen Centre's, 1976—. Recipient Chaplain's Service Recognition award Briar Glen Healthcare Centre, Rockford, Ill., 1983. Home: 2306 E Gate Pkwy Rockford IL 61108

SPENCER, MARLENE ANN, religion educator, Roman Catholic Church; b. Rutland, Vt., Jan. 29, 1947; d. Louise Ann Spencer. B.A., Berry Coll., 1971; M.A., Fla. State U., 1972, M.A., 1974, Ph.D., 1984. Prof. religion Valencia Community Coll., Orlando, Fla., 1977—, Author: The Sacred and the Profane in Flannery O'Connor's Fiction, 1984. Rockefeller fellow, 1979. Mem. AAUP, Am. Assn. Humanities Edn., Am. Assn. Community Colls., Fla. Leadership Forum, Sigma Tau Delta. Office: Valencia Jr Coll PO Box 3028 Orlando FL 32802

SPENCER, ROGER W., minister, Lutheran Church in America; b. N.Y.C., May 4, 1947; s. George W. and Florence E. (White) S.; m. Patricia J. Heinsohn, May 30, 1970; children: Cortney, Shayne. B.A., Muhlenberg Coll., 1969; M.Div., Luth. Theol. Sem., 1973. Ordained to ministry Luth. Ch. in Am., 1973. Pastor St. Stephen's Luth. Ch., Edison, N.J., 1973-83, Good Shepherd Luth. Ch., Glen Rock, N.J., 1983—; dean Central Dist. N.J. Synod, 1982-83, mem. dist. cabinet No. Dist., 1983—. Bd. dirs. Emergency Food Distbn., Edison, 1979-83, West Bergen Mental Health Clinec, Ridgewood, N.J., 1983—. Office: Good Shepherd Luth Ch 233 S Highwood Ave Glen Rock NJ 07452

SPENCER, STEPHEN ROBERT, seminary educator, minister, General Association of Regular Baptist Churches; b. Gowanda, N.Y., July 1, 1952; s. James William and Lorna Rae (Johnston) S.; m. H. Gaylynn Trueblood, Dec. 21, 1974. B.A., Cedarville Coll., 1974; M.Div., Grand Rapids Bapt. Sem., 1978, Th.M., 1981; postgrad. Mich. State U., 1980—. Lic. for ministry, 1971. Asst. in theology Grand Rapids Bapt. Sem., Mich., 1978-80, instr. philosophy/theology, 1980-82, asst. prof. philos. theology, 1982—. Contbr. articles to profl. jours. Mem. Evang. Theol. Soc., Evang. Philos. Soc., Soc. Christian Philosophers, Conf. on Faith and History. Home: 1316 Arianna NW Grand Rapids MI 49504 Office: Baptist Seminary 1001 E Beltline NE Grand Rapids MI 49505

SPENCER, THEODORE BROWN, minister, marriage and family counselor, United Meth. Ch.; b. Mexia, Tex., Oct. 12, 1932; s. Charles Roy and Bessie Adelaide (Brown) S.; B.S., Tex. Wesleyan Coll., 1954; B.D., So. Meth. U., 1957, Th.M., 1970; postgrad. So. Calif. Sch. Theology, 1970; m. Patricia Jean Allen, June 11, 1954; children—Tedi Lee, Jean Elise, Scott Allen. Ordained to ministry, 1957; asso. pastor Englewood Meth. Ch., Ft. Worth, Tex., 1954-56; pastor Eureka (Tex.) Meth. Ch., 1957-58; asso. pastor First Meth. Ch., Corsicana, Tex., 1958-59; organizer, pastor Davis Meml. Meth. Ch., Ft. Worth, Tex., 1959-63; pres. Wesleyan Enterprises, Dallas, 1963-66; asso. pastor First Meth. Ch., Corpus Christi, Tex., 1966-70; dir. Mental Health Services, Neuces County Mental Health-Mental Retardation Center, Corpus Christi, Tex., 1970-72; co-dir. Psychotherapy Assos., Houston, 1972-76. Chmn. human relations com. S.W. Tex. Conf. bd. Christian Social Concerns, 1968-70. Vice pres., bd. dirs. Suicide Prevention, Inc., Corpus Christi, 1967-70; organizer, dir. Coastal Bend Half Way House for Alcoholics, Corpus Christi, 1967-70; trustee Nueces County Mental Health-Mental Rehab. Community Center, Corpus Christi, 1972-74. Home: 1710 Castlerock St Houston TX 77090 Office: 6111 FM 1960 W Houston TX 77069

SPERL, WENZEL EARL, minister, educator, Conservative Baptist Assn. Am.; b. Bloomfield Mo., Dec. 12, 1930; s. David Earl and Fathie Bee (Holt) S.; B.A. in Bus. Adminstrn., U. Md., 1958; postgrad. in Religion and Practical Theology, U. Heidelberg, W. Ger., 1963; m. Janet Marie Elder, July 10, 1951; children—Linda Marie, Vicky Lee, Wenzel Alan, Deborah Joy, Daniel Earl, Alice Ann. Ordained to ministry, 1972; pastor English-speaking Gospel Fellowship Ch., Baulmholder, Germany, 1956-58; asso. pastor Free Meth. Ch., Barstow, Calif., 1968-70; dir. Soul Folks Inc., Youth Outreach Program, Barstow, 1970-72; pastor Lacerne Valley (Calif.) Community Ch., 1971-72; dir. Azusa Pacific Coll. Retreat and Edn. Center, Crestline, Calif., 1972—. Contbr. articles in field to religious jours. Home and Office: PO Box 753 Crestline CA 92325

SPERRY, JOHN REGINALD See *Who's Who in America*, 43rd edition.

SPEYRER, JUDE, bishop, Roman Catholic Church. Bishop of Lake Charles, La., 1980—. Office: Weber Office Bldg PO Box 3223 Lake Charles LA 70602*

SPICELAND, JAMES DARRAL, religion educator, Presbyterian Church in U.S.A.; b. Detroit, May 14, 1940; s. James Roy and Elleanore Inez (Johnson) S.; m. Annette Elizabeth Ryding, June 10, 1967; children: Tristan Mark, Allison Ruth. B.A., Bethel Coll., 1965; M.A., Western Ky. U., 1970; Ph.D., Exeter U., 1974. Commd. to ministry Presbyn. Ch., 1983. Minister, Fifth Ave Bapt. Ch., Humboldt, Iowa, 1965-66; youth minister East Park Bapt. Ch., St. Paul, 1966-67; lay minister Little Rock Presbyn. Ch., Bowling Green, Ky., 1980-81, First Presbyn. Ch., Auburn, Ky., 1982—; assoc. prof. philosophy and religion Western Ky. U., Bowling Green, 1975—. Co-editor: One God in Trinity, 1980. Contbr. articles to religious publs. Scholar-in-residence Leighton Park Sch., English Quaker Found., 1981-82; NEH summer seminar participant, 1979. Mem. Soc. Christian Philosophers, Am. Acad. Religion. Democrat. Office: West Ky U Dept Philosophy Bowling Green KY 42101

SPICER, REX DICKINSON, minister, Lutheran Church-Mo. Synod; b. Balt., Jan. 10, 1935; s. Rixey Dickinson and Ellen Roberta (Spielman) S.; B.A., U. Md., 1958; degree Valparaiso U., 1963; B.D., Concordia Sem., 1964, M.Div., 1973; D.Min., Colgate/Rochester Div. Sch., 1976; m. June Suzanne Devan, Aug. 11, 1962; children: Rexanne, Jeffrey, Nina, Katherine, Rex St. John, Amy. Ordained to ministry, 1964; pastor St. John's Luth. Ch., Fenton, Iowa, 1964-73, 74—; pastoral counselor, 1976—; workshop leader, 1976—. Contbr. articles to profl. publs. Cons. Luth. Family Service, Ft. Dodge, Iowa, 1976—; counselor Family Service Agy., Rochester, N.Y., 1973-74; chmn. Dist. Family Life com., Iowa Dist. W., 1972-76. Sec. Fenton Devel. Com., 1967-73; chaplain State House, Des Moines, 1975. Mem. Am. Assn. Marriage and Family Counselors (assoc.), Therapists Clin., Assn. for Clin. Pastoral Edn. Address: PO Box 169 Fenton IA 50539

SPICER, THOMAS OTIS, JR., minister, So. Baptist Conv.; b. Paris, Ark., Feb. 22, 1937; s. Thomas Otis and Golda Elizabeth (Norfleet) S.; B.A., U. Ark., 1960; B.D., Southwestern Bapt. Theol. Sem., 1966, Th.M., 1971; m. Martha Belle Alexander, June 30, 1957; 1 son, Thomas Otis. Ordained to ministry, 1968; pastor Bapt. Ford Ch. Washington County, Ark., 1956-57, Garland Heights Bapt. Chapel, Fayetteville, Ark., 1957-59, Liberty Bapt. Ch., Dutch Mills, Ark., 19S9-60, Johnson (Ark.) Bapt. Ch., 1961-62, Wheatland (Tex.) Bapt. Ch., 1963-67, Webster Park Bapt. Ch., Springfield, Mo., 1968-73, 1st Bapt. Ch., Walnut Ridge, Ark., 1973-77; dir. missions Spring River Bapt. Assn., Carthage, Mo., 1977—. Dir. tng. union Washington/Madison Bapt. Assn., 1961; mem. com. on race relations Tarrant Bapt. Assn., 1964-67; chmn. nominating com. Greene County Bapt. Assn., 1972, chmn. com. on stewardship, 1974-77; chmn. spl. com. mission needs and opportunities Black River Bapt. Assn., 1976-77; mem. hist commn. Ark. Bapt. State Conv., 1973-77. Mem. Kappa Kappa Psi, Phi Mu Alpha. Home: Woodland Park Route 4 Carthage MO 64836 Office: PO Box 163 Carthage MO 64836

SPIEGEL, ALBERT A., religious organization executive. Chmn. B'nai B'rith Hillet Commn. Office: B'nai B'rith Hillet Found Inc 1640 Rhode Island Ave NW Washington DC 20036*

SPIEKER, GEORGE FREDERICK, minister, Lutheran Church in America; b. Emmaus, Pa., May 9, 1930; s. Paul Frederick and Marian (Stager) S.; m. Rebecca Ann Keller, Aug. 11, 1956; children: David Charles, Jane Ann. A.B., Muhlenberg Coll., 1952; B.D., Luth. Sem., Phila., 1957. Ordained to ministry Lutheran Ch., 1957. Pastor St. Paul Luth. Ch., Gordon, Pa., 1957-59, Robeson Luth. Ch., Plowville, Pa., 1959-72, St. John Luth. Ch., Coplay, Pa., 1972—; conv. del. Luth. Ch. in Am., 1974; dir. Luth. Services, Easton, Pa., 1978-80; com. mem. Synod Parish Edn., Wescosville, Pa., 1984—. Pres. Robeson Twp. PTA, Pa., 1965-67; bd. dirs. Coplay Library, 1975—; Eagle rev. chmn., dist. 5, Minsi Trail council Boy Scouts Am., 1982—, Silver Beaver award, 1984. Served with U.S. Army, 1952-54, Korea. Decorated Bronze Star. Mem. Whitehall/Coplay Pastoral Assn. (pres. 1978-80). Republican. Home: 305 Coplay St Coplay PA 18037

SPITTLER, RUSSELL PAUL, seminary educator, Assemblies of God; b. Pitts., Aug. 6, 1931; s. Russell Paul and Helen Virginia (Maguire) S.; m. Roberta Jeane Watson, Aug. 13, 1955; children: Cheryl Ruth Spittler Azlin, Heidi Jeane Spittler Fink, Russell Watson. B.A., Fla. So. Coll., 1954; M.A., Wheaton Coll., 1957; B.D., Gordon-Conwell Theol. Sem., 1958; Ph.D., Harvard U., 1971. Ordained to ministry Assemblies of God, 1961. Asst. prof. Bible, Central Bible Coll., Springfield, Mo., 1958-62; acad. dean So. Calif. Coll., Costa Mesa, 1967-76; assoc. dean Fuller Theol. Sem., Pasadena, Calif., 1976—. Editor: Perspectives on the New Pentecostalism, 1976, others. Contbr. articles to profl. publs., chpts. to books. Served to capt. as chaplain USNR, 1963—. Mem. Soc. Pentecostal Studies (sec. 1983—), Evang. Theol. Soc., Internat. Orgn. Septuagint and Cognate Studies. Home: 2075 Fox Ridge Dr Pasadena CA 91107 Office: Fuller Theol Sem 135 N Oakland Ave Pasadena CA 91101

SPITZER, LEE BARNETT, minister, American Baptist Churches in the U.S.A. B. Bklyn., Apr. 30, 1957; s. William and Norma (Landau) S.; m. Lois Nancy Yellin, Aug. 20, 1977. B.A. in Religion, The King's Coll., 1977; M.Div., Gordon-Conwell Theol. Sem., 1981. Ordained to ministry Baptist Ch., 1981. Intern, Bethlehem Presbyn. Ch., Buffalo, summer 1976; youth minister St. Mark's Episcopal Ch., Glendale, Calif., 1977-79, Trinity Bapt. Ch., Lynnfield, Mass., 1979-80; pastor First Bapt. Ch. in East Providence, Rumford, R.I., 1981—; founder, pres. Am. Bapt. Peacemakers of R.I., 1983—; mem. social action dept. R.I. Council of Chs., 1982—; vice chmn. mission support commn. Am. Bapt. Chs. R.I., 1984—, mem. bd. of mgrs., 1981—; del. Bapt. Peace Tour to USSR, Bapt. Peace Fellowship, 1983. Editor: Peacemaking Throughout the Year, 1984. Speaker and lectr. on nuclear freeze and peace issues in R.I., 1982—. Mem. Ministers Council Am. Bapt. Chs. U.S.A., Evangelical Theol. Soc. Republican. Home: 1396 Pawtucket Ave Rumford RI 02916 Office: First Bapt Ch in East Providence 1400 Pawtucket Ave Rumford RI 02916

SPLETT, GILBERT ERNST, minister, Am. Luth. Ch.; b. Black Earth, Wis., Mar. 28, 1935; s. F. Paul and Olga Frederica (Denef) S.; B.A., U. Wis., 1956; B.D., Evangel. Luth. Theol. Sem., 1960; M.A., U. Wis., 1966, postgrad. U. So. Calif., 1970-72; m. Carolyn Joyce Mitchell, June 29, 1957; children—Kathryn Michael, Paul Malcolm, Gilbert Timothy. Ordained to ministry, 1960; pastor St. Paul Luth. Ch., Chewelah, Wash., 1960-64; parish edn. dir. Zion Luth. Ch., Madison, Wis., 1964-65; campus pastor Central Wash. State Coll., Ellensburg, Wash., 1965-69; U. So. Calif., 1969-72; U. Mont., Missoula, 1972—. Mem. standing com. office of communication and mission support, Am. Luth. Ch., 1975-78, mem. council Rocky Mountain dist., 1975—; mem. adv. bd. Center for the Study of Campus Ministry, Valparaiso U., 1974-75. Mem. City Council, Chewelah, 1962-64; mem. citizen's adv. com. Bd. Edn., Ellensburg, 1968-69. Recipient Distinguished Service award City of Chewelah Jaycees, 1964. Mem. Missoula Ministerial Assn., Nat. Luth. Campus Ministry Assn. Contbr. movie revs. and articles to religious jours. Home: 630 Dearborn Missoula MT 59801 Office: 538 University Missoula MT 59801

SPLINTER, JOHN PAUL, minister, Evangelical Presbyterian Church; b. Redwing, Minn., Aug. 18, 1945; s. Gerrald Edward and Mileen Elouise (McCreary) S.; m. Marcia Lee Carlson, Aug. 10, 1968; children: Gretchen, Kirsten, Megan. B.A., Bethel Coll., 1968; M.Christian Edn., Bethel Sem., 1970. Ordained to ministry Presbyterian Ch., 1984. Area dir. Young Life Campaign, Winnipeg, Can., 1970-75, St. Louis, 1975-80; dir. single life ministries Central Presbyn. Ch., Clayton, Mo., 1980—; dir. Second Chpt. Divorce Recovery, St. Louis, 1984—. Comml. ins. broker, 1980-84. Co-Author and editor: Second Chapter, 1985; Parent to Parent, 1980. Chmn. Parent to Parent Council, Kirkwood, 1979-80; treas. Keysor Sch. PTA, Kirkwood, 1981; campaign worker City Council election, Kirkwood, 1984; mem. adv. bd. Clayton Sch. Dist., Mo., 1980. Republican. Avocation: woodworking. Home: 452 Clemens Kirkwood MO 63122 Office: Central Presbyn Ch 7700 Davis Dr Clayton MO 63105

SPONG, JOHN SHELBY See *Who's Who in America*, 43rd edition.

SPRAGUE, STUART RUSSELL, religious educator, Southern Baptist Convention; b. Dallas, Mar. 18, 1947; s. Russell Earl and Julia Margareit (Boswell) S.; m. Sarah Lee Cellar, Aug. 14, 1971; 1 son, Drew Stuart. B.S., Duke U., 1969; M.Div., So. Bapt. Theol. Sem., Louisville, 1972, Ph.D., 1975. Ordained to ministry So. Bapt. Conv., 1977. Mem. faculty dept. religion Anderson Coll., S.C., 1977—; adj. instr. family medicine Med. U. S.C., Anderson, 1983—. Deacon, chmn. deacons Blvd. Bapt. Ch., Anderson, 1979—. Trustee Montessori Sch. Anderson, 1982-84. Mem. Am. Acd. Religion, Soc. Health and Human Values, Am. Philos. Assn., Nat. Assn. Bapt. Profs. Religion, S.C. Acad. Religion (sec. 1984). Home: 801 Camfield Rd Anderson SC 29621 Office: Anderson Coll 316 Boulevard Anderson SC 29621

SPRAGUE, WILLIAM LEIGH, minister, Disciples of Christ; b. Weatherford, Okla., July 28, 1938; s. Frank William Jr. and Eula Louise (Miley) S.; A.B., Phillips U., 1960, B.D., 1964; S.T.M., Boston U., 1966. Ordained to ministry, 1964; minister Christian Ch., Sharon, Kans., 1961-64, acting chaplain Enid (Okla.) State Sch., 1963-64; dir. pastoral services N. Conway Inst., Boston, 1966-68; chief chaplain Washingtonian Center for Addictions, field edn. supr. Boston Theol. Inst., 1969-73; asst. dir. clergy tng. program in drug abuse, Boston, 1971-73; clin. asso. Boston U. Sch. Theol., 1971—; cons. supr. Boston Theol. Inst., 1972—; dir. clergy tng. program in drug abuse McLean Hosp., Belmont, Mass., from 1973; dir. congl. men's work and resources Christian Ch., Indpls., 1977—. Pres. Waltham (Mass.) Council Chs., 1968-70; chmn. citizenship and missions commn. Covenant Congl. Ch., Waltham, 1975-76. Mem. Waltham Low-Income Housing Coalition, 1969-70. Recipient Christian Bd. Publication award, Phillips U., 1962. Mem. Coll. Chaplains, Am. Protestant Hosp. Assn., Congress of Disciples Clergy, Waltham Clergy Assn., ACLU, Common Cause. Contbr. articles to religious jours. Home: 92 Central St Waltham MA 02154 Office: 222 S Downey Ave Indianapolis IN 46206

SPRAKER, CHARLES EDWARD, minister, Lutheran Church in America; hospital administrator; b. Tazewell Va., June 5, 1933; s. Stephen Marco and Cynthia Polly (Cook) S.; m. Martha Cecelia Harris, May 26, 1956; 1 child, Cynthia Marceil. B.A., Roanoke Coll., 1955; B.D., Luth. Theol. So. Sem., 1958, M.Div., 1972; M.Edn., U. Va., 1971. Ordained to ministry Luth. Ch. in Am., 1958. Pastor, Our Saviour Luth. Ch., Norge, Va., 1958-65, Faith Luth. Ch., Staunton, Va., 1965-68; counselor, adminstr. Commonwealth of Va., Staunton, 1968—; dir. Shenandoah Geriatric Treatment Ctr., Staunton, 1981—. Home: 107 Oxford Circle Staunton VA 24401

SPRIGGS, ROBERT, minister, Holiness Ch. of God, in Christ; b. Greensboro, N.C., Jan. 7, 1928; s. John and Minnie Lillie (Shepherd) S.; gen. edn. Meml. Adult Center, 1976; m. Dorothy Jean Fortner, July 20, 1968; children—Robert Lee, Raymond Allen. Ordained to ministry, 1968; jr. ch. pastor Faith Tabernacle Ch. of God in Christ, San Diego, 1968-72; asst. pastor Community House of Prayer, San Diego, 1972-74; asst. pastor Ch. of God in Christ, San Diego, 1973-74; pastor Deliverance Ch., San Diego, 1974—. Home: 5625 Elk St San Diego CA 92114 Office: 1530 S 39th St San Diego CA 92113

SPRINGER, GARLAN LEE, minister, National American Baptist; b. Carrollton, Ga., Apr. 28, 1929; s. John and Mary Graham S.; div. B.A., ABT Coll. of Bible, Nashville, 1961; M.Div., Drew U., 1966; postgrad. Va. Union Sch. of Religion, M.Div., Ashland Theol. Sch., 1975. Ordained to ministry Bapt. Ch., 1959. Student pastor North N.J. Conf., Newark, 1964-66; co-pastor Harrison Meth. Ch., Wilmington, Del., 1966-77; community minister Antioch Bapt. Ch., Cleve., 1967-73; clin. chaplain Massilon OYC, Ohio, 1973-76, Coastal Correctional Inst., State of Ga., Columbus, Ohio, and Garden City, Ga., 1976—; chapel mgr. U.S. Air Force Res., Denver, 1957—; pres. Columbus Ministers Alliance, Ga., 1981-84; program dir. Bapt. Ministers Union, Savannah, Ga., 1984—. Bd. dirs. Caring About People, Canton, Ohio, 1972; program dir. United for Better Community, Columbus, 1983-84; chaplain Ga. wing CAP, Dobbins AFB, 1976—. Serving with USAFR, 1957—. Mem. NAACP, Am. Correctional Assn., Am. Correctional Ch. Assn. (sec. 1981-84).

SPRINGS, FRANCES STOVALL, lay church worker, Southern Baptist Convention; b. Eddyville, Ky., Dec. 28, 1916; d. William Archie and Stella Mae (Davis) Stovall; m. Edward W. Springs, Dec. 25, 1940; children: Priscilla Frances, Lance Edward, Willard Malcolm. Student Murray State Coll., 1935-37, 41. Cert. tchr., Ky. Pres., Ind. Woman's Missionary Union, 1964-67; hist. sec. Ind. State Bapt. Conv., 1977-80, 81-85, bd. dirs., 1974-79; mem. hist. commn. So. Bapt. Conv., 1975-83. Pub. sch. tchr., Lyon County, Ky., 1937-40, 43-45; substitute tchr. Hammond Pub. Schs., Ind., 1960-72. Author: (pamphlet) Fifty Years of Ministry, 1984; co-author: Hoosier Southern Baptists: Turning Points and Milestones, 1983; columnist History in Hoosierland, 1976. Democrat. Home: 1444 Michigan St Hammond IN 46320

SPROAT, ORLEN KEITH, chaplain, Christian Ch.; b. Beecher City, Ill., Dec. 19, 1936; s. Harry W. and Lelah B. (Pickel) S.; student Lincoln Christian Coll., 1954-58; A.B., St. Louis Christian Coll., 1961; postgrad. Lincoln Christian Sem., 1961-62; m. Beverly Carter, Nov. 27, 1955; children—Daniel, David, Douglas. Ordained to ministry, 1955;-pastor Oak Mound Christian Ch., Xenia, Ill., 1953-56, Red Brush Christian Ch., Louisville, Ill., 1956-58, 1st Christian Ch., Florissant, Mo., 1958-62, Meml. Park Christian Ch., Tulsa, 1962-65, Pana (Ill.) Christian Ch., 1965-68, 1st Christian Ch., Hazelwood, Mo., 1970-72; chaplain Christian Hosp., St. Louis, 1972—. Pres. Fedn. for Instl. Ministries, Greater St. Louis, 1976-77. Mem. Florissant Citizens' Participation Com., 1976-77. Contbr. articles to religious jours. Home: 1460 Saint Anthony St Florissant MO 63033 Office: 11133 Dunn Rd Saint Louis MO 63136

SPROLES, RALPH EUGENE, minister, Church of Christ (Christian); b. Bluefield, W.Va., Jan. 3, 1936; s. Raymond Herbert and Della Mae (Austin) S.; A.B., Johnson Bible Coll., Kimberlin Heights, Tenn., 1958; m. Rita Lynn Akers, June 1, 1958; children: Kathy, Paul. Ordained to ministry, 1957; pastor Duhring (W.Va.) Ch. of Christ, 1956-58, Poplar Springs Ch. of Christ, King, N.C., 1959—. Pres. Johnson Bible Coll. Alumni Assn., 1970, trustee coll., 1984; pres. Council of 70 Johnson Bible Coll., 1972; mem. Gen. Bd. Christian TV Mission, N. Am. Christian Conv. Com., continuation com. So. Christian Youth Conv.; bd. dirs. Winston Salem Bible Coll.; trustee Johnson Bible Coll. Home and Office: Rt 1 King NC 27021

SPRY, MARVIN O'DELL, minister, So. Baptist Conv.; b. Cooleemee, N.C., Apr. 26, 1928; s. Granville Hopson and Beulah Beatrice (Fletcher) S.; B.S., George Peabody Coll. for Tchrs., 1949, M.A., 1953; m. Helen Colleen Nelson, Dec. 6, 1952; children—Charisse Anne, Marvin O'Dell, Jr., Mark Nelson. Ordained to ministry, 1975; minister of music chs. in N.C. and Fla., 1953-62; minister of music Dawson Meml. Bapt. Ch., Birmingham, Ala., 1963—. Pres. Ala. Religious Edn. Assn.; mem. exec. council So. Bapt. Ch. Music Conf. Mem. Am. Guild Organists, Choristers Guild, Ala. Singing Men. Home: 1304 Parliament Ln Birmingham AL 35216 Office: 1114 Oxmoor Rd Birmingham AL 35209

SPURLOCK, EDWARD MARSHALL, JR., minister, Southern Baptist Convention; b. Baton Rouge, La., Oct. 14, 1953; s. Edward Marshall Sr. and Helen Louise (Sebastian) S.; m. Sue Ellen Grissom, Jan. 6, 1976; children: Edward Marshall III, Emily Morgan. B.S., SUNY-N.Y.C., 1983; Diploma in N.T., Moody Bible Inst., Chgo., 1984. Ordained to ministry So. Bapt. Conv., 1975. Minister, Eden Bapt. Ch., Denham Springs, La., 1973-74, Park Forest Bapt. Ch., Baton Rouge, 1974-75; staff minister Revolution Ministries, 1974-83; dir. Ctr. for Christian Research, Baton Rouge, 1981—. Recipient Outstanding Young Man in Am. award U.S. Jaycees, 1983; Presdl. Achievement award, 1982. Mem. Shared Blessings Social Services, La. for Safe Energy, Soc. Bibl. Lit., Am. Schs. Oriental Research, Bibl. Archeol. Soc. Am. Parapsychol. Research Fellowship. Republican.

SQUADRON, HOWARD MAURICE See *Who's Who in America*, 43rd edition.

SQUIRE, ANNE MARGUERITE, lay worker, United Church of Canada; b. Amherstburg, Ont., Can., Oct. 17, 1920; s. Alexander Samuel and Coral Marguerite Park; m. William Robert Squire, June 24, 1943; children: Frances, Laura, Margaret. B.A., Carleton U., Ottawa, 1972, B.A. with honors, 1974, M.A., 1975; D.D. (hon.), United Theol. Coll., 1979. Cert. tchr., Ont. Adj. prof. Carleton U., 1975-82; sec. div. ministry personnel and edn. United Ch. of Can., Toronto, 1982-85; mem. bd. mgmt. St. Andrew's Coll., Saskatoon, Sask., 1982, Queens Theol. Coll., Kingston, Ont., 1980-82. Author curriculum materials, 1959—. Contbr. articles to profl. jours. Recipient Senate medal Carleton U., 1972. Mem. Can. Research Inst. for Advancement Women, Delta Kappa Gamma. (pres. 1978-79). Office: United Ch Can 85 Saint Clair Ave E Toronto ON M4T 1M8 Canada

SQUYRES, DEWEY FRANCIS, minister, So. Bapt. Conv.; b. Lawton, Okla., Mar. 9, 1949; s. Dewey Carol and Lura Faye (Kelley) S.; B.A. magna cum laude, Calif. Bapt. Coll., 1971; M.Div. with highest honors, Midwestern Bapt. Theol. Sem., 1973; postgrad. Golden Gate Bapt. Theol. Sem., 1974—; m. Sharon Kay Gardner, Aug. 5, 1967; children—David Roy, Karen Faye. Ordained to ministry, 1969; pastor First Bapt. Ch. Rancho Calif., Temecula, 1969-71, Corder Bapt. Ch. (Mo.), 1972-73, First Bapt. Ch., Rancho Calif., Temecula, 1973—. Chaplain extern Bapt. Meml. Hosp., Kansas City, Mo., 1973; chaplain coordinator Lakeview Community Hosp., Lake Elsinore, Calif., 1974—, head dept. pastoral care, 1974—. Mem. Rancho Calif. Scholarship Com., Temecula, 1971; mem. Lakeview Hosp. Citizens' Adv. Com., 1974—. Mem. Valley Ministerial Assn., Calvary-Arrowhead Minister's Conf. Religion columnist Rancho News, Temecula, Calif., 1974—. Home: 31071 Camino del Este Temecula CA 92390 Office: PO Box 753 Temecula CA 92390

SRIGLEY-SEITSINGER, GRETCHEN HEDGES, deaconess, hospital administrator, United Methodist Church; b. Ashville, Ohio, Apr. 11, 1919; d. Richard Harrison and Sarah Anne (Millar) Hedges; m. Robert Sprague, Nov. 14, 1943 (dec. 1973); children: Robert Jr., Pamela, Penelope; m. Ralph Emerson Seitsinger, Jan. 27, 1984. B.S., Ohio State U., 1940; M.B.A., Central State U., Edmund, Okla., 1978, M.Ed., 1979. Commd. deaconess United Meth. Ch., 1982. Adminstr. Maynard McDougall Meml. Hosp., Nome, Alaska, 1975-77; exec. dir. Houchen Community and Newark Meth. Hosp., El Paso, Tex., 1979—. Mem. Am. Coll. Hosp. Adminstrs., Weslyan Hosp. Assn., P.E.O. (sec. El Paso chpt. 1982-83). Home: 11601 Trey Burton El Paso TX 79936 Office: Newark Meth Hosp 1109 E 5th Ave El Paso TX 79901

STACKHOUSE, REGINALD, priest, college administrator, Anglican Church of Canada; member of parliament; b. Toronto, Ont., Can., Apr. 30, 1925; s. Edward Ingram and Emma (McNeill) S.; m. Margaret Eleanor Allman, June 2, 1951; children: Mary, Elizabeth, Ruth, John. B.A., U. Toronto, 1946, M.A., 1951; L.Th., Wycliffe Coll. (Toronto), 1953, B.D., 1954; Ph.D., Yale U., 1962; D.D. (hon.), Huron Coll., 1982. Ordained priest Anglican Ch. Rector, St. Matthew's Ch., Islington, Ont., 1946-56, St. John's Ch., Toronto, 1956-60; prof. theology Wycliffe Coll., Toronto, 1962—, prin., 1975—; M.P. Parliament of Can., Ottawa, Ont., 1984—; trustee Wycliffe Coll. Author: Christianity and Politics, 1964, The God Nobody Knows, 1985. Office: Wycliffe Coll Hoskin Ave Toronto ON M5S 1H7 Canada

STADDON, THEARON EMERY, pastor, Seventh-day Adventists; b. Missoula, Mont., June 7, 1945; s. Harold Kenneth and Rosa Louise S.; m. Sharon Alyce McHenry, June 10, 1968; children: Jack Hiler, Jeff William. B.A., Pacific Union Coll., 1968; M.S., Loma Linda U., 1980. Ordained to gospel ministry Seventh-day Adventists, 1973. Pastor Minn. Conf. Seventh-day Adventists, Cambridge, 1968-71, Grand Rapids, 1971-75, Nebr. Conf. Seventh-day Adventists, McCook, 1975-77; pastor Alaska Conf. Seventh-day Adventists, Palmer, 1980-83, pastor, dist. leader, Nome, 1983—. Home and Office: PO Box 1748 Nome AK 99762

STADELMANN, RICHARD WILLIAM, minister, educator, Christian Church (Disciples of Christ); b. Lynn, Mass., Dec. 16, 1932; s. William Louis and Olga Anna (Halbich) S.; B.A., Earlham Coll., 1954; M.Div., Yale U., 1958; postgrad. Tulane U., 1960-65; m. Bonnie Sue Shelton, June 16, 1956 (div. Dec. 1972); children: Marcus Richard, Lowell Shelton, Mary Idell, Kristine Marie; m. Patricia Annette Perry Wall, June 12, 1976; children: Aimee Elizabeth, Lisa Annette, Olga Gertrude, Greta Katryn. Ordained to ministry, 1954. Minister Bethel Christian Ch., Fountain City, Ind., 1952-54, Perry Christian Ch., Ohio, 1958-60; instr. philosophy Tulane U., 1962-63; instr. philosophy and religion La. State U., 1963-67; prof. philosophy and humanities Tex. A & M U., 1967—; minister 1st Christian Ch., Brenham, Tex., 1968-76; chmn. United Campus Christian Fellowship, 1963-65; Ind. chaplain Order of DeMolay, 1960. Chmn. Burleson County Republican Com., 1973-74; precinct chmn. Brazos County Rep. Com., 1974-84, vice chmn., 1976-84; del. Tex. Rep. Conv., 1974-85; chmn. Reagan-Bush Com., Washington County, Tex., 1984. Mem. AAUP, Am. Philos. Assn., Metaphys. Soc. Am., Soc. Process Studies, Southwestern Philos. Soc., Am. Forensic Assn., Tau Kappa Alpha. Home: Route 5 Box 57 Brenham TX 77833 Office: Texas A & M University College Station TX 77843

STAFFORD, BRYCE FRANK, minister, educator, Southern Baptist Convention; b. Marion, N.C., June 25, 1932; s. Julius Winslow and Abilene Dare (McKinney) S.; A.A., El Camino Jr. Coll., 1951; B.A., Wayland Coll., 1960; B.D., Golden Gate Bapt. Theol. Sem., 1963, M.R.E., 1965; m. Mary Evagene Foster, Aug. 6, 1964; 1 son, Milo Winslow. Ordained deacon, 1959, to ministry, 1965; pastor chs., Calif., 1965-69, prin., tchr. Grace Christian Acad., Vallejo, Calif., 1969-72, Castlewood Christian Schs., Vallejo, 1972-76, North Hills Christian Sch., Vallejo, 1976—. Pres. Benicia (Calif.) Ministerial Assn. Active PTA. Mem. Assn. Christian Schs. Internat. Home: 2137 Casa Grande St Benicia CA 94510 Office: PO Box 4342 Vallejo CA 94590

STAFFORD, GILBERT WAYNE, minister, seminary educator, Church of God (Anderson, Ind.); b. Portageville, Mo., Dec. 30, 1938; s. Dawsey Calvin and Orell Elvesta (Smith) S.; m. Darlene Dawn Covert, Dec. 30, 1962; children: Matthew Wayne, Heather Noelle, Anne Elizabeth, Joshua Wayne Covert. A.B., Anderson Coll., 1961; student Anderson Sch. Theology, 1960-62; M.Div., Andover Newton Theol. Sch., 1964; Th.D., Boston U., 1973; postgrad. Inst. Holy Land Studies, Israel, 1976; vis. scholar Cambridge U., Eng., 1985. Ordained to ministry Ch. of God, 1965. Pastor Malden Ch. of God, Mass., 1962-66; dir. Christian edn. Hyde Park Congl. Ch., Boston, 1968-69; pastor East Ashman Ch. of God, Midland, Mich., 1969-76; faculty Anderson Sch. Theology, Ind., 1976—, now assoc. prof. Christian theology, assoc. dean, dean of chapel; mem. commn. on Christian unity Ch. of God, Anderson, 1975-78, 80—; mem. new curriculum philosophy com. Warner Press, Anderson, 1983—; convener Internat. Dialogue on Doctrinal Issues, 1980—; mem. continuation com. Believers' Ch. Conf., 1980—; founder, convener Didaskaloi, 1980-83; mem. faith and order commn. Nat. Council Chs. of Christ in U.S.A. Author: Living as Redeemed People, 1976; The Life of Salvation, 1979; Beliefs that Guide Us, 1977; The Person and Work of the Holy Spirit, 1977; The People of God, 1977; The Seven Doctrinal Leaders of the Church of God Movement, 1977; contbr. to books, articles to religious jours. Recipient Bethany Heritage award, 1979. Mem. Wesleyan Theol. Soc. (nominating com. 1977-80). Home: 2424 Albert St Anderson IN 46012 Office: Anderson Sch of Theology E 3d St Anderson IN 46012

STAFFORD, J. FRANCIS, bishop, Roman Catholic Church; b. Balt., July 26, 1932; s. Francis Emmett and Mary Dorothy (Stanton) S. B.A., St. Mary's Sem., Balt., 1954; S.T.B., S.T.L., Gregorian U., Rome, 1958; M.S.W., Cath. U. Am., 1964. Ordained priest, Roman Cath. Ch., 1957. Asst. pastor Immaculate Heart of Mary, Balt., 1958-62; asst. pastor St. Ann's, Balt., 1964-65; chaplain Villa Maria Home for Children, Balt., 1965-69; asst. in sacramental ministry Basilica of the Assumption, Balt., 1969-76; dir. Assoc. Cath. Charities, Balt., 1966-76; urban vicar, aux. bishop Archdiocese of Balt., 1976-82; bishop of Memphis, 1982—. Mem. policy bd. Center for Met. Planning and Research, Johns Hopkins U., 1973—; bd. trustees Jenkins Meml. Hosp., 1976—; chmn. bishops' com. on marriage and family life U.S. Cath. Conf.; mem. White House Com. on Families, 1979-81; co-chmn. World Meth./Roman Cath. Dialogue, 1977—, Roman Cath./Oriental Orthodox Bilateral Dialogue, 1977—. Mem. Nat. Conf. Cath. Bishops (bishops com. on ecumenical and interreligious affairs). Office: 1325 Jefferson Memphis TN 38114

STAGG, PAUL LEONARD, religious organization executive, minister, Southern Baptist Conv.; b. Eunice, La., Feb. 24, 1914; s. Paul and Della Edith (Hammers) S.; B.A., La. Coll., 1936; Th.M., So. Baptist Theol. Sem., 1939; postgrad. Union Theol. Sem. and Columbia, 1946-47; m. Margaret M. Persinger, Oct. 17, 1939; children—Brenda (Mrs. William A. Harrison), Jane (Mrs. Lester M. Brassington, Jr.). Ordained to ministry So. Baptist Conv., 1934; minister Montgomery (W.Va.) Bapt. Ch., 1939-42; chaplain USAAF, ETO, 1942-45; minister Glendale (N.Y.) Bapt. Ch., 1946-47, First Bapt. Ch., Front Royal, Va., 1947-59; program dir. Am. Bapt. Home Mission Soc. (now Am. Bapt. Chs. in U.S.A.), Valley Forge, Pa., 1959-70; gen. sec. N.J. Council Chs., East Orange, 1970—. Ecumenical cons. Roman Catholic Diocese of Newark; mem. exec. com. Jewish Christian Clergy Conf., Coalition for Fair Broadcasting in N.J. Chmn., Fair Housing Com., King of Prussia, Pa., 1962-69, N.J. Coalition on Penal Reform, 1971—; mem. Paris Peace Conf., 1971, Brussels 2d World Conf. Soviet Jewry, 1976. Trustee Bar Inst. N.J. Named Man of Year, Jr. C. of C., 1965. Author: The Converted Church: From Escape to Engagement, 1967; Preaching in the New Age, 1968; Evangelism through Small Groups, 1968. Office: 116 N Oraton Pkwy East Orange NJ 07017

STAGGEMEIER, DALE AUGUST, minister, United Church of Christ; b. St. Charles, Mo., Feb. 1, 1948; s. Wilbur Henry and Ruth Ella (Ritter) S.; A.B., U. Mo., St. Louis, 1970; M.Div., Eden Theol. Sem., 1973, D.Min., 1979; m. Marylouise Matilda Voss, Jan. 31, 1970; children—Dale August, Bethany Ann. Ordained to ministry, 1973; pastor Ebenezer United Ch. of Christ, Augusta, Mo., 1971-76, St. Peter's United Ch. of Christ, New Haven, Mo., 1976—. Del. from Mo. Conf. to 10th and 11th Gen. Synods, United Ch. of Christ, 1975-77; mem. com. on ch. and ministry Eastern Assn., Mo. Conf., 1974, chmn., 1974, mem. commn. on ch. and ministry, 1974, sec., 1975; asst. chaplain St. Charles County Sheriff's Dept., 1975. Vol. adv. bd. St. Charles County Welfare, St. Charles, Mo., 1973-74; bd. advisors Family and Children Services, St. Charles, 1973-75, Mo. Conf. Council, 1983—; v.p. Hermann Area Pastors Circle, 1978-83, pres., 1984. Home: 101 Mary Hammack St New Haven MO 63068 Office: 701 Maupin St New Haven MO 63068

STAHL, SAMUEL MORTON, rabbi, Reform Jewish Congregations; b. Sharon, Pa., Aug. 25, 1939; s. Harry Jeremiah and Pearl (Sherman) S.; A.B., U. Pitts., 1961; B.H.L., Hebrew Union Coll.-Jewish Inst. Religion, 1963, M.A. in Hebrew Lit., 1967, D.H.L., 1975; m. Lynn Ann Cohodas, Aug. 28, 1966; children: Heather Sara, Alisa Michelle. Ordained rabbi, 1967; chaplain U.S. Army, Ft. Belvoir, Va., 1967-68, Seoul, Korea, 1968-69; rabbi Temple B'nai Israel, Galveston, Tex., 1969-76, Temple Beth-El, San Antonio, Tex., 1976—. Pres., Galveston Ministerial Assn., 1971; mem. Jewish Adv. Group to Galveston-Houston Diocesan Ecumenical Council, 1975; instr. O'Connell Cath. High Sch., Galveston, 1974-75; pres. Kallah of Tex. Rabbis, 1977-78; bd. dirs. Ecumenical Ctr. for Religion and Health, 1977—; mem. instl. rev. com. St. Luke's Luth. Hosp., 1979—. Recipient Shalom award State of Israel Bonds, 1971. Mem. Central Conf. Am. Rabbis, (exec. bd. 1984—), Am. Jewish Com., Southwest Assn. Reform Rabbis (pres. 1984—), NCCJ (chpt. bd. dirs. 1983—). Home: 4218 Bluemel Rd San Antonio TX 78240 Office: 211 Belknap Pl San Antonio TX 78212

STAHL, WILLIAM MARVIN, minister, American Baptist Churches in the U.S.A.; b. Endicott, N.Y., Apr. 6, 1928; s. Raymond and Margaret (Crawford) S.; m. Romayne Arlette Fowler, June 6, 1950; children: Judith Marie Stahl Foley, William Randall, Sylvia Denise. Diploma, Providence Bible Inst., Providence, 1949; B.A., Harpur Coll., SUNY-Binghamton, 1953; B.D., Eastern Bapt. Theol. Sem., 1956, D.Min., 1976. Ordained to ministry Am. Baptist Chs. in U.S.A., 1956. Pastor First Bapt. Ch., Greene, N.Y., 1956-58, Community Bapt. Ch., Binghamton, N.Y., 1958-66; sr. pastor Hatboro Bapt. Ch., Pa., 1966-75, First Bapt. Ch., Plymouth, Mich., 1975—; chmn. inner city com. Phila. Bapt. Assn., 1971-74; bd. dirs. Upstate Bapt. Home, Oneonta, N.Y., 1960-66; pres. Am. Bapt. Ministers Council, 1973-75, 76-78; chmn. Commn. on Ministry, Mich., 1981-83; 2d v.p., chmn. program com. Am. Bapt. Chs./Mich., 1983-84. Bd. dirs. Vis. Nurse Assn., Abington, Pa., 1973-76. Mem. Profl. Soc. for Drs. of Ministry, Ministers Council (pres. 1973-78). Republican. Clubs: Kiwanis (bd. dirs. 1976—), Rotary (bd. dirs. 1967-75). Home: 45050 N Territorial Rd Plymouth MI 48170 Office: First Baptist Church 45000 N Territorial Rd Plymouth MI 48170

STAIRS, ARNOLD LEO, pastor, administrator, Wesleyan Methodist Church; b. Woodstock, N.B., Can., Oct. 11, 1926; s. Theron Earl and Gladys J. (Dickinson) S.; m. M. Leota Sears, June 3, 1948; children: Reid Arnold, Nadine Rosella. Degree, Bethany Bible Coll., N.S., 1948. Ordained to ministry, 1949. Pastor, Reformed Baptist Chs., Maine, N.S. and N.B., Can., 1948-66, Wesleyan Meth. Ch., N.B., 1966-68, Wesleyan Ch., N.B., 1968-83; regional rep. Christian Blind Mission Internat., Atlantic Provinces, Can., 1983—. Trustee Bethany Bible Coll., 1964—. Mem. Pi Alpha Mu. Office: Christian Blind Mission Internat 224 Main St Salisbury NB E0A 3E0 Canada

STALLINGS, DALLAS THURSTON, JR., minister, So. Baptist Conv.; b. Edenton, N.C., Aug. 13, 1940; s. Dallas Thurston and Gladys Virginia (Bunch) S.; B.A., Wake Forest U., 1962; B.D., Southeastern Bapt. Theol. Sem., Wake Forest, 1965, Th.M., 1970, D.Min., 1975; postgrad. Sch. Pastoral Care, Va. Bapt. Hosp., Lynchburg, 1975-76; m. Donna Catherine Raper, July 11, 1964; 1 son, Dallas Thurston. Ordained to ministry, 1963; pastor Cullen (Va.) Bapt. Ch., 1964-65, Union Grove Bapt. Ch., Keysville, Va., 1964-66; asso. minister Franklin (Va.) Bapt. Ch., 1966-68; pastor Chatham (Va.) Bapt. Ch., 1968—. Bd. dirs. Va. Bapt. Hosp., Lynchburg; mem. Va. Bapt. Pastor's Discussion Group; bible tchr. Chatham Hall, Episc. Girls' Sch., 1976; narrator religious drama All Men Shall Be Free. Pres. bd. Pittsylvania chpt. ARC; mem. Pittsylvania County Sch. Bd.; past pres. Chatham Rotary; coordinator Chatham Playground Com.; active Family Counseling Clinic, Community Ednl. Council, Boy Scouts Am., Chatham Rescue Squad, Piedmont Forum Com. Recipient Eagle Scout award, 1957; Danforth fellow, 1958. Contbr. articles to religious publs. Home: 45 Whittle St Chatham VA 24531 Office: PO Box 104 Chatham VA 24531

STALLINGS, MARK EDMOND, music educator; Methodist Church; b. Tampa, Fla., Jan. 3, 1956; s. Kindle Edmond and Rozene (Carpenter) S.; m. Terry Stehle, Mar. 2, 1985. B.M. in Music Edn., U. Miami, 1978; D.M.A. in Choral Music, 1984; Ed.M. in Music Edn., Fla. Atlantic U., 1981. Soloist Allapattah United Meth. Ch., Miami, Fla., 1974-78; dir. music Wesley United Meth. Ch., Miami, 1975-78; co-dir. Sonrise, Miami, 1976-78; dir. music and youth ministries Trinity United Meth. Ch., Lighthouse Point, Fla., 1978-82, Christ Congl. Ch., Miami, 1982-84; dir. music ministries First United Meth. Ch. of Winter Park, Fla., 1984—; mgr. U. Miami Chamber Singers, Coral Gables, Fla., 1976-78, 1981-83, dir. Mixed Chorus, 1982-84; music camp dir. Christi Congl. Ch., Miami, 1983; music clinician, adjudicator So. States; baritone soloist, Mark and Mark Sacred Concerts, Miami, 1981—; music librarian, mgr. Miami Civic Chorale, Coral Gables, 1974-84; camp dir., clinician, counselor U. Miami, 1974-78, 1982. U. Miami sch. of Music scholar, 1974-78, grad. teaching assistantship, 1981. Mem. Music Educators nat. conf., Am. Choral Dirs. Assn., Fla. Vocal Assn., Coll. Music Soc., Fellowship of United Meths. in Worship, Music, and Other Arts, Am. Guild of Organists, Am. Guild Handbell Ringers, Omicron Delta Kappa, Phi Kappa Lambda, Pi Kappa Phi. Home: 3810 Bay to Bay Blvd Tampa FL 33629 Office: First United Meth Ch PO Box 819 Winter Park FL 32789

STAM, PETER, III, missions administrator, Africa Inland Mission; b. Paterson, N.J., Apr. 26, 1917; s. Peter, Jr. and Margaret (Gardinier) S.; B.A. in Philosophy, Wheaton (Ill.) Coll., 1939; M.Div., Faith Theol. Sem., Wilmington, Del., 1942; m. Mary Louise Kennedy, Oct. 14, 1943; children: Sharon (Mrs. James Rouse), Bruce Allan, Marilyn Stam Lonander, Blair. Ordained minister Wheaton Bible Ch., 1942; gen. sec. Student Fgn. Missions Fellowship, 1942-44; pastor Western Springs (Ill.) Baptist Ch., 1944-45; radio speaker Songs in the Night, 1944-45; mem. staff Africa Inland Mission, 1946—; prin., tchr. Rethy Acad., Congo, 1946-47, Adi Bible Sch., Congo, 1948-63; sch. supr. Aba, Congo, 1947-48; dir. Canadian div., 1964-77, dir. Am. div., 1977—. Mem. exec. com. Toronto Inst. Linguistics, 1965-77; mem. corp. Ont. Bible Coll., 1966-77; mem. ofcl. bd. Interdenominational Fgn. Mission Assn., 1966—, sec. 1968-70, treas. 1973-75, v.p. 1970-72, pres., 1975-79. Author: A Pedagogical Grammer of the Bangala Language, 1955; also articles, text books. Home: 2 Prospect Ave Westwood NJ 07675 Office: Africa Inland Mission PO Box 178 Pearl River NY 10965

STAMBACH, ARTHUR WILLIAM, minister United Methodist Church; b. Spring Run, Pa., July 2, 1925; s. Charles Guy and Glenna Alice (Damuth) S.; m. Betty Mae Getz, Mar. 30, 1945; children: Susan Kay, Nancy Patricia. A.B., Lebanon Valley Coll., 1945; M.Div., United Theol. Sem., 1948; D.D., Lebanon Valley Coll., 1967. Ordained to ministry United Meth. Ch., 1948. Pastor, Park Ave. Ch., Chambersburg, Pa., 1948-51, Calvary Ch., Lemoyne, Pa., 1952-59, First Ch., York, Pa., 1959-63; assoc. program dir. Central Pa. Conf. United Meth. Ch., 1963-75; dist. supt., Chambersburg, Pa., 1975-79; sr. pastor First Church, Hershey, Pa., 1979—; mem. gen. bd. publs. United Meth. Ch., Nashville; trustee Lebanon Valley Coll.; bd. dirs. Quincy United Meth. Home; v.p. Christian Churches United, Harrisburg. Served as chaplain AUS, 1950-52, Korea. Lodge: Rotary. Address: 64 W Chocolate Ave Hershey PA 17033

STANDIFER, LAFAYETTE BOGLE, III, lay church worker, Am. Bapt. Chs. in U.S.A.; b. Jackson, Miss., Aug. 18, 1936; s. Lafayette Bogle, Jr. and Emma Louise (Barnes) S.; B.S. in Bus. Adminstrn., Cedarville Coll., 1962; m. Bonnie Louise Mayes, Nov. 17, 1961; children: Lafayette Bogle, Carolyn Annette. Youth counselor, song leader, Sunday Sch. tchr., deacon Am. Baptist Chs. in U.S.A., 1968-70; treas. First Bapt. Ch., Hamilton, O., 1970-71; accounting dir. Green Lake (Wis.) Center, Am. Bapt. Assembly, 1972-73, controller, 1973-76, dir. fin., 1976-81, dir. bus., 1982—. Mem. Nat. Assn. Accountants, Am. Bapt. Men Wis. (treas. 1975—). Alpha Chi. Home: 432 Joy Ave Ripon WI 54971 Office: Green Lake Conf Center Am Bapt Assembly Green Lake WI 54941

STANDRIDGE, FREDERICK LEE, minister, General Association of Regular Baptist Churches; b. Pontiac, Mich., Dec. 31, 1931; s. Jesse Raymond and Blanche Elizebeth (Sproule) S.; m. Celia Grace Young, Feb. 2, 1952; children: Allen Lee, Cheryl Ann, Anita Louise, Craig Andrew. Cert. Moody Bible Inst., 1953; student Detroit Conservatory Music, 1949, Grand Rapids Bapt., 1960. Ordained to ministry Gen. Assn. Regular Bapt. Chs., 1965. Youth, music pastor various chs., Mich., Ill., Ind., 1953-70; radio preacher, pastor Prison Evangelism, Grand Rapids, 1957-61; childrens choir dir. Childrens Bible House, Grand Rapids, Mich., 1959-63; pastor Faith Bapt. Ch., Kokomo, Ind., 1970—; tchr., preacher Gary Rescue Mission, Ind., 1963-67; youth, Sunday Sch. Conf. speaker Gen. Assn. Regular Bapts., Schaumburg, Ill., 1963-69; tchr. Calumet Christian, Highland, Ind., 1964-65; radio pastor Person to Person, Inc., Kokomo, Ind., 1969-81. Author: Youth Ministry, 1968; Mental Health, 1984. Recipient Excellence in Graphic Design Honor award Kimberly Clark Corp., 1971. Avocations: Antique car restoration; camping. Home: 3492 E Blvd 100 S Kokomo IN 46902 Office: Faith Bapt Ch 610 W Alto Rd Box 2192 Kokomo IN 46902

STANFEL, ALBIN J., minister, Lutheran Church-Missouri Synod; b. Laurium, Mich., Aug. 23, 1928; s. Albin Joseph and Mary Wilhelmina (Birk) S.; m. Dorothy Jean Honold, June 20, 1953; children: Julie Marie, Albin William, Jonathan David, Martin Andrew. B.A., Concordia Sem., St. Louis, 1952; D.D. (hon.), Concordia Sem., Springfield, Ill., 1976. Ordained to ministry Luth. Ch., 1955. Pastor, Our Savior Luth. Ch., Thistletown, Ont., Can., 1955-64, Hope Luth. Ch., Kitchener, Ont., 1964-68; asst. exec. sec. Ont. Dist. Luth. Ch.-Mo. Synod, Kitchener, 1969-72, pres.,

1970—, chmn. bd. dirs., 1970—; chmn. bd. regents Concordia Sem., St. Catharines, Ont., 1983—; bd. dirs. Luth. Ch.-Can., Vancouver, B.C., 1970—. Recipient Christo et Ecclesiae medal Concordia Coll., Edmonton, 1984. Home: 15 Eastwood Dr Kitchener ON N2A 2A1 Canada Office: Ont Dist Luth Ch 149 Queen St S Box 481 Kitchener ON N2G 4A2 Canada

STANFIELD, ELSTON BENTON, minister, Southern Baptist Convention; b. Lafayette, Ga., Aug. 7, 1918; s. Emory Benton and Pearl Kathern (Nation) S.; m. Rosalie Hegwood, Sept. 6, 1936 (dec. 1983); 1 child, Sandra Sue Glenn; m. Laurine Calwell, Mar. 11, 1984. A.A., Norman Jr. Coll., 1951; A.B., Mercer U., 1953. Ordained to ministry Southern Baptist Convention, 1942. Deacon, So. Bapt. Lafayette, Ga., 1938-42, pastor, 1942-57; vice moderator Mercer Bapt. Assn., 1960-63, clk., 1975-76; chmn. evangelism, 1967, Sunday sch. dir., 1975-79; minister Rest a While Nursing, 1981-82; chaplain Middle South Ga. Soil and Water Conservation Dist., 1963—; mem. exec. com. Ga. Bapt. Conv., 1969-72. Named Rural Minister of Yr., State of Ga., 1967. Mem. Barwick C. of C. (pres. 1966-69). Home and Office: Hempstead Bapt Ch Barwick GA 31720

STANLEY, CHARLES FRAZIER, minister, Southern Baptist Convention; b. Danville, Va., Sept. 25, 1932; s. Charles Stanley and Rebecca (Hardy) Hall; m. Anna Margaret Johnson, Aug. 6, 1955; children: Charles Andrew, Rebecca Louise. B.A., U. Richmond, 1954; B.Div., Southwestern Baptist, 1957; Th.M., Theol. Sem. Luther Rice Sem., 1968, D.Theology, 1971. Ordained to minister Southern Baptist Convention, 1956. Pastor, First Bapt. Ch., Fruitland, N.C., 1957-59, Fairborn, Ohio, 1959-62, Miami, Fla., 1962-68, Bartow, Fla., 1968-69, Atlanta, 1971—; prof. Fruitland Bible Inst., 1958-59; prin. George Muiller Christian Sch., Miami, Fla., 1962-68; assoc. pastor First Baptist Ch., Atlanta, 1969-71; pres. So. Bapt. Conv., Nashville, 1984—; bd. dirs. Nat. Religious Broadcasters, Morristown, N.J., 1982—; trustee Toccoa Falls Bible Coll. Ga., 1982-84. Author: A Man's Touch, 1977; The Walk of Faith, 1979; Reaching Your Goals, 1980; Stand Up, America, 1980; Handle With Prayer, 1982. Recipient George Washington Honor medal Freedoms Found., 1980. Republican. Office: First Baptist Church 754 Peachtree St NE Atlanta GA 30365

STANLEY, DONALD CLAUDE, minister, Southern Baptist Convention; b. Dixon, Nebr., Nov. 3, 1918; s. Claude Ulmont and Eva (Phipps) S.; m. Angeline June Swedberg, June 4, 1942; children: Patricia, Mary, William, Catherine, Janet, Paul. A.A., Scottsbluff Jr. Coll., 1942; B.A. in Sociology, William Jewell Coll., 1944; B.D., Central Bapt. Sem., Kansas City, Kans., 1949, Th.M., 1950. Ordained to ministry So. Bapt. Conv., 1944; pastor Paradise Bapt. Ch., Mo., 1943-44, Hopewell Bapt. Ch., Cowgill, Mo., 1943-50, 1st Bapt. Ch., Stanberry, Mo., 1950-55, Polo, Mo., 1955-60, Desloge, Mo., 1960—. Chmn. Title I com. North County Reorganized 1 Sch. Dist., Desloge, 1974-81, mem. PTA audit com., 1982. Lodge: Rotary (service com Bonne Terre, Mo. 1984-85).

STANO, LESTER PAUL, minister, Lutheran Church - Missouri Synod; b. St. Louis, Mar. 31, 1947; s. Paul and Anna (Dinga) S. B.B.A., U. Mo., 1969; M.Div., Concordia Sem., 1973. Ordained to ministry Lutheran Ch., 1974; cert. VA chaplain, 1976. Asst. pastor Immanuel Luth. Ch., Balt., 1974-75; instr. religion Balt. Luth. High Sch., Towson, Md., 1975-76, bd. dirs., 1976—; intermitent chaplain VA Med. Ctr., Balt., 1976—; pastor First Luth. Ch., Towson, 1976—; bd. dirs. Luth. Mission Soc., Balt., 1976—; circuit counselor Luth. Ch.-Mo. Synod (southeastern dist.), Alexandria, Va., 1981—. Mem. Towson Manor Village Assn., 1979—. Mem. Towson Area Ministerial Assn. (sec. 1979, v.p. 1982, pres. 1983), Am. Protestant Hosp. Assn. (Coll. Chaplains), Assn. Clin. Pastoral Edn. Home: 29 Linden Terr Towson MD 21204 Office: First Luth Ch Towson 40 E Burke Ave Towson MD 21204

STANTON, GORDON BURKE JACK, minister, Southern Baptist Ch.; b. East St. Louis, Ill., Aug. 31, 1919; s. Harmon and Lora S.; m. Mary Agnes Skrivan, Feb. 28, 1941; children: Mary Lee Lanier, Melody Ann Stephens. B.A., Shurtleff Coll., 1944; B.D., Central Bapt. Theol. Sem., 1955; Th.D., Luther Rice Sem., 1974; D.D. (hon.), S.W. Bapt. U., 1974. Ordained to ministry, 1972. Pastor, Carpenter St. Bapt. Ch., Moberly, Mo., 1947-52; dir. evangelism Kans. Bapt. Conv., Wichita, 1952-57; dir. evangelism Colo. Bapt. Gen. Conv., Denver, 1957-60; dir. personal and mass evangelism Home Mission Bd., So. Bapt. Conv., Atlanta, 1960-75; dir. Inst. Evangelism, S.W. Bapt. U., Bolivar, Mo., 1975—. Contbr. articles to profl. jours. Co-author: Southern Baptist Handbook of Evangelism, 1956; Handbook of Evangelism, 1965; We Are Witnesses, 1966; author: Teachers Manual for Lay Evangelism School, 1970, others. Mem. Acad. Evangelism, Bapt. Tchrs. Religion, Mo. Bapt. Evangelists (pres. 1978-81), Conf. So. Bapt. Evangelists. Address: 601 N Claud St Bolivar MO 65613

STAPERT, JOHN CHARLES, minister, editor, publisher, Reformed Church in America; b. Kalamazoo, Sept. 25, 1942; s. Elko M. and Martha Edith (Van Zee) S.; m. Barbara Sue Vanderlinde, Aug. 17, 1963; children: Craig William, TerriLynne. A.B., Hope Coll., 1963; M.Div., Fuller Sem., Pasadena, Calif., 1966; M.A., U. Ill., 1968, Ph.D., 1969. Ordained to ministry Reformed Ch. in Am., 1969. Exec. coordinator Synod of West, Reformed Ch. in Am., Orange City, Iowa, 1972-74; editor, pub. The Church Herald, Grand Rapids, Mich., 1974—; elder 5th Reformed Ch., Grand Rapids, 1979-82. Assoc. prof. psychology Northwestern Coll., Orange City, 1969-72. Contbr. articles to profl. jours. Mem. Mailers Tech. Adv. Com., Washington, 1981-84. Mem. Am. Psychol. Assn., Assoc. Ch. Press (pres. 1983-85), Evang. Press Assn. Home: 502 Edgeworthe Dr SE Grand Rapids MI 49506 Office: The Church Herald 1324 Lake Dr SE Grand Rapids MI 49506

STAPLES, JOHN DOUGLAS, minister, ch. ofcl., United Ch. Can.; b. Stratford, Ont., Can., Aug. 26, 1921; s. Walter Ernest and Jessie (Curtis) S.; student Queen's U., 1956-58; Testamur, Queen's Theol. Coll., 1958-61; m. Winifred D. Bonney, Nov. 17, 1945; children—Ann (Mrs. Alex Lawrence). Ordained to ministry United Ch. of Can., 1961; minister Manitowaning-Tehkummah Pastoral Charge, Ont., 1961-64, Nelson-Palermo Pastoral Charge, Ont., 1964-68; capital funds dir. United Ch. Can., Toronto, 1968-69, adminstrv. asst. dept. pensions, 1969-73; minister Westmount United Ch., Orillia, Ont., 1973-75; adminstr. div. ministry, personnel and edn. United Ch. Can., Toronto, 1975—. Mem. Civitan Internat. Home: 15-16 Normark Dr Thornhill ON L3T 3P9 Canada Office: 85 St Clair Ave E Toronto ON M4T 1M8 Canada

STAPLETON, THOMAS HOWARD, minister, Am. Bapt. Assn.; b. Mobile, Ala., Jan. 30, 1943; s. Joseph Benjamin and Edna Louisa (Terkeurst) S.; B.B.L., Little Rock Bapt. Sem. and Inst., 1970; m. Beatrice Aline Turner, Nov. 17, 1965; 1 son, Matthew Mark. Ordained to ministry, 1965; pastor chs., Overlook, Miss., 1970-74, New Home, Miss., 1974-76, Bogalusa, La., 1976—. Instr. Faith High Sch. Acad., Eight Mile, Ala., 1972-74. Moderator Ala. Miss. Baptist Assn., 1971-72. 74-75. Home: 833 Union Ave Bogalusa LA 70427 Office: 814 Union Ave Bogalusa LA 70427

STARK, ALICE REYNOLDS, lay church worker, Episcopal Church; b. Bklyn., June 16, 1930; d. T. Benton and Eleanor (Wolcott) Reynolds; m. Nils Edward Stark, May 19, 1951; 1 child, Victoria Johanna. A.B., Hofstra U., 1968. Tchr., Transfiguration Day Sch., Freeport, N.Y., 1962-65; counsellor St. Andrew's Ch., Denver, N.Y., 1970-72; dir. Prodigal House, Denver, 1972-76, Central Denver Community Service 1976—; mem. exec. council Diocese of Colo., 1983—; mem. commn. social and spl. ministries Nat. Exec. Council Episcopal Ch. in U.S., N.Y.C., 1984—. Contbr. articles to profl. jours. Mem. Mensa. Home: 2717 S Glencoe St Denver CO 80222 Office: Episcopal Pastoral Center 1300 Washington St Denver CO 80218

STARKS, HENRY LOGAN, minister, educator, A.M.E. Ch.; b. Memphis, Oct. 16, 1921; s. Harry Logan and Ella Grace (Green) S.; B.S., Le Moyne Coll., 1949; M.A., Fisk U., 1956; D.D. (hon.), Monrovia Coll., 1963, Jackson Sem., 1970; M.Div., Memphis Theol. Sem., 1968; m. Alma Edwards, Jan. 26, 1944; 1 dau., Almella Yvonne. Ordained to ministry A.M.E. Ch., 1951; pastor various chs., Hollow Rock circuit, Lexington circuit, St. James A.M.E. Ch., Dickson, Tenn., 1949-56, Clayborn Temple A.M.E. Ch., Memphis, 1956-60, St. James A.M.E. Ch., Memphis, 1960—; prof. dept. history Memphis Theol. Sem., 1969—. Pres., Interdenominational Ministers Alliance, Memphis, 1964—; chaplain Western State Mental Hosp., Bolivar, Tenn., 1956-60. Recipient plaques, civic, religious activities. Mem. Memphis Ministers Assn. (pres. 1974—). Home: 546 Stephens Pl Memphis TN 38126 Office: 600 N 4th St Memphis TN 38107

STARR, ARNON TIMOTHY, minister, religious organization executive, Fellowship of Evangelical Baptist Churches in Canada; b. Toronto, Ont., Can., Nov. 25, 1924; s. Clinton Emerson and Gladys Elizabeth (Robins) S.; m. Hazel McClure, Dec. 27, 1948; children: David, Miriam, Jonathan, Grace. Diploma Toronto Bible Coll., 1946; B.A., Coe Coll., 1948; M.A., U. Iowa, 1949; D.Min., Luther Rice Sem., 1978. Ordained to ministry Fellowship of Evang. Bapt. Chs. in Can., 1948. Pastor Calvary Bapt. Ch., St. Cloud, Minn., 1951-59, Mona Shores Bapt. Ch., Muskegon, Mich., 1959-66, Dovercourt Bapt. Ch., Toronto, 1967-71; home missions dir. Fellowship Bapt. Chs. of Can., Toronto, 1971—; prof. Central Bapt. Sem., Toronto, 1967—; vice chmn. bd. edn. Peoples Ch., Toronto, 1979-81; mem. Inter-faith Com. on Chaplaincy, Toronto, 1984. Author: Church Planting, 1978; Impressions, 1984. Contbr. articles to profl. jours. Home: 90 James Gray Dr Willowdale ON M2H 1P1 Canada Office: Fellowship of Evang Bapt Chs 74 Sheppard Ave W Willowdale ON M2N 1M3 Canada

STARR, CHARLES MARION, minister, Lutheran Church in America; b. Hickory, N.C., May 31, 1925; s. Charles Burton and Annie Iona (Abernethy) S.; m. Mary June Hollar, June 13, 1926; children: Carol Ann, Charles Emery, Mary June. A.B., Lenoir-Rhyne Coll., 1945, D.D. (hon.), 1973; M.Div., Luth. Theol. So. Sem., 1948. Ordained to ministry Luth. Ch., 1948. Pastor, St. Paul Luth. Ch., Hamlet, N.C., 1948-52, Calvary Luth. Ch., Spencer, N.C., 1952-58, Redeemer Luth. Ch., Charlotte, N.C., 1958-66, Kimball Meml. Luth. Ch., Kannapolis, N.C., 1966-76, St. Paul Luth. Ch., Wilmington, N.C., 1976-83, St. Mark Luth. Ch., Asheville, N.C., 1983—; conv. del. Luth. Ch. in Am., 1984. Trustee, sec. bd. Lenoir-Rhyne Coll., Hickory, N.C., 1980—. Home: 20 Graystone Rd Asheville NC 28804 Office: St Mark's Luth Ch Box 8608 Asheville NC 28814

STARR, EDWARD CARYL, retired minister, American Baptist Chs. in the U.S.A.; b. Yonkers, N.Y., Jan. 9, 1911; s. Edward Charles and Mary Hamilton (Reid) S.; A.B. cum laude, Colgate U., 1933; B.S. in L.S., Columbia, 1939; M.Div., Colgate-Rochester Div. Sch., 1940; m. Hilda Ruth Thomforde, Aug. 31, 1940; children: Caroline May (Mrs. Norman C. Wehmer), Edward Jonathan. Ordained to ministry, 1952; curator Samuel Colgate Bapt. Hist. Collection, Colgate U., 1935-48; librarian Crozer Theol. Sem., Chester, Pa., 1948-54; curator Am. Bapt. Hist. Soc., 1948-55; curator combined Samuel Colgate Bapt. Hist. Collection and Am. Bapt. Hist. Soc., Colgate Rochester Div. Sch., Rochester, N.Y., 1955-76; exec. dir. dept. archives and history Am. Bapt. Chs. in U.S.A., also archivist Colgate Rochester Div. Sch. Mem. Phi Beta Kappa. Editor: A Baptist Bibliography, 25 vols., 1947-76. Contbr. articles to periodicals. Home: 3215 Brookshire Dr Florissant MO 63033

STAUDENMAIER, WILBERT NORBERT VINCENT, priest, retirement home administrator, Roman Catholic Church; b. Wathena, Kans., Mar. 7, 1911; s. Anton and Clara (Kaelin) S. Ed. Kenrick Sem., 1940-43. Ordained priest Roman Cath. Ch., 1943. Pastor Sacred Heart of Jesus Cath. Ch., Appleton, Wis., 1946—; founder, pres. Keen Ager Corp., low cost retirement housing, Appleton, 1976—. Address: Sacred Heart of Jesus Ch 222 E Fremont St Appleton WI 54915

STAUDER, PAUL WENCESLAUS, priest, TV film producer, Roman Catholic Church; b. Belleville, Ill., Apr. 12, 1921; s. Raymond L. and Elizabeth (Bachinger) S.; student St. Henry's Prep. Sem., 1936-42; B.A., St. Mary of the Lake Sem., Mundelein, Ill., 1948; grad. Famous Photographers Sch., Westport, Conn., 1970. Ordained priest Roman Catholic Ch., 1948; pastor Ill. chs., 1948-60, 63-71; chaplain St. Clement's Hosp., Red Bud, Ill., 1960-62, St. Mary's Hosp., East St. Louis, Ill., 1962-63; adminstr. St. Henry's Ch., East St. Louis, 1972-75, pastor, 1975—; archivist, photographer Diocese of Belleville, 1971—; chaplain Belleville Area Cath. Boy Scouts Am., 1950-54, mem. exec. bd. Kaskaskia Council, 1950-54; photographer, editor; narrator, dir., producer Tele-Vue 1 Prodns., 1970—; producer Cath. sound films. Mem. Nat. Acad. TV Arts and Scis., AFTRA, Nat. Free Lance Photographers Am. Producer: Three Crosses on the Mohawk, 1972; The Northwest Legacy, 1973; You Are a Priest Forever, 1976. Home: 525 E Broadway Ave East St Louis IL 62201

STAUFFACHER, DAN GLEN, minister, United Church of Christ; b. Corona, Calif., Aug. 17, 1948; s. Robert Henry and Ida Merle (Lee) S.; m. Pamela A. Imwie, June 17, 1972; children: David, Paul. B.A. LaVerne Coll., 1970; M.Div., Bethany Theol. Sem., 1974. Ordained to ministry United Ch. of Christ, 1974. Cons. for planning United Ch. of Christ, Chgo., 1972—; cons. for faith devel., 1972—; pastor Burr Ridge United Ch. of Christ, Ill., 1979—; teaching pastor Bethany Theol. Sem., 1982—; chmn. Bd. Services United Ch. of Christ, Chgo., 1975-83, coordinator Conf. on Small Chs., 1984; host radio show Religion on the Line, WIND, 1979, TV show Different Drummer CBS, 1979—; lectr. developmental disabilities Chgo. Police Acad., part-time 1976-80. Coordinator, Greater Hinsdale Area Conf. on Suicide Prevention, 1982; coordinator, lectr. Suicide Prevention DuPage county, 1982—; v.p. DuPage County Child Welfare Consortium, 1975-79; chmn. personnel com. Downers Grove Youth Commn. Named Outstanding Youth Worker of Yr., DuPage County Child Welfare Consortium, 1979, Citizens of Yr., Burr Ridge Police, 1980. Mem. Suburban Health Systems Planning Bd., 1981—. Mem. Profl. Assn. Clergy, Hinsdale Ministerial Assn. (chmn. 1980-81), Ch. Fedn. Greater Chgo. (bd. dirs. 1975—). Democrat. Home: 425 S Quincy St Hinsdale IL 60521 Office: Burr Ridge United Ch Christ 15 W 100 Plainfield Rd Burr Ridge IL 60521

STAUFFER, S. ANITA, minister, Lutheran Church in America; b. Chgo., Nov. 16, 1947; d. Laverne Mahlon and Betty Marie (Grimes) S. B.A., Gustavus Adolphus Coll., 1969; M.Div., Yale Div. Sch., 1973. Ordained to ministry Luth. Ch. in Am., 1973. Pastor Good Shepherd Luth Ch., Coatesville, Pa., 1973-78; worship editor Luth. Ch. Am., Phila., 1978—; chmn. SE Pa. Synod Worship Com., 1978-79; rep. Luth. World Fedn. Consultations on Worship, 1977-83. Author: The Altar Guild, 1978; Lutherans at Worship, 1978; By Water and The Spirit, 1979; Teaching for Worship, 1981. Contbr. articles to profl. jours., chpts. to books. Recipient Mersick prize in Preaching Yale U., 1973, First Decade award Gustavus Adolphus Coll., 1979. Mem. N. Am.

40211 Office: Louisville Dist Office 971 S Preston St Louisville KY 40203

WALTON, LOUIS EDWARD, minister, Assemblies of God; b. Georgiana, Ala., Apr. 7, 1939; s. D.C. and Mary W.; B.A., N. Central Bible Coll., 1962; m. Gloria Nash, Aug. 23, 1964; children—Lisa, Louis, Timothy, Teresa. Ordained to ministry, 1964; pastor Trinity Tabernacle Assemblies God Ch., Mpls., 1970—. Counsellor young boys and teens; speaker in field. Home: 2206 N Queen Ave Minneapolis MN 55411 Office: 2314 Plymouth Ave N Minneapolis MN 55411

WAMPLER, JEFFREY RANDOLPH, minister, Presbyterian Church in the U.S.A.; b. Roanoke, Va., Aug. 25, 1942; s. Rollin Horace and Ruth Elizabeth (Layman) W.; m. Rebecca Anne Booze, July 16, 1966; children: Paul Christopher, Anne Alphin, Mary Rollin. A.B., Davidson Coll., 1964; M.Div., Princeton Theol. Sem., 1967, D.Ministry, 1975; postgrad., U. Edinburgh, Scotland, 1967-68. Ordained to ministry Presbyterian Ch., 1967. Asst. minister Bethesda Presbyn. Ch., Md., 1968-71; sr. minister First Presbyn. Ch., Concord, N.C., 1971-82, Presbyn. Ch., Westfield, N.J., 1982—; chmn. bd. trustees Presbytery Elizabeth, Plainfield, N.J., 1984—; trustee Princeton Theol. Sem., N.J., 1982—. Contbr. articles to profl. jours. Princeton Theol. Sem. fellow 1967. Mem. Acad. Parish Clergy. Democrat. Avocations: golf; tennis; woodworking. Office: Presbyn Ch Westfield 140 Mountain Ave Westfield NJ 07090

WANTLAND, THOMAS ANTHONY, priest, Roman Catholic Church; b. Kokomo, Ind., Aug. 29, 1940; s. Ivan Oswald and Irene Marie (Heritier) W.; B.A., Resurrection Coll., Kitchener, Ont., Can., 1963; postgrad. in theology St. John's Provincial Sem., Plymouth, Mich., 1963-67, M.Div., 1982. Ordained priest, 1967; asso. pastor St. Joseph-St. Patrick's Ch., Hancock, Mich., 1967-68, Am. Martyr's Ch., Kingsford, Mich., 1968-69, St. Sebastian's Ch., Bessemer, Mich., 1969-74; pastor St. Albert the Great Univ. Parish, Houghton, Mich., 1974-84; pastor St. Joseph's Ch., Sault Sainte Marie, Mich., 1984—; mem. priests' senate Diocese of Marquette, 1981-82, presbyteral council, 1984—; mem. Gogebic Range Clergy Council, Ironwood, Mich., 1969-74, pres., 1972-74; mem. Coop. Christian Campus Ministry, Mich. Tech. U., Houghton, 1974-84; mem. Copper Country Clergy Council, Houghton, 1974-84. Moderator, Bessemer (Mich.) Youth Council, 1969-74; mem. Gogebic County Assn. for Retarded Children, Inc., Ironwood, Mich., 1972-75; pres. Upper Great Lakes Human and Econ. Devel. Assn., Inc., Bessemer, 1972-74; mem. Bessemer Community Schs. Advisory Bd., 1974; mem. Gogebic Range Jaycees, Ironwood, 1970-74, internal v.p., 1974; chmn. Gogebic County Physician Recruitment Com., Ironwood, 1973-74; mem. Copper County Jaycees, Hancock, Mich., 1974-77, internal v.p., 1975-76, sec., 1976-77. Club: Elks. Contbr. articles to religious mags. and jours. Home and Office: St Joseph's Ch 606 E 4th Ave Sault Sainte Marie MI 49783

WANTLAND, WILLIAM CHARLES, priest, lawyer, Episcopal Church; b. Edmond, Okla., Apr. 14, 1934; s. William Lindsay and Edna Louise (Yost) W.; B.A. in History, Hawaii U., 1957; J.D., Oklahoma City U., 1964; D.Religion, Geneva-St. Alban's Theol. Coll., 1976; m. Mary Jo Watson, June 10, 1954; children: Timothy Doyal, Malia Katherine, Thomas Ken. Ordained deacon, 1963, priest, 1970; vicar St. Mark's Episc. Ch., Seminole, Okla., 1963-77, St. Paul's Episc. Ch., Holdenville, Okla., 1974-77; rector St. John's Episc. Ch., Oklahoma City, 1977—; prof. Christian ethics Bishop's Sch. Theol., Oklahoma City, 1972-74. Regional rural dean S.E. Okla., 1972-77; pres. standing com. Diocese Okla., 1975-76; cons. Nat. Com. Indian Work Episc. Ch.; exec. com. Am. Ch. Union, 1973-76; rep. 7th province, nat. council Coalition for Apostolic Ministry; pres. Clergy Assn. Diocese Okla., 1973-74. Prof. probate law Okla. U., Norman, 1970—; cons. Am. Indian policy rev. commn. U.S. Senate; judge Seminole Municipal Ct., 1970-77; atty. gen. Seminole Nation Okla., 1969-72, 1975-77. Recipient Best Ct. in U.S.A. award Am. Bar Assn., 1972, Outstanding Contbn. award Okla. Supreme Ct., 1975. Mem. Okla. Indian Rights Assn. (pres. 1975-76), Okla., Am. bar assns., Am. Judges Assn. Contbr. articles Vigor Episc. Mag., Am. Ch. News, Am. Indian Law Rev. Office: 5201 N Brookline Oklahoma City OK 73112

WARD, DONALD B., minister, National Association of Congregational Christian Churches; b. Boston, June 15, 1919; s. Donald Butler and Emma Alta (Lyons) W.; m. Vera Bantz, June 10, 1944; children: Vera Margaret, Laura Ann, Christopher Donald. B.S., Northwestern U., 1942; M.Div., U. Chgo., 1959; D.D., Lakeland Coll., 1964, Yankton Coll., 1982; LL.D., Morningside Coll., 1964. Ordained to ministry Congl. Christian Chs., 1959. Minister, 1st Congl. Ch., Ravenswood, Chgo., 1958-60, Kirk of Bonnie Brae, Denver, 1960-62; pres. Yankton Coll., S.D., 1962-70; sr. minister 1st Congl. Ch., Evanston, Ill., 1970-79, Los Angeles, 1980—; v.p. Alaska Pacific Univ., Anchorage, 1979-80; asso. trustee Sch. Theology, Claremont, Calif., 1981—. Author: Pray Then Like This, 1984. Contbr. articles Look Mag. Composer coll. hymn, Alaska Pacific U. Alma Mater. Named Man of Yr., 1st Congl. Ch., Evanston, 1956; recipient Disting. Alumni award Omega Sigma Chi, 1983; Order of Constantine, Sigma Chi, 1972. Mem. Mayflower Soc., Barons of Magna Charta, Acad. Magical Arts. Home: 312 S Westmoreland Ave Los Angeles CA 90020 Office: 540 S Commonwealth Ave Los Angeles CA 90020

WARD, ERNESTINE MIRIAM, minister, A.M.E. Ch.; b. Charleston, S.C., July 6, 1920; d. Solomon K. and Clara (Weston) Dailey; student Adelphi U., 1972-75; m. Joseph Ward, Dec. 16, 1936; children—Joseph, Pricilla. Ordained to ministry, 1967; pastor A.M.E. Ch., Jamaica, N.Y., 1967—. Asst. rec. sec. N.Y. Conf. A.M.E. Ch., 1969-74; counselor Family Ct., Jamaica, 1970-76; chaplain Key Woman of Am., 1973-74; dir. Dept. Evangelism, N.Y. Annual Conf., 1964-76. Mem. Community Assn. for Betterment of the People, Queens Fedn. A.M.E. Ministerial Alliance, Interfaith Clergy. Address: 14719 115 Ave Jamaica NY 11436

WARD, GORDON WILLIAM, JR., minister, Lutheran Church in America; b. Durham, N.C., Sept. 26, 1935; s. Gordon William and Gladys Harriet (Hofmann) W.; m. Lois Ann Hanewald, Sept. 10, 1960; children: Karen Andrea, Kristin Harriet, Paul Andrew. student Davidson Coll., 1953-54; B.A., Lenoir-Rhyne Coll., 1957; M.Div., Luth. Theol. Sem., Phila., 1961; M.A., U. Pa., 1962; M.A., U. Colo., 1974. Ordained to ministry Luth. Ch. in Am., 1962. Pastor Zion Luth. Ch., Spring City, Pa., 1962-65; campus pastor Luth. Student Found. of Colo., U. Colo., Boulder, 1965-74, U. Mich., Ann Arbor, 1975-81; dir. West Central region Nat. Luth. Campus Ministry, Chgo., 1982—; del. World Teaching Conf. World Student Christian Fedn., Strasburg, France, 1960; chmn. univ. com. Boulder Council Chs., 1965-66; bd. senators Nat. Luth. Campus Ministry, 1967-69; nat. adv. Luth. Student Assn. Am., 1968-70, Luth. Student Movement, Chgo., 1983-85; pres. Religious Workers Assn. U. Colo., 1968-69, Assn. Religious Counselors U. Mich., 1980-81; mem. exec. com. Rocky Mountain Synod Luth. Chs. Am., 1973-74; formerly active numerous other orgns. Mem. human relations com. Boulder Valley Schs., 1968-69, adv. com. early childhood edn., 1972-74; pres. Tappan Jr. High Sch. PTO, Ann Arbor, 1976-77. Luth. Brotherhood Fraternal Ins. Co. scholar, 1961; Danforth grantee, 1969. Mem. Luth. Acad. Scholarship, Luth. Campus Ministry Assn. (pres. 1974-75), Nat. Inst. Campus Ministry. Democrat.

WARD, JOHN J. See *Who's Who in America,* 43rd edition.

WARD, TERRY GRANVILLE, minister, So. Bapt. Conv.; b. Duncan, Okla., Jan. 15, 1941; s. Granville O'Dell and Louise (Haines) W.; B.Mus., Okla. Bapt. U., 1963; postgrad. Southwestern Bapt. Theol. Sem., 1964-65, 67-68, Dallas Theol. Sem., 1966-67; m. Karen Louise Raish, Feb. 1, 1964; children—Christopher Brock, Jeffrey Raish. Entered ministry, 1956, licensed, 1966, ordained, 1974; minister music and youth Mountain Grove (Okla.) Bapt. Ch., 1956-57, Trinity Bapt. Ch., Duncan, Okla., 1957-59, Windsor Hill Bapt. Ch., Oklahoma City, 1959-61, Crown Heights Bapt. Ch., Oklahoma City, 1961-63, Trinity Bapt. Ch., Ada, Okla., 1963-64, Lakeside Bapt. Ch., Dallas, 1964-65, MacArthur Blvd. Bapt. Ch., Irving, Tex., Green Acres Bapt. Ch., Tyler, Tex., 1969-74; asso. pastor Allandale Bapt. Ch., Austin, Tex., 1974—. Mem. youth com. Austin Bapt. Assn., 1974—, mem. Bapt. Student Union com., 1974—. Mem. Austin Civic Chorus. Mem. Christian Concered Citizens. Author: The Quiet Time, 1966; Guidelines for Disciples, 1970. Home: 5817 Westmont St Austin TX 78731 Office: 2615 Allandale Rd Austin TX 78756

WARDEN, JAMES DAVID, minister, Southern Baptist Convention; retail store training specialist; b. San Antonio, Feb. 1, 1951; s. Claude Leroy and Blondell (Bracewell) W.; m. Sara Lane Goldbaum, June 1, 1971; children: James, Claude, Jarrod. B.A., Wayland U., 1981. Ordained to ministry Seth Ward Baptist Ch., 1981. Minister of youth Seth Ward Bapt. Ch., Plainview, Tex., 1978-80; pastor First Bapt. Ch., Roaring Springs, Tex., 1980-82, Southside Bapt. Ch., San Antonio, 1982-83, Living Way Bapt. Ch., San Antonio, 1983—; dist. tng. specialist Nat. Convenience Stores, San Antonio, 1983—; counselor Billy Graham Evang. Assn., San Antonio, 1968. Contbr. articles to religious publs. Alderman City of Roaring Springs, Tex., 1982—. Served in USN, 1973-82. Decorated Nat. Def. medal USN, 1973, Navy Unit Commendation, Navy Unit Meritorious Commendation, 1975. Lodge: Lions (sec.-treas. 1981-82). Home: 4032 E Southcross Apt 4202 San Antonio TX 78222 Office: National Convenience Stores 5050 SW Military Dr San Antonio TX

WARDLE, JOHN LOUIS, minister, So. Bapt. Conv.; b. Alton, Ill., Feb. 4, 1932; s. John Daniel Bauser and Lula Bernice (Norris) Bauser Wardle; B.A., William Carey Coll., 1966; student New Orleans Bapt. Theol. Sem., 1966-68; M.Div., Luther Rice Sem.; m. Ruby Marie Parker, Feb. 21, 1950; children—Rebecca Marie, Helen Christine, John Louis. Ordained to ministry, 1959; pastor Paradise Bapt. Ch., Jersyville, Ill., 1960-62, Beacon Bapt. Ch., Hattiesburg, Miss., 1962-66, 1st Bapt. Ch., Pearlington, Miss., 1966-71, 1st Bapt. Ch., Palm City, Fla., 1971—; has held crusades throughout Am. and Asia. Chmn. evang. Indian River Bapt. Assn., 1972-73; pres. Ministerial Assn. William Carey Coll., 1962-63; founder, pres. Palm City Bapt. Acad., 1974—; chaplain Martin County (Fla.) Sheriff's Dept., 1973—. Named Citizen of Yr., Civitan Club Martin County, Fla., 1975. Author: From Gangland to Glory. Home: PO Box 672 W 34th St Palm City FL 33490 Office: Box 696 W 34th St Palm City FL 33490

WARE, JAMES HAMILTON, religious educator, minister, Southern Baptist Convention; b. Shanghai, China, June 27, 1932 (parents Am. citizens); s. James Hamilton and Mary Bibb (Long) W.; m. Emma Holmes, July 12, 1953. B.A., Baylor U., 1954, M.A., 1959; B.D., So. Bapt. Theol. Sem., 1957; Ph.D., Duke U., 1964. Ordained to ministry So. Bapt. Conv., 1957. Asst. prof. religion Bridgewater Coll., Va., 1962-64; asst. prof. philosophy and religion Clemson U., S.C., 1964-65; prof. philosophy U. Central Ark., Conway, 1965-70; prof. philosophy and religion Austin Coll., Sherman, Tex., 1970—. Author: Chinese Religion, 1972; Korean Religion, 1974; Not With Words of Wisdom, 1981. Mem. Social Services Bd. City of Sherman, 1974-78. Fund for Study of World Great Religions fellow, 1969. Mem. Am. Acad. Religion (regional v.p.), Assn. Asian Studies (SW Conf. pres. 1978-79, bd. dirs. 1971-84). Office: Box 1549 Austin Coll Sherman TX 75090

WARE, JOSEPH LOUIS, minister, So. Bapt. Conv.; b. Detroit, Nov. 28, 1938; s. Benjamin and Beulah (Blandchard) W.; B.Th., Community Sch. Bible, 1967; M.Th., Toledo Bible Coll., 1969; B.S., Wayne State U., 1977; m. Sandra Jean Anderson, Aug. 17, 1961; children—Latrice, Joseph, David, Constance, Sharon, Michele. Ordained to ministry, 1965; pastor Northwestern Community Bapt. Ch., Detroit, 1974—. Mem. Concerned Citizen's Council, Detroit, 1974—. Named Outstanding Citizen, City of Detroit, 1974. Mem. Greater Detroit Assn. Office: 14700 Puritan St Detroit MI 48227

WARE, REBECCA INEZ, minister of music, So. Baptist Conv.; b. Mobile, Mar. 13, 1952; d. Claude Oliver and Lee Aarus (Pierce) Ware; Mus.B., William Carey Coll., Hattiesburg, Miss., 1974; m. Roderick Stephen Fox, Sept. 10, 1977. Dir. children's choirs First Bapt. Ch., Hattiesburg, 1972-73; pianist, dir. children's choir Shawdowlawn Bapt. Ch., Mobile, 1973-74, minister music, 1974—, also Sunday sch. tchr. Mem. piano faculty William Carey Coll., 1976—. Mem. Music Educators Nat. Conf., Alpha Chi, Delta Omicron. Home: 202 Edington Dr Mobile AL 36607 Office: Music Dept William Carey Coll Hattiesburg MS 39401

WARFORD, WILLIAM SMITH, chaplain, church official, American Baptist Church; b. Springfield, Mo., May 13, 1921; s. Harold LeRoy and Pearl Julia (Bouldin) W.; student Carthage Coll.; B.S. in Edn., Western Ill. U., 1956; postgrad. Quincy (Ill.) Coll., Augustana Sem.; m. Twila Darlene Gooding, Feb. 28, 1954; 1 son, Robin Ray. Ordained to ministry Am. Bapt. Ch., 1961; Protestant chaplain Ill. Vets. Home, Quincy, Ill., 1962—. Pres. Quincy Council of Chs., 1972-74. Mem. Quincy Pub. Works Commn., 1971-78, chmn., 1978; sec. Ill. State Tollway Adv. Commn., 1961-65; founder, pres. western Ill. Council on Alcoholism, 1968-75; chmn. Water Commn., Quincy, 1968-78; vice chmn. West Central Ill. Council on Aging, 1974, pres., 1975-76; mem. staff Am. Theatre, St. Louis, 1948-53. Bd. dirs. ARC, 1970-83; bd. dirs. Salvation Army, 1972—, v.p., 1975, chmn., 1976-80; mem. west-central Mental Health Authority Bd., Quincy, 1973; mem. Ill. State Council on Aging, 1976—; bd. dirs. Hospice of Quincy and Adams Counties, 1983—; del. White House Conf. Aging, 1981. Recipient Best Actor award Quincy Community Little Theatre, 1972, Disting. Service award Am. Heart Assn., 1965, Disting. Alumni award Western Ill. U., 1975. Mem. Ill. (life) Hist. Soc., Kans. Hist. Soc. (life), Quincy Ministerial Assn. (pres. 1969-73 award 1973), Ill. Assn. Chaplains (treas. 1973-75), Ill. Protestant Chaplains Assn. (vice chmn. 1968-70), Ill. State Assn. Chaplains (pres. 1978-82, award 1982), Ill. Assn. Agys. Aging (v.p. 1974-76). Contbr. hist. articles to scholarly jours. Home: 2140 Hampshire St Quincy IL 62301 Office: Protestant Chaplains Office Illinois Veteran's Home Quincy IL 62301

WARMAN, JOHN BOYLE, retired bishop, United Methodist Church; b. Uniontown, Pa., Apr. 9, 1915; s. Robert Densmore and Minnie Lillian (Conaway) W.; A.B., Western Md. Coll., 1937; B.D., Andover Newton Theol. Sch., 1941; Ed.M., U. Pitts., 1951; D.D., Allegheny Coll., 1958, Western Md. Coll., 1962, Lebanon Valley Coll., 1974; m. Annie Owings Sansbury, June 15, 1939; children: John Sansbury, Irene (Mrs. Vernard Taulbee, Jr.), Oden Robert. Ordained to ministry, 1941. Pastor 1st Meth. Ch., Butler, Pa., 1950-58, 1st Meth. Ch., Pitts., 1958-62, Baldwin Community Ch., Pitts., 1965-72; bishop Harrisburg (Pa.) area United Meth. Ch., 1972-84; supt. Pitts. dist. Meth. Ch., 1962-65. Mem. Pitts. Human Relations Commn., 1962-65. Trustee Mt. Union Coll., 1962-65, Lebanon Valley Coll., 1974—, Dickinson Coll., 1974—. Served with USNR, 1945-46. Mem. Tau Kappa Alpha. Address: 262 Sansbury Rd Friendship MD 20758

WARMSLEY, ERNESTINE LAURA, church official, Church of God in Christ; b. St. Louis, Feb. 20, 1930; d. Ernest and Laura (Williams) Walker; student Mo. U., 1963, 70; B.A. in Psychology and Sociology, So. Ill. U., 1971; postgrad. Fla. State Christian Coll., 1972, Webster U.; m. Emitt Joseph Warmsely, Oct. 15, 1949 (dec. Jan. 1965); 1 son, Emit Joseph (dec.). Tchr., personal worker Home and Fgn. and Vol. Mission, Ch. of God in Christ, St. Louis, 1966—; state pres. Young Women Christian Counsel, Ch. of God in Christ, St. Louis, 1971—; organizer Community Outreach and Bible Study Project, St. Louis, 1974—; financial sec. Charles H. Mason Scholarship Found. Chs. of God in Christ, St. Louis, 1970—; mem. internat. dept. Evangelism Ch. of God in Christ; state dir. evangelism seminar Jurisdiction Eastern Mo. Chs. of God in Christ; state pres. Evangelistic Dept. Adv. Bd. Social worker St. Louis div. Children's Services, 1973—; employment and tng. rep. City of St. Louis. Bd. dirs. Homer G. Phillips Hosp. Aux., St. Louis, 1969—. Mem. Alpha Psi Omega. Editor: Periodic Mag., 1967-69. Home and Office: 1533 Gieseking Lane St Louis MO 63147

WARNECK, WALTER JOHN, JR., pastoral psychotherapist, Lutheran Church-Missouri Synod, marital and family therapist; b. St. Louis, Aug. 22, 1945; s. Walter John and Selma M. (Meier) W.; m. Janet E. Boscoe, May 31, 1969; children: Walter J. III and Stephen C. (twins). A.A. cum laude, Concordia Luth. Jr. Coll., 1965; B.A. cum laude, Concordia Sr. Coll., 1967; M.Div., Concordia Sem., 1971; Th.M., Princeton Theol. Sem., 1972, D.Min., 1985. Cert. specialized pastoral ministries Luth. Council U.S.A.; cert. marriage and family therapist, Conn. Ordained to ministry Lutheran Ch., 1971. Clin. supr. advanced pastoral counseling practicum Trinity Counseling Service, Princeton, N.J., 1971-72; clin. supr. clin. certification program Episcopal Social Service, Diocese of Conn., 1975; supr. N.E. Counseling Ctr., Found. for Religion and Mental Health, Carmel, N.Y., 1975-76; clin. intern family psychotherapy dept. psychiatry family treatment unit Bristol Hosp., Conn., 1975-77; dir. Project People Community Ctr., St. Louis, 1970-71; asst. minister Luth. Ch. of the Messiah, Princeton, N.J., 1971-72; minister Immanual Luth. Ch., Danbury, Conn., 1972-75; pastoral counselor N.E. Counseling Ctr., Found. for Religion and Mental Health, Carmel, N.Y., 1975-76; asst. pastor spl. ministries Trinity Luth. Ch., New Milford, Conn., 1978-80; adj. minister for counseling First Congl. Ch., Danbury, Conn., 1979-80; adj. faculty mem., clin. supr. Found. for Religion and Mental Health, 1979-80; clin. cons. patient, family and staff dynamics New Milford Nursing Home, Conn., 1979-80; mem. faculty Westchester Inst. for Tng. in Counseling and Psychotherapy, 1981-82; certified staff assoc., therapist Episcopal Social Service, Diocese of Conn., 1975-82; founding dir. Found. for Pastoral Care, Ridgefield, Conn., 1984—; founding pres., exec. dir. New Eng. Counseling Ltd., Ridgefield, Danbury, Bethel, Conn., 1975—. Pub., editor Pastoral Care and Clin. Practice, 1984—. Bd. dirs. Danbury YMCA, Conn., 1977-78; profl. dir. support group program, support group leader Am. Cancer Soc., Danbury, Conn., 1977—, bd. dirs., 1978—, mem. psycho-social adv. com., profl. screening com. support group leaders, Conn. div., 1979-85, tng. leader, supr. clin. tng. support group leaders, 1979—, 2d v.p., chmn. nominating com. Danbury unit, 1984—, vol. of yr. award, 1980-81. Recipient Youth Leadership Fellowship award Am. Youth Found., 1962, Dr. Meyer Hon. Scholarship, 1966. Mem. Am. Assn. Marriage and Family Therapy, Am. Assn. Pastoral Counselors, Assn. Clin. Pastoral Edn., Inc., Am. Assn. Sex Educators, Counselors and Therapists. Office: New Eng Counseling Ltd Exec Offices 339 Florida Hill Rd Ridgefield CT 06877

WARNER, HAROLD WALTON, JR., minister, Southern Baptist Convention; b. Hatboro, Pa., Nov. 15, 1929; s. Harold Walton and Marian (Hollowell) W.; m. Eleanor Mae Washington, Nov. 19, 1949; children: Philip Harold, John Keith. Student Phila. Sch. Bible, 1948, Ref. Episcopal Sem., Phila., 1949-51; D.D., Trinity Coll., Dunedin, Fla., 1967. Ordained to ministry So. Bapt. Conv., 1950. Pastor, chs., Wellsboro, Pa., 1952-55; evangelist, N. Am., W. I., Eng., 1955-60, 65-70; pastor Palm Ave Bapt. Ch., Tampa, 1960-65, West End Bapt. Ch., Mobile, Ala., 1970-75, 1st Bapt. Ch. Citrus Park, Tampa, 1980—; assoc. dir. Bay Islands Bapt. Bible Inst., Honduras, 1982—. Exec. bd. Tyoga Youth Ranch, Wellsboro, Pa., 1968-75. Author: When the World's On Fire, 1965; Dear Hunting, 1968; The American Home and Its Needs, 1968. Republican. Home: 14308 Ravenwood Ln Tampa FL 33618 Office: 1st Bapt Ch Citrus Park 7705 Gunn Hwy Tampa FL 33625

WARNER, MICHAEL DENNIS, minister, Lutheran Church-Missouri Synod; b. Mason City, Iowa, June 4, 1945; s. Gerald Edris and Catherine (Greene) W.; m. Dianne Carol Marks, June 3, 1967; children: Michelle, Jonathan, Daniel. B.A., Concordia Coll., Minn., 1967; B.D., Concordia Theol. Sem., Ill., 1971, M.Div., 1973; Ph.D., Purdue U., 1981. Ordained to ministry Lutheran Ch., 1972. Pastor, St. John Luth. Ch., Buffalo, Minn., 1972-76; prof. Concordia Theol. Sem., Fort Wayne, Ind., 1976-83; family life pastor Concordia Evang. Luth. Ch., Fort Wayne, 1982-83; sr. pastor Grace Evang. Luth. Ch., Waterloo, Iowa, 1983—; bd. dirs. Luth. Family Services, Iowa, 1984—; chmn. adult edn. task force Luth. Ch., Iowa Dist. East, 1984—; mem. adult edn. task force family life com. Luth. Ch., Ind. Dist., 1982-83. Contbr. articles to profl. jours. Grantee Aid Assn. Lutherans, 1979-81, Luth. Brotherhood Ins., 1983. Mem. Minn. Citizens Concerned for Life, Am. Assn. Marriage and Family Therapy (clin. mem.), Assn. Clin. Pastoral Edn. (clin. mem.), Nat. Council Family Relations, Iowa Assn. Marriage and Family Therapy (clin. mem.), Iowa Council on Family Relations. Republican. Home: 1405 Prospect Blvd Waterloo IA 50701 Office: Grace Evang Luth Ch W 7th & Allen St Waterloo IA 50702

WARNER, RICHARD VICTOR, priest, Roman Catholic Church; b. Cleve., June 10, 1939; s. Victor Henry and Vivian Rose (Gallagher) W. A.B., U. Notre Dame, 1962; S.T.B., Universidad Catolica, Santiago, Chile, 1964, S.T.L., 1966. Ordained to ministry, 1966. Tchr., St. George's Coll., Santiago, 1966-73; provincial treas. Congregation of Holy Cross, Ind. Province, South Bend, 1973-79, provincial superior, 1979—; trustee U. Notre Dame, Ind., 1979—; cons. ad hoc com. on war and peace Nat. Conf. Cath. Bishops, 1981-83. Regent, U. Portland, 1979—. Address: 1304 E Jefferson Blvd South Bend IN 46617

WARNER, WAYNE MARSHALL, minister, Church of God (Anderson, Indiana); b. South Haven, Mich., May 24, 1927; s. Lyle Wesley and Ruthe Adelia (Knapp) W.; m. Tommie Beatrice Leora Stiles, Mar. 20, 1926; children: Meredith Lyn, Donald Scott. B.Th., Warner Pacific Coll., 1951; M.R.E., Southwestern Bapt. Theol. Sem., Ft. Worth, 1969. Ordained to ministry Ch. of God (Anderson, Ind.), 1952. Pastor, Ridglea Ch. of God, Ft. Worth, Tex., 1972-70, First Ch. of God, Vallejo, Calif., 1972-73, Cap Ave Ch. of God, Battle Creek, Mich., 1973-77, First Ch. of God, Three Rivers, Mich., 1979—; chmn. planning and devel., also bd. dirs. Warner Meml. Conf. and Retreat Ctr., 1983—. Lt. Wells Fargo Guard, 1978—. Contbr. articles to profl. jours. Served with USAF, 1946-47. Home: 43 New England Ave Battle Creek MI 49017 Office: First Church of God 1111 S Man St Three Rivers MI 49093

WARREN, CHARLES LEROY, minister, Bapt. Missionary Assn. Am.; b. Hamilton, Mont., Aug. 4, 1930; s. Charles Anderson and Emma Fay (Bennett) W.; grad. Bible langs. Calif. Missionary Bapt. Inst. and Sem., 1965; m. Shirley Dean Russell, Feb. 2, 1957; children—Michael Austin, Cynthia Renee. Ordained to ministry, 1965; pastor Winston (Oreg.) Missionary Bapt. Ch., 1965-76, Madras (Oreg.) Bapt. Ch., 1976—. Pres., Calif. Missionary Bapt. Inst. and Sem. Extension Sch., Winston, Oreg., 1969-76. Home: 602 1st St Madras OR 97741

WARREN, EUGENE LUSTER, lay church worker, educator, administrator, Cumberland Presbyterian Church; b. Cord, Ark., Nov. 27, 1911; s. Oscar Blake and Minnie Florence (Forester) W.; m. Rosa Mae Perryman, Feb. 10, 1945; children: William Edward, Anna Rose Warren Manner. B.S.A., U. Ark., 1950, M.S., 1951; Litt.D., Bethel Coll., 1963. Exec. sec. bd. fin. Cumberland Presbyn. Ch., 1951-81, moderator gen. assembly, 1962-63; elder, Sunday sch. tchr. and supt., deacon, Memphis, 1952-84; elder, tchr., trustee Cumberland Presbyn. Ch., Memphis Presbytery, 1954-84; elder, tchr. Cumberland Presbyn. Ch., Germantown, Tenn., 1984—. Author pamphlets, articles, tracts. Mem. Germantown Cultural Arts Com., Orange Mound Day Care Nursery, Memphis, Mid-South Peace and Justice Bd. Served to chief warrant officer U.S. Army, 1942-46. Decorated Commendation medal. Spl. Commendations U.S. Forces in Can. Mem. Future Farmers Am. (nat. v.p.), Stray Future Farmer (nat. v.p.). Democrat. Lodge: Kiwanis (Germantown) (past (past pres.) (lt. gov. West Tenn.). Home: 7505 Parker Circle Germantown TN 38138

WARREN, RONALD BARRY, pastor, American Lutheran Church; b. Sandusky, Ohio, Nov. 22, 1944; s. Kenneth Henry and Evelyn Lucille (Hirt) W.; m. Neva Arlene Klepzig, June 8, 1968; children: Heather Lynn, Jeremy Todd. B.A., Capital U., 1966; M.Div., Trinity Luth. Sem., 1970; D.Ministry, Luth. Sch. Theology at Chgo., 1983. Ordained to ministry Am. Luth. Ch., 1970. Pastor, St. John Luth. Ch., Avoca, Wis., 1970-73, House of Prayer Luth. Ch., Franklin, Wis., 1976-83; assoc. pastor 1st Luth. Ch., Janesville, Wis., 1973-76; sr. pastor Ascension Luth. Ch., Memphis, 1983—; pres. Christian Ednl. Media, Inc., Burnsville, Minn., 1980-83; pres. Memphis State U. Cluster Pastors, 1983—; vice chmn. S. Wis. dist. Missions Com., 1983; bd. dirs. Wis. Interfaith Com. on Family, Inc., 1979-83, Chs. and Synagogues Serving People, Memphis, 1984. Mem. editorial bd. Seasons: The Interfaith Family Jour., 1980-83. Firefighter and chaplain Fire Dept., Franklin, Wis., 1976-83. Mem. Nat. Eagle Scout Assn. Club: Crosscut (Memphis). Home: 3117 Flint Dr Memphis TN 38115 Office: Ascension Luth Ch 961 Getwell Rd Memphis TN 38111

WARSHAW, THAYER SOLOMON, university official; b. Methuen, Mass., May 30, 1915; s. Max Moses and Rae (Brown) W.; m. Bernice Kepner, July 10, 1938; children: Elinor Warshaw Davidson, Shirley Warshaw Zarin, Margaret Warshaw Brill. B.A. cum laude in Philosophy, Harvard U., 1937, M.A. in Teaching, 1961. Assoc. dir. Ind. U. Inst. on Teaching the Bible in Secondary Schs., Bloomington, 1970—; mem. profl. adv. com. Pub. Edn. Religion Studies Ctr., Dayton, Ohio, 1972—. Author: The Bible As/In Literature, 1975; Handbook for Teaching the Bible in Literature Classes, 1979; Religion, Education and the Supreme Court, 1979; Abingdon Glossary of Religious Terms, 1980; A Compact Guide to Bible-Based Beliefs, 1981; (book series) Bible-Related Curriculum Materials: A Bibliography, 1976; Gen. co-editor The Bible in Literature Courses series, 1974—; editor: Reviews of Curricular and Resource Materials, 1981. Contbr. chpts. to books, articles to profl. jours. Chmn. bd. Pub. Welfare, Andover, Mass., 1962-67. Recipient citation of appreciation award Laymen's Nat. Bible Com., 1978, Pub. Service Spl. award Town of Andover, 1984; Warshaw Prize Essay award established by Nat. Council on Religion and Pub. Edn., 1983. Mem. Religious Edn. Assn., Soc. Bibl. Lit., Am. Acad. Religion (religion studies in edn. unit), Phi Delta Kappa. Address: 45 Clark Rd Andover MA 01810

WASH, RICHARD FORD, minister, Southern Baptist Convention; b. Greenwood, S.C., Jan. 28, 1940; s. Thomas Agustus and Louise Francis (Harrison) W.; m. Janice Anita Payne, May 28, 1960; children: Thomas Jonathan, Richard Kevin, Donald Stephen, Daniel Lanford. B.A., Mobile Coll., 1968; Th.M., New Orleans Bapt. Theol. Sem., 1971, D.Ministry, 1978. Ordained to ministry Baptist Ch., 1960. Pastor, Liberty Bapt. Ch., Thomasville, Ala., 1964-67, Axis First Bapt. Ch., Ala., 1967-71, Cedar Hill Bapt. Ch., Brewton, Ala., 1971-75, Crosscreek Bapt. Ch., Pelham, Ala., 1975—; moderator Shelby Bapt. Assn., Ala., 1982-84; chmn. Bapt. Assn. Council, Birmingham, Ala., 1984; mem. bd. ministerial aid Ala. Bapt. State Conv., 1983—. Author: Devotional Guide for Advent, 1982; (pamphlet) The Case for Women Deacons, 1982. Contbr. articles to profl. jours. Avocations: reading; golf; fishing; carpentry. Office: Crosscreek Bapt Ch 600 Crosscreek Trail Pelham AL 35124

WASHA, ROBERT ANTHONY, priest, Roman Catholic Church; clinical psychologist; b. N.Y.C., July 26, 1935; s. Anthony Phillip and Katherine (Roos) W. B.A. in Philosophy, Cathedral Coll., 1957; S.T.B. in Theology, Cath. U. Am., 1961; S.T.M. in Counseling, N.Y. Theol. Sem., 1971; M.A. in Clin. Psychology, Adelphi U., 1974, Ph.D. in Clin. Psychology, 1978. Ordained priest Roman Cath. Ch., 1961. Assoc. pastor Diocese of Bklyn., 1961-70, student priest, 1970-78; priest, psychologist Diocese of Pensacola and Tallahassee, Fla., 1978-81; assoc. pastor Diocese of Orlando, Fla., 1982; priest, psychologist Archdiocese of Miami, Fla., 1983—. Clin. psychologist in pvt. practice, Coral Gables, Fla., 1984—. Author: Dogmatism and Its Relationship to Sexual Attitudes Among Roman Catholic Priests of the Diocese of Brooklyn, 1978. Mem. Am. Psychol. Assn., Southeastern Psychol. Assn., Fla. Psychol. Assn., Dade County Psychol. Assn. Democrat.

WASHBURN, ALPHONSO VICTOR, religious assn. adminstr., So. Bapt. Conv.; b. Cleveland County, N.C., Aug. 4, 1912; s. Alphonso Victor and Mary Edith (Greene) W.; B.A., Wake Forest U., 1933; postgrad. So. Bapt. Theol. Sem., 1934-38, Southwestern Bapt. Theol. Sem., 1955-57; M.A., George Peabody Coll., 1951; Litt.D. (hon.), Georgetown Coll., 1956; m. Ethel Kate Allison, Dec. 16, 1933; children—Ann Allison, James Kent, Mary Janet. Summer field worker N.C. Bapt. Conv., 1929-32; supt. young people's Sunday sch. work Sunday Sch. Bd., So. Bapt. Conv., Nashville, 1933-43, sec. teaching and tng., 1946-57, sec. Sunday sch. dept., 1958—. Mem. coordinating com. inter-agency council So. Bapt. Conv., 1958—; mem. commn. on Christian teaching and tng. Bapt. World Alliance, 1965-75, sec. commn., 1970-75, mem. coordinating com. div. of Evangelism and Edn., 1976—. Mem. Eastern, Southwestern, So. Bapt. religious edn. assns. Author: Young People in the Sunday School, 1955, Outreach for the Unreached, 1960, Administering the Bible Teaching Program, 1969, numerous tracts; editor The Sunday School Builder, 1958-70. Home: 6420 Jocelyn Hollow Rd Nashville TN 37205 Office: 127 9th Ave N Nashville TN 37234

WASHBURN, PAUL ARTHUR, bishop, United Methodist Church; b. Aurora, Ill., Mar. 31, 1911; s. Eliot A. and Lena E. (Buhrnsen) W.; m. Kathryn Fischer, Jan. 12, 1937; children: Mary Marks, Jane Eigenbrodt (dec.), Frederick, John. B.A., North Central Coll., Naperville, Ill., 1936, L.H.D. (hon.), 1970; B.D., Evang. Theol. Sem., Naperville, 1938; D.D. (hon.), Ind. Central U., 1954, Wiley Coll., Tex., 1975, Garrett Theol. Sem., 1983; D.C.L. (hon.), Westmar Coll., Iowa, 1975. Ordained to ministry Meth. Ch., 1938, consecrated bishop, 1968. Pastor chs. in Ill., 1934-64; exec. dir. Evang. United Brethren Commn. on Union, Dayton, Ohio, 1964-68; bishop Minn. area United Meth. Ch., 1968-72, Chgo. area, 1972-80; pres. Commn. Ecumenical Affairs, N.Y.C., 1968-72, Bd. Global Ministries, 1972-76; trustee North Central Coll., 1962—, Garrett-Evang. Sem., 1960—. Author: United Methodist Primer, 1968. Recipient St. George's Gold medal St. George's United Meth. Ch., Phila., 1974;

Outstanding Alumnus award North Central Coll., 1979, Albright-Wesley award, 1980. Democrat. Home: 413 E Parkway Dr Wheaton IL 60187

WASHINGTON, FREDERICK DOUGLAS, Bishop, mem. gen. bd. The Church of God in Christ. Office: The Church of God in Christ 1328 President St Brooklyn NY 11213*

WASHINGTON, JAMES MELVIN, minister, educator Progressive National Baptist Convention; b. Knoxville, Tenn., Apr. 24, 1948; s. James William and Annie Beatrice (Moore) W.; m. Patricia Anne Alexander, Dec. 19, 1970; 1 child, Ayanna Nicole. B.A., U. Tenn., 1970; M.T.S., Harvard U., 1972; M.Phil., Yale U., 1975, Ph.D., 1979. Ordained to ministry Am. Bapt. Chs. U.S.A., 1973. Asst. pastor Mt. Olive Bapt. Ch., Knoxville, 1965-70; pastor Riverview Bapt. Ch., Lenoir City, Tenn., 1967-70; instr. Am. ch. history Yale Div. Sch., New Haven, 1974-76; assoc. prof. ch. history Union Theol. Sem., N.Y.C., 1976—. Mem. gen. bd. Am. Bapt. Chs., Valley Forge, Pa., 1982—, mem. commn. life and theology, 1980—; bd. govs. Nat. Council Chs., N.Y.C., 1984—, mem. commn on faith and order, 1984—. Author: Frustrated Fellowship, 1985. Editor: Afro American Protestant Spirituality, 1985. Cons. religious affairs dept. NAACP, Bklyn., 1982. Woodrow Wilson fellow, 1970-71; Fund Theol. Edn. fellow, 1971-72; Rockefeller doctoral fellow, 1972-74. Fellow Soc. Values in Higher Edn.; mem. Am. Soc. Ch. History, Am. Hist. Assn., Assn. Study Afro Am. Life and History, Am. Acad. Religion (chmn. Afro Am. religious history group 1980—). Democrat. Home: 99 Claremont Ave New York NY 10027 Office: Union Theol Sem 3041 Broadway New York NY 10027

WASSON, ARNOLD DOUGLAS, minister, United Church of Christ; b. Minot, N.D., Aug. 21, 1927; s. Robert Lawrence and Jennie Marguerite (Clarke) W.; m. Mary Jo Peacock, June 2, 1958. A.A., N.D. State Normal and Indsl. Coll., 1946; A.B., Case West Res. U., 1950; B.D., Oberlin Coll., 1953; M.Ed., Auburn U., 1961, M.Div. Vanderbilt Div. Sch., 1968. Acting pres. So. Union Coll., Wadley, Ala., 1955-58; asst. to pres. Snead Coll., Boaz, Ala., 1958-59; pastor 1st Congregational Ch., Rock Springs, Wyo., 1961-68, Colorado Springs, Colo., 1968-72; founding pastor The Church at Woodmoor, Monument, Colo., 1972—; bd. dirs. Christian Ministry in Nat. Parks, N.Y.C., 1965—, San Luis Valley Christian Community Services, Inc., Alamosa, Colo., 1976—, Frontier Boys Village, Larkspur, Colo., 1974-80. Mem. adv. com. State Parks and Recreation Bd., Cheyenne, Wyo., 1965-68; chmn. Sweetwater County Outdoor Recreational Bd., Rock Springs, Wyo., 1964-68; mem. adv. com. Garden of the Gods Com., . City Park and Recreational Dept., City of Colorado Springs, Colo., 1973-74. Ann. Douglas Wasson award for New Club Bldg., Circle K Internat., Indpls., named in his honor, 1981; recipient citation CROP, Ch. World Service, 1984. Mem. Rocky Mountain United Ch. Christ (mission council 1978-82, 1984—), Rock Springs C. of C. (publicity dir. 1965-68). Democrat. Lodge: Kiwanis (trustee 1974-78, dist. gov., mem. 4 internat. coms. 1969-74). Home: 1677 Shrider Rd Colorado Springs CO 80918 Office: Ch at Woodmoor 1691 Woodmoor Dr Monument CO 80132

WATERMAN, BYRON OLNEY, minister, American Baptist Churches, also United Church of Christ; b. Johnston, R.I., Nov. 23, 1909; s. Walter Day and Fannie May (Sweet) W.; A.B., Brown U., 1932; B.D., Andover-Newton Theol. Sch., 1934, M.Div., 1973; m. Marion Palmer Eddy, Aug. 24, 1934; children: Byron Eddy, Holden Tozer. Ordained to ministry, 1935; asst. minister First Calvary Bapt. Ch., Lawrence, Mass., 1935-41; minister First Bapt. Ch., Plaistow, N.H., 1941-50, Mt. Vernon Larger Parish, Greene, R.I., 1950—. Vis. chaplain R.I. Med. Center Inst. Mental Health, 1953—. Mem. Griswold (Conn.) Conservation Commn., 1971—; violinist Eastern Conn. Symphony Orch., New London, 1968—, Conn. Coll. Orch., New London, 1967—. Recipient citation R.I. Ho. of Reps., 1975. Mem. Assn. Mental Health Chaplains, Archeol. Soc. Am. Club: Brown Faculty. Home: Route 3 Norwich CT 06360 Office: POB 55 Greene RI 02827

WATERS, BILLY GLENN, minister, Ch. of God (Anderson, Ind.); b. McVeigh, Ky., June 21, 1931; s. William Armstrong and Molly (Shell) W.; B.A., Clarksville Sch. Theology, 1971; postgrad. Anderon Coll., Chgo. Evang. Inst., No. Bapt. Theol. Sem.; m. Carol Jean Stanley, July 28, 1950; children—Victoria Ann, Connie Sue. Ordained to ministry, 1951; asso. pastor, minister youth and music Ch. of God, Chgo., 1950-52; pastor First Ch. of God, Homewood-Flossmoor, Ill., 1952—. Chmn. No. Ill. Assn. of Ch. of God; treas. Ill. Ch. of God; chmn., vice chmn. bd. Ch. Extension, Ill. Ch. of God; chmn. credentials com. Ill. Ch. of God.; chaplain S. Suburban Hosp., Hazel Crest, Ill.; lectr. on charts of revelation and Bibl. trace of the ch. Home: 2841 Birch Rd Homewood IL 60430 Office: 19320 S Kedzie Ave Homewood IL 60430

WATERS, DALE CLINTON, minister, United Meth. Ch.; b. Moundsville, W.Va., Dec. 9, 1935; s. Charles Clyde and Lenna Alberta (Preston) W.; B.A., Anderson-Broaddus Coll., 1965; M.Div., United Theol. Sem., 1968; m. Pauline Elenore Goudy, Aug. 28, 1953; children—Debra, Dale, Christine, Carey. Ordained to ministry, 1968; pastor Belington circuit Evang. United Brethren Ch., 1960-65, Jacksonburg, Ohio, 1965-68, South Chestnut St. Ch., Clarksburg, W.Va., 1968, 4th Ave. Ch., Clarksburg, 1968-75; dist. supt. Lewisburg (W.Va.) Dist., 1975—. Mem. Conf. Bd. Pensions, Conf. Bd. Ordained Ministry, Conf. Bd. Higher Edn. and Ministry; del. Gen. Conf. and Jurisdictional Conf., 1976. Home and Office: 401 E Washington St Lewisburg WV 24901

WATERS, JOHN W., minister, educator, American Baptist Church; b. Atlanta, Feb. 5, 1936; s. Henry and Mary Annie (Randall) W. Cert., U. Geneva, Switzerland, 1962; B.A., Fisk U., 1957; S.T.B., Boston U., 1967, Ph.D., 1970. Ordained to ministry Bapt. Ch., 1967. Minister religious edn. Ebenezer Bapt. Ch., Boston, 1965-67, assoc. minister, 1967-69; minister Myrtle Bapt. Ch., West Newton, Mass., 1969; minister Greater Solid Rock Bapt. Ch., Atlanta, 1981—; prof. Interdenominational Theol. Ctr., Atlanta, 1976—, trustee, 1980—; bd. dirs. Habitat for Humanities, Atlanta, 1984—; chmn. S. Atlanta Joint Urban Ministries, 1983—. Contbr. articles to profl. jours. Mem. S. Atlanta Civic League, 1983, Butler St. YMCA, 1980—, Va.-Highlands Neighborhood Assn., Atlanta, 1977—. Served with U.S. Army, 1960-63. Rockefeller doctoral fellow, 1969; Nat. Fellowship Fund fellow, 1968-70; Fund for Theol. Edn. fellow, 1965-67, others. Mem. AAUP (chpt. pres. 1971-72), Am. Acad. Religion, Soc. Bibl. Lit., Blacks in Bibl. Studies, New Era Missionary Bapt. Conv. Ga. Democrat. Home: 704 Park Dr NE Atlanta GA 3036 Office: Interdenominational Theol Center 671 Beckwith St SW Atlanta GA 30314

WATERSTON, WILLIAM KING, minister, American Baptist Churches; b. Elizabeth, N.J., Feb. 12, 1937; s. John Robert and Sylvia (Eadie) W.; m. Judith Jane Schramm, Aug. 29, 1959 (div. 1983); children: John Scott, Gregory Glenn, Robert Ormsby, Chad Larsen; m. Kathryn Yuhasz Larsen, Dec. 17, 1983. A.B., Bates Coll., 1959; B.Div., Eastern Bapt. Theol. Sem., 1962, M.Div., 1969. Ordained to ministry, 1962. Bus. mgr. Missions Mag., Am. Bapt. Chs., Valley Forge, Pa., 1962-66, Crusader Mag., 1964-66, assoc. dir. radio and TV, 1966-69, dir. electronic media, 1969-74; pastor Chestnut St. Bapt. Ch., Phila., 1971-75, Parker Ford Bapt. Ch., Pa., 1975-81; dir. ch. relations/group homes Bapt. Children's Services, Phila., 1981—; mem. communications faculty Eastern Coll., 1973—, dir. media services, 1978-84; bd. dirs. Broadcasting Commn., N.Y.C. Council Chs., 1966-74; chmn. edn. com. NCC/BFC, N.Y.C., 1967-73; bd. dirs. Phila. Council Chs., broadcasting commn., 1964-70; founder, v.p. Del. Valley Media Ministry, Phila., 1973—. Author/editor: Media Think, 1972. Contbr. articles to profl. jours. Host TV religious talk show: Dialogue, 1971—. CROP walk organizer Ch. World Service, Pottstown, Pa., 1984. Democrat. Home: 528 Wilson St Pottstown PA 19464 Office: Bapt Children's Services 58th and Thomas Ave Philadelphia PA 19143

WATKINS, FORREST HENDERSON, minister, Southern Baptist Convention; b. Fairburn, Ga., July 23, 1922; s. John Condor and Harriet Eunice (Henderson) W.; A.B., Miss. Coll., 1946; M.Th., So. Bapt. Theol. Sem., 1948; m. Marian E. Caldwell, July 3, 1947; children—Faith, Hope. Ordained to ministry, 1945; pastor chs., Miami, Fla., 1952-64, Stuart, Fla., 1964-67; cons. new ch. mem. orientation Sunday Sch. Bd., Nashville, 1967-74; dir. associational evangelism Bapt. Home Mission Bd., Atlanta, 1976—; dir. of missions Hamilton County Bapt. Assn., Chattanooga, 1977—; state dir. evangelism Tenn. Bapt. Conv., Nashville, 1982—. Pres. Greater Miami Ministerial Assn., 1959-60; pastor advisor Bapt. Student Union, Fla. Editor: New Member Training Guide; LEAD: A WIN Guide. Office: Tenn Bapt Conv Brentwood TN 37027

WATKINS, H. WAYNE, youth minister, Baptist Missionary Association of America; b. Sedalia, Mo., July 21, 1946; s. Harry G. and JoElla (Johnson) W.; m. Jo Ann Wheat, Aug. 25, 1966; 1 child, Jennifer Dyan. Student So. Meth. U., 1964-66. Minister of music First Bapt. Ch., Ferris, Tex., 1970-71, Pleasant Oaks Bapt. Ch., Dallas, 1971-72, Friendship Bapt. Ch., Dallas, 1972-74; youth pastor Bryan St. Bapt. Ch., Lamesa, Tex., 1974-80, Bethel Bapt. Ch., Dallas, 1980—; bd. dirs. Friendship Day Care, Dallas, 1972-74; sec., treas. Dal-Cen-Tex Encampment, Dallas, 1972-74; trustee Nat. Youth Dept., Texarkana, Tex., 1980-82. Mem. Bapt. Music Fellowship (sec., treas. 1979-84). Home: 11315 Dumbarton St Dallas TX 75228 Office: Bethel Bapt Ch 9314 Ferguson Rd Dallas TX 75228

WATKINS, JAMES W(ALTER) II, minister, Southern Baptist Convention; b. Luxora, Ark., May 13, 1948; s. James Walter and Thelma Irene (Gillis) W.; m. Annie Fay Brown, Sept. 15, 1969; children: Jimmy, Daniel, David. A.A. in Religion, So. Bapt. Coll., Walnut Ridge, Ark., 1975; B.A. in Social Work, Ark. State U., 1977; M.Div., Midwestern Bapt. Sem., Kansas City, Mo., 1980; diploma in pastoral care Mid Mo. Mental Health Ctr., Columbia, 1980. Ordained to ministry So. Bapt. Conv., 1974. Pastor Providence Bapt. Ch., Jonesboro, Ark., 1974-75, Valley View Bapt. Ch., Harrisburg, Ark., 1975-77, Armstrong 1st Bapt. Ch., Mo., 1978-80, 1st Bapt. Ch., Jasper, Mo., 1980—; pastoral notes columnist Jasper County News, 1980-83. Alderman City of Armstrong, 1979-80. Served with U.S. Army, 1968-70, Vietnam. Decorated Bronze Star, Purple Heart; Vietnamese Accomodation medal. Mem. Spring River Bapt. Assn. (pastoral support com. 1981-82, associational missions com. 1984), VFW. Democrat. Home: 311 N 2d St Jasper MO 64755 Office: 1st Bapt Ch PO Box 115 Jasper MO 64755

WATKINS, LIZZIE L., minister, Church of God (Anderson, Indiana); b. East Earl, Pa., Dec. 3, 1943; d. Joseph N. and Mabel (Leid) Hoover; m. Curtis D. Watkins, May 24, 1968; children: Olga E., Reginald C. B.A., Wheeling Coll., 1982. Ordained to ministry Ch. of God (Anderson, Ind.), 1982. Assoc. pastor Elm Grove Ch. of God, Wheeling, W.Va., 1981-84, trustee, 1980—, dir. religious edn. program, 1981—; pastor Triadelphia Ch. of God, 1984—; vol. staff chaplain Ohio Valley Med. Ctr., 1980—. Organizer, chmn. Refugee Resettlement Task Force, Wheeling, 1979-84; mem. Clergy and Laity Concerned, Wheeling, 1982-84; 1st congl. dist. coordinator Bread for the World, 1981-84. Mem. Ch. Women United (pres. 1979-82), Ohio Valley Ministerial Assn. of Ch. of God, Instl. Ministries of Greater Wheeling Council of Chs. Democrat. Address: 5 Highland Park Wheeling WV 26003

WATKINS, MAYLON DEVAN, minister, Am. Baptist Association; b. Franklin County, N.C., Aug. 18, 1918; s. Charles Martin and Dora Jane (Curren) W.; Th.D., Bible Bapt. Sem. at Ft. Worth, 1951; postgrad. Louisburg Coll., Wake Forest Coll. Ordained minister, 1939; pastor Charlotte (N.C.) Bapt. Temple, 1940-55, Met. Bapt. Ch., Miami, Fla., 1955-64; nat. sec. Christian Crusade, Tulsa, 1965-67; asso. pastor Village Green Bapt. Ch., Miami, 1970-71; pastor Charlotte Bapt. Temple, 1973—; dir. Am. Bible Crusade, Charlotte, N.C., 1971—, also editor Bible Crusader. Sec., boys program YMCA, Charlotte, 1938-39; supreme councilor Miami Jr. Order United Am. Mechanics, 1962. Recipient Minister of Year award, Christian Crusade, Tulsa, 1964. Address: PO Box 18232 Charlotte NC 28205

WATSON, CLARENCE HERBERT, minister, Southern Baptist Convention, religion educator; b. Yazoo City, Miss., June 4, 1921; s. John Franklin and Bessie (Bridges) W.; m. Frances Hairston; children: Suzanne Watson Beach, Melanie. B.A., Miss. Coll., 1943; B.D., So. Bapt. Theol. Sem., 1947; D.R.E., Southwestern Bapt. Theol. Sem., 1950, Ed.D., 1974. Ordained to ministry Bapt. Ch., 1945. Pastor, Dixon Bapt. Ch., Ky., 1946-47, Morgan Bapt. Ch., Tex., 1948-49; minister edn. and assoc. pastor Calvary Bapt. Ch., Birmingham, Ala., 1949-50; assoc. state Sunday Sch. sec. Fla. Bapt. Conv., Jacksonville, 1950-52; assoc. prof. religion Carson-Newman Coll., Jefferson City, Tenn., 1953—. Contbr. articles to publs. in field. Home: 602 E Ellis St Jefferson City TN 37760 Office: Carson-Newman Coll Jefferson City TN 37760

WATSON, DAVID LOWES, minister, theology educator, religious organization executive; United Methodist Church. b. Newcastle upon Tyne, England, Mar. 31, 1938; came to U.S., 1971; s. Norman Lowes and Annie Ward (Grigs) W.; m. Gayle Turner, Aug. 18, 1961; children: Catherine Dessa, Timothy David. M.A., Oxford U., Eng., 1964; M.Div., Eden Theol. Sem., 1974; Ph.D., Duke U., 1978. Ordained to ministry, United Meth. Ch., 1975. Minister United Meth. Ch., East St. Louis, Ill., 1971-75, Holly Springs, N.C., 1975-78; prof. Perkins Sch. Theology, So. Meth. U., Dallas, 1978-84; dir. evangelism ministries, bd. discipleship, United Meth. Ch., Nashville, 1984—. Author: Accountable Discipleship, 1984; The Early Methodist Class Meeting, 1985. Contbr. articles to profl. jours. Bd. dirs. Lessie Bates Davis Neighborhood House, East St. Louis, 1973-75. Gurney Harris Kearns fellow, 1977. Mem. Assn. Profs. of Missions (sec. 1980-84), Am. Soc. Missiology (bd. publs. 1984—), Acad. for Evangelism (v.p. 1984—), Am. Acad. Religion, Am. Soc. Ch. History. Home: 1768 Hillmont Dr Nashville TN 37215 Office: Bd of Discipleship United Meth Ch PO Box 840 Nashville TN 37202

WATSON, GEORGE GILMAN, minister, United Methodist Ch.; b. Atlanta, Oct. 25, 1946; s. James Ralph and Virginia Paralee (Hubbard) W.; B.A., Oglethorpe U., 1968; M.Div., Emory U., 1971; D.Min., McCormick Sem., 1977; m. Carol E. Lawhorn, Mar. 9, 1968; children—Geoffrey Hamilton Hubbard, George Gilman. Ordained to ministry, 1969; pastor asso., Collins Meml. United Meth. Ch., Atlanta, 1968-70; pastor Bethel United Meth. Ch., Hiram, Ga., 1970-74, 1st United Meth. Ch., Lithonia, Ga., 1974—. Chaplain Paulding County Jail, 1970-74, O'Keefe High Sch. Football team, 1968-70, Paulding County High Sch. Team, 1970-74, Lithonia High Sch. team, 1974, Columbia High Sch. team, 1975-76; mem. bd. evangelism North Ga. Conf., 1972-76, com. on worship, 1972-76. Recipient Am. Bible Soc. award for outstanding pub. reading scriptures, 1971; named Civitan of Year, 1972. Author: Being a United Methodist Means, 1975; From Darkness into Light, 1976. Columnist, Dallas New Era, weekly, 1970-74.

Home: 2770 Davidson Dr Lithonia GA 30058 Office: 3099 Stone Mountain St Lithonia GA 30058

WATSON, JAMES THOMAS, minister, Ch. of God in Christ; b. Harvey, Ill., Mar. 19, 1911; s. Wilson Frank and Ada Leona (Faris) W.; student Chgo. Tchrs. Coll., 1930-31; D.D., Trinity Hall Coll., 1971; m. Lejeun Elizabeth McAllister, Mar. 26, 1936; 1 dau., Joan Angeline (Mrs. Joseph L. Ganns). Ordained to ministry Ch. of God in Christ, 1936; founder, pastor Paradise Temple Ch. of God in Christ, Chgo., 1941—. 2d internat. v.p. youth dept. Ch. of God in Christ, 1966; state pres. youth dept. Ill. Jurisdiction, 1955. Home: 8109 S Wabash Ave Chicago IL 60619 Office: 11445 S Forest Ave Chicago IL 60628

WATSON, JERRY DALE, minister, Nat. Assn. Free Will Baptists; b. Sulphur, Okla., Jan. 11, 1935; s. John William and Vera Maude (Roberts) W.; student C.O.S. Jr. Coll., Pacific Bible Coll., Calif. Christian Coll.; m. Betty Lois Cooley, Dec. 28, 1955; children—Kathy Ann, Gary Don. Ordained to ministry, 1960; pastor Neighborhood Free Will Bapt. Ch., Goshen, Calif., 1961-64, Calwa Ch., Fresno, Calif., 1965-66, Goshen Ch., 1966-74, Visalia (Calif.) First Ch., 1974—. Moderator Center Assn., 1964-65; exec. bd., 1963-74; mission bd., 1970-74; exec. bd. So. Assn., 1974-75. Active Visalia Little League, 1969, Goshen Little League, 1970-72; coach, treas. Visalia Pop Warner Football program, 1972-75; dir. youth camp activities, 1965, 70, tchr., 1975, activities dir., 1976. Contbr. articles to religious jours. Home: 4415 Damsen Ln Visalia CA 93277 Office: 1027 E Tulare Ave Visalia CA 93277

WATSON, MARY MCDONALD, ch. ofcl., So. Bapt. Conv.; b. Greensboro, Fla., Oct. 18, 1917; d. Joshua Gordon and Sarah Lillian (Shepard) McDonald; A.B., Fla. State U., 1944, postgrad., 1956-58; m. Beechem Lamar Watson, Mar. 8, 1945. Music coordinator First Bapt. Ch., Chattahoochee, Fla., 1948—. Curriculum coordinator Chattahoochee Elementary Sch., 1970—. Named Outstanding Music Educator, Sch. Musician's Mag., 1952. Mem. Music Educators Nat. Conf., Fla. Bandmasters Assn. Home: Box 215 Chattahoochee FL 32324 Office: Box 218 Chattahoochee FL 32324

WATSON, WILLIAM HENRY, minister, Ch. God in Christ; b. Arkansas City, Kans., May 17, 1943; s. William Lewis and Juanita Maxine (Morris) W.; A.A., Cowley County (Kans.) Community Jr. Coll., 1963; Mus.B. in Edn., Wichita (Kans.) State U., 1967, postgrad., 1970; m. Arneda Walton, Jan. 29, 1966; children—William Henry, Legena Maxine. Ordained to ministry, 1972; pastor Prayer House Ch. of God in Christ, Lamesa, Tex., 1974—; state pres. denoml. music dept. Ch. God in Christ, N.W. Tex., 1970. Coordinator manpower programs, S. Plains, Tex. Home: 1301 47th St Lubbock TX 79412

WATT, CHARLES MONTGOMERY, JR., lay ch. worker, Episcopalian Ch.; b. Pitts., May 31, 1903; s. Charles Montgomery and Nell (Robinson) W.; B.S., U. Pitts., 1924; m. Lucille Faubel, Aug. 26, 1925 (dec. Sept. 1953); children—Charles Montgomery III, Peter Faubel, Michael Arne; m. 2d, Louise Chester, May 1, 1954; stepchildren—Joan Haworth Young, Kathleen (Mrs. James Gibson). Pres., Christian Council Met. Atlanta, 1971-73, now chmn. past pres.'s adv. council, chmn. policy com.; chmn. long range planning St. Philips Episcopal Cathedral, also former mem. cathedral chpt., past chmn. every mem. canvass. Mem. trust fund com. Episcopal Diocese of Atlanta; mem. exec. bd. Ga. Assn. Pastoral Care. Mem. Ga. State Crime Commn., 1968-72, chmn., 1970-72; chmn. Ga. council Nat. Council on Crime and Delinquency, 1970-72, now vice-chmn. Bd. dirs. Ga. Mental Health Assn., Planned Parenthood Atlanta; adv. bd. League Women Voters; adv. council Ga. State U.; mem. Ga. Gov.'s Commn. Family Planning. Named Layman of Year, Northside Kiwanis, 1972; Christian Council established Charles M. Watt Jr. award for laymen contbg. most to quality of life annually in Atlanta. Mem. Service Corps Ret. Execs. (hon.), Nat. Assn. Accountants (past pres. chpt.), Beta Gamma Sigma. Kiwanian. Address: 3807 Narmore Dr NE Atlanta GA 30319

WATTERS, LORAS JOSEPH, bishop, Roman Catholic Ch.; b. Dubuque, Iowa, Oct. 15, 1915; s. Martin James and Carolyn Regina (Sisler) W.; B.A., Loras Coll., 1937; S.T.B., Gregorianum, Rome, 1940; B.A., Cath. U. Am., S.T.L., 1941, M.A., 1947, Ph.D., 1954. Ordained priest Roman Catholic Ch., 1941, consecrated bishop, 1965; asso. pastor, Cascade, Iowa, 1941-45; prin. Loras Acad., Dubuque, Iowa, 1945-46, chmn. edn. dept., 1954-56; spiritual dir. N.Am. Coll., Rome, 1956-60; dir. Am. Martyrs Retreat House, Cedar Falls, Iowa, 1960-65; aux. bishop of Dubuque, pastor Ch. of Nativity, 1965-69; bishop of Winona, Minn., 1969—; chmn. bishops' com. priestly formation Nat. Conf. Cath. Bishops, 1972-75. Trustee Loras Coll., 1966-72, St. Mary's Coll.; bd. dirs. Xavier Hosp., Dubuque, 1966-68. Address: POB 588 Winona MN 55987

WATTLEY, JAMES COOPER, priest, Episcopal Church; b. New Orleans, Dec. 12, 1925; s. Donald Hubert and Cornelia (Laurans) W.; m. Patricia Margaret Isabel Palmer, Sept. 10, 1950; children: Geoffrey James, Evelyn Anne, Catherine Cornelia. B.E. in Elec. Engring., Tulane U., 1947; B.D., Nashotah House, 1952; M.A., Oxford U., 1968; S.T.M., Gen. Theol. Sem., N.Y.C., 1968. Ordained priest Episcopal Ch., 1953. Vicar, Ch. of Incarnation, Amite, La., 1952-56, St. Alban and St. Thomas Ch., Monroe, La., 1956-61; rector St. Martha's Ch., Bronx, N.Y., 1968-75; exec. sec. CAM/ECM, N.Y.C., 1975-80; canon to ordinary Diocese of L.I., Garden City, N.Y., 1980—; bishop and council Diocese of La., New Orleans, 1958-61; nat. council CAM, N.Y.C., 1975-76; nat. council ECM, Chgo., 1976—; trustee Nashotah House, Wis., 1980—; canon Cathedral of Incarnation, 1983. Mem. Middle Atlantic Convocation of Alumni Assn. Nashtah House (pres. 1978-82). Home: 100 Stratford Ave Garden City NY 11530 Office: Diocese of Long Island 36 Cathedral Ave Garden City NY 11530

WATTS, RALPH SMEDLEY, Seventh-day Adventists; b. Seoul, Korea, Apr. 15, 1934; s. Ralph Shore and Mildred Lucille (Hoopes) W.; came to U.S., 1940; B.A., Union Coll., Lincoln, Nebr., 1956; postgrad. Loma Linda U., 1973, Andrews U., 1974; m. Patricia Ann Ortner, Aug. 17, 1952; children—Edith Delaine, Marcia Renée, Ralph Steven, Lori Ann. Ordained to ministry, 1960; staff evangelist Nebr. Conf., 1956-57; dist. pastor, Chadron, Nebr., 1957-60; pastor, Scottsbluff, Nebr., 1960-61; dir. laymen's activities and religious edn. N.D. Conf., 1961-63; dir. lay activities and religious edn., South Korea, 1963-67; dir. religious edn. Far Eastern div., 1967-69; pres. S.E. Asia Union Seventh-day Adventists, Vietnam, Cambodia, Laos, Thailand, Malaya, Singapore, Sarawak, Sabah Borneo, 1969-75; pres. N.D. Conf. Seventh-day Adventists, Jamestown, 1975—. Chmn. bd. Saigon Adventist, Bangkok Adventist, Penang Adventist and Youngberg Meml. Adventist hosps., S.E. Asia Union Coll. Recipient Presidential Citation, South Korea, 1965. Home: 413 14th Ave NE Jamestown ND 58401 Office: 1315 4th St NE Jamestown ND 58401

WAUGH, JAMES EDWARD, minister, United Methodist Church; b. Columbus, Ohio, Mar. 23, 1949; s. Alva Leroy and Ruth Eileen (Potts) W.; m. Carol Ann Carpenter, June 26, 1971; children: Lisa Renee, Laura Ann. B.A. in History, Otterbein Coll., 1971; M.Div., United Theol. Sem., 1975. Ordained to ministry United Methodist Ch. 1972. Pastor Ansonia-Rossburg Ch., Ohio, 1975-80, New Knoxville-Olive Branch, 1980—; del. N. Central Jurisdictional Conf., Duluth, Minn., 1984. Vice pres. Civic Assn., New Knoxville, 1984; 1st v.p. Auglaize County Mental Health Assn., Ohio, 1984. Mem. Nat. United Meth. Rural Fellowship (treas. 1983—). Democrat. Club: Kiwanis (pres. 1984-85). Home: 106 E Spring St New Knoxville OH 45871 Office: New Knoxville United Methodist Ch 110 S Main St New Knoxville OH 45871

WAUGH, JULIUS DAVID, minister, Southern Baptist Convention; b. Burlington, N.C., Aug. 6, 1949; s. Julius Harvey and Julia May (David) W.; m. Rebecca Lea Van Landingham, June 9, 1973; children: Kristin, Michael, Bethany, John David. B.A., Wake Forest U., 1971; M.Div., So. Bapt. Theol. Sem., 1977; postgrad. Gordon-Conwell Theol. Sem., 1984—. Ordained to ministry Bapt. Ch., 1974. Youth minister Deer Park Bapt. Ch., Louisville, 1972-74; pastor Bapt. Chapel, Montpelier, Vt., 1974-76, Woodstock Bapt. Fellowship, Woodstock, Vt., 1978—; moderator Upper New Eng. Bapt. Assn., 1980-82, Green Mountain Bapt. Assn., Vt., 1982-84; bd. dirs. Bapt. Conv. New Eng., 1982-85. Club: Lions. Office: Woodstock Bapt Fellowship Box 484 Woodstock VT 05091

WAX, SYDNEY L., religious organization executive, Jewish. Nat. pres. Labor Zionist Movement Can., Montreal, Que. Office: Labor Zionist Movement Can 4770 Kent Ave Montreal PQ H3W 1H2 Canada*

WAXMAN, MORDECAI, rabbi. Pres. World Council of Synagogues (Conservative). Office: Temple Israel of Great Neck 108 Old Mill Rd Great Neck NY 11023*

WEAKLAND, REMBERT G., archbishop, Roman Catholic Church; b. Patton, Pa., Apr. 2, 1927; s. Basil and Mary (Kane) W. A.B., St. Vincent Coll., 1948; M.S. in Piano, Juilliard Sch. Music; postgrad. Sch. Music, Columbia U., 1954-56; L.H.D. (hon.), Duquesne U., 1964, Belmont Coll., 1964, Cath. U. Am., 1975, Cardinal Stritch Coll., 1978, St. Joseph's Coll., 1979, Marquette U. Joined Order of Benedictines, 1945, ordained priest Roman Catholic Ch., 1951. Mem. faculty dept. music St. Vincent Coll., 1957-63, chmn., 1961-63, chancellor, chmn. bd. coll., 1963-67; elected co-adjutor archabbot, 1963; abbot primate Benedictine Confedn., 1967-77; consecrated bishop; archbishop of Milw., 1977—. Mem. Ch. Music Assn. Am. (pres. 1964-66), Am. Guild Organists. Office: Archdiocese Milw Chancery Office 345 N 95th St Milwaukee WI 53266

WEAVER, G(AIL) NORMAN, minister, religion educator, Southern Baptist Convention; b. Enon, Mo., Nov. 30, 1921; s. Gail James and Mary Lieurania (Enloe) W.; m. Garnet Elizabeth Newton, Oct. 1, 1942; children: Elizabeth Weaver Kronk, Marcia Sue Weaver Wood, David Norman. A.A. in Edn., Southwest Bapt. Coll., 1941; B.S. in Bus. Edn., SW Mo. State Coll., 1947; M.R.E., Southwestern Bapt. Theol. Sem., 1949, D.R.E., 1960, Ed.D., 1976; Ed.M., U. Mo., 1950; postgrad. Central Bapt. Sem., 1955-56, Hardin Simmons U., 1975-76. Ordained to ministry So. Bapt. Conv., 1959; cert. secondary tchr. Mo. Tchr. Southwest Bapt. Coll., Bolivar, Mo., 1950-57; teaching fellow Southwestern Bapt. Sem., Fort Worth, 1957-59; minister edn. First Bapt. Ch., Lake Worth, Tex., 1957-60; tchr. Hardin-Simmons U., Abilene, Tex., 1960—; interim pastor Elmdale Bapt. Ch., Abilene, 1967-69; edn. cons. Southside Bapt. Ch., Abilene, 1969-72; minister edn. Wylie Bapt. Ch., Abilene, part-time 1972-75; asst. pastor First Bapt. Ch., Clyde, Tex., 1975-79, Immanuel Bapt. Ch., Abilene, 1980-83; aux. missionary tchr. Ghana Bapt. Sem., Abuaka, 1983-84; vol. tchr., leader ch. programs Mo. and Tex., 1944-83; Bapt. Assn. moderator, Sunday Sch. and ch. tng. dir., Mo. and Tex., 1955-70; tchr. So. Bapt. Leadership Tng. Ctrs., N.Mex., N.C., 1964-65. Contbr. articles So. Bapt. Educator, Ch. Tng. Mag., others. Scout master, com. mem. Ozarks council and Chisholm Trail council Boy Scouts Am., 1955—; sec., pres. Community Action Program, Abilene, Tex., 1980-85; sec. adv. council on aging West Central Tex. Council of Govts., Abilene, 1981—; chmn. edn. cluster Abilene Coordinating Council, 1978-80; precinct chmn. Democratic Party Taylor County, Abilene, 1982-84. Served with USAAF, 1942-46. Mem. Southwestern Bapt. Religious Edn. Assn. (v.p. 1962-63), AAUP, Assn. Profs. and Researchers in Religious Edn., So. Bapt. Religious Edn. Assn., Phi Delta Kappa (pres. local chpt. 1973-74). Democrat. Club: Kiwanis (Abilene, Tex.). Home: 2302 Clinton St Abilene TX 79603 Office: Logsdon Sch of Theology Hardin-Simmons Univ PO Box 1136 Abilene TX 79698

WEAVER, KEVIN EARL, minister, United Church of Christ; b. Clinton, Iowa, Apr. 18, 1955; s. Kenneth Earl and Norma Mae (Bailey) W.; m. Debra Sue Crane, Oct. 17, 1980. A.A., Clinton Community Coll., 1975; B.A. with honors, U. Iowa, 1977; M.Div., Eden Theol. Sem., 1980. Ordained to ministry United Ch. Christ, 1980. Chaplain's asst. St. Louis City Hosp., 1977-78; student chaplain Iowa Methodist Med. Ctr., Des Moines, 1978; student asst. St. Paul United Ch. Christ, St. Louis, 1978-79, Evangelical United Ch. Christ, St. Louis, 1979-80; pastor St. John's United Ch. Christ, Owensville, Mo., 1980—; mem. Mo. Conf. Task Force on Peace and Family Life, 1982-84; del. Gen. Synod United Ch. Christ, 1983-85; chmn. nominating com. Eastern Assn. United Ch. Christ, 1984—, mem. council, 1984—. Project dir. Owensville Community Theatre Project, Mo. 1984—; dir. Owensville Community CROP walk, 1984—. Mem. Hermann Area Pastors' Circle (pres. 1984), Owensville Ministerial Alliance (sec. 1984—). Republican. Lodges: DeMolay (chpt. adv. 1983-84), Masons (jr. deacon 1982-83). Home: Route 2 Box 106 Owensville MO 65066

WEAVER, MACARTHUR, minister, So. Baptist Conv.; b. Scottsboro, Ala., June 2, 1942; s. Otis and Nancy (Dobbs) W.; A.S., Walker Jr. Coll., Jasper, Ala., 1964; B.A., McNeese State Coll., Lake Charles, La., 1967, M.Ed., 1968; M.R.E., So. Bapt. Theol. Sem., Louisville, 1971; m. Judy Kay Dennis, Aug. 29, 1964; children—Joel Arthur, Jennifer Kay, John Andrew. Ordained to ministry, 1977; youth and recreation dir. First Bapt. Ch., Jasper, 1962-64; dir. recreation First Bapt. Ch., Lake Charles, 1964-68; youth and recreation dir. Buechel Park Bapt. Ch., Louisville, 1968-69; minister edn. Bethany Bapt. Ch., Louisville, 1970-71, First Bapt. Ch., Valdosta, Ga., 1971—; pastor-adviser Bapt. Student Union, Valdosta State Coll. Vice moderator Valdosta Bapt. Assn.; chmn. membership com. Valdosta Area Ministerial Assn., 1975—. Coach, Midget Football League, Valdosta Boys Club, 1974—, coach Cadet Basketball League, 1976—; v.p. Azalea City Kiwanis Club, 1975-76, pres., 1977-78. Recipient Walk for Mankind awards, 1974, 75, 76; named Alt. Mr. Walker Coll., 1963-64. Mem. Valdosta Bapt. Ministerial Assn., Lowndes Adult Edn. Council, Assn. Couples for Marriage Enrichment, Inc. Home: 306 Simpson Pl Valdosta GA 31601 Office: PO Box 670 Valdosta GA 31601

WEAVER, RICHARD DONALD, minister, educator, United Methodist Church; b. St. Louis, Mar. 25, 1926; s. Robert Raymond and Ada Viola (Holz) W. B.S. in Commerce, St. Louis U., 1949; M.Div., Garrett Theol. Sem., 1952; postgrad., U. Chgo., 1951-53; M.A., Scarritt Coll., 1979; postgrad., San Francisco Theol. Sem., 1978-80. Ordained to ministry United Methodist Ch., 1951. Pastor, Lizton and Salem Meth. Chs., Ind., 1951-53, Centenary Meth. Ch., Veedersburg, Ind., 1953-58; sr. pastor Ind. Harbor U. Meth. Ch., East Chicago, Ind., 1958-73, First United Meth. Ch., Hobart, Ind., 1973-80, Crown Point, Ind., 1980-84, Angola United Meth. Ch., Ind., 1984—; dir. Ind. United Meth. Children's Home, Lebanon, 1965-70, 71-79, 80—; mem. Ft. Wayne Dist. Council Ministry, 1984—, Steuben County Ministerial Assn., Angola, 1984—; lectr. Calumet Coll., Whiting, Ind., 1967-84. Served to staff sgt. AUS, 1944-46, ETO. Recipient Community Leadership award Twin City Community Services, 1971. Mem. Am. Soc. Ch. History, Assn. Sociology of

Religion, Hymn Soc. Am., Religious Edn. Assn. Am. and Can., Religious Research Assn., Soc. Sci. Study Religion. Lodge: Rotary. Home: 403 Hilltop Dr Angola IN 46703-2220 Office: Angola United Meth Ch 220 W Maumee St Angola IN 46703-1497

WEBB, ALEXANDER HENDERSON, minister, Episcopal Church; b. Mt. Kisco, N.Y., Oct. 19, 1951; s. Jean Francis and Nancy (Bukeley) W.; m. Ruth Kathleen Poole, Oct. 20, 1979; 1 child, Alexander Henderson. B.A., Amherst Coll., 1973; postgrad. Gordon Conwell Theol. Sem., 1977; M.Div., Gen. Theol. Sem., 1978. Ordained priest, Episcopal Ch., 1979. Seminarian asst. Trinity Ch., Shrewsbury, Mass., 1976-77; diocesan coordinator Vacation Bible Schs., Diocese of Western Mass., 1978; asst. to rector St. Thomas Ch., Hanover, N.H., 1978-80; vicar Ch. of the Nativity, Northborough, Mass., 1980-81, rector, 1981—; mem. various commns. Diocese of Western Mass., 1980—, chmn. parish edn. commn. Diocese of N.H., Concord, 1979-80, mem. diocesan council, 1979-80. Adv. bd. Northborough Housing Authority, 1982-83; chmn. bd. dirs. Aid to Infants, Hanover, N.H., 1978-80; bd. dirs. Headrest, Inc., Lebanon, N.H., 1978-80; mem. Election Commn., Northborough, Mass., 1984—. Mem. Fellowship of the Way of the Cross. Republican. Home: 59 Howard St Northborough MA 01532-0627 Office: Ch of the Nativity 45 Howard St Northborough MA 01532-0627

WEBB, ALLEN OTIS, minister, Southern Baptist Convention; b. Walthal, Miss., Nov. 22, 1918; s. James Otis and Lottie Velma (Watson) W.; B.A., Miss. Coll., 1941; Th.M., Southwestern Bapt. Theol. Sem., 1944, Th.D., 1950; m. Leila Mae Runnels, Aug. 17, 1941; children—Beverly Ann, James Allen, Ronald Lee. Ordained to ministry, 1940; pastor chs. in Miss. and Tex., 1938—, Harlendale Bapt. Ch., San Antonio, 1958-60, Daniel Meml. Bapt. Ch., Jackson, Miss., 1960-71, Ingalls Ave. Bapt. Ch., Pascagoula, Miss., 1971—. Mem. exec. bd. Bapt. Gen. Conv. of Tex., 1954-60; bd. trustees Bapt. Standard, 1954-59, S. Tex. Children's Home, Beeville, Tex., 1956-59, Valley Bapt. Acad., Harlingen, Tex., 1956-58, U. Corpus Christi, 1954-60, Mexican Children's Home, 1958-60, Alto Frio Bapt. Encampment, 1958-60; pres. Tex. Bapt. Encampment, 1954-55, Zephr Bapt. Encampment, 1957-58, S. Tex. Bible Conf., 1957-58; mem. pioneer missions com., 1961-67; chmn. missions com., Jackson County, 1972-76; exec. dir. missions, Jackson County, 1978-84. Bd. dirs. Bapt. Med. Ctr., 1976-79, 82—. Mem. Jackson County Pastors Conf. (pres. 1972), SW Bapt. Theol. Sem. Alumni of Miss. (pres. 1976), Jackson County Bapt. Assn. (moderator 1977). Home: 4008 S Shore Dr Pascagoula MS 39567 Office: 4505 Ingalls Ave POB 358 Pascagoula MS 39567

WEBB, ANDREW HOWARD, minister, Free Methodist Church of North America; b. Monterey Park, Calif., Dec. 28, 1945; s. Samuel Gorden and Jeannie (Stewart) W.; m. Marjorie Jean Pattison, June 20, 1970; children: Karen Jean, James Patrick. A.B., San Diego State U., 1968; M.A., 1975; postgrad. Mennonite Brothern Bibl. Sem., 1982—. Ordained deacon, 1983, ordained to ministry Meth. Ch., 1983. Minister Christian edn. and outreach Modesto Free Meth. Ch., Calif., 1981-85; pastor Orangeville Free Meth. Ch., Calif., 1985—; dir. children's ministry Calif. Conf., 1978-83, bd. adminstrn., 1983—, chair bd. Christian edn., 1983—, chair camping trust fund, 1984—; v.p. Inter-Faith Ministeries, Modesto, 1985. Pres. Lemon Grove Tchrs. Assn., Calif., 1972-74, Imperial Valley Council Internat. Reading Assn., El Centro, Calif., 1969; bd. dirs. Empire Union Sch. Dist., Calif., 1979-83. Mem. Wesleyan Theol. Soc., Alpha Phi Omega, Alpha Delta. Club: Kiwanis. Home: 6815 Hazel Ave Orangevale CA 95662 Office: 8790 Oak Ave Orangevale CA 95662

WEBB, WILLIAM BRITTON, minister, Southern Baptist Convention; b. Union, Miss., May 10, 1932; s. James Doris Sr. and Ola (May) W.; m. Senita A. Wilson, Aug. 26, 1955; children: Twila Cherise Webb Massingale, Risa Michelle. B.A., Baylor U., 1954; M.Div., So. Bapt. Theol. Sem., Louisville, 1957. Ordained to ministry So. Bapt. Conv., 1952; pastor Monterey Bapt. Ch., Ky., 1954-60, Medway Bapt. Ch., Ohio, 1960-66, Midway Bapt. Ch., Meridian, Miss., 1966—; trustee So. Bapt. Theol. Sem., Louisville, 1966-67. Mem. Miss. Bapt. Conv. (exec. com. 1977-78, exec. bd. 1977-82). Home: RD 2 Box 185 Meridian MS 39305 Office: Midway Bapt Ch RD 9 Box 195 Meridian MS 39305

WEBB, WILLIAM CLEMENT, minister, Southern Baptist Convention; b. Aransas Pass, Tex., Aug. 14, 1943; s. William Vernon and Fannie Maxine (Jordon) W.; B.A., Belmont Coll., Nashville, 1968; M.Div., Midwestern Bapt. Theol. Sem., Kansas City, Mo., 1971; M.A., U. No. Colo., Greeley, 1976; m. Debra Ann Keenan, Dec. 15, 1972; children—Melinda Joy, Kristi Lin, William Robert. Pastor chs. in Tenn., W. Ger., Mo., 1968-69, Wyo., 1964-67, 74, 75-76; dir. rehab. Nashville Rescue Mission, 1965, 67-68; social worker Platte County Dept. Social Services, Wheatland, Wyo., 1975-76; counsellor-chaplain Union Missions Settlement, Charleston, W.Va., 1976-77; pastor, family service ctr. dir. Home Mission Bd., Nome, Alaska, 1977-83; dir. Nome Receiving Home, 1978-83; assoc. prof. Northwest Community Coll., Nome, 1980-81; clin. dir. Alaska Bapt. Family Service Ctr., 1983—. Bd. dirs., publicity chmn. Wyo. Human Resources Confedn., Wheatland, 1975-76; chmn. bd. Bering Strait Treatment Ctr., 1981-83. Mem. Am. Council Alcoholic Problems, Am. Personnel and Guidance Assn. Address: 13216 Elmhurst Circle Anchorage AK 99515

WEBER, ARNOLD JOHN, priest, Roman Cath. Ch.; b. St. Martin, Minn., Oct. 21, 1925; s. Ben Martin and Louise Ann (Arceneau) W.; B.A., St. John's U., Collegeville, Minn., 1948; M.A., Cath. U. Am., 1956. Ordained priest, 1952; tchr. and coach schs. in Minn., 1951-70; head religion dept. Benilde High Sch., St. Louis Park, Minn., 1970-73; pastor Holy Rosary Ch., Detroit Lakes, Minn., 1973-77; dir. Benilde High Sch., St. Louis Park, Minn., 1977—. Pres. Detroit Lakes Ministerial Assn., 1975-77; mem. priests senate Crookston Roman Cath. Diocese, 1973-75, mem. sch. bd., 1975—. Mem. Nat. Cath. Ednl. Assn. Lectr., retreat dir., author in field of family life. Address: 2501 Hwy 100 S St Louis Park MN 55416

WEBER, GLORIA RICHIE, pastor, American Lutheran Church. B. St. Louis, Apr. 4, 1933; d. George Omar and Gladys Harriet (Klein) Richie; m. John R. Weber, Mar. 5, 1954; children: Julie, Betty, Ruth, John Jr. B.A., Wash. U., 1953; M.C.E., Eden Theol. Sem., 1972, M.Div., 1974. Ordained to ministry Am. Luth. Ch., 1974. Asst. pastor St. Luke Luth. Ch., St. Louis, 1974-76, Holy Cross Luth. Ch., St. Louis, 1976-79; family life educator Luth. Family and Children's Services of Mo., St. Louis, 1979—; bd. dirs. Luth. Human Relations Assn. Am., Milw., 1979-83, Luth. Acad. Scholarship, Valparaiso, Ill., 1980-82, Eden Theol. Sem., St. Louis, 1980-82; chaplain coordinator St. Louis County Police Dept., 1980—. Mem. Mo. State Commn. on Status Women, Jefferson City, 1978—. Named Woman of Achievement, St. Louis Globe-Democrat Newspaper, 1977. Mem. Luth. Profl. Ch. Workers St. Louis (v.p. 1980—), St. Louis Women in Ministry, Phi Beta Kappa. Club: Variety (Woman of Yr., St. Louis chpt. 1976). Home: 4910 Valley Crest Dr Saint Louis MO 63128 Office: 4625 Lindell #501 Saint Louis MO 63108

WEBER, JOSEPH COTTRELL, JR., minister, educator, United Meth. Ch.; b. Pitts., Mar. 31, 1930; s. Joseph Cottrell and Esther (Morrell) W.; A.B., Ohio Wesleyan U., 1953; S.T.B., Boston U., 1957, Ph.D., 1963; m. Adelheid Lisa Haertwig, Oct. 25, 1957; children—Robert Andreas, Miriam Lisa. Ordained to ministry; asst. prof. religion Temple U., 1962-65; asso. prof. N.T., Meth. Theol. Sch. in Ohio, 1965-66; asso. dir. Ecumenical Inst., Bosey, Switzerland, 1966-69, also lectr.; asso. prof. ecumenics Boston U. Sch. Theology, 1969-73; prof. Bibl. theology Wesley Theol. Sem., 1973—. Pres., N.Am. Acad. Ecumenists. Mem. Soc. for Values in Higher Edn., Soc. Bibl. Lit. Contbr. articles to scholarly jours. Home: 8108 Hampden Ln Bethesda MD 20014 Office: 4400 Massachusetts Ave NW Washington DC 20016

WEBER, TIMOTHY PRESTON, theology educator, pastor, Conservative Baptist Assn. of Am.; b. Los Angeles, May 25, 1947; s. Jack Brown and Ruth Marie (McNutt) W.; m. Linda Lee Gryde, July 20, 1968; children: Jonathan Mark, Michael David. B.A., UCLA, 1969; M.Div., Fuller Theol. Sem., 1972; M.A., U. Chgo., 1974, Ph.D., 1976. Ordained to ministry Baptist General Conference, 1976. Asst. prof. ch. history Denver Sem., 1976-81, assoc. prof., 1981—; pastor Heritage Bapt. Ch., Aurora, Colo., 1984—; bd. dirs. Evang. Concern of Denver, 1980-83; pres. Christian Conciliation Service, Denver, 1982—. Author: The Future Explored, 1978, Living in the Shadow of the Second Coming, 1979, enlarged edit., 1983. Mem. Am. Soc. of Ch. History, Conf. on Faith and History, Am. Bapt. Hist. Soc., Christian Legal Soc. Home: 7498 E Davies Pl Englewood CO 80112 Office: Denver Sem Box 10,000 Denver CO 80210

WEBSTER, WARREN WAYNE, religious organization administrator, Conservative Baptist Foreign Mission Soc.; b. Gary, Ind., Feb. 17, 1928; s. Vance H. and Jessie I. (Wise) W.; m. Shirley Ann Finley, Dec. 23, 1951; children: Debra Ann, Cindy Lou. B.A., U. Oreg., 1949; M.Div., Fuller Theol. Sem., 1952; D.D. (hon.), Denver Sem., 1971. Field missionary Conservative Bapt. Fgn. Mission Soc., Pakistan, 1954-70, gen. dir., Wheaton, Ill., 1971—; bd. dirs. Fellowship of Faith for Muslims, Toronto, Ont., Can., 1970—; mem. Lausanne Com. for World Evangelization, London, 1978—. Mem. Evang. Fgn. Mission Assn. (bd. dirs. 1976—), Phi Beta Kappa. Office: Conservative Bapt Fgn Mission Soc PO Box 5 Wheaton IL 60189

WEDEKING, RALPH WEINBERG, minister, religion and social studies educator, United Church of Christ; b. Waverly, Iowa, Feb. 5, 1934; s. Martin and Edna (Weinberg) W. B.A., U. No. Iowa, 1956, M.A., 1971; M.Div., Eden Sem., 1959. Ordained to ministry, United Ch. Christ, 1959. Pastor St. Paul United Ch. Christ, Washington, Iowa, 1959-62, Peace United Ch. Christ, Waverly, Iowa, 1962-66; interim pastor St. Paul United Ch. Christ, Denver, Iowa, 1968-69; assoc. pastor First Pleasant Valley Ch., Clarksville, Iowa, 1966-67; part-time pastor First Congl. Ch., Nashua, Iowa, 1969—; interim pastor Little Brown Ch. in Vale, Nashua, 1969, 77-78; prof. Iowa Central Community Coll., Fort Dodge, 1971—, speakers' bur., 1971—, mem. faculty relations com., 1978—, developer courses in marriage and family relationships and religion in culture, 1971, 78; part-time instr. in sociology Wartburg Coll., Waverly, 1967-71. Organizer, bd. dirs. Waverly Sr. Citizens, 1966-71; active Fort Dodge Pre-Sch., 1974-77, Fort Dodge United Fund Com., 1976-78, Mem. Iowa Sociol. Soc. Democrat. Home: 606 S 14th St Fort Dodge IA 50501 Office: Iowa Central Community Coll 330 Ave M Fort Dodge IA 50501

WEDELL, ROGER WILLIAM, minister, Christian Church (Disciples of Christ); b. Burbank, Calif., Mar. 15, 1948; s. Jack A. and Rosetta Maxine (Davis) W. Student Calif. State U.-Fullerton, 1966-68; B.A., Tex. Christian U.,1970; U., M.Div., Brite Div. Sch., 1974; Ph.D., Grad. Theol. Union, Berkeley, Calif., 1982. Ordained to ministry Christian Ch., 1973. Assoc. pastor 1st Christian Ch., Longview, Tex., 1974-76; ednl. assoc. Good Samaritan Meth. Ch., Cupertino, Calif., 1976-78; edn. coordinator Eden United Ch. of Christ, Hayward, Calif., 1978-80; staff exec. Thanks-Giving Square, Dallas, 1980—; adj. instr. Tex. Christian U., Fort Worth, 1983—; mem. worship com. Greater Dallas Community Chs., 1980—; co-founder S.W. Ctr. for Religion and the Arts, Dallas, 1983. Mem. editorial bd. Modern Liturgy Mag., 1980—. Contbr. articles to profl. jours. Co-founder, trustee Children's Assn. Gregg County, Longview, Tex., 1975. Henson scholar Brite Div. Sch., Fort Worth, 1972,73, grantee for fgn. study Curtis Found., Longview, Tex., 1976. Mem. Memeses Inst., Am. Acad. Religion, Theta Phi. Democrat. Office: Thanks- Giving Sq POBox 1777 Dallas TX 75221

WEE, PAUL ALLEN, religious association administrator, American Lutheran Church; b. St. Paul, Feb. 6, 1937; s. Palmer and Evelyn (Hamre) W.; m. Irene Grossfuss, Dec. 28, 1958; children: Christopher, Deborah, Steven. B.A., Harvard U., 1959; postgrad. Union Theol. Sem., 1959-60; M.Div., Luther Theol. Sem., St. Paul, 1963; postgrad. Philipps U., Marburg-Lahn, Germany, 1963-64; Ph.D., Free U. Berlin, 1975. Ordained to ministry Am. Luth. Ch., 1964. Intern Luth. Ch. of Good Shepherd, Sacramento, 1961-62; pastor St. Andrew's Luth. Ch., Los Angeles, 1964-67, Trinity Luth. Ch., Park Forest, Ill., 1967-68; sr. rep. Luth. World Fedn., Berlin, 1968-74; lectr. Lutheranism, Faculty of Theology, Mansfield Coll., Oxford U., Eng., 1974-75; gen. sec. Luth. World Ministries, N.Y.C., 1975—; mem. div. overseas ministry unit com. Nat. Council Chs. U.S.A., 1976—, mem. Ch. World Service dept. com., 1976—. Author: Space and Time, 1975. Decorated Order of Merit 1st Class, Fed. Republic of Germany; Fulbright fellow, 1963-64. Office: 360 Park Ave S New York NY 10010

WEEKS, WILLIAM ROBERT, minister Southern Baptist Convention; b. N.Y.C., Nov. 8, 1935; s. Robert Leroy and Clare Bell Weeks; Grad. Theology Degree, Tenn. Temple Schs., Chattanooga, 1958; postgrad. Luther Rice Sem., Jacksonville, Fla.; m. Ruth Carol Garrison, July 13, 1958; children—Sandra Lynn, William Garrison. Ordained to ministry, 1960; asso. pastor, minister music chs. in Tex., Fla. and Ga., 1958-72; pastor Dudley (Ga.) Bapt. Ch., 1972—; chaplain Macon (Ga.) High Sch. Football Team, 1964-66, Dublin (Ga.) Civitan Club, 1968-70; evangelist in preaching and music, 1953—. Mem. exec. com. Ga. Bapt. Conv., 1979-82, 84—. Address: PO Box 316 Dudley GA 31022

WEEMS, VAIL JONES, lay church worker, United Methodist Ch.; b. Rome, Ga., Feb. 21, 1897; d. John Willie and Sarah (Quillian) Jones; A.B., Wesleyan Coll., Macon, Ga., 1918; postgrad. Columbia, summer 1919; X-ray certificate Postgrad. Sch. Atlanta, 1930; m. Howard Vincent Weems, June 29, 1921; children—Howard Vincent, Verna Vail (Mrs. Joseph O. Macbeth), Carolyn (dec.). Mem. Gen. Bd. Missions, United Methodist Ch., 1960-68; del. Gen. Conf. United Meth. Ch., 1960, 64, 66, 68, 70, 72, del. to S.E. Jurisdiction, 1960, 64, 68, 72, del. to Fla. Meth. Ann. Conf., 1956—; dir. Fla. Meth. Found., 1967-77. Pres., YWCA at Wesleyan Coll., Macon, Ga., 1917-18. Named Woman of Year, Fla. United Ch. Women, 1959; recipient Distinguished award Wesleyan Coll., Macon, 1958. Mem. Woman's Soc. Christian Service (dist. sec. student work 1950-52, Fla. conf. sec. lit. and publs. 1952-56, Fla. conf. pres., 1956-60), Alfalit Internat. (dir.), Sebring Hist. Soc., C. of C. Clubs: Woman's, Staff and Book (Sebring, Fla.). Home: 507 Lakeview Dr SE Sebring FL 33870

WEENINK, ALLAN JOHN, minister, United Presbyn. Ch. in U.S.A.; b. Kalamazoo, July 6, 1921; s. John Wilhelm and Joanna (Sinon) W.; A.B., Hope Coll., 1943, M.Div., New Brunswick Theol. Sem., 1946; M.A., Columbia, 1949; D.D., Alma Coll., 1962; L.H.D., Angeles U., Philippines, 1974; m. Virginia Ruth Heidanus, June 5, 1943; children—John Alan, James Brian, Judith Carol, Jeffrey David. Ordained to ministry, 1946; pastor Christ Ref. Ch. Newark, 1946-49; asso. pastor Westminster Ch., Detroit, 1949-58; sr. pastor First Presbyn. Ch. Battle Creek (Mich.), 1958—. Adj. prof. San Francisco Theol. Sem.; collegium group leader Continuing Edn. Center, Alma Coll.; spl. missioner to Philippines, 1966, 70, 74; trustee, mem. exec. com. Alma (Mich.) Coll., 1969—. Sec. bd. trustees Kellogg Community Coll., Battle Creek, 1972—. Contbr. articles and sermons to religious jours. Author: Running With Patience, 1971; Only the Wounded Can Serve, 1977. Home: 287 Central St Battle Creek MI 49017 Office: 111 Capital Ave NE Battle Creek MI 49017

WEER, RALPH MILTON, minister, General Association of Regular Baptist Churches; b. Phila., Jan. 7, 1929; s. Ralph and Daisy (Nicholls) W.; m. Myrtle Sarah Pidcock, Sept. 23, 1949; children: Richard, Thomas, Judith, Steven. Diploma, Phila. Coll. of Bible, 1967. Ordained to ministry, 1975. Pastor, Kendall Park Bapt. Ch., N.J., 1966-73; state rep. Garden State Fellowship of Regular Bapt. Ch., Frenchtown, N.J., 1976-84; camp dir. New Life Island, Frenchtown, 1974—; pastor Indian Creek Park, Ft. Myers, Fla., 1980-84; trustee Bapt. Bible Coll., Clarks Summit, Pa., 1976—, Spurgeon Bapt. Coll., Mulberry, Fla., 1974—. Contbr. articles to profl. jours. Served with USN, 1948-50. Republican. Address: PO Box AC Frenchtown NJ 08825 also 8 Kiowa Dr Fort Myer FL 33931

WEERTS, MILAN GENE, minister, Lutheran Church-Missouri Synod; b. Norfolk, Nebr., Nov. 20, 1936; s. Wallrich Frederick and Alta I. (Halsey) W.; m. Marjorie Ann Schmitt, Aug. 20, 1959; children: James Andrew, Sara Elizabeth Weerts Spicer. A.A., St. John's Coll., 1956; B.A., Concordia Coll., St. Louis, 1958, M.Div., 1961; postgrad. Pitts. Theol. Sem., 1983—. Ordained to ministry Luth. Ch., 1961. Pastor, Our Savior Luth. Ch., Zephyrhills, Fla., 1961-63, St. Petersburg, Fla., 1963-78, Trinity Evang. Luth. Ch., Orlando, Fla., 1978—; chmn. bd. Woodlands Luth. Ctr., Orlando, 1978—; dir. Fla.-Ga. dist. Luth. Ch.-Mo. Synod, Orlando, 1980—, Luther High Sch., Orlando, 1980—, Christian Service Ctr., Orlando, 1981—. Bd. dirs. Nat. Marriage Encounter Central Fla., Orlando, 1979—. Named Outstanding Young Men Am., Jaycees, 1970. Mem. Fla. State Assn. Dist. Mental Health Bds. (hon.). Home: 3563 Oakwater Pointe Dr Orlando FL 32806 Office: Trinity Evang Luth Ch 123 E Livingston St Orlando FL 32801

WEGNER, LAWRENCE EMIL, minister, Conservative Baptist Association of America; b. Gladwin, Mich., July 21, 1920; s. Gottlieb and Amanda (Schultz) W.; m. Muriel Elizabeth Geisler, Apr. 21, 1945; children: Vance Lester, Joy Corrine Wegner Clatterbuck. Th.B., No. Bapt. Sem., 1944; D.D. (hon.), Fort Myers Bible Inst., 1983. Ordained to ministry, 1944. Pastor 1st Bapt. Ch., Manitowoc, Wis., 1943-45, Immanuel Bapt. Ch., Wausau, Wis., 1946-51, Forrest Park Bapt. Ch., Orlando, Fla., 1951-53, Faith Bapt. Ch., Orlando, 1953-74, Kissimmee, Fla., 1974-81; new ch. coordinator Conservative Bapt. Home Mission Soc., Wheaton, Ill., 1981—. Mem. Kissimmee Ministerial Assn. (pres. 1976-77), Conservative Bapt. Assn. of Fla. (coordinator 1973—). Republican. Home and Office: 14152 Boggy Creek Rd Orlando FL 32824

WEHMEYER, WILLIAM RAYMOND, minister, Southern Baptist Convention; b. Kansas City, Kans., July 31, 1928; s. William Fredrick and Leola M. (Matthews) W.; B.A., William Jewell Coll., 1961; M.Div., Midwestern Bapt. Theol. Sem., 1967; m. Sylvia Clara Ann Hinze, July 11, 1959; children—Raymond Edmond, William Randolph, Amber Kathleen. Ordained to ministry So. Baptist Conv., 1966; pastor First Bapt. Ch., Welda, Kans., also interim pastor First Bapt. Ch., Cottonwood Falls, Kans., and Calvary Bapt. Ch., Atchison, 1964-65; pastor First Bapt. Ch., Winigan, Mo., 1966-70; supt. missions Linn and Livingston Bapt. Assns., Brookfield, Mo., 1970-74; dir. missions New Madrid Bapt. Assn., Hayti, Mo., 1974—. Vice pres. Grand Oaks Bapt. Assembly, 1973-74; v.p. Mo. Bapt. Supt. Missions Conf., 1972-73; 2d v.p. Mo. Bapt. Conv., 1984, 1st vice chmn. exec. bd., 1st v.p., 1985; mem. S.E. Mo. adv. bd. to Nat. Baptists, 1974—; v.p. dir. missions conf. Mo. Bapt. Conv., 1983-84, pres., 1984-85; area rep. Ams. United for Separation of Ch. and State, 1973—; mem. exec. bd. S. Mo. Bapt. Assembly, 1974—; pres. S.E. Mo. Ministers Conf., Mo. Bapt. Conv. Ministers, 1975—. Area educator Christian Civic Found., 1968—; soil stewardship chmn. Linn County Soil and Water Conservation, 1972-74. Trustee Mo. Bapt. Children's Home, Bridgeton, Mo., 1975—. William Jewell Coll. Walter Pope Binns fellow, 1984. Mem. Charles Hadden Spurgeon Soc. Republican. Home: 102 E 8th St Portageville MO 63873 Office: PO Drawer W 604 N 6th St Hayti MO 63851

WEIDLER, RONALD WALTER, minister, Lutheran Church-Missouri Synod; b. Chgo., July 25, 1950; s. Henry and Anna Marie (Kalchbrenner) W.; m. Jean Gail Oelrich, June 11, 1972; children: Jonathan Paul, Christa Jean, Mark Christian. A.A., summa cum laude, Concordia Coll., Ann Arbor, Mich., 1970, B.A. with high distinction, Concordia Sr. Coll., Fort Wayne, Ind., 1972; M.Div., Concordia Sem., Springfield, Ill., 1976. Ordained to ministry Luth. Ch., 1976. Pastor, Holy Cross Luth. Ch., Carlisle, Iowa, 1976-80, Holy Trinity Luth. Ch., Tampa, Fla., 1980—; dir. communications Iowa dist. W., Luth. Ch.-Mo. Synod, 1977-80, Fla.-Ga. dist., 1981—. Contbr. articles, sermons to religious publs. Mem. Luths. for Life. Republican. Lodge: Optimists (service award 1984). Home: 3705 Kensington Ave Tampa FL 33629 Office: Holy Trinity Luth Ch 3712 El Prado Blvd Tampa FL 33629

WEIER, GARY WILBERT, minister, Lutheran Church-Missouri Synod; b. Shreveport, La., Dec. 10, 1943; s. Wilbert Louis and Esther (Bellhorn) W.; m. Evelyn Kay Nortrup, Sept. 30, 1967; children: Michael, David. B.A., Concordia Sr. Coll., Fort Wayne, Ind., 1965; M.Div., Concordia Sem., St. Louis, 1969; M.A. in Christian Edn., Presbyn. Sch. Christian Edn., 1970. Ordained to ministry Luth. Ch.-Mo. Synod, 1970. Vicar St. Mark's Luth. Ch., Cleve., 1967-68; pastor Bethlehem Luth. Ch., Pleasant Dale, Nebr., 1970-77, St. Paul's Luth. Ch., Malcolm, Nebr., 1970-77; Pilgrim Luth. Ch., Bellevue, Nebr., 1977—; cons. chaplain Meth. Hosp. Midtown, Omaha, 1981—; bd. dirs. Ctr. for Indian Ministries, Seward, Nebr., 1976—, Luth. Met. Ministries, Omaha, 1977—. Chmn. Bellevue CROP walk, 1980—; co-chmn. Effort Against Video Lottery, Bellevue, 1984. Republican. Home: 817 N 4th St Bellevue NE 68005 Office: Pilgrim Luth Ch 2401 Jackson St Bellevue NE 68005

WEIGAND, WILLIAM KEITH See *Who's Who in America*, 43rd edition.

WEIL, HERMAN, educator, Jewish Congregation; b. Regisheim, Alsace-Lorraine, France, Dec. 15, 1905; s. Leopold and Selma (Israel) W.; came to U.S., 1938, naturalized, 1944; Ph.D. in Psychology, U. Marburg (Germany), 1929; German state exam. in edn., Kassel, Germany, 1931; m. Bertha Weiler, July 26, 1931; 1 son, Gunther M. Mem. of Lehrhaus staff Jewish Adult Edn. Acad., Frankfurt-Main, Germany, 1933-38; co-chmn. Wis. region NCCJ, 1952-72, chmn. edn. workshop policy com., 1958-59, mem. Wis. regional exec. bd., 1973—, nat. chmn. on Observance of Brotherhood Week in Schs. and Colls., 1957, nat. trustee, 1977-84; dir. of religious edn. Temple Emanu-El B'ne Jeshurun, Milw., 1946-56; lectr. Jewish Adult Inst. of Temple, 1953-55; dir. religious edn. North Shore Congregation Israel, Glencoe, Ill., 1948-49; dir. Milw. B'nai B'rith Hillel Counselorship for Jewish students at colls. and univs., Milw., 1950-60; pres. Wis. Soc. for Jewish Learning, Milw., 1957-59, mem. liaison com. to depts. of Hebrew studies U. Wis., Madison and Milw. campuses, 1972-80; chmn. steering com. Milw. Inst. Adult Jewish Studies, 1958; trustee Temple Emanu-El B'ne Jeshurun, 1960-68, v.p., 1965-68; chmn. Milw. chpt. Am. Jewish Com., 1973-75; mem. nat. exec. council Am. Jewish Com., 1974-80. Prof. emeritus psychology U. Wis.-Milw., 1976—, assoc. dean, 1967-71; disting. service fellow Congregation Emanu-el B'ne Jeshurun, Milw., 1976-84, emeritus, 1984—; disting. scholar in residence Milw. Jewish Community Center, 1977-80. Mem. Wis. Gov.'s Commn. on Human Rights, 1953-56. Recipient Meritorious citation Wis. Soc. for Jewish Learning, 1973, Interfaith award Milw. B'nai B'rith Council, 1952, Wis. Brotherhood award NCCJ, 1959, Disting. Merit citation NCCJ, 1973; Disting. Human Relations award (with wife Bertha) Am. Jewish Com., 1978, Century award Jewish Chautauqua Soc., 1983. Mem. Midwestern, Wis. (pres. 1962-63), Am. psychol. assns., AAUP (Disting. Service award 1975), Phi Kappa Phi. Club: Century (hon.). Author: (with others) Studien zur Psychologie Menschlicher Typen, 1930, In Quest of Excellence, 1975, Faculty Retirement Guidebook, 1975, 76; contbr. book chpts. and numerous articles on edn. to profl. jours. Address: 2027 E Lake Bluff Blvd Milwaukee WI 53211

WEINHAUER, WILLIAM GILLETTE, bishop, Episc. Ch.; b. N.Y.C., Dec. 3, 1924; s. Nicholas Alfred and Florence Anastasia (Davis) W.; B.S., Trinity Coll., 1948; S.T.B., Gen. Theol. Sem., N.Y.C., 1951, S.T.M., 1956, Th.D., 1970; m. Jean Roberta Shanks, Mar. 20, 1948; 3 children. Ordained priest, 1951; curate Ch. of the Resurrection, Queens, N.Y., 1951-52; vicar St. George's Ch., Bronx, N.Y., chaplain N.Y. U., 1952-53; chaplain Hunter Coll., Coll. City N.Y., Bronx, 1952-56; dir. religious edn. St. James Ch., Scarsdale N.Y., 1953-56; prof. St. Andrew's Theol. Sem., Philippines, 1956-60; vicar St. Paul Ch., Pleasant Valley, N.Y., 1960-61; instr. Gen. Theol. Sem., 1961-64, prof., 1964-71; rector Christ Ch., Poughkeepsie, N.Y., 1971; bishop Diocese of Western N.C., 1971—. Office: Box 368 Black Mountain NC 28711*

WEINLICK, JOHN HENRY, minister, Moravian Church; b. Rhinelander, Wis., May 27, 1942; s. Henry Christian and Elsie (Heise) W.; m. Pamela Stanoridge, Aug. 17, 1967 (div. 1984); children: Amy Rose, Benjamin John. B.S., U. Wis., 1964, B.Communication, 1965; M.Div., Moravian Theol. Sem., 1968; D.Min., St. Stephen's Coll., 1982. Ordained to ministry, 1968. Pastor, Rio Terrace Community Ch., Edmonton, Alta., Can., 1970—; pres. Moravian Ch. in Can., Edmonton, 1977-82; pastor College Hill Moravian Ch., Bethlehem, Pa., 1968-70; mem. D.Min. com. St. Stephen's Coll., Edmonton, 1984—. Founder, personal Devel. Ctr., Edmonton, 1977; bd. dirs. Minerva Found., Edmonton, 1979—. Mem. Acad. Parish Clergy. Home: 15106 76 Ave Edmonton AB T5R 2Z9 Canada Office: Rio Terrace Ch 15108 76 Ave Edmonton AB T5R 2Z9 Canada

WEIR, DANIEL SARGENT, priest, Episcopal Church; b. Ithaca, N.Y., Nov. 2, 1946; s. Charles Ignatius and Gertrude Locke (Burgess) W.; m. Janette MacLean, May 20, 1972; children: Meghan MacLean, Matthew Charles. B.A. cum laude, U. Mass., 1969; M.Div., Episcopal Theol. Sem., 1972. Ordained priest Episcopal Ch., 1973. Asst. minister St. Stephen's Ch., Pittsfield, Mass., 1973-76; rector Trinity Ch., Ware, Mass., 1976-79, Holy Trinity Ch., Southbridge, Mass., 1979—; chaplain Order of St. Luke, Ware, 1977-79, Southbridge, 1979—. Vice chmn. Southbridge Housing Authority, 1984—. Democrat. Home: 183 South St Southbridge MA 01550 Office: Holy Trinity Ch Box 685 Southbridge MA 01550

WEIS, EARL AUGUST, educator, priest, Roman Catholic Church; b. Toledo, May 5, 1923; s. Sylvester Ignatius and Louise Marie (Lammers) W.; student Xavier U., 1941-45; A.B., Loyola U., Chgo., 1946, A.M., 1948; Ph.L., W. Baden Coll., 1948; S.T.B., Weston Coll., 1953, S.T.L., 1955; S.T.D., Pontifical Gregorian U., 1958. Joined Soc. of Jesus, 1941, ordained priest Roman Catholic Ch., 1954; prof. theology W. Baden Coll., 1958-66; asso. prof. religious studies U. Detroit, 1970-71; prof., chmn. dept. theology Loyola U., Chgo., 1971—. Staff editor dogmatic theology New Cath. Ency., 1963-66; editorial bd. Cath. Theol. Ency., 1966-70; book review editor Review for Religious, 1958-63. Mem. Cath. Theol. Soc. Am., Cath. Bibl. Assn., Soc. Bibl. Lit., Coll. Theology Soc. Club: Chgo. Press. Address: Loyola Univ 820 N Michigan Ave Chicago IL 60611

WEISENSEL, MARY DELBERT, nun, Roman Catholic Church; b. Sun Prairie, Wis., Aug. 4, 1936; d. Gilbert Edward and Adeline M. (Suchomel) W. B.S., Mt. Mary Coll., Milw., 1964; M.A., Clarke Coll., 1973. Joined Sch. Sisters of Notre Dame, Roman Cath. Ch., 1956; tchr. various schs., Wis., Chgo., 1958-72; prin. St. Nicholas Sch., Freedom, Wis., 1972-76, St. Jerome Sch., Phoenix, 1976—; mem. com. Diocesan Evaluation Team, Green Bay, Wis., 1972-76, ad hoc com. Diocesan Religious Edn. Bd., Phoenix, 1981-82; coordinator, instr. Diocese of Phoenix Tchrs., 1983-84. Mem. Nat. Assn. Elem. Sch. Prins., Assn. Supervision and Curriculum Devel., Nat. Cath. Edn. Assn. Office: St Jerome Sch 10815 N 35th Ave Phoenix AZ 85029

WEISER, CHARLES BERNARD, ednl. adminstr., priest, Roman Catholic Ch.; b. Newark, May 1, 1939; s. Charles B. and Frances M. (Giblin) W.; A.B., Mt. St. Mary's Coll., 1962; postgrad. Mt. St. Mary's Sem., 1966; Th.M., Princeton Theol. Sem., 1970. Ordained priest Roman Catholic Ch., 1966; asso. pastor St. Matthias Roman Cath. Ch., Somerset, N.J., 1966-69, St. Paul's Ch., Princeton, N.J., 1969-70; dir. Aquinas Inst. Princeton U., 1970—. Prosynodal judge The Ecclesiastical Tribunal of Roman Cath. Diocese of Trenton (N.J.), 1973; mem. Liturgical Com., Roman Cath. Diocese of Trenton, 1972—, Ecumenical Commn., 1973—. Mem. Franklin Twp. Civil Rights Commn., 1968-69. Bd. dirs. Cath. Protestant Rome seminar, 1973—, Trinity Counseling, 1975—, YMCA, Princeton, 1976. Mem. Nat. Orgn. for Continuing Edn. Roman Cath. Clergy (dir.). Address: 65 Stockton St Princeton NJ 08540

WEISER, FREDERICK SHEELY, minister, Lutheran Church in America; b. Hanover, Pa., Nov. 25, 1935; s. Donald Koehler and Elizabeth Katharyn (Sheely) W. A.B., Gettysburg Coll., 1957; B.D., Luth. Theol. Sem., 1960; S.T.M., 1966. Ordained to ministry Luth. Ch. in Am., 1960. Asst. pastor Grace Luth. Ch., Lancaster, Pa., 1960-64; archivist Luth. Theol. Sem., Gettysburg, 1966-71; pastor St. Paul's Ch., Biglerville, Pa., 1971—. Author: Serving Love, 1960; Love's Response, 1961; To Serve God and His People, 1984. Mem. folklife adv. council Gov.'s Ethnic Affairs Commn., Commonwealth of Pa.; sec. Weiser Family Assn. Fellow Nat. Geneal. Soc., 1984. Mem. Phi Kappa Psi. Republican. Home: 55 Kohler Sch Rd New Oxford

PA 17350 Office: St Paul's Evang Luth Ch Franklin St PO Box 325 Biglerville PA 17307

WEISFELD, ISRAEL HAROLD, rabbi, educational director; b. Poland, Nov. 1, 1906; s. Judah Leib and Sarah (Greenblum) W.; came to U.S., 1911, naturalized, 1929; B.A., U. Miami, 1929; Ph.D., U. Chgo., 1943; m. Lillian Reva Rosen, June 30, 1929; children—Hillel Daniel, Naomi Ruth. Ordained rabbi, 1929; rabbi Congregation Beth David, Miami, Fla., 1928-30, Agudas Achim N. Shore, Chgo., 1930-38, W. Surburban Jewish Center, Oak Park, Ill., 1938-44, Shearith Israel, Dallas, 1944-54, Beth Israel, New Orleans, 1954-63, Emanu-El, Burbank, Calif., 1963-68; exec. dir. Bur. Jewish Edn., San Diego, 1968-76, ret., 1976. Pres., Kallah Tex. Rabbis, San Diego Rabbinical Assn.; dir. Hillel Found. So. Meth. U.; mem. exec. com. Am. Jewish Congress; v.p. Zionist Orgn. Los Angeles; pres. San Diego Zionist Orgn.; mem. bd. rabbis So. Calif., Rabbinical Council Am. Author: The Message of Israel, 1933; Lord, God of Hosts, 1939; My Son, 1941; The Ethics of Israel, 1948; The Pulpit Treasury of Wit and Humor, 1950; This Man Moses, 1966; Labor Legislation in the Bible and Talmud, 1974; David the King, 1984. Home and office: 4467 Dawson Ave San Diego CA 92115

WEISS, HAROLD S., Bishop, Lutheran Church in America. Office: 4865 Hamilton Blvd Wescosville PA 18106*

WEISS, HEROLD DAVID, religious studies educator; b. Montevideo, Uruguay, Sept. 5, 1934; came to U.S., 1954; s. Daniel and Maria (Riffel) W.; m. Aida Almira Acosta, July 8, 1962; children: Herold E., Carlos O. B.A., So. Coll., 1956; M.A., Andrews U., 1957, B.D., 1960; Ph.D., Duke U., 1964. Prof. religious studies St. Mary's Coll., Notre Dame, Ind., 1969—. Contbr. writings to religious jours. Lilly Endowment grantee, 1958-59; faculty devel. grantee Shell Oil, 1976. Fellow Philos. Inst.; mem. Soc. Bibl. Lit., Am. Acad. Religion. Home: Rt 1 Box 375 Berrien Springs MI 49103 Office: Box 78 Madeleva Hall St Mary's Coll Notre Dame IN 46556

WEISS, MIKA MIKSA, rabbi, Conservative Jewish; b. Hungary, Oct. 19, 1913; came to U.S., 1961, naturalized, 1967; s. Ferenc Weisz and Terez (Hollander) Weissman; m. Maria Brull, Oct. 22, 1946; 1 child, Peter Fracis. Ph.D., U. Budapest (Hungary), 1939; diploma Francis Joseph Nat. Jewish Theol. Sem. Budapest, 1941; M. Hebrew Lit., U. Judaism, 1966; D.D. (hon.), Jewish Theol. Sem. Am., 1977. Ordained rabbi, 1941. Rabbi Congregation Oroshaza, Hungary, 1939-44, Congregation Debrecen and Dist., Hungary, 1946-57; chief rabbi of Finland, Helsinki, 1957-61; rabbi Jewish Community Ctr., Flemington, N.J., 1962-63, Temple Mishkon Tefilo, Venice, Calif., 1963-66; rabbi Temple B'Nai Hayim, Sherman Oaks, Calif., 1966-83, rabbi emeritus, 1983—; chaplain East Army Corps Free Hungarian Army, 1945-48; v.p. Hungarian Rabbinical Assembly, 1955-56; on staff adult edn. Hebrew, Jewish Folklore and Jewish History, Los Angeles Unified Sch. Dist., 1974—; chaplain Los Angeles Area Hosp., 1967—, Los Angeles County Jail, 1969—, Los Angeles Police Dept., Van Nuys, Calif., 1979—. Recipient Resolution award City Council Los Angeles, 1978, cert. appreciation Los Angeles Police Dept., 1980. Mem. Rabbinical Assembly Conservative Movement (v.p. western region 1983-84). Lodge: Masons. Home: 14535 Benefit Sherman Oaks CA 91403 Office: 4302 Van Nuys Blvd Sherman Oaks CA 91403

WEISS, ROBERT FRANCIS See *Who's Who in America,* 43rd edition.

WEISSER, THOMAS HENRY, minister, United Pentecostal Church International; b. St. Paul, Apr. 3, 1954; s. Henry John and Margaret Helen (Olson) W.; m. Bonnie Lou Watts, Aug. 23, 1975; children: Cynthia Marie, Lance Douglas. B.Th., Apostolic Bible Inst., 1975. Ordained to ministry United Pentecostal Ch. Internat., 1978. Asst. pastor United Pentecostal Ch., Albany, Oreg., 1976-78, Monmouth, Oreg., 1979-80, Corvallis, Oreg., 1980-81, pastor, Monmouth, 1981—; lectr. Harvard Div. Sch., 1984. Owner, mgr. Weisser Enterprises, Monmouth, 1978—. Author: After the Way Called Heresy, 1981; Three Persons—from the Bible? or Babylon?, 1983. Mem. Oreg. Right-to-Life, Monmouth-Independence C. of C. Republican. Home: 151 Edwards Rd S #63 Monmouth OR 97361 Office: United Pentecostal Ch PO Box 53 Monmouth OR 97361

WEISZ, JAMES MILTON, minister, United Methodist Church; b. Pitts., May 11, 1945; s. Frank Howard Leroy and Ruth Carrie (Eisley) W.; m. Candice Jean Ramsay, Dec. 19, 1970; 1 son, Eric James. Student, Wayne State U., 1965-66; B.A., Otterbein Coll., 1967; postgrad., Lehigh U., 1969-72; M. Div., United Sem., 1976. Ordained to ministry United Methodist Ch. as deacon, 1975, as elder, 1977. Student pastor Okeana United Meth. Ch., Ohio, 1974-76; assoc. pastor Asbury United Meth. Ch., Uniontown, Pa., 1976-79; pastor Coolspring United Meth. Ch., Hopwood, Pa., 1976-79, Anne Ashley United Meth. Ch., Munhall, Pa., 1979-82, Kingsley United Meth. Ch., Erie, Pa., 1982—; chaplain Stairways, Erie, 1983—; chaplaincy chmn. Assn. Chs., Uniontown, 1979; mem. Com. on Ministry, Erie/Meadville Dist., 1976—. Republican. Office: Kingsley United Meth Ch 913 Cranberry St Erie PA 16502

WELCH, CLAUDE See *Who's Who in America,* 43rd edition.

WELCH, CLINE HOFF, minister, Southern Baptist Convention; b. Ft. Blackmore, Va., Aug. 10,1923; s. Samuel Richmond and Orpha Evada (Quillen) W.; m. Mabel Lorene Carter, Nov. 10, 1942; children: Patricia Ray, Sue Mosely, Deborah Rhoton, Edward, David, Michael. B.S., East Tenn. State U., 1960; D.MIn., Internat. Bible Inst. and Sem., 1981, M.Min., 1980, Dr. Letters (hon.), 1981. Ordained to Ministry, So. Bapt. Conv., 1956. Pastor, Rivermont Ch., Gate City, Va., 1956-62, Moores Meml. Ch., Gate City, 1962-68, Fall Creek Ch., Blountville, Tenn., 1968-70, Muddy Creek Ch., Blountville, 1970-74, Big Creek Ch., Rogersville, Tenn., 1974, Ft. Robinson Ch., Kingsport, Tenn., 1975, Cowans Branch Ch., Gate City, Va., 1976—; active chaplain Kingsport Vol. Chaplaincy Service; moderator, vice moderator Clinch Valley Bapt. Assn., Gate City, 1967-68; state bd. Bapt. Gen. Assn. Va., 1968; messenger to state and nat. convs., 1978,80,81, 82, 83; mem. Clinch Valley Assn. Mission Com., 1980-83. Author: Golden Pathways in the Mud (poetry), 1979. Mem. East Tenn. State U. Alumni Assn., Am. Legion, Appalachian Bapt. Pastors Conf., Clinch Valley Bapt. Assn. Pastors Conf., Va. Bapt. Pastors Conf., Am. Assn. Ret. Persons, So. Bapt. Pastors Conf., 437th Troop Carrier Assn., Tenn. Law Enforcement Officers Assn. Republican. Home: 2016 Netherland Inn Rd Kingsport TN 37660 (615) 247-6218

WELCH, JOHN RICHARD, minister, Southern Baptist Convention; b. Stockton, Calif., May 26, 1939; s. Sterling T. and Pauline Leona (Palmer) W.; B.A., Calif. Bapt. Coll., Riverside, 1969; m. Nelda Kay Cox, May 10, 1963; children—Julia Kay, James Richard. Ordained to ministry, 1970; minister music and/or edn. chs. in Calif., 1959—; minister music and edn. Harvard Terr. Bapt. Ch., Fresno, 1967-68, First Bapt. Ch., Westminster, 1968-81, 1st So. Bapt. Ch., Sacramento, Calif., 1981—. Pres. Orange County Ministers Assn., 1971; music dir. Calif. Bapt. Ministers Conf., 1971, 75; pres. Calif. Bapt. Coll. Alumni Assn., 1976—. Commnr., Westminster Merit Systems Commn., 1973—; trustee Calif. Bapt. Coll., 1980-84; pres. parent adv. council for Title I program Westminister High Sch., 1969. Mem. Council Moral Concerns. Home: 4395 Armadale Way Sacramento CA 95823 Office: 4840 Fruitridge Rd Sacramento CA 95820

WELGE, JOHN WILLIS, minister, Lutheran Church-Missouis Synod; b. Red Bud, Ill., Aug. 7, 1946; s. Harold August and Adele Sophie (Bockhorn) W.; m. Susan Joette Sandman, June 25, 1971; children: Joshua Christian, Mary Rebekah. B.A., Concordia Sr. Coll., Ft. Wayne, Ind., 1969; B.D., Concordia Sem., Springfield, Ill., 1972. Ordained to ministry, Luth. Ch., 1972. Pastor, St. Paul's Luth. Ch., Columbia, Pa., 1972-77, Immanuel Luth. Ch., Danbury, Conn., 1977-85; assoc. pastor Hope Luth. Ch., Park Forest, Ill., 1985—; mem. com. on youth New Eng. Dist. Luth. Ch.-Mo. Synod, Springfield, Mass., 1977—, mem. com. on worship, 1981—; composer Resources for Youth Ministry, 1982. Dir. Luther 500, 1983, Bach 300, 1984. Mem. Am. Guild Organists, Hymn Soc. Am. Democrat. Home: 22 King St Danbury CT 06810 Office: Immanuel Luth Ch 32 West St Danbury CT 06810

WELL, DON, rabbi; pres. Hebrew Theol. Coll., Skokie, Ill. Office: Hebrew Theol Coll Office of the Pres 7135 N Carpenter Rd Skokie IL 60077*

WELLS, GEORGE HENRY, minister, United Presbyterian Church in the U.S.A.; b. Durant, Okla., May 14, 1940; s. Philip Yancy and Delta Iona (Harlin) W.; m. Deborah Lynn Lehman, Mar. 21, 1984. B.A.Ed., Okla. U., 1961; B.D., St. Andrews U., Scotland, 1964; M.Div., San Francisco Theol. Sem., 1980, D.Ministry, 1984. Ordained to ministry So. Bapt. Conv., 1962, United Presbyn. Ch. in the U.S.A., 1980. Pastor Francis Bapt. Ch., Okla., 1960-61; minister of evangelism and youth First Bapt. Ch., Ada, Okla., 1961-63; dir. crusades haggai Evangel. Assn., Atlanta, 1965-69; pastor, chmn. edn. adminstrn. First Presbyn. Ch., Bakersfield, Calif., 1969-76; assoc. pastor Fair Oaks Presbyn. Ch., Calif., 1976-83, co-pastor, 1983-84, pastor, 1985—; bd. dirs. HIS Farm, Inc., Sacramento, 1980—; mem. council Sacramento Presbytery, 1983—. Author: Electronic Church Awareness Guide, 1983. Named Outstanding Young Men Am., U.S. Jaycees, 1974; Rotary Found. fellow St. Andrews U., 1964. Mem. Nat. Assn. Christian Bus. Adminstrs., Nat. Assn. Evangelicals, Alpha Chi. Republican. Home: 4592 Minnesota Ave Fair Oaks CA 95628 Office: Fair Oaks Presbyn Ch 11427 Fair Oaks Blvd Fair Oaks CA 95628

WELLS, PAUL MONROE, minister, educational administrator, Assemblies of God; b. Collinsville, Okla., Jan. 21, 1918; s. James Monroe and Olive Marie (Burgess) W.; m. Betty Eileen Rockwell, Sept. 28, 1940; 1 child, Sheri Lee. Th.B., Belen Meml. U., 1954, D.D. (hon.), 1956. Ordained to ministry Assembly of God Ch., 1948. Pres., founder Inter-Faith Fellowship, Ventura and Tri County, Calif., 1953-56; pastor, evangelist Assemblies of God Ch., headquartered Taft, Calif., 1946-49, dir. youth central coast dist., Calif., 1951-54, Presbyter dist., 1956-60, minister, Santa Paula, Calif., 1960—; adminstr. Santa Paula Christian Sch., Calif., 1960—; producer, dir. The Messiah Ministry Assn., Santa Paula, 1952-53; asst. producer Sta. ABC-TV Inspiration Hour, Hollywood, Calif., 1952-53; producer, speaker Sta. Ind. Network-TV Hiway to Heaven, Hollywood, 1969-76, dir., speaker, Santa Paula, 1949-75; raised funds to build 21 chs., Kenya, East Africa, 1971-81. Author numerous religious books. Musician, rec. artist Million Miles of Song (4 Star Best Country Gospel award Billboard Mag., 1970), 1970. Contbr. articles on religion to profl. jours. Pres. Inter-faith Baskets for Hungry, Santa Paula, 1958-62; dir. Crop March for Needy of World, Santa Paula, 1970-71; chaplain Santa Paula City Council 1950-75. Recipient Golden Mike radio award Santa Paula Broadcasting Corp., 1952, Mr. Motivator award Santa Paula C. of C., 1960, Leadership in Community award KC, Santa Clara County, 1974, letter of recognition for 24 yrs. outstanding service to community and day named in honor Santa Paula City Council, 1974. Mem. Am. Legion. Lodge: Kiwanis. Avocation: golf. Home: 133 Mupu St PO Box 506 Santa Paula CA 93060 Office: Assemblies of God Ch Santa Paula Christian Sch 203 S 8th St Santa Paula CA 93060

WELLS, ROBERT LOUIS, minister, So. Bapt. Conv.; b. Alexandria, La., Mar. 18, 1939; s. Charles Alexander and Marie Elouise (Hinton) W.; B.A., La. State U., 1961; M.Div., Golden Gate Bapt. Theol. Sem., 1971, B.D., 1965; m. Michal Ann McCubbin, Mar. 12, 1966; children—Stephen Christopher, Jonathan David, Melissa Renee. Ordained to ministry, 1967; asso. pastor Emmanuel Bapt. Ch., Vallejo, Calif., 1963-65; dir. Bapt. Student Ministries, Ariz. State U., 1965-66; pastor Second Bapt. Ch., Lubbock, Tex., 1966—. Sec. bd. dirs. Contact Teleministries, U.S.A., Inc., 1971-75, vice-chmn., 1975—; v.p. bd. dirs. Contact Lubbock, Inc., 1971-73, pres., 1974-76. Mem. Community Planning Council of United Way, Lubbock, 1976—; mem. City-County Child Welfare Bd., 1968-71; chmn. bd. Lubbock Interagy. Action Council, 1973-75. Rockefeller Found. parish ministers fellow, 1975-76. Mem. Internat. Transactional Analysis Assn. Home: 3810 41st St Lubbock TX 79413 Office: 5300 Elgin Ave Lubbock TX 79413

WELLS, WILLIAM THOMAS, minister, United Church of Canada; b. London, Ont., Can., Aug. 3, 1938; s. Ernest Stanley and Winnifred Agnes (Staerck) W.; m. Judith Ann Green, Sept. 25, 1965; children: Gregory, Robert. B.A., U. Western Ont., 1962; B.Div., Queen's U., 1965. Ordained to ministry United Ch. Can., 1965. Minister Plumas-Lakeshore Pastoral Charge, Man., Can., 1965-67, 1st Westminster Ch., London, 1967-71; sr. minister Northminster Ch., Peterborough, Ont., 1971—; chmn. Peterborough Presbytery, 1981-83; pres. Bay of Quinte Conf., Kingston, Ont., 1984-85. Founding mem. Telecare, Peterborough, 1977. Served to capt. Can. Air Force. Home: 1335 Amundsen Ave Peterborough ON K9H 6T6 Canada Office: Northminster Church Sunset Blvd Peterborough ON K9H 6T6 Canada

WELSH, LAWRENCE H. See *Who's Who in America,* 43rd edition.

WELSH, THOMAS J., bishop, Roman Catholic Church; b. Weatherly, Pa., Dec. 20, 1921; ed. St. Charles Borromeo Sem., also Cath. U. Am., Washington. Ordained priest, 1946; ordained titular bishop of Scattery Islands, aux. bishop of Phila., 1970; bishop of Arlington (Va.), 1974-83; bishop of Allentown, Pa., 1983—. Office: 202 N 17th St Allentown PA 18104*

WENDEL, ARTHUR GEORGE, college president, priest, Roman Catholic Church; b. N.Y.C., Apr. 2, 1933; s. Maximilian and Elizabeth (Braun) W. B.A., St. John's U., 1954; M.R.E., Mt. St. Alphonsus U., 1960; M.A., Cath. U., 1962; B.S.M., Manhattanville U., 1972. Ordained priest Roman Catholic Ch., 1959. Tchr. St. Mary's Sem., North East, Pa., 1962-73; assoc. pastor St. Clement's Ch., Saratoga Springs, N.Y., 1973-78; pastor Most Holy Redeemer Parish, N.Y.C., 1978-84; pres. Mt. St. Alphonsus, Esopus, N.Y., 1984—. Mem. Assn. Theol. Schs., Nat. Assn. Pastoral Musicians.

WENDLER, HARLAN CARL, minister, Lutheran Church-Missouri Synod; b. Collinsville, Ill., Dec. 4, 1921; s. John Carl and Martha (Sepmeyer) W.; m. Dorothy Irene Burstadt, June 23, 1946; children: Douglas, Julaine, Bruce, Marcella, Brian. B.A., Concordia Sem., 1944, M. Div., 1946, M.S.T., 1966. Ordained to ministry Luth. Ch.-Mo. Synod, 1946. Pastor various chs., Okla., Ill., 1946-70, St. John's Luth. Ch., Effingham, Ill., 1970—; chmn. regional pastoral conf. So. Ill. dist. Luth. Ch.-Mo. Synod, Harvel, 1952-56, v.p. pastoral conf. No. Ill. dist. Addison, 1967-70, circuit counsellor, 1970; bd. dirs. Luth. Child and Family Services, Effingham, 1978-81. Contbr. articles to mags. Vice pres. NE Okla. Conf. Aging, Miami, 1960-62; treas. Effingham Children's Devel. Ctr., 1971-74; invoker meetings Republican Com., Effingham, 1973-82. Lodges: Lions, Kiwanis. Home:

905 W Jefferson Effingham IL 62401 Office: St Johns Luth Ch 901 W Jefferson Effingham IL 62401

WENDT, LOWELL CHRISTOPHER, minister, Independent Fundamental Chs. Am.; b. Manzanola, Colo., Nov. 11, 1917; s. Christopher Gottlieb and Emma Alice (Michael) W.; B.Th., Bible Inst. Los Angeles, 1940; D.D., Talbot Theol. Sem., 1960; m. Marie Esther Gunther, June 21, 1941; children—Lowell Cedrick, Louise Marie Wendt Eben, Judith Ann. Ordained to ministry, 1942; pastor Montecito Park Union Ch., Los Angeles, 1941-54, Lake City Community Ch., Tacoma, Wash., 1954-59, Hope Union Ch., Rosemead, Calif., 1959-63, Reinhardt Bible Ch., Dallas, 1963-70, Alderwood Manor Community Ch., Lynnwood, Wash., 1970—. Instr., Bible Inst. Los Angeles, 1952-53, Tacoma Bible Inst., 1955-59; lectr. pastoral therology Dallas Theol. Sem.; instr., pres. Seattle Bible Inst., 1972—; mem. nat. exec. com. Ind. Fundamental Chs. Am., 1957-72, nat. pres., 1960-63, pres. Tex. region, 1968-69, nat. pres., 1969-72, pres. Pacific n.w. regional, 1975-77. Mem. Home Council of Overseas Missionary Fellowship, United Indian Mission (adv. bd.). Editorial bd. Translation fellow, Lockman Found., 1960—; editor: Standards for Ordination Councils, 1954; contbr. articles in field to profl. jours. Home: 4910 181st Pl SW Lynnwood WA 98036 Office: PO Box 2146 Lynnwood WA 98036

WENDT, THEODORE ELWOOD, minister, American Lutheran Church. B. Cleve., June 26, 1932; s. William J. and Ruth Emma (Schaedel) W.; m. Jacqueline Irene Murray, Mar. 31, 1953; children: Alan, Timothy, Amy. A.B., Capital U., 1954; B.D. with honors, Luth. Theol. Sem., Columbus, Ohio, 1958. Ordained to ministry Am. Lutheran Ch., 1958. Pastor, St. Paul Luth. Ch., Waldo, Ohio, 1958-60, Grace Luth. Ch., Eaton, Ohio, 1963-69, Faith Luth. Ch., Lakeland, Fla., 1969-79; founding pastor Christ Luth. Ch., Massillon, Ohio, 1960-63, Shepherd Woods Luth. Ch., Jacksonville, Fla., 1979—; conf. pres. Northeast Fla. Conf., Am. Luth. Ch. (Southeastern dist.), Jacksonville, 1981—; council mem. Southeastern Dist., 1981. Author: Doing the Gospel, 1977. Mem. Jacksonville Luth. Ministerial Assn. Democrat. Lodge: Rotary. Home and Office: 8441 Allerton Ln Jacksonville FL 32216

WENGER, KIM ROGER, minister, American Lutheran Church; b. Columbus, Ohio, Oct. 25, 1950; s. Frederick Theodore and Francie May (Geis) W.; m. Ann Christine Jenny, June 12, 1971; children: Katherine Elizabeth, Julianne Jenny. B.A., Ohio State U., 1973; M.Div., Trinity Luth. Sem., 1977. Ordained to ministry Am. Luth. Ch., 1977. Pastor St. John Luth. Ch., Sandusky, Ohio, 1977-81, Grace Luth. Ch., East Palestine, Ohio, 1981—; mem. Service and Mission in Am. Dist. Com., Am. Luth. Ch., 1978-81, mem. outdoor ministry commn., 1981—, chmn. program com., bd. dirs. Camp Frederick, Rogers, Ohio, 1981—; bd. dirs. chaplaincy com. Tobin Ctr., Lisbon, Ohio, 1984. Bd. dirs. East Palestine Meals-on-Wheels, 1984. Mem. Youngstown Area Luth. Pastors Assn. (treas. 1983—), East Palestine Ministers Assn. (treas. 1981-84). Democrat. Home: 439 N Walnut St East Palestine OH 44413 Office: Grace Luth Ch 439 N Walnut St East Palestine OH 44413

WENGERT, TIMOTHY JOHN, pastor, American Lutheran Church; b. Teaneck, N.J., Oct. 1, 1950; s. Norman Irving and Janet (Mueller) W.; m. Barbara Ann Farlow, Nov. 17, 1973; children: Emily Jane, David Hayworth. Student, U. Freiburg, Fed. Republic Germany, 1970-71; A.B., U. Mich., 1972, M.A., 1973; M.Div., Luther Theol. Sem., St. Paul, 1977; Ph.D., Duke U., 1984. Ordained to ministry Am. Luth. Ch., 1977. Asst. pastor Luth. Ch. of the Master, Edina, Minn., 1977-78; pastor Cross Luth. Ch., Roberts, Wis., 1983—; mem. task force on studies Commn. for Luth.-Roman Cath. Relations in Wis. and Upper Mich., 1984—; panel mem. SELECT, Columbus, Ohio, 1984—; conf. rep. Growth Learning Enrichment Enterprises, Kenosha, Wis., 1984—. Contbg. editor: Luther's Werke, Vol. 59, 1983. Contbr. articles to religious publs. Recipient scholarship Deutsche Akademische Austauschdienst, U. Tübingen, 1980-81. Office: Cross Luth Ch Rural Route 1 Box 187 Roberts WI 54023

WENKER, KEVIN LEE, minister, Lutheran Church-Missouri Synod; b. Garden City, Mich., Nov. 20, 1950; s. Frederick William and Joyce Ann (Molander) W.; m. Barbara Jane Kelly, Aug. 22, 1970; children: Keri-Lee, Sarah Abigail, Joshua Frederick Norris. B.A., U. Pitts., 1972; M.Div., Concordia Theol. Sem., 1976. Ordained to ministry Luth. Ch., 1976. Pastor, Prince of Peace Luth. Ch., Waukegan, Ill., 1976-77, St. John Luth. Ch., Munosn, Pa., 1977-78, Faith Luth. Ch., Oak Lawn, Ill., 1978-82, Zion and Christ Luth. Ch., Granton, Wis., 1982-85, Our Redeemer Luth. Ch., Bessemer, Mich., 1985—; del. Nobel Conf., St. Peter, Minn., 1975; rep. Dist. Stewardship Bd., Marshfield, Wis., 1982-84; mem. Luth. Layman's League, Oak Lawn, 1976—, advisor, 1982; mem. Luth. Cir. Stewardship Com., 1982—. Author: (with others) Mirrors for Managers, 1982; Meanings—Teacher's Guide, 1983. Co-author, editor: Meanings for Managers, 1983. Chmn. Black Bear Environ. Commn., Munosn, 1977; bd. advisors Granton Sch., Wis., 1983. Tech. student scholar Westinghouse Co., 1969-72. Mem. Luth. Pastor's Assn. (sec. 1976-77) Gogebic Woodcarvers Assn. Republican. Club: Hivernann (Marshfield) (pub. relations com. 1983-84). Home: 819 Margaret St Ironwood MI 49938 Office: Our Redeemer Luth Ch Bessemer MI

WENTHOLD, ALBERTONA MARY, nun, Roman Catholic Ch.; b. Festina, Iowa, Apr. 18, 1904; d. William and Frances (Mehs) Wenthold; B.A., U. Detroit, 1938; M.A., Cath. U., 1945; certificate in theology Mount Mary Coll., 1954; postgrad. U. Madrid, 1966. Joined Sisters of St. Dominic, 1921; high sch. tchr. Center Line, Mich., 1924-31, 35-36, St. Catherine's High Sch., Racine, Wis., 1931-35, 52-58, 62-70, Little Chute, Wis., 1936-40, Nativity of Our Lord Sch., Detroit, 1940-45; prin. Assumption Grotto, Detroit, 1945-51, Santa Fe, N.M., 1959-62, St. Sebastian, Sturtevant, Wis., 1969-71, Holy Trinity Sch., Racine, Wis., 1971-73, St. Anthony Sch., Kenosha, Wis., 1973—. Mission chmn. Milw. Archdiocesan Council Cath. Women, 1967-70. Mem. Wis. Latin Assn., Nat. Cath. Edn. Assn. Home: 5116 22nd Ave Kenosha WI 53140 Office: 5115 23rd Ave Kenosha WI 53140

WERGER, PAUL MYRON See *Who's Who in America*, 43rd edition.

WERNER, JAMES EDWARD, minister, United Church of Christ. B. Elgin, Il., Apr. 6, 1951; s. Edward Henry and Henrietta (Lichthardt) W.; m. Nancy Jo Lilly, Sept. 15, 1979; children: Megan Elizabeth, Mary Catherine, Melissa Anne. B.A., Elmhurst Coll., 1973; M. Div., Lancaster Theol. Sem., 1976. Ordained to ministry United Ch. Christ, 1976. Assoc. pastor St. Paul United Ch. Christ, 1976-82; pastor 1st Congl. Ch., Rock Falls, Ill., 1982—; recording sec. Ministerial Assn., Sterling-Rock Falls, 1983-84, pres., 1984—; dean United Ch. Mission Council, Sterling-Rock Falls, 1983—; mem. spiritual growth com. No. Ill. assn. United Ch. Christ, 1983—. Home: 907 Dixon Ave Rock Falls IL 61071 Office: First Congl United Ch Christ 905 Dixon Ave Rock Falls IL 61071

WERNETH, XAVIER, brother, educator, Roman Catholic Church; b. Mobile, Ala., Dec. 14, 1942; s. Francis Xavier and Maurine (Wilson) W. A.B., Springhill Coll., 1965; M.A., La. State U., 1971. Joined Bros. of Sacred Heart, Roman Cath. Ch., 1958. Tchr. Cath. high sch., Baton Rouge, 1965-75; prin. E.D. White High Sch., Thibodaux, La., 1975-82; provincial superior Bros. of Sacred Heart, Bay St. Louis, Miss., 1982—, del. gen. chpt., Rome, 1982. Mem. Conf. Major Superiors of Men, Chief Adminstrs. of Cath. Edn. Address: PO Box 89 Bay Saint Louis MS 39520

WERTH, LOREN JAMES, priest, Roman Cath. Ch.; b. Schoenchen, Kans., Oct. 16; s. Eddie and Sophie (Herklotz) W.; B.A., Conception (Mo.) Sem., 1952, M.A. in Theology, 1956. Ordained priest, 1956; pastor chs. in Kans., 1956—, Our Lady of Perpetual Help Ch., Concordia, 1970—. Pres. Concordia Ministerial Assn., 1977; lay adv. bd. St. Joseph's Hosp., Concordia; diocesan consultor to bishop, mem. liturgy commn. Roman Cath. Diocese of Salina (Kans.). Chmn. United Way campaign, Concordia, 1976—. Mem. Common Cause. Contbr. articles to religious jours. Address: Box 608 307 E 5th St Concordia KS 66901

WESBERRY, JAMES PICKETT, minister, author, Southern Baptist Convention; b. Bishopville, S.C., Apr. 16, 1906; s. William Mc Cleod and Lillian Ione (Galloway) W.; A.B., Mercer U., 1929, M.A., 1930, D.D., 1957; B.D., Andover Newton Theol. Sch., 1931, M.S.T., 1934; postgrad. Harvard, 1931, Union Theol. Sem., 1935, 65; LL.D., Atlanta Law Sch., 1946; L.H.D., LaGrange Coll., 1962; Litt.D., Bolen-Draughon Coll., 1967; m. Ruby Lee Perry, Sept. 5, 1929 (dec. 1941); 1 son, James P.; m. 2d, Mary Sue Latimer, June 1, 1943 (dec. 1982); m. 3d, Margaret Spratlin, Oct. 15, 1983. Ordained to ministry, 1926; pastor Kingstree (S.C.) Bapt. Ch., 1931-33, Cedar Grove Bapt. Ch., 1931-33, Bamberg Bapt. Ch., Bamberg, S.C., 1933-44, Morningside Bapt. Ch., Atlanta, 1944-75, pastor emeritus, 1975—; acting chaplain U.S. Ho. of Reps., 1949; chaplain Nat. League of Masonic Clubs, 1973; missioner to U.S. Air Bases in Japan, Okinawa, Philippines, Nfld. and Hawaii. Pres. Atlanta Bapt. Ministers Conf., 1949, Atlanta Christian Council, 1952-53; chmn. radio and TV com. Greater Atlanta Council of Chs., 1960-71; v.p. Ga. Bapt. Conv., 1946, 50, pres., 1956-57, sec. exec. com., 1971—; mem. Home Mission Bd. So. Bapt. Conv., 1944-51, v.p., 1946, mem. Sunday sch. bd., 1966-73, rec. sec.; pres. So. Bapt. Pastors' Conf., 1957; trustee Atlanta Bapt. Coll., 1964-72; exec. dir., editor The Lord's Day, Alliance of U.S. Bapt. Ctr. Mem. Atlanta Fund Rev. Bd., 1953-73; chmn. State Lit. Commn., State of Ga., 1953-74; chmn. editorial com. Citizens Penal Reform Commn., 1968; chmn. bd. of govs. Highview Nursing Home, 1947—; trustee Mercer U., 1944-49, 54-56, 72-74, Truett-McConnell Coll., 1960-65. Elected to South's Hall of Fame, Dixie Bus. Mag., 1972. Mem. Chaplains Mil. Assn., Royal Order of Scotland, Alpha Chi Omega (nat. pres. 1949-50). Clubs: Lion (chaplain), Harvard, Kiwanis, Atlanta Athletic, Atlanta Amateur Movie (pres.), Mason. Author: Life and Work of William Screven, 1941, Prayers in Congress, 1949, Rainbow Over Russia, 1963, Baptists in South Carolina Before the War Between the States, 1966, Meditations for Happy Christians, 1973, Evangelistic Sermons, 1973, Making Hell Tremble, 1974; Bread in a Barren Land, 1983; contbr. articles to newspapers and religious publs. Editor Sunday, Basharat. Home: 1715 Merton Rd NE Atlanta GA 30306 Office: Suite 107 2930 Flowers Rd S Atlanta GA 30341

WESELOH, MELVIN LESLIE, minister, Lutheran Church-Missouri Synod; b. Dickinson, N.D., Dec. 29, 1932; s. Henry John and Edith (Oehler) W.; m. Karen H. Miller, June 9, 1957; children—David, Debra, Diane, Daryl. B.A., Concordia Sem., St. Louis, 1957. Ordained to ministry Luth. Ch., 1957. Asst. pastor St. Luke's Luth. Ch., N.Y.C., 1957-58; pastor chs. in Minn., 1959-74, Trinity Luth. Ch., Coal Valley, Ill., 1974-77; missionary at-large Epiphany Luth. Ch., Dunlap, Ill., 1978-80; pastor St. Paul's Luth. Ch., Havana, Ill., 1980—; advisor Luth. Laymen's League, Central Ill., 1984—; v.p. bd. Camp Cilca, Cantrall, Ill., 1977-84. Contbr. articles to profl. jours. Bd. dirs., treas. Lakes and Pines Community Action Com., Mora, Minn., Minn., 1971-74; bd. dirs. Kanabec County Commn. on Aging, Mora, 1967-74. Mem. Havana Ministerial Assn. (pres.), Havana C. of C. (bd. dirs.). Lodge: Lions (treas. 1976). Address: 227 E Market Havana IL 62644

WESEMANN, RONALD PAUL, minister, Lutheran Church in America; b. Phila., Apr. 8, 1953; s. Elmer Frederick and Pearl Zoe (Branchide) W.; m. Catherine Marie Qquitiere, Aug. 20, 1977; 1 child, Catherine Zoe. B.A. in Philosophy, Pa. State U., 1974; M.Div., Luth. Theol. Sem., Phila., 1978, postgrad. Acad. of Preachers, 1984; postgrad. Appalachian Regional Sch., 1980. Ordained to ministry Luth. Ch., 1978. Intern St. Paul's Luth. Ch., Douglassville, Pa., 1976-77; asst. to pastor Immanuel Luth. Ch., Phila., 1977-78; pastor St. Paul's English Evang. Luth. Ch., Phila., 1978—; pastoral cons. Cheltenham Nursing Home, Phila., 1983—; mem. task force justice and social change SE Pa. Synod, Luth. Ch. Am., 1983-84, chmn., 1984—; mem. network pub. policy Luth. Ch.Am., 1984. Recipient Legion of Honor award Chapel of Four Chaplains, Phila., 1984. Mem. Olney Clergy Assn. (sec. 1980-82). Office: St Pauls English Evang Luth Ch 3d St and Cheltenham Ave Philadelphia PA 19126

WESSELSCHMIDT, QUENTIN FREDERICK, minister, Lutheran Church-Missouri Synod, educator; b. Washington, Mo., Feb. 3, 1937; s. Raenhard Henry and Thelma Corinne (Hartge) W.; m. Susan Elizabeth Susanka, Nov. 16, 1963. Diploma, St. Paul's Jr. Coll., 1957; B.A., Concordia Sr. Coll., Ft. Wayne, Ind., 1959; B.D., Concordia Sem., St. Louis, 1963, M.Div., 1963; M.A., Marquette U., 1969; Ph.D., U. Iowa, 1979. Ordained to ministry, 1963. Pastor Our Savior Luth. Ch., Hillsboro, Ill., 1963-65; asst. prof. Concordia Coll., Milw., 1965-71; lectr. in classics U. Wis., Milw., 1973-75; adminstrv. asst., instr. religion Luth. High Sch. Assn. Greater Milw., 1974-77; assoc. prof. hist. theology, chmn. hist. theology dept., Concordia Sem., St. Louis, 1977—, editor Concordia Jour., 1982—; vacancy pastor Immanuel Luth. Chapel, St. Louis, 1982—. Mem. Am. Philol. Assn., Classical Assn. Middle West and South, Concordia Hist. Inst. Home: 444 Eatherton Valley Rd Chesterfield MO 63017 Office: Concordia Seminary 801 DeMun Ave Saint Louis MO 63105

WESSLER, JEANNETTE (JANEY) WATKINS, lay church worker, retired music director, Presbyterian Church in the U.S.; b. McPherson, Kans., Apr. 27, 1925; d. George Earl and Orpha Marie (Andes) Watkins; m. Jack Copeland Wessler, Nov. 17, 1945; children: Christine Elaine Wessler Jarboe, John Watkins, Glenn Alan. Student in music North Tex. Agr. Coll., 1943-44, North Tex. State U., 1944-45. Ordained to ministry Presbyterian Ch. as ruling elder, 1977. Dir. music First Presbyn. Ch., Arlington, Tex., 1945-70, ret., 1970; chmn. com. on worship Grace Presbytery, Presbyn. Ch. in the U.S., 1980-85, cons. worship edn., 1985; commr. to Gen. Assembly, Presbyn. Ch. in the U.S., Atlanta, 1983; mem. Task Force For Liturgical Resource for Funeral Service, Presbyn. Ch. in the U.S., 1984-85; moderator com. on worship in presbyteries and synods Mid-Governing Bodies Conf., St. Charles, Mo., 1985. Vice pres. Arlington Fine Arts League, 1981. Mem. P.E.O. (pres. local club 1981-83), Arlington Music Club (v.p.), Mu Phi Epsilon. Home: 1409 Glasgow Dr Arlington TX 76015

WEST, EARL C., bishop, Ch. of God of Prophecy; b. Sampson County, N.C., June 24, 1928; s. Carl and Carrie (Moore) W.; grad. Bible Tng. Inst., Cleveland, Tenn., 1972; m. Ila Ruth Lee, Sept. 11, 1948; children—Brenda Ruth, Ronnie Earl, Pamela Kay, Sherry Melinda. Licensed evangelist, 1961, bishop, 1974; pastor chs., N.C., 1961—, Selma, N.C., 1973—. Dist. overseer chs., Johnston and Wayne Counties, N.C. Home and Office: 304 E Elizabeth Ave Selma NC 27576

WEST, EDWARD NASON, priest, Episcopal Church; b. Boston, Nov. 5, 1909; s. Edward Nason and Isadora Angelina (da Vincente-Bellizia) W. B.S., Boston U., 1931, Litt.D., 1950; S.T.B., Gen. Theol. Sem., 1934,

S.T.D., 1963; D.D., Ripon Coll., 1946; fellow Trinity Coll., London, 1948; Th.D., Russian Theol. Inst., Paris, 1953; D.D., U. Kings Coll., Halifax, N.S., 1975; L.H.D., Episcopal Sem. of Southwest, 1984. Ordained to ministry Episcopal Ch., deacon 1934, priest 1935. Curate, Trinity Ch., Ossining, N.Y., 1934-37, rector, 1937-41; sacrist Cathedral Ch. of St. John, N.Y.C., 1941-43, canon residentiary, 1943-81, subdean, 1966-81, master of ceremonies, 1981—; hon. canon of Vt., 1975—; dep. to gen. conv., 1969-81; lectr. liturgics Gen. Theol. Sem., 1957-60; Washburn lectr. Episcopal Theol. Sch., Cambridge, 1960; lectr. edn. NY U 1961-62; Purser Shortt lectr. U. Dublin, 1971; lectr. Anglican doctrine and worship Union Theol. Sem., 1965-80, Diocesan Inst. Theology, 1973—; nat. chaplain Am. Guild Organists, 1944-49, 59-60, 68-70; vice chmn. Joint Commn. Ch. Architecture and Allied Arts, 1955-82; chmn. Diocesan Commn. Ch. Bldg., 1943-83; select preacher U. Dublin, 1952, 71; cons. Trinity Corp., U.S. Mil. Acad., West Point; warden Community of Holy Spirit; trustee St. Vladimir's Orthodox Theol. Sch. and Acad., Tolstoy Found., St. Peter's Sch. Author: Meditations on the Gospel of St. John, 1955; Things I Always Thought I Knew, 1957; A Glossary of Architectural and Liturgical Terms, 1958; (with Norman Laliberte) The History of the Cross, 1960; God's Image in Us, 1960; The Far Spent Night, 1960; also monographs; contbr. Ency. Americana, Funk and Wagnells Universal Standard Ency. Designer, Emblem of Anglican Communion. Served to maj., chaplain USAR-N.G., 1947-69; lt. col. USNG, 1970—. Decorated officer Orange-Nassau (The Netherlands), officer Order Brit. Empire, chevalier Legion of Honor (France), State Conspicuous Service Cross, sub-prelate Order St. John Jerusalem (Gt. Britain), silver medal Red Cross of Japan, comdr. Order of Holy Sepulchre, Order of St. Gregory the Illuminator. Fellow Royal Soc. Arts; mem. Episcopal Soc. for Promoting Religion and Learning in State N.Y., Pilgrims of U.S., St. Andrews Soc., St. George Soc., Soc. of Cin. Clubs: Century, University, Columbia Faculty (N.Y.C.); Athenaeum (London). Home and Office: Cathedral Heights 1047 Amsterdam Ave New York NY 10025

WEST, PAUL JOSEPH, minister, Am. Bapt. Chs., U.S.A.; b. Boston, Feb. 19, 1919; s. Joseph Axel and Olga Elena (Anderson) W.; student Northeastern U., 1937-38, Gordon Coll., 1945; A.B., Gordon Div. Sch., 1946; M.A., U. N.H., 1948; postgrad. Inst. Pastoral Care, 1965; LL.D., Calif. Grad. Sch. Theology, 1971; m. Edith Holmberg, Aug. 4, 1945; children—Sandra Edith West Clark, Stephen Paul. Ordained to ministry, 1946; pastor West Falmouth (Maine) Bapt. Ch., 1945-48, St. Lawrence Congl. Ch., Portland, Maine, 1948-50, Central Bapt. Ch., Middleboro, Mass., 1950—; chaplain Lakeville (Mass.) Hosp., 1950—. Chaplain Mass. State Police, 1965—, Middleboro Police, 1965—. Bd. dirs. Middleboro YMCA, 1968—. Recipient numerous awards, including citations from Pres. U.S., Mass. Senate, Ho. of Reps., Am. Legion, Radio Sta. WPEP, Radio Sta. WRLM; Paul J. West Day was observed in Middleborough, June 1975. Mem. Lakeville Hosp. Assos., Inst. for Pastoral Care, Mass. Chaplains Assn., Am. Hosp. Protestant Chaplains Assn., Coll. Chaplains of Am. Hosp. Assn., Pi Gamma Mu. Home: 28 Heritage Hill Dr Lakeville MA 02346 Office: Central Baptist Ch Box 369 Union St Middleboro MA 02346

WESTCOTT, EDWARD AUGUST, JR., minister, church official, Lutheran Church-Missouri Synod; b. Selma, Ala., Oct. 28, 1922; s. Edward August and Louise Wilhemina (Hagemann) W.; student Concordia Coll., 1939, student Concordia Theol. Sem., 1947, D.D. (hon.), 1974; m. Sylvia Jean Hyduk, Oct. 9, 1948; children: Rebecca Westcott Virden, Deborah Westcott-Callahan, Mark, Timothy, Elizabeth Westcott Rushlo. Ordained to ministry, 1948. Missionary Nigeria, W. Africa, 1948-55; pastor Milan, Mich., 1955-57, Detroit, 1957-71, Ch. of the Holy Cross, Scottsdale, Ariz., 1971-78; exec. sec. bd. for mission services, Luth. Ch.-Mo. Synod, 1978—; mem. mission bd. Mich. dist. Luth. Ch.-Mo. Synod, Ann Arbor, Mich., 1960-68, v.p. 1968-71; mem. mission study commn. Luth. Ch.-Mo. Synod, St. Louis, 1974-75, mem. commn. on theology and ch. relations, 1975-77, bd. dirs., 1977-78. Mem. bd. control Christ Coll., Irvine, Calif., 1973—. Bd. dirs. Luth. Bible Translators, Orange, Calif., 1972—. Recipient Servus Ecclesiae Christi award Concordia Theol. Sem., 1971. Office: 1333 S Kirkwood Rd Saint Louis MO 63122

WESTENDICK, BASIL CHARLES, priest, friar, Roman Catholic Church; B. Tallahassee, Fla., July 27, 1930; s. Frank Charles and Alyce Mae (Converse) W. B.A., Duns Scotus Coll., 1953; postgrad. in philosophy and theology Holy Family Friary, 1953-57. Ordained priest Roman Catholic Ch., 1957. Asst. pastor St. Michael's Ch., Southfield, Mich., 1957-62; vocat. dir. St. Francis Sem., Cin., 1962-67; pastor St. Patrick Ch., Port Sulphur, La., 1967-76; dir. bros. tng. program St. Anthony Friary, Cin., 1976-78; pastor Corpus Christi Ch., Cin., 1978—. Home and Office: Corpus Christi Ch 2014 Springdale Rd Cincinnati OH 45231

WESTERBUHR, GERALD GENE, minister, American Lutheran Church. B. Hildreth, Nebr., May 24, 1934; s. Gerd Eilers and Marie (Quadhamer) W.; m. Brenda K. Bowker, Aug. 29, 1958 (div. May 1980); 1 child, Ms. Michal M. Smithpeters; m. Ruby N. Borel, June 29, 1980; stepchildren: Miguel J. Puckett, Scott J. Puckett. B.A., Wartburg Coll., 1956; B.D., Wartburg Sem., 1960, M.Div., 1977; cert. hypno-therapist Inst. Hypnosis, New Orleans, 1982. Ordained to ministry Am. Luth. Ch., 1960. Pastor Zion Luth. Ch., McGregor, Tex., 1960-62, Christ Luth. Ch., Syracuse, Nebr., 1962-65, Hope Luth. Ch., Tulsa, 1965-69; assoc. pastor Zion Luth. Ch., Aberdeen, S.D., 1969-75; pastor 1st Evang. Luth. Ch., Damon, Tex., 1975-77, Community Luth. Ch., Hope/Murfreesboro, Ark., 1977-78, Immanuel Evang. Luth. Ch., New Orleans, 1978—; v.p. Clifton Luth. Sunset Home, Tex., 1962-63; sec. worship com. central dist. Am. Luth. Ch., Tulsa, 1966—; chmn. Okla. conf., Tulsa, 1969; chaplain Lakeside Tng. Ctr., Tulsa, 1969; dir. Joint Luth. Choir, New Orleans, 1979-81. Vice pres. One the Bricks, Inc., Tulsa, 1968; treas. Nat. Research and Devel., Aberdeen, 1973; pres. bd. No. Alcohol and Drug Abuse Info. Ctr., Aberdeen, 1973; bd. dirs., founder Damon Community Choir, Tex., 1976-77; bd. dirs. Ecumenical Immigration Services, New Orleans, 1982-85. Mem. Greater New Orleans Fedn. Chs. Republican. Lodge: Lions (pres. 1979-80, 2d v.p. 1984—). Home: 3708 Bissonet Dr Metairie LA 70003 Office: Immanuel Evang Luth Ch 134 N Broad Ave New Orleans LA 70119

WESTERFIELD, NANCY GILLESPIE, lay church worker, Episcopal Church; b. Cin., Dec. 24, 1925; d. Charles Herman and Lilian Elizabeth (Appleton) G.; m. Hargis Westerfield, Aug. 31, 1950. B.A., U. Cin., 1947; M.A., Ind. U., 1951. Exec. council Diocese of Nebr., 1974-79, 80—, sec. dept. missions, 1975—, dep. to gen. conv. Episcopal Ch., 1982, 85. Author: (poetry) Welded Women, 1983. Contbr. articles to profl. jours. Nat. Endowment for Arts fellow, 1975; Yaddo fellow in poetry, 1979, 81; recipient award in poetry Nat. Cath. Press Assn., 1979. Mem. Phi Beta Kappa, Delta Zeta. Democrat. Home: 414 W 25th St Kearney NE 68847 Office: Saint Luke's Church PO Box 609 2304 2d Ave Kearney NE 68847

WESTERHOFF, JOHN HENRY, III, priest, educator, Episcopal Church; b. Paterson, N.J., June 28, 1933; s. John Henry, Jr. and Nona C. (Walsh) W.; B.S., Ursinus Coll., 1955; M.Div., Harvard Div. Sch., 1958; Ed.D., Columbia, 1974; m. Alberta Barnhart, Dec. 28, 1955; children: Jill, Jack, Beth. Ordained to ministry United Ch. of Christ, 1958; pastor Presque Isle (Maine) Congl. Ch., 1958-60, Needham (Mass.) Congl. Ch., 1960-64, 1st Congl. Ch., Williamstown, Mass., 1964-66; ch. exec., editor United Ch. Bd. Homeland Ministries, 1966-74; prof. religion and edn. Duke Div. Sch., Durham, N.C., 1974—, ordained priest Episcopal Ch., 1978. Mem. Am. Anthrop. Assn., Religious Edn. Assn., Assn. Profs. and Researchers in Religious Edn. Author: Values for Tomorrow's Children 1970; A Colloquy on Christian Education, 1972; Liberation Letters, 1972; (with Joseph Williams on) Learning to Be Free, 1973; (with Gwen Kennedy Neville) Generation to Generation, 1974, Learning Through Liturgy, 1978; Tomorrow's Church, 1976; Will Our Children Have Faith?, 1976; McGuffey and His Readers, 1977; Inner Growth-Outer Change, 1979; Bringing Up Children in the Christian Faith, 1980; Building God's People, 1983; A Pilgrim People, 1984; Living A Faith Community, 1985; (with Caroline Hughes) On the Threshold of God's Future, 1986, others. Editor: The Church's Ministry in Higher Education, 1978. Home: 3510 Racine St Durham NC 27707

WESTRICK, MARY COLETTE, nun, Roman Catholic Church; b. Hastings, Pa., Mar. 17, 1912; d. Augustine James and Melvina Agatha (Lantzy) W.; B.Ph., DePaul U., 1942, M.A., 1956. Joined Benedictine Sisters of Chgo., 1930; tchr. parochial schs., Chgo., 1931-46, prin., 1947-55; tchr. and prin. secondary schs., Chgo. and Canon City, Colo., 1955-59; prioress Benedictine Sisters, Chgo., 1971—; dir. consolidation of 4 Cath. elem. schs. into Lake Shore Cath. Acad. Mem. Ill. Com. for Responsible Investment. Mem. Fedn. St. Scholastica, Nat. Cath. Edn. Assn., Leadership Conf. Women Religious, Nat. Assn. Ch. Personnel Adminstrs., Nat. Smithsonian Inst. Assos., Common Cause. Home: 7430 Ridge Blvd Chicago IL 60645

WETTHER, NORMAN ARTHUR, minister, mission administrator, Conservative Baptist Association of America; b. Portland, Oreg., Oct. 22, 1921; s. Arthur F. and Julia (Mickelsen) W.; m. Joyce Elaine Reid, Jan. 29, 1945; children: Sandra Lynn, Karen Lee, Anne Marie, Carol Joyce. B.A., Linfield Coll., 1948; M.Div., Fuller Theol. Sem., 1951; D.Div. (hon.), Internat. Coll., Honolulu, 1980. Ordained to ministry, 1950. Pastor, Berean Bapt. Ch., Eugene, Oreg., 1951-56; missionary Conservative Bapt. Home Mission Soc., Agana, Guam, 1957-70, mission adminstr., Wheaton, Ill., 1970—. Mem. territorial parole bd. Govt. Guam, Agana, 1965-68, hosp. chaplain, 1966-67. Served to 1st lt. U.S. Army, 1943-46, ETO. Republican.

WETZEL, GALE THOMAS, evangelist, United Methodist Church; b. Owensboro, Ky., Sept. 29, 1937; s. Carter Thomas and Dorothy Glidden (Bennett) W.; B.A., Ky. Wesleyan Coll., 1962; M.Div., Asbury Theol. Sem., 1967; m. Nancy Duessa Gumm, June 3, 1962; children: Dorothy Pauline, Owen Thomas. Ordained deacon, 1964, elder, 1967; pastor Fordsville Circuit, 1962, New Springs-Fincastle Chs., Beattyville, Ky., 1963-65, Shiloh United Meth. Ch., Stanton, Ky., 1965-67, Bonnieville (Ky.) United Meth. Ch., 1967, Wesley-Baird St. Mission, Louisville, 1968-70, Summit Heights Ch., Louisville, 1970-72; approved evangelist, 1972—; mem. bd. evangelism Louisville Conf., 1962-72, Louisville continuing com. on memls., 1976—; mem. Louisville Conf. Bd. Global Ministries. Mem. Nat. Assn. United Meth. Evangelists. Author booklets; contbr. to Born of the Spirit, 1976. Home and Office: Rt 5 Franklin KY 42134

WHATLEY, JOHN CALHOUN, III, minister, educator, Southern Baptist Convention; b. Augusta, Ga., Feb. 7, 1935; s. John Calhoun and Marian (Wall) W. B.A., U. S.C., 1958; B.D., Southeastern Theol. Sem., 1967, M.Div., 1968; S.T.D., Emory U., 1976. Ordained to ministry Southern Baptist Conv., United Methodist Church, 1962. Instr. psychology, sr. counselor Bklyn.-Cayce Schs., West Columbia, S.C., 1960-62; assoc. minister First United Meth. Ch., Myrtle Beach, S.C., 1962-64; sr. minister Forestville Ch., Wake Forest, N.C., 1964-69; minister preaching and pastoral concerns Myers Park Bapt. Ch., Charlotte, N.C., 1969-71; prof. religion Andrew Coll., Cuthbert, Ga., 1975-77; sr. minister Ch. of the Covenant, Birmingham, Ala., 1977-83; sr. cons. Birmingham Assn. Chs., 1983—. Pres., City Council, Wake Forest, 1967-69 (recipient 2 awards). Recipient Outstanding Prof. award Andrew Coll., 1967.

WHATLEY, RAY EDWARD, minister, United Meth. Ch.; b. Whatley, Ala., Oct. 16, 1919; s. George Lemuel and Ruby (Calhoun) W.; A.B., Huntingdon Coll., 1945; B.D., Emory U., 1948; m. Irma Katherine Greene, Feb. 4, 1945; 1 son, Charles David. Admitted on trial Ala. Conf., Meth. Ch., 1943, full connection, 1945, ordained deacon, 1945, ordained elder, 1947; pastor chs., Gainesville, Ala., 1941, Shorter, Ala., 1941-43, Montgomery, Ala., 1943-45, 53-56, Inman, Ga., 1945-47, Decatur, Ga., 1947-48, Pensacola, Fla., 1948-49, Florala, Ala., 1949-51, Monroeville, Ala., 1951-53, Linden, Ala., 1956-57, Mobile, Ala., 1957-61, Evergreen, Ala., 1961-63; mem. Gen. Bd. Pensions, United Meth. Ch., Evanston, Ill., 1962—, dir. disability benefit program, 1962-74, asst. gen. sec., 1975—. Asst. Conf. statistician, 1943-56, asst. Conf. sec., 1960-62, mem. Conf. Bd. Pensions, 1949-60, 64-68; sec. Pensacola Ministerial Assn., 1948-49; pres. Covington County Ministerial Assn., 1950-51, Monroe County Ministerial Assn., 1952-53; pres. Montgomery (Ala.) Chpt. Council on Human Relations, 1955-56; sec., bd. dirs. Evanston (Ill.) Council of Chs., 1963-66. Home: 1560 Asbury Ave Evanston IL 60201 Office: 1200 Davis St Evanston IL 60201

WHEALON, JOHN FRANCIS, archbishop, Roman Catholic Church; b. Barberton, Ohio, Jan. 15, 1921; s. John J. and Mary (Zanders) W.; student St. Charles Coll., Catonsville, Md., 1940, St. Mary's Sem., Cleve., 1945; S.T.L., U. Ottawa (Can.), 1946; S.S.L., Pontifical Bibl. U., Rome, Italy, 1950; M.A. in Edn., John Carroll U., 1957. Ordained priest Roman Cath. Ch., 1945, consecrated bishop, 1961; asst. pastor Diocese of Cleve., 1945-53; founding rector Borromeo Sem., Wickliffe, Ohio, 1953, tchr. Latin, Hebrew, Sacred Scripture, 1953-61; titular bishop Andrapa, from 1961, Cleve., 1961-66; bishop of Erie, Pa., 1967-68; archbishop of Hartford, Conn., 1969—; chmn. Nat. Bishops' Com. on Ecumenism Affairs, 1981—, Revision of New Am. Bible Com., 1981—. Author: Living the Catholic Faith Today, 1974; The Teaching of Christ, 1976. Address: 134 Farmington Ave Hartford CT 06105*

WHEAT, ROBERT EDGAR, minister, Presbyterian Church in the U.S.A.; b. Miami, Fla., Oct. 4, 1939; s. Orien Robert Wheat and Frances (Spaulding) Shea; m. Deborah June Hook, Feb. 27, 1971; children: Matthew Wynne, Emily Field, Micah Jonathan. B.A. in History, Stetson U., 1962; M.Div. in Theology, So. Bapt. Theol. Sem., 1967; D.Min., Union Theol. Sem., 1984. Ordained to ministry Presbyterian Ch., 1974. Assoc. pastor Fourth Presbyn. Ch., Chgo., 1974-78; pastor First Presbyn. Ch., Oakland, Fla., 1978-85; The Presbyn. Ch., Danville, Ky., 1985—; staff Cong. World Evangelism, Berlin, 1966; mem. Chgo. Loop Clergy, 1974-78; del. Consultant World Evang., Pattaya, Thailand, 1980; pres. W.O. Ministerial Assn., Winter Garden, Fla., 1980-82; commr. Gen. Assembly Presby. Ch. U.S.A., Phoenix, 1984. Bd. dirs. Orleans Housing Project, Chgo., 1975-81. Office: The Presbyn Ch 500 W Main St Danville KY 40422

WHEATLEY, MELVIN ERNEST, JR., bishop, United Methodist Ch.; b. Lewisville, Pa., May 7, 1915; s. Melvin Ernest and Gertrude Elizabeth (Mitchell) W.; A.B. magna cum laude, Am. U., 1936; B.D. summa cum laude, Drew U., Madison, N.J., 1939; D.D., Am. U., 1958, U. of Pacific, 1948; m. Lucile Elizabeth Maris, June 15, 1939; children—Paul Melvin, James Maris, John Sherwood. Ordained to ministry United Methodist Ch., 1939; pastor, Lincoln, Del., 1939-41; asso. pastor First Meth. Ch., Fresno, Calif., 1941-43; pastor Centenary Meth. Ch., Modesto, Calif., 1943-46, Central Meth. Ch., Stockton, Calif., 1946-54, Westwood Meth. Ch., Los Angeles, 1954-72; bishop Denver Area, 1972-84; instr. philosophy Modesto Jr.

Coll., 1944; summer session instr. Hebrew-Christian Heritage, U. of Pacific; instr. homiletics Iliff Sch. of Theology, Denver; Sch. of Theology, Claremont; St. Luke's lectures, Houston, 1966. Mem. Nat. Bd. Edn., United Meth. Ch., mem. Bd. Discipleship, chmn. program-curriculum com.; condr. European Christian Heritage tour, 1961, Alaska and Hawaii Missions, 1952, 54. Chmn., Community Relations Conf. So. Calif., 1966-69. Pres., bd. dirs. Stockton Family Service Agy.; pres. Stockton Community Council, So. Calif.-Ariz. Conf. Bd. Edn., 1960-68; bd. dirs. Community Justice Center, Inc., Los Angeles; trustee U. Denver, Iliff Sch. Theology, Rocky Mountain Coll., Billings, Mont.; bd. regents U. of Pacific and Sch. Theology at Claremont. Named Young Man of Year, Stockton Jr. C. of C., 1950, Clergyman of Year, Ch. Fedn. Los Angeles for Westwood Mental Health Clinic, 1958. Author: Going His Way, 1957; Our Man and the Church, 1968; The Power of Worship, 1970; Family Ministries Manual, 1970; Christmas is for Celebrating, 1977. Contbr. articles to profl. jours. Home: 859 A Ronda Mendoza Laguna Hills CA 92653

WHEATON, ANITA, nun, educational administrator, Roman Catholic Church; b. Parkersburg, W.Va., May 19, 1920; d. Dennis Warne and Anna Mae (Doan) W. B.A., Duquesne U., 1949; postgrad. Notre Dame U., summers 1959-60, Georgetown U., summers 1966-67; M.A., Cardinal Stritch Coll., 1965. Joined Sisters of the Poor Child Jesus, Roman Catholic Ch., 1940. Tchr. Sisters of the Poor Child Jesus, Diocese of Wheeling, Parkersburg, Bluefield, Follansbee, and St. Albans, W.Va., 1945-62, prin. St. Anthony Sch., Follansbee, 1963-66, St. Stephen Sch., Columbus, Ohio, 1967-69; provincial adminstr. Sisters of the Poor Child Jesus, Columbus, 1969-75; tchr. social justice Seton Hall Prep. Sch., South Orange, N.J., 1977-79; tchr. religion St. Kevin's Sch., Flushing, N.Y., 1980-82; coordinator religious edn. Sts. Peter and Paul Parish, Towanda, Pa., 1982—; Am. del. Internat. Chpts. of Congregation of Sisters of the Poor Child Jesus, Simpelveld, The Netherlands, 1969-75; mem. Inst. Active Spirituality for Global Community, Cin., 1975, 76. NSF scholar W.Va. U., 1964, Georgetown U., 1966-67, Mich. State U., 1968. Mem. Sisters of Mercy of the Union of Mercy of the Union, Nat. Cath. Edn. Assn., Nat. Assn. Parish Coordinators and Dirs., N. Am. Forum on Catechumenate. Republican. Home: 100 Third St Towanda PA 18848 Office: Sts Peter and Paul Parish 106 Third St Towanda PA 18848

WHEDBEE, JAMES WILLIAM, educator; b. Santa Ana, Calif., Sept. 24, 1938; s. James Everett and Alta Pearl (Lewallen) W.; B.A., Westmont Coll., 1960; B.D., Fuller Theol. Sem., 1963; M.A., Yale, 1965, Ph.D., 1968; m. Bylle Kae Snyder, July 24, 1971; 1 son, David. Asso. prof. religion Pomona Coll., 1966—. Mem. Soc. Bibl. Lit., Author: Isaiah and Wisdom, 1971. Home: 981 Marymount Ln Claremont CA 91711

WHEELER, FRANCIS JEWETT WILDER WHITNEY, ch. ofcl., minister, Soc. of Friends; b. Worcester, Mass., Nov. 2, 1903; s. Fred Lincoln and Lillian Imogene (Wilder) W.; student Worcester YMCA Coll. Law, 1928-29, Babson Inst., Mass., 1931-32; m. G. Eveline Harris, Sept. 18, 1926; children—Fred Lincoln 2d, Edwin H., Faith E. Wheeler Clarke; m. 2d, Marjorie E. Taylor, Mar. 14, 1960. Local minister Religious Soc. of Friends, 1959—; presiding clk. Pleasant St. Friends Meeting, Worcester, 1952-74, Conn. Valley Quar. Meeting, 1970-72; sec. young Friends, New Eng. Yearly Meeting, 1925-33, mem. permanent bd., 1966-76. bd. mgrs. investments and permanent funds, 1971—, mem. bd. ministry and counsel, 1964-73; temp. acting chaplain Worcester City Hosp., 1952; v.p. Quaker Meeting House Assn., Uxbridge, Mass., 1971—; editor County Call, peace jour., 1960-65, New Eng. Young Friend, 1927-30; leader Am. Friends Service Com. unit, Mexico, 1949. Pres., Worcester Inter-racial Council, 1958-59; v.p. Worcester Area Co-op. Assn., 1959-61; cashier Worcester United Fund, 1942-69; treas. Worcester Home Aged Colored People, 1965-69, bd. dirs., 1956-71. Mem. Worcester Republican City Com., 1933-36; pres. Ward 9 Rep. Club, Worcester, 1937. Author: Basic Quaker Concepts, 1966; Quaker Meditations: Biblical Sources, 1976. Address: 15 Pleasant St Paxton Worcester MA 01612

WHEELER, GERALD WILLIAM, religious book editor, Seventh-day Adventists; b. Niles, Mich., Sept. 16, 1943; s. Elmer and Melva Louise (Tabb) W.; m. Penny Ann Estes, June 18, 1967; children: Robin, Noelle, Bronwen, James. B.A., Andrews U., 1966, M.A., 1981; M.A., U. Mich., 1967. Cert. Seventh-day Adventists, 1973. Asst. copy editor So. Pub. Assn., Nashville, 1967, asst. book editor, 1968-74, assoc. book editor, 1974-80; assoc. book editor Rev. and Herald Pub. Assn., Hagerstown, Md., 1980—. Author: The Two-Taled Dinosaur, 1975; Who Put the Worm in the Apple?, 1975; Is God a Committee?, 1975; God's Catalog of Gifts, 1976; Deluge, 1978. Contbr. articles and religious study lessons to religious publs. Recipient grad. scholarship U. Mich., 1966-67. Mem. Andrews Soc. Religious Studies, Hist Sci. Soc., Am. Acad. Religion/Soc. Bibl. Lit. Home: 229 Kelso Dr Hagerstown MD 21740 Office: Rev and Herald Pub Assn 55 W Oak Ridge Dr Hagerstown MD 21740

WHEELER, MARY PAUL, contemplative nun, Roman Catholic Church; b. N.Y.C., Apr. 3, 1915; d. William August Gaedeke and Florence (Pritchard) Kearns. Student New York schs., pvt. lessons. Joined Sacramentine Nuns, Roman Catholic Ch., 1936. Novice mistress Blessed Sacrament, Yonkers, N.Y., 1951-56, prioress, 1956-59, sub-prioress, prioress, 1959-83, sub-prioress, 1984—. Founder Met. Assn. Contemplative Communities, Archdiocese of N.Y., 1967. Home: 23 Park Ave Yonkers NY 10703

WHEELER, ZOE, nun, Roman Catholic Church; b. N.Y.C., May 9, 1918; d. Ferdinand Chatard and Nina Marie (Barr) W. B.S. in Bus., St. Joseph Coll., 1948; M.A. in Spl. Edn., Vanderbilt U., 1972. Joined Daus. of Charity of St. Vincent de Paul, Roman Cath. Ch., 1937. Tchr. Cath. schs., Pa., Va., Del., D.C., Ohio, 1939-76; asst. supt. Diocese of Wilmington, Del., 1976-81; prin. St. Ann Sch., Bridgeport, Conn., 1981—. Del. White House Conf. on Children, 1970, White House Conf. on Library and Info. Services, 1980. Address: St Anns Sch 42 Jetland St Bridgeport CT 06605

WHELAN, ROBERT LOUIS, bishop, Roman Catholic Church. Mem. Soc. of Jesus; ordained priest Roman Catholic Ch., 1944; titular bishop of Sicilibba and coadjutor bishop of Fairbanks, Alaska, 1967-68; bishop of Fairbanks, 1968—. Address: 1316 Peger Rd Fairbanks AK 99701

WHETSTONE, JAMES DEWITT, minister, Southern Baptist Convention; b. North, S.C., Nov. 27, 1935; s. Dewitt and Thelma (Jackson) W.; m. Sally Rodwell, July 11, 1961; children: James, Jr., David Rodwell. A.A., Mars Hill Coll., 1955; B.A., Wake Forest U., 1957; M.Div., Southwestern Bapt. Sem., 1960, Doctor of Ministry, 1978. Ordained to ministry So. Bapt. Conv., 1961. Youth pastor First Bapt. Ch., Decatur, Ga., 1961-62; assoc. pastor First Bapt. Ch., Columbia, S.C., 1974-76; pastor Parkway Bapt. Ch., Chester, S.C., 1963-65, First Bapt. Ch., Pamplico, S.C., 1966-74, West Gantt Bapt. Ch., Greenville, S.C., 1976-82, Temple Bapt. Ch., Wilmington, N.C., 1982—; trustee S.C. Bapt. Ministry to Aging, S.C. Bapt. Conv., 1969-74, chmn. S.C. Christian Life Com., 1973-81; trustee N.C. Bapt. Gen. Bd., N.C. Bapt. Conv., 1982—. Bd. dirs. Lower Cape Fear Hospice, Inc., Wilmington, 1982—, Crime-stoppers of New Hanover County, Wilmington, 1982—. Mem. Southeastern Bapt. Sem. Alumni (nat. dir. 1980-82), Execs. Club of Wilmington. Democrat. Lodge: Rotary (bd. dirs. 1982-83). Home: 2222 Market St Wilmington NC 28403 Office: Temple Bapt Ch 1801 Market St Wilmington NC 28403

WHETSTONE, RAYMOND HENRY, minister, Southern Baptist Convention; b. Kansas City, Mo., Aug. 3, 1940; s. Ben Raymond and Verlea (Leftwitch) W.; A.A., SW Bapt. Coll. of Bolivar (Mo.), 1963; B.A., Ouachita Bapt. U., Arkadelphia, Ark., 1968; M.Bible Theology, Internat. Bible Inst., 1983; children: Raymond Lee, Teresa Jean, Portia Jean. Ordained to ministry, 1965; pastor Pine Creek Bapt. Ch., Nebo and Lynchburg, Mo., 1963, Fairview Bapt. Ch., Antoine, Ark., 1963-64, Linn Creek (Mo.) Bapt. Ch., 1964-66, Pearcy (Ark.) Bapt. Ch., 1966-71, Midway Bapt. Ch., Pernell, Okla., 1971-72, First Bapt. Ch., Fox, Okla., 1972-76, First Bapt. Ch., Chetopa, Kans., 1976—. Chaplain, Chetopa City Police Dept., 1976—. Mem. Tri-County Assn. So. Bapts., Chetopa Ministerial Alliance (pres.). Office: 721 Maple St Chetopa KS 67336

WHIPPLE, GEORGE CARL, minister, educator, United Church of Christ; b. York, Nebr., Dec. 1, 1920; s. George Gorton and Hazel Dell (Scheel) W.; m. Elizabeth Elaine Hufton, June 6, 1941 (dec. Apr. 1976); children: Hazel Marie, Leslie Victor; m. Caroline Bertha Becker, June 12, 1976. B.A., Albion Coll., 1941; M.Div., Boston U., 1944, Ph.D., 1947. Ordained to ministry United Ch. of Christ, 1978. Asst. prof. Bible, Southwestern Coll., Winfield, Kans., 1947-50; minister 1st Meth. Ch., Ashland, Kans., 1950-51; assoc. prof. religion Doane Coll., Crete, Nebr., 1951-53; assoc. prof. philosophy and religion Ohio No. U., Ada, 1956-76; asst. to pres. Sch. Theology, Claremont, Calif., 1980—. Dir. Brooks Inst. Photography, Santa Barbara, Calif., 1957-66. Contbr. articles to profl. jours. Resident fellow in New Testament, Boston U., 1946. Mem. Am. Schs. Oriental Research, United Ch. of Christ Foothill Assn., Pub. Relations Assn. So. Calif. Colls. Democrat. Lodge: Rotary (pres. 1962-63). Home: 929 E Foothill Blvd #71 Upland CA 91786 Office: Sch Theology 1325 N College Ave Claremont CA 91711

WHITAKER, MILTON OLIVER, hospital chaplain; b. Sacramento, Nov. 20, 1926; s. Clement Sherman and Harriet Elizabeth (Reynolds) W.; B.S., U. Calif. at Berkeley, 1950; B.D., Berkeley Baptist Div. Sch., 1957; postgrad. Grad. Theol. Union, Berkeley, 1969-70, Pepperdine Coll., Los Angeles, 1973, Am. Inst. Family Relations, 1973; m. Colleen Miriam Rowden, July 27, 1947; children—Milton Oliver, Janine Gay, Tami Lee. Ordained minister Am. Bapt. Conv., 1957; chaplain USNR, 1959-66; pastor chs. in Calif., 1954-59, 66-69; grad. residency clin. pastoral edn. and pastoral psychology VA hosps. in Tex. and Calif., 1969-70; chaplain VA Hosp., Seattle, 1970—; vis. prof. pastoral psychology and clin. pastoral care Northwest Coll., Kirkland, Wash., 1972—; lectr. Seattle Pacific Coll., 1972—; individual practice pastoral psychology, marriage and family counseling, 1971—; cons. in field. Mem. Mayor Seattle Task Force Vietnam Vet. and Returning Servicemen, 1971—. Fellow Coll. Chaplains; clin. mem. Am. Protestant Hosp. Assn., Am. Assn. Marriage and Family Counselors, Calif. Marriage and Family Therapy Assn., Assn. Christian Marriage Counselors; mem. Assn. Clin. Pastoral Edn. Pioneer program and concept psycho-social-spiritual growth for patients and their families facing life-threatening illnesses and death through use of logos therapy and group therapy. Home: 11741 NE 150th Pl Bothell WA 98011 Office: VA Med Ctr 1660 S Columbia Way Seattle WA 98108

WHITE, A. H., bishop, House of God, Which is the Ch. of the Living God, the Pillar and Ground of the Truth, Inc. Address: 6107 Cobbs Creek Pkwy Philadelphia PA 19143

WHITE, ALBERT, pastor, Seventh-day Adventists; b. Muskogee, Okla., Dec. 11, 1937; s. Otto and Georgia White; m. Jean Haley, Dec. 24, 1961; 1 child, Annette. B.A., Oakwood Coll., 1961; M.A. in Religion, Andrew U., 1963; Ph.D., Berndean U., 1982. Pastor Lake Region Conf., Seventh-day Adventists, Chgo., 1961-80, Northeastern Conf., N.Y.C., 1980-84, Central Conf., Wichita, Kans., 1981-84, Kansas City, Mo., 1984—. Commodity distbr. U.S. Govt. Wichita, 1981—. Recipient awards, City of Bklyn., 1967, Goodwill Industry, Bridgeport, Conn., 1976, Carrier Air Conditioner, Wichita, 1981. Mem. Brit. Guild Drugless Practitioners. Democrat.

WHITE, ALFRED E., Bishop, Methodist Zion Ch. (Twelfth Episcopal Area). Office: 93 Ridgefield St Hartford CT 06112*

WHITE, C. DALE, bishop, United Methodist Church, N.Y. Conf. Office: 252 Bryan Ave White Plains NY 10605*

WHITE, C(HARLES) EDWARD, minister, Church of Christ; educator, real estate salesman; b. Alfred, Ohio, Apr. 20, 1920; s. Clyde E. and Mary L. (Stout) W.; m. Evelyn Juanita Garloch, June 30, 1942; children: R. Wayne, Charles O., Donald E., James L. B.A., Marshall U., 1959, M.A., 1961. Ordained to ministry Ch. of Christ, 1940. Minister Ch. of Christ, New Martinsville, W.Va., 1944-46, Athens, Ohio, 1946-51, Canton, Ohio, 1951-55, Huntington, W.Va., 1955-61, elder, Searcy, Ark., 1983—. Assoc. prof. English, Harding U., Searcy, 1969—; sales assoc. Lightle & Assocs., Searcy, 1978—. Co-author corr. course, 1956. Contbr. articles, tracts to profl. publs. Co-chmn. White County ARC, Searcy, 1983—; bd. dirs. White County Govt. Employees Credit Union, 1983—. Mem. Searcy C. of C., MLA (Southcentral region), Conf. Christianity and Lit. Lodge: Optimists (pres. 1977-78, dist. lt. gov. 1980-81). Home: 122 Apache Dr Searcy AR 72143 Office: Harding U Box 652 Searcy AR 72143

WHITE, HOMER DONALD, SR., minister, Southern Baptist Convention; b. Gainesville, Fla., Feb. 26, 1944; s. Terrell D. and Jeanette M. (Price) W.; m. Ethel Gardner, Sept. 29, 1963; children: Homer Donald, Laura, Mary. B.Th. in Religious Edn., Bapt. Bible Inst., Graceville, Fla., 1980; M.Ministry, So. Bapt. Ctr., Folkston, Ga., 1984. Ordained to ministry Bapt. Ch., 1970. Mem. staff Union Gospel Mission, Charleston, W.Va., 1970-72; asst. pastor Oak Park Bapt. Ch., Gainesville, 1972-76; pastor Pine Level Bapt. Ch., Jay, Fla., 1978—; vol. chaplain Jay Hosp., 1978—, organizer hosp. vols., 1980, mem. longrange planning com., 1981—. Foster parent Ema-chamee Camps, Jay, 1980—. Mem. Santa Rosa Bapt. Assn. (exec. bd. 1978—, trustee Milton, Fla. chpt. 1983—), North Santa Rosa Ministerial Assn. (sec. 1984—). Republican. Home: Rt 2 Box 142 Jay FL 32565

WHITE, JAMES FLOYD, theology educator, United Methodist Church; b. Boston, Jan. 23, 1932; s. Edwin Turner and Mary Madeline (Rinker) W.; m. Susan Jan Kendall, Oct. 28, 1982; children: Louise, Robert, Ellen, Laura, Martin, Todd. A.B., Harvard U., 1953; B.D., Union Theol. Sem., 1956; postgrad. Cambridge U., Eng., 1956-57; Ph.D., Duke U., 1958. Ordained elder, United Meth. Ch., 1961. Instr. Ohio Wesleyan U., Delaware, 1959-61; prof. Perkins Sch. Theology, Dallas, 1961-83, U. Notre Dame, Ind., 1983—, dir. grad. studies, dept. theology, 1984—; vis. instr. Meth. Theol. Sch., Delaware, 1960-61; mem. sect. on worship United Meth. Ch., Nashville, 1976-80. Author: Cambridge Movement, 1962, 2d edit. 1979; Introduction Xian Worship, 1980; Sacraments as God's Self Giving, 1983; New Forms of Worship, 1971. Mem. N. Am. Acad. Liturgy (pres. 1978, Berakah award 1983), Societas Liturgica. Office: Univ Notre Dame Notre Dame IN 46556

WHITE, JOE L., minister, So. Bapt. Conv.; b. Weaver, Tex., July 16, 1921; s. Harvey J. and Minnie May (Brewer) W.; student Southwestern Sem., 1954, Odessa Coll., 1955; m. Lorene Montgomery, Feb. 12, 1942; children—Ronnie, Rickey, Joey. Ordained to ministry, 1950; pastor Cotton Flat Bapt. Ch., Midland, Tex., 1950-53, Vine Ave. Bapt. Ch., Odessa, Tex., 1953-71;

evangelist, Odessa, 1971—. Moderator, Odessa Bapt. Assn., 1963-64, past chmn. missions and survey com., wayside mission com.; past pres. Odessa Bapt. Pastors. Past pres. Ector County chpt. Am. Heart Assn. Mem. Odessa (life), W. Tex. chambers commerce. Home: 1419 Byron St Odessa TX 79761 Office: POB 2146 Odessa TX 79760

WHITE, JOHN HUGH, minister, Reformed Presbyterian Church of North America. b. Newburgh, N.Y., June 14, 1936; s. John White and Ethel Jenny (Perry) W.; m. Norma Delores Woods, Aug. 9, 1961; children: Natalie, Stephanie. B.A., Geneva Coll., 1958; B.D. Reformed Presbyterian Sem., 1961; M.A., U. Pitts., 1962; D.Ministry, Pitts. Theol. Sem., 1975. Ordained to ministry Reformed Presbyterian Ch., 1962. Pastor, Coll. Hill Reformed Presbyn. Ch., Beaver Falls, Pa., 1962-70; dean religious services Geneva Coll., Beaver Falls, 1970—; moderator Ad-Interim Commn. Pitts. Presbytery, 1984; chmn. N. Am. Presbyn. and Reformed Council, 1979, 81. Editor, author; The Book of Books, 1975. Contbr. articles to profl. jours. Mem. Nat. Assn. Evangelicals (2d v.p. 1984), Bd. Ctr. Urban Theol. Studies (pres. 1983-84), Bd. Coalition for Christian Outreach, Presbyn. Jour. Bd. Home: Box 241 Darlington PA 16115 Office: Geneva Coll College Ave Beaver Falls PA 15010

WHITE, JOHN WALTER, Bishop, mem. gen. bd. The Church of God in Christ. Office: The Ch of God in Christ 2236 Penniston St New Orleans LA 70115*

WHITE, LELAND J., priest, religion educator, Roman Catholic Church; b. Charleston, S.C., July 25, 1940; s. Leland S. and Rose Winifred (Budds) W. B.A., St. Mary's Sem., Balt., 1962; S.T.B., S.T.L., Gregorian U., Rome, 1966; M.A., U. Mich., 1972; Ph.D., Duke U., 1974. Ordained priest Roman Cath. Ch., 1965. Instr. theology St. Thomas Sem., Kenmore, wash., 1968-69, St. John's Sem., Plymouth, Mich., 1969-70; asst. prof. religious studies Nazareth Coll., Mich., 1974-76, Siena Coll., Loudonville, N.Y., 1976-82; assoc. prof. theology St. John's U., N.Y.C., 1982—. Author: Act in Theology, 1974; Christ and the Christian Movement, 1985. Mem. editorial bd. Bibl. Theol. Bull., 1979-82, asst. editor: 1982-84, editor, 1984—. Mem. Am. Acad. Religion, Cath. Theol. Soc. Am., Coll. Theology Soc. Democrat. Office: Theology Dept St Johns U Grand Central and Utopia Jamaica NY 11439

WHITE, RICKEY LEE, minister, Southern Baptist Convention; b. Ypsilanti, Mich., Feb. 23, 1955; s. Melvin Lee and Melvene Sue (Ledford) W.; m. Marla Kay Allen, May 15, 1977; children: Matthew Allen, Joshua Lee. B.A., Carson-Newman Coll., 1977; M.Div., So. Bapt. Theol. Sem., 1980. Ordained to ministry Baptist Ch., 1979. Interim pastor Petersburg Bapt. Chapel, Mich., summer 1974; assoc. pastor Fairview Bapt. Tabernacle, Sweetwater, Tenn., summer 1977, also student missionary; pastor 1st So. Bapt. Ch., Freetown, Ind., 1978-81, 1st Bapt. Ch., Lebanon Junction, Ky., 1981—; mem. exec. bd. Ky. Bapt. Conv., 1983—, ch. relations adv. bd. Cumberland Coll., 1984. Mem. Phi Alpha Theta. Democrat. Home: 408 E Oak St Lebanon Junction KY 40150 Office: Rt 2 Box 85A Lebanon Junction KY 40150

WHITE, ROBERT CARROLL, minister, So. Bapt. Conv.; b. Edenton, N.C., Dec. 20, 1932; s. Watson Bryan and Isa Mae (Bunch) W.; B.A., Wake Forest U., 1961; B.D., Southeastern Bapt. Theol. Sem., 1965, M.Div., 1968; m. Alice Ann Tumblin, May 12, 1963; children—Betty Ann, Susan Amanda, Robert Carroll, Philip Edward. Ordained to ministry, 1964; pastor Connaritsa and Horton's Bapt. chs., Aulander, N.C., 1972—. Brotherhood dir. W. Chowan Bapt. Assn., 1976; v.p. pastor's conf., 1976-77. Chmn. Aulander Planning Bd., 1976—; trustee Bertie Meml. Hosp., Windsor, N.C., 1976—. Home: Rice Ave Aulander NC 27805 Office: PO Box 160 Aulander NC 27805

WHITE, RONALD LYNN, minister, American Lutheran Church; b. Santa Ana, Calif., Feb. 24, 1944; s. John L. and Zanelli J. (Morton) W.; m. Janis Lee Seamon, June 10, 1967; children: Kimberly Jo, Tonya Lyn, Jeremy Lee. B.A., Calif. Luth. Coll., 1965; M.Div., Wartburg Theol. Sem., 1969. Ordained to ministry Am. Luth. Ch., 1969. Asst. pastor Newport Harbor Luth. Ch., Calif., 1969-71; pastor youth and parish edn. Shepherd Valley Luth. Ch., Canoga Park, Calif., 1972-73; pastor Lord Life Luth. Ch., Spring Valley, Calif., 1973-81, Am. Luth. Ch., Burbank, Calif., 1981—; clergy del. Am. Luth. Ch. Conv., Washington, D.C., 1976 Moorhead, Minn., 1984. area clergy contact couple Luth. Marriage Encounter, San Diego, 1979-81, Los Angeles, 1982-83, clergy presenting couple, San Diego and Los Angeles, 1979—. Mem. Burbank Ministerial Assn.

WHITE, WOODIE W., bishop, United Methodist Church, So. Ill. and Central Ill. Conf. Office: 1919 Broadway Mount Vernon IL 62864*

WHITEHEAD, BRADY, BRAXTON, JR., minister, educational administrator, United Methodist Church; b. Memphis, Feb. 5, 1930; s. Brady Braxton and Gertrude (Murphy) W.; m. Emmy Lou Sessions, Sept. 9, 1955; children: Nancy Kathleen, Diana Lynn. B.S., Rhodes Coll., 1952; M.Div., Emory U., 1955, M.A., 1957; Th.D., Boston U., 1972. Ordained to ministry United Meth. Ch., 1955. Chaplain, asst. prof. religion Lambuth Coll., Jackson, Tenn., 1967-74, chaplain, assoc. prof., 1974-81, v.p. student affairs, 1981—; United Meth. Ch. del. World Meth. Council, Denver, 1971; registrar, bd. diaconal ministry Memphis Ann. Conf., 1980—; sec. bd. trustees Memphis Theol. Sem., 1981—; workshop leader Nat. Conf. on Student Services, 1983—. Author ch. sch. curriculum United Meth. Ch. Mem. So. Assn. Coll. Student Affairs, Tenn. Coll. Personnel Assn., Soc. Bibl. Lit. Democrat. Home: 30 Foxlea Dr Jackson TN 38305 Office: Lambuth Coll Lambuth Blvd Jackson TN 38301

WHITEMAN, DARRELL LAVERNE, religion and anthropology educator, Free Methodist Church; b. Lexington, Ky., Jan. 3, 1947; s. G. Edgar Whiteman and Kathleen B. (Gaddis) Whiteman Hicks; m. Delores Bishop, Aug. 7, 1984; 1 child, Geoffrey John Ryan. B.A. in Sociology-Anthropology, Seattle Pacific U., 1970; Ph.D. in Anthropology, So. Ill. U., 1980. Vis. scholar Sch. of World Mission, Fuller Theol. Sem., Pasadena, Calif., 1975-76; assoc. prof. cultural anthropology Asbury Theol. Sem., Wilmore, Ky., 1984—. Research anthropologist Melanesian Inst., Goroka, Papua New Guinea, 1980-84. Author: Melanesians and Missionaries, 1983. Editor: Introduction to Melanesian Cultures, 1984; Missionaries and Anthropologists, 1985. Contbr. articles to profl. jours. Mem. Am. Soc. Missiology, Internat. Assn. for Mission Studies, Am. Anthrop. Assn., Soc. for Applied Anthropology, Assn. Social Anthropologists in Oceania. Office: E Stanley Jones Sch World Mission and Evangelism Asbury Theol Sem Wilmore KY 40390

WHITERMORE, DAVID MALCOLM, minister, Mennonite Church General Conference; b. Zairie, Sept. 12, 1928; came to U.S., 1931; s. Frederick Lucias and Mildred M. (Yost) W.; children: Martha Susan Whitermore Dillon, David Jon, Mark Craig; m. Debra Lea Suderman, Mar. 14, 1976. Student Prairie Bible Inst., Alta., Can., 1948-53. Ordained to ministry Mennonite Ch. Gen. Conf., 1953. Missionary, W. I. Mission, Trinidad, 1953-62; pastor Gen. Conf. Mennonite Ch., Lansdale, Pa., 1962-72; exec. home ministries and ch. planting, Newton, Kans., 1972-75; coordinator Chgo. area Mennonite, Mennonite Denoms. in Chgo., 1976-81; pastor Gen. Conf. Mennonite Ch., Liberal, Kans., 1981-83; exec. dir. Ch. Fedn. of Greater Chgo., 1983—; staff Religious Leaders of Met. Chgo., 1984-85; bd. dirs. Ctr. for Religion and Psychotherapy, NCCJ, Chgo., 1984—, Chgo. Covenant, 1984. Bd. dirs. Fed. Emergency Mgmt. Agency, Chgo., 1983. Office: The Ch Fedn of Greater Chgo 111 E Wacker Dr Suite 510 Chicago IL 60601

WHITLEY, JAMES WILLIAM, minister, United Church of Christ; b. Wilson, N.C., Dec. 24, 1954; s. James Henry Whitley and Floy Norvelle (Wiggs) Whitley Coats; m. Cathy Jean Waters, May 28, 1978; children: Jennifer Jaye, Ashley Brandon. B.A., Campbell U., 1977; M.Div., Southeastern Theol. Sem., 1981. Ordained to ministry United Ch. Christ, 1981. Pastor, Turner's Chapel, United Ch. Christ, Sanford, N.C., 1977-79, Beulah United Ch. Christ, Wake Forest, N.C., 1979-81, Union United Ch. Christ, Virgilina, Va., 1981—; mem. Eastern N.C. Assn. Church and Ministry Commn., United Ch. Christ, 1982—, So. Conf. Family Life Task Force, 1982—; dir. native Am. camp So. Conf. Camps, 1983—; mem. retarded offender advocacy program of Commn. Racial Justice, United Ch. Christ, 1979-80. Student editor: North Carolina Church History, 1977. Pres. Halifax Assn. for Retarded Citizens, Va., 1982—; bd. dirs. Southside Va. Community Services, South Boston, Va., 1983—; co-coordinator Halifax County Ch. World Service Crop Walk, 1984; mem. Virgilina Vol. Fire Dept., 1981—. Recipient Disting. Service award ARC, 1982. Mem. Burlington Area Ministerium, Eastern N.C. Assn., South Boston Area Ministerium, So. Conf. United Ch. Christ, Halifax Ministerial Assn. (pres. 1984—). Democrat. Lodge: Ruritan (Virgilina pres. 1983-84). Home and Office: PO Box 148 Virgilina VA 24598

WHITLOCK, LUDER GRADICK, JR., minister, educator, Presbyterian Church in America; b. Jacksonville, Fla., June 20, 1940; s. Luder Gradick and Juanita Ostelle (Nessmith) W.; B.A., U. Fla., 1962; M.Div., Westminster Theol. Sem., 1966; D.Ministry, Vanderbilt U., 1973; m. Mary Louise Patton, Aug. 29, 1959; children: Frank Christopher, Alissa Ann, Beth LaVerne. Ordained minister, 1966. Pastor Sharon Orthodox Presbyn. Ch., Hialeah, Fla., 1966-69, West Hills Presbyn. Ch., Harriman, Tenn., 1969-75; assoc. prof. evangelism and Christian edn. Reformed Theol. Sem., Jackson, Miss., 1975-78, pres. sem., 1978—. Mem. com. on home missions and ch. extension Orthodox Presbyn. Ch., 1971-74, com. on ministerial tng., 1967-76; moderator Presbytery, 1968-69; fraternal del. Gen. Synod Reformed Presbyn. Ch., 1971; dir. Southland Bible Conf., 1967-69, 74, 75; mem. Nat. Presbyn. and Ref. Fellowship, 1971—; vis. lectr. Korea Theol. Sem., Pusan, 1976, Kobe (Japan) Theol. Sem., 1976. Bd. dirs. Roane County United Fund, 1971-73; trustee Covenant Coll., Chattanooga, 1973-78, Westminster Theol. Sem., 1973-76. Office: Reformed Theol Seminary 5422 Clinton Blvd Jackson MS 39209

WHITMAN, STEVE LYNN, youth pastor, Interdenominational Ch.; b. Bremen, Ga., Mar. 10, 1956; s. Amos L. and Elizabeth Mary (Smith) W.; m. Sharon Louise Swanson, Oct. 11, 1975. Student, Shorter Coll.; Th.M., Internat. Bible Sem., 1984, B. Bible Ministry, 1985. Ordained to ministry Southern Baptist Convention, 1981. Youth pastor First Assembly of God, Rome, Ga., 1976-78, asst. youth pastor, Baton Rouge, La., 1978-80; youth pastor Northview Assembly of God, Shreveport, 1977-78; pastor Everett Springs Bapt. Ch., Armuchee, Ga., 1980-85; youth pastor A Voice in the Wilderness, Eatonton, Ga., 1985—; missionary Evang. St. Preachers Assn., Oneonta, Ala., 1974—. Contbr. articles to profl. jours. Dir. and writer of radio programs. Recipient Dale Carnegie leadership award Leo Hawkins & Assocs. 1978, Citizenship award DAR 1974. Mem. Nat. Pro-Life Assn., North Am. Fellowship Christian Ventriloquists, Baldwin County Ministerial Fellowship, Full Gospel Businessman's Fellowship Internat. Republican. Office: A Voice in the Wilderness 242 N Jefferson St PO Box 401 Eatonton GA 31024

WHITNEY, BARRY LYN, religious studies educator, Anglican Church of Canada; b. Cornwall, Ont., Can., Dec. 10, 1947; s. Earl Stanley whittney and Gwendolyn Grace (Meldrum) Goddard; m. Mary Ellen Abernathy, May 16, 1970; children: Christopher, Matthew, Lara. B.A. with honors, Carleton U., 1971; Ph.D. in Religious Studies, McMaster U., Hamilton, Ont., 1977. Assoc. prof. religious studies U. Windsor, Ont., 1976—; lectr. pastoral edn. Southwestern Regional Ctr., Cedar Springs, Ont., 1977-79; mem. Anglican commn. Canterbury Coll., London and Windsor, 1977-79, tutor of admissions, Windsor, 1979-82, fellow, 1979-82; regional coordinator Ctr. for Process Studies, 1979—. Author: Evil and the Process God, 1985. Contbr. articles to profl. jours. Scholar Carleton U., 1967-71, McMaster U., 1971-76; Can. Council scholar McMaster U., 1972-75. Mem. Soc. for Study Process Philosophies (book reviewer), Coll. Theology Soc. (book reviewer), Am. Acad. Religion (book reviewer), Council for Study of Religion. Home: 3289 Askin Ave Windsor ON N9E 3J6 Canada Office: Univ Windsor Dept Religious Studies Sunset Ave Windsor OH N9B 3P4 Canada

WHITTEY, FREDERICK, minister, Wesleyan Church; b. Kingsclear County York, N.B., Can., Sept. 7, 1936; s. Joseph and Francis (Muzarall) W.; m. Lilyan Edna Jewett; children: Janet, Duane, Shari. Diploma Bethany Bible Coll., Yarmouth, N.S., 1959. Ordained to ministry Wesleyan Ch., 1959. Pastor Wesleyan Ch., Woods Harbour, N.S., 1959-64, Perth, N.B., 1964-71, Woodstock, N.B., 1971-81, Kings Valley Wesleyan Ch., Rothesay, N.B., 1981—; treas. Atlantic dist. Ref. Bapt. Mission, 1960-65; dist. bd. dirs. Atlantic dist. Wesleyan Ch., 1971-75, dist. Sunday Sch. sec., 1979—; Treas. N.B. Fedn. on Alcohol and Drug Problems, 1971—. Home: 111 Scarlet Dr Rothesay NB E0G 2W0 Canada Office: 332 Hampton Rd Quispamsis NB F0G 2W0 Canada

WHITTINGTON, HOWARD REID, JR., minister, So. Bapt. Conv.; b. Laurel, Miss., Feb. 2, 1945; s. Howard Reid and Anita Louise (Nicholson) W.; B.S., Miss. Coll., 1969; M.R.E., New Orleans Bapt. Theol. Sem., 1971; m. Judy Mae Chance, Jan. 21, 1968; children—Lori Mechelle, Chance Reid, Nick Anderson. Ordained to ministry, 1975; minister of youth Williams Blvd. Bapt. Ch., Kenner, La., 1969-70; chaplain intern Bapt. Rescue Mission, New Orleans, 1971; minister of youth and edn. 1st Bapt. Ch., Monroeville, Ala., 1972-75; asst. pastor, 1975—. Spl. worker Sunday sch. dept. Ala. State Bapt. Conv., 1972—; youth Sunday sch. leader Bethlehem Bapt. Assn., 1972—; chaplain Monroeville Jaycees, 1973. Named Outstanding Young Religious Leader Monroeville Jaycees, 1974. Mem. Ala. Bapt. Assn. Religious Edn. Workers. Home: 402 Kress St Monroeville AL 36460 Office: 420 Pineville Rd Monroeville AL 36460

WHYTE, JAMES MCLAURIN, minister, United Church of Canada and United Church of Christ; b. Kansas City, Mo., Feb. 6, 1933; s. James McLaurin and Harriet Marion (Mills) W.; m. Harriet Lodge Edwards, July 1, 1961; children: Martin Edwards, Matthew Ekholm. B.A., Ill. Coll., Jacksonville, 1957; B.D., Hartford Theol. Sem., 1961; S.T.M., Andover Newton Theol. Sch., 1970. Ordained to ministry United Ch. of Christ, 1962, admitted into ministry United Ch. Can., 1979. Minister, Congregational Chs., Bridport and Shoreham, Vt., 1961-67, Union Congl. Ch., Amesbury, Mass., 1968-70, Federated Ch., Ayer, Mass., 1970-77, Central Lanark Pastoral Charge (Ont., Can.), 1978—. Club: Civitan. Address: Rural Route 3 Lanark ON K0G 1K0 Canada

WICK, LAWRENCE WAYNE, minister, Lutheran Church in America; b. Sterling, Ill., Aug. 13, 1939; s. Maurice LeRoy and Alice Catherine (Johannsen) W.; B.A., Wartburg Coll., 1961; certificate Inst. Pastoral Care, Ill., 1965; M.Div., Luth. Sch. Theology, Chgo., 1966; M.S., Purdue U., 1973; D. Min., Chgo. Theol. Sem., 1976; postgrad. Seabury-Western Theol. Sem., 1980-81, Princeton U., 1983; m. Sherrill Anne Carlson, June 28, 1969; children: Anders Christopher, Annika Christina. Student asst. Martin Luther Ch., Chgo.,

1963-64; intern Frederick Luth. Ch., St. Thomas, V.I., 1964-65; chaplain Elgin (Ill.) State Hosp., 1965; ordained to ministry Luth. Ch. Am., 1966; pastor Grace Luth. Ch., Richmond, Ill., 1966-70, House of Prayer Luth. Ch., Country Club Hills, Ill., 1970-74, Wilmette (Ill.) Luth. Ch., 1974-84, St. Mark's Luth. Ch., Charlotte, N.C., 1984—. Mem. Luth. Research and Planning Council Ill., 1976—; instr. ministry Luth. Sch. Theology, Chgo., 1978-80; mem. camping com. Ill. Synod Luth. Ch., 1969-71, chmn. sub-com. on program, 1969-71, mem. spl. missions com., 1974—, mem. exec. bd., 1981-84, mem. com. on Am. missions Ill. Synod, 1972-74; sec. exec. cabinet Joliet (Ill.) dist. Ill. Synod, 1972-74; bd. dirs. Luth. Ch. in Am. Found., 1978—, chmn., 1981—; mem. devel. com. Luth. Welfare Services of Ill., 1976—. Treas. Richmond council Boy Scouts Am., 1966-70; treas. Salvation Army Service Unit, Country Club Hills, 1970-74. Mem. Wilmette Clergy Council. Clubs: Michigan Shores (Wilmette, Ill.); Myers Park Country, Foxcroft Racquet and Swim (Charlotte, N.C.). Contbr. articles to religious publs. Home: 4113 Beresford Rd Charlotte NC 28211 Office: 1001 Queens Rd Charlotte NC 28207

WICKER, JAMES ROBERT, minister, Southern Baptist Convention, magician. B. Corpus Christi, Tex., Sept. 30, 1954; s. David Elzy, III, and Carolyn (Reed) W.; m. Dana Abernathy, Dec. 22, 1978. B.A. in Oral Communication, Baylor U., 1977; M.Div., Southwestern Bapt. Theol. Sem., 1980, postgrad., 1981—. Lic., 1973, ordained, 1981. Sunday Sch. cons. Mo. Bapt. Conv., Jefferson City, 1978; asst. dir. Youth Evangelism Schs., Evangelism Div. Bapt. Gen. Conv. of Tex., Dallas, 1979-81, dir., 1982-85; pastor 1st Bapt. Ch., Lavon, Tex., 1981-84; teaching fellow Southwestern Bapt. Theol. Sem., Ft. Worth, 1982-83; pastor 1st Bapt. Ch., Farmersville, Tex., 1984—; mem. Ministerial Alliance, Farmersville, 1984—; mem. evangelism com. Collin Bapt. Assn., McKinney, Tex., 1982—, chmn., 1984—. Magician, 1974—. Author pamphlet; contbr. article to Christian Conjurer. Sch. adv. bd. Community Ind. Sch. Dist., Nevada, Tex., 1983-84. Winner awards talent shows, tng. award for religious leadership, Order Eastern Star, Lavon, 1983. Mem. Farmersville C. of C. (bd. dirs. 1985—), Tex. Assn. Magicians (awards in comedy magic 1977, 79), Internat. Brotherhood of Magicians, Fellowship of Christian Magicians, Kappa Omega Tau. Lodge: Rotary. Home: 208 Jouette Farmersville TX 75031 Office: First Bapt Ch 104 S Washington Farmersville TX 75031

WICKER, RICHARD FENTON, JR., pastoral counselor, chaplain, naval officer, United Methodist Church; b. Benton County, Miss., Mar. 27, 1929; s. Richard Fenton and Willie Thomas (Dunn) W.; B.A., U. Miss., 1952; B.D., So. Meth. U., 1955; D.Ministry, McCormick Theol. Sch., 1974; m. Louise Zeller, Mar. 29, 1953; children: Richard Fenton, Stephen Bryant, David William. Ordained to ministry, 1955; pastor Hickory Flat (Miss.) Meth. Ch., 1951-52, Richland (Tex.) Meth. Ch., 1953-54; commd. lt. (j.g.), Chaplain Corps., U.S. Navy, 1955; advanced through grades to capt., 1973, ret., 1982; staff pastoral counselor, dir. tng. Tidewater Pastoral Counseling Services, Inc., 1982—. Mem. biomed. ethics com. Eastern Va. Med. Sch., 1972—. Decorated Air medal with gold star, Meritorious Service medal, Legion of Merit. Fellow Am. Assn. Pastoral Counselors; mem. Assn. for Clin. Pastoral Edn. Home: 5136 Violet Bank Dr Virginia Beach VA 23464 Office: Tidewater Pastoral Counseling Services 495 Redgate Ave Norfolk VA 23507

WICKERT, GRANT ALAN, minister, Lutheran Church in America; b. Syracuse, N.Y., Dec. 25, 1944; s. Theodore Ralph William and Elizabeth Caroline (Probeck) W.; m. Linda Lee Croft, Aug. 17, 1968; children: Lori Lynn, William Grant, Elizabeth Ann. B.A., Syracuse U., 1966; M.Div., Luth. Theol. Sem., 1970. Ordained to ministry Luth. Ch. in Am., 1970. Pastor, St. Paul's Luth. Ch., Tannerville, Pa., 1970-80, St. Mark's Luth. Ch., Allentown, Pa., 1980—; dir. leadership edn. Northeastern Pa. Synod, Allentown, 1980-82, Allentown Area Luth. Parish, 1980—. Contbr. article to Luth. mag., 1984. Republican.

WIDEMAN, DONALD VIVIAN, minister, Southern Baptist Convention; b. St. Louis, Aug. 13, 1927; s. Emil Vivian and Katheryn Belle (Moore) W.; m. Marian Elizabeth Kiepe, Jan. 27, 1951; children: David Mark, Katheryn E. Wideman Campbell, Thomas Wayne, Rebecca Jo. Student Washington U., St. Louis, 1958, St. Louis Bapt. Coll.-Hannibal-LaGrange, 1959-61; B.A. with honors, So. Ill. U., 1966; M.Div. magna cum laude, Midwestern Bapt. Theol. Sem., 1969; D.D. (hon.), William Jewell Coll., 1980. Ordained minister Bapt. Ch., 1955. Asst. pastor 2d Bapt. Ch., Festus, Mo., 1955; pastor Oakland Bapt. Ch., DeSoto, Mo., 1955-61, 1st Bapt. Ch., Oakville, St. Louis, 1961-66, North Kansas City, Mo., 1973—; Liberty Manor Bapt. Ch., Mo., 1966-73, del. Bapt. World Alliance, Tokyo, 1970; condr. Friendship Evangelism Seminar, Bold Mission Taiwan, 1982; trustee Southwestern Bapt. Theol. Sem., 1975—, mem. com. So. Bapt. Conv., 1978, 2d v.p., 1984—, chmn. local arrangements info. com., 1977, 84; key pastor cons. Woman's Missionary Union, Birmingham, Ala., 1981; mem. transitional exec. council Hispanic Bapt. Theol. Sem., 1982; exec. bd. Mo. Bapt. Conv., 1973-76, pres., 1979-80; pres. Mo. Bapt. Pastors' Conf., 1974-75, com. on religious lit. and publs., 1972, chmn. ch. devel. com., 1974-76; trustee, sec. Bapt. Meml. Hosp., 1976-79; pres. parents assn. William Jewell Coll. 1975, trustee coll. 1979—; speaker Evangelism Conf., 1983. Salesman advt. specialties, auto parts, bookkeeper, 1946-51; time study, cost acct. Pitts. Plate Glass Co., 1952-59. Bd. dirs. Mental Health Assn. Clay-Ray Counties, 1974; mem. instl. rev. com. North Kansas City Meml. Hosp., 1980—. Served with USN, 1945-46. Recipient Am. Bible Soc. award, 1969. Mem. Jefferson County Bapt. Assn. (various coms. 1955-61), St. Louis Bapt. Assn. (various coms. 1961-66), Clay Platte Bapt. Assn. (chmn. various coms., past pres. Pastor's Conf.), Kansas City Bapt. Assn. (exec. com.), Midwestern Bapt. Theol. Sem. Alumni Assn. (past pres.), Lambda Iota Tau. Club: Kiwanis (North Kansas City) (pres. 1977-78). Home: 3314 NE Chippewa Kansas City MO 64116 Office: First Bapt Ch 2205 Iron N Kansas City MO 64116

WIEBE, PAUL G., deacon, religion educator, Mennonite Church; b. Aberdeen, Idaho, Jan. 22, 1938; s. Walter Henry and Stella (Enns) W.; m. Eleanor Sawatzky, May 26, 1959. B.A., Bethel Coll., 1960; A.M., U. Chgo., 1966, Ph.D., 1975. Ordained as deacon Mennonite Ch., 1982. Assoc. prof. religion Wichita State U., Kans., 1969—; bd. deacons Lorraine Ave. Mennonite Ch., Wichita, 1982—, chmn., 1983—. Author: The Architecture of Religion, 1984. Translator: Paul Tillich, The System of the Sciences, 1981. Contbr. articles to religious jours. Fellow Woodrow Wilson Found. 1960-61, Rockefeller Bros., 1961-62, NEH, 1976-77. Mem. Am. Acad. Religion. Home: 2313 N Bluff Wichita KS 67220 Office: Dept Religion Wichita State U Wichita KS 67208

WIEBER, ROBERT JOHN, priest, Roman Cath. Ch.; b. Farming, Minn., June 24, 1940; s. Edwin Leo and Helen Ann (Mehr) W.; B.A., St. John's U., 1963. Joined Order of St. Benedict, 1960; ordained priest; tchr. San Antonio Abad, Humanao, P.R., 1967-68; asso. pastor Sts. Peter and Paul Ch., Richmond, Minn., 1968-70; adminstr. Sacred Hearth Ch., Freeport, Minn., 1970; asso. pastor St. Boniface Ch., Hastings, Minn., 1970-71; tchr., chaplain St. Margaret's High Sch., St. Louis Park, Minn., 1971-75; pastor TriParish Community, St. Benedicts Ch., White Earth, Minn., 1975—. Vol. chaplain Hennepin County Jail, Mpls., 1973-75. Vice chmn. bd. dirs. White Earth Chem. Dependency Programs, 1976—. Address: St Benedict's Mission White Earth MN 56591

WIEDERAENDERS, ROBERT CHARLES, archivist, American Lutheran Church; b. Clinton, Iowa, June 23, 1922; s. Martin Frederick and Olivia (Mix) W.; m. Wauneta Ione Gorrell, June 15, 1951; children: Paul Catherine, Claudia, Calr. B.A., Wartburg Coll., 1943; B.D., Wartburg Sem., 1950; S.T.M., Luth. Sch. Theology, 1959. Ordained to ministry Am. Luth. Ch., 1952. Pastor Our Savior Ch., Burbank, Ill., 1952-56, Kankakee, Ill., 1956-64, Grace Luth. Ch., St. Anne, Ill., 1956-63; archivist Wartburg Theol. Sem., Dubuque, Iowa, 1964—. Editor: Microfilm Corpus of American Lutheranism, 1952-60. Author: (with W.G. Tillmanns) The Synods of American Lutheranism, 1968. Served with U.S. Army, 1943-46. Mem. Soc. Am. Archivists, Luth. Hist. Conf. (past pres.), Midwest Archives Conf. Democrat. Lodge: Lions. Home: 1769 University Ave Dubuque IA 52001 Office: Wartburg Theol Sem 333 Wartburg Pl Dubuque IA 52001

WIEKERT, NANKE RICHARD, minister, American Lutheran Church; b. Morris, Ill., Mar. 31, 1939; s. Nanke Wendell and Ethel Marie (McComas) W.; m. Arlene JoAnn Christianson, Sept. 7, 1968; children: Nanke John, Christopher Lane, Sarah Kathryn. B.A., Luther Coll., Decorah, Iowa, 1962; M.Div., Wartburg Theol. Sem., 1977. Ordained to ministry Am. Luth. Ch., 1977. Minister Scandinavia-Bethany Luth. Parish, Rural Aberdeen, S.D., 1977-81, Scandia-Immanuel Luth. Parish, Centerville, S.D., 1981—; bd. dirs. Luth. Soc. Services S.D., 1979-81; mem. dist. council, chmn. southeastern conf. S.D. dist. Am. Luth Ch., 1982-84. Served with U.S. Army, 1963-65, Korea. Home and Office: Scandia-Immanuel Luth Parish Box 147 Centerville SD 57014

WIEMER, LOYAL HULBERT, minister, Am. Bapt. Chs. in U.S.A.; b. Syracuse, N.Y., Oct. 28, 1914; s. Bernhard A. and Bertha A. (Hulbert) W.; A.B., Wheaton (Ill.) Coll., 1937; B.D., Eastern Bapt. Theol. Sem., Phila., 1941; m. Lola Myrtle Horton, May 28, 1938; children: Douglas Loyal, Carol Jane. Ordained to ministry Am. Bapt. Chs. in U.S.A., 1941; pastor chs., N.Y., 1941-43, 48-53; dir. U.S.O., Buzzards Bay, Mass., Presque Isle, Maine and East Greenwich, R.I., 1943-47; dir. camping, Detroit, 1954-59, Mass. Bapt. Conv., Grotonwood, 1959-62; pastor Clarklake (Mich.) Community Ch., 1963-79; minister-at-large Am. Bapt. Chs. U.S.A., 1979—. Exec. dir. Jackson County Interfaith Council, 1974—; bd. dirs. Mich. Bapt. Chs., 1964—, del. constn. revision com., 1968; pres. Mich. sect. Am. Camping Assn., 1964-68, chmn. standards com. Mich. sect., 1964-73; chaplain Internat. Order Foresters-Rebekah Homes, 1963-79. Bd. dirs., chmn. budget com. United Way Jackson County, 1969-79; bd. dirs. Jackson Osteo. Hosp., 1966-76, United Way of Mich., 1973—, Land O'Lakes council Boy Scouts Am.; mem. Jackson Bd. Commrs., 1980—, vice chmn., 1985; chair Jackson Transit Authority, 1985. Mem. Am. Bapt. Chs. U.S.A. Ministers Assn., Mich. Bapt. Ministers. Author: Flight of the Snow Goose, 1947. Address: 425 Oakwood Dr PO Box 156 Clarklake MI 49234

WIENER, MARVIN S., editor, rabbi, Jewish religion; b. N.Y.C., Mar. 16, 1925; s. Max and Rebecca (Dodell) W.; B.S., Coll. City N.Y., 1944, M.S., 1945; B.H.L., Jewish Theol. Sem. Am., 1947, M.H.L., 1951, D.D. (hon.), 1977; m. Sylvia Bodek, Mar. 2, 1952; children—David Hillel, Judith Rachel. Ordained rabbi, 1951; registrar, sec. faculty Rabbinical Sch., Jewish Theol. Sem. Am., 1951-57; cons. Frontiers of Faith Television Series, NBC, 1951-57; dir. Cantors Inst., Sem. Coll. Jewish Music, Jewish Theol. Sem. Am., 1954-58, faculty coordinator Sem. Sch. and Womens Inst., 1958-64; dir. Nat. Acad. for Adult Jewish Studies, United Synagogue Am., N.Y.C., 1958—; editor Burning Bush Press, 1958—. Sec., Joint Retirement Bd., Jewish Theol. Sem. Am., Rabbinical Assembly and United Synagogue Am., 1968-76, 1st vice chmn., 1976-82, chmn., 1982, treas., 1983; co-chmn. Jewish Bible Assn., 1960-64; chmn. bd. rev. Nat. Council Jewish Audio-Visual Materials, 1968-69; mem. exec. com. Nat. Council for Adult Jewish Edn., 1966—; chmn. Internat. Conf. Adult Jewish Edn., Jerusalem, Israel, 1972. Mem. Adult Edn. Assn. U.S., Am. Acad. Jewish Research, Assn. Jewish Studies, N.Y. Bd. Rabbis, Rabbinical Assembly. Editor: Adult Jewish Education, also Nat. Acad. Adult Jewish Studies Bull., 1955-78; Past and Present: Selected Essays, 1961; Jewish Tract Series, 1964-78; Talmudic Law and the Modern State, 1973. Home: 67-66 108th St Forest Hills NY 11375 Office: 155 Fifth Ave New York City NY 10010

WIENER, SIDNEY, lay worker, Jewish; b. Bklyn., Aug. 24, 1915; s. Louis and Ida (Lefkowitz) W.; m. Ruth Pressman, Nov. 16, 1940 (dec. Sept. 1970); children: Helen Wiener Friedlander, Alan; m. Shirley Pearlstein, June 17, 1973. B.S., Bklyn. Coll., 1936. Del. World Zionist Orgn., Jerusalem, 1972, 78, 82; pres. L.I. region B'nai Zion, 1978-80, nat. pres., N.Y.C., 1981—; chmn. ritual com. Jewish Ctr. Kew Gardens Hills, Flushing, N.Y., 1951-54, v.p., 1954-56; chmn. ritual com. Hewlett-East Rockaway Jewish Ctr., East Rockaway, N.Y., 1964-66, v.p., 1966-68. Subject of testimonials United Jewish Appeal, 1953, 56, 65, 79, 80, State of Israel Bonds, 1961, 66, 78, 81; named to Prime Minister's Club, State of Israel Bonds, 1983. Mem. Conf. Pres. Maj. Am. Jewish Orgns. Office: Arc Knitwear Mills Inc 32 33d St Brooklyn NY 11232

WIERENGA, EDWARD, religious studies educator, Christian Reformed Church; b. Chgo., Oct. 14, 1947; s. Lambert William and Henrietta Myrtle (Dekker) W.; m. Wilma Vierzen, July 31, 1971; children: Christina, Stephen. A.B., Calvin Coll. 1969; M.A., Ph.D. U. Mass., 1974. Assoc. prof. religious studies U. Rochester, N.Y., 1977—. Contbr. articles to profl. jours. Mem. Am. Acad. Religion, Am. Philos. Assn. Home: 171 Inglewood Dr Rochester NY 14619 Office: Dept Religious and Classical Studies U Rochester NY 14627

WIESE, RONALD JAMES, minister, Lutheran Church-Missouri Synod; b. St. Joseph, Mich., Oct. 18, 1943; s. Edward Herman and Pauline (Marske) W.; m. June Carol Van Bergen, June 3, 1967; children: Rachel Lynn, Jennifer Rebekah, Sarah Catherine. B.A., Concordia Sr. Coll., Fort Wayne, Ind., 1965; M.Div., Concordia Sem., St. Louis, 1969. Ordained to ministry Luth. Ch.-Mo. Synod, 1969. Pastor Christ and Good Shepherd Ch., Meridian, Miss., 1969-75, Our Savior Luth. Ch., Butler, Ala., 1969-75; assoc. pastor Trinity Luth. Ch., Memphis, 1976-82, sr. pastor, 1983—; chmn. bd. soc. ministry Mid-South dist. Luth. Ch.-Mo. Synod, Memphis, 1980—, pastoral del. convs., 1975, 79, 81; pastoral counselor Mid-South dist. Luth. Women's League, 1978-80; pres. Downtown Churches Assn., Memphis, 1978. Pres. Lauderdale County Mental Health Assn., Meridian, 1974, Criminal Justice Ministry, Memphis, 1979-80. Recipient service award Lauderdale County Mental Health Assn., 1975. Mem. Memphis Ministerial Assn. Republican. Home: 3276 N Waynoka Circle Memphis TN 38111 Office: 210 Washington Ave Trinity Ch Memphis TN 38102

WIGERT, LEE ROY, minister, pastoral counselor, United Methodist Church. b. Hastings, Nebr., Dec. 5, 1951; s. Robert Dale and Helen Mae (Krabel) W.; m. Diane Lynne Sackett, June 30, 1979; children: Benjamin George, Nathan Lee. Student U. Bergen, Norway, 1973; B.A., Hastings Coll., 1974;

M.Psychology in Arts, U. Nebr., 1977; M.Div., Union Theol. Sem., 1980; D.Min., Drew U., 1982. Ordained to ministry United Meth. Ch., 1978, elder, 1981; cert. pastoral counselor. Asst. minister Waverly United Meth., Nebr., 1976-77; assoc. minister St. Mark's United Meth., Rockeville Centre, N.Y., 1977-78; pastoral counselor Westside Ecumenical Ministry to Elderly, N.Y.C., 1978-79; pastor Clay County Parish, Sutton, Nebr., 1979-82, Faith United Meth., Lincoln, Nebr., 1982—; mem. adv. bd. Domestic Violence Task Force, Clay Center, Nebr., 1979-82; chmn. Crop Hunger Walk, Sutton, 1980-82, Ch. World Service, Lincoln, 1983-85. Author: A Systems Approach to Parish Planning, 1982. Contbr. articles to religious jours. Mem. adv. bd. Community Mental Health Ctr., Clay Center, 1979-82. Recipient Disting. Recognition award South Central Mental Health Assn., 1973; research grantee Nebr. Psychol. Assn., 1972. Mem. Am. Psychol. Assn. (local pres. 1975), Assn. Pastoral Counselors. Democrat. Lodges: Masons, Kiwanis. Home: 3245 Starr St Lincoln NE 68503 Office: Faith United Methodist Ch 1333 N 33d St Lincoln NE 68503

WIGGER, HARRY CHESTER, minister; b. Frankclay, Mo., Mar. 25, 1912; s. William Moses and Florence Minerva (Newcomer) W.; A.A., Will Mayfield Coll., 1931; A.B., William Jewell Coll., 1933; Th.M., So. Bapt. Theol. Sem., 1936; m. Mary Elizabeth Boren, May 25, 1936; children—Harriet, David, Mary Evelyn. Ordained to ministry So. Bapt. Conv., 1933; pastor chs., Mo., 1932-33, 36-46, 56-58, Ind., 1934-36, Tex., 1946-56, Ark., 1962-75, including Bella Vista (Ark.) Bapt. Ch., 1973-75; missionary, Antigua, W.I., 1976—. supt. missions Wyaconda and Bethel Bapt. Assns., N.E. Mo., 1958-62, Benton County, Ark., 1965-73. Mem. exec. bd. Ark. Bapt. State Conv., 1971—. Home and Office: 807 Carson Dr Bentonville AR 72712

WIGGINS, DANIEL BRAXTON, JR., minister, Southern Baptist Convention; b. Mobile, Ala., Jan. 16, 1952; s. Daniel B. and Christine L. (Dobbs) W.; m. Margaet Anne Stephens, Mar. 3, 1972; children: Karl Daniel, Matthew Braxton, Jacquelyn Christine. Student U. Ala., 1970-72. Ordained to ministry Baptist Ch., 1978. Youth preacher, Tuscaloosa, Ala., 1970; Sunday sch. tchr. Hopewell Bapt. Ch., Tuscaloosa, 1971-75, royal ambassador, dir., 1977-78; pastor Catherine Bapt. Ch., Ala., 1977-80, River Rd. Bpt. Ch., Tallassee, Ala., 1980—; mem. exec. com. Tuskegee-Lee Bapt. Assn., 1980—, messenger, 1981—; buyer/dept. mgr. Gayfers-Merc. Stores Co., Auburn, Ala., 1978—. Mem. PTA, Tallassee, 1981—. Democrat. Home: 711 Powers Extension Tallassee AL 36078 Office: Gayfers Village Mall Auburn AL 36830

WIGGINS, JAMES BRYAN, minister, United Methodist Church, religion educator, religious organization administrator; b. Mexia, Tex., Aug. 24, 1935; children: Bryan, Karis. B.A., Tex. Wesleyan U., 1957; B.D., So. Meth. U., 1959; Ph.D., Drew U., 1963; postgrad. Tubingen U., W. Ger., 1968-69. Ordained to ministry United Meth. Ch. Instr. English, Union Jr. Coll., Cranford, N.J., 1960-65; asst. prof. Syracuse U., N.Y., 1963-69, assoc. prof., 1969-75, prof. religion, 1975—; exec. dir., treas. Am. Acad. Religion, Syracuse, 1983—. Co-author: Christian Word Book; Foundations in Christianity, 1970. Editor: Readings in Judaism and Christianity, 1964. Fellow Rockefeller Found., 1962-63, Soc. Religion in Higher Edn., 1968, Danforth Assn., 1972. Mem. Soc. Arts Religion and Culture (bd. dirs.), Scholars Press (bd. dirs.), AAUP, Am. Soc. Ch. History, Am. Hist. Assn. (com. profl. devel. and research 1979—). Democrat. Office: Dept Religion Syracuse U 501 Hall of Langs Syracuse NY 13210

WIGGS, JOEL MATT, JR., priest, Roman Catholic Church; b. Nashville, Jan. 23, 1923; s. Joel Matt and Charlie (Ford) W.; B.A., St. Mary's Sem. and U., Balt., 1945, S.T.B., 1947. Ordained priest, 1949; asso. pastor St. Ann's Ch., Memphis, 1949-52, Blessed Sacrament Ch., Memphis, 1952-54, St. Mary's Ch., Oak Ridge, 1954-55; pastor St. Francis Ch., Chattanooga, 1955-57, Blessed Sacrament Ch., Harriman, Tenn., 1957-66, Sacred Heart Ch., Humboldt, Tenn., 1966—. Chaplain Diocese of Memphis Boy Scouts Am., Girl Scouts U.S.A.; mem. Nat. Cath. Disaster Relief Com., 1973—. Chmn. Humboldt Park Commn., 1974—; mem. State of Tenn. Human Services Adv. Com., 1976—; v.p. St. Matthew Manor; mem. exec. bd. W. Tenn. council Boy Scouts Am. Home and Office: 2881 E Main Humboldt TN 38343

WIKER, EDGAR GUY, minister, Lutheran Church in America; b. Phila., July 26, 1932; s. Edgar Maine and Lillian Kandle (Honeker) W.; m. Irene Haines Rae, July 12, 1958; children: Mona, Christine. B.A. in Econs., Gettysburg Coll., 1954; M.Div., Luth. Theol. Sem., 1963. Ordained to ministry Lutheran Ch. in Am., 1963. Pastor Lebanon Luth. Ch., DuBois, Pa., 1963-67; dir. camping services Luth. Social Services, Bklyn., 1967-69; pastor Emanuel Luth. Ch., Friesburg, N.J., 1969—; pres. bd. Faith Farm, Inc., Bridgeton, N.J., 1972—; bd. dirs. Spanish Christian Ch., Bridgeton, 1976—. Served with U.S. Army, 1955-57, Germany. Home and Office: Rural Route 3 Box 252 Elmer NJ 08318

WILBUR, JOHN ELDREDGE, priest, Episc. Ch.; b. Balt., Jan. 9, 1942; s. Arnold Jackson and Marjorie Creighton (Harper) W.; B.A., Moravian Coll., 1965; M.Div., Phila. Div. Sch., 1968; children—Sarah Elizabeth, Jennifer Lynn. Ordained priest, 1968; curate Holy Trinity Ch., Collingswood, N.J., 1968-69, rector, 1969-73; rector St. Mary's Ch., Washington, 1974—. Chaplain to students of George Washington U., 1974—; mem. alumni com. Phila. Div. Sch., 1968-73; mem. steering bd. Camden Episc. Community Center, 1969-73; county chmn. Spriitual Frontiers Fellowship, 1970-73; bd. dirs. St. Mary's Ct. Housing Devel. Corp.; steering com. chmn. of research Gerontology Program, George Washington U. Med. Sch., 1977-79; mem. providers Council services to the Aging for Washington, D.C.; guest lectr. George Washington U. Med. Sch.; Companies of the Soc of the Holy Cross, 1982- 84, Internat. Order of St. Luke the Physician, 1974-82; healing Missionary, Jamaica, 1979. Charter mem. Center for Study Democratic Instns. Mem. Washington Episc. Clergy Assn., Order of Holy Cross (assoc.). Home: 730 23d St NW Washington DC 20037 Office: 728 23d St NW Washington DC 20037

WILBUR, MARVIN CUMMINGS, church official, United Presbyterian Church U.S.A.; b. Sprague, Wash., July 12, 1914; s. George Henry and Harriet Starr (Nutter) W.; B.S., Oreg. State U., 1936; postgrad. George Washington U., 1937-38; M.Div., Union Theol. Sem., 1943; D.D., Alma Coll., 1956; m. G. Marie Lacy, Nov. 1, 1945; children: Judy Marie, George Marvin, John Cummings. Ordained to ministry United Presbyn. Ch. in U.S.A., 1943; chaplain USNR, 1943-46; Presbyn. chaplain Yale, 1946-49; dir. pub. info. Union Theol. Sem., N.Y.C., 1949-51; sec. program materials U.P. Ch., U.S.A., N.Y.C., 1951-64; asst. v.p. U.P. Found., 1964—. Asst. dir. pub. info. sec. to chancellor Oreg. System Higher Edn., 1936; bd. dirs. Religion in Am. Life, Inc., 1951—; sec. Presbyn. Homes N.J., 1979—. Mem. Nat. Visual Communication Assn. (Outstanding Achievement award 1954), Pub. Relations Soc. Am., Religious Pub. Relations Council (pres. 1955-57, 1st exec. sec., 1959—, editor Mediakit), Sigma Delta Chi, Phi Kappa Phi, Delta Phi Epsilon, Pi Kappa Phi. Contbg. author: Pub. Relations Handbook, 1972. Home: 32 Windsor Rd Tenafly NJ 07670 Office: 475 Riverside Dr New York NY 10115

WILBURN, JAMES RUSSELL, educator, minister, Presbyterian Ch. U.S.; b. Caneyville, Ky., Aug. 10, 1924; s. Hardy Lee and Clarcia Marie (Weedman) W.; student Wright Jr. Coll., Chgo., 1943, Grove City Coll., 1943-44; B.A., Belhaven Coll., 1960; M.Div., Columbia, 1966; postgrad., Atlanta, 1976—; m. Evelyn Phillips, Dec. 6, 1944; 1 son, James Mark. Ordained to ministry Presbyn. Ch. U.S., 1966; tchr. Belhaven Coll., Jackson, Miss., 1964-65; pastor St. Paul Presbyn. Ch., Jackson, 1966-67; prof. Bible and philosophy Belhaven Coll., 1967—; pastor Pickens (Miss.) Presbyn. Ch., 1968-76, Shelby Presbyn. Ch., 1968—. Sec. Miss. Religious and Pastoral Counseling Center. Mem. Am. Schs. Oriental Research, Oriental Inst. Club: Civitan (pres. 1974) (Jackson). Home: 1436 Kimwood Jackson MS 39211 Office: Belhaven College Jackson MS 39202

WILCOX, JOHN BANCROFT, minister, United Church of Christ; b. Norwich, Conn., Jan. 5, 1930; s. Frank Herbert and Bertha Isabel (Montgomery) W.; m. Beatrice Mae Barden, Dec. 20, 1952 (dec. Dec. 1980); children: John Bancroft, Robert, Jeffrey; m. Susan Christine Ennis, June 26, 1981. B.S.E.E., Naval Postgrad. Sch., 1965; M. Div., Andover Newton Theol. Sch., 1980. Ordained to ministry United Ch. Christ and Am. Bapt. Ch., 1980. Pastor Federated Ch. Christ, Brooklyn, Conn., 1976-81, Congl. United Ch. Christ, Kinsley, Kans., 1981-83, Kiowa, Kans., 1983—, St. John's United Ch. Christ, Hardtner, Kans., 1983—; dept. chmn. Conn. conf. United Ch. Christ, Hartford, 1975-76, chmn. dept. ministry Windham Assn., Brooklyn, 1979-80, commn. on ministry Western Assn., Kans.-Okla. Conf., 1981-83. Mcpl. judge City of Kiowa, 1984—. Served to lt. comdr. USN, 1947-70. Lodge: Masons. Home: 603 Rumsey Kiowa KS 67070 Office: Kiowa-Hardtner Parish 7th and Rumsey Sts Kiowa KS 67070

WILCOX, RONALD WAYNE, minister, Southern Baptist Convention. B. Hazlehurst, Ga., Mar. 15, 1941; s. Odis C. and Margelene (Schell) W.; m. Leita Euree Johnson, Aug. 26, 1960; children: Rhonda Ruth, LeRee DeNise, Karen LeAnne. B.A., Luther Rice Bible Coll., Jacksonville, Fla., 1983; M.Divinity, Luther Rice Sem., 1985. Ordained to ministry Southern Bapt. Conv., 1978; tchr. ch. sch. South Side Bapt. Ch., Hazlehurst, Ga., 1968-76, deacon, 1966-77, pianist, 1971-77; pastor 1st Bapt. Ch., Screven, Ga., 1977—; pres. Wayne County Ministers, Jesup, Ga., 1983-84; moderator Altamaha Bapt. Assn., Jesup, 1983-85. Pianist 9 recorded gospel albums, 1968-78; religious columnist Press-Sentinel, Jesup, 1978—. Chmn., Hazlehurst Heart Fund Dr., 1976, St. Jude's Children's Hosp., Screven, 1981. Democrat. Club: Exchange (pres. 1976-78) (Hazlehurst). Home: Grace St Screven GA 31560 Office: 1st Baptist Ch Church and School Sts Screven GA 31560

WILDIN, ROLLIN VIRGIL, minister, Am. Baptist Conv.; b. Hutchinson, Kans., Feb. 15, 1912; s. Charles Roy and Sigrid Malvida (Ogren) W.; A.B., Sioux Falls (S.D.) Coll., 1940; M.A., B.D., Berkeley (Calif.) Baptist Div. Sch., 1951; m. Martha Sylvia Hill, July 24, 1936; children—Rollin Charles, Mary Ann (Mrs. Stephen Steen), Elizabeth (Mrs. Alan Tariska). Ordained minister Am. Bapt. Conv., 1940; pastor chs. in S.D., Minn., Calif., Colo. and Iowa, 1937-45, 47-54; chaplain AUS, 1945-47; exec. dir. Christian edn. Nebr. Bapt. Conv., 1954-60, Am. Bapt. Chs. N.J., 1960-71; area rep. Kirby-Smith Assos., West Milford, N.J., 1971—. Chmn. dept. Christian edn. Nebr. Council Chs., 1958-60; treas. ministers council Am. Bapt. Chs., 1968-70; mem. field services com., dept. Christian edn. Nat. Council Chs., 1965-68; chaplain, lt. col. AUS (ret.). Address: RFD 4 Red Lion PA 17356

WILHELM, MARK NORMAN, pastor, American Lutheran Church; b. Salem, Ohio, Feb. 13, 1951; s. Norman E. and Madeleine (Bretz) W.; m. Laura Natalie Mamis, Aug. 25, 1973; children: Peter Edward, Adam Mark. B.A., St. Olaf Coll., 1973; M.Div., Luther Sem., St. Paul, 1977. Ordained to ministry Am. Luth. Ch., 1977. Pastor Martin Luther Luth. Ch., Balt., 1977-81, Bethany Luth. Ch., Bklyn., 1981—; continuing edn. coordinator, eastern dist. NE region Am. Luth Ch., Edison, N.J., 1981—; chmn. ch. in soc. com., eastern dist., Springfield, Va., 1984—. Bd. dirs. Neighborhood Housing Services, Balt., 1979-81, Housing Assistance Corp., Balt., 1979-81, Marien-Heim Housing, Bklyn., 1983—; pres. Neighborhood Rental Services, Balt., 1979-81; mem. Mayor's Task Force on Arabing, Balt., 1979-81; mem. instl. rev. bd. Johns Hopkins Hosp., Balt., 1980-81. Recipient scholarship Luther Sem., 1974; Mark N. Wilhelm Day named in his honor, City of Balt., 1981. Mem. Phi Beta Kappa. Home: 1017 84th St Brooklyn NY 11228 Office: Bethany Luth Ch 1037 72d St Brooklyn NY 11228

WILHITE, ORLAN WAYNE, minister, Gen. Assn. Regular Baptist Chs.; b. Corwith, Ia., Jan. 6, 1927; s. Earl Eli and Carrie V. (Zigler) W.; grad. Grand Rapids Theol. Sem., 1953; m. Mabel E. Harban, Jan. 16, 1948; children—Duane, Dennis, Mary, Stephen, Ronald. Ordained to ministry, 1953; interim pastor Grandview Park Bapt. Ch., Des Moines, 1953; missionary to Philippines, Assn. Bapts. for World Evangelism, 1954-67; prof. missions dept. Bapt. Bible Coll., Clarks Summit, Pa., 1968-69; pastor First Bapt. Ch., North Tonawanda, N.Y., 1969—. Adv. bd. Assn. Bapts. for World Evangelism, 1969—; exec. bd. Buffalo Hebrew Christian Mission, 1970—, Grand Rapids Bapt. Coll. and Sem., 1973—. Named Alumnus of the Year, Grand Rapids Bapt. Theol. Sem., 1963. Home: 469 Roncroff Dr North Tonawanda NY 14120 Office: 530 Meadow Dr North Tonawanda NY 14120

WILHOIT, MELVIN ROSS, minister of music, Southern Baptist Church; music educator; b. Fort Wayne, Ind., May 26, 1948; s. Bert Harvey and Vivian C. (Hitchcock) W.; m. Susan Beth Cassidy, May 27, 1970; children: Robert Christian, Christina Elizabeth, Angela Noel. B.S. in Music Edn., Bob Jones U., 1971; Mus.M. in Music History and Lit., Mankato State U., 1976; Mus.D., So. Bapt. Theol. Sem., 1982. Prof. music Pillsbury Bapt. Music Coll., Owatonna, Minn., 1971-76; prof. music Boyce Bible Sch., Louisville, 1977-80; asst. prof. music Bryan Coll., Dayton, Tenn., 1980—; minister of music Oak Park Bapt. Ch., Jeffersonville, Ind., 1977-80, Oak St. Bapt. Ch., Soddy-Daisy, Tenn., 1982—; active Am. Christian Action Council, Rhea County, Tenn., 1980-84. Contbr. articles to profl. jours. Area organizer Rhea County Republicans, 1980-84; sch. coordinator Cherokee council Boy Scouts Am., 1983. NEH grantee, 1984. Mem. Music Educators Nat. Conf., Hymn Soc. Am., Sonneck Soc., Christian Instrumental Dirs. Assn., Tenn. Music Educators. Home: Rt 6 Box 517 Dayton TN 37321 Office: Bryan Coll Box 7000 Dayton TN 37321

WILKEN, DON AL, pastor, American Lutheran Church; b. Upland, Nebr., June 13, 1937; s. Herman R. and Gretje (DeJonge) W.; m. Carol J. Sexauer, June 20, 1964; children: Robert, Mark, Deborah. B.A., Wartburg Coll., 1959; B.D., Wartburg Sem., 1963, M.Div., 1977. Ordained to ministry Am. Luth. Ch., 1963. Sr. pastor Upper Wolf Lutheran Ch., Robinson, Kans., 1963-68, Fredericksburg Luth. Ch., Minden, Nebr., 1968-73, Faith Luth. Ch., Eaton, Colo., 1973-78, St. John Luth. Ch., Sterling, Nebr., 1978-81, Zion Luth. Ch., Albion, Nebr., 1981—; chmn. bd. Circle R Luth. Camp, Omaha, 1970-73; clergy dean Central Nebr. Conf. Am. Luth. Ch., 1985—, mem. ch. council central Nebr. Dist., 1985—. Property and bldg. dir. Northeast Cove-Johnson Lake, Lexington, Nebr., 1971; dir. housing devel., Minden, Nebr., 1971—. Mem. NE Luth. Outdoor Ministries (bldg. chmn. 1982, bd. dirs. 1979—), Boone County Ministers (pres. 1983). Democrat. Club: Albion Country. Home: 426 Marengo

Albion NE 68620 Office: Zion Luth Ch 319 S 5th St Albion NE 68620

WILKERSON, JOHN ABBOTT, JR., minister, Presbyterian Ch. (U.S.A.); b. Lynchburg, Va., Sept. 16, 1937; s. John Abbott and Sarah Virginia (Allen) W.; m. Kaye Hatke, Dec. 26, 1959; children: John Kevin, Karen Marie, Joseph Kerry, Kathryn Elizabeth. B.A., Lynchburg Coll., 1959; M.Div., Union Theol. Sem., 1962, D. Ministry, 1976. Ordained to ministry Presbyn. Ch. (U.S.A.), 1962. Pastor Pink Hill Presbyn. Ch., N.C., 1962-64, Northminster Presbyn. Ch., Hickory, N.C., 1964-75, Huntersville Presbyn. Ch., N.C., 1975-83, John Calvin Presbyn. Ch., Salisbury, N.C., 1983—. Mem. Acad. of Parish Clergy, Internat. Transactional Analysis Assn. Democrat. Lodge: Lions (2d v.p. Salisbury chpt.). Home: 209 Overman Ave Salisbury NC 28144 Office: John Calvin Presbyn Ch 1620 Brenner Ave Salisbury NC 28144

WILKERSON, WILLIAM NORRIS, minister, So. Baptist Conv.; b. Snellville, Ga., Apr. 10, 1932; s. Murphy and Ethel Mae (Williams) W.; B.B.A., Ga. State U., 1954; B.D., New Orleans Bapt. Theol. Sem., 1957; m. Patsy Ann Brown, Aug. 12, 1955; children—John Mark, Lorraine May. Ordained to ministry, 1956; pastor chs. in Miss. and Ga., 1956-70; pastor Parkwood Hills Bapt. Ch., Decatur, Ga., 1971-74, Rockdale Bapt. Ch., Conyers, Ga., 1974—; dean, mem. faculty extension sch. Mercer U., Atlanta, 1960-68. Pres. Atlanta Bapt. Ministers Conf., 1969; moderator Atlanta Bapt. Assn. Chs., 1971-72, pastor-adviser Bapt. Student Union, Ga. State Coll., 1957-64. Mem. Stone Mountain Bapt. Pastors Conf., Ga. State U., New Orleans Bapt. Theol. Sem. (chpt. sec. 1970-71) alumni assns. Author newspaper columns. Home: 2145 River Acres Ct Lithonia GA 30058 Office: 1295 Upper Smyrna Rd Conyers GA 30207

WILKIN, RICHARD EDWIN, ch. ofcl., Chs. of God in N.Am.; b. nr. Paulding, Ohio, Nov. 3, 1930; s. Gaylord D. and Beulah E. (Tarlton) W.; student Giffin Jr. Coll., 1948-49; B.S., Findlay Coll., 1952, D.D., 1975; postgrad. Ind. U., 1959-60; m. Barbara A. Zehender, Aug. 10, 1952; children: Richard Edward, James Lee, Deborah Ann. Ordained to ministry Chs. of God in N.Am., 1953; pastor Neptune Ch. of God, Celina, Ohio, 1952-59, Wharton (Ohio) Ch. of God, 1959-64, Anthony Wayne Ch. of God, Ft. Wayne, Ind., 1964-70; adminstr., chief exec. Gen. Conf. Chs. of God, Findlay, Ohio, 1970—, adminstr. cross-cultural ministries in India, Bangladesh, Haiti, also Am. Indian ministries in N.Mex. and Ariz. Dir. summer youth camps, sec., mem. exec. com. Ohio Conf., 1952-59, stated clk., pres., 1959-64; chmn. Commn. on Edn., mem. exec. com. Ind. Conf., 1964-70; adv. council Am. Bible Soc., 1980—; pres. Ft. Wayne Ministerial Assn.; bd. dirs. Assoc. Chs. of Ft. Wayne and Allen County, 1966-70; tchr. Center Twp. Jr. High Sch., Celina, Mendon (Ohio) Union High Sch., Van Del High Sch., Van Wert, Ohio, 1954-59. Vice pres. bd. trustees Winebrenner Haven; trustee Winebrenner Theol. Sem., Findlay, 1980—; mem. adv. com. in race relations regarding sch. reorgn. and busing, Ft. Wayne, 1967-69. Recipient Outstanding Tchr. award, 1958, Distinguished Alumnus award Findlay Coll., 1973. Mem. Nat., Ohio edn. assns., NAACP, Farm Bur. Lodge: Lions. Contbr. numerous articles to religious periodicals. Office: 700 E Melrose Ave PO Box 926 Findlay OH 45839

WILKINSON, ELWYN NATHANIEL, JR., minister, Southern Baptist Convention; b. Louisville, May 31, 1938; s. Elwyn Nathaniel and Mary (Riley) W.; m. Nancy Lou Wade, Jan. 18, 1964; children: Elwyn, Nathalie, Jeremy. B.S. in Math., Miss. Coll., 1961; B.D., New Orleans Bapt. Theol. Sem., 1965, Th.D., 1972. Ordained to ministry Bapt. Ch., 1963. Pastor Calvary Bapt. Ch., Baton Rouge, 1963-65, Forrest Ave. Bapt. Ch., Biloxi, Miss., 1965-68; dir. religious activities Cumberland Coll., Williamsburg, Ky., 1968-75; Bapt. campus minister Western Ky. U., Bowling Green, 1975-77; pastor Perkinston Bapt. Ch., Miss., 1977—; instr. Miss. Gulf Coast Jr. Coll., Perkinston, 1978—; spl. cons. Miss. Bapt. Conv., 1984. Pres., Stone County Mental Health/Mental Retardation Adv. Com., 1983-84. Mem. Stone County Ministerial Assn. (pres. 1981—), Gulf Coast Bapt. Assn. (assoc. dir. Sunday sch. 1981—). Republican. Home: PO Box 55 Perkinston MS 39573 Office: Perkinston Baptist Ch PO Box 55 Perkinston MS 39537

WILKINSON, JOE WRIGHT, elder, chaplain, Presbyterian Church in the U.S.A., retired airline pilot; b. Tuskegee, Ala., Feb. 22, 1920; s. Joseph Brady and Mannie (Campbell) W.; m. Kathryn Randall Gill, Sept. 28, 1941; children: Joseph Gill, Wade Campbell. Student Columbia Mil. Acad., Tenn., 1935-38, Auburn U., 1939-40, Am. Bible Coll., Pine Land, Fla., 1975-78. Ordained elder Presbyn. Ch., 1956. Various positions Presbyn. Ch., Peachtree City, Ga., 1951—; ch. sec. Gideons, Fayette County, Ga., 1981-83; chaplain Atlanta Internat. Airport Chaplaincy, 1982-84; dir. vol. chaplains Christian City Convalescent Ctr., Atlanta, 1984—; chaplain Fayette County Sheriff Dept., 1983—. Ret. pilot Delta Airlines, Atlanta. Served with USAF, 1941-46, CBI. Decorated D.F.C., Air Medal; Order of Flying Cloud (Republic of China). Mem. Inst. Indsl. and Comml. Ministries (bd. dirs., unit dir. 1983-84), Atlanta Hartsfield Internat. Airport Chapel (bd. dirs. 1982-84). Republican. Lodge: Kiwanis (bd. dirs. 1982-84). Home: 608 Golf View Dr Peachtree City GA 30269 Office: Christian City Convalescent Ctr 7300 Lester Rd Atlanta GA 30349

WILKINSON, JOHN HARLEY, educator, Baptist Federation of Canada; b. Toronto, Ont., Can., Jan. 5, 1947; s. George William and Ruby Mae (Barnes) W.; m. Patricia Joan Gracie, Oct. 5, 1974; children: Matthew, Mark. B.A. (honors), U. Winnipeg, 1970; M.A., U. Toronto, 1974. Gen. dir. Canadian Keswick Conf. & Camps-Ont., 1970-75; gen. dir. Muskoka Woods Youth Camps, Ont., 1979-80; prof. Christian Edn. Ont. Bible Coll. & Sem., 1976—, chmn. Christian Edn. dept., 1983—, dir. New Staff Devel., Youth for Christ Can., 1980—; chmn. Youth for Christ, Toronto, 1978-80; pres. Kesalon Ministries, Inc., Toronto, 1976—; chmn. Spring Garden Bapt. Ch., Toronto, 1983—. Contbr. articles to profl. jours. Author: Organized Resident Camping in the 80's, 1983; Tips and Trails on Canoeing in Manitoba, 1970. Fellow Soc. Camp Dirs.; mem. Canadian Camping Assn., Nat. Assn. Profs. Christian Edn., Ont. Camping Assn., Christian Camping Internat. (dir.). Office: Ont Bible Coll Theol Sem 25 Ballyconnor Ct Willowdale ON M2M 4B3 Canada

WILLARD, CONRAD RAYMOND, minister, educator Southern Baptist Convention; b. Lebanon, Mo., May 13, 1918; s. Charles Raymond and Chloe Helena (Adams) W.; m. Lena Mae Hicks, July 21, 1940; children: Sherri, Patricia. B.A., Drury Coll., 1949; B.D., So. Bapt. Theol. Sem., 1952; Th.D., Central Bapt. Theol. Sem., 1956; D.D. (hon.), Stetson U., 1966. Ordained to ministry Baptist Ch., 1943. Pastor, Calvery Bapt. Ch., Kansas City, Mo., 1953-62, Central Bapt. Ch., Miami, Fla., 1962-83, pastor emeritus, 1983—; mem. exec. com. So. Bapt. Conv., 1955-57, 76-84, 1st v.p., 1957, pres. bd. trustees Sunday Sch. Bd., 1966-73; pres. Fla. Bapt. Conv., 1967; pres. bd. trustees Midwestern Bapt. Theol. Sem., Kansas City, Mo., 1957-62. Co-author: Southern Baptist Preaching, 1965; Is the Bible a Human Book?, 1970; Teacher's Bible Commentary, 1972. Author manual of Bible study, life and work, 1956-82. Trustee William Jewell Coll., Liberty, Mo., 1958-62, Bapt. Meml. Hosp., Kansas City, 1957-62, Bapt. Hosp. of Miami, Inc., 1971—, Stetson U., 1973-83; bank examiner Mo. Dept. Fin., Jefferson City, 1941-43; chmn. Community Relations Bd. Dade County, Miami, 1981; pres. Kansas City Assn. for Blind, 1958; mem. New World Ctr. Action Com., Miami, 1965-83. Served with U.S. Army, 1944-46, ETO. Decorated Bronze Star; recipient Medal of Honor, DAR, 1975, Life Service award Southwest Bapt. U., 1971. Republican. Lodges: Kiwanis (Miami); Masons.

WILLARD, NEIL EMERSON, chancellor, Roman Catholic Church; b. Sherbrooke, Que., Can., May 9, 1937; s. Wilbur E. and Margaret (Deacon) W. Lic. in Theology, U. Montreal, 1961; Lic. in Canon Law, Gregorian U., Rome, 1966. Ordained priest Roman Cath. Ch., 1961. Parish asst. Ascension Parish, Westmount, Que., 1961-64; vice-chancellor Diocese of Montreal, 1966-75, chancellor, 1975—; exec. dir. Diocesan Priesthood Guild, Montreal, 1967—. Named Prelate of Honor, Holy See, the Vatican, 1978. Mem. Canon Law Soc. Can. (pres.). Office: Archevêché de Montreal 2000 Sherbrooke St W Montreal PQ H3H 1G4 Canada

WILLETTE, JANICE HOUK, minister, Presbyterian Church in the U.S.; b. Merced, Calif., Mar. 15, 1939; d. Harold Francis and Alberta Irene (Peard) Houk; m. Richard D. Willette, Feb, 16, 1963; children: Steven, Trevor, Carrie. B.A., Barnard Coll., 1961; B.D., San Francisco Theol. Sem., 1964, M.A., 1969. Ordained to ministry Presbyn. Ch. in the U.S., 1971. Youth dir. Lebanon Presbyn. Ch., San Francisco, 1962-65; asst. pastor 1st Presbyn. Ch., San Anselmo, Calif., 1971-73; cons. planning Synod of Pacific, San Francisco, 1973-75; assoc. pastor Lafayette-Orinda Presbyn. Ch., Calif., 1975-81; exec. presbyter Presbytery of San Gabriel, Azusa, Calif., 1981—; adj. prof. San Francisco Theol. Sem., San Anselmo, 1976-77, 80-81; gen. council San Francisco Presbytery, Berkeley, Calif., 1979-81; bd. dirs. Vocation Agy., N.Y.C., 1981—, Bd. of Pensions, Phila., 1982—; cert. instr. Parent Effectiveness Tng., Couples Communication Program. Office: The Presbytery of San Gabriel 630 N Dalton Ave Azusa CA 91702

WILLHOITE, FREDERICK HALE, minister, Southern Baptist Convention; b. Grady, N.Mex., Apr. 12, 1913; s. Frederick and Leona (Cain) W.; A.B., Okla. Bapt. U., 1942; post-grad. Southwestern Bapt. Theol. Sem., 1946-47; m. Laura Odetta Sherrill, Sept. 9, 1935; children—Frederick Hale, David Roy, Karel Lea Clemens. Ordained to ministry, 1935; pastor Bapt. Chs., Stonewall, Okla., 1936-40, Cromwell, Okla., 1940-42; chaplain USAAF, 1942-46; pastor Broadacres Bapt. Ch., Shreveport, La., 1946-47, First Bapt. Ch., Yukon, Okla., 1947-49, Central Bapt. Ch., Lawton, Okla., 1949-51, 57-63, chaplain USAF, Rhein Main, Germany, 1951-53; pastor Meml. Bapt. Ch., Tulsa, 1953-57, Council Rd. Bapt. Ch., Bethany, Okla., 1963-75. Renewal Evang. asso. So. Bapt. Conv., 1975; trustee Okla. Bapt. U., 1950-51, 64-67, 69-73; v.p. Bapt. Gen. Conv., 1970; bd. dirs., chmn. bldg. com. Bapt. Gen. Conv., 1959-63; bd. dirs. Agy. Ch. Coop. Ministry, 1970—; chaplain Okla. Farmers Union, 1964-84. Mem. Common Cause, Ret. Officers Assn., Nat. Lay Renewal Assos., Bison Athletic Assn. Contbr. articles to religious jours. Home: 8308 NW 39th St Bethany OK 73008

WILLIAMS, A. L., Chief bishop Triumph the Church and Kingdom of God (Internat.), Birmingham, Ala. Office: Triumph the Ch and Kingdom of God PO Box 77056 Birmingham AL 35228*

WILLIAMS, ALBERT ROGER, minister, Am. Bapt. Ch.; b. Boston, Mar. 5, 1912; s. Albert W. and Mamie Elizabeth (Parker) W.; B.Th., Gordon Coll., 1934; M.Div., Andover Newton Theol. Sch., 1937; D.D., Va. Coll. and Sem., 1976; m. Hazel Elizabeth Daniel, Dec. 22, 1939; children—Albert W., Roger E., Ronald T., Phyllis L., Stephen C. Ordained to ministry, 1937; pastor St. John's Bapt. Ch., Woburn, Mass., 1932-41; chaplain U.S. Army, 1942-45; pastor Massachusetts Ave. Bapt. Ch., Cambridge, Mass., 1946-65, Union Bapt. Ch., Hartford, Conn., 1966—; lectr. Duke U. Div. Sch., 1976. Pres. Am. Bapt. Chs. of Conn., 1971-72; chaplain Conn. State Legislature, 1971; mem. personnel com. Capitol Region Conf. of Chs., Hartford, 1976-77. Mem. adv. bd. Greater Hartford Community Coll., 1970-74. Mem. Hartford Urban League (dir. 1968-70). Contbr. articles to religious publs. Office: 1913 Main St Hartford CT 06120

WILLIAMS, GENERAL ALONZO, minister, Am. Bapt. Assn.; b. Quinton, Okla., Nov. 29, 1918; s. Thomas Jefferson and Loduska Mae (New) W.; B.A., Missionary Bapt. Coll., 1967; M.A., Landmark Bapt. Coll., 1971; m. Inez Alice Ryles, June 7, 1939; children—June Marie, Robert Lynn, Brenda Sue. Ordained to ministry, 1949; rec. sec. No. Calif. Assn., 1952-53; moderator Central Calif. Assn., 1956-57, 59; pastor Landmark Missionary Bapt. Ch., Lockeford, Calif., 1973—. Home: 11011 East Hwy 12 Lockeford CA 95237

WILLIAMS, CARL CARNELIUS, JR., minister, Church of God (Anderson, Ind.); b. Jefferson City, Mo., June 29, 1926; s. Carl C. and Stella (Shikles) W.; B.Th., Anderson Theol. Sem., 1949; B.A., Anderson Coll., 1950. Ordained to ministry, 1952; pastor in Nebr., 1951-55; sec. treas. Nebr. Ch. of God Campgrounds, 1954-55; pastor Ch. of God, Lawrence, Kans., 1955-57; assoc. minister and sec. Ch. of God., Oklahoma City, 1959-62; pastor S. Agnew Ch., Oklahoma City, 1962-71, Nowata (Okla.) Ch. of God., 1971-74, supr. constrn. of ch. plants, 1970-74; mem. bd. religious edn. Ch. of God Okla., 1971-73; supply pastor Independence (Kans.) Ch. of God, 1974-75. Sec. Nowata Ministerial Assn., 1972-74. Composer: (words and music) Songbook of 52 Songs, 1974; Songs of Real Joy, 1980; composer (with Carl Williams, Sr.) over 50 hymns, 1944-58; contbr. articles to religious publs. Home: 718 S Delaware St Bartlesville OK 74003

WILLIAMS, CARL E., SR., presiding bishop Church of God in Christ, Internat. Office: 170 Adelphi St Brooklyn NY 11205*

WILLIAMS, DONALD EUGENE, minister, Church of God (Anderson, Ind.); b. DeLand, Fla., Jan. 4, 1929; s. John and Willie Bertha (Kinner) W.; grad. Shelton Coll., 1951; m. Leah Keturah Pollard, Sept. 11, 1954; children: Donald Eugene, Celeste Jean, Michele Angela. Ordained to ministry Ch. of God-Anderson, Ind., 1962; pastor N. Main St. Ch. of God, 1962-69, E. Randolph United Methodist Ch., 1968-69, Ch. of God of Detroit, 1969-76; dir. minority ministries Ch. of God World Service, 1976—. Mem. missionary bd. Ch. of God, 1966—, assoc. sec. bd., 1982—; chmn. credentials div. Ch. of God in Mich., 1972—; dep. chief police chaplain City of Detroit, 1973—; dir. Met. Jail Ministry, 1973—. Bd. dirs. Girls Club of Detroit, 1970—; corp. leader Boys Clubs Met. Detroit, 1975-76. Mem. Interdenominational Ministerial Alliance (v.p. 1974), Chautauqua County Literacy Council (v.p. 1964-69). Rotarian. Author: Mission to Kenya, 1965. Home: 406 Stuart Circle Anderson IN 46012 Office: 1303 E 5th St Anderson IN 46011

WILLIAMS, DONALD HAMMOND, minister, Lutheran Church-Missouri Synod; b. Balt., Feb. 14, 1939; s. Harry Fullenwilder and Doris Elizabeth (Hammond) W.; m. Lorna Jean Engel, July 2, 1966; children: Elizabeth Alene, Stephen Christian, Katherine Wren. B.A., Valparaiso U., 1961; M.Div., Concordia Sem.-St. Louis, 1966. Ordained to ministry Luth. Ch.-Mo. Synod. 1966. Pastor, missionary-at-large Incarnate Word Luth. Ch., Florence, S.C., 1966-74, Immanuel Luth. Ch., Valparaiso, Ind., 1974—; part-time instr. Valparaiso U., 1982—; del. Luth. Ch.-Mo. Synod, St. Louis, 1973-83; program dir. Luth. Assn. Larger Chs., St. Joseph, Mich., 1979-83; conf. chmn. SE Dist. Pastors Conf., Balt., 1973. Editor: Foolishness of God, 1977. Bd. dirs. Prisoners and Community Together, 1976-84; bd. chmn. PACT, Eng., 1984; bd. chmn. Florence Symphony Orch., S.C., 1970-74. Recipient Nat. Appreciation award, Soc. Dist. Am. High Sch. Students. 1984-84. Mem. Luth. Acad. Scholarship. Office: Immanuel Luth Ch 1700 Monticello Dr Valparaiso IN 46383

WILLIAMS, EDWARD LEE, minister, Church of God in Christ; b. Columbus, Ga., Feb. 5, 1922; s. Henry and Estelle W.; B.Th., Birmingham Bapt. Coll. Theology, 1953; cert. various certs. and diplomas profl. courses; m. Lillie M. Fletcher, Dec. 25, 1969. Ordained to ministry, 1949; tchr. Birmingham (Ala.) Bapt. Coll., 1950-52; assoc. pastor 1st Bapt. Ch., Birmingham, 1970-74; Good Samaritan Ch. of God in Christ Home Mission, La Puente, Calif., 1970-74; assoc. pastor Goodwill Ch. of God in Christ, Pomona, Calif., 1976—. Speaker, tchr. Evangelist Mission Bd. to Mex. Recipient Nat. Leadership award Ch. of God in Christ, 1984. Home: 1338 N Evanwood Ave La Puente CA 91744 Office: Good Samaritan Ch of God in Christ Home Mission La Puente CA 91744

WILLIAMS, ERVIN EUGENE, minister, educational administrator, Baptist Church; b. Corning, N.Y., Feb. 25, 1923; s. Douglas Lewis and Mina P. (Barnes) W.; student Toccoa Falls (Ga.) Bible Coll., Cornell U.; B.A., Pa. State U., 1949; M.A., Mich. State U., 1961, Ph.D. in Communication, 1971; m. Ruth Evelyn Snyder, June 12, 1945; children: Roger Eugene, Virginia Ruth. Ordained to ministry, 1950; academic dean Greensburg (Pa.) Bible Inst., 1949-51; minister Bapt. Ch., New Kensington, Pa., 1951-53; instr. Pa. State U., 1953-55; sr. minister East Lansing (Mich.) Trinity Ch., 1955-71; chaplain Mich. State U., East Lansing, 1955-71; vis. prof. Trinity Evang. Div. Sch., Deerfield, Ill., 1968-71, prof. communication and practical theology, 1971-77, dir. D.Min. program, 1975-76; gen. dir. Am. Missionary Fellowship, Villanova, Pa., 1977—; cons. Evangelism Internat., Inc., Atlanta, 1969-75; lectr. Calvary Bible Coll., Kansas City, Mo., 1962, Haggai Inst 3d World Leaders, Singapore, 1970—; Staley lectr. Roberts Wesleyan Coll., N. Chili, N.Y., 1973, Judson Coll., Elgin, Ill., 1977—; cons. to mission bds., 1967-76; asso. dir. Camp of the Woods, Speculator, N.Y., 1971-77. Mem. bd. regents Owosso (Mich.) Coll., 1971-73. Mem. Nat. Sunday Sch. Assn., Christian Assn. Psychol. Studies, Mich. Acad. Arts and Scis., Aircraft Owners and Pilots Assn., Phi Beta Kappa, Pi Gamma Mu, Phi Kappa Phi, Alpha Kappa Delta. Contbr. numerous articles to religious periodicals and monographs. Home: 19 Moores Rd Malvern PA 19355 Office: Am Missionary Fellowship Box 368 672 Conestoga Rd Villanova PA 19085

WILLIAMS, GENE MILLER, religion educator, minister, Southern Baptists; b. Corsicana, Tex., Sept. 6, 1927; s. Henry Williams and Iola (Jordan) Williams Miller; m. Dorothy Fiew, July 5, 1948; children: Sandra Jeanne, Joe Randall, Paul Timothy. B.A., Baylor U., 1950; M.Div., New Orleans Bapt. Sem., 1953, Th.D., 1955. Ordained to ministry Bapt. Ch., 1945. Pastor, Fla. Blvd. Bapt. Ch., Baton Rouge, 1950-57; pres. Gene Williams Evang. Assn., Houston, 1957-73, Fort Worth, 1976-82; dir., spl. speaker World Concern TV Ministry, Fort Worth, 1976-79; prof. Liberty Bapt. Sem., Lynchburg, Va., 1973-76; pres. Luther Rice Sem., Jacksonville, Fla., 1982—; del. So. Bapt. Conv., 1955-82. Author: Know-So Salvation, 1970; Boney and Clod, 1984. Author, editor Forward Program of Church Evangelism, 1960. Producer TV program Concern for the World, 1976-79. Home: PO Box 49090 Jacksonville Beach FL 32240 Office: 1050 Hendricks Ave Jacksonville FL 32207

WILLIAMS, GEORGE MASAYASU, church official, Nichiren Shoshu Acad.; b. Seoul, Korea, June 16, 1930; s. Masao and Yae (Yoshimoto) Sadanaga; came to U.S., 1957, naturalized, 1973; B.A., Law Meiji U., Tokyo, 1954; M.A. in Polit. Sci., U. Md., 1962; m. Virginia K. Sueta, Mar. 27, 1961; children—Andrew, Monica, David. Organizer, dir. Nichiren Shoshu Acad. in N.Am., Santa Monica, Calif., 1960—; founding editor-pub. World Tribune Daily Newspaper, 1964—, NSA Quarterly, 1973—; fellow Soka U., Tokyo, 1975—; condr. Buddhist seminars at 80 univs. Mem. Los Angeles City Schs. Clergy Adv. Com., 1971—. Named Distinguished Alumnus, U. Md., 1974. Mem. Greater Los Angeles Press Club, Santa Monica C. of C., Smithsonian Assn., Inter-Am. Soc. OAS, Pi Sigma Alpha. Author: An Introduction to True Buddhism; contbr. articles to religious publs. Home: 209 Euclid St Santa Monica CA 90402 Office: 525 Wilshire Blvd Santa Monica CA 90406

WILLIAMS, HARLAN BRYAN, minister, So. Baptist Conv.; b. Tullahoma, Tenn., June 27, 1946; s. James Harlan and Amy Jewell (Isom) W.; B.A., Belmont Coll., Nashville, 1968; postgrad. New Orleans Bapt. Theol. Sem., 1975—; m. Brenda Jeane Denton, Aug. 29, 1969; 1 son, Matthew Harlan. Ordained to ministry, 1966; pastor Dodson Br. Bapt. Ch., Cookeville, Tenn., 1965-66; interim pastor First Bapt. Ch., Christiana, Tenn., 1967; pastor Rucker Bapt. Ch., Murfreesboro, Tenn., 1967-68; asso. pastor, mission pastor, youth dir. Big Spring Bapt. Ch., Cleveland, Tenn., 1968-70; pastor Wolf Creek Bapt. Ch., Spring City, Tenn., 1970-74, Allons (Tenn.) Bapt. Ch., 1974-75, Jerusalem Bapt. Ch., Bush, La., 1976—; chaplain Rotary Club, Allons, 1974-75. Ch. tng. dir. Tenn. Valley Assn. Bapts., Dayton, 1970-72, vice-moderator, 1971-72, ann. message preacher, 1971, chmn. constl. com., 1971, chmn. promotional com., 1971-72, moderator, 1972-74; Sunday sch. dir. Riverside Assn. Bapts., Livingston, Tenn., 1974-75, hospitality chmn. World Mission Conf., 1975, chmn. adminstrv. com., 1974-75; mem. youth com. St. Tammany Parish Assn. Bapts., Covington, La., 1976—. Mem. N.Am. Assn. Ventriloquists, Lindberg, Belmont hist. socs., Collectors Guild, Belmont Alumni Assn., Nat. Locksmith Assn. Home and Office: Route 1 Box 63 Bush LA 70431

WILLIAMS, JAMES HENRY, minister, Presbyn. Ch. in Can.; b. Barney's River Station, N.S., Can., Dec. 13, 1916; s. Joseph Gaffney and Bessie Margaret (Bruce) W.; B.A., St. Francis Xavier U., 1937; D.D., Presbyn. Coll., Montreal, Que., 1967; m. Edith Willena Smith, July 4, 1942; children—Carol, Ian, James, Wayne. Ordained to ministry, 1941; pastor Sedgewick Meml. Presbyn. Ch., Tatamagouche, N.S., 1941-43, Bethel Presbyn. Ch., Scotsburn, N.S., 1943-52, Westminster Presbyn. Ch., Sault Ste. Marie, Ont., Can., 1952-60, Glenview Presbyn. Ch., Toronto, Ont., 1960—. Moderator, Presbyteries Pictou, Algoma and North Bay, 1948, 56, Synod of Toronto and Kingston, 1959; mem. adminstrv. council Presbyn. Ch. in Can., Toronto, 1959-62, mem. bd. world mission, 1963-69, mem. bd. Christian edn., 1956-59, trustee bd., 1974—; mem. bd. Fernie House, 1967—; pres. N. Toronto Ministerial Assn., 1969-70. Contbr. articles to religious jours. Home: 17 Glenview Ave Toronto ON M4R 1P5 Canada Office: 1 Glenview Ave Toronto ON M4R 1P5 Canada

WILLIAMS, JAMES KENDRICK, bishop, Roman Catholic Church. Titular bishop of Catula, aux. bishop, Covington, Ky., 1984—. Office: PO Box 192 Covington KY 41012*

WILLIAMS, JAY GOMER, minister, educator Presbyterian Church; religion educator; b. Rome, N.Y., Dec. 18, 1932; s. Jay Gomer Williams and Mary Christine (Craig) Williams Olson; m. Hermine H. Weigel, Sept. 9, 1956; children: Jay, Lynn, Daryl, Ruth. A.B., Hamilton Coll., 1954; B.D., Union Theol. Sem., 1957; Ph.D., Columbia U., 1964. Ordained to ministry Presbyterian Ch. Assoc. dir. Ministry in Nat. Parks, N.Y.C., 1958-60; from instr. to prof. religion Hamilton Coll., Clinton, N.Y., 1960—; mem. Presbytery of Utica, 1956—. Author: Ten Words of Freedom, 1970; Understanding the Old Testament, 1972; Yeshiva Buddha, 1978; Judaism, 1980. Mem. Am. Acad. Religion, Hermetic Soc., Am. Theosophical Soc. Democrat. Office: Hamilton Coll Dept Religion Clinton NY 13323

WILLIAMS, JESSE FRANKLIN, minister, United Pentecostal Church International; b. Wilmington, N.C., Aug. 3, 1927; s. Jesse Franklin Williams and Annie Isabel (King) Williams Harrell; m. Sue Collins, Sept. 19, 1947; children: Cranford Patton, Michael Jesse, Sue Ann, Fay Elizabeth. Student Wilmington pub. schs. Ordained to ministry United Pentecostal Ch., 1955. Pastor United Pentecostal Ch., Fayetteville, N.C., 1966—; exec. presbyter Southeast, United Pentecostal Ch. Internat., 1977-79, sec. N.C. dist., 1971-79, dist. supt., 1979-82, asst. gen. supt., St. Louis, 1982—. Dir. Hercules Steel Co., 1974—. Served as staff sgt. U.S. Army, 1946-47. Republican. Home: 2001 Bismark Court Fayetteville NC 28304 Office: United Pentecostal Church 2813 Cumberland Rd Fayetteville NC 28304

WILLIAMS, JOHN CHARLES, minister, Church of God, Anderson, Indiana; b. Maud, Ohio, Nov. 16, 1923; s. Carroll Lee and Frances Ann (Rosenbaum) W.; m. Bertha Elizabeth Doughman, Jan. 9, 1943; children: Joan, Beth. B.A., Anderson Coll., 1951; postgrad. Christian Theol. Sem., 1954. Ordained to ministry Ch. of God, 1952. Minister, Bell's Chapel Ch. of God, Indpls., 1951-59, Park Rd. Ch. of God, Anderson, Ind., 1959-68, Forest Ave. Ch. of God, Niagara Falls, N.Y., 1968-77, Oak Grove Ch. of God, Tampa, Fla., 1977—; chmn. credentials and ordination com. Ch. of God, Niagara Falls, 1969-77; pastoral counsellor Lelawala Manor Girls Home and Midway Manors Boys Home, Niagara Falls, 1975-77; chmn. Gen. Assembly of Ch. of God, Tampa, 1984, chmn. exec. council, 1984; chaplain CAP, N. Tampa, 1980-84; mem. chaplaincy program Niagara County Jail, 1976-77; exec. com. Niagara Council Chs., 1969-77. Bd. dirs. Big Bros., Niagara County, 1972-77, Council on Alcoholism, 1970-77. Served with U.S. Army, 1943-46; ETO. Recipient Sr. of Yr. award, N. Tampa CAP, 1981; Cert. of Honor, Big Bros. of Niagara County, 1977. Mem. Niagara Ministerial Assn. (chmn. 1976-77). Home: 406 Bullard Pkwy Tampa FL 33617 Office: Oak Grove Ch of God 6830 N Habana Tampa FL 33614

WILLIAMS, JOHN RODMAN, minister, educator, Presbyterian Ch. (U.S.A.); b. Clyde, N.C., Aug. 21, 1918; s. John Rodman and Odessa Lee (Medford) W.; A.B., Davidson Coll., 1939; B.D., Union Theol. Sem. in Va., 1943, Th.M., 1944; Ph.D., Columbia U., 1954; m. Johanna Servaas, Aug. 6, 1949; children: John Rodman, Lucinda Lee, David Bert. Ordained to ministry, 1943; chaplain USNR, 1944-46; chaplain, assoc. prof. philosophy Beloit Coll., 1949-52; pastor 1st Presbyn. Ch., Rockford, Ill., 1952-59; prof. systematic theology and philosophy of religion Austin Presbyn. Theol. Sem., 1959-72; pres., prof. Christian doctrine Melodyland Sch. Theology, Anaheim, Calif., 1972-82; prof. Christian theology CBN U., Virginia Beach, Va., 1982—. Author: Contemporary Existentialism and Christian Faith, 1965; The Era of the Spirit, 1971; The Pentecostal Reality, 1972; Ten Teachings, 1974; The Gift of the Holy Spirit Today, 1980. Home: 4105 Ace Ct Virginia Beach VA 23462 Office: CBN U Virginia Beach VA 23463

WILLIAMS, LAWRENCE WOOLLASTON, minister, Gen. Assn. Regular Baptist Chs.; b. Cedar Falls, Iowa, Oct. 12, 1915; s. Ray Dodge and Winnifred Mae (Woollaston) W.; diploma Moody Bible Inst., 1940; Th.B., Burton Coll., 1952, B.A., 1953, Th.M., 1953, Th.D., 1954; m. Anna M. Heine, Aug. 23, 1940; children—Jeneen (Mrs. Ralph Gebhardt), Lawrence Heine, Cheryl Maralee (Mrs. Stephen Michael). Ordained to ministry Gen. Assn. Regular Bapt. Churches, 1940; pastor chs. in Mich., 1941-49, Community Bapt. Ch., Silver Lake, Wis., 1949-61, 1st Bapt. Ch., Greenfield, Ind., 1961-70, Calvary Bapt. Ch., Rochester, Minn., 1970-72, Park Lane Bapt. Ch., Omaha, 1972-75, Trinity Bapt. Ch., Muskegon, Mich., 1975—. Chmn. assns. regular Bapt. chs. Eastern Mich., 1947-48, Wis., 1959-61, Minn., 1971-72, Nebr., 1973-75; dir. Bapt. Haiti Mission, Grand Rapids, Mich., 1976—. Contbr. to religious publs. Home: 4347 S Sheridan Rd Muskegon MI 49444 Office: S Sheridan Dr and Emens St Muskegon MI 49444

WILLIAMS, MAC JAMES, minister, Southern Baptist Convention; b. Rutherfordton, N.C., Dec. 11, 1929; s. Mack and Essie Mae (Green) W.; m. Rosa Lee Watts, Jan. 16, 1951 (div. 1981); children: Pamela, Essie, Mac, Brenda, Yolanda, Tonya; m. Naomi Ruth Bell, July 12, 1981; children: Roderick, Wendell. A.A., Gibbs Jr. Coll., 1963; B.S., Fla. Meml. Coll., 1965; Th.M., Internat. Bible Inst. and Sem., 1984. Ordained to ministry Baptist Ch., 1951. Interim pastor Beulah Inst. Bapt., Tampa, Fla., 1953-54; pastor Mount Olive Bapt. Ch., Tampa, 1954-58, Shiloh Bapt. Ch., Dunedin, Fla., 1959-69, Mount Carmel Bapt. Ch., Clearwater, Fla., 1969—; asst. dean edn. Progressive Bapt. State Conv., Jacksonville, Fla., 1950-75. Pres., chmn. religious affairs Clearwater br. NAACP, 1980-84. Recipient Outstanding Citizen award Pinellas County Com., 1964, Cert. of Honor, Tampa Bay Black, 1982. Mem. First South Fla. Bapt. Assn. (chmn. fin. com. 1965-75, chmn. scholarships com. 1969), Pinellas Bapt. Assn. (moderator 1978-80, Appreciation award 1980), VFW (comdr. G.D. Roger post 1956). Republican. Home: 1014 Pennsylvania Ave Clearwater FL 33515

WILLIAMS, MACK CHARLES, minister, religious organization executive, General Association of General Baptist Church; b. Bernie, Mo., June 21, 1935; s. Mack McKinley and Effie Elzady (McCain) W.; m. Thelma Beall Peck, May 18, 1953; children: Terry Wayne, Sebrina Kay. B.A., Oakland City Coll., 1959; postgrad. So. Bapt. Sem., 1961-63, SE Mo. U., 1963-64, Ark. State U., 1969-70. Ordained to ministry Gen. Assn. of Gen. Bapts., 1955. Pastor Hahn's Chapel, Marble Hill, Mo., 1963-66; sr. pastor 1st Gen. Bapt. Ch., Detroit, 1966-68; pastor White Oak Grove Ch., Bernie, 1968-73; missionary Gen. Bapt. Ch., Saipan, Micronesia, 1973-77; dir. pastoral ministries Gen. Bapt. Hdqrs., Poplar Bluff, Mo., 1977—, bd. dirs. Fgn. Missions, 1960-69, Gen. Bd., 1968, 1980, moderator, 1979-80; mem. Gen. Bapt. Presbytery, Poplar Bluff, 1968—; chaplain Micronesian Constl. Conv., Saipan, 1975, Congress of Micronesia, 1973-77. Contbr. articles to Messenger Mag. Co-chmn. Micronesian Gambling Com., 1974-75; bd. dirs. High Commr's. Disaster Com., Saipan, 1976. Recipient certs. appreciation Micronesian Constl. Conv., 1975, Chief Justice of Micronesia, 1977. Mem. Fellowship Christian Educators. Republican. Lodge: Masons. Home: 1817 Sunset Dr Poplar Bluff MO 63901 Office: Gen Bapt World Hdqrs 100 Stinson Dr Poplar Bluff MO 63901

WILLIAMS, MARION RODNEY, minister, So. Bapt. Conv.; b. Mount Belvieu, Tex., Aug. 31, 1938; s. Leslie Marion and Ruth W.; B.S., E. Tex. Bapt. Coll., Marshall, 1964; M.R.E., Southwestern Bapt. Theol. Sem., 1969; m. Virginia Ann Solice, Aug. 30, 1958; children—Anna Lee, Angela Kay. Ordained to ministry, 1959; pastor Beulah Bapt. Ch., Mansfield, La., 1959-62, Gray Bapt. Ch., Jefferson, Tex., 1963, Smyrna Bapt. Ch., 1964-66, Mimosa Ln. Bapt. Ch., Mesquite, Tex., 1966—. Pres. Mesquite Ministers Assn., 1975; v.p. Dallas Bapt. Assn. Pastor's Conf., 1974. Home: 246 Mansfield Blvd Mesquite TX 75182 Office: 1233 N Belt Line Rd Mesquite TX 75182

WILLIAMS, MICHAEL GUY, minister, Christian Church; b. Houston, Mar. 5, 1952; s. Wallace Guy and Bonnie Lee (Laughlin) W.; m. Karen Lynne Schaaf, Aug. 18, 1973; children: Joshua Guy, Jared Michael, Jeremiah Ben. B.S. in Sacred Lit., Dallas Christian Sem., 1974; M.S. in Bible Theology, Internat. Bible Sem., 1983, postgrad., 1983—. Ordained to ministry Meml. Christian Ch., 1975. Youth minister Central Christian, Portales, N.Mex., 1974-76, minister, Truth or Consequences, N.Mex., 1976-82; founder, dir. Mountain Christian Day Care, Cedar Crest, N.Mex., 1982; minister of youth and Christian edn., assoc. minister, Bay Area Christian Ch., Houston, 1983—; pres. N.Mex. Christian Conv., 1981-82, sec., treas., 1980-81; trustee El Paso Christian Coll., Tex., 1976-78; dir. Gulf Coast S.S. Conv., Houston, 1983, 84. Crisis line counselor N.Mex. State U., Truth or Consequences, 1981; police chaplain Truth or Consequences Police Dept., 1978; emergency med. technician State of N.Mex., Truth or Consequences, 1981; tester Taylor Johnson Temperment Analysis Testing, 1985. Named Humanitarian of Yr. C. of C., 1980. Democrat. Avocations: basketball, golf, tennis. Office: Bay Area Christian Ch 14550 Old Galveston Rd Houston TX 77258

WILLIAMS, MICHAEL NEAL, minister, Church of God (Anderson, Ind.); b. Nashville, May 20, 1952; s. Jesse Lee and Anna Mae (Neal) W.; m. Gwendolyn Burns, Mar. 31, 1972; children: Brian Neal, Chad Michael. B.S., Middle Tenn. State U., 1977; M.Div., Anderson Coll. and Sch. Theology, 1980. Ordained to ministry Church of God, 1977. Pastor First Ch. of God, Shelbyville, Tenn., 1976-77, Penton Ch. of God, Lafayette, Ala., 1980-83, First Ch. of God, Huntsville, Ala., 1983—; chmn. bd. Camp Chula Vista, Pell City, Ala., 1982—, mem. lodge constrn. project com., 1982—; sec. Ala. Minister's Fellowship of Ch. of God, Decatur, Ala., 1983—. Home: 8009 Warden Dr SE Huntsville AL 35802 Office: First Ch of God 8100 Whitesburg SW Huntsville AL 35802

WILLIAMS, MILTON ALLEN, minister, Southern Baptist Convention; b. Columbia, La., Jan. 16, 1925; s. George A. and Ella (McKenzie) W.; A.A., Clarke Coll., Newton, Miss., 1959; B.A., William Carey Coll., Hattiesburg, Miss., 1961; B.D., Luther Rice Sem., Jacksonville, Fla., 1966, Th.M., 1968, Th.D., 1970; D.D. (hon.), United Bapt. Theol. Sem.; m. Betty Adell Watson, July 24, 1943; children—Diane, Donny, Perry. Pastor chs. in Miss., 1956-67; pastor First Bapt. Ch., Wisner, La., 1968—. Mem. nominating com. La. Bapt. Conv., 1974—; past moderator Deer Creek Bapt. Assn. Recipient Christian Service award radio and TV commn. So. Bapt. Conv., 1963. Address: PO Box 580 Wisner LA 71378

WILLIAMS, O. L., minister, vice moderator United Free Will Baptist Church. Address: 1052 N Missouri Ave Lakeland FL 33801

WILLIAMS, RHYS, minister, Unitarian Universalist Association; b. San Francisco, Feb. 27, 1929; s. Albert R. and Lucita (Squier) W.; A.B., St. Lawrence U., 1951, B.D., 1953, D.D., 1966; LL.D. (hon.), Emerson Coll., 1962; m. Eleanor Hoyle Barnhart, Sept. 22, 1956; children—Rhys Hoyle, Eleanor Pierce. Ordained to ministry Unitarian Universalist Assn., 1954; pastor Universalist Ch., Edwards, N.Y., 1951-52, Unitarian Ch., Charleston, S.C., 1953-60, First Ch., Boston, 1960-70, First and Second Ch., Boston, 1970—; pres. Unitarian Service Pension, 1973—; supr. field work Harvard Div. Sch., 1966—. Sec. bd. trustees Emerson Coll., 1961—, v.p., 1973; trustee Franklin Inst., v.p., 1981—; trustee Edward Everett Hale House, 1964-82, Meadville Theol. Sem., 1971-77; trustee John Wintrop Sch., Opera Co. Boston, 1969—. Russell lectr. Tufts U., 1966. Mem. Continental Unitarian Universalist Ministers Assn. (pres. 1968-70), Evang. Missionary Soc. (pres. 1965—), Unitarian Hist. Soc. (sec. 1960-76), Colonial Soc., Soc. Ministerial Relief (pres. 1975—), Indian Soc. (v.p. 1975—), Colonial Wars Soc. (chaplain, v.p. 1975), Soc. of Cin. (v.p. state N.H. 1982—, chaplain gen. 1982—), Ch. of the Larger Fellowship (fin. chmn. 1982—), Beta Theta Pi. Home: 7 Chestnut St Boston MA 02108 Office: 66 Marlborough St Boston MA 02116

WILLIAMS, RICHARD JOEL, minister, Christian Ch.; b. Houston, Dec. 25, 1932; s. Neil and Annie (Johnson) W.; B.A., Ozark Bible Coll., 1956; B.A., Tulsa U., 1961; student Okla. State U., 1951-53; m. Jeannette Rutherford, June 14, 1963; children—Sonya Lynn, Timothy Joel, Joseph Jay. Ordained to ministry, 1957; minister First Christian Ch., Conway, Mo., 1954-56; asso. minister Central Ch. of Christ, Mt. Vernon, Ill., 1956-57; minister First Christian Ch., Eugene, Mo., 1957-59; pres. Ozark Coll. Alumni Assn., 1959; minister Washita (Okla.) Christian Ch., 1959-60; founding minister Western Hills Christian Ch., Lawton, Okla., 1961, minister, 1961—. Bd. dirs. S.W. Evangelizing Assn., 1961—; dir. Wichita Mountain Christian Service Camp, S.W. Okla., 1966-69; bd. dirs. Christ in Youth, Tulsa, 1968-76, v.p., 1972-74; trustee, bd. dirs. Midwest Christian Coll., Oklahoma City, 1972-76, pres. bd. dirs., 1975; condr. numerous evangelistic crusades in various communities; pres. Okla. Christian Conv., 1977—. Counselor Comanche County unit, Am. Cancer Soc., 1976—; exec. bd. dirs. Am. Trustee Life Corp., Oklahoma City, 1974—. Mem. Alumni Assn. Ozark Bible Coll. (bd. dirs. 1977—). Home: 7509 Wycliffe Ln Lawton OK 73505 Office: PO Box 5005 82d and Cache Rd Lawton OK 73501

WILLIAMS, ROBERT CARL, minister, Ch. of God (Anderson, Ind.); b. Cin., Oct. 11, 1941; s. Eddie and Iona (Scott) W.; B.Th., Bay Ridge Christian Coll., 1966; M.Ed., U. So. Miss., 1976, D.Ed., 1982. m. Joyce Odoms, Dec. 9, 1967; children—Robert Carl, Joycelyn Sheri, Roderic Karl, Margaret Iona. Ordained to ministry, 1973; pastor Doty Rd Ch. of God, Ferriday, La., 1971-80. Tchr. Ferriday Vocations Sch., 1973-80; ednl. assessment tchr., Ferriday; pastor Crossroad Ch. of God, Farmhaven, Miss.; speaker weekly radio broadcast A Time for Spiritual Inspiration and Devotion, Sta. KFNV, Ferriday, 1976-78; mem. credential and adv. com. La. Gen. Ministerial Assembly Ch. of God, mem. adv. bd. Bay Ridge Christian Coll., Kendleton, Tex., mem. adv. bd. for Spl. Edn., Ferriday; pres. Concordia Parish Assn. for Retarded Citizens; vice chmn. gen. Assembly of Ch. of God in Miss. (Farmhaven dist.); bd. dirs. Christian Campers and Crusaders, Washington Court House, Ohio. MBd. dirs. First Step, Ferriday, 1975-76. Home: 6234 Hanging Moss Rd Jackson MS 39206

WILLIAMS, ROBERT FRANKLIN, JR., minister, Southern Baptist Convention; b. Eufaula, Ala., June 7, 1942; s. Robert Franklin and Lessie (Vinson) W.; m. Rosalind Dorathea Davis, June 20, 1964; children: Carol Marie, Bryan Davis. Diploma advanced acctg. Wallace Tech. Sch., Dothan, Ala., 1963; B.S., Troy State U., 1976; M.Div., New Orleans Bapt. Theol. Sem., 1979, D.Min., 1984. Ordained to ministry So. Bapt. Conv., 1975. Pastor, Mt. Carmel Bapt. Ch., Union Springs, Ala., 1975-76, New Hope Bapt. Ch., Franklinton, La., 1977-79, Improve Bapt. Ch., Columbia, Miss., 1979-85; sec.-treas. Marion County Ministerial Assn., Columbia, 1979-80; vice moderator Marion County Bapt. Assn., Columbia, 1980-81, moderator, 1982-83, sr. adult coordinator, 1983-84. Pres. Barbour County Assn. for Retarded Citizens, Eufaula, 1973-74; scoutmaster Ala.-Fla. council Boy Scouts Am., Eufaula, 1971-74; mem. Marion County Assn. Retarded Citizens, Columbia. Mem. So. Gerontol. Soc., Sigma Delta Chi, Phi Theta Kappa. Democrat. Home: Route So Sta Box 8082 Hattiesburg MS 39406

WILLIAMS, SMALLWOOD E., presiding bishop Bible Way Church of Our Lord Jesus Christ World Wide, Inc. Address: 4720 16th St NW Washington DC 20011

WILLIAMS, STANLEY WORTH, minister, counselor, Assemblies of God; b. Achille, Okla., Jan. 21, 1917; s. Isaac Taylor and Julie Frances (Weekley) W.; student LIFE Bible Coll., 1936, So. Bible Coll., 1938-39, S. Tex. Coll., 1958, Arlington State Coll., 1963; B.A., Southwestern Assemblies of God Coll., 1966; Th.B., So. Bible Coll., 1967; m. Velma Edith Wright, Nov. 21, 1939; children: Wendell Worth, Cecil Wayne. Ordained to ministry, 1941; cert. Am. Assn. Pastoral Counselors; pastor Assembly of God Chs., Wichita Falls, Tex., 1939-47, South Houston, Tex., 1948-53, First Assembly of God, Grand Prairie, Tex., 9 yrs., Oaklawn Assembly of God Ch., Houston, 4 yrs., Berean Temple Assembly of God Ch., Houston, 1969-74; dir. counseling Evangelistic Temple, Houston, after 1975; counselor Christian Counseling Assocs., Houston, 1980-85; instr. So. Bible Coll., Houston, 1976—. Presbyter, Wichita Falls Sect., N. Tex. Dist., Assemblies of God, 1945-47; sectional Sunday sch. dir., Houston Sect., 1949-50; organizer, first asst. supt. South Tex. Dist., Assemblies of God, 1951-53; organizer, presbyter South Dallas Sect., 1955-57; chaplain, campus pastor So. Bible Coll., Houston, 1969; chaplain St. Luke's Hosp., Houston, 1970-71, Houston Meml. Hosp. System; rep. of Assemblies of God chs., on Quiz the Pastor program, radio KFMK-FM, 1972-73; faculty Baytown br. Southwestern Assemblies of God Coll., Waxahacie, Tex., 1973, chmn. staff for Houston extension, 1973-74; chaplain, dir. spiritual life staff recruiter Christian Coll. Am., Houston. Mem. Assn. Clin. Pastoral Edn., Am. Assn. Pastoral Counselors, So. Assn. Marriage Counselors. Office: 2025 W 11th St Houston TX 77008

WILLIAMS, TERRY J(EROME), pastor, Southern Baptist Convention; b. Etowah, Tenn., Mar. 30, 1941; s. Ray and Grace (Burns) W.; m. Carolyn Sue Evans, Jan. 12, 1974; 1 child, Todd. B.Th., Clear Creek Bapt. Inst., 1979. Ordained to ministry So. Bapt. Conv., 1978. Pastor New Bethel Bapt. Ch., Barbourville, Ky., 1978-81, Friendship Bapt. Ch., Jonesville, Va., 1981-84, Ferndale Bapt. Mission, Pineville, Ky., 1984—. Leader temperance Powell River Assn., 1983—. Lodge: Masons. Home: Rt 2 Box 77N Harrogate TN 37752 Office: Ferndale Bapt Mission Pineville KY 40977

WILLIAMS, THOMAS WARD, minister, United Ch. Christ; b. Birmingham, Ala., Sept. 1, 1940; s. Harry Ward and Elizabeth (Stepp) W.; B.A., Duke, 1962; M.Div., Union Theol. Sem., 1965; D.D., London Inst., 1974; m. Suzanne Van de Putte; children—Christopher Ward, Stacy Suzanne. Ordained to ministry, 1965; asst. pastor Am. Protestant Ch. of Brussels (Belgium), 1965-67; minister of Christian edn. Ch. of the Valley, Santa Clara, Calif., 1967-68; pastor Union Ch., Lima, Peru, 1968-71, Fellowship Community Ch., Sao Paulo, Brazil, 1971-76, Federated Ch., Colchester, Conn., 1976—. Observer Internat. Assembly World Council of Christian Edn., Huampani, Peru, 1971. Home: 10 Stebbins Rd Colchester CT 06415 Office: Centre Green Colchester CT 06415

WILLIAMS, WILLIAM COREY, religion educator, Assemblies of God; b. Wilkes-Barre, Pa., July 12, 1937; s. Edward Douglas and Elizabeth Irene (Schooley) W.; m. Alma Mary Simmenroth, June 27, 1959; 1 child, Linda. B.A., Central Bible Coll., 1963, M.A., 1964; M.A., NY U, 1966, Ph.D., 1975; postgrad. Semitic langs. Hebrew U., 1977-78. Reference librarian Hebraic sect. Library of Congress, Washington, 1967-69; adj. prof. O.T., Melodyland Sch., Anaheim, Calif., 1975-77; vis. prof. O.T. Fuller Theol. Sem., Pasadena, 1978-81; mem. editorial bd. The Lockman Found., 1974—; prof. O.T., So. Calif. Coll., Costa Mesa, Calif., 1969—; vis. prof. O.T. Continental Bible Coll., 1985, Mattersay Bible Coll., 1985, Inst. Holy Land Studies, 1986. translation cons. New Internat. Version, Bible, 1975-76; critic cons. Internat. Children's Version N.T., Ft. Worth, 1983; translation, rev. cons. New Am. Standard N.T., 1969—. Author: Hebrew I: A Study Guide, 1980; Hebrew II: A Study Guide, 1984. Contbr. articles to profl. jours. NDEA Fgn. Lang. fellow, 1964-65, 65-66, 66-67; N.E. Bible Inst. Alumni scholar, 1960-61. Mem. Am. Acad. Religion, Am. Oriental Soc., Am. Schs. Oriental Research, Evang. Theol. Soc. (exec. officer 1974-77), Inst. Bibl. Research, Nat. Assn. Profs. Hebrew. Republican. Office: Southern Calif Coll 55 Fair Dr Costa Mesa CA 92626

WILLIAMSON, WALTER ELLIS, minister, United Meth. Ch.; b. Seminary, Miss., Dec. 28, 1914; s. Walter Franklin and Lola Gertrude (Ellis) W.; A.B., Millsaps Coll., 1943; B.D., M.Div., Emory U., 1949; M.A., U. S.Fla., 1968; Th.D., Luther Rice Sem., 1975; m. Eugenia Laurene Hurst, Apr. 13, 1941; children—Sandra Kay, Melody Ann, Christopher Ellis, Mark Hurst. Ordained to ministry, 1944; pastor chs., Miss., 1943-44, 46-47; chaplain U.S. Army, 1944-46; dir. Wesley Found., Miss. State U., 1949-51; pastor 1st Meth. Ch., Shawano, Wis., 1951-57, Seminole Meth. Ch., St. Petersburg, Fla., 1957-61, Christ Meth. Ch., Fort Lauderdale, Fla., 1961-65; prof. Fla. So. Coll., Lakeland, 1965-70; prof. sociology and religion Fla. Jr. Coll., Jacksonville, 1970—. Vice pres. United Charities; pres. scholarship com. United Cerebral Palsy, 1951-57; bd. dirs. YMCA. Mem. Fla. Assn. Sociologists, Fla. Conf. United Meth. Ch., Omicron Delta Kappa, Pi Gamma Mu. Author: Community Power Continuity, 1968; Role of the Clergy in Community Power and Influence, 1975. Home: 1008 Lucy Ln Atlantic Beach FL 32233 Office: Fla Jr Coll Jacksonville FL 32216

WILLINGHAM, EDWARD BACON, JR., religious broadcasting adminstr., minister, Am. Baptist Ch.; b. St. Louis, July 27, 1934; s. Edward and Harriet (Sharon) W.; B.S. in Physics, U. Richmond, 1956; postgrad. U. Rochester, 1958-59; M.Div., Colgate Rochester Div. Sch., 1960; m. Angeline Walton Pettit, June 14, 1957; children: Katie, Carol. Ordained to ministry, 1960; minister Christian edn. Delaware Av. Bapt. Ch., Buffalo, 1960-62; dir. radio and TV Met. Detroit Council Chs., 1962-75; exec. dir. Christian Communication Council Met. Detroit Chs., 1976—; Broadcast cons. Mich. Council Chs., 1965-75; guest cons. religious broadcasting, Fed. Republic Germany, 1968; mem. Interfaith Broadcasting Commn. Greater Detroit, 1968—. Bd. mgrs. Broadcasting and Film Commn., Nat. Council Chs., 1965-73. Recipient Gabriel award Catholic Broadcaster Assn., 1972. Mem. Assn. Regional Religious Communicators (pres. 1969-71), World Assn. Christian Communications (central com. 1973-78, bus. mgr. N.Am. broadcasting sect. 1970—), Phi Gamma Delta, Sigma Pi Sigma. Office: 1300 Mutual Bldg Detroit MI 48226

WILLINGHAM, JIMMIE DON, minister, Southern Baptist Convention; b. Rector, Ark., Dec. 30, 1940; s. Roy D. and Mary Sue (Bankston) W.; B.S. in Edn., Lincoln U., Jefferson City, Mo., 1967; M.A., Morehead (Ky.) State U., 1971; M.Div., Southeastern Bapt. Theol. Sem., Wake Forest, N.C., 1974, D.Min., 1976; m. Rosemary Caudill, Sept. 5, 1969; children: Lisa Denise, Craig Lee. Ordained to ministry, 1962; pastor chs. in Mo., 1962-66; instr. history S.C. State Coll., 1970-72; pastor Gum Springs Bapt. Ch., Moncure, N.C., 1972-83, Heritage Bapt. Ch., Rockingham, N.C., 1984—; mem. exec. bd. Sandy Creek Bapt. Assn., 1972—; mem. hist. com. Bapt. State Conv. of N.C., 1982-85, chmn. hist. com., 1983-85; clk. Pee Dee Bapt. Assn., 1984—. Margaret B. Frasier Sem. scholar, 1975. Mem. Assn. Social and Behavioral Scientists, Orgn. Am. Historians, Assn. Study Negro Life History, Internat. Platform Assn., S.C. Soc. Philosophy, Phi Alpha Theta, Pi Gamma Mu. Author: Dynamic Gospel for a Dynamic Age, 1965; also articles, book revs. Address: 1225 Long Dr Rockingham NC 28379

WILLINGHAM, SAUNDRA ANN, lay ch. worker, Roman Cath. Ch.; b. Cin., Jan. 3, 1942; d. Jacob William and Ruby Mae (Stewart) Haslerig; B.S. in Edn., U. Dayton, 1967; postgrad. Xavier U. Mem. Sisters of Notre Dame de Namur, 1960-68; elementary sch. tchr., Dayton, Ohio, 1963-65, 68, Cin., 1967, Cleve., 1970-72; charter mem. Black Lay Cath. Caucus Cleve., 1970-72; exec. dir. On Call, Model Cities transp. program, 1972-73, Black Cath. Caucus, Archdiocese Cin., 1973—; Region IV rep. Nat. Black Lay Cath. Caucus, 1976—; sec. ecumenical commn. on minority ch. persons Ohio Council Chs., 1976—; mem. dels. council Met. Council Religious Coalition Cin., 1974—; del. at large Archiocesan Pastoral Council, 1974—; mem. edn. com. Archdiocesan Social Action Commn., 1974-76; mem. Cath. Interracial Council, Dayton, 1967-68; mem. social services div. Cath. Conf. Ohio, 1974—. Mem. spl. community resources com. programs and allocations div. Community Chest Cin., 1975—, mem. personal and social devel. com.; mem. Ohio Citizen Council,

Columbus, 1973-76; sec. treas. Findlay St. Forum, Cin., 1975-76, v.p. elect, 1976—; trustee Work Activities Center, Hamilton County Bd. Mental Retardation, 1976—, St. Joseph Infant and Maternity Home, 1977—; mem. planning bd. Cin. Coalition Operation Voter Edn.-Registration. Contbr. article to Ebony mag. Home: 1410 Marlowe Ave Cincinnati OH 45224 Office: 426 E 5th St Cincinnati OH 45202

WILLINGHAM, WILLIAM WAGNER, minister, educator, Southern Baptist Convention. B. Spencer, N.C., Jan. 1, 1929; s. William Alfred and Ola Mae (Hammett) W.; m. Evelyn Joy Smith, Nov. 22, 1956; children: William Turner, Laura Lynn, David Edward, Joel Smith, John Mark. B.S., Maryville Coll., 1951; B.D., Southwestern Bapt. Theol. Sem., 1955; M.Div., 1973. Ordained to Bapt. Ch., ministry, 1953. Pastor, So. Bapt. Chs., N.C. and S.C., 1957—, Fairview Bapt. Ch., Kinards, S.C., 1964-67, Mount Moriah Bapt. Ch., Edneyville, S.C., 1973—; tchr. Fruitland Bapt. Bible Inst., Hendersonville, N.C., 1974—; substitute tchr. Edneyville High Sch., 1973—; moderator Laurens Bapt. Assn. (S.C.), 1972-73, Carolina Bapt. Assn., Hendersonville, 1982-83; sec. Co. Bapt. Adult Edn. Assn., 1984—. Chaplain Hendersonville Police Dept., 1983—; asst. chaplain Margaret Pardee Hosp., Hendersonville, 1984. Mem. Bapt. Pastors' Conf. Republican. Home: PO Box 29 Edneyville NC 28727 Office: Mount Moriah Bapt Ch Gilliam Mountain Rd Edneyville NC 28727

WILLIS, AVERY THOMAS, JR., minister, religious organization executive, Southern Baptist Convention; b. Lepanto, Ark., Feb. 21, 1394; s. Avery Thomas and Grace (Catherine) W.; m. Shirley Jean Morris, Dec. 17, 1955; children: Randal Kean, Sherrie Dennette, Wade Avery, Krista Dawn, Brett Lane. B.A., Okla. Bapt. U., 1956; B.D., Southwestern Bapt. Theol. Sem., 1961, M.Div., 1973, Th.D., 1974. Ordained to ministry So. Bapt. Conv., 1954. Pastor Sunset Heights Bapt. Ch., Fort Worth, 1957-60, Inglewood Bapt. Ch., Grand Prairie, Tex., 1960-64; missionary fgn. service bd. So. Bapt. Conv., Bogor, Jember, Indonesia, 1964-78, interagy. work group on ministry of laity, Nashville, 1984, chmn. nat. task force Commitment Counseling, 1984—; pres. Indonesian Bapt. Theol. Sem., Semarang, 1972-78; supr. adult sect., ch. tng. dept. Bapt. Sunday Sch. Bd., Nashville, 1978-83, leadership sect., 1983—; mem. lay renewal task force Home Mission Bd., 1982—. Author: Biblical Basis of Missions, 1979; Indonesian Revival, 1977; also tng. course curriculums. Democratic campaign worker, 1984. Recipient Disting. Service award Okla. Bapt. U., 1984. Mem. So. Bapt. Religious Edn. Soc., Religious Edn. Soc. Home: 204 Rosehill Dr Goodlettsville TN 37072 Office: Bapt Sunday School Bd 127 9th Ave N Nashville TN 37234

WILLIS, CARL GARRETT, minister, Bapt. Missionary Assn. Am.; b. Wheaton, Mo., May 20, 1933; s. John Garrett and Georgia Violet (Daffern) W.; student So. State Coll., 1957-58, Columbia Bible Sch., 1957-58, U. Ark., 1959-61, Centenary Coll., 1961, La. Tech. Inst., 1962-63; m. Virginia Tonnemaker, Aug. 1, 1952; children—Gary Dale, Linda Virginia. Ordained to ministry, 1952; pastor Union Grove Bapt. Ch., Hope, Ark., 1952-53; interim pastor Temple Bapt. Ch., Bossier City, La., 1954-56, River Valley Bapt. Ch., Plain Dealing, La., 1957, Second Bapt. Ch., Huttig, Ark., 1957-58, First Bapt. Ch., Summers, Ark., 1958-61; pastor Temple Bapt. Ch., Bossier City, La., 1961-67, Beacon Bapt. Ch., Port Arthur, Tex., 1967-69, Grace Temple Bapt. Ch., Ft. Smith, Ark., 1969—. Sec.-treas. missions, La. State Assn., 1963-66; chmn. spl. missions com. from chs. Port Arthur Tex. area, 1969-70; moderator chs., Ft. Smith and Fayetteville, Ark., 1970-71; chmn. com. to oversee Bapt. Student Center on campus of U. Ark., Fayetteville, 1973; standing missionary com. Fayetteville Bapt. Assn., 1969—; evangelist revivals in Ark., La., Tex. Active Boys Club, Ft. Smith, 1969-71. Mem. Bapt. Missionary Assn. Am. (v.p. of brotherhood 1957-58). Contbr. articles to religious jours. Home: 2823 S 36th St Fort Smith AR 72903 Office: 2800 Hendricks Blvd Fort Smith AR 72903

WILLIS, JERRY EUGENE, minister, So. Bapt. Conv.; b. Akien, S.C., Oct. 26, 1952; s. Arthur Namon and Wilda Joelene (Pritchett) W.; A.A., Norman Bapt. Coll., 1971; student Valdosta (Ga.) State Coll., 1971-72; m. Donna Jean Tucker, Oct. 2, 1976. Ordained to ministry, 1971; minister music Pavo (Ga.) Bapt. Ch., 1970-71; pastor Crestwood Gardens Bapt. Ch., Moultrie, Ga., 1971-72; minister youth First Bapt. Ch., Putney, Ga., 1972-76; minister youth and music Southside Bapt. Ch., Griffin, Ga., 1976—. Youth dir. Mallary Bapt. Assn., Albany, Ga. Recipient Music award Norman Bapt. Coll., 1971; named Outstanding Youth Dir., 1976. Mem. Ministerial Assn. Flint River Bapt. Assn., Ga. Bapt. Conv. Music Dirs. Recorded album I'll Tell the World, 1975. Home: 1330 Zebulon Rd Griffin GA 30223 Office: 1332 Zebulon Rd Griffin GA 30223

WILLIS, PRUITT, minister, United Meth. Ch.; b. Ozark, Ala., Oct. 26, 1930; s. James Erastus and Sarah Bertha (Paschal) W.; A.B., Huntingdon Coll., 1959, B.D., 1962, M.D., 1972; m. Billie Gaye Cotter, Aug. 13, 1955; children—Charlotte, David, Carol. Ordained to ministry, 1962; pastor, Millbrook, Ala., 1957-59, Mt. Carmel United Meth. Ch., Montgomery, Ala., 1963-66, Whitfield Meml. United Meth. Ch., Montgomery, 1966-70, 1st United Meth. Ch., Monroeville, Ala., 1970-75, 1st United Meth. Ch., Prattville, Ala., 1975—. Mem. coms. Ala.-W. Fla. United Meth. Conf.; coordinator adult ministries Selma (Ala.) Dist.; mem. bd. ministerial advisors Huntingdon Coll. Bd. dirs. Ret. Vol. Service Program, Autauga County (Ala.); mem. project council Montgomery Area Nutrition Program for Elderly; active Montgomery County chpt. ARC; past chmn. United Services. Office: PO Box 396 Prattville AL 36067

WILLMANN, RONALD CHARLES, minister, American Lutheran Church; b. Columbus, Ohio, June 25, 1950; s. Charles Jacob and Mildred Eleanor (Haid) W.; m. Barbara E. Carter, June 30, 1973; children: Matthew, Sarah, Andrew. A.B., Capital U., 1972; M.Div., Evang. Luth. Sem. 1976. Ordained to ministry, 1976. Intern, St. Paul's Luth. Ch., Charleston, W.Va., 1974-75; acting univ. pastor Capital U., Columbus, Ohio, 1975-76; pastor St. Martin Luth. Ch., Webster, N.Y., 1976—; mem. Inter-Luth. Agy. on Campus Ministry, Rochester, N.Y., 1978-82; chmn. Western N.Y. Conf., Am. Luth. Ch. ch. in soc. com., 1984—, mem. eastern dist. ch. in soc. com., 1984—. Youth com. chmn. Webster Council Chs., 1976-81, v.p., 1977-79, coordinator, Webster Walks for Hunger, 1978-80, pres., 1982-84; treas. Rochester Area Labor/Religion Conf., 1982—. Mem. Webster Ministerial Assn. (convener 1983—). Home: 647 Bending Bough Dr Webster NY 14580 Office: Saint Martin Luth Ch 813 Bay Rd PO Box 8057 Webster NY 14580

WILLMORE, ROGER DALE, minister, Southern Baptist Convention; b. Gadsden, Ala., Aug. 14, 1951; s. Inoma P. and Mildred Marie (Tarvin) W.; m. Sandra Gail Carroll, Aug. 3, 1973; 1 son, Stephen Andrew. B.A., Jacksonville State U., 1978; M.Div., Luther Rice Sem., 1981, D.Min., 1982. Ordained to ministry Baptist Ch., 1971. Chaplain, Boy Scouts Am., Arab, Ala., 1965-67; pres. Youth for Christ, Snead St. Jr. Coll., Boaz, Ala., 1970; pastor Ephesus Bapt. Ch., Sprott, Ala., 1971, Pine Ridge Bapt. Ch., Union Grove, Ala., 1971-73, Cherry St. Bapt. Ch., Attalla, Ala., 1973-79, Locust Fork Bapt. Ch., Locust Fork, Ala., 1979—; exec. bd. State Bapt. Conv., Ala., 1983—; chmn. Keswick Christian Life Conf., Birmingham, 1982—; pres. FBA Ministerial Assn., Blount County, Ala., 1980-81. Author: Silver Dawn, 1982; The Pulpit, 1982-83. Host radio show daily devotion/The Abundant Life. Mem. Inst. Bibl. Preaching, Luther Rice Sem. Nat. Alumni Assn. (pres. state assn. 1983—). Home: Rt 1 Box 180 Cleveland AL 35049 Office: Locust Fork Bapt Ch PO Box 97 Locust Fork AL 35097

WILMER, RICHARD HOOKER, JR., educator, priest, Episcopal Church; b. Ancon, C.Z., Apr. 13, 1918 (parents Am. citizens); s. Richard Hooker and Margaret Van Dyke (Grant) W.; grad. Taft Sch., 1935; B.A., Yale, 1939; M.Div., Gen. Theol. Sem., N.Y.C., 1942, S.T.D. (hon.), 1958; D.Phil., Oxford (Eng.) U., 1948; D.D. (hon.), Berkeley Div. Sch., New Haven, 1970; m. Elisabeth F. Green, June 6, 1942; children—Richard, Margaret (Mrs. Marshall P. Bartlett), Stephen, Natalie, Rebecca (dec.), Christine; m. 2d, Sarah King, Aug. 2, 1969. Ordained deacon and priest Episcopal Ch., 1942; deacon-in-charge, vicar, rector St. John's Ch., Mt. Rainier, Md., 1942-45; chaplain USNR, 1945-46; chaplain, prof. English Bible, U. of South, Sewanee, Tenn., 1948-53; minister to Episcopal students Yale, 1953-57; prof. theology, dean Berkeley Div. Sch., 1957-69; vis. prof. religious studies U. Pitts., 1970-72, prof., 1972—, chmn. dept., 1975—. Mem. Am. Acad. Religion, Am. Soc. Ch. History, Am. Soc. for Reformation Research, Phi Beta Kappa. Author: The Doctrine of the Church in the English Reformation, 1952. Home: 1128 Heberton St Pittsburgh PA 15206

WILSON, AGNES, church official, Presbyterian Church in the U.S.A. Head of Gen. Assembly Council, Presbyn. Ch. in the U.S.A., N.Y.C. Office: 475 Riverside Dr Rm 1201 New York NY 10115*

WILSON, ANDREW GRAHAM, minister, United Church of Christ; b. Portland, Maine, May 19, 1949; s. Robert Elmer and June Roberta (Spencer) W.; m. Maria Gloria Theodos, Aug. 15, 1976; 1 child, Rebecca Marina. B.A., Colby Coll., 1971; M.Div., Bangor Theol. Sem., 1980. Ordained to ministry United Ch. Christ, 1980. Pastor Jacksonville and Whitingham Community Chs., Vt., 1975-83, White Meml. United Ch. Christ, Milroy, Pa., 1983—; treas. Milroy Ministerium, 1983-85; sec. No. Assn., Pa., 1984-85, mem. sub-com. on C. Am., 1984; trainer United Ch. Christ Network, Pa., 1984; resource Leader Community Outreach, Pa. Central Conf., 1984; chaplain Milroy Hose Co., 1983-85; Author newsletter Peace-o-Gram, 1983-84. Editor newsletter Good News, 1983-85. Del. Impact, Washington, 1984. Recipient Prix D'Honneur Concours Nat. De Francais, 1967. Mem. Delta Phi Alpha. Republican. Lodge: Masons. Office: White Meml United Ch Christ PO Box 597 Milroy PA 17063

WILSON, CARL BENOITE, church organist and pianist, Baptist Ch.; b. Cleve., Oct. 11, 1930; s. Leelis R. and Corrie B. (Crawford) W.; m. Viola Johnson, May 1, 1980; 1 child, Colin. Student Miller Acad. Fine Arts, 1951-54, Hiram House Inst. Music, 1955-58. Organist, pianist Community Bapt. Ch., Greenburgh, N.Y., 1977-78, First Bapt. Ch., Elmsford, N.Y., 1978-81, Grace Bapt. Ch., Mt. Vernon, N.Y., 1982-83, Trinity Methodist Ch., White Plains, N.Y., 1983—; writer, arranger liturgical music. Democrat. Home: 630 E Lincoln Ave Mount Vernon NY 10552

WILSON, CHARLES ALDEN, lay church worker, Southern Baptist Convention; sheeting service company executive; b. Washington County, Ind., Oct. 8, 1943; s. Alden H. and Betty Ann (Kay) W.; m. Sandra Kay Hart, June 7, 1965; children: James, Jonathan, Christopher. B.A. in Acctg., Miami U., Oxford, Ohio, 1965; postgrad. in econs. U. Ga., 1973; M.B.A., U. Pa., 1977. Ordained as deacon Bapt. Ch., 1977; C.P.A., 1978. Deacon, Emmanuel Bapt. Ch., Cherry Hill, N.J., 1977—, treas., 1979—, ch. tng. dir., 1984—. Chmn. various coms. South Jersey Bapt. Assn., Cherry Hill, 1980-84; bd. dirs., chmn. long range planning Kings Christian Sch., Haddon Heights, N.J., 1982—. Mng. ptnr. Precision Sheeting Service, Pennsauken, N.J., 1980—. Mgr., Catalina Hills Little League, Somerdale, N.J., 1980-84. Served to comdr. USN, 1965-81; capt. USNR, 1982—. Mem. N.J. Soc. C.P.A.s, Pa. Soc. C.P.A.s, GAA Credit Union (bd. dirs., v.p. 1982—). Avocations: reading; flying. Home: 228 Burleigh Dr Somerdale NJ 08083 Office: Precision Sheeting Service 751 Hylton Rd Pennsauken NJ 08110

WILSON, CHARLES ANDREW, lay church worker, Southern Baptist Convention; b. Birmingham, Ala., Aug. 6, 1930; s. Stephen Andrew and Lois Era (Threadgill) W.; B.S., U. So. Miss., 1969; m. Patricia Agnes Beaudin, Apr. 1, 1953; 1 son, Joseph Stephen Wilson. Minister youth and music Belle Fountain Bapt. Ch., Fountainbleau, Miss., 1963-66, Emmanuel Bapt. Ch., Ocean Springs, Miss., 1966-72; adv. council Jackson County Youth Rally, Pascagoula, Miss., 1968-70; dir. youth First Bapt. Ch., Palmerdale, Ala., 1972—; tchr. math. and Bible, Palmerdale Bapt. Sch., 1972-73, head master, tchr., 1973-75; exec. com. Birmingham Bapt. Assn., 1976-77; minister music and youth Hopewell Bapt. Ch., Pinson, Ala., 1977-82; minister of music Friendship Bapt. Assn., Oneonta, Ala., 1978-82; minister of music First Bapt. Ch., Palmerdale, Ala., 1982—; bd. dirs. SuArt Ministries/Sound of Joy, Pensacola, Fla., 1980—, Gideon, 1983—. Agt., Nationwide Ins. Co., Palmerdale, 1975—. Mem. Nat. Assn. Life Underwriters. Address: PO Box 225 Palmerdale AL 35123

WILSON, CHARLES LEE, minister, Christian Ch. (Disciples of Christ); b. Canton, Mo., Aug. 20, 1915; s. Charles Oakes and Nelle Edwina (Boice) W.; B.A., Tex. Christian U., 1937; B.D., Yale, 1945; S.T.M., Harvard, 1951; m. Betty Bruce Jones, Sept. 14, 1938; children—Linda Pat (Wilson) Swanson, Marilee Oaks Wilson Clark. Ordained to ministry, 1937; pastor Community Ch., Pepperell, Mass., 1949-52, 1st Christian Ch., Salina, Kans., 1951-58, 1st Christian Ch., Lincoln, Nebr., 1958-62, Forest Hill Christian Ch., Laguna Honda, San Francisco, 1961-77, Community Christian Ch., Tulsa, Okla., 1977—. Pres. Homes of No. Calif., Christian Ch. (Disciples of Christ), 1969-73, 75-76, bd. dirs. Calif., 1972-75; mem. San Francisco Bicentennial Com., 1976. Mem. Nat. Benevolent Assn., No. Calif. Ecumenical Council, Harvard Club, Yale Club. Office: 8920 E 31st St Tulsa OK 74145

WILSON, DONALD JOSEPH, religious organization executive, minister, United Presbyterian Church in the U.S.A.; b. Bklyn., July 14, 1929; s. John and Margaret Sarah (Young) W.; m. Marie Katherine Graf, Sept. 18, 1954; children: Peter Scott, Sara Janet, Rebecca Ann, Mark Mackay. B.S., Union Coll., 1950; B.Div., Presbyn. Coll., Montreal, Que., Can., 1953; Ph.D., New Coll., Edinburgh, Scotland, 1956. Ordained to ministry Presbyterian Ch., 1953. Pastor, Leggatt's Point Presbyn. Ch., Mont Joli, Que., 1956-58; prof. practical theology Taiwan Theol. Coll., 1962-64; assoc. gen. sec. Presbyn. Ch. in Taiwan, 1964-67; assoc. for internat. affairs United Presbyn. Ch. in the U.S.A., 1970-75, unit dir. for health edn. and social justice program agy., N.Y.C., 1975—; exec. com. ch. and soc. div. Nat. Council Chs., N.Y.C., 1980—; bd. dirs. Christianity and Crisis, N.Y.C., 1982—; adv. del. VI Assembly, World Council Chs., Vancouver, B.C., Can., 1983, mem. Commn. on Inter-church Aid, Refugee and World Service, 1985—. Bd. dirs. U.S./China Relations Com., N.Y.C., 1971; non-govt. orgn. rep. UN Pub. Affairs Office, N.Y.C., 1971-75. Mem. N.Y.C. Presbytery. Democrat. Office: Program Agy 475 Riverside Dr New York NY 10115

WILSON, EDWARD COX, minister, Presbyterian Church (USA); b. Danville, Va., Sept. 30, 1938; s. James Thomas and Sallie Estelle (Cox) W.; m. Nancy Alva Hudson, Aug. 9, 1960; children: Michael Edward, Suzanne Adams. A.B., Elon Coll., 1960; B.D., Union Theol. Sem., 1965. Ordained to ministry Presbyn. Ch., 1965. Pastor Meadowbrook Presbyn. Ch., Greenville, N.C., 1965-67, Indian Trail Presbyn. Ch., N.C., 1971—; assoc. pastor Selwyn Ave. Presbyn. Ch., Charlotte, N.C., 1968-71; commr. Gen. Assembly Presbyn. Ch. U.S., Atlanta, 1974, 79; mem. nominating com. Mecklenburg Presbytery, Charlotte, N.C., 1983-85, mem. ministry com., 1984—. Author (devotional) These Days, 1979; (sermons) Master Sermons Series,

1977, 80-83. Contbr. articles to Presbyn. Outlook and Survey, 1977, 79, 81. Union Theol. Sem. fellow, 1965. Mem. Alban Inst. Democrat. Avocations: Stamp collecting, sports. Home: PO Box 219 Indian Trail NC 28079 Office: Indian Trail Presbyn Ch PO Box 187 Indian Trail NC 28079

WILSON, FRANCIS LAMAR, minister, Southern Baptist Convention; b. Athens, Ga., Mar. 16, 1932; s. Eloyd Lamar and Carrie Lucile (Asbell) W.; m. Patsy Ann Hutto, Feb. 24, 1956; children: Terri, Todd, Tracey. B.A., Mercer U., 1954; B.D., Southwestern Bapt. Theol. Sem., 1958. Ordained to ministry Bapt. Ch., 1952. Pastor, Hardwick Bapt. Ch., (Ga.), 1952, Pleasant Grove Bapt. Ch., Sandersville, Ga., 1953-54, Trinity Bapt. Ch., Henderson, Tex., 1955-58, First Bapt. Ch., Troup, Tex., 1958-64, First Bapt. Ch., Monahans, Tex., 1964-67, Trinity Bapt. Ch., Lubbock, Tex., 1967-76, First Bapt. Ch., Alamogordo, N.M., 1976—; mem. exec. bd. Bapt. Gen. Conv. Tex., Dallas, 1964-67; mem. adminstrv. com., 1971-76; mem. exec. bd. Bapt. Conv. N.Mex., Albuquerque, 1978-82, chmn., 1981, 82, chmn. property-fin. com., 1981, 82; exec. com. So. Bapt. Conv., Nashville, 1980—. Contbr. articles to religious publs. Pres. Am. Cancer Soc. Otero County Alamogordo, 1981-82; bd. dirs. N.Mex. Am. Cancer Soc., Albuquerque, 1982. Mem. Biblical Archeol. Soc., Am. Sch. Oriental Research. Democrat. Lodge: Rotary. Home: 2346 Union Alamogordo NM 88310 Office: First Bapt Ch PO Box 229 Alamogordo NM 88310

WILSON, GEORGE HUGH, minister, Christian Church (Disciples of Christ). B. Muncie, Ind., Sept. 13, 1932; s. George Harley and Berenice (Andrews) W.; m. Barbara Jean McHugh, Dec. 27, 1953; children: Gregory Hugh, Scott Howard. A.B., Drury Coll., 1953; B.D., Lexington Theol. Sem., 1956; S.T.M., Hartford Theol. Sem., 1957; Ph.D., Hartford Theol. Found., 1962. Ordained, 1956. Minister, Compton Heights Christian Ch., St. Louis, 1958-68; sr. minister 1st Christian Ch., Norman, Okla., 1968—; moderator Christian Ch. in Okla., 1980-82; sec. div. higher edn. Christian Ch., St. Louis, 1969-73, 78-80, mem. nat. adv. com. dept. ministry, Indpls., 1972-77; pres. Okla. Conf. Chs., 1974-76; chmn. dept. religious edn. Christian Ch. in Mo., 1962-64, chmn. dept. ministry, 1966-68; pres. Mo. Christian Ministers Assn., 1964-66; mem. bd. Drury Sch. Religion, 1965-68, bd. Univ. Christian Ctr., Norman, 1968—, pres., 1983-84; pres. Norman Ministerial Fellowship, 1973-74, SW Pastors Colloquium, Okla. Disciples Theol. Discussion Group, pres., 1984—. Editor: The Scroll, 1967-71; contbr. articles to publs., adult uniform lessons. Pres. Norman Regional Hosp. Bd., 1981—; sec. Norman Human Rights Commn., 1972-73. Jacobus fellow, Hartford Theol. Sem., 1953. Mem. Theta Phi. Democrat. Clubs: Lions (pres. 1976-77), Kappa Alpha. Office: First Christian Ch 220 S Webster Norman OK 73069

WILSON, GERALD HENRY, religion educator; b. Beaumont, Tex., Oct. 29, 1945; s. William Elbert and Ruth (Davidson) W.; m. Diane F. Buckmaster, June 8, 1968; children: Micah Aaron, Meghan Susanne. B.A., Baylor U., 1968; M.Div., Fuller Theol. Sem., 1973, M.A., 1974; Ph.D., Yale U., 1981. Instr. Bibl. Hebrew, Yale Div. Sch., New Haven, 1976-77; tchr. religion, Northfield-Mt. Hermon, Mass., 1978-79; vis. lectr. U. Ga., Athens, 1979-82, asst. prof. religion, 1982—. Author: The Editing of the Hebrew Psalter, 1984; assoc. editor Studia Biblica et Theologica Jour., 1973-74. Contbr. articles to religious jours. Recipient LaSor award Fuller Theol. Sem., 1974. Mem. Soc. Bibl. Lit., Nat. Assn. Profs. Hebrew, Inst. Bibl. Research. Office: Univ Georgia Dept Religion Athens GA 30602

WILSON, GLENN, lay worker, teacher, United Methodist Church; teacher; b. Leesburg, Fla., July 19, 1953; s. Sherman Glenn and Ruth (Boyd) W.; m. Michielle Joy Atherton, Sept. 19, 1980. A.A., Lake-Sunter Community Coll., 1972; B.A., U. Fla., 1976. Sun. Sch. supt. Webster United Meth. Ch., Fla., 1969-71; Christian Ideals dir. Am. Youth Found., Ossipee, N.H., 1974-78, assoc. dir., St. Louis, 1980-82; exec. dir. Am. Christian Found., Webster, Fla., 1983—; lay speaker Meth. Ch., Central Fla., 1982—; song leader Linden United Meth. Ch., Fla., 1982-83; del. Am. Camping Assn. Conv., Houston, 1981, N.Y.C., 1982. Tchr. Sumter Dist. Schs., Bushnell, Fla., 1978—. Editor: Fla. Coop. News, 1975; Sumter County Times, 1975-76, Founder Fire, 1981-82, SCEA Bulletin, 1985. Named Tchr. of Yr. South Sumter High Sch., Bushnell, Fla., 1980; recipient Disting. Service award Am. Youth Found., Ossipee, 1982. Mem. Sumter County Edn. Assn. (sec. 1978-79, v.p. 1984-85, pres. 1985—), Fla. Athletic Coaches Assn. Democrat. Office: Am Christian Found PO Box 1007 Webster FL 33597

WILSON, J. W., church official. Pres. Seventh-day Adventist Church in Canada, Ottawa, Ont. Office: Seventh-day Adventist Ch in Can 1148 King St E Ottawa ON L1H 1H8 Canada*

WILSON, LLOYD LEE, church administrator, Friends General Conference; b. Elkton, Md., Sept. 14, 1947; s. Clifton Laws and Betty Raye (Bare) W.; m. Merrill Wilson Varn, May 23, 1981; 1 child, Asa Cadbury Varn. S.B., MIT, 1969, S.M., 1977. Gen. sec. Friends Gen. Conf., Phila., 1982—; corp. mem. Cambridge Friends Sch., Mass., 1970-77; mem. permanent bd. New Eng. Yearly Meeting Friends, Freeport, Maine, 1975-77; mem. stewardship and fin. com. Balt. Yearly Meeting Friends, Sandy Spring, Md., 1979—, clerk, 1980-83; bd. dirs. Am. Friends Service Com., Phila., 1980-83; adminstr. Friends Meeting House Fund, Inc., Phila., 1982—; asst. sec.-treas. Friends Meeting House Fund, Inc., 1984—. Owner apple growing company. Contbr. articles to religious publs. Conscientious objector on religious grounds. Mem. Bible Assn. Friends in Am. (bd. mgrs. 1983—). Home: Fiddle Hill Farm Route 2 Box 57H Barboursville VA 22923 Office: Friends Gen Conf 1520-B Race St Philadelphia PA 19102

WILSON, MASON, JR., priest, Episcopal Church; b. Kansas City, Mo., Aug. 31, 1924; s. Mason and Eula Jane (Bullock) W.; m. Barbara Prue Sherrill, Jan. 2, 1960; children: Mason, Henry Knox Sherrill. B.A., U. Tex.-Austin, 1948; M.Div., Episcopal Theol. Sch., 1951. Ordained priest, 1951. Rector, Ch. of Messiah, Woods Hole, Mass., 1951-61; rector St. Andrew's Ch., Framingham, Mass., 1961—; mem. standing com. of Episcopal Diocese of Mass., Boston, 1982—, chmn. ecumenical commn., 1980—; mem. Mass. Com. on Christian Unity, 1976—. Commr., Human Relations Commn., Framingham, 1970-82. Named Disting. Citizen, Jaycees, 1977; Norman Nash fellow, 1977. Mem. Mass. Episcopal Clergy Assn. Home: 72 Main St Framingham MA 01701 Office: Saint Andrews Episcopal Ch Buckminster Sq Framingham MA 01701

WILSON, MICHAEL LEWIS, lay church worker, American Baptist Association; sales person; b. Mt. Gilead, Ohio, Aug. 26, 1960; s. Verl Lewis and Bobbie Jean (Robinson) W. Bapt. youth fellowship adv. Bryn Zion Bapt. Ch., Mt. Gilead, Ohio, 1979—; sunday sch. tchr., 1979—, deacon, 1981—, mem. christian bd. edn., 1981-83, sunday sch. supt., 1983, chorister, 1983-84. Sales person Quality Farm & Fleet, Mansfield, Ohio, 1979-85. Republican. Home: 5826 Township Rd 103 Mt Gilead OH 43338

WILSON, NADINE JENNINGS, lay educator, Methodist Church; b. Augusta, Ga., Oct. 1, 1918; d. Smith Crafton and Carrie Belle (Barnes) Jennings; m. Hubert Ernest Wilson, Dec. 27, 1939; 1 child, Vivian Wilson Shackelford. B.A., Paine Coll., 1939. Dir. youth work Christian Meth. Episcopal Ch., Augusta, 1966-75; youth worker Williams Meml. Christian Meth. Episcopal Ch., Augusta, 1975—. Dir. tutoring Shiloh Community Ctr., Augusta, 1979—. Recipient Celebrate Literacy award Internat. Reading Assn., 1985; named Tchr. of Yr., Richmond County Tchrs. Assn., 1965. Mem. Nat. Assn. Univ. Women (fin. sec. 1980—), Delta Sigma Theta. Democrat.

WILSON, NEAL CLAYTON, organization executive, Seventh-day Adventist Church; b. Lodi, Calif., July 5, 1920; s. Nathaniel Carter and Nannah Myrtle (Wallin) W.; m. Elinor Esther Neumann, July 19, 1942; children: Norman C., Shirley Wilson Anderson. B.A. in Theology and History, Pacific Union Coll., 1942; postgrad. Theol. Sem., Andrews U., Barrien Springs, Mich., 1943-44, D.D. (hon.), 1976. Ordained to ministry Seventh-day Adventist Ch., 1944. Acct. So. Asia div. Seventh-day Adventist Ch., Poona, India, 1939-40; acting treas. Oriental Watchman Press, Poona, 1940; asst. to cashier St. Helena Sanitarium, Deer Park, Calif., 1941-42; pastor-evangelist, Wyo., 1942; evangelist Gen. Conf. Seventh-day Adventist Ch., 1952-55, pastor-evangelist Middle East div., Cairo, 1944-45, pres. Egyptian mission, 1945-50, pres. Nile union, 1950-58, sec. Central Calif. conf., 1959-60, sec., then pres. Columbia Union conf., Takoma Park, Md., 1960-66, v.p. for N. Am., Gen. Conf., Washington, 1966-78, pres., 1979—; dir. Pacific Press, Loma Linda Foods, Harris Pine Mills, Internat. Ins. Co., Takoma Park. Author articles in field. Bd. dirs. Loma Linda U., Andrews U., Christian Record Braille Found., Oakwood Coll., Rev. & Herald Pub. Assn., Seventh-day Adventist Radio-TV Film Center. Office: 6840 Eastern Ave NW Washington DC 20012

WILSON, OLIVER JOSEPHUS, minister, Nat. Baptist Conv., U.S.A., Inc.; b. Hamburg, Ark., Oct. 4, 1899; s. Sam and Rosy (Draton) W.; B.A., Ark. Bapt. Coll., 1932, D.D., 1976; m. Janora E. Downs, Apr. 13, 1952. Ordained to ministry, 1942; pastor First Bapt. Ch., Granite Mountain, Little Rock, 1948-55, Pilgrim Rest Bapt. Ch., Little Rock, 1958—; instr. Ark. Bapt. Coll., 1932-37, interim pres., 1937. Exec. sec. Consol. Missionary Bapt. State Conv., 1962-64. Mem. Bapt. Ministerium, NAACP. Home: 28 Detroit St Little Rock AR 72206 Office: 1421 W 16th St Little Rock AR 72202

WILSON, ROBERT ALLEN, religion educator, Church of Christ. B. Beff, Ill., Oct. 7, 1936; s. Perry Arthur and Eva Mae (Dye) W.; m. Patsy Ann Jarrett, June 1, 1957; children: Elizabeth Ann, Angela Dawn, Christine Joy. A.B., Lincoln Christian Coll., 1958, Hanover Coll., 1961; M.R.E., So. Bapt. Sem., Louisville, 1965, Ed.D., 1972. Ordained to ministry Ch. of Christ, 1957. Minister, Fowler Christian Ch., Ind., 1955-59, Zoah Christian Ch., Scottsburg, Ind., 1959-63; minister edn. and youth Shively Christian Ch., Louisville, 1964-69; prof. christian edn. and family life Lincoln Christian Sem., Ill., 1969—; interim preaching minister Jefferson St. Christian Ch., Lincoln, 1983; elder, founder Jefferson St. Christian Ch., 1972—; founder Parkway Christian Ch., Pekin, Ill.; founder, dir. Christian Marriage and Family Enrichment Services, 1978—. Contbr. youth lessons and articles to religious publs. Mem. Nat. Assn. Profs. Christian Edn. (pres. 1979-80, newsletter editor 1975-79), Religious Edn. Assn. Home: 330 Campus View Dr Lincoln IL 62656 Office: Lincoln Christian Sem Box 178 Lincoln IL 62656

WILSON, ROBERT LEROY, educator, minister, United Methodist Ch.; b. Forty Fort, Pa., Jan. 19, 1925; s. Herbert Leroy and Kathryn Crawford (Haxton) W.; A.B., Asbury Coll., 1949; M.A., Lehigh U., 1950; B.D., Garrett Theol. Sem., 1955; Ph.D., Northwestern U., 1958; m. Betty Berenthien, June 19, 1950; children: Keith Alan, Marian. Ordained to ministry, 1954; pastor, Chgo., 1952-55; instr. Garrett Theol. Sem., Evanston, Ill., 1955-58; dir. research Nat. Div. Methodist Bd. Missions, 1958-70; prof. ch. and soc., Duke U. Divinity Sch., 1970—. Mem. Religious Research Assn. Author: Questions City Churches Must Answer, 1962; The Methodist Church in Urban America, 1963; The Church in the Racially Changing Community, 1966; Conflict and Resolution, 1973; What's Ahead for Old First Church, 1974; What New Creation?, 1977; Preaching and Worship in the Small Church, 1980; Too Many Pastors?, 1980; Shaping the Congregation, 1981.

WILSON, S. DUNHAM, priest, Episcopal Church; b. N.Y.C., July 6, 1927; s. Sering Dunham and Fredricka Gertrude (Binney) W.; m. Virginia Starr Kohlsaat, July 7, 1950; children: Heather Starr, Mark Dunham, Matthew McKendry. Diploma Lawrenceville Sch., 1945. Ordained priest, 1963. Rector, St. Jude's Episcopal Ch., Burbank, Calif., 1965-73; asst. rector St. Patrick's Episcopal Ch., Thousand Oaks, Calif., 1975-77, St. John's Cathedral, Albuquerque, 1978-80; assoc. rector St. Mark's on the Mesa, Albuquerque, 1980; rector St. Christopher's Episcopal Ch., Hobbs, N.Mex., 1980—; mem. Commn. on Liturgy, Los Angeles, 1971-73, Commn. on Ministry, 1972-73, Commn. on Alcoholism, Albuquerque, 1980-82; deanery chmn. Evangelism Task Force, Hobbs, 1982—. Author one act play: Everyman, 1955; musical anthem Dawn Bears the Sun, 1960. Mem. Santa Monica Mountains Planning Commn., 1977. Recipient Alfred Noyes Prize in Poetry, Princeton U., 1946, 47. Democrat. Home: 701 W Tucker Hobbs NM 88240 Office: Saint Christophers Episcopal Church 207 E Permian Dr Hobbs NM 88240

WILSON, SCOTT FRANCIS, elder United Methodist Church; b. Canton, Ohio, Apr. 18, 1954; s. Ralph Morgan and G. June (Kelley) W.; m. Barbara Lee Beaver, July 23, 1976. B.A., Malone Coll., 1976; M.Div., Asbury Theol. Sem., 1979. Ordained deacon United Meth. Ch., 1978, elder, 1981. Co-pastor Christ United Meth. Ch., Louisville, Ohio, 1979-84; instr. Christian edn. Malone Coll., 1982-84; pastor Grace United Meth. Ch., Bucyrus, Ohio, 1984—; cons., specialist in youth ministry. Mem. Evang. Tchr. Tng. Assn. Avocations: traveling, photography, woodworking. Office: Grace United Meth Ch 320 Hopley Ave Bucyrus OH 44820

WILSON, WALTER RAYMOND, minister, Southern Baptist Convention; b. Knox County, Ky., Sept. 6, 1935; s. Claybourn Sherman and Flora Mae (Lockhart) W.; student Clear Creek Bapt. Sch., 1971; m. Juanita Baker, June 22, 1952 (dec.); children: Lynita, Lana, Lana, Ray, Nicky; m. Scotty Allen, Oct. 3, 1974; children—Donnie, Danny, Deanna. Ordained to ministry, 1969; deacon and pastor chs., Ky., 1965-76; pastor Stoney Fork Bapt. Ch., Fleming Bapt. Ch., Buck Creek Bapt. Ch., Calhoun, Ky., 1972-73, Calvary Bapt. Ch., W. Irvine, Ky., 1973-76, Providence Bapt. Ch., Winston, Ky., 1979-83, Wolf Creek Bapt. Ch., Williamsburg, Ky., 1983—; evangelist Ray Wilson Assn. Inc., 1976—; staff Ky. State Missions Bd., Home Missions Bd.; chmn. missions com. South Union Assn. Asst. moderator Boones Creek (Ky.) Assn.; mem. exec. bd. Cleark Creek Bapt. Alumni Assn. Home: PO Box 732 Williamsburg KY 40769

WILSON, WILLIAM MICHAEL, minister, So. Bapt. Conv.; b. Henryetta, Okla., May 30, 1946; s. William L. and Willie L. (Thomason) W.; B.S., Hardin-Simmons U., 1969; M.Div., Southwestern Bapt. Theol. Sem., 1974, postgrad., 1976—; m. Olivia Faye Jackson, July 19, 1969; 1 son, Mark Andrew. Ordained to ministry, 1969; minister of youth First Bapt. Ch., Lamesa, Tex., 1967; summer missionary Kenya, E. Africa, 1968; asso. pastor First Bapt. Ch., San Angelo, Tex., 1969-70; pastor First Bapt. Ch., Frost, Tex., 1970-72, Tower Bapt. Ch., Ft. Worth, 1974-75; minister evangelism First Bapt. Ch., Lubbock, Tex., 1975-76; pastor 1st So. Bapt. Ch., Yuma, Ariz., 1976—. Preacher revival crusades, E. Africa, 1968, Japan, 1969; instr. Wayland Bapt. Coll.; mem. bd. young assos. of bd. trustees Hardin-Simmons U. Del., Lubbock County (Tex.) Democratic Conv., 1976; active YMCA. Mem. Fellowship Christian Athletics, Alpha Phi Omega (recipient pres.'s award, 1969). Home: 1535 8th Ave Yuma AZ 85364 Office: PO Box 5150 Yuma AZ 85364

WILT, MATTHEW RICHARD See *Who's Who in America*, 43rd edition.

WIMMER, HAROLD R., Bishop, Lutheran Church in America. Office: 71 Lancaster St Worcester MA 01608*

WINCHELL, RICHARD MARION, minister, Evangelical Alliance Mission; b. Columbus, Ohio, Nov. 2, 1928; s. Harold Brooks and Marion (Shattuck) W.; A.B. in Theology, Gordon Coll., Beverly Farms, Mass., 1950; m. Marjorie Alice Lundquist, Dec. 26, 1949; children—Peter, Martha, Leigh, Barry. Ordained to ministry, 1950; missionary Evang. Alliance Mission (TEAM), South Africa, 1950-68; founder, dir. TEAM's Word of Life Publs., South Africa, 1957; assoc. gen. dir. TEAM, 1968-75, gen. dir., 1975—. Bd. dirs. Interdenominational Fgn. Missions Assn., 1971—, v.p., 1975-83, pres., 1983—. Home: 1720 N Washington St Wheaton IL 60187 Office: PO Box 969 Wheaton IL 60187

WINDERS, THOMAS JOLLY, JR., minister, So. Bapt. Conv.; b. Corinth, Miss., Jan. 23, 1946; s. Thomas Jolly and Eunice Evelyn (White) W.; B.S.E., Delta State U., 1967; Th.M., New Orleans Bapt. Theol. Sem., 1971; m. Diane Kathryn Koonce, Dec. 27, 1968; children—Kristi Lyn, Brian Jolly. Ordained to ministry, 1969; pres. Bapt. Student Union, pres. Inter-Faith Council, Delta State U., Cleveland, Miss., 1966-67; founder, pres. Tommy Winders Evangelism, Inc., 1972—. Home: 1404 President St Tupelo MS 38801 Office: Box 1711 Tupelo MS 38801

WINDLE, JOSEPH RAYMOND, bishop, Roman Catholic Church; b. Ashdad, Ont., Can., Aug. 28, 1917; s. James David and Bridget (Scollard) W.; student St. Alexander's Coll., Limbour, Que., 1936-39; D.D. Grand Sem., Montreal, 1943; D.C.L., Lateran U., Rome, 1953. Ordained priest Roman Cath. Ch., 1943; asst. priest, later parish priest and vice-chancellor Pembroke Diocese, 1943-61; aux. bishop Ottawa, 1961-69; coadjutor bishop Pembroke, 1969-75, bishop, 1975—. K.C. Home: 188 Remfrew St PO Box 7 Pembroke ON Canada

WINE, SHERWIN THEODORE, rabbi, Humanistic Jewish; b. Detroit, Jan. 25, 1928; s. William Harry and Tille (Israel) W. A.B., U. Mich., 1950, A.M., 1952; B.H.L., Hebrew Union Coll., 1954, M.H.L., 1956, D.D. (hon.), 1981. Ordained rabbi, 1956. Rabbi Temple Beth El, Detroit, 1956-60, Windsor, Ont., Can., 1960-64, Birmingham Temple, Farmington Hills, Mich., 1964—; pres. N. Am. Com. for Humanism, Farmington Hills, 1982—; dir. Ctr. for New Thinking, Birmingham, 1976—; chmn. Leadership Conf. for Secular and Humanistic Jews, Farmington Hills, 1983—. Author: Humanistic Judaism, 1977; Mediation Services, 1977; Judaism Without God, 1984. Bd. dirs. Mich. Found. for Arts, Detroit, 1975; founder Ams. for Religious Liberty, Washington, 1981. Served to 1st lt. U.S. Army, 1957-58, Korea. Mem. Assn. Humanistic Rabbis, Soc. for Humanistic Judaism (founder 1969). Home: 555 S Woodward Birmingham MI 48011 Office: The Birmingham Temple 28611 W Twelve Mile Farmington Hills MI 48011

WINFIELD, LOVEL VALRE, minister, United Meth. Ch.; b. League City, Tex., Feb. 28, 1907; s. John and Annie (Stepny) W.; B.S., Houston Coll. for Negroes, 1944; M. in Edn., U. Houston, 1946; D.D. (hon.) Mt. Hope Bible Coll., 1968; Sci. of Bus. degree Erma Hughes Bus. Coll., 1949; m. Elice Mae Watson, Dec. 31, 1936; adopted dau., Virginia Marie Hightower. Ordained deacon Meth. Episc. Ch., 1935, elder, 1938; pastor The Sweeney Circuit, Brazoria County, Tex., 1932-37, Ebenezer Meth. Ch., Houston, 1937-45, Mt. Vernon Meth. Ch., Houston, 1945-50; dist. supt. Beaumont Dist. Episc. Meth. Ch., 1950-56; pastor Sloan Meml. Meth. Ch., Tex., 1956-64, Trinity East Meth. Ch., Houston, 1964-72; asso. dir. Council Ministries, Tex. Ann. Conf., United Meth. Ch., Houston. Trustee Tex. Conf. United Meth. Ch., mem. Bd. Missions; chmn. State Wide Ministries Conf., 1972; chmn. conf. commn. on world service and fin. Active Boy Scouts Am., 1938-60; del. to Democratic State Conv., 1972, state of Tex.; chmn. South Union Civic League, Houston, 1970-76. Recipient Plaque award Mt. Vernon Meth. Ch., 1962, Certificate of Service award Ct. Volunteers Service of Houston; Silver Beaver award Boy Scouts Am., 1960; Distinguished Service in Christian Edn. award Tex. Ministers Conf., 1975. Mem. Citizens C. of C. (dir. 1966-72), Phi Beta Sigma. Clubs: Mason, Century. Home: 3602 Lydia Houston TX 77021 Office: 5215 S Main Houston TX 77002

WINGER, ROGER ELSON, minister, Lutheran Church-Missouri Synod; b. Fisherville, Ont., Can., Dec. 25, 1933; s. Elson Clare and Bertha Caroline (Schweyer) W.; m. Della Bertha Lebien, June 7, 1958; children: Jeffrey, Karen, David, Thomas, Susan. A.A., Concordia Jr. Coll., 1953; B.A., Theol. diploma, Concordia Sem., St. Louis, 1958. Ordained to ministry Luth. Ch., 19—. Pastor, Holy Trinity Luth. Ch., London, 1958-64, Good Shepherd Luth. Ch., Coventry, Eng., 1964-69, Immanuel Luth. Ch., Liverpool, Eng., 1969-72, Faith, St. Matthews, Dunnville and Smithville, Ont., Can., 1972-78, St. Paul's Luth. Ch., Kitchener, Ont., 1978—; editor Ont. Dist. News, Luth. Ch.-Mo. Synod, Kitchner, 1979—, 1st v.p. Ont. dist., 1982—; bd. regents Concordia Luth. Sem., Edmonton, Alta., Can., 1983—; sec., bd. dirs. Luth. Council in Can., Winnipeg, Manitoba, Can., 1983—. Bd. dirs. Elem. Sch., Liverpool, 1971. Home: 76 Deerwood Crescent Kitchener ON N2N 1R3 Canada Office: St Paul's Luth Ch 137 Queen St S Kitchener ON N2G 1W2 Canada

WINGERT, NORMAN AMBROSE, minister, Brethren in Christ Ch.; b. Chambersburg, Pa., Apr. 1, 1898; s. Daniel Hoover and Emma (Rotz) W.; student Messiah Coll., 1918-20; Litt.B., Grove City Coll., 1923, M.A., 1923; m. Eunice Mary Lady, Dec. 25, 1927; children—Lois Wingert Tidgwell, Norman Olan. Ordained to ministry, 1955; pres. Jabbok Bible Sch., Thomas, Okla., 1927-30; faculty Southwestern Tchrs. Coll., Weatherford, Okla., 1930-31, Messiah Coll., Grantham, Pa., 1932-42, Upland (Calif.) Coll., 1945-48; relief worker Mennonite Central Com., Akron, Pa., 1948-64, Germany, 1948-49, Austria, 1950-52, Japan, 1953-57, Hong Kong, 1958-60; relief worker Mennonite Central Com., Ch. World Service and World Relief Commn., Burundi, Central Africa, 1962-64. Recipient Distinguished Alumnus award Messiah Coll., 1965. Mem. Pi Gamma Mu. Author: I Was Born Again, 1946; Twice Born, 1955; A Relief Worker's Notebook, 1952; Mosaics in Verse, 1968; Belief and Relief, 1967; No Place to Stop Killing, 1974. Home and Office: 491 S Reed Ave Box 168 Reedley CA 93654

WINKELMANN, JOHN PAUL, association executive; b. St. Louis, Sept. 14, 1933; s. Clarence Henry and Alyce Marie (Pierce) W.; B.S., St. Louis U., 1955; B.S. in Pharmacy, St. Louis Coll. Pharmacy, 1960; D.Sc., London Coll. Applied Sci., 1972; m. Margaret Ann Grandy, June 16, 1967; children: John Damian and James Paul (twins), Joseph Peter, Christopher Louis, Sean Martin. Founding mem. Nat. Cath. Pharmacists Guild of U.S., 1962, sec., 1966-67, 1st v.p., 1967-68, pres., 1968-70, 79-83, co-pres., 1985—, exec. dir., 1970—, editor quar. jour. Cath. Pharmacist, 1967—. Mem. Mo. Statewide Profl. Standards Rev. Commn. Historian St. Louis Coll. Pharmacy, 1960—, trustee, 1961-84, chmn. audit com., 1968-83. Bd. dirs. St. Peter Claver Sponsors Guild. Capt. USAF Res. (ret.). Decorated Master Knight of Malta, knight comdr. Equestrian Order of Holy Sepulchre of Jerusalem, Marian Knight of Teutonic Order, Gold Papal Lateran Cross, hon. Knight Crusader Red Star, Knight Comdr., Equestrian Order Holy Cross Jerusalem, Knight Sacred Mil. Constantinian Order St. George, Knight Sts. Maurice and Lazarus, Knight comdr. with Star Order Polonia Restituta, others; named Cath. Pharmacist of Year, 1970, hon. Ky. col.; recipient Presdl. Medal of Merit. registered pharmacist, Mo.; diploma Wine Adv. Bd. Calif.; notary pub. Fellow Royal Soc. Health, Nat. Cath. Pharmacists Guild, Am. Coll. Apothecaries, Am. Coll. Pharmacists, Soc. Apothecaries of London Faculty of History of Medicine and Pharmacy; charter mem. Am. Bd. Diplomates in Pharmacy, Am. Inst. History Pharmacy (council 1977-80), Inst. Certified Profl. Mgrs. (cert. mgr.), Am. Pharm. Assn., Acad. Pharm Practice, Assn. Mil. Surgeons U.S., Rho Chi. Author: Catholic Pharmacy, 1966; History of the St. Louis College of Pharmacy, 1964; also numerous articles. Home: 1012 Surrey Hills Dr St Louis MO 63117

WINNINGHAM, GREGORY GENE, minister, educator, Southern Baptist Convention; b. New Orleans, Nov. 18, 1959; s. Zack T. and Donzie G. (Ladner) W.; m. Janet R. Braswell; 1 child, Gregory Gene II. A.A., Holmes Jr. Coll., 1980; B.S., Miss. Coll., 1982; M.Div., New Orleans Bapt. Sem., 1985. Ordained to ministry So. Bapt. Conv., 1978. Pastor, Campbell's Creek Bapt. Ch., Miss., 1978-83; counselor Central Hills Bapt. Retreat, Kosciusko, Miss., 1979-81; pastor Lee Hill Bapt. Ch., Folsom, La., 1983—; associational dir. Brotherhood Assn., St. Tammany Assn., 1983—. Clin. asst. Jo Ellen Smith Hosp., New Orleans, 1984—. Author: Sermons from Corinthians, 1978. Recipient Evangelism award Miss. Bapt. Conv., 1979, Jr. Lions award, 1978, Jr. Rotary award, 1978, Freddie Harreid Meml. award Athletic Assn. of Canton, Miss., 1978. Mem. NEA. Republican. Club: Fellowship of Christian Athletes (Miss. Coll.). Lodge: Masons. Home: 4434 Iroquois Apt D New Orleans LA 70126

WINQUIST, CHARLES EDWIN, minister, Christian Church (Disciples of Christ); b. Toledo, June 11, 1944; s. Donald Edwin and Gladys June (Bryant) W.; B.A., U. Toledo, 1965; A.M., U. Chgo., 1968, Ph.D., 1970; m. Anna Lois Davis, Nov. 8, 1963; children—Diane Chasteen, Heidi Erika. Ordained to ministry, 1973; instr. philosophy Central YMCA Community Coll., Chgo., 1965-68; asst. prof. Union Coll., Barbourville, Ky., 1968-69; asso. prof. religious studies Calif. State U., Chico, 1969—, chmn. dept. religious studies, 1974—. Pres. western region Am. Acad. Religion, 1975-77. Author: The Transcendental Imagination, 1972; The Communion of Possibility, 1975. Office: Dept Religious Studies Calif State U Chico CA 95929

WINSOR, BENJAMIN THOMAS, priest, Episc. Ch.; b. Providence, June 8, 1934; s. Andrew DeWitt and Elizabeth (Barton) W.; Ed.B., R.I. Coll. Edn., 1957; M.Div., Episc. Theol. Sch., 1962; m. Barbara Crocker, Mar. 3, 1962; children—Brian Christopher, Jeffrey David, Kimberly, Deborah Lynnn, Matthew Stephen. Ordained priest, 1962; asst. minister Grace Ch., Providence, 1960-64; rector St. Paul's Episc. Ch., Monongahela, Pa., 1964-66; rector Ch. of Nativity, Pitts., 1966—. Bd. dirs. U. Pitts. Alcohol Tng. Program, 1968-72; bd. dirs. Parents Without Partners, Nat. Assn. Mental Health Pa.; mem. Pa. Task Force on Drug Abuse. Mem. Nat. Assn. Early Childhood Devel. Home: 1701 Crafton Blvd Pittsburgh PA 15205 Office: 33 Alice St Pittsburgh PA 15205

WINSOR, GORDON CODER, educator, minister, Presbyterian Church U.S.A.; b. Bremerton, Wash., Aug. 20, 1922; s. Thomas Williams and Grace Valentine (Coder) W.; m. Wilma Beth Ollis, July 11, 1946; children: Virginia Louise, Robert Milton, Anne Elizabeth. B.S.E.E., U. Wash., 1944; B.D., San Francisco Theol. Sem., 1948, S.T.M., 1954, Th.D., 1960. Ordained to ministry, 1951. Pastor Presbyn. Ch., Friday Harbor, Wash., 1953-55; asst. prof. religion and psychology Centre Coll., Danville, Ky., 1955-62, assoc. prof., 1963-69, prof. religion, 1970—. Translator: Time and History, 1966; God's History, 1969. Mem. Am. Acad. Religion, Soc. Bibl. Lit., AAUP, Phi Beta Kappa. Democrat. Lodge: Rotary (pres. 1970-71). Home: 704 East Dr Danville KY 40422 Office: Centre Coll Danville KY 40422

WINTER, HAROLD FREDERICK, minister, Lutheran Church-Missouri Synod; b. Mpls., July 20, 1919; s. Frederick William and Wilhelmina Louise (Ahrenholz) W.; m. Hazel Marie Tegen, June 9, 1944; children: Ruth Marie, Anita Louise. B.Th., Concordia Theol. Sem., 1944. Ordained to ministry Faith Luth. Ch., 1944. Pastor, Trinity Luth. Ch., Luther Meml. Ch., Hudson and River Falls, Wis., 1948-55, Zion Luth. Ch., Turtle Lake, Wis., Immanuel Luth. Ch., Clayton, Wis., 1955-64; pastor, organizer Rib Mountain Luth. Ch., Wausau, Wis., 1964-76, Good Shepherd by the Lake Luth. Ch., Stoughton, Wis., 1976-79, Rock of Ages Luth. Ch., Minocqua, Wis., 1979-84; mem. bd. missions No. Wis. dist. Luth. Ch., 1980—, coordinator for major gifts, 1984—. Recipient Servus Ecclesiae Christi award Concordia Sem., Ft. Wayne, Ind., 1984. Republican. Home: AV 1075 Brandy Lake Rd Woodruff WI 54568

WINTER, MARK ANDREW, minister, Lutheran Church in America; b. Winnipeg, Man., Can., Feb. 19, 1953; s. Otto and Esther Henrietta (Juettner) W.; m. Deborah Marie Wolin, July 29, 1978. B.A. cum laude, Wagner Coll., 1975; M.Div., Yale U., 1977. Ordained to ministry Luth. Ch., 1978. Intern pastor St. Luke's Luth. Ch., Long Beach, Calif., 1977-78; chaplain Yale-New Haven Med. Center, 1976-77; assisting pastor Reformation Luth. Ch., Las Vegas, 1978-80; pastor, team ministry Lurenburg County Luth. Staff Ministry, New Germany, N.S., Can., 1980-82; pastor Gethsemane Luth. Ch., San Diego, 1982—; on-call chaplain Sharp Hosp., San Diego, 1982—; worship rep. San Diego Ecumenical Conf., 1984; mem. San Diego Cabinet, Luth. Social Services. Lodge: Optimists. Home: 9234 Rebecca Ave San Diego CA 92123 Office: Gethsemane Luth Ch 2696 Melbourne Dr San Diego CA 92123

WINTERMEYER, HERBERT HERMAN, minister, United Church of Christ; b. Hartsburg, Mo., Sept. 23, 1912; s. Herman F. and Emma Bertha (Schormann) W.; B.A., Elmhurst (Ill.) Coll., 1934; D.D., 1966; B.D., Eden Theol. Sem., Webster Groves, Mo., 1938; m. Henrietta Louise Matuschek, Aug. 22, 1938; children: Don Robert, Lois Ann. Ordained to ministry, 1938; pastor chs., Balt., 1936, Grand Pass, Mo., 1938-41; pastor Immanuel Ch., Latimer, Iowa, 1941-57, St. John's Ch., St. Louis, 1957—. Mem. bd. Christian edn. United Ch. Christ, 1950-57; chmn. bd. Mo. Valley Camps United Ch. Christ, 1958-63; bd. dirs. United Ch. Bd. for Homeland Ministers, United Ch., 1960-70; v.p. Iowa synod United Ch. Christ, 1954-56; bd. dirs. Evang. Synod N.Am., 1976—; dir. Eden Publishing Ho., 1969-76. Bd. dirs. Elmhurst Coll., 1954-70, Deaconess Hosp., St. Louis, 1962-67. Author: Rural Worship, 1946; also articles. Address: 5243 Caribee Saint Louis MO 63128

WINTERS, MATTHEW LITTLETON, minister, Lutheran Church in America; b. Clare, Mich., Sept. 23, 1926; s. Matthew Littleton and Bertha Alexandra (Ross) W.; m. Elizabeth Wiegand, Oct. 16, 1954; children: Deborah Anne, Matthew Littleton IV. B.A., Wittenberg U., 1950; M.Div., Hamma Div. Sch., 1954; D.D. (hon.), Gettysburg Coll., 1972. Ordained to ministry Lutheran Ch., 1954. Assoc. pastor Holy Trinity Luth. Ch., Buffalo, 1954-60, sr. pastor, 1975—; sr. pastor Trinity Luth. Ch., Camp Hill, Pa., 1960-75; bd. dirs. Buffalo Area Met. Ministries, 1981—; pres. Luth. Coordinated Ministry of Buffalo, 1982—. Bd. dirs. Loth-Lorien, West Seneca, N.Y., 1984. Served with U.S. Army, 1944-48; PTO. Republican. Lodge: Rotary. Home: 16 Huntington Ct Williamsville NY 14221 Office: Holy Trinity Lutheran Ch 1080 Main St Buffalo NY 14209

WINTZ, JACK, clergyman, writer, editor; b. Batesville, Ind., Feb. 22, 1936; s. Paul and Viola (Thalheimer) W. B.A., Duns Scotus Coll., Detroit, 1959; M.A. in Theology, St. Leonard Coll., Dayton, Ohio, 1963; M.A. in English Lit., Xavier U., Cin., 1966. Ordained

Franciscan priest Roman Catholic Ch., 1963. Pastoral work St. Boniface Parish, Louisville, 1963-64; tchr. English, journalism, religion Roger Bacon High Sch., Cin., 1964-65; tchr. English, drama, communication arts Bishop Luers High Sch., Ft. Wayne, Ind., 1965-69; tchr. lit. Franciscan Sem. Coll. and Maryknoll Coll. for Women, Manila, Philippines, 1969-72; chaplain Catholic Family Movement and Cursillo, 1970-72. Assoc. editor: St. Anthony Messinger, Cin., 1972—. Editor: Catholic Update, 1973—. Movie reviewer: Catholic Telegraph, 1975—. Contbr. articles to profl. jours. Recipient numerous awards Cath. Press Assn., Cin. Editors Assn.; Hiroshima Internat. Cultural Found. grantee, 1982.

WIRZ, GEORGE O., bishop, Roman Catholic Church. Titular bishop of Muncipa, aux. bishop, Madison, Wis. Office: St Bernard 2450 Atwood Ave Madison WI 53704*

WISE, PHILIP DOUGLAS, minister, Southern Baptist Convention; b. Andalusia, Ala., Jan. 3, 1949; s. Harold L. and Doris M. (Jones) W.; m. Cynthia Adams, June 22, 1968; children: Myra D., Philip D., Fisher E. B.A. with honors, Samford U., 1970; Th.M. with honors, New Orleans Bapt. Theol. Sem., 1973, Th.D., 1980. Ordained to ministry Baptist Ch., 1970. Dir. Parkchester Friendship House, New Orleans, 1972-73; lectr. Culham Coll., Abingdon, Eng., 1974-76, New Orleans Bapt. Theol. Sem., 1977-78; pastor Fairview Bapt. Ch., Selma, Ala., 1978-82, Morningview Bapt. Ch., Montgomery, Ala., 1982—. Co-author: Dictionary of Theological Terms, 1983. Mem. Montgomery Race Relations Com., 1984; bd. dirs. Parents Without Ptnrs., Selma, 1982; pres. Oxford U. Grad. Reps. Conf., 1975. Mem. Am. Acad. Religion. Democrat. Home: 3049 Pinehardt Dr Montgomery AL 36109 Office: Morningview Baptist Ch 125 Calhoun Rd Montgomery AL 36109

WISHNER, MAYNARD IRA, finance company executive; Jewish; b. Chgo., Sept. 17, 1923; s. Hyman L. and Frances (Fisher) W.; m. Elaine Loewenberg, July 4, 1954; children: Ellen Wishner Kenemore, Jane, Miriam. B.A., U. Chgo., 1944, J.S., 1947. Bar: Ill. 1947. Vice pres. Jewish Fedn Met. Chgo., 1969-70; chmn. nat. exec. council Am. Jewish Com., 1973—, chmn. bd. govs., 1977-80, nat. pres., 1980-83, hon. pres. recipient Human Rights medallion, 1975. Bd. dirs. Nat. Found. for Jewish Culture; commr. Hillel Found. Pres. Walter E. Heller & Co., Chgo., 1974—. Served with AUS, 1943. Home: 1410 Sheridan Rd Wilmette IL 60091 Office: Walter E Heller & Co 105 W Adams St Chicago IL 60690

WISMAR, GREGORY JUST, minister, Lutheran Ch.-Mo. Synod; b. Jersey City, Jan. 9, 1946; s. Adolph Harold and Norma Meta (Just) W.; A.A., Concordia Coll., 1965; B.A., Concordia Coll., 1967; M.Div., Concordia Sem. St. Louis, 1971; M.S., So. Conn. State Coll., 1977; m. Priscilla Emily Ames, June 7, 1969; children—Eric Andrew, Sarah Emily, Elizabeth Victoria. Ordained to ministry, 1971; asst. pastor Immanuel Luth. Ch., Danbury, Conn., 1971-72; pastor St. Paul's Luth. Ch., Naugatuck, Conn., 1972—; tchr. spl. edn., pub. schs. Naugatuck, part time, 1972—. Regional council mem. New Eng. Dist., 1974; mem., sec. Anaheim Conv. format com., 1975; mem. dist. youth bd. New Eng., 1976—, Dallas Conv. format com., 1976-77; mem. Naugatuck Ecumenical Council; chaplain Conn. Republican Conv., 1974. Mem. Citizens' Advisory Bd., U.S. 5th Congl. Dist. Mem. Conn. Assn. for Gifted, Hymn Soc. Am. Home: 167 Park Ave Naugatuck CT 06770 Office: 350 Millville Ave Naugatuck CT 06770

WITCHER, ROBERT CAMPELL, bishop, Episcopal Church; b. New Orleans, Oct. 5, 1926; s. Charles S. and Lily S. (Campbell) W.; m. Elisabeth Alice Cole, June 4, 1957; children: Elisabeth Alice, Robert Campbell. B.A., Tulane U., 1949; M.A., La. State U., 1960, Ph.D., 1968; M.Div., Seabury-Western Theol. Sem., 1952, D.D. (hon.), 1974. Ordained deacon Episcopal Ch., 1952, priest, 1953, consecrated bishop, 1975. Priest-in-charge St. Andrew's Mission, Clinton, La., 1952-55; canon pastor Christ Ch. Cathedral, New Orleans, 1961-62; rector St. James Ch., Baton Rouge, 1962-75; bishop coadjutor Diocese of L.I., Garden City, N.Y., 1975-77, bishop, 1977—; pres. Ch. Charity Found., N.Y., 1977—, Trustees of Estate of Diocesan L.I., 1977—, Mercer Sch. Theology, Garden City, 1977—; chmn. com. on structure of ch. Ho. of Bishops Pastoral Commn., 1983—. Author: Founding of the Episcopal Church in Louisiana, 1805-1838, 1960; The Episcopal Church in Louisiana, 1801-1861, 1969. Bd. dirs. L.I. Council Alcoholism, 1980—, Nat. Council Alcoholism, 1981—; mem. Breakthrough, Inc. Mem. N.Y. State Council Chs., L.I. Council Chs., Phi Kappa Phi, Phi Alpha Theta, Eta Sigma Phi. Home: 118 Dogwood Ln Manhasset NY 11030 Office: 36 Cathedral Ave Garden City NY 11530

WITKOWIAK, STANLEY BENEDICT, priest, Roman Cath. Ch.; b. Dortmund, Ger., May 18, 1909; s. Stanley Paul and Helen Barbara (Grobelna) W.; came to U.S., 1909, naturalized, 1930; B.A., St. Francis (Wis.) Sem., 1931, M.A., 1935; Ph.D., Cath. U. Am., 1942. Ordained priest, 1935; asst. pastor, athletic dir. St. Stanislaus Parish and High Sch., Milw., 1935-39; prin. St. Catherine's High Sch., Racine, Wis., 1942-72, prin. emeritus, 1972-74; pastor St. Stanislaus Parish and Grade Sch., Racine, 1974—. Bd. dirs. Racine Library, 1973-76, Racine Jr. Achievement, 1963-76. Recipient Citizen of Year award City of Racine, 1967; Jr. Achievement award Racine, 1975. Mem. Priests Forum, Racine Clergy Assn. Address: 1754 Grand Ave Racine WI 53403

WITMER, LAWRENCE EUGENE, minister, American Baptist Churches in the U.S.A.; b. Lancaster, Pa., Nov. 16, 1935; s. Omar Garman and Anna (Buckwalter) W.; m. Margaret Burhans; children: Laura, James, Thomas, Joy. B.A., Cornell U., 1957; M.Div., Colgate Rochester Div. Sch., 1963; M.A., U. Chgo., 1968. Ordained to ministry Bapt. Ch., 1963. Minister of edn. Hyde Park Union Ch., Chgo., 1963-67; community minister Monroe Bapt. Assn., Rochester, N.Y., 1968-76; exec. dir. Genesee Ecumenical Ministries, Rochester, 1976—; mem. Div. Edn. and Soc., Nat. Council Chs., 1975-77. Co-author: Edge of the Ghetto: A Study of Churches in Community Organization, 1968. Bd. dirs. United Way of Greater Rochester, 1978-84. Served to lt. (j.g.) USN, 1957-60. Mem. Nat. Assn. Ecumenical Staff (program chmn. 1985-86). Democrat.

WITT, ROBERT EDWARD, JR., priest, Episcopal Church; b. Plainfield, N.J., Sept. 15, 1946; s. Robert Edward and Nicolina (Santacroce) W.; m. Marion Frances Burdick, Dec. 27, 1967; children: Robert Edward, Andrew James, Scott Lewis. B.A., Alfred U., 1968; M.Div., Gen. Theol. Sem., 1978; cert. in Spiritual Direction, Gen. Theol. Sem., 1984. Ordained priest, Episcopal Ch., 1978. Chaplain, Bishopswood, Camden, Maine, summer 1978; vicar St. Joseph's Ch., Milo, Maine, 1978-81, St. John The Bapt. Ch., Brownville Junction, Maine, 1978-81; rector Zion Ch., Morris, N.Y., 1981—, Christ Ch., Gilbertsville, N.Y., 1981—; del. Diocesan Council, Diocese of Albany, 1981—, mem. com. on ecumenism, 1982—, mem. structure com., 1983—. Contbr. articles to profl. jours. Chaplain, Morris Vol. Fire Dept., N.Y., 1981—, sec., 1984. Served to capt. U.S. Army, 1968-73. Mem. Brotherhood of St. Andrew. Home: Box 156 24 E Main St Morris NY 13808 Office: Episcopal Parish of Zion Ch and Christ Ch Marion Ave Gilbertsville NY 13776

WIZMAN, RAPHAEL, rabbi, Orthodox Jewish Congregation; b. Casablanca, Morocco, July 25, 1943; came to U.S., 1956; s. Haim and Mazal (Levy) W.; m. Bella Gruber; children: Eliezer, Chaim-Tova. M.A. in Theology, New Brunswick, Theol. Sem., 1972; Ed.D., Rutgers U., 1976; Pastoral Degree, N.Y. Bd. Rabbis, 1974. Rabbi, 1965. Rabbi, Congregation Etz Ahaim, Highland Park, N.J., 1966-70, Sephardic Congregation, Forest Hills, N.Y., 1970-72, Young Israel of Commack, N.Y., 1972—. Bd. dirs. Rainbow Spl. Edn. Sch., Commack, 1983—. Mem. N.Y. Bd. Rabbis, Suffolk Bd. Rabbis. Office: Young Israel of Commack 40 Kings Park Rd Commack NY 11725

WOGAMAN, JOHN PHILIP, minister, United Methodist Church; b. Toledo, Mar. 18, 1932; s. Donald Ford and Ella Louise (Kilbury) W.; B.A., U. Pacific, 1954; S.T.B., Boston U., 1957, Ph.D., 1960; m. Carolyn Jane Gattis, Aug. 4, 1956; children—Stephen Neil, Donald George, Paul Joseph, Jean Ann. Ordained to ministry, 1957; pastor First Meth. Ch., Marlborough, Mass., 1956-58; staff asst., div. world missions United Meth. Ch., 1960-61; asst. prof., then asso. prof. U. Pacific, 1961-66; prof. Christian social ethics Wesley Theol. Sem., Washington, 1966—, dean, 1972—. Mem. com. religious and civil liberties Nat. Council Chs., 1966-68, mem. com. internat. affairs, 1967-69. Pres. Stockton (Calif.) Fair Housing Com., 1963-64, Suburban Md. Fair Housing, 1970; mem. Calif. Democratic Central Com., 1964-66. Lilly fellow, 1959-60; recipient Research award Assn. Theol. Schs., 1975. Mem. Am. Soc. Christian Ethics (pres. 1976-77), Am. Acad. Religion. Author: Methodism's Challenge in Race Relations, 1960; Protestant Faith and Religious Liberty, 1967; Guaranteed Annual Income: The Moral Issues, 1968; A Christian Method of Moral Judgment, 1976; Christians and the Great Economic Debate, 1977; editor: The Population Crisis and Moral Responsibility, 1973. Office: 4400 Massachusetts Ave NW Washington DC 20016

WOIKE, KAY ELIZABETH, minister, United Church of Christ; b. Temple, Tex., Jan. 13, 1944; d. Frederick Houghten and Margaret Alma (Gignac) Reinhart; m. Glenn Victor Woike, Sept. 11, 1965; children: Elizabeth, Sarah (dec.), Adrienne. B.A., DePauw U., 1965; M.Div., Yale U., 1971. Ordained to ministry United Ch. Christ, 1972. Frontier intern in mission Presbyn. Ch. E. Africa, Kenya, 1968-70; pastor Fayette Federated Ch., N.Y., 1972-75, Varick United Methodist Ch., East Varick, N.Y., 1972-75, Ch. of Nativity, Tonawanda, N.Y., 1978—; asst. moderator Western area United Ch. Christ, Buffalo, 1979-80, moderator, 1980-81, gen. synod del. from N.Y., 1980-84; chmn. Food for All Program, Buffalo, 1984—; bd. dirs. Buffalo Area Met. Ministries, 1983—. Office: Ch of Nativity 1530 Colvin Blvd Buffalo NY 14223

WOLBRINK, DEAN DANIEL, minister, Reformed Church America; b. Mobridge, S.D., May 4, 1943; s. William Gerrit and Gertrude (Hasselman) W.; A.B., U. Minn., 1965; B.D., M.Div., Western Theol. Sem., Mich., 1969; S.T.M., N.Y. Theol. Sem., 1973, D.M., 1979; m. Virginia Lynne Dalrymple, Nov. 6, 1964; children—Jeffrey, Rhonda. Ordained to ministry Ref. Ch. Am., 1969; pastor 1st Ref. Ch., Jamaica, N.Y., 1969—. Pres. classis of Queens, Ref. Ch. Am., 1973-74; v.p. S.E. Queens Ecumenical Council; bd. dirs. Queens Fedn. Chs., 1975—; mem. Queens Interfaith Clergy Council; chaplain Police Benevolent Assn., also USNR. Mem. Queens County Council on Alcoholism, Jamaica Service Program for Older Adults; pres. Low Income Housing for Elderly, 1975; bd. dirs. Central Queens YMCA. Recipient award for youth work Alpha Kappa Alpha, 1975. Mem. Jamaica C. of C. Home: 96 Tappan Landing Rd Tarrytown NY 10591 Office: 42 N Broadway Tarrytown NY 10591

WOLCOTT, ROY ANDREW, minister, Seventh-day Adventists; b. Bryan, Ohio, Mar. 11, 1921; s. Clyde Oliver and Emelia Ann (Betts) W.; B.A., Emmanuel Missionary Coll., 1945; M.A., Andrews U., 1960; m. Nancy Louise Bartlett, Aug. 12, 1945; children—Dale, Alvin, Glenn. Ordained to ministry, 1950; prin., tchr. Grand Rapids (Mich.) Adventist Elementary Sch., 1945-47; pastoral intern, Detroit, 1947-50; head Religion Dept., Korean Jr. Coll. and pastor Osaka (Japan) Ch., 1950-52; head Dept. Religion, S.E. Asian Union Coll. and pastor of coll. ch., 1952-55; pastor Regina (Sask.) Seventh-day Adventist Ch., 1955-58; tchr. Bible, English and biology Mount Aetna Seventh-day Adventist Acad., Hagerstown, Md., 1958-60, Golden Gate Acad., Oakland, Calif., 1960-63; pastor Fremont (Calif.) Seventh-day Adventist Ch., 1963-67; pastor Gilroy (Calif.) Seventh-day Adventist Ch., 1967-73, Shafter (Calif.) Seventh-day Adventist Ch., 1973-76, Morton and Onalaska (Wash.) Seventh-day Adventist Ch., 1976-81, Bremerton, Wash., 1981-85, Belfair, Wash., 1982-85. Exec. com. Shafter Ministerial Assn., 1975—; v.p. Gilroy Ministerial Assn., 1970-71. Contbr. articles to religious jours. and newspapers. Home: 4913 NW David Rd Bremerton WA 98312 Office: Wash Conf Seventh-Day Adventists 20015 Bothell Way SE Bothell WA 98011

WOLF, ARNOLD JACOB, rabbi, Reform Jewish; educator; b. Chgo., Mar. 19, 1924; s. Max A. and Nettie (Schanfarber) W.; m. Margery Steiner, Nov. 1, 1948 (div. Mar. 1960); m. Lois Blumberg, Dec. 26, 1963; children: Jonathan, Benjamin, Sara. A.A., U. Chgo., 1942; B.A., U. Cin., 1945; M. Hebrew Lit., Hebrew Union Coll., Cin., 1948; D.D. (hon.), Hebrew Union Coll., N.Y.C., 1973. Rabbi Congregation Solel, Highland Park, Ill., 1957-72; chaplain and instr. Yale U., New Haven, 1972-80; rabbi KAM-Isaiah Israel, Chgo., 1980—; chmn. Breira, N.Y.C., 1976-79; dir. Jewish Council Urban Affairs, Chgo., 1981—; mem. ethics com. City of Chgo., 1983—; Jewish rep. World Council Chs., Nairobi, Kenya, 1985. Lectr. U. Chgo., 1980—. Author: Challenge to Confirmands, 1963. Editor: What is Man?, 1968; Rediscovering Judaism, 1965; Sh'ma, 1970—. Served to lt. (j.g.) USNR, 1951-53. Recipient Brotherhood award NCCJ, 1962. Mem. Central Conf. Am. Rabbis. Home: 5000 S East End Chicago IL 60615 Office: KAM-Isaiah Israel Congregation 1000 E Hyde Park Blvd Chicago IL 60615

WOLF, FRED CARL, JR., priest, Episc. Ch.; b. Helena, Ark., Aug. 10, 1922; s. Fred Carl and Maggie Katherine (Wiggs) W.; B.S., B.A., Albright Coll., Reading, Pa., 1948; M.Div., U. South, Sewanee, Tenn., 1951; D.C.L., U. Edinburgh (Scotland), 1961; m. Mary Allison Schmidt, Dec. 29, 1953; children—Mary Katherine, Fred Carl, III. Ordained priest, 1951; pastor chs. in Tenn. and Tex., 1951-60, 63-68; mem. faculty history dept. U. Tex., 1962-63; asso. St. Martin's Ch., Metairie, La., 1968-71; rector St. Paul's Ch., Chillicothe, Ohio, 1971—. Dean No. convocation Episc. Diocese W. Tex., 1953-55; dean So. deanery Episc. Diocese Dallas, 1955-60, No. deanery, 1965-67; chmn. coms. evangelism and Christian edn. Episc. Diocese Dallas, 1955-60; pres. Ministerial Alliance, Corsicana, Tex., 1957-58; chmn. visual aids Ft. Worth Council Chs., 1967. Chmn. San Marcos (Tex.) Community Chest, 1954; chmn. fin. com. Ft. Worth Symphony and Youth Symphony, 1967-68. Grantee D.L. West Found.; mem. Exeter Coll., Oxford, Eng., 1960—. Mem. Oxford Union, Anglican Soc., Am. Ch. Union, English Speaking Union, Soc. Propagation of Gospel, Soc. Promotion Christian Knowledge. Author articles. Home: 367 Fairway Ave Chillicothe OH 45601 Office: 33 E Main St Chillicothe OH 45601

WOLF, FREDERICK BARTON, bishop, Episcopal Church; b. Cedar Rapids, Iowa, Apr. 12, 1922; s. Frederick Barton and Emily Julietta (Reynolds) W.; B.A., Grinnell Coll., 1946; B.D., Seabury-Western Theol. Sem., 1946, D.D., 1969; LL.D., St. Francis Coll., Biddeford, Maine, 1969; J.U.D., Nasson Coll., Springvale, Maine, 1969; S.T.D., Gen. Theol. Sem., N.Y.C., 1974; m. Barbara Buckley, Oct. 5, 1946; children: Mary Julietta Wolf, Martha, Jane. Ordained priest, 1946, consecrated bishop, 1968; priest-in-charge, rector Trinity Ch., Belvidere, Ill., 1946-50; rector St. Christopher's Ch., Oak Park, Ill., 1950-54; dean Cathedral Ch. of St. John, Quincy, Ill., 1954-57; asso.

sec., leadership tng. dept. Christian edn. Exec. Council, Episc. Ch., 1957-59; rector St. Peters Ch., Bennington, Vt., 1959-68; bishop of Maine, Portland, 1968—; mem. examining chaplains and exec. council Province of New Eng., 1963-68, dep. Gen. Conv., 1964-67, pres. standing com., 1966-68; chmn. Gen. Bd. Examining Chaplains, 1970-73, pres. Province of New Eng., 1974-83; chmn. bd. trustees Gen. Theol. Sem.; chmn. council of advice to presiding bishop and house of bishops, 1975-83. Author: Christian Forgiveness, 1956; (with Barbara Wolf) Journey in Faith, 1958; Exploring Faith and Life, 1962. Home: 180 High St Portland ME 04101 Office: 143 State St Portland ME 04101

WOLFE, CHARLES EDWARD, minister, writer, United Methodist Ch. B. Elk River, Minn., Nov. 7, 1931; s. Raymond Wolfe and Blanche Harriet (Marshall) Strawser; m. Anne Chamberlin, Sept. 15, 1951 (div. Apr. 1968); children: Christian, Hawley, Lewis, David; m. Helen Bickel, Sept. 13, 1968. B.A., No. Iowa U., 1952; B.D., Austin Presbyn. Theol. Sem., 1958; D.Ministry, Wesley Sem., Washington, 1977. Ordained to ministry United Methodist Ch. as elder, 1977. Pastor 1st Presbyn. Ch., Overton, Tex., 1958-60, 1st Presbyn. Ch., Killeen, Tex., 1960-66; assoc. pastor Delmar Meth. Ch., N.Y., 1969-70; pastor West End Presbyn. Ch., Albany, N.Y., 1970-76, Shiloh Meth. Ch., Hampstead, Md., 1977—; adj. prof. Western Md. Coll., Westminster, 1978—; prof. Wesley Sem., 1979—. Author: Homecoming, 1979, Seven Words From Cross (Faculty Book award Western Md. Coll., 1981), Special Days, Year B (Faculty award 1982), 1981, Special Days, Year C (Faculty award 1983), 1982, Special Days, Year A (Faculty award 1984), 1983, Flight of the Bluebirds, 1984. Contbr. articles to profl. religious jours. Served to capt. U.S. Army, 1966-68, Vietnam. Decorated Purple, Bronze Star, Army Commendation medal with oak leaf cluster. Mem. Soc. of Bibl. Lit. Home and Office: Shiloh Meth Ch 3100 Shiloh Rd Hampstead MD 21074

WOLFE, DAVID LEE, minister, philosophy educator, American Baptist Church; b. Lock Haven, Pa., Mar. 7, 1939; s. James H. and Thelma G. (Liddick) W.; m. Jean Alice Neale, Aug. 18, 1962; children: Jonathan David, Benjamin Michael, Timothy Matthew. B.A. in Anthropology, Wheaton Coll., 1961, M.A. in Theology, 1964; postgrad. New Sch. Social Research, 1964-67; Ph.D., NY U, 1969. Ordained to ministry Bapt. Ch., 1962. Pastor, W. Hill Meth. Ch., Chelsea, Vt., 1975-79, The Tunbridge Ch., Vt., 1979—; prof. philosophy Gordon Coll., Wenham, Mass., 1974—. Author: Epistemology: The Justification of Belief, 1982. Contbr. articles to profl. jours. Recipient Founders Day award NY U, 1969. Mem. Am. Philos. Assn., Philosophy of Edn. Soc. Home: Rivendell Tunbridge VT 05077 Office: Gordon Coll 225 Grapevine Rd Wenham MA 01984

WOLFF, WALTER LEO, minister, American Lutheran Church; b. Munich, Germany, June 7, 1950; came to U.S., 1952; s. Walter Leo and Viola Ellen (Boettinger) W.; m. Jennifer Marie Olson, June 14, 1975; children: Karl Walter, William, Steven Gregory James. B.A., Dana Coll., 1972; M.Div., Wartburg Sem., 1976, postgrad., 1982—. Ordained to ministry Am. Luth. Ch., 1976; registered emergency med. technician. Pastor, chaplain Kvernes Luth. Ch. and Luth. Home of Good Shepherd, New Rockford, N.D., 1976—; mem. dist. div. Service and Mission Com., Am. Luth. Ch., Fargo, N.D., 1978-82, dist. Ch. in Soc. Com., Fargo, 1983-84, del. gen. conv., Mpls., 1980; bd. dirs. Red Willow Bible Camp, Binford, N.D., 1977-84. Active Bread for World, Washington, 1976, Community Ambulance Service, New Rockford, 1980, New Rockford Park Bd., 1984. Recipient Service award Luth. Home of Good Shepherd, 1984. Mem. Soc. Bibl. Lit. Home: 1219 4th Ave N New Rockford ND 58356 Office: Luth Home of Good Shepherd 1226 1st Ave N New Rockford ND 58356

WOLK, ROBERT GASPER, priest, Latin Rite Catholic Church; b. Pitts., July 23, 1940; s. Gasper Albert and Mary (Kuzmovich) W.; B.A. in Philosophy, St. Vincent Coll., Latrobe, Pa., 1962; M.Div., St. Vincent Sem., Latrobe, 1966; license in canon law Cath. U. Am., 1974. Ordained priest, 1966; asst. St. Athanasius Ch., West View, Pitts., 1966-72; asst. chancellor Diocese of Pitts., 1974—; sec. Tribunal, 1970-72, defender of bond, 1972—, judge, 1980—; mem. speakers bur. Diocese of Pitts. Mem. Canon Law Soc. Am., Smithsonian Instn., Mellon Inst., Nat. Hist. Soc., Nat. Trust Hist. Preservation, Pitts. Symphony Soc. Author: Diocesan Pastoral Manual, 1975. Home: 4537 William Flynn Hwy Allison Park PA 15101 Office: 111 Boulevard of Allies Pittsburgh PA 15222

WOLLERSHEIM, GARY MATTHEW, minister, Lutheran Church in America; b. Chgo., Feb. 25, 1951; s. Irving Matthew and Evelyn Ovedia (Gunderson) W.; m. Paulette Ann Swanson, Aug. 25, 1972; children: Ruth, Matthew, Rachel. B.A., Augsburg Coll., 1973; M.Div., Luther/Northwestern Sem., 1977. Ordained to ministry Luth. Ch., 1977. Pastor Gehtsemane Luth. Ch., Cicero, Ill., 1977-80; pastor, developer Luth. Ch. in Am., St. Charles, Ill., 1980-81, dist. dean Ill. Synod, 1978-80, evangelism leader, 1981—; pastor Hosanna! Luth. Ch., St. Charles, 1981—. Home: 1819 Indiana St Saint Charles IL 60174 Office: Hosanna! Luth Ch Randall and Crane Rds PO Box 1100 Saint Charles IL 60174

WOLTERS, ALBERT MARTEN, religion educator, Christian Reformed Church; b. Enschede, Overijssel, The Netherlands, Sept. 9, 1942; came to Can., 1948; s. Syrt and Luchiena (Seinen) W.; m. Alice Van Andel, Sept. 28, 1968; children: Victor, Benita. B.A., Calvin Coll., 1964; Ph.D., Free U., 1972. Sr. mem. Inst. for Christian Studies, Toronto, Ont., Can., 1974-84; prof. religion and classics Redeemer Ref. Christian Coll., Hamilton Ont., 1984—. Author: Plotinus: On Eros, 1984; Creation Regained, 1985. Contbr. articles to profl. jours. Can. Council fellow, 1969-72; recipient vis. scholar's stipend Dutch govt., 1981-82. Mem. Can. Philos. Assn., Can. Soc. Renaissance Studies, Internat. Soc. Neoplatonic Studies, Soc. Bibl. Lit. Home: 131 Britten Close Hamilton ON L9C 4K1 Canada Office: Redeemer Reformed Christian Coll 467 Beach Blvd Hamilton ON L8H 6W8 Canada

WOLVEN, JOE RAY, minister, So. Bapt. Conv.; b. McFall, Mo., Apr. 1, 1939; s. Fred Ray and Edna (Benson) W.; A.A., S.W. Bapt. Coll., 1959; m. Cathy Hartzell, Aug. 2, 1959; children—Kent, Keith, Chris. Ordained to ministry, 1960; pastor Mt. Zion Ch., New Hampton, Mo., 1957, Caplinger Mills (Mo.) Ch., 1958-60, Keystone Mission, Reeds Spring, Mo., 1960-67, Verona (Mo.) Ch., 1967-72, Elsey (Mo.) Ch., 1972-74, Keystone Mission, Reeds Spring, Mo., 1975—. Associational clk., Stone-Taney County, 1974-76; interim associational missionary, Lawrence County, 1970, youth camp dir., 1969-70. Dir., Community Betterment, Reeds Spring, Mo., 1975-76; pres. Music Booster Club, Reeds Spring, Mo., 1974-76. Home: Rural Route 2 Reeds Spring MO 65737

WOMACK, FRED MICHAEL, minister, Southern Baptist Convention; b. Sylacauga, Ala., Feb. 9, 1949; s. Fred Hoyt and Willie Dean (Forbus) W.; m. Claudia Donnini, June 13, 1975; children: Catherine Elaine, Emily Elizabeth. A.A., Miami Dade Community Coll., 1974; Th.B., Miami Christian Coll., 1975; Th.M. Dallas Theol. Sem., 1982. Ordained to ministry So. Bapt. Conv., 1978. Music and youth dir. Emmanuel Bapt. Ch., Hialeah, Fla., 1973-78; outreach dir. East Grand Bapt. Ch., Dallas, 1978-80; assoc. pastor White Rock Bapt. Ch., Mesquite, Tex., 1980-82; pastor Calvary Bapt. Ch., Erwin, Tenn., 1982—. Contbr. articles to religious publs. Office: Calvary Bapt Ch 540 Adams St Erwin TN 37650

WOOD, CHARLES MONROE, minister, Christian Church (Disciples of Christ); educator, florist; b. Luray, Va., July 26, 1943; s. Charles Monroe and Mildred Elizabeth (Atkins) W.; m. Doris Rebecca Hunt, Aug. 3, 1963; children: Rebecca Lynn, Christopher Allen, Thomas Mark, Charles Monroe. A.S. in Elem. Edn., Bluefield Jr. Coll., 1963; B.S. in Elem. Edn., Madison Coll., 1965; postgrad. New Orleans So. Bapt. Theol. Sem., 1965-66; M.Div., Christian Theol. Sem., Indpls., 1975; postgrad. Longwood Coll., 1983—. Lic. Bapt. Ch., 1962, ordained to ministry, 1964; ordained to ministry Christian Ch., 1969. Pastor Bentonville Bapt. Ch., Va., 1964-65, 1st Christian Ch., Shenandoah, Va., 1967-68, Veedersburg., Ind., 1973-75, Waurika, Okla., 1984—; Crewe Christian Ch., Va., 1968-72, 75-81, Petunia Christian Ch., Wytheville, Va., 1972-73, Jeterville Christian Ch., Va., 1975-84, Liberty Christian Ch., Green Bay, Va., 1981-84; mem. Va. Evangelism Com., 1969-72; traveling ambassador Nat. Decision Evangelism Program, 1969-72; vol. chaplain Wythe Meml. Hosp., 1972-73; mem. Christian Edn. com., Ind. Region 1975-76, evangelism com., 1974-76, regional bd., 1977-79, assembly program com., 1984—. Substitute tchr. Charlottesville, Va., 1966; elem. tchr. Page County Pub. Schs., Va., 1966-68; owner, mgr. Crewe Florist & Gifts, 1979-83. Compilor: Holistic Evangelism, 1976. Council mem. Town of Crewe, 1982-84; vice chmn. Gov.'s Commn. on Comprehensive Health Planning, Indpls., 1974-76; sub-chmn. Gov.'s Commn. on Alcohol and Drugs, 1974-76; v.p. Wabash Mental Health Assn., 1974; assoc. counselor, co-dir. Wabash Mental Health Satellite Counseling Ctr., 1974-75; mem. Gov.'s Council on Teenage Drug Abuse and Aging, 1974-76; co-founder chpt. Alcoholics Anonymous, Al-Anon, Al-Teen Ctr.; bd. dirs., sponsor Meals on Wheels, 1974-75; Recipient Outstanding Community Service award County of Notoway, Crewe, 1984, Heart Fund award Am. Heart Assn., 1970. Mem. Crewe C. of C. (chmn. parade com. 1981-83, appreciation award 1984), Okla. Council of Chs. (coop. ministries com.). Home: 526 N Elm St Waurika OK 73573 Office: First Christian Ch Waurika OK 73573

WOOD, DANIEL WARREN, minister, Southern Baptist Convention; educator. B. Durham, N.C., Sept. 24, 1955; s. Warren Clemons and Helen Viola (Holmes) W.; m. Deborah Lynn Langdon, June 17, 1978; 1 dau., Lauren. B.A., U. N.C., 1977; M.Div., Southwestern Bapt. Theol. Sem., Ft. Worth, 1981. Ordained to ministry So. Bapt. Conv., 1981; pastor 1st Bapt. Ch., Franklinville, N.C., 1981—; del. Bapt. State Conv. N.C., Carey, 1981—, spl. youth worker, 1983—; instr. adult edn., Randolph Tech. Coll., Asheboro, N.C., 1984—. Mem. Randolph Bapt. Pastors' Conf. (pres. 1984), Randolph Bapt. Assn. (del. 1981—, AssisTeem mem. 1982—). Club: Bapt. Men (Franklinville). Lodge: Lions (Franklinville chaplain 1983). Home: Park St Franklinville NC 27248 Office: 1st Bapt Ch PO Box 111 Franklinville NC 27248

WOOD, DARRELL WAYNE, minister, So. Bapt. Conv.; b. Seminole, Okla., Jan. 4, 1939; s. Delmer Loyd and Neva Irene (Dillon) W.; B.F.A., U. Okla., 1961; B.D., Southwestern Bapt. Theol. Sem., Ft. Worth, 1966, M.Div., 1968; M.A., U. Mo., Columbia, 1975; m. Priscilla Louise Kelly, Dec. 22, 1964; children—Deborah Michelle, Pamela Kathleen. Campus minister Wichita State U., 1966-69; promotion specialist Kans. Conv. So. Bapts., 1966-68; missionary, Hong Kong, 1968-73; editor Bapt. Sunday Sch. Bd., Nashville, 1974—; mem. adj. faculty U. Tenn., Nashville, 1976—. Internat. corr. Bapt. Press, Hong Kong, 1969-72; dir. internat. student ministries Mo. Bapt. Conv., 1972-73; chmn. missions com. Woodmont Bapt. Ch., Nashville, 1976-77. Recipient Letzeiser Art award U. Okla., 1961. Mem. Assn. Edn. Journalism, Assn. Mass Communication Research and Info. Center, Omicron Delta Kappa, Delta Phi Delta. Author articles. Address: 5510 Country Dr 102 Nashville TN 37211

WOOD, DARRYL ROYCE, minister, Southern Baptist Convention; b. Decatur, Ala., Oct. 4, 1950; s. Royce Collier and Neria Faye (Campbell) W.; m. Marcia Sean Spurgeon, June 21, 1975; children: Neil Alan, Tyler David. B.A., Samford U., 1972; M.Div., New Orleans Bapt. Theol. Sem., 1974, D.Th., 1979. Ordained to ministry Bapt. Ch., 1974. Minister of youth 85th St. Bapt. Ch., Birmingham, Ala., 1972, Sandy Creek Bapt. Ch., Pride, La., 1972-74; pastor Bluff Creek Bapt. Ch., Clinton, La., 1974-80, Goodyear Bapt. Ch., Picayune, Miss., 1980-85, Moulton Bapt. Ch., Ala., 1985—; moderator Pearl River Bapt. Assn., Carriere, Miss., 1981-83, dir., tchr. sem. extension, 1981-82; spl. worker Sunday sch. Miss. Bapt. Conv., Jackson, 1984; adj. faculty New Orleans Bapt. Theol. Sem., 1984. Author Sunday sch. lessons; also article. Active Assn. for Retarded Citizens, Pearl River County, Miss., 1984. Office: Moulton Bapt Ch PO Box 415 Moulton AL 35650

WOOD, FRED DICKSON, III, minister, United Methodist Ch.; dentist; b. Phila., Oct. 21, 1934; s. Fred Dickson Jr. and Gladys (Clark) W.; m. Patricia Ann Haines, Sept. 29, 1958 (dec. Apr. 1980); children: Fred Dickson IV, William Wescott Woodward, John Clark, Harlan Haines Fergus, Amanda Lee; m. Lela Jean Roupp, Dec. 19, 1981. A.B., U. Pa., 1960, D.M.D., 1965; M.Div., Wesley Theol. Sem., 1979, D.Ministry, 1985. Ordained United Meth. Ch. as deacon, 1975, elder Peninsula Ann. Conf., 1983. Pastor, Bethel United Meth. Charge, Del., 1980-81, Parsonburg United Meth. Charge, Md., 1982—; missionary, dentist to Haiti, 1985. Gen. practice dentistry, Seaford, Del., 1968—. Served as chaplain CAP, 1980—. Bd. dirs. Lower Shore Sheltered Workshop, Salisbury, Md., 1984—; mem. Wicomico County Mental Health Adv. Bd., Md., 1983—. Mem. Am. Dental Assn., Del. State Dental Soc. Republican. Home: PO Box 88 Parsonburg MD 21849 Office: Nanticoke Hosp Profl Bldg Middleford Rd Seaford DE 19973

WOOD, J. M., minister, So. Bapt. Conv.; b. Manitou, Okla., July 22, 1929; s. John Sherman and Maude Esther (Alexander) W.; B.Music Edn., Okla. Bapt. U., 1957; M.Music Edn., N.Tex. State U., 1959; m. Margaret Gail Richardson, May 30, 1955; children—Gary, Don, Rita Lynn. Ordained to ministry, 1957; minister music Calvary Bapt. Ch., Sulphur, Okla., 1956-62, Eastwood Bapt. Ch., Tulsa, 1962-65, First Bapt. Ch., Muskogee, Okla., 1965-69, Met. Bapt. Ch., Wichita, Kans., 1969-73, Broadmoor Bapt. Ch., Jackson, Miss., 1973—. Pres., Singing Churchmen Okla., 1966, associational staff members, Jackson, 1976, Alumni Assn. Southwestern Bapt. Theol. Sem. for Miss., 1977. Dir. Air Force Officers Wives Chorus, 1972-73. Home: 6202 Whitestone Rd Jackson MS 39206 Office: 787 E Northside Dr Jackson MS 39206

WOOD, JAMES FRANCIS, minister, Christian Church (Disciples of Christ); b. Hubbard, Ohio, Feb. 11, 1943; s. Lawrence Tilman and Phyllis (Hunt) W.; m. Sylvia E. Froggett, Aug. 26, 1966; children: James Francis, Kenneth. B.A., Milligan Coll., 1969; M.A., U. S. Fla., 1982, M.L.S., 1985. Ordained to ministry Christian Ch., 1968. Youth minister Harrison Ch. of Christ, Johnson City, Tenn., 1968-70; minister Simms Kill Christian Ch., Elizabethtown, Tenn., 1970, Blvd. Christian Ch., Balt., 1970-73, Broad St. Christian Ch., Tampa, Fla., 1973—. Bd. dirs. Indian Lake Camp, Lake Wales, Fla., 1975—. Served with U.S. Army, 1962-66, Vietnam. Mem. Christian Ministers Assn. (pres. Tampa chpt. 1977-78), Ch. History Soc., Disciples of Christ Hist. Soc., Bibl. Archeology Soc., ALA, Fla. Library Assn. Home: 7304 Dixon Ave Tampa FL 33604 Office: Broad St Christian Ch 7401 Dixon Ave Tampa FL 33604

WOOD, JAMES LAWRENCE, evangelist, So. Baptist Conv.; b. Atlanta, Jan. 31, 1948; s. Charles Aaron and Sara (McClam) W.; B.A., John Brown U., 1970; M. Div., Southwestern Bapt. Theol. Sem., 1974; m. Paula Kay Hanson, Dec. 20, 1969; children—Nathan Lawrence, Timothy Paul. Ordained to ministry, 1970; pastor Mountain Bible Ch., Jane, Mo., 1968; asst. pastor

First Bapt. Ch., Bentonville, Ark., 1969-70; asst. dean Sch. Evangelism Greater SW Billy Graham Crusade, Dallas, 1971; evangelist, statewide coordinator Meet Jesus City-Wide Crusades Tex., Ft. Worth, 1971—; tchr. W.I.N. Lay Evangelism Sch. Tex., Ft. Worth, 1974—; dean Youth Evangelism Sch. Tex., Ft. Worth, 1974—; evangelist, tchr. Nationwide Christian Discipleship Seminar, 1975—; minister at large Internat. Evangelism Assn., Ft. Worth, 1976—. Mem. Conf. So. Bapt. Evangelists for State of Tex., Conf. Evangelists of the So. Bapt. Conv. Home: 6560 McCart Court Fort Worth TX 76133 Office: Box 22005 Fort Worth TX 76122

WOOD, JOHN ATKINS, religion educator, minister, Southern Baptist Convention; b. Birmingham, Ala., Apr. 8, 1938; s. LeRoy and Mary Grace (Stiff) W.; m. Suzanne Elizabeth Raymond, Aug. 10, 1962; children: Karl, Chad, Stephen, Kevin. B.A., Columbia Bible Coll., 1960; postgrad. Samford U., 1961, Dallas Theol. Sem., 1961-63, U. Notre Dame, 1974, 75; B.D., Southwestern Bapt. Theol. Sem., 1966; Ph.D., Baylor U., 1975. Ordained to ministry Bapt. Ch., 1966. Dir. Christian Soc. Ministries, Waco, Tex., 1968-71; dir. Caritas of Waco, Catholic Charities, 1973-76; dir. program devel. Christian Life Commn., So. Bapt. Conv., Nashville, 1976-81; asst. prof. religion Baylor U., Waco, 1981—. Contbr. articles, reviews to profl. publs. Sec. bd. Alcohol Research Info. Service, Lansing, Mich., 1981—; mem. exec. com. Econ. Opportunity Advancement Corp., Waco, 1982—; bd. dirs. Concerned Citizens on Alcoholism, Waco, 1982—, N. Conway Inst., Boston. Mem. Assn. Bapt. Profs. Religion, Am. Acad. Religion. Democrat. Home: 5014 Ridgeview Dr Waco TX 76710 Office: Baylor U Dept Religion Waco TX 76798

WOOD, JOHN RALPH, minister, General Association of Regular Baptist Churches; b. Chgo., Dec. 19, 1927; s. John Walter and Lydia Neonta (DuKate) W.; m. Anna Jean Mitchell, Oct. 1, 1949; 1 child, Ronald Mark. Student, Moody Bible Inst., 1947-49. Ordained to ministry Bapt. Ch., 1953. Pastor Lapaz Union Ch., Ind., 1952-54, Calvary Bapt. Ch., Ecorse, Mich., 1955-62, Bellefontaine, Ohio, 1962-73; state rep., editor Mich. Assn. Regular Bapt. Chs., 1973-82; pastor 1st Bapt. Ch., Cass City, Mich., 1982—; trustee Skyview Ranch Youth Camp, Millersburg, Ohio, 1971-73; council mem. Ohio Assn. Regular Bapts, 1972-73; exec. bd. dirs. Grand Rapids Bapt. Coll., Mich., 1975—. Editor Bapt. Testimony, 1974-83. Contbr. articles to religious jours. Home: 4644 Oak St Cass City MI 48726 Office: First Bapt Ch 6420 Houghton St Cass City MI 48726

WOOD, KENNETH PERRY, minister, So. Baptist Conv.; b. Corpus Christi, Sept. 28, 1948; s. Joseph Perry and Dorothy (Cox) W.; B.A., Wayland Baptist Coll., 1970; postgrad. Southwestern Baptist Theol. Sem., 1973-74, Perkins Sch. Theology So. Meth. U., 1974-75; m. Sharyn Jennette Hamphill, Aug. 22, 1970. Ordained to ministry, 1977; program dir. Sta. KHBL-FM, Plainview, Tex., 1969-71; minister youth 1st Baptist Ch., Plainview, Tex., 1970-72; minister youth edn. 1st Baptist Ch., Richardson, Tex., 1972—. Home: 2821 Lancer Ln Garland TX 75042 Office: Box 1357 Richardson TX 75081

WOOD, MILTON LEGRAND, bishop, Episcopal Ch.; b. Selma, Ala., Aug. 21, 1922; s. Milton LeGrand and Roberta Owen (Hawkins) W.; B.A., U. of South, 1943, M.Div., 1945, D.D., 1967; m. Ann Scott, May 3, 1949; children—Leigh (Mrs. Charles Pate), Ann (Mrs. Barry Benedict), Milton LeGrand IV, Roberta. Ordained to ministry Episcopal Ch., 1946, bishop, 1967; rector St. Paul's Ch., Mobile, Ala., 1946-52, All Saints Ch., Atlanta, 1952-60; dir. Appleton Home, archdeacon, Macon, Ga., 1960-63; canon to ordinary, Atlanta, 1963-67; suffragan bishop Episcopal Diocese of Atlanta, 1967-74; dep. for adminstrn. for presiding bishop Nat. Episcopal Ch., N.Y.C., from 1974; ret., 1984. Bd. dirs. Egleston Hosp., Atlanta. Mem. Ga. Interchurch Assn. (pres.). Home: PO Box 420 Elberta AL 36530

WOOD, MORRIS VERNON, minister, college president, Christian Church (Disciples of Christ); b. Oconee, Ga., July 28, 1933; s. Edgar Kindrell and Evelyn Estelle (Brantley) W.; m. Winifred Juanita Mason, Dec. 23, 1951; children: Barbara E. (Mrs. John I. Crutchfield), Vernon, Virginia A. (Mrs. C.E. Davis), Cherrie M. (Mrs. Herbert Knight), Thomas E. A.A., Ga. Mil. Coll., 1952; B.B.A., U. Ga., 1959; M.Div., Lexington Theol. Sem., 1969; D.D. (hon.), Christian Coll. of Ga., 1979. Ordained to ministry Christian Ch. (Disciples of Christ), 1969. Minister, Chapel Christian Ch., Winder, Ga., 1956-61, First Christian Ch., Wrightsville, Ga., 1961-66, Hustonville Christian Ch., Ky., 1966-69; sr. minister Central Christian Ch., Augusta, Ga., 1969-79, First Christian Ch., Charleston, S.C., 1979-82; pres. Christian Coll. of Ga., Athens, 1982—; trustee Nat. Interfaith Coalition Aging, Athens, 1982; mem. adv. bd. Dept. Pastoral Care-Gen. Hosp., Athens, 1982; pres. Metro-Athens Ministerial Assn., 1984. Served with USAR, 1954-56. Recipient Excellence award Am. Bible Soc., 1969; named Minister of Yr., Christian Ch. in Ga., 1962. Lodge: Masons. Home: 1050 Cherokee Circle Athens GA 30606 Office: Christian Coll of GA Inc 220 S Hull St Athens GA 30605

WOOD, STEPHEN WRAY, minister, religious educator, Society of Friends; b. Winston Salem, N.C., Oct. 6, 1948; s. D.W. Wood and Annie Lee (Harris) W.; m. Starr Smith, June 18, 1978; children: Allyson, Joshua. Th.B., John Wesley Coll., High Point, N.C., 1970; B.A., Asbury Coll., Ky., 1973; M.A., U. N.C., 1979; D.Min., Luther Rice Sem., Fla., 1980. Ordained minister Society of Friends. Asst. dean, asst. prof. John Wesley Coll., High Point, N.C., 1975-81; assoc. pastor Glenwood Friends Ch., Greensboro, N.C., 1979-81; pastor Deep River Friends Ch., High Point, 1981-84; adj. prof. John Wesley Coll., High Point, 1985—; pres. Remnant Assocs., High Point, 1977—; pres. Triad Christian Counseling, Greensboro, N.C., 1979; bd. trustees John Wesley Coll., High Point, 1981—; bd. dirs. Friends Ctr.-Guilford Coll., Greensboro, 1982—. Contbr. articles to religious jours. Composer, singer religious music. Vice chmn. Guilford County Republican Party, N.C., 1981-85; rep. N.C. State Ho. of Reps., 1985—. Served with U.S. Army, 1970-71. Mem. Broadcast Music Inc. (affiliate 1978). Avocations: golf; book collecting; fishing; tennis. Home: PO Box 5172 High Point NC 27262 Office: Remnant Assocs PO Box 5172 202 Blvd St High Point NC 27262

WOOD, SUZI ROBERTSON, educator, United Methodist Church; b. Ft. Worth, Jan. 10, 1952; d. Kenneth Ray and Margaret (Bell) Robertson; m. W. Dale Wood, Aug. 13, 1971; 1 child, Michael Robertson. B. Liberal Studies cum laude, St. Edward's U., Austin, Tex., 1981; M. Religious Edn., U. St. Thomas, Houston, 1983, specialization in liturgical studies, 1983—. Cert., edn. for ministry Sch. of Theology, U. of South, Sewanee. Registrar Camp Allen, Episcopal Diocese of Tex., Navasota, 1975-79; youth dir. First United Methodist Ch., Navasota, 1978-79; ednl. asst. St. John's United Meth. Ch., Richmond, Tex., 1979-82; dir. Christian edn. Klein United Meth. Ch., Spring, Tex., 1982—; council del. Episcopal Diocese of Tex., 1977-78; trustee United Meth. Army, Houston, 1982—. Bd. dirs. Meml. Chase Swim Team, Spring, 1985. Recipient Christian Devel. award So. Bapt. Conv., 1980; St. Edward's U. scholar, 1980-81, U. St. Thomas scholar, 1983-84. Mem. Nat. Christian Educator's Fellowship United Methodist Ch., Tex. Conf. Christian Educator's Fellowship United Meth. Ch. Democrat. Home: 17218 Chaseloch St Spring TX 77379 Office: Klein United Methodist Ch 5920 FM 2920 Spring TX 77388

WOOD, WILLIAM RAYMOND, minister, Baptist Convention of Ontario and Quebec. b. Toronto, Ont., Can., Feb. 15, 1931; s. Sidney and Grace May Isabel (Foster) W.; m. Joan Katherine Bradt, June 11, 1955; children: Katherine Ann, William Robert, Janice Heather. B.A., McMaster U., 1954, B.D., 1957; Th.M., Knox Coll., 1974; D. Ministry, So. Bapt. Theol. Sem., 1982. Ordained to ministry Baptist Conv. Ontario and Quebec 1957. Minister Humber Blvd. Bapt. Ch., Toronto, Ont., 1955-57, Ferndale Bapt. Ch., Toronto, 1957-64; assoc. minister Walmer Rd. Bapt. Ch., Toronto, 1964-70; sr. minister First Bapt. Ch., Saskatoon, Sask., 1970-80, Highland Bapt. Ch., Kitchener, Ont., 1980—; pres. Bapt. Union Western Can., Calgary, Alta., 1978-79, Bapt. Conv. Ont. and Que., Toronto, 1984-85; trustee McMaster Div. Coll., Hamilton, Ont., 1982—. Author: (with others) Canadian Baptist History and Polity, 1982. Home: 107 Woodington Pl Waterloo ON N2L 5X8 Canada Office: Highland Bapt Ch 135 Highland Rd W Kitchener ON N2M 3B9 Canada

WOOD, WILLIAM ROBERT, minister, United Methodist Church. b. Mt. Olivet, KY., Nov. 17, 1931; s. William Fant and Hazel Dean (Collins) W.; m. Sarah Joyce Brierly, June 2, 1950; children: Robert Lamont, Denise Lynne, William Bradley. B.A., Asbury Coll., 1954; M.Div., Emory U., 1956; D. of Ministry, Internat. Bible Inst. and Sem., 1985. Ordained to ministry United Methodist, 1950. Pastor, McKendree and Dover, Maysville, Ky., 1951-53, Morefield and Hdqrs., Carlisle, Ky., 1953-54, New Oregon Circuit, Ft. Payne, Ala., 1954-56, Mt. Pleasant, Owingsville, Ky., 1956-58, Millerburg Meth., Ky., 1958-61, Benham Community, Ky., 1961-65, Bowman Mem., Hazard, Ky., 1965-71, First United Methodist, Flemingsburg, Ky., 1971-75, Epworth, Lexington Ky., 1975-81; dist. supt. Ashland Dist. United Meth. Ch., Ky. Conf., 1981—; chaplin City of Hazard, 1966-71, Mcpl. League, State of Ky., 1969-71. Recipient Minister of Year award, Ky. Conf., 1958, 68, Plaque of Honor award, Community Action Program, 1975. Mem. Ky. Colonel. Democrat. Lodge: Lions (Benham) (chmn. eye com. 1961-65) (Hazard) (flag com. 1965-68). Home and Office: 3000 Belhaven Dr Russell KY 41169

WOODALL, HARRY ELSWORTH, missionary, So. Bapt. Conv.; b. Malvern, Ark., Aug. 19, 1929; s. Sidney Jefferson and Lora (Burns) W.; B.A., Ouachita Bapt. U., 1960, M.A., 1967; M.Div., So. Bapt. Theol. Sem., 1967; m. Geraldine Harkrider, Aug. 15, 1952; children—Melissa Jane, Melanie June. Ordained to ministry, 1960; pastor Jessieville (Ark.) Bapt. Ch., 1960-62, Brooks (Ky.) Bapt. Ch., 1962-66, Little Union Bapt. Ch., Fairfield, Ky., 1966-68; dir. Christian Social Ministries, Hot Springs, Ark., 1968-76; tchr. religion Garland County Community Coll., Hot Springs, Ark., 1975—. Mem. joint com. Nat. Bapts. and So. Bapts., 1975. Bd. dirs. Hotsprings Children's Home, 1976; mem. Juvenile Ct. Council, 1975; mem. study com. Hot Springs Pub. Schs., 1976. Recipient award City of Hotsprings, 1972. Home: 121 Nickels St Hot Springs AR 71901 Office: 2350 Central Ave Hot Springs AR 71901

WOODBRIDGE, JOHN DUNNING, theology educator, minister, Evangelical Free Church of America; b. Salisbury, N.C., May 24, 1941; s. Charles Jahleel and Ruth (Dunning) W.; m. Susan Jane Frerichs, June 28, 1970; children: Elisabeth Ann, Joshua David. B.A. in History, Wheaton Coll. (Ill.), 1963; M.A. in History, Mich. State U., 1965; Doctorat de Troisieme Cycle, U. Toulouse (France), 1969; M.Div., Trinity Evang. Divinity Sch., Deerfield, Ill., 1971. Licensed to ministry Evang. Free Ch. of Am., 1973. Vis. prof. Am. history U. Toulouse, 1969-70; asst. prof. Trinity Coll., Deerfield, 1970-74, prof. ch. history Trinity Evang. Divinity Sch., Deerfield, 1970—. Author: Biblical Authority, 1982; co-author: The Gospel in America, 1979, 82; co-editor: The Evangelicals, 1975, 77; Eardmans' Handbook to Christianity, 1983; America, 1983; Scripture and Truth, 1983. Richard Simon: Additions, 1983. Fellow Fulbright Found., 1965-66, NEH, 1973-74, Am. Council Learned Socs., 1976-77, Herzog August Bibliothek, 1982, Assn. of Theol. Schs., 1985. Mem. Am. Soc. Ch. History, Am. Soc. Eighteenth Century Studies, Société Francaise d'Étude du 18e Siecle. Republican. Office: Trinity Evang Divinity Sch Deerfield IL 60015

WOODHAM, FRED DANIEL, minister, Church of God; b. Fitzgerald, Ga., May 14, 1909; s. Beaty William and Viola (Barnes) W.; grad. high sch.; m. Thelma Doris Ingram, Nov. 15, 1936; children—Faye Woodham Woodard), Fredrick, Doris Woodham Ragalyi, Phyllis Woodham Smith. Ordained to ministry Ch. of God., 1936; pastor Chs. of God, Bainbridge, Ga., 1936-44, Whitmire, S.C., 1944-52, 67-70, Palatka, Fla., 1952-55, Valdosta, Ga., 1956-58, Moss, Miss., 1960-65, Panama City, Fla., 1965-67, Ch. of God., Aiken, S.C., 1970-80. State chmn. Ga. Ministerial Assembly, Ch. of God., 1957-58, S.C. Assembly of Ch. of God, 1968-69; pres. Whitmire Ministerial Assn., 1967-68. Lion. Editor: Booster, 1972-74. Home: 155 Sharyn Ln Aiken SC 29801

WOODIE, GLENN NORMAN, minister, Baptist Church; b. Ashe County, N.C., Nov. 21, 1935; s. Edward Hampton and Bertie Ethel (Sexton) W.; student pub. schs.; m. Hazel Arlene Paisley, June 29, 1957; children: Debra Kaye, Linda Arlene, Rebecca Ann, David Glenn. Ordained to ministry, 1951; asst. pastor Mt. Olive Bapt. Ch., Todd, N.C., 1955-62, Clifton Bapt. Ch., Warrensville, N.C., 1962-66; pastor Calvary Bapt. Ch., West Jefferson, N.C., 1963-67, Rock Creek Bapt. Ch., Creston, N.C., 1963-72, Valley Home Bapt. Ch., Todd, also Mountain View Bapt. Ch., Grayson, N.C., 1970-72, Bapt. Home Bapt. Ch., Creston, 1969-77, Temple Ind. Missionary Bapt. Ch., West Jefferson, N.C., 1982—; rep. of Bapt. Children's Home, Inc., Tomasville, N.C., 1969-71. Mem. Ashe (N.C.) Bapt. Assn. Home: 305 Hamilton Dr Jefferson NC 28640

WOODRICK, HERBERT LAVELLE, minister, United Methodist Church; b. Meridian, Miss., Mar. 27, 1930; s. James Benjamin and Marie (Wilkerson) W.; m. Patricia Banks, Sept. 7, 1954; children: Deborah, Herbert Lavelle, Rebecca. B.A., Millsaps Coll., 1952; M.Div., Emory U., 1955. Ordained to ministry Methodist Ch., 1952. Pastor Lovely Ln. United Meth. Ch., Natchez, Miss., 1955-57; assoc. pastor Capitol St. United Meth. Ch., Jackson, Miss., 1957-60; pastor Sturgis Meth. Ch., Miss., 1960-63, St. Luke United Meth. Ch., Tupelo, Miss., 1963-69, St. John United Meth. Ch., Greenwood, Miss., 1969-71, Oxford-Univ. United Meth. Ch., Oxford, Miss., 1971-78, First United Meth. Ch., New Albany, Miss., 1978-80; dist. supt. Starkville dist. No. Miss. Conf., United Meth. Ch., 1980—, chmn. Bd. Ordained Ministry, 1972-76; chmn. religious observances Bicentennial Com., Oxford, Miss., 1976. Trustee Millsaps Coll., Jackson, Miss., 1972-76, Wood Jr. Coll., Mathiston, Miss., 1980—. Lodges: Lions, Rotary, Masons, Shriners. Home and Office: PO Drawer 1329 Starkville MS 39759

WOODRING, DEWAYNE STANLEY, religious association executive; b. Gary, Ind., Nov. 10, 1931; s. J. Stanley and Vera Luella (Brown) W.; B.S., Northwestern U., 1954, postgrad. in public and community relations; M.Div., Garrett Theol. Sem., 1957; L.H.D., Mt. Union Coll., 1967; D.D., Salem Coll., 1970; m. Donna Jean Wishart, June 15, 1957; children: Judith Lynn (Mrs. Richard Bigelow), Beth Ellen. Ordained deacon, 1955, elder, 1957, minister, 1957; staff mem. radio services dept. Second Assembly, World Council Chs., Evanston, Ill., 1954; minister edn. Griffith (Ind.) Meth. Ch., 1955-57; minister adminstrn. and program First Meth. Ch., Eugene, Oreg., 1957-59; dir. pub. relations Dakotas Area, Meth. Ch., 1959-60, Ohio Area, 1960-64; adminstrv. exec. to bishop Ohio East Area, United Meth. Ch., Canton, 1964-77; asst. gen. sec. Gen. Council on Fin. and Adminstrn., United Meth. Ch., Evanston, 1977-79, assoc. gen. sec., 1979-84; exec. dir. Religious Conf. Mgmt. Assn., 1982—; writer-dir. TV series Parables in Miniature, 1957-59; originator The Word and Music nat. radio

433 WHO'S WHO IN RELIGION

series, 1963; chmn. communications com. Ohio Council Chs., 1961-65; mem. com. on entertainment and program N.Central Jurisdictional Conf., 1968-76, chmn., 1972-76; mem. Council on Ministries, 1972-76; mem. Div. of Interpretation, United Meth. Ch., 1969-72; mem. Commn. on Gen. Conf., 1972—, bus. mgr., exec. dir., 1976—; mem. exec. com. Assn. United Meth. Founds., 1968-72; del. World Meth. Conf., London, 1966, Dublin, Ireland, 1976, Honolulu, 1981; participant U.S. Dept. Def. Joint Civilian Orientation Conf., 1970; chmn. bd. mgrs. United Meth. Bldg., Evanston, 1977-84; v.p., trustee Copeland Oaks Retirement Community, 1969-76; v.p. Ohio East Area United Meth. Found., 1967-76; advisor East Ohio Conf. Communications Commn., 1968-76. Pres. Guild Assocs., 1971—; lectr., cons. fgn. travel. Mem. Am. Soc. Assn. Execs., Conv. Liaison Council (bd. dirs. exec. com.), Meeting Planners Internat., Def. Orientation Conf. Assn. (dir.), Nat. Assn. Expn. Mgrs., Cert. Meeting Profls. (exec. bd.). Editor Dakotas Area News, 1959-60, Ohio Area News, 1960-64, Ohio East Area News, 1964-73. Office: One Hoosier Dome Suite 120 Indianapolis IN 46225

WOODRUFF, FRANKLIN EUGENE, minister, Southern Baptist Convention; b. Hogansville, Ga., July 2, 1934; s. Ira and Miti Mae (Garrett) W.; m. Dianne Ramsay, Sept. 22, 1957; children: Woody, Vicki, Mark, Chad. B.A., Samford U., 1967; M.Th. with honors, New Orleans Bapt. Theol. Sem., 1971. Ordained to ministry Baptist Ch., 1965. Pastor New Bethel Bapt. Ch., Braggs, Ala., 1965-67, Mt. Nebo Bapt. Ch., Roseland, La., 1969-72, Porter Meml. Bapt. Ch., Columbus, Ga., 1972-75, Calvary Bapt. Ch., Cottonwood, Ala., 1976-80, Sister Spring Bapt. Ch., Tyler, Ala., 1980—. Chaplain Tyler Community Club, 1980—. Served with U.S. Army, 1954-56. Democrat. Home: Rt 1 Box 17A Tyler AL 36785 Office: Sister Spring Bapt Ch Rt 1 Box 6CC Tyler AL 36785

WOODRUFF, WILLIAM JENNINGS, minister, educator, Church of the Nazarene; b. Vassar, Kans., Sept. 30, 1925; s. Kenney Arthur and Carrie (Brecheisen) W.; m. Wanda Lea Shuck, Aug. 18, 1962; children: Teresa Kaye, Bruce Alan, Neal Wayne. B.A., Ottawa U., Kans., 1954; M.Div., Fuller Theol. Sem., 1958; M.R.E., M.Th., Asbury Theol. Sem., 1964; Th.D. candidate Concordia Theol. Sem., 1985—. Ordained to ministry Ch. of the Nazarene, 1960. Youth dir. Hyde Park EUB Ch., Wichita, Kans., 1958-59; pastor Attica EUB Ch., Kans., 1960-62, Salem EUB Ch., Jersey City, 1964-65, Third Ch. EUB, Phila., 1965-68; prof. Olivet Nazarene Coll., Kankakee, Ill., 1968—. Contbr. articles to profl. jours. Served with U.S. Army, 1951-53. Mem. Wesleyan Theol. Soc., Evang. Theol. Soc., Near East Archaeol. Soc., Evang. Tchr. Tng. Assn., Theta Phi. Republican. Office: Olivet Nazarene Coll Box 173 Kankakee IL 60901

WOODSON, CHARLES RAY, minister, American Baptist Churches in the U.S.A.; b. Grosse Pointe, Mich., Sept. 25, 1923; s. George Ray and Julia Mildred (Cornwell) W.; B.A., Kalamazoo Coll., 1945; B.D., Crozer Theol. Sem., Chester, Pa., 1948; m. Charlotte Edna Schwem, Feb. 23, 1946; children: Shirley Ann (Mrs. James Graham), George Ray II, Barbara Gwen (Mrs. John Collins), Marilynn Baker (Mrs. James Graves). Ordained to ministry, 1947; pastor chs., Washington, Wis., Pa., Ind., 1946-53, 59-67; dir. jr. high work, bd. edn. and publ. Am. Bapt. Chs. in U.S.A., Phila., 1953-59; sr. pastor 1st Bapt. Ch., Waukegan, Ill., 1967-82; pastor Union Ch., Lake Bluff, Ill., 1983—; mem. exec. com. Chgo. Bapt. Assn., 1968-82, chmn. dept. Christian edn., 1968-71, chmn. dept. evangelism, 1975-78, v.p., 1978-79, mem. communication commn. Ch. Fedn. Chgo., 1969-74, mem. gen. bd., 1974—; pres. Waukegan Area Ministerial Assn., 1970-71; mem. Am. Bapt. Evangelism Team, 1975—; mem. gen. bd. Am. Bapt. Chs. in U.S.A., 1980-83, mem. bd. ednl. ministries, 1980-83; chaplain Victory Meml. Hosp., Waukegan, Ill., 1974—. Mem. exec. bd. N.E. Ill. council Boy Scouts Am., 1971-74; chmn. Lake County Service for Counseling and Marriage, 1974—; bd. dirs. Waukegan Area Council Chs., 1968-72, chmn. radio ministry, 1968-70, chmn. community relations, 1970-72. Author curriculum material. Home: 531 E Prospect Ave Lake Bluff IL 60044 Office: 525 E Prospect Ave Lake Bluff IL 60044

WOODSON, RAYMOND JAMES, minister, United Pentecostal Church International; medical technologist; b. Glendale, Calif., May 18, 1954; s. Richard Arvel and Marjorie Agnes (Quirk) W.; m. Jill Marlene Ballou, Aug. 31, 1974; children: Amy Marlene, Raymond James, Timothy James. A.S., George Washington U., 1977; diploma Christian Service Tng. Inst., 1979. Ordained to ministry, United Pentecostal Ch. Internat. Sectional Sunday sch. dir., western dist. United Pentecostal Ch., Calif. and Nev., 1981-82, pastoral asst., San Diego, 1981-82, pastor, Vancouver, Wash., 1983—, dist. Sunday sch. dir. State of Wash., 1983—, mem. Gen. Sunday Sch. Bd., Hazelwood, Mo., 1983—. Nuclear medicine technologist Southwest Washington Hosps., Vancouver, 1983—. Contbr. articles to profl. jours. Served with USN, 1973-79. Home: 910A W 29th St Vancouver WA 98660 Office: United Pentecostal Ch 1110 E 33d St PO Box 2725 Vancouver WA 98668

WOODSON, WALTER BENJAMIN, JR., minister, Southern Baptist Convention; b. Lynchburg, Va., Dec. 29, 1929; s. Walter Benjamin and Flora W. (Wooldridge) W.; B.S., Hampden-Sydney Coll., 1950; M.Div., So. Bapt. Theol. Sem., Louisville, 1954; M.S., Radford (Va.) Coll., 1967; D.Min., Southeastern Bapt. Sem., 1982; m. Anna Phyllis Greenwell, June 3, 1955; children—Ben, Joe, Nathan. Ordained to ministry, 1952; pastor chs. in Ky. and Va., 1954-65; prof. English, Wingate (N.C.) Bapt. Coll., 1965—; interim pastor chs. in N.C. Address: Box 336 Wingate NC 28174

WOODWARD, ROBERT FRANKLIN, minister, Southern Baptist Convention; b. Winston-Salem, N.C., June 29, 1921; s. MacLeon and Nellie Viola (Ross) W.; m. Jean Nelson, Sept. 1, 1945; children: Robert Franklin, Claire Woodward Wiles, Peter N., Jonathan R. B.A., Wheaton Coll., 1945; M.Div., So. Bapt. Theol. Sem., 1948; D.D. (hon.), Alderson-Broaddus Coll., 1982. Ordained to ministry Baptist Ch., 1948. Pastor 1st Bapt. Ch., Princess Anne, Md., 1949-52, 1st Bapt. Ch., Frederick, Md., 1952-74, Winchester, Va., 1974—; mem. faculty U. Richmond Extension, 1952-60; mem. budget com. Bapt. Assn. Va., 1983—, mem. gen. bd., 1976-80; mem. Christian life commn. So. Bapt. Conv., 1954-56, trustee Annuity Bd., 1958-64; chmn. resoluations com. So. Bapt. Conv., 1964, mem. com. on bds., 1957, 65, mem. Bapt. edn. study task force, 1962-64; mem. minister's adv. com. Alderson-Broaddus Coll., 1979-81, 84—; mem. state mission bd. Bapt. Conv. Md., 1951-53, pres. bd., 1968, mem. exec. com., 1952-70, chmn. exec. com., 1961-63; pres. Bapt. Conv. Md., 1961-63; trustee Bapt. Home Md., 1965-74; missionary, Quito, Ecuador, 1984. Regional editor So. Bapt. Ency., 1958. Bd. dirs. chpt. ARC, 1975-84, chmn. bd., 1980-82. Mem. Winchester Ministerial Assn. (past pres.). Republican. Lodge: Rotary (Winchester). Home: 1013 Caroline St Winchester VA 22601 Office: PO Box 77 Winchester VA 22601

WOODWARD, WAYNE WILLIAM, minister, librarian, United Methodist Church; b. Greensburg, Ind., May 4, 1930; s. Arthur Coy and Hazel Prue (Ayres) W.; m. H. Corinne Vaughn, Jan. 17, 1956; children: Gail, Karen. A.B., Taylor U., 1952; B.D., Asbury Theol. Sem., 1955; M.A., Appalachian Coll., 1960; M.L.S., U. Ky., 1967. Ordained to ministry, United Meth. Ch., as elder, 1959. Minister United Meth. Ch., N.C., 1959-65; adminstrv. asst. to librarian Asbury Theol. Sem., Wilmore, Ky., 1965-67; librarian Asbury Coll., Wilmore, 1967-77, reference librarian, 1977-78; librarian Wesley Bibl. Sem., Jackson, Miss., 1978—. Mem. Am. Theol. Library Assn. Home: 1752 Waycona Dr Jackson MS 39204 Office: Wesley Bibl Sem Box 9938 Jackson MS 39206

WOODWORTH, HAROLD G., minister, Lutheran Church-Missouri Synod; b. Milw., Apr. 28, 1933; s. Harold G. and Nettie A. (Megow) W.; m. Bernice M. Livangood, June 9, 1956; children: Mark, David, Karen, Kathryn. B.Th., Concordia Sem., Springfield, Ill., 1958, M.Div., 1973; M.A., Sangamon State U., 1973; D.Ministry, Wartburg Theol. Sem., 1976. Ordained to ministry Luth. Ch., 1958. Pastor, Prince of Peace Luth. Ch., New Orleans, 1958-63, Concordia Luth. Ch., Birmingham, Ala., 1963-64, Zion Luth. Ch., Colby, Wis., 1964-65, Salem Luth. Ch., Jacksonville, Ill., 1968-76, Our Redeemer Luth. Ch., Jacksonville, 1976—; cir. counselor Luth. Ch.-Mo. Synod, New Orleans, 1960-63, sec. mission bd., 1960-64; dist. chmn. Student Aid Com., Springfield, 1982—; bd. dirs. Concordia Tract Mission, St. Louis, 1980—. Contbr. articles to mags. Bd. dirs. Sherwood Eddy YMCA, Jacksonville, 1970-76; pres. Morgan County ARC, 1972-74; v.p. Community Services Block Grant Bd., Morgan County, 1983—. Served as chaplain to capt. U.S. Army, 1965-68, Vietnam. Recipient Servus Ecclesiae Christi, Concordia Sem., 1979. Mem. Ill. Sociol. Assn., Ctr. Am. Archeology. Lodge: Kiwanis (pres. 1983—). Home: 47 Westfair Dr Jacksonville IL 62650 Office: Our Redeemer Luth Ch 405 Massey Ln Jacksonville IL 62650

WOOLFOLK, T. E., bishop. Bishop Church of Our Lord Jesus Christ of the Apostolic Faith, Inc., also gen. sec. Office: 2081 Adam Clayton Powell Jr Blvd New York NY 10027*

WOOLSEY, GARY FREDERICK, bishop, Anglican Church of Canada; b. Brantford, Ont., Can., Mar. 16, 1942; s. William Frederick and Doreen Pearl (Wood) W.; m. Marie Elaine Tooker, Aug. 4, 1967; children: Todd, Kathleen, Andrew, Tina. B.A., U. Western Ont., 1964; B.Th., Huron Coll., London, Ont., 1967, D.D. (hon.), 1984. Ordained priest Anglican Ch. of Can., 1967, bishop, 1983; cert. tchr., Winnipeg, Can. Priest, Diocese of Keewatin, Kenora, Ont., 1967-72; rector St. Mark's Ch., Norway House, Manitoba, 1972-76, St. Paul's Ch., Churchill, Manitoba, 1976-80; program dir. Diocese of Keewatin, Kenora, Ont., 1980-83; bishop Diocese of Athabasca, Peace River, Alta., 1983—; mem. World Mission Sub-Com., 1980, Nat. Exec. Council, 1983—, Provincial Exec. Council, 1982—. Office: Diocese of Athabasca Box 279 Peace River AB T0H 2X0 Canada

WOOTERS, BRIAN ALLAN, minister, Southern Baptist Convention; b. East St. Louis, Ill., Aug. 9, 1954; s. Alfred Elbert Wooters and Marjorie Lucille (Steele) McClain; m. Susan Marie Franklin, June 22, 1974; 1 child, Christina Marie. B.A., Union U., Jackson, Tenn., 1984. Ordained to ministry So. Bapt. Conv., 1978. Outreach dir. Jerome Lane Bapt. Ch., Cahokia, Ill., 1975-76; asst. music dir. 1st Bapt. Ch., Dupo, Ill., 1976-78; pastor Tumbling Creek Bapt. Ch., Gleason, Tenn., 1978-84. Recipient award Am. Bible Soc., 1984; Presdl. Preaching and Congl. Leadership scholar So. Bapt. Theol. Sem. Mem. Weakley County Bapt. Assn. (pub. relations com. 1982-84, missions com. 1982-84, preacher ann. doctrinal sermon 1982), Alpha Chi. Republican. Office: So Bapt Theol Sem 2825 Lexington Rd Louisville KY 40280

WORRELL, GEORGE EDWARD, minister, So. Baptist Conv.; b. Dalhart, Tex., Jan. 26, 1930; s. Champ Clark and Deloris (Jackson) W.; B.A., Tex. Tech. Coll., 1951; B.D., Southwestern Bapt. Theol. Sem., 1955, Th.D., 1962; m. Betty Joy Haberer, Aug. 3, 1952; children—Edith, Ed, Molody, Dawn, Stephanie. Ordained to ministry, 1953; pastor ch., Durant, Okla., 1955-57, Ft. Worth, 1958-66, 1st Bapt. Ch., Lamesa, Tex., 1966-70; asso. for youth, academic and renewal evangelism Bapt. Gen. Conf. Tex., 1970—. Author: How to Take the Worry Out of Witnessing; editor: Resources for Renewal; contbr. articles to religious jours. Address: 306 Baptist Bldg Dallas TX 75201

WORTHINGTON, MELVIN, Exec. sec. Free Will Baptists, Nashville. Office: Free Will Baptists PO Box 1088 Nashville TN 37202*

WOUDSTRA, SIERD J(AN), minister, editor, Christian Reformed Church in North America; b. Doniaga, Friesland, The Netherlands, Feb. 4, 1928; came to U.S., 1953, naturalized, 1972; s. Jan S. and Ynskje (Wielinga) W.; m. Allerdina C. Bouwkamp, Aug. 15, 1953; children: John, Kathy, Irene, Christine, Timothy, Yvonne, Ingrid. A.B., Calvin Coll., 1955; B.D., Calvin Sem., 1958; Th.M., Westminster Sem., 1959, Th.D., 1963. Ordained to ministry Christian Reformed Ch., 1961. Pastor, Calvin Christian Reformed Ch., Ottawa, Ont., Can., 1961-65; prof. of Bible, Dordt Coll., Sioux Center, Iowa, 1965-67; librarian, lectr. in Old Testament, Calvin Sem., Grand Rapids, Mich., 1967-72; prof. of systematic theology Reformed Theol. Coll., Geelong, Australia, 1972-74; pastor Hobart Reformed Ch., Tasmania, Australia, 1975-77; prof. religion and theology Calvin Coll., Grand Rapids, Mich., 1977-81; editor De Wachter, 1983—. Author: Commentary on Song of Solomon. Contbr. articles to profl. jours. Translator: Christelijk Geloof (Hendrikus Berkhof). Vice pres. Dutch Internat. Soc., Grand Rapids, 1985—. Home: 2929 Giddings SE Grand Rapids MI 49508 Office: De Wachter 2850 Kalamazoo Ave SE Grand Rapids MI 49560

WOULLARD, RALPH WALDO, minister, American Baptist Convention; b. Starkville, Miss., Oct. 11, 1918; s. Ralph Waldo and Narah Alice (Baldwin) W.; m. Annette Jewel Rogers, Aug. 13, 1937; children: Ralph, Dorothy, Veronica, Roderick, Reginald. Student, Ala. State Coll., 1936-37; grad. Welch Coll. Mortuary Sci., 1940; M.Th., Miss. Bapt. Sem., 1955. Ordained to ministry Bapt. Ch. Pastor, Macedonia Bapt. Ch., Collins, Miss., 1966—, Shady Grove Bapt. Ch., Hattiesburg, Miss., 1969—; dean Miss. Bapt. Sem., Hattiesburg, 1979—; mem. holding bd. Miss. Bapt. Sem., Hattiesburg, 1973—; instr. ministers Second Sweet Pilgrim Congress, Hattiesburg, 1980—; instr. Dist. Minister's Conf., 1983—; numerous other civic and profl. positions. Mem. Optimist Evening Club, Hattiesburg, 1985—; life mem. NAACP. Named Community Leader of Am., 1969, Outstanding Contbr., Miss. Headstart Program, 1975, Col., Miss. Gov.'s Staff, 1976. Mem. Nat. Bapt. Conv. Am., South Miss. State Conv., First Sweet Pilgrim Assn., Second Sweet Pilgrim Assn. Lodge: Masons. Avocations: reading; fishing; swimming. Home: PO Box 1294 Hattiesburg MS 39403 Office: Miss Bapt Sem 1400 Country Club Rd Hattiesburg MS 39403

WREN, JIMMY PAUL, minister, Churches of Christ; b. Leland, Miss., Jan. 4, 1945; s. Jim Roy and Pauline (George) W.; m. Janelle Jefcoat, July 12, 1963; children: Jimmy, Jr., Jason Chris, Julie, Joanthan. B.A., Internat. Bible Coll., 1978; postgrad. Harding Grad. Sch. Religion, 1981-83; M.Th., Internat. Bible Inst., 1983. Minister, Ch. of Christ, Sneed, Ala., 1976, Lancaster, S.C., 1978-80, Leland, Miss., 1980-84; dean Sch. Religious Studies, Greenville, Miss., 1980—, lectureship dir., 1982—. Cert. leader Adventures in Christian Living, West Monroe, La., 1983. Cub master Delta council Boy Scouts Am., 1972-74. Recipient Appreciation award Sch. Religious Studies, 1983, Boy Scouts Am., 1973. Office: Ch of Christ PO Box 514 Greenville MS 38702

WRIGHT, C(HARLES) CONRAD, church history educator, Unitarian Universalist Association; b. Cambridge, Mass., Feb. 9, 1917; s. Charles Henry Conrad and Elizabeth Longfellow (Woodman) W.; m. Elizabeth Jane Hilgendorff, Sept. 4, 1948; children: Conrad E., Nielson, Elizabeth L. A.B., Harvard U., 1937, A.M., 1942, Ph.D., 1946; L.H.D., Meadville

Theol. Sch., 1968. Lectr. on ch. history Harvard Div. Sch., Cambridge, Mass., 1954-69, prof. Am. ch. history, 1969—, registrar, 1955-68; pres. Unitarian Hist. Soc., 1962-78; Dudleian lectr. Harvard U., 1960, John Bartlett lectr. on New England ch. history, 1969—. Author: The Beginnings of Unitarianism in America, 1955 (Carnegie award); The Liberal Christians, 1970. Editor: Religion in American Life, 1972; A Stream of Light, 1975. Am. Council Learned Socs. fellow, 1968, NEH fellow, 1981-82. Mem. Am. Hist. Assn., Am. Soc. Ch. History (council 1976-79), Orgn. Am. Historians, Cambridge Hist. Soc., Unitarian Universalist Hist. Soc. (bd. dirs. 1978—). Home: 983 Memorial Dr Apt 102 Cambridge MA 02138 Office: Harvard Div Sch 45 Francis Ave Cambridge MA 02138

WRIGHT, CLOYD HERBERT, minister, Am. Baptist Assn.; b. Glenwood, Ark., July 14, 1922; s. Joel S. and Retter (Grant) W.; student Missionary Bapt. Inst. and Sem., Little Rock, 1951-52; m. Mildred Marie Short, Dec. 20, 1941; 1 dau., Patsy Ann Podbevsek. Ordained to ministry, 1948; pastor Mt. Pleasant Missionary Bapt. Ch., Langley, Ark., 1976—. Home: Route 1 Glenwood AR 71943

WRIGHT, EUGENE ALLEN, minister, United Presbyn. Ch. in U.S.A.; b. Toronto, Ont., Can., May 27, 1943; s. Eugene Allen and Elsie Sophia (King) W.; came to U.S., 1963; B.Th., Ont. Bible Coll., 1969; M.Div. (Byington fellow), Gordon-Conwell Theol. Sem., 1972; m. Marjorie Ann Day, May 26, 1969; children—Sherrie Elizabeth, Pamelyn Sue. Ordained to ministry, 1973; pastor English Presbyn. Ch., Marietta, Pa., 1973-75, 1st Presbyn. Ch., Douglas, Ariz., 1975—. Mem. exec. com. Christian Edn. Resource Fair, 1975. Mem. evaluation com. Lancaster (Pa.) County Bd. Mental Health and Rehab., 1973-75. Home: 1245 10th St Douglas AZ 85607 Office: Box 410 Douglas AZ 85607

WRIGHT, JEREMIAH ALVESTA, JR., minister, United Ch. of Christ; b. Phila., Sept. 22, 1941; s. Jeremiah A. and Mary Elizabeth (Henderson) W.; A.B., Howard U., 1968, M.A., 1969; M.A., U. Chgo. Div. Sch., 1974; m. Esther Janet Bowden, Dec. 16, 1962; children—Janet Marie, Jeri Lynne. Ordained to ministry, 1967; asst. pastor Mt. Calvary Bapt. Ch., Rockville, Md., 1967-69; interim pastor Zion Bapt. Ch., Hagerstown, Md., 1969; asst. pastor Beth Eden Bapt. Ch., Chgo., 1969-71; pastor Trinity United Ch. of Christ, Chgo., 1972—. Research asst. Am. Assn. Theol. Schs., Chgo., 1970-72; exec. dir. Chgo. Center for Black Religious Studies, 1974-75; adj. prof. Chgo. Theol. Sem., 1974-75, Cath. Theol. Union, 1975; lectr. Chgo. Cluster of Theol. Schs., 1975—; bd. dirs. Office of Ch. in Soc., United Ch. Christ, 1976; bd. services Chgo. Met. Assn., United Ch. Christ, 1974-76; mem. commn. for racial justice United Ch. Christ, 1976—; mem. ecumenical strategy com. Ill. Conf. United Ch. Christ, 1975-76, resolutions com., 1973-74, urban ministers task force, 1975-76. Dir. Creative Writing Workshop, Chgo., 1969-70; community rep. Neighborhood Youth Corps program, Chgo., 1970-71; proposal writer, editor, Dropout Prevention Program, Bd. Edn., City of Chgo., 1971-72; bd. dirs. Malcolm X Sch. Nursing, 1974—. Howard U. grad. fellow, 1968-69; Rockefeller fellow, 1970-72; recipient Presdl. commendations Pres. Lyndon B. Johnson, 1965-66. Mem. Ch. Fedn. Greater Chgo., Emergency Sch. Aid Act/Urban Ministerial Alliance, Ill. Conf. Chs., Ministers for Racial and Social Justice, United Black Christians, Omega Psi Phi, Alpha Kappa Mu. Author: God Will Answer Prayer, 1974; Jesus Is His Name, 1975 (songs); also articles. Home: 10850 S Wallace Ave Chicago IL 60628 Office: 532 W 95th St Chicago IL 60620

WRIGHT, PAUL ORRIN, minister, Christ Fellowship Church; b. Melrose Park, Ill., Oct. 10, 1937; s. Vale Hycle and Claudine Marie (Norris) W.; A.B., Wheaton (Ill.) Coll., 1959; Th.M., Dallas Theol. Sem., 1963, Th.D., 1968; m. Lynne Hazel Duffecy, Aug. 19, 1961; children: Lisa Joy, Hugh Latimer, Jonathan Edwards, Andrea Lynne. Began ministry, 1966; instr. So. Bible Tng. Sch., Dallas, 1963-66; teaching fellow ch. history Dallas Theol. Sem., 1964-65; acad. dean Western Bible Coll., Denver, 1966-73, acting pres., 1969-72; prof. theology Columbia (S.C.) Sch. Bible and Missions, 1972—; pastor-tchr. Christ Fellowship Ch., Columbia, 1974-80. Recipient Charles S. Nash award ch. history Dallas Theol. Sem., 1963. Mem. Soc. Bibl. Lit., Evang. Theol. Soc. Home: 2116 Cunningham Rd Columbia SC 29210 Office: PO Box 3122 Columbia SC 29230

WRIGHT, ROBERT BRADLEY, Biblical scholar, United Church of Christ; university administrator; b. Jersey City, Apr. 6, 1934; s. Leonard and Marion (Macdonald) W.; m. Mary Lynette Halterman, Dec. 27, 1956; children: Kevin, Karen. B.D., Drake U., 1960; S.T.M., Hartford Sem. Found., 1964, Ph.D., 1966. Lectr. Boston U., 1966-67; asst. prof. Gettysburg Coll., Pa., 1967-69; adj. prof. Wilson Coll, Chambersburg, Pa., 1969-72; assoc. prof. Temple U., Phila., 1972—, asst. dean for grad. affairs, 1984—; archael. staff Gezer excavations Harvard U. and Hebrew Union Coll., 1966-71. Maps and photography editor: Westminster Dictionary of the Bible, 1969. Contbr. article to ency. Mem. sch. bd. Moorestown Twp., N.J., 1975-80. Mem. Soc. Bibl. Lit., Catholic Bibl. Assn., Am. Acad. Religion (exec. assoc. 1969-72). Office: Religion Dept Temple Univ Philadelphia PA 19192

WRIGHT, SARA-ALYCE PARSON See *Who's Who in America*, 43rd edition.

WU, TED TIEN-TZE, minister, Lutheran Church in America; b. Tou-Cheng Yilan, Republic of China, Sept. 4, 1920; came to U.S., 1972, naturalized, 1981; s. Wan-Cheng and Chuan Lee Wu; m. Anna Chun-Chu Lai, Jan. 10, 1945; children: Jonathan Hsien-ming, Albert Hsien-yang, Mei-maiu. M.Div., Taiwan Theol. Coll., Taipei, 1944; B.D., Th.M., Columbia Theol. Sem., 1960. Ordained to ministry East Coast Presbytery, 1947; accepted as minister Lutheran Church in America, 1983. Pastor, Hwalien Presbyn. Ch., Republic of China, 1944-50; founder, pastor Milun Presbyn. Church, Republic of China, 1950-55, Changchun Presbyn. Ch., Taipei, 1966-72, Asian Fellowship, Park Ridge, Ill., 1972-77, Grace Christian Ch., Huntington Beach, Calif., 1979—; pres. Presbyn. Bible Inst., Hsinchu, Republic of China, 1955-67; pastor, developer Luth. Ch. in Am., Santa Ana, Calif., 1983—; chmn. bd. dirs. Taiwan Theol. Coll., Taipei, 1957-58; chmn. bd. Christian edn. Presbyn. Ch. in Taiwan, 1963-64, 65-66; moderator Seven Stars Presbytery of Presbyn. Ch. in Taiwan, 1969-70; vice moderator North Synod of Presbyn. Ch. in Taiwan, 1969-70. Home: 14081 Magnolia St Space 169 Westminster CA 92683 Office: Grace Luth Ch 1416 S Bristol St Santa Ana CA 92704

WURST, RODNEY CHESHIRE, minister, American Baptist Churches in the U.S.A.; b. Ochlochnee, Ga., Sept. 21, 1927; s. William Henry and Minnie Lee (Giles) W.; B.S., Fla. State U., 1957; M.Div., Southeastern Bapt. Theol. Sem., 1960; D.Min. San Francisco Theol. Sem., 1979; m. Frances Latrell Herring, Dec. 5, 1948; children: Rodney Cheshire, Gwendolyn Ruth Wurst Carr, Margaret Patricia. Ordained to ministry, 1954; pastor Mt. Zion Bapt. Ch., Bainbridge, Ga., 1954-56, Capitola Bapt. Ch., Tallahassee, Fla., 1956-57, Rustburg (Va.) Bapt. Ch., 1958-59; chaplain USAF, 1960-75; founder Brasilia (Brazil) Community Ch., 1967; pastor Cordova Bapt. Ch., Rancho Cordova, Calif., 1975-79, Mayhew Community Bapt. Ch., Sacramento, Calif., 1981—. Decorated D.F.C., Purple Heart, Meritorious Service medal. Mem. Am. Bapt. Chs., U.S.A. Ministers Assn., Assn. Pastoral Counselors. Home: 8265 Twin Oaks Ave Citrus Heights CA 95610 Office: 3401 Routier Rd Sacramento CA 95827

WURZBURGER, WALTER SAMUEL, rabbi, Orthodox Jewish Congregations; b. Munich, Germany, Aug. 29, 1920; s. Adolf and Hedwig (Tannenwald) W.; came to U.S., 1938, naturalized, 1943; B.A., Yeshiva U., 1943; M.A., Harvard, 1944, Ph.D., 1951; m. Naomi C. Rabinowitz, Aug. 18, 1947; children—Benjamin William, Myron Israel, Joshua Jacob. Ordained rabbi, 1944; rabbi Congregation Chai Odom, Dorchester, Mass., 1944-53, Congregation Shaarai Shomayim, Toronto, Ont., Can., 1953-67, Congregation Shaaray Tefila, Far Rockaway, N.Y., 1967—; vis. asso. prof. philosophy Yeshiva U., N.Y.C., 1967—. Pres., Rabbinical Council Am., 1976—; mem. nat. advisory bd. United Jewish Appeal Am.; past v.p. synagogue commn. Fedn. Jewish Philanthropies. Mem. Rabbinical Council Am., Am. Acad. Religion, Am. Philos. Assn. Editor: Tradition, 1961—; contbr. articles to scholarly publs. Office: 1295 Central Ave Far Rockaway NY 11691

WUSKE, TODD ALAN, minister, non-denominational Christian church; b. Canton, Ohio, Mar. 8, 1958; s. Ward Henry and Jean (Figley) W.; m. Marqueta Faye Evans, May 17, 1980; 1 child, Shawn Alan. B.S., Cin. Bible Coll., 1980. Ordained to ministry First Christian Ch., 1980. Minister of children Mt. Carmel Christian Ch., Decatur, Ga., 1980—, chaplain grades 1-4 Mt. Carmel Christian School, 1980—. Avocation: reading. Office: Mount Carmel Christian Ch 3250 Rainbow Dr Decatur GA 30034

WYATT, JOHN FRANCIS MINFORD, priest, Episcopal Ch.; b. Kansas City, Mo., Aug. 19, 1917; s. John Miller and Maude Alice (Smith) W.; student St. Augustines Coll., Canterbury, Eng., 1969, Kings Coll. U. London, 1971; m. Florence Rebecca Cohen, Jan. 1, 1946; children—Susan, Marcia, Claudia. Ordained priest, 1971; asst. to dean St. Pauls Cathedral, Oklahoma City, 1971-73; vicar St. Johns Ch., Durant, Okla., 1973-74; canon to Bishop Okla., 1974-76; founder, dir. Mission for Outreach, Renewal and Evangelism, Inc., Eureka Springs, Ark., 1976—. Founder, Zoe Community, Eureka, 1976—. Dir. Commn. Outreach and Renewal, 1971-73; producer, moderator Confession series, network TV, Young Am. Speaks, Kids and Co., Anything Goes. Formerly advt. and mktg. exec. Home and office: PO Box 550 Eureka Springs AR 72632

WYCKOFF, JOHN WESLEY, religion educator, Assemblies of God; b. Mooreland, Okla., Mar. 8, 1944; s. John Wayne and Loretta Jane (Kelso) W.; m. Myrna Loene Green, June 7, 1969; children: Ryan Keith, Bethany Dawn. B.S., Southwestern State U., Weatherford, Okla., 1966, Southwestern Assemblies of God Coll., Waxhachie, Tex., 1970; M.A., Bethany Nazarene Coll., 1972; postgrad. Baylor U., 1981—. Ordained to ministry Assemblies of God, 1972. Pastor, Assemblies of God, Humboldt, Kans., 1972-76; asst. prof. Southwestern Assemblies of God Coll., 1976—, Bibl. studies and N.T. Ministries div. chmn., 1983—; christian service dir. Southwestern Assemblies of God Coll., 1976—; local ch. leader Evangel Temple Assemblies of God, Waxahachie, 1976—. Mem. Am. Assn. Bible Colls. (hon.), Delta Epsilon Chi (hon.). Office: Southwestern Assemblies of God Coll 1200 Sycamore St Waxahachie TX 75165

WYMAN, HENRY GREGORY, minister, United Church of Christ; b. Brewer, Maine, Nov. 7, 1924; s. Samuel Deering and Ethel mary (Linscott) W.; m. Sona Averill, Aug. 29, 1948; children: Susan Elizabeth, Stephen Henry. B.Ed., U. Maine, 1949, M.Ed., 1950; M.Div., Hartford Sem. Found., 1956; D.D. (hon.), Piedmont Coll., 1975. Minister Columbia Congregation, Conn., 1952-56, United Ch. Christ, North Olmstead, Ohio, 1956-68, Congl. Ch., Patchogue, N.Y., 1968—. Author pub. sermon I Can't See the Moon Any More, 1983. Active Patchogue Cultural Arts Council, 1980. Served with U.S. Army, 1943-45, ETO. Mem. Suffolk Assn. United Ch. Christ (chmn. com. on ministry), United Conf. United Ch. Christ, Patchogue C. of C. (named Father of Yr. 1980). Lodges: Rotary, Lions (hon.). Home: 38 Rose Ave Patchogue NY 11772 Office: Congl Ch 95 E Main St Patchogue NY 11772

WYNN, CHARLES RAY, minister, Southern Baptist Convention; b. Russell County, Ala., Sept. 28, 1935; s. Bennie Sanborn and Mary Wistee (Cox) W.; m. Clara Margaret O'Rear, Aug. 1, 1958; children: Mary Elizabeth, Martha Anne. B.S. in Agrl. Edn., Auburn U., 1957; M.Div., New Orleans Bapt. Theol. Sem., 1975, D.Min., 1976. Ordained to ministry So. Bapt. Conv., 1959. Tchr. vocat. agr. Walker County Schs., Jasper, Ala., 1958-61; prin. Sewell Meml Sch., Titus, Ala., 1961-63; pastor Providence Bapt. Ch., Oakman, Ala., 1958-61, Beulah Bapt. Ch., Wetumpka, Ala., 1961-66, Carrville Bapt. Ch., East Tallassee, Ala., 1966-72, Calvary Bapt. Ch., Butler, Ala., 1972-73, Valence Street Bapt. Ch., New Orleans, 1973-75, Steve Creek Bapt. Ch., Jackson, Ala., 1975-76, Woodley East Bapt. Ch., Montgomery, Ala., 1976—; tchr. religious edn. and N.T., Howard Coll. Extension, Samford U., Montgomery, 1972-85; pres. Tuskegee-Lee Bapt. Pastors Conf., 1971-72, Tallassee Ministerial Alliance, 1970-71; vice moderator Tuskegee-Lee Bapt. Assn., 1971-72; mem. com. on commns. and bds. Ala. Bapt. State Conv. Bd. dirs. Montgomery United Way, 1980-84. Mem. Montgomery Ministerial Union (pres. 1980-82). Home: 2188 Mona Lisa Dr Montgomery AL 36111 Office: 4530 Virginia Loop Rd Montgomery AL 36116

WYNN, DANIEL WEBSTER, minister, religious orgn. exec., United Meth. Ch.; b. Wewoka, Okla., Mar. 19, 1919; s. Phay Willie and Mary (Carter) W.; A.B., Langston U., 1941; B.D., Howard U., 1944, M.A., 1945; Ph.D., Boston U., 1954; D.D. (hon.), Eden Theol. Sem., 1959; D.Humanities (hon.), Utah State U., 1975; m. Lillian Robinson, June 4, 1944; children—Marian Danita, Patricia Ann. Ordained to ministry, 1941; dean Sch. Religion, Bishop Coll., Marshall, Tex., 1946-53; chaplain, prof. philosophy Tuskegee (Ala.) Inst., 1953-54, 1955-65; dean students Langston (Okla.) Univ., 1954; dir. Office College Support United Meth. Bd. Higher Edn. and Ministry, Nashville, 1965—. Life mem. Tuskegee Civic Assn. Recipient Distinguished Alumnus award Langston U., 1963, Service award Wiley Coll., 1973, Leadership Shield, Rust Coll., 1974; named Okla. Man of Yr., Muskogee Service League, 1969. Mem. NAACP. Editor Nat. Assn. Coll. and Univ. Chaplains and Dirs. Religious Life Newsletter, 1955-62; Author: NAACP vs. Negro Revolutionary Protest, 1955; The Chaplain Speaks, 1956; Moral Behavior and the Christian Ideal, 1961; Timeless Issues, 1967; The Black Protest Movement, 1974; The Protestant Church Related College, 1975; Higher Education for Blacks, 1975; contbr. to Black Ency., 1974, also many profl. jours. and mags. Home: 3926 Drakes Branch Rd Nashville TN 37218 Office: Box 871 Nashville TN 37202

WYRICK, DANIEL JOHN, educator, Seventh-day Adventist; b. Oakland, Calif., May 22, 1952; s. Charles Truman and Thelma Lillian (White) W.; m. Christine Evelyn Ingels, Nov. 10, 1972; children: Aimee Christina, Emilie April. B.A., Pacific Union Coll., 1977, M.A., 1984. Sabbath sch. supt. Meadow Vista Seventh-day Adventist, Meadow Vista, Calif., 1978-79, youth leader, 1979-80; ch. deacon Fort Bragg Seventh-day Adventist, Calif., 1982-83, youth leader, 1982—; elem. tchr. Pine Hills Jr. Acad., Auburn, Calif., 1977-81; prin., tchr. Fort Bragg Seventh-day Adventist Elem. Sch., 1981—. Mem. Nat. Sci. Tchrs. Assn., Calif. Sci. Tchrs. Assn., Calif. Assn. Pvt. Sch. Orgns. Democrat. Home: 437 N Corry St Fort Bragg CA 95437 Office: Fort Bragg Seventh-day Adventist Elem Sch 22805 N Highway One Fort Bragg CA 95437

WYSSMANN, GENE ALAN, minister, Lutheran Church-Missouri Synod; b. Springfield, Ill., May 23, 1952; s. Robert William and Rutheleen Viola (Bargfrede) W.; m. Melinda Lou Robbins, June 15, 1974; children: Aaron Michael, Jason Andrew. B.A. in

English, SW Mo. State U., 1973; M.Div., Concordia Theol. Sem., Fort Wayne, Ind., 1978. Pastor Trinity Luth. Ch., Pinckney, Mich., 1978-81, Immanuel Luth. Ch., Crystal City, Mo., 1981—; treas. Twin-City Ministerial Alliance, Crystal City-Festus, Mo., 1984—. Home: #3 Bellamy Hills Crystal City MO 63019 Office: Immanuel Lutheran Church Ward and Brierton Ln Crystal City MO 63019

WYTON, ALEC, musician, Episcopal Church; b. London, Aug. 3, 1921; came to U.S., 1950; divorced; children: Vaughan, Richard, Patrick; m. Mary Broman, Nov. 24, 1979; 1 child, Christopher. M.A., Oxford U., Eng., 1946; Mus.D. (hon.), Susquehanna U., 1970. Asst. organist Christ Ch. Cathedral, Oxford, 1943-46; organist, choirmaster St. Matthew's Ch., Northampton, Eng., 1946-50, Christ Ch. Cathedral, St. Louis, 1950-54, Cathedral St. John the Divine, N.Y.C., 1954-74, St. James' Ch., N.Y.C., 1974—; chmn. dept. ch. music Manhattan Sch. Music, 1984—; coordinator standing commn. on ch. music, Episcopal Ch., 1974—. Composer for solo, choir, organ and instruments. Contbr. articles to religious and mus. publs. Recipient ann. awards ASCAP, 1967—. Fellow Royal Acad. Music, Royal Sch. Ch. Music; mem. Am. Guild Organists (pres. 1964-69), N.Y. Musicians Club (pres. 1976-78), Hymn Soc. Am. Home: 129 E 69th St New York NY 10021 Office: St James Ch 865 Madison Ave New York NY 10021

YAMAOKA, SEIGEN H., bishop, Buddhist Churches in America. Office: 1710 Octavia St San Francisco CA 94109*

YANOWITZ, BENNETT, lawyer, religious organization administrator; b. Cleve., Feb. 25, 1923; s. Jacob and Mollie (Berkowitz) Y.; m. Donna Karen Yanowitz, May 6, 1951; children: Gerald H., Joel H., Alan H. A.B., U. Mich., 1947; LL.B., Western Res. U. Sch. Law, 1949. Vice pres. Jewish Community Fedn. of Cleve.; trustee Council Jewish Fedns., Jewish Community Fedn. Cleve., Menorah Park Jewish Home for Aged; chmn. Nat. Jewish Community Relations Adv. Council, N.Y.C.; chmn. community relations com. Jewish Community Fedn. Cleve.; pres. Akiva High Sch.; prin. law firm Kahn, Kleinman, Yanowitz & Arnson, Cleve., 1964—. Served to capt., U.S. Army, 1943-46. Address: Kahn Kleinman Yanowitz & Arnson Co 1300 Bond Ct Bldg Cleveland OH 44114

YARBROUGH, DAVID OWEN, minister, Southern Baptist Convention; state social science administrator; b. Clarksville, Tenn., June 14, 1946; s. Roy Lee and Jessie (Ferrell) Y.; m. Sara Louise Morris, Aug. 14, 1971; children: Sara Alycia, Laura Elizabeth. B.A.Ed., Austin Peay State U., 1969; M.Div., So. Bapt. Theol. Sem., Louisville, 1977. Ordained to ministry So. Bapt. Conv., 1965. Pastor, Excell Bapt. Ch., Clarksville, Tenn., 1965-70, 1st Bapt. Ch., Odell, Oreg., 1973-74, Sulphur Bapt. Ch., Ky., 1975-78, Grace Bapt. Ch., Bend, Oreg., 1978-81, 1st Bapt. Ch., Montesano, Wash. 1981—. Adult social service worker, Bend, 1971-73; employment and tng. specialist Dept. Social and Health Services Wash., Aberdeen, 1983—. Mem. Montesano Ministerial Assn., Olympic Bapt. Asn. (vice moderator 1982-83). Democrat. Lodge: Kiwanis. Home: 1413 W Wynoochee St Montesano WA 98563 Office: 1st Bapt Ch PO Box 653 Montesano WA 98563

YARRINGTON, HAROLD DEWITT, minister, Bible Fellowship Ch.; b. Wilmington, Del., Mar. 27, 1918; s. Clifton DeWitt, and Mae (Potts) Y.; B.R.E., Shelton Coll., 1952, B.A., 1953; M.A., N.Y. U., 1959; m. Betty Lorraine Sparn, Sept. 28, 1946; children—Betty Lorraine, Harold DeWitt. Ordained to ministry, 1937; founder, pastor Mennonite Missions, Newark, 1937-40, Trenton, N.J., 1940-41, Phila., 1941-43, Binghamton, N.Y., 1943-45, Bklyn., 1945-50; pastor Mennonite Ch., Jersey City, 1950-55, Staten Island, N.Y., 1955-57; pastor Evang. Covenant Ch., New Haven, 1970-76; teaching chaplain, dir. chaplaincy tng. Conn. Valley Hosp., Middletown, 1958—. Chaplain Community Correctional Center, New Haven, 1971-76; sec. to spl. person, com. of the Conn. Council Chs., 1958-68; dir. pastoral counseling clinic, Clinton, Conn., 1972-76; vice-chmn. World Harvest Evangelism; dir. Charismatic Prayer Groups, North Branford, Conn. and New Haven. Sec. to exec. Council Clin. Pastoral Edn., 1967-68; bd. dirs. Middlesex County chpt. United Fund, 1966-68, Connection House, 1972-76; chmn. task force com., HelpLine, Middletown, Conn., 1971-76. Fellow Coll. Chaplains, Am. Assn. Pastoral Counselors, mem. Am. Protestant Chaplains Assn., Assn. Clin. Pastoral Edn., Acad. Religion and Mental Health, Am. Group Psychotherapy Assn., Mental Health Chaplains Assn., Internat. Assn. Group Psychotherapy, Am. Assn. Suicidology, Alcohol and Drug Problems Assn. N. Am., Nat. Alliance for Family Life, Found. for Christian Living, Nat. Council on Family. Home: 912 Ridgewood Rd Middletown CT 06457 Office: PO Box 351 Middletown CT 06457

YATES, JERRY LEE, minister, Southern Baptist Convention; b. Santa Anna, Tex., Sept. 11, 1944; s. Theron Lee and Gail Marie (Elkins) Y.; m. Linda Joanne Siteman, July 7, 1967; children: John Lee, William James. B.A. in Econs., Calif. State U., Fullerton, 1967; M.Div., Golden Gate Bapt. Theol. Sem., 1974. Ordained to ministry So. Bapt. Conv., 1971. Pawtor Am. Indian Bapt. Ch., San Jose, Calif., 1971-73, First Bapt. Ch., Rio Vista, Calif., 1973-77, Hillview Bapt. Ch., Union City, Calif., 1977-84, First So. Bapt. Ch., Visalia, Calif., 1984—; vice chmn. pub. affairs com. exec. bd. So. Bapt. Gen. Conv. of Calif., Fresno, 1983—; regional cons. Am. Christian TV System, Radio and TV Commn., So. Bapt. Conv., Fort Worth, 1983—; dir. Sunday Sch. dept. East Bay Bapt. Assn., Hayward, Calif., 1979—; cons. for lay evangelism Home Mission Bd. of So. Bapt. Conv., Atlanta, 1975—. Recipient Am. Bible Soc. award, 1974. Mem. Assn. for Calif. Bapt. Devel. (bd. dirs., treas. 1983—). Democrat. Home: 2326 Oakhurst Ct Visalia CA 93291 Office: First So Bapt Ch 1248 N Willis Visalia CA 93291

YATES, ORLANDO BENJAMIN, minister, Missionary Bapt. Ch.; b. Mobile, Apr. 25, 1950; s. Robert Lee and Maggie (Bumpers) Y.; B.A., Kans. State U., 1971; M.A., U. Ala., 1973; m. Margie Faye Hosea, July 14, 1973; 1 son, Kenneth Lamar. Ordained to ministry, 1971; coordinator religious activities Kans. State U., 1971-72, counselor, 1973-74; pastor Thankful Bapt. Ch., Rome, Ga., 1975—; counselor, instr. spl. studies W. Ga. Coll., Carrollton, since 1974. Mem. adv. bd. Rome (Ga.) Youth Community Choir. Mem. Rome Human Relations Bd. Martin Luther King, Jr. scholar, 1971. Mem. Am., Ga. personnel and guidance assns., NAACP, Blue Key. Home: 6 Gibbons St Rome GA 30161 Office: 132 Mandeville Hall West Georgia Coll Carrollton GA 30117

YEAKEL, JOSEPH HUGHES, bishop, United Methodist Church; b. Mahanoy City, Pa., Mar. 12, 1928; s. Claude Harrison and Florence Mae (Hughes) Y.; A.B., Lebanon Valley Coll., 1949, D.D. (hon.), 1968; M.Div., United Theol. Sem., 1952; LL.D., Otterbein Coll., 1975; m. Lois Josephine Shank, Mar. 26, 1948; children: Claudia Jo, Joseph Douglas, Joanna Irene, Mary Jo, Jody Lucile. Ordained to ministry, 1952. Student asst. pastor Euclid Av. Evang. United Brethren Ch., Dayton, Ohio, 1949-52; asst. pastor Otterbein Evang. United Brethren Ch., Hagerstown, Md., 1952-55; pastor Messiah Evang. United Brethren Ch., York, Pa., 1955-61, Meml. Evang. United Brethren Ch., Silver Spring, Md., 1961-63; asst. sec. Gen. Bd. Evangelism, Evang. United Brethren Ch., 1963-65, exec. sec., 1965-68; gen. sec., Gen. Bd. Evangelism, United Meth. Ch., Nashville, 1968-72; bishop N.Y. West area United Methodist Ch., 1972-84, bishop Washington area, 1984—. Office: 9226 Colesville Rd Silver Spring MD 20910

YODER, LAWRENCE MCCULLOH, minister, educator, Brethren in Christ Church; b. Mount Joy, Pa., Apr. 14, 1943; s. Leroy G. and Vida (McCulloh) Y.; m. Shirlee Kohler, June 18, 1966; children: Christopher Jonathan, Gregory Matthew, Bradley David. B.A., Messiah Coll., 1966; M.Div., Mennonite Bibl. Sem., 1969; Th.M., Fuller Theol. Sem., 1981, Ph.D. candidate. Lic. minister Brethren in Christ Ch., 1969. Tchr. Akademi Kristen Wiyata Wacana Sem., Pati, Indonesia, 1970-79; rep. Mennonite Central Com., Pati, 1973-77; prof. missiology Eastern Mennonite Sem., Harrisonburg, Va., 1983—, dir. Ctr. for Evang. and Ch. Planning, 1983—. Author: Sejarah Gereja Kristen Muria Indonesia, 1985; contbr. articles to profl. jours. Mem. Am. Soc. Missiology, Soc. for Sci. Study of Religion. Democrat. Home: 1301 Mount Clinton Pike Harrisonburg VA 22801 Office: Eastern Mennonite Sem Harrisonburg VA 22801

YOHO, KEVIN RICHARD, minister, Presbyterian Church in the U.S.A.; b. Cheverly, Md., Jan. 17, 1954; s. Bill Lee and Martha Sue (Carroll) Y.; m. Julie Diane Windsor, June 29, 1979; children: Kimberly, Jaime. B.A., Washington Bible Coll., 1977; M.Div., Gordon-Conwell Theol. Sem., 1980; postgrad. McCormick Theol. Sem. Ordained to ministry Presbyterian Ch. in the U.S.A., 1982. Mem. area staff Young Life, South Hamilton, Mass., 1978-80, Lanham, Md., 1980-82; asst. to pastor Largo Community Ch., Upper Marlboro, Md., 1981-82; pastor First Presbyn. Ch., Elmwood Park, N.J., 1982—; evangelism cons. Presbyn. Ch. in the U.S.A., 1983—; dir. Journey Enhancement Assocs., Elmwood Park, 1984—; chaplain Elmwood Park Fire Dept., 1984—. Mem. adj. faculty Bloomfield Coll., N.J., 1983-84. Author: TheoTech, 1985; columnist A Time For Living, 1983—. Mem. Mid-Bergen County Community Mental Health, N.J., 1983-84; dist. coordinator Bread for the World, Elmwood Park, 1984—. Recipient cert. appreciation Billy Graham Evangelistic Assn., 1984, Vol. Ambulance Corp., Elmwood Park, 1985. Mem. Presbyn. Writers Guild. Democrat. Lodge: Rotary. Home: 11 Church St Elmwood Park NJ 07407 Office: First Presbyterian Ch 11 Church St Elmwood Park NJ 07407

YORK, R(OY) IVAN, minister, Evangelical Free Church of America; b. Monticello, Ky., Aug. 13, 1935; s. Roy Elton and Rubena Finis (Campbell) Y.; m. Doris Edith Nelson, June 23, 1956; children: Brenda Joy, Lisa Diane, Julie Kay. B.A., Kings Coll., 1957; B.Div., Trinity Evang. Div. Sch., Deerfield, Ill., 1960, M.Div., 1973, D. Ministries, 1981. Ordained to ministry Evang. Free Ch. Am., 1962. Assoc. dir. Am. Inst. of Holy Land Studies, Jerusalem, 1960-63; pastor Canton Evang. Free Ch., Ill., 1963-67; sr. pastor Calvary Community Ch., Williams Bay, Wis., 1967-78, Wheaton Evang. Free Ch., Ill., 1978—; bd. dirs. Inst. Holy Land Studies, 1981—; chmn. Gt. Lakes dist. conf. Evang. Free Ch. Am., 1982—, chmn. nat. ministerial assn., 1983—. Author: Elder-Deacon Training Manual, 1981. Contbg. editor Evang. Beacon Mag. Republican. Home: 1489 McCormick Pl Wheaton IL 60187 Office: Wheaton Evang Free Ch 520 E Roosevelt Rd Wheaton IL 60187

YOSHIOKA, BARBARA SAMUELSEN, religion academy administrator; flower company executive; b. Lakeview, Oreg., July 14, 1943; d. Arnold Marinjus and Edna Belle (Frakes) Samuelsen; m. Robert Bunny Yoshioka, Aug. 10, 1968. B.A., U. So. Calif., 1966; M.A., Syracuse U., 1969, Ph.D., 1977. Mem. Princeton Inst. Mediterranean Studies, Los Angeles, 1964; teaching asst. dept. religion Syracuse U., N.Y., 1968; adminstrv. asst. SAS, AFSC, Phila., 1968; co-dir. workshop Ctr. for Intercultural Studies, Calif. State U., Chico, 1974; dir. seminar Am. Acad. Religion, Fresno, Calif., 1975, exec. assoc., Syracuse, 1985—. Pres., bus. mgr. United Lily Growers, Inc., Smith River, Calif., 1978—. Co-editor: Women's Caucus-Religious Studies newsletter, Berkeley, Calif., 1973. Mem. Del Norte County Sch. Bds., Crescent City, Calif., 1983-85. Mem. Pacific Bulb Growers, Calif. Sch. Bds. Assn. Democrat. Home: 274 Genesee Park Dr Syracuse NY 13224 Office: 501 Hall of Langs Syracuse U Syracuse NY 13210

YOST, GEORGE VICTOR, SR., ednl. adminstr. Seventh-day Adventists; b. Mumford, N.Y., Nov. 1, 1922; s. Steven James and Isa Dora Mary (Berringer) Y.; B.A., Andrews U., 1950; M.A., Peabody Tchr's. Coll., 1970; m. Marilyn Gale Ross, Feb. 25, 1945; children—George Victor, II, David Edward, Kenneth Todd. Head dept. religion Mt. Pisgah Acad., Asheville, N.C., 1955-56; supt. edn., young peoples' sec. Carolina Conf., Charlotte, N.C., 1956-62; asso. dir. youth dept. No. Calif. Conf., Oakland, 1962-65, temperance and med. sec., 1965-67; supt. edn. Ky.-Tenn. Conf., Madison, Tenn., 1967—. Home: 110 Cherry Hill Dr Hendersonville TN 37075 Office: PO Box 459 Madison TN 37115

YOUNG, CORRINE ORELIA, religious educator, Seventh-day Adventists; b. Hendersonville, N.C., Oct. 14, 1924; d. Elzie Charran and Amanda Eleanor (Schuster) Graham; m. Alvis Thomas Young, Sept. 20, 1951; 1 child, Alva Jean. B.S., So. Missionary Coll., 1964; M.Ed., Ga. State U., 1972. Bible instr. Ga. Cumberland Conf., Calhoun, Ga., 1948-53, tchr., Savannah, Columbus, Albany and Calhoun, Ga., 1953-68; tchr. Carolina Conf., Asheville-Pisqah and Candler, N.C., 1972-75, Ky.-Tenn. Conf., Memphis, 1975-84, Threshold Montessori, Memphis, 1984—. Democrat. Home: 6911 7th Rd Bartlett TN 38134

YOUNG, DANIEL MERRITT, minister, United Methodist Church; b. Flint, Mich., Jan. 17, 1953; s. George Mardlin and Madeline C. (Merritt) Y.; m. Dianne Kay Rosenberger, Aug. 11, 1973; children: Daniel Laurence, Rachael Kathleen. B.S. magna cum laude, Central Mich. U., 1975, postgrad., 1984-85; M.Div. cum laude, Boston U., 1980, D.Min., 1981. Ordained deacon United Meth. Ch., 1978, ordained elder, 1983. Ednl. asst. Alma 1st Meth. Ch., Mich., 1975-77; intern pastor St. Matthew's United Meth. Ch., Acton, Mass., 1978-81; chaplain intern Meml. Hosp., Worcester, Mass., 1980; assoc. pastor Central Meth. Ch., Detroit, 1981-84; sr. pastor Ortonville United Meth. Ch., Mich., 1984—; dean leadership camp Detroit Conf. United Meth. Ch., 1981, 82, 83. Editorial commentator Mich. Christian Advocate, 1981-84. Founding mem. Draft Resistors Def. Com., Detroit, 1982-84; bd. advisers Mich. Religious Coalition for Abortion Rights, Detroit, 1981-83, Mich. Planned Parenthood, Detroit, 1981-84; bd. dirs. Mich. Nuclear Freeze Voters, Lansing, 1984-85. Charles E. Jefferson fellow Boston U., 1979-80. Mem. Bibl. Archeology Soc., Planetary Soc., Ortonville Pastors' Assn., Conf. on Reawakening Am. Liberalism (founding mem. 1985), Sigma Iota Epsilon. Lodge: Rotary. Avocations: astronomy, photography, furniture refinishing. Home: 319 Sherman Ct Ortonville MI 48462 Office: Ortonville United Meth Ch 91 Church St Ortonville MI 48462

YOUNG, DONALD NORMAN, minister, Presbyterian Church in Canada; b. Charlottetown, P.E.I., Can., Aug. 26, 1948; s. Frederick Norman and Margaret Berneice (Cameron) Y.; m. Karen Joan Waterfield, Sept. 12, 1972; children: Stephanie, Daniel. B.A., U. Toronto, Ont., Can., 1971; M.Div., Knox Coll., Toronto, 1974. Ordained to ministry Presbyn. Ch. in Can., 1976. Minister Pine Ridge Presbyn. Ch., Toronto, 1976-80, St. John's and Sandhill Presbyn. Chs., Kingston, Ont., 1980—; clk. Presbytery of Kingston, 1983—. Mem. Pittsburgh Twp. Hist. Soc. Home: Middle Rd Rural Route 2 Kingston ON K7L 5H6 Canada

YOUNG, GEORGE DOUGLAS, minister, United Ch. of Can.; b. Margate, P.E.I., Can., Sept. 17, 1905; s. Hugh Stanley and Marjorie (Matthews) Y.; B.A., Mt. Allison U., 1929; B.D., U. Alta, 1933; D.D., St. Stephens Coll., 1970; m. Jennie Alexandra Young, Aug. 7, 1935 (dec.); children—Beverly, Stanley. Ordained to ministry, 1933; minister, Rimbey, Alta., 1933-36, Panoka, Alta.,

1936-40; supr. Shawbridge Boys Farm, 1940-46; minister, Marmora, Ont., 1946-52, Taber, Alta., 1952-58; Christian edn. field sec., Alta., 1958-64; dir. Five Oaks Christian Worker Center, Paris, Ont., Can., 1964—. Mem. bd. Christian edn. United Ch. of Can., 1952-64; chmn. Presbytery, 1957; pres. Hamilton Conf., United Ch. of Can., 1976-78. Mem. Five Oaks C. of C. Home and office: Five Oaks Center Box 216 Paris ON N3L 3E7 Canada

YOUNG, GERALD LEWIS, minister, Southern Baptist Convention; b. St. Louis, Oct. 15, 1944; s. Herbert Lewis and Ruth Ellen (Piper) Y.; B.A., Ouachita Bapt. U., 1966; M.Div., Midwestern Bapt. Theol. Sem., 1970, D.Min., 1977; m. Gerry Sue Trantham, June 20, 1964; children: Stephen Paul, Karen Sue, John Robert. Ordained to ministry, 1968; pastor Antioch Bapt. Ch., Sweet Springs, Mo., 1967-68; assoc. pastor 1st Bapt. Ch. St. Johns, St. Louis, 1970-77; pastor North Side Bapt. Ch., Florissant, Mo., 1977—; supr. doctoral candidates Midwestern Bapt. Theol. Sem., St. Louis; curriculum writer Bapt. Sunday Sch. Bd.; leader youth mission tours Mont. and Wis. Mem. Bapt. Music and Edn. Assn. Mo., St. Louis Associated Ministers Conf., Alpha Chi.

YOUNG, GLENN ALONZO, JR., minister, United Methodist Church. b. Washington, July 24, 1946; s. Glenn Alonzo Sr. and Shirley Mae (Porter) Y.; m. Siri Ann Wyman, May 23, 1970; 1 child, Jenny Marie. A.A., Montgomery Coll., 1966; B.A., W.V. Wesleyan Coll., 1970; M.Div., Wesley Sem., 1973. Ordained to ministry United Methodist Ch. 1972, ordained deacon 1972, ordained elder 1974. Assoc. pastor Faith United Meth. Ch., Rockville, Md., 1973-77; pastor Centenary United Meth. Ch., Shady Side, Md., 1977-78, Fairhaven United Meth. Ch., Gaithersburg, Md., 1978—; pres. Gaithersburg Clergy, 1979-81; sec. Community Ministry Montgomery County, Rockville, 1979-80; counselor Washington Pastoral Counseling, 1976-80. Pres., Montgomery Habitat for Humanity, Rockville, 1980—, Gaithersburg HELP, 1979-81; active in Germantown Estates Homeowners, 1983—. Pastoral Counseling and Consultation Ctr. scholar, 1982. Mem. Yokefellows Internat. Republican. Lodge: Lions. Home: 19006 Perrone Dr Germantown MD 20878 Office: Fairhaven United Meth Ch 12801 Darnestown Rd Gaithersburg MD 20874

YOUNG, GORDON JAMES, minister, Lutheran Church in America; b. Havre, Mont., July 13, 1950; s. James Gordon and Juanita Avon (Hoehner) Y.; m. Dayle Marie Bergquist, Apr. 11, 1980; 1 child, Kathryn Ruth. A.A., Concordia Coll., St. Paul, 1970; B.A., Concordia Sr. Coll., Fort Wayne, Ind., 1972; M.Div., Seminex, St. Louis, 1976. Ordained to ministry Luth. Ch. in Am., 1978. Asst. pastor Salem Luth. Ch., Mt. Vernon, Wash., 1978-79; pastor St. John Luth. Ch., Chehalis, Wash., 1979—; Protestant chief of chaplains St. Helen Hosp., Chehalis, 1983—; Bd. advisors Family Living Program, Chehalis, 1984. Mem. Wash. Assn. Chs., Lewis County Assn. Chs. (pres. 1984—). Democrat. Lodge: Rotary. Home: 585 SE Washignton Ave Chehalis WA 98532 Office: St John Luth Ch 103 Wallace Rd Chehalis WA 98532

YOUNG, H. RICHARD, minister, United Pentecostal Church; b. Springfield, Ohio, July 21, 1939; s. David Wilson and Ruth Irene (Brown) Y.; m. Charlotte Delores Ashley, June 20, 1959; children: Beverly Jo, Sherrie Lynn. Grad. Apostolic Bible Inst., 1966. Ordained to ministry United Pentecostal Ch., 1967. Pastor United Pentecostal Ch., Mankato, Minn., 1966-68, New Lexington, Ohio, 1968—, Sun. sch. sec. Ohio Dist., 1973-81, Sun. sch. dir., 1981—. Home: PO Box 23 New Lexington OH 43764 Office: United Pentecostal Ch PO Box 23 New Lexington OH 43764

YOUNG, JANELL EVANS, lay church worker, Southern Baptist Convention; artist; b. Birmingham, Ala., Mar. 12, 1948; d. James Gay and Vivian Lee (Mullins) Evans; m. John David Young, Jan. 16, 1982. B.A., U. Montevallo, Ala., 1970. Artist Woman's Missionary Union, So. Bapt. Conv., Birmingham, 1970-74, dir. art dept., 1974-83, sr. artist, 1983—. Office: PO Box C-10 Birmingham AL 35283

YOUNG, JOAN FULLER, minister, Church of God; b. Savannah, Ga., Aug. 3, 1933; d. Nathan Baker and Eva (Adams) Fuller; m. Joseph Augustus Young, June 3, 1956; children: Earl, Bernard. B.S., Savannah State Coll., 1966; grad. Anderson Sch. Theology. Ordained to ministry. Sunday sch. tchr. Thankful Bapt. Ch., Savannah, 1951-74, tchr. vacation Bible Sch., 1951-72, 81; dir., v.p. Women's Guild, Savannah Ch. of God, 1983; dir. City-Wide Youth Crusade, 1983; pres. Christians United Ministries, 1983; minister, 1976—. Mem. Chatham County Foster Parent Assn., 1980, Child Adv. Council. Home: 3309 Iantha St Savannah GA 31404

YOUNG, JOSEPH SCOTT, priest, Episcopal Church; b. Hutchinson, Kans., Nov. 15, 1915; s. Harry Wesley and Minnie Jean (Hardcastle) Y.; B.A., U. Kans., 1937; M.Div. cum laude, Seabury-Western Theol. Sem., 1940, D.D., 1965; m. Dorothy Mize, June 12, 1940; children: Harry Mize, Judith Yeats, Chester Scott. Ordained priest, 1940; vicar St. Thomas Ch., Garden City, Kans., 1939-49, rector, 1949-50; vicar St. Andrews Ch., Liberal, Kans., 1940-49, St. Augustines Ch., Meade, Kans., 1942-49; vicar St. John's Ch., Norman, Okla., 1950-52, rector, 1952-63; rector St. James Ch., Wichita, Kans., 1963-67, All Saints Ch., Portland, Oreg., 1967-74; Episcopal chaplain U. Calif. at San Diego, La Jolla, 1974-81, San Diego State U., 1977-81; vicar St. Barnabas Ch., Borrego Springs, Calif., 1981—; chmn. dept. youth Diocese of Salina, Kans., 1941-48; adult adviser Nat. Youth Com., 1949-51; examining chaplain Diocese of Okla., 1955-61, mem. standing com., 1955-57, 59-61, pres., 1961, mem. council, 1958, v.p., 1960-61; trustee Seabury-Western Theol. Sem., 1961-63, Windham House, N.Y.C., 1962-67; mem. exec. council Episcopal Ch., 1961-67, constl. standing liturgical commn., 1971-74, dept. Christian edn. of exec. council, 1961-67, gen. div. Laymens Week, exec. com., 1961-67, dep. Gen. Conv., 1949, 58, 61, 67; mem. com. on ministry Diocese of Oreg., 1972-74; bd. dirs. Greater Portland Council Chs., 1969-73, St. Francis Boys Homes, 1946-63, 65-67. Pres. USO Council, Garden City, 1942-45; mem. Cleveland County Child Welfare Commn., 1951-63; chmn. Cleveland County chpt. ARC, 1954-55, del. Nat. Conv., 1955. Mem. Phi Beta Kappa. Home: 8875 Robinhood Ln La Jolla CA 92037

YOUNG, MICHAEL JACOB, SR., minister, Southern Baptist Convention. b. Ellijay, Ga., May 4, 1953; s. Marion Calvin and Lois Carolyn (Hall) Y.; m. Sandra Joyce Masters, May 26, 1973; children: Sandra Michele, Michael Jacob, Jr. B.S. in Edn., U. Tenn.-Chattanooga, 1975; M.Div., Southern Bapt. Sem., 1977; D.Ministry, Internat. Bible Inst. and Sem., 1980. Ordained to ministry Southern Baptist Conv., 1976; cert. secondary tchr., Tenn. Children's pastor East Lake Bapt., Chattanooga, 1974-75; assoc. pastor Melbourne Heights Bapt. Ch., Louisville, 1976-77; pastor Arabi Bapt. Ch., Ga., 1977-79, Pilgrim's Rest Bapt. Ch., Soddy-Daisy, Tenn., 1979-83, Alpine Bapt. Ch., Chattanooga, 1983-84; Bapt. Student Union dir. Chattanooga State Tech. Community Coll., 1984—; dir. edn. Houston Bapt. Assn., Vienna, Ga., 1978-79; pres. Pastors Conf. Hamilton County Bapt. Assn., Chattanooga, 1979-81; program chmn. Hamilton County Bapt. Pastors Conf., Chattanooga, 1984—. Author Bible curriculum guide, 1980. Mem. Chattanooga PTA, 1979—. Mem. NEA, Tenn. Edn. Assn., Chattanooga Edn. Assn. Democrat. Home: 500 Shawnee Trail Chattanooga TN 37411 Office: Chattanooga State Tech Community Coll 4501 Amnicola Hwy Chattanooga TN 37406

YOUNG, PAUL DONALD, church administrator, Presbyterian Church U.S.A.; b. Houston, Jan. 13, 1926; s. James Gordon and Irma Louise (Schmidt) Y.; m. Mary Frances Allen, Nov. 28, 1981; children by previous marriage: Gloria Ann, William Andrew. Student, Trinity U., 1943-45; B.S., Davidson Coll., 1950; B.D., Yale Div. Sch., 1955; D.Min., McCormick Theol. Sem., 1978. Ordained to ministry, 1955. Pastor, Webster Presbyn. Ch., Tex., 1955-60, Trinity Presbyn. Ch., Denton, Tex., 1960-66, Central Presbyn. Ch., Waco, Tex., 1966-72; exec. presbyter Palo Duro Presbytery, Lubbock, Tex., 1972—; adj. faculty McCormick Theol. Sem., Chgo., 1980—, Austin Theol. Sem., 1983. Home: 5524 80th St Lubbock TX 79424 Office: Dalo Duro Presbytery 4820 19th St Lubbock TX 79407

YOUNG, WARREN CAMERON, minister, American Baptist Churches in U.S.A.; b. P.E.I., Can., Dec. 26, 1913; s. Walter Burns and Margaret Jane (Bruce) Y.; B.A., Gordon Coll., 1942; M.A., Boston U., 1944, Ph.D., 1946; B.D., No. Bapt. Theol. Sem., 1948; postgrad. Heidelberg U., 1960-61; m. Alda Helena Jones, June 9, 1943; children—Judith, Karen, Lynn. Ordained to ministry, 1944; pastor chs., Sutton and Manchang, Mass., 1943-46; faculty No. Bapt. Theol. Sem., 1946—, Disting. Prof. Christian philosophy, 1978-81, Disting. Prof. Emeritus, 1981—. Mem. Am. Philos. Assn., Am. Theol. Soc., Am. Acad. Religion, Evang. Theol. Soc., Phi Alpha Chi. Author: A Christian Approach to Philosophy, 1954; also articles and revs. Home: 1490 Briar Cove Wheaton IL 60187 Office: 660 E Butterfield Rd Lombard IL 60148

YOUNG, WILLIAM EDGAR, minister, administrator, Southern Baptist Convention; b. Whitesburg, Ga., July 28, 1930; s. Edgar Woodfin and Maude Alva (Duke) Y.; A.B., Mercer U., 1956; M.R.E., Southwestern Bapt. Theol. Sem., 1958; postgrad. Boston U., 1959, U. Tenn., 1975-76, George Peabody Coll. Tchrs., 1976—; m. Mary Todd Watts, Mar. 19, 1963; children—William Jefferson, Todd Woodfin. Ordained to ministry; minister edn. and music First Bapt. Ch., Swainsboro, Ga., 1958; tchr. English, N. Cobb High Sch., Acworth, Ga., 1959; minister edn.-adminstrn. First Bapt. Ch., Sherman, Tex., 1960-64; cons. ch. adminstrn. dept. Bapt. Sunday Sch. Bd., Nashville, 1964; dir. field services, 1965-70, supr. children's sect., ch. tng. dept., Nashville, 1970—. Mem., tchr., leader First Bapt. Ch., Nashville; adj. prof. Sch. Religious Edn., Southwestern Bapt. Theol. Sem., 1984; sec., bd. dirs. So. Bapt. Religious Edn., 1983—; sec.-treas. So. Bapt. Religious Edn. Assn., 1970-75, v.p., 1975-76, pres., 1976-77; pres. Franklin High Community Assn., 1983-84. Pres. PTA Stanford Elementary Sch., Nashville, 1973-75; mem. adv. council, dept. edn. Belmont Coll. chmn. Citizens Adv. Com. Metro Schs., Nashville, 1974-75; parent rep. curriculum assessment group Williamson County Schs., Franklin, Tenn., 1976-77. Served with USAF, 1951-55. Recipient Disting. service award Metro. Assnl. Dirs. Religious Edn., 1980; named Outstanding Sr. Mercer U., 1956. Mem. Assn. Childhood Edn. Internat., Southwestern Bapt. Religious Edn. Assn. (v.p. 1964-65), Grassland Sch. Community Assn. (pres. 1977-78), Alpha Chi Omega, Am. Soc. Curriculum Devel., Blue Key. Author: Moses-God's Helper, 1976; The Effective Church Usher, 1972; The Church Ushering Committee, 1977; Learning to Worshop God, 1977; (with others) The Equipping of Disciples, 1977, Developing Your Children's Church Training Program, 1977; Jesus, Lord and Savior, 1984; curriculum writer Bible Searchers; contbr. articles to religious jours. Home: 605 Williamsburg Dr Rt 7 Franklin TN 37064 Office: 127 Ninth Ave N Nashville TN 37234

YOUNG, WILLIAM GRAHAM, minister, Presbyterian Church in the U.S.A.; b. Goldsboro, N.C., Sept. 20, 1955; s. John Norman and Elizabeth Leah (Graham) Y.; m. Lynne Carol Edwards, Dec. 29, 1974; children: William Graham II, Elizabeth Frances. B.A. cum laude, Pembroke State U., 1977; D.Min., Union Theol. Sem., 1981. Ordained to ministry Presbyterian Ch., 1981. Pastor, Midway Presbyn. Ch., New Zion, S.C., 1981-83, Latta Presbyn. Ch., S.C., 1983—; chmn. Christian edn. com. Pee Dee Presbytery, Florence, S.C., 1985—; del. Synod of Southeast S.C./Ga., 1982, 1984. Active Young Democrats, Robeson County, N.C., 1972; vol. tutor Literacy Program, Dillon County, S.C., 1984—. Lodge: Rotary. Avocations: golf; swimming; gardening. Office: Latta Presbyn Ch PO Box 5 Latta SC 29565

YOUNGBAR, HENRY ALLEN, minister, Southern Baptist Convention. B. Bapt., Oct. 20, 1951; s. Henry Pierce and Lois Lillian (Ackerman) Y.; m. Debra Sue Jenkins, Nov. 19, 1976; children: Joshua Allen, Micah Allen. B.A., U. Md., 1972; M.Div., Southeastern Bapt. Theol. Sem., 1976. Ordained to ministry Bapt. Ch., 1977. Pastor, Greenbrier Bapt. Ch., Boonsboro, Md., 1977-84; fgn. missionary, 1984—. Republican. Address: Quinta de Marques Lote 59 2-B 2780 Oeiras Portugal

YOUNGBLOOD, THOMAS JEFFERSON, minister, Southern Baptist Church; b. Chattanooga, Feb. 5, 1934; s. Luther and Ruth Almeda (Padgett) Y.; m. Charlotte Anne Goodner, May 30, 1951; children: Thomas Jefferson, Timothy James. Cert. Tiff Coll., 1978, Med. Coll. Ga., 1978, Mercer U., 1979; A.S., Cleveland State Coll., 1980; student Chattanooga State Coll., 1980-82. Ordained to ministry So. Bapt. Ch., 1950. Pastor Stevenson Bapt. Tabernacle, Ala., 1955-56, Haynes Bapt. Ch., Chattanooga, 1956-61, Frawley Bapt. Ch., East Ridge, Tenn., 1961-64, Oak St. Bapt. Ch., Soddy, Tenn., 1964-69, Center Grove Bapt. Ch., Rock Springs, Ga., 1969-73, Maple Grove Bapt. Ch., Harrison, Tenn., 1973-77, 2d Bapt. Ch., Chattanooga, 1977—; dir. Pioneer Mission Campaign, Kern County, Calif., 1976, Promotion World Mission Conf., 1977; crusade mem. Fgn. Mission Bd., Zambia, 1977; chmn. mission com. So. Bapt. Conv., 1979—, mem. various coms., 1983—; v.p., mem. exec. bd. chaplain's assn. Tri-County Hosp., Rossville, Ga., 1970-73; mem. chaplain service Meml. Hosp., Chattanooga, 1974-83; chaplain Goodwill Industries, Chattanooga; conductor numerous revivals and Bible confs. Lodge: Ruritan (chaplain 1975-77, bd. dirs. 1976-77).

YOUNGBLOOD, THOMAS JEFFERSON, JR., minister, Christian Church (Disciples of Christ); b. Covington, Ky., Aug. 1, 1920; s. Thomas J. and Cornelia Ella (Duvall) Y.; m. Katharyn Margaret Lilly, Apr. 6, 1941; children: Thomas J., III, Judy Kaye Youngblood Banks. B.A., Tex. Christian U., 1948, LL.D., 1978; B.Div., Phillips U., 1951; D.D. (hon.), Atlantic Christian Coll., 1968, Bethany Coll., W.Va., 1981; Ordained to ministry Christian Ch. (Disciples of Christ), 1951. Minister 1st Christian Ch., Thomas, Okla., 1948-51, sr. minister, Arlington, Tex., 1951-60; sr. minister Hillyer Meml. Christian Ch., Raleigh, N.C., 1960-71, Central Christian Ch., San Antonio, 1971—; trustee Tex. Christian U., Fort Worth; pres. SW region Christian Ch. (Disciples of Christ), 1974-76, moderator U.S. and Can., 1979-81. Bd. dirs. Contact of San Antonio, Inc., 1984, Ecumenical Ctr. for Religion and Health, San Antonio, 1984. Contbr. articles to religious jours. Served as sgt. USAAF, 1942-46. Recipient honor cert. Freedoms Found., 1976; named Churchman of Yr., San Antonio Council Chs., 1979. Mem. San Antonio Met.Ministries (v.p. 1983-84). Democrat. Lodge: Kiwanis (pres. 1959). Office: Central Christian Ch 720 N Main Ave San Antonio TX 78205

YOUNGDAHL, PAUL MATTHEW, minister, Lutheran Church in America; b. St. Paul, Aug. 14, 1937; s. Reuben Kenneth and Ruth (Youngberg) Y.; m. Nancy Kay Holmstrom, June 22, 1962; children: Kristi Lee, Aaron Paul, Peter Daniel. B.A., Gustavus Adolphus Coll., 1959, Dr. (hon.), 1981; B.Div., Luth. Sch. Theology, 1963. Ordained to ministry Luth. Ch. Am., 1963. Pastor, Love Luth. Ch., New Orleans, 1963-66, Our Redeemer Luth. Ch., St. Paul, 1966-68; assoc. pastor Mt. Olivet Luth. Ch., Mpls., 1968-74, sr. pastor, 1974—; bd. dirs. Inst. for Ecumenical and Cultural Research; pres., camp dir. Cathedral of the Pines Youth

Camp, Lutsen, Minn., 1969—; bd. dirs. bd. publs. Luth. Ch. Am., 1980—; pres. bd. dirs. Mt. Olivet Rolling Acres, Mt. Olivet Home Bd., Mt. Olivet Careview Home Bd.; former mem. stewardship com. Minn. Synod, adv. mem. camp bd.; mem. Luth. Ch. Am. office for communication, commn. on ch. papers. Recipient Radio Sta. WCCO's Good Neighbor award, 1980; One of the Twin Cities Most Influential Clergy, 1981. Mem. Greater Mpls. C. of C. (bd. dirs.). Club: Dunkers. Lodge: Kiwanis. Home: 4932 James Ave S Minneapolis MN 55409 Office: Mount Olivet Lutheran Church 5025 Knox Ave South Minneapolis MN 55419

YOUNGER, DORIS ANNE, religious organization executive. Gen. dir. Church Women United in the U.S.A., 1984—. Office: Church Women United in the USA 475 Riverside Dr Room 812 New York NY 10015*

YOUNGQUIST, GERALD LEE, minister, Lutheran Church in America; b. Gowrie, Iowa, Aug. 29, 1930; s. C. Alvin and Ruby (Jacobson) Y.; m. Rozella June Youngquist, Apr. 22, 1953; children: Grant, Andrew, Karl. B.A., Gustavus Adolphus Coll., 1958; M.Div., Augustan Theol. Sem., 1962; postgrad. Inst. Advanced Pastoral Studies-Detroit, 1983—. Ordained to ministry, 1962. Pastor, First Luth. Ch., Kirkland, Ill., 1962-71; sr. pastor First Luth. Ch., Monmouth, Ill., 1971—; bd. dirs. Augustana Coll., Rock Island, Ill., 1972-82; del. Luth. Ch. Am. Conv., Chgo., Toronto, 1978, 84. Served with U.S. Army, 1951-53. Democrat. Lodge: Rotary (bull. editor). Home: 122 S 4th St Monmouth IL 61462 Office: First Luth Ch 116 S B St Monmouth IL 61462

YOUNT, ROYALL AUSTIN, bishop, Lutheran Church in America; b. Hickocy, N.C., May 19, 1922; s. Floyd Stephan and Lottie May (Austin) Y.; m. Martha Lee Townsend, June 14, 1945; children: Royall Austin, J. Timothy. A.B., Lenoir Rhyne Coll., 1942; D.D. (hon.), Newberry Coll., 1956. Ordained to ministry, Lutheran Ch. Am., 1945. Pastor St. Paul Luth. Ch., Tampa, Fla., 1945-52; pres. Fla. Synod United Luth. Ch. Am., Tampa, 1952-62; pres., bishop Fla. Synod Luth. Ch. Am., Tampa, 1962—; dir. Bd. of Pensions, Luth. Ch. Am., Mpls., 1978—; mem. com. div. service to mil. personnel, Washington, 1976—. Trustee Newberry Coll., 1950—, So. Sem., Columbia, S.C., 1950—. Democrat. Office: Fla Synod Luth Ch Am 3838 W Cypress St Tampa FL 33607

YOUNT, WILLIAM MCKINLEY, minister, librarian, Presbyterian Church in America; b. Cin., Feb. 3, 1945; s. James Niles and Daisy Norma (Kammerer) Y.; m. Helen Charlene Glover, June 24, 1966; children: William Barton, Amy Joy, Katherine Lorene, Jennifer Leigh. B.A., Asbury Coll., 1967; M.A., Trinity Evang. Div. Sch., 1970, M.Div., 1971; Th.M., Princeton Theol. Sem., 1974; M.L.S., U. So. Miss., 1982. Ordained to ministry Presbyn. Ch., 1973. Pastor 1st Presbyn. Ch., Trussville, Ala., 1973-75, Green Cove Springs, Fla., 1975-79; prof. religion Whitworth Bible Coll., Brookhaven, Miss., 1979-81; librarian, asst. prof. theol. bibliography Trinity Evang. Div. Sch., Deerfield, Ill., 1982—; minister No. Ill. Presbytery, Presbyn. Ch. in Am., 1982—, mem. Mission to N. Am. Com., 1983—. Mem. Evang. Theol. Soc., Am. Theol. Library Assn. Office: Rolfing Meml Library Trinity Evang Div Sch 2065 Half Day Rd Deerfield IL 60015

YOW, JACKIE NEIL, pastor, Southern Baptist Convention; b. Burnwell, Ala., June 29, 1949; s. Dock and Margaret Catherine (Sanders) Earnest; m. Nineveh Gail Wakefield, Dec. 27, 1966; children: Jason Neil, Jeremy Wayne. A.A. with honors, Clarke Coll., 1974; B.S., Blue Mountain Coll., 1976; M.Div., Mid-Am. Baptist Theol. Sem., 1980. Ordained to ministry Southern Baptist Conv., 1974. Pastor, Sardis Bapt. Ch., Philadelphia, Miss., 1974-75, Walnut Bapt. Ch., Miss., 1975-79, Flag Lake Baptist Ch., Sarah, Miss., 1979—. Served with U.S. Army, 1966-69. Home: Rt 1 Sarah MS 38665 Office: Flag Lake Baptist Ch Hwy 4 W Sarah MS 38665

YUHAUS, CASSIAN JOSEPH, religion educator, priest, Roman Catholic Church; b. Hazleton, Pa., July 12, 1922; s. Adam Anthony and Elizabeth Marie (Alasko) Y. M.A. in Theology, St. Michael's U., 1951; M.A. in History, Gregorian U.-Rome, 1956, Ph.D., 1962. Ordained priest, 1951. Prof. theology Cath. Sem., East Coast Schs., 1963-76, dir. formation, 1963-68; major superior Congregation of the Passion, Union City, N.J., 1968-74; pres. Ctr. for Research, Washington, 1980-85; exec. dir. Inst. for World Concerns, Duquesne U., Pitts., 1985—; mem. gen. assembly Pro Mundi Vita Research Ctr., Brussels, 1982—. Author: Compelled to Speak, 1967. Editor: Forum for Religious 1974-84. Contbr. articles to profl. jours. Mem. World Future Soc., Common Cause, Ctr. for Concern, Network Lobby for Justice, Stauros Internat. Democrat. Office: Inst for World Concerns Duquesne Univ Pittsburgh PA 15282

YUNKER, ARTHUR DAVID, minister, Lutheran Church-Missouri Synod; b. New Orleans, Aug. 18, 1945; s. Ward Stanley and Isobel Ida (Mann) Y.; m. Grace Anna Rempert, Aug. 12, 1973; children: Ward Irwin, Mark Arthur. Student Concordia Coll., St. Paul, 1963-65; B.A., Concordia Sr. Coll., Fort Wayne, Ind., 1968; M.Div., Concordia Sem., St. Louis, 1972. Ordained to ministry Luth. Ch., 1972. Asst. pastor Luth. Ch. of St. Philip, Chgo., 1972-73; pastor St. Mark's Luth. Ch. and St. John's Luth Ch., Rushford, Minn., 1973-78, Holy Cross Luth. Ch., Rochester, Minn., 1978—; counselor So. dist. Winona Cir., Luth. Ch.-Mo. Synod, Minn., 1976-78, edn. rep. So. dist. Rochester Cir., 1978—, del. conv., 1977. Author: Toward a Theology of Pipesmoking, 1970; Confession of the Son of Man, 1982; His Suffering—Our Strength (Mark 14—16), 1985.

ZABOROWSKI, ROBERT RONALD JOHN MARIA, archbishop, Mariavite Old Catholic Church Province of North America; b. Detroit, Mar. 14, 1946; s. Richard and Bernice Julia (Zaborowski) Kuhlman. D.D., Holy Cross Old Cath. Sem., 1968; S.T.D., St. Ignatius Bishop and Martyr Theol. Sch., 1974, J.C.D., 1976, Ph.D., 1977; D.S.S., D.D.M. and D.Th.D., Inst. Sainte Pierre, 1977. Ordained priest Mariavite Old Catholic Ch. of North Am., 1968, Episcopal consecration, 1972, Archipeiscopal installation, 1972. Parochial asst. Holy Cross Old Cath. Ch., Chgo., 1968-69; parochial pastor Sacred Heart Parish, Wyandotte, Mich., 1969—; aux. bishop Mariavite Old Cath. Ch., Jersey City, 1972-74; archbishop/prime bishop Mariavite Old Cath. Ch., Wyandotte, 1974—; ch. organist, choirmaster various Roman Catholic Chs., 1966-71. Editor The Mariavita Monthly, 1978—. Author booklets, also contbr. articles to profl. jours. Decorated Order of St. John of Jerusalem Knights of Malta, St. John of Jerusalem Knights Hospitaller, Teutonic Order of Levant, Imperial Byzantine Order of Contantine the Great, Valencia, Holy and Blessed Order of Sacred Cup, other decorations and knighthoods; named Hon. Consul Republic of Free Poland, London, 1983. Mem. St. Irenaeus Inst. of France (hon.), Internat. Congress of Lit. and Arts, Constantinian Acad. Letters, Arts and Scis. Home: 2803 Tenth St Wyandotte MI 48192-4994 Office: Mariavite Old Cath Ch Adminstrv Ctr 2803 Tenth St Wyandotte MI 48192-4994

ZACHARY, CHARLOTTE HOTOPP, minister, United Presbyterian Church U.S.A.; b. Jersey City, Aug. 21, 1923; d. Edwin Franz and Nanetta (Hartmann) HoTopp; R.N., Jersey City Med. Center, 1945; B.Sc., N.J. State Tchrs. Coll., 1945; M.A., N.Y. U., 1950; B.D., Oberlin Sch. Theology, 1957; D.Min., Eden Theol. Sem., St. Louis, 1985; m. Jesse Willard Zachary, Jan. 30, 1972. Ordained to ministry, 1956; pastor Congl. Ch., New England, N.D., 1957-59, Wayne (Ohio) Congl. Ch., 1959-60, New Lyme (Ohio) Presbyn. Ch., 1960-63, United Presbyn. Ch., Monon, Ind., 1963-66, Inner City Project, United Presbyn. Milligan Meml. Ch., Crawfordsville, Ind., 1966-75, Five Ch. Assn., St. Louis, 1975-77, 1st United Presbyn. Ch., Madison, Ill., 1977—. Dir. Christian Nursing Service, Vol. Christian Health Agy., Crawfordsville, Ind., 1967-76. Recipient Community Service award Bus. and Profl. Women, 1970, Ind. Community Service award Ind. Homemakers, 1974, Jane award for community service Crawfordsville-Montgomery County, 1974, Community Service award Ministerial Assn., 1975, award for Vol. Health Service to Community, Christian Nursing Service, 1975, Community Service award U.S. Dept. Agr., 1975, Disting. Service award Purdue U. Sch. Nursing, 1975, Disting. Service award Hospice of Madison County, 1982, Mem. Bus. and Profl. Women, Ind. Assn. Women Ministers, St. Louis Assn. Women in Ministry. Address: First United Presbyn Ch 1641 3d Madison IL 62060

ZACHERT, VIRGINIA, lay church worker, So. Baptist Conv.; b. Jacksonville, Ala., Mar. 1, 1920; d. Reinhold Edward and Cora Harrison (Massee) Z.; B.A., Valdosta State Coll.; M.A., Emory U., Atlanta, 1947; Ph.D., Purdue U., 1949. Bible tchr. Research prof. ob-gyn Med. Coll. Ga., Augusta, 1963-84, prof. emerita, 1984—. Chmn., Sr. Citizens Adv. Bd., 1982—. Home: 1126 Highland Ave Augusta GA 30904 Office: Dept Obstetrics and Gynecology Med Coll Ga Augusta GA 30912

ZAHNISER, ALISON HOWARD MATHIAS, religion educator, Free Methodist Church of North America; b. Washington, Jan. 10, 1938; s. Howard Clinton and Alice Bernita (Hayden) Z.; m. Elizabeth Ann Harrington, Aug. 31, 1959; children: James, David, Laura. B.A., Greenville Coll., 1960; M.S., Am. U., 1962; B.D., Asbury Theol. Sem., 1965; Ph.D., Johns Hopkins U., 1973. Missionary Free Meth. Ch., Winona Lake, Ind., 1965-67; assoc. prof. Central Mich. U., Mt. Pleasant, 1971-78; prof. Greenville Coll., Ill., 1978-83; assoc. prof. religion Asbury Theol. Sem., Wilmore, Ky., 1983—. Contbr. articles to profl. jours. Mem. Am. Acad. Religion. Democrat. Home: 110 Gaile Morris Ct Wilmore KY 40390 Office: Asbury Theol Sem 205 Lexington Ave Wilmore KY 40390

ZAKUTO, SAMUEL ISAAC, rabbi, Conservative Jewish Congregations; b. Liverpool, Eng., June 13, 1903; s. Gabriel and Leah (Zakuto) Z.; came to U.S., 1913, naturalized, 1928; A.B., U. Mich., 1927; M.Ed., U. Pitts., 1948; D.D. (hon.), Jewish Theol. Sem., N.Y., 1975; m. Dorothy Stein, Dec. 12, 1937 (dec. 1966); children—Ila Berenson; m. 2d, Minnie Stern, June 18, 1967; stepchildren—Morton, Allen. Rabbi, 1930; rabbi Agudas Achim, Austin, Tex., 1957-61, Temple Israel, Valdosta, Ga., 1961—; aux. chaplain Moody AFB; chaplain S. Ga. Med. Center. Mem. Rabbinical Assembly. Author articles. Address: 600 W Park Ave Valdosta GA 31601

ZANETOS, JOHN CONSTANTINE, priest, Greek Orthodox Archdiocese of North and South America; b. Karavas, Cyprus, Mar. 16, 1920; came to U.S., 1937, naturalized, 1945; s. Costas and Eugenia (Spanos) Z.; m. Irene Greos, July 1, 1945; children: Dena J., Eugenia Buba. Diploma, Holy Cross Sch. Theology, 1942; B.D., Hartford Sem., 1945. Ordained priest Greek Orthodox Ch., 1945. Pastor, Assumption Ch., Poughkeepsie, N.Y., 1945-49, St. Bpyridon Ch., N.Y.C., 1949-50, Sts. Constantine and Helen Ch., Bklyn., 1950-56, St. Anthony's Ch., Pasadena, Calif., 1982—; dean Annunciation Cathedral, Boston, 1956-81. Home: 2755 Diana St Pasadena CA 91107 Office: St Anthony's Ch 778 S Rosemead Blvd Pasadena CA 91107

ZAPPIA, JERRY DALE, educator, Seventh-day Adventist Church; b. Albany, Calif., July 29, 1944; s. Joseph and Doris Jean (Crosby) Z.; m. Elayne Zappia, June 11, 1967; children: Darlene, Joseph. A.A., Contra Costa Jr. Coll., 1965; B.A., Pacific Union Coll., 1968, M.A., 1969. Tchr., Pleasant Hill Jr. Acad., Calif., 1968-71, Pine Hills Jr. Acad, Auburn, Calif., 1971-77, San Gabriel Elementary Sch., Calif., 1977-81, Chico Seventh-day Adventist Elementary Sch., 1981-83; tchr., prin. Westlake Seventh-day Adventist Elementary Sch., 1983—; mem. So. Calif. Conf. Seventh-day Adventist Edn. Bd., Glendale, Calif., 1979-81. Editor curriculum: Continuous Progress in Mathematics, 1975, 76. Mem. Nat. Council Tchrs. Math. Home: PO Box 1254 Upper Lake CA 95485 Office: Westlake Seventh-day adventist Elementary Sch 6585 Westlake Rd Lakeport CA 95453

ZARFAS, MARIE ASTRID, college administrator, General Association of General Baptists; b. Tacoma, Wash., Dec. 15, 1935; d. Aslak and May (Parsons) Lauvrak; m. G. Nelson Zarfas, Mar. 14, 1959 (dec. 1973); 1 child, Nelson Taylor. Student Knapp Bus. Coll., 1954-55. Coll. sec. Western Bapt. Coll., El Cerrito, Calif., 1957-59; ch. sec. First Presbyterian Ch., Berkeley, Calif., 1961-66; pastor's wife Faith Baptist Ch., San Pablo, Calif., 1965-69; sch. sec., dir. of admissions, adminstrv. asst. to pres. Western Bapt. Coll., Salem, Oreg., 1973—; lectr. in field. Republican. Home: 3516 Turner Rd SE Salem OR 97302 Office: Western Bapt Coll 5000 Deer Park Dr Salem OR 97301

ZAWISTOWSKI, JOSEPH K., bishop, Polish National Catholic Church of America, Western Diocese. Office: 2010 W Charleston St Chicago IL 60647*

ZAYEK, FRANCIS MANSOUR, bishop, Roman Catholic Church; b. Manzaillo, Cuba, Oct. 18, 1920; s. Mansour and Mary (Coury) Z.; student St. Josephs Catholic U., Beirut, 1938; D.D., U. Propogation of Faith, 1947, Ph.D., 1947; Dr. Canon Law, Lateran U., 1951. Ordained priest Roman Catholic Ch., 1946; rector Maronite Cathedral of Holy Family, Cairo, Egypt, 1951-56; Oriental sec. to Vatican Apostolic Internunciature, mem. Archdiocesan Tribunal, 1951-56; promoter of justice Sacred Roman Rota, 1956-58; prof. Oriental canon law Internat. Coll. St. Anselm, Rome, 1958-60; prof. Oriental canon law Lateran U., Rome, 1960-61; aux. bishop to Cardinal James De Barros Camera, Archbishop of Rio de Janeiro, 1962; consecrated maronite bishop, 1962; maronite bishop, Rio de Janeiro, 1962-64; presided over First Ann. Maronite Conv., Washington, 1964; first maronite exarch of U.S.A., 1966—, also titular bishop of Callinicum; given title of Archbishop, 1982. Decorated knight comdr. Equestrian Order of Holy Sepulchre of Jerusalem; recipient medal of merit Govt. of Republic Italy, 1966. Home: 935 Three Mile Dr Grosse Pointe MI 48230 Office: 11470 Kercheval St Detroit MI 48214

ZECHMAN, DONALD EUGENE, minister, ecumenical broadcast coordinator, United Methodist Church; b. Harrisburg, Pa., Dec. 6, 1938; s. Harry William and Vesta Mae (Harner) Z.; m. Faye Elizabeth Gamber, Sept. 26, 1964; children: Scott Alan, Craig Alan. B.A., Lebanon Valley Coll., 1960; postgrad. Luth. Theol. Sem., 1960-62; B.D., United Theol. Sem., 1964; M.A. in Speech-Communication, Univ. Mich., 1969. Ordained to ministry Evang. United Brethren Ch., 1964. Organist, choir dir. St. Matthew's Ch., Livonia, Mich., 1967-70; asst. pastor Derry St. Evang. United Brethren Ch., Harrisburg, 1964-67; pastor Bethany United Meth. Ch., Lancaster, Pa., 1970-78; program coordinator TELERAD (South Central Pa. TV and Radio Ministry), Harrisburg, 1972—; assoc. pastor Salem United Meth. Ch., Manheim, Pa., 1978—; mem. planning com. Lancaster County Crop Walk for Hungry, 1973—; bd. dirs. Lancaster County Council Chs., 1983—. Author Sunday sch. curriculum materials. Exec. producer: The Magic Cocoon, Sta. WGAL-TV, Lancaster, 1971-78; Real-to-Reel, Sta. WHTM-TV, Harrisburg, 1983—. Coordinator Manheim Chem. People, 1983—. Mem. Am. Guild of Organists, Manheim Area Ministers Assn. (exec. com. 1980-84). Lodge: Rotary. Home: 110 N Grant St Manheim PA 17545 Office: Salem United Meth Ch 140 N Penn St Manheim PA 17545

ZELLMER, DAVID BRUCE, minister, American Lutheran Church; b. Mpls., Dec. 21, 1953; s. Bruce Edward and Ila Corrine (Johnson) Z.; m. LaDonna Jean Graves, Mar. 6, 1976; children: Christina, Joshua, Sarah. B.S. in Psychology, Southwestern Okla. State U., 1977; M.Div., Luther-Northwestern Theol. Sem., 1981. Ordained to ministry Am. Luth. Ch., 1981. Pastor, chaplain Scandinavia/Bethany Luth. Parish and Bethesda Nursing Home, Aberdeen, S.D., 1981—; chmn. S.D. dist. Ch. in Soc. Com., Am. Luth. Ch., 1982—. Address: Rural Route 4 Box 367 Aberdeen SD 74601

ZEMBRZUSKI, MICHAEL MARION, priest, Roman Catholic Ch.; b. Szypulki, Poland, Dec. 16, 1908; s. Maximilian and Victoria (Tanski) Z.; grad. Krakow (Poland) Coll., 1930; student Theol. and Philos. Sem., Krakow, 1930-34; L.HD. (hon.), Alliance Coll., Cambridge Springs, Pa., 1968. Joined Pauline Fathers, 1926; ordained priest, 1934; prior, Budapest, Hungary, 1934-40; provincial Pauline Fathers in Hungary, 1940-48; dir. Pontifical Aid Commn.-Polish Desk, Rome, 1948-51; missionary, U.S., 1951-53; organizer Nat. Shrine, Doylestown, Pa., 1954, vicar gen., dir., 1963-75. Chmn., Nat. Copernicus Com., 1970-73; host radio program in Polish, 1955-75. Contbr. articles to Polish lang. jours., religious jours. Address: Pauline Fathers Bunker Hill Rd Box 66 Kittanning PA 16201

ZERSEN, DAVID JOHN, minister, Lutheran Church-Missouri Synod; b. Elmhurst, Ill., Feb. 20, 1938; s. Carl W. and Alma C. (Selle) Z.; m. Julia J. Schmid, Oct. 30, 1966; children: Kristin, Rolf. B.A., Valparaiso U., 1960; B.S., Concordia Sem., Springfield, Ill., 1963, M.Div., 1973; postgrad. Georg-August U., Göttingen, Fed. Republic Germany, 1963-65; D.Ministry, Bethany Sem., Oak Brook, Ill., 1979. Ordained to ministry Luth. Ch., 1965. Pastor Trinity Luth. Ch., Tinley Park, Ill., 1963, Concordia Luth. Ch., Midlothian, Ill., 1965-71, St. Mark Luth. Ch., St. Charles, Ill., 1971-82, St. Luke Luth. Ch., Itasca, Ill., 1982—; chmn. Valley Luth. High Sch., St. Charles, 1975-78; chmn. continuing edn. com. No. Ill. dist. Luth. Ch.-Mo. Synod, 1982—. Author: Lutheran Congregation Handbook, 1968. Translator: Theological Significance of Dead Sea Scrolls, 1968. Editor continuing edn. jour. HELP, 1982—. Contbr. articles to religious publs. Mem. Soc. Advancement Continuing Edn. Ministry, St. Charles Minesterial Assn. (chmn. 1977). Home: 460 S Rush St Itasca IL 60143 Office: St Luke Luth Ch 410 S Rush St Itasca IL 60143

ZIEFLE, HELMUT WILHELM, educator, General Baptist Conference; b. Heilbronn, Württenberg, Fed. Republic Germany, Apr. 2, 1939; came to U.S., 1956; s. George and Maria (Glaser) Z.; m. Christa Lembeck; children: Helmut, Mark. B.A., SUNY-Albany, 1964, M.A., 1966; Ph.D., U. Ill., 1973. Tchr. Bethlehem Central High Sch., Delmar, N.Y., 1965-67; faculty Wheaton Coll., Ill., 1967—, prof. German, 1982—, scholar-in-residence U. Ill.-Chgo., 1979. Author: One Woman Against the Reich, 1981; Dictionary of Modern Theological German, 1982. Mem. internat. editorial bd. KOSMAS acad. jour. Contbr. articles to profl. jours. Pres. German Evening Sch., Wheaton, 1978-80. Mem. Am. Assn. German Tchrs., Ill. Fedn. Fgn. Lang. Tchrs., Czechoslovak Soc. Arts and Sci, Delta Phi Alpha. Home: ON460 Fanchon St Wheaton IL 60187 Office: Wheaton Coll 501 E Seminary Wheaton IL 60187

ZIEGLER, LEVI JOHN, minister, Church of the Brethren; b. Millbach Twp., Pa., May 17, 1931; s. Jesse Hoffman and Mary (Darkes) Z.; m. Helen Ruth Trimmer, Aug. 30, 1953; children: John L., Dale T., Robert A. B.A., Elizabethtown Coll., 1953; M.Div., Bethany Theol. Sem., 1956. Ordained to ministry Ch. of the Brethren, 1956. Pastor Greenland/Allegheny Ch. of the Brethren, Maysville, W.Va., 1956-57, Greenland Ch. of the Brethren, 1956-58, Westernport Ch. of the Brethren, Md., 1958-64, Roxbury Ch. of the Brethren, Johnstown, Pa., 1964-68, Community United Ch., Erie, Pa., 1969-78, Conewago Ch. of the Brethren, Bachmanville, Pa., 1979—; bd. dirs. Atlantic NE Dist., Harrisburg, Pa., 1983—, Germantown Ministry, 1983—; pres. Erie County Council Chs., 1972-73, Open Door Ministry-Drug Ministry, Erie, 1973-77; Hershey Ministerium, 1982-84. Home and Office: Conewago Ch of the Brethren Route 1 Box 129D Hershey PA 17033

ZIELASKO, JOHN WARLOW, minister, Fellowship of Grace Brethren Churches; b. Minersville, Pa., May 7, 1921; s. John L. and Marfel (Warlow) Z.; m. F. Jean Beveridge, 1944; children: John R., Ann L., James M., Janet S. B.S., Millersville State Coll., 1947; B.D., Grace Sem., Ind., 1950, M.Th., 1979. Ordained to ministry Fellowship of Grace Brethren Chs., 1950. Pastor Grace Brethren Ch., South Bend, Ind., 1950-52; missionary, Brazil, 1952-65; fgn. sec. Grace Brethren Fgn. Missions, Winona Lake, Ind., 1966-67, gen. dir. Fgn. Missionary Soc., 1967—, bd. dirs., 1966—. Editor sect. Herald mag., 1966—. Contbr. articles to religious jours. Served as ensign USN, 1942-45, PTO. Home: 114 15th St Winona Lake IN 46590 Office: PO Box 588 Winona Lake IN 46590

ZIEMER, MARK URBEN, pastor, American Lutheran Church; b. Port Washington, Wis., July 10, 1953; s. Urben August Valentine and Arleen Hulda Louise (Rusch) Z.; m. Claudia Lee Fischer, Aug. 14, 1977; children: Nathaniel, Andrew. A.A., Concordia Coll., Milw., 1973; B.A., Concordia Sr. Coll., Fort Wayne, Ind., 1975; M.Div., Wartburg Sem., 1979. Ordained to ministry Am. Luth. Ch., 1979. Pastor Hollandale Luth. Ch., Wis., 1979—, Trinity Luth. Ch., Blanchardville, Wis., 1979—. Mem. Iowa County Commn. on Aging, Dodgeville, Wis., 1980—, Citizens for Better Health, Blanchardville, 1983-84. Mem. Iowa County Clergy Assn., Pecatonica Area Pastoral Assn. (sec. 1979-81, pres. 1983—), Dodgeville Conf. Ministerium (sec. 1980-81, 83-84, chmn. youth com. 1981—). Home and Office: Box 96 Hollandale WI 53544

ZIGLAR, WILLIAM LARRY, religious educator, Episcopal Church; b. Yazoo City, Miss., Aug. 25, 1938; s. W. Hubert and Freida Belle (Waaser) Z.; m. Brenda Joy Helms, June 25, 1960; children: Scott Lawrence, Heidi Lynn. B.A., Miss. Coll., 1960, M.A., 1961; Ph.D., U. Maine, 1972. Ordained to ministry, So. Bapt. Conv., 1960. Music/youth dir. Midway Bapt. Ch., Jackson, Miss., 1957-59; minister Ebenezer Bapt. Ch., Ebenezer, Miss., 1959-61, Immanuel Bapt. Ch., Bangor, Maine, 1961-62; faculty Eastern Coll., St. David's, Pa., 1964—, prof., Kea chair Am. history and dean spl. programs, 1979—; Disting. Christian scholar/lectr. Staley Found., 1983—; bd. dirs. Presbyn. Hist. Commn., Phila., 1981-84; scholar-in-residence Wayne Presbyn. Ch., Pa., 1981; ch. sch. tchr. Ch. of the Good Samaritan, Paoli, Pa., 1984—. Author: Requiem for God, 1984; Battle of Trenton, 1976. Contbr. articles to profl. jours. Historian, N. Wayne Protective Assn., 1984—; scholar in residence Radnor Pub. Library/NEH, Wayne, 1980-81; v.p. Wayne PTA, 1979-80. Recipient Goddard Medal in space history, Nat. Space Assn., 1979; Legion of Honor, Chapel of Four Chaplains, 1983; Lindback Disting. Coll. Tchr., Lindback Found., 1979; Prof. of Yr., Eastern Coll., 1967, 73; Shell Found. grantee, 1970; NEH grantee, 1979-80. Mem. Yellow Springs Inst. (dir.), Am. Studies Assn., Am. Hist. Assn., Am. Assn. for State and Local History, Hist. Soc. Pa., Soc. History Tech., Inst. Study Am. Evangelicals, Am. Soc. Ch. History, Phi Alpha Theta, Pi Kappa Delta, Pi Gamma Mu, Kappa Delta Pi, Omicron Delta Kappa, Delta Mu Delta, Sigma Zeta, Alpha Chi. Home: 408 Oak Ln Wayne PA 19087 Office: Eastern Coll Saint Davids PA 19087

ZIKMUND, BARBARA BROWN, minister, seminary dean, religion educator, United Church of Christ; b. Ann Arbor, Mich., Oct. 16, 1939; d. Henry Daniels and Helen Monroe (Langworthy) Brown; m. Joseph Zikmund, Aug. 26, 1961; 1 child, Brian. B.A., Beloit Coll., 1961; B.D., Duke U., 1964, Ph.D., 1969; D.D. (hon.), Doane Coll., 1984, Chgo. Theol. Sem., 1985. Ordained to ministry United Ch. of Christ, 1964. Instr. in history and religion Albright Coll., Reading, Pa., 1966-67, Temple U., Phila., 1967-68, Ursinus Coll., Collegeville, Pa., 1968-69; asst. prof. religious studies Albion Coll., Mich., 1970-75; asst. prof., dir. religious studies Chgo. Theol. Sem., 1975-80; assoc. prof. religion, dean Pacific Sch. of Religion, Berkeley, Calif., 1981-85, prof., 1985—; chmn. UCC Hist. Council, 1984—; v.p. Assn. Theol. Schs. in U.S. and Can., 1984—; mem. council Am. Soc. Ch. History, 1984—; commr. World Council of Chs. Programme for Theol. Edn., 1984. Author: Discovering the Church, 1983; Hidden Histories in the United Church of Christ, 1984. Co-editor: The American Religious Experience, 1976. Mem. city council City of Albion, Mich., 1972-75; pres., founder Albion Montessori Assn., 1973-75; trustee Beloit Coll., Wis., 1980-83. Grantee NEH, 1974-75, Assn. Theol. Schs. in U.S. and Can., 1983-84; Woodrow Wilson fellow, 1964-66. Mem. Faith Order Commn. Nat. Council Chs., 6th Assembly World Council Chs. Vancouver (accredited visitor), Internat. Assn. Women Ministers, Am. Acad. Religion, Pacific Coast Theol. Soc. Home: 1281 Peachwood Ct San Bruno CA 94066 Office: Pacific Sch of Religion 1798 Scenic Ave Berkeley CA 94709

ZIMMERMAN, CURTIS ROY, priest, Episcopal Ch.; b. Santa Monica, Calif., Dec. 22, 1942; s. Thomas Henry and Verna Ruth (Naylor) Z.; B.Mus., U. Redlands, 1966; M.Div., Ch. Div. Sch. of Pacific, Berkeley, Calif., 1974. Ordained priest, 1974; dir. music Arlington United Meth. Ch., Riverside, Calif., 1963-66; organist-choirmaster St. George's Ch., Honolulu, 1968-70; asst. to rector St. Francis Ch., San Jose, Calif., 1971-74; canon liturgist St. Andrew's Cathedral, Honolulu, 1974—. Adviser mus. groups, Honolulu, 1974—; lectr., resource adviser Anglican liturg. renewal, 1967—. Chmn., Diocesan Liturg. Commn. Recipient Oscar Greene Meml. Preaching prize Berkeley, 1973. Mem. Am. Guild Organists, Choral Condrs. Guild. Home: 46-318 Haiku Rd Unit 75 Kaneohe HI 96744 Office: St Andrew's Cathedral Queen Emma Sq Honolulu HI 96813

ZIMMERMAN, DONALD FRANCIS, priest Roman Catholic Church; b. Dallas, Apr. 21, 1947; s. James Leonard and Ann (Lerner) Z. B.A., U. Dallas, 1969; M.Th., U. Dallas, 1973. Ordained priest Roman Catholic Church, 1973. Asst. pastor Christ the King Ch., Dallas, 1973-76, St. Luke Ch., Irving, Tex., 1977-78, St. Bernard Ch., Dallas, 1978-80; pastor Good Shepherd Ch., Garland, Tex., 1980-83, St. Monica Ch., Dallas, 1983—. Bd. dirs. Tex. Right to Life of Dallas, 1979. Pres., Senate Priests Diocese Dallas, 1977-78; rep. Presbyterial Council Diocese Dallas, 1984, consultor Coll. Consultors, 1984. Decorated knight Order Holy Sepulchre. Home: 9933 Midway Rd Dallas TX 75220 Office: St Monica Ch 9933 Midway Rd Dallas TX 75220

ZIMMERMAN, JEANNE V., lay minister, nurse, Roman Catholic Church; b. Waukegan, Ill., Mar. 2, 1942; d. Peter Christian and Lily Virginia (Rasmussen) Vig; m. Gordon Edward Zimmerman, Aug. 22, 1964; children: Stephanie, Gregory, Nancy. B.S. in Nursing, U. Mich., 1964. Tchr. 2d grade CCD, St. Ignatius Cathedral, Palm Beach Gardens, Fla., 1973-83, liturgy com., 1975-85, chmn., 1984-85; lay minister Palm Beach Diocese, Fla., 1985—. Community home health nurse Palm Beach Regional Vis. Nurse Assn., West Palm Beach, 1983—. Author: (summer program) Old Testament Roots, 1974. Contbr. to numerous religious programs. Speaker, mem. com. Jewish/Catholic Dialogue for Palm Beach, 1984-85; profl. adv. bd. March of Dimes, West Palm Beach, 1985. Recipient St. Anne medal Cath. Com. for Scouting, Miami Archdiocese, 1980. Mem. Cath. Com. for Peace and Justice, Sigma Theta Tau. Home: 208 River Dr Tequesta FL 33458

ZIMMERMAN, JOHN CURTIS, minister, Presbyterian Church in the U.S.A.; b. Spokane, Wash., May 28, 1935; s. Curtis Prang and Ruth Frances (Rickman) Z.; m. Martha Jane Gadske, Aug. 31, 1957; children: John Curtus, Richard Prang, Sarah Jane. B.A., U. Calif.-Berkeley, 1956; M.Div., Princeton Theol. Sem., 1963; D.Min., San Francisco Theol. Sem., 1977. Ordained to ministry Presbyn. Ch. in U.S.A., 1963. Student asst. Lawrenceville Presbyn. Ch., N.J., 1962-63; asst. pastor Laurelhurst Presbyn. Ch., Seattle, 1963-64; pastor Naches Presbyn. Ch., Wash., 1965-68; sr. pastor West Side Ch., Richland, Wash., 1968-84, 1st Presbyn. Ch., Miami, Fla., 1984—; moderator Synod of Alaska-NW, Seattle, 1982-83; Ga. moderator candidate Presbyn. Ch. in U.S.A., Atlanta, 1983—. Author: Seeing Through the Eyes of Michelangelo, 1977. Mem. human rights commn. City of Richland, 1973-75, Benton-Franklin Counties Juvenile Justice Commn., 1975-77. Served as chaplain USNR. Recipient Golden Acorn award Wash. State PTA, 1965. Mem. Am. Acad. Religion, Am. Schs. Oriental Research, Am. Sci. Affiliation, Am. Soc. Missiology, Soc. Bibl. Lit. Lodge: Rotary (bd. dirs. Richland 1979-81, Paul Harris fellow 1984). Home: 1801 S Bayshore Dr Miami FL 33133 Office: First Presbyn Ch Miami 609 Brickell Ave Miami FL 33131

ZIMMERMAN, JOHN MURR See *Who's Who in America,* 43rd edition.

ZIMMERMAN, SHELDON, rabbi, Reform Jewish; b. Toronto, Ont., Can., Feb. 21, 1942; came to U.S., 1965; s. Morris and Helen (Stitsky) Z.; m. Judith Elaine Baumgarten; children: Brian Howard, Kira Rahel, David Zvi, Micol Eliana. B.A., U. Toronto, 1964, M.A., 1965; B.H.L., Hebrew Union Coll., 1969, M.H.L., 1970. Ordained rabbi, 1970. Asst. rabbi Central Synagogue, N.Y.C., 1970-72, sr. rabbi, 1972—; lectr. liturgy and rabbinics Jewis Inst. Religion, Hebrew Union Coll., N.Y.C., 1979—; trustee Fedn. Jewish Philanthropies N.Y., 1975—, exec. com., 1979—; co-chmn. joint commn. on outreach Union Am. Hebrew Congregations and Central Conf. Am. Rabbis, 1981—; bd. govs. Hebrew Union Coll., 1982—; trustee Louise Wise Services; adv. bd. Learning for Living; mem. nat. rabbinic adv. com. Jewish Nat. Fund, 1975-81, many others. Author: The Threat of Mixed Marriage—A Response, 1976. Contbr. articles to profl. jours. Exec. bd. Boy Scouts Am., 1973. Recipient Samuel W. and Rose Hurowitz award Commn. on Synagogue Relations, 1975, City of Peace award, 1981. Mem. Am. Friends of Israel Interfaith Assn. (pres. 1981-82), Jewish Hist. Soc. N.Y. (bd. dirs.), Assn. Reform Zionists Am. (trustee). Lodge: B'nai B'rith (trustee World Ctr., Jerusalem, nat. commr. youth orgn., Sam Beber Disting. Alumnus award 1979). Address: Central Synagogue 123 E 55th St New York NY 10022

ZIMMERMAN, THOMAS FLETCHER, minister, church official Assemblies of God; b. Indpls., Mar. 26, 1912; s. Thomas F. and Carrie D. (Kenagy) Z.; student Ind. U.; D.D. (hon.), Northwest Assemblies of God Coll., 1964; m. Harriett Elizabeth Price, June 17, 1933; children—Betty (Mrs. Paul Tinlin), Thomas Fletcher III, David R. Ordained to ministry, 1936; pastor chs., Indpls., 1928-32, Kokomo, Ind., 1933, Harrodsburg, Ind., 1934, South Bend, Ind., 1935-39, Granite City, Ill., 1939-42, Springfield, Mo., 1943-47, Cleve., 1951-52; dist. ofcl. Ill. Assemblies of God, 1941-43, So. Mo. Assemblies of God, 1944-47, 49-51; asst. gen. supt. Assemblies of God, 1952-59, gen. supt., 1960—. Pres. Assemblies of God Grad. Sch., Springfield, 1973—; chmn. Pentecostal World Confs., 1970-85; exec. com. Nat. Religious Broadcasters; mem. World Relief Commn., Pentecostal Fellowship N.Am. Mem. religious relationships com. Boy Scouts Am., 1964—. Bd. dirs. Cox Med Center, Springfield, Evangel Coll., Springfield, Jr. Achievement, Springfield; chmn. bd. dirs. Central Bible Coll., Maranatha Village Retirement Complex, Springfield; exec. com. Lausanne Com. World

Evangelism. Recipient Silver Beaver award Boy Scouts Am., 1969, Springfieldian of Yr. award Springfield C. of C., 1974. Mem. Am. Bible Soc., Nat. Assn. Evangelicals (exec. bd. 1957—), C. of C. Springfield. Office: 1445 Boonville St Springfield MO 65802

ZIMMERMANN, BENJAMIN CHRISTIAN, minister, Lutheran Church-Missouri Synod; pilot; b. Shasi, Hupeh, China, Apr. 14, 1940; came to U.S., 1942; s. Elmer Christian and Anna Elizabeth (Backs) Z.; m. Melvia Kahale, Apr. 25, 1965; children: Eric Christian, William Stephen, Elizabeth Kahale. Student in architecture Iowa State U., 1958, in art, Boise State U., 1966-68; M.Div., Concordia Sem., 1980. Ordained to ministry Lutheran Ch., 1980. Missionary, Wilderness Ministries, Idaho Back Country, 1980—; pastor Cascade Luth. Mission, Idaho, 1980-83; asst. pastor Our Savior Luth. Ch., McCall, Idaho, 1980-82, sr. pastor, 1982-83; candidates reverendi ministerii Luth. Ch. - Mo. Synod, St. Louis, 1983—. Pilot, Trans World Airlines, N.Y.C., 1968—. Served to major USAF, 1959-65, 82—. Mem. Airline Pilots Assn., Air Force Assn., N.G. Assn., Cascade C. of C. Republican. Home: 121 Bogie Dr Cascade ID 83611-0764 Office: Trans World Airlines 605 3rd Ave New York NY also 124 TRG Gowen Field Boise ID

ZIMMERMANN, ELWOOD HENRY, church official, Lutheran Church-Missouri Synod; b. Milw., Sept. 29, 1919; s. Henry and Hildegarde (Scholz) Z.; student Concordia Jr. Coll., Milw., 1937-39; B.A., Concordia Sem., St. Louis, 1944, D.D., 1974; m. Betty Louise Jeske, Oct. 8, 1944; children—John M., Paul S., Philip J., Ruth R. Ordained to ministry Lutheran Ch.-Mo. Synod, 1944; pastor Bethel Luth. Ch., Austin, Ind., 1944-48, Grace Luth. Ch., Indpls., 1948-58; exec. sec. stewardship Central dist. Luth. Ch.-Mo. Synod, 1958-63, exec. sec. Ind. dist., 1963-66, exec. sec. missions and ch. extension, 1966-70, pres., 1970—, now chmn. nominating com., mem. council on stewardship; regional chmn. Luth. Council-U.S.A., 1968-69, chmn. conv. com. on higher edn., 1973; mem., chmn. Concordia Sr. Coll., Ft. Wayne, Ind., 1970—, chmn. com. on adminstrn., 1975—; mem. bd. of control Concordia Theol. Sem., Ft. Wayne, 1976—; council mem. Ind. Council Chs., 1970—; mem. Ind. Interreligious Commn. on Human Equality, 1970—; chmn. project com. North Am. Missions, 1978—. Bd. dirs. Luth. Child Welfare Assn., Indpls., 1949-55. Contbr. to sermon books. Home: 1928 Reed Rd Fort Wayne IN 46805 Office: 1145 S Barr St Fort Wayne IN 46802

ZINNER, DIRK KARL RONALD, minister, Seventh-Day Adventist Church; b. Hannover, Fed. Republic Germany, Dec. 6, 1947; came to Can., 1952; s. Helmut and Dorothea (Fenner) Z.; m. Jeanice Lynn Wehling, Nov. 11, 1973; children: Anita Jerilyn, Nathan Aaron Richard. B.A., Walla Walla Coll., 1971; M.Div., Andrews U., 1974. Ordained to ministry Seventh-Day Adventist Ch., 1978. Assoc. pastor 7th-Day Adventist Ch., Vancouver, B.C., Can., 1975, 84—, McBride, Prince George, Vanderhoof, B.C., 1975-77, West Kootenays, B.C., 1977-82, South Central, B.C., 1982-84; guest speaker religious programs local radio stas. Local dir. 5 Day Plan to Stop Smoking, West Kootenays, 1977-82, Prince George, 1975-77, Merritt and Ashcroft, Can., 1982-84; coach Merritt Juvenile Soccer League, 1983-84. Mem. Ministerial Assn., Castlegar Ministerial Club (v.p. 1981). Home: 1592 Blaine Ave Burnaby BC V5A 2L8 Canada Office: Box 35399 Sta E 5350 Baillie St Vancouver BC V6M 4G5 Canada

ZINZ, DAVID ALBERT, lay worker, photographer, N. Am. Baptist Conf.; b. Philipsburg, Pa., Nov. 2, 1952; s. Albert Calvin and Dolores Aleda (Helwig) Z. Student, Pa. State U., 1970-72; Diploma, Sch. Modern Photography, Little Falls, N.J., 1974; corr. study Moody Bible Inst., Chgo., 1982—. Deacon, Forest Baptist Ch., Winburne, Pa., 1981—, trustee, 1981—; del. Eastern Assn.-Am. Baptist Conf., 1983—; pres. Cross Road Riders Christian Motorcycle Club, DuBois, Pa., 1983—. Vol., West Br. Area Clothing Bank, 1983—. Mem. Christian Motorcyclists Assn. Home: PO Box 171 1 Trolley St Winburne PA 16879 Office: HRB-Singer Inc Science Park Rd State College PA 16804

ZIPPEL, MARY-ELLA HOLST, religious educator, Unitarian Universalist Association; b. Detroit, Oct. 12, 1934; d. Spencer and Ruth (McCullough) Holst; m. Philip Baker Hall, Dec. 28, 1954 (div. July 1965); children: Patricia Hall Infante, Darcy; m. Bert Zippel, Jan. 18, 1969. B.A., U. Toledo, 1959; M.A., NY U, 1970. Dir. religious edn. Unitarian Ch. of All Souls, N.Y.C., 1976—; chmn. Unitarian Universalist Youth/Adult Com., Boston, 1977-79; mem. Unitarian Universalist Hist. Scholarship Com., Boston, 1980—. Author: Chapel Talks, 1982; (with A. Utt) Unitarian Universalist Contributors to Literature for Children 1976. Contbg. editor Jour. Women and Religion, 1981—. Contbr. articles and poetry to religious jours. Bd. mgrs. Soc. for Aging, Inc., N.Y.C., 1974—; bd. dirs. Yorkville Common Pantry, N.Y.C., 1981—. Home: 150-74 Village Rd Jamaica NY 11432 Office: Unitarian Ch of All Souls 1157 Lexington Ave New York NY 10021

ZLOTOWITZ, BERNARD MALACHI, Reform Judaism; b. N.Y.C., July 11, 1925; s. Aron and Fannie (Pasternak) Z.; m. Shirley Masef, June 12, 1949; children: Debra, Robin, Richard, Alice. B.A., Bklyn. Coll., 1948; M.H.L., Hebrew Union Coll., 1955; M.A., Columbia U., 1965; D.H.L., Hebrew Union Coll., 1974, D.D. (hon.), 1980. Ordained rabbi, 1955. Rabbi, Temple Israel, Nyack, N.Y., 1955-60, Union Reform Temple, Freeport, N.Y., 1960-72, Temple Beth El, Charlotte, N.C., 1972-74; regional dir. N.J. Union of Am. Hebrew Congregations, 1975-80, N.Y. Union of Am. Hebrew Congregations, N.Y.C., 1980—; lectr. Bible, Hebrew Union Coll., 1963-72, 79—. Author: Folkways and Minhagim, 1970; Art in Judaism, 1975; The Septuagint Translation of the Hebrew Terms in Relation to God in The Book of Jeremiah, 1981. Contbr. articles to jours., chpts. to books. Editor: One People by Abraham Segal, 1982. Columnist Reform Judaism, book rev. editor 1983—. Contbg. editor Keeping Posted, 1981. Mem. Central Conf. Am. Rabbis, N.Y. Bd. Rabbis (exec. com.), Internat. Orgn. Masoretic Studies, Soc. Bible Lit. Democrat. Home: 15 Aberdeen Pl Fair Lawn NJ 07410 Office: Union of Am Hebrew Congregations 838 Fifth Ave New York NY 10021

ZODHIATES, SPIROS, religious organization executive, author, Baptist Church; b. Nicosia, Cyprus, Mar. 13, 1922; came to U.S., 1946, naturalized, 1949; s. George and Mary (Toumazou) Z.; m. Joan Carol Wassel, Jan. 10, 1948; children: Priscilla, Lois, Philip, Mary. B.Th., Am. U., Cairo, Egypt, 1945; postgrad. Nat. Bible Inst., 1946-47; M.A., NY U, 1951; Th.D., Luther Rice Sem., 1978. Pres. Advancing Ministries of Gospel Internat., Chattanooga, 1966—. Author numerous books on N.T. in both English and Greek including, The Hebrew-Greek Key Study Bible. Home: 8927 Villa Rica Circle Chattanooga TN 37421 Office: Advancing Ministries of Gospel Internat 6815 Shallow Ford Rd Chattanooga TN 37422

ZOLVINSKI, FRANK JOHN, religious education administrator, Roman Catholic Church; b. Michigan City, Ind., Jan. 8, 1950; s. Frank Zolvinski and Frances Foldenauer; m. Susan Mary Minich, Jan. 22, 1952; 1 child, Martha Eileen. B.A., St. Meinrad, 1972; cert. Religious Edn., Cal Coll., 1977; M.R.E., Loyola U., Chgo., 1981; M.R.E., U. Notre Dame, 1984. Tchr. St. Mary's Sch., Griffith, Ind., 1972-73; dir. religious edn. St. Peter Ch., La Porte, Ind., 1976—; prof. Inst. of Religion, Cal Coll., Whiting, Ind., 1979—; bd. dirs. Inst. of Religion, Whiting, 1979—. Bus driver La Porte Schs., 1975—. Contbg. author youth group meeting book, retreat book; contbr. articles to profl. publs. Mem. La Porte Bus Driver Assn. (pres. 1982-83). Club: Rotary. Office: St Peter Religious Edn 1110 Monroe St La Porte IN 46350

ZONDERVAN, PETER JOHN See *Who's Who in America*, 43rd edition.

ZORN, KENNETH LLOYD, minister, Lutheran Church-Missouri Synod; b. Oaskshella, Sask., Can., July 30, 1929; s. Henry Rudolph and Dorothea Johanna (Dech) Z.; B.A., Concordia Coll., Edmonton, Alta., 1951; M.Div., Concordia Sem., St. Louis, 1956; m. Eileen Norma Getzinger, July 31, 1954; children: Deborah, David, Donald. Ordained to ministry, 1956; asst. pastor Trinity 1st Luth. Ch., Mpls., 1954-55, Zion Luth. Ch., Dashwood, Ont., 1956-60; pastor Prince of Peace Luth. Ch., Burlington, Ont., 1960-67, Good Shepherd Luth. Ch., Regina, Sask., 1967-69, Hope Luth. Ch., Kitchener, Ont., 1969—. Dir. pub. relations, Luth. Ch. Ont. Dist.; dir. evangelism Sask. and Ont. dists.; pres., bd. dirs. Canadian Bible Soc. Hamilton Dist.; bd. govs. Canadian Home Bible League; bd. dirs. Ont. Dist. Luth. Ch.-Mo. Synod; bd. dirs. Man. and Sask. Dist. Luth. Ch.-Mo. Synod; past pastoral adviser Ont. Luth. Laymen's League; pres. Evang. Ministerial Waterloo Region, 1982-84; v.p. World Lit. Crusade-Can., 1983—; pres. Christian Film Library, 1970—; pres. Kitchener-Waterloo br. Canadian Bible Soc., 1983—. Office: 30 Shaftsbury Dr Kitchener ON N2A 1N6 Canada Home: 96 Crosby Dr Kitchener ON Canada

ZUBEK, THEODORIC JOSEPH, priest, educator, author, Roman Catholic Church; b. Malacky, Czechoslovakia, Apr. 4, 1914; s. John and Theresa (Ivan) Z.; Th.D., Cath. U., Fribourg (Switzerland), 1940; came to U.S., 1952, naturalized, 1957. Joined Franciscan Order, 1929; ordained priest, 1938; prof. systematic theology Franciscan Sem., Zilina, Czechoslovakia, 1941-50; asst. prof. theology Seton Hall U., Newark, 1956-60; provincial superior Franciscan Custody Most Holy Savior, Pitts., 1964-70. Preacher and lectr. religious topics. Author: The Church of Silence in Slovakia, 1956; Slovak Bishops—Martyrs of Christ, 1963; Slovak Clergy in History and Culture, 1970; editor Listy Sv. Frantiska, 1958-62, 79—; contbr. articles to religious jours.

ZUCK, VICTOR IRA, priest, Episcopal Church; pipe organ consultant; b. Hagerstown, Md., Jan. 29, 1908; s. Jacob Ira and Ora Alverda (Turner) Z.; m. Nathalie Amelia Peterson, July 3, 1937; 1 child, Victoria Janet. B.R.E., Blue Ridge Coll., 1927; M. Sacred Lit., Trinity Theol. Sem., 1982; D.Min., 1983. Ordained to ministry Episcopal Ch., as deacon, 1975, as priest, 1976. Warden Epiphany Ch., South Haven, Mich., 1938-45; lay evangelist St. Paul's Ch., Pitts., 1972-75, asst. 1982—; rector St. Luke's Ch., Georgetown, Pa., 1975-82; organ architect, Diocese of Pitts., 1974—; chmn. adv. Council for Holy Orders, Pitts., 1977—; mem. Cathedral Chpt., Pitts., 1978-80; vice chmn. Archtl. Commn., Pitts., 1984—. Pvt. organ cons., Pitts., 1974—. Patentee electronic organs, mus. instruments, 1942-52. Pres. Restoration Com. for Hist. Landmark, Old St. Luke's Ch., Woodville, Pa., 1974. Recipient Cert. of Merit, Am. Acad. of Organ, 1951. Mem. Automatic Mus. Instrument Collectors Assn. (hon.), Am. Guild of Organists, Organ Hist. Soc., Episcopal Hist. Soc., Pitts. History and Landmarks Soc. (pres. 1980—), Juniata Coll. Alumni Assn., Trinity Theol. Sem. Alumni Assn., Am. Bible Soc. Republican. Lodge: Masons (32 degree). Home: 212 Trotwood West Dr Pittsburgh PA 15241 Office: St Paul Episcopal Ch Pittsburgh PA 15228

ZUCKERMAN, HOWARD, Jewish organization executive. Pres. Nat. Jewish Commn. on Law and Pub. Affairs. Office: Nat Jewish Commn on Law and Pub Affairs 71 Broadway 6th Fl New York NY 10006*

ZUMBRUN, MORRIS G., bishop Lutheran Church in America, Md. Synod, Balt. Office: 7604 York Rd Baltimore MD 21204*

ZUNIGA, ABDON ANTHONY, priest, Roman Cath. Ch.; b. Puebla, Mexico, July 30, 1900; s. Anthony Adalberto and Ana Maria (Marin) Z.; came to U.S., 1932, naturalized, 1968; degree St. Louis U., 1932-36. Ordained priest, 1935; pastor LaPurisima Ch., Socorro, Tex., 1946—. Mem. Soc. Jesus. Home: 328 S Nevarez St El Paso TX 79927

ZUZIAK, JOZEF ROMAN, priest, Roman Catholic Church; b. Lipowa, Krakow, Poland, Jan. 17, 1934; came to U.S., 1969, naturalized, 1977; s. Wojciech Jan and Aniela Anna (Piotrowski) Z. Licentiate, Sem. Philos. Theology, Bagno-Wroclaw, Poland, 1966; postgrad. Inter-Religious Pastoral Sch., Krakow, 1967. Ordained priest Roman Cath. Ch., 1966. Treas. Salvatorian Fathers, Gary, Ind., 1970-73, superior Merrillville, Ind., 1973-78, regional superior, Merrillville, 1978—. Address: Salvatorian Fathers 5755 Pennsylvania St Merrillville IN 46410

ZWERNEMANN, JAMES CHARLES, minister, Luth. Ch.-Missouri Syod; b. Brenham, Tex., Jan. 15, 1938; s. Erwin Theodore and Alwine Augusta (Jatzlau) Z.; A.A., Concordia Coll., 1958; B.A., Concordia Sr. Coll., 1960; M.Div., Concordia Sem., 1964; S.T.M., N.Y. Theol. Sem., 1967, D.Min., 1976; m. Madelynn Bonnie McGinnis, Aug. 18, 1962; children: Jimmy, Kelly Jeanne, John, Lori, Christina. Intern, St. Paul's Luth. Ch. Tremont, Bronx, N.Y., 1962-63; ordained to ministry, 1964; founding pastor Good Shepherd Luth. Ch., Warwick, N.Y., 1964-69; pastor Christ Meml. Luth. Ch., Houston, 1969-74, Village Luth. Ch., Bronxville, N.Y., 1974—. Mem. bd. parish services Tex. Dist., 1972-74; Synodical Family Life dir., Tex., 1972-74; circuit counselor Tex. dist., 1972; bd. dirs. Houston Met. Campus Ministry, 1969-74; v.p., bd. dirs., mem. bd. missions Atlantic dist. Luth. Ch.-Mo. Synod, 1976—. Mem. Luth. Edn. Assn., Greater Houston Luth. Clergyman's Assn. Author: Godspeak, 1975; contbr. articles to religious jours. Home: 51 Edgewood Ln Bronxville NY 10708 Office: 172 White Plains Rd Bronxville NY 10708

ZYTKOSKEE, TATE VAN EMAN, minister, Seventh-day Adventists; b. Takoma Park, Md., Sept. 15, 1912; s. Adrian Edmond and Laura (Tate) Z.; B.A., Union Coll., 1949; M.A., U. Md., 1959; m. Mary Alice Fernald, Aug. 11, 1946; children—Jacquie Marie, Taryl Beth. Ordained to ministry, 1952; prin. tchr. Edgecombe Acad., Balt., 1949-50; supt. edn., youth dir. Chesapeake Conf., Balt., 1950-55; supt. edn. youth, temperance dir. N.J. Conf., 1955-57; youth dir., temperance dir. Potomac Conf., Staunton, Va., 1957-59; edn. dir., youth dir., Indonesia, 1959-60; pres. Korean Union Coll., Seoul, 1960-65; edn. dir. Far Eastern div., Singapore, 1965-68; civilian chaplain Korean Union Servicemen's Center, 1968-70; supt. edn. N.Y. Conf., Seventh-day Adventists, 1970—, communications dir., 1976—. Recipient Honor award Korean Union Coll., 1967. Home: 11 Tree Line Dr Liverpool NY 13088 Office: PO Box 67 Onondoga Branch Syracuse NY 13215